P9-EDX-569

DEC 2 0 2012

PETERSON'S GRADUATE PROGRAMS IN BIOLOGICAL/BIOMEDICAL SCIENCES & HEALTH-RELATED MEDICAL PROFESSIONS

2013

PETERSON'S
Publishing

About Peterson's Publishing

Peterson's Publishing provides the accurate, dependable, high-quality education content and guidance you need to succeed. No matter where you are on your academic or professional path, you can rely on Peterson's print and digital publications for the most up-to-date education exploration data, expert test-prep tools, and top-notch career success resources—everything you need to achieve your goals.

Visit us online at **www.petersonspublishing.com** and let Peterson's help you achieve your goals.

For more information, contact Peterson's Publishing, 2000 Lenox Drive, Lawrenceville, NJ 08648; 800-338-3282 Ext. 54229; or find us on the World Wide Web at www.petersonspublishing.com.

© 2013 Peterson's, a Nelnet company

Previous editions published as *Peterson's Graduate Programs in the Biological Sciences* © 1966, 1967, 1968, 1969, 1970, 1971, 1972, 1973, 1974, 1975, 1976, 1977, 1978, 1979, 1980, 1981, 1982, 1983, 1984, 1985, 1986, 1987, 1988, 1989, 1990, 1991, 1992, 1993, 1994, 1995, 1996, 1997, 1998, 1999, 2000, 2001, 2002, 2003, 2004, 2005, 2006, 2007, 2008, 2009, 2010, 2011, 2012

Facebook® and Facebook logos are registered trademarks of Facebook, Inc., which was not involved in the production of this book and makes no endorsement of this product.

Bernadette Webster, Managing Editor; Jill C. Schwartz, Editor; Ken Britschge, Research Project Manager; Amanda Ortiz, Amy L. Weber, Research Associates; Phyllis Johnson, Software Engineer; Ray Golaszewski, Publishing Operations Manager; Linda M. Williams, Composition Manager; Carrie Hansen, Christine Lucht, Bailey Williams, Client Fulfillment Team

Peterson's makes every reasonable effort to obtain accurate, complete, and timely data from reliable sources. Nevertheless, Peterson's and the third-party data suppliers make no representation or warranty, either expressed or implied, as to the accuracy, timeliness, or completeness of the data or the results to be obtained from using the data, including, but not limited to, its quality, performance, merchantability, or fitness for a particular purpose, non-infringement or otherwise.

Neither Peterson's nor the third-party data suppliers warrant, guarantee, or make any representations that the results from using the data will be successful or will satisfy users' requirements. The entire risk to the results and performance is assumed by the user.

NOTICE: Certain portions of or information contained in this book have been submitted and paid for by the educational institution identified, and such institutions take full responsibility for the accuracy, timeliness, completeness and functionality of such content. Such portions of information include (i) each display ad that comprises a half page of information covering a single educational institution or program and (ii) each two-page description or Close-Up of a graduate school or program that appear in the different sections of this guide. The "Close-Ups and Displays" are listed in various sections throughout the book.

ALL RIGHTS RESERVED. No part of this work covered by the copyright herein may be reproduced or used in any form or by any means—graphic, electronic, or mechanical, including photocopying, recording, taping, Web distribution, or information storage and retrieval systems—without the prior written permission of the publisher.

For permission to use material from this text or product, complete the Permission Request Form at http://www.petersonspublishing.com/permissions.

ISSN 1093-8443
ISBN-13: 978-0-7689-3622-3
ISBN-10: 0-7689-3622-5

Printed in the United States of America

10 9 8 7 6 5 4 3 2 1   15 14 13

Forty-seventh Edition

By producing this book on recycled paper (40% post-consumer waste) 77 trees were saved.

Certified Chain of Custody

60% Certified Fiber Sourcing and
40% Post-Consumer Recycled

www.sfiprogram.org

*This label applies to the text stock.

Sustainability—Its Importance to Peterson's Publishing

What does sustainability mean to Peterson's Publishing? As a leading publisher, we are aware that out business has a direct impact on vital resources—most especially the trees that are used to make out books. Peterson's Publishing is proud that its products are certified to the Sustainable Forestry Initiative (SFI) chain-of-custody standard and that all of its books are printed on paper that is 40 percent post-consumer waste using vegetable-based ink.

Being a part of the Sustainable Forestry Initiative (SFI) means that all of out vendors—from paper suppliers to printers—have undergone rigorous audits to demonstrate that they are maintaining a sustainable environment.

Peterson's Publishing continuously strives to find new ways to incorporate sustainability throughout all aspects of its business.

CONTENTS

CONTENTS

ACADEMIC AND PROFESSIONAL PROGRAMS IN THE MEDICAL PROFESSIONS AND SCIENCES

A Note from the Peterson's Editors

The six volumes of Peterson's *Graduate and Professional Programs*, the only annually updated reference work of its kind, provide wideranging information on the graduate and professional programs offered by accredited colleges and universities in the United States, U.S. territories, and Canada and by those institutions outside the United States that are accredited by U.S. accrediting bodies. Nearly 36,000 individual academic and professional programs at more than 2,200 institutions are listed. Peterson's *Graduate and Professional Programs* have been used for more than forty years by prospective graduate and professional students, placement counselors, faculty advisers, and all others interested in postbaccalaureate education.

Graduate & Professional Programs: An Overview contains information on institutions as a whole, while the other books in the series are devoted to specific academic and professional fields:

Graduate Programs in the Humanities, Arts & Social Sciences
Graduate Programs in the Biological/Biomedical Sciences & Health-Related Medical Professions
Graduate Programs in the Physical Sciences, Mathematics, Agricultural Sciences, the Environment & Natural Resources
Graduate Programs in Engineering & Applied Sciences
Graduate Programs in Business, Education, Information Studies, Law & Social Work

The books may be used individually or as a set. For example, if you have chosen a field of study but do not know what institution you want to attend or if you have a college or university in mind but have not chosen an academic field of study, it is best to begin with the Overview guide.

Graduate & Professional Programs: An Overview presents several directories to help you identify programs of study that might interest you; you can then research those programs further in the other books in the series by using the Directory of Graduate and Professional Programs by Field, which lists 500 fields and gives the names of those institutions that offer graduate degree programs in each.

For geographical or financial reasons, you may be interested in attending a particular institution and will want to know what it has to offer. You should turn to the Directory of Institutions and Their Offerings, which lists the degree programs available at each institution. As in the Directory of Graduate and Professional Programs by Field, the level of degrees offered is also indicated. All books in the series include advice on graduate education, including topics such as admissions tests, financial aid, and accreditation. **The Graduate Adviser** includes two essays and information about accreditation. The first essay, "The Admissions

Process," discusses general admission requirements, admission tests, factors to consider when selecting a graduate school or program, when and how to apply, and how admission decisions are made. Special information for international students and tips for minority students are also included. The second essay, "Financial Support," is an overview of the broad range of support available at the graduate level. Fellowships, scholarships, and grants; assistantships and internships; federal and private loan programs, as well as Federal Work-Study; and the GI bill are detailed. This essay concludes with advice on applying for need-based financial aid. "Accreditation and Accrediting Agencies" gives information on accreditation and its purpose and lists institutional accrediting agencies first and then specialized accrediting agencies relevant to each volume's specific fields of study.

With information on more than 44,000 graduate programs in more than 500 disciplines, Peterson's *Graduate and Professional Programs* give you all the information you need about the programs that are of interest to you in three formats: **Profiles** (capsule summaries of basic information), **Displays** (information that an institution or program wants to emphasize), and **Close-Ups** (written by administrators, with more expansive information than the **Profiles**, emphasizing different aspects of the programs). By using these various formats of program information, coupled with **Appendixes** and **Indexes** covering directories and subject areas for all six books, you will find that these guides provide the most comprehensive, accurate, and up-to-date graduate study information available.

Find Us on Facebook®

Join the grad school conversation on Facebook® at www.facebook.com/petersonspublishing. Peterson's expert resources are available to help you as you search for the right graduate program for you.

Peterson's publishes a full line of resources with information you need to guide you through the graduate admissions process. Peterson's publications can be found at college libraries and career centers and your local bookstore or library—or visit us on the Web at www. petersonspublishing.com. Peterson's books are now also available as eBooks.

Colleges and universities will be pleased to know that Peterson's helped you in your selection. Admissions staff members are more than happy to answer questions, address specific problems, and help in any way they can. The editors at Peterson's wish you great success in your graduate program search!

NOTICE: Certain portions of or information contained in this book have been submitted and paid for by the educational institution identified, and such institutions take full responsibility for the accuracy, timeliness, completeness and functionality of such contents. Such portions or information include (i) each display ad that comprises a half page of information covering a single educational institution or program and (ii) each two-page description or Close-Up of a graduate school or program that appear in the different sections of this guide. The "Close-Ups and Displays" are listed in various sections throughout the book.

THE GRADUATE ADVISER

The Admissions Process

Generalizations about graduate admissions practices are not always helpful because each institution has its own set of guidelines and procedures. Nevertheless, some broad statements can be made about the admissions process that may help you plan your strategy.

Factors Involved in Selecting a Graduate School or Program

Selecting a graduate school and a specific program of study is a complex matter. Quality of the faculty; program and course offerings; the nature, size, and location of the institution; admission requirements; cost; and the availability of financial assistance are among the many factors that affect one's choice of institution. Other considerations are job placement and achievements of the program's graduates and the institution's resources, such as libraries, laboratories, and computer facilities. If you are to make the best possible choice, you need to learn as much as you can about the schools and programs you are considering before you apply.

The following steps may help you narrow your choices.

- Talk to alumni of the programs or institutions you are considering to get their impressions of how well they were prepared for work in their fields of study.
- Remember that graduate school requirements change, so be sure to get the most up-to-date information possible.
- Talk to department faculty members and the graduate adviser at your undergraduate institution. They often have information about programs of study at other institutions.
- Visit the Web sites of the graduate schools in which you are interested to request a graduate catalog. Contact the department chair in your chosen field of study for additional information about the department and the field.
- Visit as many campuses as possible. Call ahead for an appointment with the graduate adviser in your field of interest and be sure to check out the facilities and talk to students.

General Requirements

Graduate schools and departments have requirements that applicants for admission must meet. Typically, these requirements include undergraduate transcripts (which provide information about undergraduate grade point average and course work applied toward a major), admission test scores, and letters of recommendation. Most graduate programs also ask for an essay or personal statement that describes your personal reasons for seeking graduate study. In some fields, such as art and music, portfolios or auditions may be required in addition to other evidence of talent. Some institutions require that the applicant have an undergraduate degree in the same subject as the intended graduate major.

Most institutions evaluate each applicant on the basis of the applicant's total record, and the weight accorded any given factor varies widely from institution to institution and from program to program.

The Application Process

You should begin the application process at least one year before you expect to begin your graduate study. Find out the application deadline for each institution (many are provided in the **Profile** section of this guide). Go to the institution's Web site and find out if you can apply online. If not, request a paper application form. Fill out this form thoroughly and neatly. Assume that the school needs all the information it is requesting and that the admissions officer will be sensitive to the neatness and overall quality of what you submit. Do not supply more information than the school requires.

The institution may ask at least one question that will require a threeor four-paragraph answer. Compose your response on the assumption that the admissions officer is interested in both what you think and how you express yourself. Keep your statement brief and to the point, but, at the same time, include all pertinent information about your past experiences and your educational goals. Individual statements vary greatly in style and content, which helps admissions officers differentiate among applicants. Many graduate departments give considerable weight to the statement in making their admissions decisions, so be sure to take the time to prepare a thoughtful and concise statement.

If recommendations are a part of the admissions requirements, carefully choose the individuals you ask to write them. It is generally best to ask current or former professors to write the recommendations, provided they are able to attest to your intellectual ability and motivation for doing the work required of a graduate student. It is advisable to provide stamped, preaddressed envelopes to people being asked to submit recommendations on your behalf.

Completed applications, including references, transcripts, and admission test scores, should be received at the institution by the specified date.

Be advised that institutions do not usually make admissions decisions until all materials have been received. Enclose a self-addressed postcard with your application, requesting confirmation of receipt. Allow at least ten days for the return of the postcard before making further inquiries.

If you plan to apply for financial support, it is imperative that you file your application early.

ADMISSION TESTS

The major testing program used in graduate admissions is the Graduate Record Examinations (GRE) testing program, sponsored by the GRE Board and administered by Educational Testing Service, Princeton, New Jersey.

The Graduate Record Examinations testing program consists of a General Test and eight Subject Tests. The General Test measures critical thinking, verbal reasoning, quantitative reasoning, and analytical writing skills. It is offered as an Internet-based test (iBT) in the United States, Canada, and many other countries.

The Graduate Record Examinations testing program consists of the revised General Test and eight Subject Tests. The GRE® revised General Test, introduced in August 2011, features a new test-taker friendly design and new question types. It reflects the kind of thinking students need to do in graduate or business school and demonstrates that students are indeed ready for graduate-level work.

- **Verbal Reasoning**—Measures ability to analyze and evaluate written material and synthesize information obtained from it, analyze relationships among component parts of sentences, and recognize relationships among words and concepts.
- **Quantitative Reasoning**—Measures problem-solving ability, focusing on basic concepts of arithmetic, algebra, geometry, and data analysis.
- **Analytical Writing**—Measures critical thinking and analytical writing skills, specifically the ability to articulate and support complex ideas clearly and effectively.

The GRE® revised General Test is available at about 700 test centers in more than 160 countries. It is offered as a computer-based test year-round at most locations around the world and as a paper-based test up to three times a year in areas where computer-based testing is not available.

Three scores are reported on the revised General Test:

1. A **Verbal Reasoning score** is reported on a 130–170 score scale, in 1-point increments.
2. A **Quantitative Reasoning score** is reported on a 130–170 score scale, in 1-point increments.

3. An **Analytical Writing score** is reported on a 0–6 score level, in half-point increments.

The GRE Subject Tests measure achievement and assume undergraduate majors or extensive background in the following eight disciplines:

- Biochemistry, Cell and Molecular Biology
- Biology
- Chemistry
- Computer Science
- Literature in English
- Mathematics
- Physics
- Psychology

The Subject Tests are available three times per year as paper-based administrations around the world. Testing time is approximately 2 hours and 50 minutes. You can obtain more information about the GRE by visiting the ETS Web site at www.ets.org or consulting the *GRE Information and Registration Bulletin*. The *Bulletin* can be obtained at many undergraduate colleges. You can also download it from the ETS Web site or obtain it by contacting Graduate Record Examinations, Educational Testing Service, P.O. Box 6000, Princeton, NJ 08541-6000; phone: 609-771-7670.

If you expect to apply for admission to a program that requires any of the GRE tests, you should select a test date well in advance of the application deadline. Scores on the computer-based General Test are reported within ten to fifteen days; scores on the paper-based Subject Tests are reported within six weeks.

Another testing program, the Miller Analogies Test (MAT), is administered at more than 500 Controlled Testing Centers, licensed by Harcourt Assessment, Inc., in the United States, Canada, and other countries. The MAT computer-based test is now available. Testing time is 60 minutes. The test consists of 120 partial analogies. You can obtain the *Candidate Information Booklet,* which contains a list of test centers and instructions for taking the test, from http://www.milleranalogies.com or by calling 800-622-3231 (toll-free).

Check the specific requirements of the programs to which you are applying.

How Admission Decisions Are Made

The program you apply to is directly involved in the admissions process. Although the final decision is usually made by the graduate dean (or an associate) or the faculty admissions committee, recommendations from faculty members in your intended field are important. At some institutions, an interview is incorporated into the decision process.

A Special Note for International Students

In addition to the steps already described, there are some special considerations for international students who intend to apply for graduate study in the United States. All graduate schools require an indication of competence in English. The purpose of the Test of English as a Foreign Language (TOEFL) is to evaluate the English proficiency of people who are nonnative speakers of English and want to study at colleges and universities where English is the language of instruction. The TOEFL is administered by Educational Testing Service (ETS) under the general direction of a policy board established by the College Board and the Graduate Record Examinations Board.

The TOEFL iBT assesses the four basic language skills: listening, reading, writing, and speaking. It was administered for the first time in September 2005, and ETS continues to introduce the TOEFL iBT in selected cities. The Internet-based test is administered at secure, official test centers. The testing time is approximately 4 hours. Because the TOEFL iBT includes a speaking section, the Test of Spoken English (TSE) is no longer needed.

The TOEFL is also offered in the paper-based format in areas of the world where Internet-based testing is not available. The paper-based TOEFL consists of three sections—listening comprehension, structure and written expression, and reading comprehension. The testing time is approximately 3 hours. The Test of Written English (TWE) is also given. The TWE is a 30-minute essay that measures the examinee's ability to compose in English. Examinees receive a TWE score separate from their TOEFL score. The *Information Bulletin* contains information on local fees and registration procedures.

The TOEFL® paper-based test (TOEFL PBT) began being phased out in mid-2012. For those who may have taken the TOEFL PBT, scores remain valid for two years after the test date. The Test of Written English (TWE) is also given. The TWE is a 30-minute essay that measures the examinee's ability to compose in English. Examinees receive a TWE score separate from their TOEFL score. The Information Bulletin contains information on local fees and registration procedures.

Additional information and registration materials are available from TOEFL Services, Educational Testing Service, P.O. Box 6151, Princeton, New Jersey 08541-6151. Phone: 609-771-7100. Web site: www.toefl.org.

International students should apply especially early because of the number of steps required to complete the admissions process. Furthermore, many United States graduate schools have a limited number of spaces for international students, and many more students apply than the schools can accommodate.

International students may find financial assistance from institutions very limited. The U.S. government requires international applicants to submit a certification of support, which is a statement attesting to the applicant's financial resources. In addition, international students *must* have health insurance coverage.

Tips for Minority Students

Indicators of a university's values in terms of diversity are found both in its recruitment programs and its resources directed to student success. Important questions: Does the institution vigorously recruit minorities for its graduate programs? Is there funding available to help with the costs associated with visiting the school? Are minorities represented in the institution's brochures or Web site or on their faculty rolls? What campus-based resources or services (including assistance in locating housing or career counseling and placement) are available? Is funding available to members of underrepresented groups?

At the program level, it is particularly important for minority students to investigate the "climate" of a program under consideration. How many minority students are enrolled and how many have graduated? What opportunities are there to work with diverse faculty and mentors whose research interests match yours? How are conflicts resolved or concerns addressed? How interested are faculty in building strong and supportive relations with students? "Climate" concerns should be addressed by posing questions to various individuals, including faculty members, current students, and alumni.

Information is also available through various organizations, such as the Hispanic Association of Colleges & Universities (HACU), and publications such as *Diverse Issues in Higher Education* and *Hispanic Outlook* magazine. There are also books devoted to this topic, such as *The Multicultural Student's Guide to Colleges* by Robert Mitchell.

Financial Support

The range of financial support at the graduate level is very broad. The following descriptions will give you a general idea of what you might expect and what will be expected of you as a financial support recipient.

Fellowships, Scholarships, and Grants

These are usually outright awards of a few hundred to many thousands of dollars with no service to the institution required in return. Fellowships and scholarships are usually awarded on the basis of merit and are highly competitive. Grants are made on the basis of financial need or special talent in a field of study. Many fellowships, scholarships, and grants not only cover tuition, fees, and supplies but also include stipends for living expenses with allowances for dependents. However, the terms of each should be examined because some do not permit recipients to supplement their income with outside work. Fellowships, scholarships, and grants may vary in the number of years for which they are awarded.

In addition to the availability of these funds at the university or program level, many excellent fellowship programs are available at the national level and may be applied for before and during enrollment in a graduate program. A listing of many of these programs can be found at the Council of Graduate Schools' Web site: http://www. cgsnet.org. There is a wealth of information in the "Programs" and "Awards" sections.

Assistantships and Internships

Many graduate students receive financial support through assistantships, particularly involving teaching or research duties. It is important to recognize that such appointments should not be viewed simply as employment relationships but rather should constitute an integral and important part of a student's graduate education. As such, the appointments should be accompanied by strong faculty mentoring and increasingly responsible apprenticeship experiences. The specific nature of these appointments in a given program should be considered in selecting that graduate program.

TEACHING ASSISTANTSHIPS

These usually provide a salary and full or partial tuition remission and may also provide health benefits. Unlike fellowships, scholarships, and grants, which require no service to the institution, teaching assistantships require recipients to provide the institution with a specific amount of undergraduate teaching, ideally related to the student's field of study. Some teaching assistants are limited to grading papers, compiling bibliographies, taking notes, or monitoring laboratories. At some graduate schools, teaching assistants must carry lighter course loads than regular full-time students.

RESEARCH ASSISTANTSHIPS

These are very similar to teaching assistantships in the manner in which financial assistance is provided. The difference is that recipients are given basic research assignments in their disciplines rather than teaching responsibilities. The work required is normally related to the student's field of study; in most instances, the assistantship supports the student's thesis or dissertation research.

ADMINISTRATIVE INTERNSHIPS

These are similar to assistantships in application of financial assistance funds, but the student is given an assignment on a part-time basis, usually as a special assistant with one of the university's administrative offices. The assignment may not necessarily be directly related to the recipient's discipline.

RESIDENCE HALL AND COUNSELING ASSISTANTSHIPS

These assistantships are frequently assigned to graduate students in psychology, counseling, and social work, but they may be offered to students in other disciplines, especially if the student has worked in this capacity during his or her undergraduate years. Duties can vary from being available in a dean's office for a specific number of hours for consultation with undergraduates to living in campus residences and being responsible for both counseling and administrative tasks or advising student activity groups. Residence hall assistantships often include a room and board allowance and, in some cases, tuition assistance and stipends. Contact the Housing and Student Life Office for more information.

Health Insurance

The availability and affordability of health insurance is an important issue and one that should be considered in an applicant's choice of institution and program. While often included with assistantships and fellowships, this is not always the case and, even if provided, the benefits may be limited. It is important to note that the U.S. government requires international students to have health insurance.

The GI Bill

This provides financial assistance for students who are veterans of the United States armed forces. If you are a veteran, contact your local Veterans Administration office to determine your eligibility and to get full details about benefits. There are a number of programs that offer educational benefits to current military enlistees. Some states have tuition assistance programs for members of the National Guard. Contact the VA office at the college for more information.

Federal Work-Study Program (FWS)

Employment is another way some students finance their graduate studies. The federally funded Federal Work-Study Program provides eligible students with employment opportunities, usually in public and private nonprofit organizations. Federal funds pay up to 75 percent of the wages, with the remainder paid by the employing agency. FWS is available to graduate students who demonstrate financial need. Not all schools have these funds, and some only award them to undergraduates. Each school sets its application deadline and workstudy earnings limits. Wages vary and are related to the type of work done. You must file the Free Application for Federal Student Aid (FAFSA) to be eligible for this program.

Loans

Many graduate students borrow to finance their graduate programs when other sources of assistance (which do not have to be repaid) prove insufficient. You should always read and understand the terms of any loan program before submitting your application.

FEDERAL DIRECT LOANS

Federal Direct Stafford Loans. The Federal Direct Stafford Loan Program offers 6.8 percent interest rate loans to students with the Department of Education acting as the lender.

There are two components of the Federal Stafford Loan program. Under the *subsidized* component (for loans with enrollment prior to July 1, 2012) of the program, the federal government pays the interest on the loan

while you are enrolled in graduate school on at least a half-time basis, as well as during any period of deferment. Under the *unsubsidized* component of the program, you pay the interest on the loan from the day proceeds are issued. Eligibility for the federal subsidy is based on demonstrated financial need as determined by the financial aid office from the information you provide on the FAFSA. A cosigner is not required, since the loan is not based on creditworthiness.

Although *unsubsidized* Federal Direct Stafford Loans may not be as desirable as *subsidized* Federal Direct Stafford Loans from the student's perspective, they are a useful source of support for those who may not qualify for the subsidized loans or who need additional financial assistance.

Graduate students may borrow up to $20,500 per year through the Direct Stafford Loan Program, up to a cumulative maximum of $138,500, including undergraduate borrowing. This may include up to $8,500 in *subsidized* Direct Stafford Loans annually, depending on eligibility, up to a cumulative maximum of $65,500, including undergraduate borrowing. The amount of the loan borrowed through the *unsubsidized* Direct Stafford Loan Program equals the total amount of the loan (as much as $20,500) minus your eligibility for a *subsidized* Direct Loan (as much as $8,500). You may borrow up to the cost of attendance at the school in which you are enrolled or will attend, minus estimated financial assistance from other federal, state, and private sources, up to a maximum of $20,500.

Direct Stafford Graduate Loans made on or after July 1, 2006, carry a fixed interest rate of 6.8% both for in-school and in-repayment borrowers.

A fee is deducted from the loan proceeds upon disbursement. Loans with a first disbursement on or after July 1, 2010 but before July 1, 2012, have a borrower origination fee of 1 percent. For loans disbursed after July 1, 2012, these fee deductions no longer apply. The Budget Control Act of 2011, signed into law on August 2, 2011, eliminates Direct Subsidized Loan eligibility for graduate and professional students for periods of enrollment beginning on or after July 1, 2012 and terminates the authority of the Department of Education to offer most repayment incentives to Direct Loan borrowers for loans disbursed on or after July 1, 2012.

Under the *subsidized* Federal Direct Stafford Loan Program, repayment begins six months after your last date of enrollment on at least a half-time basis. Under the *unsubsidized* program, repayment of interest begins within thirty days from disbursement of the loan proceeds, and repayment of the principal begins six months after your last enrollment on at least a half-time basis. Some borrowers may choose to defer interest payments while they are in school. The accrued interest is added to the loan balance when the borrower begins repayment. There are several repayment options.

Federal Perkins Loans. The Federal Perkins Loan is available to students demonstrating financial need and is administered directly by the school. Not all schools have these funds, and some may award them to undergraduates only. Eligibility is determined from the information you provide on the FAFSA. The school will notify you of your eligibility.

Eligible graduate students may borrow up to $6,000 per year, up to a maximum of $40,000, including undergraduate borrowing (even if your previous Perkins Loans have been repaid). The interest rate for Federal Perkins Loans is 5 percent, and no interest accrues while you remain in school at least half-time. There are no guarantee, loan, or disbursement fees. Repayment begins nine months after your last date of enrollment on at least a half-time basis and may extend over a maximum of ten years with no prepayment penalty.

Federal Direct Graduate PLUS Loans. Effective July 1, 2006, graduate and professional students are eligible for Graduate PLUS loans. This program allows students to borrow up to the cost of attendance, less any other aid received. These loans have a fixed interest rate of 7.9 percent, and interest begins to accrue at the time of disbursement. The PLUS loans do involve a credit check; a PLUS borrower may obtain a loan with a cosigner if his or her credit is not good enough. Grad PLUS loans may be deferred while a student in school and for the six months following a drop below half-time enrollment. For more information, contact your college financial aid office.

Deferring Your Federal Loan Repayments. If you borrowed under the Federal Direct Stafford Loan Program, Federal Direct PLUS Loan Program, or the Federal Perkins Loan Program for previous undergraduate or graduate study, your payments may be deferred when you return to graduate school, depending on when you borrowed and under which program.

There are other deferment options available if you are temporarily unable to repay your loan. Information about these deferments is provided at your entrance and exit interviews. If you believe you are eligible for a deferment of your loan payments, you must contact your lender or loan servicer to request a deferment. The deferment must be filed prior to the time your payment is due, and it must be refiled when it expires if you remain eligible for deferment at that time.

SUPPLEMENTAL (PRIVATE) LOANS

Many lending institutions offer supplemental loan programs and other financing plans, such as the ones described here, to students seeking additional assistance in meeting their education expenses. Some loan programs target all types of graduate students; others are designed specifically for business, law, or medical students. In addition, you can use private loans not specifically designed for education to help finance your graduate degree.

If you are considering borrowing through a supplemental or private loan program, you should carefully consider the terms and be sure to "read the fine print." Check with the program sponsor for the most current terms that will be applicable to the amounts you intend to borrow for graduate study. Most supplemental loan programs for graduate study offer unsubsidized, credit-based loans. In general, a credit-ready borrower is one who has a satisfactory credit history or no credit history at all. A creditworthy borrower generally must pass a credit test to be eligible to borrow or act as a cosigner for the loan funds.

Many supplemental loan programs have minimum and maximum annual loan limits. Some offer amounts equal to the cost of attendance minus any other aid you will receive for graduate study. If you are planning to borrow for several years of graduate study, consider whether there is a cumulative or aggregate limit on the amount you may borrow. Often this cumulative or aggregate limit will include any amounts you borrowed and have not repaid for undergraduate or previous graduate study.

The combination of the annual interest rate, loan fees, and the repayment terms you choose will determine how much you will repay over time. Compare these features in combination before you decide which loan program to use. Some loans offer interest rates that are adjusted monthly, some quarterly, some annually. Some offer interest rates that are lower during the in-school, grace, and deferment periods and then increase when you begin repayment. Some programs include a loan "origination" fee, which is usually deducted from the principal amount you receive when the loan is disbursed and must be repaid along with the interest and other principal when you graduate, withdraw from school, or drop below half-time study. Sometimes the loan fees are reduced if you borrow with a qualified cosigner. Some programs allow you to defer interest and/or principal payments while you are enrolled in graduate school. Many programs allow you to capitalize your interest payments; the interest due on your loan is added to the outstanding balance of your loan, so you don't have to repay immediately, but this increases the amount you owe. Other programs allow you to pay the interest as you go, which reduces the amount you later have to repay. The private loan market is very competitive, and your financial aid office can help you evaluate these programs.

Applying for Need-Based Financial Aid

Schools that award federal and institutional financial assistance based on need will require you to complete the FAFSA and, in some cases, an institutional financial aid application.

If you are applying for federal student assistance, you **must** complete the FAFSA. A service of the U.S. Department of Education, the FAFSA is free to all applicants. Most applicants apply online at www.fafsa.ed.gov. Paper applications are available at the financial aid office of your local college.

After your FAFSA information has been processed, you will receive a Student Aid Report (SAR). If you provided an e-mail address on the

FAFSA, this will be sent to you electronically; otherwise, it will be mailed to your home address.

Follow the instructions on the SAR if you need to correct information reported on your original application. If your situation changes after you file your FAFSA, contact your financial aid officer to discuss amending your information. You can also appeal your financial aid award if you have extenuating circumstances.

If you would like more information on federal student financial aid, visit the FAFSA Web site or download the most recent version of *Funding Education Beyond High School: The Guide to Federal Student Aid* at http://studentaid.ed.gov/sites/default/files/2012-13-funding-your-education.pdf. This guide is also available in Spanish.

The U.S. Department of Education also has a toll-free number for questions concerning federal student aid programs. The number is 1-800-4-FED AID (1-800-433-3243). If you are hearing impaired, call toll-free, 1-800-730-8913.

Summary

Remember that these are generalized statements about financial assistance at the graduate level. Because each institution allots its aid differently, you should communicate directly with the school and the specific department of interest to you. It is not unusual, for example, to find that an endowment vested within a specific department supports one or more fellowships. You may fit its requirements and specifications precisely.

Accreditation and Accrediting Agencies

Colleges and universities in the United States, and their individual academic and professional programs, are accredited by nongovernmental agencies concerned with monitoring the quality of education in this country. Agencies with both regional and national jurisdictions grant accreditation to institutions as a whole, while specialized bodies acting on a nationwide basis—often national professional associations— grant accreditation to departments and programs in specific fields.

Institutional and specialized accrediting agencies share the same basic concerns: the purpose an academic unit—whether university or program—has set for itself and how well it fulfills that purpose, the adequacy of its financial and other resources, the quality of its academic offerings, and the level of services it provides. Agencies that grant institutional accreditation take a broader view, of course, and examine university-wide or college-wide services with which a specialized agency may not concern itself.

Both types of agencies follow the same general procedures when considering an application for accreditation. The academic unit prepares a self-evaluation, focusing on the concerns mentioned above and usually including an assessment of both its strengths and weaknesses; a team of representatives of the accrediting body reviews this evaluation, visits the campus, and makes its own report; and finally, the accrediting body makes a decision on the application. Often, even when accreditation is granted, the agency makes a recommendation regarding how the institution or program can improve. All institutions and programs are also reviewed every few years to determine whether they continue to meet established standards; if they do not, they may lose their accreditation.

Accrediting agencies themselves are reviewed and evaluated periodically by the U.S. Department of Education and the Council for Higher Education Accreditation (CHEA). Recognized agencies adhere to certain standards and practices, and their authority in matters of accreditation is widely accepted in the educational community.

This does not mean, however, that accreditation is a simple matter, either for schools wishing to become accredited or for students deciding where to apply. Indeed, in certain fields the very meaning and methods of accreditation are the subject of a good deal of debate. For their part, those applying to graduate school should be aware of the safeguards provided by regional accreditation, especially in terms of degree acceptance and institutional longevity. Beyond this, applicants should understand the role that specialized accreditation plays in their field, as this varies considerably from one discipline to another. In certain professional fields, it is necessary to have graduated from a program that is accredited in order to be eligible for a license to practice, and in some fields the federal government also makes this a hiring requirement. In other disciplines, however, accreditation is not as essential, and there can be excellent programs that are not accredited. In fact, some programs choose not to seek accreditation, although most do.

Institutions and programs that present themselves for accreditation are sometimes granted the status of candidate for accreditation, or what is known as "preaccreditation." This may happen, for example, when an academic unit is too new to have met all the requirements for accreditation. Such status signifies initial recognition and indicates that the school or program in question is working to fulfill all requirements; it does not, however, guarantee that accreditation will be granted.

Institutional Accrediting Agencies—Regional

MIDDLE STATES ASSOCIATION OF COLLEGES AND SCHOOLS
Accredits institutions in Delaware, District of Columbia, Maryland, New Jersey, New York, Pennsylvania, Puerto Rico, and the Virgin Islands.
Dr. Elizabeth Sibolski, President
Middle States Commission on Higher Education
3624 Market Street, Second Floor West
Philadelphia, Pennsylvania 19104
Phone: 267-284-5000
Fax: 215-662-5501
E-mail: info@msche.org
Web: www.msche.org

NEW ENGLAND ASSOCIATION OF SCHOOLS AND COLLEGES
Accredits institutions in Connecticut, Maine, Massachusetts, New Hampshire, Rhode Island, and Vermont.
Barbara E. Brittingham, Director
Commission on Institutions of Higher Education
209 Burlington Road, Suite 201
Bedford, Massachusetts 01730-1433
Phone: 781-271-0022
Fax: 781-271-0950
E-mail: kwillis@neasc.org
Web: http://cihe.neasc.org

NORTH CENTRAL ASSOCIATION OF COLLEGES AND SCHOOLS
Accredits institutions in Arizona, Arkansas, Colorado, Illinois, Indiana, Iowa, Kansas, Michigan, Minnesota, Missouri, Nebraska, New Mexico, North Dakota, Ohio, Oklahoma, South Dakota, West Virginia, Wisconsin, and Wyoming.
Dr. Sylvia Manning, President
The Higher Learning Commission
230 South LaSalle Street, Suite 7-500
Chicago, Illinois 60604-1413
Phone: 312-263-0456
Fax: 312-263-7462
E-mail: smanning@hlcommission.org
Web: www.ncahlc.org

NORTHWEST COMMISSION ON COLLEGES AND UNIVERSITIES
Accredits institutions in Alaska, Idaho, Montana, Nevada, Oregon, Utah, and Washington.
Dr. Sandra E. Elman, President
8060 165th Avenue, NE, Suite 100
Redmond, Washington 98052
Phone: 425-558-4224
Fax: 425-376-0596
E-mail: selman@nwccu.org
Web: www.nwccu.org

SOUTHERN ASSOCIATION OF COLLEGES AND SCHOOLS
Accredits institutions in Alabama, Florida, Georgia, Kentucky, Louisiana, Mississippi, North Carolina, South Carolina, Tennessee, Texas, and Virginia.
Belle S. Wheelan, President
Commission on Colleges
1866 Southern Lane
Decatur, Georgia 30033-4097
Phone: 404-679-4500
Fax: 404-679-4558
E-mail: questions@sacscoc.org
Web: www.sacscoc.org

WESTERN ASSOCIATION OF SCHOOLS AND COLLEGES
Accredits institutions in California, Guam, and Hawaii.
Ralph A. Wolff, President and Executive Director
Accrediting Commission for Senior Colleges and Universities
985 Atlantic Avenue, Suite 100
Alameda, California 94501
Phone: 510-748-9001
Fax: 510-748-9797
E-mail: wascsr@wascsenior.org
Web: www.wascweb.org

Institutional Accrediting Agencies—Other

ACCREDITING COUNCIL FOR INDEPENDENT COLLEGES AND SCHOOLS
Albert C. Gray, Ph.D., Executive Director and CEO
750 First Street, NE, Suite 980
Washington, DC 20002-4241
Phone: 202-336-6780
Fax: 202-842-2593
E-mail: info@acics.org
Web: www.acics.org

DISTANCE EDUCATION AND TRAINING COUNCIL (DETC)
Accrediting Commission
Michael P. Lambert, Executive Director
1601 18th Street, NW, Suite 2
Washington, DC 20009
Phone: 202-234-5100
Fax: 202-332-1386
E-mail: Brianna@detc.org
Web: www.detc.org

Specialized Accrediting Agencies

ACUPUNCTURE AND ORIENTAL MEDICINE
William W. Goding, M.Ed., RRT, Interim Executive Director
Accreditation Commission for Acupuncture and Oriental Medicine
14502 Greenview Drive, Suite 300B
Laurel, Maryland 20708
Phone: 301-313-0855
Fax: 301-313-0912
E-mail: coordinator@acaom.org
Web: www.acaom.org

ART AND DESIGN
Samuel Hope, Executive Director
Karen P. Moynahan, Associate Director
National Association of Schools of Art and Design (NASAD)
Commission on Accreditation
11250 Roger Bacon Drive, Suite 21
Reston, Virginia 20190-5243
Phone: 703-437-0700
Fax: 703-437-6312
E-mail: info@arts-accredit.org
Web: http://nasad.arts-accredit.org/

BUSINESS
Jerry Trapnell, Executive Vice President/Chief Accreditation Officer
AACSB International—The Association to Advance Collegiate Schools of Business
777 South Harbour Island Boulevard, Suite 750
Tampa, Florida 33602
Phone: 813-769-6500
Fax: 813-769-6559
E-mail: jerryt@aacsb.edu
Web: www.aacsb.edu

CHIROPRACTIC
S. Ray Bennett, Director of Accreditation Services
Council on Chiropractic Education (CCE)
Commission on Accreditation
8049 North 85th Way
Scottsdale, Arizona 85258-4321
Phone: 480-443-8877
Fax: 480-483-7333
E-mail: cce@cce-usa.org
Web: www.cce-usa.org

CLINICAL LABORATORY SCIENCES
Dianne M. Cearlock, Ph.D., Chief Executive Officer
National Accrediting Agency for Clinical Laboratory Sciences
5600 North River Road, Suite 720
Rosemont, Illinois 60018-5119
Phone: 773-714-8880
Fax: 773-714-8886
E-mail: info@naacls.org
Web: www.naacls.org

CLINICAL PASTORAL EDUCATION
Deryck Durston, Interim Executive Director
Association for Clinical Pastoral Education, Inc.
1549 Claremont Road, Suite 103
Decatur, Georgia 30033-4611
Phone: 404-320-1472
Fax: 404-320-0849
E-mail: acpe@acpe.edu
Web: www.acpe.edu

DANCE
Samuel Hope, Executive Director
Karen P. Moynahan, Associate Director
National Association of Schools of Dance (NASD)
Commission on Accreditation
11250 Roger Bacon Drive, Suite 21
Reston, Virginia 20190-5248
Phone: 703-437-0700
Fax: 703-437-6312
E-mail: info@arts-accredit.org
Web: http://nasd.arts-accredit.org

DENTISTRY
Anthony Ziebert, Director
Commission on Dental Accreditation
American Dental Association
211 East Chicago Avenue, Suite 1900
Chicago, Illinois 60611
Phone: 312-440-4643
E-mail: accreditation@ada.org
Web: www.ada.org

DIETETICS
Ulric K. Chung, Ph.D., Executive Director
American Dietetic Association
Commission on Accreditation for Dietetics Education (CADE-ADA)
120 South Riverside Plaza, Suite 2000
Chicago, Illinois 60606-6995
Phone: 800-877-1600
Fax: 312-899-4817
E-mail: cade@eatright.org
Web: www.eatright.org/cade

ENGINEERING
Michael Milligan, Ph.D., PE, Executive Director
Accreditation Board for Engineering and Technology, Inc. (ABET)
111 Market Place, Suite 1050
Baltimore, Maryland 21202
Phone: 410-347-7700
Fax: 410-625-2238
E-mail: accreditation@abet.org
Web: www.abet.org

FORESTRY
Carol L. Redelsheimer
Director of Science and Education
5400 Grosvenor Lane
Bethesda, Maryland 20814-2198
Phone: 301-897-8720 Ext. 123
Fax: 301-897-3690
E-mail: redelsheimerc@safnet.org
Web: www.safnet.org

HEALTH SERVICES ADMINISTRATION
Commission on Accreditation of Healthcare Management Education
    (CAHME)
John S. Lloyd, President and CEO
2111 Wilson Boulevard, Suite 700
Arlington, Virginia 22201
Phone: 703-351-5010
Fax: 703-991-5989
E-mail: info@cahme.org
Web: www.cahme.org

INTERIOR DESIGN
Holly Mattson, Executive Director
Council for Interior Design Accreditation
206 Grandview Avenue, Suite 350
Grand Rapids, Michigan 49503-4014
Phone: 616-458-0400
Fax: 616-458-0460
E-mail: info@accredit-id.org
Web: www.accredit-id.org

JOURNALISM AND MASS COMMUNICATIONS
Susanne Shaw, Executive Director
Accrediting Council on Education in Journalism and Mass
    Communications (ACEJMC)
School of Journalism
Stauffer-Flint Hall
University of Kansas
1435 Jayhawk Boulevard
Lawrence, Kansas 66045-7575
Phone: 785-864-3973
Fax: 785-864-5225
E-mail: sshaw@ku.edu
Web: www2.ku.edu/~acejmc

LANDSCAPE ARCHITECTURE
Ronald C. Leighton, Executive Director
Landscape Architectural Accreditation Board (LAAB)
American Society of Landscape Architects (ASLA)
636 Eye Street, NW
Washington, DC 20001-3736
Phone: 202-898-2444
Fax: 202-898-1185
E-mail: info@asla.org
Web: www.asla.org

LAW
Hulett H. Askew, Consultant on Legal Education
American Bar Association
321 North Clark Street, 21st Floor
Chicago, Illinois 60654
Phone: 312-988-6738
Fax: 312-988-5681
E-mail: legaled@americanbar.org
Web: www.abanet.org/legaled/

LIBRARY
Karen O'Brien, Director
Office for Accreditation
American Library Association
50 East Huron Street
Chicago, Illinois 60611
Phone: 800-545-2433 Ext. 2432
Fax: 312-280-2433
E-mail: accred@ala.org
Web: www.ala.org/accreditation/

MARRIAGE AND FAMILY THERAPY
Tanya A. Tamarkin, Director of Educational Affairs
Commission on Accreditation for Marriage and Family Therapy
    Education
American Association for Marriage and Family Therapy
112 South Alfred Street
Alexandria, Virginia 22314-3061
Phone: 703-838-9808
Fax: 703-838-9805
E-mail: coamfte@aamft.org
Web: www.aamft.org

MEDICAL ILLUSTRATION
Commission on Accreditation of Allied Health Education Programs
    (CAAHEP)
Kathleen Megivern, Executive Director
1361 Park Street
Clearwater, Florida 33756
Phone: 727-210-2350
Fax: 727-210-2354
E-mail: mail@caahep.org
Web: www.caahep.org

MEDICINE
Liaison Committee on Medical Education (LCME)
In odd-numbered years beginning each July 1, contact:
Barbara Barzansky, Ph.D., LCME Secretary
American Medical Association
Council on Medical Education
515 North State Street
Chicago, Illinois 60654
Phone: 312-464-4933
Fax: 312-464-5830
E-mail: cme@aamc.org
Web: www.ama-assn.org

In even-numbered years beginning each July 1, contact:
Dan Hunt, M.D., LCME Secretary
Association of American Medical Colleges
2450 N Street, NW Washington, DC 20037
Phone: 202-828-0596
Fax: 202-828-1125
E-mail: dhunt@aamc.org
Web: www.lcme.org

MUSIC
Samuel Hope, Executive Director
Karen P. Moynahan, Associate Director
National Association of Schools of Music (NASM)
Commission on Accreditation
11250 Roger Bacon Drive, Suite 21
Reston, Virginia 20190-5248
Phone: 703-437-0700
Fax: 703-437-6312
E-mail: info@arts-accredit.org
Web: http://nasm.arts-accredit.org/

NATUROPATHIC MEDICINE
Daniel Seitz, J.D., Ed.D., Executive Director
Council on Naturopathic Medical Education
P.O. Box 178
Great Barrington, Massachusetts 01230
Phone: 413-528-8877
Fax: 413-528-8880
E-mail: council@cnme.org
Web: www.cnme.org

NURSE ANESTHESIA
Francis R. Gerbasi, Executive Director
Council on Accreditation of Nurse Anesthesia Educational Programs
American Association of Nurse Anesthetists
222 South Prospect Avenue, Suite 304
Park Ridge, Illinois 60068
Phone: 847-692-7050 Ext. 1154
Fax: 847-692-6968
E-mail: fgerbasi@aana.com
Web: http://home.coa.us.com

NURSE EDUCATION
Jennifer L. Butlin, Director
Commission on Collegiate Nursing Education (CCNE)
One Dupont Circle, NW, Suite 530
Washington, DC 20036-1120
Phone: 202-887-6791
Fax: 202-887-8476
E-mail: jbutlin@aacn.nche.edu
Web: www.aacn.nche.edu/accreditation

NURSE MIDWIFERY
Lorrie Kaplan, Executive Director
Accreditation Commission for Midwifery Education
American College of Nurse-Midwives
Nurse-Midwifery Program
8403 Colesville Road, Suite 1550
Silver Spring, Maryland 20910
Phone: 240-485-1800
Fax: 240-485-1818
E-mail: lkaplan@acnm.org
Web: www.midwife.org/acme.cfm

Jo Anne Myers-Ciecko, MPH, Executive Director
Midwifery Education Accreditation Council
P.O. Box 984
La Conner, Washington 98257
Phone: 360-466-2080
Fax: 480-907-2936
E-mail: info@meacschools.org
Web: www.meacschools.org

NURSE PRACTITIONER
Gay Johnson, Acting CEO
National Association of Nurse Practitioners in Women's Health
Council on Accreditation
505 C Street, NE Washington, DC 20002
Phone: 202-543-9693 Ext. 1
Fax: 202-543-9858
E-mail: info@npwh.org
Web: www.npwh.org

NURSING
Sharon J. Tanner, Ed.D., RN, Executive Director
National League for Nursing Accrediting Commission (NLNAC)
3343 Peachtree Road, NE, Suite 500
Atlanta, Georgia 30326
Phone: 404-975-5000
Fax: 404-975-5020
E-mail: nlnac@nlnac.org
Web: www.nlnac.org

OCCUPATIONAL THERAPY
Neil Harvison, Ph.D., OTR/L
Director of Accreditation and Academic Affairs
The American Occupational Therapy Association
4720 Montgomery Lane
P.O. Box 31220
Bethesda, Maryland 20824-1220
Phone: 301-652-2682 Ext. 2912
Fax: 301-652-7711
E-mail: accred@aota.org
Web: www.aota.org

OPTOMETRY
Joyce L. Urbeck, Administrative Director
Accreditation Council on Optometric Education
American Optometric Association (AOA)
243 North Lindbergh Boulevard
St. Louis, Missouri 63141
Phone: 314-991-4000 Ext. 246
Fax: 314-991-4101
E-mail: acoe@aoa.org
Web: www.theacoe.org

OSTEOPATHIC MEDICINE
Konrad C. Miskowicz-Retz, Ph.D., CAE
Director, Department of Education
Commission on Osteopathic College Accreditation
American Osteopathic Association
142 East Ontario Street
Chicago, Illinois 60611
Phone: 312-202-8048
Fax: 312-202-8202
E-mail: kretz@osteopathic.org
Web: www.osteopathic.org

PHARMACY
Peter H. Vlasses, Executive Director
Accreditation Council for Pharmacy Education
20 North Clark Street, Suite 2500
Chicago, Illinois 60602-5109
Phone: 312-664-3575
Fax: 312-664-4652
E-mail: csinfo@acpe-accredit.org
Web: www.acpe-accredit.org

PHYSICAL THERAPY
Mary Jane Harris, Director
Commission on Accreditation in Physical Therapy Education (CAPTE)
American Physical Therapy Association (APTA)
1111 North Fairfax Street
Alexandria, Virginia 22314
Phone: 703-706-3245
Fax: 703-706-3387
E-mail: accreditation@apta.org
Web: www.capteonline.org

PHYSICIAN ASSISTANT STUDIES
John E. McCarty, Executive Director
Accreditation Review Commission on Education for the Physician
    Assistant, Inc. (ARC-PA)
12000 Findley Road, Suite 150
Johns Creek, Georgia 30097
Phone: 770-476-1224
Fax: 770-476-1738
E-mail: arc-pa@arc-pa.org
Web: www.arc-pa.org

PLANNING
Shonagh Merits, Executive Director
American Institute of Certified Planners/Association of Collegiate
    Schools of Planning/American Planning Association
Planning Accreditation Board (PAB)
53 W. Jackson Boulevard, Suite 1315
Chicago, Illinois 60604
Phone: 312-334-1271
Fax: 312-334-1273
E-mail: smerits@planningaccreditationboard.org
Web: www.planningaccreditationboard.org

PODIATRIC MEDICINE
Alan R. Tinkleman, Executive Director
Council on Podiatric Medical Education (CPME)
American Podiatric Medical Association
9312 Old Georgetown Road
Bethesda, Maryland 20814-1621
Phone: 301-571-9200
Fax: 301-571-4903
E-mail: artinkleman@apma.org
Web: www.cpme.org

PSYCHOLOGY AND COUNSELING
Susan Zlotlow, Executive Director
Office of Program Consultation and Accreditation
American Psychological Association
750 First Street, NE Washington, DC 20002-4242
Phone: 202-336-5979
Fax: 202-336-5978
E-mail: apaaccred@apa.org
Web: www.apa.org/ed/accreditation

Carol L. Bobby, Executive Director
Council for Accreditation of Counseling and Related Educational
    Programs (CACREP)
1001 North Fairfax Street, Suite 510
Alexandria, Virginia 22314
Phone: 703-535-5990
Fax: 703-739-6209
E-mail: cacrep@cacrep.org
Web: www.cacrep.org

PUBLIC AFFAIRS AND ADMINISTRATION
Crystal Calarusse, Executive Director
Commission on Peer Review and Accreditation
National Association of Schools of Public Affairs and Administration
1029 Vermont Avenue, NW, Suite 1100
Washington, DC 20005
Phone: 202-628-8965
Fax: 202-626-4978
E-mail: copra@naspaa.org
Web: www.naspaa.org

PUBLIC HEALTH
Laura Rasar King, M.P.H., CHES, Executive Director
Council on Education for Public Health
800 Eye Street, NW, Suite 202
Washington, DC 20001-3710
Phone: 202-789-1050
Fax: 202-789-1895
E-mail: Lking@ceph.org
Web: www.ceph.org

REHABILITATION EDUCATION
Dr. Tom Evenson, Executive Director
Council on Rehabilitation Education (CORE)
Commission on Standards and Accreditation
1699 Woodfield Road, Suite 300
Schaumburg, Illinois 60173
Phone: 847-944-1345
Fax: 847-944-1324
E-mail: evenson@unt.edu
Web: www.core-rehab.org

SOCIAL WORK
Stephen M. Holloway, Director of Accreditation
Commission on Accreditation
Council on Social Work Education
1701 Duke Street, Suite 200
Alexandria, Virginia 22314
Phone: 703-683-8080
Fax: 703-683-8099
E-mail: sholloway@cswe.org
Web: www.cswe.org

SPEECH-LANGUAGE PATHOLOGY AND AUDIOLOGY
Patrima L. Tice, Director of Credentialing
American Speech-Language-Hearing Association
Council on Academic Accreditation in Audiology and SpeechLanguage
    Pathology
2200 Research Boulevard
Rockville, Maryland 20850-3289
Phone: 301-296-5796
Fax: 301-296-8750
E-mail: ptice@asha.org
Web: www.asha.org/academic/accreditation/default.htm

TECHNOLOGY
Michale S. McComis, Ed.D., Executive Director
Accrediting Commission of Career Schools and Colleges
2101 Wilson Boulevard, Suite 302
Arlington, Virginia 22201
Phone: 703-247-4212
Fax: 703-247-4533
E-mail: mccomis@accsc.org
Web: www.accsc.org

TEACHER EDUCATION
James G. Cibulka, President
National Council for Accreditation of Teacher Education
2010 Massachusetts Avenue, NW, Suite 500
Washington, DC 20036-1023
Phone: 202-466-7496
Fax: 202-296-6620
E-mail: ncate@ncate.org
Web: www.ncate.org

Mark LaCelle-Peterson, President
Teacher Education Accreditation Council (TEAC)
Accreditation Committee
One Dupont Circle, Suite 320
Washington, DC 20036-0110
Phone: 202-831-0400
Fax: 202-831-3013
E-mail: teac@teac.org
Web: www.teac.org

THEATER
Samuel Hope, Executive Director
Karen P. Moynahan, Associate Director
National Association of Schools of Theatre Commission on
    Accreditation
11250 Roger Bacon Drive, Suite 21
Reston, Virginia 20190
Phone: 703-437-0700
Fax: 703-437-6312
E-mail: info@arts-accredit.org
Web: http://nast.arts-accredit.org/

THEOLOGY

Bernard Fryshman, Executive Vice President
Association of Advanced Rabbinical and Talmudic Schools (AARTS)
Accreditation Commission
11 Broadway, Suite 405
New York, New York 10004
Phone: 212-363-1991
Fax: 212-533-5335
E-mail: BFryshman@nyit.edu

Daniel O. Aleshire, Executive Director
Association of Theological Schools in the United States and Canada
　(ATS)
Commission on Accrediting
10 Summit Park Drive
Pittsburgh, Pennsylvania 15275-1110
Phone: 412-788-6505
Fax: 412-788-6510
E-mail: ats@ats.edu
Web: www.ats.edu

Paul Boatner, President
Transnational Association of Christian Colleges and Schools (TRACS)
Accreditation Commission
15935 Forest Road
Forest, Virginia 24551
Phone: 434-525-9539
Fax: 434-525-9538
E-mail: info@tracs.org
Web: www.tracs.org

VETERINARY MEDICINE

Dave Granstrom, Executive Director
Education and Research Division
American Veterinary Medical Association (AVMA)
Council on Education
1931 North Meacham Road, Suite 100
Schaumburg, Illinois 60173
Phone: 847-925-8070 Ext. 6674
Fax: 847-925-9329
E-mail: info@avma.org
Web: www.avma.org

How to Use These Guides

As you identify the particular programs and institutions that interest you, you can use both the *Graduate & Professional Programs: An Overview* volume and the specialized volumes in the series to obtain detailed information.

- *Graduate Programs in the Physical Sciences, Mathematics, Agricultural Sciences, the Environment & Natural Resources*
- *Graduate Programs in Engineering & Applied Sciences*
- *Graduate Programs the Humanities, Arts & Social Sciences*
- *Graduate Programs in the Biological/Biomedical Sciences & Health-Related Professions*
- *Graduate Programs in Business, Education, Information Studies, Law & Social Work*

Each of the specialized volumes in the series is divided into sections that contain one or more directories devoted to programs in a particular field. If you do not find a directory devoted to your field of interest in a specific volume, consult "Directories and Subject Areas" (located at the end of each volume). After you have identified the correct volume, consult the "Directories and Subject Areas in This Book" index, which shows (as does the more general directory) what directories cover subjects not specifically named in a directory or section title.

Each of the specialized volumes in the series has a number of general directories. These directories have entries for the largest unit at an institution granting graduate degrees in that field. For example, the general Engineering and Applied Sciences directory in the *Graduate Programs in Engineering & Applied Sciences* volume consists of **Profiles** for colleges, schools, and departments of engineering and applied sciences.

General directories are followed by other directories, or sections, that give more detailed information about programs in particular areas of the general field that has been covered. The general Engineering and Applied Sciences directory, in the previous example, is followed by nineteen sections with directories in specific areas of engineering, such as Chemical Engineering, Industrial/Management Engineering, and Mechanical Engineering.

Because of the broad nature of many fields, any system of organization is bound to involve a certain amount of overlap. Environmental studies, for example, is a field whose various aspects are studied in several types of departments and schools. Readers interested in such studies will find information on relevant programs in the *Graduate Programs in the Biological/Biomedical Sciences & Health-Related Professions* volume under Ecology and Environmental Biology and Environmental and Occupational Health; in the *Graduate Programs in the Physical Sciences, Mathematics, Agricultural Sciences, the Environment & Natural Resources* volume under Environmental Management and Policy and Natural Resources; and in the *Graduate Programs in Engineering & Applied Sciences* volume under Energy Management and Policy and Environmental Engineering. To help you find all of the programs of interest to you, the introduction to each section within the specialized volumes includes, if applicable, a paragraph suggesting other sections and directories with information on related areas of study.

Directory of Institutions with Programs in the Biological/ Biomedical Sciences & Health-Related Medical Professions

This directory lists institutions in alphabetical order and includes beneath each name the academic fields in which each institution offers graduate programs. The degree level in each field is also indicated, provided that the institution has supplied that information in response to Peterson's Annual Survey of Graduate and Professional Institutions.

An M indicates that a master's degree program is offered; a D indicates that a doctoral degree program is offered; a P indicates that the first professional degree is offered; an O signifies that other advanced degrees (e.g., certificates or specialist degrees) are offered; and an * (asterisk) indicates that a **Close-Up** and/or **Display** is located in this volume. See the index, "Close-Ups and Displays," for the specific page number.

Profiles of Academic and Professional Programs in the Specialized Volumes

Each section of **Profiles** has a table of contents that lists the Program Directories, **Displays**, and **Close-Ups**. Program Directories consist of the **Profiles** of programs in the relevant fields, with **Displays** following if programs have chosen to include them. **Close-Ups,** which are more individualized statements, again if programs have chosen to submit them, are also listed.

The **Profiles** found in the 500 directories in the specialized volumes provide basic data about the graduate units in capsule form for quick reference. To make these directories as useful as possible, **Profiles** are generally listed for an institution's smallest academic unit within a subject area. In other words, if an institution has a College of Liberal Arts that administers many related programs, the **Profile** for the individual program (e.g., Program in History), not the entire College, appears in the directory.

There are some programs that do not fit into any current directory and are not given individual **Profiles**. The directory structure is reviewed annually in order to keep this number to a minimum and to accommodate major trends in graduate education.

The following outline describes the **Profile** information found in the guides and explains how best to use that information. Any item that does not apply to or was not provided by a graduate unit is omitted from its listing. The format of the **Profiles** is constant, making it easy to compare one institution with another and one program with another.

Identifying Information. The institution's name, in boldface type, is followed by a complete listing of the administrative structure for that field of study. (For example, University of Akron, Buchtel College of Arts and Sciences, Department of Theoretical and Applied Mathematics, Program in Mathematics.) The last unit listed is the one to which all information in the **Profile** pertains. The institution's city, state, and zip code follow.

Offerings. Each field of study offered by the unit is listed with all postbaccalaureate degrees awarded. Degrees that are not preceded by a specific concentration are awarded in the general field listed in the unit name. Frequently, fields of study are broken down into subspecializations, and those appear following the degrees awarded; for example, "Offerings in secondary education (M.Ed.), including English education, mathematics education, science education." Students enrolled in the M.Ed. program would be able to specialize in any of the three fields mentioned.

Professional Accreditation. Some **Profiles** indicate whether a program is professionally accredited. Because it is possible for a program to receive or lose professional accreditation at any time, students entering fields in which accreditation is important to a career should verify the status of programs by contacting either the chairperson or the appropriate accrediting association.

Jointly Offered Degrees. Explanatory statements concerning programs that are offered in cooperation with other institutions are included in the list of degrees offered. This occurs most commonly on a regional basis (for example, two state universities offering a cooperative Ph.D. in special education) or where the specialized nature of the institutions encourages joint efforts (a J.D./M.B.A. offered by a law school at an institution with no formal business programs and an institution with a business school but lacking a law school). Only programs that are truly cooperative are listed; those involving only limited course work at

another institution are not. Interested students should contact the heads of such units for further information.

Part-Time and Evening/Weekend Programs. When information regarding the availability of part-time or evening/weekend study appears in the **Profile**, it means that students are able to earn a degree exclusively through such study.

Postbaccalaureate Distance Learning Degrees. A post-baccalaureate distance learning degree program signifies that course requirements can be fulfilled with minimal or no on-campus study.

Faculty. Figures on the number of faculty members actively involved with graduate students through teaching or research are separated into full- and part-time as well as men and women whenever the information has been supplied.

Students. Figures for the number of students enrolled in graduate and professional programs pertain to the semester of highest enrollment from the 2011–12 academic year. These figures are broken down into full- and part-time and men and women whenever the data have been supplied. Information on the number of matriculated students enrolled in the unit who are members of a minority group or are international students appears here. The average age of the matriculated students is followed by the number of applicants, the percentage accepted, and the number enrolled for fall 2011.

Degrees Awarded. The number of degrees awarded in the calendar year is listed. Many doctoral programs offer a terminal master's degree if students leave the program after completing only part of the requirements for a doctoral degree; that is indicated here. All degrees are classified into one of four types: master's, doctoral, first professional, and other advanced degrees. A unit may award one or several degrees at a given level; however, the data are only collected by type and may therefore represent several different degree programs.

Degree Requirements. The information in this section is also broken down by type of degree, and all information for a degree level pertains to all degrees of that type unless otherwise specified. Degree requirements are collected in a simplified form to provide some very basic information on the nature of the program and on foreign language, thesis or dissertation, comprehensive exam, and registration requirements. Many units also provide a short list of additional requirements, such as fieldwork or an internship. For complete information on graduation requirements, contact the graduate school or program directly.

Entrance Requirements. Entrance requirements are broken down into the four degree levels of master's, doctoral, first professional, and other advanced degrees. Within each level, information may be provided in two basic categories: entrance exams and other requirements. The entrance exams are identified by the standard acronyms used by the testing agencies, unless they are not well known. Other entrance requirements are quite varied, but they often contain an undergraduate or graduate grade point average (GPA). Unless otherwise stated, the GPA is calculated on a 4.0 scale and is listed as a minimum required for admission. Additional exam requirements/recommendations for international students may be listed here. Application deadlines for domestic and international students, the application fee, and whether electronic applications are accepted may be listed here. Note that the deadline should be used for reference only; these dates are subject to change, and students interested in applying should always contact the graduate unit directly about application procedures and deadlines.

Expenses. The typical cost of study for the 2011–12 academic year is given in two basic categories: tuition and fees. Cost of study may be quite complex at a graduate institution. There are often sliding scales for part-time study, a different cost for first-year students, and other variables that make it impossible to completely cover the cost of study for each graduate program. To provide the most usable information, figures are given for full-time study for a full year where available and for part-time study in terms of a per-unit rate (per credit, per semester hour, etc.). Occasionally, variances may be noted in tuition and fees for reasons such as the type of program, whether courses are taken during the day or evening, whether courses are at the master's or doctoral level, or other institution-specific reasons. Expenses are usually subject to change; for exact costs at any given time, contact your chosen schools and programs directly. Keep in mind that the tuition of Canadian institutions is usually given in Canadian dollars.

Financial Support. This section contains data on the number of awards administered by the institution and given to graduate students during the 2011–12 academic year. The first figure given represents the total number of students receiving financial support enrolled in that unit. If the unit has provided information on graduate appointments, these are broken down into three major categories: fellowships give money to graduate students to cover the cost of study and living expenses and are not based on a work obligation or research commitment, research assistantships provide stipends to graduate students for assistance in a formal research project with a faculty member, and teaching assistantships provide stipends to graduate students for teaching or for assisting faculty members in teaching undergraduate classes. Within each category, figures are given for the total number of awards, the average yearly amount per award, and whether full or partial tuition reimbursements are awarded. In addition to graduate appointments, the availability of several other financial aid sources is covered in this section. Tuition waivers are routinely part of a graduate appointment, but units sometimes waive part or all of a student's tuition even if a graduate appointment is not available. Federal WorkStudy is made available to students who demonstrate need and meet the federal guidelines; this form of aid normally includes 10 or more hours of work per week in an office of the institution. Institutionally sponsored loans are low-interest loans available to graduate students to cover both educational and living expenses. Career-related internships or fieldwork offer money to students who are participating in a formal off-campus research project or practicum. Grants, scholarships, traineeships, unspecified assistantships, and other awards may also be noted. The availability of financial support to part-time students is also indicated here.

Some programs list the financial aid application deadline and the forms that need to be completed for students to be eligible for financial awards. There are two forms: FAFSA, the Free Application for Federal Student Aid, which is required for federal aid, and the CSS PROFILE®.

Faculty Research. Each unit has the opportunity to list several keyword phrases describing the current research involving faculty members and graduate students. Space limitations prevent the unit from listing complete information on all research programs. The total expenditure for funded research from the previous academic year may also be included.

Unit Head and Application Contact. The head of the graduate program for each unit is listed with academic title and telephone and fax numbers and e-mail address if available. In addition to the unit head, many graduate programs list a separate contact for application and admission information, which follows the listing for the unit head. If no unit head or application contact is given, you should contact the overall institution for information on graduate admissions.

Displays and Close-Ups

The **Displays** and **Close-Ups** are supplementary insertions submitted by deans, chairs, and other administrators who wish to offer an additional, more individualized statement to readers. A number of graduate school and program administrators have attached a **Display** ad near the **Profile** listing. Here you will find information that an institution or program wants to emphasize. The **Close-Ups** are by their very nature more expansive and flexible than the **Profiles**, and the administrators who have written them may emphasize different aspects of their programs. All of the **Close-Ups** are organized in the same way (with the exception of a few that describe research and training opportunities instead of degree programs), and in each one you will find information on the same basic topics, such as programs of study, research facilities, tuition and fees, financial aid, and application procedures. If an institution or program has submitted a **Close-Up**, a boldface cross-reference appears below its **Profile**. As with the **Displays**, all of the **Close-Ups** in the guides have been submitted by choice; the absence of a **Display** or **Close-Up** does not reflect any type of editorial judgment on the part of Peterson's, and their presence in the guides should not be taken as an indication of status, quality, or approval. Statements regarding a university's objectives and accomplishments are a reflection of its own beliefs and are not the opinions of the Peterson's editors.

Appendixes

This section contains two appendixes. The first, "Institutional Changes Since the 2012 Edition," lists institutions that have closed, merged, or changed their name or status since the last edition of the guides. The second, "Abbreviations Used in the Guides," gives abbreviations of degree names, along with what those abbreviations stand for. These appendixes are identical in all six volumes of *Peterson's Graduate and Professional Programs*.

Indexes

There are three indexes presented here. The first index, "Close-Ups and Displays," gives page references for all programs that have chosen to place **Close-Ups** and **Displays** in this volume. It is arranged alphabetically by institution; within institutions, the arrangement is alphabetical by subject area. It is not an index to all programs in the book's directories of **Profiles**; readers must refer to the directories themselves for **Profile** information on programs that have not submitted the additional, more individualized statements. The second index, "Directories and Subject Areas in Other Books in This Series", gives book references for the directories in the specialized volumes and also includes cross-references for subject area names not used in the directory structure, for example, "Computing Technology (see Computer Science)." The third index, "Directories and Subject Areas in This Book," gives page references for the directories in this volume and cross-references for subject area names not used in this volume's directory structure.

Data Collection Procedures

The information published in the directories and **Profiles** of all the books is collected through Peterson's Annual Survey of Graduate and Professional Institutions. The survey is sent each spring to nearly 2,400 institutions offering postbaccalaureate degree programs, including accredited institutions in the United States, U.S. territories, and Canada and those institutions outside the United States that are accredited by U.S. accrediting bodies. Deans and other administrators complete these surveys, providing information on programs in the 500 academic and professional fields covered in the guides as well as overall institutional information. While every effort has been made to ensure the accuracy and completeness of the data, information is sometimes unavailable or changes occur after publication deadlines. All usable information received in time for publication has been included. The omission of any particular item from a directory or **Profile** signifies either that the item is not applicable to the institution or program or that information was not available. **Profiles** of programs scheduled to begin during the 2012–13 academic year cannot, obviously, include statistics on enrollment or, in many cases, the number of faculty members. If no usable data were submitted by an institution, its name, address, and program name appear in order to indicate the availability of graduate work.

Criteria for Inclusion in This Guide

To be included in this guide, an institution must have full accreditation or be a candidate for accreditation (preaccreditation) status by an institutional or specialized accrediting body recognized by the U.S. Department of Education or the Council for Higher Education Accreditation (CHEA). Institutional accrediting bodies, which review each institution as a whole, include the six regional associations of schools and colleges (Middle States, New England, North Central, Northwest, Southern, and Western), each of which is responsible for a specified portion of the United States and its territories. Other institutional accrediting bodies are national in scope and accredit specific kinds of institutions (e.g., Bible colleges, independent colleges, and rabbinical and Talmudic schools). Program registration by the New York State Board of Regents is considered to be the equivalent of institutional accreditation, since the board requires that all programs offered by an institution meet its standards before recognition is granted. A Canadian institution must be chartered and authorized to grant degrees by the provincial government, affiliated with a chartered institution, or accredited by a recognized U.S. accrediting body. This guide also includes institutions outside the United States that are accredited by these U.S. accrediting bodies. There are recognized specialized or professional accrediting bodies in more than fifty different fields, each of which is authorized to accredit institutions or specific programs in its particular field. For specialized institutions that offer programs in one field only, we designate this to be the equivalent of institutional accreditation. A full explanation of the accrediting process and complete information on recognized institutional (regional and national) and specialized accrediting bodies can be found online at www.chea.org or at www.ed.gov/admins/finaid/accred/index.html.

NOTICE: Certain portions of or information contained in this book have been submitted and paid for by the educational institution identified, and such institutions take full responsibility for the accuracy, timeliness, completeness and functionality of such contents. Such portions or information include (i) each display ad that comprises a half page of information covering a single educational institution or program and (ii) each two-page description or Close-Up of a graduate school or program that appear in the different sections of this guide. The "Close-Ups and Displays" are listed in various sections throughout the book.

DIRECTORY OF INSTITUTIONS WITH PROGRAMS IN THE BIOLOGICAL/ BIOMEDICAL SCIENCES & HEALTH-RELATED MEDICAL PROFESSIONS

ABILENE CHRISTIAN UNIVERSITY
Communication Disorders — M
Family Nurse Practitioner Studies — M,O
Nursing and Healthcare Administration — M,O
Nursing Education — M,O
Nursing—General — M,O

ACADEMY FOR FIVE ELEMENT ACUPUNCTURE
Acupuncture and Oriental Medicine — M

ACADEMY OF CHINESE CULTURE AND HEALTH SCIENCES
Acupuncture and Oriental Medicine — M

ACADEMY OF ORIENTAL MEDICINE AT AUSTIN
Acupuncture and Oriental Medicine — M

ACADIA UNIVERSITY
Biological and Biomedical
    Sciences—General — M

ACUPUNCTURE & INTEGRATIVE MEDICINE COLLEGE, BERKELEY
Acupuncture and Oriental Medicine — M

ACUPUNCTURE AND MASSAGE COLLEGE
Acupuncture and Oriental Medicine — M

ADELPHI UNIVERSITY
Biological and Biomedical
    Sciences—General — M*
Communication Disorders — M,D
Community Health — M,O
Nursing—General — M,D,O*
Public Health—General — O

ADLER SCHOOL OF PROFESSIONAL PSYCHOLOGY
Biopsychology — M,D,O

ALABAMA AGRICULTURAL AND MECHANICAL UNIVERSITY
Biological and Biomedical
    Sciences—General — M
Communication Disorders — M

ALABAMA STATE UNIVERSITY
Allied Health—General — D
Biological and Biomedical
    Sciences—General — M,D
Physical Therapy — D

ALASKA PACIFIC UNIVERSITY
Health Services Management and
    Hospital Administration — M

ALBANY COLLEGE OF PHARMACY AND HEALTH SCIENCES
Cell Biology — M
Health Services Research — M
Pharmaceutical Sciences — M,D
Pharmacology — M,D
Pharmacy — M,D*

ALBANY MEDICAL COLLEGE
Allopathic Medicine — D
Bioethics — M,O
Cardiovascular Sciences — M,D
Cell Biology — M,D
Immunology — M,D
Microbiology — M,D
Molecular Biology — M,D
Neuroscience — M,D
Nurse Anesthesia — M
Pharmacology — M,D
Physician Assistant Studies — M

ALBANY STATE UNIVERSITY
Family Nurse Practitioner Studies — M
Health Services Management and
    Hospital Administration — M
Nursing Education — M
Nursing—General — M

ALBERT EINSTEIN COLLEGE OF MEDICINE
Allopathic Medicine — D
Anatomy — D
Biochemistry — D
Biological and Biomedical
    Sciences—General — D
Biophysics — D
Cell Biology — D
Developmental Biology — D
Genetics — D
Genomic Sciences — D
Immunology — D
Microbiology — D
Molecular Biology — D
Molecular Genetics — D
Molecular Pharmacology — D
Neurobiology — D
Pathology — D
Physiology — D

ALCORN STATE UNIVERSITY
Biological and Biomedical
    Sciences—General — M
Nursing—General — M

ALDERSON-BROADDUS COLLEGE
Physician Assistant Studies — M

ALLEN COLLEGE
Acute Care/Critical Care Nursing — M,D,O
Adult Nursing — M,D,O
Family Nurse Practitioner Studies — M,D,O
Gerontological Nursing — M,D,O
Nursing and Healthcare Administration — M,D,O
Nursing—General — M,D,O
Psychiatric Nursing — M,D,O

ALLIANT INTERNATIONAL UNIVERSITY–SAN DIEGO
Neuroscience — M,D,O

ALLIANT INTERNATIONAL UNIVERSITY–SAN FRANCISCO
Pharmacology — M

ALVERNIA UNIVERSITY
Occupational Therapy — M

ALVERNO COLLEGE
Family Nurse Practitioner Studies — M
Nursing Education — M
Nursing—General — M

AMERICAN COLLEGE OF ACUPUNCTURE AND ORIENTAL MEDICINE
Acupuncture and Oriental Medicine — M

AMERICAN COLLEGE OF HEALTHCARE SCIENCES
Allied Health—General — M,O
Nutrition — M,O

AMERICAN COLLEGE OF TRADITIONAL CHINESE MEDICINE
Acupuncture and Oriental Medicine — M,D,O

AMERICAN INTERCONTINENTAL UNIVERSITY ONLINE
Health Services Management and
    Hospital Administration — M

AMERICAN INTERNATIONAL COLLEGE
Nursing and Healthcare Administration — M
Nursing Education — M
Nursing—General — M
Occupational Therapy — M
Physical Therapy — D

AMERICAN PUBLIC UNIVERSITY SYSTEM
Environmental and Occupational
    Health — M
Health Services Management and
    Hospital Administration — M
Public Health—General — M

AMERICAN SENTINEL UNIVERSITY
Health Services Management and
    Hospital Administration — M
Nursing—General — M

AMERICAN UNIVERSITY
Biological and Biomedical
    Sciences—General — M
Biopsychology — M,D,O
Health Promotion — M,O
Neuroscience — M,D,O

THE AMERICAN UNIVERSITY IN DUBAI
Health Services Management and
    Hospital Administration — M

THE AMERICAN UNIVERSITY OF ATHENS
Biological and Biomedical
    Sciences—General — M

AMERICAN UNIVERSITY OF BEIRUT
Adult Nursing — M
Allopathic Medicine — M,D
Anatomy — M,D
Biochemistry — M,D
Biological and Biomedical
    Sciences—General — M,D
Cell Biology — M,D
Community Health Nursing — M
Community Health — M
Environmental and Occupational
    Health — M
Epidemiology — M
Genetics — M,D
Health Promotion — M
Health Services Management and
    Hospital Administration — M
Immunology — M,D
Microbiology — M,D
Neuroscience — M,D
Nursing and Healthcare Administration — M
Nursing—General — M
Nutrition — M
Pharmacology — M,D
Psychiatric Nursing — M
Public Health—General — M
Toxicology — M,D

ANDREWS UNIVERSITY
Allied Health—General — M
Biological and Biomedical
    Sciences—General — M
Nursing—General — M
Nutrition — M
Physical Therapy — D

ANGELO STATE UNIVERSITY
Adult Nursing — M
Biological and Biomedical
    Sciences—General — M
Medical/Surgical Nursing — M
Nursing Education — M
Physical Therapy — D

ANNA MARIA COLLEGE
Environmental and Occupational
    Health — M

ANTIOCH UNIVERSITY NEW ENGLAND
Conservation Biology — M

APPALACHIAN STATE UNIVERSITY
Biological and Biomedical
    Sciences—General — M
Cell Biology — M
Communication Disorders — M
Molecular Biology — M
Nutrition — M
Rehabilitation Sciences — M

AQUINAS COLLEGE
Health Services Management and
    Hospital Administration — M

AQUINAS INSTITUTE OF THEOLOGY
Health Services Management and
    Hospital Administration — M,D,O

ARCADIA UNIVERSITY
Community Health — M
Physical Therapy — D

ARGOSY UNIVERSITY, ATLANTA
Biopsychology — M,D,O
Health Services Management and
    Hospital Administration — M,D
Public Health—General — M

ARGOSY UNIVERSITY, CHICAGO
Health Services Management and
    Hospital Administration — M,D
Neuroscience — D
Public Health—General — M

ARGOSY UNIVERSITY, DALLAS
Health Services Management and
    Hospital Administration — M,D,O
Public Health—General — M

ARGOSY UNIVERSITY, DENVER
Health Services Management and
    Hospital Administration — M,D
Public Health—General — M

ARGOSY UNIVERSITY, HAWAI`I
Health Services Management and
    Hospital Administration — M,D,O
Pharmacology — M,O
Public Health—General — M

ARGOSY UNIVERSITY, INLAND EMPIRE
Health Services Management and
    Hospital Administration — M,D
Public Health—General — M

ARGOSY UNIVERSITY, LOS ANGELES
Health Services Management and
    Hospital Administration — M
Public Health—General — M

ARGOSY UNIVERSITY, NASHVILLE
Health Services Management and
    Hospital Administration — M,D
Public Health—General — M

ARGOSY UNIVERSITY, ORANGE COUNTY
Health Services Management and
    Hospital Administration — M,D,O
Public Health—General — M

ARGOSY UNIVERSITY, PHOENIX
Health Services Management and
    Hospital Administration — M,D
Neuroscience — M,D
Public Health—General — M

ARGOSY UNIVERSITY, SALT LAKE CITY
Health Services Management and
    Hospital Administration — M,D
Public Health—General — M

ARGOSY UNIVERSITY, SAN DIEGO
Public Health—General — M

ARGOSY UNIVERSITY, SAN FRANCISCO BAY AREA
Health Services Management and
    Hospital Administration — M,D
Public Health—General — M

ARGOSY UNIVERSITY, SARASOTA
Health Services Management and
    Hospital Administration — M,D,O
Public Health—General — M

ARGOSY UNIVERSITY, SCHAUMBURG
Health Services Management and
    Hospital Administration — M,D,O
Neuroscience — M,D,O
Public Health—General — M

ARGOSY UNIVERSITY, SEATTLE
Health Services Management and
    Hospital Administration — M,D
Public Health—General — M

ARGOSY UNIVERSITY, TAMPA
Health Services Management and
    Hospital Administration — M,D
Neuroscience — M,D
Public Health—General — M

ARGOSY UNIVERSITY, TWIN CITIES
Biopsychology — M,D,O
Health Services Management and
    Hospital Administration — M,D
Public Health—General — M

ARGOSY UNIVERSITY, WASHINGTON DC
Health Services Management and
    Hospital Administration — M,D,O
Public Health—General — M

ARIZONA SCHOOL OF ACUPUNCTURE AND ORIENTAL MEDICINE
Acupuncture and Oriental Medicine — M

ARIZONA STATE UNIVERSITY
Animal Behavior — M,D
Biochemistry — M,D
Biological and Biomedical
    Sciences—General — M,D
Cell Biology — M,D
Communication Disorders — M,D
Community Health Nursing — M,D,O
Community Health — M,D,O
Computational Biology — M,D
Evolutionary Biology — M,D
Family Nurse Practitioner Studies — M,D,O
International Health — M,D,O
Microbiology — M,D
Molecular Biology — M,D
Neuroscience — M,D

Nursing and Healthcare Administration — M,D,O
Nursing—General — M,D,O
Nutrition — M,D,O
Psychiatric Nursing — M,D,O
Public Health—General — M,D,O

ARKANSAS STATE UNIVERSITY
Biological and Biomedical
    Sciences—General — M,O
Communication Disorders — M
Health Services Management and
    Hospital Administration — M,O
Molecular Biology — D
Nurse Anesthesia — M,O
Nursing—General — M,O
Physical Therapy — D

ARKANSAS TECH UNIVERSITY
Nursing—General — M

ARMSTRONG ATLANTIC STATE UNIVERSITY
Communication Disorders — M
Health Services Management and
    Hospital Administration — M
Nursing—General — M
Physical Therapy — D
Public Health—General — M

ASHWORTH COLLEGE
Health Services Management and
    Hospital Administration — M

ATHABASCA UNIVERSITY
Allied Health—General — M,O
Nursing and Healthcare Administration — M,O
Nursing—General — M

ATLANTIC INSTITUTE OF ORIENTAL MEDICINE
Acupuncture and Oriental Medicine — M

A.T. STILL UNIVERSITY OF HEALTH SCIENCES
Allied Health—General — M,D
Biological and Biomedical
    Sciences—General — M,D
Communication Disorders — M,D
Health Services Management and
    Hospital Administration — M,D
Occupational Therapy — M,D
Oral and Dental Sciences — M,D,O
Osteopathic Medicine — M,D
Physical Therapy — M,D
Physician Assistant Studies — M,D
Public Health—General — M,D

AUBURN UNIVERSITY
Anatomy — M,D
Biochemistry — M,D
Biological and Biomedical
    Sciences—General — M,D
Botany — M,D
Cell Biology — M,D
Communication Disorders — M,D
Entomology — M,D
Health Promotion — M,D,O
Microbiology — M,D
Molecular Biology — M,D
Nursing Education — M
Nursing—General — M
Nutrition — M,D,O
Pathobiology — M,D
Pharmaceutical Sciences — M,D
Pharmacology — M,D
Pharmacy — D
Plant Pathology — M,D
Radiation Biology — M,D
Veterinary Medicine — D
Veterinary Sciences — M,D
Zoology — M,D

AUGSBURG COLLEGE
Community Health Nursing — M
Nursing—General — M
Physician Assistant Studies — M
Transcultural Nursing — M

AURORA UNIVERSITY
Nursing—General — M,D

AUSTIN PEAY STATE UNIVERSITY
Biological and Biomedical
    Sciences—General — M
Clinical Laboratory Sciences/Medical
    Technology — M
Community Health — M
Nursing and Healthcare Administration — M
Nursing Education — M
Nursing Informatics — M
Nursing—General — M
Public Health—General — M
Radiation Biology — M

AVILA UNIVERSITY
Health Services Management and
    Hospital Administration — M

AZUSA PACIFIC UNIVERSITY
Nursing Education — M,D
Nursing—General — M,D
Physical Therapy — D

BAKER COLLEGE CENTER FOR GRADUATE STUDIES - ONLINE
Health Services Management and
    Hospital Administration — M,D

BALDWIN WALLACE UNIVERSITY
Health Services Management and
    Hospital Administration — M

BALL STATE UNIVERSITY
Biological and Biomedical
    Sciences—General — M,D
Communication Disorders — M,D
Health Promotion — M
Nursing—General — M,D
Physiology — M

BANK STREET COLLEGE OF EDUCATION
Maternal and Child Health — M

BARRY UNIVERSITY
Acute Care/Critical Care Nursing — M,O
Anatomy — M
Biological and Biomedical Sciences—General — M
Communication Disorders — M
Family Nurse Practitioner Studies — M,O
Health Services Management and Hospital Administration — M,O
Nurse Anesthesia — M
Nursing and Healthcare Administration — M,D,O
Nursing Education — M,O
Nursing—General — M,D,O
Occupational Therapy — M
Physician Assistant Studies — M
Podiatric Medicine — D
Public Health—General — M

BASTYR UNIVERSITY
Acupuncture and Oriental Medicine — M,D,O
Naturopathic Medicine — D
Nurse Midwifery — M,O
Nutrition — M,O

BAYLOR COLLEGE OF MEDICINE
Allopathic Medicine — D
Biochemistry — D
Biological and Biomedical Sciences—General — M,D
Biophysics — D
Cancer Biology/Oncology — D
Cardiovascular Sciences — D
Cell Biology — D*
Clinical Laboratory Sciences/Medical Technology — M,D
Computational Biology — D
Developmental Biology — D*
Genetics — D
Human Genetics — D
Immunology — D
Microbiology — D
Molecular Biology — D
Molecular Biophysics — D
Molecular Medicine — D
Molecular Physiology — D
Neuroscience — M,D
Nurse Anesthesia — D
Pathology — D
Pharmacology — D
Physician Assistant Studies — M
Structural Biology — D
Translational Biology — D
Virology — D

BAYLOR UNIVERSITY
Allied Health—General — M,D
Biological and Biomedical Sciences—General — M,D
Communication Disorders — M
Ecology — D
Emergency Medical Services — D
Environmental Biology — M,D
Family Nurse Practitioner Studies — M,D
Health Services Management and Hospital Administration — M
Maternal and Child/Neonatal Nursing — M,D
Nurse Midwifery — M,D
Nursing—General — M,D
Nutrition — M,D
Physical Therapy — M,D

BAY PATH COLLEGE
Occupational Therapy — M

BELLARMINE UNIVERSITY
Family Nurse Practitioner Studies — M,D
Nursing and Healthcare Administration — M,D
Nursing Education — M,D
Nursing—General — M,D
Physical Therapy — M,D

BELLEVUE UNIVERSITY
Health Services Management and Hospital Administration — M

BELLIN COLLEGE
Nursing and Healthcare Administration — M
Nursing Education — M
Nursing—General — M

BELMONT UNIVERSITY
Allied Health—General — M,D
Family Nurse Practitioner Studies — M
Nursing—General — M
Occupational Therapy — M,D
Pharmacy — D
Physical Therapy — D

BEMIDJI STATE UNIVERSITY
Biological and Biomedical Sciences—General — M

BENEDICTINE UNIVERSITY
Health Promotion — M
Health Services Management and Hospital Administration — M
Nursing—General — M
Nutrition — M
Public Health—General — M

BENEDICTINE UNIVERSITY AT SPRINGFIELD
Health Services Management and Hospital Administration — M

BENNINGTON COLLEGE
Allied Health—General — O

BERNARD M. BARUCH COLLEGE OF THE CITY UNIVERSITY OF NEW YORK
Health Services Management and Hospital Administration — M

BETHEL COLLEGE
Nursing—General — M

BETHEL UNIVERSITY (MN)
Nursing and Healthcare Administration — M,D,O
Nursing Education — M,D,O
Nursing—General — M,D,O

BETHEL UNIVERSITY (TN)
Physician Assistant Studies — M

BLACK HILLS STATE UNIVERSITY
Genomic Sciences — M

BLESSING-RIEMAN COLLEGE OF NURSING
Nursing—General — M

BLOOMSBURG UNIVERSITY OF PENNSYLVANIA
Adult Nursing — M
Biological and Biomedical Sciences—General — M
Communication Disorders — M,D
Community Health — M
Family Nurse Practitioner Studies — M
Health Physics/Radiological Health — M
Nursing and Healthcare Administration — M
Nursing—General — M

BOISE STATE UNIVERSITY
Biological and Biomedical Sciences—General — M
Public Health—General — M

BOSTON COLLEGE
Adult Nursing — M,D
Biochemistry — D
Biological and Biomedical Sciences—General — D*
Community Health Nursing — M,D
Forensic Nursing — M,D
Gerontological Nursing — M,D
Maternal and Child/Neonatal Nursing — M,D
Medical/Surgical Nursing — M,D
Nurse Anesthesia — M,D
Nursing—General — M,D
Pediatric Nursing — M,D
Psychiatric Nursing — M,D

BOSTON UNIVERSITY
Allied Health—General — M,D,O
Allopathic Medicine — D
Anatomy — M,D
Biochemistry — M,D
Bioethics — M
Biological and Biomedical Sciences—General — M,D
Biophysics — M,D
Biopsychology — M
Cell Biology — M,D
Clinical Research — M
Communication Disorders — M,D,O
Dental Hygiene — M,D,O
Dentistry — M,D,O
Environmental and Occupational Health — M,D
Epidemiology — M,D
Genetics — D
Genomic Sciences — D
Health Promotion — D
Health Services Management and Hospital Administration — M,D
Immunology — D
International Health — M,D
Maternal and Child Health — M,D
Medical Imaging — M
Molecular Biology — M,D
Molecular Medicine — D
Neurobiology — M,D
Neuroscience — M,D
Nutrition — M,D
Occupational Therapy — M,D
Oral and Dental Sciences — M,D,O
Pathology — D
Pharmaceutical Sciences — M,D
Pharmacology — M,D
Physical Therapy — D
Physiology — M,D
Public Health—General — M,D,O
Rehabilitation Sciences — D

BOWIE STATE UNIVERSITY
Family Nurse Practitioner Studies — M
Nursing and Healthcare Administration — M
Nursing Education — M
Nursing—General — M

BOWLING GREEN STATE UNIVERSITY
Biological and Biomedical Sciences—General — M,D
Communication Disorders — M,D
Nutrition — M
Public Health—General — M

BRADLEY UNIVERSITY
Biological and Biomedical Sciences—General — M
Nurse Anesthesia — M
Nursing and Healthcare Administration — M
Nursing—General — M
Physical Therapy — D

BRANDEIS UNIVERSITY
Biochemistry — D
Biological and Biomedical Sciences—General — M,D,O
Biophysics — D
Cell Biology — M,D

Genetics — M,D
Health Services Management and Hospital Administration — M
International Health — M,D
Microbiology — M,D
Molecular Biology — M,D
Neurobiology — M,D
Neuroscience — M,D

BRANDMAN UNIVERSITY
Health Services Management and Hospital Administration — M

BRENAU UNIVERSITY
Family Nurse Practitioner Studies — M
Health Services Management and Hospital Administration — M
Nursing and Healthcare Administration — M
Nursing Education — M
Occupational Therapy — M

BRIAR CLIFF UNIVERSITY
Nursing—General — M

BRIDGEWATER STATE UNIVERSITY
Health Promotion — M

BRIGHAM YOUNG UNIVERSITY
Biochemistry — M,D
Biological and Biomedical Sciences—General — M,D
Communication Disorders — M
Developmental Biology — M,D
Family Nurse Practitioner Studies — M
Health Promotion — M,D
Microbiology — M,D
Molecular Biology — M,D
Neuroscience — M,D
Nursing—General — M*
Nutrition — M
Physiology — M,D

BROADVIEW UNIVERSITY–WEST JORDAN
Health Services Management and Hospital Administration — M

BROCK UNIVERSITY
Allied Health—General — M,D
Biological and Biomedical Sciences—General — M,D
Neuroscience — M,D

BROOKLYN COLLEGE OF THE CITY UNIVERSITY OF NEW YORK
Biological and Biomedical Sciences—General — M,D
Communication Disorders — M,D
Community Health — M
Health Services Management and Hospital Administration — M
Nutrition — M
Public Health—General — M

BROWN UNIVERSITY
Allopathic Medicine — D
Biochemistry — M,D
Biological and Biomedical Sciences—General — M,D
Biopsychology — M,D
Cancer Biology/Oncology — M,D
Cell Biology — M,D
Community Health — M,D
Developmental Biology — M,D
Ecology — D
Epidemiology — M,D
Evolutionary Biology — D
Health Services Research — M,D
Immunology — M,D
Microbiology — M,D
Molecular Biology — M,D
Molecular Pharmacology — M,D
Neuroscience — D
Pathobiology — M,D
Pathology — M,D
Physiology — M,D
Public Health—General — M
Toxicology — M,D

BRYANLGH COLLEGE OF HEALTH SCIENCES
Nurse Anesthesia — M

BUCKNELL UNIVERSITY
Animal Behavior — M
Biological and Biomedical Sciences—General — M

BUFFALO STATE COLLEGE, STATE UNIVERSITY OF NEW YORK
Biological and Biomedical Sciences—General — M
Communication Disorders — M

BUTLER UNIVERSITY
Pharmaceutical Sciences — M,D
Pharmacy — M,D
Physician Assistant Studies — M,D

CALIFORNIA BAPTIST UNIVERSITY
Nursing and Healthcare Administration — M
Nursing Education — M
Nursing—General — M

CALIFORNIA COAST UNIVERSITY
Health Services Management and Hospital Administration — M

CALIFORNIA INSTITUTE OF TECHNOLOGY
Biochemistry — M,D
Biological and Biomedical Sciences—General — D
Biophysics — D
Cell Biology — D

Genetics — M,D
Health Services Management and Hospital Administration — M
International Health — M,D
Microbiology — M,D
Molecular Biology — M,D
Neurobiology — M,D
Neuroscience — M,D
Developmental Biology — D
Genetics — D
Immunology — D
Molecular Biology — D
Molecular Biophysics — M,D
Neurobiology — D
Neuroscience — M,D

CALIFORNIA INTERCONTINENTAL UNIVERSITY
Health Services Management and Hospital Administration — M,D

CALIFORNIA POLYTECHNIC STATE UNIVERSITY, SAN LUIS OBISPO
Biochemistry — M
Biological and Biomedical Sciences—General — M

CALIFORNIA SCHOOL OF PODIATRIC MEDICINE AT SAMUEL MERRITT UNIVERSITY
Podiatric Medicine — D

CALIFORNIA STATE POLYTECHNIC UNIVERSITY, POMONA
Biological and Biomedical Sciences—General — M

CALIFORNIA STATE UNIVERSITY, BAKERSFIELD
Biological and Biomedical Sciences—General — M
Health Services Management and Hospital Administration — M

CALIFORNIA STATE UNIVERSITY, CHICO
Biological and Biomedical Sciences—General — M
Botany — M
Communication Disorders — M
Health Services Management and Hospital Administration — M
Nursing—General — M
Nutrition — M

CALIFORNIA STATE UNIVERSITY, DOMINGUEZ HILLS
Biological and Biomedical Sciences—General — M
Nursing—General — M
Occupational Therapy — M

CALIFORNIA STATE UNIVERSITY, EAST BAY
Biochemistry — M
Biological and Biomedical Sciences—General — M
Communication Disorders — M
Health Services Management and Hospital Administration — M

CALIFORNIA STATE UNIVERSITY, FRESNO
Biological and Biomedical Sciences—General — M
Communication Disorders — M
Family Nurse Practitioner Studies — M
Health Promotion — M
Health Services Management and Hospital Administration — M
Nursing Education — M
Nursing—General — M
Physical Therapy — M,D
Public Health—General — M

CALIFORNIA STATE UNIVERSITY, FULLERTON
Biological and Biomedical Sciences—General — M
Communication Disorders — M
Nursing—General — M
Public Health—General — M

CALIFORNIA STATE UNIVERSITY, LONG BEACH
Biochemistry — M
Biological and Biomedical Sciences—General — M
Communication Disorders — M
Health Services Management and Hospital Administration — M
Microbiology — M
Nursing—General — M
Nutrition — M
Physical Therapy — M

CALIFORNIA STATE UNIVERSITY, LOS ANGELES
Biochemistry — M
Biological and Biomedical Sciences—General — M
Communication Disorders — M
Health Services Management and Hospital Administration — M
Nursing—General — M
Nutrition — M

CALIFORNIA STATE UNIVERSITY, NORTHRIDGE
Biochemistry — M
Biological and Biomedical Sciences—General — M
Communication Disorders — M
Environmental and Occupational Health — M
Health Services Management and Hospital Administration — M
Industrial Hygiene — M
Physical Therapy — M
Public Health—General — M

*M—master's degree; P—first professional degree; D—doctorate; O—other advanced degree; *Close-Up and/or Display*

Peterson's Graduate Programs in the Biological/Biomedical Sciences & Health-Related Medical Professions 2013

CALIFORNIA STATE UNIVERSITY, SACRAMENTO
Biological and Biomedical Sciences—General M
Communication Disorders M
Nursing—General M

CALIFORNIA STATE UNIVERSITY, SAN BERNARDINO
Biological and Biomedical Sciences—General M
Health Services Management and Hospital Administration M
Nursing—General M
Public Health—General M

CALIFORNIA STATE UNIVERSITY, SAN MARCOS
Biological and Biomedical Sciences—General M

CALIFORNIA STATE UNIVERSITY, STANISLAUS
Conservation Biology M
Ecology M
Gerontological Nursing M
Nursing Education M
Nursing—General M

CALIFORNIA UNIVERSITY OF PENNSYLVANIA
Communication Disorders M
Rehabilitation Sciences M

CAMBRIDGE COLLEGE
Health Services Management and Hospital Administration M
School Nursing M,D,O

CAMPBELL UNIVERSITY
Pharmaceutical Sciences M,D
Pharmacy M,D

CANADIAN COLLEGE OF NATUROPATHIC MEDICINE
Naturopathic Medicine D*

CANADIAN MEMORIAL CHIROPRACTIC COLLEGE
Acupuncture and Oriental Medicine O
Chiropractic D,O

CANISIUS COLLEGE
Allied Health—General M
Communication Disorders M,O
Community Health M
Nutrition M
Zoology M

CAPELLA UNIVERSITY
Environmental and Occupational Health M,D
Health Services Management and Hospital Administration M,D,O
Nursing Education M,D

CAPITAL UNIVERSITY
Nursing and Healthcare Administration M
Nursing—General M

CARDINAL STRITCH UNIVERSITY
Nursing—General M

CARIBBEAN UNIVERSITY
Gerontological Nursing M,D
Pediatric Nursing M,D

CARLETON UNIVERSITY
Biological and Biomedical Sciences—General M,D
Neuroscience M,D

CARLOS ALBIZU UNIVERSITY
Communication Disorders M,D

CARLOW UNIVERSITY
Family Nurse Practitioner Studies M,O
Nursing and Healthcare Administration M
Nursing Education M
Nursing—General D

CARNEGIE MELLON UNIVERSITY
Biochemistry M,D
Biological and Biomedical Sciences—General M,D
Biophysics M,D
Biopsychology D
Cell Biology M,D
Computational Biology M,D
Developmental Biology M,D
Genetics M,D
Health Services Management and Hospital Administration M
Molecular Biology M,D
Molecular Biophysics D
Neurobiology M,D
Neuroscience D
Structural Biology D

CARROLL UNIVERSITY
Physical Therapy M,D
Physician Assistant Studies M

CARSON-NEWMAN COLLEGE
Family Nurse Practitioner Studies M
Nursing Education M
Nursing—General M

CASE WESTERN RESERVE UNIVERSITY
Acute Care/Critical Care Nursing M,D
Allopathic Medicine D
Anatomy M
Anesthesiologist Assistant Studies M
Biochemistry M,D
Bioethics M
Biological and Biomedical Sciences—General M,D
Biophysics M,D
Cancer Biology/Oncology D
Cell Biology M,D
Clinical Research M
Communication Disorders M,D
Dentistry D
Epidemiology M,D
Family Nurse Practitioner Studies M,D
Genetics D
Genomic Sciences D
Gerontological Nursing M,D
Health Services Research M,D
Human Genetics D
Immunology M,D
Maternal and Child/Neonatal Nursing M,D
Microbiology D
Molecular Biology D
Molecular Medicine D
Molecular Physiology M,D
Neurobiology D
Neuroscience D
Nurse Anesthesia M
Nurse Midwifery M,D
Nursing and Healthcare Administration D
Nursing Education D
Nursing—General M,D
Nutrition M,D*
Oral and Dental Sciences M,O
Pathology M,D
Pediatric Nursing M,D
Pharmacology D
Physiology M,D*
Psychiatric Nursing D
Public Health—General M
Virology D
Women's Health Nursing M,D

THE CATHOLIC UNIVERSITY OF AMERICA
Biological and Biomedical Sciences—General M,D
Cell Biology M,D
Clinical Laboratory Sciences/Medical Technology M,D
Microbiology M,D
Nursing—General M,D,O

CEDAR CREST COLLEGE
Nursing and Healthcare Administration M
Nursing Education M
Nursing—General M

CEDARS-SINAI MEDICAL CENTER
Biological and Biomedical Sciences—General D
Translational Biology D

CEDARVILLE UNIVERSITY
Family Nurse Practitioner Studies M
Nursing Education M
Nursing—General M

CENTRAL CONNECTICUT STATE UNIVERSITY
Biochemistry M,O
Biological and Biomedical Sciences—General M,O
Molecular Biology M,O
Nurse Anesthesia M,O

CENTRAL METHODIST UNIVERSITY
Nursing and Healthcare Administration M
Nursing—General M

CENTRAL MICHIGAN UNIVERSITY
Biological and Biomedical Sciences—General M
Communication Disorders M,D
Conservation Biology M
Health Services Management and Hospital Administration M,D,O
International Health M,D,O
Neuroscience M,D
Nutrition M,D,O
Physical Therapy M,D
Physician Assistant Studies M,D
Rehabilitation Sciences M,D

CENTRAL WASHINGTON UNIVERSITY
Biological and Biomedical Sciences—General M
Nutrition M

CHAMPLAIN COLLEGE
Health Services Management and Hospital Administration M

CHAPMAN UNIVERSITY
Communication Disorders M,D,O
Nutrition M
Physical Therapy D

CHARLES DREW UNIVERSITY OF MEDICINE AND SCIENCE
Allopathic Medicine D
Public Health—General M

CHARLESTON SOUTHERN UNIVERSITY
Health Services Management and Hospital Administration M

CHATHAM UNIVERSITY
Biological and Biomedical Sciences—General M
Environmental Biology M
Nursing and Healthcare Administration M,D
Nursing Education M,D
Nursing—General M,D
Occupational Therapy M,D
Physical Therapy D
Physician Assistant Studies M

CHICAGO STATE UNIVERSITY
Biological and Biomedical Sciences—General M

CHRISTIAN BROTHERS UNIVERSITY
Physician Assistant Studies M

THE CITADEL, THE MILITARY COLLEGE OF SOUTH CAROLINA
Biological and Biomedical Sciences—General M

CITY COLLEGE OF THE CITY UNIVERSITY OF NEW YORK
Biochemistry M,D
Biological and Biomedical Sciences—General M,D

CITY OF HOPE NATIONAL MEDICAL CENTER/BECKMAN RESEARCH INSTITUTE
Biological and Biomedical Sciences—General D*

CLAREMONT GRADUATE UNIVERSITY
Botany M,D
Computational Biology M,D
Health Promotion M,D
Public Health—General M,D

CLARION UNIVERSITY OF PENNSYLVANIA
Communication Disorders M
Family Nurse Practitioner Studies M,O
Nursing Education M,O
Nursing—General M,O
Rehabilitation Sciences M

CLARK ATLANTA UNIVERSITY
Biological and Biomedical Sciences—General M,D

CLARKE UNIVERSITY
Family Nurse Practitioner Studies M,O
Nursing and Healthcare Administration M,O
Nursing Education M,O
Nursing—General M,O
Physical Therapy D

CLARKSON COLLEGE
Adult Nursing M,O
Family Nurse Practitioner Studies M,O
Nursing and Healthcare Administration M,O
Nursing Education M,O
Nursing—General M,O

CLARKSON UNIVERSITY
Health Services Research M
Physical Therapy D
Physician Assistant Studies M

CLARK UNIVERSITY
Biological and Biomedical Sciences—General M,D
Health Services Management and Hospital Administration M

CLAYTON STATE UNIVERSITY
Health Services Management and Hospital Administration M
Nursing—General M

CLEMSON UNIVERSITY
Biochemistry D
Biological and Biomedical Sciences—General M,D
Biophysics M,D
Community Health M
Ecology M,D
Entomology M,D
Environmental and Occupational Health M
Evolutionary Biology M,D
Genetics M,D
Microbiology M,D
Molecular Biology D
Nursing—General M,D
Nutrition M
Plant Biology M,D
Veterinary Sciences M,D

CLEVELAND CHIROPRACTIC COLLEGE–KANSAS CITY CAMPUS
Chiropractic D
Health Promotion M

CLEVELAND STATE UNIVERSITY
Allied Health—General M
Bioethics M,O
Biological and Biomedical Sciences—General M,D
Communication Disorders M
Community Health Nursing M,D
Forensic Nursing M,D
Health Services Management and Hospital Administration M,O
Medical Imaging M
Medical Physics M
Medicinal and Pharmaceutical Chemistry M,D
Molecular Medicine M,D
Nursing Education M,D
Nursing—General M,D
Occupational Therapy M
Physical Therapy D
Physician Assistant Studies M,D
Public Health—General M

COLD SPRING HARBOR LABORATORY, WATSON SCHOOL OF BIOLOGICAL SCIENCES
Biological and Biomedical Sciences—General D*

THE COLLEGE AT BROCKPORT, STATE UNIVERSITY OF NEW YORK
Biological and Biomedical Sciences—General M
Community Health M
Health Services Management and Hospital Administration M,O

COLLEGE OF CHARLESTON
Marine Biology M

COLLEGE OF MOUNT ST. JOSEPH
Nursing and Healthcare Administration M,D
Nursing Education M
Nursing—General M,D
Physical Therapy D

COLLEGE OF MOUNT SAINT VINCENT
Adult Nursing M,O
Family Nurse Practitioner Studies M,O
Gerontological Nursing M,O
Nursing and Healthcare Administration M,O
Nursing Education M,O
Nursing—General M,O

THE COLLEGE OF NEW JERSEY
Nursing—General M,O

THE COLLEGE OF NEW ROCHELLE
Acute Care/Critical Care Nursing M,O
Family Nurse Practitioner Studies M,O
Nursing and Healthcare Administration M,O
Nursing Education M,O
Nursing—General M,O

COLLEGE OF SAINT ELIZABETH
Health Services Management and Hospital Administration M
Nursing—General M
Nutrition M,O

COLLEGE OF SAINT MARY
Nursing—General M
Occupational Therapy M

THE COLLEGE OF SAINT ROSE
Communication Disorders M

THE COLLEGE OF ST. SCHOLASTICA
Nursing—General M,O
Occupational Therapy M
Physical Therapy D

COLLEGE OF STATEN ISLAND OF THE CITY UNIVERSITY OF NEW YORK
Adult Nursing M,O
Biological and Biomedical Sciences—General M
Gerontological Nursing M,O
Neuroscience M
Nursing Education O
Nursing—General M,O

THE COLLEGE OF WILLIAM AND MARY
Biological and Biomedical Sciences—General M

COLORADO SCHOOL OF TRADITIONAL CHINESE MEDICINE
Acupuncture and Oriental Medicine M

COLORADO STATE UNIVERSITY
Biochemistry M,D
Biological and Biomedical Sciences—General M,D
Botany M,D
Cell Biology M,D
Conservation Biology M,D
Ecology M,D
Entomology M,D
Environmental and Occupational Health M,D
Immunology M,D
Microbiology M,D
Molecular Biology M,D
Neuroscience D
Nutrition M,D
Occupational Therapy M
Pathology M,D
Plant Pathology M,D
Radiation Biology M,D
Veterinary Medicine D
Veterinary Sciences M,D
Zoology M,D

COLORADO STATE UNIVERSITY–PUEBLO
Biochemistry M
Biological and Biomedical Sciences—General M
Nursing—General M

COLORADO TECHNICAL UNIVERSITY SIOUX FALLS
Health Services Management and Hospital Administration M

COLUMBIA SOUTHERN UNIVERSITY
Environmental and Occupational Health M
Health Services Management and Hospital Administration M

COLUMBIA UNIVERSITY
Acute Care/Critical Care Nursing M,O
Adult Nursing M,O
Allopathic Medicine M,D
Anatomy M,D
Biochemistry M,D
Bioethics M
Biological and Biomedical Sciences—General M,D,O*
Biophysics M,D
Biopsychology M,D
Cell Biology M,D
Community Health M,D
Conservation Biology M,D,O
Dentistry D
Developmental Biology M,D
Ecology M,D,O
Environmental and Occupational Health M,D
Epidemiology M,D
Evolutionary Biology M,D,O
Family Nurse Practitioner Studies M,O
Genetics M,D
Gerontological Nursing M,O
Health Services Management and Hospital Administration M
Maternal and Child Health M

Maternal and Child/Neonatal Nursing M,O
Medical Physics M,D,O
Medical/Surgical Nursing M,O
Microbiology M,D
Molecular Biology D
Neurobiology D
Nurse Anesthesia M,O
Nurse Midwifery M
Nursing—General M,D,O
Nutrition M,D
Occupational Therapy M,D
Oncology Nursing M,O
Oral and Dental Sciences M,D,O
Pathobiology M,D
Pathology M,D
Pediatric Nursing M,O
Pharmaceutical Administration M
Pharmacology M,D
Physical Therapy D
Physiology M,D
Psychiatric Nursing M,O
Public Health—General M,D
Structural Biology D
Toxicology M,D
Women's Health Nursing O

CONCORDIA UNIVERSITY (CANADA)
Biological and Biomedical
 Sciences—General M,D,O
Genomic Sciences M,D,O
Health Services Management and
 Hospital Administration M,D,O

CONCORDIA UNIVERSITY, ST. PAUL
Health Services Management and
 Hospital Administration M

CONCORDIA UNIVERSITY WISCONSIN
Family Nurse Practitioner Studies M
Gerontological Nursing M
Health Services Management and
 Hospital Administration M
Nursing Education M
Nursing—General M
Occupational Therapy M
Physical Therapy M,D
Rehabilitation Sciences M

CONCORD UNIVERSITY
Health Promotion M

COPENHAGEN BUSINESS SCHOOL
Health Services Management and
 Hospital Administration M,D

COPPIN STATE UNIVERSITY
Family Nurse Practitioner Studies M,O
Nursing—General M,O

CORNELL UNIVERSITY
Anatomy M,D
Animal Behavior D
Biochemistry D
Biological and Biomedical
 Sciences—General M,D
Biophysics D
Biopsychology D
Cell Biology M,D
Computational Biology D
Developmental Biology M,D
Ecology M,D
Entomology M,D
Epidemiology M,D
Evolutionary Biology D
Genetics D
Health Services Management and
 Hospital Administration M,D
Immunology M,D
Infectious Diseases M,D
Microbiology D
Molecular Biology D
Molecular Medicine M,D
Neurobiology D
Nutrition M,D
Pharmacology M,D
Physiology M,D
Plant Biology M,D
Plant Molecular Biology M,D
Plant Pathology M,D
Plant Physiology M,D
Reproductive Biology M,D
Structural Biology M,D
Toxicology M,D
Veterinary Medicine D
Zoology M,D

COX COLLEGE
Family Nurse Practitioner Studies M
Nursing and Healthcare Administration M
Nursing Education M
Nursing—General M

CREIGHTON UNIVERSITY
Allied Health—General M,D
Allopathic Medicine D
Anatomy M
Biological and Biomedical
 Sciences—General M,D
Dentistry D
Immunology M,D
Medical Microbiology M,D
Nursing—General M,D
Occupational Therapy D
Pharmaceutical Sciences M,D
Pharmacology M,D
Pharmacy D
Physical Therapy D

CURRY COLLEGE
Nursing—General M

DAEMEN COLLEGE
Adult Nursing M,D,O

Health Services Management and
 Hospital Administration M
Medical/Surgical Nursing M,D,O
Nursing and Healthcare Administration M,D,O
Nursing Education M,D,O
Nursing—General M,D,O
Physical Therapy D,O
Physician Assistant Studies M

DALHOUSIE UNIVERSITY
Allopathic Medicine M,D
Anatomy M,D
Biochemistry M,D
Biological and Biomedical
 Sciences—General M,D
Biophysics M,D
Communication Disorders M,D
Community Health M
Epidemiology M
Health Services Management and
 Hospital Administration M,D
Immunology M,D
Microbiology M,D
Neurobiology M,D
Neuroscience M,D
Nursing—General M,D
Occupational Therapy M
Oral and Dental Sciences
Pathology M,D
Pharmacology M,D
Physical Therapy M
Physiology M,D

DALLAS BAPTIST UNIVERSITY
Health Services Management and
 Hospital Administration M

DARTMOUTH COLLEGE
Allopathic Medicine D
Biochemistry D
Biological and Biomedical
 Sciences—General D
Cancer Biology/Oncology D
Cardiovascular Sciences D
Cell Biology D
Ecology D
Evolutionary Biology D
Genetics D
Health Services Management and
 Hospital Administration M,D
Health Services Research M,D
Immunology D
Microbiology D
Molecular Biology D
Molecular Medicine D
Molecular Pathogenesis D
Molecular Pharmacology D
Neuroscience D
Pharmaceutical Sciences D
Pharmacology D
Physiology D
Public Health—General M
Systems Biology D
Toxicology D

DAVENPORT UNIVERSITY
Health Services Management and
 Hospital Administration M
Public Health—General M

DAVENPORT UNIVERSITY
Health Services Management and
 Hospital Administration M
Public Health—General M

DAVENPORT UNIVERSITY
Health Services Management and
 Hospital Administration M
Public Health—General M

DEFIANCE COLLEGE
Health Services Management and
 Hospital Administration M

DELAWARE STATE UNIVERSITY
Biological and Biomedical
 Sciences—General M
Neuroscience M,D
Nursing—General M

DELTA STATE UNIVERSITY
Biological and Biomedical
 Sciences—General M
Family Nurse Practitioner Studies M
Health Services Management and
 Hospital Administration M
Nursing Education M
Nursing—General M

DEPAUL UNIVERSITY
Adult Nursing M,O
Biochemistry M
Biological and Biomedical
 Sciences—General M
Community Health M
Family Nurse Practitioner Studies M,O
Health Services Management and
 Hospital Administration M,O
Nurse Anesthesia M,O
Nursing—General M,O
Public Health—General M

DESALES UNIVERSITY
Adult Nursing M,D,O
Family Nurse Practitioner Studies M,D,O
Health Services Management and
 Hospital Administration M
Nurse Midwifery M
Nursing and Healthcare Administration M,D,O
Nursing Education M,D,O
Nursing—General M,D,O
Physician Assistant Studies M

DES MOINES UNIVERSITY
Anatomy M

Biological and Biomedical
 Sciences—General M
Health Services Management and
 Hospital Administration M
Osteopathic Medicine D
Physical Therapy D
Physician Assistant Studies M
Podiatric Medicine D
Public Health—General M

DOMINICAN COLLEGE
Allied Health—General M,D
Family Nurse Practitioner Studies M
Nursing—General M
Occupational Therapy M
Physical Therapy M,D

DOMINICAN UNIVERSITY OF CALIFORNIA
Biological and Biomedical
 Sciences—General M
Nursing and Healthcare Administration M
Nursing—General M
Occupational Therapy M

DONGGUK UNIVERSITY LOS ANGELES
Acupuncture and Oriental Medicine M

DOWLING COLLEGE
Health Services Management and
 Hospital Administration M,O

DRAKE UNIVERSITY
Pharmacy D

DREW UNIVERSITY
Bioethics M,D,O
Biological and Biomedical
 Sciences—General M

DREXEL UNIVERSITY
Acute Care/Critical Care Nursing M
Allied Health—General M,D,O
Allopathic Medicine D
Biochemistry M,D
Biological and Biomedical
 Sciences—General M,D,O
Biopsychology M,D
Cell Biology M,D
Emergency Medical Services M
Epidemiology M,D,O
Family Nurse Practitioner Studies M
Genetics M,D
Immunology M,D
Microbiology M,D
Molecular Biology M,D
Molecular Medicine M
Neuroscience M,D
Nurse Anesthesia M
Nursing and Healthcare Administration M
Nursing Education M
Nursing—General M,D
Nutrition M
Pathobiology M,D
Pediatric Nursing M
Pharmaceutical Sciences M
Pharmacology M,D
Physical Therapy M,D,O
Physician Assistant Studies M
Psychiatric Nursing M
Public Health—General M,D,O
Veterinary Sciences M
Women's Health Nursing M

DUKE UNIVERSITY
Acute Care/Critical Care Nursing M,D,O
Adult Nursing M,D,O
Allopathic Medicine D
Anatomy D
Biochemistry D
Biological and Biomedical
 Sciences—General D
Biopsychology D
Cancer Biology/Oncology D
Cell Biology D,O
Clinical Laboratory Sciences/Medical
 Technology M
Clinical Research M
Developmental Biology O
Ecology M,D,O
Environmental and Occupational
 Health M,D,O
Family Nurse Practitioner Studies M,D,O
Genetics D
Gerontological Nursing M,D,O
Immunology D
International Health M
Maternal and Child/Neonatal Nursing M,D,O
Microbiology D
Molecular Biology D,O
Molecular Biophysics O
Molecular Genetics D
Neurobiology D
Neuroscience D,O
Nurse Anesthesia M,D,O
Nursing and Healthcare Administration M,D,O
Nursing Education M,D,O
Nursing Informatics M,D,O
Nursing—General D
Oncology Nursing M,D,O
Pathology M,D
Pediatric Nursing M,D,O
Pharmacology D
Physical Therapy D
Physician Assistant Studies M
Structural Biology O
Toxicology D,O

DUQUESNE UNIVERSITY
Allied Health—General M,D
Biochemistry M,D
Bioethics M,D,O
Biological and Biomedical
 Sciences—General M,D

Communication Disorders M,D
Community Health M
Family Nurse Practitioner Studies M,O
Forensic Nursing M,O
Health Services Management and
 Hospital Administration M,D
Medicinal and Pharmaceutical
 Chemistry M,D
Nursing Education M,O
Nursing—General M,D,O
Occupational Therapy M
Pharmaceutical Administration M
Pharmaceutical Sciences M,D
Pharmacology M,D
Pharmacy D
Physical Therapy M,D
Physician Assistant Studies M,D
Rehabilitation Sciences M,D

D'YOUVILLE COLLEGE
Chiropractic D
Community Health Nursing M,O
Family Nurse Practitioner Studies M,O
Health Services Management and
 Hospital Administration M,D,O
Nursing and Healthcare Administration M,O
Nursing Education M,O
Nursing—General M,O*
Nutrition M
Occupational Therapy M
Pharmacy D
Physical Therapy M,D,O
Physician Assistant Studies M

EAST CAROLINA UNIVERSITY
Allied Health—General M,D,O
Allopathic Medicine D
Anatomy D
Biochemistry M,D
Biological and Biomedical
 Sciences—General M,D
Biophysics M,D
Cell Biology D
Communication Disorders M,D,O
Community Health M,O
Environmental and Occupational
 Health M,D
Health Physics/Radiological Health M,D
Immunology M,D
Maternal and Child Health D
Medical Physics M,D
Microbiology M,D
Molecular Biology M,D
Nursing—General M,D
Nutrition M
Occupational Therapy M,D,O
Pathology D
Pharmacology D
Physical Therapy D
Physician Assistant Studies M
Physiology D
Public Health—General M
Rehabilitation Sciences M,D,O

EASTERN ILLINOIS UNIVERSITY
Biological and Biomedical
 Sciences—General M
Communication Disorders M
Nutrition M

EASTERN KENTUCKY UNIVERSITY
Allied Health—General M
Biological and Biomedical
 Sciences—General M
Communication Disorders M
Community Health M
Ecology M
Environmental and Occupational
 Health M
Family Nurse Practitioner Studies M
Health Promotion M
Health Services Management and
 Hospital Administration M
Nursing—General M
Nutrition M
Occupational Therapy M

EASTERN MENNONITE UNIVERSITY
Biological and Biomedical
 Sciences—General M
Nursing and Healthcare Administration M
Nursing—General M
School Nursing M

EASTERN MICHIGAN UNIVERSITY
Adult Nursing M,O
Biological and Biomedical
 Sciences—General M
Cell Biology M
Clinical Research M,O
Communication Disorders M
Ecology M
Health Promotion M,O
Health Services Management and
 Hospital Administration M,O
Molecular Biology M
Nursing and Healthcare Administration M,O
Nursing Education M
Nutrition M
Occupational Therapy M
Physiology M

EASTERN NEW MEXICO UNIVERSITY
Biochemistry M
Biological and Biomedical
 Sciences—General M
Cell Biology M
Communication Disorders M
Ecology M
Microbiology M
Molecular Biology M
Plant Biology M
Zoology M

---

*M—master's degree; P—first professional degree; D—doctorate; O—other advanced degree; *Close-Up and/or Display*

EASTERN UNIVERSITY
Health Services Management and
  Hospital Administration — M
School Nursing — M,O

EASTERN VIRGINIA MEDICAL SCHOOL
Allopathic Medicine — D
Biological and Biomedical
  Sciences—General — M,D
Medical/Surgical Nursing — O
Physician Assistant Studies — M
Public Health—General — M
Reproductive Biology — M
Vision Sciences — O

EASTERN WASHINGTON UNIVERSITY
Biological and Biomedical
  Sciences—General — M
Communication Disorders — M
Dental Hygiene — M
Occupational Therapy — M
Physical Therapy — D

EAST STROUDSBURG UNIVERSITY OF PENNSYLVANIA
Biological and Biomedical
  Sciences—General — M
Communication Disorders — M
Community Health — M
Public Health—General — M
Rehabilitation Sciences — M

EAST TENNESSEE STATE UNIVERSITY
Adult Nursing — M,D
Allied Health—General — M,D,O
Allopathic Medicine — D
Anatomy — D
Biochemistry — D
Biological and Biomedical
  Sciences—General — M,D
Cell Biology — D
Communication Disorders — M,D
Community Health — M,D
Environmental and Occupational
  Health — M,D
Epidemiology — M,D,O
Family Nurse Practitioner Studies — D,O
Gerontological Nursing — D
Health Services Management and
  Hospital Administration — M,O
Microbiology — M,D
Molecular Biology — M
Nursing and Healthcare Administration — M,D,O
Nursing Education — M
Nursing Informatics — M
Nursing—General — M,D
Nutrition — M
Pharmaceutical Sciences — D
Pharmacology — D
Pharmacy — D
Physical Therapy — D
Physiology — D
Psychiatric Nursing — D
Public Health—General — D

EAST WEST COLLEGE OF NATURAL MEDICINE
Acupuncture and Oriental Medicine — M

EDGEWOOD COLLEGE
Nursing—General — M

EDINBORO UNIVERSITY OF PENNSYLVANIA
Biological and Biomedical
  Sciences—General — M
Communication Disorders — M
Nursing Education — M,O
Nursing—General — M,O

EDWARD VIA COLLEGE OF OSTEOPAHTIC MEDICINE–VIRGINIA CAMPUS
Osteopathic Medicine — D

EDWARD VIA COLLEGE OF OSTEOPATHIC MEDICINE–CAROLINAS CAMPUS
Osteopathic Medicine — D

ELIZABETH CITY STATE UNIVERSITY
Biological and Biomedical
  Sciences—General — M

ELIZABETHTOWN COLLEGE
Occupational Therapy — M

ELLIS UNIVERSITY
Health Services Management and
  Hospital Administration — M

ELMHURST COLLEGE
Nursing—General — M

ELMS COLLEGE
Communication Disorders — M,O
Nursing and Healthcare Administration — M
Nursing Education — M
Nursing—General — M

ELON UNIVERSITY
Physical Therapy — D

EMERSON COLLEGE
Communication Disorders — M

EMMANUEL COLLEGE (UNITED STATES)
Nursing and Healthcare Administration — M
Nursing Education — M
Nursing—General — M
Pharmaceutical Administration — M,O

EMORY UNIVERSITY
Adult Nursing — M
Allied Health—General — M,D
Allopathic Medicine — D
Anesthesiologist Assistant Studies — M
Animal Behavior — D
Biochemistry — D

Bioethics — M
Biological and Biomedical
  Sciences—General — D
Biophysics — D
Cancer Biology/Oncology — D
Cell Biology — D
Clinical Research — M
Developmental Biology — D
Ecology — D
Environmental and Occupational
  Health — M,D
Epidemiology — M,D
Evolutionary Biology — D
Family Nurse Practitioner Studies — M
Genetics — D
Health Promotion — M
Health Services Management and
  Hospital Administration — M,D
Health Services Research — M,D
Human Genetics — D
Immunology — D
International Health — M
Microbiology — D
Molecular Biology — D
Molecular Genetics — D
Molecular Pathogenesis — D
Neuroscience — D
Nurse Midwifery — M
Nursing and Healthcare Administration — M
Nursing—General — M
Nutrition — M,D
Pediatric Nursing — M
Pharmacology — D
Physical Therapy — M
Physician Assistant Studies — M
Public Health—General — M,D
Women's Health Nursing — M

EMPEROR'S COLLEGE OF TRADITIONAL ORIENTAL MEDICINE
Acupuncture and Oriental Medicine — M,D

EMPORIA STATE UNIVERSITY
Biological and Biomedical
  Sciences—General — M
Botany — M
Cell Biology — M
Environmental Biology — M
Microbiology — M
Zoology — M

ENDICOTT COLLEGE
Nursing—General — M

EXCELSIOR COLLEGE
Nursing Education — M
Nursing Informatics — M
Nursing—General — M

FAIRFIELD UNIVERSITY
Family Nurse Practitioner Studies — M,D
Nurse Anesthesia — M,D
Nursing and Healthcare Administration — M,D
Nursing—General — M,D
Psychiatric Nursing — M,D

FAIRLEIGH DICKINSON UNIVERSITY, COLLEGE AT FLORHAM
Biological and Biomedical
  Sciences—General — M
Health Services Management and
  Hospital Administration — M
Pharmacology — M,O

FAIRLEIGH DICKINSON UNIVERSITY, METROPOLITAN CAMPUS
Biological and Biomedical
  Sciences—General — M
Clinical Laboratory Sciences/Medical
  Technology — M
Health Services Management and
  Hospital Administration — M
Nursing—General — M,D,O
Pharmaceutical Administration — M,O

FAIRMONT STATE UNIVERSITY
Health Promotion — M

FAYETTEVILLE STATE UNIVERSITY
Biological and Biomedical
  Sciences—General — M

FELICIAN COLLEGE
Adult Nursing — M,O
Family Nurse Practitioner Studies — M,O
Health Services Management and
  Hospital Administration — M
Nursing Education — M,O
Nursing—General — M,D,O*
School Nursing — M,O

FERRIS STATE UNIVERSITY
Allied Health—General — M
Nursing and Healthcare Administration — M
Nursing Education — M
Nursing Informatics — M
Nursing—General — M
Optometry — D
Pharmacy — D

FIELDING GRADUATE UNIVERSITY
Neuroscience — M,D,O

FISK UNIVERSITY
Biological and Biomedical
  Sciences—General — M

FITCHBURG STATE UNIVERSITY
Biological and Biomedical
  Sciences—General — M,O
Forensic Nursing — M,O

FIVE BRANCHES UNIVERSITY: GRADUATE SCHOOL OF TRADITIONAL CHINESE MEDICINE
Acupuncture and Oriental Medicine — M

FLORIDA AGRICULTURAL AND MECHANICAL UNIVERSITY
Allied Health—General — M
Biological and Biomedical
  Sciences—General — M
Medicinal and Pharmaceutical
  Chemistry — M,D
Nursing and Healthcare Administration — M
Nursing—General — M
Occupational Therapy — M
Pharmaceutical Administration — M,D
Pharmaceutical Sciences — M,D
Pharmacology — M,D
Pharmacy — D
Physical Therapy — M
Public Health—General — M
Toxicology — M,D

FLORIDA ATLANTIC UNIVERSITY
Allopathic Medicine — M
Biological and Biomedical
  Sciences—General — M,D
Communication Disorders — M
Health Promotion — M
Neuroscience — D
Nursing—General — M,D,O

FLORIDA COLLEGE OF INTEGRATIVE MEDICINE
Acupuncture and Oriental Medicine — M

FLORIDA GULF COAST UNIVERSITY
Allied Health—General — M,D
Nurse Anesthesia — M
Occupational Therapy — M
Physical Therapy — M

FLORIDA HOSPITAL COLLEGE OF HEALTH SCIENCES
Nurse Anesthesia — M

FLORIDA INSTITUTE OF TECHNOLOGY
Biochemistry — M,D
Biological and Biomedical
  Sciences—General — M,D
Cell Biology — M
Conservation Biology — M,D
Ecology — M
Health Services Management and
  Hospital Administration — M
Marine Biology — M
Molecular Biology — M

FLORIDA INTERNATIONAL UNIVERSITY
Allopathic Medicine — D
Biological and Biomedical
  Sciences—General — M,D
Communication Disorders — M
Environmental and Occupational
  Health — M,D
Epidemiology — M,D
Health Promotion — M,D
Health Services Management and
  Hospital Administration — M,D
Nursing—General — M,D
Nutrition — M,D
Occupational Therapy — M
Physical Therapy — D
Public Health—General — M,D

FLORIDA SOUTHERN COLLEGE
Adult Nursing — M
Family Nurse Practitioner Studies — M
Nursing Education — M
Nursing—General — M

FLORIDA STATE UNIVERSITY
Biochemistry — M,D
Biological and Biomedical
  Sciences—General — M,D
Cell Biology — M,D
Communication Disorders — M,D
Computational Biology — D
Ecology — M,D
Evolutionary Biology — M,D
Family Nurse Practitioner Studies — M,D,O
Genetics — M,D
Health Services Management and
  Hospital Administration — M,D,O
Molecular Biology — M,D
Molecular Biophysics — D
Neuroscience — D
Nursing and Healthcare Administration — M,D,O
Nursing Education — M,D,O
Nursing—General — M,D,O
Nutrition — M,D
Plant Biology — M,D
Public Health—General — M
Structural Biology — M,D

FONTBONNE UNIVERSITY
Communication Disorders — M

FORDHAM UNIVERSITY
Biological and Biomedical
  Sciences—General — M,D

FORT HAYS STATE UNIVERSITY
Biological and Biomedical
  Sciences—General — M
Communication Disorders — M
Nursing—General — M

FORT VALLEY STATE UNIVERSITY
Environmental and Occupational
  Health — M
Public Health—General — M

FRAMINGHAM STATE UNIVERSITY
Health Services Management and
  Hospital Administration — M
Nursing and Healthcare Administration — M
Nursing Education — M
Nursing—General — M
Nutrition — M

FRANCISCAN UNIVERSITY OF STEUBENVILLE
Nursing—General — M

FRANCIS MARION UNIVERSITY
Health Services Management and
  Hospital Administration — M

FRANKLIN PIERCE UNIVERSITY
Health Services Management and
  Hospital Administration — M,D,O
Nursing—General — M,D,O
Physical Therapy — M,D,O
Physician Assistant Studies — M,D,O

FRIENDS UNIVERSITY
Health Services Management and
  Hospital Administration — M

FRONTIER NURSING UNIVERSITY
Family Nurse Practitioner Studies — M,O
Nurse Midwifery — M,O
Nursing—General — M,O
Women's Health Nursing — M,O

FROSTBURG STATE UNIVERSITY
Biological and Biomedical
  Sciences—General — M
Conservation Biology — M
Ecology — M

FUTURE GENERATIONS GRADUATE SCHOOL
Maternal and Child Health — M

GALLAUDET UNIVERSITY
Communication Disorders — M,D,O

GANNON UNIVERSITY
Environmental and Occupational
  Health — O
Family Nurse Practitioner Studies — M,O
Medical/Surgical Nursing — M,O
Nurse Anesthesia — M,O
Nursing and Healthcare Administration — M,O
Nursing—General — M,O
Occupational Therapy — M
Physical Therapy — D
Physician Assistant Studies — M

GARDNER-WEBB UNIVERSITY
Nursing—General — M,D,O

GENEVA COLLEGE
Cardiovascular Sciences — M

GEORGE FOX UNIVERSITY
Physical Therapy — D

GEORGE MASON UNIVERSITY
Biochemistry — M,D
Biological and Biomedical
  Sciences—General — M,D,O
Community Health — M,O
Computational Biology — M,D,O
Epidemiology — M,O
Forensic Nursing — M,D,O
Health Promotion — M
Health Services Management and
  Hospital Administration — M,O
International Health — M,O
Microbiology — M,D
Molecular Biology — M,D
Neuroscience — D
Nursing and Healthcare Administration — M,D,O
Nursing Education — M,D,O
Nursing—General — M,D,O
Nutrition — M,O
Public Health—General — M,O
Rehabilitation Sciences — D

GEORGETOWN UNIVERSITY
Acute Care/Critical Care Nursing — M
Allopathic Medicine — D
Biochemistry — M,D
Biological and Biomedical
  Sciences—General — M,D
Biophysics — M,D
Cell Biology — D
Community Health — M,D
Epidemiology — M
Family Nurse Practitioner Studies — M
Health Physics/Radiological Health — M
Health Promotion — M,D
Immunology — M,D
Infectious Diseases — M,D
International Health — M
Microbiology — M,D
Molecular Biology — M,D
Neuroscience — D
Nurse Anesthesia — M
Nurse Midwifery — M
Nursing Education — M
Nursing—General — M
Pathology — M,D
Pharmacology — M,D
Physiology — M,D
Public Health—General — M,D
Radiation Biology — M

THE GEORGE WASHINGTON UNIVERSITY
Adult Nursing — M,D,O
Allopathic Medicine — D
Biochemistry — M,D
Biological and Biomedical
  Sciences—General — M,D
Communication Disorders — M
Environmental and Occupational
  Health — M
Epidemiology — M,D
Family Nurse Practitioner Studies — M,D,O
Genetics — M
Health Services Management and
  Hospital Administration — M,D,O
Health Services Research — D
Immunology — M
Infectious Diseases — M
International Health — M
Microbiology — M
Molecular Biology — M,D
Molecular Genetics — M,D

Molecular Medicine — D
Nursing and Healthcare Administration — M,D,O
Nursing—General — M,D,O
Physical Therapy — D
Physician Assistant Studies — M
Public Health—General — M,O
Toxicology — M

GEORGIA CAMPUS–PHILADELPHIA COLLEGE OF OSTEOPATHIC MEDICINE
Biological and Biomedical
  Sciences—General — M,O
Osteopathic Medicine — D
Pharmacy — D

GEORGIA COLLEGE & STATE UNIVERSITY
Adult Nursing — M
Biological and Biomedical
  Sciences—General — M
Family Nurse Practitioner Studies — M
Health Promotion — M
Health Services Management and
  Hospital Administration — M
Nursing and Healthcare Administration — M
Nursing—General — M

GEORGIA HEALTH SCIENCES UNIVERSITY
Allied Health—General — M
Allopathic Medicine — D
Anatomy — M,D
Biochemistry — M,D
Biological and Biomedical
  Sciences—General — M,D,O
Cardiovascular Sciences — M,D
Cell Biology — M,D
Clinical Research — M,O
Dental Hygiene — M
Dentistry — D
Family Nurse Practitioner Studies — M,O
Genomic Sciences — M,D
Molecular Biology — M,D
Molecular Medicine — M,D
Neuroscience — M,D
Nurse Anesthesia — M
Nursing and Healthcare Administration — M
Nursing—General — D
Oral and Dental Sciences — M,D
Pediatric Nursing — M,O
Pharmacology — M,D
Physiology — M,D

GEORGIA INSTITUTE OF TECHNOLOGY
Biochemistry — M,D
Biological and Biomedical
  Sciences—General — M,D
Health Physics/Radiological Health — M,D
Health Services Management and
  Hospital Administration — M
Medical Physics — M,D
Physiology — M

GEORGIAN COURT UNIVERSITY
Biological and Biomedical
  Sciences—General — M,O

GEORGIA SOUTHERN UNIVERSITY
Allied Health—General — M,D,O
Biological and Biomedical
  Sciences—General — M
Community Health Nursing — M,D,O
Community Health — M,D
Environmental and Occupational
  Health — M,D
Epidemiology — M,D
Family Nurse Practitioner Studies — M,O
Health Services Management and
  Hospital Administration — M,D
Nursing—General — D
Public Health—General — M,D
Women's Health Nursing — M,D,O

GEORGIA STATE UNIVERSITY
Adult Nursing — M,D,O
Allied Health—General — M,D,O
Biochemistry — M,D
Biological and Biomedical
  Sciences—General — M,D
Cell Biology — M,D
Communication Disorders — M
Environmental Biology — M,D
Family Nurse Practitioner Studies — M,D,O
Health Promotion — M,D,O
Health Services Management and
  Hospital Administration — M
Microbiology — M,D
Molecular Biology — M,D
Molecular Genetics — M,D
Neurobiology — M,D
Nursing—General — M,D,O
Nutrition — M
Pediatric Nursing — M,D,O
Physical Therapy — D
Physiology — M,D
Psychiatric Nursing — M,D,O
Public Health—General — M,D,O
Women's Health Nursing — M,D,O

GERSTNER SLOAN-KETTERING GRADUATE SCHOOL OF BIOMEDICAL SCIENCES
Biological and Biomedical
  Sciences—General — D
Cancer Biology/Oncology — D*

GLOBE UNIVERSITY–WOODBURY
Health Services Management and
  Hospital Administration — M

GODDARD COLLEGE
Health Promotion — M

GOLDEY-BEACOM COLLEGE
Health Services Management and
  Hospital Administration — M

GOLDFARB SCHOOL OF NURSING AT BARNES-JEWISH COLLEGE
Adult Nursing — M
Health Services Management and
  Hospital Administration — M
Nurse Anesthesia — M
Nursing Education — M
Nursing—General — M
Oncology Nursing — M

GONZAGA UNIVERSITY
Nurse Anesthesia — M
Nursing—General — M

GOODING INSTITUTE OF NURSE ANESTHESIA
Nurse Anesthesia — M

GOSHEN COLLEGE
Family Nurse Practitioner Studies — M
Nursing—General — M

GOUCHER COLLEGE
Biological and Biomedical
  Sciences—General — O

GOVERNORS STATE UNIVERSITY
Communication Disorders — M
Environmental Biology — M
Health Services Management and
  Hospital Administration — M
Nursing—General — M
Occupational Therapy — M
Physical Therapy — M,D

GRACELAND UNIVERSITY (IA)
Family Nurse Practitioner Studies — M,O
Nursing Education — M,O
Nursing—General — M,O

GRADUATE SCHOOL AND UNIVERSITY CENTER OF THE CITY UNIVERSITY OF NEW YORK
Biochemistry — D
Biological and Biomedical
  Sciences—General — D
Biopsychology — D
Communication Disorders — D
Neuroscience — D
Nursing—General — D
Physical Therapy — D
Public Health—General — D

GRAMBLING STATE UNIVERSITY
Family Nurse Practitioner Studies — M,O
Health Services Management and
  Hospital Administration — M
Nursing Education — M,O
Nursing—General — M,O

GRAND CANYON UNIVERSITY
Acute Care/Critical Care Nursing — M,O
Family Nurse Practitioner Studies — M,O
Health Services Management and
  Hospital Administration — M,O
Nursing Education — M,O
Nursing—General — M,O
Public Health—General — M,O

GRAND VALLEY STATE UNIVERSITY
Allied Health—General — M,D
Biological and Biomedical
  Sciences—General — M
Cell Biology — M
Health Services Management and
  Hospital Administration — M,D
Molecular Biology — M
Nursing and Healthcare Administration — M,D
Nursing Education — M,D
Nursing—General — M,D
Occupational Therapy — M
Physical Therapy — D
Physician Assistant Studies — M

GRAND VIEW UNIVERSITY
Nursing—General — M

GRANTHAM UNIVERSITY
Adult Nursing — M
Health Services Management and
  Hospital Administration — M
Nursing and Healthcare Administration — M
Nursing Education — M
Nursing Informatics — M

GWYNEDD-MERCY COLLEGE
Adult Nursing — M
Family Nurse Practitioner Studies — M
Gerontological Nursing — M
Nursing—General — M
Oncology Nursing — M
Pediatric Nursing — M

HAMPTON UNIVERSITY
Adult Nursing — M
Biological and Biomedical
  Sciences—General — M
Communication Disorders — M
Community Health Nursing — M
Environmental Biology — M
Gerontological Nursing — M
Health Services Management and
  Hospital Administration — M,D
Medical Physics — M,D
Nursing—General — M,D
Pediatric Nursing — M
Pharmacy — D
Physical Therapy — D
Psychiatric Nursing — M
Women's Health Nursing — M

HARDING UNIVERSITY
Communication Disorders — M
Health Services Management and
  Hospital Administration — M
Pharmacy — D
Physician Assistant Studies — M

HARDIN-SIMMONS UNIVERSITY
Family Nurse Practitioner Studies — M
Maternal and Child/Neonatal Nursing — M
Nursing—General — M
Physical Therapy — D

HARRISBURG UNIVERSITY OF SCIENCE AND TECHNOLOGY
Health Services Management and
  Hospital Administration — M

HARVARD UNIVERSITY
Allopathic Medicine — D
Biochemistry — D
Biological and Biomedical
  Sciences—General — M,D,O
Biophysics — D*
Biopsychology — D
Cell Biology — D
Communication Disorders — D
Dentistry — M,D,O
Environmental and Occupational
  Health — M,D
Epidemiology — M,D
Evolutionary Biology — D
Genetics — D
Genomic Sciences — D
Health Promotion — M,D
Health Services Management and
  Hospital Administration — M,D
Immunology — D
Infectious Diseases — D
International Health — M,D
Medical Physics — D
Microbiology — D
Molecular Biology — D
Molecular Genetics — D
Molecular Pharmacology — D
Neurobiology — D
Neuroscience — D
Nutrition — D
Oral and Dental Sciences — M,D,O
Pathology — D
Physiology — M,D
Public Health—General — M,D*
Structural Biology — D
Systems Biology — D

HAWAI`I PACIFIC UNIVERSITY
Community Health Nursing — M
Family Nurse Practitioner Studies — M
Nursing—General — M*

HERITAGE UNIVERSITY
Biological and Biomedical
  Sciences—General — M

HERZING UNIVERSITY ONLINE
Health Services Management and
  Hospital Administration — M
Nursing and Healthcare Administration — M
Nursing Education — M
Nursing—General — M

HOFSTRA UNIVERSITY
Allopathic Medicine — D
Biological and Biomedical
  Sciences—General — M,O
Communication Disorders — M,D
Community Health — M
Health Services Management and
  Hospital Administration — M,O
Molecular Medicine — D
Physician Assistant Studies — M
Public Health—General — M

HOLY FAMILY UNIVERSITY
Community Health Nursing — M
Health Services Management and
  Hospital Administration — M
Nursing and Healthcare Administration — M
Nursing Education — M
Nursing—General — M*

HOLY NAMES UNIVERSITY
Community Health Nursing — M,O
Family Nurse Practitioner Studies — M,O
Nursing and Healthcare Administration — M,O
Nursing Education — M,O
Nursing—General — M,O

HOOD COLLEGE
Biological and Biomedical
  Sciences—General — M,O
Environmental Biology — M
Immunology — M,O
Microbiology — M,O
Molecular Biology — M,O

HOUSTON BAPTIST UNIVERSITY
Health Services Management and
  Hospital Administration — M

HOWARD UNIVERSITY
Allopathic Medicine — D*
Anatomy — M,D
Biochemistry — M,D
Biological and Biomedical
  Sciences—General — M,D
Biophysics — D
Biopsychology — M,D
Communication Disorders — M,D
Dentistry — D,O
Family Nurse Practitioner Studies — M,O
Microbiology — D
Molecular Biology — M,D
Nursing—General — M,O
Nutrition — M,D

Oral and Dental Sciences — D,O
Pharmacology — M,D
Pharmacy — D
Physiology — D
Public Health—General — M

HUMBOLDT STATE UNIVERSITY
Biological and Biomedical
  Sciences—General — M
Physical Therapy — M

HUNTER COLLEGE OF THE CITY UNIVERSITY OF NEW YORK
Adult Nursing — M
Biochemistry — M,D
Biological and Biomedical
  Sciences—General — M,D
Communication Disorders — M
Community Health Nursing — M
Community Health — M
Environmental and Occupational
  Health — M
Epidemiology — M
Gerontological Nursing — M
Health Services Management and
  Hospital Administration — M
Nursing—General — M,O
Nutrition — M
Psychiatric Nursing — M,O
Public Health—General — M

HUNTINGTON COLLEGE OF HEALTH SCIENCES
Nutrition — M

HUSSON UNIVERSITY
Community Health Nursing — M,O
Family Nurse Practitioner Studies — M,O
Health Services Management and
  Hospital Administration — M
Nursing Education — M,O
Nursing—General — M,O
Occupational Therapy — M
Physical Therapy — D
Psychiatric Nursing — M,O

ICR GRADUATE SCHOOL
Biological and Biomedical
  Sciences—General — M

IDAHO STATE UNIVERSITY
Allied Health—General — M,D,O
Biological and Biomedical
  Sciences—General — M,D
Communication Disorders — M,D,O
Community Health — O
Dental Hygiene — M
Dentistry — O
Health Physics/Radiological Health — M,D
Medical Microbiology — M,D
Medicinal and Pharmaceutical
  Chemistry — M,D
Microbiology — M,D
Nursing—General — M,O
Nutrition — M,O
Occupational Therapy — M
Oral and Dental Sciences — O
Pharmaceutical Administration — M,D
Pharmaceutical Sciences — M,D
Pharmacology — M,D
Pharmacy — M,D
Physical Therapy — D
Physician Assistant Studies — M
Public Health—General — M,O

ILLINOIS COLLEGE OF OPTOMETRY
Optometry — D

ILLINOIS INSTITUTE OF TECHNOLOGY
Biochemistry — M,D
Biological and Biomedical
  Sciences—General — M,D
Cell Biology — M,D
Health Physics/Radiological Health — M,D
Medical Imaging — M,D
Microbiology — M,D
Molecular Biology — M,D
Molecular Biophysics — M,D

ILLINOIS STATE UNIVERSITY
Animal Behavior — M,D
Bacteriology — M,D
Biochemistry — M,D
Biological and Biomedical
  Sciences—General — M,D
Biophysics — M,D
Botany — M,D
Cell Biology — M,D
Communication Disorders — M
Conservation Biology — M,D
Developmental Biology — M,D
Ecology — M,D
Entomology — M,D
Evolutionary Biology — M,D
Family Nurse Practitioner Studies — M,D,O
Genetics — M,D
Immunology — M,D
Microbiology — M,D
Molecular Biology — M,D
Molecular Genetics — M,D
Neurobiology — M,D
Neuroscience — M,D
Nursing—General — M,D,O
Parasitology — M,D
Physiology — M,D
Plant Biology — M,D
Plant Molecular Biology — M,D
Structural Biology — M,D
Zoology — M,D

IMMACULATA UNIVERSITY
Nursing—General — M
Nutrition — M

M—master's degree; P—first professional degree; D—doctorate; O—other advanced degree; *Close-Up and/or Display

INDEPENDENCE UNIVERSITY

Community Health Nursing	M
Community Health	M
Gerontological Nursing	M
Health Promotion	M
Health Services Management and Hospital Administration	M
Nursing and Healthcare Administration	M
Nursing—General	M
Public Health—General	M

INDIANA STATE UNIVERSITY

Biological and Biomedical Sciences—General	M,D
Community Health	M
Ecology	M,D
Environmental and Occupational Health	M
Health Promotion	M
Microbiology	M,D
Nursing—General	M
Nutrition	M
Physiology	M,D

INDIANA TECH

Health Services Management and Hospital Administration	M

INDIANA UNIVERSITY BLOOMINGTON

Biochemistry	M,D
Biological and Biomedical Sciences—General	M,D
Cell Biology	M,D
Communication Disorders	M,D
Community Health	M,D
Ecology	M,D
Environmental and Occupational Health	M,D
Epidemiology	M,D
Evolutionary Biology	M,D
Genetics	M,D
Health Promotion	M,D
Health Services Management and Hospital Administration	M,D
Medical Physics	M,D
Microbiology	M,D
Molecular Biology	M,D
Neuroscience	M,D
Nutrition	M,D
Optometry	M,D
Plant Biology	M,D
Public Health—General	M,D
Toxicology	M,D
Zoology	M,D

INDIANA UNIVERSITY EAST

Nursing—General	M

INDIANA UNIVERSITY OF PENNSYLVANIA

Biological and Biomedical Sciences—General	M
Communication Disorders	M
Environmental and Occupational Health	M
Health Services Management and Hospital Administration	M,D
Nursing and Healthcare Administration	M
Nursing Education	M
Nursing—General	D
Nutrition	M

INDIANA UNIVERSITY–PURDUE UNIVERSITY FORT WAYNE

Adult Nursing	M,O
Biological and Biomedical Sciences—General	M
Communication Disorders	M
Nursing and Healthcare Administration	M,O
Nursing Education	M,O
Nursing—General	M,O
Women's Health Nursing	M,O

INDIANA UNIVERSITY–PURDUE UNIVERSITY INDIANAPOLIS

Acute Care/Critical Care Nursing	M,D
Adult Nursing	M,D
Allopathic Medicine	M,D
Anatomy	M,D
Biochemistry	M,D
Bioethics	M,O
Biological and Biomedical Sciences—General	M,D
Biopsychology	D
Cell Biology	M,D
Community Health Nursing	M,D
Dentistry	M,D,O
Environmental and Occupational Health	M,O
Epidemiology	M
Family Nurse Practitioner Studies	M,D
Health Services Management and Hospital Administration	M
Immunology	M,D
Maternal and Child/Neonatal Nursing	M,D
Microbiology	M,D
Molecular Biology	D
Molecular Genetics	M,D
Nursing and Healthcare Administration	M
Nursing Education	M
Nursing—General	M,D
Nutrition	M,D
Occupational Therapy	M,D
Pathology	M,D
Pediatric Nursing	M,D
Pharmacology	M,D
Physical Therapy	M,D
Psychiatric Nursing	M,D
Public Health—General	M
Rehabilitation Sciences	M,D
Toxicology	M,D
Women's Health Nursing	M,D

INDIANA UNIVERSITY SOUTH BEND

Health Services Management and Hospital Administration	M,O

INDIANA WESLEYAN UNIVERSITY

Community Health Nursing	M,O
Nursing and Healthcare Administration	M,O
Nursing Education	M,O
Nursing—General	M,O

INSTITUTE OF CLINICAL ACUPUNCTURE AND ORIENTAL MEDICINE

Acupuncture and Oriental Medicine	M

INSTITUTE OF PUBLIC ADMINISTRATION

Health Services Management and Hospital Administration	M,O

INSTITUT FRANCO-EUROP• DE CHIROPRATIQUE

Chiropractic	D

INSTITUTO TECNOLOGICO DE SANTO DOMINGO

Allopathic Medicine	M,D
Bioethics	M,O
Health Promotion	M,O
Maternal and Child Health	M,O
Nutrition	M,O

INTER AMERICAN UNIVERSITY OF PUERTO RICO, ARECIBO CAMPUS

Acute Care/Critical Care Nursing	M
Medical/Surgical Nursing	M
Nurse Anesthesia	M
Nursing—General	M

INTER AMERICAN UNIVERSITY OF PUERTO RICO, BAYAMÓN CAMPUS

Ecology	M

INTER AMERICAN UNIVERSITY OF PUERTO RICO, METROPOLITAN CAMPUS

Clinical Laboratory Sciences/Medical Technology	M
Microbiology	M
Molecular Biology	M

INTER AMERICAN UNIVERSITY OF PUERTO RICO SCHOOL OF OPTOMETRY

Optometry	D

IONA COLLEGE

Health Services Management and Hospital Administration	M,O

IOWA STATE UNIVERSITY OF SCIENCE AND TECHNOLOGY

Biochemistry	M,D
Biological and Biomedical Sciences—General	M,D
Biophysics	D
Cell Biology	M,D
Computational Biology	M,D
Developmental Biology	M,D
Ecology	M,D
Entomology	M,D
Evolutionary Biology	M,D
Genetics	M,D
Immunology	M,D
Microbiology	M,D
Molecular Biology	M,D
Molecular Genetics	M,D
Neuroscience	M,D
Nutrition	M,D
Pathology	M,D
Plant Biology	M,D
Plant Pathology	M,D
Structural Biology	M,D
Toxicology	M,D
Veterinary Medicine	M,D
Veterinary Sciences	M,D

IRELL & MANELLA GRADUATE SCHOOL OF BIOLOGICAL SCIENCES

Biological and Biomedical Sciences—General	D*

ITHACA COLLEGE

Allied Health—General	M,D
Communication Disorders	M
Occupational Therapy	M
Physical Therapy	M,D

JACKSON STATE UNIVERSITY

Biological and Biomedical Sciences—General	M,D
Communication Disorders	M

JACKSONVILLE STATE UNIVERSITY

Biological and Biomedical Sciences—General	M
Nursing—General	M

JACKSONVILLE UNIVERSITY

Nursing—General	M,D
Oral and Dental Sciences	O

JAMES MADISON UNIVERSITY

Biological and Biomedical Sciences—General	M
Communication Disorders	M,D
Nursing—General	M
Occupational Therapy	M
Physician Assistant Studies	M

JEFFERSON COLLEGE OF HEALTH SCIENCES

Nursing and Healthcare Administration	M
Nursing Education	M
Nursing—General	M
Occupational Therapy	M
Physician Assistant Studies	M

JOHN CARROLL UNIVERSITY

Biological and Biomedical Sciences—General	M

THE JOHNS HOPKINS UNIVERSITY

Acute Care/Critical Care Nursing	M,O
Adult Nursing	M,O
Allopathic Medicine	D
Anatomy	D
Biochemistry	M,D
Bioethics	M,D
Biological and Biomedical Sciences—General	M,D
Biophysics	D
Cell Biology	D
Clinical Research	M,D
Community Health Nursing	M
Community Health	M,D
Developmental Biology	D
Environmental and Occupational Health	M,D
Epidemiology	M,D
Evolutionary Biology	D
Family Nurse Practitioner Studies	M,O
Genetics	M,D
Health Services Management and Hospital Administration	M,D,O
Health Services Research	M,D
Human Genetics	D
Immunology	M,D
Infectious Diseases	M,D
International Health	M,D
Microbiology	M,D
Molecular Biology	M,D
Molecular Biophysics	M,D
Molecular Medicine	D
Neuroscience	D
Nursing and Healthcare Administration	M,O
Nursing—General	M,D,O
Nutrition	M,D
Pathobiology	D
Pathology	D
Pediatric Nursing	M,O
Pharmaceutical Sciences	M
Pharmacology	D
Physiology	M,D
Public Health—General	M,D
Toxicology	M,D
Women's Health Nursing	M,O

JONES INTERNATIONAL UNIVERSITY

Health Services Management and Hospital Administration	M

KANSAS CITY UNIVERSITY OF MEDICINE AND BIOSCIENCES

Bioethics	M
Biological and Biomedical Sciences—General	M
Osteopathic Medicine	D

KANSAS STATE UNIVERSITY

Biochemistry	M,D
Biological and Biomedical Sciences—General	M,D
Communication Disorders	M
Entomology	M,D
Genetics	M,D
Microbiology	M,D
Nutrition	M,D
Pathobiology	M,D
Physiology	D
Plant Pathology	M,D
Veterinary Sciences	M

KAPLAN UNIVERSITY, DAVENPORT CAMPUS

Health Services Management and Hospital Administration	M,O
Nursing and Healthcare Administration	M
Nursing Education	M
Nursing—General	M

KEAN UNIVERSITY

Communication Disorders	M
Community Health Nursing	M
Health Services Management and Hospital Administration	M
Nursing and Healthcare Administration	M
Nursing—General	M
Occupational Therapy	M
School Nursing	M

KECK GRADUATE INSTITUTE OF APPLIED LIFE SCIENCES

Biological and Biomedical Sciences—General	M,D,O
Computational Biology	M,D,O

KEENE STATE COLLEGE

Environmental and Occupational Health	M,O

KEISER UNIVERSITY

Health Services Management and Hospital Administration	M
Nursing—General	M
Physician Assistant Studies	M

KENNESAW STATE UNIVERSITY

Biological and Biomedical Sciences—General	M
Health Services Management and Hospital Administration	M
Nursing—General	M,D

KENT STATE UNIVERSITY

Acute Care/Critical Care Nursing	M,D
Adult Nursing	M,D
Biochemistry	M,D
Biological and Biomedical Sciences—General	M,D
Cell Biology	M,D
Communication Disorders	M,D,O
Ecology	M,D
Family Nurse Practitioner Studies	M,D
Gerontological Nursing	M,D
Health Promotion	M,D
Molecular Biology	M,D
Neuroscience	M,D
Nursing and Healthcare Administration	M,D
Nursing Education	M,D
Nursing—General	M,D
Nutrition	M
Pediatric Nursing	M,D
Pharmacology	M,D
Physiology	M,D
Psychiatric Nursing	M,D
Women's Health Nursing	M,D

KEUKA COLLEGE

Nursing—General	M
Occupational Therapy	M

KING'S COLLEGE

Health Services Management and Hospital Administration	M
Physician Assistant Studies	M

KUTZTOWN UNIVERSITY OF PENNSYLVANIA

School Nursing	M

LAKE ERIE COLLEGE

Health Services Management and Hospital Administration	M

LAKE ERIE COLLEGE OF OSTEOPATHIC MEDICINE

Biological and Biomedical Sciences—General	M,D,O
Osteopathic Medicine	M,D,O
Pharmacy	M,D,O

LAKE FOREST GRADUATE SCHOOL OF MANAGEMENT

Health Services Management and Hospital Administration	M

LAKEHEAD UNIVERSITY

Biological and Biomedical Sciences—General	M
Health Services Research	M

LAKELAND COLLEGE

Health Services Management and Hospital Administration	M

LAMAR UNIVERSITY

Biological and Biomedical Sciences—General	M
Communication Disorders	M,D
Health Services Management and Hospital Administration	M
Nursing and Healthcare Administration	M
Nursing Education	M
Nursing—General	M

LANGSTON UNIVERSITY

Physical Therapy	D

LA ROCHE COLLEGE

Nurse Anesthesia	M
Nursing and Healthcare Administration	M
Nursing Education	M
Nursing—General	M

LA SALLE UNIVERSITY

Communication Disorders	M
Nursing—General	M,O

LAURENTIAN UNIVERSITY

Biochemistry	M
Biological and Biomedical Sciences—General	M,D
Ecology	M,D
Nursing—General	M
Public Health—General	D

LEBANESE AMERICAN UNIVERSITY

Pharmacy	D

LEBANON VALLEY COLLEGE

Physical Therapy	D

LEHIGH UNIVERSITY

Biochemistry	M,D
Biological and Biomedical Sciences—General	M,D
Health Services Management and Hospital Administration	M
Molecular Biology	M,D
Neuroscience	M,D

LEHMAN COLLEGE OF THE CITY UNIVERSITY OF NEW YORK

Adult Nursing	M
Biological and Biomedical Sciences—General	M
Communication Disorders	M
Gerontological Nursing	M
Health Promotion	M
Maternal and Child/Neonatal Nursing	M
Nursing—General	M
Nutrition	M
Pediatric Nursing	M

LE MOYNE COLLEGE

Nursing and Healthcare Administration	M,O
Nursing Education	M,O
Nursing—General	M,O
Physician Assistant Studies	M

LENOIR-RHYNE UNIVERSITY

Occupational Therapy	M

LESLEY UNIVERSITY

Ecology	M,D,O

LETOURNEAU UNIVERSITY

Health Services Management and Hospital Administration	M

LEWIS & CLARK COLLEGE

Communication Disorders	M

LEWIS UNIVERSITY

Adult Nursing	M,D
Environmental and Occupational Health	M
Health Services Management and Hospital Administration	M
Nursing and Healthcare Administration	M,D

Nursing Education M,D
Nursing—General M,D

LIBERTY UNIVERSITY
Nursing—General M,D

LIFE CHIROPRACTIC COLLEGE WEST
Chiropractic D

LIFE UNIVERSITY
Chiropractic D

LINCOLN MEMORIAL UNIVERSITY
Family Nurse Practitioner Studies M
Nurse Anesthesia M
Nursing—General M
Osteopathic Medicine D
Psychiatric Nursing M

LINDENWOOD UNIVERSITY
Health Services Management and Hospital Administration M,O

LIPSCOMB UNIVERSITY
Health Services Management and Hospital Administration M
Nutrition M
Pharmacy D

LOCK HAVEN UNIVERSITY OF PENNSYLVANIA
Physician Assistant Studies M

LOGAN UNIVERSITY–COLLEGE OF CHIROPRACTIC
Chiropractic M,D
Nutrition M
Rehabilitation Sciences M

LOMA LINDA UNIVERSITY
Adult Nursing M
Allied Health—General M,D
Allopathic Medicine M,D
Anatomy M,D
Biochemistry M,D
Bioethics M,O
Biological and Biomedical Sciences—General M,D
Communication Disorders M
Dentistry M,D,O
Environmental and Occupational Health M
Epidemiology M,D,O
Gerontological Nursing M
Health Promotion M,D
Health Services Management and Hospital Administration M
International Health M
Microbiology M,D
Nursing and Healthcare Administration M
Nursing—General M
Nutrition M,D
Occupational Therapy M,D
Oral and Dental Sciences M,O
Pathology M,D
Pediatric Nursing M
Pharmacology M,D
Pharmacy D
Physical Therapy M,D
Physician Assistant Studies M
Physiology M,D
Public Health—General M,D,O

LONG ISLAND UNIVERSITY–BROOKLYN CAMPUS
Adult Nursing M,O
Biological and Biomedical Sciences—General M
Communication Disorders M
Community Health M
Health Services Management and Hospital Administration M
Nursing and Healthcare Administration M
Nursing—General M,O
Pharmaceutical Administration M
Pharmaceutical Sciences M,D
Pharmacology M,D
Physical Therapy D
Toxicology M,D

LONG ISLAND UNIVERSITY–C. W. POST CAMPUS
Allied Health—General M,O
Biological and Biomedical Sciences—General M
Cardiovascular Sciences M
Clinical Laboratory Sciences/Medical Technology M
Communication Disorders M
Family Nurse Practitioner Studies M,O
Health Services Management and Hospital Administration M,O
Immunology M
Medicinal and Pharmaceutical Chemistry M
Microbiology M
Nursing—General M,O
Nutrition M,O
Perfusion M

LONG ISLAND UNIVERSITY–HUDSON AT ROCKLAND
Health Services Management and Hospital Administration M,O
Pharmaceutical Sciences M

LONGWOOD UNIVERSITY
Communication Disorders M

LOUISIANA STATE UNIVERSITY AND AGRICULTURAL AND MECHANICAL COLLEGE
Biochemistry M,D
Biological and Biomedical Sciences—General M,D

Biopsychology M,D
Communication Disorders M,D
Entomology M,D
Medical Physics M,D
Plant Pathology M,D
Toxicology M
Veterinary Medicine D
Veterinary Sciences M,D

LOUISIANA STATE UNIVERSITY HEALTH SCIENCES CENTER
Adult Nursing M,D
Allopathic Medicine M,D
Anatomy M,D
Biological and Biomedical Sciences—General M,D
Cell Biology M,D
Communication Disorders M,D
Community Health Nursing M,D
Community Health M,D
Dentistry D
Developmental Biology M,D
Environmental and Occupational Health M,D
Epidemiology M,D
Health Services Management and Hospital Administration M,D
Human Genetics M,D
Immunology M,D
Microbiology M,D
Neurobiology M,D
Neuroscience M,D
Nurse Anesthesia M,D
Nursing—General M,D
Occupational Therapy M
Parasitology M,D
Pharmacology M,D
Physical Therapy D
Physiology M,D
Public Health—General M,D

LOUISIANA STATE UNIVERSITY HEALTH SCIENCES CENTER AT SHREVEPORT
Allopathic Medicine D
Anatomy M,D
Biochemistry M,D
Biological and Biomedical Sciences—General M,D
Cell Biology M,D
Immunology M,D
Microbiology M,D
Molecular Biology M,D
Pharmacology D
Physiology M,D

LOUISIANA STATE UNIVERSITY IN SHREVEPORT
Health Promotion M
Health Services Management and Hospital Administration M
Public Health—General M

LOUISIANA TECH UNIVERSITY
Biological and Biomedical Sciences—General M
Communication Disorders M
Nutrition M

LOYOLA MARYMOUNT UNIVERSITY
Bioethics M

LOYOLA UNIVERSITY CHICAGO
Acute Care/Critical Care Nursing M,O
Adult Nursing M,O
Allopathic Medicine D
Anatomy M,D
Biochemistry M,D
Bioethics D,O
Biological and Biomedical Sciences—General M
Cardiovascular Sciences M,O
Cell Biology M,D
Clinical Research M
Environmental and Occupational Health M,O
Family Nurse Practitioner Studies M,O
Health Services Management and Hospital Administration M,D,O
Immunology M,D
Infectious Diseases M,O
Microbiology M,D
Molecular Biology M,D
Molecular Physiology M,D
Neurobiology M,D
Neuroscience M,D
Nursing and Healthcare Administration M
Nursing Informatics D
Nursing—General M,D
Nutrition M,O
Oncology Nursing M,O
Pharmacology M,D
Physiology M,D
Public Health—General M
Women's Health Nursing M,O

LOYOLA UNIVERSITY MARYLAND
Communication Disorders M

LOYOLA UNIVERSITY NEW ORLEANS
Adult Nursing M,D
Family Nurse Practitioner Studies M,D
Health Services Management and Hospital Administration M,D
Nursing—General M,D

LYNCHBURG COLLEGE
Nursing and Healthcare Administration M
Nursing Education M
Nursing—General M
Physical Therapy D

MADONNA UNIVERSITY
Adult Nursing M

Health Services Management and Hospital Administration M
Hospice Nursing M
Nursing and Healthcare Administration M
Nursing—General M

MALONE UNIVERSITY
Family Nurse Practitioner Studies M
Nursing—General M

MANSFIELD UNIVERSITY OF PENNSYLVANIA
Nursing—General M

MARIAN UNIVERSITY (WI)
Adult Nursing M
Nursing Education M
Nursing—General M

MARIETTA COLLEGE
Physician Assistant Studies M

MARLBORO COLLEGE
Health Services Management and Hospital Administration M

MARQUETTE UNIVERSITY
Acute Care/Critical Care Nursing M,D,O
Adult Nursing M,D,O
Biological and Biomedical Sciences—General M,D
Cardiovascular Sciences M
Cell Biology M,D
Communication Disorders M,O
Dentistry D
Developmental Biology M,D
Ecology M,D
Genetics M,D
Gerontological Nursing M,D,O
Health Services Management and Hospital Administration M,O
Maternal and Child/Neonatal Nursing M,O
Microbiology M,D
Molecular Biology M,D
Neuroscience M,D
Nurse Midwifery M,D,O
Nursing and Healthcare Administration M,D,O
Nursing—General M,D,O
Oral and Dental Sciences M,O
Pediatric Nursing M,D,O
Physical Therapy M,D
Physician Assistant Studies M
Physiology M,D
Rehabilitation Sciences M,D

MARSHALL UNIVERSITY
Allopathic Medicine D
Biological and Biomedical Sciences—General M,D
Communication Disorders M
Health Services Management and Hospital Administration M,D
Nurse Anesthesia D
Nursing—General M
Nutrition M
Pharmacy D
Physical Therapy D

MARYLHURST UNIVERSITY
Health Services Management and Hospital Administration M

MARYMOUNT UNIVERSITY
Allied Health—General M,D,O
Family Nurse Practitioner Studies M,D,O
Health Promotion M
Health Services Management and Hospital Administration M,O
Nursing Education M,D,O
Nursing—General M,D,O
Physical Therapy D

MARYVILLE UNIVERSITY OF SAINT LOUIS
Adult Nursing M,D
Allied Health—General M,D,O
Family Nurse Practitioner Studies M,D
Gerontological Nursing M,D
Nursing Education M,D
Nursing—General M,D
Occupational Therapy M
Physical Therapy D

MARYWOOD UNIVERSITY
Communication Disorders M
Health Promotion M,D,O
Health Services Management and Hospital Administration M
Nutrition M,O
Physician Assistant Studies M

MASSACHUSETTS COLLEGE OF PHARMACY AND HEALTH SCIENCES
Community Health M
Health Services Management and Hospital Administration M
Nursing—General M
Oral and Dental Sciences M
Pharmaceutical Sciences M,D
Pharmacology M,D
Pharmacy D
Physician Assistant Studies M

MASSACHUSETTS INSTITUTE OF TECHNOLOGY
Biochemistry D
Biological and Biomedical Sciences—General D
Cell Biology D
Communication Disorders D
Computational Biology D
Developmental Biology D
Environmental Biology M,D,O
Genetics D
Immunology D

Medical Physics D
Microbiology D
Molecular Biology D
Molecular Toxicology D
Neurobiology D
Neuroscience D
Structural Biology D
Systems Biology D
Toxicology M,D

MASSACHUSETTS SCHOOL OF PROFESSIONAL PSYCHOLOGY
Community Health M,D,O
International Health M,D,O

MAYO GRADUATE SCHOOL
Biochemistry D
Biological and Biomedical Sciences—General D
Cancer Biology/Oncology D
Cell Biology D
Genetics D
Immunology D
Molecular Biology D
Molecular Pharmacology D
Neuroscience D
Structural Biology D
Virology D

MAYO MEDICAL SCHOOL
Allopathic Medicine D

MAYO SCHOOL OF HEALTH SCIENCES
Nurse Anesthesia M
Physical Therapy D

MCGILL UNIVERSITY
Allopathic Medicine M,D
Anatomy M,D
Biochemistry M,D
Bioethics M,D,O
Biological and Biomedical Sciences—General M,D
Cell Biology M,D
Communication Disorders M,D
Community Health M,D,O
Dentistry M,D,O
Entomology M,D
Environmental and Occupational Health M,D,O
Epidemiology M,D,O
Family Nurse Practitioner Studies M,D,O
Health Services Management and Hospital Administration M,D,O
Human Genetics M,D
Immunology M,D
Medical Physics M,D
Microbiology M,D
Neuroscience M,D
Nursing—General M,D
Nutrition M,D,O
Oral and Dental Sciences M,D,O
Parasitology M,D,O
Pathology M,D
Pharmacology M,D
Physiology M,D
Rehabilitation Sciences M,D,O

MCKENDREE UNIVERSITY
Nursing and Healthcare Administration M
Nursing Education M
Nursing—General M

MCMASTER UNIVERSITY
Biochemistry M,D
Biological and Biomedical Sciences—General M,D
Cancer Biology/Oncology M,D
Cardiovascular Sciences M,D
Cell Biology M,D
Genetics M,D
Health Physics/Radiological Health M,D
Health Services Research M,D
Immunology M,D
Medical Physics M,D
Molecular Biology M,D
Neuroscience M,D
Nursing—General M,D
Nutrition M,D
Occupational Therapy M
Pharmacology M,D
Physical Therapy M
Physiology M,D
Rehabilitation Sciences M,D
Virology M,D

MCNEESE STATE UNIVERSITY
Family Nurse Practitioner Studies M
Health Promotion M
Nursing and Healthcare Administration M
Nursing Education M
Nursing—General M
Nutrition M

MEDICAL COLLEGE OF WISCONSIN
Allopathic Medicine D
Biochemistry D
Bioethics M,O
Biological and Biomedical Sciences—General M,D,O
Biophysics D
Clinical Laboratory Sciences/Medical Technology M,D
Clinical Research
Community Health M,D,O
Epidemiology M,D,O
Medical Imaging D
Microbiology M,D
Molecular Genetics D
Neuroscience D
Pharmacology D
Physiology D
Public Health—General M,D,O
Toxicology D

M—master's degree; P—first professional degree; D—doctorate; O—other advanced degree; *Close-Up and/or Display

MEDICAL UNIVERSITY OF SOUTH CAROLINA
Adult Nursing M
Allied Health—General M,D
Allopathic Medicine D
Biochemistry M,D
Biological and Biomedical Sciences—General M,D
Cancer Biology/Oncology D
Cardiovascular Sciences D
Cell Biology D
Clinical Research M
Dentistry D
Developmental Biology D
Epidemiology M,D
Family Nurse Practitioner Studies M
Genetics D
Health Services Management and Hospital Administration M,D
Health Services Research M
Immunology M,D
International Health M
Maternal and Child/Neonatal Nursing M
Medical Imaging D
Medicinal and Pharmaceutical Chemistry D
Microbiology M,D
Molecular Biology M,D
Molecular Pharmacology M,D
Neuroscience M,D
Nurse Anesthesia M
Nursing and Healthcare Administration M
Nursing Education M
Nursing—General D
Occupational Therapy M
Pathobiology D
Pathology M,D
Pharmacy D
Physical Therapy D
Physician Assistant Studies M
Rehabilitation Sciences D
Toxicology D

MEHARRY MEDICAL COLLEGE
Allopathic Medicine D
Biological and Biomedical Sciences—General D
Cancer Biology/Oncology D
Community Health M
Dentistry D
Environmental and Occupational Health M
Health Services Management and Hospital Administration M
Immunology D
Microbiology D
Neuroscience D
Pharmacology D

MEMORIAL UNIVERSITY OF NEWFOUNDLAND
Biochemistry M,D
Biological and Biomedical Sciences—General M,D,O
Biopsychology M,D
Cancer Biology/Oncology M,D
Cardiovascular Sciences M,D
Clinical Research M
Community Health M,D,O
Epidemiology M,D,O
Human Genetics M,D
Immunology M,D
Marine Biology M,D
Neuroscience M,D
Nursing—General M,O
Pharmaceutical Sciences M,D

MERCER UNIVERSITY
Allopathic Medicine M,D
Environmental and Occupational Health M,D
Nursing—General M,D,O
Pharmaceutical Sciences M,D
Pharmacy M,D

MERCY COLLEGE
Allied Health—General M,D,O
Communication Disorders M
Health Services Management and Hospital Administration M
Nursing and Healthcare Administration M,O
Nursing Education M,O
Nursing—General M,O
Occupational Therapy M
Physical Therapy D
Physician Assistant Studies M

MEREDITH COLLEGE
Nutrition M,O

METHODIST UNIVERSITY
Physician Assistant Studies M

METROPOLITAN STATE UNIVERSITY
Nursing and Healthcare Administration M,D
Nursing—General M,D
Oral and Dental Sciences M,D

MGH INSTITUTE OF HEALTH PROFESSIONS
Communication Disorders M,O
Gerontological Nursing M,D,O
Nursing Education M,D,O
Nursing—General M,D,O
Pediatric Nursing M,D,O
Physical Therapy M,D,O
Psychiatric Nursing M,D,O
Women's Health Nursing M,D,O

MIAMI UNIVERSITY
Biochemistry M,D
Botany M,D
Communication Disorders M
Microbiology M,D
Plant Biology M,D
Zoology M,D

MICHIGAN STATE UNIVERSITY
Allopathic Medicine D
Biochemistry M,D
Biological and Biomedical Sciences—General M,D
Cell Biology M,D
Clinical Laboratory Sciences/Medical Technology M
Communication Disorders M,D
Ecology D
Entomology M,D
Epidemiology M,D
Evolutionary Biology D
Genetics M,D
Microbiology M,D
Molecular Biology M,D
Molecular Genetics M,D
Neuroscience M,D
Nursing—General M,D
Nutrition M,D
Osteopathic Medicine D
Pathobiology M,D
Pathology M,D
Pharmacology M,D
Physiology M,D
Plant Biology M,D
Plant Pathology M,D
Public Health—General M
Structural Biology D
Systems Biology D
Toxicology M,D
Veterinary Medicine D
Veterinary Sciences M,D
Zoology M,D

MICHIGAN TECHNOLOGICAL UNIVERSITY
Biological and Biomedical Sciences—General M,D
Ecology M,D
Plant Molecular Biology M,D

MIDDLE TENNESSEE SCHOOL OF ANESTHESIA
Nurse Anesthesia M

MIDDLE TENNESSEE STATE UNIVERSITY
Biological and Biomedical Sciences—General M
Family Nurse Practitioner Studies M,O
Health Services Management and Hospital Administration O
Nursing—General M,O

MIDWEST COLLEGE OF ORIENTAL MEDICINE
Acupuncture and Oriental Medicine M,O

MIDWESTERN STATE UNIVERSITY
Biological and Biomedical Sciences—General M
Family Nurse Practitioner Studies M
Health Physics/Radiological Health M
Health Services Management and Hospital Administration M
Nursing Education M
Nursing—General M
Psychiatric Nursing M

MIDWESTERN UNIVERSITY, DOWNERS GROVE CAMPUS
Allied Health—General D
Biological and Biomedical Sciences—General M
Dentistry D
Occupational Therapy M
Osteopathic Medicine D
Pharmacy D
Physical Therapy D
Physician Assistant Studies M

MIDWESTERN UNIVERSITY, GLENDALE CAMPUS
Allied Health—General M,D
Biological and Biomedical Sciences—General M
Cardiovascular Sciences M
Dentistry D
Nurse Anesthesia M
Occupational Therapy M
Optometry D
Osteopathic Medicine D
Pharmacy D
Physical Therapy D
Physician Assistant Studies M
Podiatric Medicine D

MIDWIVES COLLEGE OF UTAH
Nurse Midwifery M

MILLERSVILLE UNIVERSITY OF PENNSYLVANIA
Nursing—General M

MILLIGAN COLLEGE
Occupational Therapy M

MILLIKIN UNIVERSITY
Nurse Anesthesia M
Nursing and Healthcare Administration M
Nursing Education M
Nursing—General M

MILLS COLLEGE
Biological and Biomedical Sciences—General O

MILWAUKEE SCHOOL OF ENGINEERING
Cardiovascular Sciences M
Clinical Laboratory Sciences/Medical Technology M
Perfusion M

MINNESOTA STATE UNIVERSITY MANKATO
Allied Health—General M,D,O
Biological and Biomedical Sciences—General M
Communication Disorders M
Community Health M,O
Family Nurse Practitioner Studies M,D
Nursing—General M,D

MINNESOTA STATE UNIVERSITY MOORHEAD
Communication Disorders M
Nursing Education M
Nursing—General M,O

MINOT STATE UNIVERSITY
Communication Disorders M

MISERICORDIA UNIVERSITY
Allied Health—General M,D
Communication Disorders M
Nursing—General M
Occupational Therapy M,D
Physical Therapy M,D

MISSISSIPPI COLLEGE
Biochemistry M
Biological and Biomedical Sciences—General M
Health Services Management and Hospital Administration M

MISSISSIPPI STATE UNIVERSITY
Biochemistry M,D
Biological and Biomedical Sciences—General M,D
Entomology M,D
Genetics M,D
Health Promotion M,D
Molecular Biology M,D
Nutrition M,D
Plant Pathology M,D
Veterinary Medicine D
Veterinary Sciences M,D

MISSISSIPPI UNIVERSITY FOR WOMEN
Communication Disorders M,O
Nursing—General M,O

MISSISSIPPI VALLEY STATE UNIVERSITY
Environmental and Occupational Health M

MISSOURI SOUTHERN STATE UNIVERSITY
Dental Hygiene M
Nursing—General M

MISSOURI STATE UNIVERSITY
Biological and Biomedical Sciences—General M
Cell Biology M
Communication Disorders M,D
Family Nurse Practitioner Studies M
Health Promotion M
Health Services Management and Hospital Administration M
Molecular Biology M
Nurse Anesthesia M
Nursing Education M
Nursing—General M
Physical Therapy D
Physician Assistant Studies M
Public Health—General M

MISSOURI UNIVERSITY OF SCIENCE AND TECHNOLOGY
Biological and Biomedical Sciences—General M
Environmental Biology M

MISSOURI WESTERN STATE UNIVERSITY
Nursing and Healthcare Administration M
Nursing—General M

MOLLOY COLLEGE
Adult Nursing M,O
Communication Disorders M
Family Nurse Practitioner Studies M,O
Nursing and Healthcare Administration M,O
Nursing Education M,O
Nursing Informatics M,O
Nursing—General M,O
Pediatric Nursing M,O
Psychiatric Nursing M,O

MONMOUTH UNIVERSITY
Adult Nursing M,D,O
Family Nurse Practitioner Studies M,D,O
Forensic Nursing M,D,O
Health Services Management and Hospital Administration M,O
Nursing and Healthcare Administration M,D,O
Nursing Education M,D,O
Nursing—General M,D,O
Psychiatric Nursing M,D,O
School Nursing M,D,O

MONTANA STATE UNIVERSITY
Biochemistry M,D
Biological and Biomedical Sciences—General M,D
Ecology M,D
Family Nurse Practitioner Studies M,O
Immunology M,D
Infectious Diseases M,D
Microbiology M,D
Neuroscience M,D
Nursing and Healthcare Administration M,O
Nursing Education M,O
Plant Pathology M,D
Psychiatric Nursing M,O

MONTANA STATE UNIVERSITY BILLINGS
Health Services Management and Hospital Administration M

MONTANA TECH OF THE UNIVERSITY OF MONTANA
Industrial Hygiene M

MONTCLAIR STATE UNIVERSITY
Biochemistry M
Biological and Biomedical Sciences—General M,O
Communication Disorders M,D
Ecology M,O
Evolutionary Biology M,O
Molecular Biology M,O
Nutrition M,O
Pharmacology M
Physiology M,O
Public Health—General M

MORAVIAN COLLEGE
Allied Health—General M
Nursing and Healthcare Administration M
Nursing Education M
Nursing—General M

MOREHEAD STATE UNIVERSITY
Biological and Biomedical Sciences—General M

MOREHOUSE SCHOOL OF MEDICINE
Allopathic Medicine D
Biological and Biomedical Sciences—General M,D
Clinical Research M
Epidemiology M
Health Promotion M
Health Services Management and Hospital Administration M
International Health M
Public Health—General M

MORGAN STATE UNIVERSITY
Biological and Biomedical Sciences—General M,D
Environmental Biology D
Nursing—General M,D
Public Health—General M,D

MOUNTAIN STATE UNIVERSITY
Allied Health—General M
Family Nurse Practitioner Studies M
Nursing and Healthcare Administration M
Nursing Education M
Nursing—General M
Physician Assistant Studies M

MOUNT ALLISON UNIVERSITY
Biological and Biomedical Sciences—General M

MOUNT CARMEL COLLEGE OF NURSING
Adult Nursing M
Family Nurse Practitioner Studies M
Nursing and Healthcare Administration M
Nursing Education M
Nursing—General M

MOUNT MARTY COLLEGE
Nurse Anesthesia M
Nursing—General M

MOUNT MARY COLLEGE
Nutrition M
Occupational Therapy M

MOUNT SAINT MARY COLLEGE
Adult Nursing M,O
Family Nurse Practitioner Studies M,O
Nursing and Healthcare Administration M,O
Nursing Education M,O
Nursing—General M,O

MOUNT ST. MARY'S COLLEGE
Health Services Management and Hospital Administration M
Nursing and Healthcare Administration M
Nursing Education M
Nursing—General M
Physical Therapy D

MOUNT ST. MARY'S UNIVERSITY
Health Services Management and Hospital Administration M

MOUNT SAINT VINCENT UNIVERSITY
Nutrition M

MOUNT SINAI SCHOOL OF MEDICINE
Allopathic Medicine D
Bioethics M
Biological and Biomedical Sciences—General M,D
Clinical Research M,D
Community Health M,D
Neuroscience M,D

MURRAY STATE UNIVERSITY
Biological and Biomedical Sciences—General M,D
Communication Disorders M
Environmental and Occupational Health M
Family Nurse Practitioner Studies M
Industrial Hygiene M
Nurse Anesthesia M
Nursing—General M

NATIONAL COLLEGE OF MIDWIFERY
Nurse Midwifery M,D

NATIONAL COLLEGE OF NATURAL MEDICINE
Acupuncture and Oriental Medicine M
Naturopathic Medicine M,D

NATIONAL UNIVERSITY
Biological and Biomedical Sciences—General M,O
Communication Disorders M,O
Community Health M,O
Health Promotion M,O

Health Services Management and
   Hospital Administration — M,O
Public Health—General — M,O

NATIONAL UNIVERSITY OF HEALTH SCIENCES
Acupuncture and Oriental Medicine — M,D
Chiropractic — M,D
Health Services Management and
   Hospital Administration — M
Medical Imaging — M
Naturopathic Medicine — M,D

NAZARETH COLLEGE OF ROCHESTER
Communication Disorders — M
Gerontological Nursing — M
Nursing—General — M
Physical Therapy — M,D

NEBRASKA METHODIST COLLEGE
Health Promotion — M
Health Services Management and
   Hospital Administration — M
Nursing and Healthcare Administration — M
Nursing Education — M
Nursing—General — M

NEBRASKA WESLEYAN UNIVERSITY
Nursing—General — M

NEUMANN UNIVERSITY
Nursing—General — M
Physical Therapy — D

NEW CHARTER UNIVERSITY
Health Services Management and
   Hospital Administration — M

NEW ENGLAND COLLEGE
Health Services Management and
   Hospital Administration — M

THE NEW ENGLAND COLLEGE OF OPTOMETRY
Optometry — M,D
Vision Sciences — M,D

NEW ENGLAND INSTITUTE OF TECHNOLOGY
Occupational Therapy — M

NEW ENGLAND SCHOOL OF ACUPUNCTURE
Acupuncture and Oriental Medicine — M

NEW JERSEY CITY UNIVERSITY
Allied Health—General — M
Community Health — M
Health Services Management and
   Hospital Administration — M

NEW JERSEY INSTITUTE OF TECHNOLOGY
Biological and Biomedical
   Sciences—General — M,D
Computational Biology — M,D
Health Services Management and
   Hospital Administration — M
Medicinal and Pharmaceutical
   Chemistry — M
Pharmaceutical Administration — M
Pharmacology — M

NEWMAN UNIVERSITY
Nurse Anesthesia — M

NEW MEXICO INSTITUTE OF MINING AND TECHNOLOGY
Biological and Biomedical
   Sciences—General — M

NEW MEXICO STATE UNIVERSITY
Adult Nursing — M,D
Biological and Biomedical
   Sciences—General — M,D
Communication Disorders — M,D
Community Health Nursing — M,D
Community Health — M
Entomology — M
Family Nurse Practitioner Studies — M,D
Gerontological Nursing — M,D
Molecular Biology — M,D
Nursing—General — M,D
Nutrition — M
Plant Pathology — M
Public Health—General — M

NEW YORK CHIROPRACTIC COLLEGE
Acupuncture and Oriental Medicine — M
Anatomy — M
Chiropractic — D
Health Physics/Radiological Health — M
Nutrition — M

NEW YORK COLLEGE OF HEALTH PROFESSIONS
Acupuncture and Oriental Medicine — M

NEW YORK COLLEGE OF PODIATRIC MEDICINE
Podiatric Medicine — D

NEW YORK COLLEGE OF TRADITIONAL CHINESE MEDICINE
Acupuncture and Oriental Medicine — M

NEW YORK INSTITUTE OF TECHNOLOGY
Nutrition — M
Occupational Therapy — M
Osteopathic Medicine — D
Physical Therapy — D
Physician Assistant Studies — M

NEW YORK MEDICAL COLLEGE
Allopathic Medicine — D
Anatomy — M,D

Biochemistry — M,D
Biological and Biomedical
   Sciences—General — M,D*
Cell Biology — M,D
Communication Disorders — M
Environmental and Occupational
   Health — M,O
Epidemiology — M
Health Promotion — M,O
Health Services Management and
   Hospital Administration — M,D,O
Immunology — M,D
Industrial Hygiene — O
International Health — O
Microbiology — M,D
Molecular Biology — M,D
Neuroscience — M,D
Pathology — M,D
Pharmacology — M,D
Physical Therapy — D
Physiology — M,D
Public Health—General — M,D,O

NEW YORK UNIVERSITY
Acute Care/Critical Care Nursing — M,D,O
Adult Nursing — M,D,O
Allopathic Medicine — D
Bioethics — M
Biological and Biomedical
   Sciences—General — M,D
Cancer Biology/Oncology — M,D
Cell Biology — M,D
Clinical Research — M,D
Communication Disorders — M,D
Community Health — D
Computational Biology — M,D
Dentistry — D
Developmental Biology — M,D
Environmental and Occupational
   Health — M,D
Epidemiology — M,D
Family Nurse Practitioner Studies — M,D,O
Genetics — M,D
Gerontological Nursing — M,D,O
Health Promotion — M,D,O
Health Services Management and
   Hospital Administration — M,O
Immunology — M,D
Medical Imaging — M,D
Microbiology — M,D
Molecular Biology — M,D
Molecular Genetics — M,D
Molecular Pharmacology — D
Molecular Toxicology — M,D
Neurobiology — M,D
Neuroscience — M,D
Nurse Midwifery — M,D,O
Nursing and Healthcare Administration — M
Nursing Education — M,O
Nursing Informatics — M,O
Nursing—General — M,D,O
Nutrition — M,D
Occupational Therapy — M,D
Oral and Dental Sciences — M,D,O
Parasitology — M,D
Pathobiology — M,D
Pediatric Nursing — M,D,O
Pharmacology — M,D
Physical Therapy — M,D,O
Physiology — M,D
Plant Biology — M,D
Psychiatric Nursing — M,D,O
Public Health—General — D
Structural Biology — M,D
Toxicology — M,D

NICHOLLS STATE UNIVERSITY
Environmental Biology — M
Marine Biology — M

NORTH CAROLINA AGRICULTURAL AND TECHNICAL STATE UNIVERSITY
Biological and Biomedical
   Sciences—General — M
Environmental and Occupational
   Health — M
Nutrition — M

NORTH CAROLINA CENTRAL UNIVERSITY
Biological and Biomedical
   Sciences—General — M
Communication Disorders — M

NORTH CAROLINA STATE UNIVERSITY
Biochemistry — D
Biological and Biomedical
   Sciences—General — M,D,O
Botany — M,D
Cell Biology — M,D
Entomology — M,D
Epidemiology — M,D
Genetics — M,D
Genomic Sciences — M,D
Immunology — M,D
Infectious Diseases — M,D
Microbiology — M,D
Molecular Toxicology — M,D
Nutrition — M,D
Pathology — M,D
Pharmacology — M,D
Physiology — M,D
Plant Biology — M,D
Plant Pathology — M,D
Toxicology — M,D
Veterinary Medicine — D
Veterinary Sciences — M,D
Zoology — M,D

NORTH DAKOTA STATE UNIVERSITY
Biochemistry — M,D
Biological and Biomedical
   Sciences—General — M,D

Botany — M,D
Cell Biology — M,D
Conservation Biology — M,D
Ecology — M,D
Entomology — M,D
Genomic Sciences — M,D
Microbiology — M,D
Molecular Biology — M,D
Molecular Pathogenesis — M,D
Nursing—General — M,D
Nutrition — M
Pathology — M,D
Pharmaceutical Sciences — M,D
Plant Pathology — M,D
Veterinary Sciences — M,D
Zoology — M,D

NORTHEASTERN ILLINOIS UNIVERSITY
Biological and Biomedical
   Sciences—General — M

NORTHEASTERN OHIO MEDICAL UNIVERSITY
Allopathic Medicine — D
Pharmacy — D

NORTHEASTERN STATE UNIVERSITY
Communication Disorders — M
Nursing Education — M
Optometry — D

NORTHEASTERN UNIVERSITY
Acute Care/Critical Care Nursing — M,O
Allied Health—General — M,D,O
Biochemistry — M,D
Biological and Biomedical
   Sciences—General — M,D
Communication Disorders — M,D
Health Services Management and
   Hospital Administration — M,D,O
Marine Biology — M,D
Maternal and Child/Neonatal Nursing — M,O
Nurse Anesthesia — M,O
Nursing and Healthcare Administration — M
Nursing—General — M,O
Pediatric Nursing — M,O
Pharmaceutical Sciences — M,D
Physical Therapy — D
Physician Assistant Studies — M
Psychiatric Nursing — M,O
Public Health—General — M

NORTHERN ARIZONA UNIVERSITY
Allied Health—General — M,D,O
Biological and Biomedical
   Sciences—General — M,D
Communication Disorders — M
Family Nurse Practitioner Studies — M,D,O
Health Services Management and
   Hospital Administration — O
Nursing—General — M,D,O
Physical Therapy — D
Physician Assistant Studies — M
Public Health—General — O

NORTHERN ILLINOIS UNIVERSITY
Biological and Biomedical
   Sciences—General — M,D
Communication Disorders — M,D
Nursing—General — M
Nutrition — M
Physical Therapy — M
Public Health—General — M

NORTHERN KENTUCKY UNIVERSITY
Nursing—General — M,D,O

NORTHERN MICHIGAN UNIVERSITY
Biological and Biomedical
   Sciences—General — M
Nursing—General — M

NORTH GEORGIA COLLEGE & STATE UNIVERSITY
Family Nurse Practitioner Studies — M
Nursing Education — M
Physical Therapy — D

NORTH PARK UNIVERSITY
Adult Nursing — M
Nursing and Healthcare Administration — M
Nursing—General — M

NORTH SHORE–LIJ GRADUATE SCHOOL OF MOLECULAR MEDICINE
Molecular Medicine — D

NORTHWESTERN HEALTH SCIENCES UNIVERSITY
Acupuncture and Oriental Medicine — M
Chiropractic — D
Medical Imaging — M
Nutrition — M

NORTHWESTERN STATE UNIVERSITY OF LOUISIANA
Health Physics/Radiological Health — M
Nursing—General — M

NORTHWESTERN UNIVERSITY
Allopathic Medicine — D
Biochemistry — D
Biological and Biomedical
   Sciences—General — D
Biophysics — D
Biopsychology — D
Cancer Biology/Oncology — D
Cell Biology — D
Clinical Laboratory Sciences/Medical
   Technology — M
Clinical Research — M,O
Communication Disorders — M,D
Developmental Biology — D
Evolutionary Biology — D
Genetics — D

Immunology — D
Microbiology — D
Molecular Biology — D
Neurobiology — M,D
Neuroscience — D
Pharmacology — D
Physical Therapy — D
Physiology — M
Public Health—General — M
Rehabilitation Sciences — D
Reproductive Biology — D
Structural Biology — D
Toxicology — D

NORTHWEST MISSOURI STATE UNIVERSITY
Biological and Biomedical
   Sciences—General — M

NORTHWEST NAZARENE UNIVERSITY
Community Health — M
Health Services Management and
   Hospital Administration — M
Nursing and Healthcare Administration — M

NORWICH UNIVERSITY
Nursing and Healthcare Administration — M
Nursing Education — M
Nursing—General — M

NOTRE DAME DE NAMUR UNIVERSITY
Biological and Biomedical
   Sciences—General — O

NOVA SCOTIA AGRICULTURAL COLLEGE
Botany — M
Ecology — M
Environmental Biology — M
Physiology — M
Plant Pathology — M
Plant Physiology — M

NOVA SOUTHEASTERN UNIVERSITY
Allied Health—General — M,D
Biological and Biomedical
   Sciences—General — M,D
Communication Disorders — M,D,O
Dentistry — M,D,O
Marine Biology — M,D
Nursing Education — M,D
Nursing—General — M,D
Occupational Therapy — M,D
Optometry — M,D
Osteopathic Medicine — M,D,O
Pharmacology — M,D,O
Pharmacy — D*
Physical Therapy — M,D
Public Health—General — M,D,O
Vision Sciences — M,D

OAKLAND UNIVERSITY
Adult Nursing — M
Allied Health—General — M,D,O
Biological and Biomedical
   Sciences—General — M,D
Environmental and Occupational
   Health — M
Family Nurse Practitioner Studies — M,O
Gerontological Nursing — M,O
Health Promotion — O
Maternal and Child Health — M,D,O
Medical Physics — M,D
Nurse Anesthesia — M,O
Nursing Education — M,O
Nursing—General — M,D,O
Physical Therapy — M,D,O

OCCIDENTAL COLLEGE
Biological and Biomedical
   Sciences—General — M

OHIO COLLEGE OF PODIATRIC MEDICINE
Podiatric Medicine — D

OHIO NORTHERN UNIVERSITY
Pharmacy — D

THE OHIO STATE UNIVERSITY
Allied Health—General — M,D
Allopathic Medicine — D
Anatomy — M,D
Biochemistry — M,D
Biological and Biomedical
   Sciences—General — D
Biophysics — M,D
Cell Biology — M,D
Communication Disorders — M,D
Dentistry — M,D
Developmental Biology — M,D
Ecology — M,D
Entomology — M,D
Evolutionary Biology — M,D
Genetics — M,D
Health Services Management and
   Hospital Administration — M,D
Immunology — D
Microbiology — M,D
Molecular Biology — M,D
Molecular Genetics — M,D
Neuroscience — M,D
Nursing—General — M,D
Nutrition — M,D
Occupational Therapy — M
Optometry — M,D
Oral and Dental Sciences — M,D
Pathobiology — M
Pathology — M,D
Pharmaceutical Administration — M,D
Pharmacology — M,D
Pharmacy — M,D
Physical Therapy — D
Plant Pathology — M,D

---

*M—master's degree; P—first professional degree; D—doctorate; O—other advanced degree; *Close-Up and/or Display*

Public Health—General M,D
Rehabilitation Sciences M,D
Veterinary Sciences M,D
Virology D

OHIO UNIVERSITY
Acute Care/Critical Care Nursing M
Biochemistry M,D
Biological and Biomedical
   Sciences—General M,D
Cell Biology M,D
Communication Disorders M,D
Ecology M,D
Environmental Biology M,D
Evolutionary Biology M,D
Family Nurse Practitioner Studies M
Health Services Management and
   Hospital Administration M
Microbiology M,D
Molecular Biology M,D
Neuroscience M,D
Nursing and Healthcare Administration M
Nursing Education M
Nursing—General M
Nutrition M
Osteopathic Medicine D
Physical Therapy D
Physiology M,D
Plant Biology M,D
Public Health—General M

OKLAHOMA CITY UNIVERSITY
Health Services Management and
   Hospital Administration M
Nursing—General M

OKLAHOMA STATE UNIVERSITY
Biochemistry M,D
Botany M,D
Communication Disorders M
Entomology M,D
Microbiology M,D
Molecular Biology M,D
Molecular Genetics M,D
Nutrition M,D
Plant Pathology M,D
Veterinary Medicine D
Veterinary Sciences M,D
Zoology M,D

**OKLAHOMA STATE UNIVERSITY
CENTER FOR HEALTH SCIENCES**
Biological and Biomedical
   Sciences—General M,D
Health Services Management and
   Hospital Administration M
Microbiology M,O
Molecular Biology M,O
Osteopathic Medicine D
Pathology M,O
Toxicology M,O

OLD DOMINION UNIVERSITY
Allied Health—General M,D
Biochemistry M,D
Biological and Biomedical
   Sciences—General M,D
Communication Disorders M
Dental Hygiene M
Ecology D
Environmental and Occupational
   Health M
Family Nurse Practitioner Studies M
Health Promotion M
Health Services Research D
Nurse Anesthesia M
Nurse Midwifery M,D
Nursing and Healthcare Administration M
Nursing Education M
Nursing—General M,D
Physical Therapy D
Public Health—General M
Women's Health Nursing M

**OREGON COLLEGE OF ORIENTAL
MEDICINE**
Acupuncture and Oriental Medicine M,D

**OREGON HEALTH & SCIENCE
UNIVERSITY**
Allopathic Medicine D
Biochemistry M,D
Biological and Biomedical
   Sciences—General M,D,O
Biopsychology D
Cancer Biology/Oncology D
Cell Biology D
Clinical Research M,O
Community Health Nursing M,O
Computational Biology M,D,O
Dentistry D,O
Developmental Biology D
Epidemiology M,O
Family Nurse Practitioner Studies M,O
Genetics D
Gerontological Nursing O
Health Services Management and
   Hospital Administration M
Immunology D
Microbiology D
Molecular Biology M,D
Neuroscience D
Nurse Anesthesia M
Nurse Midwifery M,O
Nursing Education M,O
Nursing—General M,D,O
Nutrition M,O
Oral and Dental Sciences M,D,O
Pharmacology D
Physician Assistant Studies M
Physiology D
Psychiatric Nursing M,O

OREGON STATE UNIVERSITY
Biochemistry M,D
Biophysics M,D
Botany M,D

Cell Biology M,D
Computational Biology M,D
Environmental and Occupational
   Health M,D
Epidemiology M
Genetics M,D
Genomic Sciences M,D
Health Physics/Radiological Health M,D
Health Promotion M,D
Health Services Management and
   Hospital Administration M,D
International Health M
Microbiology M,D
Molecular Biology M,D
Molecular Toxicology M,D
Pharmaceutical Sciences M,D
Pharmacy M,D
Plant Pathology M,D
Plant Physiology M,D
Toxicology M,D
Veterinary Medicine D
Veterinary Sciences M
Zoology M,D

OTTERBEIN UNIVERSITY
Family Nurse Practitioner Studies M,D,O
Nurse Anesthesia M,D,O
Nursing and Healthcare Administration M,D,O
Nursing Education M,D,O
Nursing—General M,D,O

OUR LADY OF THE LAKE COLLEGE
Nurse Anesthesia M
Nursing and Healthcare Administration M
Nursing Education M
Nursing—General M
Physician Assistant Studies M

**OUR LADY OF THE LAKE UNIVERSITY
OF SAN ANTONIO**
Communication Disorders M
Health Services Management and
   Hospital Administration M

PACE UNIVERSITY
Family Nurse Practitioner Studies M,D,O
Health Services Management and
   Hospital Administration M
Nursing and Healthcare Administration M,D,O
Nursing Education M,D,O
Nursing—General M,D,O
Physician Assistant Studies M

**PACIFIC COLLEGE OF ORIENTAL
MEDICINE**
Acupuncture and Oriental Medicine M,D

**PACIFIC COLLEGE OF ORIENTAL
MEDICINE-CHICAGO**
Acupuncture and Oriental Medicine M

**PACIFIC COLLEGE OF ORIENTAL
MEDICINE-NEW YORK**
Acupuncture and Oriental Medicine M

PACIFIC LUTHERAN UNIVERSITY
Family Nurse Practitioner Studies M
Nursing and Healthcare Administration M
Nursing—General M

PACIFIC UNIVERSITY
Health Services Management and
   Hospital Administration M
Occupational Therapy M
Pharmacy D
Physical Therapy D
Physician Assistant Studies M

PALM BEACH ATLANTIC UNIVERSITY
Pharmacy D

PALMER COLLEGE OF CHIROPRACTIC
Anatomy M
Chiropractic D
Clinical Research M

PALO ALTO UNIVERSITY
Biopsychology D

PARKER UNIVERSITY
Chiropractic D

PARK UNIVERSITY
Health Services Management and
   Hospital Administration M

PENN STATE HARRISBURG
Health Services Management and
   Hospital Administration M

**PENN STATE HERSHEY MEDICAL
CENTER**
Allopathic Medicine M,D
Anatomy M,D
Biochemistry M,D
Biological and Biomedical
   Sciences—General M,D
Genetics M,D
Health Services Research M
Immunology M,D
Microbiology M,D
Molecular Biology M,D
Molecular Genetics M,D
Molecular Medicine M,D
Molecular Toxicology M,D
Neuroscience M,D
Pharmacology M,D
Physiology M,D
Public Health—General M
Veterinary Sciences M
Virology M,D

PENN STATE UNIVERSITY PARK
Biochemistry M,D
Biological and Biomedical
   Sciences—General M,D
Biopsychology M,D
Communication Disorders M,D,O
Ecology M,D
Entomology M,D

Genetics M,D
Health Services Management and
   Hospital Administration M,D
Immunology M,D
Infectious Diseases M,D
Microbiology M,D
Molecular Biology M,D
Molecular Pharmacology M,D
Nursing—General M,D
Nutrition M,D
Pathobiology M,D
Physiology M,D
Plant Biology M,D
Plant Pathology M,D
Veterinary Sciences M,D

PFEIFFER UNIVERSITY
Health Services Management and
   Hospital Administration M

**PHILADELPHIA COLLEGE OF
OSTEOPATHIC MEDICINE**
Biological and Biomedical
   Sciences—General M,O
Osteopathic Medicine D
Physician Assistant Studies M*

PHILADELPHIA UNIVERSITY
Health Services Management and
   Hospital Administration M
Nurse Midwifery M,O
Occupational Therapy M
Physician Assistant Studies M

PITTSBURG STATE UNIVERSITY
Biological and Biomedical
   Sciences—General M
Nursing—General M

POINT LOMA NAZARENE UNIVERSITY
Biological and Biomedical
   Sciences—General M
Nursing—General M,O

**PONCE SCHOOL OF MEDICINE &
HEALTH SCIENCES**
Allopathic Medicine D
Biological and Biomedical
   Sciences—General D
Epidemiology M,D
Public Health—General M,D

**PONTIFICAL CATHOLIC UNIVERSITY OF
PUERTO RICO**
Biological and Biomedical
   Sciences—General M
Clinical Laboratory Sciences/Medical
   Technology O
Medical/Surgical Nursing M
Nursing—General M
Psychiatric Nursing M

**PONTIFICIA UNIVERSIDAD CATOLICA
MADRE Y MAESTRA**
Allopathic Medicine D

PORTLAND STATE UNIVERSITY
Biological and Biomedical
   Sciences—General M,D
Communication Disorders M
Health Promotion M,O
Health Services Management and
   Hospital Administration M
Public Health—General M,O

PRAIRIE VIEW A&M UNIVERSITY
Biological and Biomedical
   Sciences—General M
Family Nurse Practitioner Studies M
Nursing and Healthcare Administration M
Nursing Education M
Nursing—General M
Toxicology M

PRINCETON UNIVERSITY
Computational Biology D
Ecology D
Evolutionary Biology D
Marine Biology D
Molecular Biology D
Neuroscience D

PURDUE UNIVERSITY
Allied Health—General M,D
Anatomy M,D
Biochemistry M,D
Biological and Biomedical
   Sciences—General M,D
Biophysics M,D
Botany M,D
Cancer Biology/Oncology D
Cell Biology M,D
Communication Disorders M,D
Developmental Biology M,D
Ecology M,D
Entomology M,D
Environmental and Occupational
   Health M,D
Epidemiology M,D
Evolutionary Biology M,D
Genetics M,D
Genomic Sciences M,D
Health Physics/Radiological Health M,D
Immunology M,D
Medical Physics M,D
Medicinal and Pharmaceutical
   Chemistry M,D,O
Microbiology M,D
Molecular Biology M,D
Molecular Pharmacology M,D,O
Neurobiology M,D
Neuroscience D
Nutrition M,D
Pathobiology M,D
Pathology M,D
Pharmaceutical Administration M,D,O
Pharmaceutical Sciences M,D
Pharmacology M,D

Pharmacy D
Physiology M,D
Plant Pathology M,D
Plant Physiology M,D
Public Health—General M,D
Systems Biology D
Toxicology M,D
Veterinary Medicine D
Veterinary Sciences M,D
Virology M,D

PURDUE UNIVERSITY CALUMET
Acute Care/Critical Care Nursing M
Adult Nursing M
Biological and Biomedical
   Sciences—General M
Family Nurse Practitioner Studies M
Nursing and Healthcare Administration M
Nursing—General M

**QUEENS COLLEGE OF THE CITY
UNIVERSITY OF NEW YORK**
Biochemistry M
Biological and Biomedical
   Sciences—General M
Communication Disorders M

QUEEN'S UNIVERSITY AT KINGSTON
Allopathic Medicine M
Anatomy M,D
Biochemistry M,D
Biological and Biomedical
   Sciences—General M,D
Cancer Biology/Oncology M,D
Cardiovascular Sciences M,D
Cell Biology M,D
Epidemiology M,D
Family Nurse Practitioner Studies M,D,O
Health Services Management and
   Hospital Administration M,D
Immunology M,D
Microbiology M,D
Molecular Biology M,D
Molecular Medicine M,D
Neurobiology M,D
Neuroscience M,D
Nursing—General M,D,O
Occupational Therapy M,D
Pathology M,D
Pediatric Nursing M,D,O
Pharmaceutical Sciences M,D
Pharmacology M,D
Physical Therapy M,D
Physiology M,D
Public Health—General M,D
Rehabilitation Sciences M,D
Reproductive Biology M,D
Toxicology M,D
Women's Health Nursing M,D,O

QUEENS UNIVERSITY OF CHARLOTTE
Nursing and Healthcare Administration M
Nursing—General M

QUINNIPIAC UNIVERSITY
Adult Nursing D
Allied Health—General M,D
Biological and Biomedical
   Sciences—General M
Cardiovascular Sciences M
Cell Biology M
Clinical Laboratory Sciences/Medical
   Technology M
Community Health D
Family Nurse Practitioner Studies M
Health Physics/Radiological Health M
Health Services Management and
   Hospital Administration M
Microbiology M
Molecular Biology M
Nursing—General M,D
Occupational Therapy M
Pathology M
Perfusion M
Physical Therapy M,D
Physician Assistant Studies M

RADFORD UNIVERSITY
Communication Disorders M
Nursing—General M,D
Occupational Therapy M
Physical Therapy D

RAMAPO COLLEGE OF NEW JERSEY
Nursing Education M
Nursing—General M

REGIS COLLEGE (MA)
Biological and Biomedical
   Sciences—General M,D,O
Family Nurse Practitioner Studies M,D,O
Health Services Management and
   Hospital Administration M,D,O
Nursing Education M,D,O
Nursing—General M,D,O

REGIS UNIVERSITY
Allied Health—General M,D,O
Family Nurse Practitioner Studies M,D,O
Health Services Management and
   Hospital Administration M,D,O
Maternal and Child/Neonatal Nursing M,D,O
Nursing and Healthcare Administration M,D,O
Nursing—General M,D,O
Pharmacy M,D,O
Physical Therapy M,D,O

**RENSSELAER POLYTECHNIC
INSTITUTE**
Biochemistry M,D
Biological and Biomedical
   Sciences—General M,D
Biophysics M,D

RESEARCH COLLEGE OF NURSING
Family Nurse Practitioner Studies M
Nursing and Healthcare Administration M

Nursing Education M
Nursing—General M

RESURRECTION UNIVERSITY
Nursing—General M

RHODE ISLAND COLLEGE
Biological and Biomedical Sciences—General M,O
Nursing—General M

RICE UNIVERSITY
Biochemistry M,D
Cell Biology M,D
Ecology M,D
Evolutionary Biology M,D
Health Services Management and Hospital Administration M

THE RICHARD STOCKTON COLLEGE OF NEW JERSEY
Communication Disorders M
Nursing—General M
Occupational Therapy M
Physical Therapy D

RIVIER UNIVERSITY
Family Nurse Practitioner Studies M
Nursing Education M
Nursing—General M
Psychiatric Nursing M

ROBERT MORRIS UNIVERSITY
Nursing—General M,D

ROBERT MORRIS UNIVERSITY ILLINOIS
Health Services Management and Hospital Administration M

ROBERTS WESLEYAN COLLEGE
Health Services Management and Hospital Administration M
Nursing and Healthcare Administration M
Nursing Education M
Nursing—General M

ROCHESTER INSTITUTE OF TECHNOLOGY
Biological and Biomedical Sciences—General M
Environmental and Occupational Health M
Health Services Management and Hospital Administration M,O

THE ROCKEFELLER UNIVERSITY
Biological and Biomedical Sciences—General D*

ROCKHURST UNIVERSITY
Communication Disorders M
Occupational Therapy M
Physical Therapy D

ROCKY MOUNTAIN COLLEGE
Physician Assistant Studies M

ROCKY MOUNTAIN UNIVERSITY OF HEALTH PROFESSIONS
Family Nurse Practitioner Studies D
Health Promotion D
Nursing—General M,D
Occupational Therapy D
Pediatric Nursing D
Physical Therapy D
Physiology D

ROOSEVELT UNIVERSITY
Pharmacy D

ROSALIND FRANKLIN UNIVERSITY OF MEDICINE AND SCIENCE
Allied Health—General M,D,O
Allopathic Medicine D
Anatomy M,D
Biochemistry M,D
Biological and Biomedical Sciences—General M,D
Biophysics M,D
Cell Biology M,D
Health Services Management and Hospital Administration M,O
Immunology M,D
Medical Physics M
Microbiology M,D
Molecular Biology M,D
Molecular Pharmacology M,D
Neuroscience D
Nurse Anesthesia M
Nutrition M
Pathology M
Physical Therapy M,D
Physician Assistant Studies M
Physiology M,D
Podiatric Medicine D
Women's Health Nursing M,O

ROSEMAN UNIVERSITY OF HEALTH SCIENCES
Oral and Dental Sciences M
Pharmacy D

ROWAN UNIVERSITY
Health Promotion M

ROYAL ROADS UNIVERSITY
Health Services Management and Hospital Administration O

RUSH UNIVERSITY
Acute Care/Critical Care Nursing M,D,O
Adult Nursing M,D,O
Allopathic Medicine D
Anatomy M,D
Biochemistry D
Bioethics M,O
Cell Biology M,D
Clinical Laboratory Sciences/Medical Technology M
Communication Disorders M,D
Community Health Nursing M,D,O
Family Nurse Practitioner Studies M,D,O
Gerontological Nursing M,D,O
Health Services Management and Hospital Administration M,D
Immunology M,D
Maternal and Child/Neonatal Nursing M,D,O
Medical Physics M,D
Medical/Surgical Nursing M,D,O
Microbiology M,D
Neuroscience M,D
Nurse Anesthesia M,D,O
Nursing—General M,D,O
Nutrition M
Occupational Therapy M
Pediatric Nursing M,D,O
Pharmaceutical Sciences M,D
Pharmacology M,D
Physician Assistant Studies M
Physiology D
Psychiatric Nursing M,D,O
Virology M,D

RUTGERS, THE STATE UNIVERSITY OF NEW JERSEY, CAMDEN
Biological and Biomedical Sciences—General M
Computational Biology M,D
Physical Therapy D

RUTGERS, THE STATE UNIVERSITY OF NEW JERSEY, NEWARK
Adult Nursing M
Biochemistry M,D
Biological and Biomedical Sciences—General M,D
Biopsychology D
Community Health Nursing M
Computational Biology M
Family Nurse Practitioner Studies M
Gerontological Nursing M
Health Services Management and Hospital Administration M,D
Maternal and Child/Neonatal Nursing M
Neuroscience D
Nursing—General M
Psychiatric Nursing M

RUTGERS, THE STATE UNIVERSITY OF NEW JERSEY, NEW BRUNSWICK
Biochemistry M,D
Biological and Biomedical Sciences—General D
Biopsychology D
Cancer Biology/Oncology M,D
Cell Biology M,D
Computational Biology D
Developmental Biology M,D
Ecology M,D
Entomology M,D
Environmental Biology M,D
Evolutionary Biology M,D
Genetics M,D
Immunology M,D
Marine Biology M,D
Medical Microbiology M,D
Medicinal and Pharmaceutical Chemistry M,D
Microbiology M,D
Molecular Biology M,D
Molecular Biophysics D
Molecular Genetics M,D
Molecular Pharmacology D
Molecular Physiology M,D
Neuroscience M,D
Nutrition M,D
Pharmaceutical Sciences M,D
Pharmacy M,D
Physiology M,D
Plant Biology M,D
Plant Molecular Biology M,D
Plant Pathology M,D
Public Health—General M,D
Reproductive Biology M,D
Systems Biology D
Toxicology M,D
Virology M,D

SACRED HEART UNIVERSITY
Family Nurse Practitioner Studies M,D
Health Services Management and Hospital Administration M,D
Nursing and Healthcare Administration M,D
Nursing—General M,D
Occupational Therapy M
Physical Therapy D

SAGE GRADUATE SCHOOL
Adult Nursing M,O
Community Health Nursing M,O
Community Health M
Family Nurse Practitioner Studies M,O
Gerontological Nursing M,D,O
Health Services Management and Hospital Administration M,D,O
Nursing and Healthcare Administration M,D,O
Nursing Education D
Nursing—General M,D,O
Nutrition M,O
Occupational Therapy M
Physical Therapy D
Psychiatric Nursing M,O

SAGINAW VALLEY STATE UNIVERSITY
Family Nurse Practitioner Studies M
Health Services Management and Hospital Administration M
Nursing and Healthcare Administration M
Nursing—General M
Occupational Therapy M

ST. AMBROSE UNIVERSITY
Communication Disorders M
Health Services Management and Hospital Administration M,D
Nursing—General M
Occupational Therapy M
Physical Therapy D

SAINT ANTHONY COLLEGE OF NURSING
Nursing—General M

ST. CATHARINE COLLEGE
Health Promotion M

ST. CATHERINE UNIVERSITY
Adult Nursing M,D
Gerontological Nursing M,D
Maternal and Child/Neonatal Nursing M,D
Nursing Education M,D
Nursing—General M,D
Occupational Therapy M
Pediatric Nursing M,D
Physical Therapy D
Public Health—General M

ST. CLOUD STATE UNIVERSITY
Biological and Biomedical Sciences—General M
Communication Disorders M

SAINT FRANCIS MEDICAL CENTER COLLEGE OF NURSING
Family Nurse Practitioner Studies M,D,O
Maternal and Child/Neonatal Nursing M,D,O
Medical/Surgical Nursing M,D,O
Nursing and Healthcare Administration M,D,O
Nursing Education M,D,O
Nursing—General M,D,O
Psychiatric Nursing M,D,O

SAINT FRANCIS UNIVERSITY
Biological and Biomedical Sciences—General M
Occupational Therapy M
Physical Therapy D
Physician Assistant Studies M

ST. FRANCIS XAVIER UNIVERSITY
Biological and Biomedical Sciences—General M

ST. JOHN FISHER COLLEGE
Family Nurse Practitioner Studies M,O
Nursing Education M,O
Nursing—General M,D,O
Pharmacy D

ST. JOHN'S UNIVERSITY (NY)
Biological and Biomedical Sciences—General M,D
Communication Disorders M,D
Pharmaceutical Administration M
Pharmaceutical Sciences M,D
Pharmacy D
Toxicology M,D

ST. JOSEPH'S COLLEGE, LONG ISLAND CAMPUS
Health Services Management and Hospital Administration M,O
Nursing—General M

ST. JOSEPH'S COLLEGE, NEW YORK
Health Services Management and Hospital Administration M
Nursing—General M*

SAINT JOSEPH'S COLLEGE OF MAINE
Family Nurse Practitioner Studies M,O
Health Services Management and Hospital Administration M
Nursing and Healthcare Administration M,O
Nursing Education M,O
Nursing—General M,O

SAINT JOSEPH'S UNIVERSITY
Biological and Biomedical Sciences—General M
Communication Disorders M,D,O
Environmental and Occupational Health M,O
Health Services Management and Hospital Administration M,O
Nurse Anesthesia M,O
Nursing and Healthcare Administration M,O
School Nursing M,O

SAINT LEO UNIVERSITY
Health Services Management and Hospital Administration M

ST. LOUIS COLLEGE OF PHARMACY
Pharmacy D

SAINT LOUIS UNIVERSITY
Allied Health—General M,D,O
Allopathic Medicine D
Anatomy M,D
Biochemistry D
Bioethics D,O
Biological and Biomedical Sciences—General M,D
Communication Disorders M
Community Health M
Dentistry M
Health Services Management and Hospital Administration M,D
Immunology D
Microbiology D
Molecular Biology D
Nursing—General M,D,O
Nutrition M
Occupational Therapy M
Oral and Dental Sciences M
Pathology D
Pharmacology D
Physical Therapy M,D
Physician Assistant Studies M
Physiology D
Public Health—General M,D

SAINT MARY'S UNIVERSITY OF MINNESOTA
Environmental and Occupational Health M
Health Services Management and Hospital Administration M
Nurse Anesthesia M

SAINT PETER'S UNIVERSITY
Adult Nursing M,D,O
Health Services Management and Hospital Administration M
Nursing and Healthcare Administration M,D,O
Nursing—General M,D,O

ST. THOMAS UNIVERSITY
Health Services Management and Hospital Administration M,O

SAINT VINCENT COLLEGE
Nurse Anesthesia M
Nursing and Healthcare Administration M

SAINT XAVIER UNIVERSITY
Communication Disorders M
Health Services Management and Hospital Administration M,O
Nursing—General M,O

SALEM STATE UNIVERSITY
Nursing—General M
Occupational Therapy M

SALISBURY UNIVERSITY
Biological and Biomedical Sciences—General M
Nursing—General M
Physiology M

SALUS UNIVERSITY
Communication Disorders D
Optometry D
Physician Assistant Studies M
Public Health—General M
Rehabilitation Sciences M,O
Vision Sciences M,O

SALVE REGINA UNIVERSITY
Health Services Management and Hospital Administration M,O

SAMFORD UNIVERSITY
Family Nurse Practitioner Studies M,D
Nurse Anesthesia M,D
Nursing and Healthcare Administration M,D
Nursing Education M,D
Nursing—General M,D
Pharmacy D

SAM HOUSTON STATE UNIVERSITY
Biological and Biomedical Sciences—General M
Nutrition M

SAMRA UNIVERSITY OF ORIENTAL MEDICINE
Acupuncture and Oriental Medicine M,D

SAMUEL MERRITT UNIVERSITY
Family Nurse Practitioner Studies M,D,O
Nurse Anesthesia M,D,O
Nursing and Healthcare Administration M,D,O
Nursing—General M,D,O
Occupational Therapy M
Physical Therapy D
Physician Assistant Studies M

SAN DIEGO STATE UNIVERSITY
Biochemistry M,D
Biological and Biomedical Sciences—General M,D
Cell Biology M,D
Communication Disorders M,D
Ecology M,D
Emergency Medical Services M,D
Environmental and Occupational Health M,D
Epidemiology M,D
Health Physics/Radiological Health M
Health Promotion M,D
Health Services Management and Hospital Administration M,D
International Health M,D
Microbiology M
Molecular Biology M,D
Nursing—General M
Nutrition M
Pharmaceutical Administration M
Public Health—General M,D
Toxicology M,D

SAN FRANCISCO STATE UNIVERSITY
Biochemistry M
Biological and Biomedical Sciences—General M
Cell Biology M
Communication Disorders M
Community Health Nursing M,O
Conservation Biology M
Developmental Biology M
Ecology M
Family Nurse Practitioner Studies M,O
Marine Biology M
Microbiology M
Molecular Biology M
Nursing and Healthcare Administration M,O
Nursing Education M,O
Nursing—General M,O
Physical Therapy D

*M—master's degree; P—first professional degree; D—doctorate; O—other advanced degree; *Close-Up and/or Display*

Physiology M
Public Health—General M

SAN JOSE STATE UNIVERSITY
Biological and Biomedical
  Sciences—General M
Communication Disorders M
Ecology M
Gerontological Nursing M,O
Microbiology M
Molecular Biology M
Nursing and Healthcare Administration M,O
Nursing Education M
Nursing—General M
Nutrition M
Occupational Therapy M
Physiology M
Public Health—General M,O

SAN JUAN BAUTISTA SCHOOL OF MEDICINE
Allopathic Medicine D

SARAH LAWRENCE COLLEGE
Human Genetics M
Public Health—General M

SAYBROOK UNIVERSITY
Nutrition M,D,O

THE SCRIPPS RESEARCH INSTITUTE
Biological and Biomedical
  Sciences—General D

SEATTLE INSTITUTE OF ORIENTAL MEDICINE
Acupuncture and Oriental Medicine M

SEATTLE PACIFIC UNIVERSITY
Adult Nursing M,O
Family Nurse Practitioner Studies M,O
Gerontological Nursing M,O
Nursing and Healthcare Administration M,O
Nursing Education M,O
Nursing Informatics M,O
Nursing—General M,O

SEATTLE UNIVERSITY
Adult Nursing M
Community Health Nursing M
Family Nurse Practitioner Studies M
Gerontological Nursing M
Nurse Midwifery M
Nursing—General M
Psychiatric Nursing M

SETON HALL UNIVERSITY
Adult Nursing M,D
Allied Health—General D
Biochemistry M,D
Biological and Biomedical
  Sciences—General M,D
Communication Disorders M
Gerontological Nursing M,D
Health Services Management and
  Hospital Administration M,D,O
Microbiology M,D
Molecular Biology M,D
Neuroscience M,D
Nursing and Healthcare Administration M,D
Nursing Education M,D
Nursing—General M,D
Occupational Therapy M
Pediatric Nursing M,D
Physical Therapy D
Physician Assistant Studies M
School Nursing M,D

SETON HILL UNIVERSITY
Oral and Dental Sciences O
Physician Assistant Studies M

SHAWNEE STATE UNIVERSITY
Occupational Therapy M

SHENANDOAH UNIVERSITY
Allied Health—General M,D,O
Family Nurse Practitioner Studies M,D,O
Nurse Midwifery M,D,O
Nursing Education M,D,O
Nursing—General M,D,O
Occupational Therapy D
Pharmacy D
Physical Therapy D
Physician Assistant Studies M
Psychiatric Nursing M,D,O

SHERMAN COLLEGE OF CHIROPRACTIC
Chiropractic D

SHIPPENSBURG UNIVERSITY OF PENNSYLVANIA
Biological and Biomedical
  Sciences—General M

SIMMONS COLLEGE
Health Services Management and
  Hospital Administration M,O
Nursing and Healthcare Administration M,D,O
Nursing—General M,D,O
Nutrition M,D,O
Physical Therapy M,D,O

SIMON FRASER UNIVERSITY
Biochemistry M,D
Biological and Biomedical
  Sciences—General M,D
Biophysics M,D
Community Health M
Entomology M,D
Molecular Biology M,D
Public Health—General M
Toxicology M,D

SLIPPERY ROCK UNIVERSITY OF PENNSYLVANIA
Physical Therapy D

SMITH COLLEGE
Biological and Biomedical
  Sciences—General M

SONOMA STATE UNIVERSITY
Biochemistry M
Biological and Biomedical
  Sciences—General M
Environmental Biology M
Family Nurse Practitioner Studies M

SOUTH BAYLO UNIVERSITY
Acupuncture and Oriental Medicine M

SOUTH CAROLINA STATE UNIVERSITY
Allied Health—General M
Communication Disorders M
Nutrition M

SOUTH COLLEGE
Physician Assistant Studies M

SOUTH DAKOTA STATE UNIVERSITY
Biological and Biomedical
  Sciences—General M,D
Microbiology M,D
Nursing—General M,D
Nutrition M,D
Pharmaceutical Sciences M,D
Pharmacy D
Veterinary Sciences M,D

SOUTHEASTERN LOUISIANA UNIVERSITY
Adult Nursing M
Biological and Biomedical
  Sciences—General M
Communication Disorders M
Family Nurse Practitioner Studies M
Nursing and Healthcare Administration M
Nursing Education M
Nursing—General M
Psychiatric Nursing M

SOUTHEASTERN OKLAHOMA STATE UNIVERSITY
Environmental and Occupational
  Health M

SOUTHEAST MISSOURI STATE UNIVERSITY
Biological and Biomedical
  Sciences—General M
Communication Disorders M
Health Services Management and
  Hospital Administration M
Nursing—General M
Nutrition M

SOUTHERN ADVENTIST UNIVERSITY
Acute Care/Critical Care Nursing M
Adult Nursing M
Family Nurse Practitioner Studies M
Health Services Management and
  Hospital Administration M
Nursing and Healthcare Administration M
Nursing—General M

SOUTHERN ARKANSAS UNIVERSITY–MAGNOLIA
Psychiatric Nursing M

SOUTHERN CALIFORNIA COLLEGE OF OPTOMETRY
Optometry M,D
Vision Sciences M,D

SOUTHERN CALIFORNIA UNIVERSITY OF HEALTH SCIENCES
Acupuncture and Oriental Medicine M
Chiropractic D

SOUTHERN COLLEGE OF OPTOMETRY
Optometry D

SOUTHERN CONNECTICUT STATE UNIVERSITY
Biological and Biomedical
  Sciences—General M
Communication Disorders M
Nursing and Healthcare Administration M
Nursing Education M
Nursing—General M
Public Health—General M

SOUTHERN ILLINOIS UNIVERSITY CARBONDALE
Biochemistry M,D
Biological and Biomedical
  Sciences—General M,D
Communication Disorders M
Community Health M
Health Services Management and
  Hospital Administration M
Microbiology M,D
Molecular Biology M,D
Nutrition M
Pharmacology M,D
Physician Assistant Studies M
Physiology M,D
Plant Biology M,D
Zoology M,D

SOUTHERN ILLINOIS UNIVERSITY EDWARDSVILLE
Biological and Biomedical
  Sciences—General M
Communication Disorders M
Dentistry D
Family Nurse Practitioner Studies M,D,O
Nurse Anesthesia M
Nursing and Healthcare Administration M,O
Nursing Education M,O
Nursing—General M,D,O
Pharmacy D

SOUTHERN METHODIST UNIVERSITY
Biological and Biomedical
  Sciences—General M,D

SOUTHERN NAZARENE UNIVERSITY
Health Services Management and
  Hospital Administration M
Nursing and Healthcare Administration M
Nursing Education M
Nursing—General M

SOUTHERN NEW HAMPSHIRE UNIVERSITY
Community Health M,O

SOUTHERN UNIVERSITY AND AGRICULTURAL AND MECHANICAL COLLEGE
Biochemistry M
Biological and Biomedical
  Sciences—General M
Family Nurse Practitioner Studies M,D,O
Gerontological Nursing M,D,O
Nursing and Healthcare Administration M,D,O
Nursing Education M,D,O
Nursing—General M,D,O

SOUTH UNIVERSITY (AL)
Health Services Management and
  Hospital Administration M*

SOUTH UNIVERSITY
Family Nurse Practitioner Studies M
Health Services Management and
  Hospital Administration M
Nursing—General M

SOUTH UNIVERSITY (FL)
Adult Nursing M
Family Nurse Practitioner Studies M
Health Services Management and
  Hospital Administration M*
Nursing Education M
Nursing—General M

SOUTH UNIVERSITY (GA)
Anesthesiologist Assistant Studies M*
Health Services Management and
  Hospital Administration M
Nursing Education M
Nursing—General M
Pharmacy D*
Physician Assistant Studies M*

SOUTH UNIVERSITY (SC)
Health Services Management and
  Hospital Administration M*
Pharmacy D*

SOUTHWEST ACUPUNCTURE COLLEGE
Acupuncture and Oriental Medicine M

SOUTHWEST BAPTIST UNIVERSITY
Health Services Management and
  Hospital Administration M
Physical Therapy D

SOUTHWEST COLLEGE OF NATUROPATHIC MEDICINE AND HEALTH SCIENCES
Naturopathic Medicine D

SOUTHWESTERN OKLAHOMA STATE UNIVERSITY
Allied Health—General M
Microbiology M
Pharmacy D

SPALDING UNIVERSITY
Adult Nursing M
Family Nurse Practitioner Studies M
Nursing and Healthcare Administration M
Nursing—General M
Occupational Therapy M
Pediatric Nursing M

SPRING ARBOR UNIVERSITY
Nursing—General M

SPRINGFIELD COLLEGE
Health Promotion M,D
Health Services Management and
  Hospital Administration M
Occupational Therapy M,O
Physical Therapy D
Physician Assistant Studies M

SPRING HILL COLLEGE
Nursing and Healthcare Administration M,O
Nursing—General M,O

STANFORD UNIVERSITY
Allopathic Medicine D
Biochemistry D
Biological and Biomedical
  Sciences—General M,D
Biophysics D
Cancer Biology/Oncology D
Developmental Biology D
Epidemiology M,D
Genetics D
Health Services Research M
Immunology D
Microbiology D
Molecular Pharmacology D
Neuroscience D
Physiology D
Structural Biology D

STATE UNIVERSITY OF NEW YORK AT BINGHAMTON
Biological and Biomedical
  Sciences—General M,D
Biopsychology M,D
Health Services Management and
  Hospital Administration M,D
Nursing—General M,D,O

STATE UNIVERSITY OF NEW YORK AT FREDONIA
Biological and Biomedical
  Sciences—General M
Communication Disorders M

STATE UNIVERSITY OF NEW YORK AT NEW PALTZ
Biological and Biomedical
  Sciences—General M
Communication Disorders M

STATE UNIVERSITY OF NEW YORK AT PLATTSBURGH
Communication Disorders M

STATE UNIVERSITY OF NEW YORK COLLEGE AT ONEONTA
Biological and Biomedical
  Sciences—General M
Nutrition M

STATE UNIVERSITY OF NEW YORK COLLEGE OF ENVIRONMENTAL SCIENCE AND FORESTRY
Biochemistry M,D
Conservation Biology M,D
Ecology M,D
Entomology M,D
Environmental Biology M,D
Plant Pathology M,D

STATE UNIVERSITY OF NEW YORK COLLEGE OF OPTOMETRY
Optometry D
Vision Sciences M,D

STATE UNIVERSITY OF NEW YORK DOWNSTATE MEDICAL CENTER
Allopathic Medicine M,D
Biological and Biomedical
  Sciences—General M,D
Cell Biology D
Community Health M
Family Nurse Practitioner Studies M,O
Medical/Surgical Nursing M,O
Molecular Biology D
Neuroscience D
Nurse Anesthesia M
Nurse Midwifery M,O
Nursing—General M,O
Public Health—General M

STATE UNIVERSITY OF NEW YORK INSTITUTE OF TECHNOLOGY
Adult Nursing M,O
Family Nurse Practitioner Studies M,O
Gerontological Nursing M,O
Nursing and Healthcare Administration M,O
Nursing Education M,O

STATE UNIVERSITY OF NEW YORK UPSTATE MEDICAL UNIVERSITY
Allopathic Medicine D
Anatomy M,D
Biochemistry M,D
Biological and Biomedical
  Sciences—General M,D
Cancer Biology/Oncology
Cardiovascular Sciences
Cell Biology M,D
Clinical Laboratory Sciences/Medical
  Technology M
Family Nurse Practitioner Studies M,O
Immunology M,D
Infectious Diseases
Microbiology M,D
Molecular Biology M,D
Neuroscience D
Nursing—General M,O
Pharmacology D
Physical Therapy D
Physiology M,D

STEPHEN F. AUSTIN STATE UNIVERSITY
Biological and Biomedical
  Sciences—General M
Communication Disorders M

STEVENS INSTITUTE OF TECHNOLOGY
Biochemistry M,D,O
Pharmaceutical Sciences M,O

STEVENSON UNIVERSITY
Nursing—General M

STONY BROOK UNIVERSITY, STATE UNIVERSITY OF NEW YORK
Adult Nursing M,O
Allopathic Medicine D
Anatomy D
Biochemistry D
Biological and Biomedical
  Sciences—General D
Biophysics D
Biopsychology D
Cell Biology M,D
Community Health M,D
Dentistry D,O
Developmental Biology M,D
Ecology M,D
Environmental and Occupational
  Health M,O
Evolutionary Biology M,D
Family Nurse Practitioner Studies M,O
Genetics D
Health Services Management and
  Hospital Administration M,D,O
Immunology M,O
Maternal and Child/Neonatal Nursing M,O
Medical Physics M,D
Microbiology M,D
Molecular Biology M,D
Molecular Genetics M,D
Molecular Physiology M,D
Neuroscience D
Nurse Midwifery M,O
Nursing—General M,D,O
Occupational Therapy M,D,O
Oral and Dental Sciences M,D,O
Pathology M,D
Pediatric Nursing M,O
Pharmacology D

Physical Therapy | M,D,O
Physician Assistant Studies | M,D,O
Physiology | D
Psychiatric Nursing | M,O
Public Health—General | M
Structural Biology | D
Women's Health Nursing | M,O

STRAYER UNIVERSITY
Health Services Management and
  Hospital Administration | M

SUFFOLK UNIVERSITY
Health Services Management and
  Hospital Administration | M,O

SUL ROSS STATE UNIVERSITY
Biological and Biomedical
  Sciences—General | M

SWEDISH INSTITUTE, COLLEGE OF HEALTH SCIENCES
Acupuncture and Oriental Medicine | M

SYRACUSE UNIVERSITY
Biochemistry | D
Biological and Biomedical
  Sciences—General | M,D
Biophysics | D
Communication Disorders | M,D
Community Health | M
Health Services Management and
  Hospital Administration | O
International Health | O
Maternal and Child Health | M
Nutrition | M
Public Health—General | O
Structural Biology | D

TAI SOPHIA INSTITUTE
Acupuncture and Oriental Medicine | M,O

TARLETON STATE UNIVERSITY
Biological and Biomedical
  Sciences—General | M

TEACHERS COLLEGE, COLUMBIA UNIVERSITY
Communication Disorders | M,D
Neuroscience | D
Nursing and Healthcare Administration | M,D
Nutrition | M,D
Physiology | M,D
Public Health—General | M,D

TEMPLE UNIVERSITY
Allied Health—General | M,D
Allopathic Medicine | D
Anatomy | M,D
Biochemistry | M,D
Biological and Biomedical
  Sciences—General | M,D
Cell Biology | M,D
Communication Disorders | M,D
Dentistry | D
Environmental and Occupational
  Health | M,D
Epidemiology | M,D
Genetics | M,D
Health Services Management and
  Hospital Administration | M
Immunology | M,D
Medicinal and Pharmaceutical
  Chemistry | M,D
Microbiology | M,D
Molecular Biology | M,D
Neuroscience | M,D
Nursing—General | M
Occupational Therapy | M,D
Oral and Dental Sciences | M,O
Pathology | D
Pharmaceutical Administration | M
Pharmaceutical Sciences | M
Pharmacology | D
Pharmacy | D
Physical Therapy | D
Physiology | D
Podiatric Medicine | D
Public Health—General | M,D

TENNESSEE STATE UNIVERSITY
Allied Health—General | M,D
Biological and Biomedical
  Sciences—General | M,D
Communication Disorders | M
Family Nurse Practitioner Studies | M
Nursing Informatics | M
Nursing—General | M
Physical Therapy | M,D

TENNESSEE TECHNOLOGICAL UNIVERSITY
Biological and Biomedical
  Sciences—General | M,D
Family Nurse Practitioner Studies | M
Nursing and Healthcare Administration | M
Nursing Education | M
Nursing Informatics | M
Nursing—General | M

TEXAS A&M HEALTH SCIENCE CENTER
Biological and Biomedical
  Sciences—General | M,D
Cell Biology | D
Dental Hygiene | M
Dentistry | D
Environmental and Occupational
  Health | M
Epidemiology | M
Health Services Management and
  Hospital Administration | M
Immunology | D
Microbiology | D
Molecular Biology | D
Molecular Medicine | D

Molecular Pathogenesis | D
Neuroscience | D
Oral and Dental Sciences | M,D,O
Pharmacy | D
Public Health—General | M
Systems Biology | D
Translational Biology | D
Virology | D

TEXAS A&M INTERNATIONAL UNIVERSITY
Biological and Biomedical
  Sciences—General | M
Family Nurse Practitioner Studies | M
Nursing—General | M

TEXAS A&M UNIVERSITY
Biochemistry | M,D
Biological and Biomedical
  Sciences—General | M,D
Biophysics | M,D
Biopsychology | D
Botany | M,D
Cell Biology | M,D
Entomology | M,D
Epidemiology | M
Genetics | M,D
Health Physics/Radiological Health | M,D
Microbiology | M,D
Neuroscience | M,D
Nutrition | M,D
Parasitology | M,D
Pathobiology | M,D
Pathology | M,D
Physiology | M,D
Plant Biology | M,D
Plant Pathology | M,D
Public Health—General | M
Toxicology | M,D
Veterinary Medicine | M,D
Veterinary Sciences | M
Zoology | M,D

TEXAS A&M UNIVERSITY AT GALVESTON
Marine Biology | M,D

TEXAS A&M UNIVERSITY–COMMERCE
Biological and Biomedical
  Sciences—General | M,O
Health Promotion | M,D

TEXAS A&M UNIVERSITY–CORPUS CHRISTI
Biological and Biomedical
  Sciences—General | M
Family Nurse Practitioner Studies | M
Health Services Management and
  Hospital Administration | M
Nursing and Healthcare Administration | M
Nursing—General | M

TEXAS A&M UNIVERSITY–KINGSVILLE
Biological and Biomedical
  Sciences—General | M
Communication Disorders | M

TEXAS A&M UNIVERSITY– SAN ANTONIO
Health Services Management and
  Hospital Administration | M

TEXAS CHIROPRACTIC COLLEGE
Chiropractic | D

TEXAS CHRISTIAN UNIVERSITY
Adult Nursing | M,D
Allied Health—General | M,D
Biochemistry | M,D
Biological and Biomedical
  Sciences—General | M
Communication Disorders | M
Gerontological Nursing | M,D
Neuroscience | M,D
Nurse Anesthesia | M
Nursing and Healthcare Administration | M,D
Nursing Education | M,D
Nursing—General | M,D
Pediatric Nursing | M,D

TEXAS COLLEGE OF TRADITIONAL CHINESE MEDICINE
Acupuncture and Oriental Medicine | M

TEXAS SOUTHERN UNIVERSITY
Biological and Biomedical
  Sciences—General | M
Pharmacy | M,D
Toxicology | M,D

TEXAS STATE UNIVERSITY–SAN MARCOS
Allied Health—General | M,D
Biochemistry | M
Biological and Biomedical
  Sciences—General | M
Communication Disorders | M
Conservation Biology | M
Health Services Management and
  Hospital Administration | M
Health Services Research | M
Marine Biology | M,D
Nutrition | M
Physical Therapy | D

TEXAS TECH UNIVERSITY
Biological and Biomedical
  Sciences—General | M,D
Health Services Management and
  Hospital Administration | M,D
Microbiology | M,D
Nutrition | M,D
Toxicology | M,D
Zoology | M,D

TEXAS TECH UNIVERSITY HEALTH SCIENCES CENTER
Acute Care/Critical Care Nursing | M,D,O
Allied Health—General | M,D
Allopathic Medicine | D
Biochemistry | M,D
Biological and Biomedical
  Sciences—General | M,D
Cell Biology | M,D
Communication Disorders | M,D
Family Nurse Practitioner Studies | M,D,O
Gerontological Nursing | M,D,O
Health Services Management and
  Hospital Administration | M
Medical Microbiology | M,D
Molecular Biophysics | M,D
Molecular Genetics | M,D
Molecular Pathology | M
Molecular Physiology | M,D
Neuroscience | M,D
Nursing and Healthcare Administration | M,D,O
Nursing Education | M,D
Nursing—General | M,D,O
Occupational Therapy | M,D
Pediatric Nursing | M,D,O
Pharmaceutical Sciences | M,D
Pharmacology | M,D
Physical Therapy | D
Physician Assistant Studies | M
Rehabilitation Sciences | D

TEXAS WESLEYAN UNIVERSITY
Health Services Management and
  Hospital Administration | M
Nurse Anesthesia | M,D

TEXAS WOMAN'S UNIVERSITY
Acute Care/Critical Care Nursing | M,D
Adult Nursing | M,D
Allied Health—General | M,D
Biological and Biomedical
  Sciences—General | M,D
Communication Disorders | M
Family Nurse Practitioner Studies | M,D
Health Services Management and
  Hospital Administration | M
Molecular Biology | M,D
Nursing and Healthcare Administration | M,D
Nursing Education | M,D
Nursing—General | M,D
Nutrition | M,D
Occupational Therapy | M,D
Pediatric Nursing | M,D
Physical Therapy | D
Women's Health Nursing | M,D

THOMAS EDISON STATE COLLEGE
Epidemiology | O
Nursing Education | O
Nursing—General | M

THOMAS JEFFERSON UNIVERSITY
Allopathic Medicine | D
Biochemistry | D
Biological and Biomedical
  Sciences—General | M,D,O
Biophysics | D
Cell Biology | M,D
Clinical Laboratory Sciences/Medical
  Technology | M
Clinical Research | O
Developmental Biology | M,D
Epidemiology | M,D,O
Genetics | D
Health Physics/Radiological Health | M
Health Services Management and
  Hospital Administration | M,D,O
Health Services Research | M,D,O
Immunology | D
Microbiology | M,D
Molecular Biology | D
Molecular Pharmacology | D
Molecular Physiology | D
Neuroscience | D
Nursing—General | M
Occupational Therapy | M
Pharmacology | M
Pharmacy | D
Physical Therapy | D
Public Health—General | M,O
Structural Biology | D

THOMAS UNIVERSITY
Nursing—General | M

TIFFIN UNIVERSITY
Health Services Management and
  Hospital Administration | M

TOURO COLLEGE
Acupuncture and Oriental Medicine | M,D
Communication Disorders | M,D
Occupational Therapy | M,D
Physical Therapy | M,D
Public Health—General | M,D

TOURO UNIVERSITY
Osteopathic Medicine | M,D
Pharmacy | M,D
Public Health—General | M,D

TOWSON UNIVERSITY
Allied Health—General | M
Biological and Biomedical
  Sciences—General | M
Communication Disorders | M,D
Environmental and Occupational
  Health | D
Health Services Management and
  Hospital Administration | O
Nursing Education | M,O
Nursing—General | M,O
Occupational Therapy | M
Physician Assistant Studies | M

TRADITIONAL CHINESE MEDICAL COLLEGE OF HAWAII
Acupuncture and Oriental Medicine | M

TRENT UNIVERSITY
Biological and Biomedical
  Sciences—General | M,D

TREVECCA NAZARENE UNIVERSITY
Physician Assistant Studies | M

TRIDENT UNIVERSITY INTERNATIONAL
Clinical Research | M,D,O
Environmental and Occupational
  Health | M,D,O
Health Services Management and
  Hospital Administration | M,D,O
International Health | M,D,O
Nursing and Healthcare Administration | M,D,O
Public Health—General | M,D,O

TRINITY INTERNATIONAL UNIVERSITY
Bioethics | M

TRINITY UNIVERSITY
Health Services Management and
  Hospital Administration | M

TRINITY WASHINGTON UNIVERSITY
Public Health—General | M

TRINITY WESTERN UNIVERSITY
Health Services Management and
  Hospital Administration | M,O
Nursing—General | M

TRI-STATE COLLEGE OF ACUPUNCTURE
Acupuncture and Oriental Medicine | M,O

TROPICAL AGRICULTURE RESEARCH AND HIGHER EDUCATION CENTER
Conservation Biology | M,D

TROY UNIVERSITY
Adult Nursing | M,D,O
Family Nurse Practitioner Studies | M,D,O
Health Services Management and
  Hospital Administration | M
Maternal and Child Health | M,D,O
Nursing Informatics | M,D,O
Nursing—General | M,D,O

TRUMAN STATE UNIVERSITY
Biological and Biomedical
  Sciences—General | M
Communication Disorders | M

TUFTS UNIVERSITY
Allopathic Medicine | D
Biochemistry | D
Biological and Biomedical
  Sciences—General | M,D
Cell Biology | D
Clinical Research | M,D
Dentistry | D
Developmental Biology | D
Environmental and Occupational
  Health | M,D
Epidemiology | M,D,O
Genetics | D
Immunology | D
Infectious Diseases | M,D
International Health | D
Microbiology | D
Molecular Biology | D
Molecular Physiology | M,D
Neuroscience | M,D
Nutrition | M
Occupational Therapy | M,D,O
Oral and Dental Sciences | M,O
Pathology | M,D
Pharmacology | D
Public Health—General | M
Reproductive Biology | M,D
Veterinary Medicine | M,D

TULANE UNIVERSITY
Allopathic Medicine | D
Biochemistry | M,D
Biological and Biomedical
  Sciences—General | M,D
Cell Biology | M,D
Ecology | M,D
Environmental and Occupational
  Health | M,D
Epidemiology | M,D
Evolutionary Biology | M,D
Health Services Management and
  Hospital Administration | M,D
Human Genetics | M,D
Immunology | M,D
Infectious Diseases | M,D,O
International Health | M,D
Maternal and Child Health | M,D
Microbiology | M,D
Molecular Biology | M,D
Neuroscience | M,D
Nutrition | M
Parasitology | M,D,O
Pharmacology | M,D
Physiology | M,D
Public Health—General | M,D,O
Structural Biology | M,D

TUSKEGEE UNIVERSITY
Biological and Biomedical
  Sciences—General | M,D
Nutrition | M
Veterinary Medicine | M,D
Veterinary Sciences | M,D

UNIFORMED SERVICES UNIVERSITY OF THE HEALTH SCIENCES
Biological and Biomedical
  Sciences—General | M,D

M—master's degree; P—first professional degree; D—doctorate; O—other advanced degree; *Close-Up and/or Display

Cell Biology M,D
Environmental and Occupational
  Health M,D
Family Nurse Practitioner Studies M,D
Health Services Management and
  Hospital Administration M,D
Immunology D
Infectious Diseases D*
International Health M,D
Medical/Surgical Nursing M,D
Molecular Biology M,D*
Neuroscience D*
Nurse Anesthesia M,D
Nursing—General M,D
Psychiatric Nursing M,D
Public Health—General M,D
Zoology M,D

UNION COLLEGE (NE)
Physician Assistant Studies M

UNION GRADUATE COLLEGE
Bioethics M,O
Health Services Management and
  Hospital Administration M,O

UNION INSTITUTE & UNIVERSITY
Health Promotion M,D,O

UNION UNIVERSITY
Family Nurse Practitioner Studies M,D,O
Nurse Anesthesia M,D,O
Nursing and Healthcare Administration M,D,O
Nursing Education M,D,O
Nursing—General M,D,O

UNITED STATES UNIVERSITY
Family Nurse Practitioner Studies M

UNITED STATES UNIVERSITY
Nursing and Healthcare Administration M
Nursing Education M
Nursing—General M

UNIVERSIDAD ADVENTISTA DE LAS ANTILLAS
Medical/Surgical Nursing M

UNIVERSIDAD AUTONOMA DE GUADALAJARA
Allopathic Medicine D
Environmental and Occupational
  Health M,D

UNIVERSIDAD CENTRAL DEL CARIBE
Allopathic Medicine M,D
Anatomy M,D
Biochemistry M,D
Biological and Biomedical
  Sciences—General M,D
Cell Biology M,D
Immunology M,D
Microbiology M,D
Molecular Biology M,D
Pharmacology M,D
Physiology M,D

UNIVERSIDAD CENTRAL DEL ESTE
Allopathic Medicine D
Dentistry D

UNIVERSIDAD DE CIENCIAS MEDICAS
Allopathic Medicine M,D,O
Anatomy M,D,O
Biological and Biomedical
  Sciences—General M,D,O
Community Health M,D,O
Environmental and Occupational
  Health M,D,O
Health Services Management and
  Hospital Administration M,D,O
Pharmacy M,D,O

UNIVERSIDAD DE IBEROAMERICA
Acute Care/Critical Care Nursing M,D
Allopathic Medicine M,D
Health Services Management and
  Hospital Administration M,D
Neuroscience M,D

UNIVERSIDAD DE LAS AMÉRICAS–PUEBLA
Clinical Laboratory Sciences/Medical
  Technology M

UNIVERSIDAD DEL TURABO
Adult Nursing M,O
Communication Disorders M
Environmental Biology M,D
Family Nurse Practitioner Studies M
Health Promotion M
Naturopathic Medicine D
Nursing—General M

UNIVERSIDAD IBEROAMERICANA
Allopathic Medicine D
Dentistry M,D

UNIVERSIDAD METROPOLITANA
Nursing and Healthcare Administration M,O
Nursing—General M,O
Oncology Nursing M,O

UNIVERSIDAD NACIONAL PEDRO HENRIQUEZ URENA
Allopathic Medicine D
Dentistry D
Ecology M

UNIVERSITÉ DE MONCTON
Biochemistry M
Biological and Biomedical
  Sciences—General M
Nutrition M

UNIVERSITÉ DE MONTRÉAL
Allopathic Medicine D
Biochemistry M,D,O
Bioethics M,D,O

Biological and Biomedical
  Sciences—General M,D
Cell Biology M,D
Communication Disorders M,O
Community Health M,D,O
Dental Hygiene O
Environmental and Occupational
  Health M
Genetics O
Health Services Management and
  Hospital Administration M,O
Immunology M,D
Microbiology M,D
Molecular Biology M,D
Neuroscience M,D
Nursing—General M,D,O
Nutrition M,D,O
Occupational Therapy O
Optometry D
Oral and Dental Sciences M,D
Pathology M,D
Pharmaceutical Sciences M,D,O
Pharmacology M,D
Physiology M,D
Public Health—General M,D,O
Rehabilitation Sciences O
Toxicology O
Veterinary Medicine D
Veterinary Sciences D
Virology D
Vision Sciences M,O

UNIVERSITÉ DE SHERBROOKE
Allopathic Medicine D
Biochemistry M,D
Biological and Biomedical
  Sciences—General M,D
Biophysics M,D
Cell Biology M,D
Clinical Laboratory Sciences/Medical
  Technology M,D
Immunology M,D
Microbiology M,D
Pharmacology M,D
Physiology M,D
Radiation Biology M,D

UNIVERSITÉ DU QUÉBEC À CHICOUTIMI
Genetics M

UNIVERSITÉ DU QUÉBEC À MONTRÉAL
Biological and Biomedical
  Sciences—General M,D
Environmental and Occupational
  Health O

UNIVERSITÉ DU QUÉBEC À RIMOUSKI
Nursing—General M,O

UNIVERSITÉ DU QUÉBEC À TROIS-RIVIÈRES
Biophysics M,D
Chiropractic D
Nursing—General M,O

UNIVERSITÉ DU QUÉBEC EN ABITIBI-TÉMISCAMINGUE
Biological and Biomedical
  Sciences—General M,D

UNIVERSITÉ DU QUÉBEC EN OUTAOUAIS
Nursing—General M,O

UNIVERSITÉ DU QUÉBEC, INSTITUT NATIONAL DE LA RECHERCHE SCIENTIFIQUE
Biological and Biomedical
  Sciences—General M,D
Immunology M,D
Medical Microbiology M,D
Microbiology M,D
Virology M,D

UNIVERSITÉ LAVAL
Allopathic Medicine D,O
Anatomy O
Anesthesiologist Assistant Studies O
Biochemistry M,D,O
Biological and Biomedical
  Sciences—General M,D,O
Cancer Biology/Oncology O
Cardiovascular Sciences O
Cell Biology M,D
Communication Disorders M
Community Health M,D,O
Dentistry D
Emergency Medical Services O
Environmental and Occupational
  Health O
Epidemiology O
Health Physics/Radiological Health O
Immunology M,D
Infectious Diseases O
Microbiology M,D
Molecular Biology M,D
Neurobiology M,D
Nursing—General M,D,O
Nutrition M,D
Oral and Dental Sciences M,O
Pathology O
Pharmaceutical Sciences M,D,O
Physiology M,D
Plant Biology M,D

UNIVERSITY AT ALBANY, STATE UNIVERSITY OF NEW YORK
Biochemistry M,D
Biological and Biomedical
  Sciences—General M,D
Biopsychology M,D,O
Cell Biology M,D
Conservation Biology M
Developmental Biology M,D
Ecology M,D
Environmental and Occupational
  Health M,D

Epidemiology M,D
Evolutionary Biology M,D
Genetics M,D
Health Services Management and
  Hospital Administration M
Immunology M,D
Molecular Biology M,D
Molecular Pathogenesis M,D
Neurobiology M,D
Neuroscience M,D
Public Health—General M,D
Structural Biology M,D
Toxicology M,D

UNIVERSITY AT BUFFALO, THE STATE UNIVERSITY OF NEW YORK
Adult Nursing M,D,O
Allied Health—General M,D,O
Allopathic Medicine D
Anatomy M,D
Biochemistry M,D
Biological and Biomedical
  Sciences—General M,D
Biophysics M,D
Cancer Biology/Oncology M
Cell Biology D
Clinical Laboratory Sciences/Medical
  Technology M
Communication Disorders M,D
Community Health M,D
Dentistry M,D,O
Ecology M,D,O
Epidemiology M,D*
Evolutionary Biology M,D,O
Family Nurse Practitioner Studies M,D,O
Health Services Management and
  Hospital Administration M,D,O
Immunology M,D
Medicinal and Pharmaceutical
  Chemistry M,D
Microbiology M,D
Molecular Biology D
Neuroscience M,D
Nurse Anesthesia M,D,O
Nursing and Healthcare Administration M,D,O
Nursing—General M,D,O
Nutrition M,D,O
Occupational Therapy M
Oral and Dental Sciences M,D,O
Pathology M,D
Pharmaceutical Sciences M,D
Pharmacology M,D
Pharmacy D
Physical Therapy D
Physiology M,D
Psychiatric Nursing M,D,O
Public Health—General M,D
Rehabilitation Sciences M,D,O
Structural Biology M,D
Toxicology M,D

THE UNIVERSITY OF AKRON
Biological and Biomedical
  Sciences—General M,D
Communication Disorders M,D
Health Services Management and
  Hospital Administration M
Nursing—General M,D
Nutrition M
Public Health—General M,D

THE UNIVERSITY OF ALABAMA
Biological and Biomedical
  Sciences—General M,D
Communication Disorders M
Community Health M
Health Promotion M,D
Nursing—General M,D
Nutrition M

THE UNIVERSITY OF ALABAMA AT BIRMINGHAM
Allied Health—General M,D
Allopathic Medicine D
Biochemistry D
Biological and Biomedical
  Sciences—General M,D*
Cell Biology D
Clinical Laboratory Sciences/Medical
  Technology M
Dentistry D
Environmental and Occupational
  Health D
Epidemiology D
Genetics D
Health Promotion D
Health Services Management and
  Hospital Administration M,D
Microbiology D
Molecular Biology D
Molecular Genetics D
Molecular Physiology D
Neurobiology D
Nurse Anesthesia M,D
Nursing—General M,D
Nutrition D
Occupational Therapy M
Optometry D
Oral and Dental Sciences M
Pathology D
Pharmacology D
Physical Therapy D
Physician Assistant Studies M
Public Health—General M,D
Rehabilitation Sciences M
Toxicology D
Vision Sciences M,D

THE UNIVERSITY OF ALABAMA IN HUNTSVILLE
Acute Care/Critical Care Nursing M,D,O
Biological and Biomedical
  Sciences—General M
Family Nurse Practitioner Studies M,D,O

Health Services Management and
  Hospital Administration M,D,O
Nursing Education M,D,O
Nursing—General M,D,O

UNIVERSITY OF ALASKA ANCHORAGE
Biological and Biomedical
  Sciences—General M
Family Nurse Practitioner Studies M,O
Nursing Education M,O
Nursing—General M,O
Psychiatric Nursing M,O
Public Health—General M

UNIVERSITY OF ALASKA FAIRBANKS
Biochemistry M,D
Biological and Biomedical
  Sciences—General M,D
Botany M,D
Marine Biology M,D
Nutrition M,D
Zoology M,D

UNIVERSITY OF ALBERTA
Biochemistry M,D
Biological and Biomedical
  Sciences—General M,D
Cancer Biology/Oncology M,D
Cell Biology M,D
Clinical Laboratory Sciences/Medical
  Technology M,D
Communication Disorders M,D
Community Health M,D
Conservation Biology M,D
Dental Hygiene O
Dentistry D
Ecology M,D
Environmental and Occupational
  Health M,D
Environmental Biology M,D
Epidemiology M,D
Evolutionary Biology M,D
Genetics M,D
Health Physics/Radiological Health M,D
Health Promotion M,O
Health Services Management and
  Hospital Administration M,D
Health Services Research M,D
Immunology M,D
International Health M,D
Maternal and Child/Neonatal Nursing D
Medical Microbiology M,D
Medical Physics M,D
Microbiology M,D
Molecular Biology M,D
Neuroscience M,D
Nursing—General M,D
Occupational Therapy M,D
Oral and Dental Sciences M,D
Pathology M,D
Pharmaceutical Sciences M,D
Pharmacology M,D
Pharmacy D
Physical Therapy M,D
Physiology M,D
Plant Biology M,D
Public Health—General M,D
Rehabilitation Sciences D
Vision Sciences M,D

THE UNIVERSITY OF ARIZONA
Allopathic Medicine D
Anatomy D
Biochemistry D
Biological and Biomedical
  Sciences—General M
Cancer Biology/Oncology D
Cell Biology M,D
Communication Disorders M,D
Ecology M,D
Entomology M,D
Epidemiology M,D
Evolutionary Biology M,D
Family Nurse Practitioner Studies M,D,O
Genetics M,D
Immunology M,D
Microbiology M,D
Molecular Biology M,D
Neuroscience D
Nursing—General M,D,O
Nutrition M,D
Pathobiology M,D
Perfusion M,D
Pharmaceutical Sciences M,D
Pharmacology M,D
Pharmacy D
Physiology M,D
Plant Pathology M,D
Public Health—General M,D

UNIVERSITY OF ARKANSAS
Biological and Biomedical
  Sciences—General M,D
Cell Biology M,D
Communication Disorders M
Entomology M,D
Molecular Biology M,D
Nursing—General M
Plant Pathology M

UNIVERSITY OF ARKANSAS AT LITTLE ROCK
Allied Health—General M
Biological and Biomedical
  Sciences—General M

UNIVERSITY OF ARKANSAS FOR MEDICAL SCIENCES
Allopathic Medicine D
Anatomy M,D
Biochemistry M,D
Biological and Biomedical
  Sciences—General M,D,O
Biophysics M,D
Communication Disorders M,D

Environmental and Occupational
   Health — M,O
Health Promotion — D
Health Services Research — D
Immunology — M,D
Microbiology — M,D
Molecular Biology — M,D
Neurobiology — M,D
Nursing—General — D
Nutrition — M
Pathology — M
Pharmaceutical Administration — M
Pharmaceutical Sciences — M
Pharmacology — M,D
Pharmacy — M,D
Physiology — M,D
Toxicology — M,D

UNIVERSITY OF ATLANTA
Health Services Management and
   Hospital Administration — M,D,O

UNIVERSITY OF BALTIMORE
Health Services Management and
   Hospital Administration — M

UNIVERSITY OF BRIDGEPORT
Acupuncture and Oriental Medicine — M
Chiropractic — D
Dental Hygiene — M
Naturopathic Medicine — D
Nutrition — M
Physician Assistant Studies — M

THE UNIVERSITY OF BRITISH COLUMBIA
Allopathic Medicine — M,D
Anatomy — M,D
Biochemistry — M,D
Biopsychology — M,D
Botany — M,D
Cell Biology — M,D
Communication Disorders — M,D
Dentistry — D
Environmental and Occupational
   Health — M,D
Epidemiology — M,D
Genetics — M,D
Health Services Management and
   Hospital Administration — M,D
Immunology — M,D
Microbiology — M,D
Molecular Biology — M,D
Neuroscience — M,D
Nurse Anesthesia — M,D
Nursing—General — M,D
Nutrition — M,D
Occupational Therapy — M
Oral and Dental Sciences — M,D,O
Pathology — M,D
Pharmaceutical Sciences — M,D
Pharmacology — M,D
Pharmacy — M,D
Physiology — M,D
Public Health—General — M,D
Rehabilitation Sciences — M,D
Reproductive Biology — M,D
Zoology — M,D

UNIVERSITY OF CALGARY
Allopathic Medicine — D
Biochemistry — M,D
Biological and Biomedical
   Sciences—General — M,D
Cancer Biology/Oncology — M,D
Cardiovascular Sciences — M,D
Community Health — M,D,O
Epidemiology — M,D
Immunology — M,D
Infectious Diseases — M,D
Microbiology — M,D
Molecular Biology — M,D
Neuroscience — M,D
Nursing—General — M,D,O

UNIVERSITY OF CALIFORNIA, BERKELEY
Allopathic Medicine
Biochemistry — D
Biological and Biomedical
   Sciences—General — D
Biophysics — D
Cell Biology — D
Clinical Research — O
Environmental and Occupational
   Health — M,D
Epidemiology — M,D
Health Services Management and
   Hospital Administration — D
Immunology — D
Infectious Diseases — M,D
Microbiology — D
Molecular Biology — D
Molecular Toxicology — D
Neuroscience — D
Nutrition — D
Optometry — D,O
Physiology — M,D
Plant Biology — D
Public Health—General — M,D
Vision Sciences — M,D

UNIVERSITY OF CALIFORNIA, DAVIS
Allopathic Medicine — M,D
Animal Behavior — D
Biochemistry — M,D
Biophysics — M,D
Cell Biology — M,D
Clinical Research — M
Developmental Biology — M,D
Ecology — M,D
Entomology — M,D
Epidemiology — M,D

Evolutionary Biology — D
Genetics — M,D
Immunology — M,D
Maternal and Child Health — M
Microbiology — M,D
Molecular Biology — M,D
Neuroscience — D
Nutrition — M,D
Pathology — M,D
Pharmacology — M,D
Physiology — M,D
Plant Biology — M,D
Plant Pathology — M,D
Toxicology — M,D
Veterinary Medicine — D
Veterinary Sciences — M,O
Zoology — M

UNIVERSITY OF CALIFORNIA, IRVINE
Allopathic Medicine
Anatomy — M,D
Biochemistry — M,D
Biological and Biomedical
   Sciences—General — M,D
Biophysics — D
Cell Biology — M,D
Computational Biology — D
Developmental Biology — M,D
Ecology — M,D
Epidemiology — M,D
Evolutionary Biology — M,D
Genetics — D
Health Services Management and
   Hospital Administration — M
Medicinal and Pharmaceutical
   Chemistry — D
Microbiology — M,D
Molecular Biology — M,D
Molecular Genetics — M,D
Neurobiology — M,D
Neuroscience — D
Nursing—General — M
Pathology — D
Pharmacology — M,D
Physiology — D
Public Health—General — M,D
Systems Biology — D
Toxicology — M,D

UNIVERSITY OF CALIFORNIA, LOS ANGELES
Allopathic Medicine — D
Anatomy — D
Biochemistry — M,D
Biological and Biomedical
   Sciences—General — M,D
Cell Biology — D
Clinical Research — M
Community Health — M,D
Dentistry — D,O
Developmental Biology — D
Ecology — M,D
Environmental and Occupational
   Health — M,D
Epidemiology — M,D
Evolutionary Biology — M,D
Health Services Management and
   Hospital Administration — M,D
Human Genetics — M,D
Immunology — M,D
Medical Physics — M,D
Microbiology — M,D
Molecular Biology — D
Molecular Genetics — M,D
Molecular Toxicology — D
Neurobiology — D
Neuroscience — D
Nursing—General — M,D
Oral and Dental Sciences — M,D
Pathology — M,D
Pharmacology — D
Physiology — M,D
Public Health—General — M,D
Toxicology — D

UNIVERSITY OF CALIFORNIA, MERCED
Biological and Biomedical
   Sciences—General — M,D
Systems Biology — M,D

UNIVERSITY OF CALIFORNIA, RIVERSIDE
Biochemistry — M,D
Biological and Biomedical
   Sciences—General — M,D
Botany — M,D
Cell Biology — M,D
Developmental Biology — M,D
Ecology — M,D
Entomology — M,D
Evolutionary Biology — M,D
Genetics — D
Genomic Sciences — D
Microbiology — M,D
Molecular Biology — M,D
Molecular Genetics — D
Neuroscience — D
Plant Biology — M,D
Plant Molecular Biology — M,D
Plant Pathology — M,D
Toxicology — M,D

UNIVERSITY OF CALIFORNIA, SAN DIEGO
Allopathic Medicine — D
Biochemistry — M,D
Biological and Biomedical
   Sciences—General — M,D
Biophysics — M,D
Cancer Biology/Oncology — D
Cardiovascular Sciences — D
Cell Biology — D

Clinical Research — M
Communication Disorders — D
Developmental Biology — D
Ecology — D
Epidemiology — D
Evolutionary Biology — D
Genetics — D
Health Services Management and
   Hospital Administration — M
Immunology — D
Marine Biology — D
Microbiology — D
Molecular Biology — D
Molecular Pathology — D
Neurobiology — D
Neuroscience — D
Pharmacology — D
Pharmacy — D
Physiology — D
Plant Biology — D
Plant Molecular Biology — D
Public Health—General — D
Structural Biology — D
Systems Biology — D
Virology — D

UNIVERSITY OF CALIFORNIA, SAN FRANCISCO
Allopathic Medicine — D
Anatomy — D
Biochemistry — D
Biological and Biomedical
   Sciences—General — D
Biophysics — D
Cell Biology — D
Dentistry — D
Developmental Biology — D
Genetics — D
Genomic Sciences — D
Immunology — D
Medicinal and Pharmaceutical
   Chemistry — D
Microbiology — D
Molecular Biology — D
Neuroscience — D
Nursing—General — M,D
Oral and Dental Sciences — M,D
Pathology — D
Pharmaceutical Sciences — D
Pharmacology — D
Pharmacy — D
Physical Therapy — M,D
Physiology — D

UNIVERSITY OF CALIFORNIA, SANTA BARBARA
Biochemistry — D
Biophysics — D
Cell Biology — M,D
Developmental Biology — M,D
Ecology — M,D
Evolutionary Biology — M,D
Marine Biology — M,D
Molecular Biology — M,D

UNIVERSITY OF CALIFORNIA, SANTA CRUZ
Biochemistry — M,D
Cell Biology — M,D
Developmental Biology — M,D
Ecology — M,D
Environmental Biology — M,D
Evolutionary Biology — M,D
Molecular Biology — M,D
Toxicology — M,D

UNIVERSITY OF CENTRAL ARKANSAS
Biological and Biomedical
   Sciences—General — M
Communication Disorders — M,D
Family Nurse Practitioner Studies — M
Medical Physics — M
Nursing—General — M
Occupational Therapy — M
Physical Therapy — D

UNIVERSITY OF CENTRAL FLORIDA
Adult Nursing — M,D,O
Allopathic Medicine — M,D
Biological and Biomedical
   Sciences—General — M,D,O
Communication Disorders — M,D,O
Conservation Biology — M,D,O
Family Nurse Practitioner Studies — M,D,O
Gerontological Nursing — M,D,O
Health Services Management and
   Hospital Administration — M,O
Nursing and Healthcare Administration — M,D,O
Nursing Education — M,D,O
Nursing—General — M,D,O
Physical Therapy — D

UNIVERSITY OF CENTRAL MISSOURI
Biological and Biomedical
   Sciences—General — M,D
Communication Disorders — M
Environmental and Occupational
   Health — M
Industrial Hygiene — M
Nursing—General — M

UNIVERSITY OF CENTRAL OKLAHOMA
Biological and Biomedical
   Sciences—General — M
Communication Disorders — M
Health Promotion — M
Nutrition — M

UNIVERSITY OF CHARLESTON
Pharmacy — D
Physician Assistant Studies — M

UNIVERSITY OF CHICAGO
Allopathic Medicine — D

Anatomy — D
Biochemistry — D
Biological and Biomedical
   Sciences—General — D
Biophysics — D
Cancer Biology/Oncology — D
Cell Biology — D
Developmental Biology — D
Ecology — D
Evolutionary Biology — D
Genetics — D
Genomic Sciences — D
Health Promotion — M,D
Health Services Management and
   Hospital Administration — M,D,O
Human Genetics — D
Immunology — D
Medical Physics — D
Microbiology — D
Molecular Biology — D
Molecular Medicine — D
Molecular Pathogenesis — D
Molecular Physiology — D
Neurobiology — D
Neuroscience — D
Nutrition — D
Pathology — D
Pharmacology — D
Physiology — D
Systems Biology — D
Vision Sciences — D
Zoology — D

UNIVERSITY OF CINCINNATI
Acute Care/Critical Care Nursing — M,D
Adult Nursing — M,D
Allopathic Medicine — M,D
Biochemistry — M,D
Biological and Biomedical
   Sciences—General — M,D
Biophysics — D
Cancer Biology/Oncology — D
Cell Biology — D
Communication Disorders — M,D,O
Community Health Nursing — M,D
Developmental Biology — D
Environmental and Occupational
   Health — M,D
Epidemiology — M,D
Genomic Sciences — M,D
Health Physics/Radiological Health — M
Immunology — M,D
Industrial Hygiene — M,D
Maternal and Child/Neonatal Nursing — M,D
Medical Imaging — D
Medical Physics — M
Microbiology — M,D
Molecular Biology — M,D
Molecular Genetics — M,D
Molecular Medicine — D
Molecular Toxicology — M,D
Neuroscience — D
Nurse Anesthesia — M,D
Nurse Midwifery — M,D
Nursing and Healthcare Administration — M,D
Nursing—General — M,D
Nutrition — M
Occupational Health Nursing — M,D
Pathobiology — D
Pathology — D
Pediatric Nursing — M,D
Pharmaceutical Sciences — M,D
Pharmacology — D
Pharmacy — D
Physiology — D
Psychiatric Nursing — M,D
Rehabilitation Sciences — D
Women's Health Nursing — M,D

UNIVERSITY OF COLORADO AT COLORADO SPRINGS
Adult Nursing — M,D
Biological and Biomedical
   Sciences—General — M
Community Health Nursing — M,D
Family Nurse Practitioner Studies — M,D
Forensic Nursing — M,D
Health Promotion — M,D
Maternal and Child/Neonatal Nursing — M,D
Nursing and Healthcare Administration — M,D
Nursing—General — M,D
Nutrition — M
Women's Health Nursing — M,D

UNIVERSITY OF COLORADO BOULDER
Animal Behavior — M,D
Biochemistry — M,D
Cell Biology — M,D
Communication Disorders — M,D
Developmental Biology — M,D
Ecology — M,D
Evolutionary Biology — M,D
Genetics — M,D
Marine Biology — M,D
Medical Physics — M,D
Microbiology — M,D
Molecular Biology — M,D
Neurobiology — M,D
Physiology — M,D

UNIVERSITY OF COLORADO DENVER
Adult Nursing — M,D
Allopathic Medicine — D
Animal Behavior — M
Biochemistry — D
Biological and Biomedical
   Sciences—General — M,D
Biophysics — M,D
Cancer Biology/Oncology — D
Cell Biology — M,D
Clinical Laboratory Sciences/Medical
   Technology — M,D

*M—master's degree; P—first professional degree; D—doctorate; O—other advanced degree; *Close-Up and/or Display*

Clinical Research — M,D
Community Health — M,D'
Computational Biology — M,D
Dentistry — M,D
Developmental Biology — M,D
Ecology — M
Environmental and Occupational
　Health — M,D
Epidemiology — M,D
Evolutionary Biology — M,D
Family Nurse Practitioner Studies — M,D
Genetics — M,D
Health Services Management and
　Hospital Administration — M,D
Health Services Research — D
Immunology — D
International Health — M
Medical Imaging — M,D
Microbiology — M,D
Molecular Biology — M,D
Molecular Genetics — D
Neurobiology — M
Neuroscience — D
Nurse Midwifery — M,D
Nursing and Healthcare Administration — M,D
Nursing—General — M,D
Oral and Dental Sciences — M,D
Pediatric Nursing — M,D
Pharmaceutical Sciences — D
Pharmacology — D
Physical Therapy — D
Physician Assistant Studies — M
Physiology — D
Psychiatric Nursing — M,D
Public Health—General — M,D
Rehabilitation Sciences — D
Toxicology — D
Women's Health Nursing — M,D

UNIVERSITY OF CONNECTICUT
Allied Health—General — M
Biochemistry — M,D
Biological and Biomedical
　Sciences—General — D
Biophysics — M,D
Biopsychology — M,D,O
Botany — M,D
Cell Biology — M,D
Clinical Research — M
Communication Disorders — M,D
Developmental Biology — M,D
Ecology — M,D,O
Entomology — M,D
Environmental and Occupational
　Health — M
Genetics — M,D
Genomic Sciences — M
Health Services Management and
　Hospital Administration — M,D
Medicinal and Pharmaceutical
　Chemistry — M,D
Microbiology — M
Molecular Biology — M,D
Neurobiology — M,D,O
Neuroscience — M,D,O
Nursing—General — M,D,O
Nutrition — M,D
Oral and Dental Sciences — M
Pathobiology — M,D
Pharmaceutical Sciences — M,D
Pharmacology — D
Pharmacy — D
Physical Therapy — D
Physiology — M,D*
Plant Biology — M,D
Plant Molecular Biology — M,D
Public Health—General — M
Structural Biology — M,D
Toxicology — M,D
Zoology — M,D

UNIVERSITY OF CONNECTICUT HEALTH CENTER
Allopathic Medicine — D
Biochemistry — D*
Biological and Biomedical
　Sciences—General — D*
Cell Biology — D*
Clinical Research — M
Dentistry — D,O
Developmental Biology — D
Genetics — D*
Immunology — D*
Molecular Biology — D*
Neuroscience — D*
Oral and Dental Sciences — M,D*
Public Health—General — M

UNIVERSITY OF DALLAS
Health Services Management and
　Hospital Administration — M

UNIVERSITY OF DAYTON
Biological and Biomedical
　Sciences—General — M,D
Physical Therapy — M,D

UNIVERSITY OF DELAWARE
Adult Nursing — M,O
Biochemistry — M,D
Biological and Biomedical
　Sciences—General — M,D
Cancer Biology/Oncology — M,D
Cell Biology — M,D
Developmental Biology — M,D
Ecology — M,D
Entomology — M,D
Evolutionary Biology — M,D
Family Nurse Practitioner Studies — M,O
Genetics — M,D
Gerontological Nursing — M,O
Health Promotion — M
HIV/AIDS Nursing — M,O
Maternal and Child/Neonatal Nursing — M,O
Microbiology — M,D
Molecular Biology — M,D

Neuroscience — D
Nursing and Healthcare Administration — M,O
Nursing—General — M
Nutrition — M
Oncology Nursing — M,O
Pediatric Nursing — M,O
Physical Therapy — D
Physiology — M,D
Psychiatric Nursing — M,O
Women's Health Nursing — M,O

UNIVERSITY OF DENVER
Biochemistry — M,D
Biological and Biomedical
　Sciences—General — M,D
Environmental and Occupational
　Health — M,O
Health Services Management and
　Hospital Administration — M,O
International Health — M,D,O
Neuroscience — M,D

UNIVERSITY OF DETROIT MERCY
Allied Health—General — M,O
Biochemistry — M
Dentistry — D
Family Nurse Practitioner Studies — M,O
Health Services Management and
　Hospital Administration — M
Nurse Anesthesia — M
Oral and Dental Sciences — M,O
Physician Assistant Studies — M

UNIVERSITY OF EVANSVILLE
Health Services Management and
　Hospital Administration — M
Physical Therapy — D

THE UNIVERSITY OF FINDLAY
Health Services Management and
　Hospital Administration — M
Occupational Therapy — M
Pharmacy — D
Physical Therapy — D
Physician Assistant Studies — M

UNIVERSITY OF FLORIDA
Allied Health—General — M,D
Allopathic Medicine — D
Biochemistry — D
Biological and Biomedical
　Sciences—General — D
Botany — M,D
Cell Biology — M,D
Clinical Laboratory Sciences/Medical
　Technology — D
Clinical Research — M
Communication Disorders — M,D
Dentistry — D,O
Ecology — M,D
Entomology — M,D
Environmental and Occupational
　Health — M,D
Epidemiology — M,D
Genetics — D
Genomic Sciences — D
Health Services Management and
　Hospital Administration — M,D
Health Services Research — D
Immunology — D
Medicinal and Pharmaceutical
　Chemistry — M,D
Microbiology — M,D
Molecular Biology — M,D
Molecular Genetics — M,D
Neuroscience — M,D
Nursing—General — M,D
Occupational Therapy — M
Oral and Dental Sciences — M,D,O
Pathology — D
Pharmaceutical Administration — M,D
Pharmaceutical Sciences — M,D
Pharmacology — M,D
Pharmacy — M,D
Physical Therapy — D
Physician Assistant Studies — M
Physiology — M,D
Plant Biology — M,D
Plant Molecular Biology — M,D
Plant Pathology — M,D
Public Health—General — M,D
Rehabilitation Sciences — D
Toxicology — M,D,O
Veterinary Medicine — D
Veterinary Sciences — M,D,O
Zoology — M,D

UNIVERSITY OF GEORGIA
Anatomy — M
Biochemistry — M,D
Biological and Biomedical
　Sciences—General — D
Cell Biology — M,D
Communication Disorders — M,D,O
Ecology — M,D
Entomology — M,D
Environmental and Occupational
　Health — M
Genetics — M,D
Genomic Sciences — M,D
Health Promotion — M,D
Health Services Management and
　Hospital Administration — M
Infectious Diseases — M,D
Microbiology — M,D
Molecular Biology — M,D
Neuroscience — D
Nutrition — M,D
Pathology — M,D
Pharmaceutical Sciences — M,D,O
Pharmacology — M,D
Pharmacy — M,D,O
Physiology — M,D
Plant Biology — M,D
Plant Pathology — M,D
Public Health—General — D

Veterinary Medicine — M,D
Veterinary Sciences — M

UNIVERSITY OF GUAM
Biological and Biomedical
　Sciences—General — M
Marine Biology — M

UNIVERSITY OF GUELPH
Acute Care/Critical Care Nursing — M,D,O
Anatomy — M,D
Anesthesiologist Assistant Studies — M,D,O
Biochemistry — M,D
Biological and Biomedical
　Sciences—General — M,D
Biophysics — M,D
Botany — M,D
Cardiovascular Sciences — M,D,O
Cell Biology — M,D
Ecology — M,D
Emergency Medical Services — M,D,O
Entomology — M,D
Environmental Biology — M,D
Epidemiology — M,D
Evolutionary Biology — M,D
Immunology — M,D,O
Infectious Diseases — M,D
Medical Imaging — M,D,O
Microbiology — M,D
Molecular Biology — M,D
Molecular Genetics — M,D
Neuroscience — M,D,O
Nutrition — M,D
Pathology — M,D
Pharmacology — M,D
Physiology — M,D
Plant Pathology — M,D
Toxicology — M,D
Veterinary Medicine — M,D,O
Veterinary Sciences — M,D,O
Vision Sciences — M,D,O
Zoology — M,D

UNIVERSITY OF HARTFORD
Biological and Biomedical
　Sciences—General — M
Community Health Nursing — M
Neuroscience — M
Nursing Education — M
Nursing—General — M
Physical Therapy — M,D

UNIVERSITY OF HAWAII AT HILO
Conservation Biology — M
Marine Biology — M

UNIVERSITY OF HAWAII AT MANOA
Adult Nursing — M,D,O
Allopathic Medicine — D
Biological and Biomedical
　Sciences—General — M,D
Botany — M,D
Communication Disorders — M
Community Health Nursing — M,D,O
Conservation Biology — M,D
Developmental Biology — M,D
Ecology — M,D
Entomology — D
Epidemiology — M,D
Evolutionary Biology — M,D
Family Nurse Practitioner Studies — M,D,O
Genetics — M,D
Marine Biology — M,D
Medical Microbiology — M,D
Microbiology — M,D
Molecular Biology — M,D
Nursing and Healthcare Administration — M,D,O
Nursing—General — M,D
Nutrition — M,D
Physiology — M,D
Plant Pathology — M,D
Public Health—General — M,D,O
Reproductive Biology — M,D
Zoology — M,D

UNIVERSITY OF HOUSTON
Biochemistry — M,D
Biological and Biomedical
　Sciences—General — M,D
Communication Disorders — M
Nutrition — M,D
Optometry — D
Pharmaceutical Administration — M,D
Pharmaceutical Sciences — M,D
Pharmacology — M,D
Pharmacy — M,D
Vision Sciences — M,D

UNIVERSITY OF HOUSTON–CLEAR LAKE
Biological and Biomedical
　Sciences—General — M
Health Services Management and
　Hospital Administration — M

UNIVERSITY OF HOUSTON–VICTORIA
Nursing—General — M

UNIVERSITY OF IDAHO
Biochemistry — M,D
Biological and Biomedical
　Sciences—General — M,D
Computational Biology — M,D
Entomology — M,D
Microbiology — M,D
Molecular Biology — M,D
Neuroscience — M,D
Veterinary Sciences — M,D

UNIVERSITY OF ILLINOIS AT CHICAGO
Acute Care/Critical Care Nursing — M
Adult Nursing — M
Allied Health—General — M,D
Allopathic Medicine — D
Anatomy — D
Biochemistry — D

Biological and Biomedical
　Sciences—General — M,D
Biophysics — M,D
Cell Biology — D
Community Health Nursing — M
Community Health — M,D
Dentistry — D
Environmental and Occupational
　Health — M,D
Epidemiology — M,D
Family Nurse Practitioner Studies — M
Genetics — D
Gerontological Nursing — M
Health Services Management and
　Hospital Administration — M,D
Health Services Research — M,D
Immunology — D
Maternal and Child/Neonatal Nursing — M
Microbiology — D
Molecular Biology — D
Molecular Genetics — D
Neurobiology — D
Neuroscience — D
Nurse Midwifery — M
Nursing and Healthcare Administration — M
Nursing—General — M,D
Nutrition — M
Occupational Health Nursing — M
Occupational Therapy — M,D
Oral and Dental Sciences — M,D
Pediatric Nursing — M
Pharmaceutical Administration — M,D
Pharmaceutical Sciences — M,D
Pharmacology — D
Pharmacy — D
Physical Therapy — M,D
Physiology — M,D
Psychiatric Nursing — M
Public Health—General — M,D
School Nursing — M
Women's Health Nursing — M

UNIVERSITY OF ILLINOIS AT SPRINGFIELD
Biological and Biomedical
　Sciences—General — M
Public Health—General — M

UNIVERSITY OF ILLINOIS AT URBANA–CHAMPAIGN
Allopathic Medicine —
Biochemistry — M,D
Biological and Biomedical
　Sciences—General — M,D
Biophysics — M,D
Cell Biology — D
Communication Disorders — M,D
Community Health — M,D
Computational Biology — M,D
Conservation Biology — M,D
Developmental Biology — D
Ecology — M,D
Entomology — M,D
Evolutionary Biology — M,D
Microbiology — M,D
Molecular Physiology — M,D
Neuroscience — D
Nutrition — M,D
Pathobiology — M,D
Physiology — M,D
Plant Biology — M,D
Public Health—General — M,D
Rehabilitation Sciences — M,D
Veterinary Medicine — D
Veterinary Sciences — M,D
Zoology — M,D

UNIVERSITY OF INDIANAPOLIS
Biological and Biomedical
　Sciences—General — M
Nurse Midwifery — M
Nursing and Healthcare Administration — M
Nursing Education — M
Nursing—General — M
Occupational Therapy — M,D
Physical Therapy — M,D

THE UNIVERSITY OF IOWA
Allopathic Medicine — D
Anatomy — D
Bacteriology — M,D
Biochemistry — M,D
Biological and Biomedical
　Sciences—General — M,D
Biophysics — M,D
Cell Biology — M,D
Clinical Research — M,D
Communication Disorders — M,D
Community Health — M,D
Computational Biology — M,D,O
Dentistry — M,D,O
Environmental and Occupational
　Health — M,D,O
Epidemiology — M,D
Evolutionary Biology — M,D
Genetics — M,D
Health Services Management and
　Hospital Administration — M,D
Immunology — M,D
Microbiology — M,D
Molecular Biology — D
Neurobiology — M,D
Neuroscience — M,D
Nursing—General — M,D
Oral and Dental Sciences — M,D,O
Pathology — M
Pharmacology — M,D
Pharmacy — D
Physical Therapy — D
Physician Assistant Studies — M
Physiology — M,D
Public Health—General — M,D,O
Radiation Biology — M,D
Rehabilitation Sciences — D
Toxicology — M,D

Translational Biology — M,D
Virology — M,D

THE UNIVERSITY OF KANSAS
Adult Nursing — M,D,O
Allied Health—General — M,D,O
Allopathic Medicine — D
Anatomy — M,D
Biochemistry — M,D
Biological and Biomedical
  Sciences—General — M,D*
Biophysics — M,D
Botany — M,D
Cell Biology — M,D
Clinical Research — M
Communication Disorders — M,D
Community Health Nursing — M,D,O
Developmental Biology — M,D
Ecology — M,D
Entomology — M,D
Environmental and Occupational
  Health — M
Epidemiology — M
Evolutionary Biology — M,D
Family Nurse Practitioner Studies — M,D,O
Gerontological Nursing — M,D,O
Health Services Management and
  Hospital Administration — M,D
Medicinal and Pharmaceutical
  Chemistry — M,D
Microbiology — M,D
Molecular Biology — M,D
Neuroscience — M,D
Nurse Anesthesia — M
Nurse Midwifery — M,D,O
Nursing and Healthcare Administration — M,D,O
Nursing—General — M,D,O
Nutrition — M,D,O
Occupational Therapy — M,D
Pathology — M,D
Pharmaceutical Sciences — M
Pharmacology — M,D
Physical Therapy — D
Physiology — M,D
Psychiatric Nursing — M,D,O
Public Health—General — M
Rehabilitation Sciences — M,D
Toxicology — M,D

UNIVERSITY OF KENTUCKY
Allied Health—General — M,D
Allopathic Medicine — D
Anatomy — D
Biochemistry — D
Biological and Biomedical
  Sciences—General — M,D
Clinical Laboratory Sciences/Medical
  Technology — M,D
Communication Disorders — M
Dentistry — M,D
Entomology — M,D
Health Physics/Radiological Health — M,D
Health Promotion — M,D
Health Services Management and
  Hospital Administration — M
Medical Physics — M
Microbiology — D
Neurobiology — D
Nursing—General — M,D
Nutrition — M,D
Oral and Dental Sciences — M
Pharmaceutical Sciences — M,D
Pharmacology — D
Pharmacy — D
Physical Therapy — M
Physician Assistant Studies — M
Physiology — M,D
Plant Pathology — M,D
Plant Physiology — D
Public Health—General — M
Rehabilitation Sciences — D
Toxicology — M,D
Veterinary Sciences — M,D

UNIVERSITY OF LA VERNE
Health Services Management and
  Hospital Administration — M,O
Health Services Research — M

UNIVERSITY OF LETHBRIDGE
Biochemistry — M,D
Biological and Biomedical
  Sciences—General — M,D
Molecular Biology — M,D
Neuroscience — M,D
Nursing—General — M,D

UNIVERSITY OF LOUISIANA AT LAFAYETTE
Biological and Biomedical
  Sciences—General — M,D
Communication Disorders — M,D
Environmental Biology — M,D
Evolutionary Biology — M,D
Nursing—General — M

UNIVERSITY OF LOUISIANA AT MONROE
Biological and Biomedical
  Sciences—General — M
Communication Disorders — M
Pharmacy — D

UNIVERSITY OF LOUISVILLE
Adult Nursing — M,D
Allopathic Medicine — D
Anatomy — M,D
Biochemistry — M,D
Biological and Biomedical
  Sciences—General — M,D
Biophysics — M,D
Clinical Research — M,D,O
Communication Disorders — M,D

Community Health — M
Dentistry — M,D
Environmental and Occupational
  Health — M,D
Environmental Biology — M,D
Epidemiology — M,D
Family Nurse Practitioner Studies — M,D
Health Promotion — D
Health Services Management and
  Hospital Administration — M,D
Immunology — M,D
Maternal and Child/Neonatal Nursing — M,D
Microbiology — M,D
Molecular Biology — M,D
Neurobiology — M,D
Nursing—General — M,D
Oral and Dental Sciences — M,D
Pharmacology — M,D
Physiology — M,D
Psychiatric Nursing — M,D
Public Health—General — M,D
Toxicology — M,D

UNIVERSITY OF MAINE
Biochemistry — M,D
Biological and Biomedical
  Sciences—General — D
Botany — M
Cell Biology — D
Communication Disorders — M
Ecology — M,D
Entomology — M,D
Family Nurse Practitioner Studies — M,O
Genomic Sciences — D
Marine Biology — M,D
Microbiology — M,D,
Molecular Biology — M,D
Neuroscience — D
Nursing—General — M,O
Nutrition — M,D
Plant Biology — M,D
Plant Pathology — M
Toxicology — D
Zoology — M,D

THE UNIVERSITY OF MANCHESTER
Biochemistry — M,D
Biological and Biomedical
  Sciences—General — M,D
Biophysics — M,D
Cancer Biology/Oncology — M,D
Cell Biology — M,D
Communication Disorders — M,D
Dentistry — M,D
Developmental Biology — M,D
Ecology — M,D
Environmental Biology — M,D
Evolutionary Biology — M,D
Genetics — M,D
Immunology — M,D
Microbiology — M,D
Molecular Biology — M,D
Molecular Genetics — M,D
Neurobiology — M,D
Neuroscience — M,D
Nurse Midwifery — M,D
Nursing—General — M,D
Optometry — M,D
Oral and Dental Sciences — M,D
Pharmaceutical Sciences — M,D
Pharmacology — M,D
Pharmacy — M,D
Physiology — M,D
Public Health—General — M,D
Structural Biology — M,D
Toxicology — M,D
Vision Sciences — M,D

UNIVERSITY OF MANITOBA
Anatomy — M,D
Biochemistry — M,D
Biological and Biomedical
  Sciences—General — M,D,O
Botany — M,D
Cancer Biology/Oncology — M
Community Health — M,D,O
Dentistry — D
Ecology — M,D
Entomology — M,D
Human Genetics — M,D
Immunology — M,D
Medical Microbiology — M,D
Microbiology — M,D
Nursing—General — M
Nutrition — M,D
Occupational Therapy — M,D
Oral and Dental Sciences — M,D
Pathology — M
Pharmaceutical Sciences — M,D
Pharmacology — M,D
Physical Therapy — M,D
Physiology — M,D
Plant Physiology — M,D
Rehabilitation Sciences — M,D
Zoology — M,D

UNIVERSITY OF MARY
Cardiovascular Sciences — M
Family Nurse Practitioner Studies — M
Health Services Management and
  Hospital Administration — M
Nursing and Healthcare Administration — M
Nursing Education — M
Nursing—General — M
Occupational Therapy — M
Physical Therapy — M

UNIVERSITY OF MARY HARDIN-BAYLOR
Family Nurse Practitioner Studies — M
Nursing and Healthcare Administration — M
Nursing Education — M
Nursing—General — M

UNIVERSITY OF MARYLAND, BALTIMORE
Allopathic Medicine — D
Biochemistry — M,D
Biological and Biomedical
  Sciences—General — M,D
Cancer Biology/Oncology — M,D
Cell Biology — M,D
Clinical Laboratory Sciences/Medical
  Technology — M
Clinical Research — M,D
Community Health Nursing — M
Dental Hygiene — M
Dentistry — D,O
Epidemiology — M,D
Genomic Sciences — M,D
Gerontological Nursing — M
Health Services Research — M,D
Human Genetics — M,D
Immunology — D
Maternal and Child/Neonatal Nursing — M
Medical/Surgical Nursing — M
Microbiology — D
Molecular Biology — M,D
Molecular Medicine — M,D
Neurobiology — D
Neuroscience — D
Nurse Midwifery — M
Nursing and Healthcare Administration — M
Nursing Education — M
Nursing—General — M,D,O
Oral and Dental Sciences — M,D,O
Pathology — M,D
Pediatric Nursing — M
Pharmaceutical Administration — M,D
Pharmaceutical Sciences — D
Pharmacology — M,D
Pharmacy — M,D
Physical Therapy — D
Psychiatric Nursing — M
Rehabilitation Sciences — D
Toxicology — M,D

UNIVERSITY OF MARYLAND, BALTIMORE COUNTY
Biochemistry — M,D,O
Biological and Biomedical
  Sciences—General — M,D,O
Cell Biology — D
Epidemiology — M,O
Health Services Management and
  Hospital Administration — M,D,O
Molecular Biology — M,D
Neuroscience — M,D

UNIVERSITY OF MARYLAND, COLLEGE PARK
Biochemistry — M,D
Biological and Biomedical
  Sciences—General — M,D
Biophysics — D
Cell Biology — M,D
Communication Disorders — M,D
Computational Biology — D
Conservation Biology — M
Ecology — M,D
Entomology — M,D
Environmental and Occupational
  Health — M
Epidemiology — M,D
Evolutionary Biology — M,D
Genomic Sciences — M,D
Health Services Management and
  Hospital Administration — M,D
Maternal and Child Health — M,D
Molecular Biology — D
Molecular Genetics — M,D
Neuroscience — M,D
Nutrition — M,D
Plant Biology — M,D
Public Health—General — M,D
Veterinary Medicine — D
Veterinary Sciences — M,D

UNIVERSITY OF MARYLAND EASTERN SHORE
Physical Therapy — D
Rehabilitation Sciences — M
Toxicology — M,D

UNIVERSITY OF MARYLAND UNIVERSITY COLLEGE
Health Services Management and
  Hospital Administration — M,O

UNIVERSITY OF MASSACHUSETTS AMHERST
Animal Behavior — M,D
Biochemistry — M,D
Biological and Biomedical
  Sciences—General — M,D
Cell Biology — M,D
Communication Disorders — M,D
Community Health Nursing — M,D
Community Health — M,D
Developmental Biology — D
Entomology — M,D
Environmental and Occupational
  Health — M,D
Environmental Biology — M,D
Epidemiology — M,D
Evolutionary Biology — M,D
Family Nurse Practitioner Studies — M,D
Genetics — M,D
Health Services Management and
  Hospital Administration — M,D
Microbiology — M,D*
Molecular Biophysics — D
Neuroscience — M,D
Nursing and Healthcare Administration — M,D
Nursing—General — M,D
Nutrition — M,D

Physiology — M,D
Plant Biology — M,D
Plant Molecular Biology — M,D
Plant Physiology — M,D
Public Health—General — M,D

UNIVERSITY OF MASSACHUSETTS BOSTON
Biological and Biomedical
  Sciences—General — M
Cell Biology — D
Environmental Biology — D
Health Services Management and
  Hospital Administration — M,D,O
Molecular Biology — D
Nursing—General — M,D

UNIVERSITY OF MASSACHUSETTS DARTMOUTH
Adult Nursing — M,D,O
Biological and Biomedical
  Sciences—General — M
Community Health Nursing — M,D,O
Marine Biology — D
Nursing and Healthcare Administration — M,D,O
Nursing Education — M,D,O
Nursing—General — M,D,O

UNIVERSITY OF MASSACHUSETTS LOWELL
Allied Health—General — M,D,O
Biochemistry — M,D
Biological and Biomedical
  Sciences—General — M,D
Clinical Laboratory Sciences/Medical
  Technology — M,O
Epidemiology — M,D,O
Family Nurse Practitioner Studies — M
Gerontological Nursing — M,O
Health Physics/Radiological Health — M
Health Promotion — D
Health Services Management and
  Hospital Administration — M,O
Industrial Hygiene — M,D,O
Medical/Surgical Nursing — M,D,O
Nursing and Healthcare Administration — D
Nursing Education — M,D,O
Nursing—General — M,D,O
Nutrition — M,O
Pathology — M,O
Physical Therapy — D
Psychiatric Nursing — M,O
Public Health—General — M,O

UNIVERSITY OF MASSACHUSETTS WORCESTER
Acute Care/Critical Care Nursing — M,D,O
Adult Nursing — M,D,O
Allopathic Medicine — D
Biochemistry — M,D
Biological and Biomedical
  Sciences—General — M,D
Cancer Biology/Oncology — M,D
Cell Biology — M,D
Clinical Research — M,D
Computational Biology — M,D
Epidemiology — M,D
Family Nurse Practitioner Studies — M,D,O
Gerontological Nursing — M,D,O
Health Services Research — M,D
Immunology — M,D
Microbiology — M,D
Molecular Genetics — M,D
Molecular Pharmacology — M,D
Neuroscience — M,D
Nursing and Healthcare Administration — M,D,O
Nursing Education — M,D,O
Nursing—General — M,D,O
Virology — M,D

UNIVERSITY OF MEDICINE AND DENTISTRY OF NEW JERSEY
Adult Nursing — M,D,O
Allied Health—General — M,D,O
Allopathic Medicine — D
Biochemistry — M,D
Biological and Biomedical
  Sciences—General — M,D,O
Cancer Biology/Oncology — D,O
Cardiovascular Sciences — M,D
Cell Biology — M,D
Clinical Laboratory Sciences/Medical
  Technology — M,D
Dentistry — M,D,O
Developmental Biology — D,O
Environmental and Occupational
  Health — M,D,O
Epidemiology — M,D,O
Family Nurse Practitioner Studies — M,D,O
Health Physics/Radiological Health — M
Health Services Management and
  Hospital Administration — M,D,O
Immunology — M,D
Infectious Diseases — D,O
Medical Imaging — M
Microbiology — M,D
Molecular Biology — M,D
Molecular Genetics — M,D
Molecular Medicine — D
Molecular Pathology — M,D
Molecular Pharmacology — M,D
Neuroscience — M,D
Nurse Anesthesia — M,D,O
Nurse Midwifery — M,O
Nursing Informatics — M
Nursing—General — M,D,O
Nutrition — M,D,O
Occupational Health Nursing — M,D,O
Oral and Dental Sciences — M,D,O
Osteopathic Medicine — D
Pathology — M,D
Pharmacology — D

---

*M—master's degree; P—first professional degree; D—doctorate; O—other advanced degree; *Close-Up and/or Display*

Physical Therapy	M,D
Physician Assistant Studies	M
Physiology	M,D
Public Health—General	M,D,O
Toxicology	M,D
Transcultural Nursing	D
Women's Health Nursing	M,D,O

UNIVERSITY OF MEMPHIS

Biological and Biomedical Sciences—General	M,D
Communication Disorders	M,D
Environmental and Occupational Health	M
Epidemiology	M
Family Nurse Practitioner Studies	M,O
Health Promotion	M
Health Services Management and Hospital Administration	M
Nursing and Healthcare Administration	M,O
Nursing Education	M,O
Nursing Informatics	M,O
Nursing—General	M,O
Nutrition	M
Public Health—General	M

UNIVERSITY OF MIAMI

Acute Care/Critical Care Nursing	M,D
Adult Nursing	M,D
Allopathic Medicine	D
Biochemistry	D
Biological and Biomedical Sciences—General	M,D
Biophysics	D
Cancer Biology/Oncology	D
Cell Biology	D
Developmental Biology	D
Environmental and Occupational Health	M
Epidemiology	M,D
Evolutionary Biology	M,D
Family Nurse Practitioner Studies	M,D
Genetics	M,D
Immunology	D
Marine Biology	M,D
Microbiology	D
Molecular Biology	D
Neuroscience	M,D
Nurse Anesthesia	M,D
Nurse Midwifery	M,D
Nursing—General	M,D
Pharmacology	D
Physical Therapy	D
Physiology	D
Public Health—General	M,D

UNIVERSITY OF MICHIGAN

Acute Care/Critical Care Nursing	M
Adult Nursing	M,O
Allopathic Medicine	D
Biochemistry	D
Biological and Biomedical Sciences—General	M,D
Biophysics	D
Biopsychology	D
Cancer Biology/Oncology	D
Cell Biology	M,D
Clinical Research	M
Community Health Nursing	M,O
Conservation Biology	M,D
Dental Hygiene	M
Dentistry	D
Developmental Biology	M,D
Ecology	M,D
Environmental and Occupational Health	M,D
Epidemiology	M,D
Evolutionary Biology	M,D
Family Nurse Practitioner Studies	M,O
Gerontological Nursing	M
Health Physics/Radiological Health	M,D,O
Health Promotion	M,D
Health Services Management and Hospital Administration	M,D
Human Genetics	M,D
Immunology	D
Industrial Hygiene	M,D
International Health	M,D
Medical/Surgical Nursing	M
Medicinal and Pharmaceutical Chemistry	D
Microbiology	D
Molecular Biology	M,D
Molecular Pathology	D
Neuroscience	D
Nurse Midwifery	M,O
Nursing and Healthcare Administration	M
Nursing—General	M,D,O
Nutrition	M,D
Occupational Health Nursing	M,O
Oral and Dental Sciences	M,D
Pathology	D
Pediatric Nursing	M,O
Pharmaceutical Administration	D
Pharmaceutical Sciences	D
Pharmacology	M,D
Pharmacy	D
Physiology	D
Psychiatric Nursing	M
Public Health—General	M,D
Toxicology	M,D

UNIVERSITY OF MICHIGAN–FLINT

Biological and Biomedical Sciences—General	M
Nurse Anesthesia	M
Nursing—General	D
Physical Therapy	D

UNIVERSITY OF MINNESOTA, DULUTH

Allopathic Medicine	D
Biochemistry	M,D
Biological and Biomedical Sciences—General	M,D
Biophysics	M,D
Communication Disorders	M
Immunology	M,D
Medical Microbiology	M,D
Molecular Biology	M,D
Pharmacology	M,D
Pharmacy	M,D
Physiology	M,D
Toxicology	M,D

UNIVERSITY OF MINNESOTA, TWIN CITIES CAMPUS

Adult Nursing	M
Allopathic Medicine	D
Animal Behavior	M,D
Biochemistry	D
Biological and Biomedical Sciences—General	M
Biophysics	M,D
Biopsychology	D
Cancer Biology/Oncology	D
Cell Biology	M,D
Clinical Research	M
Communication Disorders	M,D
Community Health Nursing	M
Community Health	M
Conservation Biology	M,D
Dentistry	D
Developmental Biology	M,D
Ecology	M,D
Entomology	M,D
Environmental and Occupational Health	M,D,O
Epidemiology	M,D
Evolutionary Biology	M,D
Family Nurse Practitioner Studies	M
Genetics	M,D
Gerontological Nursing	M
Health Services Management and Hospital Administration	M,D
Health Services Research	M,D
Immunology	D
Industrial Hygiene	M,D
Infectious Diseases	M,D
International Health	M,D
Maternal and Child Health	M
Medical Physics	M,D
Medicinal and Pharmaceutical Chemistry	M,D
Microbiology	D
Molecular Biology	M,D
Neurobiology	M,D
Neuroscience	M,D
Nurse Anesthesia	M
Nurse Midwifery	M
Nursing and Healthcare Administration	M
Nursing—General	M,D
Nutrition	M,D
Occupational Health Nursing	M,D
Oral and Dental Sciences	M,D,O
Pediatric Nursing	M
Pharmaceutical Administration	M,D
Pharmaceutical Sciences	M,D
Pharmacology	M,D
Pharmacy	D
Physical Therapy	D
Physiology	D
Plant Biology	M,D
Plant Pathology	M,D
Psychiatric Nursing	M
Public Health—General	M,D,O
Structural Biology	D
Toxicology	M,D
Veterinary Medicine	D
Veterinary Sciences	M,D
Virology	D
Women's Health Nursing	M

UNIVERSITY OF MISSISSIPPI

Biological and Biomedical Sciences—General	M,D
Communication Disorders	M
Medicinal and Pharmaceutical Chemistry	M,D
Pharmaceutical Administration	M,D
Pharmaceutical Sciences	M,D
Pharmacology	M,D
Pharmacy	D

UNIVERSITY OF MISSISSIPPI MEDICAL CENTER

Allied Health—General	M
Allopathic Medicine	D
Anatomy	M,D
Biochemistry	M,D
Biological and Biomedical Sciences—General	M,D
Biophysics	M,D
Clinical Laboratory Sciences/Medical Technology	M,D
Dentistry	M,D
Maternal and Child Health	M
Microbiology	M,D
Nursing—General	M,D
Occupational Therapy	M
Oral and Dental Sciences	M,D
Pathology	M,D
Pharmacology	M,D
Physical Therapy	M
Physiology	M,D
Toxicology	M,D

UNIVERSITY OF MISSOURI

Allopathic Medicine	D
Anatomy	M
Biochemistry	M,D
Biological and Biomedical Sciences—General	M,D
Cell Biology	M,D
Communication Disorders	M
Conservation Biology	M,D,O
Ecology	M,D
Entomology	M,D
Evolutionary Biology	M,D
Genetics	M,D
Health Physics/Radiological Health	M,D
Health Promotion	M,O
Health Services Management and Hospital Administration	M,D,O
Immunology	M,D
Medical Physics	M,D
Microbiology	M,D
Neurobiology	M,D
Neuroscience	M,D
Nursing—General	M,D
Nutrition	M,D
Occupational Therapy	M
Pathobiology	M,D
Pathology	M
Pharmacology	M,D
Physical Therapy	M
Physiology	M,D
Plant Biology	M,D
Public Health—General	M,O
Veterinary Medicine	D
Veterinary Sciences	M,D

UNIVERSITY OF MISSOURI–KANSAS CITY

Adult Nursing	M,D
Allopathic Medicine	M,D
Anesthesiologist Assistant Studies	M,D
Biochemistry	D
Biological and Biomedical Sciences—General	M,D
Biophysics	D
Cell Biology	D*
Dental Hygiene	M,D,O
Dentistry	M,D,O
Family Nurse Practitioner Studies	M,D
Maternal and Child/Neonatal Nursing	M,D
Molecular Biology	D*
Nursing and Healthcare Administration	M,D
Nursing Education	M,D
Nursing—General	M,D
Oral and Dental Sciences	M,D,O
Pediatric Nursing	M,D
Pharmaceutical Sciences	D
Pharmacology	D
Pharmacy	D
Toxicology	D
Women's Health Nursing	M,D

UNIVERSITY OF MISSOURI–ST. LOUIS

Adult Nursing	M,D,O
Biochemistry	M,D
Biological and Biomedical Sciences—General	M,D,O
Cell Biology	M,D,O
Conservation Biology	M,D,O
Ecology	M,D,O
Evolutionary Biology	M,D,O
Family Nurse Practitioner Studies	M,D,O
Health Services Management and Hospital Administration	M,O
Maternal and Child/Neonatal Nursing	M,D,O
Molecular Biology	M,D,O
Neuroscience	M,D,O
Nursing and Healthcare Administration	M,D,O
Nursing Education	M,D,O
Nursing—General	M,D,O
Optometry	D
Pediatric Nursing	M,D,O
Psychiatric Nursing	M,D,O
Vision Sciences	M,D
Women's Health Nursing	M,D,O

UNIVERSITY OF MOBILE

Nursing—General	M

THE UNIVERSITY OF MONTANA

Animal Behavior	M,D,O
Biochemistry	M,D
Biological and Biomedical Sciences—General	M,D
Ecology	M,D
Health Promotion	M
Infectious Diseases	D
Microbiology	M,D
Neuroscience	M,D
Pharmaceutical Sciences	M,D
Pharmacy	M,D
Physical Therapy	D
Public Health—General	M,O
Toxicology	M,D
Zoology	M,D

UNIVERSITY OF MONTEVALLO

Communication Disorders	M

UNIVERSITY OF NEBRASKA AT KEARNEY

Biological and Biomedical Sciences—General	M
Communication Disorders	M

UNIVERSITY OF NEBRASKA AT OMAHA

Biological and Biomedical Sciences—General	M
Biopsychology	M,D,O
Communication Disorders	M

UNIVERSITY OF NEBRASKA–LINCOLN

Biochemistry	M,D
Biological and Biomedical Sciences—General	M,D
Biopsychology	M,D
Communication Disorders	M,D
Entomology	M,D
Health Promotion	M,D
Nutrition	M,D
Toxicology	M,D
Veterinary Sciences	M,D

UNIVERSITY OF NEBRASKA MEDICAL CENTER

Allied Health—General	M,D,O
Allopathic Medicine	D,O
Anatomy	M,D
Biochemistry	M,D
Biological and Biomedical Sciences—General	M,D
Cancer Biology/Oncology	D
Cell Biology	M,D
Clinical Laboratory Sciences/Medical Technology	M,O
Dentistry	M,D,O
Genetics	M,D
Microbiology	M,D
Molecular Biology	M,D
Neuroscience	M,D
Nursing—General	M,D
Nutrition	O
Pathology	M,D
Perfusion	M
Pharmaceutical Sciences	M,D
Pharmacology	M,D
Pharmacy	D
Physical Therapy	D
Physician Assistant Studies	M
Physiology	M,D
Public Health—General	M
Toxicology	M,D

UNIVERSITY OF NEVADA, LAS VEGAS

Allied Health—General	M,D
Biochemistry	M,D
Biological and Biomedical Sciences—General	M,D
Community Health	M,D
Family Nurse Practitioner Studies	M,D,O
Health Physics/Radiological Health	M
Health Promotion	M
Health Services Management and Hospital Administration	M
Nursing Education	M,D,O
Nursing—General	M,D,O
Pediatric Nursing	M,D,O
Physical Therapy	D
Public Health—General	M,D

UNIVERSITY OF NEVADA, RENO

Biochemistry	M,D*
Biological and Biomedical Sciences—General	M
Cell Biology	M,D
Communication Disorders	M,D
Conservation Biology	D
Ecology	D
Environmental and Occupational Health	M,D
Evolutionary Biology	D
Molecular Biology	M,D
Molecular Pharmacology	D
Nursing—General	M,D
Nutrition	M
Physiology	D
Public Health—General	M,D

UNIVERSITY OF NEW BRUNSWICK FREDERICTON

Biological and Biomedical Sciences—General	M,D
Health Services Research	M
Nursing Education	M
Nursing—General	M

UNIVERSITY OF NEW BRUNSWICK SAINT JOHN

Biological and Biomedical Sciences—General	M,D

UNIVERSITY OF NEW ENGLAND

Nurse Anesthesia	M
Occupational Therapy	M
Osteopathic Medicine	D
Pharmacy	D
Physical Therapy	D
Physician Assistant Studies	M
Public Health—General	M,O

UNIVERSITY OF NEW HAMPSHIRE

Biochemistry	M,D
Biological and Biomedical Sciences—General	M,D
Communication Disorders	M
Family Nurse Practitioner Studies	M,O
Genetics	M,D
Microbiology	M,D
Nursing—General	M,O
Nutrition	M,D
Occupational Therapy	M,O
Plant Biology	M,D
Public Health—General	M,O
Zoology	M,D

UNIVERSITY OF NEW HAVEN

Cell Biology	M
Environmental and Occupational Health	M,O
Health Services Management and Hospital Administration	M,O
Molecular Biology	M
Nutrition	M

UNIVERSITY OF NEW MEXICO

Allopathic Medicine	D
Biochemistry	M,D,O
Biological and Biomedical Sciences—General	M,D,O
Cell Biology	M,D,O
Clinical Laboratory Sciences/Medical Technology	M,O
Communication Disorders	M
Community Health	M
Dental Hygiene	M
Epidemiology	M
Genetics	M,D,O
Microbiology	M,D,O
Molecular Biology	M,D,O
Neuroscience	M,D,O
Nursing—General	M,D
Nutrition	M
Occupational Therapy	M
Pathology	M,D,O
Pharmaceutical Sciences	M,D
Pharmacy	D
Physical Therapy	D
Physician Assistant Studies	M
Physiology	M,D,O

Public Health—General M
Toxicology M,D,O

UNIVERSITY OF NEW ORLEANS
Biological and Biomedical
   Sciences—General M,D
Health Services Management and
   Hospital Administration M

UNIVERSITY OF NORTH ALABAMA
Health Promotion M
Nursing—General M

THE UNIVERSITY OF NORTH CAROLINA AT CHAPEL HILL
Adult Nursing M,D,O
Allied Health—General M,D
Allopathic Medicine D
Biochemistry M,D
Biological and Biomedical
   Sciences—General M,D
Biophysics M,D
Botany M,D
Cell Biology M,D
Communication Disorders M,D
Community Health Nursing M
Computational Biology D
Dental Hygiene M,D
Dentistry D
Developmental Biology M,D
Ecology M,D
Environmental and Occupational
   Health M,D
Epidemiology M,D
Evolutionary Biology M,D
Family Nurse Practitioner Studies M,D,O
Genetics M,D
Health Promotion M
Health Services Management and
   Hospital Administration M,D
Immunology M,D
Industrial Hygiene M,D
Maternal and Child Health M,D
Microbiology M,D
Molecular Biology M,D
Molecular Physiology D
Neurobiology M,D
Nursing and Healthcare Administration M,D,O
Nursing—General M,D,O
Nutrition M,D
Occupational Health Nursing M
Occupational Therapy M,D
Oral and Dental Sciences M,D
Pathology D
Pediatric Nursing M,D,O
Pharmaceutical Sciences M,D
Pharmacology D
Physical Therapy M,D
Psychiatric Nursing M,D,O
Public Health—General M,D
Toxicology M,D
Women's Health Nursing M,D,O

THE UNIVERSITY OF NORTH CAROLINA AT CHARLOTTE
Adult Nursing M,O
Biological and Biomedical
   Sciences—General M,D
Community Health M,D,O
Family Nurse Practitioner Studies M,O
Health Services Management and
   Hospital Administration M,D,O
Nurse Anesthesia M,O
Nursing Education M,O
Nursing—General M,O
Psychiatric Nursing M,O
Public Health—General M,D,O

THE UNIVERSITY OF NORTH CAROLINA AT GREENSBORO
Adult Nursing M,D,O
Biochemistry M
Biological and Biomedical
   Sciences—General M
Communication Disorders M,D
Community Health M,D
Gerontological Nursing M,D,O
Nurse Anesthesia M,D,O
Nursing and Healthcare Administration M,D,O
Nursing Education M,D,O
Nursing—General M,D,O
Nutrition M,D

THE UNIVERSITY OF NORTH CAROLINA WILMINGTON
Biological and Biomedical
   Sciences—General M,D
Family Nurse Practitioner Studies M
Marine Biology M,D
Nursing Education M
Nursing—General M

UNIVERSITY OF NORTH DAKOTA
Allopathic Medicine D
Anatomy M,D
Biochemistry M,D
Biological and Biomedical
   Sciences—General M,D
Botany M,D
Cell Biology M,D
Clinical Laboratory Sciences/Medical
   Technology M
Communication Disorders M,D
Community Health Nursing M,D
Ecology M,D
Entomology M,D
Environmental Biology M,D
Family Nurse Practitioner Studies M,D
Genetics M,D
Gerontological Nursing M,D
Immunology M,D
Microbiology M,D

Molecular Biology M,D
Nurse Anesthesia M,D
Nursing Education M,D
Nursing—General M,D
Occupational Therapy M
Pharmacology M,D
Physical Therapy M,D
Physician Assistant Studies M
Physiology M,D
Psychiatric Nursing M,D
Zoology M,D

UNIVERSITY OF NORTHERN BRITISH COLUMBIA
Community Health M,D,O

UNIVERSITY OF NORTHERN COLORADO
Biological and Biomedical
   Sciences—General M
Communication Disorders M,D
Family Nurse Practitioner Studies M,D
Nursing Education M,D
Nursing—General M,D
Public Health—General M

UNIVERSITY OF NORTHERN IOWA
Biochemistry M
Biological and Biomedical
   Sciences—General M
Communication Disorders M
Community Health M,D
Rehabilitation Sciences M,D

UNIVERSITY OF NORTH FLORIDA
Adult Nursing M,D,O
Allied Health—General M,D,O
Biological and Biomedical
   Sciences—General M
Communication Disorders M
Community Health M,O
Family Nurse Practitioner Studies M,D,O
Health Services Management and
   Hospital Administration M,O
Nurse Anesthesia M,D,O
Nursing and Healthcare Administration M,D,O
Nursing—General M
Nutrition M
Physical Therapy M,D
Public Health—General M,O

UNIVERSITY OF NORTH TEXAS
Biochemistry M,D
Biological and Biomedical
   Sciences—General M,D
Communication Disorders M,D
Community Health M,D
Molecular Biology M,D
Rehabilitation Sciences M

UNIVERSITY OF NORTH TEXAS HEALTH SCIENCE CENTER AT FORT WORTH
Anatomy M,D
Biochemistry M,D
Biological and Biomedical
   Sciences—General M,D
Community Health M,D
Environmental and Occupational
   Health M,D
Epidemiology M,D
Genetics M,D
Health Services Management and
   Hospital Administration M,D
Immunology M,D
Microbiology M,D
Molecular Biology M,D
Osteopathic Medicine M,D
Pharmacology M,D
Physician Assistant Studies M
Physiology M,D
Public Health—General M,D

UNIVERSITY OF NOTRE DAME
Biochemistry M,D
Biological and Biomedical
   Sciences—General M,D
Cell Biology M,D
Ecology M,D
Evolutionary Biology M,D
Genetics M,D
Molecular Biology M,D
Parasitology M,D
Physiology M,D

UNIVERSITY OF OKLAHOMA
Biochemistry M,D
Botany M,D
Ecology D
Evolutionary Biology D
Health Promotion M,D
Microbiology M,D
Neurobiology M,D
Zoology M,D

UNIVERSITY OF OKLAHOMA HEALTH SCIENCES CENTER
Allied Health—General M,D,O
Allopathic Medicine D
Biochemistry M,D
Biological and Biomedical
   Sciences—General M,D
Biopsychology M,D
Cell Biology M,D
Communication Disorders M,D,O
Dentistry D,O
Environmental and Occupational
   Health M,D
Epidemiology M,D
Health Physics/Radiological Health M,D
Health Promotion M,D
Health Services Management and
   Hospital Administration M,D
Immunology M,D

Medical Physics M,D
Microbiology M,D
Molecular Biology M,D
Neuroscience M,D
Nursing—General M
Nutrition M
Occupational Therapy M
Oral and Dental Sciences M
Pathology D
Pharmaceutical Sciences M,D
Pharmacy D
Physical Therapy M
Physiology M,D
Public Health—General M,D
Radiation Biology M,D
Rehabilitation Sciences M

UNIVERSITY OF OREGON
Biochemistry M,D
Biological and Biomedical
   Sciences—General M,D
Biopsychology M,D
Ecology M,D
Evolutionary Biology M,D
Genetics M,D
Marine Biology M,D
Molecular Biology M,D
Neuroscience M,D
Physiology M,D

UNIVERSITY OF OTTAWA
Allopathic Medicine M,D
Biochemistry M,D
Biological and Biomedical
   Sciences—General M,D
Cell Biology M,D
Communication Disorders M
Community Health M,D,O
Epidemiology M
Health Services Management and
   Hospital Administration M
Health Services Research D,O
Immunology M,D
Microbiology M,D
Molecular Biology M,D
Nursing—General M,D,O
Public Health—General D
Rehabilitation Sciences M

UNIVERSITY OF PENNSYLVANIA
Acute Care/Critical Care Nursing M
Adult Nursing M
Allopathic Medicine D
Biochemistry D
Bioethics M
Biological and Biomedical
   Sciences—General M,D
Cancer Biology/Oncology D
Cell Biology D
Clinical Laboratory Sciences/Medical
   Technology M
Computational Biology D
Dentistry D
Developmental Biology D
Environmental and Occupational
   Health M
Epidemiology M,D
Family Nurse Practitioner Studies M,O
Genetics D
Genomic Sciences D
Health Services Management and
   Hospital Administration M,D
Health Services Research D
Immunology D
International Health M
Maternal and Child/Neonatal Nursing M,O
Medical Physics M,D
Microbiology D
Molecular Biology D
Molecular Biophysics D
Neuroscience D
Nurse Anesthesia M
Nurse Midwifery M
Nursing and Healthcare Administration M,D
Nursing—General M,D,O
Pediatric Nursing M
Pharmacology D
Physiology D
Psychiatric Nursing M
Public Health—General M
Veterinary Medicine D
Virology D
Women's Health Nursing M

UNIVERSITY OF PHOENIX–ATLANTA CAMPUS
Health Services Management and
   Hospital Administration M
Nursing Education M
Nursing—General M

UNIVERSITY OF PHOENIX–AUGUSTA CAMPUS
Health Services Management and
   Hospital Administration M
Nursing Education M
Nursing—General M

UNIVERSITY OF PHOENIX–AUSTIN CAMPUS
Health Services Management and
   Hospital Administration M
Nursing—General M

UNIVERSITY OF PHOENIX–BAY AREA CAMPUS
Gerontological Nursing M,D
Health Services Management and
   Hospital Administration M,D
Nursing and Healthcare Administration M,D
Nursing Education M,D

Nursing Informatics M,D
Nursing—General M,D

UNIVERSITY OF PHOENIX–BIRMINGHAM CAMPUS
Community Health M
Health Services Management and
   Hospital Administration M
Nursing Education M
Nursing—General M

UNIVERSITY OF PHOENIX–CENTRAL FLORIDA CAMPUS
Health Services Management and
   Hospital Administration M
Nursing Education M
Nursing—General M

UNIVERSITY OF PHOENIX–CENTRAL VALLEY CAMPUS
Community Health M
Health Services Management and
   Hospital Administration M
Nursing—General M

UNIVERSITY OF PHOENIX–CHARLOTTE CAMPUS
Health Services Management and
   Hospital Administration M
Nursing Education M
Nursing Informatics M
Nursing—General M

UNIVERSITY OF PHOENIX–CHATTANOOGA CAMPUS
Community Health M
Health Services Management and
   Hospital Administration M
Nursing—General M

UNIVERSITY OF PHOENIX–CHEYENNE CAMPUS
Health Services Management and
   Hospital Administration M
Nursing Education M
Nursing—General M

UNIVERSITY OF PHOENIX–CLEVELAND CAMPUS
Nursing—General M,D

UNIVERSITY OF PHOENIX–COLUMBUS GEORGIA CAMPUS
Nursing—General M

UNIVERSITY OF PHOENIX–COLUMBUS OHIO CAMPUS
Nursing—General M,D

UNIVERSITY OF PHOENIX–DENVER CAMPUS
Health Services Management and
   Hospital Administration M
Nursing—General M

UNIVERSITY OF PHOENIX–DES MOINES CAMPUS
Health Services Management and
   Hospital Administration M,D
Nursing Education M,D
Nursing Informatics M,D
Nursing—General M,D

UNIVERSITY OF PHOENIX–HARRISBURG CAMPUS
Health Services Management and
   Hospital Administration M
Nursing Education M
Nursing—General M

UNIVERSITY OF PHOENIX–HAWAII CAMPUS
Community Health M
Family Nurse Practitioner Studies M
Health Services Management and
   Hospital Administration M
Nursing Education M
Nursing—General M

UNIVERSITY OF PHOENIX–HOUSTON CAMPUS
Health Services Management and
   Hospital Administration M
Nursing—General M

UNIVERSITY OF PHOENIX–IDAHO CAMPUS
Nursing Education M
Nursing—General M

UNIVERSITY OF PHOENIX–INDIANAPOLIS CAMPUS
Health Services Management and
   Hospital Administration M
Nursing Education M
Nursing—General M

UNIVERSITY OF PHOENIX–LAS VEGAS CAMPUS
Allied Health—General M

UNIVERSITY OF PHOENIX–LOUISIANA CAMPUS
Nursing—General M

UNIVERSITY OF PHOENIX–MEMPHIS CAMPUS
Health Services Management and
   Hospital Administration M,D
Nursing—General M,D

UNIVERSITY OF PHOENIX–METRO DETROIT CAMPUS
Nursing Education M
Nursing—General M

---

*M—master's degree; P—first professional degree; D—doctorate; O—other advanced degree; *Close-Up and/or Display*

UNIVERSITY OF PHOENIX–MILWAUKEE CAMPUS
Health Services Management and
   Hospital Administration M,D
Nursing Education M,D
Nursing Informatics M,D
Nursing—General M,D

UNIVERSITY OF PHOENIX–NASHVILLE CAMPUS
Health Services Management and
   Hospital Administration M
Nursing—General M

UNIVERSITY OF PHOENIX–NEW MEXICO CAMPUS
Health Services Management and
   Hospital Administration M
Nursing Education M
Nursing—General M

UNIVERSITY OF PHOENIX–NORTHERN NEVADA CAMPUS
Health Services Management and
   Hospital Administration M
Nursing Education M
Nursing—General M

UNIVERSITY OF PHOENIX–NORTHERN VIRGINIA CAMPUS
Health Services Management and
   Hospital Administration M
Nursing—General M

UNIVERSITY OF PHOENIX–NORTH FLORIDA CAMPUS
Health Services Management and
   Hospital Administration M
Nursing Education M
Nursing—General M

UNIVERSITY OF PHOENIX–NORTHWEST ARKANSAS CAMPUS
Health Services Management and
   Hospital Administration M
Nursing Education M
Nursing—General M

UNIVERSITY OF PHOENIX–OKLAHOMA CITY CAMPUS
Nursing—General M

UNIVERSITY OF PHOENIX–OMAHA CAMPUS
Health Services Management and
   Hospital Administration M
Nursing—General M

UNIVERSITY OF PHOENIX–ONLINE CAMPUS
Family Nurse Practitioner Studies M
Health Services Management and
   Hospital Administration M,D,O
International Health M
Nursing Education M
Nursing Informatics M
Nursing—General M,D,O

UNIVERSITY OF PHOENIX–OREGON CAMPUS
Health Services Management and
   Hospital Administration M
Nursing—General M

UNIVERSITY OF PHOENIX–PHOENIX MAIN CAMPUS
Family Nurse Practitioner Studies M,O
Gerontological Nursing M,O
Health Services Management and
   Hospital Administration M,O
Nursing Education M,O
Nursing Informatics M,O
Nursing—General M,O

UNIVERSITY OF PHOENIX–PITTSBURGH CAMPUS
Health Services Management and
   Hospital Administration M
Nursing Education M
Nursing—General M

UNIVERSITY OF PHOENIX–RALEIGH CAMPUS
Health Services Management and
   Hospital Administration M,D
Nursing Education M,D
Nursing Informatics M,D
Nursing—General M,D

UNIVERSITY OF PHOENIX–RICHMOND CAMPUS
Health Services Management and
   Hospital Administration M
Nursing Education M
Nursing—General M

UNIVERSITY OF PHOENIX–SACRAMENTO VALLEY CAMPUS
Family Nurse Practitioner Studies M
Health Services Management and
   Hospital Administration M
Nursing Education M
Nursing—General M

UNIVERSITY OF PHOENIX–SAN ANTONIO CAMPUS
Health Services Management and
   Hospital Administration M
Nursing—General M

UNIVERSITY OF PHOENIX–SAN DIEGO CAMPUS
Nursing Education M
Nursing—General M

UNIVERSITY OF PHOENIX–SAVANNAH CAMPUS
Health Services Management and
   Hospital Administration M

Nursing Education M
Nursing—General M

UNIVERSITY OF PHOENIX–SOUTHERN CALIFORNIA CAMPUS
Family Nurse Practitioner Studies M,O
Health Services Management and
   Hospital Administration M
Nursing Education M,O
Nursing Informatics M,O
Nursing—General M,O

UNIVERSITY OF PHOENIX–SOUTHERN COLORADO CAMPUS
Health Services Management and
   Hospital Administration M
Nursing—General M

UNIVERSITY OF PHOENIX–SOUTH FLORIDA CAMPUS
Health Services Management and
   Hospital Administration M
Nursing Education M
Nursing—General M

UNIVERSITY OF PHOENIX–SPRINGFIELD CAMPUS
Health Services Management and
   Hospital Administration M
Nursing—General M

UNIVERSITY OF PHOENIX–TULSA CAMPUS
Nursing—General M

UNIVERSITY OF PHOENIX–UTAH CAMPUS
Nursing Education M
Nursing—General M

UNIVERSITY OF PHOENIX–VANCOUVER CAMPUS
Health Services Management and
   Hospital Administration M
Nursing—General M

UNIVERSITY OF PHOENIX–WASHINGTON D.C. CAMPUS
Health Services Management and
   Hospital Administration M,D
Nursing and Healthcare Administration M,D
Nursing Education M,D
Nursing Informatics M,D
Nursing—General M,D

UNIVERSITY OF PHOENIX–WEST FLORIDA CAMPUS
Health Services Management and
   Hospital Administration M
Nursing Education M
Nursing—General M

UNIVERSITY OF PIKEVILLE
Osteopathic Medicine D

UNIVERSITY OF PITTSBURGH
Acute Care/Critical Care Nursing M,D
Adult Nursing M,D
Allopathic Medicine D
Bioethics M
Biological and Biomedical
   Sciences—General D
Cell Biology M,D
Clinical Laboratory Sciences/Medical
   Technology D
Clinical Research M,D,O
Communication Disorders M,D
Community Health M,D,O
Computational Biology D
Dentistry M,D,O
Developmental Biology M,D
Ecology D
Environmental and Occupational
   Health M,D,O
Epidemiology M,D
Evolutionary Biology D
Family Nurse Practitioner Studies M,D
Health Promotion M
Health Services Management and
   Hospital Administration M,D,O
Human Genetics M,D,O
Immunology M,D
Infectious Diseases M,D,O
Maternal and Child/Neonatal Nursing M
Microbiology M,D,O
Molecular Biology D
Molecular Biophysics D
Molecular Genetics M,D
Molecular Pathology M,D
Molecular Pharmacology M,D
Molecular Physiology M,D
Neuroscience D
Nurse Anesthesia M,D
Nursing and Healthcare Administration M,D
Nursing—General M,D
Nutrition M
Occupational Therapy M
Oral and Dental Sciences M,O
Pathology M,D
Pediatric Nursing M,D
Pharmaceutical Sciences M,D
Pharmacy D
Physical Therapy M,D
Physician Assistant Studies M
Psychiatric Nursing M,D
Public Health—General M,D,O
Rehabilitation Sciences M,D
Structural Biology D
Virology M,D

UNIVERSITY OF PORTLAND
Health Services Management and
   Hospital Administration M,D
Nursing—General M,D

UNIVERSITY OF PRINCE EDWARD ISLAND
Anatomy M,D

Bacteriology M,D
Biological and Biomedical
   Sciences—General M,D
Epidemiology M,D
Immunology M,D
Parasitology M,D
Pathology M,D
Pharmacology M,D
Physiology M,D
Toxicology M,D
Veterinary Medicine D
Veterinary Sciences M,D
Virology M,D

UNIVERSITY OF PUERTO RICO, MAYAGÜEZ CAMPUS
Biological and Biomedical
   Sciences—General M

UNIVERSITY OF PUERTO RICO, MEDICAL SCIENCES CAMPUS
Acute Care/Critical Care Nursing M
Adult Nursing M
Allied Health—General M,D,O
Allopathic Medicine D
Anatomy M,D
Biochemistry M,D
Biological and Biomedical
   Sciences—General M,D
Clinical Laboratory Sciences/Medical
   Technology M,O
Clinical Research M,O
Communication Disorders M,D
Community Health Nursing M
Dentistry D
Environmental and Occupational
   Health M,D
Epidemiology M
Family Nurse Practitioner Studies M
Gerontological Nursing M
Health Promotion O
Health Services Management and
   Hospital Administration M
Health Services Research M
Industrial Hygiene M
Maternal and Child Health M
Maternal and Child/Neonatal Nursing M
Microbiology M,D
Nurse Midwifery M,O
Nursing—General M
Nutrition M,D,O
Occupational Therapy M
Oral and Dental Sciences O
Pediatric Nursing M
Pharmaceutical Sciences M,D
Pharmacology M,D
Pharmacy M,D
Physical Therapy M
Physiology M,D
Psychiatric Nursing M
Toxicology M,D

UNIVERSITY OF PUERTO RICO, RÍO PIEDRAS
Biological and Biomedical
   Sciences—General M,D
Cell Biology M,D
Ecology M,D
Evolutionary Biology M,D
Genetics M,D
Molecular Biology M,D
Neuroscience M,D
Nutrition M,D

UNIVERSITY OF PUGET SOUND
Occupational Therapy M
Physical Therapy D

UNIVERSITY OF REDLANDS
Communication Disorders M

UNIVERSITY OF REGINA
Biochemistry M,D
Biological and Biomedical
   Sciences—General M,D
Biophysics M,D
Cancer Biology/Oncology M,D
Health Services Management and
   Hospital Administration M,D,O
Health Services Research M,D,O

UNIVERSITY OF RHODE ISLAND
Biochemistry M,D
Biological and Biomedical
   Sciences—General M,D
Cell Biology M,D
Clinical Laboratory Sciences/Medical
   Technology M,D
Communication Disorders M
Entomology M,D
Family Nurse Practitioner Studies M,D
Gerontological Nursing M,D
Medicinal and Pharmaceutical
   Chemistry M,D
Microbiology M,D
Molecular Biology M,D
Molecular Genetics M,D
Nursing and Healthcare Administration M,D
Nursing Education M,D
Nursing—General M,D
Nutrition M,D
Pharmaceutical Sciences M,D
Pharmacology M,D
Pharmacy M,D
Physical Therapy D
Psychiatric Nursing M,D
Toxicology M,D

UNIVERSITY OF ROCHESTER
Acute Care/Critical Care Nursing M,D
Adult Nursing M,D
Allopathic Medicine D
Anatomy D
Biochemistry D
Biological and Biomedical
   Sciences—General M,D
Biophysics D

Clinical Research M,D
Computational Biology D
Epidemiology D
Family Nurse Practitioner Studies M,D
Genetics D
Genomic Sciences D
Gerontological Nursing M,D
Health Services Management and
   Hospital Administration M,D
Health Services Research M,D
Immunology M,D
Maternal and Child/Neonatal Nursing M,D
Microbiology M,D
Molecular Biology D
Neurobiology D
Neuroscience D
Nursing and Healthcare Administration M,D
Nursing—General M,D
Oral and Dental Sciences M
Pathology D
Pediatric Nursing M,D
Pharmacology M,D
Physiology M,D
Psychiatric Nursing M,D
Public Health—General M
Structural Biology D
Toxicology D

UNIVERSITY OF ST. AUGUSTINE FOR HEALTH SCIENCES
Occupational Therapy M,D
Physical Therapy M,D,O

UNIVERSITY OF ST. FRANCIS (IL)
Adult Nursing M,D,O
Family Nurse Practitioner Studies M,D,O
Health Services Management and
   Hospital Administration M
Nursing and Healthcare Administration M,D,O
Nursing—General M,D,O
Physician Assistant Studies M,O

UNIVERSITY OF SAINT FRANCIS (IN)
Allied Health—General M
Health Services Management and
   Hospital Administration M
Nursing—General M
Physician Assistant Studies M

UNIVERSITY OF SAINT JOSEPH
Biochemistry M
Biological and Biomedical
   Sciences—General M
Nursing—General M
Nutrition M
Pharmacy M

UNIVERSITY OF ST. THOMAS (MN)
Health Services Management and
   Hospital Administration M

UNIVERSITY OF SAN DIEGO
Adult Nursing M,D
Communication Disorders M
Family Nurse Practitioner Studies M,D
Gerontological Nursing M,D
Nursing and Healthcare Administration M,D
Nursing—General M,D
Pediatric Nursing M,D
Psychiatric Nursing M,D

UNIVERSITY OF SAN FRANCISCO
Biological and Biomedical
   Sciences—General M
Family Nurse Practitioner Studies D
Health Services Management and
   Hospital Administration M
Nursing and Healthcare Administration D
Nursing—General M,D
Public Health—General M

UNIVERSITY OF SASKATCHEWAN
Allopathic Medicine D
Anatomy M,D
Biochemistry M,D
Biological and Biomedical
   Sciences—General M,D
Cell Biology M,D
Community Health M,D
Dentistry D
Epidemiology M,D
Health Services Management and
   Hospital Administration M
Immunology M,D
Microbiology M,D
Nursing—General M
Pathology M,D
Pharmaceutical Sciences M,D
Pharmacology M,D
Physiology M,D
Reproductive Biology M,D
Toxicology M,D,O
Veterinary Medicine M,D
Veterinary Sciences M,D

THE UNIVERSITY OF SCRANTON
Adult Nursing M,O
Biochemistry M
Family Nurse Practitioner Studies M,O
Health Services Management and
   Hospital Administration M
Nurse Anesthesia M,O
Nursing—General M,O
Occupational Therapy M
Physical Therapy M,D

UNIVERSITY OF SIOUX FALLS
Health Services Management and
   Hospital Administration M

UNIVERSITY OF SOUTH AFRICA
Acute Care/Critical Care Nursing M,D
Health Services Management and
   Hospital Administration M,D
Maternal and Child/Neonatal Nursing M,D
Medical/Surgical Nursing M,D
Nurse Midwifery M,D
Public Health—General M,D

UNIVERSITY OF SOUTH ALABAMA
Adult Nursing M,D
Allied Health—General M,D
Allopathic Medicine D
Biological and Biomedical Sciences—General M,D
Communication Disorders M,D
Community Health Nursing M,D
Environmental and Occupational Health M
Maternal and Child/Neonatal Nursing M,D
Nursing—General M,D
Occupational Therapy M
Physical Therapy D
Physician Assistant Studies M
Toxicology M

UNIVERSITY OF SOUTH CAROLINA
Acute Care/Critical Care Nursing M,O
Adult Nursing M
Allopathic Medicine D
Biochemistry M,D
Biological and Biomedical Sciences—General M,D,O
Cell Biology M,D
Communication Disorders M,D
Community Health Nursing M
Developmental Biology M,D
Ecology M,D
Environmental and Occupational Health M,D
Epidemiology M,D
Evolutionary Biology M,D
Family Nurse Practitioner Studies M
Health Promotion M,D,O
Health Services Management and Hospital Administration M,D
Industrial Hygiene M,D
Medical/Surgical Nursing M
Molecular Biology M,D
Nurse Anesthesia M
Nursing and Healthcare Administration M
Nursing—General M,O
Pediatric Nursing M
Pharmaceutical Sciences M,D
Pharmacy D
Psychiatric Nursing M,O
Public Health—General M
Rehabilitation Sciences M,O
Women's Health Nursing M

THE UNIVERSITY OF SOUTH DAKOTA
Allied Health—General M,D
Allopathic Medicine D
Biological and Biomedical Sciences—General M,D
Cardiovascular Sciences M,D
Cell Biology M,D
Communication Disorders M,D
Immunology M,D
Microbiology M,D
Molecular Biology M,D
Neuroscience M,D
Occupational Therapy M
Pharmacology M,D
Physical Therapy D
Physician Assistant Studies M
Physiology M,D

UNIVERSITY OF SOUTHERN CALIFORNIA
Allopathic Medicine D
Biochemistry M,D
Biological and Biomedical Sciences—General M,D
Biophysics M,D
Cell Biology M,D
Clinical Research M,D,O
Computational Biology D
Dentistry D
Environmental and Occupational Health M
Environmental Biology M,D
Epidemiology M,D
Evolutionary Biology D
Genetics M,D
Health Promotion M
Health Services Management and Hospital Administration M,O
Health Services Research D
Immunology M,D
International Health M
Marine Biology M,D
Medical Imaging M,D
Microbiology M,D
Molecular Biology M,D
Molecular Pharmacology M,D
Neurobiology M,D
Neuroscience M,D
Occupational Therapy M,D
Oral and Dental Sciences M,D,O
Pathobiology M,D
Pathology M,D
Pharmaceutical Sciences M,D,O
Pharmacy D
Physical Therapy M,D
Physician Assistant Studies M
Physiology M,D
Public Health—General D
Systems Biology D
Toxicology M,D

UNIVERSITY OF SOUTHERN INDIANA
Health Services Management and Hospital Administration M
Nursing—General M,D
Occupational Therapy M

UNIVERSITY OF SOUTHERN MAINE
Adult Nursing M,D,O
Biological and Biomedical Sciences—General M
Family Nurse Practitioner Studies M,D,O
Health Services Management and Hospital Administration M,O
Immunology M
Medical/Surgical Nursing M,D,O
Molecular Biology M
Nursing and Healthcare Administration M,D,O
Nursing Education M,D,O
Nursing—General M,D,O
Occupational Therapy M
Psychiatric Nursing M,D,O

UNIVERSITY OF SOUTHERN MISSISSIPPI
Biochemistry M,D
Biological and Biomedical Sciences—General M,D
Clinical Laboratory Sciences/Medical Technology M
Communication Disorders M,D
Environmental and Occupational Health M
Environmental Biology M,D
Epidemiology M
Family Nurse Practitioner Studies M,D
Health Services Management and Hospital Administration M
Marine Biology M,D
Maternal and Child/Neonatal Nursing M,D
Microbiology M,D
Molecular Biology M,D
Nursing and Healthcare Administration M,D
Nursing—General M,D
Nutrition M,D
Psychiatric Nursing M,D
Public Health—General M

UNIVERSITY OF SOUTH FLORIDA
Allopathic Medicine M,D
Biochemistry M,D
Bioethics M,D
Biological and Biomedical Sciences—General M,D
Cancer Biology/Oncology D
Cell Biology M,D
Communication Disorders M,D
Community Health M,D
Computational Biology M,D
Conservation Biology M,D
Environmental and Occupational Health M,D
Epidemiology M,D
Health Services Management and Hospital Administration M,D
International Health M,D
Marine Biology M,D
Molecular Biology M,D
Neuroscience D
Nursing—General M,D
Physical Therapy M,D
Public Health—General M,D

THE UNIVERSITY OF TAMPA
Adult Nursing M
Family Nurse Practitioner Studies M
Nursing—General M

THE UNIVERSITY OF TENNESSEE
Anatomy M,D
Animal Behavior M,D
Biochemistry M,D
Bioethics M,D
Biological and Biomedical Sciences—General M,D
Communication Disorders M,D,O
Community Health M,D
Ecology M,D
Entomology M,D
Evolutionary Biology M,D
Genetics M,D
Genomic Sciences M,D
Health Promotion M
Health Services Management and Hospital Administration M
Microbiology M,D
Nursing—General M,D
Nutrition M
Physiology M,D
Plant Pathology M,D
Plant Physiology M,D
Public Health—General M
Veterinary Medicine D

THE UNIVERSITY OF TENNESSEE AT CHATTANOOGA
Family Nurse Practitioner Studies M,D,O
Nurse Anesthesia M,D,O
Nursing and Healthcare Administration M,D,O
Nursing Education M,D,O
Nursing—General M,D,O
Physical Therapy D

THE UNIVERSITY OF TENNESSEE AT MARTIN
Nutrition M

THE UNIVERSITY OF TENNESSEE HEALTH SCIENCE CENTER
Allied Health—General M,D
Allopathic Medicine M,D
Dentistry M,D,O
Nursing—General M,D
Oral and Dental Sciences M,D,O
Pharmacy M,D
Physical Therapy M,D

THE UNIVERSITY OF TENNESSEE–OAK RIDGE NATIONAL LABORATORY
Biological and Biomedical Sciences—General M,D
Genomic Sciences M,D

THE UNIVERSITY OF TEXAS AT ARLINGTON
Biological and Biomedical Sciences—General M,D
Family Nurse Practitioner Studies M,D
Health Services Management and Hospital Administration M
Nursing and Healthcare Administration M,D
Nursing Education M,D
Nursing—General M,D

THE UNIVERSITY OF TEXAS AT AUSTIN
Adult Nursing M,D
Animal Behavior D
Biochemistry D
Biological and Biomedical Sciences—General M,D
Biopsychology D
Cell Biology D
Clinical Laboratory Sciences/Medical Technology M,D
Communication Disorders M,D
Community Health Nursing M,D
Ecology D
Evolutionary Biology D
Family Nurse Practitioner Studies M,D
Gerontological Nursing M,D
Maternal and Child/Neonatal Nursing M,D
Medicinal and Pharmaceutical Chemistry M,D
Microbiology D
Molecular Biology D
Neurobiology D
Neuroscience D
Nursing and Healthcare Administration M,D
Nursing Education M,D
Nursing—General M,D
Nutrition M,D
Pediatric Nursing M,D
Pharmaceutical Sciences M,D
Pharmacology M,D
Pharmacy D
Plant Biology M,D
Psychiatric Nursing M,D
Toxicology M,D

THE UNIVERSITY OF TEXAS AT BROWNSVILLE
Biological and Biomedical Sciences—General M
Community Health Nursing M

THE UNIVERSITY OF TEXAS AT DALLAS
Biological and Biomedical Sciences—General M,D
Cell Biology M,D
Communication Disorders M,D
Computational Biology M,D
Health Services Management and Hospital Administration M
Molecular Biology M,D
Neuroscience M,D

THE UNIVERSITY OF TEXAS AT EL PASO
Allied Health—General D
Biological and Biomedical Sciences—General M,D
Communication Disorders M
Family Nurse Practitioner Studies M,D,O
Health Services Management and Hospital Administration M,D,O
Nursing and Healthcare Administration M,D,O
Nursing—General M,D,O
Occupational Therapy M
Physical Therapy M

THE UNIVERSITY OF TEXAS AT SAN ANTONIO
Biological and Biomedical Sciences—General M,D
Cell Biology M,D
Molecular Biology M,D
Neurobiology M,D

THE UNIVERSITY OF TEXAS AT TYLER
Biological and Biomedical Sciences—General M
Environmental and Occupational Health M
Family Nurse Practitioner Studies M,D
Health Services Management and Hospital Administration M
Nursing and Healthcare Administration M,D
Nursing Education M,D
Nursing—General M,D

THE UNIVERSITY OF TEXAS HEALTH SCIENCE CENTER AT HOUSTON
Allopathic Medicine D
Biochemistry M,D
Biological and Biomedical Sciences—General M,D
Cancer Biology/Oncology M,D
Cell Biology M,D
Dentistry M,D
Developmental Biology M,D
Genetics M,D
Human Genetics M,D
Immunology M,D
Medical Physics M,D
Microbiology M,D
Molecular Biology M,D
Molecular Genetics M,D
Molecular Pathology M,D
Neuroscience M,D
Nursing—General M,D
Public Health—General M,D,O
Virology M,D

THE UNIVERSITY OF TEXAS HEALTH SCIENCE CENTER AT SAN ANTONIO
Allopathic Medicine M,D
Biochemistry M,D
Biological and Biomedical Sciences—General M,D
Cell Biology M,D
Clinical Laboratory Sciences/Medical Technology M
Clinical Research M
Communication Disorders M
Dental Hygiene M
Dentistry M,D,O
Immunology D
Medical Physics M,D
Microbiology D
Molecular Medicine M,D
Neuroscience D
Nursing—General M,D
Occupational Therapy M
Pharmacology D
Physical Therapy M
Physician Assistant Studies M
Physiology M,D
Structural Biology M,D

THE UNIVERSITY OF TEXAS MEDICAL BRANCH
Allied Health—General M,D
Allopathic Medicine D
Bacteriology D
Biochemistry D
Biological and Biomedical Sciences—General M,D
Biophysics D
Cell Biology D
Clinical Laboratory Sciences/Medical Technology M,D
Community Health M,D
Computational Biology D
Genetics D
Immunology M,D
Infectious Diseases D
Microbiology M,D
Molecular Biophysics M,D
Neuroscience D
Nursing—General M,D
Occupational Therapy M
Pathology D
Pharmacology M,D
Physical Therapy M,D
Physician Assistant Studies M
Physiology M,D
Public Health—General M
Structural Biology D
Toxicology M,D
Virology D

THE UNIVERSITY OF TEXAS OF THE PERMIAN BASIN
Biological and Biomedical Sciences—General M

THE UNIVERSITY OF TEXAS–PAN AMERICAN
Adult Nursing M
Biological and Biomedical Sciences—General M
Communication Disorders M
Family Nurse Practitioner Studies M
Nursing—General M
Occupational Therapy M

THE UNIVERSITY OF TEXAS SOUTHWESTERN MEDICAL CENTER
Allopathic Medicine D
Biochemistry D
Biological and Biomedical Sciences—General M,D
Cancer Biology/Oncology D
Cell Biology D
Developmental Biology D
Genetics D
Immunology D
Microbiology D
Molecular Biophysics D
Neuroscience D
Nutrition M
Physical Therapy D
Physician Assistant Studies M

UNIVERSITY OF THE CUMBERLANDS
Physician Assistant Studies M

UNIVERSITY OF THE DISTRICT OF COLUMBIA
Cancer Biology/Oncology M
Communication Disorders M
Nutrition M

UNIVERSITY OF THE INCARNATE WORD
Biological and Biomedical Sciences—General M
Health Promotion M
Health Services Management and Hospital Administration M,O
Nursing—General M,D
Nutrition M,O
Optometry D
Pharmacy D

UNIVERSITY OF THE PACIFIC
Biological and Biomedical Sciences—General M
Communication Disorders M
Dentistry M,D,O
Pharmaceutical Sciences M,D
Pharmacy D
Physical Therapy M,D

UNIVERSITY OF THE SACRED HEART
Environmental and Occupational Health M
Occupational Health Nursing M

*M—master's degree; P—first professional degree; D—doctorate; O—other advanced degree; *Close-Up and/or Display*

UNIVERSITY OF THE SCIENCES IN PHILADELPHIA
- Biochemistry — M,D
- Cell Biology — M,D
- Health Services Management and Hospital Administration — M,D
- Medicinal and Pharmaceutical Chemistry — M,D
- Molecular Biology — D
- Pharmaceutical Administration — M
- Pharmaceutical Sciences — M,D
- Pharmacology — M,D
- Pharmacy — M,D
- Public Health—General — M,D
- Toxicology — M,D

THE UNIVERSITY OF TOLEDO
- Adult Nursing — M,O
- Biochemistry — M,D
- Biological and Biomedical Sciences—General — M,D,O
- Cancer Biology/Oncology — M,D
- Cardiovascular Sciences — M,D
- Cell Biology — M,D
- Communication Disorders — M,D
- Community Health Nursing — M,D
- Ecology — M,D
- Environmental and Occupational Health — M,O
- Epidemiology — M,O
- Family Nurse Practitioner Studies — M,O
- Genomic Sciences — M,O
- Health Promotion — M,D,O
- Health Services Management and Hospital Administration — M,O
- Immunology — M,D
- International Health — M,O
- Medical Physics — M,D
- Medicinal and Pharmaceutical Chemistry — M,D
- Molecular Biology — M,D
- Neuroscience — M,D
- Nursing and Healthcare Administration — M,O
- Nursing Education — M,O
- Nursing—General — M,D,O
- Nutrition — M,O
- Occupational Therapy — M,D
- Oral and Dental Sciences — M
- Pathology — O
- Pediatric Nursing — M,O
- Pharmaceutical Administration — M
- Pharmaceutical Sciences — M
- Pharmacology — M
- Physical Therapy — M,D
- Physician Assistant Studies — M
- Psychiatric Nursing — M,O
- Public Health—General — M,O

UNIVERSITY OF TORONTO
- Allopathic Medicine — M,D
- Biochemistry — M,D
- Bioethics — M,D
- Biophysics — M,D
- Cell Biology — M,D
- Communication Disorders — M,D
- Dentistry — D
- Ecology — M,D
- Epidemiology — M,D
- Evolutionary Biology — M,D
- Health Physics/Radiological Health — M,D
- Health Promotion — M,D
- Health Services Management and Hospital Administration — M,D
- Immunology — M,D
- Molecular Genetics — M,D
- Nursing—General — M,D
- Nutrition — M,D
- Occupational Therapy — M
- Oral and Dental Sciences — M,D
- Pathobiology — M,D
- Pharmaceutical Sciences — M,D
- Pharmacology — M,D
- Physical Therapy — M
- Physiology — M,D
- Public Health—General — M,D
- Rehabilitation Sciences — M,D
- Systems Biology — M,D

UNIVERSITY OF TULSA
- Biochemistry — M
- Biological and Biomedical Sciences—General — M,D
- Communication Disorders — M

UNIVERSITY OF UTAH
- Allopathic Medicine — D
- Anatomy — D
- Biochemistry — M,D
- Biological and Biomedical Sciences—General — M,D,O
- Cancer Biology/Oncology — M,D
- Clinical Laboratory Sciences/Medical Technology — M
- Communication Disorders — M,D
- Gerontological Nursing — M,O
- Health Promotion — M,D
- Health Services Management and Hospital Administration — M
- Human Genetics — M,D
- Medical Physics — M,D
- Medicinal and Pharmaceutical Chemistry — M,D
- Molecular Biology — D
- Neurobiology — D
- Neuroscience — D
- Nursing—General — M,D
- Nutrition — M
- Occupational Therapy — M,D
- Pathology — M,D
- Pharmaceutical Sciences — M,D
- Pharmacology — D
- Pharmacy — D
- Physical Therapy — D
- Physician Assistant Studies — M
- Physiology — D

UNIVERSITY OF VERMONT
- Allied Health—General — M,D
- Allopathic Medicine — D
- Biochemistry — M,D
- Biological and Biomedical Sciences—General — M,D
- Biophysics — M,D
- Cell Biology — M,D
- Clinical Laboratory Sciences/Medical Technology — M,D
- Microbiology — M,D
- Molecular Biology — M,D
- Molecular Genetics — M,D
- Molecular Physiology — M,D
- Neuroscience — D
- Nursing—General — M
- Nutrition — M,D
- Pathology — M
- Pharmacology — M,D
- Physical Therapy — D
- Plant Biology — M,D

UNIVERSITY OF VICTORIA
- Biochemistry — M,D
- Biological and Biomedical Sciences—General — M,D
- Family Nurse Practitioner Studies — M,D
- Medical Physics — M,D
- Microbiology — M,D
- Nursing and Healthcare Administration — M,D
- Nursing Education — M,D
- Nursing—General — M,D

UNIVERSITY OF VIRGINIA
- Acute Care/Critical Care Nursing — M,D
- Allopathic Medicine — M,D
- Biochemistry — D
- Bioethics — M
- Biological and Biomedical Sciences—General — M,D
- Biophysics — M,D
- Cell Biology — D
- Clinical Research — M
- Communication Disorders — M
- Community Health — M,D
- Health Services Management and Hospital Administration — M
- Health Services Research — M
- Microbiology — D
- Molecular Genetics — D
- Molecular Physiology — M,D
- Neuroscience — D
- Nursing and Healthcare Administration — M,D
- Nursing—General — M,D
- Pathology — D
- Pharmacology — D
- Physiology — D
- Psychiatric Nursing — M,D
- Public Health—General — M,D

UNIVERSITY OF WASHINGTON
- Allopathic Medicine — D
- Animal Behavior — D
- Bacteriology — D
- Biochemistry — D
- Bioethics — M
- Biological and Biomedical Sciences—General — M,D
- Biophysics — D
- Cell Biology — D*
- Clinical Laboratory Sciences/Medical Technology — M
- Clinical Research — M,D
- Communication Disorders — M,D
- Community Health — M,D
- Dentistry — D
- Ecology — M,D
- Environmental and Occupational Health — M,D
- Epidemiology — M,D
- Genetics — M,D
- Genomic Sciences — M,D
- Health Services Management and Hospital Administration — M
- Health Services Research — M,D
- Immunology — D
- International Health — M,D
- Maternal and Child Health — M,D
- Medicinal and Pharmaceutical Chemistry — D
- Microbiology — D
- Molecular Biology — D
- Molecular Medicine — D
- Neurobiology — D
- Nursing—General — M,D,O
- Nutrition — M,D
- Occupational Therapy — M,D
- Oral and Dental Sciences — M,D,O
- Parasitology — D
- Pathobiology — D
- Pathology — D
- Pharmaceutical Sciences — M,D
- Pharmacology — D
- Pharmacy — M,D
- Physical Therapy — M,D
- Physiology — D
- Rehabilitation Sciences — M,D
- Structural Biology — D
- Toxicology — M,D
- Veterinary Sciences

UNIVERSITY OF WASHINGTON, BOTHELL
- Nursing—General — M

UNIVERSITY OF WASHINGTON, TACOMA
- Community Health Nursing — M
- Nursing and Healthcare Administration — M
- Nursing Education — M
- Nursing—General — M

UNIVERSITY OF WATERLOO
- Biochemistry — M,D
- Biological and Biomedical Sciences—General — M,D
- Optometry — M,D
- Public Health—General — M
- Vision Sciences — M,D

THE UNIVERSITY OF WESTERN ONTARIO
- Allopathic Medicine — M,D
- Anatomy — M,D
- Biochemistry — M,D
- Biophysics — M,D
- Cell Biology — M,D
- Communication Disorders — M
- Dentistry — D
- Epidemiology — M,D
- Health Services Management and Hospital Administration — M,D
- Immunology — M,D
- Microbiology — M,D
- Molecular Biology — M,D
- Neuroscience — M,D
- Nursing—General — M,D
- Occupational Therapy — M
- Oral and Dental Sciences — M
- Pathology — M,D
- Physical Therapy — M,O
- Physiology — M,D
- Plant Biology — M,D
- Zoology — M,D

UNIVERSITY OF WESTERN STATES
- Chiropractic — D

UNIVERSITY OF WEST FLORIDA
- Biochemistry — M
- Biological and Biomedical Sciences—General — M
- Community Health — M
- Environmental and Occupational Health — M
- Environmental Biology — M
- Nursing and Healthcare Administration — M,O
- Nursing—General — M
- Pharmaceutical Administration — M,O
- Public Health—General — M

UNIVERSITY OF WEST GEORGIA
- Biological and Biomedical Sciences—General — M
- Communication Disorders — M,D,O
- Health Services Management and Hospital Administration — M,O
- Nursing Education — M,O
- Nursing—General — M,O

UNIVERSITY OF WINDSOR
- Biochemistry — M,D
- Biological and Biomedical Sciences—General — M,D
- Biopsychology — M,D
- Nursing—General — M

UNIVERSITY OF WISCONSIN–EAU CLAIRE
- Adult Nursing — M,D
- Communication Disorders — M
- Family Nurse Practitioner Studies — M,D
- Gerontological Nursing — M,D
- Nursing and Healthcare Administration — M,D
- Nursing Education — M,D
- Nursing—General — M,D

UNIVERSITY OF WISCONSIN–LA CROSSE
- Biological and Biomedical Sciences—General — M
- Cancer Biology/Oncology — M
- Cell Biology — M
- Community Health — M
- Medical Microbiology — M
- Microbiology — M
- Molecular Biology — M
- Nurse Anesthesia — M
- Occupational Therapy — M
- Physical Therapy — M,D
- Physician Assistant Studies — M
- Physiology — M
- Public Health—General — M
- Rehabilitation Sciences — M

UNIVERSITY OF WISCONSIN–MADISON
- Adult Nursing — D
- Allopathic Medicine — D
- Bacteriology — M
- Biochemistry — M,D
- Biological and Biomedical Sciences—General — M,D
- Biophysics — D
- Biopsychology — D
- Botany — M,D
- Cancer Biology/Oncology — D
- Cell Biology — D
- Clinical Research — M,D
- Communication Disorders — M,D
- Community Health — M,D
- Conservation Biology — M
- Ecology — M
- Entomology — M,D
- Environmental Biology — M,D
- Epidemiology — M,D
- Genetics — M,D
- Gerontological Nursing — D
- Health Services Research — D
- Medical Microbiology — M,D
- Medical Physics — M,D
- Microbiology — D
- Molecular Biology — D
- Neurobiology — M,D
- Neuroscience — D
- Nursing—General — M,D
- Nutrition — M,D
- Occupational Therapy — M
- Pathology — D*

UNIVERSITY OF WISCONSIN–MILWAUKEE (Pediatric Nursing etc.)
- Pediatric Nursing — D
- Pharmaceutical Administration — M,D
- Pharmaceutical Sciences — M,D
- Pharmacology — D
- Pharmacy — D
- Physiology — M,D
- Plant Pathology — M,D
- Psychiatric Nursing — D
- Rehabilitation Sciences — M
- Toxicology — M,D
- Veterinary Medicine — M,D
- Veterinary Sciences — M,D
- Zoology — M,D

UNIVERSITY OF WISCONSIN–MILWAUKEE
- Allied Health—General — M,D,O
- Biochemistry — M,D
- Biological and Biomedical Sciences—General — M,D
- Communication Disorders — M,O
- Environmental and Occupational Health — D
- Family Nurse Practitioner Studies — M,D,O
- Health Promotion — M,D,O
- Nursing—General — M,D,O
- Occupational Therapy — M,O
- Physical Therapy — D
- Public Health—General — M,D,O

UNIVERSITY OF WISCONSIN–OSHKOSH
- Adult Nursing — M
- Biological and Biomedical Sciences—General — M
- Botany — M
- Family Nurse Practitioner Studies — M
- Health Services Management and Hospital Administration — M
- Microbiology — M
- Nursing—General — M
- Zoology — M

UNIVERSITY OF WISCONSIN–PARKSIDE
- Molecular Biology — M

UNIVERSITY OF WISCONSIN–RIVER FALLS
- Communication Disorders — M

UNIVERSITY OF WISCONSIN–STEVENS POINT
- Communication Disorders — M,D
- Health Promotion — M
- Nutrition — M

UNIVERSITY OF WISCONSIN–STOUT
- Industrial Hygiene — M
- Nutrition — M

UNIVERSITY OF WISCONSIN–WHITEWATER
- Communication Disorders — M
- Environmental and Occupational Health — M

UNIVERSITY OF WYOMING
- Botany — M,D
- Cell Biology — D
- Communication Disorders — M
- Community Health — M,D
- Computational Biology — D
- Ecology — M,D
- Entomology — M,D
- Genetics — D
- Health Promotion — M
- Microbiology — D
- Molecular Biology — M,D
- Nursing—General — M
- Nutrition — M
- Pathobiology — M
- Pharmacy — D
- Physiology — M,D
- Reproductive Biology — M,D
- Zoology — M,D

URBANA UNIVERSITY
- Nursing—General — M

URSULINE COLLEGE
- Medical/Surgical Nursing — M,D
- Nursing and Healthcare Administration — M,D
- Nursing Education — M,D
- Nursing—General — M,D

UTAH STATE UNIVERSITY
- Biochemistry — M,D
- Biological and Biomedical Sciences—General — M,D
- Communication Disorders — M,D,O
- Ecology — M,D
- Nutrition — M,D
- Toxicology — M,D
- Veterinary Sciences — M,D

UTAH VALLEY UNIVERSITY
- Nursing—General — M

UTICA COLLEGE
- Health Services Management and Hospital Administration — M
- Occupational Therapy — M
- Physical Therapy — D

VALPARAISO UNIVERSITY
- Nursing Education — M,O
- Nursing—General — M,O

VANDERBILT UNIVERSITY
- Acute Care/Critical Care Nursing — M,D
- Adult Nursing — M,D
- Allopathic Medicine — M,D
- Biochemistry — M,D
- Biological and Biomedical Sciences—General — M,D
- Biophysics — M,D
- Cancer Biology/Oncology — M,D
- Cell Biology — M,D
- Clinical Research — M,D
- Communication Disorders — M,D

Family Nurse Practitioner Studies — M,D
Gerontological Nursing — M,D
Human Genetics — D
Immunology — M,D
Maternal and Child/Neonatal Nursing — M,D
Medical Physics — M
Microbiology — M,D
Molecular Biology — M,D
Molecular Physiology — M,D
Nurse Midwifery — M,D
Nursing and Healthcare Administration — M,D
Nursing Informatics — M,D
Nursing—General — M,D
Pathology — D
Pediatric Nursing — M,D
Pharmacology — D
Psychiatric Nursing — M,D
Public Health—General — M
Women's Health Nursing — M,D

VILLANOVA UNIVERSITY
Adult Nursing — M,D,O
Biological and Biomedical
 Sciences—General — M
Family Nurse Practitioner Studies — M,D,O
Health Services Management and
 Hospital Administration — M,D,O
Nurse Anesthesia — M,D,O
Nursing and Healthcare Administration — M,D,O
Nursing Education — M,D,O
Nursing—General — M,D,O
Pediatric Nursing — M,D,O

VIRGINIA COLLEGE AT BIRMINGHAM
Health Services Management and
 Hospital Administration — M

VIRGINIA COMMONWEALTH UNIVERSITY
Adult Nursing — M,D,O
Allied Health—General — D
Allopathic Medicine — D,O
Anatomy — D,O
Biochemistry — M,D,O
Biological and Biomedical
 Sciences—General — M,D,O
Biopsychology — D
Clinical Laboratory Sciences/Medical
 Technology — M,D
Community Health — M,D
Dentistry — M,D
Epidemiology — M,D
Family Nurse Practitioner Studies — M,O
Genetics — M,D
Health Physics/Radiological Health — D
Health Services Management and
 Hospital Administration — M,D
Health Services Research — D
Human Genetics — M,D,O
Immunology — M,D
Medical Physics — M,D
Medicinal and Pharmaceutical
 Chemistry — M,D
Microbiology — M,D,O
Molecular Biology — M,D
Neurobiology — D
Neuroscience — M,D,O
Nurse Anesthesia — M,D
Nursing and Healthcare Administration — M,D,O
Nursing Education — M,D,O
Nursing—General — M,D,O
Occupational Therapy — M,D
Pathology — D
Pediatric Nursing — M,D,O
Pharmaceutical Administration — M,D
Pharmaceutical Sciences — M,D
Pharmacology — M,D,O
Pharmacy — D
Physical Therapy — M,D
Physiology — M,D,O
Psychiatric Nursing — M,D,O
Public Health—General — M,D
Rehabilitation Sciences — D
Systems Biology — D
Toxicology — M,D,O
Women's Health Nursing — M,D,O

VIRGINIA INTERNATIONAL UNIVERSITY
Health Services Management and
 Hospital Administration — M,O

VIRGINIA POLYTECHNIC INSTITUTE AND STATE UNIVERSITY
Biochemistry — M,D
Biological and Biomedical
 Sciences—General — M,D
Community Health — M,D
Computational Biology — D
Entomology — M,D
Genetics — D
Gerontological Nursing — M,D,O
Microbiology — D
Molecular Biology — M,D
Nutrition — M,D
Physiology — M,D
Plant Pathology — M,D
Plant Physiology — M,D
Public Health—General — M
Veterinary Medicine — D
Veterinary Sciences — M,D,O

VIRGINIA STATE UNIVERSITY
Biological and Biomedical
 Sciences—General — M
Community Health — M,D

VITERBO UNIVERSITY
Nursing—General — M

WAGNER COLLEGE
Biological and Biomedical
 Sciences—General — M
Family Nurse Practitioner Studies — O

Health Services Management and
 Hospital Administration — M
Microbiology — M
Nursing—General — M
Physician Assistant Studies — M

WAKE FOREST UNIVERSITY
Allopathic Medicine — D
Anatomy — D
Biochemistry — D
Biological and Biomedical
 Sciences—General — M,D
Cancer Biology/Oncology — D
Genomic Sciences — D
Health Services Management and
 Hospital Administration — M
Health Services Research — M
Human Genetics — D
Immunology — D
Microbiology — D
Molecular Biology — D
Molecular Genetics — D
Molecular Medicine — M,D
Neurobiology — D
Neuroscience — D
Pathobiology — M,D
Pharmacology — D
Physiology — D

WALDEN UNIVERSITY
Clinical Research — M,D,O
Community Health — M,D,O
Epidemiology — M,D,O
Health Promotion — M,D,O
Health Services Management and
 Hospital Administration — M,D,O
Nursing and Healthcare Administration — M,D,O
Nursing Education — M,D,O
Nursing Informatics — M,D,O
Nursing—General — M,D,O
Public Health—General — M,D,O

WALLA WALLA UNIVERSITY
Biological and Biomedical
 Sciences—General — M

WALSH UNIVERSITY
Health Services Management and
 Hospital Administration — M,O
Nursing and Healthcare Administration — M,D
Nursing—General — M,D
Physical Therapy — D

WASHBURN UNIVERSITY
Adult Nursing — M
Family Nurse Practitioner Studies — M
Nursing and Healthcare Administration — M
Nursing—General — M

WASHINGTON ADVENTIST UNIVERSITY
Health Services Management and
 Hospital Administration — M
Nursing and Healthcare Administration — M
Nursing Education — M
Nursing—General — M

WASHINGTON STATE UNIVERSITY
Biochemistry — M,D
Biological and Biomedical
 Sciences—General — M
Biophysics — M,D
Botany — M,D
Cell Biology — M,D
Entomology — M,D
Genetics — M,D
Health Services Management and
 Hospital Administration — M
Microbiology — M,D
Molecular Biology — M,D
Neuroscience — M,D
Nutrition — M,D
Pharmacy — D
Plant Molecular Biology — M,D
Plant Pathology — M,D
Veterinary Medicine — D
Veterinary Sciences — M,D
Zoology — M,D

WASHINGTON STATE UNIVERSITY SPOKANE
Communication Disorders — M
Health Services Management and
 Hospital Administration — M
Nursing—General — M
Pharmacy — D

WASHINGTON STATE UNIVERSITY TRI-CITIES
Nursing—General — M,D

WASHINGTON STATE UNIVERSITY VANCOUVER
Nursing—General — M

WASHINGTON UNIVERSITY IN ST. LOUIS
Allied Health—General — M,D
Allopathic Medicine — D
Biochemistry — D
Biological and Biomedical
 Sciences—General — D
Cell Biology — D
Clinical Research — M
Communication Disorders — M,D
Computational Biology — D
Developmental Biology — D
Ecology — D
Environmental Biology — D
Evolutionary Biology — D
Genetics — M,D
Genomic Sciences — M
Human Genetics — D
Immunology — D
Microbiology — D

Molecular Biology — D
Molecular Biophysics — D
Molecular Genetics — D
Molecular Pathogenesis — D
Neuroscience — D
Occupational Therapy — M,D
Physical Therapy — D
Plant Biology — D
Public Health—General — M,D
Rehabilitation Sciences — D
Systems Biology — D
Translational Biology — M

WAYLAND BAPTIST UNIVERSITY
Health Services Management and
 Hospital Administration — M

WAYNESBURG UNIVERSITY
Health Services Management and
 Hospital Administration — M
Medical/Surgical Nursing — M,D
Nursing and Healthcare Administration — M,D
Nursing Education — M,D
Nursing Informatics — M,D
Nursing—General — M,D

WAYNE STATE UNIVERSITY
Acute Care/Critical Care Nursing — M
Adult Nursing — M
Allopathic Medicine — D,O
Anatomy — M,D
Biochemistry — M,D
Biological and Biomedical
 Sciences—General — M,D
Biopsychology — M,D
Cancer Biology/Oncology — M,D
Communication Disorders — M,D
Community Health Nursing — M
Environmental and Occupational
 Health — M,O
Genetics — M,D
Gerontological Nursing — M
Health Physics/Radiological Health — M,D
Health Services Management and
 Hospital Administration — M
Immunology — M,D
Maternal and Child/Neonatal Nursing — M
Medical Physics — M,D
Medicinal and Pharmaceutical
 Chemistry — M,D
Microbiology — M,D
Molecular Biology — M,D
Neuroscience — M,D
Nurse Anesthesia — M,O
Nurse Midwifery — M,D,O
Nursing Education — M,O
Nursing—General — D
Nutrition — M,D
Occupational Therapy — M
Pathology — D
Pediatric Nursing — M
Pharmaceutical Sciences — M,D
Pharmacology — M,D
Pharmacy — M,D
Physical Therapy — D
Physician Assistant Studies — M
Physiology — M,D
Psychiatric Nursing — M,O
Public Health—General — M,O
Toxicology — M,D
Women's Health Nursing — M,D,O

WEBER STATE UNIVERSITY
Health Services Management and
 Hospital Administration — M

WEBSTER UNIVERSITY
Health Services Management and
 Hospital Administration — M,D,O
Nurse Anesthesia — M
Nursing—General — M,O

WEILL CORNELL MEDICAL COLLEGE
Biochemistry — D
Biological and Biomedical
 Sciences—General — M,D
Biophysics — M,D
Cell Biology — M,D
Computational Biology — D
Epidemiology — M
Health Services Research — M
Immunology — M,D
Molecular Biology — M,D
Neuroscience — M,D
Pharmacology — M,D
Physician Assistant Studies — M
Physiology — M,D
Structural Biology — M,D
Systems Biology — M,D

WESLEYAN UNIVERSITY
Animal Behavior — D
Biochemistry — M,D
Biological and Biomedical
 Sciences—General — D
Cell Biology — D
Developmental Biology — D
Ecology — D
Evolutionary Biology — D
Genetics — D
Genomic Sciences — D
Molecular Biology — D
Neurobiology — D

WESLEY COLLEGE
Nursing—General — M

WEST CHESTER UNIVERSITY OF PENNSYLVANIA
Biological and Biomedical
 Sciences—General — M,O
Communication Disorders — M,O
Community Health Nursing — M,O

Health Services Management and
 Hospital Administration — M,O
Nursing and Healthcare Administration — M,O
Nursing Education — M,O
Nursing—General — M,O
Public Health—General — M,O
School Nursing — M,O

WESTERN CAROLINA UNIVERSITY
Biological and Biomedical
 Sciences—General — M
Communication Disorders — M
Health Services Management and
 Hospital Administration — M
Nursing Education — M,O
Nursing—General — M,O
Physical Therapy — M,D

WESTERN CONNECTICUT STATE UNIVERSITY
Adult Nursing — M
Biological and Biomedical
 Sciences—General — M
Health Services Management and
 Hospital Administration — M
Nursing—General — M

WESTERN ILLINOIS UNIVERSITY
Biological and Biomedical
 Sciences—General — M,O
Communication Disorders — M
Health Services Management and
 Hospital Administration — M,O
Marine Biology — M,O
Zoology — M,O

WESTERN KENTUCKY UNIVERSITY
Biological and Biomedical
 Sciences—General — M
Communication Disorders — M
Health Services Management and
 Hospital Administration — M
Nursing—General — M
Public Health—General — M

WESTERN MICHIGAN UNIVERSITY
Biological and Biomedical
 Sciences—General — M,D
Communication Disorders — M,D
Health Services Management and
 Hospital Administration — M,D,O
Nursing—General — M
Occupational Therapy — M
Physician Assistant Studies — M
Physiology — M
Rehabilitation Sciences — M

WESTERN NEW MEXICO UNIVERSITY
Occupational Therapy — M

WESTERN UNIVERSITY OF HEALTH SCIENCES
Allied Health—General — M,D
Biological and Biomedical
 Sciences—General — M
Dentistry — D
Family Nurse Practitioner Studies — D
Nursing and Healthcare Administration — M
Nursing—General — M,D
Optometry — D
Osteopathic Medicine — D
Pharmaceutical Sciences — M
Pharmacy — D
Physical Therapy — M
Physician Assistant Studies — M
Veterinary Medicine — D

WESTERN WASHINGTON UNIVERSITY
Biological and Biomedical
 Sciences—General — M
Communication Disorders — M

WESTMINSTER COLLEGE (UT)
Family Nurse Practitioner Studies — M
Nurse Anesthesia — M
Nursing Education — M
Nursing—General — M
Public Health—General — M

WEST TEXAS A&M UNIVERSITY
Biological and Biomedical
 Sciences—General — M
Communication Disorders — M
Family Nurse Practitioner Studies — M
Nursing—General — M

WEST VIRGINIA SCHOOL OF OSTEOPATHIC MEDICINE
Osteopathic Medicine — D

WEST VIRGINIA UNIVERSITY
Allopathic Medicine — D
Biochemistry — M,D
Biological and Biomedical
 Sciences—General — M,D
Cancer Biology/Oncology — M,D
Cell Biology — M,D
Communication Disorders — M,D
Community Health — M
Dentistry — D
Developmental Biology — M,D
Entomology — M,D
Environmental and Occupational
 Health — D
Environmental Biology — M,D
Evolutionary Biology — M,D
Genetics — M,D
Genomic Sciences — M,D
Health Promotion — M,D
Human Genetics — M,D
Immunology — M,D
Industrial Hygiene — M
Medicinal and Pharmaceutical
 Chemistry — M,D
Microbiology — M,D

M—master's degree; P—first professional degree; D—doctorate; O—other advanced degree; *Close-Up and/or Display

Molecular Biology — M,D
Neurobiology — M,D
Neuroscience — D.
Nursing—General — M,D,O
Nutrition — M
Occupational Therapy — M
Oral and Dental Sciences — M
Pharmaceutical Administration — M,D
Pharmaceutical Sciences — M,D
Pharmacology — M,D
Pharmacy — M,D
Physical Therapy — D
Physiology — M,D
Plant Pathology — M,D
Public Health—General — M
Reproductive Biology — M,D
Teratology — M,D
Toxicology — M,D

WEST VIRGINIA WESLEYAN COLLEGE
Nursing—General — M

WHEELING JESUIT UNIVERSITY
Nursing—General — M
Physical Therapy — D

WICHITA STATE UNIVERSITY
Allied Health—General — M,D
Biological and Biomedical
   Sciences—General — M
Communication Disorders — M,D
Nursing—General — M,D
Physical Therapy — D
Physician Assistant Studies — M

WIDENER UNIVERSITY
Health Services Management and
   Hospital Administration — M
Nursing—General — M,D,O
Physical Therapy — M,D

WILFRID LAURIER UNIVERSITY
Biological and Biomedical
   Sciences—General — M
Health Promotion — M
Neuroscience — M,D

WILKES UNIVERSITY
Health Services Management and
   Hospital Administration — M
Nursing—General — M,D
Pharmacy — D

WILLIAM CAREY UNIVERSITY
Nursing—General — M

WILLIAM PATERSON UNIVERSITY OF NEW JERSEY
Biological and Biomedical
   Sciences—General — M
Communication Disorders — M
Nursing—General — M

WILLIAM WOODS UNIVERSITY
Health Services Management and
   Hospital Administration — M,O

WILMINGTON UNIVERSITY
Adult Nursing — M,D
Family Nurse Practitioner Studies — M,D
Gerontological Nursing — M,D
Health Services Management and
   Hospital Administration — M,D
Nursing and Healthcare Administration — M,D
Nursing—General — M,D

WINGATE UNIVERSITY
Pharmacy — D

WINONA STATE UNIVERSITY
Adult Nursing — M,D,O
Family Nurse Practitioner Studies — M,D,O
Nursing and Healthcare Administration — M,D,O
Nursing Education — M,D,O
Nursing—General — M,D,O

WINSTON-SALEM STATE UNIVERSITY
Nursing—General — M
Occupational Therapy — M
Physical Therapy — M

WINTHROP UNIVERSITY
Biological and Biomedical
   Sciences—General — M
Nutrition — M

WON INSTITUTE OF GRADUATE STUDIES
Acupuncture and Oriental Medicine — M

WOODS HOLE OCEANOGRAPHIC INSTITUTION
Marine Biology — D

WORCESTER POLYTECHNIC INSTITUTE
Biochemistry — M,D
Biological and Biomedical
   Sciences—General — M,D

WORCESTER STATE UNIVERSITY
Communication Disorders — M
Community Health Nursing — M
Health Services Management and
   Hospital Administration — M
Nursing Education — M
Occupational Therapy — M

WORLD MEDICINE INSTITUTE OF ACUPUNCTURE AND HERBAL MEDICINE
Acupuncture and Oriental Medicine — M

WRIGHT STATE UNIVERSITY
Acute Care/Critical Care Nursing — M
Adult Nursing — M
Allopathic Medicine — D
Anatomy — M
Biochemistry — M
Biological and Biomedical
   Sciences—General — M,D
Biophysics — M
Community Health Nursing — M
Family Nurse Practitioner Studies — M
Health Promotion — M
Health Services Management and
   Hospital Administration — M
Immunology — M
Medical Physics — M
Microbiology — M
Molecular Biology — M
Nursing and Healthcare Administration — M
Nursing—General — M
Pediatric Nursing — M
Pharmacology — M
Physiology — M
Public Health—General — M
School Nursing — M
Toxicology — M

XAVIER UNIVERSITY
Health Services Management and
   Hospital Administration — M
Nursing and Healthcare Administration — M
Nursing Education — M
Nursing Informatics — M
Nursing—General — M
Occupational Therapy — M

XAVIER UNIVERSITY OF LOUISIANA
Pharmacy — D

YALE UNIVERSITY
Allopathic Medicine — D
Biochemistry — D
Biological and Biomedical
   Sciences—General — D
Biophysics — D
Cancer Biology/Oncology — D
Cell Biology — D
Computational Biology — D
Developmental Biology — D
Ecology — D
Environmental and Occupational
   Health — M,D

Epidemiology — M,D
Evolutionary Biology — D
Genetics — D
Genomic Sciences — D
Health Services Management and
   Hospital Administration — M,D
Immunology — D
Infectious Diseases — D
International Health — M,D
Microbiology — D
Molecular Biology — D
Molecular Biophysics — D
Molecular Medicine — D
Molecular Pathology — D
Molecular Physiology — D
Neurobiology — D
Neuroscience — D
Nursing—General — M,D,O
Pathobiology — D
Pathology — M,D
Pharmacology — D
Physician Assistant Studies — M
Physiology — D
Plant Biology — D
Public Health—General — M,D
Virology — D

YORK COLLEGE OF PENNSYLVANIA
Adult Nursing — M,D
Nurse Anesthesia — M,D
Nursing and Healthcare Administration — M,D
Nursing Education — M,D
Nursing—General — M,D

YORK UNIVERSITY
Biological and Biomedical
   Sciences—General — M,D
Nursing—General — M

YO SAN UNIVERSITY OF TRADITIONAL CHINESE MEDICINE
Acupuncture and Oriental Medicine — M

YOUNGSTOWN STATE UNIVERSITY
Anatomy — M
Biochemistry — M
Biological and Biomedical
   Sciences—General — M
Environmental Biology — M
Health Services Management and
   Hospital Administration — M
Microbiology — M
Molecular Biology — M
Nursing—General — M
Physical Therapy — D
Physiology — M

ACADEMIC AND PROFESSIONAL PROGRAMS IN THE BIOLOGICAL AND BIOMEDICAL SCIENCES

Section 1
Biological and Biomedical Sciences

This section contains a directory of institutions offering graduate work in biological and biomedical sciences, followed by in-depth entries submitted by institutions that chose to prepare detailed program descriptions. Additional information about programs listed in the directory but not augmented by an in-depth entry may be obtained by writing directly to the dean of a graduate school or chair of a department at the address given in the directory.

Programs in fields related to the biological and biomedical sciences may be found throughout this book. In the other guides in this series:

Graduate Programs in the Humanities, Arts & Social Sciences

See *Psychology and Counseling* and *Sociology, Anthropology, and Archaeology*

Graduate Programs in the Physical Sciences, Mathematics, Agricultural Sciences, the Environment & Natural Resources

See *Chemistry, Marine Sciences and Oceanography,* and *Mathematical Sciences*

Graduate Programs in Engineering & Applied Sciences

See *Agricultural Engineering and Bioengineering, Biomedical Engineering and Biotechnology, Civil and Environmental Engineering, Management of Engineering and Technology,* and *Ocean Engineering*

CONTENTS

Biological and Biomedical Sciences—General

Acadia University, Faculty of Pure and Applied Science, Department of Biology, Wolfville, NS B4P 2R6, Canada. Offers M Sc. *Degree requirements:* For master's, comprehensive exam, thesis. *Entrance requirements:* For master's, minimum B-average in last 2 years of major. Additional exam requirements/recommendations for international students: Required—TOEFL (minimum score 580 paper-based; 237 computer-based; 93 iBT), IELTS (minimum score 6.5). *Faculty research:* Respiration physiology, estuaries and fisheries, limnology, plant biology, conservation biology.

Adelphi University, College of Arts and Sciences, Department of Biology, Garden City, NY 11530-0701. Offers MS. Part-time and evening/weekend programs available. *Students:* 24 full-time (12 women), 12 part-time (7 women); includes 10 minority (4 Black or African American, non-Hispanic/Latino; 5 Asian, non-Hispanic/Latino; 1 Native Hawaiian or other Pacific Islander, non-Hispanic/Latino), 11 international. Average age 25. In 2011, 19 master's awarded. *Degree requirements:* For master's, thesis or alternative. *Entrance requirements:* For master's, bachelor's degree in biology or allied sciences, essay, 3 letters of recommendation, official transcripts. Additional exam requirements/recommendations for international students: Required—TOEFL (minimum score 550 paper-based; 213 computer-based; 80 iBT). *Application deadline:* For fall admission, 5/1 for international students; for spring admission, 12/1 for international students. Applications are processed on a rolling basis. Application fee: $50. Electronic applications accepted. *Expenses: Tuition:* Full-time $29,600; part-time $930 per credit. *Required fees:* $1100. *Financial support:* Research assistantships with full and partial tuition reimbursements, teaching assistantships, career-related internships or fieldwork, Federal Work-Study, institutionally sponsored loans, and unspecified assistantships available. Financial award application deadline: 2/15; financial award applicants required to submit FAFSA. *Faculty research:* Plant-animal interactions, physiology (plant, cornea), reproductive behavior, topics in evolution, fish biology. *Unit head:* Dr. Alan Schoenfeld, Chair, 516-877-4211, E-mail: schoenfeld@adelphi.edu. *Application contact:* Christine Murphy, Director of Admissions, 516-877-3050, Fax: 516-877-3039, E-mail: graduateadmissions@adelphi.edu. Web site: http://academics.adelphi.edu/artsci/bio/index.php.

See Display below and Close-Up on page 101.

Alabama Agricultural and Mechanical University, School of Graduate Studies, School of Arts and Sciences, Department of Biology, Huntsville, AL 35811. Offers MS. Program offered jointly with The University of Alabama in Huntsville. Part-time and evening/weekend programs available. *Degree requirements:* For master's, comprehensive exam, thesis. *Entrance requirements:* For master's, GRE General Test. Additional exam requirements/recommendations for international students: Required—TOEFL (minimum score 500 paper-based; 173 computer-based; 61 iBT). Electronic applications accepted. *Faculty research:* Radiation and chemical mutagenesis, human cytogenetics, microbial biotechnology, microbial metabolism, environmental toxicology.

Alabama State University, Department of Biological Sciences, Montgomery, AL 36101-0271. Offers MS, PhD. Part-time programs available. *Faculty:* 9. *Students:* 3 full-time (2 women), 16 part-time (9 women); includes 13 minority (all Black or African American, non-Hispanic/Latino), 3 international. Average age 33. 26 applicants, 19% accepted, 2 enrolled. In 2011, 2 master's awarded. *Degree requirements:* For master's, one foreign language, comprehensive exam, thesis. *Entrance requirements:* For master's, GRE General Test, GRE Subject Test, graduate writing competency test. Additional exam requirements/recommendations for international students: Required—TOEFL (minimum score 500 paper-based; 173 computer-based). *Application deadline:* For fall admission, 7/15 for domestic students; for spring admission, 12/15 for domestic students. Applications are processed on a rolling basis. Application fee: $10. *Financial support:* In 2011–12, 4 research assistantships with tuition reimbursements (averaging $12,000 per year) were awarded. *Faculty research:* Salmonella pseudomonas, cancer cells. *Total annual research expenditures:* $125,000. *Unit head:* Dr. Karyn Scissum-Gunn, Acting Chair, 334-229-4467, Fax: 334-229-1007. *Application contact:* Dr. Doris Screws, Dean of Graduate Studies, 334-229-4274, Fax: 334-229-4928, E-mail: dscrews@alasu.edu. Web site: http://www.alasu.edu/academics/colleges—departments/science-mathematics—technology/biological-sciences-department/phd-microbiology/index.aspx.

Albert Einstein College of Medicine, Graduate Division of Biomedical Sciences, Bronx, NY 10461. Offers PhD, MD/PhD. *Degree requirements:* For doctorate, thesis/dissertation. *Entrance requirements:* For doctorate, GRE General Test. Additional exam requirements/recommendations for international students: Required—TOEFL.

Albert Einstein College of Medicine, Medical Scientist Training Program, Bronx, NY 10461. Offers MD/PhD.

Alcorn State University, School of Graduate Studies, School of Arts and Sciences, Department of Biology, Alcorn State, MS 39096-7500. Offers MS.

American University, College of Arts and Sciences, Department of Biology, Washington, DC 20016-8007. Offers applied science (MS), including biotechnology, environmental science assessment; biology (MA, MS). Part-time programs available. *Faculty:* 10 full-time (4 women), 3 part-time/adjunct (2 women). *Students:* 8 full-time (2 women), 4 part-time (1 woman); includes 4 minority (1 Black or African American, non-Hispanic/Latino; 3 Asian, non-Hispanic/Latino), 1 international. Average age 25. 15 applicants, 60% accepted, 6 enrolled. In 2011, 9 master's awarded. *Degree requirements:* For master's, comprehensive exam, thesis (for some programs). *Entrance requirements:* For master's, GRE General Test, GRE Subject Test. Additional exam requirements/recommendations for international students: Required—TOEFL. *Application deadline:* For fall admission, 2/1 for domestic students; for spring admission, 10/1 for domestic students. Application fee: $80. *Expenses: Tuition:* Full-time $24,264; part-time $1348 per credit hour. *Required fees:* $430. Tuition and fees vary according to course load and program. *Financial support:* Fellowships, research assistantships with tuition reimbursements, teaching assistantships with tuition reimbursements, career-related internships or fieldwork, Federal Work-Study, and institutionally sponsored loans available. Financial award application deadline: 2/1. *Faculty research:* Neurobiology, cave biology, population genetics, vertebrate physiology. *Unit head:* Dr. David Carlini, Chair, 202-885-2194, Fax: 202-885-2182, E-mail: carlini@american.edu. *Application contact:* Kathleen Clowery, Director, Graduate Admissions, 202-885-3621, Fax: 202-885-1505, E-mail: clowery@american.edu. Web site: http://www.american.edu/cas/biology/.

The American University of Athens, School of Graduate Studies, Athens, Greece. Offers biomedical sciences (MS); business (MBA); business communication (MA); computer sciences (MS); engineering and applied sciences (MS); politics and policy making (MA); systems engineering (MS); telecommunications (MS). *Entrance requirements:* For master's, resume, 2 recommendation letters. Additional exam requirements/recommendations for international students: Required—TOEFL (minimum score 550 paper-based; 213 computer-based). *Faculty research:* Nanotechnology,

RISE AND SHINE

Adelphi University graduate students are engaged and challenged, and our scheduling is structured to support your professional life outside of the community. As of Fall 2011, 89 percent of Adelphi students who earned a master's degree were employed within a year.

Our graduate programs include:

- Business
- Creative arts
- Education
- Healthcare
- Psychology
- Science
- Social work

ADELPHI UNIVERSITY **ADELPHI.EDU/GRADUATE**

environmental sciences, rock mechanics, human skin studies, Monte Carlo algorithms and software.

American University of Beirut, Graduate Programs, Faculty of Arts and Sciences, Beirut, Lebanon. Offers anthropology (MA); Arabic language and literature (MA); archaeology (MA); biology (MS); chemistry (MS); computational science (MS); computer science (MS); economics (MA); education (MA); English language (MA); English literature (MA); environmental policy planning (MSES); financial economics (MAFE); geology (MS); history (MA); mathematics (MA, MS); Middle Eastern studies (MA); philosophy (MA); physics (MS); political studies (MA); psychology (MA); public administration (MA); sociology (MA); statistics (MA, MS). Part-time programs available. *Faculty:* 154 full-time (44 women), 12 part-time/adjunct (2 women). *Students:* 180 full-time (122 women), 240 part-time (158 women). Average age 25. 336 applicants, 47% accepted, 86 enrolled. In 2011, 57 master's awarded. *Degree requirements:* For master's, one foreign language, comprehensive exam, thesis (for some programs). *Entrance requirements:* For master's, GRE, letter of recommendation. Additional exam requirements/recommendations for international students: Required—TOEFL (minimum score 600 paper-based; 250 computer-based; 97 iBT), IELTS (minimum score 7). *Application deadline:* For fall admission, 4/30 for domestic and international students; for spring admission, 11/1 for domestic and international students. Application fee: $50. *Expenses: Tuition:* Full-time $12,780; part-time $710 per credit. Tuition and fees vary according to course load and program. *Financial support:* In 2011–12, 33 students received support. Career-related internships or fieldwork, institutionally sponsored loans, scholarships/grants, health care benefits, and unspecified assistantships available. Financial award application deadline: 2/4; financial award applicants required to submit FAFSA. *Faculty research:* History of composition studies, syntax of Arabic dialects, Oscar Wilde, decadence, Middle Eastern and international politics, neural mechanisms of creativity and consciousness, personality and psycho-socio-cultural-spiritual correlates of negative and positive mental health, philosophy of mind, metaphysics, micropaleontology and stratigraphy, geochemistry, mineralogy and petrology, tectonophysics, Abbasid, Ottoman and Russian history, landscape, Bronze and Iron Age archaeology. *Unit head:* Dr. Patrick McGreevy, Dean, 961-1374374 Ext. 3800, Fax: 961-1744461, E-mail: pm07@aub.edu.lb. *Application contact:* Dr. Salim Kanaan, Director, Admissions Office, 961-1350000 Ext. 2594, Fax: 961-1750775, E-mail: sk00@aub.edu.lb. Web site: http://staff.aub.edu.lb/~webfas.

American University of Beirut, Graduate Programs, Faculty of Medicine, Beirut, Lebanon. Offers anatomy, cell biology and human morphology (MS); biochemistry and medical genetics (MS); biomedical sciences (PhD); experimental pathology, immunology and microbiology (MS); medicine (MD); neuroscience (MS); pharmacology and toxicology (MS). Part-time programs available. *Faculty:* 232 full-time (58 women), 68 part-time/adjunct (7 women). *Students:* 346 full-time (135 women), 69 part-time (57 women). Average age 23. In 2011, 20 master's, 82 doctorates awarded. *Degree requirements:* For master's, one foreign language, comprehensive exam, thesis (for some programs). *Entrance requirements:* For master's, letter of recommendation; for doctorate, MCAT, bachelor's degree. Additional exam requirements/recommendations for international students: Required—TOEFL (minimum score 600 paper-based; 250 computer-based; 100 iBT), IELTS (minimum score 7.5). *Application deadline:* For fall admission, 4/30 for domestic and international students; for spring admission, 11/1 for domestic and international students. Application fee: $50. *Expenses: Tuition:* Full-time $12,780; part-time $710 per credit. Tuition and fees vary according to course load and program. *Financial support:* In 2011–12, 19 students received support. Career-related internships or fieldwork, institutionally sponsored loans, scholarships/grants, health care benefits, and unspecified assistantships available. Financial award application deadline: 2/2. *Faculty research:* Cancer research (targeted therapy, mechanisms of leukemogenesis, tumor cell extravasation and metastasis, cancer stem cells); stem cell research (regenerative medicine, drug discovery); genetic research (neurogenetics, hereditary cardiomyopathy, hemoglobinopathies, pharmacogenomics, proteomics); neuroscience research (pain, neurodegenerative disorder); metabolism (inflammation and metabolism, metabolic disorder, diabetes mellitus); vascular and renal biology, signal transduction. *Total annual research expenditures:* $2.3 million. *Unit head:* Dr. Mohamed Sayegh, Dean, 961-1350000 Ext. 4700, Fax: 961-1744464, E-mail: msayegh@aub.edu.lb. *Application contact:* Dr. Salim Kanaan, Director, Admissions Office, 961-1350000 Ext. 2594, Fax: 961-1750775, E-mail: sk00@aub.edu.lb. Web site: http://www.aub.edu.lb/fm/fm_home/Pages/index.aspx.

Andrews University, School of Graduate Studies, College of Arts and Sciences, Department of Biology, Berrien Springs, MI 49104. Offers MAT, MS. *Faculty:* 7 full-time (0 women). *Students:* 3 full-time (1 woman), 4 part-time (all women), 1 international. Average age 26. 8 applicants, 25% accepted, 1 enrolled. In 2011, 1 master's awarded. *Degree requirements:* For master's, comprehensive exam, thesis. *Entrance requirements:* For master's, GRE Subject Test. Additional exam requirements/recommendations for international students: Required—TOEFL (minimum score 550 paper-based). *Application deadline:* Applications are processed on a rolling basis. Application fee: $40. *Financial support:* Fellowships, research assistantships, teaching assistantships, career-related internships or fieldwork, Federal Work-Study, and institutionally sponsored loans available. Financial award application deadline: 3/15. *Unit head:* Dr. David A. Steen, Chairman, 269-471-3243. *Application contact:* Carolyn Hurst, Supervisor of Graduate Admission, 800-253-2874, Fax: 269-471-6321, E-mail: graduate@andrews.edu.

Angelo State University, College of Graduate Studies, College of Arts and Sciences, Department of Biology, San Angelo, TX 76909. Offers MS. Part-time and evening/weekend programs available. *Faculty:* 8 full-time (2 women). *Students:* 14 full-time (6 women), 9 part-time (5 women); includes 3 minority (1 American Indian or Alaska Native, non-Hispanic/Latino; 2 Hispanic/Latino), 1 international. Average age 27. 9 applicants, 67% accepted, 5 enrolled. In 2011, 4 master's awarded. *Degree requirements:* For master's, comprehensive exam, thesis optional. *Entrance requirements:* For master's, GRE General Test, essay. Additional exam requirements/recommendations for international students: Required—TOEFL or IELTS. *Application deadline:* For fall admission, 7/15 priority date for domestic students, 6/10 for international students; for spring admission, 12/1 priority date for domestic students, 11/1 for international students. Applications are processed on a rolling basis. Application fee: $40 ($50 for international students). Electronic applications accepted. *Financial support:* In 2011–12, 12 students received support, including 1 research assistantship, 2 teaching assistantships (averaging $10,251 per year); career-related internships or fieldwork, Federal Work-Study, scholarships/grants, and unspecified assistantships also available. Support available to part-time students. Financial award application deadline: 3/1. *Faculty research:* Texas poppy-mallow project, Chisos hedgehog cactus, skunks, reptiles, amphibians, rodents, seed germination; mammals. *Unit head:* Dr. Russell Wilke, Department Head, 325-942-2189 Ext. 246, Fax: 325-942-2184, E-mail: russell.wilke@angelo.edu. *Application contact:* Dr. Bonnie B. Amos, Graduate Advisor, 325-942-2189 Ext. 256, Fax: 325-942-2184, E-mail: bonnie.amos@angelo.edu. Web site: http://www.angelo.edu/dept/biology/.

Appalachian State University, Cratis D. Williams Graduate School, Department of Biology, Boone, NC 28608. Offers cell and molecular (MS); general (MS). Part-time programs available. *Faculty:* 29 full-time (12 women), 3 part-time/adjunct (1 woman).

Students: 46 full-time (24 women), 9 part-time (7 women); includes 1 minority (Asian, non-Hispanic/Latino). 32 applicants, 63% accepted, 15 enrolled. In 2011, 11 master's awarded. *Degree requirements:* For master's, comprehensive exam, thesis. *Entrance requirements:* For master's, GRE General Test, 3 letters of recommendation. Additional exam requirements/recommendations for international students: Required—TOEFL (minimum score 570 paper-based; 230 computer-based; 79 iBT), IELTS (minimum score 6.5). *Application deadline:* For fall admission, 3/5 priority date for domestic students, 2/1 for international students; for spring admission, 11/1 for domestic students, 7/1 for international students. Applications are processed on a rolling basis. Application fee: $55. Electronic applications accepted. *Expenses:* Tuition, state resident: full-time $4040; part-time $180 per semester hour. Tuition, nonresident: full-time $15,900; part-time $760 per semester hour. *Required fees:* $2500; $20 per semester hour. Tuition and fees vary according to campus/location. *Financial support:* In 2011–12, 25 teaching assistantships (averaging $9,500 per year) were awarded; fellowships, research assistantships, career-related internships or fieldwork, Federal Work-Study, scholarships/grants, and unspecified assistantships also available. Financial award application deadline: 3/15; financial award applicants required to submit FAFSA. *Faculty research:* Aquatic and terrestrial ecology, animal and plant physiology, behavior and systematics, immunology and cell biology, molecular biology and microbiology. *Unit head:* Dr. Steven Seagle, Chairman, 828-262-3025, E-mail: seaglesw@appstate.edu. *Application contact:* Dr. Ece Karatan, Graduate Coordinator, 828-262-6742, E-mail: karatane@appstate.edu. Web site: http://www.biology.appstate.edu.

Arizona State University, College of Liberal Arts and Sciences, School of Life Sciences, Tempe, AZ 85287-4601. Offers animal behavior (PhD); applied ethics (biomedical and health ethics) (MA); biological design (PhD); biology (MS, PhD); biology (biology and society) (MS, PhD); environmental life sciences (PhD); evolutionary biology (PhD); human and social dimensions of science and technology (PhD); microbiology (PhD); molecular and cellular biology (PhD); neuroscience (PhD); philosophy (history and philosophy of science) (MA); sustainability (PhD). Terminal master's awarded for partial completion of doctoral program. *Degree requirements:* For master's, thesis (for some programs), interactive Program of Study (iPOS) submitted before completing 50 percent of required credit hours; for doctorate, variable foreign language requirement, comprehensive exam, thesis/dissertation, interactive Program of Study (iPOS) submitted before completing 50 percent of required credit hours. *Entrance requirements:* For master's and doctorate, GRE, minimum GPA of 3.0 or equivalent in last 2 years of work leading to bachelor's degree. Additional exam requirements/recommendations for international students: Required—TOEFL (minimum score 600 paper-based; 250 computer-based; 100 iBT). Electronic applications accepted.

Arizona State University, College of Technology and Innovation, Department of Applied Sciences and Mathematics, Mesa, AZ 85212. Offers applied biological sciences (MS). Part-time programs available. *Degree requirements:* For master's, thesis, oral defense, interactive Program of Study (iPOS) submitted before completing 50 percent of required credit hours. *Entrance requirements:* For master's, GRE (minimum combined score of 1080) or MAT (minimum score of 45), minimum GPA of 3.0 or equivalent in last 2 years of work leading to bachelor's degree, 3 letters of recommendation, resume, 18 hours of biological sciences or related courses, statement of intent. Additional exam requirements/recommendations for international students: Required—TOEFL (minimum score 83 iBT), TOEFL, IELTS, or Pearson Test of English. Electronic applications accepted.

Arizona State University, Graduate College, Program in Biological Design, Tempe, AZ 85287-5001. Offers PhD. *Degree requirements:* For doctorate, comprehensive exam, thesis/dissertation, interactive Program of Study (iPOS) submitted before completing 50 percent of required credit hours. *Entrance requirements:* For doctorate, GRE, minimum GPA of 3.0 in the last 2 years of work leading to the bachelor's degree, 3 letters of recommendation, personal statement containing goals and prior/current research experience, resume. Additional exam requirements/recommendations for international students: Required—TOEFL (minimum score 550 paper-based; 213 computer-based; 80 iBT), IELTS (minimum score 6.5). Electronic applications accepted.

Arkansas State University, Graduate School, College of Sciences and Mathematics, Department of Biological Sciences, Jonesboro, State University, AR 72467. Offers biological sciences (MA); biology (MS); biology education (MSE, SCCT); biotechnology (PSM). Part-time programs available. *Faculty:* 22 full-time (7 women). *Students:* 13 full-time (8 women), 22 part-time (14 women); includes 2 minority (1 Black or African American, non-Hispanic/Latino; 1 American Indian or Alaska Native, non-Hispanic/Latino), 9 international. Average age 27. 31 applicants, 71% accepted, 13 enrolled. In 2011, 14 master's awarded. *Degree requirements:* For master's, comprehensive exam, thesis (for some programs); for SCCT, comprehensive exam. *Entrance requirements:* For master's, GRE General Test, appropriate bachelor's degree, letters of reference, interview, official transcripts, immunization records, statement of educational objectives and career goals, teaching certificate (MSE); for SCCT, GRE General Test or MAT, interview, master's degree, letters of reference, official transcript, personal statement, immunization records. Additional exam requirements/recommendations for international students: Required—TOEFL (minimum score 550 paper-based; 213 computer-based; 79 iBT), IELTS (minimum score 6), Pearson Test of English Academic (minimum score 56). *Application deadline:* For fall admission, 7/1 for domestic and international students; for spring admission, 11/15 for domestic students, 11/14 for international students. Applications are processed on a rolling basis. Application fee: $30 ($40 for international students). Electronic applications accepted. *Expenses:* Tuition, state resident: full-time $4044; part-time $225 per credit hour. Tuition, nonresident: full-time $8087; part-time $449 per credit hour. *Required fees:* $936; $52 per credit hour. $25 per term. One-time fee: $30. Tuition and fees vary according to course load and program. *Financial support:* In 2011–12, 17 students received support. Research assistantships, career-related internships or fieldwork, scholarships/grants, and unspecified assistantships available. Financial award application deadline: 7/1; financial award applicants required to submit FAFSA. *Unit head:* Dr. Thomas Risch, Chair, 870-972-3082, Fax: 870-972-2638, E-mail: trisch@astate.edu. *Application contact:* Dr. Andrew Sustich, Dean of the Graduate School, 870-972-3029, Fax: 870-972-3857, E-mail: sustich@astate.edu. Web site: http://www.astate.edu/a/scimath/biology/.

A.T. Still University of Health Sciences, Kirksville College of Osteopathic Medicine, Kirksville, MO 63501. Offers biomedical sciences (MS); osteopathic medicine (DO). *Accreditation:* AOsA. *Faculty:* 43 full-time (9 women), 21 part-time/adjunct (3 women). *Students:* 706 full-time (285 women), 14 part-time (6 women); includes 116 minority (12 Black or African American, non-Hispanic/Latino; 1 American Indian or Alaska Native, non-Hispanic/Latino; 69 Asian, non-Hispanic/Latino; 19 Hispanic/Latino; 15 Two or more races, non-Hispanic/Latino), 12 international. Average age 27. 3,556 applicants, 11% accepted, 172 enrolled. In 2011, 13 master's, 176 doctorates awarded. *Degree requirements:* For master's, thesis; for doctorate, Level 1 and 2 COMLEX-PE and CE exams. *Entrance requirements:* For master's, GRE, MCAT, or DAT, minimum undergraduate GPA of 2.5 (cumulative and science); for doctorate, MCAT, bachelor's degree with minimum GPA of 2.5 (cumulative and science) or 90 semester hours with minimum GPA of 3.5 (cumulative and science) and minimum MCAT score of 28. Additional exam requirements/recommendations for international students: Recommended—TOEFL. *Application deadline:* For fall admission, 2/1 for domestic and

international students. Applications are processed on a rolling basis. Application fee: $70. Electronic applications accepted. *Expenses:* Contact institution. *Financial support:* In 2011–12, 192 students received support, including 20 fellowships with full tuition reimbursements available (averaging $16,000 per year); Federal Work-Study and scholarships/grants also available. Financial award application deadline: 5/1; financial award applicants required to submit FAFSA. *Faculty research:* Ion channels controlling neuronal excitability, osteopathic palpatory procedures, gene array studies of pain remediation, thoracic lymphatic pump techniques, animal models of manual medicine, melanoma metastasis, exercise science, orthopedics, practice-based research network, antibiotic resistance, staphylococcus aureus, bacterial virulence and environmental survival. *Total annual research expenditures:* $394,713. *Unit head:* Dr. Margaret Wilson, Dean, 660-626-2354, Fax: 660-626-2080, E-mail: jsuzewits@atsu.edu. *Application contact:* Donna Sparks, Associate Director, Admissions Processing, 660-626-2117, Fax: 660-626-2969, E-mail: admissions@atsu.edu. Web site: http://www.atsu.edu/kcom/.

Auburn University, College of Veterinary Medicine and Graduate School, Graduate Programs in Veterinary Medicine, Auburn University, AL 36849. Offers biomedical sciences (MS, PhD), including anatomy, physiology and pharmacology (MS); biomedical sciences (PhD), clinical sciences (MS), large animal surgery and medicine (MS), pathobiology (MS), radiology (MS), small animal surgery and medicine (MS); DVM/MS. Part-time programs available. *Faculty:* 100 full-time (40 women), 5 part-time/adjunct (1 woman). *Students:* 17 full-time (13 women), 59 part-time (33 women); includes 6 minority (1 Black or African American, non-Hispanic/Latino; 3 Asian, non-Hispanic/Latino; 2 Hispanic/Latino), 30 international. Average age 30. 36 applicants, 69% accepted, 11 enrolled. In 2011, 19 master's awarded. *Degree requirements:* For doctorate, thesis/dissertation. *Entrance requirements:* For master's, GRE General Test; for doctorate, GRE General Test, GRE Subject Test. *Application deadline:* For fall admission, 7/7 for domestic students; for spring admission, 11/24 for domestic students. Applications are processed on a rolling basis. Application fee: $50 ($60 for international students). Electronic applications accepted. *Expenses:* Tuition, state resident: full-time $7290; part-time $405 per credit hour. Tuition, nonresident: full-time $21,870; part-time $1215 per credit hour. *International tuition:* $22,000 full-time. *Required fees:* $1402. *Financial support:* Research assistantships, teaching assistantships, and Federal Work-Study available. Support available to part-time students. Financial award application deadline: 3/15; financial award applicants required to submit FAFSA. *Unit head:* Dr. Calvin Johnson, Acting Dean, 334-844-2650. *Application contact:* Dr. George Flowers, Dean of the Graduate School, 334-844-2125.

Auburn University, Graduate School, College of Sciences and Mathematics, Department of Biological Sciences, Auburn University, AL 36849. Offers botany (MS, PhD); microbiology (MS, PhD); zoology (MS, PhD). *Faculty:* 35 full-time (11 women). *Students:* 32 full-time (13 women), 73 part-time (33 women); includes 11 minority (3 Black or African American, non-Hispanic/Latino; 1 American Indian or Alaska Native, non-Hispanic/Latino; 5 Asian, non-Hispanic/Latino; 2 Hispanic/Latino), 24 international. Average age 29. 106 applicants, 28% accepted, 19 enrolled. In 2011, 14 master's, 9 doctorates awarded. *Entrance requirements:* For master's and doctorate, GRE General Test. Additional exam requirements/recommendations for international students: Required—TOEFL. *Application deadline:* For fall admission, 7/7 for domestic students; for spring admission, 11/24 for domestic students. Application fee: $50 ($60 for international students). Electronic applications accepted. *Expenses:* Tuition, state resident: full-time $7290; part-time $405 per credit hour. Tuition, nonresident: full-time $21,870; part-time $1215 per credit hour. *International tuition:* $22,000 full-time. *Required fees:* $1402. *Financial support:* Research assistantships and teaching assistantships available. Financial award applicants required to submit FAFSA. *Unit head:* Dr. Jack W. Feminella, Chair, 334-844-3906, Fax: 334-844-1645. *Application contact:* Dr. George Flowers, Dean of the Graduate School, 334-844-2125.

Austin Peay State University, College of Graduate Studies, College of Science and Mathematics, Department of Biology, Clarksville, TN 37044. Offers clinical laboratory science (MS); radiologic science (MS). Part-time programs available. *Faculty:* 8 full-time (3 women), 1 part-time/adjunct (0 women). *Students:* 6 full-time (2 women), 19 part-time (12 women); includes 3 minority (2 Black or African American, non-Hispanic/Latino; 1 Hispanic/Latino), 1 international. Average age 28. 13 applicants, 92% accepted, 9 enrolled. In 2011, 9 master's awarded. *Degree requirements:* For master's, comprehensive exam, thesis optional. *Entrance requirements:* For master's, GRE General Test, 3 letters of recommendation, minimum undergraduate GPA of 2.5. Additional exam requirements/recommendations for international students: Required—TOEFL (minimum score 500 paper-based; 173 computer-based). *Application deadline:* For fall admission, 8/1 priority date for domestic students. Applications are processed on a rolling basis. Application fee: $25. Electronic applications accepted. *Expenses:* Tuition, state resident: part-time $350 per credit hour. Tuition, nonresident: full-time $20,644; part-time $971 per credit hour. *Required fees:* $1224; $61.20 per credit hour. *Financial support:* In 2011–12, research assistantships with full tuition reimbursements (averaging $5,184 per year) were awarded; career-related internships or fieldwork, Federal Work-Study, institutionally sponsored loans, scholarships/grants, and unspecified assistantships also available. Support available to part-time students. Financial award application deadline: 3/1. *Faculty research:* Non-paint source pollution, amphibian biomonitoring, aquatic toxicology, biological indicators of water quality, taxonomy. *Unit head:* Dr. Don Dailey, Chair, 931-221-7781, Fax: 931-221-6323, E-mail: daileyd@apsu.edu. *Application contact:* Kendra Bryant, Graduate Admissions, 800-844-2778, Fax: 931-221-6188, E-mail: admissionsweb@apsu.edu. Web site: http://www.apsu.edu/biology.

Ball State University, Graduate School, College of Sciences and Humanities, Department of Biology, Muncie, IN 47306-1099. Offers biology (MA, MAE, MS); biology education (Ed D). *Faculty:* 22 full-time (8 women). *Students:* 26 full-time (8 women), 26 part-time (14 women); includes 3 minority (2 Asian, non-Hispanic/Latino; 1 Two or more races, non-Hispanic/Latino), 3 international. Average age 24. 47 applicants, 68% accepted, 21 enrolled. In 2011, 17 master's awarded. *Degree requirements:* For doctorate, thesis/dissertation. *Entrance requirements:* For master's, GRE General Test; for doctorate, GRE General Test, minimum graduate GPA of 3.2. Application fee: $50. Tuition and fees vary according to program and reciprocity agreements. *Financial support:* In 2011–12, 36 students received support, including 35 teaching assistantships with full and partial tuition reimbursements available (averaging $7,672 per year); research assistantships with full tuition reimbursements available and career-related internships or fieldwork also available. Financial award application deadline: 3/1. *Faculty research:* Aquatics and fisheries, tumors, water and air pollution, developmental biology and genetics. *Unit head:* Dr. Kemuel Badger, Chairman, 765-285-8820, Fax: 765-285-8804. *Application contact:* Dr. Robert Morris, Associate Provost for Research and Dean of the Graduate School, 765-285-1300, E-mail: rmorris@bsu.edu. Web site: http://cms.bsu.edu/Academics/CollegesandDepartments/Biology.aspx.

Barry University, College of Health Sciences, Programs in Biology and Biomedical Sciences, Miami Shores, FL 33161-6695. Offers biology (MS); biomedical sciences (MS). Part-time and evening/weekend programs available. *Degree requirements:* For master's, comprehensive exam, thesis (for some programs). *Entrance requirements:* For master's, GRE General Test or Florida Teacher's Certification Exam (biology); GRE

General Test, MCAT, or DAT (biomedical sciences). Electronic applications accepted. *Faculty research:* Genetics, immunology, anthropology.

Baylor College of Medicine, Graduate School of Biomedical Sciences, Houston, TX 77030-3498. Offers MS, PhD, MD/PhD. *Faculty:* 490 full-time (122 women). *Students:* 586 full-time (311 women); includes 143 minority (29 Black or African American, non-Hispanic/Latino; 2 American Indian or Alaska Native, non-Hispanic/Latino; 68 Asian, non-Hispanic/Latino; 44 Hispanic/Latino), 223 international. Average age 28. 1,169 applicants, 17% accepted, 99 enrolled. In 2011, 16 master's, 88 doctorates awarded. Terminal master's awarded for partial completion of doctoral program. *Degree requirements:* For master's, thesis; for doctorate, thesis/dissertation, public defense. *Entrance requirements:* For doctorate, GRE General Test, GRE Subject Test (strongly recommended), minimum GPA of 3.0. Additional exam requirements/recommendations for international students: Required—TOEFL. *Application deadline:* For fall admission, 1/1 priority date for domestic students. Applications are processed on a rolling basis. Application fee: $0. Electronic applications accepted. *Financial support:* In 2011–12, 100 students received support, including 190 fellowships with full tuition reimbursements available (averaging $29,000 per year), 397 research assistantships with full tuition reimbursements available (averaging $29,000 per year); teaching assistantships, career-related internships or fieldwork, Federal Work-Study, institutionally sponsored loans, health care benefits, and scholarships to all students unless there are grant funds available to pay tuition) also available. Financial award applicants required to submit FAFSA. *Faculty research:* Cell and molecular biology of cardiac muscle, structural biophysics, gene expression and regulation, human genomes, viruses. *Unit head:* Dr. Hiram F. Gilbert, Dean of Graduate Sciences, 713-798-4032, Fax: 713-798-6325, E-mail: hgilbert@bcm.edu. *Application contact:* Melissa Houghton, Administrator for GSBS Admissions, 713-798-4031, Fax: 713-798-6325, E-mail: melissah@bcm.edu. Web site: http://www.bcm.edu/gradschool/.

Baylor University, Graduate School, College of Arts and Sciences, Department of Biology, Waco, TX 76798. Offers biology (MA, MS, PhD); environmental biology (MS); limnology (MS). Part-time programs available. *Faculty:* 13 full-time (3 women). *Students:* 37 full-time (19 women), 3 part-time (1 woman); includes 8 minority (3 Asian, non-Hispanic/Latino; 1 Hispanic/Latino; 4 Two or more races, non-Hispanic/Latino), 13 international. In 2011, 5 master's, 3 doctorates awarded. *Degree requirements:* For master's, thesis (for some programs); for doctorate, thesis/dissertation. *Entrance requirements:* For master's and doctorate, GRE General Test. *Application deadline:* For fall admission, 1/31 priority date for domestic students. Applications are processed on a rolling basis. Application fee: $25. *Financial support:* Teaching assistantships, career-related internships or fieldwork, Federal Work-Study, institutionally sponsored loans, and tuition waivers (full and partial) available. Support available to part-time students. Financial award application deadline: 2/28. *Faculty research:* Terrestrial ecology, aquatic ecology, genetics. *Unit head:* Dr. Myeongwoo Lee, Graduate Program Director, 254-710-2141, Fax: 254-710-2969, E-mail: myeongwoo_lee@baylor.edu. *Application contact:* Tamara Lehmann, Administrative Assistant, 254-710-2911, Fax: 254-710-2969, E-mail: tamara_lehmann@baylor.edu. Web site: http://www.baylor.edu/biology/.

Baylor University, Graduate School, Institute of Biomedical Studies, Waco, TX 76798. Offers MS, PhD. *Students:* 27 full-time (15 women), 2 part-time (0 women); includes 4 minority (1 Asian, non-Hispanic/Latino; 2 Hispanic/Latino; 1 Two or more races, non-Hispanic/Latino), 14 international. In 2011, 4 master's, 4 doctorates awarded. *Entrance requirements:* For master's and doctorate, GRE General Test. *Application deadline:* Applications are processed on a rolling basis. Application fee: $25. *Financial support:* Research assistantships and teaching assistantships available. *Unit head:* Dr. Chris Kearney, Graduate Program Director, 254-710-2131, Fax: 254-710-3878, E-mail: chris_kearney@baylor.edu. *Application contact:* Rhonda Bellert, Administrative Assistant, 254-710-2514, Fax: 254-710-3870, E-mail: rhonda_bellert@baylor.edu. Web site: http://www.baylor.edu/biomedical_studies/.

Bemidji State University, School of Graduate Studies, Bemidji, MN 56601-2699. Offers biology (MS); counseling psychology (MS); education (M Ed, MS); English (MA, MS); environmental studies (MS); mathematics (MS); mathematics (elementary and middle level education) (MS); special education (M Sp Ed, MS). Part-time programs available. Postbaccalaureate distance learning degree programs offered (no on-campus study). *Faculty:* 114 full-time (47 women), 22 part-time/adjunct (16 women). *Students:* 68 full-time (45 women), 311 part-time (198 women); includes 21 minority (4 Black or African American, non-Hispanic/Latino; 2 American Indian or Alaska Native, non-Hispanic/Latino; 5 Asian, non-Hispanic/Latino; 5 Hispanic/Latino; 5 Two or more races, non-Hispanic/Latino), 5 international. Average age 34. 82 applicants, 98% accepted, 37 enrolled. In 2011, 72 master's awarded. *Degree requirements:* For master's, comprehensive exam, thesis (for some programs). *Entrance requirements:* For master's, GRE, letters of recommendation, letters of interest. Additional exam requirements/recommendations for international students: Required—TOEFL (minimum score 550 paper-based; 213 computer-based; 80 iBT). *Application deadline:* Applications are processed on a rolling basis. Application fee: $20. Electronic applications accepted. *Expenses:* Tuition, state resident: full-time $6182; part-time $343.45 per credit. Tuition, nonresident: full-time $6182; part-time $343.45 per credit. *Required fees:* $954. *Financial support:* In 2011–12, 253 students received support, including 36 research assistantships with partial tuition reimbursements available (averaging $7,441 per year), 36 teaching assistantships with partial tuition reimbursements available (averaging $7,441 per year); career-related internships or fieldwork, scholarships/grants, health care benefits, and unspecified assistantships also available. Support available to part-time students. Financial award application deadline: 4/15; financial award applicants required to submit FAFSA. *Unit head:* Dr. Patricia Rogers, Dean of Health Sciences and Human Ecology, 218-755-2027, Fax: 218-755-2258, E-mail: progers@bemidjistate.edu. *Application contact:* Joan Miller, Senior Office and Administrative Specialist, 218-755-2027, Fax: 218-755-2258, E-mail: jmiller@bemidjistate.edu. Web site: http://www.bemidjistate.edu/academics/graduate_studies/.

Bloomsburg University of Pennsylvania, School of Graduate Studies, College of Science and Technology, Department of Biological and Allied Health Sciences, Program in Biology, Bloomsburg, PA 17815-1301. Offers MS. *Degree requirements:* For master's, thesis or alternative. *Entrance requirements:* For master's, minimum QPA of 3.0, 2 letters of recommendation. Additional exam requirements/recommendations for international students: Required—TOEFL (minimum score 550 paper-based; 213 computer-based; 79 iBT). Electronic applications accepted.

Boise State University, Graduate College, College of Arts and Sciences, Department of Biology, Program in Biology, Boise, ID 83725-0399. Offers MA, MS. Part-time programs available. *Degree requirements:* For master's, thesis. *Entrance requirements:* For master's, GRE General Test, minimum GPA of 3.0. Electronic applications accepted.

Boston College, Graduate School of Arts and Sciences, Department of Biology, Chestnut Hill, MA 02467-3800. Offers PhD, MBA/MS. *Degree requirements:* For doctorate, thesis/dissertation. *Entrance requirements:* For doctorate, GRE General Test, GRE Subject Test. Additional exam requirements/recommendations for international students: Required—TOEFL (minimum score 600 paper-based; 250 computer-based;

100 iBT). Electronic applications accepted. *Faculty research:* DNA replication in mammalian cells, control of the cell cycle, immunology, plant genetics.

See Display below and Close-Up on page 103.

Boston University, Graduate School of Arts and Sciences, Department of Biology, Boston, MA 02215. Offers MA, PhD. *Students:* 93 full-time (59 women), 3 part-time (1 woman); includes 11 minority (1 Black or African American, non-Hispanic/Latino; 4 Asian, non-Hispanic/Latino; 3 Hispanic/Latino; 3 Two or more races, non-Hispanic/Latino), 7 international. Average age 28. 205 applicants, 18% accepted, 18 enrolled. In 2011, 206 master's, 13 doctorates awarded. Terminal master's awarded for partial completion of doctoral program. *Degree requirements:* For master's, one foreign language, thesis (for some programs); for doctorate, one foreign language, comprehensive exam, thesis/dissertation. *Entrance requirements:* For master's and doctorate, GRE General Test, GRE Subject Test, 3 letters of recommendation. Additional exam requirements/recommendations for international students: Required—TOEFL (minimum score 600 paper-based; 250 computer-based). *Application deadline:* For fall admission, 12/7 for domestic and international students. Application fee: $70. Electronic applications accepted. *Expenses: Tuition:* Full-time $40,848; part-time $1276 per credit hour. *Required fees:* $572; $286 per semester. *Financial support:* In 2011–12, 2 fellowships with full tuition reimbursements (averaging $19,800 per year), 31 research assistantships with full tuition reimbursements (averaging $19,300 per year), 52 teaching assistantships with full tuition reimbursements (averaging $19,300 per year) were awarded; Federal Work-Study, institutionally sponsored loans, scholarships/grants, and traineeships also available. Financial award application deadline: 12/7; financial award applicants required to submit FAFSA. *Unit head:* Michael Sorenson, Chairman, 617-353-3856, Fax: 617-353-6340, E-mail: msoren@bu.edu. *Application contact:* Meredith Canode, Academic Administrator, 617-353-2432, Fax: 617-353-6340, E-mail: mcanode@bu.edu. Web site: http://www.bu.edu/biology/.

Boston University, School of Medicine, Division of Graduate Medical Sciences, Boston, MA 02118. Offers MA, MS, PhD, MA/MA, MBA/MA, MD/MBA, MD/PhD, MPH/MA. Part-time programs available. *Faculty:* 1,020 full-time (460 women), 517 part-time/adjunct (212 women). *Students:* 826 full-time (482 women), 96 part-time (63 women); includes 260 minority (35 Black or African American, non-Hispanic/Latino; 2 American Indian or Alaska Native, non-Hispanic/Latino; 150 Asian, non-Hispanic/Latino; 48 Hispanic/Latino; 3 Native Hawaiian or other Pacific Islander, non-Hispanic/Latino; 22 Two or more races, non-Hispanic/Latino), 108 international. Average age 26. 1,857 applicants, 42% accepted, 363 enrolled. In 2011, 261 master's, 47 doctorates awarded. Terminal master's awarded for partial completion of doctoral program. *Degree requirements:* For master's, thesis (for some programs); for doctorate, comprehensive exam, thesis/dissertation, qualifying exam. *Entrance requirements:* For master's, GRE, MCAT; for doctorate, GRE. Additional exam requirements/recommendations for international students: Required—TOEFL; Recommended—IELTS. *Application deadline:* For fall admission, 1/31 priority date for domestic students, 1/31 for international students; for spring admission, 10/15 priority date for domestic students, 10/15 for international students. Applications are processed on a rolling basis. Application fee: $75. Electronic applications accepted. *Expenses:* Contact institution. *Financial support:* In 2011–12, 33 students received support, including 14 fellowships (averaging $30,500 per year), 44 research assistantships (averaging $30,500 per year), 2 teaching assistantships (averaging $30,500 per year); Federal Work-Study, scholarships/grants, and traineeships also available. Financial award applicants required to submit FAFSA. *Unit head:* Dr. Linda E. Hyman, Associate Provost, 617-638-5255, Fax: 617-638-5740. *Application contact:* Michelle Hall, Associate Director of Admissions, 617-638-5121, Fax: 617-638-5740, E-mail: natashah@bu.edu. Web site: http://www.bumc.bu.edu/gms.

Bowling Green State University, Graduate College, College of Arts and Sciences, Department of Biological Sciences, Bowling Green, OH 43403. Offers MAT, MS, PhD. Part-time programs available. *Degree requirements:* For master's, thesis or alternative; for doctorate, comprehensive exam, thesis/dissertation. *Entrance requirements:* For master's and doctorate, GRE General Test. Additional exam requirements/recommendations for international students: Required—TOEFL. Electronic applications accepted. *Faculty research:* Aquatic ecology, endocrinology and neurophysiology, nitrogen fixation, photosynthesis.

Bradley University, Graduate School, College of Liberal Arts and Sciences, Department of Biology, Peoria, IL 61625-0002. Offers MS. Part-time programs available. *Degree requirements:* For master's, comprehensive exam, thesis. *Entrance requirements:* For master's, GRE General Test, 2 letters of recommendation. Additional exam requirements/recommendations for international students: Required—TOEFL (minimum score 550 paper-based; 213 computer-based).

Brandeis University, Graduate School of Arts and Sciences, Department of Physics, Waltham, MA 02454-9110. Offers physics (MS, PhD); quantitative biology (PhD). Part-time programs available. *Faculty:* 17 full-time (4 women), 2 part-time/adjunct (0 women). *Students:* 44 full-time (8 women); includes 1 minority (Hispanic/Latino), 21 international. 108 applicants, 17% accepted, 10 enrolled. In 2011, 4 master's, 7 doctorates awarded. Terminal master's awarded for partial completion of doctoral program. *Degree requirements:* For master's, thesis optional, qualifying exam, 1-year residency; for doctorate, thesis/dissertation, qualifying and advanced exams; teaching requirement. *Entrance requirements:* For master's and doctorate, GRE General Test; GRE Subject Test (recommended), resume, 2 letters of recommendation, statement of purpose, transcript(s). Additional exam requirements/recommendations for international students: Required—TOEFL (minimum score 600 paper-based; 250 computer-based; 100 iBT); Recommended—IELTS (minimum score 7). *Application deadline:* For fall admission, 1/15 priority date for domestic students. Application fee: $75. Electronic applications accepted. *Financial support:* In 2011–12, 16 fellowships with full tuition reimbursements (averaging $24,480 per year), 28 research assistantships with full tuition reimbursements (averaging $24,480 per year), 4 teaching assistantships with partial tuition reimbursements (averaging $1,250 per year) were awarded; scholarships/grants, health care benefits, and tuition waivers (full and partial) also available. Support available to part-time students. Financial award application deadline: 1/15; financial award applicants required to submit FAFSA. *Faculty research:* Astrophysics, condensed-matter and biophysics, high energy and gravitational theory, particle physics, microfluidics, radio astronomy, string theory. *Unit head:* Dr. John Wardle, Director of Graduate Studies, 781-736-2800, E-mail: wardle@brandeis.edu. *Application contact:* Catherine Broderick, Department Administrator, 781-736-2800, E-mail: cbroderi@brandeis.edu. Web site: http://www.brandeis.edu/gsas.

Brandeis University, Graduate School of Arts and Sciences, Post-Baccalaureate Premedical Program, Waltham, MA 02454-9110. Offers Postbaccalaureate Certificate. Part-time programs available. *Students:* 1 full-time (0 women), 6 part-time (4 women); includes 2 minority (1 Black or African American, non-Hispanic/Latino; 1 Asian, non-Hispanic/Latino). 73 applicants, 36% accepted, 5 enrolled. In 2011, 5 Postbaccalaureate Certificates awarded. *Entrance requirements:* For degree, GRE, ACT, or SAT, resume with paid and/or volunteer work relevant to field of medicine, letters of recommendation, transcript(s), statement of purpose. *Application deadline:* For fall admission, 6/1 for domestic students. Application fee: $75. Electronic applications accepted. *Financial support:* Applicants required to submit FAFSA. *Faculty research:* Health profession preparation, pre-medical, pre-veterinary, pre-dental, pre-optometry, pre-osteopathic. *Unit head:* Judith Hudson, Director of Health Professions Advising, 781-736-3470, Fax: 781-736-3469, E-mail: hudsonj@brandeis.edu. *Application contact:* David Cotter, Assistant Dean, Graduate School of Arts and Sciences, 781-736-3410, E-mail:

BIOLOGY

BOSTON COLLEGE
GRADUATE SCHOOL OF ARTS & SCIENCES

- **Molecular Cell Biology**
- **Neuroscience**
- **Infectious Diseases**
- **Computational Biology & Bioinformatics**
- **Signal Transduction**

To learn more about our PhD program or to apply, please visit:
http://www.bc.edu/schools/cas/biology/graduate_studies.html

gradschool@brandeis.edu. Web site: http://www.brandeis.edu/gsas/programs/premed.html.

Brandeis University, Graduate School of Arts and Sciences, Program in Biochemistry and Biophysics, Waltham, MA 02454. Offers biochemistry and biophysics (PhD); quantitative biology (PhD). Part-time programs available. *Faculty:* 9 full-time (2 women), 1 (woman) part-time/adjunct. *Students:* 31 full-time (12 women); includes 4 minority (3 Asian, non-Hispanic/Latino; 1 Hispanic/Latino), 7 international. 75 applicants, 24% accepted, 4 enrolled. In 2011, 6 doctorates awarded. Terminal master's awarded for partial completion of doctoral program. *Degree requirements:* For doctorate, thesis/dissertation, qualifying exams; teaching requirement. *Entrance requirements:* For doctorate, GRE General Test, resume, 3 letters of recommendation, statement of purpose, transcript(s). Additional exam requirements/recommendations for international students: Required—TOEFL (minimum score 600 paper-based; 250 computer-based; 100 iBT); Recommended—IELTS (minimum score 7). *Application deadline:* For fall admission, 1/15 priority date for domestic students. Application fee: $75. Electronic applications accepted. *Financial support:* In 2011–12, 7 fellowships with full tuition reimbursements (averaging $29,580 per year), 14 research assistantships with full tuition reimbursements (averaging $29,580 per year), teaching assistantships with partial tuition reimbursements (averaging $3,200 per year) were awarded; career-related internships or fieldwork, scholarships/grants, health care benefits, tuition waivers (full and partial), and unspecified assistantships also available. Support available to part-time students. Financial award application deadline: 4/15; financial award applicants required to submit FAFSA. *Faculty research:* Macromolecular chemistry, structure and function, biochemistry, biophysics, biological macromolecules . *Unit head:* Prof. Christopher Miller, Director of Graduate Studies, 781-736-3100, Fax: 781-736-3107, E-mail: cmiller@brandeis.edu. *Application contact:* Carol MacKenzie, Department Administrator, 781-736-3100, Fax: 781-736-3107, E-mail: mackenzie@brandeis.edu. Web site: http://www.brandeis.edu/gsas/programs/bio.html.

Brandeis University, Graduate School of Arts and Sciences, Program in Molecular and Cell Biology, Waltham, MA 02454-9110. Offers genetics (PhD); microbiology (PhD); molecular and cell biology (MS, PhD); molecular biology (PhD); neurobiology (PhD); quantitative biology (PhD). *Faculty:* 27 full-time (11 women), 4 part-time/adjunct (1 woman). *Students:* 65 full-time (36 women); includes 8 minority (4 Black or African American, non-Hispanic/Latino; 1 American Indian or Alaska Native, non-Hispanic/Latino; 1 Asian, non-Hispanic/Latino; 2 Hispanic/Latino), 14 international. 195 applicants, 26% accepted, 21 enrolled. In 2011, 4 master's, 6 doctorates awarded. Terminal master's awarded for partial completion of doctoral program. *Degree requirements:* For master's, thesis or alternative, research project, research lab, or project lab; for doctorate, comprehensive exam, thesis/dissertation, journal clubs; research seminar; colloquia; teaching requirement; qualifying exam. *Entrance requirements:* For master's, GRE General Test; MCAT may be substituted for the GRE exam for applicants to the M.S. program., official transcript(s), resume, 3 letters of recommendation, statement of purpose; for doctorate, GRE General Test, official transcript(s), resume, 3 letters of recommendation, statement of purpose. Additional exam requirements/recommendations for international students: Required—TOEFL (minimum score 600 paper-based; 250 computer-based; 100 iBT); Recommended—IELTS (minimum score 7). *Application deadline:* For fall admission, 1/15 priority date for domestic students; for spring admission, 11/15 for domestic students. Applications are processed on a rolling basis. Application fee: $75. Electronic applications accepted. *Financial support:* In 2011–12, 17 fellowships with full tuition reimbursements (averaging $29,580 per year), 31 research assistantships with full tuition reimbursements (averaging $29,580 per year), teaching assistantships with partial tuition reimbursements (averaging $3,200 per year) were awarded; scholarships/grants, health care benefits, tuition waivers (full and partial), and unspecified assistantships also available. Financial award application deadline: 4/15; financial award applicants required to submit FAFSA. *Faculty research:* Molecular biology, cell biology, biology, structural biology, immunology, developmental biology, neurobiology, DNA, RNA. *Unit head:* Dr. Bruce Goode, Chair, 781-736-2464, Fax: 781-736-3107, E-mail: goode@brandeis.edu. *Application contact:* Dr. Jessica Maryott, Department Administrator, 781-736-3100, Fax: 781-736-3107, E-mail: jmaryott@brandeis.edu. Web site: http://www.bio.brandeis.edu/grad/mcb/mcb_phd.html.

Brandeis University, Graduate School of Arts and Sciences, Program in Neuroscience, Waltham, MA 02454-9110. Offers neuroscience (MS, PhD); quantitative biology (PhD). *Faculty:* 23 full-time (9 women). *Students:* 56 full-time (25 women); includes 13 minority (5 Black or African American, non-Hispanic/Latino; 4 Asian, non-Hispanic/Latino; 4 Hispanic/Latino), 4 international. 141 applicants, 22% accepted, 15 enrolled. In 2011, 10 master's, 6 doctorates awarded. Terminal master's awarded for partial completion of doctoral program. *Degree requirements:* For master's, thesis optional, research project; for doctorate, thesis/dissertation, qualifying exams, teaching experience, journal club, research seminars. *Entrance requirements:* For master's and doctorate, GRE General Test, official transcript(s), statement of purpose, resume, 3 letters of recommendation. Additional exam requirements/recommendations for international students: Required—TOEFL (minimum score 600 paper-based; 250 computer-based; 100 iBT); Recommended—IELTS (minimum score 7). *Application deadline:* For fall admission, 1/15 priority date for domestic students. Applications are processed on a rolling basis. Application fee: $75. Electronic applications accepted. *Financial support:* In 2011–12, 5 fellowships with full tuition reimbursements (averaging $29,580 per year), 32 research assistantships with full tuition reimbursements (averaging $29,580 per year), teaching assistantships with partial tuition reimbursements (averaging $3,200 per year) were awarded; scholarships/grants, health care benefits, tuition waivers (full and partial), and unspecified assistantships also available. Support available to part-time students. Financial award application deadline: 4/15; financial award applicants required to submit FAFSA. *Faculty research:* Behavioral neuroscience, cellular and molecular neuroscience, cognitive neuroscience, computational and integrative neuroscience, systems neuroscience. *Unit head:* Dr. Don Katz, Director of Graduate Studies, 781-736-3100, Fax: 781-736-3107, E-mail: dbkatz@brandeis.edu. *Application contact:* Dr. Maryanna Aldrich, Department Administrator, 781-736-3100, Fax: 781-736-3107, E-mail: maldrich@brandeis.edu. Web site: http://www.brandeis.edu/gsas/programs/neuroscience.html.

Brigham Young University, Graduate Studies, College of Life Sciences, Department of Biology, Provo, UT 84602. Offers biological science education (MS); biology (MS, PhD). *Faculty:* 19 full-time (2 women). *Students:* 35 full-time (12 women); includes 7 minority (2 Asian, non-Hispanic/Latino; 5 Hispanic/Latino). Average age 31. 20 applicants, 75% accepted, 11 enrolled. In 2011, 2 master's, 3 doctorates awarded. *Degree requirements:* For master's, comprehensive exam, thesis, prospectus, defense of research, defense of thesis; for doctorate, comprehensive exam, thesis/dissertation, prospectus, defense of research, defense of dissertation. *Entrance requirements:* For master's and doctorate, GRE General Test, GRE Subject Test (biology), minimum GPA of 3.0 for last 60 credit hours of course work. Additional exam requirements/recommendations for international students: Required—TOEFL (minimum score 580 paper-based; 85 iBT). *Application deadline:* For fall admission, 1/15 for domestic and international students. Application fee: $50. Electronic applications accepted. *Expenses: Tuition:* Full-time $5760; part-time $320 per credit. Tuition and fees vary according to student's religious affiliation. *Financial support:* In 2011–12, 5 fellowships with full and partial tuition reimbursements (averaging $15,000 per year) were awarded; research assistantships with full and partial tuition reimbursements, teaching assistantships with full and partial tuition reimbursements, career-related internships or fieldwork, institutionally sponsored loans, scholarships/grants, health care benefits, tuition waivers (full and partial), and unspecified assistantships also available. Financial award application deadline: 2/1; financial award applicants required to submit FAFSA. *Faculty research:* Systematics, bioinformatics, ecology, evolution. *Total annual research expenditures:* $1.1 million. *Unit head:* Dr. Keith A. Crandall, Chair, 801-422-3495, Fax: 801-422-0090, E-mail: keith_crandall@byu.edu. *Application contact:* Sarah Willardson, Graduate Secretary, 801-422-7137, Fax: 801-422-0090, E-mail: biogradsec@byu.edu. Web site: http://biology.byu.edu/.

Brock University, Faculty of Graduate Studies, Faculty of Mathematics and Science, Program in Biological Sciences, St. Catharines, ON L2S 3A1, Canada. Offers M Sc, PhD. Part-time programs available. *Degree requirements:* For master's, thesis; for doctorate, thesis/dissertation. *Entrance requirements:* For master's, honors B Sc in biology, minimum undergraduate GPA of 3.0; for doctorate, M Sc. Additional exam requirements/recommendations for international students: Required—TOEFL (minimum score 550 paper-based; 213 computer-based; 80 iBT), IELTS (minimum score 6.5), TWE (minimum score 4). Electronic applications accepted. *Faculty research:* Viticulture, neurobiology, ecology, molecular biology, molecular genetics.

Brooklyn College of the City University of New York, Division of Graduate Studies, Department of Biology, Brooklyn, NY 11210-2889. Offers MA, PhD. *Degree requirements:* For master's, one foreign language, comprehensive exam, thesis. *Entrance requirements:* For master's, minimum GPA of 3.0, 2 letters of recommendation. Additional exam requirements/recommendations for international students: Required—TOEFL (minimum score 500 paper-based; 173 computer-based; 61 iBT). Electronic applications accepted. *Faculty research:* Evolutionary biology, molecular biology of development, cell biology, comparative endocrinology, ecology.

Brooklyn College of the City University of New York, Division of Graduate Studies, School of Education, Program in Middle Childhood Education (Science), Brooklyn, NY 11210-2889. Offers biology (MA); chemistry (MA); earth science (MA); general science (MA); physics (MA). Part-time and evening/weekend programs available. *Entrance requirements:* For master's, LAST, interview, previous course work in education and mathematics, resume, 2 letters of recommendation, essay. Additional exam requirements/recommendations for international students: Required—TOEFL (minimum score 500 paper-based; 173 computer-based; 61 iBT). Electronic applications accepted. *Faculty research:* Geometric thinking, mastery of basic facts, problem-solving strategies, history of mathematics.

Brown University, Graduate School, Division of Biology and Medicine, Providence, RI 02912. Offers M Med Sc, MA, MPH, MS, Sc M, PhD, MD/PhD. Part-time programs available. Terminal master's awarded for partial completion of doctoral program. *Degree requirements:* For doctorate, thesis/dissertation. *Entrance requirements:* For master's and doctorate, GRE General Test. Additional exam requirements/recommendations for international students: Required—TOEFL. Electronic applications accepted.

Bucknell University, Graduate Studies, College of Arts and Sciences, Department of Biology, Lewisburg, PA 17837. Offers MS. *Faculty:* 16 full-time (7 women). *Students:* 3 full-time (2 women). In 2011, 2 master's awarded. *Degree requirements:* For master's, thesis. *Entrance requirements:* For master's, GRE General Test, GRE Subject Test, minimum GPA of 3.0. Additional exam requirements/recommendations for international students: Required—TOEFL (minimum score 600 paper-based). *Application deadline:* For fall admission, 2/1 priority date for domestic students, 1/1 for international students. Application fee: $25. *Financial support:* In 2011–12, 3 research assistantships with full tuition reimbursements (averaging $30,000 per year) were awarded; unspecified assistantships also available. Financial award application deadline: 2/1. *Unit head:* Dr. DeeAnn Reeder, Chair, 570-577-1124. *Application contact:* Gretchen H. Fegley, Coordinator, 570-577-3655, Fax: 570-577-3760, E-mail: gfegley@bucknell.edu. Web site: http://www.bucknell.edu/Biology.

Buffalo State College, State University of New York, The Graduate School, Faculty of Natural and Social Sciences, Department of Biology, Buffalo, NY 14222-1095. Offers biology (MA); secondary education (MS Ed), including biology. Evening/weekend programs available. *Degree requirements:* For master's, thesis (for some programs), project. *Entrance requirements:* For master's, minimum GPA of 2.75. Additional exam requirements/recommendations for international students: Required—TOEFL (minimum score 550 paper-based; 213 computer-based).

California Institute of Technology, Division of Biology, Pasadena, CA 91125-0001. Offers biochemistry and molecular biophysics (PhD); cell biology and biophysics (PhD); developmental biology (PhD); genetics (PhD); immunology (PhD); molecular biology (PhD); neurobiology (PhD). *Degree requirements:* For doctorate, thesis/dissertation, qualifying exam. *Entrance requirements:* For doctorate, GRE General Test. Additional exam requirements/recommendations for international students: Required—TOEFL. Electronic applications accepted. *Faculty research:* Molecular genetics of differentiation and development, structure of biological macromolecules, molecular and integrative neurobiology.

California Polytechnic State University, San Luis Obispo, College of Science and Mathematics, Department of Biological Sciences, San Luis Obispo, CA 93407. Offers MA, MS. Part-time programs available. *Faculty:* 3 full-time (2 women). *Students:* 10 full-time (2 women), 19 part-time (11 women); includes 9 minority (1 Asian, non-Hispanic/Latino; 5 Hispanic/Latino; 3 Two or more races, non-Hispanic/Latino). Average age 26. 44 applicants, 45% accepted, 14 enrolled. In 2011, 18 master's awarded. *Degree requirements:* For master's, comprehensive exam (for some programs), thesis (for some programs). *Entrance requirements:* For master's, GRE General Test, minimum GPA of 3.0 in last 90 quarter units. Additional exam requirements/recommendations for international students: Required—TOEFL (minimum score 550 paper-based; 213 computer-based) or IELTS (minimum score 6). *Application deadline:* For fall admission, 2/1 for domestic students, 11/30 for international students. Applications are processed on a rolling basis. Application fee: $55. Electronic applications accepted. *Expenses:* Tuition, state resident: full-time $6738. Tuition, nonresident: full-time $17,898. *Required fees:* $2449. *Financial support:* Fellowships, research assistantships, teaching assistantships, career-related internships or fieldwork, and Federal Work-Study available. Support available to part-time students. Financial award application deadline: 3/2; financial award applicants required to submit FAFSA. *Faculty research:* Ancient fossil DNA, restoration ecology microbe biodiversity indices, biological inventories. *Unit head:* Dr. Emily Taylor, Graduate Coordinator, 805-756-2616, Fax: 805-756-1419, E-mail: etaylor@calpoly.edu. *Application contact:* Dr. James Maraviglia, Associate Vice Provost for Marketing and Enrollment Development, 805-756-2311, Fax: 805-756-5400, E-mail: admissions@calpoly.edu. Web site: http://bio.calpoly.edu/.

California State Polytechnic University, Pomona, Academic Affairs, College of Science, Program in Biological Sciences, Pomona, CA 91768-2557. Offers MS. Part-time programs available. *Students:* 30 full-time (17 women), 38 part-time (23 women); includes 28 minority (2 Black or African American, non-Hispanic/Latino; 14 Asian, non-Hispanic/Latino; 10 Hispanic/Latino; 2 Two or more races, non-Hispanic/Latino), 7 international. Average age 27. 42 applicants, 36% accepted, 10 enrolled. In 2011, 21

master's awarded. *Degree requirements:* For master's, thesis. *Entrance requirements:* For master's, GRE General Test. *Application deadline:* For fall admission, 5/1 priority date for domestic students; for winter admission, 10/15 priority date for domestic students; for spring admission, 1/20 priority date for domestic students. Applications are processed on a rolling basis. Application fee: $55. Electronic applications accepted. *Expenses:* Tuition, state resident: full-time $6738. Tuition, nonresident: full-time $12,300. *Required fees:* $657. Tuition and fees vary according to course load and program. *Financial support:* Career-related internships or fieldwork, Federal Work-Study, and institutionally sponsored loans available. Support available to part-time students. Financial award application deadline: 3/2; financial award applicants required to submit FAFSA. *Unit head:* Dr. Steve Alas, Graduate Coordinator, 909-869-4546, Fax: 909-869-4078, E-mail: alas@csupomona.edu. *Application contact:* Deborah L. Brandon, Executive Director, Admissions and Outreach, 909-869-3427, Fax: 909-869-5315, E-mail: dlbrandon@csupomona.edu. Web site: http://www.csupomona.edu/~biology/gradprog/.

California State University, Bakersfield, Division of Graduate Studies, School of Natural Sciences, Mathematics, and Engineering, Program in Biology, Bakersfield, CA 93311. Offers MS. *Entrance requirements:* For master's, GRE, minimum undergraduate GPA of 3.0 in last 90 quarter units, 3 letters of recommendation. Additional exam requirements/recommendations for international students: Required—TOEFL. *Application deadline:* Applications are processed on a rolling basis. *Expenses: Required fees:* $1302 per unit. Part-time tuition and fees vary according to course load and program. *Financial support:* Teaching assistantships available. *Unit head:* Dr. Anna L. Jacobsen, Graduate Coordinator, 661-654-2572, E-mail: ajacobsen@csub.edu. Web site: http://www.csub.edu/biology/degrees/graduate.shtml.

California State University, Chico, Office of Graduate Studies, College of Natural Sciences, Department of Biological Sciences, Program in Biological Sciences, Chico, CA 95929-0722. Offers MS. *Faculty:* 10 full-time (3 women), 1 part-time/adjunct (0 women). *Students:* 14 full-time (7 women), 10 part-time (6 women); includes 3 minority (1 Asian, non-Hispanic/Latino; 2 Hispanic/Latino). Average age 28. 18 applicants, 67% accepted, 8 enrolled. In 2011, 7 master's awarded. *Degree requirements:* For master's, thesis, oral exam. *Entrance requirements:* For master's, GRE General Test, GRE Subject Test (biology), 2 letters of recommendation, statement of purpose. Additional exam requirements/recommendations for international students: Required—TOEFL (minimum score 550 paper-based; 213 computer-based; 80 iBT), IELTS (minimum score 6.5), Pearson Test of English. *Application deadline:* For fall admission, 3/1 priority date for domestic students, 3/1 for international students; for spring admission, 9/15 priority date for domestic students, 9/15 for international students. Application fee: $55. Electronic applications accepted. Tuition and fees vary according to class time, course load and degree level. *Financial support:* Fellowships, research assistantships, teaching assistantships, career-related internships or fieldwork, and scholarships/grants available. Financial award application deadline: 3/1; financial award applicants required to submit FAFSA. *Unit head:* Dr. Jeffery R. Bell, Chair, 530-898-5356, Fax: 530-898-5060, E-mail: biol@csuchico.edu. *Application contact:* Judy L. Rice, Graduate Admissions Coordinator, 530-898-5416, Fax: 530-898-3342, E-mail: jlrice@csuchico.edu.

California State University, Dominguez Hills, College of Natural and Behavioral Sciences, Department of Biology, Carson, CA 90747-0001. Offers MS. Part-time and evening/weekend programs available. *Faculty:* 10 full-time (2 women), 23 part-time/adjunct (10 women). *Students:* 13 full-time (7 women), 34 part-time (17 women); includes 29 minority (6 Black or African American, non-Hispanic/Latino; 8 Asian, non-Hispanic/Latino; 13 Hispanic/Latino; 2 Two or more races, non-Hispanic/Latino), 4 international. Average age 29. 30 applicants, 60% accepted, 15 enrolled. In 2011, 2 master's awarded. *Degree requirements:* For master's, thesis. *Entrance requirements:* For master's, minimum GPA of 2.75. Additional exam requirements/recommendations for international students: Required—TOEFL (minimum score 550 paper-based). *Application deadline:* For fall admission, 6/1 for domestic students, 5/1 for international students; for spring admission, 12/15 for domestic students, 10/1 for international students. Application fee: $55. Electronic applications accepted. *Faculty research:* Cancer biology, infectious diseases, ecology of native plants, remediation, community ecology. *Unit head:* Dr. John Thomlinson, Chair, 310-243-3381, Fax: 310-243-2350, E-mail: jthomlinson@csudh.edu. *Application contact:* Dr. Getachew Kidane, Graduate Program Coordinator, 310-243-3564, Fax: 310-243-2350, E-mail: gkidane@csudh.edu. Web site: http://www.nbs.csudh.edu/biology.

California State University, East Bay, Office of Academic Programs and Graduate Studies, College of Science, Department of Biological Sciences, Hayward, CA 94542-3000. Offers biological sciences (MA, MS); marine science (MS). Part-time programs available. *Faculty:* 3 full-time (1 woman). *Students:* 21 full-time (18 women), 14 part-time (9 women); includes 8 minority (6 Asian, non-Hispanic/Latino; 2 Hispanic/Latino), 5 international. Average age 28. 63 applicants, 29% accepted, 10 enrolled. In 2011, 20 master's awarded. *Degree requirements:* For master's, thesis. *Entrance requirements:* For master's, GRE General and Subject Tests, minimum GPA of 3.0 in field, 2.75 overall; 3 letters of reference; statement of purpose. Additional exam requirements/recommendations for international students: Required—TOEFL (minimum score 550 paper-based; 213 computer-based). *Application deadline:* For fall admission, 4/15 for domestic and international students. Applications are processed on a rolling basis. Application fee: $55. Electronic applications accepted. *Expenses:* Tuition, state resident: full-time $6738; part-time $1302 per quarter. Tuition, nonresident: full-time $12,690; part-time $2294 per quarter. *Required fees:* $449 per quarter. Tuition and fees vary according to degree level, program and reciprocity agreements. *Financial support:* Fellowships, teaching assistantships, career-related internships or fieldwork, Federal Work-Study, institutionally sponsored loans, and scholarships/grants available. Support available to part-time students. Financial award application deadline: 3/2; financial award applicants required to submit FAFSA. *Unit head:* Dr. Donald Gailey, Chair, 510-885-3471, Fax: 510-885-4747, E-mail: donald.gailey@csueastbay.edu. *Application contact:* Prof. Maria Nieto, Biology Graduate Advisor, 510-885-4757, Fax: 510-885-4747, E-mail: maria.nieto@csueastbay.edu. Web site: http://www20.csueastbay.edu/csci/departments/biology/.

California State University, Fresno, Division of Graduate Studies, College of Science and Mathematics, Department of Biology, Fresno, CA 93740-8027. Offers biology (MA); biotechnology (MBT). Part-time and evening/weekend programs available. *Degree requirements:* For master's, thesis. *Entrance requirements:* For master's, GRE General Test, GRE Subject Test, minimum GPA of 2.5 in last 60 units. Additional exam requirements/recommendations for international students: Required—TOEFL. Electronic applications accepted. *Faculty research:* Genome neuroscience, ecology conflict resolution, biomechanics, cell death, vibrio cholerae.

California State University, Fullerton, Graduate Studies, College of Natural Science and Mathematics, Department of Biological Science, Fullerton, CA 92834-9480. Offers MS. Part-time programs available. *Students:* 32 full-time (17 women), 44 part-time (25 women); includes 29 minority (12 Asian, non-Hispanic/Latino; 14 Hispanic/Latino; 3 Two or more races, non-Hispanic/Latino), 11 international. Average age 27. 111 applicants, 32% accepted, 27 enrolled. In 2011, 11 master's awarded. *Degree requirements:* For master's, thesis. *Entrance requirements:* For master's, GRE General and Subject Tests,

MCAT, or DAT, minimum GPA of 3.0 in biology. Application fee: $55. *Financial support:* Research assistantships, teaching assistantships, career-related internships or fieldwork, Federal Work-Study, institutionally sponsored loans, and scholarships/grants available. Support available to part-time students. Financial award application deadline: 3/1; financial award applicants required to submit FAFSA. *Faculty research:* Glycosidase release and the block to polyspermy in ascidian eggs. *Unit head:* Dr. Katherine Dickson, Acting Chair, 657-278-3614. *Application contact:* Admissions/Applications, 657-278-2371.

California State University, Long Beach, Graduate Studies, College of Natural Sciences and Mathematics, Department of Biological Sciences, Long Beach, CA 90840. Offers biology (MS); microbiology (MS). Part-time programs available. *Faculty:* 23 full-time (8 women). *Students:* 8 full-time (4 women), 56 part-time (31 women); includes 24 minority (1 Black or African American, non-Hispanic/Latino; 8 Asian, non-Hispanic/Latino; 9 Hispanic/Latino; 6 Two or more races, non-Hispanic/Latino), 4 international. Average age 27. 79 applicants, 25% accepted, 13 enrolled. In 2011, 19 master's awarded. *Entrance requirements:* For master's, GRE Subject Test, minimum GPA of 3.0. *Application deadline:* For fall admission, 3/15 for domestic students. Applications are processed on a rolling basis. Application fee: $55. Electronic applications accepted. *Financial support:* Teaching assistantships, Federal Work-Study, institutionally sponsored loans, scholarships/grants, traineeships, and unspecified assistantships available. Financial award application deadline: 3/2. *Unit head:* Dr. Brian Livingston, Chair, 562-985-4807, Fax: 562-985-8878, E-mail: blivings@csulb.edu. *Application contact:* Dr. Christopher Lowe, Graduate Advisor, 562-985-4918, Fax: 562-985-8878, E-mail: clowe@csulb.edu.

California State University, Los Angeles, Graduate Studies, College of Natural and Social Sciences, Department of Biological Sciences, Los Angeles, CA 90032-8530. Offers biology (MS). Part-time and evening/weekend programs available. *Faculty:* 3 full-time (all women), 7 part-time/adjunct (4 women). *Students:* 42 full-time (21 women), 36 part-time (22 women); includes 60 minority (8 Black or African American, non-Hispanic/Latino; 22 Asian, non-Hispanic/Latino; 28 Hispanic/Latino; 2 Two or more races, non-Hispanic/Latino), 4 international. Average age 27. 271 applicants, 31% accepted, 49 enrolled. In 2011, 22 master's awarded. *Degree requirements:* For master's, comprehensive exam or thesis. *Entrance requirements:* Additional exam requirements/recommendations for international students: Required—TOEFL (minimum score 500 paper-based; 173 computer-based). *Application deadline:* For fall admission, 5/1 for domestic and international students. Applications are processed on a rolling basis. Application fee: $55. *Expenses:* Tuition, state resident: full-time $8225. *Financial support:* Federal Work-Study available. Support available to part-time students. Financial award application deadline: 3/1. *Faculty research:* Ecology, environmental biology, cell and molecular biology, physiology, medical microbiology. *Unit head:* Dr. Nancy McQueen, Chair, 323-343-2050, Fax: 323-343-6451, E-mail: nmcquee@exchange.calstatela.edu. *Application contact:* Dr. Karin Brown, Acting Associate Dean of Graduate Studies, 323-343-3820, Fax: 323-343-5653, E-mail: kbrown5@calstatela.edu. Web site: http://www.calstatela.edu/academic/biol/.

California State University, Northridge, Graduate Studies, College of Science and Mathematics, Department of Biology, Northridge, CA 91330. Offers MS. *Degree requirements:* For master's, thesis, seminar. *Entrance requirements:* For master's, GRE Subject Test, GRE General Test. Additional exam requirements/recommendations for international students: Required—TOEFL. *Faculty research:* Cell adhesion, cancer research, fishery research.

California State University, Sacramento, Office of Graduate Studies, College of Natural Sciences and Mathematics, Department of Biological Sciences, Sacramento, CA 95819-6077. Offers biological sciences (MA, MS); immunohematology (MS); marine science (MS). Part-time programs available. *Faculty:* 22 full-time (10 women), 24 part-time/adjunct (11 women). *Students:* 13 full-time, 50 part-time; includes 16 minority (7 Asian, non-Hispanic/Latino; 4 Hispanic/Latino; 4 Native Hawaiian or other Pacific Islander, non-Hispanic/Latino; 1 Two or more races, non-Hispanic/Latino), 2 international. Average age 30. 85 applicants, 40% accepted, 25 enrolled. In 2011, 23 master's awarded. *Degree requirements:* For master's, thesis, writing proficiency exam. *Entrance requirements:* For master's, GRE, bachelor's degree in biology or equivalent; minimum GPA of 3.0 in biology, 2.75 overall during last 2 years of course work. Additional exam requirements/recommendations for international students: Required—TOEFL. *Application deadline:* For fall admission, 2/1 for domestic students, 3/1 for international students; for spring admission, 9/30 for international students. Applications are processed on a rolling basis. Application fee: $55. Electronic applications accepted. *Financial support:* Research assistantships, teaching assistantships, career-related internships or fieldwork, and Federal Work-Study available. Support available to part-time students. Financial award application deadline: 3/1; financial award applicants required to submit FAFSA. *Unit head:* Jennifer Lundmark, Chair, 916-278-7676, Fax: 916-278-6993, E-mail: lundmark@csus.edu. *Application contact:* Jose Martinez, Outreach and Graduate Diversity Coordinator, 916-278-6470, Fax: 916-278-5669, E-mail: martinj@skymail.csus.edu. Web site: http://www.csus.edu/bios.

California State University, San Bernardino, Graduate Studies, College of Natural Sciences, Department of Biology, San Bernardino, CA 92407-2397. Offers MS. Part-time programs available. *Students:* 19 full-time (12 women), 4 part-time (3 women); includes 10 minority (1 Black or African American, non-Hispanic/Latino; 3 Asian, non-Hispanic/Latino; 6 Hispanic/Latino). Average age 26. 32 applicants, 34% accepted, 6 enrolled. In 2011, 3 master's awarded. *Degree requirements:* For master's, thesis or alternative, advancement to candidacy. *Entrance requirements:* For master's, minimum GPA of 3.0. *Application deadline:* For fall admission, 8/31 priority date for domestic students. Application fee: $55. *Expenses:* Tuition, state resident: full-time $7356. Tuition, nonresident: full-time $7356. *Required fees:* $1077. Tuition and fees vary according to program. *Financial support:* Fellowships, research assistantships, teaching assistantships, and career-related internships or fieldwork available. *Faculty research:* Ecology, molecular biology, physiology, cell biology, neurobiology. *Unit head:* Dr. David M. Polcyn, Chair, 909-537-5313, Fax: 909-537-7038, E-mail: dpolcyn@csusb.edu. *Application contact:* Sandra Kamusikiri, Associate Vice-President/Dean of Graduate Studies, 909-537-5058, E-mail: skamusik@csusb.edu.

California State University, San Marcos, College of Arts and Sciences, Program in Biological Sciences, San Marcos, CA 92096-0001. Offers MS. Part-time programs available. *Degree requirements:* For master's, thesis. *Entrance requirements:* For master's, GRE Subject Test, minimum GPA of 2.7 in mathematics and science or minimum GPA of 3.0 in the last 35 units of mathematics and science. *Faculty research:* Gene regulation of life states, carbon cycling, genetic markers of viral infection, neurobiology.

Carleton University, Faculty of Graduate Studies, Faculty of Science, Department of Biology, Ottawa, ON K1S 5B6, Canada. Offers M Sc, PhD. Programs offered jointly with University of Ottawa. *Degree requirements:* For master's, thesis, seminar; for doctorate, comprehensive exam, thesis/dissertation, seminar. *Entrance requirements:* For master's, honors degree in science; for doctorate, M Sc. Additional exam requirements/recommendations for international students: Required—TOEFL. *Faculty research:* Biochemical, structural, and genetic regulation in cells; behavioral ecology; insect taxonomy; physiology of cells.

Biological and Biomedical Sciences—General

Carnegie Mellon University, Mellon College of Science, Department of Biological Sciences, Pittsburgh, PA 15213-3891. Offers biochemistry (PhD); biophysics (PhD); cell biology (PhD); computational biology (MS, PhD); developmental biology (PhD); genetics (PhD); molecular biology (PhD); neuroscience (PhD). *Degree requirements:* For doctorate, comprehensive exam, thesis/dissertation. *Entrance requirements:* For doctorate, GRE General Test, GRE Subject Test, interview. Electronic applications accepted. *Faculty research:* Genetic structure, function, and regulation; protein structure and function; biological membranes; biological spectroscopy.

Case Western Reserve University, School of Graduate Studies, Department of Biology, Cleveland, OH 44106. Offers MS, PhD. Part-time programs available. *Faculty:* 23 full-time (9 women). *Students:* 69 full-time (32 women), 13 part-time (4 women); includes 13 minority (4 Black or African American, non-Hispanic/Latino; 7 Asian, non-Hispanic/Latino; 2 Hispanic/Latino), 30 international. Average age 26. 131 applicants, 35% accepted, 29 enrolled. In 2011, 18 master's, 5 doctorates awarded. Terminal master's awarded for partial completion of doctoral program. *Degree requirements:* For master's, thesis or alternative; for doctorate, thesis/dissertation. *Entrance requirements:* For master's and doctorate, GRE General Test, GRE Subject Test. Additional exam requirements/recommendations for international students: Required—TOEFL (minimum score 577 paper-based; 213 computer-based; 90 iBT); Recommended—IELTS (minimum score 7). *Application deadline:* For fall admission, 1/7 priority date for domestic students. Applications are processed on a rolling basis. Application fee: $50. Electronic applications accepted. *Financial support:* Fellowships, research assistantships, teaching assistantships, career-related internships or fieldwork, Federal Work-Study, tuition waivers, and unspecified assistantships available. Financial award application deadline: 2/15; financial award applicants required to submit FAFSA. *Faculty research:* Cellular, developmental, and molecular biology; genetics; genetic engineering; biotechnology; ecology. *Unit head:* Christopher Cullis, Chairman, 216-368-3557, Fax: 216-368-4762, E-mail: christopher.cullis@case.edu. *Application contact:* Julia Brown, Program Coordinator, 216-368-3556, Fax: 216-368-4672, E-mail: jab12@case.edu. Web site: http://www.case.edu/artsci/biol/.

Case Western Reserve University, School of Medicine and School of Graduate Studies, Graduate Programs in Medicine, Biomedical Sciences Training Program, Cleveland, OH 44106. Offers PhD. *Degree requirements:* For doctorate, thesis/dissertation. *Entrance requirements:* For doctorate, GRE General Test. Additional exam requirements/recommendations for international students: Required—TOEFL. Electronic applications accepted. *Faculty research:* Biochemistry, molecular biology, immunology, genetics, neurosciences.

Case Western Reserve University, School of Medicine and School of Graduate Studies, Graduate Programs in Medicine, Department of Biochemistry, Program in RNA Biology, Cleveland, OH 44106. Offers PhD. *Degree requirements:* For doctorate, comprehensive exam, thesis/dissertation. *Entrance requirements:* For doctorate, GRE. Additional exam requirements/recommendations for international students: Required—TOEFL (minimum score 550 paper-based; 213 computer-based).

Case Western Reserve University, School of Medicine, Medical Scientist Training Program, Cleveland, OH 44106. Offers MD/PhD. Electronic applications accepted. *Faculty research:* Biomedical research.

The Catholic University of America, School of Arts and Sciences, Department of Biology, Washington, DC 20064. Offers cell and microbial biology (MS, PhD), including cell biology, microbiology; clinical laboratory science (MS, PhD); MSLS/MS. Part-time programs available. *Faculty:* 9 full-time (5 women), 3 part-time/adjunct (2 women). *Students:* 19 full-time (16 women), 26 part-time (17 women); includes 10 minority (3 Black or African American, non-Hispanic/Latino; 6 Asian, non-Hispanic/Latino; 1 Hispanic/Latino), 20 international. Average age 29. 53 applicants, 62% accepted, 15 enrolled. In 2011, 1 master's, 2 doctorates awarded. *Degree requirements:* For master's, comprehensive exam, thesis or alternative; for doctorate, comprehensive exam, thesis/dissertation. *Entrance requirements:* For master's and doctorate, GRE General Test, GRE Subject Test, statement of purpose, official copies of academic transcripts, three letters of recommendation. Additional exam requirements/recommendations for international students: Required—TOEFL (minimum score 580 paper-based; 237 computer-based). *Application deadline:* For fall admission, 8/1 priority date for domestic students, 7/15 for international students; for spring admission, 12/1 priority date for domestic students, 10/15 for international students. Applications are processed on a rolling basis. Application fee: $55. Electronic applications accepted. *Expenses: Tuition:* Full-time $35,260; part-time $1380 per credit. *Required fees:* $80; $40 per semester hour. One-time fee: $425. *Financial support:* Fellowships, research assistantships, teaching assistantships, Federal Work-Study, scholarships/grants, tuition waivers (full and partial), and unspecified assistantships available. Financial award application deadline: 2/1; financial award applicants required to submit FAFSA. *Faculty research:* Cell and microbiology, molecular biology of cell proliferation, cellular effects of electromagnetic radiation, biotechnology. *Total annual research expenditures:* $1.4 million. *Unit head:* Dr. Venigalla Rao, Chair, 202-319-5271, Fax: 202-319-5721, E-mail: rao@cua.edu. *Application contact:* Andrew Woodall, Director of Graduate Admissions, 202-319-5057, Fax: 202-319-6533, E-mail: cua-admissions@cua.edu. Web site: http://biology.cua.edu/.

Cedars-Sinai Medical Center, Graduate Program in Biomedical Sciences and Translational Medicine, Los Angeles, CA 90048. Offers PhD. *Degree requirements:* For doctorate, comprehensive exam, thesis/dissertation. *Entrance requirements:* For doctorate, GRE, 3 letters of recommendation. Additional exam requirements/recommendations for international students: Required—TOEFL (minimum score 560 paper-based; 220 computer-based; 87 iBT). *Faculty research:* Immunology and infection, neuroscience, cardiovascular science, cancer, human genetics.

Central Connecticut State University, School of Graduate Studies, School of Arts and Sciences, Department of Biology, New Britain, CT 06050-4010. Offers biological sciences (MA, MS), including anesthesia (MS), ecology and environmental sciences (MA), general biology (MA), health sciences specialization (MS), professional education program (MS); biology (Certificate). Part-time and evening/weekend programs available. *Faculty:* 13 full-time (5 women), 6 part-time/adjunct (5 women). *Students:* 133 full-time (74 women), 40 part-time (27 women); includes 35 minority (9 Black or African American, non-Hispanic/Latino; 1 American Indian or Alaska Native, non-Hispanic/Latino; 11 Asian, non-Hispanic/Latino; 11 Hispanic/Latino; 3 Two or more races, non-Hispanic/Latino). Average age 31. 25 applicants, 60% accepted, 8 enrolled. In 2011, 40 master's, 4 other advanced degrees awarded. *Degree requirements:* For master's, comprehensive exam, thesis or alternative; for Certificate, qualifying exam. *Entrance requirements:* For master's, minimum undergraduate GPA of 2.7, essay. Additional exam requirements/recommendations for international students: Required—TOEFL (minimum score 550 paper-based; 213 computer-based). *Application deadline:* For fall admission, 6/1 for domestic students, 5/1 for international students; for spring admission, 11/1 for domestic and international students. Applications are processed on a rolling basis. Application fee: $50. Electronic applications accepted. *Expenses: Tuition, area resident:* Full-time $5137; part-time $482 per credit. Tuition, state resident: full-time $7707; part-time $494 per credit. Tuition, nonresident: full-time $14,311; part-time $494 per credit. *Required fees:* $3865. One-time fee: $62 part-time. *Financial support:* In 2011–12, 6 students received support, including 3 research assistantships; career-related internships or fieldwork, Federal Work-Study, scholarships/grants, and unspecified assistantships also available. Support available to part-time students. Financial award application deadline: 4/15; financial award applicants required to submit FAFSA. *Faculty research:* Environmental science, anesthesia, health sciences, zoology, animal behavior. *Unit head:* Dr. Jeremiah Jarrett, Chair, 860-832-2645, E-mail: jarrettj@ccsu.edu. *Application contact:* Patricia Gardner, Associate Director of Graduate Studies, 860-832-2350, Fax: 860-832-2352, E-mail: graduateadmissions@ccsu.edu. Web site: http://www.biology.ccsu.edu/.

Central Michigan University, College of Graduate Studies, College of Science and Technology, Department of Biology, Mount Pleasant, MI 48859. Offers biology (MS); conservation biology (MS). Part-time programs available. *Degree requirements:* For master's, thesis or alternative. *Entrance requirements:* For master's, GRE, bachelor's degree with a major in biological science, minimum GPA of 3.0. Electronic applications accepted. *Faculty research:* Conservation biology, morphology and taxonomy of aquatic plants, molecular biology and genetics, microbials and invertebrate ecology, vertebrates.

Central Washington University, Graduate Studies and Research, College of the Sciences, Department of Biological Sciences, Ellensburg, WA 98926. Offers MS. Part-time programs available. *Faculty:* 26 full-time (9 women). *Students:* 22 full-time (12 women), 5 part-time (0 women); includes 4 minority (3 Asian, non-Hispanic/Latino; 1 Hispanic/Latino). 16 applicants, 63% accepted, 10 enrolled. In 2011, 9 master's awarded. *Degree requirements:* For master's, thesis. *Entrance requirements:* For master's, GRE General Test, minimum GPA of 3.0. Additional exam requirements/recommendations for international students: Required—TOEFL (minimum score 550 paper-based; 213 computer-based; 79 iBT). *Application deadline:* For fall admission, 2/1 priority date for domestic students; for winter admission, 10/1 for domestic students; for spring admission, 1/1 for domestic students. Applications are processed on a rolling basis. Application fee: $50. Electronic applications accepted. *Expenses:* Tuition, state resident: full-time $8112; part-time $270 per credit. Tuition, nonresident: full-time $18,069; part-time $602 per credit. *Required fees:* $924. *Financial support:* In 2011–12, 6 research assistantships with full and partial tuition reimbursements (averaging $9,234 per year), 12 teaching assistantships with full and partial tuition reimbursements (averaging $9,234 per year) were awarded; Federal Work-Study and health care benefits also available. Financial award application deadline: 3/1; financial award applicants required to submit FAFSA. *Unit head:* Dr. Jim Johnson, Program Director, 509-963-2876, E-mail: jjohnson@cwu.edu. *Application contact:* Justine Eason, Admissions Program Coordinator, 509-963-3103, Fax: 509-963-1799, E-mail: masters@cwu.edu.

Chatham University, Program in Biology, Pittsburgh, PA 15232-2826. Offers environmental biology-non-thesis track (MS); environmental biology-thesis track (MS); human biology-non-thesis track (MS); human biology-thesis track (MS). Part-time programs available. *Students:* 31 full-time (21 women), 6 part-time (all women); includes 6 minority (1 Black or African American, non-Hispanic/Latino; 1 American Indian or Alaska Native, non-Hispanic/Latino; 2 Asian, non-Hispanic/Latino; 2 Two or more races, non-Hispanic/Latino), 4 international. Average age 26. 71 applicants, 62% accepted, 22 enrolled. In 2011, 8 master's awarded. *Degree requirements:* For master's, thesis optional. *Entrance requirements:* For master's, 3 letters of recommendation. Additional exam requirements/recommendations for international students: Required—TOEFL (minimum score 600 paper-based; 250 computer-based; 100 iBT), IELTS (minimum score 7), TWE. *Application deadline:* For fall admission, 4/1 priority date for domestic students, 4/1 for international students; for spring admission, 11/1 priority date for domestic students, 10/1 for international students. Applications are processed on a rolling basis. Application fee: $45. Electronic applications accepted. Application fee is waived when completed online. *Expenses: Tuition:* Full-time $13,896. Tuition and fees vary according to program. *Financial support:* Applicants required to submit FAFSA. *Faculty research:* Molecular evolution of iron homeostasis, characteristics of soil bacterial communities, gene flow through seed movement, role of gonadotropins in spermatogonial proliferation, phosphatid/linositol metabolism in epithelial cells. *Unit head:* Dr. Lisa Lambert, Director, 412-365-1217, E-mail: lambert@chatham.edu. *Application contact:* Ashlee Bartko, Senior Assistant Director of Graduate Admission, 412-365-1115, Fax: 412-365-1609, E-mail: gradadmissions@chatham.edu. Web site: http://www.chatham.edu/departments/sciences/graduate/biology.

Chicago State University, School of Graduate and Professional Studies, College of Arts and Sciences, Department of Biological Sciences, Chicago, IL 60628. Offers MS. Part-time and evening/weekend programs available. *Degree requirements:* For master's, thesis. *Entrance requirements:* For master's, minimum GPA of 2.75, 15 credit hours in biological sciences. *Faculty research:* Molecular genetics of gene complexes, mammalian immune cell function, genetics of agriculturally important microbes, environmental toxicology, neuromuscular physiology.

The Citadel, The Military College of South Carolina, Citadel Graduate College, Department of Biology, Charleston, SC 29409. Offers MA. *Accreditation:* NCATE. Part-time and evening/weekend programs available. *Faculty:* 4 full-time (1 woman). *Students:* 4 full-time (2 women), 16 part-time (7 women); includes 3 minority (all Black or African American, non-Hispanic/Latino). Average age 28. In 2011, 8 master's awarded. *Entrance requirements:* For master's, GRE (minimum score 900) or MAT (minimum score 396), minimum undergraduate GPA of 2.5. Additional exam requirements/recommendations for international students: Required—TOEFL (minimum score 550 paper-based; 213 computer-based). *Application deadline:* Applications are processed on a rolling basis. Application fee: $30. Electronic applications accepted. *Expenses: Tuition, area resident:* Part-time $501 per credit hour. Tuition, state resident: part-time $501 per credit hour. Tuition, nonresident: part-time $824 per credit hour. *Required fees:* $40 per term. One-time fee: $30. *Financial support:* Health care benefits and unspecified assistantships available. Support available to part-time students. Financial award application deadline: 7/1; financial award applicants required to submit FAFSA. *Faculty research:* Genetic control of parasite-host interactions, mechanisms of development of antibiotic resistance in pseudomonas aeruginosa, interaction of visual and vocal signals in avian mate choice and competition, effects of pollutants on salt marsh animals, structure and function of mitochondrial histone H3 protein, development of cardiac conduction tissue in tadpoles with left-right axis perturbation, evolution and ecology of barnacles and marine hosts. *Unit head:* Dr. John E. Weinstein, Department Head, 843-953-5203, Fax: 843-953-7264, E-mail: john.weinstein@citadel.edu. *Application contact:* Dr. Steve A. Nida, Associate Provost, The Citadel Graduate College, 843-953-5089, Fax: 843-953-7630, E-mail: cgc@citadel.edu. Web site: http://www.citadel.edu/root/ssm-biology.

City College of the City University of New York, Graduate School, College of Liberal Arts and Science, Division of Science, Department of Biology, New York, NY 10031-9198. Offers MA, PhD. PhD program offered jointly with Graduate School and University Center of the City University of New York. Part-time programs available. Terminal master's awarded for partial completion of doctoral program. *Degree requirements:* For master's, thesis or alternative; for doctorate, one foreign language, thesis/dissertation, teaching experience. *Entrance requirements:* For doctorate, GRE General Test. Additional exam requirements/recommendations for international students: Required—TOEFL (minimum score 500 paper-based; 61 iBT). Electronic applications accepted. *Faculty research:* Animal behavior, ecology, genetics, neurobiology, molecular biology.

Clark Atlanta University, School of Arts and Sciences, Department of Biology, Atlanta, GA 30314. Offers MS, PhD. Part-time programs available. *Faculty:* 5 full-time (2 women). *Students:* 12 full-time (9 women), 10 part-time (8 women); includes 18 minority (16 Black or African American, non-Hispanic/Latino; 2 Asian, non-Hispanic/Latino), 4 international. Average age 28. 13 applicants, 92% accepted, 7 enrolled. In 2011, 2 master's, 3 doctorates awarded. Terminal master's awarded for partial completion of doctoral program. *Degree requirements:* For master's, one foreign language, thesis; for doctorate, 2 foreign languages, thesis/dissertation. *Entrance requirements:* For master's, GRE General Test, minimum GPA of 2.5; for doctorate, GRE General Test, minimum graduate GPA of 3.0. Additional exam requirements/recommendations for international students: Required—TOEFL (minimum score 500 paper-based; 173 computer-based; 61 iBT). *Application deadline:* For fall admission, 4/1 for domestic and international students; for spring admission, 11/1 for domestic and international students. Applications are processed on a rolling basis. Application fee: $40 ($55 for international students). Electronic applications accepted. *Expenses: Tuition:* Full-time $13,572; part-time $754 per credit hour. *Required fees:* $806; $403 per semester. *Financial support:* In 2011–12, 6 research assistantships were awarded; career-related internships or fieldwork, Federal Work-Study, scholarships/grants, traineeships, and unspecified assistantships also available. Support available to part-time students. Financial award application deadline: 4/30; financial award applicants required to submit FAFSA. *Faculty research:* Regulation of amino-DNA, cellular regulations. *Unit head:* Dr. Marjorie Campbell, Chairperson, 404-880-6190, E-mail: mcampbell@cau.edu. *Application contact:* Michelle Clark-Davis, Graduate Program Admissions, 404-880-6605, E-mail: cauadmissions@cau.edu.

Clark University, Graduate School, Department of Biology, Worcester, MA 01610-1477. Offers MA, PhD. PhD program offered jointly with University of Massachusetts Worcester. *Faculty:* 11 full-time (4 women). *Students:* 32 full-time (18 women), 1 part-time (0 women); includes 4 minority (2 Asian, non-Hispanic/Latino; 2 Hispanic/Latino), 9 international. Average age 28. 51 applicants, 35% accepted, 17 enrolled. In 2011, 2 master's, 12 doctorates awarded. *Degree requirements:* For master's, thesis; for doctorate, thesis/dissertation. *Entrance requirements:* For master's and doctorate, GRE General Test. Additional exam requirements/recommendations for international students: Required—TOEFL. *Application deadline:* For fall admission, 2/15 priority date for domestic students. Applications are processed on a rolling basis. Application fee: $50. Electronic applications accepted. *Expenses: Tuition:* Full-time $37,000; part-time $1156 per credit hour. *Financial support:* In 2011–12, 6 research assistantships with full tuition reimbursements (averaging $19,825 per year), 13 teaching assistantships with full tuition reimbursements (averaging $19,825 per year) were awarded; fellowships, scholarships/grants, and tuition waivers (full and partial) also available. *Faculty research:* Nitrogen assimilation in marine algae, polyporale taxonomies, fungal evolutionary history, drug discovery, taste sensitivities, biodiversity inventories. *Total annual research expenditures:* $900,000. *Unit head:* Dr. Todd Lidvdahl, Chair, 508-793-7173. *Application contact:* Bogna Sowinska, Department Secretary, 528-793-7173, Fax: 528-793-8861, E-mail: biology@clarku.edu. Web site: http://www.clarku.edu/departments/biology/phd/index.cfm.

Clemson University, Graduate School, College of Agriculture, Forestry and Life Sciences, Department of Biological Sciences, Program in Biological Sciences, Clemson, SC 29634. Offers MS, PhD. *Students:* 38 full-time (24 women), 37 part-time (25 women); includes 6 minority (3 Black or African American, non-Hispanic/Latino; 2 Asian, non-Hispanic/Latino; 1 Hispanic/Latino), 9 international. Average age 34. 72 applicants, 43% accepted, 23 enrolled. In 2011, 6 master's, 2 doctorates awarded. *Degree requirements:* For master's, thesis optional; for doctorate, comprehensive exam, thesis/dissertation. *Entrance requirements:* For master's and doctorate, GRE General Test. Additional exam requirements/recommendations for international students: Required—TOEFL, IELTS. *Application deadline:* For fall admission, 1/15 for domestic students, 4/15 for international students. Applications are processed on a rolling basis. Application fee: $70 ($80 for international students). Electronic applications accepted. *Financial support:* In 2011–12, 29 students received support, including 5 fellowships with full and partial tuition reimbursements available (averaging $7,200 per year), 15 research assistantships with partial tuition reimbursements available (averaging $12,300 per year), 25 teaching assistantships with partial tuition reimbursements available (averaging $13,540 per year); career-related internships or fieldwork, institutionally sponsored loans, scholarships/grants, health care benefits, and unspecified assistantships also available. Support available to part-time students. Financial award application deadline: 3/15; financial award applicants required to submit FAFSA. *Unit head:* Dr. Alfred Wheeler, Department Chair, 864-656-1415, Fax: 864-656-0435, E-mail: wheeler@clemson.edu. *Application contact:* Jay Lyn Martin, Coordinator for Graduate Program, 864-656-3587, Fax: 864-656-0435, E-mail: gradbio@clemson.edu. Web site: http://www.clemson.edu/cafls/departments/biosci/.

Cleveland State University, College of Graduate Studies, College of Sciences and Health Professions, Department of Biological, Geological, and Environmental Sciences, Cleveland, OH 44115. Offers biology (MS); environmental science (MS); museum studies for natural historians (MS); regulatory biology (PhD); JD/MS. Part-time programs available. *Faculty:* 11 full-time (3 women), 1 part-time/adjunct (0 women). *Students:* 17 full-time (9 women), 83 part-time (50 women); includes 8 minority (4 Black or African American, non-Hispanic/Latino; 2 Asian, non-Hispanic/Latino; 2 Hispanic/Latino), 42 international. Average age 30. 97 applicants, 33% accepted, 18 enrolled. In 2011, 9 master's, 8 doctorates awarded. Terminal master's awarded for partial completion of doctoral program. *Degree requirements:* For master's, comprehensive exam (for some programs), thesis (for some programs); for doctorate, comprehensive exam, thesis/dissertation. *Entrance requirements:* For master's, GRE General Test, 2 letters of recommendation; for doctorate, GRE General Test, 2 letters of recommendation; 1-2 page essay; statement of career goals and research interests. Additional exam requirements/recommendations for international students: Required—TOEFL (minimum score 525 paper-based; 197 computer-based). *Application deadline:* For fall admission, 4/1 priority date for domestic students, 4/1 for international students; for spring admission, 12/1 priority date for domestic students. Applications are processed on a rolling basis. Application fee: $30. Electronic applications accepted. *Expenses:* Tuition, state resident: full-time $6416; part-time $494 per credit hour. Tuition, nonresident: full-time $12,074; part-time $929 per credit hour. *Financial support:* In 2011–12, 29 students received support, including research assistantships with full and partial tuition reimbursements available (averaging $16,500 per year), teaching assistantships with full and partial tuition reimbursements available (averaging $16,500 per year); institutionally sponsored loans and unspecified assistantships also available. *Faculty research:* Molecular and cell biology, immunology, urban ecology. *Unit head:* Dr. Jeffrey Dean, Chair, 216-687-2120, Fax: 216-687-6972, E-mail: j.dean@csuohio.edu. *Application contact:* Dr. Deborah L. Brown, Interim Assistant Director, Graduate Admissions, 216-523-7572, Fax: 216-687-5400, E-mail: d.l.brown@csuohio.edu. Web site: http://www.csuohio.edu/sciences/dept/biology/index.html.

Cold Spring Harbor Laboratory, Watson School of Biological Sciences, Graduate Program, Cold Spring Harbor, NY 11724. Offers biological sciences (PhD). *Faculty:* 44 full-time (8 women). *Students:* 52 full-time (22 women); includes 8 minority (2 Black or African American, non-Hispanic/Latino; 2 Asian, non-Hispanic/Latino; 2 Hispanic/Latino; 1 Native Hawaiian or other Pacific Islander, non-Hispanic/Latino; 1 Two or more races, non-Hispanic/Latino), 30 international. Average age 23. 256 applicants, 10% accepted, 10 enrolled. In 2011, 2 doctorates awarded. *Degree requirements:* For doctorate, comprehensive exam, thesis/dissertation, lab rotations, teaching experience, qualifying exam, postdoctoral proposals. *Entrance requirements:* Additional exam requirements/recommendations for international students: Required—TOEFL. *Application deadline:* For fall admission, 12/1 for domestic and international students. Application fee: $60. Electronic applications accepted. *Financial support:* In 2011–12, 52 students received support, including 52 fellowships with full tuition reimbursements available (averaging $30,500 per year); health care benefits and tuition waivers (full) also available. Financial award application deadline: 12/1. *Faculty research:* Genetics, neurobiology, cancer, plant, molecular, cellular, quantitative and structural biology. *Unit head:* Dr. Leemor Joshua-Tor, Dean, 516-367-6890, Fax: 516-367-6919, E-mail: gradschool@cshl.edu. *Application contact:* Dawn Pologruto, Director of Admissions and Student Affairs, 516-367-6911, Fax: 516-367-6919, E-mail: gradschool@cshl.edu. Web site: http://gradschool.cshl.edu.

See Display on next page and Close-Up on page 107.

The College at Brockport, State University of New York, School of Science and Mathematics, Department of Biology, Brockport, NY 14420-2997. Offers MS, PSM. Part-time programs available. *Students:* 14 full-time (8 women), 3 part-time (2 women); includes 2 minority (1 Black or African American, non-Hispanic/Latino; 1 Hispanic/Latino). 12 applicants, 67% accepted, 7 enrolled. In 2011, 5 master's awarded. *Degree requirements:* For master's, comprehensive exam, thesis or alternative. *Entrance requirements:* For master's, GRE General or Subject Test (biology, biochemistry, cell and molecular biology), letters of recommendation, minimum GPA of 3.0, scientific writing sample, statement of objectives. Additional exam requirements/recommendations for international students: Required—TOEFL (minimum score 550 paper-based; 213 computer-based; 79 iBT). *Application deadline:* For fall admission, 7/15 priority date for domestic students, 7/15 for international students; for spring admission, 11/15 priority date for domestic students, 11/15 for international students. Application fee: $50. Electronic applications accepted. *Financial support:* In 2011–12, 8 teaching assistantships with full tuition reimbursements (averaging $6,000 per year) were awarded; Federal Work-Study, scholarships/grants, and unspecified assistantships also available. Support available to part-time students. Financial award application deadline: 3/15; financial award applicants required to submit FAFSA. *Faculty research:* Microbiology, molecular genetics, cellular biology developmental biology, animal physiology. *Unit head:* Dr. Rey Sia, Chairperson, 585-395-2783, Fax: 585-395-2741, E-mail: rsia@brockport.edu. *Application contact:* Dr. Huey Hing, Graduate Program Director, 585-395-5742, Fax: 585-395-2741, E-mail: hhing@brockport.edu. Web site: http://www.brockport.edu/graduate/.

College of Staten Island of the City University of New York, Graduate Programs, Program in Biology, Staten Island, NY 10314-6600. Offers MS. Part-time programs available. *Faculty:* 6 full-time (4 women), 4 part-time/adjunct (1 woman). *Students:* 6. Average age 29. 11 applicants, 27% accepted, 3 enrolled. In 2011, 2 master's awarded. *Entrance requirements:* For master's, GRE General Test, GRE Subject Test (biology), minimum GPA of 3.0 in science and math, 2.75 overall; bachelor's degree in biology; 2 letters of recommendation (preferred). Additional exam requirements/recommendations for international students: Required—TOEFL (minimum score 550 paper-based; 213 computer-based; 79 iBT), IELTS (minimum score 6.5). *Application deadline:* For fall admission, 4/15 for domestic and international students; for spring admission, 11/15 for domestic and international students. Applications are processed on a rolling basis. Application fee: $125. Electronic applications accepted. *Expenses:* Tuition, state resident: full-time $8210; part-time $345 per credit. Tuition, nonresident: part-time $640 per credit. *Required fees:* $128 per semester. *Financial support:* Federal Work-Study and scholarships/grants available. Support available to part-time students. Financial award applicants required to submit FAFSA. *Unit head:* Dr. Frank Burbrink, Coordinator, 718-982-3961, Fax: 718-982-3852, E-mail: frank.burbrink@mail.csi.cuny.edu. *Application contact:* Sasha Spence, Assistant Director for Graduate Admissions, 718-982-2699, Fax: 718-982-2500, E-mail: sasha.spence@csi.cuny.edu. Web site: http://www.csi.cuny.edu/departments/biology/graduate.html.

The College of William and Mary, Faculty of Arts and Sciences, Department of Biology, Williamsburg, VA 23187-8795. Offers MS. Part-time programs available. *Faculty:* 28 full-time (10 women), 1 part-time/adjunct (0 women). *Students:* 16 full-time (11 women); includes 1 minority (Hispanic/Latino). Average age 24. 41 applicants, 27% accepted, 6 enrolled. In 2011, 10 master's awarded. *Degree requirements:* For master's, comprehensive exam, thesis (for some programs). *Entrance requirements:* For master's, GRE Subject Test, GRE General Test, minimum GPA of 3.0. Additional exam requirements/recommendations for international students: Required—TOEFL. *Application deadline:* For fall admission, 2/1 priority date for domestic students, 2/1 for international students. Application fee: $45. Electronic applications accepted. *Expenses:* Tuition, state resident: full-time $6400; part-time $365 per credit hour. Tuition, nonresident: full-time $19,720; part-time $985 per credit hour. *Required fees:* $4562. *Financial support:* In 2011–12, 15 teaching assistantships with full tuition reimbursements (averaging $11,000 per year) were awarded; Federal Work-Study, institutionally sponsored loans, and unspecified assistantships also available. Financial award application deadline: 3/1; financial award applicants required to submit FAFSA. *Faculty research:* Cellular and molecular biology, genetics, ecology, organismal biology, physiology. *Total annual research expenditures:* $2.4 million. *Unit head:* Dr. Lizabeth A. Allison, Chair, 757-221-2207, Fax: 757-221-6483, E-mail: laalli@wm.edu. *Application contact:* Dr. Matthew Wawersik, Graduate Director, 757-221-2237, Fax: 757-221-6483, E-mail: mjwawe@wm.edu. Web site: http://www.wm.edu/biology/.

Colorado State University, College of Veterinary Medicine and Biomedical Sciences, Department of Biomedical Sciences, Fort Collins, CO 80523-1680. Offers MS, PhD. *Faculty:* 24 full-time (5 women), 2 part-time/adjunct (1 woman). *Students:* 68 full-time (43 women), 28 part-time (15 women); includes 13 minority (1 American Indian or Alaska Native, non-Hispanic/Latino; 1 Asian, non-Hispanic/Latino; 10 Hispanic/Latino; 1 Two or more races, non-Hispanic/Latino), 4 international. Average age 26. 199 applicants, 48% accepted, 58 enrolled. In 2011, 53 master's, 4 doctorates awarded. Terminal master's awarded for partial completion of doctoral program. *Degree requirements:* For master's, comprehensive exam (for some programs), thesis (for some programs); for doctorate, thesis/dissertation. *Entrance requirements:* For master's, GRE General Test, GRE Subject Test, MCAT, or other standardized test or professional school entrance exam, bachelor's degree, minimum GPA of 3.0; for doctorate, GRE General Test, GRE Subject Test, bachelor's or professional degree, minimum GPA of 3.0. Additional exam requirements/recommendations for international students: Required—TOEFL (minimum score 550 paper-based; 213 computer-based; 80 iBT). *Application deadline:* For fall admission, 4/1 for domestic and international students; for winter admission, 9/1 for domestic students. Application fee: $50. Electronic applications accepted. *Expenses:* Tuition, state resident: full-time $7992. Tuition, nonresident: full-time $19,592. *Required fees:* $1735; $58 per credit. *Financial support:* In 2011–12, 31 students received support, including 7 fellowships with full tuition reimbursements available (averaging $29,299 per year), 18 research assistantships with full and partial tuition reimbursements available (averaging $21,962 per year), 6 teaching assistantships with full tuition reimbursements available (averaging $9,300 per year);

Federal Work-Study, scholarships/grants, traineeships, and unspecified assistantships also available. Financial award application deadline: 4/1. *Faculty research:* Developmental neurobiology, reproductive physiology, equine reproduction, molecular endocrinology, neurophysiology . *Total annual research expenditures:* $5.5 million. *Unit head:* Dr. Colin M. Clay, Chair, 970-491-7571, Fax: 970-491-3557, E-mail: colin.clay@ colostate.edu. *Application contact:* Erin Bisenius, Graduate Education Coordinator, 970-491-6188, Fax: 970-491-7569, E-mail: erin.bisenius@colostate.edu. Web site: http://www.cvmbs.colostate.edu/bms/.

Colorado State University, Graduate School, College of Natural Sciences, Department of Biology, Fort Collins, CO 80523-1878. Offers botany (MS, PhD); zoology (MS, PhD). Postbaccalaureate distance learning degree programs offered (no on-campus study). *Faculty:* 26 full-time (11 women). *Students:* 17 full-time (10 women), 32 part-time (19 women); includes 8 minority (3 Asian, non-Hispanic/Latino; 4 Hispanic/Latino; 1 Two or more races, non-Hispanic/Latino), 6 international. Average age 29. 61 applicants, 15% accepted, 7 enrolled. In 2011, 6 master's, 4 doctorates awarded. Terminal master's awarded for partial completion of doctoral program. *Degree requirements:* For master's, comprehensive exam (for some programs), thesis (for some programs); for doctorate, comprehensive exam, thesis/dissertation. *Entrance requirements:* For master's, GRE General Test, minimum GPA of 3.0; 3 letters of recommendation; for doctorate, GRE General Test, minimum GPA of 3.0; statement of purpose; 2 transcripts; 3 letters of recommendation. Additional exam requirements/recommendations for international students: Required—TOEFL (minimum score 550 paper-based; 213 computer-based; 80 iBT). *Application deadline:* For fall admission, 1/15 priority date for domestic students, 1/15 for international students; for spring admission, 11/1 priority date for domestic students, 11/1 for international students. Applications are processed on a rolling basis. Application fee: $50. Electronic applications accepted. *Expenses:* Tuition, state resident: full-time $7992. Tuition, nonresident: full-time $19,592. *Required fees:* $1735; $58 per credit. *Financial support:* In 2011–12, 20 fellowships (averaging $34,499 per year), 32 research assistantships with full tuition reimbursements (averaging $12,041 per year), 59 teaching assistantships with full tuition reimbursements (averaging $12,668 per year) were awarded; health care benefits also available. Financial award application deadline: 1/15; financial award applicants required to submit FAFSA. *Faculty research:* Aquatic and terrestrial ecology, cell biology and genetics, plant/animal physiology, developmental biology, evolutionary biology. *Total annual research expenditures:* $6.1 million. *Unit head:* Dr. Daniel R. Bush, Chair, 970-491-7013, Fax: 970-491-0649, E-mail: dbush@colostate.edu. *Application contact:* Dorothy Ramirez, Graduate Coordinator, 970-491-1923, Fax: 970-491-0649, E-mail: dorothy.ramirez@colostate.edu. Web site: http://www.biology.colostate.edu/.

Colorado State University–Pueblo, College of Science and Mathematics, Pueblo, CO 81001-4901. Offers applied natural science (MS), including biochemistry, biology, chemistry. Part-time and evening/weekend programs available. *Degree requirements:* For master's, comprehensive exam (for some programs), thesis (for some programs), internship report (if non-thesis). *Entrance requirements:* For master's, GRE General Test (minimum score 1000), 2 letters of reference, minimum GPA of 3.0. Additional exam requirements/recommendations for international students: Required—TOEFL (minimum score 500 paper-based; 173 computer-based), IELTS (minimum score 5). *Faculty research:* Fungal cell walls, molecular biology, bioactive materials synthesis, atomic force microscopy-surface chemistry, nanoscience.

Columbia University, College of Physicians and Surgeons, New York, NY 10032. Offers M Phil, MA, MS, DN Sc, DPT, Ed D, MD, PhD, Adv C, MBA/MS, MD/DDS, MD/MPH, MD/MS, MD/PhD, MPH/MS. Part-time programs available. *Entrance requirements:* For master's, GRE General Test. Additional exam requirements/recommendations for international students: Required—TOEFL. *Expenses:* Contact institution.

Columbia University, Graduate School of Arts and Sciences, Division of Natural Sciences, Department of Biological Sciences, New York, NY 10027. Offers PhD, MD/PhD. *Degree requirements:* For doctorate, comprehensive exam, thesis/dissertation, teaching experience. *Entrance requirements:* For doctorate, GRE General Test, GRE Subject Test (suggested). Additional exam requirements/recommendations for international students: Required—TOEFL.

See Display on next page and Close-Up on page 109.

Concordia University, School of Graduate Studies, Faculty of Arts and Science, Department of Biology, Montréal, QC H3G 1M8, Canada. Offers biology (M Sc, PhD); biotechnology and genomics (Diploma). *Degree requirements:* For master's, thesis; for doctorate, thesis/dissertation, pedagogical training. *Entrance requirements:* For master's, honors degree in biology; for doctorate, M Sc in life science. *Faculty research:* Cell biology, animal physiology, ecology, microbiology/molecular biology, plant physiology/biochemistry and biotechnology.

Cornell University, Graduate School, Graduate Fields of Comparative Biomedical Sciences, Field of Comparative Biomedical Sciences, Ithaca, NY 14853-0001. Offers cellular and molecular medicine (MS, PhD); developmental and reproductive biology (MS, PhD); infectious diseases (MS, PhD); population medicine and epidemiology (MS, PhD); structural and functional biology (MS, PhD). *Faculty:* 97 full-time (27 women). *Students:* 38 full-time (23 women); includes 5 minority (2 Black or African American, non-Hispanic/Latino; 1 Asian, non-Hispanic/Latino; 2 Hispanic/Latino), 15 international. Average age 30. 45 applicants, 22% accepted, 9 enrolled. In 2011, 2 master's, 7 doctorates awarded. *Degree requirements:* For master's, thesis; for doctorate, comprehensive exam, thesis/dissertation. *Entrance requirements:* For master's and doctorate, GRE General Test, 2 letters of recommendation. Additional exam requirements/recommendations for international students: Required—TOEFL (minimum score 550 paper-based; 213 computer-based; 77 iBT). *Application deadline:* For fall admission, 12/15 for domestic students. Application fee: $95. Electronic applications accepted. *Financial support:* In 2011–12, 12 fellowships with full tuition reimbursements, 25 research assistantships with full tuition reimbursements were awarded; teaching assistantships with full tuition reimbursements, institutionally sponsored loans, scholarships/grants, health care benefits, tuition waivers (full and partial), and unspecified assistantships also available. Financial award applicants required to submit FAFSA. *Faculty research:* Receptors and signal transduction, viral and bacterial infectious diseases, tumor metastasis, clinical sciences/nutritional disease, developmental/neurological disorders. *Unit head:* Director of Graduate Studies, 607-253-3276, Fax: 607-253-3756. *Application contact:* Graduate Field Assistant, 607-253-3276, Fax: 607-253-3756, E-mail: graduate_edcvm@cornell.edu. Web site: http://www.gradschool.cornell.edu/fields.php?id-64&a-2.

Creighton University, School of Medicine and Graduate School, Graduate Programs in Medicine, Department of Biomedical Sciences, Omaha, NE 68178-0001. Offers MS, PhD, MD/PhD. Terminal master's awarded for partial completion of doctoral program. *Degree requirements:* For master's, thesis; for doctorate, thesis/dissertation. *Entrance requirements:* For master's, GRE General Test (minimum 50th percentile); for doctorate, GRE General Test (minimum score: 50th percentile). Additional exam requirements/recommendations for international students: Required—TOEFL. Electronic applications accepted. *Expenses: Tuition:* Full-time $12,672; part-time $704 per credit hour. *Required fees:* $1410; $136 per semester. Tuition and fees vary according to campus/location and reciprocity agreements. *Faculty research:* Molecular biology and gene transfection.

Dalhousie University, Faculty of Graduate Studies and Faculty of Medicine, Graduate Programs in Medicine, Halifax, NS B3H 4R2, Canada. Offers M Sc, PhD. *Degree requirements:* For master's, thesis; for doctorate, thesis/dissertation. *Entrance*

Watson School of Biological Sciences

Cold Spring Harbor Laboratory

The Watson School of Biological Sciences at Cold Spring Harbor Laboratory offers an innovative four-year Ph.D. program designed for exceptional students. The curriculum includes the following features:

- ◆ Approximately four years from matriculation to Ph.D. degree award
- ◆ Broad representation of the biological sciences
- ◆ A first year with course work and laboratory rotations in separate phases
- ◆ Emphasis on the principles of scientific reasoning and logic
- ◆ Continued advanced course instruction throughout graduate curriculum
- ◆ Extensive student mentoring

There is full remission of tuition fees and full stipend and research costs are provided. Summer undergraduate research program also available. Please see our websites at www.cshl.edu/gradschool and www.cshl.edu/urp.

WATSON SCHOOL OF
BIOLOGICAL SCIENCES

COLD SPRING HARBOR
LABORATORY

requirements: Additional exam requirements/recommendations for international students: Required—1 of 5 approved tests: TOEFL, IELTS, CANTEST, CAEL, Michigan English Language Assessment Battery. Electronic applications accepted. *Expenses:* Contact institution.

Dalhousie University, Faculty of Science, Department of Biology, Halifax, NS B3H 4R2, Canada. Offers M Sc, PhD. Terminal master's awarded for partial completion of doctoral program. *Degree requirements:* For master's, thesis; for doctorate, thesis/dissertation. *Entrance requirements:* Additional exam requirements/recommendations for international students: Required—TOEFL, IELTS, CANTEST, CAEL, or Michigan English Language Assessment Battery. Electronic applications accepted. *Faculty research:* Marine biology, ecology, animal physiology, plant physiology, microbiology (cell, molecular, genetics, development).

Dartmouth College, Graduate Program in Molecular and Cellular Biology, Department of Biological Sciences, Hanover, NH 03755. Offers PhD, MD/PhD. *Entrance requirements:* For doctorate, GRE General Test, letters of recommendation. Additional exam requirements/recommendations for international students: Required—TOEFL (minimum score 450 paper-based; 90 iBT) or IELTS (minimum score 7). Electronic applications accepted.

Delaware State University, Graduate Programs, Department of Biological Sciences, Program in Biological Sciences, Dover, DE 19901-2277. Offers MS. *Entrance requirements:* For master's, GRE, prerequisite undergraduate courses. Additional exam requirements/recommendations for international students: Required—TOEFL.

Delta State University, Graduate Programs, College of Arts and Sciences, Division of Biological and Physical Sciences, Cleveland, MS 38733-0001. Offers natural sciences (MSNS). Part-time programs available. *Degree requirements:* For master's, research project or thesis. *Entrance requirements:* For master's, GRE General Test. *Expenses:* Tuition, state resident: full-time $4702; part-time $294 per credit hour. Tuition, nonresident: full-time $12,516; part-time $760 per credit hour. *Required fees:* $586.

DePaul University, College of Science and Health, Department of Biological Sciences, Chicago, IL 60614. Offers MA, MS. *Faculty:* 18 full-time (13 women). *Students:* 20 full-time (15 women), 45 part-time (32 women); includes 22 minority (6 Black or African American, non-Hispanic/Latino; 3 Asian, non-Hispanic/Latino; 12 Hispanic/Latino; 1 Two or more races, non-Hispanic/Latino), 1 international. Average age 33. 50 applicants, 18% accepted, 9 enrolled. In 2011, 3 master's awarded. *Degree requirements:* For master's, comprehensive exam, thesis (for some programs). *Entrance requirements:* For master's, GRE, MCAT or DAT, minimum GPA of 3.0. Additional exam requirements/recommendations for international students: Required—TOEFL (minimum score 590 paper-based; 243 computer-based; 96 iBT). *Application deadline:* For fall admission, 2/15 priority date for domestic students, 2/15 for international students. Applications are processed on a rolling basis. Application fee: $25. Electronic applications accepted. *Financial support:* In 2011–12, 18 students received support, including 10 teaching assistantships with full tuition reimbursements available (averaging $11,000 per year); institutionally sponsored loans, scholarships/grants, and tuition waivers (partial) also available. Financial award application deadline: 4/1. *Faculty research:* Cell motility, detoxification in plant cells, molecular biology of fungi, B-lymphocyte development, physiological ecology, traumatic brain injury, bacterial pathogenicity, cancer biology, molecular evolution, Drosophila genetics. *Unit head:* Dr. John Dean, Chair, 773-325-7595, Fax: 773-325-7596, E-mail: jdean@depaul.edu. *Application contact:* Dr. Margaret Silliker, Director of Graduate Admissions, 773-325-2194, E-mail: msillike@depaul.edu. Web site: http://www.condor.depaul.edu/~biology/.

Des Moines University, College of Osteopathic Medicine, Program in Biomedical Sciences, Des Moines, IA 50312-4104. Offers MS.

Dominican University of California, Graduate Programs, School of Health and Natural Sciences, Program in Biological Sciences, San Rafael, CA 94901-2298. Offers MS. *Students:* 21 full-time (14 women); includes 8 minority (4 Asian, non-Hispanic/Latino; 4 Hispanic/Latino), 2 international. Average age 27. 21 applicants, 76% accepted, 13 enrolled. In 2011, 9 master's awarded. *Entrance requirements:* For master's, GRE or MCAT, BS in biology, biological sciences or biomedical sciences; minimum GPA of 3.0 in last 60 units. Additional exam requirements/recommendations for international students: Required—TOEFL (minimum score 550 paper-based; 80 iBT), IELTS (minimum score 7). *Application deadline:* For fall admission, 3/15 priority date for domestic students, 3/15 for international students. Applications are processed on a rolling basis. Application fee: $40. Electronic applications accepted. *Expenses: Tuition:* Full-time $15,660. *Required fees:* $300. Tuition and fees vary according to program. *Financial support:* In 2011–12, 14 students received support. Career-related internships or fieldwork, scholarships/grants, and unspecified assistantships available. Financial award application deadline: 3/2; financial award applicants required to submit FAFSA. *Unit head:* Dr. Sibdas Ghosh, Chair, Natural Science and Mathematics, 415-482-3583, Fax: 415-482-1972, E-mail: sibdas.ghosh@dominican.edu. *Application contact:* Shannon Lovelace-White, Director, 415-485-3287, Fax: 415-485-3214, E-mail: shannon.lovelace-white@dominican.edu.

Drew University, Caspersen School of Graduate Studies, Program in Education, Madison, NJ 07940-1493. Offers biology (MAT); chemistry (MAT); English (MAT); French (MAT); Italian (MAT); math (MAT); physics (MAT); social studies (MAT); Spanish (MAT); theatre arts (MAT). Part-time programs available. *Entrance requirements:* For master's, transcripts, personal statement, recommendations. Additional exam requirements/recommendations for international students: Required—TOEFL, TWE. *Expenses:* Contact institution.

Drexel University, College of Arts and Sciences, Department of Biology, Philadelphia, PA 19104-2875. Offers biological sciences (MS, PhD); human nutrition (MS). Part-time programs available. *Degree requirements:* For doctorate, thesis/dissertation. *Entrance requirements:* For master's and doctorate, GRE General Test. Additional exam requirements/recommendations for international students: Required—TOEFL. Electronic applications accepted. *Faculty research:* Genetic engineering, physiological ecology.

Drexel University, College of Medicine, Biomedical Graduate Programs, Philadelphia, PA 19129. Offers MLAS, MMS, MS, PhD, Certificate, MD/PhD. Part-time programs available. Terminal master's awarded for partial completion of doctoral program. *Degree requirements:* For master's, comprehensive exam; for doctorate, thesis/dissertation, qualifying exam. *Entrance requirements:* For master's and doctorate, GRE General Test. Additional exam requirements/recommendations for international students: Required—TOEFL. Electronic applications accepted. *Expenses:* Contact institution.

Drexel University, College of Medicine, MD/PhD Program, Philadelphia, PA 19104-2875. Offers MD/PhD. Electronic applications accepted.

Drexel University, School of Biomedical Engineering, Science and Health Systems, Program in Biomedical Science, Philadelphia, PA 19104-2875. Offers MS, PhD. *Degree requirements:* For master's, thesis (for some programs); for doctorate, thesis/dissertation. Electronic applications accepted.

Duke University, Graduate School, Department of Biology, Durham, NC 27708. Offers PhD. *Faculty:* 50 full-time. *Students:* 78 full-time (45 women); includes 8 minority (5 Asian, non-Hispanic/Latino; 3 Hispanic/Latino), 28 international. 109 applicants, 21% accepted, 12 enrolled. In 2011, 9 doctorates awarded. *Degree requirements:* For doctorate, one foreign language, thesis/dissertation. *Entrance requirements:* For doctorate, GRE General Test, GRE Subject Test (recommended). Additional exam requirements/recommendations for international students: Required—TOEFL (minimum

COLUMBIA UNIVERSITY
DEPARTMENT OF BIOLOGICAL SCIENCES

The Department of Biological Sciences at Columbia University offers training leading to Ph.D. degrees with concentrations in cellular, molecular, developmental, computational, and structural biology as well as genetics, molecular biophysics, and neurobiology. The Ph.D. program provides each student with a solid background in contemporary biology and an in-depth knowledge of one or more of the above areas. Acceptance to the program is determined by a student's academic background as well as consideration of prior research experience, GRE scores, and letters of recommendation.

Tuition, fees and a generous stipend are paid for all graduate students accepted to the program. These benefits ensure that students have the time and resources necessary to focus on study and research. Most students live in University-owned, subsidized apartments or dorms within easy walking distance of the laboratories. In addition, both the Morningside and Health Sciences campuses are easily reached by public transportation from all areas of the city.

Completed applications are due by December 1, for admission in the following Fall term.

For more information, please contact:
Sarah Kim Fein
Department of Biological Sciences
Graduate School of Arts and Sciences
Columbia University
Sherman Fairchild Center, 1212 Amsterdam Avenue, Mailcode 2402
New York, NY 10027
biology@columbia.edu
http://www.columbia.edu/cu/biology/

score 550 paper-based; 213 computer-based; 83 iBT), IELTS (minimum score 7). *Application deadline:* For fall admission, 12/8 priority date for domestic students, 12/8 for international students. Application fee: $75. Electronic applications accepted. *Expenses: Tuition:* Full-time $40,720. *Required fees:* $3107. *Financial support:* Fellowships, research assistantships, teaching assistantships, and Federal Work-Study available. Financial award application deadline: 12/8. *Unit head:* Sonke Johnsen, Director of Graduate Studies, 919-684-3649, Fax: 919-660-7293, E-mail: aslzoo@duke.edu. *Application contact:* Elizabeth Hutton, Director of Admissions, 919-684-3913, Fax: 919-684-2277, E-mail: grad-admissions@duke.edu. Web site: http://www.biology.duke.edu/.

Duquesne University, Bayer School of Natural and Environmental Sciences, Department of Biological Sciences, Pittsburgh, PA 15282-0001. Offers MS, PhD, MS/MS. Part-time programs available. *Faculty:* 17 full-time (7 women), 1 (woman) part-time/adjunct. *Students:* 31 full-time (18 women); includes 3 minority (1 Black or African American, non-Hispanic/Latino; 1 American Indian or Alaska Native, non-Hispanic/Latino; 1 Asian, non-Hispanic/Latino), 8 international. Average age 29. 39 applicants, 18% accepted, 4 enrolled. In 2011, 2 degrees awarded. Terminal master's awarded for partial completion of doctoral program. *Degree requirements:* For master's, thesis (for some programs), 32 credit hours (for non-thesis option); for doctorate, thesis/dissertation. *Entrance requirements:* For master's, GRE General Test; GRE Subject Test in biology, biochemistry, or cell and molecular biology (recommended), BS in biological sciences or related field, 3 letters of recommendation, official transcripts, statement of purpose; for doctorate, GRE General Test; GRE Subject Test in biology, biochemistry, or cell and molecular biology (recommended), BS or MS in biological sciences or related field, 3 letters of recommendation, statement of purpose, official transcripts. Additional exam requirements/recommendations for international students: Required—TOEFL (minimum score 80 iBT). *Application deadline:* For fall admission, 2/15 for domestic and international students. Applications are processed on a rolling basis. Application fee: $0 ($40 for international students). Electronic applications accepted. *Expenses:* Contact institution. *Financial support:* In 2011–12, 31 students received support, including 1 fellowship with full tuition reimbursement available (averaging $22,100 per year), 4 research assistantships with full tuition reimbursements available (averaging $21,850 per year), 25 teaching assistantships with full tuition reimbursements available (averaging $21,850 per year); scholarships/grants, tuition waivers (partial), and unspecified assistantships also available. Financial award application deadline: 5/31. *Faculty research:* Cell and developmental biology, molecular biology and genetics, evolution, ecology, physiology and microbiology. *Unit head:* Dr. Joseph McCormick, Chair, 412-396-5657, Fax: 412-396-5907, E-mail: mccormick@duq.edu. *Application contact:* Heather Costello, Graduate Academic Advisor, 412-396-6339, Fax: 412-396-4881, E-mail: costelloh@duq.edu. Web site: http://www.science.duq.edu/.

East Carolina University, Brody School of Medicine, Department of Biochemistry and Molecular Biology, Greenville, NC 27858-4353. Offers biochemistry and molecular biology (PhD); biomedical science (MS). *Degree requirements:* For doctorate, comprehensive exam, thesis/dissertation. *Entrance requirements:* For doctorate, GRE General Test. Additional exam requirements/recommendations for international students: Required—TOEFL. *Application deadline:* For fall admission, 6/1 priority date for domestic students. Applications are processed on a rolling basis. Application fee: $50. *Expenses:* Tuition, state resident: full-time $3557; part-time $444.63 per semester hour. Tuition, nonresident: full-time $14,351; part-time $1793.88 per semester hour. *Required fees:* $2016; $252 per semester hour. Part-time tuition and fees vary according to course load, campus/location and program. *Financial support:* Fellowships with full and partial tuition reimbursements available. Financial award application deadline: 6/1. *Faculty research:* Gene regulation, development and differentiation, contractility and motility, macromolecular interactions, cancer. *Unit head:* Dr. Phillip H. Pekala, Chairman, 252-744-2684, Fax: 252-744-3383, E-mail: pekalap@ecu.edu. *Application contact:* Dr. George J. Kasperek, Assistant Dean for Graduate Studies/BSOM, 252-744-3305, Fax: 252-744-0203, E-mail: kasperekg@ecu.edu. Web site: http://www.ecu.edu/cs-dhs/biochemistry/Graduate-Program-Information.cfm.

East Carolina University, Graduate School, Thomas Harriot College of Arts and Sciences, Department of Biology, Greenville, NC 27858-4353. Offers biology (MS); molecular biology/biotechnology (MS). Part-time programs available. *Degree requirements:* For master's, one foreign language, comprehensive exam, thesis. *Entrance requirements:* For master's, GRE General Test, GRE Subject Test. Additional exam requirements/recommendations for international students: Required—TOEFL. *Application deadline:* For fall admission, 6/1 priority date for domestic students; for spring admission, 10/15 for domestic students. Applications are processed on a rolling basis. Application fee: $50. *Expenses:* Tuition, state resident: full-time $3557; part-time $444.63 per semester hour. Tuition, nonresident: full-time $14,351; part-time $1793.88 per semester hour. *Required fees:* $2016; $252 per semester hour. Part-time tuition and fees vary according to course load, campus/location and program. *Financial support:* Fellowships with partial tuition reimbursements, research assistantships with partial tuition reimbursements, teaching assistantships with partial tuition reimbursements, career-related internships or fieldwork, Federal Work-Study, scholarships/grants, and unspecified assistantships available. Support available to part-time students. Financial award application deadline: 6/1. *Faculty research:* Biochemistry, microbiology, cell biology. *Application contact:* Interim Dean of Graduate School, 252-328-6012, Fax: 252-328-6071, E-mail: gradschool@ecu.edu. Web site: http://www.ecu.edu/cs-cas/biology/graduate.cfm.

Eastern Illinois University, Graduate School, College of Sciences, Department of Biological Sciences, Charleston, IL 61920-3099. Offers MS. *Degree requirements:* For master's, exam. *Expenses:* Tuition, state resident: part-time $279 per credit hour. Tuition, nonresident: part-time $670 per credit hour. *Required fees:* $179.07 per credit hour. $1253 per semester.

Eastern Kentucky University, The Graduate School, College of Arts and Sciences, Department of Biological Sciences, Richmond, KY 40475-3102. Offers biological sciences (MS); ecology (MS). Part-time programs available. *Degree requirements:* For master's, thesis. *Entrance requirements:* For master's, GRE General Test, minimum GPA of 2.5. *Faculty research:* Systematics, ecology, and biodiversity; animal behavior; protein structure and molecular genetics; biomonitoring and aquatic toxicology; pathogenesis of microbes and parasites.

Eastern Mennonite University, Program in Biomedicine, Harrisonburg, VA 22802-2462. Offers MA.

Eastern Michigan University, Graduate School, College of Arts and Sciences, Department of Biology, Ypsilanti, MI 48197. Offers cell and molecular biology (MS); community college biology teaching (MS); ecology and organismal biology (MS); general biology (MS); water resources (MS). Part-time and evening/weekend programs available. Postbaccalaureate distance learning degree programs offered (minimal on-campus study). *Faculty:* 20 full-time (4 women). *Students:* 12 full-time (7 women), 40 part-time (21 women); includes 3 minority (1 Black or African American, non-Hispanic/Latino; 1 Asian, non-Hispanic/Latino; 1 Two or more races, non-Hispanic/Latino), 12 international. Average age 27. 70 applicants, 43% accepted, 12 enrolled. In 2011, 19 degrees awarded. *Entrance requirements:* For master's, GRE General Test, GRE Subject Test. Additional exam requirements/recommendations for international students: Required—TOEFL. *Application deadline:* Applications are processed on a rolling basis. Application fee: $35. *Expenses:* Tuition, state resident: full-time $10,367; part-time $432 per credit hour. Tuition, nonresident: full-time $20,435; part-time $851 per credit hour. *Required fees:* $39 per credit hour. $46 per semester. One-time fee: $100. Tuition and fees vary according to course level, degree level and reciprocity agreements. *Financial support:* Fellowships, research assistantships with full tuition reimbursements, teaching assistantships with full tuition reimbursements, career-related internships or fieldwork, Federal Work-Study, institutionally sponsored loans, scholarships/grants, tuition waivers (partial), and unspecified assistantships available. Support available to part-time students. Financial award applicants required to submit FAFSA. *Unit head:* Dr. Marianne Laporte, Department Head, 734-487-4242, Fax: 734-487-9235, E-mail: mlaporte@emich.edu. *Application contact:* Graduate Admissions, 734-487-2400, Fax: 734-487-6559, E-mail: graduate.admissions@emich.edu. Web site: http://www.emich.edu/biology.

Eastern New Mexico University, Graduate School, College of Liberal Arts and Sciences, Department of Biology, Portales, NM 88130. Offers applied ecology (MS); cell, molecular biology and biotechnology (MS); education (non-thesis) (MS); microbiology (MS); plant biology (MS); zoology (MS). Part-time programs available. *Faculty:* 7 full-time (0 women). *Students:* 2 full-time (1 woman), 15 part-time (9 women); includes 7 minority (5 Hispanic/Latino; 2 Two or more races, non-Hispanic/Latino), 2 international. Average age 26. 17 applicants, 82% accepted, 3 enrolled. In 2011, 4 master's awarded. *Degree requirements:* For master's, comprehensive exam, thesis optional. *Entrance requirements:* For master's, GRE, minimum GPA of 3.0, 2 letters of recommendation, statement of research interest, bachelor's degree related to field of study or proof of common knowledge. Additional exam requirements/recommendations for international students: Required—TOEFL (minimum score 550 paper-based; 213 computer-based; 79 iBT), IELTS (minimum score 6). *Application deadline:* For fall admission, 7/20 priority date for domestic students, 6/20 for international students; for spring admission, 12/15 priority date for domestic students, 11/15 for international students. Applications are processed on a rolling basis. Application fee: $10. Electronic applications accepted. *Financial support:* In 2011–12, 8 teaching assistantships with partial tuition reimbursements (averaging $8,500 per year) were awarded; scholarships/grants and unspecified assistantships also available. Support available to part-time students. Financial award applicants required to submit FAFSA. *Unit head:* Dr. Zach Jones, Graduate Coordinator, 575-562-2723, Fax: 575-562-2192, E-mail: zach.jones@enmu.edu. *Application contact:* Sharon Potter, Department Secretary, Biology and Physical Sciences, 575-562-2174, Fax: 575-562-2192, E-mail: sharon.potter@enmu.edu. Web site: http://liberal-arts.enmu.edu/biology/graduate.shtml.

Eastern Virginia Medical School, Doctoral Program in Biomedical Sciences, Norfolk, VA 23501-1980. Offers PhD. *Students:* 15 full-time (14 women); includes 8 minority (3 Black or African American, non-Hispanic/Latino; 4 Asian, non-Hispanic/Latino; 1 Hispanic/Latino). 29 applicants, 7% accepted, 2 enrolled. *Degree requirements:* For doctorate, thesis/dissertation. *Entrance requirements:* For doctorate, GRE General Test. Additional exam requirements/recommendations for international students: Required—TOEFL. *Application deadline:* For fall admission, 2/1 for domestic students. Applications are processed on a rolling basis. Application fee: $60. Electronic applications accepted. *Expenses:* Contact institution. *Financial support:* Research assistantships with full tuition reimbursements available. *Faculty research:* Cancer, cardiovascular biology, diabetes, infectious disease, neuroscience, reproductive biology. *Total annual research expenditures:* $14 million. *Unit head:* Dr. Earl Godfrey, Director, 757-446-5609, Fax: 757-446-6179, E-mail: godfreew@evms.edu. *Application contact:* Michelle Hammer, Administrative Support Coordinator, 757-446-5076, Fax: 757-446-6179, E-mail: hammermr@evms.edu. Web site: http://www.evms.edu/evms-school-of-health-professions/phd-in-biomedical-sciences.html.

Eastern Virginia Medical School, Master's Program in Biomedical Sciences (Medical Master's), Norfolk, VA 23501-1980. Offers MS. *Faculty:* 25. *Students:* 28 full-time (11 women); includes 12 minority (1 Black or African American, non-Hispanic/Latino; 11 Asian, non-Hispanic/Latino). 282 applicants, 18% accepted, 28 enrolled. In 2011, 23 master's awarded. *Entrance requirements:* For master's, MCAT. *Application deadline:* For fall admission, 4/1 for domestic students. Applications are processed on a rolling basis. Application fee: $60. Electronic applications accepted. *Expenses:* Contact institution. *Financial support:* Institutionally sponsored loans available. *Unit head:* Dr. Donald Meyer, Director, 757-446-5615, Fax: 757-446-6179, E-mail: meyerdc@evms.edu. *Application contact:* Leah Solomon, Administrative Support Coordinator, 757-446-5944, Fax: 757-446-6179, E-mail: solomolj@evms.edu. Web site: http://www.evms.edu/evms-school-of-health-professions/ms-in-biomedical-sciences-medical-masters.html.

Eastern Virginia Medical School, Master's Program in Biomedical Sciences Research, Norfolk, VA 23501-1980. Offers MS. *Faculty:* 57. *Students:* 14 full-time (9 women); includes 6 minority (1 Black or African American, non-Hispanic/Latino; 5 Asian, non-Hispanic/Latino). 30 applicants, 30% accepted, 8 enrolled. In 2011, 2 master's awarded. *Degree requirements:* For master's, comprehensive exam (for some programs), thesis optional. *Entrance requirements:* For master's, GRE. Additional exam requirements/recommendations for international students: Required—TOEFL. *Application deadline:* For fall admission, 3/1 for domestic students. Applications are processed on a rolling basis. Application fee: $60. Electronic applications accepted. *Expenses:* Contact institution. *Faculty research:* Cancer, cardiovascular biology, diabetes, infectious disease, neuroscience, reproductive biology. *Unit head:* Dr. Earl Godfrey, Director, 757-446-5609, Fax: 757-624-2255, E-mail: godfreew@evms.edu. *Application contact:* Michelle Hammer, Administrative Support Coordinator, 757-446-5076, Fax: 757-446-6179, E-mail: hammermr@evms.edu. Web site: http://www.evms.edu/evms-school-of-health-professions/biomedical-sciences-research-program-home.html.

Eastern Virginia Medical School, Master's Program in Clinical Embryology and Andrology, Norfolk, VA 23501-1980. Offers MS. Postbaccalaureate distance learning degree programs offered (minimal on-campus study). *Faculty:* 12 full-time, 8 part-time/adjunct. *Students:* 66 full-time (44 women); includes 27 minority (5 Black or African American, non-Hispanic/Latino; 13 Asian, non-Hispanic/Latino; 9 Hispanic/Latino). 38 applicants, 76% accepted, 24 enrolled. In 2011, 14 master's awarded. *Entrance requirements:* Additional exam requirements/recommendations for international students: Required—TOEFL (minimum score 550 paper-based; 213 computer-based; 80 iBT). *Application deadline:* For fall admission, 1/14 for domestic and international students. Applications are processed on a rolling basis. Application fee: $60. Electronic applications accepted. *Expenses:* Contact institution. *Unit head:* Dr. Jacob Mayer, Director, 757-446-5049, Fax: 757-446-5905. *Application contact:* Nancy Garcia, Administrator, 757-446-8935, Fax: 757-446-5905, E-mail: garcianw@evms.edu. Web site: http://www.evms.edu/evms-school-of-health-professions/embryology-andrology-ms-distance-learning.html.

Eastern Washington University, Graduate Studies, College of Science, Health and Engineering, Department of Biology, Cheney, WA 99004-2431. Offers MS. *Faculty:* 15 full-time (6 women). *Students:* 17 full-time (9 women), 8 part-time (1 woman); includes 2 minority (1 Asian, non-Hispanic/Latino; 1 Hispanic/Latino), 1 international. Average age 36. 22 applicants, 45% accepted, 8 enrolled. In 2011, 10 master's awarded. *Degree requirements:* For master's, comprehensive exam, thesis. *Entrance requirements:* For

master's, GRE General Test, minimum GPA of 3.0. *Application deadline:* For fall admission, 4/1 priority date for domestic students; for spring admission, 1/15 for domestic students. Applications are processed on a rolling basis. Application fee: $50. *Financial support:* In 2011–12, 12 teaching assistantships with partial tuition reimbursements (averaging $7,000 per year) were awarded; career-related internships or fieldwork, Federal Work-Study, institutionally sponsored loans, scholarships/grants, health care benefits, tuition waivers (partial), and unspecified assistantships also available. Support available to part-time students. Financial award application deadline: 2/1; financial award applicants required to submit FAFSA. *Faculty research:* Ecology of Eastern Washington Scablands, Columbia River fisheries, biotechnology applied to vaccines, role of mycorrhiza in plant nutrition, exercise and estrous cycles. *Unit head:* Dr. Flash Gibson, Chair, 509-359-2348, Fax: 509-359-6867. *Application contact:* Dr. Ross Black, Graduate Adviser, 509-359-2339. Web site: http://www.ewu.edu/cshe/programs/biology.xml.

East Stroudsburg University of Pennsylvania, Graduate School, College of Arts and Sciences, Department of Biology, East Stroudsburg, PA 18301-2999. Offers M Ed, MS. Part-time and evening/weekend programs available. *Degree requirements:* For master's, comprehensive exam, thesis or alternative. *Entrance requirements:* For master's, GRE, resume, undergraduate major in life science (or equivalent), completion of organic chemistry (minimum two semesters), 3 letters of recommendation, letter of intent. Additional exam requirements/recommendations for international students: Required—TOEFL (minimum score 560 paper-based; 220 computer-based; 83 iBT) or IELTS.

East Tennessee State University, James H. Quillen College of Medicine, Biomedical Science Graduate Program, Johnson City, TN 37614. Offers anatomy and cell biology (PhD); biochemistry and molecular biology (PhD); microbiology (PhD); pharmaceutical sciences (PhD); pharmacology (PhD); physiology (PhD); quantitative biosciences (PhD). *Faculty:* 33 full-time (6 women). *Students:* 29 full-time (15 women), 2 part-time (both women); includes 4 minority (1 Black or African American, non-Hispanic/Latino; 1 Asian, non-Hispanic/Latino; 2 Hispanic/Latino), 6 international. Average age 29. 76 applicants, 12% accepted, 7 enrolled. In 2011, 1 doctorate awarded. *Degree requirements:* For doctorate, thesis/dissertation, comprehensive qualifying exam. *Entrance requirements:* For doctorate, GRE General Test, GRE Subject Test. Additional exam requirements/recommendations for international students: Required—TOEFL (minimum score 550 paper-based; 213 computer-based; 79 iBT). *Application deadline:* For fall admission, 3/15 priority date for domestic students, 3/1 for international students. Application fee: $35 ($45 for international students). Electronic applications accepted. *Expenses:* Contact institution. *Financial support:* In 2011–12, 29 students received support, including 29 research assistantships with full tuition reimbursements available (averaging $19,000 per year); career-related internships or fieldwork, institutionally sponsored loans, scholarships/grants, and unspecified assistantships also available. Financial award application deadline: 7/1; financial award applicants required to submit FAFSA. *Faculty research:* Cardiovascular biology, neuroscience, infectious disease, cancer, inflammatory disease. *Total annual research expenditures:* $3.6 million. *Unit head:* Dr. Mitchell E. Robinson, Associate Dean/Program Director, 423-439-2031, Fax: 423-439-2140, E-mail: robinson@etsu.edu. *Application contact:* Shella Bennett, Graduate Specialist, 423-439-4708, Fax: 423-439-5624, E-mail: bennetsg@etsu.edu.

East Tennessee State University, School of Graduate Studies, College of Arts and Sciences, Department of Biological Sciences, Johnson City, TN 37614. Offers biology (MS); biomedical sciences (MS); microbiology (MS); paleontology (MS). *Faculty:* 14 full-time (2 women), 1 part-time/adjunct (0 women). *Students:* 31 full-time (15 women), 5 part-time (3 women); includes 2 minority (1 Asian, non-Hispanic/Latino; 1 Hispanic/Latino), 12 international. Average age 26. 55 applicants, 35% accepted, 10 enrolled. In 2011, 24 master's awarded. *Degree requirements:* For master's, comprehensive exam, thesis. *Entrance requirements:* For master's, GRE General Test or GRE Subject Test, minimum GPA of 3.0, undergraduate degree in life or physical sciences, two letters of recommendation. Additional exam requirements/recommendations for international students: Required—TOEFL (minimum score 550 paper-based; 213 computer-based; 79 iBT). *Application deadline:* For fall admission, 4/1 for domestic students, 2/1 for international students; for spring admission, 9/1 for domestic students, 7/1 for international students. Application fee: $35 ($45 for international students). Electronic applications accepted. *Expenses:* Tuition, state resident: full-time $7312; part-time $350 per credit hour. Tuition, nonresident: full-time $18,490; part-time $621 per credit hour. *Required fees:* $63 per credit hour. Tuition and fees vary according to course load and program. *Financial support:* In 2011–12, 29 students received support, including 13 research assistantships with full tuition reimbursements available (averaging $9,000 per year), 14 teaching assistantships with full tuition reimbursements available (averaging $8,500 per year); institutionally sponsored loans, scholarships/grants, and unspecified assistantships also available. Financial award application deadline: 7/1; financial award applicants required to submit FAFSA. *Faculty research:* Genetics, ecology, evolutionary biology, quantitative biology and modeling, plant molecular biology, neurobiology, physiology, biomedical sciences, microbiology, paleobiology. *Total annual research expenditures:* $160,000. *Unit head:* Dr. Darrell Moore, Interim Chair, 423-439-4329, Fax: 423-439-5958, E-mail: zavadam@etsu.edu. *Application contact:* Gail Powers, Graduate Specialist, 423-439-4703, Fax: 423-439-5624, E-mail: powersg@etsu.edu.

Edinboro University of Pennsylvania, College of Arts and Sciences, Department of Biology and Health Services, Edinboro, PA 16444. Offers biology (MS). Part-time and evening/weekend programs available. *Faculty:* 4 full-time (2 women). *Students:* 6 full-time (2 women), 4 part-time (3 women); includes 1 minority (American Indian or Alaska Native, non-Hispanic/Latino). Average age 27. In 2011, 2 master's awarded. *Degree requirements:* For master's, thesis or alternative, competency exam. *Entrance requirements:* For master's, GRE or MAT, minimum QPA of 2.5. *Application deadline:* Applications are processed on a rolling basis. Application fee: $30. Electronic applications accepted. *Financial support:* In 2011–12, 2 research assistantships with full and partial tuition reimbursements (averaging $4,050 per year) were awarded; Federal Work-Study, scholarships/grants, and unspecified assistantships also available. Support available to part-time students. Financial award application deadline: 2/15; financial award applicants required to submit FAFSA. *Faculty research:* Microbiology, molecular biology, zoology, botany, ecology. *Unit head:* Dr. Peter Lindeman, Program Head, 814-732-2447, E-mail: plindeman@edinboro.edu. *Application contact:* Dr. Alan Biel, Dean, 814-732-2752, Fax: 814-732-2268, E-mail: abiel@edinboro.edu.

Elizabeth City State University, School of Mathematics, Science and Technology, Program in Biology, Elizabeth City, NC 27909-7806. Offers MS. Part-time programs available. *Degree requirements:* For master's, thesis. *Entrance requirements:* For master's, GRE. Additional exam requirements/recommendations for international students: Required—TOEFL. Electronic applications accepted. *Faculty research:* Apoptosis and cancer, plant bioengineering, development of biofuels, microbial degradation, insect cell-like discovery.

Emory University, Laney Graduate School, Division of Biological and Biomedical Sciences, Atlanta, GA 30322-1100. Offers PhD. *Faculty:* 325 full-time (80 women). *Students:* 448 full-time (284 women); includes 92 minority (25 Black or African American, non-Hispanic/Latino; 1 American Indian or Alaska Native, non-Hispanic/Latino; 31 Asian, non-Hispanic/Latino; 27 Hispanic/Latino; 1 Native Hawaiian or other

Pacific Islander, non-Hispanic/Latino; 7 Two or more races, non-Hispanic/Latino), 48 international. Average age 27. 1,239 applicants, 14% accepted, 82 enrolled. In 2011, 32 doctorates awarded. *Degree requirements:* For doctorate, comprehensive exam, thesis/dissertation. *Entrance requirements:* For doctorate, GRE General Test, minimum GPA of 3.0 in science course work (recommended). Additional exam requirements/recommendations for international students: Required—TOEFL. *Application deadline:* For fall admission, 12/1 for domestic and international students. Application fee: $75. Electronic applications accepted. *Expenses:* Contact institution. *Financial support:* In 2011–12, 162 students received support, including 162 fellowships with full tuition reimbursements available (averaging $26,500 per year); institutionally sponsored loans, scholarships/grants, health care benefits, and tuition waivers (full) also available. *Faculty research:* Biochemistry; cancer; genetics; immunology and microbiology; neuroscience and pharmacology; nutrition; population biology and ecology. *Unit head:* Dr. Keith Wilkinson, Director, 404-727-2545, Fax: 404-727-3322, E-mail: genekdw@emory.edu. *Application contact:* Kathy Smith, Director of Recruitment and Admissions, 404-727-2547, Fax: 404-727-3322, E-mail: kathy.smith@emory.edu. Web site: http://www.biomed.emory.edu/.

Emporia State University, Graduate School, College of Liberal Arts and Sciences, Department of Biological Sciences, Emporia, KS 66801-5087. Offers botany (MS); environmental biology (MS); general biology (MS); microbial and cellular biology (MS); zoology (MS). Part-time programs available. *Faculty:* 13 full-time (3 women), 1 part-time/adjunct (0 women). *Students:* 8 full-time (5 women), 21 part-time (10 women); includes 3 minority (1 Black or African American, non-Hispanic/Latino; 1 Hispanic/Latino; 1 Two or more races, non-Hispanic/Latino), 6 international. 14 applicants, 86% accepted, 7 enrolled. In 2011, 5 master's awarded. *Degree requirements:* For master's, comprehensive exam or thesis. *Entrance requirements:* For master's, GRE, appropriate undergraduate degree, interview, letters of reference. Additional exam requirements/recommendations for international students: Required—TOEFL (minimum score 520 paper-based; 133 computer-based; 68 iBT). *Application deadline:* For fall admission, 8/15 priority date for domestic students. Applications are processed on a rolling basis. Application fee: $30 ($75 for international students). Electronic applications accepted. *Expenses:* Tuition, state resident: full-time $2342; part-time $195 per credit hour. Tuition, nonresident: full-time $7254; part-time $605 per credit hour. *Required fees:* $66 per credit hour. Tuition and fees vary according to campus/location. *Financial support:* In 2011–12, 8 research assistantships with full tuition reimbursements (averaging $6,589 per year), 10 teaching assistantships with full tuition reimbursements (averaging $7,419 per year) were awarded; career-related internships or fieldwork, Federal Work-Study, institutionally sponsored loans, health care benefits, and unspecified assistantships also available. Financial award application deadline: 3/15; financial award applicants required to submit FAFSA. *Faculty research:* Fisheries, range, and wildlife management; aquatic, plant, grassland, vertebrate, and invertebrate ecology; mammalian and plant systematics, taxonomy, and evolution; immunology, virology, and molecular biology. *Unit head:* Dr. R. Brent Thomas, Chair, 620-341-5311, Fax: 620-341-5608, E-mail: rthomas2@emporia.edu. *Application contact:* Dr. Scott Crupper, Graduate Coordinator, 620-341-5621, Fax: 620-341-5607, E-mail: scrupper@emporia.edu. Web site: http://www.emporia.edu/info/degrees-courses/grad/biology.

Fairleigh Dickinson University, College at Florham, Maxwell Becton College of Arts and Sciences, Department of Biological and Allied Health Sciences, Program in Biology, Madison, NJ 07940-1099. Offers MS.

Fairleigh Dickinson University, Metropolitan Campus, University College: Arts, Sciences, and Professional Studies, School of Natural Sciences, Program in Biology, Teaneck, NJ 07666-1914. Offers MS.

Fayetteville State University, Graduate School, Department of Biological Sciences, Fayetteville, NC 28301-4298. Offers biology (MS). Part-time and evening/weekend programs available. *Faculty:* 11 full-time (4 women), 2 part-time/adjunct (1 woman). *Students:* 9 full-time (5 women), 6 part-time (3 women); includes 8 minority (all Black or African American, non-Hispanic/Latino), 1 international. Average age 27. 2 applicants, 100% accepted, 2 enrolled. In 2011, 1 master's awarded. *Degree requirements:* For master's, comprehensive exam, thesis, internship. *Entrance requirements:* For master's, GRE General Test. *Application deadline:* For fall admission, 4/15 for domestic students; for spring admission, 10/15 for domestic students. Applications are processed on a rolling basis. Application fee: $35. Electronic applications accepted. *Faculty research:* Genetic and quantitative trait loci (QTL) mapping of important agronomic traits in soybean and other plant species such as disease resistance, yield, and phyto-pharmaceuticals; dinosaur paleobiology, dinosaur systematic, and the evolution/creation controversy; coral reef toxins in education; animal behavior and physiology; forensic science, DNA fingerprinting, and latent evidence. *Total annual research expenditures:* $170,000. *Unit head:* Dr. Abdelmajid Kassem, Chairperson, 910-672-1691, E-mail: mkassem@uncfsu.edu. *Application contact:* Katrina Hoffman, Graduate Admissions Officer, 910-672-1374, Fax: 910-672-1470, E-mail: khoffma1@uncfsu.edu.

Fisk University, Division of Graduate Studies, Department of Biology, Nashville, TN 37208-3051. Offers MA. Part-time programs available. *Degree requirements:* For master's, comprehensive exam, thesis. *Entrance requirements:* For master's, GRE. Electronic applications accepted. *Faculty research:* Cell biology, topographical imaging, serotonin receptors in rats, enzyme assays, developmental biology.

Fitchburg State University, Division of Graduate and Continuing Education, Programs in Biology and Teaching Biology (Secondary Level), Fitchburg, MA 01420-2697. Offers MA, MAT, Certificate. *Accreditation:* NCATE. Part-time and evening/weekend programs available. *Students:* 2 full-time (both women), 9 part-time (4 women); includes 1 minority (Hispanic/Latino). Average age 37. 5 applicants, 100% accepted, 5 enrolled. In 2011, 1 master's awarded. *Entrance requirements:* Additional exam requirements/recommendations for international students: Required—TOEFL (minimum score 550 paper-based; 213 computer-based; 79 iBT). *Application deadline:* For fall admission, 7/15 for international students; for spring admission, 12/1 for international students. Applications are processed on a rolling basis. Application fee: $25 ($50 for international students). Electronic applications accepted. *Expenses:* Tuition, state resident: full-time $2700; part-time $150 per credit. Tuition, nonresident: full-time $2700; part-time $150 per credit. *Required fees:* $2286; $127 per credit. *Financial support:* In 2011–12, research assistantships with partial tuition reimbursements (averaging $5,500 per year) were awarded; Federal Work-Study, scholarships/grants, and unspecified assistantships also available. Support available to part-time students. Financial award application deadline: 3/1; financial award applicants required to submit FAFSA. *Unit head:* Dr. George Babich, Chair, 978-665-3245, Fax: 978-665-3658, E-mail: gce@fitchburgstate.edu. *Application contact:* Director of Admissions, 978-665-3144, Fax: 978-665-4540, E-mail: admissions@fitchburgstate.edu. Web site: http://www.fitchburgstate.edu.

Florida Agricultural and Mechanical University, Division of Graduate Studies, Research, and Continuing Education, College of Arts and Sciences, Department of Biology, Tallahassee, FL 32307-3200. Offers MS. Part-time programs available. *Degree requirements:* For master's, comprehensive exam, thesis. *Entrance requirements:* For master's, GRE General Test, minimum GPA of 3.0. Additional exam requirements/recommendations for international students: Required—TOEFL (minimum score 550 paper-based).

Biological and Biomedical Sciences—General

Florida Atlantic University, Charles E. Schmidt College of Medicine, Boca Raton, FL 33431-0991. Offers biomedical science (MS); integrative biology (PhD); medicine (MD). *Faculty:* 17 full-time (7 women), 4 part-time/adjunct (0 women). *Students:* 89 full-time (45 women), 11 part-time (6 women); includes 33 minority (3 Black or African American, non-Hispanic/Latino; 11 Asian, non-Hispanic/Latino; 15 Hispanic/Latino; 4 Two or more races, non-Hispanic/Latino), 4 international. Average age 24. 1,583 applicants, 7% accepted, 75 enrolled. In 2011, 26 master's awarded. *Degree requirements:* For master's, thesis (for some programs). *Entrance requirements:* For master's, GRE, minimum GPA of 3.0. *Application deadline:* For fall admission, 5/1 for domestic students, 3/15 for international students; for spring admission, 10/1 for domestic and international students. Application fee: $30. *Expenses: Tuition, area resident:* Part-time $343.02 per credit hour. Tuition, state resident: full-time $8232. Tuition, nonresident: full-time $23,931; part-time $997.14 per credit hour. *Financial support:* Fellowships and research assistantships available. *Faculty research:* Protein engineering, biology of mind-body interaction, neuroendocrinology, gene expression, methodologies of correction of gynecomastia. *Unit head:* Dr. David J. Bjorkman, Dean, 561-297-4341. *Application contact:* Julie Sivigny, Academic Program Specialist for Graduate Studies, 561-297-2216, E-mail: jsivigny@fau.edu. Web site: http://med.fau.edu/medicine.

Florida Atlantic University, Charles E. Schmidt College of Science, Department of Biological Sciences, Boca Raton, FL 33431-0991. Offers MS, MST. Part-time programs available. *Faculty:* 25 full-time (6 women), 8 part-time/adjunct (2 women). *Students:* 83 full-time (59 women), 37 part-time (23 women); includes 20 minority (3 Black or African American, non-Hispanic/Latino; 6 Asian, non-Hispanic/Latino; 10 Hispanic/Latino; 1 Two or more races, non-Hispanic/Latino), 18 international. Average age 30. 95 applicants, 27% accepted, 11 enrolled. In 2011, 15 master's awarded. *Degree requirements:* For master's, thesis (for some programs). *Entrance requirements:* For master's, GRE General Test, minimum GPA of 3.0. Additional exam requirements/recommendations for international students: Required—TOEFL. *Application deadline:* For fall admission, 3/15 for domestic and international students; for spring admission, 10/1 for domestic and international students. Application fee: $30. *Expenses: Tuition, area resident:* Part-time $343.02 per credit hour. Tuition, state resident: full-time $8232. Tuition, nonresident: full-time $23,931; part-time $997.14 per credit hour. *Financial support:* Fellowships, research assistantships, teaching assistantships with tuition reimbursements, career-related internships or fieldwork, and Federal Work-Study available. *Faculty research:* Ecology of the Everglades, molecular biology and biotechnology, marine biology. *Unit head:* Dr. Rodney K. Murphey, Chair, 561-297-3320, Fax: 561-297-2749. *Application contact:* Becky Dixon, Graduate Program Assistant, 561-297-3230. Web site: http://www.science.fau.edu/biology/.

Florida Institute of Technology, Graduate Programs, College of Science, Department of Biological Sciences, Melbourne, FL 32901-6975. Offers biological science (PhD); biotechnology (MS); cell and molecular biology (MS); conservation technology (MS); ecology (MS), including ecology, marine biology. Part-time programs available. *Faculty:* 16 full-time (2 women). *Students:* 84 full-time (52 women), 12 part-time (6 women); includes 6 minority (1 Asian, non-Hispanic/Latino; 3 Hispanic/Latino; 2 Two or more races, non-Hispanic/Latino), 50 international. Average age 26. 241 applicants, 35% accepted, 29 enrolled. In 2011, 21 master's, 3 doctorates awarded. *Degree requirements:* For master's, thesis (for some programs), research, seminar, internship, or summer lab; for doctorate, comprehensive exam, thesis/dissertation, dissertations seminar, publications. *Entrance requirements:* For master's, GRE General Test, 3 letters of recommendation, minimum GPA of 3.0, resume, statement of objectives; for doctorate, GRE General Test, resume, 3 letters of recommendation, minimum GPA of 3.2, statement of objectives. Additional exam requirements/recommendations for international students: Required—TOEFL (minimum score 550 paper-based; 213 computer-based; 79 iBT). *Application deadline:* For fall admission, 3/1 for domestic students, 4/1 for international students; for spring admission, 9/1 for domestic and international students. Applications are processed on a rolling basis. Electronic applications accepted. *Expenses: Tuition:* Full-time $19,620; part-time $1090 per credit hour. Tuition and fees vary according to campus/location. *Financial support:* In 2011–12, 6 fellowships (averaging $20,737 per year), 18 research assistantships with full and partial tuition reimbursements (averaging $10,742 per year), 20 teaching assistantships with full and partial tuition reimbursements (averaging $13,883 per year) were awarded; career-related internships or fieldwork, institutionally sponsored loans, tuition waivers (partial), unspecified assistantships, and tuition remissions also available. Support available to part-time students. Financial award application deadline: 3/1; financial award applicants required to submit FAFSA. *Faculty research:* Initiation of protein synthesis in eukaryotic cells, fixation of radioactive carbon, changes in DNA molecule, endangered or threatened avian and mammalian species, hydroacoustics and feeding preference of the West Indian manatee. *Total annual research expenditures:* $1.9 million. *Unit head:* Dr. Richard B. Aronson, Department Head, 321-674-8034, Fax: 321-674-7238, E-mail: raronson@fit.edu. *Application contact:* Cheryl A. Brown, Associate Director of Graduate Admissions, 321-674-7581, Fax: 321-723-9468, E-mail: cbrown@fit.edu. Web site: http://cos.fit.edu/biology/.

Florida International University, College of Arts and Sciences, Department of Biological Sciences, Miami, FL 33199. Offers MS, PhD. Part-time programs available. *Degree requirements:* For master's, thesis; for doctorate, comprehensive exam, thesis/dissertation. *Entrance requirements:* For master's, GRE General Test, 2 letters of recommendation, minimum GPA of 3.0, faculty sponsor; for doctorate, GRE General Test, 3 letters of recommendation, faculty sponsor with dissertation advisor status, minimum GPA of 3.0. Additional exam requirements/recommendations for international students: Required—TOEFL (minimum score 550 paper-based; 80 iBT). Electronic applications accepted.

Florida State University, The Graduate School, College of Arts and Sciences, Department of Biological Science, Tallahassee, FL 32306-4295. Offers cell and molecular biology and genetics (MS, PhD); ecology and evolutionary biology (MS, PhD); plant biology (MS, PhD); science teaching (MST); structural biology (MS, PhD). *Faculty:* 51 full-time (16 women). *Students:* 104 full-time (49 women); includes 11 minority (1 Asian, non-Hispanic/Latino; 10 Hispanic/Latino), 18 international. 288 applicants, 16% accepted, 19 enrolled. In 2011, 5 master's, 13 doctorates awarded. Terminal master's awarded for partial completion of doctoral program. *Degree requirements:* For master's, comprehensive exam, thesis, teaching experience, seminar presentations; for doctorate, comprehensive exam, thesis/dissertation, teaching experience; seminar presentations. *Entrance requirements:* For master's and doctorate, GRE General Test (minimum combined score 1100, 500 verbal, 500 quantitative in old version; 72% verbal, 67% quantitative in new format), minimum upper-division GPA of 3.0. Additional exam requirements/recommendations for international students: Required—TOEFL (minimum score 600 paper-based; 250 computer-based; 92 iBT). *Application deadline:* For fall admission, 12/15 for domestic and international students. Application fee: $30. Electronic applications accepted. *Expenses:* Tuition, state resident: full-time $9474; part-time $350.88 per credit hour. Tuition, nonresident: full-time $16,236; part-time $601.34 per credit hour. *Required fees:* $630 per semester. One-time fee: $20. Tuition and fees vary according to course load and campus/location. *Financial support:* In 2011–12, 99 students received support, including 6 fellowships with full tuition reimbursements available (averaging $30,000 per year), 37 research assistantships with full tuition reimbursements available (averaging $21,000 per year), 56 teaching

assistantships with full tuition reimbursements available (averaging $21,000 per year); traineeships also available. Financial award application deadline: 12/15; financial award applicants required to submit FAFSA. *Faculty research:* Cell and molecular biology and genetics, ecology and evolutionary biology, plant science, structural biology. *Total annual research expenditures:* $5.4 million. *Unit head:* Dr. George W. Bates, Professor and Associate Chairman, 850-644-5749, Fax: 850-644-9829, E-mail: bates@bio.fsu.edu. *Application contact:* Judy Bowers, Coordinator, Graduate Affairs, 850-644-3023, Fax: 850-644-9829, E-mail: gradinfo@bio.fsu.edu. Web site: http://www.bio.fsu.edu/.

Florida State University, The Graduate School, College of Arts and Sciences, Department of Mathematics, Tallahassee, FL 32306-4510. Offers applied computational mathematics (MS, PhD); biomathematics (MS, PhD); financial mathematics (MS, PhD); pure mathematics (MS, PhD). Part-time programs available. *Faculty:* 52 full-time (13 women), 1 (woman) part-time/adjunct. *Students:* 139 full-time (36 women), 7 part-time (1 woman); includes 15 minority (6 Black or African American, non-Hispanic/Latino; 4 Asian, non-Hispanic/Latino; 5 Hispanic/Latino), 99 international. Average age 27. 336 applicants, 41% accepted, 41 enrolled. In 2011, 43 master's, 14 doctorates awarded. Terminal master's awarded for partial completion of doctoral program. *Degree requirements:* For master's, comprehensive exam (for some programs), thesis optional; for doctorate, comprehensive exam, thesis/dissertation, candidacy exam including written qualifying examinations which differ by degree concentrations. *Entrance requirements:* For master's and doctorate, GRE General Test, minimum upper-division GPA of 3.0, 4-year bachelor's degree. Additional exam requirements/recommendations for international students: Required—TOEFL (minimum score 550 paper-based; 213 computer-bases; 80 iBT) or IELTS (minimum score 6.5). *Application deadline:* For fall admission, 1/1 priority date for domestic students, 1/1 for international students; for spring admission, 10/1 priority date for domestic students, 11/1 for international students. Applications are processed on a rolling basis. Application fee: $30. Electronic applications accepted. *Expenses:* Tuition, state resident: full-time $9474; part-time $350.88 per credit hour. Tuition, nonresident: full-time $16,236; part-time $601.34 per credit hour. *Required fees:* $630 per semester. One-time fee: $20. Tuition and fees vary according to course load and campus/location. *Financial support:* In 2011–12, 106 students received support, including 7 fellowships with full tuition reimbursements available (averaging $22,600 per year), 12 research assistantships with full tuition reimbursements available (averaging $22,000 per year), 78 teaching assistantships with full tuition reimbursements available (averaging $19,300 per year); career-related internships or fieldwork, institutionally sponsored loans, scholarships/grants, health care benefits, and unspecified assistantships also available. *Faculty research:* Algebra and algebraic geometry; applied, financial, numerical, and classical analysis; biomathematics, including shape analysis and anatomical imaging; computational mathematics and numerical algorithms; geometric topology. *Unit head:* Dr. Philip L. Bowers, Chairperson, 850-645-3338, Fax: 850-644-4053, E-mail: bowers@math.fsu.edu. *Application contact:* Dr. Bettye Anne Case, Associate Chair for Graduate Studies, 850-644-1586, Fax: 850-644-4053, E-mail: case@math.fsu.edu. Web site: http://www.math.fsu.edu/.

Florida State University, The Graduate School, College of Arts and Sciences, Department of Scientific Computing, Tallahassee, FL 32306-4120. Offers computational science (MS, PSM, PhD), including atmospheric science (PhD), biochemistry (PhD), biological science (PhD), computational molecular biology/bioinformatics (PSM), computational science (PhD), geological science (PhD), materials science (PhD), physics (PhD). Part-time programs available. *Faculty:* 14 full-time (2 women). *Students:* 32 full-time (6 women), 3 part-time (0 women); includes 13 minority (1 Black or African American, non-Hispanic/Latino; 11 Asian, non-Hispanic/Latino; 1 Hispanic/Latino). Average age 28. 29 applicants, 41% accepted, 9 enrolled. In 2011, 14 master's, 3 doctorates awarded. Terminal master's awarded for partial completion of doctoral program. *Degree requirements:* For master's, thesis (for some programs); for doctorate, comprehensive exam, thesis/dissertation. *Entrance requirements:* For master's and doctorate, GRE General Test, knowledge of at least one object-oriented computing language, 3 letters of recommendations. Additional exam requirements/recommendations for international students: Required—TOEFL (minimum score 550 paper-based; 80 iBT). *Application deadline:* For fall admission, 1/15 for domestic and international students. Application fee: $30. Electronic applications accepted. *Expenses:* Tuition, state resident: full-time $9474; part-time $350.88 per credit hour. Tuition, nonresident: full-time $16,236; part-time $601.34 per credit hour. *Required fees:* $630 per semester. One-time fee: $20. Tuition and fees vary according to course load and campus/location. *Financial support:* In 2011–12, 32 students received support, including 12 research assistantships with full tuition reimbursements available (averaging $20,000 per year), 18 teaching assistantships with full tuition reimbursements available (averaging $20,000 per year); unspecified assistantships also available. Financial award application deadline: 4/15. *Faculty research:* Morphometrics, mathematical and systems biology, mining proteomic and metabolic data, computational materials research at Scientific Computing, advanced 4-D Var Data-Assimilation methods in dynamic meteorology and oceanography, computational fluid dynamics, astrophysics. *Unit head:* Dr. Sam Huckaba, Interim Dean, 850-644-1081. *Application contact:* Maribel Amwake, Graduate Academic Coordinator, 850-644-0143, Fax: 850-644-0098, E-mail: mamwake@fsu.edu. Web site: http://www.sc.fsu.edu.

Fordham University, Graduate School of Arts and Sciences, Department of Biological Sciences, New York, NY 10458. Offers MS, PhD. Part-time and evening/weekend programs available. *Faculty:* 18 full-time (2 women). *Students:* 41 full-time (25 women), 14 part-time (8 women), 17 international. Average age 27. 85 applicants, 38% accepted, 18 enrolled. In 2011, 8 master's, 5 doctorates awarded. Terminal master's awarded for partial completion of doctoral program. *Degree requirements:* For master's, one foreign language, comprehensive exam, thesis optional; for doctorate, one foreign language, comprehensive exam, thesis/dissertation. *Entrance requirements:* For master's and doctorate, GRE General Test, GRE Subject Test (recommended). Additional exam requirements/recommendations for international students: Required—TOEFL (minimum score 550 paper-based; 213 computer-based). *Application deadline:* For fall admission, 1/4 priority date for domestic students; for spring admission, 11/1 for domestic students. Application fee: $70. Electronic applications accepted. *Expenses: Tuition:* Full-time $30,480; part-time $1270 per credit. *Required fees:* $586; $293 per semester. *Financial support:* In 2011–12, 28 students received support, including 3 fellowships with full and partial tuition reimbursements available (averaging $30,500 per year), 24 research assistantships with full and partial tuition reimbursements available (averaging $27,020 per year), 1 teaching assistantship with full and partial tuition reimbursement available (averaging $9,600 per year); Federal Work-Study, institutionally sponsored loans, scholarships/grants, tuition waivers (full and partial), and unspecified assistantships also available. Support available to part-time students. Financial award application deadline: 1/4; financial award applicants required to submit FAFSA. *Faculty research:* Avian ecology, behavioral ecology, and conservation biology; plant, community and ecosystem responses to invasive organisms; neurobiology and ion channel disorders; biochemical, physiological and morphological basis of pattern formation; behavioral, physiological and biochemical adaptations of mammals to extreme environments; evolutionary ecology, functional morphology and ichthyology; genotypic response to biogeographic and anthropogenic factors; community-based sustainable resource use. *Total annual*

research expenditures: $2.1 million. *Unit head:* Dr. James Lewis, Chair, 718-817-3642, Fax: 718-817-3645, E-mail: jdlewis@fordham.edu. *Application contact:* Bernadette Valentino-Morrison, Director of Graduate Admissions, 718-817-4419, Fax: 718-817-3566, E-mail: valentinomor@fordham.edu.

Fort Hays State University, Graduate School, College of Health and Life Sciences, Department of Biological Sciences, Program in Biology, Hays, KS 67601-4099. Offers MS. Part-time programs available: *Degree requirements:* For master's, comprehensive exam, thesis optional. *Entrance requirements:* Additional exam requirements/recommendations for international students: Required—TOEFL (minimum score 550 paper-based; 213 computer-based). Electronic applications accepted.

Frostburg State University, Graduate School, College of Liberal Arts and Sciences, Department of Biology, Frostburg, MD 21532-1099. Offers applied ecology and conservation biology (MS); fisheries and wildlife management (MS). Part-time and evening/weekend programs available. *Degree requirements:* For master's, thesis. *Entrance requirements:* For master's, GRE General Test, resume. Additional exam requirements/recommendations for international students: Required—TOEFL. Electronic applications accepted. *Faculty research:* Molecular and morphological evolution, ecology and behavior of birds, conservation genetics of amphibians and fishes, biology of endangered species.

George Mason University, College of Humanities and Social Sciences, Department of Public and International Affairs, Fairfax, VA 22030. Offers association management (Certificate); biodefense (MS, PhD); emergency management and homeland security (Certificate); nonprofit management (Certificate); political science (MA, PhD); public administration (MPA); public management (Certificate). *Accreditation:* NASPAA (one or more programs are accredited). *Faculty:* 37 full-time (12 women), 38 part-time/adjunct (9 women). *Students:* 139 full-time (74 women), 316 part-time (178 women); includes 92 minority (31 Black or African American, non-Hispanic/Latino; 21 Asian, non-Hispanic/Latino; 27 Hispanic/Latino; 3 Native Hawaiian or other Pacific Islander, non-Hispanic/Latino; 10 Two or more races, non-Hispanic/Latino), 14 international. Average age 31. 505 applicants, 54% accepted, 134 enrolled. In 2011, 135 master's, 3 doctorates, 8 other advanced degrees awarded. *Entrance requirements:* For master's, GRE, GMAT or LSAT (for MPA); GRE (for MS in biodefense and MA in political science), expanded goals statement; 3 letters of recommendation; official transcripts; resume (for MPA); writing sample (for MS, MA); for doctorate, GRE (taken within the last 5 years), 3 letters of recommendation; expanded goals statement; resume; official transcript; writing sample; for Certificate, GRE, GMAT or LSAT, expanded goals statement; 3 letters of recommendation; official transcripts; resume. Additional exam requirements/recommendations for international students: Required—TOEFL (minimum score 570 paper-based; 230 computer-based; 88 iBT), IELTS, Pearson Test of English. Application fee: $65 ($80 for international students). Electronic applications accepted. *Expenses:* Tuition, state resident: full-time $8750; part-time $364.58 per credit. Tuition, nonresident: full-time $24,092; part-time $1003.83 per credit. *Required fees:* $2514; $104.75 per credit. *Financial support:* In 2011–12, 30 students received support, including 3 fellowships with full tuition reimbursements available (averaging $18,000 per year), 12 research assistantships with full and partial tuition reimbursements available (averaging $11,769 per year), 15 teaching assistantships with full and partial tuition reimbursements available (averaging $11,600 per year); career-related internships or fieldwork, Federal Work-Study, scholarships/grants, unspecified assistantships, and health care benefits (full-time research or teaching assistantship recipients) also available. Support available to part-time students. Financial award application deadline: 3/1; financial award applicants required to submit FAFSA. *Faculty research:* The Rehnquist Court and economic liberties; intersection of economic development with high-tech industry, telecommunications, and entrepreneurism; political economy of development; violence, terrorism and U. S. foreign policy; international security issues. *Total annual research expenditures:* $666,214. *Unit head:* Dr. Priscilla Regan, Chair, 703-993-1419, Fax: 703-993-1399, E-mail: pregan@gmu.edu. *Application contact:* Peg Koback, Education Support Specialist, 703-993-9466, E-mail: mkoback@gmu.edu. Web site: http://pia.gmu.edu/.

George Mason University, College of Science, Programs in Biomedical Sciences, Fairfax, VA 22030. Offers MS, Advanced Certificate. Programs jointly offered with Georgetown University. *Faculty:* 4 full-time (3 women), 1 part-time/adjunct. *Students:* 90 full-time (59 women), 2 part-time (0 women); includes 51 minority (22 Black or African American, non-Hispanic/Latino; 22 Asian, non-Hispanic/Latino; 4 Hispanic/Latino; 3 Two or more races, non-Hispanic/Latino), 3 international. Average age 24. 378 applicants, 52% accepted, 90 enrolled. In 2011, 45 other advanced degrees awarded. *Entrance requirements:* For master's, MCAT or GRE, BA/BS in related field with minimum GPA of 3.0; 3 letters of recommendation; expanded goals statement; resume; 2 official copies of transcripts; department form; for Advanced Certificate, bachelor's degree in related field with minimum GPA of 3.0; 3 letters of recommendation; resume; expanded goals statement; 2 official copies of transcripts. Additional exam requirements/recommendations for international students: Required—TOEFL (minimum score 570 paper-based; 230 computer-based; 88 iBT), IELTS, Pearson Test of English. *Application deadline:* For fall admission, 4/15 priority date for domestic students. Application fee: $65 ($80 for international students). Electronic applications accepted. *Expenses:* Tuition, state resident: full-time $8750; part-time $364.58 per credit. Tuition, nonresident: full-time $24,092; part-time $1003.83 per credit. *Required fees:* $2514; $104.75 per credit. *Financial support:* Application deadline: 3/1; applicants required to submit FAFSA. *Unit head:* Dr. Vikas E. Chandhoke, Director, 703-993-3622, Fax: 703-993-1993, E-mail: cosinfo@gmu.edu. *Application contact:* Melissa C. Hayes, Graduate Program Director, 703-993-3430, Fax: 703-993-9034, E-mail: mhayes@gmu.edu. Web site: http://cos.gmu.edu/departments/biomedical-sciences-programs.

George Mason University, College of Science, School of Systems Biology, Fairfax, VA 22030. Offers bioinformatics and computational biology (MS, PhD, Graduate Certificate); biology (MS); biosciences (PhD). *Faculty:* 15 full-time (5 women), 1 part-time/adjunct. *Students:* 68 full-time (25 women), 66 part-time (36 women); includes 33 minority (3 Black or African American, non-Hispanic/Latino; 28 Asian, non-Hispanic/Latino; 1 Hispanic/Latino; 1 Two or more races, non-Hispanic/Latino), 40 international. Average age 32. 179 applicants, 49% accepted, 34 enrolled. In 2011, 23 master's, 13 doctorates, 1 other advanced degree awarded. *Degree requirements:* For master's, research project or thesis. *Entrance requirements:* For master's, GRE, resume; 3 letters of recommendation; expanded goals statement; 2 copies of official transcripts; bachelor's degree in related field with minimum GPA of 3.0 in last 60 hours; for doctorate, GRE, self-assessment form; resume; 3 letters of recommendation; expanded goals statement; 2 copies of official transcripts; bachelor's degree in related field with minimum GPA of 3.0 in last 60 hours; for Graduate Certificate, resume; 2 copies of official transcripts. Additional exam requirements/recommendations for international students: Required—TOEFL (minimum score 570 paper-based; 230 computer-based; 88 iBT), IELTS, Pearson Test of English. Application fee: $65 ($80 for international students). Electronic applications accepted. *Expenses:* Tuition, state resident: full-time $8750; part-time $364.58 per credit. Tuition, nonresident: full-time $24,092; part-time $1003.83 per credit. *Required fees:* $2514; $104.75 per credit. *Financial support:* In 2011–12, 44 students received support, including 6 fellowships with full tuition reimbursements available (averaging $18,000 per year), 9 research assistantships with

full and partial tuition reimbursements available (averaging $13,682 per year), 29 teaching assistantships with full and partial tuition reimbursements available (averaging $12,559 per year); career-related internships or fieldwork, Federal Work-Study, scholarships/grants, unspecified assistantships, and health care benefits (full-time research or teaching assistantship recipients) also available. Support available to part-time students. Financial award application deadline: 3/1; financial award applicants required to submit FAFSA. *Total annual research expenditures:* $1.3 million. *Unit head:* Dr. James D. Willett, Director, 703-993-8311, Fax: 703-993-8976, E-mail: jwillett@gmu.edu. *Application contact:* Diane St. Germain, Graduate Student Services Coordinator, 703-993-4263, Fax: 703-993-8976, E-mail: dstgerma@gmu.edu. Web site: http://ssb.gmu.edu.

Georgetown University, GeorgeSquared Special Master's Program, Washington, DC 20057. Offers MS. Program offered jointly with George Mason University.

Georgetown University, Graduate School of Arts and Sciences, Department of Biology, Washington, DC 20057. Offers MS, PhD. Terminal master's awarded for partial completion of doctoral program. *Degree requirements:* For master's, comprehensive exam, thesis; for doctorate, comprehensive exam, thesis/dissertation. *Entrance requirements:* For master's and doctorate, GRE General Test, GRE Subject Test (biology). Additional exam requirements/recommendations for international students: Required—TOEFL (minimum score 550 paper-based; 213 computer-based). Electronic applications accepted. *Faculty research:* Parasitology, ecology, evaluation and behavior, neuroscience and development, cell and molecular biology, immunology.

Georgetown University, Graduate School of Arts and Sciences, Programs in Biomedical Sciences, Washington, DC 20057. Offers MS, PhD, MD/PhD, MS/PhD. *Entrance requirements:* For doctorate, GRE General Test. Additional exam requirements/recommendations for international students: Required—TOEFL.

Georgetown University, National Institutes of Health Sponsored Programs, GU-NIH Graduate Partnership Programs in Biomedical Sciences, Washington, DC 20057. Offers MS, PhD, MD/PhD, MS/PhD. *Entrance requirements:* For doctorate, GRE General Test. Additional exam requirements/recommendations for international students: Required—TOEFL.

The George Washington University, Columbian College of Arts and Sciences, Department of Anthropology, Program in Hominid Paleobiology, Washington, DC 20052. Offers MS, PhD. Part-time and evening/weekend programs available. Terminal master's awarded for partial completion of doctoral program. *Degree requirements:* For master's, comprehensive exam, thesis; for doctorate, thesis/dissertation, general exam. *Entrance requirements:* For master's, GRE General Test, bachelor's degree in field, minimum GPA of 3.0; for doctorate, GRE General Test, minimum GPA of 3.0. Additional exam requirements/recommendations for international students: Required—TOEFL (minimum score 550 paper-based; 213 computer-based). Electronic applications accepted.

The George Washington University, Columbian College of Arts and Sciences, Department of Biological Sciences, Washington, DC 20052. Offers MS, PhD. Part-time and evening/weekend programs available. *Faculty:* 20 full-time (6 women), 6 part-time/adjunct (3 women). *Students:* 19 full-time (12 women), 12 part-time (8 women), 15 international. Average age 30. 72 applicants, 21% accepted, 7 enrolled. In 2011, 2 doctorates awarded. Terminal master's awarded for partial completion of doctoral program. *Degree requirements:* For master's, comprehensive exam; for doctorate, thesis/dissertation, general exam. *Entrance requirements:* For master's and doctorate, GRE General Test, minimum GPA of 3.0. Additional exam requirements/recommendations for international students: Required—TOEFL (minimum score 550 paper-based; 213 computer-based; 80 iBT). *Application deadline:* For fall admission, 1/2 priority date for domestic students, 1/2 for international students; for spring admission, 10/1 priority date for domestic students, 10/1 for international students. Applications are processed on a rolling basis. Application fee: $75. Electronic applications accepted. *Financial support:* In 2011–12, 25 students received support. Fellowships with full tuition reimbursements available, teaching assistantships with full tuition reimbursements available, Federal Work-Study, and tuition waivers available. Financial award application deadline: 1/2. *Faculty research:* Systematics, evolution, ecology, developmental biology, cell/molecular biology. *Total annual research expenditures:* $900,000. *Unit head:* Dr. James M. Clark, Chair, 202-994-7144, Fax: 202-994-6100, E-mail: jclark@gwu.edu. *Application contact:* Dr. John R. Burns, Professor, 202-994-7149, Fax: 202-994-6100, E-mail: jrburns@gwu.edu.

The George Washington University, Columbian College of Arts and Sciences, Institute for Biomedical Sciences, Washington, DC 20037. Offers biochemistry and molecular genetics (PhD); microbiology and immunology (PhD); molecular medicine (PhD), including molecular and cellular oncology, neurosciences, pharmacology and physiology. Part-time and evening/weekend programs available. *Students:* 13 full-time (9 women), 45 part-time (26 women); includes 7 minority (1 Black or African American, non-Hispanic/Latino; 1 American Indian or Alaska Native, non-Hispanic/Latino; 4 Asian, non-Hispanic/Latino; 1 Hispanic/Latino), 11 international. Average age 30. 188 applicants, 8% accepted. In 2011, 16 doctorates awarded. *Degree requirements:* For doctorate, thesis/dissertation. *Entrance requirements:* For doctorate, GRE General Test, minimum GPA of 3.0. Additional exam requirements/recommendations for international students: Required—TOEFL (minimum score 600 paper-based; 250 computer-based; 80 iBT). *Application deadline:* For fall admission, 12/15 priority date for domestic students, 12/15 for international students. Applications are processed on a rolling basis. Application fee: $60. Electronic applications accepted. *Financial support:* In 2011–12, 24 students received support. Fellowships with full tuition reimbursements available, Federal Work-Study, institutionally sponsored loans, and tuition waivers available. *Unit head:* Dr. Linda L. Werling, Director, 202-994-2918, Fax: 202-994-0967. *Application contact:* 202-994-2179, Fax: 202-994-0967, E-mail: gwibs@gwu.edu. Web site: http://www.gwumc.edu/ibs/.

Georgia Campus–Philadelphia College of Osteopathic Medicine, Program in Biomedical Sciences, Suwanee, GA 30024. Offers MS, Certificate.

Georgia College & State University, Graduate School, College of Arts and Sciences, Department of Biology, Milledgeville, GA 31061. Offers MS. Part-time programs available. *Students:* 27 full-time (7 women), 8 part-time (2 women); includes 2 minority (1 Black or African American, non-Hispanic/Latino; 1 Asian, non-Hispanic/Latino), 6 international. Average age 26. 29 applicants, 59% accepted, 11 enrolled. In 2011, 16 master's awarded. *Degree requirements:* For master's, thesis optional, minimum GPA of 3.0. *Entrance requirements:* For master's, GRE (minimum score of 800), 30 hours undergraduate course work in biological science. Additional exam requirements/recommendations for international students: Recommended—TOEFL (minimum score 550 paper-based; 213 computer-based; 79 iBT). *Application deadline:* For fall admission, 7/1 priority date for domestic students, 4/1 for international students; for spring admission, 11/15 priority date for domestic students, 9/1 for international students. Applications are processed on a rolling basis. Application fee: $40. Electronic applications accepted. *Expenses:* Tuition, state resident: full-time $4806; part-time $267 per credit hour. Tuition, nonresident: full-time $17,802; part-time $989 per credit hour. *Required fees:* $936 per semester. Tuition and fees vary according to course load and campus/location. *Financial support:* In 2011–12, 23 research assistantships with tuition reimbursements were awarded; career-related internships or fieldwork and unspecified

assistantships also available. Support available to part-time students. Financial award application deadline: 3/1; financial award applicants required to submit FAFSA. *Faculty research:* Molecular genetics, cell biology, environmental microbiology, microbial ecology. *Unit head:* Dr. Indiren Pillay, Chair, 478-445-0809, E-mail: indiren.pillayll@gcsu.edu. *Application contact:* Dr. Chris Skelton, Graduate Coordinator, 478-445-2440, E-mail: chris.skelton@gcsu.edu.

Georgia Health Sciences University, College of Graduate Studies, Augusta, GA 30912. Offers MCTS, MPH, MS, MSN, DNP, PhD, CCTS, Post-Master's Certificate. Part-time programs available. Postbaccalaureate distance learning degree programs offered (no on-campus study). *Faculty:* 225 full-time (74 women), 7 part-time/adjunct (4 women). *Students:* 471 full-time (355 women), 122 part-time (101 women); includes 122 minority (60 Black or African American, non-Hispanic/Latino; 2 American Indian or Alaska Native, non-Hispanic/Latino; 33 Asian, non-Hispanic/Latino; 15 Hispanic/Latino; 12 Two or more races, non-Hispanic/Latino), 81 international. Average age 31. 451 applicants, 44% accepted, 125 enrolled. In 2011, 104 master's, 33 doctorates awarded. *Degree requirements:* For doctorate, thesis/dissertation. *Entrance requirements:* For master's and doctorate, GRE General Test. Additional exam requirements/recommendations for international students: Required—TOEFL. Application fee: $50. Electronic applications accepted. *Financial support:* In 2011–12, 10 fellowships with partial tuition reimbursements (averaging $26,000 per year), 111 research assistantships with partial tuition reimbursements (averaging $23,000 per year) were awarded; teaching assistantships, career-related internships or fieldwork, Federal Work-Study, institutionally sponsored loans, scholarships/grants, traineeships, and unspecified assistantships also available. Support available to part-time students. Financial award application deadline: 5/31; financial award applicants required to submit FAFSA. *Faculty research:* Cancer, cardiovascular biology, neurosciences, inflammation/infection, diabetes. *Total annual research expenditures:* $331,986. *Unit head:* Dr. Gretchen B. Caughman, Dean, 706-721-3278, Fax: 706-721-6829, E-mail: gcaughma@mail.mcg.edu. *Application contact:* Heather Metress, Interim Director of Admissions, 706-721-2725, Fax: 706-721-7279, E-mail: hmetress@georgiahealth.edu. Web site: http://www.georgiahealth.edu/gradstudies/.

Georgia Institute of Technology, Graduate Studies and Research, College of Sciences, School of Biology, Atlanta, GA 30332-0001. Offers applied biology (MS, PhD); bioinformatics (MS, PhD); biology (MS). Part-time programs available. Terminal master's awarded for partial completion of doctoral program. *Degree requirements:* For master's, thesis; for doctorate, thesis/dissertation, qualifying exam. *Entrance requirements:* For master's, GRE General Test, minimum GPA of 2.9; for doctorate, GRE General Test, minimum GPA of 3.0. Additional exam requirements/recommendations for international students: Required—TOEFL. Electronic applications accepted. *Faculty research:* Microbiology, molecular and cell biology, ecology.

Georgian Court University, School of Arts and Sciences, Lakewood, NJ 08701-2697. Offers biology (MA); Catholic school leadership (Certificate); clinical mental health counseling (MA); holistic health studies (MA); mathematics (MA); pastoral ministry (Certificate); religious education (Certificate); school psychology (Certificate); theology (MA, Certificate). Part-time and evening/weekend programs available. *Faculty:* 21 full-time (10 women), 6 part-time/adjunct (5 women). *Students:* 88 full-time (84 women), 126 part-time (107 women); includes 29 minority (11 Black or African American, non-Hispanic/Latino; 5 Asian, non-Hispanic/Latino; 12 Hispanic/Latino; 1 Two or more races, non-Hispanic/Latino), 1 international. Average age 39. 210 applicants, 54% accepted, 79 enrolled. In 2011, 5 master's awarded. *Degree requirements:* For master's, comprehensive exam (for some programs), thesis (for some programs). *Entrance requirements:* For master's, GRE, MAT, or NTE/PRAXIS, 3 letters of recommendation. Additional exam requirements/recommendations for international students: Required—TOEFL (minimum score 550 paper-based; 213 computer-based). *Application deadline:* For fall admission, 8/1 priority date for domestic students, 4/1 for international students; for spring admission, 1/1 priority date for domestic students, 7/1 for international students. Applications are processed on a rolling basis. Application fee: $40. Electronic applications accepted. *Expenses: Tuition:* Full-time $13,410; part-time $745 per credit. *Required fees:* $450 per year. Tuition and fees vary according to campus/location and program. *Financial support:* Scholarships/grants, health care benefits, and unspecified assistantships available. Financial award application deadline: 4/15; financial award applicants required to submit FAFSA. *Unit head:* Dr. Rita Kipp, Dean, 732-987-2493, Fax: 732-987-2007. *Application contact:* Patrick Givens, Assistant Director of Graduate Admissions, 732-987-2736, Fax: 732-987-2084, E-mail: graduateadmissions@georgian.edu. Web site: http://www.georgian.edu/arts_sciences/index.htm.

Georgia Southern University, Jack N. Averitt College of Graduate Studies, Allen E. Paulson College of Science and Technology, Department of Biology, Statesboro, GA 30460. Offers MS. Part-time programs available. *Students:* 42 full-time (21 women), 6 part-time (3 women); includes 7 minority (2 Black or African American, non-Hispanic/Latino; 1 American Indian or Alaska Native, non-Hispanic/Latino; 3 Asian, non-Hispanic/Latino; 1 Hispanic/Latino), 1 international. Average age 26. 27 applicants, 74% accepted, 15 enrolled. In 2011, 8 master's awarded. *Degree requirements:* For master's, comprehensive exam, thesis optional, terminal exam. *Entrance requirements:* For master's, GRE General Test, GRE Subject Test, minimum GPA of 2.8, BS in biology, 2 letters of reference. Additional exam requirements/recommendations for international students: Required—TOEFL (minimum score 550 paper-based; 216 computer-based; 80 iBT). *Application deadline:* For fall admission, 3/1 priority date for domestic students, 3/1 for international students; for spring admission, 10/1 priority date for domestic students, 10/1 for international students. Applications are processed on a rolling basis. Application fee: $50. Electronic applications accepted. *Expenses:* Tuition, state resident: full-time $6300; part-time $263 per semester hour. Tuition, nonresident: full-time $25,174; part-time $1049 per semester hour. *Required fees:* $1872. *Financial support:* In 2011–12, 37 students received support, including research assistantships with partial tuition reimbursements available (averaging $10,000 per year), teaching assistantships with partial tuition reimbursements available (averaging $10,000 per year); career-related internships or fieldwork, Federal Work-Study, scholarships/grants, tuition waivers (partial), and unspecified assistantships also available. Support available to part-time students. Financial award application deadline: 4/15; financial award applicants required to submit FAFSA. *Faculty research:* Behavior, evolution and ecology, molecular biology, physiology, vector-borne diseases. *Total annual research expenditures:* $1.5 million. *Unit head:* Dr. Stephen Vives, Chair, 912-478-5487, Fax: 912-478-0845, E-mail: svives@georgiasouthern.edu. *Application contact:* Amanda Gilliland, Coordinator for Graduate Student Recruitment, 912-478-5384, Fax: 912-478-0740, E-mail: gradadmissions@georgiasouthern.edu. Web site: http://www.bio.georgiasouthern.edu.

Georgia State University, College of Arts and Sciences, Department of Biology, Atlanta, GA 30302-3083. Offers applied and environmental microbiology (MS, PhD); cellular and molecular biology and physiology (MS, PhD); molecular genetics and biochemistry (MS, PhD); neurobiology and behavior (MS, PhD). Part-time programs available. Terminal master's awarded for partial completion of doctoral program. *Degree requirements:* For master's, thesis or alternative; for doctorate, thesis/dissertation, exam. *Entrance requirements:* For master's and doctorate, GRE General Test. Additional exam requirements/recommendations for international students: Required—TOEFL. Electronic applications accepted. *Faculty research:* Physiological biochemistry, gene expression, molecular virology, microbial ecology, integration in neural systems.

Georgia State University, College of Arts and Sciences, MD/PhD Program, Atlanta, GA 30302-3083. Offers MD/PhD.

Gerstner Sloan-Kettering Graduate School of Biomedical Sciences, Program in Cancer Biology, New York, NY 10021. Offers PhD. *Faculty:* 118 full-time (20 women). *Students:* 52 full-time (29 women); includes 6 minority (1 Black or African American, non-Hispanic/Latino; 4 Asian, non-Hispanic/Latino; 1 Hispanic/Latino), 4 international. In 2011, 3 doctorates awarded. *Degree requirements:* For doctorate, thesis/dissertation. *Entrance requirements:* For doctorate, GRE, transcripts, letters of recommendation. Electronic applications accepted. *Financial support:* Fellowship package including stipend ($33,773), full-tuition scholarship, first-year allowance, and comprehensive medical and dental insurance available. *Faculty research:* Biochemistry and molecular biology, biophysics/structural biology, computational biology, genetics, immunology. *Unit head:* Linda Burnley, Associate Dean, 646-888-6639, E-mail: burnleyl@sloankettering.edu. *Application contact:* Main Office, 646-888-6639, Fax: 646-422-2351, E-mail: gradstudies@sloankettering.edu.

See Display on page 182 and Close-Up on page 235.

Goucher College, Program in Post-Baccalaureate Premedical Studies, Baltimore, MD 21204-2794. Offers Certificate. *Faculty:* 10 full-time (3 women). *Students:* 30 full-time (16 women); includes 3 minority (all Asian, non-Hispanic/Latino). Average age 24. In 2011, 31 Certificates awarded. *Entrance requirements:* For degree, GRE, SAT or ACT. *Application deadline:* Applications are processed on a rolling basis. Application fee: $50. *Expenses:* Contact institution. *Financial support:* In 2011–12, 5 fellowships (averaging $4,000 per year) were awarded; institutionally sponsored loans and scholarships/grants also available. Financial award application deadline: 3/1; financial award applicants required to submit FAFSA. *Unit head:* Betsy Merideth, Director, 800-414-3437, Fax: 410-337-6461, E-mail: bmerideth@goucher.edu. *Application contact:* Theresa Reifsnider, Associate Dean for Graduate and Professional Studies, 410-337-3437, Fax: 410-337-6461, E-mail: pbpm@goucher.edu. Web site: http://www.goucher.edu/postbac/.

Graduate School and University Center of the City University of New York, Graduate Studies, Program in Biology, New York, NY 10016-4039. Offers PhD. *Degree requirements:* For doctorate, thesis/dissertation, teaching experience. *Entrance requirements:* For doctorate, GRE General Test. Additional exam requirements/recommendations for international students: Required—TOEFL. Electronic applications accepted.

Grand Valley State University, College of Liberal Arts and Sciences, Biology Department, Allendale, MI 49401-9403. Offers MS. Part-time programs available. *Degree requirements:* For master's, comprehensive exam, thesis or alternative. *Entrance requirements:* For master's, GRE General Test, 3 letters of reference. Additional exam requirements/recommendations for international students: Required—TOEFL. Electronic applications accepted. *Faculty research:* Natural resources conservation biology, aquatic sciences, terrestrial ecology, behavioral biology.

Grand Valley State University, College of Liberal Arts and Sciences, Department of Biomedical Sciences, Allendale, MI 49401-9403. Offers MHS. Part-time programs available. *Degree requirements:* For master's, thesis, qualifying exam. *Entrance requirements:* For master's, GRE General Test, minimum GPA of 3.0, 3 names of references. Additional exam requirements/recommendations for international students: Required—TOEFL. Electronic applications accepted. *Faculty research:* Cell regulation, neurobiology, parasitology, virology, microbial pathogenicity.

Hampton University, Graduate College, Department of Biological Sciences, Hampton, VA 23668. Offers biology (MS); environmental science (MS); medical science (MS). Part-time and evening/weekend programs available. *Degree requirements:* For master's, thesis optional. *Entrance requirements:* For master's, GRE General Test. *Faculty research:* Marine ecology, microbial and chemical pollution, pesticide problems.

Harvard University, Extension School, Cambridge, MA 02138-3722. Offers applied sciences (CAS); biotechnology (ALM); educational technologies (ALM); educational technology (CET); English for graduate and professional studies (DGP); environmental management (ALM, CEM); information technology (ALM); journalism (ALM); liberal arts (ALM); management (ALM, CM); mathematics for teaching (ALM); museum studies (ALM); premedical studies (Diploma); publication and communication (CPC). Part-time and evening/weekend programs available. *Degree requirements:* For master's, thesis. *Entrance requirements:* For master's, 3 completed graduate courses with grade of B or higher. Additional exam requirements/recommendations for international students: Required—TOEFL (minimum score 600 paper-based; 250 computer-based), TWE (minimum score 5). *Expenses:* Contact institution.

Harvard University, Graduate School of Arts and Sciences, Department of Organismic and Evolutionary Biology, Cambridge, MA 02138. Offers biology (PhD). *Degree requirements:* For doctorate, 2 foreign languages, public presentation of thesis research, exam. *Entrance requirements:* For doctorate, GRE General Test, GRE Subject Test (recommended), 7 courses in biology, chemistry, physics, mathematics, computer science, or geology. Additional exam requirements/recommendations for international students: Required—TOEFL. *Expenses: Tuition:* Full-time $36,304. *Required fees:* $1186. Full-time tuition and fees vary according to program.

Harvard University, Graduate School of Arts and Sciences, Division of Medical Sciences, Boston, MA 02115. Offers biological chemistry and molecular pharmacology (PhD); cell biology (PhD); genetics (PhD); microbiology and molecular genetics (PhD); pathology (PhD), including experimental pathology. *Degree requirements:* For doctorate, thesis/dissertation. *Entrance requirements:* For doctorate, GRE General Test, GRE Subject Test. Additional exam requirements/recommendations for international students: Required—TOEFL. *Expenses: Tuition:* Full-time $36,304. *Required fees:* $1186. Full-time tuition and fees vary according to program.

Harvard University, Harvard Medical School and Graduate School of Arts and Sciences, Division of Health Sciences and Technology, Biomedical Enterprise Program, Cambridge, MA 02138. Offers SM. *Students:* 28 full-time (15 women); includes 8 minority (1 American Indian or Alaska Native, non-Hispanic/Latino; 6 Asian, non-Hispanic/Latino; 1 Hispanic/Latino), 5 international. Average age 30. 43 applicants, 33% accepted, 13 enrolled. In 2011, 8 master's awarded. *Degree requirements:* For master's, thesis. *Entrance requirements:* For master's, GMAT or GRE, bachelor's degree in engineering or sciences, work experience in biomedical business. Additional exam requirements/recommendations for international students: Required—TOEFL. *Application deadline:* For fall admission, 12/15 for domestic and international students. Electronic applications accepted. *Expenses:* Contact institution. *Financial support:* In 2011–12, 8 students received support, including 1 fellowship (averaging $5,000 per year), 2 research assistantships with full and partial tuition reimbursements available (averaging $34,773 per year), 6 teaching assistantships with partial tuition reimbursements available (averaging $8,637 per year); institutionally sponsored loans, health care benefits, and unspecified assistantships also available. Financial award application deadline: 12/15; financial award applicants required to submit FAFSA. *Faculty research:* Entrepreneurship, technology strategy management, organizational

strategies and models, epidemiology and biostatistics, biomedical research from the molecular to the whole-organism level. *Unit head:* Dr. Richard Cohen, Co-Director, 617-253-7430. *Application contact:* Traci Anderson, Academic Programs Administrator, 617-253-7470, Fax: 617-253-6692, E-mail: tanderso@mit.edu.

Harvard University, Harvard School of Public Health, PhD Program in Biological Sciences in Public Health, Boston, MA 02115. Offers PhD. *Students:* 53 full-time; includes 12 minority (4 Black or African American, non-Hispanic/Latino; 5 Asian, non-Hispanic/Latino; 1 Hispanic/Latino; 2 Two or more races, non-Hispanic/Latino), 17 international. 110 applicants, 13% accepted, 10 enrolled. In 2011, 4 doctorates awarded. *Degree requirements:* For doctorate, qualifying examination, dissertation/defense. *Entrance requirements:* For doctorate, GRE General Test. Additional exam requirements/recommendations for international students: Required—TOEFL. *Application deadline:* For fall admission, 12/8 for domestic students. *Expenses: Tuition:* Full-time $36,304. *Required fees:* $1186. Full-time tuition and fees vary according to program. *Financial support:* Fellowships, research assistantships, teaching assistantships, institutionally sponsored loans, and tuition waivers (full) available. Financial award application deadline: 1/1. *Faculty research:* Nutrition biochemistry, molecular and cellular toxicology, cardiovascular disease, cancer biology, immunology and infectious diseases, environmental health physiology. *Unit head:* Carole Knapp, Administrator, 617-432-2932. *Application contact:* Leah W. Simons, Student Contact, 617-495-1000.

Heritage University, Graduate Programs in Education, Program in Professional Studies, Toppenish, WA 98948-9599. Offers bilingual education/ESL (M Ed); biology (M Ed); English and literature (M Ed); reading/literacy (M Ed); special education (M Ed). Part-time and evening/weekend programs available. *Degree requirements:* For master's, comprehensive exam (for some programs), thesis (for some programs).

Hofstra University, College of Liberal Arts and Sciences, Department of Biology, Hempstead, NY 11549. Offers biology (MA, MS); physician assistant studies (MS); urban ecology (MA, MS). Part-time and evening/weekend programs available. *Faculty:* 14 full-time (7 women), 3 part-time/adjunct (2 women). *Students:* 116 full-time (81 women), 10 part-time (6 women); includes 17 minority (4 Black or African American, non-Hispanic/Latino; 10 Asian, non-Hispanic/Latino; 3 Hispanic/Latino). Average age 25. 98 applicants, 89% accepted, 60 enrolled. In 2011, 5 master's awarded. *Degree requirements:* For master's, thesis, minimum GPA of 3.0. *Entrance requirements:* For master's, GRE, bachelor's degree in biology or equivalent; 2 letters of recommendation; essay. Additional exam requirements/recommendations for international students: Required—TOEFL (minimum score 550 paper-based; 213 computer-based; 80 iBT). *Application deadline:* Applications are processed on a rolling basis. Application fee: $70 ($75 for international students). Electronic applications accepted. *Expenses: Tuition:* Full-time $18,990; part-time $1055 per credit hour. *Required fees:* $970. Tuition and fees vary according to program. *Financial support:* In 2011–12, 20 students received support, including 12 fellowships with full and partial tuition reimbursements available (averaging $4,490 per year); research assistantships with full and partial tuition reimbursements available, Federal Work-Study, institutionally sponsored loans, scholarships/grants, and tuition waivers (full and partial) also available. Support available to part-time students. Financial award applicants required to submit FAFSA. *Faculty research:* Molecular basis of sex determination in turtles; regulation of fat metabolism in Drosophimelanogaster; molecular regulation of morphological differentiation in Streptomyces; population, ecology, evolution, and behavior of mammals, reptiles, and amphibians; systematics and biology of marine polychaete worms and crustaceans. *Total annual research expenditures:* $340,650. *Unit head:* Dr. Maureen K. Krause, Program Director, 516-463-6178, Fax: 516-463-5112, E-mail: biomkk@hofstra.edu. *Application contact:* Carol Drummer, Dean of Graduate Admissions, 516-463-4876, Fax: 516-463-4664, E-mail: gradstudent@hofstra.edu. Web site: http://www.hofstra.edu/hclas.

Hofstra University, School of Education, Health, and Human Services, Programs in Teaching - Secondary Education, Hempstead, NY 11549. Offers business education (MS Ed); education technology (Advanced Certificate); English education (MA, MS Ed); foreign language and TESOL (MS Ed); foreign language education (MA, MS Ed), including French, German, Russian, Spanish; mathematics education (MA, MS Ed); science education (MA, MS Ed), including biology, chemistry, earth science, geology, physics; secondary education (Advanced Certificate); social studies education (MA, MS Ed). Part-time and evening/weekend programs available. Postbaccalaureate distance learning degree programs offered (minimal on-campus study). *Students:* 72 full-time (47 women), 51 part-time (30 women); includes 21 minority (9 Black or African American, non-Hispanic/Latino; 7 Asian, non-Hispanic/Latino; 5 Hispanic/Latino). Average age 28. 103 applicants, 91% accepted, 41 enrolled. In 2011, 86 master's, 6 other advanced degrees awarded. *Degree requirements:* For master's, one foreign language, comprehensive exam (for some programs), thesis (for some programs), exit project, electronic portfolio, student teaching, fieldwork, curriculum project, minimum GPA of 3.0; for Advanced Certificate, 3 foreign languages, comprehensive exam (for some programs), thesis project, minimum GPA of 3.0. *Entrance requirements:* For master's, 2 letters of recommendation, teacher certification (MA), essay; for Advanced Certificate, 2 letters of recommendation, essay. Additional exam requirements/recommendations for international students: Required—TOEFL (minimum score 550 paper-based; 213 computer-based; 80 iBT). *Application deadline:* Applications are processed on a rolling basis. Application fee: $70 ($75 for international students). Electronic applications accepted. *Expenses: Tuition:* Full-time $18,990; part-time $1055 per credit hour. *Required fees:* $970. Tuition and fees vary according to program. *Financial support:* In 2011–12, 90 students received support, including 13 fellowships with full and partial tuition reimbursements available (averaging $3,202 per year), 1 research assistantship with full and partial tuition reimbursement available (averaging $11,645 per year); career-related internships or fieldwork, Federal Work-Study, institutionally sponsored loans, scholarships/grants, tuition waivers (full and partial), and unspecified assistantships also available. Support available to part-time students. Financial award applicants required to submit FAFSA. *Faculty research:* Appropriate content and pedagogy in secondary school disciplines, appropriate pedagogy in secondary school disciplines, adolescent development, secondary school organization, alternative secondary school programs. *Unit head:* Dr. Esther Fusco, Chairperson, 516-463-7704, Fax: 516-463-6196, E-mail: catezf@hofstra.edu. *Application contact:* Carol Drummer, Dean of Graduate Admissions, 516-463-4876, Fax: 516-463-4664, E-mail: gradstudent@hofstra.edu. Web site: http://www.hofstra.edu/education/.

Hood College, Graduate School, Program in Biomedical Science, Frederick, MD 21701-8575. Offers biomedical science (MS), including biotechnology/molecular biology, microbiology/immunology/virology, regulatory compliance; regulatory compliance (Certificate). Part-time and evening/weekend programs available. *Degree requirements:* For master's, comprehensive exam, thesis or alternative. *Entrance requirements:* For master's, bachelor's degree in biology; minimum GPA of 2.75; undergraduate course work in cell biology, chemistry, organic chemistry, and genetics. Additional exam requirements/recommendations for international students: Required—TOEFL (minimum score 575 paper-based; 231 computer-based; 89 iBT). Electronic applications accepted.

Howard University, Graduate School, Department of Biology, Washington, DC 20059-0002. Offers MS, PhD. Part-time programs available. *Degree requirements:* For master's, thesis, qualifying exams; for doctorate, thesis/dissertation, qualifying exams. *Entrance requirements:* For master's and doctorate, GRE General Test, minimum GPA of 3.0. Additional exam requirements/recommendations for international students: Required—TOEFL. Electronic applications accepted. *Faculty research:* Physiology, molecular biology, cell biology, microbiology, environmental biology.

Humboldt State University, Academic Programs, College of Natural Resources and Sciences, Department of Biological Sciences, Arcata, CA 95521-8299. Offers MA. *Students:* 27 full-time (17 women), 30 part-time (18 women); includes 9 minority (2 Asian, non-Hispanic/Latino; 5 Hispanic/Latino; 2 Two or more races, non-Hispanic/Latino), 1 international. Average age 32. 47 applicants, 47% accepted, 14 enrolled. In 2011, 8 master's awarded. *Degree requirements:* For master's, project or thesis. *Entrance requirements:* For master's, GRE General Test, appropriate bachelor's degree, minimum GPA of 2.5, 3 letters of recommendation. Additional exam requirements/recommendations for international students: Required—TOEFL (minimum score 500 paper-based; 173 computer-based). *Application deadline:* For fall admission, 2/15 for domestic and international students. Applications are processed on a rolling basis. Application fee: $55. *Expenses:* Tuition, state resident: full-time $6734. Tuition, nonresident: full-time $15,662; part-time $372 per credit. *Required fees:* $903. Tuition and fees vary according to program. *Financial support:* Application deadline: 3/1; applicants required to submit FAFSA. *Faculty research:* Plant ecology, DNA sequencing, invertebrates. *Unit head:* Dr. John Reiss, Chair, 707-826-3245, Fax: 707-826-3201, E-mail: jor1@humboldt.edu. *Application contact:* Dr. Michael Mesler, Coordinator, 707-826-3674, Fax: 707-826-3201, E-mail: mm1@humboldt.edu. Web site: http://www.humboldt.edu/biosci/programs/grad.html.

Hunter College of the City University of New York, Graduate School, School of Arts and Sciences, Department of Biological Sciences, New York, NY 10021-5085. Offers MA, PhD. PhD offered jointly with Graduate School and University Center of the City University of New York. Part-time programs available. *Faculty:* 10 full-time (5 women). *Students:* 9 full-time (7 women), 22 part-time (11 women); includes 17 minority (3 Black or African American, non-Hispanic/Latino; 8 Asian, non-Hispanic/Latino; 6 Hispanic/Latino), 5 international. Average age 26. 41 applicants, 51% accepted, 13 enrolled. In 2011, 21 master's awarded. Terminal master's awarded for partial completion of doctoral program. *Degree requirements:* For master's, one foreign language, comprehensive exam or thesis. *Entrance requirements:* For master's, GRE, 1 year of course work in organic chemistry (including laboratory), college physics, calculus; undergraduate major in biology, botany, physiology, zoology, chemistry or physics. Additional exam requirements/recommendations for international students: Required—TOEFL. *Application deadline:* For fall admission, 4/1 for domestic students, 2/1 for international students; for spring admission, 11/1 for domestic students, 9/1 for international students. Application fee: $125. *Expenses:* Tuition, state resident: full-time $8210; part-time $345 per credit. Tuition, nonresident: full-time $15,360; part-time $640 per credit. *Required fees:* $280 per semester. One-time fee: $125. Tuition and fees vary according to class time, campus/location and program. *Financial support:* Fellowships, research assistantships, teaching assistantships, scholarships/grants, and tuition waivers (partial) available. Support available to part-time students. *Faculty research:* Analysis of prokaryotic and eukaryotic DNA, protein structure, mammalian DNA replication, oncogene expression, neuroscience. *Unit head:* Dr. Shirley Raps, Chairperson, 212-772-5293, E-mail: raps@genectr.hunter.cuny.edu. *Application contact:* William Zlata, Director for Graduate Admissions, 212-772-4482, Fax: 212-650-3336, E-mail: admissions@hunter.cuny.edu.

ICR Graduate School, Graduate Programs, Santee, CA 92071. Offers astro/geophysics (MS); biology (MS); geology (MS); science education (MS). Part-time programs available. *Degree requirements:* For master's, comprehensive exam (for some programs), thesis (for some programs). *Entrance requirements:* For master's, minimum undergraduate GPA of 3.0, bachelor's degree in science or science education. *Faculty research:* Age of the earth, limits of variation, catastrophe, optimum methods for teaching.

Idaho State University, Office of Graduate Studies, College of Science and Engineering, Department of Biological Sciences, Pocatello, ID 83209-8007. Offers biology (MNS, MS, DA, PhD); clinical laboratory science (MS); microbiology (MS). *Accreditation:* NAACLS. Part-time programs available. *Degree requirements:* For master's, comprehensive exam, thesis; for doctorate, comprehensive exam, thesis/dissertation, 9 credits of internship (for DA). *Entrance requirements:* For master's, GRE General Test, minimum GPA of 3.0 in all upper division classes; for doctorate, GRE General Test, GRE Subject Test (biology), diagnostic exam (DA), minimum GPA of 3.0 in all upper division classes. Additional exam requirements/recommendations for international students: Required—TOEFL (minimum score 550 paper-based; 213 computer-based; 80 iBT). Electronic applications accepted. *Faculty research:* Ecology, plant and animal physiology, plant and animal developmental biology, immunology, molecular biology, bioinfomatics.

Illinois Institute of Technology, Graduate College, College of Science and Letters, Department of Biological, Chemical and Physical Sciences, Biology Division, Chicago, IL 60616. Offers biochemistry (MBS, MS); biology (PhD); biotechnology (MBS, MS); cell and molecular biology (MBS, MS); microbiology (MB, MS); molecular biochemistry and biophysics (PhD); molecular biology and biophysics (MS). Part-time and evening/weekend programs available. Postbaccalaureate distance learning degree programs offered (minimal on-campus study). Terminal master's awarded for partial completion of doctoral program. *Degree requirements:* For master's, comprehensive exam, thesis (for some programs); for doctorate, comprehensive exam, thesis/dissertation. *Entrance requirements:* For master's, GRE General Test (minimum score 1000 Quantitative and Verbal, 2.5 Analytical Writing), minimum undergraduate GPA of 3.0; for doctorate, GRE General Test (minimum score 1200 Quantitative and Verbal, 3.0 Analytical Writing), minimum undergraduate GPA of 3.0. Additional exam requirements/recommendations for international students: Required—TOEFL (minimum score 523 paper-based; 213 computer-based; 70 iBT); Recommended—IELTS (minimum score 5.5). Electronic applications accepted. *Faculty research:* Structure and biophysics of macromolecular systems; efficacy and mechanism of action of chemopreventive agents in experimental carcinogenesis of breast, colon, lung and prostate; study of fundamental structural biochemistry problems that have direct links to the understanding and treatment of disease; spectroscopic techniques for the study of multi-domain proteins; molecular mechanisms of cancer and cancer gene therapy.

Illinois State University, Graduate School, College of Arts and Sciences, Department of Biological Sciences, Normal, IL 61790-2200. Offers animal behavior (MS); bacteriology (MS); biochemistry (MS); biological sciences (MS); biology (PhD); biophysics (MS); biotechnology (MS); botany (MS, PhD); cell biology (MS); conservation biology (MS); developmental biology (MS); ecology (MS, PhD); entomology (MS); evolutionary biology (MS); genetics (MS, PhD); immunology (MS); microbiology (MS, PhD); molecular biology (MS); molecular genetics (MS); neurobiology (MS); neuroscience (MS); parasitology (MS); physiology (MS, PhD); plant biology (MS); plant molecular biology (MS); plant sciences (MS); structural biology (MS); zoology (MS, PhD). Part-time programs available. *Degree requirements:* For master's, thesis or

alternative; for doctorate, variable foreign language requirement, thesis/dissertation, 2 terms of residency. *Entrance requirements:* For master's, GRE General Test, minimum GPA of 2.6 in last 60 hours of course work; for doctorate, GRE General Test. *Faculty research:* Redoc balance and drug development in schistosoma mansoni, control of the growth of listeria monocytogenes at low temperature, regulation of cell expansion and microtubule function by SPRI, CRUI: physiology and fitness consequences of different life history phenotypes.

Indiana State University, College of Graduate and Professional Studies, College of Arts and Sciences, Department of Biology, Terre Haute, IN 47809. Offers ecology (PhD); life sciences (MS); microbiology (PhD); physiology (PhD); science education (MS). *Degree requirements:* For master's, thesis (for some programs); for doctorate, comprehensive exam, thesis/dissertation. *Entrance requirements:* For master's and doctorate, GRE General Test. Electronic applications accepted.

Indiana University Bloomington, University Graduate School, College of Arts and Sciences, Department of Biology, Bloomington, IN 47405. Offers biology teaching (MAT); biotechnology (MA); evolution, ecology, and behavior (MA, PhD); genetics (PhD); microbiology (MA, PhD); molecular, cellular, and developmental biology (PhD); plant sciences (MA, PhD); zoology (MA, PhD). *Faculty:* 58 full-time (15 women), 21 part-time/adjunct (6 women). *Students:* 175 full-time (100 women), 3 part-time (all women); includes 20 minority (5 Black or African American, non-Hispanic/Latino; 8 Asian, non-Hispanic/Latino; 7 Hispanic/Latino), 55 international. Average age 27. 316 applicants, 22% accepted, 31 enrolled. In 2011, 8 master's, 20 doctorates awarded. Terminal master's awarded for partial completion of doctoral program. *Degree requirements:* For master's, thesis, oral defense; for doctorate, thesis/dissertation, oral defense. *Entrance requirements:* For master's and doctorate, GRE General Test. Additional exam requirements/recommendations for international students: Required—TOEFL (minimum score 100 iBT). *Application deadline:* For fall admission, 1/5 priority date for domestic students, 12/1 for international students. Application fee: $55 ($65 for international students). Electronic applications accepted. *Financial support:* In 2011–12, fellowships with tuition reimbursements (averaging $19,484 per year), research assistantships with tuition reimbursements (averaging $20,300 per year), teaching assistantships with tuition reimbursements (averaging $20,521 per year) were awarded; scholarships/grants, traineeships, health care benefits, and unspecified assistantships also available. Financial award application deadline: 1/5. *Faculty research:* Evolution, ecology and behavior; microbiology; molecular biology and genetics; plant biology. *Unit head:* Dr. Roger Innes, Chair, 812-855-2219, Fax: 812-855-6082, E-mail: rinnes@indiana.edu. *Application contact:* Tracey D. Stohr, Graduate Student Recruitment Coordinator, 812-856-6303, Fax: 812-855-6082, E-mail: gradbio@indiana.edu. Web site: http://www.bio.indiana.edu/.

Indiana University of Pennsylvania, School of Graduate Studies and Research, College of Natural Sciences and Mathematics, Department of Biology, Program in Biology, Indiana, PA 15705-1087. Offers MS. *Faculty:* 11 full-time (2 women). *Students:* 19 full-time (11 women), 3 part-time (all women); includes 2 minority (1 Hispanic/Latino; 1 Two or more races, non-Hispanic/Latino), 3 international. Average age 26. 39 applicants, 44% accepted, 10 enrolled. In 2011, 7 master's awarded. *Degree requirements:* For master's, comprehensive exam, thesis optional. *Entrance requirements:* For master's, 2 letters of recommendation. Additional exam requirements/recommendations for international students: Required—TOEFL (minimum score 540 paper-based; 207 computer-based). *Application deadline:* Applications are processed on a rolling basis. Application fee: $50. Electronic applications accepted. *Expenses:* Tuition, state resident: full-time $7488; part-time $416 per credit. Tuition, nonresident: full-time $11,232; part-time $624 per credit. *Required fees:* $2070; $192.20 per credit. $90 per semester. *Financial support:* In 2011–12, 1 fellowship (averaging $6,860 per year), 4 research assistantships with full and partial tuition reimbursements (averaging $4,790 per year) were awarded. Financial award application deadline: 4/15; financial award applicants required to submit FAFSA. *Unit head:* Dr. Robert Gendron, Graduate Coordinator, 724-357-2352, E-mail: robert.gendron@iup.edu. *Application contact:* Dr. Robert Hinrichsen, Graduate Coordinator, 724-357-2352, E-mail: bhinrich@iup.edu. Web site: http://www.iup.edu/grad/biology/default.aspx.

Indiana University–Purdue University Fort Wayne, College of Arts and Sciences, Department of Biology, Fort Wayne, IN 46805-1499. Offers MS. Part-time and evening/weekend programs available. *Faculty:* 16 full-time (3 women), 3 part-time/adjunct (1 woman). *Students:* 11 full-time (7 women), 27 part-time (17 women); includes 7 minority (1 Black or African American, non-Hispanic/Latino; 1 American Indian or Alaska Native, non-Hispanic/Latino; 2 Asian, non-Hispanic/Latino; 1 Hispanic/Latino; 2 Two or more races, non-Hispanic/Latino), 5 international. Average age 26. 21 applicants, 100% accepted, 12 enrolled. In 2011, 16 master's awarded. *Degree requirements:* For master's, thesis optional. *Entrance requirements:* For master's, GRE General Test, minimum GPA of 3.0, major or minor in biology, three letters of recommendation. Additional exam requirements/recommendations for international students: Required—TOEFL (minimum score 550 paper-based; 213 computer-based; 77 iBT), TWE. *Application deadline:* For fall admission, 4/15 priority date for domestic students, 2/15 for international students; for spring admission, 8/15 priority date for domestic students, 8/15 for international students. Applications are processed on a rolling basis. Application fee: $55 ($60 for international students). Electronic applications accepted. *Financial support:* In 2011–12, 7 research assistantships with partial tuition reimbursements (averaging $12,930 per year), 16 teaching assistantships with partial tuition reimbursements (averaging $12,930 per year) were awarded; scholarships/grants and unspecified assistantships also available. Support available to part-time students. Financial award application deadline: 3/1; financial award applicants required to submit FAFSA. *Faculty research:* Predator behavior, snakes and reintroduction strategies, Egyptian tortoises. *Total annual research expenditures:* $151,407. *Unit head:* Dr. Frank Paladino, Chair and Professor, 260-481-6304, Fax: 260-481-6087, E-mail: paladino@ipfw.edu. *Application contact:* Dr. George S. Mourad, Graduate Program Director, 260-481-5704, Fax: 260-481-6087, E-mail: mourad@ipfw.edu. Web site: http://www.ipfw.edu/biology.

Indiana University–Purdue University Indianapolis, School of Science, Department of Biology, Indianapolis, IN 46202-2896. Offers MS, PhD. PhD offered jointly with Purdue University. Part-time and evening/weekend programs available. *Faculty:* 7 full-time (2 women). *Students:* 105 full-time (46 women), 12 part-time (8 women); includes 19 minority (2 Black or African American, non-Hispanic/Latino; 14 Asian, non-Hispanic/Latino; 2 Hispanic/Latino; 1 Two or more races, non-Hispanic/Latino), 17 international. Average age 25. 184 applicants, 51% accepted, 84 enrolled. In 2011, 95 master's awarded. Terminal master's awarded for partial completion of doctoral program. *Degree requirements:* For master's, thesis (for some programs); for doctorate, thesis/dissertation. *Entrance requirements:* For master's and doctorate, GRE General Test. *Application deadline:* For fall admission, 6/1 for domestic students. Application fee: $55 ($65 for international students). *Financial support:* Fellowships with partial tuition reimbursements, research assistantships with partial tuition reimbursements, teaching assistantships with partial tuition reimbursements, and career-related internships or fieldwork available. Financial award application deadline: 4/1. *Faculty research:* Cell and model membranes, cell and molecular biology, immunology, oncology, developmental biology. *Unit head:* Dr. N. Douglas Lees, Chair, 317-274-0588, Fax: 317-274-2846. *Application contact:* Dr. Sherry Queener, Director, Graduate Studies and Associate Dean, 317-274-1577, Fax: 317-278-2380.

Iowa State University of Science and Technology, Department of Biomedical Sciences, Ames, IA 50011-1250. Offers MS, PhD. *Entrance requirements:* For master's and doctorate, GRE General Test. Additional exam requirements/recommendations for international students: Required—TOEFL (minimum score 590 paper-based; 94 iBT), IELTS (minimum score 6.5). *Application deadline:* For fall admission, 3/1 priority date for domestic students, 3/1 for international students; for spring admission, 9/1 priority date for domestic students, 9/1 for international students. Application fee: $40 ($90 for international students). Electronic applications accepted. *Faculty research:* Cerebella research; endocrine physiology; memory, learning and associated diseases; ion-channels and dry resistance; glia-neuron signaling; neurobiology of pain. *Unit head:* Dr. Steve Carlson, Director of Graduate Education, 515-294-2440, E-mail: biomedsci@iastate.edu. *Application contact:* Linda Erickson, Director of Graduate Education, 515-294-2441, E-mail: lericks@iastate.edu. Web site: http://vetmed.iastate.edu/bms/.

Irell & Manella Graduate School of Biological Sciences, Graduate Program, Duarte, CA 91010. Offers PhD. *Accreditation:* WASC/ACSCU. *Degree requirements:* For doctorate, comprehensive exam, thesis/dissertation. *Entrance requirements:* For doctorate, GRE General Test; GRE Subject Test (recommended), 2 years of course work in chemistry (general and organic); 1 year course work each in biochemistry, general biology, and general physics; 2 semesters of course work in mathematics; significant research laboratory experience. Additional exam requirements/recommendations for international students: Required—TOEFL. Electronic applications accepted. *Faculty research:* DNA damage and repair, protein structure, cancer biology, T cells and immunology, RNA splicing and binding.

See Display on next page and Close-Up on page 105.

Jackson State University, Graduate School, College of Science, Engineering and Technology, Department of Biology, Jackson, MS 39217. Offers environmental science (MS, PhD). Part-time and evening/weekend programs available. *Degree requirements:* For master's, comprehensive exam, thesis (alternative accepted for MST); for doctorate, comprehensive exam, thesis/dissertation. *Entrance requirements:* For master's, GRE General Test; for doctorate, MAT. Additional exam requirements/recommendations for international students: Required—TOEFL (minimum score 520 paper-based; 195 computer-based; 67 iBT). *Faculty research:* Comparative studies on the carbohydrate composition of marine macroalgae, host-parasite relationship between the spruce budworm and entomepathogen fungus.

Jacksonville State University, College of Graduate Studies and Continuing Education, College of Arts and Sciences, Department of Biology, Jacksonville, AL 36265-1602. Offers MS. Part-time and evening/weekend programs available. *Degree requirements:* For master's, comprehensive exam, thesis (for some programs). *Entrance requirements:* For master's, GRE General Test or MAT. Electronic applications accepted. *Expenses:* Tuition, state resident: part-time $336 per hour. Tuition, nonresident: part-time $672 per hour. Part-time tuition and fees vary according to degree level.

James Madison University, The Graduate School, College of Science and Mathematics, Department of Biology, Harrisonburg, VA 22807. Offers MS. Part-time programs available. *Faculty:* 18 full-time (8 women), 1 (woman) part-time/adjunct. *Students:* 11 full-time (5 women), 1 (woman) part-time; includes 1 minority (Asian, non-Hispanic/Latino). Average age 27. In 2011, 7 master's awarded. *Degree requirements:* For master's, thesis (for some programs). *Entrance requirements:* For master's, GRE General Test, GRE Subject Test, 3 letters of recommendation. Additional exam requirements/recommendations for international students: Required—TOEFL. *Application deadline:* For fall admission, 2/15 for domestic students. Applications are processed on a rolling basis. Application fee: $55. Electronic applications accepted. *Expenses:* Tuition, state resident: full-time $8016; part-time $334 per credit hour. Tuition, nonresident: full-time $22,656; part-time $944 per credit hour. *Financial support:* In 2011–12, 9 students received support. Federal Work-Study and 9 graduate assistantships ($7382) available. Financial award application deadline: 3/1; financial award applicants required to submit FAFSA. *Faculty research:* Evolutionary ecology, gene regulation, microbial ecology, plant development, biomechanics. *Unit head:* Dr. Judith A. Dilts, Interim Academic Unit Head, 540-568-3508, E-mail: diltsja@jmu.edu. *Application contact:* Dr. Jon Kastendiek, Interim Graduate Director, 540-568-6225.

John Carroll University, Graduate School, Department of Biology, University Heights, OH 44118-4581. Offers MA, MS. Part-time programs available. *Degree requirements:* For master's, essay or thesis, seminar. *Entrance requirements:* For master's, undergraduate major in biology, 1 semester of biochemistry, minimum 2.5 GPA. Electronic applications accepted. *Faculty research:* Algal ecology, systematics, molecular genetics, neurophysiology, behavioral ecology.

The Johns Hopkins University, National Institutes of Health Sponsored Programs, Baltimore, MD 21218-2699. Offers biology (PhD), including biochemistry, biophysics, cell biology, developmental biology, genetic biology, molecular biology; cell, molecular, and developmental biology and biophysics (PhD). *Degree requirements:* For doctorate, comprehensive exam, thesis/dissertation. *Entrance requirements:* For doctorate, GRE General Test. Additional exam requirements/recommendations for international students: Required—TOEFL (minimum score 600 paper-based; 250 computer-based), TWE. Electronic applications accepted. *Faculty research:* Protein and nucleic acid biochemistry and biophysical chemistry, molecular biology and development.

The Johns Hopkins University, School of Medicine, Graduate Programs in Medicine, Baltimore, MD 21218-2699. Offers MA, MS, PhD, MD/PhD. *Degree requirements:* For doctorate, thesis/dissertation. *Entrance requirements:* Additional exam requirements/recommendations for international students: Required—TOEFL. Electronic applications accepted. *Expenses:* Contact institution.

The Johns Hopkins University, Zanvyl Krieger School of Arts and Sciences, Chemistry-Biology Interface Program, Baltimore, MD 21218-2699. Offers PhD. Terminal master's awarded for partial completion of doctoral program. *Degree requirements:* For doctorate, comprehensive exam, thesis/dissertation, 8 one-semester courses, literature seminar, research proposal. *Entrance requirements:* For doctorate, GRE General Test, GRE Subject Test in biochemistry, cell and molecular biology, biology or chemistry (strongly recommended), 3 letters of recommendation, interview. Electronic applications accepted. *Faculty research:* Enzyme mechanisms, inhibitors, and metabolic pathways; DNA replication, damaged, and repair; using small molecules to probe signal transduction, gene regulation, angiogenesis, and other biological processes; synthetic methods and medicinal chemistry; synthetic modeling of metalloenzymes.

The Johns Hopkins University, Zanvyl Krieger School of Arts and Sciences, Department of Biology, Baltimore, MD 21218. Offers PhD. Terminal master's awarded for partial completion of doctoral program. *Degree requirements:* For doctorate, comprehensive exam, thesis/dissertation. *Entrance requirements:* For doctorate, GRE General Test. Additional exam requirements/recommendations for international students: Required—TOEFL (minimum score 600 paper-based; 250 computer-based), IELTS, TWE. Electronic applications accepted. *Faculty research:* Cell biology, molecular biology and development, biochemistry, developmental biology, biophysics, genetics.

IRELL & MANELLA GRADUATE SCHOOL OF BIOLOGICAL SCIENCES

Earn your doctorate where you and your research will have the greatest impact.

The Irell and Manella Graduate School of Biological Sciences at City of Hope offers a Doctor of Philosophy (Ph.D.) degree in Biological Sciences.

City of Hope ranks in the top 5 percent of U.S. institutions in NIH research funding

TRAIN IN TWO BROADLY DEFINED TRACKS:

Molecular and Cellular Biology
• Stem cell research
• Endocrinology and metabolism
• Chromatin structure and repair
• Tumor biology
• Immunology
• Virology
• Neurosciences

Chemical Biology
• Protein structure
  X-ray crystallography
  NMR
  Computational modeling
• Small molecule synthesis
• Bioconjugate chemistry
• Analytical biological instrumentation

Enjoy a $32,000 stipend per year, plus paid insurance

Publish in top-level journals

Attend national and international meetings

FOR MORE INFORMATION AND TO APPLY, VISIT www.cityofhope.org/gradschool

Kansas City University of Medicine and Biosciences, College of Biosciences, Kansas City, MO 64106-1453. Offers bioethics (MA); biomedical sciences (MS). Part-time programs available. *Degree requirements:* For master's, comprehensive exam, thesis (for some programs). *Entrance requirements:* For master's, MCAT, GRE.

Kansas State University, College of Veterinary Medicine, Department of Diagnostic Medicine/Pathobiology, Manhattan, KS 66506. Offers biomedical science (MS); diagnostic medicine/pathobiology (PhD). *Faculty:* 24 full-time (7 women), 4 part-time/adjunct (2 women). *Students:* 30 full-time (16 women), 23 part-time (15 women); includes 6 minority (1 Black or African American, non-Hispanic/Latino; 1 Asian, non-Hispanic/Latino; 3 Hispanic/Latino; 1 Native Hawaiian or other Pacific Islander, non-Hispanic/Latino), 15 international. Average age 29. 8 applicants, 50% accepted, 1 enrolled. In 2011, 16 master's, 11 doctorates awarded. Terminal master's awarded for partial completion of doctoral program. *Degree requirements:* For doctorate, thesis/dissertation. *Entrance requirements:* For master's and doctorate, interviews. Additional exam requirements/recommendations for international students: Required—TOEFL (minimum score 550 paper-based; 213 computer-based). *Application deadline:* For fall admission, 2/1 priority date for domestic students, 2/1 for international students; for spring admission, 8/1 priority date for domestic students, 8/1 for international students. Applications are processed on a rolling basis. Application fee: $40 ($55 for international students). Electronic applications accepted. *Financial support:* In 2011–12, 22 research assistantships (averaging $21,849 per year) were awarded; Federal Work-Study, institutionally sponsored loans, and scholarships/grants also available. Financial award application deadline: 3/1; financial award applicants required to submit FAFSA. *Faculty research:* Infectious disease of animals, food safety and security, epidemiology and public health, toxicology, and pathology. *Total annual research expenditures:* $6.8 million. *Unit head:* M. M. Chengappa, Head, 785-532-4403, E-mail: chengap@ksu.edu. *Application contact:* T. G. Nagaraja, Director, 785-532-1214, E-mail: tnagaraj@ksu.edu. Web site: http://www.vet.k-state.edu/depts/dmp/.

Kansas State University, Graduate School, College of Arts and Sciences, Division of Biology, Manhattan, KS 66506. Offers biology (MS, PhD); microbiology (PhD). *Faculty:* 39 full-time (12 women), 10 part-time/adjunct (3 women). *Students:* 55 full-time (29 women), 3 part-time (all women); includes 4 minority (1 Black or African American, non-Hispanic/Latino; 3 Hispanic/Latino), 14 international. Average age 27. 90 applicants, 9% accepted, 8 enrolled. In 2011, 6 master's, 6 doctorates awarded. Terminal master's awarded for partial completion of doctoral program. *Degree requirements:* For master's, thesis; for doctorate, thesis/dissertation. *Entrance requirements:* For master's, GRE General Test, minimum undergraduate GPA of 3.0; for doctorate, GRE General Test, minimum GPA of 3.0. Additional exam requirements/recommendations for international students: Required—TOEFL (minimum score 550 paper-based; 213 computer-based). *Application deadline:* For fall admission, 12/15 priority date for domestic students, 12/15 for international students; for spring admission, 8/1 priority date for domestic students, 8/1 for international students. Applications are processed on a rolling basis. Application fee: $40 ($55 for international students). Electronic applications accepted. *Financial support:* In 2011–12, 2 fellowships with full tuition reimbursements (averaging $30,000 per year), 32 research assistantships with full tuition reimbursements (averaging $21,086 per year), 23 teaching assistantships with full tuition reimbursements (averaging $19,819 per year) were awarded; institutionally sponsored loans and scholarships/grants also available. Support available to part-time students. Financial award application deadline: 3/1; financial award applicants required to submit FAFSA. *Faculty research:* Ecology, genetics, developmental biology, microbiology, cell biology. *Total annual research expenditures:* $8.3 million. *Unit head:* Brian Spooner, Director and University Distinguished Professor, Division of Biology, 785-532-6615, Fax: 785-532-6653, E-mail: biology@ksu.edu. *Application contact:* David Rintoul, Graduate Program Director, 785-532-6795, Fax: 785-532-6653, E-mail: drintoul@ksu.edu. Web site: http://www.k-state.edu/biology/.

Keck Graduate Institute of Applied Life Sciences, Bioscience Program, Claremont, CA 91711. Offers applied life science (PhD); bioscience (MBS); bioscience management (Certificate); computational systems biology (PhD). *Degree requirements:* For master's, comprehensive exam, project. *Entrance requirements:* For master's, GRE General Test or MCAT. Additional exam requirements/recommendations for international students: Required—TOEFL. Electronic applications accepted. *Faculty research:* Computational biology, drug discovery and development, molecular and cellular biology, biomedical engineering, biomaterials and tissue engineering.

Kennesaw State University, College of Science and Mathematics, Program in Integrative Biology, Kennesaw, GA 30144-5591. Offers MS. *Entrance requirements:* For master's, GRE, two letters of recommendation, official transcript, statement of interest. Electronic applications accepted. *Expenses:* Tuition, state resident: full-time $3000; part-time $250 per semester hour. Tuition, nonresident: full-time $10,836; part-time $903 per semester hour. *Required fees:* $774 per semester.

Kent State University, College of Arts and Sciences, Department of Biological Sciences, Kent, OH 44242-0001. Offers ecology (MS, PhD); physiology (MS, PhD). *Degree requirements:* For master's, thesis; for doctorate, thesis/dissertation. *Entrance requirements:* For master's, GRE General Test, minimum GPA of 3.0; for doctorate, GRE General Test, minimum GPA of 3.25. Additional exam requirements/recommendations for international students: Required—TOEFL (minimum score 600 paper-based; 257 computer-based). Electronic applications accepted. *Expenses:* Tuition, state resident: full-time $8136; part-time $452 per credit hour. Tuition, nonresident: full-time $14,292; part-time $794 per credit hour.

Kent State University, School of Biomedical Sciences, Kent, OH 44242-0001. Offers MS, PhD. Terminal master's awarded for partial completion of doctoral program. *Degree requirements:* For master's, thesis; for doctorate, thesis/dissertation. *Entrance requirements:* For master's and doctorate, GRE General Test. Electronic applications accepted. *Expenses:* Tuition, state resident: full-time $8136; part-time $452 per credit hour. Tuition, nonresident: full-time $14,292; part-time $794 per credit hour.

Lake Erie College of Osteopathic Medicine, Professional Programs, Erie, PA 16509-1025. Offers biomedical sciences (Postbaccalaureate Certificate); medical education (MS); osteopathic medicine (DO); pharmacy (Pharm D). *Accreditation:* ACPE; AOsA. *Degree requirements:* For doctorate, comprehensive exam, National Osteopathic Medical Licensing Exam, Levels 1 and 2; for Postbaccalaureate Certificate, comprehensive exam, North American Pharmacist Licensure Examination (NAPLEX). *Entrance requirements:* For doctorate, MCAT, minimum GPA of 3.2, letters of recommendation; for Postbaccalaureate Certificate, PCAT, letters of recommendation, minimum GPA of 3.5. Electronic applications accepted. *Faculty research:* Cardiac smooth and skeletal muscle mechanics, chemotherapeutics and vitamins, osteopathic manipulation.

Lakehead University, Graduate Studies, Faculty of Social Sciences and Humanities, Department of Biology, Thunder Bay, ON P7B 5E1, Canada. Offers M Sc. Part-time and evening/weekend programs available. *Degree requirements:* For master's, thesis, department seminary, oral examination. *Entrance requirements:* For master's, minimum B average. Additional exam requirements/recommendations for international students: Required—TOEFL. *Faculty research:* Systematics and biogeography, wildlife parasitology, plant physiology and biochemistry, plant ecology, fishery biology.

Biological and Biomedical Sciences—General

Lamar University, College of Graduate Studies, College of Arts and Sciences, Department of Biology, Beaumont, TX 77710. Offers MS. Part-time and evening/weekend programs available. *Faculty:* 6 full-time (2 women). *Students:* 8 full-time (4 women), 11 part-time (9 women); includes 3 minority (1 Black or African American, non-Hispanic/Latino; 2 Hispanic/Latino), 6 international. Average age 28. 17 applicants, 71% accepted, 5 enrolled. In 2011, 4 master's awarded. *Degree requirements:* For master's, thesis. *Entrance requirements:* For master's, GRE General Test, minimum GPA of 2.5 in last 60 hours of undergraduate course work. Additional exam requirements/recommendations for international students: Required—TOEFL. *Application deadline:* For fall admission, 8/1 for domestic students; for spring admission, 12/1 for domestic students. Applications are processed on a rolling basis. Application fee: $25 ($50 for international students). *Expenses:* Tuition, state resident: full-time $5430; part-time $272 per credit hour. Tuition, nonresident: full-time $11,540; part-time $577 per credit hour. *Required fees:* $1916. *Financial support:* In 2011–12, 3 teaching assistantships (averaging $6,200 per year) were awarded. Financial award application deadline: 4/1. *Faculty research:* Microbiology, limnology, vertebrate ecology, invertebrate hemoglobin, ornithology. *Unit head:* Dr. Michael E. Warren, Chair, 409-880-8262, Fax: 409-880-1827. *Application contact:* Dr. R. C. Harrel, Graduate Adviser, 409-880-8255, Fax: 409-880-1827.

Laurentian University, School of Graduate Studies and Research, Programme in Biology, Sudbury, ON P3E 2C6, Canada. Offers biology (M Sc); boreal ecology (PhD). Part-time programs available. *Degree requirements:* For master's, thesis. *Entrance requirements:* For master's, honors degree with second class or better. *Faculty research:* Recovery of acid-stressed lakes, effects of climate change, origin and maintenance of biocomplexity, radionuclide dynamics, cytogenetic studies of plants.

Lehigh University, College of Arts and Sciences, Department of Biological Sciences, Bethlehem, PA 18015. Offers biochemistry (PhD); integrative biology and neuroscience (PhD); molecular biology (MS, PhD). Part-time programs available. Postbaccalaureate distance learning degree programs offered (no on-campus study). *Faculty:* 16 full-time (7 women). *Students:* 36 full-time (19 women), 22 part-time (15 women); includes 4 minority (2 Black or African American, non-Hispanic/Latino; 2 Asian, non-Hispanic/Latino), 7 international. Average age 30. 70 applicants, 14% accepted, 9 enrolled. In 2011, 11 master's, 3 doctorates awarded. Terminal master's awarded for partial completion of doctoral program. *Degree requirements:* For master's, research report; for doctorate, comprehensive exam, thesis/dissertation. *Entrance requirements:* For doctorate, GRE General Test. Additional exam requirements/recommendations for international students: Required—TOEFL. *Application deadline:* For fall admission, 12/15 for domestic and international students. Applications are processed on a rolling basis. Application fee: $75. Electronic applications accepted. *Financial support:* In 2011–12, 4 fellowships with full tuition reimbursements (averaging $24,500 per year), 6 research assistantships with full tuition reimbursements (averaging $23,750 per year), 16 teaching assistantships with full tuition reimbursements (averaging $23,750 per year) were awarded; scholarships/grants and unspecified assistantships also available. Financial award application deadline: 12/15. *Faculty research:* Gene expression, cytoskeleton and cell structure, cell cycle and growth regulation, neuroscience, animal behavior, microbiology. *Total annual research expenditures:* $2 million. *Unit head:* Dr. Murray Itzkowitz, Chairperson, 610-758-3680, Fax: 610-758-4004, E-mail: mi00@lehigh.edu. *Application contact:* Dr. Jennifer M. Swann, Graduate Coordinator, 610-758-5484, Fax: 610-758-4004, E-mail: jms5@lehigh.edu. Web site: http://www.lehigh.edu/~inbios/.

Lehman College of the City University of New York, Division of Natural and Social Sciences, Department of Biological Sciences, Program in Biology, Bronx, NY 10468-1589. Offers MA.

Loma Linda University, School of Science and Technology, Department of Biological and Earth Sciences, Loma Linda, CA 92350. Offers MS, PhD. *Degree requirements:* For master's, comprehensive exam, thesis; for doctorate, comprehensive exam, thesis/dissertation. *Entrance requirements:* For master's, minimum GPA of 3.0. Additional exam requirements/recommendations for international students: Required—TOEFL (minimum score 550 paper-based; 213 computer-based).

Long Island University–Brooklyn Campus, Richard L. Conolly College of Liberal Arts and Sciences, Department of Biology, Brooklyn, NY 11201-8423. Offers MS. Part-time and evening/weekend programs available. *Degree requirements:* For master's, thesis or alternative. *Entrance requirements:* For master's, 2 letters of recommendation. Additional exam requirements/recommendations for international students: Required—TOEFL (minimum score 500 paper-based; 173 computer-based). Electronic applications accepted.

Long Island University–C. W. Post Campus, College of Liberal Arts and Sciences, Department of Biology, Brookville, NY 11548-1300. Offers biology (MS); biology education (MS); genetic counseling (MS). Part-time and evening/weekend programs available. *Degree requirements:* For master's, thesis optional. *Entrance requirements:* For master's, GRE General Test, minimum GPA of 2.75 in major. Electronic applications accepted. *Faculty research:* Immunology, molecular biology, systematics, behavioral ecology, microbiology.

Long Island University–C. W. Post Campus, School of Health Professions and Nursing, Department of Biomedical Sciences, Brookville, NY 11548-1300. Offers cardiovascular perfusion (MS); clinical laboratory management (MS); medical biology (MS), including hematology, immunology, medical biology, medical chemistry, medical microbiology. Part-time and evening/weekend programs available. Postbaccalaureate distance learning degree programs offered. *Degree requirements:* For master's, thesis. *Entrance requirements:* For master's, minimum GPA of 2.75 in major. Electronic applications accepted.

Louisiana State University and Agricultural and Mechanical College, Graduate School, College of Science, Department of Biological Sciences, Baton Rouge, LA 70803. Offers biochemistry (MS, PhD); biological science (MS, PhD); science (MNS). Part-time programs available. *Faculty:* 62 full-time (8 women). *Students:* 130 full-time (57 women), 8 part-time (3 women); includes 10 minority (1 Black or African American, non-Hispanic/Latino; 5 Asian, non-Hispanic/Latino; 3 Hispanic/Latino; 1 Two or more races, non-Hispanic/Latino), 57 international. Average age 29. 144 applicants, 17% accepted, 15 enrolled. In 2011, 5 master's, 18 doctorates awarded. Terminal master's awarded for partial completion of doctoral program. *Degree requirements:* For doctorate, thesis/dissertation. *Entrance requirements:* For master's and doctorate, GRE General Test, minimum GPA of 3.0. Additional exam requirements/recommendations for international students: Required—TOEFL (minimum score 550 paper-based; 213 computer-based; 79 iBT) or IELTS (minimum score 6.5). *Application deadline:* For fall admission, 5/15 for domestic and international students; for spring admission, 10/15 for domestic and international students. Applications are processed on a rolling basis. Application fee: $25. Electronic applications accepted. *Financial support:* In 2011–12, 137 students received support, including 10 fellowships with full and partial tuition reimbursements available (averaging $22,471 per year), 37 research assistantships with full and partial tuition reimbursements available (averaging $22,448 per year), 84 teaching assistantships with full and partial tuition reimbursements available (averaging $18,811 per year); Federal Work-Study, institutionally sponsored loans, health care benefits, and unspecified assistantships also available. Support available to part-time students. Financial award applicants required to submit FAFSA. *Faculty research:* Biochemistry and molecular biology, cell developmental and integrative biology, systematics, ecology and evolutionary biology. *Total annual research expenditures:* $9.6 million. *Unit head:* Dr. James Moroney, Chair, 225-578-1765, Fax: 225-578-2597. *Application contact:* Dr. Michael E. Hellberg, Associate Chairman, 225-578-1240, Fax: 225-578-7299, E-mail: biogradcoord@lsu.edu. Web site: http://www.biology.lsu.edu/.

Louisiana State University Health Sciences Center, School of Graduate Studies in New Orleans, New Orleans, LA 70112-2223. Offers MPH, MS, PhD, MD/PhD. Part-time and evening/weekend programs available. Terminal master's awarded for partial completion of doctoral program. *Degree requirements:* For master's, comprehensive exam, thesis; for doctorate, comprehensive exam, thesis/dissertation. *Entrance requirements:* For master's and doctorate, GRE General Test. Additional exam requirements/recommendations for international students: Required—TOEFL.

Louisiana State University Health Sciences Center at Shreveport, Louisiana State University Health Sciences Center at Shreveport, Shreveport, LA 71130-3932. Offers MS, PhD, MD/PhD. *Accreditation:* SACS. Terminal master's awarded for partial completion of doctoral program. *Degree requirements:* For master's, thesis; for doctorate, thesis/dissertation. *Entrance requirements:* For master's and doctorate, GRE General Test. Additional exam requirements/recommendations for international students: Required—TOEFL.

Louisiana Tech University, Graduate School, College of Applied and Natural Sciences, School of Biological Sciences, Ruston, LA 71272. Offers MS. Part-time programs available. *Degree requirements:* For master's, thesis or alternative. *Entrance requirements:* For master's, GRE General Test, GRE Subject Test. *Faculty research:* Genetics, animal biology, plant biology, physiology biocontrol.

Loyola University Chicago, Graduate School, Department of Biology, Chicago, IL 60660. Offers biology (MA, MS); medical sciences (MA). *Faculty:* 18 full-time (6 women). *Students:* 79 full-time (37 women), 3 part-time (1 woman); includes 23 minority (1 Black or African American, non-Hispanic/Latino; 17 Asian, non-Hispanic/Latino; 5 Hispanic/Latino), 1 international. Average age 25. 600 applicants, 24% accepted, 60 enrolled. In 2011, 61 master's awarded. *Degree requirements:* For master's, thesis (for some programs). *Entrance requirements:* For master's, GRE General Test, 3 letters of recommendation. Additional exam requirements/recommendations for international students: Required—TOEFL. *Application deadline:* For fall admission, 6/1 for domestic and international students. Applications are processed on a rolling basis. Application fee: $50. Electronic applications accepted. *Expenses: Tuition:* Full-time $15,660; part-time $870 per credit hour. *Required fees:* $125 per semester. Tuition and fees vary according to course load and program. *Financial support:* In 2011–12, 7 students received support, including 7 fellowships with full tuition reimbursements available (averaging $16,000 per year); Federal Work-Study and institutionally sponsored loans also available. Financial award application deadline: 2/1; financial award applicants required to submit FAFSA. *Faculty research:* Evolution, development, aquatic biology, molecular biology and genetics, cell biology, neurobiology. *Total annual research expenditures:* $2.5 million. *Unit head:* Dr. Terry Grande, Graduate Program Director, 773-583-5649, Fax: 773-508-3646, E-mail: tgrande@luc.edu. *Application contact:* Ron Martin, Assistant Director of Enrollment Management, 312-915-8950, Fax: 312-915-8905, E-mail: gradapp@luc.edu. Web site: http://www.luc.edu/biology/.

Marquette University, Graduate School, College of Arts and Sciences, Department of Biology, Milwaukee, WI 53201-1881. Offers cell biology (MS, PhD); developmental biology (MS, PhD); ecology (MS, PhD); epithelial physiology (MS, PhD); genetics (MS, PhD); microbiology (MS, PhD); molecular biology (MS, PhD); muscle and exercise physiology (MS, PhD); neuroscience (PhD). *Faculty:* 23 full-time (11 women), 1 part-time/adjunct (0 women). *Students:* 33 full-time (14 women), 6 part-time (3 women), 19 international. Average age 25. 78 applicants, 17% accepted, 5 enrolled. In 2011, 6 doctorates awarded. Terminal master's awarded for partial completion of doctoral program. *Degree requirements:* For master's, comprehensive exam, thesis, 1 year of teaching experience or equivalent; for doctorate, thesis/dissertation, 1 year of teaching experience or equivalent, qualifying exam. *Entrance requirements:* For master's and doctorate, GRE General Test, GRE Subject Test, official transcripts from all current and previous colleges/universities except Marquette, statement of professional goals and aspirations, three letters of recommendation. Additional exam requirements/recommendations for international students: Required—TOEFL (minimum score 530 paper-based; 78 computer-based). *Application deadline:* For fall admission, 12/15 for domestic and international students. Application fee: $50. Electronic applications accepted. *Expenses: Tuition:* Full-time $17,010; part-time $945 per credit hour. Tuition and fees vary according to program. *Financial support:* In 2011–12, 39 students received support, including 6 fellowships (averaging $1,208 per year), 4 research assistantships with full tuition reimbursements available (averaging $21,750 per year), 29 teaching assistantships with full tuition reimbursements available (averaging $21,750 per year); scholarships/grants, health care benefits, tuition waivers (full and partial), and unspecified assistantships also available. Support available to part-time students. Financial award application deadline: 2/15. *Faculty research:* Neurobiology, neuroendocrinology, epithelial physiology, neuropeptide interactions, synaptic transmission. *Total annual research expenditures:* $2 million. *Unit head:* Dr. Robert Fitts, Chair, 414-288-1748, Fax: 414-288-7357. *Application contact:* Debbie Weaver, Administrative Assistant, 414-288-7355, Fax: 414-288-7357. Web site: http://www.marquette.edu/biology/.

Marshall University, Academic Affairs Division, College of Science, Department of Biological Science, Huntington, WV 25755. Offers MA, MS. *Faculty:* 19 full-time (4 women). *Students:* 39 full-time (20 women), 5 part-time (3 women); includes 7 minority (3 Black or African American, non-Hispanic/Latino; 3 Asian, non-Hispanic/Latino; 1 Hispanic/Latino), 8 international. Average age 26. In 2011, 8 master's awarded. *Degree requirements:* For master's, thesis (for some programs). *Entrance requirements:* For master's, GRE General Test, GRE Subject Test. Application fee: $40. *Financial support:* Career-related internships or fieldwork available. *Unit head:* Dr. Elmer Price, Chairperson, 304-696-3611, E-mail: pricee@marshall.edu. *Application contact:* Information Contact, 304-746-1900, Fax: 304-746-1902, E-mail: services@marshall.edu.

Marshall University, Joan C. Edwards School of Medicine and Academic Affairs Division, Program in Biomedical Sciences, Huntington, WV 25755. Offers MS, PhD. Terminal master's awarded for partial completion of doctoral program. *Degree requirements:* For master's, comprehensive exam, thesis optional; for doctorate, thesis/dissertation, written and oral qualifying exams. *Entrance requirements:* For master's, GRE General Test or MCAT (medical science), 1 year of course work in biology, physics, chemistry, and organic chemistry and associated labs; for doctorate, GRE General Test, 1 year of course work in biology, physics, chemistry, and organic chemistry and associated labs. Additional exam requirements/recommendations for international students: Required—TOEFL (minimum score 525 paper-based; 216 computer-based). *Expenses:* Contact institution. *Faculty research:* Neurosciences, cardiopulmonary science, molecular biology, toxicology, endocrinology.

Massachusetts Institute of Technology, Harvard-MIT Division of Health Sciences and Technology, Program in Medical Sciences, Cambridge, MA 02139-4307. Offers MD, MD/MS, MD/PhD. *Students:* 192 full-time (73 women); includes 102 minority (4 Black or African American, non-Hispanic/Latino; 85 Asian, non-Hispanic/Latino; 10 Hispanic/Latino; 3 Two or more races, non-Hispanic/Latino), 12 international. Average age 26. 1,012 applicants, 3% accepted, 30 enrolled. In 2011, 20 doctorates awarded. *Degree requirements:* For doctorate, thesis/dissertation. *Entrance requirements:* For doctorate, MCAT. *Application deadline:* For fall admission, 10/15 for domestic students. Application fee: $85. Electronic applications accepted. *Expenses:* Contact institution. *Financial support:* In 2011–12, 66 students received support, including 3 fellowships with partial tuition reimbursements available (averaging $53,667 per year), 45 research assistantships with partial tuition reimbursements available (averaging $11,654 per year), 21 teaching assistantships with partial tuition reimbursements available (averaging $4,170 per year); career-related internships or fieldwork, scholarships/grants, health care benefits, and unspecified assistantships also available. Financial award application deadline: 10/15; financial award applicants required to submit FAFSA. *Unit head:* Dr. David Earl Cohen, Director, 617-726-5576. *Application contact:* Zara Smith, MD Admissions Coordinator, 617-432-7195, E-mail: zara_smith@hms.harvard.edu.

Massachusetts Institute of Technology, School of Science, Department of Biology, Cambridge, MA 02139. Offers biochemistry (PhD); biological oceanography (PhD); biology (PhD); biophysical chemistry and molecular structure (PhD); cell biology (PhD); computational and systems biology (PhD); developmental biology (PhD); genetics (PhD); immunology (PhD); microbiology (PhD); molecular biology (PhD); neurobiology (PhD). *Faculty:* 58 full-time (15 women). *Students:* 248 full-time (129 women); includes 69 minority (5 Black or African American, non-Hispanic/Latino; 1 American Indian or Alaska Native, non-Hispanic/Latino; 25 Asian, non-Hispanic/Latino; 31 Hispanic/Latino; 7 Two or more races, non-Hispanic/Latino), 36 international. Average age 26. 698 applicants, 15% accepted, 44 enrolled. In 2011, 38 doctorates awarded. *Degree requirements:* For doctorate, comprehensive exam, thesis/dissertation. *Entrance requirements:* For doctorate, GRE General Test. Additional exam requirements/recommendations for international students: Required—TOEFL (minimum score 577 paper-based; 233 computer-based), IELTS (minimum score 6.5). *Application deadline:* For fall admission, 12/1 for domestic and international students. Application fee: $75. Electronic applications accepted. *Expenses: Tuition:* Full-time $40,460; part-time $630 per credit hour. *Required fees:* $272. *Financial support:* In 2011–12, 214 students received support, including 129 fellowships (averaging $33,200 per year), 117 research assistantships (averaging $32,900 per year); teaching assistantships, Federal Work-Study, institutionally sponsored loans, scholarships/grants, traineeships, health care benefits, and unspecified assistantships also available. *Faculty research:* Cellular, developmental and molecular (plant and animal) biology; biochemistry, bioengineering, biophysics and structural biology; classical and molecular genetics; immunology and microbiology; cancer biology, molecular medicine, neurobiology and human disease; computational and systems biology. *Total annual research expenditures:* $53.6 million. *Unit head:* Prof. Tania A. Baker, Head, 617-253-4701, E-mail: mitbio@mit.edu. *Application contact:* Biology Education Office, 617-253-3717, Fax: 617-258-9329, E-mail: gradbio@mit.edu. Web site: https://biology.mit.edu/.

Mayo Graduate School, Graduate Programs in Biomedical Sciences, Rochester, MN 55905. Offers PhD, MD/PhD. *Degree requirements:* For doctorate, oral defense of dissertation, qualifying oral and written exam. *Entrance requirements:* For doctorate, GRE, 1 year of chemistry, biology, calculus, and physics. Additional exam requirements/recommendations for international students: Required—TOEFL. Electronic applications accepted.

McGill University, Faculty of Graduate and Postdoctoral Studies, Faculty of Medicine, Department of Medicine, Montréal, QC H3A 2T5, Canada. Offers experimental medicine (M Sc, PhD), including bioethics (M Sc), experimental medicine.

McGill University, Faculty of Graduate and Postdoctoral Studies, Faculty of Science, Department of Biology, Montréal, QC H3A 2T5, Canada. Offers bioinformatics (M Sc, PhD); environment (M Sc, PhD); neo-tropical environment (M Sc, PhD).

McMaster University, Faculty of Health Sciences, Department of Biochemistry and Biomedical Sciences, Hamilton, ON L8S 4M2, Canada. Offers M Sc, PhD. Terminal master's awarded for partial completion of doctoral program. *Degree requirements:* For master's, thesis; for doctorate, comprehensive exam, thesis/dissertation. *Entrance requirements:* For master's and doctorate, minimum B+ average. Additional exam requirements/recommendations for international students: Required—TOEFL (minimum score 550 paper-based; 213 computer-based). *Faculty research:* Molecular and cell biology, biomolecular structure and function, molecular pharmacology and toxicology.

McMaster University, Faculty of Health Sciences and School of Graduate Studies, Program in Medical Sciences, Hamilton, ON L8S 4M2, Canada. Offers blood and vascular (M Sc, PhD); genetics and cancer (M Sc, PhD); immunity and infection (M Sc, PhD); metabolism and nutrition (M Sc, PhD); neurosciences and behavioral sciences (M Sc, PhD); physiology/pharmacology (M Sc, PhD); MD/PhD. *Degree requirements:* For master's, thesis; for doctorate, comprehensive exam, thesis/dissertation. *Entrance requirements:* For master's, honors B Sc, B+ average in related field; for doctorate, M Sc, minimum B+ average. Additional exam requirements/recommendations for international students: Required—TOEFL (minimum score 580 paper-based; 237 computer-based; 92 iBT).

McMaster University, School of Graduate Studies, Faculty of Science, Department of Biology, Hamilton, ON L8S 4M2, Canada. Offers M Sc, PhD. Part-time programs available. *Degree requirements:* For master's, thesis; for doctorate, comprehensive exam, thesis/dissertation. *Entrance requirements:* Additional exam requirements/recommendations for international students: Required—TOEFL (minimum score 550 paper-based; 213 computer-based).

Medical College of Wisconsin, Graduate School of Biomedical Sciences, Milwaukee, WI 53226-0509. Offers MA, MPH, MS, PhD, Graduate Certificate, MD/PhD. Part-time and evening/weekend programs available. Postbaccalaureate distance learning degree programs offered (minimal on-campus study). *Degree requirements:* For master's, comprehensive exam (for some programs), thesis (for some programs); for doctorate, comprehensive exam, thesis/dissertation. *Entrance requirements:* For master's and doctorate, GRE General Test. Additional exam requirements/recommendations for international students: Required—TOEFL (minimum score 100 computer-based). Electronic applications accepted. *Faculty research:* Clinical and translational science, genomics and proteomics, cancer.

Medical College of Wisconsin, Interdisciplinary Program in Biomedical Sciences, Milwaukee, WI 53226-0509. Offers PhD.

Medical University of South Carolina, College of Graduate Studies, Charleston, SC 29425. Offers MS, PhD, DMD/PhD, MD/PhD, Pharm D/PhD. *Faculty:* 268 full-time (79 women), 20 part-time/adjunct (3 women). *Students:* 219 full-time (125 women), 21 part-time (12 women); includes 25 minority (15 Black or African American, non-Hispanic/Latino; 4 Asian, non-Hispanic/Latino; 6 Hispanic/Latino), 103 international. Average age 33. 272 applicants, 28% accepted, 44 enrolled. In 2011, 31 master's, 47 doctorates awarded. Terminal master's awarded for partial completion of doctoral program. *Degree requirements:* For master's, thesis; for doctorate, thesis/dissertation, oral and written exams. *Entrance requirements:* For doctorate, GRE General Test, interview. Additional exam requirements/recommendations for international students: Required—TOEFL (minimum score 600 paper-based; 250 computer-based; 100 iBT). *Application deadline:* For fall admission, 1/15 priority date for domestic students, 1/15 for international students. Applications are processed on a rolling basis. Application fee: $85 for international students. Electronic applications accepted. *Expenses:* Contact institution. *Financial support:* In 2011–12, 114 students received support, including 114 research assistantships with partial tuition reimbursements available (averaging $23,000 per year); Federal Work-Study and scholarships/grants also available. Support available to part-time students. Financial award application deadline: 3/10; financial award applicants required to submit FAFSA. *Faculty research:* Cell signaling and cancer biology, drug discovery and toxicology, biochemistry and genetics, macromolecular structure, neurosciences, microbiology and immunology. *Unit head:* Dr. Perry V. Halushka, Dean, 843-792-3012, Fax: 843-792-6590, E-mail: halushpv@musc.edu. *Application contact:* Dr. Cynthia F. Wright, Associate Dean for Career Development and Admissions, 843-792-2564, Fax: 843-792-6590, E-mail: wrightcf@musc.edu. Web site: http://www.musc.edu/grad/.

Meharry Medical College, School of Graduate Studies, Program in Biomedical Sciences, Nashville, TN 37208-9989. Offers cancer biology (PhD); microbiology and immunology (PhD); neuroscience (PhD); pharmacology (PhD); MD/PhD. *Degree requirements:* For doctorate, comprehensive exam, thesis/dissertation. *Entrance requirements:* For doctorate, GRE General Test, GRE Subject Test. *Faculty research:* Molecular mechanisms of biological systems and their relationship to human diseases, regulatory biological and cellular structure and function, genetic regulation of growth and cellular metabolisms.

Memorial University of Newfoundland, Faculty of Medicine and School of Graduate Studies, Graduate Programs in Medicine, St. John's, NL A1C 5S7, Canada. Offers M Sc, PhD, Diploma, MD/PhD. Part-time programs available. *Degree requirements:* For master's, thesis; for doctorate, comprehensive exam, thesis/dissertation, oral defense of thesis. *Entrance requirements:* For master's, MD or B Sc; for doctorate, MD or M Sc; for Diploma, bachelor's degree in health-related field. Additional exam requirements/recommendations for international students: Required—TOEFL (minimum score 550 paper-based; 213 computer-based). Electronic applications accepted. *Faculty research:* Human genetics, community health, clinical epidemial, cancer, immunology, cardiovascular and immol sciences, applied health services research, neuroscience.

Memorial University of Newfoundland, School of Graduate Studies, Department of Biology, St. John's, NL A1C 5S7, Canada. Offers biology (M Sc, PhD); marine biology (M Sc, PhD). Part-time programs available. *Degree requirements:* For master's, thesis; for doctorate, comprehensive exam, thesis/dissertation, oral defense of thesis. *Entrance requirements:* For master's, honors degree (minimum 2nd class standing) in related field. Electronic applications accepted. *Faculty research:* Northern flora and fauna, especially cold ocean and boreal environments.

Michigan State University, College of Human Medicine and The Graduate School, Graduate Programs in Human Medicine, East Lansing, MI 48824. Offers biochemistry and molecular biology (MS, PhD); epidemiology (MS, PhD); microbiology (MS); microbiology and molecular genetics (PhD); pharmacology and toxicology (MS, PhD); physiology (MS, PhD); public health (MPH). *Entrance requirements:* Additional exam requirements/recommendations for international students: Required—TOEFL.

Michigan State University, College of Osteopathic Medicine and The Graduate School, Graduate Studies in Osteopathic Medicine, East Lansing, MI 48824. Offers biochemistry and molecular biology (MS, PhD); microbiology (MS); microbiology and molecular genetics (PhD); pharmacology and toxicology (MS, PhD), including integrative pharmacology (MS), pharmacology and toxicology, pharmacology and toxicology–environmental toxicology (PhD); physiology (MS, PhD).

Michigan State University, College of Veterinary Medicine and The Graduate School, Graduate Programs in Veterinary Medicine, Program in Comparative Medicine and Integrative Biology, East Lansing, MI 48824. Offers comparative medicine and integrative biology (MS, PhD); comparative medicine and integrative biology–environmental toxicology (PhD). *Entrance requirements:* Additional exam requirements/recommendations for international students: Required—TOEFL. Electronic applications accepted.

Michigan Technological University, Graduate School, College of Sciences and Arts, Department of Biological Sciences, Houghton, MI 49931. Offers MS, PhD. Part-time programs available. *Faculty:* 20 full-time (9 women), 13 part-time/adjunct (2 women). *Students:* 29 full-time (13 women), 7 part-time (4 women); includes 1 minority (Asian, non-Hispanic/Latino), 10 international. Average age 28. 86 applicants, 20% accepted, 6 enrolled. In 2011, 2 degrees awarded. Terminal master's awarded for partial completion of doctoral program. *Degree requirements:* For master's, comprehensive exam (for some programs), thesis (for some programs); for doctorate, comprehensive exam, thesis/dissertation. *Entrance requirements:* For master's and doctorate, GRE, statement of purpose, official transcripts, 2 letters of recommendation. Additional exam requirements/recommendations for international students: Required—TOEFL (minimum score 79 iBT) or IELTS. *Application deadline:* For fall admission, 1/15 priority date for domestic students, 1/15 for international students. Applications are processed on a rolling basis. Electronic applications accepted. *Expenses: Tuition,* state resident: full-time $12,636; part-time $702 per credit. Tuition, nonresident: full-time $12,636; part-time $702 per credit. *Required fees:* $226; $226 per year. *Financial support:* In 2011–12, 32 students received support, including 3 fellowships with full tuition reimbursements available (averaging $6,065 per year), 12 research assistantships with full tuition reimbursements available (averaging $6,065 per year), 9 teaching assistantships with full tuition reimbursements available (averaging $6,065 per year); career-related internships or fieldwork, Federal Work-Study, scholarships/grants, health care benefits, tuition waivers (partial), unspecified assistantships, and cooperative program also available. Financial award applicants required to submit FAFSA. *Faculty research:* Aquatic ecology, biological control, predator-prey interactions, environmental microbiology, microbial and plant biochemistry, genomics and bioinformatics. *Total annual research expenditures:* $1 million. *Unit head:* Dr. Michael K. Gibson, Chair, 906-487-2025, Fax: 906-487-3167, E-mail: kmgibson@mtu.edu. *Application contact:* Dr. Nancy Auer, Director of Graduate Studies, 906-487-2027, Fax: 906-487-3167, E-mail: naauer@mtu.edu. Web site: http://www.bio.mtu.edu/.

Middle Tennessee State University, College of Graduate Studies, College of Basic and Applied Sciences, Department of Biology, Murfreesboro, TN 37132. Offers MS. Part-time and evening/weekend programs available. Postbaccalaureate distance learning degree programs offered. *Faculty:* 32 full-time (6 women), 3 part-time/adjunct (0 women). *Students:* 56 part-time (23 women); includes 10 minority (1 Black or African American, non-Hispanic/Latino; 1 American Indian or Alaska Native, non-Hispanic/Latino; 4 Asian, non-Hispanic/Latino; 2 Hispanic/Latino; 2 Two or more races, non-Hispanic/Latino). Average age 30. 50 applicants, 40% accepted. In 2011, 9 master's awarded. *Degree requirements:* For master's, comprehensive exam, thesis. *Entrance requirements:* For master's, GRE. Additional exam requirements/recommendations for international students: Required—TOEFL (minimum score 525 paper-based; 195

computer-based; 71 iBT) or IELTS (minimum score 6). *Application deadline:* For fall admission, 6/1 for domestic and international students. Applications are processed on a rolling basis. Application fee: $25 ($30 for international students). Electronic applications accepted. *Expenses:* Tuition, state resident: full-time $10,008. Tuition, nonresident: full-time $25,056. *Financial support:* In 2011–12, 30 students received support. Tuition waivers available. Support available to part-time students. Financial award application deadline: 5/1; financial award applicants required to submit FAFSA. *Faculty research:* Molecular biosciences. *Unit head:* Dr. Lynn Boyd, Chair, 615-898-2847, E-mail: lynn.boyd@mtsu.edu. *Application contact:* Dr. Michael D. Allen, Dean and Vice Provost for Research, 615-898-2840, Fax: 615-904-8020, E-mail: michael.allen@mtsu.edu.

Midwestern State University, Graduate Studies, College of Science and Mathematics, Program in Biology, Wichita Falls, TX 76308. Offers MS. Part-time and evening/weekend programs available. *Degree requirements:* For master's, comprehensive exam, thesis. *Entrance requirements:* For master's, GRE General Test, MAT or GMAT. Additional exam requirements/recommendations for international students: Required—TOEFL (minimum score 550 paper-based; 213 computer-based). Electronic applications accepted. *Faculty research:* Molecular analysis of flora and fauna, mineral toxicity in plants, embryonic patterning and cell signaling, animal physiology, mammalogy.

Midwestern University, Downers Grove Campus, College of Health Sciences, Illinois Campus, Master of Arts Program in Biomedical Sciences, Downers Grove, IL 60515-1235. Offers MA. *Students:* 52 full-time (21 women); includes 13 minority (1 Black or African American, non-Hispanic/Latino; 8 Asian, non-Hispanic/Latino; 1 Hispanic/Latino; 1 Native Hawaiian or other Pacific Islander, non-Hispanic/Latino; 2 Two or more races, non-Hispanic/Latino), 2 international. Average age 25. 429 applicants, 32% accepted, 52 enrolled. *Entrance requirements:* For master's, GRE General Test, MCAT, PCAT, DAT, OAT or other professional exam, bachelor's degree, minimum cumulative GPA of 2.75. *Unit head:* Dr. Jacquelyn J. Smith, Dean, 630-515-6388. *Application contact:* Michael Laken, Director of Admissions, 630-515-6171, Fax: 630-971-6086, E-mail: admissil@midwestern.edu. Web site: http://www.midwestern.edu/Programs_and_Admission/IL_Master_of_Arts_in_Biomedical_Sciences.html.

Midwestern University, Downers Grove Campus, College of Health Sciences, Illinois Campus, Master of Biomedical Sciences Program, Downers Grove, IL 60515-1235. Offers MBS. Part-time programs available. *Faculty:* 1 (woman) full-time. *Students:* 31 full-time (11 women), 22 part-time (16 women); includes 22 minority (17 Asian, non-Hispanic/Latino; 3 Hispanic/Latino; 2 Two or more races, non-Hispanic/Latino). Average age 23. 123 applicants, 58% accepted, 29 enrolled. In 2011, 13 master's awarded. *Entrance requirements:* For master's, GRE General Test, MCAT or PCAT, 2 letters of recommendation. *Application deadline:* Applications are processed on a rolling basis. Application fee: $50. *Unit head:* Dr. Michael Fay, Director, 630-515-6382. *Application contact:* Michael Laken, Director of Admissions, 630-515-6171, Fax: 630-971-6086, E-mail: admissil@midwestern.edu. Web site: http://www.midwestern.edu/Programs_and_Admission/IL_Master_of_Biomedical_Sciences.html.

Midwestern University, Glendale Campus, College of Health Sciences, Arizona Campus, MA Program in Biomedical Sciences, Glendale, AZ 85308. Offers MA. *Faculty:* 6 full-time (2 women). *Students:* 76 full-time (32 women), 1 part-time (0 women); includes 31 minority (2 Black or African American, non-Hispanic/Latino; 19 Asian, non-Hispanic/Latino; 6 Hispanic/Latino; 1 Native Hawaiian or other Pacific Islander, non-Hispanic/Latino; 3 Two or more races, non-Hispanic/Latino), 3 international. Average age 25. 301 applicants, 47% accepted, 77 enrolled. *Entrance requirements:* For master's, GRE General Test, MCAT, or other professional exam, bachelor's degree, minimum cumulative GPA of 2.75. *Unit head:* Leonard Bell, Program Director, 623-572-3622, Fax: 623-572-3647, E-mail: lbellx@midwestern.edu. *Application contact:* James Walter, Director of Admissions, 888-247-9277, Fax: 623-572-3229, E-mail: admissaz@midwestern.edu.

Midwestern University, Glendale Campus, College of Health Sciences, Arizona Campus, MBS Program in Biomedical Sciences, Glendale, AZ 85308. Offers MBS. *Faculty:* 9 full-time (3 women). *Students:* 42 full-time (30 women), 1 part-time (0 women); includes 13 minority (2 Black or African American, non-Hispanic/Latino; 6 Asian, non-Hispanic/Latino; 1 Hispanic/Latino; 1 Native Hawaiian or other Pacific Islander, non-Hispanic/Latino; 3 Two or more races, non-Hispanic/Latino), 1 international. Average age 26. 70 applicants, 56% accepted, 25 enrolled. In 2011, 9 master's awarded. Application fee: $50. *Expenses:* Contact institution. *Unit head:* Dr. William P. Baker, Director, 623-572-3666. *Application contact:* James Walter, Director of Admissions, 888-247-9277, Fax: 623-572-3229, E-mail: admissaz@midwestern.edu.

Mills College, Graduate Studies, Pre-Medical Studies Program, Oakland, CA 94613-1000. Offers Certificate. Part-time programs available. *Faculty:* 10 full-time (4 women), 6 part-time/adjunct (3 women). *Students:* 59 full-time (33 women), 2 part-time (1 woman); includes 17 minority (2 Black or African American, non-Hispanic/Latino; 2 American Indian or Alaska Native, non-Hispanic/Latino; 8 Asian, non-Hispanic/Latino; 1 Hispanic/Latino; 4 Two or more races, non-Hispanic/Latino). Average age 26. 174 applicants, 66% accepted, 41 enrolled. In 2011, 38 Certificates awarded. *Entrance requirements:* For degree, SAT/ACT or GRE General Test, bachelor's degree in a non-science area. Additional exam requirements/recommendations for international students: Required—TOEFL (minimum score 550 paper-based; 80 iBT) or IELTS (minimum score 6). *Application deadline:* For fall admission, 2/1 priority date for domestic students, 12/15 for international students. Applications are processed on a rolling basis. Application fee: $50. Electronic applications accepted. *Expenses: Tuition:* Full-time $28,280; part-time $15,640 per year. *Required fees:* $958. Tuition and fees vary according to program. *Financial support:* In 2011–12, 30 students received support, including 30 fellowships with full and partial tuition reimbursements available (averaging $4,335 per year), 24 teaching assistantships with full and partial tuition reimbursements available (averaging $12,575 per year); institutionally sponsored loans and scholarships/grants also available. Support available to part-time students. Financial award application deadline: 2/1; financial award applicants required to submit FAFSA. *Faculty research:* Antifungal compounds and their modes of action, organic chemistry-spectroscopy and organic chemistry reaction mechanisms, oceanography, physics and chemistry education, cell-cell and cell-extracellular matrix interactions. *Total annual research expenditures:* $199,168. *Unit head:* Dr. John Brabson, Head, 510-430-2203, Fax: 510-430-3314, E-mail: johnb@mills.edu. *Application contact:* Tiana Kozoil, Graduate Admission Specialist, 510-430-3305, Fax: 510-430-2159, E-mail: grad-studies@mills.edu. Web site: http://www.mills.edu/premed.

Minnesota State University Mankato, College of Graduate Studies, College of Science, Engineering and Technology, Department of Biological Sciences, Mankato, MN 56001. Offers biology (MS); biology education (MS); environmental sciences (MS). Part-time programs available. *Students:* 14 full-time (5 women), 17 part-time (9 women). *Degree requirements:* For master's, one foreign language, comprehensive exam, thesis or alternative. *Entrance requirements:* For master's, minimum GPA of 3.0 during previous 2 years of course work. Additional exam requirements/recommendations for international students: Required—TOEFL. *Application deadline:* For fall admission, 7/1 priority date for domestic students; for spring admission, 11/1 for domestic students. Applications are processed on a rolling basis. Application fee: $40. Electronic applications accepted. *Financial support:* Fellowships, research assistantships with full tuition reimbursements, teaching assistantships with full tuition reimbursements, career-related internships or fieldwork, Federal Work-Study, institutionally sponsored loans, and unspecified assistantships available. Support available to part-time students. Financial award application deadline: 3/15; financial award applicants required to submit FAFSA. *Faculty research:* Limnology, enzyme analysis, membrane engineering, converters. *Unit head:* Dr. Penny Knoblich, Graduate Coordinator, 507-389-5736. *Application contact:* 507-389-2321, E-mail: grad@mnsu.edu.

Mississippi College, Graduate School, College of Arts and Sciences, School of Science and Mathematics, Department of Biological Sciences, Clinton, MS 39058. Offers biological science (M Ed); biology (MCS); biology-biological sciences (MS); biology-medical sciences (MS). Part-time programs available. *Degree requirements:* For master's, comprehensive exam, thesis optional. *Entrance requirements:* For master's, GRE General Test, minimum GPA of 2.5. Additional exam requirements/recommendations for international students: Recommended—TOEFL, IELTS. Electronic applications accepted.

Mississippi State University, College of Arts and Sciences, Department of Biological Sciences, Mississippi State, MS 39762. Offers MS, PhD. MS in general biology and MA only offered online. Postbaccalaureate distance learning degree programs offered (minimal on-campus study). *Faculty:* 11 full-time (5 women). *Students:* 33 full-time (16 women), 129 part-time (92 women); includes 15 minority (8 Black or African American, non-Hispanic/Latino; 1 Asian, non-Hispanic/Latino; 3 Hispanic/Latino; 3 Two or more races, non-Hispanic/Latino), 16 international. Average age 33. 164 applicants, 51% accepted, 77 enrolled. In 2011, 28 master's, 4 doctorates awarded. Terminal master's awarded for partial completion of doctoral program. *Degree requirements:* For master's, one foreign language, thesis, comprehensive oral or written exam; for doctorate, one foreign language, thesis/dissertation, comprehensive oral or written exam. *Entrance requirements:* For master's, GRE General Test, minimum GPA of 2.75 on last two years of undergraduate courses; for doctorate, GRE General Test. Additional exam requirements/recommendations for international students: Required—TOEFL (minimum score 550 paper-based; 213 computer-based; 79 iBT). *Application deadline:* For fall admission, 7/1 for domestic students, 5/1 for international students; for spring admission, 11/1 for domestic students, 9/1 for international students. Applications are processed on a rolling basis. Application fee: $40. Electronic applications accepted. *Expenses:* Tuition, state resident: full-time $5805; part-time $322.50 per credit hour. Tuition, nonresident: full-time $14,670; part-time $815 per credit hour. *Financial support:* In 2011–12, 6 research assistantships with full and partial tuition reimbursements (averaging $14,353 per year), 23 teaching assistantships with full and partial tuition reimbursements (averaging $14,865 per year) were awarded; Federal Work-Study, institutionally sponsored loans, scholarships/grants, and unspecified assistantships also available. Financial award applicants required to submit FAFSA. *Faculty research:* Botany, zoology, microbiology, ecology. *Total annual research expenditures:* $5.2 million. *Unit head:* Dr. Nancy Reichert, Professor/Head, 662-325-3483, Fax: 662-325-7939, E-mail: nreichert@biology.msstate.edu. *Application contact:* Dr. Gary Ervin, Associate Dean/Graduate Coordinator, 662-325-1203, Fax: 662-325-7939, E-mail: gervin@biology.msstate.edu. Web site: http://www.msstate.edu/dept/biosciences/.

Missouri State University, Graduate College, College of Natural and Applied Sciences, Department of Biology, Springfield, MO 65897. Offers biology (MS); natural and applied science (MNAS), including biology (MNAS, MS Ed); secondary education (MS Ed), including biology (MNAS, MS Ed). *Faculty:* 19 full-time (4 women), 6 part-time/adjunct (1 woman). *Students:* 21 full-time (9 women), 37 part-time (18 women); includes 3 minority (all Two or more races, non-Hispanic/Latino), 2 international. Average age 28. 18 applicants, 94% accepted, 15 enrolled. In 2011, 14 master's awarded. *Degree requirements:* For master's, comprehensive exam, thesis or alternative. *Entrance requirements:* For master's, GRE (MS, MNAS), 24 hours of course work in biology (MS); minimum GPA of 3.0 (MS, MNAS), 9-12 teacher certification (MS Ed). Additional exam requirements/recommendations for international students: Required—TOEFL (minimum score 550 paper-based; 213 computer-based; 79 iBT). *Application deadline:* For fall admission, 7/20 priority date for domestic students, 5/1 for international students; for spring admission, 12/20 priority date for domestic students, 9/1 for international students. Applications are processed on a rolling basis. Application fee: $35 ($50 for international students). Electronic applications accepted. *Expenses:* Tuition, state resident: full-time $4086; part-time $227 per credit hour. Tuition, nonresident: full-time $8172; part-time $454 per credit hour. *Required fees:* $275 per semester. Tuition and fees vary according to course load, campus/location and program. *Financial support:* In 2011–12, 3 research assistantships with full tuition reimbursements (averaging $8,865 per year), 12 teaching assistantships with full tuition reimbursements (averaging $9,730 per year) were awarded; Federal Work-Study, institutionally sponsored loans, scholarships/grants, and unspecified assistantships also available. Financial award application deadline: 3/31; financial award applicants required to submit FAFSA. *Faculty research:* Hibernation physiology of bats, behavioral ecology of salamanders, mussel conservation, plant evolution and systematics, cellular/molecular mechanisms involved in migraine pathology. *Unit head:* Dr. S. Alicia Mathis, Head, 417-836-5126, Fax: 417-836-6934, E-mail: biology@missouristate.edu. *Application contact:* Misty Stewart, Coordinator of Graduate Recruitment, 417-836-6079, Fax: 417-836-6200, E-mail: mistystewart@missouristate.edu. Web site: http://biology.missouristate.edu/.

Missouri University of Science and Technology, Graduate School, Department of Biological Sciences, Rolla, MO 65409. Offers applied and environmental biology (MS). *Entrance requirements:* For master's, GRE (minimum score 600 quantitative, 4 writing). Additional exam requirements/recommendations for international students: Required—TOEFL (minimum score 570 paper-based; 230 computer-based).

Montana State University, College of Graduate Studies, College of Letters and Science, Department of Cell Biology and Neuroscience, Bozeman, MT 59717. Offers biological sciences (PhD); neuroscience (MS, PhD). Part-time programs available. *Degree requirements:* For master's, comprehensive exam; for doctorate, comprehensive exam, thesis/dissertation. *Entrance requirements:* For master's and doctorate, GRE General Test. Additional exam requirements/recommendations for international students: Required—TOEFL (minimum score 550 paper-based; 213 computer-based). Electronic applications accepted. *Faculty research:* Development of the nervous system, neuronal mechanisms of visual perception, ion channel biophysics, mechanisms of sensory coding, neuroinformatics.

Montclair State University, The Graduate School, College of Science and Mathematics, Department of Biology and Molecular Biology, Montclair, NJ 07043-1624. Offers biology (MS), including biological science education, biology, ecology and evolution, physiology; molecular biology (MS, Certificate). Part-time and evening/weekend programs available. *Students:* 15 full-time (10 women), 33 part-time (23 women); includes 3 minority (all Hispanic/Latino), 1 international. Average age 28. 53 applicants, 47% accepted, 14 enrolled. In 2011, 14 degrees awarded. *Degree requirements:* For master's, comprehensive exam, thesis or alternative. *Entrance requirements:* For master's, GRE General Test, 24 credits of course work in undergraduate biology, 2 letters of recommendation, teaching certificate (biology sciences education concentration); for Certificate, 2 letters of recommendation, essay. Additional exam requirements/recommendations for international students: Required—TOEFL (minimum score 83 iBT) or IELTS. *Application deadline:* For fall admission, 6/1 for international students; for spring admission, 10/1 for international students.

Applications are processed on a rolling basis. Application fee: $60. Electronic applications accepted. *Financial support:* In 2011–12, 16 research assistantships with full tuition reimbursements (averaging $7,000 per year), 3 teaching assistantships (averaging $7,000 per year) were awarded; Federal Work-Study, scholarships/grants, and unspecified assistantships also available. Support available to part-time students. Financial award application deadline: 3/1; financial award applicants required to submit FAFSA. *Faculty research:* Ecosystem biology, molecular biology, signal transduction, neuroscience, aquatic and coastal biology. *Total annual research expenditures:* $1.3 million. *Unit head:* Dr. Quinn Vega, Chairperson, 973-655-7178. *Application contact:* Amy Aiello, Director of Graduate Admissions and Operations, 973-655-5147, Fax: 973-655-7869, E-mail: graduate.school@montclair.edu. Web site: http://www.montclair.edu/csam/biology/.

Morehead State University, Graduate Programs, College of Science and Technology, Department of Biology and Chemistry, Morehead, KY 40351. Offers biology (MS); biology regional analysis (MS). Part-time programs available. *Degree requirements:* For master's, comprehensive exam, thesis optional, oral and written final exams. *Entrance requirements:* For master's, GRE General Test, minimum GPA of 3.0 in biology, 2.5 overall; undergraduate major/minor in biology, environmental science, or equivalent. Additional exam requirements/recommendations for international students: Required—TOEFL (minimum score 525 paper-based; 173 computer-based). Electronic applications accepted. *Faculty research:* Atherosclerosis, RNA evolution, cancer biology, water quality/ecology, immunoparasitology.

Morehouse School of Medicine, Graduate Programs in Biomedical Sciences, Atlanta, GA 30310-1495. Offers biomedical research (MS); biomedical sciences (PhD); biomedical technology (MS). *Degree requirements:* For master's, thesis (for some programs); for doctorate, thesis/dissertation. *Entrance requirements:* For doctorate, GRE General Test. Additional exam requirements/recommendations for international students: Required—TOEFL (minimum score 550 paper-based; 200 computer-based). Electronic applications accepted. *Expenses:* Contact institution.

Morgan State University, School of Graduate Studies, School of Computer, Mathematical, and Natural Sciences, Department of Biology, Baltimore, MD 21251. Offers bioenvironmental science (PhD); biology (MS). *Degree requirements:* For master's, comprehensive exam, thesis. *Entrance requirements:* For master's, minimum GPA of 3.0.

Mount Allison University, Department of Biology, Sackville, NB E4L 1E4, Canada. Offers M Sc. *Degree requirements:* For master's, thesis. *Entrance requirements:* For master's, honors degree. *Faculty research:* Ecology, evolution, physiology, behavior, biochemistry.

Mount Sinai School of Medicine, Graduate School of Biological Sciences, New York, NY 10029-6504. Offers biomedical sciences (MS, PhD); clinical research education (MS, PhD); community medicine (MPH); genetic counseling (MS); neurosciences (PhD); MD/PhD. Terminal master's awarded for partial completion of doctoral program. *Degree requirements:* For master's, thesis; for doctorate, comprehensive exam, thesis/dissertation. *Entrance requirements:* For master's, GRE General Test; for doctorate, GRE General Test, GRE Subject Test, 3 years of college pre-med course work. Additional exam requirements/recommendations for international students: Required—TOEFL. Electronic applications accepted. *Faculty research:* Cancer, genetics and genomics, immunology, neuroscience, developmental and stem cell biology, translational research.

Murray State University, College of Science, Engineering and Technology, Program in Biological Sciences, Murray, KY 42071. Offers MAT, MS, PhD. PhD offered jointly with University of Louisville. Part-time programs available. *Degree requirements:* For master's, comprehensive exam, thesis optional. *Entrance requirements:* For master's, GRE General Test. Additional exam requirements/recommendations for international students: Required—TOEFL. *Faculty research:* Aquatic and terrestrial ecology, molecular systematics, micro ecology, cell biology and metabolism, palentology.

National University, Academic Affairs, College of Letters and Sciences, Department of Mathematics and Natural Sciences, La Jolla, CA 92037-1011. Offers biology (MS); forensic and crime scene investigation (Certificate); forensic sciences (MFS). Part-time and evening/weekend programs available. Postbaccalaureate distance learning degree programs offered (no on-campus study). *Degree requirements:* For master's, thesis (for some programs). *Entrance requirements:* For master's, interview, minimum GPA of 2.5. Additional exam requirements/recommendations for international students: Required—TOEFL (minimum score 550 paper-based; 213 computer-based; 79 iBT), IELTS (minimum score 6). *Application deadline:* Applications are processed on a rolling basis. Application fee: $60 ($65 for international students). Electronic applications accepted. *Financial support:* Career-related internships or fieldwork, institutionally sponsored loans, scholarships/grants, and tuition waivers (partial) available. Support available to part-time students. Financial award application deadline: 6/30; financial award applicants required to submit FAFSA. *Unit head:* Dr. Michael R. Maxwell, Head, 858-642-8413, Fax: 858-642-8715, E-mail: mmaxwell@nu.edu. *Application contact:* Dominick Giovanniello, Associate Regional Dean, 800-NAT-UNIV, Fax: 858-541-7792, E-mail: dgiovann@nu.edu. Web site: http://www.nu.edu/OurPrograms/CollegeOfLettersAndSciences/MathematicsAndNaturalSciences.html.

New Jersey Institute of Technology, Office of Graduate Studies, College of Science and Liberal Arts, Federated Department of Biological Sciences, Program in Biology, Newark, NJ 07102. Offers MS, PhD. Part-time and evening/weekend programs available. *Faculty:* 5 full-time (1 woman). *Students:* 9 full-time (5 women), 7 part-time (4 women); includes 2 minority (1 Black or African American, non-Hispanic/Latino; 1 Asian, non-Hispanic/Latino), 9 international. Average age 26. 97 applicants, 28% accepted, 3 enrolled. *Entrance requirements:* For master's, GRE General Test. Additional exam requirements/recommendations for international students: Required—TOEFL (minimum score 550 paper-based; 213 computer-based; 79 iBT). *Application deadline:* For fall admission, 6/1 priority date for domestic students, 5/1 for international students; for spring admission, 11/15 priority date for domestic students, 11/15 for international students. Applications are processed on a rolling basis. Application fee: $65. Electronic applications accepted. *Expenses:* Tuition, state resident: full-time $7980; part-time $867 per credit. Tuition, nonresident: full-time $11,336; part-time $1196 per credit. *Required fees:* $230 per credit. *Financial support:* Fellowships with full and partial tuition reimbursements, research assistantships with full and partial tuition reimbursements, teaching assistantships with full and partial tuition reimbursements, career-related internships or fieldwork, Federal Work-Study, institutionally sponsored loans, and unspecified assistantships available. Financial award application deadline: 1/15. *Faculty research:* Realistic building codes, optimization of training programs, effect of physical and mental fatigue of training. *Unit head:* Dr. Karen Roach, Academic Coordinator, 973-596-5612, E-mail: karen.roach@njit.edu. *Application contact:* Kathryn Kelly, Director of Admissions, 973-596-3300, Fax: 973-596-3461, E-mail: admissions@njit.edu.

New Mexico Institute of Mining and Technology, Graduate Studies, Department of Biology, Socorro, NM 87801. Offers MS. Part-time programs available. *Faculty:* 4 full-time (2 women), 2 part-time/adjunct (both women). *Students:* 6 full-time (3 women); includes 3 minority (all Hispanic/Latino). Average age 29. 4 applicants, 50% accepted, 1 enrolled. In 2011, 1 master's awarded. *Degree requirements:* For master's, thesis. *Entrance requirements:* For master's, GRE General Test. Additional exam requirements/recommendations for international students: Required—TOEFL (minimum score 540 paper-based; 207 computer-based). *Application deadline:* For fall admission, 3/1 priority date for domestic students; for spring admission, 6/1 priority date for domestic students. Applications are processed on a rolling basis. Application fee: $16 ($30 for international students). Electronic applications accepted. *Expenses:* Tuition, state resident: full-time $4849; part-time $269.41 per credit hour. Tuition, nonresident: full-time $16,041; part-time $891.15 per credit hour. *Required fees:* $622; $65 per credit hour. $20 per semester. Part-time tuition and fees vary according to course load. *Financial support:* In 2011–12, 4 teaching assistantships with full and partial tuition reimbursements (averaging $41,800 per year) were awarded; fellowships, research assistantships, Federal Work-Study, institutionally sponsored loans, and unspecified assistantships also available. Financial award application deadline: 3/1; financial award applicants required to submit CSS PROFILE or FAFSA. *Faculty research:* Molecular biology, evolution and evolutionary ecology, immunology, endocrinology. *Unit head:* Dr. Snezna Rogelj, Chair, 575-835-5608, Fax: 575-835-5668, E-mail: snezna@nmt.edu. *Application contact:* Dr. Lorie Liebrock, Dean of Graduate Studies, 575-835-5513, Fax: 575-835-5476, E-mail: graduate@nmt.edu. Web site: http://www.nmt.edu/~biology/biologyfrontpage.html.

New Mexico State University, Graduate School, College of Agricultural, Consumer and Environmental Sciences, Department of Animal and Range Sciences, Las Cruces, NM 88003-8001. Offers animal science (MS, PhD); domestic animal biology (M Ag); range science (M Ag, MS, PhD). Part-time programs available. *Faculty:* 15 full-time (3 women). *Students:* 33 full-time (19 women), 5 part-time (3 women); includes 4 minority (all Hispanic/Latino), 7 international. Average age 28. 23 applicants, 30% accepted, 4 enrolled. In 2011, 7 master's, 3 doctorates awarded. *Degree requirements:* For master's, thesis, seminar, experimental statistics; for doctorate, thesis/dissertation, research tool. *Entrance requirements:* For master's, minimum GPA of 3.0 in last 60 hours of undergraduate course work (MS); for doctorate, minimum graduate GPA of 3.2. Additional exam requirements/recommendations for international students: Required—TOEFL (minimum score 530 paper-based; 0 computer-based; 71 iBT), IELTS (minimum score 6). *Application deadline:* For fall admission, 7/1 priority date for domestic students, 7/1 for international students; for spring admission, 11/1 for domestic and international students. Applications are processed on a rolling basis. Application fee: $40 ($50 for international students). Electronic applications accepted. *Expenses:* Tuition, state resident: full-time $5004; part-time $208.50 per credit. Tuition, nonresident: full-time $17,446; part-time $726.90 per credit. *Financial support:* In 2011–12, 31 students received support, including 1 fellowship (averaging $3,754 per year), 8 research assistantships (averaging $21,980 per year), 19 teaching assistantships (averaging $22,750 per year); career-related internships or fieldwork, Federal Work-Study, scholarships/grants, traineeships, health care benefits, and unspecified assistantships also available. Support available to part-time students. Financial award application deadline: 3/15. *Faculty research:* Reproductive physiology, ruminant nutrition, nutrition toxicology, range ecology, wildland hydrology. *Unit head:* Dr. Tim Ross, Interim Head, 575-646-2514, Fax: 575-646-5441, E-mail: tross@nmsu.edu. *Application contact:* Dr. Tim Ross, Interim Head, 575-646-2514, Fax: 575-646-5441, E-mail: tross@nmsu.edu. Web site: http://aces.nmsu.edu/academics/anrs.

New Mexico State University, Graduate School, College of Arts and Sciences, Department of Biology, Las Cruces, NM 88003-8001. Offers biology (MS, PhD); biotechnology and business (MS). Part-time programs available. *Faculty:* 21 full-time (9 women). *Students:* 71 full-time (42 women), 15 part-time (12 women); includes 26 minority (3 Black or African American, non-Hispanic/Latino; 3 American Indian or Alaska Native, non-Hispanic/Latino; 1 Asian, non-Hispanic/Latino; 18 Hispanic/Latino; 1 Two or more races, non-Hispanic/Latino), 22 international. Average age 30. 41 applicants, 44% accepted, 12 enrolled. In 2011, 11 master's, 7 doctorates awarded. *Degree requirements:* For master's, thesis (for some programs), defense or oral exam; for doctorate, comprehensive exam, thesis/dissertation, qualifying exam, defense. *Entrance requirements:* Additional exam requirements/recommendations for international students: Required—TOEFL (minimum score 550 paper-based; 0 computer-based; 79 iBT), IELTS (minimum score 6.5). *Application deadline:* For fall admission, 1/15 priority date for domestic students, 1/15 for international students; for spring admission, 10/4 priority date for domestic students, 10/4 for international students. Applications are processed on a rolling basis. Application fee: $40 ($50 for international students). Electronic applications accepted. *Expenses:* Tuition, state resident: full-time $5004; part-time $208.50 per credit. Tuition, nonresident: full-time $17,446; part-time $726.90 per credit. *Financial support:* In 2011–12, 12 fellowships (averaging $9,914 per year), 30 research assistantships (averaging $22,031 per year), 28 teaching assistantships (averaging $22,625 per year) were awarded; Federal Work-Study and health care benefits also available. Support available to part-time students. Financial award application deadline: 1/15. *Faculty research:* Microbiology, cell and organismal physiology, ecology and ethology, evolution, genetics, developmental biology. *Total annual research expenditures:* $4.4 million. *Unit head:* Dr. John Gustafson, Head, 575-646-3611, Fax: 575-646-5665, E-mail: jgustafs@nmsu.edu. *Application contact:* Gloria Valencia, Administration Assistant, 575-646-3611, Fax: 575-646-5665, E-mail: gvalenci@nmsu.edu. Web site: http://biology-web.nmsu.edu/.

New York Medical College, Graduate School of Basic Medical Sciences, Valhalla, NY 10595-1691. Offers MS, PhD, MD/PhD. Part-time and evening/weekend programs available. *Faculty:* 91 full-time (16 women), 5 part-time/adjunct (2 women). *Students:* 165 full-time (97 women), 26 part-time (18 women); includes 88 minority (14 Black or African American, non-Hispanic/Latino; 59 Asian, non-Hispanic/Latino; 14 Hispanic/Latino; 1 Native Hawaiian or other Pacific Islander, non-Hispanic/Latino). Average age 26. 472 applicants, 39% accepted, 62 enrolled. In 2011, 41 master's, 5 doctorates awarded. Terminal master's awarded for partial completion of doctoral program. *Median time to degree:* Of those who began their doctoral program in fall 2003, 50% received their degree in 8 years or less. *Degree requirements:* For master's, thesis; for doctorate, comprehensive exam, thesis/dissertation. *Entrance requirements:* For master's, GRE General Test, MCAT or DAT; for doctorate, GRE General Test. Additional exam requirements/recommendations for international students: Required—TOEFL. *Application deadline:* For fall admission, 7/1 priority date for domestic students, 5/1 for international students; for spring admission, 12/1 priority date for domestic students, 10/1 for international students. Applications are processed on a rolling basis. Application fee: $50 ($75 for international students). Electronic applications accepted. *Financial support:* In 2011–12, 24 fellowships with tuition reimbursements (averaging $24,000 per year), 24 research assistantships with full tuition reimbursements (averaging $24,000 per year) were awarded; Federal Work-Study, institutionally sponsored loans, scholarships/grants, tuition waivers (full), and health benefits (for PhD candidates only) also available. Financial award applicants required to submit FAFSA. *Faculty research:* Cardiovascular science, infectious diseases, neuroscience, cancer, and cell signaling. *Unit head:* Dr. Francis L. Belloni, Dean, 914-594-4110, Fax: 914-594-4944, E-mail: francis_belloni@nymc.edu. *Application contact:* Valerie Romeo-Messana, Admission Coordinator, 914-594-4110, Fax: 914-594-4944, E-mail: v_romeomessana@nymc.edu.

See Display on next page and Close-Up on page 111.

New York University, Graduate School of Arts and Science, Department of Biology, New York, NY 10012-1019. Offers biology (PhD); biomedical journalism (MS); cancer

Biological and Biomedical Sciences—General

and molecular biology (PhD); computational biology (PhD); computers in biological research (MS); developmental genetics (PhD); general biology (MS); immunology and microbiology (PhD); molecular genetics (PhD); neurobiology (PhD); oral biology (MS); plant biology (PhD); recombinant DNA technology (MS); MS/MBA. Part-time programs available. *Faculty:* 24 full-time (5 women). *Students:* 146 full-time (90 women), 54 part-time (36 women); includes 49 minority (1 Black or African American, non-Hispanic/Latino; 33 Asian, non-Hispanic/Latino; 12 Hispanic/Latino; 3 Two or more races, non-Hispanic/Latino), 89 international. Average age 27. 394 applicants, 62% accepted, 82 enrolled. In 2011, 68 master's, 6 doctorates awarded. Terminal master's awarded for partial completion of doctoral program. *Degree requirements:* For master's, thesis or alternative, qualifying paper; for doctorate, comprehensive exam, thesis/dissertation. *Entrance requirements:* For master's, GRE General Test; for doctorate, GRE General Test, GRE Subject Test. Additional exam requirements/recommendations for international students: Required—TOEFL. *Application deadline:* For fall admission, 12/1 priority date for domestic students, 12/1 for international students. Application fee: $90. *Financial support:* Fellowships with tuition reimbursements, research assistantships with tuition reimbursements, teaching assistantships with tuition reimbursements, career-related internships or fieldwork, Federal Work-Study, institutionally sponsored loans, scholarships/grants, health care benefits, and unspecified assistantships available. Financial award application deadline: 12/1; financial award applicants required to submit FAFSA. *Faculty research:* Genomics, molecular and cell biology, development and molecular genetics, molecular evolution of plants and animals. *Unit head:* Stephen Small, Chair, 212-998-8200, Fax: 212-995-4015, E-mail: biology@nyu.edu. *Application contact:* Justin Blau, Director of Graduate Studies, 212-998-8200, Fax: 212-995-4015, E-mail: biology@nyu.edu. Web site: http://biology.as.nyu.edu/.

New York University, Graduate School of Arts and Science, Department of Environmental Medicine, New York, NY 10012-1019. Offers environmental health sciences (MS, PhD), including biostatistics (PhD), environmental hygiene (MS), epidemiology (PhD), ergonomics and biomechanics (PhD), exposure assessment and health effects (PhD), molecular toxicology/carcinogenesis (PhD), toxicology. Part-time programs available. *Faculty:* 26 full-time (7 women). *Students:* 62 full-time (43 women), 9 part-time (4 women); includes 12 minority (2 Black or African American, non-Hispanic/Latino; 3 Asian, non-Hispanic/Latino; 7 Hispanic/Latino), 27 international. Average age 30. 70 applicants, 56% accepted, 26 enrolled. In 2011, 9 master's, 8 doctorates awarded. Terminal master's awarded for partial completion of doctoral program. *Degree requirements:* For master's, thesis or alternative; for doctorate, one foreign language, thesis/dissertation, oral and written exams. *Entrance requirements:* For master's and doctorate, GRE General Test, GRE Subject Test, minimum GPA of 3.0; bachelor's degree in biological, physical, or engineering science. Additional exam requirements/recommendations for international students: Required—TOEFL. *Application deadline:* For fall admission, 12/12 for domestic and international students. Application fee: $90. *Financial support:* Fellowships with tuition reimbursements, teaching assistantships with tuition reimbursements, career-related internships or fieldwork, Federal Work-Study, institutionally sponsored loans, and health care benefits available. Financial award application deadline: 12/12; financial award applicants required to submit FAFSA. *Unit head:* Dr. Max Costa, Chair, 845-731-3661, Fax: 845-351-4510, E-mail: ehs@env.med.nyu.edu. *Application contact:* Dr. Jerome J. Solomon, Director of Graduate Studies, 845-731-3661, Fax: 845-351-4510, E-mail: ehs@env.med.nyu.edu. Web site: http://environmental-medicine.med.nyu.edu/.

New York University, School of Medicine and Graduate School of Arts and Science, Medical Scientist Training Program, New York, NY 10012-1019. Offers MD/MS, MD/PhD. Students must be accepted by both the School of Medicine and the Graduate School of Arts and Science. Electronic applications accepted. *Expenses:* Contact institution. *Faculty research:* Neurosciences, cell biology and molecular genetics, structural biology, microbial pathogenesis and host defense.

North Carolina Agricultural and Technical State University, School of Graduate Studies, College of Arts and Sciences, Department of Biology, Greensboro, NC 27411. Offers biology (MS); biology education (MAT). Part-time and evening/weekend programs available. *Degree requirements:* For master's, comprehensive exam, thesis (for some programs), qualifying exam. *Entrance requirements:* For master's, GRE General Test, personal statement. *Faculty research:* Physical ecology, cytochemistry, botany, parasitology, microbiology.

North Carolina Central University, Division of Academic Affairs, College of Science and Technology, Department of Biology, Durham, NC 27707-3129. Offers MS. *Degree requirements:* For master's, one foreign language, comprehensive exam, thesis. *Entrance requirements:* For master's, GRE, minimum GPA of 3.0 in major, 2.5 overall. Additional exam requirements/recommendations for international students: Required—TOEFL.

North Carolina State University, College of Veterinary Medicine, Program in Comparative Biomedical Sciences, Raleigh, NC 27695. Offers cell biology (MS, PhD); infectious disease (MS, PhD); pathology (MS, PhD); pharmacology (MS, PhD); population medicine (MS, PhD). Part-time programs available. *Degree requirements:* For master's, thesis; for doctorate, thesis/dissertation. *Entrance requirements:* For master's and doctorate, GRE General Test. Additional exam requirements/recommendations for international students: Required—TOEFL (minimum score 550 paper-based; 213 computer-based). Electronic applications accepted. *Expenses:* Contact institution. *Faculty research:* Infectious diseases, cell biology, pharmacology and toxicology, genomics, pathology and population medicine.

North Carolina State University, Graduate School, College of Agriculture and Life Sciences, Raleigh, NC 27695. Offers M Tox, MAE, MB, MBAE, MFG, MFM, MFS, MG, MMB, MN, MP, MS, MZS, Ed D, PhD, Certificate. Part-time programs available. Electronic applications accepted.

North Dakota State University, College of Graduate and Interdisciplinary Studies, College of Science and Mathematics, Department of Biological Sciences, Fargo, ND 58108. Offers biology (MS); botany (MS, PhD); cellular and molecular biology (PhD); environmental and conservation sciences (MS, PhD); genomics (PhD); natural resources management (MS, PhD); zoology (MS, PhD). *Faculty:* 13 full-time (7 women), 3 part-time/adjunct (1 woman). *Students:* 20 full-time (10 women), 2 part-time (both women); includes 1 minority (American Indian or Alaska Native, non-Hispanic/Latino), 2 international. 12 applicants, 33% accepted, 4 enrolled. In 2011, 3 degrees awarded. *Degree requirements:* For master's, thesis; for doctorate, thesis/dissertation. *Entrance requirements:* For master's and doctorate, GRE General Test. Additional exam requirements/recommendations for international students: Required—TOEFL. *Application deadline:* For fall admission, 1/15 for domestic students. Applications are processed on a rolling basis. Application fee: $35. Electronic applications accepted. *Financial support:* Fellowships with full tuition reimbursements, research assistantships with full tuition reimbursements, teaching assistantships with full tuition reimbursements, career-related internships or fieldwork, Federal Work-Study, institutionally sponsored loans, scholarships/grants, tuition waivers (full), and unspecified assistantships available. Support available to part-time students. Financial award application deadline: 4/15; financial award applicants required to submit FAFSA. *Faculty research:* Comparative endocrinology, physiology, behavioral ecology, plant cell biology, aquatic biology. *Unit head:* Dr. Wendy Reed, Head, 701-231-7087, E-mail: wendy.reed@ndsu.edu. *Application contact:* Sonya Goergen, Marketing, Recruitment, and Public Relations Coordinator, 701-231-7033, Fax: 701-231-6524. Web site: http://biology.ndsu.nodak.edu/.

YOUR BREAKTHROUGH IN SCIENCE **starts here**

NEW YORK MEDICAL COLLEGE
A Member of the Touro College and University System
Graduate School of Basic Medical Sciences

With a **student-to-faculty ratio of 2:1**, the Graduate School of Basic Medical Sciences offers students an exceptional opportunity for hands-on scientific discovery.

Degree Programs

■ **Integrated PhD**   ■ **MD/PhD**

■ **Master of Science**

• Interdisciplinary Basic Medical Sciences
  Accelerated Track (1-year)
  & Traditional Track (2-year)

• Biochemistry & Molecular Biology

• Cell Biology

• Pathology

• Microbiology & Immunology

• Pharmacology

• Physiology

Graduate School of
Basic Medical Sciences
NEW YORK MEDICAL COLLEGE

Celebrating 50 years in 2013!
www.nymc.edu • 914-594-4110

Our beautiful campus is located just 25 miles north of New York City. On-campus housing available for full-time students.

For more information, please contact us at gsbms_apply@nymc.edu.

Northeastern Illinois University, Graduate College, College of Arts and Sciences, Department of Biology, Program in Biology, Chicago, IL 60625-4699. Offers MS. Part-time and evening/weekend programs available. *Degree requirements:* For master's, comprehensive exam, thesis optional. *Entrance requirements:* For master's, minimum GPA of 2.75. Additional exam requirements/recommendations for international students: Required—TOEFL (minimum score 550 paper-based; 213 computer-based; 79 iBT). Electronic applications accepted. *Faculty research:* Paleoecology and freshwater biology, protein biosynthesis and targeting, microbial growth and physiology, molecular biology of antibody production, reptilian neurobiology.

Northeastern University, College of Science, Department of Biology, Boston, MA 02115-5096. Offers bioinformatics (PMS); biology (MS, PhD); biotechnology (MS, PSM); marine biology (MS). Part-time programs available. *Faculty:* 27 full-time, 5 part-time/adjunct. *Students:* 112 full-time, 4 part-time. 255 applicants, 73% accepted. In 2011, 21 master's, 5 doctorates awarded. Terminal master's awarded for partial completion of doctoral program. *Degree requirements:* For master's, thesis (for some programs); for doctorate, thesis/dissertation, qualifying exam. *Entrance requirements:* For master's and doctorate, GRE General Test. Additional exam requirements/recommendations for international students: Required—TOEFL (minimum score 250 computer-based). *Application deadline:* For fall admission, 1/1 priority date for domestic students, 1/1 for international students. Applications are processed on a rolling basis. Application fee: $50. Electronic applications accepted. *Financial support:* In 2011–12, 19 research assistantships with tuition reimbursements (averaging $18,285 per year), 41 teaching assistantships with tuition reimbursements (averaging $18,285 per year) were awarded; fellowships with tuition reimbursements, career-related internships or fieldwork, Federal Work-Study, tuition waivers (full and partial), and unspecified assistantships also available. Financial award application deadline: 3/1; financial award applicants required to submit FAFSA. *Faculty research:* Biochemistry, marine sciences, molecular biology, microbiology and immunology neurobiology, cellular and molecular biology, biochemistry, marine biochemistry and ecology, microbiology, neurobiology, biotechnology. *Unit head:* Dr. Wendy Smith, Graduate Coordinator, 617-373-2260, Fax: 617-373-3724, E-mail: gradbio@neu.edu. *Application contact:* Jo-Anne Dickinson, Admissions Assistant, 617-373-5990, Fax: 617-373-7281, E-mail: gsas@neu.edu. Web site: http://www.biology.neu.edu/.

Northern Arizona University, Graduate College, College of Engineering, Forestry and Natural Sciences, Department of Biological Sciences, Flagstaff, AZ 86011. Offers MS, PhD. *Faculty:* 42 full-time (14 women). *Students:* 82 full-time (49 women), 15 part-time (7 women); includes 13 minority (2 American Indian or Alaska Native, non-Hispanic/Latino; 3 Asian, non-Hispanic/Latino; 6 Hispanic/Latino; 2 Two or more races, non-Hispanic/Latino), 3 international. Average age 30. 77 applicants, 22% accepted, 15 enrolled. In 2011, 19 master's, 10 doctorates awarded. *Degree requirements:* For master's, thesis, oral exam; for doctorate, thesis/dissertation. *Entrance requirements:* For master's and doctorate, GRE General Test. Additional exam requirements/recommendations for international students: Required—TOEFL (minimum score 550 paper-based; 213 computer-based; 80 iBT), IELTS (minimum score 7). *Application deadline:* For fall admission, 2/15 priority date for domestic students, 2/15 for international students. Application fee: $65. Electronic applications accepted. *Expenses:* Tuition, state resident: full-time $7190; part-time $355 per credit hour. Tuition, nonresident: full-time $18,092; part-time $1005 per credit hour. *Required fees:* $818; $328 per semester. *Financial support:* In 2011–12, 17 fellowships, 20 research assistantships with partial tuition reimbursements (averaging $21,271 per year), 32 teaching assistantships with partial tuition reimbursements (averaging $13,164 per year) were awarded; Federal Work-Study, scholarships/grants, traineeships, health care benefits, tuition waivers (full and partial), and unspecified assistantships also available. Financial award applicants required to submit FAFSA. *Faculty research:* Genetic levels of trophic levels, plant hybrid zones, insect biodiversity, natural history and cognition of wild jays. *Total annual research expenditures:* $2.2 million. *Unit head:* Dr. Maribeth Watwood, Chair, 928-523-9322, Fax: 928-523-7500, E-mail: maribeth.watwood@nau.edu. *Application contact:* Arline Lonon, Administrative Assistant, 928-523-7164, Fax: 928-523-7500, E-mail: arline.lonon@nau.edu. Web site: http://www.cefns.nau.edu/Academic/Biology/Graduate/.

Northern Illinois University, Graduate School, College of Liberal Arts and Sciences, Department of Biological Sciences, De Kalb, IL 60115-2854. Offers MS, PhD. Part-time programs available. *Faculty:* 30 full-time (6 women), 7 part-time/adjunct (1 woman). *Students:* 49 full-time (22 women), 37 part-time (25 women); includes 8 minority (1 American Indian or Alaska Native, non-Hispanic/Latino; 1 Asian, non-Hispanic/Latino; 4 Hispanic/Latino; 2 Two or more races, non-Hispanic/Latino), 11 international. Average age 31. 72 applicants, 17% accepted, 11 enrolled. In 2011, 17 master's, 3 doctorates awarded. Terminal master's awarded for partial completion of doctoral program. *Degree requirements:* For master's, comprehensive exam, thesis optional; for doctorate, thesis/dissertation, candidacy exam, dissertation defense. *Entrance requirements:* For master's, GRE General Test, bachelor's degree in related field, minimum GPA of 2.75; for doctorate, GRE General Test, bachelor's or master's degree in related field; minimum undergraduate GPA of 2.75, graduate 3.2. Additional exam requirements/recommendations for international students: Required—TOEFL (minimum score 550 paper-based; 213 computer-based). *Application deadline:* For fall admission, 6/1 for domestic students, 5/1 for international students; for spring admission, 11/1 for domestic students, 10/1 for international students. Applications are processed on a rolling basis. Application fee: $40. Electronic applications accepted. *Financial support:* In 2011–12, 12 research assistantships with full tuition reimbursements, 39 teaching assistantships with full tuition reimbursements were awarded; fellowships with full tuition reimbursements, career-related internships or fieldwork, Federal Work-Study, scholarships/grants, tuition waivers (full), and unspecified assistantships also available. Support available to part-time students. Financial award applicants required to submit FAFSA. *Faculty research:* Plant molecular biology, neurosecretory control, ethnobotany, organellar genomes, carbon metabolism. *Unit head:* Dr. Barrie P. Bode, Chair, 815-753-1753, Fax: 815-753-0461, E-mail: bodebp@niu.edu. *Application contact:* Dr. Thomas Sims, Director of Graduate Studies, 815-753-7873. Web site: http://www.bios.niu.edu/.

Northern Michigan University, College of Graduate Studies, College of Arts and Sciences, Department of Biology, Marquette, MI 49855-5301. Offers MS. Part-time programs available. Postbaccalaureate distance learning degree programs offered (minimal on-campus study). *Degree requirements:* For master's, thesis or alternative. *Entrance requirements:* For master's, GRE, minimum GPA of 3.0. *Faculty research:* Molecular genetics of sex-linked genes, biology of protozoan parasites, wildlife ecology, organochlorines in the environment, insect development.

Northwestern University, The Graduate School, Interdepartmental Biological Sciences Program (IBiS), Evanston, IL 60208. Offers biochemistry, molecular biology, and cell biology (PhD), including biochemistry, cell and molecular biology, molecular biophysics, structural biology; biotechnology (PhD); cell and molecular biology (PhD); developmental biology and genetics (PhD); hormone action and signal transduction (PhD); neuroscience (PhD); structural biology, biochemistry, and biophysics (PhD). Program participants include the Departments of Biochemistry, Molecular Biology, and Cell Biology; Chemistry; Neurobiology and Physiology; Chemical Engineering; Civil Engineering; and Evanston Hospital. *Degree requirements:* For doctorate, thesis/dissertation, qualifying exam. *Entrance requirements:* For doctorate, GRE General Test. Additional exam requirements/recommendations for international students: Required—TOEFL (minimum score 600 paper-based). Electronic applications accepted. *Faculty research:* Developmental genetics, gene regulation, DNA-protein interactions, biological clocks, bioremediation.

Northwestern University, Northwestern University Feinberg School of Medicine, Combined MD/PhD Medical Scientist Training Program, Evanston, IL 60208. Offers MD/PhD. Application must be made to both The Graduate School and the Medical School. *Accreditation:* LCME/AMA. Electronic applications accepted. *Faculty research:* Cardiovascular epidemiology, cancer epidemiology, nutritional interventions for the prevention of cardiovascular disease and cancer, women's health, outcomes research.

Northwestern University, Northwestern University Feinberg School of Medicine and Interdepartmental Programs, Integrated Graduate Programs in the Life Sciences, Chicago, IL 60611. Offers cancer biology (PhD); cell biology (PhD); developmental biology (PhD); evolutionary biology (PhD); immunology and microbial pathogenesis (PhD); molecular biology and genetics (PhD); neurobiology (PhD); pharmacology and toxicology (PhD); structural biology and biochemistry (PhD). *Degree requirements:* For doctorate, comprehensive exam, thesis/dissertation, written and oral qualifying exams. *Entrance requirements:* For doctorate, GRE General Test. Additional exam requirements/recommendations for international students: Required—TOEFL (minimum score 600 paper-based; 250 computer-based). Electronic applications accepted.

Northwest Missouri State University, Graduate School, College of Arts and Sciences, Department of Biology, Maryville, MO 64468-6001. Offers MS. Part-time programs available. *Faculty:* 10 full-time (3 women). *Students:* 9 full-time (4 women), 5 part-time (3 women); includes 1 minority (Two or more races, non-Hispanic/Latino), 1 international. 6 applicants, 17% accepted, 0 enrolled. In 2011, 1 master's awarded. *Degree requirements:* For master's, comprehensive exam, thesis. *Entrance requirements:* For master's, GRE General Test, minimum GPA of 3.0 in last 60 hours or 2.75 overall, writing sample. Additional exam requirements/recommendations for international students: Required—TOEFL (minimum score 550 paper-based; 213 computer-based). *Application deadline:* For fall admission, 7/1 for domestic and international students; for spring admission, 11/15 for domestic and international students. Applications are processed on a rolling basis. Application fee: $0 ($50 for international students). *Financial support:* In 2011–12, 5 teaching assistantships with full tuition reimbursements (averaging $6,000 per year) were awarded; tutorial assistantships also available. Financial award application deadline: 4/1; financial award applicants required to submit FAFSA. *Unit head:* Dr. Gregg Dieringer, Chairperson, 660-562-1812. *Application contact:* Dr. Gregory Haddock, Dean of Graduate School, 660-562-1145, Fax: 660-562-1096, E-mail: gradsch@nwmissouri.edu.

Notre Dame de Namur University, Division of Academic Affairs, College of Arts and Sciences, Department of Natural Sciences, Belmont, CA 94002-1908. Offers premedical studies (Certificate). *Students:* 10 full-time (7 women), 8 part-time (6 women); includes 10 minority (1 Black or African American, non-Hispanic/Latino; 6 Asian, non-Hispanic/Latino; 2 Hispanic/Latino; 1 Two or more races, non-Hispanic/Latino). Average age 26. 28 applicants, 68% accepted, 12 enrolled. Application fee: $60. *Expenses: Tuition:* Full-time $14,220; part-time $790 per credit. *Required fees:* $35 per semester. Tuition and fees vary according to program. *Financial support:* Available to part-time students. Applicants required to submit FAFSA. *Unit head:* Dr. Isabelle Haithcox, Chair, 650-508-3496, E-mail: ihaithcox@ndnu.edu. *Application contact:* Candace Hallmark, Associate Director of Admissions, 650-508-3600, Fax: 650-508-3426, E-mail: grad.admit@ndnu.edu.

Nova Southeastern University, Health Professions Division, College of Medical Sciences, Fort Lauderdale, FL 33314-7796. Offers biomedical sciences (MBS). *Students:* 29 full-time (15 women); includes 15 minority (2 Black or African American, non-Hispanic/Latino; 3 Asian, non-Hispanic/Latino; 8 Hispanic/Latino; 2 Two or more races, non-Hispanic/Latino), 2 international. Average age 26. *Degree requirements:* For master's, thesis. *Entrance requirements:* For master's, MCAT, DAT, minimum GPA of 2.5. *Application deadline:* For spring admission, 4/15 for domestic students. Applications are processed on a rolling basis. Application fee: $50. *Expenses:* Contact institution. *Financial support:* Applicants required to submit FAFSA. *Faculty research:* Neurophysiology, mucosal immunology, allergies involving the lungs, cardiovascular physiology parasitology. *Unit head:* Dr. Harold E. Laubach, Dean, 954-262-1303, Fax: 954-262-1802, E-mail: harold@nsu.nova.edu. *Application contact:* Richard Wilson, Admissions Counselor, 954-262-1111, Fax: 954-262-1802, E-mail: rwilson@nsu.nova.edu.

Nova Southeastern University, Oceanographic Center, Fort Lauderdale, FL 33314-7796. Offers biological sciences (MS); coastal zone management (MS); marine and coastal studies (MA); marine biology (MS); marine biology and oceanography (PhD), including marine biology, oceanography; marine environmental science (MS). Part-time and evening/weekend programs available. *Faculty:* 15 full-time (1 woman), 5 part-time/adjunct (0 women). *Students:* 130 full-time (86 women), 135 part-time (87 women); includes 34 minority (5 Black or African American, non-Hispanic/Latino; 5 Asian, non-Hispanic/Latino; 22 Hispanic/Latino; 2 Two or more races, non-Hispanic/Latino), 7 international. Average age 29. 98 applicants, 82% accepted, 67 enrolled. In 2011, 30 master's, 1 doctorate awarded. *Degree requirements:* For master's, thesis; for doctorate, comprehensive exam, thesis/dissertation, departmental qualifying exam. *Entrance requirements:* For master's, GRE General Test; for doctorate, GRE General Test, master's degree. Additional exam requirements/recommendations for international students: Required—TOEFL (minimum score 550 paper-based). *Application deadline:* Applications are processed on a rolling basis. Application fee: $50. *Expenses:* Contact institution. *Financial support:* In 2011–12, 25 research assistantships (averaging $4,000 per year), 3 teaching assistantships (averaging $3,500 per year) were awarded; career-related internships or fieldwork, Federal Work-Study, scholarships/grants, tuition waivers (partial), and unspecified assistantships also available. Support available to part-time students. Financial award applicants required to submit FAFSA. *Faculty research:* Physical, geological, chemical, and biological oceanography. *Unit head:* Dr. Richard Dodge, Dean, 954-262-3600, Fax: 954-262-4020, E-mail: dodge@nsu.nova.edu. *Application contact:* Dr. Richard Spieler, Director of Academic Programs, 954-262-3600, Fax: 954-262-4020, E-mail: spieler@nova.edu. Web site: http://www.nova.edu/ocean/.

Oakland University, Graduate Study and Lifelong Learning, College of Arts and Sciences, Department of Biological Sciences, Rochester, MI 48309-4401. Offers biological sciences (MA, MS); biomedical sciences: biological communications (PhD). *Degree requirements:* For master's, thesis. *Entrance requirements:* For master's, GRE Subject Test, GRE General Test, minimum GPA of 3.0 for unconditional admission. Additional exam requirements/recommendations for international students: Required—TOEFL (minimum score 550 paper-based; 213 computer-based). Electronic applications accepted. *Expenses:* Contact institution. *Faculty research:* Mechanism producing rhythmic beating in cilia and flagella, biochemical characterization of carbofuron hydroxylase, maize as a model system to study helitron-related transposable elements, genetic mapping of estrogen-induced endothelial growth factor on rat chromosomes.

Biological and Biomedical Sciences—General

Occidental College, Graduate Studies, Department of Biology, Los Angeles, CA 90041-3314. Offers MA. Part-time programs available. *Degree requirements:* For master's, thesis, final exam. *Entrance requirements:* For master's, GRE General Test, GRE Subject Test, minimum GPA of 3.0. Additional exam requirements/recommendations for international students: Required—TOEFL (minimum score 625 paper-based; 263 computer-based). *Expenses:* Contact institution.

The Ohio State University, College of Medicine, School of Biomedical Science, Integrated Biomedical Science Graduate Program, Columbus, OH 43210. Offers immunology (PhD); medical genetics (PhD); molecular virology (PhD); pharmacology (PhD). *Degree requirements:* For doctorate, thesis/dissertation. *Entrance requirements:* For doctorate, GRE, GRE Subject Test in biochemistry, cell and molecular biology (recommended for some). Additional exam requirements/recommendations for international students: Required—TOEFL (minimum score 600 paper-based; 250 computer-based). Electronic applications accepted. *Expenses:* Tuition, state resident: full-time $11,400. Tuition, nonresident: full-time $28,125. Tuition and fees vary according to course load, degree level, campus/location and program.

Ohio University, Graduate College, College of Arts and Sciences, Department of Biological Sciences, Athens, OH 45701-2979. Offers biological sciences (MS, PhD); cell biology and physiology (MS, PhD); ecology and evolutionary biology (MS, PhD); exercise physiology and muscle biology (MS, PhD); microbiology (MS, PhD); neuroscience (MS, PhD). *Students:* 35 full-time (12 women), 4 part-time (1 woman), 14 international. 62 applicants, 10% accepted, 5 enrolled. In 2011, 2 master's, 8 doctorates awarded. Terminal master's awarded for partial completion of doctoral program. *Degree requirements:* For master's, comprehensive exam, thesis, 1 quarter of teaching experience; for doctorate, comprehensive exam, thesis/dissertation, 2 quarters of teaching experience. *Entrance requirements:* For master's, GRE General Test, names of three faculty members whose research interests most closely match the applicant's interest; for doctorate, GRE General Test, essay concerning prior training, research interest and career goals, plus names of three faculty members whose research interests most closely match the applicant's interest. Additional exam requirements/recommendations for international students: Required—TOEFL (minimum score 620 paper-based; 105 iBT) or IELTS (minimum score 7.5). *Application deadline:* For fall admission, 1/15 for domestic and international students. Application fee: $50 ($55 for international students). Electronic applications accepted. *Financial support:* In 2011–12, 1 fellowship with full tuition reimbursement (averaging $18,957 per year), 10 research assistantships with full tuition reimbursements (averaging $18,957 per year), 42 teaching assistantships with full tuition reimbursements (averaging $18,957 per year) were awarded; Federal Work-Study and institutionally sponsored loans also available. Financial award application deadline: 1/15. *Faculty research:* Ecology and evolutionary biology, exercise physiology and muscle biology, neurobiology, cell biology, physiology. *Total annual research expenditures:* $2.8 million. *Unit head:* Dr. Ralph DiCaprio, Chair, 740-593-2290, Fax: 740-593-0300, E-mail: dicaprir@ohio.edu. *Application contact:* Dr. Patrick Hassett, Graduate Chair, 740-593-4793, Fax: 740-593-0300, E-mail: hassett@ohio.edu. Web site: http://www.biosci.ohiou.edu/.

Oklahoma State University Center for Health Sciences, Program in Biomedical Sciences, Tulsa, OK 74107-1898. Offers MS, PhD, DO/PhD. Part-time programs available. *Faculty:* 25 full-time (6 women), 2 part-time/adjunct (1 woman). *Students:* 19 full-time (13 women), 5 part-time (1 woman); includes 8 minority (2 Black or African American, non-Hispanic/Latino; 4 American Indian or Alaska Native, non-Hispanic/Latino; 1 Asian, non-Hispanic/Latino; 1 Hispanic/Latino), 4 international. Average age 31. 36 applicants, 61% accepted, 18 enrolled. In 2011, 8 master's, 4 doctorates awarded. *Degree requirements:* For master's, thesis; for doctorate, thesis/dissertation, comprehensive, oral and written exam. *Entrance requirements:* For master's, GRE General Test, minimum GPA of 3.0; for doctorate, GRE General Test, MCAT, minimum GPA of 3.0. Additional exam requirements/recommendations for international students: Required—TOEFL (minimum score 213 computer-based). *Application deadline:* For fall admission, 2/15 for domestic students, 2/18 for international students; for winter admission, 9/15 for domestic and international students. Application fee: $40 ($75 for international students). *Financial support:* In 2011–12, 9 students received support, including 12 research assistantships with full tuition reimbursements available (averaging $21,180 per year), 2 teaching assistantships with full tuition reimbursements available (averaging $21,180 per year); Federal Work-Study and scholarships/grants also available. Financial award application deadline: 4/10; financial award applicants required to submit FAFSA. *Faculty research:* Neuroscience, cell biology, cell signaling, infectious disease, virology, neurotoxicology. *Total annual research expenditures:* $1.7 million. *Unit head:* Dr. Greg L. Sawyer, Director, 918-561-1221, Fax: 918-561-8276. *Application contact:* Patrick Anderson, Coordinator of Graduate Admissions, 800-677-1972, Fax: 918-561-8243, E-mail: patrick.anderson@okstate.edu.

Old Dominion University, College of Sciences, Master of Science in Biology Program, Norfolk, VA 23529. Offers MS. Part-time programs available. *Faculty:* 22 full-time (4 women), 23 part-time/adjunct (2 women). *Students:* 24 full-time (12 women), 19 part-time (8 women); includes 4 minority (2 Black or African American, non-Hispanic/Latino; 2 Asian, non-Hispanic/Latino), 3 international. Average age 28. 41 applicants, 34% accepted, 11 enrolled. In 2011, 13 master's awarded. *Degree requirements:* For master's, comprehensive exam, thesis optional. *Entrance requirements:* For master's, GRE General Test, MCAT, minimum GPA of 3.0 in major, 2.7 overall. Additional exam requirements/recommendations for international students: Required—TOEFL (minimum score 550 paper-based; 213 computer-based; 79 iBT). *Application deadline:* For fall admission, 2/1 priority date for domestic students, 2/1 for international students; for winter admission, 6/1 priority date for domestic students, 6/1 for international students; for spring admission, 10/1 priority date for domestic students, 10/1 for international students. Application fee: $50. Electronic applications accepted. *Expenses:* Tuition, state resident: full-time $9096; part-time $379 per credit. Tuition, nonresident: full-time $23,064; part-time $961 per credit. *Required fees:* $127 per semester. One-time fee: $50. *Financial support:* In 2011–12, 2 fellowships (averaging $6,575 per year), 10 research assistantships with partial tuition reimbursements (averaging $15,000 per year), 8 teaching assistantships with partial tuition reimbursements (averaging $15,000 per year) were awarded; career-related internships or fieldwork and scholarships/grants also available. Support available to part-time students. Financial award application deadline: 2/1; financial award applicants required to submit FAFSA. *Faculty research:* Wetland ecology, systematics and ecology of vertebrates, marine biology, molecular and cellular microbiology, cell biology, immunology, physiological and reproductive biology. *Total annual research expenditures:* $2 million. *Unit head:* Dr. Robert Ratzlaff, Graduate Program Director, 757-683-4361, Fax: 757-683-5283, E-mail: biolgpd@odu.edu. *Application contact:* William Heffelfinger, Director of Graduate Admissions, 757-683-5554, Fax: 757-683-3255, E-mail: gradadmit@odu.edu. Web site: http://sci.odu.edu/biology/academics/bio-ms.shtml.

Old Dominion University, College of Sciences, Program in Biomedical Sciences, Norfolk, VA 23529. Offers PhD. Program offered jointly with Eastern Virginia Medical School. *Faculty:* 29 full-time (8 women). *Students:* 21 full-time (13 women), 6 part-time (3 women); includes 2 minority (both Hispanic/Latino), 13 international. Average age 33. 18 applicants, 22% accepted, 4 enrolled. In 2011, 3 doctorates awarded. *Degree requirements:* For doctorate, comprehensive exam, thesis/dissertation. *Entrance*

requirements: For doctorate, GRE General Test, minimum GPA of 3.0. Additional exam requirements/recommendations for international students: Required—TOEFL (minimum score 213 computer-based; 79 iBT). *Application deadline:* For fall admission, 2/1 priority date for domestic students, 2/1 for international students. Application fee: $50. Electronic applications accepted. *Expenses:* Tuition, state resident: full-time $9096; part-time $379 per credit. Tuition, nonresident: full-time $23,064; part-time $961 per credit. *Required fees:* $127 per semester. One-time fee: $50. *Financial support:* In 2011–12, 2 fellowships with full tuition reimbursements (averaging $18,000 per year), 2 research assistantships with full tuition reimbursements (averaging $18,000 per year), 4 teaching assistantships with full tuition reimbursements (averaging $15,000 per year) were awarded; career-related internships or fieldwork, scholarships/grants, tuition waivers (partial), and unspecified assistantships also available. Support available to part-time students. Financial award application deadline: 2/15; financial award applicants required to submit FAFSA. *Faculty research:* Systems biology and biophysics, pure and applied biomedical sciences, biological chemistry, clinical chemistry, cell biology and molecular pathogenesis. *Total annual research expenditures:* $3.7 million. *Unit head:* Dr. Robert Ratzlaff, Graduate Program Director, 757-683-4361, Fax: 757-683-5283, E-mail: bimdgpd@odu.edu. *Application contact:* Dr. Robert Ratzlaff, Graduate Program Director, 757-683-4361, Fax: 757-683-5283, E-mail: chpgpd@odu.edu. Web site: http://sci.odu.edu/biology/academics/phdmed.shtml.

Oregon Health & Science University, School of Medicine, Graduate Programs in Medicine, Portland, OR 97239-3098. Offers MBA, MBST, MCR, MPAS, MPH, MS, MSCNU, PhD, Certificate. Part-time programs available. *Faculty:* 512. *Students:* 420 full-time (245 women), 459 part-time (250 women); includes 173 minority (24 Black or African American, non-Hispanic/Latino; 12 American Indian or Alaska Native, non-Hispanic/Latino; 78 Asian, non-Hispanic/Latino; 33 Hispanic/Latino; 3 Native Hawaiian or other Pacific Islander, non-Hispanic/Latino; 23 Two or more races, non-Hispanic/Latino), 72 international. Average age 34. 1,704 applicants, 21% accepted, 256 enrolled. In 2011, 114 master's, 51 doctorates, 75 other advanced degrees awarded. Terminal master's awarded for partial completion of doctoral program. *Degree requirements:* For master's, thesis or capstone experience; for doctorate, comprehensive exam, thesis/dissertation, qualifying exam. *Entrance requirements:* For master's, GRE General Test (minimum scores: 153 [500 old version] Verbal/148 [600 old version] Quantitative/4.5 Analytical), MCAT or GMAT (for some programs); for doctorate, GRE General Test (minimum scores: 153 [500 old version] Verbal/148 [600 old version] Quantitative/4.5 Analytical). Additional exam requirements/recommendations for international students: Required—TOEFL. *Application deadline:* Applications are processed on a rolling basis. Application fee: $70. Electronic applications accepted. *Expenses:* Contact institution. *Financial support:* Fellowships, research assistantships, teaching assistantships, scholarships/grants, health care benefits, and full tuition and stipends for PhD, some Master's scholarships available. *Unit head:* Dr. Allison Fryer, Associate Dean for Graduate Studies, 503-494-6222, Fax: 503-494-3400, E-mail: somgrad@ohsu.edu. *Application contact:* Lorie Gookin, Admissions Coordinator, 503-494-6222, Fax: 503-494-3400, E-mail: somgrad@ohsu.edu.

Penn State Hershey Medical Center, College of Medicine, Graduate School Programs in the Biomedical Sciences, Hershey, PA 17033. Offers MPH, MS, PhD, MD/PhD, PhD/MBA. Terminal master's awarded for partial completion of doctoral program. *Degree requirements:* For master's, thesis or alternative; for doctorate, comprehensive exam, thesis/dissertation, oral exam. *Entrance requirements:* For master's, GRE; for doctorate, GRE, minimum GPA of 3.0. Additional exam requirements/recommendations for international students: Required—TOEFL (minimum score 550 paper-based; 213 computer-based; 80 iBT). *Application deadline:* For fall admission, 1/31 priority date for domestic students, 2/1 for international students. Applications are processed on a rolling basis. Application fee: $65. Electronic applications accepted. *Expenses:* Contact institution. *Financial support:* In 2011–12, 3 fellowships with full tuition reimbursements (averaging $26,500 per year), 37 research assistantships with full tuition reimbursements (averaging $23,028 per year) were awarded; career-related internships or fieldwork, scholarships/grants, health care benefits, tuition waivers (full), and unspecified assistantships also available. Financial award applicants required to submit FAFSA. *Unit head:* Dr. Michael F. Verderame, Associate Dean of Graduate Studies, 717-531-8892, Fax: 717-531-0786, E-mail: grad-hmc@psu.edu. *Application contact:* Kathleen M. Simon, Administrative Assistant, 717-531-8892, Fax: 717-531-0786, E-mail: grad-hmc@psu.edu. Web site: http://www.pennstatehershey.org/web/gsa/home.

Penn State University Park, Graduate School, Eberly College of Science, Department of Biology, State College, University Park, PA 16802-1503. Offers MS, PhD. *Unit head:* Dr. Douglas R. Cavener, Head, 814-865-4562, Fax: 814-865-9131, E-mail: drc9@psu.edu. *Application contact:* Kathryn McClintock, Graduate Programs Secretary, 814-863-7034, E-mail: biokat@psu.edu. Web site: http://bio.psu.edu/.

Penn State University Park, Graduate School, Intercollege Graduate Programs, Intercollege Graduate Program in Integrative Biosciences, State College, University Park, PA 16802-1503. Offers integrative biosciences (MS, PhD), including biomolecular transport dynamics (PhD), integrative biosciences (MS). *Unit head:* Dr. Peter J. Hudson, Director, 814-865-6057, Fax: 814-863-1357. *Application contact:* Cynthia E. Nicosia, Director, Graduate Enrollment Services, 814-865-1795, Fax: 814-865-4627, E-mail: cey1@psu.edu.

Philadelphia College of Osteopathic Medicine, Graduate and Professional Programs, Program in Biomedical Sciences, Philadelphia, PA 19131-1694. Offers MS, Certificate. *Degree requirements:* For master's, thesis. *Entrance requirements:* For master's, GRE, MCAT, DAT, OAT, minimum GPA of 3.0, course work in biology, chemistry, English, physics. *Faculty research:* Developmental biology, cytokines and inflammation, neurobiology of aging, pain mechanisms, cell death.

Pittsburg State University, Graduate School, College of Arts and Sciences, Department of Biology, Pittsburg, KS 66762. Offers MS. *Degree requirements:* For master's, thesis or alternative. *Expenses:* Tuition, state resident: full-time $5056; part-time $211 per credit hour. Tuition, nonresident: full-time $13,410; part-time $559 per credit hour. *Required fees:* $50 per credit hour.

Point Loma Nazarene University, Program in Biology, San Diego, CA 92106-2899. Offers MA, MS. Part-time programs available. *Entrance requirements:* For master's, GRE Subject Test, BA/BS in science field, letters of recommendation, writing sample, interview, minimum GPA of 3.0.

Ponce School of Medicine & Health Sciences, Program in Biomedical Sciences, Ponce, PR 00732-7004. Offers PhD. *Degree requirements:* For doctorate, one foreign language, comprehensive exam, thesis/dissertation. *Entrance requirements:* For doctorate, GRE General Test, proficiency in Spanish and English, minimum overall GPA of 3.0, 3 letters of recommendation, minimum of 35 credits in science.

Pontifical Catholic University of Puerto Rico, College of Sciences, Department of Biology, Ponce, PR 00717-0777. Offers environmental sciences (MS). *Degree requirements:* For master's, thesis. *Entrance requirements:* For master's, GRE, 2 letters of recommendation, interview, minimum GPA of 2.75.

Portland State University, Graduate Studies, College of Liberal Arts and Sciences, Department of Biology, Portland, OR 97207-0751. Offers MA, MS, PhD. *Degree*

requirements: For master's, one foreign language, thesis; for doctorate, thesis/dissertation. *Entrance requirements:* For master's, GRE General Test, GRE Subject Test, minimum GPA of 3.0 in upper-division course work or 2.75 overall, 2 letters of reference; for doctorate, GRE General Test, GRE Subject Test, minimum GPA of 3.5 in science. Additional exam requirements/recommendations for international students: Required—TOEFL (minimum score 550 paper-based; 213 computer-based). *Faculty research:* Genetic diversity and natural population, vertebrate temperature regulation, water balance and sensory physiology, trace elements and aquatic ecology, molecular genetics.

Prairie View A&M University, College of Arts and Sciences, Department of Biology, Prairie View, TX 77446-0519. Offers bio- environmental toxicology (MS); biology (MS). Part-time and evening/weekend programs available. *Degree requirements:* For master's, comprehensive exam, thesis optional. *Entrance requirements:* For master's, GRE General Test. Additional exam requirements/recommendations for international students: Required—TOEFL. *Faculty research:* Genomics, hypertension, control of gene express, proteins, kigands that interact with hormone receptors, prostate cancer, renin-angiotensin yeast metabolism.

Purdue University, Graduate School, College of Science, Department of Biological Sciences, West Lafayette, IN 47907. Offers biochemistry (PhD); biophysics (PhD); cell and developmental biology (PhD); ecology, evolutionary and population biology (MS, PhD), including ecology, evolutionary biology, population biology; genetics (MS, PhD); microbiology (MS, PhD); molecular biology (PhD); neurobiology (MS, PhD); plant physiology (PhD). *Faculty:* 57 full-time (15 women), 4 part-time/adjunct (1 woman). *Students:* 94 full-time (54 women), 9 part-time (5 women); includes 7 minority (2 Black or African American, non-Hispanic/Latino; 3 Asian, non-Hispanic/Latino; 2 Hispanic/Latino), 51 international. Average age 27. 246 applicants, 11% accepted, 18 enrolled. In 2011, 9 master's, 23 doctorates awarded. Terminal master's awarded for partial completion of doctoral program. *Degree requirements:* For master's, thesis (for some programs); for doctorate, thesis/dissertation, seminars, teaching experience. *Entrance requirements:* For master's, GRE General Test, minimum analytical writing score of 3.5, minimum undergraduate GPA of 3.0; for doctorate, GRE General Test, minimum analytical writing score of 3.5, minimum undergraduate GPA of 3.5. Additional exam requirements/recommendations for international students: Required—T.OEFL (minimum score 600 paper-based; 107 iBT) for MS; TOEFL (minimum score 600 paper-based; 80 iBT) for Ph D. *Application deadline:* For fall admission, 12/7 for domestic and international students. Applications are processed on a rolling basis. Application fee: $60 ($75 for international students). Electronic applications accepted. *Financial support:* Fellowships, research assistantships, and teaching assistantships available. Support available to part-time students. Financial award application deadline: 2/15; financial award applicants required to submit FAFSA. *Unit head:* Dr. Richard J. Kuhn, Head, 765-494-4407, E-mail: kuhnr@purdue.edu. *Application contact:* Georgina E. Rupp, Graduate Coordinator, 765-494-8142, Fax: 765-494-0876, E-mail: ruppg@purdue.edu. Web site: http://www.bio.purdue.edu/.

Purdue University, Graduate School, PULSe - Purdue University Life Sciences Program, West Lafayette, IN 47907. Offers biomolecular structure and biophysics (PhD); biotechnology (PhD); chemical biology (PhD); chromatin and regulation of gene expression (PhD); integrative neuroscience (PhD); integrative plant sciences (PhD); membrane biology (PhD); microbiology (PhD); molecular evolutionary and cancer biology (PhD); molecular evolutionary genetics (PhD); molecular virology (PhD). *Students:* 90 full-time (45 women); includes 7 minority (3 Black or African American, non-Hispanic/Latino; 1 Asian, non-Hispanic/Latino; 2 Hispanic/Latino; 1 Two or more races, non-Hispanic/Latino), 40 international. Average age 26. 427 applicants, 24% accepted, 35 enrolled. *Entrance requirements:* For doctorate, GRE test required, minimum undergraduate GPA of 3.0. Additional exam requirements/recommendations for international students: Required—TOEFL (minimum score 550 paper-based; 77 iBT). *Application deadline:* For fall admission, 1/15 priority date for domestic students, 1/15 for international students. Applications are processed on a rolling basis. Application fee: $60 ($75 for international students). Electronic applications accepted. *Financial support:* In 2011–12, research assistantships with tuition reimbursements (averaging $22,500 per year), teaching assistantships with tuition reimbursements (averaging $22,500 per year) were awarded. *Unit head:* Dr. Christine A. Hrycyna, Head, 765-494-7322, E-mail: hrycyna@purdue.edu. *Application contact:* Emily E. Bramson, Graduate Contact, 765-494-5865, E-mail: bramson@purdue.edu. Web site: http://www.gradschool.purdue.edu/pulse.

Purdue University Calumet, Graduate Studies Office, School of Engineering, Mathematics, and Science, Department of Biological Sciences, Hammond, IN 46323-2094. Offers biology (MS); biology teaching (MS); biotechnology (MS). *Entrance requirements:* For master's, GRE. Additional exam requirements/recommendations for international students: Required—TOEFL. Electronic applications accepted. *Faculty research:* Cell biology, molecular biology, genetics, microbiology, neurophysiology.

Queens College of the City University of New York, Division of Graduate Studies, Mathematics and Natural Sciences Division, Department of Biology, Flushing, NY 11367-1597. Offers MA. Part-time and evening/weekend programs available. *Faculty:* 18 full-time (6 women). *Students:* 6 full-time (4 women), 45 part-time (29 women); includes 27 minority (6 Black or African American, non-Hispanic/Latino; 1 American Indian or Alaska Native, non-Hispanic/Latino; 11 Asian, non-Hispanic/Latino; 9 Hispanic/Latino), 5 international. 50 applicants, 50% accepted, 15 enrolled. In 2011, 9 master's awarded. *Degree requirements:* For master's, comprehensive exam, thesis or alternative, qualifying exam. *Entrance requirements:* For master's, minimum GPA of 3.0. Additional exam requirements/recommendations for international students: Required—TOEFL. *Application deadline:* For fall admission, 4/1 for domestic students; for spring admission, 11/1 for domestic students. Applications are processed on a rolling basis. Application fee: $125. *Expenses:* Tuition, state resident: part-time $345 per credit. Tuition, nonresident: part-time $640 per credit. *Required fees:* $145.25 per semester. *Financial support:* Career-related internships or fieldwork, Federal Work-Study, institutionally sponsored loans, tuition waivers (partial), and unspecified assistantships available. Support available to part-time students. Financial award application deadline: 4/1; financial award applicants required to submit FAFSA. *Faculty research:* Cell biology, evolutionary biology, environmental biology, microbiology. *Unit head:* Dr. Corrine Michels, Chairperson, 718-997-3400, E-mail: corinne_michels@qc.edu. *Application contact:* Dr. Jeanne Szalay, Graduate Adviser, 718-997-3400, E-mail: jeanne_szalay@qc.edu.

Queen's University at Kingston, School of Graduate Studies and Research, Faculty of Arts and Sciences, Department of Biology, Kingston, ON K7L 3N6, Canada. Offers M Sc, PhD. Part-time programs available. *Degree requirements:* For master's, thesis; for doctorate, comprehensive exam, thesis/dissertation. *Entrance requirements:* Additional exam requirements/recommendations for international students: Required—TOEFL. *Faculty research:* Limnology, plant morphogenesis, nitrogen fixation, cell cycle, genetics.

Quinnipiac University, School of Health Sciences, Program in Medical Laboratory Sciences, Hamden, CT 06518-1940. Offers biomedical sciences (MHS); laboratory management (MHS); microbiology (MHS). Part-time programs available. *Faculty:* 13 full-time (7 women), 17 part-time/adjunct (7 women). *Students:* 46 full-time (30 women), 31 part-time (13 women); includes 14 minority (8 Black or African American, non-Hispanic/Latino; 4 Asian, non-Hispanic/Latino; 2 Hispanic/Latino), 34 international. 67 applicants, 79% accepted, 46 enrolled. In 2011, 33 master's awarded. *Degree requirements:* For master's, comprehensive exam, thesis optional. *Entrance requirements:* For master's, minimum GPA of 2.75; bachelor's degree in biological, medical, or health sciences. Additional exam requirements/recommendations for international students: Required—TOEFL (minimum score 575 paper-based; 233 computer-based; 90 iBT), IELTS (minimum score 6.5). *Application deadline:* For fall admission, 7/30 priority date for domestic students, 4/30 for international students; for spring admission, 12/15 priority date for domestic students, 9/15 for international students. Applications are processed on a rolling basis. Application fee: $45. Electronic applications accepted. *Expenses:* Tuition: Part-time $855 per credit. *Required fees:* $35 per credit. *Financial support:* In 2011–12, 8 students received support. Federal Work-Study, tuition waivers (partial), and unspecified assistantships available. Support available to part-time students. Financial award application deadline: 4/15; financial award applicants required to submit FAFSA. *Faculty research:* Microbial physiology, fermentation technology. *Unit head:* Dr. Kenneth Kaloustian, Director, 203-582-8676, Fax: 203-582-3443, E-mail: ken.kaloustian@quinnipiac.edu. *Application contact:* Kristin Parent, Assistant Director of Graduate Health Sciences Admissions, 800-462-1944, Fax: 203-582-3443, E-mail: kristin.parent@quinnipiac.edu. Web site: http://www.quinnipiac.edu/gradmedlab.

Regis College, School of Nursing, Science and Health Professions, Weston, MA 02493. Offers biomedical sciences (MS); health administration (MS); nurse practitioner (Certificate); nursing (MS, DNP); nursing education (Certificate). *Accreditation:* NLN. Part-time and evening/weekend programs available. *Degree requirements:* For master's, thesis. *Entrance requirements:* For master's, GRE General Test or MAT, minimum GPA of 3.0; for doctorate, MAT or GRE if GPA from master's lower than 3.5. Additional exam requirements/recommendations for international students: Required—TOEFL (minimum score 550 paper-based; 213 computer-based). Electronic applications accepted. *Faculty research:* Health policy, education, aging, job satisfaction, psychiatric nursing, critical thinking.

Rensselaer Polytechnic Institute, Graduate School, School of Science, Program in Biology, Troy, NY 12180-3590. Offers MS, PhD. Part-time programs available. Terminal master's awarded for partial completion of doctoral program. *Degree requirements:* For master's, comprehensive exam, thesis optional; for doctorate, comprehensive exam, thesis/dissertation. *Entrance requirements:* Additional exam requirements/recommendations for international students: Required—TOEFL. Electronic applications accepted. *Faculty research:* Bioinformatics, molecular biology/biochemistry, cell and tissue biology, environment, ecology.

Rhode Island College, School of Graduate Studies, Faculty of Arts and Sciences, Department of Biology, Providence, RI 02908-1991. Offers biology (MA); modern biological sciences (CGS). Part-time programs available. *Faculty:* 5 full-time (4 women). *Students:* 1 (woman) full-time, 5 part-time (1 woman); includes 2 minority (1 Black or African American, non-Hispanic/Latino; 1 Asian, non-Hispanic/Latino). Average age 31. In 2011, 1 master's awarded. *Degree requirements:* For master's, thesis. *Entrance requirements:* For master's, GRE General and Subject Tests. Additional exam requirements/recommendations for international students: Recommended—TOEFL (minimum score 550 paper-based; 213 computer-based; 79 iBT). *Application deadline:* For fall admission, 3/1 for domestic students. Applications are processed on a rolling basis. Application fee: $50. *Expenses:* Tuition, state resident: full-time $8592; part-time $358 per credit hour. Tuition, nonresident: full-time $16,800; part-time $700 per credit hour. *Required fees:* $602; $22 per credit. $72 per term. *Financial support:* In 2011–12, 1 teaching assistantship with full tuition reimbursement (averaging $4,550 per year) was awarded; career-related internships or fieldwork, Federal Work-Study, scholarships/grants, health care benefits, and unspecified assistantships also available. Support available to part-time students. Financial award application deadline: 5/15; financial award applicants required to submit FAFSA. *Unit head:* Dr. Eric Hall, Chair, 401-456-8010, E-mail: biology@ric.edu. *Application contact:* Graduate Studies, 401-456-8700. Web site: http://www.ric.edu/biology/index.php.

Rochester Institute of Technology, Graduate Enrollment Services, College of Science, School of Life Sciences, Rochester, NY 14623-5603. Offers bioinformatics (MS); environmental science (MS). Part-time programs available. *Students:* 21 full-time (8 women), 14 part-time (7 women), 12 international. Average age 26. 70 applicants, 34% accepted, 8 enrolled. In 2011, 15 degrees awarded. *Degree requirements:* For master's, thesis or alternative. *Entrance requirements:* Additional exam requirements/recommendations for international students: Required—TOEFL (minimum score 570 paper-based; 230 computer-based; 88 iBT) or IELTS (minimum score 6.5). *Application deadline:* For fall admission, 2/15 priority date for domestic students, 2/15 for international students. Application fee: $50. *Expenses:* Tuition: Full-time $34,659; part-time $963 per credit hour. *Required fees:* $228; $76 per quarter. *Financial support:* Fellowships with partial tuition reimbursements, research assistantships with partial tuition reimbursements, teaching assistantships with partial tuition reimbursements, career-related internships or fieldwork, scholarships/grants, and unspecified assistantships available. Support available to part-time students. Financial award applicants required to submit FAFSA. *Faculty research:* Bioinformatic software development, bioscience, biomedical research, environmental research examining the human relationship to nature and developing solutions that prevent or reverse environmental deterioration. *Unit head:* Gary Skuse, Associate Head, School of Life Sciences, 585-475-6725, Fax: 585-475-2533, E-mail: biology@rit.edu. *Application contact:* Diane Ellison, Assistant Vice President, Graduate Enrollment Services, 585-475-2229, Fax: 585-475-7164, E-mail: gradinfo@rit.edu.

The Rockefeller University, Graduate Program in Biomedical Sciences, New York, NY 10021-6399. Offers PhD, MD/PhD. *Faculty:* 96 full-time (22 women), 158 part-time/adjunct (41 women). *Students:* 207 full-time (91 women); includes 27 minority (8 Black or African American, non-Hispanic/Latino; 15 Asian, non-Hispanic/Latino; 4 Hispanic/Latino), 78 international. Average age 28. 732 applicants, 10% accepted, 30 enrolled. In 2011, 37 doctorates awarded. Terminal master's awarded for partial completion of doctoral program. *Degree requirements:* For doctorate, thesis/dissertation. *Entrance requirements:* Additional exam requirements/recommendations for international students: Required—TOEFL. *Application deadline:* For winter admission, 12/5 for domestic and international students. Application fee: $80. Electronic applications accepted. *Financial support:* In 2011–12, 193 students received support. Fellowships with full tuition reimbursements available, institutionally sponsored loans, scholarships/grants, traineeships, and health care benefits available. *Unit head:* Dr. Sidney Strickland, Dean of Graduate Studies, 212-327-8086, Fax: 212-327-8505, E-mail: phd@rockefeller.edu. *Application contact:* Kristen Cullen, Graduate Admissions Administrator and Registrar, 212-327-8088, Fax: 212-327-8505, E-mail: kristen.cullen@rockefeller.edu. Web site: http://www.rockefeller.edu/graduate/.

See Display on next page and Close-Up on page 113.

Rosalind Franklin University of Medicine and Science, College of Health Professions, Department of Interprofessional Healthcare Studies, Biomedical Sciences Program, North Chicago, IL 60064-3095. Offers MS. *Entrance requirements:* For master's, MCAT, DAT, OAT, PCAT or GRE, BS in chemistry, physics, biology.

SCIENCE FOR THE BENEFIT OF HUMANITY

The David Rockefeller Graduate Program
Ph.D. Program in the Biological Sciences

The Rockefeller University is a world-renowned center for research and graduate education in the biomedical sciences. The university's Ph.D. program, whose hallmark is learning science by doing science, offers:

- a flexible academic experience with freedom to explore different areas of science
- interdisciplinary research and collaboration
- close mentoring by faculty
- unique environment without academic departments
- modern facilities and state-of-the-art research support in its more than 70 labs.

Graduate students receive a yearly stipend, free health and dental insurance, subsidized housing on or adjacent to the university's lush 14-acre campus and an annual research allowance for travel and lab support.

Founded by John D. Rockefeller in 1901 as the nation's first institute for medical research, the university's world-class faculty, with innovative approaches to scientific discovery, have produced pioneering achievements in biology and medicine. Numerous prestigious awards have been given to Rockefeller faculty, including 24 Nobel Prizes—most recently, to the late Ralph Steinman, the 2011 recipient in Physiology and Medicine.

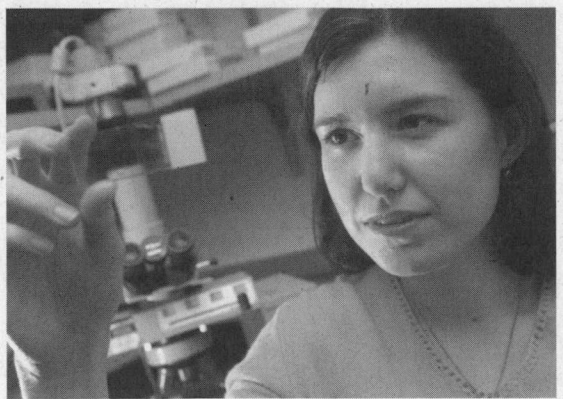

Additional exam requirements/recommendations for international students: Required—TOEFL.

Rosalind Franklin University of Medicine and Science, School of Graduate and Postdoctoral Studies - Interdisciplinary Graduate Program in Biomedical Sciences, North Chicago, IL 60064-3095. Offers MS, PhD, DPM/PhD, MD/PhD. *Students:* 65 applicants, 25% accepted, 10 enrolled. Terminal master's awarded for partial completion of doctoral program. *Degree requirements:* For master's, comprehensive exam, thesis, publication; for doctorate, comprehensive exam, thesis/dissertation. *Entrance requirements:* For master's and doctorate, GRE General Test. Additional exam requirements/recommendations for international students: Required—TOEFL, TWE. *Application deadline:* For fall admission, 12/15 priority date for domestic students, 12/15 for international students. Application fee: $0. Electronic applications accepted. *Expenses:* Contact institution. *Financial support:* In 2011–12, fellowships (averaging $23,665 per year), research assistantships (averaging $23,665 per year) were awarded; career-related internships or fieldwork, Federal Work-Study, traineeships, health care benefits, tuition waivers (full and partial), and unspecified assistantships also available. Financial award applicants required to submit FAFSA. *Faculty research:* Extracellular matrix, nutrition and mood, neuropsychopharmacology, membrane transport, brain metabolism. *Unit head:* Dr. Joseph X. DiMario, Dean, 847-578-8493, E-mail: joseph.dimario@rosalindfranklin.edu. *Application contact:* Caryn F. Wickersheim, Senior Administrative Assistant, SGPS Dean's Office, 847-578-8493, E-mail: igpbs@rosalindfranklin.edu. Web site: http://www.rosalindfranklin.edu/SGPS.

Rutgers, The State University of New Jersey, Camden, Graduate School of Arts and Sciences, Program in Biology, Camden, NJ 08102. Offers MS. Part-time and evening/weekend programs available. *Degree requirements:* For master's, comprehensive exam, thesis (for some programs), 30 credits. *Entrance requirements:* For master's; GRE General Test, GRE Subject Test (recommended), 3 letters of recommendation; statement of personal, professional and academic goals; biology or related undergraduate degree (preferred). Additional exam requirements/recommendations for international students: Required—TOEFL, IELTS. Electronic applications accepted. *Faculty research:* Neurobiology, biochemistry, ecology, developmental biology, biological signaling mechanisms.

Rutgers, The State University of New Jersey, Newark, Graduate School, Program in Biology, Newark, NJ 07102. Offers MS, PhD. Part-time and evening/weekend programs available. Terminal master's awarded for partial completion of doctoral program. *Degree requirements:* For master's, comprehensive exam, thesis optional; for doctorate, thesis/dissertation, qualifying exam. *Entrance requirements:* For master's, GRE General Test, minimum undergraduate B average; for doctorate, GRE General Test, GRE Subject Test, minimum B average. Electronic applications accepted. *Faculty research:* Cell-cytoskeletal elements, development and regeneration in the nervous system, cellular trafficking, environmental stressors and their impact on development, opportunistic parasitic infections in AIDS.

Rutgers, The State University of New Jersey, Newark, Graduate School, Program in Computational Biology, Newark, NJ 07102. Offers MS. Program offered jointly with New Jersey Institute of Technology. *Entrance requirements:* For master's, GRE, minimum undergraduate B average. Additional exam requirements/recommendations for international students: Required—TOEFL.

Rutgers, The State University of New Jersey, New Brunswick, Graduate School-New Brunswick, BioMaPS Institute for Quantitative Biology, Piscataway, NJ 08854-8097. Offers computational biology and molecular biophysics (PhD). *Degree requirements:* For doctorate, comprehensive exam, thesis/dissertation. *Entrance requirements:* For doctorate, GRE. Additional exam requirements/recommendations for international students: Required—TOEFL. Electronic applications accepted. *Faculty research:* Structural biology, systems biology, bioinformatics, translational medicine, genomics.

St. Cloud State University, School of Graduate Studies, College of Science and Engineering, Department of Biological Sciences, St. Cloud, MN 56301-4498. Offers MA, MS. *Degree requirements:* For master's, comprehensive exam (for some programs), thesis or alternative. *Entrance requirements:* For master's, GRE General Test, minimum GPA of 2.75. Additional exam requirements/recommendations for international students: Recommended—TOEFL (minimum score 550 paper-based; 213 computer-based), IELTS (minimum score 6.5). Electronic applications accepted.

Saint Francis University, Department of Physician Assistant Sciences, Medical Science Program, Loretto, PA 15940-0600. Offers MMS. Part-time and evening/weekend programs available. Postbaccalaureate distance learning degree programs offered (no on-campus study). *Faculty:* 2 full-time (both women), 5 part-time/adjunct (3 women). *Students:* 90 part-time (70 women); includes 30 minority (12 Black or African American, non-Hispanic/Latino; 13 Asian, non-Hispanic/Latino; 2 Hispanic/Latino; 3 Two or more races, non-Hispanic/Latino). Average age 34. 91 applicants, 99% accepted, 90 enrolled. In 2011, 85 master's awarded. *Degree requirements:* For master's, thesis or alternative. *Entrance requirements:* For master's, minimum GPA of 2.5, resume. *Application deadline:* For fall admission, 7/21 for domestic students; for spring admission, 11/25 for domestic students. Applications are processed on a rolling basis. Application fee: $0. Electronic applications accepted. *Expenses:* Contact institution. *Financial support:* Available to part-time students. Applicants required to submit FAFSA. *Faculty research:* Health care policy, physician assistant practice roles, health promotion/disease prevention, public health epidemiology. *Unit head:* Deborah E. Budash, Director, 814-472-3919, Fax: 814-472-3137, E-mail: dbudash@francis.edu. *Application contact:* Cheryl Strittmatter, Office Assistant, 814-472-3357, Fax: 814-472-3137, E-mail: cstrittmatter@francis.edu. Web site: http://www.francis.edu/MMShome.htm.

St. Francis Xavier University, Graduate Studies, Department of Biology, Antigonish, NS B2G 2W5, Canada. Offers M Sc. *Degree requirements:* For master's, thesis. *Entrance requirements:* For master's, 2 letters of recommendation. Additional exam requirements/recommendations for international students: Required—TOEFL (minimum score 580 paper-based; 236 computer-based). *Faculty research:* Cellular, whole organism, and population levels; marine photosynthesis; biophysical mechanisms; aquatic biology.

St. John's University, St. John's College of Liberal Arts and Sciences, Department of Biological Sciences, Queens, NY 11439. Offers MS, PhD. Part-time and evening/weekend programs available. *Students:* 31 full-time (14 women), 5 part-time (2 women); includes 6 minority (4 Black or African American, non-Hispanic/Latino; 2 Hispanic/Latino), 21 international. Average age 28. 47 applicants, 51% accepted, 8 enrolled. In 2011, 9 master's, 8 doctorates awarded. *Degree requirements:* For master's, comprehensive exam, thesis optional, residency; for doctorate, comprehensive exam, thesis/dissertation, residency. *Entrance requirements:* For master's, GRE General Test, minimum GPA of 3.0, 2 letters of recommendation; for doctorate, GRE General Test, minimum GPA of 3.0 (undergraduate), 3.5 (graduate); 2 letters of recommendation, writing sample, MS in biology or related. Additional exam requirements/recommendations for international students: Required—TOEFL (minimum score 600 paper-based; 250 computer-based; 100 iBT), IELTS (minimum score 5.5). *Application deadline:* For fall admission, 5/1 priority date for domestic students, 5/1 for international

students; for spring admission, 11/1 priority date for domestic students, 11/1 for international students. Applications are processed on a rolling basis. Application fee: $70. Electronic applications accepted. *Expenses: Tuition:* Full-time $18,000; part-time $1000 per credit. *Required fees:* $170 per semester. Tuition and fees vary according to program. *Financial support:* Fellowships, research assistantships, and scholarships/grants available. Support available to part-time students. Financial award application deadline: 3/1; financial award applicants required to submit FAFSA. *Faculty research:* Regulation of gene transcription, immunology and inflammation, cancer research, infectious diseases, molecular control of developmental processes, signal transduction, neurobiology and neurodegenerative diseases. *Total annual research expenditures:* $300,000. *Unit head:* Dr. Ales Vancura, Chair, 718-990-1679, E-mail: vancuraa@stjohns.edu. *Application contact:* Robert Medrano, Director of Graduate Admission, 718-990-1601, Fax: 718-990-5686, E-mail: gradhelp@stjohns.edu.

Saint Joseph's University, College of Arts and Sciences, Department of Biology, Philadelphia, PA 19131-1395. Offers MA, MS. Part-time programs available. *Faculty:* 12 full-time (3 women), 1 (woman) part-time/adjunct. *Students:* 3 full-time (2 women), 24 part-time (17 women); includes 7 minority (2 Black or African American, non-Hispanic/Latino; 3 Hispanic/Latino; 2 Two or more races, non-Hispanic/Latino), 2 international. Average age 25. 32 applicants, 84% accepted, 17 enrolled. In 2011, 10 master's awarded. *Degree requirements:* For master's, comprehensive exam (for some programs), thesis (for some programs), minimum GPA of 3.0, completion of degree within 5 years. *Entrance requirements:* For master's, GRE, 2 letters of recommendation, transcript, personal statement, resume. Additional exam requirements/recommendations for international students: Required—TOEFL (minimum score 550 paper-based; 213 computer-based; 79 iBT), IELTS (minimum score 6.5). *Application deadline:* For fall admission, 7/15 priority date for domestic students, 7/15 for international students; for spring admission, 11/15 priority date for domestic students, 11/15 for international students. Applications are processed on a rolling basis. Application fee: $35. Electronic applications accepted. *Expenses: Tuition:* Part-time $735 per credit hour. Tuition and fees vary according to degree level and program. *Financial support:* Research assistantships with tuition reimbursements and unspecified assistantships available. Financial award applicants required to submit FAFSA. *Faculty research:* Life science, undergraduate science education, confocal microscope for research and training. *Total annual research expenditures:* $865,347. *Unit head:* Dr. James Watrous, Director, 610-660-1829, E-mail: jwatrous@sju.edu. *Application contact:* Kate McConnell, Director, Graduate College of Arts and Sciences Admissions and Retention, 610-660-3184, Fax: 610-660-3230, E-mail: kate.mcconnell@sju.edu.

Saint Louis University, Graduate Education, College of Arts and Sciences and Graduate Education, Department of Biology, St. Louis, MO 63103-2097. Offers MS, MS-R, PhD. *Degree requirements:* For master's, comprehensive exam, thesis (for some programs); for doctorate, thesis/dissertation, preliminary exams. *Entrance requirements:* For master's, GRE General Test, letters of recommendation, resume; for doctorate, GRE General Test, letters of recommendation, resumé, statement, transcripts. Additional exam requirements/recommendations for international students: Required—TOEFL (minimum score 550 paper-based; 213 computer-based). Electronic applications accepted. *Faculty research:* Systematics, speciation, evolution, community ecology, conservation biology, molecular signaling.

Saint Louis University, Graduate Education and School of Medicine, Graduate Program in Biomedical Sciences, St. Louis, MO 63103-2097. Offers MS-R, PhD. *Degree requirements:* For doctorate, comprehensive exam, thesis/dissertation. *Entrance requirements:* For doctorate, GRE. Additional exam requirements/recommendations for international students: Required—TOEFL. Electronic applications accepted. *Faculty research:* Biochemistry and molecular biology, physiology and pharmacology, virology, pathology, immunology.

Salisbury University, Graduate Division, Program in Applied Biology, Salisbury, MD 21801-6837. Offers MS. Part-time programs available. *Faculty:* 10 full-time (3 women). *Students:* 5 full-time (1 woman), 6 part-time (3 women), 1 international. Average age 29. 5 applicants, 80% accepted, 4 enrolled. *Degree requirements:* For master's, thesis optional. *Entrance requirements:* For master's, GRE General Test, undergraduate degree with minimum cumulative GPA of 3.0, three letters of recommendation, personal statement. Additional exam requirements/recommendations for international students: Required—TOEFL (minimum score 550 paper-based; 79 iBT). *Application deadline:* Applications are processed on a rolling basis. Application fee: $45. Electronic applications accepted. *Expenses: Tuition, area resident:* Part-time $306 per credit hour. Tuition, state resident: part-time $306 per credit hour. Tuition, nonresident: part-time $595 per credit hour. *Required fees:* $68 per credit hour. *Financial support:* In 2011–12, 6 students received support, including 7 teaching assistantships with full tuition reimbursements available (averaging $6,304 per year); career-related internships or fieldwork, institutionally sponsored loans, and unspecified assistantships also available. Support available to part-time students. Financial award application deadline: 3/1; financial award applicants required to submit FAFSA. *Faculty research:* Collaborative research: multimodal communication and sexual selection. *Total annual research expenditures:* $124,044. *Unit head:* Mark Holland, Associate Chair, 410-543-6490, E-mail: maholland@salisbury.edu. Web site: http://www.salisbury.edu/biology/MS_Applied_Biology.html.

Sam Houston State University, College of Sciences, Department of Biology, Huntsville, TX 77341. Offers MA, MS. *Expenses:* Tuition, state resident: full-time $4420; part-time $221 per credit hour. Tuition, nonresident: full-time $10,680; part-time $534 per credit hour. *Required fees:* $329 per credit hour. *Application contact:* Tammy Gray, Advisor, 936-294-1230, E-mail: dca_tag@shsu.edu.

San Diego State University, Graduate and Research Affairs, College of Sciences, Department of Biology, San Diego, CA 92182. Offers biology (MA, MS), including ecology (MS), molecular biology (MS), physiology (MS), systematics/evolution (MS); cell and molecular biology (PhD); ecology (MS, PhD); microbiology (MS). Terminal master's awarded for partial completion of doctoral program. *Degree requirements:* For master's, thesis; for doctorate, thesis/dissertation. *Entrance requirements:* For master's, GRE General Test, GRE Subject Test, resume or curriculum vitae, 2 letters of recommendation. Additional exam requirements/recommendations for international students: Required—TOEFL. Electronic applications accepted.

San Francisco State University, Division of Graduate Studies, College of Science and Engineering, Department of Biology, San Francisco, CA 94132-1722. Offers biomedical science (MS); cell and molecular biology (MS); conservation biology (MS); ecology and systematic biology (MS); marine biology (MS); marine science (MS); microbiology (MS); physiology and behavioral biology (MS); science (PSM), including biotechnology, stem cell science. *Application deadline:* Applications are processed on a rolling basis. *Unit head:* Dr. Michael A. Goldman, Chair, 415-338-1548. *Application contact:* Dr. Robert Patterson, Graduate Coordinator, 415-338-1100, E-mail: patters@sfsu.edu. Web site: http://www.sfsu.edu/~biology.

San Jose State University, Graduate Studies and Research, College of Science, Department of Biological Sciences, San Jose, CA 95192-0001. Offers biological sciences (MA, MS); molecular biology and microbiology (MS); organismal biology, conservation and ecology (MS); physiology (MS). Part-time programs available.

Entrance requirements: For master's, GRE. Electronic applications accepted. *Faculty research:* Systemic physiology, molecular genetics, SEM studies, toxicology, large mammal ecology.

The Scripps Research Institute, Kellogg School of Science and Technology, La Jolla, CA 92037. Offers chemical and biological sciences (PhD). *Degree requirements:* For doctorate, thesis/dissertation. *Entrance requirements:* For doctorate, GRE General Test, GRE Subject Test, 3 letters of recommendation. Additional exam requirements/recommendations for international students: Required—TOEFL. Electronic applications accepted. *Faculty research:* Molecular structure and function, plant biology, immunology, bioorganic chemistry and molecular design, synthetic organic chemistry and natural product synthesis.

Seton Hall University, College of Arts and Sciences, Department of Biological Sciences, South Orange, NJ 07079-2697. Offers biology (MS); biology/business administration (MS); microbiology (MS); molecular bioscience (PhD); molecular bioscience/neuroscience (PhD). Part-time and evening/weekend programs available. *Degree requirements:* For master's, thesis optional; for doctorate, comprehensive exam, thesis/dissertation. *Entrance requirements:* For master's and doctorate, GRE or MS from accredited university in the U.S. Additional exam requirements/recommendations for international students: Required—TOEFL. Electronic applications accepted. *Expenses: Tuition:* Part-time $1033 per credit hour. *Required fees:* $85 per semester. *Faculty research:* Neurobiology, genetics, immunology, molecular biology, cellular physiology, toxicology, microbiology, bioinformatics.

Shippensburg University of Pennsylvania, School of Graduate Studies, College of Arts and Sciences, Department of Biology, Shippensburg, PA 17257-2299. Offers MS. Part-time and evening/weekend programs available. *Faculty:* 10 full-time (5 women). *Students:* 20 full-time (13 women), 9 part-time (7 women); includes 5 minority (1 Black or African American, non-Hispanic/Latino; 2 Hispanic/Latino; 2 Two or more races, non-Hispanic/Latino), 1 international. Average age 30. 28 applicants, 64% accepted, 12 enrolled. In 2011, 11 master's awarded. *Degree requirements:* For master's, thesis optional, oral thesis defense, seminar, minimum QPA of 3.0. *Entrance requirements:* For master's, minimum GPA of 2.75; essay; 400-500 word statement of purpose; 33 credits of course work in biology; minimum 4 courses/labs in chemistry including both inorganic and organic chemistry or biochemistry; calculus I and two lab courses in physics (recommended). Additional exam requirements/recommendations for international students: Required—TOEFL (minimum score 580 paper-based; 237 computer-based); Recommended—IELTS (minimum score 6). *Application deadline:* For fall admission, 4/30 for international students; for spring admission, 9/30 for international students. Applications are processed on a rolling basis. Application fee: $30. Electronic applications accepted. *Expenses: Tuition, area resident:* Part-time $416 per credit. Tuition, state resident: part-time $416 per credit. Tuition, nonresident: part-time $624 per credit. *Required fees:* $119 per credit. *Financial support:* In 2011–12, 11 research assistantships with full tuition reimbursements (averaging $5,000 per year) were awarded; career-related internships or fieldwork, scholarships/grants, unspecified assistantships, and resident hall director and student payroll positions also available. Support available to part-time students. Financial award application deadline: 3/1; financial award applicants required to submit FAFSA. *Unit head:* Dr. Theo Light, Graduate Coordinator, 717-477-1401, Fax: 717-477-4064, E-mail: tsligh@ship.edu. *Application contact:* Jeremy R. Goshorn, Assistant Dean of Graduate Admissions, 717-477-1231, Fax: 717-477-4016, E-mail: jrgoshorn@ship.edu. Web site: http://www.ship.edu/biology/.

Simon Fraser University, Graduate Studies, Faculty of Science, Department of Biological Sciences, Burnaby, BC V5A 1S6, Canada. Offers biological sciences (M Sc, PhD); environmental toxicology (MET); pest management (MPM). *Degree requirements:* For master's, thesis; for doctorate, thesis/dissertation. *Entrance requirements:* For master's, minimum GPA of 3.0; for doctorate, minimum GPA of 3.5. Additional exam requirements/recommendations for international students: Required—TOEFL or IELTS. Electronic applications accepted. *Faculty research:* Molecular biology, marine biology, ecology, wildlife biology, endocrinology.

Smith College, Graduate and Special Programs, Department of Biological Sciences, Northampton, MA 01063. Offers MAT, MS. Part-time programs available. *Faculty:* 14 full-time (5 women), 3 part-time/adjunct (1 woman). *Students:* 3 full-time (1 woman), 7 part-time (all women); includes 2 minority (1 Asian, non-Hispanic/Latino; 1 Hispanic/Latino). Average age 28. 11 applicants, 82% accepted, 7 enrolled. In 2011, 2 master's awarded. *Degree requirements:* For master's, one foreign language, thesis (for some programs). *Entrance requirements:* For master's, GRE General Test, GRE Subject Test. Additional exam requirements/recommendations for international students: Required—TOEFL (minimum score 590 paper-based; 243 computer-based; 97 iBT). *Application deadline:* For fall admission, 1/15 for domestic and international students; for spring admission, 12/1 for domestic students. Application fee: $60. *Expenses: Tuition:* Full-time $14,925; part-time $1245 per credit. *Financial support:* In 2011–12, 4 students received support, including 5 research assistantships with full tuition reimbursements available (averaging $12,090 per year); institutionally sponsored loans and scholarships/grants also available. Support available to part-time students. Financial award application deadline: 1/15; financial award applicants required to submit CSS PROFILE or FAFSA. *Unit head:* Stephen Tilley, Chair, 413-585-3817, E-mail: stilley@smith.edu. *Application contact:* Steven Williams, Graduate Student Advisor, 413-585-3826, E-mail: swilliam@smith.edu. Web site: http://www.smith.edu/biology/.

Sonoma State University, School of Science and Technology, Department of Biology, Rohnert Park, CA 94928-3609. Offers biochemistry (MA); environmental biology (MA). Part-time programs available. *Faculty:* 10 full-time (2 women). *Students:* 4 full-time (2 women), 14 part-time (9 women); includes 3 minority (1 American Indian or Alaska Native, non-Hispanic/Latino; 1 Asian, non-Hispanic/Latino; 1 Hispanic/Latino), 1 international. Average age 29. 23 applicants, 26% accepted, 3 enrolled. In 2011, 10 master's awarded. *Degree requirements:* For master's, thesis or alternative, oral exam. *Entrance requirements:* For master's, GRE General Test, GRE Subject Test, minimum GPA of 3.0. Additional exam requirements/recommendations for international students: Required—TOEFL (minimum score 500 paper-based; 173 computer-based). *Application deadline:* For fall admission, 11/30 for domestic students. Applications are processed on a rolling basis. Application fee: $55. *Financial support:* In 2011–12, 3 teaching assistantships (averaging $5,343 per year) were awarded; fellowships, research assistantships, career-related internships or fieldwork, Federal Work-Study, and tuition waivers (full) also available. Financial award application deadline: 3/2; financial award applicants required to submit FAFSA. *Faculty research:* Plant physiology, comparative physiology, community ecology, restoration ecology, marine ecology, conservation genetics, primate behavior, behavioral ecology, developmental biology, plant and animal systematics. *Total annual research expenditures:* $238,000. *Unit head:* Chair, 707-664-, E-mail: james.christmann@sonoma.edu. *Application contact:* Dr. Derek Girman, Graduate Adviser, 707-664-3055, E-mail: derek.girman@sonoma.edu. Web site: http://www.sonoma.edu/biology/graduate.

South Dakota State University, Graduate School, College of Agriculture and Biological Sciences, Department of Animal and Range Sciences, Brookings, SD 57007. Offers animal science (MS, PhD); biological sciences (PhD). Part-time programs available. *Degree requirements:* For master's, thesis, oral exam; for doctorate, comprehensive

exam, thesis/dissertation, preliminary oral and written exams. *Entrance requirements:* Additional exam requirements/recommendations for international students: Required—TOEFL (minimum score 550 paper-based; 213 computer-based; 79 iBT). *Faculty research:* Ruminant and nonruminant nutrition, meat science, reproductive physiology, range utilization, ecology genetics, muscle biology, animal production.

South Dakota State University, Graduate School, College of Agriculture and Biological Sciences, Department of Biology and Microbiology, Brookings, SD 57007. Offers biological sciences (MS, PhD). Part-time programs available. *Degree requirements:* For master's, thesis (for some programs), oral exam; for doctorate, comprehensive exam, thesis/dissertation, oral exam. *Entrance requirements:* For master's and doctorate, GRE General Test. Additional exam requirements/recommendations for international students: Required—TOEFL (minimum score 600 paper-based; 250 computer-based; 100 iBT). *Faculty research:* Ecosystem ecology; plant, animal and microbial genomics; animal infectious disease, microbial bioproducts.

South Dakota State University, Graduate School, College of Agriculture and Biological Sciences, Department of Dairy Science, Brookings, SD 57007. Offers animal sciences (MS, PhD); biological sciences (MS, PhD). Part-time programs available. *Degree requirements:* For master's, thesis, oral exam; for doctorate, comprehensive exam, thesis/dissertation, preliminary oral and written exams. *Entrance requirements:* Additional exam requirements/recommendations for international students: Required—TOEFL (minimum score 550 paper-based; 213 computer-based). *Faculty research:* Dairy cattle nutrition, energy metabolism, food safety, dairy processing technology.

South Dakota State University, Graduate School, College of Agriculture and Biological Sciences, Department of Veterinary and Biomedical Sciences, Brookings, SD 57007. Offers biological sciences (MS, PhD). Part-time and evening/weekend programs available. *Degree requirements:* For master's, thesis (for some programs), oral exam; for doctorate, comprehensive exam, thesis/dissertation, preliminary oral and written exams. *Entrance requirements:* Additional exam requirements/recommendations for international students: Required—TOEFL (minimum score 525 paper-based; 197 computer-based; 71 iBT). *Faculty research:* Infectious disease, food animal, virology, immunology.

South Dakota State University, Graduate School, College of Engineering, Department of Agricultural and Biosystems Engineering, Brookings, SD 57007. Offers biological sciences (MS, PhD); engineering (MS). PhD offered jointly with Iowa State University of Science and Technology. Part-time programs available. *Degree requirements:* For master's, thesis (for some programs), oral exam; for doctorate, thesis/dissertation, preliminary oral and written exams. *Entrance requirements:* For master's and doctorate, engineering degree. Additional exam requirements/recommendations for international students: Required—TOEFL (minimum score 550 paper-based; 213 computer-based; 79 iBT). *Faculty research:* Water resources, food engineering, natural resources engineering, machine design, bioprocess engineering.

South Dakota State University, Graduate School, College of Pharmacy, Department of Pharmaceutical Sciences, Brookings, SD 57007. Offers biological science (MS); pharmaceutical sciences (PhD). *Degree requirements:* For master's, thesis, oral exam; for doctorate, comprehensive exam, thesis/dissertation, oral exam. *Entrance requirements:* For master's and doctorate, GRE General Test. Additional exam requirements/recommendations for international students: Required—TOEFL (minimum score 550 paper-based; 213 computer-based). *Faculty research:* Drugs of abuse, anti-cancer drugs, sustained drug delivery, drug metabolism.

Southeastern Louisiana University, College of Science and Technology, Department of Biological Sciences, Hammond, LA 70402. Offers biology (MS). Part-time programs available. *Faculty:* 5 full-time (2 women). *Students:* 17 full-time (10 women), 8 part-time (5 women); includes 2 minority (1 Black or African American, non-Hispanic/Latino; 1 Two or more races, non-Hispanic/Latino), 2 international. Average age 25. 14 applicants, 100% accepted, 9 enrolled. In 2011, 10 degrees awarded. *Degree requirements:* For master's, comprehensive exam, thesis (for some programs). *Entrance requirements:* For master's, GRE General Test (minimum score 1000), minimum GPA of 3.0; 30 hours of undergraduate biology courses; two letters of recommendation; curriculum vitae; letter of intent. Additional exam requirements/recommendations for international students: Required—TOEFL (minimum score 500 paper-based; 173 computer-based; 61 iBT). *Application deadline:* For fall admission, 7/15 priority date for domestic students, 6/1 for international students; for spring admission, 12/1 priority date for domestic students, 10/1 for international students. Applications are processed on a rolling basis. Application fee: $20 ($30 for international students). Electronic applications accepted. *Expenses:* Tuition, state resident: full-time $3977; part-time $283 per semester hour. Tuition, nonresident: full-time $13,482; part-time $811 per semester hour. *Financial support:* In 2011–12, 2 fellowships (averaging $10,450 per year), 4 research assistantships (averaging $11,250 per year), 13 teaching assistantships (averaging $10,123 per year) were awarded; career-related internships or fieldwork, Federal Work-Study, institutionally sponsored loans, scholarships/grants, traineeships, and unspecified assistantships also available. Support available to part-time students. Financial award application deadline: 5/1; financial award applicants required to submit FAFSA. *Faculty research:* Evolutionary biology, ecology, molecular biology, morphology and phsiology, microbiology and immunology. *Total annual research expenditures:* $939,759. *Unit head:* Dr. Brian Crothers, Interim Department Head, 985-549-3741, Fax: 985-549-3851, E-mail: bcrother@selu.edu. *Application contact:* Sandra Meyers, Graduate Admissions Analyst, 985-549-5620, Fax: 985-549-5632, E-mail: admissions@selu.edu. Web site: http://www.selu.edu/acad_research/depts/biol.

Southeast Missouri State University, School of Graduate Studies, Department of Biology, Cape Girardeau, MO 63701-4799. Offers MNS. Part-time programs available. *Faculty:* 13 full-time (4 women). *Students:* 12 full-time (6 women), 15 part-time (11 women), 6 international. Average age 25. 17 applicants, 94% accepted, 9 enrolled. In 2011, 12 master's awarded. *Degree requirements:* For master's, comprehensive exam (for some programs), thesis (for some programs), either thesis or oral defense, or research paper and comprehensive exam. *Entrance requirements:* For master's, GRE General Test, minimum undergraduate GPA of 2.5, 2.75 in last 30 hours of undergraduate course work in science and mathematics; 2 letters of recommendation; faculty sponsor agreement. Additional exam requirements/recommendations for international students: Required—TOEFL (minimum score 550 paper-based; 213 computer-based; 79 iBT); Recommended—IELTS (minimum score 6). *Application deadline:* For fall admission, 8/1 for domestic students, 7/1 for international students; for spring admission, 11/21 for domestic students, 11/1 for international students. Applications are processed on a rolling basis. Application fee: $30 ($40 for international students). Electronic applications accepted. *Expenses:* Tuition, state resident: full-time $4896; part-time $272 per credit hour. Tuition, nonresident: full-time $8649; part-time $480.50 per credit hour. *Financial support:* In 2011–12, 18 students received support, including 19 teaching assistantships with full tuition reimbursements available (averaging $7,600 per year); career-related internships or fieldwork, Federal Work-Study, scholarships/grants, tuition waivers (full), and unspecified assistantships also available. Financial award application deadline: 6/30; financial award applicants required to submit FAFSA. *Faculty research:* Wildlife and conservation biology; microbiology and epidemiology; ecology, animal behavior and marine biology; case-based learning; plant systematics and physiology. *Total annual research expenditures:* $1.1 million. *Unit*

head: Dr. James Champine, Chairperson, 573-651-2171, Fax: 573-651-2382, E-mail: jchampine@semo.edu. *Application contact:* Alisa Aleen McFerron, Assistant Director of Admissions for Operations, 573-651-5937, Fax: 573-651-5936, E-mail: amcferron@semo.edu. Web site: http://www.semo.edu/biology/.

Southern Connecticut State University, School of Graduate Studies, School of Arts and Sciences, Department of Biology, New Haven, CT 06515-1355. Offers MS. Part-time and evening/weekend programs available. *Faculty:* 5 full-time (3 women). *Students:* 8 full-time (5 women), 19 part-time (12 women); includes 3 minority (all Asian, non-Hispanic/Latino. 55 applicants, 20% accepted, 7 enrolled. In 2011, 9 master's awarded. *Degree requirements:* For master's, thesis optional. *Entrance requirements:* For master's, previous course work in biology, chemistry, and mathematics; interview. *Application deadline:* Applications are processed on a rolling basis. Application fee: $50. Electronic applications accepted. *Expenses:* Tuition, state resident: full-time $5137; part-time $413 per credit. *Required fees:* $4008; $55 per term. *Financial support:* Application deadline: 4/15; applicants required to submit FAFSA. *Unit head:* Dr. Dwight Smith, Chairperson, 203-392-6222, Fax: 203-392-5364, E-mail: smithd1@southernct.edu. *Application contact:* Dr. Sean Grace, Graduate Coordinator, 203-392-6216, Fax: 203-392-5364, E-mail: graces2@southernct.edu.

Southern Illinois University Carbondale, Graduate School, College of Science, Biological Sciences Program, Carbondale, IL 62901-4701. Offers MS. *Students:* 1 (woman) part-time, all international. Average age 25. 1 applicant, 0% accepted, 0 enrolled. *Degree requirements:* For master's, thesis or alternative. *Entrance requirements:* For master's, GRE General Test, minimum GPA of 2.7. Additional exam requirements/recommendations for international students: Required—TOEFL. *Application deadline:* Applications are processed on a rolling basis. Application fee: $0. *Financial support:* Fellowships with full tuition reimbursements, research assistantships with full tuition reimbursements, teaching assistantships with full tuition reimbursements, Federal Work-Study, institutionally sponsored loans, and tuition waivers (full) available. Support available to part-time students. *Faculty research:* Molecular mechanisms of mutagenesis, reproductive endocrinology, avian energetics and nutrition, developmental plant physiology. *Unit head:* Dr. Brooks Burr, Director, 618-453-4112, E-mail: burr@zoology.siu.edu. *Application contact:* Linda Gassel, Administrative Clerk, 618-453-7079, E-mail: lgassel@cos.siu.edu.

Southern Illinois University Carbondale, Graduate School, Graduate Program in Medicine, Carbondale, IL 62901-4701. Offers molecular, cellular and systemic physiology (MS); pharmacology (MS, PhD); physiology (MS, PhD). *Faculty:* 31 full-time (5 women). *Students:* 27 full-time (14 women), 17 part-time (9 women); includes 3 minority (1 Black or African American, non-Hispanic/Latino; 1 American Indian or Alaska Native, non-Hispanic/Latino; 1 Asian, non-Hispanic/Latino), 24 international. 52 applicants, 13% accepted, 6 enrolled. In 2011, 3 master's, 1 doctorate awarded. Terminal master's awarded for partial completion of doctoral program. *Degree requirements:* For master's, thesis; for doctorate, thesis/dissertation. *Entrance requirements:* For master's, minimum GPA of 3.0; for doctorate, minimum GPA of 3.25. Additional exam requirements/recommendations for international students: Required—TOEFL. Application fee: $0. *Financial support:* In 2011–12, 27 students received support, including 12 fellowships with full tuition reimbursements available, 1 research assistantship with full tuition reimbursement available, 10 teaching assistantships with full tuition reimbursements available; institutionally sponsored loans and tuition waivers (full) also available. *Faculty research:* Cardiovascular physiology, neurophysiology of hearing. *Unit head:* Dr. John Koropchak, Dean, 618-536-7791. *Application contact:* Graduate Program Committee, 618-536-5513.

Southern Illinois University Edwardsville, Graduate School, College of Arts and Sciences, Department of Biological Sciences, Program in Biology, Edwardsville, IL 62026-0001. Offers MA, MS. Part-time programs available. *Faculty:* 26 full-time (4 women). *Students:* 25 full-time (15 women), 34 part-time (23 women); includes 4 minority (2 Black or African American, non-Hispanic/Latino; 2 Asian, non-Hispanic/Latino), 1 international. 59 applicants, 49% accepted. In 2011, 17 master's awarded. *Degree requirements:* For master's, thesis (for some programs). *Entrance requirements:* For master's, GRE. Additional exam requirements/recommendations for international students: Required—TOEFL (minimum score 550 paper-based; 213 computer-based; 79 iBT), IELTS (minimum score 6.5). *Application deadline:* For fall admission, 7/22 for domestic students, 6/1 for international students; for spring admission, 12/9 for domestic students, 10/1 for international students. Applications are processed on a rolling basis. Application fee: $30. Electronic applications accepted. Tuition and fees vary according to course load and program. *Financial support:* In 2011–12, 1 research assistantship with full tuition reimbursement (averaging $9,927 per year), 30 teaching assistantships with full tuition reimbursements (averaging $9,927 per year) were awarded; fellowships with full tuition reimbursements, institutionally sponsored loans, scholarships/grants, and unspecified assistantships also available. Financial award application deadline: 3/1; financial award applicants required to submit FAFSA. *Unit head:* Dr. Dave Duvernell, Director, 618-650-3468, E-mail: dduvern@siue.edu. *Application contact:* Michelle Robinson, Coordinator of Graduate Recruitment, 618-650-2811, Fax: 618-650-3523, E-mail: michero@siue.edu. Web site: http://www.siue.edu/BIOLOGY/graduate.htm.

Southern Methodist University, Dedman College, Department of Biological Sciences, Dallas, TX 75275. Offers MA, MS, PhD. Terminal master's awarded for partial completion of doctoral program. *Degree requirements:* For master's, thesis (MS), oral exam; for doctorate, thesis/dissertation, qualifying exam. *Entrance requirements:* For master's, GRE General Test (minimum score 1200), minimum GPA of 3.0; for doctorate, GRE General Test (minimum score: 1200), minimum GPA of 3.0. Additional exam requirements/recommendations for international students: Required—TOEFL (minimum score 550 paper-based; 217 computer-based). Electronic applications accepted. *Faculty research:* Free radicals and aging, protein structure, chromatin structure, signal processes, retroviral pathogenesis.

Southern University and Agricultural and Mechanical College, Graduate School, College of Sciences, Department of Biology, Baton Rouge, LA 70813. Offers MS. *Degree requirements:* For master's, comprehensive exam, thesis. *Entrance requirements:* For master's, GRE General Test. Additional exam requirements/recommendations for international students: Required—TOEFL (minimum score 525 paper-based; 193 computer-based). *Faculty research:* Toxicology, neuroendocrinology, mycotoxin, virology.

Stanford University, School of Humanities and Sciences, Department of Biological Sciences, Stanford, CA 94305-9991. Offers MS, PhD. Terminal master's awarded for partial completion of doctoral program. *Degree requirements:* For doctorate, thesis/dissertation, oral exam. *Entrance requirements:* For master's, GRE General Test; for doctorate, GRE General Test, GRE Subject Test. Additional exam requirements/recommendations for international students: Required—TOEFL. Electronic applications accepted. *Expenses:* Tuition: Full-time $40,050; part-time $890 per credit.

Stanford University, School of Medicine, Graduate Programs in Medicine, Stanford, CA 94305-9991. Offers MS, PhD. Terminal master's awarded for partial completion of doctoral program. *Degree requirements:* For master's, thesis; for doctorate, thesis/dissertation. *Entrance requirements:* For master's, GRE General Test or MCAT. Additional exam requirements/recommendations for international students: Required—

TOEFL. Electronic applications accepted. *Expenses: Tuition:* Full-time $40,050; part-time $890 per credit.

State University of New York at Binghamton, Graduate School, School of Arts and Sciences, Department of Biological Sciences, Binghamton, NY 13902-6000. Offers MA, PhD. *Faculty:* 26 full-time (10 women), 5 part-time/adjunct (2 women). *Students:* 37 full-time (21 women), 34 part-time (18 women); includes 11 minority (2 Black or African American, non-Hispanic/Latino; 1 American Indian or Alaska Native, non-Hispanic/Latino; 1 Asian, non-Hispanic/Latino; 3 Hispanic/Latino; 4 Native Hawaiian or other Pacific Islander, non-Hispanic/Latino), 17 international. Average age 28. 107 applicants, 31% accepted, 16 enrolled. In 2011, 19 master's, 2 doctorates awarded. Terminal master's awarded for partial completion of doctoral program. *Degree requirements:* For master's, thesis, oral exam, seminar presentation; for doctorate, comprehensive exam, thesis/dissertation. *Entrance requirements:* For master's and doctorate, GRE General Test, GRE Subject Test. Additional exam requirements/recommendations for international students: Required—TOEFL (minimum score 550 paper-based; 213 computer-based; 80 iBT). *Application deadline:* For fall admission, 1/15 priority date for domestic students, 1/15 for international students; for spring admission, 10/15 priority date for domestic students, 10/15 for international students. Applications are processed on a rolling basis. Application fee: $60. Electronic applications accepted. *Financial support:* In 2011–12, 43 students received support, including 4 fellowships with full tuition reimbursements available (averaging $17,500 per year), 7 research assistantships with full tuition reimbursements available (averaging $17,500 per year), 27 teaching assistantships with full tuition reimbursements available (averaging $17,500 per year); career-related internships or fieldwork, Federal Work-Study, institutionally sponsored loans, scholarships/grants, health care benefits, tuition waivers (full and partial), and unspecified assistantships also available. Financial award application deadline: 2/15; financial award applicants required to submit FAFSA. *Unit head:* Dr. John G. Baust, Chairperson, 607-777-24387, E-mail: jgbaust@binghamton.edu. *Application contact:* Catherine Smith, Recruiting and Admissions Coordinator, 607-777-2151, Fax: 607-777-2501, E-mail: cmsmith@binghamton.edu.

State University of New York at Fredonia, Graduate Studies, Department of Biology, Fredonia, NY 14063-1136. Offers MS, MS Ed. Part-time and evening/weekend programs available. *Degree requirements:* For master's, thesis optional. *Expenses:* Tuition, state resident: full-time $6666; part-time $370 per credit hour. Tuition, nonresident: full-time $11,376; part-time $632 per credit hour. *Required fees:* $1059.30; $58.85 per credit hour. Tuition and fees vary according to course load.

State University of New York at New Paltz, Graduate School, School of Science and Engineering, Department of Biology, New Paltz, NY 12561. Offers MA. Part-time and evening/weekend programs available. *Faculty:* 4 full-time. *Students:* 1 (woman) full-time, 3 part-time (2 women). Average age 30. 7 applicants, 29% accepted, 1 enrolled. In 2011, 4 master's awarded. *Degree requirements:* For master's, comprehensive exam, thesis (for some programs). *Entrance requirements:* For master's, GRE General Test, GRE Subject Test, minimum GPA of 3.0. Additional exam requirements/recommendations for international students: Required—TOEFL (minimum score 550 paper-based; 213 computer-based; 80 iBT), IELTS (minimum score 6.5). *Application deadline:* For fall admission, 5/15 for domestic and international students; for spring admission, 11/15 for domestic and international students. Application fee: $50. Electronic applications accepted. *Expenses:* Tuition, state resident: full-time $8870; part-time $370 per credit. Tuition, nonresident: full-time $15,160; part-time $632 per credit. *Required fees:* $1188; $34 per credit. $184 per semester. *Financial support:* In 2011–12, 3 students received support, including 3 teaching assistantships with partial tuition reimbursements available (averaging $5,000 per year); Federal Work-Study, institutionally sponsored loans, and unspecified assistantships also available. Financial award application deadline: 8/1; financial award applicants required to submit FAFSA. *Faculty research:* Neurohormonal regulation of feeding in insects. *Unit head:* Dr. Thomas Nolen, Chair, 845-257-3770, E-mail: nolent@newpaltz.edu. *Application contact:* Prof. Jeffrey Reinking, Coordinator, 845-257-3771, E-mail: reinkinj@newpaltz.edu. Web site: http://www.newpaltz.edu/biology/.

State University of New York College at Oneonta, Graduate Education, Department of Biology, Oneonta, NY 13820-4015. Offers MA. Part-time and evening/weekend programs available. *Degree requirements:* For master's, comprehensive exam. *Entrance requirements:* For master's, GRE General Test, GRE Subject Test.

State University of New York Downstate Medical Center, School of Graduate Studies, Brooklyn, NY 11203-2098. Offers MS, PhD, MD/PhD. *Degree requirements:* For doctorate, thesis/dissertation. *Entrance requirements:* For doctorate, GRE. Additional exam requirements/recommendations for international students: Required—TOEFL. *Faculty research:* Cellular and molecular neurobiology, role of oncogenes in early cardiogenesis, mechanism of gene regulation, cardiovascular physiology, yeast molecular genetics.

State University of New York Upstate Medical University, College of Graduate Studies, Syracuse, NY 13210-2334. Offers MS, PhD, MD/PhD. Terminal master's awarded for partial completion of doctoral program. *Degree requirements:* For master's, thesis; for doctorate, comprehensive exam, thesis/dissertation. *Entrance requirements:* For master's, GRE General Test, interview; for doctorate, GRE General Test, telephone interview. Additional exam requirements/recommendations for international students: Required—TOEFL. Electronic applications accepted. *Faculty research:* Cancer, disorders of the nervous system, infectious diseases, diabetes/metabolic disorders/cardiovascular diseases.

Stephen F. Austin State University, Graduate School, College of Sciences and Mathematics, Department of Biology, Nacogdoches, TX 75962. Offers MS. *Degree requirements:* For master's, comprehensive exam, thesis optional. *Entrance requirements:* For master's, GRE General Test, minimum GPA of 2.8 in last 60 hours, 2.5 overall. Additional exam requirements/recommendations for international students. Required—TOEFL.

Stony Brook University, State University of New York, Stony Brook University Medical Center, Health Sciences Center, School of Medicine and Graduate School, Graduate Programs in Medicine, Stony Brook, NY 11794. Offers PhD. *Degree requirements:* For doctorate, thesis/dissertation, exam. *Entrance requirements:* For doctorate, GRE General Test. Additional exam requirements/recommendations for international students: Required—TOEFL. Electronic applications accepted. *Expenses:* Contact institution.

Stony Brook University, State University of New York, Stony Brook University Medical Center, Health Sciences Center, School of Medicine, Medical Scientist Training Program, Stony Brook, NY 11794. Offers MD/PhD.

Sul Ross State University, School of Arts and Sciences, Department of Biology, Alpine, TX 79832. Offers MS. Part-time programs available. *Degree requirements:* For master's, thesis optional. *Entrance requirements:* For master's, GRE General Test, minimum GPA of 2.5 in last 60 hours of undergraduate work. *Faculty research:* Plant-animal interaction, Chihuahuan desert biology, insect biological control, plant and animal systematics, wildlife biology.

Syracuse University, College of Arts and Sciences, Program in Biology, Syracuse, NY 13244. Offers MS, PhD. Part-time programs available. *Students:* 29 full-time (17 women), 1 (woman) part-time, 12 international. Average age 28. 95 applicants, 13% accepted, 5 enrolled. In 2011, 5 master's, 6 doctorates awarded. Terminal master's awarded for partial completion of doctoral program. *Degree requirements:* For master's, thesis; for doctorate, thesis/dissertation. *Entrance requirements:* For master's and doctorate, GRE General Test, GRE Subject Test (recommended). Additional exam requirements/recommendations for international students: Required—TOEFL (minimum score 100 iBT). *Application deadline:* For fall admission, 1/10 priority date for domestic students, 1/10 for international students. Application fee: $75. Electronic applications accepted. *Expenses: Tuition:* Part-time $1206 per credit. *Financial support:* Fellowships with full tuition reimbursements, research assistantships with full and partial tuition reimbursements, and teaching assistantships with full tuition reimbursements available. Financial award application deadline: 1/10; financial award applicants required to submit FAFSA. *Faculty research:* Cell signaling, plant ecosystem ecology, aquatic ecology, genetics and molecular biology of color vision, ion transport by cell membranes. *Unit head:* Dr. Scott Pitnick, Graduate Program Director, 315-443-9145, E-mail: biology@syr.edu. *Application contact:* Evelyn Lott, Information Contact, 315-443-9154, Fax: 315-443-2012, E-mail: ealott@syr.edu. Web site: http://biology.syr.edu/.

Tarleton State University, College of Graduate Studies, College of Science and Technology, Department of Biological Sciences, Stephenville, TX 76402. Offers biology (MS). Part-time and evening/weekend programs available. *Faculty:* 7 full-time (0 women), 1 part-time/adjunct (0 women). *Students:* 5 full-time (3 women), 14 part-time (8 women); includes 3 minority (2 Hispanic/Latino; 1 Two or more races, non-Hispanic/Latino), 1 international. Average age 29. 9 applicants, 100% accepted, 8 enrolled. In 2011, 2 master's awarded. *Degree requirements:* For master's, comprehensive exam, thesis (for some programs). *Entrance requirements:* For master's, GRE General Test, minimum GPA of 3.0. Additional exam requirements/recommendations for international students: Required—TOEFL (minimum score 550 paper-based; 213 computer-based; 80 iBT). *Application deadline:* For fall admission, 8/5 priority date for domestic students; for spring admission, 12/1 for domestic students. Applications are processed on a rolling basis. Application fee: $30 ($130 for international students). Electronic applications accepted. *Expenses:* Tuition, state resident: full-time $3131.46; part-time $174 per credit hour. Tuition, nonresident: full-time $8225; part-time $457 per credit hour. *Required fees:* $1446. Tuition and fees vary according to course load and campus/location. *Financial support:* Research assistantships, teaching assistantships, career-related internships or fieldwork, and Federal Work-Study available. Support available to part-time students. Financial award application deadline: 5/1; financial award applicants required to submit FAFSA. *Unit head:* Dr. John Calahan, Head, 254-968-9159, Fax: 254-968-9157, E-mail: calahan@tarleton.edu. *Application contact:* Information Contact, 254-968-9104, Fax: 254-968-9670, E-mail: gradoffice@tarleton.edu. Web site: http://www.tarleton.edu/~biologyweb.

Temple University, College of Science and Technology, Department of Biology, Philadelphia, PA 19122-6096. Offers MS, PhD. *Faculty:* 19 full-time (5 women). *Students:* 29 full-time (15 women), 4 part-time (1 woman); includes 4 minority (2 Black or African American, non-Hispanic/Latino; 1 Asian, non-Hispanic/Latino; 1 Hispanic/Latino), 13 international. Average age 29. 32 applicants, 19% accepted, 5 enrolled. In 2011, 2 master's, 4 doctorates awarded. Terminal master's awarded for partial completion of doctoral program. *Degree requirements:* For master's, thesis; for doctorate, thesis/dissertation. *Entrance requirements:* For master's and doctorate, GRE General Test, minimum GPA of 3.0. Additional exam requirements/recommendations for international students: Required—TOEFL (minimum score 550 paper-based; 213 computer-based; 79 iBT). *Application deadline:* For fall admission, 4/15 for domestic students, 12/15 for international students; for spring admission, 11/15 for domestic students, 8/1 for international students. Applications are processed on a rolling basis. Application fee: $50. *Expenses:* Tuition, state resident: full-time $12,366; part-time $687 per credit hour. Tuition, nonresident: full-time $17,298; part-time $961 per credit hour. *Required fees:* $590; $213 per year. *Financial support:* Fellowships, research assistantships, teaching assistantships, Federal Work-Study, and tuition waivers (full) available. Financial award application deadline: 1/15; financial award applicants required to submit FAFSA. *Faculty research:* Membrane proteins, genetics, molecular biology, neuroscience, aquatic biology. *Unit head:* Dr. Allen Nicholson, Chair, 215-204-8854, Fax: 215-204-6646, E-mail: biology@temple.edu. *Application contact:* Tara Schumacher, Coordinator of Outreach, 215-204-6575, Fax: 215-204-8781, E-mail: tara.schumacher@temple.edu. Web site: http://www.temple.edu/biology/.

Temple University, Health Sciences Center, School of Medicine and Graduate School, Graduate Programs in Medicine, Philadelphia, PA 19122-6096. Offers MS, PhD, MD/MS, MD/PhD. *Students:* 134 full-time (71 women), 3 part-time (1 woman); includes 20 minority (5 Black or African American, non-Hispanic/Latino; 10 Asian, non-Hispanic/Latino; 3 Hispanic/Latino; 2 Two or more races, non-Hispanic/Latino), 43 international. Average age 28. 129 applicants, 35% accepted, 28 enrolled. In 2011, 6 master's, 22 doctorates awarded. Terminal master's awarded for partial completion of doctoral program. *Degree requirements:* For master's, thesis; for doctorate, thesis/dissertation, research seminars. *Entrance requirements:* For master's and doctorate, GRE General Test. Additional exam requirements/recommendations for international students: Required—TOEFL. Application fee: $50. Electronic applications accepted. *Expenses:* Contact institution. *Financial support:* Fellowships, research assistantships, career-related internships or fieldwork, Federal Work-Study, institutionally sponsored loans, scholarships/grants, and tuition waivers (full and partial) available. Support available to part-time students. Financial award application deadline: 1/15; financial award applicants required to submit FAFSA. *Faculty research:* Molecular biology and biochemistry; cardiovascular, renal, and neurophysiological pharmacology; reproductive and developmental biology; immunology and microbiology; cancer research. *Unit head:* Dr. Larry R. Kaiser, Dean, 215-707-7000, Fax: 215-707-8431, E-mail: kaiser@temple.edu. *Application contact:* Office of Admissions, 215-707-3656, Fax: 215-707-6932, E-mail: medadmissions@temple.edu.

Tennessee State University, The School of Graduate Studies and Research, College of Arts and Sciences, Department of Biological Sciences, Nashville, TN 37209-1561. Offers MS, PhD. *Degree requirements:* For master's, thesis optional; for doctorate, thesis/dissertation. *Entrance requirements:* For master's, GRE General Test, GRE Subject Test, minimum GPA of 2.5; for doctorate, GRE General Test, GRE Subject Test. *Faculty research:* Cellular and molecular biology and agribiology.

Tennessee Technological University, Graduate School, College of Arts and Sciences, Department of Biology, Cookeville, TN 38505. Offers fish, game, and wildlife management (MS). Part-time programs available. *Faculty:* 22 full-time (2 women). *Students:* 4 full-time (3 women), 12 part-time (8 women), 1 international. Average age 25. 12 applicants, 42% accepted, 5 enrolled. In 2011, 12 master's awarded. *Degree requirements:* For master's, thesis. *Entrance requirements:* For master's, GRE. Additional exam requirements/recommendations for international students: Required—TOEFL (minimum score 550 paper-based; 79 iBT), IELTS (minimum score 5.5), Pearson Test of English Academic. *Application deadline:* For fall admission, 8/1 for domestic students, 5/1 for international students; for spring admission, 12/1 for domestic students, 10/1 for international students. Application fee: $25 ($30 for international

students). Electronic applications accepted. *Expenses:* Tuition, state resident: full-time $8094; part-time $422 per credit hour. Tuition, nonresident: full-time $20,574; part-time $1046 per credit hour. *Financial support:* In 2011–12, 17 research assistantships (averaging $9,000 per year), 8 teaching assistantships (averaging $7,500 per year) were awarded. Financial award application deadline: 4/1. *Faculty research:* Aquatics, environmental studies. *Unit head:* Dr. Daniel Combs, Interim Chairperson, 931-372-3134, Fax: 931-372-6257, E-mail: dlcombs@tntech.edu. *Application contact:* Shelia K. Kendrick, Coordinator of Graduate Admissions, 931-372-3808, Fax: 931-372-3497, E-mail: skendrick@tntech.edu.

Tennessee Technological University, Graduate School, College of Arts and Sciences, Department of Environmental Sciences, Cookeville, TN 38505. Offers biology (PhD); chemistry (PhD). Part-time programs available. *Students:* 4 full-time (2 women), 12 part-time (5 women); includes 3 minority (1 Black or African American, non-Hispanic/Latino; 1 American Indian or Alaska Native, non-Hispanic/Latino; 1 Hispanic/Latino), 4 international. 8 applicants, 50% accepted, 2 enrolled. In 2011, 1 doctorate awarded. *Degree requirements:* For doctorate, comprehensive exam, thesis/dissertation. *Entrance requirements:* For doctorate, GRE. Additional exam requirements/recommendations for international students: Required—TOEFL (minimum score 550 paper-based; 79 iBT), IELTS (minimum score 5.5), Pearson Test of English Academic. *Application deadline:* For fall admission, 8/1 for domestic students, 5/1 for international students; for spring admission, 12/1 for domestic students, 10/2 for international students. Application fee: $25 ($30 for international students). Electronic applications accepted. *Expenses:* Tuition, state resident: full-time $8094; part-time $422 per credit hour. Tuition, nonresident: full-time $20,574; part-time $1046 per credit hour. *Financial support:* In 2011–12, 5 research assistantships (averaging $10,000 per year), 3 teaching assistantships (averaging $10,000 per year) were awarded; fellowships also available. Financial award application deadline: 4/1. *Application contact:* Shelia K. Kendrick, Coordinator of Graduate Admissions, 931-372-3808, Fax: 931-372-3497, E-mail: skendrick@tntech.edu.

Texas A&M Health Science Center, Baylor College of Dentistry, Department of Biomedical Sciences, College Station, TX 77840. Offers MS, PhD. Part-time programs available. Terminal master's awarded for partial completion of doctoral program. *Degree requirements:* For master's, thesis; for doctorate, thesis/dissertation. *Entrance requirements:* For master's, GRE General Test; for doctorate, GRE General Test, DDS or DMD. Additional exam requirements/recommendations for international students: Required—TOEFL. *Faculty research:* Craniofacial biology, aging, neuroscience, physiology, molecular/cellular biology.

Texas A&M Health Science Center, Institute of Biosciences and Technology, Houston, TX 77030-3303. Offers medical sciences (PhD). Degree awarded by the Graduate School for Biomedical Sciences. *Degree requirements:* For doctorate, thesis/dissertation. *Entrance requirements:* For doctorate, GRE General Test. Additional exam requirements/recommendations for international students: Required—TOEFL, TWE. *Expenses:* Contact institution. *Faculty research:* Cancer biology, DNA structure, extracellular matrix biology, development, birth defects.

Texas A&M International University, Office of Graduate Studies and Research, College of Arts and Sciences, Department of Biology and Chemistry, Laredo, TX 78041-1900. Offers biology (MS). *Faculty:* 3 full-time (0 women). *Students:* 16 full-time (11 women), 13 part-time (6 women); includes 25 minority (all Hispanic/Latino), 3 international. Average age 27. 18 applicants, 67% accepted, 9 enrolled. In 2011, 8 master's awarded. *Degree requirements:* For master's, comprehensive exam, thesis (for some programs). *Entrance requirements:* Additional exam requirements/recommendations for international students: Required—TOEFL (minimum score 79 iBT). *Application deadline:* For fall admission, 4/30 for domestic and international students; for spring admission, 11/30 for domestic students, 10/1 for international students. Applications are processed on a rolling basis. Application fee: $35 ($50 for international students). *Expenses:* Tuition, state resident: full-time $5063. *Financial support:* In 2011–12, 6 students received support, including 4 research assistantships, 2 teaching assistantships. *Unit head:* Dr. Daniel Mott, Chair, 956-326-2583. *Application contact:* Suzanne Hansen-Alford, Director of Graduate Recruiting, 956-326-3023, E-mail: salford@tamiu.edu. Web site: http://www.tamiu.edu/coas/depts/biochem/.

Texas A&M University, College of Science, Department of Biology, College Station, TX 77843. Offers biology (MS, PhD); botany (MS, PhD); microbiology (MS, PhD); molecular and cell biology (PhD); neuroscience (MS, PhD); zoology (MS, PhD). *Faculty:* 41. *Students:* 99 full-time (60 women), 8 part-time (4 women); includes 11 minority (1 Black or African American, non-Hispanic/Latino; 5 Asian, non-Hispanic/Latino; 4 Hispanic/Latino; 1 Two or more races, non-Hispanic/Latino), 46 international. Average age 28. In 2011, 5 master's, 7 doctorates awarded. *Degree requirements:* For master's, thesis or alternative; for doctorate, comprehensive exam, thesis/dissertation. *Entrance requirements:* For master's and doctorate, GRE General Test. Additional exam requirements/recommendations for international students: Required—TOEFL. *Application deadline:* For fall admission, 1/15 for domestic students. Applications are processed on a rolling basis. Application fee: $50 ($75 for international students). Electronic applications accepted. *Expenses:* Tuition, state resident: full-time $5437; part-time $226.55 per credit hour. Tuition, nonresident: full-time $12,949; part-time $539.55 per credit hour. *Required fees:* $2741. *Financial support:* Fellowships, research assistantships, and teaching assistantships available. Financial award application deadline: 4/1; financial award applicants required to submit FAFSA. *Unit head:* Dr. Jack McMahan, Department Head, 979-845-2301, E-mail: granster@mail.bio.tamu.edu. *Application contact:* 979-845-7755, Fax: 979-845-2891, E-mail: graduate@bio.tamu.edu. Web site: http://www.bio.tamu.edu/index.html.

Texas A&M University, College of Veterinary Medicine and Biomedical Sciences, Department of Veterinary Physiology and Pharmacology, College Station, TX 77843. Offers biomedical science (MS, PhD); toxicology (PhD). *Faculty:* 14. *Students:* 27 full-time (17 women), 2 part-time (1 woman); includes 3 minority (1 Black or African American, non-Hispanic/Latino; 2 Asian, non-Hispanic/Latino), 9 international. Average age 30. *Entrance requirements:* For master's and doctorate, GRE General Test. Additional exam requirements/recommendations for international students: Required—TOEFL. Application fee: $50 ($75 for international students). *Expenses:* Tuition, state resident: full-time $5437; part-time $226.55 per credit hour. Tuition, nonresident: full-time $12,949; part-time $539.55 per credit hour. *Required fees:* $2741. *Financial support:* Fellowships, research assistantships, and teaching assistantships available. Financial award application deadline: 4/1; financial award applicants required to submit FAFSA. *Faculty research:* Gamete and embryo physiology, endocrinology, equine laminitis. *Unit head:* Glen Laine, Head, 979-845-7261, E-mail: glaine@tamu.edu. *Application contact:* Graduate Admissions, 979-845-1044, E-mail: admissions@tamu.edu. Web site: http://vetmed.tamu.edu/vtpp.

Texas A&M University–Commerce, Graduate School, College of Science, Engineering and Agriculture, Department of Biological and Environmental Sciences, Commerce, TX 75429-3011. Offers biological sciences (M Ed, MS); environmental sciences (Certificate). *Degree requirements:* For master's, comprehensive exam, thesis (for some programs). *Entrance requirements:* For master's, GRE General Test. Electronic applications accepted. *Faculty research:* Microbiology, botany, environmental science, birds.

Texas A&M University–Corpus Christi, Graduate Studies and Research, College of Science and Technology, Program in Biology, Corpus Christi, TX 78412-5503. Offers MS.

Texas A&M University–Kingsville, College of Graduate Studies, College of Arts and Sciences, Department of Biology, Kingsville, TX 78363. Offers MS. Part-time programs available. *Degree requirements:* For master's, comprehensive exam, thesis or alternative. *Entrance requirements:* For master's, GRE General Test, minimum GPA of 3.0. Additional exam requirements/recommendations for international students: Required—TOEFL. *Faculty research:* Venom physiology, monoclonal research with venom, shore bird ecology, metabolism of foreign amino acids.

Texas Christian University, College of Science and Engineering, Department of Biology, Fort Worth, TX 76129. Offers MA, MS. Part-time programs available. *Faculty:* 13 full-time (2 women). *Students:* 5 full-time (3 women), 8 part-time (1 woman); includes 2 minority (both Asian, non-Hispanic/Latino), 2 international. Average age 26. 13 applicants, 77% accepted, 9 enrolled. In 2011, 4 master's awarded. *Degree requirements:* For master's, comprehensive exam, thesis (for some programs). *Entrance requirements:* For master's, GRE General Test. Additional exam requirements/recommendations for international students: Required—TOEFL (minimum score 560 paper-based; 82 computer-based). *Application deadline:* For fall admission, 1/15 priority date for domestic students, 1/15 for international students; for spring admission, 7/15 priority date for domestic students, 7/15 for international students. Applications are processed on a rolling basis. Application fee: $60. Electronic applications accepted. *Expenses: Tuition:* Full-time $20,250; part-time $1125 per credit hour. Part-time tuition and fees vary according to course load and program. *Financial support:* In 2011–12, 12 students received support, including 12 teaching assistantships with full tuition reimbursements available (averaging $14,000 per year). Financial award application deadline: 1/15. *Faculty research:* Invasive species, anthrax, mercury in biota, ecological impact of wind turbines, aging. *Total annual research expenditures:* $460,351. *Unit head:* Dr. Ray Drenner, Chairperson, 817-257-7165, E-mail: r.drenner@tcu.edu. *Application contact:* Dr. Magnus Rittby, Associate Dean, College of Science and Engineering, 817-257-7729, E-mail: m.rittby@tcu.edu. Web site: http://www.bio.tcu.edu/

Texas Southern University, School of Science and Technology, Department of Biology, Houston, TX 77004-4584. Offers MS. Part-time and evening/weekend programs available. *Degree requirements:* For master's, one foreign language, comprehensive exam, thesis. *Entrance requirements:* For master's, GRE General Test, minimum GPA of 2.5. Additional exam requirements/recommendations for international students: Required—TOEFL. Electronic applications accepted. *Faculty research:* Microbiology, cell and molecular biology, biochemistry, biochemical virology, biophysics.

Texas State University–San Marcos, Graduate School, College of Science and Engineering, Department of Biology, Program in Biology, San Marcos, TX 78666. Offers M Ed, MA, MS. *Faculty:* 10 full-time (2 women), 1 part-time/adjunct. *Students:* 42 full-time (19 women), 17 part-time (8 women); includes 19 minority (2 Black or African American, non-Hispanic/Latino; 2 Asian, non-Hispanic/Latino; 14 Hispanic/Latino; 1 Two or more races, non-Hispanic/Latino), 7 international. Average age 29. 34 applicants, 38% accepted, 11 enrolled. In 2011, 14 master's awarded. *Degree requirements:* For master's, comprehensive exam, thesis (for some programs). *Entrance requirements:* For master's, GRE General Test (minimum score 1000 preferred), minimum GPA of 3.0 in last 60 hours of undergraduate work. Additional exam requirements/recommendations for international students: Required—TOEFL (minimum score 550 paper-based; 213 computer-based; 78 iBT). *Application deadline:* For fall admission, 6/15 for domestic students, 6/1 for international students; for spring admission, 10/15 for domestic students, 10/1 for international students. Applications are processed on a rolling basis. Application fee: $40 ($90 for international students). Electronic applications accepted. *Expenses:* Tuition, state resident: full-time $6408; part-time $3204 per semester. Tuition, nonresident: full-time $14,832; part-time $7416 per semester. *Required fees:* $1824; $912 per semester. Tuition and fees vary according to course load. *Financial support:* In 2011–12, 47 students received support, including 2 research assistantships (averaging $5,139 per year), 23 teaching assistantships (averaging $12,033 per year); Federal Work-Study, institutionally sponsored loans, scholarships/grants, health care benefits, and unspecified assistantships also available. Support available to part-time students. Financial award application deadline: 4/1. *Unit head:* Dr. David Lemke, Graduate Advisor, 512-245-2178, E-mail: dl10@txstate.edu. *Application contact:* Dr. J. Michael Willoughby, Dean of the Graduate School, 512-245-2581, Fax: 512-245-8365, E-mail: jw02@swt.edu. Web site: http://www.bio.txstate.edu/.

Texas State University–San Marcos, Graduate School, Interdisciplinary Studies Program in Biology, San Marcos, TX 78666. Offers MSIS. *Degree requirements:* For master's, comprehensive exam, thesis optional. *Entrance requirements:* For master's, GRE (minimum score 1000 verbal and quantitative preferred), bachelor's degree in biology or related field, minimum GPA of 3.0 in last 60 hours of undergraduate work. Additional exam requirements/recommendations for international students: Required—TOEFL (minimum score 550 paper-based; 213 computer-based; 78 iBT). *Application deadline:* For fall admission, 6/15 priority date for domestic students, 6/1 for international students; for spring admission, 10/15 priority date for domestic students, 10/1 for international students. Applications are processed on a rolling basis. Application fee: $40 ($90 for international students). *Expenses:* Tuition, state resident: full-time $6408; part-time $3204 per semester. Tuition, nonresident: full-time $14,832; part-time $7416 per semester. *Required fees:* $1824; $912 per semester. Tuition and fees vary according to course load. *Financial support:* Research assistantships, teaching assistantships, Federal Work-Study, institutionally sponsored loans, scholarships/grants, health care benefits, and unspecified assistantships available. Support available to part-time students. Financial award application deadline: 4/1; financial award applicants required to submit FAFSA. *Unit head:* Dr. David Lemker, Graduate Advisor, 512-245-2178, E-mail: dl10@txstate.edu. *Application contact:* Dr. J. Michael Willoughby, Dean of Graduate School, 512-245-2581, Fax: 512-245-8365, E-mail: gradcollege@txstate.edu. Web site: http://www.cj.txstate.edu/.

Texas Tech University, Graduate School, College of Arts and Sciences, Department of Biological Sciences, Lubbock, TX 79409-3131. Offers biology (MS, PhD); microbiology (MS); zoology (MS, PhD). Part-time programs available. *Faculty:* 37 full-time (6 women), 2 part-time/adjunct (1 woman). *Students:* 101 full-time (54 women), 11 part-time (7 women); includes 6 minority (1 Asian, non-Hispanic/Latino; 3 Hispanic/Latino; 2 Two or more races, non-Hispanic/Latino), 54 international. Average age 29. 79 applicants, 25% accepted, 11 enrolled. In 2011, 16 master's, 9 doctorates awarded. *Degree requirements:* For master's, thesis or alternative; for doctorate, thesis/dissertation. *Entrance requirements:* For master's and doctorate, GRE General Test. Additional exam requirements/recommendations for international students: Required—TOEFL (minimum score 550 paper-based; 213 computer-based; 79 iBT). *Application deadline:* For fall admission, 6/1 priority date for domestic students, 1/15 for international students; for spring admission, 9/1 priority date for domestic students, 6/15 for international students. Applications are processed on a rolling basis. Application fee: $50 ($75 for international students). Electronic applications accepted. *Expenses:* Tuition, state resident: full-time $5899; part-time $245.80 per credit hour. Tuition, nonresident: full-time $13,411; part-time $558.80 per credit hour. *Required fees:* $2680.60; $86.50 per credit hour. $920.30

per semester. *Financial support:* In 2011–12, 33 students received support. Application deadline: 4/15; applicants required to submit FAFSA. *Faculty research:* Biodiversity and evolution, climate change in arid ecosystems, plant biology and biotechnology, animal communication and behavior, zoonotic and emerging diseases. *Total annual research expenditures:* $2.8 million. *Unit head:* Dr. Llewellyn D. Densmore, Chair, 806-742-2715, Fax: 806-742-2963, E-mail: lou.densmore@ttu.edu. *Application contact:* Dr. Randall M. Jeter, Graduate Adviser, 806-742-2710 Ext. 270, Fax: 806-742-2963, E-mail: randall.jeter@ttu.edu. Web site: http://www.biol.ttu.edu/.

Texas Tech University Health Sciences Center, Graduate School of Biomedical Sciences, Lubbock, TX 79430-0002. Offers MS, PhD, MD/PhD, MS/PhD. Terminal master's awarded for partial completion of doctoral program. *Degree requirements:* For master's, thesis; for doctorate, thesis/dissertation. *Entrance requirements:* For master's and doctorate, GRE General Test, minimum GPA of 3.0. Additional exam requirements/recommendations for international students: Required—TOEFL (minimum score 550 paper-based; 213 computer-based). Electronic applications accepted. *Faculty research:* Genetics of neurological disorders, hemodynamics to prevent DVT, toxin A synthesis, DA neurons, peroxidases.

Texas Woman's University, Graduate School, College of Arts and Sciences, Department of Biology, Denton, TX 76201. Offers biology (MS); molecular biology (PhD). Part-time programs available. *Faculty:* 14 full-time (10 women). *Students:* 26 full-time (18 women), 20 part-time (14 women); includes 8 minority (5 Black or African American, non-Hispanic/Latino; 1 Asian, non-Hispanic/Latino; 2 Hispanic/Latino), 28 international. Average age 30. 30 applicants, 73% accepted, 8 enrolled. In 2011, 1 master's, 2 doctorates awarded. Terminal master's awarded for partial completion of doctoral program. *Degree requirements:* For master's, comprehensive exam, thesis; for doctorate, comprehensive exam, thesis/dissertation, residency. *Entrance requirements:* For master's, GRE General Test (preferred minimum score 149 [425 old version] verbal, 141 [425 old version] quantitative), 3 letters of reference; letter of interest; for doctorate, GRE General Test (preferred minimum score 153 [500 old version] verbal, 144 [500 old version] quantitative), 3 letters of reference, letter of interest. Additional exam requirements/recommendations for international students: Required—TOEFL (minimum score 550 paper-based; 213 computer-based; 79 iBT). *Application deadline:* For fall admission, 2/1 priority date for domestic students, 2/1 for international students. Applications are processed on a rolling basis. Application fee: $50 ($75 for international students). Electronic applications accepted. *Expenses:* Tuition, state resident: full-time $3834; part-time $213 per credit hour. Tuition, nonresident: full-time $9468; part-time $526 per credit hour. *Required fees:* $213 per credit hour. Tuition and fees vary according to course load. *Financial support:* In 2011–12, 7 students received support, including 51 research assistantships (averaging $14,418 per year); career-related internships or fieldwork, Federal Work-Study, institutionally sponsored loans, scholarships/grants, traineeships, health care benefits, and unspecified assistantships also available. Support available to part-time students. Financial award application deadline: 3/1; financial award applicants required to submit FAFSA. *Faculty research:* Computational biology, protein-protein Interactions, chromatin structure and regulation, regulation of RNA synthesis, virus-host interactions, regulation of axon growth and guidance in neurons, estrogen compounds in plants, regulation of gene expression in male reproductive tissues, female gonadal hormones in the development of anxiety and depression, electron microscopy. *Total annual research expenditures:* $407,203. *Unit head:* Dr. Sarah McIntire, Chair, 940-898-2352, Fax: 940-898-2382, E-mail: smcintire@twu.edu. *Application contact:* Dr. Samuel Wheeler, Assistant Director of Admissions, 940-898-3188, Fax: 940-898-3081, E-mail: wheelersr@twu.edu. Web site: http://www.twu.edu/biology.

Thomas Jefferson University, Jefferson College of Graduate Studies, Philadelphia, PA 19107. Offers MS, PhD, Certificate, MD/PhD. Part-time and evening/weekend programs available. *Faculty:* 178 full-time (47 women), 30 part-time/adjunct (10 women). *Students:* 127 full-time (70 women), 132 part-time (83 women); includes 58 minority (19 Black or African American, non-Hispanic/Latino; 32 Asian, non-Hispanic/Latino; 7 Hispanic/Latino), 35 international. Average age 29. 449 applicants, 31% accepted, 95 enrolled. In 2011, 28 master's, 24 doctorates, 6 other advanced degrees awarded. Terminal master's awarded for partial completion of doctoral program. *Degree requirements:* For master's, thesis; for doctorate, comprehensive exam, thesis/dissertation. *Entrance requirements:* For master's, GRE or MCAT; for doctorate, GRE or MCAT, minimum GPA of 3.2. Additional exam requirements/recommendations for international students: Required—TOEFL (minimum score 250 computer-based; 100 iBT). *Application deadline:* For fall admission, 1/15 priority date for domestic students, 1/15 for international students; for winter admission, 6/1 for international students; for spring admission, 9/1 for international students. Applications are processed on a rolling basis. Application fee: $50. Electronic applications accepted. *Financial support:* In 2011–12, 190 students received support, including 127 fellowships with full tuition reimbursements available (averaging $54,758 per year); Federal Work-Study, institutionally sponsored loans, scholarships/grants, and traineeships also available. Support available to part-time students. Financial award application deadline: 5/1; financial award applicants required to submit FAFSA. *Unit head:* Dr. Gerald B. Grunwald, Dean, 215-503-4191, Fax: 215-503-6690, E-mail: gerald.grunwald@jefferson.edu. *Application contact:* Marc E. Stearns, Director of Admissions, 215-503-0155, Fax: 215-503-9920, E-mail: jcgs-info@jefferson.edu. Web site: http://www.jefferson.edu/jcgs/.

Towson University, Program in Biology, Towson, MD 21252-0001. Offers MS. Part-time and evening/weekend programs available. *Students:* 34 full-time (20 women), 29 part-time (19 women); includes 21 minority (12 Black or African American, non-Hispanic/Latino; 7 Asian, non-Hispanic/Latino; 1 Hispanic/Latino; 1 Two or more races, non-Hispanic/Latino), 3 international. *Degree requirements:* For master's, thesis optional, exam. *Entrance requirements:* For master's, GRE General Test (for thesis students), minimum GPA of 3.0, 24 credits in related course work, 3 letters of recommendation, minimum 24 units in biology, coursework in chemistry, organic chemistry, and physics. Additional exam requirements/recommendations for international students: Required—TOEFL. *Application deadline:* Applications are processed on a rolling basis. Application fee: $50. Electronic applications accepted. *Expenses:* Tuition, state resident: part-time $337 per credit. Tuition, nonresident: part-time $709 per credit. *Required fees:* $99 per credit. *Financial support:* Application deadline: 4/1; applicants required to submit FAFSA. *Unit head:* John Lapolla, Graduate Program Co-Director, 410-704-3121, Fax: 410-704-2405, E-mail: jlapolla@towson.edu. *Application contact:* Jack Shepherd, Graduate Program Co-Director, 410-704-2394, E-mail: jshepherd@towson.edu.

Trent University, Graduate Studies, Program in Applications of Modeling in the Natural and Social Sciences, Peterborough, ON K9J 7B8, Canada. Offers applications of modeling in the natural and social sciences (MA); biology (M Sc, PhD); chemistry (M Sc); computer studies (M Sc); geography (M Sc, PhD); physics (M Sc). Part-time programs available. *Degree requirements:* For master's, thesis. *Entrance requirements:* For master's, honours degree. *Faculty research:* Computation of heat transfer, atmospheric physics, statistical mechanics, stress and coping, evolutionary ecology.

Trent University, Graduate Studies, Program in Environmental and Life Sciences and Program in Applications of Modeling in the Natural and Social Sciences, Department of Biology, Peterborough, ON K9J 7B8, Canada. Offers M Sc, PhD. Part-time programs available. *Degree requirements:* For master's, thesis; for doctorate, thesis/dissertation. *Entrance requirements:* For master's, honours degree; for doctorate, master's degree. *Faculty research:* Aquatic and behavioral ecology, hydrology and limnology, human impact on ecosystems, behavioral ecology of birds, ecology of fish.

Truman State University, Graduate School, School of Arts and Letters, Program in Biology, Kirksville, MO 63501-4221. Offers MS. *Degree requirements:* For master's, comprehensive exam, thesis. *Entrance requirements:* For master's, GRE General Test, minimum GPA of 3.0. Additional exam requirements/recommendations for international students: Required—TOEFL (minimum score 550 paper-based; 213 computer-based). Electronic applications accepted.

Tufts University, Cummings School of Veterinary Medicine, North Grafton, MA 01536. Offers animals and public policy (MS); biomedical sciences (PhD), including digestive diseases, infectious diseases, neuroscience and reproductive biology, pathology; conservation medicine (MS); veterinary medicine (DVM); DVM/MPH; DVM/MS. *Accreditation:* AVMA (one or more programs are accredited). *Faculty:* 93 full-time (42 women), 14 part-time/adjunct (7 women). *Students:* 381 full-time (326 women); includes 47 minority (3 Black or African American, non-Hispanic/Latino; 4 American Indian or Alaska Native, non-Hispanic/Latino; 23 Asian, non-Hispanic/Latino; 16 Hispanic/Latino; 1 Two or more races, non-Hispanic/Latino), 7 international. Average age 25. 762 applicants, 33% accepted, 122 enrolled. In 2011, 8 master's, 80 doctorates awarded. *Degree requirements:* For master's, thesis (for some programs); for doctorate, comprehensive exam, thesis/dissertation (for some programs). *Entrance requirements:* For master's and doctorate, GRE General Test. Additional exam requirements/recommendations for international students: Required—TOEFL or IELTS. *Application deadline:* For fall admission, 11/1 for domestic and international students. Application fee: $70. Electronic applications accepted. *Expenses:* Contact institution. *Financial support:* In 2011–12, 245 students received support, including 6 research assistantships with full tuition reimbursements available (averaging $25,000 per year), 4 teaching assistantships (averaging $5,000 per year); career-related internships or fieldwork, Federal Work-Study, institutionally sponsored loans, scholarships/grants, and institutional aid awards; health care benefits for PhD students also available. Financial award application deadline: 5/15; financial award applicants required to submit FAFSA. *Faculty research:* Oncology, veterinary ethics, international veterinary medicine, veterinary genomics, pathogenesis of Clostridium difficile, wildlife fertility control. *Unit head:* Dr. Deborah T. Kochevar, Dean, 508-839-5302, Fax: 508-839-2953, E-mail: deborah.kochevar@tufts.edu. *Application contact:* Rebecca Russo, Director of Admissions, 508-839-7920, Fax: 508-887-4820, E-mail: vetadmissions@tufts.edu. Web site: http://www.tufts.edu/.

Tufts University, Graduate School of Arts and Sciences, Department of Biology, Medford, MA 02155. Offers MS, PhD. Part-time programs available. *Faculty:* 23 full-time. *Students:* 40 full-time (24 women); includes 1 minority (Asian, non-Hispanic/Latino), 9 international. Average age 27. 171 applicants, 15% accepted, 12 enrolled. In 2011, 6 master's, 9 doctorates awarded. Terminal master's awarded for partial completion of doctoral program. *Degree requirements:* For master's, thesis (for some programs); for doctorate, thesis/dissertation. *Entrance requirements:* For master's and doctorate, GRE General Test. Additional exam requirements/recommendations for international students: Required—TOEFL (minimum score 550 paper-based; 213 computer-based; 80 iBT). *Application deadline:* For fall admission, 1/15 for domestic students, 12/15 for international students; for spring admission, 10/15 for domestic students, 9/15 for international students. Applications are processed on a rolling basis. Application fee: $75. Electronic applications accepted. *Expenses: Tuition:* Full-time $41,208; part-time $1030 per credit hour. Full-time tuition and fees vary according to degree level, program and student level. Part-time tuition and fees vary according to course load. *Financial support:* Fellowships, research assistantships with full and partial tuition reimbursements, teaching assistantships with full and partial tuition reimbursements, Federal Work-Study, scholarships/grants, tuition waivers (partial), and unspecified assistantships available. Financial award application deadline: 1/15; financial award applicants required to submit FAFSA. *Unit head:* Dr. Juliet Fuhrman, Chair, 617-627-3195. *Application contact:* Kelly McLaughlin, Graduate Advisor, 617-627-3195. Web site: http://www.ase.tufts.edu/biology.

Tufts University, Sackler School of Graduate Biomedical Sciences, Boston, MA 02111. Offers MS, PhD, DVM/PhD, MD/PhD. *Faculty:* 186 full-time (57 women). *Students:* 208 full-time (123 women); includes 41 minority (4 Black or African American, non-Hispanic/Latino; 19 Asian, non-Hispanic/Latino; 10 Hispanic/Latino; 8 Two or more races, non-Hispanic/Latino), 40 international. Average age 29. 600 applicants, 13% accepted, 32 enrolled. In 2011, 11 master's, 43 doctorates awarded. Terminal master's awarded for partial completion of doctoral program. *Degree requirements:* For master's, comprehensive exam (for some programs), thesis; for doctorate, thesis/dissertation. *Entrance requirements:* For doctorate, GRE General Test, 3 letters of reference. Additional exam requirements/recommendations for international students: Required—TOEFL (minimum score 600 paper-based; 250 computer-based; 100 iBT). *Application deadline:* For fall admission, 12/15 for domestic and international students. Application fee: $70. Electronic applications accepted. *Expenses:* Contact institution. *Financial support:* In 2011–12, 171 research assistantships with full tuition reimbursements (averaging $30,000 per year) were awarded; health care benefits also available. Financial award application deadline: 12/15. *Unit head:* Dr. Naomi Rosenberg, Dean, 617-636-6767, Fax: 617-636-0375, E-mail: naomi.rosenberg@tufts.edu. *Application contact:* Kellie Melchin, Associate Director of Admissions, 617-636-6767, Fax: 617-636-0375, E-mail: sackler-school@tufts.edu. Web site: http://sackler.tufts.edu/.

Tulane University, School of Medicine and School of Liberal Arts, Graduate Programs in Biomedical Sciences, New Orleans, LA 70118-5669. Offers MBS, MS, PhD, MD/MS, MD/PhD. *Degree requirements:* For doctorate, thesis/dissertation. *Entrance requirements:* For master's, GRE General Test, minimum B average in undergraduate course work; for doctorate, GRE General Test. Additional exam requirements/recommendations for international students: Required—TOEFL. *Expenses:* Contact institution.

Tuskegee University, Graduate Programs, College of Agricultural, Environmental and Natural Sciences, Department of Agricultural Sciences, Tuskegee, AL 36088. Offers agricultural and resource economics (MS); animal and poultry sciences (MS); environmental sciences (MS); integrative bio-science (PhD); plant and soil sciences (MS). *Faculty:* 26 full-time (12 women), 1 part-time/adjunct (0 women). *Students:* 55 full-time (38 women), 6 part-time (5 women); includes 40 minority (39 Black or African American, non-Hispanic/Latino; 1 Two or more races, non-Hispanic/Latino), 17 international. Average age 30. In 2011, 28 master's, 3 doctorates awarded. *Degree requirements:* For master's, thesis. *Entrance requirements:* For master's, GRE General Test. Additional exam requirements/recommendations for international students: Required—TOEFL (minimum score 500 paper-based; 69 computer-based). *Application deadline:* For fall admission, 7/15 for domestic students. Applications are processed on a rolling basis. Application fee: $25 ($35 for international students). *Expenses: Tuition:* Full-time $17,070; part-time $705 per credit hour. *Financial support:* In 2011–12, 5 fellowships, 4 research assistantships were awarded. Financial award application deadline: 4/15. *Unit head:* Dr. P. K. Biswas, Head, 334-727-8446. *Application contact:*

Biological and Biomedical Sciences—General

Dr. Robert L. Laney, Jr., Vice President/Director of Admissions and Enrollment Management, 334-727-8580, Fax: 334-727-5750, E-mail: planey@tuskegee.edu.

Tuskegee University, Graduate Programs, College of Agricultural, Environmental and Natural Sciences, Department of Biology, Tuskegee, AL 36088. Offers MS. *Faculty:* 12 full-time (3 women). *Students:* 11 full-time (9 women), 1 (woman) part-time; includes 8 minority (all Black or African American, non-Hispanic/Latino), 2 international. Average age 25. In 2011, 3 master's awarded. *Degree requirements:* For master's, thesis. *Entrance requirements:* For master's, GRE General Test, GRE Subject Test. Additional exam requirements/recommendations for international students: Required—TOEFL (minimum score 500 paper-based; 69 computer-based). *Application deadline:* For fall admission, 7/15 for domestic students. Applications are processed on a rolling basis. Application fee: $25 ($35 for international students). *Expenses: Tuition:* Full-time $17,070; part-time $705 per credit hour. *Financial support:* Fellowships, teaching assistantships, Federal Work-Study, and institutionally sponsored loans available. Support available to part-time students. Financial award application deadline: 4/15. *Unit head:* Dr. Roberta Troy, Head, 334-727-8829. *Application contact:* Dr. Robert L. Laney, Jr., Vice President/Director of Admissions and Enrollment Management, 334-727-8580, Fax: 334-727-5750, E-mail: planey@tuskegee.edu.

Tuskegee University, Graduate Programs, College of Agricultural, Environmental and Natural Sciences, Program in Integrative Biosciences, Tuskegee, AL 36088. Offers PhD. *Faculty:* 30. *Students:* 13 full-time (6 women), 4 part-time (2 women); includes 12 minority (all Black or African American, non-Hispanic/Latino), 4 international. Average age 33. In 2011, 3 doctorates awarded. *Degree requirements:* For doctorate, thesis/dissertation. *Entrance requirements:* For doctorate, GRE General Test, GRE Subject Test, minimum cumulative GPA of 3.0, 3.4 in upper-division courses; 3 letters of recommendation; resume or curriculum vitae. Additional exam requirements/recommendations for international students: Required—TOEFL (minimum score 500 paper-based; 69 computer-based). *Application deadline:* For fall admission, 3/30 for domestic students, 3/1 for international students. Application fee: $35. Electronic applications accepted. *Expenses: Tuition:* Full-time $17,070; part-time $705 per credit hour. *Unit head:* Dr. Deloris Alexander, Associate Director, 334-552-0690, E-mail: dalexander@tuskegee.edu. *Application contact:* Dr. Robert L. Laney, Jr., Vice President/Director of Admissions and Enrollment Management, 334-727-8580, Fax: 334-727-5750, E-mail: planey@tuskegee.edu.

Uniformed Services University of the Health Sciences, School of Medicine, Graduate Programs in the Biomedical Sciences and Public Health, Bethesda, MD 20814. Offers emerging infectious diseases (PhD); medical and clinical psychology (PhD), including clinical psychology, medical and clinical psychology, medical psychology; molecular and cell biology (MS, PhD); neuroscience (PhD); preventive medicine and biometrics (MPH, MS, MSPH, MTMH, Dr PH, PhD), including environmental health sciences (PhD), healthcare administration and policy (MS), medical zoology (PhD), public health (MPH, MSPH, Dr PH), tropical medicine and hygiene (MTMH). *Faculty:* 372 full-time (119 women), 4,044 part-time/adjunct (908 women). *Students:* 176 full-time (96 women); includes 31 minority (6 Black or African American, non-Hispanic/Latino; 4 American Indian or Alaska Native, non-Hispanic/Latino; 14 Asian, non-Hispanic/Latino; 7 Hispanic/Latino), 11 international. Average age 28. 278 applicants, 20% accepted, 47 enrolled. In 2011, 36 master's, 17 doctorates awarded. Terminal master's awarded for partial completion of doctoral program. *Degree requirements:* For master's, comprehensive exam, thesis or alternative; for doctorate, comprehensive exam, thesis/dissertation, qualifying exam. *Entrance requirements:* For master's, GRE General Test; for doctorate, GRE General Test, minimum GPA of 3.0. Additional exam requirements/recommendations for international students: Required—TOEFL. *Application deadline:* For fall admission, 1/1 priority date for domestic students, 1/1 for international students. Applications are processed on a rolling basis. Application fee: $0. Electronic applications accepted. *Financial support:* In 2011–12, fellowships with full tuition reimbursements (averaging $26,000 per year), research assistantships with full tuition reimbursements (averaging $26,000 per year) were awarded; career-related internships or fieldwork, scholarships/grants, health care benefits, and tuition waivers (full) also available. *Unit head:* Dr. Eleanor S. Metcalf, Associate Dean, 301-295-1104, E-mail: emetcalf@usuhs.edu. *Application contact:* Elena Marina Sherman, Program Administrative Specialist, 301-295-3913, Fax: 301-295-6772, E-mail: elena.sherman@usuhs.mil. Web site: http://www.usuhs.mil/graded.

Universidad Central del Caribe, School of Medicine, Program in Biomedical Sciences, Bayamón, PR 00960-6032. Offers anatomy and cell biology (MA, MS); biochemistry (MS); biomedical sciences (MA); cellular and molecular biology (PhD); microbiology and immunology (MA, MS); pharmacology (MS); physiology (MS).

Universidad de Ciencias Medicas, Graduate Programs, San Jose, Costa Rica. Offers dermatology (SP); family health (MS); health service center administration (MHA); human anatomy (MS); medical and surgery (MD); occupational medicine (MS); pharmacy (Pharm D). Part-time programs available. *Degree requirements:* For master's, thesis; for doctorate and SP, comprehensive exam. *Entrance requirements:* For master's, MD or bachelor's degree; for doctorate, admissions test; for SP, admissions test, MD.

Université de Moncton, Faculty of Sciences, Department of Biology, Moncton, NB E1A 3E9, Canada. Offers M Sc. *Degree requirements:* For master's, one foreign language, thesis. *Entrance requirements:* For master's, minimum GPA of 3.0. Electronic applications accepted. *Faculty research:* Terrestrial ecology, aquatic ecology, marine biology, aquaculture, ethology, biotechnology.

Université de Montréal, Faculty of Arts and Sciences, Department of Biological Sciences, Montréal, QC H3C 3J7, Canada. Offers M Sc, PhD. Part-time programs available. *Degree requirements:* For master's, thesis; for doctorate, thesis/dissertation, general exam. *Entrance requirements:* For doctorate, MS in biology or related field. Electronic applications accepted. *Faculty research:* Fresh water ecology, plant biotechnology, neurobiology, genetics, cell physiology.

Université de Montréal, Faculty of Medicine, Programs in Biomedical Sciences, Montréal, QC H3C 3J7, Canada. Offers M Sc, PhD. *Degree requirements:* For master's, thesis; for doctorate, thesis/dissertation, general exam. *Entrance requirements:* For master's and doctorate, proficiency in French, knowledge of English. Electronic applications accepted.

Université de Sherbrooke, Faculty of Medicine and Health Sciences, Graduate Programs in Medicine, Sherbrooke, QC J1H 5N4, Canada. Offers M Sc, PhD. Part-time programs available. Terminal master's awarded for partial completion of doctoral program. *Degree requirements:* For master's, thesis; for doctorate, thesis/dissertation. Electronic applications accepted. *Expenses:* Contact institution.

Université de Sherbrooke, Faculty of Sciences, Department of Biology, Sherbrooke, QC J1K 2R1, Canada. Offers M Sc, PhD, Diploma. *Degree requirements:* For master's, thesis; for doctorate, comprehensive exam, thesis/dissertation. *Entrance requirements:* For doctorate, master's degree. Electronic applications accepted. *Faculty research:* Microbiology, ecology, molecular biology, cell biology, biotechnology.

Université du Québec à Montréal, Graduate Programs, Program in Biology, Montréal, QC H3C 3P8, Canada. Offers M Sc, PhD. Part-time programs available. *Degree requirements:* For master's, thesis; for doctorate, thesis/dissertation. *Entrance requirements:* For master's, appropriate bachelor's degree or equivalent, proficiency in French; for doctorate, appropriate master's degree or equivalent, proficiency in French.

Université du Québec en Abitibi-Témiscamingue, Graduate Programs, Program in Environmental Sciences, Rouyn-Noranda, QC J9X 5E4, Canada. Offers biology (MS); environmental sciences (PhD); sustainable forest ecosystem management (MS).

Université du Québec, Institut National de la Recherche Scientifique, Graduate Programs, Research Center - INRS - Institut Armand-Frappier - Human Health, Québec, QC G1K 9A9, Canada. Offers applied microbiology (M Sc); biology (PhD); experimental health sciences (M Sc); virology and immunology (M Sc, PhD). Programs given in French. Part-time programs available. *Faculty:* 41. *Students:* 158 full-time (93 women), 11 part-time (5 women), 52 international. Average age 30. In 2011, 17 master's, 9 doctorates awarded. *Degree requirements:* For master's, thesis optional; for doctorate, thesis/dissertation. *Entrance requirements:* For master's and doctorate, appropriate bachelor's degree, proficiency in French. *Application deadline:* For fall admission, 3/30 for domestic and international students; for winter admission, 11/1 for domestic and international students; for spring admission, 3/1 for domestic and international students. Application fee: $45 Canadian dollars. *Financial support:* In 2011–12, 128 students received support, including fellowships (averaging $16,500 per year); research assistantships also available. *Faculty research:* Immunity, infection and cancer; toxicology and environmental biotechnology; molecular pharmacochemistry. *Unit head:* Charles Dozois, Director, 450-687-5010, Fax: 450-686-5566, E-mail: charles.dozois@iaf.inrs.ca. *Application contact:* Yvonne Boisvert, Registrar, 418-654-3861, Fax: 418-654-3858, E-mail: registrariat@adm.inrs.ca. Web site: http://www.iaf.inrs.ca.

Université Laval, Faculty of Medicine, Graduate Programs in Medicine, Québec, QC G1K 7P4, Canada. Offers M Sc, PhD, Diploma. *Degree requirements:* For doctorate, comprehensive exam, thesis/dissertation. *Entrance requirements:* For doctorate, knowledge of French, comprehension of written English; for Diploma, knowledge of French. Electronic applications accepted.

Université Laval, Faculty of Sciences and Engineering, Department of Biology, Programs in Biology, Québec, QC G1K 7P4, Canada. Offers M Sc, PhD. Terminal master's awarded for partial completion of doctoral program. *Degree requirements:* For master's, thesis; for doctorate, comprehensive exam, thesis/dissertation. *Entrance requirements:* For master's and doctorate, knowledge of French and English. Electronic applications accepted.

University at Albany, State University of New York, College of Arts and Sciences, Department of Biological Sciences, Albany, NY 12222-0001. Offers biodiversity, conservation, and policy (MS); ecology, evolution, and behavior (MS, PhD); forensic molecular biology (MS); molecular, cellular, developmental, and neural biology (MS, PhD). *Degree requirements:* For master's, one foreign language; for doctorate, one foreign language, thesis/dissertation. *Entrance requirements:* For master's and doctorate, GRE General Test. Additional exam requirements/recommendations for international students: Required—TOEFL (minimum score 550 paper-based; 213 computer-based). Electronic applications accepted. *Faculty research:* Interferon, neural development, RNA self-splicing, behavioral ecology, DNA repair enzymes.

University at Albany, State University of New York, School of Public Health, Department of Biomedical Sciences, Albany, NY 12222-0001. Offers biochemistry, molecular biology, and genetics (MS, PhD); cell and molecular structure (MS, PhD); immunobiology and immunochemistry (MS, PhD); molecular pathogenesis (MS, PhD); neuroscience (MS, PhD). *Degree requirements:* For master's, thesis; for doctorate, comprehensive exam, thesis/dissertation. *Entrance requirements:* For master's and doctorate, GRE General Test, 3 letters of reference. Additional exam requirements/recommendations for international students: Required—TOEFL (minimum score 600 paper-based; 213 computer-based). Electronic applications accepted. *Faculty research:* Geno expression; RNA processing; membrane transport; immune response regulation; etiology of AIDS, Lyme disease, epilepsy.

University at Buffalo, the State University of New York, Graduate School, College of Arts and Sciences, Department of Biological Sciences, Buffalo, NY 14260. Offers MA, MS, PhD. Terminal master's awarded for partial completion of doctoral program. *Degree requirements:* For master's, thesis, research rotation, seminar; for doctorate, comprehensive exam, thesis/dissertation, oral candidacy exam, research, seminar. *Entrance requirements:* For master's and doctorate, GRE General Test, 2 semesters of course work in calculus, course work in chemistry through organic chemistry, strong biology background. Additional exam requirements/recommendations for international students: Required—TOEFL (minimum score 600 paper-based; 240 computer-based; 100 iBT). Electronic applications accepted. *Faculty research:* Biochemistry, bioinformatics, biophysics, biotechnology, botany, cell biology, developmental biology, evolutionary biology, genetics, genomics, molecular biology, microbiology, neuroscience, physiology, plant physiology, plant sciences, structural biology, virology, zoology.

University at Buffalo, the State University of New York, Graduate School, Graduate Programs in Cancer Research and Biomedical Sciences at Roswell Park Cancer Institute, Interdisciplinary Master of Science Program in Natural and Biomedical Sciences at Roswell Park Cancer Institute, Buffalo, NY 14260. Offers biomedical sciences and cancer research (MS). Part-time programs available. *Degree requirements:* For master's, thesis, defense of thesis, research project. *Entrance requirements:* For master's, GRE General Test, MCAT, DAT, PCAT. Additional exam requirements/recommendations for international students: Required—TOEFL (minimum score 600 paper-based; 250 computer-based; 100 iBT). Electronic applications accepted. *Faculty research:* Biochemistry, oncology, pathology, biophysics, pharmacology, molecular biology, cellular biology, genetics, bioinformatics, immunology, therapeutic development, epidemiology.

University at Buffalo, the State University of New York, Graduate School, School of Medicine and Biomedical Sciences, Graduate Programs in Medicine and Biomedical Sciences, Buffalo, NY 14260. Offers MA, MS, PhD, MD/PhD. *Faculty:* 94 full-time (22 women), 12 part-time/adjunct (2 women). *Students:* 171 full-time (75 women), 2 part-time (both women); includes 13 minority (6 Black or African American, non-Hispanic/Latino; 1 American Indian or Alaska Native, non-Hispanic/Latino; 5 Asian, non-Hispanic/Latino; 1 Hispanic/Latino), 64 international. Average age 25. 572 applicants, 20% accepted, 54 enrolled. In 2011, 22 master's, 21 doctorates awarded. Terminal master's awarded for partial completion of doctoral program. *Degree requirements:* For master's, comprehensive exam (for some programs), thesis (for some programs); for doctorate, comprehensive exam, thesis/dissertation. *Entrance requirements:* For master's, GRE General Test; for doctorate, GRE General Test, 3 letters of recommendation. Additional exam requirements/recommendations for international students: Required—TOEFL (minimum score 600 paper-based; 250 computer-based; 100 iBT). *Application deadline:* For fall admission, 2/1 priority date for domestic students, 2/1 for international students. Applications are processed on a rolling basis. Application fee: $50. Electronic applications accepted. *Expenses:* Contact institution. *Financial support:* In 2011–12, 35 students received support, including 4 fellowships with full tuition reimbursements available (averaging $25,000 per year), 30 research assistantships with full tuition reimbursements available (averaging $21,000 per year), 31 teaching assistantships with

full tuition reimbursements available (averaging $2,000 per year); career-related internships or fieldwork, Federal Work-Study, institutionally sponsored loans, scholarships/grants, traineeships, health care benefits, and unspecified assistantships also available. Financial award application deadline: 2/1; financial award applicants required to submit FAFSA. *Faculty research:* Neuroscience; molecular, cell, and structural biology; microbial pathogenesis; cardiopulmonary physiology; biochemistry, biotechnology and clinical laboratory science. *Total annual research expenditures:* $22.5 million. *Unit head:* Dr. Kenneth Blumenthal, Senior Associate Dean for Research and Graduate Education, 716-829-3398, Fax: 716-829-2437, E-mail: laychock@ acsu.buffalo.edu. *Application contact:* Elizabeth A. White, Administrative Director, 716-829-3399, Fax: 716-829-2437, E-mail: bethw@buffalo.edu.

University at Buffalo, the State University of New York, Graduate School, School of Medicine and Biomedical Sciences, PhD Program in Biomedical Sciences, Buffalo, NY 14260. Offers PhD. *Students:* 14 full-time (8 women); includes 1 minority (Black or African American, non-Hispanic/Latino), 5 international. 297 applicants, 15% accepted, 14 enrolled. *Degree requirements:* For doctorate, comprehensive exam, thesis/dissertation. *Entrance requirements:* For doctorate, GRE General Test, 3 letters of recommendation. Additional exam requirements/recommendations for international students: Required—TOEFL (minimum score 600 paper-based; 250 computer-based; 100 iBT). *Application deadline:* For fall admission, 2/1 priority date for domestic students, 2/1 for international students. Applications are processed on a rolling basis. Application fee: $50. Electronic applications accepted. *Financial support:* In 2011–12, 14 students received support. Federal Work-Study, scholarships/grants, traineeships, health care benefits, and unspecified assistantships available. Financial award application deadline: 2/1. *Faculty research:* Molecular, cell and structural biology; pharmacology and toxicology; neurosciences; microbiology; pathogenesis and disease. *Unit head:* Dr. Laurie A. Read, Director, 716-829-3398, Fax: 716-829-2437, E-mail: smbs-gradprog@buffalo.edu. *Application contact:* Elizabeth A. White, Administrative Director, 716-829-3399, Fax: 716-829-2437, E-mail: bethw@buffalo.edu. Web site: http://medicine.buffalo.edu/phdprogram.

The University of Akron, Graduate School, Buchtel College of Arts and Sciences, Department of Biology, Akron, OH 44325. Offers biology (MS); integrated bioscience (PhD). Part-time programs available. *Faculty:* 22 full-time (3 women), 3 part-time/adjunct (1 woman). *Students:* 56 full-time (20 women), 2 part-time (1 woman); includes 6 minority (2 Black or African American, non-Hispanic/Latino; 1 Asian, non-Hispanic/Latino; 1 Hispanic/Latino; 2 Two or more races, non-Hispanic/Latino), 12 international. Average age 29. 52 applicants, 46% accepted, 16 enrolled. In 2011, 7 master's awarded. *Degree requirements:* For master's, thesis optional, oral defense of thesis, oral exam, seminars; for doctorate, thesis/dissertation, oral defense of dissertation, seminars. *Entrance requirements:* For master's, GRE, baccalaureate degree in biology or the equivalent; minimum GPA of 3.0 overall and in biology; letter of interest; letter from potential biology adviser; for doctorate, GRE, minimum overall GPA of 3.0, letters of recommendation, personal statement of career goals and research interest. Additional exam requirements/recommendations for international students: Required—TOEFL (minimum score 550 paper-based; 213 computer-based; 79 iBT). *Application deadline:* Applications are processed on a rolling basis. Application fee: $30 ($40 for international students). Electronic applications accepted. *Expenses:* Tuition, state resident: full-time $7038; part-time $391 per credit hour. Tuition, nonresident: full-time $12,051; part-time $670 per credit hour. *Required fees:* $1274; $34 per credit hour. *Financial support:* In 2011–12, 2 research assistantships, 20 teaching assistantships with full tuition reimbursements were awarded. *Faculty research:* Behavior/neuroscience, ecology-evolution, genetics, molecular biology, physiology. *Total annual research expenditures:* $683,115. *Unit head:* Dr. Monte Turner, Interim Chair, 330-972-7155, E-mail: meturner@uakron.edu. *Application contact:* Dr. Mark Tausig, Associate Dean, 330-972-6266, Fax: 330-972-6475, E-mail: mtausig@uakron.edu. Web site: http://www.uakron.edu/biology/.

The University of Alabama, Graduate School, College of Arts and Sciences, Department of Biological Sciences, Tuscaloosa, AL 35487. Offers MS, PhD. *Faculty:* 39 full-time (14 women), 1 (woman) part-time/adjunct. *Students:* 99 full-time (48 women), 9 part-time (2 women); includes 17 minority (11 Black or African American, non-Hispanic/Latino; 2 Asian, non-Hispanic/Latino; 3 Hispanic/Latino; 1 Two or more races, non-Hispanic/Latino), 24 international. Average age 27. 95 applicants, 41% accepted, 28 enrolled. In 2011, 12 master's, 9 doctorates awarded. Terminal master's awarded for partial completion of doctoral program. *Median time to degree:* Of those who began their doctoral program in fall 2003, 100% received their degree in 8 years or less. *Degree requirements:* For master's, comprehensive exam, thesis optional; for doctorate, thesis/dissertation, preliminary written and oral exams. *Entrance requirements:* For master's and doctorate, GRE General Test, minimum GPA of 3.0. Additional exam requirements/recommendations for international students: Required—TOEFL (minimum score 550 paper-based; 79 iBT). *Application deadline:* For fall admission, 12/5 priority date for domestic students, 12/5 for international students; for spring admission, 12/5 priority date for domestic students, 12/5 for international students. Applications are processed on a rolling basis. Application fee: $50 ($60 for international students). Electronic applications accepted. *Expenses:* Tuition, state resident: full-time $8600. Tuition, nonresident: full-time $21,900. *Financial support:* In 2011–12, 23 fellowships with full tuition reimbursements (averaging $15,000 per year), 21 research assistantships with full tuition reimbursements (averaging $20,000 per year), 44 teaching assistantships with full tuition reimbursements (averaging $16,002 per year) were awarded; scholarships/grants, health care benefits, and unspecified assistantships also available. Financial award application deadline: 7/1; financial award applicants required to submit FAFSA. *Faculty research:* Molecular and developmental genetics, limnology, microbiology, systematics, neurobiology. *Total annual research expenditures:* $3.6 million. *Unit head:* Dr. Patrica A. Sobecky, Chair, 205-348-1807, Fax: 205-348-1786, E-mail: psobecky@as.ua.edu. *Application contact:* Dr. Stevan Marcus, Graduate Program Director, 205-348-8094, Fax: 205-348-1786, E-mail: smarcus@as.ua.edu. Web site: http://web.as.ua.edu/bsc.

The University of Alabama at Birmingham, College of Arts and Sciences, Program in Biology, Birmingham, AL 35294. Offers MS, PhD. Terminal master's awarded for partial completion of doctoral program. *Degree requirements:* For master's, thesis; for doctorate, thesis/dissertation. *Entrance requirements:* For master's and doctorate, GRE General Test, previous course work in biology, calculus, organic chemistry, and physics. Additional exam requirements/recommendations for international students: Required—TOEFL. *Application deadline:* Applications are processed on a rolling basis. Electronic applications accepted. *Expenses:* Tuition, state resident: full-time $5922; part-time $309 per hour. Tuition, nonresident: full-time $13,428; part-time $726 per hour. Tuition and fees vary according to program. *Financial support:* Fellowships with full tuition reimbursements, research assistantships with full tuition reimbursements, teaching assistantships with full tuition reimbursements, career-related internships or fieldwork, Federal Work-Study, institutionally sponsored loans, scholarships/grants, traineeships, tuition waivers (full), and unspecified assistantships available. Support available to part-time students. *Unit head:* Dr. Robert U. Fischer, Jr., Chair, 205-934-3582, Fax: 205-975-6097. Web site: http://www.uab.edu/biology/.

See Display below and Close-Up on page 115.

The University of Alabama at Birmingham, Graduate Programs in Joint Health Sciences, Program in Basic Medical Sciences, Birmingham, AL 35294. Offers MSBMS.

UAB THE UNIVERSITY OF ALABAMA AT BIRMINGHAM

GRADUATE STUDIES IN BIOLOGY

Offering Masters and PhD programs
in the Department of Biology

Research activities at all levels of biological
organization, with emphasis on:

Biology of Extremophiles
Cellular and Molecular Biology
Ecology, Chemical Ecology and Nutrition of Aquatic Organisms
Ecophysiology
Environmental Microbiology
Genetics/Epigenetics/Systems Biology
Integrative and Comparative Biology

www.uab.edu/biology   www.uab.edu/graduate

Entrance requirements: For master's, GRE. *Application deadline:* Applications are processed on a rolling basis. Electronic applications accepted. *Expenses:* Tuition, state resident: full-time $5922; part-time $309 per hour. Tuition, nonresident: full-time $13,428; part-time $726 per hour. Tuition and fees vary according to program. *Unit head:* Dr. Ray L. Watts, Vice President/Dean, School of Medicine, 205-934-1111, Fax: 205-934-0333.

The University of Alabama in Huntsville, School of Graduate Studies, College of Science, Department of Biological Sciences, Huntsville, AL 35899. Offers biology (MS); education (MS). Part-time and evening/weekend programs available. *Faculty:* 9 full-time (2 women), 4 part-time/adjunct (1 woman). *Students:* 16 full-time (9 women), 15 part-time (11 women); includes 10 minority (4 Black or African American, non-Hispanic/Latino; 2 American Indian or Alaska Native, non-Hispanic/Latino; 3 Asian, non-Hispanic/Latino; 1 Hispanic/Latino), 5 international. Average age 31. 38 applicants, 55% accepted, 14 enrolled. In 2011, 10 master's awarded. *Degree requirements:* For master's, comprehensive exam, thesis or alternative, oral and written exams. *Entrance requirements:* For master's, GRE General Test, previous course work in biochemistry and organic chemistry, minimum GPA of 3.0. Additional exam requirements/recommendations for international students: Required—TOEFL (minimum score 550 paper-based; 213 computer-based; 62 iBT). *Application deadline:* For fall admission, 7/15 for domestic students, 4/1 for international students; for spring admission, 11/30 for domestic students, 9/1 for international students. Applications are processed on a rolling basis. Application fee: $40 ($50 for international students). Electronic applications accepted. *Expenses:* Tuition, state resident: full-time $7830; part-time $473.50 per credit. Tuition, nonresident: full-time $18,748; part-time $1128.33 per credit. Tuition and fees vary according to course load and program. *Financial support:* In 2011–12, 16 students received support, including 2 fellowships with full tuition reimbursements available (averaging $12,000 per year), 14 teaching assistantships with full and partial tuition reimbursements available (averaging $8,278 per year); career-related internships or fieldwork, Federal Work-Study, institutionally sponsored loans, scholarships/grants, health care benefits, and unspecified assistantships also available. Support available to part-time students. Financial award application deadline: 4/1; financial award applicants required to submit FAFSA. *Faculty research:* Physiology and developmental biology, functional genomics, biotechnology, proteomics, microbiology. *Total annual research expenditures:* $898,355. *Unit head:* Dr. Debra M. Moriarity, Interim Chair, 256-824-6045, Fax: 256-824-6305, E-mail: moriard@uah.edu. *Application contact:* Kim Gray, Graduate Studies Admissions Manager, 256-824-6002, Fax: 256-824-6405, E-mail: deangrad@uah.edu. Web site: http://www.uah.edu/colleges/science/biology/.

University of Alaska Anchorage, College of Arts and Sciences, Department of Biological Sciences, Anchorage, AK 99508. Offers MS. Part-time programs available. *Degree requirements:* For master's, comprehensive exam; thesis. *Entrance requirements:* For master's, GRE General Test, GRE Subject Test, bachelor's degree in biology, chemistry or equivalent science. Additional exam requirements/recommendations for international students: Required—TOEFL (minimum score 550 paper-based; 213 computer-based). *Faculty research:* Taxonomy and vegetative analysis in Alaskan ecosystems, fish environment and seafood, biochemistry, arctic ecology, vertebrate ecology.

University of Alaska Fairbanks, College of Natural Sciences and Mathematics, Department of Biology and Wildlife, Fairbanks, AK 99775-6100. Offers biological sciences (MS, PhD), including biology, botany, wildlife biology (PhD), zoology; biology (MAT, MS); wildlife biology (MS). Part-time programs available. *Faculty:* 20 full-time (10 women). *Students:* 74 full-time (43 women), 29 part-time (18 women); includes 12 minority (1 Asian, non-Hispanic/Latino; 6 Hispanic/Latino; 5 Two or more races, non-Hispanic/Latino), 4 international. Average age 29. 45 applicants, 40% accepted, 15 enrolled. In 2011, 12 master's, 11 doctorates awarded. *Degree requirements:* For master's, comprehensive exam, thesis, oral exam, oral defense; for doctorate, comprehensive exam, thesis/dissertation, oral exam, oral defense. *Entrance requirements:* For master's and doctorate, GRE General Test, GRE Subject Test (biology). Additional exam requirements/recommendations for international students: Required—TOEFL (minimum score 550 paper-based; 213 computer-based; 80 iBT), TWE. *Application deadline:* For fall admission, 6/1 for domestic students, 3/1 for international students; for spring admission, 10/15 for domestic students, 9/1 for international students. Applications are processed on a rolling basis. Application fee: $60. Electronic applications accepted. *Expenses:* Tuition, state resident: full-time $6696; part-time $372 per credit. Tuition, nonresident: full-time $13,680; part-time $760 per credit. Tuition and fees vary according to course load and reciprocity agreements. *Financial support:* In 2011–12, 26 research assistantships with tuition reimbursements (averaging $13,976 per year), 26 teaching assistantships with tuition reimbursements (averaging $14,955 per year) were awarded; fellowships with tuition reimbursements, career-related internships or fieldwork, Federal Work-Study, scholarships/grants, health care benefits, and unspecified assistantships also available. Support available to part-time students. Financial award application deadline: 7/1; financial award applicants required to submit FAFSA. *Faculty research:* Plant-herbivore interactions, plant metabolic defenses, insect manufacture of glycerol, ice nucleators, structure and functions of arctic and subarctic freshwater ecosystems. *Unit head:* Christa Mulder, Department Chair, 907-474-7671, Fax: 907-474-6716, E-mail: fybio@uaf.edu. *Application contact:* Mike Earnest, Director of Admissions, 907-474-7500, Fax: 907-474-5379, E-mail: admissions@uaf.edu. Web site: http://www.bw.uaf.edu.

University of Alberta, Faculty of Graduate Studies and Research, Department of Biological Sciences, Edmonton, AB T6G 2E1, Canada. Offers environmental biology and ecology (M Sc, PhD); microbiology and biotechnology (M Sc, PhD); molecular biology and genetics (M Sc, PhD); physiology and cell biology (M Sc, PhD); plant biology (M Sc, PhD); systematics and evolution (M Sc, PhD). Terminal master's awarded for partial completion of doctoral program. *Degree requirements:* For master's, thesis; for doctorate, thesis/dissertation. *Entrance requirements:* Additional exam requirements/recommendations for international students: Required—TOEFL.

University of Alberta, Faculty of Medicine and Dentistry and Faculty of Graduate Studies and Research, Graduate Programs in Medicine, Edmonton, AB T6G 2E1, Canada. Offers M Sc, MD, PhD. Part-time programs available. *Degree requirements:* For doctorate, thesis/dissertation (for some programs). *Faculty research:* Basic, clinical, and applied biomedicine.

The University of Arizona, College of Science, Department of Molecular and Cellular Biology and Eller College of Management, Program in Applied Biosciences, Tucson, AZ 85721. Offers PSM. Part-time programs available. *Students:* 7 full-time (4 women), 4 part-time (1 woman), 1 international. Average age 29. 22 applicants, 27% accepted, 4 enrolled. In 2011, 8 master's awarded. *Degree requirements:* For master's, thesis or alternative, internship, colloquium, business courses. *Entrance requirements:* For master's, 3 letters of recommendation. Additional exam requirements/recommendations for international students: Required—TOEFL (minimum score 600 paper-based; 250 computer-based; 90 iBT). *Application deadline:* For fall admission, 2/1 for domestic students, 12/1 for international students. Application fee: $75. Electronic applications accepted. *Expenses:* Tuition, state resident: full-time $10,840. Tuition, nonresident: full-time $25,802. *Financial support:* Career-related internships or fieldwork, Federal Work-Study, scholarships/grants, health care benefits, and unspecified assistantships available. *Faculty research:* Biotechnology, bioinformatics, pharmaceuticals, agriculture, oncology. *Unit head:* Dr. Kathleen Dixon, Department Head, 520-621-7563, Fax: 520-621-3709, E-mail: dixonk@email.arizona.edu. *Application contact:* Marilyn Kramer, Graduate Coordinator, 520-621-1519, Fax: 520-621-3709, E-mail: mjkramer@u.arizona.edu. Web site: http://bmcb.biology.arizona.edu/.

University of Arkansas, Graduate School, J. William Fulbright College of Arts and Sciences, Department of Biological Sciences, Fayetteville, AR 72701-1201. Offers MA, MS, PhD. *Students:* 6 full-time (5 women), 41 part-time (18 women); includes 3 minority (1 Asian, non-Hispanic/Latino; 1 Hispanic/Latino; 1 Two or more races, non-Hispanic/Latino), 6 international. In 2011, 3 master's, 4 doctorates awarded. *Degree requirements:* For doctorate, one foreign language, thesis/dissertation. *Entrance requirements:* For master's and doctorate, GRE Subject Test. *Application deadline:* For fall admission, 4/1 for international students; for spring admission, 10/1 for international students. Applications are processed on a rolling basis. Application fee: $40 ($50 for international students). Electronic applications accepted. *Financial support:* In 2011–12, 27 research assistantships, 8 teaching assistantships were awarded; fellowships with tuition reimbursements, career-related internships or fieldwork, and Federal Work-Study also available. Support available to part-time students. Financial award application deadline: 4/1; financial award applicants required to submit FAFSA. *Unit head:* Dr. Fred Spiegel, Department Chairperson, 479-575-3251, Fax: 479-575-4010, E-mail: fspiegel@uark.edu. *Application contact:* Dr. David McNabb, Graduate Coordinator, 479-575-3797, Fax: 479-575-4010, E-mail: dmcnabb@uark.edu. Web site: http://biology.uark.edu/.

University of Arkansas at Little Rock, Graduate School, College of Science and Mathematics, Program in Biology, Little Rock, AR 72204-1099. Offers MS.

University of Arkansas for Medical Sciences, Graduate School, Graduate Programs in Biomedical Sciences, Little Rock, AR 72205. Offers MS, PhD, Certificate, MD/PhD. *Degree requirements:* For doctorate, thesis/dissertation. *Entrance requirements:* For master's and doctorate, GRE General Test. Additional exam requirements/recommendations for international students: Required—TOEFL. Electronic applications accepted. *Expenses:* Contact institution.

University of Calgary, Faculty of Graduate Studies, Faculty of Science, Department of Biological Sciences, Calgary, AB T2N 1N4, Canada. Offers M Sc, PhD. Part-time programs available. *Degree requirements:* For master's, thesis; for doctorate, thesis/dissertation, candidacy exam. *Entrance requirements:* Additional exam requirements/recommendations for international students: Required—TOEFL. Electronic applications accepted. *Faculty research:* Biochemistry; cellular, molecular, and microbial biology; botany; ecology; zoology.

University of Calgary, Faculty of Medicine and Faculty of Graduate Studies, Department of Medical Science, Calgary, AB T2N 1N4, Canada. Offers cancer biology (M Sc, PhD); immunology (M Sc, PhD); joint injury and arthritis research (M Sc, PhD); medical education (M Sc, PhD); medical science (M Sc, PhD); mountain medicine and high altitude physiology (M Sc). *Degree requirements:* For master's, thesis; for doctorate, thesis/dissertation, candidacy exam. *Entrance requirements:* For master's, minimum undergraduate GPA of 3.2; for doctorate, minimum graduate GPA of 3.2. Additional exam requirements/recommendations for international students: Required—TOEFL (minimum score 600 paper-based; 250 computer-based). Electronic applications accepted. *Faculty research:* Cancer biology, immunology, joint injury and arthritis, medical education, population genomics.

University of California, Berkeley, Graduate Division, College of Letters and Science, Department of Integrative Biology, Berkeley, CA 94720-1500. Offers PhD. *Degree requirements:* For doctorate, thesis/dissertation, oral qualifying exam. *Entrance requirements:* For doctorate, GRE General Test, GRE Subject Test, 3 letters of recommendation. Additional exam requirements/recommendations for international students: Required—TOEFL. *Faculty research:* Morphology, physiology, development of plants and animals, behavior, ecology.

University of California, Irvine, School of Biological Sciences, Irvine, CA 92697. Offers MS, PhD, MD/PhD. *Students:* 284 full-time (148 women), 4 part-time (2 women); includes 118 minority (7 Black or African American, non-Hispanic/Latino; 3 American Indian or Alaska Native, non-Hispanic/Latino; 56 Asian, non-Hispanic/Latino; 42 Hispanic/Latino; 1 Native Hawaiian or other Pacific Islander, non-Hispanic/Latino; 9 Two or more races, non-Hispanic/Latino), 25 international. Average age 26. 841 applicants, 24% accepted, 91 enrolled. In 2011, 21 master's, 41 doctorates awarded. *Degree requirements:* For doctorate, thesis/dissertation. *Entrance requirements:* For master's and doctorate, GRE General Test, GRE Subject Test, minimum GPA of 3.0. Additional exam requirements/recommendations for international students: Required—TOEFL (minimum score 550 paper-based; 213 computer-based). *Application deadline:* For fall admission, 12/15 for domestic and international students. Applications are processed on a rolling basis. Application fee: $80 ($100 for international students). Electronic applications accepted. *Financial support:* Fellowships with full tuition reimbursements, research assistantships with full tuition reimbursements, teaching assistantships with full tuition reimbursements, career-related internships or fieldwork, institutionally sponsored loans, scholarships/grants, traineeships, health care benefits, and unspecified assistantships available. Financial award application deadline: 3/1; financial award applicants required to submit FAFSA. *Faculty research:* Molecular biology and biochemistry, developmental and cell biology, physiology and biophysics, neurosciences, ecology and evolutionary biology. *Unit head:* Prof. Albert F. Bennett, Dean, 949-824-5315, Fax: 949-824-3035, E-mail: abennett@uci.edu. *Application contact:* Prof. R. Michael Mulligan, Associate Dean, 949-824-8433, Fax: 949-824-4709, E-mail: rmmullig@uci.edu. Web site: http://www.bio.uci.edu/.

University of California, Los Angeles, David Geffen School of Medicine and Graduate Division, Graduate Programs in Medicine, Los Angeles, CA 90095. Offers MS, PhD, MD/PhD. *Faculty:* 350 full-time (72 women). *Students:* 341 full-time (165 women); includes 107 minority (6 Black or African American, non-Hispanic/Latino; 1 American Indian or Alaska Native, non-Hispanic/Latino; 63 Asian, non-Hispanic/Latino; 29 Hispanic/Latino; 1 Native Hawaiian or other Pacific Islander, non-Hispanic/Latino; 7 Two or more races, non-Hispanic/Latino), 52 international. Average age 28. 468 applicants, 18% accepted, 43 enrolled. In 2011, 18 master's, 62 doctorates awarded. Terminal master's awarded for partial completion of doctoral program. *Degree requirements:* For doctorate, thesis/dissertation, qualifying exams. *Entrance requirements:* For master's, GRE General Test. Application fee: $70 ($90 for international students). Electronic applications accepted. *Financial support:* In 2011–12, 299 fellowships, 260 research assistantships, 67 teaching assistantships were awarded; career-related internships or fieldwork, Federal Work-Study, institutionally sponsored loans, scholarships/grants, and tuition waivers (full and partial) also available. Financial award application deadline: 3/1. *Unit head:* Dr. Neil H. Parker, Senior Associate Dean for Student Affairs and Graduate Medical Education, 310-825-6774, E-mail: nhparker@mednet.ucla.edu. *Application contact:* Office of Continuing Medical Education, 310-794-2620.

University of California, Los Angeles, Graduate Division, College of Letters and Science, Department of Ecology and Evolutionary Biology, Los Angeles, CA 90095. Offers MA, PhD. *Faculty:* 23 full-time (5 women). *Students:* 71 full-time (48 women); includes 20 minority (2 Black or African American, non-Hispanic/Latino; 8 Asian, non-Hispanic/Latino; 8 Hispanic/Latino; 2 Two or more races, non-Hispanic/Latino), 9

international. Average age 29. 92 applicants, 26% accepted, 16 enrolled. In 2011, 2 master's, 11 doctorates awarded. Terminal master's awarded for partial completion of doctoral program. *Degree requirements:* For master's, comprehensive exam or thesis; for doctorate, thesis/dissertation, oral and written qualifying exams; teaching experience. *Entrance requirements:* For master's and doctorate, GRE General Test, GRE Subject Test (biology), minimum GPA of 3.0, 3 letters of recommendation. *Application deadline:* For fall admission, 12/1 for domestic and international students. Application fee: $70 ($90 for international students). Electronic applications accepted. *Financial support:* In 2011–12, 64 fellowships with full and partial tuition reimbursements, 20 research assistantships with full and partial tuition reimbursements, 38 teaching assistantships with full and partial tuition reimbursements were awarded; Federal Work-Study, institutionally sponsored loans, scholarships/grants, health care benefits, tuition waivers (full and partial), and unspecified assistantships also available. Financial award application deadline: 3/1; financial award applicants required to submit FAFSA. *Faculty research:* Molecular, cell, and developmental biology; interactive biology; organisms and populations. *Unit head:* Dr. Daniel T. Blumstein, Chair, 310-267-4746, Fax: 310-206-3987, E-mail: marmots@ucla.edu. *Application contact:* Jocelyn Yamadera, Student Affairs Officer, 310-825-1959, Fax: 310-206-5280, E-mail: jocelyny@lifesci.ucla.edu. Web site: http://www.eeb.ucla.edu/.

University of California, Merced, Division of Graduate Studies, School of Natural Sciences, Merced, CA 95343. Offers applied mathematics (MS, PhD); biological engineering and small-scale technologies (MS, PhD); environmental systems (MS, PhD); mechanical engineering and applied mechanics (MS, PhD); physics and chemistry (PhD); quantitative and systems biology (MS, PhD). *Unit head:* Dr. Samuel J. Traina, Dean, 209-228-4723, Fax: 209-228-6906, E-mail: grad.dean@ucmerced.edu. *Application contact:* Tsu Ya, Graduate Admissions and Academic Services Manager, 209-228-4723, Fax: 209-228-6906, E-mail: tya@ucmerced.edu.

University of California, Riverside, Graduate Division, Department of Biology, Riverside, CA 92521-0102. Offers evolution, ecology and organismal biology (MS, PhD). Terminal master's awarded for partial completion of doctoral program. *Degree requirements:* For master's, thesis, oral defense of thesis; for doctorate, thesis/dissertation, 3 quarters of teaching experience, qualifying exams. *Entrance requirements:* For master's and doctorate, GRE General Test, minimum GPA of 3.2. Additional exam requirements/recommendations for international students: Required—TOEFL (minimum score 550 paper-based, 213 computer-based, 80 iBT) or IELTS. Electronic applications accepted. *Faculty research:* Ecology, evolutionary biology, physiology, quantitative genetics, conservation biology.

University of California, Riverside, Graduate Division, Program in Biomedical Sciences, Riverside, CA 92521-0102. Offers PhD, MD/PhD. *Degree requirements:* For doctorate, thesis/dissertation, qualifying exams. *Entrance requirements:* For doctorate, GRE General Test, minimum GPA of 3.2. Additional exam requirements/recommendations for international students: Required—TOEFL (minimum score 550 paper-based; 213 computer-based; 80 iBT). Electronic applications accepted. *Faculty research:* Cancer, receptor biology, developmental disorders, molecular basis of disease, neurodegeneration.

University of California, San Diego, Office of Graduate Studies, Division of Biological Sciences, La Jolla, CA 92093-0348. Offers biochemistry (PhD); biology (MS); cell and developmental biology (PhD); ecology, behavior, and evolution (PhD); genetics and molecular biology (PhD); immunology, virology, and cancer biology (PhD); molecular and cellular biology (PhD); neurobiology (PhD); plant molecular biology (PhD); plant systems biology (PhD); signal transduction (PhD). Offered in association with the Salk Institute; fall admission only. *Degree requirements:* For doctorate, thesis/dissertation, qualifying exam. *Entrance requirements:* For doctorate, GRE General Test; GRE Subject Test (recommended). Additional exam requirements/recommendations for international students: Required—TOEFL. Electronic applications accepted.

University of California, San Diego, School of Medicine and Office of Graduate Studies, Graduate Studies in Biomedical Sciences, La Jolla, CA 92093-0685. Offers molecular cell biology (PhD); pharmacology (PhD); physiology (PhD); regulatory biology (PhD). *Degree requirements:* For doctorate, thesis/dissertation, qualifying exam. *Entrance requirements:* For doctorate, GRE General Test. Additional exam requirements/recommendations for international students: Required—TOEFL. Electronic applications accepted. *Faculty research:* Molecular and cellular biology, molecular and cellular pharmacology, cell and organ physiology.

University of California, San Diego, School of Medicine, Medical Scientist Training Program, La Jolla, CA 92093. Offers MD/PhD.

University of California, San Francisco, Graduate Division, Biomedical Sciences Graduate Group, San Francisco, CA 94143. Offers anatomy (PhD); endocrinology (PhD); experimental pathology (PhD); physiology (PhD). *Degree requirements:* For doctorate, thesis/dissertation. *Entrance requirements:* For doctorate, GRE General Test.

University of California, San Francisco, School of Medicine, San Francisco, CA 94143-0410. Offers MD, PhD, MD/MPH, MD/MS, MD/PhD. *Accreditation:* LCME/AMA (one or more programs are accredited). *Faculty:* 2,031 full-time (678 women), 128 part-time/adjunct (41 women). *Students:* 634 full-time (354 women); includes 331 minority (44 Black or African American, non-Hispanic/Latino; 124 Asian, non-Hispanic/Latino; 100 Hispanic/Latino; 24 Native Hawaiian or other Pacific Islander, non-Hispanic/Latino; 39 Two or more races, non-Hispanic/Latino). Average age 24. 6,767 applicants, 4% accepted, 149 enrolled. In 2011, 163 doctorates awarded. *Entrance requirements:* For doctorate, MCAT (for MD), interview (for MD). *Application deadline:* For fall admission, 10/15 for domestic students. Applications are processed on a rolling basis. Application fee: $60 ($80 for international students). Electronic applications accepted. *Expenses:* Contact institution. *Financial support:* In 2011–12, 543 students received support. Federal Work-Study, institutionally sponsored loans, scholarships/grants, and tuition waivers (partial) available. Financial award application deadline: 2/1; financial award applicants required to submit FAFSA. *Faculty research:* Neurosciences, human genetics, developmental biology, social/behavioral/policy sciences, immunology. *Total annual research expenditures:* $414.4 million. *Unit head:* Dr. Sam Hawgood, Dean, 415-476-2342, Fax: 415-476-0689, E-mail: sam.hawgood@ucsf.edu. *Application contact:* Hallen Chung, Director of Admissions, 415-476-8090, Fax: 415-476-5490, E-mail: chungh@medsch.ucsf.edu. Web site: http://www.medschool.ucsf.edu/.

University of Central Arkansas, Graduate School, College of Natural Sciences and Math, Department of Biological Science, Conway, AR 72035-0001. Offers MS. Part-time programs available. *Faculty:* 19 full-time (6 women). *Students:* 22 full-time (8 women), 11 part-time (7 women); includes 1 minority (American Indian or Alaska Native, non-Hispanic/Latino), 1 international. Average age 26. 15 applicants, 87% accepted, 12 enrolled. In 2011, 11 master's awarded. *Degree requirements:* For master's, comprehensive exam, thesis optional. *Entrance requirements:* For master's, GRE General Test, minimum GPA of 2.7. Additional exam requirements/recommendations for international students: Required—TOEFL (minimum score 550 paper-based; 213 computer-based). *Application deadline:* For fall admission, 3/1 priority date for domestic students; for spring admission, 10/1 priority date for domestic students. Applications are processed on a rolling basis. Application fee: $25 ($50 for international students). *Expenses:* Tuition, state resident: full-time $4834; part-time $398.35 per credit hour. Tuition, nonresident: full-time $8686. *Financial support:* In 2011–12, 4 research assistantships with partial tuition reimbursements (averaging $8,500 per year), 21 teaching assistantships with partial tuition reimbursements (averaging $8,500 per year) were awarded; unspecified assistantships also available. Financial award application deadline: 2/15; financial award applicants required to submit FAFSA. *Unit head:* Dr. Reid Adams, Associate Chair and Graduate Coordinator, 501-450-5933, Fax: 501-450-5914, E-mail: radams@uca.edu. *Application contact:* Susan Wood, Admissions Assistant, 501-450-3124, Fax: 501-450-5678, E-mail: swood@uca.edu. Web site: http://uca.edu/biology/.

University of Central Florida, College of Medicine, Burnett School of Biomedical Sciences, Orlando, FL 32816. Offers biomedical sciences (MS, PhD); biotechnology (MS). *Faculty:* 41 full-time (13 women), 6 part-time/adjunct (3 women). *Students:* 105 full-time (62 women), 16 part-time (11 women); includes 20 minority (3 Black or African American, non-Hispanic/Latino; 10 Asian, non-Hispanic/Latino; 7 Hispanic/Latino), 54 international. Average age 27. 208 applicants, 35% accepted, 40 enrolled. In 2011, 38 master's, 9 doctorates awarded. *Expenses:* Tuition, state resident: part-time $277.08 per credit hour. Tuition, nonresident: part-time $277.08 per credit hour. Part-time tuition and fees vary according to degree level and program. *Financial support:* In 2011–12, 85 students received support, including 10 fellowships (averaging $10,800 per year), 55 research assistantships (averaging $10,000 per year), 51 teaching assistantships (averaging $8,500 per year). *Unit head:* Dr. Pappachan E. Kolattukudy, Director, 407-823-2357, Fax: 407-823-0956, E-mail: pk@ucf.edu. *Application contact:* Barbara Rodriguez, Director, Admissions and Registration, 407-823-2766, Fax: 407-823-6442, E-mail: gradadmissions@ucf.edu. Web site: http://www.biomed.ucf.edu/.

University of Central Florida, College of Sciences, Department of Biology, Orlando, FL 32816. Offers biology (MS); conservation biology (PSM, PhD, Certificate). Part-time and evening/weekend programs available. *Faculty:* 21 full-time (5 women), 9 part-time/adjunct (5 women). *Students:* 56 full-time (35 women), 18 part-time (12 women); includes 5 minority (2 Asian, non-Hispanic/Latino; 2 Hispanic/Latino; 1 Two or more races, non-Hispanic/Latino), 4 international. Average age 30. 78 applicants, 37% accepted, 17 enrolled. In 2011, 19 master's, 2 doctorates awarded. *Degree requirements:* For master's, comprehensive exam, thesis or alternative, field exam. *Entrance requirements:* For master's, GRE General Test, minimum GPA of 3.0 in last 60 hours. Additional exam requirements/recommendations for international students: Required—TOEFL. *Application deadline:* For fall admission, 3/1 priority date for domestic students; for spring admission, 10/15 for domestic students. Application fee: $30. Electronic applications accepted. *Expenses:* Tuition, state resident: part-time $277.08 per credit hour. Tuition, nonresident: part-time $277.08 per credit hour. Part-time tuition and fees vary according to degree level and program. *Financial support:* In 2011–12, 50 students received support, including 11 fellowships with partial tuition reimbursements available (averaging $1,500 per year), 14 research assistantships with partial tuition reimbursements available (averaging $9,100 per year), 41 teaching assistantships with partial tuition reimbursements available (averaging $11,600 per year); career-related internships or fieldwork, Federal Work-Study, institutionally sponsored loans, tuition waivers (partial), and unspecified assistantships also available. Financial award application deadline: 3/1; financial award applicants required to submit FAFSA. *Unit head:* Dr. Ross Hinkle, Chair, 407-823-2141, Fax: 407-823-5769, E-mail: rhinkle@ucf.edu. *Application contact:* Barbara Rodriguez, Associate Director, Admissions and Registration, 407-823-2766, Fax: 407-823-6442, E-mail: gradadmissions@ucf.edu. Web site: http://biology.cos.ucf.edu/.

University of Central Missouri, The Graduate School, College of Science and Technology, Warrensburg, MO 64093. Offers applied mathematics (MS); aviation safety (MS); biology (MS); computer science (MS); environmental studies (MA); industrial management (MS); mathematics (MS); technology (MS); technology management (PhD). PhD is offered jointly with Indiana State University. Part-time programs available. Postbaccalaureate distance learning degree programs offered. *Entrance requirements:* Additional exam requirements/recommendations for international students: Required—TOEFL (minimum score 550 paper-based; 79 computer-based). Electronic applications accepted.

University of Central Oklahoma, College of Graduate Studies and Research, College of Mathematics and Science, Department of Biology, Edmond, OK 73034-5209. Offers MS. Part-time programs available. *Faculty:* 10 full-time (3 women), 5 part-time/adjunct (1 woman). *Students:* 6 full-time (4 women), 9 part-time (7 women); includes 2 minority (1 Black or African American, non-Hispanic/Latino; 1 American Indian or Alaska Native, non-Hispanic/Latino), 1 international. Average age 28. *Degree requirements:* For master's, thesis. *Entrance requirements:* For master's, GRE General Test, GRE Subject Test (biology). Additional exam requirements/recommendations for international students: Required—TOEFL (minimum score 550 paper-based; 213 computer-based). *Application deadline:* Applications are processed on a rolling basis. Application fee: $50. Electronic applications accepted. *Expenses:* Tuition, state resident: full-time $3901; part-time $218.30 per credit hour. Tuition, nonresident: full-time $9198; part-time $511.20 per credit hour. Tuition and fees vary according to program. *Financial support:* Federal Work-Study and unspecified assistantships available. Financial award application deadline: 3/31; financial award applicants required to submit FAFSA. *Faculty research:* Environmental (&ITlegionella&RO), aquatic biology (ecological), mammalogy field studies, microbiology, genetics. *Unit head:* Dr. Clark Ovrebo, 405-974-5783, Fax: 405-974-3824, E-mail: covrebo@uco.edu. *Application contact:* Dr. Richard Bernard, Dean, Graduate College, 405-974-3493, Fax: 405-974-3852, E-mail: gradcoll@uco.edu.

University of Chicago, Division of Biological Sciences, The Interdisciplinary Scientist Training Program, Chicago, IL 60637-1513. Offers PhD. *Degree requirements:* For doctorate, thesis/dissertation, ethics class, 2 teaching assistantships. *Entrance requirements:* Additional exam requirements/recommendations for international students: Required—TOEFL (minimum score 600 paper-based; 250 computer-based; 104 iBT), IELTS (minimum score 7). Electronic applications accepted.

University of Cincinnati, Graduate School, College of Medicine, Biomedical Sciences Flex Option Program, Cincinnati, OH 45221. Offers PhD. *Degree requirements:* For doctorate, thesis/dissertation, qualifying exam. *Entrance requirements:* For doctorate, GRE, 2 letters of recommendation. Additional exam requirements/recommendations for international students: Required—TOEFL. Electronic applications accepted. *Faculty research:* Environmental health, developmental biology, cell and molecular biology, immunobiology, molecular genetics.

University of Cincinnati, Graduate School, College of Medicine, Graduate Programs in Biomedical Sciences, Cincinnati, OH 45221. Offers MS, PhD. Terminal master's awarded for partial completion of doctoral program. *Degree requirements:* For master's, thesis; for doctorate, thesis/dissertation, qualifying exam. *Entrance requirements:* For master's and doctorate, GRE General Test. Additional exam requirements/recommendations for international students: Required—TOEFL (minimum score 600 paper-based; 250 computer-based; 100 iBT). Electronic applications accepted. *Expenses:* Contact institution. *Faculty research:* Cancer, cardiovascular, metabolic disorders, neuroscience, computational medicine.

University of Cincinnati, Graduate School, College of Medicine, Physician Scientist Training Program, Cincinnati, OH 45221. Offers MD/PhD. *Entrance requirements:*

Biological and Biomedical Sciences—General

Additional exam requirements/recommendations for international students: Required—TOEFL. Electronic applications accepted.

University of Cincinnati, Graduate School, McMicken College of Arts and Sciences, Department of Biological Sciences, Cincinnati, OH 45221-0006. Offers MS, PhD. Part-time programs available. Terminal master's awarded for partial completion of doctoral program. *Degree requirements:* For master's, thesis; for doctorate, comprehensive exam, thesis/dissertation. *Entrance requirements:* For master's and doctorate, GRE General Test, BS in biology, chemistry, or equivalent. Additional exam requirements/recommendations for international students: Required—TOEFL (minimum score 600 paper-based; 250 computer-based; 100 iBT). Electronic applications accepted. *Faculty research:* Physiology and development, cell and molecular, ecology and evolutionary.

University of Colorado at Colorado Springs, College of Letters, Arts and Sciences, Master of Sciences Program, Colorado Springs, CO 80933-7150. Offers applied science - bioscience (M Sc); applied science - physics (M Sc); biology (M Sc); chemistry (M Sc); health promotion (M Sc); mathematics (M Sc); physics (M Sc); sports medicine (M Sc); sports nutrition (M Sc). Part-time programs available. *Students:* 13 full-time (5 women), 11 part-time (6 women); includes 3 minority (2 Asian, non-Hispanic/Latino; 1 Hispanic/Latino). Average age 33. 15 applicants, 53% accepted, 3 enrolled. In 2011, 39 degrees awarded. *Degree requirements:* For master's, thesis or alternative. *Entrance requirements:* For master's, minimum GPA of 2.75. Additional exam requirements/recommendations for international students: Recommended—TOEFL. *Application deadline:* For fall admission, 6/1 priority date for domestic students; for spring admission, 12/1 for domestic students. Application fee: $60 ($75 for international students). *Expenses:* Contact institution. *Financial support:* In 2011–12, 5 students received support. Fellowships, research assistantships, teaching assistantships, career-related internships or fieldwork, Federal Work-Study, and scholarships/grants available. Support available to part-time students. Financial award application deadline: 3/1; financial award applicants required to submit FAFSA. *Faculty research:* Biomechanics and physiology of elite athletic training, genetic engineering in yeast and bacteria including phage display and DNA repair, immunology and cell biology, synthetic organic chemistry. *Unit head:* Dr. Tom Christensen, Dean, 719-255-4550, Fax: 719-255-4200, E-mail: tchriste@uccs.edu. *Application contact:* Taryn Bailey, Information Contact, 719-255-3702, Fax: 719-255-3037, E-mail: gradinfo@uccs.edu.

University of Colorado Denver, College of Liberal Arts and Sciences, Department of Integrative Biology, Denver, CO 80217. Offers animal behavior (MS); biology (MS); cell and developmental biology (MS); ecology (MS); evolutionary biology (MS); genetics (MS); microbiology (MS); molecular biology (MS); neurobiology (MS); plant systematics (MS). Part-time programs available. *Faculty:* 16 full-time (8 women). *Students:* 20 full-time (13 women), 5 part-time (4 women); includes 1 minority (Hispanic/Latino), 1 international. Average age 29. 21 applicants, 43% accepted, 5 enrolled. In 2011, 7 master's awarded. *Degree requirements:* For master's, comprehensive exam, thesis or alternative, 30-32 credit hours. *Entrance requirements:* For master's, GRE General Test (minimum score in 50% percentile in each section), BA/BS from accredited institution awarded within the last 10 years; minimum undergraduate GPA of 3.0; prerequisite courses: 1 year each of general biology and general chemistry, and 1 semester each of general genetics, general ecology, cell biology, and a structure/function course. Additional exam requirements/recommendations for international students: Required—TOEFL (minimum score 525 paper-based; 197 computer-based; 71 iBT). *Application deadline:* For fall admission, 2/1 for domestic and international students. Application fee: $50 ($75 for international students). Electronic applications accepted. *Financial support:* Research assistantships, teaching assistantships, Federal Work-Study, scholarships/grants, and unspecified assistantships available. Financial award application deadline: 4/1; financial award applicants required to submit FAFSA. *Faculty research:* Molecular developmental biology; quantitative ecology, biogeography, and population dynamics;

environmental signaling and endocrine disruption; speciation, the evolution of reproductive isolation, and hybrid zones; evolutionary, behavioral, and conservation ecology. *Unit head:* Dr. Diana Tomback, Acting Chair, 303-556-2657, E-mail: diana.tomback@ucdenver.edu. *Application contact:* Timberley Roane, Associate Professor/Associate Chair, 303-556-6592, E-mail: timberley.roane@ucdenver.edu. Web site: http://www.ucdenver.edu/academics/colleges/CLAS/Departments/biology/Pages/Biology.aspx.

University of Colorado Denver, School of Medicine, Biomedical Sciences Program, Aurora, CO 80045. Offers MS, PhD. *Students:* 15 full-time (7 women); includes 1 minority (Asian, non-Hispanic/Latino), 3 international. Average age 26. 140 applicants, 14% accepted, 9 enrolled. In 2011, 5 master's awarded. Terminal master's awarded for partial completion of doctoral program. *Degree requirements:* For master's and doctorate, comprehensive exam. *Entrance requirements:* For master's, GRE, three letters of recommendation; for doctorate, GRE, minimum undergraduate GPA of 3.0; prerequisite coursework in organic chemistry, biology, biochemistry, physics, and calculus; letters of recommendation; interview. Additional exam requirements/recommendations for international students: Required—TOEFL (minimum score 550 paper-based; 213 computer-based). *Application deadline:* For fall admission, 12/1 for domestic students, 11/1 for international students. Application fee: $65. Electronic applications accepted. *Expenses:* Contact institution. *Financial support:* Fellowships, research assistantships, teaching assistantships, health care benefits, tuition waivers (full), and stipend available. Financial award applicants required to submit FAFSA. *Unit head:* Heide Ford, Director, 303-724-3509, E-mail: heide.ford@ucdenver.edu. *Application contact:* Di Collingwood, Program Administrator, 303-724-3278, E-mail: dianna.collingwood@ucdenver.edu. Web site: http://www.ucdenver.edu/academics/colleges/Graduate-School/academic-programs/Biomedical/Pages/Welcome.aspx.

University of Connecticut, Graduate School, University of Connecticut Health Center, Field of Biomedical Science, Storrs, CT 06269. Offers PhD. *Degree requirements:* For doctorate, thesis/dissertation. *Entrance requirements:* For doctorate, GRE General Test, GRE Subject Test. Additional exam requirements/recommendations for international students: Required—TOEFL (minimum score 550 paper-based; 213 computer-based). Electronic applications accepted.

University of Connecticut Health Center, Graduate School and School of Medicine, Combined Degree Program in Biomedical Sciences, Farmington, CT 06030. Offers MD/PhD. *Entrance requirements:* Additional exam requirements/recommendations for international students: Required—TOEFL (minimum score 600 paper-based; 250 computer-based). *Expenses:* Contact institution.

University of Connecticut Health Center, Graduate School, Programs in Biomedical Sciences, Farmington, CT 06030. Offers PhD, DMD/PhD, MD/PhD. *Degree requirements:* For doctorate, comprehensive exam, thesis/dissertation. *Entrance requirements:* For doctorate, GRE General Test. Additional exam requirements/recommendations for international students: Required—TOEFL (minimum score 600 paper-based; 250 computer-based). Electronic applications accepted.

See Display below and Close-Up on page 117.

University of Connecticut Health Center, Graduate School, Programs in Biomedical Sciences - Integrated, Farmington, CT 06030. Offers PhD, DMD/PhD, MD/PhD. *Degree requirements:* For doctorate, comprehensive exam, thesis/dissertation. *Entrance requirements:* For doctorate, GRE General Test. Additional exam requirements/recommendations for international students: Required—TOEFL (minimum score 600 paper-based; 250 computer-based). Electronic applications accepted.

University of Dayton, Department of Biology, Dayton, OH 45469-1300. Offers MS, PhD. *Faculty:* 17 full-time (5 women). *Students:* 19 full-time (11 women), 1 part-time (0

University of Connecticut Health Center

UCHC offers you exceptional research opportunities spanning **Cell Analysis and Modeling; Cell Biology; Genetics and Developmental Biology; Immunology; Molecular Biology and Biochemistry; Neuroscience;** and **Skeletal, Craniofacial and Oral Biology**.

Key features of our program include:
- ❖ Integrated admissions with access to more than 100 laboratories.
- ❖ Flexible educational program tailored to the interests of each student.
- ❖ Excellent education in a stimulating, cutting edge research environment.
- ❖ Competitive stipend ($28,000 for 2012–13 year), tuition waiver, and availability of student health plan.
- ❖ State-of-the-art research facilities, including the new Cell and Genome Sciences Building, which houses the UConn Stem Cell Institute, the Center for Cell Analysis and Modeling, and the Department of Genetics and Developmental Biology.

For more information, please contact:
Stephanie Rauch, Biomedical Science Admissions Coordinator
University of Connecticut Health Center
263 Farmington Ave., MC 3906
Farmington, CT 06030
BiomedSciAdmissions@uchc.edu
http://grad.uchc.edu/prospective/programs/phd_biosci/index.html

women), 8 international. Average age 26. 38 applicants, 16% accepted, 6 enrolled. In 2011, 1 master's, 3 doctorates awarded. Terminal master's awarded for partial completion of doctoral program. *Degree requirements:* For master's, comprehensive exam, thesis; for doctorate, comprehensive exam, thesis/dissertation. *Entrance requirements:* For master's and doctorate, GRE General Test, minimum undergraduate GPA of 3.0. Additional exam requirements/recommendations for international students: Required—TOEFL (minimum score 550 paper-based; 213 computer-based; 80 iBT). *Application deadline:* For fall admission, 3/1 priority date for domestic students, 3/1 for international students; for winter admission, 10/15 priority date for domestic students, 10/15 for international students; for spring admission, 1/1 for international students. Applications are processed on a rolling basis. Application fee: $50. Electronic applications accepted. *Expenses: Tuition:* Full-time $8400; part-time $700 per credit hour. *Required fees:* $25 per semester. Tuition and fees vary according to degree level. *Financial support:* In 2011–12, 2 research assistantships with full tuition reimbursements (averaging $15,260 per year), 16 teaching assistantships with full tuition reimbursements (averaging $15,470 per year) were awarded; institutionally sponsored loans, health care benefits, and unspecified assistantships also available. Financial award application deadline: 3/1; financial award applicants required to submit FAFSA. *Faculty research:* Tissue regeneration and developmental biology; cancer and stem cell biology; microbiology and immunology; molecular genetics, evolution and bioinformatics; environmental and restoration ecology. *Unit head:* Dr. Jayne B. Robinson, Chair, 937-229-2521, Fax: 937-229-2021. *Application contact:* Dr. Mark Nielsen, Director, Biology Graduate Programs, 937-229-2587, Fax: 937-229-2021, E-mail: mnielsen1@udayton.edu. Web site: http://biology.udayton.edu.

University of Delaware, College of Arts and Sciences, Department of Biological Sciences, Newark, DE 19716. Offers biotechnology (MS); cancer biology (MS, PhD); cell and extracellular matrix biology (MS, PhD); cell and systems physiology (MS, PhD); developmental biology (MS, PhD); ecology and evolution (MS, PhD); microbiology (MS, PhD); molecular biology and genetics (MS, PhD). Terminal master's awarded for partial completion of doctoral program. *Degree requirements:* For master's, thesis, preliminary exam; for doctorate, comprehensive exam, thesis/dissertation, preliminary exam. *Entrance requirements:* For master's and doctorate, GRE General Test. Additional exam requirements/recommendations for international students: Required—TOEFL (minimum score 600 paper-based; 250 computer-based); Recommended—TWE. Electronic applications accepted. *Faculty research:* Microorganisms, bone, cancer metastasis, developmental biology, cell biology, DNA.

University of Denver, Faculty of Natural Sciences and Mathematics, Department of Biological Sciences, Denver, CO 80208. Offers MS, PhD. Part-time programs available. *Faculty:* 20 full-time (5 women), 3 part-time/adjunct (1 woman). *Students:* 1 full-time (0 women), 28 part-time (22 women); includes 4 minority (1 American Indian or Alaska Native, non-Hispanic/Latino; 1 Asian, non-Hispanic/Latino; 2 Hispanic/Latino), 2 international. Average age 26. 68 applicants, 26% accepted, 14 enrolled. In 2011, 7 master's, 3 doctorates awarded. Terminal master's awarded for partial completion of doctoral program. *Median time to degree:* Of those who began their doctoral program in fall 2003, 100% received their degree in 8 years or less. *Degree requirements:* For master's, comprehensive exam (for some programs), thesis; for doctorate, one foreign language, comprehensive exam (for some programs), thesis/dissertation. *Entrance requirements:* For master's, GRE General Test, BA or BS in biology or related field; for doctorate, GRE General Test, GRE Subject Test (biology). Additional exam requirements/recommendations for international students: Required—TOEFL (minimum score 570 paper-based; 88 iBT). *Application deadline:* For fall admission, 1/15 priority date for domestic students. Applications are processed on a rolling basis. Application fee: $60. Electronic applications accepted. *Financial support:* In 2011–12, 27 students received support, including 8 research assistantships with full and partial tuition reimbursements available (averaging $18,300 per year), 22 teaching assistantships with full and partial tuition reimbursements available (averaging $17,745 per year); Federal Work-Study, institutionally sponsored loans, and unspecified assistantships also available. Support available to part-time students. Financial award application deadline: 2/15; financial award applicants required to submit FAFSA. *Faculty research:* Molecular biology, cell biology, neurobiology, ecology, molecular evolution. *Unit head:* Dr. Joseph Angleson, Chair, 303-871-3463, E-mail: jangleso@du.edu. *Application contact:* Randi Flageolle, Assistant to the Chair, 303-871-3457, E-mail: rflageol@du.edu. Web site: http://www.du.edu/biology/.

University of Florida, College of Medicine and Graduate School, Interdisciplinary Program in Biomedical Sciences, Gainesville, FL 32611. Offers PhD, JD/MS, JD/PhD, MBA/MS, MBA/PhD, MS/M Ed. *Degree requirements:* For doctorate, thesis/dissertation. *Entrance requirements:* For doctorate, GRE General Test, minimum GPA of 3.0. Additional exam requirements/recommendations for international students: Required—TOEFL. Electronic applications accepted. *Expenses:* Contact institution.

University of Georgia, Biomedical and Health Sciences Institute, Athens, GA 30602. Offers neuroscience (PhD). *Students:* 21 full-time (13 women), 2 part-time (both women); includes 3 minority (1 Black or African American, non-Hispanic/Latino; 1 Asian, non-Hispanic/Latino; 1 Hispanic/Latino), 5 international. Average age 30. 42 applicants, 29% accepted, 9 enrolled. In 2011, 1 doctorate awarded. *Entrance requirements:* For doctorate, GRE, official transcripts, 3 letters of recommendation, statement of interest. Additional exam requirements/recommendations for international students: Required—TOEFL. *Financial support:* Unspecified assistantships available. Financial award application deadline: 12/31. *Unit head:* Dr. Harry Dailey, Director, 706-542-5922, Fax: 706-542-5285, E-mail: hdailey@uga.edu. *Application contact:* Joy Peterson, Graduate Coordinator, 706-542-2684, E-mail: biomfg@uga.edu. Web site: http://biomed.uga.edu.

University of Guam, Office of Graduate Studies, College of Natural and Applied Sciences, Program in Biology, Mangilao, GU 96923. Offers tropical marine biology (MS). *Degree requirements:* For master's, comprehensive exam, thesis. *Entrance requirements:* For master's, GRE General Test, GRE Subject Test. Additional exam requirements/recommendations for international students: Required—TOEFL. *Faculty research:* Maintenance and ecology of coral reefs.

University of Guelph, Graduate Studies, College of Biological Science, Guelph, ON N1G 2W1, Canada. Offers M Sc, PhD. Part-time programs available. *Degree requirements:* For master's, thesis (for some programs); for doctorate, comprehensive exam (for some programs), thesis/dissertation. *Entrance requirements:* Additional exam requirements/recommendations for international students: Required—TOEFL (minimum score 550 paper-based; 213 computer-based). Electronic applications accepted.

University of Hartford, College of Arts and Sciences, Department of Biology, West Hartford, CT 06117-1599. Offers biology (MS); neuroscience (MS). Part-time and evening/weekend programs available. *Degree requirements:* For master's, comprehensive exam, thesis optional, oral exams. *Entrance requirements:* For master's, GRE or MCAT. Additional exam requirements/recommendations for international students: Required—TOEFL (minimum score 550 paper-based; 213 computer-based). Electronic applications accepted. *Faculty research:* Neurobiology of aging, central actions of neural steroids, neuroendocrine control of reproduction, retinopathies in sharks, plasticity in the central nervous system.

University of Hawaii at Manoa, John A. Burns School of Medicine and Graduate Division, Graduate Programs in Biomedical Sciences, Honolulu, HI 96822. Offers MS, PhD. Part-time programs available. Terminal master's awarded for partial completion of doctoral program. *Degree requirements:* For master's, thesis optional; for doctorate, comprehensive exam, thesis/dissertation. *Entrance requirements:* For master's and doctorate, GRE General Test. Additional exam requirements/recommendations for international students: Required—TOEFL (minimum score 500 paper-based; 173 computer-based; 61 iBT), IELTS (minimum score 5). *Expenses:* Contact institution.

University of Houston, College of Natural Sciences and Mathematics, Department of Biology and Biochemistry, Houston, TX 77204. Offers biochemistry (MA, PhD); biology (MA). Terminal master's awarded for partial completion of doctoral program. *Degree requirements:* For master's, comprehensive exam (for some programs), thesis optional; for doctorate, comprehensive exam (for some programs), thesis/dissertation. *Entrance requirements:* For master's and doctorate, GRE. Additional exam requirements/recommendations for international students: Required—TOEFL (minimum score 550 paper-based; 213 computer-based; 79 iBT), IELTS (minimum score 6.5). Electronic applications accepted. *Faculty research:* Cell and molecular biology, ecology and evolution, biochemical and biophysical sciences, chemical biology.

University of Houston–Clear Lake, School of Science and Computer Engineering, Program in Biological Sciences, Houston, TX 77058-1098. Offers MS. Part-time and evening/weekend programs available. *Entrance requirements:* For master's, GRE General Test. Additional exam requirements/recommendations for international students: Required—TOEFL (minimum score 550 paper-based; 213 computer-based).

University of Idaho, College of Graduate Studies, College of Science, Department of Biological Sciences, Moscow, ID 83844-3051. Offers biology (MS, PhD); microbiology, molecular biology and biochemistry (MS, PhD). *Faculty:* 12 full-time. *Students:* 29 full-time, 6 part-time. Average age 28. In 2011, 2 master's, 2 doctorates awarded. *Degree requirements:* For doctorate, one foreign language, thesis/dissertation. *Entrance requirements:* For master's, GRE, minimum GPA of 2.8; for doctorate, GRE, minimum undergraduate GPA of 2.8, 3.0 graduate. *Application deadline:* For fall admission, 8/1 for domestic students; for spring admission, 12/15 for domestic students. Applications are processed on a rolling basis. Application fee: $60. Electronic applications accepted. *Expenses:* Tuition, state resident: full-time $3874; part-time $334 per credit hour. Tuition, nonresident: full-time $16,394; part-time $861 per credit hour. *Required fees:* $2808; $99 per credit hour. Tuition and fees vary according to program. *Financial support:* Research assistantships and teaching assistantships available. Financial award applicants required to submit FAFSA. *Faculty research:* Animal behavior development, germ cell development, evolutionary biology, fish reproductive biology, molecular mechanisms. *Unit head:* John Byers, Acting Chair, 208-885-6280. *Application contact:* Erick Larson, Director of Graduate Admissions, 208-885-4723, E-mail: gadms@uidaho.edu. Web site: http://www.uidaho.edu/sci/biology.

University of Illinois at Chicago, College of Medicine and Graduate College, Graduate Programs in Medicine, Chicago, IL 60607-7128. Offers MHPE, MS, PhD, MD/MS, MD/PhD. Part-time programs available. Terminal master's awarded for partial completion of doctoral program. *Degree requirements:* For master's, thesis; for doctorate, thesis/dissertation. *Entrance requirements:* For master's and doctorate, GRE General Test. *Expenses:* Contact institution.

University of Illinois at Chicago, Graduate College, College of Liberal Arts and Sciences, Department of Biological Sciences, Chicago, IL 60607-7128. Offers MS, PhD. *Degree requirements:* For master's, thesis; for doctorate, thesis/dissertation, preliminary exam. *Entrance requirements:* For master's and doctorate, GRE General Test, GRE Subject Test, previous course work in physics, calculus, and organic chemistry; minimum GPA of 2.75. Additional exam requirements/recommendations for international students: Required—TOEFL. Electronic applications accepted.

University of Illinois at Springfield, Graduate Programs, College of Liberal Arts and Sciences, Program in Biology, Springfield, IL 62703-5407. Offers MS. Part-time and evening/weekend programs available. *Faculty:* 3 full-time (2 women). *Students:* 18 full-time (10 women), 12 part-time (7 women); includes 1 minority (Black or African American, non-Hispanic/Latino), 2 international. Average age 28. 37 applicants, 43% accepted, 13 enrolled. In 2011, 6 master's awarded. *Degree requirements:* For master's, project or thesis. *Entrance requirements:* For master's, GRE General Test, GRE Subject Test (biology), minimum undergraduate GPA of 3.0, 3 letters of reference. Additional exam requirements/recommendations for international students: Required—TOEFL (minimum score 500 paper-based; 176 computer-based; 61 iBT). *Application deadline:* Applications are processed on a rolling basis. Application fee: $50 ($60 for international students). Electronic applications accepted. *Expenses:* Tuition, state resident: full-time $6978; part-time $290.75 per credit hour. Tuition, nonresident: full-time $15,282; part-time $636.75 per credit hour. *Required fees:* $2106; $87.75 per credit hour. *Financial support:* In 2011–12, fellowships with full tuition reimbursements (averaging $8,550 per year), research assistantships with full tuition reimbursements (averaging $8,550 per year), teaching assistantships with full tuition reimbursements (averaging $8,550 per year) were awarded; career-related internships or fieldwork, Federal Work-Study, scholarships/grants, health care benefits, and unspecified assistantships also available. Support available to part-time students. Financial award application deadline: 11/15; financial award applicants required to submit FAFSA. *Unit head:* Dr. Lucia Vazquez, Program Administrator, 217-206-7337, Fax: 217-206-6217, E-mail: lvazq1@uis.edu. *Application contact:* Dr. Lynn Pardie, Office of Graduate Studies, 800-252-8533, Fax: 217-206-7623, E-mail: lpard1@uis.edu. Web site: http://www.uis.edu/biology.

University of Illinois at Urbana–Champaign, Graduate College, College of Liberal Arts and Sciences, School of Chemical Sciences, Champaign, IL 61820. Offers MA, MS, PhD, MS/JD, MS/MBA. *Faculty:* 42 full-time (7 women), 2 part-time/adjunct (1 woman). *Students:* 382 full-time (132 women), 5 part-time (1 woman); includes 51 minority (4 Black or African American, non-Hispanic/Latino; 1 American Indian or Alaska Native, non-Hispanic/Latino; 28 Asian, non-Hispanic/Latino; 9 Hispanic/Latino; 9 Two or more races, non-Hispanic/Latino), 122 international. 853 applicants, 11% accepted, 90 enrolled. In 2011, 39 master's, 65 doctorates awarded. *Entrance requirements:* For master's, minimum GPA of 3.0. *Application deadline:* Applications are processed on a rolling basis. Application fee: $75 ($90 for international students). Electronic applications accepted. *Expenses:* Contact institution. *Financial support:* In 2011–12, 146 fellowships, 247 research assistantships, 201 teaching assistantships were awarded; tuition waivers (full and partial) also available. *Unit head:* Andrew A. Gewirth, Director, 217-333-8329, Fax: 217-333-2685, E-mail: agewirth@illinois.edu. *Application contact:* Cheryl Kappes, Office Manager, 217-333-5070, Fax: 217-333-3120, E-mail: dambache@illinois.edu. Web site: http://www.scs.illinois.edu/.

University of Illinois at Urbana–Champaign, Graduate College, College of Liberal Arts and Sciences, School of Integrative Biology, Champaign, IL 61820. Offers MS, MST, PSM, PhD. *Faculty:* 32 full-time (11 women). *Students:* 48 full-time (29 women), 14 part-time (3 women); includes 14 minority (1 Black or African American, non-Hispanic/Latino; 1 American Indian or Alaska Native, non-Hispanic/Latino; 8 Asian, non-Hispanic/Latino; 1 Hispanic/Latino; 3 Two or more races, non-Hispanic/Latino), 7 international. 98 applicants, 27% accepted, 12 enrolled. In 2011, 31 master's, 11 doctorates awarded. *Application deadline:* Applications are processed on a rolling basis.

Biological and Biomedical Sciences—General

Application fee: $75 ($90 for international students). Electronic applications accepted. *Financial support:* In 2011–12, 19 fellowships, 79 research assistantships, 81 teaching assistantships were awarded; tuition waivers (full and partial) also available. *Unit head:* Evan De Lucia, Director, 217-333-6177, Fax: 217-244-1224, E-mail: delucia@illinois.edu. *Application contact:* Carol Hall, Office Manager, 217-333-8208, Fax: 217-244-1224, E-mail: cahall@illinois.edu. Web site: http://sib.illinois.edu/.

University of Indianapolis, Graduate Programs, College of Arts and Sciences, Department of Biology, Indianapolis, IN 46227-3697. Offers human biology (MS). Part-time and evening/weekend programs available. *Faculty:* 4 full-time (1 woman). *Students:* 9 full-time (8 women), 9 part-time (all women), 1 international. Average age 26. In 2011, 3 master's awarded. *Degree requirements:* For master's, thesis. *Entrance requirements:* For master's, GRE General Test, 3 letters of recommendation; minimum GPA of 3.0; BA/BS in anthropology, biology, human biology or closely-related field, resume. Additional exam requirements/recommendations for international students: Required—TOEFL (minimum score 550 paper-based). *Application deadline:* For fall admission, 1/15 for domestic and international students. Applications are processed on a rolling basis. Application fee: $30. Tuition and fees vary according to degree level and program. *Financial support:* Federal Work-Study, scholarships/grants, and tuition waivers (full and partial) available. Support available to part-time students. Financial award application deadline: 5/1; financial award applicants required to submit FAFSA. *Unit head:* Dr. L. Mark Harrison, Chairperson, 317-788-3264, E-mail: harrison@uindy.edu. *Application contact:* Dr. Stephen P. Nawrocki, Director, Graduate Program in Human Biology, 317-788-3486, Fax: 317-788-3480, E-mail: snawrocki@uindy.edu. Web site: http://biology.uindy.edu/mshumanbio/.

The University of Iowa, Graduate College, College of Liberal Arts and Sciences, Department of Biology, Iowa City, IA 52242-1324. Offers biology (MS, PhD); cell and developmental biology (MS, PhD); evolution (MS, PhD); genetics (MS, PhD); neurobiology (MS, PhD). Terminal master's awarded for partial completion of doctoral program. *Degree requirements:* For master's, thesis optional, exam; for doctorate, comprehensive exam, thesis/dissertation. *Entrance requirements:* For master's and doctorate, GRE General Test, minimum GPA of 3.0. Additional exam requirements/recommendations for international students: Required—TOEFL (minimum score 600 paper-based; 250 computer-based; 100 iBT). Electronic applications accepted. *Faculty research:* Neurobiology, evolutionary biology, genetics, cell and developmental biology.

The University of Iowa, Roy J. and Lucille A. Carver College of Medicine and Graduate College, Biosciences Program, Iowa City, IA 52242-1316. Offers anatomy and biology (PhD); biochemistry (PhD); biology (PhD); biomedical engineering (PhD); chemistry (PhD); free radical and radiation biology (PhD); genetics (PhD); human toxicology (PhD); immunology (PhD); microbiology (PhD); molecular and cellular biology (PhD); molecular physiology and biophysics (PhD); neuroscience (PhD); pharmacology (PhD); physical therapy and rehabilitation science (PhD); speech and hearing (PhD). *Faculty:* 310 full-time. *Students:* 9 full-time (5 women); includes 4 minority (1 Black or African American, non-Hispanic/Latino; 2 Asian, non-Hispanic/Latino; 1 Hispanic/Latino). 225 applicants. *Degree requirements:* For doctorate, thesis/dissertation. *Entrance requirements:* For doctorate, GRE General Test, minimum GPA of 3.0. Additional exam requirements/recommendations for international students: Required—TOEFL (minimum score 600 paper-based; 250 computer-based; 100 iBT). *Application deadline:* For fall admission, 1/15 priority date for domestic students, 1/15 for international students. Applications are processed on a rolling basis. Application fee: $60 ($100 for international students). Electronic applications accepted. *Expenses:* Contact institution. *Financial support:* In 2011–12, 9 students received support, including 9 research assistantships with full tuition reimbursements available (averaging $25,000 per year); fellowships, teaching assistantships, and health care benefits also available. *Unit head:* Dr. Douglas Spitz, Director, 319-335-8001, Fax: 319-335-7656, E-mail: andrew-russo@uiowa.edu.

Application contact: Jodi M. Graff, Program Associate, 319-335-8305, Fax: 319-335-7656, E-mail: biosciences-admissions@uiowa.edu. Web site: http://www.biology.uiowa.edu/graduate.php.

The University of Iowa, Roy J. and Lucille A. Carver College of Medicine and Graduate College, Graduate Programs in Medicine, Iowa City, IA 52242-1316. Offers MA, MPAS, MS, DPT, PhD, JD/MHA, MBA/MHA, MD/JD, MD/PhD, MHA/MA, MHA/MS, MPH/MHA, MS/MA, MS/MS. Part-time programs available. *Faculty:* 130 full-time (31 women), 94 part-time/adjunct (41 women). *Students:* 301 full-time (175 women), 4 part-time (1 woman); includes 24 minority (3 Black or African American, non-Hispanic/Latino; 6 American Indian or Alaska Native, non-Hispanic/Latino; 10 Asian, non-Hispanic/Latino; 4 Hispanic/Latino; 1 Two or more races, non-Hispanic/Latino), 25 international. 1,219 applicants, 8% accepted, 74 enrolled. In 2011, 27 master's, 21 doctorates awarded. *Degree requirements:* For doctorate, thesis/dissertation. Electronic applications accepted. *Expenses:* Contact institution. *Financial support:* In 2011–12, 162 students received support, including fellowships (averaging $25,500 per year), research assistantships (averaging $25,500 per year), teaching assistantships (averaging $25,500 per year); career-related internships or fieldwork, Federal Work-Study, institutionally sponsored loans, health care benefits, and tuition waivers (full and partial) also available. Support available to part-time students. Financial award applicants required to submit FAFSA. *Unit head:* Dr. Paul B. Rothman, Dean, 319-384-4590, Fax: 319-335-8318, E-mail: paul-rothman@uiowa.edu. *Application contact:* Betty Wood, Associate Director of Admissions, 319-335-1525, Fax: 319-335-1535, E-mail: admissions@uiowa.edu.

The University of Kansas, University of Kansas Medical Center, School of Medicine, Interdisciplinary Graduate Program in Biomedical Sciences (IGPBS), Kansas City, KS 66160. Offers MA, MPH, MS, PhD, MD/MPH, MD/MS, MD/PhD. *Students:* 19 full-time (10 women), 9 international. Average age 26, 180 applicants, 22% accepted, 17 enrolled. Terminal master's awarded for partial completion of doctoral program. *Degree requirements:* For master's, thesis; for doctorate, comprehensive exam, thesis/dissertation. *Entrance requirements:* For master's and doctorate, GRE. Additional exam requirements/recommendations for international students: Required—TOEFL. *Application deadline:* For fall admission, 1/15 priority date for domestic students, 1/15 for international students. Applications are processed on a rolling basis. Application fee: $60. Electronic applications accepted. Tuition and fees vary according to course load, campus/location, program and reciprocity agreements. *Financial support:* In 2011–12, 3 research assistantships with full tuition reimbursements (averaging $24,000 per year), 18 teaching assistantships with full tuition reimbursements (averaging $24,000 per year) were awarded; scholarships/grants and unspecified assistantships also available. Financial award application deadline: 2/14; financial award applicants required to submit FAFSA. *Faculty research:* Cardiovascular biology, neurosciences, signal transduction and cancer biology, molecular biology and genetics, developmental biology. *Unit head:* Dr. Michael J. Werle, Director, 913-588-7491, Fax: 913-588-2710, E-mail: mwerle@kumc.edu. *Application contact:* Miranda Olenhouse, Coordinator, 913-588-2719, Fax: 913-588-2711, E-mail: molenhouse@kumc.edu. Web site: http://www.kumc.edu/igpbs/.

See Display below and Close-Up on page 119.

University of Kentucky, Graduate School, College of Arts and Sciences, Program in Biology, Lexington, KY 40506-0032. Offers MS, PhD. *Degree requirements:* For master's, comprehensive exam, thesis optional; for doctorate, comprehensive exam, thesis/dissertation. *Entrance requirements:* For master's, GRE General Test, minimum undergraduate GPA of 2.75; for doctorate, GRE General Test, minimum graduate GPA of 3.0. Additional exam requirements/recommendations for international students: Required—TOEFL (minimum score 550 paper-based; 213 computer-based). Electronic

You make the Choice

In the Interdisciplinary Graduate Program
you choose research rotations and which lab to join.
You will receive a stipend of $24,000 per year.

For more Information:

Michael J. Werle, Ph.D., Director
Interdisciplinary Graduate Program
in the Biomedical Sciences
University of Kansas Medical Center
Kansas City, KS 66160
IGPBS@kumc.edu
www.kumc.edu/igpbs

applications accepted. *Faculty research:* General biology, microbiology, &ITDrosophila&RO molecular genetics, molecular virology, multiple loci inheritance.

University of Kentucky, Graduate School, Graduate School Programs from the College of Medicine, Lexington, KY 40506-0032. Offers MS, PhD, MD/PhD. *Degree requirements:* For master's, comprehensive exam, thesis (for some programs); for doctorate, comprehensive exam, thesis/dissertation. *Entrance requirements:* For master's, GRE General Test, minimum undergraduate GPA of 2.75; for doctorate, GRE General Test, minimum undergraduate GPA of 3.0. Additional exam requirements/recommendations for international students: Required—TOEFL (minimum score 550 paper-based; 213 computer-based). Electronic applications accepted.

University of Lethbridge, School of Graduate Studies, Lethbridge, AB T1K 3M4, Canada. Offers accounting (MScM); addictions counseling (M Sc); agricultural biotechnology (M Sc); agricultural studies (M Sc, MA); anthropology (MA); archaeology (MA); art (MA, MFA); biochemistry (M Sc); biological sciences (M Sc); biomolecular science (PhD); biosystems and biodiversity (PhD); Canadian studies (MA); chemistry (M Sc); computer science (M Sc); computer science and geographical information science (M Sc); counseling psychology (M Ed); dramatic arts (MA); earth, space, and physical science (PhD); economics (MA); educational leadership (M Ed); English (MA); environmental science (M Sc); evolution and behavior (PhD); exercise science (M Sc); finance (MScM); French (MA); French/German (MA); French/Spanish (MA); general education (M Ed); general management (MScM); geography (M Sc, MA); German (MA); health science (M Sc); history (MA); human resource management and labour relations (MScM); individualized multidisciplinary (M Sc, MA); information systems (MScM); international management (MScM); kinesiology (M Sc, MA); management (M Sc, MA); marketing (MScM); mathematics (M Sc); music (M Mus, MA); Native American studies (MA); neuroscience (M Sc, PhD); new media (MA); nursing (M Sc); philosophy (MA); physics (M Sc); policy and strategy (MScM); political science (MA); psychology (M Sc, MA); religious studies (MA); social sciences (MA); sociology (MA); theatre and dramatic arts (MFA); theoretical and computational science (PhD); urban and regional studies (MA); women's studies (MA). Part-time and evening/weekend programs available. *Degree requirements:* For doctorate, comprehensive exam, thesis/dissertation. *Entrance requirements:* For master's, GMAT (M Sc in management), bachelor's degree in related field, minimum GPA of 3.0 during previous 20 graded semester courses, 2 years teaching or related experience (M Ed); for doctorate, master's degree, minimum graduate GPA of 3.5. Additional exam requirements/recommendations for international students: Required—TOEFL. *Faculty research:* Movement and brain plasticity, gibberellin physiology, photosynthesis, carbon cycling, molecular properties of main-group ring components.

University of Louisiana at Lafayette, College of Sciences, Department of Biology, Lafayette, LA 70504. Offers biology (MS); environmental and evolutionary biology (PhD). Terminal master's awarded for partial completion of doctoral program. *Degree requirements:* For master's, thesis; for doctorate, 2 foreign languages, comprehensive exam, thesis/dissertation. *Entrance requirements:* For master's, GRE General Test, minimum GPA of 2.75; for doctorate, GRE General Test, GRE Subject Test, minimum GPA of 3.0. Additional exam requirements/recommendations for international students: Required—TOEFL (minimum score 550 paper-based; 213 computer-based). Electronic applications accepted. *Faculty research:* Structure and ultrastructure, system biology, ecology, processes, environmental physiology.

University of Louisiana at Monroe, Graduate School, College of Arts and Sciences, Department of Biology, Monroe, LA 71209-0001. Offers MS. *Faculty:* 12 full-time (6 women). *Students:* 21 full-time (11 women), 7 part-time (5 women); includes 8 minority (2 Black or African American, non-Hispanic/Latino; 3 Asian, non-Hispanic/Latino; 3 Two or more races, non-Hispanic/Latino), 1 international. Average age 25. 14 applicants, 50% accepted, 5 enrolled. In 2011, 13 master's awarded. *Entrance requirements:* For master's, GRE General Test, minimum GPA of 2.8 overall or 3.0 during last 21 hours of biology. Additional exam requirements/recommendations for international students: Required—TOEFL (minimum score 500 paper-based; 113 computer-based; 61 iBT). *Application deadline:* For fall admission, 8/24 priority date for domestic students, 7/1 for international students; for winter admission, 12/14 priority date for domestic students; for spring admission, 1/19 for domestic students, 11/1 for international students. Applications are processed on a rolling basis. Application fee: $20 ($30 for international students). Electronic applications accepted. *Expenses:* Tuition, state resident: full-time $3436; part-time $240 per credit hour. Tuition, nonresident: full-time $3436; part-time $240 per credit hour. *International tuition:* $10,733 full-time. *Required fees:* $1460.90. *Financial support:* In 2011–12, 17 teaching assistantships with full tuition reimbursements (averaging $4,000 per year) were awarded; career-related internships or fieldwork, Federal Work-Study, and unspecified assistantships also available. Financial award application deadline: 4/1; financial award applicants required to submit FAFSA. *Faculty research:* Fish systematics and zoogeography, taxonomy and distribution of Louisiana plants, aquatic biology, secondary succession, microbial ecology. *Unit head:* Dr. Sushma Krishnamurthy, Department Head, 318-342-1813, Fax: 318-342-3312, E-mail: krishnamurthy@ulm.edu. *Application contact:* Dr. Kim M. Tolson, Professor, 318-342-1805, Fax: 318-342-3312, E-mail: tolson@ulm.edu. Web site: http://www.ulm.edu/biology.

University of Louisville, Graduate School, College of Arts and Sciences, Department of Biology, Louisville, KY 40292-0001. Offers biology (MS); environmental biology (PhD). *Degree requirements:* For master's, thesis (for some programs); for doctorate, thesis/dissertation. *Entrance requirements:* For master's and doctorate, GRE General Test. *Expenses:* Tuition, state resident: full-time $9692; part-time $539 per credit hour. Tuition, nonresident: full-time $20,168; part-time $1121 per credit hour. Tuition and fees vary according to program and reciprocity agreements.

University of Maine, Graduate School, College of Natural Sciences, Forestry, and Agriculture, Department of Biological Sciences, Program in Biological Sciences, Orono, ME 04469. Offers PhD. *Students:* 7 full-time (3 women), 5 part-time (2 women); includes 1 minority (Asian, non-Hispanic/Latino). Average age 32. 2 applicants, 50% accepted, 1 enrolled. In 2011, 2 degrees awarded. *Degree requirements:* For doctorate, thesis/dissertation. *Entrance requirements:* For doctorate, GRE General Test. Additional exam requirements/recommendations for international students: Required—TOEFL. *Application deadline:* For fall admission, 2/1 priority date for domestic students. Applications are processed on a rolling basis. Application fee: $65. Electronic applications accepted. *Expenses:* Tuition, state resident: full-time $5016. Tuition, nonresident: full-time $14,424. *Financial support:* Application deadline: 3/1. *Unit head:* Dr. Jody Jellison, Coordinator, 207-581-2551. *Application contact:* Scott G. Delcourt, Associate Dean of the Graduate School, 207-581-3291, Fax: 207-581-3232, E-mail: graduate@maine.edu. Web site: http://www2.umaine.edu/graduate/.

University of Maine, Graduate School, Program in Biomedical Sciences, Orono, ME 04469. Offers biomedical engineering (PhD); cell and molecular biology (PhD); neuroscience (PhD); toxicology (PhD). *Students:* 11 full-time (7 women), 19 part-time (11 women), 8 international. Average age 29. 32 applicants, 31% accepted, 8 enrolled. In 2011, 3 degrees awarded. Application fee: $65. *Expenses:* Tuition, state resident: full-time $5016. Tuition, nonresident: full-time $14,424. *Financial support:* In 2011–12, 2 fellowships with full tuition reimbursements (averaging $18,000 per year), 8 research assistantships with full tuition reimbursements (averaging $23,000 per year) were awarded. *Unit head:* Dr. Carol Kim, Unit Head, 207-581-2803. *Application contact:* Scott G. Delcourt, Associate Dean of the Graduate School, 207-581-3291, Fax: 207-581-3232, E-mail: graduate@maine.edu. Web site: http://www2.umaine.edu/graduate.

The University of Manchester, Faculty of Life Sciences, Manchester, United Kingdom. Offers adaptive organismal biology (M Phil, PhD); animal biology (M Phil, PhD); biochemistry (M Phil, PhD); bioinformatics (M Phil, PhD); biomolecular sciences (M Phil, PhD); biotechnology (M Phil, PhD); cell biology (M Phil, PhD); cell matrix research (M Phil, PhD); channels and transporters (M Phil, PhD); developmental biology (M Phil, PhD); Egyptology (M Phil, PhD); environmental biology (M Phil, PhD); evolutionary biology (M Phil, PhD); gene expression (M Phil, PhD); genetics (M Phil, PhD); history of science, technology and medicine (M Phil, PhD); immunology (M Phil, PhD); integrative neurobiology and behavior (M Phil, PhD); membrane trafficking (M Phil, PhD); microbiology (M Phil, PhD); molecular and cellular neuroscience (M Phil, PhD); molecular biology (M Phil, PhD); molecular cancer studies (M Phil, PhD); neuroscience (M Phil, PhD); ophthalmology (M Phil, PhD); optometry (M Phil, PhD); organelle function (M Phil, PhD); pharmacology (M Phil, PhD); physiology (M Phil, PhD); plant sciences (M Phil, PhD); stem cell research (M Phil, PhD); structural biology (M Phil, PhD); systems neuroscience (M Phil, PhD); toxicology (M Phil, PhD).

The University of Manchester, School of Chemical Engineering and Analytical Science, Manchester, United Kingdom. Offers biocatalysis (M Phil, PhD); chemical engineering (M Phil, PhD); chemical engineering and analytical science (M Phil, D Eng, PhD); colloids, crystals, interfaces and materials (M Phil, PhD); environment and sustainable technology (M Phil, PhD); instrumentation (M Phil, PhD); multi-scale modeling (M Phil, PhD); process integration (M Phil, PhD); systems biology (M Phil, PhD).

The University of Manchester, School of Materials, Manchester, United Kingdom. Offers advanced aerospace materials engineering (M Sc); advanced metallic systems (PhD); biomedical materials (M Phil, M Sc, PhD); ceramics and glass (M Phil, M Sc, PhD); composite materials (M Sc, PhD); corrosion and protection (M Phil, M Sc, PhD); materials (M Phil, PhD); metallic materials (M Phil, M Sc, PhD); nanostructural materials (M Phil, M Sc, PhD); paper science (M Phil, M Sc, PhD); polymer science and engineering (M Phil, M Sc, PhD); technical textiles (M Sc); textile design, fashion and management (M Phil, M Sc, PhD); textile science and technology (M Phil, M Sc, PhD); textiles (M Phil, PhD); textiles and fashion (M Ent).

The University of Manchester, School of Medicine, Manchester, United Kingdom. Offers M Phil, PhD.

University of Manitoba, Faculty of Graduate Studies, Faculty of Science, Department of Biological Sciences, Winnipeg, MB R3T 2N2, Canada. Offers botany (M Sc, PhD); ecology (M Sc, PhD); zoology (M Sc, PhD).

University of Manitoba, Faculty of Medicine and Faculty of Graduate Studies, Graduate Programs in Medicine, Winnipeg, MB R3T 2N2, Canada. Offers M Sc, MPH, PhD, G Dip, MD/PhD. *Accreditation:* LCME/AMA. Part-time programs available. *Expenses:* Contact institution.

University of Maryland, Baltimore, Graduate School, Graduate Program in Life Sciences, Baltimore, MD 21201. Offers biochemistry and molecular biology (MS, PhD), including biochemistry; epidemiology (PhD); gerontology (PhD); molecular medicine (MS, PhD), including cancer biology (PhD), cell and molecular physiology (PhD), human genetics and genomic medicine (PhD), molecular medicine (MS), molecular toxicology and pharmacology (PhD); molecular microbiology and immunology (PhD); neuroscience (PhD); physical rehabilitation science (PhD); toxicology (MS, PhD); MD/MS; MD/PhD. *Students:* 262 full-time (164 women), 49 part-time (30 women); includes 74 minority (21 Black or African American, non-Hispanic/Latino; 1 American Indian or Alaska Native, non-Hispanic/Latino; 30 Asian, non-Hispanic/Latino; 14 Hispanic/Latino; 8 Two or more races, non-Hispanic/Latino), 46 international. Average age 29. 719 applicants, 22% accepted, 64 enrolled. In 2011, 20 master's, 35 doctorates awarded. *Degree requirements:* For master's, comprehensive exam (for some programs), thesis (for some programs); for doctorate, comprehensive exam, thesis/dissertation. *Entrance requirements:* For master's and doctorate, GRE. Additional exam requirements/recommendations for international students: Required—TOEFL (minimum score 550 paper-based; 80 iBT); Recommended—IELTS (minimum score 7). *Application deadline:* For fall admission, 1/15 for domestic and international students. Application fee: $50. Electronic applications accepted. *Financial support:* In 2011–12, research assistantships with partial tuition reimbursements (averaging $25,000 per year) were awarded; fellowships, scholarships/grants, health care benefits, and unspecified assistantships also available. Financial award application deadline: 3/1. *Faculty research:* Cancer, reproduction, cardiovascular, immunology. *Unit head:* Dr. Margaret Merryl McCarthy, Assistant Dean for Graduate Studies, 410-706-2655, Fax: 410-706-8341, E-mail: mmcarthy@umaryland.edu. *Application contact:* Keith T. Brooks, Assistant Dean, 410-706-7131, Fax: 410-706-3473, E-mail: kbrooks@umaryland.edu. Web site: http://lifesciences.umaryland.edu.

University of Maryland, Baltimore County, Graduate School, College of Arts, Humanities and Social Sciences, Department of Education, Program in Teaching, Baltimore, MD 21250. Offers early childhood education (MAT); elementary education (MAT); secondary education (MAT), including social studies; secondary education (MAT), including art, biology, chemistry, dance, earth/space science, English, foreign language, mathematics, music, physics, theatre. Part-time and evening/weekend programs available. *Faculty:* 24 full-time (18 women), 25 part-time/adjunct (19 women). *Students:* 46 full-time (35 women), 64 part-time (39 women); includes 24 minority (8 Black or African American, non-Hispanic/Latino; 7 Asian, non-Hispanic/Latino; 6 Hispanic/Latino; 1 Native Hawaiian or other Pacific Islander, non-Hispanic/Latino; 2 Two or more races, non-Hispanic/Latino), 4 international. Average age 31. 88 applicants, 57% accepted, 39 enrolled. In 2011, 106 master's awarded. *Degree requirements:* For master's, comprehensive exam (for some programs), thesis (for some programs). *Entrance requirements:* For master's, PRAXIS I or GRE (minimum score of 1000), minimum GPA of 3.0. Additional exam requirements/recommendations for international students: Required—TOEFL. *Application deadline:* For fall admission, 6/1 for domestic students; for spring admission, 11/1 for domestic students. Applications are processed on a rolling basis. Application fee: $50. Electronic applications accepted. *Financial support:* In 2011–12, 6 students received support, including teaching assistantships with full and partial tuition reimbursements available (averaging $12,000 per year); career-related internships or fieldwork, Federal Work-Study, scholarships/grants, tuition waivers, and unspecified assistantships also available. Financial award application deadline: 3/1. *Faculty research:* STEM teacher education, culturally sensitive pedagogy, ESOL/bilingual education, early childhood education, language, literacy and culture. *Unit head:* Dr. Susan M. Blunck, Graduate Program Director, 410-455-2869, Fax: 410-455-3986, E-mail: blunck@umbc.edu. *Application contact:* Cheryl Johnson, 410-455-3388, E-mail: blackwel@umbc.edu. Web site: http://www.umbc.edu/education/.

University of Maryland, Baltimore County, Graduate School, College of Natural and Mathematical Sciences, Department of Biological Sciences, Baltimore, MD 21250. Offers applied molecular biology (MS); biological sciences (MS, PhD); biotechnology management (MPS, Graduate Certificate); marine-estuarine-environmental sciences (MS); molecular and cell biology (PhD); neuroscience and cognitive sciences (PhD).

Part-time programs available. *Entrance requirements:* For master's and doctorate, GRE General Test, minimum GPA of 3.0. Additional exam requirements/recommendations for international students: Required—TOEFL. *Application deadline:* For fall admission, 1/15 for domestic students, 12/15 for international students. Applications are processed on a rolling basis. Application fee: $50. Electronic applications accepted. *Financial support:* Career-related internships or fieldwork and tuition waivers (partial) available. *Unit head:* Dr. Lasse Lindahl, Chairman, 410-455-2261, Fax: 410-455-3875. *Application contact:* Dr. Jeff Leips, Director, 410-455-3669, Fax: 410-455-3875, E-mail: biograd@umbc.edu.

University of Maryland, College Park, Academic Affairs, College of Computer, Mathematical and Natural Sciences, Department of Biology, PhD Program in Biological Sciences, College Park, MD 20742. Offers behavior, ecology, evolution, and systematics (PhD); computational biology, bioinformatics, and genomics (PhD); molecular and cellular biology (PhD); physiological systems (PhD). *Students:* 68 full-time (41 women), 4 part-time (2 women); includes 13 minority (3 Black or African American, non-Hispanic/Latino; 4 Asian, non-Hispanic/Latino; 5 Hispanic/Latino; 1 Two or more races, non-Hispanic/Latino), 21 international. 380 applicants, 15% accepted, 22 enrolled. *Degree requirements:* For doctorate, comprehensive exam, thesis/dissertation, present thesis work in seminar. *Entrance requirements:* For doctorate, GRE General Test; GRE Subject Test in biology (recommended), academic transcripts, statement of purpose/research interests, 3 letters of recommendation. Additional exam requirements/recommendations for international students: Required—TOEFL. *Application deadline:* For fall admission, 12/15 for domestic and international students. Applications are processed on a rolling basis. Application fee: $75. Electronic applications accepted. *Expenses:* Tuition, state resident: part-time $525 per credit hour. Tuition, nonresident: part-time $1131 per credit hour. *Required fees:* $386.31 per term. Tuition and fees vary according to program. *Financial support:* In 2011–12, 11 fellowships with full and partial tuition reimbursements (averaging $14,406 per year), 16 research assistantships (averaging $19,495 per year), 41 teaching assistantships (averaging $18,734 per year) were awarded. *Unit head:* Dr. Barbara Thorne, Director, 301-405-6905, E-mail: bthorne@umd.edu. *Application contact:* Dr. Charles A. Caramello, Dean of Graduate School, 301-405-0358, Fax: 301-314-9305. Web site: http://bisi.umd.edu/biologicalsciencesgraduateprogrambisi.

University of Maryland, College Park, Academic Affairs, College of Computer, Mathematical and Natural Sciences, Department of Biology, Program in Biology, College Park, MD 20742. Offers MS, PhD. Part-time and evening/weekend programs available. *Students:* 38 full-time (25 women), 1 (woman) part-time; includes 4 minority (1 Black or African American, non-Hispanic/Latino; 1 Asian, non-Hispanic/Latino; 2 Two or more races, non-Hispanic/Latino), 11 international. In 2011, 5 master's, 4 doctorates awarded. Terminal master's awarded for partial completion of doctoral program. *Degree requirements:* For master's, comprehensive exam, thesis optional; for doctorate, thesis/dissertation, oral exam. *Expenses:* Tuition, state resident: part-time $525 per credit hour. Tuition, nonresident: part-time $1131 per credit hour. *Required fees:* $386.31 per term. Tuition and fees vary according to program. *Financial support:* In 2011–12, 6 fellowships with full and partial tuition reimbursements (averaging $24,843 per year), 6 research assistantships with tuition reimbursements (averaging $19,721 per year), 6 teaching assistantships with tuition reimbursements (averaging $19,550 per year) were awarded. Financial award application deadline: 2/1; financial award applicants required to submit FAFSA. *Unit head:* Dr. Barbara Thorne, Director, 301-405-7947, E-mail: bthorne@umd.edu. *Application contact:* Dr. Charles A. Caramello, Dean of Graduate School, 301-405-0358, Fax: 301-314-9305.

University of Maryland, College Park, Academic Affairs, College of Computer, Mathematical and Natural Sciences, Program in Life Sciences, College Park, MD 20742. Offers MLS. *Students:* 1 (woman) full-time, 97 part-time (76 women); includes 21 minority (12 Black or African American, non-Hispanic/Latino; 2 Asian, non-Hispanic/Latino; 5 Hispanic/Latino; 2 Two or more races, non-Hispanic/Latino), 1 international. 44 applicants, 91% accepted, 25 enrolled. In 2011, 41 master's awarded. *Degree requirements:* For master's, scholarly paper. *Entrance requirements:* For master's, 1 year of teaching experience, letters of recommendation. *Application deadline:* Applications are processed on a rolling basis. Application fee: $75. Electronic applications accepted. *Expenses:* Tuition, state resident: part-time $525 per credit hour. Tuition, nonresident: part-time $1131 per credit hour. *Required fees:* $386.31 per term. Tuition and fees vary according to program. *Financial support:* Fellowships, research assistantships, teaching assistantships, Federal Work-Study, and scholarships/grants available. Support available to part-time students. Financial award applicants required to submit FAFSA. *Faculty research:* Genetic engineering, gene therapy, ecology, biocomplexity. *Unit head:* Dr. Paul Mazzocchi, Director, 301-405-8482, E-mail: pmazzocc@deans.umd.edu. *Application contact:* Dr. Charles A. Caramello, Dean of Graduate School, 301-405-0358, Fax: 301-314-9305.

University of Massachusetts Amherst, Graduate School, College of Natural Sciences, Department of Animal Biotechnology and Biomedical Sciences, Amherst, MA 01003. Offers MS, PhD. Part-time programs available. *Faculty:* 23 full-time (10 women). *Students:* 27 full-time (16 women), 9 international. Average age 30. 51 applicants, 18% accepted, 6 enrolled. In 2011, 6 master's, 2 doctorates awarded. Terminal master's awarded for partial completion of doctoral program. *Degree requirements:* For master's, thesis or alternative; for doctorate, comprehensive exam, thesis/dissertation. *Entrance requirements:* For master's and doctorate, GRE General Test. Additional exam requirements/recommendations for international students: Required—TOEFL (minimum score 550 paper-based; 213 computer-based; 80 iBT), IELTS (minimum score 6.5). *Application deadline:* For fall admission, 2/1 for domestic and international students; for spring admission, 10/1 for domestic and international students. Applications are processed on a rolling basis. Application fee: $50 ($65 for international students). Electronic applications accepted. Tuition and fees vary according to course load, campus/location and program. *Financial support:* Fellowships with full and partial tuition reimbursements, research assistantships with full and partial tuition reimbursements, teaching assistantships with full and partial tuition reimbursements, career-related internships or fieldwork, Federal Work-Study, scholarships/grants, traineeships, health care benefits, tuition waivers (full and partial), and unspecified assistantships available. Support available to part-time students. Financial award application deadline: 2/1. *Unit head:* Dr. Lisa Minter, Graduate Program Director, 413-577-1193, Fax: 413-577-1150. *Application contact:* Lindsay DeSantis, Interim Supervisor of Admissions, 413-545-0722, Fax: 413-577-0010, E-mail: gradadm@grad.umass.edu. Web site: http://www.vasci.umass.edu/graduate-program-overview.

University of Massachusetts Boston, Office of Graduate Studies, College of Science and Mathematics, Program in Biology, Boston, MA 02125-3393. Offers MS. Part-time and evening/weekend programs available. *Degree requirements:* For master's, thesis, oral exams. *Entrance requirements:* For master's, GRE General Test, GRE Subject Test, minimum GPA of 2.75. *Faculty research:* Microbial ecology, population and conservation genetics energetics of insect locomotion, science education, evolution and ecology of marine invertebrates.

University of Massachusetts Boston, Office of Graduate Studies, College of Science and Mathematics, Program in Biotechnology and Biomedical Science, Boston, MA 02125-3393. Offers MS. Part-time and evening/weekend programs available. *Degree requirements:* For master's, comprehensive exam, thesis optional, oral exams. *Entrance requirements:* For master's, GRE General Test, GRE Subject Test, minimum GPA of 2.75, 3.0 in science and math. *Faculty research:* Evolutionary and molecular immunology, molecular genetics, tissue culture, computerized laboratory technology.

University of Massachusetts Dartmouth, Graduate School, College of Arts and Sciences, Department of Biology, North Dartmouth, MA 02747-2300. Offers biology (MS); marine biology (MS). Part-time programs available. *Faculty:* 16 full-time (6 women), 4 part-time/adjunct (1 woman). *Students:* 15 full-time (10 women), 9 part-time (7 women); includes 2 minority (1 Asian, non-Hispanic/Latino; 1 Hispanic/Latino). Average age 28. 38 applicants, 50% accepted, 8 enrolled. In 2011, 3 degrees awarded. *Degree requirements:* For master's, thesis. *Entrance requirements:* For master's, GRE General Test, GRE Subject Test, statement of intent, resume, 3 letters of recommendation. Additional exam requirements/recommendations for international students: Required—TOEFL (minimum score 533 paper-based; 200 computer-based; 72 iBT). *Application deadline:* For fall admission, 2/15 for domestic students, 1/15 for international students. Application fee: $40 ($60 for international students). Electronic applications accepted. *Expenses:* Tuition, state resident: full-time $2071; part-time $86.29 per credit. Tuition, nonresident: full-time $8099; part-time $337.46 per credit. *Required fees:* $438.58 per credit. Part-time tuition and fees vary according to class time, course load, degree level and reciprocity agreements. *Financial support:* In 2011–12, 1 research assistantship with full tuition reimbursement (averaging $4,500 per year), 10 teaching assistantships with full tuition reimbursements (averaging $15,000 per year) were awarded; Federal Work-Study and unspecified assistantships also available. Support available to part-time students. Financial award application deadline: 3/1; financial award applicants required to submit FAFSA. *Faculty research:* Fish biology, antibody-mediated protection, bottlenose dolphins, adaptations in fish via genetics, evolutionary biology. *Total annual research expenditures:* $789,879. *Unit head:* Dr. Diego Bernal, Graduate Program Director, 508-999-8307, Fax: 508-999-8196, E-mail: dbernal@umassd.edu. *Application contact:* Elan Turcotte-Shamski, Graduate Admissions Officer, 508-999-8604, Fax: 508-999-8183, E-mail: graduate@umassd.edu. Web site: http://www.umassd.edu/cas/biology/.

University of Massachusetts Lowell, College of Sciences, Department of Biological Sciences, Lowell, MA 01854-2881. Offers biochemistry (PhD); biological sciences (MS); biotechnology (MS). Part-time programs available. *Degree requirements:* For master's, thesis; for doctorate, thesis/dissertation. *Entrance requirements:* For master's and doctorate, GRE General Test. Electronic applications accepted.

University of Massachusetts Worcester, Graduate School of Biomedical Sciences, Worcester, MA 01655-0115. Offers biochemistry and molecular pharmacology (PhD); bioinformatics and computational biology (PhD); cancer biology (PhD); cell biology (PhD); clinical and population health research (PhD); clinical investigation (MS); immunology and virology (PhD); interdisciplinary graduate program (PhD); molecular genetics and microbiology (PhD); neuroscience (PhD); DVM/PhD; MD/PhD. *Faculty:* 1,427 full-time (526 women), 309 part-time/adjunct (196 women). *Students:* 416 full-time (225 women); includes 47 minority (12 Black or African American, non-Hispanic/Latino; 32 Asian, non-Hispanic/Latino; 3 Hispanic/Latino), 144 international. Average age 29. 623 applicants, 17% accepted, 54 enrolled. In 2011, 5 master's, 63 doctorates awarded. Terminal master's awarded for partial completion of doctoral program. *Degree requirements:* For master's, comprehensive exam, thesis; for doctorate, comprehensive exam, thesis/dissertation. *Entrance requirements:* For master's, bachelor's degree; for doctorate, GRE General Test. Additional exam requirements/recommendations for international students: Required—TOEFL (minimum score 600 paper-based; 250 computer-based; 100 iBT) or IELTS (minimum score 7.5). *Application deadline:* For fall admission, 12/15 for domestic and international students; for spring admission, 5/15 for domestic students. Application fee: $50. Electronic applications accepted. *Expenses:* Contact institution. *Financial support:* In 2011–12, 416 students received support, including 416 research assistantships with full tuition reimbursements available (averaging $29,200 per year); scholarships/grants, health care benefits, tuition waivers (full), and unspecified assistantships also available. Financial award application deadline: 4/16. *Faculty research:* RNA interference, cell biology, bioinformatics, clinical research, infectious disease. *Total annual research expenditures:* $262.7 million. *Unit head:* Dr. Anthony Carruthers, Dean, 508-856-4135, E-mail: anthony.carruthers@umassmed.edu. *Application contact:* Dr. Kendall Knight, Associate Dean and Interim Director of Admissions and Recruitment, 508-856-5628, Fax: 508-856-3659, E-mail: kendall.knight@umassmed.edu. Web site: http://www.umassmed.edu/gsbs/.

University of Medicine and Dentistry of New Jersey, Graduate School of Biomedical Sciences, Graduate Programs in Biomedical Sciences–Newark, Newark, NJ 07107. Offers biodefense (Certificate); biomedical engineering (PhD); biomedical sciences (multidisciplinary) (PhD); cellular biology, neuroscience and physiology (PhD), including neuroscience, physiology, biophysics, cardiovascular biology, molecular pharmacology, stem cell biology; infection, immunity and inflammation (PhD), including immunology, infectious disease, microbiology, oral biology; molecular biology, genetics and cancer (PhD), including biochemistry, molecular genetics, cancer biology, radiation biology, bioinformatics; neuroscience (Certificate); pharmacological sciences (Certificate); stem cell (Certificate); DMD/PhD; MD/PhD. PhD in biomedical engineering offered jointly with New Jersey Institute of Technology. Part-time and evening/weekend programs available. Terminal master's awarded for partial completion of doctoral program. *Degree requirements:* For doctorate, thesis/dissertation, qualifying exam. *Entrance requirements:* For doctorate, GRE General Test. Additional exam requirements/recommendations for international students: Required—TOEFL. Electronic applications accepted.

University of Medicine and Dentistry of New Jersey, Graduate School of Biomedical Sciences, Graduate Programs in Biomedical Sciences–Piscataway, Piscataway, NJ 08854-5635. Offers biochemistry and molecular biology (MS, PhD); biomedical engineering (MS, PhD); biomedical science (MS); cellular and molecular pharmacology (MS, PhD); clinical and translational science (MS); environmental sciences/exposure assessment (PhD); molecular genetics, microbiology and immunology (MS, PhD); neuroscience (MS, PhD); physiology and integrative biology (MS, PhD); toxicology (PhD); MD/PhD. Terminal master's awarded for partial completion of doctoral program. *Degree requirements:* For master's, thesis (for some programs), ethics training; for doctorate, comprehensive exam, thesis/dissertation, ethics training. *Entrance requirements:* For master's, GRE General Test, MCAT, DAT; for doctorate, GRE General Test. Additional exam requirements/recommendations for international students: Required—TOEFL. Electronic applications accepted.

University of Medicine and Dentistry of New Jersey, Graduate School of Biomedical Sciences, Graduate Programs in Biomedical Sciences–Stratford, Stratford, NJ 08084-5634. Offers biomedical sciences (MBS, MS); cell and molecular biology (MS, PhD); molecular pathology and immunology (MS); DO/MS; DO/PhD; MBS/MPH; MS/MPH. Part-time and evening/weekend programs available. Terminal master's awarded for partial completion of doctoral program. *Degree requirements:* For master's, thesis (for some programs); for doctorate, thesis/dissertation, qualifying exam. *Entrance requirements:* For master's, GRE General Test, MCAT or DAT; for doctorate, GRE General Test. Additional exam requirements/recommendations for international students: Required—TOEFL. Electronic applications accepted.

University of Memphis, Graduate School, College of Arts and Sciences, Department of Biology, Memphis, TN 38152. Offers MS, PhD. Terminal master's awarded for partial completion of doctoral program. *Degree requirements:* For master's, comprehensive exam, thesis (for some programs); for doctorate, one foreign language, comprehensive exam, thesis/dissertation. *Entrance requirements:* For master's, GRE General Test; for doctorate, GRE General Test, master's degree. Additional exam requirements/recommendations for international students: Required—TOEFL (minimum score 550 paper-based; 210 computer-based; 79 iBT). Electronic applications accepted. *Faculty research:* Protein trafficking and signal transduction; animal behavior and communication, neurobiology, and circadian clock function; phylogenetics, evolution, and ecology; causation and prevention of cancer; reproductive biology.

University of Miami, Graduate School, College of Arts and Sciences, Department of Biology, Coral Gables, FL 33124. Offers biology (MS, PhD); genetics and evolution (MS, PhD). Terminal master's awarded for partial completion of doctoral program. *Degree requirements:* For master's, comprehensive exam (for some programs), thesis (for some programs); for doctorate, thesis/dissertation, oral and written qualifying exam. *Entrance requirements:* For master's, GRE General Test, 3 letters of recommendation, research papers; for doctorate, GRE General Test, 3 letters of recommendation, research papers, sponsor letter. Additional exam requirements/recommendations for international students: Required—TOEFL (minimum score 550 paper-based; 213 computer-based; 59 iBT). Electronic applications accepted. *Faculty research:* Neuroscience to ethology; plants, vertebrates and mycorrhizae; phylogenies, life histories and species interactions; molecular biology, gene expression and populations; cells, auditory neurons and vertebrate locomotion.

University of Michigan, Horace H. Rackham School of Graduate Studies, Program in Biomedical Sciences (PIBS), Ann Arbor, MI 48109-5619. Offers MS, PhD. *Faculty:* 475 full-time. *Students:* 86 full-time (46 women); includes 25 minority (8 Black or African American, non-Hispanic/Latino; 1 American Indian or Alaska Native, non-Hispanic/Latino; 9 Asian, non-Hispanic/Latino; 7 Hispanic/Latino), 6 international. Average age 24. 718 applicants, 30% accepted, 86 enrolled. *Degree requirements:* For doctorate, thesis/dissertation, oral defense of dissertation, preliminary exam. *Entrance requirements:* For doctorate, GRE General Test, 3 letters of recommendation, research experience. Additional exam requirements/recommendations for international students: Required—TOEFL (minimum score 84 iBT). *Application deadline:* For fall admission, 12/1 for domestic and international students. Application fee: $60 ($75 for international students). Electronic applications accepted. *Financial support:* In 2011–12, 86 students received support, including 86 fellowships with full tuition reimbursements available (averaging $26,500 per year); scholarships/grants, health care benefits, tuition waivers (full), and unspecified assistantships also available. Financial award application deadline: 12/1. *Faculty research:* Genetics, cellular and molecular biology, microbial pathogenesis, cancer biology, neuroscience. *Unit head:* Dr. Lori L. Isom, Assistant Dean/Director/Professor of Molecular and Integrative Physiology and Pharmacology, 734-615-7005, Fax: 734-647-7022, E-mail: lisom@umich.edu. *Application contact:* Michelle S. Melis, Director of Student Life, 734-615-6538, Fax: 734-647-7022, E-mail: pibs@umich.edu. Web site: http://www.med.umich.edu/pibs/.

University of Michigan, Medical School and Horace H. Rackham School of Graduate Studies, Medical Scientist Training Program, Ann Arbor, MI 48109. Offers MD/PhD. *Accreditation:* LCME/AMA. *Students:* 86 full-time (28 women); includes 35 minority (3 Black or African American, non-Hispanic/Latino; 31 Asian, non-Hispanic/Latino; 1 Hispanic/Latino). 276 applicants, 15% accepted, 13 enrolled. *Application deadline:* For fall admission, 10/15 for domestic students. Applications are processed on a rolling basis. Application fee: $150. Electronic applications accepted. *Financial support:* In 2011–12, 86 students received support, including 69 fellowships with full tuition reimbursements available (averaging $26,500 per year), 15 research assistantships with full tuition reimbursements available (averaging $26,500 per year), 2 teaching assistantships with full tuition reimbursements available (averaging $26,500 per year); scholarships/grants, traineeships, and health care benefits also available. *Unit head:* Dr. Ronald J. Koenig, Director, 734-764-6176, Fax: 734-764-8180, E-mail: rkoenig@umich.edu. *Application contact:* Laurie Koivupalo, Administrative Associate, 734-764-6176, Fax: 734-764-8180, E-mail: lkoivupl@umich.edu. Web site: http://www.med.umich.edu/medschool/mstp/.

University of Michigan–Flint, College of Arts and Sciences, Program in Biology, Flint, MI 48502-1950. Offers MS. Part-time programs available. *Degree requirements:* For master's, thesis or alternative. *Entrance requirements:* For master's, GRE, minimum undergraduate GPA of 3.0 in prerequisites. Additional exam requirements/recommendations for international students: Required—TOEFL (minimum score 560 paper-based; 220 computer-based; 84 iBT), IELTS (minimum score 6.5). *Expenses:* Contact institution.

University of Minnesota, Duluth, Graduate School, Swenson College of Science and Engineering, Department of Biology, Integrated Biosciences Program, Duluth, MN 55812-2496. Offers MS, PhD. Terminal master's awarded for partial completion of doctoral program. *Degree requirements:* For master's, thesis, seminar; for doctorate, comprehensive exam, thesis/dissertation, written and oral exam, seminar, written thesis. *Entrance requirements:* For master's, GRE, 1 year of biology, physics, and chemistry; 1 semester of calculus; for doctorate, GRE, 1 year each of chemistry, biology, physics, calculus, and advanced chemistry. Additional exam requirements/recommendations for international students: Required—TOEFL (minimum score 550 paper-based; 79 iBT). Electronic applications accepted. *Faculty research:* Ecology, organizational and population biology; cell, molecular and physiological biology.

University of Minnesota, Twin Cities Campus, Graduate School, College of Biological Sciences, Biological Science Program, Minneapolis, MN 55455-0213. Offers MBS. Part-time and evening/weekend programs available. *Entrance requirements:* For master's, 2 years of work experience. Electronic applications accepted. *Expenses:* Contact institution.

University of Minnesota, Twin Cities Campus, Graduate School, Stem Cell Biology Graduate Program, Minneapolis, MN 55455-3007. Offers MS. *Degree requirements:* For master's, thesis. *Entrance requirements:* For master's, GRE, BS, BA, or foreign equivalent in biological sciences or related field; minimum undergraduate GPA of 3.2. Additional exam requirements/recommendations for international students: Required—TOEFL (minimum score 580 paper-based, with a minimum score of 4 in the TWE, or 94 Internet-based, with a minimum score of 22 on each of the reading and listening, 26 on the speaking, and 26 on the writing section. *Faculty research:* Stem cell and developmental biology; embryonic stem cells; iPS cells; muscle satellite cells; hematopoietic stem cells; neuronal stem cells; cardiovascular, kidney and limb development; regenerating systems.

University of Minnesota, Twin Cities Campus, Medical School and Graduate School, Graduate Programs in Medicine, Minneapolis, MN 55455-0213. Offers MA. Part-time and evening/weekend programs available. *Expenses:* Contact institution.

University of Mississippi, Graduate School, College of Liberal Arts, Department of Biology, Oxford, University, MS 38677. Offers MS, PhD. *Students:* 28 full-time (12 women), 1 (woman) part-time; includes 1 minority (Hispanic/Latino), 5 international. In 2011, 1 master's, 2 doctorates awarded. *Degree requirements:* For master's, thesis; for doctorate, thesis/dissertation. *Entrance requirements:* For master's and doctorate, GRE General Test, GRE Subject Test, minimum GPA of 3.0. Additional exam requirements/recommendations for international students: Required—TOEFL. *Application deadline:* For fall admission, 4/1 for domestic students; for spring admission, 10/1 for domestic students. Applications are processed on a rolling basis. Application fee: $25. Electronic applications accepted. *Financial support:* Research assistantships, teaching assistantships, and scholarships/grants available. Financial award application deadline: 3/1; financial award applicants required to submit FAFSA. *Faculty research:* Freshwater biology, including ecology and evolutionary biology; environmental and applied biology. *Unit head:* Dr. Paul Lago, Interim Chair, 662-915-7203, Fax: 662-915-5144, E-mail: biology@olemiss.edu. *Application contact:* Dr. Christy M. Wyandt, Associate Dean, 662-915-7474, Fax: 662-915-7577, E-mail: cwyandt@olemiss.edu.

University of Mississippi Medical Center, School of Graduate Studies in the Health Sciences, Jackson, MS 39216-4505. Offers MS, MSN, PhD, MD/PhD. Terminal master's awarded for partial completion of doctoral program. *Degree requirements:* For master's, thesis; for doctorate, thesis/dissertation, first authored publication. *Faculty research:* Immunology; protein chemistry and biosynthesis; cardiovascular, renal, and endocrine physiology; rehabilitation therapy on immune system/hypothalamic/adrenal axis interaction.

University of Missouri, Graduate School, College of Arts and Sciences, Division of Biological Sciences, Columbia, MO 65211. Offers evolutionary biology and ecology (MA, PhD); genetic, cellular and developmental biology (MA, PhD); neurobiology and behavior (MA, PhD). *Faculty:* 40 full-time (11 women), 1 part-time/adjunct (0 women). *Students:* 87 full-time (47 women), 2 part-time (1 woman); includes 14 minority (4 Black or African American, non-Hispanic/Latino; 5 Asian, non-Hispanic/Latino; 2 Hispanic/Latino; 3 Two or more races, non-Hispanic/Latino), 5 international. Average age 29. 45 applicants, 31% accepted, 14 enrolled. In 2011, 1 master's, 9 doctorates awarded. Terminal master's awarded for partial completion of doctoral program. *Degree requirements:* For master's, thesis; for doctorate, comprehensive exam, thesis/dissertation. *Entrance requirements:* For master's and doctorate, GRE General Test (minimum score 1200 verbal and quantitative), minimum GPA of 3.0. Additional exam requirements/recommendations for international students: Required—TOEFL (minimum score 600 paper-based; 100 iBT). *Application deadline:* For fall admission, 1/15 priority date for domestic students. Applications are processed on a rolling basis. Application fee: $55 ($75 for international students). Electronic applications accepted. *Expenses:* Tuition, state resident: full-time $5881. Tuition, nonresident: full-time $15,183. *Required fees:* $952. Tuition and fees vary according to campus/location and program. *Financial support:* In 2011–12, 34 fellowships with full tuition reimbursements, 9 research assistantships with full tuition reimbursements, 33 teaching assistantships with full tuition reimbursements were awarded; institutionally sponsored loans, traineeships, health care benefits, and unspecified assistantships also available. *Faculty research:* Evolutionary biology, ecology and behavior; genetic, cellular, molecular and developmental biology; neurobiology and behavior; plant sciences. *Unit head:* Dr. John David, Division Director, 573-882-6659, E-mail: davidj@missouri.edu. *Application contact:* Nila Emerich, Application Contact, 800-553-5698, E-mail: emerichn@missouri.edu. Web site: http://biology.missouri.edu/graduate-studies/.

University of Missouri, School of Medicine and Graduate School, Graduate Programs in Medicine, Columbia, MO 65211. Offers MS, PhD. Part-time programs available. *Faculty:* 72 full-time (19 women), 6 part-time/adjunct (2 women). *Students:* 67 full-time (33 women), 9 part-time (4 women); includes 6 minority (5 Black or African American, non-Hispanic/Latino; 1 American Indian or Alaska Native, non-Hispanic/Latino), 31 international. Average age 28. 50 applicants, 46% accepted, 22 enrolled. In 2011, 5 master's, 7 doctorates awarded. *Degree requirements:* For doctorate, thesis/dissertation. *Entrance requirements:* For master's and doctorate, GRE General Test, minimum GPA of 3.0. Additional exam requirements/recommendations for international students: Required—TOEFL. *Application deadline:* Applications are processed on a rolling basis. Application fee: $55 ($75 for international students). *Expenses:* Contact institution. *Financial support:* Fellowships, research assistantships, teaching assistantships, career-related internships or fieldwork, and institutionally sponsored loans available. *Unit head:* Dr. Roberta Churchill, Interim Dean, 573-884-8733, E-mail: churchillr@missouri.edu. *Application contact:* Dr. John Gay, Associate Dean for Graduate Medical Education, 573-882-4637, E-mail: gayj@health.missouri.edu. Web site: http://som.missouri.edu/departments.shtml.

University of Missouri–Kansas City, School of Biological Sciences, Kansas City, MO 64110-2499. Offers biology (MA); cell biology and biophysics (PhD); cellular and molecular biology (MS); molecular biology and biochemistry (PhD). PhD (interdisciplinary) offered through the School of Graduate Studies. Part-time and evening/weekend programs available. *Faculty:* 40 full-time (10 women), 3 part-time/adjunct (2 women). *Students:* 24 full-time (15 women), 34 part-time (22 women); includes 10 minority (2 Black or African American, non-Hispanic/Latino; 5 Asian, non-Hispanic/Latino; 2 Hispanic/Latino; 1 Two or more races, non-Hispanic/Latino), 1 international. Average age 30. 44 applicants, 61% accepted, 23 enrolled. In 2011, 21 degrees awarded. *Degree requirements:* For doctorate, comprehensive exam, thesis/dissertation. *Entrance requirements:* For master's, GRE, minimum GPA of 3.0; for doctorate, GRE General Test. Additional exam requirements/recommendations for international students: Required—TOEFL (minimum score 550 paper-based; 213 computer-based; 80 iBT). *Application deadline:* For fall admission, 2/15 priority date for domestic students, 2/15 for international students. Applications are processed on a rolling basis. Application fee: $45 ($50 for international students). *Expenses:* Tuition, state resident: full-time $5798; part-time $322.10 per credit hour. Tuition, nonresident: full-time $14,969; part-time $831.60 per credit hour. *Required fees:* $93.51 per credit hour. *Financial support:* In 2011–12, 20 research assistantships with full tuition reimbursements (averaging $22,690 per year), 18 teaching assistantships with full tuition reimbursements (averaging $18,809 per year) were awarded; Federal Work-Study, institutionally sponsored loans, scholarships/grants, tuition waivers (full and partial), and unspecified assistantships also available. Support available to part-time students. Financial award application deadline: 3/1; financial award applicants required to submit FAFSA. *Faculty research:* Structural biology, molecular genetics. *Unit head:* Dr. Lawrence A. Dreyfus, Dean, 816-235-5246, Fax: 816-235-5158, E-mail: dreyfusl@umkc.edu. *Application contact:* Laura Batenic, Information Contact, 816-235-2352, Fax: 816-235-5158, E-mail: batenicl@umkc.edu. Web site: http://sbs.umkc.edu/.

University of Missouri–St. Louis, College of Arts and Sciences, Department of Biology, St. Louis, MO 63121. Offers biotechnology (Certificate); cell and molecular biology (MS, PhD); ecology, evolution and systematics (MS, PhD); tropical biology and conservation (Certificate). Part-time programs available. *Faculty:* 43 full-time (13 women), 4 part-time/adjunct (1 woman). *Students:* 68 full-time (33 women), 64 part-time (28 women); includes 20 minority (9 Black or African American, non-Hispanic/Latino; 7 Asian, non-Hispanic/Latino; 3 Hispanic/Latino; 1 Two or more races, non-Hispanic/Latino), 43 international. Average age 28. 122 applicants, 48% accepted, 36 enrolled. In 2011, 20 master's, 3 doctorates, 11 other advanced degrees awarded. *Degree requirements:* For master's, thesis or alternative; for doctorate, thesis/dissertation, 1 semester of teaching experience. *Entrance requirements:* For master's, 3 letters of recommendation; for doctorate, GRE General Test, 3 letters of recommendation.

Additional exam requirements/recommendations for international students: Required—TOEFL. *Application deadline:* For fall admission, 12/15 priority date for domestic students, 12/15 for international students; for spring admission, 12/1 priority date for domestic students, 12/1 for international students. Applications are processed on a rolling basis. Application fee: $35 ($40 for international students). Electronic applications accepted. *Expenses:* Tuition, state resident: full-time $6273; part-time $3866 per year. Tuition, nonresident: full-time $14,969; part-time $9980 per year. *Required fees:* $315 per year. *Financial support:* In 2011–12, 13 research assistantships with full and partial tuition reimbursements (averaging $15,300 per year), 27 teaching assistantships with full and partial tuition reimbursements (averaging $15,300 per year) were awarded; fellowships with full tuition reimbursements, career-related internships or fieldwork, and Federal Work-Study also available. Support available to part-time students. Financial award application deadline: 2/1. *Faculty research:* Molecular biology, microbial genetics, animal behavior, tropical ecology, plant systematics. *Unit head:* Dr. Wendy Olivas, Director of Graduate Studies, 314-516-6200, Fax: 314-516-6233, E-mail: olivasw@umsl.edu. *Application contact:* 314-516-5458, Fax: 314-516-6996, E-mail: gradadm@umsl.edu. Web site: http://www.umsl.edu/divisions/artscience/biology/.

The University of Montana, Graduate School, College of Arts and Sciences, Division of Biological Sciences, Missoula, MT 59812-0002. Offers biochemistry and microbiology (MS, PhD), including biochemistry (MS), integrative microbiology and biochemistry (PhD), microbial ecology, microbiology (MS); organismal biology and ecology (MS, PhD). Terminal master's awarded for partial completion of doctoral program. *Degree requirements:* For master's, thesis; for doctorate, thesis/dissertation. *Entrance requirements:* For master's and doctorate, GRE General Test. Additional exam requirements/recommendations for international students: Required—TOEFL. *Faculty research:* Biochemistry/microbiology, organismal biology, ecology.

The University of Montana, Graduate School, College of Health Professions and Biomedical Sciences, Skaggs School of Pharmacy, Department of Biomedical and Pharmaceutical Sciences, Missoula, MT 59812-0002. Offers biomedical sciences (PhD); neuroscience (MS, PhD); pharmaceutical sciences (MS); toxicology (MS, PhD). *Accreditation:* ACPE. *Degree requirements:* For master's, oral defense of thesis; for doctorate, research dissertation defense. *Entrance requirements:* For master's and doctorate, GRE General Test. Additional exam requirements/recommendations for international students: Required—TOEFL (minimum score 540 paper-based; 210 computer-based). Electronic applications accepted. *Faculty research:* Cardiovascular pharmacology, medicinal chemistry, neurosciences, environmental toxicology, pharmacogenetics, cancer.

University of Nebraska at Kearney, Graduate Studies, College of Natural and Social Sciences, Department of Biology, Kearney, NE 68849-0001. Offers biology (MS); science education (MS Ed). Part-time and evening/weekend programs available. *Degree requirements:* For master's, thesis optional. *Entrance requirements:* For master's, GRE General Test. Additional exam requirements/recommendations for international students: Required—TOEFL (minimum score 550 paper-based; 213 computer-based). Electronic applications accepted. *Faculty research:* Pollution injury, molecular biology-viral gene expression, prairie range condition modeling, evolution of symbiotic nitrogen fixation.

University of Nebraska at Omaha, Graduate Studies, College of Arts and Sciences, Department of Biology, Omaha, NE 68182. Offers MS. Part-time programs available. *Faculty:* 21 full-time (6 women). *Students:* 5 full-time (all women), 19 part-time (10 women); includes 3 minority (1 Black or African American, non-Hispanic/Latino; 1 American Indian or Alaska Native, non-Hispanic/Latino; 1 Hispanic/Latino), 2 international. Average age 27. 14 applicants, 64% accepted, 7 enrolled. In 2011, 10 master's awarded. *Degree requirements:* For master's, comprehensive exam (for some programs), thesis (for some programs). *Entrance requirements:* For master's, GRE General Test, minimum GPA of 3.0, 24 undergraduate biology hours, 3 letters of recommendation, statement of purpose. Additional exam requirements/recommendations for international students: Required—TOEFL (minimum score 550 paper-based; 173 computer-based; 80 iBT). *Application deadline:* For fall admission, 2/15 priority date for domestic students; for spring admission, 10/15 priority date for domestic students. Applications are processed on a rolling basis. Application fee: $45. Electronic applications accepted. *Financial support:* In 2011–12, 23 students received support, including 1 fellowship, 1 research assistantship with tuition reimbursement available, 21 teaching assistantships with tuition reimbursements available; Federal Work-Study, institutionally sponsored loans, scholarships/grants, tuition waivers (partial), and unspecified assistantships also available. Support available to part-time students. Financial award application deadline: 3/1; financial award applicants required to submit FAFSA. *Unit head:* Dr. William Tapprich, Chairperson, 402-554-2641. *Application contact:* Dr. Ann Antlfinger, Student Contact, 402-554-2641.

University of Nebraska–Lincoln, Graduate College, College of Agricultural Sciences and Natural Resources, School of Veterinary Medicine and Biomedical Sciences, Lincoln, NE 68588. Offers veterinary science (MS). MS, PhD offered jointly with University of Nebraska Medical Center. Postbaccalaureate distance learning degree programs offered (minimal on-campus study). *Degree requirements:* For master's, thesis optional; for doctorate, comprehensive exam, thesis/dissertation. *Entrance requirements:* For master's, GRE General Test; for doctorate, GRE General Test, MCAT, or VCAT. Additional exam requirements/recommendations for international students: Required—TOEFL (minimum score 550 paper-based; 213 computer-based). Electronic applications accepted. *Faculty research:* Virology, immunobiology, molecular biology, mycotoxins, ocular degeneration.

University of Nebraska–Lincoln, Graduate College, College of Arts and Sciences, School of Biological Sciences, Lincoln, NE 68588. Offers MA, MS, PhD. *Degree requirements:* For master's, thesis optional; for doctorate, comprehensive exam, thesis/dissertation. *Entrance requirements:* For master's and doctorate, GRE General Test. Additional exam requirements/recommendations for international students: Required—TOEFL (minimum score 550 paper-based; 213 computer-based). Electronic applications accepted. *Faculty research:* Behavior, botany, and zoology; ecology and evolutionary biology; genetics; cellular and molecular biology; microbiology.

University of Nebraska Medical Center, Graduate Studies, Biomedical Research Training Program, Omaha, NE 68198. Offers MD/PhD. *Entrance requirements:* Additional exam requirements/recommendations for international students: Required—TOEFL (minimum score 600 paper-based; 250 computer-based). Electronic applications accepted. *Faculty research:* Neuroscience, cancer, cardiovascular immunology, genetics.

University of Nebraska Medical Center, Graduate Studies, Medical Sciences Interdepartmental Area, Omaha, NE 68198. Offers MS, PhD. Part-time programs available. Terminal master's awarded for partial completion of doctoral program. *Degree requirements:* For master's, comprehensive exam, thesis; for doctorate, comprehensive exam, thesis/dissertation. *Entrance requirements:* For master's and doctorate, GRE General Test. Additional exam requirements/recommendations for international students: Required—TOEFL (minimum score 550 paper-based; 213 computer-based). *Faculty research:* Molecular genetics, oral biology, veterinary pathology, newborn medicine, immunology.

University of Nevada, Las Vegas, Graduate College, College of Science, School of Life Sciences, Las Vegas, NV 89154-4004. Offers biological sciences (MS, PhD). Part-time programs available. *Faculty:* 31 full-time (8 women), 20 part-time/adjunct (1 woman). *Students:* 16 full-time (8 women), 23 part-time (12 women); includes 9 minority (1 Black or African American, non-Hispanic/Latino; 1 Asian, non-Hispanic/Latino; 5 Hispanic/Latino; 1 Native Hawaiian or other Pacific Islander, non-Hispanic/Latino; 1 Two or more races, non-Hispanic/Latino), 4 international. Average age 31. 27 applicants, 52% accepted, 10 enrolled. In 2011, 4 master's, 7 doctorates awarded. *Degree requirements:* For master's, thesis, oral exam; for doctorate, one foreign language, comprehensive exam, thesis/dissertation. *Entrance requirements:* For master's and doctorate, GRE General Test. Additional exam requirements/recommendations for international students: Required—TOEFL (minimum score 550 paper-based; 213 computer-based; 80 iBT), IELTS (minimum score 7). *Application deadline:* For fall admission, 1/15 priority date for domestic students, 5/1 for international students; for spring admission, 10/1 for international students. Applications are processed on a rolling basis. Application fee: $60 ($95 for international students). Electronic applications accepted. *Financial support:* In 2011–12, 35 students received support, including 12 research assistantships with full tuition reimbursements available (averaging $12,260 per year), 23 teaching assistantships with partial tuition reimbursements available (averaging $13,332 per year); institutionally sponsored loans, scholarships/grants, health care benefits, and unspecified assistantships also available. Financial award application deadline: 3/1. *Faculty research:* Environmental and medical microbiology; biodiversity, evolution, and ecological sustainability; cell and molecular biology; integrative physiology. *Total annual research expenditures:* $3 million. *Unit head:* Dr. Dennis Bazylinski, Chair, 702-895-3399, Fax: 702-895-3956, E-mail: dennis.bazylinski@unlv.edu. *Application contact:* Graduate College Admissions Evaluator, 702-895-3320, Fax: 702-895-4180, E-mail: gradcollege@unlv.edu. Web site: http://sols.unlv.edu/.

University of Nevada, Reno, Graduate School, College of Science, Department of Biology, Reno, NV 89557. Offers MS. *Degree requirements:* For master's, thesis optional. *Entrance requirements:* For master's, GRE General Test, minimum GPA of 2.75. Additional exam requirements/recommendations for international students: Required—TOEFL (minimum score 500 paper-based; 173 computer-based; 61 iBT), IELTS (minimum score 6). Electronic applications accepted. *Faculty research:* Gene expression, stress protein genes, secretory proteins, conservation biology, behavioral ecology.

University of New Brunswick Fredericton, School of Graduate Studies, Faculty of Science, Department of Biology, Fredericton, NB E3B 5A3, Canada. Offers M Sc, PhD. Part-time programs available. *Faculty:* 25 full-time (6 women), 1 part-time/adjunct (0 women). *Students:* 58 full-time (32 women), 13 part-time (7 women). In 2011, 12 master's, 4 doctorates awarded. *Degree requirements:* For master's, thesis; for doctorate, thesis/dissertation. *Entrance requirements:* For master's, minimum GPA of 3.0; undergraduate degree (B Sc or equivalent preferred); for doctorate, minimum GPA of 3.0; undergraduate and/or master's degree in related discipline. Additional exam requirements/recommendations for international students: Required—TWE (minimum score 4), TOEFL (minimum score 600 paper-based; 250 computer-based) or IELTS (minimum score 7). *Application deadline:* For fall admission, 3/1 priority date for domestic students. Applications are processed on a rolling basis. Application fee: $50 Canadian dollars. Electronic applications accepted. *Financial support:* In 2011–12, 27 fellowships, 42 research assistantships with tuition reimbursements, 26 teaching assistantships were awarded. *Faculty research:* Evolutionary biology, aquatic ecology, wildlife and conservation biology, marine biology, algae and plant biology. *Unit head:* Dr. Les C. Cwynar, Director of Graduate Studies, 506-452-6197, Fax: 506-453-4583, E-mail: biodogs@unb.ca. *Application contact:* Rose Comeau, Graduate Secretary, 506-452-6052, Fax: 506-453-3583, E-mail: rcomeau@unb.ca. Web site: http://www.unb.ca/fredericton/science/biology/.

University of New Brunswick Saint John, Department of Biology, Saint John, NB E2L 4L5, Canada. Offers biology (M Sc, PhD). Part-time programs available. *Faculty:* 14 full-time (1 woman). *Students:* 50 full-time (27 women), 4 part-time (3 women). In 2011, 5 master's, 1 doctorate awarded. *Degree requirements:* For master's, thesis; for doctorate, comprehensive exam, thesis/dissertation. *Entrance requirements:* For master's, B Sc, minimum GPA of 3.0; for doctorate, M Sc, minimum GPA of 3.0. *Application deadline:* For fall admission, 2/15 for domestic and international students. Applications are processed on a rolling basis. Application fee: $50 Canadian dollars. *Financial support:* In 2011–12, research assistantships (averaging $4,000 per year), teaching assistantships (averaging $4,000 per year) were awarded; fellowships, scholarships/grants, and unspecified assistantships also available. *Faculty research:* Community ecology, marine biology and aquaculture, physiology, ecotoxicology, molecular/chemical ecology. *Unit head:* Dr. Kate Frego, Director of Graduate Studies, 506-648-5967, Fax: 506-648-5811, E-mail: frego@unbsj.ca. *Application contact:* Kim Banks, Secretary, 506-648-5605, Fax: 506-648-5811, E-mail: kbanks@unb.ca. Web site: http://www.unbsj.ca/sase/biology/.

University of New Hampshire, Graduate School, College of Life Sciences and Agriculture, Department of Biological Sciences, Durham, NH 03824. Offers animal science (MS); plant biology (MS, PhD); zoology (MS, PhD). Part-time programs available. *Faculty:* 31 full-time (7 women). *Students:* 31 full-time (18 women), 32 part-time (19 women); includes 4 minority (2 Asian, non-Hispanic/Latino; 2 Two or more races, non-Hispanic/Latino), 6 international. Average age 31. 56 applicants, 29% accepted, 15 enrolled. In 2011, 3 master's, 1 doctorate awarded. *Degree requirements:* For doctorate, thesis/dissertation. *Entrance requirements:* For master's and doctorate, GRE General Test. Additional exam requirements/recommendations for international students: Required—TOEFL (minimum score 550 paper-based; 215 computer-based; 80 iBT). *Application deadline:* For fall admission, 6/1 for domestic students, 4/1 for international students; for spring admission, 12/1 for domestic students. Application fee: $65. *Expenses:* Tuition, state resident: full-time $12,360; part-time $687 per credit hour. Tuition, nonresident: full-time $25,680; part-time $1058 per credit hour. *International tuition:* $29,550 full-time. *Required fees:* $1666; $833 per course. $416.50 per semester. Tuition and fees vary according to course load and degree level. *Financial support:* In 2011–12, 41 students received support, including 3 fellowships, 12 research assistantships, 23 teaching assistantships. *Unit head:* Chris Neefus, Dean, 603-862-1990. *Application contact:* Dianne Lavalliere, Administrative Assistant, 603-862-2100, Fax: 603-862-0275, E-mail: grad.school@unh.edu. Web site: http://www.biolsci.unh.edu/.

University of New Mexico, Graduate School, College of Arts and Sciences, Department of Biology, Albuquerque, NM 87131. Offers MS, PhD. *Faculty:* 73 full-time (28 women), 15 part-time/adjunct (4 women). *Students:* 68 full-time (38 women), 50 part-time (26 women); includes 23 minority (1 American Indian or Alaska Native, non-Hispanic/Latino; 3 Asian, non-Hispanic/Latino; 17 Hispanic/Latino; 2 Two or more races, non-Hispanic/Latino), 9 international. Average age 33. 91 applicants, 30% accepted, 25 enrolled. In 2011, 4 master's, 7 doctorates awarded. *Degree requirements:* For master's, comprehensive exam, thesis optional; for doctorate, comprehensive exam, thesis/dissertation. *Entrance requirements:* For master's and doctorate, GRE General Test, minimum GPA of 3.2, letters of recommendation. Additional exam requirements/

recommendations for international students: Required—TOEFL (minimum score 550 paper-based; 213 computer-based; 79 iBT). *Application deadline:* For fall admission, 1/3 priority date for domestic students, 1/3 for international students. Applications are processed on a rolling basis. Application fee: $50. Electronic applications accepted. *Financial support:* In 2011–12, 94 students received support, including 5 fellowships with full tuition reimbursements available (averaging $13,267 per year), 50 research assistantships with full tuition reimbursements available (averaging $12,045 per year), 56 teaching assistantships with full tuition reimbursements available (averaging $11,214 per year); Federal Work-Study, scholarships/grants, health care benefits, and unspecified assistantships also available. Financial award application deadline: 3/1; financial award applicants required to submit FAFSA. *Faculty research:* Aquatic ecology, behavioral ecology, botany, cell biology, comparative biology, conservation biology, developmental biology, ecology, evolutionary biology, genetics, genomics, global change biology, immunology, invertebrate biology, mathematical biology, microbiology, molecular evolution, paleobiology, parasitology, physiological ecology, plant biology, systematics, vertebrate biology. *Total annual research expenditures:* $10.8 million. *Unit head:* Dr. Richard Cripps, Chair, 505-277-2496, Fax: 505-277-0304, E-mail: rcripps@unm.edu. *Application contact:* Cheryl Martin, Graduate Program Coordinator, 505-277-1712, Fax: 505-277-0304, E-mail: cherylm@unm.edu. Web site: http://biology.unm.edu/

University of New Mexico, Health Sciences Center Graduate Programs, Program in Biomedical Sciences, Albuquerque, NM 87131-5196. Offers biochemistry and molecular biology (MS, PhD); cell biology and physiology (MS, PhD); clinical and translational science (Certificate); molecular genetics and microbiology (MS, PhD); neuroscience (MS, PhD); pathology (MS, PhD); toxicology (MS, PhD); university science teaching (Certificate). Part-time programs available. *Faculty:* 64 full-time (26 women), 9 part-time/adjunct (4 women). *Students:* 45 full-time (27 women), 56 part-time (28 women); includes 24 minority (3 Black or African American, non-Hispanic/Latino; 1 American Indian or Alaska Native, non-Hispanic/Latino; 4 Asian, non-Hispanic/Latino; 14 Hispanic/Latino; 1 Native Hawaiian or other Pacific Islander, non-Hispanic/Latino; 1 Two or more races, non-Hispanic/Latino), 18 international. Average age 30. 110 applicants, 18% accepted, 17 enrolled. In 2011, 14 master's, 5 doctorates awarded. Terminal master's awarded for partial completion of doctoral program. *Degree requirements:* For master's, thesis; for doctorate, comprehensive exam, thesis/dissertation. *Entrance requirements:* For master's and doctorate, GRE General Test, minimum undergraduate GPA of 3.0. Additional exam requirements/recommendations for international students: Required—TOEFL. *Application deadline:* For fall admission, 3/1 priority date for domestic students, 3/1 for international students. Applications are processed on a rolling basis. Application fee: $50. Electronic applications accepted. *Financial support:* In 2011–12, 99 students received support, including 28 fellowships with full and partial tuition reimbursements available (averaging $22,000 per year), 73 research assistantships with full tuition reimbursements available (averaging $23,000 per year), 8 teaching assistantships (averaging $2,800 per year); career-related internships or fieldwork, Federal Work-Study, institutionally sponsored loans, scholarships/grants, traineeships, health care benefits, and unspecified assistantships also available. Financial award application deadline: 1/1; financial award applicants required to submit FAFSA. *Faculty research:* Infectious disease/Immunity, cancer biology, cardiovascular and metabolic diseases, brain and behavioral illness, environmental health. *Unit head:* Dr. Helen J. Hathaway, BSGP Program Director, 505-272-1887, Fax: 505-272-2412, E-mail: hhathaway@salud.unm.edu. *Application contact:* Mary Fenton, Admissions Coordinator, 505-272-1887, Fax: 505-272-2412, E-mail: mfenton@salud.unm.edu. Web site: http://hsc.unm.edu/som/research/brep/bsgpabout.shtm.

University of New Orleans, Graduate School, College of Sciences, Department of Biological Sciences, New Orleans, LA 70148. Offers MS, PhD. *Degree requirements:* For master's, one foreign language, thesis. *Entrance requirements:* For master's, GRE General Test. Additional exam requirements/recommendations for international students: Required—TOEFL (minimum score 550 paper-based; 213 computer-based; 79 iBT). Electronic applications accepted. *Faculty research:* Biochemistry, genetics, vertebrate and invertebrate systematics and ecology, cell and mammalian physiology, morphology.

The University of North Carolina at Chapel Hill, Graduate School, College of Arts and Sciences, Department of Biology, Chapel Hill, NC 27599. Offers botany (MA, MS, PhD); cell biology, development, and physiology (MA, MS, PhD); cell motility and cytoskeleton (PhD); ecology and behavior (MA, MS, PhD); genetics and molecular biology (MA, MS, PhD); morphology, systematics, and evolution (MA, MS, PhD). Terminal master's awarded for partial completion of doctoral program. *Degree requirements:* For master's, comprehensive exam, thesis (for some programs); for doctorate, comprehensive exam, thesis/dissertation. *Entrance requirements:* For master's, GRE General Test, GRE Subject Test, 2 semesters of calculus or statistics; 2 semesters of physics, organic chemistry; 3 semesters of biology; for doctorate, GRE General Test, GRE Subject Test, 2 semesters calculus or statistics, 2 semesters physics, organic chemistry, 3 semesters of biology. Additional exam requirements/recommendations for international students: Required—TOEFL (minimum score 550 paper-based; 213 computer-based). Electronic applications accepted. *Faculty research:* Gene expression, biomechanics, yeast genetics, plant ecology, plant molecular biology.

The University of North Carolina at Chapel Hill, School of Medicine and Graduate School, Graduate Programs in Medicine, Chapel Hill, NC 27599. Offers allied health sciences (MPT, MS, Au D, DPT, PhD), including human movement science (MS, PhD), occupational science (MS, PhD), physical therapy (MPT, MS, DPT), rehabilitation counseling and psychology (MS), speech and hearing sciences (MS, Au D, PhD); biochemistry and biophysics (MS, PhD); bioinformatics and computational biology (PhD); biomedical engineering (MS, PhD); cell and developmental biology (PhD); cell and molecular physiology (PhD); genetics and molecular biology (PhD); microbiology and immunology (MS, PhD), including immunology, microbiology; neurobiology (PhD); pathology and laboratory medicine (PhD), including experimental pathology; pharmacology (PhD); MD/PhD. Postbaccalaureate distance learning degree programs offered. Terminal master's awarded for partial completion of doctoral program. *Degree requirements:* For master's, comprehensive exam; for doctorate, thesis/dissertation. Electronic applications accepted. *Expenses:* Contact institution.

The University of North Carolina at Charlotte, Graduate School, College of Liberal Arts and Sciences, Department of Biology, Charlotte, NC 28223-0001. Offers MA, MS, PhD. Part-time and evening/weekend programs available. *Faculty:* 23 full-time (8 women), 1 part-time/adjunct (0 women). *Students:* 27 full-time (13 women), 25 part-time (13 women); includes 1 minority (Black or African American, non-Hispanic/Latino), 14 international. Average age 29. 58 applicants, 17% accepted, 6 enrolled. In 2011, 5 master's, 2 doctorates awarded. Terminal master's awarded for partial completion of doctoral program. *Degree requirements:* For master's, thesis, 30-32 semester hours with a minimum GPA of 3.0; for doctorate, thesis/dissertation. *Entrance requirements:* For master's, GRE General Test, minimum GPA of 3.0 in undergraduate major, 2.75 overall; for doctorate, GRE General Test, minimum GPA of 3.5 in biology; 3.0 in chemistry, math, and overall. Additional exam requirements/recommendations for international students: Required—TOEFL (minimum score 557 paper-based; 220 computer-based; 83 iBT). *Application deadline:* For fall admission, 7/15 for domestic students, 5/1 for international students; for spring admission, 11/15 for domestic students, 10/1 for international students. Applications are processed on a rolling basis. Application fee: $65 ($75 for international students). Electronic applications accepted. *Expenses:* Tuition, state resident: full-time $3689. Tuition, nonresident: full-time $15,226. *Required fees:* $2198. Tuition and fees vary according to course load and program. *Financial support:* In 2011–12, 44 students received support, including 5 fellowships (averaging $37,974 per year), 13 research assistantships (averaging $7,274 per year), 26 teaching assistantships (averaging $7,467 per year); career-related internships or fieldwork, institutionally sponsored loans, and scholarships/grants also available. Support available to part-time students. Financial award application deadline: 4/1; financial award applicants required to submit FAFSA. *Faculty research:* Liver blood flow in response to stress/injury, host response to bacterial and viral infection, mechanisms of cancer development and spread, stress responses in marine organisms as a measure of environmental change. *Total annual research expenditures:* $2.2 million. *Unit head:* Dr. Cy Knoblauch, Acting Chair, 704-687-5465, Fax: 704-687-3128, E-mail: chknobla@uncc.edu. *Application contact:* Kathy B. Giddings, Director of Graduate Admissions, 704-687-5503, Fax: 704-687-3279, E-mail: gradadm@uncc.edu. Web site: http://www.bioweb/uncc.edu/.

The University of North Carolina at Greensboro, Graduate School, College of Arts and Sciences, Department of Biology, Greensboro, NC 27412-5001. Offers MS. *Degree requirements:* For master's, thesis. *Entrance requirements:* For master's, GRE General Test, GRE Subject Test. Additional exam requirements/recommendations for international students: Required—TOEFL. Electronic applications accepted. *Faculty research:* Environmental biology, biochemistry, animal ecology, vertebrate reproduction.

The University of North Carolina Wilmington, College of Arts and Sciences, Department of Biology and Marine Biology, Wilmington, NC 28403-3297. Offers biology (MS); marine biology (MS, PhD). Part-time programs available. *Degree requirements:* For master's, comprehensive exam, thesis; for doctorate, comprehensive exam, thesis/dissertation. *Entrance requirements:* For master's, GRE General Test, GRE Subject Test, minimum B average in undergraduate major; for doctorate, GRE General Test, minimum B average in undergraduate major and graduate courses. Additional exam requirements/recommendations for international students: Required—TOEFL (minimum score 550 paper-based; 217 computer-based; 79 iBT), IELTS (minimum score 6.5). Electronic applications accepted. *Faculty research:* Ecology, physiology, cell and molecular biology, systematics, biomechanics.

University of North Dakota, Graduate School, College of Arts and Sciences, Department of Biology, Grand Forks, ND 58202. Offers botany (MS, PhD); ecology (MS, PhD); entomology (MS, PhD); environmental biology (MS, PhD); fisheries/wildlife (MS, PhD); genetics (MS, PhD); zoology (MS, PhD). Terminal master's awarded for partial completion of doctoral program. *Degree requirements:* For master's, thesis, final exam; for doctorate, comprehensive exam, thesis/dissertation, final exam. *Entrance requirements:* For master's, GRE General Test, GRE Subject Test, minimum GPA of 3.0; for doctorate, GRE General Test, GRE Subject Test, minimum GPA of 3.5. Additional exam requirements/recommendations for international students: Required—TOEFL (minimum score 550 paper-based; 213 computer-based; 79 iBT), IELTS (minimum score 6.5). Electronic applications accepted. *Faculty research:* Population biology, wildlife ecology, RNA processing, hormonal control of behavior.

University of Northern Colorado, Graduate School, College of Natural and Health Sciences, School of Biological Sciences, Program in Biological Sciences, Greeley, CO 80639. Offers MS. Part-time programs available. *Degree requirements:* For master's, comprehensive exam. *Entrance requirements:* For master's, GRE General Test, 3 letters of recommendation. Electronic applications accepted.

University of Northern Iowa, Graduate College, College of Humanities, Arts and Sciences, Department of Biology, Cedar Falls, IA 50614. Offers biology (MA, MS); biotechnology (PSM); ecosystem management (PSM). Part-time programs available. *Students:* 30 full-time (11 women), 4 part-time (2 women); includes 1 minority (Asian, non-Hispanic/Latino), 4 international. 57 applicants, 60% accepted, 23 enrolled. In 2011, 19 master's awarded. *Degree requirements:* For master's, comprehensive exam (for some programs), thesis or alternative. *Entrance requirements:* For master's, minimum GPA of 3.0; 3 letters of recommendation. Additional exam requirements/recommendations for international students: Required—TOEFL (minimum score 500 paper-based; 180 computer-based; 61 iBT). *Application deadline:* For fall admission, 8/1 priority date for domestic students. Applications are processed on a rolling basis. Application fee: $50 ($70 for international students). Electronic applications accepted. *Expenses:* Tuition, state resident: full-time $7476. Tuition, nonresident: full-time $16,410. *Required fees:* $942. *Financial support:* Scholarships/grants available. Financial award application deadline: 2/1. *Unit head:* Dr. David Saunders, Head, 319-273-2456, Fax: 319-273-7125, E-mail: david.saunders@uni.edu. *Application contact:* Laurie S. Russell, Record Analyst, 319-273-2623, Fax: 319-273-2885, E-mail: laurie.russell@uni.edu. Web site: http://www.biology.uni.edu/.

University of North Florida, College of Arts and Sciences, Department of Biology, Jacksonville, FL 32224. Offers MA, MS. Part-time programs available. *Faculty:* 21 full-time (6 women), 1 (woman) part-time/adjunct. *Students:* 26 full-time (14 women), 23 part-time (15 women); includes 7 minority (3 Black or African American, non-Hispanic/Latino; 1 Asian, non-Hispanic/Latino; 1 Hispanic/Latino; 2 Two or more races, non-Hispanic/Latino), 2 international. Average age 28. 28 applicants, 57% accepted, 15 enrolled. In 2011, 7 master's awarded. *Degree requirements:* For master's, thesis (for some programs). *Entrance requirements:* For master's, GRE General Test, minimum GPA of 3.0 in last 60 hours, letters of recommendation. Additional exam requirements/recommendations for international students: Required—TOEFL (minimum score 570 paper-based; 230 computer-based). Application fee: $30. Electronic applications accepted. *Expenses:* Tuition, state resident: full-time $8793; part-time $366.38 per credit hour. Tuition, nonresident: full-time $23,502; part-time $979.24 per credit hour. *Required fees:* $1384; $57.66 per credit hour. Tuition and fees vary according to course load and program. *Financial support:* In 2011–12, 14 students received support, including 5 research assistantships (averaging $2,961 per year), 18 teaching assistantships (averaging $5,244 per year); Federal Work-Study, scholarships/grants, and unspecified assistantships also available. Support available to part-time students. Financial award application deadline: 4/1; financial award applicants required to submit FAFSA. *Total annual research expenditures:* $560,906. *Unit head:* Dr. Courtney Hackney, Chair, 904-620-2830, Fax: 904-620-3885, E-mail: c.hackney@unf.edu. *Application contact:* Lillith Richardson, Assistant Director, The Graduate School, 904-620-1360, Fax: 904-620-1362, E-mail: graduateschool@unf.edu. Web site: http://www.unf.edu/coas/biology/.

University of North Texas, Toulouse Graduate School, College of Arts and Sciences, Department of Biological Sciences, Program in Biology, Denton, TX 76203. Offers MA, MS, PhD. Terminal master's awarded for partial completion of doctoral program. *Degree requirements:* For master's, variable foreign language requirement, comprehensive exam, thesis (for some programs), oral defense of thesis; for doctorate, one foreign language, comprehensive exam, thesis/dissertation, oral defense of dissertation. *Entrance requirements:* For master's and doctorate, GRE General Test, letters of recommendation. *Expenses:* Tuition, state resident: part-time $100 per credit hour.

Tuition, nonresident: part-time $413 per credit hour. *Faculty research:* Animal physiology, plant science, biochemistry, environmental science.

University of North Texas Health Science Center at Fort Worth, Graduate School of Biomedical Sciences, Fort Worth, TX 76107-2699. Offers anatomy and cell biology (MS, PhD); biochemistry and molecular biology (MS, PhD); biomedical sciences (MS, PhD); biotechnology (MS); forensic genetics (MS); integrative physiology (MS, PhD); medical science (MS); microbiology and immunology (MS, PhD); pharmacology (MS, PhD); science education (MS); DO/MS; DO/PhD. Terminal master's awarded for partial completion of doctoral program. *Degree requirements:* For master's, thesis; for doctorate, thesis/dissertation. *Entrance requirements:* For master's and doctorate, GRE General Test. Additional exam requirements/recommendations for international students: Required—TOEFL. *Expenses:* Contact institution. *Faculty research:* Alzheimer's disease, aging, eye diseases, cancer, cardiovascular disease.

University of Notre Dame, Graduate School, College of Science, Department of Biological Sciences, Notre Dame, IN 46556. Offers aquatic ecology, evolution and environmental biology (MS, PhD); cellular and molecular biology (MS, PhD); genetics (MS, PhD); physiology (MS, PhD); vector biology and parasitology (MS, PhD). Terminal master's awarded for partial completion of doctoral program. *Degree requirements:* For master's, comprehensive exam, thesis; for doctorate, comprehensive exam, thesis/dissertation, candidacy exam. *Entrance requirements:* For master's and doctorate, GRE General Test. Additional exam requirements/recommendations for international students: Required—TOEFL (minimum score 600 paper-based; 250 computer-based; 80 iBT). Electronic applications accepted. *Faculty research:* Tropical disease, molecular genetics, neurobiology, evolutionary biology, aquatic biology.

University of Oklahoma Health Sciences Center, College of Medicine and Graduate College, Graduate Programs in Medicine, Oklahoma City, OK 73190. Offers biochemistry and molecular biology (MS, PhD), including biochemistry, molecular biology; cell biology (MS, PhD); medical sciences (MS); microbiology and immunology (MS, PhD), including immunology, microbiology; neuroscience (MS, PhD); pathology (PhD); physiology (MS, PhD); psychiatry and behavioral sciences (MS, PhD), including biological psychology; radiological sciences (MS, PhD), including medical radiation physics; MD/PhD. Part-time programs available. Terminal master's awarded for partial completion of doctoral program. *Degree requirements:* For doctorate, thesis/dissertation. *Entrance requirements:* For doctorate, GRE General Test, 3 letters of recommendation. Additional exam requirements/recommendations for international students: Required—TOEFL. *Expenses:* Contact institution. *Faculty research:* Behavior and drugs, structure and function of endothelium, genetics and behavior, gene structure and function, action of antibiotics.

University of Oregon, Graduate School, College of Arts and Sciences, Department of Biology, Eugene, OR 97403. Offers ecology and evolution (MA, MS, PhD); marine biology (MA, MS, PhD); molecular, cellular and genetic biology (PhD); neuroscience and development (PhD). Terminal master's awarded for partial completion of doctoral program. *Degree requirements:* For master's, thesis (for some programs); for doctorate, thesis/dissertation. *Entrance requirements:* For master's and doctorate, GRE General Test, minimum GPA of 3.2. Additional exam requirements/recommendations for international students: Required—TOEFL. *Faculty research:* Developmental neurobiology; evolution, population biology, and quantitative genetics; regulation of gene expression; biochemistry of marine organisms.

University of Ottawa, Faculty of Graduate and Postdoctoral Studies, Faculty of Science, Ottawa-Carleton Institute of Biology, Ottawa, ON K1N 6N5, Canada. Offers M Sc, PhD. M Sc, PhD offered jointly with Carleton University. Part-time programs available. *Degree requirements:* For master's, thesis, seminar; for doctorate, comprehensive exam, thesis/dissertation, seminar. *Entrance requirements:* For master's, honors B Sc degree or equivalent, minimum B average; for doctorate, honors B Sc with minimum B+ average or M Sc with minimum B+ average. Electronic applications accepted. *Faculty research:* Physiology/biochemistry, cellular and molecular biology, ecology, behavior and systematics.

University of Pennsylvania, Perelman School of Medicine, Biomedical Graduate Studies, Philadelphia, PA 19104. Offers MS, PhD, MD/PhD, VMD/PhD. *Faculty:* 853. *Students:* 820 full-time (428 women), 120 part-time (73 women); includes 267 minority (49 Black or African American, non-Hispanic/Latino; 150 Asian, non-Hispanic/Latino; 42 Hispanic/Latino; 26 Two or more races, non-Hispanic/Latino), 81 international. 1,306 applicants, 26% accepted, 187 enrolled. In 2011, 74 master's, 86 doctorates awarded. Terminal master's awarded for partial completion of doctoral program. *Degree requirements:* For doctorate, thesis/dissertation. *Entrance requirements:* For doctorate, GRE General Test. Additional exam requirements/recommendations for international students: Required—TOEFL. *Application deadline:* For fall admission, 12/1 priority date for domestic students, 12/1 for international students. Applications are processed on a rolling basis. Application fee: $80. Electronic applications accepted. *Expenses:* Contact institution. *Financial support:* In 2011–12, 721 students received support. Fellowships, research assistantships, scholarships/grants, traineeships, and unspecified assistantships available. *Unit head:* Dr. Susan R. Ross, Director, 215-898-1030. *Application contact:* Sarah Gormley, Admissions Coordinator, 215-898-1030, Fax: 215-898-2671, E-mail: gormley@mail.med.upenn.edu. Web site: http://www.med.upenn.edu/bgs/.

University of Pennsylvania, School of Arts and Sciences, Graduate Group in Biology, Philadelphia, PA 19104. Offers PhD. *Faculty:* 47 full-time (11 women), 7 part-time/adjunct (1 woman). *Students:* 61 full-time (33 women); includes 9 minority (6 Asian, non-Hispanic/Latino; 1 Hispanic/Latino; 2 Two or more races, non-Hispanic/Latino), 33 international. 242 applicants, 9% accepted, 12 enrolled. In 2011, 8 doctorates awarded. *Degree requirements:* For doctorate, thesis/dissertation. *Entrance requirements:* For doctorate, GRE General Test, GRE Subject Test. Additional exam requirements/recommendations for international students: Required—TOEFL. *Application deadline:* For fall admission, 12/1 priority date for domestic students. Application fee: $70. Electronic applications accepted. *Expenses: Tuition:* Full-time $26,660; part-time $4944 per course. *Required fees:* $2318; $291 per course. Tuition and fees vary according to course load, degree level and program. *Financial support:* Fellowships, research assistantships, teaching assistantships, institutionally sponsored loans, scholarships/grants, traineeships, health care benefits, and unspecified assistantships available. Financial award application deadline: 12/15. *Unit head:* Greg Guild, Department Chair, 215-898-3433, E-mail: gguild@sas.upenn.edu. *Application contact:* Patricia Rea, Associate Director for Admissions, 215-573-5816, Fax: 215-573-8068, E-mail: gdasadmis@sas.upenn.edu. Web site: http://www.bio.upenn.edu/.

University of Pittsburgh, Dietrich School of Arts and Sciences, Department of Biological Sciences, Pittsburgh, PA 15260. Offers ecology and evolution (PhD); molecular, cellular, and developmental biology (PhD). *Faculty:* 31 full-time (6 women). *Students:* 72 full-time (38 women); includes 7 minority (1 Black or African American, non-Hispanic/Latino; 1 American Indian or Alaska Native, non-Hispanic/Latino; 3 Asian, non-Hispanic/Latino; 2 Hispanic/Latino), 19 international. Average age 23. 238 applicants, 13% accepted, 11 enrolled. In 2011, 11 degrees awarded. *Median time to degree:* Of those who began their doctoral program in fall 2003, 100% received their degree in 8 years or less. *Degree requirements:* For doctorate, comprehensive exam, thesis/dissertation, completion of research integrity module. *Entrance requirements:* For doctorate, GRE General Test, GRE Subject Test. Additional exam requirements/recommendations for international students: Required—TOEFL (minimum score 550 paper-based; 213 computer-based; 80 iBT). *Application deadline:* For fall admission, 1/15 priority date for domestic students, 12/15 for international students. Applications are processed on a rolling basis. Application fee: $0 ($50 for international students). Electronic applications accepted. *Expenses:* Tuition, state resident: full-time $18,774; part-time $760 per credit. Tuition, nonresident: full-time $30,736; part-time $1258 per credit. *Required fees:* $740; $200 per term. Tuition and fees vary according to program. *Financial support:* In 2011–12, 44 fellowships with full tuition reimbursements (averaging $28,790 per year), 120 research assistantships with full tuition reimbursements (averaging $25,809 per year), 40 teaching assistantships with full tuition reimbursements (averaging $24,489 per year) were awarded; Federal Work-Study, scholarships/grants, traineeships, and health care benefits also available. *Faculty research:* Molecular biology, cell biology, molecular biophysics, developmental biology, ecology and evolution. *Total annual research expenditures:* $9.5 million. *Unit head:* Dr. Paula J. Grabowski, Professor and Chair, 412-624-4350, Fax: 412-624-4759, E-mail: pag4@pitt.edu. *Application contact:* Cathleen M. Barr, Graduate Administrator, 412-624-4268, Fax: 412-624-4759, E-mail: cbarr@pitt.edu. Web site: http://www.biology.pitt.edu/.

University of Pittsburgh, School of Medicine, Graduate Programs in Medicine, Interdisciplinary Biomedical Sciences Program, Pittsburgh, PA 15260. Offers PhD. *Faculty:* 271 full-time (65 women). *Students:* 29 full-time (10 women); includes 3 minority (2 Black or African American, non-Hispanic/Latino; 1 Asian, non-Hispanic/Latino), 7 international. Average age 27. 514 applicants, 12% accepted, 28 enrolled. In 2011, 25 doctorates awarded. *Degree requirements:* For doctorate, comprehensive exam, thesis/dissertation. *Entrance requirements:* For doctorate, GRE General Test, GRE Subject Test, minimum QPA of 3.0. Additional exam requirements/recommendations for international students: Required—TOEFL (minimum score 600 paper-based; 100 iBT), IELTS (minimum score 7). *Application deadline:* For fall admission, 12/15 priority date for domestic students, 12/15 for international students. Application fee: $50. Electronic applications accepted. *Expenses:* Tuition, state resident: full-time $18,774; part-time $760 per credit. Tuition, nonresident: full-time $30,736; part-time $1258 per credit. *Required fees:* $740; $200 per term. Tuition and fees vary according to program. *Financial support:* In 2011–12, 29 research assistantships with full tuition reimbursements (averaging $25,500 per year) were awarded; institutionally sponsored loans, scholarships/grants, traineeships, and unspecified assistantships also available. *Faculty research:* Cell biology and molecular physiology, cellular and molecular pathology, immunology, molecular genetics and developmental biology, molecular pharmacology and molecular virology and microbiology. *Unit head:* Dr. John P. Horn, Associate Dean for Graduate Studies, 412-648-8957, Fax: 412-648-1077, E-mail: gradstudies@medschool.pitt.edu. *Application contact:* Graduate Studies Administrator, 412-648-8957, Fax: 412-648-1077, E-mail: gradstudies@medschool.pitt.edu. Web site: http://www.gradbiomed.pitt.edu/.

University of Prince Edward Island, Faculty of Science, Charlottetown, PE C1A 4P3, Canada. Offers biology (M Sc); chemistry (M Sc). *Degree requirements:* For master's, thesis. *Entrance requirements:* Additional exam requirements/recommendations for international students: Required—TOEFL (minimum score 550 paper-based; 213 computer-based; 80 iBT), Canadian Academic English Language Assessment, Michigan English Language Assessment Battery, Canadian Test of English for Scholars and Trainees. *Faculty research:* Ecology and wildlife biology, molecular, genetics and biotechnology, organametallic, bio-organic, supramolecular and synthetic organic chemistry, neurobiology and stoke materials science.

University of Puerto Rico, Mayagüez Campus, Graduate Studies, College of Arts and Sciences, Department of Biology, Mayagüez, PR 00681-9000. Offers MS. Part-time programs available. *Students:* 76 full-time (50 women), 1 (woman) part-time; includes 65 minority (all Hispanic/Latino), 12 international. 32 applicants, 47% accepted, 13 enrolled. In 2011, 15 master's awarded. *Degree requirements:* For master's, one foreign language, comprehensive exam, thesis. *Entrance requirements:* For master's, GRE General Test, BS in biology or its equivalent; minimum GPA of 3.0 in biology courses. Additional exam requirements/recommendations for international students: Required—TOEFL. *Application deadline:* For fall admission, 2/15 for domestic and international students; for spring admission, 9/15 for domestic and international students. Applications are processed on a rolling basis. Application fee: $25. Tuition and fees vary according to course level and course load. *Financial support:* In 2011–12, 59 students received support, including 6 research assistantships with tuition reimbursements available (averaging $15,000 per year), 53 teaching assistantships with tuition reimbursements available (averaging $8,500 per year); Federal Work-Study and institutionally sponsored loans also available. *Faculty research:* Herpetology, entomology, microbiology, immunology, botany. *Total annual research expenditures:* $2.1 million. *Unit head:* Dr. Nannette Difoot, Director, 787-265-3837, Fax: 787-834-3673, E-mail: nanette.difoot@upr.edu. *Application contact:* Maria Mendez, Secretary, 787-832-4040 Ext. 3828, Fax: 787-265-1225, E-mail: maria.mendez6@upr.edu. Web site: http://biology.uprm.edu.

University of Puerto Rico, Medical Sciences Campus, School of Medicine, Division of Graduate Studies, San Juan, PR 00936-5067. Offers MS, PhD. Terminal master's awarded for partial completion of doctoral program. *Degree requirements:* For master's, one foreign language, thesis; for doctorate, one foreign language, comprehensive exam, thesis/dissertation. *Entrance requirements:* For master's and doctorate, GRE General Test, GRE Subject Test, interview, 3 letters of recommendation, minimum GPA of 3.0. Electronic applications accepted. *Expenses:* Contact institution.

University of Puerto Rico, Río Piedras, College of Natural Sciences, Department of Biology, San Juan, PR 00931-3300. Offers ecology/systematics (MS, PhD); evolution/genetics (MS, PhD); molecular/cellular biology (MS, PhD); neuroscience (MS, PhD). Part-time programs available. *Degree requirements:* For master's, one foreign language, comprehensive exam, thesis; for doctorate, one foreign language, comprehensive exam, thesis/dissertation. *Entrance requirements:* For master's, GRE Subject Test, interview, minimum GPA of 3.0, letter of recommendation; for doctorate, GRE Subject Test, interview, master's degree, minimum GPA of 3.0, letter of recommendation. *Faculty research:* Environmental, poblational and systematic biology.

University of Regina, Faculty of Graduate Studies and Research, Faculty of Science, Department of Biology, Regina, SK S4S 0A2, Canada. Offers M Sc, PhD. *Faculty:* 15 full-time (3 women). *Students:* 29 full-time (18 women), 3 part-time (2 women). 11 applicants, 55% accepted. In 2011, 3 master's, 1 doctorate awarded. *Degree requirements:* For master's, thesis; for doctorate, comprehensive exam, thesis/dissertation. *Entrance requirements:* Additional exam requirements/recommendations for international students: Required—TOEFL (minimum score 580 paper-based; 80 iBT), IELTS (minimum score 6.5). *Application deadline:* Applications are processed on a rolling basis. Application fee: $100. Electronic applications accepted. *Financial support:* In 2011–12, 4 fellowships (averaging $6,000 per year), 1 research assistantship (averaging $5,500 per year), 10 teaching assistantships (averaging $2,298 per year) were awarded; scholarships/grants also available. Financial award application deadline: 6/15. *Faculty research:* Aquatic and terrestrial ecology, molecular and population

genetics, developmental biology, microbiology, plant physiology and morphology. *Unit head:* Dr. Mark Brigham, Head, 306-585-4255, Fax: 306-337-2410, E-mail: mark.brigham@uregina.ca. *Application contact:* Dr. Harold Weger, Graduate Program Coordinator, 306-585-4479, Fax: 306-337-2410, E-mail: harold.weger@uregina.ca. Web site: http://www.uregina.ca/biology/.

University of Rhode Island, Graduate School, College of the Environment and Life Sciences, Department of Biological Sciences, Kingston, RI 02881. Offers MS, PhD. Part-time programs available. *Faculty:* 19 full-time (9 women), 1 part-time/adjunct (0 women). *Students:* 12 full-time (6 women), 3 part-time (2 women); includes 3 minority (2 Asian, non-Hispanic/Latino; 1 Hispanic/Latino), 3 international. In 2011, 5 master's, 1 doctorate awarded. *Degree requirements:* For master's, comprehensive exam (for some programs), thesis optional; for doctorate, comprehensive exam, thesis/dissertation. *Entrance requirements:* For master's and doctorate, GRE, 2 letters of recommendation. Additional exam requirements/recommendations for international students: Required—TOEFL (minimum score 550 paper-based; 213 computer-based). *Application deadline:* For fall admission, 4/15 for domestic students, 1/15 for international students. Application fee: $65. Electronic applications accepted. *Expenses:* Tuition, state resident: full-time $10,432; part-time $580 per credit hour. Tuition, nonresident: full-time $23,130; part-time $1285 per credit hour. *Required fees:* $1362; $36 per credit hour. $35 per semester. One-time fee: $130. *Financial support:* In 2011–12, 1 research assistantship with partial tuition reimbursement (averaging $6,947 per year), 4 teaching assistantships with full and partial tuition reimbursements (averaging $9,817 per year) were awarded. Financial award application deadline: 1/15; financial award applicants required to submit FAFSA. *Faculty research:* Physiological constraints on predators in Antarctics, effects of CO2 absorption in salt water particularly as it impacts pteropods. *Unit head:* Dr. Marian Goldsmith, Chairperson, 401-874-2373, Fax: 401-874-2065, E-mail: mrgoldsmith@mail.uri.edu. *Application contact:* Nasser H. Zawia, Dean of the Graduate School, 401-874-5909, Fax: 401-874-5787, E-mail: nzawia@uri.edu. Web site: http://www.uri.edu/cels/bio/.

University of Rochester, School of Arts and Sciences, Department of Biology, Rochester, NY 14627. Offers MS, PhD. *Faculty:* 20 full-time (5 women). *Students:* 50 full-time (25 women), 1 (woman) part-time; includes 1 minority (Hispanic/Latino), 35 international. 148 applicants, 16% accepted, 11 enrolled. In 2011, 10 master's, 4 doctorates awarded. Terminal master's awarded for partial completion of doctoral program. *Degree requirements:* For doctorate, thesis/dissertation, qualifying exam. *Entrance requirements:* For master's and doctorate, GRE General Test, GRE Subject Test (highly recommended). Additional exam requirements/recommendations for international students: Required—TOEFL. *Application deadline:* For fall admission, 1/1 priority date for domestic students, 1/1 for international students. Application fee: $0. Electronic applications accepted. *Expenses: Tuition:* Full-time $41,040. *Financial support:* Fellowships, research assistantships, teaching assistantships, and tuition scholarships for PhD students available. Financial award application deadline: 1/1. *Faculty research:* Molecular, cellular, and developmental biology; genetics, ecology and evolutionary biology. *Unit head:* Gloria Culver, Chair, 585-276-3602. *Application contact:* Cindy Landry, Graduate Program Administrative Assistant, 585-275-7991. Web site: http://www.rochester.edu/College/BIO/graduate.html.

University of Rochester, School of Medicine and Dentistry, Graduate Programs in Medicine and Dentistry, Interdepartmental Program in Translational Biomedical Science, Rochester, NY 14627. Offers PhD. *Expenses: Tuition:* Full-time $41,040.

University of Saint Joseph, Department of Biology, West Hartford, CT 06117-2700. Offers MS. Part-time programs available. Postbaccalaureate distance learning degree programs offered (no on-campus study). *Students:* 3 full-time (all women), 77 part-time (60 women); includes 9 minority (5 Black or African American, non-Hispanic/Latino; 2 Asian, non-Hispanic/Latino; 2 Hispanic/Latino), 1 international. Average age 34. *Degree requirements:* For master's, comprehensive exam, thesis or alternative. *Entrance requirements:* For master's, 2 letters of recommendation. *Application deadline:* Applications are processed on a rolling basis. Application fee: $50. Electronic applications accepted. Application fee is waived when completed online. *Expenses: Tuition:* Part-time $670 per credit. *Required fees:* $40 per credit. Tuition and fees vary according to course load, degree level, campus/location and program. *Financial support:* Unspecified assistantships available. Support available to part-time students. Financial award applicants required to submit FAFSA. *Application contact:* Graduate Admissions Office, 860-231-5261, E-mail: graduate@usj.edu.

University of San Francisco, College of Arts and Sciences, Biology Program, San Francisco, CA 94117-1080. Offers MS. *Faculty:* 8 full-time (6 women). *Students:* 6 full-time (4 women), 1 part-time (0 women); includes 2 minority (1 Hispanic/Latino; 1 Two or more races, non-Hispanic/Latino). Average age 26. 39 applicants, 10% accepted, 3 enrolled. In 2011, 3 master's awarded. *Degree requirements:* For master's, thesis. *Entrance requirements:* For master's, GRE General Test, GRE Subject Test, BS in biology or the equivalent. *Application deadline:* For fall admission, 4/15 for domestic students; for spring admission, 10/15 for domestic students. Application fee: $55 ($65 for international students). *Expenses: Tuition:* Full-time $20,070; part-time $1115 per unit. Tuition and fees vary according to course load, campus/location and program. *Financial support:* In 2011–12, 6 students received support. Teaching assistantships, career-related internships or fieldwork, Federal Work-Study, institutionally sponsored loans, and tuition waivers available. Financial award application deadline: 3/2; financial award applicants required to submit FAFSA. *Unit head:* Dr. Jennifer Dever, Chair, 415-422-6755, Fax: 415-422-6363. *Application contact:* Information Contact, 415-422-5135, Fax: 415-422-2217, E-mail: asgraduate@usfca.edu. Web site: http://www.usfca.edu/artsci/biog/.

University of Saskatchewan, College of Graduate Studies and Research, College of Arts and Science, Department of Biology, Saskatoon, SK S7N 5A2, Canada. Offers M Sc, PhD. *Degree requirements:* For master's, thesis (for some programs); for doctorate, comprehensive exam (for some programs), thesis/dissertation. *Entrance requirements:* Additional exam requirements/recommendations for international students: Required—TOEFL (minimum score 80 iBT); Recommended—IELTS (minimum score 6.5). Electronic applications accepted.

University of Saskatchewan, Western College of Veterinary Medicine and College of Graduate Studies and Research, Graduate Programs in Veterinary Medicine, Department of Veterinary Biomedical Sciences, Saskatoon, SK S7N 5A2, Canada. Offers veterinary anatomy (M Sc); veterinary biomedical sciences (M Vet Sc); veterinary physiological sciences (M Sc, PhD). *Degree requirements:* For master's, thesis; for doctorate, comprehensive exam (for some programs), thesis/dissertation. *Entrance requirements:* Additional exam requirements/recommendations for international students: Required—TOEFL (minimum score 80 iBT); Recommended—IELTS (minimum score 6.5). Electronic applications accepted. *Faculty research:* Toxicology, animal reproduction, pharmacology, chloride channels, pulmonary pathobiology.

University of South Alabama, College of Medicine and Graduate School, Interdisciplinary Graduate Program in Basic Medical Sciences, Mobile, AL 36688-0002. Offers PhD. *Faculty:* 45 full-time (10 women), 1 part-time/adjunct (0 women). *Students:* 54 full-time (28 women); includes 14 minority (5 Black or African American, non-Hispanic/Latino; 3 American Indian or Alaska Native, non-Hispanic/Latino; 3 Asian, non-

Hispanic/Latino; 3 Hispanic/Latino), 11 international. 59 applicants, 24% accepted, 13 enrolled. In 2011, 9 doctorates awarded. *Degree requirements:* For doctorate, comprehensive exam, thesis/dissertation. *Entrance requirements:* For doctorate, GRE, three semesters or quarters of undergraduate work in physics, general chemistry, organic chemistry, biology, English composition, and mathematics (including statistics and calculus) with minimum GPA of 3.0. Additional exam requirements/recommendations for international students: Required—TOEFL. *Application deadline:* For fall admission, 4/1 for domestic students, 3/31 for international students. Applications are processed on a rolling basis. Application fee: $25. *Expenses:* Contact institution. *Financial support:* Fellowships, research assistantships, and institutionally sponsored loans available. Financial award application deadline: 4/1; financial award applicants required to submit FAFSA. *Faculty research:* Microcirculation, molecular biology, cell biology, growth control. *Unit head:* Dr. Ronald Balczon, Director of College of Medicine Graduate Studies, 251-460-6153, Fax: 251-460-6071, E-mail: rbalzon@usouthal.edu. *Application contact:* Dr. B. Keith Harrison, Dean of the Graduate School, 251-460-6310, Fax: 251-461-1513, E-mail: kharriso@usouthal.edu. Web site: http://www.southalabama.edu/com/.

University of South Alabama, Graduate School, College of Arts and Sciences, Department of Biological Sciences, Mobile, AL 36688-0002. Offers MS. Part-time programs available. *Faculty:* 6 full-time (2 women). *Students:* 10 full-time (7 women), 8 part-time (5 women); includes 2 minority (1 Asian, non-Hispanic/Latino; 1 Hispanic/Latino), 3 international. 17 applicants, 35% accepted, 6 enrolled. In 2011, 3 master's awarded. *Degree requirements:* For master's, one foreign language, comprehensive exam, thesis optional. *Entrance requirements:* For master's, GRE Subject Test, minimum GPA of 3.0. Additional exam requirements/recommendations for international students: Required—TOEFL (minimum score 600 paper-based). *Application deadline:* For fall admission, 7/15 priority date for domestic students, 6/15 for international students; for spring admission, 12/1 for domestic students, 11/1 for international students. Applications are processed on a rolling basis. Application fee: $35. *Expenses:* Tuition, state resident: full-time $7968; part-time $332 per credit hour. Tuition, nonresident: full-time $15,936; part-time $664 per credit hour. *Financial support:* Fellowships, research assistantships, and teaching assistantships available. Support available to part-time students. Financial award application deadline: 4/1. *Faculty research:* Aquatic and marine biology, molecular biochemistry, plant and animal taxonomy. *Unit head:* Dr. John Freeman, Chair, 251-460-6331. *Application contact:* Dr. Brian Axsmith, Graduate Coordinator, 251-460-6331, E-mail: baxsmith@jaguar1.usouthal.edu. Web site: http://www.southalabama.edu/biology.

University of South Carolina, The Graduate School, College of Arts and Sciences, Department of Biological Sciences, Columbia, SC 29208. Offers biology (MS, PhD); biology education (IMA, MAT); ecology, evolution and organismal biology (MS, PhD); molecular, cellular, and developmental biology (MS, PhD). IMA and MAT offered in cooperation with the College of Education. Terminal master's awarded for partial completion of doctoral program. *Degree requirements:* For master's, one foreign language, thesis (for some programs); for doctorate, one foreign language, thesis/dissertation. *Entrance requirements:* For master's and doctorate, GRE General Test, minimum GPA of 3.0 in science. Electronic applications accepted. *Faculty research:* Marine ecology, population and evolutionary biology, molecular biology and genetics, development.

University of South Carolina, School of Medicine and The Graduate School, Graduate Programs in Medicine, Columbia, SC 29208. Offers biomedical science (MBS, PhD); genetic counseling (MS); nurse anesthesia (MNA); rehabilitation counseling (MRC, Certificate), including psychiatric rehabilitation (Certificate), rehabilitation counseling (MRC). Terminal master's awarded for partial completion of doctoral program. *Degree requirements:* For master's, comprehensive exam, thesis (for some programs), practicum; for doctorate, comprehensive exam, thesis/dissertation. *Entrance requirements:* For master's, doctorate, and Certificate, GRE General Test. Electronic applications accepted. *Expenses:* Contact institution. *Faculty research:* Cardiovascular diseases, oncology, neuroscience, psychiatric rehabilitation, genetics.

University of South Carolina, School of Medicine and The Graduate School, Graduate Programs in Medicine, Graduate Program in Biomedical Science, Doctoral Program in Biomedical Science, Columbia, SC 29208. Offers PhD. *Degree requirements:* For doctorate, comprehensive exam, thesis/dissertation. *Entrance requirements:* For doctorate, GRE General Test. Electronic applications accepted. *Faculty research:* Cancer, neuroscience, cardiovascular, reproductive, immunology.

University of South Carolina, School of Medicine and The Graduate School, Graduate Programs in Medicine, Graduate Program in Biomedical Science, Master's Program in Biomedical Science, Columbia, SC 29208. Offers MBS. *Degree requirements:* For master's, comprehensive exam, thesis. *Entrance requirements:* For master's, GRE General Test. Electronic applications accepted. *Faculty research:* Cardiovascular diseases, oncology, reproductive biology, neuroscience, microbiology.

The University of South Dakota, Graduate School, College of Arts and Sciences, Department of Biology, Vermillion, SD 57069-2390. Offers MA, MNS, MS, PhD. *Degree requirements:* For master's, comprehensive exam (for some programs), thesis (for some programs); for doctorate, comprehensive exam, thesis/dissertation. *Entrance requirements:* For master's, GRE Subject Test, GRE General Test, minimum GPA of 2.7; for doctorate, GRE General Test, GRE Subject Test, minimum GPA of 2.7. Additional exam requirements/recommendations for international students: Required—TOEFL (minimum score 550 paper-based; 213 computer-based; 70 iBT). Electronic applications accepted. *Expenses:* Tuition, state resident: full-time $3118.50; part-time $173.25 per credit hour. Tuition, nonresident: full-time $6601; part-time $366.70 per credit hour. *Required fees:* $2268; $126 per credit hour. Tuition and fees vary according to program. *Faculty research:* Evolutionary and ecological informatics, neuroscience, stress physiology.

The University of South Dakota, Graduate School, School of Medicine and Graduate School, Biomedical Sciences Graduate Program, Vermillion, SD 57069-2390. Offers cardiovascular research (MS, PhD); cellular and molecular biology (MS, PhD); molecular microbiology and immunology (MS, PhD); neuroscience (MS, PhD); physiology and pharmacology (MS, PhD). Terminal master's awarded for partial completion of doctoral program. *Degree requirements:* For master's, thesis; for doctorate, comprehensive exam, thesis/dissertation. *Entrance requirements:* For master's and doctorate, GRE General Test, minimum GPA of 3.0. Additional exam requirements/recommendations for international students: Required—TOEFL (minimum score 550 paper-based; 213 computer-based; 80 iBT), IELTS (minimum score 6). Electronic applications accepted. *Expenses:* Contact institution. *Faculty research:* Molecular biology, microbiology, neuroscience, cellular biology, physiology.

University of Southern California, Graduate School, Dana and David Dornsife College of Letters, Arts and Sciences, Department of Biological Sciences, Los Angeles, CA 90089. Offers biology (MS); computational molecular biology (MS); integrative and evolutionary biology (PhD); marine biology and biological oceanography (MS, PhD), including marine and environmental biology (MS), marine biology and biological oceanography (PhD); molecular and computational biology (PhD), including biology, computational biology and bioinformatics, molecular biology; neurobiology (PhD).

Biological and Biomedical Sciences—General

Terminal master's awarded for partial completion of doctoral program. *Degree requirements:* For master's, comprehensive exam (for some programs), research paper; for doctorate, thesis/dissertation, qualifying examination, dissertation defense. *Entrance requirements:* For master's, GRE, 3 letters of recommendation, personal statement, resume, minimum GPA of 3.0; for doctorate, GRE, 3 letters of recommendation, resume, minimum GPA of 3.0. Additional exam requirements/recommendations for international students: Required—TOEFL (minimum score 600 paper-based; 250 computer-based; 100 iBT). Electronic applications accepted. *Faculty research:* Microarray data analysis, microbial ecology and genetics, integrative organismal and behavioral biology and ecology, stem cell pluipotency, cancer cell biology.

University of Southern California, Keck School of Medicine and Graduate School, Graduate Programs in Medicine, Los Angeles, CA 90089. Offers MPAP, MPH, MS, PhD, MD/PhD. *Faculty:* 468 full-time (143 women), 17 part-time/adjunct (2 women). *Students:* 670 full-time (448 women), 35 part-time (23 women); includes 268 minority (14 Black or African American, non-Hispanic/Latino; 5 American Indian or Alaska Native, non-Hispanic/Latino; 166 Asian, non-Hispanic/Latino; 70 Hispanic/Latino; 5 Native Hawaiian or other Pacific Islander, non-Hispanic/Latino; 8 Two or more races, non-Hispanic/Latino), 222 international. Average age 27. 1,539 applicants, 27% accepted, 238 enrolled. In 2011, 156 master's, 36 doctorates awarded. Terminal master's awarded for partial completion of doctoral program. *Entrance requirements:* For master's, GRE General Test, minimum GPA of 3.0; for doctorate, GRE General Test (minimum combined Verbal and Quantitative score of 1000), minimum GPA of 3.0. Additional exam requirements/recommendations for international students: Required—TOEFL (minimum score 600 paper-based; 250 computer-based; 100 iBT). *Application deadline:* Applications are processed on a rolling basis. Application fee: $85. Electronic applications accepted. *Financial support:* In 2011–12, 335 students received support, including 30 fellowships with tuition reimbursements available, 203 research assistantships with full and partial tuition reimbursements available (averaging $29,100 per year), 34 teaching assistantships with full and partial tuition reimbursements available (averaging $29,100 per year); career-related internships or fieldwork, Federal Work-Study, institutionally sponsored loans, scholarships/grants, traineeships, health care benefits, and unspecified assistantships also available. Support available to part-time students. Financial award application deadline: 5/4; financial award applicants required to submit CSS PROFILE or FAFSA. *Unit head:* Dr. Debbie Johnson, Associate Dean for Graduate Affairs, 323-442-1446, Fax: 323-442-1199, E-mail: johnsond@usc.edu. *Application contact:* Marisela Zuniga, Administrative Coordinator, 323-442-1607, Fax: 323-442-1199, E-mail: mzuniga@usc.edu. Web site: http://www.usc.edu/medicine/scientific_affairs/.

University of Southern Maine, College of Arts and Sciences, Program in Biology, Portland, ME 04104-9300. Offers MS.

University of Southern Mississippi, Graduate School, College of Science and Technology, Department of Biological Sciences, Hattiesburg, MS 39406-0001. Offers environmental biology (MS, PhD); marine biology (MS, PhD); microbiology (MS, PhD); molecular biology (MS, PhD). *Faculty:* 27 full-time (6 women). *Students:* 57 full-time (28 women), 4 part-time (2 women); includes 5 minority (2 Black or African American, non-Hispanic/Latino; 3 Two or more races, non-Hispanic/Latino), 18 international. Average age 32. 50 applicants, 32% accepted, 12 enrolled. In 2011, 7 master's, 8 doctorates awarded. Terminal master's awarded for partial completion of doctoral program. *Degree requirements:* For master's, comprehensive exam, thesis; for doctorate, comprehensive exam, thesis/dissertation. *Entrance requirements:* For master's, GRE General Test, minimum GPA of 3.0 on last 60 hours; for doctorate, GRE General Test, minimum GPA of 3.5. Additional exam requirements/recommendations for international students: Required—TOEFL, IELTS. *Application deadline:* For fall admission, 3/1 priority date for domestic students, 3/1 for international students; for spring admission, 1/10 priority date for domestic students, 1/10 for international students. Applications are processed on a rolling basis. Application fee: $50. *Financial support:* In 2011–12, 25 research assistantships with full tuition reimbursements (averaging $9,700 per year), 33 teaching assistantships with full tuition reimbursements (averaging $10,600 per year) were awarded; Federal Work-Study, scholarships/grants, health care benefits, and unspecified assistantships also available. Financial award application deadline: 3/15; financial award applicants required to submit FAFSA. *Unit head:* Dr. Glenmore Shearer, Chair, 601-266-4748, Fax: 601-266-5797. *Application contact:* Dr. Jake Schaefer, Director of Graduate Studies, 601-266-4748, Fax: 601-266-5797. Web site: http://www.usm.edu/graduateschool/table.php.

University of South Florida, Graduate School, College of Arts and Sciences, Department of Biology, Tampa, FL 33620-9951. Offers cell biology and molecular biology (MS); coastal marine biology (MS); coastal marine biology and ecology (PhD); conservation biology (MS, PhD); molecular and cell biology (PhD). Part-time programs available. *Faculty:* 35 full-time (11 women), 16 part-time/adjunct (5 women). *Students:* 126 full-time (75 women), 24 part-time (17 women); includes 13 minority (1 Black or African American, non-Hispanic/Latino; 4 Asian, non-Hispanic/Latino; 8 Hispanic/Latino), 17 international. Average age 30. 235 applicants, 21% accepted, 30 enrolled. In 2011, 7 master's, 11 doctorates awarded. *Degree requirements:* For master's, comprehensive exam, thesis (for some programs); for doctorate, comprehensive exam, thesis/dissertation. *Entrance requirements:* For master's and doctorate, GRE General Test, minimum GPA of 3.0. Additional exam requirements/recommendations for international students: Required—TOEFL (minimum score 570 paper-based; 213 computer-based). *Application deadline:* For fall admission, 2/15 priority date for domestic students, 1/2 for international students; for spring admission, 8/1 for domestic students, 6/1 for international students. Application fee: $30. Electronic applications accepted. *Financial support:* In 2011–12, 122 students received support, including 46 research assistantships (averaging $24,716 per year), 76 teaching assistantships with tuition reimbursements available (averaging $28,434 per year); unspecified assistantships also available. Financial award application deadline: 6/30; financial award applicants required to submit FAFSA. *Total annual research expenditures:* $5.2 million. *Unit head:* Susan Bell, Co-Chairperson, 813-974-6210, Fax: 813-974-2876, E-mail: sbell@cas.usf.edu. *Application contact:* James Garey, Graduate Advisor, 813-974-8434, Fax: 813-974-3263, E-mail: grarey@cas.usf.edu. Web site: http://www.cas.usf.edu/biology/.

University of South Florida, Graduate School, College of Medicine and Graduate School, Graduate Programs in Medical Sciences, Tampa, FL 33620-9951. Offers bioethics and medical humanities (MABMH); bioinformatics and computational biology (MSBCB); biotechnology (MSB); medical sciences (MSMS, PhD). *Students:* 439 full-time (235 women), 111 part-time (65 women); includes 258 minority (82 Black or African American, non-Hispanic/Latino; 2 American Indian or Alaska Native, non-Hispanic/Latino; 85 Asian, non-Hispanic/Latino; 77 Hispanic/Latino; 12 Two or more races, non-Hispanic/Latino), 24 international. Average age 27. 1,032 applicants, 53% accepted, 364 enrolled. In 2011, 167 master's, 14 doctorates awarded. Terminal master's awarded for partial completion of doctoral program. *Degree requirements:* For master's, comprehensive exam, thesis; for doctorate, comprehensive exam, thesis/dissertation. *Entrance requirements:* For master's, GRE, MCAT, or GMAT, minimum GPA of 3.0 in last 60 hours of coursework; for doctorate, GRE, minimum GPA of 3.0 in last 60 hours of coursework, three letters of recommendation, personal statement, interview. Additional exam requirements/recommendations for international students: Required—TOEFL (minimum score 550 paper-based; 213 computer-based; 79 iBT) or IELTS (minimum score 6.5). *Application deadline:* For fall admission, 2/15 for domestic students, 1/2 for international students. Application fee: $30. *Expenses:* Contact institution. *Unit head:* Dr. Michael Barber, Program Director, 813-974-9702, Fax: 813-974-4317, E-mail: mbarber@health.usf.edu. *Application contact:* Francisco Vera, Assistant Director for Admissions, 813-974-8800, E-mail: fvera@usf.edu. Web site: http://health.usf.edu/medicine/graduatestudies.

The University of Tennessee, Graduate School, College of Arts and Sciences, Program in Life Sciences, Knoxville, TN 37996. Offers genome science and technology (MS, PhD); plant physiology and genetics (MS, PhD). *Degree requirements:* For doctorate, one foreign language, thesis/dissertation. *Entrance requirements:* For master's and doctorate, GRE General Test, minimum GPA of 2.7. Additional exam requirements/recommendations for international students: Required—TOEFL. Electronic applications accepted. *Expenses:* Tuition, state resident: full-time $8332; part-time $464 per credit hour. Tuition, nonresident: full-time $25,174; part-time $1400 per credit hour. *Required fees:* $1162; $56 per credit hour. Tuition and fees vary according to program.

The University of Tennessee, Graduate School, Intercollegiate Programs, Program in Comparative and Experimental Medicine, Knoxville, TN 37996. Offers MS, PhD. *Degree requirements:* For master's, thesis; for doctorate, thesis/dissertation. *Entrance requirements:* For master's and doctorate, GRE General Test, minimum GPA of 2.7. Additional exam requirements/recommendations for international students: Required—TOEFL. Electronic applications accepted. *Expenses:* Tuition, state resident: full-time $8332; part-time $464 per credit hour. Tuition, nonresident: full-time $25,174; part-time $1400 per credit hour. *Required fees:* $1162; $56 per credit hour. Tuition and fees vary according to program.

The University of Tennessee–Oak Ridge National Laboratory, Graduate Program in Genome Science and Technology, Oak Ridge, TN 37830-8026. Offers life sciences (MS, PhD). *Degree requirements:* For master's, thesis; for doctorate, comprehensive exam, thesis/dissertation. *Entrance requirements:* For master's and doctorate, GRE General Test. Additional exam requirements/recommendations for international students: Required—TOEFL (minimum score 550 paper-based; 213 computer-based). Electronic applications accepted. *Faculty research:* Genetics/genomics, structural biology/proteomics, computational biology/bioinformatics, bioanalytical technologies.

The University of Texas at Arlington, Graduate School, College of Science, Department of Biology, Arlington, TX 76019. Offers biology (MS); quantitative biology (PhD). Part-time and evening/weekend programs available. *Faculty:* 24 full-time (6 women). *Students:* 58 full-time (28 women), 15 part-time (11 women); includes 10 minority (3 Black or African American, non-Hispanic/Latino; 4 Asian, non-Hispanic/Latino; 3 Hispanic/Latino), 22 international. Average age 25. 65 applicants, 38% accepted, 12 enrolled. In 2011, 18 master's, 6 doctorates awarded. *Degree requirements:* For master's, thesis, oral defense of thesis; for doctorate, comprehensive exam, thesis/dissertation, oral defense of dissertation. *Entrance requirements:* For master's and doctorate, GRE General Test. Additional exam requirements/recommendations for international students: Required—TOEFL (minimum score 550 paper-based; 213 computer-based; 79 iBT). *Application deadline:* For fall admission, 6/15 for domestic students, 4/3 for international students; for spring admission, 10/15 for domestic students, 9/11 for international students. Applications are processed on a rolling basis. Application fee: $35 ($50 for international students). Electronic applications accepted. *Financial support:* In 2011–12, 52 students received support, including 4 fellowships (averaging $1,000 per year), 4 research assistantships (averaging $15,500 per year), 26 teaching assistantships (averaging $15,500 per year); Federal Work-Study and institutionally sponsored loans also available. Financial award application deadline: 6/1; financial award applicants required to submit FAFSA. *Faculty research:* Cellular and microbiology, comparative genomics, evolution and ecology. *Total annual research expenditures:* $1.9 million. *Unit head:* Dr. Johnathan Campbell, Chair, 817-272-2871, Fax: 817-272-2855, E-mail: campbell@exchange.uta.edu. *Application contact:* Dr. Laura Gough, Graduate Adviser, 817-272-2871, Fax: 817-272-2855, E-mail: gough@uta.edu. Web site: http://www.uta.edu/biology/home.html.

The University of Texas at Austin, Graduate School, College of Natural Sciences, School of Biological Sciences, Austin, TX 78712-1111. Offers ecology, evolution and behavior (PhD); microbiology (PhD); plant biology (MA, PhD). *Entrance requirements:* For master's and doctorate, GRE General Test. *Application deadline:* Applications are processed on a rolling basis. Application fee: $50 ($75 for international students). Electronic applications accepted. *Financial support:* Fellowships, research assistantships, and teaching assistantships available. Financial award application deadline: 2/1. *Unit head:* Dr. Hank Bose, Director, 512-471-5525, E-mail: bose@mail.utexas.edu. Web site: http://www.biosci.utexas.edu/graduate/.

The University of Texas at Brownsville, Graduate Studies, College of Science, Mathematics and Technology, Brownsville, TX 78520-4991. Offers biological sciences (MS, MSIS); mathematics (MS); physics (MS). Part-time and evening/weekend programs available. *Degree requirements:* For master's, comprehensive exam, thesis optional. *Entrance requirements:* For master's, GRE General Test. Additional exam requirements/recommendations for international students: Required—TOEFL. *Faculty research:* Fish, insects, barrier islands, algae, curlits.

The University of Texas at Dallas, School of Natural Sciences and Mathematics, Department of Biology, Richardson, TX 75080. Offers bioinformatics and computational biology (MS); biotechnology (MS); molecular and cell biology (MS, PhD). Part-time and evening/weekend programs available. *Faculty:* 18 full-time (2 women), 1 part-time/adjunct (0 women). *Students:* 111 full-time (59 women), 13 part-time (6 women); includes 19 minority (2 Black or African American, non-Hispanic/Latino; 14 Asian, non-Hispanic/Latino; 3 Hispanic/Latino), 86 international. Average age 27. 483 applicants, 31% accepted, 67 enrolled. In 2011, 39 master's, 7 doctorates awarded. *Degree requirements:* For master's, thesis optional; for doctorate, thesis/dissertation, publishable paper. *Entrance requirements:* For master's and doctorate, GRE (minimum combined score of 1000 on verbal and quantitative). Additional exam requirements/recommendations for international students: Required—TOEFL (minimum score 550 paper-based; 215 computer-based; 80 iBT). *Application deadline:* For fall admission, 7/15 for domestic students, 5/1 for international students; for spring admission, 11/15 for domestic students, 9/1 for international students. Applications are processed on a rolling basis. Application fee: $50 ($100 for international students). Electronic applications accepted. *Expenses:* Tuition, state resident: full-time $11,170; part-time $620.56 per credit hour. Tuition, nonresident: full-time $20,212; part-time $1122.89 per credit hour. *Financial support:* In 2011–12, 49 students received support, including 18 research assistantships with partial tuition reimbursements available (averaging $20,911 per year), 36 teaching assistantships with partial tuition reimbursements available (averaging $15,300 per year); career-related internships or fieldwork, Federal Work-Study, institutionally sponsored loans, scholarships/grants, and unspecified assistantships also available. Support available to part-time students. Financial award application deadline: 4/30; financial award applicants required to submit FAFSA. *Faculty research:* Role of mitochondria in neurodegenerative diseases, protein-DNA interactions in site-specific recombination, eukaryotic gene expression, bio-nanotechnology, sickle

cell research. *Unit head:* Dr. Stephen Spiro, Department Head, 972-883-6032, Fax: 972-883-2502, E-mail: stephen.spiro@utdallas.edu. *Application contact:* Dr. Lawrence Reitzer, Graduate Advisor, 972-883-2502, Fax: 972-883-2402, E-mail: reitzer@utdallas.edu. Web site: http://www.utdallas.edu/biology/.

The University of Texas at El Paso, Graduate School, College of Science, Department of Biological Sciences, El Paso, TX 79968-0001. Offers bioinformatics (MS); biological sciences (MS, PhD). Part-time and evening/weekend programs available. *Students:* 76 (43 women); includes 49 minority (3 Black or African American, non-Hispanic/Latino; 3 Asian, non-Hispanic/Latino; 42 Hispanic/Latino; 1 Two or more races, non-Hispanic/Latino), 14 international. Average age 34. 38 applicants, 45% accepted, 16 enrolled. In 2011, 4 master's, 1 doctorate awarded. *Degree requirements:* For master's, thesis; for doctorate, thesis/dissertation. *Entrance requirements:* For master's, GRE, minimum GPA of 3.0, letters of recommendation; for doctorate, GRE, statement of purpose, letters of recommendation. Additional exam requirements/recommendations for international students: Required—TOEFL; Recommended—IELTS. *Application deadline:* For fall admission, 8/1 priority date for domestic students, 3/1 for international students; for spring admission, 11/1 priority date for domestic students, 9/1 for international students. Applications are processed on a rolling basis. Application fee: $45 ($80 for international students). Electronic applications accepted. *Financial support:* In 2011–12, research assistantships with partial tuition reimbursements (averaging $22,500 per year), teaching assistantships with partial tuition reimbursements (averaging $18,000 per year) were awarded; fellowships with partial tuition reimbursements, institutionally sponsored loans, scholarships/grants, health care benefits, tuition waivers (partial), and unspecified assistantships also available. Support available to part-time students. Financial award application deadline: 3/15; financial award applicants required to submit FAFSA. *Unit head:* Dr. Robert Kirken, Chair, 915-747-5844, Fax: 915-747-5808, E-mail: rkirken@utep.edu. *Application contact:* Dr. Benjamin Flores, Interim Dean of Graduate School, 915-747-5491, Fax: 915-747-5788, E-mail: bflores@utep.edu.

The University of Texas at San Antonio, College of Sciences, Department of Biology, San Antonio, TX 78249-0617. Offers biology (MS); biotechnology (MS), including bioprocessing technician, biotechnology; cell and molecular biology (PhD); environmental science (MS); neurobiology (PhD). *Faculty:* 34 full-time (6 women), 7 part-time/adjunct (1 woman). *Students:* 117 full-time (62 women), 64 part-time (35 women); includes 63 minority (10 Black or African American, non-Hispanic/Latino; 10 Asian, non-Hispanic/Latino; 36 Hispanic/Latino; 7 Two or more races, non-Hispanic/Latino), 54 international. Average age 27. 239 applicants, 45% accepted, 50 enrolled. In 2011, 62 master's, 3 doctorates awarded. Terminal master's awarded for partial completion of doctoral program. *Degree requirements:* For master's, comprehensive exam, thesis or alternative; for doctorate, thesis/dissertation. *Entrance requirements:* For master's, GRE General Test, bachelor's degree with 18 credit hours in field of study or in another appropriate field of study; for doctorate, GRE General Test, 3 letters of recommendation, statement of purpose, resume. Additional exam requirements/recommendations for international students: Required—TOEFL (minimum score 500 paper-based; 100 iBT), IELTS (minimum score 5). *Application deadline:* For fall admission, 7/1 for domestic students, 4/1 for international students; for spring admission, 11/1 for domestic students, 9/1 for international students. Application fee: $45 ($85 for international students). *Expenses:* Tuition, state resident: full-time $3148; part-time $2176 per semester. Tuition, nonresident: full-time $8782; part-time $5932 per semester. *Required fees:* $719 per semester. *Financial support:* In 2011–12, 66 students received support, including 4 fellowships (averaging $22,350 per year), 34 research assistantships (averaging $22,350 per year), 8 teaching assistantships (averaging $22,350 per year). *Faculty research:* Development of human and veterinary vaccines against a fungal disease, mammalian germ cells and stem cells, dopamine neuron physiology and addiction, plant biochemistry, dendritic computation and synaptic plasticity. *Total annual research expenditures:* $2.8 million. *Unit head:* Dr. Edwin J. Barea-Rodriguez, Chair, 210-458-4511, Fax: 210-458-5658, E-mail: edwin.barea@utsa.edu. *Application contact:* Rene Munguia, Program Coordinator, 210-458-4642, Fax: 210-458-5658, E-mail: rene.munguia@utsa.edu.

The University of Texas at Tyler, College of Arts and Sciences, Department of Biology, Tyler, TX 75799-0001. Offers biology (MS); interdisciplinary studies (MSIS). *Degree requirements:* For master's, comprehensive exam, thesis, oral qualifying exam, thesis defense. *Entrance requirements:* For master's, GRE General Test, GRE Subject Test, bachelor's degree in biology or equivalent. Additional exam requirements/recommendations for international students: Required—TOEFL (minimum score 79 computer-based). Electronic applications accepted. *Faculty research:* Phenotypic plasticity and heritability of life history traits, invertebrate ecology and genetics, systematics and phylogenetics of reptiles, hibernation physiology in turtles, landscape ecology, host-microbe interaction, outer membrane proteins in bacteria.

The University of Texas Health Science Center at Houston, Graduate School of Biomedical Sciences, Houston, TX 77225-0036. Offers MS, PhD, MD/PhD. Terminal master's awarded for partial completion of doctoral program. *Degree requirements:* For master's, thesis; for doctorate, thesis/dissertation. *Entrance requirements:* For master's and doctorate, GRE General Test. Additional exam requirements/recommendations for international students: Required—TOEFL. Electronic applications accepted. *Faculty research:* Biomedical sciences.

The University of Texas Health Science Center at San Antonio, Graduate School of Biomedical Sciences, San Antonio, TX 78229-3900. Offers MS, MSN, PhD. *Degree requirements:* For master's, comprehensive exam (for some programs), thesis; for doctorate, comprehensive exam, thesis/dissertation. *Entrance requirements:* For master's and doctorate, GRE General Test. Additional exam requirements/recommendations for international students: Required—TOEFL (minimum score 560 paper-based; 220 computer-based; 68 iBT). Electronic applications accepted. *Expenses:* Contact institution. *Faculty research:* Biochemistry, cellular and structural biology, molecular medicine, microbiology and immunology, pathology, pharmacology, physiology, neuroscience, aging, cancer, genetics.

The University of Texas Medical Branch, Graduate School of Biomedical Sciences, Galveston, TX 77555. Offers MA, MMS, MPH, MS, PhD, MD/PhD. Terminal master's awarded for partial completion of doctoral program. *Degree requirements:* For master's, comprehensive exam (for some programs), thesis or alternative; for doctorate, comprehensive exam, thesis/dissertation. *Entrance requirements:* For master's and doctorate, GRE General Test, 3 letters of recommendation. Additional exam requirements/recommendations for international students: Required—TOEFL (minimum score 550 paper-based; 213 computer-based; 80 iBT), IELTS (minimum score 6.5). Electronic applications accepted. *Expenses:* Contact institution.

The University of Texas of the Permian Basin, Office of Graduate Studies, College of Arts and Sciences, Department of Biology, Odessa, TX 79762-0001. Offers MS. Part-time and evening/weekend programs available. *Degree requirements:* For master's, comprehensive exam, thesis or alternative. *Entrance requirements:* For master's, GRE General Test. Additional exam requirements/recommendations for international students: Required—TOEFL (minimum score 550 paper-based; 213 computer-based).

The University of Texas–Pan American, College of Science and Mathematics, Department of Biology, Edinburg, TX 78539. Offers MS. Part-time and evening/weekend programs available. *Degree requirements:* For master's, comprehensive exam. *Entrance requirements:* For master's, GRE General Test, minimum GPA of 2.75 in biology. Application fee: $0. Tuition and fees vary according to course load, program and student level. *Financial support:* Teaching assistantships, Federal Work-Study, institutionally sponsored loans, and tuition waivers (partial) available. Support available to part-time students. Financial award application deadline: 6/1. *Faculty research:* Flora and fauna of South Padre Island, plant taxonomy of Rio Grande Valley. *Unit head:* Dr. Mohammed Farooqui, Chair, 956-665-3543, E-mail: farooqui@utpa.edu. Web site: http://portal.utpa.edu/utpa_main/daa_home/cose_home/biology_home/biology_graduate.

The University of Texas Southwestern Medical Center, Southwestern Graduate School of Biomedical Sciences, Division of Basic Science, Dallas, TX 75390. Offers biological chemistry (PhD); biomedical engineering (MS, PhD); cancer biology (PhD); cell regulation (PhD); genetics and development (PhD); immunology (PhD); integrative biology (PhD); molecular biophysics (PhD); molecular microbiology (PhD); neuroscience (PhD); MD/PhD. *Degree requirements:* For doctorate, thesis/dissertation, qualifying exam. *Entrance requirements:* For doctorate, GRE General Test, research experience. Additional exam requirements/recommendations for international students: Required—TOEFL. Electronic applications accepted.

The University of Texas Southwestern Medical Center, Southwestern Graduate School of Biomedical Sciences, Division of Clinical Science, Clinical Science Program, Dallas, TX 75390. Offers MCS, MSCS. Part-time programs available. *Degree requirements:* For master's, 1 year clinical research project. *Entrance requirements:* For master's, graduate degree in biomedical science. Electronic applications accepted.

The University of Texas Southwestern Medical Center, Southwestern Graduate School of Biomedical Sciences, Medical Scientist Training Program, Dallas, TX 75390. Offers PhD, MD/PhD. Electronic applications accepted.

University of the Incarnate Word, School of Graduate Studies and Research, School of Mathematics, Science, and Engineering, Program in Biology, San Antonio, TX 78209-6397. Offers MA, MS. Part-time and evening/weekend programs available. *Faculty:* 4 full-time (2 women), 3 part-time/adjunct (all women). *Students:* 5 full-time (4 women), 5 part-time (all women); includes 6 minority (all Hispanic/Latino), 2 international. Average age 27. 15 applicants, 80% accepted, 4 enrolled. In 2011, 7 master's awarded. *Degree requirements:* For master's, comprehensive exam (for MA); thesis defense (for MS). *Entrance requirements:* For master's, GRE Subject Test (biology), minimum GPA of 3.0 in biology or GRE (minimum combined score 1,000 Verbal and Quantitative), 8 hours principles of chemistry, 6 hours organic chemistry, 12 upper-division hours in biology. Additional exam requirements/recommendations for international students: Required—TOEFL (minimum score 560 paper-based; 220 computer-based; 83 iBT). *Application deadline:* Applications are processed on a rolling basis. Application fee: $20. Electronic applications accepted. *Expenses: Tuition:* Part-time $725 per credit hour. Tuition and fees vary according to degree level. *Financial support:* Federal Work-Study and scholarships/grants available. Financial award applicants required to submit FAFSA. *Faculty research:* Regeneration of nervous system elements, social behaviors of electric fish, gene expression in human cells, transmission of pathogenic protozoa, human DNA response to cancer fighting molecules. *Total annual research expenditures:* $1.2 million. *Unit head:* Dr. David Foglesong, Graduate Program Director, 210-283-5033, Fax: 210-829-3153, E-mail: davidf@uiwtx.edu. *Application contact:* Andrea Cyterski-Acosta, Dean of Enrollment, 210-829-6005, Fax: 210-829-3921, E-mail: admis@uiwtx.edu. Web site: http://www.uiw.edu/biology/graduate_program.htm.

University of the Pacific, College of the Pacific, Department of Biological Sciences, Stockton, CA 95211-0197. Offers MS. *Faculty:* 16 full-time (5 women), 1 (woman) part-time/adjunct. *Students:* 24 part-time (12 women); includes 16 minority (1 Black or African American, non-Hispanic/Latino; 15 Asian, non-Hispanic/Latino), 3 international. Average age 24. 24 applicants, 58% accepted, 12 enrolled. In 2011, 8 master's awarded. *Degree requirements:* For master's, thesis. *Entrance requirements:* For master's, GRE General Test, GRE Subject Test. Additional exam requirements/recommendations for international students: Required—TOEFL. *Application deadline:* For fall admission, 3/1 priority date for domestic students; for spring admission, 10/1 priority date for domestic students. Applications are processed on a rolling basis. Application fee: $75. *Expenses: Tuition:* Full-time $18,900; part-time $1181 per unit. *Required fees:* $949. *Financial support:* In 2011–12, 22 teaching assistantships were awarded; institutionally sponsored loans also available. Support available to part-time students. Financial award application deadline: 3/1; financial award applicants required to submit FAFSA. *Unit head:* Dr. Gregg Jongeward, Chairman, 209-946-2181. *Application contact:* Information Contact, 209-946-2261.

The University of Toledo, College of Graduate Studies, College of Medicine and Life Sciences, Interdepartmental Programs, Toledo, OH 43606-3390. Offers bioinformatics/proteomics/genomics (MSBS, Certificate); human donation sciences (MSBS); medical sciences (MSBS). *Faculty:* 37. *Students:* 66 full-time (26 women), 3 part-time (1 woman); includes 17 minority (2 Black or African American, non-Hispanic/Latino; 12 Asian, non-Hispanic/Latino; 2 Hispanic/Latino; 1 Two or more races, non-Hispanic/Latino), 1 international. Average age 25. 12 applicants, 92% accepted, 10 enrolled. In 2011, 54 master's, 1 Certificate awarded. *Degree requirements:* For master's, thesis or alternative. *Entrance requirements:* For master's, GRE, minimum undergraduate GPA of 3.0, three letters of recommendation, statement of purpose, transcripts from all prior institutions attended, resume; for Certificate, minimum undergraduate GPA of 3.0, three letters of recommendation, statement of purpose, transcripts from all prior institutions attended, resume. Additional exam requirements/recommendations for international students: Required—TOEFL (minimum score 550 paper-based; 213 computer-based; 80 iBT), IELTS (minimum score 6.5). *Application deadline:* For fall admission, 1/15 priority date for domestic students, 1/15 for international students. Application fee: $45 ($75 for international students). Electronic applications accepted. *Financial support:* Tuition scholarships available. *Unit head:* Dr. Randall Ruch, Assistant Dean of Admissions for Biomedical Graduate programs. *Application contact:* Admissions Analyst, 419-383-4116, Fax: 419-383-6140. Web site: http://www.utoledo.edu/med/grad/.

The University of Toledo, College of Graduate Studies, College of Natural Sciences and Mathematics, Department of Biological Sciences, Toledo, OH 43606-3390. Offers cell/molecular biology (MS, PhD). Part-time programs available. *Faculty:* 19. *Students:* 70 full-time (34 women), 28 part-time (20 women); includes 6 minority (1 Black or African American, non-Hispanic/Latino; 2 Asian, non-Hispanic/Latino; 1 Hispanic/Latino; 2 Two or more races, non-Hispanic/Latino), 30 international. Average age 29. 110 applicants, 16% accepted, 16 enrolled. In 2011, 13 master's, 6 doctorates awarded. *Degree requirements:* For master's, thesis or alternative; for doctorate, thesis/dissertation. *Entrance requirements:* For master's and doctorate, GRE General Test, GRE Subject Test, minimum cumulative point-hour ratio of 2.7 for all previous academic work, three letters of recommendation, statement of purpose, transcripts from all prior institutions attended. Additional exam requirements/recommendations for international students: Required—TOEFL (minimum score 550 paper-based; 213 computer-based; 80 iBT), IELTS (minimum score 6.5). *Application deadline:* For fall admission, 1/15 priority date for domestic students, 1/15 for international students. Applications are processed on a rolling basis. Application fee: $45 ($75 for international students). Electronic applications

accepted. *Financial support:* In 2011–12, 31 research assistantships with full and partial tuition reimbursements (averaging $17,292 per year), 38 teaching assistantships with full and partial tuition reimbursements (averaging $18,011 per year) were awarded; fellowships, Federal Work-Study, institutionally sponsored loans, scholarships/grants, tuition waivers (full), and unspecified assistantships also available. Support available to part-time students. *Faculty research:* Biochemical parasitology, physiological ecology, animal physiology. *Unit head:* Dr. Doug Leaman, Chair, 419-530-2066, E-mail: douglas.leaman@utoledo.edu. *Application contact:* Graduate School Office, 419-530-4723, Fax: 419-530-4724, E-mail: grdsch@utnet.utoledo.edu. Web site: http://www.utoledo.edu/nsm/.

The University of Toledo, College of Graduate Studies, College of Natural Sciences and Mathematics, Department of Environmental Sciences, Toledo, OH 43606-3390. Offers biology (MS, PhD), including ecology. Part-time programs available. *Faculty:* 26. *Students:* 9 full-time (4 women), 2 part-time (1 woman); includes 1 minority (Black or African American, non-Hispanic/Latino), 1 international. Average age 30. 9 applicants, 56% accepted, 5 enrolled. In 2011, 3 master's awarded. *Degree requirements:* For master's, thesis (for some programs). *Entrance requirements:* For master's, GRE General Test, minimum cumulative point-hour ratio of 2.7 for all previous academic work, three letters of recommendation, statement of purpose, transcripts from all prior institutions attended. Additional exam requirements/recommendations for international students: Required—TOEFL (minimum score 550 paper-based; 213 computer-based; 80 iBT), IELTS (minimum score 6.5). *Application deadline:* For fall admission, 1/15 priority date for domestic students, 1/15 for international students. Applications are processed on a rolling basis. Application fee: $45 ($75 for international students). Electronic applications accepted. *Financial support:* In 2011–12, 5 research assistantships with full and partial tuition reimbursements (averaging $18,126 per year), 12 teaching assistantships with full and partial tuition reimbursements (averaging $12,850 per year) were awarded; Federal Work-Study, institutionally sponsored loans, scholarships/grants, tuition waivers (full), and unspecified assistantships also available. Support available to part-time students. *Faculty research:* Environmental geochemistry, geophysics, petrology and mineralogy, paleontology, geohydrology. *Unit head:* Dr. Timothy G. Fisher, Chair, 419-530-2883, E-mail: timothy.fisher@utoledo.edu. *Application contact:* Graduate School Office, 419-530-4723, Fax: 419-530-4724, E-mail: grdsch@utnet.utoledo.edu. Web site: http://www.utoledo.edu/nsm/.

University of Tulsa, Graduate School, College of Arts and Sciences, School of Education, Program in Teaching Arts, Tulsa, OK 74104-3189. Offers art (MTA); biology (MTA); English (MTA); history (MTA); mathematics (MTA); theatre (MTA). Part-time programs available. *Students:* 2 applicants, 0% accepted, 0 enrolled. In 2011, 1 master's awarded. *Entrance requirements:* For master's, GRE General Test. Additional exam requirements/recommendations for international students: Required—TOEFL (minimum score 577 paper-based; 233 computer-based), IELTS (minimum score 6.5). *Application deadline:* Applications are processed on a rolling basis. Application fee: $40. Electronic applications accepted. *Expenses: Tuition:* Full-time $17,748; part-time $986 per hour. *Required fees:* $5 per contact hour. $75 per semester. Tuition and fees vary according to program. *Financial support:* Fellowships with full and partial tuition reimbursements, research assistantships with full and partial tuition reimbursements, teaching assistantships with full and partial tuition reimbursements, career-related internships or fieldwork, Federal Work-Study, scholarships/grants, health care benefits, tuition waivers (full and partial), and unspecified assistantships available. Support available to part-time students. Financial award application deadline: 2/1; financial award applicants required to submit FAFSA. *Unit head:* Dr. David Brown, Advisor, 918-631-2719, Fax: 918-631-2133, E-mail: david-brown@utulsa.edu. *Application contact:* Dr. David Brown, Advisor, 918-631-2719, Fax: 918-631-2133, E-mail: david-brown@utulsa.edu.

University of Tulsa, Graduate School, College of Engineering and Natural Sciences, Department of Biological Science, Tulsa, OK 74104-3189. Offers MS, MTA, PhD, JD/MS. Part-time programs available. *Faculty:* 13 full-time (3 women). *Students:* 17 full-time (6 women), 2 part-time (both women); includes 2 minority (1 American Indian or Alaska Native, non-Hispanic/Latino; 1 Asian, non-Hispanic/Latino), 7 international. Average age 29. 30 applicants, 30% accepted, 6 enrolled. In 2011, 3 master's, 1 doctorate awarded. Terminal master's awarded for partial completion of doctoral program. *Degree requirements:* For master's, thesis, oral exams; for doctorate, comprehensive exam, thesis/dissertation. *Entrance requirements:* For master's and doctorate, GRE General Test. Additional exam requirements/recommendations for international students: Required—TOEFL (minimum score 550 paper-based; 213 computer-based; 80 iBT), IELTS (minimum score 6). *Application deadline:* Applications are processed on a rolling basis. Application fee: $40. Electronic applications accepted. *Expenses: Tuition:* Full-time $17,748; part-time $986 per hour. *Required fees:* $5 per contact hour. $75 per semester. Tuition and fees vary according to program. *Financial support:* In 2011–12, 17 students received support, including 8 fellowships with full and partial tuition reimbursements available (averaging $1,780 per year), 4 research assistantships with full and partial tuition reimbursements available (averaging $15,523 per year), 13 teaching assistantships with full and partial tuition reimbursements available (averaging $11,736 per year); career-related internships or fieldwork, Federal Work-Study, scholarships/grants, health care benefits, tuition waivers (full and partial), and unspecified assistantships also available. Support available to part-time students. Financial award application deadline: 2/1; financial award applicants required to submit FAFSA. *Faculty research:* Aerobiology, animal behavior and behavioral ecology, cell and molecular biology, ecology, developmental biology, genetics, herpetology, glycobiology, immunology, microbiology, morphology, mycology, ornithology, molecular systematic and virology. *Total annual research expenditures:* $1.9 million. *Unit head:* Dr. Estelle Levetin, Chairperson, 918-631-2764, Fax: 918-631-2762, E-mail: estelle-levetin@utulsa.edu. *Application contact:* Dr. Harrington Wells, Advisor, 918-631-3071, Fax: 918-631-2762, E-mail: harrington-wells@utulsa.edu. Web site: http://www.bio.utulsa.edu/.

University of Utah, Graduate School, College of Science, Department of Biology, Salt Lake City, UT 84112. Offers MS, PhD. Part-time programs available. *Faculty:* 47 full-time (10 women), 1 (woman) part-time/adjunct. *Students:* 52 full-time (22 women), 26 part-time (11 women); includes 3 minority (1 Asian, non-Hispanic/Latino; 1 Hispanic/Latino; 1 Two or more races, non-Hispanic/Latino), 24 international. Average age 29. 108 applicants, 22% accepted, 13 enrolled. In 2011, 4 master's, 6 doctorates awarded. Terminal master's awarded for partial completion of doctoral program. *Median time to degree:* Of those who began their doctoral program in fall 2003, 70% received their degree in 8 years or less. *Degree requirements:* For master's, comprehensive exam, thesis; for doctorate, comprehensive exam, thesis/dissertation. *Entrance requirements:* For master's and doctorate, GRE General Test, minimum GPA of 3.0. Additional exam requirements/recommendations for international students: Required—TOEFL (minimum score 500 paper-based; 173 computer-based; 61 iBT). *Application deadline:* For fall admission, 1/7 for domestic and international students. Application fee: $55 ($65 for international students). *Financial support:* In 2011–12, 79 students received support, including 19 fellowships with full tuition reimbursements available (averaging $25,000 per year), 23 research assistantships with full tuition reimbursements available (averaging $25,000 per year), 37 teaching assistantships with full tuition reimbursements available (averaging $16,500 per year); career-related internships or fieldwork, scholarships/grants, traineeships, and health care benefits also available. Financial award application deadline: 3/15; financial award applicants required to submit FAFSA. *Faculty research:* Ecology, evolutionary biology, cell and developmental biology, physiology and organismal biology, molecular biology, biochemistry, microbiology, plant biology, neurobiology, genetics. *Total annual research expenditures:* $12 million. *Application contact:* Shannon Nielsen, Administrative Program Coordinator, 801-581-5636, Fax: 801-581-4668, E-mail: shannon.nielsen@bioscience.utah.edu. Web site: http://www.biology.utah.edu.

University of Utah, School of Medicine and Graduate School, Graduate Programs in Medicine, Salt Lake City, UT 84112-1107. Offers M Phil, M Stat, MPAS, MPH, MS, MSPH, PhD, Certificate. Part-time programs available. *Degree requirements:* For doctorate, thesis/dissertation. *Entrance requirements:* For doctorate, MCAT. Electronic applications accepted. *Faculty research:* Molecular biology, biochemistry, cell biology, immunology, bioengineering.

University of Vermont, College of Medicine and Graduate College, Graduate Programs in Medicine, Burlington, VT 05405. Offers biochemistry (MS, PhD); clinical and translational science (MS, PhD); microbiology and molecular genetics (MS, PhD); molecular physiology and biophysics (MS, PhD); neuroscience (PhD); pathology (MS); pharmacology (MS, PhD); MD/MS; MD/PhD. *Students:* 88 (47 women); includes 9 minority (2 Asian, non-Hispanic/Latino; 7 Hispanic/Latino), 15 international. 168 applicants, 16% accepted, 10 enrolled. In 2011, 2 master's, 8 doctorates awarded. *Degree requirements:* For master's, thesis; for doctorate, thesis/dissertation. *Entrance requirements:* For master's and doctorate, GRE General Test. Additional exam requirements/recommendations for international students: Required—TOEFL (minimum score 550 paper-based; 213 computer-based; 80 iBT). *Application deadline:* For fall admission, 4/1 priority date for domestic students, 4/1 for international students. Applications are processed on a rolling basis. Application fee: $40. Electronic applications accepted. *Financial support:* Fellowships, research assistantships, teaching assistantships, traineeships, and analytical assistantships available. Financial award application deadline: 3/1. *Unit head:* Dr. Frederick C. Morin, Dean, 802-656-2156.

University of Vermont, Graduate College, College of Arts and Sciences, Department of Biology, Burlington, VT 05405. Offers biology (MS, PhD); biology education (MST). *Faculty:* 17. *Students:* 32 (14 women); includes 5 minority (1 Black or African American, non-Hispanic/Latino; 4 Hispanic/Latino), 11 international. 43 applicants, 33% accepted, 5 enrolled. In 2011, 2 master's, 3 doctorates awarded. *Degree requirements:* For master's, thesis; for doctorate, thesis/dissertation. *Entrance requirements:* For master's and doctorate, GRE General Test. Additional exam requirements/recommendations for international students: Required—TOEFL (minimum score 550 paper-based; 213 computer-based; 80 iBT). *Application deadline:* For fall admission, 1/15 priority date for domestic students, 1/15 for international students. Applications are processed on a rolling basis. Application fee: $40. Electronic applications accepted. *Financial support:* Fellowships, research assistantships, and teaching assistantships available. Financial award application deadline: 3/1. *Unit head:* Dr. Jim Vigoreaux, Chairperson, 802-656-2922. *Application contact:* Dr. Judith Van Houten, Coordinator, 802-656-2922.

University of Victoria, Faculty of Graduate Studies, Faculty of Science, Department of Biology, Victoria, BC V8W 2Y2, Canada. Offers M Sc, PhD. *Degree requirements:* For master's, thesis, seminar; for doctorate, thesis/dissertation, seminar, candidacy exam. *Entrance requirements:* For master's and doctorate, GRE General Test, minimum B+ average in previous 2 years of biology course work. Additional exam requirements/recommendations for international students: Required—TOEFL (minimum score 575 paper-based; 233 computer-based), IELTS (minimum score 7). Electronic applications accepted. *Faculty research:* Neurobiology of vertebrates and invertebrates, physiology, reproduction and tissue culture of forest trees, evolution and ecology, cell and molecular biology, molecular biology of environmental health.

University of Virginia, College and Graduate School of Arts and Sciences, Department of Biology, Charlottesville, VA 22903. Offers MA, MS, PhD. *Faculty:* 35 full-time (6 women), 2 part-time/adjunct (1 woman). *Students:* 49 full-time (35 women); includes 5 minority (1 Black or African American, non-Hispanic/Latino; 3 Asian, non-Hispanic/Latino; 1 Hispanic/Latino), 17 international. Average age 26. 84 applicants, 24% accepted, 11 enrolled. In 2011, 4 master's, 13 doctorates awarded. *Degree requirements:* For master's, thesis; for doctorate, thesis/dissertation. *Entrance requirements:* For master's and doctorate, GRE General Test, GRE Subject Test (recommended), 2 letters of recommendation. Additional exam requirements/recommendations for international students: Required—TOEFL (minimum score 600 paper-based; 250 computer-based; 90 iBT), IELTS (minimum score 7). *Application deadline:* For fall admission, 12/21 for domestic and international students. Applications are processed on a rolling basis. Application fee: $60. Electronic applications accepted. *Financial support:* Fellowships, research assistantships, and teaching assistantships available. Financial award applicants required to submit FAFSA. *Faculty research:* Ecology and evolution, neurobiology and behavior, molecular genetics, cell development. *Unit head:* Douglas Taylor, Chair, 434-982-5474, Fax: 434-982-5626, E-mail: drt3b@virginia.edu. *Application contact:* Dorothy Schafer, Director of Graduate Studies, 434-982-5297, Fax: 434-982-5626, E-mail: das9w@virginia.edu. Web site: http://www.virginia.edu/biology/.

University of Virginia, School of Medicine, Department of Molecular Physiology and Biological Physics, Program in Biological and Physical Sciences, Charlottesville, VA 22903. Offers MS. *Students:* 7 full-time (5 women). Average age 26. In 2011, 14 master's awarded. *Entrance requirements:* For master's, GRE General Test. Additional exam requirements/recommendations for international students: Required—TOEFL. *Application deadline:* Applications are processed on a rolling basis. Application fee: $60. Electronic applications accepted. *Financial support:* Applicants required to submit FAFSA. *Unit head:* Dr. Mark Yeager, Chair, 434-924-5108, Fax: 434-982-1616, E-mail: my3r@virginia.edu. *Application contact:* Lesley L. Thomas, Director, Admissions Office, 434-924-5571, Fax: 434-982-2586, E-mail: medsch-adm@virginia.edu. Web site: http://www.healthsystem.virginia.edu/internet/physio/.

University of Washington, Graduate School, College of Arts and Sciences, Department of Biology, Seattle, WA 98195. Offers PhD.

University of Washington, Graduate School, School of Medicine, Graduate Programs in Medicine, Seattle, WA 98195. Offers MA, MOT, MPO, MS, DPT, PhD. Part-time programs available. *Degree requirements:* For doctorate, thesis/dissertation. *Entrance requirements:* For doctorate, GRE. Electronic applications accepted. *Expenses:* Contact institution.

University of Waterloo, Graduate Studies, Faculty of Science, Department of Biology, Waterloo, ON N2L 3G1, Canada. Offers M Sc, PhD. Part-time programs available. *Degree requirements:* For master's, thesis, seminar, proposal; for doctorate, comprehensive exam, thesis/dissertation, seminar, proposal. *Entrance requirements:* For master's, honor's degree; for doctorate, master's degree. Additional exam requirements/recommendations for international students: Required—TOEFL (minimum score 580 paper-based; 237 computer-based; 90 iBT), TWE (minimum score 4). Electronic applications accepted. *Faculty research:* Biosystematics, ecology and limnology, molecular and cellular biology, biochemistry, physiology.

University of West Florida, College of Arts and Sciences: Sciences, School of Allied Health and Life Sciences, Department of Biology, Pensacola, FL 32514-5750. Offers biological chemistry (MS); biology (MS); biology education (MST); biotechnology (MS); coastal zone studies (MS); environmental biology (MS). *Faculty:* 12 full-time (3 women), 1 part-time/adjunct (0 women). *Students:* 9 full-time (7 women), 30 part-time (16 women); includes 2 minority (both Hispanic/Latino), 3 international. Average age 29. 21 applicants, 48% accepted, 5 enrolled. In 2011, 4 master's awarded. *Degree requirements:* For master's, thesis. *Entrance requirements:* For master's, GRE (minimum score: verbal 450, quantitative 550), official transcripts; BS in biology or related field; letter of interest; relevant past experience; three letters of recommendation from individuals who can evaluate applicant's academic ability. Additional exam requirements/recommendations for international students: Required—TOEFL (minimum score 550 paper-based; 213 computer-based). *Application deadline:* For fall admission, 6/1 for domestic and international students; for spring admission, 10/1 for domestic and international students. Applications are processed on a rolling basis. Application fee: $30. *Expenses:* Tuition, state resident: full-time $5729; part-time $302 per credit hour. Tuition, nonresident: full-time $20,059; part-time $961 per credit hour. *Required fees:* $1509; $63 per credit hour. *Financial support:* In 2011–12, 18 fellowships with partial tuition reimbursements (averaging $126 per year), 14 research assistantships with partial tuition reimbursements (averaging $5,980 per year), 4 teaching assistantships with partial tuition reimbursements (averaging $7,858 per year) were awarded; unspecified assistantships also available. Financial award application deadline: 4/15; financial award applicants required to submit FAFSA. *Unit head:* Dr. George L. Stewart, Chairperson, 850-474-2748. *Application contact:* Terry McCray, Assistant Director of Graduate Admissions, 850-473-7718, Fax: 850-473-7714, E-mail: gradadmissions@uwf.edu.

University of West Georgia, College of Science and Mathematics, Department of Biology, Carrollton, GA 30118. Offers MS. Part-time programs available. *Faculty:* 9 full-time (2 women), 1 part-time/adjunct (0 women). *Students:* 11 full-time (6 women), 7 part-time (4 women); includes 3 minority (all Black or African American, non-Hispanic/Latino), 1 international. Average age 26. 19 applicants, 42% accepted, 3 enrolled. In 2011, 4 master's awarded. *Degree requirements:* For master's, comprehensive exam (for some programs), thesis (for some programs). *Entrance requirements:* For master's, GRE General Test, minimum GPA of 2.5, undergraduate degree in biology. Additional exam requirements/recommendations for international students: Required—TOEFL (minimum score 523 paper-based; 193 computer-based; 69 iBT); Recommended—IELTS (minimum score 6). *Application deadline:* For fall admission, 6/1 for domestic and international students; for spring admission, 11/15 for domestic students, 10/15 for international students. Applications are processed on a rolling basis. Application fee: $30. Electronic applications accepted. *Expenses:* Tuition, state resident: full-time $4336; part-time $181 per credit hour. Tuition, nonresident: full-time $17,362; part-time $724 per credit hour. Tuition and fees vary according to course load, degree level, campus/location and program. *Financial support:* In 2011–12, 8 teaching assistantships with full tuition reimbursements (averaging $8,000 per year) were awarded; scholarships/grants and unspecified assistantships also available. Financial award application deadline: 7/1; financial award applicants required to submit FAFSA. *Faculty research:* Molecular systematics, animal physiology, marine ecology, plant ecology, animal behavior. *Unit head:* Dr. Henry G. Zot, Chair, 678-839-6547, Fax: 678-839-6548, E-mail: hzot@westga.edu. *Application contact:* Alice Wesley, Departmental Assistant, 678-839-5192, E-mail: awesley@westga.edu. Web site: http://www.westga.edu/biology/.

University of Windsor, Faculty of Graduate Studies, Faculty of Science, Department of Biological Sciences, Windsor, ON N9B 3P4, Canada. Offers M Sc, PhD. Part-time programs available. *Degree requirements:* For master's, thesis; for doctorate, comprehensive exam, thesis/dissertation. *Entrance requirements:* For master's and doctorate, minimum B average. Additional exam requirements/recommendations for international students: Required—TOEFL (minimum score 560 paper-based; 220 computer-based). Electronic applications accepted. *Faculty research:* Great Lakes Institute: aquatic ecotoxicology, regulation and development of the olfactory system, mating system evolution, signal transduction, aquatic ecology.

University of Wisconsin–La Crosse, Office of University Graduate Studies, College of Science and Health, Department of Biology, La Crosse, WI 54601-3742. Offers aquatic sciences (MS); biology (MS); cellular and molecular biology (MS); clinical microbiology (MS); microbiology (MS); nurse anesthesia (MS); physiology (MS). Part-time programs available. *Faculty:* 21 full-time (8 women), 3 part-time/adjunct (1 woman). *Students:* 45 full-time (30 women), 47 part-time (22 women); includes 10 minority (1 Black or African American, non-Hispanic/Latino; 5 Asian, non-Hispanic/Latino; 3 Hispanic/Latino; 1 Two or more races, non-Hispanic/Latino), 3 international. Average age 28. 63 applicants, 46% accepted, 24 enrolled. In 2011, 23 master's awarded. *Degree requirements:* For master's, comprehensive exam, thesis. *Entrance requirements:* For master's, GRE General Test, minimum GPA of 2.85. Additional exam requirements/recommendations for international students: Required—TOEFL (minimum score 550 paper-based; 213 computer-based; 79 iBT). *Application deadline:* For fall admission, 2/1 priority date for domestic students, 2/1 for international students; for spring admission, 1/4 priority date for domestic students, 1/4 for international students. Applications are processed on a rolling basis. Application fee: $56. Electronic applications accepted. *Expenses:* Tuition, state resident: full-time $8391; part-time $481.17 per credit. Tuition, nonresident: full-time $17,850; part-time $1006.68 per credit. *Required fees:* $2 per credit. $18.25 per semester. Tuition and fees vary according to course load, program, reciprocity agreements and student level. *Financial support:* In 2011–12, 29 research assistantships with partial tuition reimbursements (averaging $9,712 per year) were awarded; Federal Work-Study, scholarships/grants, health care benefits, and tuition waivers (partial) also available. Support available to part-time students. Financial award application deadline: 3/15; financial award applicants required to submit FAFSA. *Unit head:* Dr. Thomas Volk, Coordinator of Graduate Studies, 608-785-6972, Fax: 608-785-6959, E-mail: volk.thom@uwlax.edu. *Application contact:* Kathryn Kiefer, Director of Admissions, 608-785-8939, E-mail: admissions@uwlax.edu. Web site: http://uwlax.edu/biology/.

University of Wisconsin–Madison, School of Medicine and Public Health and Graduate School, Graduate Programs in Medicine, Madison, WI 53705. Offers biomolecular chemistry (MS, PhD); cancer biology (PhD); genetics and medical genetics (MS, PhD), including genetics (PhD), medical genetics (MS); medical physics (MS, PhD), including health physics (MS), medical physics; microbiology (PhD); molecular and cellular pharmacology (PhD); pathology and laboratory medicine (PhD); physiology (PhD); population health sciences (MPH, MS, PhD), including clinical research (MS, PhD), epidemiology (MS, PhD), health services research (MS, PhD), population health sciences (MPH), social and behavioral health sciences (MS, PhD); DPT/MPH; DVM/MPH; MD/MPH; MD/PhD; MPA/MPH; MS/MPH; Pharm D/MPH. Part-time programs available. Postbaccalaureate distance learning degree programs offered (minimal on-campus study). Terminal master's awarded for partial completion of doctoral program. Application fee: $45. Electronic applications accepted. *Expenses:* Contact institution. *Financial support:* Fellowships with full tuition reimbursements, research assistantships with full tuition reimbursements, teaching assistantships with full tuition reimbursements, scholarships/grants, traineeships, and tuition waivers (full) available. *Unit head:* Dr. Richard L. Moss, Senior Associate Dean for Basic Research, Biotechnology and Graduate Studies, 608-265-0523, Fax: 608-265-0522, E-mail: rlmoss@wisc.edu. *Application contact:* Information Contact, 608-262-2433, Fax: 608-262-5134, E-mail: gradadmiss@mail.bascom.wisc.edu. Web site: http://www.med.wisc.edu.

University of Wisconsin–Madison, School of Medicine and Public Health, Medical Scientist Training Program, Madison, WI 53705-2221. Offers MD/PhD. *Accreditation:* LCME/AMA. *Faculty:* 380 full-time (80 women). *Students:* 76 full-time (29 women); includes 25 minority (6 Black or African American, non-Hispanic/Latino; 1 American Indian or Alaska Native, non-Hispanic/Latino; 17 Asian, non-Hispanic/Latino; 1 Hispanic/Latino). 222 applicants, 13% accepted, 12 enrolled. *Application deadline:* For fall admission, 12/1 for domestic students. Applications are processed on a rolling basis. Application fee: $54. Electronic applications accepted. *Expenses:* Tuition, state resident: full-time $10,296; part-time $643.51 per credit. Tuition, nonresident: full-time $24,054; part-time $1503.40 per credit. *Required fees:* $70.06 per credit. Tuition and fees vary according to course load, campus/location, program and reciprocity agreements. *Financial support:* In 2011–12, fellowships with full tuition reimbursements (averaging $24,500 per year), research assistantships with full tuition reimbursements (averaging $24,500 per year) were awarded; traineeships and health care benefits also available. *Unit head:* Dr. Anna Huttenlocher, Director, 608-265-4642, Fax: 608-262-8418, E-mail: huttenlocher@wisc.edu. *Application contact:* Paul Cook, Program Administrator, 608-262-6321, Fax: 608-262-4226, E-mail: pscook@wisc.edu. Web site: http://mstp.med.wisc.edu/.

University of Wisconsin–Milwaukee, Graduate School, College of Health Sciences, PhD Program in Health Sciences, Milwaukee, WI 53201-0413. Offers PhD. *Faculty:* 8 full-time (4 women), 1 part-time/adjunct (0 women). *Students:* 17 full-time (10 women), 4 part-time (3 women); includes 1 minority (Two or more races, non-Hispanic/Latino), 1 international. Average age 29. 18 applicants, 44% accepted, 4 enrolled. In 2011, 3 degrees awarded. *Degree requirements:* For doctorate, comprehensive exam, thesis/dissertation. *Entrance requirements:* For doctorate, GRE. Additional exam requirements/recommendations for international students: Required—TOEFL (minimum score 600 paper-based; 250 computer-based), IELTS (minimum score 6.5). Application fee: $56 ($96 for international students). One-time fee: $506.10 full-time. Tuition and fees vary according to course load and reciprocity agreements. *Financial support:* In 2011–12, 4 fellowships, 5 research assistantships, 3 teaching assistantships were awarded; project assistantships also available. *Total annual research expenditures:* $625,094. *Unit head:* Jerry-Annette Lyons, Department Chair, 414-229-3812, E-mail: jlyons@uwm.edu. Web site: http://www4.uwm.edu/chs/academics/doctoral/hs_phd/index.html.

University of Wisconsin–Milwaukee, Graduate School, College of Health Sciences, Program in Biomedical Sciences, Milwaukee, WI 53211. Offers MS. *Accreditation:* NAACLS. Part-time programs available. *Faculty:* 8 full-time (4 women). *Students:* 13 full-time (10 women), 3 part-time (all women); includes 3 minority (1 Black or African American, non-Hispanic/Latino; 1 Hispanic/Latino; 1 Two or more races, non-Hispanic/Latino). Average age 32. 39 applicants, 31% accepted, 5 enrolled. *Degree requirements:* For master's, thesis. *Entrance requirements:* For master's, GRE General Test. Additional exam requirements/recommendations for international students: Required—TOEFL (minimum score 550 paper-based; 79 iBT), IELTS (minimum score 6.5). *Application deadline:* For fall admission, 1/1 priority date for domestic students; for spring admission, 9/1 for domestic students. Applications are processed on a rolling basis. Application fee: $56 ($96 for international students). One-time fee: $506.10 full-time. Tuition and fees vary according to course load and reciprocity agreements. *Financial support:* In 2011–12, 6 teaching assistantships were awarded; fellowships, research assistantships, career-related internships or fieldwork, and unspecified assistantships also available. Support available to part-time students. Financial award application deadline: 4/15. *Total annual research expenditures:* $136,824. *Unit head:* Jeri-Anne Lyons, Representative, 414-229-3812, E-mail: jlyons@uwm.edu. Web site: http://www4.uwm.edu/chs/academics/health_sciences/bms_masters/.

University of Wisconsin–Milwaukee, Graduate School, College of Letters and Sciences, Department of Biological Sciences, Milwaukee, WI 53201-0413. Offers MS, PhD. *Faculty:* 31 full-time (10 women). *Students:* 49 full-time (24 women), 27 part-time (16 women); includes 8 minority (2 Black or African American, non-Hispanic/Latino; 2 American Indian or Alaska Native, non-Hispanic/Latino; 2 Asian, non-Hispanic/Latino; 2 Two or more races, non-Hispanic/Latino), 25 international. Average age 31. 105 applicants, 26% accepted, 15 enrolled. In 2011, 9 master's, 5 doctorates awarded. *Degree requirements:* For master's, thesis; for doctorate, thesis/dissertation, 1 foreign language or data analysis proficiency. *Entrance requirements:* For master's and doctorate, GRE General Test. Additional exam requirements/recommendations for international students: Required—TOEFL (minimum score 550 paper-based; 79 iBT), IELTS (minimum score 6.5). *Application deadline:* For fall admission, 3/1 priority date for domestic students. Applications are processed on a rolling basis. Application fee: $56 ($96 for international students). One-time fee: $506.10 full-time. Tuition and fees vary according to course load and reciprocity agreements. *Financial support:* In 2011–12, 3 fellowships, 9 research assistantships, 67 teaching assistantships were awarded; career-related internships or fieldwork, unspecified assistantships, and project assistantships also available. Support available to part-time students. Financial award application deadline: 4/15; financial award applicants required to submit FAFSA. *Total annual research expenditures:* $2.9 million. *Unit head:* Daad Saffarini, Department Chair, 414-229-4279, E-mail: daads@uwm.edu. *Application contact:* General Information Contact, 414-229-4982, Fax: 414-229-6967, E-mail: gradschool@uwm.edu. Web site: http://www.uwm.edu/dept/biology/.

University of Wisconsin–Oshkosh, Graduate Studies, College of Letters and Science, Department of Biology and Microbiology, Oshkosh, WI 54901. Offers biology (MS), including botany, microbiology, zoology. *Degree requirements:* For master's, comprehensive exam, thesis. *Entrance requirements:* For master's, GRE General Test, minimum GPA of 3.0, BS in biology. Additional exam requirements/recommendations for international students: Required—TOEFL (minimum score 550 paper-based; 213 computer-based; 79 iBT). Electronic applications accepted.

Utah State University, School of Graduate Studies, College of Science, Department of Biology, Logan, UT 84322. Offers biology (MS, PhD); ecology (MS, PhD). Part-time programs available. *Degree requirements:* For master's, thesis; for doctorate, thesis/dissertation. *Entrance requirements:* For master's and doctorate, GRE General Test, minimum GPA of 3.0. Additional exam requirements/recommendations for international students: Required—TOEFL (minimum score 575 paper-based). *Faculty research:* Plant, insect, microbial, and animal biology.

Vanderbilt University, Graduate School, Department of Biological Sciences, Nashville, TN 37240-1001. Offers MS, PhD, MD/PhD. *Faculty:* 26 full-time (3 women), 1 (woman) part-time/adjunct. *Students:* 47 full-time (22 women); includes 10 minority (2 Black or African American, non-Hispanic/Latino; 4 Asian, non-Hispanic/Latino; 4 Hispanic/Latino), 14 international. Average age 27. 145 applicants, 11% accepted, 13 enrolled. In 2011, 2 master's, 6 doctorates awarded. Terminal master's awarded for partial completion of doctoral program. *Degree requirements:* For master's, thesis; for doctorate, thesis/dissertation, final and qualifying exams. *Entrance requirements:* For master's and doctorate, GRE General Test. Additional exam requirements/

recommendations for international students: Required—TOEFL (minimum score 570 paper-based; 230 computer-based; 88 iBT). *Application deadline:* For fall admission, 1/15 for domestic and international students. Application fee: $0. Electronic applications accepted. *Financial support:* Fellowships with full and partial tuition reimbursements, research assistantships with full tuition reimbursements, teaching assistantships with full tuition reimbursements, Federal Work-Study, institutionally sponsored loans, scholarships/grants, traineeships, and health care benefits available. Financial award application deadline: 1/15; financial award applicants required to submit CSS PROFILE or FAFSA. *Faculty research:* Protein structure and function, protein transport, membrane ion channels and receptors, signal transduction, posttranscriptional control of gene expression, DNA replication and recombination, biological clocks, development, neurobiology, vector biology, insect physiology, ecology and evolution, bioinformatics. *Unit head:* Dr. Charles Singleton, Chair, 615-322-2008, E-mail: charles.k.singleton@vanderbilt.edu. *Application contact:* Dr. Katherine Friedman, Director of Graduate Studies, 615-322-5143, Fax: 615-343-6707, E-mail: katherine.friedman@vanderbilt.edu. Web site: http://sitemason.vanderbilt.edu/biosci/grad/.

Vanderbilt University, School of Medicine and Graduate School, Medical Scientist Training Program, Nashville, TN 37240-1001. Offers MD/PhD. *Entrance requirements:* Additional exam requirements/recommendations for international students: Recommended—TOEFL. Electronic applications accepted. *Expenses:* Contact institution. *Faculty research:* Cancer biology, neurosciences, microbiology, biochemistry, metabolism/diabetics.

Villanova University, Graduate School of Liberal Arts and Sciences, Department of Biology, Villanova, PA 19085-1699. Offers MA, MS. Part-time and evening/weekend programs available. *Faculty:* 10 full-time (4 women). *Students:* 42 full-time (18 women), 6 part-time (3 women); includes 5 minority (1 Asian, non-Hispanic/Latino; 4 Hispanic/Latino), 4 international. Average age 26. 41 applicants, 80% accepted, 20 enrolled. In 2011, 28 master's awarded. *Degree requirements:* For master's, comprehensive exam (for some programs), thesis (for some programs). *Entrance requirements:* For master's, GRE General Test, minimum GPA of 3.0. Additional exam requirements/recommendations for international students: Required—TOEFL. *Application deadline:* For fall admission, 5/1 for international students; for spring admission, 10/15 for international students. Applications are processed on a rolling basis. Application fee: $50. Electronic applications accepted. *Expenses:* Contact institution. *Financial support:* Research assistantships with tuition reimbursements, teaching assistantships with tuition reimbursements, scholarships/grants, and unspecified assistantships available. Financial award applicants required to submit FAFSA. *Unit head:* Dr. Russell Gardner, Chair, 610-519-4830. *Application contact:* Dr. Adele Lindenmeyr, Dean, Graduate School of Liberal Arts and Sciences, 610-519-7093, Fax: 610-519-7096. Web site: http://www.villanova.edu/artsci/biology/graduate/.

Virginia Commonwealth University, Graduate School, College of Humanities and Sciences, Department of Biology, Richmond, VA 23284-9005. Offers MS. Part-time programs available. *Students:* 22 full-time (13 women), 11 part-time (5 women); includes 2 minority (1 Asian, non-Hispanic/Latino; 1 Hispanic/Latino), 2 international. 32 applicants, 28% accepted, 8 enrolled. In 2011, 15 master's awarded. *Degree requirements:* For master's, thesis. *Entrance requirements:* For master's, GRE General Test, BS in biology or related field. Additional exam requirements/recommendations for international students: Required—TOEFL (minimum score 600 paper-based; 250 computer-based; 100 iBT) or IELTS (minimum score 6.5). *Application deadline:* For fall admission, 1/15 for domestic students; for spring admission, 11/15 for domestic students. Applications are processed on a rolling basis. Application fee: $50. *Expenses:* Tuition, state resident: full-time $9133; part-time $507 per credit. Tuition, nonresident: full-time $18,777; part-time $1043 per credit. *Required fees:* $77 per credit. Tuition and fees vary according to degree level, campus/location, program and student level. *Financial support:* Fellowships, research assistantships, teaching assistantships, Federal Work-Study, institutionally sponsored loans, and tuition waivers (full and partial) available. Support available to part-time students. Financial award applicants required to submit FAFSA. *Faculty research:* Molecular and cellular biology, terrestrial and aquatic ecology, systematics, physiology and developmental biology. *Unit head:* Dr. Donald R. Young, Chair, 804-828-1562, E-mail: dyoung@vcu.edu. *Application contact:* Dr. Jennifer K. Stewart, Program Director, 804-828-1562, Fax: 804-828-0503, E-mail: jstewart@vcu.edu. Web site: http://www.has.vcu.edu/bio/graduate/.

Virginia Commonwealth University, Graduate School, School of Life Sciences, Richmond, VA 23284-9005. Offers M Env Sc, MB, MS, PhD. *Entrance requirements:* For master's and doctorate, GRE. Additional exam requirements/recommendations for international students: Required—TOEFL (minimum score 600 paper-based; 250 computer-based; 100 iBT). Electronic applications accepted. *Expenses:* Tuition, state resident: full-time $9133; part-time $507 per credit. Tuition, nonresident: full-time $18,777; part-time $1043 per credit. *Required fees:* $77 per credit. Tuition and fees vary according to degree level, campus/location, program and student level.

Virginia Commonwealth University, Medical College of Virginia-Professional Programs, School of Medicine, School of Medicine Graduate Programs, Richmond, VA 23284-9005. Offers MPH, MS, PhD, Certificate, MD/MPH, MD/PhD. Part-time programs available. Terminal master's awarded for partial completion of doctoral program. *Degree requirements:* For doctorate, thesis/dissertation, comprehensive oral and written exams. *Entrance requirements:* For doctorate, GRE General Test, MCAT. *Expenses:* Tuition, state resident: full-time $9133; part-time $507 per credit. Tuition, nonresident: full-time $18,777; part-time $1043 per credit. *Required fees:* $77 per credit. Tuition and fees vary according to degree level, campus/location, program and student level.

Virginia Commonwealth University, Program in Pre-Medical Basic Health Sciences, Richmond, VA 23284-9005. Offers anatomy (CBHS); biochemistry (CBHS); human genetics (CBHS); microbiology (CBHS); pharmacology (CBHS); physiology (CBHS). *Entrance requirements:* For degree, GRE, MCAT or DAT, course work in organic chemistry, minimum undergraduate GPA of 2.8. Additional exam requirements/recommendations for international students: Required—TOEFL (minimum score 600 paper-based). Electronic applications accepted. *Expenses:* Tuition, state resident: full-time $9133; part-time $507 per credit. Tuition, nonresident: full-time $18,777; part-time $1043 per credit. *Required fees:* $77 per credit. Tuition and fees vary according to degree level, campus/location, program and student level.

Virginia Polytechnic Institute and State University, Graduate School, College of Science, Department of Biological Sciences, Blacksburg, VA 24061. Offers MS, PhD. *Degree requirements:* For master's, comprehensive exam (for some programs), thesis (for some programs); for doctorate, comprehensive exam (for some programs), thesis/dissertation (for some programs). *Entrance requirements:* For master's and doctorate, GRE. Additional exam requirements/recommendations for international students: Required—TOEFL (minimum score 550 paper-based; 213 computer-based). *Application deadline:* For fall admission, 7/1 for domestic and international students; for spring admission, 12/1 for domestic and international students. Applications are processed on a rolling basis. Application fee: $65. Electronic applications accepted. *Expenses:* Tuition, state resident: full-time $10,048; part-time $558.25 per credit hour. Tuition, nonresident: full-time $19,497; part-time $1083.25 per credit hour. *Required fees:* $405 per semester. Tuition and fees vary according to course load, campus/location and program. *Financial support:* Research assistantships with full tuition reimbursements, teaching assistantships with full tuition reimbursements, career-related internships or fieldwork, Federal Work-Study, scholarships/grants, health care benefits, and unspecified assistantships available. Financial award application deadline: 1/15. *Faculty research:* Freshwater ecology, cell cycle regulation, behavioral ecology, motor proteins. *Unit head:* Dr. Brenda S. Winkel, Unit Head, 540-231-3013, Fax: 540-231-9307, E-mail: winkel@vt.edu. *Application contact:* Ernest Benfield, Information Contact, 540-231-5802, Fax: 540-231-9307, E-mail: benfield@vt.edu. Web site: http://www.biol.vt.edu/graduates/index.html.

Virginia State University, School of Graduate Studies, Research, and Outreach, School of Engineering, Science and Technology, Department of Biology, Petersburg, VA 23806-0001. Offers MS. *Degree requirements:* For master's, one foreign language, thesis. *Entrance requirements:* For master's, GRE General Test. *Faculty research:* Schwann cell cultures, selection of apios as an alternative crop, systematic botany, flowers of three species of wild ginger.

Wagner College, Division of Graduate Studies, Department of Biological Sciences, Staten Island, NY 10301-4495. Offers advanced physician assistant studies (MS); microbiology (MS). Part-time and evening/weekend programs available. *Faculty:* 8 full-time (4 women), 13 part-time/adjunct (8 women). *Students:* 35 full-time (29 women), 3 part-time (0 women); includes 10 minority (2 Black or African American, non-Hispanic/Latino; 4 Asian, non-Hispanic/Latino; 4 Hispanic/Latino). Average age 27. 36 applicants, 97% accepted, 31 enrolled. In 2011, 25 master's awarded. *Degree requirements:* For master's, comprehensive exam or thesis. *Entrance requirements:* For master's, GRE, MCAT, minimum GPA of 2.5, proficiency in statistics, undergraduate major in science; completion of ARC-PA accredited physician assistant program with minimum GPA of 3.0 (for advanced physician assistant studies). Additional exam requirements/recommendations for international students: Required—TOEFL. *Application deadline:* For fall admission, 5/1 priority date for domestic students, 3/1 for international students; for spring admission, 12/1 for domestic students, 10/1 for international students. Applications are processed on a rolling basis. Application fee: $50 ($85 for international students). *Expenses:* *Tuition:* Full-time $16,200; part-time $890 per credit. *Financial support:* Federal Work-Study, tuition waivers, unspecified assistantships, and alumni fellowship grant available. Financial award applicants required to submit FAFSA. *Unit head:* Dr. Brian Palestis, Chair, 718-390-3197, E-mail: bpalesti@wagner.edu. *Application contact:* Patricia Clancy, Assistant Coordinator of Graduate Studies, 718-420-4464, E-mail: patricia.clancy@wagner.edu.

Wake Forest University, Graduate School of Arts and Sciences, Department of Biology, Winston-Salem, NC 27109. Offers MS, PhD. Part-time programs available. *Degree requirements:* For master's, one foreign language, thesis; for doctorate, 2 foreign languages, comprehensive exam, thesis/dissertation. *Entrance requirements:* For master's and doctorate, GRE General Test. Additional exam requirements/recommendations for international students: Required—TOEFL (minimum score 213 computer-based; 79 iBT). Electronic applications accepted. *Faculty research:* Cell biology, ecology, parasitology, immunology.

Wake Forest University, School of Medicine and Graduate School of Arts and Sciences, Graduate Programs in Medicine, Winston-Salem, NC 27109. Offers MS, PhD, MD/PhD. *Degree requirements:* For master's, thesis; for doctorate, thesis/dissertation. *Entrance requirements:* For master's and doctorate, GRE General Test. Additional exam requirements/recommendations for international students: Required—TOEFL. Electronic applications accepted. *Expenses:* Contact institution. *Faculty research:* Atherosclerosis, cardiovascular physiology, pharmacology, neuroanatomy, endocrinology.

Walla Walla University, Graduate School, Department of Biological Sciences, College Place, WA 99324-1198. Offers biology (MS). *Degree requirements:* For master's, thesis. *Entrance requirements:* For master's, GRE General Test, GRE Subject Test, minimum GPA of 2.75. Additional exam requirements/recommendations for international students: Required—TOEFL (minimum score 550 paper-based; 213 computer-based; 79 iBT). Electronic applications accepted. *Faculty research:* Marine biology, plant development, neurobiology, animal physiology, behavior.

Washington State University, Graduate School, College of Sciences, School of Biological Sciences, Program in Biology, Pullman, WA 99164. Offers MS. *Faculty:* 33. *Degree requirements:* For master's, comprehensive exam (for some programs), thesis. *Entrance requirements:* For master's, GRE, three letters of recommendation, official transcripts from each university-level school attended. Additional exam requirements/recommendations for international students: Required—TOEFL, IELTS. *Application deadline:* For fall admission, 1/10 for domestic and international students; for spring admission, 7/1 for domestic and international students. Application fee: $75. *Financial support:* In 2011–12, 1 research assistantship with tuition reimbursement (averaging $13,917 per year), 1 teaching assistantship with tuition reimbursement (averaging $13,056 per year) were awarded. Financial award application deadline: 2/15. *Faculty research:* Inter-intra-cellular signaling in plant reproduction, biodiversity. *Unit head:* Dr. Gary Thorgaard, Director, 509-335-7438, Fax: 509-335-3184, E-mail: thorglab@wsu.edu. *Application contact:* Graduate School Admissions, 800-GRADWSU, Fax: 509-335-1949, E-mail: gradsch@wsu.edu. Web site: http://www.sci.wsu.edu/sbs/gradstudies.php3?pageID-4.

Washington University in St. Louis, Graduate School of Arts and Sciences, Division of Biology and Biomedical Sciences, St. Louis, MO 63130-4899. Offers biochemistry (PhD); computational and molecular biophysics (PhD); computational and systems biology (PhD); developmental, regenerative, and stem cell biology (PhD); evolution, ecology and population biology (PhD), including ecology, environmental biology, evolutionary biology, genetics; human and statistical genetics (PhD); immunology (PhD); molecular cell biology (PhD); molecular genetics and genomics (PhD); molecular microbiology and microbial pathogenesis (PhD); neurosciences (PhD); plant biology (PhD); MD/PhD. *Degree requirements:* For doctorate, thesis/dissertation. *Entrance requirements:* For doctorate, GRE General Test, GRE Subject Test. Electronic applications accepted.

Wayne State University, College of Liberal Arts and Sciences, Department of Biological Sciences, Detroit, MI 48202. Offers biological sciences (MA, MS, PhD); molecular biotechnology (MS). *Students:* 87 full-time (52 women), 17 part-time (9 women); includes 10 minority (3 Black or African American, non-Hispanic/Latino; 1 American Indian or Alaska Native, non-Hispanic/Latino; 4 Asian, non-Hispanic/Latino; 1 Hispanic/Latino; 1 Two or more races, non-Hispanic/Latino), 56 international. Average age 27. 266 applicants, 17% accepted, 29 enrolled. In 2011, 11 master's, 5 doctorates awarded. Terminal master's awarded for partial completion of doctoral program. *Degree requirements:* For master's, thesis (for some programs); for doctorate, thesis/dissertation. *Entrance requirements:* For master's, GRE (for MS applicants), minimum GPA of 3.0; adequate preparation in biological sciences and supporting courses in chemistry, physics and mathematics; curriculum vitae; for doctorate, GRE, three letters of reference, statement of goals and career objectives, curriculum vitae. Additional exam requirements/recommendations for international students: Required—TOEFL (minimum score 550 paper-based; 213 computer-based); Recommended—TWE (minimum score 5.5). *Application deadline:* For fall admission, 4/1 for domestic students, 3/1 for international students. Applications are processed on a rolling basis. Application fee:

$50. Electronic applications accepted. *Expenses:* Tuition, state resident: part-time $512.85 per credit. Tuition, nonresident: part-time $1132.65 per credit. *Required fees:* $26.60 per credit. $199.65 per semester. Tuition and fees vary according to course load and program. *Financial support:* In 2011–12, 70 students received support, including 4 fellowships with tuition reimbursements available (averaging $19,015 per year), 16 research assistantships with tuition reimbursements available (averaging $18,321 per year), 53 teaching assistantships with tuition reimbursements available (averaging $17,971 per year); Federal Work-Study, institutionally sponsored loans, scholarships/grants, health care benefits, and unspecified assistantships also available. *Faculty research:* Cell and developmental biology, neurobiology, molecular biology and biotechnology, evolutionary biology, ecology. *Total annual research expenditures:* $2.2 million. *Unit head:* David Njus, Chair, 313-577-3105, E-mail: dnjus@wayne.edu. *Application contact:* Rose Mary Priest, 313-577-2873, Fax: 313-577-6891, E-mail: rpriest@wayne.edu. Web site: http://www.science.wayne.edu/~biology/.

Weill Cornell Medical College, Weill Cornell Graduate School of Medical Sciences, New York, NY 10065. Offers MS, PhD. *Faculty:* 266 full-time (78 women). *Students:* 517 full-time (305 women); includes 81 minority (11 Black or African American, non-Hispanic/Latino; 50 Asian, non-Hispanic/Latino; 15 Hispanic/Latino; 5 Native Hawaiian or other Pacific Islander, non-Hispanic/Latino), 184 international. Average age 24. 758 applicants, 21% accepted, 62 enrolled. In 2011, 90 master's, 60 doctorates awarded. Terminal master's awarded for partial completion of doctoral program. *Degree requirements:* For master's, comprehensive exam, thesis (for some programs); for doctorate, thesis/dissertation, final exam. *Entrance requirements:* For doctorate, GRE General Test. Additional exam requirements/recommendations for international students: Required—TOEFL. *Application deadline:* For fall admission, 12/1 for domestic students. Application fee: $60. Electronic applications accepted. *Expenses:* Contact institution. *Financial support:* In 2011–12, 34 fellowships (averaging $22,380 per year) were awarded; scholarships/grants, health care benefits, and stipends (given to all students) also available. *Unit head:* Dr. David P. Hajjar, Dean, 212-746-6900, E-mail: dphajjar@med.cornell.edu. *Application contact:* Dr. Randi Silver, Associate Dean, 212-746-6565, Fax: 212-746-8906, E-mail: gsms@med.cornell.edu. Web site: http://weill.cornell.edu/gradschool/.

Weill Cornell Medical College, Weill Cornell/Rockefeller/Sloan-Kettering Tri-Institutional MD-PhD Program, New York, NY 10065. Offers MD/PhD. Offered jointly with The Rockefeller University and Sloan-Kettering Institute. *Faculty:* 278 full-time (83 women). *Students:* 106 full-time (40 women); includes 39 minority (15 Black or African American, non-Hispanic/Latino; 11 Asian, non-Hispanic/Latino; 13 Hispanic/Latino). 483 applicants, 7% accepted, 12 enrolled. *Application deadline:* For fall admission, 10/15 for domestic and international students. Applications are processed on a rolling basis. Application fee: $0. Electronic applications accepted. *Expenses:* Contact institution. *Financial support:* In 2011–12, 106 students received support, including 106 fellowships with full tuition reimbursements available (averaging $33,000 per year); health care benefits, tuition waivers (full), and stipends, research supplements, dental insurance also available. *Faculty research:* Neuroscience, pharmacology, immunology, structural biology, genetics. *Unit head:* Dr. Olaf S. Andersen, Director, 212-746-6023, Fax: 212-746-8678, E-mail: mdphd@med.cornell.edu. *Application contact:* Ruth Gotian, Administrative Director, 212-746-6023, Fax: 212-746-8678, E-mail: mdphd@med.cornell.edu. Web site: http://weill.cornell.edu/mdphd/.

Wesleyan University, Graduate Programs, Department of Biology, Middletown, CT 06459. Offers animal behavior (PhD); bioformatics/genomics (PhD); cell biology (PhD); developmental biology (PhD); evolution/ecology (PhD); genetics (PhD); neurobiology (PhD); population biology (PhD). *Degree requirements:* For doctorate, variable foreign language requirement, thesis/dissertation. *Entrance requirements:* For doctorate, GRE. Additional exam requirements/recommendations for international students: Required—TOEFL. *Faculty research:* Microbial population genetics, genetic basis of evolutionary adaptation, genetic regulation of differentiation and pattern formation in &ITdrosophila&RO.

West Chester University of Pennsylvania, College of Arts and Sciences, Department of Biology, West Chester, PA 19383. Offers biology (Teaching Certificate); biology - non-thesis (MS); biology - thesis (MS). Part-time and evening/weekend programs available. *Faculty:* 7 part-time/adjunct (0 women). *Students:* 22 full-time (12 women), 21 part-time (11 women); includes 7 minority (1 Black or African American, non-Hispanic/Latino; 2 Asian, non-Hispanic/Latino; 4 Hispanic/Latino). Average age 29. 29 applicants, 24% accepted, 7 enrolled. In 2011, 5 degrees awarded. *Degree requirements:* For master's, comprehensive exam, thesis (for some programs). *Entrance requirements:* For master's, two letters of reference. Additional exam requirements/recommendations for international students: Required—TOEFL (minimum score 550 paper-based; 213 computer-based; 80 iBT). *Application deadline:* For fall admission, 4/15 priority date for domestic students, 3/15 for international students; for spring admission, 10/15 priority date for domestic students, 9/1 for international students. Applications are processed on a rolling basis. Application fee: $45. Electronic applications accepted. *Expenses:* Tuition, state resident: full-time $7488; part-time $416 per credit. Tuition, nonresident: full-time $11,232; part-time $624 per credit. *Required fees:* $1784.64; $67.59 per credit. Tuition and fees vary according to program. *Financial support:* Unspecified assistantships available. Support available to part-time students. Financial award application deadline: 2/15; financial award applicants required to submit FAFSA. *Faculty research:* Medical microbiology, molecular genetics and physiology of living systems, mammalian biomechanics, invertebrate and vertebrate animal systems, aquatic and terrestrial ecology. *Unit head:* Dr. Jack Waber, Chair, 610-436-2319, E-mail: jwaber@wcupa.edu. *Application contact:* Dr. Xin Fan, Graduate Coordinator, 610-436-2281, E-mail: xfan@wcupa.edu. Web site: http://bio.wcupa.edu/biology/index.php.

Western Carolina University, Graduate School, College of Arts and Sciences, Department of Biology, Cullowhee, NC 28723. Offers MS. Part-time and evening/weekend programs available. *Students:* 20 full-time (11 women), 10 part-time (6 women), 1 international. Average age 28. 19 applicants, 74% accepted, 14 enrolled. In 2011, 8 master's awarded. *Degree requirements:* For master's, thesis. *Entrance requirements:* For master's, GRE General Test, appropriate undergraduate degree, 3 letters of recommendation. Additional exam requirements/recommendations for international students: Required—TOEFL (minimum score 550 paper-based; 270 computer-based; 79 iBT). *Application deadline:* For fall admission, 5/1 priority date for domestic students; for spring admission, 9/1 priority date for domestic students. Applications are processed on a rolling basis. Application fee: $50. *Expenses:* Tuition, state resident: full-time $3348. Tuition, nonresident: full-time $12,933. *Required fees:* $3155. *Financial support:* Fellowships, research assistantships with full and partial tuition reimbursements, teaching assistantships with full and partial tuition reimbursements, career-related internships or fieldwork, institutionally sponsored loans, scholarships/grants, and unspecified assistantships available. Financial award application deadline: 3/31; financial award applicants required to submit FAFSA. *Faculty research:* Pathogen interactions, gene expression, plant community ecology, restoration ecology, ornithology, herpetology. *Unit head:* Dr. Sean O'Connell, Head, 828-227-2203, Fax: 828-227-7066, E-mail: soconnell@email.wcu.edu. *Application contact:* Admission Specialist for Biology, 828-227-7398, Fax: 828-227-7480, E-mail: gradsch@email.wcu.edu. Web site: http://www.wcu.edu/as/biology/index.html.

Western Connecticut State University, Division of Graduate Studies, School of Arts and Sciences, Department of Biological and Environmental Sciences, Danbury, CT 06810-6885. Offers MA. Part-time programs available. *Faculty:* 3 full-time (1 woman). *Students:* 6 part-time (4 women); includes 1 minority (Black or African American, non-Hispanic/Latino). Average age 27. In 2011, 6 degrees awarded. *Degree requirements:* For master's, comprehensive exam or thesis, completion of program in 6 years. *Entrance requirements:* For master's, minimum GPA of 2.5. Additional exam requirements/recommendations for international students: Recommended—TOEFL (minimum score 550 paper-based; 213 computer-based; 79 iBT), IELTS (minimum score 6). *Application deadline:* For fall admission, 8/5 priority date for domestic students; for spring admission, 1/5 priority date for domestic students. Applications are processed on a rolling basis. Application fee: $50. *Expenses:* Contact institution. *Financial support:* Application deadline: 5/1; applicants required to submit FAFSA. *Faculty research:* Biology, taxonomy and evolution of aquatic flowering plants; aquatic plant reproductive systems, the spread of invasive aquatic plants, aquatic plant structure, and the taxonomy of water starworts (Callitrichaceae) and riverweeds (Podostemaceae). *Unit head:* Dr. Richard Halliburton, Graduate Coordinator, 203-837-8233, Fax: 203-837-8525, E-mail: halliburtonr@wcsu.edu. *Application contact:* Chris Shankle, Associate Director of Graduate Studies, 203-837-9005, Fax: 203-837-8326, E-mail: shanklec@wcsu.edu. Web site: http://www.wcsu.edu/biology/.

Western Illinois University, School of Graduate Studies, College of Arts and Sciences, Department of Biological Sciences, Macomb, IL 61455-1390. Offers biological sciences (MS); environmental geographic information systems (Certificate); zoo and aquarium studies (Certificate). Part-time programs available. *Students:* 55 full-time (38 women), 30 part-time (25 women); includes 6 minority (4 Black or African American, non-Hispanic/Latino; 1 Hispanic/Latino; 1 Two or more races, non-Hispanic/Latino), 4 international. Average age 26. 50 applicants, 60% accepted. In 2011, 30 master's, 19 other advanced degrees awarded. *Degree requirements:* For master's, thesis or alternative. *Entrance requirements:* Additional exam requirements/recommendations for international students: Required—TOEFL (minimum score 550 paper-based; 213 computer-based; 80 iBT); Recommended—IELTS. *Application deadline:* Applications are processed on a rolling basis. Application fee: $30. Electronic applications accepted. *Expenses:* Tuition, state resident: part-time $281.16 per credit hour. Tuition, nonresident: part-time $562.32 per credit hour. Part-time tuition and fees vary according to campus/location and reciprocity agreements. *Financial support:* In 2011–12, 28 students received support, including 9 research assistantships with full tuition reimbursements available (averaging $7,360 per year), 19 teaching assistantships with full tuition reimbursements available (averaging $8,480 per year). Financial award applicants required to submit FAFSA. *Unit head:* Dr. Michael Romano, Chairperson, 309-298-1546. *Application contact:* Nancy Parsons, Interim Associate Provost and Director of Graduate Studies, 309-298-1806, Fax: 309-298-2345, E-mail: grad-office@wiu.edu. Web site: http://wiu.edu/biology.

Western Kentucky University, Graduate Studies, Ogden College of Science and Engineering, Department of Biology, Bowling Green, KY 42101. Offers MS. Postbaccalaureate distance learning degree programs offered. *Degree requirements:* For master's, comprehensive exam, thesis optional, research tool. *Entrance requirements:* For master's, GRE General Test, minimum GPA of 2.75. Additional exam requirements/recommendations for international students: Required—TOEFL (minimum score 555 paper-based; 213 computer-based; 79 iBT). *Faculty research:* Phytoremediation, culturing of salt water organisms, PCR-based standards, biological monitoring (water) bioremediation, genetic diversity.

Western Michigan University, Graduate College, College of Arts and Sciences, Department of Biological Sciences, Kalamazoo, MI 49008. Offers MS, PhD. *Degree requirements:* For master's, thesis, oral exam; for doctorate, thesis/dissertation, oral exam. *Entrance requirements:* For master's and doctorate, GRE General Test.

Western Michigan University, Graduate College, College of Arts and Sciences, Mallinson Institute for Science Education, Kalamazoo, MI 49008. Offers science education (MA, PhD); science education: biological sciences (PhD); science education: chemistry (PhD); science education: geosciences (PhD); science education: physical geography (PhD); science education: physics (PhD). *Degree requirements:* For doctorate, thesis/dissertation, oral and written exams. *Entrance requirements:* For master's, undergraduate degree in a science or science education, teacher certification (or appropriate education courses); for doctorate, GRE General Test, master's degree in a science or science education. Additional exam requirements/recommendations for international students: Recommended—TOEFL. Electronic applications accepted. *Faculty research:* History and philosophy of science, curriculum and instruction, science content learning, college science teaching and learning, social and cultural factors in science education.

Western University of Health Sciences, Graduate College of Biomedical Sciences, Program in Masters of Science in Biomedical Sciences, Pomona, CA 91766-1854. Offers MS. *Faculty:* 4 full-time (1 woman). *Students:* 8 full-time (3 women); includes 6 minority (1 Black or African American, non-Hispanic/Latino; 1 Asian, non-Hispanic/Latino; 3 Hispanic/Latino; 1 Two or more races, non-Hispanic/Latino), 1 international. Average age 27. 20 applicants, 20% accepted, 4 enrolled. In 2011, 4 master's awarded. *Degree requirements:* For master's, comprehensive exam (for some programs), thesis. *Entrance requirements:* For master's, GRE, minimum overall GPA of 3.0; letters of recommendation; personal statement; resume; BS in pharmacy, chemistry, biology or related scientific area. Additional exam requirements/recommendations for international students: Required—TOEFL. *Application deadline:* For fall admission, 5/16 for domestic students. Application fee: $50. Electronic applications accepted. *Unit head:* Dr. Guru Betageri, Assistant Dean, Graduate College of Biomedical Sciences, 909-469-5682, E-mail: gbetageri@westernu.edu. *Application contact:* Information Contact, 909-469-5335, Fax: 909-469-5570, E-mail: admissions@westernu.edu. Web site: http://www.westernu.edu/biomedical-sciences-msbs.

Western University of Health Sciences, Graduate College of Biomedical Sciences, Program in Masters of Science in Medical Sciences, Pomona, CA 91766-1854. Offers MS. *Students:* 32 full-time (15 women); includes 18 minority (3 Black or African American, non-Hispanic/Latino; 12 Asian, non-Hispanic/Latino; 2 Hispanic/Latino; 1 Two or more races, non-Hispanic/Latino). Average age 26. 342 applicants, 11% accepted, 30 enrolled. In 2011, 24 master's awarded. *Degree requirements:* For master's, comprehensive exam (for some programs). *Entrance requirements:* For master's, GRE, MCAT, OAT, or DAT, minimum overall GPA of 2.5; letters of recommendation; personal statement; resume; transcripts; bachelor's degree. Additional exam requirements/recommendations for international students: Required—TOEFL. *Application deadline:* For fall admission, 4/1 for domestic students. Application fee: $50. Electronic applications accepted. *Unit head:* Jodi Olson, Director, Master's Program in Clinical Sciences, 909-469-3842, E-mail: olsonj@westernu.edu. *Application contact:* Information Contact, 909-469-5335, Fax: 909-469-5570, E-mail: admissions@westernu.edu. Web site: http://www.westernu.edu/biomedical-sciences-msms.

Western Washington University, Graduate School, College of Sciences and Technology, Department of Biology, Bellingham, WA 98225-5996. Offers MS. Part-time programs available. *Degree requirements:* For master's, thesis. *Entrance requirements:* For master's, GRE General Test, GRE Subject Test (biology), minimum GPA of 3.0 in

Biological and Biomedical Sciences—General

last 60 semester hours or last 90 quarter hours. Additional exam requirements/recommendations for international students: Required—TOEFL (minimum score 567 paper-based; 227 computer-based). Electronic applications accepted. *Faculty research:* Organismal biology, ecology and evolutionary biology, marine biology, cell and molecular biology, developmental biology, larval ecology, microzoo planton, symbiosis.

West Texas A&M University, College of Agriculture, Science and Engineering, Department of Life, Earth, and Environmental Sciences, Program in Biology, Canyon, TX 79016-0001. Offers MS. Part-time programs available. *Degree requirements:* For master's, comprehensive exam, thesis optional. *Entrance requirements:* For master's, GRE General Test. Additional exam requirements/recommendations for international students: Required—TOEFL (minimum score 550 paper-based). Electronic applications accepted. *Faculty research:* Aeroallergen concentration, scorpions, kangaroo mice, seed anatomy with light and scanning electron microscope.

West Virginia University, Eberly College of Arts and Sciences, Department of Biology, Morgantown, WV 26506. Offers cell and molecular biology (MS, PhD); environmental and evolutionary biology (MS, PhD); forensic biology (MS, PhD); genomic biology (MS, PhD); neurobiology (MS, PhD). Terminal master's awarded for partial completion of doctoral program. *Degree requirements:* For master's, thesis, final exam; for doctorate, thesis/dissertation, preliminary and final exams. *Entrance requirements:* For master's, GRE General Test, GRE Subject Test, minimum GPA of 3.0; for doctorate, GRE General Test, minimum GPA of 3.0. Additional exam requirements/recommendations for international students: Required—TOEFL. *Faculty research:* Environmental biology, genetic engineering, developmental biology, global change, biodiversity.

West Virginia University, School of Medicine, Graduate Programs at the Health Sciences Center, Morgantown, WV 26506. Offers MS, PhD, MD/PhD. Part-time and evening/weekend programs available. Postbaccalaureate distance learning degree programs offered (minimal on-campus study). *Expenses:* Contact institution.

Wichita State University, Graduate School, Fairmount College of Liberal Arts and Sciences, Department of Biological Sciences, Wichita, KS 67260. Offers MS. Part-time programs available. *Expenses:* Tuition, state resident: full-time $4746; part-time $263.65 per credit. Tuition, nonresident: full-time $11,669; part-time $648.30 per credit. *Unit head:* Dr. William J. Hendry, III, Chair, 316-978-3111, Fax: 316-978-3772, E-mail: william.hendry@wichita.edu. *Application contact:* Dr. Leland Russell, Graduate Coordinator, 316-978-3111, E-mail: leland.russell@wichita.edu. Web site: http://www.wichita.edu/.

Wilfrid Laurier University, Faculty of Graduate and Postdoctoral Studies, Faculty of Science, Department of Biology, Waterloo, ON N2L 3C5, Canada. Offers integrative biology (M Sc). *Degree requirements:* For master's, thesis. *Entrance requirements:* For master's, honours BA in last two years of undergraduate studies with a minimum B average. Additional exam requirements/recommendations for international students: Required—TOEFL (minimum score 89 iBT). Electronic applications accepted. *Faculty research:* Genetic/development, anatomy/physiology, ecology/environment, evolution.

William Paterson University of New Jersey, College of Science and Health, General Biology Program, Wayne, NJ 07470-8420. Offers MS. Part-time and evening/weekend programs available. *Degree requirements:* For master's, comprehensive exam, independent study or thesis. *Entrance requirements:* For master's, GRE General Test, minimum GPA of 2.75. Electronic applications accepted.

Winthrop University, College of Arts and Sciences, Department of Biology, Rock Hill, SC 29733. Offers MS. Part-time programs available. *Degree requirements:* For master's, thesis optional. *Entrance requirements:* For master's, GRE General Test. Electronic applications accepted. *Faculty research:* Anatomy of marsupials; oxygen consumption, respiratory quotient and mechanical efficiency; bioremediation with microbial mats; floristic survey.

Worcester Polytechnic Institute, Graduate Studies and Research, Department of Biology and Biotechnology, Worcester, MA 01609-2280. Offers biology and biotechnology (MS); biotechnology (PhD). *Faculty:* 20 full-time (9 women). *Students:* 13 full-time (9 women); includes 1 minority (Asian, non-Hispanic/Latino), 5 international. 86 applicants, 8% accepted, 4 enrolled. In 2011, 3 degrees awarded. Terminal master's awarded for partial completion of doctoral program. *Degree requirements:* For master's, thesis; for doctorate, comprehensive exam, thesis/dissertation, qualifying exam. *Entrance requirements:* For master's and doctorate, GRE General Test, 3 letters of recommendation, statement of purpose. Additional exam requirements/recommendations for international students: Required—TOEFL (minimum score 563 paper-based; 223 computer-based; 84 iBT), IELTS (minimum score 7). *Application deadline:* For fall admission, 1/1 priority date for domestic students, 1/1 for international students. Application fee: $70. Electronic applications accepted. *Financial support:* Research assistantships, teaching assistantships, career-related internships or fieldwork, institutionally sponsored loans, scholarships/grants, and unspecified assistantships available. Financial award application deadline: 1/1; financial award applicants required to submit FAFSA. *Faculty research:* Cellular, developmental and molecular biology; neuro and regenerative biology; behavioral and environmental biology; plant biology; immunology and microbiology. *Unit head:* Dr. Joseph Duffy, Head, 508-831-4111, Fax: 508-831-5936, E-mail: jduffy@wpi.edu. *Application contact:* Dr. Reeta Rao, Graduate Coordinator, 508-831-4111, Fax: 508-831-5936, E-mail: rpr@wpi.edu. Web site: http://www.wpi.edu/Academics/Depts/BBT/.

Wright State University, School of Graduate Studies, College of Science and Mathematics, Department of Biological Sciences, Dayton, OH 45435. Offers biological sciences (MS); environmental sciences (MS). *Degree requirements:* For master's, thesis optional. *Entrance requirements:* Additional exam requirements/recommendations for international students: Required—TOEFL.

Wright State University, School of Graduate Studies, College of Science and Mathematics and School of Medicine, Program in Biomedical Sciences, Dayton, OH 45435. Offers PhD. *Degree requirements:* For doctorate, thesis/dissertation. *Entrance requirements:* For doctorate, GRE General Test. Additional exam requirements/recommendations for international students: Required—TOEFL.

Yale University, School of Medicine and Graduate School of Arts and Sciences, Combined Program in Biological and Biomedical Sciences (BBS), New Haven, CT 06520. Offers PhD, MD/PhD. *Degree requirements:* For doctorate, thesis/dissertation. *Entrance requirements:* For doctorate, GRE General Test. Additional exam requirements/recommendations for international students: Required—TOEFL. Electronic applications accepted. *Expenses:* Contact institution.

York University, Faculty of Graduate Studies, Faculty of Science and Engineering, Program in Biology, Toronto, ON M3J 1P3, Canada. Offers M Sc, PhD. Part-time and evening/weekend programs available. *Degree requirements:* For master's, thesis or alternative; for doctorate, comprehensive exam, thesis/dissertation, preliminary exam. Electronic applications accepted.

Youngstown State University, Graduate School, College of Science, Technology, Engineering and Mathematics, Department of Biological Sciences, Youngstown, OH 44555-0001. Offers environmental biology (MS); molecular biology, microbiology, and genetic (MS); physiology and anatomy (MS). Part-time programs available. *Degree requirements:* For master's, comprehensive exam, thesis, oral review. *Entrance requirements:* For master's, GRE General Test, minimum GPA of 2.7. Additional exam requirements/recommendations for international students: Required—TOEFL. *Faculty research:* Cell biology, neurophysiology, molecular biology, neurobiology, gene regulation.

ADELPHI UNIVERSITY
College of the Arts and Sciences
Program in Biology

Program of Study

Adelphi's Master of Science in biology prepares students for doctoral study and entrance into professional schools of medicine, dentistry, and veterinary medicine. The program also qualifies future educators for certification and expands the knowledge base of experienced teachers. Other graduates acquire the tools and skills necessary for successful careers in research, public health, and environmental law. At Adelphi, students gain a broad foundation in biology, practical experience, and the fundamental skills of scientific research. Laboratory courses emphasize contemporary scientific techniques and integrate technology into the learning experience. Faculty members work closely with students as mentors, ensuring a personal academic experience and career guidance. It is possible to fulfill degree requirements on the basis of either full- or part-time study, with completion in one to two years of full-time study.

There are two paths to the M.S. in biology—the research thesis (33 credits) and the nonthesis option (36 credits). Requirements are subject to change. Most courses are offered in the evening for the convenience of the working student. Adelphi students have opportunities to gain professional experience through internships at many hospitals, laboratories, private medical and dental practices, and research institutions in the area.

Students seeking a graduate degree and New York State teaching certification for secondary-level teaching (grades 7 through 12) can complete required course work for a Master of Arts degree through Adelphi's graduate program in biology in conjunction with the Ruth S. Ammon School of Education. Students who successfully complete the program are awarded a Master of Arts from the Ammon School of Education.

Adelphi also offers a M.S. in biology with a concentration in biotechnology. This innovative program prepares students for careers in this rapidly expanding and dynamic discipline of biotechnology and in the related fields of pharmaceuticals, biomedical research, cancer research, and laboratory medicine. Students may pursue a research thesis track or a scholarly paper track; a limited number of teaching assistantships are available.

Research Facilities

Departmental laboratory facilities include modern equipment for the study of molecular biology, cell and tissue culture, and scanning and transmission electron microscopy. Students use these facilities for graduate research in cellular and molecular biology, immunology, genetics, evolution, and ecology.

The University's primary research holdings are at Swirbul Library and include 600,000 volumes (including bound periodicals and government publications), 806,000 items in microformats, 33,000 audiovisual items, and online access to more than 61,000 electronic journal titles and 221 research databases.

Financial Aid

Adelphi University offers a wide variety of federal aid programs, state grants, scholarship and fellowship programs, on- and off-campus employment, and teaching and research assistantships.

Cost of Study

For the 2012–13 academic year, the tuition rate is $965 per credit. University fees range from $315 to $550 per semester.

Living and Housing Costs

The University assists single and married students in finding suitable accommodations whenever possible. The cost of living is dependent on location and the number of rooms rented.

Location

Located in Garden City, New York, 45 minutes from Manhattan and 20 minutes from Queens, Adelphi's 75-acre suburban campus is known for the beauty of its landscape and architecture. The campus is a short walk from the Long Island Rail Road and is convenient to New York's major airports and several major highways. Off-campus centers are located in Manhattan, Hauppauge, and Poughkeepsie.

The University and The College

Founded in 1896, Adelphi is a fully accredited, private university with nearly 8,000 undergraduate, graduate, and returning-adult students in the arts and sciences, business, clinical psychology, education, nursing, and social work. Students come from forty-three states and forty-five countries. The Princeton Review named Adelphi University a Best College in the Northeastern Region, and the *Fiske Guide to Colleges* recognized Adelphi as a Best Buy in higher education for six years in a row. The University is one of only twenty-five private institutions in the nation to earn this recognition.

Mindful of the cultural inheritance of the past, the College of Arts and Sciences encompasses those realms of inquiry that have characterized the modern pursuit of knowledge. The faculty members of the College place a high priority on students' intellectual development in and out of the classroom and structure programs to foster that growth. Students analyze original research and other creative work, develop firsthand facility with creative and research methodologies, undertake collaborative work with peers and mentors, engage in serious internships, and hone communicative skills.

Applying

Applicants must hold a bachelor's degree in biology or an allied field (or its equivalent) and show promise of successful achievement in the field. A student must submit a completed application, a $50 application fee, official college transcripts and two letters of recommendation. For more information, students should contact the director of graduate studies.

Correspondence and Information

George Russell, Director
Graduate Biology Program
Science Building, Room 103
College of Arts and Sciences
Adelphi University
One South Avenue
Garden City, New York 11530
Phone: 516-877-4200
Fax: 516-877-4209
E-mail: russell@adelphi.edu
Web site: http://academics.adelphi.edu/artsci/bio/graduate-biology.php

THE FACULTY AND THEIR RESEARCH

Tandra Chakraborty, Ph.D., Calcutta, India. Interplay between endocrinology and neurobiology; estrogen metabolism; obesity, hypoglycemia.

Jonna Coombs, Ph.D., Penn State. Bioremediation; microbial ecology.

Deborah Cooperstein, Ph.D., CUNY. Cellular physiology; biochemistry.

Matthias Foellmer, Ph.D., Concordia. Behavioral ecology: mating systems in spiders; salt marsh community ecology; biostatistics.

Aaren Freeman, Ph.D., New Hampshire. Marine biology and ecology; evolutionary processes.

Heather Liwanag, Ph.D., California, Santa Cruz. Comparative physiology in ecological and evolutionary context.

George Russell, Ph.D., Harvard. Genetics; biochemistry; molecular genetics.

Alan Schoenfeld, Ph.D., Yeshiva (Einstein). Cancer biology; cell biology; molecular genetics.

Aram Stump, Ph.D., Notre Dame. Genomics; molecular genetics; genetics and evolution.

Eugenia Villa-Cuesta, Ph.D., Universidad Autonoma de Madrid. Genetics; molecular biology.

Andrea Ward, Ph.D., Massachusetts Amherst. Functional morphology in fishes; comparative vertebrate anatomy; evolution and development.

Benjamin Weeks, Ph.D., Connecticut. Developmental biology; environmental toxicology; developmental neurotoxicology.

Adelphi's campus is located in historic Garden City, Long Island, New York.

A registered arboretum, Adelphi is truly a green campus.

BOSTON COLLEGE
Biology Department

Programs of Study

The Department offers a program of study leading to a Ph.D. degree in biology. Basic areas of study include biochemistry, cellular and developmental biology, genetics, cell cycle, vector biology, neurobiology, bioinformatics, and structural biology.

The Ph.D. degree provides an in-depth training experience. Core course work is provided in cell biology, biochemistry, molecular biology, and genetics. Advanced electives are available in all areas of faculty expertise. Seminar courses provide students with ongoing training in critical thinking and oral presentation of scientific data. Research experience is provided by working in close cooperation with faculty members, postdoctoral fellows, and senior students in a collaborative, supportive environment. In cooperation with the School of Education, the Master of Science in Teaching (M.S.T.) degree in biology is also offered.

Research Facilities

The Biology Department occupies more than 30,000 square feet of research space in Higgins Hall. Faculty laboratories have state-of-the-art equipment. Shared facilities include several tissue-culture rooms; common equipment rooms; TEM, fluorescence, and confocal microscopes; X-ray diffraction and a capillary DNA sequencer; machine and electronic workshops; and state-of-the-art computers for online data analysis, production of publication-quality figures, and bioinformatic research and analysis. The university science library subscribes to more than 600 scientific journals. Access to libraries of institutions in the greater Boston area is available through consortium arrangements.

Financial Aid

Graduate assistantships (teaching and research based) are available with full tuition remission. Stipends are $30,000 per calendar year.

Cost of Study

For the 2012–13 academic year, tuition and fees for a full-time student are $1292 per credit, 100 percent of which is covered by tuition remission for students receiving financial aid.

Living and Housing Costs

The Housing Office provides an extensive list of off-campus housing options, including off-campus graduate housing. Most graduate students rent rooms or apartments near Chestnut Hill; many biology students share apartments with other students in

the program. Average monthly expenses (rent, food, utilities) for the academic year (nine months) are $2105 for students.

Student Group

The enrollment at Boston College is 14,500, including 4,200 students enrolled in the various graduate schools. There are 45 graduate students in the Ph.D. program. The graduate students are geographically and ethnically diverse.

Location

Boston College is located in the Chestnut Hill section of Newton, an attractive residential area about 5 miles from the heart of Boston, with easy access to the city by public transportation. The Boston area, with its numerous educational and biomedical research institutions, offers countless outstanding seminars, lectures, colloquia, and concerts throughout the year. A wide variety of cultural and recreational opportunities can be found close to the campus.

The College

Founded in Massachusetts in 1863, Boston College currently includes the Graduate School of Arts and Sciences and graduate schools of law, social work, management, nursing, and education. Its expanding campus is graced with many attractive Gothic buildings. Boston College has a strong tradition of academic excellence and service to the community.

Applying

Preference is given to completed applications received prior to January 1. Admission is granted on the basis of academic background and demonstrated aptitude in biology and related disciplines. A year of organic chemistry, physics, and mathematics and a solid background in biology are highly recommended for admission. Scores on the Graduate Record Examinations General Test and the Subject Test in biology are required.

Correspondence and Information

Professor Charles Hoffman
Director, Graduate Program
Biology Department
Higgins Hall
Boston College
Chestnut Hill, Massachusetts 02467-3961
Phone: 617-552-3540
E-mail: gradbio@bc.edu
Web site: http://www.bc.edu/biology

Boston College

THE GRADUATE RESEARCH FACULTY

Anthony T. Annunziato, Professor; Ph.D., Massachusetts Amherst, 1979. Biochemistry/molecular biology; DNA replication and nucleosome assembly in mammalian cells.

David R. Burgess, Professor; Ph.D., California, Davis, 1974. Spatial and temporal regulation of cytokinesis; role of the actin- and microtubule-based cytoskeletons in early development.

Hugh P. Cam, Assistant Professor; Ph.D., Harvard 2003. Epigenetic control of higher-order genome organization and chromatin structures.

Thomas C. Chiles, Professor and Chairman of Biology; Ph.D., Florida, 1988. Cell biology, signal transduction; cell-cycle control, gene regulation in mature B lymphocytes.

Jeffrey Chuang, Assistant Professor; Ph.D., MIT, 2001. Computational approaches to comparative genomics, gene regulation, and molecular evolution.

Peter G. Clote, Professor; Ph.D., Duke, 1979. Algorithms and mathematical modeling in computational biology: genomic motif detection, protein folding on lattice models, RNA secondary structure, functional genomics via gene expression profile.

Kathleen Dunn, Associate Professor; Ph.D., North Carolina at Chapel Hill, 1982. Plant molecular biology; cloning and characterization of genes induced during alfalfa nodulation.

Marc-Jan Gubbels, Assistant Professor; Ph.D., Utrecht (Netherlands), 2000. Genetics and cell biology of the apicomplexan parasite *Toxoplasma gondii*.

Laura E. Hake, Associate Professor; Ph.D., Tufts, 1992. Molecular control of early development in *Xenopus;* protein degradation; RNA-protein interactions; translational regulation during gametogenesis.

Charles Hoffman, Professor; Ph.D., Tufts, 1986. Signal transduction and transcriptional regulation in fission yeast; analysis of PKA and MAPK signal pathways in nutrient monitoring.

Welkin Johnson, Professor; Ph.D., Tufts, 1998. Retroviruses; primate lentiviruses (HIV and SIV); co-evolution of viruses and their hosts.

Daniel Kirschner, Professor; Ph.D., Harvard, 1972. Structural biochemistry of amyloids and myelin sheath; neurodegenerative diseases; peripheral demyelinating neuropathies.

Gabor T. Marth, Assistant Professor; D.Sc., Washington (St. Louis), 1994. DNA polymorphism discovery and analysis; genomic and algorithmic approaches to population genetics; long-term human demography, haplotype structure, and medical genetics.

Michelle Meyer, Assistant Professor; Ph.D., Caltech, 2006. Bioinformatic discovery and experimental characterization of RNA-based gene regulatory mechanisms.

Junona Moroianu, Associate Professor; Ph.D., Rockefeller, 1996. Cell biology; molecular mechanisms of nucleocytoplasmic transport of cellular and viral macromolecules in mammalian cells.

Marc A. T. Muskavitch, Professor; Ph.D., Stanford, 1981. Developmental biology: intercellular signaling and cell-fate specification in *Drosophila;* host-parasite interactions in *Anopheles.*

Clare M. O'Connor, Associate Professor and Associate Chair; Ph.D., Purdue, 1977. Cellular biochemistry.

Thomas N. Seyfried, Professor; Ph.D., Illinois, 1976. Neurogenetics: use of genetics and neurochemistry in neural membrane function and developmental neurobiology.

Kenneth C. Williams, Associate Professor; Ph.D., McGill, 1993. Central nervous system macrophages; neuroAIDS; AIDS pathogenesis; monocyte/macrophage biology.

Higgins Hall, home of the Biology Department.

Students find a blend of the old and the new at Boston College.

CITY OF HOPE NATIONAL MEDICAL CENTER
BECKMAN RESEARCH INSTITUTE

Irell & Manella Graduate School of Biological Sciences

Programs of Study

The mission of the City of Hope Graduate School of Biological Sciences is to train students to be outstanding research scientists in chemical, molecular, and cellular biology. Graduates of this program are awarded the degree of Doctor of Philosophy in biological sciences and are equipped to address fundamental questions in the life sciences and biomedicine for careers in academia, industry, and government. The time spent in the program is devoted to full-time study and research. During the first year, the student completes the core curriculum and two laboratory rotations (eight to ten weeks each). The core curriculum contains biochemistry, molecular biology, cell biology, and biostatistics/bioinformatics. One Advanced Topics course is taken during spring of the first year. After the first year, the student prepares and orally defends a research proposal based on an original topic not related to previous work conducted by the student, and in the second year students prepare and defend a research proposal based on their actual thesis topic. Two additional Advanced Topics courses are required after the first year and students are required to take a literature-based journal club every year after the first year. Students also participate in courses on scientific communication and on the responsible conduct of research. After successfully completing the core curriculum and research proposal, students concentrate the majority of their time on their individual dissertation laboratory research project. The written thesis/dissertation must be presented by the student for examination by 4 members of the City of Hope staff and 1 qualified member from an outside institution.

Research Facilities

City of Hope is a premier medical center, one of forty National Cancer Institute–designated Comprehensive Cancer Centers. Its Beckman Research Institute launched the biotech industry by creating the first human recombinant gene products, insulin and growth hormone, which are now used by millions of people worldwide. State-of-the-art facilities include mass spectrometry, NMR, molecular modeling, cell sorting, DNA sequencing, molecular pathology, scanning and transmission electron microscopy, confocal microscopy, and molecular imaging. The Lee Graff Medical and Scientific Library allows access to the latest biomedical information via its journal and book collection, document delivery, interlibrary loans, and searches of online databases.

Financial Aid

All students in the Graduate School receive a fellowship of $32,000 per year as well as paid health and dental insurance.

Cost of Study

There are no tuition charges. A student services fee of $50 per semester ($150 per year) is the student's only financial obligation to City of Hope.

Living and Housing Costs

The School has limited, low-cost housing available. Living in student housing provides easy access to campus resources and a connection to the vibrant campus community. Additional housing is available within the immediate area at an average cost of $700 to $1000 per month.

Student Group

The Graduate School faculty consists of 76 of City of Hope's investigators. Eighty-five graduate students were working toward the Ph.D. degree in biological sciences in 2011–12.

Student Outcomes

Graduates have gone on to work as postdoctoral fellows at California Institute of Technology; Harvard University; Scripps Research Institute; Stanford University; University of California, Los Angeles; University of California, San Diego; University of California, Irvine; Genentech; University of Southern California; and Washington University in St. Louis. Graduates have also found positions with Wyeth-Ayerst Research; Allergan, Inc.; and the U.S. Biodefense and its subsidiary, Stem Cell Research Institute of California, Inc.

Location

City of Hope is located 25 miles northeast of downtown Los Angeles, minutes away from Pasadena and close to beaches, mountains, and many recreational and cultural activities.

The Medical Center and The Institute

City of Hope was founded in 1913, initially as a tuberculosis sanatorium. Research programs were initiated in 1951, and, in 1983, the Beckman Research Institute of City of Hope was established with support from the Arnold and Mabel Beckman Foundation. The Institute comprises basic science research groups within the Divisions of Biology, Immunology, Molecular Medicine, and Neurosciences, among others.

Applying

The deadline for application is January 1 for classes starting in August. Applying early is advisable. Candidates must submit transcripts, three letters of recommendation, and take the Graduate Record Examination (General Test required, Subject Test recommended). For further information and an application, students should contact the School at the address listed in this description.

Correspondence and Information

City of Hope
Irell & Manuella Graduate School of Biological Sciences
1500 East Duarte Road
Duarte, California 91010
United States
Phone: 877-715-GRAD or 626-256-4673 Ext. 63899
Fax: 626-301-8105
E-mail: gradschool@coh.org
Web site: http://www.cityofhope.org/gradschool

City of Hope National Medical Center

THE FACULTY AND THEIR RESEARCH

Professors

David K. Ann, Ph.D. Molecular mechanisms of maintaining genomic integrity.

Michael E. Barish, Ph.D. Physiological and imaging studies of brain tumors and their interactions with neural stem cells.

Ravi Bhatia, M.D. Regulation of normal and malignant hematopoietic stem cell growth.

Edouard M. Cantin, Ph.D. Herpes simplex virus infections in the nervous system.

Saswati Chatterjee, Ph.D. Adeno-associated virus vectors for stem-cell gene therapy.

Shiuan Chen, Ph.D. Hormones and cancer.

Yuan Chen, Ph.D. Ubiquitin-like modifications.

Don J. Diamond, Ph.D. Translational research in cancer vaccines.

Richard W. Ermel, D.V.M., Ph.D. Comparative medicine.

Stephen J. Forman, M.D. T-Cell immunotherapy for treatment of cancer.

David Horne, Ph.D. Developing natural products as novel anticancer agents.

Keiichi Itakura, Ph.D. Functions of Mrf-1 and Mrf-2.

Linda Iverson, Ph.D. Stem cells and cancer.

Richard Jove, Ph.D. Development of molecular targeted therapeutics.

Susan E. Kane, Ph.D. Drug resistance and cancer.

Theodore G. Krontiris, M.D., Ph.D. Genetic risk and disease.

Peter P. Lee, Ph.D. The impact of cancer on immune system.

Terry D. Lee, Ph.D. Mass spectrometry of biomolecules.

Ren-Jang Lin, Ph.D. RNA splicing and post-transcriptional gene regulation.

Chih-Pin Liu, Ph.D. Immune regulation of autoimmune disease and tumor.

Linda Malkas, Ph.D. The selective targeting of cancer cells.

Marcia M. Miller, Ph.D. Molecular immunogenetics.

Rama Natarajan, Ph.D. Diabetic vascular complications.

Susan Neuhausen, Ph.D. Genetic epidemiology of complex diseases.

Timothy R. O'Connor, Ph.D. DNA repair.

Gerd P. Pfeifer, Ph.D. Molecular mechanisms of cancer.

Andrew Raubitschek, M.D. Immunotherapy.

Arthur D. Riggs, Ph.D. Epigenetics, chromatin structure, and X chromosome inactivation.

John J. Rossi, Ph.D. The biology and applications of small RNAs.

Paul M. Salvaterra, Ph.D. Modeling Alzheimer-type neurogeneration.

Binghui Shen, Ph.D. The study of DNA replication and repair nucleases in genome stability and cancers.

John E. Shively, Ph.D. Structure, function, and regulation of carcinoembryonic antigen genes.

Judith Singer-Sam, Ph.D. Epigenetics and disorders of the CNS.

Steven S. Smith, Ph.D. Cancer epigenetics.

Cy A. Stein, M.D, Ph.D. Cellular delivery of therapeutic oligonucleotides.

John Termini, Ph.D. Mutagenesis and carcinogenesis.

Nagarajan Vaidehi, Ph.D. Predicting protein structure and dynamics for drug discovery.

Jeffrey N. Weitzel, M.D. Genetic predisposition to cancer.

Jiing-Kuan Yee, Ph.D. Vectors for gene therapy.

Yun Yen, M.D., Ph.D. Novel molecular-targeted cancer therapies.

Hua Yu, Ph.D. Stat 3 and the tumor microenvironment.

John A. Zaia, M.D. Genetic and other anti-HIV therapy.

Associate and Assistant Professors

Karen S. Aboody, M.D. Neural stem cells—therapeutic applications.

Adam M. Bailis, Ph.D. Homologous recombination governs genome dynamics and tumor suppression.

Jacob Berlin, Ph.D. Nanoparticles for the diagnosis and treatment of cancer.

Mark Boldin, Ph.D. Noncoding RNA control of inflammation and cancer.

Ching-Cheng Chen, Ph.D. Cellular and molecular characterization of the hematopoietic niche.

Wen Yong Chen, Ph.D. Epigenetics, cancer, and aging.

Warren Chow, M.D., FACP. Cell signaling and cancer.

Fong-Fong Chu, Ph.D. The role of oxidative stress in inflammatory bowel disease and cancer.

Carlotta A. Glackin, Ph.D. Understanding gene regulation from stem cells.

Robert Hickey, Ph.D. Identification and clinical translation of molecular signatures of disease.

Wendong Huang, Ph.D. Metabolic regulation, cancer, and aging.

Janice Huss, Ph.D. The role of orphan nuclear receptors in cardiac and skeletal muscle biology.

Rahul Jandial, M.D, Ph.D. Breast-to-brain cancer metastasis.

Jeremy Jones, Ph.D. The androgen receptor in human disease.

Markus Kalkum, Dr. Rer. Nat. (Ph.D.) Biodefense and emerging infectious diseases.

Joseph Kim, M.D. Uncovering the roots of pancreatic cancer.

Mei Kong, Ph.D. Signal transduction and cancer metabolism.

Marcin Kortylewski, Ph.D. Immune cells as targets for cancer therapy.

Hsun Teresa Ku, Ph.D. Pancreatic endocrine stem cells.

Ya-Huei Kuo, Ph.D. Molecular genetics of hematopoietic stem cells and leukemia stem cells.

Yilun Liu, Ph.D. Human RECQ helicases in aging and cancer prevention.

Qiang Lu, Ph.D. Understanding the mechanisms that control self-renewal and differentiation of neural progenitor/stem cells.

Edward M. Newman, Ph.D. Biochemical pharmacology of antimetabolites.

Vu Ngo, Ph.D. Molecular pathogenesis of lymphoid malignancies.

Dustin E. Schones, Ph.D. Epigenomics of development and disease.

Yanhong Shi, Ph.D. Nuclear receptors in neural stem cells and adult neurogenesis.

Jeremy M. Stark, Ph.D. Factors and pathways that influence mammalian chromosomal stability.

Zuoming Sun, Ph.D. Mechanisms regulating T cell-mediated immunity.

Timothy W. Synold, Pharm.D. Pharmacokinetics and pharmacodynamics of anti-cancer drugs.

Piroska E. Szabó, Ph.D. Mechanisms of genomic imprinting and environmental reproductive biology.

Toshifumi Tomoda, M.D., Ph.D. Organelle transport during neuronal development and diseases.

Shizhen Emily Wang, Ph.D. Outsmarting breast cancer.

John C. Williams, Ph.D. Structural biology and biophysics.

Defu Zeng, M.D. Transplantation immune tolerance.

COLD SPRING HARBOR LABORATORY
Watson School of Biological Sciences

Program of Study

The Watson School of Biological Sciences at Cold Spring Harbor Laboratory (CSHL) offers an accredited graduate training program, which leads to the Ph.D. degree, to a select group of self-motivated students of outstanding ability and intellect. The curriculum takes advantage of the unique and flexible environment of CSHL and includes the following innovative features: approximately four years from matriculation to Ph.D. degree award, broad representation of the biological sciences, a first year with course work and laboratory rotations in separate phases, emphasis on the principles of scientific reasoning and logic, continued advanced course instruction throughout the graduate curriculum, and two-tier mentoring.

The program provides an exciting and intensive educational experience. The curriculum is designed to train self-reliant students who, under their own guidance, can acquire and assimilate the knowledge that their research or career demands require. The course work is varied, involving core courses, focused topic courses, and CSHL postgraduate courses.

The current fields of research expertise of CSHL faculty members are cancer, neuroscience, quantitative biology, plant biology, and bioinformatics and genomics. The laboratories of all CSHL research faculty members are available to students in the program.

Requirements for the award of the Ph.D. degree are successful completion of all course work, laboratory rotations, teaching (at the Laboratory's Dolan DNA Learning Center), the Ph.D. qualifying exam, thesis research and postdoctoral proposals, and defense of a written thesis that describes original research. The program aims to train future leaders in the biological sciences.

Research Facilities

Cold Spring Harbor Laboratory has state-of-the-art facilities for research in cancer, neuroscience, quantitative biology, plant biology, and bioinformatics and genomics. As a National Cancer Institute–designated Cancer Center, there is an extensive set of shared resources. There are several libraries and one archive on campus. Library services, such as database searching and reference and interlibrary loan services, are available. An information technology department provides campuswide support of computing.

Financial Aid

The Watson School of Biological Sciences supports each student with an annual stipend, health benefits, affordable housing, subsidized food, and funds for tuition and research costs. To enhance their careers, students are encouraged to seek independent funding through predoctoral fellowships from federal and private sources such as the National Science Foundation.

Cost of Study

The Watson School of Biological Sciences provides full remission of all tuition fees for all accepted students. The School also supports the stipend and research costs of each student for four years.

Living and Housing Costs

The Laboratory provides affordable housing to all graduate students through a network of on-site and off-site housing. Single graduate students are offered single rooms in shared houses with house-cleaning services; married students are housed in apartments. First-year students of the Watson School are offered housing in the Townsend Knight House, a renovated house from 1810 that is located on the shore of Cold Spring Harbor opposite the Laboratory.

Student Group

The class size is approximately 10 to 15 students per year. Over the years students have come to the School from the United States, Italy, Poland, Singapore, China, England, Germany, Argentina, Mexico, Australia, Canada, India, France, and Russia. The School aims to produce graduates in the biological sciences who are likely to become ethical world leaders in science and society.

Location

The Laboratory is located on the wooded north shore of Long Island, 35 miles east of Manhattan in New York City, and offers many amenities, both cultural and recreational. Recreational activities at CSHL include a fitness room, tennis and volleyball courts, a private beach, sailboats, and many quiet back roads for running or walking. Students may also attend classical music performances and art exhibitions sponsored by the Laboratory for scientists and the neighboring community.

The Laboratory

Since its inception in 1890, CSHL has been involved in higher education and is today a world leader in biology education. The CSHL Press publishes internationally recognized books and journals. The Dolan DNA Learning Center educates students and teachers about the world of DNA. The Undergraduate Research Program, started in 1959, hosts exceptional undergraduates from around the world for a summer research experience. CSHL is also involved in education at the highest levels through a postgraduate program of twenty-five advanced courses in biology and many large and small international conferences. These meetings and courses attract 8,000 scientists annually to the Laboratory. The Laboratory has also been involved in graduate education leading to the Ph.D. degree for more than twenty-five years, particularly through shared graduate programs with Stony Brook University.

Applying

Applicants must have received a baccalaureate degree from an accredited university or college prior to matriculation. Admission is based on the perceived ability of the applicant to excel in this doctoral program, without regard to gender, race, color, ethnic origin, sexual orientation, disability, or marital status. Suitable applicants are assessed on the basis of their academic record, recommendations from their mentors, and an on-site interview. Students should ensure that the school receives all application materials (transcripts, examination scores, letters of recommendation, etc.) no later than December 1 for the following fall term. Early application is advisable. All applicants must apply online. Further information about the School and the application procedure may be requested by mail or obtained from the Web site at http://www.cshl.edu/gradschool.

Correspondence and Information

Dawn M. Pologruto
Director of Admissions and Student Affairs
Watson School of Biological Sciences
Cold Spring Harbor Laboratory
One Bungtown Road
Cold Spring Harbor, New York 11724
Phone: 516-367-6911
Fax: 516-367-6919
E-mail: gradschool@cshl.edu
Web site: http://www.cshl.edu/gradschool

THE FACULTY AND THEIR RESEARCH

Research Faculty

Dinu Florin Albeanu, Assistant Professor; Ph.D., Harvard, 2008. Neuronal circuits; sensory coding and synaptic plasticity; neuronal correlates of behavior; olfactory processing.

Gurinder Singh Atwal, Assistant Professor; Ph.D., Cornell, 2002. Population genetics; bioinformatics; cancer; stochastic processes; statistical mechanics and information theory.

Anne Churchland, Assistant Professor; Ph.D., California, San Francisco, 2003. Behavior in awake animals; neuroscience and electrophysiology.

Josh Dubnau, Assistant Professor; Ph.D., Columbia, 1995. Learning; memory; genetics; behavior.

Mikala Egeblad, Assistant Professor, Ph.D., Copenhagen, 2000. Tumor microenvironment; intravital imaging; tumor-associated myeloid cells; breast cancer.

Grigori Enikolopov, Associate Professor; Ph.D., Russian Academy of Sciences (Moscow), 1978. Signal transduction in neurons; development; gene expression; nitric oxide.

Hiro Furukawa, Assistant Professor; Ph.D., Tokyo, 2001. Structural biology; neurodegenerative diseases; intramembrane proteolysis; ion channels; membrane proteins; X-ray crystallography.

Jesse Gillis, Assistant Professor; Ph.D., Toronto, 2007. Gene networks; gene function prediction; guilt by association; neuropsychiatric; hub genes; multifunctionality; computational genomics.

Thomas Gingeras, Professor; Ph.D., NYU, 1976. Organization and regulation of eukaryotic transcription; classification and function of non–protein coding RNAs.

Chris Hammell, Assistant Professor; Ph.D., Dartmouth, 2002. MicroRNA-mediated gene regulation of *C. elegans* developmental timing; genetics; development.

Gregory Hannon, Professor; Ph.D., Case Western Reserve, 1992. Growth control in mammalian cells.

SECTION 1: BIOLOGICAL AND BIOMEDICAL SCIENCES

Cold Spring Harbor Laboratory

Z. Josh Huang, Professor; Ph.D., Brandeis, 1994. Neuroscience; experience-dependent development and plasticity of the neocortex; mouse genetics.

Ivan Iossifov, Assistant Professor; Ph.D., Columbia, 2008. Computational biology; molecular networks; human genetics; human disease; applied statistical and machine learning; biomedical text-mining; molecular evolution.

David Jackson, Professor; Ph.D., East Anglia (England), 1991. Plant development; genetics; cell-to-cell mRNA and protein trafficking.

Leemor Joshua-Tor, Professor; Ph.D., Weizmann (Israel), 1991. Structural biology; X-ray crystallography; molecular recognition; transcription; proteases.

Adam Kepecs, Assistant Professor; Ph.D., Brandeis, 2002. Decision-making; neural circuits; behavioral electrophysiology; theoretical neuroscience; neuroeconomics.

Alexei Koulakov, Associate Professor; Ph.D., Minnesota, 1998. Theoretical neurobiology; quantitative principles of cortical design.

Adrian R. Krainer, Professor; Ph.D., Harvard, 1986. Posttranscriptional regulation of gene expression; pre-mRNA splicing mechanisms; alternative splicing; RNA-protein interactions; cell-free systems.

Alexander Krasnitz, Assistant Professor; Ph.D., Tel Aviv University, 1990. High-level analysis of microarray-derived data in cancer biology; bioinformatics.

Bo Li, Assistant Professor; Ph.D., British Columbia, 2003. Neuroscience; glutamatergic synapse; synaptic plasticity; schizophrenia; depression; rodent models of psychiatric disorders.

Zachary Lippman, Assistant Professor; Ph.D., Watson School of Biological Sciences at Cold Spring Harbor Laboratory, 2004. Plant development; genetics; flowering; inflorescence architecture; sympodial growth, phase transition; heterosis; quantitative genetics.

Gholson Lyon, Assistant Professor; M.D., Cornell, Weill, 2004; Ph.D., Rockefeller, 2003. Human genetics; neuropsychiatric diseases; whole genome sequencing; ethics.

Robert Martienssen, Professor; Ph.D., Cambridge, 1986. Plant genetics; transposons; development; gene regulation; DNA methylation.

W. Richard McCombie, Professor; Ph.D., Michigan, 1982. Genome structure; DNA sequencing; computational molecular biology; Human Genome Project.

Alea A. Mills, Associate Professor; Ph.D., California, Irvine, 1997. Functional genomics; tumorigenesis; development.

Partha P. Mitra, Professor; Ph.D., Harvard, 1993. Neuroinformatics; theoretical engineering; animal communications; neural prostheses; brain imaging; developmental linguistics.

Pavel Osten, Associate Professor; M.D., Charles University (Prague), 1991; Ph.D., SUNY Downstate Medical Center, 1995. Neurobiology of autism and schizophrenia; gene expression-based mapping of brain activity; anatomical mapping of brain connectivity; high throughput microscopy.

Darryl J. Pappin, Associate Professor; Ph.D., Leeds (United Kingdom), 1984. Proteomics; mass spectrometry; protein chemistry.

Scott Powers, Associate Professor; Ph.D., Columbia, 1983. Cancer gene discovery; cancer diagnostics and therapeutics; cancer biology.

Michael C. Schatz, Assistant Professor; Ph.D., Maryland, College Park. DNA sequence data concentrating on the alignment and assembly of short reads; bioinformatics.

Stephen Shea, Assistant Professor; Ph.D., Chicago, 2004. Olfaction; audition; communication behaviors; *in vivo* electrophysiology; individual recognition.

Raffaella Sordella, Assistant Professor; Ph.D., Turin, 1998. Molecular therapeutics; signal transduction.

David L. Spector, Professor; Ph.D., Rutgers, 1980. Cell biology; nuclear structure; microscopy; pre-mRNA splicing.

Arne Stenlund, Associate Professor; Ph.D., Uppsala (Sweden), 1984. Papillomavirus; cancer; DNA replication.

Bruce Stillman, President and CEO; Ph.D., Australian National, 1979. DNA replication; chromatin assembly; biochemistry; yeast genetics; cancer; cell cycle.

Marja Timmermans, Associate Professor; Ph.D., Rutgers, 1996. Plant development; axis specification; homeobox genes; stem cell function.

Nicholas Tonks, Professor; Ph.D., Dundee (Scotland), 1985. Posttranslational modification; phosphorylation; phosphatases; signal transduction; protein structure and function.

Lloyd Trotman, Assistant Professor; Ph.D., Zurich, 2001. Molecular mechanisms of tumor suppression; cancer modeling and treatment; molecular cancer visualization; PTEN regulation.

Glenn Turner, Assistant Professor; Ph.D., Caltech, 2000. Neural coding; learning and memory; sensory processing; *Drosophila;* electrophysiology.

David Tuveson, Professor; M.D., Ph.D., Johns Hopkins, 1994. Pancreatic cancer; experimental therapeutics; diagnostics; mouse models; cancer genetics.

Linda Van Aelst, Professor; Ph.D., Leuven (Belgium), 1991. Signal transduction; Ras and Rac proteins; tumorigenesis; metastasis.

Doreen Ware, Assistant Professor; Ph.D., Ohio State, 2000. Computational biology; comparative genomics; genome evolution; diversity; gene regulation; plant biology.

Michael Wigler, Professor; Ph.D., Columbia, 1978. Cancer; genomics; oncogenes; signal transduction; Ras; yeast genetics.

Anthony Zador, Professor; M.D./Ph.D., Yale, 1994. Computational neuroscience; synaptic plasticity; auditory processing; cortical circuitry.

Hongwu Zheng, Assistant Professor; Ph.D., Boston University, 2003. Cellular renewal and differentiation in stem cells and glioma genesis; cancer development; stem cells.

Yi Zhong, Professor; Ph.D., Iowa, 1991. Neurophysiology; *Drosophila;* learning and memory; neurofibromatosis; signal transduction.

Non-Research Faculty

Alexander A. F. Gann, Dean and Editorial Director, Cold Spring Harbor Laboratory Press; Ph.D., Edinburgh, 1989.

Terri Grodzicker, Dean, Academic Affairs; Ph.D., Columbia, 1969.

John R. Inglis, Executive Director, Cold Spring Harbor Laboratory Press; Ph.D., Edinburgh, 1976.

David A. Micklos, Executive Director, DNA Learning Center; M.A., Maryland, 1982.

David J. Stewart, Director, Meetings and Courses; Ph.D., Cambridge, 1988.

Jan A. Witkowski, Executive Director, Banbury Center; Ph.D., London, 1972.

The campus of Cold Spring Harbor Laboratory.

Urey Cottage, home of the Watson School of Biological Sciences.

Peterson's Graduate Programs in the Biological/Biomedical Sciences & Health-Related Professions 2013

COLUMBIA UNIVERSITY
Graduate School of Arts and Sciences
Department of Biological Sciences

Program of Study

The Department offers training leading to a Ph.D. in cellular, molecular, developmental, computational, and structural biology as well as genetics, molecular biophysics, and neurobiology. The graduate program provides each student with a solid background in contemporary biology and an in-depth knowledge of one or more of the above areas. The specific nature and scheduling of courses taken during the first two graduate years are determined by the student's consultation with the graduate student adviser, taking into account the background and specific research interests of the student. During the first year, all students take an intensive core course that provides a solid background in structural biology, cell biology, genetics, molecular biology, and bioinformatics.

Beginning in the first year, graduate students attend advanced seminar courses, including the preresearch seminar, which is a forum for faculty-student research discussion. Important components of graduate education include the ability to analyze critically the contemporary research literature and to present such analyses effectively through oral and written presentations. Students acquire training in these skills through participation in advanced-level seminars and journal clubs, as well as through presentation and defense of original research proposals during the spring semester of the second year of graduate study or the fall semester of the third year.

Beginning in the first year of graduate work, students also engage in research training. Students may choose laboratories in the Department of Biological Sciences on Columbia's main Morningside Heights Campus or in about twenty-five other laboratories, including many at Columbia's Health Sciences Campus. To inform incoming students of research opportunities, faculty members discuss ongoing research projects with them in the preresearch seminar held in the autumn term of the first year. All students are required to participate in ongoing research in up to three different laboratories during the first year. The choice of a dissertation sponsor is made after consultation between the student and potential faculty advisers, and intensive research begins following the spring term of the student's first year. Each student is assigned a Ph.D. Advisory Committee made up of the student's sponsor and 2 other faculty members.

Research Facilities

The Department of Biological Sciences is located in the Sherman Fairchild Center for the Life Sciences. The building provides nearly 78,000 square feet of laboratory space for the Department's laboratories, as well as extensive shared instrument facilities, including extensive sophisticated microscopy, X-ray diffraction, fluorescence-activated cell sorting (FACS), real-time PCR analysis, mass spectrometry, infrared scanning, phosphorimaging, and microinjection, as well as housing and care of research animals, including transgenic mice. In addition, several laboratories are located in the nearby new state-of-the-art Northwest Corner interdisciplinary science building.

Financial Aid

All accepted students receive generous stipends, complete tuition exemption, and medical insurance. Special fellowships with larger stipends are also available (e.g., to members of minority groups).

Cost of Study

Tuition and fees are paid for all graduate students accepted into the Department.

Living and Housing Costs

Most students live in University-owned, subsidized apartments or dormitories within easy walking distance of the laboratories. In addition, both the Morningside and Health Sciences Campuses are easily reached by public transportation from all areas of the city.

Student Group

There are about 105 graduate students and 60 postdoctoral fellows in the Department.

Location

New York is the cultural center of the country and offers unrivaled opportunities for attending concerts, operas, plays, and sporting events, for visiting outstanding museums, and for varied, affordable dining. Many excellent beaches, ski slopes, and state and national parks are within reasonable driving distance.

The University and The Department

Columbia was established as King's College in 1754 and has grown into one of the major universities of the world. The Department is located on the beautiful main campus in Morningside Heights, which combines the advantages of an urban setting and a peaceful college-town atmosphere.

Applying

Undergraduate training in one of the natural or physical sciences is recommended, although successful students have come from computer science or engineering backgrounds, as well. It is desirable for students to have had at least one year of calculus, as well as courses in organic and physical chemistry, physics, genetics, biochemistry, and cell biology. Any deficiencies may be made up while in graduate school. The Graduate Record Examinations (GRE) is required, as is the Test of English as a Foreign Language (TOEFL) for international applicants whose native language is not English and who do not hold an undergraduate degree from a U.S. college. The GRE Subject Test in biology, biochemistry, chemistry, computer science, or physics is highly recommended. Completed applications should be returned by January 4 for admission to the fall semester. Applications will be reviewed in the order received, so those submitting complete applications earlier have a better chance of being invited for an interview. Application forms and additional information can be obtained from the Department's Web site.

Columbia University is an Equal Opportunity/Affirmative Action institution.

Correspondence and Information

Graduate Student Adviser
Department of Biological Sciences
Columbia University
1212 Amsterdam Avenue, Mail Code 2402
Sherman Fairchild Center, Room 600
New York, New York 10027
United States
Phone: 212-854-2313
Fax: 212-865-8246
E-mail: biology@columbia.edu
Web site: http://www.columbia.edu/cu/biology/

Columbia University

THE FACULTY AND THEIR RESEARCH

J. Chloë Bulinski, Professor; Ph.D., Wisconsin, 1980. Dynamics and functions of microtubules during myogenic differentiation and cell-cycle progression.

Harmen Bussemaker, Associate Professor; Ph.D., Utrecht (Netherlands), 1995. Data-driven modeling of transcriptional and posttranscriptional networks based on biophysical principles.

Martin Chalfie, Professor; Ph.D., Harvard, 1977; Member, National Academy of Sciences and Nobel Laureate in Chemistry 2008. Developmental genetics of identified nerve cells in *Caenorhabditis elegans;* genetic analysis of cell differentiation, mechanosensory transduction, synapse specification, and aging.

Lawrence A. Chasin, Professor; Ph.D., MIT, 1967. Pre-mRNA splicing in cultured mammalian cells.

Lars Dietrich, Assistant Professor, Ph.D., Heidelberg (Germany), 2004. Bacterial models for biological shape and pattern formation.

Julio Fernandez, Professor; Ph.D., Berkeley, 1982. Study of the cellular events that lead to the release of histamine or catecholamine-containing secretory granules from single, isolated mast cells or chromaffin cells; analysis of single-protein elasticity by atomic force microscopy (AFM).

Stuart Firestein, Professor; Ph.D., Berkeley, 1988. Cellular and molecular physiology of transduction; coding and neuronal regeneration in the vertebrate olfactory system.

Joachim Frank, Professor and Howard Hughes Medical Institute Investigator; Ph.D., Munich Technical, 1970; Member, National Academy of Sciences. Cryoelectron microscopy and three-dimensional reconstruction for the study of the mechanism of protein biosynthesis.

Tulle Hazelrigg, Professor; Ph.D., Indiana, 1982. mRNA localization in *Drosophila* oocytes.

John F. Hunt, Associate Professor; Ph.D., Yale, 1993. Structural genomics and biophysical studies of the molecular mechanism of transmembrane transport.

Songtao Jia, Associate Professor; Ph.D., UCLA, 2003. Epigenetic regulation of the genome.

Daniel D. Kalderon, Professor; Ph.D., London, 1984. Molecular mechanisms of cellular interactions mediated by cAMP-dependent protein kinase (PKA) in *Drosophila;* roles of PKA in hedgehog signaling and in generating anterior/posterior polarity in oocytes.

Darcy B. Kelley, Professor and Howard Hughes Medical Institute Professor; Ph.D., Rockefeller, 1975. Sexual differentiation of the nervous system; molecular analyses of androgen-regulated development in neurons and muscle; neuroethology of vocal communication; evolution of the nuclear receptor family.

James L. Manley, Professor; Ph.D., SUNY at Stony Brook, 1976. Regulation of mRNA synthesis in animal cells; biochemical and genetic analysis of mechanisms and control of mRNA transcription, splicing, and polyadenylation; developmental control of gene expression.

Elizabeth Miller, Associate Professor; Ph.D., La Trobe (Australia), 1999. Protein folding, assembly, and the regulation of intracellular protein transport.

Dana Pe'er, Assistant Professor; Ph.D., Hebrew (Israel), 2003. Function and organization of molecular networks.

Carol L. Prives, Professor; Ph.D., McGill, 1968; Member, National Academy of Sciences and National Institute of Medicine. Structure and function of the p53 tumor suppressor protein and p53 family members; studies on cell cycle and apoptosis; stress-activated signaling and control of proteolysis.

Ron Prywes, Professor; Ph.D., MIT, 1984. Normal and cancerous mechanisms of regulation of cellular proliferation and gene expression; signal transduction and activation of transcription factors; activation of transcription by the ER stress/unfolded protein response.

Ozgur Sahin, Associate Professor of Biological Sciences and Physics; Ph.D., Stanford, 2005. Mechanical investigations of biological systems for energy, environment, and biological research.

Michael P. Sheetz, Professor; Ph.D., Caltech, 1972. Motility studies of cells and microtubule motor proteins, with an emphasis on the force-dependent interactions relevant to transformed cells and neuron pathfinding, using laser tweezers.

Brent Stockwell, Associate Professor and Howard Hughes Medical Institute Investigator; Ph.D., Harvard, 1997. Diagramming disease networks with chemical and biological tools.

Liang Tong, Professor; Ph.D., Berkeley, 1989. Structural biology of proteins involved in human diseases (obesity, diabetes, cancer); structural biology of proteins involved in pre-mRNA 3'-end processing.

Alexander A. Tzagoloff, Professor of Biological Sciences; Ph.D., Columbia, 1962. Energy-coupling mechanisms; structure of membrane enzymes; biogenesis of mitochondria; genetics of mitochondria in yeast.

Jian Yang, Professor; Ph.D., Washington (Seattle), 1991. Structure and function of ion channels; molecular mechanisms of ion channel regulation and localization.

Rafael Yuste, Professor and Howard Hughes Medical Institute Investigator; M.D., Madrid, 1987; Ph.D., Rockefeller, 1992. Development and function of the cortical microcircuitry.

Additional Faculty Sponsors for Ph.D. Research

Richard Axel, Biochemistry and Molecular Biophysics/Pathology and Cell Biology; Howard Hughes Medical Institute Investigator and Nobel Laureate in Physiology or Medicine 2004; Member, National Academy of Sciences. Central and peripheral organization of the olfactory system.

Richard J. Baer, Pathology and Cell Biology. The pathogenesis of hereditary breast cancer.

Andrea Califano, Biomedical Informatics. Study of gene regulatory and signaling networks in mammalian cellular contexts using computational methods.

Virginia Cornish, Chemistry. Development of in vivo selection strategies for evolving proteins with novel catalytic properties.

Riccardo Dalla-Favera, Genetics and Development, and Microbiology and Immunology. Molecular genetics of cancer; molecular pathogenesis of lymphoma and leukemia.

Jonathan E. Dworkin, Microbiology and Immunology. Bacterial signaling and interactions with the host.

Jean Gautier, Genetics and Development/Institute for Cancer Genetics. Cell cycle and cell death during early development.

Ruben L. Gonzalez Jr., Chemistry. Single molecule biophysics.

Eric C. Greene, Biochemistry and Molecular Biophysics; Howard Hughes Medical Institute Investigator. Molecular mechanisms of DNA recombination and repair; single-molecule fluorescence microscopy and other biochemical approaches.

Lloyd Greene, Pathology and Cell Biology. Mechanisms of neuronal differentiation and degeneration and their regulation by external growth factors.

Iva Greenwald, Biochemistry and Molecular Biophysics; Howard Hughes Medical Institute Investigator; Member, National Academy of Sciences, Development and cell-cell interactions.

Wei Gu, Pathology and Cell Biology. P53 in tumor suppression and aging.

René Hen, Pharmacology. Serotonin receptors and behavior.

Wayne Hendrickson, Biochemistry and Molecular Biophysics; Howard Hughes Medical Institute Investigator; Member, National Academy of Sciences. Macromolecular structure; X-ray crystallography.

Oliver Hobert, Biochemistry and Molecular Biophysics; Howard Hughes Medical Institute Investigator. Nervous system development and function.

Thomas Jessell, Biochemistry and Molecular Biophysics; Howard Hughes Medical Institute Investigator; Member, National Academy of Sciences. Molecular mechanisms of neural differentiation.

Laura Johnston, Genetics and Development. Control of growth and cell division during development.

Eric Kandel, Physiology and Cellular Biophysics/Psychiatry/Biochemistry and Molecular Biophysics; Howard Hughes Medical Institute Investigator and Nobel Laureate in Physiology or Medicine 2000; Member, National Academy of Sciences. Cell and molecular mechanisms of associative and nonassociative learning.

Arthur Karlin, Biochemistry and Molecular Biophysics/Physiology and Cellular Biophysics/Center for Molecular Recognition; Member, National Academy of Sciences. Molecular mechanisms of receptor function.

Richard Mann, Biochemistry and Molecular Biophysics. Transcriptional control.

Ann McDermott, Chemistry/Biological Sciences/Chemical Engineering; Member, National Academy of Sciences. Solid-state NMR of enzyme active sites and model systems.

Arthur G. Palmer, Biochemistry and Molecular Biophysics. Biomolecular dynamics, structure, and function; NMR spectroscopy.

Virginia Papaioannou, Genetics and Development. Genetic control of mammalian development in the peri-implantation period.

Ramon E. Parsons, Pathology and Cell Biology. The genetics of breast cancer tumorigenesis.

Rodney Rothstein, Genetics and Development. Yeast genetics; mechanisms of genetic recombination; control of genome stability; functional genomics.

Christian Schindler, Microbiology/Medicine. JAK-STAT signaling and immune response.

Steve Siegelbaum, Pharmacology; Howard Hughes Medical Institute Investigator. Molecular studies of ion channel structure and function; synaptic transmission and plasticity in the mammalian brain.

Gary Struhl, Genetics and Development; Howard Hughes Medical Institute Investigator; Member, National Academy of Sciences. Developmental genetics in *Drosophila.*

Lorraine Symington, Microbiology. Homologous recombination in the yeast *Saccharomyces cerevisiae.*

Richard Vallee, Pathology and Cell Biology. Motor proteins in axonal transport, brain developmental disease, and synaptic function.

NEW YORK MEDICAL COLLEGE
Graduate School of Basic Medical Sciences

Programs of Study

The Graduate School of Basic Medical Sciences (GSBMS) of New York Medical College offers programs leading to the M.S. and Ph.D. degrees in biochemistry and molecular biology, cell biology, pathology, microbiology and immunology, pharmacology, and physiology plus an interdisciplinary M.S. degree in basic medical sciences. The full-time faculty of 80 basic medical scientists, with their individual and collaborative research programs, great depth of knowledge, and classroom experience, provide an intellectually challenging yet supportive environment to those students with the requisite talent and motivation. These internal assets are supplemented by the Graduate School's plentiful access to other experts in clinical research, the pharmaceutical and biotechnology industry, and public health—who are available to participate in its research and educational activities.

Ph.D. degrees are awarded in six basic medical sciences. During the first year, students undertake an interdisciplinary core curriculum of courses and rotate through laboratories throughout the Graduate School. After this first year, students choose their major discipline and dissertation sponsor, complete the remaining didactic requirements in the chosen discipline, and begin intensive research training. Formal course work is usually substantially completed within two years, after which the student completes the qualifying exam, forms a dissertation advisory committee, presents a formal thesis proposal, and devotes his or her primary effort to the dissertation research project.

The M.S. degree requires completion of 30 to 32 credits, depending upon the discipline and specific track chosen. Two M.S. degree sequences are available: (1) a research program consisting of 25 didactic (i.e., classroom-based) and up to 5 research credits and a research thesis or (2) a program consisting of 29 to 32 didactic credits and a scholarly literature review. The M.S. degree is earned on a full- or part-time basis in evening classes. The interdisciplinary M.S. program is particularly suitable for students wishing to prepare for a career in medicine, dentistry, or other health professions. An accelerated track within this program allows completion of the degree requirements within one year for highly qualified candidates.

The Department of Cell Biology offers training in cell biology and neuroscience leading to careers in academia and industry. Ongoing research includes studies of oncogene expression and cytokines; intracellular mechanisms of pulmonary arterial hypertension; modulation of neuronal and astrocytic signaling; hemorrhage and neuroprotection in the developing brain; aging and preservation of oocytes and ovarian tissue; growth control in skeletal muscle; signal transduction in a variety of tissues, including platelets, the retina, muscle cells, and the *Drosophila* nervous system; intracellular protein trafficking and degradation; cytoskeletal and receptor function; the development and regeneration of the visual system; apoptosis in glaucoma; extracellular matrices and limb development; spinal cord injury; molecular mechanisms of neuroplasticity; learning and memory; Alzheimer's disease; and modulation of seizures.

The Department of Biochemistry and Molecular Biology provides students with a solid foundation in the concepts and applications of modern biochemistry and molecular biology. Areas of research include protein structure and function, enzyme reaction mechanisms, regulation of gene expression, mechanisms of hormone action and cell signaling, enzymology, mechanisms of DNA replication and repair, cell-cycle regulation, control of cell growth, molecular biology of cancer cells and the cancer process, mechanisms of nutrition and cancer prevention, molecular neurobiology and studies of neurodegenerative disorders, and the aging process.

The Department of Pathology offers a vigorous multidisciplinary milieu for training in experimental pathology. The programs focus on the comprehensive study of pathogenic mechanisms of human disease. Areas of interest in the department include examination of the underlying mechanisms involved in biochemical toxicology, cancer cell biology, cell-cycle regulation and apoptosis, chemical carcinogenesis, and tissue engineering.

In the Department of Microbiology and Immunology, students acquire a broad acquaintance with microbiology, molecular biology, and immunology as well as depth in an elective field. Areas available for thesis research include molecular biology of tumor cells, cancer vaccines, the role of stem cells in cancer, bacterial genetics, pathogenesis of infectious disease, structure and function of influenza virus antigens, molecular virology, and the biochemistry and genetics of emerging bacterial pathogens.

The Department of Pharmacology emphasizes training in research methods for examining the mechanism of action of drugs at the systemic, cellular, and subcellular levels. Areas of research include investigation into the therapeutic and pathophysiologic role of bioactive lipids (eicosanoids) in cancer, ophthalmology, and cardiovascular diseases including hypertension, kidney disease, stroke, diabetes, atherosclerosis and inflammatory conditions, cytochrome P-450 function and control, patch-clamp analysis of ion transport, and the roles of vasoactive hormones and inflammatory cytokines in hypertension end-organ damage and cardiovascular function.

The Department of Physiology provides students with an understanding of the function of the body's cells and organ systems and the mechanisms for regulation of these functions. Research opportunities include cellular neurophysiology, regulation of sleep and awake states, neural and endocrine control of the heart and circulation, microcirculation, the physiology of gene expression, heart failure, and the physiological effects of oxygen metabolites.

Research Facilities

The College has an extensive laboratory complex in the basic medical and clinical sciences. The Basic Sciences Building houses the medical sciences library, which maintains 200,000 volumes, an extensive collection of print and electronic journals, and a variety of online databases and search engines. There are also a fully accredited comparative medicine facility, a well-equipped and staffed instrumentation shop, a variety of classrooms, a bookstore, a cafeteria, and student lounges.

Financial Aid

Federal and state loan programs are available for M.S. students. Ph.D. students receive a stipend and tuition remission, medical insurance, and combinations of College fellowships and research assistantships. The Office of Student Financial Planning should be consulted for information on federal and state loan programs.

Cost of Study

In 2012–13, tuition is $875 per credit, or $14,000 annually, for a full-time master's student taking 8 credits per semester. The Accelerated Master's Program has an annual tuition rate of $32,950. Annual Ph.D. tuition is $21,000 before candidacy (first two years) and $4000 after candidacy. Comprehensive medical insurance is available on an annual basis for individuals ($4006), student plus spouse ($7666), or family ($11,214) coverage.

Living and Housing Costs

The student residences on the Valhalla campus are comprised of a garden-style apartment complex and a five-building suite-style complex. The costs range from $770 to $825 per month for furnished suite-style apartments and $585 to $965 for unfurnished single-student apartments. Married student apartment costs range from $1265 for a one-bedroom apartment, $1420 to $1445 for a two-bedroom apartment, and $1740 for a three-bedroom apartment (families with children). All apartments include kitchens with a full-size refrigerator, microwave, and an oven/stove. A student center, in the center of the complex, offers a coin-operated laundry room and an exercise center with a weight room and cardio-fitness room equipped with Stairmasters, treadmills, and stationary bicycles. Students interested in applying for housing should contact the Associate Director of Student and Residential Life, Administration Building (phone: 914-594-4832 or e-mail: housing@nymc.edu), well in advance in order to make housing arrangements. Housing is not guaranteed; there are a limited number of rooms and apartments available for graduate students on campus.

Student Group

The total College enrollment in fall 2011 was 1,438. There were 49 Ph.D. and 117 M.S. students in the Graduate School of Basic Medical Sciences.

Location

The College campus is located in the Westchester Medical Center campus, 5 miles from White Plains and 28 miles north of New York City.

The College

New York Medical College, a member of the Touro College and University System, is one of the largest medical schools in the country and was established in 1860. Graduate education at the College began informally in 1910. Graduate degrees were offered as early as 1938, and a graduate division was established in 1963.

Applying

Applications for admission may be submitted from October 1 through July 1. For optimal review of credentials and consideration for financial aid and housing, however, applications for fall enrollment into Ph.D. programs should be received by January 1. International applicants to the Master's program should complete their application no later than May 1. Specific program requirements are available on the College Web site at: http://www.nymc.edu/Academics/SchoolOfBasicMedicalSciences/Admissions/Requirements.htm. Students must apply online at the College Web site. Ph.D. applicants must submit GRE General Test scores. Applicants for the Accelerated Master's Program must submit scores for the Medical College Admission Test (MCAT). Applicants for other M.S. programs may submit GRE, MCAT, or DAT (Dental Admission Test) scores. International students are required to submit results of the TOEFL. Transcripts from all post-secondary institutions attended (undergraduate and graduate) and two letters of recommendation from teachers or scientists personally familiar with the applicant must be submitted directly by the school or recommenders separately.

Correspondence and Information

Francis L. Belloni, Ph.D., Dean
Graduate School of Basic Medical Sciences
Basic Sciences Building, Room A41
New York Medical College
Valhalla, New York 10595
United States
E-mail: gsbms_apply@nymc.edu
Web site: http://www.nymc.edu/gsbms/

THE GRADUATE FACULTY AND THEIR RESEARCH

Biochemistry and Molecular Biology. E. Y. C. Lee, Ph.D., Professor and Chairman: enzymology, structure-function relationships, and regulation of ser/thr protein phosphatases. A. J. L. Cooper, Ph.D., Professor: amino acid chemistry and biochemistry; biochemical mechanisms underlying neurological diseases. M. Y. W. Lee, Ph.D., Professor: DNA replication, polymerases, and repair; cell-cycle regulation. S. C. Olson, Ph.D., Associate Professor: signal transduction; regulation of phospholipase D pathway by protein kinase C and G proteins. J. T. Pinto, Ph.D., Professor: effects of chemopreventive agents, dietary factors, and xenobiotic substances on oxidation/reduction capacity in human cells. E. L. Sabban, Ph.D., Professor: molecular neurobiology; molecular mechanisms of stress; cloning and regulation of gene expression for catecholamine-synthesizing enzymes and neuropeptides. J. M. Wu, Ph.D., Professor and Master's Program Director: regulation of gene expression in leukemic and prostate cancer cells; cell-cycle control; chemoprevention by fenretinide and resveratrol. Z. Zhang, Ph.D., Assistant Professor and Ph.D. Program Director: X-ray crystallography; stem cell factor; quinone reductase 2.

Cell Biology and Anatomy. J. D. Etlinger, Ph.D., Professor and Chairman: skeletal muscle growth and atrophy; intracellular proteolysis in erythroid and muscle cells; role of proteasomes and ubiquitin; spinal cord injury. P. Ballabh, M.D., Professor: germinal matrix hemorrhage, pericytes. V. A. Fried, Ph.D., Professor and Graduate Program Director: ubiquitin and cellular regulation; cytoskeletal structure and functions. F. L. Hannan, Ph.D., Assistant Professor: *Drosophila melanogaster;* learning and memory; Ras-MAPK and mTOR pathways in neurological disorders, including neurofibromatosis; J. Kang, M.D., Ph.D., Associate Professor: astrocyte-mediated modulation of inhibitory synaptic transmission; interplay between excitatory and inhibitory synapses; properties of gap junction, K+, and GABA-A channels. M. Kumarasiri, Ph.D., Assistant Professor: protein turnover, ubiquitin-conjugated enzymes. K. M. Lerea, Ph.D., Associate Professor and Interdisciplinary Program Director: mechanisms of signal transduction; role of protein ser/thr kinases and phosphatases in integrin functions and platelet activation. S. A. Newman, Ph.D., Professor: physical and molecular mechanisms of development and evolution; pattern formation in the vertebrate limb; collagen assembly. K. Oktay, M.D., Professor: preservation by freezing and transplantation of oocytes and ovarian tissues to protect these cells from damage due to radiation and chemotherapy. P. B. Sehgal, M.D., Ph.D., Professor: interleukin-6; p53; gene expression; signal transduction (STAT3); cellular mechanisms of pulmonary arterial hypertension. S. C. Sharma, Ph.D., Professor: genetic approaches to regeneration of adult CNS neurons. A. D. Springer, Ph.D., Professor: engineering models of retinal development; optic nerve regeneration. P. K. Stanton, Ph.D., Professor: neuronal plasticity; long-term depression and potentiation of synaptic strength; synaptic functional changes in epilepsy; mechanisms of ischemia-induced delayed neuronal death. L. Velíšek, M.D., Ph.D., Professor and M.D./Ph.D. Program Director: epilepsy and epileptogenesis; epileptic syndromes of childhood; role of prenatal corticosteroids and stress in brain development and function; hypothalamic peptides and neuronal excitability. J. Velíšková, M.D., Ph.D., Professor: mechanisms of estrogen effects on neuronal excitability; seizures and epilepsy; neuroprotection; and synaptic plasticity; estrogen regulation of neuropeptideY and metabotropic glutamate receptor-NR2B subunit-containing NMDA receptor interactions. R. J. Zeman, Ph.D., Associate Professor: $_2$-adrenoceptors in musculoskeletal growth; mechanisms of spinal cord injury; regulation of intracellular calcium.

Pathology. J. T. Fallon, M.D., Ph.D., Professor and Chairman: cardiovascular pathology; ischemic heart disease; experimental vascular injury; immunopathology of human myocarditis and allograft rejection. A. N. Arnold, Ph.D., Assistant Professor: transplantation immunology and histocompatibility. A. Bokhari, M.B.B.S., Assistant Clinical Professor: neomatal and pediatric pathology. P. M. Chander, M.B.B.S., Professor: pathogenesis of renal and vascular damage in stroke-prone spontaneously hypertensive rats; pathogenesis of HIV-associated nephropathy. Z. Darzynkiewicz, M.D., Ph.D., Professor: development of new methods of cell analysis using flow cytometry; analysis of cell-cycle specificity of antitumor drugs. M. I. Iatropoulos, M.D., Research Professor: comparative mechanisms of toxicity and carcinogenesis. A. M. Jeffrey, Ph.D., Research Professor: toxicology and chronic carcinogenesis. P. A. Lucas, Ph.D., Research Associate Professor: wound healing and tissue engineering. F. H. Moy, Ph.D., Associate Professor of Clinical Pathology and Graduate Program Director: biostatistics and epidemiology, methodology, and applications in clinical trials and risk assessment. G. Wang, M.D., Clinical Assistant Professor: cytokines in Lyme carditis; antibacterial properties of treated fabrics; daptomycin-nonsusceptible enterococci. J. H. Weisburger, Ph.D., M.D. (hon.), Research Professor: mechanisms of toxicity and carcinogenicity; mechanisms and role of promoters in major human cancers; role of nutrition in human carcinogenesis; rational means of prevention of cancer, coronary heart disease, and stroke. G. M. Williams, M.D., Professor: mechanisms of carcinogenesis; metabolic and genetic effects of chemical carcinogens.

Microbiology and Immunology. I. S. Schwartz, Ph.D., Professor and Chairman: molecular pathogenesis of Lyme disease and other emerging bacterial pathogens; functional genomics. C. S. Bakshi, D.V.M., Ph.D., Assistant Professor: immunopathogenesis of *Francisella tularensis*, respiratory infection. R. Banerjee, Ph.D., Assistant Professor: molecular virology and molecular oncology. D. Bessen, Ph.D., Professor: molecular pathogenesis, epidemiology, and evolutionary biology of group A *Streptococcus* (GAS); role of GAS infection in pediatric neuropsychiatric disorders. D. J. Bucher, Ph.D., Associate Professor: structure, function, and immunochemistry of viral antigens. F. Cabello, M.D., Professor: microbial genetics; infectious disease; recombinant DNA. R. Dattwyler, M.D., Professor: oral wildlife bait vaccine, Lyme disease, Yersinia pestis. J. Geliebter, Ph.D., Professor: immunology and molecular biology of thyroid and prostate cancer. C. V. Hamby, Ph.D., Associate Professor: molecular biology and immunology of human tumors. D. Mordue, Ph.D., Assistant Professor: cellular and molecular strategies used by intracellular pathogens to establish and maintain infection. M. M. Petzke, Ph.D., Assistant Professor: Lyme disease; bacterial pathogenesis; innate immunity; dendritic cells; interferons; pattern recognition receptors; functional genomics. R. K. Tiwari, Ph.D., Professor and Graduate Program Director: tumor immunology and chemoprevention and therapy using stem cells and tumor microenvironment in thyroid cancer, breast cancer, prostate cancer and melanoma. X. Zhou, Ph.D., Associate Professor: tumor immunology; immunotherapy; adoptive cell therapy; Sleeping Beauty transposon; micro RNAs; lymphozyte development; hematopoietic stem cells; stem cell transplantation.

Pharmacology. M. L. Schwartzman, Ph.D., Professor and Chairwoman: cytochrome P-450 metabolism of arachidonic acid in inflammation and hypertension. M. A. Carroll, Ph.D., Professor: renal cytochrome P-450 metabolites of arachidonic acid. N. R. Ferreri, Ph.D., Professor: cytokine production and function in the kidney and vascular smooth muscle. M. S. Goligorsky, M.D., Ph.D., Professor: basic mechanisms of endothelial dysfunction, its prevention and reversal; translation of bench findings to clinical physiology and pharmacology. A. M. Guo, Ph.D., Assistant Professor: cytochrome P-450-derived eicosanoids (20-HETE) in angiogenesis and cancer growth; regulation of endothelial precursor cell function. M. A. Inchiosa Jr., Ph.D., Professor: biochemical pharmacology of muscle. D. Lin, M.D., Ph.D., Research Assistant Professor: microRNA, renal K^+ secretion and Na^+ reabsorption. A. Nasjletti, M.D., Professor and Ph.D. Program Director: hormonal mediators of blood pressure regulation. C. A. Powers, Ph.D., Associate Professor: neuroendocrinology. C. T. Stier, Ph.D., Associate Professor and M.S. Program Director: pharmacological protection against vascular damage and stroke. W. Wang, M.D., Professor: regulation of renal electrolytes transport.

Physiology. T. H. Hintze, Ph.D., Professor and Chairman: cardiovascular functions in chronically instrumented animals. F. L. Belloni, Ph.D., Professor: vascular and cardiac actions of adenosine; biomedical and research ethics. M. Boligorsky, M.D., Ph.D., Professor of Medicine and Physiology: endothelial cell dysfunction in renal disease. John G. Edwards, Ph.D., Associate Professor: physiological control of gene transcription; regulation of transcription factors; cardiac hypertrophy; exercise biochemistry and overload alterations of the myocardial phenotype. C. Eisenberg, Ph.D., Associate Professor: phenotypic potential of "adult" stem cells. L. Eisenberg, Ph.D., Professor: molecular mechanisms controlling the phenotypic direction of differentiating stem cells. A. Huang, M.D., Ph.D., Associate Professor of Physiology: role of estrogens in vascular function. A. Koller, M.D., Professor: regulation of blood flow in the microcirculation. C. S. Leonard, Ph.D., Professor: neuronal integration; synaptic and nonsynaptic neuromodulation; nitric oxide in the CNS; brain cholinergic systems; neural basis of sleep and wakefulness. N. Levine, Ph.D., Professor and Accelerated Master's Program Director: fluid and electrolyte secretion in the male reproductive system. E. J. Messina, Ph.D., Professor: microvascular control and regulation of smooth-muscle reactivity. M. Mozzor, B.A., Instructor: radiation physics. C. Ojaimi, Ph.D., Assistant Professor: gene array technology; functional genomics in vascular biology; gene expression of normal and diseased heart. S. S. Passo, Ph.D., Professor: neuroendocrine control of blood pressure. S. J. Popilskis, D.V.M., DACLAM, Assistant Professor: comparative medicine. W. N. Ross, Ph.D., Professor: regional properties of neurons. J. M. Stewart, M.D., Ph.D., Professor: orthostatic hypotension. D. Sun, M.D., Ph.D., Associate Professor: role of endothelial stress on coronary arteriolar function. C. I. Thompson, Ph.D., Professor and Graduate Program Director: renal hemodynamics and GFR control. M. S. Wolin, Ph.D., Professor: vascular regulation via cyclic GMP, metabolites, and oxygen tension.

THE ROCKEFELLER UNIVERSITY
Graduate Programs

Programs of Study

Graduate education leading to the Ph.D. is offered to outstanding students regarded as potential leaders in their scientific fields. The University's research covers a wide range of biomedical and related sciences, including biochemistry, structural biology, biophysics, and chemistry; molecular, cell, and developmental biology; medical sciences and human genetics; immunology and microbiology; neurosciences; and bioinformatics, biophysics, and computational neuroscience, as summarized by the faculty list in this description. Students work closely with a faculty of active scientists and are encouraged to learn through a combination of course work, tutorial guidance, and apprenticeship in research laboratories. Graduate Fellows spend the first two years engaged in a flexible combination of courses geared toward academic qualification while conducting research in laboratories pertaining to their area of scientific interest. They choose a laboratory for thesis research by the end of the first year and devote their remaining time to pursuit of significant experimental or theoretical research, culminating in a dissertation and thesis defense. Students can spend full time in research; there are no teaching or other service obligations.

The faculties of the Rockefeller University, Weill Medical College of Cornell University, the Weill Graduate School of Medical Sciences of Cornell University, and Sloan-Kettering Institute collaborate in offering a combined M.D./Ph.D. program in the biomedical sciences to about 90 students. This program, conducted on the adjacent campuses of these three institutions in New York City, normally requires six or seven years of study and leads to an M.D. degree conferred by Cornell University and a Ph.D. degree conferred by either the Rockefeller University or the Weill Graduate School of Cornell University, depending upon the organizational affiliation of the student's adviser.

Research Facilities

The University and its affiliate Howard Hughes Medical Institute maintain a full range of laboratories and services for the research activities of the professional staff and students. Facilities include clinical and animal research centers on campus, a library, computing services, a field research center in Dutchess County, the Aaron Diamond AIDS Research Center (ADARC), as well as new centers for human genetics, studies in physics and biology, biochemistry and structural biology, immunology and immune diseases, sensory neuroscience, and Alzheimer's disease research.

Financial Aid

Each student accepted into the Ph.D. program receives a stipend ($34,000 in 2012–13) that is adequate to meet all living expenses. Students also receive an annual budget of $1500 that can be used for travel, books and journals, computer purchases, and lab supplies.

Cost of Study

The University provides full remission of all tuition and fees for all accepted students.

Living and Housing Costs

On-campus housing is available for all students at subsidized rates. The stipend is designed to cover the cost of food, housing, and other basic living expenses. Students may elect to live off campus, but rents in the vicinity are very high.

Student Group

There are 198 graduate students, of whom 172 are enrolled in the Ph.D. program and 26 in the Ph.D. phase of the combined M.D./Ph.D. program. It is the policy of the Rockefeller University to support equality of educational opportunity. No individual is denied admission to the University or otherwise discriminated against with respect to any program of the University because of creed, color, national or ethnic origin, race, sex, or disability.

Student Outcomes

Graduates of the Rockefeller University have excelled in their professions. Two graduates have been awarded the Nobel Prize, and 27 graduates are members of the National Academy of Sciences. Most Ph.D. graduates move to postdoctoral positions at academic and research centers and subsequently have careers in academics, biotechnology, and the pharmaceutical industry. A few have pursued careers in medicine, law, and business. Almost all M.D./Ph.D. graduates first complete residencies in medical specialties, and most become medical scientists at major academic and medical research centers.

Location

The University is situated between 62nd and 68th streets in Manhattan, overlooking the East River. Despite its central metropolitan location, the 15-acre campus has a distinctive nonurban character, featuring gardens, picnic areas, fountains, and a tennis court. In addition to administrative and residential buildings, there are seven large laboratory buildings and a forty-bed hospital that serves as a clinical research center. Immediate neighbors are the New York Hospital, the Weill Medical College of Cornell University, Memorial Hospital, and the Sloan-Kettering Institute for Cancer Research. The wide range of institutions in New York City affords unlimited opportunities in research specialties, library facilities, and cultural resources.

The University

The Rockefeller University is dedicated to benefiting humankind through scientific research and its application. Founded in 1901 by John D. Rockefeller as the Rockefeller Institute for Medical Research, it rapidly became a source of major scientific innovation in treating and preventing human disease. Since 1954, the institute has extended its function by offering graduate work at the doctoral level to a select group of qualified students.

Laboratories, rather than departments, are the fundamental units of the University. The absence of departmental barriers between laboratories encourages interdisciplinary, problem-oriented approaches to research and facilitates intellectual interaction and collaboration. The collegial atmosphere fosters independence and initiative in students. In addition to the 198 doctoral students, there are 350 postdoctoral associates and fellows and a faculty of 72 full, associate, and assistant professors on campus who head laboratories.

Applying

Applications for the M.D./Ph.D. program must be completed by October 15; those for the Ph.D. program must be completed by December 3. Applicants are required to submit a personal statement describing research experience and goals as well as reasons for pursuing graduate study at the Rockefeller University. Also required are official transcripts and at least three letters of recommendation. Official GRE General Test scores are required and Subject Test scores are highly recommended for admission to the Ph.D. program. MCAT scores are required for the M.D./Ph.D. program. Further information about each program and details on application procedures may be obtained from the programs' respective Web sites. This information is also available on the University Web site, from which application forms and instructions can be downloaded.

Correspondence and Information

For the Ph.D. program:
Office of Graduate Studies
The Rockefeller University
1230 York Avenue
New York, New York 10065
Phone: 212-327-8086
E-mail: phd@rockefeller.edu
Web site: http://www.rockefeller.edu

For the M.D./Ph.D. program:
Tri-Institutional M.D./Ph.D. Program
Weill Cornell/Rockefeller/Sloan-Kettering
1300 York Avenue, Room C-103
New York, New York 10065
Phone: 212-746-6023
        888-U2-MD-PHD (toll-free)
E-mail: mdphd@mail.med.cornell.edu
Web site: http://www.med.cornell.edu/mdphd

LABORATORY HEADS AND THEIR RESEARCH

C. David Allis, Ph.D. (Histone Modifications and Chromatin Biology). Enzymology and function of covalent histone modifications; histone code and epigenetic regulation.

Cori Bargmann, Ph.D. (Neuroscience). Genetic analysis of olfactory behavior and neural development.

Günter Blobel, M.D., Ph.D. (Cell Biology). Protein translocation across membranes; macromolecular traffic into and out of the nucleus.

Sean Brady, Ph.D. (Genetically Encoded Small Molecules). Structure and function of genetically encoded small molecules.

The Rockefeller University

Jan L. Breslow, M.D. (Biochemical Genetics and Metabolism). Identifying the genes that control atherosclerosis susceptibility.

Jean-Laurent Casanova, M.D., Ph.D. (Human Genetics of Infectious Diseases). Genetics of human predisposition to pediatric infectious diseases, particularly mycobacterial diseases.

Brian T. Chait, D.Phil. (Mass Spectrometry and Gaseous Ion Chemistry). Protein mass spectrometry.

Nam-Hai Chua, Ph.D. (Plant Molecular Biology). Gene regulation and signal transduction in plants.

Joel Cohen, Ph.D., Dr.P.H. (Populations). Population dynamics; ecology; epidemiology.

Barry Coller, M.D. (Clinical Hematology). Biochemistry of platelet disorders; study of heritable coagulopathies.

Frederick P. Cross, Ph.D. (Molecular Genetics). Cell-cycle control in budding yeast.

George A. M. Cross, Ph.D. (Molecular Parasitology). Regulation of gene and surface glycoprotein expression in trypanosomes.

James E. Darnell Jr., M.D. (Molecular Cell Biology). Signal transduction and gene control in mammalian differentiation.

Robert B. Darnell, M.D., Ph.D. (Molecular Neuro-Oncology). Neuro-oncology and autoimmunity; molecular neurobiology.

Seth Darst, Ph.D. (Molecular Biophysics). Protein crystallography and electron microscopy of macromolecular assemblies.

Titia de Lange, Ph.D. (Cell Biology and Genetics). Chromosome function in vertebrates.

Mitchell J. Feigenbaum, Ph.D. (Mathematical Physics).

Vincent A. Fischetti, Ph.D. (Bacterial Pathogenesis). Pathogenesis of streptococcal diseases and mucosal vaccine development.

Jeffrey M. Friedman, M.D., Ph.D. (Molecular Genetics). Genes controlling food intake and body weight; mouse genetics.

Winrich Freiwald, Ph.D. (Neural Systems). Neural processes that form object representations, as well as those that allow attention to make those representations available for cognition.

Elaine Fuchs, Ph.D. (Mammalian Cell Biology and Development). Molecular mechanisms underlying the coordination of proliferation, transcription, and cell adhesion in tissue morphogenesis and in cancer.

Hinonori Funabiki, Ph.D. (Chromosome and Cell Biology). Mechanisms controlling accurate chromosome segregation during the cell division cycle.

David C. Gadsby, Ph.D. (Cardiac and Membrane Physiology). Mechanism and function of ion pumps and channels.

Charles D. Gilbert, M.D., Ph.D. (Neurobiology). Visual spatial integration and cortical dynamics.

Konstantin A. Goulianos, Ph.D. (Experimental High-Energy Physics).

Paul Greengard, Ph.D. (Molecular and Cellular Neuroscience). Role of phosphoproteins in signal transduction in the developing and adult nervous system.

Howard C. Hang, Ph.D. (Chemical Biology and Microbial Pathogenesis). Chemical tools for studying posttranslational modifications in living cells.

Mary E. Hatten, Ph.D. (Developmental Neurobiology). Control of CNS neuronal specification and migration during vertebrate brain development.

Nathaniel Heintz, Ph.D. (Molecular Biology). Cell-cycle regulation; molecular neurobiology; mammalian neurogenetics.

Ali Hemmati-Brivanlou, Ph.D. (Molecular Embryology). Molecular embryology of vertebrates.

David D. Ho, M.D. (Dynamics of HIV/SIV Replication). Kinetics of CD4 lymphocyte turnover; determinants of disease progression; therapy of HIV infection.

A. James Hudspeth, M.D., Ph.D. (Sensory Neuroscience). Transduction and synaptic signaling by hair cells of the inner ear.

Tarun Kapoor, Ph.D. (Chemistry and Cell Biology). Small-molecule probes of cellular processes.

Bruce W. Knight Jr. (Biophysics). Neurophysiology and applied mathematics.

M. Magda Konarska, Ph.D. (Molecular Biology and Biochemistry). Splicing of mRNA precursors and replication of hepatitis delta virus.

Mary Jeanne Kreek, M.D. (Neuroscience). Neurobiology and molecular genetics of addictive diseases; endogenous opioid system.

Daniel Kronauer, Ph.D. (Insect Social Evolution). Molecular basis of social behavior in *Cerapachys biroi.*

James G. Krueger, M.D., Ph.D. (Investigative Dermatology). Cutaneous pathobiology.

Stanislas Leibler, Ph.D. (Physics and Mathematical Biology). Analysis of biological networks.

Albert J. Libchaber, Ph.D. (Experimental Condensed-Matter Physics).

Roderick MacKinnon, M.D. (Molecular Neurobiology and Biophysics). Structure and function of ion channels and associated regulatory proteins.

Marcelo Magnasco, Ph.D. (Mathematical Physics). Stochastic processes in biology systems.

Gaby Maimon, Ph.D. (Integrative Brain Function). Neural basis of decision making in *Drosophila melanogaster.*

Luciano Marraffini, Ph.D. (Bacteriology). Mechanisms that control the traffic of DNA molecules between bacteria.

Bruce S. McEwen, Ph.D. (Neuroendocrinology). Hormonal regulation of neural plasticity.

Daniel Mucida, Ph.D. (Mucosal Immunology). Mechanisms of intestinal immunity.

Fernando Nottebohm, Ph.D. (Animal Behavior). Animal communication; mechanisms of learning, memory duration, and brain repair.

Michel C. Nussenzweig, M.D., Ph.D. (Molecular Immunology). Molecular basis of B-cell development.

Michael O'Donnell, Ph.D. (DNA Replication). Underlying principles of DNA replication in the human and *E. coli* systems.

Jürg Ott, Ph.D. (Statistical Genetics). Developing, implementing, and applying statistical methods of human genetic mapping.

F. Nina Papavasiliou, Ph.D. (Molecular Immunology). Molecular mechanisms of lymphocyte diversity.

Donald W. Pfaff, Ph.D. (Neurobiology and Behavior). Gene expression in brain; hormone action; brain control of behavior.

Jeffrey V. Ravetch, M.D., Ph.D. (Molecular Genetics and Immunology). Genetics of the humoral immune response; genetic variation in malaria parasite.

George N. Reeke Jr., Ph.D. (Biological Modeling). Theoretical models of brain functions; protein structure.

Charles Rice, Ph.D. (Virology). Molecular genetics of animal RNA viruses (alphaviruses and flaviviruses, in particular hepatitis C virus); replication and pathogenesis.

Robert G. Roeder, Ph.D. (Biochemistry and Molecular Biology). Transcriptional regulatory mechanisms in animal cells.

Michael P. Rout, Ph.D. (Structural Cell Biology). Nucleocytoplasmic transport; nuclear pore complex structure, function, and assembly.

Vanessa Ruta, Ph.D. (Neurophysiology and Behavior).Neural mechanisms and behavior modification in *Drosophila melanogaster.*

Thomas P. Sakmar, M.D. (Molecular Biology and Biochemistry). Biochemistry and molecular biology of transmembrane signal transduction and visual phototransduction.

Shai Shaham, Ph.D. (Cancer Biology). Programmed cell death in the nematode *Caenorhabditis elegans.*

Eric Siggia, Ph.D. (Theoretical Condensed-Matter Physics). Statistical physics and dynamical systems to cellular biophysics and bioinformatics.

Sanford M. Simon, Ph.D. (Cellular Biophysics). Protein biogenesis, membrane protein assembly, tumorigenesis, and drug resistance.

Agata Smogorzewska, M.D., Ph.D. (Genome Maintenance). Elucidating pathways that prevent cancer development by using Fanconi anemia as a backdrop for understanding aging and cancer.

C. Erec Stebbins, Ph.D. (Structural Microbiology). Structural studies of bacterial virulence factors and their host cell targets.

Hermann Steller, Ph.D. Molecular biology of apoptosis and cancer biology.

Sidney Strickland, Ph.D. (Neurobiology and Genetics). Genetics of neuronal function and dysfunction; genetics of early development.

Alexander Tarakhovsky, M.D., Ph.D. (Immunology). Mechanisms of the dynamic tuning of antigen receptor-mediated signaling in lymphocytes.

Sohail Tavazoie, M.D., Ph.D. (Systems Cancer Biology). Using a systems biological approach to identify and characterize key molecular regulators of metastasis.

Alexander Tomasz, Ph.D. (Microbiology). Mechanisms of antibiotic resistance and virulence in bacteria.

Thomas Tuschl, Ph.D. (Chemistry). Regulation of gene expression by double-stranded RNA in humans.

Leslie Vosshall, Ph.D. (Sensory Neuroscience). Molecular genetics of olfaction in *Drosophila melanogaster.*

Michael W. Young, Ph.D. (Genetics). Genes controlling behavior and development in *Drosophila;* molecular control of circadian rhythms.

THE UNIVERSITY OF ALABAMA AT BIRMINGHAM

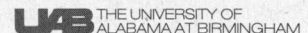

College of Arts and Sciences
Department of Biology

Programs of Study

The Department of Biology offers programs of study leading to the M.S. and Ph.D. degrees. Graduate students may specialize in research activities at all levels of biological organization, with emphases on ecophysiology, cellular and molecular biology, endocrinology, and ecology of aquatic organisms, plant biology, or on models related to human disease. The aim of the Department is to provide a broad background and a field of specialty that prepare the student for a professional career in research and/or teaching.

Two types of master's programs are available. A student may choose a research-based program that requires, in addition to a thesis, a minimum of 24 hours of committee-approved course work. The nonresearch plan requires a minimum of 30 hours of approved course work and a thesis incorporating a review and analysis of a topic of current or historical interest in biology. Either plan of study can be completed in approximately two years.

Course work requirements for the Ph.D. programs are individually designed to meet the needs of the student and to fulfill the aims of the Department and Graduate School. However, a dissertation embodying the results and analysis of an original experimental investigation is required.

Seminars and teaching experience are part of the training program for both the M.S. and Ph.D. degrees. To qualify for candidacy, the student in the master's program must take either a written or an oral comprehensive examination. The Ph.D. student must take both written and oral examinations. The final examination for all candidates consists of an oral defense of the research thesis.

Research Facilities

Well-equipped research laboratories for the Department are located in Campbell Hall. Facilities are available for vertebrates and invertebrates, including marine and freshwater forms, and for botanical specimens. The University operates a farm suitable for field studies. For students interested in marine biology, the University is a member of the Marine Environmental Science Program at Dauphin Island near Mobile, Alabama. The Medical Center library and the University College library have extensive holdings in biological and related sciences.

Financial Aid

Teaching assistantships, graduate assistantships, and fellowships are available. Stipends are awarded on a yearly basis; for 2011–12, they were $15,000 for the master's program and $19,000 to $21,000 for the doctoral program. Tuition and other fees are paid for all students who are awarded stipends. Health insurance is provided for qualified individuals. Fellowships can require teaching on a regular basis, and assistantships typically require teaching a maximum of 9 contact hours per week. Students not receiving stipends may teach laboratory sections on a fee-for-service basis.

Cost of Study

Graduate tuition for in-state students was $309 per credit hour in 2011–12. Out-of-state students were charged $726 per credit hour. Tuition and fees are paid for stipend recipients.

Living and Housing Costs

The cost of living in Birmingham is slightly lower than the average for major American cities. Many reasonably priced apartments are available near campus, and some University apartments are available.

Student Group

The total enrollment at the University of Alabama at Birmingham is approximately 17,000; 11,400 are undergraduates and more than 5,700 are in graduate and professional school programs. The Department of Biology averages about 50 graduate students in M.S. or Ph.D. programs.

Student Outcomes

Recent graduates have assumed professorships in departments such as biology, zoology, immunology, or marine science at various academic institutions. Some have chosen a career in the medical or dental profession. Other positions assumed recently by graduates include staff scientists at NASA, the Army Corps of Engineers, CDC, FDA, and marine research laboratories. In addition, different environmental consulting companies and biotechnology companies have employed graduates as technicians, staff scientists, or laboratory directors.

Location

The University of Alabama at Birmingham is a comprehensive urban university situated on a campus that occupies an eighty-block area in the southern section of Birmingham. Many cultural resources are available, including the Alys Robinson Stephens Performing Arts Center, museums, the Jimmy Morgan Zoo, and the Botanical Gardens. Recreational opportunities include athletic events and a variety of outdoor activities at nearby lakes and parks or along the Gulf Coast, which is 5 hours away by car. The city has a mild climate throughout the year.

The University

The University of Alabama at Birmingham has forty-six master's and thirty-three doctoral programs. Students benefit from the active research programs that attract $500 million in research funds each year, making the University one of the highest-ranked institutions in receipt of federal research support.

Applying

Application forms are available online. Other information can be obtained from the Dean of the Graduate School, the University of Alabama at Birmingham, UAB Station, Birmingham, Alabama 35294-1150. For admission in good standing, students should have a baccalaureate degree in biology or a related field, an overall B average in undergraduate courses, and a satisfactory score on the General Test of the Graduate Record Examinations or an equivalent test. It is also desirable that entering students have completed two years of chemistry (including a year of organic chemistry), a year of physics, and mathematics through calculus. A statement of career objectives, three letters of evaluation, and an official copy of transcripts should be included with the application.

Correspondence and Information

Dr. Stephen A. Watts, Program Director for Biology
Department of Biology
CH 375
The University of Alabama at Birmingham
1720 2nd Avenue South
Birmingham, Alabama 35294-1170
Phone: 205-934-2045
Fax: 205-975-6097
E-mail: sawatts@uab.edu
Web site: http://www.uab.edu/biology/

The University of Alabama at Birmingham

THE FACULTY AND THEIR RESEARCH

Charles D. Amsler, Professor; Ph.D., California, Santa Barbara. Phycology and chemical ecology.

Robert A. Angus, Professor; Ph.D., Connecticut. Aquatic ecology and toxicology.

Asim K. Bej, Professor; Ph.D., Louisville. Microbial molecular genetics and extremophiles.

Peggy R. Biga, Assistant Professor; Ph.D., Idaho. Comparative developmental physiology; muscle biology.

James A. Coker, Assistant Professor; Ph.D., Penn State. Microbial biochemistry.

Vithal K. Ghanta, Professor; Ph.D., Southern Illinois at Carbondale. Immunology.

David T. Jenkins, Associate Professor; Ph.D., Tennessee. *Basidiomycete* taxonomy.

Daniel D. Jones, Professor Emeritus; Ph.D., Michigan State. Plant physiology; microbial ecology.

Ken R. Marion, Professor Emeritus; Ph.D., Washington (St. Louis). Vertebrate ecology.

James B. McClintock, Endowed University Professor; Ph.D., South Florida. Invertebrate zoology; marine chemical ecology; ocean acidification; polar ecology; climate change.

Karolina M. Mukhtar, Assistant Professor; Ph.D., Max Planck Institute for Plant Breeding Research (Germany). Genetics; plant molecular biology.

Shahid M. Mukhtar, Research Assistant Professor; Ph.D., Max Planck Institute for Plant Breeding Research (Germany). Genetics; systems biology.

Timothy Nagy, Adjunct Associate Professor; Ph.D., Utah. Nutritional physiology.

Mickie L. Powell, Research Assistant Professor; Ph.D., Alabama at Birmingham. Aquatic nutritional physiology.

Nicole C. Riddle, Research Assistant Professor; Ph.D., Washington (St. Louis). Epigenetics and chromatin structure.

Robert W. Thacker, Professor; Ph.D., Michigan. Marine and freshwater ecology.

Trygve Tollefsbol, Professor; Ph.D., North Texas; D.O., North Texas Health Science at Fort Worth. Molecular biology; telomerase and DNA methylation.

Daniel A. Warner, Assistant Professor; Ph.D., Sydney. Evolutionary ecology.

R. Douglas Watson, Professor; Ph.D., Iowa. Developmental endocrinology.

Stephen A. Watts, Professor; Ph.D., South Florida. Ecology and systematics.

Thane Wibbels, Professor; Ph.D., Texas A&M. Comparative reproductive physiology of vertebrates.

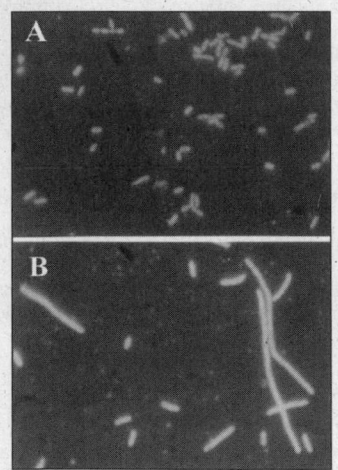

Salmonella—How expression of selected genes and their regulation enable microbes to survive in hostile environments is one area of prokaryotic research. For example, note the influence of cold temperature on morphology of *Salmonella typhimurium* LT2 grown for 78 hours at 37°C (panel A) or 10°C (panel B).

Population dynamics, reproductive ecology, and conservation of several species, including sea turtles, are studied

UNIVERSITY OF CONNECTICUT HEALTH CENTER
Graduate Programs in Biomedical Sciences

Programs of Study

Work leading to the Ph.D. degree in biomedical sciences and master's degrees in dental sciences, public health, and clinical and translational research is offered through Graduate School faculty members associated with the Schools of Medicine and Dental Medicine at the University of Connecticut Health Center in Farmington. A combined-degree program with the School of Medicine offers an M.D./Ph.D. degree to qualified students interested in academic medicine and research. In addition, the Schools of Medicine and Dental Medicine, in conjunction with the Public Health Program, offer a combined program leading to the M.D./M.P.H. or D.M.D./M.P.H. The School of Dental Medicine offers a D.M.D./Ph.D. and a Combined Certificate Training Ph.D. program for students with advanced dental degrees. Ph.D. students apply to the Integrated Admissions Mode, which offers a first year of study in the basic science curriculum prior to the selection of an area of concentration in which to pursue the Ph.D. thesis work.

Research Facilities

The program offices and laboratories are part of the University of Connecticut Health Center. A wide range of general and specialized equipment and expertise in the biological, biochemical, and biophysical sciences is available. Students have access to all facilities and equipment necessary for the pursuit of their research programs. In addition, major institutional resources include central small-animal facilities and a library that contains approximately 200,000 volumes and 450 CAI programs and subscribes to more than 1,400 current periodicals.

Financial Aid

Support for doctoral students engaged in full-time degree programs at the Health Center is provided on a competitive basis. Graduate research assistantships for 2012–13 provide a stipend of $28,000 per year, which includes a waiver of tuition/University fees for the fall and spring semesters and a student health insurance plan. While financial aid is offered competitively, the Health Center makes every possible effort to address the financial needs of all doctoral students during their period of training.

Cost of Study

For 2012–13, tuition is $10,836 per year for full-time students who are Connecticut residents and $28,116 per year for full-time students who are out-of-state residents. General University fees are added to the cost of tuition for students who do not receive a tuition waiver. These costs are usually met by traineeships or research assistantships for doctoral students.

Living and Housing Costs

There is a wide range of affordable housing options in the greater Hartford area within easy commuting distance of the campus, including an extensive complex that is adjacent to the Health Center. Costs range from $600 to $900 per month for a one-bedroom unit; 2 or more students sharing an apartment usually pay less. University housing is not available at the Health Center.

Student Group

Approximately 550 students in the Schools of Medicine and Dental Medicine, 400 graduate students in the Ph.D. and master's programs, and numerous postdoctoral fellows use the facilities in Farmington.

Location

The Health Center is located in the historic town of Farmington, Connecticut. Set in the beautiful New England countryside on a hill overlooking the Farmington Valley, it is close to ski areas, hiking trails, and facilities for boating, fishing, and swimming. Connecticut's capital city of Hartford, 7 miles east of Farmington, is the center of an urban region of approximately 800,000 people. The beaches of the Long Island Sound are about 50 minutes away to the south, and the beautiful Berkshires are a short drive to the northwest. New York City and Boston can be reached within 2½ hours by car. Hartford is the home of the acclaimed Hartford Stage Company, TheatreWorks, the Hartford Symphony and Chamber orchestras, two ballet companies, an opera company, the Wadsworth Athenaeum (the oldest public art museum in the nation), the Mark Twain house, the Hartford Civic Center, and many other interesting cultural and recreational facilities. The area is also home to several branches of the University of Connecticut, Trinity College, and the University of Hartford, which includes the Hartt School of Music. Bradley International Airport (about 30 minutes from campus) serves the Hartford/Springfield area with frequent airline connections to major cities in this country and abroad. Frequent bus and rail service is also available from Hartford.

The Health Center

The 200-acre Health Center campus at Farmington houses a division of the University of Connecticut Graduate School, as well as the School of Medicine and Dental Medicine. The campus also includes the John Dempsey Hospital, associated clinics, and extensive medical research facilities, all in a centralized facility with more than 1 million square feet of floor space. The Health Center's newest research addition, the Academic Research Building, was opened in 1999. This impressive eleven-story structure provides 170,000 square feet of state-of-the-art laboratory space. The faculty at the center includes more than 260 full-time members. The institution has a strong commitment to graduate study within an environment that promotes social and intellectual interaction among the various educational programs. Graduate students are represented on various administrative committees concerned with curricular affairs, and the Graduate Student Organization (GSO) represents graduate students' needs and concerns to the faculty and administration, in addition to fostering social contact among graduate students at the Health Center.

Applying

Applications for admission should be submitted via the online application system and should be filed together with transcripts, three letters of recommendation, a personal statement, and recent results from the General Test of the Graduate Record Examinations. International students must take the Test of English as a Foreign Language (TOEFL) to satisfy Graduate School requirements. The deadline for completed applications and receipt of all supplemental materials is **December 1**. Please note that GRE and TOEFL exams taken after the due date will not be accepted for consideration for admission. In accordance with the laws of the state of Connecticut and of the United States, the University of Connecticut Health Center does not discriminate against any person in its educational and employment activities on the grounds of race, color, creed, national origin, sex, age, or physical disability.

Correspondence and Information

Graduate Admissions Office
Ph.D. in Biomedical Science Program
University of Connecticut Health Center
263 Farmington Ave., MC 3906
Farmington, Connecticut 06030-3906
United States
Phone: 860-679-4509
E-mail: BiomedSciAdmissions@uchc.edu
Web site: http://grad.uchc.edu/prospective/programs/phd_biosci/index.html

University of Connecticut Health Center

FACULTY AND RESEARCH AREAS

The Health Center's graduate faculty of more than 150 members is drawn from both the basic and clinical departments of the Schools of Medicine and Dental Medicine.

Cell Biology. This interdisciplinary program offers the student the opportunity to bring modern molecular and physical techniques to bear on problems in cell biology. Faculty members' research spans a broad range of interests in the areas of eukaryotic cell biology and related clinical aspects. The program is particularly strong in the following areas of research: angiogenesis, cancer biology, gene expression, molecular medicine, reproductive biology, signal transduction, vascular biology, optical methods, proteomics, and computer modeling of complex biological systems. Kevin Claffey, Associate Professor of Cell Biology and Program Director.

Genetics and Developmental Biology. This program emphasizes cellular and molecular bases of differentiation and development and includes opportunities in molecular human genetics. Research opportunities are available in the biology of human embryonic stem cells, mapping and cloning of genes responsible for human disease, RNA processing (including RNA editing, alternative splicing, antisense regulation, and RNA interference), the molecular mechanisms of aging, signal transduction pathways, microbial pathogenesis, developmental neurobiology, cell differentiation, musculoskeletal development, morphogenesis and pattern formation, reproductive biology, and endocrinology. William Mohler, Assistant Professor of Genetics and Developmental Biology and Program Director; Arthur Günzl, Professor of Genetics and Developmental Biology and Associate Program Director; Blanka Rogina, Assistant Professor of Genetics and Developmental Biology and Associate Program Director.

Immunology. The central focus of this program is to train the student to become an independent investigator and educator who will provide research and educational contributions to basic, applied, or clinical immunology through lectures, seminars, laboratory rotations, research presentations, and a concentration on laboratory research. Research in the program is focused on the cellular and molecular aspects of immune system structure and function in animal models and in humans. Areas of emphasis include molecular immunology (mechanisms of antigen presentation, major histocompatibility complex genetics and function, cytokines and cytokine receptors, and tumor antigens), cellular immunology (biochemical mechanisms and biological aspects of signal transduction of lymphocytes and granulocytes; cellular and molecular requirements for thymic T-lymphocyte development, selection, and activation; cytokines in B- and T-cell development; regulation of antitumor immunity; immunoparasitology, including parasite genetics and immune recognition of parasite antigens; and mechanisms of inflammation), organ-based immunology (immune effector mechanisms of the intestine, lymphocyte interactions in the lung, and immune regulation of the eye), immunity to infectious agents (viruses, bacteria, and parasites, including vector-borne organisms), and autoimmunity (animal models of autoimmune disease and effector mechanisms in human autoimmunity). Adam Adler, Associate Professor of Immunology and Program Director; H. Leonardo Aguila, Associate Professor of Immunology and Associate Program Director.

Molecular Biology and Biochemistry. This program uniquely bridges modern molecular biology, microbiology, biochemistry, cell biology, and structural biology. Research in this program is directed toward explaining biological phenomena at the molecular level. The program includes four major areas of concentration and research: relation of the structure of macromolecules to their function, biosynthesis of macromolecules, biochemical genetics, and assembly of macromolecules into complex cellular structures. Chris Heinen, Assistant Professor of Medicine and Program Director; Bing Hao, Assistant Professor of Molecular, Microbial and Structural Biology and Associate Program Director.

Neuroscience. This interdepartmental program offers comprehensive conceptual and experimental training in molecular, systems, and behavioral neuroscience. The faculty members of the neuroscience program engage in research that involves cellular, molecular, and developmental neurobiology; neuroanatomy; neuroimaging; neurophysiology; neurochemistry; neuroendocrinology; neuropharmacology; and neuropathology. Richard Mains, Professor of Neuroscience and Program Director; Zhao-Wen Wang, Assistant Professor of Genetics and Developmental Biology and Associate Program Director.

Skeletal, Craniofacial, and Oral Biology. This program offers interdisciplinary research training in the areas of skeletal, craniofacial, and oral biology, emphasizing contemporary research technologies in cell, molecular, and developmental biology; genetics; and biochemistry. Areas of research include regulation of the formation, outgrowth, and patterning of the developing limb; control of cartilage differentiation, endochondral ossification, osteogenesis, and joint formation; molecular regulation of gene expression in bone; homeobox gene regulation of osteoblast differentiation; gene therapy of bone diseases; hormonal and cytokine regulation of bone growth, formation, and remodeling; control of craniofacial skeletogenesis and tooth development; signal transduction and intracellular signaling pathways; cellular and molecular aspects of the pathogenesis of inflammatory disease; microbiology, pathogenesis, and immunology of caries and periodontal disease; neural structure and function in the gustatory system; biomaterial development for tissue engineering; bone cell–implant interactions; differentiation of human embryonic stem cells into skeletal tissues; and analysis of oral and mucosal function and disease. Gloria Gronowicz, Professor, Department of Surgery and Program Director; Caroline Dealy, Associate Professor, Center for Regenerative Medicine and Skeletal Development and Associate Program Director.

Combined M.D./Ph.D. Program. This program is designed for students interested in careers in medical research and academic medicine. It enables students to acquire competence in both the basic science and clinical aspects of their chosen fields. The program allows a student to combine the curricula of two schools in a way that meets the specific degree requirements of each, and yet it allows the completion of both in a period less than that needed if the two curricula were taken in sequence. Entry into the program is limited to a small number of unusually well qualified students who are either currently enrolled in the medical school or who have been accepted into the first-year class. Carol Pilbeam, Professor of Medicine and Program Director.

Combined D.M.D./Ph.D. Program. This program is designed for students interested in careers in dental research and academic dental medicine. It enables students to acquire competence in both the basic science and clinical aspects of their chosen fields. The program allows a student to combine the curricula of two schools in a way that meets the specific degree requirements of each, and yet it allows the completion of both in a period less than that needed if the two curricula were taken in sequence. Entry into the program is limited to a small number of unusually well qualified students who are either currently enrolled in the dental school or who have been accepted into the first-year class. Mina Mina, Professor of Orthodontics, Oral and Maxillofacial Surgery, Pediatric Dentistry, and Advanced Education and Program Director.

Combined M.D./M.P.H. or D.M.D./M.P.H. Program. A joint-degree program leading to the Master of Public Health in addition to the Doctor of Medicine or the Doctor of Dental Medicine is sponsored by the Graduate Program in Public Health and the Schools of Medicine and Dental Medicine. The joint-degree program has been developed to prepare future physicians and dentists to deal creatively with the rapidly changing environment of medicine and health care. It is possible to complete the degree requirements for both programs during the four years of medical or dental school. David Gregorio, Professor of Community Medicine and Health Care and Program Director.

Clinical and Translational Research. The Master of Science degree program in clinical and translational research is administered in the Department of Medicine and stresses clinical research methods and research practicum in order to provide practical research training in preparation for independent research. The program is offered to individuals who have a health-related terminal degree (M.D., D.M.D., or Ph.D.) or who are involved in an M.D., D.M.D., or Ph.D. program in a health-related field and are in good standing. The master's program is based on both course work and research experience, but no research thesis is required. Students are required to sit for a final examination, which may entail the oral defense of a grant application and a manuscript. Lisa Godin (godin@nso.uchc.edu).

Dental Science. The Master of Dental Science degree program is an interdepartmental program whose primary objective is to provide instruction in dental science that will enhance the student's ability to instruct and undertake research in dental schools. This program provides an opportunity for cooperative study and research between dentistry, the basic sciences, and allied health fields. Both M.Dent.Sc. and oral biology Ph.D. students may combine their work in these programs with advanced clinical training in endodontics, orthodontics, oral pathology, pedodontics, periodontics, oral medicine, oral radiology, and oral and maxillofacial surgery. Arthur Hand, Assistant Dean for Medical and Graduate Education.

Public Health. This multidisciplinary master's program, accredited by the Council for Education in Public Health, is based in the Department of Community Medicine and Health Care. It offers a core curriculum in epidemiology, biostatistics, health administration, environmental health, the sociomedical sciences, health law, and electives in these and related areas. A Ph.D. program in public health is also offered. David Gregorio, Professor of Community Medicine and Health Care and Program Director.

THE UNIVERSITY OF KANSAS MEDICAL CENTER
Interdisciplinary Graduate Program in Biomedical Sciences

Programs of Study

Presidential and Congressional commissions have identified biomedicine and biotechnology as leading growth sectors of the American and world economies. Students can pursue graduate studies on the cutting edge of biomedical research at the University of Kansas Medical Center (KUMC) and place themselves in a competitive position. Students have the opportunity to develop research skills and earn a Ph.D. degree in a broad range of biomedical research areas, including neuroscience, protein structure and function, and pharmacology and toxicology, as well as viral, microbial, molecular, cellular, developmental, reproductive, immunological, renal, and physiological biology. Research also includes many clinically related studies focusing on a wide range of human diseases. The graduate program is a partnership between KUMC (http://www.kumc.edu/igpbs) and the nearby Stowers Institute for Medical Research (http://www.stowers-institute.org); students may conduct their research at either institution.

Graduate students pursuing a Ph.D. degree in biomedical sciences are admitted through the Interdisciplinary Graduate Program in Biomedical Sciences (IGPBS). This program is responsible for the first-year curriculum and allows each student to study in the most current areas of the biomedical sciences before selecting a laboratory in which to carry out his or her research program. Each student entering the IGPBS takes a state-of-the-art, highly integrated core curriculum. In addition to courses that provide the fundamental principles essential for understanding the biomedical sciences, students receive an introduction to practical aspects of research, including biographics, bioethics, appropriate use of animals in research, laboratory safety, and procedures for human studies research. Faculty members also present their research programs to students through a research seminar series, giving students the opportunity to evaluate each research program. Following this introduction, each student selects three laboratory rotations that are completed during the first year. Laboratory rotations expose students to potential research advisers and to the principles and procedures of cutting-edge laboratory techniques, and they allow students to decide which laboratory best fits their needs. At the beginning of the second year, each student selects a research adviser, in whose laboratory her or his doctoral research project is carried out. At this time, the student also enters one of eight graduate programs.

Research Facilities

State-of-the-art technology and equipment is available through a variety of core research facilities, including DNA microarray technology, laser capture microdissection, rodent behavioral testing facilities, bioinformatics, transgenic mouse laboratories, fluorescence-activated cell sorting, molecular neurobiology, mass spectrometry, a highly automated histological and immunohistochemistry core, FT-IR microspectroscopy, electron microscopy, confocal microscopes for live cell imaging and spectral separation, noninvasive magnetic resonance spectroscopy, functional magnetic resonance imaging, and magnetoencephalography.

Financial Aid

Teaching and research assistantships are available. Students admitted into the IGPBS are awarded $24,000 in financial support and given a tuition waiver. Student travel awards are also available as pupils progress through the program.

Cost of Study

Students accepted into the IGPBS receive a tuition waiver upon meeting enrollment requirements. Students are responsible for campus and library fees, estimated at $473 per academic year.

Living and Housing Costs

A multitude of options are available to KUMC students near the campus. Current housing costs are between $450 and $800 per month.

Student Group

Twenty-five percent of the students enrolled in the IGPBS are from international locales. The age range of students generally falls between 22 and 32 years.

Student Outcomes

Upon graduation from KUMC, students can expect to obtain a position in the biotechnology, academic, or governmental career fields.

Location

The University of Kansas Medical Center is located at 39th Avenue and Rainbow Boulevard in Kansas City, Kansas. It is on the border of Kansas and Missouri, with quick access to Westport, the Country Club Plaza, the Nelson-Atkins Museum of Art, and the Kansas City Art Institute.

The University of Kansas Medical Center

The Graduate Program

The Interdisciplinary Graduate Program in Biomedical Sciences is an educational program within the School of Medicine at the University of Kansas Medical Center. It consists of eight degree-granting departments or programs. The IGPBS is made up of the Departments of Anatomy and Cell Biology; Biochemistry and Molecular Biology; Microbiology, Molecular Genetics, and Immunology; Pathology and Laboratory Medicine; Molecular and Integrative Physiology; Pharmacology, Toxicology, and Therapeutics; the Neuroscience Graduate Program; and the Training Program in Environmental Toxicology.

Applying

Students who are interested in the IGPBS may apply online at http://www.kumc.edu/igpbs. Applications must be received by January 4, although applications received after that date are considered until the class is filled.

Correspondence and Information

Director
Interdisciplinary Graduate Program in Biomedical Sciences
5015 Wescoe, MS3025
The University of Kansas Medical Center
3901 Rainbow Boulevard
Kansas City, Kansas 66160-7836
Phone: 913-588-2719
          800-408-2039 (toll-free)
Fax: 913-588-2711
E-mail: igpbs@kumc.edu
Web site: http://www.kumc.edu/igpbs

AREAS OF RESEARCH

Faculty members at KUMC have seventeen areas of research emphasis:
- Cardiovascular biology
- Cell and developmental biology
- Imaging
- Molecular and cellular biophysics
- Molecular and cellular immunology
- Molecular biology and genetics
- Molecular pathogenesis of infectious diseases
- Molecular toxicology and environmental health
- Molecular virology
- Muscle biology
- Neurosciences
- Pharmacological sciences
- Proteomics
- Renal biology
- Reproductive biology
- Signal transduction and cancer biology
- Structural biology

Section 2
Anatomy

This section contains a directory of institutions offering graduate work in anatomy. Additional information about programs listed in the directory but not augmented by an in-depth entry may be obtained by writing directly to the dean of a graduate school or chair of a department at the address given in the directory.

For programs offering related work, see also in this book *Allied Health; Biomedical Sciences; Cell, Molecular, and Structural Biology; Dentistry and Dental Sciences; Genetics, Developmental Biology, and Reproductive Biology; Neuroscience and Neurobiology; Pathology and* *Pathobiology; Physiology; Veterinary Medicine and Sciences;* and *Zoology.* In another guide in this series:

Graduate Programs in the Humanities, Arts & Social Sciences
See *Sociology, Anthropology, and Archaeology*

CONTENTS

Program Directory

Anatomy

Albert Einstein College of Medicine, Graduate Division of Biomedical Sciences, Department of Anatomy and Structural Biology, Bronx, NY 10461. Offers anatomy (PhD); cell and developmental biology (PhD); MD/PhD. *Degree requirements:* For doctorate, thesis/dissertation. *Entrance requirements:* For doctorate, GRE General Test. Additional exam requirements/recommendations for international students: Required—TOEFL. Electronic applications accepted. *Faculty research:* Cell motility, cell membranes and membrane-cytoskeletal interactions as applied to processing of pancreatic hormones, mechanisms of secretion.

American University of Beirut, Graduate Programs, Faculty of Medicine, Beirut, Lebanon. Offers anatomy, cell biology and human morphology (MS); biochemistry and medical genetics (MS); biomedical sciences (PhD); experimental pathology, immunology and microbiology (MS); medicine (MD); neuroscience (MS); pharmacology and toxicology (MS). Part-time programs available. *Faculty:* 232 full-time (58 women), 68 part-time/adjunct (7 women). *Students:* 346 full-time (135 women), 69 part-time (57 women). Average age 23. In 2011, 20 master's, 82 doctorates awarded. *Degree requirements:* For master's, one foreign language, comprehensive exam, thesis (for some programs). *Entrance requirements:* For master's, letter of recommendation; for doctorate, MCAT, bachelor's degree. Additional exam requirements/recommendations for international students: Required—TOEFL (minimum score 600 paper-based; 250 computer-based; 100 iBT), IELTS (minimum score 7.5). *Application deadline:* For fall admission, 4/30 for domestic and international students; for spring admission, 11/1 for domestic and international students. Application fee: $50. *Expenses: Tuition:* Full-time $12,780; part-time $710 per credit. Tuition and fees vary according to course load and program. *Financial support:* In 2011–12, 19 students received support. Career-related internships or fieldwork, institutionally sponsored loans, scholarships/grants, health care benefits, and unspecified assistantships available. Financial award application deadline: 2/2. *Faculty research:* Cancer research (targeted therapy, mechanisms of leukemogenesis, tumor cell extravasation and metastasis, cancer stem cells); stem cell research (regenerative medicine, drug discovery); genetic research (neurogenetics, hereditary cardiomyopathy, hemoglobinopathies, pharmacogenomics, proteomics); neuroscience research (pain, neurodegenerative disorder); metabolism (inflammation and metabolism, metabolic disorder, diabetes mellitus); vascular and renal biology, signal transduction. *Total annual research expenditures:* $2.3 million. *Unit head:* Dr. Mohamed Sayegh, Dean, 961-1350000 Ext. 4700, Fax: 961-1744464, E-mail: msayegh@aub.edu.lb. *Application contact:* Dr. Salim Kanaan, Director, Admissions Office, 961-1350000 Ext. 2594, Fax: 961-1750775, E-mail: sk00@aub.edu.lb. Web site: http://www.aub.edu.lb/fm/fm_home/Pages/index.aspx.

Auburn University, College of Veterinary Medicine and Graduate School, Graduate Programs in Veterinary Medicine, Auburn University, AL 36849. Offers biomedical sciences (MS, PhD), including anatomy, physiology and pharmacology (MS), biomedical sciences (PhD), clinical sciences (MS), large animal surgery and medicine (MS), pathobiology (MS), radiology (MS), small animal surgery and medicine (MS); DVM/MS. Part-time programs available. *Faculty:* 100 full-time (40 women), 5 part-time/adjunct (1 woman). *Students:* 17 full-time (13 women), 59 part-time (33 women); includes 6 minority (1 Black or African American, non-Hispanic/Latino; 3 Asian, non-Hispanic/Latino; 2 Hispanic/Latino), 30 international. Average age 30. 36 applicants, 69% accepted, 11 enrolled. In 2011, 19 master's awarded. *Degree requirements:* For doctorate, thesis/dissertation. *Entrance requirements:* For master's, GRE General Test; for doctorate, GRE General Test, GRE Subject Test. *Application deadline:* For fall admission, 7/7 for domestic students; for spring admission, 11/24 for domestic students. Applications are processed on a rolling basis. Application fee: $50 ($60 for international students). Electronic applications accepted. *Expenses:* Tuition, state resident: full-time $7290; part-time $405 per credit hour. Tuition, nonresident: full-time $21,870; part-time $1215 per credit hour. International tuition: $22,000 full-time. Required fees: $1402. *Financial support:* Research assistantships, teaching assistantships, and Federal Work-Study available. Support available to part-time students. Financial award application deadline: 3/15; financial award applicants required to submit FAFSA. *Unit head:* Dr. Calvin Johnson, Acting Dean, 334-844-2650. *Application contact:* Dr. George Flowers, Dean of the Graduate School, 334-844-2125.

Barry University, School of Podiatric Medicine, Program in Anatomy, Miami Shores, FL 33161-6695. Offers MS. *Entrance requirements:* For master's, GRE.

Boston University, College of Health and Rehabilitation Sciences: Sargent College, Department of Health Sciences, Programs in Applied Anatomy and Physiology, Boston, MA 02215. Offers MS, PhD. *Faculty:* 10 full-time (9 women), 5 part-time/adjunct (2 women). *Students:* 4 full-time (2 women), 4 part-time (all women), 1 international. Average age 27. 37 applicants, 41% accepted. In 2011, 11 degrees awarded. Terminal master's awarded for partial completion of doctoral program. *Degree requirements:* For master's, thesis or alternative; for doctorate, comprehensive exam, thesis/dissertation. *Entrance requirements:* For master's, GRE General Test, minimum GPA of 3.0; for doctorate, GRE General Test. Additional exam requirements/recommendations for international students: Required—TOEFL (minimum score 550 paper-based; 84 iBT). *Application deadline:* For fall admission, 1/15 priority date for domestic students, 1/15 for international students; for spring admission, 10/1 for domestic and international students. Applications are processed on a rolling basis. Application fee: $70. Electronic applications accepted. *Expenses: Tuition:* Full-time $40,848; part-time $1276 per credit hour. *Required fees:* $572; $286 per semester. *Financial support:* In 2011–12, 2 fellowships (averaging $21,000 per year), 1 research assistantship with full tuition reimbursement (averaging $18,000 per year), 3 teaching assistantships with full and partial tuition reimbursements were awarded; career-related internships or fieldwork, Federal Work-Study, institutionally sponsored loans, scholarships/grants, and tuition waivers (partial) also available. Support available to part-time students. Financial award application deadline: 4/15; financial award applicants required to submit FAFSA. *Faculty research:* Skeletal muscle, neural systems, smooth muscle, muscular dystrophy. *Total annual research expenditures:* $3 million. *Unit head:* Dr. Kathleen Morgan, Chair, 617-353-2717, E-mail: kmorgan@bu.edu. *Application contact:* Sharon Sankey, Director, Student Services, 617-353-2713, Fax: 617-353-7500, E-mail: ssankey@bu.edu.

Boston University, School of Medicine, Division of Graduate Medical Sciences, Department of Anatomy and Neurobiology, Boston, MA 02118. Offers MA, PhD, MD/PhD. Part-time programs available. *Faculty:* 29 full-time (14 women), 16 part-time/adjunct (4 women). *Students:* 33 full-time (15 women), 1 (woman) part-time; includes 4 minority (3 Asian, non-Hispanic/Latino; 1 Hispanic/Latino), 2 international. Average age 27. 38 applicants, 53% accepted, 11 enrolled. In 2011, 4 master's, 10 doctorates awarded. Terminal master's awarded for partial completion of doctoral program. *Degree requirements:* For master's, thesis, qualifying exam; for doctorate, thesis/dissertation, qualifying exam. *Entrance requirements:* For master's and doctorate, GRE General Test, GRE Subject Test. Additional exam requirements/recommendations for international students: Required—TOEFL. *Application deadline:* For fall admission, 1/15 priority date for domestic students; for spring admission, 10/15 priority date for domestic

students. Application fee: $75. Electronic applications accepted. *Expenses: Tuition:* Full-time $40,848; part-time $1276 per credit hour. *Required fees:* $572; $286 per semester. *Financial support:* In 2011–12, fellowships (averaging $30,500 per year), research assistantships (averaging $30,500 per year) were awarded; Federal Work-Study, scholarships/grants, and traineeships also available. Financial award applicants required to submit FAFSA. *Faculty research:* Neuroanatomy, development of the nervous system, aging, respiratory system, reproductive system. *Unit head:* Dr. Mark Moss, Chairman, 617-638-4200, Fax: 617-638-4216. *Application contact:* Dr. Jarrett Rushmore, Director of Graduate Program, 617-638-4188, E-mail: rushmore@bu.edu. Web site: http://www.bumc.bu.edu/anatneuro/.

Case Western Reserve University, School of Medicine and School of Graduate Studies, Graduate Programs in Medicine, Department of Anatomy, Cleveland, OH 44106. Offers applied anatomy (MS); biological anthropology (MS); cellular biology (MS); MD/MS. Part-time programs available. *Degree requirements:* For master's, comprehensive exam, thesis (for some programs). *Entrance requirements:* For master's, GRE General Test. Additional exam requirements/recommendations for international students: Required—TOEFL. *Faculty research:* Hypoxia, cell injury, biochemical aberration occurrences in ischemic tissue, human functional morphology, evolutionary morphology.

Columbia University, College of Physicians and Surgeons, Department of Anatomy and Cell Biology, New York, NY 10032. Offers anatomy (M Phil, MA, PhD); anatomy and cell biology (PhD); MD/PhD. Only candidates for the PhD are admitted. Terminal master's awarded for partial completion of doctoral program. *Degree requirements:* For doctorate, thesis/dissertation, oral exam. *Entrance requirements:* For master's and doctorate, GRE General Test. Additional exam requirements/recommendations for international students: Required—TOEFL. *Faculty research:* Protein sorting, membrane biophysics, muscle energetics, neuroendocrinology, developmental biology, cytoskeleton, transcription factors.

Cornell University, Graduate School, Graduate Fields of Agriculture and Life Sciences, Field of Zoology and Wildlife Conservation, Ithaca, NY 14853-0001. Offers animal cytology (MS, PhD); comparative and functional anatomy (MS, PhD); developmental biology (MS, PhD); ecology (MS, PhD); histology (MS, PhD). *Faculty:* 24 full-time (7 women). *Students:* 5 full-time (4 women); includes 1 minority (Two or more races, non-Hispanic/Latino), 2 international. Average age 29. 7 applicants, 14% accepted, 1 enrolled. In 2011, 2 doctorates awarded. *Degree requirements:* For doctorate, comprehensive exam, thesis/dissertation, 2 semesters of teaching experience. *Entrance requirements:* For doctorate, GRE General Test, GRE Subject Test (biology), 2 letters of recommendation. Additional exam requirements/recommendations for international students: Required—TOEFL (minimum score 550 paper-based; 213 computer-based; 77 iBT). *Application deadline:* For fall admission, 2/1 priority date for domestic students. Application fee: $95. Electronic applications accepted. *Financial support:* In 2011–12, 3 research assistantships with full tuition reimbursements, 1 teaching assistantship with full tuition reimbursement were awarded; fellowships with full tuition reimbursements, institutionally sponsored loans, scholarships/grants, health care benefits, tuition waivers (full and partial), and unspecified assistantships also available. Financial award applicants required to submit FAFSA. *Faculty research:* Organismal biology, functional morphology, biomechanics, comparative vertebrate anatomy, comparative invertebrate anatomy, paleontology. *Unit head:* Director of Graduate Studies, 607-253-3276, Fax: 607-253-3756. *Application contact:* Graduate Field Assistant, 607-253-3276, Fax: 607-253-3756, E-mail: graduate_edcvm@cornell.edu. Web site: http://www.gradschool.cornell.edu/fields.php?id-65&a-2.

Creighton University, School of Medicine and Graduate School, Graduate Programs in Medicine, Program in Clinical Anatomy, Omaha, NE 68178-0001. Offers MS. *Degree requirements:* For master's, comprehensive exam, thesis or alternative. *Entrance requirements:* For master's, GRE, MCAT or DAT. Additional exam requirements/recommendations for international students: Required—TOEFL. Electronic applications accepted. *Expenses: Tuition:* Full-time $12,672; part-time $704 per credit hour. *Required fees:* $1410; $136 per semester. Tuition and fees vary according to campus/location and reciprocity agreements. *Faculty research:* Neural crest cell migration; ontogenetic and phylogenetic nervous system development; skeletal biology.

Dalhousie University, Faculty of Graduate Studies and Faculty of Medicine, Graduate Programs in Medicine, Department of Anatomy and Neurobiology, Halifax, NS B3H 4R2, Canada. Offers M Sc, PhD. *Degree requirements:* For master's, thesis; for doctorate, thesis/dissertation. *Entrance requirements:* For master's and doctorate, GRE (recommended), minimum A- average. Additional exam requirements/recommendations for international students: Required—1 of 5 approved tests: TOEFL, IELTS, CANTEST, CAEL, Michigan English Language Assessment Battery. Electronic applications accepted. *Faculty research:* Neuroscience histology, cell biology, neuroendocrinology, evolutionary biology.

Des Moines University, College of Osteopathic Medicine, Program in Anatomy, Des Moines, IA 50312-4104. Offers MS.

Duke University, Graduate School, Department of Biological Anthropology and Anatomy, Durham, NC 27710. Offers cellular and molecular biology (PhD); gross anatomy and physical anthropology (PhD), including comparative morphology of human and non-human primates, primate social behavior, vertebrate paleontology; neuroanatomy (PhD). *Faculty:* 9 full-time. *Students:* 16 full-time (10 women); includes 3 minority (1 Black or African American, non-Hispanic/Latino; 2 Hispanic/Latino), 1 international. 71 applicants, 7% accepted, 4 enrolled. In 2011, 2 doctorates awarded. *Degree requirements:* For doctorate, one foreign language, thesis/dissertation. *Entrance requirements:* For doctorate, GRE General Test. Additional exam requirements/recommendations for international students: Required—TOEFL (minimum score 550 paper-based; 213 computer-based; 83 iBT), IELTS (minimum score 7). *Application deadline:* For fall admission, 12/8 priority date for domestic students, 12/8 for international students. Application fee: $75. Electronic applications accepted. *Expenses: Tuition:* Full-time $40,720. *Required fees:* $3107. *Financial support:* Fellowships, teaching assistantships, and Federal Work-Study available. Financial award application deadline: 12/31. *Unit head:* Daniel Schmitt, Director of Graduate Studies, 919-684-4124, Fax: 919-684-8542, E-mail: mlsquire@duke.edu. *Application contact:* Elizabeth Hutton, Director of Admissions, 919-684-3913, Fax: 919-684-2277, E-mail: grad-admissions@duke.edu. Web site: http://www.baa.duke.edu/.

East Carolina University, Brody School of Medicine, Department of Anatomy and Cell Biology, Greenville, NC 27858-4353. Offers PhD. *Degree requirements:* For doctorate, comprehensive exam, thesis/dissertation. *Entrance requirements:* For doctorate, GRE General Test. Additional exam requirements/recommendations for international students: Required—TOEFL. *Application deadline:* For fall admission, 6/1 priority date for domestic students. Applications are processed on a rolling basis. Application fee: $50. *Expenses:* Tuition, state resident: full-time $3557; part-time $444.63 per semester

hour. Tuition, nonresident: full-time $14,351; part-time $1793.88 per semester hour. *Required fees:* $2016; $252 per semester hour. Part-time tuition and fees vary according to course load, campus/location and program. *Financial support:* Fellowships with full tuition reimbursements and health care benefits available. Financial award application deadline: 6/1. *Faculty research:* Kinesin motors during slow matogensis, mitochondria and peroxisomes in obesity, ovarian innervation, tight junction function and regulation. *Unit head:* Dr. Cheryl Knudson, Chairman, 252-744-2852, Fax: 252-744-2850, E-mail: knudsonc@ecu.edu. *Application contact:* Dr. Ron Dudek, Senior Director of Graduate Studies, 252-744-2863, Fax: 252-744-2850, E-mail: dudekr@ecu.edu. Web site: http://www.ecu.edu/cs-dhs/anatomy/gradProg.cfm.

East Tennessee State University, James H. Quillen College of Medicine, Biomedical Science Graduate Program, Johnson City, TN 37614. Offers anatomy and cell biology (PhD); biochemistry and molecular biology (PhD); microbiology (PhD); pharmaceutical sciences (PhD); pharmacology (PhD); physiology (PhD); quantitative biosciences (PhD). *Faculty:* 33 full-time (6 women). *Students:* 29 full-time (15 women), 2 part-time (both women); includes 4 minority (1 Black or African American, non-Hispanic/Latino; 1 Asian, non-Hispanic/Latino; 2 Hispanic/Latino), 6 international. Average age 29. 76 applicants, 12% accepted, 7 enrolled. In 2011, 1 doctorate awarded. *Degree requirements:* For doctorate, thesis/dissertation, comprehensive qualifying exam. *Entrance requirements:* For doctorate, GRE General Test, GRE Subject Test. Additional exam requirements/recommendations for international students: Required—TOEFL (minimum score 550 paper-based; 213 computer-based; 79 iBT). *Application deadline:* For fall admission, 3/15 priority date for domestic students, 3/1 for international students. Application fee: $35 ($45 for international students). Electronic applications accepted. *Expenses:* Contact institution. *Financial support:* In 2011–12, 29 students received support, including 29 research assistantships with full tuition reimbursements available (averaging $19,000 per year); career-related internships or fieldwork, institutionally sponsored loans, scholarships/grants, and unspecified assistantships also available. Financial award application deadline: 7/1; financial award applicants required to submit FAFSA. *Faculty research:* Cardiovascular biology, neuroscience, infectious disease, cancer, inflammatory disease. *Total annual research expenditures:* $3.6 million. *Unit head:* Dr. Mitchell E. Robinson, Associate Dean/Program Director, 423-439-2031, Fax: 423-439-2140, E-mail: robinson@etsu.edu. *Application contact:* Shella Bennett, Graduate Specialist, 423-439-4708, Fax: 423-439-5624, E-mail: bennetsg@etsu.edu.

Georgia Health Sciences University, College of Graduate Studies, Program in Cellular Biology and Anatomy, Augusta, GA 30912. Offers MS, PhD. *Faculty:* 15 full-time (6 women), 3 part-time/adjunct (1 woman). *Students:* 11 full-time (7 women); includes 1 minority (Asian, non-Hispanic/Latino), 7 international. Average age 30. In 2011, 2 degrees awarded. *Degree requirements:* For doctorate, comprehensive exam, thesis/dissertation. *Entrance requirements:* For doctorate, GRE General Test. Additional exam requirements/recommendations for international students: Required—TOEFL (minimum score 550 paper-based; 213 computer-based; 79 iBT). *Application deadline:* For fall admission, 1/15 for domestic and international students. Applications are processed on a rolling basis. Application fee: $50. *Financial support:* In 2011–12, 2 students received support, including 1 fellowship with partial tuition reimbursement available (averaging $26,000 per year), 9 research assistantships with partial tuition reimbursements available (averaging $23,000 per year); teaching assistantships with partial tuition reimbursements available, Federal Work-Study, institutionally sponsored loans, and scholarships/grants also available. Support available to part-time students. Financial award application deadline: 5/31; financial award applicants required to submit FAFSA. *Faculty research:* Eye disease, developmental biology, cell injury and death, stroke and neurotoxicity, diabetic complications. *Total annual research expenditures:* $2.8 million. *Unit head:* Dr. Sally S. Atherton, Chair and Professor, 706-721-3731, Fax: 706-721-6120, E-mail: satherton@georgiahealth.edu. *Application contact:* Dr. Patricia L. Cameron, Acting Vice Dean, 706-721-3279, E-mail: pcameron@georgiahealth.edu. Web site: http://www.georgiahealth.edu/medicine/cba/index.html.

Howard University, Graduate School, Department of Anatomy, Washington, DC 20059-0002. Offers MS, PhD. *Degree requirements:* For master's, comprehensive exam, thesis, teaching experience; for doctorate, comprehensive exam, thesis/dissertation, teaching experience. *Entrance requirements:* For master's and doctorate, GRE General Test, minimum GPA of 3.0. Additional exam requirements/recommendations for international students: Required—TOEFL (minimum score 550 paper-based; 213 computer-based). Electronic applications accepted. *Faculty research:* Neural control of function, mammalian evolution and paleontology, cellular differentiation, cellular and neuronal communication, development, cell biology, molecular biology, anatomy.

Indiana University–Purdue University Indianapolis, Indiana University School of Medicine, Department of Anatomy and Cell Biology, Indianapolis, IN 46202-2896. Offers MS, PhD, MD/PhD. *Faculty:* 14 full-time (1 woman). *Students:* 12 full-time (6 women), 3 part-time (2 women); includes 1 minority (Black or African American, non-Hispanic/Latino), 4 international. Average age 29. 8 applicants, 50% accepted, 2 enrolled. In 2011, 2 degrees awarded. *Degree requirements:* For master's, thesis or alternative; for doctorate, thesis/dissertation. *Entrance requirements:* For master's and doctorate, GRE General Test. *Application deadline:* For fall admission, 1/15 priority date for domestic students. Application fee: $55 ($65 for international students). *Financial support:* Fellowships, research assistantships, Federal Work-Study, institutionally sponsored loans, tuition waivers (partial), and stipends available. Financial award application deadline: 2/15. *Faculty research:* Acoustic reflex control, osteoarthritis and bone disease, diabetes, kidney diseases, cellular and molecular neurobiology. *Unit head:* Dr. David B. Burr, Chairman, 317-274-7494, Fax: 317-278-2040, E-mail: dburr@indyvax.iupui.edu. *Application contact:* Dr. James Williams, Graduate Adviser, 317-274-3423, Fax: 317-278-2040, E-mail: williams@anatomy.iupui.edu.

The Johns Hopkins University, School of Medicine, Graduate Programs in Medicine, Center for Functional Anatomy and Evolution, Baltimore, MD 21218-2699. Offers PhD. *Degree requirements:* For doctorate, comprehensive exam, thesis/dissertation, oral exams. *Entrance requirements:* For doctorate, GRE. Additional exam requirements/recommendations for international students: Required—TOEFL. *Faculty research:* Vertebrate evolution, functional anatomy, primate evolution, vertebrate paleobiology, vertebrate morphology.

Loma Linda University, School of Medicine, Department of Pathology and Human Anatomy, Loma Linda, CA 92350. Offers MS, PhD. Part-time programs available. Terminal master's awarded for partial completion of doctoral program. *Degree requirements:* For master's, thesis; for doctorate, 2 foreign languages, thesis/dissertation. *Entrance requirements:* For master's and doctorate, GRE General Test. Additional exam requirements/recommendations for international students: Required—TOEFL (minimum score 550 paper-based; 213 computer-based). *Faculty research:* Neuroendocrine system, histochemistry and image analysis, effect of age and diabetes on PNS, electron microscopy, histology.

Louisiana State University Health Sciences Center, School of Graduate Studies in New Orleans, Department of Cell Biology and Anatomy, New Orleans, LA 70112-2223. Offers cell biology and anatomy (MS, PhD), including cell biology, developmental biology, neurobiology and anatomy; MD/PhD. *Degree requirements:* For master's, comprehensive exam, thesis; for doctorate, comprehensive exam, thesis/dissertation.

Entrance requirements: For master's and doctorate, GRE General Test, GRE Subject Test, minimum undergraduate GPA of 3.0. Additional exam requirements/recommendations for international students: Required—TOEFL. *Faculty research:* Visual system organization, neural development, plasticity of sensory systems, information processing through the nervous system, visuomotor integration.

Louisiana State University Health Sciences Center at Shreveport, Department of Cellular Biology and Anatomy, Shreveport, LA 71130-3932. Offers MS, PhD, MD/PhD. Terminal master's awarded for partial completion of doctoral program. *Degree requirements:* For master's, thesis; for doctorate, thesis/dissertation. *Entrance requirements:* For master's and doctorate, GRE General Test. Additional exam requirements/recommendations for international students: Required—TOEFL. *Faculty research:* Alcohol and immunity, neuroscience, olfactory physiology, extracellular matrix, cancer cell biology and gene therapy.

Loyola University Chicago, Graduate School, Department of Cell Biology, Neurobiology and Anatomy, Chicago, IL 60660. Offers MS, PhD. Part-time programs available. *Faculty:* 16 full-time (6 women), 9 part-time/adjunct (4 women). *Students:* 21 full-time (11 women); includes 4 minority (3 Hispanic/Latino; 1 Two or more races, non-Hispanic/Latino), 1 international. Average age 27. 28 applicants, 29% accepted, 4 enrolled. In 2011, 1 master's, 2 doctorates awarded. Terminal master's awarded for partial completion of doctoral program. *Degree requirements:* For master's, thesis; for doctorate, comprehensive exam, thesis/dissertation. *Entrance requirements:* For master's, GRE General Test, minimum GPA of 3.0; for doctorate, GRE General Test, GRE Subject Test (biology), minimum GPA of 3.0. Additional exam requirements/recommendations for international students: Required—TOEFL (minimum score 600 paper-based; 250 computer-based). *Application deadline:* For fall admission, 5/1 priority date for domestic students, 5/1 for international students. Applications are processed on a rolling basis. Application fee: $50. Electronic applications accepted. *Expenses: Tuition:* Full-time $15,660; part-time $870 per credit hour. *Required fees:* $125 per semester. Tuition and fees vary according to course load and program. *Financial support:* In 2011–12, 5 fellowships with full tuition reimbursements (averaging $23,000 per year), 5 research assistantships with full tuition reimbursements (averaging $23,000 per year) were awarded; Federal Work-Study and unspecified assistantships also available. Financial award application deadline: 5/1; financial award applicants required to submit FAFSA. *Faculty research:* Brain steroids, immunology, neuroregeneration, cytokines. *Total annual research expenditures:* $1 million. *Unit head:* Dr. Phong Le, Head, 708-216-3603, Fax: 708-216-3913, E-mail: ple@lumc.edu. *Application contact:* Ginny Hayes, Graduate Program Secretary, 708-216-3353, Fax: 708-216-3913, E-mail: vhayes@lumc.edu.

McGill University, Faculty of Graduate and Postdoctoral Studies, Faculty of Medicine, Department of Anatomy and Cell Biology, Montréal, QC H3A 2T5, Canada. Offers M Sc, PhD.

New York Chiropractic College, Program in Clinical Anatomy, Seneca Falls, NY 13148-0800. Offers MS. *Degree requirements:* For master's, thesis. *Entrance requirements:* For master's, minimum GPA of 3.0, DC, interview. *Faculty research:* Bone histology, biomechanics, craniofacial growth and anatomy, skeletal morphology.

New York Chiropractic College, Program in Human Anatomy and Physiology Instruction, Seneca Falls, NY 13148-0800. Offers MS. Postbaccalaureate distance learning degree programs offered.

New York Medical College, Graduate School of Basic Medical Sciences, Department of Cell Biology, Valhalla, NY 10595-1691. Offers cell biology and neuroscience (MS, PhD); MD/PhD. Part-time and evening/weekend programs available. *Faculty:* 16 full-time (2 women), 2 part-time/adjunct (1 woman). *Students:* 4 full-time (3 women); includes 1 minority (Asian, non-Hispanic/Latino). Average age 26. 2 applicants, 50% accepted, 0 enrolled. In 2011, 1 master's awarded. Terminal master's awarded for partial completion of doctoral program. *Degree requirements:* For master's, thesis; for doctorate, comprehensive exam, thesis/dissertation. *Entrance requirements:* For master's, GRE General Test, MCAT, DATGRE General, MCAT, DAT; for doctorate, GRE General Test. Additional exam requirements/recommendations for international students: Required—TOEFL. *Application deadline:* For fall admission, 7/1 priority date for domestic students, 5/1 for international students; for spring admission, 12/1 priority date for domestic students, 10/1 for international students. Applications are processed on a rolling basis. Application fee: $50 ($75 for international students). Electronic applications accepted. *Financial support:* In 2011–12, 4 fellowships (averaging $24,000 per year), 1 research assistantship with full tuition reimbursement (averaging $24,000 per year) were awarded; Federal Work-Study, institutionally sponsored loans, scholarships/grants, traineeships, tuition waivers (full), unspecified assistantships, and health benefits (for PhD candidates only) also available. Financial award applicants required to submit FAFSA. *Faculty research:* Mechanisms of growth control in skeletal muscle, cartilage differentiation, cytoskeletal functions, signal transduction pathways, neuronal development and plasticity. *Unit head:* Dr. Victor Fried, Director, 914-594-4036. *Application contact:* Valerie Romeo-Messana, Admission Coordinator, 914-594-4110, Fax: 914-594-4944, E-mail: v_romeomessana@nymc.edu.

The Ohio State University, College of Medicine, School of Biomedical Science, Department of Anatomy, Columbus, OH 43210. Offers MS, PhD. Terminal master's awarded for partial completion of doctoral program. *Degree requirements:* For doctorate, thesis/dissertation. *Entrance requirements:* For master's and doctorate, GRE General Test, GRE Subject Test in biology, biochemistry, chemistry, CIS, physics, or engineering. Additional exam requirements/recommendations for international students: Required—TOEFL (paper-based 600, computer-based 250) or Michigan English Language Assessment Battery (86). Electronic applications accepted. *Expenses:* Tuition, state resident: full-time $11,400. Tuition, nonresident: full-time $28,125. Tuition and fees vary according to course load, degree level, campus/location and program. *Faculty research:* Cell biology, biomechanical trauma, computer-assisted instruction.

Palmer College of Chiropractic, Division of Graduate Studies, Davenport, IA 52803-5287. Offers clinical research (MS). *Degree requirements:* For master's, 2 mentored practicum projects. *Entrance requirements:* For master's, GRE General Test, minimum GPA of 2.5, bachelor's and doctoral-level health professions degrees. Additional exam requirements/recommendations for international students: Required—TOEFL. Electronic applications accepted. *Expenses:* Contact institution. *Faculty research:* Chiropractic clinical research.

Penn State Hershey Medical Center, College of Medicine, Graduate School Programs in the Biomedical Sciences, Program in Anatomy, Hershey, PA 17033. Offers MS, PhD. *Students:* 15 full-time (11 women), 2 international. 26 applicants, 31% accepted, 6 enrolled. In 2011, 2 master's, 1 doctorate awarded. Terminal master's awarded for partial completion of doctoral program. *Degree requirements:* For master's, thesis or alternative; for doctorate, comprehensive exam, thesis/dissertation. *Entrance requirements:* For master's and doctorate, GRE General Test or MCAT, minimum GPA of 3.0. Additional exam requirements/recommendations for international students: Required—TOEFL (minimum score 500 paper-based; 213 computer-based). *Application deadline:* For fall admission, 1/31 priority date for domestic students, 2/1 for international students. Applications are processed on a rolling basis. Application fee: $65. Electronic applications accepted. *Financial support:* In 2011–12, research assistantships with full

tuition reimbursements (averaging $23,028 per year) were awarded; fellowships with full tuition reimbursements, scholarships/grants, health care benefits, and unspecified assistantships also available. Financial award applicants required to submit FAFSA. *Faculty research:* Developmental biology, stem cell, cancer-basic science and clinical application, wound healing, angiogenesis. *Unit head:* Dr. Patricia J. McLaughlin, Program Director, 717-531-0003, Fax: 717-531-0306, E-mail: anat-grad-hmc@psu.edu. *Application contact:* Dee Clarke, Program Assistant, 717-531-0003, Fax: 717-531-0306, E-mail: anat-grad-hmc@psu.edu. Web site: http://www.pennstatehershey.org/web/anatomy/home.

Purdue University, School of Veterinary Medicine and Graduate School, Graduate Programs in Veterinary Medicine, Department of Basic Medical Sciences, West Lafayette, IN 47907. Offers anatomy (MS, PhD); pharmacology (MS, PhD); physiology (MS, PhD). Part-time programs available. Terminal master's awarded for partial completion of doctoral program. *Degree requirements:* For master's, thesis; for doctorate, thesis/dissertation. *Entrance requirements:* For master's and doctorate, GRE General Test. Additional exam requirements/recommendations for international students: Required—TOEFL. Electronic applications accepted. *Faculty research:* Development and regeneration, tissue injury and shock, biomedical engineering, ovarian function, bone and cartilage biology, cell and molecular biology.

Queen's University at Kingston, School of Graduate Studies and Research, Faculty of Health Sciences, Department of Anatomy and Cell Biology, Kingston, ON K7L 3N6, Canada. Offers biology of reproduction (M Sc, PhD); cancer (M Sc, PhD); cardiovascular pathophysiology (M Sc, PhD); cell and molecular biology (M Sc, PhD); drug metabolism (M Sc, PhD); endocrinology (M Sc, PhD); motor control (M Sc, PhD); neural regeneration (M Sc, PhD); neurophysiology (M Sc, PhD). Part-time programs available. *Degree requirements:* For master's, thesis; for doctorate, one foreign language, comprehensive exam, thesis/dissertation. *Entrance requirements:* Additional exam requirements/recommendations for international students: Required—TOEFL. Electronic applications accepted. *Faculty research:* Human kinetics, neuroscience, reproductive biology, cardiovascular.

Rosalind Franklin University of Medicine and Science, School of Graduate and Postdoctoral Studies - Interdisciplinary Graduate Program in Biomedical Sciences, Department of Cell Biology and Anatomy, North Chicago, IL 60064-3095. Offers MS, PhD, MD/PhD. Terminal master's awarded for partial completion of doctoral program. *Degree requirements:* For master's, comprehensive exam, thesis, qualifying exam; for doctorate, comprehensive exam, thesis/dissertation, original research project. *Entrance requirements:* For master's and doctorate, GRE General Test, minimum GPA of 3.0. Additional exam requirements/recommendations for international students: Required—TOEFL, TWE. *Faculty research:* Neuroscience, molecular biology.

Rush University, Graduate College, Division of Anatomy and Cell Biology, Chicago, IL 60612-3832. Offers MS, PhD, MD/MS, MD/PhD. Terminal master's awarded for partial completion of doctoral program. *Degree requirements:* For master's, thesis; for doctorate, comprehensive exam, thesis/dissertation, preliminary exam, dissertation proposal. *Entrance requirements:* For master's, GRE General Test, minimum GPA of 3.0, bachelor's degree in biology or chemistry (preferred), interview; for doctorate, GRE General Test, minimum GPA of 3.0, interview. Additional exam requirements/recommendations for international students: Required—TOEFL. Electronic applications accepted. *Faculty research:* Incontinence following vaginal distension, knee replacement, biomimetric materials, injured spinal motoneurons, implant fixation.

Saint Louis University, Graduate Education and School of Medicine, Graduate Program in Biomedical Sciences and Graduate Education, Center for Anatomical Science and Education, St. Louis, MO 63103-2097. Offers anatomy (MS-R, PhD). *Degree requirements:* For master's, comprehensive exam, thesis; for doctorate, comprehensive exam, thesis/dissertation, departmental qualifying exams. *Entrance requirements:* For master's, GRE General Test, letters of recommendation, resume; for doctorate, GRE General Test, letters of recommendation, resumé, goal statement, transcripts. Additional exam requirements/recommendations for international students: Required—TOEFL (minimum score 525 paper-based; 194 computer-based). *Faculty research:* Neurodegenerative diseases, cerebellar cortical circuitry, neurogenesis, evolutionary anatomy.

State University of New York Upstate Medical University, College of Graduate Studies, Program in Cell and Developmental Biology, Syracuse, NY 13210-2334. Offers anatomy (MS, PhD); MD/PhD. Terminal master's awarded for partial completion of doctoral program. *Degree requirements:* For master's, thesis; for doctorate, comprehensive exam, thesis/dissertation. *Entrance requirements:* For master's, GRE General Test, interview; for doctorate, GRE General Test, telephone interview. Additional exam requirements/recommendations for international students: Required—TOEFL. Electronic applications accepted. *Faculty research:* Cancer, disorders of the nervous system, infectious diseases, diabetes/metabolic disorders/cardiovascular diseases.

Stony Brook University, State University of New York, Stony Brook University Medical Center, Health Sciences Center, School of Medicine and Graduate School, Graduate Programs in Medicine, Department of Anatomical Sciences, Stony Brook, NY 11794. Offers PhD. *Degree requirements:* For doctorate, comprehensive exam, thesis/dissertation. *Entrance requirements:* For doctorate, GRE General Test, GRE Subject Test, BA in life sciences, minimum GPA of 3.0. Additional exam requirements/recommendations for international students: Required—TOEFL. *Faculty research:* Biological membranes, biomechanics of locomotion, systematics and evolutionary history of primates.

Temple University, Health Sciences Center, School of Medicine and Graduate School, Graduate Programs in Medicine, Department of Anatomy and Cell Biology, Philadelphia, PA 19122-6096. Offers MS, PhD. *Faculty:* 21 full-time (6 women). *Students:* 15 full-time (5 women), 1 part-time (0 women); includes 2 minority (1 Black or African American, non-Hispanic/Latino; 1 Hispanic/Latino), 3 international. Average age 30. 9 applicants, 44% accepted, 2 enrolled. In 2011, 2 doctorates awarded. *Degree requirements:* For doctorate, thesis/dissertation, research seminars. *Entrance requirements:* For master's and doctorate, GRE General Test, GRE Subject Test, minimum GPA of 3.0. Additional exam requirements/recommendations for international students: Required—TOEFL. *Application deadline:* For fall admission, 1/15 for domestic students, 12/15 for international students; for spring admission, 9/1 for domestic students, 8/1 for international students. Application fee: $50. Electronic applications accepted. *Expenses:* Tuition, state resident: full-time $12,366; part-time $687 per credit hour. Tuition, nonresident: full-time $17,298; part-time $961 per credit hour. *Required fees:* $590; $213 per year. *Financial support:* Fellowships and Federal Work-Study available. Financial award application deadline: 1/15; financial award applicants required to submit FAFSA. *Faculty research:* Neurobiology, reproductive biology, cardiovascular system, musculoskeletal biology, developmental biology. *Unit head:* Dr. Steven Popoff, Chair, 215-707-3161, Fax: 215-707-2966, E-mail: spopoff@temple.edu. *Application contact:* Office of Admissions, 215-707-3656, Fax: 215-707-6932, E-mail: medadmissions@temple.edu. Web site: http://www.temple.edu/medicine/departments_centers/basic_science/anatomy.htm.

Universidad Central del Caribe, School of Medicine, Program in Biomedical Sciences, Bayamón, PR 00960-6032. Offers anatomy and cell biology (MA, MS); biochemistry (MS); biomedical sciences (MA); cellular and molecular biology (PhD); microbiology and immunology (MA, MS); pharmacology (MS); physiology (MS).

Universidad de Ciencias Medicas, Graduate Programs, San Jose, Costa Rica. Offers dermatology (SP); family health (MS); health service center administration (MHA); human anatomy (MS); medical and surgery (MD); occupational medicine (MS); pharmacy (Pharm D). Part-time programs available. *Degree requirements:* For master's, thesis; for doctorate and SP, comprehensive exam. *Entrance requirements:* For master's, MD or bachelor's degree; for doctorate, admissions test; for SP, admissions test, MD.

Université Laval, Faculty of Medicine, Post-Professional Programs in Medical Studies, Québec, QC G1K 7P4, Canada. Offers anatomy–pathology (DESS); anesthesiology (DESS); cardiology (DESS); care of older people (Diploma); clinical research (DESS); community health (DESS); dermatology (DESS); diagnostic radiology (DESS); emergency medicine (Diploma); family medicine (DESS); general surgery (DESS); geriatrics (DESS); hematology (DESS); internal medicine (DESS); maternal and fetal medicine (Diploma); medical biochemistry (DESS); medical microbiology and infectious diseases (DESS); medical oncology (DESS); nephrology (DESS); neurology (DESS); neurosurgery (DESS); obstetrics and gynecology (DESS); ophthalmology (DESS); orthopedic surgery (DESS); oto-rhino-laryngology (DESS); palliative medicine (Diploma); pediatrics (DESS); plastic surgery (DESS); psychiatry (DESS); pulmonary medicine (DESS); radiology–oncology (DESS); thoracic surgery (DESS); urology (DESS). *Degree requirements:* For other advanced degree, comprehensive exam. *Entrance requirements:* For degree, knowledge of French. Electronic applications accepted.

University at Buffalo, the State University of New York, Graduate School, School of Medicine and Biomedical Sciences, Graduate Programs in Medicine and Biomedical Sciences, Department of Pathology and Anatomical Sciences, Buffalo, NY 14260. Offers anatomical sciences (MA, PhD); pathology (MA, PhD). Part-time programs available. *Faculty:* 14 full-time (3 women). *Students:* 7 full-time (2 women); includes 2 minority (both Asian, non-Hispanic/Latino), 2 international. Average age 29. 11 applicants, 27% accepted, 1 enrolled. In 2011, 3 doctorates awarded. *Degree requirements:* For master's, thesis; for doctorate, comprehensive exam, thesis/dissertation. *Entrance requirements:* For master's, GRE, MCAT, or DAT, 3 letters of recommendation; for doctorate, GRE, 3 letters of recommendation. Additional exam requirements/recommendations for international students: Required—TOEFL (minimum score 600 paper-based; 250 computer-based; 100 iBT). *Application deadline:* For fall admission, 3/1 priority date for domestic students, 3/1 for international students. Application fee: $50. *Financial support:* In 2011–12, 2 students received support, including 1 fellowship with full tuition reimbursement available (averaging $24,000 per year), 1 research assistantship with full tuition reimbursement available (averaging $22,000 per year); health care benefits also available. Financial award application deadline: 2/1; financial award applicants required to submit FAFSA. *Faculty research:* Immunopathology-immunobiology, experimental hypertension, neuromuscular disease, molecular pathology, cell motility and cytoskeleton. *Unit head:* Dr. John E. Tomaszewski, Chairman, 716-829-2847, Fax: 716-829-2086, E-mail: johntoma@buffalo.edu. *Application contact:* Patricia Simons, Graduate Program Secretary, 716-829-2846, Fax: 716-829-2086, E-mail: pesimons@buffalo.edu. Web site: http://wings.buffalo.edu/smbs/path/.

The University of Arizona, College of Medicine, Department of Cell Biology and Anatomy, Tucson, AZ 85721. Offers PhD. *Faculty:* 15 full-time (3 women), 1 (woman) part-time/adjunct. *Students:* 15 full-time (8 women); includes 5 minority (1 Black or African American, non-Hispanic/Latino; 1 Asian, non-Hispanic/Latino; 1 Hispanic/Latino; 2 Two or more races, non-Hispanic/Latino), 2 international. Average age 29. 30 applicants, 10% accepted. In 2011, 3 degrees awarded. *Degree requirements:* For doctorate, thesis/dissertation. *Entrance requirements:* For doctorate, GRE General Test. *Application deadline:* For fall admission, 1/15 priority date for domestic students. Application fee: $75. *Expenses:* Tuition, state resident: full-time $10,840. Tuition, nonresident: full-time $25,802. *Financial support:* In 2011–12, 11 research assistantships with partial tuition reimbursements (averaging $25,000 per year) were awarded; fellowships with full and partial tuition reimbursements, teaching assistantships, institutionally sponsored loans, scholarships/grants, traineeships, tuition waivers (full), and unspecified assistantships also available. Support available to part-time students. Financial award application deadline: 1/15. *Faculty research:* Heart development, neural development, cellular toxicology and microcirculation; membrane traffic and cytoskeleton; cell-surface receptors. *Total annual research expenditures:* $4.6 million. *Unit head:* Dr. Carol Gregorio, Head, 520-626-8113, Fax: 520-626-2097, E-mail: gregorio@email.arizona.edu. *Application contact:* Dr. Jean M. Wilson, Chairperson, Graduate Studies Committee, 520-626-2553, Fax: 520-626-2097. Web site: http://www.cba.arizona.edu/.

University of Arkansas for Medical Sciences, Graduate School, Graduate Programs in Biomedical Sciences, Department of Neurobiology and Developmental Sciences, Little Rock, AR 72205-7199. Offers MS, PhD, MD/PhD. *Degree requirements:* For master's, thesis; for doctorate, thesis/dissertation. *Entrance requirements:* For master's, GRE General Test; for doctorate, GRE General Test, GRE Subject Test. Additional exam requirements/recommendations for international students: Required—TOEFL. *Faculty research:* Cellular and molecular neuroscience, translation neuroscience.

The University of British Columbia, Faculty of Medicine, Department of Cellular and Physiological Sciences, Division of Anatomy and Cell Biology, Vancouver, BC V6T 1Z1, Canada. Offers M Sc, PhD. *Degree requirements:* For master's, thesis, oral defense; for doctorate, comprehensive exam, thesis/dissertation, oral defense. *Entrance requirements:* Additional exam requirements/recommendations for international students: Required—TOEFL (minimum score 550 paper-based; 213 computer-based), IELTS (minimum score 6.2). Electronic applications accepted. *Faculty research:* Cell and developmental biology, membrane biophysics, cellular immunology, cancer, fetal alcohol syndrome.

University of California, Irvine, School of Medicine and School of Biological Sciences, Department of Anatomy and Neurobiology, Irvine, CA 92697. Offers biological sciences (MS, PhD); MD/PhD. *Students:* 25 full-time (15 women), 4 part-time (all women); includes 11 minority (1 Black or African American, non-Hispanic/Latino; 5 Asian, non-Hispanic/Latino; 5 Hispanic/Latino), 2 international. Average age 28. 1 applicant, 100% accepted, 1 enrolled. In 2011, 1 master's, 6 doctorates awarded. *Degree requirements:* For doctorate, thesis/dissertation. *Entrance requirements:* For master's and doctorate, GRE General Test, GRE Subject Test. Additional exam requirements/recommendations for international students: Required—TOEFL (minimum score 550 paper-based; 213 computer-based). *Application deadline:* For fall admission, 1/15 priority date for domestic students, 1/15 for international students. Applications are processed on a rolling basis. Application fee: $80 ($100 for international students). Electronic applications accepted. *Financial support:* Fellowships, research assistantships with full tuition reimbursements, teaching assistantships, institutionally sponsored loans, traineeships, health care benefits, and unspecified assistantships available. Financial award application deadline: 3/1; financial award applicants required to submit FAFSA.

Faculty research: Neurotransmitter immunocytochemistry, intracellular physiology, molecular neurobiology, forebrain organization and development, structure and function of sensory and motor systems. *Unit head:* Prof. Ivan Soltesz, Professor and Chair, 949-824-3957, Fax: 949-824-9860, E-mail: isoltesz@uci.edu. *Application contact:* Debra S. Caputo, Chief Administrative Officer, 949-824-6340, Fax: 949-824-8549, E-mail: dscaputo@uci.edu.

University of California, Los Angeles, David Geffen School of Medicine and Graduate Division, Graduate Programs in Medicine, Department of Neurobiology, Los Angeles, CA 90095. Offers PhD. *Faculty:* 21 full-time (0 women). *Students:* 9 full-time (6 women); includes 2 minority (1 Asian, non-Hispanic/Latino; 1 Hispanic/Latino), 1 international. Average age 27. In 2011, 6 degrees awarded. *Median time to degree:* Of those who began their doctoral program in fall 2003, 100% received their degree in 8 years or less. *Degree requirements:* For doctorate, thesis/dissertation, oral and written qualifying exams. *Entrance requirements:* For doctorate, GRE General Test, GRE Subject Test, bachelor's degree in physical or biological science. Application fee: $70 ($90 for international students). Electronic applications accepted. *Financial support:* In 2011–12, 14 fellowships, 12 research assistantships, 3 teaching assistantships were awarded; Federal Work-Study, institutionally sponsored loans, scholarships/grants, and tuition waivers (full and partial) also available. Financial award application deadline: 3/1. *Faculty research:* Neuroendocrinology, neurophysiology. *Unit head:* Dr. Marie-Francoise Chesselet, Chair, 310-267-1781, Fax: 310-267-1786, E-mail: mchesselet@mednet.ucla.edu. *Application contact:* UCLA ACCESS Coordinator, 310-206-1845, Fax: 310-206-1636, E-mail: uclaaccess@mednet.ucla.edu.

University of California, San Francisco, Graduate Division, Biomedical Sciences Graduate Group, San Francisco, CA 94143. Offers anatomy (PhD); endocrinology (PhD); experimental pathology (PhD); physiology (PhD). *Degree requirements:* For doctorate, thesis/dissertation. *Entrance requirements:* For doctorate, GRE General Test.

University of Chicago, Division of Biological Sciences, Darwinian Sciences Cluster: Ecological, Integrative and Evolutionary Biology, Department of Organismal Biology and Anatomy, Chicago, IL 60637-1513. Offers integrative biology (PhD). *Degree requirements:* For doctorate, thesis/dissertation, ethics class, 2 teaching assistantships. *Entrance requirements:* For doctorate, GRE General Test. Additional exam requirements/recommendations for international students: Required—TOEFL (minimum score 600 paper-based; 250 computer-based; 104 iBT), IELTS (minimum score 7). Electronic applications accepted. *Faculty research:* Ecological physiology, evolution of fossil reptiles, vertebrate paleontology.

University of Georgia, College of Veterinary Medicine, Department of Veterinary Anatomy and Radiology, Athens, GA 30602. Offers veterinary anatomy (MS). *Faculty:* 7 full-time (3 women). *Students:* 2 full-time (1 woman). Average age 31. 1 applicant, 100% accepted, 1 enrolled. *Degree requirements:* For master's, thesis. *Entrance requirements:* For master's, GRE General Test. *Application deadline:* For fall admission, 7/1 priority date for domestic students; for spring admission, 11/15 for domestic students. Application fee: $50. Electronic applications accepted. *Financial support:* Fellowships, research assistantships, teaching assistantships, and unspecified assistantships available. *Unit head:* Dr. Steven D. Holladay, Head, 706-542-8305, E-mail: sdholl@uga.edu. *Application contact:* Dr. Sharon Crowell-Davis, Graduate Coordinator, 706-542-8343, Fax: 706-542-0051, E-mail: scrowell@uga.edu. Web site: http://www.vet.uga.edu/var/.

University of Guelph, Ontario Veterinary College and Graduate Studies, Graduate Programs in Veterinary Sciences, Department of Biomedical Sciences, Guelph, ON N1G 2W1, Canada. Offers morphology (M Sc, DV Sc, PhD); neuroscience (M Sc, DV Sc, PhD); pharmacology (M Sc, DV Sc, PhD); physiology (M Sc, DV Sc, PhD); toxicology (M Sc, DV Sc, PhD). Part-time programs available. *Degree requirements:* For master's, thesis; for doctorate, comprehensive exam, thesis/dissertation. *Entrance requirements:* For master's, honors B Sc, minimum 75% average in last 20 courses; for doctorate, M Sc with thesis from accredited institution. Additional exam requirements/recommendations for international students: Required—TOEFL (minimum score 550 paper-based; 213 computer-based; 89 iBT). Electronic applications accepted. *Faculty research:* Cellular morphology; endocrine, vascular and reproductive physiology; clinical pharmacology; veterinary toxicology; developmental biology, neuroscience.

University of Illinois at Chicago, College of Medicine and Graduate College, Graduate Programs in Medicine, Department of Anatomy and Cell Biology, Chicago, IL 60612. Offers neuroscience (PhD), including cellular and systems neuroscience and cell biology; MD/PhD. *Degree requirements:* For doctorate, preliminary oral examination, dissertation and oral defense. *Entrance requirements:* For doctorate, GRE General Test, minimum GPA of 2.75, 3 letters of recommendation, personal statement. Additional exam requirements/recommendations for international students: Required—TOEFL (minimum score 550 paper-based; 213 computer-based). Electronic applications accepted. *Faculty research:* Synapses, axonal transport, neurodegenerative diseases.

The University of Iowa, Roy J. and Lucille A. Carver College of Medicine and Graduate College, Graduate Programs in Medicine, Department of Anatomy and Cell Biology, Iowa City, IA 52242-1316. Offers PhD. *Faculty:* 22 full-time (4 women). *Students:* 14 full-time (6 women); includes 2 minority (1 American Indian or Alaska Native, non-Hispanic/Latino; 1 Asian, non-Hispanic/Latino), 1 international. Average age 28. 113 applicants, 0% accepted. In 2011, 2 doctorates awarded. *Degree requirements:* For doctorate, comprehensive exam, thesis/dissertation. *Entrance requirements:* For doctorate, GRE General Test, minimum GPA of 3.0. Additional exam requirements/recommendations for international students: Required—TOEFL (minimum score 600 paper-based; 250 computer-based; 100 iBT). *Application deadline:* For fall admission, 1/15 priority date for domestic students, 1/15 for international students. Applications are processed on a rolling basis. Application fee: $60 ($100 for international students). Electronic applications accepted. *Financial support:* In 2011–12, 14 students received support, including 1 fellowship with full tuition reimbursement available (averaging $25,000 per year), 12 research assistantships with full tuition reimbursements available (averaging $25,000 per year), teaching assistantships with full tuition reimbursements available (averaging $25,000 per year); institutionally sponsored loans, scholarships/grants, and health care benefits also available. Financial award application deadline: 3/1. *Faculty research:* Biology of differentiation and transformation, developmental and vascular cell biology, neurobiology. *Total annual research expenditures:* $3.4 million. *Unit head:* Dr. John F. Engelhardt, Professor and Head, 319-335-7744, Fax: 319-335-7770, E-mail: john-engelhardt@uiowa.edu. *Application contact:* Julie A. Stark, Program Assistant, 319-335-7744, Fax: 319-335-7770, E-mail: julie-stark@uiowa.edu. Web site: http://www.anatomy.uiowa.edu/.

The University of Kansas, University of Kansas Medical Center, School of Medicine, Department of Anatomy and Cell Biology, Kansas City, KS 66160. Offers MA, PhD, MD/PhD. *Faculty:* 33. *Students:* 14 full-time (9 women), 1 (woman) part-time; includes 2 minority (1 Asian, non-Hispanic/Latino; 1 Hispanic/Latino), 5 international. Average age 27. In 2011, 1 doctorate awarded. Terminal master's awarded for partial completion of doctoral program. *Degree requirements:* For doctorate, comprehensive exam, thesis/dissertation. *Entrance requirements:* For doctorate, GRE. Additional exam requirements/recommendations for international students: Required—TOEFL. *Application deadline:* For fall admission, 1/15 priority date for domestic students.

Applications are processed on a rolling basis. Application fee: $0. Electronic applications accepted. Tuition and fees vary according to course load, campus/location, program and reciprocity agreements. *Financial support:* Fellowships, research assistantships with full tuition reimbursements, teaching assistantships with full tuition reimbursements, institutionally sponsored loans, health care benefits, and unspecified assistantships available. Financial award application deadline: 2/14; financial award applicants required to submit FAFSA. *Faculty research:* Development of the synapse and neuromuscular junction, pain perception and diabetic neuropathies, cardiovascular and kidney development, reproductive immunology, post-fertilization signaling events. *Total annual research expenditures:* $10.5 million. *Unit head:* Dr. Dale R. Abrahamson, Chairman, 913-588-7000, Fax: 913-588-2710, E-mail: dabrahamson@kumc.edu. *Application contact:* Dr. Brenda Rongish, Associate Professor, 913-588-1878, Fax: 913-588-2710, E-mail: brongish@kumc.edu. Web site: http://www.kumc.edu/school-of-medicine/anatomy-and-cell-biology.html.

University of Kentucky, Graduate School, Graduate School Programs from the College of Medicine, Program in Anatomy and Neurobiology, Lexington, KY 40506-0032. Offers anatomy (PhD). *Degree requirements:* For doctorate, comprehensive exam, thesis/dissertation. *Entrance requirements:* For doctorate, GRE General Test, minimum undergraduate GPA of 2.75. Additional exam requirements/recommendations for international students: Required—TOEFL (minimum score 550 paper-based; 213 computer-based). Electronic applications accepted. *Faculty research:* Neuroendocrinology, developmental neurobiology, neurotrophic substances, neural plasticity and trauma, neurobiology of aging.

University of Louisville, School of Medicine, Department of Anatomical Sciences and Neurobiology, Louisville, KY 40292-0001. Offers MS, PhD, MD/PhD. Terminal master's awarded for partial completion of doctoral program. *Degree requirements:* For master's, thesis; for doctorate, comprehensive exam, thesis/dissertation. *Entrance requirements:* For master's and doctorate, GRE General Test (minimum score of 1000 verbal and quantitative), minimum GPA of 3.0. Additional exam requirements/recommendations for international students: Required—TOEFL. Electronic applications accepted. *Expenses:* Tuition, state resident: full-time $9692; part-time $539 per credit hour. Tuition, nonresident: full-time $20,168; part-time $1121 per credit hour. Tuition and fees vary according to program and reciprocity agreements. *Faculty research:* Human adult neural stem cells, development and plasticity of the nervous system, organization of the dorsal thalamus, electrophysiology/neuroanatomy of central neurons mediating control of reproductive and pelvic organs, normal neural mechanisms and plasticity following injury and/or chronic pain, differentiation and regeneration of motor neurons and oligodendrocytes.

University of Manitoba, Faculty of Medicine and Faculty of Graduate Studies, Graduate Programs in Medicine, Department of Human Anatomy and Cell Science, Winnipeg, MB R3T 2N2, Canada. Offers M Sc, PhD. *Degree requirements:* For master's, thesis; for doctorate, one foreign language, thesis/dissertation.

University of Mississippi Medical Center, School of Graduate Studies in the Health Sciences, Department of Anatomy, Jackson, MS 39216-4505. Offers MS, PhD, MD/PhD. Terminal master's awarded for partial completion of doctoral program. *Degree requirements:* For master's, thesis; for doctorate, comprehensive exam, thesis/dissertation, first authored publication. *Entrance requirements:* For master's and doctorate, GRE General Test, minimum GPA of 3.0. Additional exam requirements/recommendations for international students: Required—TOEFL. *Faculty research:* Systems neuroscience with emphasis on motor and sensory, cell biology with emphasis on cell-matrix interactions, development of cardiovascular system, biology of glial cells.

University of Missouri, School of Medicine and Graduate School, Graduate Programs in Medicine, Department of Pathology and Anatomical Sciences, Columbia, MO 65211. Offers MS. *Faculty:* 22 full-time (8 women), 7 part-time/adjunct (3 women). *Students:* 3 full-time (1 woman), 1 part-time (0 women), 1 international. Average age 28. 4 applicants, 50% accepted, 2 enrolled. In 2011, 3 degrees awarded. *Entrance requirements:* For master's, GRE (minimum Verbal and Analytical score of 1250), letters of recommendation, minimum GPA of 3.5. Additional exam requirements/recommendations for international students: Required—TOEFL. *Expenses:* Tuition, state resident: full-time $5881. Tuition, nonresident: full-time $15,183. *Required fees:* $952. Tuition and fees vary according to campus/location and program. *Faculty research:* Anatomic pathology, cancer biology, diabetes, integrative anatomy, laboratory medicine, neurobiology, tissue procurement core. *Unit head:* Dr. Douglas Anthony, Chair, 573-882-1205, E-mail: anthonydc@missouri.edu. *Application contact:* Dr. Carol V. Ward, Director of Graduate Studies, 573-884-7303, E-mail: wardcv@missouri.edu. Web site: http://pathology-anatomy.missouri.edu/.

University of Nebraska Medical Center, Graduate Studies, Department of Genetics, Cell Biology and Anatomy, Omaha, NE 68198. Offers MS, PhD. Part-time programs available. Terminal master's awarded for partial completion of doctoral program. *Degree requirements:* For master's, comprehensive exam, thesis; for doctorate, comprehensive exam, thesis/dissertation. *Entrance requirements:* For master's and doctorate, GRE General Test. Additional exam requirements/recommendations for international students: Required—TOEFL (minimum score 550 paper-based; 213 computer-based). Electronic applications accepted. *Faculty research:* Hematology, immunology, developmental biology, genetics cancer biology, neuroscience.

University of North Dakota, Graduate School and Graduate School, Graduate Programs in Medicine, Department of Anatomy and Cell Biology, Grand Forks, ND 58202. Offers MS, PhD. *Degree requirements:* For master's, thesis, final exam; for doctorate, comprehensive exam, thesis/dissertation, final exam. *Entrance requirements:* For master's and doctorate, GRE General Test, minimum GPA of 3.0. Additional exam requirements/recommendations for international students: Required—TOEFL (minimum score 550 paper-based; 213 computer-based; 79 iBT), IELTS (minimum score 6.5). Electronic applications accepted. *Faculty research:* Coronary vessel, vasculogenesis, acellular glomerular and retinal microvessel membranes, ependymal cells, cardiac muscle.

University of North Texas Health Science Center at Fort Worth, Graduate School of Biomedical Sciences, Fort Worth, TX 76107-2699. Offers anatomy and cell biology (MS, PhD); biochemistry and molecular biology (MS, PhD); biomedical sciences (MS, PhD); biotechnology (MS); forensic genetics (MS); integrative physiology (MS, PhD); medical science (MS); microbiology and immunology (MS, PhD); pharmacology (MS, PhD); science education (MS); DO/MS; DO/PhD. Terminal master's awarded for partial completion of doctoral program. *Degree requirements:* For master's, thesis; for doctorate, thesis/dissertation. *Entrance requirements:* For master's and doctorate, GRE General Test. Additional exam requirements/recommendations for international students: Required—TOEFL. *Expenses:* Contact institution. *Faculty research:* Alzheimer's disease, aging, eye diseases, cancer, cardiovascular disease.

University of Prince Edward Island, Atlantic Veterinary College, Graduate Program in Veterinary Medicine, Charlottetown, PE C1A 4P3, Canada. Offers anatomy (M Sc, PhD); bacteriology (M Sc, PhD); clinical pharmacology (M Sc, PhD); clinical sciences (M Sc, PhD); epidemiology (M Sc, PhD), including reproduction; fish health (M Sc, PhD); food animal nutrition (M Sc, PhD); immunology (M Sc, PhD); microanatomy (M Sc, PhD); parasitology (M Sc, PhD); pathology (M Sc, PhD); pharmacology (M Sc, PhD);

Anatomy

physiology (M Sc, PhD); toxicology (M Sc, PhD); veterinary science (M Vet Sc); virology (M Sc, PhD). Part-time programs available. *Degree requirements:* For master's, thesis; for doctorate, thesis/dissertation. *Entrance requirements:* For master's, DVM, B Sc honors degree, or equivalent; for doctorate, M Sc. Additional exam requirements/recommendations for international students: Required—TOEFL (minimum score 550 paper-based; 213 computer-based; 80 iBT). *Expenses:* Contact institution. *Faculty research:* Animal health management, infectious diseases, fin fish and shellfish health, basic biomedical sciences, ecosystem health.

University of Puerto Rico, Medical Sciences Campus, School of Medicine, Division of Graduate Studies, Department of Anatomy and Neurobiology, San Juan, PR 00936-5067. Offers anatomy (MS, PhD). *Degree requirements:* For master's, one foreign language, comprehensive exam, thesis; for doctorate, one foreign language, comprehensive exam, thesis/dissertation. *Entrance requirements:* For master's and doctorate, GRE General Test, GRE Subject Test, interview, minimum GPA of 3.0, 3 letters of recommendation. Electronic applications accepted. *Faculty research:* Neurobiology, primatology, visual system, muscle structure.

University of Rochester, School of Medicine and Dentistry, Graduate Programs in Medicine and Dentistry, Department of Neurobiology and Anatomy, Programs in Neurobiology and Anatomy, Rochester, NY 14627. Offers PhD, MD/MS. *Degree requirements:* For doctorate, thesis/dissertation, qualifying exam. *Entrance requirements:* For doctorate, GRE General Test. *Expenses: Tuition:* Full-time $41,040.

University of Saskatchewan, College of Medicine, Department of Anatomy and Cell Biology, Saskatoon, SK S7N 5A2, Canada. Offers M Sc, PhD. *Degree requirements:* For master's, thesis; for doctorate, thesis/dissertation. *Entrance requirements:* Additional exam requirements/recommendations for international students: Required—TOEFL.

University of Saskatchewan, Western College of Veterinary Medicine and College of Graduate Studies and Research, Graduate Programs in Veterinary Medicine, Department of Veterinary Biomedical Sciences, Saskatoon, SK S7N 5A2, Canada. Offers veterinary anatomy (M Sc); veterinary biomedical sciences (M Vet Sc); veterinary physiological sciences (M Sc, PhD). *Degree requirements:* For master's, thesis; for doctorate, comprehensive exam (for some programs), thesis/dissertation. *Entrance requirements:* Additional exam requirements/recommendations for international students: Required—TOEFL (minimum score 80 iBT); Recommended—IELTS (minimum score 6.5). Electronic applications accepted. *Faculty research:* Toxicology, animal reproduction, pharmacology, chloride channels, pulmonary pathobiology.

The University of Tennessee, Graduate School, College of Agricultural Sciences and Natural Resources, Department of Animal Science, Knoxville, TN 37996. Offers animal anatomy (PhD); breeding (MS, PhD); management (MS, PhD); nutrition (MS, PhD); physiology (MS, PhD). Part-time programs available. *Degree requirements:* For master's, thesis; for doctorate, thesis/dissertation. *Entrance requirements:* For master's and doctorate, GRE General Test, minimum GPA of 2.7. Additional exam requirements/recommendations for international students: Required—TOEFL. Electronic applications accepted. *Expenses:* Tuition, state resident: full-time $8332; part-time $464 per credit hour. Tuition, nonresident: full-time $25,174; part-time $1400 per credit hour. *Required fees:* $1162; $56 per credit hour. Tuition and fees vary according to program.

University of Utah, School of Medicine and Graduate School, Graduate Programs in Medicine, Department of Neurobiology and Anatomy, Salt Lake City, UT 84112-1107. Offers PhD. Part-time programs available. Terminal master's awarded for partial completion of doctoral program. *Degree requirements:* For doctorate, comprehensive exam, thesis/dissertation. *Entrance requirements:* For doctorate, GRE General Test. Additional exam requirements/recommendations for international students: Required—TOEFL. *Faculty research:* Neuroscience, neuroanatomy, developmental neurobiology, neurogenetics.

The University of Western Ontario, Faculty of Graduate Studies, Biosciences Division, Department of Biology, London, ON N6A 5B8, Canada. Offers M Sc, PhD. *Degree requirements:* For master's, thesis; for doctorate, comprehensive exam, thesis/dissertation. *Entrance requirements:* For master's, honors degree or equivalent in biological sciences; for doctorate, master's degree. Additional exam requirements/recommendations for international students: Required—TOEFL. *Faculty research:* Cell and molecular biology, developmental biology, neuroscience, immunobiology and cancer.

Virginia Commonwealth University, Medical College of Virginia-Professional Programs, School of Medicine, School of Medicine Graduate Programs, Department of Anatomy and Neurobiology, Program in Anatomy and Neurobiology, Richmond, VA 23284-9005. Offers PhD. *Accreditation:* APTA. *Degree requirements:* For doctorate, thesis/dissertation. *Entrance requirements:* For doctorate, GRE, MCAT or DAT. Electronic applications accepted. *Expenses:* Tuition, state resident: full-time $9133; part-time $507 per credit. Tuition, nonresident: full-time $18,777; part-time $1043 per credit. *Required fees:* $77 per credit. Tuition and fees vary according to degree level, campus/location, program and student level.

Virginia Commonwealth University, Program in Pre-Medical Basic Health Sciences, Richmond, VA 23284-9005. Offers anatomy (CBHS); biochemistry (CBHS); human genetics (CBHS); microbiology (CBHS); pharmacology (CBHS); physiology (CBHS). *Entrance requirements:* For degree, GRE, MCAT or DAT, course work in organic chemistry, minimum undergraduate GPA of 2.8. Additional exam requirements/recommendations for international students: Required—TOEFL (minimum score 600 paper-based). Electronic applications accepted. *Expenses:* Tuition, state resident: full-time $9133; part-time $507 per credit. Tuition, nonresident: full-time $18,777; part-time $1043 per credit. *Required fees:* $77 per credit. Tuition and fees vary according to degree level, campus/location, program and student level.

Wake Forest University, School of Medicine and Graduate School of Arts and Sciences, Graduate Programs in Medicine, Department of Neurobiology and Anatomy, Winston-Salem, NC 27109. Offers PhD, MD/PhD. *Degree requirements:* For doctorate, thesis/dissertation. *Entrance requirements:* For doctorate, GRE General Test. Additional exam requirements/recommendations for international students: Required—TOEFL. Electronic applications accepted. *Faculty research:* Sensory neurobiology, reproductive endocrinology, regulatory processes in cell biology.

Wayne State University, School of Medicine, Department of Anatomy and Cell Biology, Detroit, MI 48202. Offers anatomy (MS, PhD); MD/PhD. *Students:* 9 full-time (6 women), 1 part-time (0 women), 5 international. Average age 30. 11 applicants, 9% accepted, 1 enrolled. *Degree requirements:* For doctorate, thesis/dissertation. *Entrance requirements:* For master's and doctorate, GRE General Test, minimum GPA of 3.0 undergraduate and in life science coursework, research experience, three letters of faculty recommendation, personal statement, resume. Additional exam requirements/recommendations for international students: Required—TOEFL (minimum score 600 paper-based; 260 computer-based; 100 iBT); Recommended—TWE (minimum score 6). *Application deadline:* For fall admission, 6/1 priority date for domestic students, 5/1 for international students; for winter admission, 10/1 priority date for domestic students, 9/1 for international students; for spring admission, 2/1 priority date for domestic students, 1/1 for international students. Applications are processed on a rolling basis. Application fee: $50. Electronic applications accepted. *Expenses:* Tuition, state resident: part-time $512.85 per credit. Tuition, nonresident: part-time $1132.65 per credit. *Required fees:* $26.60 per credit. $199.65 per semester. Tuition and fees vary according to course load and program. *Financial support:* In 2011–12, 6 students received support, including 2 fellowships with tuition reimbursements available (averaging $33,516 per year), 8 research assistantships with tuition reimbursements available (averaging $22,389 per year); teaching assistantships with tuition reimbursements available, Federal Work-Study, scholarships/grants, and unspecified assistantships also available. Financial award application deadline: 2/1. *Faculty research:* Inflammation and inflammatory mediators, neuronal plasticity, neural connections and glia, vision and visual neurosciences, cell signaling and receptor interactions. *Unit head:* Dr. Linda Hazlett, Chair, 313-577-1061, E-mail: lhazlett@med.wayne.edu. *Application contact:* Dr. Paul D. Walker, Graduate Director, 313-577-5678, E-mail: pdwalker@med.wayne.edu. Web site: http://anatomy.med.wayne.edu/.

Wright State University, School of Graduate Studies, College of Science and Mathematics, Department of Neuroscience, Cell Biology, and Physiology, Dayton, OH 45435. Offers anatomy (MS); physiology and biophysics (MS). *Degree requirements:* For master's, thesis optional. *Entrance requirements:* Additional exam requirements/recommendations for international students: Required—TOEFL. *Faculty research:* Reproductive cell biology, neurobiology of pain, neurohistochemistry.

Youngstown State University, Graduate School, College of Science, Technology, Engineering and Mathematics, Department of Biological Sciences, Youngstown, OH 44555-0001. Offers environmental biology (MS); molecular biology, microbiology, and genetic (MS); physiology and anatomy (MS). Part-time programs available. *Degree requirements:* For master's, comprehensive exam, thesis, oral review. *Entrance requirements:* For master's, GRE General Test, minimum GPA of 2.7. Additional exam requirements/recommendations for international students: Required—TOEFL. *Faculty research:* Cell biology, neurophysiology, molecular biology, neurobiology, gene regulation.

Section 3
Biochemistry

This section contains a directory of institutions offering graduate work in biochemistry, followed by an in-depth entry submitted by an institution that chose to prepare a detailed program description. Additional information about programs listed in the directory but not augmented by an in-depth entry may be obtained by writing directly to the dean of a graduate school or chair of a department at the address given in the directory.

For programs offering related work, see also in this book *Allied Health; Biological and Biomedical Sciences; Biophysics; Botany and Plant Biology; Cell, Molecular, and Structural Biology; Genetics, Developmental Biology, and Reproductive Biology; Microbiological Sciences; Neuroscience and Neurobiology; Nutrition; Pathology and Pathobiology; Pharmacology and Toxicology; Pharmacy and Pharmaceutical Sciences;* and *Physiology.* In the other guides in this series:

Graduate Programs in the Physical Sciences, Mathematics, Agricultural Sciences, the Environment & Natural Resources

See *Agricultural and Food Sciences, Chemistry,* and *Physics*

Graduate Programs in Engineering & Applied Sciences

See *Agricultural Engineering and Bioengineering, Biomedical Engineering and Biotechnology, Chemical Engineering,* and *Materials Sciences and Engineering*

CONTENTS

Biochemistry

Albert Einstein College of Medicine, Graduate Division of Biomedical Sciences, Department of Biochemistry, Bronx, NY 10461-1602. Offers PhD, MD/PhD. *Degree requirements:* For doctorate, thesis/dissertation. *Entrance requirements:* For doctorate, GRE General Test. Additional exam requirements/recommendations for international students: Required—TOEFL. *Faculty research:* Biochemical mechanisms, enzymology, protein chemistry, bio-organic chemistry, molecular genetics.

American University of Beirut, Graduate Programs, Faculty of Medicine, Beirut, Lebanon. Offers anatomy, cell biology and human morphology (MS); biochemistry and medical genetics (MS); biomedical sciences (PhD); experimental pathology, immunology and microbiology (MS); medicine (MD); neuroscience (MS); pharmacology and toxicology (MS). Part-time programs available. *Faculty:* 232 full-time (58 women), 68 part-time/adjunct (7 women). *Students:* 346 full-time (135 women), 69 part-time (57 women). Average age 23. In 2011, 20 master's, 82 doctorates awarded. *Degree requirements:* For master's, one foreign language, comprehensive exam, thesis (for some programs). *Entrance requirements:* For master's, letter of recommendation; for doctorate, MCAT, bachelor's degree. Additional exam requirements/recommendations for international students: Required—TOEFL (minimum score 600 paper-based; 250 computer-based; 100 iBT), IELTS (minimum score 7.5). *Application deadline:* For fall admission, 4/30 for domestic and international students; for spring admission, 11/1 for domestic and international students. Application fee: $50. *Expenses: Tuition:* Full-time $12,780; part-time $710 per credit. Tuition and fees vary according to course load and program. *Financial support:* In 2011–12, 19 students received support. Career-related internships or fieldwork, institutionally sponsored loans, scholarships/grants, health care benefits, and unspecified assistantships available. Financial award application deadline: 2/2. *Faculty research:* Cancer research (targeted therapy, mechanisms of leukemogenesis, tumor cell extravasation and metastasis, cancer stem cells); stem cell research (regenerative medicine, drug discovery); genetic research (neurogenetics, hereditary cardiomyopathy, hemoglobinopathies, pharmacogenomics, proteomics); neuroscience research (pain, neurodegenerative disorder); metabolism (inflammation and metabolism, metabolic disorder, diabetes mellitus); vascular and renal biology, signal transduction. *Total annual research expenditures:* $2.3 million. *Unit head:* Dr. Mohamed Sayegh, Dean, 961-1350000 Ext. 4700, Fax: 961-1744464, E-mail: msayegh@aub.edu.lb. *Application contact:* Dr. Salim Kanaan, Director, Admissions Office, 961-1350000 Ext. 2594, Fax: 961-1750775, E-mail: sk00@aub.edu.lb. Web site: http://www.aub.edu.lb/fm/fm_home/Pages/index.aspx.

Arizona State University, College of Liberal Arts and Sciences, Department of Chemistry and Biochemistry, Tempe, AZ 85287-1604. Offers biochemistry (MS, PhD); chemistry (MS, PhD); nanoscience (PSM). Terminal master's awarded for partial completion of doctoral program. *Degree requirements:* For master's, thesis, interactive Program of Study (iPOS) submitted before completing 50 percent of required credit hours; for doctorate, comprehensive exam, thesis/dissertation, interactive Program of Study (iPOS) submitted before completing 50 percent of required credit hours. *Entrance requirements:* For master's and doctorate, GRE, minimum GPA of 3.0 or equivalent in last 2 years of work leading to bachelor's degree. Additional exam requirements/recommendations for international students: Required—TOEFL (minimum score 80 iBT), TOEFL, IELTS, or Pearson Test of English. Electronic applications accepted.

Auburn University, Graduate School, College of Sciences and Mathematics, Department of Chemistry and Biochemistry, Auburn University, AL 36849. Offers analytical chemistry (MS, PhD); biochemistry (MS, PhD); inorganic chemistry (MS, PhD); organic chemistry (MS, PhD); physical chemistry (MS, PhD). Part-time programs available. *Faculty:* 28 full-time (5 women), 1 part-time/adjunct (0 women). *Students:* 37 full-time (14 women), 30 part-time (15 women); includes 6 minority (3 Black or African American, non-Hispanic/Latino; 1 American Indian or Alaska Native, non-Hispanic/Latino; 1 Asian, non-Hispanic/Latino; 1 Hispanic/Latino), 41 international. Average age 28. 38 applicants, 39% accepted, 12 enrolled. In 2011, 1 master's, 9 doctorates awarded. *Degree requirements:* For master's, thesis (for some programs); for doctorate, thesis/dissertation, oral and written exams. *Entrance requirements:* For master's and doctorate, GRE General Test. *Application deadline:* For fall admission, 7/7 for domestic students; for spring admission, 11/24 for domestic students. Applications are processed on a rolling basis. Application fee: $50 ($60 for international students). Electronic applications accepted. *Expenses:* Tuition, state resident: full-time $7290; part-time $405 per credit hour. Tuition, nonresident: full-time $21,870; part-time $1215 per credit hour. *International tuition:* $22,000 full-time. *Required fees:* $1402. *Financial support:* Fellowships, research assistantships, and teaching assistantships available. Financial award application deadline: 3/15; financial award applicants required to submit FAFSA. *Unit head:* Dr. J. V. Ortiz, Chair, 334-844-4043, Fax: 334-844-4043. *Application contact:* Dr. George Flowers, Dean of the Graduate School, 334-844-2125. Web site: http://www.auburn.edu/cosam/departments/chemistry/.

Baylor College of Medicine, Graduate School of Biomedical Sciences, Department of Biochemistry and Molecular Biology, Houston, TX 77030-3498. Offers PhD, MD/PhD. *Faculty:* 38 full-time (7 women). *Students:* 50 full-time (26 women); includes 6 minority (1 Black or African American, non-Hispanic/Latino; 1 American Indian or Alaska Native, non-Hispanic/Latino; 2 Asian, non-Hispanic/Latino; 2 Hispanic/Latino), 31 international. Average age 28. 105 applicants, 13% accepted, 8 enrolled. In 2011, 9 doctorates awarded. *Degree requirements:* For doctorate, thesis/dissertation, public defense. *Entrance requirements:* For doctorate, GRE General Test, GRE Subject Test (strongly recommended), minimum GPA of 3.0. Additional exam requirements/recommendations for international students: Required—TOEFL. *Application deadline:* For fall admission, 1/1 priority date for domestic students. Application fee: $0. Electronic applications accepted. *Financial support:* In 2011–12, 17 fellowships with full tuition reimbursements (averaging $29,000 per year), 33 research assistantships with full tuition reimbursements (averaging $29,000 per year) were awarded; career-related internships or fieldwork, Federal Work-Study, institutionally sponsored loans, health care benefits, and scholarships (to all students unless there are grant funds available to pay tuition) also available. Financial award applicants required to submit FAFSA. *Faculty research:* DNA repair, homologous recombination, gene therapy, trinucleotide repeat diseases, retinitis pigmentosa. *Unit head:* Dr. John Wilson, Director, 713-798-5760. *Application contact:* Ruth Reeves, Graduate Program Administrator, 713-798-0124, Fax: 713-796-9438, E-mail: rareeves@bcm.edu. Web site: http://www.bcm.edu/biochem/.

Baylor College of Medicine, Graduate School of Biomedical Sciences, Interdepartmental Program in Cell and Molecular Biology, Houston, TX 77030-3498. Offers biochemistry (PhD); cell and molecular biology (PhD); genetics (PhD); human genetics (PhD); immunology (PhD); microbiology (PhD); virology (PhD); MD/PhD. *Faculty:* 112 full-time (30 women). *Students:* 66 full-time (42 women); includes 21 minority (5 Black or African American, non-Hispanic/Latino; 1 American Indian or Alaska Native, non-Hispanic/Latino; 7 Asian, non-Hispanic/Latino; 8 Hispanic/Latino), 14 international. Average age 27. 126 applicants, 25% accepted, 14 enrolled. In 2011, 7 degrees awarded. *Median time to degree:* Of those who began their doctoral program in

fall 2003, 82% received their degree in 8 years or less. *Degree requirements:* For doctorate, thesis/dissertation, public defense. *Entrance requirements:* For doctorate, GRE General Test, GRE Subject Test (strongly recommended), minimum GPA of 3.0. Additional exam requirements/recommendations for international students: Required—TOEFL. *Application deadline:* For fall admission, 1/1 priority date for domestic students. Applications are processed on a rolling basis. Application fee: $0. Electronic applications accepted. *Financial support:* In 2011–12, 66 students received support, including 30 fellowships with full tuition reimbursements available (averaging $29,000 per year), 36 research assistantships with full tuition reimbursements available (averaging $29,000 per year); teaching assistantships, Federal Work-Study, institutionally sponsored loans, health care benefits, and tuition waivers (full) also available. Financial award applicants required to submit FAFSA. *Faculty research:* Molecular and cellular biology; cancer, aging and stem cells; genomics and proteomics; microbiome, molecular microbiology; infectious disease, immunology and translational research. *Unit head:* Dr. Susan Marriott, Director, 713-798-6557. *Application contact:* Lourdes Fernandez, Graduate Program Administrator, 713-798-6557, Fax: 713-798-6325, E-mail: cmbprog@bcm.edu. Web site: http://bcm.edu/cmb/.

Boston College, Graduate School of Arts and Sciences, Department of Chemistry, Program in Biochemistry, Chestnut Hill, MA 02467-3800. Offers PhD. *Degree requirements:* For doctorate, 2 foreign languages, comprehensive exam, thesis/dissertation. *Entrance requirements:* For doctorate, GRE General Test, GRE Subject Test.

Boston University, Graduate School of Arts and Sciences, Molecular Biology, Cell Biology, and Biochemistry Program (MCBB), Boston, MA 02215. Offers MA, PhD. *Students:* 36 full-time (17 women), 3 part-time (2 women); includes 8 minority (3 Black or African American, non-Hispanic/Latino; 2 Asian, non-Hispanic/Latino; 3 Hispanic/Latino), 9 international. Average age 29. 126 applicants, 13% accepted, 4 enrolled. In 2011, 6 master's, 20 doctorates awarded. Terminal master's awarded for partial completion of doctoral program. *Degree requirements:* For master's, one foreign language, thesis (for some programs); for doctorate, one foreign language, comprehensive exam, thesis/dissertation. *Entrance requirements:* For master's and doctorate, GRE General Test, GRE Subject Test. Additional exam requirements/recommendations for international students: Required—TOEFL (minimum score 600 paper-based; 250 computer-based). *Application deadline:* For fall admission, 12/7 for domestic and international students. Application fee: $70. Electronic applications accepted. *Expenses: Tuition:* Full-time $40,848; part-time $1276 per credit hour. *Required fees:* $572; $286 per semester. *Financial support:* In 2011–12, 10 students received support, including 1 fellowship with full tuition reimbursement available (averaging $18,300 per year), 8 research assistantships with full tuition reimbursements available (averaging $19,300 per year), 1 teaching assistantship with full tuition reimbursement available (averaging $19,300 per year); Federal Work-Study, scholarships/grants, and traineeships also available. Financial award application deadline: 12/7; financial award applicants required to submit FAFSA. *Unit head:* Dr. Ulla Hansen, Director, 617-353-2432, Fax: 617-353-6340, E-mail: uhansen@bu.edu. *Application contact:* Meredith Canode, Academic Administrator, 617-353-2432, Fax: 617-353-6340, E-mail: mcanode@bu.edu. Web site: http://www.bu.edu/mcbb/.

Brandeis University, Graduate School of Arts and Sciences, Program in Biochemistry and Biophysics, Waltham, MA 02454. Offers biochemistry and biophysics (PhD); quantitative biology (PhD). Part-time programs available. *Faculty:* 9 full-time (2 women), 1 (woman) part-time/adjunct. *Students:* 31 full-time (12 women); includes 4 minority (3 Asian, non-Hispanic/Latino; 1 Hispanic/Latino), 7 international. 75 applicants, 24% accepted, 4 enrolled. In 2011, 6 doctorates awarded. Terminal master's awarded for partial completion of doctoral program. *Degree requirements:* For doctorate, thesis/dissertation, qualifying exams; teaching requirement. *Entrance requirements:* For doctorate, GRE General Test, resume, 3 letters of recommendation, statement of purpose, transcript(s). Additional exam requirements/recommendations for international students: Required—TOEFL (minimum score 600 paper-based; 250 computer-based; 100 iBT); Recommended—IELTS (minimum score 7). *Application deadline:* For fall admission, 1/15 priority date for domestic students. Application fee: $75. Electronic applications accepted. *Financial support:* In 2011–12, 7 fellowships with full tuition reimbursements (averaging $29,580 per year), 14 research assistantships with full tuition reimbursements (averaging $29,580 per year), teaching assistantships with partial tuition reimbursements (averaging $3,200 per year) were awarded; career-related internships or fieldwork, scholarships/grants, health care benefits, tuition waivers (full and partial), and unspecified assistantships also available. Support available to part-time students. Financial award application deadline: 4/15; financial award applicants required to submit FAFSA. *Faculty research:* Macromolecular chemistry, structure and function, biochemistry, biophysics, biological macromolecules. *Unit head:* Prof. Christopher Miller, Director of Graduate Studies, 781-736-3100, Fax: 781-736-3107, E-mail: cmiller@brandeis.edu. *Application contact:* Carol MacKenzie, Department Administrator, 781-736-3100, Fax: 781-736-3107, E-mail: mackenzie@brandeis.edu. Web site: http://www.brandeis.edu/gsas/programs/bio.html.

Brigham Young University, Graduate Studies, College of Physical and Mathematical Sciences, Department of Chemistry and Biochemistry, Provo, UT 84602. Offers biochemistry (MS, PhD); chemistry (MS, PhD). *Faculty:* 33 full-time (2 women). *Students:* 104 full-time (39 women); includes 3 minority (2 Asian, non-Hispanic/Latino; 1 Native Hawaiian or other Pacific Islander, non-Hispanic/Latino), 53 international. Average age 28. 93 applicants, 41% accepted, 19 enrolled. In 2011, 5 master's, 11 doctorates awarded. *Median time to degree:* Of those who began their doctoral program in fall 2003, 50% received their degree in 8 years or less. *Degree requirements:* For master's, thesis; for doctorate, comprehensive exam, thesis/dissertation, qualifying exam. *Entrance requirements:* For master's and doctorate, GRE General Test, minimum GPA of 3.0 in last 60 hours. Additional exam requirements/recommendations for international students: Required—TOEFL (minimum score 580 paper-based; 237 computer-based; 85 iBT), IELTS (minimum score 7); Recommended—TWE. *Application deadline:* For fall admission, 2/1 priority date for domestic students, 2/1 for international students. Applications are processed on a rolling basis. Application fee: $50. Electronic applications accepted. *Expenses: Tuition:* Full-time $5760; part-time $320 per credit. Tuition and fees vary according to student's religious affiliation. *Financial support:* In 2011–12, 104 students received support, including 10 fellowships with full tuition reimbursements available (averaging $21,250 per year), 59 research assistantships with full tuition reimbursements available (averaging $21,250 per year), 35 teaching assistantships with full tuition reimbursements available (averaging $21,250 per year); institutionally sponsored loans, scholarships/grants, health care benefits, tuition waivers (full), and unspecified assistantships also available. Financial award application deadline: 2/1. *Faculty research:* Separation science, molecular recognition, organic synthesis and biomedical application, biochemistry and molecular biology, molecular spectroscopy. *Total annual research expenditures:* $5.6 million. *Unit head:* Dr.

Gregory F. Burton, Chair, 801-422-4917, Fax: 801-422-0153, E-mail: gburton@byu.edu. *Application contact:* Dr. Paul B. Farnsworth, Graduate Coordinator, 801-422-6502, Fax: 801-422-0153, E-mail: pbfarnsw@byu.edu. Web site: http://www.chem.byu.edu/.

Brown University, Graduate School, Department of Chemistry, Providence, RI 02912. Offers biochemistry (PhD); chemistry (AM, Sc M, PhD). *Degree requirements:* For master's, thesis; for doctorate, one foreign language, thesis/dissertation, cumulative exam.

Brown University, Graduate School, Division of Biology and Medicine, Program in Molecular Biology, Cell Biology, and Biochemistry, Providence, RI 02912. Offers biochemistry (M Med Sc, Sc M, PhD), including biochemistry (Sc M, PhD), biology (Sc M, PhD), medical science (M Med Sc, PhD); biology (MA); cell biology (M Med Sc, Sc M, PhD), including biochemistry (Sc M, PhD), biology (Sc M, PhD), medical science (M Med Sc, PhD); developmental biology (M Med Sc, Sc M, PhD), including biochemistry (Sc M, PhD), biology (Sc M, PhD), medical science (M Med Sc, PhD); immunology (M Med Sc, Sc M, PhD), including biochemistry (Sc M, PhD), biology (Sc M, PhD), medical science (M Med Sc, PhD); molecular microbiology (M Med Sc, Sc M, PhD), including biochemistry (Sc M, PhD), biology (Sc M, PhD), medical science (M Med Sc, PhD); MD/PhD. Part-time programs available. Terminal master's awarded for partial completion of doctoral program. *Degree requirements:* For master's, thesis (for some programs); for doctorate, one foreign language, thesis/dissertation, preliminary exam. *Entrance requirements:* For master's and doctorate, GRE General Test, GRE Subject Test. Additional exam requirements/recommendations for international students: Required—TOEFL. Electronic applications accepted. *Faculty research:* Molecular genetics, gene regulation.

California Institute of Technology, Division of Biology and Division of Chemistry and Chemical Engineering, Biochemistry and Molecular Biophysics Graduate Option, Pasadena, CA 91125-0001. Offers PhD. *Degree requirements:* For doctorate, thesis/dissertation, qualifying exam. *Entrance requirements:* For doctorate, GRE General Test. Additional exam requirements/recommendations for international students: Required—TOEFL. Electronic applications accepted.

California Institute of Technology, Division of Chemistry and Chemical Engineering, Pasadena, CA 91125-0001. Offers biochemistry and molecular biophysics (MS, PhD); chemical engineering (MS, PhD); chemistry (MS, PhD). Part-time and evening/weekend programs available. Postbaccalaureate distance learning degree programs offered (minimal on-campus study). *Faculty:* 40 full-time (7 women). *Students:* 315 full-time (116 women); includes 26 minority (2 Black or African American, non-Hispanic/Latino; 15 Asian, non-Hispanic/Latino; 5 Hispanic/Latino; 1 Native Hawaiian or other Pacific Islander, non-Hispanic/Latino; 3 Two or more races, non-Hispanic/Latino). Average age 26. 704 applicants, 18% accepted, 46 enrolled. In 2011, 10 master's, 46 doctorates awarded. Terminal master's awarded for partial completion of doctoral program. *Degree requirements:* For master's, thesis; for doctorate, thesis/dissertation. *Entrance requirements:* Additional exam requirements/recommendations for international students: Required—TOEFL; Recommended—IELTS, TWE. *Application deadline:* For fall admission, 1/1 for domestic and international students. Application fee: $80. Electronic applications accepted. *Financial support:* In 2011–12, 9 students received support. Fellowships, research assistantships, teaching assistantships, Federal Work-Study, institutionally sponsored loans, scholarships/grants, traineeships, health care benefits, and unspecified assistantships available. Financial award application deadline: 1/1. *Unit head:* Prof. Jacqueline K. Barton, Chair, 626-395-3646, Fax: 626-395-6948, E-mail: jkbarton@caltech.edu. *Application contact:* Natalie Gilmore, Graduate Office, 626-395-3812, Fax: 626-577-9246, E-mail: ngilmore@its.caltech.edu. Web site: http://cce.caltech.edu/index.html.

California Polytechnic State University, San Luis Obispo, College of Science and Mathematics, Department of Chemistry and Biochemistry, San Luis Obispo, CA 93407. Offers polymers and coating science (MS). Part-time programs available. *Faculty:* 1 full-time (0 women). *Students:* 2 full-time (1 woman), 3 part-time (0 women); includes 2 minority (both Asian, non-Hispanic/Latino). Average age 24. 5 applicants, 40% accepted, 1 enrolled. In 2011, 3 master's awarded. *Degree requirements:* For master's, comprehensive exam (for some programs), thesis (for some programs), comprehensive oral exam. *Entrance requirements:* For master's, minimum GPA of 2.5 in last 90 quarter units of course work. Additional exam requirements/recommendations for international students: Required—TOEFL (minimum score 550 paper-based; 213 computer-based) or IELTS (minimum score 6). *Application deadline:* For fall admission, 7/1 for domestic students, 11/30 for international students; for winter admission, 11/1 for domestic students, 6/30 for international students; for spring admission, 2/1 for domestic students. Applications are processed on a rolling basis. Application fee: $55. Electronic applications accepted. *Expenses:* Tuition, state resident: full-time $6738. Tuition, nonresident: full-time $17,898. *Required fees:* $2449. *Financial support:* Fellowships, research assistantships, career-related internships or fieldwork, Federal Work-Study, and scholarships/grants available. Support available to part-time students. Financial award application deadline: 3/2; financial award applicants required to submit FAFSA. *Faculty research:* Polymer physical chemistry and analysis, polymer synthesis, coatings formulation. *Unit head:* Dr. Ray Fernando, Graduate Coordinator, 805-756-2395, Fax: 805-756-5500, E-mail: rhfernan@calpoly.edu. *Application contact:* Dr. James Maraviglia, Associate Vice Provost for Marketing and Enrollment Development, 805-756-2311, Fax: 805-756-5400, E-mail: admissions@calpoly.edu. Web site: http://polymerscoatings.calpoly.edu/graduate.htm.

California State University, East Bay, Office of Academic Programs and Graduate Studies, College of Science, Department of Chemistry, Hayward, CA 94542-3000. Offers biochemistry (MS); chemistry (MS). *Faculty:* 3 full-time (2 women), 2 part-time/adjunct (1 woman). *Students:* 23 full-time (14 women), 31 part-time (19 women); includes 24 minority (3 Black or African American, non-Hispanic/Latino; 18 Asian, non-Hispanic/Latino; 3 Hispanic/Latino), 15 international. Average age 28. 57 applicants, 68% accepted, 22 enrolled. In 2011, 13 master's awarded. *Degree requirements:* For master's, comprehensive exam or thesis. *Entrance requirements:* For master's, minimum GPA of 2.6 in field during previous 2 years of course work. Additional exam requirements/recommendations for international students: Required—TOEFL (minimum score 550 paper-based; 213 computer-based). *Application deadline:* For fall admission, 6/30 for domestic and international students. Application fee: $55. Electronic applications accepted. *Expenses:* Tuition, state resident: full-time $6738; part-time $1302 per quarter. Tuition, nonresident: full-time $12,690; part-time $2294 per quarter. *Required fees:* $449 per quarter. Tuition and fees vary according to degree level, program and reciprocity agreements. *Financial support:* Fellowships, career-related internships or fieldwork, Federal Work-Study, institutionally sponsored loans, and scholarships/grants available. Support available to part-time students. Financial award application deadline: 3/2; financial award applicants required to submit FAFSA. *Unit head:* Dr. Ann McPartland, Chair, 510-885-3452, Fax: 510-885-4675, E-mail: ann.mcpartland@csueastbay.edu. *Application contact:* Prof. Chul Kim, Chemistry Graduate Advisor, 510-885-3490, Fax: 510-885-4675, E-mail: chul.kim@csueastbay.edu. Web site: http://www20.csueastbay.edu/csci/departments/chemistry.

California State University, Long Beach, Graduate Studies, College of Natural Sciences and Mathematics, Department of Chemistry and Biochemistry, Long Beach, CA 90840. Offers biochemistry (MS); chemistry (MS). Part-time programs available.

Faculty: 15 full-time (3 women). *Students:* 12 full-time (5 women), 24 part-time (10 women); includes 13 minority (7 Asian, non-Hispanic/Latino; 6 Hispanic/Latino), 6 international. Average age 26. 75 applicants, 16% accepted, 10 enrolled. In 2011, 5 master's awarded. *Degree requirements:* For master's, thesis, departmental qualifying exam. *Application deadline:* For fall admission, 6/1 for domestic students. Applications are processed on a rolling basis. Application fee: $55. Electronic applications accepted. *Financial support:* Research assistantships, teaching assistantships, Federal Work-Study, institutionally sponsored loans, scholarships/grants, and unspecified assistantships available. Financial award application deadline: 3/2. *Faculty research:* Enzymology, organic synthesis, molecular modeling, environmental chemistry, reaction kinetics. *Unit head:* Dr. Jeffrey Cohlberg, Chair, 562-985-4944, Fax: 562-985-8557, E-mail: cohlberg@csulb.edu. *Application contact:* Dr. Lijuan Li, Graduate Advisor, 562-985-5068, Fax: 562-985-8557, E-mail: lli@csulb.edu.

California State University, Los Angeles, Graduate Studies, College of Natural and Social Sciences, Department of Chemistry and Biochemistry, Los Angeles, CA 90032-8530. Offers analytical chemistry (MS); biochemistry (MS); chemistry (MS); inorganic chemistry (MS); organic chemistry (MS); physical chemistry (MS). Part-time and evening/weekend programs available. *Faculty:* 4 part-time/adjunct (1 woman). *Students:* 22 full-time (14 women), 24 part-time (11 women); includes 30 minority (4 Black or African American, non-Hispanic/Latino; 7 Asian, non-Hispanic/Latino; 19 Hispanic/Latino), 7 international. Average age 29. 60 applicants, 48% accepted, 17 enrolled. In 2011, 15 master's awarded. *Degree requirements:* For master's, one foreign language, comprehensive exam or thesis. *Entrance requirements:* Additional exam requirements/recommendations for international students: Required—TOEFL. *Application deadline:* For fall admission, 5/1 for domestic and international students. Applications are processed on a rolling basis. Application fee: $55. *Expenses:* Tuition, state resident: full-time $8225. *Financial support:* Federal Work-Study available. Support available to part-time students. Financial award application deadline: 3/1. *Faculty research:* Intercalation of heavy metal, carborane chemistry, conductive polymers and fabrics, titanium reagents, computer modeling and synthesis. *Unit head:* Dr. Robert L. Vellanoweth, Chair, 323-343-2300, Fax: 323-343-6490, E-mail: rvellan@calstatela.edu. *Application contact:* Dr. Karin Brown, Acting Associate Dean of Graduate Studies, 323-343-3820 Ext. 3827, Fax: 323-343-5653, E-mail: kbrown5@calstatela.edu. Web site: http://www.calstatela.edu/dept/chem/index.htm.

California State University, Northridge, Graduate Studies, College of Science and Mathematics, Department of Chemistry and Biochemistry, Northridge, CA 91330. Offers biochemistry (MS); chemistry (MS), including chemistry, environmental chemistry. *Degree requirements:* For master's, thesis. *Entrance requirements:* For master's, GRE General Test or minimum GPA of 3.0. Additional exam requirements/recommendations for international students: Required—TOEFL. Electronic applications accepted.

Carnegie Mellon University, Mellon College of Science, Department of Biological Sciences, Pittsburgh, PA 15213-3891. Offers biochemistry (PhD); biophysics (PhD); cell biology (PhD); computational biology (MS, PhD); developmental biology (PhD); genetics (PhD); molecular biology (PhD); neuroscience (PhD). *Degree requirements:* For doctorate, comprehensive exam, thesis/dissertation. *Entrance requirements:* For doctorate, GRE General Test, GRE Subject Test, interview. Electronic applications accepted. *Faculty research:* Genetic structure, function, and regulation; protein structure and function; biological membranes; biological spectroscopy.

Case Western Reserve University, School of Medicine and School of Graduate Studies, Graduate Programs in Medicine, Department of Biochemistry, Cleveland, OH 44106. Offers biochemical research (MS); biochemistry (MS, PhD); RNA biology (PhD); MD/PhD. Part-time programs available. Terminal master's awarded for partial completion of doctoral program. *Degree requirements:* For master's, thesis (for some programs); for doctorate, thesis/dissertation. *Entrance requirements:* For master's and doctorate, GRE General Test. Additional exam requirements/recommendations for international students: Required—TOEFL. Electronic applications accepted. *Faculty research:* Regulation of metabolism, regulation of gene expression and protein synthesis, cell biology, molecular biology, structural biology.

Case Western Reserve University, School of Medicine and School of Graduate Studies, Graduate Programs in Medicine, Department of Nutrition, Cleveland, OH 44106. Offers dietetics (MS); nutrition (MS, PhD), including molecular nutrition (PhD), nutrition and biochemistry (PhD); public health nutrition (MS). Part-time programs available. Terminal master's awarded for partial completion of doctoral program. *Degree requirements:* For master's, thesis (for some programs); for doctorate, thesis/dissertation. *Entrance requirements:* For master's, GRE General Test; for doctorate, GRE General Test, GRE Subject Test. Additional exam requirements/recommendations for international students: Required—TOEFL. *Faculty research:* Fatty acid metabolism, application of gene therapy to nutritional problems, dietary intake methodology, nutrition and physical fitness, metabolism during infancy and pregnancy.

See Display on page 390 and Close-Up on page 407.

Central Connecticut State University, School of Graduate Studies, School of Arts and Sciences, Department of Chemistry and Biochemistry, New Britain, CT 06050-4010. Offers natural sciences (MS). Part-time and evening/weekend programs available. *Students:* 1 (woman) part-time. 1 applicant, 100% accepted, 1 enrolled. *Degree requirements:* For master's, comprehensive exam, thesis or alternative; for Certificate, qualifying exam. *Entrance requirements:* For master's, minimum undergraduate GPA of 2.7. Additional exam requirements/recommendations for international students: Required—TOEFL (minimum score 550 paper-based; 213 computer-based). *Application deadline:* For fall admission, 6/1 for domestic students, 5/1 for international students; for spring admission, 11/1 for domestic and international students. Applications are processed on a rolling basis. Application fee: $50. Electronic applications accepted. *Expenses:* Tuition, area resident: Full-time $5137; part-time $482 per credit. Tuition, state resident: full-time $7707; part-time $494 per credit. Tuition, nonresident: full-time $14,311; part-time $494 per credit. *Required fees:* $3865. One-time fee: $62 part-time. *Unit head:* Dr. Thomas Burkholder, Chair, 860-832-2675, E-mail: burkholder@ccsu.edu. *Application contact:* Patricia Gardner, Associate Director of Graduate Studies, 860-832-2350, Fax: 860-832-2352, E-mail: graduateadmissions@ccsu.edu. Web site: http://www.chemistry.ccsu.edu/.

City College of the City University of New York, Graduate School, College of Liberal Arts and Science, Division of Science, Department of Chemistry, Program in Biochemistry, New York, NY 10031-9198. Offers MA, PhD. PhD program offered jointly with Graduate School and University Center of the City University of New York. Terminal master's awarded for partial completion of doctoral program. *Degree requirements:* For doctorate, one foreign language, thesis/dissertation. *Entrance requirements:* For doctorate, GRE. Additional exam requirements/recommendations for international students: Required—TOEFL (minimum score 550 paper-based; 79 iBT). Electronic applications accepted. *Faculty research:* Fatty acid metabolism, lectins, gene structure.

Clemson University, Graduate School, College of Agriculture, Forestry and Life Sciences, Department of Genetics and Biochemistry, Program in Biochemistry and Molecular Biology, Clemson, SC 29634. Offers PhD. *Students:* 16 full-time (13 women), 1 (woman) part-time, 8 international. Average age 28. 22 applicants, 18% accepted, 2 enrolled. In 2011, 6 doctorates awarded. *Degree requirements:* For doctorate,

comprehensive exam, thesis/dissertation. *Entrance requirements:* For doctorate, GRE General Test. Additional exam requirements/recommendations for international students: Required—TOEFL. *Application deadline:* For fall admission, 1/1 for domestic students; for spring admission, 9/1 for domestic students. Applications are processed on a rolling basis. Application fee: $70 ($80 for international students). Electronic applications accepted. *Expenses:* Contact institution. *Financial support:* In 2011–12, 16 students received support, including 11 research assistantships with partial tuition reimbursements available (averaging $17,091 per year), 7 teaching assistantships with partial tuition reimbursements available (averaging $19,429 per year); fellowships with full and partial tuition reimbursements available, career-related internships or fieldwork, institutionally sponsored loans, scholarships/grants, health care benefits, and unspecified assistantships also available. Support available to part-time students. Financial award application deadline: 3/15; financial award applicants required to submit FAFSA. *Faculty research:* Biomembranes, protein structure, molecular biology of plants, APYA and stress response. *Total annual research expenditures:* $670,000. *Unit head:* Dr. Keith Murphy, Chair, 864-656-6237, Fax: 864-656-0435, E-mail: kmurph2@clemson.edu. *Application contact:* Sheryl Banks, Administrative Coordinator, 864-656-6878, E-mail: sherylb@clemson.edu. Web site: http://www.clemson.edu/genbiochem.

Colorado State University, Graduate School, College of Natural Sciences, Department of Biochemistry and Molecular Biology, Fort Collins, CO 80523-1870. Offers biochemistry (MS, PhD). Postbaccalaureate distance learning degree programs offered (no on-campus study). *Faculty:* 12 full-time (5 women), 2 part-time/adjunct (0 women). *Students:* 20 full-time (7 women), 24 part-time (15 women); includes 2 minority (1 Asian, non-Hispanic/Latino; 1 Hispanic/Latino), 16 international. Average age 26. 52 applicants, 25% accepted, 13 enrolled. In 2011, 8 master's, 3 doctorates awarded. Terminal master's awarded for partial completion of doctoral program. *Degree requirements:* For master's, comprehensive exam (for some programs), thesis (for some programs); for doctorate, thesis/dissertation, comprehensive oral exam at the end of second year. *Entrance requirements:* For master's, GRE General Test, minimum GPA of 3.0; 3 letters of recommendation; resume; for doctorate, GRE General Test, minimum GPA of 3.0; one year of biology, organic chemistry, physics, calculus, and biochemistry; 3 letters of recommendation; bachelor's degree. Additional exam requirements/recommendations for international students: Required—TOEFL (minimum score 550 paper-based; 213 computer-based; 80 iBT). *Application deadline:* For fall admission, 1/7 priority date for domestic students, 1/7 for international students; for spring admission, 9/15 priority date for domestic students, 9/15 for international students. Applications are processed on a rolling basis. Application fee: $50. Electronic applications accepted. *Expenses:* Tuition, state resident: full-time $7992. Tuition, nonresident: full-time $19,592. *Required fees:* $1735; $58 per credit. *Financial support:* In 2011–12, 43 students received support, including 9 fellowships (averaging $33,516 per year), 23 research assistantships with full tuition reimbursements available (averaging $19,973 per year), 11 teaching assistantships with full tuition reimbursements available (averaging $16,881 per year); health care benefits also available. Financial award application deadline: 1/15; financial award applicants required to submit FAFSA. *Faculty research:* Cellular biology, molecular gene expression, neurobiology, structural biology, yeast genetics. *Total annual research expenditures:* $5.1 million. *Unit head:* Dr. P. Shing Ho, Chair, 970-491-0569, Fax: 970-491-0494, E-mail: shing.ho@colostate.edu. *Application contact:* Neda Amidon, Graduate Contact, 970-491-5566, Fax: 970-491-0494, E-mail: neda.amidon@colostate.edu. Web site: http://www.bmb.colostate.edu/.

Colorado State University–Pueblo, College of Science and Mathematics, Pueblo, CO 81001-4901. Offers applied natural science (MS), including biochemistry, biology, chemistry. Part-time and evening/weekend programs available. *Degree requirements:* For master's, comprehensive exam (for some programs), thesis (for some programs), internship report (if non-thesis). *Entrance requirements:* For master's, GRE General Test (minimum score 1000), 2 letters of reference, minimum GPA of 3.0. Additional exam requirements/recommendations for international students: Required—TOEFL (minimum score 500 paper-based; 173 computer-based), IELTS (minimum score 5). *Faculty research:* Fungal cell walls, molecular biology, bioactive materials synthesis, atomic force microscopy-surface chemistry, nanoscience.

Columbia University, College of Physicians and Surgeons, Department of Biochemistry and Molecular Biophysics, New York, NY 10032. Offers biochemistry and molecular biophysics (M Phil, PhD); biophysics (PhD); MD/PhD. Only candidates for the PhD are admitted. *Degree requirements:* For doctorate, one foreign language, thesis/dissertation. *Entrance requirements:* For master's and doctorate, GRE General Test. Additional exam requirements/recommendations for international students: Required—TOEFL.

Cornell University, Graduate School, Graduate Fields of Agriculture and Life Sciences, Field of Biochemistry, Molecular and Cell Biology, Ithaca, NY 14853-0001. Offers biochemistry (PhD); biophysics (PhD); cell biology (PhD); molecular and cell biology (PhD); molecular biology (PhD). *Faculty:* 62 full-time (17 women). *Students:* 91 full-time (46 women); includes 12 minority (1 Black or African American, non-Hispanic/Latino; 8 Asian, non-Hispanic/Latino; 2 Hispanic/Latino; 1 Two or more races, non-Hispanic/Latino), 34 international. Average age 26. 247 applicants, 8% accepted, 17 enrolled. In 2011, 11 doctorates awarded. *Degree requirements:* For doctorate, comprehensive exam, thesis/dissertation, 2 semesters of teaching experience. *Entrance requirements:* For doctorate, GRE General Test, GRE Subject Test (biology, chemistry, physics, biochemistry, cell and molecular biology), 3 letters of recommendation. Additional exam requirements/recommendations for international students: Required—TOEFL (minimum score 600 paper-based; 250 computer-based; 77 iBT). *Application deadline:* For fall admission, 1/5 for domestic students. Application fee: $95. Electronic applications accepted. *Financial support:* In 2011–12, 88 students received support, including 26 fellowships with full tuition reimbursements available, 46 research assistantships with full tuition reimbursements available, 14 teaching assistantships with full tuition reimbursements available; institutionally sponsored loans, scholarships/grants, health care benefits, tuition waivers (full and partial), and unspecified assistantships also available. Financial award applicants required to submit FAFSA. *Faculty research:* Biophysics, structural biology. *Unit head:* Director of Graduate Studies, 607-255-2100, Fax: 607-255-2100. *Application contact:* Graduate Field Assistant, 607-255-2100, Fax: 607-255-2100, E-mail: bmcb@cornell.edu. Web site: http://www.gradschool.cornell.edu/fields.php?id-43&a-2.

Cornell University, Graduate School, Graduate Fields of Arts and Sciences, Field of Chemistry and Chemical Biology, Ithaca, NY 14853-0001. Offers analytical chemistry (PhD); bio-organic chemistry (PhD); biophysical chemistry (PhD); chemical biology (PhD); chemical physics (PhD); inorganic chemistry (PhD); materials chemistry (PhD); organic chemistry (PhD); organometallic chemistry (PhD); physical chemistry (PhD); polymer chemistry (PhD); theoretical chemistry (PhD). *Faculty:* 46 full-time (3 women). *Students:* 151 full-time (67 women); includes 16 minority (13 Asian, non-Hispanic/Latino; 2 Hispanic/Latino; 1 Two or more races, non-Hispanic/Latino), 48 international. Average age 25. 297 applicants, 35% accepted, 29 enrolled. In 2011, 22 doctorates awarded. *Degree requirements:* For doctorate, comprehensive exam, thesis/dissertation. *Entrance requirements:* For doctorate, GRE General Test, GRE Subject Test (chemistry), 3 letters of recommendation. Additional exam requirements/recommendations for international students: Required—TOEFL (minimum score 600 paper-based; 250 computer-based; 77 iBT). *Application deadline:* For fall admission, 1/10 for domestic students. Application fee: $95. Electronic applications accepted. *Financial support:* In 2011–12, 21 fellowships with full tuition reimbursements, 63 research assistantships with full tuition reimbursements, 59 teaching assistantships with full tuition reimbursements were awarded; institutionally sponsored loans, scholarships/grants, health care benefits, tuition waivers (full and partial), and unspecified assistantships also available. Financial award applicants required to submit FAFSA. *Faculty research:* Analytical, organic, inorganic, physical, materials, chemical biology. *Unit head:* Director of Graduate Studies, 607-255-4139, Fax: 607-255-4137. *Application contact:* Graduate Field Assistant, 607-255-4139, Fax: 607-255-4137, E-mail: chemgrad@cornell.edu. Web site: http://www.gradschool.cornell.edu/fields.php?id-26&a-2.

Dalhousie University, Faculty of Medicine, Department of Biochemistry and Molecular Biology, Halifax, NS B3H 4R2, Canada. Offers M Sc, PhD. *Degree requirements:* For master's, thesis, demonstrating/teaching experience, oral defense, seminar; for doctorate, comprehensive exam, thesis/dissertation, demonstrating/teaching experience, oral defense, seminar, 2 short grant proposals in year 3. *Entrance requirements:* For master's and doctorate, GRE. Additional exam requirements/recommendations for international students: Required—1 of 5 approved tests: TOEFL, IELTS, CANTEST, CAEL, Michigan English Language Assessment Battery. Electronic applications accepted. *Expenses:* Contact institution. *Faculty research:* Gene expression and cell regulation; lipids, lipoproteins, and membranes; molecular evolution; proteins, molecular cell biology and molecular genetics; structure, function, and metabolism of biomolecules.

Dartmouth College, Graduate Program in Molecular and Cellular Biology, Department of Biochemistry, Hanover, NH 03755. Offers PhD, MD/PhD. *Entrance requirements:* For doctorate, GRE General Test, letters of recommendation. Additional exam requirements/recommendations for international students: Required—TOEFL (minimum score 450 paper-based; 90 iBT) or IELTS (minimum score 7). Electronic applications accepted.

DePaul University, College of Science and Health, Department of Chemistry, Chicago, IL 60614. Offers biochemistry (MS); chemistry (MS); polymer chemistry and coatings technology (MS). Part-time and evening/weekend programs available. *Faculty:* 13 full-time (7 women), 4 part-time/adjunct (1 woman). *Students:* 11 full-time (6 women), 3 part-time (2 women); includes 5 minority (1 Asian, non-Hispanic/Latino; 3 Hispanic/Latino; 1 Two or more races, non-Hispanic/Latino), 1 international. Average age 26. 6 applicants, 100% accepted, 4 enrolled. In 2011, 2 master's awarded. *Degree requirements:* For master's, thesis (for some programs), oral exam (for select programs). *Entrance requirements:* For master's, GRE Subject Test (chemistry), GRE General Test, BS in chemistry or equivalent. Additional exam requirements/recommendations for international students: Required—TOEFL (minimum score 590 paper-based; 243 computer-based). *Application deadline:* For fall admission, 7/15 for domestic students, 5/1 for international students; for winter admission, 11/15 for domestic students, 9/1 for international students; for spring admission, 2/15 for domestic students, 12/1 for international students. Applications are processed on a rolling basis. Application fee: $40. Electronic applications accepted. *Financial support:* In 2011–12, 4 students received support, including 6 teaching assistantships with partial tuition reimbursements available (averaging $9,000 per year). Financial award application deadline: 6/1. *Faculty research:* Computational chemistry, organic synthesis, inorganic synthesis, polymer synthesis, biochemistry. *Total annual research expenditures:* $30,000. *Unit head:* Dr. Richard F. Niedziela, Chair, 773-325-7307, Fax: 773-325-7421, E-mail: rniedzie@condor.depaul.edu. *Application contact:* Dr. Matthew Dintzner, Director of Graduate Studies, 773-325-4726, Fax: 773-325-7421, E-mail: mdintzne@depaul.edu. Web site: http://chemistry.depaul.edu.

Drexel University, College of Medicine, Biomedical Graduate Programs, Program in Biochemistry, Philadelphia, PA 19104-2875. Offers MS, PhD, MD/PhD. Part-time programs available. Terminal master's awarded for partial completion of doctoral program. *Degree requirements:* For master's, comprehensive exam, thesis; for doctorate, thesis/dissertation, qualifying exam. *Entrance requirements:* For master's, GRE General Test, minimum GPA of 2.75; for doctorate, GRE General Test, minimum GPA of 3.0. Additional exam requirements/recommendations for international students: Required—TOEFL. Electronic applications accepted.

Duke University, Graduate School, Department of Biochemistry, Durham, NC 27710. Offers crystallography of macromolecules (PhD); enzyme mechanisms (PhD); lipid biochemistry (PhD); membrane structure and function (PhD); molecular genetics (PhD); neurochemistry (PhD); nucleic acid structure and function (PhD); protein structure and function (PhD). *Faculty:* 28 full-time. *Students:* 73 full-time (28 women); includes 6 minority (4 Black or African American, non-Hispanic/Latino; 2 Asian, non-Hispanic/Latino), 29 international. 76 applicants, 17% accepted, 3 enrolled. In 2011, 7 doctorates awarded. *Degree requirements:* For doctorate, thesis/dissertation. *Entrance requirements:* For doctorate, GRE General Test, GRE Subject Test (recommended). Additional exam requirements/recommendations for international students: Required—TOEFL (minimum score 550 paper-based; 213 computer-based; 83 iBT), IELTS (minimum score 7). *Application deadline:* For fall admission, 12/8 priority date for domestic students, 12/8 for international students. Application fee: $75. Electronic applications accepted. *Expenses: Tuition:* Full-time $40,720. *Required fees:* $3107. *Financial support:* Fellowships, research assistantships, teaching assistantships, and Federal Work-Study available. Financial award application deadline: 12/8. *Unit head:* Leonard Spicer, Director of Graduate Studies, 919-681-8770, Fax: 919-684-8885, E-mail: anorfleet@biochem.duke.edu. *Application contact:* Elizabeth Hutton, Director of Admissions, 919-684-3913, Fax: 919-684-2277, E-mail: grad-admissions@duke.edu. Web site: http://www.biochem.duke.edu/.

Duquesne University, Bayer School of Natural and Environmental Sciences, Department of Chemistry and Biochemistry, Pittsburgh, PA 15282-0001. Offers chemistry (MS, PhD). Part-time programs available. *Faculty:* 16 full-time (5 women), 17 part-time/adjunct (8 women). *Students:* 45 full-time (19 women), 3 part-time (0 women); includes 5 minority (3 Black or African American, non-Hispanic/Latino; 1 Asian, non-Hispanic/Latino; 1 Two or more races, non-Hispanic/Latino), 12 international. Average age 28. 50 applicants, 38% accepted, 4 enrolled. In 2011, 2 master's, 6 doctorates awarded. Terminal master's awarded for partial completion of doctoral program. *Degree requirements:* For master's, thesis (for some programs); for doctorate, thesis/dissertation. *Entrance requirements:* For master's, GRE General Test, BS in chemistry or related field, 3 letters of recommendation, official transcripts, statement of purpose; for doctorate, GRE General Test, BS in chemistry or related field, statement of purpose, official transcripts, 3 letters of recommendation with recommendation forms. Additional exam requirements/recommendations for international students: Required—TOEFL (minimum score 100 iBT). *Application deadline:* For fall admission, 2/15 priority date for domestic students, 2/15 for international students; for spring admission, 10/1 priority date for domestic students, 10/1 for international students. Applications are processed on a rolling basis. Application fee: $0 ($40 for international students). Electronic applications accepted. *Expenses:* Contact institution. *Financial support:* In 2011–12, 43 students received support, including 1 fellowship with tuition reimbursement available (averaging $22,100 per year), 11 research assistantships with full tuition

reimbursements available (averaging $21,850 per year), 28 teaching assistantships with full tuition reimbursements available (averaging $21,850 per year); scholarships/grants and unspecified assistantships also available. Financial award application deadline: 5/31. *Faculty research:* Computational physical chemistry, bioinorganic chemistry, analytical chemistry, biophysics, synthetic organic chemistry. *Unit head:* Dr. Ralph Wheeler, Chair, 412-396-6341, Fax: 412-396-5683, E-mail: wheeler7@duq.edu. *Application contact:* Heather Costello, Graduate Academic Advisor, 412-396-6339, Fax: 412-396-4881, E-mail: costelloh@duq.edu. Web site: http://www.science.duq.edu/.

East Carolina University, Brody School of Medicine, Department of Biochemistry and Molecular Biology, Greenville, NC 27858-4353. Offers biochemistry and molecular biology (PhD); biomedical science (MS). *Degree requirements:* For doctorate, comprehensive exam, thesis/dissertation. *Entrance requirements:* For doctorate, GRE General Test. Additional exam requirements/recommendations for international students: Required—TOEFL. *Application deadline:* For fall admission, 6/1 priority date for domestic students. Applications are processed on a rolling basis. Application fee: $50. *Expenses:* Tuition, state resident: full-time $3557; part-time $444.63 per semester hour. Tuition, nonresident: full-time $14,351; part-time $1793.88 per semester hour. *Required fees:* $2016; $252 per semester hour. Part-time tuition and fees vary according to course load, campus/location and program. *Financial support:* Fellowships with full and partial tuition reimbursements available. Financial award application deadline: 6/1. *Faculty research:* Gene regulation, development and differentiation, contractility and motility, macromolecular interactions, cancer. *Unit head:* Dr. Phillip H. Pekala, Chairman, 252-744-2684, Fax: 252-744-3383, E-mail: pekalap@ecu.edu. *Application contact:* Dr. George J. Kasperek, Assistant Dean for Graduate Studies/BSOM, 252-744-3305, Fax: 252-744-0203, E-mail: kasperekg@ecu.edu. Web site: http://www.ecu.edu/cs-dhs/biochemistry/Graduate-Program-Information.cfm.

Eastern New Mexico University, Graduate School, College of Liberal Arts and Sciences, Department of Physical Sciences, Portales, NM 88130. Offers chemistry (MS), including analytical, biochemistry, inorganic, organic, physical. Part-time programs available. *Faculty:* 6 full-time (0 women). *Students:* 11 part-time (5 women), 9 international. Average age 25. 25 applicants, 44% accepted, 4 enrolled. In 2011, 5 master's awarded. *Degree requirements:* For master's, thesis optional, seminar, oral and written comprehensive exams. *Entrance requirements:* For master's, ACS placement examination, minimum GPA of 3.0; 2 letters of recommendation; personal statement of career goals; bachelor's degree with one year minimum each of general, organic, and analytical chemistry. Additional exam requirements/recommendations for international students: Required—TOEFL (minimum score 550 paper-based; 213 computer-based; 79 iBT), IELTS (minimum score 6). *Application deadline:* For fall admission, 7/20 priority date for domestic students, 6/20 for international students; for spring admission, 12/15 priority date for domestic students, 11/15 for international students. Applications are processed on a rolling basis. Application fee: $10. Electronic applications accepted. *Financial support:* In 2011–12, 1 research assistantship with partial tuition reimbursement (averaging $8,500 per year), 10 teaching assistantships with partial tuition reimbursements (averaging $8,500 per year) were awarded; career-related internships or fieldwork and unspecified assistantships also available. Support available to part-time students. Financial award application deadline: 3/1; financial award applicants required to submit FAFSA. *Faculty research:* Synfuel, electrochemistry, protein chemistry. *Unit head:* Dr. Juacho Yan, Graduate Coordinator, 575-562-2494, Fax: 575-562-2192, E-mail: juacho.yan@enmu.edu. *Application contact:* Sharon Potter, Department Secretary, Biology and Physical Sciences, 575-562-2174, Fax: 575-562-2192, E-mail: sharon.potter@enmu.edu. Web site: http://liberal-arts.enmu.edu/sciences/grad-chemistry.shtml.

East Tennessee State University, James H. Quillen College of Medicine, Biomedical Science Graduate Program, Johnson City, TN 37614. Offers anatomy and cell biology (PhD); biochemistry and molecular biology (PhD); microbiology (PhD); pharmaceutical sciences (PhD); pharmacology (PhD); physiology (PhD); quantitative biosciences (PhD). *Faculty:* 33 full-time (6 women). *Students:* 29 full-time (15 women), 2 part-time (both women); includes 4 minority (1 Black or African American, non-Hispanic/Latino; 1 Asian, non-Hispanic/Latino; 2 Hispanic/Latino), 6 international. Average age 29. 76 applicants, 12% accepted, 7 enrolled. In 2011, 1 doctorate awarded. *Degree requirements:* For doctorate, thesis/dissertation, comprehensive qualifying exam. *Entrance requirements:* For doctorate, GRE General Test, GRE Subject Test. Additional exam requirements/recommendations for international students: Required—TOEFL (minimum score 550 paper-based; 213 computer-based; 79 iBT). *Application deadline:* For fall admission, 3/15 priority date for domestic students, 3/1 for international students. Application fee: $35 ($45 for international students). Electronic applications accepted. *Expenses:* Contact institution. *Financial support:* In 2011–12, 29 students received support, including 29 research assistantships with full tuition reimbursements available (averaging $19,000 per year); career-related internships or fieldwork, institutionally sponsored loans, scholarships/grants, and unspecified assistantships also available. Financial award application deadline: 7/1; financial award applicants required to submit FAFSA. *Faculty research:* Cardiovascular biology, neuroscience, infectious disease, cancer, inflammatory disease. *Total annual research expenditures:* $3.6 million. *Unit head:* Dr. Mitchell E. Robinson, Associate Dean/Program Director, 423-439-2031, Fax: 423-439-2140, E-mail: robinson@etsu.edu. *Application contact:* Shella Bennett, Graduate Specialist, 423-439-4708, Fax: 423-439-5624, E-mail: bennetsg@etsu.edu.

Emory University, Laney Graduate School, Division of Biological and Biomedical Sciences, Program in Biochemistry, Cell and Developmental Biology, Atlanta, GA 30322. Offers PhD. *Faculty:* 52 full-time (10 women). *Students:* 53 full-time (34 women); includes 9 minority (1 Black or African American, non-Hispanic/Latino; 4 Asian, non-Hispanic/Latino; 4 Hispanic/Latino), 10 international. Average age 27. 147 applicants, 11% accepted, 7 enrolled. In 2011, 5 doctorates awarded. *Degree requirements:* For doctorate, comprehensive exam, thesis/dissertation. *Entrance requirements:* For doctorate, GRE General Test, minimum GPA of 3.0 in science course work (recommended). Additional exam requirements/recommendations for international students: Required—TOEFL. *Application deadline:* For fall admission, 1/3 for domestic students, 1/1 for international students. Application fee: $75. Electronic applications accepted. *Expenses: Tuition:* Full-time $34,800. *Required fees:* $1300. *Financial support:* In 2011–12, 18 students received support, including 18 fellowships with full tuition reimbursements available (averaging $26,500 per year); institutionally sponsored loans, scholarships/grants, health care benefits, and tuition waivers (full) also available. *Faculty research:* Signal transduction, molecular biology, enzymes and cofactors, receptor and ion channel function, membrane biology. *Unit head:* Dr. Richard Kahn, Program Director, 404-727-3561, Fax: 404-727-3746, E-mail: rkahn@emory.edu. *Application contact:* Kathy Smith, Director of Recruitment and Admissions, 404-727-2547, Fax: 404-727-3322, E-mail: kathy.smith@emory.edu. Web site: http://www.biomed.emory.edu/PROGRAM_SITES/BCDB/.

Florida Institute of Technology, Graduate Programs, College of Science, Department of Chemistry, Melbourne, FL 32901-6975. Offers biochemistry (MS); chemistry (MS, PhD). Part-time programs available. *Faculty:* 5 full-time (0 women). *Students:* 44 full-time (22 women), 1 (woman) part-time; includes 1 minority (Black or African American, non-Hispanic/Latino), 34 international. Average age 29. 79 applicants, 57% accepted, 13 enrolled. In 2011, 1 degree awarded. Terminal master's awarded for partial completion of doctoral program. *Median time to degree:* Of those who began their doctoral program in fall 2003, 100% received their degree in 8 years or less. *Degree requirements:* For master's, comprehensive exam, research proposal, thesis and oral examination in defense of the thesis, proficiency examination; for doctorate, comprehensive exam, thesis/dissertation, oral defense of dissertation, dissertation research publishable to standards, complete original research study. *Entrance requirements:* For master's, proficiency exams, minimum GPA of 3.0; for doctorate, minimum GPA of 3.3, resume, 3 letters of recommendation, statement of objectives. Additional exam requirements/recommendations for international students: Required—TOEFL (minimum score 550 paper-based; 213 computer-based; 79 iBT). *Application deadline:* For fall admission, 4/1 for international students; for spring admission, 9/30 for international students. Applications are processed on a rolling basis. Electronic applications accepted. *Expenses: Tuition:* Full-time $19,620; part-time $1090 per credit hour. Tuition and fees vary according to campus/location. *Financial support:* In 2011–12, 4 research assistantships with full and partial tuition reimbursements (averaging $11,704 per year), 15 teaching assistantships with full and partial tuition reimbursements (averaging $10,318 per year) were awarded; career-related internships or fieldwork, institutionally sponsored loans, tuition waivers (partial), unspecified assistantships, and tuition remissions also available. Support available to part-time students. Financial award application deadline: 3/1; financial award applicants required to submit FAFSA. *Faculty research:* Energy storage applications, marine and organic chemistry, stereochemistry, medicinal chemistry, environmental chemistry. *Total annual research expenditures:* $772,720. *Unit head:* Dr. Michael W. Babich, Department Head, 321-674-8046, Fax: 321-674-8951, E-mail: babich@fit.edu. *Application contact:* Cheryl A. Brown, Associate Director of Graduate Admissions, 321-674-7581, Fax: 321-723-9468, E-mail: cbrown@fit.edu. Web site: http://cos.fit.edu/chemistry/.

Florida State University, The Graduate School, College of Arts and Sciences, Department of Chemistry and Biochemistry, Specialization in Biochemistry, Tallahassee, FL 32306-4390. Offers MS, PhD. *Faculty:* 8 full-time (3 women), 1 (woman) part-time/adjunct. *Students:* 25 full-time (11 women), 1 (woman) part-time; includes 2 minority (1 Black or African American, non-Hispanic/Latino; 1 Hispanic/Latino), 14 international. Average age 25. Terminal master's awarded for partial completion of doctoral program. *Degree requirements:* For master's, comprehensive exam (for some programs), thesis (for some programs), cumulative exams; for doctorate, comprehensive exam (for some programs), thesis/dissertation, cumulative exams. *Entrance requirements:* For master's and doctorate, GRE General Test, minimum B average in undergraduate course work. Additional exam requirements/recommendations for international students: Required—TOEFL (minimum score 550 paper-based; 213 computer-based; 80 iBT). *Application deadline:* For fall admission, 12/15 priority date for domestic students, 12/15 for international students; for spring admission, 9/15 priority date for domestic students, 9/15 for international students. Applications are processed on a rolling basis. Application fee: $30. Electronic applications accepted. *Expenses:* Tuition, state resident: full-time $9474; part-time $350.88 per credit hour. Tuition, nonresident: full-time $16,236; part-time $601.34 per credit hour. *Required fees:* $630 per semester. One-time fee: $20. Tuition and fees vary according to course load and campus/location. *Financial support:* In 2011–12, 25 students received support, including fellowships with tuition reimbursements available (averaging $20,000 per year), research assistantships with tuition reimbursements available (averaging $20,000 per year), teaching assistantships with tuition reimbursements available (averaging $20,000 per year); traineeships also available. Financial award application deadline: 12/15; financial award applicants required to submit FAFSA. *Faculty research:* Metalloenzymes, gene regulation, DNA structure, NMR of synthetic membranes, secondary metabolites. *Unit head:* Dr. Timothy Logan, Interim Chairman, 850-644-1244, Fax: 850-644-8281, E-mail: gradinfo@chem.fsu.edu. *Application contact:* Dr. Tyler McQuade, Chair, Graduate Admissions Committee, 888-525-9281, Fax: 850-644-0465, E-mail: gradinfo@chem.fsu.edu. Web site: http://www.chem.fsu.edu.

Florida State University, The Graduate School, College of Arts and Sciences, Department of Scientific Computing, Tallahassee, FL 32306-4120. Offers computational science (MS, PSM, PhD), including atmospheric science (PhD), biochemistry (PhD), biological science (PhD), computational molecular biology/bioinformatics (PSM), computational science (PhD), geological science (PhD), materials science (PhD), physics (PhD). Part-time programs available. *Faculty:* 14 full-time (2 women). *Students:* 32 full-time (6 women), 3 part-time (0 women); includes 13 minority (1 Black or African American, non-Hispanic/Latino; 11 Asian, non-Hispanic/Latino; 1 Hispanic/Latino). Average age 28. 29 applicants, 41% accepted, 9 enrolled. In 2011, 14 master's, 3 doctorates awarded. Terminal master's awarded for partial completion of doctoral program. *Degree requirements:* For master's, thesis (for some programs); for doctorate, comprehensive exam, thesis/dissertation. *Entrance requirements:* For master's and doctorate, GRE General Test, knowledge of at least one object-oriented computing language, 3 letters of recommendations. Additional exam requirements/recommendations for international students: Required—TOEFL (minimum score 550 paper-based; 80 iBT). *Application deadline:* For fall admission, 1/15 for domestic and international students. Application fee: $30. Electronic applications accepted. *Expenses:* Tuition, state resident: full-time $9474; part-time $350.88 per credit hour. Tuition, nonresident: full-time $16,236; part-time $601.34 per credit hour. *Required fees:* $630 per semester. One-time fee: $20. Tuition and fees vary according to course load and campus/location. *Financial support:* In 2011–12, 32 students received support, including 12 research assistantships with full tuition reimbursements available (averaging $20,000 per year), 18 teaching assistantships with full tuition reimbursements available (averaging $20,000 per year); unspecified assistantships also available. Financial award application deadline: 4/15. *Faculty research:* Morphometrics, mathematical and systems biology, mining proteomic and metabolic data, computational materials research at Scientific Computing, advanced 4-D Var Data-Assimilation methods in dynamic meteorology and oceanography, computational fluid dynamics, astrophysics. *Unit head:* Dr. Sam Huckaba, Interim Dean, 850-644-1081. *Application contact:* Maribel Amwake, Graduate Academic Coordinator, 850-644-0143, Fax: 850-644-0098, E-mail: mamwake@fsu.edu. Web site: http://www.sc.fsu.edu.

George Mason University, College of Science, Department of Chemistry and Biochemistry, Fairfax, VA 22030. Offers chemistry (MS); chemistry and biochemistry (PhD). *Faculty:* 17 full-time (3 women), 5 part-time/adjunct (3 women). *Students:* 20 full-time (7 women), 31 part-time (14 women); includes 17 minority (3 Black or African American, non-Hispanic/Latino; 1 American Indian or Alaska Native, non-Hispanic/Latino; 10 Asian, non-Hispanic/Latino; 3 Hispanic/Latino), 5 international. Average age 29. 58 applicants, 50% accepted, 11 enrolled. In 2011, 14 master's, 1 doctorate awarded. *Degree requirements:* For master's, thesis or alternative. *Entrance requirements:* For master's, GRE, bachelor's degree in related field; 2 official copies of transcripts; expanded goals statement; 3 letters of recommendation; resume for those whose bachelor's degree is 5 years or older; for doctorate, GRE, undergraduate degree in related field; BS with minimum GPA of 3.0; 3 letters of recommendation; 2 copies of official transcripts; expanded goals statement; resume. Additional exam requirements/recommendations for international students: Required—TOEFL (minimum score 570 paper-based; 230 computer-based; 88 iBT), IELTS, Pearson Test of English. *Application deadline:* For fall admission, 4/15 priority date for domestic students; for spring

admission, 11/1 priority date for domestic students. Application fee: $65 ($80 for international students). Electronic applications accepted. *Expenses:* Tuition, state resident: full-time $8750; part-time $364.58 per credit. Tuition, nonresident: full-time $24,092; part-time $1003.83 per credit. *Required fees:* $2514; $104.75 per credit. *Financial support:* In 2011–12, 15 students received support, including 1 fellowship with full tuition reimbursement available (averaging $18,000 per year), 1 research assistantship with full and partial tuition reimbursement available (averaging $11,329 per year), 13 teaching assistantships with full and partial tuition reimbursements available (averaging $16,002 per year); career-related internships or fieldwork, Federal Work-Study, scholarships/grants, unspecified assistantships, and health care benefits (full-time research or teaching assistantship recipients) also available. Financial award application deadline: 3/1; financial award applicants required to submit FAFSA. *Total annual research expenditures:* $61,378. *Unit head:* John A. Schreifels, Chair, 703-993-1082, Fax: 703-993-1055, E-mail: jschreif@gmu.edu. *Application contact:* Mery Tucker, Administrative Specialist, 703-993-1070, Fax: 703-993-1055, E-mail: mtucker2@gmu.edu. Web site: http://chemistry.gmu.edu/.

Georgetown University, Graduate School of Arts and Sciences, Department of Chemistry, Washington, DC 20057. Offers analytical chemistry (PhD); biochemistry (PhD); computational chemistry (PhD); inorganic chemistry (PhD); materials chemistry (PhD); organic chemistry (PhD); physical chemistry (PhD); theoretical chemistry (PhD). Terminal master's awarded for partial completion of doctoral program. *Degree requirements:* For doctorate, comprehensive exam, thesis/dissertation. *Entrance requirements:* For doctorate, GRE General Test. Additional exam requirements/recommendations for international students: Required—TOEFL.

Georgetown University, Graduate School of Arts and Sciences, Programs in Biomedical Sciences, Department of Biochemistry and Molecular Biology, Washington, DC 20057. Offers MS, PhD. *Degree requirements:* For doctorate, comprehensive exam, thesis/dissertation. *Entrance requirements:* For doctorate, GRE General Test. Additional exam requirements/recommendations for international students: Required—TOEFL.

The George Washington University, Columbian College of Arts and Sciences, Institute for Biomedical Sciences, Program in Biochemistry and Molecular Genetics, Washington, DC 20052. Offers PhD. *Students:* 6 part-time (3 women), 1 international. Average age 28. In 2011, 3 degrees awarded. Terminal master's awarded for partial completion of doctoral program. *Degree requirements:* For doctorate, thesis/dissertation, general exam. *Entrance requirements:* For doctorate, GRE General Test, interview, minimum GPA of 3.0. Additional exam requirements/recommendations for international students: Required—TOEFL (minimum score 600 paper-based; 250 computer-based). *Application deadline:* For fall admission, 12/15 priority date for domestic students, 12/15 for international students; for spring admission, 10/1 priority date for domestic students, 10/1 for international students. Applications are processed on a rolling basis. Application fee: $75. Electronic applications accepted. *Financial support:* In 2011–12, 4 students received support. Fellowships, Federal Work-Study, institutionally sponsored loans, and tuition waivers available. Financial award application deadline: 2/1. *Unit head:* Valerie W. Hu, Director, 202-994-8431, E-mail: valhu@gwu.edu. *Application contact:* Information Contact, 202-994-7120, Fax: 202-994-6100, E-mail: genetics@gwu.edu. Web site: http://www.gwumc.edu/ibs/fields/biochemgenetics.html.

The George Washington University, School of Medicine and Health Sciences, Department of Biochemistry and Molecular Biology, Washington, DC 20037. Offers biochemistry and molecular biology (MS); biochemistry and molecular genetics (PhD); molecular biochemistry and bioinformatics (MS). *Degree requirements:* For master's, comprehensive exam; for doctorate, thesis/dissertation, general exam. *Entrance requirements:* For master's, GRE General Test, interview, minimum GPA of 3.0; for doctorate, GRE General Test, minimum GPA of 3.0. Additional exam requirements/recommendations for international students: Required—TOEFL (minimum score 550 paper-based; 213 computer-based).

Georgia Health Sciences University, College of Graduate Studies, Program in Biochemistry and Molecular Biology, Augusta, GA 30912. Offers MS, PhD. *Faculty:* 13 full-time (2 women). *Students:* 20 full-time (10 women); includes 1 minority (Hispanic/Latino), 9 international. Average age 27. In 2011, 4 doctorates awarded. *Degree requirements:* For doctorate, comprehensive exam, thesis/dissertation. *Entrance requirements:* For doctorate, GRE General Test. Additional exam requirements/recommendations for international students: Required—TOEFL (minimum score 550 paper-based; 213 computer-based; 79 iBT). *Application deadline:* For fall admission, 1/15 for domestic and international students. Application fee: $50. Electronic applications accepted. *Financial support:* In 2011–12, 8 research assistantships with partial tuition reimbursements (averaging $23,000 per year) were awarded; Federal Work-Study, institutionally sponsored loans, and scholarships/grants also available. Support available to part-time students. Financial award application deadline: 5/31; financial award applicants required to submit FAFSA. *Faculty research:* Bacterial pathogenesis, eye diseases, vitamins and amino acid transporters, transcriptional control and molecular oncology, tumor biology. *Total annual research expenditures:* $3.8 million. *Unit head:* Dr. Vadivel Ganapathy, Chair/Professor, 706-721-7652, Fax: 706-721-9947, E-mail: vganapat@georgiahealth.edu. *Application contact:* Dr. Patricia L. Cameron, Acting Vice Dean, 706-721-3279, E-mail: pcameron@georgiahealth.edu. Web site: http://www.georgiahealth.edu/bmb/.

Georgia Institute of Technology, Graduate Studies and Research, College of Sciences, School of Chemistry and Biochemistry, Atlanta, GA 30332-0001. Offers MS, MS Chem, PhD. Terminal master's awarded for partial completion of doctoral program. *Degree requirements:* For master's, thesis (for some programs); for doctorate, thesis/dissertation. *Entrance requirements:* For master's and doctorate, GRE General Test, GRE Subject Test, minimum GPA of 2.7. Additional exam requirements/recommendations for international students: Required—TOEFL. Electronic applications accepted. *Faculty research:* Inorganic, organic, physical, and analytical chemistry.

Georgia State University, College of Arts and Sciences, Department of Biology, Program in Molecular Genetics and Biochemistry, Atlanta, GA 30302-3083. Offers MS, PhD. Part-time programs available. Terminal master's awarded for partial completion of doctoral program. *Degree requirements:* For master's, thesis or alternative; for doctorate, thesis/dissertation, exam. *Entrance requirements:* For master's and doctorate, GRE General Test. Additional exam requirements/recommendations for international students: Required—TOEFL. Electronic applications accepted.

Graduate School and University Center of the City University of New York, Graduate Studies, Program in Biochemistry, New York, NY 10016-4039. Offers PhD. *Degree requirements:* For doctorate, thesis/dissertation, field experience. *Entrance requirements:* For doctorate, GRE General Test. Additional exam requirements/recommendations for international students: Required—TOEFL. Electronic applications accepted.

Harvard University, Graduate School of Arts and Sciences, Department of Chemistry and Chemical Biology, Cambridge, MA 02138. Offers biochemical chemistry (PhD); inorganic chemistry (PhD); organic chemistry (PhD); physical chemistry (PhD). *Degree requirements:* For doctorate, thesis/dissertation, cumulative exams. *Entrance requirements:* For doctorate, GRE General Test, GRE Subject Test. Additional exam requirements/recommendations for international students: Required—TOEFL. *Expenses: Tuition:* Full-time $36,304. *Required fees:* $1186. Full-time tuition and fees vary according to program.

Harvard University, Graduate School of Arts and Sciences, Division of Medical Sciences, Boston, MA 02115. Offers biological chemistry and molecular pharmacology (PhD); cell biology (PhD); genetics (PhD); microbiology and molecular genetics (PhD); pathology (PhD), including experimental pathology. *Degree requirements:* For doctorate, thesis/dissertation. *Entrance requirements:* For doctorate, GRE General Test, GRE Subject Test. Additional exam requirements/recommendations for international students: Required—TOEFL. *Expenses: Tuition:* Full-time $36,304. *Required fees:* $1186. Full-time tuition and fees vary according to program.

Howard University, College of Medicine, Department of Biochemistry and Molecular Biology, Washington, DC 20059-0002. Offers biochemistry and molecular biology (PhD); biotechnology (MS); MD/PhD. Part-time programs available. *Degree requirements:* For master's, externship; for doctorate, comprehensive exam, thesis/dissertation. *Entrance requirements:* For master's and doctorate, GRE General Test, minimum GPA of 3.0. *Faculty research:* Cellular and molecular biology of olfaction, gene regulation and expression, enzymology, NMR spectroscopy of molecular structure, hormone regulation/metabolism.

Howard University, Graduate School, Department of Chemistry, Washington, DC 20059-0002. Offers analytical chemistry (MS, PhD); atmospheric (MS, PhD); biochemistry (MS, PhD); environmental (MS, PhD); inorganic chemistry (MS, PhD); organic chemistry (MS, PhD); physical chemistry (MS, PhD). Terminal master's awarded for partial completion of doctoral program. *Degree requirements:* For master's, comprehensive exam, thesis, teaching experience; for doctorate, comprehensive exam, thesis/dissertation, teaching experience. *Entrance requirements:* For master's, GRE General Test, minimum GPA of 2.7; for doctorate, GRE General Test, minimum GPA of 3.0. Additional exam requirements/recommendations for international students: Required—TOEFL. Electronic applications accepted. *Faculty research:* Synthetic organics, materials, natural products, mass spectrometry.

Hunter College of the City University of New York, Graduate School, School of Arts and Sciences, Department of Chemistry, Program in Biochemistry, New York, NY 10021-5085. Offers MA, PhD. Part-time programs available. *Faculty:* 3 full-time (2 women). *Students:* 3 full-time (0 women), 8 part-time (6 women); includes 4 minority (3 Asian, non-Hispanic/Latino; 1 Hispanic/Latino), 3 international. Average age 26. 13 applicants, 54% accepted, 6 enrolled. In 2011, 5 master's awarded. *Degree requirements:* For master's, comprehensive exam or thesis. *Entrance requirements:* For master's, GRE General Test, 1 year of course work in chemistry, quantitative analysis, organic chemistry, physical chemistry, biology, biochemistry lecture and laboratory. Additional exam requirements/recommendations for international students: Required—TOEFL. *Application deadline:* For fall admission, 4/1 for domestic students; for spring admission, 11/1 for domestic students. Application fee: $125. *Expenses:* Tuition, state resident: full-time $8210; part-time $345 per credit. Tuition, nonresident: full-time $15,360; part-time $640 per credit. *Required fees:* $280 per semester. One-time fee: $125. Tuition and fees vary according to class time, campus/location and program. *Financial support:* Teaching assistantships, Federal Work-Study, scholarships/grants, and tuition waivers (partial) available. Support available to part-time students. *Faculty research:* Protein/nucleic acid interactions, physical properties of iron-sulfur proteins, neurotransmitter receptors and ion channels Drosophila melanogaster, requirements of DNA synthesis, oncogenes. *Unit head:* Yuiia Xu, Adviser, 212-772-4310. *Application contact:* William Zlata, Director for Graduate Admissions, 212-772-4482, Fax: 212-650-3336, E-mail: admissions@hunter.cuny.edu.

Illinois Institute of Technology, Graduate College, College of Science and Letters, Department of Biological, Chemical and Physical Sciences, Biology Division, Chicago, IL 60616. Offers biochemistry (MBS, MS); biology (PhD); biotechnology (MBS, MS); cell and molecular biology (MBS, MS); microbiology (MB, MS); molecular biochemistry and biophysics (PhD); molecular biology and biophysics (MS). Part-time and evening/weekend programs available. Postbaccalaureate distance learning degree programs offered (minimal on-campus study). Terminal master's awarded for partial completion of doctoral program. *Degree requirements:* For master's, comprehensive exam, thesis (for some programs); for doctorate, comprehensive exam, thesis/dissertation. *Entrance requirements:* For master's, GRE General Test (minimum score 1000 Quantitative and Verbal, 2.5 Analytical Writing), minimum undergraduate GPA of 3.0; for doctorate, GRE General Test (minimum score 1200 Quantitative and Verbal, 3.0 Analytical Writing), minimum undergraduate GPA of 3.0. Additional exam requirements/recommendations for international students: Required—TOEFL (minimum score 523 paper-based; 213 computer-based; 70 iBT); Recommended—IELTS (minimum score 5.5). Electronic applications accepted. *Faculty research:* Structure and biophysics of macromolecular systems; efficacy and mechanism of action of chemopreventive agents in experimental carcinogenesis of breast, colon, lung and prostate; study of fundamental structural biochemistry problems that have direct links to the understanding and treatment of disease; spectroscopic techniques for the study of multi-domain proteins; molecular mechanisms of cancer and cancer gene therapy.

Illinois State University, Graduate School, College of Arts and Sciences, Department of Biological Sciences, Normal, IL 61790-2200. Offers animal behavior (MS); bacteriology (MS); biochemistry (MS); biological sciences (MS); biology (PhD); biophysics (MS); biotechnology (MS); botany (MS, PhD); cell biology (MS); conservation biology (MS); developmental biology (MS); ecology (MS, PhD); entomology (MS); evolutionary biology (MS); genetics (MS, PhD); immunology (MS); microbiology (MS, PhD); molecular biology (MS); molecular genetics (MS); neurobiology (MS); neuroscience (MS); parasitology (MS); physiology (MS, PhD); plant biology (MS); plant molecular biology (MS); plant sciences (MS); structural biology (MS); zoology (MS, PhD). Part-time programs available. *Degree requirements:* For master's, thesis or alternative; for doctorate, variable foreign language requirement, thesis/dissertation, 2 terms of residency. *Entrance requirements:* For master's, GRE General Test, minimum GPA of 2.6 in last 60 hours of course work; for doctorate, GRE General Test. *Faculty research:* Redoc balance and drug development in schistosoma mansoni, control of the growth of listeria monocytogenes at low temperature, regulation of cell expansion and microtubule function by SPRI, CRUI: physiology and fitness consequences of different life history phenotypes.

Indiana University Bloomington, University Graduate School, College of Arts and Sciences, Department of Chemistry, Bloomington, IN 47405. Offers analytical chemistry (PhD); chemical biology chemistry (PhD); chemistry (MAT); inorganic chemistry (PhD); materials chemistry (PhD); organic chemistry (PhD); physical chemistry (PhD). *Faculty:* 42 full-time (4 women). *Students:* 200 full-time (82 women), 3 part-time (0 women); includes 18 minority (7 Black or African American, non-Hispanic/Latino; 8 Asian, non-Hispanic/Latino; 1 Hispanic/Latino; 1 Native Hawaiian or other Pacific Islander, non-Hispanic/Latino; 1 Two or more races, non-Hispanic/Latino), 63 international. Average age 27. 290 applicants, 49% accepted, 46 enrolled. In 2011, 11 master's, 20 doctorates awarded. Terminal master's awarded for partial completion of doctoral program. *Median time to degree:* Of those who began their doctoral program in fall 2003, 49% received their degree in 8 years or less. *Degree requirements:* For master's, thesis; for doctorate, thesis/dissertation. *Entrance requirements:* For master's and doctorate, GRE General

Test, GRE Subject Test. Additional exam requirements/recommendations for international students: Required—TOEFL. *Application deadline:* For fall admission, 1/15 priority date for domestic students, 12/15 for international students. Applications are processed on a rolling basis. Application fee: $55 ($65 for international students). *Financial support:* In 2011–12, 200 students received support, including 10 fellowships with full tuition reimbursements available, 76 research assistantships with full tuition reimbursements available, 111 teaching assistantships with full tuition reimbursements available; Federal Work-Study and institutionally sponsored loans also available. *Faculty research:* Synthesis of complex natural products, organic reaction mechanisms, organic electrochemistry, transitive-metal chemistry, solid-state and surface chemistry. *Total annual research expenditures:* $7.7 million. *Unit head:* David Giedroc, Chairperson, 812-855-6239, E-mail: chemchair@indiana.edu. *Application contact:* Daniel Mindiola, Director of Graduate Admissions, 812-855-2069, Fax: 812-855-8385, E-mail: mindiola@indiana.edu. Web site: http://www.chem.indiana.edu/.

Indiana University Bloomington, University Graduate School, College of Arts and Sciences, Interdisciplinary Biochemistry Graduate Program, Bloomington, IN 47405. Offers PhD. *Faculty:* 59 full-time (16 women). *Students:* 59 full-time (35 women); includes 6 minority (1 Black or African American, non-Hispanic/Latino; 1 American Indian or Alaska Native, non-Hispanic/Latino; 1 Asian, non-Hispanic/Latino; 1 Hispanic/Latino; 2 Two or more races, non-Hispanic/Latino), 34 international. Average age 26. 66 applicants, 36% accepted, 10 enrolled. In 2011, 3 doctorates awarded. Terminal master's awarded for partial completion of doctoral program. *Degree requirements:* For doctorate, comprehensive exam, thesis/dissertation, Test of English Proficiency for International Associate Instructor Candidates (TEPAIC)(for international students). *Entrance requirements:* For doctorate, GRE. Additional exam requirements/recommendations for international students: Required—TOEFL (minimum score 550 paper-based; 213 computer-based; 79 iBT). *Application deadline:* For fall admission, 1/15 priority date for domestic students, 12/1 for international students. Application fee: $55 ($65 for international students). Electronic applications accepted. *Financial support:* In 2011–12, 10 students received support, including 10 fellowships with full tuition reimbursements available (averaging $25,000 per year), 21 research assistantships with full tuition reimbursements available (averaging $20,500 per year), 27 teaching assistantships with full tuition reimbursements available (averaging $20,500 per year); scholarships/grants, health care benefits, tuition waivers (full), and unspecified assistantships also available. *Faculty research:* Biochemistry of genes and genomes, microbial biochemistry and virology, structural biology, chemical biology, cellular and medicinal biochemistry, plant biochemistry. *Unit head:* Dr. Carl E. Bauer, Chair, Molecular and Cellular Biochemistry Department, 812-856-0192, Fax: 812-856-5710, E-mail: bchem@indiana.edu. *Application contact:* Susanne Kindred, Administrative Assistant, 812-856-1301, Fax: 812-856-5710, E-mail: bchem@indiana.edu. Web site: http://www.indiana.edu/~mcbdept/graduate/#3.

Indiana University–Purdue University Indianapolis, Indiana University School of Medicine, Department of Biochemistry and Molecular Biology, Indianapolis, IN 46202-2896. Offers PhD, MD/MS, MD/PhD. *Faculty:* 17 full-time (4 women). *Students:* 29 full-time (16 women), 20 part-time (7 women); includes 5 minority (1 Black or African American, non-Hispanic/Latino; 3 Asian, non-Hispanic/Latino; 1 Hispanic/Latino), 20 international. Average age 32. 2 applicants, 50% accepted, 1 enrolled. In 2011, 5 doctorates awarded. Terminal master's awarded for partial completion of doctoral program. *Degree requirements:* For doctorate, thesis/dissertation. *Entrance requirements:* For doctorate, GRE General Test, GRE Subject Test (recommended), previous course work in organic chemistry. *Application deadline:* For fall admission, 1/15 priority date for domestic students. Applications are processed on a rolling basis. Application fee: $55 ($65 for international students). *Financial support:* In 2011–12, teaching assistantships (averaging $14,949 per year) were awarded; fellowships with tuition reimbursements, research assistantships with tuition reimbursements, Federal Work-Study, institutionally sponsored loans, scholarships/grants, and tuition waivers (partial) also available. Support available to part-time students. Financial award application deadline: 2/1. *Faculty research:* Metabolic regulation, enzymology, peptide and protein chemistry, cell biology, signal transduction. *Unit head:* Dr. Zhong-Yin Zhang, Chairman, 317-274-7151. *Application contact:* Robert M. Stump, Jr., Director of Admissions, 317-274-3772, E-mail: inmedadm@iupui.edu. Web site: http://www.biochemistry.iu.edu/.

Indiana University–Purdue University Indianapolis, School of Science, Department of Chemistry and Chemical Biology, Indianapolis, IN 46202-2896. Offers MS, PhD, MD/PhD. MD/PhD offered jointly with Indiana University School of Medicine and Purdue University. Part-time and evening/weekend programs available. *Faculty:* 10 full-time (2 women). *Students:* 21 full-time (11 women), 22 part-time (10 women); includes 4 minority (1 Asian, non-Hispanic/Latino; 1 Hispanic/Latino; 2 Two or more races, non-Hispanic/Latino), 7 international. Average age 31. 21 applicants, 71% accepted, 15 enrolled. In 2011, 8 master's awarded. Terminal master's awarded for partial completion of doctoral program. *Degree requirements:* For master's, thesis (for some programs); for doctorate, thesis/dissertation. *Entrance requirements:* For master's and doctorate, minimum GPA of 3.0. Additional exam requirements/recommendations for international students: Required—TOEFL. *Application deadline:* Applications are processed on a rolling basis. Application fee: $55 ($65 for international students). *Financial support:* In 2011–12, fellowships with partial tuition reimbursements (averaging $13,500 per year), teaching assistantships with partial tuition reimbursements (averaging $17,440 per year) were awarded; research assistantships with partial tuition reimbursements, career-related internships or fieldwork, institutionally sponsored loans, tuition waivers (partial), and cooperative positions also available. Financial award application deadline: 3/1. *Faculty research:* Analytical, biological, inorganic, organic, and physical chemistry. *Total annual research expenditures:* $1.6 million. *Unit head:* Jay A. Siegel, Chair, 317-274-6872. *Application contact:* Eric Long, Associate Chair, 317-274-6888, Fax: 317-274-4701, E-mail: long@chem.iupui.edu. Web site: http://www.chem.iupui.edu/.

Iowa State University of Science and Technology, Department of Biochemistry, Biophysics, and Molecular Biology, Ames, IA 50011. Offers biochemistry (MS, PhD); biophysics (MS, PhD); genetics (MS, PhD); molecular, cellular, and developmental biology (MS, PhD); toxicology (MS, PhD). *Degree requirements:* For master's, thesis; for doctorate, thesis/dissertation. *Entrance requirements:* For master's and doctorate, GRE General Test. Additional exam requirements/recommendations for international students: Required—TOEFL (minimum score 550 paper-based; 79 iBT), IELTS (minimum score 6.5). *Application deadline:* For fall admission, 1/1 priority date for domestic students, 1/1 for international students. Application fee: $40 ($90 for international students). Electronic applications accepted. *Unit head:* Dr. Reuben Peters, Director of Graduate Education, 515-294-6116, Fax: 515-294-0453, E-mail: biochem@iastate.edu. *Application contact:* Connie Garnett, Application Contact, 515-294-6116, Fax: 515-294-0453, E-mail: biochem@iastate.edu. Web site: http://www.bbmb.iastate.edu/index.php?.

The Johns Hopkins University, Bloomberg School of Public Health, Department of Biochemistry and Molecular Biology, Baltimore, MD 21205. Offers MHS, Sc M, PhD. Part-time programs available. *Degree requirements:* For master's, thesis; for doctorate, comprehensive exam, thesis/dissertation, oral and written exams. *Entrance requirements:* For master's, MCAT or GRE, 3 letters of recommendation, curriculum

vitae; for doctorate, GRE General Test, 3 letters of recommendation, curriculum vitae. Additional exam requirements/recommendations for international students: Required—TOEFL (minimum score 600 paper-based; 250 computer-based). Electronic applications accepted. *Faculty research:* DNA replication, repair, structure, carcinogenesis, protein structure, enzyme catalysts, reproductive biology.

The Johns Hopkins University, National Institutes of Health Sponsored Programs, Baltimore, MD 21218-2699. Offers biology (PhD), including biochemistry, biophysics, cell biology, developmental biology, genetic biology, molecular biology; cell, molecular, and developmental biology and biophysics (PhD). *Degree requirements:* For doctorate, comprehensive exam, thesis/dissertation. *Entrance requirements:* For doctorate, GRE General Test. Additional exam requirements/recommendations for international students: Required—TOEFL (minimum score 600 paper-based; 250 computer-based), TWE. Electronic applications accepted. *Faculty research:* Protein and nucleic acid biochemistry and biophysical chemistry, molecular biology and development.

The Johns Hopkins University, School of Medicine, Graduate Programs in Medicine, Department of Biological Chemistry, Baltimore, MD 21205. Offers PhD. *Degree requirements:* For doctorate, thesis/dissertation. *Entrance requirements:* For doctorate, GRE General Test. Additional exam requirements/recommendations for international students: Required—TOEFL. Electronic applications accepted. *Faculty research:* Cell adhesion, genetics, signal transduction and RNA metabolism, enzyme structure and function, gene expression.

The Johns Hopkins University, School of Medicine, Graduate Programs in Medicine, Program in Biochemistry, Cellular and Molecular Biology, Baltimore, MD 21205. Offers PhD. *Degree requirements:* For doctorate, comprehensive exam, thesis/dissertation. *Entrance requirements:* For doctorate, GRE General Test. Additional exam requirements/recommendations for international students: Required—TOEFL. Electronic applications accepted. *Faculty research:* Developmental biology, genomics/proteomics, protein targeting, signal transduction, structural biology.

Kansas State University, Graduate School, College of Arts and Sciences, Department of Biochemistry, Manhattan, KS 66506. Offers MS, PhD. Part-time programs available. *Faculty:* 14 full-time (2 women), 3 part-time/adjunct (0 women). *Students:* 31 full-time (15 women), 1 part-time (0 women); includes 2 minority (1 Black or African American, non-Hispanic/Latino; 1 Hispanic/Latino), 25 international. Average age 28. 27 applicants, 19% accepted, 2 enrolled. In 2011, 2 master's, 4 doctorates awarded. *Degree requirements:* For master's, thesis; for doctorate, thesis/dissertation. *Entrance requirements:* For master's, GRE General Test, minimum GPA of 3.0 for junior and senior year; for doctorate, GRE General Test, minimum undergraduate GPA of 3.0 or an excellent postgraduate record. Additional exam requirements/recommendations for international students: Required—TOEFL (minimum score 550 paper-based; 213 computer-based; 79 iBT). *Application deadline:* For fall admission, 2/1 priority date for domestic students, 2/1 for international students; for spring admission, 8/1 priority date for domestic students, 8/1 for international students. Applications are processed on a rolling basis. Application fee: $40 ($55 for international students). Electronic applications accepted. *Financial support:* In 2011–12, 27 research assistantships (averaging $18,080 per year), 12 teaching assistantships (averaging $19,243 per year) were awarded; Federal Work-Study, institutionally sponsored loans, and scholarships/grants also available. Support available to part-time students. Financial award application deadline: 3/1; financial award applicants required to submit FAFSA. *Faculty research:* Protein structure/function, insect biochemistry, computational biochemistry, molecular mechanisms in cancer, membrane and lipids biochemistry. *Total annual research expenditures:* $2.2 million. *Unit head:* Michael Kanost, Head, 785-532-6964, Fax: 785-532-7278, E-mail: kanost@ksu.edu. *Application contact:* Michal Zolkiewski, Director, 785-532-3083, Fax: 785-532-7278, E-mail: michalz@ksu.edu. Web site: http://www.k-state.edu/bchem/.

Kansas State University, Graduate School, College of Arts and Sciences, Department of Chemistry, Manhattan, KS 66506. Offers analytical chemistry (MS); biological chemistry (MS); chemistry (PhD); inorganic chemistry (MS); materials chemistry (MS); organic chemistry (MS); physical chemistry (MS). *Faculty:* 17 full-time (2 women). *Students:* 63 full-time (28 women), 4 part-time (0 women); includes 2 minority (1 Black or African American, non-Hispanic/Latino; 1 Asian, non-Hispanic/Latino), 55 international. Average age 28. 119 applicants, 34% accepted, 15 enrolled. In 2011, 2 master's, 10 doctorates awarded. Terminal master's awarded for partial completion of doctoral program. *Degree requirements:* For master's, thesis; for doctorate, thesis/dissertation. *Entrance requirements:* For master's and doctorate, GRE, minimum GPA of 3.0. Additional exam requirements/recommendations for international students: Required—TOEFL (minimum score 550 paper-based; 213 computer-based). *Application deadline:* For fall admission, 2/1 priority date for domestic students, 2/1 for international students; for spring admission, 8/1 priority date for domestic students, 8/1 for international students. Applications are processed on a rolling basis. Application fee: $40 ($55 for international students). Electronic applications accepted. *Financial support:* In 2011–12, 39 research assistantships (averaging $18,182 per year), 24 teaching assistantships with full tuition reimbursements (averaging $18,106 per year) were awarded; institutionally sponsored loans and scholarships/grants also available. Support available to part-time students. Financial award application deadline: 3/1; financial award applicants required to submit FAFSA. *Faculty research:* Inorganic chemistry, organic and biological chemistry, analytical chemistry, physical chemistry, materials chemistry and nanotechnology. *Total annual research expenditures:* $2.4 million. *Unit head:* Eric Maatta, Head, 785-532-6665, Fax: 785-532-6666, E-mail: eam@ksu.edu. *Application contact:* Christer Aakeroy, Director, 785-532-6096, Fax: 785-532-6666, E-mail: aakeroy@ksu.edu. Web site: http://www.k-state.edu/chem/.

Kent State University, College of Arts and Sciences, Department of Chemistry and Biochemistry, Kent, OH 44242-0001. Offers analytical chemistry (MS, PhD); biochemistry (MS, PhD); chemistry (MA); inorganic chemistry (MS, PhD); organic chemistry (MS, PhD); physical chemistry (MS, PhD). Terminal master's awarded for partial completion of doctoral program. *Degree requirements:* For master's, comprehensive exam, thesis; for doctorate, comprehensive exam, thesis/dissertation. *Entrance requirements:* For master's and doctorate, placement exam, GRE General Test, GRE Subject Test (recommended), minimum GPA of 2.75. Additional exam requirements/recommendations for international students: Required—TOEFL (minimum score 525 paper-based; 71 iBT). Electronic applications accepted. *Expenses:* Tuition, state resident: full-time $8136; part-time $452 per credit hour. Tuition, nonresident: full-time $14,292; part-time $794 per credit hour. *Faculty research:* Biological chemistry, materials chemistry, molecular spectroscopy.

Laurentian University, School of Graduate Studies and Research, Programme in Chemistry and Biochemistry, Sudbury, ON P3E 2C6, Canada. Offers analytical chemistry (M Sc); biochemistry (M Sc); environmental chemistry (M Sc); organic chemistry (M Sc); physical/theoretical chemistry (M Sc). Part-time programs available. *Degree requirements:* For master's, thesis or alternative. *Entrance requirements:* For master's, honors degree with minimum second class. *Faculty research:* Cell cycle checkpoints, kinetic modeling, toxicology to metal stress, quantum chemistry, biogeochemistry metal speciation.

Biochemistry

Lehigh University, College of Arts and Sciences, Department of Biological Sciences, Bethlehem, PA 18015. Offers biochemistry (PhD); integrative biology and neuroscience (PhD); molecular biology (MS, PhD). Part-time programs available. Postbaccalaureate distance learning degree programs offered (no on-campus study). *Faculty:* 16 full-time (7 women). *Students:* 36 full-time (19 women), 22 part-time (15 women); includes 4 minority (2 Black or African American, non-Hispanic/Latino; 2 Asian, non-Hispanic/Latino), 7 international. Average age 30. 70 applicants, 14% accepted, 9 enrolled. In 2011, 11 master's, 3 doctorates awarded. Terminal master's awarded for partial completion of doctoral program. *Degree requirements:* For master's, research report; for doctorate, comprehensive exam, thesis/dissertation. *Entrance requirements:* For doctorate, GRE General Test. Additional exam requirements/recommendations for international students: Required—TOEFL. *Application deadline:* For fall admission, 12/15 for domestic and international students. Applications are processed on a rolling basis. Application fee: $75. Electronic applications accepted. *Financial support:* In 2011–12, 4 fellowships with full tuition reimbursements (averaging $24,500 per year), 6 research assistantships with full tuition reimbursements (averaging $23,750 per year), 16 teaching assistantships with full tuition reimbursements (averaging $23,750 per year) were awarded; scholarships/grants and unspecified assistantships also available. Financial award application deadline: 12/15. *Faculty research:* Gene expression, cytoskeleton and cell structure, cell cycle and growth regulation, neuroscience, animal behavior, microbiology. *Total annual research expenditures:* $2 million. *Unit head:* Dr. Murray Itzkowitz, Chairperson, 610-758-3680, Fax: 610-758-4004, E-mail: mi00@lehigh.edu. *Application contact:* Dr. Jennifer M. Swann, Graduate Coordinator, 610-758-5484, Fax: 610-758-4004, E-mail: jms5@lehigh.edu. Web site: http://www.lehigh.edu/~inbios/.

Loma Linda University, School of Medicine, Department of Biochemistry/Microbiology, Loma Linda, CA 92350. Offers MS, PhD. Part-time programs available. *Degree requirements:* For master's, thesis or alternative; for doctorate, thesis/dissertation. *Entrance requirements:* For master's and doctorate, GRE General Test. Additional exam requirements/recommendations for international students: Required—TOEFL (minimum score 550 paper-based; 213 computer-based). *Faculty research:* Physical chemistry of macromolecules, biochemistry of endocrine system, biochemical mechanism of bone volume regulation.

Louisiana State University and Agricultural and Mechanical College, Graduate School, College of Science, Department of Biological Sciences, Baton Rouge, LA 70803. Offers biochemistry (MS, PhD); biological science (MS, PhD); science (MNS). Part-time programs available. *Faculty:* 62 full-time (8 women). *Students:* 130 full-time (57 women), 8 part-time (3 women); includes 10 minority (1 Black or African American, non-Hispanic/Latino; 5 Asian, non-Hispanic/Latino; 3 Hispanic/Latino; 1 Two or more races, non-Hispanic/Latino), 57 international. Average age 29. 144 applicants, 17% accepted, 15 enrolled. In 2011, 5 master's, 18 doctorates awarded. Terminal master's awarded for partial completion of doctoral program. *Degree requirements:* For doctorate, thesis/dissertation. *Entrance requirements:* For master's and doctorate, GRE General Test, minimum GPA of 3.0. Additional exam requirements/recommendations for international students: Required—TOEFL (minimum score 550 paper-based; 213 computer-based; 79 iBT) or IELTS (minimum score 6.5). *Application deadline:* For fall admission, 5/15 for domestic and international students; for spring admission, 10/15 for domestic and international students. Applications are processed on a rolling basis. Application fee: $25. Electronic applications accepted. *Financial support:* In 2011–12, 137 students received support, including 10 fellowships with full and partial tuition reimbursements available (averaging $22,471 per year), 37 research assistantships with full and partial tuition reimbursements available (averaging $22,448 per year), 84 teaching assistantships with full and partial tuition reimbursements available (averaging $18,811 per year); Federal Work-Study, institutionally sponsored loans, health care benefits, and unspecified assistantships also available. Support available to part-time students. Financial award applicants required to submit FAFSA. *Faculty research:* Biochemistry and molecular biology, cell developmental and integrative biology, systematics, ecology and evolutionary biology. *Total annual research expenditures:* $9.6 million. *Unit head:* Dr. James Moroney, Chair, 225-578-1765, Fax: 225-578-2597. *Application contact:* Dr. Michael E. Hellberg, Associate Chairman, 225-578-1240, Fax: 225-578-7299, E-mail: biogradcoord@lsu.edu. Web site: http://www.biology.lsu.edu/.

Louisiana State University Health Sciences Center at Shreveport, Department of Biochemistry and Molecular Biology, Shreveport, LA 71130-3932. Offers MS, PhD, MD/PhD. *Degree requirements:* For master's, thesis; for doctorate, thesis/dissertation. *Entrance requirements:* For master's and doctorate, GRE General Test. Additional exam requirements/recommendations for international students: Required—TOEFL. *Faculty research:* Metabolite transport, regulation of translation and transcription, prokaryotic molecular genetics, cell matrix biochemistry, yeast molecular genetics, oncogenes.

Loyola University Chicago, Graduate School, Program in Molecular and Cellular Biochemistry, Chicago, IL 60660. Offers MS, PhD, MD/PhD. *Faculty:* 23 full-time (11 women). *Students:* 10 full-time (6 women); includes 1 minority (Asian, non-Hispanic/Latino), 5 international. Average age 28. 2 applicants, 50% accepted, 0 enrolled. In 2011, 5 degrees awarded. *Median time to degree:* Of those who began their doctoral program in fall 2003, 100% received their degree in 8 years or less. *Degree requirements:* For master's, oral and written reports; for doctorate, comprehensive exam, thesis/dissertation. *Entrance requirements:* For master's and doctorate, GRE General Test. Additional exam requirements/recommendations for international students: Required—TOEFL (minimum score 600 paper-based; 250 computer-based). *Application deadline:* For fall admission, 3/30 priority date for domestic students, 3/30 for international students. Applications are processed on a rolling basis. Application fee: $50. Electronic applications accepted. *Expenses: Tuition:* Full-time $15,660; part-time $870 per credit hour. *Required fees:* $125 per semester. Tuition and fees vary according to course load and program. *Financial support:* In 2011–12, 5 students received support, including 5 fellowships with full tuition reimbursements available, 11 research assistantships with full tuition reimbursements available; Federal Work-Study, institutionally sponsored loans, and scholarships/grants also available. Financial award application deadline: 3/30. *Faculty research:* Molecular oncology, molecular neurochemical mechanisms of brain development and alcohol addiction, biochemistry of RNA and protein synthesis and intracellular protein degradation, developmentally regulated genes, neurotransmitters and cell-cell interactions. *Unit head:* Dr. William H. Simmons, Chief, 708-216-3362, Fax: 708-216-8523, E-mail: hsimmon@lumc.edu. *Application contact:* Ashyia D. Paul, Administrative Secretary, 708-216-3360, Fax: 708-216-8523, E-mail: apaul@lumc.edu.

Massachusetts Institute of Technology, School of Science, Department of Biology, Cambridge, MA 02139. Offers biochemistry (PhD); biological oceanography (PhD); biology (PhD); biophysical chemistry and molecular structure (PhD); cell biology (PhD); computational and systems biology (PhD); developmental biology (PhD); genetics (PhD); immunology (PhD); microbiology (PhD); molecular biology (PhD); neurobiology (PhD). *Faculty:* 58 full-time (15 women). *Students:* 248 full-time (129 women); includes 69 minority (5 Black or African American, non-Hispanic/Latino; 1 American Indian or Alaska Native, non-Hispanic/Latino; 25 Asian, non-Hispanic/Latino; 31 Hispanic/Latino; 7 Two or more races, non-Hispanic/Latino), 36 international. Average age 26. 698 applicants, 15% accepted, 44 enrolled. In 2011, 38 doctorates awarded. *Degree requirements:* For doctorate, comprehensive exam, thesis/dissertation. *Entrance requirements:* For doctorate, GRE General Test. Additional exam requirements/recommendations for international students: Required—TOEFL (minimum score 577 paper-based; 233 computer-based), IELTS (minimum score 6.5). *Application deadline:* For fall admission, 12/1 for domestic and international students. Application fee: $75. Electronic applications accepted. *Expenses: Tuition:* Full-time $40,460; part-time $630 per credit hour. *Required fees:* $272. *Financial support:* In 2011–12, 214 students received support, including 129 fellowships (averaging $33,200 per year), 117 research assistantships (averaging $32,900 per year); teaching assistantships, Federal Work-Study, institutionally sponsored loans, scholarships/grants, traineeships, health care benefits, and unspecified assistantships also available. *Faculty research:* Cellular, developmental and molecular (plant and animal) biology; biochemistry, bioengineering, biophysics and structural biology; classical and molecular genetics; immunology and microbiology; cancer biology, molecular medicine, neurobiology and human disease; computational and systems biology. *Total annual research expenditures:* $53.6 million. *Unit head:* Prof. Tania A. Baker, Head, 617-253-4701, E-mail: mitbio@mit.edu. *Application contact:* Biology Education Office, 617-253-3717, Fax: 617-258-9329, E-mail: gradbio@mit.edu. Web site: https://biology.mit.edu/.

Massachusetts Institute of Technology, School of Science, Department of Chemistry, Cambridge, MA 02139. Offers biological chemistry (PhD, Sc D); inorganic chemistry (PhD, Sc D); organic chemistry (PhD, Sc D); physical chemistry (PhD, Sc D). *Faculty:* 26 full-time (5 women). *Students:* 221 full-time (73 women), 1 (woman) part-time; includes 48 minority (5 Black or African American, non-Hispanic/Latino; 1 American Indian or Alaska Native, non-Hispanic/Latino; 24 Asian, non-Hispanic/Latino; 14 Hispanic/Latino; 4 Two or more races, non-Hispanic/Latino), 64 international. Average age 25. 570 applicants, 20% accepted, 43 enrolled. In 2011, 45 doctorates awarded. *Degree requirements:* For doctorate, comprehensive exam, thesis/dissertation. *Entrance requirements:* For doctorate, GRE General Test. Additional exam requirements/recommendations for international students: Required—IELTS (minimum score 7); Recommended—TOEFL (minimum score 600 paper-based; 250 computer-based). *Application deadline:* For fall admission, 12/15 for domestic and international students. Application fee: $75. Electronic applications accepted. *Expenses: Tuition:* Full-time $40,460; part-time $630 per credit hour. *Required fees:* $272. *Financial support:* In 2011–12, 216 students received support, including 79 fellowships (averaging $34,800 per year), 127 research assistantships (averaging $31,400 per year), 16 teaching assistantships (averaging $32,600 per year); Federal Work-Study, institutionally sponsored loans, scholarships/grants, traineeships, health care benefits, and unspecified assistantships also available. *Faculty research:* Synthetic organic and organometallic chemistry including catalysis; biological chemistry including bioorganic chemistry; physical chemistry including chemical dynamics and biophysical chemistry; inorganic chemistry including synthesis, catalysis, bioinorganic and physical inorganic chemistry; materials chemistry including surface science, nanoscience and polymers. *Total annual research expenditures:* $31.1 million. *Unit head:* Prof. Sylvia T. Ceyer, Head, 617-253-1803, Fax: 617-258-7500. *Application contact:* Graduate Administrator, 617-253-1845, Fax: 617-258-0241, E-mail: chemgradeducation@mit.edu. Web site: http://web.mit.edu/chemistry/www/.

Mayo Graduate School, Graduate Programs in Biomedical Sciences, Programs in Biochemistry, Structural Biology, Cell Biology, and Genetics, Rochester, MN 55905. Offers biochemistry and structural biology (PhD); cell biology and genetics (PhD); molecular biology (PhD). *Degree requirements:* For doctorate, oral defense of dissertation, qualifying oral and written exam. *Entrance requirements:* For doctorate, GRE, 1 year of chemistry, biology, calculus, and physics. Additional exam requirements/recommendations for international students: Required—TOEFL. Electronic applications accepted. *Faculty research:* Gene structure and function, membranes and receptors/cytoskeleton, oncogenes and growth factors, protein structure and function, steroid hormonal action.

McGill University, Faculty of Graduate and Postdoctoral Studies, Faculty of Medicine, Department of Biochemistry, Montréal, QC H3A 2T5, Canada. Offers M Sc, PhD.

McGill University, Faculty of Graduate and Postdoctoral Studies, Faculty of Science, Department of Chemistry, Montréal, QC H3A 2T5, Canada. Offers chemical biology (M Sc, PhD); chemistry (M Sc, PhD).

McMaster University, Faculty of Health Sciences, Department of Biochemistry and Biomedical Sciences, Hamilton, ON L8S 4M2, Canada. Offers M Sc, PhD. Terminal master's awarded for partial completion of doctoral program. *Degree requirements:* For master's, thesis; for doctorate, comprehensive exam, thesis/dissertation. *Entrance requirements:* For master's and doctorate, minimum B+ average. Additional exam requirements/recommendations for international students: Required—TOEFL (minimum score 550 paper-based; 213 computer-based). *Faculty research:* Molecular and cell biology, biomolecular structure and function, molecular pharmacology and toxicology.

Medical College of Wisconsin, Graduate School of Biomedical Sciences, Department of Biochemistry, Milwaukee, WI 53226-0509. Offers PhD, MD/PhD. *Degree requirements:* For doctorate, comprehensive exam, thesis/dissertation. *Entrance requirements:* For doctorate, GRE, official transcripts, three letters of recommendation. Additional exam requirements/recommendations for international students: Required—TOEFL. *Faculty research:* Enzymology, macromolecular structure and synthesis, nucleic acids, molecular and cell biology.

Medical University of South Carolina, College of Graduate Studies, Department of Biochemistry and Molecular Biology, Charleston, SC 29425. Offers MS, PhD, MD/PhD. *Faculty:* 24 full-time (9 women), 3 part-time/adjunct (1 woman). *Students:* 15 full-time (8 women), 1 (woman) part-time; includes 1 minority (Hispanic/Latino), 7 international. Average age 30. 9 applicants, 22% accepted, 2 enrolled. In 2011, 1 master's, 2 doctorates awarded. Terminal master's awarded for partial completion of doctoral program. *Degree requirements:* For master's, thesis, oral exam/thesis defense; for doctorate, thesis/dissertation, oral and written exams/dissertation defense. *Entrance requirements:* For master's, GRE General Test; for doctorate, GRE General Test, interview, minimum GPA of 3.0. Additional exam requirements/recommendations for international students: Required—TOEFL (minimum score 600 paper-based; 250 computer-based; 100 iBT). *Application deadline:* For fall admission, 1/15 priority date for domestic students, 1/15 for international students. Applications are processed on a rolling basis. Application fee: $0 ($85 for international students). Electronic applications accepted. *Financial support:* In 2011–12, 10 research assistantships with partial tuition reimbursements (averaging $23,000 per year) were awarded; Federal Work-Study and scholarships/grants also available. Support available to part-time students. Financial award applicants required to submit FAFSA. *Faculty research:* Lipid biochemistry, DNA replication, nucleic acids, protein structure. *Unit head:* Dr. Yusuf A. Hannun, Chairman, 843-792-9318, Fax: 843-792-6590, E-mail: hannun@musc.edu. *Application contact:* Dr. Maurizio Del Poeta, Associate Professor, 843-792-8381, Fax: 843-792-6590, E-mail: delpoeta@musc.edu. Web site: http://www.musc.edu/BCMB/.

Memorial University of Newfoundland, School of Graduate Studies, Department of Biochemistry, St. John's, NL A1C 5S7, Canada. Offers biochemistry (M Sc, PhD); food science (M Sc, PhD). Part-time programs available. *Degree requirements:* For master's, thesis; for doctorate, comprehensive exam, thesis/dissertation, oral defense of thesis.

Entrance requirements: For master's, 2nd class degree in related field; for doctorate, M Sc. Electronic applications accepted. *Faculty research:* Toxicology, cell and molecular biology, food engineering, marine biotechnology, lipid biology.

Miami University, College of Arts and Science, Department of Chemistry and Biochemistry, Oxford, OH 45056. Offers MS, PhD. *Students:* 67 full-time (32 women), 1 part-time (0 women); includes 5 minority (1 Black or African American, non-Hispanic/Latino; 3 Asian, non-Hispanic/Latino; 1 Hispanic/Latino), 30 international. Average age 26. In 2011, 3 master's, 4 doctorates awarded. *Entrance requirements:* For master's, GRE General Test; GRE Subject Test (recommended), minimum undergraduate GPA of 3.0 during previous 2 years or 2.75 overall; for doctorate, GRE General Test, minimum undergraduate GPA of 2.75, 3.0 graduate. Additional exam requirements/recommendations for international students: Required—TOEFL. *Application deadline:* Applications are processed on a rolling basis. Application fee: $50. Electronic applications accepted. *Expenses:* Tuition, state resident: full-time $12,023; part-time $501 per credit hour. Tuition, nonresident: full-time $26,554; part-time $1107 per credit hour. *Required fees:* $528. *Financial support:* Fellowships with full tuition reimbursements, research assistantships with full tuition reimbursements, teaching assistantships with full tuition reimbursements, Federal Work-Study, institutionally sponsored loans, tuition waivers (full), and unspecified assistantships available. Financial award application deadline: 2/15; financial award applicants required to submit FAFSA. *Unit head:* Dr. Chris Makaroff, Chair, 513-529-1659, E-mail: makaroca@muohio.edu. *Application contact:* Dr. Stacey Lowery Bretz, Professor, 513-529-3731, E-mail: bretzsl@muohio.edu. Web site: http://chemistry.muohio.edu/.

Michigan State University, College of Human Medicine and The Graduate School, Graduate Programs in Human Medicine, East Lansing, MI 48824. Offers biochemistry and molecular biology (MS, PhD); epidemiology (MS, PhD); microbiology (MS); microbiology and molecular genetics (PhD); pharmacology and toxicology (MS, PhD); physiology (MS, PhD); public health (MPH). *Entrance requirements:* Additional exam requirements/recommendations for international students: Required—TOEFL.

Michigan State University, College of Osteopathic Medicine and The Graduate School, Graduate Studies in Osteopathic Medicine, East Lansing, MI 48824. Offers biochemistry and molecular biology (MS, PhD); microbiology (MS); microbiology and molecular genetics (PhD); pharmacology and toxicology (MS, PhD), including integrative pharmacology (MS), pharmacology and toxicology, pharmacology and toxicology-environmental toxicology (PhD); physiology (MS, PhD).

Michigan State University, The Graduate School, College of Agriculture and Natural Resources, MSU-DOE Plant Research Laboratory, East Lansing, MI 48824. Offers biochemistry and molecular biology (PhD); cellular and molecular biology (PhD); crop and soil sciences (PhD); genetics (PhD); microbiology and molecular genetics (PhD); plant biology (PhD); plant physiology (PhD). Offered jointly with the Department of Energy. *Degree requirements:* For doctorate, comprehensive exam, thesis/dissertation, laboratory rotation, defense of dissertation. *Entrance requirements:* For doctorate, GRE General Test, acceptance into one of the affiliated department programs; 3 letters of recommendation; bachelor's degree or equivalent in life sciences, chemistry, biochemistry, or biophysics; research experience. Electronic applications accepted. *Faculty research:* Role of hormones in the regulation of plant development and physiology, molecular mechanisms associated with signal recognition, development and application of genetic methods and materials, protein routing and function.

Michigan State University, The Graduate School, College of Natural Science and Graduate Programs in Human Medicine and Graduate Studies in Osteopathic Medicine, Department of Biochemistry and Molecular Biology, East Lansing, MI 48824. Offers biochemistry and molecular biology (MS, PhD); biochemistry and molecular biology/environmental toxicology (PhD). *Entrance requirements:* Additional exam requirements/recommendations for international students: Required—TOEFL. Electronic applications accepted.

Mississippi College, Graduate School, College of Arts and Sciences, School of Science and Mathematics, Department of Chemistry and Biochemistry, Clinton, MS 39058. Offers MCS, MS. Part-time programs available. *Degree requirements:* For master's, comprehensive exam, thesis (for some programs). *Entrance requirements:* For master's, GRE. Additional exam requirements/recommendations for international students: Recommended—TOEFL, IELTS. Electronic applications accepted.

Mississippi State University, College of Agriculture and Life Sciences, Department of Biochemistry, Molecular Biology, Entomology and Plant Pathology, Mississippi State, MS 39762. Offers agriculture life sciences (MS), including entomology and plant pathology; molecular biology (PhD). *Faculty:* 25 full-time (1 woman). *Students:* 46 full-time (17 women), 14 part-time (6 women); includes 4 minority (2 Black or African American, non-Hispanic/Latino; 2 Two or more races, non-Hispanic/Latino), 18 international. Average age 30. 43 applicants, 33% accepted, 13 enrolled. In 2011, 7 master's, 5 doctorates awarded. Terminal master's awarded for partial completion of doctoral program. *Degree requirements:* For master's, thesis (for some programs), comprehensive oral or written exam; for doctorate, thesis/dissertation, comprehensive oral and written exam. *Entrance requirements:* For master's, GRE General Test, minimum GPA of 2.75; for doctorate, GRE. Additional exam requirements/recommendations for international students: Required—TOEFL (minimum score 550 paper-based; 213 computer-based; 79 iBT); Recommended—IELTS (minimum score 6.5). *Application deadline:* For fall admission, 7/1 for domestic students, 5/1 for international students; for spring admission, 11/1 for domestic students, 9/1 for international students. Applications are processed on a rolling basis. Application fee: $40. Electronic applications accepted. *Expenses:* Tuition, state resident: full-time $5805; part-time $322.50 per credit hour. Tuition, nonresident: full-time $14,670; part-time $815 per credit hour. *Financial support:* In 2011–12, 41 research assistantships with full tuition reimbursements (averaging $15,714 per year) were awarded; Federal Work-Study, institutionally sponsored loans, and unspecified assistantships also available. Financial award application deadline: 4/1; financial award applicants required to submit FAFSA. *Faculty research:* Fish nutrition, plant and animal molecular biology, plant biochemistry, enzymology, lipid metabolism, chromatin, cell wall synthesis in rice, a model grass bioenergy species and the source of rice stover residues, using reverse genetic and functional genomic and proteomic approaches. *Unit head:* Dr. Scott T. Willard, Professor and Department Head, 662-325-2640, Fax: 662-325-8664, E-mail: swilliard@ads.msstate.edu. *Application contact:* Dr. Din-Pow Ma, Professor/Graduate Coordinator, 662-325-7739, Fax: 662-325-8664, E-mail: dm1@ra.msstate.edu.

Montana State University, College of Graduate Studies, College of Letters and Science, Department of Chemistry and Biochemistry, Bozeman, MT 59717. Offers biochemistry (MS, PhD); chemistry (MS, PhD). Part-time programs available. *Degree requirements:* For master's, comprehensive exam, thesis (for some programs); for doctorate, comprehensive exam, thesis/dissertation. *Entrance requirements:* For master's and doctorate, GRE General Test, transcripts, letter of recommendation. Additional exam requirements/recommendations for international students: Required—TOEFL (minimum score 550 paper-based; 213 computer-based). Electronic applications accepted. *Faculty research:* Proteomics, nano-materials chemistry, computational chemistry, optical spectroscopy, photochemistry.

Montclair State University, The Graduate School, College of Science and Mathematics, Department of Chemistry and Biochemistry, Program in Pharmaceutical Biochemistry, Montclair, NJ 07043-1624. Offers MS. Part-time and evening/weekend programs available. *Students:* 6 full-time (4 women), 3 part-time (2 women); includes 3 minority (2 Asian, non-Hispanic/Latino; 1 Hispanic/Latino), 2 international. Average age 28. 14 applicants, 43% accepted, 4 enrolled. *Entrance requirements:* For master's, GRE General Test, 24 undergraduate credits in chemistry, 2 letters of recommendation, essay. *Application deadline:* Applications are processed on a rolling basis. Application fee: $60. Electronic applications accepted. *Financial support:* Federal Work-Study, scholarships/grants, and unspecified assistantships available. Support available to part-time students. Financial award application deadline: 3/1. *Faculty research:* Enzyme kinetics, enzyme expression, pharmaceutical biochemistry, medicinal chemistry, biophysical chemistry. *Unit head:* Dr. Marc Kasner, Chair, 973-655-6864. *Application contact:* Amy Aiello, Executive Director of The Graduate School, 973-655-5147, E-mail: graduate.school@montclair.edu. Web site: http://www.montclair.edu/csam/chemistry-biochemistry/graduate-programs/ms-pharmaceutical-biochemistry/.

New York Medical College, Graduate School of Basic Medical Sciences, Program in Biochemistry and Molecular Biology, Valhalla, NY 10595-1691. Offers MS, PhD, MD/PhD. Part-time and evening/weekend programs available. *Faculty:* 10 full-time (4 women), 2 part-time/adjunct (0 women). *Students:* 8 full-time (6 women); includes 2 minority (both Asian, non-Hispanic/Latino). Average age 27. 11 applicants, 73% accepted, 2 enrolled. In 2011, 1 master's, 1 doctorate awarded. Terminal master's awarded for partial completion of doctoral program. *Median time to degree:* Of those who began their doctoral program in fall 2003, 100% received their degree in 8 years or less. *Degree requirements:* For master's, thesis; for doctorate, comprehensive exam, thesis/dissertation. *Entrance requirements:* For master's and doctorate, GRE General Test. Additional exam requirements/recommendations for international students: Required—TOEFL. *Application deadline:* For fall admission, 7/1 priority date for domestic students, 5/1 for international students; for spring admission, 12/1 priority date for domestic students, 10/1 for international students. Applications are processed on a rolling basis. Application fee: $50 ($75 for international students). Electronic applications accepted. *Financial support:* In 2011–12, 2 fellowships, 5 research assistantships with full tuition reimbursements (averaging $24,000 per year) were awarded; Federal Work-Study, institutionally sponsored loans, scholarships/grants, traineeships, tuition waivers (full), unspecified assistantships, and health benefits (for PhD candidates only) also available. Financial award applicants required to submit FAFSA. *Faculty research:* Expression, mechanisms of hormone action and cell signaling, enzymology, mechanisms of DNA replication and repair, cell cycle regulation, control of cell growth, molecular biology of cancer cells and the cancer process, mechanisms of nutrition and cancer prevention, molecular neurobiology and studies of neurodegenerative disorders, the aging process. *Unit head:* Dr. Joseph Wu, Director, 914-594-4891, Fax: 914-594-4944, E-mail: joseph_wu@nymc.edu. *Application contact:* Valerie Romeo-Messana, Admission Coordinator, 914-594-4110, Fax: 914-594-4944, E-mail: v_romeomessana@nymc.edu.

North Carolina State University, Graduate School, College of Agriculture and Life Sciences, Department of Biochemistry, Raleigh, NC 27695. Offers PhD. *Degree requirements:* For doctorate, thesis/dissertation. *Entrance requirements:* For doctorate, GRE General Test. Additional exam requirements/recommendations for international students: Required—TOEFL. Electronic applications accepted. *Faculty research:* Regulation of gene expression, structure and function of proteins and nucleic acids, molecular biology, high-field NMR, bioinorganic chemistry.

North Dakota State University, College of Graduate and Interdisciplinary Studies, College of Science and Mathematics, Department of Biochemistry and Molecular Biology, Program in Biochemistry, Fargo, ND 58108. Offers MS, PhD. Part-time programs available. *Students:* 13 full-time (6 women), 10 international. Average age 24. 17 applicants, 18% accepted, 0 enrolled. In 2011, 1 master's, 4 doctorates awarded. *Degree requirements:* For master's, thesis; for doctorate, thesis/dissertation. *Entrance requirements:* Additional exam requirements/recommendations for international students: Required—TOEFL (minimum score 550 paper-based). *Application deadline:* For fall admission, 3/1 priority date for domestic students, 3/1 for international students; for spring admission, 9/1 priority date for domestic students, 9/1 for international students. Applications are processed on a rolling basis. Application fee: $35. Electronic applications accepted. *Financial support:* In 2011–12, 4 research assistantships with full tuition reimbursements (averaging $19,000 per year), 5 teaching assistantships with full tuition reimbursements (averaging $19,000 per year) were awarded; career-related internships or fieldwork, Federal Work-Study, and institutionally sponsored loans also available. Financial award application deadline: 4/15. *Unit head:* Dr. Gregory Cook, Chair, 701-231-8694, Fax: 701-231-8831, E-mail: gregory.cook@ndsu.edu.

Northeastern University, College of Science, Department of Chemistry and Chemical Biology, Boston, MA 02115-5096. Offers analytical chemistry (PhD); chemistry (MS, PhD); inorganic chemistry (PhD); organic chemistry (PhD); physical chemistry (PhD). Part-time and evening/weekend programs available. *Faculty:* 24 full-time, 7 part-time/adjunct. *Students:* 98 full-time (58 women), 31 part-time (15 women). 190 applicants, 32% accepted, 34 enrolled. In 2011, 16 master's, 6 doctorates awarded. Terminal master's awarded for partial completion of doctoral program. *Degree requirements:* For master's, thesis (for some programs); for doctorate, thesis/dissertation, qualifying exam in specialty area. *Entrance requirements:* Additional exam requirements/recommendations for international students: Required—TOEFL. *Application deadline:* For fall admission, 2/1 priority date for domestic students, 2/1 for international students. Applications are processed on a rolling basis. Application fee: $50. Electronic applications accepted. *Financial support:* In 2011–12, 41 research assistantships with tuition reimbursements (averaging $18,285 per year), 38 teaching assistantships with tuition reimbursements (averaging $18,285 per year) were awarded; fellowships with tuition reimbursements, career-related internships or fieldwork, Federal Work-Study, scholarships/grants, tuition waivers (partial), and unspecified assistantships also available. Financial award application deadline: 3/1; financial award applicants required to submit FAFSA. *Faculty research:* Bioanalysis, biorganic and medicinal chemistry, biophysical chemistry, nanomaterials, proteonics. *Unit head:* Dr. Robert N. Hanson, Graduate Coordinator, 617-373-3313, Fax: 617-373-8795, E-mail: chemistry-grad-info@neu.edu. *Application contact:* Jo-Anne Dickinson, Admissions Contact, 617-373-5990, Fax: 617-373-7281, E-mail: gsas@neu.edu. Web site: http://www.northeastern.edu/chem/.

Northwestern University, The Graduate School, Interdepartmental Biological Sciences Program (IBiS), Evanston, IL 60208. Offers biochemistry, molecular biology, and cell biology (PhD), including biochemistry, cell and molecular biology, molecular biophysics, structural biology; biotechnology (PhD); cell and molecular biology (PhD); developmental biology and genetics (PhD); hormone action and signal transduction (PhD); neuroscience (PhD); structural biology, biochemistry, and biophysics (PhD). Program participants include the Departments of Biochemistry, Molecular Biology, and Cell Biology; Chemistry; Neurobiology and Physiology; Chemical Engineering; Civil Engineering; and Evanston Hospital. *Degree requirements:* For doctorate, thesis/dissertation, qualifying exam. *Entrance requirements:* For doctorate, GRE General Test. Additional exam requirements/recommendations for international students: Required—

TOEFL (minimum score 600 paper-based). Electronic applications accepted. *Faculty research:* Developmental genetics, gene regulation, DNA-protein interactions, biological clocks, bioremediation.

Northwestern University, Northwestern University Feinberg School of Medicine and Interdepartmental Programs, Integrated Graduate Programs in the Life Sciences, Chicago, IL 60611. Offers cancer biology (PhD); cell biology (PhD); developmental biology (PhD); evolutionary biology (PhD); immunology and microbial pathogenesis (PhD); molecular biology and genetics (PhD); neurobiology (PhD); pharmacology and toxicology (PhD); structural biology and biochemistry (PhD). *Degree requirements:* For doctorate, comprehensive exam, thesis/dissertation, written and oral qualifying exams. *Entrance requirements:* For doctorate, GRE General Test. Additional exam requirements/recommendations for international students: Required—TOEFL (minimum score 600 paper-based; 250 computer-based). Electronic applications accepted.

The Ohio State University, Graduate School, College of Arts and Sciences, Division of Natural and Mathematical Sciences, Biochemistry Program, Columbus, OH 43210. Offers PhD. *Faculty:* 102. *Students:* 42 full-time (19 women), 42 part-time (13 women); includes 2 minority (1 Black or African American, non-Hispanic/Latino; 1 Asian, non-Hispanic/Latino), 44 international. Average age 27. In 2011, 12 doctorates awarded. *Entrance requirements:* Additional exam requirements/recommendations for international students: Required—TOEFL (minimum score 550 paper-based; 250 computer-based; 79 iBT), Michigan English Language Assessment Battery (minimum score 82). *Application deadline:* Applications are processed on a rolling basis. Application fee: $40 ($50 for international students). Electronic applications accepted. *Expenses:* Tuition, state resident: full-time $11,400. Tuition, nonresident: full-time $28,125. Tuition and fees vary according to course load, degree level, campus/location and program. *Financial support:* Fellowships, research assistantships, and teaching assistantships available. *Unit head:* Dr. Jill Rafael-Fortney, Program Director, 614-292-1463, Fax: 614-292-6511, E-mail: rafael-fortney.1@osu.edu. Web site: http://www.biosci.ohio-state.edu/~osbp/.

The Ohio State University, Graduate School, College of Arts and Sciences, Division of Natural and Mathematical Sciences, Departments of Chemistry and Biochemistry, Columbus, OH 43210. Offers biochemistry (MS); chemistry (MS, PhD). *Faculty:* 45. *Students:* 76 full-time (24 women), 144 part-time (54 women); includes 21 minority (6 Black or African American, non-Hispanic/Latino; 1 American Indian or Alaska Native, non-Hispanic/Latino; 8 Asian, non-Hispanic/Latino; 4 Hispanic/Latino; 2 Two or more races, non-Hispanic/Latino), 111 international. Average age 26. In 2011, 15 master's, 35 doctorates awarded. *Degree requirements:* For master's, thesis optional; for doctorate, thesis/dissertation. *Entrance requirements:* For master's and doctorate, GRE General Test, GRE Subject Test (chemistry). Additional exam requirements/recommendations for international students: Required—TOEFL (minimum score 550 paper-based; 250 computer-based; 79 iBT), Michigan English Language Assessment Battery (minimum score 82). *Application deadline:* For fall admission, 8/15 priority date for domestic students, 7/1 for international students; for winter admission, 12/1 priority date for domestic students, 11/1 for international students; for spring admission, 3/1 priority date for domestic students, 2/1 for international students. Applications are processed on a rolling basis. Application fee: $40 ($50 for international students). Electronic applications accepted. *Expenses:* Tuition, state resident: full-time $11,400. Tuition, nonresident: full-time $28,125. Tuition and fees vary according to course load, degree level, campus/location and program. *Financial support:* Fellowships, research assistantships, teaching assistantships, Federal Work-Study, and institutionally sponsored loans available. Support available to part-time students. *Unit head:* Dr. Susan V. Olesik, Chair, 614-292-0733, E-mail: olesik.1@osu.edu. *Application contact:* Dr. Claudia Turro, Vice Chair, 614-292-8917, Fax: 614-292-1685, E-mail: turro.1@osu.edu. Web site: https://chemistry.osu.edu/.

Ohio University, Graduate College, College of Arts and Sciences, Department of Chemistry and Biochemistry, Athens, OH 45701-2979. Offers MS, PhD. *Students:* 57 full-time (25 women), 6 part-time (4 women); includes 3 minority (all Two or more races, non-Hispanic/Latino), 44 international. 113 applicants, 6% accepted, 7 enrolled. In 2011, 9 degrees awarded. *Degree requirements:* For master's, comprehensive exam, thesis, exam; for doctorate, comprehensive exam, thesis/dissertation, exam. *Entrance requirements:* For master's and doctorate, GRE. Additional exam requirements/recommendations for international students: Required—TOEFL (minimum score 550 paper-based; 80 iBT) or IELTS (minimum score 6.5). *Application deadline:* For fall admission, 2/1 priority date for domestic students, 2/1 for international students. Application fee: $50 ($55 for international students). Electronic applications accepted. *Financial support:* Fellowships, research assistantships with full tuition reimbursements, teaching assistantships with full tuition reimbursements, Federal Work-Study, and institutionally sponsored loans available. Financial award application deadline: 2/1. *Faculty research:* Materials, RNA, synthesis, carbohydrate, mass spectrometry. *Total annual research expenditures:* $3.5 million. *Unit head:* Dr. Tadeusz Malinski, Chair, 740-593-1737, Fax: 740-593-0148, E-mail: malinski@ohio.edu. *Application contact:* Dr. Stephen C. Bergmeier, Graduate Chair, 740-597-6949, Fax: 740-593-0148, E-mail: bergmeis@ohio.edu. Web site: http://www.ohio.edu/chemistry/.

Oklahoma State University, College of Agricultural Science and Natural Resources, Department of Biochemistry and Molecular Biology, Stillwater, OK 74078. Offers MS, PhD. *Faculty:* 27 full-time (11 women), 1 part-time/adjunct (0 women). *Students:* 3 full-time (0 women), 34 part-time (17 women); includes 5 minority (1 Asian, non-Hispanic/Latino; 4 Hispanic/Latino), 22 international. Average age 28. 88 applicants, 13% accepted, 10 enrolled. In 2011, 1 master's, 4 doctorates awarded. *Degree requirements:* For master's, thesis, oral exam; for doctorate, comprehensive exam, thesis/dissertation. *Entrance requirements:* For master's and doctorate, GRE or GMAT. Additional exam requirements/recommendations for international students: Required—TOEFL (minimum score 550 paper-based; 79 iBT). *Application deadline:* For fall admission, 3/1 for international students; for spring admission, 8/1 for international students. Applications are processed on a rolling basis. Application fee: $40 ($75 for international students). Electronic applications accepted. *Expenses:* Tuition, state resident: full-time $4044; part-time $168.50 per credit hour. Tuition, nonresident: full-time $16,008; part-time $667 per credit hour. *Required fees:* $2122; $88.45 per credit hour. One-time fee: $50. Tuition and fees vary according to course load and campus/location. *Financial support:* In 2011–12, 34 research assistantships (averaging $19,233 per year), 2 teaching assistantships (averaging $18,699 per year) were awarded; career-related internships or fieldwork, Federal Work-Study, scholarships/grants, health care benefits, tuition waivers (partial), and unspecified assistantships also available. Support available to part-time students. Financial award application deadline: 3/1; financial award applicants required to submit FAFSA. *Unit head:* Dr. Dale Thomas, Interim Head, 405-744-5431, Fax: 405-744-7799. *Application contact:* Dr. Sheryl Tucker, Dean, 405-744-7099, Fax: 405-744-0355, E-mail: grad-i@okstate.edu. Web site: http://biochemistry.okstate.edu/.

Old Dominion University, College of Sciences, Program in Chemistry, Norfolk, VA 23529. Offers analytical chemistry (MS); biochemistry (MS); chemistry (PhD); environmental chemistry (MS); organic chemistry (MS); physical chemistry (MS). Part-time and evening/weekend programs available. *Faculty:* 14 full-time (5 women), 2 part-time/adjunct (0 women). *Students:* 34 full-time (17 women), 2 part-time (1 woman); includes 2 minority (1 Black or African American, non-Hispanic/Latino; 1 Asian, non-Hispanic/Latino), 17 international. Average age 28. 35 applicants, 60% accepted, 8 enrolled. In 2011, 3 master's, 2 doctorates awarded. *Degree requirements:* For master's, comprehensive exam, thesis. *Entrance requirements:* For master's, GRE General Test, minimum GPA of 3.0 in major, 2.5 overall; for doctorate, GRE General Test. Additional exam requirements/recommendations for international students: Required—TOEFL. *Application deadline:* For fall admission, 7/1 for domestic students, 1/15 for international students; for spring admission, 11/1 for domestic students, 8/15 for international students. Applications are processed on a rolling basis. Application fee: $30. Electronic applications accepted. *Expenses:* Tuition, state resident: full-time $9096; part-time $379 per credit. Tuition, nonresident: full-time $23,064; part-time $961 per credit. *Required fees:* $127 per semester. One-time fee: $50. *Financial support:* In 2011–12, 6 students received support, including fellowships (averaging $18,000 per year), research assistantships with tuition reimbursements available (averaging $21,000 per year), teaching assistantships with tuition reimbursements available (averaging $18,000 per year); career-related internships or fieldwork, scholarships/grants, and unspecified assistantships also available. Financial award application deadline: 2/15; financial award applicants required to submit FAFSA. *Faculty research:* Biogeochemistry, materials chemistry, bioanalytical chemistry, computational chemistry, organic chemistry. *Total annual research expenditures:* $2.6 million. *Unit head:* Dr. Craig A. Bayse, Graduate Program Director, 757-683-4097, Fax: 757-683-4628, E-mail: chemgpd@odu.edu. *Application contact:* Valerie DeCosta, Grants and Graduate Program Assistant, 757-683-6979, Fax: 757-683-4628, E-mail: chemgpd@odu.edu.

Oregon Health & Science University, School of Medicine, Graduate Programs in Medicine, Department of Environmental and Biomolecular Systems, Portland, OR 97239-3098. Offers biochemistry and molecular biology (MS, PhD); environmental science and engineering (MS, PhD). Part-time programs available. *Faculty:* 14 full-time (4 women), 1 (woman) part-time/adjunct. *Students:* 28 full-time (20 women), 5 part-time (3 women); includes 11 minority (1 Black or African American, non-Hispanic/Latino; 3 American Indian or Alaska Native, non-Hispanic/Latino; 2 Asian, non-Hispanic/Latino; 4 Hispanic/Latino; 1 Two or more races, non-Hispanic/Latino), 5 international. Average age 30. 36 applicants, 25% accepted, 5 enrolled. In 2011, 9 master's, 2 doctorates awarded. Terminal master's awarded for partial completion of doctoral program. *Degree requirements:* For master's, thesis (for some programs); for doctorate, comprehensive exam, thesis/dissertation, qualifying exam. *Entrance requirements:* For master's and doctorate, GRE General Test (minimum scores: 500 Verbal/600 Quantitative/4.5 Analytical) or MCAT (for some programs). Additional exam requirements/recommendations for international students: Required—TOEFL. *Application deadline:* For fall admission, 7/15 for domestic students, 5/15 for international students; for winter admission, 10/15 for domestic students, 9/15 for international students; for spring admission, 1/15 for domestic students, 12/15 for international students. Applications are processed on a rolling basis. Application fee: $70. Electronic applications accepted. *Financial support:* Health care benefits and full tuition and stipends for PhD students available. *Unit head:* Dr. Paul Tratnyek, Program Director, 503-748-1070, E-mail: info@ebs.ogi.edu. *Application contact:* Nancy Christie, Program Coordinator, 503-748-1070, E-mail: info@ebs.ogi.edu.

Oregon Health & Science University, School of Medicine, Graduate Programs in Medicine, Program in Molecular and Cellular Biosciences, Department of Biochemistry and Molecular Biology, Portland, OR 97239-3098. Offers PhD. *Faculty:* 13 full-time (4 women), 1 part-time/adjunct (0 women). *Students:* 14 full-time (6 women), 3 international. Average age 30. In 2011, 1 doctorate awarded. *Degree requirements:* For doctorate, comprehensive exam, thesis/dissertation, qualifying exam. *Entrance requirements:* For doctorate, GRE General Test (minimum scores: 153 Verbal/148 Quantitative/4.5 Analytical). Additional exam requirements/recommendations for international students: Required—TOEFL. Electronic applications accepted. *Financial support:* Health care benefits, tuition waivers (full), and full tuition and stipends available. *Faculty research:* Protein structure, membrane proteins, metabolic regulation, molecular basis of disease, signal transduction mechanisms. *Unit head:* Dr. David Farrens, Program Director, 503-494-7781, E-mail: farrensd@ohsu.edu. *Application contact:* Jeni Wroblewski, Administrative Coordinator, 503-494-2541, E-mail: wroblews@ohsu.edu. Web site: http://www.ohsu.edu/som-biochem/.

Oregon State University, Graduate School, College of Science, Department of Biochemistry and Biophysics, Corvallis, OR 97331. Offers MA, MAIS, MS, PhD. *Degree requirements:* For master's, thesis optional; for doctorate, thesis/dissertation, exams. *Entrance requirements:* For master's, GRE General Test, minimum GPA of 3.0; for doctorate, GRE Subject Test, minimum GPA of 3.0. Additional exam requirements/recommendations for international students: Required—TOEFL. *Faculty research:* DNA and deoxyribonucleotide metabolism, cell growth control, receptors and membranes, protein structure and function.

Penn State Hershey Medical Center, College of Medicine, Graduate School Programs in the Biomedical Sciences, Graduate Program in Biomedical Sciences, Hershey, PA 17033. Offers biochemistry and molecular genetics (PhD); biomedical sciences (MS, PhD); translational therapeutics (MS, PhD); virology and immunology (MS, PhD); MD/PhD; PhD/MBA. *Students:* 12 full-time (6 women); includes 2 minority (1 Black or African American, non-Hispanic/Latino; 1 Asian, non-Hispanic/Latino), 1 international. 211 applicants, 16% accepted, 12 enrolled. Terminal master's awarded for partial completion of doctoral program. *Degree requirements:* For master's, thesis (for some programs); for doctorate, comprehensive exam, thesis/dissertation, candidacy exam. *Entrance requirements:* For doctorate, GRE General Test. Additional exam requirements/recommendations for international students: Required—TOEFL (minimum score 550 paper-based; 213 computer-based; 80 iBT). *Application deadline:* For fall admission, 1/1 for domestic students, 2/1 for international students. Applications are processed on a rolling basis. Application fee: $65. Electronic applications accepted. *Financial support:* In 2011–12, research assistantships (averaging $23,028 per year) were awarded; fellowships, scholarships/grants, health care benefits, and unspecified assistantships also available. Financial award applicants required to submit FAFSA. *Unit head:* Dr. Ralph L. Keil, Chair, 717-531-8595, Fax: 717-531-0388, E-mail: rlk9@psu.edu. *Application contact:* Karen Shields, Administrative Support Coordinator, 717-531-1045, Fax: 717-531-0388, E-mail: kpb2@psu.edu. Web site: http://med.psu.edu/web/biomedical-sciences/home.

Penn State University Park, Graduate School, Eberly College of Science, Department of Biochemistry and Molecular Biology, State College, University Park, PA 16802-1503. Offers biochemistry, microbiology, and molecular biology (MS, PhD); biotechnology (MBIOT). *Unit head:* Dr. Richard J. Frisque, Head, 814-863-1851, E-mail: rjf6@psu.edu. *Application contact:* Dr. Ronald Porter, Director of Graduate Studies, 814-863-4903, E-mail: rdp1@psu.edu. Web site: http://bmb.psu.edu.

Purdue University, College of Pharmacy and Pharmacal Sciences and Graduate School, Graduate Programs in Pharmacy and Pharmacal Sciences, Department of Medicinal Chemistry and Molecular Pharmacology, West Lafayette, IN 47907. Offers biophysical and computational chemistry (PhD); cancer research (PhD); immunology and infectious disease (PhD); medicinal biochemistry and molecular biology (PhD); medicinal chemistry and chemical biology (PhD); molecular pharmacology (PhD); neuropharmacology, neurodegeneration, and neurotoxicity (PhD); systems biology and functional genomics (PhD). *Faculty:* 22 full-time (2 women), 4 part-time/adjunct (1

woman). *Students:* 49 full-time (18 women); includes 3 minority (1 Asian, non-Hispanic/Latino; 2 Hispanic/Latino), 26 international. Average age 27. 250 applicants, 12% accepted, 9 enrolled. In 2011, 10 doctorates awarded. *Degree requirements:* For doctorate, thesis/dissertation. *Entrance requirements:* For doctorate, GRE General Test; GRE Subject Test in biology, biochemistry, and chemistry (recommended), minimum undergraduate GPA of 3.0. Additional exam requirements/recommendations for international students: Required—TOEFL (minimum score 550 paper-based; 77 iBT); Recommended—TWE. *Application deadline:* For fall admission, 2/1 for domestic and international students. Applications are processed on a rolling basis. Application fee: $60 ($75 for international students). Electronic applications accepted. *Financial support:* Fellowships, research assistantships, teaching assistantships, and traineeships available. Support available to part-time students. Financial award applicants required to submit FAFSA. *Faculty research:* Drug design and development, cancer research, drug synthesis and analysis, chemical pharmacology, environmental toxicology. *Unit head:* Dr. Richard F. Borch, Head, 765-494-1403, E-mail: borch@purdue.edu. *Application contact:* Janine C. Mott, Graduate Contact, 765-494-1269, E-mail: jmott@purdue.edu.

Purdue University, Graduate School, College of Agriculture, Department of Biochemistry, West Lafayette, IN 47907. Offers MS, PhD. *Faculty:* 17 full-time (4 women). *Students:* 38 full-time (17 women); includes 4 minority (3 Asian, non-Hispanic/Latino; 1 Hispanic/Latino), 20 international. Average age 26. 135 applicants, 21% accepted, 13 enrolled. In 2011, 1 master's, 5 doctorates awarded. Terminal master's awarded for partial completion of doctoral program. *Degree requirements:* For doctorate, thesis/dissertation, preliminary and qualifying exams. *Entrance requirements:* For doctorate, GRE General Test, minimum undergraduate GPA of 3.0 or equivalent. Additional exam requirements/recommendations for international students: Required—TOEFL (minimum score 600 paper-based; 77 iBT). *Application deadline:* For fall admission, 1/15 priority date for domestic students, 1/15 for international students; for spring admission, 9/30 for domestic and international students. Applications are processed on a rolling basis. Application fee: $60 ($75 for international students). Electronic applications accepted. *Financial support:* Fellowships, research assistantships, and teaching assistantships available. Support available to part-time students. Financial award application deadline: 4/15; financial award applicants required to submit FAFSA. *Faculty research:* Molecular biology and post-translational modifications of neuropeptides, membrane transport proteins. *Unit head:* Dr. C. C. Chapple, Head, 765-494-0494, E-mail: chapple@purdue.edu. *Application contact:* Kristi L. Trimble, Graduate Contact for Admissions, 765-494-1636, E-mail: trimblek@purdue.edu. Web site: http://www.biochem.purdue.edu/.

Purdue University, Graduate School, PULSe - Purdue University Life Sciences Program, West Lafayette, IN 47907. Offers biomolecular structure and biophysics (PhD); biotechnology (PhD); chemical biology (PhD); chromatin and regulation of gene expression (PhD); integrative neuroscience (PhD); integrative plant sciences (PhD); membrane biology (PhD); microbiology (PhD); molecular evolutionary and cancer biology (PhD); molecular evolutionary genetics (PhD); molecular virology (PhD). *Students:* 90 full-time (45 women); includes 7 minority (3 Black or African American, non-Hispanic/Latino; 1 Asian, non-Hispanic/Latino; 2 Hispanic/Latino; 1 Two or more races, non-Hispanic/Latino), 40 international. Average age 26. 427 applicants, 24% accepted, 35 enrolled. *Entrance requirements:* For doctorate, GRE test required, minimum undergraduate GPA of 3.0. Additional exam requirements/recommendations for international students: Required—TOEFL (minimum score 550 paper-based; 77 iBT). *Application deadline:* For fall admission, 1/15 priority date for domestic students, 1/15 for international students. Applications are processed on a rolling basis. Application fee: $60 ($75 for international students). Electronic applications accepted. *Financial support:* In 2011–12, research assistantships with tuition reimbursements (averaging $22,500 per year), teaching assistantships with tuition reimbursements (averaging $22,500 per year) were awarded. *Unit head:* Dr. Christine A. Hrycyna, Head, 765-494-7322, E-mail: hrycyna@purdue.edu. *Application contact:* Emily E. Bramson, Graduate Contact, 765-494-5865, E-mail: bramson@purdue.edu. Web site: http://www.gradschool.purdue.edu/pulse.

Queens College of the City University of New York, Division of Graduate Studies, Mathematics and Natural Sciences Division, Department of Chemistry and Biochemistry, Flushing, NY 11367-1597. Offers biochemistry (MA); chemistry (MA). Part-time and evening/weekend programs available. *Faculty:* 14 full-time (4 women). *Students:* 3 full-time (1 woman), 14 part-time (3 women); includes 9 minority (1 Black or African American, non-Hispanic/Latino; 5 Asian, non-Hispanic/Latino; 3 Hispanic/Latino), 3 international. 13 applicants, 38% accepted, 2 enrolled. In 2011, 3 master's awarded. *Degree requirements:* For master's, comprehensive exam. *Entrance requirements:* For master's, GRE, previous course work in calculus and physics, minimum GPA of 3.0. Additional exam requirements/recommendations for international students: Required—TOEFL. *Application deadline:* For fall admission, 4/1 for domestic students; for spring admission, 11/1 for domestic students. Applications are processed on a rolling basis. Application fee: $125. *Expenses:* Tuition, state resident: part-time $345 per credit. Tuition, nonresident: part-time $640 per credit. *Required fees:* $145.25 per semester. *Financial support:* Career-related internships or fieldwork, Federal Work-Study, institutionally sponsored loans, and tuition waivers (partial) available. Support available to part-time students. Financial award application deadline: 4/1; financial award applicants required to submit FAFSA. *Unit head:* Dr. William Hersh, Chairperson, 718-997-4144. *Application contact:* Graduate Adviser, 718-997-4100.

Queen's University at Kingston, School of Graduate Studies and Research, Faculty of Health Sciences, Department of Biochemistry, Kingston, ON K7L 3N6, Canada. Offers M Sc, PhD. Part-time programs available. *Degree requirements:* For master's, thesis, research proposal; for doctorate, comprehensive exam, thesis/dissertation, research proposal. *Entrance requirements:* For master's, GRE (if undergraduate degree is not from a Canadian University); for doctorate, GRE required if undergraduate degree is not from a Canadian University. Additional exam requirements/recommendations for international students: Required—TOEFL (minimum score 580 paper-based; 237 computer-based). Electronic applications accepted. *Faculty research:* Gene expression, protein structure, enzyme activity, signal transduction.

Rensselaer Polytechnic Institute, Graduate School, School of Science, Program in Biochemistry and Biophysics, Troy, NY 12180-3590. Offers MS, PhD. Part-time programs available. Terminal master's awarded for partial completion of doctoral program. *Degree requirements:* For master's, thesis optional; for doctorate, comprehensive exam, thesis/dissertation. *Entrance requirements:* For doctorate, GRE General Test. Additional exam requirements/recommendations for international students: Required—TOEFL. Electronic applications accepted. *Faculty research:* Biopolymers, photosynthesis, cellular bioengineering.

Rensselaer Polytechnic Institute, Graduate School, School of Science, Program in Chemistry, Troy, NY 12180-3590. Offers analytical chemistry (MS, PhD); biochemistry (MS, PhD); inorganic chemistry (MS, PhD); organic chemistry (MS, PhD); physical chemistry (MS, PhD); polymer chemistry (MS, PhD). Part-time and evening/weekend programs available. Terminal master's awarded for partial completion of doctoral program. *Degree requirements:* For master's, thesis (for some programs); for doctorate, comprehensive exam, thesis/dissertation. *Entrance requirements:* For master's, GRE General Test, GRE Subject Test (strongly recommended); for doctorate, GRE General Test, GRE Subject Test (chemistry or biochemistry strongly recommended). Additional exam requirements/recommendations for international students: Required—TOEFL (minimum score 570 paper-based; 230 computer-based; 88 iBT). Electronic applications accepted. *Faculty research:* Synthetic polymer and biopolymer chemistry, physical chemistry of polymeric systems, bioanalytical chemistry, synthetic and computational drug design, protein folding and protein design.

Rice University, Graduate Programs, Wiess School of Natural Sciences, Department of Biochemistry and Cell Biology, Houston, TX 77251-1892. Offers MA, PhD. Terminal master's awarded for partial completion of doctoral program. *Degree requirements:* For master's, thesis; for doctorate, thesis/dissertation. *Entrance requirements:* For master's and doctorate, GRE. Additional exam requirements/recommendations for international students: Required—TOEFL (minimum score 600 paper-based; 250 computer-based; 90 iBT). Electronic applications accepted. *Expenses:* Contact institution. *Faculty research:* Steroid metabolism, protein structure NMR, biophysics, cell growth and movement.

Rosalind Franklin University of Medicine and Science, School of Graduate and Postdoctoral Studies - Interdisciplinary Graduate Program in Biomedical Sciences, Department of Biochemistry and Molecular Biology, North Chicago, IL 60064-3095. Offers MS, PhD, MD/PhD. Terminal master's awarded for partial completion of doctoral program. *Degree requirements:* For master's, comprehensive exam, thesis; for doctorate, comprehensive exam, thesis/dissertation. *Entrance requirements:* For master's and doctorate, GRE General Test, minimum GPA of 3.0. Additional exam requirements/recommendations for international students: Required—TOEFL, TWE. Electronic applications accepted. *Faculty research:* Structure of control enzymes, extracellular matrix, glucose metabolism, gene expression, ATP synthesis.

Rush University, Graduate College, Division of Biochemistry, Chicago, IL 60612-3832. Offers PhD, MD/PhD. *Degree requirements:* For doctorate, thesis/dissertation, preliminary exam. *Entrance requirements:* For doctorate, GRE General Test. Additional exam requirements/recommendations for international students: Required—TOEFL. Electronic applications accepted. *Faculty research:* Biochemistry of extracellular matrix, connective tissue biosynthesis and degradation, molecular biology of connective tissue components, cartilage, arthritis.

Rutgers, The State University of New Jersey, Newark, Graduate School, Program in Chemistry, Newark, NJ 07102. Offers analytical chemistry (MS, PhD); biochemistry (MS, PhD); inorganic chemistry (MS, PhD); organic chemistry (MS, PhD); physical chemistry (MS, PhD). Part-time and evening/weekend programs available. Terminal master's awarded for partial completion of doctoral program. *Degree requirements:* For master's, thesis optional, cumulative exams; for doctorate, thesis/dissertation, exams, research proposal. *Entrance requirements:* For master's and doctorate, GRE General Test, minimum undergraduate B average. Additional exam requirements/recommendations for international students: Required—TOEFL. Electronic applications accepted. *Faculty research:* Medicinal chemistry, natural products, isotope effects, biophysics and biorganic approaches to enzyme mechanisms, organic and organometallic synthesis.

Rutgers, The State University of New Jersey, New Brunswick, Graduate School-New Brunswick, Department of Chemistry and Chemical Biology, Piscataway, NJ 08854-8097. Offers biological chemistry (MS, PhD); inorganic chemistry (MS, PhD); organic chemistry (MS, PhD); physical chemistry (MS, PhD). Part-time and evening/weekend programs available. Terminal master's awarded for partial completion of doctoral program. *Degree requirements:* For master's, thesis or alternative, exam; for doctorate, thesis/dissertation, 1 year residency. *Entrance requirements:* For master's and doctorate, GRE General Test, GRE Subject Test. Additional exam requirements/recommendations for international students: Required—TOEFL. Electronic applications accepted. *Faculty research:* Biophysical organic/bioorganic, inorganic/bioinorganic, theoretical, and solid-state/surface chemistry.

Rutgers, The State University of New Jersey, New Brunswick, Graduate School-New Brunswick, Programs in the Molecular Biosciences, Program in Biochemistry, Piscataway, NJ 08854-8097. Offers PhD. Program offered jointly with University of Medicine and Dentistry of New Jersey. *Degree requirements:* For doctorate, thesis/dissertation, written qualifying exam. *Entrance requirements:* For doctorate, GRE General Test, GRE Subject Test (recommended), minimum GPA of 3.0. Additional exam requirements/recommendations for international students: Required—TOEFL. Electronic applications accepted. *Faculty research:* DNA replication and transcription, virus gene expression, tumor biology, structural biochemistry, signal transduction and molecular targeting.

Saint Louis University, Graduate Education and School of Medicine, Graduate Program in Biomedical Sciences and Graduate Education, Department of Biochemistry and Molecular Biology, St. Louis, MO 63103-2097. Offers PhD. *Degree requirements:* For doctorate, comprehensive exam, thesis/dissertation, departmental qualifying exams. *Entrance requirements:* For doctorate, GRE General Test, GRE Subject Test (optional), letters of recommendation, resume, interview. Additional exam requirements/recommendations for international students: Required—TOEFL (minimum score 525 paper-based; 194 computer-based). Electronic applications accepted. *Faculty research:* Transcription, chromatin modification and regulation of gene expression; structure/function of proteins and enzymes, including x-ray crystallography; inflammatory mediators in pathenogenesis of diabetes and arteriosclerosis; cellular signaling in response to growth factors, opiates and angiogenic mediators; genomics and proteomics of Cryptococcus neoformans.

San Diego State University, Graduate and Research Affairs, College of Sciences, Department of Chemistry and Biochemistry, San Diego, CA 92182. Offers MA, MS, PhD. PhD offered jointly with University of California, San Diego. Terminal master's awarded for partial completion of doctoral program. *Degree requirements:* For doctorate, thesis/dissertation. *Entrance requirements:* For master's, GRE General Test, bachelor's degree in related field, 3 letters of reference; for doctorate, GRE General Test, GRE Subject Test. Additional exam requirements/recommendations for international students: Required—TOEFL. Electronic applications accepted. *Faculty research:* Nonlinear, laser, and electrochemistry; surface reaction dynamics; catalysis, synthesis, and organometallics; proteins, enzymology, and gene expression regulation.

San Francisco State University, Division of Graduate Studies, College of Science and Engineering, Department of Chemistry and Biochemistry, San Francisco, CA 94132-1722. Offers chemistry (MS), including biochemistry. Part-time programs available. *Application deadline:* Applications are processed on a rolling basis. Electronic applications accepted. *Unit head:* Dr. Jane DeWitt, Chair, 415-338-1288, Fax: 415-338-2384, E-mail: gradchem@sfsu.edu. *Application contact:* Dr. Bruce Manning, Graduate Coordinator, 415-338-1288, Fax: 415-338-2384, E-mail: bmanning@sfsu.edu. Web site: http://lewis.sfsu.edu.

Seton Hall University, College of Arts and Sciences, Department of Chemistry and Biochemistry, South Orange, NJ 07079-2697. Offers analytical chemistry (MS, PhD); biochemistry (MS, PhD); chemistry (MS); inorganic chemistry (MS, PhD); organic chemistry (MS, PhD); physical chemistry (MS, PhD). Part-time and evening/weekend programs available. Terminal master's awarded for partial completion of doctoral program. *Degree requirements:* For master's, thesis optional; for doctorate, comprehensive exam, thesis/dissertation. *Entrance requirements:* Additional exam

requirements/recommendations for international students: Required—TOEFL. Electronic applications accepted. *Expenses: Tuition:* Part-time $1033 per credit hour. *Required fees:* $85 per semester. *Faculty research:* DNA metal reactions; chromatography; bioinorganic, biophysical, organometallic, polymer chemistry; heterogeneous catalyst; synthetic organic and carbohydrate chemistry.

Simon Fraser University, Graduate Studies, Faculty of Science, Department of Molecular Biology and Biochemistry, Burnaby, BC V5A 1S6, Canada. Offers M Sc, PhD. *Degree requirements:* For master's, thesis; for doctorate, thesis/dissertation. *Entrance requirements:* For master's, minimum GPA of 3.0; for doctorate, minimum GPA of 3.5. Additional exam requirements/recommendations for international students: Required—TWE or IELTS. *Faculty research:* Molecular genetics and development, biochemistry, molecular physiology, genomics, molecular phylogenetics and population genetics, bioinformation.

Sonoma State University, School of Science and Technology, Department of Biology, Rohnert Park, CA 94928-3609. Offers biochemistry (MA); environmental biology (MA). Part-time programs available. *Faculty:* 10 full-time (2 women). *Students:* 4 full-time (2 women), 14 part-time (9 women); includes 3 minority (1 American Indian or Alaska Native, non-Hispanic/Latino; 1 Asian, non-Hispanic/Latino; 1 Hispanic/Latino), 1 international. Average age 29. 23 applicants, 26% accepted, 3 enrolled. In 2011, 10 master's awarded. *Degree requirements:* For master's, thesis or alternative, oral exam. *Entrance requirements:* For master's, GRE General Test, GRE Subject Test, minimum GPA of 3.0. Additional exam requirements/recommendations for international students: Required—TOEFL (minimum score 500 paper-based; 173 computer-based). *Application deadline:* For fall admission, 11/30 for domestic students. Applications are processed on a rolling basis. Application fee: $55. *Financial support:* In 2011–12, 3 teaching assistantships (averaging $5,343 per year) were awarded; fellowships, research assistantships, career-related internships or fieldwork, Federal Work-Study, and tuition waivers (full) also available. Financial award application deadline: 3/2; financial award applicants required to submit FAFSA. *Faculty research:* Plant physiology, comparative physiology, community ecology, restoration ecology, marine ecology, conservation genetics, primate behavior, behavioral ecology, developmental biology, plant and animal systematics. *Total annual research expenditures:* $238,000. *Unit head:* Chair, 707-664-, E-mail: james.christmann@sonoma.edu. *Application contact:* Dr. Derek Girman, Graduate Adviser, 707-664-3055, E-mail: derek.girman@sonoma.edu. Web site: http://www.sonoma.edu/biology/graduate.

Southern Illinois University Carbondale, Graduate School, College of Science, Department of Chemistry and Biochemistry, Carbondale, IL 62901-4701. Offers MS, PhD. Part-time programs available. *Faculty:* 18 full-time (1 woman), 2 part-time/adjunct (0 women). *Students:* 49 full-time (24 women), 9 part-time (3 women); includes 1 minority (Black or African American, non-Hispanic/Latino), 37 international. Average age 25. 59 applicants, 10% accepted, 4 enrolled. In 2011, 2 master's, 4 doctorates awarded. Terminal master's awarded for partial completion of doctoral program. *Degree requirements:* For master's, one foreign language, thesis; for doctorate, variable foreign language requirement, thesis/dissertation. *Entrance requirements:* For master's, minimum GPA of 2.7; for doctorate, GRE General Test, minimum GPA of 3.25. Additional exam requirements/recommendations for international students: Required—TOEFL. *Application deadline:* Applications are processed on a rolling basis. Application fee: $0. *Financial support:* In 2011–12, 17 research assistantships with full tuition reimbursements, 23 teaching assistantships with full tuition reimbursements were awarded; fellowships with full tuition reimbursements, Federal Work-Study, institutionally sponsored loans, and tuition waivers (full) also available. Support available to part-time students. *Faculty research:* Materials, separations, computational chemistry, synthetics. *Total annual research expenditures:* $1 million. *Unit head:* Gary Kinsel, Chair, 618-453-6482, Fax: 618-453-6408. *Application contact:* Kristen Burton, Office Specialist, 618-453-6494, Fax: 618-453-6408, E-mail: kburton@chem.siu.edu.

Southern Illinois University Carbondale, Graduate School, College of Science, Program in Molecular Biology, Microbiology, and Biochemistry, Carbondale, IL 62901-4701. Offers MS, PhD. *Faculty:* 16 full-time (2 women). *Students:* 52 full-time (27 women), 42 part-time (25 women); includes 10 minority (5 Black or African American, non-Hispanic/Latino; 5 Asian, non-Hispanic/Latino), 64 international. Average age 25. 139 applicants, 12% accepted, 12 enrolled. In 2011, 14 master's, 8 doctorates awarded. *Degree requirements:* For master's, thesis; for doctorate, thesis/dissertation. *Entrance requirements:* For master's, GRE, minimum GPA of 2.7; for doctorate, GRE, minimum GPA of 3.25. Additional exam requirements/recommendations for international students: Required—TOEFL. *Application deadline:* Applications are processed on a rolling basis. Application fee: $20. *Financial support:* In 2011–12, 40 students received support, including 3 fellowships with full tuition reimbursements available, 24 research assistantships with full tuition reimbursements available, 12 teaching assistantships with full tuition reimbursements available; Federal Work-Study and institutionally sponsored loans also available. Support available to part-time students. Financial award application deadline: 3/1. *Faculty research:* Prokaryotic gene regulation and expression; eukaryotic gene regulation; microbial, phylogenetic, and metabolic diversity; immune responses to tumors, pathogens, and autoantigens; protein folding and structure. *Unit head:* Dr. John Martinko, Director, 618-453-8116, Fax: 618-453-8036, E-mail: martinko.mbmb@science.siu.edu. *Application contact:* Charlotte Keller, Office Systems Specialist, 618-453-7071, Fax: 618-453-8036, E-mail: ckeller@siumed.edu. Web site: http://mbmb.siu.edu/.

Southern University and Agricultural and Mechanical College, Graduate School, College of Sciences, Department of Chemistry, Baton Rouge, LA 70813. Offers analytical chemistry (MS); biochemistry (MS); environmental sciences (MS); inorganic chemistry (MS); organic chemistry (MS); physical chemistry (MS). *Degree requirements:* For master's, thesis. *Entrance requirements:* For master's, GMAT or GRE General Test. Additional exam requirements/recommendations for international students: Required—TOEFL (minimum score 525 paper-based; 193 computer-based). *Faculty research:* Synthesis of macrocyclic ligands, latex accelerators, anticancer drugs, biosensors, absorption isotheums, isolation of specific enzymes from plants.

Stanford University, School of Medicine, Graduate Programs in Medicine, Department of Biochemistry, Stanford, CA 94305-9991. Offers PhD. *Degree requirements:* For doctorate, thesis/dissertation. *Entrance requirements:* For doctorate, GRE General Test, GRE Subject Test (biology or chemistry). Additional exam requirements/recommendations for international students: Required—TOEFL. Electronic applications accepted. *Expenses: Tuition:* Full-time $40,050; part-time $890 per credit. *Faculty research:* DNA replication, recombination, and gene regulation; methods of isolating, analyzing, and altering genes and genomes; protein structure, protein folding, and protein processing; protein targeting and transport in the cell; intercellular signaling.

State University of New York College of Environmental Science and Forestry, Department of Chemistry, Syracuse, NY 13210-2779. Offers biochemistry (MPS, MS, PhD); environmental chemistry (MPS, MS, PhD); organic chemistry of natural products (MPS, MS, PhD); polymer chemistry (MPS, MS, PhD). *Degree requirements:* For master's, thesis; for doctorate, comprehensive exam, thesis/dissertation. *Entrance requirements:* For master's and doctorate, GRE General Test, GRE Subject Test, minimum GPA of 3.0. Additional exam requirements/recommendations for international students: Required—TOEFL (minimum score 550 paper-based; 213 computer-based; 80 iBT), IELTS (minimum score 6). *Application deadline:* For fall admission, 2/1 priority date for domestic students, 2/1 for international students; for spring admission, 11/1 priority date for domestic students, 11/1 for international students. Applications are processed on a rolling basis. Application fee: $60. Electronic applications accepted. *Expenses:* Tuition, state resident: full-time $8870; part-time $370 per credit hour. Tuition, nonresident: full-time $15,160; part-time $632 per credit hour. *Required fees:* $60; $370 per credit hour. $350 per semester. One-time fee: $85. *Financial support:* Fellowships with full tuition reimbursements, research assistantships with full tuition reimbursements, teaching assistantships with full tuition reimbursements, Federal Work-Study, institutionally sponsored loans, scholarships/grants, health care benefits, and unspecified assistantships available. Financial award application deadline: 6/30; financial award applicants required to submit FAFSA. *Faculty research:* Polymer chemistry, biochemistry. *Total annual research expenditures:* $1.8 million. *Unit head:* Prof. Gregory Boyer, Chair, 315-470-6825, Fax: 315-470-6856, E-mail: glboyer@esf.edu. *Application contact:* Scott Shannon, Associate Provost for Instruction/Dean of the Graduate School, 315-470-6599, Fax: 315-470-6978, E-mail: sshannon@esf.edu. Web site: http://www.esf.edu/chemistry.

State University of New York Upstate Medical University, College of Graduate Studies, Program in Biochemistry and Molecular Biology, Syracuse, NY 13210-2334. Offers biochemistry (MS); biochemistry and molecular biology (PhD); MD/PhD. Terminal master's awarded for partial completion of doctoral program. *Degree requirements:* For master's, thesis; for doctorate, comprehensive exam, thesis/dissertation. *Entrance requirements:* For master's, GRE General Test, interview; for doctorate, GRE General Test, telephone interview. Additional exam requirements/recommendations for international students: Required—TOEFL. Electronic applications accepted. *Faculty research:* Enzymology, membrane structure and functions, developmental biochemistry.

Stevens Institute of Technology, Graduate School, Charles V. Schaefer Jr. School of Engineering, Department of Chemistry, Chemical Biology and Biomedical Engineering, Hoboken, NJ 07030. Offers analytical chemistry (PhD, Certificate); bioinformatics (PhD, Certificate); biomedical chemistry (Certificate); biomedical engineering (M Eng, Certificate); chemical biology (MS, PhD, Certificate); chemical physiology (Certificate); chemistry (MS, PhD); organic chemistry (PhD); physical chemistry (PhD); polymer chemistry (PhD, Certificate). Part-time and evening/weekend programs available. Postbaccalaureate distance learning degree programs offered (no on-campus study). Terminal master's awarded for partial completion of doctoral program. *Degree requirements:* For master's, thesis or alternative; for doctorate, one foreign language, thesis/dissertation; for Certificate, project or thesis. *Entrance requirements:* Additional exam requirements/recommendations for international students: Required—TOEFL. Electronic applications accepted. *Faculty research:* Biochemical reaction engineering, polymerization engineering, reactor design, biochemical process control and synthesis.

Stony Brook University, State University of New York, Graduate School, College of Arts and Sciences, Department of Biochemistry and Cell Biology, Molecular and Cellular Biology Program, Specialization in Biochemistry and Molecular Biology, Stony Brook, NY 11794. Offers PhD. *Degree requirements:* For doctorate, comprehensive exam, thesis/dissertation, teaching experience. *Entrance requirements:* For doctorate, GRE General Test, GRE Subject Test. Additional exam requirements/recommendations for international students: Required—TOEFL.

Stony Brook University, State University of New York, Graduate School, College of Arts and Sciences, Department of Biochemistry and Cell Biology, Program in Biochemistry and Structural Biology, Stony Brook, NY 11794. Offers PhD.

Syracuse University, College of Arts and Sciences, Program in Structural Biology, Biochemistry and Biophysics, Syracuse, NY 13244. Offers PhD. *Students:* 5 full-time (3 women); includes 1 minority (Black or African American, non-Hispanic/Latino), 2 international. Average age 30. 10 applicants, 10% accepted, 1 enrolled. In 2011, 1 degree awarded. *Degree requirements:* For doctorate, comprehensive exam, thesis/dissertation, exam. *Entrance requirements:* For doctorate, GRE General Test, GRE Subject Test. Additional exam requirements/recommendations for international students: Required—TOEFL (minimum score 100 iBT). *Application deadline:* For fall admission, 1/10 priority date for domestic students, 1/10 for international students. Application fee: $75. Electronic applications accepted. *Expenses: Tuition:* Part-time $1206 per credit. *Financial support:* Fellowships with full tuition reimbursements, research assistantships with full and partial tuition reimbursements, teaching assistantships with full and partial tuition reimbursements, and tuition waivers available. Financial award application deadline: 1/1; financial award applicants required to submit FAFSA. *Unit head:* Prof. Scott Pitnick, Director, 315-443-5128, Fax: 315-443-2012, E-mail: sspitnic@syr.edu. *Application contact:* Evelyn Lott, Information Contact, 315-443-9154, Fax: 315-443-2012, E-mail: ealott@syr.edu. Web site: http://sb3.syr.edu/.

Temple University, Health Sciences Center, School of Medicine and Graduate School, Graduate Programs in Medicine, Department of Biochemistry, Philadelphia, PA 19122-6096. Offers MS, PhD. *Faculty:* 16 full-time (4 women). *Students:* 15 full-time (8 women); includes 3 minority (1 Black or African American, non-Hispanic/Latino; 2 Asian, non-Hispanic/Latino), 6 international. Average age 28. 3 applicants, 100% accepted, 2 enrolled. In 2011, 2 degrees awarded. *Degree requirements:* For master's, thesis, research seminar; for doctorate, thesis/dissertation, research seminars. *Entrance requirements:* For master's and doctorate, GRE General Test, GRE Subject Test, minimum GPA of 3.0. Additional exam requirements/recommendations for international students: Required—TOEFL (minimum score 650 paper-based; 280 computer-based). *Application deadline:* For fall admission, 4/15 priority date for domestic students, 12/15 for international students; for spring admission, 11/15 priority date for domestic students, 8/1 for international students. Applications are processed on a rolling basis. Application fee: $50. Electronic applications accepted. *Expenses:* Tuition, state resident: full-time $12,366; part-time $687 per credit hour. Tuition, nonresident: full-time $17,298; part-time $961 per credit hour. *Required fees:* $590; $213 per year. *Financial support:* Fellowships, research assistantships, Federal Work-Study, and institutionally sponsored loans available. Financial award application deadline: 1/15; financial award applicants required to submit FAFSA. *Faculty research:* Metabolism, enzymology, molecular biology, membranology, biophysics. *Unit head:* Dr. Donald L. Gill, Acting Chair, 215-707-3979, Fax: 215-707-7536, E-mail: dgill@temple.edu. *Application contact:* Office of Admissions, 215-707-3656, Fax: 215-707-6932, E-mail: medadmissions@temple.edu. Web site: http://www.temple.edu/medicine/departments_centers/basic_science/biochemistry.htm.

Texas A&M University, College of Agriculture and Life Sciences, Department of Biochemistry and Biophysics, College Station, TX 77843. Offers biochemistry (MS, PhD); biophysics (MS). *Faculty:* 34. *Students:* 138 full-time (55 women), 6 part-time (3 women); includes 17 minority (2 Black or African American, non-Hispanic/Latino; 1 American Indian or Alaska Native, non-Hispanic/Latino; 2 Asian, non-Hispanic/Latino; 10 Hispanic/Latino; 2 Two or more races, non-Hispanic/Latino), 55 international. Average age 27. In 2011, 3 master's, 14 doctorates awarded. *Entrance requirements:* For master's and doctorate, GRE General Test. Additional exam requirements/recommendations for international students: Required—TOEFL. *Application deadline:* For fall admission, 2/1 priority date for domestic students, 12/1 for international students. Applications are processed on a rolling basis. Application fee: $50 ($75 for international students). Electronic applications accepted. *Expenses:* Tuition, state resident: full-time

$5437; part-time $226.55 per credit hour. Tuition, nonresident: full-time $12,949; part-time $539.55 per credit hour. *Required fees:* $2741. *Financial support:* In 2011–12, 6 fellowships with tuition reimbursements (averaging $20,000 per year), 70 research assistantships with partial tuition reimbursements (averaging $20,000 per year) were awarded; teaching assistantships with partial tuition reimbursements, institutionally sponsored loans, scholarships/grants, traineeships, and unspecified assistantships also available. Financial award application deadline: 2/1; financial award applicants required to submit FAFSA. *Faculty research:* Enzymology, gene expression, protein structure, plant biochemistry. *Unit head:* Dr. Gregory D. Reinhart, Department Head, 979-862-2263, Fax: 979-845-9274, E-mail: gdr@tamu.edu. *Application contact:* Pat Swigert, Graduate Advisor, 979-845-1779, Fax: 979-845-9274. Web site: http://biochemistry.tamu.edu/.

Texas Christian University, College of Science and Engineering, Department of Chemistry, Fort Worth, TX 76129. Offers biochemistry (MS, PhD); chemistry (MA); inorganic (MS, PhD); organic (MS, PhD); physical (MS, PhD). Part-time programs available. *Faculty:* 11 full-time (2 women). *Students:* 4 full-time (2 women), 16 part-time (10 women); includes 3 minority (1 Asian, non-Hispanic/Latino; 2 Hispanic/Latino), 11 international. Average age 27. 5 applicants, 100% accepted, 4 enrolled. In 2011, 1 master's, 3 doctorates awarded. *Degree requirements:* For master's, thesis; for doctorate, thesis/dissertation, literature seminar, cumulative exams, research progress report, original proposal. *Entrance requirements:* For master's and doctorate, GRE General Test. Additional exam requirements/recommendations for international students: Required—TOEFL. *Application deadline:* For fall admission, 3/1 priority date for domestic students, 3/1 for international students; for spring admission, 9/1 priority date for domestic students, 9/1 for international students. Application fee: $50. Electronic applications accepted. *Expenses: Tuition:* Full-time $20,250; part-time $1125 per credit hour. Part-time tuition and fees vary according to course load and program. *Financial support:* In 2011–12, 11 students received support, including 11 teaching assistantships with full tuition reimbursements available; tuition waivers (full and partial) and unspecified assistantships also available. Financial award application deadline: 3/1. *Faculty research:* Phase transitions and transport properties of bio/macromolecular solutions, nanoscale biomaterials, electronic structure theory, synthetic methodology and total synthesis of natural products, chemistry and biology of (bio)polymers. *Unit head:* Dr. Robert Neilson, Chairperson/Professor, 817-257-7345, Fax: 817-257-5851, E-mail: r.neilson@tcu.edu. *Application contact:* Dr. Sergei V. Dzyuba, Director of Graduate Studies/Assistant Professor, 817-257-6218, Fax: 817-257-5851, E-mail: s.dzyuba@tcu.edu. Web site: http://www.chm.tcu.edu/.

Texas State University–San Marcos, Graduate School, College of Science and Engineering, Department of Chemistry and Biochemistry, Program in Biochemistry, San Marcos, TX 78666. Offers MS. *Faculty:* 7 full-time (3 women), 1 part-time/adjunct. *Students:* 21 full-time (9 women), 5 part-time (2 women); includes 11 minority (1 Black or African American, non-Hispanic/Latino; 1 Asian, non-Hispanic/Latino; 9 Hispanic/Latino), 2 international. Average age 27. 20 applicants, 45% accepted, 4 enrolled. In 2011, 5 master's awarded. *Degree requirements:* For master's, thesis. *Entrance requirements:* For master's, minimum GPA of 2.75 in last 60 hours of course work. Additional exam requirements/recommendations for international students: Required—TOEFL (minimum score 550 paper-based; 213 computer-based; 78 iBT). *Application deadline:* For fall admission, 6/15 priority date for domestic students, 6/1 for international students; for spring admission, 10/15 priority date for domestic students, 10/1 for international students. Applications are processed on a rolling basis. Application fee: $40 ($90 for international students). Electronic applications accepted. *Expenses:* Tuition, state resident: full-time $6408; part-time $3204 per semester. Tuition, nonresident: full-time $14,832; part-time $7416 per semester. *Required fees:* $1824; $912 per semester. Tuition and fees vary according to course load. *Financial support:* In 2011–12, 20 students received support, including 15 teaching assistantships (averaging $11,475 per year); research assistantships, Federal Work-Study, institutionally sponsored loans, scholarships/grants, health care benefits, and unspecified assistantships also available. Support available to part-time students. Financial award application deadline: 4/1; financial award applicants required to submit FAFSA. *Unit head:* Dr. Chad Booth, Graduate Advisor, 512-245-2156, Fax: 512-245-2374, E-mail: chadbooth@txstate.edu. *Application contact:* Dr. J. Michael Willoughby, Dean of Graduate School, 512-245-2581, Fax: 512-245-8365, E-mail: gradcollege@txstate.edu. Web site: http://www.txstate.edu/chemistry/.

Texas Tech University Health Sciences Center, Graduate School of Biomedical Sciences, Department of Cell Biology and Biochemistry, Program in Biochemistry and Molecular Genetics, Lubbock, TX 79430. Offers MS, PhD, MD/PhD, MS/PhD. Terminal master's awarded for partial completion of doctoral program. *Degree requirements:* For master's, comprehensive exam, thesis, preliminary, comprehensive, and final exams; for doctorate, comprehensive exam, thesis/dissertation, preliminary, comprehensive, and final exams. *Entrance requirements:* For master's and doctorate, GRE General Test, minimum GPA of 3.0. Additional exam requirements/recommendations for international students: Required—TOEFL. Electronic applications accepted. *Faculty research:* Reproductive endocrinology, immunology, developmental biochemistry, biochemistry and genetics of cancer, molecular genetics and cell cycle.

Thomas Jefferson University, Jefferson College of Graduate Studies, PhD Program in Biochemistry and Molecular Biology, Philadelphia, PA 19107. Offers PhD. *Faculty:* 48 full-time (15 women), 1 (woman) part-time/adjunct. *Students:* 17 full-time (11 women); includes 2 minority (both Asian, non-Hispanic/Latino), 3 international. Average age 24. 40 applicants, 20% accepted, 3 enrolled. In 2011, 4 doctorates awarded. *Degree requirements:* For doctorate, comprehensive exam, thesis/dissertation. *Entrance requirements:* For doctorate, GRE General Test or MCAT, minimum GPA of 3.2. Additional exam requirements/recommendations for international students: Required—TOEFL (minimum score 250 computer-based; 100 iBT) or IELTS. *Application deadline:* For fall admission, 1/2 priority date for domestic students, 1/2 for international students. Applications are processed on a rolling basis. Application fee: $50. Electronic applications accepted. *Financial support:* In 2011–12, 17 students received support, including 17 fellowships with full tuition reimbursements available (averaging $54,758 per year); Federal Work-Study, institutionally sponsored loans, scholarships/grants, traineeships, and stipends also available. Financial award application deadline: 5/1; financial award applicants required to submit FAFSA. *Faculty research:* Signal transduction and molecular genetics, translational biochemistry, human mitochondrial genetics, molecular biology of protein-RNA interaction, mammalian mitochondrial biogenesis and function. *Total annual research expenditures:* $26.8 million. *Unit head:* Dr. Diane E. Merry, Program Director, 215-503-4907, Fax: 215-923-9162, E-mail: diane.merry@jefferson.edu. *Application contact:* Marc E. Stearns, Director of Admissions, 215-503-0155, Fax: 215-503-9920, E-mail: jcgs-info@jefferson.edu. Web site: http://www.jefferson.edu/jcgs/phd/bmb/.

Tufts University, Sackler School of Graduate Biomedical Sciences, Biochemistry Program, Medford, MA 02155. Offers PhD. *Faculty:* 25 full-time (6 women). *Students:* 11 full-time (5 women); includes 2 minority (both Asian, non-Hispanic/Latino), 1 international. Average age 29. In 2011, 6 doctorates awarded. Terminal master's awarded for partial completion of doctoral program. *Degree requirements:* For doctorate, thesis/dissertation. *Entrance requirements:* For doctorate, GRE, 3 letters of recommendation. Additional exam requirements/recommendations for international students: Required—TOEFL (minimum score 600 paper-based; 250 computer-based; 100 iBT). *Application deadline:* For fall admission, 12/15 for domestic and international students. Application fee: $70. Electronic applications accepted. *Expenses: Tuition:* Full-time $41,208; part-time $1030 per credit hour. Full-time tuition and fees vary according to degree level, program and student level. Part-time tuition and fees vary according to course load. *Financial support:* In 2011–12, 11 students received support, including 11 research assistantships with full tuition reimbursements available (averaging $30,000 per year); health care benefits also available. *Faculty research:* Structure-based drug design based on nuclear magnetic resonance (NMR) analysis; mechanism of protein action using x-ray crystallography; biochemical basis of cell death; molecular basis of gene function including DNA replication, molecular bases of cancer. *Unit head:* Dr. Larry Feig, Program Director, 617-636-6956, Fax: 617-636-2409, E-mail: larry.feig@tufts.edu. *Application contact:* Kellie Melchin, Associate Director of Admissions, 617-636-6767, Fax: 617-636-0375, E-mail: sackler-school@tufts.edu. Web site: http://sackler.tufts.edu/Academics/Degree-Programs/PhD-Programs/Biochemistry.

Tulane University, School of Medicine and School of Liberal Arts, Graduate Programs in Biomedical Sciences, Department of Biochemistry, New Orleans, LA 70118-5669. Offers MS, PhD, MD/PhD. MS and PhD offered through the Graduate School. *Degree requirements:* For master's, thesis; for doctorate, 2 foreign languages, thesis/dissertation. *Entrance requirements:* For master's, GRE General Test, GRE Subject Test, minimum B average in undergraduate course work; for doctorate, GRE General Test, GRE Subject Test. Additional exam requirements/recommendations for international students: Required—TOEFL. Electronic applications accepted. *Faculty research:* Nucleic acid chemistry, complex carbohydrates biochemistry.

Universidad Central del Caribe, School of Medicine, Program in Biomedical Sciences, Bayamón, PR 00960-6032. Offers anatomy and cell biology (MA, MS); biochemistry (MS); biomedical sciences (MA); cellular and molecular biology (PhD); microbiology and immunology (MA, MS); pharmacology (MS); physiology (MS).

Université de Moncton, Faculty of Sciences, Department of Chemistry and Biochemistry, Moncton, NB E1A 3E9, Canada. Offers biochemistry (M Sc); chemistry (M Sc). Part-time programs available. *Degree requirements:* For master's, one foreign language, thesis. *Entrance requirements:* For master's, minimum GPA of 3.0. Electronic applications accepted. *Faculty research:* Environmental contaminants, natural products synthesis, nutraceutical, organic catalysis, molecular biology of cancer.

Université de Montréal, Faculty of Medicine, Department of Biochemistry, Montréal, QC H3C 3J7, Canada. Offers biochemistry (M Sc, PhD); clinical biochemistry (DEPD). Terminal master's awarded for partial completion of doctoral program. *Degree requirements:* For master's, thesis; for doctorate, thesis/dissertation, general exam. *Entrance requirements:* For master's and doctorate, proficiency in French, knowledge of English; for DEPD, proficiency in French. Electronic applications accepted.

Université de Sherbrooke, Faculty of Medicine and Health Sciences, Graduate Programs in Medicine, Department of Biochemistry, Sherbrooke, QC J1H 5N4, Canada. Offers M Sc, PhD. Terminal master's awarded for partial completion of doctoral program. *Degree requirements:* For master's, thesis; for doctorate, thesis/dissertation. Electronic applications accepted. *Faculty research:* RNA structure-function, chromatin and gene expression, genetic diseases.

Université Laval, Faculty of Medicine, Post-Professional Programs in Medical Studies, Québec, QC G1K 7P4, Canada. Offers anatomy–pathology (DESS); anesthesiology (DESS); cardiology (DESS); care of older people (Diploma); clinical research (DESS); community health (DESS); dermatology (DESS); diagnostic radiology (DESS); emergency medicine (Diploma); family medicine (DESS); general surgery (DESS); geriatrics (DESS); hematology (DESS); internal medicine (DESS); maternal and fetal medicine (Diploma); medical biochemistry (DESS); medical microbiology and infectious diseases (DESS); medical oncology (DESS); nephrology (DESS); neurology (DESS); neurosurgery (DESS); obstetrics and gynecology (DESS); ophthalmology (DESS); orthopedic surgery (DESS); oto-rhino-laryngology (DESS); palliative medicine (Diploma); pediatrics (DESS); plastic surgery (DESS); psychiatry (DESS); pulmonary medicine (DESS); radiology–oncology (DESS); thoracic surgery (DESS); urology (DESS). *Degree requirements:* For other advanced degree, comprehensive exam. *Entrance requirements:* For degree, knowledge of French. Electronic applications accepted.

Université Laval, Faculty of Sciences and Engineering, Department of Biochemistry and Microbiology, Programs in Biochemistry, Québec, QC G1K 7P4, Canada. Offers M Sc, PhD. Terminal master's awarded for partial completion of doctoral program. *Degree requirements:* For master's, thesis; for doctorate, comprehensive exam, thesis/dissertation. *Entrance requirements:* For master's and doctorate, knowledge of French, comprehension of written English. Electronic applications accepted.

University at Albany, State University of New York, School of Public Health, Department of Biomedical Sciences, Program in Biochemistry, Molecular Biology, and Genetics, Albany, NY 12222-0001. Offers MS, PhD. *Degree requirements:* For master's, thesis; for doctorate, thesis/dissertation. *Entrance requirements:* For master's and doctorate, GRE General Test, GRE Subject Test.

University at Buffalo, the State University of New York, Graduate School, School of Medicine and Biomedical Sciences, Graduate Programs in Medicine and Biomedical Sciences, Department of Biochemistry, Buffalo, NY 14260. Offers MA, PhD. *Faculty:* 18 full-time (6 women), 1 (woman) part-time/adjunct. *Students:* 29 full-time (12 women); includes 1 minority (American Indian or Alaska Native, non-Hispanic/Latino), 17 international. Average age 26. 25 applicants, 28% accepted, 4 enrolled. In 2011, 4 master's, 6 doctorates awarded. Terminal master's awarded for partial completion of doctoral program. *Degree requirements:* For master's, thesis optional; for doctorate, comprehensive exam, thesis/dissertation. *Entrance requirements:* For master's, GRE General Test; for doctorate, GRE General Test, 3 letters of recommendation. Additional exam requirements/recommendations for international students: Required—TOEFL (minimum score 600 paper-based; 250 computer-based; 100 iBT). *Application deadline:* For fall admission, 2/1 priority date for domestic students, 2/1 for international students. Applications are processed on a rolling basis. Application fee: $50. Electronic applications accepted. *Financial support:* In 2011–12, 1 fellowship with full tuition reimbursement (averaging $4,000 per year), 25 research assistantships with full tuition reimbursements (averaging $24,000 per year), 2 teaching assistantships with full tuition reimbursements (averaging $24,000 per year) were awarded; Federal Work-Study, institutionally sponsored loans, scholarships/grants, health care benefits, and unspecified assistantships also available. Financial award application deadline: 2/1; financial award applicants required to submit FAFSA. *Faculty research:* Gene expression, proteins and metalloenzymes, biochemical endocrinology. *Total annual research expenditures:* $2.5 million. *Unit head:* Dr. Kenneth M. Blumenthal, Chair, 716-829-2727, Fax: 716-829-2725, E-mail: kblumen@buffalo.edu. *Application contact:* Dr. Mark R. O'Brian, Director of Graduate Studies, 716-829-3200, Fax: 716-829-2725, E-mail: mrobrian@buffalo.edu. Web site: http://www.smbs.buffalo.edu/bch/.

The University of Alabama at Birmingham, Graduate Programs in Joint Health Sciences, Program in Biochemistry and Molecular Genetics, Birmingham, AL 35294. Offers PhD. *Degree requirements:* For doctorate, thesis/dissertation. *Entrance*

requirements: For doctorate, GRE General Test, interview. *Application deadline:* Applications are processed on a rolling basis. Electronic applications accepted. *Expenses:* Tuition, state resident: full-time $5922; part-time $309 per hour. Tuition, nonresident: full-time $13,428; part-time $726 per hour. Tuition and fees vary according to program. *Financial support:* In 2011–12, 8 fellowships were awarded. *Unit head:* Dr. Tim M. Townes, Chair, 205-934-5294, E-mail: ttownes@uab.edu. *Application contact:* Information Contact, 205-934-6034, Fax: 205-975-2547.

University of Alaska Fairbanks, College of Natural Sciences and Mathematics, Department of Chemistry and Biochemistry, Fairbanks, AK 99775-6160. Offers biochemistry and molecular biology (MS, PhD); chemistry (MA, MS); environmental chemistry (MS, PhD). Part-time programs available. *Faculty:* 7 full-time (0 women). *Students:* 26 full-time (11 women), 5 part-time (3 women); includes 4 minority (1 American Indian or Alaska Native, non-Hispanic/Latino; 2 Asian, non-Hispanic/Latino; 1 Hispanic/Latino), 7 international. Average age 27. 28 applicants, 29% accepted, 6 enrolled. In 2011, 4 master's, 3 doctorates awarded. *Degree requirements:* For master's, comprehensive exam, thesis or alternative; for doctorate, comprehensive exam, thesis/dissertation, oral defense. *Entrance requirements:* Additional exam requirements/recommendations for international students: Required—TOEFL (minimum score 550 paper-based; 213 computer-based). *Application deadline:* For fall admission, 6/1 for domestic students, 3/1 for international students; for spring admission, 10/15 for domestic students, 9/1 for international students. Applications are processed on a rolling basis. Application fee: $60. Electronic applications accepted. *Expenses:* Tuition, state resident: full-time $6696; part-time $372 per credit. Tuition, nonresident: full-time $13,680; part-time $760 per credit. Tuition and fees vary according to course load and reciprocity agreements. *Financial support:* In 2011–12, 8 research assistantships with tuition reimbursements (averaging $12,759 per year), 16 teaching assistantships with tuition reimbursements (averaging $17,112 per year) were awarded; fellowships with tuition reimbursements, Federal Work-Study, scholarships/grants, health care benefits, and unspecified assistantships also available. Support available to part-time students. Financial award application deadline: 7/1; financial award applicants required to submit FAFSA. *Faculty research:* Atmospheric aerosols, cold adaptation, hibernation and neuroprotection, liganogated ion channels, arctic contaminants. *Unit head:* Bill Simpson, Department Chair, 907-474-5510, Fax: 907-474-5640, E-mail: fychem@uaf.edu. *Application contact:* Mike Earnest, Director of Admissions, 907-474-7500, Fax: 907-474-5379, E-mail: admissions@uaf.edu. Web site: http://www.uaf.edu/chem.

University of Alberta, Faculty of Medicine and Dentistry and Faculty of Graduate Studies and Research, Graduate Programs in Medicine, Department of Biochemistry, Edmonton, AB T6G 2E1, Canada. Offers M Sc, PhD. Terminal master's awarded for partial completion of doctoral program. *Degree requirements:* For master's, thesis; for doctorate, thesis/dissertation. *Entrance requirements:* For master's and doctorate, minimum GPA of 3.3. Additional exam requirements/recommendations for international students: Required—TOEFL (minimum score 550 paper-based). *Faculty research:* Proteins, nucleic acids, membranes, regulation of gene expression, receptors.

The University of Arizona, College of Science, Department of Chemistry and Biochemistry, Tucson, AZ 85721. Offers biochemistry (PhD); chemistry (PhD). Part-time programs available. *Faculty:* 34 full-time (7 women), 4 part-time/adjunct (2 women). *Students:* 193 full-time (86 women), 12 part-time (4 women); includes 22 minority (1 Black or African American, non-Hispanic/Latino; 2 American Indian or Alaska Native, non-Hispanic/Latino; 10 Hispanic/Latino; 1 Native Hawaiian or other Pacific Islander, non-Hispanic/Latino; 8 Two or more races, non-Hispanic/Latino), 78 international. Average age 29. 124 applicants, 31% accepted, 34 enrolled. In 2011, 31 doctorates awarded. *Degree requirements:* For doctorate, comprehensive exam, thesis/dissertation. *Entrance requirements:* For doctorate, GRE General Test, 3 letters of recommendation, statement of purpose. Additional exam requirements/recommendations for international students: Required—TOEFL (minimum score 550 paper-based; 213 computer-based; 79 iBT). *Application deadline:* For fall admission, 2/1 for domestic students, 1/1 for international students; for spring admission, 10/15 for domestic and international students. Applications are processed on a rolling basis. Application fee: $75. Electronic applications accepted. *Expenses:* Tuition, state resident: full-time $10,840. Tuition, nonresident: full-time $25,802. *Financial support:* In 2011–12, 56 research assistantships with full tuition reimbursements (averaging $24,349 per year), 107 teaching assistantships with full tuition reimbursements (averaging $24,878 per year) were awarded; institutionally sponsored loans, scholarships/grants, health care benefits, tuition waivers (partial), and unspecified assistantships also available. Financial award applicants required to submit FAFSA. *Faculty research:* Analytical, inorganic, organic, physical chemistry, biological chemistry. *Total annual research expenditures:* $14.7 million. *Unit head:* Dr. Vicki Wysocki, Head, 520-621-2628, Fax: 520-621-8407, E-mail: vwysocki@u.arizona.edu. *Application contact:* Lori Boyd, 800-545-5814, Fax: 520-621-8407, E-mail: chemistry@arizona.edu. Web site: http://www.chem.arizona.edu/.

University of Arkansas for Medical Sciences, Graduate School, Graduate Programs in Biomedical Sciences, Program in Biochemistry and Molecular Biology, Little Rock, AR 72205-7199. Offers MS, PhD, MD/PhD. *Degree requirements:* For master's, comprehensive exam, thesis; for doctorate, thesis/dissertation, qualifying exam. *Entrance requirements:* For master's, GRE General Test, bachelor's degree in biology, chemistry, or related field; for doctorate, GRE General Test. Additional exam requirements/recommendations for international students: Required—TOEFL. *Faculty research:* Gene regulation, growth factors, oncogenes, metabolic diseases, hormone regulation.

The University of British Columbia, Faculty of Medicine, Department of Biochemistry and Molecular Biology, Vancouver, BC V6T 1Z1, Canada. Offers M Sc, PhD. *Degree requirements:* For master's, thesis; for doctorate, comprehensive exam, thesis/dissertation. *Entrance requirements:* For master's, first class B Sc; for doctorate, master's or first class honors bachelor's degree in biochemistry. Additional exam requirements/recommendations for international students: Required—TOEFL (minimum score 625 paper-based; 263 computer-based). Electronic applications accepted. *Faculty research:* Membrane biochemistry, protein structure/function, signal transduction, biochemistry.

University of Calgary, Faculty of Medicine and Faculty of Graduate Studies, Department of Biochemistry and Molecular Biology, Calgary, AB T2N 1N4, Canada. Offers M Sc, PhD. *Degree requirements:* For master's, thesis; for doctorate, thesis/dissertation, candidacy exam. *Entrance requirements:* For master's and doctorate, GRE General Test, minimum GPA of 3.2. Additional exam requirements/recommendations for international students: Required—TOEFL. Electronic applications accepted. *Faculty research:* Molecular and developmental genetics; molecular biology of disease; genomics, proteomics and bioinformatics; ceu signaling and structure.

University of California, Berkeley, Graduate Division, Group in Comparative Biochemistry, Berkeley, CA 94720-1500. Offers PhD. *Degree requirements:* For doctorate, thesis/dissertation, qualifying exam. *Entrance requirements:* For doctorate, GRE General Test, GRE Subject Test, minimum GPA of 3.0, 3 letters of recommendation. Additional exam requirements/recommendations for international students: Required—TOEFL.

University of California, Davis, Graduate Studies, Graduate Group in Biochemistry and Molecular Biology, Davis, CA 95616. Offers MS, PhD. Terminal master's awarded for partial completion of doctoral program. *Degree requirements:* For master's, comprehensive exam (for some programs), thesis (for some programs); for doctorate, thesis/dissertation. *Entrance requirements:* For master's and doctorate, GRE General Test, GRE Subject Test. Additional exam requirements/recommendations for international students: Required—TOEFL (minimum score 550 paper-based; 213 computer-based). Electronic applications accepted. *Faculty research:* Gene expression, protein structure, molecular virology, protein synthesis, enzymology, membrane transport and structural biology.

University of California, Irvine, School of Biological Sciences, Department of Molecular Biology and Biochemistry, Irvine, CA 92697. Offers biological science (MS); biological sciences (PhD); biotechnology (MS); MD/PhD. *Students:* 62 full-time (30 women), 1 part-time (0 women); includes 29 minority (4 Black or African American, non-Hispanic/Latino; 13 Asian, non-Hispanic/Latino; 12 Hispanic/Latino), 3 international. Average age 28. 1 applicant, 100% accepted, 1 enrolled. In 2011, 14 degrees awarded. *Degree requirements:* For doctorate, thesis/dissertation. *Entrance requirements:* For master's, GRE, minimum GPA of 3.0; for doctorate, GRE General Test, GRE Subject Test, minimum GPA of 3.0. Additional exam requirements/recommendations for international students: Required—TOEFL (minimum score 550 paper-based; 213 computer-based). *Application deadline:* For fall admission, 12/15 priority date for domestic students, 12/15 for international students. Applications are processed on a rolling basis. Application fee: $80 ($100 for international students). Electronic applications accepted. *Financial support:* Fellowships, research assistantships with full tuition reimbursements, teaching assistantships, institutionally sponsored loans, traineeships, health care benefits, and unspecified assistantships available. Financial award application deadline: 3/1; financial award applicants required to submit FAFSA. *Faculty research:* Structure and synthesis of nucleic acids and proteins, regulation, virology, biochemical genetics, gene organization. *Unit head:* Prof. Christopher C. Hughes, Chair, 949-824-8771, Fax: 949-824-8551, E-mail: cchughes@uci.edu. *Application contact:* Rene Frigo, CMB Program Manager, 949-824-8145, Fax: 949-824-1965, E-mail: rfrigo@uci.edu. Web site: http://www.bio.uci.edu/.

University of California, Irvine, School of Biological Sciences and School of Medicine, Interdisciplinary Graduate Program in Cellular and Molecular Biosciences, Irvine, CA 92697. Offers PhD. *Faculty:* 138 full-time (35 women). *Students:* 59 full-time (33 women); includes 16 minority (8 Asian, non-Hispanic/Latino; 8 Hispanic/Latino), 6 international. Average age 25. In 2011, 19 doctorates awarded. *Degree requirements:* For doctorate, thesis/dissertation, teaching assignment, preliminary exam. *Entrance requirements:* For doctorate, GRE General Test, minimum GPA of 3.0, research experience. Additional exam requirements/recommendations for international students: Required—TOEFL, IELTS, SPEAK. *Application deadline:* For fall admission, 1/1 for domestic and international students. Application fee: $60 ($80 for international students). Electronic applications accepted. *Expenses:* Contact institution. *Financial support:* In 2011–12, 56 fellowships with full tuition reimbursements (averaging $26,250 per year) were awarded; institutionally sponsored loans, scholarships/grants, tuition waivers (full), unspecified assistantships, and stipends also available. Financial award application deadline: 1/1; financial award applicants required to submit FAFSA. *Faculty research:* Cellular biochemistry; gene structure and expression; protein structure, function, and design; molecular genetics; pathogenesis and inherited disease. *Unit head:* Dr. David Fruman, Director, 949-824-3431, Fax: 949-824-1965, E-mail: gp-mbgb@uci.edu. *Application contact:* Renee Frigo, Administrator, 949-824-8145, Fax: 949-824-1965, E-mail: rfrigo@uci.edu. Web site: http://cmb.uci.edu/.

University of California, Irvine, School of Medicine and School of Biological Sciences, Department of Biological Chemistry, Irvine, CA 92697. Offers biological sciences (MS, PhD). *Students:* 38 full-time (23 women), 1 part-time (0 women); includes 15 minority (1 Black or African American, non-Hispanic/Latino; 11 Asian, non-Hispanic/Latino; 3 Hispanic/Latino), 4 international. Average age 29. In 2011, 1 master's, 9 doctorates awarded. *Degree requirements:* For doctorate, thesis/dissertation. *Entrance requirements:* For master's, minimum GPA of 3.0; for doctorate, GRE General Test, GRE Subject Test, minimum GPA of 3.0. Additional exam requirements/recommendations for international students: Required—TOEFL (minimum score 550 paper-based; 213 computer-based). *Application deadline:* For fall admission, 1/15 priority date for domestic students, 1/15 for international students. Application fee: $80 ($100 for international students). Electronic applications accepted. *Financial support:* Fellowships, research assistantships with full tuition reimbursements, teaching assistantships, institutionally sponsored loans, traineeships, health care benefits, and unspecified assistantships available. Financial award application deadline: 3/1; financial award applicants required to submit FAFSA. *Faculty research:* RNA splicing, mammalian chromosomal organization, membrane-hormone interactions, regulation of protein synthesis, molecular genetics of metabolic processes. *Unit head:* Dr. Eva Yhp Lee, Chair/Professor, 949-824-9766, Fax: 949-824-9767, E-mail: elee@uci.edu. *Application contact:* Aaron M. Goddman, Administrative Assistant, 949-824-6051, Fax: 949-824-2688, E-mail: amgoodma@uci.edu. Web site: http://www.bio.uci.edu/.

University of California, Los Angeles, David Geffen School of Medicine and Graduate Division, Graduate Programs in Medicine, Department of Biological Chemistry, Los Angeles, CA 90095. Offers MS, PhD. *Faculty:* 20 full-time (3 women). *Students:* 27 full-time (14 women); includes 7 minority (1 Black or African American, non-Hispanic/Latino; 4 Asian, non-Hispanic/Latino; 1 Hispanic/Latino; 1 Native Hawaiian or other Pacific Islander, non-Hispanic/Latino), 7 international. Average age 28. In 2011, 3 master's, 4 doctorates awarded. *Degree requirements:* For master's, comprehensive exam or thesis; for doctorate, thesis/dissertation, oral and written qualifying exams. *Entrance requirements:* For master's and doctorate, GRE General Test. Application fee: $70 ($90 for international students). Electronic applications accepted. *Financial support:* In 2011–12, 36 fellowships, 31 research assistantships, 10 teaching assistantships were awarded; Federal Work-Study, institutionally sponsored loans, scholarships/grants, and tuition waivers (full and partial) also available. Financial award application deadline: 3/1. *Unit head:* Dr. Carey F. Michael, Head, 310-206-7859, E-mail: mcarey@mednet.ucla.edu. *Application contact:* UCLA ACCESS Coordinator, 310-206-1845, Fax: 310-206-1636, E-mail: uclaaccess@mednet.ucla.edu. Web site: http://www.biolchem.ucla.edu/.

University of California, Los Angeles, Graduate Division, College of Letters and Science, Department of Chemistry and Biochemistry, Program in Biochemistry and Molecular Biology, Los Angeles, CA 90034. Offers PhD. *Students:* 71 full-time (31 women); includes 28 minority (1 Black or African American, non-Hispanic/Latino; 22 Asian, non-Hispanic/Latino; 5 Hispanic/Latino), 8 international. Average age 27. 139 applicants, 15% accepted, 10 enrolled. In 2011, 16 doctorates awarded. Terminal master's awarded for partial completion of doctoral program. *Degree requirements:* For doctorate, thesis/dissertation, oral and written exams, 1 year teaching experience. *Entrance requirements:* For doctorate, GRE General Test, GRE Subject Test, minimum undergraduate GPA of 3.0. *Application deadline:* For fall admission, 1/15 for domestic and international students. Application fee: $70 ($90 for international students). Electronic applications accepted. *Financial support:* In 2011–12, 77 fellowships with full and partial tuition reimbursements, 53 research assistantships with full and partial tuition

reimbursements, 38 teaching assistantships with full and partial tuition reimbursements were awarded; Federal Work-Study, scholarships/grants, health care benefits, tuition waivers (full and partial), and unspecified assistantships also available. Financial award applicants required to submit FAFSA. *Unit head:* Dr. Albert Courey, 310-825-3958, E-mail: courey@chem.ucla.edu. *Application contact:* Departmental Office, 310-825-2645, E-mail: bmbgrad@chem.ucla.edu. Web site: http://www.biochemistry.ucla.edu.

University of California, Los Angeles, Graduate Division, College of Letters and Science and David Geffen School of Medicine, UCLA ACCESS to Programs in the Molecular, Cellular and Integrative Life Sciences, Los Angeles, CA 90095. Offers biochemistry and molecular biology (PhD); biological chemistry (PhD); cellular and molecular pathology (PhD); human genetics (PhD); microbiology, immunology, and molecular genetics (PhD); molecular biology (PhD); molecular toxicology (PhD); molecular, cellular and integrative physiology (PhD); neurobiology (PhD); oral biology (PhD); physiology (PhD). *Students:* 44 full-time (30 women); includes 18 minority (11 Asian, non-Hispanic/Latino; 6 Hispanic/Latino; 1 Two or more races, non-Hispanic/Latino), 9 international. Average age 25. 495 applicants, 18% accepted, 41 enrolled. *Degree requirements:* For doctorate, thesis/dissertation, oral and written qualifying exams. *Entrance requirements:* For doctorate, GRE General Test, minimum undergraduate GPA of 3.0. Additional exam requirements/recommendations for international students: Required—TOEFL. *Application deadline:* For fall admission, 12/15 for domestic and international students. Application fee: $70 ($90 for international students). Electronic applications accepted. *Financial support:* In 2011–12, 51 fellowships with full and partial tuition reimbursements, 9 research assistantships with full and partial tuition reimbursements were awarded; teaching assistantships with full and partial tuition reimbursements, Federal Work-Study, institutionally sponsored loans, scholarships/grants, health care benefits, tuition waivers (full and partial), and unspecified assistantships also available. Financial award application deadline: 3/1; financial award applicants required to submit FAFSA. *Faculty research:* Molecular, cellular, and developmental biology; immunology; microbiology; integrative biology. *Unit head:* Jody Spillane, Project Coordinator, 310-206-1845, E-mail: jspillane@mednet.ucla.edu. *Application contact:* UCLA ACCESS Admissions, 310-206-1845, E-mail: uclaaccess@mednet.ucla.edu. Web site: https://www.uclaaccess.ucla.edu/.

University of California, Riverside, Graduate Division, Department of Biochemistry, Riverside, CA 92521-0102. Offers biochemistry and molecular biology (MS, PhD). Part-time programs available. Terminal master's awarded for partial completion of doctoral program. *Degree requirements:* For master's, comprehensive exams or thesis; for doctorate, comprehensive exam, thesis/dissertation, 2 quarters of teaching experience, qualifying exams. *Entrance requirements:* For master's and doctorate, GRE General Test, minimum GPA of 3.25. Additional exam requirements/recommendations for international students: Required—TOEFL (minimum score 550 paper-based; 213 computer-based; 80 iBT). Electronic applications accepted. *Faculty research:* Structural biology and molecular biophysics, signal transduction, plant biochemistry and molecular biology, gene expression and metabolic regulation, molecular toxicology and pathogenesis.

University of California, San Diego, Office of Graduate Studies, Department of Chemistry and Biochemistry, La Jolla, CA 92093. Offers chemistry (MS, PhD). *Degree requirements:* For doctorate, thesis/dissertation. *Entrance requirements:* For doctorate, GRE General Test, GRE Subject Test. Electronic applications accepted.

University of California, San Diego, Office of Graduate Studies, Division of Biological Sciences, Program in Biochemistry, La Jolla, CA 92093-0348. Offers PhD. Offered in association with the Salk Institute. *Degree requirements:* For doctorate, thesis/dissertation, qualifying exam. Electronic applications accepted.

University of California, San Francisco, Graduate Division and School of Medicine, Department of Biochemistry and Biophysics, Program in Biochemistry and Molecular Biology, San Francisco, CA 94143. Offers PhD, MD/PhD. *Degree requirements:* For doctorate, thesis/dissertation. *Entrance requirements:* For doctorate, GRE General Test, GRE Subject Test. Additional exam requirements/recommendations for international students: Required—TOEFL. *Expenses:* Contact institution. *Faculty research:* Structural biology, genetics, cell biology, cell physiology, metabolism.

University of California, San Francisco, School of Pharmacy and Graduate Division, Chemistry and Chemical Biology Graduate Program, San Francisco, CA 94143. Offers PhD. *Faculty:* 45 full-time (11 women). *Students:* 52 full-time (30 women); includes 17 minority (4 Black or African American, non-Hispanic/Latino; 8 Asian, non-Hispanic/Latino; 5 Hispanic/Latino), 4 international. Average age 27. 95 applicants, 23% accepted, 7 enrolled. In 2011, 7 degrees awarded. *Median time to degree:* Of those who began their doctoral program in fall 2003, 100% received their degree in 8 years or less. *Degree requirements:* For doctorate, thesis/dissertation. *Entrance requirements:* For doctorate, GRE General Test, GRE Subject Test, minimum GPA of 3.0. Additional exam requirements/recommendations for international students: Required—TOEFL (minimum score 550 paper-based; 213 computer-based; 80 iBT). *Application deadline:* For fall admission, 12/1 for domestic and international students. Applications are processed on a rolling basis. Application fee: $80 ($100 for international students). Electronic applications accepted. *Financial support:* In 2011–12, 52 students received support, including 9 fellowships with full tuition reimbursements available (averaging $29,500 per year), 43 research assistantships with full tuition reimbursements available (averaging $29,500 per year); teaching assistantships with partial tuition reimbursements available, institutionally sponsored loans, scholarships/grants, traineeships, and tuition waivers (full) also available. Financial award application deadline: 5/15. *Faculty research:* Biochemistry, macromolecular structure, cellular and molecular pharmacology, physical chemistry and computational biology, synthetic chemistry. *Unit head:* Dr. Charles S. Craik, Director, 415-476-8146, E-mail: craik@cgl.ucsf.edu. *Application contact:* Julia Molla, Senior Administrative Analyst, 415-476-1914, Fax: 415-514-1546, E-mail: julia.molla@ucsf.edu. Web site: http://ccb.ucsf.edu/.

University of California, Santa Barbara, Graduate Division, College of Letters and Sciences, Division of Mathematics, Life, and Physical Sciences, Interdepartmental Graduate Program in Biomolecular Science and Engineering, Santa Barbara, CA 93106-2014. Offers biochemistry and molecular biology (PhD), including biochemistry and molecular biology, biophysics and bioengineering. *Faculty:* 38 full-time (5 women), 1 (woman) part-time/adjunct. *Students:* 29 full-time (14 women); includes 3 minority (2 Asian, non-Hispanic/Latino; 1 Two or more races, non-Hispanic/Latino), 3 international. Average age 28. 83 applicants, 20% accepted, 4 enrolled. In 2011, 4 degrees awarded. Terminal master's awarded for partial completion of doctoral program. *Median time to degree:* Of those who began their doctoral program in fall 2003, 100% received their degree in 8 years or less. *Degree requirements:* For doctorate, thesis/dissertation. *Entrance requirements:* For doctorate, GRE General Test. Additional exam requirements/recommendations for international students: Required—TOEFL (minimum score 630 paper-based; 109 iBT), IELTS (minimum score 7). *Application deadline:* For fall admission, 12/15 for domestic and international students. Application fee: $80 ($100 for international students). Electronic applications accepted. *Expenses:* Tuition, state resident: full-time $12,192. Tuition, nonresident: full-time $27,294. *Required fees:* $764.13. *Financial support:* In 2011–12, 29 students received support, including 16 fellowships with full and partial tuition reimbursements available (averaging $11,321 per year), 31 research assistantships with full and partial tuition reimbursements available (averaging $14,777 per year), 16 teaching assistantships with full and partial tuition reimbursements available (averaging $6,307 per year); Federal Work-Study, traineeships, health care benefits, tuition waivers (full and partial), and unspecified assistantships also available. Financial award application deadline: 12/15; financial award applicants required to submit FAFSA. *Faculty research:* Biochemistry and molecular biology, biophysics, biomaterials, bioengineering, systems biology. *Unit head:* Prof. Philip A. Pincus, Director/Professor, 805-893-4685, E-mail: fyl@mrl.ucsb.edu. *Application contact:* Graduate Admissions Coordinator, 805-893-2278, Fax: 805-893-8259, E-mail: gradadmissions@graddiv.ucsb.edu. Web site: http://www.bmse.ucsb.edu/.

University of California, Santa Cruz, Division of Graduate Studies, Division of Physical and Biological Sciences, Department of Chemistry and Biochemistry, Santa Cruz, CA 95064. Offers MS, PhD. *Degree requirements:* For master's, thesis optional; for doctorate, one foreign language, thesis/dissertation, qualifying exam. *Entrance requirements:* For master's and doctorate, GRE General Test, GRE Subject Test. Additional exam requirements/recommendations for international students: Required—TOEFL (minimum score 570 paper-based; 230 computer-based; 89 iBT); Recommended—IELTS (minimum score 8). Electronic applications accepted. *Faculty research:* Marine chemistry; biochemistry; inorganic, organic, and physical chemistry.

University of Chicago, Division of Biological Sciences, Molecular Biosciences Cluster, Department of Biochemistry and Molecular Biology, Chicago, IL 60637-1513. Offers PhD, MD/PhD. *Degree requirements:* For doctorate, thesis/dissertation, ethics class, 2 teaching assistantships. *Entrance requirements:* For doctorate, GRE General Test, GRE Subject Test. Additional exam requirements/recommendations for international students: Required—TOEFL (minimum score 600 paper-based; 250 computer-based; 104 iBT), IELTS (minimum score 7). Electronic applications accepted. *Faculty research:* Molecular biology, gene expression, and DNA-protein interactions; membrane biochemistry, molecular endocrinology, and transmembrane signaling; enzyme mechanisms, physical biochemistry, and structural biology.

University of Cincinnati, Graduate School, College of Medicine, Graduate Programs in Biomedical Sciences, Department of Molecular Genetics, Biochemistry and Microbiology, Cincinnati, OH 45221. Offers MS, PhD. Terminal master's awarded for partial completion of doctoral program. *Degree requirements:* For master's, thesis or alternative; for doctorate, thesis/dissertation, qualifying exam. *Entrance requirements:* For master's and doctorate, GRE General Test. Additional exam requirements/recommendations for international students: Required—TOEFL (minimum score 600 paper-based; 250 computer-based; 100 iBT), TWE. Electronic applications accepted. *Faculty research:* Cancer biology and developmental genetics, gene regulation and chromosome structure, microbiology and pathogenic mechanisms, structural biology, membrane biochemistry and signal transduction.

University of Cincinnati, Graduate School, McMicken College of Arts and Sciences, Department of Chemistry, Cincinnati, OH 45221. Offers analytical chemistry (MS, PhD); biochemistry (MS, PhD); inorganic chemistry (MS, PhD); organic chemistry (MS, PhD); physical chemistry (MS, PhD); polymer chemistry (MS, PhD); sensors (PhD). Part-time and evening/weekend programs available. Terminal master's awarded for partial completion of doctoral program. *Degree requirements:* For master's, thesis optional; for doctorate, comprehensive exam, thesis/dissertation. *Entrance requirements:* For master's and doctorate, GRE General Test. Additional exam requirements/recommendations for international students: Required—TOEFL (minimum score 580 paper-based; 237 computer-based). Electronic applications accepted. *Faculty research:* Biomedical chemistry, laser chemistry, surface science, chemical sensors, synthesis.

University of Colorado Boulder, Graduate School, College of Arts and Sciences, Department of Chemistry and Biochemistry, Boulder, CO 80309. Offers biochemistry (PhD); chemistry (MS). *Faculty:* 40 full-time (7 women). *Students:* 210 full-time (83 women), 2 part-time; includes 20 minority (3 Black or African American, non-Hispanic/Latino; 7 Asian, non-Hispanic/Latino; 9 Hispanic/Latino; 1 Two or more races, non-Hispanic/Latino), 38 international. Average age 27. 451 applicants, 10% accepted, 42 enrolled. In 2011, 3 master's, 26 doctorates awarded. Terminal master's awarded for partial completion of doctoral program. *Degree requirements:* For master's, comprehensive exam or thesis; for doctorate, comprehensive exam, thesis/dissertation, cumulative exam. *Entrance requirements:* For master's, GRE General Test, GRE Subject Test, minimum undergraduate GPA of 2.75; for doctorate, GRE General Test, GRE Subject Test, minimum GPA of 3.0. *Application deadline:* For fall admission, 1/15 priority date for domestic students, 1/15 for international students. Applications are processed on a rolling basis. Application fee: $50 ($60 for international students). Electronic applications accepted. *Financial support:* In 2011–12, 265 students received support, including 119 fellowships (averaging $8,382 per year), 125 research assistantships with full and partial tuition reimbursements available (averaging $21,743 per year), 53 teaching assistantships with full and partial tuition reimbursements available (averaging $20,060 per year); institutionally sponsored loans, scholarships/grants, health care benefits, and unspecified assistantships also available. Financial award applicants required to submit FAFSA. *Faculty research:* Analytical, atmospheric, biochemistry, biophysical, chemical physics, environmental, inorganic, organic and physical chemistry. *Total annual research expenditures:* $26.7 million. *Application contact:* E-mail: gradassist.chembiochem@colorado.edu. Web site: http://chem.colorado.edu.

University of Colorado Denver, School of Medicine, Biochemistry Program, Aurora, CO 80045. Offers biochemistry and molecular genetics (PhD). *Students:* 19 full-time (7 women), 3 international. Average age 30. 28 applicants, 4% accepted, 1 enrolled. In 2011, 6 doctorates awarded. *Degree requirements:* For doctorate, comprehensive exam, thesis/dissertation, 30 credit hours each of coursework and thesis research. *Entrance requirements:* For doctorate, GRE (minimum combined score of 1200 on Verbal and Quantitative portions and at least 4.0 on the Analytical Writing section), minimum of three letters of recommendation from qualified referees. Additional exam requirements/recommendations for international students: Required—TOEFL (minimum score 570 paper-based; 230 computer-based). *Application deadline:* For fall admission, 12/1 for domestic students. Applications are processed on a rolling basis. Application fee: $50. Electronic applications accepted. *Expenses:* Contact institution. *Financial support:* In 2011–12, 6 students received support. Fellowships, health care benefits, tuition waivers (full), and stipend available. Financial award application deadline: 3/15; financial award applicants required to submit FAFSA. *Faculty research:* DNA damage, cancer and neurodegeneration, molecular mechanisms of pro-MRNA splicing, yeast RNA polymerases, DNA replication. *Total annual research expenditures:* $8.6 million. *Unit head:* Dr. Paul Megee, Associate Professor, Department of Biochemistry and Molecular Genetics, 303-724-3270, Fax: 303-724-3215, E-mail: paul.megee@ucdenver.edu. *Application contact:* Jennifer Spaulding, Administrative Assistant, 303-724-3201, Fax: 303-724-3215, E-mail: jennifer.spaulding@ucdenver.edu. Web site: http://www.uchsc.edu/sm/bbgn.

University of Connecticut, Graduate School, College of Liberal Arts and Sciences, Department of Molecular and Cell Biology, Field of Biochemistry, Storrs, CT 06269. Offers MS, PhD. Terminal master's awarded for partial completion of doctoral program. *Degree requirements:* For master's, comprehensive exam; for doctorate, thesis/dissertation. *Entrance requirements:* For master's and doctorate, GRE General Test,

GRE Subject Test. Additional exam requirements/recommendations for international students: Required—TOEFL (minimum score 550 paper-based; 213 computer-based). Electronic applications accepted.

University of Connecticut Health Center, Graduate School, Programs in Biomedical Sciences, Graduate Program in Molecular Biology and Biochemistry, Farmington, CT 06030. Offers PhD, DMD/PhD, MD/PhD. *Degree requirements:* For doctorate, comprehensive exam, thesis/dissertation. *Entrance requirements:* For doctorate, GRE General Test. Additional exam requirements/recommendations for international students: Required—TOEFL (minimum score 600 paper-based; 250 computer-based). Electronic applications accepted. *Faculty research:* Molecular biology, structural biology, protein biochemistry, microbial physiology and pathogenesis.

See Display on page 219 and Close-Up on page 243.

University of Delaware, College of Arts and Sciences, Department of Chemistry and Biochemistry, Newark, DE 19716. Offers biochemistry (MA, MS, PhD); chemistry (MA, MS, PhD). Part-time programs available. Terminal master's awarded for partial completion of doctoral program. *Degree requirements:* For master's, one foreign language, thesis (for some programs); for doctorate, one foreign language, thesis/dissertation, cumulative exam. *Entrance requirements:* For master's and doctorate, GRE General Test. Additional exam requirements/recommendations for international students: Required—TOEFL (minimum score 600 paper-based; 260 computer-based). Electronic applications accepted. *Faculty research:* Micro-organisms, bone, cancer metastosis, developmental biology, cell biology, molecular biology.

University of Denver, Faculty of Natural Sciences and Mathematics, Department of Chemistry and Biochemistry, Denver, CO 80208. Offers MA, MS, PhD. Part-time programs available. *Faculty:* 16 full-time (2 women), 4 part-time/adjunct (1 woman). *Students:* 13 full-time (9 women), 12 part-time (6 women); includes 1 minority (Black or African American, non-Hispanic/Latino), 11 international. Average age 28. 41 applicants, 41% accepted, 10 enrolled. In 2011, 1 degree awarded. Terminal master's awarded for partial completion of doctoral program. *Median time to degree:* Of those who began their doctoral program in fall 2003, 100% received their degree in 8 years or less. *Degree requirements:* For master's, comprehensive exam (for some programs), thesis; for doctorate, comprehensive exam, thesis/dissertation. *Entrance requirements:* For master's, GRE General Test (for MS). Additional exam requirements/recommendations for international students: Required—TOEFL (minimum score 550 paper-based; 80 iBT). *Application deadline:* For fall admission, 3/1 priority date for domestic students. Applications are processed on a rolling basis. Application fee: $60. Electronic applications accepted. *Financial support:* In 2011–12, 19 students received support, including 12 research assistantships with full and partial tuition reimbursements available (averaging $19,300 per year), 13 teaching assistantships with full and partial tuition reimbursements available (averaging $18,310 per year); career-related internships or fieldwork, Federal Work-Study, institutionally sponsored loans, and scholarships/grants also available. Support available to part-time students. Financial award application deadline: 2/15; financial award applicants required to submit FAFSA. *Faculty research:* Atmospheric chemistry, magnetic resonance, molecular spectroscopy, laser photolysis, biophysical chemistry. *Unit head:* Dr. Sandra S. Eaton, Chair, 303-871-3100, Fax: 303-871-2254, E-mail: seaton@du.edu. *Application contact:* Information Contact, 303-871-2435, Fax: 303-871-2254, E-mail: cheminfo@du.edu. Web site: http://www.du.edu/nsm/departments/chemistryandbiochemistry/.

University of Detroit Mercy, College of Engineering and Science, Department of Chemistry and Biochemistry, Detroit, MI 48221. Offers chemistry (MS). Evening/weekend programs available. *Degree requirements:* For master's, thesis. *Entrance requirements:* For master's, GRE General Test, minimum GPA of 3.0. *Faculty research:* Polymer and physical chemistry, industrial aspects of chemistry.

University of Florida, College of Medicine and Graduate School, Interdisciplinary Program in Biomedical Sciences, Concentration in Biochemistry and Molecular Biology, Gainesville, FL 32611. Offers PhD. *Degree requirements:* For doctorate, thesis/dissertation. *Entrance requirements:* For doctorate, GRE General Test, minimum GPA of 3.0. Additional exam requirements/recommendations for international students: Required—TOEFL. Electronic applications accepted. *Faculty research:* Gene expression, metabolic regulation, structural biology, enzyme mechanism, membrane transporters.

University of Georgia, Franklin College of Arts and Sciences, Department of Biochemistry and Molecular Biology, Athens, GA 30602. Offers MS, PhD. *Faculty:* 35 full-time (5 women). *Students:* 68 full-time (23 women), 2 part-time (both women); includes 7 minority (3 Black or African American, non-Hispanic/Latino; 3 Asian, non-Hispanic/Latino; 1 Hispanic/Latino), 21 international. Average age 29. 119 applicants, 11% accepted, 6 enrolled. In 2011, 1 master's, 8 doctorates awarded. *Degree requirements:* For master's, one foreign language, thesis; for doctorate, one foreign language, thesis/dissertation. *Entrance requirements:* For master's and doctorate, GRE General Test. Additional exam requirements/recommendations for international students: Required—TOEFL. *Application deadline:* For fall admission, 1/1 priority date for domestic students, 1/1 for international students. Application fee: $50. Electronic applications accepted. *Financial support:* Fellowships, research assistantships, teaching assistantships, scholarships/grants, and unspecified assistantships available. Financial award application deadline: 1/1. *Unit head:* Dr. Stephen L. Hajduk, Head, 706-542-1676, Fax: 706-542-0182, E-mail: shajduk@bmb.uga.edu. *Application contact:* Dr. Lance Wells, Graduate Coordinator, 706-583-7806, Fax: 706-542-1738, E-mail: lwells@ccr..uga.edu. Web site: http://www.bmb.uga.edu/home/.

University of Guelph, Graduate Studies, College of Biological Science, Department of Molecular and Cellular Biology, Guelph, ON N1G 2W1, Canada. Offers biochemistry (M Sc, PhD); biophysics (M Sc, PhD); botany (M Sc, PhD); microbiology (M Sc, PhD); molecular biology and genetics (M Sc, PhD). *Degree requirements:* For master's, thesis, research proposal; for doctorate, comprehensive exam, thesis/dissertation, research proposal. *Entrance requirements:* For master's, minimum B-average during previous 2 years of coursework; for doctorate, minimum A-average. Additional exam requirements/recommendations for international students: Required—TOEFL (minimum score 550 paper-based; 213 computer-based), IELTS (minimum score 6.5). Electronic applications accepted. *Faculty research:* Physiology, structure, genetics, and ecology of microbes; virology and microbial technology.

University of Guelph, Graduate Studies, College of Physical and Engineering Science, Guelph-Waterloo Centre for Graduate Work in Chemistry and Biochemistry, Guelph, ON N1G 2W1, Canada. Offers M Sc, PhD. M Sc, PhD offered jointly with University of Waterloo. Part-time programs available. *Degree requirements:* For master's, thesis; for doctorate, thesis/dissertation. *Faculty research:* Inorganic, analytical, biological, physical/theoretical, polymer, and organic chemistry.

University of Houston, College of Natural Sciences and Mathematics, Department of Biology and Biochemistry, Houston, TX 77204. Offers biochemistry (MA, PhD); biology (MA). Terminal master's awarded for partial completion of doctoral program. *Degree requirements:* For master's, comprehensive exam (for some programs), thesis optional; for doctorate, comprehensive exam (for some programs), thesis/dissertation. *Entrance requirements:* For master's and doctorate, GRE. Additional exam requirements/recommendations for international students: Required—TOEFL (minimum score 550 paper-based; 213 computer-based; 79 iBT), IELTS (minimum score 6.5). Electronic applications accepted. *Faculty research:* Cell and molecular biology, ecology and evolution, biochemical and biophysical sciences, chemical biology.

University of Idaho, College of Graduate Studies, College of Science, Department of Biological Sciences, Moscow, ID 83844-3051. Offers biology (MS, PhD); microbiology, molecular biology and biochemistry (MS, PhD). *Faculty:* 12 full-time. *Students:* 29 full-time, 6 part-time. Average age 28. In 2011, 2 master's, 2 doctorates awarded. *Degree requirements:* For doctorate, one foreign language, thesis/dissertation. *Entrance requirements:* For master's, GRE, minimum GPA of 2.8; for doctorate, GRE, minimum undergraduate GPA of 2.8, 3.0 graduate. *Application deadline:* For fall admission, 8/1 for domestic students; for spring admission, 12/15 for domestic students. Applications are processed on a rolling basis. Application fee: $60. Electronic applications accepted. *Expenses:* Tuition, state resident: full-time $3874; part-time $334 per credit hour. Tuition, nonresident: full-time $16,394; part-time $861 per credit hour. *Required fees:* $2808; $99 per credit hour. Tuition and fees vary according to program. *Financial support:* Research assistantships and teaching assistantships available. Financial award applicants required to submit FAFSA. *Faculty research:* Animal behavior development, germ cell development, evolutionary biology, fish reproductive biology, molecular mechanisms. *Unit head:* John Byers, Acting Chair, 208-885-6280. *Application contact:* Erick Larson, Director of Graduate Admissions, 208-885-4723, E-mail: gadms@uidaho.edu. Web site: http://www.uidaho.edu/sci/biology.

University of Illinois at Chicago, College of Medicine and Graduate College, Graduate Programs in Medicine, Department of Biochemistry and Molecular Genetics, Chicago, IL 60607-7128. Offers PhD, MD/PhD. Terminal master's awarded for partial completion of doctoral program. *Degree requirements:* For doctorate, thesis/dissertation. *Entrance requirements:* For doctorate, GRE General Test. Additional exam requirements/recommendations for international students: Required—TOEFL. Electronic applications accepted. *Faculty research:* Nature of cellular components, control of metabolic processes, regulation of gene expression.

University of Illinois at Urbana–Champaign, Graduate College, College of Liberal Arts and Sciences, School of Chemical Sciences, Champaign, IL 61820. Offers MA, MS, PhD, MS/JD, MS/MBA. *Faculty:* 42 full-time (7 women), 2 part-time/adjunct (1 woman). *Students:* 382 full-time (132 women), 5 part-time (1 woman); includes 51 minority (4 Black or African American, non-Hispanic/Latino; 1 American Indian or Alaska Native, non-Hispanic/Latino; 28 Asian, non-Hispanic/Latino; 9 Hispanic/Latino; 9 Two or more races, non-Hispanic/Latino), 122 international. 853 applicants, 11% accepted, 90 enrolled. In 2011, 39 master's, 65 doctorates awarded. *Entrance requirements:* For master's, minimum GPA of 3.0. *Application deadline:* Applications are processed on a rolling basis. Application fee: $75 ($90 for international students). Electronic applications accepted. *Expenses:* Contact institution. *Financial support:* In 2011–12, 146 fellowships, 247 research assistantships, 201 teaching assistantships were awarded; tuition waivers (full and partial) also available. *Unit head:* Andrew A. Gewirth, Director, 217-333-8329, Fax: 217-333-2685, E-mail: agewirth@illinois.edu. *Application contact:* Cheryl Kappes, Office Manager, 217-333-5070, Fax: 217-333-3120, E-mail: dambache@illinois.edu. Web site: http://www.scs.illinois.edu/.

University of Illinois at Urbana–Champaign, Graduate College, College of Liberal Arts and Sciences, School of Molecular and Cellular Biology, Department of Biochemistry, Champaign, IL 61820. Offers MS, PhD. *Faculty:* 11 full-time (2 women). *Students:* 66 full-time (34 women), 1 part-time (0 women); includes 14 minority (8 Asian, non-Hispanic/Latino; 5 Hispanic/Latino; 1 Two or more races, non-Hispanic/Latino), 33 international. In 2011, 4 master's, 10 doctorates awarded. *Entrance requirements:* For master's, GRE General Test, minimum GPA of 3.0; for doctorate, GRE General Test, minimum GPA of 3.0. Additional exam requirements/recommendations for international students: Required—TOEFL (minimum score 590 paper-based; 243 computer-based; 96 iBT). *Application deadline:* Applications are processed on a rolling basis. Application fee: $75 ($90 for international students). Electronic applications accepted. *Financial support:* In 2011–12, 16 fellowships, 49 research assistantships, 42 teaching assistantships were awarded; tuition waivers (full and partial) also available. *Unit head:* Susan A. Martinis, Head, 217-333-3945, Fax: 217-333-8920, E-mail: martinis@illinois.edu. *Application contact:* Satish K. Nair, Associate Professor, 217-333-6041, Fax: 217-244-5858, E-mail: snair@illinois.edu. Web site: http://mcb.illinois.edu/departments/biochemistry/index.html.

The University of Iowa, Roy J. and Lucille A. Carver College of Medicine and Graduate College, Graduate Programs in Medicine, Department of Biochemistry, Iowa City, IA 52242. Offers MS, PhD, MD/PhD. *Faculty:* 19 full-time (7 women), 6 part-time/adjunct (2 women). *Students:* 16 full-time (7 women), 9 international. Average age 27. 49 applicants, 2% accepted, 1 enrolled. Terminal master's awarded for partial completion of doctoral program. *Degree requirements:* For master's, thesis; for doctorate, comprehensive exam, thesis/dissertation, research project, one semester of teaching. *Entrance requirements:* For master's and doctorate, GRE General Test. Additional exam requirements/recommendations for international students: Required—TOEFL (minimum score 600 paper-based; 250 computer-based; 100 iBT). *Application deadline:* For winter admission, 11/15 priority date for domestic students, 12/15 for international students. Applications are processed on a rolling basis. Application fee: $30 ($67 for international students). Electronic applications accepted. *Financial support:* In 2011–12, research assistantships with full tuition reimbursements (averaging $25,500 per year) were awarded; institutionally sponsored loans, scholarships/grants, traineeships, tuition waivers, and unspecified assistantships also available. *Faculty research:* Regulation of gene expression, protein structure, membrane structure/function, DNA structure and replication. *Total annual research expenditures:* $6.1 million. *Unit head:* Dr. Charles M. Brenner, Head, 319-335-7934, Fax: 319-335-9570, E-mail: charles-brenner@uiowa.edu. *Application contact:* Admissions Committee, 319-335-7932, Fax: 319-335-9570, E-mail: biochem@uiowa.edu. Web site: http://www.biochem.uiowa.edu/.

The University of Kansas, Graduate Studies, College of Liberal Arts and Sciences, Department of Molecular Biosciences, Lawrence, KS 66044. Offers biochemistry and biophysics (MA, PhD); microbiology (MA, PhD); molecular, cellular, and developmental biology (MA, PhD). *Faculty:* 34. *Students:* 57 full-time (29 women), 2 part-time (1 woman); includes 6 minority (2 Asian, non-Hispanic/Latino; 3 Hispanic/Latino; 1 Two or more races, non-Hispanic/Latino), 26 international. Average age 28. 60 applicants, 30% accepted, 10 enrolled. In 2011, 1 master's, 12 doctorates awarded. Terminal master's awarded for partial completion of doctoral program. *Degree requirements:* For master's, comprehensive exam, thesis; for doctorate, comprehensive exam, thesis/dissertation. *Entrance requirements:* For master's and doctorate, GRE General Test. Additional exam requirements/recommendations for international students: Required—TOEFL or IELTS. *Application deadline:* For fall admission, 12/15 for domestic and international students. Application fee: $55 ($65 for international students). Electronic applications accepted. Tuition and fees vary according to course load, campus/location, program and reciprocity agreements. *Financial support:* Fellowships with tuition reimbursements, research assistantships with tuition reimbursements, teaching assistantships with tuition reimbursements, health care benefits, and unspecified assistantships available. Financial award application deadline: 3/1. *Faculty research:* Structure and function of proteins, genetics of organism development, molecular genetics, neurophysiology,

molecular virology and pathogenics, developmental biology, cell biology. *Unit head:* Dr. Mark Richter, Chair, 785-864-3334, Fax: 785-864-5294, E-mail: richter@ku.edu. *Application contact:* John P. Connolly, Graduate Program Assistant, 785-864-4311, Fax: 785-864-5294, E-mail: jconnolly@ku.edu. Web site: http://www.molecularbiosciences.ku.edu/.

The University of Kansas, University of Kansas Medical Center, School of Medicine, Department of Biochemistry and Molecular Biology, Kansas City, KS 66160. Offers MS, PhD, MD/PhD. *Faculty:* 17. *Students:* 6 full-time (1 woman), 5 international. Average age 27. In 2011, 2 doctorates awarded. Terminal master's awarded for partial completion of doctoral program. *Degree requirements:* For master's, thesis, oral defense of thesis; for doctorate, thesis/dissertation, comprehensive oral and written exam. *Entrance requirements:* Additional exam requirements/recommendations for international students: Required—TOEFL. Application fee: $0. Electronic applications accepted. Tuition and fees vary according to course load, campus/location, program and reciprocity agreements. *Financial support:* In 2011–12, 5 teaching assistantships with full and partial tuition reimbursements were awarded; fellowships, research assistantships with partial tuition reimbursements, traineeships, health care benefits, and unspecified assistantships also available. Financial award application deadline: 2/14; financial award applicants required to submit FAFSA. *Faculty research:* Determination of portion structure, underlying bases for interaction of proteins with their target, mapping allosteric circuiting within proteins, mechanism of action of transcription factors, renal signal transduction. *Total annual research expenditures:* $3 million. *Unit head:* Dr. Gerald M. Carlson, Chairman, 913-588-7005, Fax: 913-588-9896, E-mail: gcarlson@kumc.edu. *Application contact:* Dr. Liskin Swint-Kruse, Associate Professor, 913-588-0399, Fax: 913-588-9896, E-mail: lswint-kruse@kumc.edu. Web site: http://www.kumc.edu/biochemistry/.

University of Kentucky, Graduate School, Graduate School Programs from the College of Medicine, Program in Molecular and Cellular Biochemistry, Lexington, KY 40506-0032. Offers biochemistry (PhD); MD/PhD. *Degree requirements:* For doctorate, comprehensive exam, thesis/dissertation. *Entrance requirements:* For doctorate, GRE General Test, minimum undergraduate GPA of 2.75. Additional exam requirements/recommendations for international students: Required—TOEFL (minimum score 550 paper-based; 213 computer-based). Electronic applications accepted.

University of Lethbridge, School of Graduate Studies, Lethbridge, AB T1K 3M4, Canada. Offers accounting (MScM); addictions counseling (M Sc); agricultural biotechnology (M Sc); agricultural studies (M Sc, MA); anthropology (MA); archaeology (MA); art (MA, MFA); biochemistry (M Sc); biological sciences (M Sc); biomolecular science (PhD); biosystems and biodiversity (PhD); Canadian studies (MA); chemistry (M Sc); computer science (M Sc); computer science and geographical information science (M Sc); counseling psychology (M Ed); dramatic arts (MA); earth, space, and physical science (PhD); economics (MA); educational leadership (M Ed); English (MA); environmental science (M Sc); evolution and behavior (PhD); exercise science (M Sc); finance (MScM); French (MA); French/German (MA); French/Spanish (MA); general education (M Ed); general management (MScM); geography (M Sc, MA); German (MA); health science (M Sc); history (MA); human resource management and labour relations (MScM); individualized multidisciplinary (M Sc, MA); information systems (MScM); international management (MScM); kinesiology (M Sc, MA); management (M Sc, MA); marketing (MScM); mathematics (M Sc); music (M Mus, MA); Native American studies (MA); neuroscience (M Sc, PhD); new media (MA); nursing (M Sc); philosophy (MA); physics (M Sc); policy and strategy (MScM); political science (MA); psychology (M Sc, MA); religious studies (MA); social sciences (MA); sociology (MA); theatre and dramatic arts (MFA); theoretical and computational science (PhD); urban and regional studies (MA); women's studies (MA). Part-time and evening/weekend programs available. *Degree requirements:* For doctorate, comprehensive exam, thesis/dissertation. *Entrance requirements:* For master's, GMAT (M Sc in management), bachelor's degree in related field, minimum GPA of 3.0 during previous 20 graded semester courses, 2 years teaching or related experience (M Ed); for doctorate, master's degree, minimum graduate GPA of 3.5. Additional exam requirements/recommendations for international students: Required—TOEFL. *Faculty research:* Movement and brain plasticity, gibberellin physiology, photosynthesis, carbon cycling, molecular properties of main-group ring components.

University of Louisville, Graduate School, College of Arts and Sciences, Department of Chemistry, Louisville, KY 40292-0001. Offers analytical chemistry (MS, PhD); biochemistry (MS, PhD); chemical physics (PhD); inorganic chemistry (MS, PhD); organic chemistry (MS, PhD); physical chemistry (MS, PhD). Terminal master's awarded for partial completion of doctoral program. *Degree requirements:* For master's, variable foreign language requirement, comprehensive exam, thesis optional; for doctorate, variable foreign language requirement, comprehensive exam, thesis/dissertation. *Entrance requirements:* For master's and doctorate, BA or BS coursework. Additional exam requirements/recommendations for international students: Required—TOEFL. Electronic applications accepted. *Expenses:* Tuition, state resident: full-time $9692; part-time $539 per credit hour. Tuition, nonresident: full-time $20,168; part-time $1121 per credit hour. Tuition and fees vary according to program and reciprocity agreements. *Faculty research:* Computational chemistry, biophysics nuclear magnetic resonance, synthetic organic chemistry, synthetic inorganic chemistry, medicinal chemistry, protein chemistry, enzymology, nanochemistry, electrochemistry, analytical chemistry, synthetic biology, bioinformatics.

University of Louisville, School of Medicine, Department of Biochemistry and Molecular Biology, Louisville, KY 40292-0001. Offers MS, PhD, MD/PhD. Terminal master's awarded for partial completion of doctoral program. *Degree requirements:* For master's, thesis; for doctorate, comprehensive exam, thesis/dissertation, one first author publication. *Entrance requirements:* For master's and doctorate, GRE General Test (minimum score of 1000 verbal and quantitative), minimum GPA of 3.0. Additional exam requirements/recommendations for international students: Required—TOEFL. Electronic applications accepted. *Expenses:* Tuition, state resident: full-time $9692; part-time $539 per credit hour. Tuition, nonresident: full-time $20,168; part-time $1121 per credit hour. Tuition and fees vary according to program and reciprocity agreements. *Faculty research:* Genetic regulatory mechanisms, microRNAs, vesicular trafficking in cancer metastasis and angiogenesis, ribosome biogenesis and disease, regulation of foreign compound metabolism/lipid and steroid metabolism.

University of Maine, Graduate School, College of Natural Sciences, Forestry, and Agriculture, Department of Biochemistry, Molecular Biology, and Microbiology, Orono, ME 04469. Offers biochemistry (MPS, MS); biochemistry and molecular biology (PhD); microbiology (MPS, MS, PhD). *Faculty:* 11 full-time (6 women), 3 part-time/adjunct (2 women). *Students:* 25 full-time (15 women), 35 part-time (23 women); includes 4 minority (2 Asian, non-Hispanic/Latino; 1 Hispanic/Latino; 1 Two or more races, non-Hispanic/Latino), 13 international. Average age 31. 41 applicants, 29% accepted, 11 enrolled. In 2011, 6 master's, 6 doctorates awarded. *Degree requirements:* For doctorate, thesis/dissertation. *Entrance requirements:* For master's and doctorate, GRE General Test. Additional exam requirements/recommendations for international students: Required—TOEFL. *Application deadline:* For fall admission, 2/1 priority date for domestic students. Applications are processed on a rolling basis. Application fee: $65. Electronic applications accepted. *Expenses:* Tuition, state resident: full-time

$5016. Tuition, nonresident: full-time $14,424. *Financial support:* In 2011–12, 5 research assistantships with full tuition reimbursements (averaging $25,368 per year), 12 teaching assistantships with full tuition reimbursements (averaging $20,106 per year) were awarded; tuition waivers (full and partial) also available. Financial award application deadline: 3/1. *Total annual research expenditures:* $242,844. *Unit head:* Dr. Robert Gundersen, Chair, 207-581-2802, Fax: 207-581-2801. *Application contact:* Scott G. Delcourt, Associate Dean of the Graduate School, 207-581-3291, Fax: 207-581-3232, E-mail: graduate@maine.edu. Web site: http://www2.umaine.edu/graduate/.

The University of Manchester, Faculty of Life Sciences, Manchester, United Kingdom. Offers adaptive organismal biology (M Phil, PhD); animal biology (M Phil, PhD); biochemistry (M Phil, PhD); bioinformatics (M Phil, PhD); biomolecular sciences (M Phil, PhD); biotechnology (M Phil, PhD); cell biology (M Phil, PhD); cell matrix research (M Phil, PhD); channels and transporters (M Phil, PhD); developmental biology (M Phil, PhD); Egyptology (M Phil, PhD); environmental biology (M Phil, PhD); evolutionary biology (M Phil, PhD); gene expression (M Phil, PhD); genetics (M Phil, PhD); history of science, technology and medicine (M Phil, PhD); immunology (M Phil, PhD); integrative neurobiology and behavior (M Phil, PhD); membrane trafficking (M Phil, PhD); microbiology (M Phil, PhD); molecular and cellular neuroscience (M Phil, PhD); molecular biology (M Phil, PhD); molecular cancer studies (M Phil, PhD); neuroscience (M Phil, PhD); ophthalmology (M Phil, PhD); optometry (M Phil, PhD); organelle function (M Phil, PhD); pharmacology (M Phil, PhD); physiology (M Phil, PhD); plant sciences (M Phil, PhD); stem cell research (M Phil, PhD); structural biology (M Phil, PhD); systems neuroscience (M Phil, PhD); toxicology (M Phil, PhD).

The University of Manchester, School of Chemistry, Manchester, United Kingdom. Offers biological chemistry (PhD); chemistry (M Ent, M Phil, M Sc, D Ent, PhD); inorganic chemistry (PhD); materials chemistry (PhD); nanoscience (PhD); nuclear fission (PhD); organic chemistry (PhD); physical chemistry (PhD); theoretical chemistry (PhD).

University of Manitoba, Faculty of Medicine and Faculty of Graduate Studies, Graduate Programs in Medicine, Department of Biochemistry and Medical Genetics, Winnipeg, MB R3T 2N2, Canada. Offers M Sc, PhD. Terminal master's awarded for partial completion of doctoral program. *Degree requirements:* For master's, thesis; for doctorate, thesis/dissertation. *Faculty research:* Cancer, gene expression, membrane lipids, metabolic control, genetic diseases.

University of Maryland, Baltimore, Graduate School, Graduate Program in Life Sciences, Program in Biochemistry and Molecular Biology, Baltimore, MD 21201. Offers biochemistry (MS, PhD); MD/PhD. *Students:* 28 full-time (15 women), 2 part-time (1 woman); includes 11 minority (2 Black or African American, non-Hispanic/Latino; 1 American Indian or Alaska Native, non-Hispanic/Latino; 3 Asian, non-Hispanic/Latino; 3 Hispanic/Latino; 2 Two or more races, non-Hispanic/Latino), 3 international. Average age 27. 62 applicants, 3% accepted, 2 enrolled. In 2011, 1 master's, 4 doctorates awarded. *Entrance requirements:* For doctorate, GRE General Test. Additional exam requirements/recommendations for international students: Required—TOEFL (minimum score 550 paper-based; 80 iBT); Recommended—IELTS (minimum score 7). *Application deadline:* For fall admission, 1/15 for domestic and international students. Application fee: $50. Electronic applications accepted. *Financial support:* In 2011–12, research assistantships with full tuition reimbursements (averaging $25,000 per year) were awarded; fellowships, health care benefits, and unspecified assistantships also available. Financial award application deadline: 3/1. *Faculty research:* Membrane transport, hormonal regulation, protein structure, molecular virology. *Unit head:* Dr. Gerald Wilson, Professor/Director, 410-706-8904. *Application contact:* Foyeke Daramola, Program Coordinator, 410-706-8417, Fax: 410-706-8297, E-mail: fdaramola@som.umaryland.edu. Web site: http://biochemistry.umaryland.edu.

University of Maryland, Baltimore County, Graduate School, College of Natural and Mathematical Sciences, Department of Chemistry and Biochemistry, Baltimore, MD 21250. Offers biochemistry (PhD); chemistry (MS, PhD); chemistry and biochemistry (Postbaccalaureate Certificate). Part-time programs available. *Faculty:* 77 full-time (11 women). *Students:* 90 full-time (51 women), 2 part-time (0 women); includes 24 minority (10 Black or African American, non-Hispanic/Latino; 1 American Indian or Alaska Native, non-Hispanic/Latino; 6 Asian, non-Hispanic/Latino; 6 Hispanic/Latino; 1 Two or more races, non-Hispanic/Latino), 26 international. Average age 27. 142 applicants, 30% accepted, 27 enrolled. In 2011, 4 master's, 5 doctorates awarded. Terminal master's awarded for partial completion of doctoral program. *Degree requirements:* For master's, comprehensive exam (for some programs), thesis (for some programs); for doctorate, comprehensive exam, thesis/dissertation. *Entrance requirements:* For master's, GRE General Test, minimum GPA of 3.0; for doctorate, GRE General Test, GRE Subject Test (recommended), minimum GPA of 3.0. Additional exam requirements/recommendations for international students: Required—TOEFL (minimum score 550 paper-based; 213 computer-based). *Application deadline:* For fall admission, 6/1 priority date for domestic students, 1/1 for international students; for spring admission, 11/1 priority date for domestic students, 5/1 for international students. Applications are processed on a rolling basis. Application fee: $50. Electronic applications accepted. *Financial support:* In 2011–12, 13 fellowships with full tuition reimbursements (averaging $24,000 per year), 41 research assistantships with full tuition reimbursements (averaging $21,000 per year), 35 teaching assistantships with full tuition reimbursements (averaging $21,000 per year) were awarded; health care benefits also available. *Faculty research:* Protein structures, bio-organic chemistry, enzyme catalysis, molecular biology, metabolism. *Total annual research expenditures:* $3.3 million. *Unit head:* Dr. Dale R. Whalen, Director, Graduate Program, 410-455-2491, Fax: 410-455-2608, E-mail: chemgrad@umbc.edu. *Application contact:* Patricia Gagne, Graduate Coordinator, 410-455-2491, Fax: 410-455-2608, E-mail: pgagne1@umbc.edu. Web site: http://www.umbc.edu/chem.

University of Maryland, College Park, Academic Affairs, College of Computer, Mathematical and Natural Sciences, Department of Chemistry and Biochemistry, Biochemistry Program, College Park, MD 20742. Offers MS, PhD. Part-time and evening/weekend programs available. *Students:* 48 full-time (25 women), 1 (woman) part-time; includes 8 minority (4 Black or African American, non-Hispanic/Latino; 3 Asian, non-Hispanic/Latino; 1 Two or more races, non-Hispanic/Latino), 21 international. 101 applicants, 13% accepted, 9 enrolled. In 2011, 1 master's, 4 doctorates awarded. Terminal master's awarded for partial completion of doctoral program. *Degree requirements:* For master's, thesis or alternative; for doctorate, thesis/dissertation, 2 seminar presentations, oral exam. *Entrance requirements:* For master's and doctorate, GRE General Test, GRE Subject Test (recommended), minimum GPA of 3.0, 3 letters of recommendation. Additional exam requirements/recommendations for international students: Required—TOEFL. *Application deadline:* For fall admission, 2/1 for domestic and international students; for spring admission, 6/1 for domestic and international students. Applications are processed on a rolling basis. Application fee: $75. Electronic applications accepted. *Expenses:* Tuition, state resident: part-time $525 per credit hour. Tuition, nonresident: part-time $1131 per credit hour. *Required fees:* $386.31 per term. Tuition and fees vary according to program. *Financial support:* In 2011–12, 2 fellowships with partial tuition reimbursements (averaging $9,765 per year), 17 research assistantships (averaging $19,418 per year), 29 teaching assistantships with tuition reimbursements (averaging $19,525 per year) were awarded; Federal Work-Study also

available. Support available to part-time students. Financial award applicants required to submit FAFSA. *Faculty research:* Analytical biochemistry, immunochemistry, drug metabolism, biosynthesis of proteins, mass spectrometry. *Unit head:* Dr. Michael Doyle, Chairperson, 301-405-1795, Fax: 301-314-2779, E-mail: mdoyle3@umd.edu. *Application contact:* Dr. Charles A. Caramello, Dean of Graduate School, 301-405-0358, Fax: 301-314-9305.

University of Massachusetts Amherst, Graduate School, College of Natural Sciences, Department of Biochemistry and Molecular Biology, Amherst, MA 01003. Offers MS. Part-time programs available. *Faculty:* 20 full-time (9 women). *Students:* 1 (woman) full-time. Average age 22. 1 applicant, 100% accepted, 1 enrolled. In 2011, 2 master's awarded. Terminal master's awarded for partial completion of doctoral program. *Degree requirements:* For master's, thesis or alternative. *Entrance requirements:* Additional exam requirements/recommendations for international students: Required—TOEFL (minimum score 550 paper-based; 213 computer-based; 80 iBT), IELTS (minimum score 6.5). *Application deadline:* For fall admission, 2/1 for domestic and international students; for spring admission, 10/1 for domestic and international students. Applications are processed on a rolling basis. Application fee: $50 ($65 for international students). Electronic applications accepted. Tuition and fees vary according to course load, campus/location and program. *Financial support:* Fellowships with full and partial tuition reimbursements, research assistantships with full and partial tuition reimbursements, teaching assistantships with full and partial tuition reimbursements, career-related internships or fieldwork, Federal Work-Study, scholarships/grants, traineeships, health care benefits, tuition waivers (full and partial), and unspecified assistantships available. Support available to part-time students. Financial award application deadline: 2/1. *Unit head:* Dr. Danny Schnell, Graduate Program Director, 413-545-0352, Fax: 413-545-3291. *Application contact:* Lindsay DeSantis, Interim Supervisor of Admissions, 413-545-0722, Fax: 413-577-0010, E-mail: gradadm@grad.umass.edu. Web site: http://www.biochem.umass.edu/graduate.

University of Massachusetts Amherst, Graduate School, Interdisciplinary Programs, Program in Molecular and Cellular Biology, Amherst, MA 01003. Offers biological chemistry and molecular biophysics (PhD); biomedicine (PhD); cellular and developmental biology (PhD). Part-time programs available. *Students:* 62 full-time (40 women), 18 part-time (9 women); includes 14 minority (2 Black or African American, non-Hispanic/Latino; 4 Asian, non-Hispanic/Latino; 7 Hispanic/Latino; 1 Two or more races, non-Hispanic/Latino), 28 international. Average age 27. 138 applicants, 36% accepted, 22 enrolled. In 2011, 8 doctorates awarded. Terminal master's awarded for partial completion of doctoral program. *Degree requirements:* For doctorate, comprehensive exam, thesis/dissertation. *Entrance requirements:* For doctorate, GRE General Test. Additional exam requirements/recommendations for international students: Required—TOEFL (minimum score 550 paper-based; 213 computer-based; 80 iBT), IELTS (minimum score 6.5). *Application deadline:* For fall admission, 12/1 for domestic and international students. Applications are processed on a rolling basis. Application fee: $50 ($65 for international students). Electronic applications accepted. Tuition and fees vary according to course load, campus/location and program. *Financial support:* Fellowships with full and partial tuition reimbursements, research assistantships with full and partial tuition reimbursements, teaching assistantships with full and partial tuition reimbursements, career-related internships or fieldwork, Federal Work-Study, scholarships/grants, traineeships, health care benefits, tuition waivers (full and partial), and unspecified assistantships available. Support available to part-time students. Financial award application deadline: 12/1. *Unit head:* Dr. Barbara Osborne, Graduate Program Director, 413-545-3246, Fax: 413-545-1812. *Application contact:* Lindsay DeSantis, Interim Supervisor of Admissions, 413-545-0722, Fax: 413-577-0010, E-mail: gradadm@grad.umass.edu. Web site: http://www.bio.umass.edu/mcb/.

University of Massachusetts Amherst, Graduate School, Interdisciplinary Programs, Program in Plant Biology, Amherst, MA 01003. Offers biochemistry and metabolism (MS, PhD); cell biology and physiology (MS, PhD); environmental, ecological and integrative (PhD); environmental, ecological and integrative biology (MS); genetics and evolution (MS, PhD). *Students:* 16 full-time (7 women), 1 (woman) part-time, 7 international. Average age 27. 22 applicants, 50% accepted, 5 enrolled. In 2011, 3 degrees awarded. *Median time to degree:* Of those who began their doctoral program in fall 2003, 100% received their degree in 8 years or less. *Degree requirements:* For master's, thesis; for doctorate, 2 foreign languages, comprehensive exam, thesis/dissertation. *Entrance requirements:* For master's and doctorate, GRE General Test. Additional exam requirements/recommendations for international students: Required—TOEFL (minimum score 550 paper-based; 213 computer-based; 80 iBT), IELTS (minimum score 6.5). *Application deadline:* For fall admission, 12/15 for domestic and international students; for spring admission, 10/1 for domestic and international students. Applications are processed on a rolling basis. Application fee: $50 ($65 for international students). Electronic applications accepted. Tuition and fees vary according to course load, campus/location and program. *Financial support:* Fellowships with full and partial tuition reimbursements, research assistantships with full and partial tuition reimbursements, teaching assistantships with full and partial tuition reimbursements, career-related internships or fieldwork, Federal Work-Study, scholarships/grants, traineeships, health care benefits, tuition waivers (full and partial), and unspecified assistantships available. Support available to part-time students. Financial award application deadline: 12/15. *Unit head:* Dr. Elsbeth L. Walker, Graduate Program Director, 413-577-3217, Fax: 413-545-3243. *Application contact:* Lindsay DeSantis, Interim Supervisor of Admissions, 413-545—0722, Fax: 413-577-0010, E-mail: gradadm@grad.umass.edu. Web site: http://www.bio.umass.edu/plantbio/.

University of Massachusetts Lowell, College of Sciences, Department of Biological Sciences, Lowell, MA 01854-2881. Offers biochemistry (PhD); biological sciences (MS); biotechnology (MS). Part-time programs available. *Degree requirements:* For master's, thesis; for doctorate, thesis/dissertation. *Entrance requirements:* For master's and doctorate, GRE General Test. Electronic applications accepted.

University of Massachusetts Lowell, College of Sciences, Department of Chemistry, Lowell, MA 01854-2881. Offers analytical chemistry (PhD); biochemistry (PhD); chemistry (MS, PhD); environmental studies (PhD); green chemistry (PhD); inorganic chemistry (PhD); organic chemistry (PhD); polymer science (MS). Terminal master's awarded for partial completion of doctoral program. *Degree requirements:* For master's, thesis; for doctorate, 2 foreign languages, thesis/dissertation. *Entrance requirements:* For master's and doctorate, GRE General Test. Electronic applications accepted.

University of Massachusetts Worcester, Graduate School of Biomedical Sciences, Worcester, MA 01655-0115. Offers biochemistry and molecular pharmacology (PhD); bioinformatics and computational biology (PhD); cancer biology (PhD); cell biology (PhD); clinical and population health research (PhD); clinical investigation (MS); immunology and virology (PhD); interdisciplinary graduate program (PhD); molecular genetics and microbiology (PhD); neuroscience (PhD); DVM/PhD; MD/PhD. *Faculty:* 1,427 full-time (526 women), 309 part-time/adjunct (196 women). *Students:* 416 full-time (225 women); includes 47 minority (12 Black or African American, non-Hispanic/Latino; 32 Asian, non-Hispanic/Latino; 3 Hispanic/Latino), 144 international. Average age 29. 623 applicants, 17% accepted, 54 enrolled. In 2011, 5 master's, 63 doctorates awarded. Terminal master's awarded for partial completion of doctoral program. *Degree requirements:* For master's, comprehensive exam, thesis; for doctorate, comprehensive exam, thesis/dissertation. *Entrance requirements:* For master's, bachelor's degree; for doctorate, GRE General Test. Additional exam requirements/recommendations for international students: Required—TOEFL (minimum score 600 paper-based; 250 computer-based; 100 iBT) or IELTS (minimum score 7.5). *Application deadline:* For fall admission, 12/15 for domestic and international students; for spring admission, 5/15 for domestic students. Application fee: $50. Electronic applications accepted. *Expenses:* Contact institution. *Financial support:* In 2011–12, 416 students received support, including 416 research assistantships with full tuition reimbursements available (averaging $29,200 per year); scholarships/grants, health care benefits, tuition waivers (full), and unspecified assistantships also available. Financial award application deadline: 4/16. *Faculty research:* RNA interference, cell biology, bioinformatics, clinical research, infectious disease. *Total annual research expenditures:* $262.7 million. *Unit head:* Dr. Anthony Carruthers, Dean, 508-856-4135, E-mail: anthony.carruthers@umassmed.edu. *Application contact:* Dr. Kendall Knight, Associate Dean and Interim Director of Admissions and Recruitment, 508-856-5628, Fax: 508-856-3659, E-mail: kendall.knight@umassmed.edu. Web site: http://www.umassmed.edu/gsbs/.

University of Medicine and Dentistry of New Jersey, Graduate School of Biomedical Sciences, Graduate Programs in Biomedical Sciences–Newark, Department of Biochemistry and Molecular Biology, Newark, NJ 07107. Offers MS, PhD. *Degree requirements:* For master's, thesis; for doctorate, thesis/dissertation, qualifying exam. *Entrance requirements:* For master's and doctorate, GRE General Test. Additional exam requirements/recommendations for international students: Required—TOEFL. Electronic applications accepted.

University of Medicine and Dentistry of New Jersey, Graduate School of Biomedical Sciences, Graduate Programs in Biomedical Sciences–Piscataway, Program in Biochemistry and Molecular Biology, Piscataway, NJ 08854-5635. Offers MS, PhD, MD/PhD. PhD, MS offered jointly with Rutgers, The State University of New Jersey, New Brunswick. Terminal master's awarded for partial completion of doctoral program. *Degree requirements:* For master's, thesis, qualifying exam; for doctorate, thesis/dissertation, qualifying exam. *Entrance requirements:* For master's and doctorate, GRE General Test. Additional exam requirements/recommendations for international students: Required—TOEFL. Electronic applications accepted. *Faculty research:* Signal transduction, regulation of RNA, polymerase II transcribed genes, developmental gene expression.

University of Miami, Graduate School, Miller School of Medicine, Graduate Programs in Medicine, Department of Biochemistry and Molecular Biology, Coral Gables, FL 33124. Offers PhD, MD/PhD. *Degree requirements:* For doctorate, comprehensive exam, thesis/dissertation, proposition exams. *Faculty research:* Macromolecule metabolism, molecular genetics, protein folding and 3-D structure, regulation of gene expression and enzyme function, signal transduction and developmental biology.

University of Michigan, Horace H. Rackham School of Graduate Studies, Chemical Biology Program, Ann Arbor, MI 48109. Offers PhD. *Faculty:* 51 full-time (11 women). *Students:* 50 full-time (24 women). 64 applicants, 30% accepted, 7 enrolled. In 2011, 12 doctorates awarded. *Degree requirements:* For doctorate, thesis/dissertation. *Entrance requirements:* Additional exam requirements/recommendations for international students: Required—TOEFL (minimum score 600 paper-based; 250 computer-based; 102 iBT). *Application deadline:* For fall admission, 1/1 priority date for domestic students, 1/1 for international students. Application fee: $0 ($75 for international students). Electronic applications accepted. *Financial support:* In 2011–12, 50 students received support, including fellowships with full tuition reimbursements available (averaging $26,500 per year), research assistantships with full tuition reimbursements available (averaging $26,500 per year); career-related internships or fieldwork, scholarships/grants, traineeships, health care benefits, and unspecified assistantships also available. *Faculty research:* Chemical genetics, structural enzymology, signal transduction, biological catalysis, biomolecular structure, function and recognition. *Unit head:* Prof. Anna Mapp, Program Director, 734-763-7175, Fax: 734-615-1252, E-mail: chemicalbiology@umich.edu. *Application contact:* Admissions Office, 734-764-8129, E-mail: rackadmis@umich.edu. Web site: http://www.chembio.umich.edu/.

University of Michigan, Horace H. Rackham School of Graduate Studies, College of Literature, Science, and the Arts, Department of Chemistry, Ann Arbor, MI 48109-1055. Offers analytical chemistry (PhD); chemical biology (PhD); inorganic chemistry (PhD); material chemistry (PhD); organic chemistry (PhD); physical chemistry (PhD). *Faculty:* 39 full-time (9 women). *Students:* 221 full-time (114 women); includes 24 minority (1 Black or African American, non-Hispanic/Latino; 15 Asian, non-Hispanic/Latino; 4 Hispanic/Latino; 4 Two or more races, non-Hispanic/Latino), 66 international. Average age 26. 608 applicants, 27% accepted, 39 enrolled. In 2011, 39 doctorates awarded. *Degree requirements:* For doctorate, thesis/dissertation, oral defense of dissertation, organic cumulative proficiency exams. *Entrance requirements:* For doctorate, GRE General Test, GRE Subject Test (recommended), 3 letters of recommendation. Additional exam requirements/recommendations for international students: Required—TOEFL (minimum score 560 paper-based; 220 computer-based; 84 iBT). *Application deadline:* For fall admission, 12/31 for domestic students, 12/15 for international students. Applications are processed on a rolling basis. Application fee: $0 ($75 for international students). Electronic applications accepted. *Financial support:* In 2011–12, 221 students received support, including 25 fellowships with full tuition reimbursements available (averaging $26,553 per year), 86 research assistantships with full tuition reimbursements available (averaging $26,553 per year), 110 teaching assistantships with full tuition reimbursements available (averaging $26,553 per year); career-related internships or fieldwork, scholarships/grants, traineeships, health care benefits, and unspecified assistantships also available. *Faculty research:* Biological catalysis, protein engineering, chemical sensors, de novo metalloprotein design, supramolecular architecture. *Unit head:* Dr. Carol A. Fierke, Chair, 734-763-9681, Fax: 734-647-4847. *Application contact:* Margarita Bekiares, Graduate Program Coordinator, 734-764-7278, Fax: 734-647-4865, E-mail: chemadmissions@umich.edu. Web site: http://www.umich.edu/~michchem/.

University of Michigan, Horace H. Rackham School of Graduate Studies, Program in Biomedical Sciences (PIBS), Department of Biological Chemistry, Ann Arbor, MI 48109-0600. Offers PhD. *Faculty:* 46 full-time (10 women), 1 part-time/adjunct (0 women). *Students:* 35 full-time (17 women); includes 9 minority (4 Black or African American, non-Hispanic/Latino; 1 Asian, non-Hispanic/Latino; 2 Hispanic/Latino; 2 Two or more races, non-Hispanic/Latino), 5 international. Average age 27. 49 applicants, 51% accepted, 11 enrolled. In 2011, 10 doctorates awarded. *Degree requirements:* For doctorate, comprehensive exam, thesis/dissertation. *Entrance requirements:* For doctorate, GRE General Test, bachelor's degree. Additional exam requirements/recommendations for international students: Required—TOEFL (minimum score 84 iBT). *Application deadline:* For fall admission, 12/1 for domestic and international students. Application fee: $65 ($75 for international students). Electronic applications accepted. *Expenses:* Contact institution. *Financial support:* In 2011–12, 2 students received support, including 2 fellowships with full tuition reimbursements available (averaging $28,200 per year), 33 research assistantships with full tuition reimbursements available (averaging $26,500 per year), 10 teaching assistantships with partial tuition reimbursements available; traineeships, health care benefits, tuition waivers, and unspecified assistantships also available. *Faculty research:* Regulation of

gene expression, structural enzymology, protein processing and folding, biochemical signaling. *Total annual research expenditures:* $8.1 million. *Unit head:* Craig A. Reynolds, Administrative Director, Healthcare, 734-763-0185, Fax: 734-763-4581, E-mail: creyno@umich.edu. *Application contact:* Elizabeth L. Goodwin, Graduate Program Manager, 734-764-8594, Fax: 734-763-4581, E-mail: egoodwin@umich.edu. Web site: http://www.biochem.med.umich.edu/.

University of Minnesota, Duluth, Graduate School, Swenson College of Science and Engineering, Department of Chemistry and Biochemistry, Duluth, MN 55812-2496. Offers MS. Part-time programs available. *Degree requirements:* For master's, thesis. *Entrance requirements:* For master's, bachelor's degree in chemistry, minimum GPA of 3.0. Additional exam requirements/recommendations for international students: Required—TOEFL (minimum score 550 paper-based; 213 computer-based; 79 iBT), IELTS (minimum score 6.5). *Faculty research:* Physical, inorganic, organic, and analytical chemistry; biochemistry and molecular biology.

University of Minnesota, Duluth, Medical School, Department of Biochemistry, Molecular Biology and Biophysics, Duluth, MN 55812-2496. Offers biochemistry, molecular biology and biophysics (MS); biology and biophysics (PhD); social, administrative, and clinical pharmacy (MS, PhD); toxicology (MS, PhD). Terminal master's awarded for partial completion of doctoral program. *Degree requirements:* For master's, comprehensive exam, thesis; for doctorate, comprehensive exam, thesis/dissertation. *Entrance requirements:* For master's and doctorate, GRE General Test. Additional exam requirements/recommendations for international students: Required—TOEFL. Electronic applications accepted. *Faculty research:* Intestinal cancer biology; hepatotoxins and mitochondriopathies; toxicology; cell cycle regulation in stem cells; neurobiology of brain development, trace metal function and blood-brain barrier; hibernation biology.

University of Minnesota, Twin Cities Campus, Graduate School, College of Biological Sciences, Biochemistry, Molecular Biology and Biophysics Graduate Program, Minneapolis, MN 55455-0213. Offers PhD. *Degree requirements:* For doctorate, thesis/dissertation. *Entrance requirements:* For doctorate, GRE, 3 letters of recommendation, more than 1 semester of laboratory experience. Additional exam requirements/recommendations for international students: Required—TOEFL (minimum score 625 paper-based; 263 computer-based; 108 iBT with writing subsection 25 and reading subsection 25) or IELTS (minimum score 7). Electronic applications accepted. *Faculty research:* Microbial biochemistry, biotechnology, molecular biology, regulatory biochemistry, structural biology and biophysics, physical biochemistry, enzymology, physiological chemistry.

University of Mississippi Medical Center, School of Graduate Studies in the Health Sciences, Department of Biochemistry, Jackson, MS 39216-4505. Offers MS, PhD, MD/PhD. Terminal master's awarded for partial completion of doctoral program. *Degree requirements:* For master's, thesis; for doctorate, thesis/dissertation, first authored publication. *Entrance requirements:* For doctorate, GRE General Test, minimum GPA of 3.0. Additional exam requirements/recommendations for international students: Required—TOEFL. *Faculty research:* Structural biology, regulation of gene expression, enzymology of redox reactions, mechanism of anti cancer drugs, function of nuclear substructure.

University of Missouri, Graduate School, College of Agriculture, Food and Natural Resources, Department of Biochemistry, Columbia, MO 65211. Offers MS, PhD. *Faculty:* 32 full-time (11 women), 5 part-time/adjunct (2 women). *Students:* 47 full-time (18 women), 1 part-time (0 women); includes 5 minority (2 Asian, non-Hispanic/Latino; 2 Hispanic/Latino; 1 Two or more races, non-Hispanic/Latino), 21 international. Average age 26. 53 applicants, 19% accepted, 9 enrolled. In 2011, 3 master's, 1 doctorate awarded. Terminal master's awarded for partial completion of doctoral program. *Degree requirements:* For master's, thesis; for doctorate, comprehensive exam, thesis/dissertation. *Entrance requirements:* For master's and doctorate, minimum GPA of 3.0; undergraduate research. Additional exam requirements/recommendations for international students: Required—TOEFL (minimum score 620 paper-based; 95 iBT). *Application deadline:* For fall admission, 1/15 priority date for domestic students, 1/15 for international students. Application fee: $55 ($75 for international students). Electronic applications accepted. *Expenses:* Tuition, state resident: full-time $5881. Tuition, nonresident: full-time $15,183. *Required fees:* $952. Tuition and fees vary according to campus/location and program. *Financial support:* Fellowships with tuition reimbursements, research assistantships with tuition reimbursements, teaching assistantships with tuition reimbursements, institutionally sponsored loans, scholarships/grants, health care benefits, and unspecified assistantships available. Support available to part-time students. *Faculty research:* Gene expression; molecular medicine; plant sciences; receptors and signaling; macromolecular synthesis, assembly and localization; structural and chemical biology; proteomics, genomics and combinatorial chemistry; enzymology, nutrition and metabolism. *Unit head:* Dr. Gerald Hazelbauer, Department Chair, 573-882-4845, E-mail: hazelbauerg@missouri.edu. *Application contact:* Ryan Duncan, Executive Staff Assistant, 573-882-4845, E-mail: duncancd@missouri.edu. Web site: http://biochem.missouri.edu/grad-program/index.php.

University of Missouri–Kansas City, School of Biological Sciences, Program in Molecular Biology and Biochemistry, Kansas City, MO 64110-2499. Offers PhD. Offered through the School of Graduate Studies. *Faculty:* 40 full-time (10 women), 3 part-time/adjunct (2 women). *Students:* 6 full-time (4 women), 7 part-time (6 women), 7 international. Average age 31. 8 applicants, 100% accepted, 3 enrolled. *Degree requirements:* For doctorate, comprehensive exam, thesis/dissertation. *Entrance requirements:* For doctorate, GRE General Test, bachelor's degree in chemistry, biology, or a related discipline; minimum GPA of 3.0. Additional exam requirements/recommendations for international students: Required—TOEFL (minimum score 550 paper-based; 213 computer-based; 80 iBT). *Application deadline:* For fall admission, 2/15 priority date for domestic students, 2/15 for international students. Application fee: $45 ($50 for international students). *Expenses:* Tuition, state resident: full-time $5798; part-time $322.10 per credit hour. Tuition, nonresident: full-time $14,969; part-time $831.60 per credit hour. *Required fees:* $93.51 per credit hour. *Financial support:* Research assistantships with full tuition reimbursements, teaching assistantships with full and partial tuition reimbursements, scholarships/grants, tuition waivers (full and partial), and unspecified assistantships available. Financial award application deadline: 3/1; financial award applicants required to submit FAFSA. *Unit head:* Dr. Henry Miziorko, Head, 816-235-2235, E-mail: miziorkoh@umkc.edu. *Application contact:* Laura Batenic, Information Contact, 816-235-2352, Fax: 816-235-5158, E-mail: batenicl@umkc.edu. Web site: http://sbs.umkc.edu/.

See Display on page 222 and Close-Up on page 247.

University of Missouri–St. Louis, College of Arts and Sciences, Department of Chemistry and Biochemistry, St. Louis, MO 63121. Offers chemistry (MS, PhD), including biochemistry, inorganic chemistry, organic chemistry, physical chemistry. Part-time and evening/weekend programs available. *Faculty:* 18 full-time (3 women), 4 part-time/adjunct (1 woman). *Students:* 37 full-time (18 women), 28 part-time (11 women); includes 4 minority (1 Black or African American, non-Hispanic/Latino; 2 Asian, non-Hispanic/Latino; 1 Hispanic/Latino), 22 international. Average age 30. 73 applicants, 30% accepted, 11 enrolled. In 2011, 16 master's, 4 doctorates awarded. Terminal master's awarded for partial completion of doctoral program. *Degree requirements:* For master's, thesis optional; for doctorate, thesis/dissertation. *Entrance requirements:* For master's, 2 letters of recommendation; for doctorate, GRE General Test, 3 letters of recommendation. Additional exam requirements/recommendations for international students: Required—TOEFL (minimum score 550 paper-based; 213 computer-based). *Application deadline:* For fall admission, 7/1 priority date for domestic students, 7/1 for international students; for spring admission, 12/1 priority date for domestic students, 12/1 for international students. Applications are processed on a rolling basis. Application fee: $35 ($40 for international students). Electronic applications accepted. *Expenses:* Tuition, state resident: full-time $6273; part-time $3866 per year. Tuition, nonresident: full-time $14,969; part-time $9980 per year. *Required fees:* $315 per year. *Financial support:* In 2011–12, 19 research assistantships with full and partial tuition reimbursements (averaging $13,500 per year), 19 teaching assistantships with full and partial tuition reimbursements (averaging $13,500 per year) were awarded; fellowships with full and partial tuition reimbursements also available. *Faculty research:* Metallaborane chemistry, serum transferrin chemistry, natural products chemistry, organic synthesis. *Unit head:* Dr. Janet Wilking, Director of Graduate Studies, 314-516-5311, Fax: 314-516-5342, E-mail: gradchem@umsl.edu. *Application contact:* Graduate Admissions, 314-516-5458, Fax: 314-516-6996, E-mail: gradadm@umsl.edu. Web site: http://www.umsl.edu/chemistry/.

The University of Montana, Graduate School, College of Arts and Sciences, Division of Biological Sciences, Program in Biochemistry and Microbiology, Missoula, MT 59812-0002. Offers biochemistry (MS); integrative microbiology and biochemistry (PhD); microbial ecology (MS, PhD); microbiology (MS). Terminal master's awarded for partial completion of doctoral program. *Degree requirements:* For master's, thesis; for doctorate, variable foreign language requirement, thesis/dissertation. *Entrance requirements:* For master's and doctorate, GRE General Test. *Faculty research:* Ribosome structure, medical microbiology/pathogenesis, microbial ecology/environmental microbiology.

University of Nebraska–Lincoln, Graduate College, College of Agricultural Sciences and Natural Resources and College of Arts and Sciences, Department of Biochemistry, Lincoln, NE 68588. Offers MS, PhD. Terminal master's awarded for partial completion of doctoral program. *Degree requirements:* For master's, thesis optional; for doctorate, comprehensive exam, thesis/dissertation. *Entrance requirements:* For master's and doctorate, GRE General Test, GRE Subject Test. Additional exam requirements/recommendations for international students: Required—TOEFL (minimum score 550 paper-based; 213 computer-based). Electronic applications accepted. *Faculty research:* Molecular genetics, enzymology, photosynthesis, molecular virology, structural biology.

University of Nebraska–Lincoln, Graduate College, College of Arts and Sciences, Department of Chemistry, Lincoln, NE 68588. Offers analytical chemistry (PhD); biochemistry (PhD); chemistry (MS); inorganic chemistry (PhD); materials chemistry (PhD); organic chemistry (PhD); physical chemistry (PhD). *Degree requirements:* For master's, one foreign language, thesis optional, departmental qualifying exam; for doctorate, one foreign language, comprehensive exam, thesis/dissertation, departmental qualifying exams. *Entrance requirements:* For master's and doctorate, GRE. Additional exam requirements/recommendations for international students: Required—TOEFL (minimum score 550 paper-based; 213 computer-based). Electronic applications accepted. *Faculty research:* Bioorganic and bioinorganic chemistry, biophysical and bioanalytical chemistry, structure-function of DNA and proteins, organometallics, mass spectrometry.

University of Nebraska Medical Center, Graduate Studies, Department of Biochemistry and Molecular Biology, Omaha, NE 68198. Offers MS, PhD. Terminal master's awarded for partial completion of doctoral program. *Degree requirements:* For master's, comprehensive exam, thesis; for doctorate, comprehensive exam, thesis/dissertation. *Entrance requirements:* For master's and doctorate, GRE General Test. Additional exam requirements/recommendations for international students: Required—TOEFL (minimum score 550 paper-based; 213 computer-based). Electronic applications accepted. *Faculty research:* Recombinant DNA, cancer biology, diabetes and drug metabolism, biochemical endocrinology.

University of Nevada, Las Vegas, Graduate College, College of Science, Department of Chemistry, Las Vegas, NV 89154-4003. Offers biochemistry (MS); chemistry (MS, PhD); radiochemistry (PhD). Part-time programs available. *Faculty:* 15 full-time (2 women), 6 part-time/adjunct (1 woman). *Students:* 10 full-time (3 women), 34 part-time (18 women); includes 7 minority (2 Black or African American, non-Hispanic/Latino; 2 Asian, non-Hispanic/Latino; 1 Hispanic/Latino; 2 Two or more races, non-Hispanic/Latino), 9 international. Average age 30. 22 applicants, 41% accepted, 5 enrolled. In 2011, 3 master's, 7 doctorates awarded. *Degree requirements:* For master's, thesis. *Entrance requirements:* For master's and doctorate, GRE General Test. Additional exam requirements/recommendations for international students: Required—TOEFL (minimum score 550 paper-based; 213 computer-based; 80 iBT), IELTS (minimum score 7). *Application deadline:* For fall admission, 2/1 priority date for domestic students, 5/1 for international students; for spring admission, 10/1 priority date for domestic students, 10/1 for international students. Applications are processed on a rolling basis. Application fee: $60 ($95 for international students). Electronic applications accepted. *Financial support:* In 2011–12, 44 students received support, including 33 research assistantships with partial tuition reimbursements available (averaging $13,346 per year), 11 teaching assistantships with partial tuition reimbursements available (averaging $16,397 per year); institutionally sponsored loans, scholarships/grants, health care benefits, and unspecified assistantships also available. Financial award application deadline: 3/1. *Faculty research:* Material science, biochemistry, chemical education, physical chemistry and theoretical computation, analytical and organic chemistry. *Total annual research expenditures:* $2.4 million. *Unit head:* Dr. Dennis Lindle, Chair/Professor, 702-895-4426, Fax: 702-895-4072, E-mail: lindle@unlv.nevada.edu. *Application contact:* Graduate Coordinator, 702-895-3320, Fax: 702-895-4180, E-mail: gradcollege@unlv.edu. Web site: http://sciences.unlv.edu/Chemistry/index.htm.

University of Nevada, Reno, Graduate School, College of Agriculture, Biotechnology and Natural Resources, Program in Biochemistry, Reno, NV 89557. Offers MS, PhD. Terminal master's awarded for partial completion of doctoral program. *Degree requirements:* For master's, thesis; for doctorate, thesis/dissertation. *Entrance requirements:* For master's, GRE General Test, minimum GPA of 2.75; for doctorate, GRE General Test, minimum GPA of 3.0. Additional exam requirements/recommendations for international students: Required—TOEFL (minimum score 500 paper-based; 173 computer-based; 61 iBT), IELTS (minimum score 6). Electronic applications accepted. *Faculty research:* Cancer research, insect biochemistry, plant biochemistry, enzymology.

See Display on next page and Close-Up on page 153.

University of New Hampshire, Graduate School, College of Life Sciences and Agriculture, Department of Molecular, Cellular and Biomedical Sciences, Program in Biochemistry, Durham, NH 03824. Offers MS, PhD. Part-time programs available. *Faculty:* 12 full-time. *Students:* 10 full-time (1 woman), 10 part-time (4 women); includes 3 minority (1 Asian, non-Hispanic/Latino; 2 Hispanic/Latino), 7 international. Average

Biochemistry

age 29. 39 applicants, 15% accepted, 4 enrolled. In 2011, 2 doctorates awarded. Terminal master's awarded for partial completion of doctoral program. *Degree requirements:* For master's, thesis; for doctorate, one foreign language, thesis/dissertation. *Entrance requirements:* For master's and doctorate, GRE General Test. Additional exam requirements/recommendations for international students: Required—TOEFL (minimum score 550 paper-based; 213 computer-based; 80 iBT). *Application deadline:* For fall admission, 6/1 priority date for domestic students, 4/1 for international students; for spring admission, 12/1 for domestic students. Applications are processed on a rolling basis. Application fee: $65. Electronic applications accepted. *Expenses:* Tuition, state resident: full-time $12,360; part-time $687 per credit hour. Tuition, nonresident: full-time $25,680; part-time $1058 per credit hour. *International tuition:* $29,550 full-time. *Required fees:* $1666; $833 per course. $416.50 per semester. Tuition and fees vary according to course load and degree level. *Financial support:* In 2011–12, 14 students received support, including 4 research assistantships, 10 teaching assistantships; fellowships, career-related internships or fieldwork, Federal Work-Study, scholarships/grants, and tuition waivers (full and partial) also available. Support available to part-time students. Financial award application deadline: 2/15. *Faculty research:* Developmental biochemistry, biochemistry of natural products, physical biochemistry, biochemical genetics, structure and metabolism of macromolecules. *Unit head:* Rick Cote, Chairperson, 603-862-2470. *Application contact:* Flora Joyal, Administrative Assistant, 603-862-2103, E-mail: biochemistry.dept@unh.edu. Web site: http://biochemistry.unh.edu/.

University of New Mexico, Health Sciences Center Graduate Programs, Program in Biomedical Sciences, Albuquerque, NM 87131-5196. Offers biochemistry and molecular biology (MS, PhD); cell biology and physiology (MS, PhD); clinical and translational science (Certificate); molecular genetics and microbiology (MS, PhD); neuroscience (MS, PhD); pathology (MS, PhD); toxicology (MS, PhD); university science teaching (Certificate). Part-time programs available. *Faculty:* 64 full-time (26 women), 9 part-time/adjunct (4 women). *Students:* 45 full-time (27 women), 56 part-time (28 women); includes 24 minority (3 Black or African American, non-Hispanic/Latino; 1 American Indian or Alaska Native, non-Hispanic/Latino; 4 Asian, non-Hispanic/Latino; 14 Hispanic/Latino; 1 Native Hawaiian or other Pacific Islander, non-Hispanic/Latino; 1 Two or more races, non-Hispanic/Latino), 18 international. Average age 30. 110 applicants, 18% accepted, 17 enrolled. In 2011, 14 master's, 5 doctorates awarded. Terminal master's awarded for partial completion of doctoral program. *Degree requirements:* For master's, thesis; for doctorate, comprehensive exam, thesis/dissertation. *Entrance requirements:* For master's and doctorate, GRE General Test, minimum undergraduate GPA of 3.0. Additional exam requirements/recommendations for international students: Required—TOEFL. *Application deadline:* For fall admission, 3/1 priority date for domestic students, 3/1 for international students. Applications are processed on a rolling basis. Application fee: $50. Electronic applications accepted. *Financial support:* In 2011–12, 99 students received support, including 28 fellowships with full and partial tuition reimbursements available (averaging $22,000 per year), 73 research assistantships with full tuition reimbursements available (averaging $23,000 per year), 8 teaching assistantships (averaging $2,800 per year); career-related internships or fieldwork, Federal Work-Study, institutionally sponsored loans, scholarships/grants, traineeships, health care benefits, and unspecified assistantships also available. Financial award application deadline: 1/1; financial award applicants required to submit FAFSA. *Faculty research:* Infectious disease/immunity, cancer biology, cardiovascular and metabolic diseases, brain and behavioral illness, environmental health. *Unit head:* Dr. Helen J. Hathaway, BSGP Program Director, 505-272-1887, Fax: 505-272-2412, E-mail: hhathaway@salud.unm.edu. *Application contact:* Mary Fenton, Admissions Coordinator, 505-272-1887, Fax: 505-272-2412, E-mail: mfenton@salud.unm.edu. Web site: http://hsc.unm.edu/som/research/brep/bsgpabout.shtm.

The University of North Carolina at Chapel Hill, School of Medicine and Graduate School, Graduate Programs in Medicine, Department of Biochemistry and Biophysics, Chapel Hill, NC 27599. Offers MS, PhD. Terminal master's awarded for partial completion of doctoral program. *Degree requirements:* For master's, comprehensive exam, thesis; for doctorate, comprehensive exam, thesis/dissertation. *Entrance requirements:* For master's and doctorate, GRE General Test, GRE Subject Test (recommended), minimum GPA of 3.0. Additional exam requirements/recommendations for international students: Required—TOEFL. Electronic applications accepted.

The University of North Carolina at Greensboro, Graduate School, College of Arts and Sciences, Department of Chemistry and Biochemistry, Greensboro, NC 27412-5001. Offers biochemistry (MS); chemistry (MS). *Degree requirements:* For master's, one foreign language, thesis. *Entrance requirements:* For master's, GRE General Test. Additional exam requirements/recommendations for international students: Required—TOEFL. Electronic applications accepted. *Faculty research:* Synthesis of novel cyclopentadienes, molybdenum hydroxylase-cata ladder polymers, vinyl silicones.

University of North Dakota, Graduate School and Graduate School, Graduate Programs in Medicine, Department of Biochemistry and Molecular Biology, Grand Forks, ND 58202. Offers MS, PhD. *Degree requirements:* For master's, thesis, final exam; for doctorate, comprehensive exam, thesis/dissertation, final exam. *Entrance requirements:* For master's and doctorate, GRE General Test, minimum GPA of 3.0. Additional exam requirements/recommendations for international students: Required—TOEFL (minimum score 550 paper-based; 213 computer-based; 79 iBT), IELTS (minimum score 6.5). Electronic applications accepted. *Faculty research:* Glucose-6-phosphatase, guanine nucleotides, carbohydrate and lipid metabolism, cytoskeletal proteins, chromatin structure.

University of Northern Iowa, Graduate College, College of Humanities, Arts and Sciences, Department of Chemistry, Cedar Falls, IA 50614. Offers applied chemistry and biochemistry (PSM); chemistry (MA, MS). Part-time programs available. *Students:* 2 full-time (0 women), 1 part-time (0 women). 16 applicants, 19% accepted, 0 enrolled. In 2011, 4 master's awarded. *Degree requirements:* For master's, comprehensive exam (for some programs), thesis (for some programs). *Entrance requirements:* For master's, minimum GPA of 3.0, 3 letters of recommendation. Additional exam requirements/recommendations for international students: Required—TOEFL (minimum score 500 paper-based; 180 computer-based; 61 iBT). *Application deadline:* For fall admission, 8/1 priority date for domestic students. Applications are processed on a rolling basis. Application fee: $50 ($70 for international students). Electronic applications accepted. *Expenses:* Tuition, state resident: full-time $7476. Tuition, nonresident: full-time $16,410. *Required fees:* $942. *Financial support:* Career-related internships or fieldwork, Federal Work-Study, scholarships/grants, and tuition waivers (full and partial) available. Support available to part-time students. Financial award application deadline: 2/1. *Unit head:* Dr. William S. Harwood, Head, 319-273-2437, Fax: 319-273-7127, E-mail: bill.harwood@uni.edu. *Application contact:* Laurie S. Russell, Record Analyst, 319-273-2623, Fax: 319-273-2885, E-mail: laurie.russell@uni.edu. Web site: http://www.chem.uni.edu/.

University of North Texas, Toulouse Graduate School, College of Arts and Sciences, Program in Biochemistry, Denton, TX 76203. Offers MS, PhD. Terminal master's awarded for partial completion of doctoral program. *Degree requirements:* For master's, comprehensive exam, thesis (for some programs), oral defense of thesis; for doctorate, one foreign language, comprehensive exam, thesis/dissertation, oral defense of dissertation. *Entrance requirements:* For master's, GRE General Test, placement exams in 3 areas, letters of recommendation; for doctorate, GRE General Test, placement exams in 4 areas. Additional exam requirements/recommendations for international students: Recommended—TOEFL (minimum score

Graduate Program in Biochemistry (BCH)

The University of Nevada, Reno ranks among the top 100 Public Research Schools in the U.S. according to a recent survey by U.S. News and World Report. Biochemistry graduate students have opportunities to conduct research either in the College of Agriculture, Biotechnology and Natural Resources (CABNR) or the School of Medicine (SOM) with access to state-of-the-art federally funded research centers in genomics, proteomics, bioinformatics, flow cytometry and *in vivo* imaging. Graduate student have a broad range of research areas from which to choose spanning human biomedicine and disease, insect biochemistry and signaling, and plant and microbial genomics and biotechnology.

The University is situated within an unusually attractive natural setting on the eastern slopes of the majestic Sierra Nevada mountain range. Reno-Sparks benefits from a comfortable climate marked by generally cool and dry weather with more than 300 sunny days per year. The area is a haven for those who love the four seasons, an active live style, and it offers many diverse recreational activities including Lake Tahoe and many world-class ski resorts.

Interdisciplinary Graduate Programs in Molecular Biosciences (MB)

All first year Ph.D. candidates are provided research stipends and have the opportunity to conduct research rotations within interdisciplinary graduate programs in the molecular biosciences with more than 65 active research faculty.

Contact: John C. Cushman, Ph.D.
Professor, Graduate Program Director
Department of Biochemistry & Molecular Biology
Reno, NV 89557
Email: jcushman@unr.edu
BCH: http://www.cabnr.unr.edu/bmb/default.aspx
MB: http://www.unr.edu/mb/index.html

 University of Nevada, Reno

550 paper-based; 213 computer-based; 79 iBT). *Expenses:* Tuition, state resident: part-time $100 per credit hour. Tuition, nonresident: part-time $413 per credit hour. *Faculty research:* Microbial and plant metabolism, regulation of prokaryotic and eukarytoic gene expression, protein interaction.

University of North Texas Health Science Center at Fort Worth, Graduate School of Biomedical Sciences, Fort Worth, TX 76107-2699. Offers anatomy and cell biology (MS, PhD); biochemistry and molecular biology (MS, PhD); biomedical sciences (MS, PhD); biotechnology (MS); forensic genetics (MS); integrative physiology (MS, PhD); medical science (MS); microbiology and immunology (MS, PhD); pharmacology (MS, PhD); science education (MS); DO/MS; DO/PhD. Terminal master's awarded for partial completion of doctoral program. *Degree requirements:* For master's, thesis; for doctorate, thesis/dissertation. *Entrance requirements:* For master's and doctorate, GRE General Test. Additional exam requirements/recommendations for international students: Required—TOEFL. *Expenses:* Contact institution. *Faculty research:* Alzheimer's disease, aging, eye diseases, cancer, cardiovascular disease.

University of Notre Dame, Graduate School, College of Science, Department of Chemistry and Biochemistry, Notre Dame, IN 46556. Offers biochemistry (MS, PhD); inorganic chemistry (MS, PhD); organic chemistry (MS, PhD); physical chemistry (MS, PhD). Terminal master's awarded for partial completion of doctoral program. *Degree requirements:* For master's, comprehensive exam, thesis; for doctorate, thesis/dissertation, qualifying exam. *Entrance requirements:* For master's and doctorate, GRE General Test, GRE Subject Test (strongly recommended). Additional exam requirements/recommendations for international students: Required—TOEFL (minimum score 600 paper-based; 250 computer-based; 80 iBT). Electronic applications accepted. *Faculty research:* Reaction design and mechanistic studies; reactive intermediates; synthesis, structure and reactivity of organometallic cluster complexes and biologically active natural products; bioorganic chemistry; enzymology.

University of Oklahoma, College of Arts and Sciences, Department of Chemistry and Biochemistry, Norman, OK 73019. Offers chemistry and biochemistry (MS, PhD), including bioinformatics, cellular and behavioral neurobiology (PhD), chemistry. Part-time programs available. *Faculty:* 27 full-time (6 women). *Students:* 67 full-time (25 women), 22 part-time (9 women); includes 15 minority (5 Black or African American, non-Hispanic/Latino; 1 American Indian or Alaska Native, non-Hispanic/Latino; 3 Asian, non-Hispanic/Latino; 4 Hispanic/Latino; 2 Two or more races, non-Hispanic/Latino), 40 international. Average age 28. 92 applicants, 17% accepted, 15 enrolled. In 2011, 17 master's, 17 doctorates awarded. Terminal master's awarded for partial completion of doctoral program. *Degree requirements:* For master's, thesis optional; for doctorate, thesis/dissertation. *Entrance requirements:* For master's, GRE, BS in chemistry; for doctorate, GRE. Additional exam requirements/recommendations for international students: Required—TOEFL (minimum score 550 paper-based; 79 iBT). *Application deadline:* For fall admission, 4/1 priority date for domestic students, 3/1 for international students; for spring admission, 9/1 priority date for domestic students, 9/1 for international students. Applications are processed on a rolling basis. Application fee: $40 ($90 for international students). Electronic applications accepted. *Expenses:* Tuition, state resident: full-time $4087; part-time $170.30 per credit hour. Tuition, nonresident: full-time $14,875; part-time $619.80 per credit hour. *Required fees:* $2659; $100.25 per credit hour. Tuition and fees vary according to course load and degree level. *Financial support:* In 2011–12, 89 students received support, including 1 fellowship with full tuition reimbursement available (averaging $5,000 per year), 19 research assistantships with partial tuition reimbursements available (averaging $15,794 per year), 58 teaching assistantships with partial tuition reimbursements available (averaging $16,776 per year); scholarships/grants, tuition waivers (full), and unspecified assistantships also available. Financial award applicants required to submit FAFSA. *Faculty research:* Structural biology, synthesis and catalysis, biomaterials, membrane biochemistry, genomics. *Total annual research expenditures:* $7 million. *Unit head:* Dr. George Richter-Addo, Chair, 405-325-4811, Fax: 405-325-6111, E-mail: grichteraddo@ou.edu. *Application contact:* Angelika Tietz, Graduate Program Assistant, 405-325-4811 Ext. 62946, Fax: 405-325-6111, E-mail: atietz@ou.edu. Web site: http://chem.ou.edu.

University of Oklahoma Health Sciences Center, College of Medicine and Graduate College, Graduate Programs in Medicine, Department of Biochemistry and Molecular Biology, Oklahoma City, OK 73190. Offers biochemistry (MS, PhD); molecular biology (MS, PhD). Part-time programs available. Terminal master's awarded for partial completion of doctoral program. *Degree requirements:* For master's, thesis; for doctorate, thesis/dissertation. *Entrance requirements:* For master's, GRE General Test, 2 letters of recommendation; for doctorate, GRE General Test, 3 letters of recommendation. Additional exam requirements/recommendations for international students: Required—TOEFL. *Faculty research:* Gene expression, regulation of transcription, enzyme evolution, melanogenesis, signal transduction.

University of Oregon, Graduate School, College of Arts and Sciences, Department of Chemistry, Eugene, OR 97403. Offers biochemistry (MA, MS, PhD); chemistry (MA, MS, PhD). Terminal master's awarded for partial completion of doctoral program. *Degree requirements:* For doctorate, thesis/dissertation. *Entrance requirements:* For master's and doctorate, GRE General Test, minimum GPA of 3.0. Additional exam requirements/recommendations for international students: Required—TOEFL. *Faculty research:* Organic chemistry, organometallic chemistry, inorganic chemistry, physical chemistry, materials science, biochemistry, chemical physics, molecular or cell biology.

University of Ottawa, Faculty of Graduate and Postdoctoral Studies, Faculty of Medicine, Department of Biochemistry, Microbiology and Immunology, Ottawa, ON K1N 6N5, Canada. Offers biochemistry (M Sc, PhD); microbiology and immunology (M Sc, PhD). *Degree requirements:* For master's, thesis; for doctorate, comprehensive exam, thesis/dissertation, seminar. *Entrance requirements:* For master's, honors degree or equivalent, minimum B average; for doctorate, master's degree, minimum B+ average. Electronic applications accepted. *Faculty research:* General biochemistry, molecular biology, microbiology, host biology, nutrition and metabolism.

University of Pennsylvania, Perelman School of Medicine, Biomedical Graduate Studies, Graduate Group in Biochemistry and Molecular Biophysics, Philadelphia, PA 19104. Offers PhD, MD/PhD, VMD/PhD. *Faculty:* 74. *Students:* 81 full-time (30 women); includes 22 minority (3 Black or African American, non-Hispanic/Latino; 11 Asian, non-Hispanic/Latino; 8 Hispanic/Latino), 8 international. 122 applicants, 30% accepted, 14 enrolled. In 2011, 4 doctorates awarded. *Degree requirements:* For doctorate, thesis/dissertation. *Entrance requirements:* For doctorate, GRE General Test. Additional exam requirements/recommendations for international students: Required—TOEFL. *Application deadline:* For fall admission, 12/1 priority date for domestic students, 12/1 for international students. Applications are processed on a rolling basis. Application fee: $80. Electronic applications accepted. *Expenses: Tuition:* Full-time $26,660; part-time $4944 per course. *Required fees:* $2318; $291 per course. Tuition and fees vary according to course load, degree level and program. *Financial support:* In 2011–12, 81 students received support. Fellowships, research assistantships, scholarships/grants, traineeships, and unspecified assistantships available. *Faculty research:* Biochemistry of cell differentiation, tissue culture, intermediary metabolism, structure of proteins and nucleic acids, biochemical genetics. *Unit head:* Dr. Kathryn Ferguson, Chairperson, 215-573-1207, E-mail: ferguso2@mail.med.upenn.edu. *Application contact:* Ruth Keris, Administrator. Web site: http://www.med.upenn.edu/bmbgrad/.

University of Puerto Rico, Medical Sciences Campus, School of Medicine, Division of Graduate Studies, Department of Biochemistry, San Juan, PR 00936-5067. Offers MS, PhD. *Degree requirements:* For master's, thesis; for doctorate, comprehensive exam, thesis/dissertation. *Entrance requirements:* For master's and doctorate, GRE General Test, GRE Subject Test, interview, minimum GPA of 3.0. Electronic applications accepted. *Faculty research:* Genetics, cell and molecular biology, cancer biology, protein structure/function, glycosilation of proteins.

University of Regina, Faculty of Graduate Studies and Research, Faculty of Science, Department of Chemistry and Biochemistry, Regina, SK S4S 0A2, Canada. Offers analytical/environmental chemistry (M Sc, PhD); biophysics of biological interfaces (M Sc, PhD); enzymology/chemical biology (M Sc, PhD); inorganic/organometallic chemistry (M Sc, PhD); signal transduction and mechanisms of cancer cell regulation (M Sc, PhD); supramolecular organic photochemistry and photophysics (M Sc, PhD); synthetic organic chemistry (M Sc, PhD); theoretical/computational chemistry (M Sc, PhD). *Faculty:* 12 full-time (2 women). *Students:* 13 full-time (4 women), 1 (woman) part-time. 22 applicants, 50% accepted. In 2011, 1 master's, 2 doctorates awarded. *Degree requirements:* For master's, thesis; for doctorate, thesis/dissertation. *Entrance requirements:* Additional exam requirements/recommendations for international students: Required—TOEFL (minimum score 580 paper-based; 80 iBT), IELTS (minimum score 6.5). *Application deadline:* Applications are processed on a rolling basis. Application fee: $100. Electronic applications accepted. *Financial support:* In 2011–12, 3 fellowships (averaging $6,500 per year), 1 research assistantship (averaging $5,500 per year), 7 teaching assistantships (averaging $2,298 per year) were awarded; scholarships/grants also available. Financial award application deadline: 6/15. *Faculty research:* Asymmetric synthesis and methodology, theoretical and computational chemistry, biophysical biochemistry, analytical and environmental chemistry, chemical biology. *Unit head:* Dr. Lynn Mihichuk, Head, 306-585-4793, Fax: 306-337-2409, E-mail: lynn.mihichuk@uregina.ca. *Application contact:* Dr. Tanya Dahms, Graduate Program Coordinator, 306-585-4246, Fax: 306-337-2409, E-mail: tanya.dahms@uregina.ca. Web site: http://www.chem.uregina.ca/.

University of Rhode Island, Graduate School, College of the Environment and Life Sciences, Department of Cell and Molecular Biology, Kingston, RI 02881. Offers biochemistry (MS, PhD); clinical laboratory sciences (MS), including biotechnology, clinical laboratory science, cytopathology; microbiology (MS, PhD); molecular genetics (MS, PhD). Part-time programs available. *Faculty:* 14 full-time (5 women), 3 part-time/adjunct (2 women). *Students:* 32 full-time (15 women), 37 part-time (23 women); includes 2 minority (1 Asian, non-Hispanic/Latino; 1 Hispanic/Latino), 1 international. In 2011, 2 master's, 2 doctorates awarded. *Degree requirements:* For master's, comprehensive exam (for some programs); for doctorate, comprehensive exam. *Entrance requirements:* For master's and doctorate, GRE, 2 letters of recommendation. Additional exam requirements/recommendations for international students: Required—TOEFL (minimum score 550 paper-based; 213 computer-based). *Application deadline:* For fall admission, 7/15 for domestic students, 2/1 for international students; for spring admission, 11/15 for domestic students, 7/15 for international students. Application fee: $65. Electronic applications accepted. *Expenses:* Tuition, state resident: full-time $10,432; part-time $580 per credit hour. Tuition, nonresident: full-time $23,130; part-time $1285 per credit hour. *Required fees:* $1362; $36 per credit hour. $35 per semester. One-time fee: $130. *Financial support:* In 2011–12, 2 research assistantships with full and partial tuition reimbursements (averaging $13,894 per year), 6 teaching assistantships with full and partial tuition reimbursements (averaging $12,850 per year) were awarded. Financial award application deadline: 7/15; financial award applicants required to submit FAFSA. *Faculty research:* Genomics and Sequencing Center: an interdisciplinary genomics research and undergraduate and graduate student training program which provides researchers access to cutting-edge technologies in the field of genomics. *Unit head:* Dr. Jay Sperry, Chairperson, 401-874-2201, Fax: 401-874-2202, E-mail: jsperry@mail.uri.edu. *Application contact:* Nasser H. Zawia, Dean of the Graduate School, 401-874-5909, Fax: 401-874-5787, E-mail: nzawia@uri.edu. Web site: http://cels.uri.edu/cmb/.

University of Rochester, School of Medicine and Dentistry, Graduate Programs in Medicine and Dentistry, Department of Biochemistry and Biophysics, Programs in Biochemistry, Rochester, NY 14627. Offers biochemistry and molecular biology (PhD). Terminal master's awarded for partial completion of doctoral program. *Degree requirements:* For doctorate, thesis/dissertation, qualifying exam. *Entrance requirements:* For doctorate, GRE General Test. *Expenses: Tuition:* Full-time $41,040.

University of Saint Joseph, Department of Chemistry, West Hartford, CT 06117-2700. Offers biochemistry (MS); chemistry (MS). Part-time and evening/weekend programs available. Postbaccalaureate distance learning degree programs offered. *Students:* 33 part-time (20 women); includes 8 minority (3 Black or African American, non-Hispanic/Latino; 2 Asian, non-Hispanic/Latino; 3 Hispanic/Latino). Average age 30. *Degree requirements:* For master's, comprehensive exam, thesis optional. *Entrance requirements:* For master's, 2 letters of recommendation. *Application deadline:* Applications are processed on a rolling basis. Application fee: $50. Electronic applications accepted. Application fee is waived when completed online. *Expenses: Tuition:* Part-time $670 per credit. *Required fees:* $40 per credit. Tuition and fees vary according to course load, degree level, campus/location and program. *Financial support:* Career-related internships or fieldwork and unspecified assistantships available. Support available to part-time students. Financial award applicants required to submit FAFSA. *Application contact:* Graduate Admissions Office, 860-231-5261, E-mail: graduate@usj.edu.

University of Saskatchewan, College of Medicine, Department of Biochemistry, Saskatoon, SK S7N 5A2, Canada. Offers M Sc, PhD. *Degree requirements:* For master's, thesis; for doctorate, thesis/dissertation. *Entrance requirements:* Additional exam requirements/recommendations for international students: Required—TOEFL.

The University of Scranton, College of Graduate and Continuing Education, Department of Chemistry, Program in Biochemistry, Scranton, PA 18510. Offers MA, MS. Part-time and evening/weekend programs available. *Faculty:* 10 full-time (3 women), 1 part-time/adjunct (0 women). *Students:* 25 full-time (8 women), 5 part-time (1 woman); includes 2 minority (both Asian, non-Hispanic/Latino), 6 international. Average age 24. 38 applicants, 58% accepted. In 2011, 3 master's awarded. *Degree requirements:* For master's, comprehensive exam (for some programs), thesis (for some programs), capstone experience. *Entrance requirements:* For master's, minimum GPA of 2.75. Additional exam requirements/recommendations for international students: Required—TOEFL (minimum score 500 paper-based; 173 computer-based), IELTS (minimum score 5.5). *Application deadline:* Applications are processed on a rolling basis. Application fee: $0. *Financial support:* Fellowships, teaching assistantships with full and partial tuition reimbursements, career-related internships or fieldwork, Federal Work-Study, and unspecified assistantships available. Support available to part-time students. Financial award application deadline: 3/1. *Unit head:* Dr. Christopher A. Baumann, Director, 570-941-6389, Fax: 570-941-7510, E-mail: cab@scranton.edu. *Application contact:* Dr. Christopher A. Baumann, Director, 570-941-6389, Fax: 570-941-7510, E-mail: cab@scranton.edu.

University of South Carolina, The Graduate School, College of Arts and Sciences, Department of Chemistry and Biochemistry, Columbia, SC 29208. Offers IMA, MAT,

Biochemistry

MS, PhD. IMA and MAT offered in cooperation with the College of Education. Part-time programs available. Terminal master's awarded for partial completion of doctoral program. *Degree requirements:* For master's, comprehensive exam, thesis; for doctorate, comprehensive exam, thesis/dissertation. *Entrance requirements:* For master's and doctorate, GRE General Test. Additional exam requirements/recommendations for international students: Required—TOEFL. Electronic applications accepted. *Faculty research:* Spectroscopy, crystallography, organic and organometallic synthesis, analytical chemistry, materials.

University of Southern California, Keck School of Medicine and Graduate School, Graduate Programs in Medicine, Department of Biochemistry and Molecular Biology, Los Angeles, CA 90089. Offers MS, PhD. *Faculty:* 24 full-time (5 women). *Students:* 43 full-time (25 women); includes 4 minority (2 Asian, non-Hispanic/Latino; 1 Hispanic/Latino; 1 Native Hawaiian or other Pacific Islander, non-Hispanic/Latino), 34 international. Average age 27. 61 applicants, 51% accepted, 22 enrolled. In 2011, 3 master's, 1 doctorate awarded. Terminal master's awarded for partial completion of doctoral program. *Median time to degree:* Of those who began their doctoral program in fall 2003, 100% received their degree in 8 years or less. *Degree requirements:* For master's, thesis; for doctorate, comprehensive exam, thesis/dissertation. *Entrance requirements:* For master's and doctorate, GRE General Test, minimum GPA of 3.0. Additional exam requirements/recommendations for international students: Required—TOEFL (minimum score 600 paper-based; 250 computer-based; 100 iBT). *Application deadline:* For fall admission, 4/15 priority date for domestic students, 4/15 for international students. Applications are processed on a rolling basis. Application fee: $85. Electronic applications accepted. *Financial support:* In 2011–12, 2 fellowships with full tuition reimbursements (averaging $29,100 per year), 2 research assistantships with full tuition reimbursements (averaging $29,100 per year) were awarded; Federal Work-Study, institutionally sponsored loans, scholarships/grants, health care benefits, tuition waivers (full), and unspecified assistantships also available. Financial award application deadline: 5/4. *Faculty research:* Molecular genetics, gene expression, membrane biochemistry, metabolic regulation, cancer biology. *Total annual research expenditures:* $4.4 million. *Unit head:* Dr. Michael R. Stallcup, Chair, 323-442-1145, Fax: 323-442-1224, E-mail: stallcup@usc.edu. *Application contact:* Janet Stoeckert, Administrative Director, Basic Science Departments, 323-442-3568, Fax: 323-442-1610, E-mail: janet.stoeckert@usc.edu. Web site: http://www.usc.edu/medicine/biochemistry/.

University of Southern Mississippi, Graduate School, College of Science and Technology, Department of Chemistry and Biochemistry, Hattiesburg, MS 39406-0001. Offers analytical chemistry (MS, PhD); biochemistry (MS, PhD); inorganic chemistry (MS, PhD); organic chemistry (MS, PhD); physical chemistry (MS, PhD). *Faculty:* 16 full-time (4 women). *Students:* 22 full-time (9 women), 4 part-time (3 women); includes 1 minority (Black or African American, non-Hispanic/Latino), 9 international. Average age 29. 43 applicants, 19% accepted, 5 enrolled. In 2011, 1 master's, 4 doctorates awarded. *Degree requirements:* For master's, comprehensive exam, thesis; for doctorate, comprehensive exam, thesis/dissertation. *Entrance requirements:* For master's, GRE General Test, minimum GPA of 2.75 in last 60 hours; for doctorate, GRE General Test, minimum GPA of 3.5. Additional exam requirements/recommendations for international students: Required—TOEFL, IELTS. *Application deadline:* For fall admission, 3/1 priority date for domestic students, 3/1 for international students. Applications are processed on a rolling basis. Application fee: $50. *Financial support:* In 2011–12, 3 research assistantships with full tuition reimbursements (averaging $17,000 per year), 19 teaching assistantships with full tuition reimbursements (averaging $20,700 per year) were awarded; fellowships, Federal Work-Study, institutionally sponsored loans, scholarships/grants, health care benefits, and unspecified assistantships also available. Support available to part-time students. Financial award application deadline: 3/15; financial award applicants required to submit FAFSA. *Faculty research:* Plant biochemistry, photo chemistry, polymer chemistry, x-ray analysis, enzyme chemistry. *Unit head:* Dr. Sabine Heinhorst, Chair, 601-266-4701, Fax: 601-266-6075. *Application contact:* Dr. Sabine Heinhorst, Graduate Coordinator, 601-266-4702, Fax: 601-266-6075. Web site: http://www.usm.edu/graduateschool/table.php.

University of South Florida, Graduate School, College of Arts and Sciences, Department of Chemistry, Tampa, FL 33620-9951. Offers analytical chemistry (MS, PhD); biochemistry (MS, PhD); computational chemistry (MS, PhD); environmental chemistry (MS, PhD); inorganic chemistry (MS, PhD); organic chemistry (MS); physical chemistry (MS, PhD); polymer chemistry (PhD). Part-time programs available. *Faculty:* 25 full-time (4 women), 9 part-time/adjunct (1 woman). *Students:* 118 full-time (46 women), 14 part-time (7 women); includes 28 minority (8 Black or African American, non-Hispanic/Latino; 11 Asian, non-Hispanic/Latino; 9 Hispanic/Latino), 58 international. Average age 29. 127 applicants, 31% accepted, 19 enrolled. In 2011, 3 master's, 16 doctorates awarded. Terminal master's awarded for partial completion of doctoral program. *Degree requirements:* For master's, comprehensive exam, thesis (for some programs); for doctorate, comprehensive exam, thesis/dissertation. *Entrance requirements:* For master's and doctorate, GRE General Test, minimum GPA of 3.0. Additional exam requirements/recommendations for international students: Required—TOEFL (minimum score 550 paper-based; 213 computer-based; 79 iBT) or IELTS (minimum score 6.5). *Application deadline:* For fall admission, 2/15 priority date for domestic students, 1/2 for international students; for spring admission, 10/1 priority date for domestic students, 6/1 for international students. Applications are processed on a rolling basis. Application fee: $30. Electronic applications accepted. *Financial support:* In 2011–12, 136 students received support, including 28 research assistantships with tuition reimbursements available (averaging $15,020 per year), 108 teaching assistantships with tuition reimbursements available (averaging $15,164 per year); unspecified assistantships also available. Financial award application deadline: 6/30. *Faculty research:* Synthesis, bio-organic chemistry, bioinorganic chemistry, environmental chemistry, NMR. *Total annual research expenditures:* $3.1 million. *Unit head:* Dr. Randy Larsen, Chairperson, 813-974-4129, Fax: 813-974-3203, E-mail: rlarsen@cas.usf.edu. *Application contact:* Patricia Muisener, Director, 813-974-1730, Fax: 813-974-3203, E-mail: muisener@cas.usf.edu. Web site: http://chemistry.usf.edu/.

The University of Tennessee, Graduate School, College of Arts and Sciences, Department of Biochemistry, Cellular and Molecular Biology, Knoxville, TN 37996. Offers MS, PhD. Terminal master's awarded for partial completion of doctoral program. *Degree requirements:* For master's, thesis; for doctorate, thesis/dissertation. *Entrance requirements:* For master's and doctorate, GRE General Test, minimum GPA of 2.7. Additional exam requirements/recommendations for international students: Required—TOEFL. Electronic applications accepted. *Expenses:* Tuition, state resident: full-time $8332; part-time $464 per credit hour. Tuition, nonresident: full-time $25,174; part-time $1400 per credit hour. *Required fees:* $1162; $56 per credit hour. Tuition and fees vary according to program.

The University of Texas at Austin, Graduate School, College of Natural Sciences, Department of Chemistry and Biochemistry, Program in Biochemistry, Austin, TX 78712-1111. Offers PhD. *Entrance requirements:* For doctorate, GRE General Test. Application fee: $50 ($75 for international students). *Financial support:* Fellowships, research assistantships, teaching assistantships, and scholarships/grants available. Financial award application deadline: 2/1. *Unit head:* Dr. David W. Hoffman, Graduate Advisor, 512-471-7859, E-mail: dhoffman@mail.utexas.edu. *Application contact:* Rick Russell, Faculty Chair, Admissions Committee, 512-471-1514, E-mail: rick_russell@mail.utexas.edu. Web site: http://www.icmb.utexas.edu/Biochemistry/.

The University of Texas Health Science Center at Houston, Graduate School of Biomedical Sciences, Program in Biochemistry and Molecular Biology, Houston, TX 77225-0036. Offers MS, PhD, MD/PhD. Terminal master's awarded for partial completion of doctoral program. *Degree requirements:* For master's, thesis; for doctorate, thesis/dissertation. *Entrance requirements:* For master's and doctorate, GRE General Test. Additional exam requirements/recommendations for international students: Required—TOEFL. Electronic applications accepted. *Faculty research:* Biochemistry, membrane biology, macromolecular structure, structural biophysics, molecular models of human disease, molecular biology of the cell.

The University of Texas Health Science Center at San Antonio, Graduate School of Biomedical Sciences, Department of Biochemistry, San Antonio, TX 78229. Offers MS, PhD. *Degree requirements:* For master's, thesis; for doctorate, comprehensive exam, thesis/dissertation. *Entrance requirements:* For master's and doctorate, GRE General Test. Additional exam requirements/recommendations for international students: Required—TOEFL (minimum score 560 paper-based; 220 computer-based; 68 iBT). Electronic applications accepted. *Faculty research:* Protein structure and function, lipid biochemistry, metabolic regulation, immunology, membrane assembly.

The University of Texas Medical Branch, Graduate School of Biomedical Sciences, Program in Biochemistry and Molecular Biology, Galveston, TX 77555. Offers biochemistry (PhD); bioinformatics (PhD); biophysics (PhD); cell biology (PhD); computational biology (PhD); structural biology (PhD). *Degree requirements:* For doctorate, thesis/dissertation. *Entrance requirements:* Additional exam requirements/recommendations for international students: Required—TOEFL (minimum score 550 paper-based; 213 computer-based). Electronic applications accepted.

The University of Texas Southwestern Medical Center, Southwestern Graduate School of Biomedical Sciences, Division of Basic Science, Program in Biological Chemistry, Dallas, TX 75390. Offers PhD. *Degree requirements:* For doctorate, thesis/dissertation, qualifying exam. *Entrance requirements:* For doctorate, GRE General Test, minimum GPA of 3.0. Additional exam requirements/recommendations for international students: Required—TOEFL. Electronic applications accepted. *Faculty research:* Regulation of gene expression, protein trafficking, molecular neurobiology, protein structure and function, metabolic regulation.

University of the Sciences in Philadelphia, College of Graduate Studies, Program in Chemistry, Biochemistry and Pharmacognosy, Philadelphia, PA 19104-4495. Offers biochemistry (MS, PhD); chemistry (MS, PhD); pharmacognosy (MS, PhD). Part-time programs available. *Degree requirements:* For master's, thesis, qualifying exams; for doctorate, comprehensive exam, thesis/dissertation, qualifying exams. *Entrance requirements:* For master's and doctorate, GRE General Test, GRE Subject Test. Additional exam requirements/recommendations for international students: Required—TOEFL, TWE. *Expenses:* Contact institution. *Faculty research:* Organic and medicinal synthesis, mass spectroscopy use in protein analysis, study of analogues of taxol, cholesteryl esters.

The University of Toledo, College of Graduate Studies, College of Natural Sciences and Mathematics, Department of Chemistry, Toledo, OH 43606-3390. Offers analytical chemistry (MS, PhD); biological chemistry (MS, PhD); inorganic chemistry (MS, PhD); organic chemistry (MS, PhD); physical chemistry (MS, PhD). Part-time programs available. *Faculty:* 22. *Students:* 56 full-time (18 women), 18 part-time (10 women); includes 4 minority (1 Black or African American, non-Hispanic/Latino; 1 Asian, non-Hispanic/Latino; 2 Hispanic/Latino), 43 international. Average age 27. 111 applicants, 17% accepted, 16 enrolled. In 2011, 4 master's, 6 doctorates awarded. *Degree requirements:* For master's, thesis (for some programs); for doctorate, thesis/dissertation. *Entrance requirements:* For master's and doctorate, GRE General Test, GRE Subject Test, minimum cumulative point-hour ratio of 2.7 for all previous academic work, three letters of recommendation, statement of purpose, transcripts from all prior institutions attended. Additional exam requirements/recommendations for international students: Required—TOEFL (minimum score 550 paper-based; 213 computer-based; 80 iBT), IELTS (minimum score 6.5). *Application deadline:* For fall admission, 1/15 priority date for domestic students, 1/15 for international students. Applications are processed on a rolling basis. Application fee: $45 ($75 for international students). Electronic applications accepted. *Financial support:* In 2011–12, 24 research assistantships with full and partial tuition reimbursements (averaging $17,218 per year) were awarded; fellowships with tuition reimbursements, Federal Work-Study, institutionally sponsored loans, scholarships/grants, tuition waivers (full), and unspecified assistantships also available. Support available to part-time students. *Faculty research:* Enzymology, materials chemistry, crystallography, theoretical chemistry. *Unit head:* Dr. Alan Pinkerton, Chair, 419-530-7902, Fax: 419-530-4033, E-mail: alan.pinkerton@utoledo.edu. *Application contact:* Graduate School Office, 419-530-4723, Fax: 419-530-4724, E-mail: grdsch@utnet.utoledo.edu. Web site: http://www.utoledo.edu/nsm/.

The University of Toledo, College of Graduate Studies, College of Pharmacy and Pharmaceutical Sciences, Program in Medicinal and Biological Chemistry, Toledo, OH 43606-3390. Offers MS, PhD. Terminal master's awarded for partial completion of doctoral program. *Degree requirements:* For master's, thesis; for doctorate, thesis/dissertation. *Entrance requirements:* For master's and doctorate, GRE General Test. Additional exam requirements/recommendations for international students: Required—TOEFL (minimum score 550 paper-based; 213 computer-based; 80 iBT). Electronic applications accepted. *Faculty research:* Neuroscience, molecular modeling, immunotoxicology, organic synthesis, peptide biochemistry.

University of Toronto, Faculty of Medicine, Department of Biochemistry, Toronto, ON M5S 1A1, Canada. Offers M Sc, PhD. *Degree requirements:* For master's, thesis, oral examination of thesis; for doctorate, thesis/dissertation, oral defense of thesis. *Entrance requirements:* For master's, B Sc in biochemistry or molecular biology, minimum B+ average, letters of reference. Additional exam requirements/recommendations for international students: Required—TOEFL (minimum score 580 paper-based; 237 computer-based; 93 iBT), TWE (minimum score 5). Electronic applications accepted.

University of Tulsa, Graduate School, College of Engineering and Natural Sciences, Department of Chemistry and Biochemistry, Program in Biochemistry, Tulsa, OK 74104-3189. Offers MS. Part-time programs available. *Faculty:* 2 full-time (0 women). *Students:* 4 full-time (3 women), 2 part-time (both women); includes 1 minority (American Indian or Alaska Native, non-Hispanic/Latino), 3 international. Average age 25. 7 applicants, 86% accepted, 1 enrolled. In 2011, 1 master's awarded. *Degree requirements:* For master's, thesis (for some programs). *Entrance requirements:* For master's, GRE General Test. Additional exam requirements/recommendations for international students: Required—TOEFL (minimum score 550 paper-based; 213 computer-based; 80 iBT), IELTS (minimum score 6). *Application deadline:* Applications are processed on a rolling basis. Application fee: $40. Electronic applications accepted. *Expenses: Tuition:* Full-time $17,748; part-time $986 per hour. *Required fees:* $5 per contact hour. $75 per semester. Tuition and fees vary according to program. *Financial support:* In 2011–12, 4 students received support, including 4 teaching assistantships (averaging $10,662 per year); career-related internships or fieldwork, Federal Work-Study, scholarships/grants, health

care benefits, and unspecified assistantships also available. Support available to part-time students. Financial award application deadline: 2/1; financial award applicants required to submit FAFSA. *Unit head:* Dr. Dale C. Teeters, Chairperson and Advisor, 918-631-2515, Fax: 918-631-3404, E-mail: dale-teeters@utulsa.edu. *Application contact:* Dr. Robert Sheaff, Advisor, 918-631-2319, Fax: 918-631-3404, E-mail: robert-sheaff@utulsa.edu.

University of Utah, Graduate School and Graduate Programs in Medicine, Program in Biological Chemistry, Salt Lake City, UT 84112-1107. Offers PhD. *Students:* 15 full-time (6 women), 1 part-time (0 women), 6 international. Average age 24. 210 applicants, 13% accepted, 13 enrolled. *Degree requirements:* For doctorate, thesis/dissertation. *Entrance requirements:* For doctorate, GRE General Test. Additional exam requirements/recommendations for international students: Required—TOEFL (minimum score 500 paper-based; 173 computer-based; 60 iBT). *Application deadline:* For fall admission, 12/15 for domestic and international students. Application fee: $55 ($65 for international students). *Financial support:* In 2011–12, 12 research assistantships with full tuition reimbursements (averaging $25,000 per year) were awarded; health care benefits also available. *Faculty research:* Protein structure, nucleic acid, enzymes, proteolysis, HIV. *Unit head:* Dr. Dennis Winge, Director, 801-581-5207, Fax: 801-585-2465. *Application contact:* Jamie Lodermeier, Administrative Program Coordinator, 801-587-5677, Fax: 801-585-2465.

University of Utah, School of Medicine and Graduate School, Graduate Programs in Medicine, Department of Biochemistry, Salt Lake City, UT 84112-1107. Offers MS, PhD. Terminal master's awarded for partial completion of doctoral program. *Degree requirements:* For master's, thesis; for doctorate, thesis/dissertation. *Entrance requirements:* For doctorate, GRE Subject Test, minimum GPA of 3.0. Additional exam requirements/recommendations for international students: Required—TOEFL. Electronic applications accepted. *Faculty research:* Protein structure and function, nucleic acid structure and function, nucleic acid enzymology, RNA modification, protein turnover.

University of Vermont, College of Medicine and Graduate College, Graduate Programs in Medicine, Department of Biochemistry, Burlington, VT 05405. Offers MS, PhD, MD/MS, MD/PhD. *Students:* 15 (9 women), 3 international. 31 applicants, 13% accepted, 2 enrolled. In 2011, 1 master's, 2 doctorates awarded. *Degree requirements:* For master's, thesis; for doctorate, thesis/dissertation. *Entrance requirements:* For master's and doctorate, GRE General Test. Additional exam requirements/recommendations for international students: Required—TOEFL (minimum score 550 paper-based; 213 computer-based; 80 iBT). *Application deadline:* For fall admission, 3/1 priority date for domestic students, 3/1 for international students. Applications are processed on a rolling basis. Application fee: $40. Electronic applications accepted. *Financial support:* Fellowships, research assistantships, teaching assistantships, and analytical assistantships available. Financial award application deadline: 3/1. *Faculty research:* Endocrinology, protein chemistry, cell-surface signaling. *Unit head:* Dr. Paula Tracy, Interim Chairperson, 802-656-2220. *Application contact:* Anne B. Mason, Coordinator, 802-656-2220.

University of Victoria, Faculty of Graduate Studies, Faculty of Science, Department of Biochemistry and Microbiology, Victoria, BC V8W 2Y2, Canada. Offers biochemistry (M Sc, PhD); microbiology (M Sc, PhD). *Degree requirements:* For master's, thesis, seminar; for doctorate, thesis/dissertation, seminar, candidacy exam. *Entrance requirements:* For master's, GRE General Test, minimum B+ average; for doctorate, GRE General Test, minimum B+ average, M Sc. Additional exam requirements/recommendations for international students: Required—TOEFL (minimum score 600 paper-based; 250 computer-based). Electronic applications accepted. *Faculty research:* Molecular pathogenesis, prokaryotic, eukaryotic, macromolecular interactions, microbial surfaces, virology, molecular genetics.

University of Virginia, School of Medicine, Department of Biochemistry and Molecular Genetics, Charlottesville, VA 22903. Offers biochemistry (PhD); MD/PhD. *Faculty:* 24 full-time (3 women), 1 (woman) part-time/adjunct. *Students:* 32 full-time (13 women); includes 2 minority (1 Black or African American, non-Hispanic/Latino; 1 Two or more races, non-Hispanic/Latino), 12 international. Average age 26. 150 applicants, 19% accepted, 10 enrolled. In 2011, 7 doctorates awarded. *Degree requirements:* For doctorate, thesis/dissertation, written research proposal and defense. *Entrance requirements:* For doctorate, GRE General Test, 3 letters of recommendation. Additional exam requirements/recommendations for international students: Recommended—TOEFL (minimum score 630 paper-based; 250 computer-based; 90 iBT). Application fee: $60. Electronic applications accepted. *Financial support:* Fellowships, health care benefits, and tuition waivers (full) available. Financial award applicants required to submit FAFSA. *Unit head:* Joel Hockensmith, Faculty Director, 434-924-1230, Fax: 434-924-5069, E-mail: jwh6f@virginia.edu. *Application contact:* Biomedical Sciences Graduate Studies, E-mail: bims@virginia.edu. Web site: http://www.virginia.edu/artsandsciences/.

University of Washington, Graduate School, School of Medicine, Graduate Programs in Medicine, Department of Biochemistry, Seattle, WA 98195. Offers PhD. *Degree requirements:* For doctorate, thesis/dissertation. *Entrance requirements:* For doctorate, GRE General Test, GRE Subject Test (biology, chemistry, biochemistry, or cell and molecular biology), minimum GPA of 3.0. Additional exam requirements/recommendations for international students: Required—TOEFL. Electronic applications accepted. *Faculty research:* Blood coagulation, structure and function of enzymes, fertilization events, interaction of plants with bacteria, protein structure.

University of Waterloo, Graduate Studies, Faculty of Science, Guelph-Waterloo Centre for Graduate Work in Chemistry and Biochemistry, Waterloo, ON N2L 3G1, Canada. Offers M Sc, PhD. M Sc, PhD offered jointly with University of Guelph. Part-time programs available. *Degree requirements:* For master's and doctorate, project or thesis. *Entrance requirements:* For master's, GRE, honors degree, minimum B average; for doctorate, GRE, master's degree, minimum B average. Additional exam requirements/recommendations for international students: Required—TOEFL, TWE. Electronic applications accepted. *Faculty research:* Polymer, physical, inorganic, organic, and theoretical chemistry.

The University of Western Ontario, Faculty of Graduate Studies, Biosciences Division, Department of Biochemistry, London, ON N6A 5B8, Canada. Offers M Sc, PhD. *Degree requirements:* For master's, thesis; for doctorate, thesis/dissertation. *Entrance requirements:* For master's, minimum B+ average in last 2 years of undergraduate study; for doctorate, M Sc or an external scholarship winner.

University of West Florida, College of Arts and Sciences: Sciences, School of Allied Health and Life Sciences, Department of Biology, Pensacola, FL 32514-5750. Offers biological chemistry (MS); biology (MS); biology education (MST); biotechnology (MS); coastal zone studies (MS); environmental biology (MS). *Faculty:* 12 full-time (3 women), 1 part-time/adjunct (0 women). *Students:* 9 full-time (7 women), 30 part-time (16 women); includes 2 minority (both Hispanic/Latino), 3 international. Average age 29. 21 applicants, 48% accepted, 5 enrolled. In 2011, 4 master's awarded. *Degree requirements:* For master's, thesis. *Entrance requirements:* For master's, GRE (minimum score: verbal 450, quantitative 550), official transcripts; BS in biology or related field; letter of interest; relevant past experience; three letters of recommendation from individuals who can evaluate applicant's academic ability. Additional exam requirements/recommendations for international students: Required—TOEFL (minimum score 550 paper-based; 213 computer-based). *Application deadline:* For fall admission, 6/1 for domestic and international students; for spring admission, 10/1 for domestic and international students. Applications are processed on a rolling basis. Application fee: $30. *Expenses:* Tuition, state resident: full-time $5729; part-time $302 per credit hour. Tuition, nonresident: full-time $20,059; part-time $961 per credit hour. *Required fees:* $1509; $63 per credit hour. *Financial support:* In 2011–12, 18 fellowships with partial tuition reimbursements (averaging $126 per year), 14 research assistantships with partial tuition reimbursements (averaging $5,980 per year), 4 teaching assistantships with partial tuition reimbursements (averaging $7,858 per year) were awarded; unspecified assistantships also available. Financial award application deadline: 4/15; financial award applicants required to submit FAFSA. *Unit head:* Dr. George L. Stewart, Chairperson, 850-474-2748. *Application contact:* Terry McCray, Assistant Director of Graduate Admissions, 850-473-7718, Fax: 850-473-7714, E-mail: gradadmissions@uwf.edu.

University of Windsor, Faculty of Graduate Studies, Faculty of Science, Department of Chemistry and Biochemistry, Windsor, ON N9B 3P4, Canada. Offers M Sc, PhD. Part-time programs available. *Degree requirements:* For master's, thesis; for doctorate, comprehensive exam, thesis/dissertation. *Entrance requirements:* For master's and doctorate, minimum B average. Additional exam requirements/recommendations for international students: Required—TOEFL (minimum score 560 paper-based; 220 computer-based). Electronic applications accepted. *Faculty research:* Molecular biology/recombinant DNA techniques (PCR, cloning mutagenesis), No/02 detectors, western immunoblotting and detection, CD/NMR protein/peptide structure determination, confocal/electron microscopes.

University of Wisconsin–Madison, Graduate School, College of Agricultural and Life Sciences, Department of Biochemistry, Madison, WI 53706. Offers PhD. Terminal master's awarded for partial completion of doctoral program. *Degree requirements:* For doctorate, thesis/dissertation. *Entrance requirements:* For doctorate, GRE General Test, GRE Subject Test (recommended). Additional exam requirements/recommendations for international students: Required—TOEFL. Electronic applications accepted. *Expenses:* Tuition, state resident: full-time $10,296; part-time $643.51 per credit. Tuition, nonresident: full-time $24,054; part-time $1503.40 per credit. *Required fees:* $70.06 per credit. Tuition and fees vary according to course load, campus/location, program and reciprocity agreements. *Faculty research:* Molecular structure of vitamins and hormones, enzymology, NMR spectroscopy, protein structure, molecular genetics.

University of Wisconsin–Madison, School of Medicine and Public Health and Graduate School, Graduate Programs in Medicine, Department of Biomolecular Chemistry, Madison, WI 53706-1380. Offers MS, PhD. *Faculty:* 14 full-time (4 women). *Students:* 24 full-time (10 women); includes 1 minority (Hispanic/Latino), 4 international. Average age 25. 273 applicants, 14% accepted, 15 enrolled. In 2011, 10 doctorates awarded. Terminal master's awarded for partial completion of doctoral program. *Degree requirements:* For master's, thesis; for doctorate, thesis/dissertation. *Entrance requirements:* For doctorate, GRE. *Application deadline:* For fall admission, 12/1 priority date for domestic students. Application fee: $56. Electronic applications accepted. *Expenses:* Tuition, state resident: full-time $10,296; part-time $643.51 per credit. Tuition, nonresident: full-time $24,054; part-time $1503.40 per credit. *Required fees:* $70.06 per credit. Tuition and fees vary according to course load, campus/location, program and reciprocity agreements. *Financial support:* In 2011–12, fellowships with full tuition reimbursements (averaging $20,000 per year), research assistantships with full tuition reimbursements (averaging $24,000 per year), teaching assistantships with full tuition reimbursements (averaging $27,640 per year) were awarded; traineeships, health care benefits, and tuition waivers (full) also available. *Faculty research:* Membrane biochemistry, protein folding and translocation, gene expression, signal transduction, cell growth and differentiation. *Total annual research expenditures:* $3.4 million. *Unit head:* Dr. Robert H. Fillingame, Chair, 608-262-1347, Fax: 608-262-5253, E-mail: rhfillin@wisc.edu. *Application contact:* Elyse Meuer, Student Services Coordinator, 608-262-1347, Fax: 608-262-5253, E-mail: eemeuer@wisc.edu. Web site: http://www.bmolchem.wisc.edu.

University of Wisconsin–Milwaukee, Graduate School, College of Letters and Sciences, Department of Chemistry, Milwaukee, WI 53201-0413. Offers biogeochemistry (PhD); chemistry (MS, PhD). *Faculty:* 20 full-time (4 women). *Students:* 58 full-time (25 women), 16 part-time (8 women); includes 12 minority (2 Black or African American, non-Hispanic/Latino; 5 Asian, non-Hispanic/Latino; 4 Hispanic/Latino; 1 Two or more races, non-Hispanic/Latino), 7 international. Average age 32. 46 applicants, 30% accepted, 9 enrolled. In 2011, 4 master's, 6 doctorates awarded. *Degree requirements:* For master's, thesis or alternative; for doctorate, thesis/dissertation. *Entrance requirements:* For doctorate, GRE General Test. Additional exam requirements/recommendations for international students: Required—TOEFL (minimum score 600 paper-based; 79 iBT), IELTS (minimum score 6.5). *Application deadline:* For fall admission, 1/1 priority date for domestic students; for spring admission, 9/1 for domestic students. Applications are processed on a rolling basis. Application fee: $56 ($96 for international students). One-time fee: $506.10 full-time. Tuition and fees vary according to course load and reciprocity agreements. *Financial support:* In 2011–12, 3 fellowships, 30 research assistantships, 46 teaching assistantships were awarded; career-related internships or fieldwork, unspecified assistantships, and project assistantships also available. Support available to part-time students. Financial award application deadline: 4/15; financial award applicants required to submit FAFSA. *Faculty research:* Analytical chemistry, biochemistry, inorganic chemistry, organic chemistry, physical chemistry. *Total annual research expenditures:* $4 million. *Unit head:* Peter Geissinger, Department Chair, 414-229-5230, Fax: 414-229-5530, E-mail: geissing@uwm.edu. *Application contact:* General Information Contact, 414-229-4982, Fax: 414-229-6967, E-mail: gradschool@uwm.edu. Web site: http://www.uwm.edu/dept/chemistry/.

Utah State University, School of Graduate Studies, College of Science, Department of Chemistry and Biochemistry, Logan, UT 84322. Offers biochemistry (MS, PhD); chemistry (MS, PhD). Part-time programs available. Terminal master's awarded for partial completion of doctoral program. *Degree requirements:* For master's, thesis, oral and written exams; for doctorate, thesis/dissertation, oral and written exams. *Entrance requirements:* For master's and doctorate, GRE General Test, minimum GPA of 3.0. Additional exam requirements/recommendations for international students: Required—TOEFL. *Faculty research:* Analytical, inorganic, organic, and physical chemistry; iron in asbestos chemistry and carcinogenicity; dicopper complexes; photothermal spectrometry; metal molecule clusters.

Vanderbilt University, Graduate School and School of Medicine, Department of Biochemistry, Nashville, TN 37240-1001. Offers MS, PhD, MD/PhD. *Faculty:* 21 full-time (1 woman). *Students:* 36 full-time (18 women); includes 5 minority (2 Black or African American, non-Hispanic/Latino; 1 Asian, non-Hispanic/Latino; 1 Hispanic/Latino; 1 Two or more races, non-Hispanic/Latino), 3 international. Average age 27. In 2011, 7 degrees awarded. Terminal master's awarded for partial completion of doctoral program. *Degree requirements:* For master's, thesis; for doctorate, thesis/dissertation, preliminary, qualifying, and final exams. *Entrance requirements:* For master's, GRE

Biochemistry

General Test; for doctorate, GRE General Test, GRE Subject Test (recommended). Additional exam requirements/recommendations for international students: Required—TOEFL (minimum score 570 paper-based; 230 computer-based; 88 iBT). *Application deadline:* For fall admission, 1/15 for domestic and international students. Application fee: $0. Electronic applications accepted. *Financial support:* Fellowships with full tuition reimbursements, research assistantships with full tuition reimbursements, Federal Work-Study, institutionally sponsored loans, scholarships/grants, traineeships, and tuition waivers (partial) available. Financial award application deadline: 1/15; financial award applicants required to submit CSS PROFILE or FAFSA. *Faculty research:* Protein chemistry, carcinogenesis, metabolism, toxicology, receptors and signaling, DNA recognition and transcription. *Unit head:* Dr. Peter F. Guengerich, Interim Chair, 615-322-2261, Fax: 615-322-4349, E-mail: f.guengerich@vanderbilt.edu. *Application contact:* Marlene Jayne, Department Administrator and Director of Graduate Studies, 615-322-3318, Fax: 615-322-4349, E-mail: marlene.jayne@vanderbilt.edu. Web site: http://medschool.mc.vanderbilt.edu/biochemistry/.

Vanderbilt University, School of Medicine, Program in Chemical and Physical Biology, Nashville, TN 37240-1001. Offers PhD. *Degree requirements:* For doctorate, comprehensive exam, thesis/dissertation, dissertation defense. *Entrance requirements:* For doctorate, GRE, 3 letters of recommendation, official transcripts. Additional exam requirements/recommendations for international students: Required—TOEFL. Electronic applications accepted. *Faculty research:* Mathematical modeling, enzyme kinetics, structural biology, genomics, proteomics and mass spectrometry.

Virginia Commonwealth University, Medical College of Virginia-Professional Programs, School of Medicine, School of Medicine Graduate Programs, Department of Biochemistry, Richmond, VA 23284-9005. Offers biochemistry (MS, PhD); molecular biology (MS, PhD); MD/PhD. *Degree requirements:* For master's, thesis; for doctorate, thesis/dissertation, comprehensive oral and written exams. *Entrance requirements:* For master's and doctorate, GRE, MCAT or DAT. Electronic applications accepted. *Expenses:* Tuition, state resident: full-time $9133; part-time $507 per credit. Tuition, nonresident: full-time $18,777; part-time $1043 per credit. *Required fees:* $77 per credit. Tuition and fees vary according to degree level, campus/location, program and student level. *Faculty research:* Molecular biology, peptide/protein chemistry, neurochemistry, enzyme mechanisms, macromolecular structure determination.

Virginia Commonwealth University, Program in Pre-Medical Basic Health Sciences, Richmond, VA 23284-9005. Offers anatomy (CBHS); biochemistry (CBHS); human genetics (CBHS); microbiology (CBHS); pharmacology (CBHS); physiology (CBHS). *Entrance requirements:* For degree, GRE, MCAT or DAT, course work in organic chemistry, minimum undergraduate GPA of 2.8. Additional exam requirements/recommendations for international students: Required—TOEFL (minimum score 600 paper-based). Electronic applications accepted. *Expenses:* Tuition, state resident: full-time $9133; part-time $507 per credit. Tuition, nonresident: full-time $18,777; part-time $1043 per credit. *Required fees:* $77 per credit. Tuition and fees vary according to degree level, campus/location, program and student level.

Virginia Polytechnic Institute and State University, Graduate School, College of Agriculture and Life Sciences, Department of Biochemistry, Blacksburg, VA 24061. Offers MSLFS, PhD. *Degree requirements:* For master's, comprehensive exam (for some programs), thesis (for some programs); for doctorate, comprehensive exam (for some programs), thesis/dissertation (for some programs). *Entrance requirements:* For master's and doctorate, GRE. Additional exam requirements/recommendations for international students: Required—TOEFL (minimum score 550 paper-based; 213 computer-based). *Application deadline:* For fall admission, 7/1 for domestic and international students; for spring admission, 12/1 for domestic and international students. Applications are processed on a rolling basis. Application fee: $65. Electronic applications accepted. *Expenses:* Contact institution. *Financial support:* Research assistantships with full tuition reimbursements, teaching assistantships with full tuition reimbursements, career-related internships or fieldwork, Federal Work-Study, scholarships/grants, health care benefits, and unspecified assistantships available. Financial award application deadline: 1/15. *Faculty research:* Molecular biology, molecular entomology, enzymology, signal transduction, protein structure-function. *Unit head:* Dr. Peter J. Kennelly, Unit Head, 540-231-6315, Fax: 540-231-6315, E-mail: pjkennel@vt.edu. *Application contact:* Tim Larson, Information Contact, 540-231-7060, Fax: 540-231-6315, E-mail: tilarson@vt.edu. Web site: http://www.biochem.vt.edu/.

Wake Forest University, School of Medicine and Graduate School of Arts and Sciences, Graduate Programs in Medicine, Department of Biochemistry, Winston-Salem, NC 27109. Offers PhD, MD/PhD. *Degree requirements:* For doctorate, thesis/dissertation. *Entrance requirements:* For doctorate, GRE General Test. Additional exam requirements/recommendations for international students: Required—TOEFL. Electronic applications accepted. *Faculty research:* Biomembranes, cancer, biophysics.

Washington State University, Graduate School, College of Sciences, School of Molecular Biosciences, Program in Biochemistry and Biophysics, Pullman, WA 99164. Offers MS, PhD. *Faculty:* 23 full-time (5 women), 21 part-time/adjunct (4 women). *Students:* 53 full-time (24 women), 9 part-time (3 women); includes 7 minority (4 Asian, non-Hispanic/Latino; 3 Hispanic/Latino), 4 international. Average age 26. 116 applicants, 22% accepted, 15 enrolled. In 2011, 3 master's awarded. Terminal master's awarded for partial completion of doctoral program. *Degree requirements:* For master's, thesis or alternative, oral exam; for doctorate, comprehensive exam, thesis/dissertation, oral exam, written exam. *Entrance requirements:* For master's and doctorate, GRE General Test, minimum GPA of 3.0. Additional exam requirements/recommendations for international students: Required—TOEFL (minimum score 550 paper-based; 213 computer-based). *Application deadline:* For fall admission, 12/15 for domestic and international students. Application fee: $75. Electronic applications accepted. *Financial support:* In 2011–12, 5 fellowships with full tuition reimbursements (averaging $18,384 per year), 11 research assistantships with full tuition reimbursements (averaging $18,384 per year), 10 teaching assistantships with full tuition reimbursements (averaging $18,384 per year) were awarded; career-related internships or fieldwork, Federal Work-Study, institutionally sponsored loans, traineeships, and health care benefits also available. Financial award application deadline: 4/1; financial award applicants required to submit FAFSA. *Faculty research:* Gene regulation, signal transduction, protein export, reproductive biology, DNA repair. *Total annual research expenditures:* $5.8 million. *Unit head:* Dr. John H. Nilson, Director, 509-335-8724, Fax: 509-335-9688, E-mail: jhn@wsu.edu. *Application contact:* Kelly G. McGovern, 509-335-6424, E-mail: mcgnerk@wsu.edu. Web site: http://molecular.biosciences.wsu.edu/.

Washington University in St. Louis, Graduate School of Arts and Sciences, Division of Biology and Biomedical Sciences, Program in Biochemistry, St. Louis, MO 63130-4899. Offers PhD. *Degree requirements:* For doctorate, thesis/dissertation. *Entrance requirements:* For doctorate, GRE General Test, GRE Subject Test. Electronic applications accepted.

Wayne State University, School of Medicine, Department of Biochemistry and Molecular Biology, Detroit, MI 48202. Offers MS, PhD, MD/PhD. *Students:* 29 full-time (17 women), 1 part-time (0 women); includes 4 minority (1 Black or African American, non-Hispanic/Latino; 3 Asian, non-Hispanic/Latino), 16 international. Average age 27. 84 applicants, 10% accepted, 7 enrolled. In 2011, 2 master's, 4 doctorates awarded.

Terminal master's awarded for partial completion of doctoral program. *Degree requirements:* For master's, thesis; for doctorate, thesis/dissertation. *Entrance requirements:* For master's, BA or BS in biology, chemistry, or (if approved) physics or mathematics with minimum GPA of 2.6 from accredited university; three letters of recommendation; personal statement; for doctorate, GRE, undergraduate degree with minimum GPA of 3.0. Additional exam requirements/recommendations for international students: Required—TOEFL (minimum score 600 paper-based; 250 computer-based; 100 iBT). *Application deadline:* For fall admission, 5/1 priority date for domestic students, 5/1 for international students. Application fee: $50. Electronic applications accepted. *Expenses:* Tuition, state resident: part-time $512.85 per credit. Tuition, nonresident: part-time $1132.65 per credit. *Required fees:* $26.60 per credit. $199.65 per semester. Tuition and fees vary according to course load and program. *Financial support:* In 2011–12, 17 students received support, including 1 fellowship with tuition reimbursement available (averaging $18,000 per year), 14 research assistantships with tuition reimbursements available (averaging $21,144 per year); scholarships/grants and unspecified assistantships also available. Financial award application deadline: 2/1. *Faculty research:* Protein structure, molecular biology, molecular genetics, enzymology, x-ray crystallography. *Unit head:* Dr. Bharati Mitra, Interim Chair, 313-577-0400, E-mail: bmitra@med.wayne.edu. *Application contact:* Dr. Marilyn Doscher, Graduate Director, 313-577-1295, E-mail: mdoscher@med.wayne.edu. Web site: http://gradprograms.med.wayne.edu/program-spotlight.php?id=28.

Weill Cornell Medical College, Weill Cornell Graduate School of Medical Sciences, Biochemistry, Cell and Molecular Biology Allied Program, New York, NY 10065. Offers MS, PhD. *Faculty:* 111 full-time (32 women). *Students:* 152 full-time (95 women); includes 19 minority (2 Black or African American, non-Hispanic/Latino; 5 Asian, non-Hispanic/Latino; 8 Hispanic/Latino; 4 Native Hawaiian or other Pacific Islander, non-Hispanic/Latino), 82 international. Average age 22. 374 applicants, 23% accepted, 30 enrolled. In 2011, 2 master's, 19 doctorates awarded. Terminal master's awarded for partial completion of doctoral program. *Degree requirements:* For master's, comprehensive exam; for doctorate, thesis/dissertation, final exam. *Entrance requirements:* For doctorate, GRE General Test, background in genetics, molecular biology, chemistry, or biochemistry. Additional exam requirements/recommendations for international students: Required—TOEFL. *Application deadline:* For fall admission, 12/1 for domestic students. Application fee: $60. Electronic applications accepted. *Expenses: Tuition:* Full-time $46,001. *Financial support:* In 2011–12, 16 fellowships (averaging $22,600 per year) were awarded; scholarships/grants, health care benefits, and stipends (given to all students) also available. *Faculty research:* Molecular structure determination, protein structure, gene structure, stem cell biology, control of gene expression, DNA replication, chromosome maintenance, RNA biosynthesis. *Unit head:* Dr. Kirk Deitsch, Co-Director, 212-746-4976, Fax: 212-746-8906, E-mail: kwd2001@med.cornell.edu. *Application contact:* Rosalia Mora, Program Coordinator, 212-746-6058, Fax: 212-746-8906, E-mail: rmora@med.cornell.edu. Web site: http://weill.cornell.edu/gradschool/program/cell.html.

Weill Cornell Medical College, Weill Cornell Graduate School of Medical Sciences, Tri-Institutional Training Program in Chemical Biology, New York, NY 10065. Offers PhD. Program offered jointly with The Rockefeller University and Sloan-Kettering Institute. *Faculty:* 37 full-time (4 women). *Students:* 42 full-time (15 women); includes 24 minority (20 Asian, non-Hispanic/Latino; 3 Hispanic/Latino; 1 Native Hawaiian or other Pacific Islander, non-Hispanic/Latino). Average age 23. 59 applicants, 27% accepted, 6 enrolled. In 2011, 8 doctorates awarded. *Degree requirements:* For doctorate, comprehensive exam, thesis/dissertation. *Entrance requirements:* For doctorate, GRE General Test, 3 letters of recommendation. Additional exam requirements/recommendations for international students: Required—TOEFL (minimum score 600 paper-based; 250 computer-based; 90 iBT). *Application deadline:* For winter admission, 12/15 for domestic and international students. Application fee: $80. Electronic applications accepted. *Expenses: Tuition:* Full-time $46,001. *Financial support:* In 2011–12, 42 students received support, including 42 fellowships with full tuition reimbursements available (averaging $40,000 per year). *Faculty research:* Bio-organic chemistry, biological chemistry/biochemistry, biophysical chemistry, bio-analytical chemistry, computational chemistry and biology. *Unit head:* Kathleen E. Pickering, Executive Director, 212-746-6049, Fax: 212-746-8992, E-mail: kap2013@med.cornell.edu. *Application contact:* Margie H. Mendoza, Program Coordinator, 212-746-5267, Fax: 212-746-8992, E-mail: mah2036@med.cornell.edu. Web site: http://www.triiprograms.org/tpcb/.

Wesleyan University, Graduate Programs, Department of Chemistry, Middletown, CT 06459. Offers biochemistry (MA, PhD); chemical physics (MA, PhD); inorganic chemistry (MA, PhD); organic chemistry (MA, PhD); physical chemistry (MA, PhD); theoretical chemistry (MA, PhD). Terminal master's awarded for partial completion of doctoral program. *Degree requirements:* For master's, thesis, proposal; for doctorate, thesis/dissertation, proposal. *Entrance requirements:* For doctorate, GRE General Test, 3 recommendations. Additional exam requirements/recommendations for international students: Required—TOEFL. Electronic applications accepted.

Wesleyan University, Graduate Programs, Department of Molecular Biology and Biochemistry, Middletown, CT 06459. Offers biochemistry (PhD); molecular biology (PhD). *Degree requirements:* For doctorate, comprehensive exam, thesis/dissertation. *Entrance requirements:* For doctorate, GRE General Test, GRE Subject Test. Additional exam requirements/recommendations for international students: Required—TOEFL. Electronic applications accepted. *Faculty research:* Genome organization, regulation of gene expression, molecular biology of development, physical biochemistry.

West Virginia University, School of Medicine, Graduate Programs at the Health Sciences Center, Interdisciplinary Graduate Programs in Biomedical Sciences, Program in Biochemistry and Molecular Biology, Morgantown, WV 26506. Offers MS, PhD, MD/PhD. *Degree requirements:* For doctorate, comprehensive exam, thesis/dissertation. *Entrance requirements:* For doctorate, GRE General Test, minimum GPA of 3.0. Additional exam requirements/recommendations for international students: Required—TOEFL. Electronic applications accepted. *Faculty research:* Regulation of gene expression, cell survival mechanisms, signal transduction, regulation of metabolism, sensory neuroscience.

Worcester Polytechnic Institute, Graduate Studies and Research, Department of Chemistry and Biochemistry, Worcester, MA 01609-2280. Offers biochemistry (MS, PhD); chemistry (MS, PhD). Evening/weekend programs available. *Faculty:* 8 full-time (1 woman), 1 part-time/adjunct (0 women). *Students:* 14 full-time (5 women), 16 part-time (4 women); includes 5 minority (3 Asian, non-Hispanic/Latino; 1 Hispanic/Latino; 1 Two or more races, non-Hispanic/Latino), 7 international. 37 applicants, 16% accepted, 3 enrolled. In 2011, 5 degrees awarded. *Degree requirements:* For master's, thesis; for doctorate, comprehensive exam, thesis/dissertation. *Entrance requirements:* For master's and doctorate, GRE General Test, 3 letters of recommendation, statement of purpose. Additional exam requirements/recommendations for international students: Required—TOEFL (minimum score 563 paper-based; 223 computer-based; 84 iBT), IELTS (minimum score 7). *Application deadline:* For fall admission, 1/1 priority date for domestic students, 1/1 for international students; for spring admission, 10/1 priority date for domestic students, 10/1 for international students. Applications are processed on a rolling basis. Application fee: $70. Electronic applications accepted. *Financial support:*

Research assistantships, teaching assistantships, career-related internships or fieldwork, institutionally sponsored loans, scholarships/grants, and unspecified assistantships available. Financial award application deadline: 1/1; financial award applicants required to submit FAFSA. *Faculty research:* Catalysis experimental and computational protein biophysics, biological metals, synthetic methods, surface chemistry, computational chemistry. *Unit head:* Dr. Arne Gericke, Department Head, 508-831-5371, Fax: 508-831-5933, E-mail: agericke@wpi.edu. *Application contact:* Dr. George Kaminski, Graduate Coordinator, 508-831-5371, Fax: 508-831-5933, E-mail: gkaminski@wpi.edu. Web site: http://www.wpi.edu/Academics/Depts/Chemistry/.

Wright State University, School of Graduate Studies, College of Science and Mathematics, Department of Biochemistry and Molecular Biology, Dayton, OH 45435. Offers MS. *Degree requirements:* For master's, thesis. *Entrance requirements:* Additional exam requirements/recommendations for international students: Required—TOEFL. *Faculty research:* Regulation of gene expression, macromolecular structural function, NMR imaging, visual biochemistry.

Yale University, Graduate School of Arts and Sciences, Department of Geology and Geophysics, New Haven, CT 06520. Offers biogeochemistry (PhD); climate dynamics (PhD); geochemistry (PhD); geophysics (PhD); meteorology (PhD); oceanography (PhD); paleontology (PhD); paleooceanography (PhD); petrology (PhD); tectonics (PhD). *Degree requirements:* For doctorate, thesis/dissertation. *Entrance requirements:* For doctorate, GRE General Test. Additional exam requirements/recommendations for international students: Required—TOEFL.

Yale University, Graduate School of Arts and Sciences, Department of Molecular Biophysics and Biochemistry, New Haven, CT 06520. Offers PhD. *Degree requirements:* For doctorate, thesis/dissertation. *Entrance requirements:* For doctorate, GRE General Test, GRE Subject Test.

Yale University, Graduate School of Arts and Sciences, Department of Molecular, Cellular, and Developmental Biology, Program in Biochemistry, Molecular Biology and Chemical Biology, New Haven, CT 06520. Offers PhD. *Degree requirements:* For doctorate, thesis/dissertation. *Entrance requirements:* For doctorate, GRE General Test, GRE Subject Test.

Yale University, School of Medicine and Graduate School of Arts and Sciences, Combined Program in Biological and Biomedical Sciences (BBS), Molecular Biophysics and Biochemistry Track, New Haven, CT 06520. Offers PhD, MD/PhD. *Degree requirements:* For doctorate, thesis/dissertation. *Entrance requirements:* For doctorate, GRE General Test. Additional exam requirements/recommendations for international students: Required—TOEFL. Electronic applications accepted.

Youngstown State University, Graduate School, College of Science, Technology, Engineering and Mathematics, Department of Chemistry, Youngstown, OH 44555-0001. Offers analytical chemistry (MS); biochemistry (MS); chemistry education (MS); inorganic chemistry (MS); organic chemistry (MS); physical chemistry (MS). Part-time programs available. *Degree requirements:* For master's, thesis. *Entrance requirements:* For master's, bachelor's degree in chemistry, minimum GPA of 2.7. Additional exam requirements/recommendations for international students: Required—TOEFL. *Faculty research:* Analysis of antioxidants, chromatography, defects and disorder in crystalline oxides, hydrogen bonding, novel organic and organometallic materials.

UNIVERSITY OF NEVADA, RENO

Department of Biochemistry and Molecular Biology
Graduate Programs in Biochemistry

Programs of Study

The Department of Biochemistry and Molecular Biology at the University of Nevada, Reno (UNR), offers a challenging and broad-based graduate program of research and course studies leading to the M.S. or Ph.D. in biochemistry. The aim of the graduate program is to train scientists for critical analysis and solution of biochemical problems at the molecular level. The diverse research areas represented by the faculty have the common theme of understanding the structures and roles of macromolecules in complex biological systems. Students benefit from exposure to faculty members appointed in both the College of Agriculture, Biotechnology and Natural Resources (CABNR) and the School of Medicine as well as the Desert Research Institute. They have an opportunity for multidisciplinary interactions with graduate students and faculty members in related departments, including the Departments of Physiology and Anatomy; Microbiology and Immunology; Pharmacology and Cell Biology; Chemistry; Biological Sciences; and Agriculture, Nutrition, and Veterinary Sciences. The academic environment is lively and highly interactive, as represented by a diverse, interdisciplinary seminar program sponsored in conjunction with other related departments. The program of study includes lecture courses, laboratory rotations, journal club presentations and discussion groups, a qualifying written and oral examination, thesis or dissertation research, and one or more semesters of teaching experience. First-year students take a core curriculum and gain research experience by rotating through student-selected research laboratories. Laboratory rotations facilitate the choice of a dissertation adviser. Doctoral and master's research projects are selected by the student in consultation with a major dissertation adviser and an advisory committee. The requirements for the Ph.D. can generally be completed in four or five years. The program, which is designed to prepare students for careers in research and/or teaching, emphasizes a cooperative, personal working environment between students and members of the faculty.

Faculty interests cover a wide range of disciplines in the biomedical sciences and life sciences. Research interests include metagenomics analysis of extreme microbial ecosystems; environmental and biotic stress functional genomics, rubber, and vitamin biosynthesis, and biofuel feedstock production in plants and algae; functional genomics of insect peptide and lipid hormones and pheromones, and lipid metabolism; insect chromatin structure and remodeling; muscle protein enzymology, structure, and signaling; muscle contraction and excitation-contraction coupling; cell motility; insulin signaling pathways and glucose transport; receptor structure and transmembrane signal transduction mechanisms; membrane-cytoskeletal interactions; oxygen toxicity; mammalian lipid metabolism in cancer; receptor-mediated endocytosis; and computational methods in database mining and macromolecular structure. Each faculty member directs an active research program and is dedicated to training postdoctoral associates and doctoral- and master's-level graduate students as well as undergraduate students. Faculty members are funded by the National Institutes of Health, National Science Foundation, Department of Energy, United States Department of Agriculture, and other extramural sources of about $4 million per year.

Research Facilities

Research in UNR's Department of Biochemistry and Molecular Biology is supported by state-of-the-art approaches to genomics, proteomics, gene transfer, recombinant techniques, bioinformatics, computational biology, electrophysiology, spectroscopy, single-molecule biophysics, protein analytical biochemistry, and mass spectrometry, among others. Facilities and technical staff members are available for analysis of samples by electron, confocal, two-photon confocal, single-molecule, and atomic force microscopy; flow cytometry; mass spectrometry; high-throughput DNA sequence and mRNA, and protein expression analysis. In addition, research centers for genomics, monoclonal antibody production, construction of viral vectors, calcium imaging, proteomics analysis, bioinformatics and molecular modeling including more than 1 TB of RAM for computational use through the University Research Grid. Transgenic mouse generation and housing are also available.

The Mathewson-IGT Knowledge Center that integrates a modern library with extensive digital retrieval of information serves as the primary center for information resources and services in support of teaching and research. The Savitt Medical Library is located in close proximity to the Biochemistry Department. The libraries' Web-based information delivery system provides access to the libraries' physical collections (more than 1.2 million books, 20,000 videos and DVDs, and 3.7 million microforms); course reserves, most of which are available online; full-text articles from a growing number of electronic journals and magazines (currently around 38,000); approximately 115,000 electronic books; more than 417 general and specialized databases; and high-quality Internet resources selected and organized for the UNR community.

Financial Aid

Graduate fellowships, assistantships, and research awards are available to students admitted to the Graduate School on a competitive basis. Both fellowships and assistantships carry a stipend and a tuition waiver. Assistantship stipends currently start at $22,000. Information is available from the Graduate School (http://www.unr.edu/grad/) or the Department of Biochemistry and Molecular Biology (http://www.ag.unr.edu/bmb/).

Cost of Study

Nevada residents pay registration fees only. The registration fee is $246 per credit. Nonresidents pay tuition in addition to registration fees. In 2012–13, part-time tuition (1–6 credits) is $263 per credit and full-time tuition (7 credits or more) is $6955 per semester. Students awarded research fellowships or teaching assistantships are entitled to a partial fee waiver of nonresident tuition rates and pay only $187 per credit. Residents of neighboring Arizona and California counties are eligible for reduced "Good Neighbor" nonresident tuition fees of $482 per credit. Additional fees and student insurance costs also apply.

Living and Housing Costs

A room in the residence halls ranges from $4750 to $7450 per academic year, depending on location. Meal plans range from $3708 to $4768. A listing of off-campus housing—including rooms, apartments, and houses—is also available.

Student Group

There are approximately 30 students enrolled in the graduate biochemistry program within a larger cohort of approximately 100 graduate students in molecular biosciences disciplines.

Student Outcomes

Ph.D. graduates from the Department of Biochemistry and Molecular Biology now hold professional positions in universities, industry, and government, including federal science administration. These include faculty members at leading universities and medical schools and research scientists at pharmaceutical companies. Many other former students hold positions in biotechnology start-up companies.

Location

The University of Nevada, Reno, is a center of innovation and energy for the thriving Reno-Sparks metropolitan area. Its 290-acre campus of rolling hills features a blend of ivy-covered buildings, sweeping lawns, and functional, progressive architecture. Reno-Sparks is in an unusually attractive natural setting. It is bounded on the west by the majestic Sierra Nevada range and on the east by a rolling basin and range province. Reno-Sparks benefits from a comfortable climate marked by generally cool and dry weather with more than 300 sunny days per year. The area is a haven for those who love the four seasons and outdoor activities. Recreational activities are easy to find. Students are within less than an hour's driving distance of the many world-class ski resorts of Lake Tahoe and the historic Western realm of Virginia City.

The University

The University of Nevada, Reno, is a constitutionally established land-grant university founded in 1874. The University served the state of Nevada as its only state-supported institution of higher education for almost seventy-five years. In that historical role, it has emerged as a doctoral-granting university that focuses its resources on doing a select number of things well. A diverse student body strengthens the academic atmosphere for the cultural and intellectual development of the student. By fostering creative and scholarly activity, the University encourages and supports faculty research and the application of that research to state and national problems. UNR is growing rapidly and currently enrolls more than 17,000 students, including 3,300 enrolled in graduate programs. The University houses a School of Medicine with a class of 65 medical students. The Northwest Commission on Colleges and Universities (NWCCU) accredits the University.

Applying

There is a $90 nonrefundable graduate program application fee. All GPA and test score information must be included on the application. Interested students should submit two copies of their official undergraduate and graduate school transcripts directly from the institutions previously attended to the

University of Nevada, Reno

University of Nevada, Reno. Applicants who are applying must also submit GRE scores, three letters of recommendation, and a statement of purpose as part of the online application process. All accepted students are automatically granted a graduate or teaching assistantship during the first year.

Correspondence and Information

Dr. John C. Cushman
Graduate Program Director
Department of Biochemistry and Molecular Biology
University of Nevada, Reno
1664 North Virginia Street, MS 330
Reno, Nevada 89557-0330
Phone: 775-784-1918
Fax: 775-784-1419
E-mail: jcushman@unr.edu
Web site: http://www.ag.unr.edu/biochemistry/

THE FACULTY AND THEIR RESEARCH

Josh E. Baker, Associate Professor; Ph.D., Minnesota, Twin Cities, 1999. Use of optical traps, fluorescence microscopy, and single-molecule imaging techniques to study the molecular basis for cell motility.

Gary Blomquist, Professor and Department Chair; Ph.D., Montana State, 1973. Biosynthesis and molecular biology of pheromone production; insect hydrocarbons and lipid metabolism.

Grant R. Cramer, Professor; Ph.D., California, Davis, 1985. Systems biology of grapes; abiotic stress effects on vines and berries; influence of water deficit on wine flavors.

Christine Cremo, Professor; Ph.D., Oregon State, 1983. Structure, function, and regulation of motor proteins in smooth muscle.

John C. Cushman, Professor; Ph.D., Rutgers, 1987. Molecular and evolutionary genetics of Crassulacean acid metabolism; functional genomics of environmental stress tolerance in plants; biofuel production from algal and plant feedstocks.

Hanna Damke, Assistant Professor; Ph.D., Marburg (Germany), 1992. Role of the signaling GTPase dynamin in coordinating endocytosis with other cellular functions to maintain homeostasis.

Patricia Ellison, Associate Professor; Ph.D., Sheffield, 1981. Regulation of smooth muscle myosins by phosphorylation and dephosphorylation; interaction between myosin and actin, myosin light chain kinase, and phosphatase.

Kevin Facemyer, Research Assistant Professor; Ph.D., Washington State, 1996. Computational analysis of motor proteins; development of novel computational methods of detecting and quantifying interfacial binding energy.

Joseph J. Grzymski, Adjunct Assistant Research Professor, Desert Research Institute; Ph.D., Rutgers, 2002. Computational and synthetic biology; genome and protein adaptations to the environment; protein cost minimization.

Jeffrey Harper, Professor; Ph.D., Washington (St. Louis), 1985. Calcium signaling in plants; engineering plants to better tolerate abiotic and biotic stress; plant mineral nutrition.

Christie Howard, Associate Professor; Ph.D., Michigan State, 1996. Director of the BS-MS Biotechnology program and faculty advisor for the University of Nevada International Genetically Engineered Machine (iGEM) Program.

Susan W. Liebman, Research Professor; Ph.D., Rochester, 1974. Using yeast genetics and molecular biology to study protein misfolding diseases.

Cynthia Corley Mastick, Associate Professor; Ph.D., Carnegie Mellon, 1990. Cellular mechanisms of insulin action and peripheral insulin resistance; molecular mechanisms of signal transduction and signaling specificity; cellular basis of insulin action and peripheral insulin resistance; regulation of glucose and lipid uptake/metabolism; cell biology of adipocytes and muscle.

Kunio Misono, Adjunct Professor; Ph.D., Vanderbilt, 1978. Structure of cell membrane receptors and signal transduction mechanisms.

Alison Murray, Adjunct Associate Research Professor, Desert Research Institute; Ph.D., California, Santa Barbara, 1998. Metagenomics of aquatic and symbiotic microbial communities in Antarctic and deep sea environments; environmental adaptation, biogeochemical cycling, and metabolic plasticity.

Ronald S. Pardini, Professor and Interim Dean of the College of Agriculture, Biotechnology, and Natural Resources; and Director, Nevada Agriculture Experiment Station; Ph.D., Illinois, 1965. Nutritional intervention with omega-3 fatty acids in the treatment of cancer; understanding mechanisms of omega-3 fatty acid–induced growth inhibition and enhanced response to cancer therapy.

David Quilici, Manager, Nevada Proteomics Center; Ph.D., Nevada, Reno, 1997. Identifying unknown compounds; quantifying known compounds; elucidating structure and chemical properties of molecules.

Kathleen M. Schegg, Research Biochemist, Nevada Proteomics Center; Ph.D., Nevada, Reno, 1980. Proteomics; 2-D gel separation of proteins; amino acid analysis; protein sequencing; peptide synthesis.

Karen A. Schlauch, Associate Professor; Ph.D., New Mexico State, 1998. Bioinformatic analysis of gene interactions and biological expression data using novel clustering algorithms and graph-theoretic approaches; mathematical models.

David A. Schooley, Professor; Ph.D., Stanford, 1968. Structural, biosynthetic, and metabolic studies on physiologically active materials, chiefly insect juvenile hormones and peptide hormones; mechanism of signal transduction of peptide hormones.

David Shintani, Associate Professor; Ph.D., Michigan State, 1996. Plant biochemistry and genome research; metabolic and developmental regulation of plant isoprenoid metabolism; vitamin and cofactor biosynthesis in plants.

Claus Tittiger, Associate Professor; Ph.D., Queen's at Kingston, 1994. Insect molecular biology and genomics; isoprenoid metabolism and pheromone biosynthesis; cytochromes P450; hydrocarbon and lipid metabolism.

Maria L. Valencik, Associate Professor; Ph.D., UCLA, 1991. Cardiovascular research; integrins and natriuretic peptides in cardiac myocytes.

William H. Welch, Professor (Emeritus); Ph.D., Kansas, 1968. Molecular modeling of enzymes and ion channels; enzymology; ryanodine receptor function; immunology of pathogen capsules.

The 290-acre University of Nevada, Reno, campus is located next to downtown Reno, pictured here against the eastern slope of the Sierra Nevada mountain range.

The Reno-Sparks metropolitan area is located within 1 hour of Lake Tahoe, nicknamed the "Jewel of the Sierra" for its pristine, crystal-clear waters and many summertime recreational opportunities. More than a dozen world-class ski resorts surround Lake Tahoe for winter sports activities.

Section 4
Biophysics

This section contains a directory of institutions offering graduate work in biophysics, followed by an in-depth entry submitted by an institution that chose to prepare a detailed program description. Additional information about programs listed in the directory but not augmented by an in-depth entry may be obtained by writing directly to the dean of a graduate school or chair of a department at the address given in the directory.

For programs offering related work, see also in this book *Allied Health; Biochemistry; Biological and Biomedical Sciences; Cell, Molecular, and Structural Biology; Optometry and Vision Sciences; Neuroscience and Neurobiology; Physiology;* and *Public Health.* In the other guides in this series:

Graduate Programs in the Physical Sciences, Mathematics, Agricultural Sciences, the Environment & Natural Resources

See *Chemistry* and *Physics*

Graduate Programs in Engineering & Applied Sciences

See *Agricultural Engineering and Bioengineering* and *Biomedical Engineering and Biotechnology*

CONTENTS

Biophysics

Albert Einstein College of Medicine, Graduate Division of Biomedical Sciences, Department of Physiology and Biophysics, Bronx, NY 10461. Offers PhD, MD/PhD. *Degree requirements:* For doctorate, thesis/dissertation. *Entrance requirements:* For doctorate, GRE General Test. Additional exam requirements/recommendations for international students: Required—TOEFL. *Faculty research:* Biophysical and biochemical basis of body function at the subcellular, cellular, organ, and whole-body level.

Baylor College of Medicine, Graduate School of Biomedical Sciences, Department of Molecular Physiology and Biophysics, Houston, TX 77030-3498. Offers cardiovascular sciences (PhD); molecular physiology and biophysics (PhD); MD/PhD. *Faculty:* 110 full-time (23 women). *Students:* 30 full-time (12 women); includes 7 minority (4 Black or African American, non-Hispanic/Latino; 2 Asian, non-Hispanic/Latino; 1 Hispanic/Latino), 9 international. Average age 27. 39 applicants, 26% accepted, 4 enrolled. In 2011, 3 doctorates awarded. *Degree requirements:* For doctorate, thesis/dissertation, public defense. *Entrance requirements:* For doctorate, GRE General Test, GRE Subject Test (strongly recommended), minimum GPA of 3.0. Additional exam requirements/recommendations for international students: Required—TOEFL. *Application deadline:* For fall admission, 1/1 priority date for domestic students. Electronic applications accepted. *Financial support:* In 2011–12, 10 fellowships with full tuition reimbursements (averaging $29,000 per year), 20 research assistantships with full tuition reimbursements (averaging $29,000 per year) were awarded; career-related internships or fieldwork, Federal Work-Study, institutionally sponsored loans, health care benefits, and scholarships (to all students unless there are grant funds available to pay tuition) also available. Financial award applicants required to submit FAFSA. *Faculty research:* Cardiovascular disease; skeletal muscle disease (myasthenia gravis, muscular dystrophy, malignant hyperthermia, central core disease); cancer; Alzheimer's disease; developmental diseases of the nervous system, eye and heart; diabetes; motor neuron disease (amyotrophic lateral sclerosis and spinal muscular atrophy); asthma; autoimmune diseases. *Unit head:* Dr. Robia Pautler, Co-Director, 713-798-3892, E-mail: rpautler@bcm.edu. *Application contact:* Dr. Steen Pedersen, Co-Director, 713-798-3888, E-mail: pedersen@bcm.edu. Web site: http://www.bcm.edu/physio/.

Boston University, Graduate School of Arts and Sciences, Program in Cellular Biophysics, Boston, MA 02215. Offers PhD. *Students:* 8 full-time (6 women); includes 3 minority (1 Black or African American, non-Hispanic/Latino; 1 Asian, non-Hispanic/Latino; 1 Hispanic/Latino). Average age 25. 6 applicants, 0% accepted. In 2011, 4 doctorates awarded. *Degree requirements:* For doctorate, one foreign language, comprehensive exam, thesis/dissertation. *Entrance requirements:* For doctorate, GRE General Test, GRE Subject Test, 3 letters of recommendation. Additional exam requirements/recommendations for international students: Required—TOEFL (minimum score 550 paper-based; 213 computer-based; 84 iBT). *Application deadline:* For fall admission, 7/1 for domestic and international students; for spring admission, 10/15 for domestic and international students. Application fee: $70. Electronic applications accepted. *Expenses: Tuition:* Full-time $40,848; part-time $1276 per credit hour. *Required fees:* $572; $286 per semester. *Financial support:* Career-related internships or fieldwork available. Support available to part-time students. Financial award application deadline: 1/15; financial award applicants required to submit FAFSA. *Unit head:* Dr. M. Carter Cornwall, Director, 617-638-4256, Fax: 617-638-4273, E-mail: cornwall@bu.edu. *Application contact:* Rebekah Alexander, Assistant Director of Admissions and Financial Aid, 617-353-2696, Fax: 617-358-5492, E-mail: grs@bu.edu. Web site: http://www.bu.edu/academics/grs/programs/cellular-biophysics/.

Boston University, School of Medicine, Division of Graduate Medical Sciences, Department of Physiology and Biophysics, Boston, MA 02118. Offers MA, PhD, MD/PhD. Part-time programs available. *Faculty:* 21 full-time (6 women), 1 part-time/adjunct. *Students:* 14 full-time (7 women), 3 part-time (1 woman); includes 3 minority (2 Asian, non-Hispanic/Latino; 1 Hispanic/Latino), 5 international. Average age 26. 18 applicants, 44% accepted, 4 enrolled. In 2011, 1 master's, 4 doctorates awarded. Terminal master's awarded for partial completion of doctoral program. *Degree requirements:* For master's, thesis, qualifying exam; for doctorate, thesis/dissertation, qualifying exam. *Entrance requirements:* For master's and doctorate, GRE General Test, GRE Subject Test (strongly recommended). Additional exam requirements/recommendations for international students: Required—TOEFL. *Application deadline:* For fall admission, 1/15 priority date for domestic students; for spring admission, 10/15 priority date for domestic students. Application fee: $75. Electronic applications accepted. *Expenses: Tuition:* Full-time $40,848; part-time $1276 per credit hour. *Required fees:* $572; $286 per semester. *Financial support:* In 2011–12, 5 research assistantships (averaging $30,500 per year) were awarded; fellowships, scholarships/grants, and traineeships also available. *Faculty research:* X-ray scattering, NMR spectroscopy, protein crystallography, structural electron microscopy, molecular modeling. *Unit head:* Dr. David Atkinson, Chairman, 617-638-4015, Fax: 617-638-4041, E-mail: atkinson@bu.edu. *Application contact:* Dr. Esther Bullitt, 617-638-5037, E-mail: bullitt@bu.edu. Web site: http://www.bumc.bu.edu/phys-biophys/.

Brandeis University, Graduate School of Arts and Sciences, Program in Biochemistry and Biophysics, Waltham, MA 02454. Offers biochemistry and biophysics (PhD); quantitative biology (PhD). Part-time programs available. *Faculty:* 9 full-time (2 women), 1 (woman) part-time/adjunct. *Students:* 31 full-time (12 women); includes 4 minority (3 Asian, non-Hispanic/Latino; 1 Hispanic/Latino), 7 international. 75 applicants, 24% accepted, 4 enrolled. In 2011, 6 doctorates awarded. Terminal master's awarded for partial completion of doctoral program. *Degree requirements:* For doctorate, thesis/dissertation, qualifying exams; teaching requirement. *Entrance requirements:* For doctorate, GRE General Test, resume, 3 letters of recommendation, statement of purpose, transcript(s). Additional exam requirements/recommendations for international students: Required—TOEFL (minimum score 600 paper-based; 250 computer-based; 100 iBT); Recommended—IELTS (minimum score 7). *Application deadline:* For fall admission, 1/15 priority date for domestic students. Application fee: $75. Electronic applications accepted. *Financial support:* In 2011–12, 7 fellowships with full tuition reimbursements (averaging $29,580 per year), 14 research assistantships with full tuition reimbursements (averaging $29,580 per year), teaching assistantships with partial tuition reimbursements (averaging $3,200 per year) were awarded; career-related internships or fieldwork, scholarships/grants, health care benefits, tuition waivers (full and partial), and unspecified assistantships also available. Support available to part-time students. Financial award application deadline: 4/15; financial award applicants required to submit FAFSA. *Faculty research:* Macromolecular chemistry, structure and function, biochemistry, biophysics, biological macromolecules. *Unit head:* Prof. Christopher Miller, Director of Graduate Studies, 781-736-3100, Fax: 781-736-3107, E-mail: cmiller@brandeis.edu. *Application contact:* Carol MacKenzie, Department Administrator, 781-736-3100, Fax: 781-736-3107, E-mail: mackenzie@brandeis.edu. Web site: http://www.brandeis.edu/gsas/programs/bio.html.

California Institute of Technology, Division of Biology, Program in Cell Biology and Biophysics, Pasadena, CA 91125-0001. Offers PhD. *Degree requirements:* For doctorate, thesis/dissertation, qualifying exam. *Entrance requirements:* For doctorate, GRE General Test.

Carnegie Mellon University, Mellon College of Science, Department of Biological Sciences, Pittsburgh, PA 15213-3891. Offers biochemistry (PhD); biophysics (PhD); cell biology (PhD); computational biology (MS, PhD); developmental biology (PhD); genetics (PhD); molecular biology (PhD); neuroscience (PhD). *Degree requirements:* For doctorate, comprehensive exam, thesis/dissertation. *Entrance requirements:* For doctorate, GRE General Test, GRE Subject Test, interview. Electronic applications accepted. *Faculty research:* Genetic structure, function, and regulation; protein structure and function; biological membranes; biological spectroscopy.

Carnegie Mellon University, Mellon College of Science, Department of Chemistry, Pittsburgh, PA 15213-3891. Offers biotechnology and management (MS); chemistry (PhD), including bioinorganic, bioorganic, organic and materials, biophysics and spectroscopy, computational and theoretical, polymer; colloids, polymers and surfaces (MS). Part-time programs available. Terminal master's awarded for partial completion of doctoral program. *Degree requirements:* For doctorate, thesis/dissertation, departmental qualifying and oral exams, teaching experience. *Entrance requirements:* For master's, GRE General Test; for doctorate, GRE General Test, GRE Subject Test. Additional exam requirements/recommendations for international students: Required—TOEFL. Electronic applications accepted. *Faculty research:* Physical and theoretical chemistry, chemical synthesis, biophysical/bioinorganic chemistry.

Case Western Reserve University, School of Medicine and School of Graduate Studies, Graduate Programs in Medicine, Department of Physiology and Biophysics, Cleveland, OH 44106. Offers cell and molecular physiology (MS); cell physiology (PhD); molecular/cellular biophysics (PhD); physiology and biophysics (PhD); systems physiology (PhD); MD/PhD. Terminal master's awarded for partial completion of doctoral program. *Degree requirements:* For master's, thesis; for doctorate, thesis/dissertation. *Entrance requirements:* For master's, GRE General Test, minimum GPA of 3.28; for doctorate, GRE General Test, minimum GPA of 3.6. Additional exam requirements/recommendations for international students: Required—TOEFL. Electronic applications accepted. *Faculty research:* Cardiovascular physiology, calcium metabolism, epithelial cell biology.

See Display on page 450 and Close-Up on page 461.

Clemson University, Graduate School, College of Engineering and Science, Department of Physics and Astronomy, Clemson, SC 29634. Offers physics (MS, PhD), including astronomy and astrophysics, atmospheric physics, biophysics. Part-time programs available. *Faculty:* 27 full-time (3 women). *Students:* 67 full-time (21 women); includes 3 minority (2 Black or African American, non-Hispanic/Latino; 1 Hispanic/Latino), 27 international. Average age 27. 133 applicants, 75% accepted, 31 enrolled. In 2011, 4 master's, 6 doctorates awarded. Terminal master's awarded for partial completion of doctoral program. *Median time to degree:* Of those who began their doctoral program in fall 2003, 100% received their degree in 8 years or less. *Degree requirements:* For master's, thesis or alternative; for doctorate, thesis/dissertation. *Entrance requirements:* For master's and doctorate, GRE General Test. Additional exam requirements/recommendations for international students: Required—TOEFL. *Application deadline:* For fall admission, 1/15 priority date for domestic students; for spring admission, 9/15 priority date for domestic students. Applications are processed on a rolling basis. Application fee: $70 ($80 for international students). Electronic applications accepted. *Financial support:* In 2011–12, 58 students received support, including 1 fellowship with full and partial tuition reimbursement available (averaging $8,000 per year), 24 research assistantships with partial tuition reimbursements available (averaging $13,653 per year), 50 teaching assistantships with partial tuition reimbursements available (averaging $13,265 per year); career-related internships or fieldwork, institutionally sponsored loans, scholarships/grants, health care benefits, and unspecified assistantships also available. Support available to part-time students. Financial award application deadline: 6/1; financial award applicants required to submit FAFSA. *Faculty research:* Radiation physics, solid-state physics, nuclear physics, radar and lidar studies of atmosphere. Total annual research expenditures: $2.6 million. *Unit head:* Dr. Peter Barnes, Chair, 864-656-3419, Fax: 864-656-0805, E-mail: peterb@clemson.edu. *Application contact:* Graduate Coordinator, 864-656-6702, Fax: 864-656-0805, E-mail: physgradinfo-l@clemson.edu. Web site: http://physicsnt.clemson.edu/.

Columbia University, College of Physicians and Surgeons, Department of Biochemistry and Molecular Biophysics, New York, NY 10032. Offers biochemistry and molecular biophysics (M Phil, PhD); biophysics (PhD); MD/PhD. Only candidates for the PhD are admitted. *Degree requirements:* For doctorate, one foreign language, thesis/dissertation. *Entrance requirements:* For master's and doctorate, GRE General Test. Additional exam requirements/recommendations for international students: Required—TOEFL.

Columbia University, College of Physicians and Surgeons, Department of Physiology and Cellular Biophysics, New York, NY 10032. Offers M Phil, MA, PhD, MD/PhD. Only candidates for the PhD are admitted. Terminal master's awarded for partial completion of doctoral program. *Degree requirements:* For doctorate, thesis/dissertation. *Entrance requirements:* For master's and doctorate, GRE General Test. Additional exam requirements/recommendations for international students: Required—TOEFL. *Faculty research:* Membrane physiology, cellular biology, cardiovascular physiology, neurophysiology.

Columbia University, College of Physicians and Surgeons, Integrated Program in Cellular, Molecular, Structural and Genetic Studies, New York, NY 10032. Offers PhD. Terminal master's awarded for partial completion of doctoral program. *Degree requirements:* For doctorate, thesis/dissertation. *Entrance requirements:* For doctorate, GRE General Test, GRE Subject Test. Additional exam requirements/recommendations for international students: Required—TOEFL. *Expenses:* Contact institution. *Faculty research:* Transcription, macromolecular sorting, gene expression during development, cellular interaction.

Cornell University, Graduate School, Graduate Fields of Agriculture and Life Sciences, Field of Biochemistry, Molecular and Cell Biology, Ithaca, NY 14853-0001. Offers biochemistry (PhD); biophysics (PhD); cell biology (PhD); molecular and cell biology (PhD); molecular biology (PhD). *Faculty:* 62 full-time (17 women). *Students:* 91 full-time (46 women); includes 12 minority (1 Black or African American, non-Hispanic/Latino; 8 Asian, non-Hispanic/Latino; 2 Hispanic/Latino; 1 Two or more races, non-Hispanic/Latino), 34 international. Average age 26. 247 applicants, 8% accepted, 17 enrolled. In 2011, 11 doctorates awarded. *Degree requirements:* For doctorate, comprehensive exam, thesis/dissertation, 2 semesters of teaching experience. *Entrance requirements:* For doctorate, GRE General Test, GRE Subject Test (biology, chemistry, physics,

biochemistry, cell and molecular biology), 3 letters of recommendation. Additional exam requirements/recommendations for international students: Required—TOEFL (minimum score 600 paper-based; 250 computer-based; 77 iBT). *Application deadline:* For fall admission, 1/5 for domestic students. Application fee: $95. Electronic applications accepted. *Financial support:* In 2011–12, 88 students received support, including 26 fellowships with full tuition reimbursements available, 46 research assistantships with full tuition reimbursements available, 14 teaching assistantships with full tuition reimbursements available; institutionally sponsored loans, scholarships/grants, health care benefits, tuition waivers (full and partial), and unspecified assistantships also available. Financial award applicants required to submit FAFSA. *Faculty research:* Biophysics, structural biology. *Unit head:* Director of Graduate Studies, 607-255-2100, Fax: 607-255-2100. *Application contact:* Graduate Field Assistant, 607-255-2100, Fax: 607-255-2100, E-mail: bmcb@cornell.edu. Web site: http://www.gradschool.cornell.edu/fields.php?id-43&a-2.

Cornell University, Graduate School, Graduate Fields of Agriculture and Life Sciences, Graduate Field of Biophysics, Ithaca, NY 14853-0001. Offers PhD. *Faculty:* 32 full-time (4 women). *Students:* 18 full-time (8 women); includes 2 minority (both Asian, non-Hispanic/Latino), 5 international. Average age 26. 13 applicants, 31% accepted, 4 enrolled. In 2011, 5 doctorates awarded. *Degree requirements:* For doctorate, comprehensive exam, thesis/dissertation. *Entrance requirements:* For doctorate, GRE General Test, GRE Subject Test (physics or chemistry preferred), 3 letters of recommendation. Additional exam requirements/recommendations for international students: Required—TOEFL (minimum score 550 paper-based; 213 computer-based; 77 iBT). *Application deadline:* For fall admission, 1/15 for domestic students. Application fee: $95. Electronic applications accepted. *Financial support:* In 2011–12, 2 fellowships with full tuition reimbursements, 8 research assistantships with full tuition reimbursements, 1 teaching assistantship with full tuition reimbursement were awarded; institutionally sponsored loans, scholarships/grants, health care benefits, tuition waivers (full and partial), and unspecified assistantships also available. Financial award applicants required to submit FAFSA. *Faculty research:* Protein structure and function, biomolecular and cellular function, membrane biophysics, signal transduction, computational biology. *Unit head:* Director of Graduate Studies, 607-255-2100, E-mail: biophysics@cornell.edu. *Application contact:* Graduate Field Assistant, 610-255-2100, E-mail: biophysics@cornell.edu. Web site: http://www.gradschool.cornell.edu/fields.php?id-68&a-2.

Dalhousie University, Faculty of Medicine, Department of Physiology and Biophysics, Halifax, NS B3H 1X5, Canada. Offers M Sc, PhD, M Sc/PhD. *Degree requirements:* For master's, thesis; for doctorate, thesis/dissertation. *Entrance requirements:* For master's and doctorate, GRE Subject Test (for international students). Additional exam requirements/recommendations for international students: Required—1 of 5 approved tests: TOEFL, IELTS, CANTEST, CAEL, Michigan English Language Assessment Battery. Electronic applications accepted. *Faculty research:* Computer modeling, reproductive and endocrine physiology, cardiovascular physiology, neurophysiology, membrane biophysics.

East Carolina University, Graduate School, Thomas Harriot College of Arts and Sciences, Department of Physics, Greenville, NC 27858-4353. Offers applied physics (MS); biomedical physics (PhD); health physics (MS); medical physics (MS). Part-time programs available. *Degree requirements:* For master's, one foreign language, comprehensive exam. *Entrance requirements:* For master's, GRE General Test. Additional exam requirements/recommendations for international students: Required—TOEFL. *Application deadline:* Applications are processed on a rolling basis. Application fee: $50. *Expenses:* Tuition, state resident: full-time $3557; part-time $444.63 per semester hour. Tuition, nonresident: full-time $14,351; part-time $1793.88 per semester hour. *Required fees:* $2016; $252 per semester hour. Part-time tuition and fees vary according to course load, campus/location and program. *Financial support:* Research assistantships with partial tuition reimbursements, teaching assistantships with partial tuition reimbursements, and Federal Work-Study available. Support available to part-time students. Financial award application deadline: 6/1. *Unit head:* Dr. John Sutherland, Chair, 252-328-2023, E-mail: sutherlandj@ecu.edu. *Application contact:* Dean of Graduate School, 252-328-6012, Fax: 252-328-6071, E-mail: gradschool@ecu.edu. Web site: http://www.ecu.edu/cs-cas/physics/Graduate-Program.cfm#.

Emory University, Laney Graduate School, Department of Physics, Atlanta, GA 30322-1100. Offers biophysics (PhD); experimental condensed matter physics (PhD); theoretical and computational statistical physics (PhD); MS/PhD. *Faculty:* 19 full-time (2 women). *Students:* 17 full-time (4 women); includes 2 minority (1 Black or African American, non-Hispanic/Latino; 1 Hispanic/Latino), 13 international. Average age 24. 48 applicants, 27% accepted, 10 enrolled. *Degree requirements:* For doctorate, thesis/dissertation, qualifier proposal. *Entrance requirements:* For doctorate, GRE General Test, minimum GPA of 3.0. Additional exam requirements/recommendations for international students: Required—TOEFL (minimum score 600 paper-based). *Application deadline:* For fall admission, 1/3 priority date for domestic students, 1/3 for international students. Application fee: $50. Electronic applications accepted. *Expenses:* Tuition: Full-time $34,800. *Required fees:* $1300. *Financial support:* In 2011–12, 17 students received support. Fellowships, teaching assistantships, institutionally sponsored loans, scholarships/grants, health care benefits, and tuition waivers (full) available. Financial award application deadline: 1/3; financial award applicants required to submit FAFSA. *Faculty research:* Experimental studies of the structure and function of metalloproteins, soft condensed matter, granular materials, biophotonics and fluorescence correlation spectroscopy, single molecule studies of DNA-protein systems. *Total annual research expenditures:* $1.5 million. *Unit head:* Kurt Warncke, Chair, 404-727-4296, Fax: 404-727-0873, E-mail: kwarncke@physics.emory.edu. *Application contact:* Stefan Boettcher, Director of Graduate Studies, 404-727-4298, Fax: 404-727-0873, E-mail: sboettc@emory.edu. Web site: http://www.physics.emory.edu.

Georgetown University, Graduate School of Arts and Sciences, Programs in Biomedical Sciences, Department of Physiology and Biophysics, Washington, DC 20057. Offers MS, PhD, MD/PhD. *Degree requirements:* For doctorate, thesis/dissertation. *Entrance requirements:* For master's, GRE General Test, MCAT; for doctorate, GRE General Test. Additional exam requirements/recommendations for international students: Required—TOEFL.

Harvard University, Graduate School of Arts and Sciences, Committee on Biophysics, Cambridge, MA 02138. Offers PhD. *Degree requirements:* For doctorate, thesis/dissertation, exam, qualifying paper. *Entrance requirements:* For doctorate, GRE General Test, GRE Subject Test (recommended). Additional exam requirements/recommendations for international students: Required—TOEFL. *Expenses: Tuition:* Full-time $36,304. *Required fees:* $1186. Full-time tuition and fees vary according to program. *Faculty research:* Structural molecular biology, cell and membrane biophysics, molecular genetics, physical biochemistry, mathematical biophysics.

See Display on this page and Close-Up on page 165.

Howard University, Graduate School, Department of Physiology and Biophysics, Washington, DC 20059-0002. Offers biophysics (PhD); physiology (PhD). *Degree requirements:* For doctorate, comprehensive exam, thesis/dissertation. *Entrance requirements:* For doctorate, GRE General Test, minimum B average in field. *Faculty*

Harvard University
Graduate Program in Biophysics

Initiated in 1959, the Committee on Higher Degrees in Biophysics at Harvard University has a long history of important research achievements.

Designed to nurture independent, creative scientists, the program is for students with sound preliminary training in a physical or quantitative science; such as chemistry, physics, mathematics, or computer science. The primary objective of the program is to educate and train individuals with this background to apply the concepts and methods of the physical sciences to the solution of biological problems.

Structural Biology
- X-ray crystallography
- NMR
- Electron microscopy
- Computational chemistry

Imaging
- Medical Imaging
  fMRI
  Magnetoencephalography
- Cellular Imaging
  Confocal microscopy
  Multiphoton microscopy
  Advance sub-Rayleigh approaches
- Molecular imaging
  Single molecule methods

Computational Biology
- Bioinformatics
- Genomics
- Proteomics

Computational Modeling
- Molecules
- Networks

Neurobiology
- Molecular
- Cellular
- Systems

Biophysics Program
HMS Campus, 240 Longwood Ave, Boston, MA 02115
Phone: 617-495-3360 Fax: 617-432-4360
http://www.fas.harvard.edu/~biophys/

Application Information:
http://www.gsas.harvard.edu/

research: Cardiovascular physiology, pulmonary physiology, renal physiology, neurophysiology, endocrinology.

Illinois State University, Graduate School, College of Arts and Sciences, Department of Biological Sciences, Normal, IL 61790-2200. Offers animal behavior (MS); bacteriology (MS); biochemistry (MS); biological sciences (MS); biology (PhD); biophysics (MS); biotechnology (MS); botany (MS, PhD); cell biology (MS); conservation biology (MS); developmental biology (MS); ecology (MS, PhD); entomology (MS); evolutionary biology (MS); genetics (MS, PhD); immunology (MS); microbiology (MS, PhD); molecular biology (MS); molecular genetics (MS); neurobiology (MS); neuroscience (MS); parasitology (MS); physiology (MS, PhD); plant biology (MS); plant molecular biology (MS); plant sciences (MS); structural biology (MS); zoology (MS, PhD). Part-time programs available. *Degree requirements:* For master's, thesis or alternative; for doctorate, variable foreign language requirement, thesis/dissertation, 2 terms of residency. *Entrance requirements:* For master's, GRE General Test, minimum GPA of 2.6 in last 60 hours of course work; for doctorate, GRE General Test. *Faculty research:* Redoc balance and drug development in schistosoma mansoni, control of the growth of listeria monocytogenes at low temperature, regulation of cell expansion and microtubule function by SPRI, CRUI: physiology and fitness consequences of different life history phenotypes.

Iowa State University of Science and Technology, Program in Biophysics, Ames, IA 50011. Offers PhD. *Entrance requirements:* Additional exam requirements/recommendations for international students: Required—TOEFL (minimum score 550 paper-based; 79 iBT), IELTS (minimum score 6.5). *Application deadline:* For fall admission, 2/1 priority date for domestic students, 1/1 for international students. Electronic applications accepted. *Unit head:* Reuben Peters, Director of Graduate Education, 515-294-6116, Fax: 515-294-0453, E-mail: biochem@iastate.edu. *Application contact:* Connie Garnett, Information Contact, 515-294-6116, Fax: 515-294-0453, E-mail: biochem@iastate.edu. Web site: http://www.bbmb.iastate.edu/index.php?.

The Johns Hopkins University, National Institutes of Health Sponsored Programs, Baltimore, MD 21218-2699. Offers biology (PhD), including biochemistry, biophysics, cell biology, developmental biology, genetic biology, molecular biology; cell, molecular, and developmental biology and biophysics (PhD). *Degree requirements:* For doctorate, comprehensive exam, thesis/dissertation. *Entrance requirements:* For doctorate, GRE General Test. Additional exam requirements/recommendations for international students: Required—TOEFL (minimum score 600 paper-based; 250 computer-based), TWE. Electronic applications accepted. *Faculty research:* Protein and nucleic acid biochemistry and biophysical chemistry, molecular biology and development.

The Johns Hopkins University, Zanvyl Krieger School of Arts and Sciences, Program in Molecular Biophysics, Baltimore, MD 21218-2699. Offers PhD. *Degree requirements:* For doctorate, comprehensive exam, thesis/dissertation. *Entrance requirements:* For doctorate, GRE General Test. Additional exam requirements/recommendations for international students: Required—TOEFL (minimum score 600 paper-based; 250 computer-based), IELTS; Recommended—TWE. Electronic applications accepted. *Faculty research:* Protein folding and dynamics, membranes and membrane proteins, structural biology and prediction, RNA biophysics, enzymes and metabolic pathways, single molecule studies, DNA-protein interactions.

Medical College of Wisconsin, Graduate School of Biomedical Sciences, Department of Biophysics, Milwaukee, WI 53226-0509. Offers PhD, MD/PhD. *Degree requirements:* For doctorate, comprehensive exam, thesis/dissertation. *Entrance requirements:* For doctorate, GRE, official transcripts, three letters of recommendation. Additional exam requirements/recommendations for international students: Required—TOEFL. Electronic applications accepted.

Medical College of Wisconsin, Graduate School of Biomedical Sciences, Program in Biophysics, Milwaukee, WI 53226-0509. Offers PhD, MD/PhD. Part-time programs available. *Degree requirements:* For doctorate, thesis/dissertation, oral exam. *Entrance requirements:* For doctorate, GRE General Test. Additional exam requirements/recommendations for international students: Required—TOEFL. Electronic applications accepted. *Faculty research:* X-ray crystallography, electron spin resonance and membrane structure, protein and membrane dynamics, magnetic resonance imaging, free radical biology.

Northwestern University, The Graduate School, Interdepartmental Biological Sciences Program (IBiS), Evanston, IL 60208. Offers biochemistry, molecular biology, and cell biology (PhD), including biochemistry, cell and molecular biology, molecular biophysics, structural biology; biotechnology (PhD); cell and molecular biology (PhD); developmental biology and genetics (PhD); hormone action and signal transduction (PhD); neuroscience (PhD); structural biology, biochemistry, and biophysics (PhD). Program participants include the Departments of Biochemistry, Molecular Biology, and Cell Biology; Chemistry; Neurobiology and Physiology; Chemical Engineering; Civil Engineering; and Evanston Hospital. *Degree requirements:* For doctorate, thesis/dissertation, qualifying exam. *Entrance requirements:* For doctorate, GRE General Test. Additional exam requirements/recommendations for international students: Required—TOEFL (minimum score 600 paper-based). Electronic applications accepted. *Faculty research:* Developmental genetics, gene regulation, DNA-protein interactions, biological clocks, bioremediation.

The Ohio State University, Graduate School, College of Arts and Sciences, Division of Natural and Mathematical Sciences, Program in Biophysics, Columbus, OH 43210. Offers MS, PhD. *Faculty:* 93. *Students:* 20 full-time (5 women), 25 part-time (10 women); includes 2 minority (both Asian, non-Hispanic/Latino), 24 international. Average age 28. In 2011, 4 master's, 9 doctorates awarded. *Degree requirements:* For master's, thesis optional; for doctorate, thesis/dissertation. *Entrance requirements:* For master's and doctorate, GRE General Test. Additional exam requirements/recommendations for international students: Required—TOEFL (minimum score 550 paper-based; 250 computer-based; 79 iBT), Michigan English Language Assessment Battery (minimum score 82). *Application deadline:* For fall admission, 8/15 priority date for domestic students, 7/1 for international students; for winter admission, 12/1 priority date for domestic students, 11/1 for international students; for spring admission, 3/1 priority date for domestic students, 2/1 for international students. Applications are processed on a rolling basis. Application fee: $40 ($50 for international students). Electronic applications accepted. *Expenses:* Tuition, state resident: full-time $11,400. Tuition, nonresident: full-time $28,125. Tuition and fees vary according to course load, degree level, campus/location and program. *Financial support:* Fellowships, research assistantships, teaching assistantships, Federal Work-Study, and institutionally sponsored loans available. Support available to part-time students. *Unit head:* Richard Swenson, Chair, 614-292-9428, E-mail: swenson.1@osu.edu. *Application contact:* Susan Hauser, Program Administrator, 614-292-5626, Fax: 614-688-3555, E-mail: hauser.1@osu.edu. Web site: http://biophysics.osu.edu/.

Oregon State University, Graduate School, College of Science, Department of Biochemistry and Biophysics, Corvallis, OR 97331. Offers MA, MAIS, MS, PhD. *Degree requirements:* For master's, thesis optional; for doctorate, thesis/dissertation, exams. *Entrance requirements:* For master's, GRE General Test, minimum GPA of 3.0; for doctorate, GRE Subject Test, minimum GPA of 3.0. Additional exam requirements/recommendations for international students: Required—TOEFL. *Faculty research:* DNA and deoxyribonucleotide metabolism, cell growth control, receptors and membranes, protein structure and function.

Purdue University, Graduate School, College of Science, Department of Biological Sciences, West Lafayette, IN 47907. Offers biochemistry (PhD); biophysics (PhD); cell and developmental biology (PhD); ecology, evolutionary and population biology (MS, PhD), including ecology, evolutionary biology, population biology; genetics (MS, PhD); microbiology (MS, PhD); molecular biology (PhD); neurobiology (MS, PhD); plant physiology (PhD). *Faculty:* 57 full-time (15 women), 4 part-time/adjunct (1 woman). *Students:* 94 full-time (54 women), 9 part-time (5 women); includes 7 minority (2 Black or African American, non-Hispanic/Latino; 3 Asian, non-Hispanic/Latino; 2 Hispanic/Latino), 51 international. Average age 27. 246 applicants, 11% accepted, 18 enrolled. In 2011, 9 master's, 23 doctorates awarded. Terminal master's awarded for partial completion of doctoral program. *Degree requirements:* For master's, thesis (for some programs); for doctorate, thesis/dissertation, seminars, teaching experience. *Entrance requirements:* For master's, GRE General Test, minimum analytical writing score of 3.5, minimum undergraduate GPA of 3.0; for doctorate, GRE General Test, minimum analytical writing score of 3.5, minimum undergraduate GPA of 3.5. Additional exam requirements/recommendations for international students: Required—TOEFL (minimum score 600 paper-based; 107 iBT) for MS; TOEFL (minimum score 600 paper-based; 80 iBT) for Ph D. *Application deadline:* For fall admission, 12/7 for domestic and international students. Applications are processed on a rolling basis. Application fee: $60 ($75 for international students). Electronic applications accepted. *Financial support:* Fellowships, research assistantships, and teaching assistantships available. Support available to part-time students. Financial award application deadline: 2/15; financial award applicants required to submit FAFSA. *Unit head:* Dr. Richard J. Kuhn, Head, 765-494-4407, E-mail: kuhnr@purdue.edu. *Application contact:* Georgina E. Rupp, Graduate Coordinator, 765-494-8142, Fax: 765-494-0876, E-mail: ruppg@purdue.edu. Web site: http://www.bio.purdue.edu/.

Purdue University, Graduate School, PULSe - Purdue University Life Sciences Program, West Lafayette, IN 47907. Offers biomolecular structure and biophysics (PhD); biotechnology (PhD); chemical biology (PhD); chromatin and regulation of gene expression (PhD); integrative neuroscience (PhD); integrative plant sciences (PhD); membrane biology (PhD); microbiology (PhD); molecular evolutionary and cancer biology (PhD); molecular evolutionary genetics (PhD); molecular virology (PhD). *Students:* 90 full-time (45 women); includes 7 minority (3 Black or African American, non-Hispanic/Latino; 1 Asian, non-Hispanic/Latino; 2 Hispanic/Latino; 1 Two or more races, non-Hispanic/Latino), 40 international. Average age 26. 427 applicants, 24% accepted, 35 enrolled. *Entrance requirements:* For doctorate, GRE test required, minimum undergraduate GPA of 3.0. Additional exam requirements/recommendations for international students: Required—TOEFL (minimum score 550 paper-based; 77 iBT). *Application deadline:* For fall admission, 1/15 priority date for domestic students, 1/15 for international students. Applications are processed on a rolling basis. Application fee: $60 ($75 for international students). Electronic applications accepted. *Financial support:* In 2011–12, research assistantships with tuition reimbursements (averaging $22,500 per year), teaching assistantships with tuition reimbursements (averaging $22,500 per year) were awarded. *Unit head:* Dr. Christine A. Hrycyna, Head, 765-494-7322, E-mail: hrycyna@purdue.edu. *Application contact:* Emily E. Bramson, Graduate Contact, 765-494-5865, E-mail: bramson@purdue.edu. Web site: http://www.gradschool.purdue.edu/pulse.

Rensselaer Polytechnic Institute, Graduate School, School of Science, Program in Biochemistry and Biophysics, Troy, NY 12180-3590. Offers MS, PhD. Part-time programs available. Terminal master's awarded for partial completion of doctoral program. *Degree requirements:* For master's, thesis optional; for doctorate, comprehensive exam, thesis/dissertation. *Entrance requirements:* For doctorate, GRE General Test. Additional exam requirements/recommendations for international students: Required—TOEFL. Electronic applications accepted. *Faculty research:* Biopolymers, photosynthesis, cellular bioengineering.

Rosalind Franklin University of Medicine and Science, School of Graduate and Postdoctoral Studies - Interdisciplinary Graduate Program in Biomedical Sciences, Department of Physiology and Biophysics, North Chicago, IL 60064-3095. Offers MS, PhD, MD/PhD. Terminal master's awarded for partial completion of doctoral program. *Degree requirements:* For master's, comprehensive exam, thesis; for doctorate, comprehensive exam, thesis/dissertation. *Entrance requirements:* For master's and doctorate, GRE General Test. Additional exam requirements/recommendations for international students: Required—TOEFL, TWE. *Faculty research:* Membrane transport, mechanisms of cellular regulation, brain metabolism, peptide metabolism.

Simon Fraser University, Graduate Studies, Faculty of Science, Department of Physics, Burnaby, BC V5A 1S6, Canada. Offers biophysics (M Sc, PhD); chemical physics (M Sc, PhD); physics (M Sc, PhD). *Degree requirements:* For master's, thesis; for doctorate, thesis/dissertation. *Entrance requirements:* For master's, minimum GPA of 3.0; for doctorate, minimum GPA of 3.5. Additional exam requirements/recommendations for international students: Required—TOEFL or IELTS. *Faculty research:* Solid-state physics, magnetism, energy research, superconductivity, nuclear physics.

Stanford University, School of Humanities and Sciences, Program in Biophysics, Stanford, CA 94305-9991. Offers PhD. *Degree requirements:* For doctorate, thesis/dissertation, oral exam. *Entrance requirements:* For doctorate, GRE General Test, GRE Subject Test. Additional exam requirements/recommendations for international students: Required—TOEFL. Electronic applications accepted. *Expenses:* Tuition: Full-time $40,050; part-time $890 per credit.

Stony Brook University, State University of New York, Stony Brook University Medical Center, Health Sciences Center, School of Medicine and Graduate School, Graduate Programs in Medicine, Department of Physiology and Biophysics, Stony Brook, NY 11794. Offers PhD. *Degree requirements:* For doctorate, comprehensive exam, thesis/dissertation. *Entrance requirements:* For doctorate, GRE General Test, GRE Subject Test, BS in related field, minimum GPA of 3.0. Additional exam requirements/recommendations for international students: Required—TOEFL. *Faculty research:* Cellular electrophysiology, membrane permeation and transport, metabolic endocrinology.

Syracuse University, College of Arts and Sciences, Program in Structural Biology, Biochemistry and Biophysics, Syracuse, NY 13244. Offers PhD. *Students:* 5 full-time (3 women); includes 1 minority (Black or African American, non-Hispanic/Latino), 2 international. Average age 30. 10 applicants, 10% accepted, 1 enrolled. In 2011, 1 degree awarded. *Degree requirements:* For doctorate, comprehensive exam, thesis/dissertation, exam. *Entrance requirements:* For doctorate, GRE General Test, GRE Subject Test. Additional exam requirements/recommendations for international students: Required—TOEFL (minimum score 100 iBT). *Application deadline:* For fall admission, 1/10 priority date for domestic students, 1/10 for international students. Application fee: $75. Electronic applications accepted. *Expenses:* Tuition: Part-time $1206 per credit. *Financial support:* Fellowships with full tuition reimbursements, research assistantships with full and partial tuition reimbursements, teaching

assistantships with full and partial tuition reimbursements, and tuition waivers available. Financial award application deadline: 1/1; financial award applicants required to submit FAFSA. *Unit head:* Prof. Scott Pitnick, Director, 315-443-5128, Fax: 315-443-2012, E-mail: sspitnic@syr.edu. *Application contact:* Evelyn Lott, Information Contact, 315-443-9154, Fax: 315-443-2012, E-mail: ealott@syr.edu. Web site: http://sb3.syr.edu/.

Texas A&M University, College of Agriculture and Life Sciences, Department of Biochemistry and Biophysics, College Station, TX 77843. Offers biochemistry (MS, PhD); biophysics (MS). *Faculty:* 34. *Students:* 138 full-time (55 women), 6 part-time (3 women); includes 17 minority (2 Black or African American, non-Hispanic/Latino; 1 American Indian or Alaska Native, non-Hispanic/Latino; 2 Asian, non-Hispanic/Latino; 10 Hispanic/Latino; 2 Two or more races, non-Hispanic/Latino), 55 international. Average age 27. In 2011, 3 master's, 14 doctorates awarded. *Entrance requirements:* For master's and doctorate, GRE General Test. Additional exam requirements/recommendations for international students: Required—TOEFL. *Application deadline:* For fall admission, 2/1 priority date for domestic students, 12/1 for international students. Applications are processed on a rolling basis. Application fee: $50 ($75 for international students). Electronic applications accepted. *Expenses:* Tuition, state resident: full-time $5437; part-time $226.55 per credit hour. Tuition, nonresident: full-time $12,949; part-time $539.55 per credit hour. *Required fees:* $2741. *Financial support:* In 2011–12, 6 fellowships with tuition reimbursements (averaging $20,000 per year), 70 research assistantships with partial tuition reimbursements (averaging $20,000 per year) were awarded; teaching assistantships with partial tuition reimbursements, institutionally sponsored loans, scholarships/grants, traineeships, and unspecified assistantships also available. Financial award application deadline: 2/1; financial award applicants required to submit FAFSA. *Faculty research:* Enzymology, gene expression, protein structure, plant biochemistry. *Unit head:* Dr. Gregory D. Reinhart, Department Head, 979-862-2263, Fax: 979-845-9274, E-mail: gdr@tamu.edu. *Application contact:* Pat Swigert, Graduate Advisor, 979-845-1779, Fax: 979-845-9274. Web site: http://biochemistry.tamu.edu/.

Thomas Jefferson University, Jefferson College of Graduate Studies, Program in Molecular Physiology and Biophysics, Philadelphia, PA 19107. Offers PhD. *Faculty:* 10 full-time (5 women). *Students:* 1 full-time (0 women). *Degree requirements:* For doctorate, comprehensive exam, thesis/dissertation. *Entrance requirements:* For doctorate, GRE General Test, minimum GPA of 3.2. Additional exam requirements/recommendations for international students: Required—TOEFL (minimum score 250 computer-based; 100 iBT). *Application deadline:* For fall admission, 1/15 priority date for domestic students, 1/15 for international students. Applications are processed on a rolling basis. Application fee: $50. Electronic applications accepted. *Financial support:* In 2011–12, 1 student received support, including 1 fellowship with full tuition reimbursement available (averaging $54,758 per year); Federal Work-Study, institutionally sponsored loans, scholarships/grants, traineeships, and stipends also available. Support available to part-time students. Financial award application deadline: 5/1; financial award applicants required to submit FAFSA. *Faculty research:* Cardiovascular physiology, smooth muscle physiology, pathophysiology of myocardial ischemia, endothelial cell physiology, molecular biology of ion channel physiology. *Total annual research expenditures:* $893,526. *Unit head:* Dr. Thomas M. Butler, Program Director, 215-503-6583, E-mail: thomas.butler@jefferson.edu. *Application contact:* Marc E. Stearns, Director of Admissions, 215-503-0155, Fax: 215-503-9920, E-mail: jcgs-info@jefferson.edu. Web site: http://www.jefferson.edu/physiology/.

Université de Sherbrooke, Faculty of Medicine and Health Sciences, Graduate Programs in Medicine, Department of Physiology and Biophysics, Sherbrooke, QC J1H 5N4, Canada. Offers M Sc, PhD. Terminal master's awarded for partial completion of doctoral program. *Degree requirements:* For master's, thesis; for doctorate, thesis/dissertation. Electronic applications accepted. *Faculty research:* Ion channels, neurological basis of pain, insulin resistance, obesity.

Université du Québec à Trois-Rivières, Graduate Programs, Program in Biophysics and Cellular Biology, Trois-Rivières, QC G9A 5H7, Canada. Offers M Sc, PhD. Part-time programs available. *Degree requirements:* For master's, thesis; for doctorate, thesis/dissertation. *Entrance requirements:* For master's, appropriate bachelor's degree, proficiency in French; for doctorate, appropriate master's degree, proficiency in French.

University at Buffalo, the State University of New York, Graduate School, Graduate Programs in Cancer Research and Biomedical Sciences at Roswell Park Cancer Institute, Department of Molecular and Cellular Biophysics and Biochemistry at Roswell Park Cancer Institute, Buffalo, NY 14260. Offers PhD. *Degree requirements:* For doctorate, comprehensive exam, thesis/dissertation. *Entrance requirements:* For doctorate, GRE General Test. Additional exam requirements/recommendations for international students: Required—TOEFL (minimum score 600 paper-based; 250 computer-based; 100 iBT). Electronic applications accepted. *Faculty research:* MRI research, structural and function of biomolecules, photodynamic therapy, DNA damage and repair, heat-shock proteins and vaccine research.

University at Buffalo, the State University of New York, Graduate School, School of Medicine and Biomedical Sciences, Graduate Programs in Medicine and Biomedical Sciences, Department of Physiology and Biophysics, Buffalo, NY 14260. Offers biophysics (MS, PhD); physiology (MA, PhD). *Faculty:* 19 full-time (4 women). *Students:* 30 full-time (11 women); includes 1 minority (Asian, non-Hispanic/Latino), 14 international. Average age 29. 38 applicants, 21% accepted, 4 enrolled. In 2011, 2 master's, 2 doctorates awarded. Terminal master's awarded for partial completion of doctoral program. *Degree requirements:* For master's, thesis, oral exam, project; for doctorate, thesis/dissertation, oral and written qualifying exam or 2 research proposals. *Entrance requirements:* For master's and doctorate, GRE General Test. Additional exam requirements/recommendations for international students: Required—TOEFL (minimum score 600 paper-based; 250 computer-based; 100 iBT). *Application deadline:* For fall admission, 2/1 priority date for domestic students, 2/1 for international students. Applications are processed on a rolling basis. Application fee: $50. Electronic applications accepted. *Financial support:* In 2011–12, fellowships with tuition reimbursements (averaging $21,000 per year), 17 research assistantships with tuition reimbursements (averaging $21,000 per year) were awarded; Federal Work-Study, institutionally sponsored loans, health care benefits, and unspecified assistantships also available. Financial award application deadline: 2/1; financial award applicants required to submit FAFSA. *Faculty research:* Neurosciences, ion channels, cardiac physiology, renal/epithelial transport, cardiopulmonary exercise. *Total annual research expenditures:* $5.4 million. *Unit head:* Dr. Perry M. Hogan, Chair, 716-829-2738, Fax: 716-829-2344, E-mail: phogan@buffalo.edu. *Application contact:* Shaun C. Hoppel, Academic Coordinator, 716-829-2417, Fax: 716-829-2344, E-mail: schoppel@buffalo.edu.

University of Arkansas for Medical Sciences, Graduate School, Graduate Programs in Biomedical Sciences, Department of Physiology and Biophysics, Little Rock, AR 72205-7199. Offers MS, PhD, MD/PhD. *Degree requirements:* For master's, thesis; for doctorate, thesis/dissertation. *Entrance requirements:* For master's and doctorate, GRE General Test. Additional exam requirements/recommendations for international students: Required—TOEFL. *Faculty research:* Gene transcription, protein targeting, membrane biology, cell-cell communication.

University of California, Berkeley, Graduate Division, College of Letters and Science, Group in Biophysics, Berkeley, CA 94720-1500. Offers PhD. *Degree requirements:* For doctorate, thesis/dissertation, qualifying exam. *Entrance requirements:* For doctorate, GRE General Test, minimum GPA of 3.0, 3 letters of recommendation.

University of California, Davis, Graduate Studies, Graduate Group in Biophysics, Davis, CA 95616. Offers MS, PhD. *Degree requirements:* For doctorate, thesis/dissertation. *Entrance requirements:* For master's and doctorate, GRE General Test, GRE Subject Test. Additional exam requirements/recommendations for international students: Required—TOEFL (minimum score 550 paper-based; 213 computer-based). Electronic applications accepted. *Faculty research:* Molecular structure, protein structure/function relationships, spectroscopy.

University of California, Irvine, School of Medicine and School of Biological Sciences, Department of Physiology and Biophysics, Irvine, CA 92697. Offers biological sciences (PhD); MD/PhD. *Students:* 12 full-time (6 women); includes 5 minority (1 American Indian or Alaska Native, non-Hispanic/Latino; 3 Asian, non-Hispanic/Latino; 1 Hispanic/Latino), 1 international. Average age 28. 1 applicant, 100% accepted, 1 enrolled. In 2011, 1 degree awarded. *Degree requirements:* For doctorate, thesis/dissertation. *Entrance requirements:* For doctorate, GRE General Test, GRE Subject Test, minimum GPA of 3.0. Additional exam requirements/recommendations for international students: Required—TOEFL (minimum score 550 paper-based; 213 computer-based). *Application deadline:* For fall admission, 1/15 priority date for domestic students, 1/15 for international students. Application fee: $80 ($100 for international students). Electronic applications accepted. *Financial support:* Fellowships, research assistantships with full tuition reimbursements, teaching assistantships, institutionally sponsored loans, traineeships, health care benefits, and unspecified assistantships available. Financial award application deadline: 3/1; financial award applicants required to submit FAFSA. *Faculty research:* Membrane physiology, exercise physiology, regulation of hormone biosynthesis and action, endocrinology, ion channels and signal transduction. *Unit head:* Prof. Michael Cahalan, Chairman, 949-824-7776, Fax: 949-824-3143, E-mail: mcahalan@uci.edu. *Application contact:* Vicki C. Ledray, Chief Administrative Officer, 949-824-5865, Fax: 949-824-0019, E-mail: ledray@uci.edu. Web site: http://www.physiology.uci.edu/.

University of California, San Diego, Office of Graduate Studies, Department of Physics, La Jolla, CA 92093. Offers biophysics (MS, PhD); physics (MS, PhD); physics/materials physics (MS). *Degree requirements:* For doctorate, thesis/dissertation. *Entrance requirements:* For master's and doctorate, GRE General Test, GRE Subject Test. Additional exam requirements/recommendations for international students: Required—TOEFL. Electronic applications accepted.

University of California, San Francisco, School of Pharmacy and School of Medicine, Graduate Group in Biophysics, San Francisco, CA 94143. Offers PhD. *Faculty:* 47 full-time (13 women). *Students:* 55 full-time (19 women); includes 14 minority (9 Asian, non-Hispanic/Latino; 5 Hispanic/Latino), 6 international. Average age 25. 152 applicants, 36% accepted, 28 enrolled. In 2011, 4 doctorates awarded. *Degree requirements:* For doctorate, thesis/dissertation. *Entrance requirements:* For doctorate, GRE General Test; GRE Subject Test (recommended). Additional exam requirements/recommendations for international students: Required—TOEFL. *Application deadline:* For fall admission, 12/1 for domestic students. Application fee: $70 ($90 for international students). Electronic applications accepted. *Financial support:* In 2011–12, fellowships with full tuition reimbursements (averaging $29,500 per year), research assistantships with full tuition reimbursements (averaging $29,500 per year) were awarded; traineeships, health care benefits, tuition waivers (full), unspecified assistantships, and stipends also available. *Faculty research:* Structural and computational biology; proteomic, genomic, and cell biology; chemistry; systems biology. *Unit head:* Dr. Matthew Jacobson, Program Director, 415-514-9881, E-mail: matt.jacobson@ucsf.edu. *Application contact:* Rebecca Brown, Program Administrator, 415-476-6671, Fax: 415-476-1902, E-mail: rbrown@cgl.ucsf.edu. Web site: http://biophysics.ucsf.edu/.

University of California, Santa Barbara, Graduate Division, College of Letters and Sciences, Division of Mathematics, Life, and Physical Sciences, Interdepartmental Graduate Program in Biomolecular Science and Engineering, Santa Barbara, CA 93106-2014. Offers biochemistry and molecular biology (PhD), including biochemistry and molecular biology, biophysics and bioengineering. *Faculty:* 38 full-time (5 women), 1 (woman) part-time/adjunct. *Students:* 29 full-time (14 women); includes 3 minority (2 Asian, non-Hispanic/Latino; 1 Two or more races, non-Hispanic/Latino), 3 international. Average age 28. 83 applicants, 20% accepted, 4 enrolled. In 2011, 4 degrees awarded. Terminal master's awarded for partial completion of doctoral program. *Median time to degree:* Of those who began their doctoral program in fall 2003, 100% received their degree in 8 years or less. *Degree requirements:* For doctorate, thesis/dissertation. *Entrance requirements:* For doctorate, GRE General Test. Additional exam requirements/recommendations for international students: Required—TOEFL (minimum score 630 paper-based; 109 iBT), IELTS (minimum score 7). *Application deadline:* For fall admission, 12/15 for domestic and international students. Application fee: $80 ($100 for international students). Electronic applications accepted. *Expenses:* Tuition, state resident: full-time $12,192. Tuition, nonresident: full-time $27,294. *Required fees:* $764.13. *Financial support:* In 2011–12, 29 students received support, including 16 fellowships with full and partial tuition reimbursements available (averaging $11,321 per year), 31 research assistantships with full and partial tuition reimbursements available (averaging $14,777 per year), 16 teaching assistantships with full and partial tuition reimbursements available (averaging $6,307 per year); Federal Work-Study, traineeships, health care benefits, tuition waivers (full and partial), and unspecified assistantships also available. Financial award application deadline: 12/15; financial award applicants required to submit FAFSA. *Faculty research:* Biochemistry and molecular biology, biophysics, biomaterials, bioengineering, systems biology. *Unit head:* Prof. Philip A. Pincus, Director/Professor, 805-893-4685, E-mail: fyl@mrl.ucsb.edu. *Application contact:* Graduate Admissions Coordinator, 805-893-2278, Fax: 805-893-8259, E-mail: gradadmissions@graddiv.ucsb.edu. Web site: http://www.bmse.ucsb.edu/.

University of Chicago, Division of the Physical Sciences, Graduate Program in Biophysical Science, Chicago, IL 60637-1513. Offers PhD. *Degree requirements:* For doctorate, comprehensive exam, thesis/dissertation, ethics class, 2 teaching assistantships. *Entrance requirements:* Additional exam requirements/recommendations for international students: Required—IELTS (minimum score 7); Recommended—TOEFL (minimum score 600 paper-based; 250 computer-based; 104 iBT). Electronic applications accepted.

University of Cincinnati, Graduate School, College of Medicine, Graduate Programs in Biomedical Sciences, Department of Pharmacology and Cell Biophysics, Cincinnati, OH 45221. Offers cell biophysics (PhD); pharmacology (PhD). *Degree requirements:* For doctorate, thesis/dissertation, qualifying exam. *Entrance requirements:* For doctorate, GRE General Test. Additional exam requirements/recommendations for international students: Required—TOEFL. Electronic applications accepted. *Faculty research:* Lipoprotein research, enzyme regulation, electrophysiology, gene actuation.

University of Colorado Denver, School of Medicine, Graduate Program in Genetic Counseling, Aurora, CO 80045. Offers biophysics and genetics (MS, PhD). *Students:* 12

full-time (all women), 2 international. Average age 24. 80 applicants, 9% accepted, 6 enrolled. In 2011, 6 master's awarded. *Degree requirements:* For master's, 44 core semester hours, project or thesis; for doctorate, comprehensive exam, thesis/dissertation, 30 hours of didactic course work, 30 hours of research credits. *Entrance requirements:* For master's, GRE, minimum undergraduate GPA of 3.0; 4 letters of recommendation; prerequisite coursework in biology, general chemistry, general biochemistry, general genetics, general psychology; experience in counseling and laboratory settings and strong understanding of genetic counseling field (highly recommended); for doctorate, GRE, three letters of recommendation, laboratory research experience and solid undergraduate foundation in mathematics and biological sciences. Additional exam requirements/recommendations for international students: Required—TOEFL (minimum score 570 paper-based; 230 computer-based; 89 iBT). *Application deadline:* For fall admission, 1/1 for domestic students, 12/1 for international students. Application fee: $65. Electronic applications accepted. *Expenses:* Contact institution. *Financial support:* Career-related internships or fieldwork and Federal Work-Study available. Financial award application deadline: 4/1; financial award applicants required to submit FAFSA. *Faculty research:* Psychosocial aspects of genetic counseling, clinical cytogenetics and molecular genetics, human inborn errors of metabolism, congenital malformations and disorders of the newborn, cancer genetics and genetic counseling. *Unit head:* Carol Walton, Director, 303-724-2370, E-mail: walton.carol@tchden.org. *Application contact:* Dr. Norma Wagoner, Associate Dean for Admissions, 303-724-8025, E-mail: somadmin@ucdenver.edu. Web site: http://www.ucdenver.edu/academics/colleges/Graduate-School/academic-programs/genetic-counseling/Pages/default.aspx.

University of Connecticut, Graduate School, College of Liberal Arts and Sciences, Department of Molecular and Cell Biology, Field of Biophysics and Structural Biology, Storrs, CT 06269. Offers MS, PhD. Terminal master's awarded for partial completion of doctoral program. *Degree requirements:* For master's, comprehensive exam; for doctorate, thesis/dissertation. *Entrance requirements:* For master's and doctorate, GRE General Test, GRE Subject Test. Additional exam requirements/recommendations for international students: Required—TOEFL (minimum score 550 paper-based; 213 computer-based). Electronic applications accepted.

University of Guelph, Graduate Studies, Biophysics Interdepartmental Group, Guelph, ON N1G 2W1, Canada. Offers M Sc, PhD. *Degree requirements:* For master's, thesis; for doctorate, comprehensive exam, thesis/dissertation. *Entrance requirements:* For master's, minimum B average during previous 2 years of course work; for doctorate, minimum B+ average. Additional exam requirements/recommendations for international students: Required—TOEFL (minimum score 550 paper-based; 213 computer-based). Electronic applications accepted. *Faculty research:* Molecular, cellular, structural, and computational biophysics.

University of Guelph, Graduate Studies, College of Biological Science, Department of Molecular and Cellular Biology, Guelph, ON N1G 2W1, Canada. Offers biochemistry (M Sc, PhD); biophysics (M Sc, PhD); botany (M Sc, PhD); microbiology (M Sc, PhD); molecular biology and genetics (M Sc, PhD). *Degree requirements:* For master's, thesis, research proposal; for doctorate, comprehensive exam, thesis/dissertation, research proposal. *Entrance requirements:* For master's, minimum B-average during previous 2 years of coursework; for doctorate, minimum A-average. Additional exam requirements/recommendations for international students: Required—TOEFL (minimum score 550 paper-based; 213 computer-based), IELTS (minimum score 6.5). Electronic applications accepted. *Faculty research:* Physiology, structure, genetics, and ecology of microbes; virology and microbial technology.

University of Illinois at Chicago, College of Medicine and Graduate College, Graduate Programs in Medicine, Department of Physiology and Biophysics, Chicago, IL 60607-7128. Offers MS, PhD. Terminal master's awarded for partial completion of doctoral program. *Degree requirements:* For master's, thesis; for doctorate, thesis/dissertation. *Entrance requirements:* For master's and doctorate, GRE General Test. Additional exam requirements/recommendations for international students: Required—TOEFL. Electronic applications accepted. *Faculty research:* Neuroscience, endocrinology and reproduction, cell physiology, exercise physiology, NMR.

University of Illinois at Urbana–Champaign, Graduate College, College of Liberal Arts and Sciences, School of Molecular and Cellular Biology, Center for Biophysics and Computational Biology, Champaign, IL 61820. Offers MS, PhD. *Students:* 68 full-time (13 women), 4 part-time (2 women); includes 9 minority (6 Asian, non-Hispanic/Latino; 2 Hispanic/Latino; 1 Two or more races, non-Hispanic/Latino), 44 international. 93 applicants, 9% accepted, 8 enrolled. In 2011, 2 master's, 7 doctorates awarded. *Entrance requirements:* For doctorate, GRE, minimum GPA of 3.0. Additional exam requirements/recommendations for international students: Required—TOEFL. *Application deadline:* Applications are processed on a rolling basis. Application fee: $75 ($90 for international students). Electronic applications accepted. *Financial support:* In 2011–12, 14 fellowships, 60 research assistantships, 22 teaching assistantships were awarded; tuition waivers (full and partial) also available. *Unit head:* Robert M. Clegg, Director, 217-244-8143, Fax: 217-244-3186, E-mail: rclegg@illinois.edu. *Application contact:* Cynthia Dodds, Office Administrator, 217-333-1630, Fax: 217-244-6615, E-mail: dodds@illinois.edu. Web site: http://www.life.illinois.edu/biophysics/.

The University of Iowa, Roy J. and Lucille A. Carver College of Medicine and Graduate College, Graduate Programs in Medicine, Department of Molecular Physiology and Biophysics, Iowa City, IA 52242-1316. Offers MS, PhD. *Faculty:* 16 full-time (2 women), 17 part-time/adjunct (2 women). *Students:* 22 full-time (5 women); includes 8 minority (1 American Indian or Alaska Native, non-Hispanic/Latino; 7 Asian, non-Hispanic/Latino). Average age 25. In 2011, 4 degrees awarded. Terminal master's awarded for partial completion of doctoral program. *Median time to degree:* Of those who began their doctoral program in fall 2003, 100% received their degree in 8 years or less. *Degree requirements:* For master's, comprehensive exam; for doctorate, comprehensive exam, thesis/dissertation, teaching experience. *Entrance requirements:* For master's, GRE General Test; for doctorate, GRE General Test, minimum GPA of 3.0. Additional exam requirements/recommendations for international students: Required—TOEFL. *Application deadline:* For fall admission, 4/1 for domestic students, 3/1 for international students; for spring admission, 10/1 for domestic students, 9/1 for international students. Applications are processed on a rolling basis. Application fee: $60 ($80 for international students). Electronic applications accepted. *Financial support:* In 2011–12, 2 fellowships with full tuition reimbursements (averaging $25,500 per year), 20 research assistantships with full tuition reimbursements (averaging $25,500 per year) were awarded; traineeships also available. Financial award application deadline: 4/1. *Faculty research:* Cellular and molecular endocrinology, membrane structure and function, cardiac cell electrophysiology, regulation of gene expression, neurophysiology. *Unit head:* Dr. Kevin P. Campbell, Head, 319-335-7800, Fax: 319-335-7330, E-mail: kevin-campbell@uiowa.edu. *Application contact:* Dr. Michael Anderson, Director of Graduate Studies, 319-335-7839, Fax: 319-335-7330, E-mail: michael-g-anderson@uiowa.edu. Web site: http://www.physiology.uiowa.edu/.

The University of Kansas, Graduate Studies, College of Liberal Arts and Sciences, Department of Molecular Biosciences, Lawrence, KS 66044. Offers biochemistry and biophysics (MA, PhD); microbiology (MA, PhD); molecular, cellular, and developmental biology (MA, PhD). *Faculty:* 34. *Students:* 57 full-time (29 women), 2 part-time (1 woman); includes 6 minority (2 Asian, non-Hispanic/Latino; 3 Hispanic/Latino; 1 Two or more races, non-Hispanic/Latino), 26 international. Average age 28. 60 applicants, 30% accepted, 10 enrolled. In 2011, 1 master's, 12 doctorates awarded. Terminal master's awarded for partial completion of doctoral program. *Degree requirements:* For master's, comprehensive exam, thesis; for doctorate, comprehensive exam, thesis/dissertation. *Entrance requirements:* For master's and doctorate, GRE General Test. Additional exam requirements/recommendations for international students: Required—TOEFL or IELTS. *Application deadline:* For fall admission, 12/15 for domestic and international students. Application fee: $55 ($65 for international students). Electronic applications accepted. Tuition and fees vary according to course load, campus/location, program and reciprocity agreements. *Financial support:* Fellowships with tuition reimbursements, research assistantships with tuition reimbursements, teaching assistantships with tuition reimbursements, health care benefits, and unspecified assistantships available. Financial award application deadline: 3/1. *Faculty research:* Structure and function of proteins, genetics of organism development, molecular genetics, neurophysiology, molecular virology and pathogenics, developmental biology, cell biology. *Unit head:* Dr. Mark Richter, Chair, 785-864-3334, Fax: 785-864-5294, E-mail: richter@ku.edu. *Application contact:* John P. Connolly, Graduate Program Assistant, 785-864-4311, Fax: 785-864-5294, E-mail: jconnolly@ku.edu. Web site: http://www.molecularbiosciences.ku.edu/.

University of Louisville, School of Medicine, Department of Physiology and Biophysics, Louisville, KY 40292-0001. Offers MS, PhD, MD/PhD. Terminal master's awarded for partial completion of doctoral program. *Degree requirements:* For master's, thesis; for doctorate, comprehensive exam, thesis/dissertation. *Entrance requirements:* For master's and doctorate, GRE General Test (minimum score of 1000 verbal and quantitative), minimum GPA of 3.0. Additional exam requirements/recommendations for international students: Required—TOEFL. Electronic applications accepted. *Expenses:* Tuition, state resident: full-time $9692; part-time $539 per credit hour. Tuition, nonresident: full-time $20,168; part-time $1121 per credit hour. Tuition and fees vary according to program and reciprocity agreements. *Faculty research:* Control of microvascular function during normal and disease states; mechanisms of cellular adhesive interactions on endothelial cells lining blood vessels; changes in blood rheological properties and mechanisms associated with increased blood fibrinogen content; role of nutrition in microvascular control mechanisms; mechanism of cardiovascular-renal remodeling in hypertension, diabetes, and heart failure.

The University of Manchester, School of Physics and Astronomy, Manchester, United Kingdom. Offers astronomy and astrophysics (M Sc, PhD); biological physics (M Sc, PhD); condensed matter physics (M Sc, PhD); nonlinear and liquid crystals physics (M Sc, PhD); nuclear physics (M Sc, PhD); particle physics (M Sc, PhD); photon physics (M Sc, PhD); physics (M Sc, PhD); theoretical physics (M Sc, PhD).

University of Maryland, College Park, Academic Affairs, College of Computer, Mathematical and Natural Sciences, Department of Biology, PhD Program in Biological Sciences, College Park, MD 20742. Offers behavior, ecology, evolution, and systematics (PhD); computational biology, bioinformatics, and genomics (PhD); molecular and cellular biology (PhD); physiological systems (PhD). *Students:* 68 full-time (41 women), 4 part-time (2 women); includes 13 minority (3 Black or African American, non-Hispanic/Latino; 4 Asian, non-Hispanic/Latino; 5 Hispanic/Latino; 1 Two or more races, non-Hispanic/Latino), 21 international. 380 applicants, 15% accepted, 22 enrolled. *Degree requirements:* For doctorate, comprehensive exam, thesis/dissertation, present thesis work in seminar. *Entrance requirements:* For doctorate, GRE General Test; GRE Subject Test in biology (recommended), academic transcripts, statement of purpose/research interests, 3 letters of recommendation. Additional exam requirements/recommendations for international students: Required—TOEFL. *Application deadline:* For fall admission, 12/15 for domestic and international students. Applications are processed on a rolling basis. Application fee: $75. Electronic applications accepted. *Expenses:* Tuition, state resident: part-time $525 per credit hour. Tuition, nonresident: part-time $1131 per credit hour. *Required fees:* $386.31 per term. Tuition and fees vary according to program. *Financial support:* In 2011–12, 11 fellowships with full and partial tuition reimbursements (averaging $14,406 per year), 16 research assistantships (averaging $19,495 per year), 41 teaching assistantships (averaging $18,734 per year) were awarded. *Unit head:* Dr. Barbara Thorne, Director, 301-405-6905, E-mail: bthorne@umd.edu. *Application contact:* Dr. Charles A. Caramello, Dean of Graduate School, 301-405-0358, Fax: 301-314-9305. Web site: http://bisi.umd.edu/biologicalsciencesgraduateprogrambisi.

University of Maryland, College Park, Academic Affairs, College of Computer, Mathematical and Natural Sciences, Institute for Physical Science and Technology, Program in Biophysics, College Park, MD 20742. Offers PhD. *Students:* 13 full-time (5 women), 1 (woman) part-time; includes 2 minority (1 Black or African American, non-Hispanic/Latino; 1 Two or more races, non-Hispanic/Latino), 9 international. 33 applicants, 30% accepted, 6 enrolled. *Application deadline:* For fall admission, 1/15 for domestic and international students. Application fee: $75. *Expenses:* Tuition, state resident: part-time $525 per credit hour. Tuition, nonresident: part-time $1131 per credit hour. *Required fees:* $386.31 per term. Tuition and fees vary according to program. *Financial support:* In 2011–12, 1 fellowship with full tuition reimbursement (averaging $18,000 per year), 4 research assistantships (averaging $19,782 per year), 8 teaching assistantships (averaging $18,109 per year) were awarded; Federal Work-Study and scholarships/grants also available. Support available to part-time students. Financial award applicants required to submit FAFSA. *Unit head:* Dr. Wolfgang Losert, Director, 301-405-0629, E-mail: dirbiph@umd.edu. *Application contact:* Dr. Charles A. Caramello, Dean of the Graduate School, 301-405-0376.

University of Miami, Graduate School, Miller School of Medicine, Graduate Programs in Medicine, Department of Physiology and Biophysics, Coral Gables, FL 33124. Offers PhD, MD/PhD. *Degree requirements:* For doctorate, thesis/dissertation, qualifying exam. *Entrance requirements:* For doctorate, GRE General Test, minimum GPA of 3.0 in sciences. Additional exam requirements/recommendations for international students: Required—TOEFL. *Faculty research:* Cell and membrane physiology, cell-to-cell communication, molecular neurobiology, neuroimmunology, neural development.

University of Michigan, Horace H. Rackham School of Graduate Studies, College of Literature, Science, and the Arts, Department of Biophysics, Ann Arbor, MI 48109. Offers PhD. *Faculty:* 45 full-time (7 women). *Students:* 30 full-time (8 women); includes 5 minority (1 Black or African American, non-Hispanic/Latino; 3 Asian, non-Hispanic/Latino; 1 Hispanic/Latino), 8 international. Average age 22. 34 applicants, 26% accepted, 4 enrolled. In 2011, 2 doctorates awarded. *Degree requirements:* For doctorate, thesis/dissertation, oral defense of dissertation, preliminary exam. *Entrance requirements:* For doctorate, GRE General Test, GRE Subject Test. Additional exam requirements/recommendations for international students: Required—TOEFL. *Application deadline:* For fall admission, 12/15 for domestic and international students. Application fee: $65 ($75 for international students). Electronic applications accepted. *Financial support:* In 2011–12, 14 fellowships with full tuition reimbursements (averaging $26,553 per year), 6 research assistantships with full tuition reimbursements (averaging $26,553 per year), 7 teaching assistantships with full tuition reimbursements (averaging $26,553 per year) were awarded; scholarships/grants, traineeships, health care benefits, and unspecified assistantships also available. Financial award application

deadline: 3/15. *Faculty research:* Structural biology, computational biophysics, physical chemistry, cellular biophysics. *Unit head:* Dr. Jens-Christian Meiners, Program Director, 734-764-1146, E-mail: meiners@umich.edu. *Application contact:* Sara Grosky, Student Services Administrator, 734-763-6722, E-mail: saramin@umich.edu. Web site: http://biop.lsa.umich.edu/.

University of Minnesota, Duluth, Medical School, Department of Biochemistry, Molecular Biology and Biophysics, Duluth, MN 55812-2496. Offers biochemistry, molecular biology and biophysics (MS); biology and biophysics (PhD); social, administrative, and clinical pharmacy (MS, PhD); toxicology (MS, PhD). Terminal master's awarded for partial completion of doctoral program. *Degree requirements:* For master's, comprehensive exam, thesis; for doctorate, comprehensive exam, thesis/dissertation. *Entrance requirements:* For master's and doctorate, GRE General Test. Additional exam requirements/recommendations for international students: Required—TOEFL. Electronic applications accepted. *Faculty research:* Intestinal cancer biology; hepatotoxins and mitochondriopathies; toxicology; cell cycle regulation in stem cells; neurobiology of brain development, trace metal function and blood-brain barrier; hibernation biology.

University of Minnesota, Twin Cities Campus, Graduate School, College of Biological Sciences, Biochemistry, Molecular Biology and Biophysics Graduate Program, Minneapolis, MN 55455-0213. Offers PhD. *Degree requirements:* For doctorate, thesis/dissertation. *Entrance requirements:* For doctorate, GRE, 3 letters of recommendation, more than 1 semester of laboratory experience. Additional exam requirements/recommendations for international students: Required—TOEFL (minimum score 625 paper-based; 263 computer-based; 108 iBT with writing subsection 25 and reading subsection 25) or IELTS (minimum score 7). Electronic applications accepted. *Faculty research:* Microbial biochemistry, biotechnology, molecular biology, regulatory biochemistry, structural biology and biophysics, physical biochemistry, enzymology, physiological chemistry.

University of Minnesota, Twin Cities Campus, Graduate School, Program in Biophysical Sciences and Medical Physics, Minneapolis, MN 55455-0213. Offers MS, PhD. Part-time programs available. *Degree requirements:* For master's, thesis optional, research paper, oral exam; for doctorate, thesis/dissertation, oral/written preliminary exam, oral final exam. *Faculty research:* Theoretical biophysics, radiological physics, cellular and molecular biophysics.

University of Mississippi Medical Center, School of Graduate Studies in the Health Sciences, Department of Physiology and Biophysics, Jackson, MS 39216-4505. Offers MS, PhD, MD/PhD. *Degree requirements:* For master's, thesis; for doctorate, thesis/dissertation, first authored publication. *Entrance requirements:* For master's and doctorate, GRE General Test, minimum GPA of 3.0. *Faculty research:* Cardiovascular, renal, endocrine, and cellular neurophysiology; molecular physiology.

University of Missouri–Kansas City, School of Biological Sciences, Program in Cell Biology and Biophysics, Kansas City, MO 64110-2499. Offers PhD. Offered through the School of Graduate Studies. *Faculty:* 40 full-time (10 women), 3 part-time/adjunct (2 women). *Students:* 4 full-time (1 woman), 15 part-time (7 women), 10 international. Average age 27. 5 applicants, 100% accepted, 3 enrolled. *Degree requirements:* For doctorate, comprehensive exam, thesis/dissertation. *Entrance requirements:* For doctorate, GRE General Test, bachelor's degree in chemistry, biology or related field; minimum GPA of 3.0. Additional exam requirements/recommendations for international students: Required—TOEFL (minimum score 550 paper-based; 213 computer-based; 80 iBT). *Application deadline:* For fall admission, 2/15 priority date for domestic students, 2/15 for international students. Applications are processed on a rolling basis. Application fee: $45 ($50 for international students). Electronic applications accepted. *Expenses:* Tuition, state resident: full-time $5798; part-time $322.10 per credit hour. Tuition, nonresident: full-time $14,969; part-time $831.60 per credit hour. *Required fees:* $93.51 per credit hour. *Financial support:* Fellowships with full tuition reimbursements, research assistantships with full tuition reimbursements, teaching assistantships with full and partial tuition reimbursements, scholarships/grants, tuition waivers (full and partial), and unspecified assistantships available. Financial award application deadline: 3/1; financial award applicants required to submit FAFSA. *Unit head:* Dr. G. Sullivan Read, Interim Head, 816-235-5247, E-mail: sbsgradrecruit@umkc.edu. *Application contact:* Laura Batenic, Information Contact, 816-235-2352, Fax: 816-235-5158, E-mail: batenicl@umkc.edu. Web site: http://sbs.umkc.edu/.

See Display on page 201 and Close-Up on page 245.

The University of North Carolina at Chapel Hill, School of Medicine and Graduate School, Graduate Programs in Medicine, Department of Biochemistry and Biophysics, Chapel Hill, NC 27599. Offers MS, PhD. Terminal master's awarded for partial completion of doctoral program. *Degree requirements:* For master's, comprehensive exam, thesis; for doctorate, comprehensive exam, thesis/dissertation. *Entrance requirements:* For master's and doctorate, GRE General Test, GRE Subject Test (recommended), minimum GPA of 3.0. Additional exam requirements/recommendations for international students: Required—TOEFL. Electronic applications accepted.

University of Regina, Faculty of Graduate Studies and Research, Faculty of Science, Department of Chemistry and Biochemistry, Regina, SK S4S 0A2, Canada. Offers analytical/environmental chemistry (M Sc, PhD); biophysics of biological interfaces (M Sc, PhD); enzymology/chemical biology (M Sc, PhD); inorganic/organometallic chemistry (M Sc, PhD); signal transduction and mechanisms of cancer cell regulation (M Sc, PhD); supramolecular organic photochemistry and photophysics (M Sc, PhD); synthetic organic chemistry (M Sc, PhD); theoretical/computational chemistry (M Sc, PhD). *Faculty:* 12 full-time (2 women). *Students:* 13 full-time (4 women), 1 (woman) part-time. 22 applicants, 50% accepted. In 2011, 1 master's, 2 doctorates awarded. *Degree requirements:* For master's, thesis; for doctorate, thesis/dissertation. *Entrance requirements:* Additional exam requirements/recommendations for international students: Required—TOEFL (minimum score 580 paper-based; 80 iBT), IELTS (minimum score 6.5). *Application deadline:* Applications are processed on a rolling basis. Application fee: $100. Electronic applications accepted. *Financial support:* In 2011–12, 3 fellowships (averaging $6,500 per year), 1 research assistantship (averaging $5,500 per year), 7 teaching assistantships (averaging $2,298 per year) were awarded; scholarships/grants also available. Financial award application deadline: 6/15. *Faculty research:* Asymmetric synthesis and methodology, theoretical and computational chemistry, biophysical biochemistry, analytical and environmental chemistry, chemical biology. *Unit head:* Dr. Lynn Mihichuk, Head, 306-585-4793, Fax: 306-337-2409, E-mail: lynn.mihichuk@uregina.ca. *Application contact:* Dr. Tanya Dahms, Graduate Program Coordinator, 306-585-4246, Fax: 306-337-2409, E-mail: tanya.dahms@uregina.ca. Web site: http://www.chem.uregina.ca/.

University of Rochester, School of Medicine and Dentistry, Graduate Programs in Medicine and Dentistry, Department of Biochemistry and Biophysics, Programs in Biophysics, Rochester, NY 14627. Offers biophysics, structural and computational biology (PhD). Terminal master's awarded for partial completion of doctoral program. *Degree requirements:* For doctorate, thesis/dissertation, qualifying exam. *Entrance requirements:* For doctorate, GRE General Test. *Expenses: Tuition:* Full-time $41,040.

University of Southern California, Keck School of Medicine and Graduate School, Graduate Programs in Medicine, Department of Physiology and Biophysics, Los Angeles, CA 90089. Offers MS, PhD, MD/PhD. *Faculty:* 9 full-time (1 woman). *Students:* 8 full-time (4 women), 5 international. Average age 29. 1 applicant, 100% accepted, 1 enrolled. Terminal master's awarded for partial completion of doctoral program. *Degree requirements:* For master's, thesis optional; for doctorate, comprehensive exam, thesis/dissertation. *Entrance requirements:* For master's and doctorate, GRE General Test, minimum GPA of 3.0. Additional exam requirements/recommendations for international students: Required—TOEFL (minimum score 600 paper-based; 250 computer-based; 100 iBT). *Application deadline:* For fall admission, 12/1 priority date for domestic students, 12/1 for international students. Application fee: $85. Electronic applications accepted. *Financial support:* In 2011–12, 5 research assistantships with full tuition reimbursements (averaging $29,100 per year) were awarded; Federal Work-Study, institutionally sponsored loans, scholarships/grants, traineeships, health care benefits, and unspecified assistantships also available. Financial award application deadline: 5/4. *Faculty research:* Endocrinology and metabolism, neurophysiology, mathematical modeling, cell transport, autoimmunity and cancer immunotherapy. *Total annual research expenditures:* $2.1 million. *Unit head:* Dr. Berislav Zlokovic, Chair, 323-442-2566, Fax: 323-442-2230, E-mail: zlokovic@usc.edu. *Application contact:* Janet Stoeckert, Administrative Director, Basic Sciences Departments, 323-442-3568, Fax: 323-442-1610, E-mail: janet.stoeckert@usc.edu.

The University of Texas Medical Branch, Graduate School of Biomedical Sciences, Program in Biochemistry and Molecular Biology, Galveston, TX 77555. Offers biochemistry (PhD); bioinformatics (PhD); biophysics (PhD); cell biology (PhD); computational biology (PhD); structural biology (PhD). *Degree requirements:* For doctorate, thesis/dissertation. *Entrance requirements:* Additional exam requirements/recommendations for international students: Required—TOEFL (minimum score 550 paper-based; 213 computer-based). Electronic applications accepted.

University of Toronto, Faculty of Medicine, Department of Medical Biophysics, Toronto, ON M5S 1A1, Canada. Offers M Sc, PhD. *Degree requirements:* For master's, thesis; for doctorate, thesis/dissertation. *Entrance requirements:* For master's and doctorate, resume, 2 letters of reference. Additional exam requirements/recommendations for international students: Required—TOEFL (minimum score 620 paper-based; 260 computer-based), TWE (minimum score 5). Electronic applications accepted.

University of Vermont, College of Medicine and Graduate College, Graduate Programs in Medicine, Department of Molecular Physiology and Biophysics, Burlington, VT 05405. Offers MS, PhD, MD/MS, MD/PhD. *Students:* 5 (2 women), 1 international. 4 applicants, 25% accepted, 1 enrolled. *Degree requirements:* For master's, thesis; for doctorate, thesis/dissertation. *Entrance requirements:* For master's and doctorate, GRE General Test. Additional exam requirements/recommendations for international students: Required—TOEFL (minimum score 550 paper-based; 213 computer-based; 80 iBT). *Application deadline:* For fall admission, 2/15 priority date for domestic students, 2/15 for international students. Applications are processed on a rolling basis. Application fee: $40. Electronic applications accepted. *Financial support:* Fellowships, research assistantships, and teaching assistantships available. Financial award application deadline: 3/1. *Unit head:* Dr. D. Warshaw, Chairperson, 802-656-2540. *Application contact:* Dr. Terese Ruiz, Coordinator, 802-656-2540.

University of Virginia, School of Medicine, Department of Molecular Physiology and Biological Physics, Charlottesville, VA 22903. Offers biological and physical sciences (MS); physiology (PhD); MD/PhD. *Faculty:* 29 full-time (5 women), 2 part-time/adjunct (0 women). *Students:* 19 full-time (10 women); includes 2 minority (both Black or African American, non-Hispanic/Latino). Average age 28. In 2011, 14 master's, 2 doctorates awarded. *Entrance requirements:* For doctorate, GRE General Test, GRE Subject Test. Additional exam requirements/recommendations for international students: Required—TOEFL. *Application deadline:* For fall admission, 2/15 for domestic and international students. Applications are processed on a rolling basis. Application fee: $60. Electronic applications accepted. *Financial support:* Fellowships, research assistantships, and teaching assistantships available. Financial award applicants required to submit FAFSA. *Unit head:* Dr. Mark Yeager, Chair, 434-924-5108, Fax: 434-982-1616, E-mail: my3r@virginia.edu. *Application contact:* Lesley L. Thomas, Director, Admissions Office, 434-924-5571, Fax: 434-982-2586, E-mail: medsch-adm@virginia.edu. Web site: http://www.healthsystem.virginia.edu/internet/physio/.

University of Virginia, School of Medicine, Interdisciplinary Program in Biophysics, Charlottesville, VA 22908. Offers PhD. *Students:* 12 full-time (3 women); includes 2 minority (both Asian, non-Hispanic/Latino), 6 international. Average age 28. In 2011, 5 doctorates awarded. *Degree requirements:* For doctorate, thesis/dissertation, research proposal, oral defense. *Entrance requirements:* For doctorate, GRE General Test, GRE Subject Test (recommended), 2 or more letters of recommendation. Additional exam requirements/recommendations for international students: Required—TOEFL. *Application deadline:* For fall admission, 4/15 for domestic and international students. Applications are processed on a rolling basis. Application fee: $60. Electronic applications accepted. *Financial support:* Fellowships with full tuition reimbursements, research assistantships with full tuition reimbursements, teaching assistantships with full tuition reimbursements, and tuition waivers (full) available. Financial award application deadline: 1/15; financial award applicants required to submit FAFSA. *Faculty research:* Structural biology and structural genomics, structural biology of membrane proteins and membrane biophysics, spectroscopy and thermodynamics of macromolecular interactions, high resolution imaging and cell biophysics. *Unit head:* Robert K. Nakamoto, Director, 434-982-6390. *Application contact:* Pam Mullinex, Graduate Program Administrator, 434-243-7248, Fax: 434-982-1616, E-mail: prm8b@virginia.edu. Web site: http://www.healthsystem.virginia.edu/internet/biophysics/.

University of Washington, Graduate School, School of Medicine, Graduate Programs in Medicine, Department of Physiology and Biophysics, Seattle, WA 98195. Offers PhD. *Degree requirements:* For doctorate, thesis/dissertation. *Entrance requirements:* For doctorate, GRE General Test. Additional exam requirements/recommendations for international students: Required—TOEFL (minimum score 580 paper-based; 237 computer-based; 70 iBT). *Faculty research:* Membrane and cell biophysics, neuroendocrinology, cardiovascular and respiratory physiology, systems neurophysiology and behavior, molecular physiology.

The University of Western Ontario, Faculty of Graduate Studies, Biosciences Division, Department of Medical Biophysics, London, ON N6A 5B8, Canada. Offers M Sc, PhD. *Degree requirements:* For master's, thesis; for doctorate, thesis/dissertation. *Entrance requirements:* Additional exam requirements/recommendations for international students: Required—TOEFL. *Faculty research:* Haemodynamics and cardiovascular biomechanics, microcirculation, orthopedic biomechanics, radiobiology, medical imaging.

University of Wisconsin–Madison, Graduate School, Program in Biophysics, Madison, WI 53706-1380. Offers PhD. *Degree requirements:* For doctorate, comprehensive exam, thesis/dissertation. *Entrance requirements:* For doctorate, GRE General Test, minimum GPA of 3.0. Additional exam requirements/recommendations for international students: Required—TOEFL (minimum score 600 paper-based). Electronic

applications accepted. *Expenses:* Tuition, state resident: full-time $10,296; part-time $643.51 per credit. Tuition, nonresident: full-time $24,054; part-time $1503.40 per credit. *Required fees:* $70.06 per credit. Tuition and fees vary according to course load, campus/location, program and reciprocity agreements. *Faculty research:* NMR spectroscopy, high-speed automated DNA sequencing, x-ray crystallography, neuronal signaling and exocytosis, protein structure.

Vanderbilt University, Graduate School and School of Medicine, Department of Molecular Physiology and Biophysics, Nashville, TN 37240-1001. Offers MS, PhD, MD/PhD. *Faculty:* 37 full-time (8 women). *Students:* 39 full-time (25 women); includes 10 minority (4 Black or African American, non-Hispanic/Latino; 1 American Indian or Alaska Native, non-Hispanic/Latino; 3 Hispanic/Latino; 2 Two or more races, non-Hispanic/Latino), 4 international. Average age 28. In 2011, 3 doctorates awarded. *Degree requirements:* For doctorate, comprehensive exam, thesis/dissertation, preliminary, qualifying, and final exams. *Entrance requirements:* For doctorate, GRE General Test, GRE Subject Test (recommended). Additional exam requirements/recommendations for international students: Required—TOEFL (minimum score 570 paper-based; 230 computer-based; 88 iBT). *Application deadline:* For fall admission, 1/15 for domestic and international students. Application fee: $0. Electronic applications accepted. *Financial support:* Fellowships with full tuition reimbursements, research assistantships with full tuition reimbursements, Federal Work-Study, institutionally sponsored loans, scholarships/grants, traineeships, health care benefits, and tuition waivers (partial) available. Financial award application deadline: 1/15; financial award applicants required to submit CSS PROFILE or FAFSA. *Faculty research:* Biophysics, cell signaling and gene regulation, human genetics, diabetes and obesity, neuroscience. *Unit head:* Dr. Roger Cone, Chair, 615-936-7085, Fax: 615-343-4075, E-mail: roger.cone@vanderbilt.edu. *Application contact:* Angie Pernell, Administrative Assistant/Director of Graduate Studies Assistant, 615-322-7001, Fax: 615-343-0490, E-mail: angie.pernell@vanderbilt.edu. Web site: http://www.mc.vanderbilt.edu/medschool/mpb/.

Vanderbilt University, School of Medicine, Program in Chemical and Physical Biology, Nashville, TN 37240-1001. Offers PhD. *Degree requirements:* For doctorate, comprehensive exam, thesis/dissertation, dissertation defense. *Entrance requirements:* For doctorate, GRE, 3 letters of recommendation, official transcripts. Additional exam requirements/recommendations for international students: Required—TOEFL. Electronic applications accepted. *Faculty research:* Mathematical modeling, enzyme kinetics, structural biology, genomics, proteomics and mass spectrometry.

Washington State University, Graduate School, College of Sciences, School of Molecular Biosciences, Program in Biochemistry and Biophysics, Pullman, WA 99164. Offers MS, PhD. *Faculty:* 23 full-time (5 women), 21 part-time/adjunct (4 women). *Students:* 53 full-time (24 women), 9 part-time (3 women); includes 7 minority (4 Asian, non-Hispanic/Latino; 3 Hispanic/Latino), 4 international. Average age 26. 116 applicants, 22% accepted, 15 enrolled. In 2011, 3 master's awarded. Terminal master's awarded for partial completion of doctoral program. *Degree requirements:* For master's, thesis or alternative, oral exam; for doctorate, comprehensive exam, thesis/dissertation, oral exam, written exam. *Entrance requirements:* For master's and doctorate, GRE General Test, minimum GPA of 3.0. Additional exam requirements/recommendations for international students: Required—TOEFL (minimum score 550 paper-based; 213 computer-based). *Application deadline:* For fall admission, 12/15 for domestic and international students. Application fee: $75. Electronic applications accepted. *Financial support:* In 2011–12, 5 fellowships with full tuition reimbursements (averaging $18,384 per year), 11 research assistantships with full tuition reimbursements (averaging $18,384 per year), 10 teaching assistantships with full tuition reimbursements (averaging $18,384 per year) were awarded; career-related internships or fieldwork, Federal Work-Study, institutionally sponsored loans, traineeships, and health care benefits also available. Financial award application deadline: 4/1; financial award applicants required to submit FAFSA. *Faculty research:* Gene regulation, signal transduction, protein export, reproductive biology, DNA repair. *Total annual research expenditures:* $5.8 million. *Unit head:* Dr. John H. Nilson, Director, 509-335-8724, Fax: 509-335-9688, E-mail: jhn@wsu.edu. *Application contact:* Kelly G. McGovern, 509-335-6424, E-mail: mcgnerk@wsu.edu. Web site: http://molecular.biosciences.wsu.edu/.

Weill Cornell Medical College, Weill Cornell Graduate School of Medical Sciences, Physiology, Biophysics and Systems Biology Program, New York, NY 10065. Offers MS, PhD. *Faculty:* 36 full-time (9 women). *Students:* 48 full-time (15 women); includes 7 minority (1 Black or African American, non-Hispanic/Latino; 4 Asian, non-Hispanic/Latino; 1 Hispanic/Latino; 1 Native Hawaiian or other Pacific Islander, non-Hispanic/Latino), 26 international. Average age 23. 37 applicants, 32% accepted, 5 enrolled. In 2011, 12 doctorates awarded. Terminal master's awarded for partial completion of doctoral program. *Degree requirements:* For master's, comprehensive exam; for doctorate, thesis/dissertation, final exam. *Entrance requirements:* For doctorate, GRE General Test, introductory courses in biology, inorganic and organic chemistry, physics, and mathematics. Additional exam requirements/recommendations for international students: Required—TOEFL. *Application deadline:* For fall admission, 12/1 for domestic students. Application fee: $60. *Expenses: Tuition:* Full-time $46,001. *Financial support:* In 2011–12, 4 fellowships (averaging $21,210 per year) were awarded; scholarships/grants, health care benefits, and stipends (given to all students) also available. *Faculty research:* Receptor-mediated regulation of cell function, molecular properties of channels or receptors, bioinformatics, mathematical modeling. *Unit head:* Dr. Emre Aksay, Co-Director, 212-746-6207, E-mail: ema2004@med.cornell.edu. *Application contact:* Audrey Rivera, Program Coordinator, 212-746-6361, E-mail: ajr2004@med.cornell.edu. Web site: http://weill.cornell.edu/gradschool/program/physiology.html.

Wright State University, School of Graduate Studies, College of Science and Mathematics, Department of Neuroscience, Cell Biology, and Physiology, Dayton, OH 45435. Offers anatomy (MS); physiology and biophysics (MS). *Degree requirements:* For master's, thesis optional. *Entrance requirements:* Additional exam requirements/recommendations for international students: Required—TOEFL. *Faculty research:* Reproductive cell biology, neurobiology of pain, neurohistochemistry.

Yale University, Graduate School of Arts and Sciences, Department of Molecular Biophysics and Biochemistry, New Haven, CT 06520. Offers PhD. *Degree requirements:* For doctorate, thesis/dissertation. *Entrance requirements:* For doctorate, GRE General Test, GRE Subject Test.

Molecular Biophysics

Baylor College of Medicine, Graduate School of Biomedical Sciences, Program in Structural and Computational Biology and Molecular Biophysics, Houston, TX 77030-3498. Offers PhD, MD/PhD. MD/PhD offered jointly with Rice University and University of Houston. *Faculty:* 84 full-time (10 women). *Students:* 38 full-time (12 women); includes 4 minority (1 Black or African American, non-Hispanic/Latino; 2 Asian, non-Hispanic/Latino; 1 Hispanic/Latino), 19 international. Average age 28. 74 applicants, 14% accepted, 8 enrolled. In 2011, 6 doctorates awarded. *Degree requirements:* For doctorate, thesis/dissertation, public defense. *Entrance requirements:* For doctorate, GRE General Test, GRE Subject Test (strongly recommended), minimum GPA of 3.0. Additional exam requirements/recommendations for international students: Required—TOEFL. *Application deadline:* For fall admission, 1/1 for domestic students. Application fee: $0. Electronic applications accepted. *Financial support:* In 2011–12, 38 students received support, including 21 fellowships with full tuition reimbursements available (averaging $29,000 per year), 17 research assistantships with full tuition reimbursements available (averaging $29,000 per year); career-related internships or fieldwork, Federal Work-Study, institutionally sponsored loans, health care benefits, and scholarships (to all students unless there are grant funds available to pay tuition) also available. Financial award applicants required to submit FAFSA. *Faculty research:* Computational biology, structural biology, biophysics. *Unit head:* Dr. Wah Chiu, Director, 713-798-6985. *Application contact:* Amber Eakin, Administrative Coordinator, 713-798-5197, Fax: 713-798-6325, E-mail: ameakin@bcm.edu.

California Institute of Technology, Division of Biology and Division of Chemistry and Chemical Engineering, Biochemistry and Molecular Biophysics Graduate Option, Pasadena, CA 91125-0001. Offers PhD. *Degree requirements:* For doctorate, thesis/dissertation, qualifying exam. *Entrance requirements:* For doctorate, GRE General Test. Additional exam requirements/recommendations for international students: Required—TOEFL. Electronic applications accepted.

California Institute of Technology, Division of Chemistry and Chemical Engineering, Pasadena, CA 91125-0001. Offers biochemistry and molecular biophysics (MS, PhD); chemical engineering (MS, PhD); chemistry (MS, PhD). Part-time and evening/weekend programs available. Postbaccalaureate distance learning degree programs offered (minimal on-campus study). *Faculty:* 40 full-time (7 women). *Students:* 315 full-time (116 women); includes 26 minority (2 Black or African American, non-Hispanic/Latino; 15 Asian, non-Hispanic/Latino; 5 Hispanic/Latino; 1 Native Hawaiian or other Pacific Islander, non-Hispanic/Latino; 3 Two or more races, non-Hispanic/Latino). Average age 26. 704 applicants, 18% accepted, 46 enrolled. In 2011, 10 master's, 46 doctorates awarded. Terminal master's awarded for partial completion of doctoral program. *Degree requirements:* For master's, thesis; for doctorate, thesis/dissertation. *Entrance requirements:* Additional exam requirements/recommendations for international students: Required—TOEFL; Recommended—IELTS, TWE. *Application deadline:* For fall admission, 1/1 for domestic and international students. Application fee: $80. Electronic applications accepted. *Financial support:* In 2011–12, 9 students received support. Fellowships, research assistantships, teaching assistantships, Federal Work-Study, institutionally sponsored loans, scholarships/grants, traineeships, health care benefits, and unspecified assistantships available. Financial award application deadline: 1/1. *Unit head:* Prof. Jacqueline K. Barton, Chair, 626-395-3646, Fax: 626-395-6948, E-mail: jkbarton@caltech.edu. *Application contact:* Natalie Gilmore, Graduate Office, 626-395-3812, Fax: 626-577-9246, E-mail: ngilmore@its.caltech.edu. Web site: http://cce.caltech.edu/index.html.

Carnegie Mellon University, Mellon College of Science, Joint Pitt + CMU Molecular Biophysics and Structural Biology Graduate Program, Pittsburgh, PA 15213-3891. Offers PhD. Program offered jointly with University of Pittsburgh. *Degree requirements:* For doctorate, comprehensive exam, thesis/dissertation. *Entrance requirements:* For doctorate, GRE General Test. Additional exam requirements/recommendations for international students: Required—TOEFL (minimum score 600 paper-based; 250 computer-based; 100 iBT), IELTS (minimum score 7). Electronic applications accepted. *Faculty research:* Structural biology, protein dynamics and folding, computational biophysics, molecular informatics, membrane biophysics and ion channels, NMR, x-ray crystallography cryaelectron microscopy.

Duke University, Graduate School, Program in Structural Biology and Biophysics, Durham, NC 27710. Offers Certificate. Students must be enrolled in a participating PhD program (biochemistry, cell biology, chemistry, molecular genetics, neurobiology, pharmacology). *Faculty:* 25 full-time. *Students:* 3 full-time (2 women), 2 international. 21 applicants, 24% accepted, 3 enrolled. *Entrance requirements:* For degree, GRE General Test. Additional exam requirements/recommendations for international students: Required—TOEFL (minimum score 550 paper-based; 213 computer-based; 83 iBT), IELTS (minimum score 7). *Application deadline:* For fall admission, 12/8 priority date for domestic students, 12/8 for international students. Application fee: $75. *Expenses: Tuition:* Full-time $40,720. *Required fees:* $3107. *Financial support:* Application deadline: 12/8. *Unit head:* David Richardson, Director of Graduate Studies, 919-684-6559, Fax: 919-684-8346, E-mail: carol.richardson@duke.edu. *Application contact:* Elizabeth Hutton, Director of Admissions, 919-684-3913, Fax: 919-684-2277, E-mail: grad-admissions@duke.edu. Web site: http://sbb.duke.edu.

Florida State University, The Graduate School, College of Arts and Sciences, Program in Molecular Biophysics, Tallahassee, FL 32306. Offers computational structural biology (PhD); molecular biophysics (PhD). *Faculty:* 50 full-time (8 women). *Students:* 24 full-time (10 women); includes 7 minority (4 Asian, non-Hispanic/Latino; 3 Hispanic/Latino), 8 international. Average age 28. 35 applicants, 29% accepted, 5 enrolled. In 2011, 3 doctorates awarded. *Degree requirements:* For doctorate, comprehensive exam, thesis/dissertation, teaching 1 term in professor's major department. *Entrance requirements:* For doctorate, GRE General Test. Additional exam requirements/recommendations for international students: Required—TOEFL (minimum score 600 paper-based; 250 computer-based; 90 iBT). *Application deadline:* For fall admission, 1/15 for domestic students, 2/15 for international students. Applications are processed on a rolling basis. Application fee: $30. Electronic applications accepted. *Expenses:* Tuition, state resident: full-time $9474; part-time $350.88 per credit hour. Tuition, nonresident: full-time $16,236; part-time $601.34 per credit hour. *Required fees:* $630 per semester. One-time fee: $20. Tuition and fees vary according to course load and campus/location. *Financial support:* In 2011–12, 23 students received support, including 1 fellowship with partial tuition reimbursement available (averaging $10,000 per year), 19 research assistantships with partial tuition reimbursements available (averaging $22,050 per year), 4 teaching assistantships with partial tuition reimbursements available (averaging $22,050 per year); scholarships/grants, health care benefits, and unspecified assistantships also available. Financial award applicants required to submit FAFSA. *Faculty research:* Protein and nucleic acid structure and function, membrane protein

structure, computational biophysics, 3-D image reconstruction. *Total annual research expenditures:* $1.7 million. *Unit head:* Dr. Hong Li, Director, 850-644-6785, Fax: 850-644-7244, E-mail: hongli@sb.fsu.edu. *Application contact:* Lyn Kittle, Academic Coordinator, Graduate Programs, 850-644-1012, Fax: 850-644-7244, E-mail: lkittle@fsu.edu. Web site: http://www.sb.fsu.edu/mob/.

Illinois Institute of Technology, Graduate College, College of Science and Letters, Department of Biological, Chemical and Physical Sciences, Biology Division, Chicago, IL 60616. Offers biochemistry (MBS, MS); biology (PhD); biotechnology (MBS, MS); cell and molecular biology (MBS, MS); microbiology (MB, MS); molecular biochemistry and biophysics (PhD); molecular biology and biophysics (MS). Part-time and evening/weekend programs available. Postbaccalaureate distance learning degree programs offered (minimal on-campus study). Terminal master's awarded for partial completion of doctoral program. *Degree requirements:* For master's, comprehensive exam, thesis (for some programs); for doctorate, comprehensive exam, thesis/dissertation. *Entrance requirements:* For master's, GRE General Test (minimum score 1000 Quantitative and Verbal, 2.5 Analytical Writing), minimum undergraduate GPA of 3.0; for doctorate, GRE General Test (minimum score 1200 Quantitative and Verbal, 3.0 Analytical Writing), minimum undergraduate GPA of 3.0. Additional exam requirements/recommendations for international students: Required—TOEFL (minimum score 523 paper-based; 213 computer-based; 70 iBT); Recommended—IELTS (minimum score 5.5). Electronic applications accepted. *Faculty research:* Structure and biophysics of macromolecular systems; efficacy and mechanism of action of chemopreventive agents in experimental carcinogenesis of breast, colon, lung and prostate; study of fundamental structural biochemistry problems that have direct links to the understanding and treatment of disease; spectroscopic techniques for the study of multi-domain proteins; molecular mechanisms of cancer and cancer gene therapy.

The Johns Hopkins University, School of Medicine, Graduate Programs in Medicine, Program in Molecular Biophysics, Baltimore, MD 21218-2699. Offers MS, PhD. Program held jointly with Zanvyl Krieger School of Arts and Sciences and G. W. C. Whiting School of Engineering. *Degree requirements:* For doctorate, comprehensive exam, thesis/dissertation, oral exam, thesis defense. *Entrance requirements:* For doctorate, GRE. Additional exam requirements/recommendations for international students: Required—TOEFL (minimum score 600 paper-based; 250 computer-based), IELTS; Recommended—TWE. Electronic applications accepted. *Faculty research:* Protein folding and dynamics; membranes and membrane proteins; structural biology; RNA biophysics; enzymes and metabolic pathways; computation, theory and prediction; DNA protein interactions; single molecule studies; protein design and evolution.

Rutgers, The State University of New Jersey, New Brunswick, Graduate School-New Brunswick, BioMaPS Institute for Quantitative Biology, Piscataway, NJ 08854-8097. Offers computational biology and molecular biophysics (PhD). *Degree requirements:* For doctorate, comprehensive exam, thesis/dissertation. *Entrance requirements:* For doctorate, GRE. Additional exam requirements/recommendations for international students: Required—TOEFL. Electronic applications accepted. *Faculty research:* Structural biology, systems biology, bioinformatics, translational medicine, genomics.

Texas Tech University Health Sciences Center, Graduate School of Biomedical Sciences, Department of Cell Physiology and Molecular Biophysics, Lubbock, TX 79430. Offers MS, PhD, MD/PhD. Terminal master's awarded for partial completion of doctoral program. *Degree requirements:* For master's, thesis; for doctorate, thesis/dissertation. *Entrance requirements:* For master's and doctorate, GRE General Test, minimum GPA of 3.4. Additional exam requirements/recommendations for international students: Required—TOEFL. Electronic applications accepted. *Faculty research:* Cardiovascular physiology, neurophysiology, renal physiology, respiratory physiology.

University of Massachusetts Amherst, Graduate School, Interdisciplinary Programs, Program in Molecular and Cellular Biology, Amherst, MA 01003. Offers biological chemistry and molecular biophysics (PhD); biomedicine (PhD); cellular and developmental biology (PhD). Part-time programs available. *Students:* 62 full-time (40 women), 18 part-time (9 women); includes 14 minority (2 Black or African American, non-Hispanic/Latino; 4 Asian, non-Hispanic/Latino; 7 Hispanic/Latino; 1 Two or more races, non-Hispanic/Latino), 28 international. Average age 27. 138 applicants, 36% accepted, 22 enrolled. In 2011, 8 doctorates awarded. Terminal master's awarded for partial completion of doctoral program. *Degree requirements:* For doctorate, comprehensive exam, thesis/dissertation. *Entrance requirements:* For doctorate, GRE General Test. Additional exam requirements/recommendations for international students: Required—TOEFL (minimum score 550 paper-based; 213 computer-based; 80 iBT), IELTS (minimum score 6.5). *Application deadline:* For fall admission, 12/1 for domestic and international students. Applications are processed on a rolling basis. Application fee: $50 ($65 for international students). Electronic applications accepted. Tuition and fees vary according to course load, campus/location and program. *Financial support:* Fellowships with full and partial tuition reimbursements, research assistantships with full and partial tuition reimbursements, teaching assistantships with full and partial tuition reimbursements, career-related internships or fieldwork, Federal Work-Study, scholarships/grants, traineeships, health care benefits, tuition waivers (full and partial), and unspecified assistantships available. Support available to part-time students. Financial award application deadline: 12/1. *Unit head:* Dr. Barbara Osborne,

Graduate Program Director, 413-545-3246, Fax: 413-545-1812. *Application contact:* Lindsay DeSantis, Interim Supervisor of Admissions, 413-545-0722, Fax: 413-577-0010, E-mail: gradadm@grad.umass.edu. Web site: http://www.bio.umass.edu/mcb/.

University of Pennsylvania, Perelman School of Medicine, Biomedical Graduate Studies, Graduate Group in Biochemistry and Molecular Biophysics, Philadelphia, PA 19104. Offers PhD, MD/PhD, VMD/PhD. *Faculty:* 74. *Students:* 81 full-time (30 women); includes 22 minority (3 Black or African American, non-Hispanic/Latino; 11 Asian, non-Hispanic/Latino; 8 Hispanic/Latino), 8 international. 122 applicants, 30% accepted, 14 enrolled. In 2011, 4 doctorates awarded. *Degree requirements:* For doctorate, thesis/dissertation. *Entrance requirements:* For doctorate, GRE General Test. Additional exam requirements/recommendations for international students: Required—TOEFL. *Application deadline:* For fall admission, 12/1 priority date for domestic students, 12/1 for international students. Applications are processed on a rolling basis. Application fee: $80. Electronic applications accepted. *Expenses: Tuition:* Full-time $26,660; part-time $4944 per course. *Required fees:* $2318; $291 per course. Tuition and fees vary according to course load, degree level and program. *Financial support:* In 2011–12, 81 students received support. Fellowships, research assistantships, scholarships/grants, traineeships, and unspecified assistantships available. *Faculty research:* Biochemistry of cell differentiation, tissue culture, intermediary metabolism, structure of proteins and nucleic acids, biochemical genetics. *Unit head:* Dr. Kathryn Ferguson, Chairperson, 215-573-1207, E-mail: ferguso2@mail.med.upenn.edu. *Application contact:* Ruth Keris, Administrator. Web site: http://www.med.upenn.edu/bmbgrad/.

University of Pittsburgh, School of Medicine and Dietrich School of Arts and Sciences, Joint Pitt + CMU Molecular Biophysics and Structural Biology Graduate Program, Pittsburgh, PA 15260. Offers PhD. *Faculty:* 54 full-time (16 women). *Students:* 19 full-time (5 women); includes 3 minority (1 Asian, non-Hispanic/Latino; 1 Hispanic/Latino; 1 Native Hawaiian or other Pacific Islander, non-Hispanic/Latino), 6 international. Average age 26. 63 applicants, 10% accepted, 5 enrolled. In 2011, 3 doctorates awarded. *Degree requirements:* For doctorate, comprehensive exam, thesis/dissertation. *Entrance requirements:* For doctorate, GRE General Test. Additional exam requirements/recommendations for international students: Required—TOEFL (minimum score 600 paper-based; 250 computer-based; 100 iBT), IELTS (minimum score 7). *Application deadline:* For fall admission, 12/15 priority date for domestic students, 12/15 for international students. Application fee: $0. Electronic applications accepted. *Expenses:* Tuition, state resident: full-time $18,774; part-time $760 per credit. Tuition, nonresident: full-time $30,736; part-time $1258 per credit. *Required fees:* $740; $200 per term. Tuition and fees vary according to program. *Financial support:* In 2011–12, 5 fellowships with full tuition reimbursements (averaging $28,646 per year), 14 research assistantships with full tuition reimbursements (averaging $25,500 per year) were awarded; institutionally sponsored loans, scholarships/grants, traineeships, and unspecified assistantships also available. *Faculty research:* Structural biology, protein dynamics and folding, computational biophysics, molecular informatics, membrane biophysics and ion channels, x-ray crystallography cryaelectron microscopy. *Unit head:* Dr. Angela M. Gronenborn, Director, 412-648-8957, Fax: 412-648-1077, E-mail: mbsbinfo@medschool.pitt.edu. *Application contact:* Jennifer L. Walker, Program Coordinator, 412-648-8957, Fax: 412-648-1077, E-mail: mbsbinfo@medschool.pitt.edu. Web site: http://www.mbsb.pitt.edu.

The University of Texas Medical Branch, Graduate School of Biomedical Sciences, Program in Cellular Physiology and Molecular Biophysics, Galveston, TX 77555. Offers MS, PhD. *Degree requirements:* For master's, thesis or alternative; for doctorate, thesis/dissertation. *Entrance requirements:* For master's and doctorate, GRE General Test. Additional exam requirements/recommendations for international students: Required—TOEFL (minimum score 550 paper-based; 213 computer-based). Electronic applications accepted.

The University of Texas Southwestern Medical Center, Southwestern Graduate School of Biomedical Sciences, Division of Basic Science, Program in Molecular Biophysics, Dallas, TX 75390. Offers PhD. *Degree requirements:* For doctorate, thesis/dissertation, qualifying exam. *Entrance requirements:* For doctorate, GRE General Test, minimum GPA of 3.0. Additional exam requirements/recommendations for international students: Required—TOEFL. Electronic applications accepted. *Faculty research:* Optical spectroscopy, x-ray crystallography, protein chemistry, ion channels, contractile and cytoskeletal proteins.

Washington University in St. Louis, Graduate School of Arts and Sciences, Division of Biology and Biomedical Sciences, Program in Computational and Molecular Biophysics, St. Louis, MO 63130-4899. Offers PhD. *Degree requirements:* For doctorate, thesis/dissertation. *Entrance requirements:* For doctorate, GRE General Test, GRE Subject Test. Electronic applications accepted.

Yale University, School of Medicine and Graduate School of Arts and Sciences, Combined Program in Biological and Biomedical Sciences (BBS), Molecular Biophysics and Biochemistry Track, New Haven, CT 06520. Offers PhD, MD/PhD. *Degree requirements:* For doctorate, thesis/dissertation. *Entrance requirements:* For doctorate, GRE General Test. Additional exam requirements/recommendations for international students: Required—TOEFL. Electronic applications accepted.

Radiation Biology

Auburn University, College of Veterinary Medicine and Graduate School, Graduate Programs in Veterinary Medicine, Auburn University, AL 36849. Offers biomedical sciences (MS, PhD), including anatomy, physiology and pharmacology (MS), biomedical sciences (PhD), clinical sciences (MS), large animal surgery and medicine (MS), pathobiology (MS), radiology (MS), small animal surgery and medicine (MS); DVM/MS. Part-time programs available. *Faculty:* 100 full-time (40 women), 5 part-time/adjunct (1 woman). *Students:* 17 full-time (13 women), 59 part-time (33 women); includes 6 minority (1 Black or African American, non-Hispanic/Latino; 3 Asian, non-Hispanic/Latino; 2 Hispanic/Latino), 30 international. Average age 30. 36 applicants, 69% accepted, 11 enrolled. In 2011, 19 master's awarded. *Degree requirements:* For doctorate, thesis/dissertation. *Entrance requirements:* For master's, GRE General Test; for doctorate, GRE General Test, GRE Subject Test. *Application deadline:* For fall admission, 7/7 for domestic students; for spring admission, 11/24 for domestic students. Applications are processed on a rolling basis. Application fee: $50 ($60 for international students). Electronic applications accepted. *Expenses:* Tuition, state resident: full-time $7290; part-time $405 per credit hour. Tuition, nonresident: full-time $21,870; part-time $1215 per credit hour. International tuition: $22,000 full-time. *Required fees:* $1402. *Financial support:* Research assistantships, teaching assistantships, and Federal Work-

Study available. Support available to part-time students. Financial award application deadline: 3/15; financial award applicants required to submit FAFSA. *Unit head:* Dr. Calvin Johnson, Acting Dean, 334-844-2650. *Application contact:* Dr. George Flowers, Dean of the Graduate School, 334-844-2125.

Austin Peay State University, College of Graduate Studies, College of Science and Mathematics, Department of Biology, Clarksville, TN 37044. Offers clinical laboratory science (MS); radiologic science (MS). Part-time programs available. *Faculty:* 8 full-time (3 women), 1 part-time/adjunct (0 women). *Students:* 6 full-time (2 women), 19 part-time (12 women); includes 3 minority (2 Black or African American, non-Hispanic/Latino; 1 Hispanic/Latino), 1 international. Average age 28. 13 applicants, 92% accepted, 9 enrolled. In 2011, 9 master's awarded. *Degree requirements:* For master's, comprehensive exam, thesis optional. *Entrance requirements:* For master's, GRE General Test, 3 letters of recommendation, minimum undergraduate GPA of 2.5. Additional exam requirements/recommendations for international students: Required—TOEFL (minimum score 500 paper-based; 173 computer-based). *Application deadline:* For fall admission, 8/1 priority date for domestic students. Applications are processed on a rolling basis. Application fee: $25. Electronic applications accepted. *Expenses:* Tuition, state resident: part-time $350 per credit hour. Tuition, nonresident: full-time

Radiation Biology

$20,644; part-time $971 per credit hour. *Required fees:* $1224; $61.20 per credit hour. *Financial support:* In 2011–12, research assistantships with full tuition reimbursements (averaging $5,184 per year) were awarded; career-related internships or fieldwork, Federal Work-Study, institutionally sponsored loans, scholarships/grants, and unspecified assistantships also available. Support available to part-time students. Financial award application deadline: 3/1. *Faculty research:* Non-paint source pollution, amphibian biomonitoring, aquatic toxicology, biological indicators of water quality, taxonomy. *Unit head:* Dr. Don Dailey, Chair, 931-221-7781, Fax: 931-221-6323, E-mail: daileyd@apsu.edu. *Application contact:* Kendra Bryant, Graduate Admissions, 800-844-2778, Fax: 931-221-6188, E-mail: admissionsweb@apsu.edu. Web site: http://www.apsu.edu/biology.

Colorado State University, College of Veterinary Medicine and Biomedical Sciences, Department of Environmental and Radiological Health Sciences, Fort Collins, CO 80523-1681. Offers environmental health (MS, PhD); radiological health sciences (MS, PhD). Part-time programs available. *Faculty:* 26 full-time (7 women), 3 part-time/adjunct (0 women). *Students:* 105 full-time (66 women), 28 part-time (14 women); includes 20 minority (5 Black or African American, non-Hispanic/Latino; 1 American Indian or Alaska Native, non-Hispanic/Latino; 10 Hispanic/Latino; 4 Two or more races, non-Hispanic/Latino), 7 international. Average age 28. 92 applicants, 82% accepted, 56 enrolled. In 2011, 39 master's, 23 doctorates awarded. Terminal master's awarded for partial completion of doctoral program. *Degree requirements:* For master's, comprehensive exam (for some programs), thesis (for some programs), publishable paper; for doctorate, comprehensive exam, thesis/dissertation, publishable paper. *Entrance requirements:* For master's, GRE General Test, 1 year of course work in biology lab and chemistry lab, 1 semester of course work in organic chemistry, course work in calculus, resume, letters of recommendation; for doctorate, GRE General Test, 1 year of course work in biology lab and chemistry lab, 1 semester of course work in organic chemistry, course work in calculus, resume, letters of recommendation, evidence of research capability. Additional exam requirements/recommendations for international students: Required—TOEFL (minimum score 550 paper-based; 213 computer-based). *Application deadline:* For fall admission, 6/1 for domestic and international students; for spring admission, 11/1 for domestic and international students. Applications are processed on a rolling basis. Application fee: $50. Electronic applications accepted. *Expenses:* Tuition, state resident: full-time $7992. Tuition, nonresident: full-time $19,592. *Required fees:* $1735; $58 per credit. *Financial support:* In 2011–12, 20 students received support, including 5 fellowships with full and partial tuition reimbursements available (averaging $45,693 per year), 13 research assistantships with full and partial tuition reimbursements available (averaging $18,772 per year), 2 teaching assistantships with full and partial tuition reimbursements available (averaging $12,330 per year); career-related internships or fieldwork, Federal Work-Study, institutionally sponsored loans, traineeships, and unspecified assistantships also available. Support available to part-time students. Financial award application deadline: 2/1; financial award applicants required to submit FAFSA. *Faculty research:* Epidemiology, toxicology, industrial hygiene, occupational health, radiation therapy. *Total annual research expenditures:* $7.8 million. *Unit head:* Dr. Jac A. Nickoloff, Head, 970-491-6674, Fax: 970-491-0623, E-mail: j.nickoloff@colostate.edu. *Application contact:* Jeanne A. Brockway, Graduate Program Coordinator, 970-491-5003, Fax: 970-491-0623, E-mail: jeanne.brockway@colostate.edu. Web site: http://www.cvmbs.colostate.edu/erhs/.

Georgetown University, Graduate School of Arts and Sciences, Programs in Biomedical Sciences, Department of Health Physics, Washington, DC 20057. Offers health physics (MS); radiobiology (MS). *Degree requirements:* For master's, thesis. *Entrance requirements:* Additional exam requirements/recommendations for international students: Required—TOEFL.

Université de Sherbrooke, Faculty of Medicine and Health Sciences, Graduate Programs in Medicine, Program in Radiobiology, Sherbrooke, QC J1H 5N4, Canada. Offers M Sc, PhD. Terminal master's awarded for partial completion of doctoral program. *Degree requirements:* For master's, thesis; for doctorate, thesis/dissertation. Electronic applications accepted. *Faculty research:* DNA repair, physiochemical actions of radiation, radiopharmacy, phototherapy, imaging.

The University of Iowa, Roy J. and Lucille A. Carver College of Medicine and Graduate College, Graduate Programs in Medicine, Program in Free Radical and Radiation Biology, Iowa City, IA 52242-1316. Offers MS, PhD. Part-time programs available. *Faculty:* 5 full-time (1 woman). *Students:* 17 full-time (4 women). Average age 26. 6 applicants, 67% accepted, 4 enrolled. In 2011, 1 degree awarded. *Degree requirements:* For doctorate, thesis/dissertation. *Entrance requirements:* For master's and doctorate, GRE. Additional exam requirements/recommendations for international students: Required—TOEFL. *Application deadline:* For fall admission, 5/31 priority date for domestic students, 5/31 for international students; for spring admission, 10/31 for domestic and international students. Applications are processed on a rolling basis. Application fee: $60 ($85 for international students). *Financial support:* In 2011–12, fellowships with partial tuition reimbursements (averaging $25,000 per year), research assistantships with tuition reimbursements (averaging $25,000 per year) were awarded; traineeships, health care benefits, tuition waivers (partial), and unspecified assistantships also available. *Faculty research:* Radiation injury and cellular repair, cell proliferation kinetics, free radical biology, tumor control, PET imaging, EPR. *Total annual research expenditures:* $1 million. *Unit head:* Dr. Douglas R. Spitz, Head, 319-335-8019, Fax: 319-335-8039. *Application contact:* Jennifer K. DeWitte, Grant and Program Administrator, 319-335-8164, Fax: 319-335-8039, E-mail: jennifer-dewitte@uiowa.edu. Web site: http://radiology.uiowa.edu/.

University of Oklahoma Health Sciences Center, College of Medicine and Graduate College, Graduate Programs in Medicine, Department of Radiological Sciences, Oklahoma City, OK 73190. Offers medical radiation physics (MS, PhD), including diagnostic radiology, nuclear medicine, radiation therapy, ultrasound. Part-time programs available. Terminal master's awarded for partial completion of doctoral program. *Degree requirements:* For master's, thesis; for doctorate, thesis/dissertation. *Entrance requirements:* For master's, GRE General Test; for doctorate, GRE General Test, 3 letters of recommendation. Additional exam requirements/recommendations for international students: Required—TOEFL. *Faculty research:* Monte Carlo applications in radiation therapy, observer-performed studies in diagnostic radiology, error analysis in gated cardiac nuclear medicine studies, nuclear medicine absorbed fraction determinations.

HARVARD UNIVERSITY
Biophysics Program

Program of Study

The Committee on Higher Degrees in Biophysics offers a program of study leading to the Ph.D. degree. The committee comprises senior representatives of the Departments of Chemistry and Chemical Biology, Physics, and Molecular and Cellular Biology; the School of Engineering and Applied Physics; and the Division of Medical Sciences. Students receive sufficient training in physics, biology, and chemistry to enable them to apply the concepts and methods of the physical sciences to the solution of biological problems.

An initial goal of the Biophysics Program is to provide an introduction through courses and seminars to several of the diverse areas of biophysics, such as structural molecular biology, cell and membrane biophysics, neurobiology, molecular genetics, physical biochemistry, and theoretical biophysics. The program is flexible, and special effort has been devoted to minimizing course work and other formal requirements. Students engage in several research rotations during their first two years. The qualifying examination is taken at the end of the second year to determine admission to candidacy. Students undertake dissertation research as early as possible in the field and subject of their choice. Opportunities for dissertation research are available in a number of special fields. The Ph.D. requires not less than three years devoted to advanced studies, including dissertation research and the dissertation. The Committee on Higher Degrees in Biophysics anticipates that it takes an average of five years, with the maximum being six years, to complete this program.

Research Facilities

Many more of the University's modern research facilities are available to the biophysics student because of the interdepartmental nature of the program. Research programs may be pursued in the Departments of Chemistry and Chemical Biology, Molecular and Cellular Biology, Applied Physics, and Engineering Sciences in Cambridge as well as in the Departments of Biological Chemistry and Molecular Pharmacology, Genetics, Microbiology and Molecular Genetics, Neurobiology, Virology, and Cell Biology in the Harvard Medical School Division of Medical Sciences. Research may also be pursued in the Harvard School of Public Health, the Dana Farber Cancer Institute, Children's Hospital, Massachusetts General Hospital, Beth Israel Hospital, and more than ten other Harvard-affiliated institutions located throughout the cities.

Financial Aid

In 2012–13, all graduate students receive a stipend ($32,616 for twelve months) and full tuition and health fees ($40,674). A semester of teaching is required in the second year. Students are strongly encouraged to apply for fellowships from such sources as the National Science Foundation, the NDSEG, the Hertz Foundation, and the Ford Foundation. Full-time Ph.D. candidates in good academic standing are guaranteed full financial support through their sixth year of study or throughout their academic program if less than six years.

Cost of Study

Tuition and health fees for the 2012–13 academic year are $40,674. After two years in residence, students are eligible for a reduced rate (currently $12,868).

Living and Housing Costs

Accommodations in graduate residence halls are available at rents ranging from $5900 to $9266 per academic year. In addition, there are approximately 1,500 apartments available for graduate students in Harvard-owned buildings. Applications may be obtained from the Harvard University Housing Office, which also maintains a list of available private rooms, houses, and apartments in the vicinity.

Student Group

On average, the program enrolls 50 students annually. Currently, 18 women and 9 international students are enrolled in the program. Biophysics students intermingle in both their research and their social life with graduate students from the many other departments where research in the biophysical sciences is carried out.

Location

The Biophysics Program maintains a dual-campus orientation in the neighboring cities of Cambridge and Boston. Their proximity provides for a wide range of academic, cultural, extracurricular, and recreational opportunities, and the large numbers of theaters, museums, libraries, and universities contribute to enrich the scientific and cultural life of students. Because New England is compact in area, it is easy to reach countryside, mountains, and seacoast for winter and summer sports or just for a change of scenery.

The University

Established in 1636 in the Massachusetts Bay Colony, Harvard has grown to become a complex of many facilities whose educational vitality, social commitment, and level of cultural achievement contribute to make the University a leader in the academic world. Comprising more than 15,000 students and 3,000 faculty members, Harvard appeals to self-directed, resourceful students of diverse beliefs and backgrounds.

Applying

Students must apply by December 1, 2012, to be considered for admission in September 2013. Scores on the General Test of the Graduate Record Examinations are required except in rare circumstances. GRE Subject Tests are recommended. Due to the early application deadline, applicants should plan to take the GRE test no later than October to ensure that original scores are received by December 1. Information about Graduate School fellowships and scholarships, admission procedures, and graduate study at Harvard may be obtained by writing to the Admissions Office.

Correspondence and Information

For information on the program:
Harvard Biophysics Program
Building C2, Room 122
Harvard Medical School Campus
240 Longwood Avenue
Boston, Massachusetts 02115
United States
E-mail: biophys@fas.harvard.edu
Web site: http://fas.harvard.edu/~biophys

For application forms for admission and financial aid:
Admissions Office
Graduate School of Arts and Sciences
Holyoke Center
Harvard University
1350 Massachusetts Avenue
Cambridge, Massachusetts 02138
United States
E-mail: admiss@fas.harvard.edu
Web site: http://www.gsas.harvard.edu

THE FACULTY AND THEIR RESEARCH

The following faculty members accept students for degree work in biophysics. Thesis research with other faculty members is possible by arrangement.

John Assad, Ph.D., Professor of Neurobiology. Mechanisms of visual processing in the visual cortex of awake behaving monkeys.

Frederick M. Ausubel, Ph.D., Professor of Genetics. Molecular biology of microbial pathogenesis in plants and animals.

Howard Berg, Ph.D., Herchel Smith Professor of Physics and Professor of Molecular and Cellular Biology. Motile behavior of bacteria.

Harvard University

Stephen C. Blacklow, M.D., Ph.D., Professor of Pathology. Molecular basis for specificity in protein folding and protein-protein interactions.

Martha L. Bulyk, Ph.D., Associate Professor of Medicine and Health Sciences and Technology and of Pathology. Computational methods; genomic and proteomic technologies in the study of DNA-protein interactions.

Lewis Cantley, Ph.D., Professor of Cell Biology and Systems Biology. Structural basis for specificity in eukaryotic signal transduction pathways.

James J. Chou, Ph.D., Associate Professor of Biological Chemistry and Molecular Pharmacology. NMR spectroscopy on membrane-associated proteins and peptides.

George McDonald Church, Ph.D., Professor of Genetics. Human and microbial functional genomics; genotyping; gene expression regulatory network models.

David E. Clapham, M.D., Ph.D., Professor of Pediatrics and of Neurobiology. Intracellular signal transduction.

Jon Clardy, Ph.D., Professor of Biological Chemistry and Molecular Pharmacology. Chemical ecology; biosynthesis; structure-based design.

Adam E. Cohen, Ph.D., Assistant Professor of Chemistry and Chemical Biology and of Physics. Analysis of structure and function of nicotinic acetylcholine receptors.

Jonathan B. Cohen, Ph.D., Professor of Neurobiology. Structure and function of ligand-gated ion channels.

David P. Corey, Ph.D., Professor of Neurobiology. Ion channels in neural cell membranes.

Vladimir Denic, Ph.D., Assistant Professor of Molecular and Cellular Biology. Structural diversification of very long-chain fatty acids.

Michael M. Desai, Ph.D., Assistant Professor of Organismic and Evolutionary Biology and of Physics. Theoretical and experimental approaches to study genetic variation within populations.

Michael J. Eck, M.D., Ph.D., Professor of Biological Chemistry and Molecular Pharmacology. Structural studies of proteins involved in signal transduction pathways.

Conor L. Evans, Ph.D., Assistant Professor of Dermatology. Development and application of optical detection, treatment, and monitoring approaches targeting major human diseases.

Florian Engert, Ph.D., Associate Professor of Molecular and Cellular Biology. Synaptic plasticity and neuronal networks.

Rachelle Gaudet, Ph.D., Associate Professor of Molecular and Cellular Biology. Structural studies of the stereochemistry of signaling and transport through biological membranes.

David E. Golan, M.D., Ph.D., Professor of Biological Chemistry and Molecular Pharmacology and of Medicine. Membrane dynamics; membrane structure; cellular adhesion.

Stephen C. Harrison, Ph.D., Professor of Biological Chemistry and Molecular Pharmacology. Structure of viruses and viral membranes; protein-DNA interactions; structural aspects of signal transduction and membrane traffic; X-ray diffraction.

James M. Hogle, Ph.D., Professor of Biological Chemistry and Molecular Pharmacology. Structure and function of viruses and virus-related proteins; X-ray crystallography.

Sun Hur, Ph.D., Assistant Professor of Biological Chemistry and Molecular Pharmacology. Principles of self versus nonself RNA discrimination by the immune system.

Donald E. Ingber, M.D., Ph.D., Professor of Bioengineering and Judah Folkman Professor of Vascular Biology. Research in integrin signaling, cytoskeleton, and control of angiogenesis.

Tomas Kirchhausen, Ph.D., Professor of Cell Biology. Molecular mechanisms of membrane traffic; X-ray crystallography; chemical genetics.

Andrew J. M. Kiruluta, Ph.D., Associate Professor of Radiology. Novel theory and experiments in NMR spectroscopy.

Roy Kishony, Ph.D., Associate Professor of Systems Biology. System-level genetic networks.

Nancy Kleckner, Ph.D., Herchel Smith Professor of Molecular Biology. Chromosome metabolism in bacteria and yeast.

Roberto D. Kolter, Ph.D., Professor of Microbiology and Molecular Genetics. DNA protection from oxidative damage; cell-cell communication in biofilms; microbial evolution.

Gabriel Kreiman, Ph.D., Assistant Professor of Neurology. Transcriptional regulatory circuits and neuronal circuits in visual recognition.

Galit Lahav, Ph.D., Assistant Professor of Systems Biology. Dynamics of network motifs in single living human cells.

Andres Leschziner, Ph.D., Assistant Professor of Molecular and Cellular Biology. Structural biology of ATP-dependent chromatin remodeling.

Erel Levine, Ph.D., Assistant Professor of Physics. Communication in and between cells and organisms.

David R. Liu, Ph.D., Professor of Chemistry and Chemical Biology. Organic chemistry and chemical biology.

Jun S. Liu, Ph.D., Professor of Statistics. Stochastic processes, probability theory, and statistical inference.

Joseph J. Loparo, Ph.D., Assistant Professor of Biological Chemistry and Molecular Pharmacology. Developing novel single-molecule methods to study multiprotein complexes.

Keith W. Miller, Ph.D., Mallinckrodt Professor of Pharmacology, Department of Anesthesia. Molecular mechanisms of regulatory conformation changes and drug action on membrane receptors and channels, using rapid kinetics, time-resolved photolabeling, and spectroscopy (EPR, fluorescence, NMR); characterization of lipid-protein interactions in membrane proteins.

Timothy Mitchison, Ph.D., Hasib Sabbagh Professor of Systems Biology. Cytoskeleton dynamics; mechanism of mitosis and cell locomotion; small-molecule inhibitors.

Venkatesh N. Murthy, Ph.D., Morris Khan Associate Professor of Molecular and Cellular Biology. Mechanisms of synaptic transmission and plasticity.

Daniel J. Needleman, Ph.D., Assistant Professor of Applied Physics. Physics of macromolecular assemblies and subcellular organization.

Bence P. Olveczky, Ph.D., Assistant Professor of Organismic and Evolutionary Biology. Neurobiology of vocal learning.

Erin K. O'Shea, Ph.D., Professor of Molecular and Cellular Biology and of Chemistry and Chemical Biology. Quantitative analysis of regulatory networks.

David Pellman, M.D., Professor of Cell Biology. The mechanics and regulation of mitosis.

Mara Prentiss, Ph.D., Professor of Physics. Exploitation of optical manipulation to measure adhesion properties, including virus cell binding.

Tom A. Rapoport, Ph.D., Professor of Cell Biology. Mechanism of how proteins are transported across the endoplasmic reticulum membrane.

Samara L. Reck-Peterson, Ph.D., Assistant Professor of Cell Biology. Single molecule studies of cellular motors.

Gary Ruvkun, Ph.D., Professor of Genetics. Genetic control of developmental timing, neurogenesis, and neural function.

Bernardo L. Sabatini, Ph.D., Associate Professor of Neurobiology. Regulation of synaptic transmission and dendritic function in the mammalian brain.

Aravinthan D. T. Samuel, Ph.D., Associate Professor of Physics. Topics in biophysics, neurobiology, and animal behavior.

Stuart L. Schreiber, Ph.D., Morris Loeb Professor of Chemistry and Chemical Biology. Forward and reverse chemical genetics: using small molecules to explore biology.

Brian Seed, Ph.D., Professor of Genetics. Genetic analysis of signal transduction in the immune system.

Eugene Shakhnovich, Ph.D., Professor of Chemistry and Chemical Biology. Theory and experiments in protein folding and design; theory of molecular evolution; rational drug design and physical chemistry of protein-ligand interactions; theory of complex systems.

William Shih, Ph.D., Assistant Professor of Biological Chemistry and Molecular Pharmacology. Biomolecular nanotechnology.

Steven E. Shoelson, M.D., Ph.D., Professor of Medicine. Structural and cellular biology of insulin signal transduction, insulin, resistance, diabetes, and obesity.

Pamela Silver, Ph.D., Professor of Systems Biology. Nucleocytoplasmic transport; RNA-protein interactions; protein methylation; cell-based small-molecule screens.

Timothy A. Springer, Ph.D., Latham Family Professor of Pathology. Molecular biology of immune cell interactions.

Shamil R. Sunyaev, Ph.D., Assistant Professor of Genetics. Population genetic variation and genomic divergence, with a focus on protein coding regions.

Jack W. Szostak, Ph.D., Professor of Genetics. Directed evolution; information content and molecular function; self-replicating systems.

Gregory L. Verdine, Ph.D., Erving Professor of Chemistry. Protein–nucleic acid interactions; transcriptional regulation; X-ray crystallography.

Gerhard Wagner, Ph.D., Elkan Blout Professor of Biological Chemistry and Molecular Pharmacology. Protein and nucleic acid structure, interaction, and mobility; NMR spectroscopy.

John R. Wakeley, Ph.D., Professor of Organismic and Evolutionary Biology. Theoretical population genetics.

Thomas Walz, Ph.D., Professor of Cell Biology. High-resolution electron microscopy.

George M. Whitesides, Ph.D., Mallinckrodt Professor of Chemistry. Molecular pharmacology; biosurface chemistry; virology.

Wesley P. Wong, Ph.D., Assistant Professor of Biological Chemistry and Molecular Pharmacology. Understanding physical basis of how biological systems work at the nanoscale, focused on the role of mechanical force.

Xiaoliang Sunney Xie, Ph.D., Mallinckrodt Professor of Chemistry and Chemical Biology. Single-molecule spectroscopy and dynamics; molecular interaction and chemical dynamics in biological systems.

Gary Yellen, Ph.D., Professor of Neurobiology. Molecular physiology of ion channels: functional motions, drug interactions, and electrophysiological mechanisms.

Xaiowei Zhuang, Ph.D., Professor of Chemistry and Chemical Biology and of Physics. Single-molecule biophysics.

Section 5
Botany and Plant Biology

This section contains a directory of institutions offering graduate work in botany and plant biology. Additional information about programs listed in the directory but not augmented by an in-depth entry may be obtained by writing directly to the dean of a graduate school or chair of a department at the address given in the directory.

For programs offering related work, see also in this book *Biochemistry; Biological and Biomedical Sciences; Cell, Molecular, and Structural Biology; Ecology, Environmental Biology, and Evolutionary Biology; Entomology; Genetics, Developmental Biology, and Reproductive Biology;* and *Microbiological Sciences.* In the other guides in this series:

Graduate Programs in the Humanities, Arts & Social Sciences

See *Architecture (Landscape Architecture)* and *Economics (Agricultural Economics and Agribusiness)*

Graduate Programs in the Physical Sciences, Mathematics, Agricultural Sciences, the Environment & Natural Resources
See *Agricultural and Food Sciences*
Graduate Programs in Engineering & Applied Sciences
See *Agricultural Engineering* and *Bioengineering*

CONTENTS

Program Directories

Botany

Auburn University, Graduate School, College of Sciences and Mathematics, Department of Biological Sciences, Auburn University, AL 36849. Offers botany (MS, PhD); microbiology (MS, PhD); zoology (MS, PhD). *Faculty:* 35 full-time (11 women). *Students:* 32 full-time (13 women), 73 part-time (33 women); includes 11 minority (3 Black or African American, non-Hispanic/Latino; 1 American Indian or Alaska Native, non-Hispanic/Latino; 5 Asian, non-Hispanic/Latino; 2 Hispanic/Latino), 24 international. Average age 29. 106 applicants, 28% accepted, 19 enrolled. In 2011, 14 master's, 9 doctorates awarded. *Entrance requirements:* For master's and doctorate, GRE General Test. Additional exam requirements/recommendations for international students: Required—TOEFL. *Application deadline:* For fall admission, 7/7 for domestic students; for spring admission, 11/24 for domestic students. Application fee: $50 ($60 for international students). Electronic applications accepted. *Expenses:* Tuition, state resident: full-time $7290; part-time $405 per credit hour. Tuition, nonresident: full-time $21,870; part-time $1215 per credit hour. *International tuition:* $22,000 full-time. *Required fees:* $1402. *Financial support:* Research assistantships and teaching assistantships available. Financial award applicants required to submit FAFSA. *Unit head:* Dr. Jack W. Feminella, Chair, 334-844-3906, Fax: 334-844-1645. *Application contact:* Dr. George Flowers, Dean of the Graduate School, 334-844-2125.

California State University, Chico, Office of Graduate Studies, College of Natural Sciences, Department of Biological Sciences, Program in Botany, Chico, CA 95929-0722. Offers MS. *Students:* 1 (woman) part-time. Average age 32. *Degree requirements:* For master's, thesis, seminar presentation. *Entrance requirements:* For master's, GRE General Test, GRE Subject Test (biology), two letters of recommendation, statement of purpose. Additional exam requirements/recommendations for international students: Required—TOEFL (minimum score 550 paper-based; 213 computer-based; 80 iBT), IELTS (minimum score 6.5), Pearson Test of English. *Application deadline:* For fall admission, 3/1 priority date for domestic students, 3/1 for international students; for spring admission, 9/15 priority date for domestic students, 9/15 for international students. Application fee: $55. Electronic applications accepted. Tuition and fees vary according to class time, course load and degree level. *Financial support:* Fellowships, teaching assistantships, career-related internships or fieldwork, and scholarships/grants available. *Unit head:* Dr. Jeffery R. Bell, Chair, 530-898-5356, Fax: 530-898-3342, E-mail: biol@csuchico.edu. *Application contact:* Judy L. Rice, Graduate Admissions Coordinator, 530-898-5416, Fax: 530-898-3342, E-mail: jlrice@csuchico.edu.

Claremont Graduate University, Graduate Programs, Program in Botany, Claremont, CA 91711-6160. Offers MS, PhD. Part-time programs available. *Faculty:* 5 full-time (3 women). *Students:* 14 full-time (10 women); includes 1 minority (Hispanic/Latino), 4 international. Average age 31. In 2011, 2 master's, 2 doctorates awarded. Terminal master's awarded for partial completion of doctoral program. *Entrance requirements:* For master's and doctorate, GRE General Test. Additional exam requirements/recommendations for international students: Required—TOEFL (minimum score 550 paper-based; 213 computer-based; 80 iBT). *Application deadline:* For fall admission, 2/1 priority date for domestic students. Applications are processed on a rolling basis. Application fee: $60. Electronic applications accepted. *Expenses: Tuition:* Full-time $36,374; part-time $1581 per unit. *Required fees:* $165 per semester. *Financial support:* Fellowships, research assistantships, Federal Work-Study, institutionally sponsored loans, scholarships/grants, and tuition waivers (full) available. Support available to part-time students. Financial award application deadline: 2/15; financial award applicants required to submit FAFSA. *Unit head:* Lucinda McDade, Director of Research/Chair, 909-625-8767 Ext. 234, Fax: 909-626-3489, E-mail: lucinda.mcdade@cgu.edu. *Application contact:* Linda Worlow, Program Coordinator, 909-625-8767 Ext. 241, Fax: 909-626-3489, E-mail: botany@cgu.edu. Web site: http://www.cgu.edu/pages/1311.asp.

Colorado State University, Graduate School, College of Natural Sciences, Department of Biology, Fort Collins, CO 80523-1878. Offers botany (MS, PhD); zoology (MS, PhD). Postbaccalaureate distance learning degree programs offered (no on-campus study). *Faculty:* 26 full-time (11 women). *Students:* 17 full-time (10 women), 32 part-time (19 women); includes 8 minority (3 Asian, non-Hispanic/Latino; 4 Hispanic/Latino; 1 Two or more races, non-Hispanic/Latino), 6 international. Average age 29. 61 applicants, 15% accepted, 7 enrolled. In 2011, 6 master's, 4 doctorates awarded. Terminal master's awarded for partial completion of doctoral program. *Degree requirements:* For master's, comprehensive exam (for some programs), thesis (for some programs); for doctorate, comprehensive exam, thesis/dissertation. *Entrance requirements:* For master's, GRE General Test, minimum GPA of 3.0; 3 letters of recommendation; for doctorate, GRE General Test, minimum GPA of 3.0; statement of purpose; 2 transcripts; 3 letters of recommendation. Additional exam requirements/recommendations for international students: Required—TOEFL (minimum score 550 paper-based; 213 computer-based; 80 iBT). *Application deadline:* For fall admission, 1/15 priority date for domestic students, 1/15 for international students; for spring admission, 11/1 priority date for domestic students, 11/1 for international students. Applications are processed on a rolling basis. Application fee: $50. Electronic applications accepted. *Expenses:* Tuition, state resident: full-time $7992. Tuition, nonresident: full-time $19,592. *Required fees:* $1735; $58 per credit. *Financial support:* In 2011–12, 20 fellowships (averaging $34,499 per year), 32 research assistantships with full tuition reimbursements (averaging $12,041 per year), 59 teaching assistantships with full tuition reimbursements (averaging $12,668 per year) were awarded; health care benefits also available. Financial award application deadline: 1/15; financial award applicants required to submit FAFSA. *Faculty research:* Aquatic and terrestrial ecology, cell biology and genetics, plant/animal physiology, developmental biology, evolutionary biology. *Total annual research expenditures:* $6.1 million. *Unit head:* Dr. Daniel R. Bush, Chair, 970-491-7013, Fax: 970-491-0649, E-mail: dbush@colostate.edu. *Application contact:* Dorothy Ramirez, Graduate Coordinator, 970-491-1923, Fax: 970-491-0649, E-mail: dorothy.ramirez@colostate.edu. Web site: http://www.biology.colostate.edu/.

Emporia State University, Graduate School, College of Liberal Arts and Sciences, Department of Biological Sciences, Emporia, KS 66801-5087. Offers botany (MS); environmental biology (MS); general biology (MS); microbial and cellular biology (MS); zoology (MS). Part-time programs available. *Faculty:* 13 full-time (3 women), 1 part-time/adjunct (0 women). *Students:* 8 full-time (5 women), 21 part-time (10 women); includes 3 minority (1 Black or African American, non-Hispanic/Latino; 1 Hispanic/Latino; 1 Two or more races, non-Hispanic/Latino), 6 international. 14 applicants, 86% accepted, 7 enrolled. In 2011, 5 master's awarded. *Degree requirements:* For master's, comprehensive exam or thesis. *Entrance requirements:* For master's, GRE, appropriate undergraduate degree, interview, letters of reference. Additional exam requirements/recommendations for international students: Required—TOEFL (minimum score 520 paper-based; 133 computer-based; 68 iBT). *Application deadline:* For fall admission, 8/15 priority date for domestic students. Applications are processed on a rolling basis. Application fee: $30 ($75 for international students). Electronic applications accepted. *Expenses:* Tuition, state resident: full-time $2342; part-time $195 per credit hour. Tuition, nonresident: full-time $7254; part-time $605 per credit hour. *Required fees:* $66 per credit hour. Tuition and fees vary according to campus/location. *Financial support:* In 2011–12, 8 research assistantships with full tuition reimbursements (averaging $6,589 per year), 10 teaching assistantships with full tuition reimbursements (averaging $7,419 per year) were awarded; career-related internships or fieldwork, Federal Work-Study, institutionally sponsored loans, health care benefits, and unspecified assistantships also available. Financial award application deadline: 3/15; financial award applicants required to submit FAFSA. *Faculty research:* Fisheries, range, and wildlife management; aquatic, plant, grassland, vertebrate, and invertebrate ecology; mammalian and plant systematics, taxonomy, and evolution; immunology, virology, and molecular biology. *Unit head:* Dr. R. Brent Thomas, Chair, 620-341-5311, Fax: 620-341-5608, E-mail: rthomas2@emporia.edu. *Application contact:* Dr. Scott Crupper, Graduate Coordinator, 620-341-5621, Fax: 620-341-5607, E-mail: scrupper@emporia.edu. Web site: http://www.emporia.edu/info/degrees-courses/grad/biology.

Illinois State University, Graduate School, College of Arts and Sciences, Department of Biological Sciences, Normal, IL 61790-2200. Offers animal behavior (MS); bacteriology (MS); biochemistry (MS); biological sciences (MS); biology (PhD); biophysics (MS); biotechnology (MS); botany (MS, PhD); cell biology (MS); conservation biology (MS); developmental biology (MS); ecology (MS, PhD); entomology (MS); evolutionary biology (MS); genetics (MS, PhD); immunology (MS); microbiology (MS, PhD); molecular biology (MS); molecular genetics (MS); neurobiology (MS); neuroscience (MS); parasitology (MS); physiology (MS, PhD); plant biology (MS); plant molecular biology (MS); plant sciences (MS); structural biology (MS); zoology (MS, PhD). Part-time programs available. *Degree requirements:* For master's, thesis or alternative; for doctorate, variable foreign language requirement, thesis/dissertation, 2 terms of residency. *Entrance requirements:* For master's, GRE General Test, minimum GPA of 2.6 in last 60 hours of course work; for doctorate, GRE General Test. *Faculty research:* Redoc balance and drug development in schistosoma mansoni, control of the growth of listeria monocytogenes at low temperature, regulation of cell expansion and microtubule function by SPRI, CRUI: physiology and fitness consequences of different life history phenotypes.

Miami University, College of Arts and Science, Department of Botany, Oxford, OH 45056. Offers MA, MAT, MS, PhD. Part-time programs available. *Students:* 59 full-time (30 women), 183 part-time (142 women); includes 15 minority (3 Black or African American, non-Hispanic/Latino; 2 Asian, non-Hispanic/Latino; 5 Hispanic/Latino; 5 Two or more races, non-Hispanic/Latino), 22 international. Average age 34. In 2011, 11 master's, 4 doctorates awarded. *Entrance requirements:* For master's, GRE General Test, minimum undergraduate GPA of 3.0 during previous 2 years or 2.75 overall; for doctorate, GRE General Test, minimum undergraduate GPA of 2.75, 3.0 graduate. Additional exam requirements/recommendations for international students: Required—TOEFL (minimum score 550 paper-based). *Application deadline:* For fall admission, 1/1 for domestic and international students. Applications are processed on a rolling basis. Application fee: $50. Electronic applications accepted. *Expenses:* Tuition, state resident: full-time $12,023; part-time $501 per credit hour. Tuition, nonresident: full-time $26,554; part-time $1107 per credit hour. *Required fees:* $528. *Financial support:* Research assistantships, teaching assistantships with full tuition reimbursements, Federal Work-Study, institutionally sponsored loans, health care benefits, and unspecified assistantships available. Financial award application deadline: 2/15; financial award applicants required to submit FAFSA. *Faculty research:* Evolution of plants, fungi and algae; bioinformatics; molecular biology of plants and cyanobacteria; food web dynamics; plant science education. *Unit head:* Dr. John Kiss, Chair, 513-529-4200, E-mail: kissjz@muohio.edu. *Application contact:* Dr. Richard C. Moore, Graduate Coordinator, 513-529-4278, E-mail: moorerc@muohio.edu. Web site: http://www.muohio.edu/botany/.

North Carolina State University, Graduate School, College of Agriculture and Life Sciences, Department of Plant Biology, Raleigh, NC 27695. Offers MS, PhD. Part-time programs available. Terminal master's awarded for partial completion of doctoral program. *Degree requirements:* For master's, thesis (for some programs); for doctorate, thesis/dissertation. *Entrance requirements:* For master's and doctorate, GRE. Additional exam requirements/recommendations for international students: Required—TOEFL. Electronic applications accepted. *Faculty research:* Plant molecular and cell biology, aquatic ecology, community ecology, restoration, systematics plant pathogen and environmental interactions.

North Dakota State University, College of Graduate and Interdisciplinary Studies, College of Science and Mathematics, Department of Biological Sciences, Fargo, ND 58108. Offers biology (MS); botany (MS, PhD); cellular and molecular biology (PhD); environmental and conservation sciences (MS, PhD); genomics (PhD); natural resources management (MS, PhD); zoology (MS, PhD). *Faculty:* 13 full-time (7 women), 3 part-time/adjunct (1 woman). *Students:* 20 full-time (10 women), 2 part-time (both women); includes 1 minority (American Indian or Alaska Native, non-Hispanic/Latino), 2 international. 12 applicants, 33% accepted, 4 enrolled. In 2011, 3 degrees awarded. *Degree requirements:* For master's, thesis; for doctorate, thesis/dissertation. *Entrance requirements:* For master's and doctorate, GRE General Test. Additional exam requirements/recommendations for international students: Required—TOEFL. *Application deadline:* For fall admission, 1/15 for domestic students. Applications are processed on a rolling basis. Application fee: $35. Electronic applications accepted. *Financial support:* Fellowships with full tuition reimbursements, research assistantships with full tuition reimbursements, teaching assistantships with full tuition reimbursements, career-related internships or fieldwork, Federal Work-Study, institutionally sponsored loans, scholarships/grants, tuition waivers (full), and unspecified assistantships available. Support available to part-time students. Financial award application deadline: 4/15; financial award applicants required to submit FAFSA. *Faculty research:* Comparative endocrinology, physiology, behavioral ecology, plant cell biology, aquatic biology. *Unit head:* Dr. Wendy Reed, Head, 701-231-7087, E-mail: wendy.reed@ndsu.edu. *Application contact:* Sonya Goergen, Marketing, Recruitment, and Public Relations Coordinator, 701-231-7033, Fax: 701-231-6524. Web site: http://biology.ndsu.nodak.edu/.

Nova Scotia Agricultural College, Research and Graduate Studies, Truro, NS B2N 5E3, Canada. Offers agriculture (M Sc), including air quality, animal behavior, animal molecular genetics, animal nutrition, animal technology, aquaculture, botany, crop management, crop physiology, ecology, environmental microbiology, food science, horticulture, nutrient management, pest management, physiology, plant biotechnology, plant pathology, soil chemistry, soil fertility, waste management and composting, water quality. Program offered jointly with Dalhousie University. Part-time programs available. *Degree requirements:* For master's, thesis, ATC Exam Teaching Assistantship. *Entrance requirements:* For master's, honors B Sc, minimum GPA of 3.0. Additional exam requirements/recommendations for international students: Required—TOEFL (minimum score 580 paper-based; 237 computer-based; 92 iBT), IELTS, Michigan

English Language Assessment Battery, CanTEST, CAEL. *Faculty research:* Bio-product development, organic agriculture, nutrient management, air and water quality, agricultural biotechnology.

Oklahoma State University, College of Arts and Sciences, Department of Botany, Stillwater, OK 74078. Offers botany (MS); environmental science (MS, PhD); plant science (PhD). *Faculty:* 15 full-time (6 women), 3 part-time/adjunct (1 woman). *Students:* 1 full-time (0 women), 9 part-time (5 women); includes 3 minority (1 American Indian or Alaska Native, non-Hispanic/Latino; 1 Hispanic/Latino; 1 Two or more races, non-Hispanic/Latino). Average age 28. 9 applicants, 22% accepted, 2 enrolled. In 2011, 1 degree awarded. *Degree requirements:* For master's, thesis; for doctorate, comprehensive exam, thesis/dissertation. *Entrance requirements:* For master's and doctorate, GRE or GMAT. Additional exam requirements/recommendations for international students: Required—TOEFL (minimum score 550 paper-based; 79 iBT). *Application deadline:* For fall admission, 3/1 for international students; for spring admission, 8/1 for international students. Applications are processed on a rolling basis. Application fee: $40 ($75 for international students). Electronic applications accepted. *Expenses:* Tuition, state resident: full-time $4044; part-time $168.50 per credit hour. Tuition, nonresident: full-time $16,008; part-time $667 per credit hour. *Required fees:* $2122; $88.45 per credit hour. One-time fee: $50. Tuition and fees vary according to course load and campus/location. *Financial support:* In 2011–12, 3 research assistantships (averaging $16,004 per year), 9 teaching assistantships (averaging $15,405 per year) were awarded; career-related internships or fieldwork, Federal Work-Study, scholarships/grants, health care benefits, tuition waivers (partial), and unspecified assistantships also available. Support available to part-time students. Financial award application deadline: 3/1; financial award applicants required to submit FAFSA. *Faculty research:* Ethnobotany, developmental genetics of Arabidopsis, biological roles of Plasmodesmata, community ecology and biodiversity, nutrient cycling in grassland ecosystems. *Unit head:* Dr. Linda Watson, Head, 405-744-5559, Fax: 405-744-7074. *Application contact:* Dr. Sheryl Tucker, Dean, 405-744-7099, Fax: 405-744-0355, E-mail: grad-i@okstate.edu. Web site: http://botany.okstate.edu.

Oregon State University, Graduate School, College of Science, Department of Botany and Plant Pathology, Corvallis, OR 97331. Offers applied systematics (MA, MAIS, MS, PhD); ecology (MA, MAIS, MS, PhD); genetics (MA, MAIS, MS, PhD); genomics and computational biology (MA, MAIS, MS, PhD); molecular and cellular biology (MA, MAIS, MS, PhD); mycology (MA, MAIS, MS, PhD); plant pathology (MA, MAIS, MS, PhD); plant physiology (MA, MAIS, MS, PhD); systematics (MA, MAIS, MS, PhD). Part-time programs available. *Degree requirements:* For master's, variable foreign language requirement, thesis optional; for doctorate, thesis/dissertation. *Entrance requirements:* For master's and doctorate, GRE General Test, minimum GPA of 3.0 in last 90 hours. *Faculty research:* Plant ecology, plant molecular biology, systematic botany, epidemiology, host-pathogen interaction.

Purdue University, Graduate School, College of Agriculture, Department of Botany and Plant Pathology, West Lafayette, IN 47907. Offers MS, PhD. Part-time programs available. *Faculty:* 20 full-time (5 women), 2 part-time/adjunct (1 woman). *Students:* 34 full-time (17 women), 3 part-time (2 women); includes 3 minority (2 American Indian or Alaska Native, non-Hispanic/Latino; 1 Asian, non-Hispanic/Latino), 15 international. Average age 27. 61 applicants, 31% accepted, 9 enrolled. In 2011, 6 master's awarded. Terminal master's awarded for partial completion of doctoral program. *Degree requirements:* For master's, thesis; for doctorate, thesis/dissertation. *Entrance requirements:* For master's, GRE General Test, minimum undergraduate GPA of 3.0 or equivalent; for doctorate, GRE, minimum undergraduate GPA of 3.0 or equivalent. Additional exam requirements/recommendations for international students: Required—TOEFL (minimum score 550 paper-based; 77 iBT); Recommended—TWE. *Application deadline:* For fall admission, 4/15 priority date for domestic students, 4/15 for international students; for spring admission, 12/15 for domestic students, 9/15 for international students. Applications are processed on a rolling basis. Application fee: $60 ($75 for international students). Electronic applications accepted. *Financial support:* In 2011–12, 30 students received support. Fellowships with full tuition reimbursements available, research assistantships with full tuition reimbursements available, teaching assistantships with full tuition reimbursements available, and career-related internships or fieldwork available. Support available to part-time students. Financial award application deadline: 3/1; financial award applicants required to submit FAFSA. *Faculty research:* Biotechnology, plant growth, weed control, crop improvement, plant physiology. *Unit head:* Dr. Peter B. Goldsbrough, Head, 765-494-4615, Fax: 765-494-0363, E-mail: goldsbrough@purdue.edu. *Application contact:* Tyson J. McFall, Graduate Contact, 765-494-0352, E-mail: tjmcfall@purdue.edu. Web site: http://www.btny.purdue.edu/.

Texas A&M University, College of Science, Department of Biology, College Station, TX 77843. Offers biology (MS, PhD); botany (MS, PhD); microbiology (MS, PhD); molecular and cell biology (PhD); neuroscience (MS, PhD); zoology (MS, PhD). *Faculty:* 41. *Students:* 99 full-time (60 women), 8 part-time (4 women); includes 11 minority (1 Black or African American, non-Hispanic/Latino; 5 Asian, non-Hispanic/Latino; 4 Hispanic/Latino; 1 Two or more races, non-Hispanic/Latino), 46 international. Average age 28. In 2011, 5 master's, 7 doctorates awarded. *Degree requirements:* For master's, thesis or alternative; for doctorate, comprehensive exam, thesis/dissertation. *Entrance requirements:* For master's and doctorate, GRE General Test. Additional exam requirements/recommendations for international students: Required—TOEFL. *Application deadline:* For fall admission, 1/15 for domestic students. Applications are processed on a rolling basis. Application fee: $50 ($75 for international students). Electronic applications accepted. *Expenses:* Tuition, state resident: full-time $5437; part-time $226.55 per credit hour. Tuition, nonresident: full-time $12,949; part-time $539.55 per credit hour. *Required fees:* $2741. *Financial support:* Fellowships, research assistantships, and teaching assistantships available. Financial award application deadline: 4/1; financial award applicants required to submit FAFSA. *Unit head:* Dr. Jack McMahan, Department Head, 979-845-2301, E-mail: granster@mail.bio.tamu.edu. *Application contact:* 979-845-7755, Fax: 979-845-2891, E-mail: graduate@bio.tamu.edu. Web site: http://www.bio.tamu.edu/index.html.

University of Alaska Fairbanks, College of Natural Sciences and Mathematics, Department of Biology and Wildlife, Fairbanks, AK 99775-6100. Offers biological sciences (MS, PhD), including biology, botany, wildlife biology (PhD), zoology; biology (MAT, MS); wildlife biology (MS). Part-time programs available. *Faculty:* 20 full-time (10 women). *Students:* 74 full-time (43 women), 29 part-time (18 women); includes 12 minority (1 Asian, non-Hispanic/Latino; 6 Hispanic/Latino; 5 Two or more races, non-Hispanic/Latino), 4 international. Average age 29. 45 applicants, 40% accepted, 15 enrolled. In 2011, 12 master's, 11 doctorates awarded. *Degree requirements:* For master's, comprehensive exam, thesis, oral exam, oral defense; for doctorate, comprehensive exam, thesis/dissertation, oral exam, oral defense. *Entrance requirements:* For master's and doctorate, GRE General Test, GRE Subject Test (biology). Additional exam requirements/recommendations for international students: Required—TOEFL (minimum score 550 paper-based; 213 computer-based; 80 iBT), TWE. *Application deadline:* For fall admission, 6/1 for domestic students, 3/1 for international students; for spring admission, 10/15 for domestic students, 9/1 for international students. Applications are processed on a rolling basis. Application fee: $60. Electronic applications accepted. *Expenses:* Tuition, state resident: full-time $6696; part-time $372 per credit. Tuition, nonresident: full-time $13,680; part-time $760 per credit. Tuition and fees vary according to course load and reciprocity agreements. *Financial support:* In 2011–12, 26 research assistantships with tuition reimbursements (averaging $13,976 per year), 26 teaching assistantships with tuition reimbursements (averaging $14,955 per year) were awarded; fellowships with tuition reimbursements, career-related internships or fieldwork, Federal Work-Study, scholarships/grants, health care benefits, and unspecified assistantships also available. Support available to part-time students. Financial award application deadline: 7/1; financial award applicants required to submit FAFSA. *Faculty research:* Plant-herbivore interactions, plant metabolic defenses, insect manufacture of glycerol, ice nucleators, structure and functions of arctic and subarctic freshwater ecosystems. *Unit head:* Christa Mulder, Department Chair, 907-474-7671, Fax: 907-474-6716, E-mail: fybio@uaf.edu. *Application contact:* Mike Earnest, Director of Admissions, 907-474-7500, Fax: 907-474-5379, E-mail: admissions@uaf.edu. Web site: http://www.bw.uaf.edu.

The University of British Columbia, Faculty of Science, Department of Botany, Vancouver, BC V6T 1Z1, Canada. Offers M Sc, PhD. *Degree requirements:* For master's, thesis; for doctorate, comprehensive exam, thesis/dissertation. *Entrance requirements:* Additional exam requirements/recommendations for international students: Required—TOEFL. Electronic applications accepted. *Faculty research:* Plant ecology, evolution and systematics, cell and developmental biology, plant physiology/biochemistry, genetics.

University of California, Riverside, Graduate Division, Department of Botany and Plant Sciences, Riverside, CA 92521-0102. Offers plant biology (MS, PhD), including plant cell, molecular, and developmental biology (PhD), plant ecology (PhD), plant genetics (PhD). Part-time programs available. *Faculty:* 40 full-time (13 women). *Students:* 66 full-time (40 women); includes 12 minority (5 Asian, non-Hispanic/Latino; 7 Hispanic/Latino), 24 international. Average age 29. In 2011, 3 master's, 3 doctorates awarded. Terminal master's awarded for partial completion of doctoral program. *Degree requirements:* For master's, comprehensive exams or thesis; for doctorate, thesis/dissertation, qualifying exams. *Entrance requirements:* For master's and doctorate, GRE General Test, minimum GPA of 3.2. Additional exam requirements/recommendations for international students: Required—TOEFL (minimum score 550 paper-based; 213 computer-based; 80 iBT). *Application deadline:* For fall admission, 5/1 for domestic students, 2/1 for international students; for winter admission, 2/1 for domestic students, 7/1 for international students; for spring admission, 12/1 for domestic students, 10/1 for international students. Applications are processed on a rolling basis. Application fee: $80 ($100 for international students). Electronic applications accepted. *Financial support:* In 2011–12, fellowships with tuition reimbursements (averaging $12,000 per year), research assistantships with tuition reimbursements (averaging $23,000 per year), teaching assistantships with tuition reimbursements (averaging $16,500 per year) were awarded; career-related internships or fieldwork, Federal Work-Study, institutionally sponsored loans, scholarships/grants, and tuition waivers (full and partial) also available. *Faculty research:* Agricultural plant biology; biochemistry and physiology; cellular, molecular and developmental biology; ecology, evolution, systematics and ethnobotany; genetics, genomics and bioinformatics. *Unit head:* Dr. Mikeal Roose, Chair, 951-827-4413. *Application contact:* Deidra Kornfeld, Graduate Program Assistant, 800-735-0717, Fax: 951-827-5517, E-mail: deidra.kornfeld@ucr.edu. Web site: http://www.plantbiology.ucr.edu/.

University of Connecticut, Graduate School, College of Liberal Arts and Sciences, Department of Ecology and Evolutionary Biology, Storrs, CT 06269. Offers botany (MS, PhD); ecology (MS, PhD); entomology (MS, PhD); zoology (MS, PhD). Terminal master's awarded for partial completion of doctoral program. *Degree requirements:* For master's, comprehensive exam; for doctorate, thesis/dissertation. *Entrance requirements:* For master's and doctorate, GRE General Test, GRE Subject Test. Additional exam requirements/recommendations for international students: Required—TOEFL (minimum score 550 paper-based; 213 computer-based). Electronic applications accepted.

University of Florida, Graduate School, College of Liberal Arts and Sciences and College of Agricultural and Life Sciences, Department of Botany, Gainesville, FL 32611. Offers M Ag, MS, MST, PhD. Part-time programs available. *Entrance requirements:* Additional exam requirements/recommendations for international students: Required—TOEFL, IELTS. *Application deadline:* Applications are processed on a rolling basis. Electronic applications accepted. *Financial support:* Federal Work-Study and institutionally sponsored loans available. Support available to part-time students.

University of Guelph, Graduate Studies, College of Biological Science, Department of Integrative Biology, Botany and Zoology, Guelph, ON N1G 2W1, Canada. Offers botany (M Sc, PhD); zoology (M Sc, PhD). Part-time programs available. *Degree requirements:* For master's, thesis, research proposal; for doctorate, thesis/dissertation, research proposal, qualifying exam. *Entrance requirements:* For master's, minimum B average during previous 2 years of course work. Additional exam requirements/recommendations for international students: Required—TOEFL (minimum score 550 paper-based; 213 computer-based), IELTS (minimum score 6.5). Electronic applications accepted. *Faculty research:* Aquatic science, environmental physiology, parasitology, wildlife biology, management.

University of Guelph, Graduate Studies, College of Biological Science, Department of Molecular and Cellular Biology, Guelph, ON N1G 2W1, Canada. Offers biochemistry (M Sc, PhD); biophysics (M Sc, PhD); botany (M Sc, PhD); microbiology (M Sc, PhD); molecular biology and genetics (M Sc, PhD). *Degree requirements:* For master's, thesis, research proposal; for doctorate, comprehensive exam, thesis/dissertation, research proposal. *Entrance requirements:* For master's, minimum B-average during previous 2 years of coursework; for doctorate, minimum A-average. Additional exam requirements/recommendations for international students: Required—TOEFL (minimum score 550 paper-based; 213 computer-based), IELTS (minimum score 6.5). Electronic applications accepted. *Faculty research:* Physiology, structure, genetics, and ecology of microbes; virology and microbial technology.

University of Hawaii at Manoa, Graduate Division, College of Natural Sciences, Department of Botany, Honolulu, HI 96822. Offers MS, PhD. Part-time programs available. Terminal master's awarded for partial completion of doctoral program. *Degree requirements:* For master's, one foreign language, thesis optional, presentation; for doctorate, one foreign language, comprehensive exam, thesis/dissertation, presentation. *Entrance requirements:* For master's and doctorate, GRE General Test, GRE Subject Test (biology). Additional exam requirements/recommendations for international students: Required—TOEFL (minimum score 540 paper-based; 207 computer-based; 76 iBT), IELTS (minimum score 5). *Faculty research:* Plant ecology, evolution, systematics, conservation biology, ethnobotany.

The University of Kansas, Graduate Studies, College of Liberal Arts and Sciences, Department of Ecology and Evolutionary Biology, Lawrence, KS 66045. Offers botany (MA, PhD); ecology and evolutionary biology (MA, PhD); entomology (MA, PhD). *Faculty:* 15 full-time (6 women), 25 part-time/adjunct (6 women). *Students:* 64 full-time (31 women), 1 part-time (0 women); includes 4 minority (1 Hispanic/Latino; 3 Two or more races, non-Hispanic/Latino), 20 international. Average age 28. 67 applicants, 34%

accepted, 18 enrolled. In 2011, 6 master's, 9 doctorates awarded. Terminal master's awarded for partial completion of doctoral program. *Degree requirements:* For master's, comprehensive exam, thesis (for some programs), 30-36 credits, thesis presentation; for doctorate, comprehensive exam, thesis/dissertation, residency, responsible scholarship and research skills, final exam, dissertation defense. *Entrance requirements:* For master's, GRE General Test, bachelor's degree with minimum undergraduate GPA of 3.0; for doctorate, GRE General Test, bachelor's degree; minimum undergraduate/graduate GPA of 3.0. Additional exam requirements/recommendations for international students: Required—TOEFL or IELTS. *Application deadline:* For fall admission, 12/1 for domestic students, 12/15 for international students; for spring admission, 9/15 for domestic and international students. Application fee: $55 ($65 for international students). Electronic applications accepted. Tuition and fees vary according to course load, campus/location, program and reciprocity agreements. *Financial support:* In 2011–12, 8 fellowships with full and partial tuition reimbursements, 22 research assistantships with full and partial tuition reimbursements, 32 teaching assistantships with full and partial tuition reimbursements were awarded; scholarships/grants, traineeships, health care benefits, and unspecified assistantships also available. Financial award application deadline: 12/1. *Faculty research:* Biodiversity and macroevolution, ecology and global change, evolutionary mechanisms. *Unit head:* Dr. Christopher H. Haufler, Chair, 785-864-3255, Fax: 785-864-5860, E-mail: vulgare@ku.edu. *Application contact:* Jaime Rochelle Keeler, Graduate Coordinator, 785-864-2362, Fax: 785-864-5860, E-mail: jrkeeler@ku.edu. Web site: http://www.ku.edu/~eeb/.

University of Maine, Graduate School, College of Natural Sciences, Forestry, and Agriculture, Department of Biological Sciences, Program in Botany and Plant Pathology, Orono, ME 04469. Offers MS. Part-time programs available. *Students:* 2 full-time (1 woman), 1 international. Average age 30. 1 applicant, 0% accepted, 0 enrolled. In 2011, 1 degree awarded. *Degree requirements:* For master's, thesis. *Entrance requirements:* For master's, GRE General Test. Additional exam requirements/recommendations for international students: Required—TOEFL. *Application deadline:* For fall admission, 2/1 priority date for domestic students. Applications are processed on a rolling basis. Application fee: $65. Electronic applications accepted. *Expenses:* Tuition, state resident: full-time $5016. Tuition, nonresident: full-time $14,424. *Financial support:* Career-related internships or fieldwork, Federal Work-Study, institutionally sponsored loans, and tuition waivers (full) available. Financial award application deadline: 3/1. *Faculty research:* Molecular biology of viral and fungal pathogens, marine ecology, paleoecology and acid systematics and evolution. *Unit head:* Dr. Jody Jellison, Coordinator, 207-581-2551. *Application contact:* Scott G. Delcourt, Associate Dean of the Graduate School, 207-581-3291, Fax: 207-581-3232, E-mail: graduate@maine.edu. Web site: http://www2.umaine.edu/graduate/.

University of Manitoba, Faculty of Graduate Studies, Faculty of Science, Department of Biological Sciences, Winnipeg, MB R3T 2N2, Canada. Offers botany (M Sc, PhD); ecology (M Sc, PhD); zoology (M Sc, PhD).

The University of North Carolina at Chapel Hill, Graduate School, College of Arts and Sciences, Department of Biology, Chapel Hill, NC 27599. Offers botany (MA, MS, PhD); cell biology, development, and physiology (MA, MS, PhD); cell motility and cytoskeleton (PhD); ecology and behavior (MA, MS, PhD); genetics and molecular biology (MA, MS, PhD); morphology, systematics, and evolution (MA, MS, PhD). Terminal master's awarded for partial completion of doctoral program. *Degree requirements:* For master's, comprehensive exam, thesis (for some programs); for doctorate, comprehensive exam, thesis/dissertation. *Entrance requirements:* For master's, GRE General Test, GRE Subject Test, 2 semesters of calculus or statistics; 2 semesters of physics, organic chemistry; 3 semesters of biology; for doctorate, GRE General Test, GRE Subject Test, 2 semesters calculus or statistics, 2 semesters physics, organic chemistry, 3 semesters of biology. Additional exam requirements/recommendations for international students: Required—TOEFL (minimum score 550 paper-based; 213 computer-based). Electronic applications accepted. *Faculty research:* Gene expression, biomechanics, yeast genetics, plant ecology, plant molecular biology.

University of North Dakota, Graduate School, College of Arts and Sciences, Department of Biology, Grand Forks, ND 58202. Offers botany (MS, PhD); ecology (MS, PhD); entomology (MS, PhD); environmental biology (MS, PhD); fisheries/wildlife (MS, PhD); genetics (MS, PhD); zoology (MS, PhD). Terminal master's awarded for partial completion of doctoral program. *Degree requirements:* For master's, thesis, final exam; for doctorate, comprehensive exam, thesis/dissertation, final exam. *Entrance requirements:* For master's, GRE General Test, GRE Subject Test, minimum GPA of 3.0; for doctorate, GRE General Test, GRE Subject Test, minimum GPA of 3.5. Additional exam requirements/recommendations for international students: Required—TOEFL (minimum score 550 paper-based; 213 computer-based; 79 iBT), IELTS (minimum score 6.5). Electronic applications accepted. *Faculty research:* Population biology, wildlife ecology, RNA processing, hormonal control of behavior.

University of Oklahoma, College of Arts and Sciences, Department of Microbiology and Plant Biology, Program in Plant Biology, Norman, OK 73019. Offers MS, PhD. *Students:* 18 full-time (10 women), 3 part-time (0 women); includes 2 minority (1 Asian, non-Hispanic/Latino; 1 Hispanic/Latino), 12 international. Average age 27. 18 applicants, 56% accepted, 7 enrolled. In 2011, 4 master's, 2 doctorates awarded. Terminal master's awarded for partial completion of doctoral program. *Degree requirements:* For master's, thesis, oral exam; for doctorate, one foreign language, thesis/dissertation, general exam. *Entrance requirements:* Additional exam requirements/recommendations for international students: Required—TOEFL (minimum score 550 paper-based; 79 iBT). *Application deadline:* For fall admission, 4/1 for domestic students, 3/1 for international students; for spring admission, 9/1 for domestic and international students. Applications are processed on a rolling basis. Application fee: $40 ($90 for international students). Electronic applications accepted. *Expenses:* Tuition, state resident: full-time $4087; part-time $170.30 per credit hour. Tuition, nonresident: full-time $14,875; part-time $619.80 per credit hour. *Required fees:* $2659; $100.25 per credit hour. Tuition and fees vary according to course load and degree level. *Financial support:* In 2011–12, 21 students received support. Federal Work-Study, institutionally sponsored loans, scholarships/grants, health care benefits, and unspecified assistantships available. Support available to part-time students. Financial award applicants required to submit FAFSA. *Faculty research:* Ecology, evolution and systematics of plants; molecular biology of plant stress and reproduction; global change biology and ecosystem modeling; plant structure and development; science education. *Unit head:* Dr. Gordon Uno, Chair, 405-325-4321, Fax: 405-325-7619, E-mail: guno@ou.edu. *Application contact:* Adell Hopper, Staff Assistant, 405-325-4322, Fax: 405-325-7619, E-mail: ahopper@ou.edu. Web site: http://mpbio.ou.edu/.

University of Wisconsin–Madison, Graduate School, College of Letters and Science, Department of Botany, Madison, WI 53706-1380. Offers MS, PhD. Part-time programs available. Terminal master's awarded for partial completion of doctoral program. *Degree requirements:* For master's, thesis; for doctorate, one foreign language, thesis/dissertation. *Entrance requirements:* For master's and doctorate, GRE General Test. Electronic applications accepted. *Expenses:* Tuition, state resident: full-time $10,296; part-time $643.51 per credit. Tuition, nonresident: full-time $24,054; part-time $1503.40 per credit. *Required fees:* $70.06 per credit. Tuition and fees vary according to course load, campus/location, program and reciprocity agreements. *Faculty research:* Taxonomy and systematics; ecology; structural botany; physiological, cellular, and molecular biology.

University of Wisconsin–Oshkosh, Graduate Studies, College of Letters and Science, Department of Biology and Microbiology, Oshkosh, WI 54901. Offers biology (MS), including botany, microbiology, zoology. *Degree requirements:* For master's, comprehensive exam, thesis. *Entrance requirements:* For master's, GRE General Test, minimum GPA of 3.0, BS in biology. Additional exam requirements/recommendations for international students: Required—TOEFL (minimum score 550 paper-based; 213 computer-based; 79 iBT). Electronic applications accepted.

University of Wyoming, College of Arts and Sciences, Department of Botany, Laramie, WY 82070. Offers botany (MS, PhD); botany/water resources (MS). Part-time programs available. Terminal master's awarded for partial completion of doctoral program. *Degree requirements:* For master's, thesis; for doctorate, thesis/dissertation. *Entrance requirements:* For master's and doctorate, GRE General Test, minimum GPA of 3.0. Additional exam requirements/recommendations for international students: Required—TOEFL. Electronic applications accepted. *Faculty research:* Ecology, systematics, physiology, mycology, genetics.

Washington State University, Graduate School, College of Sciences, School of Biological Sciences, Department of Botany, Pullman, WA 99164. Offers MS, PhD. *Faculty:* 33. *Students:* 23 full-time (7 women); includes 1 minority (Hispanic/Latino), 2 international. Average age 27. 31 applicants, 13% accepted, 4 enrolled. In 2011, 3 master's, 1 doctorate awarded. *Degree requirements:* For master's, comprehensive exam (for some programs), thesis (for some programs), oral exam; for doctorate, comprehensive exam, thesis/dissertation, oral exam. *Entrance requirements:* For master's and doctorate, GRE General Test, GRE Subject Test (recommended), three letters of recommendation, official transcripts from each university-level school attended, minimum GPA of 3.0. Additional exam requirements/recommendations for international students: Required—TOEFL, IELTS. *Application deadline:* For fall admission, 1/10 priority date for domestic students, 1/15 for international students; for spring admission, 9/15 for domestic students, 7/1 for international students. Applications are processed on a rolling basis. Application fee: $75. *Financial support:* In 2011–12, 3 fellowships (averaging $4,000 per year), 4 research assistantships with full and partial tuition reimbursements (averaging $13,917 per year), 21 teaching assistantships with full and partial tuition reimbursements (averaging $13,056 per year) were awarded; career-related internships or fieldwork, Federal Work-Study, institutionally sponsored loans, health care benefits, and tuition waivers (partial) also available. Financial award application deadline: 2/15; financial award applicants required to submit FAFSA. *Unit head:* Dr. Gary Thorgaard, Director, 509-335-3553, Fax: 509-335-3184, E-mail: sbs@wsu.edu. *Application contact:* Graduate School Admissions, 800-GRADWSU, Fax: 509-335-1949, E-mail: gradsch@wsu.edu.

Plant Biology

Clemson University, Graduate School, College of Agriculture, Forestry and Life Sciences, Department of Forestry and Natural Resources, Program in Plant and Environmental Sciences, Clemson, SC 29634. Offers MS, PhD. *Students:* 43 full-time (16 women), 10 part-time (1 woman); includes 2 minority (1 Hispanic/Latino; 1 Two or more races, non-Hispanic/Latino), 16 international. Average age 31. 36 applicants, 47% accepted, 16 enrolled. In 2011, 12 master's, 3 doctorates awarded. *Degree requirements:* For master's, thesis; for doctorate, comprehensive exam, thesis/dissertation. *Entrance requirements:* For master's, GRE General Test, bachelor's degree in biological science or related disciplines; for doctorate, GRE General Test. Additional exam requirements/recommendations for international students: Required—TOEFL, IELTS. *Application deadline:* Applications are processed on a rolling basis. Electronic applications accepted. *Expenses:* Contact institution. *Financial support:* In 2011–12, 37 students received support, including 3 fellowships with full and partial tuition reimbursements available (averaging $9,667 per year), 29 research assistantships with partial tuition reimbursements available (averaging $16,876 per year), 10 teaching assistantships with partial tuition reimbursements available (averaging $12,424 per year); career-related internships or fieldwork, institutionally sponsored loans, scholarships/grants, health care benefits, and unspecified assistantships also available. Support available to part-time students. Financial award application deadline: 3/15; financial award applicants required to submit FAFSA. *Faculty research:* Sustainable agroecology, horticulture and turfgrass, physiology and pathology of plants. *Unit head:* Dr. Patricia Layton, School Director, 864-656-3302, Fax: 864-656-3304, E-mail: playton@clemson.edu. *Application contact:* Dr. Halina Knap, Coordinator, 864-656-3523, Fax: 864-656-3443, E-mail: hskrpsk@clemson.edu. Web site: http://www.clemson.edu/cafls/departments/pes/.

Cornell University, Graduate School, Graduate Fields of Agriculture and Life Sciences, Field of Plant Biology, Ithaca, NY 14853-0001. Offers cytology (MS, PhD); paleobotany (MS, PhD); plant cell biology (MS, PhD); plant ecology (MS, PhD); plant molecular biology (MS, PhD); plant morphology, anatomy and biomechanics (MS, PhD); plant physiology (MS, PhD); systematic botany (MS, PhD). *Faculty:* 49 full-time (14 women). *Students:* 33 full-time (18 women); includes 4 minority (2 Black or African American, non-Hispanic/Latino; 1 Hispanic/Latino; 1 Two or more races, non-Hispanic/Latino), 15 international. Average age 27. 54 applicants, 20% accepted, 6 enrolled. In 2011, 1 master's, 3 doctorates awarded. *Degree requirements:* For doctorate, comprehensive exam, thesis/dissertation. *Entrance requirements:* For doctorate, GRE General Test, GRE Subject Test in biology (recommended), 3 letters of recommendation. Additional exam requirements/recommendations for international students: Required—TOEFL (minimum score 610 paper-based; 253 computer-based; 77 iBT). *Application deadline:* For fall admission, 1/15 priority date for domestic students. Application fee: $95. Electronic applications accepted. *Financial support:* In 2011–12, 7 fellowships with full tuition reimbursements, 15 research assistantships with full tuition reimbursements, 9 teaching assistantships with full tuition reimbursements were awarded; institutionally

sponsored loans, scholarships/grants, health care benefits, tuition waivers (full and partial), and unspecified assistantships also available. Financial award applicants required to submit FAFSA. *Faculty research:* Plant cell biology/cytology; plant molecular biology; plant morphology/anatomy/biomechanics; plant physiology, systematic botany, paleobotany; plant ecology, ethnobotany, plant biochemistry, photosynthesis. *Unit head:* Director of Graduate Studies, 607-255-2131. *Application contact:* Graduate Field Assistant, 607-255-2131, E-mail: plbio@cornell.edu. Web site: http://www.gradschool.cornell.edu/fields.php?id-45&a-2.

Eastern New Mexico University, Graduate School, College of Liberal Arts and Sciences, Department of Biology, Portales, NM 88130. Offers applied ecology (MS); cell, molecular biology and biotechnology (MS); education (non-thesis) (MS); microbiology (MS); plant biology (MS); zoology (MS). Part-time programs available. *Faculty:* 7 full-time (0 women). *Students:* 2 full-time (1 woman), 15 part-time (9 women); includes 7 minority (5 Hispanic/Latino; 2 Two or more races, non-Hispanic/Latino), 2 international. Average age 26. 17 applicants, 82% accepted, 3 enrolled. In 2011, 4 master's awarded. *Degree requirements:* For master's, comprehensive exam, thesis optional. *Entrance requirements:* For master's, GRE, minimum GPA of 3.0, 2 letters of recommendation, statement of research interest, bachelor's degree related to field of study or proof of common knowledge. Additional exam requirements/recommendations for international students: Required—TOEFL (minimum score 550 paper-based; 213 computer-based; 79 iBT), IELTS (minimum score 6). *Application deadline:* For fall admission, 7/20 priority date for domestic students, 6/20 for international students; for spring admission, 12/15 priority date for domestic students, 11/15 for international students. Applications are processed on a rolling basis. Application fee: $10. Electronic applications accepted. *Financial support:* In 2011–12, 8 teaching assistantships with partial tuition reimbursements (averaging $8,500 per year) were awarded; scholarships/grants and unspecified assistantships also available. Support available to part-time students. Financial award applicants required to submit FAFSA. *Unit head:* Dr. Zach Jones, Graduate Coordinator, 575-562-2723, Fax: 575-562-2192, E-mail: zach.jones@enmu.edu. *Application contact:* Sharon Potter, Department Secretary, Biology and Physical Sciences, 575-562-2174, Fax: 575-562-2192, E-mail: sharon.potter@enmu.edu. Web site: http://liberal-arts.enmu.edu/biology/graduate.shtml.

Florida State University, The Graduate School, College of Arts and Sciences, Department of Biological Science, Specialization in Plant Biology, Tallahassee, FL 32306-4295. Offers MS, PhD. *Faculty:* 10 full-time (5 women). *Students:* 17 full-time (10 women); includes 2 minority (both Hispanic/Latino), 2 international. In 2011, 1 master's, 3 doctorates awarded. Terminal master's awarded for partial completion of doctoral program. *Degree requirements:* For master's, comprehensive exam, thesis, teaching experience, seminar presentation; for doctorate, comprehensive exam, thesis/dissertation, teaching experience, seminar presentation. *Entrance requirements:* For master's and doctorate, GRE General Test (minimum combined score 1100, 500 verbal, 500 quantitative in old version; 72% verbal, 67% quantitative in new format), minimum upper-division GPA of 3.0. Additional exam requirements/recommendations for international students: Required—TOEFL (minimum score 600 paper-based; 250 computer-based; 92 iBT). *Application deadline:* For fall admission, 12/15 for domestic and international students. Application fee: $30. Electronic applications accepted. *Expenses:* Tuition, state resident: full-time $9474; part-time $350.88 per credit hour. Tuition, nonresident: full-time $16,236; part-time $601.34 per credit hour. *Required fees:* $630 per semester. One-time fee: $20. Tuition and fees vary according to course load and campus/location. *Financial support:* In 2011–12, 17 students received support, including 1 fellowship (averaging $30,000 per year), 5 research assistantships with full tuition reimbursements available (averaging $21,000 per year), 11 teaching assistantships with full tuition reimbursements available (averaging $21,000 per year). Financial award application deadline: 12/15; financial award applicants required to submit FAFSA. *Faculty research:* Plant cell and molecular biology; plant population ecology and evolution; meiosis in higher plants; 7pPlant systematics, evolution, ecology, and biogeography; plant-environment interaction; community ecology; plant-insect interactions; rhizobial/plant symbiotic interactions; cell fate specification and reprogramming in plants; evolutionary and developmental biology; plant-environment interaction. *Unit head:* Professor and Associate Chairman for Graduate Studies. *Application contact:* Judy Bowers, Coordinator, Graduate Affairs, 850-644-3023, Fax: 850-644-9829, E-mail: gradinfo@bio.fsu.edu. Web site: http://bio.fsu.edu.

Illinois State University, Graduate School, College of Arts and Sciences, Department of Biological Sciences, Normal, IL 61790-2200. Offers animal behavior (MS); bacteriology (MS); biochemistry (MS); biological sciences (MS); biology (PhD); biophysics (MS); biotechnology (MS); botany (MS, PhD); cell biology (MS); conservation biology (MS); developmental biology (MS); ecology (MS, PhD); entomology (MS); evolutionary biology (MS); genetics (MS, PhD); immunology (MS); microbiology (MS, PhD); molecular biology (MS); molecular genetics (MS); neurobiology (MS); neuroscience (MS); parasitology (MS); physiology (MS, PhD); plant biology (MS); plant molecular biology (MS); plant sciences (MS); structural biology (MS); zoology (MS, PhD). Part-time programs available. *Degree requirements:* For master's, thesis or alternative; for doctorate, variable foreign language requirement, thesis/dissertation, 2 terms of residency. *Entrance requirements:* For master's, GRE General Test, minimum GPA of 2.6 in last 60 hours of course work; for doctorate, GRE General Test. *Faculty research:* Redoc balance and drug development in schistosoma mansoni, control of the growth of listeria monocytogenes at low temperature, regulation of cell expansion and microtubule function by SPRI, CRUI: physiology and fitness consequences of different life history phenotypes.

Indiana University Bloomington, University Graduate School, College of Arts and Sciences, Department of Biology, Bloomington, IN 47405. Offers biology teaching (MAT); biotechnology (MA); evolution, ecology, and behavior (MA, PhD); genetics (PhD); microbiology (MA, PhD); molecular, cellular, and developmental biology (PhD); plant sciences (MA, PhD); zoology (MA, PhD). *Faculty:* 58 full time (15 women), 21 part-time/adjunct (6 women). *Students:* 175 full-time (100 women), 3 part-time (all women); includes 20 minority (5 Black or African American, non-Hispanic/Latino; 8 Asian, non-Hispanic/Latino; 7 Hispanic/Latino), 55 international. Average age 27. 316 applicants, 22% accepted, 31 enrolled. In 2011, 8 master's, 20 doctorates awarded. Terminal master's awarded for partial completion of doctoral program. *Degree requirements:* For master's, thesis, oral defense; for doctorate, thesis/dissertation, oral defense. *Entrance requirements:* For master's and doctorate, GRE General Test. Additional exam requirements/recommendations for international students: Required—TOEFL (minimum score 100 iBT). *Application deadline:* For fall admission, 1/5 priority date for domestic students, 12/1 for international students. Application fee: $55 ($65 for international students). Electronic applications accepted. *Financial support:* In 2011–12, fellowships with tuition reimbursements (averaging $19,484 per year), research assistantships with tuition reimbursements (averaging $20,300 per year), teaching assistantships with tuition reimbursements (averaging $20,521 per year) were awarded; scholarships/grants, traineeships, health care benefits, and unspecified assistantships also available. Financial award application deadline: 1/5. *Faculty research:* Evolution, ecology and behavior; microbiology; molecular biology and genetics; plant biology. *Unit head:* Dr. Roger Innes, Chair, 812-855-2219, Fax: 812-855-6082, E-mail: rinnes@indiana.edu. *Application contact:* Tracey D. Stohr, Graduate Student Recruitment Coordinator, 812-856-6303, Fax: 812-855-6082, E-mail: gradbio@indiana.edu. Web site: http://www.bio.indiana.edu/.

Iowa State University of Science and Technology, Program in Plant Biology, Ames, IA 50011-3211. Offers MS, PhD. *Degree requirements:* For master's, thesis; for doctorate, thesis/dissertation. *Entrance requirements:* For master's and doctorate, GRE General Test. Additional exam requirements/recommendations for international students: Required—TOEFL (minimum score 550 paper-based; 79 iBT), IELTS (minimum score 6.5). *Application deadline:* For fall admission, 1/16 priority date for domestic students, 1/16 for international students. Applications are processed on a rolling basis. Application fee: $40 ($90 for international students). Electronic applications accepted. *Unit head:* Dr. Steven Whitman, Director of Graduate Education, 515-294-9052, Fax: 515-294-6019, E-mail: ipb@iastate.edu. *Application contact:* Dai Nhuyen, Application Contact, 515-294-9052, Fax: 515-294-6019, E-mail: ipb@iastate.edu. Web site: http://www.ipb.iastate.edu/.

Miami University, College of Arts and Science, Department of Botany, Oxford, OH 45056. Offers MA, MAT, MS, PhD. Part-time programs available. *Students:* 59 full-time (30 women), 183 part-time (142 women); includes 15 minority (3 Black or African American, non-Hispanic/Latino; 2 Asian, non-Hispanic/Latino; 5 Hispanic/Latino; 5 Two or more races, non-Hispanic/Latino), 22 international. Average age 34. In 2011, 11 master's, 4 doctorates awarded. *Entrance requirements:* For master's, GRE General Test, minimum undergraduate GPA of 3.0 during previous 2 years or 2.75 overall; for doctorate, GRE General Test, minimum undergraduate GPA of 2.75, 3.0 graduate. Additional exam requirements/recommendations for international students: Required—TOEFL (minimum score 550 paper-based). *Application deadline:* For fall admission, 1/1 for domestic and international students. Applications are processed on a rolling basis. Application fee: $50. Electronic applications accepted. *Expenses:* Tuition, state resident: full-time $12,023; part-time $501 per credit hour. Tuition, nonresident: full-time $26,554; part-time $1107 per credit hour. *Required fees:* $528. *Financial support:* Research assistantships, teaching assistantships with full tuition reimbursements, Federal Work-Study, institutionally sponsored loans, health care benefits, and unspecified assistantships available. Financial award application deadline: 2/15; financial award applicants required to submit FAFSA. *Faculty research:* Evolution of plants, fungi and algae; bioinformatics; molecular biology of plants and cyanobacteria; food web dynamics; plant science education. *Unit head:* Dr. John Kiss, Chair, 513-529-4200, E-mail: kissjz@muohio.edu. *Application contact:* Dr. Richard C. Moore, Graduate Coordinator, 513-529-4278, E-mail: moorerc@muohio.edu. Web site: http://www.muohio.edu/botany/.

Michigan State University, The Graduate School, College of Agriculture and Natural Resources, MSU-DOE Plant Research Laboratory, East Lansing, MI 48824. Offers biochemistry and molecular biology (PhD); cellular and molecular biology (PhD); crop and soil sciences (PhD); genetics (PhD); microbiology and molecular genetics (PhD); plant biology (PhD); plant physiology (PhD). Offered jointly with the Department of Energy. *Degree requirements:* For doctorate, comprehensive exam, thesis/dissertation, laboratory rotation, defense of dissertation. *Entrance requirements:* For doctorate, GRE General Test, acceptance into one of the affiliated department programs; 3 letters of recommendation; bachelor's degree or equivalent in life sciences, chemistry, biochemistry, or biophysics; research experience. Electronic applications accepted. *Faculty research:* Role of hormones in the regulation of plant development and physiology, molecular mechanisms associated with signal recognition, development and application of genetic methods and materials, protein routing and function.

Michigan State University, The Graduate School, College of Natural Science and College of Agriculture and Natural Resources, Department of Plant Biology, East Lansing, MI 48824. Offers plant biology (MS, PhD); plant breeding, genetics and biotechnology - plant biology (MS, PhD). *Entrance requirements:* Additional exam requirements/recommendations for international students: Required—TOEFL. Electronic applications accepted. *Faculty research:* Physiological, molecular, and biochemical mechanisms; systematics; inheritance; ecology and geohistory.

New York University, Graduate School of Arts and Science, Department of Biology, New York, NY 10012-1019. Offers biology (PhD); biomedical journalism (MS); cancer and molecular biology (PhD); computational biology (PhD); computers in biological research (MS); developmental genetics (PhD); general biology (MS); immunology and microbiology (PhD); molecular genetics (PhD); neurobiology (PhD); oral biology (MS); plant biology (PhD); recombinant DNA technology (MS); MS/MBA. Part-time programs available. *Faculty:* 24 full-time (5 women). *Students:* 146 full-time (90 women), 54 part-time (36 women); includes 49 minority (1 Black or African American, non-Hispanic/Latino; 33 Asian, non-Hispanic/Latino; 12 Hispanic/Latino; 3 Two or more races, non-Hispanic/Latino), 89 international. Average age 27. 394 applicants, 62% accepted, 82 enrolled. In 2011, 68 master's, 6 doctorates awarded. Terminal master's awarded for partial completion of doctoral program. *Degree requirements:* For master's, thesis or alternative, qualifying paper; for doctorate, comprehensive exam, thesis/dissertation. *Entrance requirements:* For master's, GRE General Test; for doctorate, GRE General Test, GRE Subject Test. Additional exam requirements/recommendations for international students: Required—TOEFL. *Application deadline:* For fall admission, 12/1 priority date for domestic students, 12/1 for international students. Application fee: $90. *Financial support:* Fellowships with tuition reimbursements, research assistantships with tuition reimbursements, teaching assistantships with tuition reimbursements, career-related internships or fieldwork, Federal Work-Study, institutionally sponsored loans, scholarships/grants, health care benefits, and unspecified assistantships available. Financial award application deadline: 12/1; financial award applicants required to submit FAFSA. *Faculty research:* Genomics, molecular and cell biology, development and molecular genetics, molecular evolution of plants and animals. *Unit head:* Stephen Small, Chair, 212-998-8200, Fax: 212-995-4015, E-mail: biology@nyu.edu. *Application contact:* Justin Blau, Director of Graduate Studies, 212-998-8200, Fax: 212-995-4015, E-mail: biology@nyu.edu. Web site: http://biology.as.nyu.edu/.

North Carolina State University, Graduate School, College of Agriculture and Life Sciences, Department of Plant Biology, Raleigh, NC 27695. Offers MS, PhD. Part-time programs available. Terminal master's awarded for partial completion of doctoral program. *Degree requirements:* For master's, thesis (for some programs); for doctorate, thesis/dissertation. *Entrance requirements:* For master's and doctorate, GRE. Additional exam requirements/recommendations for international students: Required—TOEFL. Electronic applications accepted. *Faculty research:* Plant molecular and cell biology, aquatic ecology, community ecology, restoration, systematics plant pathogen and environmental interactions.

Ohio University, Graduate College, College of Arts and Sciences, Department of Environmental and Plant Biology, Athens, OH 45701-2979. Offers MS, PhD. Part-time programs available. *Students:* 20 full-time (5 women); includes 2 minority (1 Black or African American, non-Hispanic/Latino; 1 Two or more races, non-Hispanic/Latino), 1 international. 21 applicants, 24% accepted, 5 enrolled. In 2011, 5 master's, 1 doctorate awarded. *Degree requirements:* For master's, thesis, 2 quarters of teaching experience; for doctorate, comprehensive exam, thesis/dissertation, 2 quarters of teaching experience. *Entrance requirements:* For master's, GRE General Test, minimum GPA of 3.0; for doctorate, GRE General Test, minimum GPA of 3.2. Additional exam requirements/recommendations for international students: Required—TOEFL (minimum

score 620 paper-based; 260 computer-based; 105 iBT) or IELTS (minimum score 7.5). *Application deadline:* For fall admission, 1/15 priority date for domestic students, 1/15 for international students. Applications are processed on a rolling basis. Application fee: $50 ($55 for international students). Electronic applications accepted. *Financial support:* Fellowships with full tuition reimbursements, research assistantships with full tuition reimbursements, teaching assistantships with full tuition reimbursements, Federal Work-Study, institutionally sponsored loans, and scholarships/grants available. Financial award application deadline: 1/15. *Faculty research:* Eastern deciduous forest ecology, evolutionary developmental plant biology, phylogenetic systematics, plant cell wall biotechnology. *Total annual research expenditures:* $859,166. *Unit head:* Dr. Allan C. Showalter, Chair, 740-593-1135, Fax: 740-593-1130, E-mail: showalte@ohio.edu. *Application contact:* Dr. Glenn Matlack, Graduate Chair, 740-593-1131, Fax: 740-593-1130, E-mail: matlack@ohio.edu. Web site: http://www.plantbio.ohiou.edu/.

Penn State University Park, Graduate School, Intercollege Graduate Programs, Intercollege Graduate Program in Plant Biology, State College, University Park, PA 16802-1503. Offers MS, PhD. *Unit head:* Dr. Teh-hui Kao, Head, 814-823-1042, Fax: 814-863-9416, E-mail: txk3@psu.edu. *Application contact:* Cynthia E. Nicosia, Director, Graduate Enrollment Services, 814-865-1795, Fax: 814-865-4627, E-mail: cey1@psu.edu.

Rutgers, The State University of New Jersey, New Brunswick, Graduate School-New Brunswick, Program in Plant Biology, Piscataway, NJ 08854-8097. Offers horticulture and plant technology (MS, PhD); molecular and cellular biology (MS, PhD); organismal and population biology (MS, PhD); plant pathology (MS, PhD). Part-time programs available. Terminal master's awarded for partial completion of doctoral program. *Degree requirements:* For master's, comprehensive exam, thesis or alternative; for doctorate, comprehensive exam, thesis/dissertation. *Entrance requirements:* For master's and doctorate, GRE General Test, GRE Subject Test (recommended). Additional exam requirements/recommendations for international students: Required—TOEFL (minimum score 600 paper-based; 250 computer-based). Electronic applications accepted. *Faculty research:* Molecular biology and biochemistry of plants, plant development and genomics, plant protection, plant improvement, plant management of horticultural and field crops.

Southern Illinois University Carbondale, Graduate School, College of Science, Department of Plant Biology, Carbondale, IL 62901-4701. Offers MS, PhD. *Faculty:* 13 full-time (2 women). *Students:* 11 full-time (7 women), 34 part-time (20 women); includes 5 minority (1 Black or African American, non-Hispanic/Latino; 2 Asian, non-Hispanic/Latino; 2 Hispanic/Latino), 7 international. Average age 25. 17 applicants, 53% accepted, 6 enrolled. In 2011, 3 master's, 2 doctorates awarded. *Degree requirements:* For master's, thesis; for doctorate, one foreign language, thesis/dissertation. *Entrance requirements:* For master's, GRE General Test, minimum GPA of 2.7; for doctorate, GRE General Test, minimum GPA of 3.25. Additional exam requirements/recommendations for international students: Required—TOEFL. *Application deadline:* Applications are processed on a rolling basis. Application fee: $20. *Financial support:* In 2011–12, 24 students received support, including 4 fellowships with full tuition reimbursements available, 6 research assistantships with full tuition reimbursements available, 13 teaching assistantships with full tuition reimbursements available; Federal Work-Study, institutionally sponsored loans, and tuition waivers (full) also available. Support available to part-time students. *Faculty research:* Algal toxins, ethnobotany, community and wetland ecology, morphogenesis, systematics and evolution. *Total annual research expenditures:* $524,140. *Unit head:* Dr. Dale Vitt, Chairperson, 618-453-3210, E-mail: dvitt@plant.siu.edu. *Application contact:* William G. Dyer, Associate Dean, 618-536-6666.

Texas A&M University, College of Agriculture and Life Sciences, Department of Soil and Crop Sciences, College Station, TX 77843. Offers agronomy (M Agr, MS, PhD); food science and technology (MS, PhD); genetics (PhD); molecular and environmental plant sciences (MS, PhD); plant breeding (MS, PhD); soil science (MS, PhD). *Faculty:* 37. *Students:* 98 full-time (36 women), 29 part-time (4 women); includes 12 minority (4 Black or African American, non-Hispanic/Latino; 3 Asian, non-Hispanic/Latino; 5 Hispanic/Latino), 42 international. Average age 26. In 2011, 4 master's, 8 doctorates awarded. *Degree requirements:* For master's, thesis; for doctorate, thesis/dissertation. *Entrance requirements:* For master's and doctorate, GRE General Test. Additional exam requirements/recommendations for international students: Required—TOEFL. *Application deadline:* For fall admission, 3/1 priority date for domestic students; for spring admission, 8/1 for domestic students. Applications are processed on a rolling basis. Application fee: $50 ($75 for international students). *Expenses:* Tuition, state resident: full-time $5437; part-time $226.55 per credit hour. Tuition, nonresident: full-time $12,949; part-time $539.55 per credit hour. *Required fees:* $2741. *Financial support:* In 2011–12, fellowships (averaging $16,000 per year), research assistantships with partial tuition reimbursements (averaging $15,000 per year) were awarded; career-related internships or fieldwork, Federal Work-Study, and institutionally sponsored loans also available. *Faculty research:* Soil and crop management, turfgrass science, weed science, cereal chemistry, food protein chemistry. *Unit head:* Dr. David D. Baltensperger, Department Head, 979-845-3001, E-mail: dbaltensperger@ag.tamu.edu. *Application contact:* Graduate Admissions, 979-845-1044, E-mail: admissions@tamu.edu. Web site: http://soilcrop.tamu.edu.

Université Laval, Faculty of Agricultural and Food Sciences, Program in Plant Biology, Québec, QC G1K 7P4, Canada. Offers M Sc, PhD. Terminal master's awarded for partial completion of doctoral program. *Degree requirements:* For master's, thesis (for some programs); for doctorate, comprehensive exam, thesis/dissertation. *Entrance requirements:* For master's and doctorate, knowledge of French and English. Electronic applications accepted.

University of Alberta, Faculty of Graduate Studies and Research, Department of Biological Sciences, Edmonton, AB T6G 2E1, Canada. Offers environmental biology and ecology (M Sc, PhD); microbiology and biotechnology (M Sc, PhD); molecular biology and genetics (M Sc, PhD); physiology and cell biology (M Sc, PhD); plant biology (M Sc, PhD); systematics and evolution (M Sc, PhD). Terminal master's awarded for partial completion of doctoral program. *Degree requirements:* For master's, thesis; for doctorate, thesis/dissertation. *Entrance requirements:* Additional exam requirements/recommendations for international students: Required—TOEFL.

University of California, Berkeley, Graduate Division, College of Natural Resources, Department of Plant and Microbial Biology, Berkeley, CA 94720-1500. Offers plant biology (PhD). *Degree requirements:* For doctorate, thesis/dissertation, qualifying exam, seminar presentation. *Entrance requirements:* For doctorate, GRE General Test, minimum GPA of 3.0, 3 letters of recommendation. *Faculty research:* Development, molecular biology, genetics, microbial biology, mycology.

University of California, Davis, Graduate Studies, Graduate Group in Plant Biology, Davis, CA 95616. Offers MS, PhD. *Degree requirements:* For master's, comprehensive exam (for some programs), thesis (for some programs); for doctorate, thesis/dissertation. *Entrance requirements:* For master's, GRE General Test, GRE Subject Test (biology), minimum GPA of 3.0; for doctorate, GRE General Test, GRE Subject Test (biology). Additional exam requirements/recommendations for international students: Required—TOEFL (minimum score 550 paper-based; 213 computer-based). Electronic applications accepted. *Faculty research:* Cell and molecular biology, ecology, systematics and evolution, integrative plant and crop physiology, plant development and structure.

University of California, Riverside, Graduate Division, Department of Botany and Plant Sciences, Riverside, CA 92521-0102. Offers plant biology (MS, PhD), including plant cell, molecular, and developmental biology (PhD), plant ecology (PhD), plant genetics (PhD). Part-time programs available. *Faculty:* 40 full-time (13 women). *Students:* 66 full-time (40 women); includes 12 minority (5 Asian, non-Hispanic/Latino; 7 Hispanic/Latino), 24 international. Average age 29. In 2011, 3 master's, 3 doctorates awarded. Terminal master's awarded for partial completion of doctoral program. *Degree requirements:* For master's, comprehensive exams or thesis; for doctorate, thesis/dissertation, qualifying exams. *Entrance requirements:* For master's and doctorate, GRE General Test, minimum GPA of 3.2. Additional exam requirements/recommendations for international students: Required—TOEFL (minimum score 550 paper-based; 213 computer-based; 80 iBT). *Application deadline:* For fall admission, 5/1 for domestic students, 2/1 for international students; for winter admission, 2/1 for domestic students, 7/1 for international students; for spring admission, 12/1 for domestic students, 10/1 for international students. Applications are processed on a rolling basis. Application fee: $80 ($100 for international students). Electronic applications accepted. *Financial support:* In 2011–12, fellowships with tuition reimbursements (averaging $12,000 per year), research assistantships with tuition reimbursements (averaging $23,000 per year), teaching assistantships with tuition reimbursements (averaging $16,500 per year) were awarded; career-related internships or fieldwork, Federal Work-Study, institutionally sponsored loans, scholarships/grants, and tuition waivers (full and partial) also available. *Faculty research:* Agricultural plant biology; biochemistry and physiology; cellular, molecular and developmental biology; ecology, evolution, systematics and ethnobotany; genetics, genomics and bioinformatics. *Unit head:* Dr. Mikeal Roose, Chair, 951-827-4413. *Application contact:* Deidra Kornfeld, Graduate Program Assistant, 800-735-0717, Fax: 951-827-5517, E-mail: deidra.kornfeld@ucr.edu. Web site: http://www.plantbiology.ucr.edu/.

University of California, San Diego, Office of Graduate Studies, Division of Biological Sciences, Program in Plant Systems Biology, La Jolla, CA 92093. Offers PhD.

University of Connecticut, Graduate School, College of Liberal Arts and Sciences, Department of Molecular and Cell Biology, Field of Plant Cell and Molecular Biology, Storrs, CT 06269. Offers MS, PhD. *Degree requirements:* For doctorate, thesis/dissertation. *Entrance requirements:* For master's and doctorate, GRE General Test, GRE Subject Test. Additional exam requirements/recommendations for international students: Required—TOEFL.

University of Florida, Graduate School, College of Agricultural and Life Sciences and College of Liberal Arts and Sciences, Program in Plant Molecular and Cellular Biology, Gainesville, FL 32611. Offers MS, PhD. *Students:* 27 full-time (11 women), 1 (woman) part-time; includes 3 minority (all Asian, non-Hispanic/Latino), 16 international. Average age 28. 69 applicants, 9% accepted, 6 enrolled. In 2011, 1 master's, 2 doctorates awarded. *Degree requirements:* For master's, thesis; for doctorate, comprehensive exam, thesis/dissertation, first author peer-reviewed publication. *Entrance requirements:* For master's and doctorate, GRE General Test (minimum combined score 1100 verbal and quantitative), minimum GPA of 3.0. Additional exam requirements/recommendations for international students: Required—TOEFL (minimum score 550 paper-based; 213 computer-based; 80 iBT), IELTS (minimum score 6). *Application deadline:* For fall admission, 1/1 priority date for domestic students, 1/1 for international students; for spring admission, 8/1 for domestic and international students. Applications are processed on a rolling basis. Application fee: $30. Electronic applications accepted. *Financial support:* Fellowships, research assistantships, and unspecified assistantships available. Financial award applicants required to submit FAFSA. *Faculty research:* The understanding of molecular and cellular mechanisms that mediate plant development, adaptation, and evolution including bioinformatics, genomics, proteomics, genetics, biochemistry, breeding, physiology and molecular and cellular biology. *Unit head:* Dr. Gary F. Peter, Director, 352-846-0896, E-mail: gfpeter@ufl.edu. *Application contact:* Dr. A. Mark Settles, Graduate Coordinator, 352-392-7571, E-mail: settles@ufl.edu. Web site: http://pmcb.ifas.ufl.edu/.

University of Georgia, Franklin College of Arts and Sciences, Department of Plant Biology, Athens, GA 30602. Offers MS, PhD. *Faculty:* 22 full-time (8 women). *Students:* 45 full-time (25 women), 2 part-time (1 woman); includes 5 minority (1 Black or African American, non-Hispanic/Latino; 1 Hispanic/Latino; 3 Two or more races, non-Hispanic/Latino), 12 international. Average age 26. 35 applicants, 60% accepted, 16 enrolled. In 2011, 1 master's, 6 doctorates awarded. *Degree requirements:* For master's, thesis; for doctorate, one foreign language, thesis/dissertation. *Entrance requirements:* For master's and doctorate, GRE General Test. *Application deadline:* For fall admission, 1/1 priority date for domestic students. Application fee: $50. Electronic applications accepted. *Financial support:* Fellowships, research assistantships, teaching assistantships, and unspecified assistantships available. *Unit head:* Dr. Michelle Momany, Head, 706-542-1811, Fax: 706-542-1805, E-mail: depthead@plantbio.uga.edu. *Application contact:* Dr. Lisa Donovan, Graduate Coordinator, 706-542-2969, Fax: 706-542-1805, E-mail: donovan@plantbio.uga.edu. Web site: http://www.plantbio.uga.edu/.

University of Illinois at Urbana–Champaign, Graduate College, College of Liberal Arts and Sciences, School of Integrative Biology, Department of Plant Biology, Champaign, IL 61820. Offers MS, PSM, PhD. *Faculty:* 13 full-time (3 women). *Students:* 38 full-time (24 women), 3 part-time (1 woman); includes 7 minority (2 Black or African American, non-Hispanic/Latino; 1 American Indian or Alaska Native, non-Hispanic/Latino; 3 Asian, non-Hispanic/Latino; 1 Hispanic/Latino), 6 international. 47 applicants, 19% accepted, 8 enrolled. In 2011, 3 degrees awarded. *Entrance requirements:* For master's, GRE General Test, minimum GPA of 3.0; for doctorate, GRE, minimum GPA of 3.0. Additional exam requirements/recommendations for international students: Required—TOEFL (minimum score 600 paper-based; 250 computer-based; 102 iBT). *Application deadline:* Applications are processed on a rolling basis. Application fee: $75 ($90 for international students). Electronic applications accepted. *Financial support:* In 2011–12, 2 fellowships, 25 research assistantships, 16 teaching assistantships were awarded; tuition waivers (full and partial) also available. *Unit head:* Feng Sheng Hu, Head, 217-244-2982, Fax: 217-244-7246, E-mail: fhu@illinois.edu. *Application contact:* Martha Plummer, Office Administrator, 217-333-2377, Fax: 217-244-7246, E-mail: marthapl@illinois.edu. Web site: http://www.life.illinois.edu/plantbio/.

University of Illinois at Urbana–Champaign, Graduate College, College of Liberal Arts and Sciences, School of Integrative Biology, Program in Physiological and Molecular Plant Biology, Champaign, IL 61820. Offers PhD. *Students:* 3 full-time (1 woman), 2 international. In 2011, 6 doctorates awarded. *Entrance requirements:* For doctorate, GRE, minimum GPA of 3.0. Additional exam requirements/recommendations for international students: Required—TOEFL (minimum score 570 paper-based; 230 computer-based; 89 iBT). *Application deadline:* Applications are processed on a rolling basis. Application fee: $75 ($90 for international students). Electronic applications accepted. *Financial support:* In 2011–12, 2 research assistantships, 2 teaching assistantships were awarded; fellowships and tuition waivers (full and partial) also available. *Unit head:* Stephen Moose, Director, 217-244-6308, Fax: 217-244-1224,

E-mail: smoose@illinois.edu. *Application contact:* Carol Hall, Office Manager, 217-333-8208, Fax: 217-244-1224, E-mail: cahall@illinois.edu. Web site: http://www.life.illinois.edu/plantbio/pmpb/.

University of Maine, Graduate School, College of Natural Sciences, Forestry, and Agriculture, Department of Biological Sciences, Program in Plant Science, Orono, ME 04469. Offers PhD. Part-time programs available. *Students:* 2 full-time (1 woman), 1 (woman) part-time, 2 international. Average age 30. *Degree requirements:* For doctorate, thesis/dissertation. *Entrance requirements:* For doctorate, GRE General Test. Additional exam requirements/recommendations for international students: Required—TOEFL. *Application deadline:* For fall admission, 2/1 priority date for domestic students. Applications are processed on a rolling basis. Application fee: $65. Electronic applications accepted. *Expenses:* Tuition, state resident: full-time $5016. Tuition, nonresident: full-time $14,424. *Financial support:* Career-related internships or fieldwork, Federal Work-Study, institutionally sponsored loans, and tuition waivers (full) available. Financial award application deadline: 3/1. *Unit head:* Dr. Jody Jellison, Coordinator, 207-581-2551. *Application contact:* Scott G. Delcourt, Associate Dean of the Graduate School, 207-581-3291, Fax: 207-581-3232, E-mail: graduate@maine.edu. Web site: http://www2.umaine.edu/graduate/.

University of Maine, Graduate School, College of Natural Sciences, Forestry, and Agriculture, Department of Plant, Soil, and Environmental Sciences, Orono, ME 04469. Offers biological sciences (PhD); ecology and environmental sciences (MS, PhD); forest resources (PhD); horticulture (MS); plant science (PhD); plant, soil, and environmental sciences (MS); resource utilization (MS). *Faculty:* 9 full-time (3 women), 7 part-time/adjunct (3 women). *Students:* 7 full-time (4 women), 2 part-time (0 women), 2 international. Average age 30. 14 applicants, 50% accepted, 5 enrolled. In 2011, 4 degrees awarded. *Entrance requirements:* For master's and doctorate, GRE General Test. Additional exam requirements/recommendations for international students: Required—TOEFL. *Application deadline:* Applications are processed on a rolling basis. Application fee: $65. Electronic applications accepted. *Expenses:* Tuition, state resident: full-time $5016. Tuition, nonresident: full-time $14,424. *Financial support:* In 2011–12, 16 research assistantships with full tuition reimbursements (averaging $17,336 per year), 1 teaching assistantship with full tuition reimbursement (averaging $13,600 per year) were awarded; scholarships/grants, tuition waivers (full and partial), and unspecified assistantships also available. *Total annual research expenditures:* $179,065. *Unit head:* Dr. Gregory Porter, Chair, 207-581-2943, Fax: 207-581-3207. *Application contact:* Scott G. Delcourt, Associate Dean of the Graduate School, 207-581-3291, Fax: 207-581-3232, E-mail: graduate@maine.edu. Web site: http://www2.umaine.edu/graduate/.

University of Maryland, College Park, Academic Affairs, College of Computer, Mathematical and Natural Sciences, Department of Cell Biology and Molecular Genetics, College Park, MD 20742. Offers cell biology and molecular genetics (MS, PhD); molecular and cellular biology (PhD); plant biology (MS, PhD). Part-time and evening/weekend programs available. *Faculty:* 81 full-time (31 women), 7 part-time/adjunct (6 women). *Students:* 72 full-time (40 women), 3 part-time (all women); includes 10 minority (2 Black or African American, non-Hispanic/Latino; 5 Asian, non-Hispanic/Latino; 3 Hispanic/Latino), 33 international. In 2011, 5 master's, 14 doctorates awarded. Terminal master's awarded for partial completion of doctoral program. *Degree requirements:* For master's, thesis; for doctorate, thesis/dissertation. *Entrance requirements:* For master's, GRE General Test, minimum GPA of 3.0, 3 letters of recommendation; for doctorate, GRE General Test. Additional exam requirements/recommendations for international students: Required—TOEFL. *Application deadline:* Applications are processed on a rolling basis. Application fee: $75. Electronic applications accepted. *Expenses:* Tuition, state resident: part-time $525 per credit hour. Tuition, nonresident: part-time $1131 per credit hour. *Required fees:* $386.31 per term. Tuition and fees vary according to program. *Financial support:* In 2011–12, 7 fellowships with full and partial tuition reimbursements (averaging $23,147 per year), 20 research assistantships (averaging $19,591 per year), 38 teaching assistantships (averaging $19,458 per year) were awarded; Federal Work-Study and scholarships/grants also available. Support available to part-time students. Financial award applicants required to submit FAFSA. *Faculty research:* Cytoskeletal activity, membrane biology, cell division, genetics and genomics, virology. *Total annual research expenditures:* $7.8 million. *Unit head:* Dr. Norma Andrews, Chair, 301-405-8418, E-mail: andrewsn@umd.edu. *Application contact:* Dr. Charles A. Caramello, Dean of Graduate School, 301-405-0358, Fax: 301-314-9305.

University of Massachusetts Amherst, Graduate School, Interdisciplinary Programs, Program in Plant Biology, Amherst, MA 01003. Offers biochemistry and metabolism (MS, PhD); cell biology and physiology (MS, PhD); environmental, ecological and integrative (PhD); environmental, ecological and integrative biology (MS); genetics and evolution (MS, PhD). *Students:* 16 full-time (7 women), 1 (woman) part-time, 7 international. Average age 27. 22 applicants, 50% accepted, 5 enrolled. In 2011, 3 degrees awarded. *Median time to degree:* Of those who began their doctoral program in fall 2003, 100% received their degree in 8 years or less. *Degree requirements:* For master's, thesis; for doctorate, 2 foreign languages, comprehensive exam, thesis/dissertation. *Entrance requirements:* For master's and doctorate, GRE General Test. Additional exam requirements/recommendations for international students: Required—TOEFL (minimum score 550 paper-based; 213 computer-based; 80 iBT), IELTS (minimum score 6.5). *Application deadline:* For fall admission, 12/15 for domestic and international students; for spring admission, 10/1 for domestic and international students. Applications are processed on a rolling basis. Application fee: $50 ($65 for international students). Electronic applications accepted. Tuition and fees vary according to course load, campus/location and program. *Financial support:* Fellowships with full and partial tuition reimbursements, research assistantships with full and partial tuition reimbursements, teaching assistantships with full and partial tuition reimbursements, career-related internships or fieldwork, Federal Work-Study, scholarships/grants, traineeships, health care benefits, tuition waivers (full and partial), and unspecified assistantships available. Support available to part-time students. Financial award application deadline: 12/15. *Unit head:* Dr. Elsbeth L. Walker, Graduate Program Director, 413-577-3217, Fax: 413-545-3243. *Application contact:* Lindsay DeSantis, Interim Supervisor of Admissions, 413-545—0722, Fax: 413-577-0010, E-mail: gradadm@grad.umass.edu. Web site: http://www.bio.umass.edu/plantbio/.

University of Minnesota, Twin Cities Campus, Graduate School, College of Biological Sciences, Program in Plant Biological Sciences, Minneapolis, MN 55455-0213. Offers MS, PhD. Part-time programs available. Terminal master's awarded for partial completion of doctoral program. *Degree requirements:* For master's, thesis or alternative; for doctorate, thesis/dissertation, written and oral preliminary exams. *Entrance requirements:* For master's and doctorate, GRE General Test. Additional exam requirements/recommendations for international students: Required—TOEFL. Electronic applications accepted. *Faculty research:* Cell and molecular biology; plant physiology; plant structure, diversity, and development; ecology, systematics, evolution and genomics.

University of Missouri, Graduate School, College of Agriculture, Food and Natural Resources, Division of Plant Sciences, Program in Plant Biology and Genetics, Columbia, MO 65211. Offers MS, PhD. Terminal master's awarded for partial completion of doctoral program. *Degree requirements:* For master's, thesis; for doctorate, thesis/dissertation. *Entrance requirements:* For master's and doctorate, GRE General Test, minimum GPA of 3.0. *Application deadline:* For fall admission, 3/1 priority date for domestic students. Applications are processed on a rolling basis. Application fee: $55 ($75 for international students). *Expenses:* Tuition, state resident: full-time $5881. Tuition, nonresident: full-time $15,183. *Required fees:* $952. Tuition and fees vary according to campus/location and program. *Financial support:* Research assistantships, teaching assistantships, and institutionally sponsored loans available. *Unit head:* Dr. Jeanne Mihail, Director of Graduate Studies, 573-882-0574, E-mail: mihailj@missouri.edu. *Application contact:* Dr. Jeanne Mihail, Director of Graduate Studies, 573-882-0574, E-mail: mihailj@missouri.edu.

University of New Hampshire, Graduate School, College of Life Sciences and Agriculture, Department of Biological Sciences, Program in Plant Biology, Durham, NH 03824. Offers MS, PhD. Part-time programs available. *Faculty:* 22 full-time. *Students:* 11 full-time (9 women), 10 part-time (3 women); includes 3 minority (1 Asian, non-Hispanic/Latino; 2 Two or more races, non-Hispanic/Latino), 4 international. Average age 30. 13 applicants, 38% accepted, 4 enrolled. In 2011, 1 doctorate awarded. Terminal master's awarded for partial completion of doctoral program. *Degree requirements:* For master's, thesis; for doctorate, thesis/dissertation. *Entrance requirements:* For master's and doctorate, GRE General Test, GRE Subject Test. Additional exam requirements/recommendations for international students: Required—TOEFL (minimum score 550 paper-based; 213 computer-based; 80 iBT). *Application deadline:* For fall admission, 6/1 priority date for domestic students, 4/1 for international students; for spring admission, 12/1 for domestic students. Applications are processed on a rolling basis. Application fee: $65. Electronic applications accepted. *Expenses:* Tuition, state resident: full-time $12,360; part-time $687 per credit hour. Tuition, nonresident: full-time $25,680; part-time $1058 per credit hour. *International tuition:* $29,550 full-time. *Required fees:* $1666; $833 per course. $416.50 per semester. Tuition and fees vary according to course load and degree level. *Financial support:* In 2011–12, 14 students received support, including 1 fellowship, 5 research assistantships, 8 teaching assistantships; career-related internships or fieldwork, Federal Work-Study, scholarships/grants, and tuition waivers (full and partial) also available. Support available to part-time students. Financial award application deadline: 2/15. *Unit head:* Larry Harris, Chairperson, 603-862-3897. *Application contact:* Diane Lavalliere, Administrative Assistant, 603-862-4095, E-mail: diane.lavallier@unh.edu. Web site: http://www.plant.unh.edu/.

The University of Texas at Austin, Graduate School, College of Natural Sciences, School of Biological Sciences, Program in Plant Biology, Austin, TX 78712-1111. Offers MA, PhD. *Entrance requirements:* For master's and doctorate, GRE General Test, minimum GPA of 3.0. Additional exam requirements/recommendations for international students: Required—TOEFL. *Application deadline:* For fall admission, 1/15 priority date for domestic students, 1/15 for international students. Applications are processed on a rolling basis. Application fee: $50 ($75 for international students). Electronic applications accepted. *Financial support:* Fellowships, research assistantships, and teaching assistantships with tuition reimbursements available. Financial award applicants required to submit FAFSA. *Faculty research:* Systematics, plant molecular biology, psychology, ecology, evolution. *Unit head:* Karen S. Browning, Chair, 512-471-4562, E-mail: kbrowning@mail.utexas.edu. Web site: http://www.biosci.utexas.edu/graduate/plantbio/.

University of Vermont, Graduate College, College of Agriculture and Life Sciences, Department of Plant Biology, Burlington, VT 05405. Offers field naturalist (MS); plant biology (MS, PhD). *Students:* 14 (12 women), 4 international. 38 applicants, 24% accepted, 1 enrolled. In 2011, 7 degrees awarded. *Entrance requirements:* Additional exam requirements/recommendations for international students: Required—TOEFL (minimum score 550 paper-based; 213 computer-based; 80 iBT). *Application deadline:* For fall admission, 1/1 priority date for domestic students, 1/1 for international students. Application fee: $40. Electronic applications accepted. *Unit head:* Dr. David Barrington, Interim Chairperson, 802-656-2930. *Application contact:* Mary Tierney, Director and Coordinator, 802-656-2930.

The University of Western Ontario, Faculty of Graduate Studies, Biosciences Division, Department of Plant Sciences, London, ON N6A 5B8, Canada. Offers plant and environmental sciences (M Sc); plant sciences (M Sc, PhD); plant sciences and environmental sciences (PhD); plant sciences and molecular biology (M Sc, PhD). *Degree requirements:* For master's, thesis; for doctorate, thesis/dissertation. *Entrance requirements:* For doctorate, M Sc or equivalent. Additional exam requirements/recommendations for international students: Required—TOEFL. *Faculty research:* Ecology systematics, plant biochemistry and physiology, yeast genetics, molecular biology.

Washington University in St. Louis, Graduate School of Arts and Sciences, Division of Biology and Biomedical Sciences, Program in Plant Biology, St. Louis, MO 63130-4899. Offers PhD. *Degree requirements:* For doctorate, thesis/dissertation. *Entrance requirements:* For doctorate, GRE General Test, GRE Subject Test. Electronic applications accepted.

Yale University, Graduate School of Arts and Sciences, Department of Molecular, Cellular, and Developmental Biology, Program in Plant Sciences, New Haven, CT 06520. Offers PhD. *Degree requirements:* For doctorate, thesis/dissertation. *Entrance requirements:* For doctorate, GRE General Test, GRE Subject Test.

Plant Molecular Biology

Cornell University, Graduate School, Graduate Fields of Agriculture and Life Sciences, Field of Plant Biology, Ithaca, NY 14853-0001. Offers cytology (MS, PhD); paleobotany (MS, PhD); plant cell biology (MS, PhD); plant ecology (MS, PhD); plant molecular biology (MS, PhD); plant morphology, anatomy and biomechanics (MS, PhD); plant physiology (MS, PhD); systematic botany (MS, PhD). *Faculty:* 49 full-time (14 women). *Students:* 33 full-time (18 women); includes 4 minority (2 Black or African American,

non-Hispanic/Latino; 1 Hispanic/Latino; 1 Two or more races, non-Hispanic/Latino), 15 international. Average age 27. 54 applicants, 20% accepted, 6 enrolled. In 2011, 1 master's, 3 doctorates awarded. *Degree requirements:* For doctorate, comprehensive exam, thesis/dissertation. *Entrance requirements:* For doctorate, GRE General Test, GRE Subject Test in biology (recommended), 3 letters of recommendation. Additional exam requirements/recommendations for international students: Required—TOEFL (minimum score 610 paper-based; 253 computer-based; 77 iBT). *Application deadline:* For fall admission, 1/15 priority date for domestic students. Application fee: $95. Electronic applications accepted. *Financial support:* In 2011–12, 7 fellowships with full tuition reimbursements, 15 research assistantships with full tuition reimbursements, 9 teaching assistantships with full tuition reimbursements were awarded; institutionally sponsored loans, scholarships/grants, health care benefits, tuition waivers (full and partial), and unspecified assistantships also available. Financial award applicants required to submit FAFSA. *Faculty research:* Plant cell biology/cytology; plant molecular biology; plant morphology/anatomy/biomechanics; plant physiology, systematic botany, paleobotany; plant ecology, ethnobotany, plant biochemistry, photosynthesis. *Unit head:* Director of Graduate Studies, 607-255-2131. *Application contact:* Graduate Field Assistant, 607-255-2131, E-mail: plbio@cornell.edu. Web site: http://www.gradschool.cornell.edu/fields.php?id-45&a-2.

Illinois State University, Graduate School, College of Arts and Sciences, Department of Biological Sciences, Normal, IL 61790-2200. Offers animal behavior (MS); bacteriology (MS); biochemistry (MS); biological sciences (MS); biology (PhD); biophysics (MS); biotechnology (MS); botany (MS, PhD); cell biology (MS); conservation biology (MS); developmental biology (MS); ecology (MS, PhD); entomology (MS); evolutionary biology (MS); genetics (MS, PhD); immunology (MS); microbiology (MS, PhD); molecular biology (MS); molecular genetics (MS); neurobiology (MS); neuroscience (MS); parasitology (MS); physiology (MS, PhD); plant biology (MS); plant molecular biology (MS); plant sciences (MS); structural biology (MS); zoology (MS, PhD). Part-time programs available. *Degree requirements:* For master's, thesis or alternative; for doctorate, variable foreign language requirement, thesis/dissertation, 2 terms of residency. *Entrance requirements:* For master's, GRE General Test, minimum GPA of 2.6 in last 60 hours of course work; for doctorate, GRE General Test. *Faculty research:* Redoc balance and drug development in schistosoma mansoni, control of the growth of listeria monocytogenes at low temperature, regulation of cell expansion and microtubule function by SPRI, CRUI: physiology and fitness consequences of different life history phenotypes.

Michigan Technological University, Graduate School, School of Forest Resources and Environmental Science, Houghton, MI 49931. Offers applied ecology (MS); forest ecology and management (MS); forest science (PhD); forestry (MF, MS); molecular genetics and biotechnology (MS, PhD). *Accreditation:* SAF. Part-time programs available. *Faculty:* 26 full-time (5 women), 37 part-time/adjunct (13 women). *Students:* 67 full-time (37 women), 18 part-time (8 women), 15 international. Average age 30. 72 applicants, 39% accepted, 24 enrolled. In 2011, 24 degrees awarded. Terminal master's awarded for partial completion of doctoral program. *Degree requirements:* For master's, comprehensive exam (for some programs), thesis (for some programs); for doctorate, comprehensive exam, thesis/dissertation. *Entrance requirements:* For master's and doctorate, GRE (minimum scores: 500 in verbal, 500 quantitative, 3.5 in analytical), statement of purpose, official transcripts, 3 letters of recommendation, resume/curriculum vitae. Additional exam requirements/recommendations for international students: Required—TOEFL (minimum score 79 iBT) or IELTS. *Application deadline:* Applications are processed on a rolling basis. Electronic applications accepted. *Expenses:* Tuition, state resident: full-time $12,636; part-time $702 per credit. Tuition, nonresident: full-time $12,636; part-time $702 per credit. *Required fees:* $226; $226 per year. *Financial support:* In 2011–12, 78 students received support, including 16 fellowships with full tuition reimbursements available (averaging $6,065 per year), 36 research assistantships with full tuition reimbursements available (averaging $6,065 per year), 2 teaching assistantships with full tuition reimbursements available (averaging $6,065 per year); career-related internships or fieldwork, Federal Work-Study, scholarships/grants, health care benefits, tuition waivers (partial), unspecified assistantships, and cooperative program also available. Financial award applicants required to submit FAFSA. *Faculty research:* Forest molecular genetics and biotechnology, forestry, forest ecology and management, applied ecology, wood science. *Total annual research expenditures:* $5.9 million. *Unit head:* Dr. Terry Sharik, Dean, 906-487-2352, Fax: 906-487-2915. *Application contact:* 906-487-2352, Fax: 906-487-2915. Web site: http://www.mtu.edu/forest/.

Rutgers, The State University of New Jersey, New Brunswick, Graduate School-New Brunswick, Program in Plant Biology, Piscataway, NJ 08854-8097. Offers horticulture and plant technology (MS, PhD); molecular and cellular biology (MS, PhD); organismal and population biology (MS, PhD); plant pathology (MS, PhD). Part-time programs available. Terminal master's awarded for partial completion of doctoral program. *Degree requirements:* For master's, comprehensive exam, thesis or alternative; for doctorate, comprehensive exam, thesis/dissertation. *Entrance requirements:* For master's and doctorate, GRE General Test, GRE Subject Test (recommended). Additional exam requirements/recommendations for international students: Required—TOEFL (minimum score 600 paper-based; 250 computer-based). Electronic applications accepted. *Faculty research:* Molecular biology and biochemistry of plants, plant development and genomics, plant protection, plant improvement, plant management of horticultural and field crops.

University of California, Riverside, Graduate Division, Department of Botany and Plant Sciences, Riverside, CA 92521-0102. Offers plant biology (MS, PhD), including plant cell, molecular, and developmental biology (PhD), plant ecology (PhD), plant genetics (PhD). Part-time programs available. *Faculty:* 40 full-time (13 women). *Students:* 66 full-time (40 women); includes 12 minority (5 Asian, non-Hispanic/Latino; 7 Hispanic/Latino), 24 international. Average age 29. In 2011, 3 master's, 3 doctorates awarded. Terminal master's awarded for partial completion of doctoral program. *Degree requirements:* For master's, comprehensive exams or thesis; for doctorate, thesis/dissertation, qualifying exams. *Entrance requirements:* For master's and doctorate, GRE General Test, minimum GPA of 3.2. Additional exam requirements/recommendations for international students: Required—TOEFL (minimum score 550 paper-based; 213 computer-based; 80 iBT). *Application deadline:* For fall admission, 5/1 for domestic students, 2/1 for international students; for winter admission, 2/1 for domestic students, 7/1 for international students; for spring admission, 12/1 for domestic students, 10/1 for international students. Applications are processed on a rolling basis. Application fee: $80 ($100 for international students). Electronic applications accepted. *Financial support:* In 2011–12, fellowships with tuition reimbursements (averaging $12,000 per year), research assistantships with tuition reimbursements (averaging $23,000 per year), teaching assistantships with tuition reimbursements (averaging $16,500 per year) were awarded; career-related internships or fieldwork, Federal Work-Study, institutionally sponsored loans, scholarships/grants, and tuition waivers (full and partial) also available. *Faculty research:* Agricultural plant biology; biochemistry and physiology; cellular, molecular and developmental biology; ecology, evolution, systematics and ethnobotany; genetics, genomics and bioinformatics. *Unit head:* Dr. Mikeal Roose, Chair, 951-827-4413. *Application contact:* Deidra Kornfeld, Graduate Program Assistant, 800-735-0717, Fax: 951-827-5517, E-mail: deidra.kornfeld@ucr.edu. Web site: http://www.plantbiology.ucr.edu/.

University of California, San Diego, Office of Graduate Studies, Division of Biological Sciences, Program in Plant Molecular Biology, La Jolla, CA 92093. Offers PhD. Offered in association with the Salk Institute. *Degree requirements:* For doctorate, thesis/dissertation, qualifying exam. Electronic applications accepted.

University of Connecticut, Graduate School, College of Liberal Arts and Sciences, Department of Molecular and Cell Biology, Field of Plant Cell and Molecular Biology, Storrs, CT 06269. Offers MS, PhD. *Degree requirements:* For doctorate, thesis/dissertation. *Entrance requirements:* For master's and doctorate, GRE General Test, GRE Subject Test. Additional exam requirements/recommendations for international students: Required—TOEFL.

University of Florida, Graduate School, College of Agricultural and Life Sciences and College of Liberal Arts and Sciences, Program in Plant Molecular and Cellular Biology, Gainesville, FL 32611. Offers MS, PhD. *Students:* 27 full-time (11 women), 1 (woman) part-time; includes 3 minority (all Asian, non-Hispanic/Latino), 16 international. Average age 28. 69 applicants, 9% accepted, 6 enrolled. In 2011, 1 master's, 2 doctorates awarded. *Degree requirements:* For master's, thesis; for doctorate, comprehensive exam, thesis/dissertation, first author peer-reviewed publication. *Entrance requirements:* For master's and doctorate, GRE General Test (minimum combined score 1100 verbal and quantitative), minimum GPA of 3.0. Additional exam requirements/recommendations for international students: Required—TOEFL (minimum score 550 paper-based; 213 computer-based; 80 iBT), IELTS (minimum score 6). *Application deadline:* For fall admission, 1/1 priority date for domestic students, 1/1 for international students; for spring admission, 8/1 for domestic and international students. Applications are processed on a rolling basis. Application fee: $30. Electronic applications accepted. *Financial support:* Fellowships, research assistantships, and unspecified assistantships available. Financial award applicants required to submit FAFSA. *Faculty research:* The understanding of molecular and cellular mechanisms that mediate plant development, adaptation, and evolution including bioinformatics, genomics, proteomics, genetics, biochemistry, breeding, physiology and molecular and cellular biology. *Unit head:* Dr. Gary F. Peter, Director, 352-846-0896, E-mail: gfpeter@ufl.edu. *Application contact:* Dr. A. Mark Settles, Graduate Coordinator, 352-392-7571, E-mail: settles@ufl.edu. Web site: http://pmcb.ifas.ufl.edu/.

University of Massachusetts Amherst, Graduate School, Interdisciplinary Programs, Program in Plant Biology, Amherst, MA 01003. Offers biochemistry and metabolism (MS, PhD); cell biology and physiology (MS, PhD); environmental, ecological and integrative (PhD); environmental, ecological and integrative biology (MS); genetics and evolution (MS, PhD). *Students:* 16 full-time (7 women), 1 (woman) part-time, 7 international. Average age 27. 22 applicants, 50% accepted, 5 enrolled. In 2011, 3 degrees awarded. *Median time to degree:* Of those who began their doctoral program in fall 2003, 100% received their degree in 8 years or less. *Degree requirements:* For master's, thesis; for doctorate, 2 foreign languages, comprehensive exam, thesis/dissertation. *Entrance requirements:* For master's and doctorate, GRE General Test. Additional exam requirements/recommendations for international students: Required—TOEFL (minimum score 550 paper-based; 213 computer-based; 80 iBT), IELTS (minimum score 6.5). *Application deadline:* For fall admission, 12/15 for domestic and international students; for spring admission, 10/1 for domestic and international students. Applications are processed on a rolling basis. Application fee: $50 ($65 for international students). Electronic applications accepted. Tuition and fees vary according to course load, campus/location and program. *Financial support:* Fellowships with full and partial tuition reimbursements, research assistantships with full and partial tuition reimbursements, teaching assistantships with full and partial tuition reimbursements, career-related internships or fieldwork, Federal Work-Study, scholarships/grants, traineeships, health care benefits, tuition waivers (full and partial), and unspecified assistantships available. Support available to part-time students. Financial award application deadline: 12/15. *Unit head:* Dr. Elsbeth L. Walker, Graduate Program Director, 413-577-3217, Fax: 413-545-3243. *Application contact:* Lindsay DeSantis, Interim Supervisor of Admissions, 413-545—0722, Fax: 413-577-0010, E-mail: gradadm@grad.umass.edu. Web site: http://www.bio.umass.edu/plantbio/.

Washington State University, Graduate School, College of Agricultural, Human, and Natural Resource Sciences, Program in Molecular Plant Sciences, Pullman, WA 99164. Offers MS, PhD. *Faculty:* 28. *Students:* 48 full-time (20 women), 3 part-time (2 women); includes 2 minority (1 Asian, non-Hispanic/Latino; 1 Two or more races, non-Hispanic/Latino), 23 international. Average age 29. 58 applicants, 16% accepted, 6 enrolled. In 2011, 5 doctorates awarded. Terminal master's awarded for partial completion of doctoral program. *Degree requirements:* For master's, comprehensive exam (for some programs), thesis (for some programs), oral exam, written exam; for doctorate, comprehensive exam, thesis/dissertation, oral exam, written exam. *Entrance requirements:* For master's and doctorate, GRE General Test. Additional exam requirements/recommendations for international students: Required—TOEFL, IELTS. *Application deadline:* For fall admission, 1/1 priority date for domestic students, 1/1 for international students. Applications are processed on a rolling basis. Application fee: $75. *Financial support:* In 2011–12, 40 research assistantships with full and partial tuition reimbursements (averaging $18,204 per year), 5 teaching assistantships with full and partial tuition reimbursements (averaging $18,204 per year) were awarded; career-related internships or fieldwork, Federal Work-Study, institutionally sponsored loans, and tuition waivers (partial) also available. Financial award application deadline: 4/1; financial award applicants required to submit FAFSA. *Faculty research:* Cell response to environmental signals, transport of amino acids, regulation of synthesis of defense proteins. *Unit head:* Dr. Michael Neff, Chair, 509-335-7705, Fax: 509-335-1949, E-mail: mmneff@wsu.edu. *Application contact:* Graduate School Admissions, 800-GRADWSU, Fax: 509-335-1949, E-mail: gradsch@wsu.edu. Web site: http://www.wsu.edu/molecular-plants/.

Plant Pathology

Auburn University, Graduate School, College of Agriculture, Department of Entomology and Plant Pathology, Auburn University, AL 36849. Offers entomology (M Ag, MS, PhD); plant pathology (M Ag, MS, PhD). Part-time programs available. *Faculty:* 17 full-time (6 women). *Students:* 25 full-time (9 women), 13 part-time (6 women); includes 1 minority (Black or African American, non-Hispanic/Latino), 18 international. Average age 28. 19 applicants, 63% accepted, 11 enrolled. In 2011, 2 master's, 5 doctorates awarded. *Degree requirements:* For master's, thesis (for some programs); for doctorate, one foreign language, thesis/dissertation. *Entrance requirements:* For master's, GRE General Test; for doctorate, GRE General Test, GRE Subject Test, master's degree with thesis. *Application deadline:* For fall admission, 7/7 for domestic students; for spring admission, 11/24 for domestic students. Applications are processed on a rolling basis. Application fee: $50 ($60 for international students). Electronic applications accepted. *Expenses:* Tuition, state resident: full-time $7290; part-time $405 per credit hour. Tuition, nonresident: full-time $21,870; part-time $1215 per credit hour. *International tuition:* $22,000 full-time. *Required fees:* $1402. *Financial support:* Research assistantships, teaching assistantships, and Federal Work-Study available. Support available to part-time students. Financial award application deadline: 3/15; financial award applicants required to submit FAFSA. *Faculty research:* Pest management, biological control, systematics, medical entomology. *Unit head:* Dr. Arthur Appel, Chair, 334-844-5006. *Application contact:* Dr. George Flowers, Dean of the Graduate School, 334-844-2125.

Colorado State University, Graduate School, College of Agricultural Sciences, Department of Bioagricultural Sciences and Pest Management, Fort Collins, CO 80523-1177. Offers entomology (MS, PhD); plant pathology and weed science (MS, PhD). Part-time programs available. *Faculty:* 20 full-time (5 women). *Students:* 8 full-time (5 women), 26 part-time (10 women); includes 2 minority (1 American Indian or Alaska Native, non-Hispanic/Latino; 1 Hispanic/Latino), 4 international. Average age 33. 7 applicants, 43% accepted, 1 enrolled. In 2011, 2 master's, 1 doctorate awarded. *Degree requirements:* For master's, comprehensive exam, thesis; for doctorate, comprehensive exam, thesis/dissertation. *Entrance requirements:* For master's, GRE General Test, minimum GPA of 3.0, letters of recommendation; for doctorate, GRE General Test, minimum GPA of 3.0, letters of recommendation, essay. Additional exam requirements/recommendations for international students: Required—TOEFL (minimum score 550 paper-based; 213 computer-based; 80 iBT). *Application deadline:* For fall admission, 1/15 priority date for domestic students, 1/1 for international students; for spring admission, 9/1 priority date for domestic students, 9/1 for international students. Applications are processed on a rolling basis. Application fee: $50. Electronic applications accepted. *Expenses:* Tuition, state resident: full-time $7992. Tuition, nonresident: full-time $19,592. *Required fees:* $1735; $58 per credit. *Financial support:* In 2011–12, 10 fellowships with partial tuition reimbursements (averaging $29,548 per year), 18 research assistantships with full tuition reimbursements (averaging $15,794 per year), 12 teaching assistantships with full tuition reimbursements (averaging $10,933 per year) were awarded; unspecified assistantships also available. Financial award application deadline: 1/15; financial award applicants required to submit FAFSA. *Faculty research:* Entomology specialization, plant pathology specialization, weed science specialization, ecology and biodiversity, integrated pest management. *Total annual research expenditures:* $3 million. *Unit head:* Dr. Thomas O. Holtzer, Head, 970-491-5261, Fax: 970-491-3862, E-mail: tholtzer@lamar.colostate.edu. *Application contact:* Janet Dill, Education Coordinator, 970-491-0402, Fax: 970-491-3862, E-mail: janet.dill@colostate.edu. Web site: http://www.colostate.edu/Depts/bspm/.

Cornell University, Graduate School, Graduate Fields of Agriculture and Life Sciences, Field of Plant Pathology and Plant-Microbe Biology, Ithaca, NY 14853-0001. Offers ecological and environmental plant pathology (MPS, MS, PhD); epidemiological plant pathology (MPS, MS, PhD); molecular plant pathology (MPS, MS, PhD); mycology (MPS, MS, PhD); plant disease epidemiology (MPS, MS, PhD); plant pathology (MPS, MS, PhD). *Faculty:* 46 full-time (16 women). *Students:* 28 full-time (16 women); includes 3 minority (2 Hispanic/Latino; 1 Two or more races, non-Hispanic/Latino), 8 international. Average age 28. 49 applicants, 16% accepted, 7 enrolled. In 2011, 1 master's, 5 doctorates awarded. *Degree requirements:* For master's, thesis (MS), project paper (MPS); for doctorate, comprehensive exam, thesis/dissertation. *Entrance requirements:* For master's and doctorate, GRE General Test, GRE Subject Test (biology recommended), 3 letters of recommendation. Additional exam requirements/recommendations for international students: Required—TOEFL (minimum score 550 paper-based; 213 computer-based; 77 iBT). *Application deadline:* For fall admission, 1/15 priority date for domestic students. Applications are processed on a rolling basis. Application fee: $95. Electronic applications accepted. *Financial support:* In 2011–12, 3 fellowships with full tuition reimbursements, 21 research assistantships with full tuition reimbursements, 1 teaching assistantship with full tuition reimbursement were awarded; institutionally sponsored loans, scholarships/grants, health care benefits, tuition waivers (full and partial), and unspecified assistantships also available. Financial award applicants required to submit FAFSA. *Faculty research:* Plant pathology; mycology; molecular plant pathology; plant disease epidemiology, ecological and environmental plant pathology; plant disease epidemiology and simulation modeling. *Unit head:* Director of Graduate Studies, 607-255-3259, Fax: 607-255-4471. *Application contact:* Graduate Field Assistant, 607-255-3259, Fax: 607-255-4471, E-mail: plpathology@cornell.edu. Web site: http://www.gradschool.cornell.edu/fields.php?id-59&a-2.

Iowa State University of Science and Technology, Department of Plant Pathology, Ames, IA 50011. Offers MS, PhD. *Entrance requirements:* For master's and doctorate, GRE General Test, resume. Additional exam requirements/recommendations for international students: Required—TOEFL (minimum score 550 paper-based; 79 iBT), IELTS (minimum score 6.5). *Application deadline:* For fall admission, 3/15 priority date for domestic students, 3/15 for international students; for spring admission, 9/1 for domestic and international students. Applications are processed on a rolling basis. Application fee: $40 ($90 for international students). Electronic applications accepted. *Unit head:* Dr. Gary Munkvold, Director of Graduate Education, 515-294-7159, Fax: 515-294-9420, E-mail: plantpath@iastate.edu. *Application contact:* Dai Nguyen, Information Contact, 515-294-7159, Fax: 515-294-9420, E-mail: plantpath@iastate.edu. Web site: http://www.plantpath.iastate.edu/.

Kansas State University, Graduate School, College of Agriculture, Department of Plant Pathology, Manhattan, KS 66506. Offers genetics (MS, PhD); plant pathology (MS, PhD). *Faculty:* 19 full-time (5 women), 2 part-time/adjunct (0 women). *Students:* 33 full-time (13 women), 1 (woman) part-time; includes 3 minority (1 Black or African American, non-Hispanic/Latino; 2 Hispanic/Latino), 18 international. Average age 28. 26 applicants, 23% accepted, 4 enrolled. In 2011, 5 doctorates awarded. Terminal master's awarded for partial completion of doctoral program. *Degree requirements:* For master's, thesis, oral exam; for doctorate, thesis/dissertation, preliminary exams. *Entrance requirements:* For master's and doctorate, minimum undergraduate GPA of 3.0.

Additional exam requirements/recommendations for international students: Required—TOEFL (minimum score 550 paper-based; 213 computer-based; 79 iBT). *Application deadline:* For fall admission, 5/15 priority date for domestic students, 12/1 for international students; for spring admission, 10/15 priority date for domestic students, 6/1 for international students. Applications are processed on a rolling basis. Application fee: $40 ($55 for international students). Electronic applications accepted. *Financial support:* In 2011–12, 32 research assistantships (averaging $23,845 per year) were awarded; Federal Work-Study, institutionally sponsored loans, and scholarships/grants also available. Support available to part-time students. Financial award application deadline: 3/1; financial award applicants required to submit FAFSA. *Faculty research:* Applied microbiology, microbial genetics, microbial ecology/epidemiology, integrated pest management, plant genetics/genomics/molecular biology. *Total annual research expenditures:* $6.5 million. *Unit head:* Dr. John Leslie, Head, 785-532-6176, Fax: 785-532-5692, E-mail: jfl@ksu.edu. *Application contact:* Dr. Bill Bockus, Director, 785-532-1378, Fax: 785-532-5692, E-mail: bockus@ksu.edu. Web site: http://www.plantpath.k-state.edu/DesktopDefault.aspx.

Louisiana State University and Agricultural and Mechanical College, Graduate School, College of Agriculture, Department of Plant Pathology and Crop Physiology, Baton Rouge, LA 70803. Offers plant health (MS, PhD). *Faculty:* 19 full-time (1 woman). *Students:* 28 full-time (9 women), 2 part-time (0 women); includes 2 minority (both Hispanic/Latino), 18 international. Average age 30. 17 applicants, 47% accepted, 4 enrolled. In 2011, 5 master's, 2 doctorates awarded. Terminal master's awarded for partial completion of doctoral program. *Degree requirements:* For master's, thesis; for doctorate, thesis/dissertation. *Entrance requirements:* For master's and doctorate, GRE General Test, minimum GPA of 3.0. Additional exam requirements/recommendations for international students: Required—TOEFL (minimum score 550 paper-based; 213 computer-based; 79 iBT) or IELTS (minimum score 6.5). *Application deadline:* For fall admission, 1/25 priority date for domestic students, 5/15 for international students; for spring admission, 10/15 for international students. Applications are processed on a rolling basis. Application fee: $50 ($70 for international students). Electronic applications accepted. *Financial support:* In 2011–12, 29 students received support, including 26 research assistantships with partial tuition reimbursements available (averaging $18,232 per year); fellowships, teaching assistantships with partial tuition reimbursements available, career-related internships or fieldwork, Federal Work-Study, health care benefits, and tuition waivers (full) also available. Support available to part-time students. Financial award applicants required to submit FAFSA. *Faculty research:* Plant health and protection, weed biology and management, crop physiology and biotechnology. *Total annual research expenditures:* $1,000. *Unit head:* Dr. Lawrence Datnoff, Chair, 225-578-1464, Fax: 225-763 5573, E-mail: ldatno1@lsu.edu. *Application contact:* Dr. Raymond Schneider, Graduate Adviser, 225-578-4880, Fax: 225-578-1415, E-mail: rschneider@agcenter.lsu.edu. Web site: http://www.lsu.edu/ppcp/.

Michigan State University, The Graduate School, College of Agriculture and Natural Resources and College of Natural Science, Department of Plant Pathology, East Lansing, MI 48824. Offers MS, PhD. *Entrance requirements:* Additional exam requirements/recommendations for international students: Required—TOEFL.

Mississippi State University, College of Agriculture and Life Sciences, Department of Biochemistry, Molecular Biology, Entomology and Plant Pathology, Mississippi State, MS 39762. Offers agriculture life sciences (MS), including entomology and plant pathology; molecular biology (PhD). *Faculty:* 25 full-time (1 woman). *Students:* 46 full-time (17 women), 14 part-time (6 women); includes 4 minority (2 Black or African American, non-Hispanic/Latino; 2 Two or more races, non-Hispanic/Latino), 18 international. Average age 30. 43 applicants, 33% accepted, 13 enrolled. In 2011, 7 master's, 5 doctorates awarded. Terminal master's awarded for partial completion of doctoral program. *Degree requirements:* For master's, thesis (for some programs), comprehensive oral or written exam; for doctorate, thesis/dissertation, comprehensive oral and written exam. *Entrance requirements:* For master's, GRE General Test, minimum GPA of 2.75; for doctorate, GRE. Additional exam requirements/recommendations for international students: Required—TOEFL (minimum score 550 paper-based; 213 computer-based; 79 iBT); Recommended—IELTS (minimum score 6.5). *Application deadline:* For fall admission, 7/1 for domestic students, 5/1 for international students; for spring admission, 11/1 for domestic students, 9/1 for international students. Applications are processed on a rolling basis. Application fee: $40. Electronic applications accepted. *Expenses:* Tuition, state resident: full-time $5805; part-time $322.50 per credit hour. Tuition, nonresident: full-time $14,670; part-time $815 per credit hour. *Financial support:* In 2011–12, 41 research assistantships with full tuition reimbursements (averaging $15,714 per year) were awarded; Federal Work-Study, institutionally sponsored loans, and unspecified assistantships also available. Financial award application deadline: 4/1; financial award applicants required to submit FAFSA. *Faculty research:* Fish nutrition, plant and animal molecular biology, plant biochemistry, enzymology, lipid metabolism, chromatin, cell wall synthesis in rice, a model grass bioenergy species and the source of rice stover residues, using reverse genetic and functional genomic and proteomic approaches. *Unit head:* Dr. Scott T. Willard, Professor and Department Head, 662-325-2640, Fax: 662-325-8664, E-mail: swilliard@ads.msstate.edu. *Application contact:* Dr. Din-Pow Ma, Professor/Graduate Coordinator, 662-325-7739, Fax: 662-325-8664, E-mail: dm1@ra.msstate.edu.

Montana State University, College of Graduate Studies, College of Agriculture, Department of Plant Sciences and Plant Pathology, Bozeman, MT 59717. Offers plant pathology (MS); plant sciences (MS, PhD), including plant genetics (PhD), plant pathology (PhD). Part-time programs available. *Degree requirements:* For master's, comprehensive exam; for doctorate, comprehensive exam, thesis/dissertation. *Entrance requirements:* For master's, GRE General Test, minimum GPA of 3.0; for doctorate, GRE General Test. Additional exam requirements/recommendations for international students: Required—TOEFL (minimum score 550 paper-based; 213 computer-based). Electronic applications accepted. *Faculty research:* Plant genetics, plant metabolism, plant microbe interactions, plant pathology, entomology research.

New Mexico State University, Graduate School, College of Agricultural, Consumer and Environmental Sciences, Department of Entomology, Plant Pathology and Weed Science, Las Cruces, NM 88003-8001. Offers agricultural biology (MS). Part-time programs available. *Faculty:* 6 full-time (2 women), 2 part-time/adjunct (0 women). *Students:* 11 full-time (3 women), 5 part-time (2 women); includes 5 minority (4 Hispanic/Latino; 1 Two or more races, non-Hispanic/Latino), 3 international. Average age 26. 6 applicants, 67% accepted, 4 enrolled. In 2011, 5 master's awarded. *Degree requirements:* For master's, comprehensive exam, thesis. *Entrance requirements:* For master's, GRE General Test. Additional exam requirements/recommendations for international students: Required—TOEFL (minimum score 550 paper-based; 0 computer-based; 79 iBT), IELTS (minimum score 6.5). *Application deadline:* For fall admission, 7/1 priority date for domestic students; for spring admission, 11/1 priority

date for domestic students. Applications are processed on a rolling basis. Application fee: $40 ($50 for international students). Electronic applications accepted. *Expenses:* Tuition, state resident: full-time $5004; part-time $208.50 per credit. Tuition, nonresident: full-time $17,446; part-time $726.90 per credit. *Financial support:* In 2011–12, 9 students received support, including 2 fellowships (averaging $4,304 per year), 9 research assistantships with full tuition reimbursements available (averaging $20,235 per year); teaching assistantships with partial tuition reimbursements available, career-related internships or fieldwork, and health care benefits also available. Financial award application deadline: 3/1. *Faculty research:* Integrated pest management, pesticide application and safety, livestock ectoparasite research, biotechnology, nematology. *Unit head:* Dr. Jill Schroeder, Interim Head, 575-646-3225, Fax: 575-646-8087, E-mail: jischroe@nmsu.edu. *Application contact:* Cindy Bullard, Intermediate Administrative Assistant, 575-646-1145, Fax: 575-646-8087, E-mail: cbullard@nmsu.edu. Web site: http://eppws.nmsu.edu/.

North Carolina State University, Graduate School, College of Agriculture and Life Sciences, Department of Plant Pathology, Raleigh, NC 27695. Offers MS, PhD. Terminal master's awarded for partial completion of doctoral program. *Degree requirements:* For master's, thesis (for some programs); for doctorate, thesis/dissertation. *Entrance requirements:* For master's and doctorate, GRE. Additional exam requirements/recommendations for international students: Required—TOEFL. Electronic applications accepted. *Faculty research:* Microbe-plant interactions, biology of plant pathogens, pathogen evaluation, host-plant resistance, genomics.

North Dakota State University, College of Graduate and Interdisciplinary Studies, College of Agriculture, Food Systems, and Natural Resources, Department of Plant Pathology, Fargo, ND 58108. Offers MS, PhD. Part-time programs available. *Faculty:* 12 full-time (2 women). *Students:* 25 full-time (12 women), 11 part-time (4 women), 25 international. Average age 23. 12 applicants, 92% accepted, 8 enrolled. In 2011, 2 master's, 3 doctorates awarded. *Degree requirements:* For master's, thesis; for doctorate, thesis/dissertation. *Entrance requirements:* Additional exam requirements/recommendations for international students: Required—TOEFL (minimum score 550 paper-based; 213 computer-based; 79 iBT). *Application deadline:* For fall admission, 5/1 for international students; for winter admission, 8/1 for international students. Applications are processed on a rolling basis. Application fee: $35. Electronic applications accepted. *Financial support:* In 2011–12, 19 research assistantships with full tuition reimbursements were awarded; Federal Work-Study and institutionally sponsored loans also available. Financial award application deadline: 4/15. *Faculty research:* Electron microscopy, disease physiology, molecular biology, genetic resistance, tissue culture. *Unit head:* Dr. Jack Rasmussen, Chair, 701-231-8362, Fax: 701-231-7851, E-mail: jack.rasmussen@ndsu.edu. *Application contact:* Sonya Goergen, Marketing, Recruitment, and Public Relations Coordinator, 701-231-7033, Fax: 701-231-6524.

Nova Scotia Agricultural College, Research and Graduate Studies, Truro, NS B2N 5E3, Canada. Offers agriculture (M Sc), including air quality, animal behavior, animal molecular genetics, animal nutrition, animal technology, aquaculture, botany, crop management, crop physiology, ecology, environmental microbiology, food science, horticulture, nutrient management, pest management, physiology, plant biotechnology, plant pathology, soil chemistry, soil fertility, waste management and composting, water quality. Program offered jointly with Dalhousie University. Part-time programs available. *Degree requirements:* For master's, thesis, ATC Exam Teaching Assistantship. *Entrance requirements:* For master's, honors B Sc, minimum GPA of 3.0. Additional exam requirements/recommendations for international students: Required—TOEFL (minimum score 580 paper-based; 237 computer-based; 92 iBT), IELTS, Michigan English Language Assessment Battery, CanTEST, CAEL. *Faculty research:* Bio-product development, organic agriculture, nutrient management, air and water quality, agricultural biotechnology.

The Ohio State University, Graduate School, College of Food, Agricultural, and Environmental Sciences, Department of Plant Pathology, Columbus, OH 43210. Offers MS, PhD. *Faculty:* 16. *Students:* 25 full-time (13 women), 10 part-time (6 women); includes 1 minority (Asian, non-Hispanic/Latino), 19 international. Average age 28. In 2011, 4 master's, 3 doctorates awarded. *Degree requirements:* For master's, thesis optional; for doctorate, thesis/dissertation. *Entrance requirements:* For master's and doctorate, GRE General Test. Additional exam requirements/recommendations for international students: Required—TOEFL (minimum score 550 paper-based; 213 computer-based), IELTS (minimum score 6.5), or Michigan English Language Assessment Battery (minimum score 82). *Application deadline:* For fall admission, 8/15 priority date for domestic students, 7/1 for international students; for winter admission, 12/1 priority date for domestic students, 11/1 for international students; for spring admission, 3/1 priority date for domestic students, 2/1 for international students. Applications are processed on a rolling basis. Application fee: $40 ($50 for international students). Electronic applications accepted. *Expenses:* Tuition, state resident: full-time $11,400. Tuition, nonresident: full-time $28,125. Tuition and fees vary according to course load, degree level, campus/location and program. *Financial support:* Fellowships, research assistantships, teaching assistantships, Federal Work-Study, and institutionally sponsored loans available. Support available to part-time students. *Unit head:* Terry L. Niblack, Chair, 614-292-8038, E-mail: niblack.2@osu.edu. *Application contact:* Graduate Admissions, 614-292-6031, Fax: 614-292-3656, E-mail: gradadmissions@osu.edu. Web site: http://plantpath.osu.edu/.

Oklahoma State University, College of Agricultural Science and Natural Resources, Department of Entomology and Plant Pathology, Stillwater, OK 74078. Offers entomology (PhD); entomology and plant pathology (MS); plant pathology (PhD). *Faculty:* 33 full-time (13 women). *Students:* 4 full-time (1 woman), 24 part-time (11 women); includes 2 minority (1 American Indian or Alaska Native, non-Hispanic/Latino; 1 Asian, non-Hispanic/Latino), 13 international. Average age 29. 21 applicants, 24% accepted, 3 enrolled. In 2011, 4 master's, 2 doctorates awarded. *Degree requirements:* For master's, thesis or alternative; for doctorate, comprehensive exam, thesis/dissertation. *Entrance requirements:* For master's and doctorate, GRE or GMAT. Additional exam requirements/recommendations for international students: Required—TOEFL (minimum score 550 paper-based; 79 iBT). *Application deadline:* For fall admission, 3/1 for international students; for spring admission, 8/1 for international students. Applications are processed on a rolling basis. Application fee: $40 ($75 for international students). Electronic applications accepted. *Expenses:* Tuition, state resident: full-time $4044; part-time $168.50 per credit hour. Tuition, nonresident: full-time $16,008; part-time $667 per credit hour. *Required fees:* $2122; $88.45 per credit hour. One-time fee: $50. Tuition and fees vary according to course load and campus/location. *Financial support:* In 2011–12, 27 research assistantships (averaging $17,665 per year), 1 teaching assistantship (averaging $16,584 per year) were awarded; career-related internships or fieldwork, Federal Work-Study, scholarships/grants, health care benefits, tuition waivers (partial), and unspecified assistantships also available. Support available to part-time students. Financial award application deadline: 3/1; financial award applicants required to submit FAFSA. *Unit head:* Dr. Phil Mulder, Jr., Head, 405-744-5527, Fax: 405-744-6039. *Application contact:* Dr. Brad Kard, Graduate Coordinator, 405-744-2142, Fax: 405-744-6039, E-mail: brad.kard@okstate.edu. Web site: http://www.ento.okstate.edu/.

Oregon State University, Graduate School, College of Science, Department of Botany and Plant Pathology, Corvallis, OR 97331. Offers applied systematics (MA, MAIS, MS, PhD); ecology (MA, MAIS, MS, PhD); genetics (MA, MAIS, MS, PhD); genomics and computational biology (MA, MAIS, MS, PhD); molecular and cellular biology (MA, MAIS, MS, PhD); mycology (MA, MAIS, MS, PhD); plant pathology (MA, MAIS, MS, PhD); plant physiology (MA, MAIS, MS, PhD); systematics (MA, MAIS, MS, PhD). Part-time programs available. *Degree requirements:* For master's, variable foreign language requirement, thesis optional; for doctorate, thesis/dissertation. *Entrance requirements:* For master's and doctorate, GRE General Test, minimum GPA of 3.0 in last 90 hours. *Faculty research:* Plant ecology, plant molecular biology, systematic botany, epidemiology, host-pathogen interaction.

Penn State University Park, Graduate School, College of Agricultural Sciences, Department of Plant Pathology, State College, University Park, PA 16802-1503. Offers MS, PhD. *Unit head:* Dr. Bruce A. McPheron, Dean, 814-865-2541, Fax: 814-865-3103, E-mail: bam10@psu.edu. *Application contact:* Cynthia E. Nicosia, Director of Graduate Enrollment Services, 814-865-1834, E-mail: cey1@psu.edu. Web site: http://plantpath.psu.edu/.

Purdue University, Graduate School, College of Agriculture, Department of Botany and Plant Pathology, West Lafayette, IN 47907. Offers MS, PhD. Part-time programs available. *Faculty:* 20 full-time (5 women), 2 part-time/adjunct (1 woman). *Students:* 34 full-time (17 women), 3 part-time (2 women); includes 3 minority (2 American Indian or Alaska Native, non-Hispanic/Latino; 1 Asian, non-Hispanic/Latino), 15 international. Average age 27. 61 applicants, 31% accepted, 9 enrolled. In 2011, 6 master's awarded. Terminal master's awarded for partial completion of doctoral program. *Degree requirements:* For master's, thesis; for doctorate, thesis/dissertation. *Entrance requirements:* For master's, GRE General Test, minimum undergraduate GPA of 3.0 or equivalent; for doctorate, GRE, minimum undergraduate GPA of 3.0 or equivalent. Additional exam requirements/recommendations for international students: Required—TOEFL (minimum score 550 paper-based; 77 iBT); Recommended—TWE. *Application deadline:* For fall admission, 4/15 priority date for domestic students, 4/15 for international students; for spring admission, 12/15 for domestic students, 9/15 for international students. Applications are processed on a rolling basis. Application fee: $60 ($75 for international students). Electronic applications accepted. *Financial support:* In 2011–12, 30 students received support. Fellowships with full tuition reimbursements available, research assistantships with full tuition reimbursements available, teaching assistantships with full tuition reimbursements available, and career-related internships or fieldwork available. Support available to part-time students. Financial award application deadline: 3/1; financial award applicants required to submit FAFSA. *Faculty research:* Biotechnology, plant growth, weed control, crop improvement, plant physiology. *Unit head:* Dr. Peter B. Goldsbrough, Head, 765-494-4615, Fax: 765-494-0363, E-mail: goldsbrough@purdue.edu. *Application contact:* Tyson J. McFall, Graduate Contact, 765-494-0352, E-mail: tjmcfall@purdue.edu. Web site: http://www.btny.purdue.edu/.

Rutgers, The State University of New Jersey, New Brunswick, Graduate School-New Brunswick, Program in Plant Biology, Piscataway, NJ 08854-8097. Offers horticulture and plant technology (MS, PhD); molecular and cellular biology (MS, PhD); organismal and population biology (MS, PhD); plant pathology (MS, PhD). Part-time programs available. Terminal master's awarded for partial completion of doctoral program. *Degree requirements:* For master's, comprehensive exam, thesis or alternative; for doctorate, comprehensive exam, thesis/dissertation. *Entrance requirements:* For master's and doctorate, GRE General Test, GRE Subject Test (recommended). Additional exam requirements/recommendations for international students: Required—TOEFL (minimum score 600 paper-based; 250 computer-based). Electronic applications accepted. *Faculty research:* Molecular biology and biochemistry of plants, plant development and genomics, plant protection, plant improvement, plant management of horticultural and field crops.

State University of New York College of Environmental Science and Forestry, Department of Environmental and Forest Biology, Syracuse, NY 13210-2779. Offers applied ecology (MPS); chemical ecology (MPS, MS, PhD); conservation biology (MPS, MS, PhD); ecology (MPS, MS, PhD); entomology (MPS, MS, PhD); environmental interpretation (MPS, MS, PhD); environmental physiology (MPS, MS, PhD); fish and wildlife biology and management (MPS, MS, PhD); forest pathology and mycology (MPS, MS, PhD); plant biotechnology (MPS); plant science and biotechnology (MPS, MS, PhD). *Degree requirements:* For master's, thesis (for some programs); for doctorate, comprehensive exam, thesis/dissertation. *Entrance requirements:* For master's and doctorate, GRE General Test, GRE Subject Test, minimum GPA of 3.0. Additional exam requirements/recommendations for international students: Required—TOEFL (minimum score 550 paper-based; 213 computer-based; 80 iBT), IELTS (minimum score 6). *Application deadline:* For fall admission, 2/1 priority date for domestic students, 2/1 for international students; for spring admission, 11/1 priority date for domestic students, 11/1 for international students. Applications are processed on a rolling basis. Application fee: $60. *Expenses:* Tuition, state resident: full-time $8870; part-time $370 per credit hour. Tuition, nonresident: full-time $15,160; part-time $632 per credit hour. *Required fees:* $60; $370 per credit hour. $350 per semester. One-time fee: $85. *Financial support:* Fellowships with full and partial tuition reimbursements, research assistantships with full and partial tuition reimbursements, teaching assistantships with full and partial tuition reimbursements, Federal Work-Study, institutionally sponsored loans, scholarships/grants, health care benefits, and unspecified assistantships available. Financial award application deadline: 6/30. *Faculty research:* Ecology, fish and wildlife biology and management, plant science, entomology. *Total annual research expenditures:* $4.1 million. *Unit head:* Dr. Donald J. Leopold, Chair, 315-470-6760, Fax: 315-470-6934. *Application contact:* Dr. Dudley J. Raynal, Dean, Instruction and Graduate Studies, 315-470-6599, Fax: 315-470-6978, E-mail: esfgrad@esf.edu. Web site: http://www.esf.edu/efb/.

Texas A&M University, College of Agriculture and Life Sciences, Department of Plant Pathology and Microbiology, College Station, TX 77843. Offers M Agr, MS, PhD. Part-time programs available. Postbaccalaureate distance learning degree programs offered. *Faculty:* 16. *Students:* 31 full-time (14 women), 3 part-time (2 women); includes 11 minority (1 Black or African American, non-Hispanic/Latino; 9 Hispanic/Latino; 1 Two or more races, non-Hispanic/Latino), 13 international. Average age 31. In 2011, 2 master's, 7 doctorates awarded. *Degree requirements:* For master's, comprehensive exam (for some programs), thesis; for doctorate, comprehensive exam, thesis/dissertation. *Entrance requirements:* For master's and doctorate, GRE General Test, letters of recommendation, BS/BA in biological sciences. *Application deadline:* Applications are processed on a rolling basis. Application fee: $50 ($75 for international students). *Expenses:* Tuition, state resident: full-time $5437; part-time $226.55 per credit hour. Tuition, nonresident: full-time $12,949; part-time $539.55 per credit hour. *Required fees:* $2741. *Financial support:* In 2011–12, research assistantships with partial tuition reimbursements (averaging $16,800 per year), teaching assistantships with partial tuition reimbursements (averaging $16,800 per year) were awarded; fellowships, career-related internships or fieldwork, Federal Work-Study, institutionally sponsored loans, and unspecified assistantships also available. Support available to part-time students. Financial award application deadline: 4/1; financial award applicants required to submit

FAFSA. *Faculty research:* Plant disease control, population biology of plant pathogens, disease epidemiology, molecular genetics of host/parasite interactions. *Unit head:* Leland S. Pierson, III, Professor and Head, 979-845-8288, Fax: 979-845-6483, E-mail: lspierson@tamu.edu. *Application contact:* Graduate Admissions, 979-845-1044, E-mail: admissions@tamu.edu. Web site: http://plantpathology.tamu.edu/.

The University of Arizona, College of Agriculture and Life Sciences, School of Plant Sciences, Program in Plant Pathology, Tucson, AZ 85721. Offers MS, PhD. Part-time programs available. *Faculty:* 19 full-time (6 women), 3 part-time/adjunct (1 woman). *Students:* 12 full-time (7 women); includes 1 minority (Asian, non-Hispanic/Latino), 5 international. Average age 30. 6 applicants. In 2011, 4 master's, 3 doctorates awarded. *Degree requirements:* For master's, thesis optional; for doctorate, thesis/dissertation. *Entrance requirements:* For master's, GRE (recommended), minimum GPA of 3.0, academic resume, 3 letters of recommendation; for doctorate, GRE (recommended), minimum GPA of 3.0, academic resume, statement of purpose, 3 letters of recommendation. Additional exam requirements/recommendations for international students: Required—TOEFL. *Application deadline:* For fall admission, 12/1 for domestic and international students; for spring admission, 6/1 for domestic and international students. Applications are processed on a rolling basis. Application fee: $75. *Expenses:* Tuition, state resident: full-time $10,840. Tuition, nonresident: full-time $25,802. *Financial support:* Fellowships, research assistantships, teaching assistantships, Federal Work-Study, and institutionally sponsored loans available. *Faculty research:* Fungal molecular biology, ecology of soil-borne plant pathogens, plant virology, plant bacteriology, plant/pathogen interactions. *Unit head:* Dr. Leland S. Pierson, III, Chair, 520-621-1828, E-mail: lsp@u.arizona.edu. *Application contact:* Dr. Rachel W. Pfister, Graduate Coordinator/Advisor, 520-621-8423, Fax: 520-621-7186, E-mail: pfister@ag.arizona.edu. Web site: http://cals.arizona.edu/spls/graduate.

University of Arkansas, Graduate School, Dale Bumpers College of Agricultural, Food and Life Sciences, Department of Plant Pathology, Fayetteville, AR 72701-1201. Offers MS. *Students:* 11 part-time (6 women); includes 1 minority (Two or more races, non-Hispanic/Latino), 3 international. In 2011, 3 degrees awarded. *Degree requirements:* For master's, thesis. *Application deadline:* For fall admission, 4/1 for international students; for spring admission, 10/1 for international students. Applications are processed on a rolling basis. Application fee: $40 ($50 for international students). Electronic applications accepted. *Financial support:* In 2011–12, 10 research assistantships were awarded; fellowships, teaching assistantships, career-related internships or fieldwork, and Federal Work-Study also available. Support available to part-time students. Financial award application deadline: 4/1; financial award applicants required to submit FAFSA. *Unit head:* Dr. A. Rick Bennett, Department Head, 479-575-2445, E-mail: rbennett@uark.edu. *Application contact:* Dr. Ioannis Tzanetakis, Graduate Coordinator, 479-575-3180, E-mail: itzaneta@uark.edu. Web site: http://plantpathology.uark.edu/.

University of California, Davis, Graduate Studies, Program in Plant Pathology, Davis, CA 95616. Offers MS, PhD. Terminal master's awarded for partial completion of doctoral program. *Degree requirements:* For master's, comprehensive exam (for some programs), thesis (for some programs); for doctorate, thesis/dissertation. *Entrance requirements:* For master's and doctorate, GRE General Test. Additional exam requirements/recommendations for international students: Required—TOEFL (minimum score 550 paper-based; 213 computer-based). Electronic applications accepted. *Faculty research:* Soil microbiology; diagnosis etiology and control of plant diseases; genomics and molecular biology of plant microbe interactions; biotechnology, ecology of plant pathogens and epidemiology of diseases in agricultural and native ecosystems.

University of California, Riverside, Graduate Division, Department of Plant Pathology, Riverside, CA 92521-0102. Offers MS, PhD. *Faculty:* 15 full-time (3 women). *Students:* 15 full-time (6 women); includes 3 minority (1 Asian, non-Hispanic/Latino; 2 Hispanic/Latino), 10 international. Average age 30. 21 applicants, 19% accepted, 2 enrolled. In 2011, 1 master's, 3 doctorates awarded. Terminal master's awarded for partial completion of doctoral program. *Degree requirements:* For master's, comprehensive exams or thesis; for doctorate, thesis/dissertation, qualifying exams. *Entrance requirements:* For master's, GRE General Test (minimum score 1100 or approximately 300 on the new GRE scoring scale), minimum GPA of 3.2; for doctorate, GRE General Test (minimum score 1100 or approximately 300 on the new GRE scoring scale)), minimum GPA of 3.2. Additional exam requirements/recommendations for international students: Required—TOEFL (minimum score 550 paper-based; 213 computer-based; 80 iBT). *Application deadline:* For fall admission, 5/1 for domestic students, 2/1 for international students; for winter admission, 9/1 for domestic students, 7/1 for international students; for spring admission, 12/1 for domestic students, 10/1 for international students. Applications are processed on a rolling basis. Application fee: $85 ($100 for international students). Electronic applications accepted. *Financial support:* In 2011–12, 7 students received support, including fellowships with full and partial tuition reimbursements available (averaging $12,000 per year), research assistantships with full and partial tuition reimbursements available (averaging $18,081 per year), teaching assistantships with full and partial tuition reimbursements available (averaging $16,500 per year); career-related internships or fieldwork, institutionally sponsored loans, scholarships/grants, health care benefits, tuition waivers (full and partial), and unspecified assistantships also available. *Faculty research:* Host-pathogen interactions, biological control and integrated approaches to disease management, fungicide behavior, molecular genetics. *Unit head:* Dr. Michael Allen, Chair, 951-827-5494. *Application contact:* Deidra Kornfeld, Student Affairs Officer, 800-735-0717, Fax: 951-827-5688, E-mail: plantpa@urc.edu. Web site: http://www.plantpathology.ucr.edu/.

University of Florida, Graduate School, College of Agricultural and Life Sciences, Department of Plant Pathology, Gainesville, FL 32611. Offers plant pathology (MS); toxicology (PhD). Part-time programs available. *Faculty:* 13 full-time (3 women). *Students:* 29 full-time (14 women), 6 part-time (4 women); includes 4 minority (1 Asian, non-Hispanic/Latino; 3 Hispanic/Latino), 20 international. Average age 31. 22 applicants, 14% accepted, 2 enrolled. In 2011, 1 master's, 6 doctorates awarded. Terminal master's awarded for partial completion of doctoral program. *Degree requirements:* For master's, comprehensive exam (for some programs), thesis optional; for doctorate, comprehensive exam, thesis/dissertation. *Entrance requirements:* For master's and doctorate, GRE General Test, minimum GPA of 3.0. Additional exam requirements/recommendations for international students: Required—TOEFL (minimum score 550 paper-based; 213 computer-based; 80 iBT), IELTS (minimum score 6). *Application deadline:* For fall admission, 2/1 priority date for domestic students, 2/1 for international students; for winter admission, 2/1 for domestic and international students; for spring admission, 10/1 for domestic students, 9/1 for international students. Applications are processed on a rolling basis. Application fee: $30. Electronic applications accepted. *Financial support:* Fellowships, research assistantships, and career-related internships or fieldwork available. Financial award application deadline: 2/1; financial award applicants required to submit FAFSA. *Faculty research:* Epidemiology, molecular biology of host-parasite interactions, bacteriology, virology, post-harvest diseases. *Total annual research expenditures:* $4.3 million. *Unit head:* Dr. Eric Triplett, Chair, 352-392-5430, E-mail: ewt@ufl.edu. *Application contact:* Dr. Robert J. McGovern, Graduate Coordinator, 352-392-3631 Ext. 213, Fax: 352-392-6532, E-mail: rjmcgov@ufl.edu. Web site: http://plantpath.ifas.ufl.edu/.

University of Georgia, College of Agricultural and Environmental Sciences, Department of Plant Pathology, Athens, GA 30602. Offers MS, PhD. *Faculty:* 20 full-time (5 women), 3 part-time/adjunct (1 woman). *Students:* 29 full-time (16 women), 2 part-time (1 woman); includes 3 minority (1 Black or African American, non-Hispanic/Latino; 2 Hispanic/Latino), 15 international. Average age 28. 23 applicants, 35% accepted, 7 enrolled. In 2011, 5 master's, 4 doctorates awarded. *Degree requirements:* For master's, thesis (MS); for doctorate, one foreign language, thesis/dissertation. *Entrance requirements:* For master's and doctorate, GRE General Test. *Application deadline:* For fall admission, 7/1 priority date for domestic students; for spring admission, 11/15 for domestic students. Application fee: $50. Electronic applications accepted. *Financial support:* Fellowships, research assistantships, teaching assistantships, and unspecified assistantships available. *Unit head:* Dr. John L. Sherwood, Head, 706-542-1246, E-mail: sherwood@uga.edu. *Application contact:* Dr. Harald Scherm, Graduate Coordinator, 706-542-1258, Fax: 706-542-1262, E-mail: scherm@uga.edu. Web site: http://plantpath.caes.uga.edu/.

University of Guelph, Graduate Studies, Ontario Agricultural College, Department of Environmental Biology, Guelph, ON N1G 2W1, Canada. Offers entomology (M Sc, PhD); environmental microbiology and biotechnology (M Sc, PhD); environmental toxicology (M Sc, PhD); plant and forest systems (M Sc, PhD); plant pathology (M Sc, PhD). Part-time programs available. *Degree requirements:* For master's, thesis; for doctorate, comprehensive exam, thesis/dissertation. *Entrance requirements:* For master's, minimum 75% average during previous 2 years of course work; for doctorate, minimum 75% average. Additional exam requirements/recommendations for international students: Required—TOEFL or IELTS. Electronic applications accepted. *Faculty research:* Entomology, environmental microbiology and biotechnology, environmental toxicology, forest ecology, plant pathology.

University of Hawaii at Manoa, Graduate Division, College of Tropical Agriculture and Human Resources, Department of Plant and Environmental Protection Sciences, Program in Tropical Plant Pathology, Honolulu, HI 96822. Offers MS, PhD. Part-time programs available. *Degree requirements:* For master's, thesis optional; for doctorate, comprehensive exam, thesis/dissertation. *Entrance requirements:* For master's and doctorate, GRE General Test. Additional exam requirements/recommendations for international students: Required—TOEFL (minimum score 540 paper-based; 207 computer-based; 76 iBT), IELTS (minimum score 5).

University of Kentucky, Graduate School, College of Agriculture, Program in Plant Pathology, Lexington, KY 40506-0032. Offers MS, PhD. *Degree requirements:* For master's, comprehensive exam, thesis; for doctorate, comprehensive exam, thesis/dissertation. *Entrance requirements:* For master's, GRE General Test, minimum undergraduate GPA of 2.75; for doctorate, GRE General Test, minimum graduate GPA of 3.0. Additional exam requirements/recommendations for international students: Required—TOEFL (minimum score 550 paper-based; 213 computer-based). Electronic applications accepted. *Faculty research:* Molecular biology of viruses and fungi, biochemistry and physiology of disease resistance, plant transformation, disease ecology, forest pathology.

University of Maine, Graduate School, College of Natural Sciences, Forestry, and Agriculture, Department of Biological Sciences, Program in Botany and Plant Pathology, Orono, ME 04469. Offers MS. Part-time programs available. *Students:* 2 full-time (1 woman), 1 international. Average age 30. 1 applicant, 0% accepted, 0 enrolled. In 2011, 1 degree awarded. *Degree requirements:* For master's, thesis. *Entrance requirements:* For master's, GRE General Test. Additional exam requirements/recommendations for international students: Required—TOEFL. *Application deadline:* For fall admission, 2/1 priority date for domestic students. Applications are processed on a rolling basis. Application fee: $65. Electronic applications accepted. *Expenses:* Tuition, state resident: full-time $5016. Tuition, nonresident: full-time $14,424. *Financial support:* Career-related internships or fieldwork, Federal Work-Study, institutionally sponsored loans, and tuition waivers (full) available. Financial award application deadline: 3/1. *Faculty research:* Molecular biology of viral and fungal pathogens, marine ecology, paleoecology and acid systematics and evolution. *Unit head:* Dr. Jody Jellison, Coordinator, 207-581-2551. *Application contact:* Scott G. Delcourt, Associate Dean of the Graduate School, 207-581-3291, Fax: 207-581-3232, E-mail: graduate@maine.edu. Web site: http://www2.umaine.edu/graduate/.

University of Minnesota, Twin Cities Campus, Graduate School, College of Food, Agricultural and Natural Resource Sciences, Department of Plant Pathology, Saint Paul, MN 55108. Offers MS, PhD. Part-time programs available. *Faculty:* 28 full-time (7 women). *Students:* 15 full-time (5 women), 1 part-time (0 women), 6 international. Average age 30. 13 applicants, 54% accepted, 4 enrolled. In 2011, 1 master's, 5 doctorates awarded. Terminal master's awarded for partial completion of doctoral program. *Degree requirements:* For master's, comprehensive exam, thesis; for doctorate, comprehensive exam, thesis/dissertation. *Entrance requirements:* For master's and doctorate, GRE General Test. Additional exam requirements/recommendations for international students: Required—TOEFL (minimum score 550 paper-based; 213 computer-based; 79 iBT), IELTS (minimum score 6.5), TOEFL preferred. *Application deadline:* For fall admission, 1/10 priority date for domestic students, 1/10 for international students; for spring admission, 5/1 priority date for domestic students, 5/10 for international students. Applications are processed on a rolling basis. Application fee: $75 ($95 for international students). Electronic applications accepted. *Financial support:* In 2011–12, 3 students received support, including fellowships with full tuition reimbursements available (averaging $23,500 per year), research assistantships with full and partial tuition reimbursements available (averaging $18,000 per year), teaching assistantships with full and partial tuition reimbursements available (averaging $18,000 per year); scholarships/grants, health care benefits, and unspecified assistantships also available. Support available to part-time students. Financial award application deadline: 1/10. *Faculty research:* Plant disease management, disease resistance, product deterioration, international agriculture, molecular biology. *Total annual research expenditures:* $4.9 million. *Unit head:* Dr. Robert Blanchette, Director of Graduate Studies, 612-625-4735, Fax: 612-625-0202, E-mail: robertb@umn.edu. *Application contact:* Anne Lageson, Program Coordinator, 612-625-8200, Fax: 612-625-9728, E-mail: anna@umn.edu. Web site: http://plpa.cfans.umn.edu/.

The University of Tennessee, Graduate School, College of Agricultural Sciences and Natural Resources, Department of Entomology and Plant Pathology, Knoxville, TN 37996. Offers entomology (MS, PhD); integrated pest management and bioactive natural products (PhD); plant pathology (MS, PhD). Part-time programs available. *Degree requirements:* For master's, thesis, seminar. *Entrance requirements:* For master's, GRE General Test, minimum GPA of 2.7, 3 reference letters, letter of intent; for doctorate, GRE General Test, minimum GPA of 2.7, 3 reference letters, letter of intent, proposed dissertation research. Additional exam requirements/recommendations for international students: Required—TOEFL. Electronic applications accepted. *Expenses:* Tuition, state resident: full-time $8332; part-time $464 per credit hour. Tuition, nonresident: full-time $25,174; part-time $1400 per credit hour. *Required fees:* $1162; $56 per credit hour. Tuition and fees vary according to program.

University of Wisconsin–Madison, Graduate School, College of Agricultural and Life Sciences, Department of Plant Pathology, Madison, WI 53706-1380. Offers MS, PhD.

Part-time programs available. Terminal master's awarded for partial completion of doctoral program. *Degree requirements:* For master's, thesis; for doctorate, thesis/dissertation. *Entrance requirements:* For master's and doctorate, GRE. Additional exam requirements/recommendations for international students: Required—TOEFL. Electronic applications accepted. *Expenses:* Tuition, state resident: full-time $10,296; part-time $643.51 per credit. Tuition, nonresident: full-time $24,054; part-time $1503.40 per credit. *Required fees:* $70.06 per credit. Tuition and fees vary according to course load, campus/location, program and reciprocity agreements. *Faculty research:* Plant disease, plant health, plant-microbe interactions, plant disease management, biological control.

Virginia Polytechnic Institute and State University, Graduate School, College of Agriculture and Life Sciences, Department of Plant Pathology, Physiology and Weed Science, Blacksburg, VA 24061. Offers plant pathology (MS); plant physiology (MS); weed science (PhD). *Degree requirements:* For master's, comprehensive exam (for some programs), thesis (for some programs); for doctorate, comprehensive exam (for some programs), thesis/dissertation (for some programs). *Entrance requirements:* For master's and doctorate, GRE. Additional exam requirements/recommendations for international students: Required—TOEFL (minimum score 550 paper-based; 213 computer-based). *Application deadline:* For fall admission, 7/1 for domestic and international students; for spring admission, 12/1 for domestic students, 12/15 for international students. Applications are processed on a rolling basis. Application fee: $65. Electronic applications accepted. *Expenses:* Tuition, state resident: full-time $10,048; part-time $558.25 per credit hour. Tuition, nonresident: full-time $19,497; part-time $1083.25 per credit hour. *Required fees:* $405 per semester. Tuition and fees vary according to course load, campus/location and program. *Financial support:* In 2011–12, 15 research assistantships with full tuition reimbursements (averaging $21,551 per year) were awarded; career-related internships or fieldwork, Federal Work-Study, scholarships/grants, health care benefits, and unspecified assistantships also available. Financial award application deadline: 1/15. *Faculty research:* Biotechnology, Dutch elm disease, weed control, plant pathogenic microorganisms, agronomic crop resistance to fungal and viral pathogens. *Unit head:* Dr. Elizabeth A. Grabau, Unit Head, 540-231-6361, Fax: 540-231-7477, E-mail: egrabau@vt.edu. *Application contact:* Anton Baudoin, Information Contact, 540-231-5757, Fax: 540-231-7477, E-mail: abaudoin@vt.edu. Web site: http://www.ppws.vt.edu/.

Washington State University, Graduate School, College of Agricultural, Human, and Natural Resource Sciences, Department of Plant Pathology, Pullman, WA 99164. Offers MS, PhD. *Faculty:* 11. *Students:* 45 full-time (25 women), 1 (woman) part-time; includes 4 minority (3 Asian, non-Hispanic/Latino; 1 Hispanic/Latino), 28 international. Average age 31. 16 applicants, 88% accepted, 14 enrolled. In 2011, 6 master's, 5 doctorates awarded. Terminal master's awarded for partial completion of doctoral program. *Degree requirements:* For master's, comprehensive exam (for some programs), thesis (for some programs), oral exam; for doctorate, comprehensive exam, thesis/dissertation, oral exam. *Entrance requirements:* For master's and doctorate, GRE, statement of purpose. Additional exam requirements/recommendations for international students: Required—TOEFL (minimum score 550 paper-based; 213 computer-based), IELTS. *Application deadline:* For fall admission, 1/10 priority date for domestic students, 1/10 for international students; for spring admission, 7/1 for domestic and international students. Applications are processed on a rolling basis. Application fee: $75. Electronic applications accepted. *Financial support:* In 2011–12, 25 students received support, including 16 research assistantships with full and partial tuition reimbursements available (averaging $18,204 per year), 1 teaching assistantship with full and partial tuition reimbursement available (averaging $18,204 per year); career-related internships or fieldwork, Federal Work-Study, institutionally sponsored loans, scholarships/grants, and teaching associateships also available. Financial award application deadline: 4/1; financial award applicants required to submit FAFSA. *Faculty research:* Biology of fungi, bacteria, and viruses; diseases of plants; genetics of fungi, bacteria, and viruses. *Total annual research expenditures:* $4.6 million. *Unit head:* Dr. Hanu R. Pappu, Chair, 509-335-9541, Fax: 509-335-9581, E-mail: hrp@wsu.edu. *Application contact:* Graduate School Admissions, 800-GRADWSU, Fax: 509-335-1949, E-mail: gradsch@wsu.edu. Web site: http://plantpath.wsu.edu/.

West Virginia University, Davis College of Agriculture, Forestry and Consumer Sciences, Division of Plant and Soil Sciences, Morgantown, WV 26506. Offers agricultural sciences (PhD), including animal and food sciences, plant and soil sciences; agronomy (MS); entomology (MS); environmental microbiology (MS); horticulture (MS); plant pathology (MS). *Degree requirements:* For master's, thesis. *Entrance requirements:* For master's, GRE, minimum GPA of 2.5. Additional exam requirements/recommendations for international students: Required—TOEFL. *Faculty research:* Water quality, reclamation of disturbed land, crop production, pest control, environmental protection.

Plant Physiology

Cornell University, Graduate School, Graduate Fields of Agriculture and Life Sciences, Field of Plant Biology, Ithaca, NY 14853-0001. Offers cytology (MS, PhD); paleobotany (MS, PhD); plant cell biology (MS, PhD); plant ecology (MS, PhD); plant molecular biology (MS, PhD); plant morphology, anatomy and biomechanics (MS, PhD); plant physiology (MS, PhD); systematic botany (MS, PhD). *Faculty:* 49 full-time (14 women). *Students:* 33 full-time (18 women); includes 4 minority (2 Black or African American, non-Hispanic/Latino; 1 Hispanic/Latino; 1 Two or more races, non-Hispanic/Latino), 15 international. Average age 27. 54 applicants, 20% accepted, 6 enrolled. In 2011, 1 master's, 3 doctorates awarded. *Degree requirements:* For doctorate, comprehensive exam, thesis/dissertation. *Entrance requirements:* For doctorate, GRE General Test, GRE Subject Test in biology (recommended), 3 letters of recommendation. Additional exam requirements/recommendations for international students: Required—TOEFL (minimum score 610 paper-based; 253 computer-based; 77 iBT). *Application deadline:* For fall admission, 1/15 priority date for domestic students. Application fee: $95. Electronic applications accepted. *Financial support:* In 2011–12, 7 fellowships with full tuition reimbursements, 15 research assistantships with full tuition reimbursements, 9 teaching assistantships with full tuition reimbursements were awarded; institutionally sponsored loans, scholarships/grants, health care benefits, tuition waivers (full and partial), and unspecified assistantships also available. Financial award applicants required to submit FAFSA. *Faculty research:* Plant cell biology/cytology; plant molecular biology; plant morphology/anatomy/biomechanics; plant physiology, systematic botany, paleobotany; plant ecology, ethnobotany, plant biochemistry, photosynthesis. *Unit head:* Director of Graduate Studies, 607-255-2131. *Application contact:* Graduate Field Assistant, 607-255-2131, E-mail: plbio@cornell.edu. Web site: http://www.gradschool.cornell.edu/fields.php?id-45&a-2.

Nova Scotia Agricultural College, Research and Graduate Studies, Truro, NS B2N 5E3, Canada. Offers agriculture (M Sc), including air quality, animal behavior, animal molecular genetics, animal nutrition, animal technology, aquaculture, botany, crop management, crop physiology, ecology, environmental microbiology, food science, horticulture, nutrient management, pest management, physiology, plant biotechnology, plant pathology, soil chemistry, soil fertility, waste management and composting, water quality. Program offered jointly with Dalhousie University. Part-time programs available. *Degree requirements:* For master's, thesis, ATC Exam Teaching Assistantship. *Entrance requirements:* For master's, honors B Sc, minimum GPA of 3.0. Additional exam requirements/recommendations for international students: Required—TOEFL (minimum score 580 paper-based; 237 computer-based; 92 iBT), IELTS, Michigan English Language Assessment Battery, CanTEST, CAEL. *Faculty research:* Bio-product development, organic agriculture, nutrient management, air and water quality, agricultural biotechnology.

Oregon State University, Graduate School, College of Science, Department of Botany and Plant Pathology, Corvallis, OR 97331. Offers applied systematics (MA, MAIS, MS, PhD); ecology (MA, MAIS, MS, PhD); genetics (MA, MAIS, MS, PhD); genomics and computational biology (MA, MAIS, MS, PhD); molecular and cellular biology (MA, MAIS, MS, PhD); mycology (MA, MAIS, MS, PhD); plant pathology (MA, MAIS, MS, PhD); plant physiology (MA, MAIS, MS, PhD); systematics (MA, MAIS, MS, PhD). Part-time programs available. *Degree requirements:* For master's, variable foreign language requirement, thesis optional; for doctorate, thesis/dissertation. *Entrance requirements:* For master's and doctorate, GRE General Test, minimum GPA of 3.0 in last 90 hours. *Faculty research:* Plant ecology, plant molecular biology, systematic botany, epidemiology, host-pathogen interaction.

Oregon State University, Graduate School, Program in Plant Physiology, Corvallis, OR 97331. Offers MS, PhD. *Degree requirements:* For master's, thesis; for doctorate, thesis/dissertation. *Entrance requirements:* For master's, BS in related area; for doctorate, BS or MS in related area, minimum GPA of 3.0 in last 90 hours of course work. Additional exam requirements/recommendations for international students: Required—TOEFL. *Faculty research:* Nitrogen metabolism, physiological ecology, phloem transport, mineral nutrition, plant hormones.

Purdue University, Graduate School, College of Science, Department of Biological Sciences, West Lafayette, IN 47907. Offers biochemistry (PhD); biophysics (PhD); cell and developmental biology (PhD); ecology, evolutionary and population biology (MS, PhD), including ecology, evolutionary biology, population biology; genetics (MS, PhD); microbiology (MS, PhD); molecular biology (PhD); neurobiology (MS, PhD); plant physiology (PhD). *Faculty:* 57 full-time (15 women), 4 part-time/adjunct (1 woman). *Students:* 94 full-time (54 women), 9 part-time (5 women); includes 7 minority (2 Black or African American, non-Hispanic/Latino; 3 Asian, non-Hispanic/Latino; 2 Hispanic/Latino), 51 international. Average age 27. 246 applicants, 11% accepted, 18 enrolled. In 2011, 9 master's, 23 doctorates awarded. Terminal master's awarded for partial completion of doctoral program. *Degree requirements:* For master's, thesis (for some programs); for doctorate, thesis/dissertation, seminars, teaching experience. *Entrance requirements:* For master's, GRE General Test, minimum analytical writing score of 3.5, minimum undergraduate GPA of 3.0; for doctorate, GRE General Test, minimum analytical writing score of 3.5, minimum undergraduate GPA of 3.5. Additional exam requirements/recommendations for international students: Required—TOEFL (minimum score 600 paper-based; 107 iBT) for MS; TOEFL (minimum score 600 paper-based; 80 iBT) for Ph D. *Application deadline:* For fall admission, 12/7 for domestic and international students. Applications are processed on a rolling basis. Application fee: $60 ($75 for international students). Electronic applications accepted. *Financial support:* Fellowships, research assistantships, and teaching assistantships available. Support available to part-time students. Financial award application deadline: 2/15; financial award applicants required to submit FAFSA. *Unit head:* Dr. Richard J. Kuhn, Head, 765-494-4407, E-mail: kuhnr@purdue.edu. *Application contact:* Georgina E. Rupp, Graduate Coordinator, 765-494-8142, Fax: 765-494-0876, E-mail: ruppg@purdue.edu. Web site: http://www.bio.purdue.edu/.

University of Kentucky, Graduate School, College of Agriculture, Program in Plant Physiology, Lexington, KY 40506-0032. Offers PhD. *Degree requirements:* For doctorate, comprehensive exam, thesis/dissertation. *Entrance requirements:* For doctorate, GRE General Test, minimum graduate GPA of 3.0, undergraduate 2.75. Additional exam requirements/recommendations for international students: Required—TOEFL (minimum score 550 paper-based; 213 computer-based). Electronic applications accepted. *Faculty research:* Biochemistry and biophysics of photosynthesis, biochemical and molecular basis for resistance of plants to pathogens, plant gene expression, physiological aspects of crop production.

University of Manitoba, Faculty of Graduate Studies, Faculty of Agricultural and Food Sciences, Department of Plant Science, Winnipeg, MB R3T 2N2, Canada. Offers agronomy and plant protection (M Sc, PhD); horticulture (M Sc, PhD); plant breeding and genetics (M Sc, PhD); plant physiology-biochemistry (M Sc, PhD). *Degree requirements:* For master's, thesis; for doctorate, one foreign language, thesis/dissertation.

University of Massachusetts Amherst, Graduate School, Interdisciplinary Programs, Program in Plant Biology, Amherst, MA 01003. Offers biochemistry and metabolism (MS, PhD); cell biology and physiology (MS, PhD); environmental, ecological and integrative (PhD); environmental, ecological and integrative biology (MS); genetics and evolution (MS, PhD). *Students:* 16 full-time (7 women), 1 (woman) part-time, 7 international. Average age 27. 22 applicants, 50% accepted, 5 enrolled. In 2011, 3 degrees awarded. *Median time to degree:* Of those who began their doctoral program in fall 2003, 100% received their degree in 8 years or less. *Degree requirements:* For master's, thesis; for doctorate, 2 foreign languages, comprehensive exam, thesis/dissertation. *Entrance requirements:* For master's and doctorate, GRE General Test. Additional exam requirements/recommendations for international students: Required—TOEFL (minimum score 550 paper-based; 213 computer-based; 80 iBT), IELTS (minimum score 6.5). *Application deadline:* For fall admission, 12/15 for domestic and international students; for spring admission, 10/1 for domestic and international students. Applications are processed on a rolling basis. Application fee: $50 ($65 for international students). Electronic applications accepted. Tuition and fees vary according to course load, campus/location and program. *Financial support:* Fellowships

with full and partial tuition reimbursements, research assistantships with full and partial tuition reimbursements, teaching assistantships with full and partial tuition reimbursements, career-related internships or fieldwork, Federal Work-Study, scholarships/grants, traineeships, health care benefits, tuition waivers (full and partial), and unspecified assistantships available. Support available to part-time students. Financial award application deadline: 12/15. *Unit head:* Dr. Elsbeth L. Walker, Graduate Program Director, 413-577-3217, Fax: 413-545-3243. *Application contact:* Lindsay DeSantis, Interim Supervisor of Admissions, 413-545—0722, Fax: 413-577-0010, E-mail: gradadm@grad.umass.edu. Web site: http://www.bio.umass.edu/plantbio/.

The University of Tennessee, Graduate School, College of Arts and Sciences, Program in Life Sciences, Knoxville, TN 37996. Offers genome science and technology (MS, PhD); plant physiology and genetics (MS, PhD). *Degree requirements:* For doctorate, one foreign language, thesis/dissertation. *Entrance requirements:* For master's and doctorate, GRE General Test, minimum GPA of 2.7. Additional exam requirements/recommendations for international students: Required—TOEFL. Electronic applications accepted. *Expenses:* Tuition, state resident: full-time $8332; part-time $464 per credit hour. Tuition, nonresident: full-time $25,174; part-time $1400 per credit hour. *Required fees:* $1162; $56 per credit hour. Tuition and fees vary according to program.

Virginia Polytechnic Institute and State University, Graduate School, College of Agriculture and Life Sciences, Department of Plant Pathology, Physiology and Weed Science, Blacksburg, VA 24061. Offers plant pathology (MS); plant physiology (MS); weed science (PhD). *Degree requirements:* For master's, comprehensive exam (for some programs), thesis (for some programs); for doctorate, comprehensive exam (for some programs), thesis/dissertation (for some programs). *Entrance requirements:* For master's and doctorate, GRE. Additional exam requirements/recommendations for international students: Required—TOEFL (minimum score 550 paper-based; 213 computer-based). *Application deadline:* For fall admission, 7/1 for domestic and international students; for spring admission, 12/1 for domestic students, 12/15 for international students. Applications are processed on a rolling basis. Application fee: $65. Electronic applications accepted. *Expenses:* Tuition, state resident: full-time $10,048; part-time $558.25 per credit hour. Tuition, nonresident: full-time $19,497; part-time $1083.25 per credit hour. *Required fees:* $405 per semester. Tuition and fees vary according to course load, campus/location and program. *Financial support:* In 2011–12, 15 research assistantships with full tuition reimbursements (averaging $21,551 per year) were awarded; career-related internships or fieldwork, Federal Work-Study, scholarships/grants, health care benefits, and unspecified assistantships also available. Financial award application deadline: 1/15. *Faculty research:* Biotechnology, Dutch elm disease, weed control, plant pathogenic microorganisms, agronomic crop resistance to fungal and viral pathogens. *Unit head:* Dr. Elizabeth A. Grabau, Unit Head, 540-231-6361, Fax: 540-231-7477, E-mail: egrabau@vt.edu. *Application contact:* Anton Baudoin, Information Contact, 540-231-5757, Fax: 540-231-7477, E-mail: abaudoin@vt.edu. Web site: http://www.ppws.vt.edu/.

Section 6
Cell, Molecular, and Structural Biology

This section contains a directory of institutions offering graduate work in cell, molecular, and structural biology, followed by in-depth entries submitted by institutions that chose to prepare detailed program descriptions. Additional information about programs listed in the directory but not augmented by an in-depth entry may be obtained by writing directly to the dean of a graduate school or chair of a department at the address given in the directory.

For programs offering related work, see also in this book *Anatomy; Biochemistry; Biological and Biomedical Sciences; Biophysics; Botany and Plant Biology; Genetics, Developmental Biology, and Reproductive Biology; Microbiological Sciences; Pathology and Pathobiology; Pharmacology and Toxicology; Pharmacy and Pharmaceutical Sciences; Physiology;* and *Veterinary Medicine and Sciences.* In the other guides in this series:

Graduate Programs in the Physical Sciences, Mathematics, Agricultural Sciences, the Environment & Natural Resources
See *Chemistry*

Graduate Programs in Engineering & Applied Sciences
See *Agricultural Engineering and Bioengineering* and *Biomedical Engineering and Biotechnology*

CONTENTS

Cancer Biology/Oncology

Baylor College of Medicine, Graduate School of Biomedical Sciences, Program in Translational Biology and Molecular Medicine, Houston, TX 77030-3498. Offers PhD. *Faculty:* 192 full-time (56 women). *Students:* 63 full-time (35 women); includes 24 minority (10 Black or African American, non-Hispanic/Latino; 9 Asian, non-Hispanic/Latino; 5 Hispanic/Latino), 17 international. Average age 27. 133 applicants, 17% accepted, 12 enrolled. In 2011, 1 doctorate awarded. *Degree requirements:* For doctorate, thesis/dissertation, public defense. *Entrance requirements:* For doctorate, GRE, minimum GPA of 3.0. Additional exam requirements/recommendations for international students: Required—TOEFL. *Application deadline:* For fall admission, 1/1 for domestic students. Application fee: $0. Electronic applications accepted. *Financial support:* In 2011–12, 63 students received support, including 36 fellowships with full tuition reimbursements available (averaging $29,000 per year), 27 research assistantships with full tuition reimbursements available (averaging $29,000 per year); career-related internships or fieldwork, Federal Work-Study, health care benefits, and scholarships (to all students unless there are grant funds available to pay tuition) also available. Financial award applicants required to submit FAFSA. *Faculty research:* Molecular medicine, translational biology, human disease biology and therapy. *Unit head:* Dr. Mary Estes, Director, 713-798-3585, Fax: 713-798-3586, E-mail: tbmm@bcm.edu. *Application contact:* Wanda Waguespack, Graduate Program Administrator, 713-798-1077, Fax: 713-798-3586, E-mail: wandaw@bcm.edu. Web site: http://www.bcm.edu/tbmm.

Brown University, Graduate School, Division of Biology and Medicine, Program in Pathology and Laboratory Medicine, Providence, RI 02912. Offers biology (PhD); cancer biology (PhD); immunology and infection (PhD); medical science (PhD); pathobiology (Sc M); toxicology and environmental pathology (PhD). Terminal master's awarded for partial completion of doctoral program. *Degree requirements:* For doctorate, thesis/dissertation, preliminary exam. *Entrance requirements:* For master's and doctorate, GRE General Test, GRE Subject Test. Additional exam requirements/recommendations for international students: Required—TOEFL. Electronic applications accepted. *Faculty research:* Environmental pathology, carcinogenesis, immunopathology, signal transduction, innate immunity.

Case Western Reserve University, School of Medicine and School of Graduate Studies, Graduate Programs in Medicine, Programs in Molecular and Cellular Basis of Disease/Pathology, Cancer Biology Training Program, Cleveland, OH 44106. Offers PhD, MD/PhD. *Degree requirements:* For doctorate, comprehensive exam, thesis/dissertation. *Entrance requirements:* For doctorate, GRE. Additional exam requirements/recommendations for international students: Required—TOEFL (minimum score 550 paper-based; 213 computer-based).

Dartmouth College, Program in Experimental and Molecular Medicine, Cancer Biology and Molecular Therapeutics Track, Hanover, NH 03755. Offers PhD.

Duke University, Graduate School, University Program in Molecular Cancer Biology, Durham, NC 27710. Offers PhD. *Faculty:* 50 full-time (28 women). *Students:* 48 full-time (28 women); includes 4 minority (1 Black or African American, non-Hispanic/Latino; 2 Asian, non-Hispanic/Latino; 1 Hispanic/Latino), 18 international. 75 applicants, 12% accepted, 6 enrolled. In 2011, 6 doctorates awarded. *Degree requirements:* For doctorate, thesis/dissertation. *Entrance requirements:* For doctorate, GRE General Test, GRE Subject Test in biology or biochemistry, cell and molecular biology (recommended). Additional exam requirements/recommendations for international students: Required—TOEFL (minimum score 550 paper-based; 213 computer-based; 83 iBT), IELTS (minimum score 7). *Application deadline:* For fall admission, 12/8 priority date for domestic students, 12/8 for international students. Application fee: $75. Electronic applications accepted. *Expenses: Tuition:* Full-time $40,720. *Required fees:* $3107. *Financial support:* Fellowships and research assistantships available. Financial award application deadline: 12/31. *Unit head:* Ann Marie Pendergast, Director of Graduate Studies, 919-613-8600, Fax: 919-681-7767, E-mail: baize@duke.edu. *Application contact:* Elizabeth Hutton, Director of Admissions, 919-684-3913, Fax: 919-684-2277, E-mail: grad-admissions@duke.edu. Web site: http://cancerbio.mc.duke.edu/.

Emory University, Laney Graduate School, Division of Biological and Biomedical Sciences, Program in Cancer Biology, Atlanta, GA 30322. Offers PhD. *Faculty:* 27 full-time (4 women). *Students:* 10 full-time (7 women); includes 5 minority (4 Black or African American, non-Hispanic/Latino; 1 Hispanic/Latino). 147 applicants, 10% accepted, 10 enrolled. *Degree requirements:* For doctorate, comprehensive exam, thesis/dissertation. *Entrance requirements:* For doctorate, GRE General Test, minimum GPA of 3.0 in science course work (recommended). Additional exam requirements/recommendations for international students: Required—TOEFL. *Application deadline:* For fall admission, 12/1 for domestic and international students. Application fee: $75. Electronic applications accepted. *Expenses:* Contact institution. *Financial support:* In 2011–12, 9 students received support, including 9 fellowships with tuition reimbursements available (averaging $26,500 per year); institutionally sponsored loans, scholarships/grants, health care benefits, and tuition waivers (full) also available. *Faculty research:* Basic and translational cancer research, molecular and cellular biology, genetics and epigenetics, signal transduction, genetic engineering and nanotechnologies. *Unit head:* Dr. Erwin Van Meir, Program Director, 404-778-5563, Fax: 404-778-5550, E-mail: evanmei@emory.edu. *Application contact:* Kathy Smith, Director of Recruitment and Admissions, 404-727-2547, Fax: 404-727-3322, E-mail: kathy.smith@emory.edu. Web site: http://www.biomed.emory.edu/PROGRAM_SITES/CB/.

Gerstner Sloan-Kettering Graduate School of Biomedical Sciences, Program in Cancer Biology, New York, NY 10021. Offers PhD. *Faculty:* 118 full-time (20 women). *Students:* 52 full-time (29 women); includes 6 minority (1 Black or African American, non-Hispanic/Latino; 4 Asian, non-Hispanic/Latino; 1 Hispanic/Latino), 4 international. In 2011, 3 doctorates awarded. *Degree requirements:* For doctorate, thesis/dissertation. *Entrance requirements:* For doctorate, GRE, transcripts, letters of recommendation. Electronic applications accepted. *Financial support:* Fellowship package including stipend ($33,773), full-tuition scholarship, first-year allowance, and comprehensive medical and dental insurance available. *Faculty research:* Biochemistry and molecular biology, biophysics/structural biology, computational biology, genetics, immunology. *Unit head:* Linda Burnley, Associate Dean, 646-888-6639, E-mail: burnleyl@sloankettering.edu. *Application contact:* Main Office, 646-888-6639, Fax: 646-422-2351, E-mail: gradstudies@sloankettering.edu.

See Display below and Close-Up on page 235.

Mayo Graduate School, Graduate Programs in Biomedical Sciences, Program in Tumor Biology, Rochester, MN 55905. Offers PhD. *Degree requirements:* For doctorate, oral defense of dissertation, qualifying oral and written exam. *Entrance requirements:* For doctorate, GRE, 1 year of chemistry, biology, calculus, and physics. Additional exam requirements/recommendations for international students: Required—TOEFL. Electronic applications accepted.

The Gerstner Sloan-Kettering Graduate School of Biomedical Sciences offers the next generation of basic scientists a program to study the biological sciences through the lens of cancer — while giving students the tools they will need to put them in the vanguard of research that can be applied in any area of human disease.

Gerstner Sloan-Kettering
Graduate School of Biomedical Sciences

Memorial Sloan-Kettering Cancer Center | New York City

PhD Program in Cancer Biology

An Internationally Recognized Research Faculty in:

- Cancer genetics
- Genomic integrity
- Cell signaling and regulation
- Structural biology
- Immunology
- Chemical biology
- Developmental biology
- Computational biology
- Experimental therapeutics
- Experimental pathology
- Imaging and radiation sciences
- Oncology
- Genomics
- Animal models of disease

An Innovative, Integrated Curriculum Provides a Fundamental Understanding of:

- The nature of genes and gene expression
- Cellular organization
- Tissue and organ formation
- Cell-cell interactions
- Cellular response to the environment
- Enzyme activity

All Matriculated Students Receive a Full Fellowship Package for the Duration of Study.

Please visit our Web site to learn how to apply, for application deadlines, and for more information about our PhD program.

www.sloankettering.edu

gradstudies@sloankettering.edu | 646.888.6639

McMaster University, Faculty of Health Sciences and School of Graduate Studies, Program in Medical Sciences, Genetics and Cancer Area, Hamilton, ON L8S 4M2, Canada. Offers M Sc, PhD, MD/PhD. *Degree requirements:* For master's, thesis; for doctorate, comprehensive exam, thesis/dissertation. *Entrance requirements:* For master's, honors B Sc, B+ average in related field; for doctorate, M Sc, minimum B+ average, students with proven research experience and an A average may be admitted with a B Sc degree. Additional exam requirements/recommendations for international students: Required—TOEFL (minimum score 580 paper-based; 237 computer-based; 92 iBT).

Medical University of South Carolina, College of Graduate Studies, Program in Molecular and Cellular Biology and Pathobiology, Charleston, SC 29425. Offers cancer biology (PhD); cardiovascular biology (PhD); cardiovascular imaging (PhD); cell regulation (PhD); craniofacial biology (PhD); genetics and development (PhD); marine biomedicine (PhD); DMD/PhD; MD/PhD. *Faculty:* 137 full-time (33 women). *Students:* 28 full-time (23 women); includes 5 minority (4 Black or African American, non-Hispanic/Latino; 1 Hispanic/Latino), 5 international. Average age 30. In 2011, 16 doctorates awarded. *Degree requirements:* For doctorate, thesis/dissertation, oral and written exams. *Entrance requirements:* For doctorate, GRE General Test, interview, minimum GPA of 3.0. Additional exam requirements/recommendations for international students: Required—TOEFL (minimum score 600 paper-based; 250 computer-based; 100 iBT). *Application deadline:* For fall admission, 1/15 priority date for domestic students, 1/15 for international students. Applications are processed on a rolling basis. Application fee: $0 ($85 for international students). Electronic applications accepted. *Financial support:* In 2011–12, 39 research assistantships with partial tuition reimbursements (averaging $23,000 per year) were awarded; Federal Work-Study and scholarships/grants also available. Support available to part-time students. Financial award application deadline: 3/10; financial award applicants required to submit FAFSA. *Unit head:* Dr. Donald R. Menick, Director, 843-876-5045, Fax: 843-792-6590, E-mail: menickd@musc.edu. *Application contact:* Dr. Cynthia F. Wright, Associate Dean for Admissions and Career Development, 843-792-2564, Fax: 843-792-6590, E-mail: wrightcf@musc.edu. Web site: http://www.musc.edu/mcbp/.

Meharry Medical College, School of Graduate Studies, Program in Biomedical Sciences, Cancer Biology Emphasis, Nashville, TN 37208-9989. Offers PhD, MD/PhD. *Degree requirements:* For doctorate, comprehensive exam, thesis/dissertation. *Entrance requirements:* For doctorate, GRE. *Faculty research:* Regulation of metabolism, enzymology, signal transduction, physical biochemistry.

Memorial University of Newfoundland, Faculty of Medicine and School of Graduate Studies, Graduate Programs in Medicine, Division of Biomedical Sciences, St. John's, NL A1C 5S7, Canada. Offers cancer (M Sc, PhD); cardiovascular (M Sc, PhD); immunology (M Sc, PhD); neuroscience (M Sc, PhD). Part-time programs available. *Degree requirements:* For master's, thesis; for doctorate, comprehensive exam, thesis/dissertation, oral defense of thesis. *Entrance requirements:* For master's, MD or B Sc; for doctorate, MD or M Sc. Additional exam requirements/recommendations for international students: Required—TOEFL. *Faculty research:* Neuroscience, immunology, cardiovascular, and cancer.

New York University, Graduate School of Arts and Science, Department of Biology, New York, NY 10012-1019. Offers biology (PhD); biomedical journalism (MS); cancer and molecular biology (PhD); computational biology (PhD); computers in biological research (MS); developmental genetics (PhD); general biology (MS); immunology and microbiology (PhD); molecular genetics (PhD); neurobiology (PhD); oral biology (MS); plant biology (PhD); recombinant DNA technology (MS); MS/MBA. Part-time programs available. *Faculty:* 24 full-time (5 women). *Students:* 146 full-time (90 women), 54 part-time (36 women); includes 49 minority (1 Black or African American, non-Hispanic/Latino; 33 Asian, non-Hispanic/Latino; 12 Hispanic/Latino; 3 Two or more races, non-Hispanic/Latino), 89 international. Average age 27. 394 applicants, 62% accepted, 82 enrolled. In 2011, 68 master's, 6 doctorates awarded. Terminal master's awarded for partial completion of doctoral program. *Degree requirements:* For master's, thesis or alternative, qualifying paper; for doctorate, comprehensive exam, thesis/dissertation. *Entrance requirements:* For master's, GRE General Test; for doctorate, GRE General Test, GRE Subject Test. Additional exam requirements/recommendations for international students: Required—TOEFL. *Application deadline:* For fall admission, 12/1 priority date for domestic students, 12/1 for international students. Application fee: $90. *Financial support:* Fellowships with tuition reimbursements, research assistantships with tuition reimbursements, teaching assistantships with tuition reimbursements, career-related internships or fieldwork, Federal Work-Study, institutionally sponsored loans, scholarships/grants, health care benefits, and unspecified assistantships available. Financial award application deadline: 12/1; financial award applicants required to submit FAFSA. *Faculty research:* Genomics, molecular and cell biology, development and molecular genetics, molecular evolution of plants and animals. *Unit head:* Stephen Small, Chair, 212-998-8200, Fax: 212-995-4015, E-mail: biology@nyu.edu. *Application contact:* Justin Blau, Director of Graduate Studies, 212-998-8200, Fax: 212-995-4015, E-mail: biology@nyu.edu. Web site: http://biology.as.nyu.edu/.

New York University, School of Medicine, New York, NY 10012-1019. Offers biomedical sciences (PhD), including biomedical imaging, cellular and molecular biology, computational biology, developmental genetics, medical and molecular parasitology, microbiology, molecular oncobiology and immunology, neuroscience and physiology, pathobiology, pharmacology, structural biology; clinical investigation (MS); medicine (MD); MD/MA; MD/MPA; MD/MS; MD/PhD. *Accreditation:* LCME/AMA (one or more programs are accredited). *Degree requirements:* For master's, comprehensive exam, thesis; for doctorate, comprehensive exam (for some programs), thesis/dissertation (for some programs). *Entrance requirements:* For doctorate, MCAT (for MD). Additional exam requirements/recommendations for international students: Required—TOEFL. *Expenses:* Contact institution. *Faculty research:* AIDS, cancer, neuroscience, molecular biology, neuroscience, cell biology and molecular genetics, structural biology, microbial pathogenesis and host defense, pharmacology, molecular oncology and immunology.

New York University, School of Medicine and Graduate School of Arts and Science, Sackler Institute of Graduate Biomedical Sciences, Program in Molecular Oncology and Tumor Immunology, New York, NY 10012-1019. Offers immunology (PhD); molecular oncology (PhD); MD/PhD. *Faculty:* 52 full-time (16 women). *Students:* 29 full-time (17 women); includes 8 minority (3 Black or African American, non-Hispanic/Latino; 2 Asian, non-Hispanic/Latino; 3 Hispanic/Latino), 9 international. Average age 28. In 2011, 2 doctorates awarded. *Degree requirements:* For doctorate, one foreign language, thesis/dissertation, qualifying exam. *Entrance requirements:* For doctorate, GRE General Test, GRE Subject Test. Additional exam requirements/recommendations for international students: Required—TOEFL. *Application deadline:* For fall admission, 2/1 for domestic students. Applications are processed on a rolling basis. Application fee: $85. Electronic applications accepted. *Financial support:* Tuition waivers (full) available. *Faculty research:* Stem cells, immunology, genome instability, DNA damage checkpoints. *Unit head:* Dr. Joel D. Oppenheim, Senior Associate Dean for Graduate Studies, 212-263-8001, Fax: 212-263-7600. *Application contact:* Dr. David Levy, Graduate Adviser, 212-263-8192, Fax: 212-263-8211, E-mail: david.levy@med.nyu.edu.

Northwestern University, Northwestern University Feinberg School of Medicine and Interdepartmental Programs, Integrated Graduate Programs in the Life Sciences, Chicago, IL 60611. Offers cancer biology (PhD); cell biology (PhD); developmental biology (PhD); evolutionary biology (PhD); immunology and microbial pathogenesis (PhD); molecular biology and genetics (PhD); neurobiology (PhD); pharmacology and toxicology (PhD); structural biology and biochemistry (PhD). *Degree requirements:* For doctorate, comprehensive exam, thesis/dissertation, written and oral qualifying exams. *Entrance requirements:* For doctorate, GRE General Test. Additional exam requirements/recommendations for international students: Required—TOEFL (minimum score 600 paper-based; 250 computer-based). Electronic applications accepted.

Oregon Health & Science University, School of Medicine, Graduate Programs in Medicine, Program in Molecular and Cellular Biosciences, Cancer Biology Program, Portland, OR 97239-3098. Offers PhD. *Faculty:* 27 full-time (6 women). *Students:* 8 full-time (4 women); includes 2 minority (1 Black or African American, non-Hispanic/Latino; 1 Hispanic/Latino), 4 international. Average age 28. *Degree requirements:* For doctorate, comprehensive exam, thesis/dissertation, qualifying exam. *Entrance requirements:* For doctorate, GRE General Test (minimum scores: 158 Verbal/148 Quantitative/4.5 Analytical). Additional exam requirements/recommendations for international students: Required—TOEFL. Electronic applications accepted. *Financial support:* Health care benefits and full tuition and stipends for PhD students available. *Faculty research:* Signal transduction, apoptosis, carcinogenesis, genome integrity, tumor micro-environment. *Unit head:* Dr. Matthew Thayer, Program Leader, 503-494-2447, E-mail: thayerm@ohsu.edu. *Application contact:* Jeni Wroblewski, Program Coordinator, 503-494-2541, Fax: 503-494-8393, E-mail: wroblews@ohsu.edu. Web site: http://www.ohsu.edu/cancerbio.

Purdue University, Graduate School, PULSe - Purdue University Life Sciences Program, West Lafayette, IN 47907. Offers biomolecular structure and biophysics (PhD); biotechnology (PhD); chemical biology (PhD); chromatin and regulation of gene expression (PhD); integrative neuroscience (PhD); integrative plant sciences (PhD); membrane biology (PhD); microbiology (PhD); molecular evolutionary and cancer biology (PhD); molecular evolutionary genetics (PhD); molecular virology (PhD). *Students:* 90 full-time (45 women); includes 7 minority (3 Black or African American, non-Hispanic/Latino; 1 Asian, non-Hispanic/Latino; 2 Hispanic/Latino; 1 Two or more races, non-Hispanic/Latino), 40 international. Average age 26. 427 applicants, 24% accepted, 35 enrolled. *Entrance requirements:* For doctorate, GRE test required, minimum undergraduate GPA of 3.0. Additional exam requirements/recommendations for international students: Required—TOEFL (minimum score 550 paper-based; 77 iBT). *Application deadline:* For fall admission, 1/15 priority date for domestic students, 1/15 for international students. Applications are processed on a rolling basis. Application fee: $60 ($75 for international students). Electronic applications accepted. *Financial support:* In 2011–12, research assistantships with tuition reimbursements (averaging $22,500 per year), teaching assistantships with tuition reimbursements (averaging $22,500 per year) were awarded. *Unit head:* Dr. Christine A. Hrycyna, Head, 765-494-7322, E-mail: hrycyna@purdue.edu. *Application contact:* Emily E. Bramson, Graduate Contact, 765-494-5865, E-mail: bramson@purdue.edu. Web site: http://www.gradschool.purdue.edu/pulse.

Queen's University at Kingston, School of Graduate Studies and Research, Faculty of Health Sciences, Department of Anatomy and Cell Biology, Kingston, ON K7L 3N6, Canada. Offers biology of reproduction (M Sc, PhD); cancer (M Sc, PhD); cardiovascular pathophysiology (M Sc, PhD); cell and molecular biology (M Sc, PhD); drug metabolism (M Sc, PhD); endocrinology (M Sc, PhD); motor control (M Sc, PhD); neural regeneration (M Sc, PhD); neurophysiology (M Sc, PhD). Part-time programs available. *Degree requirements:* For master's, thesis; for doctorate, one foreign language, comprehensive exam, thesis/dissertation. *Entrance requirements:* Additional exam requirements/recommendations for international students: Required—TOEFL. Electronic applications accepted. *Faculty research:* Human kinetics, neuroscience, reproductive biology, cardiovascular.

Rutgers, The State University of New Jersey, New Brunswick, Graduate School-New Brunswick, Program in Endocrinology and Animal Biosciences, Piscataway, NJ 08854-8097. Offers MS, PhD. Terminal master's awarded for partial completion of doctoral program. *Degree requirements:* For master's, thesis; for doctorate, comprehensive exam, thesis/dissertation. *Entrance requirements:* For master's and doctorate, GRE General Test. Additional exam requirements/recommendations for international students: Required—TOEFL. Electronic applications accepted. *Faculty research:* Comparative and behavioral endocrinology, epigenetic regulation of the endocrine system, exercise physiology and immunology, fetal and neonatal developmental programming, mammary gland biology and breast cancer, neuroendocrinology and alcohol studies, reproductive and developmental toxicology.

Stanford University, School of Medicine, Graduate Programs in Medicine, Program in Cancer Biology, Stanford, CA 94305-9991. Offers PhD. *Degree requirements:* For doctorate, thesis/dissertation, qualifying examination. *Entrance requirements:* For doctorate, GRE General Test, GRE Subject Test. Additional exam requirements/recommendations for international students: Required—TOEFL. Electronic applications accepted. *Expenses: Tuition:* Full-time $40,050; part-time $890 per credit.

State University of New York Upstate Medical University, College of Graduate Studies, Major Research Areas of the College of Graduate Studies, Syracuse, NY 13210-2334.

Université Laval, Faculty of Medicine, Post-Professional Programs in Medical Studies, Québec, QC G1K 7P4, Canada. Offers anatomy–pathology (DESS); anesthesiology (DESS); cardiology (DESS); care of older people (Diploma); clinical research (DESS); community health (DESS); dermatology (DESS); diagnostic radiology (DESS); emergency medicine (Diploma); family medicine (DESS); general surgery (DESS); geriatrics (DESS); hematology (DESS); internal medicine (DESS); maternal and fetal medicine (Diploma); medical biochemistry (DESS); medical microbiology and infectious diseases (DESS); medical oncology (DESS); nephrology (DESS); neurology (DESS); neurosurgery (DESS); obstetrics and gynecology (DESS); ophthalmology (DESS); orthopedic surgery (DESS); oto-rhino-laryngology (DESS); palliative medicine (Diploma); pediatrics (DESS); plastic surgery (DESS); psychiatry (DESS); pulmonary medicine (DESS); radiology–oncology (DESS); thoracic surgery (DESS); urology (DESS). *Degree requirements:* For other advanced degree, comprehensive exam. *Entrance requirements:* For degree, knowledge of French. Electronic applications accepted.

University at Buffalo, the State University of New York, Graduate School, Graduate Programs in Cancer Research and Biomedical Sciences at Roswell Park Cancer Institute, Interdisciplinary Master of Science Program in Natural and Biomedical Sciences at Roswell Park Cancer Institute, Buffalo, NY 14260. Offers biomedical sciences and cancer research (MS). Part-time programs available. *Degree requirements:* For master's, thesis, defense of thesis, research project. *Entrance requirements:* For master's, GRE General Test, MCAT, DAT, PCAT. Additional exam requirements/recommendations for international students: Required—TOEFL (minimum score 600 paper-based; 250 computer-based; 100 iBT). Electronic applications accepted. *Faculty research:* Biochemistry, oncology, pathology, biophysics,

pharmacology, molecular biology, cellular biology, genetics, bioinformatics, immunology, therapeutic development, epidemiology.

University of Alberta, Faculty of Medicine and Dentistry and Faculty of Graduate Studies and Research, Graduate Programs in Medicine, Department of Oncology, Edmonton, AB T6G 2E1, Canada. Offers M Sc, PhD. Terminal master's awarded for partial completion of doctoral program. *Degree requirements:* For master's, thesis; for doctorate, thesis/dissertation. *Entrance requirements:* For master's and doctorate, minimum GPA of 7.0 on a 9.0 scale, B SC. Additional exam requirements/recommendations for international students: Required—TOEFL (minimum score 600 paper-based). Electronic applications accepted. *Faculty research:* Experimental oncology, radiation oncology, medical physics, medical oncology.

The University of Arizona, Graduate Interdisciplinary Programs, Graduate Interdisciplinary Program in Cancer Biology, Tucson, AZ 85721. Offers PhD. *Students:* 16 full-time (9 women); includes 4 minority (1 Black or African American, non-Hispanic/Latino; 2 Hispanic/Latino; 1 Two or more races, non-Hispanic/Latino), 1 international. Average age 30. 49 applicants, 6% accepted, 3 enrolled. In 2011, 4 degrees awarded. *Degree requirements:* For doctorate, comprehensive exam, thesis/dissertation. *Entrance requirements:* For doctorate, GRE General Test, 3 letters of recommendation. Additional exam requirements/recommendations for international students: Required—TOEFL (minimum score 550 paper-based; 213 computer-based; 79 iBT). *Application deadline:* For fall admission, 12/1 for domestic and international students. Applications are processed on a rolling basis. Application fee: $75. Electronic applications accepted. *Expenses:* Tuition, state resident: full-time $10,840. Tuition, nonresident: full-time $25,802. *Financial support:* Institutionally sponsored loans, scholarships/grants, traineeships, health care benefits, tuition waivers (full), and unspecified assistantships available. *Faculty research:* Differential gene expression, DNA-protein cross linking, cell growth regulation steroid, receptor proteins. *Unit head:* Dr. G. Tim Bowden, Chairman, 520-626-7479, E-mail: bowden@azcc.arizona.edu. *Application contact:* Anne Cione, Senior Program Coordinator, 520-626-7479, Fax: 520-626-4979, E-mail: acione@azcc.arizona.edu.

University of Calgary, Faculty of Medicine and Faculty of Graduate Studies, Department of Medical Science, Calgary, AB T2N 1N4, Canada. Offers cancer biology (M Sc, PhD); immunology (M Sc, PhD); joint injury and arthritis research (M Sc, PhD); medical education (M Sc, PhD); medical science (M Sc, PhD); mountain medicine and high altitude physiology (M Sc). *Degree requirements:* For master's, thesis; for doctorate, thesis/dissertation, candidacy exam. *Entrance requirements:* For master's, minimum undergraduate GPA of 3.2; for doctorate, minimum graduate GPA of 3.2. Additional exam requirements/recommendations for international students: Required—TOEFL (minimum score 600 paper-based; 250 computer-based). Electronic applications accepted. *Faculty research:* Cancer biology, immunology, joint injury and arthritis, medical education, population genomics.

University of California, San Diego, Office of Graduate Studies, Division of Biological Sciences, Program in Immunology, Virology, and Cancer Biology, La Jolla, CA 92093. Offers PhD. Offered in association with the Salk Institute. *Degree requirements:* For doctorate, thesis/dissertation, qualifying exam. Electronic applications accepted.

University of California, San Diego, School of Medicine and Office of Graduate Studies, Molecular Pathology Program, La Jolla, CA 92093. Offers bioinformatics (PhD); cancer biology/oncology (PhD); cardiovascular sciences and disease (PhD); microbiology (PhD); molecular pathology (PhD); neurological disease (PhD); stem cell and developmental biology (PhD); structural biology/drug design (PhD). *Entrance requirements:* For doctorate, GRE General Test, GRE Subject Test. Additional exam requirements/recommendations for international students: Required—TOEFL. Electronic applications accepted.

University of Chicago, Division of Biological Sciences, Biomedical Sciences Cluster: Cancer Biology, Immunology, Molecular Metabolism and Nutrition, Pathology, and Microbiology, Committee on Cancer Biology, Chicago, IL 60637-1513. Offers PhD. *Degree requirements:* For doctorate, thesis/dissertation, ethics class, 2 teaching assistantships. *Entrance requirements:* For doctorate, GRE General Test. Additional exam requirements/recommendations for international students: Required—TOEFL (minimum score 600 paper-based; 250 computer-based; 104 iBT), IELTS (minimum score 7). Electronic applications accepted. *Faculty research:* Cancer genetics, apoptosis, signal transduction, tumor biology, cell cycle regulation.

University of Cincinnati, Graduate School, College of Medicine, Graduate Programs in Biomedical Sciences, Graduate Program in Cell and Cancer Biology, Cincinnati, OH 45221. Offers PhD. *Degree requirements:* For doctorate, thesis/dissertation, qualifying exam. *Entrance requirements:* For doctorate, GRE General Test. Additional exam requirements/recommendations for international students: Required—TOEFL. Electronic applications accepted. *Faculty research:* Cancer biology, cell and molecular biology, breast cancer, pancreatic cancer, drug discovery.

University of Colorado Denver, School of Medicine, Program in Cancer Biology, Denver, CO 80217-3364. Offers PhD. *Students:* 20 full-time (16 women); includes 2 minority (1 Asian, non-Hispanic/Latino; 1 Hispanic/Latino), 3 international. Average age 26. 42 applicants, 12% accepted, 5 enrolled. In 2011, 1 doctorate awarded. *Degree requirements:* For doctorate, comprehensive exam, thesis/dissertation, 3 laboratory rotations. *Entrance requirements:* For doctorate, GRE General Test, interview, minimum undergraduate GPA of 3.0. Additional exam requirements/recommendations for international students: Required—TOEFL (minimum score 550 paper-based; 213 computer-based). *Application deadline:* For fall admission, 12/1 for domestic students, 11/1 for international students. Application fee: $50 ($75 for international students). Electronic applications accepted. *Expenses:* Contact institution. *Financial support:* In 2011–12, 2 students received support. Fellowships with full tuition reimbursements available, health care benefits, tuition waivers (full), and stipend available. Financial award application deadline: 3/15; financial award applicants required to submit FAFSA. *Faculty research:* Signal transduction by tyrosine kinases, estrogen and progesterone receptors in breast cancer, mechanism of mitochondrial DNA replication in the mammalian cell. *Total annual research expenditures:* $9 million. *Unit head:* Dr. Mary Reyland, Director, 303-724-4572, E-mail: mary.reyland@ucdenver.edu. *Application contact:* Deanne Sylvester, Program Administrator, 303-724-3244, E-mail: deanne.sylvester@ucdenver.edu.

University of Delaware, College of Arts and Sciences, Department of Biological Sciences, Newark, DE 19716. Offers biotechnology (MS); cancer biology (MS, PhD); cell and extracellular matrix biology (MS, PhD); cell and systems physiology (MS, PhD); developmental biology (MS, PhD); ecology and evolution (MS, PhD); microbiology (MS, PhD); molecular biology and genetics (MS, PhD). Terminal master's awarded for partial completion of doctoral program. *Degree requirements:* For master's, thesis, preliminary exam; for doctorate, comprehensive exam, thesis/dissertation, preliminary exam. *Entrance requirements:* For master's and doctorate, GRE General Test. Additional exam requirements/recommendations for international students: Required—TOEFL (minimum score 600 paper-based; 250 computer-based); Recommended—TWE. Electronic applications accepted. *Faculty research:* Microorganisms, bone, cancer metastasis, developmental biology, cell biology, DNA.

The University of Manchester, Faculty of Life Sciences, Manchester, United Kingdom. Offers adaptive organismal biology (M Phil, PhD); animal biology (M Phil, PhD); biochemistry (M Phil, PhD); bioinformatics (M Phil, PhD); biomolecular sciences (M Phil, PhD); biotechnology (M Phil, PhD); cell biology (M Phil, PhD); cell matrix research (M Phil, PhD); channels and transporters (M Phil, PhD); developmental biology (M Phil, PhD); Egyptology (M Phil, PhD); environmental biology (M Phil, PhD); evolutionary biology (M Phil, PhD); gene expression (M Phil, PhD); genetics (M Phil, PhD); history of science, technology and medicine (M Phil, PhD); immunology (M Phil, PhD); integrative neurobiology and behavior (M Phil, PhD); membrane trafficking (M Phil, PhD); microbiology (M Phil, PhD); molecular and cellular neuroscience (M Phil, PhD); molecular biology (M Phil, PhD); molecular cancer studies (M Phil, PhD); neuroscience (M Phil, PhD); ophthalmology (M Phil, PhD); optometry (M Phil, PhD); organelle function (M Phil, PhD); pharmacology (M Phil, PhD); physiology (M Phil, PhD); plant sciences (M Phil, PhD); stem cell research (M Phil, PhD); structural biology (M Phil, PhD); systems neuroscience (M Phil, PhD); toxicology (M Phil, PhD).

The University of Manchester, School of Dentistry, Manchester, United Kingdom. Offers basic dental sciences (cancer studies) (M Phil, PhD); basic dental sciences (molecular genetics) (M Phil, PhD); basic dental sciences (stem cell biology) (M Phil, PhD); biomaterials sciences and dental technology (M Phil, PhD); dental public health/community dentistry (M Phil, PhD); dental science (clinical) (PhD); endodontology (M Phil, PhD); fixed and removable prosthodontics (M Phil, PhD); operative dentistry (M Phil, PhD); oral and maxillofacial surgery (M Phil, PhD); oral radiology (M Phil, PhD); orthodontics (M Phil, PhD); restorative dentistry (M Phil, PhD).

University of Manitoba, Faculty of Graduate Studies, Faculty of Nursing, Winnipeg, MB R3T 2N2, Canada. Offers cancer nursing (MN); nursing (MN). *Degree requirements:* For master's, thesis.

University of Maryland, Baltimore, Graduate School, Graduate Program in Life Sciences, Program in Molecular Medicine, Baltimore, MD 21201. Offers cancer biology (PhD); cell and molecular physiology (PhD); human genetics and genomic medicine (PhD); molecular medicine (MS); molecular toxicology and pharmacology (PhD); MD/PhD. *Students:* 80 full-time (53 women), 11 part-time (4 women); includes 21 minority (8 Black or African American, non-Hispanic/Latino; 6 Asian, non-Hispanic/Latino; 4 Hispanic/Latino; 3 Two or more races, non-Hispanic/Latino), 13 international. Average age 27. 207 applicants, 24% accepted, 15 enrolled. In 2011, 3 master's, 5 doctorates awarded. *Entrance requirements:* Additional exam requirements/recommendations for international students: Required—TOEFL (minimum score 600 paper-based; 100 iBT); Recommended—IELTS (minimum score 7). *Application deadline:* For fall admission, 1/15 for domestic and international students. Application fee: $50. Electronic applications accepted. *Financial support:* In 2011–12, research assistantships with partial tuition reimbursements (averaging $25,000 per year) were awarded; fellowships also available. Financial award application deadline: 3/1. *Unit head:* Dr. Toni Antalis, Director, 410-706-8222, E-mail: tantalis@som.umaryland.edu. *Application contact:* Sharron Graves, Program Coordinator, 410-706-6044, Fax: 410-706-6040, E-mail: sgraves@som.umaryland.edu. Web site: http://molecularmedicine.umaryland.edu.

University of Massachusetts Worcester, Graduate School of Biomedical Sciences, Worcester, MA 01655-0115. Offers biochemistry and molecular pharmacology (PhD); bioinformatics and computational biology (PhD); cancer biology (PhD); cell biology (PhD); clinical and population health research (PhD); clinical investigation (MS); immunology and virology (PhD); interdisciplinary graduate program (PhD); molecular genetics and microbiology (PhD); neuroscience (PhD); DVM/PhD; MD/PhD. *Faculty:* 1,427 full-time (526 women), 309 part-time/adjunct (196 women). *Students:* 416 full-time (225 women); includes 47 minority (12 Black or African American, non-Hispanic/Latino; 32 Asian, non-Hispanic/Latino; 3 Hispanic/Latino), 144 international. Average age 29. 623 applicants, 17% accepted, 54 enrolled. In 2011, 5 master's, 63 doctorates awarded. Terminal master's awarded for partial completion of doctoral program. *Degree requirements:* For master's, comprehensive exam, thesis; for doctorate, comprehensive exam, thesis/dissertation. *Entrance requirements:* For master's, bachelor's degree; for doctorate, GRE General Test. Additional exam requirements/recommendations for international students: Required—TOEFL (minimum score 600 paper-based; 250 computer-based; 100 iBT) or IELTS (minimum score 7.5). *Application deadline:* For fall admission, 12/15 for domestic and international students; for spring admission, 5/15 for domestic students. Application fee: $50. Electronic applications accepted. *Expenses:* Contact institution. *Financial support:* In 2011–12, 416 students received support, including 416 research assistantships with full tuition reimbursements available (averaging $29,200 per year); scholarships/grants, health care benefits, tuition waivers (full), and unspecified assistantships also available. Financial award application deadline: 4/16. *Faculty research:* RNA interference, cell biology, bioinformatics, clinical research, infectious disease. *Total annual research expenditures:* $262.7 million. *Unit head:* Dr. Anthony Carruthers, Dean, 508-856-4135, E-mail: anthony.carruthers@umassmed.edu. *Application contact:* Dr. Kendall Knight, Associate Dean and Interim Director of Admissions and Recruitment, 508-856-5628, Fax: 508-856-3659, E-mail: kendall.knight@umassmed.edu. Web site: http://www.umassmed.edu/gsbs/.

University of Medicine and Dentistry of New Jersey, Graduate School of Biomedical Sciences, Graduate Programs in Biomedical Sciences–Newark, Newark, NJ 07107. Offers biodefense (Certificate); biomedical engineering (PhD); biomedical sciences (multidisciplinary) (PhD); cellular biology, neuroscience and physiology (PhD), including neuroscience, physiology, biophysics, cardiovascular biology, molecular pharmacology, stem cell biology; infection, immunity and inflammation (PhD), including immunology, infectious disease, microbiology, oral biology; molecular biology, genetics and cancer (PhD), including biochemistry, molecular genetics, cancer biology, radiation biology, bioinformatics; neuroscience (Certificate); pharmacological sciences (Certificate); stem cell (Certificate); DMD/PhD; MD/PhD. PhD in biomedical engineering offered jointly with New Jersey Institute of Technology. Part-time and evening/weekend programs available. Terminal master's awarded for partial completion of doctoral program. *Degree requirements:* For doctorate, thesis/dissertation, qualifying exam. *Entrance requirements:* For doctorate, GRE General Test. Additional exam requirements/recommendations for international students: Required—TOEFL. Electronic applications accepted.

University of Miami, Graduate School, Miller School of Medicine, Program in Cancer Biology, Coral Gables, FL 33124. Offers PhD, MD/PhD.

University of Michigan, Horace H. Rackham School of Graduate Studies, Program in Biomedical Sciences (PIBS), Program in Cancer Biology, Ann Arbor, MI 48109. Offers PhD. *Faculty:* 44 full-time (10 women). *Students:* 1 (woman) full-time. Average age 36. 50 applicants, 20% accepted, 1 enrolled. *Degree requirements:* For doctorate, thesis/dissertation, preliminary examination, oral defense of dissertation. *Entrance requirements:* For doctorate, GRE General Test, three letters of recommendation, research experience. Additional exam requirements/recommendations for international students: Required—TOEFL (minimum score 84 iBT). *Application deadline:* For fall admission, 12/1 for domestic and international students. Application fee: $60 ($75 for international students). Electronic applications accepted. *Financial support:* In 2011–12, 1 student received support, including 1 fellowship with full tuition reimbursement available (averaging $26,500 per year); scholarships/grants, health care benefits, tuition waivers (full), and unspecified assistantships also available. Financial award application

deadline: 12/1. *Faculty research:* Tumor immunology, viral oncogenesis, cell biology, genetics, epidemiology, pathology, bioinformatics. *Unit head:* Dr. Michael Imperiale, Director, 734-763-9162, E-mail: imperial@umich.edu. *Application contact:* Michelle S. Melis, Director of Student Life, Programs in Biomedical Sciences (PIBS), 734-615-6538, Fax: 734-647-7022, E-mail: pibs@umich.edu. Web site: http://www.med.umich.edu/cancerbio/.

University of Minnesota, Twin Cities Campus, Graduate School, PhD Program in Microbiology, Immunology and Cancer Biology, Minneapolis, MN 55455-0213. Offers PhD. *Degree requirements:* For doctorate, thesis/dissertation. *Entrance requirements:* For doctorate, GRE General Test. Additional exam requirements/recommendations for international students: Required—TOEFL (minimum score 600 paper-based; 250 computer-based). Electronic applications accepted. *Faculty research:* Virology, microbiology, cancer biology, immunology.

University of Nebraska Medical Center, Graduate Studies, Program in Cancer Research, Omaha, NE 68198. Offers PhD. Terminal master's awarded for partial completion of doctoral program. *Degree requirements:* For doctorate, comprehensive exam, thesis/dissertation. *Entrance requirements:* For doctorate, GRE, 3 letters of reference; course work in chemistry, biology, physics and mathematics. Additional exam requirements/recommendations for international students: Required—TOEFL (minimum score 550 paper-based; 213 computer-based). Electronic applications accepted. *Faculty research:* DNA repair, tumor immunology, signal transduction, structural biology, gene expression.

University of Pennsylvania, Perelman School of Medicine, Biomedical Graduate Studies, Graduate Group in Cell and Molecular Biology, Philadelphia, PA 19104. Offers cancer biology (PhD); cell biology and physiology (PhD); developmental stem cell regenerative biology (PhD); gene therapy and vaccines (PhD); genetics and gene regulation (PhD); microbiology, virology, and parasitology (PhD); MD/PhD; VMD/PhD. *Faculty:* 306. *Students:* 337 full-time (186 women); includes 81 minority (16 Black or African American, non-Hispanic/Latino; 43 Asian, non-Hispanic/Latino; 16 Hispanic/Latino; 6 Two or more races, non-Hispanic/Latino), 41 international. 585 applicants, 21% accepted, 58 enrolled. In 2011, 42 doctorates awarded. *Degree requirements:* For doctorate, thesis/dissertation. *Entrance requirements:* For doctorate, GRE General Test. Additional exam requirements/recommendations for international students: Required—TOEFL. *Application deadline:* For fall admission, 12/1 priority date for domestic students, 12/1 for international students. Applications are processed on a rolling basis. Application fee: $80. Electronic applications accepted. *Expenses:* Tuition: Full-time $26,660; part-time $4944 per course. *Required fees:* $2318; $291 per course. Tuition and fees vary according to course load, degree level and program. *Financial support:* In 2011–12, 337 students received support. Fellowships, research assistantships, scholarships/grants, traineeships, and unspecified assistantships available. *Unit head:* Dr. Daniel Kessler, Graduate Group Chair. *Application contact:* Meagan Schofer, Coordinator. Web site: http://www.med.upenn.edu/camb/.

University of Regina, Faculty of Graduate Studies and Research, Faculty of Science, Department of Chemistry and Biochemistry, Regina, SK S4S 0A2, Canada. Offers analytical/environmental chemistry (M Sc, PhD); biophysics of biological interfaces (M Sc, PhD); enzymology/chemical biology (M Sc, PhD); inorganic/organometallic chemistry (M Sc, PhD); signal transduction and mechanisms of cancer cell regulation (M Sc, PhD); supramolecular organic photochemistry and photophysics (M Sc, PhD); synthetic organic chemistry (M Sc, PhD); theoretical/computational chemistry (M Sc, PhD). *Faculty:* 12 full-time (2 women). *Students:* 13 full-time (4 women), 1 (woman) part-time. 22 applicants, 50% accepted. In 2011, 1 master's, 2 doctorates awarded. *Degree requirements:* For master's, thesis; for doctorate, thesis/dissertation. *Entrance requirements:* Additional exam requirements/recommendations for international students: Required—TOEFL (minimum score 580 paper-based; 80 iBT), IELTS (minimum score 6.5). *Application deadline:* Applications are processed on a rolling basis. Application fee: $100. Electronic applications accepted. *Financial support:* In 2011–12, 3 fellowships (averaging $6,500 per year), 1 research assistantship (averaging $5,500 per year), 7 teaching assistantships (averaging $2,298 per year) were awarded; scholarships/grants also available. Financial award application deadline: 6/15. *Faculty research:* Asymmetric synthesis and methodology, theoretical and computational chemistry, biophysical biochemistry, analytical and environmental chemistry, chemical biology. *Unit head:* Dr. Lynn Mihichuk, Head, 306-585-4793, Fax: 306-337-2409, E-mail: lynn.mihichuk@uregina.ca. *Application contact:* Dr. Tanya Dahms, Graduate Program Coordinator, 306-585-4246, Fax: 306-337-2409, E-mail: tanya.dahms@uregina.ca. Web site: http://www.chem.uregina.ca/.

University of South Florida, Graduate School, College of Arts and Sciences, Cancer Biology Program, Tampa, FL 33620-9951. Offers PhD. *Students:* 30 full-time (23 women), 1 (woman) part-time; includes 2 minority (both Hispanic/Latino), 6 international. Average age 29. 72 applicants, 13% accepted, 4 enrolled. In 2011, 4 doctorates awarded. *Degree requirements:* For doctorate, comprehensive exam, thesis/dissertation. *Entrance requirements:* For doctorate, GRE, minimum GPA of 3.0. Additional exam requirements/recommendations for international students: Required—TOEFL (minimum score 550 paper-based; 213 computer-based; 79 iBT) or IELTS (minimum score 6.5). *Application deadline:* For fall admission, 2/1 for domestic students, 1/1 for international students. Application fee: $30. *Financial support:* Career-related internships or fieldwork, health care benefits, and unspecified assistantships available. Financial award application deadline: 4/1. *Faculty research:* Immunology, cancer control, signal transduction, drug discovery, genomics. *Unit head:* James Gary, Chair, 813-974-7103, Fax: 813-745-7264, E-mail: gary@usf.edu. *Application contact:* Kenneth Wright, Director, 813-745-6876, Fax: 813-745-7264, E-mail: ken.wright@moffitt.org. Web site: http://www.cancerbiology.usf.edu/.

The University of Texas Health Science Center at Houston, Graduate School of Biomedical Sciences, Program in Cancer Biology, Houston, TX 77225-0036. Offers MS, PhD, MD/PhD. Terminal master's awarded for partial completion of doctoral program. *Degree requirements:* For master's, thesis; for doctorate, thesis/dissertation. *Entrance requirements:* For master's and doctorate, GRE General Test. Additional exam requirements/recommendations for international students: Required—TOEFL. Electronic applications accepted. *Faculty research:* Cancer metastasis, signal transduction, therapeutic resistance, cell cycle deregulation, cancer markers and target.

The University of Texas Health Science Center at Houston, Graduate School of Biomedical Sciences, Program in Molecular Carcinogenesis, Houston, TX 77225-0036. Offers MS, PhD, MD/PhD. Terminal master's awarded for partial completion of doctoral program. *Degree requirements:* For master's, thesis; for doctorate, thesis/dissertation. *Entrance requirements:* For master's and doctorate, GRE General Test. Additional exam requirements/recommendations for international students: Required—TOEFL. Electronic applications accepted. *Faculty research:* Carcinogenesis, mutagenesis, epigenetics, mouse models, cancer prevention.

The University of Texas Southwestern Medical Center, Southwestern Graduate School of Biomedical Sciences, Division of Basic Science, Program in Cancer Biology, Dallas, TX 75390. Offers PhD. *Degree requirements:* For doctorate, thesis/dissertation, qualifying examination.

University of the District of Columbia, College of Arts and Sciences, Department of Biological and Environmental Sciences, Program in Cancer Biology, Prevention and Control, Washington, DC 20008-1175. Offers MS. Program offered in partnership with Lombardi Comprehensive Cancer Center at Georgetown University. *Expenses: Tuition, area resident:* Full-time $7580; part-time $421 per credit hour. Tuition, state resident: full-time $8580; part-time $477 per credit hour. Tuition, nonresident: full-time $14,580; part-time $810 per credit hour. *Required fees:* $620; $30 per credit hour. $310 per semester.

The University of Toledo, College of Graduate Studies, College of Medicine and Life Sciences, Department of Biochemistry and Cancer Biology, Toledo, OH 43606-3390. Offers cancer biology (MSBS, PhD); MD/MSBS; MD/PhD. *Faculty:* 17. *Students:* 21 full-time (16 women), 1 (woman) part-time; includes 2 minority (1 Black or African American, non-Hispanic/Latino; 1 Asian, non-Hispanic/Latino), 15 international. Average age 26. 12 applicants, 83% accepted, 6 enrolled. In 2011, 3 degrees awarded. Terminal master's awarded for partial completion of doctoral program. *Degree requirements:* For master's, thesis, qualifying exam; for doctorate, thesis/dissertation, qualifying exam. *Entrance requirements:* For master's and doctorate, GRE, minimum undergraduate GPA of 3.0, three letters of recommendation, statement of purpose, transcripts from all prior institutions attended; resume. Additional exam requirements/recommendations for international students: Required—TOEFL (minimum score 550 paper-based; 213 computer-based; 80 iBT), IELTS (minimum score 6.5). *Application deadline:* For fall admission, 1/15 priority date for domestic students, 1/15 for international students. Application fee: $45 ($75 for international students). Electronic applications accepted. *Financial support:* In 2011–12, 19 research assistantships with full tuition reimbursements (averaging $21,180 per year) were awarded; fellowships with tuition reimbursements, Federal Work-Study, institutionally sponsored loans, scholarships/grants, tuition waivers (full), and unspecified assistantships also available. *Unit head:* Dr. James Trempe, Track Director, 419-383-4103, E-mail: james.trempe@utoledo.edu. *Application contact:* Admissions Analyst, 419-383-4116, Fax: 419-383-6140, E-mail: christine.wile@utoledo.edu. Web site: http://www.utoledo.edu/med/grad/.

University of Utah, School of Medicine and Graduate School, Graduate Programs in Medicine, Department of Oncological Sciences, Salt Lake City, UT 84112-1107. Offers M Phil, MS, PhD. Terminal master's awarded for partial completion of doctoral program. *Degree requirements:* For master's, thesis (for some programs); for doctorate, thesis/dissertation. *Entrance requirements:* For master's and doctorate, GRE General Test, GRE Subject Test, minimum GPA of 3.0. Additional exam requirements/recommendations for international students: Required—TOEFL. *Faculty research:* Molecular basis of cell growth and differences, regulation of gene expression, biochemical mechanics of DNA replication, molecular biology and biochemistry of signal transduction, somatic cell genetics.

University of Wisconsin–La Crosse, Office of University Graduate Studies, College of Science and Health, Department of Health Professions, Program in Medical Dosimetry, La Crosse, WI 54601-3742. Offers MS. Postbaccalaureate distance learning degree programs offered (no on-campus study). *Faculty:* 2 full-time (both women). *Students:* 15 full-time (7 women); includes 4 minority (1 Black or African American, non-Hispanic/Latino; 3 Asian, non-Hispanic/Latino). Average age 32. 13 applicants, 62% accepted, 7 enrolled. In 2011, 5 master's awarded. *Entrance requirements:* For master's, American Registry of Radiologic Technologists test, Medical Dosimetrist Certification Board Exam. Additional exam requirements/recommendations for international students: Required—TOEFL (minimum score 600 paper-based; 250 computer-based; 100 iBT). *Application deadline:* For fall admission, 12/1 priority date for domestic students, 11/1 for international students. Application fee: $56. Electronic applications accepted. *Expenses:* Contact institution. *Financial support:* Federal Work-Study and scholarships/grants available. Support available to part-time students. Financial award applicants required to submit FAFSA. *Unit head:* Nishele Lenards, Program Director, 608-785-8470, E-mail: nlenards@uwlax.edu. *Application contact:* Kathryn Kiefer, Director of Admissions, 608-785-8939, E-mail: admissions@uwlax.edu. Web site: http://www.uwlax.edu/md/.

University of Wisconsin–Madison, School of Medicine and Public Health and Graduate School, Graduate Programs in Medicine, Program in Cancer Biology, Madison, WI 53706. Offers PhD. *Faculty:* 48 full-time (15 women). *Students:* 33 full-time (18 women); includes 2 minority (1 Black or African American, non-Hispanic/Latino; 1 Hispanic/Latino), 8 international. 186 applicants, 10% accepted, 6 enrolled. In 2011, 5 doctorates awarded. *Degree requirements:* For doctorate, comprehensive exam, thesis/dissertation. *Entrance requirements:* For doctorate, GRE General Test. Additional exam requirements/recommendations for international students: Required—TOEFL (minimum score 580 paper-based; 237 computer-based; 92 iBT). *Application deadline:* For fall admission, 12/3 priority date for domestic students, 12/3 for international students. Application fee: $56. Electronic applications accepted. *Expenses:* Tuition, state resident: full-time $10,296; part-time $643.51 per credit. Tuition, nonresident: full-time $24,054; part-time $1503.40 per credit. *Required fees:* $70.06 per credit. Tuition and fees vary according to course load, campus/location, program and reciprocity agreements. *Financial support:* In 2011–12, 33 students received support, including 4 fellowships with full tuition reimbursements available (averaging $24,480 per year), 24 research assistantships with full tuition reimbursements available (averaging $24,480 per year); traineeships, health care benefits, and unspecified assistantships also available. Financial award application deadline: 12/3. *Faculty research:* Cancer genetics, tumor virology, chemical carcinogenesis, signal transduction, cell cycle. *Total annual research expenditures:* $18 million. *Unit head:* Dr. James Shull, Director, 608-262-2177, Fax: 608-262-2824, E-mail: shull@oncology.wisc.edu. *Application contact:* Katie Roemer, Administrative Program Manager, 608-262-4682, Fax: 608-262-2824, E-mail: kjroemer@oncology.wisc.edu. Web site: http://www.cancerbiology.wisc.edu/.

Vanderbilt University, Graduate School, Department of Cancer Biology, Nashville, TN 37240-1001. Offers MS, PhD, MD/PhD. *Faculty:* 12 full-time (7 women). *Students:* 48 full-time (35 women); includes 14 minority (8 Black or African American, non-Hispanic/Latino; 2 Asian, non-Hispanic/Latino; 3 Hispanic/Latino; 1 Two or more races, non-Hispanic/Latino), 12 international. Average age 28. In 2011, 7 doctorates awarded. *Degree requirements:* For doctorate, thesis/dissertation, final and qualifying exams. *Entrance requirements:* For master's and doctorate, GRE General Test. Additional exam requirements/recommendations for international students: Required—TOEFL (minimum score 570 paper-based; 230 computer-based; 88 iBT). *Application deadline:* For fall admission, 1/15 for domestic and international students. Application fee: $0. Electronic applications accepted. *Financial support:* Fellowships with full and partial tuition reimbursements, research assistantships with full and partial tuition reimbursements, Federal Work-Study, institutionally sponsored loans, scholarships/grants, traineeships, and health care benefits available. Financial award application deadline: 1/15; financial award applicants required to submit CSS PROFILE or FAFSA. *Faculty research:* Microenvironmental influences on cellular phenotype, in particular as it relates to host/tumor interactions, tumor-stroma interactions, angiogenesis, growth factor and cytokine signaling, oncogenes, tumor suppressors, matrix and matrix degradation, cell adhesion, metastasis. *Unit head:* Dr. Harold L. Moses, Interim Chair, 615-936-1374, Fax: 615-936-1790, E-mail: hal.moses@vanderbilt.edu. *Application contact:* Dr. Jin Chen, Director of Graduate Studies, 615-343-3819, Fax: 615-343-7392, E-mail: jin.chen@vanderbilt.edu. Web site: https://medschool.vanderbilt.edu/cancer-biology/.

Wake Forest University, School of Medicine and Graduate School of Arts and Sciences, Graduate Programs in Medicine, Department of Cancer Biology, Winston-Salem, NC 27109. Offers PhD, MD/PhD. *Degree requirements:* For doctorate, thesis/dissertation. *Entrance requirements:* For doctorate, GRE General Test. Additional exam requirements/recommendations for international students: Required—TOEFL. Electronic applications accepted. *Faculty research:* Cancer research, mechanisms of carcinogenesis, signal transduction and regulation of cell growth.

Wayne State University, School of Medicine, Cancer Biology Graduate Program, Detroit, MI 48202. Offers MS, PhD. *Students:* 29 full-time (20 women); includes 5 minority (3 Black or African American, non-Hispanic/Latino; 1 American Indian or Alaska Native, non-Hispanic/Latino; 1 Asian, non-Hispanic/Latino), 4 international. Average age 27. 74 applicants, 9% accepted, 4 enrolled. In 2011, 8 doctorates awarded. *Degree requirements:* For doctorate, thesis/dissertation. *Entrance requirements:* For master's and doctorate, GRE General Test, statement of purpose, detailed description of research experience, resume, three letters of recommendation. Additional exam requirements/recommendations for international students: Required—TOEFL (minimum score 550 paper-based; 213 computer-based; 100 iBT); Recommended—TWE (minimum score 6). *Application deadline:* For fall admission, 3/1 for domestic and international students. Application fee: $50. Electronic applications accepted. *Expenses:* Tuition, state resident: part-time $512.85 per credit. Tuition, nonresident: part-time $1132.65 per credit. *Required fees:* $26.60 per credit. $199.65 per semester. Tuition and fees vary according to course load and program. *Financial support:* In 2011–12, 23 students received support, including 7 fellowships with tuition reimbursements available (averaging $22,342 per year), 16 research assistantships with tuition reimbursements available (averaging $21,287 per year); scholarships/grants, unspecified assistantships, and 4 external fellowships (averaging over $20,000 per year), 5 training grant appointments also available. *Faculty research:* Molecular oncology and carcinogenesis, cellular interactions and signaling, proteases in neoplasia, therapeutics and prevention, translational research. *Unit head:* Dr. Larry Matherly, Director, Cancer Biology Graduate Program and Program Leader, Molecular Therapeutics Program, 313-578-4280, E-mail: matherly@karmanos.org. *Application contact:* Jill de Jesus, CB Program Coordinator, E-mail: jdejesus@med.wayne.edu. Web site: http://www.med.wayne.edu/cancer/.

Wayne State University, School of Medicine, Graduate Programs in Medicine, Department of Radiation Oncology, Detroit, MI 48202. Offers medical physics (PhD); radiological physics (MS). Part-time and evening/weekend programs available. In 2011, 1 doctorate awarded. Terminal master's awarded for partial completion of doctoral program. *Degree requirements:* For master's, thesis, essay, exit exam; for doctorate, thesis/dissertation, qualifying exam. *Entrance requirements:* For master's, GRE General Test, BS in physics or related area; for doctorate, GRE General Test, GRE Subject Test, BS in physics or related area. Additional exam requirements/recommendations for international students: Required—TOEFL (minimum score 550 paper-based; 213 computer-based); Recommended—TWE (minimum score 6). *Application deadline:* For fall admission, 1/15 for domestic students, 6/1 for international students; for winter admission, 10/1 for international students; for spring admission, 2/1 for international students. Applications are processed on a rolling basis. Application fee: $50. Electronic applications accepted. *Expenses:* Tuition, state resident: part-time $512.85 per credit. Tuition, nonresident: part-time $1132.65 per credit. *Required fees:* $26.60 per credit. $199.65 per semester. Tuition and fees vary according to course load and program. *Financial support:* In 2011–12, 1 research assistantship (averaging $20,787 per year) was awarded; fellowships, teaching assistantships, and career-related internships or fieldwork also available. Support available to part-time students. Financial award application deadline: 1/15. *Unit head:* Maria Vlachaki, Chair, 313-966-2774, Fax: 313-745-2314, E-mail: 661250@wayne.edu. *Application contact:* Michael Joiner, Professor, 313-745-2489, E-mail: joinerm@kci.wayne.edu. Web site: http://gradprograms.med.wayne.edu/program-spotlight.php?id=30.

West Virginia University, Davis College of Agriculture, Forestry and Consumer Sciences, Interdisciplinary Program in Genetics and Developmental Biology, Morgantown, WV 26506. Offers animal breeding (MS, PhD); biochemical and molecular genetics (MS, PhD); cytogenetics (MS, PhD); descriptive embryology (MS, PhD); developmental genetics (MS); experimental morphogenesis/teratology (MS); human genetics (MS, PhD); immunogenetics (MS, PhD); life cycles of animals and plants (MS, PhD); molecular aspects of development (MS, PhD); mutagenesis (MS, PhD); oncology (MS, PhD); plant genetics (MS, PhD); population and quantitative genetics (MS, PhD); regeneration (MS, PhD); teratology (PhD); toxicology (MS, PhD). *Degree requirements:* For master's, thesis; for doctorate, comprehensive exam, thesis/dissertation. *Entrance requirements:* For master's, GRE or MCAT, minimum GPA of 2.75. Additional exam requirements/recommendations for international students: Required—TOEFL.

West Virginia University, School of Medicine, Graduate Programs at the Health Sciences Center, Interdisciplinary Graduate Programs in Biomedical Sciences, Program in Cancer Cell Biology, Morgantown, WV 26506. Offers PhD, MD/PhD. *Degree requirements:* For doctorate, comprehensive exam, thesis/dissertation. *Entrance requirements:* For doctorate, GRE General Test, minimum GPA of 3.0. Additional exam requirements/recommendations for international students: Required—TOEFL. Electronic applications accepted. *Faculty research:* Cellular signaling, tumor microenvironment, cancer therapeutics.

Yale University, School of Medicine and Graduate School of Arts and Sciences, Combined Program in Biological and Biomedical Sciences (BBS), Pharmacological Sciences and Molecular Medicine Track, New Haven, CT 06520. Offers PhD, MD/PhD. *Degree requirements:* For doctorate, thesis/dissertation. *Entrance requirements:* For doctorate, GRE General Test. Additional exam requirements/recommendations for international students: Required—TOEFL. Electronic applications accepted.

Cell Biology

Albany College of Pharmacy and Health Sciences, School of Health Sciences, Albany, NY 12208. Offers biotechnology (MS); cytotechnology and molecular cytology (MS); health outcomes research (MS). *Faculty:* 8 full-time (3 women), 6 part-time/adjunct (5 women). *Students:* 47 full-time (22 women), 2 part-time (both women); includes 1 minority (Asian, non-Hispanic/Latino), 29 international. 49 applicants, 94% accepted, 32 enrolled. *Degree requirements:* For master's, thesis. *Entrance requirements:* For master's, GRE, minimum GPA of 3.0. Additional exam requirements/recommendations for international students: Required—TOEFL (minimum score 474 paper-based; 84 iBT). *Application deadline:* For fall admission, 3/1 for domestic and international students. Applications are processed on a rolling basis. Application fee: $75. Electronic applications accepted. *Expenses: Tuition:* Full-time $29,100; part-time $855 per credit hour. *Required fees:* $1230; $680. Tuition and fees vary according to degree level. *Financial support:* Federal Work-Study and scholarships/grants available. Support available to part-time students. Financial award application deadline: 3/1; financial award applicants required to submit FAFSA. *Unit head:* Dr. Hassan El-Fawal, Dean, 888-203-8010. *Application contact:* Donna Myers, Director of Pharmacy and Graduate Admissions, 518-694-7186, Fax: 518-694-7929, E-mail: graduate@acphs.edu.

Albany Medical College, Center for Cell Biology and Cancer Research, Albany, NY 12208-3479. Offers MS, PhD. Part-time programs available. Terminal master's awarded for partial completion of doctoral program. *Degree requirements:* For master's, thesis; for doctorate, comprehensive exam, thesis/dissertation. *Entrance requirements:* For master's and doctorate, GRE General Test, all transcripts, letters of recommendation. Additional exam requirements/recommendations for international students: Required—TOEFL. *Faculty research:* Cancer cell biology, tissue remodeling, signal transduction, gene regulation, cell adhesion, angiogenesis.

Albert Einstein College of Medicine, Graduate Division of Biomedical Sciences, Department of Anatomy and Structural Biology, Bronx, NY 10461. Offers anatomy (PhD); cell and developmental biology (PhD); MD/PhD. *Degree requirements:* For doctorate, thesis/dissertation. *Entrance requirements:* For doctorate, GRE General Test. Additional exam requirements/recommendations for international students: Required—TOEFL. Electronic applications accepted. *Faculty research:* Cell motility, cell membranes and membrane-cytoskeletal interactions as applied to processing of pancreatic hormones, mechanisms of secretion.

Albert Einstein College of Medicine, Graduate Division of Biomedical Sciences, Division of Biological Sciences, Department of Cell Biology, Bronx, NY 10461. Offers PhD, MD/PhD. *Degree requirements:* For doctorate, thesis/dissertation. *Entrance requirements:* For doctorate, GRE General Test. Additional exam requirements/recommendations for international students: Required—TOEFL. *Faculty research:* Molecular and genetic basis of gene expression in animal cells; expression of differentiated traits of albumin, hemoglobin, myosin, and immunoglobin.

American University of Beirut, Graduate Programs, Faculty of Medicine, Beirut, Lebanon. Offers anatomy, cell biology and human morphology (MS); biochemistry and medical genetics (MS); biomedical sciences (PhD); experimental pathology, immunology and microbiology (MS); medicine (MD); neuroscience (MS); pharmacology and toxicology (MS). Part-time programs available. *Faculty:* 232 full-time (58 women), 68 part-time/adjunct (7 women). *Students:* 346 full-time (135 women), 69 part-time (57 women). Average age 23. In 2011, 20 master's, 82 doctorates awarded. *Degree requirements:* For master's, one foreign language, comprehensive exam, thesis (for some programs). *Entrance requirements:* For master's, letter of recommendation; for doctorate, MCAT, bachelor's degree. Additional exam requirements/recommendations for international students: Required—TOEFL (minimum score 600 paper-based; 250 computer-based; 100 iBT), IELTS (minimum score 7.5). *Application deadline:* For fall admission, 4/30 for domestic and international students; for spring admission, 11/1 for domestic and international students. Application fee: $50. *Expenses: Tuition:* Full-time $12,780; part-time $710 per credit. Tuition and fees vary according to course load and program. *Financial support:* In 2011–12, 19 students received support. Career-related internships or fieldwork, institutionally sponsored loans, scholarships/grants, health care benefits, and unspecified assistantships available. Financial award application deadline: 2/2. *Faculty research:* Cancer research (targeted therapy, mechanisms of leukemogenesis, tumor cell extravasation and metastasis, cancer stem cells); stem cell research (regenerative medicine, drug discovery); genetic research (neurogenetics, hereditary cardiomyopathy, hemoglobinopathies, pharmacogenomics, proteomics); neuroscience research (pain, neurodegenerative disorder); metabolism (inflammation and metabolism, metabolic disorder, diabetes mellitus); vascular and renal biology, signal transduction. *Total annual research expenditures:* $2.3 million. *Unit head:* Dr. Mohamed Sayegh, Dean, 961-1350000 Ext. 4700, Fax: 961-1744464, E-mail: msayegh@aub.edu.lb. *Application contact:* Dr. Salim Kanaan, Director, Admissions Office, 961-1350000 Ext. 2594, Fax: 961-1750775, E-mail: sk00@aub.edu.lb. Web site: http://www.aub.edu.lb/fm/fm_home/Pages/index.aspx.

Appalachian State University, Cratis D. Williams Graduate School, Department of Biology, Boone, NC 28608. Offers cell and molecular (MS); general (MS). Part-time programs available. *Faculty:* 29 full-time (12 women), 3 part-time/adjunct (1 woman). *Students:* 46 full-time (24 women), 9 part-time (7 women); includes 1 minority (Asian, non-Hispanic/Latino). 32 applicants, 63% accepted, 15 enrolled. In 2011, 11 master's awarded. *Degree requirements:* For master's, comprehensive exam, thesis. *Entrance requirements:* For master's, GRE General Test, 3 letters of recommendation. Additional exam requirements/recommendations for international students: Required—TOEFL (minimum score 570 paper-based; 230 computer-based; 79 iBT), IELTS (minimum score 6.5). *Application deadline:* For fall admission, 3/5 priority date for domestic students, 2/1 for international students; for spring admission, 11/1 for domestic students, 7/1 for international students. Applications are processed on a rolling basis. Application fee: $55. Electronic applications accepted. *Expenses:* Tuition, state resident: full-time $4040; part-time $180 per semester hour. Tuition, nonresident: full-time $15,900; part-time $760 per semester hour. *Required fees:* $2500; $20 per semester hour. Tuition and fees vary according to campus/location. *Financial support:* In 2011–12, 25 teaching assistantships (averaging $9,500 per year) were awarded; fellowships, research assistantships, career-related internships or fieldwork, Federal Work-Study, scholarships/grants, and unspecified assistantships also available. Financial award application deadline: 3/15; financial award applicants required to submit FAFSA. *Faculty research:* Aquatic and terrestrial ecology, animal and plant physiology, behavior and systematics, immunology and cell biology, molecular biology and microbiology. *Unit head:* Dr. Steven Seagle, Chairman, 828-262-3025, E-mail: seaglesw@appstate.edu. *Application contact:* Dr. Ece Karatan, Graduate Coordinator, 828-262-6742, E-mail: karatane@appstate.edu. Web site: http://www.biology.appstate.edu.

Arizona State University, College of Liberal Arts and Sciences, School of Life Sciences, Tempe, AZ 85287-4601. Offers animal behavior (PhD); applied ethics (biomedical and health ethics) (MA); biological design (PhD); biology (MS, PhD); biology (biology and society) (MS, PhD); environmental life sciences (PhD); evolutionary biology (PhD); human and social dimensions of science and technology (PhD); microbiology (PhD); molecular and cellular biology (PhD); neuroscience (PhD); philosophy (history and philosophy of science) (MA); sustainability (PhD). Terminal master's awarded for partial completion of doctoral program. *Degree requirements:* For master's, thesis (for some programs), interactive Program of Study (iPOS) submitted before completing 50

percent of required credit hours; for doctorate, variable foreign language requirement, comprehensive exam, thesis/dissertation, interactive Program of Study (iPOS) submitted before completing 50 percent of required credit hours. *Entrance requirements:* For master's and doctorate, GRE, minimum GPA of 3.0 or equivalent in last 2 years of work leading to bachelor's degree. Additional exam requirements/recommendations for international students: Required—TOEFL (minimum score 600 paper-based; 250 computer-based; 100 iBT). Electronic applications accepted.

Auburn University, Graduate School, Interdepartmental Programs, Auburn University, AL 36849. Offers applied economics (PhD); cell and molecular biology (PhD); integrated textile and apparel sciences (PhD); real estate development (MRED); sociology and rural sociology (MA, MS), including rural sociology (MS), sociology. Part-time programs available. *Students:* 25 full-time (12 women), 19 part-time (13 women); includes 4 minority (1 Black or African American, non-Hispanic/Latino; 1 American Indian or Alaska Native, non-Hispanic/Latino; 2 Asian, non-Hispanic/Latino), 26 international. Average age 28. 88 applicants, 35% accepted, 12 enrolled. In 2011, 4 master's, 3 doctorates awarded. *Entrance requirements:* For master's, GRE General Test. *Application deadline:* For fall admission, 7/7 for domestic students; for spring admission, 11/24 for domestic students. Applications are processed on a rolling basis. Application fee: $50 ($60 for international students). Electronic applications accepted. *Expenses:* Tuition, state resident: full-time $7290; part-time $405 per credit hour. Tuition, nonresident: full-time $21,870; part-time $1215 per credit hour. *International tuition:* $22,000 full-time. *Required fees:* $1402. *Financial support:* Fellowships, research assistantships, teaching assistantships, and Federal Work-Study available. Support available to part-time students. Financial award application deadline: 3/15; financial award applicants required to submit FAFSA. *Unit head:* Interim Dean of the Graduate School. *Application contact:* Dr. George Flowers, Dean of the Graduate School, 334-844-2125.

Baylor College of Medicine, Graduate School of Biomedical Sciences, Department of Molecular and Cellular Biology, Houston, TX 77030-3498. Offers PhD, MD/PhD. *Faculty:* 81 full-time (23 women). *Students:* 55 full-time (35 women); includes 12 minority (1 Black or African American, non-Hispanic/Latino; 5 Asian, non-Hispanic/Latino; 6 Hispanic/Latino), 15 international. Average age 27. 145 applicants, 14% accepted, 8 enrolled. In 2011, 12 degrees awarded. *Median time to degree:* Of those who began their doctoral program in fall 2003, 69% received their degree in 8 years or less. *Degree requirements:* For doctorate, thesis/dissertation, public defense, qualifying exam. *Entrance requirements:* For doctorate, GRE General Test, GRE Subject Test (strongly recommended), minimum GPA of 3.0. Additional exam requirements/recommendations for international students: Required—TOEFL. *Application deadline:* For fall admission, 1/1 priority date for domestic students. Application fee: $0. Electronic applications accepted. *Financial support:* In 2011–12, 14 fellowships with full tuition reimbursements (averaging $29,000 per year), 41 research assistantships with full tuition reimbursements (averaging $29,000 per year) were awarded; career-related internships or fieldwork, Federal Work-Study, institutionally sponsored loans, health care benefits, and tuition waivers (full) also available. Financial award applicants required to submit FAFSA. *Faculty research:* Hormone action, development, cancer, gene therapy, neurobiology. *Unit head:* Dr. JoAnne Richards, Director, 713-798-4598. *Application contact:* Caroline Kosnik, Graduate Program Administrator, 713-798-4598, Fax: 713-790-0545, E-mail: ckosnik@bcm.edu. Web site: http://www.bcm.edu/mcb/.

Baylor College of Medicine, Graduate School of Biomedical Sciences, Interdepartmental Program in Cell and Molecular Biology, Houston, TX 77030-3498. Offers biochemistry (PhD); cell and molecular biology (PhD); genetics (PhD); human genetics (PhD); immunology (PhD); microbiology (PhD); virology (PhD); MD/PhD. *Faculty:* 112 full-time (30 women). *Students:* 66 full-time (42 women); includes 21 minority (5 Black or African American, non-Hispanic/Latino; 1 American Indian or Alaska Native, non-Hispanic/Latino; 7 Asian, non-Hispanic/Latino; 8 Hispanic/Latino), 14

international. Average age 27. 126 applicants, 25% accepted, 14 enrolled. In 2011, 7 degrees awarded. *Median time to degree:* Of those who began their doctoral program in fall 2003, 82% received their degree in 8 years or less. *Degree requirements:* For doctorate, thesis/dissertation, public defense. *Entrance requirements:* For doctorate, GRE General Test, GRE Subject Test (strongly recommended), minimum GPA of 3.0. Additional exam requirements/recommendations for international students: Required—TOEFL. *Application deadline:* For fall admission, 1/1 priority date for domestic students. Applications are processed on a rolling basis. Application fee: $0. Electronic applications accepted. *Financial support:* In 2011–12, 66 students received support, including 30 fellowships with full tuition reimbursements available (averaging $29,000 per year), 36 research assistantships with full tuition reimbursements available (averaging $29,000 per year); teaching assistantships, Federal Work-Study, institutionally sponsored loans, health care benefits, and tuition waivers (full) also available. Financial award applicants required to submit FAFSA. *Faculty research:* Molecular and cellular biology; cancer, aging and stem cells; genomics and proteomics; microbiome, molecular microbiology; infectious disease, immunology and translational research. *Unit head:* Dr. Susan Marriott, Director, 713-798-6557. *Application contact:* Lourdes Fernandez, Graduate Program Administrator, 713-798-6557, Fax: 713-798-6325, E-mail: cmbprog@bcm.edu. Web site: http://bcm.edu/cmb/.

Baylor College of Medicine, Graduate School of Biomedical Sciences, Program in Developmental Biology, Houston, TX 77030-3498. Offers PhD, MD/PhD. *Faculty:* 68 full-time (20 women). *Students:* 55 full-time (28 women); includes 9 minority (7 Asian, non-Hispanic/Latino; 2 Hispanic/Latino), 37 international. Average age 28. 771 applicants, 2% accepted, 10 enrolled. In 2011, 5 degrees awarded. *Median time to degree:* Of those who began their doctoral program in fall 2003, 100% received their degree in 8 years or less. *Degree requirements:* For doctorate, thesis/dissertation, public defense. *Entrance requirements:* For doctorate, GRE General Test, GRE Subject Test (strongly recommended), minimum GPA of 3.0. Additional exam requirements/recommendations for international students: Required—TOEFL. *Application deadline:* For fall admission, 1/1 priority date for domestic students. Application fee: $0. Electronic applications accepted. *Financial support:* In 2011–12, 55 students received support, including 6 fellowships with full tuition reimbursements available (averaging $29,000 per year), 49 research assistantships with full tuition reimbursements available (averaging $29,000 per year); career-related internships or fieldwork, Federal Work-Study, institutionally sponsored loans, health care benefits, tuition waivers (full), and stipends also available. *Faculty research:* Stem cells, cancer, neurobiology, organogenesis, genetics of model organisms. *Unit head:* Dr. Hugo Bellen, Director, 713-798-6410. *Application contact:* Catherine Tasnier, Graduate Program Administrator, 713-798-6410, Fax: 713-798-5386, E-mail: cat@bcm.edu. Web site: http://www.bcm.edu/db/.

See Display on page 287 and Close-Up on page 311.

Baylor College of Medicine, Program in Cell and Molecular Biology of Aging, Houston, TX 77030-3498. Offers PhD, MD/PhD. *Application contact:* Dr. Lloyd H. Michael, Senior Associate Dean of the Medical School, 713-798-4842, Fax: 713-798-5563, E-mail: lmichael@bcm.edu.

See Display below and Close-Up on page 233.

Boston University, Graduate School of Arts and Sciences, Molecular Biology, Cell Biology, and Biochemistry Program (MCBB), Boston, MA 02215. Offers MA, PhD. *Students:* 36 full-time (17 women), 3 part-time (2 women); includes 8 minority (3 Black or African American, non-Hispanic/Latino; 2 Asian, non-Hispanic/Latino; 3 Hispanic/Latino), 9 international. Average age 29. 126 applicants, 13% accepted, 4 enrolled. In 2011, 6 master's, 20 doctorates awarded. Terminal master's awarded for partial completion of doctoral program. *Degree requirements:* For master's, one foreign language, thesis (for some programs); for doctorate, one foreign language,

BAYLOR COLLEGE OF MEDICINE

Graduate School of Biomedical Sciences

In the world of scientific exploration, there are many mysteries to unravel. What areas of research fascinate you?

- The Graduate School of Biomedical Sciences at Baylor College of Medicine offers 12 Ph.D. programs, as well as a highly competitive M.D., Ph.D. program. Each of these paths has internationally recognized faculty, including members of the National Academy of Sciences, investigators in the Howard Hughes Medical Institute, and recipients of a variety of other prestigious awards.
- Ranked 1st in Texas in funding from the National Institutes of Health
- Ranked 2nd in the nation in federal funding for research and development in the biological sciences at universities and colleges by the National Science Foundation
- Ranked as one of the top 25 medical schools for research in *U.S. News & World Report*'s America's Best Graduate Schools 2013
- Total research support: $363 million ($280 million from federal sources)
- $38 million in the first year of funding from CPRIT, the Cancer Prevention and Research Institute of Texas

BCM
Baylor College *of* Medicine

www.bcm.edu/gradschool

comprehensive exam, thesis/dissertation. *Entrance requirements:* For master's and doctorate, GRE General Test, GRE Subject Test. Additional exam requirements/recommendations for international students: Required—TOEFL (minimum score 600 paper-based; 250 computer-based). *Application deadline:* For fall admission, 12/7 for domestic and international students. Application fee: $70. Electronic applications accepted. *Expenses: Tuition:* Full-time $40,848; part-time $1276 per credit hour. *Required fees:* $572; $286 per semester. *Financial support:* In 2011–12, 10 students received support, including 1 fellowship with full tuition reimbursement available (averaging $18,300 per year), 8 research assistantships with full tuition reimbursements available (averaging $19,300 per year), 1 teaching assistantship with full tuition reimbursement available (averaging $19,300 per year); Federal Work-Study, scholarships/grants, and traineeships also available. Financial award application deadline: 12/7; financial award applicants required to submit FAFSA. *Unit head:* Dr. Ulla Hansen, Director, 617-353-2432, Fax: 617-353-6340, E-mail: uhansen@bu.edu. *Application contact:* Meredith Canode, Academic Administrator, 617-353-2432, Fax: 617-353-6340, E-mail: mcanode@bu.edu. Web site: http://www.bu.edu/mcbb/.

Boston University, School of Medicine, Division of Graduate Medical Sciences, Department of Biochemistry, Boston, MA 02118. Offers MA, PhD, MD/PhD. Part-time programs available. *Faculty:* 41 full-time (17 women), 11 part-time/adjunct (5 women). *Students:* 29 full-time (15 women), 2 part-time (1 woman); includes 4 minority (3 Asian, non-Hispanic/Latino; 1 Hispanic/Latino), 14 international. Average age 28. 32 applicants, 25% accepted, 4 enrolled. In 2011, 2 master's, 4 doctorates awarded. Terminal master's awarded for partial completion of doctoral program. *Degree requirements:* For master's, thesis or alternative, qualifying exam; for doctorate, thesis/dissertation, qualifying exam. *Entrance requirements:* For master's and doctorate, GRE General Test, GRE Subject Test. Additional exam requirements/recommendations for international students: Required—TOEFL. *Application deadline:* For fall admission, 1/15 priority date for domestic students; for spring admission, 10/15 priority date for domestic students. Application fee: $75. Electronic applications accepted. *Expenses: Tuition:* Full-time $40,848; part-time $1276 per credit hour. *Required fees:* $572; $286 per semester. *Financial support:* In 2011–12, 2 fellowships (averaging $30,500 per year), research assistantships (averaging $30,500 per year) were awarded; Federal Work-Study, scholarships/grants, and traineeships also available. Financial award applicants required to submit FAFSA. *Faculty research:* Extracellular matrix, gene expression, receptors, growth control. *Unit head:* Dr. David A. Harris, Chair, 617-638-5090. *Application contact:* Dr. Barbara Schreiber, Director of the Graduate Program, 617-638-5094, E-mail: schreibe@bu.edu. Web site: http://www.bumc.bu.edu/biochemistry/.

Boston University, School of Medicine, Division of Graduate Medical Sciences, Program in Cell and Molecular Biology, Boston, MA 02118. Offers PhD, MD/PhD. *Faculty:* 10 full-time (5 women). *Students:* 35 full-time (20 women); includes 5 minority (1 Black or African American, non-Hispanic/Latino; 2 Asian, non-Hispanic/Latino; 1 Hispanic/Latino; 1 Two or more races, non-Hispanic/Latino), 6 international. Average age 27. 52 applicants, 19% accepted, 7 enrolled. In 2011, 7 doctorates awarded. *Degree requirements:* For doctorate, thesis/dissertation. *Entrance requirements:* For doctorate, GRE General Test, GRE Subject Test. Additional exam requirements/recommendations for international students: Required—TOEFL. *Application deadline:* For fall admission, 1/15 priority date for domestic students; for spring admission, 10/15 priority date for domestic students. Application fee: $75. Electronic applications accepted. *Expenses: Tuition:* Full-time $40,848; part-time $1276 per credit hour. *Required fees:* $572; $286 per semester. *Financial support:* In 2011–12, 8 fellowships (averaging $30,500 per year), 6 research assistantships (averaging $30,500 per year) were awarded; Federal Work-Study, scholarships/grants, and traineeships also available. Financial award applicants required to submit FAFSA. *Unit head:* Dr. Vickery Trinkaus Randall, Director, 617-638-6099, Fax: 617-638-5337, E-mail: vickery@bu.edu. *Application contact:* Dr. Vickery Trinkaus-Randall, Program Director, 617-638-6099, Fax: 617-638-5337, E-mail: vickery@bu.edu. Web site: http://www.bumc.bu.edu/cmbio/.

Brandeis University, Graduate School of Arts and Sciences, Program in Molecular and Cell Biology, Waltham, MA 02454-9110. Offers genetics (PhD); microbiology (PhD); molecular and cell biology (MS, PhD); molecular biology (PhD); neurobiology (PhD); quantitative biology (PhD). *Faculty:* 27 full-time (11 women), 4 part-time/adjunct (1 woman). *Students:* 65 full-time (36 women); includes 8 minority (4 Black or African American, non-Hispanic/Latino; 1 American Indian or Alaska Native, non-Hispanic/Latino; 1 Asian, non-Hispanic/Latino; 2 Hispanic/Latino), 14 international. 195 applicants, 26% accepted, 21 enrolled. In 2011, 4 master's, 6 doctorates awarded. Terminal master's awarded for partial completion of doctoral program. *Degree requirements:* For master's, thesis or alternative, research project, research lab, or project lab; for doctorate, comprehensive exam, thesis/dissertation, journal clubs; research seminar; colloquia; teaching requirement; qualifying exam. *Entrance requirements:* For master's, GRE General Test; MCAT may be substituted for the GRE exam for applicants to the M.S. program., official transcript(s), resume, 3 letters of recommendation, statement of purpose; for doctorate, GRE General Test, official transcript(s), resume, 3 letters of recommendation, statement of purpose. Additional exam requirements/recommendations for international students: Required—TOEFL (minimum score 600 paper-based; 250 computer-based; 100 iBT); Recommended—IELTS (minimum score 7). *Application deadline:* For fall admission, 1/15 priority date for domestic students; for spring admission, 11/15 for domestic students. Applications are processed on a rolling basis. Application fee: $75. Electronic applications accepted. *Financial support:* In 2011–12, 17 fellowships with full tuition reimbursements (averaging $29,580 per year), 31 research assistantships with full tuition reimbursements (averaging $29,580 per year), teaching assistantships with partial tuition reimbursements (averaging $3,200 per year) were awarded; scholarships/grants, health care benefits, tuition waivers (full and partial), and unspecified assistantships also available. Financial award application deadline: 4/15; financial award applicants required to submit FAFSA. *Faculty research:* Molecular biology, cell biology, biology, structural biology, immunology, developmental biology, neurobiology, DNA, RNA. *Unit head:* Dr. Bruce Goode, Chair, 781-736-2464, Fax: 781-736-3107, E-mail: goode@brandeis.edu. *Application contact:* Dr. Jessica Maryott, Department Administrator, 781-736-3100, Fax: 781-736-3107, E-mail: jmaryott@brandeis.edu. Web site: http://www.bio.brandeis.edu/grad/mcb/mcb_phd.html.

Brown University, Graduate School, Division of Biology and Medicine, Program in Molecular Biology, Cell Biology, and Biochemistry, Providence, RI 02912. Offers biochemistry (M Med Sc, Sc M, PhD), including biochemistry (Sc M, PhD), biology (Sc M, PhD), medical science (M Med Sc, PhD); biology (MA); cell biology (M Med Sc, Sc M, PhD), including biochemistry (Sc M, PhD), biology (Sc M, PhD), medical science (M Med Sc, PhD); developmental biology (M Med Sc, Sc M, PhD), including biochemistry (Sc M, PhD), biology (Sc M, PhD), medical science (M Med Sc, PhD); immunology (M Med Sc, Sc M, PhD), including biochemistry (Sc M, PhD), biology (Sc M, PhD), medical science (M Med Sc, PhD); molecular microbiology (M Med Sc, Sc M, PhD), including biochemistry (Sc M, PhD), biology (Sc M, PhD), medical science (M Med Sc, PhD); MD/PhD. Part-time programs available. Terminal master's awarded for partial completion of doctoral program. *Degree requirements:* For master's, thesis (for some programs); for doctorate, one foreign language, thesis/dissertation, preliminary exam. *Entrance requirements:* For master's and doctorate, GRE General Test, GRE Subject Test. Additional exam requirements/recommendations for international students: Required—TOEFL. Electronic applications accepted. *Faculty research:* Molecular genetics, gene regulation.

California Institute of Technology, Division of Biology, Program in Cell Biology and Biophysics, Pasadena, CA 91125-0001. Offers PhD. *Degree requirements:* For doctorate, thesis/dissertation, qualifying exam. *Entrance requirements:* For doctorate, GRE General Test.

Carnegie Mellon University, Mellon College of Science, Department of Biological Sciences, Pittsburgh, PA 15213-3891. Offers biochemistry (PhD); biophysics (PhD); cell biology (PhD); computational biology (MS, PhD); developmental biology (PhD); genetics (PhD); molecular biology (PhD); neuroscience (PhD). *Degree requirements:* For doctorate, comprehensive exam, thesis/dissertation. *Entrance requirements:* For doctorate, GRE General Test, GRE Subject Test, interview. Electronic applications accepted. *Faculty research:* Genetic structure, function, and regulation; protein structure and function; biological membranes; biological spectroscopy.

Case Western Reserve University, School of Medicine and School of Graduate Studies, Graduate Programs in Medicine, Department of Anatomy, Cleveland, OH 44106. Offers applied anatomy (MS); biological anthropology (MS); cellular biology (MS); MD/MS. Part-time programs available. *Degree requirements:* For master's, comprehensive exam, thesis (for some programs). *Entrance requirements:* For master's, GRE General Test. Additional exam requirements/recommendations for international students: Required—TOEFL. *Faculty research:* Hypoxia, cell injury, biochemical aberration occurrences in ischemic tissue, human functional morphology, evolutionary morphology.

Case Western Reserve University, School of Medicine and School of Graduate Studies, Graduate Programs in Medicine, Department of Molecular Biology and Microbiology, Cleveland, OH 44106-4960. Offers cellular biology (PhD); microbiology (PhD); molecular biology (PhD); molecular virology (PhD); MD/PhD. Students are admitted to an integrated Biomedical Sciences Training Program involving 11 basic science programs at Case Western Reserve University. *Degree requirements:* For doctorate, thesis/dissertation. *Entrance requirements:* For doctorate, GRE General Test, GRE Subject Test. Additional exam requirements/recommendations for international students: Required—TOEFL. Electronic applications accepted. *Faculty research:* Gene expression in eukaryotic and prokaryotic systems; microbial physiology; intracellular transport and signaling; mechanisms of oncogenesis; molecular mechanisms of RNA processing, editing, and catalysis.

Case Western Reserve University, School of Medicine and School of Graduate Studies, Graduate Programs in Medicine, Program in Cell Biology, Cleveland, OH 44106. Offers PhD. *Degree requirements:* For doctorate, thesis/dissertation. *Entrance requirements:* For doctorate, GRE General Test, GRE Subject Test, previous course work in biochemistry. Additional exam requirements/recommendations for international students: Required—TOEFL. Electronic applications accepted. *Faculty research:* Macromolecular transport, membrane traffic, signal transduction, nuclear organization, lipid metabolism.

Case Western Reserve University, School of Medicine and School of Graduate Studies, Graduate Programs in Medicine, Programs in Molecular and Cellular Basis of Disease/Pathology, Cleveland, OH 44106. Offers cancer biology (PhD); cell biology (MS, PhD); immunology (MS, PhD); pathology (MS, PhD); MD/PhD. Terminal master's awarded for partial completion of doctoral program. *Degree requirements:* For master's, thesis; for doctorate, thesis/dissertation. *Entrance requirements:* For master's and doctorate, GRE General Test, GRE Subject Test. Additional exam requirements/recommendations for international students: Required—TOEFL (minimum score 550 paper-based; 213 computer-based). Electronic applications accepted. *Faculty research:* Neurobiology, molecular biology, cancer biology, biomaterials, biocompatibility.

The Catholic University of America, School of Arts and Sciences, Department of Biology, Washington, DC 20064. Offers cell and microbial biology (MS, PhD), including cell biology, microbiology; clinical laboratory science (MS, PhD); MSLS/MS. Part-time programs available. *Faculty:* 9 full-time (5 women), 3 part-time/adjunct (2 women). *Students:* 19 full-time (16 women), 26 part-time (17 women); includes 10 minority (3 Black or African American, non-Hispanic/Latino; 6 Asian, non-Hispanic/Latino; 1 Hispanic/Latino), 20 international. Average age 29. 53 applicants, 62% accepted, 15 enrolled. In 2011, 1 master's, 2 doctorates awarded. *Degree requirements:* For master's, comprehensive exam, thesis or alternative; for doctorate, comprehensive exam, thesis/dissertation. *Entrance requirements:* For master's and doctorate, GRE General Test, GRE Subject Test, statement of purpose, official copies of academic transcripts, three letters of recommendation. Additional exam requirements/recommendations for international students: Required—TOEFL (minimum score 580 paper-based; 237 computer-based). *Application deadline:* For fall admission, 8/1 priority date for domestic students, 7/15 for international students; for spring admission, 12/1 priority date for domestic students, 10/15 for international students. Applications are processed on a rolling basis. Application fee: $55. Electronic applications accepted. *Expenses: Tuition:* Full-time $35,260; part-time $1380 per credit. *Required fees:* $80; $40 per semester hour. One-time fee: $425. *Financial support:* Fellowships, research assistantships, teaching assistantships, Federal Work-Study, scholarships/grants, tuition waivers (full and partial), and unspecified assistantships available. Financial award application deadline: 2/1; financial award applicants required to submit FAFSA. *Faculty research:* Cell and microbiology, molecular biology of cell proliferation, cellular effects of electromagnetic radiation, biotechnology. *Total annual research expenditures:* $1.4 million. *Unit head:* Dr. Venigalla Rao, Chair, 202-319-5271, Fax: 202-319-5721, E-mail: rao@cua.edu. *Application contact:* Andrew Woodall, Director of Graduate Admissions, 202-319-5057, Fax: 202-319-6533, E-mail: cua-admissions@cua.edu. Web site: http://biology.cua.edu/.

Colorado State University, Graduate School, Program in Cell and Molecular Biology, Fort Collins, CO 80523-1618. Offers MS, PhD. *Students:* 34 full-time (20 women), 29 part-time (14 women); includes 10 minority (2 Black or African American, non-Hispanic/Latino; 2 Asian, non-Hispanic/Latino; 5 Hispanic/Latino; 1 Two or more races, non-Hispanic/Latino), 19 international. Average age 30. 79 applicants, 19% accepted, 14 enrolled. In 2011, 2 master's, 4 doctorates awarded. *Degree requirements:* For master's, comprehensive exam, thesis; for doctorate, comprehensive exam, thesis/dissertation. *Entrance requirements:* For master's and doctorate, GRE General Test, GRE Subject Test in biology (strongly recommended), minimum GPA of 3.0; BA/BS in biology, biochemistry, physics; calculus sequence, letters of recommendation. Additional exam requirements/recommendations for international students: Required—TOEFL (minimum score 625 paper-based; 263 computer-based; 107 iBT). *Application deadline:* For fall admission, 1/1 priority date for domestic students, 1/1 for international students. Application fee: $50. Electronic applications accepted. *Expenses:* Tuition, state resident: full-time $7992. Tuition, nonresident: full-time $19,592. *Required fees:* $1735; $58 per credit. *Financial support:* In 2011–12, 8 students received support, including 3 research assistantships with full tuition reimbursements available (averaging $11,147 per year), 5 teaching assistantships with full tuition reimbursements available (averaging $15,015 per year); fellowships with partial tuition reimbursements available, traineeships, and unspecified assistantships also available. Financial award application

deadline: 1/1; financial award applicants required to submit FAFSA. *Faculty research:* Regulation of gene expression, cancer biology, plant molecular genetics, reproductive physiology, infectious diseases. *Total annual research expenditures:* $2,294. *Unit head:* Dr. Paul J. Laybourn, Director, 970-491-5100, Fax: 970-491-0623, E-mail: paul.laybourn@colostate.edu. *Application contact:* Lori Williams, Administrative Assistant, 970-491-0241, Fax: 970-491-0623, E-mail: cmb@colostate.edu. Web site: http://cmb.colostate.edu/.

Columbia University, College of Physicians and Surgeons, Department of Anatomy and Cell Biology, New York, NY 10032. Offers anatomy (M Phil, MA, PhD); anatomy and cell biology (PhD); MD/PhD. Only candidates for the PhD are admitted. Terminal master's awarded for partial completion of doctoral program. *Degree requirements:* For doctorate, thesis/dissertation, oral exam. *Entrance requirements:* For master's and doctorate, GRE General Test. Additional exam requirements/recommendations for international students: Required—TOEFL. *Faculty research:* Protein sorting, membrane biophysics, muscle energetics, neuroendocrinology, developmental biology, cytoskeleton, transcription factors.

Columbia University, College of Physicians and Surgeons, Integrated Program in Cellular, Molecular, Structural and Genetic Studies, New York, NY 10032. Offers PhD. Terminal master's awarded for partial completion of doctoral program. *Degree requirements:* For doctorate, thesis/dissertation. *Entrance requirements:* For doctorate, GRE General Test, GRE Subject Test. Additional exam requirements/recommendations for international students: Required—TOEFL. *Expenses:* Contact institution. *Faculty research:* Transcription, macromolecular sorting, gene expression during development, cellular interaction.

Cornell University, Graduate School, Graduate Fields of Agriculture and Life Sciences, Field of Biochemistry, Molecular and Cell Biology, Ithaca, NY 14853-0001. Offers biochemistry (PhD); biophysics (PhD); cell biology (PhD); molecular and cell biology (PhD); molecular biology (PhD). *Faculty:* 62 full-time (17 women). *Students:* 91 full-time (46 women); includes 12 minority (1 Black or African American, non-Hispanic/Latino; 8 Asian, non-Hispanic/Latino; 2 Hispanic/Latino; 1 Two or more races, non-Hispanic/Latino), 34 international. Average age 26. 247 applicants, 8% accepted, 17 enrolled. In 2011, 11 doctorates awarded. *Degree requirements:* For doctorate, comprehensive exam, thesis/dissertation, 2 semesters of teaching experience. *Entrance requirements:* For doctorate, GRE General Test, GRE Subject Test (biology, chemistry, physics, biochemistry, cell and molecular biology), 3 letters of recommendation. Additional exam requirements/recommendations for international students: Required—TOEFL (minimum score 600 paper-based; 250 computer-based; 77 iBT). *Application deadline:* For fall admission, 1/5 for domestic students. Application fee: $95. Electronic applications accepted. *Financial support:* In 2011–12, 88 students received support, including 26 fellowships with full tuition reimbursements available, 46 research assistantships with full tuition reimbursements available, 14 teaching assistantships with full tuition reimbursements available; institutionally sponsored loans, scholarships/grants, health care benefits, tuition waivers (full and partial), and unspecified assistantships also available. Financial award applicants required to submit FAFSA. *Faculty research:* Biophysics, structural biology. *Unit head:* Director of Graduate Studies, 607-255-2100, Fax: 607-255-2100. *Application contact:* Graduate Field Assistant, 607-255-2100, Fax: 607-255-2100, E-mail: bmcb@cornell.edu. Web site: http://www.gradschool.cornell.edu/fields.php?id-43&a-2.

Cornell University, Graduate School, Graduate Fields of Agriculture and Life Sciences, Field of Computational Biology, Ithaca, NY 14853-0001. Offers computational behavioral biology (PhD); computational biology (PhD); computational cell biology (PhD); computational ecology (PhD); computational macromolecular biology (PhD); computational organismal biology (PhD). *Faculty:* 37 full-time (5 women). *Students:* 22 full-time (8 women); includes 4 minority (3 Asian, non-Hispanic/Latino; 1 Native Hawaiian or other Pacific Islander, non-Hispanic/Latino), 9 international. Average age 26. 145 applicants, 7% accepted, 10 enrolled. In 2011, 2 doctorates awarded. *Degree requirements:* For doctorate, comprehensive exam, thesis/dissertation, 2 semesters of teaching experience. *Entrance requirements:* For doctorate, GRE General Test, GRE Subject Test (biology), 2 letters of recommendation. Additional exam requirements/recommendations for international students: Required—TOEFL (minimum score 550 paper-based; 213 computer-based; 77 iBT). *Application deadline:* For fall admission, 2/1 priority date for domestic students. Application fee: $95. Electronic applications accepted. *Financial support:* In 2011–12, 17 fellowships with full tuition reimbursements, 4 research assistantships with full tuition reimbursements, 1 teaching assistantship with full tuition reimbursement were awarded; institutionally sponsored loans, scholarships/grants, health care benefits, tuition waivers (full and partial), and unspecified assistantships also available. Financial award applicants required to submit FAFSA. *Faculty research:* Computational behavioral biology, computational biology, computational cell biology, computational ecology, computational genetics, computational macromolecular biology, computational organismal biology. *Unit head:* Dr. Andrew Clark, Director of Graduate Studies, 607-255-5488, E-mail: ac347@cornell.edu. *Application contact:* Graduate School Application Requests, 607-255-5816, E-mail: gradadmissions@cornell.edu. Web site: http://www.gradschool.cornell.edu/fields.php?id-4A.

Cornell University, Graduate School, Graduate Fields of Agriculture and Life Sciences, Field of Zoology and Wildlife Conservation, Ithaca, NY 14853-0001. Offers animal cytology (MS, PhD); comparative and functional anatomy (MS, PhD); developmental biology (MS, PhD); ecology (MS, PhD); histology (MS, PhD). *Faculty:* 24 full-time (7 women). *Students:* 5 full-time (4 women); includes 1 minority (Two or more races, non-Hispanic/Latino), 2 international. Average age 29. 7 applicants, 14% accepted, 1 enrolled. In 2011, 2 doctorates awarded. *Degree requirements:* For doctorate, comprehensive exam, thesis/dissertation, 2 semesters of teaching experience. *Entrance requirements:* For doctorate, GRE General Test, GRE Subject Test (biology), 2 letters of recommendation. Additional exam requirements/recommendations for international students: Required—TOEFL (minimum score 550 paper-based; 213 computer-based; 77 iBT). *Application deadline:* For fall admission, 2/1 priority date for domestic students. Application fee: $95. Electronic applications accepted. *Financial support:* In 2011–12, 3 research assistantships with full tuition reimbursements, 1 teaching assistantship with full tuition reimbursement were awarded; fellowships with full tuition reimbursements, institutionally sponsored loans, scholarships/grants, health care benefits, tuition waivers (full and partial), and unspecified assistantships also available. Financial award applicants required to submit FAFSA. *Faculty research:* Organismal biology, functional morphology, biomechanics, comparative vertebrate anatomy, comparative invertebrate anatomy, paleontology. *Unit head:* Director of Graduate Studies, 607-253-3276, Fax: 607-253-3756. *Application contact:* Graduate Field Assistant, 607-253-3276, Fax: 607-253-3756, E-mail: graduate_edcvm@cornell.edu. Web site: http://www.gradschool.cornell.edu/fields.php?id-65&a-2.

Dartmouth College, Graduate Program in Molecular and Cellular Biology, Hanover, NH 03755. Offers PhD, MD/PhD. *Entrance requirements:* For doctorate, GRE General Test, letters of recommendation. Additional exam requirements/recommendations for international students: Required—TOEFL (minimum score 450 paper-based; 90 iBT) or IELTS (minimum score 7). Electronic applications accepted.

Drexel University, College of Medicine, Biomedical Graduate Programs, Interdisciplinary Program in Molecular and Cell Biology and Genetics, Philadelphia, PA 19104-2875. Offers MS, PhD, MD/PhD. Terminal master's awarded for partial completion of doctoral program. *Degree requirements:* For master's, comprehensive exam, thesis; for doctorate, thesis/dissertation, qualifying exam. *Entrance requirements:* For master's, GRE General Test, minimum GPA of 2.75; for doctorate, GRE General Test, minimum GPA of 3.0. Additional exam requirements/recommendations for international students: Required—TOEFL. Electronic applications accepted. *Faculty research:* Molecular anatomy, biochemistry, medical biotechnology, molecular pathology, microbiology and immunology.

Duke University, Graduate School, Department of Biological Anthropology and Anatomy, Durham, NC 27710. Offers cellular and molecular biology (PhD); gross anatomy and physical anthropology (PhD), including comparative morphology of human and non-human primates, primate social behavior, vertebrate paleontology; neuroanatomy (PhD). *Faculty:* 9 full-time. *Students:* 16 full-time (10 women); includes 3 minority (1 Black or African American, non Hispanic/Latino; 2 Hispanic/Latino), 1 international. 71 applicants, 7% accepted, 4 enrolled. In 2011, 2 doctorates awarded. *Degree requirements:* For doctorate, one foreign language, thesis/dissertation. *Entrance requirements:* For doctorate, GRE General Test. Additional exam requirements/recommendations for international students: Required—TOEFL (minimum score 550 paper-based; 213 computer-based; 83 iBT), IELTS (minimum score 7). *Application deadline:* For fall admission, 12/8 priority date for domestic students, 12/8 for international students. Application fee: $75. Electronic applications accepted. *Expenses: Tuition:* Full-time $40,720. *Required fees:* $3107. *Financial support:* Fellowships, teaching assistantships, and Federal Work-Study available. Financial award application deadline: 12/31. *Unit head:* Daniel Schmitt, Director of Graduate Studies, 919-684-4124, Fax: 919-684-8542, E-mail: mlsquire@duke.edu. *Application contact:* Elizabeth Hutton, Director of Admissions, 919-684-3913, Fax: 919-684-2277, E-mail: grad-admissions@duke.edu. Web site: http://www.baa.duke.edu/.

Duke University, Graduate School, Department of Cell Biology, Durham, NC 27710. Offers PhD. *Faculty:* 21 full-time. *Students:* 51 full-time (27 women); includes 12 minority (1 Black or African American, non-Hispanic/Latino; 5 Asian, non-Hispanic/Latino; 6 Hispanic/Latino), 8 international. 218 applicants, 24% accepted, 16 enrolled. In 2011, 6 doctorates awarded. *Degree requirements:* For doctorate, thesis/dissertation. *Entrance requirements:* For doctorate, GRE General Test, GRE Subject Test in biology, chemistry, cell and molecular biology (recommended). Additional exam requirements/recommendations for international students: Required—TOEFL (minimum score 550 paper-based; 213 computer-based; 83 iBT), IELTS (minimum score 7). *Application deadline:* For fall admission, 12/8 priority date for domestic students, 12/8 for international students. Applications are processed on a rolling basis. Application fee: $75. Electronic applications accepted. *Expenses: Tuition:* Full-time $40,720. *Required fees:* $3107. *Financial support:* Fellowships, research assistantships, teaching assistantships, and Federal Work-Study available. Financial award application deadline: 12/8. *Unit head:* Chris Nicchitta, Director of Graduate Studies, 919-684-8085, Fax: 919-684-8592, E-mail: teresa.jenkins@duke.edu. *Application contact:* Elizabeth Hutton, Director of Admissions, 919-684-3913, Fax: 919-684-2277, E-mail: grad-admissions@duke.edu. Web site: http://www.cellbio.duke.edu/graduate/gradprogram.html.

Duke University, Graduate School, Program in Cellular and Molecular Biology, Durham, NC 27710. Offers Certificate. Students must be enrolled in a participating PhD program (biology, cell biology, immunology, molecular genetics, neurobiology, pathology, pharmacology). *Faculty:* 144 full-time. *Students:* 17 full-time (4 women); includes 6 minority (2 Asian, non-Hispanic/Latino; 4 Hispanic/Latino), 3 international. 218 applicants, 24% accepted, 16 enrolled. *Entrance requirements:* Additional exam requirements/recommendations for international students: Required—TOEFL (minimum score 550 paper-based; 213 computer-based; 83 iBT), IELTS (minimum score 7). *Application deadline:* For fall admission, 12/8 priority date for domestic students, 12/8 for international students. Application fee: $75. Electronic applications accepted. *Expenses: Tuition:* Full-time $40,720. *Required fees:* $3107. *Financial support:* Fellowships available. Financial award application deadline: 12/8. *Unit head:* Dr. Margarethe Kuehn, Director of Graduate Studies, 919-684-6559, Fax: 919-684-8346, E-mail: carol.richardson@duke.edu. *Application contact:* Elizabeth Hutton, Director of Admissions, 919-684-3913, Fax: 919-684-3913, E-mail: grad-admissions@duke.edu. Web site: http://cmb.duke.edu/.

East Carolina University, Brody School of Medicine, Department of Anatomy and Cell Biology, Greenville, NC 27858-4353. Offers PhD. *Degree requirements:* For doctorate, comprehensive exam, thesis/dissertation. *Entrance requirements:* For doctorate, GRE General Test. Additional exam requirements/recommendations for international students: Required—TOEFL. *Application deadline:* For fall admission, 6/1 priority date for domestic students. Applications are processed on a rolling basis. Application fee: $50. *Expenses:* Tuition, state resident: full-time $3557; part-time $444.63 per semester hour. Tuition, nonresident: full-time $14,351; part-time $1793.88 per semester hour. *Required fees:* $2016; $252 per semester hour. Part-time tuition and fees vary according to course load, campus/location and program. *Financial support:* Fellowships with full tuition reimbursements and health care benefits available. Financial award application deadline: 6/1. *Faculty research:* Kinesin motors during slow matogensis, mitochondria and peroxisomes in obesity, ovarian innervation, tight junction function and regulation. *Unit head:* Dr. Cheryl Knudson, Chairman, 252-744-2852, Fax: 252-744-2850, E-mail: knudsonc@ecu.edu. *Application contact:* Dr. Ron Dudek, Senior Director of Graduate Studies, 252-744-2863, Fax: 252-744-2850, E-mail: dudekr@ecu.edu. Web site: http://www.ecu.edu/cs-dhs/anatomy/gradProg.cfm.

Eastern Michigan University, Graduate School, College of Arts and Sciences, Department of Biology, Ypsilanti, MI 48197. Offers cell and molecular biology (MS); community college biology teaching (MS); ecology and organismal biology (MS); general biology (MS); water resources (MS). Part-time and evening/weekend programs available. Postbaccalaureate distance learning degree programs offered (minimal on-campus study). *Faculty:* 20 full-time (4 women). *Students:* 12 full-time (7 women), 40 part-time (21 women); includes 3 minority (1 Black or African American, non-Hispanic/Latino; 1 Asian, non-Hispanic/Latino; 1 Two or more races, non-Hispanic/Latino), 12 international. Average age 27. 70 applicants, 43% accepted, 12 enrolled. In 2011, 19 degrees awarded. *Entrance requirements:* For master's, GRE General Test, GRE Subject Test. Additional exam requirements/recommendations for international students: Required—TOEFL. *Application deadline:* Applications are processed on a rolling basis. Application fee: $35. *Expenses:* Tuition, state resident: full-time $10,367; part-time $432 per credit hour. Tuition, nonresident: full-time $20,435; part-time $851 per credit hour. *Required fees:* $39 per credit hour. $46 per semester. One-time fee: $100. Tuition and fees vary according to course level, degree level and reciprocity agreements. *Financial support:* Fellowships, research assistantships with full tuition reimbursements, teaching assistantships with full tuition reimbursements, career-related internships or fieldwork, Federal Work-Study, institutionally sponsored loans, scholarships/grants, tuition waivers (partial), and unspecified assistantships available. Support available to part-time students. Financial award applicants required to submit FAFSA. *Unit head:* Dr. Marianne Laporte, Department Head, 734-487-4242, Fax: 734-487-9235, E-mail: mlaporte@emich.edu. *Application contact:* Graduate Admissions,

734-487-2400, Fax: 734-487-6559, E-mail: graduate.admissions@emich.edu. Web site: http://www.emich.edu/biology.

Eastern New Mexico University, Graduate School, College of Liberal Arts and Sciences, Department of Biology, Portales, NM 88130. Offers applied ecology (MS); cell, molecular biology and biotechnology (MS); education (non-thesis) (MS); microbiology (MS); plant biology (MS); zoology (MS). Part-time programs available. *Faculty:* 7 full-time (0 women). *Students:* 2 full-time (1 woman), 15 part-time (9 women); includes 7 minority (5 Hispanic/Latino; 2 Two or more races, non-Hispanic/Latino), 2 international. Average age 26. 17 applicants, 82% accepted, 3 enrolled. In 2011, 4 master's awarded. *Degree requirements:* For master's, comprehensive exam, thesis optional. *Entrance requirements:* For master's, GRE, minimum GPA of 3.0, 2 letters of recommendation, statement of research interest, bachelor's degree related to field of study or proof of common knowledge. Additional exam requirements/recommendations for international students: Required—TOEFL (minimum score 550 paper-based; 213 computer-based; 79 iBT), IELTS (minimum score 6). *Application deadline:* For fall admission, 7/20 priority date for domestic students, 6/20 for international students; for spring admission, 12/15 priority date for domestic students, 11/15 for international students. Applications are processed on a rolling basis. Application fee: $10. Electronic applications accepted. *Financial support:* In 2011–12, 8 teaching assistantships with partial tuition reimbursements (averaging $8,500 per year) were awarded; scholarships/grants and unspecified assistantships also available. Support available to part-time students. Financial award applicants required to submit FAFSA. *Unit head:* Dr. Zach Jones, Graduate Coordinator, 575-562-2723, Fax: 575-562-2192, E-mail: zach.jones@enmu.edu. *Application contact:* Sharon Potter, Department Secretary, Biology and Physical Sciences, 575-562-2174, Fax: 575-562-2192, E-mail: sharon.potter@enmu.edu. Web site: http://liberal-arts.enmu.edu/biology/graduate.shtml.

East Tennessee State University, James H. Quillen College of Medicine, Biomedical Science Graduate Program, Johnson City, TN 37614. Offers anatomy and cell biology (PhD); biochemistry and molecular biology (PhD); microbiology (PhD); pharmaceutical sciences (PhD); pharmacology (PhD); physiology (PhD); quantitative biosciences (PhD). *Faculty:* 33 full-time (6 women). *Students:* 29 full-time (15 women), 2 part-time (both women); includes 4 minority (1 Black or African American, non-Hispanic/Latino; 1 Asian, non-Hispanic/Latino; 2 Hispanic/Latino), 6 international. Average age 29. 76 applicants, 12% accepted, 7 enrolled. In 2011, 1 doctorate awarded. *Degree requirements:* For doctorate, thesis/dissertation, comprehensive qualifying exam. *Entrance requirements:* For doctorate, GRE General Test, GRE Subject Test. Additional exam requirements/recommendations for international students: Required—TOEFL (minimum score 550 paper-based; 213 computer-based; 79 iBT). *Application deadline:* For fall admission, 3/15 priority date for domestic students, 3/1 for international students. Application fee: $35 ($45 for international students). Electronic applications accepted. *Expenses:* Contact institution. *Financial support:* In 2011–12, 29 students received support, including 29 research assistantships with full tuition reimbursements available (averaging $19,000 per year); career-related internships or fieldwork, institutionally sponsored loans, scholarships/grants, and unspecified assistantships also available. Financial award application deadline: 7/1; financial award applicants required to submit FAFSA. *Faculty research:* Cardiovascular biology, neuroscience, infectious disease, cancer, inflammatory disease. *Total annual research expenditures:* $3.6 million. *Unit head:* Dr. Mitchell E. Robinson, Associate Dean/Program Director, 423-439-2031, Fax: 423-439-2140, E-mail: robinson@etsu.edu. *Application contact:* Shella Bennett, Graduate Specialist, 423-439-4708, Fax: 423-439-5624, E-mail: bennetsg@etsu.edu.

Emory University, Laney Graduate School, Division of Biological and Biomedical Sciences, Program in Biochemistry, Cell and Developmental Biology, Atlanta, GA 30322. Offers PhD. *Faculty:* 52 full-time (10 women). *Students:* 53 full-time (34 women); includes 9 minority (1 Black or African American, non-Hispanic/Latino; 4 Asian, non-Hispanic/Latino; 4 Hispanic/Latino), 10 international. Average age 27. 147 applicants, 11% accepted, 7 enrolled. In 2011, 5 doctorates awarded. *Degree requirements:* For doctorate, comprehensive exam, thesis/dissertation. *Entrance requirements:* For doctorate, GRE General Test, minimum GPA of 3.0 in science course work (recommended). Additional exam requirements/recommendations for international students: Required—TOEFL. *Application deadline:* For fall admission, 1/3 for domestic students, 1/1 for international students. Application fee: $75. Electronic applications accepted. *Expenses: Tuition:* Full-time $34,800. *Required fees:* $1300. *Financial support:* In 2011–12, 18 students received support, including 18 fellowships with full tuition reimbursements available (averaging $26,500 per year); institutionally sponsored loans, scholarships/grants, health care benefits, and tuition waivers (full) also available. *Faculty research:* Signal transduction, molecular biology, enzymes and cofactors, receptor and ion channel function, membrane biology. *Unit head:* Dr. Richard Kahn, Program Director, 404-727-3561, Fax: 404-727-3746, E-mail: rkahn@emory.edu. *Application contact:* Kathy Smith, Director of Recruitment and Admissions, 404-727-2547, Fax: 404-727-3322, E-mail: kathy.smith@emory.edu. Web site: http://www.biomed.emory.edu/PROGRAM_SITES/BCDB/.

Emporia State University, Graduate School, College of Liberal Arts and Sciences, Department of Biological Sciences, Emporia, KS 66801-5087. Offers botany (MS); environmental biology (MS); general biology (MS); microbial and cellular biology (MS); zoology (MS). Part-time programs available. *Faculty:* 13 full-time (3 women), 1 part-time/adjunct (0 women). *Students:* 8 full-time (5 women), 21 part-time (10 women); includes 3 minority (1 Black or African American, non-Hispanic/Latino; 1 Hispanic/Latino; 1 Two or more races, non-Hispanic/Latino), 6 international. 14 applicants, 86% accepted, 7 enrolled. In 2011, 5 master's awarded. *Degree requirements:* For master's, comprehensive exam or thesis. *Entrance requirements:* For master's, GRE, appropriate undergraduate degree, interview, letters of reference. Additional exam requirements/recommendations for international students: Required—TOEFL (minimum score 520 paper-based; 133 computer-based; 68 iBT). *Application deadline:* For fall admission, 8/15 priority date for domestic students. Applications are processed on a rolling basis. Application fee: $30 ($75 for international students). Electronic applications accepted. *Expenses:* Tuition, state resident: full-time $2342; part-time $195 per credit hour. Tuition, nonresident: full-time $7254; part-time $605 per credit hour. *Required fees:* $66 per credit hour. Tuition and fees vary according to campus/location. *Financial support:* In 2011–12, 8 research assistantships with full tuition reimbursements (averaging $6,589 per year), 10 teaching assistantships with full tuition reimbursements (averaging $7,419 per year) were awarded; career-related internships or fieldwork, Federal Work-Study, institutionally sponsored loans, health care benefits, and unspecified assistantships also available. Financial award application deadline: 3/15; financial award applicants required to submit FAFSA. *Faculty research:* Fisheries, range, and wildlife management; aquatic, plant, grassland, vertebrate, and invertebrate ecology; mammalian and plant systematics, taxonomy, and evolution; immunology, virology, and molecular biology. *Unit head:* Dr. R. Brent Thomas, Chair, 620-341-5311, Fax: 620-341-5608, E-mail: rthomas2@emporia.edu. *Application contact:* Dr. Scott Crupper, Graduate Coordinator, 620-341-5621, Fax: 620-341-5607, E-mail: scrupper@emporia.edu. Web site: http://www.emporia.edu/info/degrees-courses/grad/biology.

Florida Institute of Technology, Graduate Programs, College of Science, Department of Biological Sciences, Program in Cell and Molecular Biology, Melbourne, FL 32901-6975. Offers MS. Part-time programs available. *Faculty:* 16 full-time (2 women). *Students:* 5 full-time (3 women), 2 part-time (1 woman); includes 1 minority (Hispanic/Latino), 1 international. Average age 27. 56 applicants, 5% accepted, 3 enrolled. In 2011, 2 master's awarded. *Degree requirements:* For master's, research, seminar, internship, or summer lab. *Entrance requirements:* For master's, GRE General Test, 3 letters of recommendation, minimum GPA of 3.0, resume, statement of objectives. Additional exam requirements/recommendations for international students: Required—TOEFL (minimum score 550 paper-based; 213 computer-based; 79 iBT). *Application deadline:* Applications are processed on a rolling basis. Application fee: $0. Electronic applications accepted. *Expenses: Tuition:* Full-time $19,620; part-time $1090 per credit hour. Tuition and fees vary according to campus/location. *Financial support:* Career-related internships or fieldwork, institutionally sponsored loans, tuition waivers (partial), unspecified assistantships, and tuition remissions available. Support available to part-time students. Financial award application deadline: 3/1; financial award applicants required to submit FAFSA. *Faculty research:* Changes in DNA molecule and differential expression of genetic information during aging. *Total annual research expenditures:* $1.9 million. *Unit head:* Dr. Richard B. Aronson, Department Head, 321-674-8034, Fax: 321-674-7238, E-mail: raronson@fit.edu. *Application contact:* Cheryl A. Brown, Associate Director of Graduate Admission, 321-674-7581, Fax: 321-723-9468, E-mail: cbrown@fit.edu. Web site: http://www.cos.fit.edu/biology/.

Florida State University, The Graduate School, College of Arts and Sciences, Department of Biological Science, Specialization in Cell and Molecular Biology and Genetics, Tallahassee, FL 32306-4295. Offers MS, PhD. *Faculty:* 28 full-time (7 women). *Students:* 44 full-time (19 women); includes 6 minority (all Hispanic/Latino), 15 international. 152 applicants, 16% accepted, 11 enrolled. In 2011, 3 master's, 8 doctorates awarded. Terminal master's awarded for partial completion of doctoral program. *Degree requirements:* For master's, comprehensive exam, thesis, teaching experience, seminar presentation; for doctorate, comprehensive exam, thesis/dissertation, teaching experience; seminar presentation. *Entrance requirements:* For master's and doctorate, GRE General Test (minimum combined score 1100, 500 verbal, 500 quantitative in old version; 72% verbal, 67% quantitative in new format), minimum upper-division GPA of 3.0. Additional exam requirements/recommendations for international students: Required—TOEFL (minimum score 600 paper-based; 250 computer-based; 92 iBT). *Application deadline:* For fall admission, 12/15 for domestic and international students. Application fee: $30. Electronic applications accepted. *Expenses:* Tuition, state resident: full-time $9474; part-time $350.88 per credit hour. Tuition, nonresident: full-time $16,236; part-time $601.34 per credit hour. *Required fees:* $630 per semester. One-time fee: $20. Tuition and fees vary according to course load and campus/location. *Financial support:* In 2011–12, 43 students received support, including 17 research assistantships with full tuition reimbursements available (averaging $21,000 per year), 26 teaching assistantships with full tuition reimbursements available (averaging $21,000 per year); fellowships and unspecified assistantships also available. Financial award application deadline: 12/15; financial award applicants required to submit FAFSA. *Faculty research:* Molecular biology; genetics and genomics; developmental biology and gene expression; cell structure, function, and motility; cellular and organismal physiology; biophysical and structural biology. *Unit head:* Dr. George W. Bates, Professor and Associate Chairman, 850-644-5749, Fax: 850-644-9829, E-mail: bates@bio.fsu.edu. *Application contact:* Judy Bowers, Coordinator, Graduate Affairs, 850-644-3023, Fax: 850-644-9829, E-mail: gradinfo@bio.fsu.edu. Web site: http://www.bio.fsu.edu/.

Georgetown University, Graduate School of Arts and Sciences, Programs in Biomedical Sciences, Department of Cell Biology, Washington, DC 20057. Offers PhD, MD/PhD. *Degree requirements:* For doctorate, comprehensive exam, thesis/dissertation. *Entrance requirements:* For doctorate, GRE General Test. Additional exam requirements/recommendations for international students: Required—TOEFL.

Georgia Health Sciences University, College of Graduate Studies, Program in Cellular Biology and Anatomy, Augusta, GA 30912. Offers MS, PhD. *Faculty:* 15 full-time (6 women), 3 part-time/adjunct (1 woman). *Students:* 11 full-time (7 women); includes 1 minority (Asian, non-Hispanic/Latino), 7 international. Average age 30. In 2011, 2 degrees awarded. *Degree requirements:* For doctorate, comprehensive exam, thesis/dissertation. *Entrance requirements:* For doctorate, GRE General Test. Additional exam requirements/recommendations for international students: Required—TOEFL (minimum score 550 paper-based; 213 computer-based; 79 iBT). *Application deadline:* For fall admission, 1/15 for domestic and international students. Applications are processed on a rolling basis. Application fee: $50. *Financial support:* In 2011–12, 2 students received support, including 1 fellowship with partial tuition reimbursement available (averaging $26,000 per year), 9 research assistantships with partial tuition reimbursements available (averaging $23,000 per year); teaching assistantships with partial tuition reimbursements available, Federal Work-Study, institutionally sponsored loans, and scholarships/grants also available. Support available to part-time students. Financial award application deadline: 5/31; financial award applicants required to submit FAFSA. *Faculty research:* Eye disease, developmental biology, cell injury and death, stroke and neurotoxicity, diabetic complications. *Total annual research expenditures:* $2.8 million. *Unit head:* Dr. Sally S. Atherton, Chair and Professor, 706-721-3731, Fax: 706-721-6120, E-mail: satherton@georgiahealth.edu. *Application contact:* Dr. Patricia L. Cameron, Acting Vice Dean, 706-721-3279, E-mail: pcameron@georgiahealth.edu. Web site: http://www.georgiahealth.edu/medicine/cba/index.html.

Georgia State University, College of Arts and Sciences, Department of Biology, Program in Cellular and Molecular Biology and Physiology, Atlanta, GA 30302-3083. Offers MS, PhD. Part-time programs available. Terminal master's awarded for partial completion of doctoral program. *Degree requirements:* For master's, thesis or alternative; for doctorate, thesis/dissertation, exam. *Entrance requirements:* For master's and doctorate, GRE General Test. Additional exam requirements/recommendations for international students: Required—TOEFL.

Grand Valley State University, College of Liberal Arts and Sciences, Program in Cell and Molecular Biology, Allendale, MI 49401-9403. Offers MS. *Entrance requirements:* For master's, minimum GPA of 3.0. *Faculty research:* Plant cell biology, plant development, cell/signal integration.

Harvard University, Graduate School of Arts and Sciences, Department of Molecular and Cellular Biology, Cambridge, MA 02138. Offers PhD. *Degree requirements:* For doctorate, thesis/dissertation, oral exam. *Entrance requirements:* For doctorate, GRE General Test, GRE Subject Test (recommended). Additional exam requirements/recommendations for international students: Required—TOEFL. *Expenses: Tuition:* Full-time $36,304. *Required fees:* $1186. Full-time tuition and fees vary according to program.

Harvard University, Graduate School of Arts and Sciences, Division of Medical Sciences, Boston, MA 02115. Offers biological chemistry and molecular pharmacology (PhD); cell biology (PhD); genetics (PhD); microbiology and molecular genetics (PhD); pathology (PhD), including experimental pathology. *Degree requirements:* For doctorate, thesis/dissertation. *Entrance requirements:* For doctorate, GRE General Test, GRE Subject Test. Additional exam requirements/recommendations for international students: Required—TOEFL. *Expenses: Tuition:* Full-time $36,304. *Required fees:* $1186. Full-time tuition and fees vary according to program.

Illinois Institute of Technology, Graduate College, College of Science and Letters, Department of Biological, Chemical and Physical Sciences, Biology Division, Chicago, IL 60616. Offers biochemistry (MBS, MS); biology (PhD); biotechnology (MBS, MS); cell and molecular biology (MBS, MS); microbiology (MB, MS); molecular biochemistry and biophysics (PhD); molecular biology and biophysics (MS). Part-time and evening/weekend programs available. Postbaccalaureate distance learning degree programs offered (minimal on-campus study). Terminal master's awarded for partial completion of doctoral program. *Degree requirements:* For master's, comprehensive exam, thesis (for some programs); for doctorate, comprehensive exam, thesis/dissertation. *Entrance requirements:* For master's, GRE General Test (minimum score 1000 Quantitative and Verbal, 2.5 Analytical Writing), minimum undergraduate GPA of 3.0; for doctorate, GRE General Test (minimum score 1200 Quantitative and Verbal, 3.0 Analytical Writing), minimum undergraduate GPA of 3.0. Additional exam requirements/recommendations for international students: Required—TOEFL (minimum score 523 paper-based; 213 computer-based; 70 iBT); Recommended—IELTS (minimum score 5.5). Electronic applications accepted. *Faculty research:* Structure and biophysics of macromolecular systems; efficacy and mechanism of action of chemopreventive agents in experimental carcinogenesis of breast, colon, lung and prostate; study of fundamental structural biochemistry problems that have direct links to the understanding and treatment of disease; spectroscopic techniques for the study of multi-domain proteins; molecular mechanisms of cancer and cancer gene therapy.

Illinois State University, Graduate School, College of Arts and Sciences, Department of Biological Sciences, Normal, IL 61790-2200. Offers animal behavior (MS); bacteriology (MS); biochemistry (MS); biological sciences (MS); biology (PhD); biophysics (MS); biotechnology (MS); botany (MS, PhD); cell biology (MS); conservation biology (MS); developmental biology (MS); ecology (MS, PhD); entomology (MS); evolutionary biology (MS); genetics (MS, PhD); immunology (MS); microbiology (MS, PhD); molecular biology (MS); molecular genetics (MS); neurobiology (MS); neuroscience (MS); parasitology (MS); physiology (MS, PhD); plant biology (MS); plant molecular biology (MS); plant sciences (MS); structural biology (MS); zoology (MS, PhD). Part-time programs available. *Degree requirements:* For master's, thesis or alternative; for doctorate, variable foreign language requirement, thesis/dissertation, 2 terms of residency. *Entrance requirements:* For master's, GRE General Test, minimum GPA of 2.6 in last 60 hours of course work; for doctorate, GRE General Test. *Faculty research:* Redoc balance and drug development in schistosoma mansoni, control of the growth of listeria monocytogenes at low temperature, regulation of cell expansion and microtubule function by SPRI, CRUI: physiology and fitness consequences of different life history phenotypes.

Indiana University Bloomington, University Graduate School, College of Arts and Sciences, Department of Biology, Bloomington, IN 47405. Offers biology teaching (MAT); biotechnology (MA); evolution, ecology, and behavior (MA, PhD); genetics (PhD); microbiology (MA, PhD); molecular, cellular, and developmental biology (PhD); plant sciences (MA, PhD); zoology (MA, PhD). *Faculty:* 58 full-time (15 women), 21 part-time/adjunct (6 women). *Students:* 175 full-time (100 women), 3 part-time (all women); includes 20 minority (5 Black or African American, non-Hispanic/Latino; 8 Asian, non-Hispanic/Latino; 7 Hispanic/Latino), 55 international. Average age 27. 316 applicants, 22% accepted, 31 enrolled. In 2011, 8 master's, 20 doctorates awarded. Terminal master's awarded for partial completion of doctoral program. *Degree requirements:* For master's, thesis, oral defense; for doctorate, thesis/dissertation, oral defense. *Entrance requirements:* For master's and doctorate, GRE General Test. Additional exam requirements/recommendations for international students: Required—TOEFL (minimum score 100 iBT). *Application deadline:* For fall admission, 1/5 priority date for domestic students, 12/1 for international students. Application fee: $55 ($65 for international students). Electronic applications accepted. *Financial support:* In 2011–12, fellowships with tuition reimbursements (averaging $19,484 per year), research assistantships with tuition reimbursements (averaging $20,300 per year), teaching assistantships with tuition reimbursements (averaging $20,521 per year) were awarded; scholarships/grants, traineeships, health care benefits, and unspecified assistantships also available. Financial award application deadline: 1/5. *Faculty research:* Evolution, ecology and behavior; microbiology; molecular biology and genetics; plant biology. *Unit head:* Dr. Roger Innes, Chair, 812-855-2219, Fax: 812-855-6082, E-mail: rinnes@indiana.edu. *Application contact:* Tracey D. Stohr, Graduate Student Recruitment Coordinator, 812-856-6303, Fax: 812-855-6082, E-mail: gradbio@indiana.edu. Web site: http://www.bio.indiana.edu/.

Indiana University–Purdue University Indianapolis, Indiana University School of Medicine, Department of Anatomy and Cell Biology, Indianapolis, IN 46202-2896. Offers MS, PhD, MD/PhD. *Faculty:* 14 full-time (1 woman). *Students:* 12 full-time (6 women), 3 part-time (2 women); includes 1 minority (Black or African American, non-Hispanic/Latino), 4 international. Average age 29. 8 applicants, 50% accepted, 2 enrolled. In 2011, 2 degrees awarded. *Degree requirements:* For master's, thesis or alternative; for doctorate, thesis/dissertation. *Entrance requirements:* For master's and doctorate, GRE General Test. *Application deadline:* For fall admission, 1/15 priority date for domestic students. Application fee: $55 ($65 for international students). *Financial support:* Fellowships, research assistantships, Federal Work-Study, institutionally sponsored loans, tuition waivers (partial), and stipends available. Financial award application deadline: 2/15. *Faculty research:* Acoustic reflex control, osteoarthritis and bone disease, diabetes, kidney diseases, cellular and molecular neurobiology. *Unit head:* Dr. David B. Burr, Chairman, 317-274-7494, Fax: 317-278-2040, E-mail: dburr@indyvax.iupui.edu. *Application contact:* Dr. James Williams, Graduate Adviser, 317-274-3423, Fax: 317-278-2040, E-mail: williams@anatomy.iupui.edu.

Iowa State University of Science and Technology, Department of Biochemistry, Biophysics, and Molecular Biology, Ames, IA 50011. Offers biochemistry (MS, PhD); biophysics (MS, PhD); genetics (MS, PhD); molecular, cellular, and developmental biology (MS, PhD); toxicology (MS, PhD). *Degree requirements:* For master's, thesis; for doctorate, thesis/dissertation. *Entrance requirements:* For master's and doctorate, GRE General Test. Additional exam requirements/recommendations for international students: Required—TOEFL (minimum score 550 paper-based; 79 iBT), IELTS (minimum score 6.5). *Application deadline:* For fall admission, 1/1 priority date for domestic students, 1/1 for international students. Application fee: $40 ($90 for international students). Electronic applications accepted. *Unit head:* Dr. Reuben Peters, Director of Graduate Education, 515-294-6116, Fax: 515-294-0453, E-mail: biochem@iastate.edu. *Application contact:* Connie Garnett, Application Contact, 515-294-6116, Fax: 515-294-0453, E-mail: biochem@iastate.edu. Web site: http://www.bbmb.iastate.edu/index.php?.

Iowa State University of Science and Technology, Program in Molecular, Cellular, and Developmental Biology, Ames, IA 50011. Offers MS, PhD. *Entrance requirements:* For master's and doctorate, GRE General Test. Additional exam requirements/recommendations for international students: Required—TOEFL (minimum score 580 paper-based; 85 iBT), IELTS (minimum score 7). *Application deadline:* For fall admission, 1/15 priority date for domestic students, 1/15 for international students. Application fee: $40 ($90 for international students). Electronic applications accepted. *Unit head:* Dr. Clark Ford, Director of Graduate Education, 515-294-7252, Fax: 515-294-6790, E-mail: idgp@iastate.edu. *Application contact:* Katie Blair, Application Contact, 515-294-7252, Fax: 515-924-6790, E-mail: idgp@iastate.edu. Web site: http://www.mcdb.iastate.edu.

The Johns Hopkins University, National Institutes of Health Sponsored Programs, Baltimore, MD 21218-2699. Offers biology (PhD), including biochemistry, biophysics, cell biology, developmental biology, genetic biology, molecular biology; cell, molecular, and developmental biology and biophysics (PhD). *Degree requirements:* For doctorate, comprehensive exam, thesis/dissertation. *Entrance requirements:* For doctorate, GRE General Test. Additional exam requirements/recommendations for international students: Required—TOEFL (minimum score 600 paper-based; 250 computer-based), TWE. Electronic applications accepted. *Faculty research:* Protein and nucleic acid biochemistry and biophysical chemistry, molecular biology and development.

The Johns Hopkins University, School of Medicine, Graduate Programs in Medicine, Graduate Program in Cellular and Molecular Medicine, Baltimore, MD 21218-2699. Offers PhD. *Degree requirements:* For doctorate, comprehensive exam, thesis/dissertation, oral exam. *Entrance requirements:* For doctorate, GRE. Additional exam requirements/recommendations for international students: Required—TOEFL. Electronic applications accepted. *Faculty research:* Cellular and molecular basis of disease.

The Johns Hopkins University, School of Medicine, Graduate Programs in Medicine, Program in Biochemistry, Cellular and Molecular Biology, Baltimore, MD 21205. Offers PhD. *Degree requirements:* For doctorate, comprehensive exam, thesis/dissertation. *Entrance requirements:* For doctorate, GRE General Test. Additional exam requirements/recommendations for international students: Required—TOEFL. Electronic applications accepted. *Faculty research:* Developmental biology, genomics/proteomics, protein targeting, signal transduction, structural biology.

Kent State University, School of Biomedical Sciences, Program in Cellular and Molecular Biology, Kent, OH 44242-0001. Offers MS, PhD. Offered in cooperation with Northeastern Ohio Universities College of Medicine. Terminal master's awarded for partial completion of doctoral program. *Degree requirements:* For master's, thesis; for doctorate, thesis/dissertation. *Entrance requirements:* For master's, GRE General Test, letter of recommendation, minimum GPA of 3.0; for doctorate, GRE General Test, letter of recommendation, minimum GPA of 3.0, MS. Additional exam requirements/recommendations for international students: Required—TOEFL. Electronic applications accepted. *Expenses:* Tuition, state resident: full-time $8136; part-time $452 per credit hour. Tuition, nonresident: full-time $14,292; part-time $794 per credit hour. *Faculty research:* Molecular genetics, molecular endocrinology, virology and tumor biology, P450 enzymology and catalysis, membrane structure and function.

Louisiana State University Health Sciences Center, School of Graduate Studies in New Orleans, Department of Cell Biology and Anatomy, New Orleans, LA 70112-2223. Offers cell biology and anatomy (MS, PhD), including cell biology, developmental biology, neurobiology and anatomy; MD/PhD. *Degree requirements:* For master's, comprehensive exam, thesis; for doctorate, comprehensive exam, thesis/dissertation. *Entrance requirements:* For master's and doctorate, GRE General Test, GRE Subject Test, minimum undergraduate GPA of 3.0. Additional exam requirements/recommendations for international students: Required—TOEFL. *Faculty research:* Visual system organization, neural development, plasticity of sensory systems, information processing through the nervous system, visuomotor integration.

Louisiana State University Health Sciences Center at Shreveport, Department of Cellular Biology and Anatomy, Shreveport, LA 71130-3932. Offers MS, PhD, MD/PhD. Terminal master's awarded for partial completion of doctoral program. *Degree requirements:* For master's, thesis; for doctorate, thesis/dissertation. *Entrance requirements:* For master's and doctorate, GRE General Test. Additional exam requirements/recommendations for international students: Required—TOEFL. *Faculty research:* Alcohol and immunity, neuroscience, olfactory physiology, extracellular matrix, cancer cell biology and gene therapy.

Loyola University Chicago, Graduate School, Department of Cell Biology, Neurobiology and Anatomy, Chicago, IL 60660. Offers MS, PhD. Part-time programs available. *Faculty:* 16 full-time (6 women), 9 part-time/adjunct (4 women). *Students:* 21 full-time (11 women); includes 4 minority (3 Hispanic/Latino; 1 Two or more races, non-Hispanic/Latino), 1 international. Average age 27. 28 applicants, 29% accepted, 4 enrolled. In 2011, 1 master's, 2 doctorates awarded. Terminal master's awarded for partial completion of doctoral program. *Degree requirements:* For master's, thesis; for doctorate, comprehensive exam, thesis/dissertation. *Entrance requirements:* For master's, GRE General Test, minimum GPA of 3.0; for doctorate, GRE General Test, GRE Subject Test (biology), minimum GPA of 3.0. Additional exam requirements/recommendations for international students: Required—TOEFL (minimum score 600 paper-based; 250 computer-based). *Application deadline:* For fall admission, 5/1 priority date for domestic students, 5/1 for international students. Applications are processed on a rolling basis. Application fee: $50. Electronic applications accepted. *Expenses: Tuition:* Full-time $15,660; part-time $870 per credit hour. *Required fees:* $125 per semester. Tuition and fees vary according to course load and program. *Financial support:* In 2011–12, 5 fellowships with full tuition reimbursements (averaging $23,000 per year), 5 research assistantships with full tuition reimbursements (averaging $23,000 per year) were awarded; Federal Work-Study and unspecified assistantships also available. Financial award application deadline: 5/1; financial award applicants required to submit FAFSA. *Faculty research:* Brain steroids, immunology, neuroregeneration, cytokines. *Total annual research expenditures:* $1 million. *Unit head:* Dr. Phong Le, Head, 708-216-3603, Fax: 708-216-3913, E-mail: ple@lumc.edu. *Application contact:* Ginny Hayes, Graduate Program Secretary, 708-216-3353, Fax: 708-216-3913, E-mail: vhayes@lumc.edu.

Marquette University, Graduate School, College of Arts and Sciences, Department of Biology, Milwaukee, WI 53201-1881. Offers cell biology (MS, PhD); developmental biology (MS, PhD); ecology (MS, PhD); epithelial physiology (MS, PhD); genetics (MS, PhD); microbiology (MS, PhD); molecular biology (MS, PhD); muscle and exercise physiology (MS, PhD); neuroscience (PhD). *Faculty:* 23 full-time (11 women), 1 part-time/adjunct (0 women). *Students:* 33 full-time (14 women), 6 part-time (3 women), 19 international. Average age 25. 78 applicants, 17% accepted, 5 enrolled. In 2011, 6 doctorates awarded. Terminal master's awarded for partial completion of doctoral program. *Degree requirements:* For master's, comprehensive exam, thesis, 1 year of teaching experience or equivalent; for doctorate, thesis/dissertation, 1 year of teaching experience or equivalent, qualifying exam. *Entrance requirements:* For master's and doctorate, GRE General Test, GRE Subject Test, official transcripts from all current and previous colleges/universities except Marquette, statement of professional goals and aspirations, three letters of recommendation. Additional exam requirements/recommendations for international students: Required—TOEFL (minimum score 530 paper-based; 78 computer-based). *Application deadline:* For fall admission, 12/15 for domestic and international students. Application fee: $50. Electronic applications accepted. *Expenses: Tuition:* Full-time $17,010; part-time $945 per credit hour. Tuition and fees vary according to program. *Financial support:* In 2011–12, 39 students received support, including 6 fellowships (averaging $1,208 per year), 4 research assistantships with full tuition reimbursements available (averaging $21,750 per year), 29 teaching assistantships with full tuition reimbursements available (averaging $21,750

per year); scholarships/grants, health care benefits, tuition waivers (full and partial), and unspecified assistantships also available. Support available to part-time students. Financial award application deadline: 2/15. *Faculty research:* Neurobiology, neuroendocrinology, epithelial physiology, neuropeptide interactions, synaptic transmission. *Total annual research expenditures:* $2 million. *Unit head:* Dr. Robert Fitts, Chair, 414-288-1748, Fax: 414-288-7357. *Application contact:* Debbie Weaver, Administrative Assistant, 414-288-7355, Fax: 414-288-7357. Web site: http://www.marquette.edu/biology/.

Massachusetts Institute of Technology, School of Science, Department of Biology, Cambridge, MA 02139. Offers biochemistry (PhD); biological oceanography (PhD); biology (PhD); biophysical chemistry and molecular structure (PhD); cell biology (PhD); computational and systems biology (PhD); developmental biology (PhD); genetics (PhD); immunology (PhD); microbiology (PhD); molecular biology (PhD); neurobiology (PhD). *Faculty:* 58 full-time (15 women). *Students:* 248 full-time (129 women); includes 69 minority (5 Black or African American, non-Hispanic/Latino; 1 American Indian or Alaska Native, non-Hispanic/Latino; 25 Asian, non-Hispanic/Latino; 31 Hispanic/Latino; 7 Two or more races, non-Hispanic/Latino), 36 international. Average age 26. 698 applicants, 15% accepted, 44 enrolled. In 2011, 38 doctorates awarded. *Degree requirements:* For doctorate, comprehensive exam, thesis/dissertation. *Entrance requirements:* For doctorate, GRE General Test. Additional exam requirements/recommendations for international students: Required—TOEFL (minimum score 577 paper-based; 233 computer-based), IELTS (minimum score 6.5). *Application deadline:* For fall admission, 12/1 for domestic and international students. Application fee: $75. Electronic applications accepted. *Expenses: Tuition:* Full-time $40,460; part-time $630 per credit hour. *Required fees:* $272. *Financial support:* In 2011–12, 214 students received support, including 129 fellowships (averaging $33,200 per year), 117 research assistantships (averaging $32,900 per year); teaching assistantships, Federal Work-Study, institutionally sponsored loans, scholarships/grants, traineeships, health care benefits, and unspecified assistantships also available. *Faculty research:* Cellular, developmental and molecular (plant and animal) biology; biochemistry, bioengineering, biophysics and structural biology; classical and molecular genetics; immunology and microbiology; cancer biology, molecular medicine, neurobiology and human disease; computational and systems biology. *Total annual research expenditures:* $53.6 million. *Unit head:* Prof. Tania A. Baker, Head, 617-253-4701, E-mail: mitbio@mit.edu. *Application contact:* Biology Education Office, 617-253-3717, Fax: 617-258-9329, E-mail: gradbio@mit.edu. Web site: https://biology.mit.edu/.

Mayo Graduate School, Graduate Programs in Biomedical Sciences, Programs in Biochemistry, Structural Biology, Cell Biology, and Genetics, Rochester, MN 55905. Offers biochemistry and structural biology (PhD); cell biology and genetics (PhD); molecular biology (PhD). *Degree requirements:* For doctorate, oral defense of dissertation, qualifying oral and written exam. *Entrance requirements:* For doctorate, GRE, 1 year of chemistry, biology, calculus, and physics. Additional exam requirements/recommendations for international students: Required—TOEFL. Electronic applications accepted. *Faculty research:* Gene structure and function, membranes and receptors/cytoskeleton, oncogenes and growth factors, protein structure and function, steroid hormonal action.

McGill University, Faculty of Graduate and Postdoctoral Studies, Faculty of Medicine, Department of Anatomy and Cell Biology, Montréal, QC H3A 2T5, Canada. Offers M Sc, PhD.

McMaster University, Faculty of Health Sciences and School of Graduate Studies, Program in Medical Sciences, Metabolism and Nutrition Area, Hamilton, ON L8S 4M2, Canada. Offers M Sc, PhD, MD/PhD. *Degree requirements:* For master's, thesis; for doctorate, comprehensive exam, thesis/dissertation. *Entrance requirements:* For master's, honors B Sc, B+ average in related field; for doctorate, M Sc, minimum B+ average, students with proven research experience and an A average may be admitted with a B Sc degree. Additional exam requirements/recommendations for international students: Required—TOEFL (minimum score 580 paper-based; 237 computer-based; 92 iBT).

Medical University of South Carolina, College of Graduate Studies, Program in Molecular and Cellular Biology and Pathobiology, Charleston, SC 29425. Offers cancer biology (PhD); cardiovascular biology (PhD); cardiovascular imaging (PhD); cell regulation (PhD); craniofacial biology (PhD); genetics and development (PhD); marine biomedicine (PhD); DMD/PhD; MD/PhD. *Faculty:* 137 full-time (33 women). *Students:* 28 full-time (23 women); includes 5 minority (4 Black or African American, non-Hispanic/Latino; 1 Hispanic/Latino), 5 international. Average age 30. In 2011, 16 doctorates awarded. *Degree requirements:* For doctorate, thesis/dissertation, oral and written exams. *Entrance requirements:* For doctorate, GRE General Test, interview, minimum GPA of 3.0. Additional exam requirements/recommendations for international students: Required—TOEFL (minimum score 600 paper-based; 250 computer-based; 100 iBT). *Application deadline:* For fall admission, 1/15 priority date for domestic students, 1/15 for international students. Applications are processed on a rolling basis. Application fee: $0 ($85 for international students). Electronic applications accepted. *Financial support:* In 2011–12, 39 research assistantships with partial tuition reimbursements (averaging $23,000 per year) were awarded; Federal Work-Study and scholarships/grants also available. Support available to part-time students. Financial award application deadline: 3/10; financial award applicants required to submit FAFSA. *Unit head:* Dr. Donald R. Menick, Director, 843-876-5045, Fax: 843-792-6590, E-mail: menickd@musc.edu. *Application contact:* Dr. Cynthia F. Wright, Associate Dean for Admissions and Career Development, 843-792-2564, Fax: 843-792-6590, E-mail: wrightcf@musc.edu. Web site: http://www.musc.edu/mcbp/.

Michigan State University, The Graduate School, College of Agriculture and Natural Resources, MSU-DOE Plant Research Laboratory, East Lansing, MI 48824. Offers biochemistry and molecular biology (PhD); cellular and molecular biology (PhD); crop and soil sciences (PhD); genetics (PhD); microbiology and molecular genetics (PhD); plant biology (PhD); plant physiology (PhD). Offered jointly with the Department of Energy. *Degree requirements:* For doctorate, comprehensive exam, thesis/dissertation, laboratory rotation, defense of dissertation. *Entrance requirements:* For doctorate, GRE General Test, acceptance into one of the affiliated department programs; 3 letters of recommendation; bachelor's degree or equivalent in life sciences, chemistry, biochemistry, or biophysics; research experience. Electronic applications accepted. *Faculty research:* Role of hormones in the regulation of plant development and physiology, molecular mechanisms associated with signal recognition, development and application of genetic methods and materials, protein routing and function.

Michigan State University, The Graduate School, College of Natural Science, Program in Cell and Molecular Biology, East Lansing, MI 48824. Offers cell and molecular biology (MS, PhD); cell and molecular biology/environmental toxicology (PhD). *Entrance requirements:* Additional exam requirements/recommendations for international students: Required—TOEFL. Electronic applications accepted.

Missouri State University, Graduate College, College of Health and Human Services, Department of Biomedical Sciences, Program in Cell and Molecular Biology, Springfield, MO 65897. Offers MS. Part-time programs available. *Students:* 7 full-time (4 women), 6 part-time (3 women); includes 2 minority (1 Asian, non-Hispanic/Latino; 1 Hispanic/Latino), 2 international. Average age 24. 7 applicants, 57% accepted, 4 enrolled. In 2011, 10 master's awarded. *Degree requirements:* For master's, thesis or alternative, oral and written exams. *Entrance requirements:* For master's, GRE General Test, 2 semesters of course work in organic chemistry and physics, 1 semester of course work in calculus, minimum GPA of 3.0 in last 60 hours of course work. Additional exam requirements/recommendations for international students: Required—TOEFL (minimum score 550 paper-based; 213 computer-based; 79 iBT). *Application deadline:* For fall admission, 7/20 priority date for domestic students, 5/1 for international students; for spring admission, 12/20 priority date for domestic students, 9/1 for international students. Applications are processed on a rolling basis. Application fee: $35 ($50 for international students). Electronic applications accepted. *Expenses:* Tuition, state resident: full-time $4086; part-time $227 per credit hour. Tuition, nonresident: full-time $8172; part-time $454 per credit hour. *Required fees:* $275 per semester. Tuition and fees vary according to course load, campus/location and program. *Financial support:* In 2011–12, 4 teaching assistantships with full tuition reimbursements (averaging $7,340 per year) were awarded; career-related internships or fieldwork, Federal Work-Study, institutionally sponsored loans, scholarships/grants, and unspecified assistantships also available. Support available to part-time students. Financial award application deadline: 3/31; financial award applicants required to submit FAFSA. *Faculty research:* Extracellular matrix membrane protein, P2 nucleotide receptors, double stranded RNA viruses. *Unit head:* Dr. Scott Zimmernan, Program Director, 417-836-5478, E-mail: scottzimmerman@missouristate.edu. *Application contact:* Misty Stewart, Coordinator of Graduate Admissions and Recruitment, 417-836-6079, Fax: 417-836-6200, E-mail: mistystewart@missouristate.edu. Web site: http://www.missouristate.edu/bms/CMB/.

New York Medical College, Graduate School of Basic Medical Sciences, Department of Cell Biology, Valhalla, NY 10595-1691. Offers cell biology and neuroscience (MS, PhD); MD/PhD. Part-time and evening/weekend programs available. *Faculty:* 16 full-time (2 women), 2 part-time/adjunct (1 woman). *Students:* 4 full-time (3 women); includes 1 minority (Asian, non-Hispanic/Latino). Average age 26. 2 applicants, 50% accepted, 0 enrolled. In 2011, 1 master's awarded. Terminal master's awarded for partial completion of doctoral program. *Degree requirements:* For master's, thesis; for doctorate, comprehensive exam, thesis/dissertation. *Entrance requirements:* For master's, GRE General Test, MCAT, DATGRE General, MCAT, DAT; for doctorate, GRE General Test. Additional exam requirements/recommendations for international students: Required—TOEFL. *Application deadline:* For fall admission, 7/1 priority date for domestic students, 5/1 for international students; for spring admission, 12/1 priority date for domestic students, 10/1 for international students. Applications are processed on a rolling basis. Application fee: $50 ($75 for international students). Electronic applications accepted. *Financial support:* In 2011–12, 4 fellowships (averaging $24,000 per year), 1 research assistantship with full tuition reimbursement (averaging $24,000 per year) were awarded; Federal Work-Study, institutionally sponsored loans, scholarships/grants, traineeships, tuition waivers (full), unspecified assistantships, and health benefits (for PhD candidates only) also available. Financial award applicants required to submit FAFSA. *Faculty research:* Mechanisms of growth control in skeletal muscle, cartilage differentiation, cytoskeletal functions, signal transduction pathways, neuronal development and plasticity. *Unit head:* Dr. Victor Fried, Director, 914-594-4036. *Application contact:* Valerie Romeo-Messana, Admission Coordinator, 914-594-4110, Fax: 914-594-4944, E-mail: v_romeomessana@nymc.edu.

New York University, School of Medicine, New York, NY 10012-1019. Offers biomedical sciences (PhD), including biomedical imaging, cellular and molecular biology, computational biology, developmental genetics, medical and molecular parasitology, microbiology, molecular oncobiology and immunology, neuroscience and physiology, pathobiology, pharmacology, structural biology; clinical investigation (MS); medicine (MD); MD/MA; MD/MPA; MD/MS; MD/PhD. *Accreditation:* LCME/AMA (one or more programs are accredited). *Degree requirements:* For master's, comprehensive exam, thesis; for doctorate, comprehensive exam (for some programs), thesis/dissertation (for some programs). *Entrance requirements:* For doctorate, MCAT (for MD). Additional exam requirements/recommendations for international students: Required—TOEFL. *Expenses:* Contact institution. *Faculty research:* AIDS, cancer, neuroscience, molecular biology, neuroscience, cell biology and molecular genetics, structural biology, microbial pathogenesis and host defense, pharmacology, molecular oncology and immunology.

New York University, School of Medicine and Graduate School of Arts and Science, Sackler Institute of Graduate Biomedical Sciences, Program in Cellular and Molecular Biology, New York, NY 10012-1019. Offers PhD, MD/PhD. *Faculty:* 58 full-time (14 women). *Students:* 33 full-time (17 women); includes 13 minority (2 Black or African American, non-Hispanic/Latino; 8 Asian, non-Hispanic/Latino; 3 Hispanic/Latino), 10 international. Average age 28. In 2011, 9 doctorates awarded. *Degree requirements:* For doctorate, comprehensive exam, thesis/dissertation, qualifying exams. *Entrance requirements:* For doctorate, GRE General Test. Additional exam requirements/recommendations for international students: Required—TOEFL. *Application deadline:* For fall admission, 1/4 priority date for domestic students. Applications are processed on a rolling basis. Application fee: $85. *Financial support:* Fellowships with tuition reimbursements, research assistantships with tuition reimbursements, and teaching assistantships with tuition reimbursements available. *Faculty research:* Membrane and organelle structure and biogenesis, intracellular transport and processing of proteins, cellular recognition and cell adhesion, oncogene structure and function, action of growth factors. *Total annual research expenditures:* $1.9 million. *Unit head:* Dr. Daniel Rifkin, Director, 212-263-5109, E-mail: rifkind01@popmail.med.nyu.edu. *Application contact:* Lynette Wilson, Information Contact, 212-263-7684, Fax: 212-263-8139, E-mail: wilsoe01@popmail.med.nyu.edu.

North Carolina State University, College of Veterinary Medicine, Program in Comparative Biomedical Sciences, Raleigh, NC 27695. Offers cell biology (MS, PhD); infectious disease (MS, PhD); pathology (MS, PhD); pharmacology (MS, PhD); population medicine (MS, PhD). Part-time programs available. *Degree requirements:* For master's, thesis; for doctorate, thesis/dissertation. *Entrance requirements:* For master's and doctorate, GRE General Test. Additional exam requirements/recommendations for international students: Required—TOEFL (minimum score 550 paper-based; 213 computer-based). Electronic applications accepted. *Expenses:* Contact institution. *Faculty research:* Infectious diseases, cell biology, pharmacology and toxicology, genomics, pathology and population medicine.

North Dakota State University, College of Graduate and Interdisciplinary Studies, College of Science and Mathematics, Department of Biological Sciences, Fargo, ND 58108. Offers biology (MS); botany (MS, PhD); cellular and molecular biology (PhD); environmental and conservation sciences (MS, PhD); genomics (PhD); natural resources management (MS, PhD); zoology (MS, PhD). *Faculty:* 13 full-time (7 women), 3 part-time/adjunct (1 woman). *Students:* 20 full-time (10 women), 2 part-time (both women); includes 1 minority (American Indian or Alaska Native, non-Hispanic/Latino), 2 international. 12 applicants, 33% accepted, 4 enrolled. In 2011, 3 degrees awarded. *Degree requirements:* For master's, thesis; for doctorate, thesis/dissertation. *Entrance requirements:* For master's and doctorate, GRE General Test. Additional exam requirements/recommendations for international students: Required—TOEFL. *Application deadline:* For fall admission, 1/15 for domestic students. Applications are

processed on a rolling basis. Application fee: $35. Electronic applications accepted. *Financial support:* Fellowships with full tuition reimbursements, research assistantships with full tuition reimbursements, teaching assistantships with full tuition reimbursements, career-related internships or fieldwork, Federal Work-Study, institutionally sponsored loans, scholarships/grants, tuition waivers (full), and unspecified assistantships available. Support available to part-time students. Financial award application deadline: 4/15; financial award applicants required to submit FAFSA. *Faculty research:* Comparative endocrinology, physiology, behavioral ecology, plant cell biology, aquatic biology. *Unit head:* Dr. Wendy Reed, Head, 701-231-7087, E-mail: wendy.reed@ndsu.edu. *Application contact:* Sonya Goergen, Marketing, Recruitment, and Public Relations Coordinator, 701-231-7033, Fax: 701-231-6524. Web site: http://biology.ndsu.nodak.edu/.

North Dakota State University, College of Graduate and Interdisciplinary Studies, Interdisciplinary Program in Cellular and Molecular Biology, Fargo, ND 58108. Offers PhD. PhD offered in cooperation with 11 departments in the university. *Students:* 9 full-time (7 women), 4 part-time (1 woman), 8 international. 33 applicants, 0% accepted, 0 enrolled. *Degree requirements:* For doctorate, thesis/dissertation. *Entrance requirements:* For doctorate, GRE. Additional exam requirements/recommendations for international students: Required—TOEFL (minimum score 525 paper-based; 197 computer-based; 71 iBT). *Application deadline:* Applications are processed on a rolling basis. Application fee: $35. Electronic applications accepted. *Financial support:* Fellowships with full tuition reimbursements, research assistantships with full tuition reimbursements, teaching assistantships with full tuition reimbursements, and unspecified assistantships available. Financial award application deadline: 3/15. *Faculty research:* Plant and animal cell biology, gene regulation, molecular genetics, plant and animal virology. *Unit head:* Dr. Mark Sheridan, Director, 701-231-7087, E-mail: ndsu.cmb@ndsu.edu. *Application contact:* Sonya Goergen, Marketing, Recruitment, and Public Relations Coordinator, 701-231-7033, Fax: 701-231-6524. Web site: http://www.ndsu.edu/cellularmolecularbiology/.

Northwestern University, The Graduate School, Interdepartmental Biological Sciences Program (IBiS), Evanston, IL 60208. Offers biochemistry, molecular biology, and cell biology (PhD), including biochemistry, cell and molecular biology, molecular biophysics, structural biology; biotechnology (PhD); cell and molecular biology (PhD); developmental biology and genetics (PhD); hormone action and signal transduction (PhD); neuroscience (PhD); structural biology, biochemistry, and biophysics (PhD). Program participants include the Departments of Biochemistry, Molecular Biology, and Cell Biology; Chemistry; Neurobiology and Physiology; Chemical Engineering; Civil Engineering; and Evanston Hospital. *Degree requirements:* For doctorate, thesis/dissertation, qualifying exam. *Entrance requirements:* For doctorate, GRE General Test. Additional exam requirements/recommendations for international students: Required—TOEFL (minimum score 600 paper-based). Electronic applications accepted. *Faculty research:* Developmental genetics, gene regulation, DNA-protein interactions, biological clocks, bioremediation.

Northwestern University, Northwestern University Feinberg School of Medicine and Interdepartmental Programs, Integrated Graduate Programs in the Life Sciences, Chicago, IL 60611. Offers cancer biology (PhD); cell biology (PhD); developmental biology (PhD); evolutionary biology (PhD); immunology and microbial pathogenesis (PhD); molecular biology and genetics (PhD); neurobiology (PhD); pharmacology and toxicology (PhD); structural biology and biochemistry (PhD). *Degree requirements:* For doctorate, comprehensive exam, thesis/dissertation, written and oral qualifying exams. *Entrance requirements:* For doctorate, GRE General Test. Additional exam requirements/recommendations for international students: Required—TOEFL (minimum score 600 paper-based; 250 computer-based). Electronic applications accepted.

The Ohio State University, Graduate School, College of Arts and Sciences, Division of Natural and Mathematical Sciences, Department of Molecular Genetics, Columbus, OH 43210. Offers cell and developmental biology (MS, PhD); genetics (MS, PhD); molecular biology (MS, PhD). *Faculty:* 23. *Students:* 11 full-time (5 women), 23 part-time (11 women); includes 1 minority (Black or African American, non-Hispanic/Latino), 15 international. Average age 26. In 2011, 8 doctorates awarded. *Degree requirements:* For master's, thesis; for doctorate, thesis/dissertation. *Entrance requirements:* For master's and doctorate, GRE General Test, GRE Subject Test in biology or biochemistry (recommended). Additional exam requirements/recommendations for international students: Required—TOEFL (minimum score 550 paper-based; 250 computer-based; 79 iBT), Michigan English Language Assessment Battery (minimum score 82). *Application deadline:* For fall admission, 8/15 priority date for domestic students, 7/1 for international students; for winter admission, 12/1 priority date for domestic students, 11/1 for international students; for spring admission, 3/1 priority date for domestic students, 2/1 for international students. Applications are processed on a rolling basis. Application fee: $40 ($50 for international students). Electronic applications accepted. *Expenses:* Tuition, state resident: full-time $11,400. Tuition, nonresident: full-time $28,125. Tuition and fees vary according to course load, degree level, campus/location and program. *Financial support:* Fellowships, research assistantships, teaching assistantships, Federal Work-Study, and institutionally sponsored loans available. Support available to part-time students. *Unit head:* Dr. Anita Hopper, Chair, 614-688-3306, Fax: 614-292-4466, E-mail: hopper.64@osu.edu. *Application contact:* Graduate Admissions, 614-292-6031, Fax: 614-292-3656, E-mail: gradadmissions@osu.edu. Web site: https://molgen.osu.edu/.

The Ohio State University, Graduate School, College of Arts and Sciences, Division of Natural and Mathematical Sciences, Program in Molecular, Cellular and Developmental Biology, Columbus, OH 43210. Offers MS, PhD. *Faculty:* 169. *Students:* 62 full-time (38 women), 66 part-time (36 women); includes 17 minority (8 Asian, non-Hispanic/Latino; 7 Hispanic/Latino; 2 Two or more races, non-Hispanic/Latino), 70 international. Average age 27. In 2011, 6 master's, 19 doctorates awarded. *Degree requirements:* For master's, thesis; for doctorate, thesis/dissertation. *Entrance requirements:* For master's and doctorate, GRE General Test, GRE Subject Test (biology or biochemistry, cell and molecular biology). Additional exam requirements/recommendations for international students: Required—TOEFL (minimum score 550 paper-based; 250 computer-based; 79 iBT), Michigan English Language Assessment Battery (minimum score 82). *Application deadline:* For fall admission, 8/15 priority date for domestic students, 7/1 for international students; for winter admission, 12/1 priority date for domestic students, 11/1 for international students; for spring admission, 3/1 priority date for domestic students, 2/1 for international students. Applications are processed on a rolling basis. Application fee: $40 ($50 for international students). Electronic applications accepted. *Expenses:* Tuition, state resident: full-time $11,400. Tuition, nonresident: full-time $28,125. Tuition and fees vary according to course load, degree level, campus/location and program. *Unit head:* David M. Bisaro, Director, 614-292-3281, Fax: 614-292-4466, E-mail: bisaro.1@osu.edu. *Application contact:* Graduate Admissions, 614-292-6031, Fax: 614-292-3656, E-mail: gradadmissions@osu.edu. Web site: http://www.biosci.ohio-state.edu/~mcdb/.

Ohio University, Graduate College, College of Arts and Sciences, Department of Biological Sciences, Athens, OH 45701-2979. Offers biological sciences (MS, PhD); cell biology and physiology (MS, PhD); ecology and evolutionary biology (MS, PhD); exercise physiology and muscle biology (MS, PhD); microbiology (MS, PhD); neuroscience (MS, PhD). *Students:* 35 full-time (12 women), 4 part-time (1 woman), 14 international. 62 applicants, 10% accepted, 5 enrolled. In 2011, 2 master's, 8 doctorates awarded. Terminal master's awarded for partial completion of doctoral program. *Degree requirements:* For master's, comprehensive exam, thesis, 1 quarter of teaching experience; for doctorate, comprehensive exam, thesis/dissertation, 2 quarters of teaching experience. *Entrance requirements:* For master's, GRE General Test, names of three faculty members whose research interests most closely match the applicant's interest; for doctorate, GRE General Test, essay concerning prior training, research interest and career goals, plus names of three faculty members whose research interests most closely match the applicant's interest. Additional exam requirements/recommendations for international students: Required—TOEFL (minimum score 620 paper-based; 105 iBT) or IELTS (minimum score 7.5). *Application deadline:* For fall admission, 1/15 for domestic and international students. Application fee: $50 ($55 for international students). Electronic applications accepted. *Financial support:* In 2011–12, 1 fellowship with full tuition reimbursement (averaging $18,957 per year), 10 research assistantships with full tuition reimbursements (averaging $18,957 per year), 42 teaching assistantships with full tuition reimbursements (averaging $18,957 per year) were awarded; Federal Work-Study and institutionally sponsored loans also available. Financial award application deadline: 1/15. *Faculty research:* Ecology and evolutionary biology, exercise physiology and muscle biology, neurobiology, cell biology, physiology. *Total annual research expenditures:* $2.8 million. *Unit head:* Dr. Ralph DiCaprio, Chair, 740-593-2290, Fax: 740-593-0300, E-mail: dicapri@ohio.edu. *Application contact:* Dr. Patrick Hassett, Graduate Chair, 740-593-4793, Fax: 740-593-0300, E-mail: hassett@ohio.edu. Web site: http://www.biosci.ohiou.edu/.

Ohio University, Graduate College, College of Arts and Sciences, Interdisciplinary Graduate Program in Molecular and Cellular Biology, Athens, OH 45701-2979. Offers MS, PhD. *Students:* 23 full-time (11 women), 2 part-time (1 woman); includes 1 minority (Hispanic/Latino), 20 international. 45 applicants, 4% accepted, 2 enrolled. In 2011, 6 doctorates awarded. *Degree requirements:* For master's, comprehensive exam, thesis, research proposal, teaching experience; for doctorate, comprehensive exam, thesis/dissertation, research proposal, teaching experience. *Entrance requirements:* For master's and doctorate, GRE General Test. Additional exam requirements/recommendations for international students: Required—TOEFL (minimum score 620 paper-based; 260 computer-based; 105 iBT); Recommended—TWE. *Application deadline:* For fall admission, 12/30 priority date for domestic students, 12/30 for international students. Application fee: $50 ($55 for international students). Electronic applications accepted. *Financial support:* In 2011–12, 25 students received support, including research assistantships with full tuition reimbursements available (averaging $19,500 per year), teaching assistantships with full tuition reimbursements available (averaging $19,500 per year); Federal Work-Study, institutionally sponsored loans, traineeships, and unspecified assistantships also available. Financial award application deadline: 12/30. *Faculty research:* Animal biotechnology, plant molecular biology RNA, immunology, cellular genetics, biochemistry of signal transduction, cancer research, membrane transport, bioinformatics, bioengineering, chemical biology and drug discovery, diabetes, microbiology, neuroscience. *Total annual research expenditures:* $4.4 million. *Unit head:* Dr. Robert A. Colvin, Chair, 740-593-0198, Fax: 740-593-1569, E-mail: colvin@ohio.edu. *Application contact:* Dr. Xiaozhuo Chen, Graduate Chair, 740-593-9699, Fax: 740-593-1569, E-mail: chenx@ohio.edu. Web site: http://www.ohio.edu/mcb.

Oregon Health & Science University, School of Medicine, Graduate Programs in Medicine, Program in Molecular and Cellular Biosciences, Department of Cell and Developmental Biology, Portland, OR 97239-3098. Offers PhD. *Faculty:* 10 full-time (2 women), 1 part-time/adjunct. *Students:* 27 full-time (12 women); includes 3 minority (1 Asian, non-Hispanic/Latino; 1 Native Hawaiian or other Pacific Islander, non-Hispanic/Latino; 1 Two or more races, non-Hispanic/Latino), 9 international. Average age 30. In 2011, 5 doctorates awarded. *Degree requirements:* For doctorate, comprehensive exam, thesis/dissertation, qualifying exam. *Entrance requirements:* For doctorate, GRE General Test (minimum scores: 153 Verbal/148 Quantitative/4.5 Analytical) or MCAT. Additional exam requirements/recommendations for international students: Required—TOEFL. *Financial support:* Health care benefits, tuition waivers (full), and full tuition and stipends available. *Faculty research:* Developmental mechanisms, molecular biology of cancer, molecular neurobiology, intracellular signaling, growth factors and development. *Unit head:* Dr. Richard Maurer, Program Director, 503-494-7811, E-mail: maurerr@ohsu.edu. *Application contact:* Elaine Offield, Program Coordinator, 503-494-5824, E-mail: offielde@ohsu.edu. Web site: http://www.ohsu.edu/cellbio.

Oregon State University, Graduate School, Program in Molecular and Cellular Biology, Corvallis, OR 97331. Offers MS, PhD. *Degree requirements:* For doctorate, thesis/dissertation, oral and written qualifying exams. *Entrance requirements:* For doctorate, minimum GPA of 3.0 in last 90 hours. Additional exam requirements/recommendations for international students: Required—TOEFL.

Purdue University, Graduate School, College of Science, Department of Biological Sciences, West Lafayette, IN 47907. Offers biochemistry (PhD); biophysics (PhD); cell and developmental biology (PhD); ecology, evolutionary and population biology (MS, PhD), including ecology, evolutionary biology, population biology; genetics (MS, PhD); microbiology (MS, PhD); molecular biology (PhD); neurobiology (MS, PhD); plant physiology (PhD). *Faculty:* 57 full-time (15 women), 4 part-time/adjunct (1 woman). *Students:* 94 full-time (54 women), 9 part-time (5 women); includes 7 minority (2 Black or African American, non-Hispanic/Latino; 3 Asian, non-Hispanic/Latino; 2 Hispanic/Latino), 51 international. Average age 27. 246 applicants, 11% accepted, 18 enrolled. In 2011, 9 master's, 23 doctorates awarded. Terminal master's awarded for partial completion of doctoral program. *Degree requirements:* For master's, thesis (for some programs); for doctorate, thesis/dissertation, seminars, teaching experience. *Entrance requirements:* For master's, GRE General Test, minimum analytical writing score of 3.5, minimum undergraduate GPA of 3.0; for doctorate, GRE General Test, minimum analytical writing score of 3.5, minimum undergraduate GPA of 3.5. Additional exam requirements/recommendations for international students: Required—TOEFL (minimum score 600 paper-based; 107 iBT) for MS; TOEFL (minimum score 600 paper-based; 80 iBT) for Ph D. *Application deadline:* For fall admission, 12/7 for domestic and international students. Applications are processed on a rolling basis. Application fee: $60 ($75 for international students). Electronic applications accepted. *Financial support:* Fellowships, research assistantships, and teaching assistantships available. Support available to part-time students. Financial award application deadline: 2/15; financial award applicants required to submit FAFSA. *Unit head:* Dr. Richard J. Kuhn, Head, 765-494-4407, E-mail: kuhnr@purdue.edu. *Application contact:* Georgina E. Rupp, Graduate Coordinator, 765-494-8142, Fax: 765-494-0876, E-mail: ruppg@purdue.edu. Web site: http://www.bio.purdue.edu/.

Queen's University at Kingston, School of Graduate Studies and Research, Faculty of Health Sciences, Department of Anatomy and Cell Biology, Kingston, ON K7L 3N6, Canada. Offers biology of reproduction (M Sc, PhD); cancer (M Sc, PhD); cardiovascular pathophysiology (M Sc, PhD); cell and molecular biology (M Sc, PhD); drug metabolism (M Sc, PhD); endocrinology (M Sc, PhD); motor control (M Sc, PhD); neural regeneration (M Sc, PhD); neurophysiology (M Sc, PhD). Part-time programs available. *Degree requirements:* For master's, thesis; for doctorate, one foreign

Cell Biology

language, comprehensive exam, thesis/dissertation. *Entrance requirements:* Additional exam requirements/recommendations for international students: Required—TOEFL. Electronic applications accepted. *Faculty research:* Human kinetics, neuroscience, reproductive biology, cardiovascular.

Quinnipiac University, School of Health Sciences, Program in Molecular and Cell Biology, Hamden, CT 06518-1940. Offers MS. Part-time programs available. *Faculty:* 9 full-time (6 women), 17 part-time/adjunct (7 women). *Students:* 22 (18 women); includes 4 minority (2 Black or African American, non-Hispanic/Latino; 1 Asian, non-Hispanic/Latino; 1 Hispanic/Latino), 4 international. Average age 26. 44 applicants, 68% accepted, 18 enrolled. In 2011, 12 master's awarded. *Degree requirements:* For master's, thesis optional. *Entrance requirements:* For master's, bachelor's degree in biological, medical, or health sciences; minimum GPA of 2.75. Additional exam requirements/recommendations for international students: Required—TOEFL (minimum score 575 paper-based; 233 computer-based; 90 iBT), IELTS (minimum score 6.5). *Application deadline:* For fall admission, 7/30 priority date for domestic students, 4/30 for international students; for spring admission, 12/15 priority date for domestic students, 9/15 for international students. Applications are processed on a rolling basis. Application fee: $45. Electronic applications accepted. *Expenses: Tuition:* Part-time $855 per credit. *Required fees:* $35 per credit. *Financial support:* In 2011–12, 6 students received support. Federal Work-Study, tuition waivers, and unspecified assistantships available. Support available to part-time students. Financial award application deadline: 4/15; financial award applicants required to submit FAFSA. *Unit head:* Dr. Sarah Berke, Director, 203-582-6431, E-mail: sarah.berke@quinnipiac.edu. *Application contact:* Kristin Parent, Assistant Director of Graduate Health Sciences Admissions, 800-462-1944, Fax: 203-582-3443, E-mail: kristin.parent@quinnipiac.edu. Web site: http://www.quinnipiac.edu/gradmolecular.

Rice University, Graduate Programs, Wiess School of Natural Sciences, Department of Biochemistry and Cell Biology, Houston, TX 77251-1892. Offers MA, PhD. Terminal master's awarded for partial completion of doctoral program. *Degree requirements:* For master's, thesis; for doctorate, thesis/dissertation. *Entrance requirements:* For master's and doctorate, GRE. Additional exam requirements/recommendations for international students: Required—TOEFL (minimum score 600 paper-based; 250 computer-based; 90 iBT). Electronic applications accepted. *Expenses:* Contact institution. *Faculty research:* Steroid metabolism, protein structure NMR, biophysics, cell growth and movement.

Rosalind Franklin University of Medicine and Science, School of Graduate and Postdoctoral Studies - Interdisciplinary Graduate Program in Biomedical Sciences, Department of Cell Biology and Anatomy, North Chicago, IL 60064-3095. Offers MS, PhD, MD/PhD. Terminal master's awarded for partial completion of doctoral program. *Degree requirements:* For master's, comprehensive exam, thesis, qualifying exam; for doctorate, comprehensive exam, thesis/dissertation, original research project. *Entrance requirements:* For master's and doctorate, GRE General Test, minimum GPA of 3.0. Additional exam requirements/recommendations for international students: Required—TOEFL, TWE. *Faculty research:* Neuroscience, molecular biology.

Rush University, Graduate College, Division of Anatomy and Cell Biology, Chicago, IL 60612-3832. Offers MS, PhD, MD/MS, MD/PhD. Terminal master's awarded for partial completion of doctoral program. *Degree requirements:* For master's, thesis; for doctorate, comprehensive exam, thesis/dissertation, preliminary exam, dissertation proposal. *Entrance requirements:* For master's, GRE General Test, minimum GPA of 3.0, bachelor's degree in biology or chemistry (preferred), interview; for doctorate, GRE General Test, minimum GPA of 3.0, interview. Additional exam requirements/recommendations for international students: Required—TOEFL. Electronic applications accepted. *Faculty research:* Incontinence following vaginal distension, knee replacement, biomimetric materials, injured spinal motoneurons, implant fixation.

Rutgers, The State University of New Jersey, New Brunswick, Graduate School-New Brunswick, Programs in the Molecular Biosciences, Program in Cell and Developmental Biology, Piscataway, NJ 08854-8097. Offers MS, PhD. MS, PhD offered jointly with University of Medicine and Dentistry of New Jersey. Part-time programs available. Terminal master's awarded for partial completion of doctoral program. *Degree requirements:* For master's, thesis; for doctorate, thesis/dissertation, written qualifying exam. *Entrance requirements:* For master's, GRE General Test; for doctorate, GRE General Test, GRE Subject Test (recommended), minimum GPA of 3.0. Additional exam requirements/recommendations for international students: Required—TOEFL. Electronic applications accepted. *Faculty research:* Signal transduction and regulation of gene expression, developmental biology, cellular biology, developmental genetics, neurobiology.

San Diego State University, Graduate and Research Affairs, College of Sciences, Department of Biology, San Diego, CA 92182. Offers biology (MA, MS), including ecology (MS), molecular biology (MS), physiology (MS), systematics/evolution (MS); cell and molecular biology (PhD); ecology (MS, PhD); microbiology (MS). Terminal master's awarded for partial completion of doctoral program. *Degree requirements:* For master's, thesis; for doctorate, thesis/dissertation. *Entrance requirements:* For master's, GRE General Test, GRE Subject Test, resume or curriculum vitae, 2 letters of recommendation. Additional exam requirements/recommendations for international students: Required—TOEFL. Electronic applications accepted.

San Diego State University, Graduate and Research Affairs, College of Sciences, Molecular Biology Institute, Program in Cell and Molecular Biology, San Diego, CA 92182. Offers PhD. Program offered jointly with University of California, San Diego. *Degree requirements:* For doctorate, thesis/dissertation, oral comprehensive qualifying exam. *Entrance requirements:* For doctorate, GRE General Test, GRE Subject Test, resumé or curriculum vitae, 3 letters of recommendation. Electronic applications accepted. *Faculty research:* Structure/dynamics of protein kinesis, chromatin structure and DNA methylation membrane biochemistry, secretory protein targeting, molecular biology of cardiac myocytes.

San Francisco State University, Division of Graduate Studies, College of Science and Engineering, Department of Biology, Program in Cell and Molecular Biology, San Francisco, CA 94132-1722. Offers MS. *Application deadline:* Applications are processed on a rolling basis. *Unit head:* Dr. Diana Chu, Program Coordinator, 415-405-3487, E-mail: chud@sfsu.edu. *Application contact:* Dr. Robert Patterson, Graduate Coordinator, 415-338-1100, E-mail: patters@sfsu.edu. Web site: http://biology.sfsu.edu/programs/graduate.

State University of New York Downstate Medical Center, School of Graduate Studies, Program in Molecular and Cellular Biology, Brooklyn, NY 11203-2098. Offers PhD, MD/PhD. Affiliation with a particular PhD degree-granting program is deferred to the second year. *Degree requirements:* For doctorate, comprehensive exam, thesis/dissertation. *Entrance requirements:* For doctorate, GRE General Test. Additional exam requirements/recommendations for international students: Recommended—TOEFL. *Faculty research:* Mechanism of gene regulation, molecular virology.

State University of New York Upstate Medical University, College of Graduate Studies, Program in Cell and Developmental Biology, Syracuse, NY 13210-2334. Offers anatomy (MS, PhD); MD/PhD. Terminal master's awarded for partial completion of doctoral program. *Degree requirements:* For master's, thesis; for doctorate,

comprehensive exam, thesis/dissertation. *Entrance requirements:* For master's, GRE General Test, interview; for doctorate, GRE General Test, telephone interview. Additional exam requirements/recommendations for international students: Required—TOEFL. Electronic applications accepted. *Faculty research:* Cancer, disorders of the nervous system, infectious diseases, diabetes/metabolic disorders/cardiovascular diseases.

Stony Brook University, State University of New York, Graduate School, College of Arts and Sciences, Department of Biochemistry and Cell Biology, Molecular and Cellular Biology Program, Stony Brook, NY 11794. Offers biochemistry and molecular biology (PhD); biological sciences (MA); cellular and developmental biology (PhD); immunology and pathology (PhD); molecular and cellular biology (PhD). *Degree requirements:* For doctorate, comprehensive exam, thesis/dissertation, teaching experience. *Entrance requirements:* For doctorate, GRE General Test, GRE Subject Test. Additional exam requirements/recommendations for international students: Required—TOEFL.

Temple University, Health Sciences Center, School of Medicine and Graduate School, Graduate Programs in Medicine, Department of Anatomy and Cell Biology, Philadelphia, PA 19122-6096. Offers MS, PhD. *Faculty:* 21 full-time (6 women). *Students:* 15 full-time (5 women), 1 part-time (0 women); includes 2 minority (1 Black or African American, non-Hispanic/Latino; 1 Hispanic/Latino), 3 international. Average age 30. 9 applicants, 44% accepted, 2 enrolled. In 2011, 2 doctorates awarded. *Degree requirements:* For doctorate, thesis/dissertation, research seminars. *Entrance requirements:* For master's and doctorate, GRE General Test, GRE Subject Test, minimum GPA of 3.0. Additional exam requirements/recommendations for international students: Required—TOEFL. *Application deadline:* For fall admission, 1/15 for domestic students, 12/15 for international students; for spring admission, 9/1 for domestic students, 8/1 for international students. Application fee: $50. Electronic applications accepted. *Expenses:* Tuition, state resident: full-time $12,366; part-time $687 per credit hour. Tuition, nonresident: full-time $17,298; part-time $961 per credit hour. *Required fees:* $590; $213 per year. *Financial support:* Fellowships and Federal Work-Study available. Financial award application deadline: 1/15; financial award applicants required to submit FAFSA. *Faculty research:* Neurobiology, reproductive biology, cardiovascular system, musculoskeletal biology, developmental biology. *Unit head:* Dr. Steven Popoff, Chair, 215-707-3161, Fax: 215-707-2966, E-mail: spopoff@temple.edu. *Application contact:* Office of Admissions, 215-707-3656, Fax: 215-707-6932, E-mail: medadmissions@temple.edu. Web site: http://www.temple.edu/medicine/departments_centers/basic_science/anatomy.htm.

Texas A&M Health Science Center, College of Medicine, Department of Molecular and Cellular Medicine, College Station, TX 77840. Offers PhD. *Degree requirements:* For doctorate, thesis/dissertation. *Entrance requirements:* For doctorate, GRE General Test. *Faculty research:* Immunology, cell and membrane biology, protein biochemistry, molecular genetics, parasitology, vertebrate embryogenesis and microbiology.

Texas A&M Health Science Center, College of Medicine, Program in Cell and Molecular Biology, College Station, TX 77840. Offers PhD.

Texas A&M University, College of Science, Department of Biology, College Station, TX 77843. Offers biology (MS, PhD); botany (MS, PhD); microbiology (MS, PhD); molecular and cell biology (PhD); neuroscience (MS, PhD); zoology (MS, PhD). *Faculty:* 41. *Students:* 99 full-time (60 women), 8 part-time (4 women); includes 11 minority (1 Black or African American, non-Hispanic/Latino; 5 Asian, non-Hispanic/Latino; 4 Hispanic/Latino; 1 Two or more races, non-Hispanic/Latino), 46 international. Average age 28. In 2011, 5 master's, 7 doctorates awarded. *Degree requirements:* For master's, thesis or alternative; for doctorate, comprehensive exam, thesis/dissertation. *Entrance requirements:* For master's and doctorate, GRE General Test. Additional exam requirements/recommendations for international students: Required—TOEFL. *Application deadline:* For fall admission, 1/15 for domestic students. Applications are processed on a rolling basis. Application fee: $50 ($75 for international students). Electronic applications accepted. *Expenses:* Tuition, state resident: full-time $5437; part-time $226.55 per credit hour. Tuition, nonresident: full-time $12,949; part-time $539.55 per credit hour. *Required fees:* $2741. *Financial support:* Fellowships, research assistantships, and teaching assistantships available. Financial award application deadline: 4/1; financial award applicants required to submit FAFSA. *Unit head:* Dr. Jack McMahan, Department Head, 979-845-2301, E-mail: granster@mail.bio.tamu.edu. *Application contact:* 979-845-7755, Fax: 979-845-2891, E-mail: graduate@bio.tamu.edu. Web site: http://www.bio.tamu.edu/index.html.

Texas Tech University Health Sciences Center, Graduate School of Biomedical Sciences, Department of Cell Biology and Biochemistry, Program in Cell and Molecular Biology, Lubbock, TX 79430. Offers MS, PhD, MD/PhD, MS/PhD. Terminal master's awarded for partial completion of doctoral program. *Degree requirements:* For master's, comprehensive exam, thesis; for doctorate, comprehensive exam, thesis/dissertation. *Entrance requirements:* For master's and doctorate, GRE General Test, minimum GPA of 3.0. Additional exam requirements/recommendations for international students: Required—TOEFL. *Faculty research:* Biochemical endocrinology, neurobiology, molecular biology, reproductive biology, biology of developing systems.

Thomas Jefferson University, Jefferson College of Graduate Studies, MS Program in Cell and Developmental Biology, Philadelphia, PA 19107. Offers MS. Part-time and evening/weekend programs available. *Faculty:* 22 full-time (7 women), 23 part-time/adjunct (6 women). *Students:* 17 part-time (11 women); includes 2 minority (both Asian, non-Hispanic/Latino), 1 international. 19 applicants, 58% accepted, 10 enrolled. In 2011, 3 master's awarded. *Degree requirements:* For master's, thesis, clerkship. *Entrance requirements:* For master's, GRE General Test or MCAT, minimum GPA of 3.0. Additional exam requirements/recommendations for international students: Required—TOEFL (minimum score 100 iBT) or IELTS (minimum score 7). *Application deadline:* For fall admission, 8/1 priority date for domestic students, 3/1 for international students; for winter admission, 12/1 priority date for domestic students, 6/1 for international students; for spring admission, 4/1 priority date for domestic students. Applications are processed on a rolling basis. Application fee: $50. Electronic applications accepted. *Financial support:* In 2011–12, 7 students received support. Federal Work-Study and institutionally sponsored loans available. Support available to part-time students. Financial award application deadline: 5/1; financial award applicants required to submit FAFSA. *Faculty research:* Developmental biology, cell biology, planning and management, drug development. *Unit head:* Dr. Gerald B. Grunwald, Dean and Program Director, 215-503-4191, Fax: 215-503-6690, E-mail: gerald.grunwald@jefferson.edu. *Application contact:* Eleanor M. Gorman, Assistant Coordinator, Graduate Center Programs, 215-503-5799, Fax: 215-503-3433, E-mail: eleanor.gorman@jefferson.edu. Web site: http://www.jefferson.edu/jcgs/msbs/.

Thomas Jefferson University, Jefferson College of Graduate Studies, PhD Program in Cell and Developmental Biology, Philadelphia, PA 19107. Offers PhD. *Faculty:* 73 full-time (17 women). *Students:* 28 full-time (15 women); includes 4 minority (2 Asian, non-Hispanic/Latino; 2 Hispanic/Latino), 4 international. 58 applicants, 12% accepted, 5 enrolled. In 2011, 3 doctorates awarded. *Degree requirements:* For doctorate, comprehensive exam, thesis/dissertation. *Entrance requirements:* For doctorate, GRE General Test, minimum GPA of 3.2. Additional exam requirements/recommendations for international students: Required—TOEFL (minimum score 250 computer-based; 100

iBT). *Application deadline:* For fall admission, 1/5 priority date for domestic students, 1/5 for international students. Applications are processed on a rolling basis. Application fee: $50. Electronic applications accepted. *Financial support:* In 2011–12, 28 students received support, including 28 fellowships with full tuition reimbursements available (averaging $54,758 per year); Federal Work-Study, institutionally sponsored loans, scholarships/grants, traineeships, and stipends also available. Support available to part-time students. Financial award application deadline: 5/1; financial award applicants required to submit FAFSA. *Total annual research expenditures:* $31.8 million. *Unit head:* Dr. Theodore F. Taraschi, Program Director, 215-503-5020, Fax: 215-503-0206, E-mail: theodore.taraschi@jefferson.edu. *Application contact:* Marc E. Stearns, Director of Admissions, 215-503-0155, Fax: 215-503-9920, E-mail: jcgs-info@jefferson.edu. Web site: http://www.jefferson.edu/jcgs/phd/mcb/.

Tufts University, Sackler School of Graduate Biomedical Sciences, Cell, Molecular and Developmental Biology Program, Medford, MA 02155. Offers PhD. *Faculty:* 39 full-time (15 women). *Students:* 26 full-time (12 women); includes 5 minority (3 Asian, non-Hispanic/Latino; 1 Hispanic/Latino; 1 Two or more races, non-Hispanic/Latino), 4 international. Average age 29. In 2011, 8 doctorates awarded. Terminal master's awarded for partial completion of doctoral program. *Degree requirements:* For doctorate, thesis/dissertation. *Entrance requirements:* For doctorate, GRE General Test, 3 letters of reference. Additional exam requirements/recommendations for international students: Required—TOEFL (minimum score 600 paper-based; 250 computer-based; 100 iBT). *Application deadline:* For fall admission, 12/15 for domestic and international students. Application fee: $70. Electronic applications accepted. *Expenses: Tuition:* Full-time $41,208; part-time $1030 per credit hour. Full-time tuition and fees vary according to degree level, program and student level. Part-time tuition and fees vary according to course load. *Financial support:* In 2011–12, 25 students received support, including 25 research assistantships with full tuition reimbursements available (averaging $30,000 per year); fellowships and health care benefits also available. *Faculty research:* Reproduction and hormone action, control of gene expression, cell-matrix and cell-cell interactions, growth control and tumorigenesis, cytoskeleton and contractile proteins. *Unit head:* Dr. John Castellot, Program Director, 617-636-0303, Fax: 617-636-0375. *Application contact:* Kellie Johnston, Associate Director of Admissions, 617-636-6767, Fax: 617-636-0375, E-mail: sackler-school@tufts.edu. Web site: http://sackler.tufts.edu/Academics/Degree-Programs/PhD-Programs/Cell-Molecular-and-Developmental-Biology.

Tulane University, School of Medicine and School of Liberal Arts, Graduate Programs in Biomedical Sciences, Department of Structural and Cellular Biology, New Orleans, LA 70118-5669. Offers MS, PhD, MD/PhD. MS and PhD offered through the Graduate School. *Degree requirements:* For master's, one foreign language, thesis; for doctorate, 2 foreign languages, thesis/dissertation. *Entrance requirements:* For master's, GRE General Test, minimum B average in undergraduate course work; for doctorate, GRE General Test. Additional exam requirements/recommendations for international students: Required—TOEFL. Electronic applications accepted. *Faculty research:* Reproductive endocrinology, visual neuroscience, neural response to altered hormones.

Tulane University, School of Medicine and School of Liberal Arts, Graduate Programs in Biomedical Sciences, Interdisciplinary Graduate Program in Molecular and Cellular Biology, New Orleans, LA 70118-5669. Offers PhD, MD/PhD. PhD offered through the Graduate School. *Degree requirements:* For doctorate, thesis/dissertation. *Entrance requirements:* For doctorate, GRE General Test, GRE Subject Test. Additional exam requirements/recommendations for international students: Required—TOEFL. Electronic applications accepted. *Faculty research:* Developmental biology, neuroscience, virology.

Tulane University, School of Science and Engineering, Department of Cell and Molecular Biology, New Orleans, LA 70118-5669. Offers MS, PhD. Terminal master's awarded for partial completion of doctoral program. *Degree requirements:* For doctorate, thesis/dissertation. *Entrance requirements:* For master's, GRE General Test, minimum B average in undergraduate course work; for doctorate, GRE General Test. Additional exam requirements/recommendations for international students: Required—TOEFL. Electronic applications accepted.

Uniformed Services University of the Health Sciences, School of Medicine, Graduate Programs in the Biomedical Sciences and Public Health, Graduate Program in Molecular and Cell Biology, Bethesda, MD 20814-4799. Offers MS, PhD. *Faculty:* 43 full-time (11 women), 3 part-time/adjunct (0 women). *Students:* 22 full-time (11 women); includes 10 minority (5 Asian, non-Hispanic/Latino; 5 Hispanic/Latino), 6 international. Average age 26. 30 applicants, 43% accepted, 8 enrolled. In 2011, 2 doctorates awarded. *Degree requirements:* For doctorate, comprehensive exam, thesis/dissertation, qualifying exam. *Entrance requirements:* For doctorate, GRE General Test, minimum GPA of 3.0. Additional exam requirements/recommendations for international students: Required—TOEFL. *Application deadline:* For fall admission, 1/1 priority date for domestic students, 1/1 for international students. Applications are processed on a rolling basis. Application fee: $0. Electronic applications accepted. *Financial support:* In 2011–12, fellowships with full tuition reimbursements (averaging $27,000 per year) were awarded; scholarships/grants, health care benefits, and tuition waivers (full) also available. *Faculty research:* Immunology, biochemistry, cancer biology, stem cell biology. *Unit head:* Dr. Mary Lou Cutler, Director, 301-295-3248, Fax: 301-295-1996. *Application contact:* Tina Finley, Administrative Assistant, 301-295-3642, Fax: 301-295-1996, E-mail: nfinley@usuhs.mil. Web site: http://www.usuhs.mil/mcb/index.html.

See Display on page 216 and Close-Up on page 237.

Universidad Central del Caribe, School of Medicine, Program in Biomedical Sciences, Bayamón, PR 00960-6032. Offers anatomy and cell biology (MA, MS); biochemistry (MS); biomedical sciences (MA); cellular and molecular biology (PhD); microbiology and immunology (MA, MS); pharmacology (MS); physiology (MS).

Université de Montréal, Faculty of Medicine, Department of Pathology and Cellular Biology, Montréal, QC H3C 3J7, Canada. Offers M Sc, PhD. Terminal master's awarded for partial completion of doctoral program. *Degree requirements:* For master's, thesis; for doctorate, thesis/dissertation, general exam. *Entrance requirements:* For master's and doctorate, proficiency in French, knowledge of English. Electronic applications accepted. *Faculty research:* Immunopathology, cardiovascular pathology, oncogenetics, cellular neurocytology, muscular dystrophy.

Université de Sherbrooke, Faculty of Medicine and Health Sciences, Graduate Programs in Medicine, Department of Anatomy and Cell Biology, Sherbrooke, QC J1H 5N4, Canada. Offers cell biology (M Sc, PhD). Terminal master's awarded for partial completion of doctoral program. *Degree requirements:* For master's, thesis; for doctorate, thesis/dissertation. Electronic applications accepted. *Faculty research:* Biology of the gut epithelium, signal transduction, gene expression and differentiation, intestinal inflammation, vascular and skeletal muscle cell biology.

Université Laval, Faculty of Medicine, Graduate Programs in Medicine, Programs in Cellular and Molecular Biology, Québec, QC G1K 7P4, Canada. Offers M Sc, PhD. Terminal master's awarded for partial completion of doctoral program. *Degree requirements:* For master's, thesis; for doctorate, comprehensive exam, thesis/dissertation. *Entrance requirements:* For master's and doctorate, knowledge of French,

comprehension of written English. Electronic applications accepted. *Faculty research:* Oral bacterial metabolism, sugar transport.

University at Albany, State University of New York, College of Arts and Sciences, Department of Biological Sciences, Specialization in Molecular, Cellular, Developmental, and Neural Biology, Albany, NY 12222-0001. Offers MS, PhD. *Degree requirements:* For master's, one foreign language; for doctorate, one foreign language, thesis/dissertation. *Entrance requirements:* For master's and doctorate, GRE General Test.

University at Albany, State University of New York, School of Public Health, Department of Biomedical Sciences, Program in Cell and Molecular Structure, Albany, NY 12222-0001. Offers MS, PhD. *Degree requirements:* For master's, thesis; for doctorate, thesis/dissertation. *Entrance requirements:* For master's and doctorate, GRE General Test, GRE Subject Test.

University at Buffalo, the State University of New York, Graduate School, Graduate Programs in Cancer Research and Biomedical Sciences at Roswell Park Cancer Institute, Department of Cellular and Molecular Biology at Roswell Park Cancer Institute, Buffalo, NY 14260. Offers PhD. *Degree requirements:* For doctorate, thesis/dissertation, exam, project. *Entrance requirements:* For doctorate, GRE General Test, minimum B average in undergraduate coursework. Additional exam requirements/recommendations for international students: Required—TOEFL (minimum score 600 paper-based; 250 computer-based; 100 iBT) or IELTS. Electronic applications accepted. *Faculty research:* Cancer genetics, chromatin structure and replication, regulation of transcription, human gene mapping, genetic and structural approaches to regulation of gene expression.

The University of Alabama at Birmingham, Graduate Programs in Joint Health Sciences, Program in Cell Biology, Birmingham, AL 35294. Offers PhD. *Degree requirements:* For doctorate, variable foreign language requirement, thesis/dissertation, qualifying exam. *Entrance requirements:* For doctorate, GRE General Test, interview. *Application deadline:* Applications are processed on a rolling basis. Electronic applications accepted. *Expenses:* Tuition, state resident: full-time $5922; part-time $309 per hour. Tuition, nonresident: full-time $13,428; part-time $726 per hour. Tuition and fees vary according to program. *Financial support:* Fellowships available. *Unit head:* Dr. Etty Benveniste, Chair, 205-934-7667, Fax: 205-975-6748, E-mail: tika@uab.edu. *Application contact:* Information Contact, 205-975-7145, Fax: 205-975-6748.

The University of Alabama at Birmingham, Graduate Programs in Joint Health Sciences, Program in Cellular and Molecular Physiology, Birmingham, AL 35294. Offers PhD. Application fee: $35 ($60 for international students). *Expenses:* Tuition, state resident: full-time $5922; part-time $309 per hour. Tuition, nonresident: full-time $13,428; part-time $726 per hour. Tuition and fees vary according to program. *Unit head:* Dr. Etty Benvenister, Chair, 205-934-7667, Fax: 205-975-6748, E-mail: tika@uab.edu.

University of Alberta, Faculty of Graduate Studies and Research, Department of Biological Sciences, Edmonton, AB T6G 2E1, Canada. Offers environmental biology and ecology (M Sc, PhD); microbiology and biotechnology (M Sc, PhD); molecular biology and genetics (M Sc, PhD); physiology and cell biology (M Sc, PhD); plant biology (M Sc, PhD); systematics and evolution (M Sc, PhD). Terminal master's awarded for partial completion of doctoral program. *Degree requirements:* For master's, thesis; for doctorate, thesis/dissertation. *Entrance requirements:* Additional exam requirements/recommendations for international students: Required—TOEFL.

University of Alberta, Faculty of Medicine and Dentistry and Faculty of Graduate Studies and Research, Graduate Programs in Medicine, Department of Cell Biology, Edmonton, AB T6G 2E1, Canada. Offers cell and molecular biology (M Sc, PhD). Terminal master's awarded for partial completion of doctoral program. *Degree requirements:* For master's, thesis; for doctorate, thesis/dissertation. *Entrance requirements:* For master's and doctorate, 3 letters of reference, curriculum vitae. Additional exam requirements/recommendations for international students: Required—TOEFL (minimum score 600 paper-based; 250 computer-based). *Faculty research:* Protein targeting, membrane trafficking, signal transduction, cell growth and division, cell-cell interaction and development.

The University of Arizona, College of Medicine, Department of Cell Biology and Anatomy, Tucson, AZ 85721. Offers PhD. *Faculty:* 15 full-time (3 women), 1 (woman) part-time/adjunct. *Students:* 15 full-time (8 women); includes 5 minority (1 Black or African American, non-Hispanic/Latino; 1 Asian, non-Hispanic/Latino; 1 Hispanic/Latino; 2 Two or more races, non-Hispanic/Latino), 2 international. Average age 29. 30 applicants, 10% accepted. In 2011, 3 degrees awarded. *Degree requirements:* For doctorate, thesis/dissertation. *Entrance requirements:* For doctorate, GRE General Test. *Application deadline:* For fall admission, 1/15 priority date for domestic students. Application fee: $75. *Expenses:* Tuition, state resident: full-time $10,840. Tuition, nonresident: full-time $25,802. *Financial support:* In 2011–12, 11 research assistantships with partial tuition reimbursements (averaging $25,000 per year) were awarded; fellowships with full and partial tuition reimbursements, teaching assistantships, institutionally sponsored loans, scholarships/grants, traineeships, tuition waivers (full), and unspecified assistantships also available. Support available to part-time students. Financial award application deadline: 1/15. *Faculty research:* Heart development, neural development, cellular toxicology and microcirculation; membrane traffic and cytoskeleton; cell-surface receptors. *Total annual research expenditures:* $4.6 million. *Unit head:* Dr. Carol Gregorio, Head, 520-626-8113, Fax: 520-626-2097, E-mail: gregorio@email.arizona.edu. *Application contact:* Dr. Jean M. Wilson, Chairperson, Graduate Studies Committee, 520-626-2553, Fax: 520-626-2097. Web site: http://www.cba.arizona.edu/.

The University of Arizona, College of Science, Department of Molecular and Cellular Biology, Tucson, AZ 85721. Offers applied biosciences (PSM); molecular and cellular biology (MS, PhD). Evening/weekend programs available. *Faculty:* 13 full-time (5 women), 1 (woman) part-time/adjunct. *Students:* 26 full-time (14 women), 1 part-time (0 women); includes 8 minority (1 Asian, non-Hispanic/Latino; 3 Hispanic/Latino; 4 Two or more races, non-Hispanic/Latino), 5 international. Average age 28. 160 applicants, 11% accepted, 9 enrolled. In 2011, 2 master's, 9 doctorates awarded. Terminal master's awarded for partial completion of doctoral program. *Degree requirements:* For master's, thesis; for doctorate, thesis/dissertation. *Entrance requirements:* For master's, 3 letters of recommendation; for doctorate, 3 letters of recommendation, statement of purpose. Additional exam requirements/recommendations for international students: Required—TOEFL (minimum score 600 paper-based; 250 computer-based; 90 iBT), IELTS (minimum score 7). *Application deadline:* For fall admission, 1/1 for domestic and international students. Applications are processed on a rolling basis. Application fee: $75. Electronic applications accepted. *Expenses:* Tuition, state resident: full-time $10,840. Tuition, nonresident: full-time $25,802. *Financial support:* In 2011–12, 13 research assistantships with full tuition reimbursements (averaging $24,286 per year), 4 teaching assistantships with full tuition reimbursements (averaging $19,145 per year) were awarded; career-related internships or fieldwork, scholarships/grants, health care benefits, and unspecified assistantships also available. *Faculty research:* Plant molecular biology, cellular and molecular aspects of development, genetics of bacteria and lower eukaryotes. *Total annual research expenditures:* $3.2 million. *Unit head:* Kathleen Dixon, Department Head, 520-621-7563, Fax: 520-621-3709, E-mail: dixonk@

email.arizona.edu. *Application contact:* 520-621-3569, E-mail: bmcb@email.arizona.edu. Web site: http://bmcb.biology.arizona.edu/.

University of Arkansas, Graduate School, Interdisciplinary Program in Cell and Molecular Biology, Fayetteville, AR 72701-1201. Offers MS, PhD. *Students:* 11 full-time (6 women), 45 part-time (23 women); includes 5 minority (1 Black or African American, non-Hispanic/Latino; 3 Asian, non-Hispanic/Latino; 1 Hispanic/Latino), 38 international. In 2011, 5 master's, 3 doctorates awarded. *Degree requirements:* For doctorate, thesis/dissertation. *Application deadline:* For fall admission, 4/1 for international students; for spring admission, 10/1 for international students. Applications are processed on a rolling basis. Application fee: $40 ($50 for international students). Electronic applications accepted. *Financial support:* In 2011–12, 31 research assistantships, 12 teaching assistantships were awarded; fellowships with tuition reimbursements also available. Financial award application deadline: 4/1; financial award applicants required to submit FAFSA. *Unit head:* Dr. Douglas Rhoads, Head, 479-575-7396, Fax: 479-575-5908, E-mail: drhoads@uark.edu. *Application contact:* Graduate Admissions, 479-575-6246, Fax: 479-575-5908, E-mail: gradinfo@uark.edu. Web site: http://www.uark.edu/depts/cemb/.

The University of British Columbia, Faculty of Medicine, Department of Cellular and Physiological Sciences, Division of Anatomy and Cell Biology, Vancouver, BC V6T 1Z1, Canada. Offers M Sc, PhD. *Degree requirements:* For master's, thesis, oral defense; for doctorate, comprehensive exam, thesis/dissertation, oral defense. *Entrance requirements:* Additional exam requirements/recommendations for international students: Required—TOEFL (minimum score 550 paper-based; 213 computer-based), IELTS (minimum score 6.2). Electronic applications accepted. *Faculty research:* Cell and developmental biology, membrane biophysics, cellular immunology, cancer, fetal alcohol syndrome.

University of California, Berkeley, Graduate Division, College of Letters and Science, Department of Molecular and Cell Biology, Berkeley, CA 94720-1500. Offers PhD. *Degree requirements:* For doctorate, comprehensive exam, thesis/dissertation, qualifying exam, 2 semesters of teaching, 3 seminars. *Entrance requirements:* For doctorate, GRE General Test, GRE Subject Test (recommended), minimum GPA of 3.0. Additional exam requirements/recommendations for international students: Required—TOEFL (minimum score 570 paper-based; 230 computer-based; 68 iBT), IELTS (minimum score 7). Electronic applications accepted. *Faculty research:* Biochemistry and molecular biology, cell and developmental biology, genetics, immunology, neurobiology, genomics.

University of California, Davis, Graduate Studies, Graduate Group in Cell and Developmental Biology, Davis, CA 95616. Offers MS, PhD. *Degree requirements:* For master's, comprehensive exam (for some programs), thesis (for some programs); for doctorate, thesis/dissertation. *Entrance requirements:* For doctorate, GRE General Test, GRE Subject Test. Additional exam requirements/recommendations for international students: Required—TOEFL (minimum score 550 paper-based; 213 computer-based). Electronic applications accepted. *Faculty research:* Molecular basis of cell function and development.

University of California, Irvine, School of Biological Sciences, Department of Developmental and Cell Biology, Irvine, CA 92697. Offers biological sciences (MS, PhD). *Students:* 36 full-time (20 women), 2 part-time (1 woman); includes 22 minority (1 American Indian or Alaska Native, non-Hispanic/Latino; 13 Asian, non-Hispanic/Latino; 8 Hispanic/Latino), 2 international. Average age 28. In 2011, 10 degrees awarded. *Degree requirements:* For doctorate, thesis/dissertation. *Entrance requirements:* For master's and doctorate, GRE General Test, GRE Subject Test, minimum GPA of 3.0. Additional exam requirements/recommendations for international students: Required—TOEFL (minimum score 550 paper-based; 213 computer-based). *Application deadline:* For fall admission, 12/15 priority date for domestic students, 12/15 for international students. Application fee: $80 ($100 for international students). Electronic applications accepted. *Financial support:* Fellowships, research assistantships with full tuition reimbursements, teaching assistantships, institutionally sponsored loans, traineeships, health care benefits, and unspecified assistantships available. Financial award application deadline: 3/1; financial award applicants required to submit FAFSA. *Faculty research:* Genetics and development, oncogene signaling pathways, gene regulation, tissue regeneration and molecular genetics. *Unit head:* Prof. Ken W. Cho, Chair, 949-824-7950, Fax: 949-824-4709, E-mail: kwcho@uci.edu. *Application contact:* Renee Marie Frigo, Program Manager, 949-824-8145, Fax: 949-824-1965, E-mail: rfrigo@uci.edu. Web site: http://devcell.bio.uci.edu/.

University of California, Irvine, School of Biological Sciences and School of Medicine, Interdisciplinary Graduate Program in Cellular and Molecular Biosciences, Irvine, CA 92697. Offers PhD. *Faculty:* 138 full-time (35 women). *Students:* 59 full-time (33 women); includes 16 minority (8 Asian, non-Hispanic/Latino; 8 Hispanic/Latino), 6 international. Average age 25. In 2011, 19 doctorates awarded. *Degree requirements:* For doctorate, thesis/dissertation, teaching assignment, preliminary exam. *Entrance requirements:* For doctorate, GRE General Test, minimum GPA of 3.0, research experience. Additional exam requirements/recommendations for international students: Required—TOEFL, IELTS, SPEAK. *Application deadline:* For fall admission, 1/1 for domestic and international students. Application fee: $60 ($80 for international students). Electronic applications accepted. *Expenses:* Contact institution. *Financial support:* In 2011–12, 56 fellowships with full tuition reimbursements (averaging $26,250 per year) were awarded; institutionally sponsored loans, scholarships/grants, tuition waivers (full), unspecified assistantships, and stipends also available. Financial award application deadline: 1/1; financial award applicants required to submit FAFSA. *Faculty research:* Cellular biochemistry; gene structure and expression; protein structure, function, and design; molecular genetics; pathogenesis and inherited disease. *Unit head:* Dr. David Fruman, Director, 949-824-3431, Fax: 949-824-1965, E-mail: gp-mbgb@uci.edu. *Application contact:* Renee Frigo, Administrator, 949-824-8145, Fax: 949-824-1965, E-mail: rfrigo@uci.edu. Web site: http://cmb.uci.edu/.

University of California, Los Angeles, David Geffen School of Medicine and Graduate Division, Graduate Programs in Medicine, Department of Neurobiology, Los Angeles, CA 90095. Offers PhD. *Faculty:* 21 full-time (0 women). *Students:* 9 full-time (6 women); includes 2 minority (1 Asian, non-Hispanic/Latino; 1 Hispanic/Latino), 1 international. Average age 27. In 2011, 6 degrees awarded. *Median time to degree:* Of those who began their doctoral program in fall 2003, 100% received their degree in 8 years or less. *Degree requirements:* For doctorate, thesis/dissertation, oral and written qualifying exams. *Entrance requirements:* For doctorate, GRE General Test, GRE Subject Test, bachelor's degree in physical or biological science. Application fee: $70 ($90 for international students). Electronic applications accepted. *Financial support:* In 2011–12, 14 fellowships, 12 research assistantships, 3 teaching assistantships were awarded; Federal Work-Study, institutionally sponsored loans, scholarships/grants, and tuition waivers (full and partial) also available. Financial award application deadline: 3/1. *Faculty research:* Neuroendocrinology, neurophysiology. *Unit head:* Dr. Marie-Francoise Chesselet, Chair, 310-267-1781, Fax: 310-267-1786, E-mail: mchesselet@mednet.ucla.edu. *Application contact:* UCLA ACCESS Coordinator, 310-206-1845, Fax: 310-206-1636, E-mail: uclaaccess@mednet.ucla.edu.

University of California, Los Angeles, Graduate Division, College of Letters and Science, Department of Molecular, Cell and Developmental Biology, Los Angeles, CA 90095. Offers PhD. *Faculty:* 23 full-time (8 women). *Students:* 35 full-time (20 women); includes 16 minority (3 Black or African American, non-Hispanic/Latino; 8 Asian, non-Hispanic/Latino; 5 Hispanic/Latino), 8 international. Average age 28. 1 applicant, 100% accepted, 1 enrolled. In 2011, 7 degrees awarded. *Median time to degree:* Of those who began their doctoral program in fall 2003, 67% received their degree in 8 years or less. *Degree requirements:* For doctorate, thesis/dissertation, qualifying exams. *Entrance requirements:* For doctorate, GRE General Test, GRE Subject Test. Additional exam requirements/recommendations for international students: Required—TOEFL. Application fee: $70 ($90 for international students). Electronic applications accepted. *Financial support:* In 2011–12, 28 fellowships, 29 research assistantships, 9 teaching assistantships were awarded; scholarships/grants, traineeships, and unspecified assistantships also available. Financial award application deadline: 3/1. *Unit head:* Dr. Utpal Banerjee, Chair, 310-206-5439, Fax: 310-206-3987, E-mail: banerjee@mbi.ucla.edu. *Application contact:* UCLA ACCESS Coordinator, 310-206-1845, Fax: 310-206-1636, E-mail: uclaaccess@mednet.ucla.edu. Web site: http://www.mcdb.ucla.edu.

University of California, Los Angeles, Graduate Division, College of Letters and Science and David Geffen School of Medicine, UCLA ACCESS to Programs in the Molecular, Cellular and Integrative Life Sciences, Los Angeles, CA 90095. Offers biochemistry and molecular biology (PhD); biological chemistry (PhD); cellular and molecular pathology (PhD); human genetics (PhD); microbiology, immunology, and molecular genetics (PhD); molecular biology (PhD); molecular toxicology (PhD); molecular, cellular and integrative physiology (PhD); neurobiology (PhD); oral biology (PhD); physiology (PhD). *Students:* 44 full-time (30 women); includes 18 minority (11 Asian, non-Hispanic/Latino; 6 Hispanic/Latino; 1 Two or more races, non-Hispanic/Latino), 9 international. Average age 25. 495 applicants, 18% accepted, 41 enrolled. *Degree requirements:* For doctorate, thesis/dissertation, oral and written qualifying exams. *Entrance requirements:* For doctorate, GRE General Test, minimum undergraduate GPA of 3.0. Additional exam requirements/recommendations for international students: Required—TOEFL. *Application deadline:* For fall admission, 12/15 for domestic and international students. Application fee: $70 ($90 for international students). Electronic applications accepted. *Financial support:* In 2011–12, 51 fellowships with full and partial tuition reimbursements, 9 research assistantships with full and partial tuition reimbursements were awarded; teaching assistantships with full and partial tuition reimbursements, Federal Work-Study, institutionally sponsored loans, scholarships/grants, health care benefits, tuition waivers (full and partial), and unspecified assistantships also available. Financial award application deadline: 3/1; financial award applicants required to submit FAFSA. *Faculty research:* Molecular, cellular, and developmental biology; immunology; microbiology; integrative biology. *Unit head:* Jody Spillane, Project Coordinator, 310-206-1845, E-mail: jspillane@mednet.ucla.edu. *Application contact:* UCLA ACCESS Admissions, 310-206-1845, E-mail: uclaaccess@mednet.ucla.edu. Web site: https://www.uclaaccess.ucla.edu/.

University of California, Riverside, Graduate Division, Program in Cell, Molecular, and Developmental Biology, Riverside, CA 92521-0102. Offers MS, PhD. Terminal master's awarded for partial completion of doctoral program. *Degree requirements:* For master's, thesis, oral defense of thesis; for doctorate, thesis/dissertation, oral defense of thesis, qualifying exams, 2 quarters of teaching experience. *Entrance requirements:* For master's and doctorate, GRE General Test, minimum GPA of 3.2. Additional exam requirements/recommendations for international students: Required—TOEFL (minimum score 550 paper-based; 213 computer-based; 80 iBT). Electronic applications accepted.

University of California, San Diego, Office of Graduate Studies, Division of Biological Sciences, Program in Cell and Developmental Biology, La Jolla, CA 92093-0348. Offers PhD. Offered in association with the Salk Institute. *Degree requirements:* For doctorate, thesis/dissertation, qualifying exam. Electronic applications accepted.

University of California, San Diego, Office of Graduate Studies, Division of Biological Sciences, Program in Molecular and Cellular Biology, La Jolla, CA 92093. Offers PhD. Offered in association with the Salk Institute. *Degree requirements:* For doctorate, thesis/dissertation, qualifying exam. Electronic applications accepted.

University of California, San Diego, School of Medicine and Office of Graduate Studies, Graduate Studies in Biomedical Sciences, Program in Molecular Cell Biology, La Jolla, CA 92093. Offers PhD. *Degree requirements:* For doctorate, thesis/dissertation, qualifying exam. *Entrance requirements:* For doctorate, GRE General Test. Additional exam requirements/recommendations for international students: Required—TOEFL. Electronic applications accepted. *Faculty research:* Molecular and cellular pharmacology, cell and organ physiology.

University of California, San Diego, School of Medicine and Office of Graduate Studies, Graduate Studies in Biomedical Sciences, Regulatory Biology Program, La Jolla, CA 92093. Offers PhD. *Degree requirements:* For doctorate, thesis/dissertation, 2 qualifying exams. *Entrance requirements:* For doctorate, GRE General Test, GRE Subject Test. Additional exam requirements/recommendations for international students: Required—TOEFL. Electronic applications accepted. *Faculty research:* Eukaryotic regulatory and molecular biology, molecular and cellular pharmacology, cell and organ physiology.

University of California, San Francisco, Graduate Division and School of Medicine, Department of Biochemistry and Biophysics, Program in Cell Biology, San Francisco, CA 94143. Offers PhD, MD/PhD. *Degree requirements:* For doctorate, thesis/dissertation. *Entrance requirements:* For doctorate, GRE General Test, GRE Subject Test. Additional exam requirements/recommendations for international students: Required—TOEFL. *Expenses:* Contact institution.

University of California, Santa Barbara, Graduate Division, College of Letters and Sciences, Division of Mathematics, Life, and Physical Sciences, Department of Molecular, Cellular, and Developmental Biology, Santa Barbara, CA 93106-9625. Offers MA, PhD, MA/PhD. *Faculty:* 21 full-time (3 women), 7 part-time/adjunct (2 women). *Students:* 52 full-time (29 women); includes 10 minority (1 Black or African American, non-Hispanic/Latino; 8 Asian, non-Hispanic/Latino; 1 Hispanic/Latino), 2 international. Average age 28. 115 applicants, 18% accepted, 9 enrolled. In 2011, 8 master's, 8 doctorates awarded. Terminal master's awarded for partial completion of doctoral program. *Median time to degree:* Of those who began their doctoral program in fall 2003, 100% received their degree in 8 years or less. *Degree requirements:* For master's, comprehensive exam (for some programs), thesis (for some programs); for doctorate, comprehensive exam, thesis/dissertation. *Entrance requirements:* For master's, GRE General Test, 3 letters of recommendation, resume/curriculum vitae; for doctorate, GRE General Test, 3 letters of recommendation, statement of purpose, personal achievements/contributions statement, resume/curriculum vitae, transcripts for post-secondary institutions attended. Additional exam requirements/recommendations for international students: Required—TOEFL (minimum score 610 paper-based; 102 iBT), IELTS (minimum score 7). *Application deadline:* For fall admission, 12/20 priority date for domestic students, 12/20 for international students. Application fee: $80 ($100 for international students). Electronic applications accepted. *Expenses:* Tuition, state resident: full-time $12,192. Tuition, nonresident: full-time $27,294. *Required fees:*

$764.13. *Financial support:* In 2011–12, 14 students received support, including 14 fellowships with full and partial tuition reimbursements available (averaging $6,562 per year), 40 research assistantships with full and partial tuition reimbursements available (averaging $15,250 per year), 46 teaching assistantships with partial tuition reimbursements available (averaging $10,500 per year); career-related internships or fieldwork, Federal Work-Study, institutionally sponsored loans, scholarships/grants, traineeships, health care benefits, and unspecified assistantships also available. Financial award application deadline: 12/20; financial award applicants required to submit FAFSA. *Faculty research:* Microbiology, neurobiology (including stem cell research), developmental, virology, cell biology. *Unit head:* Dr. Joel H. Rothman, Chair, 805-893-7885, E-mail: joel.rothman@lifesci.ucsb.edu. *Application contact:* Nicole McCoy, Graduate Program Advisor, 805-893-8499, E-mail: nicole.mccoy@lifesci.ucsb.edu. Web site: http://www.lifesci.ucsb.edu/mcdb/programs/graduate/graduate.html.

University of California, Santa Cruz, Division of Graduate Studies, Division of Physical and Biological Sciences, Program in Molecular, Cellular, and Developmental Biology, Santa Cruz, CA 95064. Offers MA, PhD. Terminal master's awarded for partial completion of doctoral program. *Degree requirements:* For master's, thesis; for doctorate, thesis/dissertation, qualifying exam. *Entrance requirements:* For master's and doctorate, GRE General Test, 3 letters of recommendation, interview. Additional exam requirements/recommendations for international students: Required—TOEFL (minimum score 550 paper-based; 220 computer-based; 83 iBT); Recommended—IELTS (minimum score 8). Electronic applications accepted. *Faculty research:* RNA biology, chromatin and chromosome biology, neurobiology, stem cell biology and differentiation, cell structure and function.

University of Chicago, Division of Biological Sciences, Molecular Biosciences Cluster, Graduate Program in Cell and Molecular Biology, Chicago, IL 60637-1513. Offers PhD. *Degree requirements:* For doctorate, thesis/dissertation, ethics class, 2 teaching assistantships. *Entrance requirements:* For doctorate, GRE General Test. Additional exam requirements/recommendations for international students: Required—TOEFL (minimum score 600 paper-based; 250 computer-based; 104 iBT), IELTS (minimum score 7). Electronic applications accepted. *Faculty research:* Gene expression, chromosome structure, animal viruses, plant molecular genetics.

University of Cincinnati, Graduate School, College of Medicine, Graduate Programs in Biomedical Sciences, Graduate Program in Cell and Cancer Biology, Cincinnati, OH 45221. Offers PhD. *Degree requirements:* For doctorate, thesis/dissertation, qualifying exam. *Entrance requirements:* For doctorate, GRE General Test. Additional exam requirements/recommendations for international students: Required—TOEFL. Electronic applications accepted. *Faculty research:* Cancer biology, cell and molecular biology, breast cancer, pancreatic cancer, drug discovery.

University of Colorado Boulder, Graduate School, College of Arts and Sciences, Department of Molecular, Cellular, and Developmental Biology, Boulder, CO 80309. Offers cellular structure and function (MA, PhD); developmental biology (MA, PhD); molecular biology (MA, PhD). *Faculty:* 16 full-time (6 women). *Students:* 71 full-time (36 women); includes 4 minority (1 American Indian or Alaska Native, non-Hispanic/Latino; 1 Asian, non-Hispanic/Latino; 2 Hispanic/Latino), 13 international. Average age 28. 259 applicants, 13% accepted, 14 enrolled. In 2011, 3 master's, 11 doctorates awarded. Terminal master's awarded for partial completion of doctoral program. *Degree requirements:* For master's, comprehensive exam, thesis or alternative; for doctorate, comprehensive exam, thesis/dissertation. *Entrance requirements:* For master's, GRE General Test, GRE Subject Test, minimum undergraduate GPA of 3.0; for doctorate, GRE General Test, GRE Subject Test. *Application deadline:* For fall admission, 1/1 for domestic students, 12/1 for international students. Application fee: $50 ($60 for international students). *Financial support:* In 2011–12, 86 students received support, including 44 fellowships (averaging $12,916 per year), 48 research assistantships with tuition reimbursements available (averaging $18,648 per year), 15 teaching assistantships with tuition reimbursements available (averaging $19,818 per year); institutionally sponsored loans, scholarships/grants, health care benefits, and unspecified assistantships also available. Financial award application deadline: 2/1; financial award applicants required to submit FAFSA. *Faculty research:* Molecular biology of RNA and DNA, molecular genetics, cell motility and cytoskeleton, cell membranes, developmental genetics, human genetics. *Total annual research expenditures:* $16.2 million. *Application contact:* E-mail: mcdbgrad@colorado.edu. Web site: http://mcdb.colorado.edu/.

University of Colorado Denver, College of Liberal Arts and Sciences, Department of Integrative Biology, Denver, CO 80217. Offers animal behavior (MS); biology (MS); cell and developmental biology (MS); ecology (MS); evolutionary biology (MS); genetics (MS); microbiology (MS); molecular biology (MS); neurobiology (MS); plant systematics (MS). Part-time programs available. *Faculty:* 16 full-time (8 women). *Students:* 20 full-time (13 women), 5 part-time (4 women); includes 1 minority (Hispanic/Latino), 1 international. Average age 29. 21 applicants, 43% accepted, 5 enrolled. In 2011, 7 master's awarded. *Degree requirements:* For master's, comprehensive exam, thesis or alternative, 30-32 credit hours. *Entrance requirements:* For master's, GRE General Test (minimum score in 50% percentile in each section), BA/BS from accredited institution awarded within the last 10 years; minimum undergraduate GPA of 3.0; prerequisite courses: 1 year each of general biology and general chemistry, and 1 semester each of general genetics, general ecology, cell biology, and a structure/function course. Additional exam requirements/recommendations for international students: Required—TOEFL (minimum score 525 paper-based; 197 computer-based; 71 iBT). *Application deadline:* For fall admission, 2/1 for domestic and international students. Application fee: $50 ($75 for international students). Electronic applications accepted. *Financial support:* Research assistantships, teaching assistantships, Federal Work-Study, scholarships/grants, and unspecified assistantships available. Financial award application deadline: 4/1; financial award applicants required to submit FAFSA. *Faculty research:* Molecular developmental biology; quantitative ecology, biogeography, and population dynamics; environmental signaling and endocrine disruption; speciation, the evolution of reproductive isolation, and hybrid zones; evolutionary, behavioral, and conservation ecology. *Unit head:* Dr. Diana Tomback, Acting Chair, 303-556-2657, E-mail: diana.tomback@ucdenver.edu. *Application contact:* Timberley Roane, Associate Professor/Associate Chair, 303-556-6592, E-mail: timberley.roane@ucdenver.edu. Web site: http://www.ucdenver.edu/academics/colleges/CLAS/Departments/biology/Pages/Biology.aspx.

University of Colorado Denver, School of Medicine, Program in Cell Biology, Stem Cells, and Developmental Biology, Aurora, CO 80045. Offers PhD. *Students:* 28 full-time (17 women); includes 2 minority (both Hispanic/Latino), 4 international. Average age 27. 42 applicants, 12% accepted, 5 enrolled. In 2011, 5 doctorates awarded. *Degree requirements:* For doctorate, comprehensive exam, thesis/dissertation, at least 30 credit hours of coursework and 30 credit hours of thesis research; laboratory rotations. *Entrance requirements:* For doctorate, GRE, minimum GPA of 3.0; 3 letters of reference; prerequisite coursework in organic chemistry, biology, biochemistry, physics and calculus; research experience (highly recommended). Additional exam requirements/recommendations for international students: Required—TOEFL (minimum score 550 paper-based; 213 computer-based). *Application deadline:* For fall admission, 12/1 for domestic students, 11/1 for international students. Application fee: $65. Electronic applications accepted. *Expenses:* Contact institution. *Financial support:* Fellowships, research assistantships, teaching assistantships, health care benefits, tuition waivers (full), and stipend available. Financial award application deadline: 3/15; financial award

University of Connecticut Health Center

UCHC offers you exceptional research opportunities spanning **Cell Analysis and Modeling; Cell Biology; Genetics and Developmental Biology; Immunology; Molecular Biology and Biochemistry; Neuroscience;** and **Skeletal, Craniofacial and Oral Biology**.

Key features of our program include:

❖ Integrated admissions with access to more than 100 laboratories.

❖ Flexible educational program tailored to the interests of each student.

❖ Excellent education in a stimulating, cutting edge research environment.

❖ Competitive stipend ($28,000 for 2012–13 year), tuition waiver, and availability of student health plan.

❖ State-of-the-art research facilities, including the new Cell and Genome Sciences Building, which houses the UConn Stem Cell Institute, the Center for Cell Analysis and Modeling, and the Department of Genetics and Developmental Biology.

For more information, please contact:
Stephanie Rauch, Biomedical Science Admissions Coordinator
University of Connecticut Health Center
263 Farmington Ave., MC 3906
Farmington, CT 06030
BiomedSciAdmissions@uchc.edu
http://grad.uchc.edu/prospective/programs/phd_biosci/index.html

applicants required to submit FAFSA. *Faculty research:* Development and repair of the vertebrate nervous system; molecular, genetic and developmental mechanisms involved in the patterning of the early spinal cord (neural plate) during vertebrate embryogenesis; structural analysis of protein glycosylation using NMR and mass spectrometry; small RNAs and post-transcriptional gene regulation during nematode gametogenesis and early development; diabetes-mediated changes in cardiovascular gene expression and functional exercise capacity. *Total annual research expenditures:* $5.7 million. *Unit head:* Dr. Wendy Macklin, Department Chair, 303-724-3426, E-mail: wendy.macklin@ucdenver.edu. *Application contact:* Jennifer Thurston, Program Manager, 303-724-5902, Fax: 303-724-3420, E-mail: jennifer.thurston@ucdenver.edu. Web site: http://www.ucdenver.edu/academics/colleges/medicalschool/departments/CellDevelopmentalBiology/Pages/CellDevelopmentalBioHome.aspx.

University of Connecticut, Graduate School, College of Liberal Arts and Sciences, Department of Molecular and Cell Biology, Field of Cell and Developmental Biology, Storrs, CT 06269. Offers MS, PhD. *Degree requirements:* For doctorate, thesis/dissertation. *Entrance requirements:* For master's and doctorate, GRE General Test, GRE Subject Test. Additional exam requirements/recommendations for international students: Required—TOEFL (minimum score 550 paper-based; 213 computer-based). Electronic applications accepted.

University of Connecticut Health Center, Graduate School, Graduate Program in Cell Analysis and Modeling, Farmington, CT 06030. Offers PhD. *Degree requirements:* For doctorate, comprehensive exam, thesis/dissertation. *Entrance requirements:* For doctorate, GRE General Test. Additional exam requirements/recommendations for international students: Required—TOEFL (minimum score 600 paper-based; 250 computer-based). Electronic applications accepted.

See Display below and Close-Up on page 239.

University of Connecticut Health Center, Graduate School, Programs in Biomedical Sciences, Graduate Program in Cell Biology, Farmington, CT 06030. Offers PhD, DMD/PhD, MD/PhD. *Degree requirements:* For doctorate, comprehensive exam, thesis/dissertation. *Entrance requirements:* For doctorate, GRE General Test. Additional exam requirements/recommendations for international students: Required—TOEFL (minimum score 600 paper-based; 250 computer-based). Electronic applications accepted. *Faculty research:* Vascular biology, computational biology, cytoskeleton and molecular motors, reproductive biology, signal transduction.

See Display below and Close-Up on page 241.

University of Delaware, College of Arts and Sciences, Department of Biological Sciences, Newark, DE 19716. Offers biotechnology (MS); cancer biology (MS, PhD); cell and extracellular matrix biology (MS, PhD); cell and systems physiology (MS, PhD); developmental biology (MS, PhD); ecology and evolution (MS, PhD); microbiology (MS, PhD); molecular biology and genetics (MS, PhD). Terminal master's awarded for partial completion of doctoral program. *Degree requirements:* For master's, thesis, preliminary exam; for doctorate, comprehensive exam, thesis/dissertation, preliminary exam. *Entrance requirements:* For master's and doctorate, GRE General Test. Additional exam requirements/recommendations for international students: Required—TOEFL (minimum score 600 paper-based; 250 computer-based); Recommended—TWE. Electronic applications accepted. *Faculty research:* Microorganisms, bone, cancer metastasis, developmental biology, cell biology, DNA.

University of Florida, College of Medicine and Graduate School, Interdisciplinary Program in Biomedical Sciences, Concentration in Molecular Cell Biology, Gainesville, FL 32611. Offers PhD. *Degree requirements:* For doctorate, thesis/dissertation. *Entrance requirements:* For doctorate, GRE General Test, minimum GPA of 3.0.

Additional exam requirements/recommendations for international students: Required—TOEFL. Electronic applications accepted.

University of Florida, Graduate School, College of Agricultural and Life Sciences, Department of Microbiology and Cell Science, Gainesville, FL 32611. Offers MS, PhD. *Faculty:* 22 full-time (7 women), 1 part-time/adjunct (0 women). *Students:* 36 full-time (17 women), 1 part-time (0 women); includes 7 minority (4 Asian, non-Hispanic/Latino; 3 Hispanic/Latino), 14 international. Average age 27. 74 applicants, 19% accepted, 9 enrolled. In 2011, 6 master's, 9 doctorates awarded. *Degree requirements:* For master's, comprehensive exam, thesis (for some programs); for doctorate, comprehensive exam, thesis/dissertation. *Entrance requirements:* For master's and doctorate, GRE General Test (minimum score 1000), minimum GPA of 3.0. Additional exam requirements/recommendations for international students: Required—TOEFL (minimum score 550 paper-based; 213 computer-based; 80 iBT), IELTS (minimum score 6). *Application deadline:* For fall admission, 6/1 priority date for domestic students. Applications are processed on a rolling basis. Application fee: $30. Electronic applications accepted. *Financial support:* Fellowships, research assistantships, and teaching assistantships available. Financial award applicants required to submit FAFSA. *Faculty research:* Biomass conversion, membrane and cell wall chemistry, plant biochemistry and genetics. *Unit head:* Dr. Eric Triplett, Chair, 352-392-1906, Fax: 352-392-5922, E-mail: ewt@ufl.edu. *Application contact:* Dr. Tony Romeo, Graduate Coordinator, 352-392-2400, Fax: 352-392-5922, E-mail: tromeo@ufl.edu. Web site: http://microcell.ufl.edu/.

University of Florida, Interdisciplinary Concentration in Animal Molecular and Cellular Biology, Gainesville, FL 32611. Offers MS, PhD. Program offered jointly by College of Agricultural and Life Sciences, College of Liberal Arts and Sciences, College of Medicine, and College of Veterinary Medicine. *Students:* 12 full-time (7 women); includes 1 minority (Hispanic/Latino), 7 international. Average age 30. 7 applicants, 0% accepted, 0 enrolled. In 2011, 1 master's, 1 doctorate awarded. *Entrance requirements:* For master's and doctorate, GRE General Test (minimum score 1000), minimum GPA of 3.0. Additional exam requirements/recommendations for international students: Required—TOEFL (minimum score 550 paper-based; 213 computer-based; 80 iBT), IELTS (minimum score 6). Application fee: $30. Electronic applications accepted. *Financial support:* Fellowships and research assistantships available. Financial award applicants required to submit FAFSA. *Unit head:* Dr. Alan D. Ealy, Director, 352-392-5590, Fax: 352-392-5595, E-mail: ealy@ufl.edu. *Application contact:* Dr. Joel H. Brendemuhl, Assistant Chair, 352-392-8073, Fax: 352-392-5595, E-mail: brendj@ufl.edu. Web site: http://www.animal.ufl.edu/amcb/.

University of Georgia, Franklin College of Arts and Sciences, Department of Cellular Biology, Athens, GA 30602. Offers MS, PhD. *Faculty:* 18 full-time (6 women), 1 part-time/adjunct (0 women). *Students:* 44 full-time (25 women), 1 part-time (0 women); includes 9 minority (5 Black or African American, non-Hispanic/Latino; 1 Asian, non-Hispanic/Latino; 3 Hispanic/Latino), 21 international. Average age 27. 58 applicants, 28% accepted, 10 enrolled. In 2011, 3 master's, 5 doctorates awarded. *Degree requirements:* For master's, thesis; for doctorate, one foreign language, thesis/dissertation. *Entrance requirements:* For master's and doctorate, GRE General Test. *Application deadline:* For fall admission, 7/1 priority date for domestic students; for spring admission, 11/15 for domestic students. Application fee: $50. Electronic applications accepted. *Financial support:* Fellowships, research assistantships, teaching assistantships, and unspecified assistantships available. *Unit head:* Dr. Kojo Mensa-Wilmot, Head, 706-542-3383, E-mail: head@cb.uga.edu. *Application contact:* Dr. Scott T. Dougan, Graduate Coordinator, 706-543-8194, Fax: 706-542-4271, E-mail: dougan@cb.uga.edu. Web site: http://www.uga.edu/~cellbio/.

University of Guelph, Graduate Studies, College of Biological Science, Department of Molecular and Cellular Biology, Guelph, ON N1G 2W1, Canada. Offers biochemistry

University of Connecticut Health Center

UCHC offers you exceptional research opportunities spanning **Cell Analysis and Modeling; Cell Biology; Genetics and Developmental Biology; Immunology; Molecular Biology and Biochemistry; Neuroscience;** and **Skeletal, Craniofacial and Oral Biology**.

Key features of our program include:
- ❖ Integrated admissions with access to more than 100 laboratories.
- ❖ Flexible educational program tailored to the interests of each student.
- ❖ Excellent education in a stimulating, cutting edge research environment.
- ❖ Competitive stipend ($28,000 for 2012–13 year), tuition waiver, and availability of student health plan.
- ❖ State-of-the-art research facilities, including the new Cell and Genome Sciences Building, which houses the UConn Stem Cell Institute, the Center for Cell Analysis and Modeling, and the Department of Genetics and Developmental Biology.

For more information, please contact:
Stephanie Rauch, Biomedical Science Admissions Coordinator
University of Connecticut Health Center
263 Farmington Ave., MC 3906
Farmington, CT 06030
BiomedSciAdmissions@uchc.edu
http://grad.uchc.edu/prospective/programs/phd_biosci/index.html

(M Sc, PhD); biophysics (M Sc, PhD); botany (M Sc, PhD); microbiology (M Sc, PhD); molecular biology and genetics (M Sc, PhD). *Degree requirements:* For master's, thesis, research proposal; for doctorate, comprehensive exam, thesis/dissertation, research proposal. *Entrance requirements:* For master's, minimum B-average during previous 2 years of coursework; for doctorate, minimum A-average. Additional exam requirements/recommendations for international students: Required—TOEFL (minimum score 550 paper-based; 213 computer-based), IELTS (minimum score 6.5). Electronic applications accepted. *Faculty research:* Physiology, structure, genetics, and ecology of microbes; virology and microbial technology.

University of Illinois at Chicago, College of Medicine and Graduate College, Graduate Programs in Medicine, Department of Anatomy and Cell Biology, Chicago, IL 60612. Offers neuroscience (PhD), including cellular and systems neuroscience and cell biology; MD/PhD. *Degree requirements:* For doctorate, preliminary oral examination, dissertation and oral defense. *Entrance requirements:* For doctorate, GRE General Test, minimum GPA of 2.75, 3 letters of recommendation, personal statement. Additional exam requirements/recommendations for international students: Required—TOEFL (minimum score 550 paper-based; 213 computer-based). Electronic applications accepted. *Faculty research:* Synapses, axonal transport, neurodegenerative diseases.

University of Illinois at Urbana–Champaign, Graduate College, College of Liberal Arts and Sciences, School of Molecular and Cellular Biology, Department of Cell and Developmental Biology, Champaign, IL 61820. Offers PhD. *Faculty:* 14 full-time (5 women), 1 (woman) part-time/adjunct. *Students:* 40 full-time (21 women), 1 part-time (0 women); includes 7 minority (6 Asian, non-Hispanic/Latino; 1 Hispanic/Latino), 24 international. In 2011, 10 doctorates awarded. *Entrance requirements:* For doctorate, GRE, minimum GPA of 3.0. Additional exam requirements/recommendations for international students: Required—TOEFL (minimum score 590 paper-based; 243 computer-based). *Application deadline:* Applications are processed on a rolling basis. Application fee: $75 ($90 for international students). Electronic applications accepted. *Financial support:* In 2011–12, 6 fellowships, 37 research assistantships, 17 teaching assistantships were awarded; tuition waivers (full and partial) also available. *Unit head:* Andrew Belmont, Head, 217-244-2311, Fax: 217-244-1648, E-mail: asbel@illinois.edu. *Application contact:* Delynn Carter, Assistant to the Head, 217-244-8116, Fax: 217-244-1648, E-mail: dmcarter@illinois.edu. Web site: http://mcb.illinois.edu/departments/cdb/.

The University of Iowa, Graduate College, College of Liberal Arts and Sciences, Department of Biology, Iowa City, IA 52242-1324. Offers biology (MS, PhD); cell and developmental biology (MS, PhD); evolution (MS, PhD); genetics (MS, PhD); neurobiology (MS, PhD). Terminal master's awarded for partial completion of doctoral program. *Degree requirements:* For master's, thesis optional, exam; for doctorate, comprehensive exam, thesis/dissertation. *Entrance requirements:* For master's and doctorate, GRE General Test, minimum GPA of 3.0. Additional exam requirements/recommendations for international students: Required—TOEFL (minimum score 600 paper-based; 250 computer-based; 100 iBT). Electronic applications accepted. *Faculty research:* Neurobiology, evolutionary biology, genetics, cell and developmental biology.

The University of Iowa, Graduate College, Program in Molecular and Cellular Biology, Iowa City, IA 52242-1316. Offers PhD, MD/PhD. *Degree requirements:* For doctorate, comprehensive exam, thesis/dissertation. *Entrance requirements:* For doctorate, GRE General Test, minimum GPA of 3.0. Additional exam requirements/recommendations for international students: Required—TOEFL (minimum score 600 paper-based; 250 computer-based; 100 iBT). Electronic applications accepted. *Faculty research:* Regulation of gene expression, inherited human genetic diseases, signal transduction mechanisms, structural biology and function.

The University of Iowa, Roy J. and Lucille A. Carver College of Medicine and Graduate College, Graduate Programs in Medicine, Department of Anatomy and Cell Biology, Iowa City, IA 52242-1316. Offers PhD. *Faculty:* 22 full-time (4 women). *Students:* 14 full-time (6 women); includes 2 minority (1 American Indian or Alaska Native, non-Hispanic/Latino; 1 Asian, non-Hispanic/Latino), 1 international. Average age 28. 113 applicants, 0% accepted. In 2011, 2 doctorates awarded. *Degree requirements:* For doctorate, comprehensive exam, thesis/dissertation. *Entrance requirements:* For doctorate, GRE General Test, minimum GPA of 3.0. Additional exam requirements/recommendations for international students: Required—TOEFL (minimum score 600 paper-based; 250 computer-based; 100 iBT). *Application deadline:* For fall admission, 1/15 priority date for domestic students, 1/15 for international students. Applications are processed on a rolling basis. Application fee: $60 ($100 for international students). Electronic applications accepted. *Financial support:* In 2011–12, 14 students received support, including 1 fellowship with full tuition reimbursement available (averaging $25,000 per year), 12 research assistantships with full tuition reimbursements available (averaging $25,000 per year), teaching assistantships with full tuition reimbursements available (averaging $25,000 per year); institutionally sponsored loans, scholarships/grants, and health care benefits also available. Financial award application deadline: 3/1. *Faculty research:* Biology of differentiation and transformation, developmental and vascular cell biology, neurobiology. *Total annual research expenditures:* $3.4 million. *Unit head:* Dr. John F. Engelhardt, Professor and Head, 319-335-7744, Fax: 319-335-7770, E-mail: john-engelhardt@uiowa.edu. *Application contact:* Julie A. Stark, Program Assistant, 319-335-7744, Fax: 319-335-7770, E-mail: julie-stark@uiowa.edu. Web site: http://www.anatomy.uiowa.edu/.

The University of Kansas, Graduate Studies, College of Liberal Arts and Sciences, Department of Molecular Biosciences, Lawrence, KS 66044. Offers biochemistry and biophysics (MA, PhD); microbiology (MA, PhD); molecular, cellular, and developmental biology (MA, PhD). *Faculty:* 34. *Students:* 57 full-time (29 women), 2 part-time (1 woman); includes 6 minority (2 Asian, non-Hispanic/Latino; 3 Hispanic/Latino; 1 Two or more races, non-Hispanic/Latino), 26 international. Average age 28. 60 applicants, 30% accepted, 10 enrolled. In 2011, 1 master's, 12 doctorates awarded. Terminal master's awarded for partial completion of doctoral program. *Degree requirements:* For master's, comprehensive exam, thesis; for doctorate, comprehensive exam, thesis/dissertation. *Entrance requirements:* For master's and doctorate, GRE General Test. Additional exam requirements/recommendations for international students: Required—TOEFL or IELTS. *Application deadline:* For fall admission, 12/15 for domestic and international students. Application fee: $55 ($65 for international students). Electronic applications accepted. Tuition and fees vary according to course load, campus/location, program and reciprocity agreements. *Financial support:* Fellowships with tuition reimbursements, research assistantships with tuition reimbursements, teaching assistantships with tuition reimbursements, health care benefits, and unspecified assistantships available. Financial award application deadline: 3/1. *Faculty research:* Structure and function of proteins, genetics of organism development, molecular genetics, neurophysiology, molecular virology and pathogenics, developmental biology, cell biology. *Unit head:* Dr. Mark Richter, Chair, 785-864-3334, Fax: 785-864-5294, E-mail: richter@ku.edu. *Application contact:* John P. Connolly, Graduate Program Assistant, 785-864-4311, Fax: 785-864-5294, E-mail: jconnolly@ku.edu. Web site: http://www.molecularbiosciences.ku.edu/.

The University of Kansas, University of Kansas Medical Center, School of Medicine, Department of Anatomy and Cell Biology, Kansas City, KS 66160. Offers MA, PhD, MD/PhD. *Faculty:* 33. *Students:* 14 full-time (9 women), 1 (woman) part-time; includes 2 minority (1 Asian, non-Hispanic/Latino; 1 Hispanic/Latino), 5 international. Average age

27. In 2011, 1 doctorate awarded. Terminal master's awarded for partial completion of doctoral program. *Degree requirements:* For doctorate, comprehensive exam, thesis/dissertation. *Entrance requirements:* For doctorate, GRE. Additional exam requirements/recommendations for international students: Required—TOEFL. *Application deadline:* For fall admission, 1/15 priority date for domestic students. Applications are processed on a rolling basis. Application fee: $0. Electronic applications accepted. Tuition and fees vary according to course load, campus/location, program and reciprocity agreements. *Financial support:* Fellowships, research assistantships with full tuition reimbursements, teaching assistantships with full tuition reimbursements, institutionally sponsored loans, health care benefits, and unspecified assistantships available. Financial award application deadline: 2/14; financial award applicants required to submit FAFSA. *Faculty research:* Development of the synapse and neuromuscular junction, pain perception and diabetic neuropathies, cardiovascular and kidney development, reproductive immunology, post-fertilization signaling events. *Total annual research expenditures:* $10.5 million. *Unit head:* Dr. Dale R. Abrahamson, Chairman, 913 588 7000, Fax: 913 588-2710, E-mail: dabrahamson@kumc.edu. *Application contact:* Dr. Brenda Rongish, Associate Professor, 913-588-1878, Fax: 913-588-2710, E-mail: brongish@kumc.edu. Web site: http://www.kumc.edu/school-of-medicine/anatomy-and-cell-biology.html.

University of Maine, Graduate School, Program in Biomedical Sciences, Orono, ME 04469. Offers biomedical engineering (PhD); cell and molecular biology (PhD); neuroscience (PhD); toxicology (PhD). *Students:* 11 full-time (7 women), 19 part-time (11 women), 8 international. Average age 29. 32 applicants, 31% accepted, 8 enrolled. In 2011, 3 degrees awarded. Application fee: $65. *Expenses:* Tuition, state resident: full-time $5016. Tuition, nonresident: full-time $14,424. *Financial support:* In 2011–12, 2 fellowships with full tuition reimbursements (averaging $18,000 per year), 8 research assistantships with full tuition reimbursements (averaging $23,000 per year) were awarded. *Unit head:* Dr. Carol Kim, Unit Head, 207-581-2803. *Application contact:* Scott G. Delcourt, Associate Dean of the Graduate School, 207-581-3291, Fax: 207-581-3232, E-mail: graduate@maine.edu. Web site: http://www2.umaine.edu/graduate.

The University of Manchester, Faculty of Life Sciences, Manchester, United Kingdom. Offers adaptive organismal biology (M Phil, PhD); animal biology (M Phil, PhD); biochemistry (M Phil, PhD); bioinformatics (M Phil, PhD); biomolecular sciences (M Phil, PhD); biotechnology (M Phil, PhD); cell biology (M Phil, PhD); cell matrix research (M Phil, PhD); channels and transporters (M Phil, PhD); developmental biology (M Phil, PhD); Egyptology (M Phil, PhD); environmental biology (M Phil, PhD); evolutionary biology (M Phil, PhD); gene expression (M Phil, PhD); genetics (M Phil, PhD); history of science, technology and medicine (M Phil, PhD); immunology (M Phil, PhD); integrative neurobiology and behavior (M Phil, PhD); membrane trafficking (M Phil, PhD); microbiology (M Phil, PhD); molecular and cellular neuroscience (M Phil, PhD); molecular biology (M Phil, PhD); molecular cancer studies (M Phil, PhD); neuroscience (M Phil, PhD); ophthalmology (M Phil, PhD); optometry (M Phil, PhD); organelle function (M Phil, PhD); pharmacology (M Phil, PhD); physiology (M Phil, PhD); plant sciences (M Phil, PhD); stem cell research (M Phil, PhD); structural biology (M Phil, PhD); systems neuroscience (M Phil, PhD); toxicology (M Phil, PhD).

University of Maryland, Baltimore, Graduate School, Graduate Program in Life Sciences, Program in Molecular Medicine, Baltimore, MD 21201. Offers cancer biology (PhD); cell and molecular physiology (PhD); human genetics and genomic medicine (PhD); molecular medicine (MS); molecular toxicology and pharmacology (PhD); MD/PhD. *Students:* 80 full-time (53 women), 11 part-time (4 women); includes 21 minority (8 Black or African American, non-Hispanic/Latino; 6 Asian, non-Hispanic/Latino; 4 Hispanic/Latino; 3 Two or more races, non-Hispanic/Latino), 13 international. Average age 27. 207 applicants, 24% accepted, 15 enrolled. In 2011, 3 master's, 5 doctorates awarded. *Entrance requirements:* Additional exam requirements/recommendations for international students: Required—TOEFL (minimum score 600 paper-based; 100 iBT); Recommended—IELTS (minimum score 7). *Application deadline:* For fall admission, 1/15 for domestic and international students. Application fee: $50. Electronic applications accepted. *Financial support:* In 2011–12, research assistantships with partial tuition reimbursements (averaging $25,000 per year) were awarded; fellowships also available. Financial award application deadline: 3/1. *Unit head:* Dr. Toni Antalis, Director, 410-706-8222, E-mail: tantalis@som.umaryland.edu. *Application contact:* Sharron Graves, Program Coordinator, 410-706-6044, Fax: 410-706-6040, E-mail: sgraves@som.umaryland.edu. Web site: http://molecularmedicine.umaryland.edu.

University of Maryland, Baltimore County, Graduate School, College of Natural and Mathematical Sciences, Department of Biological Sciences, Program in Molecular and Cell Biology, Baltimore, MD 21250. Offers PhD. *Faculty:* 26 full-time (9 women). *Students:* 21 full-time (13 women); includes 8 minority (2 Black or African American, non-Hispanic/Latino; 6 Asian, non-Hispanic/Latino). Average age 27. 13 applicants, 23% accepted, 2 enrolled. In 2011, 1 doctorate awarded. *Degree requirements:* For doctorate, thesis/dissertation. *Entrance requirements:* For doctorate, GRE General Test, GRE Subject Test, minimum GPA of 3.0. Additional exam requirements/recommendations for international students: Required—TOEFL. *Application deadline:* For fall admission, 1/15 for domestic students, 12/15 for international students. Applications are processed on a rolling basis. Application fee: $50. Electronic applications accepted. *Financial support:* In 2011–12, fellowships with full tuition reimbursements (averaging $22,300 per year), research assistantships with full tuition reimbursements (averaging $22,300 per year), teaching assistantships with full tuition reimbursements (averaging $22,300 per year) were awarded. *Unit head:* Dr. Stephen Miller, Graduate Program Director, 410-455-3669, Fax: 410-455-3875, E-mail: biograd@umbc.edu. *Application contact:* Dr. Stephen Miller, Graduate Program Director, 410-455-3669, Fax: 410-455-3875, E-mail: biograd@umbc.edu. Web site: http://www.umbc.edu/biosci/.

University of Maryland, College Park, Academic Affairs, College of Computer, Mathematical and Natural Sciences, Department of Biology, PhD Program in Biological Sciences, College Park, MD 20742. Offers behavior, ecology, evolution, and systematics (PhD); computational biology, bioinformatics, and genomics (PhD); molecular and cellular biology (PhD); physiological systems (PhD). *Students:* 68 full-time (41 women), 4 part-time (2 women); includes 13 minority (3 Black or African American, non-Hispanic/Latino; 4 Asian, non-Hispanic/Latino; 5 Hispanic/Latino; 1 Two or more races, non-Hispanic/Latino), 21 international. 380 applicants, 15% accepted, 22 enrolled. *Degree requirements:* For doctorate, comprehensive exam, thesis/dissertation, present thesis work in seminar. *Entrance requirements:* For doctorate, GRE General Test; GRE Subject Test in biology (recommended), academic transcripts, statement of purpose/research interests, 3 letters of recommendation. Additional exam requirements/recommendations for international students: Required—TOEFL. *Application deadline:* For fall admission, 12/15 for domestic and international students. Applications are processed on a rolling basis. Application fee: $75. Electronic applications accepted. *Expenses:* Tuition, state resident: part-time $525 per credit hour. Tuition, nonresident: part-time $1131 per credit hour. Required fees: $386.31 per term. Tuition and fees vary according to program. *Financial support:* In 2011–12, 11 fellowships with full and partial tuition reimbursements (averaging $14,406 per year), 16 research assistantships (averaging $19,495 per year), 41 teaching assistantships (averaging $18,734 per year) were awarded. *Unit head:* Dr. Barbara Thorne, Director, 301-405-6905, E-mail:

bthorne@umd.edu. *Application contact:* Dr. Charles A. Caramello, Dean of Graduate School, 301-405-0358, Fax: 301-314-9305. Web site: http://bisi.umd.edu/biologicalsciencesgraduateprogrambisi.

University of Maryland, College Park, Academic Affairs, College of Computer, Mathematical and Natural Sciences, Department of Cell Biology and Molecular Genetics, Program in Cell Biology and Molecular Genetics, College Park, MD 20742. Offers MS, PhD. *Students:* 42 full-time (20 women), 1 (woman) part-time; includes 4 minority (2 Asian, non-Hispanic/Latino; 2 Hispanic/Latino), 16 international. In 2011, 5 master's, 8 doctorates awarded. *Degree requirements:* For master's, thesis; for doctorate, thesis/dissertation, exams. *Expenses:* Tuition, state resident: part-time $525 per credit hour. Tuition, nonresident: part-time $1131 per credit hour. *Required fees:* $386.31 per term. Tuition and fees vary according to program. *Financial support:* In 2011–12, 5 fellowships with full tuition reimbursements (averaging $28,086 per year), 10 research assistantships (averaging $19,519 per year), 21 teaching assistantships (averaging $19,520 per year) were awarded. Financial award applicants required to submit FAFSA. *Faculty research:* Cytoskeletal activity, membrane biology, cell division, genetics and genomics, virology. *Unit head:* Dr. Barbara Thorne, Director, 301-405-7947, E-mail: bthorne@umd.edu. *Application contact:* Dr. Charles A. Caramello, Dean of Graduate School, 301-405-0358, Fax: 301-314-9305.

University of Maryland, College Park, Academic Affairs, College of Computer, Mathematical and Natural Sciences, Department of Cell Biology and Molecular Genetics, Program in Molecular and Cellular Biology, College Park, MD 20742. Offers PhD. Part-time and evening/weekend programs available. *Students:* 30 full-time (20 women), 2 part-time (both women); includes 6 minority (2 Black or African American, non-Hispanic/Latino; 3 Asian, non-Hispanic/Latino; 1 Hispanic/Latino), 17 international. In 2011, 6 doctorates awarded. *Degree requirements:* For doctorate, thesis/dissertation, exam, public service. *Expenses:* Tuition, state resident: part-time $525 per credit hour. Tuition, nonresident: part-time $1131 per credit hour. *Required fees:* $386.31 per term. Tuition and fees vary according to program. *Financial support:* In 2011–12, 2 fellowships with partial tuition reimbursements (averaging $10,800 per year), 10 research assistantships (averaging $19,663 per year), 17 teaching assistantships (averaging $19,382 per year) were awarded. Financial award applicants required to submit FAFSA. *Faculty research:* Monoclonal antibody production, oligonucleotide synthesis, macronolular processing, signal transduction, developmental biology. *Unit head:* Dr. Barbara Thorne, Director, 301-405-7947, E-mail: bthorne@umd.edu. *Application contact:* Dr. Charles A. Caramello, Dean of Graduate School, 301-405-0358, Fax: 301-314-9305.

University of Massachusetts Amherst, Graduate School, Interdisciplinary Programs, Program in Molecular and Cellular Biology, Amherst, MA 01003. Offers biological chemistry and molecular biophysics (PhD); biomedicine (PhD); cellular and developmental biology (PhD). Part-time programs available. *Students:* 62 full-time (40 women), 18 part-time (9 women); includes 14 minority (2 Black or African American, non-Hispanic/Latino; 4 Asian, non-Hispanic/Latino; 7 Hispanic/Latino; 1 Two or more races, non-Hispanic/Latino), 28 international. Average age 27. 138 applicants, 36% accepted, 22 enrolled. In 2011, 8 doctorates awarded. Terminal master's awarded for partial completion of doctoral program. *Degree requirements:* For doctorate, comprehensive exam, thesis/dissertation. *Entrance requirements:* For doctorate, GRE General Test. Additional exam requirements/recommendations for international students: Required—TOEFL (minimum score 550 paper-based; 213 computer-based; 80 iBT), IELTS (minimum score 6.5). *Application deadline:* For fall admission, 12/1 for domestic and international students. Applications are processed on a rolling basis. Application fee: $50 ($65 for international students). Electronic applications accepted. Tuition and fees vary according to course load, campus/location and program. *Financial support:* Fellowships with full and partial tuition reimbursements, research assistantships with full and partial tuition reimbursements, teaching assistantships with full and partial tuition reimbursements, career-related internships or fieldwork, Federal Work-Study, scholarships/grants, traineeships, health care benefits, tuition waivers (full and partial), and unspecified assistantships available. Support available to part-time students. Financial award application deadline: 12/1. *Unit head:* Dr. Barbara Osborne, Graduate Program Director, 413-545-3246, Fax: 413-545-1812. *Application contact:* Lindsay DeSantis, Interim Supervisor of Admissions, 413-545-0722, Fax: 413-577-0010, E-mail: gradadm@grad.umass.edu. Web site: http://www.bio.umass.edu/mcb/.

University of Massachusetts Amherst, Graduate School, Interdisciplinary Programs, Program in Plant Biology, Amherst, MA 01003. Offers biochemistry and metabolism (MS, PhD); cell biology and physiology (MS, PhD); environmental, ecological and integrative (PhD); environmental, ecological and integrative biology (MS); genetics and evolution (MS, PhD). *Students:* 16 full-time (7 women), 1 (woman) part-time, 7 international. Average age 27. 22 applicants, 50% accepted, 5 enrolled. In 2011, 3 degrees awarded. *Median time to degree:* Of those who began their doctoral program in fall 2003, 100% received their degree in 8 years or less. *Degree requirements:* For master's, thesis; for doctorate, 2 foreign languages, comprehensive exam, thesis/dissertation. *Entrance requirements:* For master's and doctorate, GRE General Test. Additional exam requirements/recommendations for international students: Required—TOEFL (minimum score 550 paper-based; 213 computer-based; 80 iBT), IELTS (minimum score 6.5). *Application deadline:* For fall admission, 12/15 for domestic and international students; for spring admission, 10/1 for domestic and international students. Applications are processed on a rolling basis. Application fee: $50 ($65 for international students). Electronic applications accepted. Tuition and fees vary according to course load, campus/location and program. *Financial support:* Fellowships with full and partial tuition reimbursements, research assistantships with full and partial tuition reimbursements, teaching assistantships with full and partial tuition reimbursements, career-related internships or fieldwork, Federal Work-Study, scholarships/grants, traineeships, health care benefits, tuition waivers (full and partial), and unspecified assistantships available. Support available to part-time students. Financial award application deadline: 12/15. *Unit head:* Dr. Elsbeth L. Walker, Graduate Program Director, 413-577-3217, Fax: 413-545-3243. *Application contact:* Lindsay DeSantis, Interim Supervisor of Admissions, 413-545—0722, Fax: 413-577-0010, E-mail: gradadm@grad.umass.edu. Web site: http://www.bio.umass.edu/plantbio/.

University of Massachusetts Boston, Office of Graduate Studies, College of Science and Mathematics, Track in Molecular, Cellular and Organismal Biology, Boston, MA 02125-3393. Offers PhD.

University of Massachusetts Worcester, Graduate School of Biomedical Sciences, Worcester, MA 01655-0115. Offers biochemistry and molecular pharmacology (PhD); bioinformatics and computational biology (PhD); cancer biology (PhD); cell biology (PhD); clinical and population health research (PhD); clinical investigation (MS); immunology and virology (PhD); interdisciplinary graduate program (PhD); molecular genetics and microbiology (PhD); neuroscience (PhD); DVM/PhD; MD/PhD. *Faculty:* 1,427 full-time (526 women), 309 part-time/adjunct (196 women). *Students:* 416 full-time (225 women); includes 47 minority (12 Black or African American, non-Hispanic/Latino; 32 Asian, non-Hispanic/Latino; 3 Hispanic/Latino), 144 international. Average age 29. 623 applicants, 17% accepted, 54 enrolled. In 2011, 5 master's, 63 doctorates awarded. Terminal master's awarded for partial completion of doctoral program. *Degree requirements:* For master's, comprehensive exam, thesis; for doctorate, comprehensive exam, thesis/dissertation. *Entrance requirements:* For master's, bachelor's degree; for doctorate, GRE General Test. Additional exam requirements/recommendations for international students: Required—TOEFL (minimum score 600 paper-based; 250 computer-based; 100 iBT) or IELTS (minimum score 7.5). *Application deadline:* For fall admission, 12/15 for domestic and international students; for spring admission, 5/15 for domestic students. Application fee: $50. Electronic applications accepted. *Expenses:* Contact institution. *Financial support:* In 2011–12, 416 students received support, including 416 research assistantships with full tuition reimbursements available (averaging $29,200 per year); scholarships/grants, health care benefits, tuition waivers (full), and unspecified assistantships also available. Financial award application deadline: 4/16. *Faculty research:* RNA interference, cell biology, bioinformatics, clinical research, infectious disease. *Total annual research expenditures:* $262.7 million. *Unit head:* Dr. Anthony Carruthers, Dean, 508-856-4135, E-mail: anthony.carruthers@umassmed.edu. *Application contact:* Dr. Kendall Knight, Associate Dean and Interim Director of Admissions and Recruitment, 508-856-5628, Fax: 508-856-3659, E-mail: kendall.knight@umassmed.edu. Web site: http://www.umassmed.edu/gsbs/.

University of Medicine and Dentistry of New Jersey, Graduate School of Biomedical Sciences, Graduate Programs in Biomedical Sciences–Newark, Department of Cell Biology and Molecular Medicine, Newark, NJ 07107. Offers PhD. *Degree requirements:* For doctorate, thesis/dissertation, qualifying exam. *Entrance requirements:* For doctorate, GRE General Test. Additional exam requirements/recommendations for international students: Required—TOEFL. Electronic applications accepted.

University of Medicine and Dentistry of New Jersey, Graduate School of Biomedical Sciences, Graduate Programs in Biomedical Sciences–Stratford, Program in Cell and Molecular Biology, Stratford, NJ 08084-5634. Offers MS, PhD, DO/PhD. *Degree requirements:* For master's, thesis; for doctorate, thesis/dissertation, qualifying exam. *Entrance requirements:* For master's and doctorate, GRE General Test. Additional exam requirements/recommendations for international students: Required—TOEFL. Electronic applications accepted.

University of Miami, Graduate School, Miller School of Medicine, Graduate Programs in Medicine, Department of Cell Biology and Anatomy, Coral Gables, FL 33124. Offers molecular cell and developmental biology (PhD); MD/PhD. *Degree requirements:* For doctorate, thesis/dissertation. *Entrance requirements:* For doctorate, GRE General Test, GRE Subject Test. Additional exam requirements/recommendations for international students: Required—TOEFL. Electronic applications accepted.

University of Michigan, Horace H. Rackham School of Graduate Studies, College of Literature, Science, and the Arts, Department of Molecular, Cellular, and Developmental Biology, Ann Arbor, MI 48109. Offers MS, PhD. Part-time programs available. *Faculty:* 33 full-time (10 women). *Students:* 78 full-time (39 women), 5 part-time (2 women); includes 5 minority (3 Asian, non-Hispanic/Latino; 2 Hispanic/Latino), 40 international. Average age 27. 137 applicants, 17% accepted, 12 enrolled. In 2011, 7 master's, 7 doctorates awarded. Terminal master's awarded for partial completion of doctoral program. *Degree requirements:* For master's, 24 credits with at least 16 in molecular, cellular, and developmental biology and 4 in a cognate field; for doctorate, thesis/dissertation, preliminary exam, oral defense. *Entrance requirements:* For master's and doctorate, GRE General Test. Additional exam requirements/recommendations for international students: Required—TOEFL (minimum score 560 paper-based; 220 computer-based; 83 iBT). *Application deadline:* For fall admission, 1/5 for domestic and international students; for winter admission, 11/1 for domestic and international students; for spring admission, 4/1 for domestic and international students. Applications are processed on a rolling basis. Application fee: $65 ($75 for international students). Electronic applications accepted. *Financial support:* In 2011–12, 55 students received support, including 12 fellowships with full tuition reimbursements available (averaging $26,500 per year), 30 research assistantships with full tuition reimbursements available (averaging $26,500 per year), 13 teaching assistantships with full tuition reimbursements available (averaging $26,500 per year); health care benefits also available. *Faculty research:* Cell biology, microbiology, neurobiology and physiology, developmental biology and plant molecular biology. *Unit head:* Dr. Pamela A. Raymond, Department Chair, 734-764-7476, Fax: 734-615-6337, E-mail: praymond@umich.edu. *Application contact:* Mary Carr, Graduate Coordinator, 734-615-1635, Fax: 734-764-0884, E-mail: carrmm@umich.edu. Web site: http://www.mcdb.lsa.umich.edu.

University of Michigan, Horace H. Rackham School of Graduate Studies, Program in Biomedical Sciences (PIBS), Department of Cell and Developmental Biology, Ann Arbor, MI 48109. Offers PhD. *Faculty:* 29 full-time (10 women). *Students:* 15 full-time (7 women); includes 8 minority (all Asian, non-Hispanic/Latino), 3 international. Average age 30. 28 applicants, 25% accepted, 4 enrolled. In 2011, 6 doctorates awarded. *Degree requirements:* For doctorate, thesis/dissertation, oral defense of dissertation, preliminary exam. *Entrance requirements:* For doctorate, GRE General Test, 3 letters of recommendation, research experience. Additional exam requirements/recommendations for international students: Required—TOEFL (minimum score 84 iBT). *Application deadline:* For fall admission, 12/1 for domestic and international students. Application fee: $60 ($75 for international students). Electronic applications accepted. *Financial support:* In 2011–12, 21 students received support, including 21 fellowships (averaging $26,500 per year); scholarships/grants, health care benefits, tuition waivers (full), and unspecified assistantships also available. Financial award application deadline: 12/1. *Faculty research:* Small stress proteins, cellular stress response, muscle, male reproductive, toxicology, cell cytoskeleton. *Total annual research expenditures:* $3.8 million. *Unit head:* Dr. James Douglas Engel, Chair, 734-615-7509, Fax: 734-763-1166, E-mail: engel@umich.edu. *Application contact:* Michelle S. Melis, Director of Student Life, 734-615-6538, Fax: 734-647-7022, E-mail: msmtegan@umich.edu. Web site: http://www.med.umich.edu/cdb/.

University of Michigan, Horace H. Rackham School of Graduate Studies, Program in Biomedical Sciences (PIBS), Interdisciplinary Program in Cellular and Molecular Biology, Ann Arbor, MI 48109. Offers PhD. *Faculty:* 161 part-time/adjunct (44 women). *Students:* 74 full-time (40 women); includes 21 minority (2 Black or African American, non-Hispanic/Latino; 1 American Indian or Alaska Native, non-Hispanic/Latino; 10 Asian, non-Hispanic/Latino; 8 Hispanic/Latino). Average age 26. In 2011, 12 doctorates awarded. *Degree requirements:* For doctorate, comprehensive exam, thesis/dissertation, oral defense of dissertation, preliminary exam. *Entrance requirements:* For doctorate, GRE General Test, GRE Subject Test. *Financial support:* In 2011–12, 74 students received support, including 21 fellowships with tuition reimbursements available (averaging $26,500 per year), 53 research assistantships with tuition reimbursements available (averaging $26,500 per year); teaching assistantships and scholarships/grants also available. *Faculty research:* Genetics, genomics, gene regulation, models of disease, microbes. *Total annual research expenditures:* $20 million. *Unit head:* Dr. Jessica Schwartz, Director, 734-764-5428, Fax: 734-647-6232, E-mail: jeschwar@umich.edu. *Application contact:* Catherine A. Mitchell, Senior Student Services Associate I, 734-764-5428, Fax: 734-647-6232, E-mail: cmbgrad@umich.edu. Web site: http://www.med.umich.edu/cmb/.

University of Minnesota, Twin Cities Campus, Graduate School, Program in Molecular, Cellular, Developmental Biology and Genetics, Minneapolis, MN 55455-0213. Offers genetic counseling (MS); molecular, cellular, developmental biology and genetics (PhD). Terminal master's awarded for partial completion of doctoral program.

Degree requirements: For master's, thesis optional; for doctorate, thesis/dissertation. *Entrance requirements:* For master's and doctorate, GRE General Test. Additional exam requirements/recommendations for international students: Required—TOEFL (minimum score 625 paper-based; 263 computer-based; 80 iBT). Electronic applications accepted. *Faculty research:* Membrane receptors and membrane transport, cell interactions, cytoskeleton and cell mobility, regulation of gene expression, plant cell and molecular biology.

University of Minnesota, Twin Cities Campus, Graduate School, Stem Cell Biology Graduate Program, Minneapolis, MN 55455-3007. Offers MS. *Degree requirements:* For master's, thesis. *Entrance requirements:* For master's, GRE, BS, BA, or foreign equivalent in biological sciences or related field; minimum undergraduate GPA of 3.2. Additional exam requirements/recommendations for international students: Required— TOEFL (minimum score 580 paper-based, with a minimum score of 4 in the TWE, or 94 Internet-based, with a minimum score of 22 on each of the reading and listening, 26 on the speaking, and 26 on the writing section. *Faculty research:* Stem cell and developmental biology; embryonic stem cells; iPS cells; muscle satellite cells; hematopoietic stem cells; neuronal stem cells; cardiovascular, kidney and limb development; regenerating systems.

University of Missouri, Graduate School, College of Arts and Sciences, Division of Biological Sciences, Program in Genetic, Cellular and Developmental Biology, Columbia, MO 65211. Offers MA, PhD. *Faculty:* 23. *Expenses:* Tuition, state resident: full-time $5881. Tuition, nonresident: full-time $15,183. *Required fees:* $952. Tuition and fees vary according to campus/location and program. *Financial support:* In 2011– 12, fellowships (averaging $21,000 per year), teaching assistantships (averaging $16,300 per year) were awarded; research assistantships, scholarships/grants, health care benefits, and tuition waivers (full) also available. *Total annual research expenditures:* $6.1 million. *Unit head:* Dr. Ray Semlitsch, Director of Graduate Studies, 573-884-6396, E-mail: semlitschr@missouri.edu. *Application contact:* Nila Emerich, Application Contact, 800-553-5698.

University of Missouri–Kansas City, School of Biological Sciences, Program in Cell Biology and Biophysics, Kansas City, MO 64110-2499. Offers PhD. Offered through the School of Graduate Studies. *Faculty:* 40 full-time (10 women), 3 part-time/adjunct (2 women). *Students:* 4 full-time (1 woman), 15 part-time (7 women), 10 international. Average age 27. 5 applicants, 100% accepted, 3 enrolled. *Degree requirements:* For doctorate, comprehensive exam, thesis/dissertation. *Entrance requirements:* For doctorate, GRE General Test, bachelor's degree in chemistry, biology or related field; minimum GPA of 3.0. Additional exam requirements/recommendations for international students: Required—TOEFL (minimum score 550 paper-based; 213 computer-based; 80 iBT). *Application deadline:* For fall admission, 2/15 priority date for domestic students, 2/15 for international students. Applications are processed on a rolling basis. Application fee: $45 ($50 for international students). Electronic applications accepted. *Expenses:* Tuition, state resident: full-time $5798; part-time $322.10 per credit hour. Tuition, nonresident: full-time $14,969; part-time $831.60 per credit hour. *Required fees:* $93.51 per credit hour. *Financial support:* Fellowships with full tuition reimbursements, research assistantships with full tuition reimbursements, teaching assistantships with full and partial tuition reimbursements, scholarships/grants, tuition waivers (full and partial), and unspecified assistantships available. Financial award application deadline: 3/1; financial award applicants required to submit FAFSA. *Unit head:* Dr. G. Sullivan Read, Interim Head, 816-235-5247, E-mail: sbsgradrecruit@umkc.edu. *Application contact:* Laura Batenic, Information Contact, 816-235-2352, Fax: 816-235-5158, E-mail: batenicl@umkc.edu. Web site: http://sbs.umkc.edu/.

See Display on this page and Close-Up on page 245.

University of Missouri–St. Louis, College of Arts and Sciences, Department of Biology, St. Louis, MO 63121. Offers biotechnology (Certificate); cell and molecular biology (MS, PhD); ecology, evolution and systematics (MS, PhD); tropical biology and conservation (Certificate). Part-time programs available. *Faculty:* 43 full-time (13 women), 4 part-time/adjunct (1 woman). *Students:* 68 full-time (33 women), 64 part-time (28 women); includes 20 minority (9 Black or African American, non-Hispanic/Latino; 7 Asian, non-Hispanic/Latino; 3 Hispanic/Latino; 1 Two or more races, non-Hispanic/ Latino), 43 international. Average age 28. 122 applicants, 48% accepted, 36 enrolled. In 2011, 20 master's, 3 doctorates, 11 other advanced degrees awarded. *Degree requirements:* For master's, thesis or alternative; for doctorate, thesis/dissertation, 1 semester of teaching experience. *Entrance requirements:* For master's, 3 letters of recommendation; for doctorate, GRE General Test, 3 letters of recommendation. Additional exam requirements/recommendations for international students: Required— TOEFL. *Application deadline:* For fall admission, 12/15 priority date for domestic students, 12/15 for international students; for spring admission, 12/1 priority date for domestic students, 12/1 for international students. Applications are processed on a rolling basis. Application fee: $35 ($40 for international students). Electronic applications accepted. *Expenses:* Tuition, state resident: full-time $6273; part-time $3866 per year. Tuition, nonresident: full-time $14,969; part-time $9980 per year. *Required fees:* $315 per year. *Financial support:* In 2011–12, 13 research assistantships with full and partial tuition reimbursements (averaging $15,300 per year), 27 teaching assistantships with full and partial tuition reimbursements (averaging $15,300 per year) were awarded; fellowships with full tuition reimbursements, career-related internships or fieldwork, and Federal Work-Study also available. Support available to part-time students, Financial award application deadline: 2/1. *Faculty research:* Molecular biology, microbial genetics, animal behavior, tropical ecology, plant systematics. *Unit head:* Dr. Wendy Olivas, Director of Graduate Studies, 314-516-6200, Fax: 314-516-6233, E-mail: olivasw@ umsl.edu. *Application contact:* 314-516-5458, Fax: 314-516-6996, E-mail: gradadm@ umsl.edu. Web site: http://www.umsl.edu/divisions/artscience/biology/.

University of Nebraska Medical Center, Graduate Studies, Department of Genetics, Cell Biology and Anatomy, Omaha, NE 68198. Offers MS, PhD. Part-time programs available. Terminal master's awarded for partial completion of doctoral program. *Degree requirements:* For master's, comprehensive exam, thesis; for doctorate, comprehensive exam, thesis/dissertation. *Entrance requirements:* For master's and doctorate, GRE General Test. Additional exam requirements/recommendations for international students: Required—TOEFL (minimum score 550 paper-based; 213 computer-based). Electronic applications accepted. *Faculty research:* Hematology, immunology, developmental biology, genetics cancer biology, neuroscience.

University of Nevada, Reno, Graduate School, Interdisciplinary Program in Cell and Molecular Biology, Reno, NV 89557. Offers MS, PhD. Terminal master's awarded for partial completion of doctoral program. *Degree requirements:* For master's, thesis; for doctorate, thesis/dissertation. *Entrance requirements:* For master's, GRE Subject Test (recommended), minimum GPA of 2.75; for doctorate, GRE Subject Test (recommended), minimum GPA of 3.0. Additional exam requirements/recommendations for international students: Required—TOEFL (minimum score 500 paper-based; 173 computer-based; 61 iBT), IELTS (minimum score 6). Electronic applications accepted. *Faculty research:* Cellular biology, biophysics, cancer, microbiology, insect biochemistry.

University of New Haven, Graduate School, College of Arts and Sciences, Program in Cellular and Molecular Biology, West Haven, CT 06516-1916. Offers MS. *Students:* 29

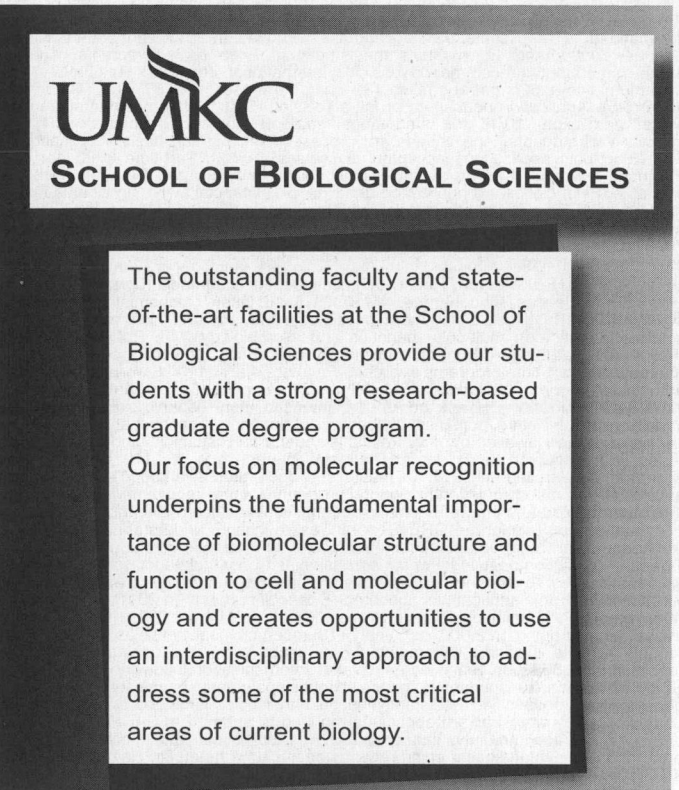

UMKC
SCHOOL OF BIOLOGICAL SCIENCES

The outstanding faculty and state-of-the-art facilities at the School of Biological Sciences provide our students with a strong research-based graduate degree program.

Our focus on molecular recognition underpins the fundamental importance of biomolecular structure and function to cell and molecular biology and creates opportunities to use an interdisciplinary approach to address some of the most critical areas of current biology.

Graduate degree programs:

http://sbs.umkc.edu/graduate_overview.cfm

UNIVERSITY OF MISSOURI
KANSAS CITY

sbsgradrecruit@umkc.edu   **www.umkc.edu/sbs**

full-time (21 women), 19 part-time (12 women); includes 4 minority (1 Black or African American, non-Hispanic/Latino; 2 Asian, non-Hispanic/Latino; 1 Hispanic/Latino), 24 international. 41 applicants, 93% accepted, 12 enrolled. In 2011, 22 master's awarded. *Degree requirements:* For master's, thesis optional. *Entrance requirements:* Additional exam requirements/recommendations for international students: Required—TOEFL (minimum score 520 paper-based; 190 computer-based; 70 iBT), IELTS (minimum score 5.5). *Application deadline:* For fall admission, 5/31 for international students; for winter admission, 10/15 for international students; for spring admission, 1/15 for international students. Applications are processed on a rolling basis. Application fee: $50. Electronic applications accepted. *Expenses: Tuition:* Part-time $750 per credit. *Financial support:* Career-related internships or fieldwork and Federal Work-Study available. Financial award application deadline: 5/1; financial award applicants required to submit FAFSA. *Unit head:* Dr. Michael Rossi, Chair, 203-932-7125, E-mail: mrossi@newhaven.edu. *Application contact:* Eloise Gormley, Director of Graduate Admissions, 203-932-7449, Fax: 203-932-7137, E-mail: gradinfo@newhaven.edu. Web site: http://www.newhaven.edu/4724/.

University of New Mexico, Health Sciences Center Graduate Programs, Program in Biomedical Sciences, Albuquerque, NM 87131-5196. Offers biochemistry and molecular biology (MS, PhD); cell biology and physiology (MS, PhD); clinical and translational science (Certificate); molecular genetics and microbiology (MS, PhD); neuroscience (MS, PhD); pathology (MS, PhD); toxicology (MS, PhD); university science teaching (Certificate). Part-time programs available. *Faculty:* 64 full-time (26 women), 9 part-time/adjunct (4 women). *Students:* 45 full-time (27 women), 56 part-time (28 women); includes 24 minority (3 Black or African American, non-Hispanic/Latino; 1 American Indian or Alaska Native, non-Hispanic/Latino; 4 Asian, non-Hispanic/Latino; 14 Hispanic/Latino; 1 Native Hawaiian or other Pacific Islander, non-Hispanic/Latino; 1 Two or more races, non-Hispanic/Latino), 18 international. Average age 30. 110 applicants, 18% accepted, 17 enrolled. In 2011, 14 master's, 5 doctorates awarded. Terminal master's awarded for partial completion of doctoral program. *Degree requirements:* For master's, thesis; for doctorate, comprehensive exam, thesis/dissertation. *Entrance requirements:* For master's and doctorate, GRE General Test, minimum undergraduate GPA of 3.0. Additional exam requirements/recommendations for international students: Required—TOEFL. *Application deadline:* For fall admission, 3/1 priority date for domestic students, 3/1 for international students. Applications are processed on a rolling basis. Application fee: $50. Electronic applications accepted. *Financial support:* In 2011–12, 99 students received support, including 28 fellowships with full and partial tuition reimbursements available (averaging $22,000 per year), 73 research assistantships with full tuition reimbursements available (averaging $23,000 per year), 8 teaching assistantships (averaging $2,800 per year); career-related internships or fieldwork, Federal Work-Study, institutionally sponsored loans, scholarships/grants, traineeships, health care benefits, and unspecified assistantships also available. Financial award application deadline: 1/1; financial award applicants required to submit FAFSA. *Faculty research:* Infectious disease/Immunity, cancer biology, cardiovascular and metabolic diseases, brain and behavioral illness, environmental health. *Unit head:* Dr. Helen J. Hathaway, BSGP Program Director, 505-272-1887, Fax: 505-272-2412, E-mail: hhathaway@salud.unm.edu. *Application contact:* Mary Fenton, Admissions Coordinator, 505-272-1887, Fax: 505-272-2412, E-mail: mfenton@salud.unm.edu. Web site: http://hsc.unm.edu/som/research/brep/bsgpabout.shtm.

The University of North Carolina at Chapel Hill, Graduate School, College of Arts and Sciences, Department of Biology, Chapel Hill, NC 27599. Offers botany (MA, MS, PhD); cell biology, development, and physiology (MA, MS, PhD); cell motility and cytoskeleton (PhD); ecology and behavior (MA, MS, PhD); genetics and molecular biology (MA, MS, PhD); morphology, systematics, and evolution (MA, MS, PhD). Terminal master's awarded for partial completion of doctoral program. *Degree requirements:* For master's, comprehensive exam, thesis (for some programs); for doctorate, comprehensive exam, thesis/dissertation. *Entrance requirements:* For master's, GRE General Test, GRE Subject Test, 2 semesters of calculus or statistics; 2 semesters of physics, organic chemistry; 3 semesters of biology; for doctorate, GRE General Test, GRE Subject Test, 2 semesters calculus or statistics, 2 semesters physics, organic chemistry, 3 semesters of biology. Additional exam requirements/recommendations for international students: Required—TOEFL (minimum score 550 paper-based; 213 computer-based). Electronic applications accepted. *Faculty research:* Gene expression, biomechanics, yeast genetics, plant ecology, plant molecular biology.

The University of North Carolina at Chapel Hill, School of Medicine and Graduate School, Graduate Programs in Medicine, Department of Cell and Developmental Biology, Chapel Hill, NC 27599. Offers PhD. *Degree requirements:* For doctorate, comprehensive exam, thesis/dissertation. *Entrance requirements:* For doctorate, GRE General Test, GRE Subject Test. Electronic applications accepted. *Faculty research:* Cell adhesion, motility and cytoskeleton; molecular analysis of signal transduction; development biology and toxicology; reproductive biology; cell and molecular imaging.

University of North Dakota, Graduate School and Graduate School, Graduate Programs in Medicine, Department of Anatomy and Cell Biology, Grand Forks, ND 58202. Offers MS, PhD. *Degree requirements:* For master's, thesis, final exam; for doctorate, comprehensive exam, thesis/dissertation, final exam. *Entrance requirements:* For master's and doctorate, GRE General Test, minimum GPA of 3.0. Additional exam requirements/recommendations for international students: Required—TOEFL (minimum score 550 paper-based; 213 computer-based; 79 iBT), IELTS (minimum score 6.5). Electronic applications accepted. *Faculty research:* Coronary vessel, vasculogenesis, acellular glomerular and retinal microvessel membranes, ependymal cells, cardiac muscle.

University of Notre Dame, Graduate School, College of Science, Department of Biological Sciences, Notre Dame, IN 46556. Offers aquatic ecology, evolution and environmental biology (MS, PhD); cellular and molecular biology (MS, PhD); genetics (MS, PhD); physiology (MS, PhD); vector biology and parasitology (MS, PhD). Terminal master's awarded for partial completion of doctoral program. *Degree requirements:* For master's, comprehensive exam, thesis; for doctorate, comprehensive exam, thesis/dissertation, candidacy exam. *Entrance requirements:* For master's and doctorate, GRE General Test. Additional exam requirements/recommendations for international students: Required—TOEFL (minimum score 600 paper-based; 250 computer-based; 80 iBT). Electronic applications accepted. *Faculty research:* Tropical disease, molecular genetics, neurobiology, evolutionary biology, aquatic biology.

University of Oklahoma Health Sciences Center, College of Medicine and Graduate College, Graduate Programs in Medicine, Department of Cell Biology, Oklahoma City, OK 73190. Offers MS, PhD. *Degree requirements:* For master's, thesis; for doctorate, thesis/dissertation. *Entrance requirements:* For doctorate, GRE General Test, GRE Subject Test, 3 letters of recommendation. Additional exam requirements/recommendations for international students: Required—TOEFL. *Faculty research:* Neurobiology, reproductive, neuronal plasticity, extracellular matrix, neuroendocrinology.

University of Ottawa, Faculty of Graduate and Postdoctoral Studies, Faculty of Medicine, Department of Cellular and Molecular Medicine, Ottawa, ON K1H 8M5, Canada. Offers M Sc, PhD. *Degree requirements:* For master's, thesis, seminar; for doctorate, comprehensive exam, thesis/dissertation, seminar. *Entrance requirements:*

For master's, honors degree or equivalent, minimum B average; for doctorate, master's degree, minimum B+ average. Electronic applications accepted. *Faculty research:* Physiology, pharmacology, growth and development.

University of Pennsylvania, Perelman School of Medicine, Biomedical Graduate Studies, Graduate Group in Cell and Molecular Biology, Philadelphia, PA 19104. Offers cancer biology (PhD); cell biology and physiology (PhD); developmental stem cell regenerative biology (PhD); gene therapy and vaccines (PhD); genetics and gene regulation (PhD); microbiology, virology, and parasitology (PhD); MD/PhD; VMD/PhD. *Faculty:* 306. *Students:* 337 full-time (186 women); includes 81 minority (16 Black or African American, non-Hispanic/Latino; 43 Asian, non-Hispanic/Latino; 16 Hispanic/Latino; 6 Two or more races, non-Hispanic/Latino), 41 international. 585 applicants, 21% accepted, 58 enrolled. In 2011, 42 doctorates awarded. *Degree requirements:* For doctorate, thesis/dissertation. *Entrance requirements:* For doctorate, GRE General Test. Additional exam requirements/recommendations for international students: Required—TOEFL. *Application deadline:* For fall admission, 12/1 priority date for domestic students, 12/1 for international students. Applications are processed on a rolling basis. Application fee: $80. Electronic applications accepted. *Expenses: Tuition:* Full-time $26,660; part-time $4944 per course. *Required fees:* $2318; $291 per course. Tuition and fees vary according to course load, degree level and program. *Financial support:* In 2011–12, 337 students received support. Fellowships, research assistantships, scholarships/grants, traineeships, and unspecified assistantships available. *Unit head:* Dr. Daniel Kessler, Graduate Group Chair. *Application contact:* Meagan Schofer, Coordinator. Web site: http://www.med.upenn.edu/camb/.

University of Pittsburgh, Dietrich School of Arts and Sciences, Department of Biological Sciences, Program in Molecular, Cellular, and Developmental Biology, Pittsburgh, PA 15260. Offers PhD. *Faculty:* 22 full-time (4 women). *Students:* 56 full-time (33 women); includes 4 minority (1 Black or African American, non-Hispanic/Latino; 2 Asian, non-Hispanic/Latino; 1 Hispanic/Latino), 17 international. Average age 23. 202 applicants, 10% accepted, 8 enrolled. In 2011, 9 doctorates awarded. *Degree requirements:* For doctorate, comprehensive exam, thesis/dissertation, completion of research integrity module. *Entrance requirements:* For doctorate, GRE General Test, GRE Subject Test. Additional exam requirements/recommendations for international students: Required—TOEFL (minimum score 550 paper-based; 213 computer-based; 80 iBT). *Application deadline:* For fall admission, 1/15 priority date for domestic students, 12/15 for international students. Applications are processed on a rolling basis. Application fee: $0 ($50 for international students). Electronic applications accepted. *Expenses:* Tuition, state resident: full-time $18,774; part-time $760 per credit. Tuition, nonresident: full-time $30,736; part-time $1258 per credit. *Required fees:* $740; $200 per term. Tuition and fees vary according to program. *Financial support:* In 2011–12, 24 fellowships with full tuition reimbursements (averaging $28,790 per year), 111 research assistantships with full tuition reimbursements (averaging $25,793 per year), 24 teaching assistantships with full tuition reimbursements (averaging $24,414 per year) were awarded; Federal Work-Study, scholarships/grants, traineeships, health care benefits, and tuition waivers (full) also available. *Unit head:* Dr. Jeffrey G. Lawrence, Professor, 412-624-4204, Fax: 412-624-4759, E-mail: jlawrenc@pitt.edu. *Application contact:* Cathleen M. Barr, Graduate Administrator, 412-624-4268, Fax: 412-624-4759, E-mail: cbarr@pitt.edu. Web site: http://www.biology.pitt.edu/.

University of Pittsburgh, School of Medicine, Graduate Programs in Medicine, Program in Cell Biology and Molecular Physiology, Pittsburgh, PA 15260. Offers MS, PhD. *Faculty:* 45 full-time (12 women). *Students:* 8 full-time (6 women); includes 1 minority (Asian, non-Hispanic/Latino), 3 international. Average age 27. 514 applicants, 12% accepted, 8 enrolled. In 2011, 4 doctorates awarded. *Degree requirements:* For doctorate, comprehensive exam, thesis/dissertation. *Entrance requirements:* For doctorate, GRE General Test, GRE Subject Test, minimum QPA of 3.0. Additional exam requirements/recommendations for international students: Required—TOEFL (minimum score 600 paper-based; 100 iBT), IELTS (minimum score 7). *Application deadline:* For fall admission, 12/15 priority date for domestic students, 12/15 for international students. Application fee: $50. Electronic applications accepted. *Expenses:* Tuition, state resident: full-time $18,774; part-time $760 per credit. Tuition, nonresident: full-time $30,736; part-time $1258 per credit. *Required fees:* $740; $200 per term. Tuition and fees vary according to program. *Financial support:* In 2011–12, 3 research assistantships with full tuition reimbursements (averaging $25,500 per year), 5 teaching assistantships with full tuition reimbursements (averaging $25,500 per year) were awarded; institutionally sponsored loans, scholarships/grants, traineeships, health care benefits, and unspecified assistantships also available. *Faculty research:* Genetic disorders of ion channels, regulation of gene expression/development, membrane traffic of proteins and lipids, reproductive biology, signal transduction in diabetes and metabolism. *Unit head:* Dr. William H. Walker, Graduate Program Director, 412-641-7672, Fax: 412-641-7676, E-mail: walkerw@pitt.edu. *Application contact:* Graduate Studies Administrator, 412-648-8957, Fax: 412-648-1077, E-mail: gradstudies@medschool.pitt.edu. Web site: http://www.gradbiomed.pitt.edu.

University of Puerto Rico, Río Piedras, College of Natural Sciences, Department of Biology, San Juan, PR 00931-3300. Offers ecology/systematics (MS, PhD); evolution/genetics (MS, PhD); molecular/cellular biology (MS, PhD); neuroscience (MS, PhD). Part-time programs available. *Degree requirements:* For master's, one foreign language, comprehensive exam, thesis; for doctorate, one foreign language, comprehensive exam, thesis/dissertation. *Entrance requirements:* For master's, GRE Subject Test, interview, minimum GPA of 3.0, letter of recommendation; for doctorate, GRE Subject Test, interview, master's degree, minimum GPA of 3.0, letter of recommendation. *Faculty research:* Environmental, poblational and systematic biology.

University of Rhode Island, Graduate School, College of the Environment and Life Sciences, Department of Cell and Molecular Biology, Kingston, RI 02881. Offers biochemistry (MS, PhD); clinical laboratory sciences (MS), including biotechnology, clinical laboratory science, cytopathology; microbiology (MS, PhD); molecular genetics (MS, PhD). Part-time programs available. *Faculty:* 14 full-time (5 women), 3 part-time/adjunct (2 women). *Students:* 32 full-time (15 women), 37 part-time (23 women); includes 2 minority (1 Asian, non-Hispanic/Latino; 1 Hispanic/Latino), 1 international. In 2011, 2 master's, 2 doctorates awarded. *Degree requirements:* For master's, comprehensive exam (for some programs); for doctorate, comprehensive exam. *Entrance requirements:* For master's and doctorate, GRE, 2 letters of recommendation. Additional exam requirements/recommendations for international students: Required—TOEFL (minimum score 550 paper-based; 213 computer-based). *Application deadline:* For fall admission, 7/15 for domestic students, 2/1 for international students; for spring admission, 11/15 for domestic students, 7/15 for international students. Application fee: $65. Electronic applications accepted. *Expenses:* Tuition, state resident: full-time $10,432; part-time $580 per credit hour. Tuition, nonresident: full-time $23,130; part-time $1285 per credit hour. *Required fees:* $1362; $36 per credit hour. $35 per semester. One-time fee: $130. *Financial support:* In 2011–12, 2 research assistantships with full and partial tuition reimbursements (averaging $13,894 per year), 6 teaching assistantships with full and partial tuition reimbursements (averaging $12,850 per year) were awarded. Financial award application deadline: 7/15; financial award applicants required to submit FAFSA. *Faculty research:* Genomics and Sequencing Center: an interdisciplinary genomics research and undergraduate and graduate student training

program which provides researchers access to cutting-edge technologies in the field of genomics. *Unit head:* Dr. Jay Sperry, Chairperson, 401-874-2201, Fax: 401-874-2202, E-mail: jsperry@mail.uri.edu. *Application contact:* Nasser H. Zawia, Dean of the Graduate School, 401-874-5909, Fax: 401-874-5787, E-mail: nzawia@uri.edu. Web site: http://cels.uri.edu/cmb/.

University of Saskatchewan, College of Medicine, Department of Anatomy and Cell Biology, Saskatoon, SK S7N 5A2, Canada. Offers M Sc, PhD. *Degree requirements:* For master's, thesis; for doctorate, thesis/dissertation. *Entrance requirements:* Additional exam requirements/recommendations for international students: Required—TOEFL.

University of South Carolina, The Graduate School, College of Arts and Sciences, Department of Biological Sciences, Graduate Training Program in Molecular, Cellular, and Developmental Biology, Columbia, SC 29208. Offers MS, PhD. *Degree requirements:* For master's, one foreign language, thesis; for doctorate, one foreign language, thesis/dissertation. *Entrance requirements:* For master's and doctorate, GRE General Test, minimum GPA of 3.0 in science. Electronic applications accepted. *Faculty research:* Marine ecology, population and evolutionary biology, molecular biology and genetics, development.

The University of South Dakota, Graduate School, School of Medicine and Graduate School, Biomedical Sciences Graduate Program, Cellular and Molecular Biology Group, Vermillion, SD 57069-2390. Offers MS, PhD. Terminal master's awarded for partial completion of doctoral program. *Degree requirements:* For master's, thesis; for doctorate, comprehensive exam, thesis/dissertation. *Entrance requirements:* For master's and doctorate, GRE General Test, GRE Subject Test, minimum GPA of 3.0. Additional exam requirements/recommendations for international students: Required—TOEFL (minimum score 550 paper-based; 213 computer-based; 80 iBT), IELTS (minimum score 6). Electronic applications accepted. *Expenses:* Contact institution. *Faculty research:* Molecular aspects of protein and DNA, neurochemistry and energy transduction, gene regulation, cellular development.

University of Southern California, Keck School of Medicine and Graduate School, Graduate Programs in Medicine, Department of Cell and Neurobiology, Los Angeles, CA 90089. Offers MS, PhD. *Faculty:* 32 full-time (10 women). *Students:* 1 (woman) full-time; minority (Asian, non-Hispanic/Latino). In 2011, 1 degree awarded. Terminal master's awarded for partial completion of doctoral program. *Degree requirements:* For master's, thesis or alternative; for doctorate, thesis/dissertation. *Entrance requirements:* For master's, GRE General Test, minimum GPA of 3.0; for doctorate, GRE General Test. Additional exam requirements/recommendations for international students: Recommended—TOEFL (minimum score 600 paper-based; 250 computer-based; 100 iBT). *Application deadline:* For fall admission, 12/1 priority date for domestic students, 12/1 for international students. Application fee: $85. Electronic applications accepted. *Financial support:* In 2011–12, 1 research assistantship (averaging $29,100 per year) was awarded; health care benefits and unspecified assistantships also available. *Faculty research:* Neurobiology and development, gene therapy in vision, lachrymal glands, neuroendocrinology, signal transduction mechanisms. *Total annual research expenditures:* $1.7 million. *Unit head:* Dr. Mikel Henry Snow, Vice-Chair, 323-442-1881, Fax: 323-442-3466. *Application contact:* Janet Stoeckert, Administrative Director, Basic Science Departments, 323-442-3568, Fax: 323-442-1610, E-mail: janet.stoeckert@usc.edu.

University of South Florida, Graduate School, College of Arts and Sciences, Department of Biology, Tampa, FL 33620-9951. Offers cell biology and molecular biology (MS); coastal marine biology (MS); coastal marine biology and ecology (PhD); conservation biology (MS, PhD); molecular and cell biology (PhD). Part-time programs available. *Faculty:* 35 full-time (11 women), 16 part-time/adjunct (5 women). *Students:* 126 full-time (75 women), 24 part-time (17 women); includes 13 minority (1 Black or African American, non-Hispanic/Latino; 4 Asian, non-Hispanic/Latino; 8 Hispanic/Latino), 17 international. Average age 30. 235 applicants, 21% accepted, 30 enrolled. In 2011, 7 master's, 11 doctorates awarded. *Degree requirements:* For master's, comprehensive exam, thesis (for some programs); for doctorate, comprehensive exam, thesis/dissertation. *Entrance requirements:* For master's and doctorate, GRE General Test, minimum GPA of 3.0. Additional exam requirements/recommendations for international students: Required—TOEFL (minimum score 570 paper-based; 213 computer-based). *Application deadline:* For fall admission, 2/15 priority date for domestic students, 1/2 for international students; for spring admission, 8/1 for domestic students, 6/1 for international students. Application fee: $30. Electronic applications accepted. *Financial support:* In 2011–12, 122 students received support, including 46 research assistantships (averaging $24,716 per year), 76 teaching assistantships with tuition reimbursements available (averaging $28,434 per year); unspecified assistantships also available. Financial award application deadline: 6/30; financial award applicants required to submit FAFSA. *Total annual research expenditures:* $5.2 million. *Unit head:* Susan Bell, Co-Chairperson, 813-974-6210, Fax: 813-974-2876, E-mail: sbell@cas.usf.edu. *Application contact:* James Garey, Graduate Advisor, 813-974-8434, Fax: 813-974-3263, E-mail: grarey@cas.usf.edu. Web site: http://www.cas.usf.edu/biology/.

The University of Texas at Austin, Graduate School, Institute for Cellular and Molecular Biology, Austin, TX 78712-1111. Offers PhD. *Financial support:* Fellowships, research assistantships, teaching assistantships, institutionally sponsored loans, and traineeships available. *Unit head:* Alan M. Lambowitz, Director, 512-232-3418, E-mail: lambowitz@mail.utexas.edu. *Application contact:* Information Contact, 512-471-1156, Fax: 512-471-2149. Web site: http://www.icmb.utexas.edu/.

The University of Texas at Dallas, School of Natural Sciences and Mathematics, Department of Biology, Richardson, TX 75080. Offers bioinformatics and computational biology (MS); biotechnology (MS); molecular and cell biology (MS, PhD). Part-time and evening/weekend programs available. *Faculty:* 18 full-time (2 women), 1 part-time/adjunct (0 women). *Students:* 111 full-time (59 women), 13 part-time (6 women); includes 19 minority (2 Black or African American, non-Hispanic/Latino; 14 Asian, non-Hispanic/Latino; 3 Hispanic/Latino), 86 international. Average age 27. 483 applicants, 31% accepted, 67 enrolled. In 2011, 39 master's, 7 doctorates awarded. *Degree requirements:* For master's, thesis optional; for doctorate, thesis/dissertation, publishable paper. *Entrance requirements:* For master's and doctorate, GRE (minimum combined score of 1000 on verbal and quantitative). Additional exam requirements/recommendations for international students: Required—TOEFL (minimum score 550 paper-based; 215 computer-based; 80 iBT). *Application deadline:* For fall admission, 7/15 for domestic students, 5/1 for international students; for spring admission, 11/15 for domestic students, 9/1 for international students. Applications are processed on a rolling basis. Application fee: $50 ($100 for international students). Electronic applications accepted. *Expenses:* Tuition, state resident: full-time $11,170; part-time $620.56 per credit hour. Tuition, nonresident: full-time $20,212; part-time $1122.89 per credit hour. *Financial support:* In 2011–12, 49 students received support, including 18 research assistantships with partial tuition reimbursements available (averaging $20,911 per year), 36 teaching assistantships with partial tuition reimbursements available (averaging $15,300 per year); career-related internships or fieldwork, Federal Work-Study, institutionally sponsored loans, scholarships/grants, and unspecified assistantships also available. Support available to part-time students. Financial award application deadline: 4/30; financial award applicants required to submit FAFSA. *Faculty research:* Role of mitochondria in neurodegenerative diseases, protein-DNA interactions in site-specific recombination, eukaryotic gene expression, bio-nanotechnology, sickle cell research. *Unit head:* Dr. Stephen Spiro, Department Head, 972-883-6032, Fax: 972-883-2502, E-mail: stephen.spiro@utdallas.edu. *Application contact:* Dr. Lawrence Reitzer, Graduate Advisor, 972-883-2502, Fax: 972-883-2402, E-mail: reitzer@utdallas.edu. Web site: http://www.utdallas.edu/biology/.

The University of Texas at San Antonio, College of Sciences, Department of Biology, San Antonio, TX 78249-0617. Offers biology (MS); biotechnology (MS), including bioprocessing technician, biotechnology; cell and molecular biology (PhD); environmental science (MS); neurobiology (PhD). *Faculty:* 34 full-time (6 women), 7 part-time/adjunct (1 woman). *Students:* 117 full-time (62 women), 64 part-time (35 women); includes 63 minority (10 Black or African American, non-Hispanic/Latino; 16 Asian, non-Hispanic/Latino; 36 Hispanic/Latino; 7 Two or more races, non-Hispanic/Latino), 54 international. Average age 27. 239 applicants, 45% accepted, 50 enrolled. In 2011, 62 master's, 3 doctorates awarded. Terminal master's awarded for partial completion of doctoral program. *Degree requirements:* For master's, comprehensive exam, thesis or alternative; for doctorate, thesis/dissertation. *Entrance requirements:* For master's, GRE General Test, bachelor's degree with 18 credit hours in field of study or in another appropriate field of study; for doctorate, GRE General Test, 3 letters of recommendation, statement of purpose, resume. Additional exam requirements/recommendations for international students: Required—TOEFL (minimum score 500 paper-based; 100 iBT), IELTS (minimum score 5). *Application deadline:* For fall admission, 7/1 for domestic students, 4/1 for international students; for spring admission, 11/1 for domestic students, 9/1 for international students. Application fee: $45 ($85 for international students). *Expenses:* Tuition, state resident: full-time $3148; part-time $2176 per semester. Tuition, nonresident: full-time $8782; part-time $5932 per semester. *Required fees:* $719 per semester. *Financial support:* In 2011–12, 66 students received support, including 4 fellowships (averaging $22,350 per year), 34 research assistantships (averaging $22,350 per year), 8 teaching assistantships (averaging $22,350 per year). *Faculty research:* Development of human and veterinary vaccines against a fungal disease, mammalian germ cells and stem cells, dopamine neuron physiology and addiction, plant biochemistry, dendritic computation and synaptic plasticity. *Total annual research expenditures:* $2.8 million. *Unit head:* Dr. Edwin J. Barea-Rodriguez, Chair, 210-458-4511, Fax: 210-458-5658, E-mail: edwin.barea@utsa.edu. *Application contact:* Rene Munguia, Program Coordinator, 210-458-4642, Fax: 210-458-5658, E-mail: rene.munguia@utsa.edu.

The University of Texas Health Science Center at Houston, Graduate School of Biomedical Sciences, Program in Cell and Regulatory Biology, Houston, TX 77225-0036. Offers MS, PhD, MD/PhD. Terminal master's awarded for partial completion of doctoral program. *Degree requirements:* For master's, thesis; for doctorate, thesis/dissertation. *Entrance requirements:* For master's and doctorate, GRE General Test. Additional exam requirements/recommendations for international students: Required—TOEFL. Electronic applications accepted. *Faculty research:* Pharmacology, cell biology, physiology, signal transduction, systems biology.

The University of Texas Health Science Center at San Antonio, Graduate School of Biomedical Sciences, Department of Cellular and Structural Biology, San Antonio, TX 78229-3900. Offers MS, PhD. *Degree requirements:* For master's, thesis; for doctorate, comprehensive exam, thesis/dissertation. *Entrance requirements:* For doctorate, GRE General Test, previous course work in biology, chemistry, physics, and calculus. Additional exam requirements/recommendations for international students: Required—TOEFL (minimum score 550 paper-based; 213 computer-based; 68 iBT). Electronic applications accepted. *Faculty research:* Human/molecular genetics, endocrinology and neurobiology, cell biology, stem cell biology, cancer biology, biology of aging.

The University of Texas Medical Branch, Graduate School of Biomedical Sciences, Program in Biochemistry and Molecular Biology, Galveston, TX 77555. Offers biochemistry (PhD); bioinformatics (PhD); biophysics (PhD); cell biology (PhD); computational biology (PhD); structural biology (PhD). *Degree requirements:* For doctorate, thesis/dissertation. *Entrance requirements:* Additional exam requirements/recommendations for international students: Required—TOEFL (minimum score 550 paper-based; 213 computer-based). Electronic applications accepted.

The University of Texas Southwestern Medical Center, Southwestern Graduate School of Biomedical Sciences, Division of Basic Science, Program in Cell Regulation, Dallas, TX 75390. Offers PhD. *Degree requirements:* For doctorate, thesis/dissertation, qualifying exam. *Entrance requirements:* For doctorate, GRE General Test, minimum GPA of 3.0. Additional exam requirements/recommendations for international students: Required—TOEFL. Electronic applications accepted. *Faculty research:* Molecular and cellular approaches to regulatory biology, receptor-effector coupling, membrane structure, function, and assembly.

University of the Sciences in Philadelphia, College of Graduate Studies, Misher College of Arts and Sciences, Program in Cell and Molecular Biology, Philadelphia, PA 19104-4495. Offers PhD.

University of the Sciences in Philadelphia, College of Graduate Studies, Program in Cell Biology and Biotechnology, Philadelphia, PA 19104-4495. Offers cell and molecular biology (PhD); cell biology (MS). Part-time and evening/weekend programs available. *Degree requirements:* For master's, thesis (for some programs). *Entrance requirements:* For master's, GRE General Test. Additional exam requirements/recommendations for international students: Required—TOEFL, TWE. *Expenses:* Contact institution. *Faculty research:* Invertebrate cell adhesion, plant-microbe interactions, natural product mechanisms, cell signal transduction, gene regulation and organization.

The University of Toledo, College of Graduate Studies, College of Natural Sciences and Mathematics, Department of Biological Sciences, Toledo, OH 43606-3390. Offers cell/molecular biology (MS, PhD). Part-time programs available. *Faculty:* 19. *Students:* 70 full-time (34 women), 28 part-time (20 women); includes 6 minority (1 Black or African American, non-Hispanic/Latino; 2 Asian, non-Hispanic/Latino; 1 Hispanic/Latino; 2 Two or more races, non-Hispanic/Latino), 30 international. Average age 29. 110 applicants, 16% accepted, 16 enrolled. In 2011, 13 master's, 6 doctorates awarded. *Degree requirements:* For master's, thesis or alternative; for doctorate, thesis/dissertation. *Entrance requirements:* For master's and doctorate, GRE General Test, GRE Subject Test, minimum cumulative point-hour ratio of 2.7 for all previous academic work, three letters of recommendation, statement of purpose, transcripts from all prior institutions attended. Additional exam requirements/recommendations for international students: Required—TOEFL (minimum score 550 paper-based; 213 computer-based; 80 iBT), IELTS (minimum score 6.5). *Application deadline:* For fall admission, 1/15 priority date for domestic students, 1/15 for international students. Applications are processed on a rolling basis. Application fee: $45 ($75 for international students). Electronic applications accepted. *Financial support:* In 2011–12, 31 research assistantships with full and partial tuition reimbursements (averaging $17,292 per year), 38 teaching assistantships with full and partial tuition reimbursements (averaging $18,011 per year) were awarded; fellowships, Federal Work-Study, institutionally sponsored loans, scholarships/grants, tuition waivers (full), and unspecified assistantships also available. Support available to part-time students. *Faculty research:* Biochemical parasitology, physiological ecology, animal physiology. *Unit head:* Dr. Doug Leaman, Chair, 419-530-2066, E-mail:

Cell Biology

douglas.leaman@utoledo.edu. *Application contact:* Graduate School Office, 419-530-4723, Fax: 419-530-4724, E-mail: grdsch@utnet.utoledo.edu. Web site: http://www.utoledo.edu/nsm/.

University of Toronto, School of Graduate Studies, Faculty of Arts and Science, Department of Cell and Systems Biology, Toronto, ON M5S 1A1, Canada. Offers M Sc, PhD. *Degree requirements:* For master's, thesis, thesis defense; for doctorate, thesis/dissertation, thesis defense, oral thesis examination. *Entrance requirements:* For master's, minimum B+ average in final year, B overall, 3 letters of reference. Additional exam requirements/recommendations for international students: Required—TOEFL (minimum score 580 paper-based; 237 computer-based; 93 iBT), TWE (minimum score 5). Electronic applications accepted.

University of Vermont, Graduate College, Cell and Molecular Biology Program, Burlington, VT 05405. Offers MS, PhD. *Students:* 37 (14 women); includes 7 minority (2 Asian, non-Hispanic/Latino; 5 Hispanic/Latino), 5 international. 68 applicants, 25% accepted, 4 enrolled. In 2011, 1 master's, 2 doctorates awarded. *Degree requirements:* For master's, thesis; for doctorate, thesis/dissertation. *Entrance requirements:* For master's and doctorate, GRE General Test. Additional exam requirements/recommendations for international students: Required—TOEFL (minimum score 550 paper-based; 213 computer-based; 80 iBT). *Application deadline:* For fall admission, 1/15 priority date for domestic students, 1/15 for international students. Applications are processed on a rolling basis. Application fee: $40. Electronic applications accepted. *Financial support:* Fellowships, research assistantships, teaching assistantships, and career-related internships or fieldwork available. Financial award application deadline: 3/1. *Unit head:* Dr. Mary Tierney, Coordinator, 802-656-9673.

University of Virginia, School of Medicine, Department of Cell Biology, Charlottesville, VA 22903. Offers PhD, MD/PhD. *Faculty:* 22 full-time (7 women), 3 part-time/adjunct (1 woman). *Students:* 26 full-time (13 women); includes 4 minority (3 Black or African American, non-Hispanic/Latino; 1 Hispanic/Latino), 7 international. Average age 28. In 2011, 4 doctorates awarded. *Degree requirements:* For doctorate, one foreign language, thesis/dissertation. *Entrance requirements:* For doctorate, GRE General Test, GRE Subject Test (recommended), 2 letters of recommendation. Additional exam requirements/recommendations for international students: Required—TOEFL. *Application deadline:* For fall admission, 4/15 for domestic and international students. Applications are processed on a rolling basis. Application fee: $60. Electronic applications accepted. *Financial support:* Application deadline: 1/15; applicants required to submit FAFSA. *Unit head:* Dr. Barry M. Gumbiner, Chairman, 434-924-2731, Fax: 434-982-3912, E-mail: bmg4n@virginia.edu. *Application contact:* Lesley L. Thomas, Director, Admissions Office, 434-924-5571, Fax: 434-982-2586, E-mail: medsch-adm@virginia.edu. Web site: http://www.virginia.edu/cellbiology/.

University of Washington, Graduate School, School of Medicine, Graduate Programs in Medicine, Program in Molecular and Cellular Biology, Seattle, WA 98195. Offers PhD. Offered jointly with Fred Hutchinson Cancer Research Center. *Degree requirements:* For doctorate, thesis/dissertation. *Entrance requirements:* For doctorate, GRE General Test. Additional exam requirements/recommendations for international students: Required—TOEFL. Electronic applications accepted.

See Display on this page and Close-Up on page 249.

The University of Western Ontario, Faculty of Graduate Studies, Biosciences Division, Department of Biology, London, ON N6A 5B8, Canada. Offers M Sc, PhD. *Degree requirements:* For master's, thesis; for doctorate, comprehensive exam, thesis/dissertation. *Entrance requirements:* For master's, honors degree or equivalent in biological sciences; for doctorate, master's degree. Additional exam requirements/recommendations for international students: Required—TOEFL. *Faculty research:* Cell and molecular biology, developmental biology, neuroscience, immunobiology and cancer.

University of Wisconsin–La Crosse, Office of University Graduate Studies, College of Science and Health, Department of Biology, La Crosse, WI 54601-3742. Offers aquatic sciences (MS); biology (MS); cellular and molecular biology (MS); clinical microbiology (MS); microbiology (MS); nurse anesthesia (MS); physiology (MS). Part-time programs available. *Faculty:* 21 full-time (8 women), 3 part-time/adjunct (1 woman). *Students:* 45 full-time (30 women), 47 part-time (22 women); includes 10 minority (1 Black or African American, non-Hispanic/Latino; 5 Asian, non-Hispanic/Latino; 3 Hispanic/Latino; 1 Two or more races, non-Hispanic/Latino), 3 international. Average age 28. 63 applicants, 46% accepted, 24 enrolled. In 2011, 23 master's awarded. *Degree requirements:* For master's, comprehensive exam, thesis. *Entrance requirements:* For master's, GRE General Test, minimum GPA of 2.85. Additional exam requirements/recommendations for international students: Required—TOEFL (minimum score 550 paper-based; 213 computer-based; 79 iBT). *Application deadline:* For fall admission, 2/1 priority date for domestic students, 2/1 for international students; for spring admission, 1/4 priority date for domestic students, 1/4 for international students. Applications are processed on a rolling basis. Application fee: $56. Electronic applications accepted. *Expenses:* Tuition, state resident: full-time $8391; part-time $481.17 per credit. Tuition, nonresident: full-time $17,850; part-time $1006.68 per credit. *Required fees:* $2 per credit. $18.25 per semester. Tuition and fees vary according to course load, program, reciprocity agreements and student level. *Financial support:* In 2011–12, 29 research assistantships with partial tuition reimbursements (averaging $9,712 per year) were awarded; Federal Work-Study, scholarships/grants, health care benefits, and tuition waivers (partial) also available. Support available to part-time students. Financial award application deadline: 3/15; financial award applicants required to submit FAFSA. *Unit head:* Dr. Thomas Volk, Coordinator of Graduate Studies, 608-785-6972, Fax: 608-785-6959, E-mail: volk.thom@uwlax.edu. *Application contact:* Kathryn Kiefer, Director of Admissions, 608-785-8939, E-mail: admissions@uwlax.edu. Web site: http://uwlax.edu/biology/.

University of Wisconsin–Madison, Graduate School, Program in Cellular and Molecular Biology, Madison, WI 53706-1596. Offers PhD. *Degree requirements:* For doctorate, comprehensive exam, thesis/dissertation. *Entrance requirements:* For doctorate, GRE General Test, GRE Subject Test (recommended), minimum GPA of 3.0, lab experience. Additional exam requirements/recommendations for international students: Required—TOEFL (minimum score 580 paper-based; 237 computer-based; 92 iBT). Electronic applications accepted. *Expenses:* Tuition, state resident: full-time $10,296; part-time $643.51 per credit. Tuition, nonresident: full-time $24,054; part-time $1503.40 per credit. *Required fees:* $70.06 per credit. Tuition and fees vary according to course load, campus/location, program and reciprocity agreements. *Faculty research:* Virology, cancer biology, transcriptional mechanisms, plant biology, immunology.

University of Wyoming, Graduate Program in Molecular and Cellular Life Sciences, Laramie, WY 82070. Offers PhD. *Degree requirements:* For doctorate, thesis/dissertation, four eight-week laboratory rotations, comprehensive basic practical exam, two-part qualifying exam, seminars, symposium.

Vanderbilt University, Graduate School and School of Medicine, Department of Cell and Developmental Biology, Nashville, TN 37240-1001. Offers MS, PhD, MD/PhD. *Faculty:* 20 full-time (10 women). *Students:* 84 full-time (45 women); includes 14 minority (3 Black or African American, non-Hispanic/Latino; 7 Asian, non-Hispanic/Latino; 1

W

UNIVERSITY *of* WASHINGTON

www.mcb-seattle.org

Molecular & Cellular Biology

A PhD Program in Seattle Washington

MCB is an interdisciplinary research program fostering an innovative and flexible graduate program with a broad range of research in all areas of biomedical science.

Partners:

**FRED HUTCHINSON CANCER RESEARCH CENTER
SEATTLE BIOMEDICAL RESEARCH CENTER
INSTITUTE FOR SYSTEMS BIOLOGY
UNIVERSITY OF WASHINGTON**

Hispanic/Latino; 3 Two or more races, non-Hispanic/Latino), 8 international. Average age 27. In 2011, 1 master's, 7 doctorates awarded. Terminal master's awarded for partial completion of doctoral program. *Degree requirements:* For master's, thesis or alternative; for doctorate, thesis/dissertation, preliminary, qualifying, and final exams. *Entrance requirements:* For master's, GRE General Test; for doctorate, GRE General Test, GRE Subject Test (recommended). Additional exam requirements/recommendations for international students: Required—TOEFL (minimum score 570 paper-based; 230 computer-based; 88 iBT). *Application deadline:* For fall admission, 1/15 for domestic and international students. Application fee: $0. Electronic applications accepted. *Financial support:* Fellowships with full and partial tuition reimbursements, research assistantships with full and partial tuition reimbursements, career-related internships or fieldwork, Federal Work-Study, institutionally sponsored loans, scholarships/grants, traineeships, health care benefits, and tuition waivers (partial) available. Financial award application deadline: 1/15; financial award applicants required to submit CSS PROFILE or FAFSA. *Faculty research:* Cancer biology, cell cycle regulation, cell signaling, cytoskeletal biology, developmental biology, neurobiology, proteomics, stem cell biology, structural biology, reproductive biology, trafficking and transport, medical education and gross anatomy. *Unit head:* Dr. Susan R. Wente, Chair, 615-936-3455, Fax: 615-343-4539, E-mail: susan.wente@vanderbilt.edu. *Application contact:* Dr. Kathy Gould, Director of Graduate Studies, 615-343-9502, Fax: 615-343-4539, E-mail: kathy.gould@vanderbilt.edu. Web site: http://www.mc.vanderbilt.edu/vumcdept/cellbio/.

Washington State University, Graduate School, College of Sciences, School of Molecular Biosciences, Program in Genetics and Cell Biology, Pullman, WA 99164. Offers MS, PhD. *Faculty:* 23 full-time (5 women), 21 part-time/adjunct (4 women). *Students:* 9 full-time (6 women); includes 2 minority (1 Hispanic/Latino; 1 Two or more races, non-Hispanic/Latino), 3 international. Average age 29. In 2011, 3 doctorates awarded. Terminal master's awarded for partial completion of doctoral program. *Degree requirements:* For master's, thesis or alternative, oral exam; for doctorate, comprehensive exam, thesis/dissertation, oral exam. *Entrance requirements:* For master's and doctorate, GRE General Test, minimum GPA of 3.0. Additional exam requirements/recommendations for international students: Required—TOEFL (minimum score 550 paper-based; 213 computer-based). *Application deadline:* For fall admission, 12/15 for domestic and international students. Application fee: $75. Electronic applications accepted. *Financial support:* In 2011–12, 1 fellowship with full tuition reimbursement (averaging $18,852 per year), 16 research assistantships with full tuition reimbursements (averaging $18,852 per year), 6 teaching assistantships with full tuition reimbursements (averaging $18,852 per year) were awarded; Federal Work-Study, institutionally sponsored loans, health care benefits, and unspecified assistantships also available. Financial award application deadline: 4/1; financial award applicants required to submit FAFSA. *Faculty research:* Plant molecular biology, growth factors, cancer induction and DNA repair, gene regulation and genetic engineering. *Total annual research expenditures:* $5.8 million. *Unit head:* Dr. John H. Nilson, Director, 509-335-8724, Fax: 509-335-9688, E-mail: jhn@wsu.edu. *Application contact:* Kelly G. McGovern, Academic Coordinator, 509-335-4566, Fax: 509-335-1907, E-mail: smbgrad@wsu.edu. Web site: http://molecular.biosciences.wsu.edu/.

Washington University in St. Louis, Graduate School of Arts and Sciences, Division of Biology and Biomedical Sciences, Program in Molecular Cell Biology, St. Louis, MO 63130-4899. Offers PhD. *Degree requirements:* For doctorate, thesis/dissertation. *Entrance requirements:* For doctorate, GRE General Test, GRE Subject Test. Electronic applications accepted.

Weill Cornell Medical College, Weill Cornell Graduate School of Medical Sciences, Biochemistry, Cell and Molecular Biology Allied Program, New York, NY 10065. Offers MS, PhD. *Faculty:* 111 full-time (32 women). *Students:* 152 full-time (95 women); includes 19 minority (2 Black or African American, non-Hispanic/Latino; 5 Asian, non-Hispanic/Latino; 8 Hispanic/Latino; 4 Native Hawaiian or other Pacific Islander, non-Hispanic/Latino), 82 international. Average age 22. 374 applicants, 23% accepted, 30 enrolled. In 2011, 2 master's, 19 doctorates awarded. Terminal master's awarded for partial completion of doctoral program. *Degree requirements:* For master's, comprehensive exam; for doctorate, thesis/dissertation, final exam. *Entrance requirements:* For doctorate, GRE General Test, background in genetics, molecular biology, chemistry, or biochemistry. Additional exam requirements/recommendations for international students: Required—TOEFL. *Application deadline:* For fall admission, 12/1 for domestic students. Application fee: $60. Electronic applications accepted. *Expenses: Tuition:* Full-time $46,001. *Financial support:* In 2011–12, 16 fellowships (averaging $22,600 per year) were awarded; scholarships/grants, health care benefits, and stipends (given to all students) also available. *Faculty research:* Molecular structure determination, protein structure, gene structure, stem cell biology, control of gene expression, DNA replication, chromosome maintenance, RNA biosynthesis. *Unit head:* Dr. Kirk Deitsch, Co-Director, 212-746-4976, Fax: 212-746-8906, E-mail: kwd2001@med.cornell.edu. *Application contact:* Rosalia Mora, Program Coordinator, 212-746-6058, Fax: 212-746-8906, E-mail: rmora@med.cornell.edu. Web site: http://weill.cornell.edu/gradschool/program/cell.html.

Wesleyan University, Graduate Programs, Department of Biology, Middletown, CT 06459. Offers animal behavior (PhD); bioformatics/genomics (PhD); cell biology (PhD); developmental biology (PhD); evolution/ecology (PhD); genetics (PhD); neurobiology (PhD); population biology (PhD). *Degree requirements:* For doctorate, variable foreign language requirement, thesis/dissertation. *Entrance requirements:* For doctorate, GRE. Additional exam requirements/recommendations for international students: Required—TOEFL. *Faculty research:* Microbial population genetics, genetic basis of evolutionary adaptation, genetic regulation of differentiation and pattern formation in &ITdrosophila&RO.

West Virginia University, Eberly College of Arts and Sciences, Department of Biology, Morgantown, WV 26506. Offers cell and molecular biology (MS, PhD); environmental and evolutionary biology (MS, PhD); forensic biology (MS, PhD); genomic biology (MS, PhD); neurobiology (MS, PhD). Terminal master's awarded for partial completion of doctoral program. *Degree requirements:* For master's, thesis, final exam; for doctorate, thesis/dissertation, preliminary and final exams. *Entrance requirements:* For master's, GRE General Test, GRE Subject Test, minimum GPA of 3.0; for doctorate, GRE General Test, minimum GPA of 3.0. Additional exam requirements/recommendations for international students: Required—TOEFL. *Faculty research:* Environmental biology, genetic engineering, developmental biology, global change, biodiversity.

Yale University, Graduate School of Arts and Sciences, Department of Cell Biology, New Haven, CT 06520. Offers PhD. *Degree requirements:* For doctorate, thesis/dissertation. *Entrance requirements:* For doctorate, GRE General Test. *Expenses:* Contact institution.

Yale University, Graduate School of Arts and Sciences, Department of Molecular, Cellular, and Developmental Biology, Program in Cellular and Developmental Biology, New Haven, CT 06520. Offers PhD. *Degree requirements:* For doctorate, thesis/dissertation. *Entrance requirements:* For doctorate, GRE General Test, GRE Subject Test.

Yale University, School of Medicine and Graduate School of Arts and Sciences, Combined Program in Biological and Biomedical Sciences (BBS), Molecular Cell Biology, Genetics, and Development Track, New Haven, CT 06520. Offers PhD, MD/PhD. *Entrance requirements:* Additional exam requirements/recommendations for international students: Required—TOEFL.

Molecular Biology

Albany Medical College, Center for Cell Biology and Cancer Research, Albany, NY 12208-3479. Offers MS, PhD. Part-time programs available. Terminal master's awarded for partial completion of doctoral program. *Degree requirements:* For master's, thesis; for doctorate, comprehensive exam, thesis/dissertation. *Entrance requirements:* For master's and doctorate, GRE General Test, all transcripts, letters of recommendation. Additional exam requirements/recommendations for international students: Required—TOEFL. *Faculty research:* Cancer cell biology, tissue remodeling, signal transduction, gene regulation, cell adhesion, angiogenesis.

Albert Einstein College of Medicine, Graduate Division of Biomedical Sciences, Division of Biological Sciences, Department of Developmental and Molecular Biology, Bronx, NY 10461. Offers PhD, MD/PhD. *Degree requirements:* For doctorate, thesis/dissertation. *Entrance requirements:* For doctorate, GRE General Test. Additional exam requirements/recommendations for international students: Required—TOEFL. *Faculty research:* DNA, RNA, and protein synthesis in prokaryotes and eukaryotes; chemical and enzymatic alteration of RNA; glycoproteins.

Appalachian State University, Cratis D. Williams Graduate School, Department of Biology, Boone, NC 28608. Offers cell and molecular (MS); general (MS). Part-time programs available. *Faculty:* 29 full-time (12 women), 3 part-time/adjunct (1 woman). *Students:* 46 full-time (24 women), 9 part-time (7 women); includes 1 minority (Asian, non-Hispanic/Latino). 32 applicants, 63% accepted, 15 enrolled. In 2011, 11 master's awarded. *Degree requirements:* For master's, comprehensive exam, thesis. *Entrance requirements:* For master's, GRE General Test, 3 letters of recommendation. Additional exam requirements/recommendations for international students: Required—TOEFL (minimum score 570 paper-based; 230 computer-based; 79 iBT), IELTS (minimum score 6.5). *Application deadline:* For fall admission, 3/5 priority date for domestic students, 2/1 for international students; for spring admission, 11/1 for domestic students, 7/1 for international students. Applications are processed on a rolling basis. Application fee: $55. Electronic applications accepted. *Expenses:* Tuition, state resident: full-time $4040; part-time $180 per semester hour. Tuition, nonresident: full-time $15,900; part-time $760 per semester hour. *Required fees:* $2500; $20 per semester hour. Tuition and fees vary according to campus/location. *Financial support:* In 2011–12, 25 teaching assistantships (averaging $9,500 per year) were awarded; fellowships, research assistantships, career-related internships or fieldwork, Federal Work-Study, scholarships/grants, and unspecified assistantships also available. Financial award application deadline: 3/15; financial award applicants required to submit FAFSA. *Faculty research:* Aquatic and terrestrial ecology, animal and plant physiology, behavior and systematics, immunology and cell biology, molecular biology and microbiology. *Unit head:* Dr. Steven Seagle, Chairman, 828-262-3025, E-mail: seaglesw@appstate.edu. *Application contact:* Dr. Ece Karatan, Graduate Coordinator, 828-262-6742, E-mail: karatane@appstate.edu. Web site: http://www.biology.appstate.edu.

Arizona State University, College of Liberal Arts and Sciences, School of Life Sciences, Tempe, AZ 85287-4601. Offers animal behavior (PhD); applied ethics (biomedical and health ethics) (MA); biological design (PhD); biology (MS, PhD); biology (biology and society) (MS, PhD); environmental life sciences (PhD); evolutionary biology (PhD); human and social dimensions of science and technology (PhD); microbiology (PhD); molecular and cellular biology (PhD); neuroscience (PhD); philosophy (history and philosophy of science) (MA); sustainability (PhD). Terminal master's awarded for partial completion of doctoral program. *Degree requirements:* For master's, thesis (for some programs), interactive Program of Study (iPOS) submitted before completing 50 percent of required credit hours; for doctorate, variable foreign language requirement, comprehensive exam, thesis/dissertation, interactive Program of Study (iPOS) submitted before completing 50 percent of required credit hours. *Entrance requirements:* For master's and doctorate, GRE, minimum GPA of 3.0 or equivalent in last 2 years of work leading to bachelor's degree. Additional exam requirements/recommendations for international students: Required—TOEFL (minimum score 600 paper-based; 250 computer-based; 100 iBT). Electronic applications accepted.

Arkansas State University, Graduate School, College of Sciences and Mathematics, Program in Molecular Biosciences, Jonesboro, State University, AR 72467. Offers PhD. Part-time programs available. *Faculty:* 1 full-time (0 women). *Students:* 15 full-time (4 women); includes 3 minority (1 American Indian or Alaska Native, non-Hispanic/Latino; 1 Asian, non-Hispanic/Latino; 1 Two or more races, non-Hispanic/Latino), 8 international. Average age 29. 2 applicants, 0% accepted, 0 enrolled. In 2011, 1 doctorate awarded. *Degree requirements:* For doctorate, comprehensive exam, thesis/dissertation. *Entrance requirements:* For doctorate, GRE, appropriate bachelor's or master's degree, interview, letters of reference, official transcripts, personal statement, immunization records. Additional exam requirements/recommendations for international students: Required—TOEFL (minimum score 550 paper-based; 213 computer-based; 79 iBT), IELTS (minimum score 6), Pearson Test of English Academic (minimum score 56). *Application deadline:* For fall admission, 2/15 for domestic and international students; for spring admission, 11/15 for domestic students, 11/14 for international students. Applications are processed on a rolling basis. Application fee: $50. Electronic applications accepted. *Expenses:* Tuition, state resident: full-time $4044; part-time $225 per credit hour. Tuition, nonresident: full-time $8087; part-time $449 per credit hour. *Required fees:* $936; $52 per credit hour. $25 per term. One-time fee: $30. Tuition and fees vary according to course load and program. *Financial support:* In 2011–12, 11 students received support. Fellowships, research assistantships, teaching assistantships, career-related internships or fieldwork, scholarships/grants, and

unspecified assistantships available. Financial award application deadline: 7/1; financial award applicants required to submit FAFSA. *Unit head:* Dr. Roger Buchanan, Director, 870-972-2007, Fax: 870-972-2008, E-mail: rbuck@astate.edu. *Application contact:* Dr. Andrew Sustich, Dean of the Graduate School, 870-972-3029, Fax: 870-972-3857, E-mail: sustich@astate.edu. Web site: http://www.astate.edu/scimath/mbs.

Auburn University, Graduate School, Interdepartmental Programs, Auburn University, AL 36849. Offers applied economics (PhD); cell and molecular biology (PhD); integrated textile and apparel sciences (PhD); real estate development (MRED); sociology and rural sociology (MA, MS), including rural sociology (MS), sociology. Part-time programs available. *Students:* 25 full-time (12 women), 19 part-time (13 women); includes 4 minority (1 Black or African American, non-Hispanic/Latino; 1 American Indian or Alaska Native, non-Hispanic/Latino; 2 Asian, non-Hispanic/Latino), 26 international. Average age 28. 88 applicants, 35% accepted, 12 enrolled. In 2011, 4 master's, 3 doctorates awarded. *Entrance requirements:* For master's, GRE General Test. *Application deadline:* For fall admission, 7/7 for domestic students; for spring admission, 11/24 for domestic students. Applications are processed on a rolling basis. Application fee: $50 ($60 for international students). Electronic applications accepted. *Expenses:* Tuition, state resident: full-time $7290; part-time $405 per credit hour. Tuition, nonresident: full-time $21,870; part-time $1215 per credit hour. *International tuition:* $22,000 full-time. *Required fees:* $1402. *Financial support:* Fellowships, research assistantships, teaching assistantships, and Federal Work-Study available. Support available to part-time students. Financial award application deadline: 3/15; financial award applicants required to submit FAFSA. *Unit head:* Interim Dean of the Graduate School. *Application contact:* Dr. George Flowers, Dean of the Graduate School, 334-844-2125.

Baylor College of Medicine, Graduate School of Biomedical Sciences, Department of Biochemistry and Molecular Biology, Houston, TX 77030-3498. Offers PhD, MD/PhD. *Faculty:* 38 full-time (7 women). *Students:* 50 full-time (26 women); includes 6 minority (1 Black or African American, non-Hispanic/Latino; 1 American Indian or Alaska Native, non-Hispanic/Latino; 2 Asian, non-Hispanic/Latino; 2 Hispanic/Latino), 31 international. Average age 28. 105 applicants, 13% accepted, 8 enrolled. In 2011, 9 doctorates awarded. *Degree requirements:* For doctorate, thesis/dissertation, public defense. *Entrance requirements:* For doctorate, GRE General Test, GRE Subject Test (strongly recommended), minimum GPA of 3.0. Additional exam requirements/recommendations for international students: Required—TOEFL. *Application deadline:* For fall admission, 1/1 priority date for domestic students. Application fee: $0. Electronic applications accepted. *Financial support:* In 2011–12, 17 fellowships with full tuition reimbursements (averaging $29,000 per year), 33 research assistantships with full tuition reimbursements (averaging $29,000 per year) were awarded; career-related internships or fieldwork, Federal Work-Study, institutionally sponsored loans, health care benefits, and scholarships (to all students unless there are grant funds available to pay tuition) also available. Financial award applicants required to submit FAFSA. *Faculty research:* DNA repair, homologous recombination, gene therapy, trinucleotide repeat diseases, retinitis pigmentosa. *Unit head:* Dr. John Wilson, Director, 713-798-5760. *Application contact:* Ruth Reeves, Graduate Program Administrator, 713-798-0124, Fax: 713-796-9438, E-mail: rareeves@bcm.edu. Web site: http://www.bcm.edu/biochem/.

Baylor College of Medicine, Graduate School of Biomedical Sciences, Department of Molecular and Cellular Biology, Houston, TX 77030-3498. Offers PhD, MD/PhD. *Faculty:* 81 full-time (23 women). *Students:* 55 full-time (35 women); includes 12 minority (1 Black or African American, non-Hispanic/Latino; 5 Asian, non-Hispanic/Latino; 6 Hispanic/Latino), 15 international. Average age 27. 145 applicants, 14% accepted, 8 enrolled. In 2011, 12 degrees awarded. *Median time to degree:* Of those who began their doctoral program in fall 2003, 69% received their degree in 8 years or less. *Degree requirements:* For doctorate, thesis/dissertation, public defense, qualifying exam. *Entrance requirements:* For doctorate, GRE General Test, GRE Subject Test (strongly recommended), minimum GPA of 3.0. Additional exam requirements/recommendations for international students: Required—TOEFL. *Application deadline:* For fall admission, 1/1 priority date for domestic students. Application fee: $0. Electronic applications accepted. *Financial support:* In 2011–12, 14 fellowships with full tuition reimbursements (averaging $29,000 per year), 41 research assistantships with full tuition reimbursements (averaging $29,000 per year) were awarded; career-related internships or fieldwork, Federal Work-Study, institutionally sponsored loans, health care benefits, and tuition waivers (full) also available. Financial award applicants required to submit FAFSA. *Faculty research:* Hormone action, development, cancer, gene therapy, neurobiology. *Unit head:* Dr. JoAnne Richards, Director, 713-798-4598. *Application contact:* Caroline Kosnik, Graduate Program Administrator, 713-798-4598, Fax: 713-790-0545, E-mail: ckosnik@bcm.edu. Web site: http://www.bcm.edu/mcb/.

Baylor College of Medicine, Graduate School of Biomedical Sciences, Interdepartmental Program in Cell and Molecular Biology, Houston, TX 77030-3498. Offers biochemistry (PhD); cell and molecular biology (PhD); genetics (PhD); human genetics (PhD); immunology (PhD); microbiology (PhD); virology (PhD); MD/PhD. *Faculty:* 112 full-time (30 women). *Students:* 66 full-time (42 women); includes 21 minority (5 Black or African American, non-Hispanic/Latino; 1 American Indian or Alaska Native, non-Hispanic/Latino; 7 Asian, non-Hispanic/Latino; 8 Hispanic/Latino), 14 international. Average age 27. 126 applicants, 25% accepted, 14 enrolled. In 2011, 7 degrees awarded. *Median time to degree:* Of those who began their doctoral program in fall 2003, 82% received their degree in 8 years or less. *Degree requirements:* For doctorate, thesis/dissertation, public defense. *Entrance requirements:* For doctorate, GRE General Test, GRE Subject Test (strongly recommended), minimum GPA of 3.0. Additional exam requirements/recommendations for international students: Required—TOEFL. *Application deadline:* For fall admission, 1/1 priority date for domestic students. Applications are processed on a rolling basis. Application fee: $0. Electronic applications accepted. *Financial support:* In 2011–12, 66 students received support, including 30 fellowships with full tuition reimbursements available (averaging $29,000 per year), 36 research assistantships with full tuition reimbursements available (averaging $29,000 per year); teaching assistantships, Federal Work-Study, institutionally sponsored loans, health care benefits, and tuition waivers (full) also available. Financial award applicants required to submit FAFSA. *Faculty research:* Molecular and cellular biology; cancer, aging and stem cells; genomics and proteomics; microbiome, molecular microbiology; infectious disease, immunology and translational research. *Unit head:* Dr. Susan Marriott, Director, 713-798-6557. *Application contact:* Lourdes Fernandez, Graduate Program Administrator, 713-798-6557, Fax: 713-798-6325, E-mail: cmbprog@bcm.edu. Web site: http://bcm.edu/cmb/.

Baylor College of Medicine, Graduate School of Biomedical Sciences, Program in Developmental Biology, Houston, TX 77030-3498. Offers PhD, MD/PhD. *Faculty:* 68 full-time (20 women). *Students:* 55 full-time (28 women); includes 9 minority (7 Asian, non-Hispanic/Latino; 2 Hispanic/Latino), 37 international. Average age 28. 771 applicants, 2% accepted, 10 enrolled. In 2011, 5 degrees awarded. *Median time to degree:* Of those who began their doctoral program in fall 2003, 100% received their degree in 8 years or less. *Degree requirements:* For doctorate, thesis/dissertation, public defense. *Entrance requirements:* For doctorate, GRE General Test, GRE Subject Test (strongly recommended), minimum GPA of 3.0. Additional exam requirements/recommendations for international students: Required—TOEFL. *Application deadline:* For fall admission, 1/1 priority date for domestic students. Application fee: $0. Electronic applications accepted. *Financial support:* In 2011–12, 55 students received support, including 6 fellowships with full tuition reimbursements available (averaging $29,000 per year), 49 research assistantships with full tuition reimbursements available (averaging $29,000 per year); career-related internships or fieldwork, Federal Work-Study, institutionally sponsored loans, health care benefits, tuition waivers (full), and stipends also available. *Faculty research:* Stem cells, cancer, neurobiology, organogenesis, genetics of model organisms. *Unit head:* Dr. Hugo Bellen, Director, 713-798-6410. *Application contact:* Catherine Tasnier, Graduate Program Administrator, 713-798-6410, Fax: 713-798-5386, E-mail: cat@bcm.edu. Web site: http://www.bcm.edu/db/.

See Display on page 287 and Close-Up on page 311.

Boston University, Graduate School of Arts and Sciences, Molecular Biology, Cell Biology, and Biochemistry Program (MCBB), Boston, MA 02215. Offers MA, PhD. *Students:* 36 full-time (17 women), 3 part-time (2 women); includes 8 minority (3 Black or African American, non-Hispanic/Latino; 2 Asian, non-Hispanic/Latino; 3 Hispanic/Latino), 9 international. Average age 29. 126 applicants, 13% accepted, 4 enrolled. In 2011, 6 master's, 20 doctorates awarded. Terminal master's awarded for partial completion of doctoral program. *Degree requirements:* For master's, one foreign language, thesis (for some programs); for doctorate, one foreign language, comprehensive exam, thesis/dissertation. *Entrance requirements:* For master's and doctorate, GRE General Test, GRE Subject Test. Additional exam requirements/recommendations for international students: Required—TOEFL (minimum score 600 paper-based; 250 computer-based). *Application deadline:* For fall admission, 12/7 for domestic and international students. Application fee: $70. Electronic applications accepted. *Expenses: Tuition:* Full-time $40,848; part-time $1276 per credit hour. *Required fees:* $572; $286 per semester. *Financial support:* In 2011–12, 10 students received support, including 1 fellowship with full tuition reimbursement available (averaging $18,300 per year), 8 research assistantships with full tuition reimbursements available (averaging $19,300 per year), 1 teaching assistantship with full tuition reimbursement available (averaging $19,300 per year); Federal Work-Study, scholarships/grants, and traineeships also available. Financial award application deadline: 12/7; financial award applicants required to submit FAFSA. *Unit head:* Dr. Ulla Hansen, Director, 617-353-2432, Fax: 617-353-6340, E-mail: uhansen@bu.edu. *Application contact:* Meredith Canode, Academic Administrator, 617-353-2432, Fax: 617-353-6340, E-mail: mcanode@bu.edu. Web site: http://www.bu.edu/mcbb/.

Boston University, School of Medicine, Division of Graduate Medical Sciences, Department of Biochemistry, Boston, MA 02118. Offers MA, PhD, MD/PhD. Part-time programs available. *Faculty:* 41 full-time (17 women), 11 part-time/adjunct (5 women). *Students:* 29 full-time (15 women), 2 part-time (1 woman); includes 4 minority (3 Asian, non-Hispanic/Latino; 1 Hispanic/Latino), 14 international. Average age 28. 32 applicants, 25% accepted, 4 enrolled. In 2011, 2 master's, 4 doctorates awarded. Terminal master's awarded for partial completion of doctoral program. *Degree requirements:* For master's, thesis or alternative, qualifying exam; for doctorate, thesis/dissertation, qualifying exam. *Entrance requirements:* For master's and doctorate, GRE General Test, GRE Subject Test. Additional exam requirements/recommendations for international students: Required—TOEFL. *Application deadline:* For fall admission, 1/15 priority date for domestic students; for spring admission, 10/15 priority date for domestic students. Application fee: $75. Electronic applications accepted. *Expenses: Tuition:* Full-time $40,848; part-time $1276 per credit hour. *Required fees:* $572; $286 per semester. *Financial support:* In 2011–12, 2 fellowships (averaging $30,500 per year), research assistantships (averaging $30,500 per year) were awarded; Federal Work-Study, scholarships/grants, and traineeships also available. Financial award applicants required to submit FAFSA. *Faculty research:* Extracellular matrix, gene expression, receptors, growth control. *Unit head:* Dr. David A. Harris, Chair, 617-638-5090. *Application contact:* Dr. Barbara Schreiber, Director of the Graduate Program, 617-638-5094, E-mail: schreibe@bu.edu. Web site: http://www.bumc.bu.edu/biochemistry/.

Boston University, School of Medicine, Division of Graduate Medical Sciences, Program in Cell and Molecular Biology, Boston, MA 02118. Offers PhD, MD/PhD. *Faculty:* 10 full-time (5 women). *Students:* 35 full-time (20 women); includes 5 minority (1 Black or African American, non-Hispanic/Latino; 2 Asian, non-Hispanic/Latino; 1 Hispanic/Latino; 1 Two or more races, non-Hispanic/Latino), 6 international. Average age 27. 52 applicants, 19% accepted, 7 enrolled. In 2011, 7 doctorates awarded. *Degree requirements:* For doctorate, thesis/dissertation. *Entrance requirements:* For doctorate, GRE General Test, GRE Subject Test. Additional exam requirements/recommendations for international students: Required—TOEFL. *Application deadline:* For fall admission, 1/15 priority date for domestic students; for spring admission, 10/15 priority date for domestic students. Application fee: $75. Electronic applications accepted. *Expenses: Tuition:* Full-time $40,848; part-time $1276 per credit hour. *Required fees:* $572; $286 per semester. *Financial support:* In 2011–12, 8 fellowships (averaging $30,500 per year), 6 research assistantships (averaging $30,500 per year) were awarded; Federal Work-Study, scholarships/grants, and traineeships also available. Financial award applicants required to submit FAFSA. *Unit head:* Dr. Vickery Trinkaus Randall, Director, 617-638-6099, Fax: 617-638-5337, E-mail: vickery@bu.edu. *Application contact:* Dr. Vickery Trinkaus-Randall, Program Director, 617-638-6099, Fax: 617-638-5337, E-mail: vickery@bu.edu. Web site: http://www.bumc.bu.edu/cmbio/.

Brandeis University, Graduate School of Arts and Sciences, Program in Molecular and Cell Biology, Waltham, MA 02454-9110. Offers genetics (PhD); microbiology (PhD); molecular and cell biology (MS, PhD); molecular biology (PhD); neurobiology (PhD); quantitative biology (PhD). *Faculty:* 27 full-time (11 women), 4 part-time/adjunct (1 woman). *Students:* 65 full-time (36 women); includes 8 minority (4 Black or African American, non-Hispanic/Latino; 1 American Indian or Alaska Native, non-Hispanic/Latino; 1 Asian, non-Hispanic/Latino; 2 Hispanic/Latino), 14 international. 195 applicants, 26% accepted, 21 enrolled. In 2011, 4 master's, 6 doctorates awarded. Terminal master's awarded for partial completion of doctoral program. *Degree requirements:* For master's, thesis or alternative, research project, research lab, or project lab; for doctorate, comprehensive exam, thesis/dissertation, journal clubs; research seminar; colloquia; teaching requirement; qualifying exam. *Entrance requirements:* For master's, GRE General Test; MCAT may be substituted for the GRE exam for applicants to the M.S. program., official transcript(s), resume, 3 letters of recommendation, statement of purpose; for doctorate, GRE General Test, official transcript(s), resume, 3 letters of recommendation, statement of purpose. Additional exam requirements/recommendations for international students: Required—TOEFL (minimum score 600 paper-based; 250 computer-based; 100 iBT); Recommended—IELTS (minimum score 7). *Application deadline:* For fall admission, 1/15 priority date for domestic students; for spring admission, 11/15 for domestic students. Applications are processed on a rolling basis. Application fee: $75. Electronic applications accepted. *Financial support:* In 2011–12, 17 fellowships with full tuition reimbursements (averaging $29,580 per year), 31 research assistantships with full tuition reimbursements (averaging $29,580 per year), teaching assistantships with partial tuition reimbursements (averaging $3,200 per year) were awarded; scholarships/grants, health care benefits, tuition waivers (full and partial), and unspecified assistantships also available. Financial award application deadline: 4/15; financial award applicants required to submit FAFSA. *Faculty research:* Molecular biology, cell biology, biology, structural biology, immunology, developmental biology, neurobiology, DNA, RNA. *Unit head:* Dr.

Bruce Goode, Chair, 781-736-2464, Fax: 781-736-3107, E-mail: goode@brandeis.edu. *Application contact:* Dr. Jessica Maryott, Department Administrator, 781-736-3100, Fax: 781-736-3107, E-mail: jmaryott@brandeis.edu. Web site: http://www.bio.brandeis.edu/grad/mcb/mcb_phd.html.

Brigham Young University, Graduate Studies, College of Life Sciences, Department of Microbiology and Molecular Biology, Provo, UT 84602-1001. Offers microbiology (MS, PhD); molecular biology (MS, PhD). *Faculty:* 15 full-time (3 women). *Students:* 32 full-time (13 women); includes 4 minority (3 Asian, non-Hispanic/Latino; 1 Hispanic/Latino), 5 international. Average age 28. 25 applicants, 60% accepted, 13 enrolled. In 2011, 1 degree awarded. Terminal master's awarded for partial completion of doctoral program. *Degree requirements:* For master's, comprehensive exam, thesis; for doctorate, comprehensive exam, thesis/dissertation. *Entrance requirements:* For master's, GRE General Test, minimum GPA of 3.0 during previous 2 years; for doctorate, GRE General Test, minimum GPA of 3.0. Additional exam requirements/recommendations for international students: Required—TOEFL (minimum score 580 paper-based; 85 iBT), IELTS (minimum score 7). *Application deadline:* For fall admission, 12/15 priority date for domestic students, 12/15 for international students. Application fee: $50. Electronic applications accepted. *Expenses: Tuition:* Full-time $5760; part-time $320 per credit. Tuition and fees vary according to student's religious affiliation. *Financial support:* In 2011–12, 18 students received support, including 6 research assistantships with full and partial tuition reimbursements available (averaging $18,000 per year), 6 teaching assistantships with full and partial tuition reimbursements available (averaging $18,000 per year); institutionally sponsored loans, scholarships/grants, health care benefits, and unspecified assistantships also available. Financial award application deadline: 2/1. *Faculty research:* Immunobiology, molecular genetics, molecular virology, cancer biology, pathogenic and environmental microbiology. *Total annual research expenditures:* $645,068. *Unit head:* Dr. Laura Bridgewater, Chair, 801-422-2434, Fax: 801-422-0519, E-mail: laura_bridgewater@byu.edu. *Application contact:* Dr. Richard A. Robison, Graduate Coordinator, 801-422-2416, Fax: 801-422-0519, E-mail: richard_robison@byu.edu. Web site: http://mmbio.byu.edu/.

Brown University, Graduate School, Division of Biology and Medicine, Program in Molecular Biology, Cell Biology, and Biochemistry, Providence, RI 02912. Offers biochemistry (M Med Sc, Sc M, PhD), including biochemistry (Sc M, PhD), biology (Sc M, PhD), medical science (M Med Sc, PhD); biology (MA); cell biology (M Med Sc, Sc M, PhD), including biochemistry (Sc M, PhD), biology (Sc M, PhD), medical science (M Med Sc, PhD); developmental biology (M Med Sc, Sc M, PhD), including biochemistry (Sc M, PhD), biology (Sc M, PhD), medical science (M Med Sc, PhD); immunology (M Med Sc, Sc M, PhD), including biochemistry (Sc M, PhD), biology (Sc M, PhD), medical science (M Med Sc, PhD); molecular microbiology (M Med Sc, Sc M, PhD), including biochemistry (Sc M, PhD), biology (Sc M, PhD), medical science (M Med Sc, PhD); MD/PhD. Part-time programs available. Terminal master's awarded for partial completion of doctoral program. *Degree requirements:* For master's, thesis (for some programs); for doctorate, one foreign language, thesis/dissertation, preliminary exam. *Entrance requirements:* For master's and doctorate, GRE General Test, GRE Subject Test. Additional exam requirements/recommendations for international students: Required—TOEFL. Electronic applications accepted. *Faculty research:* Molecular genetics, gene regulation.

California Institute of Technology, Division of Biology, Program in Molecular Biology, Pasadena, CA 91125-0001. Offers PhD. *Degree requirements:* For doctorate, thesis/dissertation, qualifying exam. *Entrance requirements:* For doctorate, GRE General Test.

Carnegie Mellon University, Mellon College of Science, Department of Biological Sciences, Pittsburgh, PA 15213-3891. Offers biochemistry (PhD); biophysics (PhD); cell biology (PhD); computational biology (MS, PhD); developmental biology (PhD); genetics (PhD); molecular biology (PhD); neuroscience (PhD). *Degree requirements:* For doctorate, comprehensive exam, thesis/dissertation. *Entrance requirements:* For doctorate, GRE General Test, GRE Subject Test, interview. Electronic applications accepted. *Faculty research:* Genetic structure, function, and regulation; protein structure and function; biological membranes; biological spectroscopy.

Case Western Reserve University, School of Medicine and School of Graduate Studies, Graduate Programs in Medicine, Department of Molecular Biology and Microbiology, Cleveland, OH 44106-4960. Offers cellular biology (PhD); microbiology (PhD); molecular biology (PhD); molecular virology (PhD); MD/PhD. Students are admitted to an integrated Biomedical Sciences Training Program involving 11 basic science programs at Case Western Reserve University. *Degree requirements:* For doctorate, thesis/dissertation. *Entrance requirements:* For doctorate, GRE General Test, GRE Subject Test. Additional exam requirements/recommendations for international students: Required—TOEFL. Electronic applications accepted. *Faculty research:* Gene expression in eukaryotic and prokaryotic systems; microbial physiology; intracellular transport and signaling; mechanisms of oncogenesis; molecular mechanisms of RNA processing, editing, and catalysis.

Central Connecticut State University, School of Graduate Studies, School of Technology, Department of Biomolecular Sciences, New Britain, CT 06050-4010. Offers MS, Certificate. Part-time and evening/weekend programs available. *Faculty:* 8 full-time (3 women), 7 part-time/adjunct (5 women). *Students:* 11 full-time (7 women), 21 part-time (15 women); includes 11 minority (3 Black or African American, non-Hispanic/Latino; 5 Asian, non-Hispanic/Latino; 3 Hispanic/Latino), 3 international. Average age 30. 43 applicants, 67% accepted, 25 enrolled. In 2011, 18 master's, 1 other advanced degree awarded. *Degree requirements:* For master's, comprehensive exam, thesis or alternative; for Certificate, qualifying exam. *Entrance requirements:* For master's, minimum undergraduate GPA of 2.7, essay; for Certificate, essay. Additional exam requirements/recommendations for international students: Required—TOEFL (minimum score 550 paper-based; 213 computer-based). *Application deadline:* For fall admission, 6/1 for domestic students, 5/1 for international students; for spring admission, 11/1 for domestic and international students. Applications are processed on a rolling basis. Application fee: $50. Electronic applications accepted. *Expenses: Tuition, area resident:* Full-time $5137; part-time $482 per credit. Tuition, state resident: full-time $7707; part-time $494 per credit. Tuition, nonresident: full-time $14,311; part-time $494 per credit. *Required fees:* $3865. One-time fee: $62 part-time. *Financial support:* In 2011–12, 6 students received support, including 2 research assistantships; career-related internships or fieldwork, Federal Work-Study, scholarships/grants, and unspecified assistantships also available. Support available to part-time students. Financial award application deadline: 4/15; financial award applicants required to submit FAFSA. *Unit head:* Dr. James Mulrooney, Chair, 860-832-3560, E-mail: mulrooneyj@ccsu.edu. *Application contact:* Patricia Gardner, Associate Director of Graduate Studies, 860-832-2350, Fax: 860-832-2352, E-mail: graduateadmissions@ccsu.edu. Web site: http://www.ccsu.edu/page.cfm?p=6494.

Clemson University, Graduate School, College of Agriculture, Forestry and Life Sciences, Department of Genetics and Biochemistry, Program in Biochemistry and Molecular Biology, Clemson, SC 29634. Offers PhD. *Students:* 16 full-time (13 women), 1 (woman) part-time, 8 international. Average age 28. 22 applicants, 18% accepted, 2 enrolled. In 2011, 6 doctorates awarded. *Degree requirements:* For doctorate, comprehensive exam, thesis/dissertation. *Entrance requirements:* For doctorate, GRE General Test. Additional exam requirements/recommendations for international

students: Required—TOEFL. *Application deadline:* For fall admission, 1/1 for domestic students; for spring admission, 9/1 for domestic students. Applications are processed on a rolling basis. Application fee: $70 ($80 for international students). Electronic applications accepted. *Expenses:* Contact institution. *Financial support:* In 2011–12, 16 students received support, including 11 research assistantships with partial tuition reimbursements available (averaging $17,091 per year), 7 teaching assistantships with partial tuition reimbursements available (averaging $19,429 per year); fellowships with full and partial tuition reimbursements available, career-related internships or fieldwork, institutionally sponsored loans, scholarships/grants, health care benefits, and unspecified assistantships also available. Support available to part-time students. Financial award application deadline: 3/15; financial award applicants required to submit FAFSA. *Faculty research:* Biomembranes, protein structure, molecular biology of plants, APYA and stress response. *Total annual research expenditures:* $670,000. *Unit head:* Dr. Keith Murphy, Chair, 864-656-6237, Fax: 864-656-0435, E-mail: kmurph2@clemson.edu. *Application contact:* Sheryl Banks, Administrative Coordinator, 864-656-6878, E-mail: sherylb@clemson.edu. Web site: http://www.clemson.edu/genbiochem.

Colorado State University, Graduate School, Program in Cell and Molecular Biology, Fort Collins, CO 80523-1618. Offers MS, PhD. *Students:* 34 full-time (20 women), 29 part-time (14 women); includes 10 minority (2 Black or African American, non-Hispanic/Latino; 2 Asian, non-Hispanic/Latino; 5 Hispanic/Latino; 1 Two or more races, non-Hispanic/Latino), 19 international. Average age 30. 79 applicants, 19% accepted, 14 enrolled. In 2011, 2 master's, 4 doctorates awarded. *Degree requirements:* For master's, comprehensive exam, thesis; for doctorate, comprehensive exam, thesis/dissertation. *Entrance requirements:* For master's and doctorate, GRE General Test, GRE Subject Test in biology (strongly recommended), minimum GPA of 3.0. BA/BS in biology, biochemistry, physics; calculus sequence, letters of recommendation. Additional exam requirements/recommendations for international students: Required—TOEFL (minimum score 625 paper-based; 263 computer-based; 107 iBT). *Application deadline:* For fall admission, 1/1 priority date for domestic students, 1/1 for international students. Application fee: $50. Electronic applications accepted. *Expenses:* Tuition, state resident: full-time $7992. Tuition, nonresident: full-time $19,592. *Required fees:* $1735; $58 per credit. *Financial support:* In 2011–12, 8 students received support, including 3 research assistantships with full tuition reimbursements available (averaging $11,147 per year), 5 teaching assistantships with full tuition reimbursements available (averaging $15,015 per year); fellowships with partial tuition reimbursements available, traineeships, and unspecified assistantships also available. Financial award application deadline: 1/1; financial award applicants required to submit FAFSA. *Faculty research:* Regulation of gene expression, cancer biology, plant molecular genetics, reproductive physiology, infectious diseases. *Total annual research expenditures:* $2,294. *Unit head:* Dr. Paul J. Laybourn, Director, 970-491-5100, Fax: 970-491-0623, E-mail: paul.laybourn@colostate.edu. *Application contact:* Lori Williams, Administrative Assistant, 970-491-0241, Fax: 970-491-0623, E-mail: cmb@colostate.edu. Web site: http://cmb.colostate.edu/.

Columbia University, College of Physicians and Surgeons, Integrated Program in Cellular, Molecular, Structural and Genetic Studies, New York, NY 10032. Offers PhD. Terminal master's awarded for partial completion of doctoral program. *Degree requirements:* For doctorate, thesis/dissertation. *Entrance requirements:* For doctorate, GRE General Test, GRE Subject Test. Additional exam requirements/recommendations for international students: Required—TOEFL. *Expenses:* Contact institution. *Faculty research:* Transcription, macromolecular sorting, gene expression during development, cellular interaction.

Cornell University, Graduate School, Graduate Fields of Agriculture and Life Sciences, Field of Biochemistry, Molecular and Cell Biology, Ithaca, NY 14853-0001. Offers biochemistry (PhD); biophysics (PhD); cell biology (PhD); molecular and cell biology (PhD); molecular biology (PhD). *Faculty:* 62 full-time (17 women). *Students:* 91 full-time (46 women); includes 12 minority (1 Black or African American, non-Hispanic/Latino; 8 Asian, non-Hispanic/Latino; 2 Hispanic/Latino; 1 Two or more races, non-Hispanic/Latino), 34 international. Average age 26. 247 applicants, 8% accepted, 17 enrolled. In 2011, 11 doctorates awarded. *Degree requirements:* For doctorate, comprehensive exam, thesis/dissertation, 2 semesters of teaching experience. *Entrance requirements:* For doctorate, GRE General Test, GRE Subject Test (biology, chemistry, physics, biochemistry, cell and molecular biology), 3 letters of recommendation. Additional exam requirements/recommendations for international students: Required—TOEFL (minimum score 600 paper-based; 250 computer-based; 77 iBT). *Application deadline:* For fall admission, 1/5 for domestic students. Application fee: $95. Electronic applications accepted. *Financial support:* In 2011–12, 88 students received support, including 26 fellowships with full tuition reimbursements available, 46 research assistantships with full tuition reimbursements available, 14 teaching assistantships with full tuition reimbursements available; institutionally sponsored loans, scholarships/grants, health care benefits, tuition waivers (full and partial), and unspecified assistantships also available. Financial award applicants required to submit FAFSA. *Faculty research:* Biophysics, structural biology. *Unit head:* Director of Graduate Studies, 607-255-2100, Fax: 607-255-2100. *Application contact:* Graduate Field Assistant, 607-255-2100, Fax: 607-255-2100, E-mail: bmcb@cornell.edu. Web site: http://www.gradschool.cornell.edu/fields.php?id-43&a-2.

Dartmouth College, Graduate Program in Molecular and Cellular Biology, Hanover, NH 03755. Offers PhD, MD/PhD. *Entrance requirements:* For doctorate, GRE General Test, letters of recommendation. Additional exam requirements/recommendations for international students: Required—TOEFL (minimum score 450 paper-based; 90 iBT) or IELTS (minimum score 7). Electronic applications accepted.

Drexel University, College of Medicine, Biomedical Graduate Programs, Interdisciplinary Program in Molecular and Cell Biology and Genetics, Philadelphia, PA 19104-2875. Offers MS, PhD, MD/PhD. Terminal master's awarded for partial completion of doctoral program. *Degree requirements:* For master's, comprehensive exam, thesis; for doctorate, thesis/dissertation, qualifying exam. *Entrance requirements:* For master's, GRE General Test, minimum GPA of 2.75; for doctorate, GRE General Test, minimum GPA of 3.0. Additional exam requirements/recommendations for international students: Required—TOEFL. Electronic applications accepted. *Faculty research:* Molecular anatomy, biochemistry, medical biotechnology, molecular pathology, microbiology and immunology.

Duke University, Graduate School, Department of Biological Anthropology and Anatomy, Durham, NC 27710. Offers cellular and molecular biology (PhD); gross anatomy and physical anthropology (PhD), including comparative morphology of human and non-human primates, primate social behavior, vertebrate paleontology; neuroanatomy (PhD). *Faculty:* 9 full-time. *Students:* 16 full-time (10 women); includes 3 minority (1 Black or African American, non-Hispanic/Latino; 2 Hispanic/Latino), 1 international. 71 applicants, 7% accepted, 4 enrolled. In 2011, 2 doctorates awarded. *Degree requirements:* For doctorate, one foreign language, thesis/dissertation. *Entrance requirements:* For doctorate, GRE General Test. Additional exam requirements/recommendations for international students: Required—TOEFL (minimum score 550 paper-based; 213 computer-based; 83 iBT), IELTS (minimum score 7). *Application deadline:* For fall admission, 12/8 priority date for domestic students, 12/8 for international students. Application fee: $75. Electronic applications accepted. *Expenses:*

Tuition: Full-time $40,720. *Required fees:* $3107. *Financial support:* Fellowships, teaching assistantships, and Federal Work-Study available. Financial award application deadline: 12/31. *Unit head:* Daniel Schmitt, Director of Graduate Studies, 919-684-4124, Fax: 919-684-8542, E-mail: mlsquire@duke.edu. *Application contact:* Elizabeth Hutton, Director of Admissions, 919-684-3913, Fax: 919-684-2277, E-mail: grad-admissions@duke.edu. Web site: http://www.baa.duke.edu/.

Duke University, Graduate School, Program in Cellular and Molecular Biology, Durham, NC 27710. Offers Certificate. Students must be enrolled in a participating PhD program (biology, cell biology, immunology, molecular genetics, neurobiology, pathology, pharmacology). *Faculty:* 144 full-time. *Students:* 17 full-time (4 women); includes 6 minority (2 Asian, non-Hispanic/Latino; 4 Hispanic/Latino), 3 international. 218 applicants, 24% accepted, 16 enrolled. *Entrance requirements:* Additional exam requirements/recommendations for international students: Required—TOEFL (minimum score 550 paper-based; 213 computer-based; 83 iBT), IELTS (minimum score 7). *Application deadline:* For fall admission, 12/8 priority date for domestic students, 12/8 for international students. Application fee: $75. Electronic applications accepted. *Expenses: Tuition:* Full-time $40,720. *Required fees:* $3107. *Financial support:* Fellowships available. Financial award application deadline: 12/8. *Unit head:* Dr. Margarethe Kuehn, Director of Graduate Studies, 919-684-6559, Fax: 919-684-8346, E-mail: carol.richardson@duke.edu. *Application contact:* Elizabeth Hutton, Director of Admissions, 919-684-3913, Fax: 919-684-3913, E-mail: grad-admissions@duke.edu. Web site: http://cmb.duke.edu/.

East Carolina University, Brody School of Medicine, Department of Biochemistry and Molecular Biology, Greenville, NC 27858-4353. Offers biochemistry and molecular biology (PhD); biomedical science (MS). *Degree requirements:* For doctorate, comprehensive exam, thesis/dissertation. *Entrance requirements:* For doctorate, GRE General Test. Additional exam requirements/recommendations for international students: Required—TOEFL. *Application deadline:* For fall admission, 6/1 priority date for domestic students. Applications are processed on a rolling basis. Application fee: $50. *Expenses:* Tuition, state resident: full-time $3557; part-time $444.63 per semester hour. Tuition, nonresident: full-time $14,351; part-time $1793.88 per semester hour. *Required fees:* $2016; $252 per semester hour. Part-time tuition and fees vary according to course load, campus/location and program. *Financial support:* Fellowships with full and partial tuition reimbursements available. Financial award application deadline: 6/1. *Faculty research:* Gene regulation, development and differentiation, contractility and motility, macromolecular interactions, cancer. *Unit head:* Dr. Phillip H. Pekala, Chairman, 252-744-2684, Fax: 252-744-3383, E-mail: pekalap@ecu.edu. *Application contact:* Dr. George J. Kasperek, Assistant Dean for Graduate Studies/BSOM, 252-744-3305, Fax: 252-744-0203, E-mail: kasperekg@ecu.edu. Web site: http://www.ecu.edu/cs-dhs/biochemistry/Graduate-Program-Information.cfm.

East Carolina University, Graduate School, Thomas Harriot College of Arts and Sciences, Department of Biology, Greenville, NC 27858-4353. Offers biology (MS); molecular biology/biotechnology (MS). Part-time programs available. *Degree requirements:* For master's, one foreign language, comprehensive exam, thesis. *Entrance requirements:* For master's, GRE General Test, GRE Subject Test. Additional exam requirements/recommendations for international students: Required—TOEFL. *Application deadline:* For fall admission, 6/1 priority date for domestic students; for spring admission, 10/15 for domestic students. Applications are processed on a rolling basis. Application fee: $50. *Expenses:* Tuition, state resident: full-time $3557; part-time $444.63 per semester hour. Tuition, nonresident: full-time $14,351; part-time $1793.88 per semester hour. *Required fees:* $2016; $252 per semester hour. Part-time tuition and fees vary according to course load, campus/location and program. *Financial support:* Fellowships with partial tuition reimbursements, research assistantships with partial tuition reimbursements, teaching assistantships with partial tuition reimbursements, career-related internships or fieldwork, Federal Work-Study, scholarships/grants, and unspecified assistantships available. Support available to part-time students. Financial award application deadline: 6/1. *Faculty research:* Biochemistry, microbiology, cell biology. *Application contact:* Interim Dean of Graduate School, 252-328-6012, Fax: 252-328-6071, E-mail: gradschool@ecu.edu. Web site: http://www.ecu.edu/cs-cas/biology/graduate.cfm.

Eastern Michigan University, Graduate School, College of Arts and Sciences, Department of Biology, Ypsilanti, MI 48197. Offers cell and molecular biology (MS); community college biology teaching (MS); ecology and organismal biology (MS); general biology (MS); water resources (MS). Part-time and evening/weekend programs available. Postbaccalaureate distance learning degree programs offered (minimal on-campus study). *Faculty:* 20 full-time (4 women). *Students:* 12 full-time (7 women), 40 part-time (21 women); includes 3 minority (1 Black or African American, non-Hispanic/Latino; 1 Asian, non-Hispanic/Latino; 1 Two or more races, non-Hispanic/Latino), 12 international. Average age 27. 70 applicants, 43% accepted, 12 enrolled. In 2011, 19 degrees awarded. *Entrance requirements:* For master's, GRE General Test, GRE Subject Test. Additional exam requirements/recommendations for international students: Required—TOEFL. *Application deadline:* Applications are processed on a rolling basis. Application fee: $35. *Expenses:* Tuition, state resident: full-time $10,367; part-time $432 per credit hour. Tuition, nonresident: full-time $20,435; part-time $851 per credit hour. *Required fees:* $39 per credit hour. $46 per semester. One-time fee: $100. Tuition and fees vary according to course level, degree level and reciprocity agreements. *Financial support:* Fellowships, research assistantships with full tuition reimbursements, teaching assistantships with full tuition reimbursements, career-related internships or fieldwork, Federal Work-Study, institutionally sponsored loans, scholarships/grants, tuition waivers (partial), and unspecified assistantships available. Support available to part-time students. Financial award applicants required to submit FAFSA. *Unit head:* Dr. Marianne Laporte, Department Head, 734-487-4242, Fax: 734-487-9235, E-mail: mlaporte@emich.edu. *Application contact:* Graduate Admissions, 734-487-2400, Fax: 734-487-6559, E-mail: graduate.admissions@emich.edu. Web site: http://www.emich.edu/biology.

Eastern New Mexico University, Graduate School, College of Liberal Arts and Sciences, Department of Biology, Portales, NM 88130. Offers applied ecology (MS); cell, molecular biology and biotechnology (MS); education (non-thesis) (MS); microbiology (MS); plant biology (MS); zoology (MS). Part-time programs available. *Faculty:* 7 full-time (0 women). *Students:* 2 full-time (1 woman), 15 part-time (9 women); includes 7 minority (5 Hispanic/Latino; 2 Two or more races, non-Hispanic/Latino), 2 international. Average age 26. 17 applicants, 82% accepted, 3 enrolled. In 2011, 4 master's awarded. *Degree requirements:* For master's, comprehensive exam, thesis optional. *Entrance requirements:* For master's, GRE, minimum GPA of 3.0, 2 letters of recommendation, statement of research interest, bachelor's degree related to field of study or proof of common knowledge. Additional exam requirements/recommendations for international students: Required—TOEFL (minimum score 550 paper-based; 213 computer-based; 79 iBT), IELTS (minimum score 6). *Application deadline:* For fall admission, 7/20 priority date for domestic students, 6/20 for international students; for spring admission, 12/15 priority date for domestic students, 11/15 for international students. Applications are processed on a rolling basis. Application fee: $10. Electronic applications accepted. *Financial support:* In 2011–12, 8 teaching assistantships with partial tuition reimbursements (averaging $8,500 per year) were awarded; scholarships/grants and unspecified assistantships also available. Support available to part-time students. Financial award applicants required to submit FAFSA. *Unit head:* Dr. Zach Jones, Graduate Coordinator, 575-562-2723, Fax: 575-562-2192, E-mail: zach.jones@enmu.edu. *Application contact:* Sharon Potter, Department Secretary, Biology and Physical Sciences, 575-562-2174, Fax: 575-562-2192, E-mail: sharon.potter@enmu.edu. Web site: http://liberal-arts.enmu.edu/biology/graduate.shtml.

East Tennessee State University, James H. Quillen College of Medicine, Biomedical Science Graduate Program, Johnson City, TN 37614. Offers anatomy and cell biology (PhD); biochemistry and molecular biology (PhD); microbiology (PhD); pharmaceutical sciences (PhD); pharmacology (PhD); physiology (PhD); quantitative biosciences (PhD). *Faculty:* 33 full-time (6 women). *Students:* 29 full-time (15 women), 2 part-time (both women); includes 4 minority (1 Black or African American, non-Hispanic/Latino; 1 Asian, non-Hispanic/Latino; 2 Hispanic/Latino), 6 international. Average age 29. 76 applicants, 12% accepted, 7 enrolled. In 2011, 1 doctorate awarded. *Degree requirements:* For doctorate, thesis/dissertation, comprehensive qualifying exam. *Entrance requirements:* For doctorate, GRE General Test, GRE Subject Test. Additional exam requirements/recommendations for international students: Required—TOEFL (minimum score 550 paper-based; 213 computer-based; 79 iBT). *Application deadline:* For fall admission, 3/15 priority date for domestic students, 3/1 for international students. Application fee: $35 ($45 for international students). Electronic applications accepted. *Expenses:* Contact institution. *Financial support:* In 2011–12, 29 students received support, including 29 research assistantships with full tuition reimbursements available (averaging $19,000 per year); career-related internships or fieldwork, institutionally sponsored loans, scholarships/grants, and unspecified assistantships also available. Financial award application deadline: 7/1; financial award applicants required to submit FAFSA. *Faculty research:* Cardiovascular biology, neuroscience, infectious disease, cancer, inflammatory disease. *Total annual research expenditures:* $3.6 million. *Unit head:* Dr. Mitchell E. Robinson, Associate Dean/Program Director, 423-439-2031, Fax: 423-439-2140, E-mail: robinson@etsu.edu. *Application contact:* Shella Bennett, Graduate Specialist, 423-439-4708, Fax: 423-439-5624, E-mail: bennetsg@etsu.edu.

Emory University, Laney Graduate School, Division of Biological and Biomedical Sciences, Program in Genetics and Molecular Biology, Atlanta, GA 30322-1100. Offers PhD. *Faculty:* 44 full-time (8 women). *Students:* 51 full-time (29 women); includes 11 minority (5 Black or African American, non-Hispanic/Latino; 3 Asian, non-Hispanic/Latino; 3 Hispanic/Latino), 8 international. Average age 27. 134 applicants, 16% accepted, 8 enrolled. In 2011, 7 degrees awarded. *Median time to degree:* Of those who began their doctoral program in fall 2003, 100% received their degree in 8 years or less. *Degree requirements:* For doctorate, comprehensive exam, thesis/dissertation. *Entrance requirements:* For doctorate, GRE General Test, minimum GPA of 3.0 in science course work (recommended). Additional exam requirements/recommendations for international students: Required—TOEFL. *Application deadline:* For fall admission, 12/1 for domestic and international students. Application fee: $75. Electronic applications accepted. *Expenses: Tuition:* Full-time $34,800. *Required fees:* $1300. *Financial support:* In 2011–12, 18 students received support, including 18 fellowships with full tuition reimbursements available (averaging $26,500 per year); institutionally sponsored loans, scholarships/grants, health care benefits, and tuition waivers (full) also available. *Faculty research:* Gene regulation, genetic combination, developmental regulation. *Unit head:* Dr. Bill Kelly, Director, 404-727-6461, Fax: 404-727-2880, E-mail: william.kelly@emory.edu. *Application contact:* Kathy Smith, Director of Recruitment and Admissions, 404-727-2547, Fax: 404-727-3322, E-mail: kathy.smith@emory.edu. Web site: http://www.biomed.emory.edu/.

Florida Institute of Technology, Graduate Programs, College of Science, Department of Biological Sciences, Program in Cell and Molecular Biology, Melbourne, FL 32901-6975. Offers MS. Part-time programs available. *Faculty:* 16 full-time (2 women). *Students:* 5 full-time (3 women), 2 part-time (1 woman); includes 1 minority (Hispanic/Latino), 1 international. Average age 27. 56 applicants, 5% accepted, 3 enrolled. In 2011, 2 master's awarded. *Degree requirements:* For master's, research, seminar, internship, or summer lab. *Entrance requirements:* For master's, GRE General Test, 3 letters of recommendation, minimum GPA of 3.0, resume, statement of objectives. Additional exam requirements/recommendations for international students: Required—TOEFL (minimum score 550 paper-based; 213 computer-based; 79 iBT). *Application deadline:* Applications are processed on a rolling basis. Application fee: $0. Electronic applications accepted. *Expenses: Tuition:* Full-time $19,620; part-time $1090 per credit hour. Tuition and fees vary according to campus/location. *Financial support:* Career-related internships or fieldwork, institutionally sponsored loans, tuition waivers (partial), unspecified assistantships, and tuition remissions available. Support available to part-time students. Financial award application deadline: 3/1; financial award applicants required to submit FAFSA. *Faculty research:* Changes in DNA molecule and differential expression of genetic information during aging. *Total annual research expenditures:* $1.9 million. *Unit head:* Dr. Richard B. Aronson, Department Head, 321-674-8034, Fax: 321-674-7238, E-mail: raronson@fit.edu. *Application contact:* Cheryl A. Brown, Associate Director of Graduate Admission, 321-674-7581, Fax: 321-723-9468, E-mail: cbrown@fit.edu. Web site: http://www.cos.fit.edu/biology/.

Florida State University, The Graduate School, College of Arts and Sciences, Department of Biological Science, Specialization in Cell and Molecular Biology and Genetics, Tallahassee, FL 32306-4295. Offers MS, PhD. *Faculty:* 28 full-time (7 women). *Students:* 44 full-time (19 women); includes 6 minority (all Hispanic/Latino), 15 international. 152 applicants, 16% accepted, 11 enrolled. In 2011, 3 master's, 8 doctorates awarded. Terminal master's awarded for partial completion of doctoral program. *Degree requirements:* For master's, comprehensive exam, thesis, teaching experience, seminar presentation; for doctorate, comprehensive exam, thesis/dissertation, teaching experience; seminar presentation. *Entrance requirements:* For master's and doctorate, GRE General Test (minimum combined score 1100, 500 verbal, 500 quantitative in old version; 72% verbal, 67% quantitative in new format), minimum upper-division GPA of 3.0. Additional exam requirements/recommendations for international students: Required—TOEFL (minimum score 600 paper-based; 250 computer-based; 92 iBT). *Application deadline:* For fall admission, 12/15 for domestic and international students. Application fee: $30. Electronic applications accepted. *Expenses:* Tuition, state resident: full-time $9474; part-time $350.88 per credit hour. Tuition, nonresident: full-time $16,236; part-time $601.34 per credit hour. *Required fees:* $630 per semester. One-time fee: $20. Tuition and fees vary according to course load and campus/location. *Financial support:* In 2011–12, 43 students received support, including 17 research assistantships with full tuition reimbursements available (averaging $21,000 per year), 26 teaching assistantships with full tuition reimbursements available (averaging $21,000 per year); fellowships and unspecified assistantships also available. Financial award application deadline: 12/15; financial award applicants required to submit FAFSA. *Faculty research:* Molecular biology; genetics and genomics; developmental biology and gene expression; cell structure, function, and motility; cellular and organismal physiology; biophysical and structural biology. *Unit head:* Dr. George W. Bates, Professor and Associate Chairman, 850-644-5749, Fax: 850-644-9829, E-mail: bates@bio.fsu.edu. *Application contact:* Judy Bowers, Coordinator, Graduate Affairs, 850-644-3023, Fax: 850-644-9829, E-mail: gradinfo@bio.fsu.edu. Web site: http://www.bio.fsu.edu/.

Florida State University, The Graduate School, College of Arts and Sciences, Department of Scientific Computing, Tallahassee, FL 32306-4120. Offers computational science (MS, PSM, PhD), including atmospheric science (PhD), biochemistry (PhD), biological science (PhD), computational molecular biology/bioinformatics (PSM), computational science (PhD), geological science (PhD), materials science (PhD), physics (PhD). Part-time programs available. *Faculty:* 14 full-time (2 women). *Students:* 32 full-time (6 women), 3 part-time (0 women); includes 13 minority (1 Black or African American, non-Hispanic/Latino; 11 Asian, non-Hispanic/Latino; 1 Hispanic/Latino). Average age 28. 29 applicants, 41% accepted, 9 enrolled. In 2011, 14 master's, 3 doctorates awarded. Terminal master's awarded for partial completion of doctoral program. *Degree requirements:* For master's, thesis (for some programs); for doctorate, comprehensive exam, thesis/dissertation. *Entrance requirements:* For master's and doctorate, GRE General Test, knowledge of at least one object-oriented computing language, 3 letters of recommendations. Additional exam requirements/recommendations for international students: Required—TOEFL (minimum score 550 paper-based; 80 iBT). *Application deadline:* For fall admission, 1/15 for domestic and international students. Application fee: $30. Electronic applications accepted. *Expenses:* Tuition, state resident: full-time $9474; part-time $350.88 per credit hour. Tuition, nonresident: full-time $16,236; part-time $601.34 per credit hour. *Required fees:* $630 per semester. One-time fee: $20. Tuition and fees vary according to course load and campus/location. *Financial support:* In 2011–12, 32 students received support, including 12 research assistantships with full tuition reimbursements available (averaging $20,000 per year), 18 teaching assistantships with full tuition reimbursements available (averaging $20,000 per year); unspecified assistantships also available. Financial award application deadline: 4/15. *Faculty research:* Morphometrics, mathematical and systems biology, mining proteomic and metabolic data, computational materials research at Scientific Computing, advanced 4-D Var Data-Assimilation methods in dynamic meteorology and oceanography, computational fluid dynamics, astrophysics. *Unit head:* Dr. Sam Huckaba, Interim Dean, 850-644-1081. *Application contact:* Maribel Amwake, Graduate Academic Coordinator, 850-644-0143, Fax: 850-644-0098, E-mail: mamwake@fsu.edu. Web site: http://www.sc.fsu.edu.

George Mason University, College of Science, Department of Molecular and Microbiology, Fairfax, VA 22030. Offers biology (MS); biosciences (PhD). *Expenses:* Tuition, state resident: full-time $8750; part-time $364.58 per credit. Tuition, nonresident: full-time $24,092; part-time $1003.83 per credit. *Required fees:* $2514; $104.75 per credit. *Financial support:* Scholarships/grants and unspecified assistantships available. Financial award applicants required to submit FAFSA.

Georgetown University, Graduate School of Arts and Sciences, Programs in Biomedical Sciences, Department of Biochemistry and Molecular Biology, Washington, DC 20057. Offers MS, PhD. *Degree requirements:* For doctorate, comprehensive exam, thesis/dissertation. *Entrance requirements:* For doctorate, GRE General Test. Additional exam requirements/recommendations for international students: Required—TOEFL.

The George Washington University, School of Medicine and Health Sciences, Department of Biochemistry and Molecular Biology, Washington, DC 20037. Offers biochemistry and molecular biology (MS); biochemistry and molecular genetics (PhD); molecular biochemistry and bioinformatics (MS). *Degree requirements:* For master's, comprehensive exam; for doctorate, thesis/dissertation, general exam. *Entrance requirements:* For master's, GRE General Test, interview, minimum GPA of 3.0; for doctorate, GRE General Test, minimum GPA of 3.0. Additional exam requirements/recommendations for international students: Required—TOEFL (minimum score 550 paper-based; 213 computer-based).

Georgia Health Sciences University, College of Graduate Studies, Program in Biochemistry and Molecular Biology, Augusta, GA 30912. Offers MS, PhD. *Faculty:* 13 full-time (2 women). *Students:* 20 full-time (10 women); includes 1 minority (Hispanic/Latino), 9 international. Average age 27. In 2011, 4 doctorates awarded. *Degree requirements:* For doctorate, comprehensive exam, thesis/dissertation. *Entrance requirements:* For doctorate, GRE General Test. Additional exam requirements/recommendations for international students: Required—TOEFL (minimum score 550 paper-based; 213 computer-based; 79 iBT). *Application deadline:* For fall admission, 1/15 for domestic and international students. Application fee: $50. Electronic applications accepted. *Financial support:* In 2011–12, 8 research assistantships with partial tuition reimbursements (averaging $23,000 per year) were awarded; Federal Work-Study, institutionally sponsored loans, and scholarships/grants also available. Support available to part-time students. Financial award application deadline: 5/31; financial award applicants required to submit FAFSA. *Faculty research:* Bacterial pathogenesis, eye diseases, vitamins and amino acid transporters, transcriptional control and molecular oncology, tumor biology. *Total annual research expenditures:* $3.8 million. *Unit head:* Dr. Vadivel Ganapathy, Chair/Professor, 706-721-7652, Fax: 706-721-9947, E-mail: vganapat@georgiahealth.edu. *Application contact:* Dr. Patricia L. Cameron, Acting Vice Dean, 706-721-3279, E-mail: pcameron@georgiahealth.edu. Web site: http://www.georgiahealth.edu/bmb/.

Georgia State University, College of Arts and Sciences, Department of Biology, Program in Cellular and Molecular Biology and Physiology, Atlanta, GA 30302-3083. Offers MS, PhD. Part-time programs available. Terminal master's awarded for partial completion of doctoral program. *Degree requirements:* For master's, thesis or alternative; for doctorate, thesis/dissertation, exam. *Entrance requirements:* For master's and doctorate, GRE General Test. Additional exam requirements/recommendations for international students: Required—TOEFL.

Grand Valley State University, College of Liberal Arts and Sciences, Program in Cell and Molecular Biology, Allendale, MI 49401-9403. Offers MS. *Entrance requirements:* For master's, minimum GPA of 3.0. *Faculty research:* Plant cell biology, plant development, cell/signal integration.

Harvard University, Graduate School of Arts and Sciences, Department of Molecular and Cellular Biology, Cambridge, MA 02138. Offers PhD. *Degree requirements:* For doctorate, thesis/dissertation, oral exam. *Entrance requirements:* For doctorate, GRE General Test, GRE Subject Test (recommended). Additional exam requirements/recommendations for international students: Required—TOEFL. *Expenses: Tuition:* Full-time $36,304. *Required fees:* $1186. Full-time tuition and fees vary according to program.

Harvard University, Graduate School of Arts and Sciences, Program in Chemical Biology, Cambridge, MA 02138. Offers PhD. *Expenses: Tuition:* Full-time $36,304. *Required fees:* $1186. Full-time tuition and fees vary according to program.

Hood College, Graduate School, Program in Biomedical Science, Frederick, MD 21701-8575. Offers biomedical science (MS), including biotechnology/molecular biology, microbiology/immunology/virology, regulatory compliance; regulatory compliance (Certificate). Part-time and evening/weekend programs available. *Degree requirements:* For master's, comprehensive exam, thesis or alternative. *Entrance requirements:* For master's, bachelor's degree in biology; minimum GPA of 2.75; undergraduate course work in cell biology, chemistry, organic chemistry, and genetics. Additional exam requirements/recommendations for international students: Required—TOEFL (minimum score 575 paper-based; 231 computer-based; 89 iBT). Electronic applications accepted.

Howard University, College of Medicine, Department of Biochemistry and Molecular Biology, Washington, DC 20059-0002. Offers biochemistry and molecular biology (PhD); biotechnology (MS); MD/PhD. Part-time programs available. *Degree requirements:* For master's, externship; for doctorate, comprehensive exam, thesis/dissertation. *Entrance requirements:* For master's and doctorate, GRE General Test, minimum GPA of 3.0. *Faculty research:* Cellular and molecular biology of olfaction, gene regulation and expression, enzymology, NMR spectroscopy of molecular structure, hormone regulation/metabolism.

Illinois Institute of Technology, Graduate College, College of Science and Letters, Department of Biological, Chemical and Physical Sciences, Biology Division, Chicago, IL 60616. Offers biochemistry (MBS, MS); biology (PhD); biotechnology (MBS, MS); cell and molecular biology (MBS, MS); microbiology (MB, MS); molecular biochemistry and biophysics (PhD); molecular biology and biophysics (MS). Part-time and evening/weekend programs available. Postbaccalaureate distance learning degree programs offered (minimal on-campus study). Terminal master's awarded for partial completion of doctoral program. *Degree requirements:* For master's, comprehensive exam, thesis (for some programs); for doctorate, comprehensive exam, thesis/dissertation. *Entrance requirements:* For master's, GRE General Test (minimum score 1000 Quantitative and Verbal, 2.5 Analytical Writing), minimum undergraduate GPA of 3.0; for doctorate, GRE General Test (minimum score 1200 Quantitative and Verbal, 3.0 Analytical Writing), minimum undergraduate GPA of 3.0. Additional exam requirements/recommendations for international students: Required—TOEFL (minimum score 523 paper-based; 213 computer-based; 70 iBT); Recommended—IELTS (minimum score 5.5). Electronic applications accepted. *Faculty research:* Structure and biophysics of macromolecular systems; efficacy and mechanism of action of chemopreventive agents in experimental carcinogenesis of breast, colon, lung and prostate; study of fundamental structural biochemistry problems that have direct links to the understanding and treatment of disease; spectroscopic techniques for the study of multi-domain proteins; molecular mechanisms of cancer and cancer gene therapy.

Illinois State University, Graduate School, College of Arts and Sciences, Department of Biological Sciences, Normal, IL 61790-2200. Offers animal behavior (MS); bacteriology (MS); biochemistry (MS); biological sciences (MS); biology (PhD); biophysics (MS); biotechnology (MS); botany (MS, PhD); cell biology (MS); conservation biology (MS); developmental biology (MS); ecology (MS, PhD); entomology (MS); evolutionary biology (MS); genetics (MS, PhD); immunology (MS); microbiology (MS, PhD); molecular biology (MS); molecular genetics (MS); neurobiology (MS); neuroscience (MS); parasitology (MS); physiology (MS, PhD); plant biology (MS); plant molecular biology (MS); plant sciences (MS); structural biology (MS); zoology (MS, PhD). Part-time programs available. *Degree requirements:* For master's, thesis or alternative; for doctorate, variable foreign language requirement, thesis/dissertation, 2 terms of residency. *Entrance requirements:* For master's, GRE General Test, minimum GPA of 2.6 in last 60 hours of course work; for doctorate, GRE General Test. *Faculty research:* Redoc balance and drug development in schistosoma mansoni, control of the growth of listeria monocytogenes at low temperature, regulation of cell expansion and microtubule function by SPRI, CRUI: physiology and fitness consequences of different life history phenotypes.

Indiana University Bloomington, University Graduate School, College of Arts and Sciences, Department of Biology, Bloomington, IN 47405. Offers biology teaching (MAT); biotechnology (MA); evolution, ecology, and behavior (MA, PhD); genetics (PhD); microbiology (MA, PhD); molecular, cellular, and developmental biology (PhD); plant sciences (MA, PhD); zoology (MA, PhD). *Faculty:* 58 full-time (15 women), 21 part-time/adjunct (6 women). *Students:* 175 full-time (100 women), 3 part-time (all women); includes 20 minority (5 Black or African American, non-Hispanic/Latino; 8 Asian, non-Hispanic/Latino; 7 Hispanic/Latino), 55 international. Average age 27. 316 applicants, 22% accepted, 31 enrolled. In 2011, 8 master's, 20 doctorates awarded. Terminal master's awarded for partial completion of doctoral program. *Degree requirements:* For master's, thesis, oral defense; for doctorate, thesis/dissertation, oral defense. *Entrance requirements:* For master's and doctorate, GRE General Test. Additional exam requirements/recommendations for international students: Required—TOEFL (minimum score 100 iBT). *Application deadline:* For fall admission, 1/5 priority date for domestic students, 12/1 for international students. Application fee: $55 ($65 for international students). Electronic applications accepted. *Financial support:* In 2011–12, fellowships with tuition reimbursements (averaging $19,484 per year), research assistantships with tuition reimbursements (averaging $20,300 per year), teaching assistantships with tuition reimbursements (averaging $20,521 per year) were awarded; scholarships/grants, traineeships, health care benefits, and unspecified assistantships also available. Financial award application deadline: 1/5. *Faculty research:* Evolution, ecology and behavior; microbiology; molecular biology and genetics; plant biology. *Unit head:* Dr. Roger Innes, Chair, 812-855-2219, Fax: 812-855-6082, E-mail: rinnes@indiana.edu. *Application contact:* Tracey D. Stohr, Graduate Student Recruitment Coordinator, 812-856-6303, Fax: 812-855-6082, E-mail: gradbio@indiana.edu. Web site: http://www.bio.indiana.edu/.

Indiana University–Purdue University Indianapolis, Indiana University School of Medicine, Department of Biochemistry and Molecular Biology, Indianapolis, IN 46202-2896. Offers PhD, MD/MS, MD/PhD. *Faculty:* 17 full-time (4 women). *Students:* 29 full-time (16 women), 20 part-time (7 women); includes 5 minority (1 Black or African American, non-Hispanic/Latino; 3 Asian, non-Hispanic/Latino; 1 Hispanic/Latino), 20 international. Average age 32. 2 applicants, 50% accepted, 1 enrolled. In 2011, 5 doctorates awarded. Terminal master's awarded for partial completion of doctoral program. *Degree requirements:* For doctorate, thesis/dissertation. *Entrance requirements:* For doctorate, GRE General Test, GRE Subject Test (recommended), previous course work in organic chemistry. *Application deadline:* For fall admission, 1/15 priority date for domestic students. Applications are processed on a rolling basis. Application fee: $55 ($65 for international students). *Financial support:* In 2011–12, teaching assistantships (averaging $14,949 per year) were awarded; fellowships with tuition reimbursements, research assistantships with tuition reimbursements, Federal Work-Study, institutionally sponsored loans, scholarships/grants, and tuition waivers (partial) also available. Support available to part-time students. Financial award application deadline: 2/1. *Faculty research:* Metabolic regulation, enzymology, peptide and protein chemistry, cell biology, signal transduction. *Unit head:* Dr. Zhong-Yin Zhang, Chairman, 317-274-7151. *Application contact:* Robert M. Stump, Jr., Director of Admissions, 317-274-3772, E-mail: inmedadm@iupui.edu. Web site: http://www.biochemistry.iu.edu/.

Inter American University of Puerto Rico, Metropolitan Campus, Graduate Programs, Program in Medical Technology, San Juan, PR 00919-1293. Offers administration of clinical laboratories (MS); molecular microbiology (MS). *Accreditation:* NAACLS. Part-time programs available. *Degree requirements:* For master's, comprehensive exam. *Entrance requirements:* For master's, BS in medical technology, minimum GPA of 2.5. Electronic applications accepted.

Iowa State University of Science and Technology, Bioinformatics and Computational Biology Program, Ames, IA 50011-3260. Offers MS, PhD. *Degree requirements:* For doctorate, thesis/dissertation. *Entrance requirements:* For master's and doctorate, GRE General Test. Additional exam requirements/recommendations for international

students: Recommended—TOEFL, IELTS. *Application deadline:* For fall admission, 1/15 priority date for domestic students, 1/15 for international students; for spring admission, 10/15 for domestic and international students. Application fee: $40 ($90 for international students). Electronic applications accepted. *Faculty research:* Functional and structural genomics, genome evolution, macromolecular structure and function, mathematical biology and biological statistics, metabolic and developmental networks. *Unit head:* Dr. Julie Dickerson, Chair, Supervising Committee, 515-294-5122, Fax: 515-294-6790, E-mail: bcb@iastate.edu. *Application contact:* Information Contact, 515-294-5836, Fax: 515-294-2592, E-mail: grad_admissions@iastate.edu. Web site: http://www.bcb.iastate.edu/.

Iowa State University of Science and Technology, Department of Biochemistry, Biophysics, and Molecular Biology, Ames, IA 50011. Offers biochemistry (MS, PhD); biophysics (MS, PhD); genetics (MS, PhD); molecular, cellular, and developmental biology (MS, PhD); toxicology (MS, PhD). *Degree requirements:* For master's, thesis; for doctorate, thesis/dissertation. *Entrance requirements:* For master's and doctorate, GRE General Test. Additional exam requirements/recommendations for international students: Required—TOEFL (minimum score 550 paper-based; 79 iBT), IELTS (minimum score 6.5). *Application deadline:* For fall admission, 1/1 priority date for domestic students, 1/1 for international students. Application fee: $40 ($90 for international students). Electronic applications accepted. *Unit head:* Dr. Reuben Peters, Director of Graduate Education, 515-294-6116, Fax: 515-294-0453, E-mail: biochem@iastate.edu. *Application contact:* Connie Garnett, Application Contact, 515-294-6116, Fax: 515-294-0453, E-mail: biochem@iastate.edu. Web site: http://www.bbmb.iastate.edu/index.php?.

Iowa State University of Science and Technology, Program in Molecular, Cellular, and Developmental Biology, Ames, IA 50011. Offers MS, PhD. *Entrance requirements:* For master's and doctorate, GRE General Test. Additional exam requirements/recommendations for international students: Required—TOEFL (minimum score 580 paper-based; 85 iBT), IELTS (minimum score 7). *Application deadline:* For fall admission, 1/15 priority date for domestic students, 1/15 for international students. Application fee: $40 ($90 for international students). Electronic applications accepted. *Unit head:* Dr. Clark Ford, Director of Graduate Education, 515-294-7252, Fax: 515-294-6790, E-mail: idgp@iastate.edu. *Application contact:* Katie Blair, Application Contact, 515-294-7252, Fax: 515-924-6790, E-mail: idgp@iastate.edu. Web site: http://www.mcdb.iastate.edu.

The Johns Hopkins University, Bloomberg School of Public Health, Department of Biochemistry and Molecular Biology, Baltimore, MD 21205. Offers MHS, Sc M, PhD. Part-time programs available. *Degree requirements:* For master's, thesis; for doctorate, comprehensive exam, thesis/dissertation, oral and written exams. *Entrance requirements:* For master's, MCAT or GRE, 3 letters of recommendation, curriculum vitae; for doctorate, GRE General Test, 3 letters of recommendation, curriculum vitae. Additional exam requirements/recommendations for international students: Required—TOEFL (minimum score 600 paper-based; 250 computer-based). Electronic applications accepted. *Faculty research:* DNA replication, repair, structure, carcinogenesis, protein structure, enzyme catalysts, reproductive biology.

The Johns Hopkins University, National Institutes of Health Sponsored Programs, Baltimore, MD 21218-2699. Offers biology (PhD), including biochemistry, biophysics, cell biology, developmental biology, genetic biology, molecular biology; cell, molecular, and developmental biology and biophysics (PhD). *Degree requirements:* For doctorate, comprehensive exam, thesis/dissertation. *Entrance requirements:* For doctorate, GRE General Test. Additional exam requirements/recommendations for international students: Required—TOEFL (minimum score 600 paper-based; 250 computer-based), TWE. Electronic applications accepted. *Faculty research:* Protein and nucleic acid biochemistry and biophysical chemistry, molecular biology and development.

The Johns Hopkins University, School of Medicine, Graduate Programs in Medicine, Department of Pharmacology and Molecular Sciences, Baltimore, MD 21205. Offers PhD. *Degree requirements:* For doctorate, comprehensive exam, thesis/dissertation, departmental seminar. *Entrance requirements:* For doctorate, GRE General Test. Additional exam requirements/recommendations for international students: Required—TOEFL. Electronic applications accepted.

The Johns Hopkins University, School of Medicine, Graduate Programs in Medicine, Predoctoral Training Program in Human Genetics, Baltimore, MD 21218-2699. Offers PhD, MD/PhD. Terminal master's awarded for partial completion of doctoral program. *Degree requirements:* For doctorate, comprehensive exam, thesis/dissertation. *Entrance requirements:* For doctorate, GRE General Test, GRE Subject Test. Additional exam requirements/recommendations for international students: Recommended—TOEFL. Electronic applications accepted. *Faculty research:* Human, mammalian, and molecular genetics, bioinformatics, genomics.

The Johns Hopkins University, School of Medicine, Graduate Programs in Medicine, Program in Biochemistry, Cellular and Molecular Biology, Baltimore, MD 21205. Offers PhD. *Degree requirements:* For doctorate, comprehensive exam, thesis/dissertation. *Entrance requirements:* For doctorate, GRE General Test. Additional exam requirements/recommendations for international students: Required—TOEFL. Electronic applications accepted. *Faculty research:* Developmental biology, genomics/proteomics, protein targeting, signal transduction, structural biology.

Kent State University, School of Biomedical Sciences, Program in Cellular and Molecular Biology, Kent, OH 44242-0001. Offers MS, PhD. Offered in cooperation with Northeastern Ohio Universities College of Medicine. Terminal master's awarded for partial completion of doctoral program. *Degree requirements:* For master's, thesis; for doctorate, thesis/dissertation. *Entrance requirements:* For master's, GRE General Test, letter of recommendation, minimum GPA of 3.0; for doctorate, GRE General Test, letter of recommendation, minimum GPA of 3.0, MS. Additional exam requirements/recommendations for international students: Required—TOEFL. Electronic applications accepted. *Expenses:* Tuition, state resident: full-time $8136; part-time $452 per credit hour. Tuition, nonresident: full-time $14,292; part-time $794 per credit hour. *Faculty research:* Molecular genetics, molecular endocrinology, virology and tumor biology, P450 enzymology and catalysis, membrane structure and function.

Lehigh University, College of Arts and Sciences, Department of Biological Sciences, Bethlehem, PA 18015. Offers biochemistry (PhD); integrative biology and neuroscience (PhD); molecular biology (MS, PhD). Part-time programs available. Postbaccalaureate distance learning degree programs offered (no on-campus study). *Faculty:* 16 full-time (7 women). *Students:* 36 full-time (19 women), 22 part-time (15 women); includes 4 minority (2 Black or African American, non-Hispanic/Latino; 2 Asian, non-Hispanic/Latino), 7 international. Average age 30. 70 applicants, 14% accepted, 9 enrolled. In 2011, 11 master's, 3 doctorates awarded. Terminal master's awarded for partial completion of doctoral program. *Degree requirements:* For master's, research report; for doctorate, comprehensive exam, thesis/dissertation. *Entrance requirements:* For doctorate, GRE General Test. Additional exam requirements/recommendations for international students: Required—TOEFL. *Application deadline:* For fall admission, 12/15 for domestic and international students. Applications are processed on a rolling basis. Application fee: $75. Electronic applications accepted. *Financial support:* In 2011–12, 4 fellowships with full tuition reimbursements (averaging $24,500 per year), 6 research assistantships with full tuition reimbursements (averaging $23,750 per year), 16 teaching assistantships with full tuition reimbursements (averaging $23,750 per year) were awarded; scholarships/grants and unspecified assistantships also available. Financial award application deadline: 12/15. *Faculty research:* Gene expression, cytoskeleton and cell structure, cell cycle and growth regulation, neuroscience, animal behavior, microbiology. *Total annual research expenditures:* $2 million. *Unit head:* Dr. Murray Itzkowitz, Chairperson, 610-758-3680, Fax: 610-758-4004, E-mail: mi00@lehigh.edu. *Application contact:* Dr. Jennifer M. Swann, Graduate Coordinator, 610-758-5484, Fax: 610-758-4004, E-mail: jms5@lehigh.edu. Web site: http://www.lehigh.edu/~inbios/.

Louisiana State University Health Sciences Center at Shreveport, Department of Biochemistry and Molecular Biology, Shreveport, LA 71130-3932. Offers MS, PhD, MD/PhD. *Degree requirements:* For master's, thesis; for doctorate, thesis/dissertation. *Entrance requirements:* For master's and doctorate, GRE General Test. Additional exam requirements/recommendations for international students: Required—TOEFL. *Faculty research:* Metabolite transport, regulation of translation and transcription, prokaryotic molecular genetics, cell matrix biochemistry, yeast molecular genetics, oncogenes.

Loyola University Chicago, Graduate School, Program in Molecular Biology, Maywood, IL 60153. Offers MS, PhD, MD/PhD. *Faculty:* 28 full-time (5 women). *Students:* 14 full-time (9 women); includes 1 minority (Two or more races, non-Hispanic/Latino), 6 international. Average age 28. 54 applicants, 7% accepted, 2 enrolled. In 2011, 1 doctorate awarded. Terminal master's awarded for partial completion of doctoral program. *Degree requirements:* For master's, comprehensive exam (for some programs), thesis; for doctorate, comprehensive exam, thesis/dissertation, 48 credit hours. *Entrance requirements:* For master's, GRE General Test, statement of purpose, transcripts, 3 letters of recommendation; for doctorate, GRE General Test, 3 letters of recommendation. Additional exam requirements/recommendations for international students: Required—TOEFL (minimum score 600 paper-based; 250 computer-based). *Application deadline:* For fall admission, 3/1 for domestic and international students. Applications are processed on a rolling basis. Application fee: $40. Electronic applications accepted. *Expenses: Tuition:* Full-time $15,660; part-time $870 per credit hour. *Required fees:* $125 per semester. Tuition and fees vary according to course load and program. *Financial support:* In 2011–12, 7 students received support, including fellowships (averaging $23,000 per year); research assistantships, Federal Work-Study, institutionally sponsored loans, scholarships/grants, and health care benefits also available. Financial award application deadline: 2/15; financial award applicants required to submit FAFSA. *Faculty research:* Cell cycle regulation, molecular immunology, molecular genetics, molecular oncology, molecular virology. *Total annual research expenditures:* $3,500. *Unit head:* Dr. Manuel O. Diaz, Director, 708-327-3172, Fax: 708-216-6505, E-mail: mdiaz@luc.edu. *Application contact:* Dr. Mitchell Denning, Graduate Program Director, 708-327-3358, E-mail: mdennin@lumc.edu. Web site: http://www.luc.edu/biomed.

Marquette University, Graduate School, College of Arts and Sciences, Department of Biology, Milwaukee, WI 53201-1881. Offers cell biology (MS, PhD); developmental biology (MS, PhD); ecology (MS, PhD); epithelial physiology (MS, PhD); genetics (MS, PhD); microbiology (MS, PhD); molecular biology (MS, PhD); muscle and exercise physiology (MS, PhD); neuroscience (PhD). *Faculty:* 23 full-time (11 women), 1 part-time/adjunct (0 women). *Students:* 33 full-time (14 women), 6 part-time (3 women), 19 international. Average age 25. 78 applicants, 17% accepted, 5 enrolled. In 2011, 6 doctorates awarded. Terminal master's awarded for partial completion of doctoral program. *Degree requirements:* For master's, comprehensive exam, thesis, 1 year of teaching experience or equivalent; for doctorate, thesis/dissertation, 1 year of teaching experience or equivalent, qualifying exam. *Entrance requirements:* For master's and doctorate, GRE General Test, GRE Subject Test, official transcripts from all current and previous colleges/universities except Marquette, statement of professional goals and aspirations, three letters of recommendation. Additional exam requirements/recommendations for international students: Required—TOEFL (minimum score 530 paper-based; 78 computer-based). *Application deadline:* For fall admission, 12/15 for domestic and international students. Application fee: $50. Electronic applications accepted. *Expenses: Tuition:* Full-time $17,010; part-time $945 per credit hour. Tuition and fees vary according to program. *Financial support:* In 2011–12, 39 students received support, including 6 fellowships (averaging $1,208 per year), 4 research assistantships with full tuition reimbursements available (averaging $21,750 per year), 29 teaching assistantships with full tuition reimbursements available (averaging $21,750 per year); scholarships/grants, health care benefits, tuition waivers (full and partial), and unspecified assistantships also available. Support available to part-time students. Financial award application deadline: 2/15. *Faculty research:* Neurobiology, neuroendocrinology, epithelial physiology, neuropeptide interactions, synaptic transmission. *Total annual research expenditures:* $2 million. *Unit head:* Dr. Robert Fitts, Chair, 414-288-1748, Fax: 414-288-7357. *Application contact:* Debbie Weaver, Administrative Assistant, 414-288-7355, Fax: 414-288-7357. Web site: http://www.marquette.edu/biology/.

Massachusetts Institute of Technology, School of Science, Department of Biology, Cambridge, MA 02139. Offers biochemistry (PhD); biological oceanography (PhD); biology (PhD); biophysical chemistry and molecular structure (PhD); cell biology (PhD); computational and systems biology (PhD); developmental biology (PhD); genetics (PhD); immunology (PhD); microbiology (PhD); molecular biology (PhD); neurobiology (PhD). *Faculty:* 58 full-time (15 women). *Students:* 248 full-time (129 women); includes 69 minority (5 Black or African American, non-Hispanic/Latino; 1 American Indian or Alaska Native, non-Hispanic/Latino; 25 Asian, non-Hispanic/Latino; 31 Hispanic/Latino; 7 Two or more races, non-Hispanic/Latino), 36 international. Average age 26. 698 applicants, 15% accepted, 44 enrolled. In 2011, 38 doctorates awarded. *Degree requirements:* For doctorate, comprehensive exam, thesis/dissertation. *Entrance requirements:* For doctorate, GRE General Test. Additional exam requirements/recommendations for international students: Required—TOEFL (minimum score 577 paper-based; 233 computer-based), IELTS (minimum score 6.5). *Application deadline:* For fall admission, 12/1 for domestic and international students. Application fee: $75. Electronic applications accepted. *Expenses: Tuition:* Full-time $40,460; part-time $630 per credit hour. *Required fees:* $272. *Financial support:* In 2011–12, 214 students received support, including 129 fellowships (averaging $33,200 per year), 117 research assistantships (averaging $32,900 per year); teaching assistantships, Federal Work-Study, institutionally sponsored loans, scholarships/grants, traineeships, health care benefits, and unspecified assistantships also available. *Faculty research:* Cellular, developmental and molecular (plant and animal) biology; biochemistry, bioengineering, biophysics and structural biology; classical and molecular genetics; immunology and microbiology; cancer biology, molecular medicine, neurobiology and human disease; computational and systems biology. *Total annual research expenditures:* $53.6 million. *Unit head:* Prof. Tania A. Baker, Head, 617-253-4701, E-mail: mitbio@mit.edu. *Application contact:* Biology Education Office, 617-253-3717, Fax: 617-258-9329, E-mail: gradbio@mit.edu. Web site: https://biology.mit.edu/.

Mayo Graduate School, Graduate Programs in Biomedical Sciences, Programs in Biochemistry, Structural Biology, Cell Biology, and Genetics, Rochester, MN 55905. Offers biochemistry and structural biology (PhD); cell biology and genetics (PhD);

molecular biology (PhD). *Degree requirements:* For doctorate, oral defense of dissertation, qualifying oral and written exam. *Entrance requirements:* For doctorate, GRE, 1 year of chemistry, biology, calculus, and physics. Additional exam requirements/recommendations for international students: Required—TOEFL. Electronic applications accepted. *Faculty research:* Gene structure and function, membranes and receptors/cytoskeleton, oncogenes and growth factors, protein structure and function, steroid hormonal action.

McMaster University, Faculty of Health Sciences and School of Graduate Studies, Program in Medical Sciences, Hamilton, ON L8S 4M2, Canada. Offers blood and vascular (M Sc, PhD); genetics and cancer (M Sc, PhD); immunity and infection (M Sc, PhD); metabolism and nutrition (M Sc, PhD); neurosciences and behavioral sciences (M Sc, PhD); physiology/pharmacology (M Sc, PhD); MD/PhD. *Degree requirements:* For master's, thesis; for doctorate, comprehensive exam, thesis/dissertation. *Entrance requirements:* For master's, honors B Sc, B+ average in related field; for doctorate, M Sc, minimum B+ average. Additional exam requirements/recommendations for international students: Required—TOEFL (minimum score 580 paper-based; 237 computer-based; 92 iBT).

Medical University of South Carolina, College of Graduate Studies, Department of Biochemistry and Molecular Biology, Charleston, SC 29425. Offers MS, PhD, MD/PhD. *Faculty:* 24 full-time (9 women), 3 part-time/adjunct (1 woman). *Students:* 15 full-time (8 women), 1 (woman) part-time; includes 1 minority (Hispanic/Latino), 7 international. Average age 30. 9 applicants, 22% accepted, 2 enrolled. In 2011, 1 master's, 2 doctorates awarded. Terminal master's awarded for partial completion of doctoral program. *Degree requirements:* For master's, thesis, oral exam/thesis defense; for doctorate, thesis/dissertation, oral and written exams/dissertation defense. *Entrance requirements:* For master's, GRE General Test; for doctorate, GRE General Test, interview, minimum GPA of 3.0. Additional exam requirements/recommendations for international students: Required—TOEFL (minimum score 600 paper-based; 250 computer-based; 100 iBT). *Application deadline:* For fall admission, 1/15 priority date for domestic students, 1/15 for international students. Applications are processed on a rolling basis. Application fee: $0 ($85 for international students). Electronic applications accepted. *Financial support:* In 2011–12, 10 research assistantships with partial tuition reimbursements (averaging $23,000 per year) were awarded; Federal Work-Study and scholarships/grants also available. Support available to part-time students. Financial award applicants required to submit FAFSA. *Faculty research:* Lipid biochemistry, DNA replication, nucleic acids, protein structure. *Unit head:* Dr. Yusuf A. Hannun, Chairman, 843-792-9318, Fax: 843-792-6590, E-mail: hannun@musc.edu. *Application contact:* Dr. Maurizio Del Poeta, Associate Professor, 843-792-8381, Fax: 843-792-6590, E-mail: delpoeta@musc.edu. Web site: http://www.musc.edu/BCMB/.

Medical University of South Carolina, College of Graduate Studies, Program in Molecular and Cellular Biology and Pathobiology, Charleston, SC 29425. Offers cancer biology (PhD); cardiovascular biology (PhD); cardiovascular imaging (PhD); cell regulation (PhD); craniofacial biology (PhD); genetics and development (PhD); marine biomedicine (PhD); DMD/PhD; MD/PhD. *Faculty:* 137 full-time (33 women). *Students:* 28 full-time (23 women); includes 5 minority (4 Black or African American, non-Hispanic/Latino; 1 Hispanic/Latino), 5 international. Average age 30. In 2011, 16 doctorates awarded. *Degree requirements:* For doctorate, thesis/dissertation, oral and written exams. *Entrance requirements:* For doctorate, GRE General Test, interview, minimum GPA of 3.0. Additional exam requirements/recommendations for international students: Required—TOEFL (minimum score 600 paper-based; 250 computer-based; 100 iBT). *Application deadline:* For fall admission, 1/15 priority date for domestic students, 1/15 for international students. Applications are processed on a rolling basis. Application fee: $0 ($85 for international students). Electronic applications accepted. *Financial support:* In 2011–12, 39 research assistantships with partial tuition reimbursements (averaging $23,000 per year) were awarded; Federal Work-Study and scholarships/grants also available. Support available to part-time students. Financial award application deadline: 3/10; financial award applicants required to submit FAFSA. *Unit head:* Dr. Donald R. Menick, Director, 843-876-5045, Fax: 843-792-6590, E-mail: menickd@musc.edu. *Application contact:* Dr. Cynthia F. Wright, Associate Dean for Admissions and Career Development, 843-792-2564, Fax: 843-792-6590, E-mail: wrightcf@musc.edu. Web site: http://www.musc.edu/mcbp/.

Michigan State University, The Graduate School, College of Agriculture and Natural Resources, MSU-DOE Plant Research Laboratory, East Lansing, MI 48824. Offers biochemistry and molecular biology (PhD); cellular and molecular biology (PhD); crop and soil sciences (PhD); genetics (PhD); microbiology and molecular genetics (PhD); plant biology (PhD); plant physiology (PhD). Offered jointly with the Department of Energy. *Degree requirements:* For doctorate, comprehensive exam, thesis/dissertation, laboratory rotation, defense of dissertation. *Entrance requirements:* For doctorate, GRE General Test, acceptance into one of the affiliated department programs; 3 letters of recommendation; bachelor's degree or equivalent in life sciences, chemistry, biochemistry, or biophysics; research experience. Electronic applications accepted. *Faculty research:* Role of hormones in the regulation of plant development and physiology, molecular mechanisms associated with signal recognition, development and application of genetic methods and materials, protein routing and function.

Michigan State University, The Graduate School, College of Natural Science and Graduate Programs in Human Medicine and Graduate Studies in Osteopathic Medicine, Department of Biochemistry and Molecular Biology, East Lansing, MI 48824. Offers biochemistry and molecular biology (MS, PhD); biochemistry and molecular biology/environmental toxicology (PhD). *Entrance requirements:* Additional exam requirements/recommendations for international students: Required—TOEFL. Electronic applications accepted.

Michigan State University, The Graduate School, College of Natural Science, Program in Cell and Molecular Biology, East Lansing, MI 48824. Offers cell and molecular biology (MS, PhD); cell and molecular biology/environmental toxicology (PhD). *Entrance requirements:* Additional exam requirements/recommendations for international students: Required—TOEFL. Electronic applications accepted.

Mississippi State University, College of Agriculture and Life Sciences, Department of Biochemistry, Molecular Biology, Entomology and Plant Pathology, Mississippi State, MS 39762. Offers agriculture life sciences (MS), including entomology and plant pathology; molecular biology (PhD). *Faculty:* 25 full-time (1 woman). *Students:* 46 full-time (17 women), 14 part-time (6 women); includes 4 minority (2 Black or African American, non-Hispanic/Latino; 2 Two or more races, non-Hispanic/Latino), 18 international. Average age 30. 43 applicants, 33% accepted, 13 enrolled. In 2011, 7 master's, 5 doctorates awarded. Terminal master's awarded for partial completion of doctoral program. *Degree requirements:* For master's, thesis (for some programs), comprehensive oral or written exam; for doctorate, thesis/dissertation, comprehensive oral and written exam. *Entrance requirements:* For master's, GRE General Test, minimum GPA of 2.75; for doctorate, GRE. Additional exam requirements/recommendations for international students: Required—TOEFL (minimum score 550 paper-based; 213 computer-based; 79 iBT); Recommended—IELTS (minimum score 6.5). *Application deadline:* For fall admission, 7/1 for domestic students, 5/1 for international students; for spring admission, 11/1 for domestic students, 9/1 for international students. Applications are processed on a rolling basis. Application fee: $40. Electronic applications accepted. *Expenses:* Tuition, state resident: full-time $5805; part-time $322.50 per credit hour. Tuition, nonresident: full-time $14,670; part-time $815 per credit hour. *Financial support:* In 2011–12, 41 research assistantships with full tuition reimbursements (averaging $15,714 per year) were awarded; Federal Work-Study, institutionally sponsored loans, and unspecified assistantships also available. Financial award application deadline: 4/1; financial award applicants required to submit FAFSA. *Faculty research:* Fish nutrition, plant and animal molecular biology, plant biochemistry, enzymology, lipid metabolism, chromatin, cell wall synthesis in rice, a model grass bioenergy species and the source of rice stover residues, using reverse genetic and functional genomic and proteomic approaches. *Unit head:* Dr. Scott T. Willard, Professor and Department Head, 662-325-2640, Fax: 662-325-8664, E-mail: swilliard@ads.msstate.edu. *Application contact:* Dr. Din-Pow Ma, Professor/Graduate Coordinator, 662-325-7739, Fax: 662-325-8664, E-mail: dm1@ra.msstate.edu.

Missouri State University, Graduate College, College of Health and Human Services, Department of Biomedical Sciences, Program in Cell and Molecular Biology, Springfield, MO 65897. Offers MS. Part-time programs available. *Students:* 7 full-time (4 women), 6 part-time (3 women); includes 2 minority (1 Asian, non-Hispanic/Latino; 1 Hispanic/Latino), 2 international. Average age 24. 7 applicants, 57% accepted, 4 enrolled. In 2011, 10 master's awarded. *Degree requirements:* For master's, thesis or alternative, oral and written exams. *Entrance requirements:* For master's, GRE General Test, 2 semesters of course work in organic chemistry and physics, 1 semester of course work in calculus, minimum GPA of 3.0 in last 60 hours of course work. Additional exam requirements/recommendations for international students: Required—TOEFL (minimum score 550 paper-based; 213 computer-based; 79 iBT). *Application deadline:* For fall admission, 7/20 priority date for domestic students, 5/1 for international students; for spring admission, 12/20 priority date for domestic students, 9/1 for international students. Applications are processed on a rolling basis. Application fee: $35 ($50 for international students). Electronic applications accepted. *Expenses:* Tuition, state resident: full-time $4086; part-time $227 per credit hour. Tuition, nonresident: full-time $8172; part-time $454 per credit hour. *Required fees:* $275 per semester. Tuition and fees vary according to course load, campus/location and program. *Financial support:* In 2011–12, 4 teaching assistantships with full tuition reimbursements (averaging $7,340 per year) were awarded; career-related internships or fieldwork, Federal Work-Study, institutionally sponsored loans, scholarships/grants, and unspecified assistantships also available. Support available to part-time students. Financial award application deadline: 3/31; financial award applicants required to submit FAFSA. *Faculty research:* Extracellular matrix membrane protein, P2 nucleotide receptors, double stranded RNA viruses. *Unit head:* Dr. Scott Zimmerman, Program Director, 417-836-5478, E-mail: scottzimmerman@missouristate.edu. *Application contact:* Misty Stewart, Coordinator of Graduate Admissions and Recruitment, 417-836-6079, Fax: 417-836-6200, E-mail: mistystewart@missouristate.edu. Web site: http://www.missouristate.edu/bms/CMB/.

Montclair State University, The Graduate School, College of Science and Mathematics, Department of Biology and Molecular Biology, Montclair, NJ 07043-1624. Offers biology (MS), including biological science education, biology, ecology and evolution, physiology; molecular biology (MS, Certificate). Part-time and evening/weekend programs available. *Students:* 15 full-time (10 women), 33 part-time (23 women); includes 3 minority (all Hispanic/Latino), 1 international. Average age 28. 53 applicants, 47% accepted, 14 enrolled. In 2011, 14 degrees awarded. *Degree requirements:* For master's, comprehensive exam, thesis or alternative. *Entrance requirements:* For master's, GRE General Test, 24 credits of course work in undergraduate biology, 2 letters of recommendation, teaching certificate (biology sciences education concentration); for Certificate, 2 letters of recommendation, essay. Additional exam requirements/recommendations for international students: Required—TOEFL (minimum score 83 iBT) or IELTS. *Application deadline:* For fall admission, 6/1 for international students; for spring admission, 10/1 for international students. Applications are processed on a rolling basis. Application fee: $60. Electronic applications accepted. *Financial support:* In 2011–12, 16 research assistantships with full tuition reimbursements (averaging $7,000 per year), 3 teaching assistantships (averaging $7,000 per year) were awarded; Federal Work-Study, scholarships/grants, and unspecified assistantships also available. Support available to part-time students. Financial award application deadline: 3/1; financial award applicants required to submit FAFSA. *Faculty research:* Ecosystem biology, molecular biology, signal transduction, neuroscience, aquatic and coastal biology. *Total annual research expenditures:* $1.3 million. *Unit head:* Dr. Quinn Vega, Chairperson, 973-655-7178. *Application contact:* Amy Aiello, Director of Graduate Admissions and Operations, 973-655-5147, Fax: 973-655-7869, E-mail: graduate.school@montclair.edu. Web site: http://www.montclair.edu/csam/biology/.

New Mexico State University, Graduate School, Program in Molecular Biology, Las Cruces, NM 88003-8001. Offers MS, PhD. *Faculty:* 1 (woman) full-time. *Students:* 18 full-time (10 women), 5 part-time (3 women); includes 8 minority (1 Black or African American, non-Hispanic/Latino; 1 American Indian or Alaska Native, non-Hispanic/Latino; 6 Hispanic/Latino), 7 international. Average age 31. 10 applicants, 20% accepted, 2 enrolled. In 2011, 1 master's, 5 doctorates awarded. *Degree requirements:* For master's, thesis, oral seminars; for doctorate, comprehensive exam, thesis/dissertation, oral seminars. *Entrance requirements:* For master's and doctorate, GRE General Test, minimum GPA of 3.3. Additional exam requirements/recommendations for international students: Required—TOEFL (minimum score 550 paper-based; 79 iBT), IELTS (minimum score 6.5). *Application deadline:* For fall admission, 12/15 for domestic and international students; for spring admission, 1/15 for domestic and international students. Applications are processed on a rolling basis. Application fee: $40 ($50 for international students). Electronic applications accepted. *Expenses:* Tuition, state resident: full-time $5004; part-time $208.50 per credit. Tuition, nonresident: full-time $17,446; part-time $726.90 per credit. *Financial support:* In 2011–12, 6 research assistantships (averaging $24,046 per year), 10 teaching assistantships (averaging $21,757 per year) were awarded; fellowships, career-related internships or fieldwork, health care benefits, and unspecified assistantships also available. Financial award application deadline: 2/1. *Faculty research:* Emerging pathogens, plant-molecular biology and virology, molecular symbiotic interactions, cell and organismal biology, applied and environmental microbiology. *Unit head:* Dr. Rebecca Creamer, Director, 575-646-3068, Fax: 575-646-8087, E-mail: creamer@nmsu.edu. *Application contact:* Nancy McDow, Program Secretary, 575-646-3437, Fax: 575-646-5170, E-mail: nancyt@nmsu.edu. Web site: http://molb.research.nmsu.edu.

New York Medical College, Graduate School of Basic Medical Sciences, Program in Biochemistry and Molecular Biology, Valhalla, NY 10595-1691. Offers MS, PhD, MD/PhD. Part-time and evening/weekend programs available. *Faculty:* 10 full-time (4 women), 2 part-time/adjunct (0 women). *Students:* 8 full-time (6 women); includes 2 minority (both Asian, non-Hispanic/Latino). Average age 27. 11 applicants, 73% accepted, 2 enrolled. In 2011, 1 master's, 1 doctorate awarded. Terminal master's awarded for partial completion of doctoral program. *Median time to degree:* Of those who began their doctoral program in fall 2003, 100% received their degree in 8 years or less. *Degree requirements:* For master's, thesis; for doctorate, comprehensive exam, thesis/dissertation. *Entrance requirements:* For master's and doctorate, GRE General Test. Additional exam requirements/recommendations for international students: Required—TOEFL. *Application deadline:* For fall admission, 7/1 priority date for

domestic students, 5/1 for international students; for spring admission, 12/1 priority date for domestic students, 10/1 for international students. Applications are processed on a rolling basis. Application fee: $50 ($75 for international students). Electronic applications accepted. *Financial support:* In 2011–12, 2 fellowships, 5 research assistantships with full tuition reimbursements (averaging $24,000 per year) were awarded; Federal Work-Study, institutionally sponsored loans, scholarships/grants, traineeships, tuition waivers (full), unspecified assistantships, and health benefits (for PhD candidates only) also available. Financial award applicants required to submit FAFSA. *Faculty research:* Expression, mechanisms of hormone action and cell signaling, enzymology, mechanisms of DNA replication and repair, cell cycle regulation, control of cell growth, molecular biology of cancer cells and the cancer process, mechanisms of nutrition and cancer prevention, molecular neurobiology and studies of neurodegenerative disorders, the aging process. *Unit head:* Dr. Joseph Wu, Director, 914-594-4891, Fax: 914-594-4944, E-mail: joseph_wu@nymc.edu. *Application contact:* Valerie Romeo-Messana, Admission Coordinator, 914-594-4110, Fax: 914-594-4944, E-mail: v_romeomessana@nymc.edu.

New York University, Graduate School of Arts and Science, Department of Biology, New York, NY 10012-1019. Offers biology (PhD); biomedical journalism (MS); cancer and molecular biology (PhD); computational biology (PhD); computers in biological research (MS); developmental genetics (PhD); general biology (MS); immunology and microbiology (PhD); molecular genetics (PhD); neurobiology (PhD); oral biology (MS); plant biology (PhD); recombinant DNA technology (MS); MS/MBA. Part-time programs available. *Faculty:* 24 full-time (5 women). *Students:* 146 full-time (90 women), 54 part-time (36 women); includes 49 minority (1 Black or African American, non-Hispanic/Latino; 33 Asian, non-Hispanic/Latino; 12 Hispanic/Latino; 3 Two or more races, non-Hispanic/Latino), 89 international. Average age 27. 394 applicants, 62% accepted, 82 enrolled. In 2011, 68 master's, 6 doctorates awarded. Terminal master's awarded for partial completion of doctoral program. *Degree requirements:* For master's, thesis or alternative, qualifying paper; for doctorate, comprehensive exam, thesis/dissertation. *Entrance requirements:* For master's, GRE General Test; for doctorate, GRE General Test, GRE Subject Test. Additional exam requirements/recommendations for international students: Required—TOEFL. *Application deadline:* For fall admission, 12/1 priority date for domestic students, 12/1 for international students. Application fee: $90. *Financial support:* Fellowships with tuition reimbursements, research assistantships with tuition reimbursements, teaching assistantships with tuition reimbursements, career-related internships or fieldwork, Federal Work-Study, institutionally sponsored loans, scholarships/grants, health care benefits, and unspecified assistantships available. Financial award application deadline: 12/1; financial award applicants required to submit FAFSA. *Faculty research:* Genomics, molecular and cell biology, development and molecular genetics, molecular evolution of plants and animals. *Unit head:* Stephen Small, Chair, 212-998-8200, Fax: 212-995-4015, E-mail: biology@nyu.edu. *Application contact:* Justin Blau, Director of Graduate Studies, 212-998-8200, Fax: 212-995-4015, E-mail: biology@nyu.edu. Web site: http://biology.as.nyu.edu/.

New York University, School of Medicine, New York, NY 10012-1019. Offers biomedical sciences (PhD), including biomedical imaging, cellular and molecular biology, computational biology, developmental genetics, medical and molecular parasitology, microbiology, molecular oncobiology and immunology, neuroscience and physiology, pathobiology, pharmacology, structural biology; clinical investigation (MS); medicine (MD); MD/MA; MD/MPA; MD/MS; MD/PhD. *Accreditation:* LCME/AMA (one or more programs are accredited). *Degree requirements:* For master's, comprehensive exam, thesis; for doctorate, comprehensive exam (for some programs), thesis/dissertation (for some programs). *Entrance requirements:* For doctorate, MCAT (for MD). Additional exam requirements/recommendations for international students: Required—TOEFL. *Expenses:* Contact institution. *Faculty research:* AIDS, cancer, neuroscience, molecular biology, neuroscience, cell biology and molecular genetics, structural biology, microbial pathogenesis and host defense, pharmacology, molecular oncology and immunology.

New York University, School of Medicine and Graduate School of Arts and Science, Sackler Institute of Graduate Biomedical Sciences, Program in Cellular and Molecular Biology, New York, NY 10012-1019. Offers PhD, MD/PhD. *Faculty:* 58 full-time (14 women). *Students:* 33 full-time (17 women); includes 13 minority (2 Black or African American, non-Hispanic/Latino; 8 Asian, non-Hispanic/Latino; 3 Hispanic/Latino), 10 international. Average age 28. In 2011, 9 doctorates awarded. *Degree requirements:* For doctorate, comprehensive exam, thesis/dissertation, qualifying exams. *Entrance requirements:* For doctorate, GRE General Test. Additional exam requirements/recommendations for international students: Required—TOEFL. *Application deadline:* For fall admission, 1/4 priority date for domestic students. Applications are processed on a rolling basis. Application fee: $85. *Financial support:* Fellowships with tuition reimbursements, research assistantships with tuition reimbursements, and teaching assistantships with tuition reimbursements available. *Faculty research:* Membrane and organelle structure and biogenesis, intracellular transport and processing of proteins, cellular recognition and cell adhesion, oncogene structure and function, action of growth factors. *Total annual research expenditures:* $1.9 million. *Unit head:* Dr. Daniel Rifkin, Director, 212-263-5109, E-mail: rifkind01@popmail.med.nyu.edu. *Application contact:* Lynette Wilson, Information Contact, 212-263-7684, Fax: 212-263-8139, E-mail: wilsoe01@popmail.med.nyu.edu.

North Dakota State University, College of Graduate and Interdisciplinary Studies, College of Science and Mathematics, Department of Biological Sciences, Fargo, ND 58108. Offers biology (MS); botany (MS, PhD); cellular and molecular biology (PhD); environmental and conservation sciences (MS, PhD); genomics (PhD); natural resources management (MS, PhD); zoology (MS, PhD). *Faculty:* 13 full-time (7 women), 3 part-time/adjunct (1 woman). *Students:* 20 full-time (10 women), 2 part-time (both women); includes 1 minority (American Indian or Alaska Native, non-Hispanic/Latino), 2 international. 12 applicants, 33% accepted, 4 enrolled. In 2011, 3 degrees awarded. *Degree requirements:* For master's, thesis; for doctorate, thesis/dissertation. *Entrance requirements:* For master's and doctorate, GRE General Test. Additional exam requirements/recommendations for international students: Required—TOEFL. *Application deadline:* For fall admission, 1/15 for domestic students. Applications are processed on a rolling basis. Application fee: $35. Electronic applications accepted. *Financial support:* Fellowships with full tuition reimbursements, research assistantships with full tuition reimbursements, teaching assistantships with full tuition reimbursements, career-related internships or fieldwork, Federal Work-Study, institutionally sponsored loans, scholarships/grants, tuition waivers (full), and unspecified assistantships available. Support available to part-time students. Financial award application deadline: 4/15; financial award applicants required to submit FAFSA. *Faculty research:* Comparative endocrinology, physiology, behavioral ecology, plant cell biology, aquatic biology. *Unit head:* Dr. Wendy Reed, Head, 701-231-7087, E-mail: wendy.reed@ndsu.edu. *Application contact:* Sonya Goergen, Marketing, Recruitment, and Public Relations Coordinator, 701-231-7033, Fax: 701-231-6524. Web site: http://biology.ndsu.nodak.edu/.

North Dakota State University, College of Graduate and Interdisciplinary Studies, Interdisciplinary Program in Cellular and Molecular Biology, Fargo, ND 58108. Offers PhD. PhD offered in cooperation with 11 departments in the university. *Students:* 9 full-time (7 women), 4 part-time (1 woman), 8 international. 33 applicants, 0% accepted, 0 enrolled. *Degree requirements:* For doctorate, thesis/dissertation. *Entrance requirements:* For doctorate, GRE. Additional exam requirements/recommendations for international students: Required—TOEFL (minimum score 525 paper-based; 197 computer-based; 71 iBT). *Application deadline:* Applications are processed on a rolling basis. Application fee: $35. Electronic applications accepted. *Financial support:* Fellowships with full tuition reimbursements, research assistantships with full tuition reimbursements, teaching assistantships with full tuition reimbursements, and unspecified assistantships available. Financial award application deadline: 3/15. *Faculty research:* Plant and animal cell biology, gene regulation, molecular genetics, plant and animal virology. *Unit head:* Dr. Mark Sheridan, Director, 701-231-7087, E-mail: ndsu.cmb@ndsu.edu. *Application contact:* Sonya Goergen, Marketing, Recruitment, and Public Relations Coordinator, 701-231-7033, Fax: 701-231-6524. Web site: http://www.ndsu.edu/cellularmolecularbiology/.

Northwestern University, The Graduate School, Interdepartmental Biological Sciences Program (IBiS), Evanston, IL 60208. Offers biochemistry, molecular biology, and cell biology (PhD), including biochemistry, cell and molecular biology, molecular biophysics, structural biology; biotechnology (PhD); cell and molecular biology (PhD); developmental biology and genetics (PhD); hormone action and signal transduction (PhD); neuroscience (PhD); structural biology, biochemistry, and biophysics (PhD). Program participants include the Departments of Biochemistry, Molecular Biology, and Cell Biology; Chemistry; Neurobiology and Physiology; Chemical Engineering; Civil Engineering; and Evanston Hospital. *Degree requirements:* For doctorate, thesis/dissertation, qualifying exam. *Entrance requirements:* For doctorate, GRE General Test. Additional exam requirements/recommendations for international students: Required—TOEFL (minimum score 600 paper-based). Electronic applications accepted. *Faculty research:* Developmental genetics, gene regulation, DNA-protein interactions, biological clocks, bioremediation.

Northwestern University, Northwestern University Feinberg School of Medicine and Interdepartmental Programs, Integrated Graduate Programs in the Life Sciences, Chicago, IL 60611. Offers cancer biology (PhD); cell biology (PhD); developmental biology (PhD); evolutionary biology (PhD); immunology and microbial pathogenesis (PhD); molecular biology and genetics (PhD); neurobiology (PhD); pharmacology and toxicology (PhD); structural biology and biochemistry (PhD). *Degree requirements:* For doctorate, comprehensive exam, thesis/dissertation, written and oral qualifying exams. *Entrance requirements:* For doctorate, GRE General Test. Additional exam requirements/recommendations for international students: Required—TOEFL (minimum score 600 paper-based; 250 computer-based). Electronic applications accepted.

The Ohio State University, Graduate School, College of Arts and Sciences, Division of Natural and Mathematical Sciences, Department of Molecular Genetics, Columbus, OH 43210. Offers cell and developmental biology (MS, PhD); genetics (MS, PhD); molecular biology (MS, PhD). *Faculty:* 23. *Students:* 11 full-time (5 women), 23 part-time (11 women); includes 1 minority (Black or African American, non-Hispanic/Latino), 15 international. Average age 26. In 2011, 8 doctorates awarded. *Degree requirements:* For master's, thesis; for doctorate, thesis/dissertation. *Entrance requirements:* For master's and doctorate, GRE General Test, GRE Subject Test in biology or biochemistry (recommended). Additional exam requirements/recommendations for international students: Required—TOEFL (minimum score 550 paper-based; 250 computer-based; 79 iBT), Michigan English Language Assessment Battery (minimum score 82). *Application deadline:* For fall admission, 8/15 priority date for domestic students, 7/1 for international students; for winter admission, 12/1 priority date for domestic students, 11/1 for international students; for spring admission, 3/1 priority date for domestic students, 2/1 for international students. Applications are processed on a rolling basis. Application fee: $40 ($50 for international students). Electronic applications accepted. *Expenses:* Tuition, state resident: full-time $11,400. Tuition, nonresident: full-time $28,125. Tuition and fees vary according to course load, degree level, campus/location and program. *Financial support:* Fellowships, research assistantships, teaching assistantships, Federal Work-Study, and institutionally sponsored loans available. Support available to part-time students. *Unit head:* Dr. Anita Hopper, Chair, 614-688-3306, Fax: 614-292-4466, E-mail: hopper.64@osu.edu. *Application contact:* Graduate Admissions, 614-292-6031, Fax: 614-292-3656, E-mail: gradadmissions@osu.edu. Web site: https://molgen.osu.edu/.

The Ohio State University, Graduate School, College of Arts and Sciences, Division of Natural and Mathematical Sciences, Program in Molecular, Cellular and Developmental Biology, Columbus, OH 43210. Offers MS, PhD. *Faculty:* 169. *Students:* 62 full-time (38 women), 66 part-time (36 women); includes 17 minority (8 Asian, non-Hispanic/Latino; 7 Hispanic/Latino; 2 Two or more races, non-Hispanic/Latino), 70 international. Average age 27. In 2011, 6 master's, 19 doctorates awarded. *Degree requirements:* For master's, thesis; for doctorate, thesis/dissertation. *Entrance requirements:* For master's and doctorate, GRE General Test, GRE Subject Test (biology or biochemistry, cell and molecular biology). Additional exam requirements/recommendations for international students: Required—TOEFL (minimum score 550 paper-based; 250 computer-based; 79 iBT), Michigan English Language Assessment Battery (minimum score 82). *Application deadline:* For fall admission, 8/15 priority date for domestic students, 7/1 for international students; for winter admission, 12/1 priority date for domestic students, 11/1 for international students; for spring admission, 3/1 priority date for domestic students, 2/1 for international students. Applications are processed on a rolling basis. Application fee: $40 ($50 for international students). Electronic applications accepted. *Expenses:* Tuition, state resident: full-time $11,400. Tuition, nonresident: full-time $28,125. Tuition and fees vary according to course load, degree level, campus/location and program. *Unit head:* David M. Bisaro, Director, 614-292-3281, Fax: 614-292-4466, E-mail: bisaro.1@osu.edu. *Application contact:* Graduate Admissions, 614-292-6031, Fax: 614-292-3656, E-mail: gradadmissions@osu.edu. Web site: http://www.biosci.ohio-state.edu/~mcdb/.

Ohio University, Graduate College, College of Arts and Sciences, Interdisciplinary Graduate Program in Molecular and Cellular Biology, Athens, OH 45701-2979. Offers MS, PhD. *Students:* 23 full-time (11 women), 2 part-time (1 woman); includes 1 minority (Hispanic/Latino), 20 international. 45 applicants, 4% accepted, 2 enrolled. In 2011, 6 doctorates awarded. *Degree requirements:* For master's, comprehensive exam, thesis, research proposal, teaching experience; for doctorate, comprehensive exam, thesis/dissertation, research proposal, teaching experience. *Entrance requirements:* For master's and doctorate, GRE General Test. Additional exam requirements/recommendations for international students: Required—TOEFL (minimum score 620 paper-based; 260 computer-based; 105 iBT); Recommended—TWE. *Application deadline:* For fall admission, 12/30 priority date for domestic students, 12/30 for international students. Application fee: $50 ($55 for international students). Electronic applications accepted. *Financial support:* In 2011–12, 25 students received support, including research assistantships with full tuition reimbursements available (averaging $19,500 per year), teaching assistantships with full tuition reimbursements available (averaging $19,500 per year); Federal Work-Study, institutionally sponsored loans, traineeships, and unspecified assistantships also available. Financial award application deadline: 12/30. *Faculty research:* Animal biotechnology, plant molecular biology RNA, immunology, cellular genetics, biochemistry of signal transduction, cancer research,

membrane transport, bioinformatics, bioengineering, chemical biology and drug discovery, diabetes, microbiology, neuroscience. *Total annual research expenditures:* $4.4 million. *Unit head:* Dr. Robert A. Colvin, Chair, 740-593-0198, Fax: 740-593-1569, E-mail: colvin@ohio.edu. *Application contact:* Dr. Xiaozhuo Chen, Graduate Chair, 740-593-9699, Fax: 740-593-1569, E-mail: chenx@ohio.edu. Web site: http://www.ohio.edu/mcb.

Oklahoma State University, College of Agricultural Science and Natural Resources, Department of Biochemistry and Molecular Biology, Stillwater, OK 74078. Offers MS, PhD. *Faculty:* 27 full-time (11 women), 1 part-time/adjunct (0 women). *Students:* 3 full-time (0 women), 34 part-time (17 women); includes 5 minority (1 Asian, non-Hispanic/Latino; 4 Hispanic/Latino), 22 international. Average age 28. 88 applicants, 13% accepted, 10 enrolled. In 2011, 1 master's, 4 doctorates awarded. *Degree requirements:* For master's, thesis, oral exam; for doctorate, comprehensive exam, thesis/dissertation. *Entrance requirements:* For master's and doctorate, GRE or GMAT. Additional exam requirements/recommendations for international students: Required—TOEFL (minimum score 550 paper-based; 79 iBT). *Application deadline:* For fall admission, 3/1 for international students; for spring admission, 8/1 for international students. Applications are processed on a rolling basis. Application fee: $40 ($75 for international students). Electronic applications accepted. *Expenses:* Tuition, state resident: full-time $4044; part-time $168.50 per credit hour. Tuition, nonresident: full-time $16,008; part-time $667 per credit hour. *Required fees:* $2122; $88.45 per credit hour. One-time fee: $50. Tuition and fees vary according to course load and campus/location. *Financial support:* In 2011–12, 34 research assistantships (averaging $19,233 per year), 2 teaching assistantships (averaging $18,699 per year) were awarded; career-related internships or fieldwork, Federal Work-Study, scholarships/grants, health care benefits, tuition waivers (partial), and unspecified assistantships also available. Support available to part-time students. Financial award application deadline: 3/1; financial award applicants required to submit FAFSA. *Unit head:* Dr. Dale Thomas, Interim Head, 405-744-5431, Fax: 405-744-7799. *Application contact:* Dr. Sheryl Tucker, Dean, 405-744-7099, Fax: 405-744-0355, E-mail: grad-i@okstate.edu. Web site: http://biochemistry.okstate.edu/.

Oklahoma State University Center for Health Sciences, Graduate Program in Forensic Sciences, Tulsa, OK 74107-1898. Offers forensic DNA/molecular biology (MS); forensic document examination (MS, Graduate Certificate); forensic pathology/microbiology (MS); forensic psychology (MS); forensic science administration (MS); forensic toxicology (MS). Part-time and evening/weekend programs available. Postbaccalaureate distance learning degree programs offered (no on-campus study). *Faculty:* 2 full-time (0 women), 14 part-time/adjunct (5 women). *Students:* 7 full-time (5 women), 22 part-time (12 women); includes 4 minority (3 American Indian or Alaska Native, non-Hispanic/Latino; 1 Hispanic/Latino), 1 international. Average age 34. 12 applicants, 50% accepted, 5 enrolled. In 2011, 7 degrees awarded. *Degree requirements:* For master's, comprehensive exam (for some programs), thesis (for some programs). *Entrance requirements:* For master's, MAT (for MFSA) or GRE General Test, professional experience (MFSA). Additional exam requirements/recommendations for international students: Required—TOEFL (minimum score 600 paper-based; 250 computer-based), TWE (minimum score 5). *Application deadline:* For fall admission, 3/1 for domestic and international students; for spring admission, 10/1 for domestic and international students. Application fee: $40 ($75 for international students). *Financial support:* In 2011–12, 10 students received support, including 2 research assistantships (averaging $12,000 per year); career-related internships or fieldwork, Federal Work-Study, and tuition waivers (partial) also available. Support available to part-time students. Financial award application deadline: 4/1; financial award applicants required to submit FAFSA. *Faculty research:* Studies on the variability in chromosomal DNA; development/enhancement of accessory methods useful for forensic DNA typing; development of universal methods useful for discriminating pathogenic bacteria; forensic dentistry; transmission of microbial diseases by dentures, protective athletic mouth-guards, band wind instruments, and infant pacifiers; changes in ecologies and antibiotic sensitivities of aerobic microorganisms; forensic toxicology and trace chemical method development. *Total annual research expenditures:* $58,000. *Unit head:* Dr. Robert T. Allen, Director, 918-561-1108, Fax: 918-561-8414. *Application contact:* Cathy Newsome, Coordinator, 918-561-1108, Fax: 918-561-8414, E-mail: cathy.newsome@okstate.edu.

Oregon Health & Science University, School of Medicine, Graduate Programs in Medicine, Department of Environmental and Biomolecular Systems, Portland, OR 97239-3098. Offers biochemistry and molecular biology (MS, PhD); environmental science and engineering (MS, PhD). Part-time programs available. *Faculty:* 14 full-time (4 women), 1 (woman) part-time/adjunct. *Students:* 28 full-time (20 women), 5 part-time (3 women); includes 11 minority (1 Black or African American, non-Hispanic/Latino; 3 American Indian or Alaska Native, non-Hispanic/Latino; 2 Asian, non-Hispanic/Latino; 4 Hispanic/Latino; 1 Two or more races, non-Hispanic/Latino), 5 international. Average age 30. 36 applicants, 25% accepted, 5 enrolled. In 2011, 9 master's, 2 doctorates awarded. Terminal master's awarded for partial completion of doctoral program. *Degree requirements:* For master's, thesis (for some programs); for doctorate, comprehensive exam, thesis/dissertation, qualifying exam. *Entrance requirements:* For master's and doctorate, GRE General Test (minimum scores: 500 Verbal/600 Quantitative/4.5 Analytical) or MCAT (for some programs). Additional exam requirements/recommendations for international students: Required—TOEFL. *Application deadline:* For fall admission, 7/15 for domestic students, 5/15 for international students; for winter admission, 10/15 for domestic students, 9/15 for international students; for spring admission, 1/15 for domestic students, 12/15 for international students. Applications are processed on a rolling basis. Application fee: $70. Electronic applications accepted. *Financial support:* Health care benefits and full tuition and stipends for PhD students available. *Unit head:* Dr. Paul Tratnyek, Program Director, 503-748-1070, E-mail: info@ebs.ogi.edu. *Application contact:* Nancy Christie, Program Coordinator, 503-748-1070, E-mail: info@ebs.ogi.edu.

Oregon Health & Science University, School of Medicine, Graduate Programs in Medicine, Program in Molecular and Cellular Biosciences, Department of Biochemistry and Molecular Biology, Portland, OR 97239-3098. Offers PhD. *Faculty:* 13 full-time (4 women), 1 part-time/adjunct (0 women). *Students:* 14 full-time (6 women), 3 international. Average age 30. In 2011, 1 doctorate awarded. *Degree requirements:* For doctorate, comprehensive exam, thesis/dissertation, qualifying exam. *Entrance requirements:* For doctorate, GRE General Test (minimum scores: 153 Verbal/148 Quantitative/4.5 Analytical). Additional exam requirements/recommendations for international students: Required—TOEFL. Electronic applications accepted. *Financial support:* Health care benefits, tuition waivers (full), and full tuition and stipends available. *Faculty research:* Protein structure, membrane proteins, metabolic regulation, molecular basis of disease, signal transduction mechanisms. *Unit head:* Dr. David Farrens, Program Director, 503-494-7781, E-mail: farrensd@ohsu.edu. *Application contact:* Jeni Wroblewski, Administrative Coordinator, 503-494-2541, E-mail: wroblews@ohsu.edu. Web site: http://www.ohsu.edu/som-biochem/.

Oregon State University, Graduate School, Program in Molecular and Cellular Biology, Corvallis, OR 97331. Offers MS, PhD. *Degree requirements:* For doctorate, thesis/dissertation, oral and written qualifying exams. *Entrance requirements:* For doctorate,

minimum GPA of 3.0 in last 90 hours. Additional exam requirements/recommendations for international students: Required—TOEFL.

Penn State Hershey Medical Center, College of Medicine, Graduate School Programs in the Biomedical Sciences, Graduate Program in Microbiology and Immunology, Hershey, PA 17033. Offers genetics (PhD); immunology (MS, PhD); microbiology (MS); microbiology/virology (PhD); molecular biology (PhD); MD/PhD. *Students:* 18 full-time (9 women), 6 international. 59 applicants, 5% accepted, 3 enrolled. In 2011, 1 master's, 3 doctorates awarded. Terminal master's awarded for partial completion of doctoral program. *Degree requirements:* For master's, thesis or alternative; for doctorate, comprehensive exam, thesis/dissertation, oral exam. *Entrance requirements:* For doctorate, GRE General Test, minimum GPA of 3.0. Additional exam requirements/recommendations for international students: Required—TOEFL. *Application deadline:* For fall admission, 1/31 priority date for domestic students, 2/1 for international students. Applications are processed on a rolling basis. Application fee: $65. Electronic applications accepted. *Financial support:* In 2011–12, research assistantships with full tuition reimbursements (averaging $23,028 per year) were awarded; fellowships with full tuition reimbursements, scholarships/grants, health care benefits, and unspecified assistantships also available. Financial award applicants required to submit FAFSA. *Faculty research:* Virus replication and assembly, oncogenesis, interactions of viruses with host cells and animal model systems. *Unit head:* Dr. Aron Luckacher, Chair, 717-531-7659, Fax: 717-531-6522, E-mail: micro-grad-hmc@psu.edu. *Application contact:* Billie Burns, Secretary, 717-531-7659, Fax: 717-531-6522, E-mail: micro-grad-hmc@psu.edu. Web site: http://www.pennstatehershey.org/web/microbiology/programs.

Penn State University Park, Graduate School, Eberly College of Science, Department of Biochemistry and Molecular Biology, State College, University Park, PA 16802-1503. Offers biochemistry, microbiology, and molecular biology (MS, PhD); biotechnology (MBIOT). *Unit head:* Dr. Richard J. Frisque, Head, 814-863-1851, E-mail: rjf6@psu.edu. *Application contact:* Dr. Ronald Porter, Director of Graduate Studies, 814-863-4903, E-mail: rdp1@psu.edu. Web site: http://bmb.psu.edu.

Princeton University, Graduate School, Department of Molecular Biology, Princeton, NJ 08544-1019. Offers PhD. *Degree requirements:* For doctorate, thesis/dissertation. *Entrance requirements:* For doctorate, GRE General Test. Additional exam requirements/recommendations for international students: Required—TOEFL (minimum score 600 paper-based; 250 computer-based). Electronic applications accepted. *Faculty research:* Genetics, virology, biochemistry.

Purdue University, College of Pharmacy and Pharmacal Sciences and Graduate School, Graduate Programs in Pharmacy and Pharmacal Sciences, Department of Medicinal Chemistry and Molecular Pharmacology, West Lafayette, IN 47907. Offers biophysical and computational chemistry (PhD); cancer research (PhD); immunology and infectious disease (PhD); medicinal biochemistry and molecular biology (PhD); medicinal chemistry and chemical biology (PhD); molecular pharmacology (PhD); neuropharmacology, neurodegeneration, and neurotoxicity (PhD); systems biology and functional genomics (PhD). *Faculty:* 22 full-time (2 women), 4 part-time/adjunct (1 woman). *Students:* 49 full-time (18 women); includes 3 minority (1 Asian, non-Hispanic/Latino; 2 Hispanic/Latino), 26 international. Average age 27. 250 applicants, 12% accepted, 9 enrolled. In 2011, 10 doctorates awarded. *Degree requirements:* For doctorate, thesis/dissertation. *Entrance requirements:* For doctorate, GRE General Test; GRE Subject Test in biology, biochemistry, and chemistry (recommended), minimum undergraduate GPA of 3.0. Additional exam requirements/recommendations for international students: Required—TOEFL (minimum score 550 paper-based; 77 iBT); Recommended—TWE. *Application deadline:* For fall admission, 2/1 for domestic and international students. Applications are processed on a rolling basis. Application fee: $60 ($75 for international students). Electronic applications accepted. *Financial support:* Fellowships, research assistantships, teaching assistantships, and traineeships available. Support available to part-time students. Financial award applicants required to submit FAFSA. *Faculty research:* Drug design and development, cancer research, drug synthesis and analysis, chemical pharmacology, environmental toxicology. *Unit head:* Dr. Richard F. Borch, Head, 765-494-1403, E-mail: borch@purdue.edu. *Application contact:* Janine C. Mott, Graduate Contact, 765-494-1269, E-mail: jmott@purdue.edu.

Purdue University, Graduate School, College of Science, Department of Biological Sciences, West Lafayette, IN 47907. Offers biochemistry (PhD); biophysics (PhD); cell and developmental biology (PhD); ecology, evolutionary and population biology (MS, PhD), including ecology, evolutionary biology, population biology; genetics (MS, PhD); microbiology (MS, PhD); molecular biology (PhD); neurobiology (MS, PhD); plant physiology (PhD). *Faculty:* 57 full-time (15 women), 4 part-time/adjunct (1 woman). *Students:* 94 full-time (54 women), 9 part-time (5 women); includes 7 minority (2 Black or African American, non-Hispanic/Latino; 3 Asian, non-Hispanic/Latino; 2 Hispanic/Latino), 51 international. Average age 27. 246 applicants, 11% accepted, 18 enrolled. In 2011, 9 master's, 23 doctorates awarded. Terminal master's awarded for partial completion of doctoral program. *Degree requirements:* For master's, thesis (for some programs); for doctorate, thesis/dissertation, seminars, teaching experience. *Entrance requirements:* For master's, GRE General Test, minimum analytical writing score of 3.5, minimum undergraduate GPA of 3.0; for doctorate, GRE General Test, minimum analytical writing score of 3.5, minimum undergraduate GPA of 3.5. Additional exam requirements/recommendations for international students: Required—TOEFL (minimum score 600 paper-based; 107 iBT) for MS; TOEFL (minimum score 600 paper-based; 80 iBT) for Ph D. *Application deadline:* For fall admission, 12/7 for domestic and international students. Applications are processed on a rolling basis. Application fee: $60 ($75 for international students). Electronic applications accepted. *Financial support:* Fellowships, research assistantships, and teaching assistantships available. Support available to part-time students. Financial award application deadline: 2/15; financial award applicants required to submit FAFSA. *Unit head:* Dr. Richard J. Kuhn, Head, 765-494-4407, E-mail: kuhnr@purdue.edu. *Application contact:* Georgina E. Rupp, Graduate Coordinator, 765-494-8142, Fax: 765-494-0876, E-mail: ruppg@purdue.edu. Web site: http://www.bio.purdue.edu/.

Purdue University, Graduate School, PULSe - Purdue University Life Sciences Program, West Lafayette, IN 47907. Offers biomolecular structure and biophysics (PhD); biotechnology (PhD); chemical biology (PhD); chromatin and regulation of gene expression (PhD); integrative neuroscience (PhD); integrative plant sciences (PhD); membrane biology (PhD); microbiology (PhD); molecular evolutionary and cancer biology (PhD); molecular evolutionary genetics (PhD); molecular virology (PhD). *Students:* 90 full-time (45 women); includes 7 minority (3 Black or African American, non-Hispanic/Latino; 1 Asian, non-Hispanic/Latino; 2 Hispanic/Latino; 1 Two or more races, non-Hispanic/Latino), 40 international. Average age 26. 427 applicants, 24% accepted, 35 enrolled. *Entrance requirements:* For doctorate, GRE test required, minimum undergraduate GPA of 3.0. Additional exam requirements/recommendations for international students: Required—TOEFL (minimum score 550 paper-based; 77 iBT). *Application deadline:* For fall admission, 1/15 priority date for domestic students, 1/15 for international students. Applications are processed on a rolling basis. Application fee: $60 ($75 for international students). Electronic applications accepted. *Financial support:* In 2011–12, research assistantships with tuition reimbursements (averaging $22,500 per year), teaching assistantships with tuition reimbursements (averaging $22,500 per year) were awarded. *Unit head:* Dr. Christine A. Hrycyna, Head, 765-494-7322, E-mail:

hrycyna@purdue.edu. *Application contact:* Emily E. Bramson, Graduate Contact, 765-494-5865, E-mail: bramson@purdue.edu. Web site: http://www.gradschool.purdue.edu/pulse.

Queen's University at Kingston, School of Graduate Studies and Research, Faculty of Health Sciences, Department of Anatomy and Cell Biology, Kingston, ON K7L 3N6, Canada. Offers biology of reproduction (M Sc, PhD); cancer (M Sc, PhD); cardiovascular pathophysiology (M Sc, PhD); cell and molecular biology (M Sc, PhD); drug metabolism (M Sc, PhD); endocrinology (M Sc, PhD); motor control (M Sc, PhD); neural regeneration (M Sc, PhD); neurophysiology (M Sc, PhD). Part-time programs available. *Degree requirements:* For master's, thesis; for doctorate, one foreign language, comprehensive exam, thesis/dissertation. *Entrance requirements:* Additional exam requirements/recommendations for international students: Required—TOEFL. Electronic applications accepted. *Faculty research:* Human kinetics, neuroscience, reproductive biology, cardiovascular.

Quinnipiac University, School of Health Sciences, Program in Molecular and Cell Biology, Hamden, CT 06518-1940. Offers MS. Part-time programs available. *Faculty:* 9 full-time (6 women), 17 part-time/adjunct (7 women). *Students:* 22 (18 women); includes 4 minority (2 Black or African American, non-Hispanic/Latino; 1 Asian, non-Hispanic/Latino; 1 Hispanic/Latino), 4 international. Average age 26. 44 applicants, 68% accepted, 18 enrolled. In 2011, 12 master's awarded. *Degree requirements:* For master's, thesis optional. *Entrance requirements:* For master's, bachelor's degree in biological, medical, or health sciences; minimum GPA of 2.75. Additional exam requirements/recommendations for international students: Required—TOEFL (minimum score 575 paper-based; 233 computer-based; 90 iBT), IELTS (minimum score 6.5). *Application deadline:* For fall admission, 7/30 priority date for domestic students, 4/30 for international students; for spring admission, 12/15 priority date for domestic students, 9/15 for international students. Applications are processed on a rolling basis. Application fee: $45. Electronic applications accepted. *Expenses: Tuition:* Part-time $855 per credit. *Required fees:* $35 per credit. *Financial support:* In 2011–12, 6 students received support. Federal Work-Study, tuition waivers, and unspecified assistantships available. Support available to part-time students. Financial award application deadline: 4/15; financial award applicants required to submit FAFSA. *Unit head:* Dr. Sarah Berke, Director, 203-582-6431, E-mail: sarah.berke@quinnipiac.edu. *Application contact:* Kristin Parent, Assistant Director of Graduate Health Sciences Admissions, 800-462-1944, Fax: 203-582-3443, E-mail: kristin.parent@quinnipiac.edu. Web site: http://www.quinnipiac.edu/gradmolecular.

Rosalind Franklin University of Medicine and Science, School of Graduate and Postdoctoral Studies - Interdisciplinary Graduate Program in Biomedical Sciences, Department of Biochemistry and Molecular Biology, North Chicago, IL 60064-3095. Offers MS, PhD, MD/PhD. Terminal master's awarded for partial completion of doctoral program. *Degree requirements:* For master's, comprehensive exam, thesis; for doctorate, comprehensive exam, thesis/dissertation. *Entrance requirements:* For master's and doctorate, GRE General Test, minimum GPA of 3.0. Additional exam requirements/recommendations for international students: Required—TOEFL, TWE. Electronic applications accepted. *Faculty research:* Structure of control enzymes, extracellular matrix, glucose metabolism, gene expression, ATP synthesis.

Rutgers, The State University of New Jersey, New Brunswick, Graduate School-New Brunswick, Programs in the Molecular Biosciences, Piscataway, NJ 08854-8097. Offers biochemistry (PhD); cell and developmental biology (MS, PhD); microbiology and molecular genetics (MS, PhD), including applied microbiology, clinical microbiology (MS), clinical mircobiology (PhD), computational molecular biology (PhD), immunology, microbial biochemistry, molecular genetics, virology. MS, PhD offered jointly with University of Medicine and Dentistry of New Jersey.

Saint Louis University, Graduate Education and School of Medicine, Graduate Program in Biomedical Sciences and Graduate Education, Department of Biochemistry and Molecular Biology, St. Louis, MO 63103-2097. Offers PhD. *Degree requirements:* For doctorate, comprehensive exam, thesis/dissertation, departmental qualifying exams. *Entrance requirements:* For doctorate, GRE General Test, GRE Subject Test (optional), letters of recommendation, resume, interview. Additional exam requirements/recommendations for international students: Required—TOEFL (minimum score 525 paper-based; 194 computer-based). Electronic applications accepted. *Faculty research:* Transcription, chromatin modification and regulation of gene expression; structure/function of proteins and enzymes, including x-ray crystallography; inflammatory mediators in pathenogenesis of diabetes and arteriosclerosis; cellular signaling in response to growth factors, opiates and angiogenic mediators; genomics and proteomics of Cryptococcus neoformans.

San Diego State University, Graduate and Research Affairs, College of Sciences, Department of Biology, San Diego, CA 92182. Offers biology (MA, MS), including ecology (MS), molecular biology (MS), physiology (MS), systematics/evolution (MS); cell and molecular biology (PhD); ecology (MS, PhD); microbiology (MS). Terminal master's awarded for partial completion of doctoral program. *Degree requirements:* For master's, thesis; for doctorate, thesis/dissertation. *Entrance requirements:* For master's, GRE General Test, GRE Subject Test, resume or curriculum vitae, 2 letters of recommendation. Additional exam requirements/recommendations for international students: Required—TOEFL. Electronic applications accepted.

San Diego State University, Graduate and Research Affairs, College of Sciences, Molecular Biology Institute, Program in Cell and Molecular Biology, San Diego, CA 92182. Offers PhD. Program offered jointly with University of California, San Diego. *Degree requirements:* For doctorate, thesis/dissertation, oral comprehensive qualifying exam. *Entrance requirements:* For doctorate, GRE General Test, GRE Subject Test, resumé or curriculum vitae, 3 letters of recommendation. Electronic applications accepted. *Faculty research:* Structure/dynamics of protein kinesis, chromatin structure and DNA methylation membrane biochemistry, secretory protein targeting, molecular biology of cardiac myocytes.

San Francisco State University, Division of Graduate Studies, College of Science and Engineering, Department of Biology, Program in Cell and Molecular Biology, San Francisco, CA 94132-1722. Offers MS. *Application deadline:* Applications are processed on a rolling basis. *Unit head:* Dr. Diana Chu, Program Coordinator, 415-405-3487, E-mail: chud@sfsu.edu. *Application contact:* Dr. Robert Patterson, Graduate Coordinator, 415-338-1100, E-mail: patters@sfsu.edu. Web site: http://biology.sfsu.edu/programs/graduate.

San Jose State University, Graduate Studies and Research, College of Science, Department of Biological Sciences, San Jose, CA 95192-0001. Offers biological sciences (MA, MS); molecular biology and microbiology (MS); organismal biology, conservation and ecology (MS); physiology (MS). Part-time programs available. *Entrance requirements:* For master's, GRE. Electronic applications accepted. *Faculty research:* Systemic physiology, molecular genetics, SEM studies, toxicology, large mammal ecology.

Seton Hall University, College of Arts and Sciences, Department of Biological Sciences, South Orange, NJ 07079-2697. Offers biology (MS); biology/business administration (MS); microbiology (MS); molecular bioscience (PhD); molecular bioscience/neuroscience (PhD). Part-time and evening/weekend programs available. *Degree requirements:* For master's, thesis optional; for doctorate, comprehensive exam, thesis/dissertation. *Entrance requirements:* For master's and doctorate, GRE or MS from accredited university in the U.S.. Additional exam requirements/recommendations for international students: Required—TOEFL. Electronic applications accepted. *Expenses: Tuition:* Part-time $1033 per credit hour. *Required fees:* $85 per semester. *Faculty research:* Neurobiology, genetics, immunology, molecular biology, cellular physiology, toxicology, microbiology, bioinformatics.

Simon Fraser University, Graduate Studies, Faculty of Science, Department of Molecular Biology and Biochemistry, Burnaby, BC V5A 1S6, Canada. Offers M Sc, PhD. *Degree requirements:* For master's, thesis; for doctorate, thesis/dissertation. *Entrance requirements:* For master's, minimum GPA of 3.0; for doctorate, minimum GPA of 3.5. Additional exam requirements/recommendations for international students: Required—TWE or IELTS. *Faculty research:* Molecular genetics and development, biochemistry, molecular physiology, genomics, molecular phylogenetics and population genetics, bioinformation.

Southern Illinois University Carbondale, Graduate School, College of Science, Program in Molecular Biology, Microbiology, and Biochemistry, Carbondale, IL 62901-4701. Offers MS, PhD. *Faculty:* 16 full-time (2 women). *Students:* 52 full-time (27 women), 42 part-time (25 women); includes 10 minority (5 Black or African American, non-Hispanic/Latino; 5 Asian, non-Hispanic/Latino), 64 international. Average age 25. 139 applicants, 12% accepted, 12 enrolled. In 2011, 14 master's, 8 doctorates awarded. *Degree requirements:* For master's, thesis; for doctorate, thesis/dissertation. *Entrance requirements:* For master's, GRE, minimum GPA of 2.7; for doctorate, GRE, minimum GPA of 3.25. Additional exam requirements/recommendations for international students: Required—TOEFL. *Application deadline:* Applications are processed on a rolling basis. Application fee: $20. *Financial support:* In 2011–12, 40 students received support, including 3 fellowships with full tuition reimbursements available, 24 research assistantships with full tuition reimbursements available, 12 teaching assistantships with full tuition reimbursements available; Federal Work-Study and institutionally sponsored loans also available. Support available to part-time students. Financial award application deadline: 3/1. *Faculty research:* Prokaryotic gene regulation and expression; eukaryotic gene regulation; microbial, phylogenetic, and metabolic diversity; immune responses to tumors, pathogens, and autoantigens; protein folding and structure. *Unit head:* Dr. John Martinko, Director, 618-453-8116, Fax: 618-453-8036, E-mail: martinko.mbmb@science.siu.edu. *Application contact:* Charlotte Keller, Office Systems Specialist, 618-453-7071, Fax: 618-453-8036, E-mail: ckeller@siumed.edu. Web site: http://mbmb.siu.edu/.

State University of New York Downstate Medical Center, School of Graduate Studies, Program in Molecular and Cellular Biology, Brooklyn, NY 11203-2098. Offers PhD, MD/PhD. Affiliation with a particular PhD degree-granting program is deferred to the second year. *Degree requirements:* For doctorate, comprehensive exam, thesis/dissertation. *Entrance requirements:* For doctorate, GRE General Test. Additional exam requirements/recommendations for international students: Recommended—TOEFL. *Faculty research:* Mechanism of gene regulation, molecular virology.

State University of New York Upstate Medical University, College of Graduate Studies, Program in Biochemistry and Molecular Biology, Syracuse, NY 13210-2334. Offers biochemistry (MS); biochemistry and molecular biology (PhD); MD/PhD. Terminal master's awarded for partial completion of doctoral program. *Degree requirements:* For master's, thesis; for doctorate, comprehensive exam, thesis/dissertation. *Entrance requirements:* For master's, GRE General Test, interview; for doctorate, GRE General Test, telephone interview. Additional exam requirements/recommendations for international students: Required—TOEFL. Electronic applications accepted. *Faculty research:* Enzymology, membrane structure and functions, developmental biochemistry.

Stony Brook University, State University of New York, Graduate School, College of Arts and Sciences, Department of Biochemistry and Cell Biology, Molecular and Cellular Biology Program, Stony Brook, NY 11794. Offers biochemistry and molecular biology (PhD); biological sciences (MA); cellular and developmental biology (PhD); immunology and pathology (PhD); molecular and cellular biology (PhD). *Degree requirements:* For doctorate, comprehensive exam, thesis/dissertation, teaching experience. *Entrance requirements:* For doctorate, GRE General Test, GRE Subject Test. Additional exam requirements/recommendations for international students: Required—TOEFL.

Temple University, Health Sciences Center, School of Medicine and Graduate School, Graduate Programs in Medicine, Program in Molecular Biology and Genetics, Philadelphia, PA 19122-6096. Offers MS, PhD, MD/PhD. *Students:* 21 full-time (11 women); includes 1 minority (Asian, non-Hispanic/Latino), 11 international. Average age 27. 7 applicants, 86% accepted, 4 enrolled. In 2011, 2 master's, 2 doctorates awarded. *Degree requirements:* For doctorate, thesis/dissertation, presentation research/literature seminars distinct from area of concentration. *Entrance requirements:* For doctorate, GRE General Test, GRE Subject Test, minimum GPA of 3.0. Additional exam requirements/recommendations for international students: Required—TOEFL (minimum score 620 paper-based; 260 computer-based). *Application deadline:* For fall admission, 1/15 for domestic students, 12/15 for international students. Application fee: $50. Electronic applications accepted. *Expenses:* Tuition, state resident: full-time $12,366; part-time $687 per credit hour. Tuition, nonresident: full-time $17,298; part-time $961 per credit hour. *Required fees:* $590; $213 per year. *Financial support:* Fellowships, research assistantships, Federal Work-Study, institutionally sponsored loans, and tuition waivers (full) available. Financial award application deadline: 1/15; financial award applicants required to submit FAFSA. *Faculty research:* Molecular genetics of normal and malignant cell growth, regulation of gene expression, DNA repair systems and carcinogenesis, hormone-receptor interactions and signal transduction systems, structural biology. *Unit head:* Dr. Scott Shore, Chair, 215-707-3359, Fax: 215-707-2805, E-mail: sks@temple.edu. *Application contact:* Office of Admissions, 215-707-3656, Fax: 215-707-6932, E-mail: medadmissions@temple.edu.

Texas A&M Health Science Center, College of Medicine, Department of Microbial and Molecular Pathogenesis, College Station, TX 77840. Offers immunology (PhD); microbiology (PhD); molecular biology (PhD); virology (PhD). *Degree requirements:* For doctorate, thesis/dissertation. *Entrance requirements:* For doctorate, GRE General Test, minimum GPA of 3.0. *Faculty research:* Molecular pathogenesis, microbial therapeutics.

Texas A&M Health Science Center, College of Medicine, Program in Cell and Molecular Biology, College Station, TX 77840. Offers PhD.

Texas Woman's University, Graduate School, College of Arts and Sciences, Department of Biology, Denton, TX 76201. Offers biology (MS); molecular biology (PhD). Part-time programs available. *Faculty:* 14 full-time (10 women). *Students:* 26 full-time (18 women), 20 part-time (14 women); includes 8 minority (5 Black or African American, non-Hispanic/Latino; 1 Asian, non-Hispanic/Latino; 2 Hispanic/Latino), 28 international. Average age 30. 30 applicants, 73% accepted, 8 enrolled. In 2011, 1 master's, 2 doctorates awarded. Terminal master's awarded for partial completion of doctoral program. *Degree requirements:* For master's, comprehensive exam, thesis; for doctorate, comprehensive exam, thesis/dissertation, residency. *Entrance requirements:* For master's, GRE General Test (preferred minimum score 149 [425 old version] verbal, 141 [425 old version] quantitative), 3 letters of reference; letter of interest; for doctorate, GRE General Test (preferred minimum score 153 [500 old version] verbal, 144 [500 old

version] quantitative), 3 letters of reference, letter of interest. Additional exam requirements/recommendations for international students: Required—TOEFL (minimum score 550 paper-based; 213 computer-based; 79 iBT). *Application deadline:* For fall admission, 2/1 priority date for domestic students, 2/1 for international students. Applications are processed on a rolling basis. Application fee: $50 ($75 for international students). Electronic applications accepted. *Expenses:* Tuition, state resident: full-time $3834; part-time $213 per credit hour. Tuition, nonresident: full-time $9468; part-time $526 per credit hour. *Required fees:* $213 per credit hour. Tuition and fees vary according to course load. *Financial support:* In 2011–12, 7 students received support, including 51 research assistantships (averaging $14,418 per year); career-related internships or fieldwork, Federal Work-Study, institutionally sponsored loans, scholarships/grants, traineeships, health care benefits, and unspecified assistantships also available. Support available to part-time students. Financial award application deadline: 3/1; financial award applicants required to submit FAFSA. *Faculty research:* Computational biology, protein-protein Interactions, chromatin structure and regulation, regulation of RNA synthesis, virus-host interactions, regulation of axon growth and guidance in neurons, estrogen compounds in plants, regulation of gene expression in male reproductive tissues, female gonadal hormones in the development of anxiety and depression, electron microscopy. *Total annual research expenditures:* $407,203. *Unit head:* Dr. Sarah McIntire, Chair, 940-898-2352, Fax: 940-898-2382, E-mail: smcintire@twu.edu. *Application contact:* Dr. Samuel Wheeler, Assistant Director of Admissions, 940-898-3188, Fax: 940-898-3081, E-mail: wheelersr@twu.edu. Web site: http://www.twu.edu/biology.

Thomas Jefferson University, Jefferson College of Graduate Studies, PhD Program in Biochemistry and Molecular Biology, Philadelphia, PA 19107. Offers PhD. *Faculty:* 48 full-time (15 women), 1 (woman) part-time/adjunct. *Students:* 17 full-time (11 women); includes 2 minority (both Asian, non-Hispanic/Latino), 3 international. Average age 24. 40 applicants, 20% accepted, 3 enrolled. In 2011, 4 doctorates awarded. *Degree requirements:* For doctorate, comprehensive exam, thesis/dissertation. *Entrance requirements:* For doctorate, GRE General Test or MCAT, minimum GPA of 3.2. Additional exam requirements/recommendations for international students: Required—TOEFL (minimum score 250 computer-based; 100 iBT) or IELTS. *Application deadline:* For fall admission, 1/2 priority date for domestic students, 1/2 for international students. Applications are processed on a rolling basis. Application fee: $50. Electronic applications accepted. *Financial support:* In 2011–12, 17 students received support, including 17 fellowships with full tuition reimbursements available (averaging $54,758 per year); Federal Work-Study, institutionally sponsored loans, scholarships/grants, traineeships, and stipends also available. Financial award application deadline: 5/1; financial award applicants required to submit FAFSA. *Faculty research:* Signal transduction and molecular genetics, translational biochemistry, human mitochondrial genetics, molecular biology of protein-RNA interaction, mammalian mitochondrial biogenesis and function. *Total annual research expenditures:* $26.8 million. *Unit head:* Dr. Diane E. Merry, Program Director, 215-503-4907, Fax: 215-923-9162, E-mail: diane.merry@jefferson.edu. *Application contact:* Marc E. Stearns, Director of Admissions, 215-503-0155, Fax: 215-503-9920, E-mail: jcgs-info@jefferson.edu. Web site: http://www.jefferson.edu/jcgs/phd/bmb/.

Tufts University, Sackler School of Graduate Biomedical Sciences, Cell, Molecular and Developmental Biology Program, Medford, MA 02155. Offers PhD. *Faculty:* 39 full-time (15 women). *Students:* 26 full-time (12 women); includes 5 minority (3 Asian, non-Hispanic/Latino; 1 Hispanic/Latino; 1 Two or more races, non-Hispanic/Latino), 4 international. Average age 29. In 2011, 8 doctorates awarded. Terminal master's awarded for partial completion of doctoral program. *Degree requirements:* For doctorate, thesis/dissertation. *Entrance requirements:* For doctorate, GRE General Test, 3 letters of reference. Additional exam requirements/recommendations for international students: Required—TOEFL (minimum score 600 paper-based; 250 computer-based; 100 iBT). *Application deadline:* For fall admission, 12/15 for domestic and international students. Application fee: $70. Electronic applications accepted. *Expenses: Tuition:* Full-time $41,208; part-time $1030 per credit hour. Full-time tuition and fees vary according to degree level, program and student level. Part-time tuition and fees vary according to course load. *Financial support:* In 2011–12, 25 students received support, including 25 research assistantships with full tuition reimbursements available (averaging $30,000 per year); fellowships and health care benefits also available. *Faculty research:* Reproduction and hormone action, control of gene expression, cell-matrix and cell-cell interactions, growth control and tumorigenesis, cytoskeleton and contractile proteins. *Unit head:* Dr. John Castellot, Program Director, 617-636-0303, Fax: 617-636-0375. *Application contact:* Kellie Johnston, Associate Director of Admissions, 617-636-6767, Fax: 617-636-0375, E-mail: sackler-school@tufts.edu. Web site: http://sackler.tufts.edu/Academics/Degree-Programs/PhD-Programs/Cell-Molecular-and-Developmental-Biology.

Tufts University, Sackler School of Graduate Biomedical Sciences, Molecular Microbiology Program, Medford, MA 02155. Offers PhD. *Faculty:* 15 full-time (6 women). *Students:* 29 full-time (23 women); includes 5 minority (2 Asian, non-Hispanic/Latino; 1 Hispanic/Latino; 2 Two or more races, non-Hispanic/Latino), 1 international. Average age 26. 98 applicants, 15% accepted, 5 enrolled. In 2011, 9 doctorates awarded. Terminal master's awarded for partial completion of doctoral program. *Degree requirements:* For doctorate, thesis/dissertation. *Entrance requirements:* For doctorate, GRE General Test, 3 letters of reference. Additional exam requirements/recommendations for international students: Required—TOEFL (minimum score 600 paper-based; 250 computer-based; 100 iBT). *Application deadline:* For fall admission, 12/15 for domestic and international students. Application fee: $70. Electronic applications accepted. *Expenses: Tuition:* Full-time $41,208; part-time $1030 per credit hour. Full-time tuition and fees vary according to degree level, program and student level. Part-time tuition and fees vary according to course load. *Financial support:* In 2011–12, 29 students received support, including 29 research assistantships with full tuition reimbursements available (averaging $30,000 per year); traineeships and health care benefits also available. Financial award application deadline: 12/15. *Faculty research:* Mechanisms of gene regulation, interactions of microorganisms and viruses with host cells, infection response. *Unit head:* Dr. Michael Malamy, Director, 617-636-6750, Fax: 617-636-0337, E-mail: michael.malamy@tufts.edu. *Application contact:* Kellie Melchin, Associate Director of Admissions, 617-636-6767, Fax: 617-636-0375, E-mail: sackler-school@tufts.edu. Web site: http://sackler.tufts.edu/Academics/Degree-Programs/PhD-Programs/Molecular-Microbiology.

Tulane University, School of Medicine and School of Liberal Arts, Graduate Programs in Biomedical Sciences, Interdisciplinary Graduate Program in Molecular and Cellular Biology, New Orleans, LA 70118-5669. Offers PhD, MD/PhD. PhD offered through the Graduate School. *Degree requirements:* For doctorate, thesis/dissertation. *Entrance requirements:* For doctorate, GRE General Test, GRE Subject Test. Additional exam requirements/recommendations for international students: Required—TOEFL. Electronic applications accepted. *Faculty research:* Developmental biology, neuroscience, virology.

Tulane University, School of Science and Engineering, Department of Cell and Molecular Biology, New Orleans, LA 70118-5669. Offers MS, PhD. Terminal master's awarded for partial completion of doctoral program. *Degree requirements:* For doctorate, thesis/dissertation. *Entrance requirements:* For master's, GRE General Test, minimum B average in undergraduate course work; for doctorate, GRE General Test. Additional exam requirements/recommendations for international students: Required—TOEFL. Electronic applications accepted.

Uniformed Services University of the Health Sciences, School of Medicine, Graduate Programs in the Biomedical Sciences and Public Health, Graduate Program in Molecular and Cell Biology, Bethesda, MD 20814-4799. Offers MS, PhD. *Faculty:* 43 full-time (11 women), 3 part-time/adjunct (0 women). *Students:* 22 full-time (11 women); includes 10 minority (5 Asian, non-Hispanic/Latino; 5 Hispanic/Latino), 6 international. Average age 26. 30 applicants, 43% accepted, 8 enrolled. In 2011, 2 doctorates awarded. *Degree requirements:* For doctorate, comprehensive exam, thesis/dissertation, qualifying exam. *Entrance requirements:* For doctorate, GRE General Test, minimum GPA of 3.0. Additional exam requirements/recommendations for international students: Required—TOEFL. *Application deadline:* For fall admission, 1/1 priority date for domestic students, 1/1 for international students. Applications are processed on a rolling basis. Application fee: $0. Electronic applications accepted. *Financial support:* In 2011–12, fellowships with full tuition reimbursements (averaging $27,000 per year) were awarded; scholarships/grants, health care benefits, and tuition waivers (full) also available. *Faculty research:* Immunology, biochemistry, cancer biology, stem cell biology. *Unit head:* Dr. Mary Lou Cutler, Director, 301-295-3248, Fax: 301-295-1996. *Application contact:* Tina Finley, Administrative Assistant, 301-295-3642, Fax: 301-295-1996, E-mail: nfinley@usuhs.mil. Web site: http://www.usuhs.mil/mcb/index.html.

See Display on next page and Close-Up on page 237.

Universidad Central del Caribe, School of Medicine, Program in Biomedical Sciences, Bayamón, PR 00960-6032. Offers anatomy and cell biology (MA, MS); biochemistry (MS); biomedical sciences (MA); cellular and molecular biology (PhD); microbiology and immunology (MA, MS); pharmacology (MS); physiology (MS).

Université de Montréal, Faculty of Medicine, Program in Molecular Biology, Montréal, QC H3C 3J7, Canada. Offers M Sc, PhD. Terminal master's awarded for partial completion of doctoral program. *Degree requirements:* For master's, thesis; for doctorate, thesis/dissertation, general exam. *Entrance requirements:* For master's and doctorate, proficiency in French, knowledge of English. Electronic applications accepted. *Faculty research:* Protein interactions, intracellular signaling, development and differentiation, hematopoiesis, stem cells.

Université Laval, Faculty of Medicine, Graduate Programs in Medicine, Programs in Cellular and Molecular Biology, Québec, QC G1K 7P4, Canada. Offers M Sc, PhD. Terminal master's awarded for partial completion of doctoral program. *Degree requirements:* For master's, thesis; for doctorate, comprehensive exam, thesis/dissertation. *Entrance requirements:* For master's and doctorate, knowledge of French, comprehension of written English. Electronic applications accepted. *Faculty research:* Oral bacterial metabolism, sugar transport.

University at Albany, State University of New York, College of Arts and Sciences, Department of Biological Sciences, Specialization in Molecular, Cellular, Developmental, and Neural Biology, Albany, NY 12222-0001. Offers MS, PhD. *Degree requirements:* For master's, one foreign language; for doctorate, one foreign language, thesis/dissertation. *Entrance requirements:* For master's and doctorate, GRE General Test.

University at Albany, State University of New York, School of Public Health, Department of Biomedical Sciences, Program in Biochemistry, Molecular Biology, and Genetics, Albany, NY 12222-0001. Offers MS, PhD. *Degree requirements:* For master's, thesis; for doctorate, thesis/dissertation. *Entrance requirements:* For master's and doctorate, GRE General Test, GRE Subject Test.

University at Buffalo, the State University of New York, Graduate School, Graduate Programs in Cancer Research and Biomedical Sciences at Roswell Park Cancer Institute, Department of Cellular and Molecular Biology at Roswell Park Cancer Institute, Buffalo, NY 14260. Offers PhD. *Degree requirements:* For doctorate, thesis/dissertation, exam, project. *Entrance requirements:* For doctorate, GRE General Test, minimum B average in undergraduate coursework. Additional exam requirements/recommendations for international students: Required—TOEFL (minimum score 600 paper-based; 250 computer-based; 100 iBT) or IELTS. Electronic applications accepted. *Faculty research:* Cancer genetics, chromatin structure and replication, regulation of transcription, human gene mapping, genetic and structural approaches to regulation of gene expression.

The University of Alabama at Birmingham, Graduate Programs in Joint Health Sciences, Program in Cellular and Molecular Physiology, Birmingham, AL 35294. Offers PhD. Application fee: $35 ($60 for international students). *Expenses:* Tuition, state resident: full-time $5922; part-time $309 per hour. Tuition, nonresident: full-time $13,428; part-time $726 per hour. Tuition and fees vary according to program. *Unit head:* Dr. Etty Benvenister, Chair, 205-934-7667, Fax: 205-975-6748, E-mail: tika@uab.edu.

University of Alberta, Faculty of Graduate Studies and Research, Department of Biological Sciences, Edmonton, AB T6G 2E1, Canada. Offers environmental biology and ecology (M Sc, PhD); microbiology and biotechnology (M Sc, PhD); molecular biology and genetics (M Sc, PhD); physiology and cell biology (M Sc, PhD); plant biology (M Sc, PhD); systematics and evolution (M Sc, PhD). Terminal master's awarded for partial completion of doctoral program. *Degree requirements:* For master's, thesis; for doctorate, thesis/dissertation. *Entrance requirements:* Additional exam requirements/recommendations for international students: Required—TOEFL.

University of Alberta, Faculty of Medicine and Dentistry and Faculty of Graduate Studies and Research, Graduate Programs in Medicine, Department of Cell Biology, Edmonton, AB T6G 2E1, Canada. Offers cell and molecular biology (M Sc, PhD). Terminal master's awarded for partial completion of doctoral program. *Degree requirements:* For master's, thesis; for doctorate, thesis/dissertation. *Entrance requirements:* For master's and doctorate, 3 letters of reference, curriculum vitae. Additional exam requirements/recommendations for international students: Required—TOEFL (minimum score 600 paper-based; 250 computer-based). *Faculty research:* Protein targeting, membrane trafficking, signal transduction, cell growth and division, cell-cell interaction and development.

The University of Arizona, College of Science, Department of Molecular and Cellular Biology, Tucson, AZ 85721. Offers applied biosciences (PSM); molecular and cellular biology (MS, PhD). Evening/weekend programs available. *Faculty:* 13 full-time (5 women), 1 (woman) part-time/adjunct. *Students:* 26 full-time (14 women), 1 part-time (0 women); includes 8 minority (1 Asian, non-Hispanic/Latino; 3 Hispanic/Latino; 4 Two or more races, non-Hispanic/Latino), 5 international. Average age 28. 160 applicants, 11% accepted, 9 enrolled. In 2011, 2 master's, 9 doctorates awarded. Terminal master's awarded for partial completion of doctoral program. *Degree requirements:* For master's, thesis; for doctorate, thesis/dissertation. *Entrance requirements:* For master's, 3 letters of recommendation; for doctorate, 3 letters of recommendation, statement of purpose. Additional exam requirements/recommendations for international students: Required—TOEFL (minimum score 600 paper-based; 250 computer-based; 90 iBT), IELTS (minimum score 7). *Application deadline:* For fall admission, 1/1 for domestic and international students. Applications are processed on a rolling basis. Application fee:

$75. Electronic applications accepted. *Expenses:* Tuition, state resident: full-time $10,840. Tuition, nonresident: full-time $25,802. *Financial support:* In 2011–12, 13 research assistantships with full tuition reimbursements (averaging $24,286 per year), 4 teaching assistantships with full tuition reimbursements (averaging $19,145 per year) were awarded; career-related internships or fieldwork, scholarships/grants, health care benefits, and unspecified assistantships also available. *Faculty research:* Plant molecular biology, cellular and molecular aspects of development, genetics of bacteria and lower eukaryotes. *Total annual research expenditures:* $3.2 million. *Unit head:* Kathleen Dixon, Department Head, 520-621-7563, Fax: 520-621-3709, E-mail: dixonk@email.arizona.edu. *Application contact:* 520-621-3569, E-mail: bmcb@email.arizona.edu. Web site: http://bmcb.biology.arizona.edu/.

University of Arkansas, Graduate School, Interdisciplinary Program in Cell and Molecular Biology, Fayetteville, AR 72701-1201. Offers MS, PhD. *Students:* 11 full-time (6 women), 45 part-time (23 women); includes 5 minority (1 Black or African American, non-Hispanic/Latino; 3 Asian, non-Hispanic/Latino; 1 Hispanic/Latino), 38 international. In 2011, 5 master's, 3 doctorates awarded. *Degree requirements:* For doctorate, thesis/dissertation. *Application deadline:* For fall admission, 4/1 for international students; for spring admission, 10/1 for international students. Applications are processed on a rolling basis. Application fee: $40 ($50 for international students). Electronic applications accepted. *Financial support:* In 2011–12, 31 research assistantships, 12 teaching assistantships were awarded; fellowships with tuition reimbursements also available. Financial award application deadline: 4/1; financial award applicants required to submit FAFSA. *Unit head:* Dr. Douglas Rhoads, Head, 479-575-7396, Fax: 479-575-5908, E-mail: drhoads@uark.edu. *Application contact:* Graduate Admissions, 479-575-6246, Fax: 479-575-5908, E-mail: gradinfo@uark.edu. Web site: http://www.uark.edu/depts/cemb/.

University of Arkansas for Medical Sciences, Graduate School, Graduate Programs in Biomedical Sciences, Program in Biochemistry and Molecular Biology, Little Rock, AR 72205-7199. Offers MS, PhD, MD/PhD. *Degree requirements:* For master's, comprehensive exam, thesis; for doctorate, thesis/dissertation, qualifying exam. *Entrance requirements:* For master's, GRE General Test, bachelor's degree in biology, chemistry, or related field; for doctorate, GRE General Test. Additional exam requirements/recommendations for international students: Required—TOEFL. *Faculty research:* Gene regulation, growth factors, oncogenes, metabolic diseases, hormone regulation.

The University of British Columbia, Faculty of Medicine, Department of Biochemistry and Molecular Biology, Vancouver, BC V6T 1Z1, Canada. Offers M Sc, PhD. *Degree requirements:* For master's, thesis; for doctorate, comprehensive exam, thesis/dissertation. *Entrance requirements:* For master's, first class B Sc; for doctorate, master's or first class honors bachelor's degree in biochemistry. Additional exam requirements/recommendations for international students: Required—TOEFL (minimum score 625 paper-based; 263 computer-based). Electronic applications accepted. *Faculty research:* Membrane biochemistry, protein structure/function, signal transduction, biochemistry.

University of Calgary, Faculty of Medicine and Faculty of Graduate Studies, Department of Biochemistry and Molecular Biology, Calgary, AB T2N 1N4, Canada. Offers M Sc, PhD. *Degree requirements:* For master's, thesis; for doctorate, thesis/dissertation, candidacy exam. *Entrance requirements:* For master's and doctorate, GRE General Test, minimum GPA of 3.2. Additional exam requirements/recommendations for international students: Required—TOEFL. Electronic applications accepted. *Faculty research:* Molecular and developmental genetics; molecular biology of disease; genomics, proteomics and bioinformatics; ceu signaling and structure.

University of California, Berkeley, Graduate Division, College of Letters and Science, Department of Molecular and Cell Biology, Berkeley, CA 94720-1500. Offers PhD. *Degree requirements:* For doctorate, comprehensive exam, thesis/dissertation, qualifying exam, 2 semesters of teaching, 3 seminars. *Entrance requirements:* For doctorate, GRE General Test, GRE Subject Test (recommended), minimum GPA of 3.0. Additional exam requirements/recommendations for international students: Required—TOEFL (minimum score 570 paper-based; 230 computer-based; 68 iBT), IELTS (minimum score 7). Electronic applications accepted. *Faculty research:* Biochemistry and molecular biology, cell and developmental biology, genetics, immunology, neurobiology, genomics.

University of California, Davis, Graduate Studies, Graduate Group in Biochemistry and Molecular Biology, Davis, CA 95616. Offers MS, PhD. Terminal master's awarded for partial completion of doctoral program. *Degree requirements:* For master's, comprehensive exam (for some programs), thesis (for some programs); for doctorate, thesis/dissertation. *Entrance requirements:* For master's and doctorate, GRE General Test, GRE Subject Test. Additional exam requirements/recommendations for international students: Required—TOEFL (minimum score 550 paper-based; 213 computer-based). Electronic applications accepted. *Faculty research:* Gene expression, protein structure, molecular virology, protein synthesis, enzymology, membrane transport and structural biology.

University of California, Irvine, School of Biological Sciences, Department of Molecular Biology and Biochemistry, Irvine, CA 92697. Offers biological science (MS); biological sciences (PhD); biotechnology (MS); MD/PhD. *Students:* 62 full-time (30 women), 1 part-time (0 women); includes 29 minority (4 Black or African American, non-Hispanic/Latino; 13 Asian, non-Hispanic/Latino; 12 Hispanic/Latino), 3 international. Average age 28. 1 applicant, 100% accepted, 1 enrolled. In 2011, 14 degrees awarded. *Degree requirements:* For doctorate, thesis/dissertation. *Entrance requirements:* For master's, GRE, minimum GPA of 3.0; for doctorate, GRE General Test, GRE Subject Test, minimum GPA of 3.0. Additional exam requirements/recommendations for international students: Required—TOEFL (minimum score 550 paper-based; 213 computer-based). *Application deadline:* For fall admission, 12/15 priority date for domestic students, 12/15 for international students. Applications are processed on a rolling basis. Application fee: $80 ($100 for international students). Electronic applications accepted. *Financial support:* Fellowships, research assistantships with full tuition reimbursements, teaching assistantships, institutionally sponsored loans, traineeships, health care benefits, and unspecified assistantships available. Financial award application deadline: 3/1; financial award applicants required to submit FAFSA. *Faculty research:* Structure and synthesis of nucleic acids and proteins, regulation, virology, biochemical genetics, gene organization. *Unit head:* Prof. Christopher C. Hughes, Chair, 949-824-8771, Fax: 949-824-8551, E-mail: cchughes@uci.edu. *Application contact:* Rene Frigo, CMB Program Manager, 949-824-8145, Fax: 949-824-1965, E-mail: rfrigo@uci.edu. Web site: http://www.bio.uci.edu/.

University of California, Irvine, School of Biological Sciences and School of Medicine, Interdisciplinary Graduate Program in Cellular and Molecular Biosciences, Irvine, CA 92697. Offers PhD. *Faculty:* 138 full-time (35 women). *Students:* 59 full-time (33 women); includes 16 minority (8 Asian, non-Hispanic/Latino; 8 Hispanic/Latino), 6 international. Average age 25. In 2011, 19 doctorates awarded. *Degree requirements:* For doctorate, thesis/dissertation, teaching assignment, preliminary exam. *Entrance requirements:* For doctorate, GRE General Test, minimum GPA of 3.0, research experience. Additional exam requirements/recommendations for international students: Required—TOEFL, IELTS, SPEAK. *Application deadline:* For fall admission, 1/1 for domestic and international students. Application fee: $60 ($80 for international students). Electronic applications accepted. *Expenses:* Contact institution. *Financial support:* In 2011–12, 56 fellowships with full tuition reimbursements (averaging $26,250

UNIFORMED SERVICES UNIVERSITY

The Uniformed Services University of the Health Sciences is the nation's federal health sciences university and is committed to excellence in military medicine and public health during peace and war.

We provide the nation with health professionals who are dedicated to both civilian and military career service in the Department of Defense and the United States Public Health Service and with scientists who serve the common good.

We serve the uniformed services and the nation as an outstanding academic health sciences center with a worldwide perspective for education, research, service, and consultation. We are unique in relating these activities to military medicine, disaster medicine, and military medical readiness.

For more information, contact:

Uniformed Services University
4301 Jones Bridge Road
Bethesda, Maryland 20814-4799
Phone: 301-295-3913 or 800-772-1747 (toll-free)

http://www.usuhs.mil

per year) were awarded; institutionally sponsored loans, scholarships/grants, tuition waivers (full), unspecified assistantships, and stipends also available. Financial award application deadline: 1/1; financial award applicants required to submit FAFSA. *Faculty research:* Cellular biochemistry; gene structure and expression; protein structure, function, and design; molecular genetics; pathogenesis and inherited disease. *Unit head:* Dr. David Fruman, Director, 949-824-3431, Fax: 949-824-1965, E-mail: gp-mbgb@uci.edu. *Application contact:* Renee Frigo, Administrator, 949-824-8145, Fax: 949-824-1965, E-mail: rfrigo@uci.edu. Web site: http://cmb.uci.edu/.

University of California, Los Angeles, Graduate Division, College of Letters and Science, Department of Chemistry and Biochemistry, Program in Biochemistry and Molecular Biology, Los Angeles, CA 90034. Offers PhD. *Students:* 71 full-time (31 women); includes 28 minority (1 Black or African American, non-Hispanic/Latino; 22 Asian, non-Hispanic/Latino; 5 Hispanic/Latino), 8 international. Average age 27. 139 applicants, 15% accepted, 10 enrolled. In 2011, 16 doctorates awarded. Terminal master's awarded for partial completion of doctoral program. *Degree requirements:* For doctorate, thesis/dissertation, oral and written exams, 1 year teaching experience. *Entrance requirements:* For doctorate, GRE General Test, GRE Subject Test, minimum undergraduate GPA of 3.0. *Application deadline:* For fall admission, 1/15 for domestic and international students. Application fee: $70 ($90 for international students). Electronic applications accepted. *Financial support:* In 2011–12, 77 fellowships with full and partial tuition reimbursements, 53 research assistantships with full and partial tuition reimbursements, 38 teaching assistantships with full and partial tuition reimbursements were awarded; Federal Work-Study, scholarships/grants, health care benefits, tuition waivers (full and partial), and unspecified assistantships also available. Financial award applicants required to submit FAFSA. *Unit head:* Dr. Albert Courey, 310-825-3958, E-mail: courey@chem.ucla.edu. *Application contact:* Departmental Office, 310-825-2645, E-mail: bmbgrad@chem.ucla.edu. Web site: http://www.biochemistry.ucla.edu.

University of California, Los Angeles, Graduate Division, College of Letters and Science, Department of Molecular, Cell and Developmental Biology, Los Angeles, CA 90095. Offers PhD. *Faculty:* 23 full-time (8 women). *Students:* 35 full-time (20 women); includes 16 minority (3 Black or African American, non-Hispanic/Latino; 8 Asian, non-Hispanic/Latino; 5 Hispanic/Latino), 8 international. Average age 28. 1 applicant, 100% accepted, 1 enrolled. In 2011, 7 degrees awarded. *Median time to degree:* Of those who began their doctoral program in fall 2003, 67% received their degree in 8 years or less. *Degree requirements:* For doctorate, thesis/dissertation, qualifying exams. *Entrance requirements:* For doctorate, GRE General Test, GRE Subject Test. Additional exam requirements/recommendations for international students: Required—TOEFL. Application fee: $70 ($90 for international students). Electronic applications accepted. *Financial support:* In 2011–12, 28 fellowships, 29 research assistantships, 9 teaching assistantships were awarded; scholarships/grants, traineeships, and unspecified assistantships also available. Financial award application deadline: 3/1. *Unit head:* Dr. Utpal Banerjee, Chair, 310-206-5439, Fax: 310-206-3987, E-mail: banerjee@mbi.ucla.edu. *Application contact:* UCLA ACCESS Coordinator, 310-206-1845, Fax: 310-206-1636, E-mail: uclaaccess@mednet.ucla.edu. Web site: http://www.mcdb.ucla.edu.

University of California, Los Angeles, Graduate Division, College of Letters and Science, Program in Molecular Biology, Los Angeles, CA 90095. Offers PhD, MD/PhD. *Students:* 76 full-time (36 women); includes 27 minority (2 Black or African American, non-Hispanic/Latino; 20 Asian, non-Hispanic/Latino; 4 Hispanic/Latino; 1 Two or more races, non-Hispanic/Latino), 8 international. Average age 28. 12 applicants, 25% accepted, 3 enrolled. In 2011, 15 doctorates awarded. *Degree requirements:* For doctorate, thesis/dissertation, oral and written qualifying exams, teaching experience. *Entrance requirements:* For doctorate, GRE General Test, GRE Subject Test (biochemistry, chemistry, biology, or physics). *Application deadline:* For fall admission, 1/10 for domestic and international students. Application fee: $70 ($90 for international students). Electronic applications accepted. *Financial support:* In 2011–12, 75 fellowships with full and partial tuition reimbursements, 60 research assistantships with full and partial tuition reimbursements, 26 teaching assistantships with full and partial tuition reimbursements were awarded; Federal Work-Study, institutionally sponsored loans, scholarships/grants, health care benefits, tuition waivers (full and partial), and unspecified assistantships also available. Financial award application deadline: 3/1; financial award applicants required to submit FAFSA. *Unit head:* Dr. Luisa Iruela-Arispe, Interim Director, 310-794-5763, E-mail: arispe@mcdb.ucla.edu. *Application contact:* Sue Ellen Parsee, Department Office, 310-825-1018, E-mail: mbigrad@mednet.ucla.edu. Web site: http://www.mbidp.mbi.ucla.edu/.

University of California, Los Angeles, Graduate Division, College of Letters and Science, Program in Molecular, Cellular and Integrative Physiology, Los Angeles, CA 90095. Offers PhD. *Faculty:* 19 full-time (6 women). *Students:* 46 full-time (25 women); includes 12 minority (1 Black or African American, non-Hispanic/Latino; 9 Asian, non-Hispanic/Latino; 2 Hispanic/Latino), 15 international. Average age 29. 26 applicants, 42% accepted, 7 enrolled. In 2011, 6 doctorates awarded. *Degree requirements:* For doctorate, thesis/dissertation, oral and written exams, student teaching. *Entrance requirements:* For doctorate, GRE General Test, GRE Subject Test (biology or applicant's undergraduate major), minimum GPA of 3.0, bachelor's degree in biological or physical sciences. Application fee: $70 ($90 for international students). Electronic applications accepted. *Financial support:* In 2011–12, 34 fellowships with full and partial tuition reimbursements, 29 research assistantships with full and partial tuition reimbursements, 13 teaching assistantships with full and partial tuition reimbursements were awarded; Federal Work-Study, institutionally sponsored loans, scholarships/grants, health care benefits, tuition waivers (full and partial), and unspecified assistantships also available. Financial award applicants required to submit FAFSA. *Unit head:* Dr. James Tidball, Chair, 310-825-3891, E-mail: jtidball@physci.ucla.edu. *Application contact:* Michael Carr, Department Office, 310-825-3891, E-mail: mcarr@physci.ucla.edu. Web site: http://www.mcip.ucla.edu.

University of California, Los Angeles, Graduate Division, College of Letters and Science and David Geffen School of Medicine, UCLA ACCESS to Programs in the Molecular, Cellular and Integrative Life Sciences, Los Angeles, CA 90095. Offers biochemistry and molecular biology (PhD); biological chemistry (PhD); cellular and molecular pathology (PhD); human genetics (PhD); microbiology, immunology, and molecular genetics (PhD); molecular biology (PhD); molecular toxicology (PhD); molecular, cellular and integrative physiology (PhD); neurobiology (PhD); oral biology (PhD); physiology (PhD). *Students:* 44 full-time (30 women); includes 18 minority (11 Asian, non-Hispanic/Latino; 6 Hispanic/Latino; 1 Two or more races, non-Hispanic/Latino), 9 international. Average age 25. 495 applicants, 18% accepted, 41 enrolled. *Degree requirements:* For doctorate, thesis/dissertation, oral and written qualifying exams. *Entrance requirements:* For doctorate, GRE General Test, minimum undergraduate GPA of 3.0. Additional exam requirements/recommendations for international students: Required—TOEFL. *Application deadline:* For fall admission, 12/15 for domestic and international students. Application fee: $70 ($90 for international students). Electronic applications accepted. *Financial support:* In 2011–12, 51 fellowships with full and partial tuition reimbursements, 9 research assistantships with full and partial tuition reimbursements were awarded; teaching assistantships with full and partial tuition reimbursements, Federal Work-Study, institutionally sponsored loans, scholarships/grants, health care benefits, tuition waivers (full and partial), and unspecified assistantships also available. Financial award application deadline: 3/1; financial award applicants required to submit FAFSA. *Faculty research:* Molecular, cellular, and developmental biology; immunology; microbiology; integrative biology. *Unit head:* Jody Spillane, Project Coordinator, 310-206-1845, E-mail: jspillane@mednet.ucla.edu. *Application contact:* UCLA ACCESS Admissions, 310-206-1845, E-mail: uclaaccess@mednet.ucla.edu. Web site: https://www.uclaaccess.ucla.edu/.

University of California, Riverside, Graduate Division, Program in Cell, Molecular, and Developmental Biology, Riverside, CA 92521-0102. Offers MS, PhD. Terminal master's awarded for partial completion of doctoral program. *Degree requirements:* For master's, thesis, oral defense of thesis; for doctorate, thesis/dissertation, oral defense of thesis, qualifying exams, 2 quarters of teaching experience. *Entrance requirements:* For master's and doctorate, GRE General Test, minimum GPA of 3.2. Additional exam requirements/recommendations for international students: Required—TOEFL (minimum score 550 paper-based; 213 computer-based; 80 iBT). Electronic applications accepted.

University of California, San Diego, Office of Graduate Studies, Division of Biological Sciences, Program in Genetics and Molecular Biology, La Jolla, CA 92093-0348. Offers PhD. Offered in association with the Salk Institute. *Degree requirements:* For doctorate, thesis/dissertation, qualifying exam. Electronic applications accepted.

University of California, San Diego, Office of Graduate Studies, Division of Biological Sciences, Program in Molecular and Cellular Biology, La Jolla, CA 92093. Offers PhD. Offered in association with the Salk Institute. *Degree requirements:* For doctorate, thesis/dissertation, qualifying exam. Electronic applications accepted.

University of California, San Diego, School of Medicine and Office of Graduate Studies, Graduate Studies in Biomedical Sciences, Program in Molecular Cell Biology, La Jolla, CA 92093. Offers PhD. *Degree requirements:* For doctorate, thesis/dissertation, qualifying exam. *Entrance requirements:* For doctorate, GRE General Test. Additional exam requirements/recommendations for international students: Required—TOEFL. Electronic applications accepted. *Faculty research:* Molecular and cellular pharmacology, cell and organ physiology.

University of California, San Diego, School of Medicine and Office of Graduate Studies, Graduate Studies in Biomedical Sciences, Regulatory Biology Program, La Jolla, CA 92093. Offers PhD. *Degree requirements:* For doctorate, thesis/dissertation, 2 qualifying exams. *Entrance requirements:* For doctorate, GRE General Test, GRE Subject Test. Additional exam requirements/recommendations for international students: Required—TOEFL. Electronic applications accepted. *Faculty research:* Eukaryotic regulatory and molecular biology, molecular and cellular pharmacology, cell and organ physiology.

University of California, San Francisco, Graduate Division and School of Medicine, Department of Biochemistry and Biophysics, Program in Biochemistry and Molecular Biology, San Francisco, CA 94143. Offers PhD, MD/PhD. *Degree requirements:* For doctorate, thesis/dissertation. *Entrance requirements:* For doctorate, GRE General Test, GRE Subject Test. Additional exam requirements/recommendations for international students: Required—TOEFL. *Expenses:* Contact institution. *Faculty research:* Structural biology, genetics, cell biology, cell physiology, metabolism.

University of California, Santa Barbara, Graduate Division, College of Letters and Sciences, Division of Mathematics, Life, and Physical Sciences, Department of Molecular, Cellular, and Developmental Biology, Santa Barbara, CA 93106-9625. Offers MA, PhD, MA/PhD. *Faculty:* 21 full-time (3 women), 7 part-time/adjunct (2 women). *Students:* 52 full-time (29 women); includes 10 minority (1 Black or African American, non-Hispanic/Latino; 8 Asian, non-Hispanic/Latino; 1 Hispanic/Latino), 2 international. Average age 28. 115 applicants, 18% accepted, 9 enrolled. In 2011, 8 master's, 8 doctorates awarded. Terminal master's awarded for partial completion of doctoral program. *Median time to degree:* Of those who began their doctoral program in fall 2003, 100% received their degree in 8 years or less. *Degree requirements:* For master's, comprehensive exam (for some programs), thesis (for some programs); for doctorate, comprehensive exam, thesis/dissertation. *Entrance requirements:* For master's, GRE General Test, 3 letters of recommendation, resume/curriculum vitae; for doctorate, GRE General Test, 3 letters of recommendation, statement of purpose, personal achievements/contributions statement, resume/curriculum vitae, transcripts for post-secondary institutions attended. Additional exam requirements/recommendations for international students: Required—TOEFL (minimum score 610 paper-based; 102 iBT), IELTS (minimum score 7). *Application deadline:* For fall admission, 12/20 priority date for domestic students, 12/20 for international students. Application fee: $80 ($100 for international students). Electronic applications accepted. *Expenses:* Tuition, state resident: full-time $12,192. Tuition, nonresident: full-time $27,294. *Required fees:* $764.13. *Financial support:* In 2011–12, 14 students received support, including 14 fellowships with full and partial tuition reimbursements available (averaging $6,562 per year), 40 research assistantships with full and partial tuition reimbursements available (averaging $15,250 per year), 46 teaching assistantships with partial tuition reimbursements available (averaging $10,500 per year); career-related internships or fieldwork, Federal Work-Study, institutionally sponsored loans, scholarships/grants, traineeships, health care benefits, and unspecified assistantships also available. Financial award application deadline: 12/20; financial award applicants required to submit FAFSA. *Faculty research:* Microbiology, neurobiology (including stem cell research), developmental, virology, cell biology. *Unit head:* Dr. Joel H. Rothman, Chair, 805-893-7885, E-mail: joel.rothman@lifesci.ucsb.edu. *Application contact:* Nicole McCoy, Graduate Program Advisor, 805-893-8499, E-mail: nicole.mccoy@lifesci.ucsb.edu. Web site: http://www.lifesci.ucsb.edu/mcdb/programs/graduate/graduate.html.

University of California, Santa Barbara, Graduate Division, College of Letters and Sciences, Division of Mathematics, Life, and Physical Sciences, Interdepartmental Graduate Program in Biomolecular Science and Engineering, Santa Barbara, CA 93106-2014. Offers biochemistry and molecular biology (PhD), including biochemistry and molecular biology, biophysics and bioengineering. *Faculty:* 38 full-time (5 women), 1 (woman) part-time/adjunct. *Students:* 29 full-time (14 women); includes 3 minority (2 Asian, non-Hispanic/Latino; 1 Two or more races, non-Hispanic/Latino), 3 international. Average age 28. 83 applicants, 20% accepted, 4 enrolled. In 2011, 4 degrees awarded. Terminal master's awarded for partial completion of doctoral program. *Median time to degree:* Of those who began their doctoral program in fall 2003, 100% received their degree in 8 years or less. *Degree requirements:* For doctorate, thesis/dissertation. *Entrance requirements:* For doctorate, GRE General Test. Additional exam requirements/recommendations for international students: Required—TOEFL (minimum score 630 paper-based; 109 iBT), IELTS (minimum score 7). *Application deadline:* For fall admission, 12/15 for domestic and international students. Application fee: $80 ($100 for international students). Electronic applications accepted. *Expenses:* Tuition, state resident: full-time $12,192. Tuition, nonresident: full-time $27,294. *Required fees:* $764.13. *Financial support:* In 2011–12, 29 students received support, including 16 fellowships with full and partial tuition reimbursements available (averaging $11,321 per year), 31 research assistantships with full and partial tuition reimbursements available (averaging $14,777 per year), 16 teaching assistantships with full and partial tuition reimbursements available (averaging $6,307 per year); Federal Work-Study,

traineeships, health care benefits, tuition waivers (full and partial), and unspecified assistantships also available. Financial award application deadline: 12/15; financial award applicants required to submit FAFSA. *Faculty research:* Biochemistry and molecular biology, biophysics, biomaterials, bioengineering, systems biology. *Unit head:* Prof. Philip A. Pincus, Director/Professor, 805-893-4685, E-mail: fyl@mrl.ucsb.edu. *Application contact:* Graduate Admissions Coordinator, 805-893-2278, Fax: 805-893-8259, E-mail: gradadmissions@graddiv.ucsb.edu. Web site: http://www.bmse.ucsb.edu/.

University of California, Santa Cruz, Division of Graduate Studies, Division of Physical and Biological Sciences, Program in Molecular, Cellular, and Developmental Biology, Santa Cruz, CA 95064. Offers MA, PhD. Terminal master's awarded for partial completion of doctoral program. *Degree requirements:* For master's, thesis; for doctorate, thesis/dissertation, qualifying exam. *Entrance requirements:* For master's and doctorate, GRE General Test, 3 letters of recommendation, interview. Additional exam requirements/recommendations for international students: Required—TOEFL (minimum score 550 paper-based; 220 computer-based; 83 iBT); Recommended—IELTS (minimum score 8). Electronic applications accepted. *Faculty research:* RNA biology, chromatin and chromosome biology, neurobiology, stem cell biology and differentiation, cell structure and function.

University of Chicago, Division of Biological Sciences, Molecular Biosciences Cluster, Department of Biochemistry and Molecular Biology, Chicago, IL 60637-1513. Offers PhD, MD/PhD. *Degree requirements:* For doctorate, thesis/dissertation, ethics class, 2 teaching assistantships. *Entrance requirements:* For doctorate, GRE General Test, GRE Subject Test. Additional exam requirements/recommendations for international students: Required—TOEFL (minimum score 600 paper-based; 250 computer-based; 104 iBT), IELTS (minimum score 7). Electronic applications accepted. *Faculty research:* Molecular biology, gene expression, and DNA-protein interactions; membrane biochemistry, molecular endocrinology, and transmembrane signaling; enzyme mechanisms, physical biochemistry, and structural biology.

University of Chicago, Division of Biological Sciences, Molecular Biosciences Cluster, Graduate Program in Cell and Molecular Biology, Chicago, IL 60637-1513. Offers PhD. *Degree requirements:* For doctorate, thesis/dissertation, ethics class, 2 teaching assistantships. *Entrance requirements:* For doctorate, GRE General Test. Additional exam requirements/recommendations for international students: Required—TOEFL (minimum score 600 paper-based; 250 computer-based; 104 iBT), IELTS (minimum score 7). Electronic applications accepted. *Faculty research:* Gene expression, chromosome structure, animal viruses, plant molecular genetics.

University of Cincinnati, Graduate School, College of Medicine, Graduate Programs in Biomedical Sciences, Department of Environmental Health, Programs in Environmental Genetics and Molecular Toxicology, Cincinnati, OH 45221. Offers MS, PhD. *Degree requirements:* For doctorate, thesis/dissertation. *Entrance requirements:* For master's, GRE, minimum GPA of 3.0, 3 letters of recommendation. Additional exam requirements/recommendations for international students: Required—TOEFL (minimum score 520 paper-based; 190 computer-based).

University of Cincinnati, Graduate School, College of Medicine, Graduate Programs in Biomedical Sciences, Department of Molecular Genetics, Biochemistry and Microbiology, Cincinnati, OH 45221. Offers MS, PhD. Terminal master's awarded for partial completion of doctoral program. *Degree requirements:* For master's, thesis or alternative; for doctorate, thesis/dissertation, qualifying exam. *Entrance requirements:* For master's and doctorate, GRE General Test. Additional exam requirements/recommendations for international students: Required—TOEFL (minimum score 600 paper-based; 250 computer-based; 100 iBT), TWE. Electronic applications accepted. *Faculty research:* Cancer biology and developmental genetics, gene regulation and chromosome structure, microbiology and pathogenic mechanisms, structural biology, membrane biochemistry and signal transduction.

University of Cincinnati, Graduate School, College of Medicine, Graduate Programs in Biomedical Sciences, Department of Pediatrics, Program in Molecular and Developmental Biology, Cincinnati, OH 45221. Offers PhD. *Degree requirements:* For doctorate, thesis/dissertation, qualifying exam. *Entrance requirements:* For doctorate, GRE General Test, minimum GPA of 3.2. Additional exam requirements/recommendations for international students: Required—TOEFL (minimum score 520 paper-based; 190 computer-based). Electronic applications accepted. *Faculty research:* Cancer biology, cardiovascular biology, developmental biology, human genetics, gene therapy, genomics and bioinformatics, immunobiology, molecular medicine, neuroscience, pulmonary biology, reproductive biology, stem cell biology.

University of Colorado Boulder, Graduate School, College of Arts and Sciences, Department of Molecular, Cellular, and Developmental Biology, Boulder, CO 80309. Offers cellular structure and function (MA, PhD); developmental biology (MA, PhD); molecular biology (MA, PhD). *Faculty:* 16 full-time (6 women). *Students:* 71 full-time (36 women); includes 4 minority (1 American Indian or Alaska Native, non-Hispanic/Latino; 1 Asian, non-Hispanic/Latino; 2 Hispanic/Latino), 13 international. Average age 28. 259 applicants, 13% accepted, 14 enrolled. In 2011, 3 master's, 11 doctorates awarded. Terminal master's awarded for partial completion of doctoral program. *Degree requirements:* For master's, comprehensive exam, thesis or alternative; for doctorate, comprehensive exam, thesis/dissertation. *Entrance requirements:* For master's, GRE General Test, GRE Subject Test, minimum undergraduate GPA of 3.0; for doctorate, GRE General Test, GRE Subject Test. *Application deadline:* For fall admission, 1/1 for domestic students, 12/1 for international students. Application fee: $50 ($60 for international students). *Financial support:* In 2011–12, 86 students received support, including 44 fellowships (averaging $12,916 per year), 48 research assistantships with tuition reimbursements available (averaging $18,648 per year), 15 teaching assistantships with tuition reimbursements available (averaging $19,818 per year); institutionally sponsored loans, scholarships/grants, health care benefits, and unspecified assistantships also available. Financial award application deadline: 2/1; financial award applicants required to submit FAFSA. *Faculty research:* Molecular biology of RNA and DNA, molecular genetics, cell motility and cytoskeleton, cell membranes, developmental genetics, human genetics. *Total annual research expenditures:* $16.2 million. *Application contact:* E-mail: mcdbgrad@colorado.edu. Web site: http://mcdb.colorado.edu/.

University of Colorado Denver, College of Liberal Arts and Sciences, Department of Integrative Biology, Denver, CO 80217. Offers animal behavior (MS); biology (MS); cell and developmental biology (MS); ecology (MS); evolutionary biology (MS); genetics (MS); microbiology (MS); molecular biology (MS); neurobiology (MS); plant systematics (MS). Part-time programs available. *Faculty:* 16 full-time (8 women). *Students:* 20 full-time (13 women), 5 part-time (4 women); includes 1 minority (Hispanic/Latino), 1 international. Average age 29. 21 applicants, 43% accepted, 5 enrolled. In 2011, 7 master's awarded. *Degree requirements:* For master's, comprehensive exam, thesis or alternative, 30-32 credit hours. *Entrance requirements:* For master's, GRE General Test (minimum score in 50% percentile in each section), BA/BS from accredited institution awarded within the last 10 years; minimum undergraduate GPA of 3.0; prerequisite courses: 1 year each of general biology and general chemistry, and 1 semester each of general genetics, general ecology, cell biology, and a structure/function course.

Additional exam requirements/recommendations for international students: Required—TOEFL (minimum score 525 paper-based; 197 computer-based; 71 iBT). *Application deadline:* For fall admission, 2/1 for domestic and international students. Application fee: $50 ($75 for international students). Electronic applications accepted. *Financial support:* Research assistantships, teaching assistantships, Federal Work-Study, scholarships/grants, and unspecified assistantships available. Financial award application deadline: 4/1; financial award applicants required to submit FAFSA. *Faculty research:* Molecular developmental biology; quantitative ecology, biogeography, and population dynamics; environmental signaling and endocrine disruption; speciation, the evolution of reproductive isolation, and hybrid zones; evolutionary, behavioral, and conservation ecology. *Unit head:* Dr. Diana Tomback, Acting Chair, 303-556-2657, E-mail: diana.tomback@ucdenver.edu. *Application contact:* Timberley Roane, Associate Professor/Associate Chair, 303-556-6592, E-mail: timberley.roane@ucdenver.edu. Web site: http://www.ucdenver.edu/academics/colleges/CLAS/Departments/biology/Pages/Biology.aspx.

University of Colorado Denver, School of Medicine, Program in Molecular Biology, Aurora, CO 80045. Offers biomolecular structure (PhD); molecular biology (PhD). *Students:* 42 full-time (27 women); includes 6 minority (1 Black or African American, non-Hispanic/Latino; 3 Asian, non-Hispanic/Latino; 2 Hispanic/Latino), 4 international. Average age 28. 20 applicants, 15% accepted, 3 enrolled. In 2011, 8 doctorates awarded. *Degree requirements:* For doctorate, comprehensive exam, thesis/dissertation, 2 years of structured didactic courses, 2-3 years of research, laboratory work, thesis project. *Entrance requirements:* For doctorate, GRE, organic chemistry (2 semesters, including 1 semester of laboratory), biology, general physics, college-level mathematics through calculus. Additional exam requirements/recommendations for international students: Required—TOEFL (minimum score 550 paper-based; 213 computer-based). *Application deadline:* For fall admission, 12/1 for domestic students. Application fee: $50 ($75 for international students). Electronic applications accepted. *Expenses:* Contact institution. *Financial support:* Fellowships, research assistantships, teaching assistantships, health care benefits, tuition waivers (full), and stipend available. Financial award application deadline: 3/15; financial award applicants required to submit FAFSA. *Faculty research:* Gene transcription, RNA processing, chromosome dynamics, DNA damage and repair, chromatin assembly. *Unit head:* Dr. Mark Johnston, Chair, 303-724-3203, E-mail: mark.johnston@ucdenver.edu. *Application contact:* Jean Sibley, Administrator, 303-724-3245, Fax: 303-724-3247, E-mail: jean.sibley@uchsc.edu. Web site: http://www.ucdenver.edu/academics/colleges/medicalschool/programs/Molbio/Pages/MolecularBiology.aspx.

University of Colorado Denver, School of Medicine, Program in Pharmacology, Aurora, CO 80045. Offers bioinformatics (PhD); biomolecular structure (PhD); pharmacology (PhD). *Students:* 24 full-time (15 women); includes 4 minority (1 Black or African American, non-Hispanic/Latino; 2 Asian, non-Hispanic/Latino; 1 Hispanic/Latino). Average age 28. 18 applicants, 17% accepted, 3 enrolled. In 2011, 4 doctorates awarded. *Degree requirements:* For doctorate, comprehensive exam, thesis/dissertation, major seminar, 3 research rotations in the first year, 30 hours each of course work and thesis. *Entrance requirements:* For doctorate, GRE General Test. Additional exam requirements/recommendations for international students: Required—TOEFL (minimum score 550 paper-based; 213 computer-based; 80 iBT). *Application deadline:* For fall admission, 12/15 for domestic students, 11/15 for international students. Application fee: $50 ($75 for international students). Electronic applications accepted. *Expenses:* Contact institution. *Financial support:* Fellowships, research assistantships, teaching assistantships, health care benefits, tuition waivers (full), and stipend available. Financial award application deadline: 3/15; financial award applicants required to submit FAFSA. *Faculty research:* Cancer biology, drugs of abuse, neuroscience, signal transduction, structural biology. *Total annual research expenditures:* $16.7 million. *Unit head:* Dr. Andrew Thorburn, Interim Chair, 303-724-3290, Fax: 303-724-3663, E-mail: andrew.thorburn@ucdenver.edu. *Application contact:* Elizabeth Bowen, Graduate Training Coordinator, 303-724-3565, E-mail: elizabeth.bowen@ucdenver.edu. Web site: http://pharmacology.ucdenver.edu/.

University of Connecticut, Graduate School, College of Liberal Arts and Sciences, Department of Molecular and Cell Biology, Field of Microbial Systems Analysis, Storrs, CT 06269. Offers MS, PSM. *Degree requirements:* For master's, comprehensive exam. *Entrance requirements:* For master's, GRE General Test, GRE Subject Test. Additional exam requirements/recommendations for international students: Required—TOEFL (minimum score 550 paper-based; 213 computer-based). Electronic applications accepted.

University of Connecticut Health Center, Graduate School, Programs in Biomedical Sciences, Graduate Program in Molecular Biology and Biochemistry, Farmington, CT 06030. Offers PhD, DMD/PhD, MD/PhD. *Degree requirements:* For doctorate, comprehensive exam, thesis/dissertation. *Entrance requirements:* For doctorate, GRE General Test. Additional exam requirements/recommendations for international students: Required—TOEFL (minimum score 600 paper-based; 250 computer-based). Electronic applications accepted. *Faculty research:* Molecular biology, structural biology, protein biochemistry, microbial physiology and pathogenesis.

See Display on next page and Close-Up on page 243.

University of Delaware, College of Arts and Sciences, Department of Biological Sciences, Newark, DE 19716. Offers biotechnology (MS); cancer biology (MS, PhD); cell and extracellular matrix biology (MS, PhD); cell and systems physiology (MS, PhD); developmental biology (MS, PhD); ecology and evolution (MS, PhD); microbiology (MS, PhD); molecular biology and genetics (MS, PhD). Terminal master's awarded for partial completion of doctoral program. *Degree requirements:* For master's, thesis, preliminary exam; for doctorate, comprehensive exam, thesis/dissertation, preliminary exam. *Entrance requirements:* For master's and doctorate, GRE General Test. Additional exam requirements/recommendations for international students: Required—TOEFL (minimum score 600 paper-based; 250 computer-based); Recommended—TWE. Electronic applications accepted. *Faculty research:* Microorganisms, bone, cancer metastasis, developmental biology, cell biology, DNA.

University of Florida, College of Medicine and Graduate School, Interdisciplinary Program in Biomedical Sciences, Concentration in Biochemistry and Molecular Biology, Gainesville, FL 32611. Offers PhD. *Degree requirements:* For doctorate, thesis/dissertation. *Entrance requirements:* For doctorate, GRE General Test, minimum GPA of 3.0. Additional exam requirements/recommendations for international students: Required—TOEFL. Electronic applications accepted. *Faculty research:* Gene expression, metabolic regulation, structural biology, enzyme mechanism, membrane transporters.

University of Florida, Interdisciplinary Concentration in Animal Molecular and Cellular Biology, Gainesville, FL 32611. Offers MS, PhD. Program offered jointly by College of Agricultural and Life Sciences, College of Liberal Arts and Sciences, College of Medicine, and College of Veterinary Medicine. *Students:* 12 full-time (7 women); includes 1 minority (Hispanic/Latino), 7 international. Average age 30. 7 applicants, 0% accepted, 0 enrolled. In 2011, 1 master's, 1 doctorate awarded. *Entrance requirements:* For master's and doctorate, GRE General Test (minimum score 1000), minimum GPA of 3.0. Additional exam requirements/recommendations for international students:

Required—TOEFL (minimum score 550 paper-based; 213 computer-based; 80 iBT), IELTS (minimum score 6). Application fee: $30. Electronic applications accepted. *Financial support:* Fellowships and research assistantships available. Financial award applicants required to submit FAFSA. *Unit head:* Dr. Alan D. Ealy, Director, 352-392-5590, Fax: 352-392-5595, E-mail: ealy@ufl.edu. *Application contact:* Dr. Joel H. Brendemuhl, Assistant Chair, 352-392-8073, Fax: 352-392-5595, E-mail: brendj@ufl.edu. Web site: http://www.animal.ufl.edu/amcb/.

University of Georgia, Franklin College of Arts and Sciences, Department of Biochemistry and Molecular Biology, Athens, GA 30602. Offers MS, PhD. *Faculty:* 35 full-time (5 women). *Students:* 68 full-time (23 women), 2 part-time (both women); includes 7 minority (3 Black or African American, non-Hispanic/Latino; 3 Asian, non-Hispanic/Latino; 1 Hispanic/Latino), 21 international. Average age 29. 119 applicants, 11% accepted, 6 enrolled. In 2011, 1 master's, 8 doctorates awarded. *Degree requirements:* For master's, one foreign language, thesis; for doctorate, one foreign language, thesis/dissertation. *Entrance requirements:* For master's and doctorate, GRE General Test. Additional exam requirements/recommendations for international students: Required—TOEFL. *Application deadline:* For fall admission, 1/1 priority date for domestic students, 1/1 for international students. Application fee: $50. Electronic applications accepted. *Financial support:* Fellowships, research assistantships, teaching assistantships, scholarships/grants, and unspecified assistantships available. Financial award application deadline: 1/1. *Unit head:* Dr. Stephen L. Hajduk, Head, 706-542-1676, Fax: 706-542-0182, E-mail: shajduk@bmb.uga.edu. *Application contact:* Dr. Lance Wells, Graduate Coordinator, 706-583-7806, Fax: 706-542-1738, E-mail: lwells@ccr.uga.edu. Web site: http://www.bmb.uga.edu/home/.

University of Guelph, Graduate Studies, College of Biological Science, Department of Molecular and Cellular Biology, Guelph, ON N1G 2W1, Canada. Offers biochemistry (M Sc, PhD); biophysics (M Sc, PhD); botany (M Sc, PhD); microbiology (M Sc, PhD); molecular biology and genetics (M Sc, PhD). *Degree requirements:* For master's, thesis, research proposal; for doctorate, comprehensive exam, thesis/dissertation, research proposal. *Entrance requirements:* For master's, minimum B-average during previous 2 years of coursework; for doctorate, minimum A-average. Additional exam requirements/recommendations for international students: Required—TOEFL (minimum score 550 paper-based; 213 computer-based), IELTS (minimum score 6.5). Electronic applications accepted. *Faculty research:* Physiology, structure, genetics, and ecology of microbes; virology and microbial technology.

University of Hawaii at Manoa, Graduate Division, College of Tropical Agriculture and Human Resources, Department of Molecular Biosciences and Bioengineering, Honolulu, HI 96822. Offers bioengineering (MS); molecular bioscience and bioengineering (MS); molecular biosciences and bioengineering (PhD). Part-time programs available. *Degree requirements:* For master's, thesis optional; for doctorate, comprehensive exam, thesis/dissertation. *Entrance requirements:* For master's and doctorate, GRE General Test. Additional exam requirements/recommendations for international students: Required—TOEFL (minimum score 550 paper-based; 213 computer-based; 79 iBT), IELTS (minimum score 5). *Faculty research:* Mechanization, agricultural systems, waste management, water management, cell culture.

University of Hawaii at Manoa, John A. Burns School of Medicine, Department of Cell and Molecular Biology, Honolulu, HI 96813. Offers MS, PhD. Part-time programs available. Terminal master's awarded for partial completion of doctoral program. *Degree requirements:* For master's, thesis optional; for doctorate, comprehensive exam, thesis/dissertation. *Entrance requirements:* For master's and doctorate, GRE General Test, minimum GPA of 3.0. Additional exam requirements/recommendations for international students: Required—TOEFL (minimum score 500 paper-based; 173 computer-based; 61 iBT), IELTS (minimum score 5).

University of Idaho, College of Graduate Studies, College of Science, Department of Biological Sciences, Moscow, ID 83844-3051. Offers biology (MS, PhD); microbiology, molecular biology and biochemistry (MS, PhD). *Faculty:* 12 full-time. *Students:* 29 full-time, 6 part-time. Average age 28. In 2011, 2 master's, 2 doctorates awarded. *Degree requirements:* For doctorate, one foreign language, thesis/dissertation. *Entrance requirements:* For master's, GRE, minimum GPA of 2.8; for doctorate, GRE, minimum undergraduate GPA of 2.8, 3.0 graduate. *Application deadline:* For fall admission, 8/1 for domestic students; for spring admission, 12/15 for domestic students. Applications are processed on a rolling basis. Application fee: $60. Electronic applications accepted. *Expenses:* Tuition, state resident: full-time $3874; part-time $334 per credit hour. Tuition, nonresident: full-time $16,394; part-time $861 per credit hour. *Required fees:* $2808; $99 per credit hour. Tuition and fees vary according to program. *Financial support:* Research assistantships and teaching assistantships available. Financial award applicants required to submit FAFSA. *Faculty research:* Animal behavior development, germ cell development, evolutionary biology, fish reproductive biology, molecular mechanisms. *Unit head:* John Byers, Acting Chair, 208-885-6280. *Application contact:* Erick Larson, Director of Graduate Admissions, 208-885-4723, E-mail: gadms@uidaho.edu. Web site: http://www.uidaho.edu/sci/biology.

University of Illinois at Chicago, College of Medicine and Graduate College, Graduate Programs in Medicine, Department of Biochemistry and Molecular Genetics, Chicago, IL 60607-7128. Offers PhD, MD/PhD. Terminal master's awarded for partial completion of doctoral program. *Degree requirements:* For doctorate, thesis/dissertation. *Entrance requirements:* For doctorate, GRE General Test. Additional exam requirements/recommendations for international students: Required—TOEFL. Electronic applications accepted. *Faculty research:* Nature of cellular components, control of metabolic processes, regulation of gene expression.

The University of Iowa, Graduate College, Program in Molecular and Cellular Biology, Iowa City, IA 52242-1316. Offers PhD, MD/PhD. *Degree requirements:* For doctorate, comprehensive exam, thesis/dissertation. *Entrance requirements:* For doctorate, GRE General Test, minimum GPA of 3.0. Additional exam requirements/recommendations for international students: Required—TOEFL (minimum score 600 paper-based; 250 computer-based; 100 iBT). Electronic applications accepted. *Faculty research:* Regulation of gene expression, inherited human genetic diseases, signal transduction mechanisms, structural biology and function.

The University of Kansas, Graduate Studies, College of Liberal Arts and Sciences, Department of Molecular Biosciences, Lawrence, KS 66044. Offers biochemistry and biophysics (MA, PhD); microbiology (MA, PhD); molecular, cellular, and developmental biology (MA, PhD). *Faculty:* 34. *Students:* 57 full-time (29 women), 2 part-time (1 woman); includes 6 minority (2 Asian, non-Hispanic/Latino; 3 Hispanic/Latino; 1 Two or more races, non-Hispanic/Latino), 26 international. Average age 28. 60 applicants, 30% accepted, 10 enrolled. In 2011, 1 master's, 12 doctorates awarded. Terminal master's awarded for partial completion of doctoral program. *Degree requirements:* For master's, comprehensive exam, thesis; for doctorate, comprehensive exam, thesis/dissertation. *Entrance requirements:* For master's and doctorate, GRE General Test. Additional exam requirements/recommendations for international students: Required—TOEFL or IELTS. *Application deadline:* For fall admission, 12/15 for domestic and international students. Application fee: $55 ($65 for international students). Electronic applications accepted. Tuition and fees vary according to course load, campus/location, program and reciprocity agreements. *Financial support:* Fellowships with tuition reimbursements, research assistantships with tuition reimbursements, teaching assistantships with tuition reimbursements, health care benefits, and unspecified assistantships available. Financial award application deadline: 3/1. *Faculty research:* Structure and function of proteins, genetics of organism development, molecular genetics, neurophysiology, molecular virology and pathogenics, developmental biology, cell biology. *Unit head:* Dr.

University of Connecticut Health Center

UCHC offers you exceptional research opportunities spanning **Cell Analysis and Modeling; Cell Biology; Genetics and Developmental Biology; Immunology; Molecular Biology and Biochemistry; Neuroscience;** and **Skeletal, Craniofacial and Oral Biology**.

Key features of our program include:
- ❖ Integrated admissions with access to more than 100 laboratories.
- ❖ Flexible educational program tailored to the interests of each student.
- ❖ Excellent education in a stimulating, cutting edge research environment.
- ❖ Competitive stipend ($28,000 for 2012–13 year), tuition waiver, and availability of student health plan.
- ❖ State-of-the-art research facilities, including the new Cell and Genome Sciences Building, which houses the UConn Stem Cell Institute, the Center for Cell Analysis and Modeling, and the Department of Genetics and Developmental Biology.

For more information, please contact:
Stephanie Rauch, Biomedical Science Admissions Coordinator
University of Connecticut Health Center
263 Farmington Ave., MC 3906
Farmington, CT 06030
BiomedSciAdmissions@uchc.edu
http://grad.uchc.edu/prospective/programs/phd_biosci/index.html

Mark Richter, Chair, 785-864-3334, Fax: 785-864-5294, E-mail: richter@ku.edu. *Application contact:* John P. Connolly, Graduate Program Assistant, 785-864-4311, Fax: 785-864-5294, E-mail: jconnolly@ku.edu. Web site: http://www.molecularbiosciences.ku.edu/.

The University of Kansas, University of Kansas Medical Center, School of Medicine, Department of Biochemistry and Molecular Biology, Kansas City, KS 66160. Offers MS, PhD, MD/PhD. *Faculty:* 17. *Students:* 6 full-time (1 woman), 5 international. Average age 27. In 2011, 2 doctorates awarded. Terminal master's awarded for partial completion of doctoral program. *Degree requirements:* For master's, thesis, oral defense of thesis; for doctorate, thesis/dissertation, comprehensive oral and written exam. *Entrance requirements:* Additional exam requirements/recommendations for international students: Required—TOEFL. Application fee: $0. Electronic applications accepted. Tuition and fees vary according to course load, campus/location, program and reciprocity agreements. *Financial support:* In 2011–12, 5 teaching assistantships with full and partial tuition reimbursements were awarded; fellowships, research assistantships with partial tuition reimbursements, traineeships, health care benefits, and unspecified assistantships also available. Financial award application deadline: 2/14; financial award applicants required to submit FAFSA. *Faculty research:* Determination of portion structure, underlying bases for interaction of proteins with their target, mapping allosteric circuiting within proteins, mechanism of action of transcription factors, renal signal transduction. *Total annual research expenditures:* $3 million. *Unit head:* Dr. Gerald M. Carlson, Chairman, 913-588-7005, Fax: 913-588-9896, E-mail: gcarlson@kumc.edu. *Application contact:* Dr. Liskin Swint-Kruse, Associate Professor, 913-588-0399, Fax: 913-588-9896, E-mail: lswint-kruse@kumc.edu. Web site: http://www.kumc.edu/biochemistry/.

University of Lethbridge, School of Graduate Studies, Lethbridge, AB T1K 3M4, Canada. Offers accounting (MScM); addictions counseling (M Sc); agricultural biotechnology (M Sc); agricultural studies (M Sc, MA); anthropology (MA); archaeology (MA); art (MA, MFA); biochemistry (M Sc); biological sciences (M Sc); biomolecular science (PhD); biosystems and biodiversity (PhD); Canadian studies (MA); chemistry (M Sc); computer science (M Sc); computer science and geographical information science (M Sc); counseling psychology (M Ed); dramatic arts (MA); earth, space, and physical science (PhD); economics (MA); educational leadership (M Ed); English (MA); environmental science (M Sc); evolution and behavior (PhD); exercise science (M Sc); finance (MScM); French (MA); French/German (MA); French/Spanish (MA); general education (M Ed); general management (MScM); geography (M Sc, MA); German (MA); health science (M Sc); history (MA); human resource management and labour relations (MScM); individualized multidisciplinary (M Sc, MA); information systems (MScM); international management (MScM); kinesiology (M Sc, MA); management (M Sc, MA); marketing (MScM); mathematics (M Sc); music (M Mus, MA); Native American studies (MA); neuroscience (M Sc, PhD); new media (MA); nursing (M Sc); philosophy (MA); physics (M Sc); policy and strategy (MScM); political science (MA); psychology (M Sc, MA); religious studies (MA); social sciences (MA); sociology (MA); theatre and dramatic arts (MFA); theoretical and computational science (PhD); urban and regional studies (MA); women's studies (MA). Part-time and evening/weekend programs available. *Degree requirements:* For doctorate, comprehensive exam, thesis/dissertation. *Entrance requirements:* For master's, GMAT (M Sc in management), bachelor's degree in related field, minimum GPA of 3.0 during previous 20 graded semester courses, 2 years teaching or related experience (M Ed); for doctorate, master's degree, minimum graduate GPA of 3.5. Additional exam requirements/recommendations for international students: Required—TOEFL. *Faculty research:* Movement and brain plasticity, gibberellin physiology, photosynthesis, carbon cycling, molecular properties of main-group ring components.

University of Louisville, School of Medicine, Department of Biochemistry and Molecular Biology, Louisville, KY 40292-0001. Offers MS, PhD, MD/PhD. Terminal master's awarded for partial completion of doctoral program. *Degree requirements:* For master's, thesis; for doctorate, comprehensive exam, thesis/dissertation, one first author publication. *Entrance requirements:* For master's and doctorate, GRE General Test (minimum score of 1000 verbal and quantitative), minimum GPA of 3.0. Additional exam requirements/recommendations for international students: Required—TOEFL. Electronic applications accepted. *Expenses:* Tuition, state resident: full-time $9692; part-time $539 per credit hour. Tuition, nonresident: full-time $20,168; part-time $1121 per credit hour. Tuition and fees vary according to program and reciprocity agreements. *Faculty research:* Genetic regulatory mechanisms, microRNAs, vesicular trafficking in cancer metastasis and angiogenesis, ribosome biogenesis and disease, regulation of foreign compound metabolism/lipid and steroid metabolism.

University of Maine, Graduate School, College of Natural Sciences, Forestry, and Agriculture, Department of Biochemistry, Molecular Biology, and Microbiology, Orono, ME 04469. Offers biochemistry (MPS, MS); biochemistry and molecular biology (PhD); microbiology (MPS, MS, PhD). *Faculty:* 11 full-time (6 women), 3 part-time/adjunct (2 women). *Students:* 25 full-time (15 women), 35 part-time (23 women); includes 4 minority (2 Asian, non-Hispanic/Latino; 1 Hispanic/Latino; 1 Two or more races, non-Hispanic/Latino), 13 international. Average age 31. 41 applicants, 29% accepted, 11 enrolled. In 2011, 6 master's, 6 doctorates awarded. *Degree requirements:* For doctorate, thesis/dissertation. *Entrance requirements:* For master's and doctorate, GRE General Test. Additional exam requirements/recommendations for international students: Required—TOEFL. *Application deadline:* For fall admission, 2/1 priority date for domestic students. Applications are processed on a rolling basis. Application fee: $65. Electronic applications accepted. *Expenses:* Tuition, state resident: full-time $5016. Tuition, nonresident: full-time $14,424. *Financial support:* In 2011–12, 5 research assistantships with full tuition reimbursements (averaging $25,368 per year), 12 teaching assistantships with full tuition reimbursements (averaging $20,106 per year) were awarded; tuition waivers (full and partial) also available. Financial award application deadline: 3/1. *Total annual research expenditures:* $242,844. *Unit head:* Dr. Robert Gundersen, Chair, 207-581-2802, Fax: 207-581-2801. *Application contact:* Scott G. Delcourt, Associate Dean of the Graduate School, 207-581-3291, Fax: 207-581-3232, E-mail: graduate@maine.edu. Web site: http://www2.umaine.edu/graduate/.

University of Maine, Graduate School, Program in Biomedical Sciences, Orono, ME 04469. Offers biomedical engineering (PhD); cell and molecular biology (PhD); neuroscience (PhD); toxicology (PhD). *Students:* 11 full-time (7 women), 19 part-time (11 women), 8 international. Average age 29. 32 applicants, 31% accepted, 8 enrolled. In 2011, 3 degrees awarded. Application fee: $65. *Expenses:* Tuition, state resident: full-time $5016. Tuition, nonresident: full-time $14,424. *Financial support:* In 2011–12, 2 fellowships with full tuition reimbursements (averaging $18,000 per year), 8 research assistantships with full tuition reimbursements (averaging $23,000 per year) were awarded. *Unit head:* Dr. Carol Kim, Unit Head, 207-581-2803. *Application contact:* Scott G. Delcourt, Associate Dean of the Graduate School, 207-581-3291, Fax: 207-581-3232, E-mail: graduate@maine.edu. Web site: http://www2.umaine.edu/graduate.

The University of Manchester, Faculty of Life Sciences, Manchester, United Kingdom. Offers adaptive organismal biology (M Phil, PhD); animal biology (M Phil, PhD); biochemistry (M Phil, PhD); bioinformatics (M Phil, PhD); biomolecular sciences (M Phil, PhD); biotechnology (M Phil, PhD); cell biology (M Phil, PhD); cell matrix research (M Phil, PhD); channels and transporters (M Phil, PhD); developmental biology (M Phil, PhD); Egyptology (M Phil, PhD); environmental biology (M Phil, PhD); evolutionary biology (M Phil, PhD); gene expression (M Phil, PhD); genetics (M Phil, PhD); history of science, technology and medicine (M Phil, PhD); immunology (M Phil, PhD); integrative neurobiology and behavior (M Phil, PhD); membrane trafficking (M Phil, PhD); microbiology (M Phil, PhD); molecular and cellular neuroscience (M Phil, PhD); molecular biology (M Phil, PhD); molecular cancer studies (M Phil, PhD); neuroscience (M Phil, PhD); ophthalmology (M Phil, PhD); optometry (M Phil, PhD); organelle function (M Phil, PhD); pharmacology (M Phil, PhD); physiology (M Phil, PhD); plant sciences (M Phil, PhD); stem cell research (M Phil, PhD); structural biology (M Phil, PhD); systems neuroscience (M Phil, PhD); toxicology (M Phil, PhD).

The University of Manchester, School of Dentistry, Manchester, United Kingdom. Offers basic dental sciences (cancer studies) (M Phil, PhD); basic dental sciences (molecular genetics) (M Phil, PhD); basic dental sciences (stem cell biology) (M Phil, PhD); biomaterials sciences and dental technology (M Phil, PhD); dental public health/community dentistry (M Phil, PhD); dental science (clinical) (PhD); endodontology (M Phil, PhD); fixed and removable prosthodontics (M Phil, PhD); operative dentistry (M Phil, PhD); oral and maxillofacial surgery (M Phil, PhD); oral radiology (M Phil, PhD); orthodontics (M Phil, PhD); restorative dentistry (M Phil, PhD).

University of Maryland, Baltimore, Graduate School, Graduate Program in Life Sciences, Program in Biochemistry and Molecular Biology, Baltimore, MD 21201. Offers biochemistry (MS, PhD); MD/PhD. *Students:* 28 full-time (15 women), 2 part-time (1 woman); includes 11 minority (2 Black or African American, non-Hispanic/Latino; 1 American Indian or Alaska Native, non-Hispanic/Latino; 3 Asian, non-Hispanic/Latino; 3 Hispanic/Latino; 2 Two or more races, non-Hispanic/Latino), 3 international. Average age 27. 62 applicants, 3% accepted, 2 enrolled. In 2011, 1 master's, 4 doctorates awarded. *Entrance requirements:* For doctorate, GRE General Test. Additional exam requirements/recommendations for international students: Required—TOEFL (minimum score 550 paper-based; 80 iBT); Recommended—IELTS (minimum score 7). *Application deadline:* For fall admission, 1/15 for domestic and international students. Application fee: $50. Electronic applications accepted. *Financial support:* In 2011–12, research assistantships with full tuition reimbursements (averaging $25,000 per year) were awarded; fellowships, health care benefits, and unspecified assistantships also available. Financial award application deadline: 3/1. *Faculty research:* Membrane transport, hormonal regulation, protein structure, molecular virology. *Unit head:* Dr. Gerald Wilson, Professor/Director, 410-706-8904. *Application contact:* Foyeke Daramola, Program Coordinator, 410-706-8417, Fax: 410-706-8297, E-mail: fdaramola@som.umaryland.edu. Web site: http://biochemistry.umaryland.edu.

University of Maryland, Baltimore, Graduate School, Graduate Program in Life Sciences, Program in Molecular Medicine, Baltimore, MD 21201. Offers cancer biology (PhD); cell and molecular physiology (PhD); human genetics and genomic medicine (PhD); molecular medicine (MS); molecular toxicology and pharmacology (PhD); MD/PhD. *Students:* 80 full-time (53 women), 11 part-time (4 women); includes 21 minority (8 Black or African American, non-Hispanic/Latino; 6 Asian, non-Hispanic/Latino; 4 Hispanic/Latino; 3 Two or more races, non-Hispanic/Latino), 13 international. Average age 27. 207 applicants, 24% accepted, 15 enrolled. In 2011, 3 master's, 5 doctorates awarded. *Entrance requirements:* Additional exam requirements/recommendations for international students: Required—TOEFL (minimum score 600 paper-based; 100 iBT); Recommended—IELTS (minimum score 7). *Application deadline:* For fall admission, 1/15 for domestic and international students. Application fee: $50. Electronic applications accepted. *Financial support:* In 2011–12, research assistantships with partial tuition reimbursements (averaging $25,000 per year) were awarded; fellowships also available. Financial award application deadline: 3/1. *Unit head:* Dr. Toni Antalis, Director, 410-706-8222, E-mail: tantalis@som.umaryland.edu. *Application contact:* Sharron Graves, Program Coordinator, 410-706-6044, Fax: 410-706-6040, E-mail: sgraves@som.umaryland.edu. Web site: http://molecularmedicine.umaryland.edu.

University of Maryland, Baltimore County, Graduate School, College of Natural and Mathematical Sciences, Department of Biological Sciences, Program in Applied Molecular Biology, Baltimore, MD 21250. Offers MS. *Faculty:* 26 full-time (9 women). *Students:* 9 full-time (2 women), 1 (woman) part-time; includes 2 minority (1 Black or African American, non-Hispanic/Latino; 1 Asian, non-Hispanic/Latino). Average age 24. 41 applicants, 56% accepted, 10 enrolled. In 2011, 9 master's awarded. *Entrance requirements:* For master's, GRE General Test, GRE Subject Test (recommended), minimum GPA of 3.0. Additional exam requirements/recommendations for international students: Required—TOEFL. *Application deadline:* For fall admission, 4/1 priority date for domestic students, 4/1 for international students. Applications are processed on a rolling basis. Application fee: $50. Electronic applications accepted. *Financial support:* In 2011–12, 1 student received support, including 4 teaching assistantships with full and partial tuition reimbursements available (averaging $12,000 per year); tuition waivers (partial) also available. Financial award applicants required to submit FAFSA. *Faculty research:* Structure-function of RNA, genetics and molecular biology, biological chemistry. *Unit head:* Dr. Richard E. Wolf, Director, Applied Molecular Biology Graduate Program, 410-455-3669, Fax: 410-455-3875, E-mail: biograd@umbc.edu. *Application contact:* Dr. Richard E. Wolf, Director, Applied Molecular Biology Graduate Program, 410-455-3669, Fax: 410-455-3875, E-mail: biograd@umbc.edu. Web site: http://www.umbc.edu/biosci.

University of Maryland, Baltimore County, Graduate School, College of Natural and Mathematical Sciences, Department of Biological Sciences, Program in Molecular and Cell Biology, Baltimore, MD 21250. Offers PhD. *Faculty:* 26 full-time (9 women). *Students:* 21 full-time (13 women); includes 8 minority (2 Black or African American, non-Hispanic/Latino; 6 Asian, non-Hispanic/Latino). Average age 27. 13 applicants, 23% accepted, 2 enrolled. In 2011, 1 doctorate awarded. *Degree requirements:* For doctorate, thesis/dissertation. *Entrance requirements:* For doctorate, GRE General Test, GRE Subject Test, minimum GPA of 3.0. Additional exam requirements/recommendations for international students: Required—TOEFL. *Application deadline:* For fall admission, 1/15 for domestic students, 12/15 for international students. Applications are processed on a rolling basis. Application fee: $50. Electronic applications accepted. *Financial support:* In 2011–12, fellowships with full tuition reimbursements (averaging $22,300 per year), research assistantships with full tuition reimbursements (averaging $22,300 per year), teaching assistantships with full tuition reimbursements (averaging $22,300 per year) were awarded. *Unit head:* Dr. Stephen Miller, Graduate Program Director, 410-455-3669, Fax: 410-455-3875, E-mail: biograd@umbc.edu. *Application contact:* Dr. Stephen Miller, Graduate Program Director, 410-455-3669, Fax: 410-455-3875, E-mail: biograd@umbc.edu. Web site: http://www.umbc.edu/biosci/.

University of Maryland, College Park, Academic Affairs, College of Computer, Mathematical and Natural Sciences, Department of Biology, PhD Program in Biological Sciences, College Park, MD 20742. Offers behavior, ecology, evolution, and systematics (PhD); computational biology, bioinformatics, and genomics (PhD); molecular and cellular biology (PhD); physiological systems (PhD). *Students:* 68 full-time (41 women), 4 part-time (2 women); includes 13 minority (3 Black or African American, non-Hispanic/Latino; 4 Asian, non-Hispanic/Latino; 5 Hispanic/Latino; 1 Two or more races, non-Hispanic/Latino), 21 international. 380 applicants, 15% accepted, 22 enrolled. *Degree requirements:* For doctorate, comprehensive exam, thesis/dissertation,

present thesis work in seminar. *Entrance requirements:* For doctorate, GRE General Test; GRE Subject Test in biology (recommended), academic transcripts, statement of purpose/research interests, 3 letters of recommendation. Additional exam requirements/recommendations for international students: Required—TOEFL. *Application deadline:* For fall admission, 12/15 for domestic and international students. Applications are processed on a rolling basis. Application fee: $75. Electronic applications accepted. *Expenses:* Tuition, state resident: part-time $525 per credit hour. Tuition, nonresident: part-time $1131 per credit hour. *Required fees:* $386.31 per term. Tuition and fees vary according to program. *Financial support:* In 2011–12, 11 fellowships with full and partial tuition reimbursements (averaging $14,406 per year), 16 research assistantships (averaging $19,495 per year), 41 teaching assistantships (averaging $18,734 per year) were awarded. *Unit head:* Dr. Barbara Thorne, Director, 301-405-6905, E-mail: bthorne@umd.edu. *Application contact:* Dr. Charles A. Caramello, Dean of Graduate School, 301-405-0358, Fax: 301-314-9305. Web site: http://bisi.umd.edu/biologicalsciencesgraduateprogrambisi.

University of Maryland, College Park, Academic Affairs, College of Computer, Mathematical and Natural Sciences, Department of Cell Biology and Molecular Genetics, Program in Molecular and Cellular Biology, College Park, MD 20742. Offers PhD. Part-time and evening/weekend programs available. *Students:* 30 full-time (20 women), 2 part-time (both women); includes 6 minority (2 Black or African American, non-Hispanic/Latino; 3 Asian, non-Hispanic/Latino; 1 Hispanic/Latino), 17 international. In 2011, 6 doctorates awarded. *Degree requirements:* For doctorate, thesis/dissertation, exam, public service. *Expenses:* Tuition, state resident: part-time $525 per credit hour. Tuition, nonresident: part-time $1131 per credit hour. *Required fees:* $386.31 per term. Tuition and fees vary according to program. *Financial support:* In 2011–12, 2 fellowships with partial tuition reimbursements (averaging $10,800 per year), 10 research assistantships (averaging $19,663 per year), 17 teaching assistantships (averaging $19,382 per year) were awarded. Financial award applicants required to submit FAFSA. *Faculty research:* Monoclonal antibody production, oligonucleotide synthesis, macromolecular processing, signal transduction, developmental biology. *Unit head:* Dr. Barbara Thorne, Director, 301-405-7947, E-mail: bthorne@umd.edu. *Application contact:* Dr. Charles A. Caramello, Dean of Graduate School, 301-405-0358, Fax: 301-314-9305.

University of Massachusetts Boston, Office of Graduate Studies, College of Science and Mathematics, Track in Molecular, Cellular and Organismal Biology, Boston, MA 02125-3393. Offers PhD.

University of Medicine and Dentistry of New Jersey, Graduate School of Biomedical Sciences, Graduate Programs in Biomedical Sciences–Newark, Department of Biochemistry and Molecular Biology, Newark, NJ 07107. Offers MS, PhD. *Degree requirements:* For master's, thesis; for doctorate, thesis/dissertation, qualifying exam. *Entrance requirements:* For master's and doctorate, GRE General Test. Additional exam requirements/recommendations for international students: Required—TOEFL. Electronic applications accepted.

University of Medicine and Dentistry of New Jersey, Graduate School of Biomedical Sciences, Graduate Programs in Biomedical Sciences–Piscataway, Program in Biochemistry and Molecular Biology, Piscataway, NJ 08854-5635. Offers MS, PhD, MD/PhD. PhD, MS offered jointly with Rutgers, The State University of New Jersey, New Brunswick. Terminal master's awarded for partial completion of doctoral program. *Degree requirements:* For master's, thesis, qualifying exam; for doctorate, thesis/dissertation, qualifying exam. *Entrance requirements:* For master's and doctorate, GRE General Test. Additional exam requirements/recommendations for international students: Required—TOEFL. Electronic applications accepted. *Faculty research:* Signal transduction, regulation of RNA, polymerase II transcribed genes, developmental gene expression.

University of Medicine and Dentistry of New Jersey, Graduate School of Biomedical Sciences, Graduate Programs in Biomedical Sciences–Stratford, Program in Cell and Molecular Biology, Stratford, NJ 08084-5634. Offers MS, PhD, DO/PhD. *Degree requirements:* For master's, thesis; for doctorate, thesis/dissertation, qualifying exam. *Entrance requirements:* For master's and doctorate, GRE General Test. Additional exam requirements/recommendations for international students: Required—TOEFL. Electronic applications accepted.

University of Medicine and Dentistry of New Jersey, Graduate School of Biomedical Sciences, Programs in the Molecular Biosciences, Piscataway, NJ 08854-5696. Offers PhD. Program offered jointly with Rutgers, The State University of New Jersey, New Brunswick. *Entrance requirements:* Additional exam requirements/recommendations for international students: Required—TOEFL. Electronic applications accepted.

University of Miami, Graduate School, Miller School of Medicine, Graduate Programs in Medicine, Department of Biochemistry and Molecular Biology, Coral Gables, FL 33124. Offers PhD, MD/PhD. *Degree requirements:* For doctorate, comprehensive exam, thesis/dissertation, proposition exams. *Faculty research:* Macromolecule metabolism, molecular genetics, protein folding and 3-D structure, regulation of gene expression and enzyme function, signal transduction and developmental biology.

University of Miami, Graduate School, Miller School of Medicine, Graduate Programs in Medicine, Department of Cell Biology and Anatomy, Coral Gables, FL 33124. Offers molecular cell and developmental biology (PhD); MD/PhD. *Degree requirements:* For doctorate, thesis/dissertation. *Entrance requirements:* For doctorate, GRE General Test, GRE Subject Test. Additional exam requirements/recommendations for international students: Required—TOEFL. Electronic applications accepted.

University of Michigan, Horace H. Rackham School of Graduate Studies, College of Literature, Science, and the Arts, Department of Molecular, Cellular, and Developmental Biology, Ann Arbor, MI 48109. Offers MS, PhD. Part-time programs available. *Faculty:* 33 full-time (10 women). *Students:* 78 full-time (39 women), 5 part-time (2 women); includes 5 minority (3 Asian, non-Hispanic/Latino; 2 Hispanic/Latino), 40 international. Average age 27. 137 applicants, 17% accepted, 12 enrolled. In 2011, 7 master's, 7 doctorates awarded. Terminal master's awarded for partial completion of doctoral program. *Degree requirements:* For master's, 24 credits with at least 16 in molecular, cellular, and developmental biology and 4 in a cognate field; for doctorate, thesis/dissertation, preliminary exam, oral defense. *Entrance requirements:* For master's and doctorate, GRE General Test. Additional exam requirements/recommendations for international students: Required—TOEFL (minimum score 560 paper-based; 220 computer-based; 83 iBT). *Application deadline:* For fall admission, 1/5 for domestic and international students; for winter admission, 11/1 for domestic and international students; for spring admission, 4/1 for domestic and international students. Applications are processed on a rolling basis. Application fee: $65 ($75 for international students). Electronic applications accepted. *Financial support:* In 2011–12, 55 students received support, including 12 fellowships with full tuition reimbursements available (averaging $26,500 per year), 30 research assistantships with full tuition reimbursements available (averaging $26,500 per year), 13 teaching assistantships with full tuition reimbursements available (averaging $26,500 per year); health care benefits also available. *Faculty research:* Cell biology, microbiology, neurobiology and physiology, developmental biology and plant molecular biology. *Unit head:* Dr. Pamela A. Raymond, Department Chair, 734-764-7476, Fax: 734-615-6337, E-mail: praymond@umich.edu. *Application contact:* Mary Carr, Graduate Coordinator, 734-615-1635, Fax: 734-764-0884, E-mail: carrmm@umich.edu. Web site: http://www.mcdb.lsa.umich.edu.

University of Michigan, Horace H. Rackham School of Graduate Studies, Program in Biomedical Sciences (PIBS), Interdisciplinary Program in Cellular and Molecular Biology, Ann Arbor, MI 48109. Offers PhD. *Faculty:* 161 part-time/adjunct (44 women). *Students:* 74 full-time (40 women); includes 21 minority (2 Black or African American, non-Hispanic/Latino; 1 American Indian or Alaska Native, non-Hispanic/Latino; 10 Asian, non-Hispanic/Latino; 8 Hispanic/Latino). Average age 26. In 2011, 12 doctorates awarded. *Degree requirements:* For doctorate, comprehensive exam, thesis/dissertation, oral defense of dissertation, preliminary exam. *Entrance requirements:* For doctorate, GRE General Test, GRE Subject Test. *Financial support:* In 2011–12, 74 students received support, including 21 fellowships with tuition reimbursements available (averaging $26,500 per year), 53 research assistantships with tuition reimbursements available (averaging $26,500 per year); teaching assistantships and scholarships/grants also available. *Faculty research:* Genetics, genomics, gene regulation, models of disease, microbes. *Total annual research expenditures:* $20 million. *Unit head:* Dr. Jessica Schwartz, Director, 734-764-5428, Fax: 734-647-6232, E-mail: jeschwar@umich.edu. *Application contact:* Catherine A. Mitchell, Senior Student Services Associate I, 734-764-5428, Fax: 734-647-6232, E-mail: cmbgrad@umich.edu. Web site: http://www.med.umich.edu/cmb/.

University of Minnesota, Duluth, Medical School, Department of Biochemistry, Molecular Biology and Biophysics, Duluth, MN 55812-2496. Offers biochemistry, molecular biology and biophysics (MS); biology and biophysics (PhD); social, administrative, and clinical pharmacy (MS, PhD); toxicology (MS, PhD). Terminal master's awarded for partial completion of doctoral program. *Degree requirements:* For master's, comprehensive exam, thesis; for doctorate, comprehensive exam, thesis/dissertation. *Entrance requirements:* For master's and doctorate, GRE General Test. Additional exam requirements/recommendations for international students: Required—TOEFL. Electronic applications accepted. *Faculty research:* Intestinal cancer biology; hepatotoxins and mitochondriopathies; toxicology; cell cycle regulation in stem cells; neurobiology of brain development, trace metal function and blood-brain barrier; hibernation biology.

University of Minnesota, Twin Cities Campus, Graduate School, College of Biological Sciences, Biochemistry, Molecular Biology and Biophysics Graduate Program, Minneapolis, MN 55455-0213. Offers PhD. *Degree requirements:* For doctorate, thesis/dissertation. *Entrance requirements:* For doctorate, GRE, 3 letters of recommendation, more than 1 semester of laboratory experience. Additional exam requirements/recommendations for international students: Required—TOEFL (minimum score 625 paper-based; 263 computer-based; 108 iBT with writing subsection 25 and reading subsection 25) or IELTS (minimum score 7). Electronic applications accepted. *Faculty research:* Microbial biochemistry, biotechnology, molecular biology, regulatory biochemistry, structural biology and biophysics, physical biochemistry, enzymology, physiological chemistry.

University of Minnesota, Twin Cities Campus, Graduate School, Program in Molecular, Cellular, Developmental Biology and Genetics, Minneapolis, MN 55455-0213. Offers genetic counseling (MS); molecular, cellular, developmental biology and genetics (PhD). Terminal master's awarded for partial completion of doctoral program. *Degree requirements:* For master's, thesis optional; for doctorate, thesis/dissertation. *Entrance requirements:* For master's and doctorate, GRE General Test. Additional exam requirements/recommendations for international students: Required—TOEFL (minimum score 625 paper-based; 263 computer-based; 80 iBT). Electronic applications accepted. *Faculty research:* Membrane receptors and membrane transport, cell interactions, cytoskeleton and cell mobility, regulation of gene expression, plant cell and molecular biology.

University of Missouri–Kansas City, School of Biological Sciences, Program in Molecular Biology and Biochemistry, Kansas City, MO 64110-2499. Offers PhD. Offered through the School of Graduate Studies. *Faculty:* 40 full-time (10 women), 3 part-time/adjunct (2 women). *Students:* 6 full-time (4 women), 7 part-time (6 women), 7 international. Average age 31. 8 applicants, 100% accepted, 3 enrolled. *Degree requirements:* For doctorate, comprehensive exam, thesis/dissertation. *Entrance requirements:* For doctorate, GRE General Test, bachelor's degree in chemistry, biology, or a related discipline; minimum GPA of 3.0. Additional exam requirements/recommendations for international students: Required—TOEFL (minimum score 550 paper-based; 213 computer-based; 80 iBT). *Application deadline:* For fall admission, 2/15 priority date for domestic students, 2/15 for international students. Application fee: $45 ($50 for international students). *Expenses:* Tuition, state resident: full-time $5798; part-time $322.10 per credit hour. Tuition, nonresident: full-time $14,969; part-time $831.60 per credit hour. *Required fees:* $93.51 per credit hour. *Financial support:* Research assistantships with full tuition reimbursements, teaching assistantships with full and partial tuition reimbursements, scholarships/grants, tuition waivers (full and partial), and unspecified assistantships available. Financial award application deadline: 3/1; financial award applicants required to submit FAFSA. *Unit head:* Dr. Henry Miziorko, Head, 816-235-2235, E-mail: miziorkoh@umkc.edu. *Application contact:* Laura Batenic, Information Contact, 816-235-2352, Fax: 816-235-5158, E-mail: batenicl@umkc.edu. Web site: http://sbs.umkc.edu/.

See Display on next page and Close-Up on page 247.

University of Missouri–St. Louis, College of Arts and Sciences, Department of Biology, St. Louis, MO 63121. Offers biotechnology (Certificate); cell and molecular biology (MS, PhD); ecology, evolution and systematics (MS, PhD); tropical biology and conservation (Certificate). Part-time programs available. *Faculty:* 43 full-time (13 women), 4 part-time/adjunct (1 woman). *Students:* 68 full-time (33 women), 64 part-time (28 women); includes 20 minority (9 Black or African American, non-Hispanic/Latino; 7 Asian, non-Hispanic/Latino; 3 Hispanic/Latino; 1 Two or more races, non-Hispanic/Latino), 43 international. Average age 28. 122 applicants, 48% accepted, 36 enrolled. In 2011, 20 master's, 3 doctorates, 11 other advanced degrees awarded. *Degree requirements:* For master's, thesis or alternative; for doctorate, thesis/dissertation, 1 semester of teaching experience. *Entrance requirements:* For master's, 3 letters of recommendation; for doctorate, GRE General Test, 3 letters of recommendation. Additional exam requirements/recommendations for international students: Required—TOEFL. *Application deadline:* For fall admission, 12/15 priority date for domestic students, 12/15 for international students; for spring admission, 12/1 priority date for domestic students, 12/1 for international students. Applications are processed on a rolling basis. Application fee: $35 ($40 for international students). Electronic applications accepted. *Expenses:* Tuition, state resident: full-time $6273; part-time $3866 per year. Tuition, nonresident: full-time $14,969; part-time $9980 per year. *Required fees:* $315 per year. *Financial support:* In 2011–12, 13 research assistantships with full and partial tuition reimbursements (averaging $15,300 per year), 27 teaching assistantships with full and partial tuition reimbursements (averaging $15,300 per year) were awarded; fellowships with full tuition reimbursements, career-related internships or fieldwork, and Federal Work-Study also available. Support available to part-time students. Financial award application deadline: 2/1. *Faculty research:* Molecular biology, microbial genetics, animal behavior, tropical ecology, plant systematics. *Unit head:* Dr. Wendy Olivas,

UMKC

SCHOOL OF BIOLOGICAL SCIENCES

The outstanding faculty and state-of-the-art facilities at the School of Biological Sciences provide our students with a strong research-based graduate degree program.

Our focus on molecular recognition underpins the fundamental importance of biomolecular structure and function to cell and molecular biology and creates opportunities to use an interdisciplinary approach to address some of the most critical areas of current biology.

Graduate degree programs:

http://sbs.umkc.edu/graduate_overview.cfm

UNIVERSITY OF MISSOURI

KANSAS CITY

sbsgradrecruit@umkc.edu   www.umkc.edu/sbs

Director of Graduate Studies, 314-516-6200, Fax: 314-516-6233, E-mail: olivasw@umsl.edu. *Application contact:* 314-516-5458, Fax: 314-516-6996, E-mail: gradadm@umsl.edu. Web site: http://www.umsl.edu/divisions/artscience/biology/.

University of Nebraska Medical Center, Graduate Studies, Department of Biochemistry and Molecular Biology, Omaha, NE 68198. Offers MS, PhD. Terminal master's awarded for partial completion of doctoral program. *Degree requirements:* For master's, comprehensive exam, thesis; for doctorate, comprehensive exam, thesis/dissertation. *Entrance requirements:* For master's and doctorate, GRE General Test. Additional exam requirements/recommendations for international students: Required—TOEFL (minimum score 550 paper-based; 213 computer-based). Electronic applications accepted. *Faculty research:* Recombinant DNA, cancer biology, diabetes and drug metabolism, biochemical endocrinology.

University of Nevada, Reno, Graduate School, Interdisciplinary Program in Cell and Molecular Biology, Reno, NV 89557. Offers MS, PhD. Terminal master's awarded for partial completion of doctoral program. *Degree requirements:* For master's, thesis; for doctorate, thesis/dissertation. *Entrance requirements:* For master's, GRE Subject Test (recommended), minimum GPA of 2.75; for doctorate, GRE Subject Test (recommended), minimum GPA of 3.0. Additional exam requirements/recommendations for international students: Required—TOEFL (minimum score 500 paper-based; 173 computer-based; 61 iBT), IELTS (minimum score 6). Electronic applications accepted. *Faculty research:* Cellular biology, biophysics, cancer, microbiology, insect biochemistry.

University of New Haven, Graduate School, College of Arts and Sciences, Program in Cellular and Molecular Biology, West Haven, CT 06516-1916. Offers MS. *Students:* 29 full-time (21 women), 19 part-time (12 women); includes 4 minority (1 Black or African American, non-Hispanic/Latino; 2 Asian, non-Hispanic/Latino; 1 Hispanic/Latino), 24 international. 41 applicants, 93% accepted, 12 enrolled. In 2011, 22 master's awarded. *Degree requirements:* For master's, thesis optional. *Entrance requirements:* Additional exam requirements/recommendations for international students: Required—TOEFL (minimum score 520 paper-based; 190 computer-based; 70 iBT), IELTS (minimum score 5.5). *Application deadline:* For fall admission, 5/31 for international students; for winter admission, 10/15 for international students; for spring admission, 1/15 for international students. Applications are processed on a rolling basis. Application fee: $50. Electronic applications accepted. *Expenses:* Tuition: Part-time $750 per credit. *Financial support:* Career-related internships or fieldwork and Federal Work-Study available. Financial award application deadline: 5/1; financial award applicants required to submit FAFSA. *Unit head:* Dr. Michael Rossi, Chair, 203-932-7125, E-mail: mrossi@newhaven.edu. *Application contact:* Eloise Gormley, Director of Graduate Admissions, 203-932-7449, Fax: 203-932-7137, E-mail: gradinfo@newhaven.edu. Web site: http://www.newhaven.edu/4724/.

University of New Mexico, Health Sciences Center Graduate Programs, Program in Biomedical Sciences, Albuquerque, NM 87131-5196. Offers biochemistry and molecular biology (MS, PhD); cell biology and physiology (MS, PhD); clinical and translational science (Certificate); molecular genetics and microbiology (MS, PhD); neuroscience (MS, PhD); pathology (MS, PhD); toxicology (MS, PhD); university science teaching (Certificate). Part-time programs available. *Faculty:* 64 full-time (26 women), 9 part-time/adjunct (4 women). *Students:* 45 full-time (27 women), 56 part-time (28 women); includes 24 minority (3 Black or African American, non-Hispanic/Latino; 1 American Indian or Alaska Native, non-Hispanic/Latino; 4 Asian, non-Hispanic/Latino; 14 Hispanic/Latino; 1 Native Hawaiian or other Pacific Islander, non-Hispanic/Latino; 1 Two or more races, non-Hispanic/Latino), 18 international. Average age 30. 110 applicants, 18% accepted, 17 enrolled. In 2011, 14 master's, 5 doctorates awarded. Terminal master's awarded for partial completion of doctoral program. *Degree requirements:* For master's, thesis; for doctorate, comprehensive exam, thesis/dissertation. *Entrance requirements:* For master's and doctorate, GRE General Test, minimum undergraduate GPA of 3.0. Additional exam requirements/recommendations for international students: Required—TOEFL. *Application deadline:* For fall admission, 3/1 priority date for domestic students, 3/1 for international students. Applications are processed on a rolling basis. Application fee: $50. Electronic applications accepted. *Financial support:* In 2011–12, 99 students received support, including 28 fellowships with full and partial tuition reimbursements available (averaging $22,000 per year), 73 research assistantships with full tuition reimbursements available (averaging $23,000 per year), 8 teaching assistantships (averaging $2,800 per year); career-related internships or fieldwork, Federal Work-Study, institutionally sponsored loans, scholarships/grants, traineeships, health care benefits, and unspecified assistantships also available. Financial award application deadline: 1/1; financial award applicants required to submit FAFSA. *Faculty research:* Infectious disease/Immunity, cancer biology, cardiovascular and metabolic diseases, brain and behavioral illness, environmental health. *Unit head:* Dr. Helen J. Hathaway, BSGP Program Director, 505-272-1887, Fax: 505-272-2412, E-mail: hhathaway@salud.unm.edu. *Application contact:* Mary Fenton, Admissions Coordinator, 505-272-1887, Fax: 505-272-2412, E-mail: mfenton@salud.unm.edu. Web site: http://hsc.unm.edu/som/research/brep/bsgpabout.shtm.

The University of North Carolina at Chapel Hill, Graduate School, College of Arts and Sciences, Department of Biology, Chapel Hill, NC 27599. Offers botany (MA, MS, PhD); cell biology, development, and physiology (MA, MS, PhD); cell motility and cytoskeleton (PhD); ecology and behavior (MA, MS, PhD); genetics and molecular biology (MA, MS, PhD); morphology, systematics, and evolution (MA, MS, PhD). Terminal master's awarded for partial completion of doctoral program. *Degree requirements:* For master's, comprehensive exam, thesis (for some programs); for doctorate, comprehensive exam, thesis/dissertation. *Entrance requirements:* For master's, GRE General Test, GRE Subject Test, 2 semesters of calculus or statistics; 2 semesters of physics, organic chemistry; 3 semesters of biology; for doctorate, GRE General Test, GRE Subject Test, 2 semesters calculus or statistics, 2 semesters physics, organic chemistry, 3 semesters of biology. Additional exam requirements/recommendations for international students: Required—TOEFL (minimum score 550 paper-based; 213 computer-based). Electronic applications accepted. *Faculty research:* Gene expression, biomechanics, yeast genetics, plant ecology, plant molecular biology.

The University of North Carolina at Chapel Hill, School of Medicine and Graduate School, Graduate Programs in Medicine, Curriculum in Genetics and Molecular Biology, Chapel Hill, NC 27599. Offers MS, PhD. *Degree requirements:* For doctorate, comprehensive exam, thesis/dissertation. *Entrance requirements:* For doctorate, GRE, minimum GPA of 3.0. Additional exam requirements/recommendations for international students: Required—TOEFL. Electronic applications accepted. *Faculty research:* Telomere replication and germline immortality, experimental evolution in microorganisms, genetic vulnerabilities in tumor genomes, genetics of cell cycle control during Drosophila development, mammalian genetics.

University of North Dakota, Graduate School and Graduate School, Graduate Programs in Medicine, Department of Biochemistry and Molecular Biology, Grand Forks, ND 58202. Offers MS, PhD. *Degree requirements:* For master's, thesis, final exam; for doctorate, comprehensive exam, thesis/dissertation, final exam. *Entrance requirements:* For master's and doctorate, GRE General Test, minimum GPA of 3.0. Additional exam requirements/recommendations for international students: Required—TOEFL (minimum score 550 paper-based; 213 computer-based; 79 iBT), IELTS (minimum score 6.5).

Electronic applications accepted. *Faculty research:* Glucose-6-phosphatase, guanine nucleotides, carbohydrate and lipid metabolism, cytoskeletal proteins, chromatin structure.

University of North Texas, Toulouse Graduate School, College of Arts and Sciences, Department of Biological Sciences, Program in Molecular Biology, Denton, TX 76203. Offers MA, MS, PhD. *Degree requirements:* For master's, variable foreign language requirement, comprehensive exam, thesis (for some programs), oral defense of thesis; for doctorate, one foreign language, comprehensive exam, thesis/dissertation, oral defense of dissertation. *Entrance requirements:* For master's and doctorate, GRE General Test, letters of recommendation. Additional exam requirements/recommendations for international students: Recommended—TOEFL (minimum score 550 paper-based; 213 computer-based). *Expenses:* Tuition, state resident: part-time $100 per credit hour. Tuition, nonresident: part-time $413 per credit hour. *Faculty research:* Pyrimidine metabolism, enzymology mammalian/plant gene structure, organization and expression.

University of North Texas Health Science Center at Fort Worth, Graduate School of Biomedical Sciences, Fort Worth, TX 76107-2699. Offers anatomy and cell biology (MS, PhD); biochemistry and molecular biology (MS, PhD); biomedical sciences (MS, PhD); biotechnology (MS); forensic genetics (MS); integrative physiology (MS, PhD); medical science (MS); microbiology and immunology (MS, PhD); pharmacology (MS, PhD); science education (MS); DO/MS; DO/PhD. Terminal master's awarded for partial completion of doctoral program. *Degree requirements:* For master's, thesis; for doctorate, thesis/dissertation. *Entrance requirements:* For master's and doctorate, GRE General Test. Additional exam requirements/recommendations for international students: Required—TOEFL. *Expenses:* Contact institution. *Faculty research:* Alzheimer's disease, aging, eye diseases, cancer, cardiovascular disease.

University of Notre Dame, Graduate School, College of Science, Department of Biological Sciences, Notre Dame, IN 46556. Offers aquatic ecology, evolution and environmental biology (MS, PhD); cellular and molecular biology (MS, PhD); genetics (MS, PhD); physiology (MS, PhD); vector biology and parasitology (MS, PhD). Terminal master's awarded for partial completion of doctoral program. *Degree requirements:* For master's, comprehensive exam, thesis; for doctorate, comprehensive exam, thesis/dissertation, candidacy exam. *Entrance requirements:* For master's and doctorate, GRE General Test. Additional exam requirements/recommendations for international students: Required—TOEFL (minimum score 600 paper-based; 250 computer-based; 80 iBT). Electronic applications accepted. *Faculty research:* Tropical disease, molecular genetics, neurobiology, evolutionary biology, aquatic biology.

University of Oklahoma Health Sciences Center, College of Medicine and Graduate College, Graduate Programs in Medicine, Department of Biochemistry and Molecular Biology, Oklahoma City, OK 73190. Offers biochemistry (MS, PhD); molecular biology (MS, PhD). Part-time programs available. Terminal master's awarded for partial completion of doctoral program. *Degree requirements:* For master's, thesis; for doctorate, thesis/dissertation. *Entrance requirements:* For master's, GRE General Test, 2 letters of recommendation; for doctorate, GRE General Test, 3 letters of recommendation. Additional exam requirements/recommendations for international students: Required—TOEFL. *Faculty research:* Gene expression, regulation of transcription, enzyme evolution, melanogenesis, signal transduction.

University of Oregon, Graduate School, College of Arts and Sciences, Department of Biology, Eugene, OR 97403. Offers ecology and evolution (MA, MS, PhD); marine biology (MA, MS, PhD); molecular, cellular and genetic biology (PhD); neuroscience and development (PhD). Terminal master's awarded for partial completion of doctoral program. *Degree requirements:* For master's, thesis (for some programs); for doctorate, thesis/dissertation. *Entrance requirements:* For master's and doctorate, GRE General Test, minimum GPA of 3.2. Additional exam requirements/recommendations for international students: Required—TOEFL. *Faculty research:* Developmental neurobiology; evolution, population biology, and quantitative genetics; regulation of gene expression; biochemistry of marine organisms.

University of Ottawa, Faculty of Graduate and Postdoctoral Studies, Faculty of Medicine, Department of Cellular and Molecular Medicine, Ottawa, ON K1H 8M5, Canada. Offers M Sc, PhD. *Degree requirements:* For master's, thesis, seminar; for doctorate, comprehensive exam, thesis/dissertation, seminar. *Entrance requirements:* For master's, honors degree or equivalent, minimum B average; for doctorate, master's degree, minimum B+ average. Electronic applications accepted. *Faculty research:* Physiology, pharmacology, growth and development.

University of Pennsylvania, Perelman School of Medicine, Biomedical Graduate Studies, Graduate Group in Cell and Molecular Biology, Philadelphia, PA 19104. Offers cancer biology (PhD); cell biology and physiology (PhD); developmental stem cell regenerative biology (PhD); gene therapy and vaccines (PhD); genetics and gene regulation (PhD); microbiology, virology, and parasitology (PhD); MD/PhD; VMD/PhD. *Faculty:* 306. *Students:* 337 full-time (186 women); includes 81 minority (16 Black or African American, non-Hispanic/Latino; 43 Asian, non-Hispanic/Latino; 16 Hispanic/Latino; 6 Two or more races, non-Hispanic/Latino), 41 international. 585 applicants, 21% accepted, 58 enrolled. In 2011, 42 doctorates awarded. *Degree requirements:* For doctorate, thesis/dissertation. *Entrance requirements:* For doctorate, GRE General Test. Additional exam requirements/recommendations for international students: Required—TOEFL. *Application deadline:* For fall admission, 12/1 priority date for domestic students, 12/1 for international students. Applications are processed on a rolling basis. Application fee: $80. Electronic applications accepted. *Expenses:* Tuition: Full-time $26,660; part-time $4944 per course. *Required fees:* $2318; $291 per course. Tuition and fees vary according to course load, degree level and program. *Financial support:* In 2011–12, 337 students received support. Fellowships, research assistantships, scholarships/grants, traineeships, and unspecified assistantships available. *Unit head:* Dr. Daniel Kessler, Graduate Group Chair. *Application contact:* Meagan Schofer, Coordinator. Web site: http://www.med.upenn.edu/camb/.

University of Pittsburgh, Dietrich School of Arts and Sciences, Department of Biological Sciences, Program in Molecular, Cellular, and Developmental Biology, Pittsburgh, PA 15260. Offers PhD. *Faculty:* 22 full-time (4 women). *Students:* 56 full-time (33 women); includes 4 minority (1 Black or African American, non-Hispanic/Latino; 2 Asian, non-Hispanic/Latino; 1 Hispanic/Latino), 17 international. Average age 23. 202 applicants, 10% accepted, 8 enrolled. In 2011, 9 doctorates awarded. *Degree requirements:* For doctorate, comprehensive exam, thesis/dissertation, completion of research integrity module. *Entrance requirements:* For doctorate, GRE General Test, GRE Subject Test. Additional exam requirements/recommendations for international students: Required—TOEFL (minimum score 550 paper-based; 213 computer-based; 80 iBT). *Application deadline:* For fall admission, 1/15 priority date for domestic students, 12/15 for international students. Applications are processed on a rolling basis. Application fee: $0 ($50 for international students). Electronic applications accepted. *Expenses:* Tuition, state resident: full-time $18,774; part-time $760 per credit. Tuition, nonresident: full-time $30,736; part-time $1258 per credit. *Required fees:* $740; $200 per term. Tuition and fees vary according to program. *Financial support:* In 2011–12, 24 fellowships with full tuition reimbursements (averaging $28,790 per year), 111 research assistantships with full tuition reimbursements (averaging $25,793 per year), 24

teaching assistantships with full tuition reimbursements (averaging $24,414 per year) were awarded; Federal Work-Study, scholarships/grants, traineeships, health care benefits, and tuition waivers (full) also available. *Unit head:* Dr. Jeffrey G. Lawrence, Professor, 412-624-4204, Fax: 412-624-4759, E-mail: jlawrenc@pitt.edu. *Application contact:* Cathleen M. Barr, Graduate Administrator, 412-624-4268, Fax: 412-624-4759, E-mail: cbarr@pitt.edu. Web site: http://www.biology.pitt.edu/.

University of Pittsburgh, School of Medicine and Dietrich School of Arts and Sciences, Program in Integrative Molecular Biology, Pittsburgh, PA 15260. Offers PhD. *Faculty:* 28 full-time (9 women). *Students:* 18 full-time (9 women); includes 1 minority (Asian, non-Hispanic/Latino), 9 international. Average age 25. 23 applicants, 26% accepted, 4 enrolled. In 2011, 2 doctorates awarded. *Degree requirements:* For doctorate, comprehensive exam, thesis/dissertation. *Entrance requirements:* For doctorate, GRE, minimum GPA of 3.7, 3 letters of reference. Additional exam requirements/recommendations for international students: Required—TOEFL (minimum score 650 paper-based; 280 computer-based; 114 iBT), IELTS (minimum score 7.5). *Application deadline:* For fall admission, 1/16 for domestic and international students. Application fee: $0. Electronic applications accepted. *Expenses:* Tuition, state resident: full-time $18,774; part-time $760 per credit. Tuition, nonresident: full-time $30,736; part-time $1258 per credit. *Required fees:* $740; $200 per term. Tuition and fees vary according to program. *Financial support:* In 2011–12, 4 fellowships with full tuition reimbursements (averaging $28,646 per year), 14 research assistantships with full tuition reimbursements (averaging $25,500 per year) were awarded; institutionally sponsored loans, scholarships/grants, traineeships, and unspecified assistantships also available. *Faculty research:* Cellular, molecular, developmental biology; genomics; proteomics and gene function. *Unit head:* Dr. Alan Wells, Program Director, 412-648-8975, Fax: 412-648-1077, E-mail: pimbinfo@medschool.pitt.edu. *Application contact:* Jennifer L. Walker, Program Coordinator, 412-648-8957, Fax: 412-648-1077, E-mail: pimbinfo@medschool.pitt.edu. Web site: http://www.pimb.pitt.edu.

University of Puerto Rico, Río Piedras, College of Natural Sciences, Department of Biology, San Juan, PR 00931-3300. Offers ecology/systematics (MS, PhD); evolution/genetics (MS, PhD); molecular/cellular biology (MS, PhD); neuroscience (MS, PhD). Part-time programs available. *Degree requirements:* For master's, one foreign language, comprehensive exam, thesis; for doctorate, one foreign language, comprehensive exam, thesis/dissertation. *Entrance requirements:* For master's, GRE Subject Test, interview, minimum GPA of 3.0, letter of recommendation; for doctorate, GRE Subject Test, interview, master's degree, minimum GPA of 3.0, letter of recommendation. *Faculty research:* Environmental, poblational and systematic biology.

University of Rhode Island, Graduate School, College of the Environment and Life Sciences, Department of Cell and Molecular Biology, Kingston, RI 02881. Offers biochemistry (MS, PhD); clinical laboratory sciences (MS), including biotechnology, clinical laboratory science, cytopathology; microbiology (MS, PhD); molecular genetics (MS, PhD). Part-time programs available. *Faculty:* 14 full-time (5 women), 3 part-time/adjunct (2 women). *Students:* 32 full-time (15 women), 37 part-time (23 women); includes 2 minority (1 Asian, non-Hispanic/Latino; 1 Hispanic/Latino), 1 international. In 2011, 2 master's, 2 doctorates awarded. *Degree requirements:* For master's, comprehensive exam (for some programs); for doctorate, comprehensive exam. *Entrance requirements:* For master's and doctorate, GRE, 2 letters of recommendation. Additional exam requirements/recommendations for international students: Required—TOEFL (minimum score 550 paper-based; 213 computer-based). *Application deadline:* For fall admission, 7/15 for domestic students, 2/1 for international students; for spring admission, 11/15 for domestic students, 7/15 for international students. Application fee: $65. Electronic applications accepted. *Expenses:* Tuition, state resident: full-time $10,432; part-time $580 per credit hour. Tuition, nonresident: full-time $23,130; part-time $1285 per credit hour. *Required fees:* $1362; $36 per credit hour. $35 per semester. One-time fee: $130. *Financial support:* In 2011–12, 2 research assistantships with full and partial tuition reimbursements (averaging $13,894 per year), 6 teaching assistantships with full and partial tuition reimbursements (averaging $12,850 per year) were awarded. Financial award application deadline: 7/15; financial award applicants required to submit FAFSA. *Faculty research:* Genomics and Sequencing Center: an interdisciplinary genomics research and undergraduate and graduate student training program which provides researchers access to cutting-edge technologies in the field of genomics. *Unit head:* Dr. Jay Sperry, Chairperson, 401-874-2201, Fax: 401-874-2202, E-mail: jsperry@mail.uri.edu. *Application contact:* Nasser H. Zawia, Dean of the Graduate School, 401-874-5909, Fax: 401-874-5787, E-mail: nzawia@uri.edu. Web site: http://cels.uri.edu/cmb/.

University of Rochester, School of Medicine and Dentistry, Graduate Programs in Medicine and Dentistry, Department of Biochemistry and Biophysics, Programs in Biochemistry, Rochester, NY 14627. Offers biochemistry and molecular biology (PhD). Terminal master's awarded for partial completion of doctoral program. *Degree requirements:* For doctorate, thesis/dissertation, qualifying exam. *Entrance requirements:* For doctorate, GRE General Test. *Expenses:* Tuition: Full-time $41,040.

University of South Carolina, The Graduate School, College of Arts and Sciences, Department of Biological Sciences, Graduate Training Program in Molecular, Cellular, and Developmental Biology, Columbia, SC 29208. Offers MS, PhD. *Degree requirements:* For master's, one foreign language, thesis; for doctorate, one foreign language, thesis/dissertation. *Entrance requirements:* For master's and doctorate, GRE General Test, minimum GPA of 3.0 in science. Electronic applications accepted. *Faculty research:* Marine ecology, population and evolutionary biology, molecular biology and genetics, development.

The University of South Dakota, Graduate School, School of Medicine and Graduate School, Biomedical Sciences Graduate Program, Cellular and Molecular Biology Group, Vermillion, SD 57069-2390. Offers MS, PhD. Terminal master's awarded for partial completion of doctoral program. *Degree requirements:* For master's, thesis; for doctorate, comprehensive exam, thesis/dissertation. *Entrance requirements:* For master's and doctorate, GRE General Test, GRE Subject Test, minimum GPA of 3.0. Additional exam requirements/recommendations for international students: Required—TOEFL (minimum score 550 paper-based; 213 computer-based; 80 iBT), IELTS (minimum score 6). Electronic applications accepted. *Expenses:* Contact institution. *Faculty research:* Molecular aspects of protein and DNA, neurochemistry and energy transduction, gene regulation, cellular development.

University of Southern California, Graduate School, Dana and David Dornsife College of Letters, Arts and Sciences, Department of Biological Sciences, Program in Molecular and Computational Biology, Los Angeles, CA 90089. Offers computational biology and bioinformatics (PhD); molecular biology (PhD). *Degree requirements:* For doctorate, comprehensive exam, thesis/dissertation, qualifying examination, dissertation defense. *Entrance requirements:* For doctorate, GRE, 3 letters of recommendation, personal statement, resume, minimum GPA of 3.0. Additional exam requirements/recommendations for international students: Required—TOEFL (minimum score 600 paper-based; 250 computer-based; 100 iBT). Electronic applications accepted. *Faculty research:* Biochemistry and molecular biology; genomics; computational biology and bioinformatics; cell and developmental biology, and genetics; DNA replication and repair, and cancer biology.

Molecular Biology

University of Southern California, Keck School of Medicine and Graduate School, Graduate Programs in Medicine, Department of Biochemistry and Molecular Biology, Los Angeles, CA 90089. Offers MS, PhD. *Faculty:* 24 full-time (5 women). *Students:* 43 full-time (25 women); includes 4 minority (2 Asian, non-Hispanic/Latino; 1 Hispanic/Latino; 1 Native Hawaiian or other Pacific Islander, non-Hispanic/Latino), 34 international. Average age 27. 61 applicants, 51% accepted, 22 enrolled. In 2011, 3 master's, 1 doctorate awarded. Terminal master's awarded for partial completion of doctoral program. *Median time to degree:* Of those who began their doctoral program in fall 2003, 100% received their degree in 8 years or less. *Degree requirements:* For master's, thesis; for doctorate, comprehensive exam, thesis/dissertation. *Entrance requirements:* For master's and doctorate, GRE General Test, minimum GPA of 3.0. Additional exam requirements/recommendations for international students: Required—TOEFL (minimum score 600 paper-based; 250 computer-based; 100 iBT). *Application deadline:* For fall admission, 4/15 priority date for domestic students, 4/15 for international students. Applications are processed on a rolling basis. Application fee: $85. Electronic applications accepted. *Financial support:* In 2011–12, 2 fellowships with full tuition reimbursements (averaging $29,100 per year), 2 research assistantships with full tuition reimbursements (averaging $29,100 per year) were awarded; Federal Work-Study, institutionally sponsored loans, scholarships/grants, health care benefits, tuition waivers (full), and unspecified assistantships also available. Financial award application deadline: 5/4. *Faculty research:* Molecular genetics, gene expression, membrane biochemistry, metabolic regulation, cancer biology. *Total annual research expenditures:* $4.4 million. *Unit head:* Dr. Michael R. Stallcup, Chair, 323-442-1145, Fax: 323-442-1224, E-mail: stallcup@usc.edu. *Application contact:* Janet Stoeckert, Administrative Director, Basic Science Departments, 323-442-3568, Fax: 323-442-1610, E-mail: janet.stoeckert@usc.edu. Web site: http://www.usc.edu/medicine/biochemistry/.

University of Southern California, Keck School of Medicine and Graduate School, Graduate Programs in Medicine, Department of Preventive Medicine, Division of Biostatistics, Los Angeles, CA 90089. Offers applied biostatistics/epidemiology (MS); biostatistics (MS, PhD); epidemiology (PhD); genetic epidemiology and statistical genetics (PhD); molecular epidemiology (MS, PhD). *Faculty:* 71 full-time (30 women). *Students:* 97 full-time (51 women); includes 24 minority (18 Asian, non-Hispanic/Latino; 3 Hispanic/Latino; 3 Two or more races, non-Hispanic/Latino), 56 international. Average age 29. 68 applicants, 62% accepted, 17 enrolled. In 2011, 7 master's, 8 doctorates awarded. Terminal master's awarded for partial completion of doctoral program. *Degree requirements:* For master's, thesis; for doctorate, thesis/dissertation. *Entrance requirements:* For master's and doctorate, GRE General Test, GRE Subject Test, minimum GPA of 3.0. Additional exam requirements/recommendations for international students: Required—TOEFL (minimum score 600 paper-based; 300 computer-based; 100 iBT). *Application deadline:* For fall admission, 12/1 priority date for domestic students, 12/1 for international students. Application fee: $85. Electronic applications accepted. *Financial support:* In 2011–12, 3 fellowships with full tuition reimbursements (averaging $29,100 per year), 43 research assistantships with full tuition reimbursements (averaging $29,100 per year), 22 teaching assistantships with full and partial tuition reimbursements (averaging $14,550 per year) were awarded; career-related internships or fieldwork, Federal Work-Study, institutionally sponsored loans, scholarships/grants, traineeships, health care benefits, and unspecified assistantships also available. Financial award application deadline: 5/4; financial award applicants required to submit CSS PROFILE or FAFSA. *Faculty research:* Clinical trials in ophthalmology and cancer research, methods of analysis for epidemiological studies, genetic epidemiology. *Total annual research expenditures:* $1.3 million. *Unit head:* Dr. William Gauderman, Director, 323-442-2633, Fax: 323-442-2993, E-mail: mtrujill@usc.edu. *Application contact:* Mary L. Trujillo, Student Adviser, 323-442-2633, Fax: 323-442-2993, E-mail: mtrujill@usc.edu. Web site: http://keck.usc.edu/Education/Academic_Department_and_Divisions/Department_of_Preventive_Medicine/Divisions/Biostatistics.aspx.

University of Southern California, Keck School of Medicine and Graduate School, Program in Genetic, Molecular and Cellular Biology, Los Angeles, CA 90089. Offers PhD. *Faculty:* 224 full-time (56 women). *Students:* 120 full-time (69 women); includes 29 minority (2 Black or African American, non-Hispanic/Latino; 19 Asian, non-Hispanic/Latino; 6 Hispanic/Latino; 2 Native Hawaiian or other Pacific Islander, non-Hispanic/Latino), 65 international. Average age 29. 360 applicants, 20% accepted, 28 enrolled. In 2011, 11 doctorates awarded. *Degree requirements:* For doctorate, comprehensive exam, thesis/dissertation. *Entrance requirements:* For doctorate, GRE, minimum GPA of 3.0. Additional exam requirements/recommendations for international students: Required—TOEFL (minimum score 600 paper-based; 250 computer-based; 100 iBT). *Application deadline:* For fall admission, 12/1 priority date for domestic students, 12/1 for international students. Application fee: $85. Electronic applications accepted. *Financial support:* In 2011–12, 120 students received support, including 12 fellowships (averaging $29,100 per year), 106 research assistantships with full tuition reimbursements available (averaging $29,100 per year), 2 teaching assistantships with full tuition reimbursements available (averaging $29,100 per year); institutionally sponsored loans, scholarships/grants, traineeships, health care benefits, and unspecified assistantships also available. Financial award application deadline: 5/4; financial award applicants required to submit FAFSA. *Unit head:* Dr. Henry Sucov, Director, 323-442-1475, Fax: 323-442-1199, E-mail: sucov@usc.edu. *Application contact:* Dawn Burke, Student Program Coordinator, 323-442-1475, Fax: 323-442-1199, E-mail: pibbs@usc.edu. Web site: http://www.usc.edu/intbio.

University of Southern Maine, School of Applied Science, Engineering, and Technology, Program in Applied Medical Sciences, Portland, ME 04104-9300. Offers MS. Part-time programs available. *Degree requirements:* For master's, thesis. *Entrance requirements:* For master's, GRE General Test, minimum GPA of 3.0. Additional exam requirements/recommendations for international students: Required—TOEFL. Electronic applications accepted. *Faculty research:* Flow cytometry, cancer, epidemiology, monoclonal antibodies, DNA diagnostics.

University of Southern Mississippi, Graduate School, College of Science and Technology, Department of Biological Sciences, Hattiesburg, MS 39406-0001. Offers environmental biology (MS, PhD); marine biology (MS, PhD); microbiology (MS, PhD); molecular biology (MS, PhD). *Faculty:* 27 full-time (6 women). *Students:* 57 full-time (28 women), 4 part-time (2 women); includes 5 minority (2 Black or African American, non-Hispanic/Latino; 3 Two or more races, non-Hispanic/Latino), 18 international. Average age 32. 50 applicants, 32% accepted, 12 enrolled. In 2011, 7 master's, 8 doctorates awarded. Terminal master's awarded for partial completion of doctoral program. *Degree requirements:* For master's, comprehensive exam, thesis; for doctorate, comprehensive exam, thesis/dissertation. *Entrance requirements:* For master's, GRE General Test, minimum GPA of 3.0 on last 60 hours; for doctorate, GRE General Test, minimum GPA of 3.5. Additional exam requirements/recommendations for international students: Required—TOEFL, IELTS. *Application deadline:* For fall admission, 3/1 priority date for domestic students, 3/1 for international students; for spring admission, 1/10 priority date for domestic students, 1/10 for international students. Applications are processed on a rolling basis. Application fee: $50. *Financial support:* In 2011–12, 25 research assistantships with full tuition reimbursements (averaging $9,700 per year), 33 teaching assistantships with full tuition reimbursements (averaging $10,600 per year) were awarded; Federal Work-Study, scholarships/grants, health care benefits, and unspecified assistantships also available. Financial award application deadline: 3/15; financial award applicants required to submit FAFSA. *Unit head:* Dr. Glenmore Shearer, Chair, 601-266-4748, Fax: 601-266-5797. *Application contact:* Dr. Jake Schaefer, Director of Graduate Studies, 601-266-4748, Fax: 601-266-5797. Web site: http://www.usm.edu/graduateschool/table.php.

University of South Florida, Graduate School, College of Arts and Sciences, Department of Biology, Tampa, FL 33620-9951. Offers cell biology and molecular biology (MS); coastal marine biology (MS); coastal marine biology and ecology (PhD); conservation biology (MS, PhD); molecular and cell biology (PhD). Part-time programs available. *Faculty:* 35 full-time (11 women), 16 part-time/adjunct (5 women). *Students:* 126 full-time (75 women), 24 part-time (17 women); includes 13 minority (1 Black or African American, non-Hispanic/Latino; 4 Asian, non-Hispanic/Latino; 8 Hispanic/Latino), 17 international. Average age 30. 235 applicants, 21% accepted, 30 enrolled. In 2011, 7 master's, 11 doctorates awarded. *Degree requirements:* For master's, comprehensive exam, thesis (for some programs); for doctorate, comprehensive exam, thesis/dissertation. *Entrance requirements:* For master's and doctorate, GRE General Test, minimum GPA of 3.0. Additional exam requirements/recommendations for international students: Required—TOEFL (minimum score 570 paper-based; 213 computer-based). *Application deadline:* For fall admission, 2/15 priority date for domestic students, 1/2 for international students; for spring admission, 8/1 for domestic students, 6/1 for international students. Application fee: $30. Electronic applications accepted. *Financial support:* In 2011–12, 122 students received support, including 46 research assistantships (averaging $24,716 per year), 76 teaching assistantships with tuition reimbursements available (averaging $28,434 per year); unspecified assistantships also available. Financial award application deadline: 6/30; financial award applicants required to submit FAFSA. *Total annual research expenditures:* $5.2 million. *Unit head:* Susan Bell, Co-Chairperson, 813-974-6210, Fax: 813-974-2876, E-mail: sbell@cas.usf.edu. *Application contact:* James Garey, Graduate Advisor, 813-974-8434, Fax: 813-974-3263, E-mail: grarey@cas.usf.edu. Web site: http://www.cas.usf.edu/biology/.

The University of Texas at Austin, Graduate School, Institute for Cellular and Molecular Biology, Austin, TX 78712-1111. Offers PhD. *Financial support:* Fellowships, research assistantships, teaching assistantships, institutionally sponsored loans, and traineeships available. *Unit head:* Alan M. Lambowitz, Director, 512-232-3418, E-mail: lambowitz@mail.utexas.edu. *Application contact:* Information Contact, 512-471-1156, Fax: 512-471-2149. Web site: http://www.icmb.utexas.edu/.

The University of Texas at Dallas, School of Natural Sciences and Mathematics, Department of Biology, Richardson, TX 75080. Offers bioinformatics and computational biology (MS); biotechnology (MS); molecular and cell biology (MS, PhD). Part-time and evening/weekend programs available. *Faculty:* 18 full-time (2 women), 1 part-time/adjunct (0 women). *Students:* 111 full-time (59 women), 13 part-time (6 women); includes 19 minority (2 Black or African American, non-Hispanic/Latino; 14 Asian, non-Hispanic/Latino; 3 Hispanic/Latino), 86 international. Average age 27. 483 applicants, 31% accepted, 67 enrolled. In 2011, 39 master's, 7 doctorates awarded. *Degree requirements:* For master's, thesis optional; for doctorate, thesis/dissertation, publishable paper. *Entrance requirements:* For master's and doctorate, GRE (minimum combined score of 1000 on verbal and quantitative). Additional exam requirements/recommendations for international students: Required—TOEFL (minimum score 550 paper-based; 215 computer-based; 80 iBT). *Application deadline:* For fall admission, 7/15 for domestic students, 5/1 for international students; for spring admission, 11/15 for domestic students, 9/1 for international students. Applications are processed on a rolling basis. Application fee: $50 ($100 for international students). Electronic applications accepted. *Expenses:* Tuition, state resident: full-time $11,170; part-time $620.56 per credit hour. Tuition, nonresident: full-time $20,212; part-time $1122.89 per credit hour. *Financial support:* In 2011–12, 49 students received support, including 18 research assistantships with partial tuition reimbursements available (averaging $20,911 per year), 36 teaching assistantships with partial tuition reimbursements available (averaging $15,300 per year); career-related internships or fieldwork, Federal Work-Study, institutionally sponsored loans, scholarships/grants, and unspecified assistantships also available. Support available to part-time students. Financial award application deadline: 4/30; financial award applicants required to submit FAFSA. *Faculty research:* Role of mitochondria in neurodegenerative diseases, protein-DNA interactions in site-specific recombination, eukaryotic gene expression, bio-nanotechnology, sickle cell research. *Unit head:* Dr. Stephen Spiro, Department Head, 972-883-6032, Fax: 972-883-2502, E-mail: stephen.spiro@utdallas.edu. *Application contact:* Dr. Lawrence Reitzer, Graduate Advisor, 972-883-2502, Fax: 972-883-2402, E-mail: reitzer@utdallas.edu. Web site: http://www.utdallas.edu/biology/.

The University of Texas at San Antonio, College of Sciences, Department of Biology, San Antonio, TX 78249-0617. Offers biology (MS); biotechnology (MS), including bioprocessing technician, biotechnology; cell and molecular biology (PhD); environmental science (MS); neurobiology (PhD). *Faculty:* 34 full-time (6 women), 7 part-time/adjunct (1 woman). *Students:* 117 full-time (62 women), 64 part-time (35 women); includes 63 minority (10 Black or African American, non-Hispanic/Latino; 10 Asian, non-Hispanic/Latino; 36 Hispanic/Latino; 7 Two or more races, non-Hispanic/Latino), 54 international. Average age 27. 239 applicants, 45% accepted, 50 enrolled. In 2011, 62 master's, 3 doctorates awarded. Terminal master's awarded for partial completion of doctoral program. *Degree requirements:* For master's, comprehensive exam, thesis or alternative; for doctorate, thesis/dissertation. *Entrance requirements:* For master's, GRE General Test, bachelor's degree with 18 credit hours in field of study or in another appropriate field of study; for doctorate, GRE General Test, 3 letters of recommendation, statement of purpose, resume. Additional exam requirements/recommendations for international students: Required—TOEFL (minimum score 500 paper-based; 100 iBT), IELTS (minimum score 5). *Application deadline:* For fall admission, 7/1 for domestic students, 4/1 for international students; for spring admission, 11/1 for domestic students, 9/1 for international students. Application fee: $45 ($85 for international students). *Expenses:* Tuition, state resident: full-time $3148; part-time $2176 per semester. Tuition, nonresident: full-time $8782; part-time $5932 per semester. *Required fees:* $719 per semester. *Financial support:* In 2011–12, 66 students received support, including 4 fellowships (averaging $22,350 per year), 34 research assistantships (averaging $22,350 per year), 8 teaching assistantships (averaging $22,350 per year). *Faculty research:* Development of human and veterinary vaccines against a fungal disease, mammalian germ cells and stem cells, dopamine neuron physiology and addiction, plant biochemistry, dendritic computation and synaptic plasticity. *Total annual research expenditures:* $2.8 million. *Unit head:* Dr. Edwin J. Barea-Rodriguez, Chair, 210-458-4511, Fax: 210-458-5658, E-mail: edwin.barea@utsa.edu. *Application contact:* Rene Munguia, Program Coordinator, 210-458-4642, Fax: 210-458-5658, E-mail: rene.munguia@utsa.edu.

The University of Texas Health Science Center at Houston, Graduate School of Biomedical Sciences, Program in Biochemistry and Molecular Biology, Houston, TX 77225-0036. Offers MS, PhD, MD/PhD. Terminal master's awarded for partial completion of doctoral program. *Degree requirements:* For master's, thesis; for doctorate, thesis/dissertation. *Entrance requirements:* For master's and doctorate, GRE General Test. Additional exam requirements/recommendations for international

students: Required—TOEFL. Electronic applications accepted. *Faculty research:* Biochemistry, membrane biology, macromolecular structure, structural biophysics, molecular models of human disease, molecular biology of the cell.

The University of Texas Health Science Center at Houston, Graduate School of Biomedical Sciences, Program in Cell and Regulatory Biology, Houston, TX 77225-0036. Offers MS, PhD, MD/PhD. Terminal master's awarded for partial completion of doctoral program. *Degree requirements:* For master's, thesis; for doctorate, thesis/dissertation. *Entrance requirements:* For master's and doctorate, GRE General Test. Additional exam requirements/recommendations for international students: Required—TOEFL. Electronic applications accepted. *Faculty research:* Pharmacology, cell biology, physiology, signal transduction, systems biology.

University of the Sciences in Philadelphia, College of Graduate Studies, Misher College of Arts and Sciences, Program in Cell and Molecular Biology, Philadelphia, PA 19104-4495. Offers PhD.

The University of Toledo, College of Graduate Studies, College of Natural Sciences and Mathematics, Department of Biological Sciences, Toledo, OH 43606-3390. Offers cell/molecular biology (MS, PhD). Part-time programs available. *Faculty:* 19. *Students:* 70 full-time (34 women), 28 part-time (20 women); includes 6 minority (1 Black or African American, non-Hispanic/Latino; 2 Asian, non-Hispanic/Latino; 1 Hispanic/Latino; 2 Two or more races, non-Hispanic/Latino), 30 international. Average age 29. 110 applicants, 16% accepted, 16 enrolled. In 2011, 13 master's, 6 doctorates awarded. *Degree requirements:* For master's, thesis or alternative; for doctorate, thesis/dissertation. *Entrance requirements:* For master's and doctorate, GRE General Test, GRE Subject Test, minimum cumulative point-hour ratio of 2.7 for all previous academic work, three letters of recommendation, statement of purpose, transcripts from all prior institutions attended. Additional exam requirements/recommendations for international students: Required—TOEFL (minimum score 550 paper-based; 213 computer-based; 80 iBT), IELTS (minimum score 6.5). *Application deadline:* For fall admission, 1/15 priority date for domestic students, 1/15 for international students. Applications are processed on a rolling basis. Application fee: $45 ($75 for international students). Electronic applications accepted. *Financial support:* In 2011–12, 31 research assistantships with full and partial tuition reimbursements (averaging $17,292 per year), 38 teaching assistantships with full and partial tuition reimbursements (averaging $18,011 per year) were awarded; fellowships, Federal Work-Study, institutionally sponsored loans, scholarships/grants, tuition waivers (full), and unspecified assistantships also available. Support available to part-time students. *Faculty research:* Biochemical parasitology, physiological ecology, animal physiology. *Unit head:* Dr. Doug Leaman, Chair, 419-530-2066, E-mail: douglas.leaman@utoledo.edu. *Application contact:* Graduate School Office, 419-530-4723, Fax: 419-530-4724, E-mail: grdsch@utnet.utoledo.edu. Web site: http://www.utoledo.edu/nsm/.

University of Utah, School of Medicine, Program in Molecular Biology, Salt Lake City, UT 84132. Offers PhD. *Degree requirements:* For doctorate, thesis/dissertation, preliminary exams. *Entrance requirements:* For doctorate, GRE General Test, personal statement, transcripts, letters of recommendation. Additional exam requirements/recommendations for international students: Required—TOEFL (minimum score 500 paper-based; 173 computer-based; 60 iBT). Electronic applications accepted. *Faculty research:* Biochemistry/structural biology; cancer/cell biology; genetics; developmental biology; gene expression; microbiology/immunology and neurobiology.

University of Vermont, Graduate College, Cell and Molecular Biology Program, Burlington, VT 05405. Offers MS, PhD. *Students:* 37 (14 women); includes 7 minority (2 Asian, non-Hispanic/Latino; 5 Hispanic/Latino), 5 international. 68 applicants, 25% accepted, 4 enrolled. In 2011, 1 master's, 2 doctorates awarded. *Degree requirements:* For master's, thesis; for doctorate, thesis/dissertation. *Entrance requirements:* For master's and doctorate, GRE General Test. Additional exam requirements/recommendations for international students: Required—TOEFL (minimum score 550 paper-based; 213 computer-based; 80 iBT). *Application deadline:* For fall admission, 1/15 priority date for domestic students, 1/15 for international students. Applications are processed on a rolling basis. Application fee: $40. Electronic applications accepted. *Financial support:* Fellowships, research assistantships, teaching assistantships, and career-related internships or fieldwork available. Financial award application deadline: 3/1. *Unit head:* Dr. Mary Tierney, Coordinator, 802-656-9673.

University of Washington, Graduate School, School of Medicine, Graduate Programs in Medicine, Program in Molecular and Cellular Biology, Seattle, WA 98195. Offers PhD. Offered jointly with Fred Hutchinson Cancer Research Center. *Degree requirements:* For doctorate, thesis/dissertation. *Entrance requirements:* For doctorate, GRE General Test. Additional exam requirements/recommendations for international students: Required—TOEFL. Electronic applications accepted.

See Display on page 204 and Close-Up on page 249.

The University of Western Ontario, Faculty of Graduate Studies, Biosciences Division, Department of Plant Sciences, London, ON N6A 5B8, Canada. Offers plant and environmental sciences (M Sc); plant sciences (M Sc, PhD); plant sciences and environmental sciences (PhD); plant sciences and molecular biology (M Sc, PhD). *Degree requirements:* For master's, thesis; for doctorate, thesis/dissertation. *Entrance requirements:* For doctorate, M Sc or equivalent. Additional exam requirements/recommendations for international students: Required—TOEFL. *Faculty research:* Ecology systematics, plant biochemistry and physiology, yeast genetics, molecular biology.

University of Wisconsin–La Crosse, Office of University Graduate Studies, College of Science and Health, Department of Biology, La Crosse, WI 54601-3742. Offers aquatic sciences (MS); biology (MS); cellular and molecular biology (MS); clinical microbiology (MS); microbiology (MS); nurse anesthesia (MS); physiology (MS). Part-time programs available. *Faculty:* 21 full-time (8 women), 3 part-time/adjunct (1 woman). *Students:* 45 full-time (30 women), 47 part-time (22 women); includes 10 minority (1 Black or African American, non-Hispanic/Latino; 5 Asian, non-Hispanic/Latino; 3 Hispanic/Latino; 1 Two or more races, non-Hispanic/Latino), 3 international. Average age 28. 63 applicants, 46% accepted, 24 enrolled. In 2011, 23 master's awarded. *Degree requirements:* For master's, comprehensive exam, thesis. *Entrance requirements:* For master's, GRE General Test, minimum GPA of 2.85. Additional exam requirements/recommendations for international students: Required—TOEFL (minimum score 550 paper-based; 213 computer-based; 79 iBT). *Application deadline:* For fall admission, 2/1 priority date for domestic students, 2/1 for international students; for spring admission, 1/4 priority date for domestic students, 1/4 for international students. Applications are processed on a rolling basis. Application fee: $56. Electronic applications accepted. *Expenses:* Tuition, state resident: full-time $8391; part-time $481.17 per credit. Tuition, nonresident: full-time $17,850; part-time $1006.68 per credit. *Required fees:* $2 per credit. $18.25 per semester. Tuition and fees vary according to course load, program, reciprocity agreements and student level. *Financial support:* In 2011–12, 29 research assistantships with partial tuition reimbursements (averaging $9,712 per year) were awarded; Federal Work-Study, scholarships/grants, health care benefits, and tuition waivers (partial) also available. Support available to part-time students. Financial award application deadline: 3/15; financial award applicants required to submit FAFSA. *Unit head:* Dr. Thomas Volk, Coordinator of Graduate Studies, 608-785-6972, Fax: 608-785-6959, E-mail: volk.thom@uwlax.edu. *Application contact:* Kathryn Kiefer, Director of Admissions, 608-785-8939, E-mail: admissions@uwlax.edu. Web site: http://uwlax.edu/biology/.

University of Wisconsin–Madison, Graduate School, Program in Cellular and Molecular Biology, Madison, WI 53706-1596. Offers PhD. *Degree requirements:* For doctorate, comprehensive exam, thesis/dissertation. *Entrance requirements:* For doctorate, GRE General Test, GRE Subject Test (recommended), minimum GPA of 3.0, lab experience. Additional exam requirements/recommendations for international students: Required—TOEFL (minimum score 580 paper-based; 237 computer-based; 92 iBT). Electronic applications accepted. *Expenses:* Tuition, state resident: full-time $10,296; part-time $643.51 per credit. Tuition, nonresident: full-time $24,054; part-time $1503.40 per credit. *Required fees:* $70.06 per credit. Tuition and fees vary according to course load, campus/location, program and reciprocity agreements. *Faculty research:* Virology, cancer biology, transcriptional mechanisms, plant biology, immunology.

University of Wisconsin–Parkside, College of Arts and Sciences, Program in Applied Molecular Biology, Kenosha, WI 53141-2000. Offers MAMB. Part-time programs available. *Degree requirements:* For master's, thesis, oral exam. *Entrance requirements:* For master's, GRE General Test, minimum GPA of 3.0; course work in biology, chemistry, math, physics. Additional exam requirements/recommendations for international students: Required—TOEFL (minimum score 550 paper-based; 213 computer-based). Electronic applications accepted. *Faculty research:* Gene cloning, genome structure, cell cycle effects on gene expression, molecular biology of plant hormones, laboratory toxin production and resistance, RNA stability, pathogencity.

University of Wyoming, College of Agriculture and Natural Resources, Department of Molecular Biology, Laramie, WY 82070. Offers MA, MS, PhD. Terminal master's awarded for partial completion of doctoral program. *Degree requirements:* For master's, comprehensive exam (for some programs), thesis; for doctorate, comprehensive exam, thesis/dissertation. *Entrance requirements:* For master's and doctorate, GRE General Test, GRE Subject Test (recommended), minimum GPA of 3.0. Additional exam requirements/recommendations for international students: Required—TOEFL. Electronic applications accepted. *Faculty research:* Protein structure/function, developmental regulation, yeast genetics, bacterial pathogenesis.

University of Wyoming, Graduate Program in Molecular and Cellular Life Sciences, Laramie, WY 82070. Offers PhD. *Degree requirements:* For doctorate, thesis/dissertation, four eight-week laboratory rotations, comprehensive basic practical exam, two-part qualifying exam, seminars, symposium.

Vanderbilt University, Graduate School and School of Medicine, Department of Molecular Physiology and Biophysics, Nashville, TN 37240-1001. Offers MS, PhD, MD/PhD. *Faculty:* 37 full-time (8 women). *Students:* 39 full-time (25 women); includes 10 minority (4 Black or African American, non-Hispanic/Latino; 1 American Indian or Alaska Native, non-Hispanic/Latino; 3 Hispanic/Latino; 2 Two or more races, non-Hispanic/Latino), 4 international. Average age 28. In 2011, 3 doctorates awarded. *Degree requirements:* For doctorate, comprehensive exam, thesis/dissertation, preliminary, qualifying, and final exams. *Entrance requirements:* For doctorate, GRE General Test, GRE Subject Test (recommended). Additional exam requirements/recommendations for international students: Required—TOEFL (minimum score 570 paper-based; 230 computer-based; 88 iBT). *Application deadline:* For fall admission, 1/15 for domestic and international students. Application fee: $0. Electronic applications accepted. *Financial support:* Fellowships with full tuition reimbursements, research assistantships with full tuition reimbursements, Federal Work-Study, institutionally sponsored loans, scholarships/grants, traineeships, health care benefits, and tuition waivers (partial) available. Financial award application deadline: 1/15; financial award applicants required to submit CSS PROFILE or FAFSA. *Faculty research:* Biophysics, cell signaling and gene regulation, human genetics, diabetes and obesity, neuroscience. *Unit head:* Dr. Roger Cone, Chair, 615-936-7085, Fax: 615-343-4075, E-mail: roger.cone@vanderbilt.edu. *Application contact:* Angie Pernell, Administrative Assistant/Director of Graduate Studies Assistant, 615-322-7001, Fax: 615-343-0490, E-mail: angie.pernell@vanderbilt.edu. Web site: http://www.mc.vanderbilt.edu/medschool/mpb/.

Virginia Commonwealth University, Medical College of Virginia-Professional Programs, School of Medicine, School of Medicine Graduate Programs, Department of Biochemistry, Richmond, VA 23284-9005. Offers biochemistry (MS, PhD); molecular biology (MS, PhD); MD/PhD. *Degree requirements:* For master's, thesis; for doctorate, thesis/dissertation, comprehensive oral and written exams. *Entrance requirements:* For master's and doctorate, GRE, MCAT or DAT. Electronic applications accepted. *Expenses:* Tuition, state resident: full-time $9133; part-time $507 per credit. Tuition, nonresident: full-time $18,777; part-time $1043 per credit. *Required fees:* $77 per credit. Tuition and fees vary according to degree level, campus/location, program and student level. *Faculty research:* Molecular biology, peptide/protein chemistry, neurochemistry, enzyme mechanisms, macromolecular structure determination.

Virginia Commonwealth University, Medical College of Virginia-Professional Programs, School of Medicine, School of Medicine Graduate Programs, Department of Human and Molecular Genetics, Richmond, VA 23284-9005. Offers genetic counseling (MS); human genetics (PhD); molecular biology and genetics (MS, PhD); MD/PhD. *Degree requirements:* For master's, thesis; for doctorate, thesis/dissertation, comprehensive oral and written exams. *Entrance requirements:* For master's, GRE; for doctorate, GRE General Test. Additional exam requirements/recommendations for international students: Required—TOEFL (minimum score 600 paper-based; 250 computer-based; 100 iBT). Electronic applications accepted. *Expenses:* Tuition, state resident: full-time $9133; part-time $507 per credit. Tuition, nonresident: full-time $18,777; part-time $1043 per credit. *Required fees:* $77 per credit. Tuition and fees vary according to degree level, campus/location, program and student level. *Faculty research:* Genetic epidemiology, biochemical genetics, quantitative genetics, human cytogenetics, molecular genetics.

Virginia Polytechnic Institute and State University, Graduate School, College of Agriculture and Life Sciences, Department of Human Nutrition, Foods and Exercise, Blacksburg, VA 24061. Offers behavioral and community science (MS, PhD); clinical physiology and metabolism (MS, PhD); molecular and cellular science (MS, PhD). *Degree requirements:* For master's, comprehensive exam (for some programs), thesis (for some programs); for doctorate, comprehensive exam (for some programs), thesis/dissertation (for some programs). *Entrance requirements:* For master's and doctorate, GRE. Additional exam requirements/recommendations for international students: Required—TOEFL (minimum score 550 paper-based; 213 computer-based). *Application deadline:* For fall admission, 7/1 for domestic and international students; for spring admission, 12/1 for domestic and international students. Applications are processed on a rolling basis. Application fee: $65. Electronic applications accepted. *Expenses:* Tuition, state resident: full-time $10,048; part-time $558.25 per credit hour. Tuition, nonresident: full-time $19,497; part-time $1083.25 per credit hour. *Required fees:* $405 per semester. Tuition and fees vary according to course load, campus/location and program. *Financial support:* Fellowships with full tuition reimbursements, research assistantships with full tuition reimbursements, teaching assistantships with full tuition reimbursements, career-related internships or fieldwork, Federal Work-Study, scholarships/grants, health care benefits, and unspecified assistantships available.

Financial award application deadline: 1/15. *Faculty research:* Nutrition and food science research. *Unit head:* Dr. Susan M. Hutson, Unit Head, 540-231-8766, Fax: 540-231-3916, E-mail: susanh5@vt.edu. *Application contact:* Robert Grange, Information Contact, 540-231-2725, Fax: 540-231-3916, E-mail: rgrange@vt.edu. Web site: http://www.hnfe.vt.edu/.

Virginia Polytechnic Institute and State University, Graduate School, Intercollege, Program in Molecular Plant Sciences, Blacksburg, VA 24061. Offers PhD. *Degree requirements:* For doctorate, comprehensive exam (for some programs), thesis/dissertation (for some programs). *Entrance requirements:* For doctorate, GRE. Additional exam requirements/recommendations for international students: Required—TOEFL (minimum score 550 paper-based; 213 computer-based). *Application deadline:* For fall admission, 7/1 for domestic and international students; for spring admission, 12/1 for domestic and international students. Application fee: $65. *Expenses:* Tuition, state resident: full-time $10,048; part-time $558.25 per credit hour. Tuition, nonresident: full-time $19,497; part-time $1083.25 per credit hour. *Required fees:* $405 per semester. Tuition and fees vary according to course load, campus/location and program. *Financial support:* Career-related internships or fieldwork, Federal Work-Study, scholarships/grants, health care benefits, and unspecified assistantships available. Financial award application deadline: 1/15. *Unit head:* Dr. Karen P. DePauw, Vice President and Dean for Graduate Education, 540-231-7581, Fax: 540-231-1670, E-mail: kpdepauw@vt.edu. *Application contact:* Jacqueline Nottingham, Director of Graduate Admissions and Academic Progress, 540-231-3092, Fax: 540-231-3750, E-mail: ntnghm@vt.edu.

Wake Forest University, School of Medicine and Graduate School of Arts and Sciences, Graduate Programs in Medicine, Molecular Genetics and Genomics Program, Winston-Salem, NC 27109. Offers PhD, MD/PhD. *Degree requirements:* For doctorate, thesis/dissertation. *Entrance requirements:* For doctorate, GRE General Test. Additional exam requirements/recommendations for international students: Required—TOEFL. Electronic applications accepted. *Faculty research:* Control of gene expression, molecular pathogenesis, protein biosynthesis, cell development, clinical cytogenetics.

Washington State University, Graduate School, College of Sciences, School of Molecular Biosciences, Pullman, WA 99164. Offers MS, PhD. *Faculty:* 30. *Students:* 64 full-time (30 women), 9 part-time (3 women); includes 9 minority (4 Asian, non-Hispanic/Latino; 4 Hispanic/Latino; 1 Two or more races, non-Hispanic/Latino), 7 international. Average age 27. 116 applicants, 22% accepted, 16 enrolled. In 2011, 3 master's, 3 doctorates awarded. *Entrance requirements:* For master's and doctorate, GRE, personal statement describing qualifications, goals, and objectives in pursuing graduate research in molecular biosciences; official transcripts from all colleges attended; three letters of recommendation. Additional exam requirements/recommendations for international students: Required—TOEFL, IELTS. *Application deadline:* For fall admission, 12/15 for domestic students. Application fee: $75. *Financial support:* In 2011–12, research assistantships (averaging $13,917 per year), teaching assistantships (averaging $13,056 per year) were awarded. Financial award application deadline: 2/15; financial award applicants required to submit FAFSA. *Total annual research expenditures:* $8 million. *Unit head:* Dr. John H. Nilson, Director, 509-335-8724, Fax: 509-335-9688, E-mail: jhn@wsu.edu. *Application contact:* Graduate School Admissions, 800-GRADWSU, Fax: 509-335-1949, E-mail: gradsch@wsu.edu.

Washington University in St. Louis, Graduate School of Arts and Sciences, Division of Biology and Biomedical Sciences, Program in Molecular Cell Biology, St. Louis, MO 63130-4899. Offers PhD. *Degree requirements:* For doctorate, thesis/dissertation. *Entrance requirements:* For doctorate, GRE General Test, GRE Subject Test. Electronic applications accepted.

Wayne State University, Graduate School, Program in Molecular Biology and Genetics, Detroit, MI 48202. Offers MS, PhD, MD/PhD. *Students:* 25 full-time (13 women), 1 part-time (0 women); includes 1 minority (Asian, non-Hispanic/Latino), 7 international. Average age 28. 41 applicants, 17% accepted, 4 enrolled. In 2011, 3 doctorates awarded. Terminal master's awarded for partial completion of doctoral program. *Degree requirements:* For master's, thesis; for doctorate, thesis/dissertation. *Entrance requirements:* For master's and doctorate, GRE General Test, GRE Subject Test (chemistry or biology), minimum GPA of 3.0, strong background in one of the chemical or biological sciences, three letters of recommendation, personal statement, interview. Additional exam requirements/recommendations for international students: Required—TOEFL (minimum score 550 paper-based; 213 computer-based); Recommended—TWE (minimum score 5.5). *Application deadline:* For fall admission, 6/1 priority date for domestic students, 5/1 for international students; for winter admission, 10/1 priority date for domestic students, 9/1 for international students; for spring admission, 2/1 priority date for domestic students, 1/1 for international students. Applications are processed on a rolling basis. Application fee: $50. Electronic applications accepted. *Expenses:* Tuition, state resident: part-time $512.85 per credit. Tuition, nonresident: part-time $1132.65 per credit. *Required fees:* $26.60 per credit. $199.65 per semester. Tuition and fees vary according to course load and program. *Financial support:* In 2011–12, 23 students received support. Fellowships with tuition reimbursements available, research assistantships with tuition reimbursements available, teaching assistantships with tuition reimbursements available, scholarships/grants, and unspecified assistantships available. Financial award application deadline: 2/1. *Faculty research:* Human gene mapping, genome organization and sequencing, gene regulation, molecular evolution. *Unit head:* Dr. Lawrence Grossman, Director, 313-577-5326, E-mail: l.grossman@wayne.edu.

Wayne State University, School of Medicine, Department of Biochemistry and Molecular Biology, Detroit, MI 48202. Offers MS, PhD, MD/PhD. *Students:* 29 full-time (17 women), 1 part-time (0 women); includes 4 minority (1 Black or African American, non-Hispanic/Latino; 3 Asian, non-Hispanic/Latino), 16 international. Average age 27. 84 applicants, 10% accepted, 7 enrolled. In 2011, 2 master's, 4 doctorates awarded. Terminal master's awarded for partial completion of doctoral program. *Degree requirements:* For master's, thesis; for doctorate, thesis/dissertation. *Entrance requirements:* For master's, BA or BS in biology, chemistry, or (if approved) physics or mathematics with minimum GPA of 2.6 from accredited university; three letters of recommendation; personal statement; for doctorate, GRE, undergraduate degree with minimum GPA of 3.0. Additional exam requirements/recommendations for international students: Required—TOEFL (minimum score 600 paper-based; 250 computer-based; 100 iBT). *Application deadline:* For fall admission, 5/1 priority date for domestic students, 5/1 for international students. Application fee: $50. Electronic applications accepted. *Expenses:* Tuition, state resident: part-time $512.85 per credit. Tuition, nonresident: part-time $1132.65 per credit. *Required fees:* $26.60 per credit. $199.65 per semester. Tuition and fees vary according to course load and program. *Financial support:* In 2011–12, 17 students received support, including 1 fellowship with tuition reimbursement available (averaging $18,000 per year), 14 research assistantships with tuition reimbursements available (averaging $21,144 per year); scholarships/grants and unspecified assistantships also available. Financial award application deadline: 2/1. *Faculty research:* Protein structure, molecular biology, molecular genetics, enzymology, x-ray crystallography. *Unit head:* Dr. Bharati Mitra, Interim Chair, 313-577-0400, E-mail: bmitra@med.wayne.edu. *Application contact:* Dr. Marilyn Doscher, Graduate Director, 313-577-1295, E-mail: mdoscher@med.wayne.edu. Web site: http://gradprograms.med.wayne.edu/program-spotlight.php?id=28.

Weill Cornell Medical College, Weill Cornell Graduate School of Medical Sciences, Biochemistry, Cell and Molecular Biology Allied Program, New York, NY 10065. Offers MS, PhD. *Faculty:* 111 full-time (32 women). *Students:* 152 full-time (95 women); includes 19 minority (2 Black or African American, non-Hispanic/Latino; 5 Asian, non-Hispanic/Latino; 8 Hispanic/Latino; 4 Native Hawaiian or other Pacific Islander, non-Hispanic/Latino), 82 international. Average age 22. 374 applicants, 23% accepted, 30 enrolled. In 2011, 2 master's, 19 doctorates awarded. Terminal master's awarded for partial completion of doctoral program. *Degree requirements:* For master's, comprehensive exam; for doctorate, thesis/dissertation, final exam. *Entrance requirements:* For doctorate, GRE General Test, background in genetics, molecular biology, chemistry, or biochemistry. Additional exam requirements/recommendations for international students: Required—TOEFL. *Application deadline:* For fall admission, 12/1 for domestic students. Application fee: $60. Electronic applications accepted. *Expenses: Tuition:* Full-time $46,001. *Financial support:* In 2011–12, 16 fellowships (averaging $22,600 per year) were awarded; scholarships/grants, health care benefits, and stipends (given to all students) also available. *Faculty research:* Molecular structure determination, protein structure, gene structure, stem cell biology, control of gene expression, DNA replication, chromosome maintenance, RNA biosynthesis. *Unit head:* Dr. Kirk Deitsch, Co-Director, 212-746-4976, Fax: 212-746-8906, E-mail: kwd2001@med.cornell.edu. *Application contact:* Rosalia Mora, Program Coordinator, 212-746-6058, Fax: 212-746-8906, E-mail: rmora@med.cornell.edu. Web site: http://weill.cornell.edu/gradschool/program/cell.html.

Wesleyan University, Graduate Programs, Department of Molecular Biology and Biochemistry, Middletown, CT 06459. Offers biochemistry (PhD); molecular biology (PhD). *Degree requirements:* For doctorate, comprehensive exam, thesis/dissertation. *Entrance requirements:* For doctorate, GRE General Test, GRE Subject Test. Additional exam requirements/recommendations for international students: Required—TOEFL. Electronic applications accepted. *Faculty research:* Genome organization, regulation of gene expression, molecular biology of development, physical biochemistry.

West Virginia University, Eberly College of Arts and Sciences, Department of Biology, Morgantown, WV 26506. Offers cell and molecular biology (MS, PhD); environmental and evolutionary biology (MS, PhD); forensic biology (MS, PhD); genomic biology (MS, PhD); neurobiology (MS, PhD). Terminal master's awarded for partial completion of doctoral program. *Degree requirements:* For master's, thesis, final exam; for doctorate, thesis/dissertation, preliminary and final exams. *Entrance requirements:* For master's, GRE General Test, GRE Subject Test, minimum GPA of 3.0; for doctorate, GRE General Test, minimum GPA of 3.0. Additional exam requirements/recommendations for international students: Required—TOEFL. *Faculty research:* Environmental biology, genetic engineering, developmental biology, global change, biodiversity.

West Virginia University, School of Medicine, Graduate Programs at the Health Sciences Center, Interdisciplinary Graduate Programs in Biomedical Sciences, Program in Biochemistry and Molecular Biology, Morgantown, WV 26506. Offers MS, PhD, MD/PhD. *Degree requirements:* For doctorate, comprehensive exam, thesis/dissertation. *Entrance requirements:* For doctorate, GRE General Test, minimum GPA of 3.0. Additional exam requirements/recommendations for international students: Required—TOEFL. Electronic applications accepted. *Faculty research:* Regulation of gene expression, cell survival mechanisms, signal transduction, regulation of metabolism, sensory neuroscience.

Wright State University, School of Graduate Studies, College of Science and Mathematics, Department of Biochemistry and Molecular Biology, Dayton, OH 45435. Offers MS. *Degree requirements:* For master's, thesis. *Entrance requirements:* Additional exam requirements/recommendations for international students: Required—TOEFL. *Faculty research:* Regulation of gene expression, macromolecular structural function, NMR imaging, visual biochemistry.

Yale University, Graduate School of Arts and Sciences, Department of Molecular, Cellular, and Developmental Biology, Program in Biochemistry, Molecular Biology and Chemical Biology, New Haven, CT 06520. Offers PhD. *Degree requirements:* For doctorate, thesis/dissertation. *Entrance requirements:* For doctorate, GRE General Test, GRE Subject Test.

Yale University, School of Medicine and Graduate School of Arts and Sciences, Combined Program in Biological and Biomedical Sciences (BBS), Molecular Cell Biology, Genetics, and Development Track, New Haven, CT 06520. Offers PhD, MD/PhD. *Entrance requirements:* Additional exam requirements/recommendations for international students: Required—TOEFL.

Youngstown State University, Graduate School, College of Science, Technology, Engineering and Mathematics, Department of Biological Sciences, Youngstown, OH 44555-0001. Offers environmental biology (MS); molecular biology, microbiology, and genetic (MS); physiology and anatomy (MS). Part-time programs available. *Degree requirements:* For master's, comprehensive exam, thesis, oral review. *Entrance requirements:* For master's, GRE General Test, minimum GPA of 2.7. Additional exam requirements/recommendations for international students: Required—TOEFL. *Faculty research:* Cell biology, neurophysiology, molecular biology, neurobiology, gene regulation.

Molecular Medicine

Baylor College of Medicine, Graduate School of Biomedical Sciences, Program in Translational Biology and Molecular Medicine, Houston, TX 77030-3498. Offers PhD. *Faculty:* 192 full-time (56 women). *Students:* 63 full-time (35 women); includes 24 minority (10 Black or African American, non-Hispanic/Latino; 9 Asian, non-Hispanic/Latino; 5 Hispanic/Latino), 17 international. Average age 27. 133 applicants, 17% accepted, 12 enrolled. In 2011, 1 doctorate awarded. *Degree requirements:* For doctorate, thesis/dissertation, public defense. *Entrance requirements:* For doctorate, GRE, minimum GPA of 3.0. Additional exam requirements/recommendations for

international students: Required—TOEFL. *Application deadline:* For fall admission, 1/1 for domestic students. Application fee: $0. Electronic applications accepted. *Financial support:* In 2011–12, 63 students received support, including 36 fellowships with full tuition reimbursements available (averaging $29,000 per year), 27 research assistantships with full tuition reimbursements available (averaging $29,000 per year); career-related internships or fieldwork, Federal Work-Study, health care benefits, and scholarships (to all students unless there are grant funds available to pay tuition) also available. Financial award applicants required to submit FAFSA. *Faculty research:* Molecular medicine, translational biology, human disease biology and therapy. *Unit head:* Dr. Mary Estes, Director, 713-798-3585, Fax: 713-798-3586, E-mail: tbmm@bcm.edu. *Application contact:* Wanda Waguespack, Graduate Program Administrator, 713-798-1077, Fax: 713-798-3586, E-mail: wandaw@bcm.edu. Web site: http://www.bcm.edu/tbmm.

Boston University, School of Medicine, Division of Graduate Medical Sciences, Program in Molecular Medicine, Boston, MA 02215. Offers PhD, MD/PhD. *Faculty:* 76 full-time (25 women), 1 (woman) part-time/adjunct. *Students:* 21 full-time (15 women); includes 1 minority (Black or African American, non-Hispanic/Latino), 6 international. Average age 27. 44 applicants, 32% accepted, 3 enrolled. In 2011, 7 doctorates awarded. *Degree requirements:* For doctorate, thesis/dissertation, qualifying exam. *Entrance requirements:* For doctorate, GRE. Additional exam requirements/recommendations for international students: Required—TOEFL. *Application deadline:* For fall admission, 1/15 priority date for domestic students; for spring admission, 10/15 priority date for domestic students. Application fee: $75. Electronic applications accepted. *Expenses: Tuition:* Full-time $40,848; part-time $1276 per credit hour. *Required fees:* $572; $286 per semester. *Financial support:* In 2011–12, fellowships (averaging $30,500 per year), 4 research assistantships (averaging $30,500 per year) were awarded; Federal Work-Study, scholarships/grants, and traineeships also available. Financial award applicants required to submit FAFSA. *Unit head:* Dr. Herbert Cohen, Director, 617-638-7322, E-mail: gpmm@med-med1.bu.edu. *Application contact:* Mary-Kathleen Delooge, Administrative Coordinator, 617-414-1519, E-mail: mkdeloge@bu.edu. Web site: http://www.bumc.bu.edu/gpmm.

Case Western Reserve University, School of Graduate Studies, Cleveland Clinic Lerner Research Institute–Molecular Medicine PhD Program, Cleveland, OH 44106. Offers PhD. *Faculty:* 138 full-time (42 women). *Students:* 34 full-time (18 women), 2 part-time (0 women); includes 9 minority (5 Black or African American, non-Hispanic/Latino; 4 Asian, non-Hispanic/Latino), 8 international. Average age 26. 320 applicants, 12% accepted, 13 enrolled. In 2011, 1 doctorate awarded. *Degree requirements:* For doctorate, comprehensive exam, thesis/dissertation, seminar. *Entrance requirements:* For doctorate, GRE, 3 letters of reference, prior research experience, interview. Additional exam requirements/recommendations for international students: Required—TOEFL (minimum score 577 paper-based; 213 computer-based; 90 iBT); Recommended—IELTS (minimum score 7). *Application deadline:* For fall admission, 11/1 priority date for domestic students, 11/1 for international students. Application fee: $50. Electronic applications accepted. *Financial support:* Fellowships with full tuition reimbursements, health care benefits, and stipends available. *Faculty research:* Cancer, cardiovascular disease, neuroscience, molecular biology, genetics. *Unit head:* Dr. Marcia Tackacs Jarrett, Director of Research Education, 216-444-4860, E-mail: jarretm@ccf.org. *Application contact:* Robin Crotty, Recruiting and Development Coordinator, 216-445-4917, E-mail: crottyr@ccf.org. Web site: http://www.lerner.ccf.org/molecmed/phd/.

Case Western Reserve University, School of Medicine and School of Graduate Studies, Graduate Programs in Medicine, Department of Molecular Medicine at the Lerner Research Institute, Cleveland, OH 44106. Offers PhD. *Degree requirements:* For doctorate, comprehensive exam, thesis/dissertation. *Entrance requirements:* For doctorate, GRE. Additional exam requirements/recommendations for international students: Required—TOEFL. Electronic applications accepted.

Cleveland State University, College of Graduate Studies, College of Sciences and Health Professions, Department of Chemistry, Cleveland, OH 44115. Offers analytical chemistry (MS); clinical chemistry (MS); clinical/bioanalytical chemistry (PhD), including cellular and molecular medicine, clinical chemistry, clinical/bioanalytical chemistry; environmental chemistry (MS); inorganic chemistry (MS); pharmaceutical/organic chemistry (MS); physical chemistry (MS). Part-time and evening/weekend programs available. *Faculty:* 12 full-time (0 women). *Students:* 17 full-time (8 women), 87 part-time (36 women); includes 6 minority (5 Black or African American, non-Hispanic/Latino; 1 Asian, non-Hispanic/Latino), 74 international. Average age 27. 143 applicants, 59% accepted, 22 enrolled. In 2011, 14 master's, 10 doctorates awarded. *Median time to degree:* Of those who began their doctoral program in fall 2003, 67% received their degree in 8 years or less. *Degree requirements:* For master's, thesis optional; for doctorate, comprehensive exam, thesis/dissertation. *Entrance requirements:* For master's and doctorate, GRE General Test. Additional exam requirements/recommendations for international students: Required—TOEFL (minimum score 525 paper-based; 197 computer-based; 65 iBT). *Application deadline:* For fall admission, 1/15 priority date for domestic students, 1/15 for international students. Applications are processed on a rolling basis. Application fee: $30. Electronic applications accepted. *Expenses:* Tuition, state resident: full-time $6416; part-time $494 per credit hour. Tuition, nonresident: full-time $12,074; part-time $929 per credit hour. *Financial support:* In 2011–12, 44 students received support, including 5 fellowships with full tuition reimbursements available (averaging $30,000 per year), 13 research assistantships with full tuition reimbursements available (averaging $20,000 per year), 24 teaching assistantships with full tuition reimbursements available (averaging $18,500 per year); scholarships/grants and unspecified assistantships also available. Financial award application deadline: 1/15. *Faculty research:* Bioanalytical techniques and molecular diagnostics, glycoproteomics and antithrombotic agents, drug discovery and innovation, analytical pharmacology, inflammatory disease research. *Total annual research expenditures:* $3 million. *Unit head:* Dr. David J. Anderson, Interim Chair, 216-687-2467, Fax: 216-687-9298, E-mail: d.anderson@csuohio.edu. *Application contact:* Richelle P. Emery, Administrative Coordinator, 216-687-2457, Fax: 216-687-9298, E-mail: r.emery@csuohio.edu. Web site: http://www.csuohio.edu/chemistry/.

Cornell University, Graduate School, Graduate Fields of Comparative Biomedical Sciences, Field of Comparative Biomedical Sciences, Ithaca, NY 14853-0001. Offers cellular and molecular medicine (MS, PhD); developmental and reproductive biology (MS, PhD); infectious diseases (MS, PhD); population medicine and epidemiology (MS, PhD); structural and functional biology (MS, PhD). *Faculty:* 97 full-time (27 women). *Students:* 38 full-time (23 women); includes 5 minority (2 Black or African American, non-Hispanic/Latino; 1 Asian, non-Hispanic/Latino; 2 Hispanic/Latino), 15 international. Average age 30. 45 applicants, 22% accepted, 9 enrolled. In 2011, 2 master's, 7 doctorates awarded. *Degree requirements:* For master's, thesis; for doctorate, comprehensive exam, thesis/dissertation. *Entrance requirements:* For master's and doctorate, GRE General Test, 2 letters of recommendation. Additional exam requirements/recommendations for international students: Required—TOEFL (minimum score 550 paper-based; 213 computer-based; 77 iBT). *Application deadline:* For fall admission, 12/15 for domestic students. Application fee: $95. Electronic applications accepted. *Financial support:* In 2011–12, 12 fellowships with full tuition reimbursements, 25 research assistantships with full tuition reimbursements were awarded; teaching assistantships with full tuition reimbursements, institutionally sponsored loans, scholarships/grants, health care benefits, tuition waivers (full and partial), and unspecified assistantships also available. Financial award applicants required to submit FAFSA. *Faculty research:* Receptors and signal transduction, viral and bacterial infectious diseases, tumor metastasis, clinical sciences/nutritional disease, developmental/neurological disorders. *Unit head:* Director of Graduate Studies, 607-253-3276, Fax: 607-253-3756. *Application contact:* Graduate Field Assistant, 607-253-3276, Fax: 607-253-3756, E-mail: graduate_edcvm@cornell.edu. Web site: http://www.gradschool.cornell.edu/fields.php?id-64&a-2.

Dartmouth College, Arts and Sciences Graduate Programs, Program in Experimental and Molecular Medicine, Hanover, NH 03755. Offers biomedical physiology (PhD); cancer biology and molecular therapeutics (PhD); cardiovascular diseases (PhD); molecular pharmacology, toxicology and experimental therapeutics (PhD); neuroscience (PhD); MD/PhD. *Degree requirements:* For doctorate, comprehensive exam, thesis/dissertation. *Entrance requirements:* For doctorate, GRE, 3 letters of recommendation, interview, minimum GPA of 3.0. Additional exam requirements/recommendations for international students: Required—TOEFL (minimum score 620 paper-based; 260 computer-based; 105 iBT). Electronic applications accepted.

Dartmouth College, Program in Experimental and Molecular Medicine, Hanover, NH 03755. Offers biomedical physiology (PhD); cancer biology and molecular therapeutics (PhD); cardiovascular diseases (PhD); molecular pharmacology, toxicology and experimental therapeutics (PhD); neuroscience (PhD); MD/PhD. *Degree requirements:* For doctorate, comprehensive exam, thesis/dissertation. *Entrance requirements:* For doctorate, GRE General Test, 3 letters of recommendation. Additional exam requirements/recommendations for international students: Required—TOEFL (minimum score 620 paper-based; 260 computer-based; 105 iBT). Electronic applications accepted.

Drexel University, College of Medicine, Biomedical Graduate Programs, Molecular Medicine Program, Philadelphia, PA 19129. Offers MS.

The George Washington University, Columbian College of Arts and Sciences, Institute for Biomedical Sciences, Program in Molecular Medicine, Washington, DC 20037. Offers molecular and cellular oncology (PhD); neurosciences (PhD); pharmacology and physiology (PhD). *Students:* 6 full-time (4 women), 24 part-time (13 women); includes 4 minority (1 Black or African American, non-Hispanic/Latino; 3 Asian, non-Hispanic/Latino), 8 international. Average age 31. In 2011, 7 doctorates awarded. *Degree requirements:* For doctorate, comprehensive exam, thesis/dissertation, general exams. *Entrance requirements:* For doctorate, GRE General Test, interview, minimum GPA of 3.0. Additional exam requirements/recommendations for international students: Required—TOEFL (minimum score 600 paper-based; 250 computer-based). *Application deadline:* For fall admission, 12/15 priority date for domestic students, 12/15 for international students. Applications are processed on a rolling basis. Application fee: $75. Electronic applications accepted. *Financial support:* In 2011–12, 10 students received support. Fellowships with tuition reimbursements available, Federal Work-Study, institutionally sponsored loans, and tuition waivers available. Financial award application deadline: 2/1. *Unit head:* Dr. Norman Lee, Director, 202-994-2114, E-mail: beb@gwu.edu. *Application contact:* 202-994-2179, Fax: 202-994-0967, E-mail: gwibs@gwu.edu. Web site: http://www.gwumc.edu/ibs/.

Georgia Health Sciences University, College of Graduate Studies, Program in Molecular Medicine, Augusta, GA 30912. Offers MS, PhD. *Faculty:* 50 full-time (7 women), 2 part-time/adjunct (0 women). *Students:* 21 full-time (12 women), 1 part-time (0 women); includes 5 minority (3 Black or African American, non-Hispanic/Latino; 2 Asian, non-Hispanic/Latino), 14 international. Average age 29. In 2011, 3 doctorates awarded. *Degree requirements:* For doctorate, comprehensive exam, thesis/dissertation. *Entrance requirements:* For doctorate, GRE General Test. Additional exam requirements/recommendations for international students: Required—TOEFL (minimum score 550 paper-based; 213 computer-based; 79 iBT). *Application deadline:* For fall admission, 1/15 for domestic and international students. Application fee: $50. Electronic applications accepted. *Financial support:* In 2011–12, 4 students received support, including fellowships with partial tuition reimbursements available (averaging $26,000 per year), 17 research assistantships with partial tuition reimbursements available (averaging $23,000 per year); teaching assistantships, Federal Work-Study, institutionally sponsored loans, and scholarships/grants also available. Support available to part-time students. Financial award application deadline: 5/31; financial award applicants required to submit FAFSA. *Faculty research:* Developmental neurobiology, cancer, regenerative medicine, molecular chaperones, molecular immunology. *Total annual research expenditures:* $11.9 million. *Unit head:* Dr. Lin Mei, Director of Institute of Molecular Medicine and Genetics, 706-721-8775, Fax: 706-721-8685, E-mail: lmie@georgiahealth.edu. *Application contact:* Dr. Patricia L. Cameron, Associate Dean, 706-721-3279, E-mail: pcameron@georgiahealth.edu. Web site: http://www.georgiahealth.edu/gradmm/.

Hofstra University, School of Medicine, Hempstead, NY 11549. Offers medicine (MD); molecular basis of medicine (PhD); MD/PhD. *Accreditation:* LCME/AMA. *Faculty:* 8 full-time (3 women). *Students:* 43 full-time (22 women); includes 16 minority (3 Black or African American, non-Hispanic/Latino; 6 Asian, non-Hispanic/Latino; 2 Hispanic/Latino; 2 Native Hawaiian or other Pacific Islander, non-Hispanic/Latino; 3 Two or more races, non-Hispanic/Latino). Average age 25. *Entrance requirements:* For doctorate, MCAT. Additional exam requirements/recommendations for international students: Required—TOEFL (minimum score 600 paper-based; 250 computer-based; 100 iBT). *Application deadline:* For fall admission, 12/1 priority date for domestic students. Application fee: $100. Electronic applications accepted. *Expenses:* Contact institution. *Financial support:* In 2011–12, 43 students received support, including 43 fellowships with full and partial tuition reimbursements available (averaging $31,287 per year); research assistantships with full and partial tuition reimbursements available, Federal Work-Study, institutionally sponsored loans, scholarships/grants, and tuition waivers (full and partial) also available. Support available to part-time students. Financial award applicants required to submit FAFSA. *Faculty research:* Pathogenesis of sepsis, autoimmune disease, pathogenesis of schizophrenia and movement disorder, pathogenesis and treatment of chronic leukemia, population health: healthcare quality and effectiveness. *Unit head:* Dr. Lawrence Smith, Dean, 516-463-7577, Fax: 516-463-5631, E-mail: medlgs@hofstra.edu. *Application contact:* Carol Drummer, Dean of Graduate Admissions, 516-463-4876, Fax: 516-463-4664, E-mail: gradstudent@hofstra.edu. Web site: http://medicine.hofstra.edu/.

The Johns Hopkins University, School of Medicine, Graduate Programs in Medicine, Graduate Program in Cellular and Molecular Medicine, Baltimore, MD 21218-2699. Offers PhD. *Degree requirements:* For doctorate, comprehensive exam, thesis/dissertation, oral exam. *Entrance requirements:* For doctorate, GRE. Additional exam requirements/recommendations for international students: Required—TOEFL. Electronic applications accepted. *Faculty research:* Cellular and molecular basis of disease.

North Shore–LIJ Graduate School of Molecular Medicine, Graduate Program, Manhasset, NY 11030. Offers PhD. *Degree requirements:* For doctorate,

comprehensive exam, thesis/dissertation. *Entrance requirements:* For doctorate, MD or equivalent. *Faculty research:* Cardiopulmonary disease, cancer, inflammation, genetics of complex disorders, cytokine biology.

Penn State Hershey Medical Center, College of Medicine, Graduate School Programs in the Biomedical Sciences, The Huck Institutes of the Life Sciences, Intercollege Graduate Program in Molecular Medicine, Hershey, PA 17033. Offers MS, PhD, MD/PhD. *Students:* 10 full-time (7 women); includes 1 minority (Asian, non-Hispanic/Latino), 6 international. 25 applicants, 28% accepted, 1 enrolled. Terminal master's awarded for partial completion of doctoral program. *Degree requirements:* For master's, thesis or alternative; for doctorate, comprehensive exam, thesis/dissertation. *Application deadline:* For fall admission, 1/31 for domestic students, 2/1 for international students. Applications are processed on a rolling basis. Application fee: $65. Electronic applications accepted. *Financial support:* In 2011–12, research assistantships with full tuition reimbursements (averaging $23,028 per year) were awarded; fellowships with full tuition reimbursements, career-related internships or fieldwork, scholarships/grants, health care benefits, and unspecified assistantships also available. *Faculty research:* Transitional research, diabetes and retinal vessels, stem cell differentiation/osteogenesis, cancer, malaria. *Unit head:* Dr. Charles Lang, Head, 717-531-8982, E-mail: grad-hmc@psu.edu. *Application contact:* Kathy Shuey, Administrative Assistant, 717-531-8982, Fax: 717-531-0786, E-mail: grad-hmc@psu.edu. Web site: http://www.huck.psu.edu/education/molecular-medicine.

Queen's University at Kingston, School of Graduate Studies and Research, Faculty of Health Sciences, Department of Pathology and Molecular Medicine, Kingston, ON K7L 3N6, Canada. Offers M Sc, PhD. Part-time programs available. *Degree requirements:* For master's, thesis; for doctorate, comprehensive exam, thesis/dissertation. *Entrance requirements:* Additional exam requirements/recommendations for international students: Required—TOEFL. *Faculty research:* Immunopathology, cancer biology, immunology and metastases, cell differentiation, blood coagulation.

Texas A&M Health Science Center, College of Medicine, Department of Molecular and Cellular Medicine, College Station, TX 77840. Offers PhD. *Degree requirements:* For doctorate, thesis/dissertation. *Entrance requirements:* For doctorate, GRE General Test. *Faculty research:* Immunology, cell and membrane biology, protein biochemistry, molecular genetics, parasitology, vertebrate embryogenesis and microbiology.

University of Chicago, Division of Biological Sciences, Biomedical Sciences Cluster: Cancer Biology, Immunology, Molecular Metabolism and Nutrition, Pathology, and Microbiology, Department of Pathology, Chicago, IL 60637-1513. Offers molecular pathogenesis and molecular medicine (PhD). *Degree requirements:* For doctorate, thesis/dissertation, ethics class, 2 teaching assistantships. *Entrance requirements:* For doctorate, GRE General Test. Additional exam requirements/recommendations for international students: Required—IELTS (minimum score 7); Recommended—TOEFL (minimum score 600 paper-based; 250 computer-based; 104 iBT). Electronic applications accepted. *Faculty research:* Vascular biology, apolipoproteins, cardiovascular disease, immunopathology.

University of Cincinnati, Graduate School, College of Medicine, Graduate Programs in Biomedical Sciences, Program in Pathobiology and Molecular Medicine, Cincinnati, OH 45221. Offers pathology (PhD), including anatomic pathology, laboratory medicine, pathobiology and molecular medicine. *Degree requirements:* For doctorate, thesis/dissertation, qualifying exam. *Entrance requirements:* For doctorate, GRE General Test. Additional exam requirements/recommendations for international students: Required—TOEFL (minimum score 620 paper-based; 260 computer-based). Electronic applications accepted. *Faculty research:* Cardiovascular and lipid disorders, digestive and kidney disease, endocrine and metabolic disorders, hematologic and oncogenic, immunology and infectious disease.

University of Maryland, Baltimore, Graduate School, Graduate Program in Life Sciences, Program in Molecular Medicine, Baltimore, MD 21201. Offers cancer biology (PhD); cell and molecular physiology (PhD); human genetics and genomic medicine (PhD); molecular medicine (MS); molecular toxicology and pharmacology (PhD); MD/PhD. *Students:* 80 full-time (53 women), 11 part-time (4 women); includes 21 minority (8 Black or African American, non-Hispanic/Latino; 6 Asian, non-Hispanic/Latino; 4 Hispanic/Latino; 3 Two or more races, non-Hispanic/Latino), 13 international. Average age 27. 207 applicants, 24% accepted, 15 enrolled. In 2011, 3 master's, 5 doctorates awarded. *Entrance requirements:* Additional exam requirements/recommendations for international students: Required—TOEFL (minimum score 600 paper-based; 100 iBT); Recommended—IELTS (minimum score 7). *Application deadline:* For fall admission, 1/15 for domestic and international students. Application fee: $50. Electronic applications

accepted. *Financial support:* In 2011–12, research assistantships with partial tuition reimbursements (averaging $25,000 per year) were awarded; fellowships also available. Financial award application deadline: 3/1. *Unit head:* Dr. Toni Antalis, Director, 410-706-8222, E-mail: tantalis@som.umaryland.edu. *Application contact:* Sharron Graves, Program Coordinator, 410-706-6044, Fax: 410-706-6040, E-mail: sgraves@som.umaryland.edu. Web site: http://molecularmedicine.umaryland.edu.

University of Medicine and Dentistry of New Jersey, Graduate School of Biomedical Sciences, Graduate Programs in Biomedical Sciences–Newark, Department of Cell Biology and Molecular Medicine, Newark, NJ 07107. Offers PhD. *Degree requirements:* For doctorate, thesis/dissertation, qualifying exam. *Entrance requirements:* For doctorate, GRE General Test. Additional exam requirements/recommendations for international students: Required—TOEFL. Electronic applications accepted.

The University of Texas Health Science Center at San Antonio, Graduate School of Biomedical Sciences, Program in Molecular Medicine, San Antonio, TX 78245-3207. Offers MS, PhD. Terminal master's awarded for partial completion of doctoral program. *Degree requirements:* For master's, comprehensive exam, thesis, written and oral qualifying exam; for doctorate, comprehensive exam, thesis/dissertation, written and oral qualifying exam. *Entrance requirements:* For master's and doctorate, GRE General Test. Additional exam requirements/recommendations for international students: Required—TOEFL (minimum score 560 paper-based; 220 computer-based; 68 iBT). Electronic applications accepted. *Faculty research:* DNA repair, tumor suppressor genes, vision in drosophila, gene expression (nervous system), cell-type specific gene regulation and development.

University of Washington, Graduate School, School of Public Health, Department of Global Health, Graduate Program in Pathobiology, Seattle, WA 98195. Offers PhD. *Students:* 32 full-time (25 women), 3 part-time (all women); includes 7 minority (2 Black or African American, non-Hispanic/Latino; 3 Asian, non-Hispanic/Latino; 2 Hispanic/Latino), 5 international. Average age 29. 75 applicants, 20% accepted, 5 enrolled. In 2011, 3 doctorates awarded. *Degree requirements:* For doctorate, comprehensive exam, thesis/dissertation, published paper from thesis work. *Entrance requirements:* For doctorate, GRE General Test, minimum GPA of 3.0. Additional exam requirements/recommendations for international students: Required—TOEFL, IELTS. *Application deadline:* For fall admission, 12/1 for domestic students, 11/1 for international students. Application fee: $75. Electronic applications accepted. *Financial support:* In 2011–12, 34 students received support, including 34 research assistantships with full tuition reimbursements available (averaging $27,348 per year); traineeships and unspecified assistantships also available. *Faculty research:* Malaria, immunological response to mycobacteria infections, HIV-cell interaction and the development of an anti-HIV vaccine, regulation of intercellular communication via gap junctions, genetic and nutritional regulation of proteins involved in lipid transport. *Unit head:* Dr. King Holmes, Chair, 206-744-3620, Fax: 206-744-3694. *Application contact:* Rachel Reichert, Program Manager, 206-543-4338, Fax: 206-543-3873, E-mail: pabio@u.washington.edu.

Wake Forest University, School of Medicine and Graduate School of Arts and Sciences, Graduate Programs in Medicine, Molecular Genetics and Genomics Program, Winston-Salem, NC 27109. Offers PhD, MD/PhD. *Degree requirements:* For doctorate, thesis/dissertation. *Entrance requirements:* For doctorate, GRE General Test. Additional exam requirements/recommendations for international students: Required—TOEFL. Electronic applications accepted. *Faculty research:* Control of gene expression, molecular pathogenesis, protein biosynthesis, cell development, clinical cytogenetics.

Wake Forest University, School of Medicine and Graduate School of Arts and Sciences, Graduate Programs in Medicine, Program in Molecular Medicine, Winston-Salem, NC 27109. Offers MS, PhD, MD/PhD. *Degree requirements:* For master's, thesis; for doctorate, thesis/dissertation. *Entrance requirements:* For master's and doctorate, GRE General Test. Additional exam requirements/recommendations for international students: Required—TOEFL. Electronic applications accepted. *Faculty research:* Human biology and disease, scientific basis of medicine, cellular and molecular mechanisms of health and disease.

Yale University, School of Medicine and Graduate School of Arts and Sciences, Combined Program in Biological and Biomedical Sciences (BBS), Pharmacological Sciences and Molecular Medicine Track, New Haven, CT 06520. Offers PhD, MD/PhD. *Degree requirements:* For doctorate, thesis/dissertation. *Entrance requirements:* For doctorate, GRE General Test. Additional exam requirements/recommendations for international students: Required—TOEFL. Electronic applications accepted.

Structural Biology

Baylor College of Medicine, Graduate School of Biomedical Sciences, Program in Structural and Computational Biology and Molecular Biophysics, Houston, TX 77030-3498. Offers PhD, MD/PhD. MD/PhD offered jointly with Rice University and University of Houston. *Faculty:* 84 full-time (10 women). *Students:* 38 full-time (12 women); includes 4 minority (1 Black or African American, non-Hispanic/Latino; 2 Asian, non-Hispanic/Latino; 1 Hispanic/Latino), 19 international. Average age 28. 74 applicants, 14% accepted, 8 enrolled. In 2011, 6 doctorates awarded. *Degree requirements:* For doctorate, thesis/dissertation, public defense. *Entrance requirements:* For doctorate, GRE General Test, GRE Subject Test (strongly recommended), minimum GPA of 3.0. Additional exam requirements/recommendations for international students: Required—TOEFL. *Application deadline:* For fall admission, 1/1 for domestic students. Application fee: $0. Electronic applications accepted. *Financial support:* In 2011–12, 38 students received support, including 21 fellowships with full tuition reimbursements available (averaging $29,000 per year), 17 research assistantships with full tuition reimbursements available (averaging $29,000 per year); career-related internships or fieldwork, Federal Work-Study, institutionally sponsored loans, health care benefits, and scholarships (to all students unless there are grant funds available to pay tuition) also available. Financial award applicants required to submit FAFSA. *Faculty research:* Computational biology, structural biology, biophysics. *Unit head:* Dr. Wah Chiu, Director, 713-798-6985. *Application contact:* Amber Eakin, Administrative Coordinator, 713-798-5197, Fax: 713-798-6325, E-mail: ameakin@bcm.edu.

Carnegie Mellon University, Mellon College of Science, Joint Pitt + CMU Molecular Biophysics and Structural Biology Graduate Program, Pittsburgh, PA 15213-3891. Offers PhD. Program offered jointly with University of Pittsburgh. *Degree requirements:* For doctorate, comprehensive exam, thesis/dissertation. *Entrance requirements:* For doctorate, GRE General Test. Additional exam requirements/recommendations for international students: Required—TOEFL (minimum score 600 paper-based; 250

computer-based; 100 iBT), IELTS (minimum score 7). Electronic applications accepted. *Faculty research:* Structural biology, protein dynamics and folding, computational biophysics, molecular informatics, membrane biophysics and ion channels, NMR, X-ray crystallography cryaelectron microscopy.

Columbia University, College of Physicians and Surgeons, Integrated Program in Cellular, Molecular, Structural and Genetic Studies, New York, NY 10032. Offers PhD. Terminal master's awarded for partial completion of doctoral program. *Degree requirements:* For doctorate, thesis/dissertation. *Entrance requirements:* For doctorate, GRE General Test, GRE Subject Test. Additional exam requirements/recommendations for international students: Required—TOEFL. *Expenses:* Contact institution. *Faculty research:* Transcription, macromolecular sorting, gene expression during development, cellular interaction.

Cornell University, Graduate School, Graduate Fields of Comparative Biomedical Sciences, Field of Comparative Biomedical Sciences, Ithaca, NY 14853-0001. Offers cellular and molecular medicine (MS, PhD); developmental and reproductive biology (MS, PhD); infectious diseases (MS, PhD); population medicine and epidemiology (MS, PhD); structural and functional biology (MS, PhD). *Faculty:* 97 full-time (27 women). *Students:* 38 full-time (23 women); includes 5 minority (2 Black or African American, non-Hispanic/Latino; 1 Asian, non-Hispanic/Latino; 2 Hispanic/Latino), 15 international. Average age 30. 45 applicants, 22% accepted, 9 enrolled. In 2011, 2 master's, 7 doctorates awarded. *Degree requirements:* For master's, thesis; for doctorate, comprehensive exam, thesis/dissertation. *Entrance requirements:* For master's and doctorate, GRE General Test, 2 letters of recommendation. Additional exam requirements/recommendations for international students: Required—TOEFL (minimum score 550 paper-based; 213 computer-based; 77 iBT). *Application deadline:* For fall admission, 12/15 for domestic students. Application fee: $95. Electronic applications

accepted. *Financial support:* In 2011–12, 12 fellowships with full tuition reimbursements, 25 research assistantships with full tuition reimbursements were awarded; teaching assistantships with full tuition reimbursements, institutionally sponsored loans, scholarships/grants, health care benefits, tuition waivers (full and partial), and unspecified assistantships also available. Financial award applicants required to submit FAFSA. *Faculty research:* Receptors and signal transduction, viral and bacterial infectious diseases, tumor metastasis, clinical sciences/nutritional disease, developmental/neurological disorders. *Unit head:* Director of Graduate Studies, 607-253-3276, Fax: 607-253-3756. *Application contact:* Graduate Field Assistant, 607-253-3276, Fax: 607-253-3756, E-mail: graduate_cdcvm@cornell.edu. Web site: http://www.gradschool.cornell.edu/fields.php?id=64&a-2.

Duke University, Graduate School, Program in Structural Biology and Biophysics, Durham, NC 27710. Offers Certificate. Students must be enrolled in a participating PhD program (biochemistry, cell biology, chemistry, molecular genetics, neurobiology, pharmacology). *Faculty:* 25 full-time. *Students:* 3 full-time (2 women), 2 international. 21 applicants, 24% accepted, 3 enrolled. *Entrance requirements:* For degree, GRE General Test. Additional exam requirements/recommendations for international students: Required—TOEFL (minimum score 550 paper-based; 213 computer-based; 83 iBT), IELTS (minimum score 7). *Application deadline:* For fall admission, 12/8 priority date for domestic students, 12/8 for international students. Application fee: $75. *Expenses: Tuition:* Full-time $40,720. *Required fees:* $3107. *Financial support:* Application deadline: 12/8. *Unit head:* David Richardson, Director of Graduate Studies, 919-684-6559, Fax: 919-684-8346, E-mail: carol.richardson@duke.edu. *Application contact:* Elizabeth Hutton, Director of Admissions, 919-684-3913, Fax: 919-684-2277, E-mail: grad-admissions@duke.edu. Web site: http://sbb.duke.edu.

Florida State University, The Graduate School, College of Arts and Sciences, Department of Biological Science, Specialization in Structural Biology, Tallahassee, FL 32306-4295. Offers MS, PhD. *Faculty:* 14 full-time (4 women). *Students:* 18 full-time (10 women); includes 2 minority (both Hispanic/Latino), 5 international. In 2011, 1 master's, 4 doctorates awarded. Terminal master's awarded for partial completion of doctoral program. *Degree requirements:* For master's, comprehensive exam, thesis, teaching experience, seminar presentation; for doctorate, comprehensive exam, thesis/dissertation, teaching experience, seminar presentation. *Entrance requirements:* For master's and doctorate, GRE General Test (minimum combined score 1100, 500 verbal, 500 quantitative in old version; 72% verbal, 67% quantitative in new format), minimum upper-division GPA of 3.0. Additional exam requirements/recommendations for international students: Required—TOEFL (minimum score 600 paper-based; 250 computer-based; 92 iBT). *Application deadline:* For fall admission, 12/15 for domestic and international students. Application fee: $30. Electronic applications accepted. *Expenses:* Tuition, state resident: full-time $9474; part-time $350.88 per credit hour. Tuition, nonresident: full-time $16,236; part-time $601.34 per credit hour. *Required fees:* $630 per semester. One-time fee: $20. Tuition and fees vary according to course load and campus/location. *Financial support:* In 2011–12, 17 students received support, including 1 fellowship with full tuition reimbursement available (averaging $24,000 per year), 8 research assistantships with full tuition reimbursements available (averaging $21,000 per year), 8 teaching assistantships with full tuition reimbursements available (averaging $21,000 per year); traineeships also available. Financial award application deadline: 12/15; financial award applicants required to submit FAFSA. *Faculty research:* Molecular genetics, signal transduction and regulation of gene expression, cell and molecular biology of the cytoskeleton, olfactory signal transduction, ion channel structure-function, neuromodulation, 3-D electron microscopy and x-ray crystallography of protein complexes involved in mRNA and sulfur metabolism, olfaction, synaptic physiology and plasticity, ion channel modulation, biomechanics of cardiac and skeletal muscle, magnetic resonance of proteins. *Unit head:* Professor and Associate Chairman for Graduate Studies. *Application contact:* Judy Bowers, Coordinator, Graduate Affairs, 850-644-3023, Fax: 850-644-9829, E-mail: gradinfo@bio.fsu.edu. Web site: http://www.bio.fsu.edu/.

Florida State University, The Graduate School, College of Arts and Sciences, Program in Molecular Biophysics, Tallahassee, FL 32306. Offers computational structural biology (PhD); molecular biophysics (PhD). *Faculty:* 50 full-time (8 women). *Students:* 24 full-time (10 women); includes 7 minority (4 Asian, non-Hispanic/Latino; 3 Hispanic/Latino), 8 international. Average age 28. 35 applicants, 29% accepted, 5 enrolled. In 2011, 3 doctorates awarded. *Degree requirements:* For doctorate, comprehensive exam, thesis/dissertation, teaching 1 term in professor's major department. *Entrance requirements:* For doctorate, GRE General Test. Additional exam requirements/recommendations for international students: Required—TOEFL (minimum score 600 paper-based; 250 computer-based; 90 iBT). *Application deadline:* For fall admission, 1/15 for domestic students, 2/15 for international students. Applications are processed on a rolling basis. Application fee: $30. Electronic applications accepted. *Expenses:* Tuition, state resident: full-time $9474; part-time $350.88 per credit hour. Tuition, nonresident: full-time $16,236; part-time $601.34 per credit hour. *Required fees:* $630 per semester. One-time fee: $20. Tuition and fees vary according to course load and campus/location. *Financial support:* In 2011–12, 23 students received support, including 1 fellowship with partial tuition reimbursement available (averaging $10,000 per year), 19 research assistantships with partial tuition reimbursements available (averaging $22,050 per year), 4 teaching assistantships with partial tuition reimbursements available (averaging $22,050 per year); scholarships/grants, health care benefits, and unspecified assistantships also available. Financial award applicants required to submit FAFSA. *Faculty research:* Protein and nucleic acid structure and function, membrane protein structure, computational biophysics, 3-D image reconstruction. *Total annual research expenditures:* $1.7 million. *Unit head:* Dr. Hong Li, Director, 850-644-6785, Fax: 850-644-7244, E-mail: hongli@sb.fsu.edu. *Application contact:* Lyn Kittle, Academic Coordinator, Graduate Programs, 850-644-1012, Fax: 850-644-7244, E-mail: lkittle@fsu.edu. Web site: http://www.sb.fsu.edu/mob/.

Harvard University, Graduate School of Arts and Sciences, Department of Systems Biology, Cambridge, MA 02138. Offers PhD. *Degree requirements:* For doctorate, thesis/dissertation, lab rotation, qualifying examination. *Entrance requirements:* For doctorate, GRE. Additional exam requirements/recommendations for international students: Required—TOEFL. Electronic applications accepted. *Expenses: Tuition:* Full-time $36,304. *Required fees:* $1186. Full-time tuition and fees vary according to program.

Illinois State University, Graduate School, College of Arts and Sciences, Department of Biological Sciences, Normal, IL 61790-2200. Offers animal behavior (MS); bacteriology (MS); biochemistry (MS); biological sciences (MS); biology (PhD); biophysics (MS); biotechnology (MS); botany (MS, PhD); cell biology (MS); conservation biology (MS); developmental biology (MS); ecology (MS, PhD); entomology (MS); evolutionary biology (MS); genetics (MS, PhD); immunology (MS); microbiology (MS, PhD); molecular biology (MS); molecular genetics (MS); neurobiology (MS); neuroscience (MS); parasitology (MS); physiology (MS, PhD); plant biology (MS); plant molecular biology (MS); plant sciences (MS); structural biology (MS); zoology (MS, PhD). Part-time programs available. *Degree requirements:* For master's, thesis or

alternative; for doctorate, variable foreign language requirement, thesis/dissertation, 2 terms of residency. *Entrance requirements:* For master's, GRE General Test, minimum GPA of 2.6 in last 60 hours of course work; for doctorate, GRE General Test. *Faculty research:* Redoc balance and drug development in schistosoma mansoni, control of the growth of listeria monocytogenes at low temperature, regulation of cell expansion and microtubule function by SPRI, CRUI: physiology and fitness consequences of different life history phenotypes.

Iowa State University of Science and Technology, Bioinformatics and Computational Biology Program, Ames, IA 50011-3260. Offers MS, PhD. *Degree requirements:* For doctorate, thesis/dissertation. *Entrance requirements:* For master's and doctorate, GRE General Test. Additional exam requirements/recommendations for international students: Recommended—TOEFL, IELTS. *Application deadline:* For fall admission, 1/15 priority date for domestic students, 1/15 for international students; for spring admission, 10/15 for domestic and international students. Application fee: $40 ($90 for international students). Electronic applications accepted. *Faculty research:* Functional and structural genomics, genome evolution, macromolecular structure and function, mathematical biology and biological statistics, metabolic and developmental networks. *Unit head:* Dr. Julie Dickerson, Chair, Supervising Committee, 515-294-5122, Fax: 515-294-6790, E-mail: bcb@iastate.edu. *Application contact:* Information Contact, 515-294-5836, Fax: 515-294-2592, E-mail: grad_admissions@iastate.edu. Web site: http://www.bcb.iastate.edu/.

Massachusetts Institute of Technology, School of Science, Department of Biology, Cambridge, MA 02139. Offers biochemistry (PhD); biological oceanography (PhD); biology (PhD); biophysical chemistry and molecular structure (PhD); cell biology (PhD); computational and systems biology (PhD); developmental biology (PhD); genetics (PhD); immunology (PhD); microbiology (PhD); molecular biology (PhD); neurobiology (PhD). *Faculty:* 58 full-time (15 women). *Students:* 248 full-time (129 women); includes 69 minority (5 Black or African American, non-Hispanic/Latino; 1 American Indian or Alaska Native, non-Hispanic/Latino; 25 Asian, non-Hispanic/Latino; 31 Hispanic/Latino; 7 Two or more races, non-Hispanic/Latino), 36 international. Average age 26. 698 applicants, 15% accepted, 44 enrolled. In 2011, 38 doctorates awarded. *Degree requirements:* For doctorate, comprehensive exam, thesis/dissertation. *Entrance requirements:* For doctorate, GRE General Test. Additional exam requirements/recommendations for international students: Required—TOEFL (minimum score 577 paper-based; 233 computer-based), IELTS (minimum score 6.5). *Application deadline:* For fall admission, 12/1 for domestic and international students. Application fee: $75. Electronic applications accepted. *Expenses: Tuition:* Full-time $40,460; part-time $630 per credit hour. *Required fees:* $272. *Financial support:* In 2011–12, 214 students received support, including 129 fellowships (averaging $33,200 per year), 117 research assistantships (averaging $32,900 per year); teaching assistantships, Federal Work-Study, institutionally sponsored loans, scholarships/grants, traineeships, health care benefits, and unspecified assistantships also available. *Faculty research:* Cellular, developmental and molecular (plant and animal) biology; biochemistry, bioengineering, biophysics and structural biology; classical and molecular genetics; immunology and microbiology; cancer biology, molecular medicine, neurobiology and human disease; computational and systems biology. *Total annual research expenditures:* $53.6 million. *Unit head:* Prof. Tania A. Baker, Head, 617-253-4701, E-mail: mitbio@mit.edu. *Application contact:* Biology Education Office, 617-253-3717, Fax: 617-258-9329, E-mail: gradbio@mit.edu. Web site: https://biology.mit.edu/.

Mayo Graduate School, Graduate Programs in Biomedical Sciences, Programs in Biochemistry, Structural Biology, Cell Biology, and Genetics, Rochester, MN 55905. Offers biochemistry and structural biology (PhD); cell biology and genetics (PhD); molecular biology (PhD). *Degree requirements:* For doctorate, oral defense of dissertation, qualifying oral and written exam. *Entrance requirements:* For doctorate, GRE, 1 year of chemistry, biology, calculus, and physics. Additional exam requirements/recommendations for international students: Required—TOEFL. Electronic applications accepted. *Faculty research:* Gene structure and function, membranes and receptors/cytoskeleton, oncogenes and growth factors, protein structure and function, steroid hormonal action.

Michigan State University, The Graduate School, College of Natural Science, Quantitative Biology Program, East Lansing, MI 48824. Offers PhD.

New York University, School of Medicine, New York, NY 10012-1019. Offers biomedical sciences (PhD), including biomedical imaging, cellular and molecular biology, computational biology, developmental genetics, medical and molecular parasitology, microbiology, molecular oncobiology and immunology, neuroscience and physiology, pathobiology, pharmacology, structural biology; clinical investigation (MS); medicine (MD); MD/MA; MD/MPA; MD/MS; MD/PhD. *Accreditation:* LCME/AMA (one or more programs are accredited). *Degree requirements:* For master's, comprehensive exam, thesis; for doctorate, comprehensive exam (for some programs), thesis/dissertation (for some programs). *Entrance requirements:* For doctorate, MCAT (for MD). Additional exam requirements/recommendations for international students: Required—TOEFL. *Expenses:* Contact institution. *Faculty research:* AIDS, cancer, neuroscience, molecular biology, neuroscience, cell biology and molecular genetics, structural biology, microbial pathogenesis and host defense, pharmacology, molecular oncology and immunology.

New York University, School of Medicine and Graduate School of Arts and Science, Sackler Institute of Graduate Biomedical Sciences, Program in Molecular Biophysics, New York, NY 10012-1019. Offers PhD. *Students:* 16 full-time (8 women); includes 2 minority (1 American Indian or Alaska Native, non-Hispanic/Latino; 1 Asian, non-Hispanic/Latino), 7 international. *Degree requirements:* For doctorate, thesis/dissertation, qualifying examination. *Entrance requirements:* For doctorate, GRE General Test, GRE Subject Test in biology or chemistry (recommended). Additional exam requirements/recommendations for international students: Required—TOEFL. *Application deadline:* For fall admission, 2/1 for domestic students. Application fee: $85. *Financial support:* Research assistantships with full tuition reimbursements, institutionally sponsored loans, and health care benefits available. *Unit head:* Dr. Joel D. Oppenheim, Senior Associate Dean for Graduate Studies, 212-263-8001, Fax: 212-263-7600. *Application contact:* Dr. David L. Stokes, Associate Professor, 212-263-1580, E-mail: stokes@saturn.med.nyu.edu. Web site: http://www.med.nyu.edu/Sackler/.

Northwestern University, The Graduate School, Interdepartmental Biological Sciences Program (IBiS), Evanston, IL 60208. Offers biochemistry, molecular biology, and cell biology (PhD), including biochemistry, cell and molecular biology, molecular biophysics, structural biology; biotechnology (PhD); cell and molecular biology (PhD); developmental biology and genetics (PhD); hormone action and signal transduction (PhD); neuroscience (PhD); structural biology, biochemistry, and biophysics (PhD). Program participants include the Departments of Biochemistry, Molecular Biology, and Cell Biology; Chemistry; Neurobiology and Physiology; Chemical Engineering; Civil Engineering; and Evanston Hospital. *Degree requirements:* For doctorate, thesis/dissertation, qualifying exam. *Entrance requirements:* For doctorate, GRE General Test.

Additional exam requirements/recommendations for international students: Required—TOEFL (minimum score 600 paper-based). Electronic applications accepted. *Faculty research:* Developmental genetics, gene regulation, DNA-protein interactions, biological clocks, bioremediation.

Northwestern University, Northwestern University Feinberg School of Medicine and Interdepartmental Programs, Integrated Graduate Programs in the Life Sciences, Chicago, IL 60611. Offers cancer biology (PhD); cell biology (PhD); developmental biology (PhD); evolutionary biology (PhD); immunology and microbial pathogenesis (PhD); molecular biology and genetics (PhD); neurobiology (PhD); pharmacology and toxicology (PhD); structural biology and biochemistry (PhD). *Degree requirements:* For doctorate, comprehensive exam, thesis/dissertation, written and oral qualifying exams. *Entrance requirements:* For doctorate, GRE General Test. Additional exam requirements/recommendations for international students: Required—TOEFL (minimum score 600 paper-based; 250 computer-based). Electronic applications accepted.

Stanford University, School of Medicine, Graduate Programs in Medicine, Department of Structural Biology, Stanford, CA 94305-9991. Offers PhD. *Degree requirements:* For doctorate, thesis/dissertation. *Entrance requirements:* For doctorate, GRE General Test, GRE Subject Test. Additional exam requirements/recommendations for international students: Required—TOEFL. Electronic applications accepted. *Expenses: Tuition:* Full-time $40,050; part-time $890 per credit.

Stony Brook University, State University of New York, Graduate School, College of Arts and Sciences, Department of Biochemistry and Cell Biology, Program in Biochemistry and Structural Biology, Stony Brook, NY 11794. Offers PhD.

Syracuse University, College of Arts and Sciences, Program in Structural Biology, Biochemistry and Biophysics, Syracuse, NY 13244. Offers PhD. *Students:* 5 full-time (3 women); includes 1 minority (Black or African American, non-Hispanic/Latino), 2 international. Average age 30. 10 applicants, 10% accepted, 1 enrolled. In 2011, 1 degree awarded. *Degree requirements:* For doctorate, comprehensive exam, thesis/dissertation, exam. *Entrance requirements:* For doctorate, GRE General Test, GRE Subject Test. Additional exam requirements/recommendations for international students: Required—TOEFL (minimum score 100 iBT). *Application deadline:* For fall admission, 1/10 priority date for domestic students, 1/10 for international students. Application fee: $75. Electronic applications accepted. *Expenses: Tuition:* Part-time $1206 per credit. *Financial support:* Fellowships with full tuition reimbursements, research assistantships with full and partial tuition reimbursements, teaching assistantships with full and partial tuition reimbursements, and tuition waivers available. Financial award application deadline: 1/1; financial award applicants required to submit FAFSA. *Unit head:* Prof. Scott Pitnick, Director, 315-443-5128, Fax: 315-443-2012, E-mail: sspitnic@syr.edu. *Application contact:* Evelyn Lott, Information Contact, 315-443-9154, Fax: 315-443-2012, E-mail: ealott@syr.edu. Web site: http://sb3.syr.edu/.

Thomas Jefferson University, Jefferson College of Graduate Studies, PhD Program in Molecular Pharmacology and Structural Biology, Philadelphia, PA 19107. Offers PhD. *Faculty:* 39 full-time (8 women). *Students:* 18 full-time (9 women); includes 5 minority (all Asian, non-Hispanic/Latino), 5 international. 34 applicants, 18% accepted, 3 enrolled. In 2011, 1 doctorate awarded. *Degree requirements:* For doctorate, comprehensive exam, thesis/dissertation. *Entrance requirements:* For doctorate, GRE General Test, minimum GPA of 3.2. Additional exam requirements/recommendations for international students: Required—TOEFL (minimum score 250 computer-based; 100 iBT) or IELTS. *Application deadline:* For fall admission, 1/2 priority date for domestic students, 1/2 for international students. Applications are processed on a rolling basis. Application fee: $50. Electronic applications accepted. *Financial support:* In 2011–12, 18 students received support, including 18 fellowships with full tuition reimbursements available (averaging $54,758 per year); Federal Work-Study, institutionally sponsored loans, scholarships/grants, traineeships, and stipends also available. Support available to part-time students. Financial award application deadline: 5/1; financial award applicants required to submit FAFSA. *Faculty research:* Biochemistry and cell, molecular and structural biology of cell-surface and intracellular receptors; molecular modeling; signal transduction. *Total annual research expenditures:* $22.7 million. *Unit head:* Dr. Philip Wedegaertner, Program Director, 215-503-3137, Fax: 215-923-2117, E-mail: philip.wedegaertner@mail.tju.edu. *Application contact:* Marc E. Stearns, Director of Admissions, 215-503-0155, Fax: 215-503-9920, E-mail: jcgs-info@jefferson.edu. Web site: http://www.jefferson.edu/jcgs/phd/mpsb/.

Tulane University, School of Medicine and School of Liberal Arts, Graduate Programs in Biomedical Sciences, Department of Structural and Cellular Biology, New Orleans, LA 70118-5669. Offers MS, PhD, MD/PhD. MS and PhD offered through the Graduate School. *Degree requirements:* For master's, one foreign language, thesis; for doctorate, 2 foreign languages, thesis/dissertation. *Entrance requirements:* For master's, GRE General Test, minimum B average in undergraduate course work; for doctorate, GRE General Test. Additional exam requirements/recommendations for international students: Required—TOEFL. Electronic applications accepted. *Faculty research:* Reproductive endocrinology, visual neuroscience, neural response to altered hormones.

University at Albany, State University of New York, School of Public Health, Department of Biomedical Sciences, Program in Cell and Molecular Structure, Albany, NY 12222-0001. Offers MS, PhD. *Degree requirements:* For master's, thesis; for doctorate, thesis/dissertation. *Entrance requirements:* For master's and doctorate, GRE General Test, GRE Subject Test.

University at Buffalo, the State University of New York, Graduate School, School of Medicine and Biomedical Sciences, Graduate Programs in Medicine and Biomedical Sciences, Department of Structural Biology, Buffalo, NY 14260. Offers MS, PhD. *Faculty:* 6 part-time/adjunct (1 woman). *Students:* 9 full-time (1 woman); includes 1 minority (Hispanic/Latino). Average age 27. 2 applicants, 100% accepted. In 2011, 2 doctorates awarded. *Degree requirements:* For master's, comprehensive exam, thesis; for doctorate, comprehensive exam, thesis/dissertation. *Entrance requirements:* For master's, BS or BA in science, engineering, or math; for doctorate, GRE General Test, BS or BA in science, engineering, or math. Additional exam requirements/recommendations for international students: Required—TOEFL (minimum score 600 paper-based; 250 computer-based; 100 iBT). *Application deadline:* For fall admission, 2/1 priority date for domestic students, 2/1 for international students. Applications are processed on a rolling basis. Application fee: $50. Electronic applications accepted. *Financial support:* Federal Work-Study, scholarships/grants, traineeships, and unspecified assistantships available. Financial award application deadline: 2/1; financial award applicants required to submit FAFSA. *Faculty research:* Biomacromolecular structure and function at the level of three-dimensional atomic architecture. *Total annual research expenditures:* $3.5 million. *Unit head:* Dr. Robert H. Blessing, Interim Chair/Professor, 716-898-8613, Fax: 716-898-8660, E-mail: blessing@hwi.buffalo.edu.

University of California, San Diego, School of Medicine and Office of Graduate Studies, Molecular Pathology Program, La Jolla, CA 92093. Offers bioinformatics (PhD); cancer biology/oncology (PhD); cardiovascular sciences and disease (PhD); microbiology (PhD); molecular pathology (PhD); neurological disease (PhD); stem cell and developmental biology (PhD); structural biology/drug design (PhD). *Entrance requirements:* For doctorate, GRE General Test, GRE Subject Test. Additional exam requirements/recommendations for international students: Required—TOEFL. Electronic applications accepted.

University of Connecticut, Graduate School, College of Liberal Arts and Sciences, Department of Molecular and Cell Biology, Field of Biophysics and Structural Biology, Storrs, CT 06269. Offers MS, PhD. Terminal master's awarded for partial completion of doctoral program. *Degree requirements:* For master's, comprehensive exam; for doctorate, thesis/dissertation. *Entrance requirements:* For master's and doctorate, GRE General Test, GRE Subject Test. Additional exam requirements/recommendations for international students: Required—TOEFL (minimum score 550 paper-based; 213 computer-based). Electronic applications accepted.

The University of Manchester, Faculty of Life Sciences, Manchester, United Kingdom. Offers adaptive organismal biology (M Phil, PhD); animal biology (M Phil, PhD); biochemistry (M Phil, PhD); bioinformatics (M Phil, PhD); biomolecular sciences (M Phil, PhD); biotechnology (M Phil, PhD); cell biology (M Phil, PhD); cell matrix research (M Phil, PhD); channels and transporters (M Phil, PhD); developmental biology (M Phil, PhD); Egyptology (M Phil, PhD); environmental biology (M Phil, PhD); evolutionary biology (M Phil, PhD); gene expression (M Phil, PhD); genetics (M Phil, PhD); history of science, technology and medicine (M Phil, PhD); immunology (M Phil, PhD); integrative neurobiology and behavior (M Phil, PhD); membrane trafficking (M Phil, PhD); microbiology (M Phil, PhD); molecular and cellular neuroscience (M Phil, PhD); molecular biology (M Phil, PhD); molecular cancer studies (M Phil, PhD); neuroscience (M Phil, PhD); ophthalmology (M Phil, PhD); optometry (M Phil, PhD); organelle function (M Phil, PhD); pharmacology (M Phil, PhD); physiology (M Phil, PhD); plant sciences (M Phil, PhD); stem cell research (M Phil, PhD); structural biology (M Phil, PhD); systems neuroscience (M Phil, PhD); toxicology (M Phil, PhD).

University of Minnesota, Twin Cities Campus, Graduate School, College of Biological Sciences, Biochemistry, Molecular Biology and Biophysics Graduate Program, Minneapolis, MN 55455-0213. Offers PhD. *Degree requirements:* For doctorate, thesis/dissertation. *Entrance requirements:* For doctorate, GRE, 3 letters of recommendation, more than 1 semester of laboratory experience. Additional exam requirements/recommendations for international students: Required—TOEFL (minimum score 625 paper-based; 263 computer-based; 108 iBT with writing subsection 25 and reading subsection 25) or IELTS (minimum score 7). Electronic applications accepted. *Faculty research:* Microbial biochemistry, biotechnology, molecular biology, regulatory biochemistry, structural biology and biophysics, physical biochemistry, enzymology, physiological chemistry.

University of Pittsburgh, School of Medicine and Dietrich School of Arts and Sciences, Joint Pitt + CMU Molecular Biophysics and Structural Biology Graduate Program, Pittsburgh, PA 15260. Offers PhD. *Faculty:* 54 full-time (16 women). *Students:* 19 full-time (5 women); includes 3 minority (1 Asian, non-Hispanic/Latino; 1 Hispanic/Latino; 1 Native Hawaiian or other Pacific Islander, non-Hispanic/Latino), 6 international. Average age 26. 63 applicants, 10% accepted, 5 enrolled. In 2011, 3 doctorates awarded. *Degree requirements:* For doctorate, comprehensive exam, thesis/dissertation. *Entrance requirements:* For doctorate, GRE General Test. Additional exam requirements/recommendations for international students: Required—TOEFL (minimum score 600 paper-based; 250 computer-based; 100 iBT), IELTS (minimum score 7). *Application deadline:* For fall admission, 12/15 priority date for domestic students, 12/15 for international students. Application fee: $0. Electronic applications accepted. *Expenses:* Tuition, state resident: full-time $18,774; part-time $760 per credit. Tuition, nonresident: full-time $30,736; part-time $1258 per credit. *Required fees:* $740; $200 per term. Tuition and fees vary according to program. *Financial support:* In 2011–12, 5 fellowships with full tuition reimbursements (averaging $28,646 per year), 14 research assistantships with full tuition reimbursements (averaging $25,500 per year) were awarded; institutionally sponsored loans, scholarships/grants, traineeships, and unspecified assistantships also available. *Faculty research:* Structural biology, protein dynamics and folding, computational biophysics, molecular informatics, membrane biophysics and ion channels, x-ray crystallography cryaelectron microscopy. *Unit head:* Dr. Angela M. Gronenborn, Director, 412-648-8957, Fax: 412-648-1077, E-mail: mbsbinfo@medschool.pitt.edu. *Application contact:* Jennifer L. Walker, Program Coordinator, 412-648-8957, Fax: 412-648-1077, E-mail: mbsbinfo@medschool.pitt.edu. Web site: http://www.mbsb.pitt.edu.

University of Rochester, School of Medicine and Dentistry, Graduate Programs in Medicine and Dentistry, Department of Biochemistry and Biophysics, Programs in Biophysics, Rochester, NY 14627. Offers biophysics, structural and computational biology (PhD). Terminal master's awarded for partial completion of doctoral program. *Degree requirements:* For doctorate, thesis/dissertation, qualifying exam. *Entrance requirements:* For doctorate, GRE General Test. *Expenses: Tuition:* Full-time $41,040.

The University of Texas Health Science Center at San Antonio, Graduate School of Biomedical Sciences, Department of Cellular and Structural Biology, San Antonio, TX 78229-3900. Offers MS, PhD. *Degree requirements:* For master's, thesis; for doctorate, comprehensive exam, thesis/dissertation. *Entrance requirements:* For doctorate, GRE General Test, previous course work in biology, chemistry, physics, and calculus. Additional exam requirements/recommendations for international students: Required—TOEFL (minimum score 550 paper-based; 213 computer-based; 68 iBT). Electronic applications accepted. *Faculty research:* Human/molecular genetics, endocrinology and neurobiology, cell biology, stem cell biology, cancer biology, biology of aging.

The University of Texas Medical Branch, Graduate School of Biomedical Sciences, Program in Biochemistry and Molecular Biology, Galveston, TX 77555. Offers biochemistry (PhD); bioinformatics (PhD); biophysics (PhD); cell biology (PhD); computational biology (PhD); structural biology (PhD). *Degree requirements:* For doctorate, thesis/dissertation. *Entrance requirements:* Additional exam requirements/recommendations for international students: Required—TOEFL (minimum score 550 paper-based; 213 computer-based). Electronic applications accepted.

University of Washington, Graduate School, School of Medicine, Graduate Programs in Medicine, Department of Biological Structure, Seattle, WA 98195. Offers PhD. *Degree requirements:* For doctorate, thesis/dissertation. *Faculty research:* Cellular and developmental biology, experimental immunology and hematology, molecular structure and molecular biology, neurobiology, x-rays.

Weill Cornell Medical College, Weill Cornell Graduate School of Medical Sciences, Biochemistry, Cell and Molecular Biology Allied Program, New York, NY 10065. Offers MS, PhD. *Faculty:* 111 full-time (32 women). *Students:* 152 full-time (95 women); includes 19 minority (2 Black or African American, non-Hispanic/Latino; 5 Asian, non-Hispanic/Latino; 8 Hispanic/Latino; 4 Native Hawaiian or other Pacific Islander, non-Hispanic/Latino), 82 international. Average age 22. 374 applicants, 23% accepted, 30 enrolled. In 2011, 2 master's, 19 doctorates awarded. Terminal master's awarded for

partial completion of doctoral program. *Degree requirements:* For master's, comprehensive exam; for doctorate, thesis/dissertation, final exam. *Entrance requirements:* For doctorate, GRE General Test, background in genetics, molecular biology, chemistry, or biochemistry. Additional exam requirements/recommendations for international students: Required—TOEFL. *Application deadline:* For fall admission, 12/1 for domestic students. Application fee: $60. Electronic applications accepted. *Expenses: Tuition:* Full-time $46,001. *Financial support:* In 2011–12, 16 fellowships (averaging $22,600 per year) were awarded; scholarships/grants, health care benefits, and stipends (given to all students) also available. *Faculty research:* Molecular structure determination, protein structure, gene structure, stem cell biology, control of gene expression, DNA replication, chromosome maintenance, RNA biosynthesis. *Unit head:* Dr. Kirk Deitsch, Co-Director, 212-746-4976, Fax: 212-746-8906, E-mail: kwd2001@ med.cornell.edu. *Application contact:* Rosalia Mora, Program Coordinator, 212-746-6058, Fax: 212-746-8906, E-mail: rmora@med.cornell.edu. Web site: http:// weill.cornell.edu/gradschool/program/cell.html.

BAYLOR COLLEGE OF MEDICINE

Huffington Center on Aging
Program in Cell and Molecular Biology of Aging

Program of Study

The Program in Cell and Molecular Biology of Aging is a subspecialty of the Interdepartmental Program in Cell and Molecular Biology (CMB). The goal of this training program is to provide predoctoral and postdoctoral training in the field of aging at the molecular and cellular levels. A training grant award from the National Institute on Aging provides resources for trainees and program support. Participating faculty members hold appointments in several of the basic science departments, including the Departments of Molecular and Cellular Biology, Molecular and Human Genetics, Pathology, Cardiovascular Sciences, and Molecular Virology and in clinical departments, including Medicine. The faculty members are actively engaged in various aspects of modern cell and molecular biology research in aging, are well supported by federal grants, and are experienced in graduate education training in their respective departments.

The first year of the graduate program includes didactic courses, seminars, and laboratory rotations. During the second year, laboratory work commences, and qualifying examination requirements are fulfilled. The remainder of the graduate education program is oriented toward full-time laboratory work with participation in departmental and collegewide seminars and student-oriented functions. In addition, students attend the Biology of Aging seminar series and the Journal Club in Aging.

Students seeking a Ph.D. or M.D./Ph.D. degree may enter the program in their first year of graduate school through the Interdepartmental Program in Cell and Molecular Biology or in the second year of graduate school by matriculating in one of the graduate school departments in which aging training mentors hold a primary appointment.

Research Facilities

The program faculty members occupy extensive research space with state-of-the-art laboratory and routine equipment such as micro- and ultra-centrifuges, scintillation counters, spectrophotometers, epifluorescence and confocal imaging, and cell-culture facilities.

To maximize research efficiency, quality, and utilization of state-of-the-art instrumentation and technologies, the Office of the Vice President of Research at Baylor College of Medicine established Advanced Technology Core (ATC) facilities that have adopted and adhere to uniform policies for operation and governance. ATC labs are staffed by a scientific director and dedicated technical personnel who provide the highest quality laboratory work plus consultation on experimental design, data analysis, and training. ATC labs include those for genetically engineered mouse models, mouse and human embryonic stem cells, genomic and RNA profiling, pathway discovery, phenotyping and metabolism, integrated imaging, optical imaging and vital microscopy, genome-wide chemical and shRNA screening, monoclonal antibody/protein production, cytometry and cell sorting, mass-spectrometry proteomics, and population biosciences biorepository.

Financial Aid

Predoctoral students enrolled in the program receive initial annual stipends of $29,000. Baylor College of Medicine also maintains a financial aid office.

Cost of Study

A tuition scholarship covers the yearly tuition costs of $22,000, as well as the matriculation and learning resources center fees. Medical insurance coverage is also provided by the program.

Living and Housing Costs

There are many affordable homes, apartments, townhouses, and condominiums for lease or purchase near the Texas Medical Center (TMC). Many of these living options are close to a light rail system that provides access to the TMC and to the museum district and downtown Houston. On-campus parking garages are available for a fee—after hours and on weekends at reduced rates.

A limited number of on-campus apartments are available for single students to rent. There are two dormitories for unmarried women students. Apartments that are in the same price range are also available near the Texas Medical Center, which is located in a pleasant residential section of south-central Houston. Job opportunities for spouses are available at the many institutions of the Texas Medical Center.

Student Group

Approximately 582 students are enrolled in the Graduate School, the Medical School has more than 728 students, and there are more than 977 postdoctoral fellows in the College as a whole.

Location

The College, part of the world's largest medical center, is located in Houston, Texas. The greater Houston metropolitan area, with a population of more than 5.6 million, offers diverse urban amenities, including the symphony, ballet, live theater, year-round professional and college sports, parks and recreation centers, and many ethnic restaurants. There is very pleasant weather from fall through spring, and the temperature rarely drops below freezing in winter. Gulf Coast beaches are within an hour's drive.

The College

Baylor College of Medicine, the only private, nonsectarian, nonprofit medical school in the greater Southwest, is dedicated to excellence in graduate and medical education. Baylor is committed to major growth in the Graduate School. For 2012, *U.S. News & World Report* ranked BCM twenty-first overall among the nation's top medical schools for research. BCM also is listed seventeenth among all U.S. medical schools for National Institutes of Health funding and second in the nation in federal funding for research and development in the biological sciences at universities and colleges by the National Science Foundation. There is a high degree of interdisciplinary cooperation among the basic science and clinical departments within the College and with other institutions in the Texas Medical Center. A reciprocity agreement allows Baylor graduate students to take courses at Rice University, the University of Texas Health Science Center at Houston, and the University of Houston.

Applying

Applicants must have earned a baccalaureate degree and have a strong background in biology and biochemistry. Candidates for Graduate School admission must complete the free application form found online at http://www.bcm.edu/gradschool/index.cfm?PMID=2880. The application must contain current Graduate Record Examinations (GRE) scores, letters of recommendation, and official undergraduate transcripts. Applications receive three reviews, one by the Admissions Committee of the Graduate School, a second by the Cell and Molecular Biology Interdepartmental Program or other departmental program, and a third by faculty committee of the Aging Training Program. The Graduate School application deadline is January 1. The academic year begins July 31. Applicants are responsible for monitoring the progress of their applications. Admission policies at Baylor College of Medicine offer equal opportunity without regard to race, sex, age, religion, or handicap.

Correspondence and Information

Office of Admissions
Baylor College of Medicine
One Baylor Plaza, N104
Houston, Texas 77030
Phone: 713-798-4842
E-mail: admissions@bcm.edu

For program information, prospective students should contact:

Lawrence A. Donehower Ph.D.
Director, Aging Training Program
Huffington Center on Aging
Baylor College of Medicine
One Baylor Plaza, BCMD-819DB
Houston, Texas 77030
United States
Phone: 713-798-13594
E-mail: larryd@bcm.edu
Web site: http://www.bcm.edu/hcoa/

THE FACULTY AND THEIR RESEARCH

Adam Antebi, Ph.D., Associate Professor, Huffington Center on Aging, and Molecular and Cellular Biology. The Antebi laboratory uses the small roundworm, *Caenorhabditis elegans* to dissect evolutionarily conserved pathways that regulate developmental timing, life stages, and longevity. These studies have led them to the discovery that nuclear hormone receptors play an important role in these processes. A novel 3-hydroxysteroid dehydrogenase that regulates reproductive development and

longevity. *PloS Biology* 10:e1001305, 2012. Nuclear hormone receptor regulation of microRNAs controls developmental progression. *Science* 324:95–98, 2009. DRE-1, an evolutionarily conserved F-box protein that regulates *C. elegans* developmental age. *Dev. Cell* 12:443–455, 2007. A bile acid-like steroid modulates *C. elegans* life span through nuclear receptor signaling. *Proc. Natl. Acad. Sci. USA* 104:5014–9, 2007. Identification of hormonal ligands for DAF-12 that govern dauer formation and reproduction in *C. elegans*. *Cell* 124:1209–23, 2006.

Gretchen J. Darlington, Ph.D., Professor, Huffington Center on Aging, Pathology and Immunology, Molecular and Human Genetics, and Molecular and Cell Biology. The Darlington laboratory studies the molecular mechanisms of aging employing normal and long-lived mouse models. Dnmt3a is essential for hematopoietic stem cell differentiation. *Nat. Genet.* 44(1):23–31, 2011. Elevated interferon gamma signaling contributes to impaired regeneration in the aged liver. *J. Gerontol. Biol. Med. Sci.* 66(9):944–56, 2011. CD24-positive cells from normal adult mouse liver are hepatocyte progenitor cells. *Stem Cell. Dev.* 20(12):2177–88, 2011. Lymphoid neogenesis and immune infiltration in aged liver. *Hepatology* 47(5):1680–90, 2008. Transcriptional profiling of bipotential embryonic liver cells to identify liver progenitor cell surface markers. *Stem Cell* 25(10):2476–87, 2007.

Lawrence A. Donehower, Ph.D., Professor of Molecular Virology and Microbiology, Molecular and Cellular Biology, and Pediatrics. Functions of the tumor suppressor p53 and the cancer/aging interface. Timed somatic deletion of p53 in mice reveals age-associated differences in tumor progression. *PLoS One* 4:e6654, 2009. Altered senescence, apoptosis, and DNA damage response in a mutant p53 model of accelerated aging. *Mechanisms of Ageing and Development* 130:262–71, 2009. Altered mammary gland development in the p53+/m mouse, a model of accelerated aging. *Dev. Biol.* 313:130–41, 2008. p53: Guardian AND suppressor of longevity? *Exp. Gerontol.* 40:7–9, 2005. p53 mutant mice that display early aging-associated phenotypes. *Nature* 415:45–53, 2002.

N. Tony Eissa, M.D., Nancy Chang, Ph.D. Chair for the Biology of Inflammation Center. Professor of Medicine, Molecular and Cell Biology, Pathology and Immunology, and Molecular Physiology and Biophysics. Dr. Eissa is interested in the role of autophagy in immunity and inflammation in general and in lung diseases in particular. The Eissa lab is also interested in the inflammatory responses to misfolded proteins. The effect of aging on these pathways is being studied. Transient aggregation of ubiquitinated proteins is a cytosolic unfolded protein response to inflammation and ER stress. *J. Biol. Chem.* 2012. doi:10.1074/jbc.M112.35093. Regulation of NF-{kappa}B activity and inducible nitric oxide synthase by regulatory particle non-ATPase subunit 13 (Rpn13). *Proc. Natl. Acad. Sci. USA* 107:13854–9, 2010. Autophagy enhances the efficacy of BCG vaccine by increasing peptide presentation in mouse dendritic cells. *Nat. Med.* 15:267–76, 2009. The physiologic aggresome mediates cellular inactivation of iNOS. *Proc. Nat. Acad. Sci. USA* 106:1211–15, 2009. Toll-like receptor 4 is a sensor for autophagy associated with innate immunity. *Immunity* 27:135–44, 2007.

Jose M. Garcia, M.D., Ph.D., Assistant Professor of Medicine, Molecular and Cellular Biology, and the Huffington Center on Aging; staff endocrinologist, Michael E. DeBakey VA Medical Center. Dr. Garcia's current research focuses on the role of ghrelin and other anabolic pathways in different wasting conditions. The Garcia lab is currently involved in several human trials using different anabolic therapies for the treatment of wasting as well as in the development of different animal models to unravel the physiology of wasting and the mechanisms of action of different potential therapies. Low testosterone levels and increased inflammatory markers in patients with cancer and relationship with cachexia. *J. Clin. Endocrinol. Metab.* 97(5):E700–9, 2012. Pharmacodynamic hormonal effects, a novel oral ghrelin mimetic and growth hormone secretagogue in healthy volunteers. *Growth Hormone & IGF Research* 19(3):267–73, 2009. Ghrelin prevents cisplatin-induced mechanical hyperalgesia and cachexia. *Endocrinology* 149:455–60, 2008. Effect on body weight and safety of RC-1291, a novel, orally available ghrelin mimetic and growth hormone secretagogue: Results of a phase I, randomized, placebo-controlled, multiple-dose study in healthy volunteers. *Oncologist* 12:594–600, 2007. Hypogonadism in male patients with cancer. *Cancer* 106:2583–91, 2006.

Margaret A. Goodell, Ph.D., Professor of Pediatrics and Molecular and Human Genetics–Stem Cells and Regenerative Medicine Center. Dr. Goodell's laboratory focuses on hematopoietic stem cells, basic biology, aging, and gene therapy. Rantes/Ccl5 influences hematopoietic stem cell subtypes and causes myeloid skewing. *Blood* 119:2500–9, 2012. Dnmt3a is essential for hematopoietic stem cell differentiation. *Nat. Genet.* 44:23–31, 2011. The p47 GTPase Irg47 links host defense and hematopoietic stem cell proliferation. *Cell Stem Cell* 2(1):83–9, 2008. Aging hematopoietic stem cells decline in function and exhibit epigenetic dysregulation. *PLoS Biology* 5:e201, 2007. Hematopoietic fingerprints: An expression database of stem cells and their progeny. *Cell Stem Cell* 1:578–91, 2007.

Michael Ittmann, M.D., Ph.D., William D. Tigertt Professor of Pathology and Immunology. Dr. Ittman is interested in cellular senescence in the pathogenesis of prostate cancer and benign prostatic hyperplasia. Interleukin-8 expression is increased in senescent prostatic epithelial cells and promotes the development of benign prostatic hyperplasia. *Prostate* 60:153–9, 2004. Cellular senescence in the pathogenesis of benign prostatic hyperplasia. *Prostate* 55:30–8, 2003. IL-8 is a paracrine inducer of FGF2, a stromal and epithelial growth factor in benign prostatic hyperplasia. *Am. J. Pathol.* 159:139–47, 2001. IL-1a is a paracrine inducer of FGF-7, a key epithelial growth factor in benign prostatic hyperplasia. *Am. J. Pathol.* 157:249–55, 2000.

Joanna Jankowsky, Ph.D., Assistant Professor of Neuroscience, Neurology, and Neurosurgery. Dr. Jankowsky's interest is Alzheimer's disease: using transgenic mouse models to study basic pathogenesis and potential therapeutics. Combination therapy to improve amyloid clearance. *J. Neurosci.* 31:4124–36, 2011. Changes in brain volume begin prior to overt pathology in APP trangsenic mice. *NeuroImage* 50:416–27, 2009. Impaired survival of adultborn hippocampal neurons in amyloid-bearing APP/PS1 transgenic mice. *J. Neurosci.* 27:6771–80, 2007. Controllable APP transgenic mice suggest Ab suppression slows subsequent amyloid formation but does not remove pre-existing deposits. *PLoS Medicine* 2:e355, 2005. Environmental enrichment attenuates cognitive decline—but worsens pathology—in a mouse model of Alzheimer's disease. *J. Neurosci.* 25:5217–24, 2005.

Yi Li, Ph.D., Associate Professor of Breast Center and Department of Molecular and Cell Biology. The Li lab studies breast cancer initiation and prevention using mouse models and human tissues. In particular, the lab investigates the molecular and cellular mechanism by which breast cancer risk is increased in women who have had a pregnancy at an older age. Evidence that an early pregnancy causes a persistent decrease in the number of functional mammary epithelial stem cells—implications for pregnancy-induced protection against breast cancer. *Stem Cell.* 26:3205–9, 2008. Defining the ATM-mediated barrier to tumorigenesis in somatic mammary cells following ErbB2 activation. *Proc. Nat. Acad. Sci. USA* 107:3728–33, 2010. Genetic manipulation of individual somatic mammary cells in vivo reveals a master role of STAT5a in inducing alveolar fate commitment and lactogenesis even in the absence of ovarian hormones. *Dev. Biol.* 345:196–203, 2010. Keratin 6a marks mammary bipotential progenitor cells that can give rise to a unique tumor model resembling human normal-like breast cancer. *Oncogene* 30:4399–409, 2011. ID4 regulates mammary gland development by suppressing p38MAPK activity. *Development* 138:5247–56, 2011.

Robia G. Pautler, Ph.D., Associate Professor of Molecular Physiology and Biophysics, Neuroscience, Radiology, TBMM Graduate Program, and Huffington Center on Aging. Dr. Pautler develops and applies methodologies that permit high-resolution images of the structure and function of the brain in intact, living animals. Her current research efforts build upon the new technique that she helped develop known as manganese-enhanced MRI (MEMRI) neuronal tract tracing to assess and define the mechanisms of in vivo axonal transport deficits in mouse models of Alzheimer's disease. Additionally, Dr. Pautler is interested in using nanotechnology to monitor and also treat neurodegenerative diseases. Manganese-enhanced MRI (MEMRI): Neurophysiological Applications. *Neuroscience*, in press, 2012. R-flurbiprofen differentially rescues axonal transport deficits in mouse models of Alzheimer's disease. *Magn. Reson. Med.*, in press. Overexpression of SOD-2 rescues axonal transport deficits in the central nervous system in diabetic mice. *PLoS One* 5(10):e13463, 2010. Overexpression of SOD-2 improves axonal transport rates and cerebral blood flow in the Tg2576 Mouse model of Alzheimer's disease. *PlosOne* 5(5):e10561, 2010. In vivo neuronal tract tracing using manganese-enhanced magnetic resonance imaging. *Magn. Reson. Med.* 40:740–8. 1998.

Fred A. Pereira, Ph.D., Associate Professor, Huffington Center on Aging, Molecular and Cellular Biology, and Otolaryngology–Head and Neck Surgery. Signaling pathways in auditory development, aging and cancer. COUP-TFI controls Notch regulation of hair cell and support cell differentiation. *Development* 133:3683–93, 2006. Tuning of the outer hair cell motor by membrane cholesterol. *J. Biol. Chem.* 282(50):36659–70, 2007. Glycosylation regulates prestin cellular activity. *JARO: Journal of the Association for Research in Otolaryngology* 11(1):39–51, 2009. Genome-wide analysis of binding sites and direct target genes of the orphan nuclear receptor NR2F1/COUP-TFI. *PLoS ONE* 5(1):e8910, 2010. Head bobber: An insertional mutation on chromosome 7 causes inner ear patterning defects, hyperactive circling, and deafness. *JARO: Journal of the Association for Research in Otolaryngology* March 2:1–15, 2012.

Ergun Sahin, M.D., Ph.D., Assistant Professor, Huffington Center on Aging and Molecular Physiology and Biophysics. Dr. Sahin's laboratory is interested in understanding the mechanisms of telomere driven aging and cancer using sophisticated mouse models and in vitro based approaches. Specifically, the Sahin lab is studying how telomeres and telomerase regulate metabolic and mitochondrial pathways during ageing and cancer formation. Antitelomerase therapy provokes ALT and mitochondrial adaptive mechanisms in cancer. *Cell* 148(4):651–63, 2012. Telomere dysfunction induces metabolic and mitochondrial compromise. *Nature* 470(7334):359–65, 2011. Linking functional decline of telomeres, mitochondria and stem cells during ageing. *Nature* 464(7288):520–8, 2010.

Richard N. Sifers, Ph.D., Professor and Assistant Dean of Pathology and Immunology, Molecular and Cellular Biology, and Molecular Physiology and Biophysics. Centers: Huffington on Aging, Human Genome Sequencing Center, Dan L. Duncan Cancer Center, and Digestive Disease Center. Dr. Sifers is interested in the areas of intracellular protein trafficking, protein folding and quality control, glycobiology, and cellular proteostasis. The Sifers lab is particularly interested in understanding how these interconnected networks participate as modifiers of age-related diseases. The mammalian UPR boosts glycoprotein ERAD by suppressing the proteolytic down-regulation of ER mannosidase I. *J. Cell Sci.* 122(7):976–84, 2009. Single nucleotide polymorphism—mediated translational suppression of endoplasmic reticulum mannosidase I modifies the onset of end-stage liver disease in alpha1-antitrypsin deficiency. *Hepatology* 50(1):275–81, 2009. Golgi localization of ERManI defines spatial separation of the mammalian glycoprotein quality control system. *Mol. Biol. Cell* 22(16):2810–22, 2009. Beta-N-acetylglucosamine (O-GlcNAc) is a novel regulator of mitosis-specific phophorylations on histone H3. *J. Biol. Chem.* 287:12195–203, 2009. Human endoplasmic reticulum mannosidase I is subject to regulated proteolysis. *J. Biol. Chem.* 282:4841–9, 2007.

George E. Taffet, M.D., Associate Professor and Chief of Medicine, Geriatrics, and Cardiovascular Sciences. Physiology and biochemistry of aging cardiovascular system. Cardiac function in young and old *Little* mice. *J. Gerontol. Biol. Med. Sci.* 62(12):1319–25, 2007. Noninvasive ultrasonic measurement of arterial wall motion in mice. *Am. J. Physiol. Heart Circ. Physiol.* 287:H1426–32, 2004. The age-associated alterations in late diastolic function in mice are improved by caloric restriction. *J. Gerontol. Biol. Sci. Med. Sci.* 52(6):B285–90, 1997. Noninvasive indexes of cardiac systolic and diastolic function in hyperthyroid and senescent mouse. *Am. J. Physiol.* 270:H2204–9, 1996. CaATPase content is lower in cardiac sarcoplasmic reticulum isolated from old rats. *Am. J. Physiol.* 264:H1609–14, 1993.

Nikolai Timchenko, Ph.D., Professor, Huffington Center on Aging, Pathology and Immunology, and Molecular and Cellular Biology. The Timchenko laboratory investigates molecular mechanisms of liver cancer and mechanisms by which aging reduces liver functions. Dr. Timchenko has found that aging causes alterations in epigenetic control of gene expression leading to a global change of signaling pathways. These alterations result in development of liver cancer and hepatic steatosis and in impaired liver regeneration. The reduction of SIRT1 in livers of old mice leads to impaired body homeostasis and to inhibition of liver proliferation. *Hepatology* 54:898–998, 2011. Epigenetic changes play critical role in age-associated dysfunction of the liver. *Aging Cell* 9:895–910, 2010. Elimination of C/EBPa through the ubiquitin-proteasome system promotes the development of liver cancer in mice *J. Clin. Investig.* 120:2549–62, 2010. Liver tumors escape negative control of proliferation via PI3K/Akt-mediated block of C/EBPa growth inhibitory activity. *Genes & Development* 18:912–25, 2004. Aging reduces proliferative capacities of liver by switching pathways of C/EBPa growth arrest. *Cell* 113:495–506, 2003.

Qiang Tong, Ph.D., Associate Professor, Children's Nutrition Research Center. Dr. Tong's lab studies the molecular mechanism of caloric restriction, which extends life span and decreases the onset of obesity, diabetes, cancer, and neurodegenerative and cardiovascular diseases. The Tong lab is investigating how sirtuin genes, which might mediate the action of caloric restriction, regulate cellular function and metabolism. Another research direction of his lab is to study how mature adipocytes are derived from multi-potent precursor cells and how adipose tissue in obese individuals influences whole body metabolism, leading to insulin resistance and type-2 diabetes. Adipocyte expression of PU.1 transcription factor causes insulin resistance through up-regulation of inflammatory cytokine gene expression and ROS production. *Am. J. Physiol. Endocrinol. Metabol.*, in press. SIRT2 deacetylates FOXO3a in response to oxidative stress and caloric restriction. *Aging Cell* 6:505–14, 2007, 2009. SIRT2 suppresses adipocyte differentiation by deacetylating FOXO1 and enhancing FOXO1's repressive interaction with PPAR . *Mol. Biol. Cell* 20:801–8, 2008. Deacetylation of FOXO3 by SIRT1 or SIRT2 leads to Skp2-mediated FOXO3 ubiquitination and degradation. *Oncogene* 31:1546–57, 2008. SIRT3, a mitochondrial sirtuin deacetylase, regulates mitochondrial function and thermogenesis in brown adipocytes. *J. Biol. Chem.* 280(14):13560–7, 2005.

Meng Wang, Ph.D., Assistant Professor, Huffington Center on Aging, Molecular and Human Genetics, and Molecular and Cellular Biology. Dr. Wang's laboratory is interested in understanding the molecular genetics of aging and age-associated degenerative changes, with focus on lipid metabolism, germline stem cell homeostasis and neuroendocrine regulation. These multidisciplinary researches utilize lipidomics, metabolomics, proteomics and label-free chemical imaging techniques together with powerful *C. elegans* and *drosophila* genetic approaches. JNK extends life span and limits growth by antagonizing cellular and organism-wide responses to insulin signaling. *Cell* 121(1):115–28, 2005. Fat metabolism links germline stem cells and longevity in *C. elegans*. *Science* 322(5903):957–60, 2008. RNAi screening for fat regulatory genes with SRS microscopy. *Nature Methods* 8(2):135–8, 2011. Label-free imaging of lipid dynamics using coherent anti-Stokes Raman scattering (CARS) and stimulated Raman scattering (SRS) microscopy. *Curr. Opin. Genet. Dev.* 21(5):585–90, 2011.

Hui Zheng, Ph.D., Director of the Huffington Center on Aging and Professor of Molecular and Human Genetics, Molecular and Cellular Biology, and Neuroscience. Dr. Zheng's laboratory is interested in understanding the physiological functions of the amyloid precursor protein and presenilins, elucidating their pathogenic mechanisms in Alzheimer's disease, and identifying novel pathways for therapeutic intervention using mouse models and with a combination of molecular, cellular, electrophysiological, and behavioral approaches. Amyloid precursor protein revisited: Neuronal-specific expression and the highly stable nature of soluble derivatives. *J. Biol. Chem.* 287(4):2437–45, 2012. Convergence of presenilin- and tau-mediated pathways on axonal trafficking and neuronal function. *J. Neurosci.* 30(40):13409–18, 2010. Soluble amyloid precursor protein (APP) regulates transthyretin and Klotho gene expression without rescuing the essential function of APP. *Proc. Natl. Acad. Sci. USA* 107(40):17362–7, 2010. Presynaptic and postsynaptic interaction of the amyloid precursor protein promotes peripheral and central synaptogenesis. *J. Neurosci.* 29(35):10788–801, 2009. Amyloid precursor protein regulates Cav1.2 L-type calcium channel levels and function to influence GABAergic short-term plasticity. *J. Neurosci.* 29(50):15660–8, 2009.

GERSTNER SLOAN-KETTERING GRADUATE SCHOOL OF BIOMEDICAL SCIENCES

Ph.D. in Cancer Biology Program

Gerstner Sloan-Kettering
Graduate School of Biomedical Sciences

Program of Study

The Louis V. Gerstner, Jr. Graduate School of Biomedical Sciences, Memorial Sloan-Kettering Cancer Center offers a doctoral program that trains laboratory scientists to work in research areas directly applicable to human disease and in particular, cancer.

Much of the recent explosion in new knowledge about normal biological functions and disease is rooted in laboratory discoveries. The unique curriculum integrates Memorial Sloan-Kettering's basic science and clinical arms to maximize the potential of future basic scientists to improve human health.

During the first year, students complete a thirty-two-week core course (sixteen weeks per semester) that introduces recent findings in relevant topics through didactic lecture and discussion of research papers. Students will also complete three 5-week laboratory rotations, with each one culminating in an oral presentation of their findings; three visits with clinicians; course work in logic and critical analysis; and two semesters of the President's Research Seminar Series Journal Club, which introduces students to the published works of world-renowned speakers.

After completing the didactic portion of their education in the first year, students focus full time on thesis research at the beginning of the second year. Students are expected to present a written and oral thesis proposal by March 31 of the second year. Continuing throughout their graduate careers, students take part in the Current Topics Journal Club, along with the Graduate Student Seminar, in which students present their own research.

Students also have the opportunity to select a clinical mentor who directs the student in participating in hospital-based academic activities such as grand rounds and conferences with pathology and disease management teams.

Research Facilities

Memorial Sloan-Kettering's research space totals approximately 575,000 square feet, with many cutting-edge laboratories and facilities housed within the Rockefeller Research Laboratories building and the Zuckerman Research Center, a building with open, spacious floors designed to encourage collaboration.

There are dozens of research core facilities—ranging from bioinformatics to high-throughput drug screening and x-ray crystallography—that serve both basic and clinical research needs, offering state-of-the-art instruments and technical staff support to graduate students as they train and conduct research projects. Core facilities are staffed by research experts in the technologies offered, and training is available in select cores.

The Memorial Sloan-Kettering Cancer Center library subscribes to a full range of science, medical, and healthcare resources. Students have access to more than 2,800 journals, with the majority of these titles available electronically. The library's Web site provides access to an extensive collection of resources, including an online catalog, databases, electronic books, and electronic journals.

Financial Aid

All matriculated students receive a fellowship package that includes an annual stipend ($34,000 for 2012–13); a first-year allowance to be used for books, journals, and other school expenses; a scholarship that covers the full cost of tuition and fees; comprehensive medical and dental insurance; a laptop computer; relocation costs (up to $500); and membership in the New York Academy of Sciences.

Students may also apply for independent funding from agencies such as the National Institutes of Health and the National Science Foundation. Recipients of one of these fellowships receive an additional award of $5000 from the school; this is in addition to any supplement necessary to bring the stipend to the common level. Travel awards are given to students who present a poster or a short talk at a scientific meeting.

Cost of Study

All tuition expenses are covered by a full fellowship, which is awarded to all students who matriculate in the school. Students are also provided with health insurance at no cost to them. Additional details are available in the Financial Aid section above.

Living and Housing Costs

Affordable housing in proximity to the research buildings is provided to all students by Memorial Sloan-Kettering. Housing units are located in safe, family-oriented neighborhoods on or near Manhattan's Upper East Side. Students who have spouses or significant others can apply for family units. There is a wide range of costs, which vary depending on the size of the housing unit. The housing contract runs for the student's duration of study and is automatically renewed each year.

Student Group

There are 60 full-time students (35 women, 25 men), with 16 percent minority and 25 percent international. The graduate students enrolled at Gerstner Sloan-Kettering are drawn from a pool of applicants who comprise a variety of backgrounds and nationalities. Applicants are expected to hold an undergraduate degree from an accredited institution and have significant basic science research experience. College-level coursework in the following areas is required: biology, chemistry, physics, organic chemistry, mathematics, and biochemistry.

Student Outcomes

Graduates of the program are expected to enter into careers as researchers, scientists, and educators in excellent laboratories, hospitals, medical schools, and research institutions throughout the country and around the world.

Gerstner Sloan-Kettering Graduate School of Biomedical Sciences

Location

The campus is located on Manhattan's Upper East Side, home to some of New York City's best shopping and dining. Several world-famous museums are within walking distance, and Central Park is a few blocks away. New York also offers theater, live music, outdoor recreation, and cultural attractions such as the Metropolitan Museum of Art, all accessible by public transportation.

The Graduate School

The Louis V. Gerstner, Jr. Graduate School of Biomedical Sciences, Memorial Sloan-Kettering Cancer Center, offers the next generation of basic scientists an intensive Ph.D. program to study the biological sciences through the lens of cancer—while giving students the tools they need to put them in the vanguard of research that can be applied in any area of human disease. Students are part of a community of outstanding scientists who have extensive experience in postgraduate education and maintain a strong commitment to training and mentoring the next generation of leaders in biomedical research.

Applying

Prospective students must complete and submit the online application form and submit the following: official transcripts from all colleges previously attended, three letters of recommendation from advisers and/or research mentors, and official GRE scores. An in-person interview is requested from those applicants being seriously considered for admission, but the requirement may be waived if geographical constraints are overwhelming and may be substituted with video interviews. The deadline to apply is December 1, and interviews take place the following January.

Correspondence and Information

Gerstner Sloan-Kettering Graduate School of Biomedical Sciences
1275 York Avenue, Box 441
New York, New York 10065
Phone: 646-888-6639
Fax: 646-422-2351
E-mail: gradstudies@sloankettering.edu
Web site: http://www.sloankettering.edu

THE FACULTY AND THEIR RESEARCH

Information regarding the faculty members is available online at: http://www.sloankettering.edu/research/faculty.

UNIFORMED SERVICES UNIVERSITY OF THE HEALTH SCIENCES

F. Edward Hébert School of Medicine
Graduate Program in Molecular and Cell Biology

Program of Study

The program of study is designed for full-time students who wish to obtain a Ph.D. degree in the area of molecular and cell biology. This interdepartmental graduate program, which includes faculty members from both basic and clinical departments, offers research expertise in a wide range of areas, including bacteriology, immunology, genetics, biochemistry, regulation of gene expression, and cancer biology. The program includes core courses in molecular and cell biology that provide necessary knowledge for modern biomedical research, as well as advanced electives in areas of faculty expertise. The first-year curriculum includes courses in biochemistry, cell biology, experimental methodology, genetics, and immunology. During the first summer, students participate in laboratory rotations in two laboratories of their choice, leading to the choice of a mentor for their doctoral research. The second-year curriculum offers advanced elective courses in a variety of disciplines, including biochemistry, cell biology, immunology, molecular endocrinology, and virology, and marks the transition from classwork to original laboratory research. Throughout their graduate experience, students participate in journal clubs designed to foster interaction across disciplines and to develop the critical skills needed for data presentation and analysis. A year-round seminar series brings renowned scientists to the Uniformed Services University of the Health Sciences (USUHS) to share their results and to meet with students and faculty members. Students may also take advantage of seminars hosted by other programs and departments as well as those presented at the National Institutes of Health. Completion of the research project and preparation and successful defense of a written dissertation leads to the degree of Doctor of Philosophy.

Research Facilities

The University possesses outstanding facilities for research in molecular and cell biology. Well-equipped laboratories and extramurally funded faculty members provide an outstanding environment in which to pursue state-of-the-art research. Shared equipment in a modern biomedical instrumentation core facility includes oligonucleotide and peptide synthesizers and sequencers; a variety of imaging equipment, including laser confocal and electron microscopes; fluorescent-activated cell sorters; and an ACAS workstation. A recently added proteomics facility contains both MADLI-TOF and ESI tandem mass spectrometers. All offices, laboratories, and the Learning Resource Center are equipped with high-speed Internet connectivity and have access to an extensive online journal collection.

Financial Aid

Stipends are available for civilian applicants. Awards of stipends are competitive and may be renewed. For the 2012–13 academic year, stipends for entering students begin at $27,000. Outstanding students may be nominated for the Dean's Special Fellowship, which supports a stipend of $32,000.

Cost of Study

Graduate students are not required to pay tuition. Civilian graduate students do not incur any obligation to the United States government for service after completion of their graduate training programs. Active-duty military personnel incur an obligation for additional military service by Department of Defense regulations that govern sponsored graduate education. Students are required to maintain health insurance.

Living and Housing Costs

The University does not have housing for graduate students. However, there is an abundant supply of rental housing in the area. Living costs in the greater Washington, D.C., area are comparable to those of other East Coast metropolitan areas.

Student Group

The first graduate students in the interdisciplinary Graduate Program in Molecular and Cell Biology at USUHS were admitted in 1995. Over the last decade, the Graduate Program in Molecular and Cell Biology has grown significantly; 23 students are currently enrolled. Twenty-five Ph.D. degrees in molecular and cell biology have been awarded over the past nine years.

Location

Metropolitan Washington has a population of about 2.7 million residents in the District of Columbia and the surrounding areas of Maryland and Virginia. The region is a center of education and research and is home to five major universities, four medical schools, the National Library of Medicine and the National Institutes of Health (next to the USUHS campus), Walter Reed National Military Medical Center, the Armed Forces Institute of Pathology, the Library of Congress, the Smithsonian Institution, the National Bureau of Standards, and many other private and government research centers. Many cultural advantages of the area include the theater, a major symphony orchestra, major-league sports, and world-famous museums. The Metro subway system has a station near campus and provides a convenient connection from the University to the museums and cultural attractions of downtown Washington. For outdoor activities, the Blue Ridge Mountains, the Chesapeake Bay, and the Atlantic coast beaches are all within a few hours' drive.

The University

USUHS is located just outside Washington, D.C., in Bethesda, Maryland. The campus is situated on an attractive, wooded site at the Walter Reed National Military Medical Center and is close to several major federal health research facilities. Through various affiliation agreements, these institutes provide additional resources to enhance the educational experience of graduate students at USUHS.

Applying

Both civilians and military personnel are eligible to apply for graduate study at USUHS. Before matriculation, each applicant must complete a baccalaureate degree that includes college-level courses in biology, inorganic chemistry, mathematics, organic chemistry, and physics. Advanced courses in biology, chemistry, or related fields, such as biochemistry, cell biology, genetics, immunology, microbiology, molecular biology, and physical chemistry, are desirable but not essential. Each applicant must submit a USUHS graduate training application form, complete academic transcripts of postsecondary education, GRE scores (in addition to the aptitude sections, one advanced examination is recommended), three letters of recommendation from individuals familiar with the academic achievements or research experience of the applicant, and a personal statement expressing the applicant's career objectives. Active-duty military personnel must obtain the approval and sponsorship of their parent military department in addition to acceptance from USUHS. USUHS subscribes fully to the policy of equal educational opportunity and selects students on a competitive basis without regard to race, sex, creed, or national origin. Application forms may be obtained from the Web site at http://www.usuhs.mil/mcb/gradapp.html#applynow. Completed applications must be received before January 1 for matriculation in August.

Correspondence and Information

Associate Dean for Graduate Education
Uniformed Services University of the Health Sciences
4301 Jones Bridge Road
Bethesda, Maryland 20814
United States
Phone: 301-295-3913
800-772-1747 (toll-free)
Web site: http://www.usuhs.mil/graded/

For an application and information about the molecular and cell biology program:

Dr. Mary Lou Cutler, Director
Graduate Program in Molecular and Cell Biology
Uniformed Services University of the Health Sciences
4301 Jones Bridge Road
Bethesda, Maryland 20814
United States
Phone: 301-295-3642
Fax: 301-295-1996
E-mail: netina.finley@usuhs.edu
Web site: http://www.usuhs.mil/mcb/

Uniformed Services University of the Health Sciences

THE FACULTY AND THEIR RESEARCH

Regina C. Armstrong, Professor; Ph.D., North Carolina at Chapel Hill, 1987. Cellular and molecular mechanisms of neural stem/progenitor cell development and regeneration in demyelinating diseases and brain injury models.

Roopa Biswas, Adjunct Assistant Professor, PhD. Ohio State, 1997. Mechanisms of regulation of inflammation; http://www.usuhs.mil/gsn/abdellah/faculty.html.

Jorge Blanco, Adjunct Assistant Professor; Ph.D., Buenos Aires, 1991. Molecular mechanisms of pathogenesis of respiratory viruses. *J. Infect. Dis.* 185(12):1780–5, 2002.

Christopher C. Broder, Professor and Director; Ph.D., Florida, 1989. Virus-host cell interactions; vaccines and therapeutics; HIV, Hendra and Nipah viruses, Australian bat lyssavirus.

Teodor Brumeanu, Professor; M.D., Carol Davila (Romania), 1978. Medicine.

Rolf Bünger, Professor; M.D./Ph.D., Munich, 1979. Cellular, molecular, and metabolic mechanisms of heart and brain circulation and resuscitation at various levels of organization: intact animal/isolated perfused organs/subcellular compartments of cytosol and mitochondria. *NMR Biomed.*, doi: 10.1002/nbm.1717; *Exp. Biol. Med. 234(12):1395–416, 2009; in Recent Research Developments in Physiology, Vol. 4, ed. S. G. Pandalai, 2006;Exerc. Sport Sci. Rev.* 32(4):174–9, 2004.

Rachel Cox, Assistant Professor, Ph.D., North Carolina at Chapel Hill, 1998. Mitochondrial dynamics and inheritance during development. *Disease Models & Mechanisms* 2(9/10):490–9, 2009.

Mary Lou Cutler, Professor and Director; Ph.D., Hahnemann, 1980. Role of molecules that suppress transformation by the Ras oncogene; Ras signal transduction and human carcinogenesis. *Eur. J. Cell Biol.* 87:721–34, 2008; *J. Cell. Physiol.* 214:38–46, 2007; *BMC Cell Biol.* 7:34, 2006; *Exp. Cell Res.* 306:168–79, 2005.

Clifton Dalgard, Assistant Professor; Ph.D., Uniformed Services University of the Health Sciences, 2005. Molecular mechanisms of damage-associated inflammation.

Michael Daly, Professor; Ph.D., London, 1988. Pathology.

Thomas N. Darling, Professor; M.D./Ph.D., Duke, 1990. *Ann. Intern. Med.* 154(12):806–13, 2011; *Nat. Commun.* doi: 10.1038/ncomms1236, 2011.

Stephen Davies, Assistant Professor; Ph.D., Cornell. Microbiology.

Regina Day, Associate Professor; Ph.D., Tufts, 1995. Angiotensin-II-induced apoptosis requires regulation of nucleolin and Bcl-xL by SHP-2 in primary lung endothelial cells *J. Cell Sci.* 123(10):1634–43, 2010.

Saibal Dey, Associate Professor; Ph.D., Wayne State (Michigan), 1995. Allosteric modulation of the human multidrug transporter P-glycoprotein (MDR1 or ABCB1), which confers multidrug resistance in cancer cells and alters bioavailability of many anticancer and antimicrobial agents. *J. Biol. Chem.* 281(16):10699–777, 2006; *Biochemistry* 45:2739–51, 2006; *J. Biol. Chem.* 278(20):18132–9, 2003.

Yang Du, Assistant Professor; Ph.D., Texas Tech, 2000. Leukemia development mechanisms.

Teresa M. Dunn, Professor; Ph.D., Brandeis, 1984. Sphingolipid synthesis and function. *J. Biol. Chem.* 277:11481–8, 2002 and 277:10194–200, 2002; *Mol. Cell Biol.* 21:109–25, 2001; *Methods Enzymol.* 312:317–30, 2000.

Gabriela S. Dveksler, Professor; Ph.D., Uniformed Services University of the Health Sciences, 1991. *J. Biol. Chem.* 286(9):7577–86, 2011; *Biol. Reprod.* 83(1):27–35, 2010.

Ying-Hong Feng, Associate Professor; Ph.D., Oxford, 1993. Pharmacology.

Zygmund Galdzicki, Assistant Professor, Ph.D., Wroclaw (Poland), 1982. Molecular and electrophysiological approach to understanding mental retardation in trisomy 21/Down syndrome

Chou Zen Giam, Professor; Ph.D., Connecticut Health Center, 1983. Human T-lymphotropic virus type I, Kaposi's sarcoma herpes virus, and hepatitis C virus; cellular senescence, cell-cycle controls, I-kappa B kinases, cell transformation, viral oncogenesis, HTLV-1 pathogenesis, and transcriptional regulation. *PLoS Pathog.* 7(4):e1002025, 2011; *J. Virol.* 85(6):3001–9, 2011; *J. Virol.* 82(17):8442–55, 2008; *EMBO J.* 25:1741–52, 2006.

David A. Grahame, Professor; Ph.D., Ohio State, 1984. Metalloenzyme structure and function in Archaea. *J. Biol. Chem.* 285(20):15450–63, 2010; *Biochemistry* 47:5544–55, 2008; *Arch. Microbiol.* 184:32–40, 2005; *J. Am. Chem. Soc.* 126:88–95, 2004; *J. Biol. Chem.* 278:6101–10, 2003.

Philip M. Grimley, Professor; M.D., Albany Medical College, 1961. Population studies relevant to the pathogenesis and molecular biology of ovarian and mammary epithelial cancers.

Jeffrey M. Harmon, Professor and Chair of Pharmacology; Ph.D., Rochester, 1976. Mechanism(s) by which steroid hormones regulate gene expression and the role of steroid hormones in the development and treatment of malignant tumors. *Cancer Res.* 60:2056–62, 2000.

David Horowitz, Associate Professor; Ph.D., Harvard, 1986. Biochemistry of pre-mRNA splicing.

Ann E. Jerse, Associate Professor; Ph.D., Maryland, Baltimore, 1991. Estradiol-treated female mice as surrogate hosts for *Neisseria gonorrhoeae* genital-tract infections. *Front. Microbio.* 2:107, 2011, doi: 10.3389/fmicb.2011.00107.

Sharon L. Juliano, Professor; Ph.D., Pennsylvania, 1982. Mechanisms of development and plasticity in the cerebral cortex, with particular emphasis on the migration of neurons into the cortical plate; factors maintaining the function and morphology of radial glia and Cajal-Retzius cells.

Johnan Kaleeba, Assistant Professor, Ph.D. Mechanisms of infection and disease pathogenesis of oncogenic viruses (EBV and HHV-8); epidemiology and genetic markers of virus-induced cancer in high-risk populations; influences of parasitic inflammation on viral oncogenesis. *PLoS Pathog.* 6(1):e1000742, 2010; *Science* 311(5769):1921–24, 2006.

Radha K. Maheshwari, Professor; Ph.D., Kanpur (India), 1974. Alphaviruses as biothreat agents: Novel approaches for studying the pathogenesis for the development of diagnostic biomarkers, antivirals, and vaccines.

Joseph Mattapallil, Assistant Professor; Ph.D., California Davis, 1997. Molecular and cellular mechanisms of HIV and EBV pathogenesis using nonhuman primate models. *AIDS Res. Hum. Retroviruses* 27(7):763–75, 2011; *Mucosal Immunol.* 2(5):439–49, 2009; *J. Immunol.* 182(3):1439–48, 2009; *J. Virol.* 82(22):11467–71, 2008; *Nature* 434(7037):1093–7, 2005.

Anthony T. Maurelli, Professor; Ph.D., Alabama at Birmingham, 1983. Molecular genetics of bacterial pathogens; molecular biology and pathogenesis of the intracellular pathogens *Shigella* and *Chlamydia*. *BMC Genom.* 11:272, 2010; *Proc. Natl. Acad. Sci. U.S.A.* 106:292–7, 2009.

Ernest Maynard, Assistant Professor; Ph.D., Texas A&M, 2001. Zinc binding to the HCCH motif of HIV-1 virion infectivity factor induces a conformational change that mediates protein-protein interactions. *Proc. Natl. Acad. Sci. U.S.A.* 103:18475–80, 2006.

Joseph T. McCabe, Professor and Vice Chair; Ph.D., CUNY Graduate Center, 1983. Diazoxide, as a postconditioning and delayed preconditioner trigger, increases HSP25 and HSP70 in the central nervous system following combined cerebral stroke and hemorrhagic shock. *J. Neurotrauma* 24(3):532–46. 2007.

D. Scott Merrell, Associate Professor; Ph.D., Tufts, 2001. *H. pylori,* gene regulation and gastric cancer; http://www.usuhs.mil/mic/Merrell/index.html. *Infect. Immun.* 78(7):3073–82, 2010.

Eleanor S. Metcalf, Associate Dean; Ph.D., Pennsylvania, 1976. *J. Immun.*, in press; *Infect. Immun.* 72(5):2843–9, 2004.

Alexandra C. Miller, Assistant Professor; Ph.D., SUNY, 1986. Radiation and heavy metal exposure induced late effects: mechanisms and prevention. A review of depleted uranium biological effects: In vitro and in vivo studies. *Rev. Environ. Health* 22(1):75–94, 2007.

Edward Mitre, Assistant Professor; M.D., Johns Hopkins, 1995. Immune modulation by parasitic helminthes; www.usuhs.mil/mic/mitre.html.

Paul Mongan, Associate Professor and Chair; M.D., Uniformed Services University of the Health Sciences, 1987. Anesthesiology.

Aryan Namboodiri, Assistant Professor; Ph.D., Indian Institute of Science, 1977. Anatomy, physiology, and genetics.

Alison D. O'Brien, Professor and Chair; Ph.D., Ohio State, 1976. The role of *E. coli* shiga toxins in the pathogenesis of hemorrhagic colitis and the hemolytic uremic syndrome; analysis of the mode of action of the Rho-modifying cytotoxic necrotizing factor and its role in the pathogenesis of *E. coli*–mediated urinary-tract infections; identification of spore-surface antigens of *Bacillus anthracis* as potential vaccine candidates. *Infect. Immun.* 79(8):3012–9, 2011.

Galina Petukhova, Assistant Professor, Ph.D., Shemyakin & Ovchinnikov Institute of Bioorganic Chemistry, Moscow, 1994. Molecular mechanisms of genetic recombination in mammals. *Nature* 472:375–78, 2011.

Harvey Pollard, Professor and Chair; Ph.D., 1969, M.D., 1973, Chicago. Molecular biology of secretory processes. *Proc. Natl. Acad. Sci. U.S.A.* 98:4575–80, 2001.

Gerald Quinnan, Professor; M.D., Saint Louis, 1973. Understanding the significance of mutations in the envelope gene of HIV in determining the resistance of virus to neutralization; induction of neutralizing antibody responses using novel HIV-1 envelope glycoproteins and methods of administration with the goal of inducing protection against infection; attempting to understand the factors that limit B cell responses to neutralization epitopes on HIV envelope glycoproteins.

Brian C. Schaefer, Associate Professor; Ph.D., Harvard, 1995. Biology of lymphocyte activation, particularly the antigen regulated NF-kappa B pathway; role of inflammation in traumatic brain injury; imaging, biochemical, and cellular approaches to elucidate signal transduction mechanisms. *J. Immunol.* 185:4520–4, 2010; *J. Immunol.* 181(9):6244–54, 2008; *Mol. Biol. Cell* 17:2166–76, 2006.

Michael Shamblott, Assistant Professor; Ph.D., Johns Hopkins, 2001. Human stem cells and regenerative medicine; development of new tools for bioinformatic research. *Proc. Natl. Acad. Sci. U.S.A.* 98:113–8, 2001.

Ishaiahu Shechter, Professor and Chair; Ph.D., UCLA, 1969. Regulation of cholesterogenesis both in hepatic and nonhepatic cells/tissues; cholesterol homeostasis. *J. Lipid Res.* 37:1406–21, 1996.

Frank Shewmaker, Assistant Professor, Ph.D., Tulane.

Vijay K. Singh, Assistant Professor, Ph.D. Preclinical development of a bridging therapy for radiation casualties. *Exp. Hematol.* 38(1):61–70, 2010.

Clifford M. Snapper, Professor; M.D., Albany Medical College, 1981. In vivo regulation of protein- and polysaccharide-specific humoral immunity to extracellular bacteria and conjugate vaccines. *J. Immunol.* 183(3):1551–59, 2009.

Andrew Snow, Assistant Professor; Ph.D., Stanford, 2005. Control of human lymphocyte homeostasis via antigen receptor signaling and apoptosis. *J. Clin. Investig.* 119(10): 2976–89, 2009.

Shiv Srivastava, Professor and Co-Director, Center for Prostate Disease Research, Department of Surgery; Ph.D., Indian Institute of Technology (New Delhi), 1980. Molecular genetics of human cancer; prostate cancer. *Clin. Chem.* 51:102–12, 2005; *Oncogene* 23:605–11, 2004; *Cancer Res.* 63:4299–304, 2003.

Tharun Sundaresan, Assistant Professor; Ph.D., Centre for Cellular and Molecular Biology (India), 1995. Mechanism of eukaryotic mRNA decay, with particular focus on the role of Lsm1p-7p-Pat1p complex.

Viqar Syed, Assistant Professor, Ph.D., Karolinska Institute, Stockholm.

Aviva Symes, Associate Professor; Ph.D., University College (London), 1990. The role of the TGF-beta superfamily of cytokines in the central nervous system after injury. *J. Mol. Neurosci.* 41:383–96, 2010.

Charles S. Via, Professor; M.D., Virginia, 1973.

Shuishu Wang, Assistant Professor, Ph.D., Purdue, 1999. Structural and functional studies of potential drug target proteins from *Mycobacterium tuberculosis* by x-ray crystallography and biochemical techniques.

Robert W. Williams, Associate Professor; Ph.D., Washington State, 1980. Inelastic neutron scattering, Raman, vibrational analysis with anharmonic corrections, and scaled quantum mechanical force field for polycrystalline L-alanine. *Chem. Phys.* 343(1):1–18, 2008.

T. John Wu, Associate Professor; Ph.D., Texas A&M, 1991. Molecular and cellular neuroendocrinology of reproduction and stress. *Reproduction* 139(2):319–30, 2010; *Endocrinology* 150(4):1817–25, 2009; *Endocrinology* 146:280–6, 2005.

Xin Xiang, Associate Professor; Ph.D., University of Medicine and Dentistry of New Jersey, 1991. The p25 subunit of the dynactin complex is required for dynein–early endosome interaction. *J. Cell Biol.* 193(7):1245–55, 2011.

UNIVERSITY OF CONNECTICUT HEALTH CENTER

Graduate Program in Cell Analysis and Modeling

Program of Study

The University of Connecticut Health Center's (UCHC) quantitative cell biology research has expanded into the area in cell analysis and modeling. Faculty members associated with this area explore complex biological systems using computational cell biology, optical imaging, and other quantitative approaches to analyze processes in living cells. The program in cell analysis and modeling is designed to train students from diverse disciplinary backgrounds in the cutting-edge research techniques that comprise the interdisciplinary research of modern cell biology. Students are provided with rigorous cross-training in areas of mathematical, physical, and computational sciences as well as biology. Students in the program take courses, attend seminars, and work on interdisciplinary research projects to broaden and strengthen their abilities to conduct quantitative cell biology research.

The cell analysis and modeling (CAM) area of concentration is based at the Richard D. Berlin Center for Cell Analysis and Modeling (CCAM) at UCHC. Established in 1994, CCAM has emerged as a center that promotes the application of physics, chemistry, and computation to cell biology. The environment of CCAM is designed to promote interdisciplinary interactions and its cadre of physical scientists are supported and valued in a way that is unique for a medical school.

The CAM program is particularly strong in the following areas of research: cellular modeling (analysis and simulation, data integration, modeling movies boundaries, modularity and multistate complexes, molecular flux in crowded spaces, stochastic modeling and discrete particles); biophysics (biological signaling platforms, in vivo nanofabrication); optical imaging (fluorescent correlation spectroscopy, optical probe development, second harmonic generation, single-molecule imaging); cell biology (cellular tissues and development, cytoskeletal dynamics, RNA trafficking, signal transduction, molecular medicine).

Research Facilities

The program is situated in the modern Health Center in Farmington. This complex provides excellent physical facilities for research in both basic and clinical sciences, a computer center, and the Lyman Maynard Stowe Library. The program provides research facilities and guidance for graduate and postdoctoral work in cell biology—particularly membrane and surface function, membrane protein synthesis and turnover, cytoskeleton structure and function, stimulus-response coupling, gene expression and regulation, vascular biology, fertilization, bone biology, molecular medicine, early development, signal transduction, angiogenesis, computer modeling, and tumor biology. Facilities for training in cell culture, electron microscopy, electrophysiology, fluorescence spectroscopy, molecular biology, molecular modeling, fluorescence imaging, and intravital microscopy are available.

Financial Aid

Support for doctoral students engaged in full-time degree programs at the Health Center is provided on a competitive basis. Graduate research assistantships for 2012–13 provide a stipend of $28,000 per year, which includes a waiver of tuition/University fees for the fall and spring semesters and a student health insurance plan. While financial aid is offered competitively, the Health Center makes every possible effort to address the financial needs of all students during their period of training.

Cost of Study

For 2012–13, tuition is $10,836 per year for full-time students who are Connecticut residents and $28,116 per year for full-time students who are out-of-state residents. General University fees are added to the cost of tuition for students who do not receive a tuition waiver. These costs are usually met by traineeships or research assistantships for doctoral students.

Living and Housing Costs

There is a wide range of affordable housing options in the greater Hartford area within easy commuting distance of the campus, including an extensive complex that is adjacent to the Health Center. Costs range from $600 to $900 per month for a one-bedroom unit; 2 or more students sharing an apartment usually pay less. University housing is not available at the Health Center.

Student Group

The total number of Ph.D. students at the Health Center is approximately 150, while the medical and dental schools combined currently enroll 130 students per class.

Location

The Health Center is located in the historic town of Farmington, Connecticut. Set in the beautiful New England countryside on a hill overlooking the Farmington Valley, it is close to ski areas, hiking trails, and facilities for boating, fishing, and swimming. Connecticut's capital city of Hartford, 7 miles east of Farmington, is the center of an urban region of approximately 800,000 people. The beaches of the Long Island Sound are about 50 minutes away to the south, and the beautiful Berkshires are a short drive to the northwest. New York City and Boston can be reached within 2½ hours by car. Hartford is the home of the acclaimed Hartford Stage Company, TheatreWorks, the Hartford Symphony and Chamber orchestras, two ballet companies, an opera company, the Wadsworth Athenaeum (the oldest public art museum in the nation), the Mark Twain house, the Hartford Civic Center, and many other interesting cultural and recreational facilities. The area is also home to several branches of the University of Connecticut, Trinity College, and the University of Hartford, which includes the Hartt School of Music. Bradley International Airport (about 30 minutes from campus) serves the Hartford/Springfield area with frequent airline connections to major cities in this country and abroad. Frequent bus and rail service is also available from Hartford.

University of Connecticut Health Center

The Health Center

The 200-acre Health Center campus at Farmington houses a division of the University of Connecticut Graduate School, as well as the School of Medicine and Dental Medicine. The campus also includes the John Dempsey Hospital, associated clinics, and extensive medical research facilities, all in a centralized facility with more than 1 million square feet of floor space. The Health Center's newest research addition, the Academic Research Building, was opened in 1999. This impressive eleven-story structure provides 170,000 square feet of state-of-the-art laboratory space. The faculty at the center includes more than 260 full-time members. The institution has a strong commitment to graduate study within an environment that promotes social and intellectual interaction among the various educational programs. Graduate students are represented on various administrative committees concerned with curricular affairs, and the Graduate Student Organization (GSO) represents graduate students' needs and concerns to the faculty and administration, in addition to fostering social contact among graduate students in the Health Center.

Applying

Applications for admission should be submitted via the online application system and should be filed together with transcripts, three letters of recommendation, a personal statement, and recent results from the General Test of the Graduate Record Examinations. International students must take the Test of English as a Foreign Language (TOEFL) to satisfy Graduate School requirements. The deadline for completed applications and receipt of all supplemental materials is **December 1**. Please note that GRE and TOEFL exams taken after the due date will not be accepted for consideration for admission. In accordance with the laws of the state of Connecticut and of the United States, the University of Connecticut Health Center does not discriminate against any person in its educational and employment activities on the grounds of race, color, creed, national origin, sex, age, or physical disability.

Correspondence and Information

Graduate Admissions Office
Ph.D. in Biomedical Science Program
University of Connecticut Health Center
263 Farmington Ave., MC 3906
Farmington, Connecticut 06030-3906
United States
Phone: 860-679-4509
E-mail: BiomedSciAdmissions@uchc.edu
Web site: http://grad.uchc.edu/prospective/programs/phd_biosci/index.html
http://www.ccam.uchc.edu

THE FACULTY AND THEIR RESEARCH

Michael Blinov, Assistant Professor of Genetics and Developmental Biology; Ph.D., Weizmann Institute (Israel). Computational biology: modeling of signal transcription systems and protein-DNA interactions; bioinformatics: data mining and visualization; developing software tools and mathematical methods for rule-based modeling of signal transduction systems.

John H. Carson, Professor of Molecular, Microbial and Structural Biology; Ph.D., MIT. RNA transport in cells of the nervous system.

Ann E. Cowan, Associate Professor of Molecular, Microbial, and Structural Biology; Deputy Director, Center for Biomedical Imaging Technology; Ph.D., Colorado, 1984. Research encompassing several areas of mammalian sperm development.

Greg Huber, Assistant Professor of Cell Biology; Ph.D., Boston University. Problems in biological physics, with an emphasis on the interplay of statistical mechanics, biomechanics, and fluid dynamics.

Leslie M. Loew, Professor of Cell Biology and of Computer Science and Engineering; Ph.D., Cornell, 1974. Morphological determinants of cell physiology; image-based computational models of cellular biology; spatial variations of cell membrane electrophysiology; new optical methods for probing living cells.

Bruce J. Mayer, Associate Professor of Genetics and Developmental Biology; Ph.D., Rockefeller. Mechanisms of signal transduction.

William A. Mohler, Ph.D., Stanford. Assistant Professor of Genetics and Developmental Biology. Developmental cell fusion; *C. elegans* genetics; multidimensional imaging of developmental and cell biological processes.

Ion I. Moraru, Associate Professor of Cell Biology; M.D., Ph.D., Carol Davila (Romania). Understanding signal transduction mechanisms, in particular those related to calcium and phosphoinositides.

Vladimir Rodionov, Assistant Professor of Cell Biology; Ph.D., Moscow; 1980. Molecular mechanisms of intracellular transport; organization of microtubule cytoskeleton.

Ji Yu, Assistant Professor of Genetics and Developmental Biology; Ph.D., Texas at Austin. Optical imaging technology; regulation mechanisms in dendritic RNA translation; cytoskeletal dynamics.

UNIVERSITY OF CONNECTICUT HEALTH CENTER

Graduate Program in Cell Biology

Program of Study

The program offers training leading to a Ph.D. in biomedical sciences and includes faculty members from the Department of Cell Biology as well as eight other Health Center departments. Faculty members' research spans a broad range of interests in the areas of eukaryotic cell biology and related clinical aspects. The program is particularly strong in the following areas of research: angiogenesis, cancer biology, gene expression, molecular medicine, reproductive biology, signal transduction, vascular biology, optical methods, proteomics, and computer modeling of complex biological systems. The curriculum for the first year is tailored to the individual student and can include core courses in the basic biomedical sciences that have been specially formulated to acquaint the student with the principles and practice of modern biomedical research as well as more specialized, analytical courses. In consultation with their advisory committee, students work out a supplementary program of advanced courses, laboratory experiences, and independent study designed to prepare them for general examinations near the end of their second year. Thesis research begins in the second or third year, and research and thesis writing normally occupy the third and fourth years.

Research Facilities

The program is situated in the modern Health Center in Farmington. This complex provides excellent physical facilities for research in both basic and clinical sciences, a computer center, and the Lyman Maynard Stowe Library. The program provides research facilities and guidance for graduate and postdoctoral work in cell biology—particularly membrane and surface function, membrane protein synthesis and turnover, cytoskeleton structure and function, stimulus-response coupling, gene expression and regulation, vascular biology, fertilization, bone biology, molecular medicine, early development, signal transduction, angiogenesis, computer modeling, and tumor biology. Facilities for training in cell culture, electron microscopy, electrophysiology, fluorescence spectroscopy, molecular biology, molecular modeling, fluorescence imaging, and intravital microscopy are available.

Financial Aid

Support for doctoral students engaged in full-time degree programs at the Health Center is provided on a competitive basis. Graduate research assistantships for 2012–13 provide a stipend of $28,000 per year, which includes a waiver of tuition/University fees for the fall and spring semesters and a student health insurance plan. While financial aid is offered competitively, the Health Center makes every possible effort to address the financial needs of all students during their period of training.

Cost of Study

For 2012–13, tuition is $10,836 per year for full-time students who are Connecticut residents and $28,116 per year for full-time students who are out-of-state residents. General University fees are added to the cost of tuition for students who do not receive a tuition waiver. These costs are usually met by traineeships or research assistantships for doctoral students.

Living and Housing Costs

There is a wide range of affordable housing options in the greater Hartford area within easy commuting distance of the campus, including an extensive complex that is adjacent to the Health Center. Costs range from $600 to $900 per month for a one-bedroom unit; 2 or more students sharing an apartment usually pay less. University housing is not available at the Health Center.

Student Group

Currently, approximately 10 students are pursuing doctoral studies in the program. The total number of Ph.D. students at the Health Center is approximately 150, while the medical and dental schools combined currently enroll 130 students per class.

Location

The Health Center is located in the historic town of Farmington, Connecticut. Set in the beautiful New England countryside on a hill overlooking the Farmington Valley, it is close to ski areas, hiking trails, and facilities for boating, fishing, and swimming. Connecticut's capital city of Hartford, 7 miles east of Farmington, is the center of an urban region of approximately 800,000 people. The beaches of the Long Island Sound are about 50 minutes away to the south, and the beautiful Berkshires are a short drive to the northwest. New York City and Boston can be reached within 2½ hours by car. Hartford is the home of the acclaimed Hartford Stage Company, TheatreWorks, the Hartford Symphony and Chamber orchestras, two ballet companies, an opera company, the Wadsworth Athenaeum (the oldest public art museum in the nation), the Mark Twain house, the Hartford Civic Center, and many other interesting cultural and recreational facilities. The area is also home to several branches of the University of Connecticut, Trinity College, and the University of Hartford, which includes the Hartt School of Music. Bradley International Airport (about 30 minutes from campus) serves the Hartford/Springfield area with frequent airline connections to major cities in this country and abroad. Frequent bus and rail service is also available from Hartford.

The Health Center

The 200-acre Health Center campus at Farmington houses a division of the University of Connecticut Graduate School, as well as the School of Medicine and Dental Medicine. The campus also includes the John Dempsey Hospital, associated clinics, and extensive medical research facilities, all in a centralized facility with more than 1 million square feet of floor space. The Health Center's newest research addition, the Academic Research Building, was opened in 1999. This impressive eleven-story structure provides 170,000 square feet of state-of-the-art laboratory space. The faculty at the center includes more than 260 full-time members. The institution has a strong commitment to graduate study within an environment that promotes social and intellectual interaction among the various educational programs. Graduate students are represented on various administrative committees concerned with curricular affairs, and the Graduate Student Organization (GSO) represents graduate students' needs and concerns to the faculty and administration, in addition to fostering social contact among graduate students in the Health Center.

Applying

Applications for admission should be submitted via the online application system and should be filed together with transcripts, three letters of recommendation, a personal statement, and recent results from the General Test of the Graduate Record Examinations. International students must take the Test of English as a Foreign Language (TOEFL) to satisfy Graduate School requirements. The deadline for completed applications and receipt of all supplemental materials is **December 1**. Please note that GRE and TOEFL exams taken after the due date will not be accepted for consideration for admission. In accordance with the laws of the state of Connecticut and of the United States, the University of Connecticut Health Center does not discriminate against any person in its educational and employment activities on the grounds of race, color, creed, national origin, sex, age, or physical disability.

University of Connecticut Health Center

Correspondence and Information

Graduate Admissions Office

Ph.D. in Biomedical Science Program
University of Connecticut Health Center
263 Farmington Ave., MC 3906
Farmington, Connecticut 06030-3906
United States
Phone: 860-679-4509
E-mail: BiomedSciAdmissions@uchc.edu
Web site: http://grad.uchc.edu/prospective/programs/phd_biosci/index.html

THE FACULTY AND THEIR RESEARCH

Andrew Arnold, Professor and Director, Center for Molecular Medicine; M.D., Harvard, 1978. Structure and function of the cyclin D1 oncogene and cell-cycle regulator; molecular genetics and biology of endocrine tumors; inherited endocrine neoplastic diseases.

Rashmi Bansal, Associate Professor of Neuroscience; Ph.D., Central Drug Research Institute, 1976. Developmental, cellular, and molecular biology of oligodendrocytes (OLs), the cells that synthesize myelin membrane in the central nervous system.

Gordon G. Carmichael, Professor of Microbiology; Ph.D., Harvard, 1975. Regulation of gene expression in eukaryotes.

Joan M. Caron, Assistant Professor of Cell Biology; Ph.D., Connecticut, 1982. Biochemistry and cell biology of microtubules; palmitoylation of tubulin and cell function; functional role of palmitoylation of signaling proteins.

Kevin P. Claffey, Associate Professor of Cell Biology and Center for Vascular Biology; Ph.D., Boston University, 1989. Angiogenesis in human cancer progression and metastasis; vascular endothelial growth factor (VEGF) expression; hypoxia-mediated gene regulation.

Robert B. Clark, Associate Professor of Medicine, Division of Rheumatic Diseases; M.D., Stanford, 1975. Basic T-lymphocyte biology, especially as it relates to autoimmune diseases, such as multiple sclerosis and rheumatoid arthritis; molecular biology and structure of the T-cell antigen receptor; T-cell function; T-cell activation.

Ann Cowan, Assistant Professor of Biochemistry and Deputy Director of the Center for Biomedical Imaging Technology; Ph.D., Colorado, 1984. Mammalian sperm development.

Anne Delany, Assistant Professor of Medicine; Ph.D., Dartmouth, 1991. Function and regulation of the noncollagen matrix protein osteonectin/SPARC in bone; regulation of osteoblast gene expression by microRNAs; exploring how the extracellular matrix regulates gene expression in bone-metastatic prostate carcinoma.

Kimberly Dodge-Kafka, Assistant Professor of Cell Biology, Center for Cardiology and Cardiovascular Research; Ph.D., Texas–Houston Health Science Center, 1999. Molecular mechanism of signaling pathways in the heart.

David I. Dorsky, Assistant Professor of Medicine; M.D./Ph.D., Harvard, 1982. The structure and function of herpesvirus DNA polymerases and their roles in viral DNA replication.

Paul Epstein, Associate Professor of Cell Biology; Ph.D., Yeshiva (Einstein), 1975. Signal transduction in relation to leukemia and breast cancer; purification and cloning of cyclic nucleotide phosphodiesterases.

Alan Fein, Professor of Cell Biology; Ph.D., Johns Hopkins, 1973. Molecular basis of visual excitation and adaptation; signal transduction and calcium homeostasis in platelets.

Guo-Hua Fong, Associate Professor of Cell Biology and Center for Vascular Biology; Ph.D., Illinois, 1988. Cardiovascular biology.

Brenton R. Graveley, Assistant Professor, Department of Genetics and Developmental Biology; Ph.D., Vermont, 1996. Regulation of alternative splicing in the mammalian nervous system and mechanisms of alternative splicing.

David Han, Associate Professor of Cell Biology and Center for Vascular Biology; Ph.D., George Washington, 1994. Proteomic analysis of complex protein mixtures.

Arthur R. Hand, Professor of Craniofacial Sciences and Cell Biology; D.D.S., UCLA, 1968. Study of protein and gene expression in rodent salivary glands during normal growth and development and in various experimental conditions employing morphological, immunological, and biochemical methodology.

Marc Hansen, Professor of Medicine; Ph.D., Cincinnati, 1986. Analysis of genes involved in the development of the bone tumor osteosarcoma.

Greg Huber, Assistant Professor of Cell Biology; Ph.D., Boston University. Problems in biological physics, with an emphasis on the interplay of statistical mechanics, biomechanics, and fluid dynamics.

Marja Hurley, Professor of Medicine; M.D., Connecticut Health Center, 1972. Molecular mechanisms by which members of the fibroblast growth factor (FGFs) and fibroblast growth factor receptor (FGFR) families (produced by osteoblasts, osteoclasts, and stromal cells) regulate bone development, remodeling, and disorders of bone: Fgf2 knockout and Fgf2 transgenic mice are utilized in loss and gain of function experiments to elucidate the role of FGF-2 in disorders of bone, including osteoporosis.

Laurinda A. Jaffe, Professor of Cell Biology; Ph.D., UCLA, 1977. Physiology of fertilization, in particular the mechanisms by which membrane potential regulates sperm-egg fusion; transduction mechanisms coupling sperm-egg interaction to egg exocytosis; opening of ion channels in the egg membrane.

Ingela Jansson, Assistant Professor of Cell Biology; Ph.D., Stockholm. DNA-binding proteins in metallothionine induction and cytochrome P450–cytochrome b5 interactions.

Stephen M. King, Associate Professor of Biochemistry; Ph.D., London, 1982. Cell biology; biochemistry and function of molecular motors; dynein structure and function.

Eric S. Levine, Associate Professor of Neuroscience; Ph.D., Princeton. Synaptic physiology and plasticity; roles of nerve growth factors and endogenous cannabinoids in hippocampus and cortex.

Bruce Liang, Professor of Cardiopulmonary Medicine; M.D., Harvard, 1982. Signal transduction; cardiac and vascular cell biology; receptors; G proteins; transgenic mice.

Leslie M. Loew, Professor of Cell Biology and Director, Center for Cell Analysis and Modeling; Ph.D., Cornell, 1974. Spectroscopic methods for measuring spatial and temporal variations in membrane potential; electric field effects on cell membranes; membrane pores induced by toxins and antibiotics.

Nilanjana Maulik, Associate Professor of Surgery; Ph.D., Calcutta, 1990. Molecular and cellular signaling during myocardial ischemia and reperfusion.

Lisa Mehlman, Assistant Professor of Cell Biology; Ph.D., Kent State, 1996. Cell signaling events that regulate oocyte maturation and fertilization; maintenance of oocyte meiotic arrest by G-protein receptors; hormonal regulation of oocyte maturation.

Ion I. Moraru, Associate Professor of Cell Biology; M.D., Ph.D., Carol Davila (Romania). Understanding signal transduction mechanisms, in particular related to calcium and phosphoinositides.

Joel Pachter, Professor of Cell Biology; Ph.D., NYU, 1983. Elucidating the mechanisms by which leukocytes and pathogens invade the central nervous system.

John J. Peluso, Professor of Cell Biology and Obstetrics and Gynecology; Ph.D., West Virginia, 1974. Cell and molecular mechanisms involving the regulating ovarian cell mitosis and apoptosis; cell-cell interaction as a regulator of ovarian cell function; identification and characterization of a putative membrane receptor for progesterone.

Carol C. Pilbeam, Associate Professor of Medicine; M.D./Ph.D., Yale, 1982. Regulation and function of prostaglandins in bone; transcriptional regulation of cyclooxygenase-2; role of cytokines and estrogen in bone physiology and osteoporosis.

Vladimir Rodionov, Assistant Professor of Cell Biology; Ph.D., Moscow, 1980. Dynamics of cytoskeleton; self-organization of microtubule arrays; regulation of the activity of microtubule motors.

Daniel Rosenberg, Professor of Medicine; Ph.D., Michigan. Molecular genetics of colorectal cancer; signaling pathways in the development of tumors; toxicogenomics.

Linda H. Shapiro, Associate Professor of Cell Biology and Center for Vascular Biology; Ph.D., Michigan, 1984. Regulation and function of CD 13/aminopeptidase N in angiogenic vasculature and early myeloid cells; control of tumor and myocardial angiogenesis by peptidases; inflammatory regulation of angiogenesis.

Mark R. Terasaki, Assistant Professor of Cell Biology; Ph.D., Berkeley, 1983. Structure and function of the endoplasmic reticulum; confocal microscopy.

James Watras, Associate Professor of Medicine; Ph.D., Washington State, 1979. The mechanisms by which the sarcoplasmic reticulum regulates intracellular calcium concentration in vascular smooth muscle.

Bruce A. White, Professor of Cell Biology; Ph.D., Berkeley, 1980. Regulation of prolactin gene expression by Ca and calmodulin in rat pituitary tumor cells; examination of nuclear DNA-binding proteins, nuclear calmodulin-binding proteins, and nuclear Ca-calmodulin-dependent protein kinase activity.

Catherine H.-y. Wu, Associate Professor of Medicine; Ph.D., CUNY, Brooklyn, 1976. Mechanisms of procollagen propeptide feedback inhibition of collagen synthesis; pretranslational control.

George Y. Wu, Professor of Medicine; M.D./Ph.D., Yeshiva (Einstein), 1976. Receptor-mediated endocytosis of glycoproteins; drug delivery by endocytic targeting; targeted gene delivery and expression.

Lixia Yue, Assistant Professor of Cell Biology and Center for Cardiovascular Research; Ph.D., McGill, 1999. TRP channels and Ca^{2+} signaling mechanisms in cardiac remodeling.

UNIVERSITY OF CONNECTICUT HEALTH CENTER

Graduate Program in Molecular Biology and Biochemistry

Program of Study

The Graduate Program in Molecular Biology and Biochemistry uniquely bridges modern molecular biology, microbiology, biochemistry, cell biology, and structural biology, leading to a Ph.D. in the biomedical sciences. The goals of the graduate program are to provide rigorous research training in an environment dedicated to advancing excellence in teaching and research. Whether graduates enter academic research, the biotechnology industry, liberal arts college teaching, patent law, or other disciplines, they bring to that career a solid base of knowledge, an ability to learn independently and think independently, and an enduring desire to use their full range of professional skills and experience in creative ways. Graduates are expected to have demonstrated a high degree of competence in research, as judged by publications in first-rank journals, and to have developed essential skills in identifying important research problems, planning research projects and scientific writing. In addition, students are expected to have incorporated ethical principles of scientific conduct into their professional attitudes and activities and to be sensitive to such issues throughout their careers. The success of this training approach is indicated by the high percentage of students who have developed successful independent careers in biomedical research. The current program offers an unparalleled opportunity to study a wide variety of biological problems at the biochemical, molecular, cellular, and structural levels. The interests of the faculty are summarized below.

Research Facilities

In addition to the general facilities of the Health Center (see page describing programs in the Biological and Biomedical Sciences), the program offers complete physical research facilities. There is research equipment, as well as expertise, for all areas of genetic, biochemical, molecular, cellular, and biophysical investigation. The department houses the UConn Health Center NMR Structural Biology Facility (http://structbio. uchc.edu), which includes a 400-MHz NMR spectrometer and cryoprobe-equipped 500- and 600-MHz NMR spectrometers, as well as a circular dichroism spectropolarimeter, isothermal titration calorimeter, and multi-angle laser light scattering facilities. An 800-MHz NMR spectrometer and X-ray crystallography facilities are planned. The department also houses the UConn Health Center Structural Biology Computational Facility, which includes a bank of Mac and Linux desktop computers connected to ultrafast servers with the latest structural biology software. Facilities are also available for electron and confocal laser scanning microscopy, low-light-level imaging microscopy (in the state-of-the-art Center for Cell Analysis and Modeling), protein purification and sequencing, cell culture, monoclonal antibody production, DNA oligonucleotide and peptide synthesis and sequencing, and gene silencing using RNAi.

Financial Aid

Support for doctoral students engaged in full-time degree programs at the Health Center is provided on a competitive basis. Graduate research assistantships for 2012–13 provide a stipend of $28,000 per year, which includes a waiver of tuition/University fees for the fall and spring semesters and a student health insurance plan. While financial aid is offered competitively, the Health Center makes every possible effort to address the financial needs of all students during their period of training.

Cost of Study

For 2012–13, tuition is $10,836 per year for full-time students who are Connecticut residents and $28,116 per year for full-time out-of-state residents. General University fees are added to the cost of tuition for students who do not receive a tuition waiver. These costs are usually met by traineeships or research assistantships for doctoral students.

Living and Housing Costs

There is a wide range of affordable housing options in the greater Hartford area within easy commuting distance of the campus, including an extensive complex that is adjacent to the Health Center. Costs range from $600 to $900 per month for a one-bedroom unit; 2 or more students sharing an apartment usually pay less. University housing is not available at the Health Center.

Student Group

There are approximately 20 graduate students in the molecular biology and biochemistry program. There are approximately 150 graduate students in Ph.D. programs on the Health Center campus, and the total enrollment is about 1,000.

Location

The Health Center is located in the historic town of Farmington, Connecticut. Set in the beautiful New England countryside on a hill overlooking the Farmington Valley, it is close to ski areas, hiking trails, and facilities for boating, fishing, and swimming. Connecticut's capital city of Hartford, 7 miles east of Farmington, is the center of an urban region of approximately 800,000 people. The beaches of the Long Island Sound are about 50 minutes away to the south, and the beautiful Berkshires are a short drive to the northwest. New York City and Boston can be reached within 2½ hours by car. Hartford is the home of the acclaimed Hartford Stage Company, TheatreWorks, the Hartford Symphony and Chamber orchestras, two ballet companies, an opera company, the Wadsworth Athenaeum (the oldest public art museum in the nation), the Mark Twain house, the Hartford Civic Center, and many other interesting cultural and recreational facilities. The area is also home to several branches of the University of Connecticut, Trinity College, and the University of Hartford, which includes the Hartt School of Music. Bradley International Airport (about 30 minutes from campus) serves the Hartford/Springfield area with frequent airline connections to major cities in this country and abroad. Frequent bus and rail service is also available from Hartford.

University of Connecticut Health Center

The Health Center

The 200-acre Health Center campus at Farmington houses a division of the University of Connecticut Graduate School, as well as the School of Medicine and Dental Medicine. The campus also includes the John Dempsey Hospital, associated clinics, and extensive medical research facilities, all in a centralized facility with more than 1 million square feet of floor space. The Health Center's newest research addition, the Academic Research Building, was opened in 1999. This impressive eleven-story structure provides 170,000 square feet of state-of-the-art laboratory space. The faculty at the center includes more than 260 full-time members. The institution has a strong commitment to graduate study within an environment that promotes social and intellectual interaction among the various educational programs. Graduate students are represented on various administrative committees concerned with curricular affairs, and the Graduate Student Organization (GSO) represents graduate students' needs and concerns to the faculty and administration, in addition to fostering social contact among graduate students in the Health Center.

Applying

Applications for admission should be submitted via the online application system and should be filed together with transcripts, three letters of recommendation, a personal statement, and recent results from the General Test of the Graduate Record Examinations. International students must take the Test of English as a Foreign Language (TOEFL) to satisfy Graduate School requirements. The deadline for completed applications and receipt of all supplemental materials is **December 1**. Please note that GRE and TOEFL exams taken after the due date will not be accepted for consideration for admission. In accordance with the laws of the state of Connecticut and of the United States, the University of Connecticut Health Center does not discriminate against any person in its educational and employment activities on the grounds of race, color, creed, national origin, sex, age, or physical disability.

Correspondence and Information

Graduate Admissions Office
Ph.D. in Biomedical Science Program
University of Connecticut Health Center
263 Farmington Ave., MC 3906
Farmington, Connecticut 06030-3906
United States
Phone: 860-679-4509
E-mail: BiomedSciAdmissions@uchc.edu
Web site: http://grad.uchc.edu/prospective/programs/phd_biosci/index.html

THE FACULTY AND THEIR RESEARCH

Irina Besonova, Assistant Professor of Molecular, Microbial, and Structural Biology; Ph.D., Toronto. Structural and biochemical characterization of proteins and protein complexes of p53 pathway, especially, proteins responsible for maintenance of an appropriate level of p53 in the cell.

Gordon G. Carmichael, Professor; Ph.D., Harvard. Regulation of viral gene expression and function.

John H. Carson, Professor; Ph.D., MIT. RNA transport in cells of the nervous system.

Ann Cowan, Associate Professor; Ph.D., Colorado at Boulder. Plasma membrane proteins in sperm.

Asis Das, Professor; Ph.D., Calcutta. Gene control in bacterial adaptive response.

Kimberly Dodge-Kafka, Assistant Professor of Cell Biology/Center for Cardiology and Cardiovascular Research; Ph.D., Texas Health Science Center at Houston, 1999. Molecular mechanism of signaling pathways in the heart.

Betty Eipper, Professor; Ph.D., Harvard. Biosynthesis and secretion of peptides by neurons and endocrine cells.

Shlomo Eisenberg, Professor; Ph.D., McGill. Biochemistry of DNA replication in yeast.

Richard Everson, Deputy Director for Cancer Prevention and Control, Neag Comprehensive Cancer Center; M.D., Rochester; M.P.H., North Carolina at Chapel Hill. Conducting large-scale cancer genomic clinical research and population studies by developing a statewide biorepository of tumor tissue with analysis by high-throughput arrays and next-generation sequencing.

Michael Gryk, Assistant Professor; Ph.D., Stanford. Three-dimensional structure and function of proteins involved in DNA repair.

Arthur Günzl, Associate Professor; Ph.D., Tübingen (Germany). Transcription and antigenic variation in the mammalian parasite *Trypanosoma brucei.*

Bing Hao, Assistant Professor of Molecular, Microbial, and Structural Biology; Ph.D., Ohio State. Understanding how the cell cycle is regulated by ubiquitin-mediated proteolysis using X-ray crystallography as a primary tool.

Christopher Heinen, Assistant Professor of Medicine; Ph.D., Cincinnati. Biochemical and cellular defects of the DNA mismatch repair pathway during tumorigenesis.

Jeffrey Hoch, Associate Professor; Ph.D., Harvard. Biophysical chemistry of proteins.

Stephen M. King, Associate Professor; Ph.D., University College, London. Structure and function of microtubule-based molecular motor proteins.

Lawrence A. Klobutcher, Professor and Associate Dean of the Graduate School; Ph.D., Yale. DNA rearrangement, programmed translational frameshifting, and phagocytosis in ciliated protozoa.

Dmitry Korzhnev, Assistant Professor, Molecular, Microbial, and Structural Biology; Ph.D., Moscow Institute of Physics and Technology. Liquid-state nuclear magnetic resonance (NMR) studies of structure and dynamics of proteins and their assemblies; multiprotein complexes involved in DNA replication and repair; protein folding.

Mark Maciejewski, Assistant Professor; Ph.D., Ohio State. Enzymes of DNA replication, repair, and recombination.

Peter Setlow, Professor; Ph.D., Brandeis. Biochemistry of bacterial spore germination.

Aziz Taghbalout, Assistant Professor of Molecular, Microbial, and Structural Biology; Ph.D., Hassan II University (Morocco). Understanding the molecular organization of the RNA degradosome, a multiprotein complex that plays essential role in the normal RNA degradation and processing in *Escherichia coli.*

Sandra K. Weller, Professor and Department Head; Ph.D., Wisconsin. Mechanisms of DNA replication and DNA encapsidation in herpes simplex virus; virus-host interactions.

UNIVERSITY OF MISSOURI–KANSAS CITY

School of Biological Sciences
Program in Cell Biology and Biophysics

Program of Study

The graduate program in cell biology and biophysics at the University of Missouri–Kansas City (UMKC) leads to the Ph.D. degree. The program functions within the interdisciplinary Ph.D. framework of the University and is associated with the M.S. program in cell and molecular biology. The graduate program is designed to prepare students for research-oriented careers in academia, government, or the private sector. An original independent research project under the supervision of a faculty adviser is the core of these programs.

Programs of study provide a background of course work tailored to the interests of each student. Opportunity for research experience begins immediately as a component of the first-year curriculum, with each student being assigned short research projects. By the end of the first academic year, the student is also expected to have acquired a general understanding of the basis of molecular and cellular biology. At that time, the student selects a faculty research adviser and makes further course selections. To qualify for doctoral degree candidacy, students prepare and defend an original research proposal. The culmination of the graduate degree programs is the preparation and oral defense of a research dissertation, typically five years after entry into the program.

The areas of research interest of participating faculty members are included in the Faculty and Their Research section. Extensive possibilities for collaboration exist with the School's program in molecular biology and biochemistry and with regional research associates. Opportunities for postdoctoral research are abundant.

Research Facilities

Research facilities for cell, molecular and structural biology, and biochemistry are primarily located in the Biological Sciences and Chemistry buildings. Modern research is conducted in laboratories assigned to individual faculty members and in specialized central facilities. Sophisticated instrumentation in these facilities includes automated DNA and protein synthesizers and sequencers, mass spectrometers, macromolecular X-ray, low-intensity electron microscope and 600-MHz NMR imaging facilities, molecular graphics equipment, and Fourier-transform infrared and EPR spectrometers. Raman and UV-resonance Raman spectrometers, differential scanning and titration microcalorimeters, analytical ultracentrifuge, HPLCs, amino acid and carbohydrate analyzers, low-intensity fluorescence imaging and confocal microscopes, and a large assortment of scanning spectrophotometers, ELISA readers, gel scanners, centrifuges, and related instrumentation associated with modern biochemical research are available. Students also enjoy the use of Linda Hall Library, one of the country's premier private science libraries; central animal facilities; and a fully integrated computer network with on-site and off-site access to national and international databases and the Internet.

Financial Aid

All fully admitted U.S. citizen and resident doctoral students receive financial support as teaching or research assistants.

Support is provided for up to five years for students who are progressing satisfactorily. For the 2012–13 year, stipends are $23,000. Other forms of financial aid may be available through the Student Financial Aid Office. The metropolitan area offers many career and educational opportunities for spouses and other family members.

Cost of Study

In 2012–13, in-state tuition is about $6900 per year, while out-of-state fees are approximately $16,500 per year. Full-time doctoral students, as a general rule, receive basic tuition support.

Living and Housing Costs

A wide variety of off-campus housing is available in every price range. The overall cost of living in Kansas City is low compared with metropolitan areas in other parts of the country.

Student Group

The cell biology and biophysics graduate program has a very active graduate student organization. UMKC has approximately 10,000 students, of whom about half are graduate and professional students. The School of Biological Sciences currently has about 80 graduate students and 15 postdoctoral fellows as well as more than 200 undergraduate majors. Eight to 12 new doctoral students are admitted each year.

Student Outcomes

The majority of doctoral graduates transfer to nationally known research institutions, typically as postdoctoral associates, or undertake advanced professional training. A short transitional postdoctoral research period within the School is not uncommon.

Location

Kansas City, "The Heart of America," is the center of a metropolitan area with a population of more than 1 million. The University is adjacent to the elegant Country Club Plaza, the city's entertainment and shopping center. Major-league sports, historical and art museums, and many musical, theatrical, and cultural events as well as an extensive parks system provide entertainment throughout the year. A relaxed, Midwestern lifestyle is also an advantage of the setting, which, with its many fountains, boulevards, unusually clean air, and more days of sunshine than in most large U.S. cities, provides an enjoyable quality of life.

The University and The School

UMKC is part of the four-campus University of Missouri System, and it is the only comprehensive research university in western Missouri. It has a strong life science mission. The School of Biological Sciences was established in 1985 to develop strong research and graduate programs in the modern life sciences. The School has been cited by the Board of Curators of the University of Missouri System as an area of eminence for its programs in molecular biology and biochemistry and in cell

biology and biophysics. Program improvement funds have facilitated the hiring of many research-oriented faculty members and the creation of excellent research facilities. An innovative interdisciplinary doctoral program has also been initiated, creating a stimulating environment that offers outstanding research opportunities to graduate students.

Applying

The deadline for applications from U.S. applicants is July 1, but applications received before March 1 have priority for financial support. The deadline for international applications is February 15. A bachelor's degree in biology, chemistry, physics, or a related discipline with a minimum 3.0 grade point average is required for full admission. The General Test of the Graduate Record Examinations is also required. The TOEFL is required for international applicants whose native language is not English.

Correspondence and Information

Graduate Adviser
School of Biological Sciences
University of Missouri–Kansas City
Kansas City, Missouri 64110-2499
United States
Phone: 816-235-2352
Fax: 816-235-5158
E-mail: sbs-grad@umkc.edu
Web site: http://sbs.umkc.edu/graduate/

THE FACULTY AND THEIR RESEARCH

Professors

Lawrence A. Dreyfus, Ph.D., Kansas. Molecular biology; bacterial toxin structure-function.

Henry M. Miziorko, Ph.D., Pennsylvania. Study of enzyme catalysis and regulation using chemical, biophysical, and molecular biology approaches; lipid biosynthesis; enzymes in inherited disease.

Anthony J. Persechini, Ph.D., Carnegie Mellon. Calcium-calmodulin signaling pathways; intracellular interactions.

G. Sullivan Read, Ph.D., Penn State. RNA turnover control; gene regulation; herpes virus.

Ann Smith, Ph.D., London. Receptor-mediated endocytosis; protein-receptor interactions; intercellular heme transport.

Theodore White, Ph.D., Michigan. Virulence and drug resistance in medically important fungi.

Associate Professors

Karen J. Bame, Ph.D., UCLA. Metabolism of heparan sulfate proteoglycans.

Samuel Bouyain, D.Phil., Oxford. Structure and function of the protein tyrosine phosphatase family of cell surface receptors; X-ray crystallography.

Leonard L. Dobens Jr., Ph.D., Dartmouth. Pattern formation; cell-cell signaling.

Brian Geisbrecht, Ph.D., Johns Hopkins. Structure and function studies of bacterial virulence factors; X-ray crystallography.

Edward P. Gogol, Ph.D., Yale. Structure of macromolecular assemblies; cryoelectron microscopy.

Saul M. Honigberg, Ph.D., Yale. Signal transduction; cell-cycle control and cell differentiation.

Chi-ming Huang, Ph.D., UCLA. Evolution neurobiology of the cerebellum.

John H. Laity, Ph.D., Cornell. Molecular recognition; NMR spectroscopy; protein biophysical chemistry.

Thomas M. Menees, Ph.D., Yale. Replication of retroviral elements and transposons; yeast molecular genetics.

Michael O'Connor, Ph.D., Ireland. Structure and function of the bacterial ribosome, ribosomal subunits, and the translational reading frame.

Lynda S. Plamann, Ph.D., Iowa. Cell-cell communication during fruiting body formation and sporulation in the soil bacterium *Myxococcus xanthus.*

Michael D. Plamann, Ph.D., Iowa. Microtubule-associated motors; organelle movement; growth polarity; cytoskeleton.

Jeffrey L. Price, Ph.D., Johns Hopkins. *Drosophila* genes involved in chronobiology and circadian rhythms.

Garth Resch, Ph.D., Missouri–Columbia. Neurophysiology and behavior patterns of alcoholism.

Jakob H. Waterborg, Ph.D., Nijmegen (Netherlands). Plant histones; chromatin conformation and gene expression.

Gerald J. Wyckoff, Ph.D., Chicago. Bioinformatics and study of molecular evolution through large-scale comparative genomics in sexual selection.

Marilyn D. Yoder, Ph.D., California, Riverside. X-ray crystallography; protein structure.

Xiao-Qiang Yu, Ph.D., Kansas State. Insect molecular biology and biochemistry of immune responses, pattern recognition proteins, and protein-protein–protein-ligand interactions.

Assistant Professors

Julia Chekanova, Ph.D. Moscow State. Relationships between mRNA quality control, processing, and export in *Saccharomyces cerevisiae.*

Erika Geisbrecht, Ph.D., Johns Hopkins. Myoblast fusion in *Drosophila* embryogenesis.

Alexander Idnurm, Ph.D., Melbourne. Molecular pathogenesis of fungal parasites.

Xiaolan Yao, Ph.D., Iowa State. Structure and dynamic bases of protein function; NMR spectroscopy.

Regional Associates

Mark Fisher, Ph.D., Illinois. Chaperonin-assisted protein folding and oligomer assembly.

UNIVERSITY OF MISSOURI–KANSAS CITY

School of Biological Sciences
Program in Molecular Biology and Biochemistry

Programs of Study

The graduate program in molecular biology and biochemistry at the University of Missouri–Kansas City (UMKC) leads to the Ph.D. degree. The program functions within the interdisciplinary Ph.D. framework of the University and is associated with the M.S. program in cell and molecular biology. The graduate program is designed to prepare students for research-oriented careers in academia, government, or the private sector. An original independent research project under the supervision of a faculty adviser is the core of these programs.

Programs of study provide a background of course work tailored to the interests of each student. Opportunity for research experience begins immediately as a component of the first-year curriculum, with each student being assigned short research projects. By the end of the first academic year, the student is also expected to have acquired a general understanding of the basis of molecular and cellular biology. At that time, the student selects a faculty research adviser and makes further course selections. To qualify for doctoral degree candidacy, students prepare and defend an original research proposal. The culmination of the graduate degree programs is the preparation and oral defense of a research dissertation, typically five years after entry into the program.

The areas of research interest of participating faculty members are included in the Faculty and Their Research section. Extensive possibilities for collaboration exist with the School's program in cell biology and biophysics and with regional research associates. Opportunities for postdoctoral research are abundant.

Research Facilities

Research facilities for cell, molecular, and structural biology and biochemistry are located primarily in the Biological Sciences and Chemistry buildings. Modern research is done in laboratories assigned to individual faculty members or in specialized central facilities. Sophisticated instrumentation in these facilities includes automated DNA and protein synthesizers and sequencers, mass spectrometers, macromolecular X-ray, low-intensity electron microscope and 600-MHz NMR imaging facilities, molecular graphics equipment, and Fourier-transform infrared and EPR spectrometers. Raman and UV-resonance Raman spectrometers, differential scanning and titration microcalorimeters, analytical ultracentrifuge, HPLCs, amino-acid and carbohydrate analyzers, low-intensity fluorescence imaging and confocal microscopes, and a large assortment of scanning spectrophotometers, ELISA readers, gel scanners, centrifuges, and related instrumentation associated with modern biochemical research are also available. Students enjoy the use of Linda Hall Library, one of the country's premier private science libraries; central animal facilities; and a fully integrated computer network with on-site and off-site access to national and international databases and the Internet.

Financial Aid

All fully admitted U.S. citizen and resident doctoral students receive financial support as teaching or research assistants.

Support is provided up to five years for students who are progressing satisfactorily. For the 2012–13 year, stipends are $23,000. Other forms of financial aid may be available through the Student Financial Aid Office. The metropolitan area offers many career and educational opportunities for spouses and other family members.

Cost of Study

In 2012–13, in-state tuition is about $6900 per year, while out-of-state fees are approximately $16,500 per year. Full-time doctoral students, as a general rule, receive basic tuition support.

Living and Housing Costs

A wide variety of off-campus housing is available in every price range. The overall cost of living in Kansas City is low compared with metropolitan areas in other parts of the country.

Student Group

The molecular biology and biochemistry graduate program has a very active graduate student organization. UMKC has approximately 10,000 students, of whom about half are graduate and professional students. The School of Biological Sciences currently has about 80 graduate students and 15 postdoctoral fellows as well as more than 200 undergraduate majors. Eight to 12 new doctoral students are admitted each year.

Student Outcomes

The majority of doctoral graduates transfer to nationally known research institutions, typically as postdoctoral associates, or undertake advanced professional training. A short transitional postdoctoral research period within the School is not uncommon.

Location

Kansas City, "The Heart of America," is the center of a metropolitan area with a population of more than 1 million. The University is adjacent to the elegant Country Club Plaza, the city's entertainment and shopping center. Major-league sports, historical and art museums, and many musical, theatrical, and cultural events as well as an extensive parks system provide entertainment throughout the year. A relaxed, Midwestern lifestyle is also an advantage of the setting, which, with its many fountains, boulevards, unusually clean air, and more days of sunshine than in most large U.S. cities, provides an enjoyable quality of life.

The University and The School

UMKC is part of the four-campus University of Missouri System, and it is the only comprehensive research university in western Missouri. It has a strong life science mission. The School of Biological Sciences was established in 1985 to develop strong research and graduate programs in the modern life sciences. The School has been cited by the Board of Curators of the University of Missouri System as an area of eminence for its programs in molecular biology and biochemistry and in cell

University of Missouri–Kansas City

biology and biophysics. Program improvement funds have facilitated the hiring of many research-oriented faculty members and the creation of excellent research facilities. An innovative interdisciplinary doctoral program has also been initiated, creating a stimulating environment that offers outstanding research opportunities to graduate students.

Applying

The deadline for applications from U.S. applicants is July 1, but applications received before March 1 have priority for financial support. The deadline for international applications is February 15. A bachelor's degree in biology, chemistry, physics, or a related discipline with a minimum 3.0 grade point average is required for full admission. The General Test of the Graduate Record Examinations is also required. The TOEFL is required for international applicants whose native language is not English.

Correspondence and Information

Graduate Adviser
School of Biological Sciences
University of Missouri–Kansas City
Kansas City, Missouri 64110-2499
United States
Phone: 816-235-2352
Fax: 816-235-5158
E-mail: sbs-grad@umkc.edu
Web site: http://sbs.umkc.edu/graduate/

THE FACULTY AND THEIR RESEARCH

Professors

Lawrence A. Dreyfus, Ph.D., Kansas. Molecular biology; bacterial toxin structure-function.

Henry M. Miziorko, Ph.D., Pennsylvania. Study of enzyme catalysis and regulation using chemical, biophysical, and molecular biology approaches; lipid biosynthesis; enzymes in inherited disease.

Anthony J. Persechini, Ph.D., Carnegie Mellon. Calcium-calmodulin signaling pathways; intracellular interactions.

G. Sullivan Read, Ph.D., Penn State. RNA turnover control; gene regulation; herpes virus.

Ann Smith, Ph.D., London. Receptor-mediated endocytosis; protein-receptor interactions; intercellular heme transport.

Theodore White, Ph.D., Michigan. Virulence and drug resistance in medically important fungi.

Associate Professors

Karen J. Bame, Ph.D., UCLA. Metabolism of heparan sulfate proteoglycans.

Samuel Bouyain, D.Phil., Oxford. Structure and function of the protein tyrosine phosphatase family of cell surface receptors; X-ray crystallography.

Leonard L. Dobens Jr., Ph.D., Dartmouth. Pattern formation; cell-cell signaling.

Brian Geisbrecht, Ph.D., Johns Hopkins. Structure and function studies of bacterial virulence factors; X-ray crystallography.

Edward P. Gogol, Ph.D., Yale. Structure of macromolecular assemblies; cryoelectron microscopy.

Saul M. Honigberg, Ph.D., Yale. Signal transduction; cell-cycle control and cell differentiation.

Chi-ming Huang, Ph.D., UCLA. Evolution neurobiology of the cerebellum.

John H. Laity, Ph.D., Cornell. Molecular recognition; NMR spectroscopy; protein biophysical chemistry.

Thomas M. Menees, Ph.D., Yale. Replication of retroviral elements and transposons; yeast molecular genetics.

Michael O'Connor, Ph.D., Ireland. Structure and function of the bacterial ribosome, ribosomal subunits, and the translational reading frame.

Lynda S. Plamann, Ph.D., Iowa. Cell-cell communication during fruiting body formation and sporulation in the soil bacterium *Myxococcus xanthus*.

Michael D. Plamann, Ph.D., Iowa. Microtubule-associated motors; organelle movement; growth polarity; cytoskeleton.

Jeffrey L. Price, Ph.D., Johns Hopkins. *Drosophila* genes involved in chronobiology and circadian rhythms.

Garth Resch, Ph.D., Missouri–Columbia. Neurophysiology and behavior patterns of alcoholism.

Jakob H. Waterborg, Ph.D., Nijmegen (Netherlands). Plant histones; chromatin conformation and gene expression.

Gerald J. Wyckoff, Ph.D., Chicago. Bioinformatics and study of molecular evolution through large-scale comparative genomics in sexual selection.

Marilyn D. Yoder, Ph.D., California, Riverside. X-ray crystallography; protein structure.

Xiao-Qiang Yu, Ph.D., Kansas State. Insect molecular biology and biochemistry of immune responses, pattern recognition proteins, and protein-protein–protein-ligand interactions.

Assistant Professors

Julia Chekanova, Ph.D. Moscow State. Relationships between mRNA quality control, processing, and export in *Saccharomyces cerevisiae*.

Erika Geisbrecht, Ph.D., Johns Hopkins. Myoblast fusion in *Drosophila* embryogenesis.

Alexander Idnurm, Ph.D., Melbourne. Molecular pathogenesis of fungal parasites.

Xiaolan Yao, Ph.D., Iowa State. Structure and dynamic bases of protein function; NMR spectroscopy.

Regional Associates

Gerald M. Carlson, Ph.D., Iowa State. Biophysical, biochemical, and chemical approaches in the study of macromolecular assemblies.

UNIVERSITY OF WASHINGTON/ FRED HUTCHINSON CANCER RESEARCH CENTER

Molecular and Cellular Biology Program

UNIVERSITY *of* WASHINGTON

FRED **HUTCHINSON** CANCER RESEARCH **CENTER**
A LIFE OF SCIENCE

Program of Study

The University of Washington and the Fred Hutchinson Cancer Research Center offer a program of graduate studies in molecular and cellular biology leading to the Ph.D. degree. More than 200 faculty members participate in the program and are located on the University of Washington campus in the Departments of Biochemistry, Biological Structure, Biology, Genome Sciences, Immunology, Microbiology, Global Health, Pathology, Pharmacology, and Physiology and Biophysics, as well as on the Day campus at the Hutchinson Center, primarily in the Division of Basic Sciences and the Division of Human Biology. Recently, the Institute for Systems Biology (ISB), a nonprofit research institute headed by Dr. Leroy Hood, and the Seattle Biomedical Research Institute (Seattle BioMed), an infectious disease research center led by Dr. Alan Aderem, have joined the Molecular and Cellular Biology (MCB) program.

The goals of the program are to give the student a sound background in molecular and cellular biology and to provide access to the research expertise of all faculty members and laboratories working in this area. These goals are accomplished through the basic elements of the program, which include keystone courses in a student's area of interest, advanced elective courses in molecular and cellular biology, a two-quarter literature review course, one quarter of grant writing, three or more quarter-long lab rotations, two quarters of varied teaching experience, and a series of informal workshops and seminars on topics in diverse areas of molecular biology and cellular biology. Emphasis is placed on critical evaluation of the literature, exposure to current research methods, and creative thinking through independent research. Students are expected to begin active research in their first year through their lab rotations and to choose a permanent thesis adviser at the end of their first year.

Research Facilities

The program uses the research facilities of the individual departments, Hutchinson Center, ISB, and Seattle BioMed. The School of Medicine is housed in the Health Sciences Center and the South Lake Union research hub (SLU). The University Hospital and the College of Arts and Sciences are located in adjoining or nearby buildings. The Hutchinson Center's Day campus and SLU are a 15-minute shuttle ride from the University. The laboratories of participating faculty members are well equipped with the latest in research equipment and are funded by external support. The ISB and Seattle BioMed are located within easy commuting distance. Some of the other facilities available are two Howard Hughes Medical Institute research units, the Markey Molecular Medicine Center, animal quarters, shared major instrument facilities, oligonucleotide and peptide synthesis facilities, a marine biology station at Friday Harbor in the San Juan Islands, and an extensive Health Sciences Library.

Financial Aid

The program offers a salary of approximately $27,348 for twelve months. Students with satisfactory academic progress can anticipate funding that includes tuition and health insurance for the duration of their studies.

Cost of Study

Tuition, salary, and medical, dental, and vision benefits are funded for the duration of the program for students in good standing.

Living and Housing Costs

The University has a wide variety of housing available for single and married students as well as families. Students should call the University Housing Office at 206-543-4059 for further information. Private accommodations may be found within easy walking or bicycling distance.

Student Group

At the University of Washington, approximately 2,500 full-time faculty members serve a student population of 35,000 that is drawn from all over the United States and many other countries.

An average of 20 new students are admitted to the program each year. There are approximately 500 graduate students in the biological sciences at the University of Washington.

Student Outcomes

The Molecular and Cellular Biology Program received degree-granting status in 1994. The majority of students, upon earning Ph.D. degrees, secure postdoctoral research positions.

Location

All around Seattle, there is an abundance of opportunity for outdoor recreation. Unsurpassed sailing, hiking, mountain climbing, skiing, and camping are all a short distance away. Because of the saltwater expanse of the Puget Sound and the mountains both to the east and to the west, Seattle enjoys a moderate climate, with precipitation averaging 32 inches per year, mostly during the winter and early spring. The city's downtown area offers many cultural and educational advantages, including theater, museums, symphony, films, and opera, while the waterfront is home to a large marketplace, galleries, and fresh seafood restaurants. The University itself sponsors many public lectures, concerts, exhibits, film festivals, and theatrical performances.

The University

The University of Washington is located in a residential section of Seattle near the downtown area. It is bordered by two lakes and is one of the largest and most scenic institutions of higher education in the country. The University is a research-intensive institution, regularly ranking first overall among public universities in externally funded research programs. It is recognized for graduate instruction of high quality, offering more than ninety graduate and professional programs that enroll more than 7,300 graduate students on campus. The Hutchinson Center's research laboratories are located near Lake Union just north of downtown Seattle. It is the largest independent cancer research center in the country.

Applying

Applicants must have completed a baccalaureate or advanced degree by the time of matriculation; degrees emphasizing biology, physical or natural sciences, and mathematics are preferred. It is advisable to take the GRE (the General Test) no later than the end of September so that scores can be recorded before the deadline (code for MCB is 0206, code for UW is 4854, on the GRE registration form). New students enter the graduate program in the autumn quarter. The deadline for completion of applications is currently December 1 of the academic year preceding entrance. Students must apply via the online application available at the MCB Program Web site (http://depts.washington.edu/mcb/applicantsinfo.php).

Correspondence and Information

Graduate Program Specialist
Molecular and Cellular Biology Program, Box 357275
University of Washington
Seattle, Washington 98195-7275
United States
Phone: 206-685-3155
Fax: 206-685-8174
E-mail: mcb@u.washington.edu
Web site: http://www.mcb-seattle.edu

THE FACULTY AND THEIR RESEARCH

UNIVERSITY OF WASHINGTON

Cancer Biology

Charles Asbury, C. Anthony Blau, Richard Gardner, Philip Greenberg, Brian Iritani, Lawrence Loeb, Nancy Maizels, Raymond Monnat, Junko Oshima, Stephen Plymate, Bradley Preston, Timothy Rose, Judit Villen, Edith Wang, Alejandro Wolf-Yadlin, Linda Wordeman.

Cell Signaling and Cell/Environment Interactions

Michael Ailion, John Aitchison, Charles Asbury, Sandra Bajjalieh, Nitin Baliga, Celeste Berg, Karol Bomsztyk, Karin Bornfeldt, Mark Bothwell, Daniel Bowen-Pope, Susan Brockerhoff, Peter Byers, Steven Carlson, William Catterall, John Clark, Trisha Davis, Jeremy Duffield, Andrew Farr, Elaine Faustman, Stanley Froehner, Clement Furlong, Richard Gardner, Michael Gelb, Cecilia Giachelli, Sharona Gordon, E. Peter Greenberg, Ted Gross, Chris Hague, Bertil Hille, Takato Imaizumi, Matthew Kaeberlein, David Kimelman, Michael Laflamme, John Leigh, Weiqing Li, Jaisri Lingappa, Qinghang Liu, Stanley McKnight, Alexey Merz, Dana Miller, Randall Moon, Neil Nathanson, Jennifer Nemhauser, Leo Pallanck, William Parks, Marilyn Parsons, Stephen Plymate, Christine Queitsch, Hannele Ruohola-Baker, Andrew Scharenberg, Lynn Schnapp, Debra Schwinn, John Scott, Daniel Storm, Rong Tian, Keiko Torii, Judit Villen, Edith Wang, Alejandro Wolf-Yadlin, Zhengui Xia, Wenqing Xu, Zipora Yablonka-Reuveni, William Zagotta.

University of Washington/Fred Hutchinson Cancer Research Center

Developmental Biology, Stem Cells, and Aging

Chris Amemiya, Celeste Berg, Olivia Bermingham-McDonogh, Mark Bothwell, Steven Carlson, Jeffrey Chamberlain, Michael Cunningham, Ajay Dhaka, Christine Disteche, Cecilia Giachelli, Marshall Horwitz, David Kimelman, Michael Laflamme, Weiqing Li, Alexey Merz, Dana Miller, William Moody, Randall Moon, Charles Murry, David Parichy, Jay Parrish, Peter Rabinovitch, David Raible, Thomas Reh, Hannele Ruohola-Baker, Billie Swalla, Keiko Torii, Barbara Wakimoto, Robert Waterston, Linda Wordeman, Zhengui Xia, Zipora Yablonka-Reuveni.

Gene Expression, Cell Cycle, and Chromosome Biology

John Aitchison, Charles Asbury, Nitin Baliga, Karol Bomsztyk, Bonita Brewer, Daniel Campbell, Christine Disteche, Maitreya Dunham, Stanley Fields, Takato Imaizumi, Houra Merrikh, Raymond Monnat, David Morris, Peter Myler, Shao-En Ong, Debra Schwinn, Keiko Torii, Edith Wang, Robert Waterston, Alan Weiner, Amy Weinmann, Zipora Yablonka-Reuveni.

Genetics, Genomics, and Evolution

Michael Ailion, Chris Amemiya, Nitin Baliga, Celeste Berg, Elhanan Borenstein, Bonita Brewer, Peter Byers, Jeffrey Chamberlain, Michael Cunningham, Trisha Davis, Christine Disteche, Aimee Dudley, Maitreya Dunham, Stanley Fields, Richard Gardner, Marshall Horwitz, Matthew Kaeberlein, Mary-Claire King, Brian Kraemer, Charles Laird, John Leigh, Weiqing Li, Mary Lidstrom, Lawrence Loeb, Houra Merrikh, Dana Miller, Raymond Monnat, Shao-En Ong, Junko Oshima, Leo Pallanck, David Parichy, Jay Parrish, Bradley Preston, Christine Queitsch, David Raible, Lalita Ramakrishnan, Debra Schwinn, Jay Shendure, David Sherman, Ilya Shmulevich, Kenneth Stuart, Billie Swalla, Bruce Tempel, Rong Tian, Keiko Torii, Judit Villen, Barbara Wakimoto, Robert Waterston, Alan Weiner, Zipora Yablonka-Reuveni.

Microbiology, Infection, and Immunity

Alan Aderem, Nitin Baliga, Elhanan Borenstein, Daniel Campbell, Lee Ann Campbell, James Champoux, Edward Clark, Brad Cookson, Nicholas Crispe, Richard Darveau, Sharon Doty, Jeremy Duffield, Keith Elkon, Ferric Fang, Pamela Fink, Michael Gale, Michael Gelb, Joan Goverman, E. Peter Greenberg, Philip Greenberg, Christoph Grundner, Jessica Hamerman, Caroline Harwood, Jay Heinecke, Helen Horton, Michael Katze, Michael Lagunoff, Mary Lidstrom, Jaisri Lingappa, Nancy Maizels, Houra Merrikh, Samuel Miller, Steven Moseley, Joseph Mougous, James Mullins, William Parks, Matthew Parsek, Marilyn Parsons, Lakshmi Rajgopal, Lalita Ramakrishnan, David Rawlings, Marilyn Roberts, Timothy Rose, Jay Shendure, David Sherman, Pradeep Singh, Jason Smith, Joseph Smith, Kelly Smith, Donald Sodora, Leonidas Stamatatos, Daniel Stetson, Kenneth Stuart, Wendy Thomas, Beth Traxler, Kenneth Urdahl, Jeffrey Vieira, Wesley Van Voorhis, Amy Weinmann, Joshua Woodward, Tuofu Zhu, Steven Ziegler.

Molecular Structure and Computational Biology

John Aitchison, Charles Asbury, David Baker, Elhanan Borenstein, James Champoux, John Clark, Michael Gelb, Jay Heinecke, Bertil Hille, Rachel Klevit, Michael MacCoss, Raymond Monnat, Peter Myler, Shao-En Ong, Ram Samudrala, Ilya Shmulevich, Wendy Thomas, Gabriele Varani, Liguo Wang, Wenqing Xu, William Zagotta, Ning Zheng.

Neuroscience

Michael Ailion, Sandra Bajjalieh, Andres Barria, Joseph Beavo, Olivia Bermingham-McDonogh, Eliot Brenowitz, Susan Brockerhoff, Steven Carlson, William Catterall, Jeffrey Chamberlain, Charles Chavkin, Horacio de la Iglesia, Ajay Dhaka, Clement Furlong, Sharona Gordon, Robert Hevner, James Hurley, Matthew Kaeberlein, Brian Kraemer, Stanley McKnight, William Moody, David Morris, Neil Nathanson, John Neumaier, Leo Pallanck, Richard Palmiter, Jay Parrish, Paul Phillips, Nicholas Poolos, David Raible, Thomas Reh, Fred Rieke, Hannele Ruohola-Baker, Debra Schwinn, Robert Steiner, Nephi Stella, Daniel Storm, Bruce Tempel, Rachel Wong, Zhengui Xia, William Zagotta.

FRED HUTCHINSON CANCER RESEARCH CENTER

Cancer Biology

Antonio Bedalov, Jason Bielas, William Carter, Bruce Clurman, Robert Eisenman, Matthew Fero, Denise Galloway, William Grady, David Hockenbery, Christopher Kemp, Hans-Peter Kiem, Paul Lampe, Peter Nelson, James Olson, Susan Parkhurst, Amanda Paulovich, Peggy Porter, Martin Prlic, James Roberts, Nina Salama, Akiko Shimamura, Julian Simon, Toshiyasu Taniguchi, Stephen Tapscott, Muneesh Tewari, Valeri Vasioukhin, Edus Warren, Cassian Yee.

Cell Signaling and Cell/Environment Interactions

Jihong Bai, Linda Breeden, William Carter, Jonathan Cooper, Robert Eisenman, Daniel Gottschling, David Hockenbery, Paul Lampe, Susan Parkhurst, Amanda Paulovich, James Priess, Mark Roth, Wenying Shou, Valeri Vasioukhin.

Developmental Biology, Stem Cells, and Aging

Jihong Bai, Jonathan Cooper, Robert Eisenman, Matthew Fero, Dan Gottschling, Hans-Peter Kiem, Cecilia Moens, Patrick Paddison, Susan Parkhurst, James Priess.

Gene Expression, Cell Cycle, and Chromosome Biology

Antonio Bedalov, Sue Biggins, Robert Bradley, Linda Breeden, Bruce Clurman, Robert Eisenman, Matthew Fero, Adam Geballe, Daniel Gottschling, William Grady, Mark Groudine, Steven Henikoff, Harmit Malik, Susan Parkhurst, Amanda Paulovich, James Roberts, Mark Roth, Gerald Smith, Stephen Tapscott, Muneesh Tewari, Toshio Tsukiyama.

Genetics, Genomics, and Evolution

Antonio Bedalov, Jesse Bloom, Robert Bradley, Michael Emerman, Adam Geballe, Daniel Gottschling, Steven Henikoff, Harmit Malik, J. Lee Nelson, Peter Nelson, Amanda Paulovich, Katie Peichel, Wenying Shou, Muneesh Tewari.

Microbiology, Infection, and Immunity

Jesse Bloom, William Carter, Lawrence Corey, Michael Emerman, David Fredricks, Denise Galloway, Adam Geballe, Tobias Hohl, Keith Jerome, Hans-Peter Kiem, Julie McElrath, Harmit Malik, Dusty Miller, Julie Overbaugh, Martin Prlic, Nina Salama, Roland Strong, Edus Warren.

Molecular Structure and Computational Biology

Jesse Bloom, Robert Bradley, Steven Hahn, Wenying Shou, Barry Stoddard, Roland Strong.

Neuroscience

Jihong Bai, Linda Buck, Cecilia Moens, James Olson.

Model organism: fruit fly.

Section 7
Computational, Systems, and Translational Biology

This section contains a directory of institutions offering graduate work in computational, systems, and translational biology. Additional information about programs listed in the directory but not augmented by an in-depth entry may be obtained by writing directly to the dean of a graduate school or chair of a department at the address given in the directory.

CONTENTS

Computational Biology

Arizona State University, College of Liberal Arts and Sciences, Department of Mathematics and Statistics, Tempe, AZ 85287-1804. Offers applied mathematics (PhD); computational biosciences (PhD); mathematics (MA, MNS, PhD); mathematics education (PhD); statistics (PhD). Part-time programs available. Terminal master's awarded for partial completion of doctoral program. *Degree requirements:* For master's, thesis or alternative, interactive Program of Study (iPOS) submitted before completing 50 percent of required credit hours; for doctorate, comprehensive exam, thesis/dissertation, interactive Program of Study (iPOS) submitted before completing 50 percent of required credit hours. *Entrance requirements:* For master's and doctorate, GRE General Test, minimum GPA of 3.0 or equivalent in last 2 years of work leading to bachelor's degree. Additional exam requirements/recommendations for international students: Required—TOEFL (minimum score 80 iBT), TOEFL, IELTS, or Pearson Test of English. Electronic applications accepted. *Expenses:* Contact institution.

Baylor College of Medicine, Graduate School of Biomedical Sciences, Program in Structural and Computational Biology and Molecular Biophysics, Houston, TX 77030-3498. Offers PhD, MD/PhD. MD/PhD offered jointly with Rice University and University of Houston. *Faculty:* 84 full-time (10 women). *Students:* 38 full-time (12 women); includes 4 minority (1 Black or African American, non-Hispanic/Latino; 2 Asian, non-Hispanic/Latino; 1 Hispanic/Latino), 19 international. Average age 28. 74 applicants, 14% accepted, 8 enrolled. In 2011, 6 doctorates awarded. *Degree requirements:* For doctorate, thesis/dissertation, public defense. *Entrance requirements:* For doctorate, GRE General Test, GRE Subject Test (strongly recommended), minimum GPA of 3.0. Additional exam requirements/recommendations for international students: Required—TOEFL. *Application deadline:* For fall admission, 1/1 for domestic students. Application fee: $0. Electronic applications accepted. *Financial support:* In 2011–12, 38 students received support, including 21 fellowships with full tuition reimbursements available (averaging $29,000 per year), 17 research assistantships with full tuition reimbursements available (averaging $29,000 per year); career-related internships or fieldwork, Federal Work-Study, institutionally sponsored loans, health care benefits, and scholarships (to all students unless there are grant funds available to pay tuition) also available. Financial award applicants required to submit FAFSA. *Faculty research:* Computational biology, structural biology, biophysics. *Unit head:* Dr. Wah Chiu, Director, 713-798-6985. *Application contact:* Amber Eakin, Administrative Coordinator, 713-798-5197, Fax: 713-798-6325, E-mail: ameakin@bcm.edu.

Carnegie Mellon University, Joint CMU-Pitt PhD Program in Computational Biology, Pittsburgh, PA 15213-3891. Offers PhD.

Carnegie Mellon University, Mellon College of Science, Department of Biological Sciences, Program in Computational Biology, Pittsburgh, PA 15213-3891. Offers MS. *Entrance requirements:* For master's, GRE General Test, GRE Subject Test, interview.

Claremont Graduate University, Graduate Programs, School of Mathematical Sciences, Claremont, CA 91711-6160. Offers computational and systems biology (PhD); computational mathematics and numerical analysis (MA, MS); computational science (PhD); engineering and industrial applied mathematics (PhD); mathematics (PhD); operations research and statistics (MA, MS); physical applied mathematics (MA, MS); pure mathematics (MA, MS); scientific computing (MA, MS); systems and control theory (MA, MS). Part-time programs available. *Faculty:* 6 full-time (0 women), 1 part-time/adjunct (0 women). *Students:* 52 full-time (16 women), 24 part-time (9 women); includes 25 minority (3 Black or African American, non-Hispanic/Latino; 10 Asian, non-Hispanic/Latino; 11 Hispanic/Latino; 1 Two or more races, non-Hispanic/Latino), 17 international. Average age 33. In 2011, 15 master's, 3 doctorates awarded. Terminal master's awarded for partial completion of doctoral program. *Entrance requirements:* For master's and doctorate, GRE General Test. Additional exam requirements/recommendations for international students: Required—TOEFL (minimum score 550 paper-based; 213 computer-based; 80 iBT). *Application deadline:* For fall admission, 2/1 priority date for domestic students. Applications are processed on a rolling basis. Application fee: $60. Electronic applications accepted. *Expenses: Tuition:* Full-time $36,374; part-time $1581 per unit. *Required fees:* $165 per semester. *Financial support:* Fellowships, research assistantships, Federal Work-Study, institutionally sponsored loans, scholarships/grants, and tuition waivers (full and partial) available. Support available to part-time students. Financial award application deadline: 2/15; financial award applicants required to submit FAFSA. *Unit head:* Ellis Cumberbatch, Dean, 909-607-3369, Fax: 909-607-8261, E-mail: ellis.cumberbatch@cgu.edu. *Application contact:* Susan Townzen, Program Coordinator, 909-621-8080, Fax: 909-607-8261, E-mail: susan.n.townzen@cgu.edu. Web site: http://www.cgu.edu/pages/168.asp.

Cornell University, Graduate School, Graduate Fields of Agriculture and Life Sciences, Field of Computational Biology, Ithaca, NY 14853-0001. Offers computational behavioral biology (PhD); computational biology (PhD); computational cell biology (PhD); computational ecology (PhD); computational macromolecular biology (PhD); computational organismal biology (PhD). *Faculty:* 37 full-time (5 women). *Students:* 22 full-time (8 women); includes 4 minority (3 Asian, non-Hispanic/Latino; 1 Native Hawaiian or other Pacific Islander, non-Hispanic/Latino), 9 international. Average age 26. 145 applicants, 7% accepted, 10 enrolled. In 2011, 2 doctorates awarded. *Degree requirements:* For doctorate, comprehensive exam, thesis/dissertation, 2 semesters of teaching experience. *Entrance requirements:* For doctorate, GRE General Test, GRE Subject Test (biology), 2 letters of recommendation. Additional exam requirements/recommendations for international students: Required—TOEFL (minimum score 550 paper-based; 213 computer-based; 77 iBT). *Application deadline:* For fall admission, 2/1 priority date for domestic students. Application fee: $95. Electronic applications accepted. *Financial support:* In 2011–12, 17 fellowships with full tuition reimbursements, 4 research assistantships with full tuition reimbursements, 1 teaching assistantship with full tuition reimbursement were awarded; institutionally sponsored loans, scholarships/grants, health care benefits, tuition waivers (full and partial), and unspecified assistantships also available. Financial award applicants required to submit FAFSA. *Faculty research:* Computational behavioral biology, computational biology, computational cell biology, computational ecology, computational genetics, computational macromolecular biology, computational organismal biology. *Unit head:* Dr. Andrew Clark, Director of Graduate Studies, 607-255-5488, E-mail: ac347@cornell.edu. *Application contact:* Graduate School Application Requests, 607-255-5816, E-mail: gradadmissions@cornell.edu. Web site: http://www.gradschool.cornell.edu/fields.php?id-4A.

Florida State University, The Graduate School, College of Arts and Sciences, Program in Molecular Biophysics, Tallahassee, FL 32306. Offers computational structural biology (PhD); molecular biophysics (PhD). *Faculty:* 50 full-time (8 women). *Students:* 24 full-time (10 women); includes 7 minority (4 Asian, non-Hispanic/Latino; 3 Hispanic/Latino), 8 international. Average age 28. 35 applicants, 29% accepted, 5 enrolled. In 2011, 3 doctorates awarded. *Degree requirements:* For doctorate, comprehensive exam, thesis/dissertation, teaching 1 term in professor's major department. *Entrance requirements:* For doctorate, GRE General Test. Additional exam requirements/recommendations for international students: Required—TOEFL (minimum score 600 paper-based; 250 computer-based; 90 iBT). *Application deadline:* For fall admission, 1/15 for domestic students, 2/15 for international students. Applications are processed on a rolling basis. Application fee: $30. Electronic applications accepted. *Expenses:* Tuition, state resident: full-time $9474; part-time $350.88 per credit hour. Tuition, nonresident: full-time $16,236; part-time $601.34 per credit hour. *Required fees:* $630 per semester. One-time fee: $20. Tuition and fees vary according to course load and campus/location. *Financial support:* In 2011–12, 23 students received support, including 1 fellowship with partial tuition reimbursement available (averaging $10,000 per year), 19 research assistantships with partial tuition reimbursements available (averaging $22,050 per year), 4 teaching assistantships with partial tuition reimbursements available (averaging $22,050 per year); scholarships/grants, health care benefits, and unspecified assistantships also available. Financial award applicants required to submit FAFSA. *Faculty research:* Protein and nucleic acid structure and function, membrane protein structure, computational biophysics, 3-D image reconstruction. *Total annual research expenditures:* $1.7 million. *Unit head:* Dr. Hong Li, Director, 850-644-6785, Fax: 850-644-7244, E-mail: hongli@sb.fsu.edu. *Application contact:* Lyn Kittle, Academic Coordinator, Graduate Programs, 850-644-1012, Fax: 850-644-7244, E-mail: lkittle@fsu.edu. Web site: http://www.sb.fsu.edu/mob/.

George Mason University, College of Science, School of Systems Biology, Fairfax, VA 22030. Offers bioinformatics and computational biology (MS, PhD, Graduate Certificate); biology (MS); biosciences (PhD). *Faculty:* 15 full-time (5 women), 1 part-time/adjunct. *Students:* 68 full-time (25 women), 66 part-time (36 women); includes 33 minority (3 Black or African American, non-Hispanic/Latino; 28 Asian, non-Hispanic/Latino; 1 Hispanic/Latino; 1 Two or more races, non-Hispanic/Latino), 40 international. Average age 32. 179 applicants, 49% accepted, 34 enrolled. In 2011, 23 master's, 13 doctorates, 1 other advanced degree awarded. *Degree requirements:* For master's, research project or thesis. *Entrance requirements:* For master's, GRE, resume; 3 letters of recommendation; expanded goals statement; 2 copies of official transcripts; bachelor's degree in related field with minimum GPA of 3.0 in last 60 hours; for doctorate, GRE, self-assessment form; resume; 3 letters of recommendation; expanded goals statement; 2 copies of official transcripts; bachelor's degree in related field with minimum GPA of 3.0 in last 60 hours; for Graduate Certificate, resume; 2 copies of official transcripts. Additional exam requirements/recommendations for international students: Required—TOEFL (minimum score 570 paper-based; 230 computer-based; 88 iBT), IELTS, Pearson Test of English. Application fee: $65 ($80 for international students). Electronic applications accepted. *Expenses:* Tuition, state resident: full-time $8750; part-time $364.58 per credit. Tuition, nonresident: full-time $24,092; part-time $1003.83 per credit. *Required fees:* $2514; $104.75 per credit. *Financial support:* In 2011–12, 44 students received support, including 6 fellowships with full tuition reimbursements available (averaging $18,000 per year), 9 research assistantships with full and partial tuition reimbursements available (averaging $13,682 per year), 29 teaching assistantships with full and partial tuition reimbursements available (averaging $12,559 per year); career-related internships or fieldwork, Federal Work-Study, scholarships/grants, unspecified assistantships, and health care benefits (full-time research or teaching assistantship recipients) also available. Support available to part-time students. Financial award application deadline: 3/1; financial award applicants required to submit FAFSA. *Total annual research expenditures:* $1.3 million. *Unit head:* Dr. James D. Willett, Director, 703-993-8311, Fax: 703-993-8976, E-mail: jwillett@gmu.edu. *Application contact:* Diane St. Germain, Graduate Student Services Coordinator, 703-993-4263, Fax: 703-993-8976, E-mail: dstgerma@gmu.edu. Web site: http://ssb.gmu.edu/.

Iowa State University of Science and Technology, Bioinformatics and Computational Biology Program, Ames, IA 50011-3260. Offers MS, PhD. *Degree requirements:* For doctorate, thesis/dissertation. *Entrance requirements:* For master's and doctorate, GRE General Test. Additional exam requirements/recommendations for international students: Recommended—TOEFL, IELTS. *Application deadline:* For fall admission, 1/15 priority date for domestic students, 1/15 for international students; for spring admission, 10/15 for domestic and international students. Application fee: $40 ($90 for international students). Electronic applications accepted. *Faculty research:* Functional and structural genomics, genome evolution, macromolecular structure and function, mathematical biology and biological statistics, metabolic and developmental networks. *Unit head:* Dr. Julie Dickerson, Chair, Supervising Committee, 515-294-5122, Fax: 515-294-6790, E-mail: bcb@iastate.edu. *Application contact:* Information Contact, 515-294-5836, Fax: 515-294-2592, E-mail: grad_admissions@iastate.edu. Web site: http://www.bcb.iastate.edu/.

Keck Graduate Institute of Applied Life Sciences, Bioscience Program, Claremont, CA 91711. Offers applied life science (PhD); bioscience (MBS); bioscience management (Certificate); computational systems biology (PhD). *Degree requirements:* For master's, comprehensive exam, project. *Entrance requirements:* For master's, GRE General Test or MCAT. Additional exam requirements/recommendations for international students: Required—TOEFL. Electronic applications accepted. *Faculty research:* Computational biology, drug discovery and development, molecular and cellular biology, biomedical engineering, biomaterials and tissue engineering.

Massachusetts Institute of Technology, School of Engineering and School of Science, Program in Computational and Systems Biology, Cambridge, MA 02139. Offers PhD. *Faculty:* 100 full-time (19 women). *Students:* 39 full-time (14 women); includes 11 minority (2 Black or African American, non-Hispanic/Latino; 1 American Indian or Alaska Native, non-Hispanic/Latino; 7 Asian, non-Hispanic/Latino; 1 Hispanic/Latino), 13 international. Average age 26. 163 applicants, 12% accepted, 7 enrolled. In 2011, 6 doctorates awarded. *Degree requirements:* For doctorate, comprehensive exam, thesis/dissertation. *Entrance requirements:* For doctorate, GRE General Test. Additional exam requirements/recommendations for international students: Required—IELTS (minimum score 6). *Application deadline:* For fall admission, 12/1 for domestic and international students. Application fee: $75. Electronic applications accepted. *Expenses: Tuition:* Full-time $40,460; part-time $630 per credit hour. *Required fees:* $272. *Financial support:* In 2011–12, 38 students received support, including 17 fellowships (averaging $37,900 per year), 22 research assistantships (averaging $32,200 per year); teaching assistantships, Federal Work-Study, institutionally sponsored loans, scholarships/grants, traineeships, health care benefits, and unspecified assistantships also available. *Faculty research:* Computational biology and bioinformatics, biological design and synthetic biology, gene and protein networks, systems biology of cancer, nanobiology and microsystems. *Unit head:* Prof. Douglas A. Lauffenberger, Director, 617-252-1629, E-mail: csbi@mit.edu. *Application contact:* Academic Office, 617-324-0055, Fax: 617-253-8699, E-mail: csbphd@mit.edu. Web site: http://csbi.mit.edu/.

Massachusetts Institute of Technology, School of Science, Department of Biology, Cambridge, MA 02139. Offers biochemistry (PhD); biological oceanography (PhD); biology (PhD); biophysical chemistry and molecular structure (PhD); cell biology (PhD); computational and systems biology (PhD); developmental biology (PhD); genetics (PhD); immunology (PhD); microbiology (PhD); molecular biology (PhD); neurobiology (PhD). *Faculty:* 58 full-time (15 women). *Students:* 248 full-time (129 women); includes 69 minority (5 Black or African American, non-Hispanic/Latino; 1 American Indian or Alaska Native, non-Hispanic/Latino; 25 Asian, non-Hispanic/Latino; 31 Hispanic/Latino; 7 Two or more races, non-Hispanic/Latino), 36 international. Average age 26. 698 applicants, 15% accepted, 44 enrolled. In 2011, 38 doctorates awarded. *Degree requirements:* For doctorate, comprehensive exam, thesis/dissertation. *Entrance requirements:* For doctorate, GRE General Test. Additional exam requirements/recommendations for international students: Required—TOEFL (minimum score 577 paper-based; 233 computer-based), IELTS (minimum score 6.5). *Application deadline:* For fall admission, 12/1 for domestic and international students. Application fee: $75. Electronic applications accepted. *Expenses: Tuition:* Full-time $40,460; part-time $630 per credit hour. *Required fees:* $272. *Financial support:* In 2011–12, 214 students received support, including 129 fellowships (averaging $33,200 per year), 117 research assistantships (averaging $32,900 per year); teaching assistantships, Federal Work-Study, institutionally sponsored loans, scholarships/grants, traineeships, health care benefits, and unspecified assistantships also available. *Faculty research:* Cellular, developmental and molecular (plant and animal) biology; biochemistry, bioengineering, biophysics and structural biology; classical and molecular genetics; immunology and microbiology; cancer biology, molecular medicine, neurobiology and human disease; computational and systems biology. *Total annual research expenditures:* $53.6 million. *Unit head:* Prof. Tania A. Baker, Head, 617-253-4701, E-mail: mitbio@mit.edu. *Application contact:* Biology Education Office, 617-253-3717, Fax: 617-258-9329, E-mail: gradbio@mit.edu. Web site: https://biology.mit.edu/.

New Jersey Institute of Technology, Office of Graduate Studies, College of Science and Liberal Arts, Department of Mathematical Science, Program in Computational Biology, Newark, NJ 07102. Offers MS. Part-time and evening/weekend programs available. *Students:* Average age 24. 4 applicants, 0% accepted, 0 enrolled. In 2011, 1 master's awarded. *Entrance requirements:* For master's, GRE General Test. Additional exam requirements/recommendations for international students: Required—TOEFL (minimum score 550 paper-based; 213 computer-based; 79 iBT). *Application deadline:* For fall admission, 6/1 priority date for domestic students, 5/1 for international students; for spring admission, 11/15 for domestic and international students. Applications are processed on a rolling basis. Application fee: $65. Electronic applications accepted. *Expenses:* Tuition, state resident: full-time $7980; part-time $867 per credit. Tuition, nonresident: full-time $11,336; part-time $1196 per credit. *Required fees:* $230 per credit. *Financial support:* Fellowships with full and partial tuition reimbursements, research assistantships with full and partial tuition reimbursements, teaching assistantships with full and partial tuition reimbursements, career-related internships or fieldwork, Federal Work-Study, institutionally sponsored loans, and unspecified assistantships available. Financial award application deadline: 3/15. *Faculty research:* Technological, computational, and mathematical aspects of biology and bioengineering. *Unit head:* Dr. Daljit S. Ahluwalia, Chair, 973-596-8465, E-mail: daljit.ahluwalia@njit.edu. *Application contact:* Kathryn Kelly, Director of Admissions, 973-596-3300, Fax: 973-596-3461, E-mail: admissions@njit.edu.

New Jersey Institute of Technology, Office of Graduate Studies, College of Science and Liberal Arts, Federated Department of Biological Sciences, Newark, NJ 07102. Offers biology (MS, PhD); computational biology (MS). Part-time and evening/weekend programs available. *Faculty:* 10 full-time (3 women). *Students:* 9 full-time (5 women), 7 part-time (4 women); includes 2 minority (1 Black or African American, non-Hispanic/Latino; 1 Asian, non-Hispanic/Latino), 9 international. Average age 28. 97 applicants, 28% accepted, 3 enrolled. *Entrance requirements:* For master's, GRE General Test. Additional exam requirements/recommendations for international students: Required—TOEFL (minimum score 550 paper-based; 213 computer-based; 79 iBT). *Application deadline:* For fall admission, 6/1 priority date for domestic students, 5/1 for international students; for spring admission, 11/15 for domestic and international students. Applications are processed on a rolling basis. Application fee: $65. Electronic applications accepted. *Expenses:* Tuition, state resident: full-time $7980; part-time $867 per credit. Tuition, nonresident: full-time $11,336; part-time $1196 per credit. *Required fees:* $230 per credit. *Financial support:* Fellowships with full and partial tuition reimbursements, research assistantships with full and partial tuition reimbursements, teaching assistantships with full and partial tuition reimbursements, career-related internships or fieldwork, Federal Work-Study, institutionally sponsored loans, and unspecified assistantships available. Financial award application deadline: 1/15. *Total annual research expenditures:* $353,727. *Unit head:* Dr. Jorge P. Golowasch, Chair, 973-596-5404, E-mail: orge.p.golowasch@njit.edu. *Application contact:* Kathryn Kelly, Director of Admissions, 973-596-3300, Fax: 973-596-3461, E-mail: admissions@njit.edu. Web site: http://biology.njit.edu/.

New York University, Graduate School of Arts and Science, Department of Biology, Program in Computational Biology, New York, NY 10012-1019. Offers PhD. *Students:* 21 full-time (8 women), 6 part-time (3 women); includes 2 minority (both Asian, non-Hispanic/Latino), 8 international. Average age 30. 74 applicants, 14% accepted, 7 enrolled. In 2011, 2 doctorates awarded. *Entrance requirements:* For doctorate, GRE. Additional exam requirements/recommendations for international students: Required—TOEFL. *Application deadline:* For fall admission, 12/1 for domestic and international students. Application fee: $90. *Financial support:* Fellowships, research assistantships, teaching assistantships, Federal Work-Study, institutionally sponsored loans, scholarships/grants, health care benefits, and unspecified assistantships available. *Unit head:* Mike Shelley, Director, 212-998-4856, Fax: 212-995-4121, E-mail: fas.computational.biology@nyu.edu. *Application contact:* Brittany Shields, Graduate Department Administrator, 212-998-4856, Fax: 212-995-4121, E-mail: fas.computational.biology@nyu.edu.

New York University, School of Medicine, New York, NY 10012-1019. Offers biomedical sciences (PhD), including biomedical imaging, cellular and molecular biology, computational biology, developmental genetics, medical and molecular parasitology, microbiology, molecular oncobiology and immunology, neuroscience and physiology, pathobiology, pharmacology, structural biology; clinical investigation (MS); medicine (MD); MD/MA; MD/MPA; MD/MS; MD/PhD. *Accreditation:* LCME/AMA (one or more programs are accredited). *Degree requirements:* For master's, comprehensive exam, thesis; for doctorate, comprehensive exam (for some programs), thesis/dissertation (for some programs). *Entrance requirements:* For doctorate, MCAT (for MD). Additional exam requirements/recommendations for international students: Required—TOEFL. *Expenses:* Contact institution. *Faculty research:* AIDS, cancer, neuroscience, molecular biology, neuroscience, cell biology and molecular genetics, structural biology, microbial pathogenesis and host defense, pharmacology, molecular oncology and immunology.

New York University, School of Medicine and Graduate School of Arts and Science, Sackler Institute of Graduate Biomedical Sciences, Program in Computational Biology, New York, NY 10012-1019. Offers PhD. *Students:* 8 full-time (4 women); includes 3 minority (all Asian, non-Hispanic/Latino), 1 international. *Unit head:* Dr. Joel D. Oppenheim, Senior Associate Dean for Graduate Studies, 212-263-8001, Fax: 212-263-7600. *Application contact:* Lisabeth Greene, Program Coordinator, 212-263-5648, Fax: 212-263-7600, E-mail: sackler-info@med.nyu.edu. Web site: http://cob.as.nyu.edu/page/home.

Oregon Health & Science University, School of Medicine, Graduate Programs in Medicine, Department of Medical Informatics and Clinical Epidemiology, Portland, OR 97239-3098. Offers clinical informatics (MS, PhD, Certificate); computational biology (MS, PhD); health information management (Certificate). Part-time programs available. Postbaccalaureate distance learning degree programs offered (minimal on-campus study). *Faculty:* 10 full-time (3 women), 13 part-time/adjunct (8 women). *Students:* 40 full-time (18 women), 151 part-time (61 women); includes 46 minority (7 Black or African American, non-Hispanic/Latino; 4 American Indian or Alaska Native, non-Hispanic/Latino; 23 Asian, non-Hispanic/Latino; 2 Hispanic/Latino; 1 Native Hawaiian or other Pacific Islander, non-Hispanic/Latino; 9 Two or more races, non-Hispanic/Latino), 9 international. Average age 41. 78 applicants, 44% accepted, 34 enrolled. In 2011, 12 master's, 6 doctorates, 32 other advanced degrees awarded. Terminal master's awarded for partial completion of doctoral program. *Degree requirements:* For master's, thesis optional, thesis or capstone project; for doctorate, comprehensive exam, thesis/dissertation, qualifying exam. *Entrance requirements:* For master's and doctorate, GRE General Test (minimum scores: 153 Verbal/148 Quantitative/4.5 Analytical), coursework in computer programming, human anatomy and physiology. Additional exam requirements/recommendations for international students: Required—TOEFL. *Application deadline:* For fall admission, 12/1 for domestic students; for winter admission, 11/1 for domestic students; for spring admission, 2/1 for domestic students. Applications are processed on a rolling basis. Application fee: $70. Electronic applications accepted. *Expenses:* Contact institution. *Financial support:* Fellowships with full tuition reimbursements, research assistantships, Federal Work-Study, institutionally sponsored loans, scholarships/grants, health care benefits, and full tuition and stipends for PhD students available. Financial award application deadline: 3/1; financial award applicants required to submit FAFSA. *Faculty research:* Use of knowledge-based information by healthcare practitioners and researchers, application of text mining and machine learning techniques to the scientific literature curated databases, examining factors that affect quality of data collected in healthcare databases and the subsequent uses of that data, statistical analysis of microarray data with emphasis on time series analysis, computational biology and automatic speech recognition. *Unit head:* Andrea Ilg, 503-494-2547, E-mail: informat@ohsu.edu. *Application contact:* Lauren Ludwig, 503-494-2547, E-mail: informat@ohsu.edu. Web site: http://www.ohsu.edu/dmice/.

Oregon State University, Graduate School, College of Science, Department of Botany and Plant Pathology, Corvallis, OR 97331. Offers applied systematics (MA, MAIS, MS, PhD); ecology (MA, MAIS, MS, PhD); genetics (MA, MAIS, MS, PhD); genomics and computational biology (MA, MAIS, MS, PhD); molecular and cellular biology (MA, MAIS, MS, PhD); mycology (MA, MAIS, MS, PhD); plant pathology (MA, MAIS, MS, PhD); plant physiology (MA, MAIS, MS, PhD); systematics (MA, MAIS, MS, PhD). Part-time programs available. *Degree requirements:* For master's, variable foreign language requirement, thesis optional; for doctorate, thesis/dissertation. *Entrance requirements:* For master's and doctorate, GRE General Test, minimum GPA of 3.0 in last 90 hours. *Faculty research:* Plant ecology, plant molecular biology, systematic botany, epidemiology, host-pathogen interaction.

Princeton University, Graduate School, Department of Molecular Biology, Princeton, NJ 08544-1019. Offers PhD. *Degree requirements:* For doctorate, thesis/dissertation. *Entrance requirements:* For doctorate, GRE General Test. Additional exam requirements/recommendations for international students: Required—TOEFL (minimum score 600 paper-based; 250 computer-based). Electronic applications accepted. *Faculty research:* Genetics, virology, biochemistry.

Rutgers, The State University of New Jersey, Camden, Graduate School of Arts and Sciences, Program in Computational and Integrative Biology, Camden, NJ 08102-1401. Offers MS, PhD. *Degree requirements:* For doctorate, original research, oral defense. *Entrance requirements:* For master's and doctorate, GRE General Test; GRE Subject Test (recommended), transcripts, personal statement, three letters of recommendation. Additional exam requirements/recommendations for international students: Required—TOEFL. Electronic applications accepted.

Rutgers, The State University of New Jersey, Newark, Graduate School, Program in Computational Biology, Newark, NJ 07102. Offers MS. Program offered jointly with New Jersey Institute of Technology. *Entrance requirements:* For master's, GRE, minimum undergraduate B average. Additional exam requirements/recommendations for international students: Required—TOEFL.

Rutgers, The State University of New Jersey, New Brunswick, Graduate School-New Brunswick, BioMaPS Institute for Quantitative Biology, Piscataway, NJ 08854-8097. Offers computational biology and molecular biophysics (PhD). *Degree requirements:* For doctorate, comprehensive exam, thesis/dissertation. *Entrance requirements:* For doctorate, GRE. Additional exam requirements/recommendations for international students: Required—TOEFL. Electronic applications accepted. *Faculty research:* Structural biology, systems biology, bioinformatics, translational medicine, genomics.

University of California, Irvine, School of Biological Sciences, Program in Mathematical, Computational and Systems Biology, Irvine, CA 92697. Offers PhD. *Students:* 10 full-time (3 women); includes 4 minority (1 Black or African American, non-Hispanic/Latino; 2 Asian, non-Hispanic/Latino; 1 Hispanic/Latino), 2 international. Average age 24. 93 applicants, 23% accepted, 9 enrolled. Application fee: $80 ($100 for international students). *Unit head:* Prof. Frederic Yui-Ming Wan, Director, 949-824-5529, Fax: 949-824-7993, E-mail: fwan@math.uci.edu. *Application contact:* Prof. R. Michael Mulligan, Associate Dean, 949-824-8433, Fax: 949-824-4709, E-mail: rmmullig@uci.edu. Web site: http://mcsb.bio.uci.edu/.

University of Colorado Denver, College of Liberal Arts and Sciences, Department of Mathematical and Statistical Sciences, Denver, CO 80217. Offers applied mathematics (MS, PhD), including applied mathematics, applied probability (MS), applied statistics (MS), computational biology, computational mathematics (PhD), discrete mathematics, finite geometry (PhD), mathematics education (PhD), mathematics of engineering and science (MS), numerical analysis, operations research (MS), optimization and operations research (PhD), probability (PhD), statistics (PhD). Part-time programs available. *Faculty:* 26 full-time (4 women), 2 part-time/adjunct (1 woman). *Students:* 44 full-time (14 women), 14 part-time (5 women); includes 6 minority (4 Asian, non-Hispanic/Latino; 2 Hispanic/Latino), 10 international. Average age 33. 66 applicants, 79% accepted, 17 enrolled. In 2011, 6 master's, 6 doctorates awarded. *Degree requirements:* For master's, comprehensive exam, thesis optional, 30 hours of course work with minimum GPA of 3.0; for doctorate, comprehensive exam, thesis/dissertation. *Entrance requirements:* For master's and doctorate, GRE General Test; GRE Subject Test in math (recommended), 30 hours of course work in mathematics (24 of which must be upper-division mathematics), minimum GPA of 3.0. Additional exam requirements/recommendations for international students: Required—TOEFL (minimum score 525

paper-based; 192 computer-based; 71 iBT). *Application deadline:* For fall admission, 4/1 for domestic students, 3/1 for international students; for spring admission, 11/1 for domestic students, 10/1 for international students. Application fee: $50 ($75 for international students). Electronic applications accepted. *Financial support:* Fellowships with partial tuition reimbursements, research assistantships with full tuition reimbursements, teaching assistantships with full tuition reimbursements, Federal Work-Study, scholarships/grants, and unspecified assistantships available. Financial award application deadline: 4/1; financial award applicants required to submit FAFSA. *Faculty research:* Computational mathematics, computational biology, discrete mathematics and geometry, probability and statistics, optimization. *Unit head:* Dr. Stephen Billups, Graduate Chair, 303-556-4814, E-mail: stephen.billups@ucdenver.edu. *Application contact:* Lisa Herbert, Graduate Program Assistant, 303-556-2341, E-mail: lisa.herbert@ucdenver.edu. Web site: http://www.ucdenver.edu/academics/colleges/CLAS/Departments/math/Pages/MathStats.aspx.

University of Colorado Denver, School of Medicine, Program in Computational Bioscience, Aurora, CO 80045-0511. Offers PhD. Part-time programs available. *Students:* 13 full-time (4 women), 1 part-time; includes 2 minority (both Black or African American, non-Hispanic/Latino), 2 international. Average age 32. 13 applicants, 23% accepted, 3 enrolled. *Degree requirements:* For doctorate, comprehensive exam, thesis/dissertation, minimum of 30 semester credit hours of course work and 30 semester hours of doctoral dissertation research. *Entrance requirements:* For doctorate, GRE General Test, GRE Subject Test in computer science (recommended), demonstrated adequate computational and biological backgrounds, interviews for finalists. Additional exam requirements/recommendations for international students: Required—TOEFL. *Application deadline:* For fall admission, 12/1 for domestic students. Application fee: $65. Electronic applications accepted. *Expenses:* Contact institution. *Financial support:* Fellowships, research assistantships, teaching assistantships, scholarships/grants, health care benefits, tuition waivers (full), unspecified assistantships, and stipend available. Financial award application deadline: 4/1; financial award applicants required to submit FAFSA. *Faculty research:* Physical simulations of biological macromolecules and their dynamics, gene expression array analysis and interpretation of expression data, natural language processing in the biomedical literature, metabolic and signaling pathway analysis, evolutionary reconstruction and disease gene finding. *Unit head:* Dr. Larry Hunter, Director, 303-724-3574, E-mail: larry.hunter@ucdenver.edu. *Application contact:* Liz Pruett, Student Coordinator, 303-724-3399, E-mail: liz.pruett@ucdenver.edu. Web site: http://compbio.ucdenver.edu/.

University of Idaho, College of Graduate Studies, Program in Bioinformatics and Computational Biology, Moscow, ID 83844-3051. Offers MS, PhD. *Faculty:* 11 full-time. *Students:* 12 full-time, 4 part-time. Average age 29. *Entrance requirements:* For master's, GRE, minimum GPA of 2.8. *Application deadline:* For fall admission, 8/1 for domestic students; for spring admission, 12/15 for domestic students. Applications are processed on a rolling basis. Application fee: $60. Electronic applications accepted. *Expenses:* Tuition, state resident: full-time $3874; part-time $334 per credit hour. Tuition, nonresident: full-time $16,394; part-time $861 per credit hour. *Required fees:* $2808; $99 per credit hour. Tuition and fees vary according to program. *Financial support:* Applicants required to submit FAFSA. *Unit head:* Dr. Paul Joyce, Director, 208-885-6010, E-mail: bcb@uidaho.edu. *Application contact:* Erick Larson, Director of Graduate Admissions, 208-885-4723, E-mail: gadms@uidaho.edu. Web site: http://www.uidaho.edu/cogs/bcb.

University of Illinois at Urbana–Champaign, Graduate College, College of Liberal Arts and Sciences, School of Molecular and Cellular Biology, Center for Biophysics and Computational Biology, Champaign, IL 61820. Offers MS, PhD. *Students:* 68 full-time (13 women), 4 part-time (2 women); includes 9 minority (6 Asian, non-Hispanic/Latino; 2 Hispanic/Latino; 1 Two or more races, non-Hispanic/Latino), 44 international. 93 applicants, 9% accepted, 8 enrolled. In 2011, 2 master's, 7 doctorates awarded. *Entrance requirements:* For doctorate, GRE, minimum GPA of 3.0. Additional exam requirements/recommendations for international students: Required—TOEFL. *Application deadline:* Applications are processed on a rolling basis. Application fee: $75 ($90 for international students). Electronic applications accepted. *Financial support:* In 2011–12, 14 fellowships, 60 research assistantships, 22 teaching assistantships were awarded; tuition waivers (full and partial) also available. *Unit head:* Robert M. Clegg, Director, 217-244-8143, Fax: 217-244-3186, E-mail: rclegg@illinois.edu. *Application contact:* Cynthia Dodds, Office Administrator, 217-333-1630, Fax: 217-244-6615, E-mail: dodds@illinois.edu. Web site: http://www.life.illinois.edu/biophysics/.

The University of Iowa, Graduate College, Program in Informatics, Iowa City, IA 52242-1316. Offers bioinformatics and computational biology (Certificate); health informatics (MS, PhD, Certificate); information science (MS, PhD, Certificate). *Degree requirements:* For master's, thesis optional; for doctorate, comprehensive exam, thesis/dissertation. *Entrance requirements:* For master's and doctorate, GRE General Test, minimum GPA of 3.0. Additional exam requirements/recommendations for international students: Required—TOEFL (minimum score 550 paper-based; 213 computer-based; 81 iBT). Electronic applications accepted.

University of Maryland, College Park, Academic Affairs, College of Computer, Mathematical and Natural Sciences, Department of Biology, PhD Program in Biological Sciences, College Park, MD 20742. Offers behavior, ecology, evolution, and systematics (PhD); computational biology, bioinformatics, and genomics (PhD); molecular and cellular biology (PhD); physiological systems (PhD). *Students:* 68 full-time (41 women), 4 part-time (2 women); includes 13 minority (3 Black or African American, non-Hispanic/Latino; 4 Asian, non-Hispanic/Latino; 5 Hispanic/Latino; 1 Two or more races, non-Hispanic/Latino), 21 international. 380 applicants, 15% accepted, 22 enrolled. *Degree requirements:* For doctorate, comprehensive exam, thesis/dissertation, present thesis work in seminar. *Entrance requirements:* For doctorate, GRE General Test; GRE Subject Test in biology (recommended), academic transcripts, statement of purpose/research interests, 3 letters of recommendation. Additional exam requirements/recommendations for international students: Required—TOEFL. *Application deadline:* For fall admission, 12/15 for domestic and international students. Applications are processed on a rolling basis. Application fee: $75. Electronic applications accepted. *Expenses:* Tuition, state resident: part-time $525 per credit hour. Tuition, nonresident: part-time $1131 per credit hour. *Required fees:* $386.31 per term. Tuition and fees vary according to program. *Financial support:* In 2011–12, 11 fellowships with full and partial tuition reimbursements (averaging $14,406 per year), 16 research assistantships (averaging $19,495 per year), 41 teaching assistantships (averaging $18,734 per year) were awarded. *Unit head:* Dr. Barbara Thorne, Director, 301-405-6905, E-mail: bthorne@umd.edu. *Application contact:* Dr. Charles A. Caramello, Dean of Graduate School, 301-405-0358, Fax: 301-314-9305. Web site: http://bisi.umd.edu/biologicalsciencesgraduateprogrambisi.

University of Massachusetts Worcester, Graduate School of Biomedical Sciences, Worcester, MA 01655-0115. Offers biochemistry and molecular pharmacology (PhD); bioinformatics and computational biology (PhD); cancer biology (PhD); cell biology (PhD); clinical and population health research (PhD); clinical investigation (MS); immunology and virology (PhD); interdisciplinary graduate program (PhD); molecular genetics and microbiology (PhD); neuroscience (PhD); DVM/PhD; MD/PhD. *Faculty:* 1,427 full-time (526 women), 309 part-time/adjunct (196 women). *Students:* 416 full-time (225 women); includes 47 minority (12 Black or African American, non-Hispanic/Latino; 32 Asian, non-Hispanic/Latino; 3 Hispanic/Latino), 144 international. Average age 29. 623 applicants, 17% accepted, 54 enrolled. In 2011, 5 master's, 63 doctorates awarded. Terminal master's awarded for partial completion of doctoral program. *Degree requirements:* For master's, comprehensive exam, thesis; for doctorate, comprehensive exam, thesis/dissertation. *Entrance requirements:* For master's, bachelor's degree; for doctorate, GRE General Test. Additional exam requirements/recommendations for international students: Required—TOEFL (minimum score 600 paper-based; 250 computer-based; 100 iBT) or IELTS (minimum score 7.5). *Application deadline:* For fall admission, 12/15 for domestic and international students; for spring admission, 5/15 for domestic students. Application fee: $50. Electronic applications accepted. *Expenses:* Contact institution. *Financial support:* In 2011–12, 416 students received support, including 416 research assistantships with full tuition reimbursements available (averaging $29,200 per year); scholarships/grants, health care benefits, tuition waivers (full), and unspecified assistantships also available. Financial award application deadline: 4/16. *Faculty research:* RNA interference, cell biology, bioinformatics, clinical research, infectious disease. *Total annual research expenditures:* $262.7 million. *Unit head:* Dr. Anthony Carruthers, Dean, 508-856-4135, E-mail: anthony.carruthers@umassmed.edu. *Application contact:* Dr. Kendall Knight, Associate Dean and Interim Director of Admissions and Recruitment, 508-856-5628, Fax: 508-856-3659, E-mail: kendall.knight@umassmed.edu. Web site: http://www.umassmed.edu/gsbs/.

The University of North Carolina at Chapel Hill, School of Medicine and Graduate School, Graduate Programs in Medicine, Curriculum in Bioinformatics and Computational Biology, Chapel Hill, NC 27599. Offers PhD. *Degree requirements:* For doctorate, comprehensive exam, thesis/dissertation. *Entrance requirements:* For doctorate, GRE, minimum GPA of 3.0. Additional exam requirements/recommendations for international students: Required—TOEFL. Electronic applications accepted. *Faculty research:* Protein folding, design and evolution and molecular biophysics of disease; mathematical modeling of signaling pathways and regulatory networks; bioinformatics, medical informatics, user interface design; statistical genetics and genetic epidemiology datamining, classification and clustering analysis of gene-expression data.

University of Pennsylvania, Perelman School of Medicine, Biomedical Graduate Studies, Graduate Group in Genomics and Computational Biology, Philadelphia, PA 19104. Offers PhD, MD/PhD, VMD/PhD. *Faculty:* 60. *Students:* 33 full-time (8 women); includes 13 minority (2 Black or African American, non-Hispanic/Latino; 9 Asian, non-Hispanic/Latino; 2 Hispanic/Latino), 8 international. 69 applicants, 23% accepted, 6 enrolled. In 2011, 2 doctorates awarded. *Degree requirements:* For doctorate, thesis/dissertation optional. *Entrance requirements:* For doctorate, GRE. Additional exam requirements/recommendations for international students: Required—TOEFL. *Application deadline:* For fall admission, 12/1 priority date for domestic students, 12/1 for international students. Applications are processed on a rolling basis. Application fee: $80. Electronic applications accepted. *Expenses: Tuition:* Full-time $26,660; part-time $4944 per course. *Required fees:* $2318; $291 per course. Tuition and fees vary according to course load, degree level and program. *Financial support:* In 2011–12, 33 students received support. Fellowships, research assistantships, scholarships/grants, traineeships, and unspecified assistantships available. *Unit head:* Dr. Maja Bucan, Chairperson, 215-898-0020, E-mail: bucan@pobox.upenn.edu. *Application contact:* Hannah Chervitz, Graduate Coordinator. Web site: http://www.med.upenn.edu/gcb/.

University of Pittsburgh, Joint CMU-Pitt PhD Program in Computational Biology, Pittsburgh, PA 15260. Offers PhD. *Faculty:* 83 full-time (17 women). *Students:* 51 full-time (11 women); includes 25 minority (22 Asian, non-Hispanic/Latino; 2 Hispanic/Latino; 1 Native Hawaiian or other Pacific Islander, non-Hispanic/Latino), 18 international. Average age 25. 140 applicants, 17% accepted, 11 enrolled. In 2011, 5 degrees awarded. Terminal master's awarded for partial completion of doctoral program. *Median time to degree:* Of those who began their doctoral program in fall 2003, 100% received their degree in 8 years or less. *Degree requirements:* For doctorate, comprehensive exam, thesis/dissertation, ethics training service as course assistant, seminar. *Entrance requirements:* For doctorate, GRE Subject Test (recommended), GRE General Test, 3 letters of recommendation, resume. Additional exam requirements/recommendations for international students: Required—TOEFL (minimum score 600 paper-based; 250 computer-based; 100 iBT). *Application deadline:* For fall admission, 12/15 priority date for domestic students, 12/15 for international students. Application fee: $50. Electronic applications accepted. *Expenses:* Tuition, state resident: full-time $18,774; part-time $760 per credit. Tuition, nonresident: full-time $30,736; part-time $1258 per credit. *Required fees:* $740; $200 per term. Tuition and fees vary according to program. *Financial support:* In 2011–12, 46 students received support, including 9 fellowships with full tuition reimbursements available, 42 research assistantships with full tuition reimbursements available (averaging $25,500 per year). *Faculty research:* Computational structural biology, computational genomics, cell and systems modeling, bioimage informatics, computational neurobiology. *Unit head:* Dr. Takis Benos, Director, 412-648-3315, Fax: 412-648-3163, E-mail: benos@pitt.edu. *Application contact:* Kelly Gentille, Assistant Programs Coordinator, 412-648-8107, Fax: 412-648-3163, E-mail: kmg120@pitt.edu. Web site: http://www.compbio.cmu.edu/.

University of Rochester, School of Medicine and Dentistry, Graduate Programs in Medicine and Dentistry, Department of Biochemistry and Biophysics, Programs in Biophysics, Rochester, NY 14627. Offers biophysics, structural and computational biology (PhD). Terminal master's awarded for partial completion of doctoral program. *Degree requirements:* For doctorate, thesis/dissertation, qualifying exam. *Entrance requirements:* For doctorate, GRE General Test. *Expenses: Tuition:* Full-time $41,040.

University of Southern California, Graduate School, Dana and David Dornsife College of Letters, Arts and Sciences, Department of Biological Sciences, Program in Molecular and Computational Biology, Los Angeles, CA 90089. Offers computational biology and bioinformatics (PhD); molecular biology (PhD). *Degree requirements:* For doctorate, comprehensive exam, thesis/dissertation, qualifying examination, dissertation defense. *Entrance requirements:* For doctorate, GRE, 3 letters of recommendation, personal statement, resume, minimum GPA of 3.0. Additional exam requirements/recommendations for international students: Required—TOEFL (minimum score 600 paper-based; 250 computer-based; 100 iBT). Electronic applications accepted. *Faculty research:* Biochemistry and molecular biology; genomics; computational biology and bioinformatics; cell and developmental biology, and genetics; DNA replication and repair, and cancer biology.

University of South Florida, Graduate School, College of Medicine and Graduate School, Graduate Programs in Medical Sciences, Tampa, FL 33620-9951. Offers bioethics and medical humanities (MABMH); bioinformatics and computational biology (MSBCB); biotechnology (MSB); medical sciences (MSMS, PhD). *Students:* 439 full-time (235 women), 111 part-time (65 women); includes 258 minority (82 Black or African American, non-Hispanic/Latino; 2 American Indian or Alaska Native, non-Hispanic/Latino; 85 Asian, non-Hispanic/Latino; 77 Hispanic/Latino; 12 Two or more races, non-Hispanic/Latino), 24 international. Average age 27. 1,032 applicants, 53% accepted, 364 enrolled. In 2011, 167 master's, 14 doctorates awarded. Terminal master's awarded for partial completion of doctoral program. *Degree requirements:* For master's, comprehensive exam, thesis; for doctorate, comprehensive exam, thesis/dissertation. *Entrance requirements:* For master's, GRE, MCAT, or GMAT, minimum GPA of 3.0 in

last 60 hours of coursework; for doctorate, GRE, minimum GPA of 3.0 in last 60 hours of coursework, three letters of recommendation, personal statement, interview. Additional exam requirements/recommendations for international students: Required—TOEFL (minimum score 550 paper-based; 213 computer-based; 79 iBT) or IELTS (minimum score 6.5). *Application deadline:* For fall admission, 2/15 for domestic students, 1/2 for international students. Application fee: $30. *Expenses:* Contact institution. *Unit head:* Dr. Michael Barber, Program Director, 813-974-9702, Fax: 813-974-4317, E-mail: mbarber@health.usf.edu. *Application contact:* Francisco Vera, Assistant Director for Admissions, 813-974-8800, E-mail: fvera@usf.edu. Web site: http://health.usf.edu/medicine/graduatestudies.

The University of Texas at Dallas, School of Natural Sciences and Mathematics, Department of Mathematical Sciences, Richardson, TX 75080. Offers applied mathematics (MS, PhD); bioinformatics and computational biology (MS); engineering mathematics (MS); mathematics (MS); statistics (MS, PhD). Part-time and evening/weekend programs available. *Faculty:* 15 full-time (2 women). *Students:* 53 full-time (21 women), 17 part-time (3 women); includes 21 minority (5 Black or African American, non-Hispanic/Latino; 12 Asian, non-Hispanic/Latino; 4 Hispanic/Latino), 31 international. Average age 31. 127 applicants, 32% accepted, 28 enrolled. In 2011, 16 master's, 7 doctorates awarded. *Degree requirements:* For master's, thesis optional; for doctorate, thesis/dissertation. *Entrance requirements:* For master's, GRE General Test, minimum GPA of 3.0 in upper-level course work in field; for doctorate, GRE General Test, minimum GPA of 3.5 in upper-level course work in field. Additional exam requirements/recommendations for international students: Required—TOEFL (minimum score 550 paper-based; 215 computer-based). *Application deadline:* For fall admission, 7/15 for domestic students, 5/1 for international students; for spring admission, 11/15 for domestic students, 9/1 for international students. Applications are processed on a rolling basis. Application fee: $50 ($100 for international students). Electronic applications accepted. *Expenses:* Tuition, state resident: full-time $11,170; part-time $620.56 per credit hour. Tuition, nonresident: full-time $20,212; part-time $1122.89 per credit hour. *Financial support:* In 2011–12, 39 students received support, including 2 research assistantships (averaging $20,700 per year), 31 teaching assistantships with partial tuition reimbursements available (averaging $15,503 per year); career-related internships or fieldwork, Federal Work-Study, institutionally sponsored loans, scholarships/grants, and unspecified assistantships also available. Support available to part-time students. Financial award application deadline: 4/30; financial award applicants required to submit FAFSA. *Faculty research:* Sequential analysis, applications in semiconductor manufacturing, medical image analysis, computational anatomy, information theory, probability theory. *Unit head:* Dr. Matthew Goeckner, Department Head, 972-883-4292, Fax: 972-883-6622, E-mail: goeckner@utdallas.edu. *Application contact:* Claire C. Troy, Graduate Support Assistant, 972-883-2163, Fax: 972-883-6622, E-mail: utdmath@utdallas.edu. Web site: http://www.utdallas.edu/math.

The University of Texas Medical Branch, Graduate School of Biomedical Sciences, Program in Biochemistry and Molecular Biology, Galveston, TX 77555. Offers biochemistry (PhD); bioinformatics (PhD); biophysics (PhD); cell biology (PhD); computational biology (PhD); structural biology (PhD). *Degree requirements:* For doctorate, thesis/dissertation. *Entrance requirements:* Additional exam requirements/recommendations for international students: Required—TOEFL (minimum score 550 paper-based; 213 computer-based). Electronic applications accepted.

University of Wyoming, Graduate Program in Molecular and Cellular Life Sciences, Laramie, WY 82070. Offers PhD. *Degree requirements:* For doctorate, thesis/dissertation, four eight-week laboratory rotations, comprehensive basic practical exam, two-part qualifying exam, seminars, symposium.

Virginia Polytechnic Institute and State University, Graduate School, Intercollege, Program in Genetics, Bioinformatics and Computational Biology, Blacksburg, VA 24061. Offers PhD. *Degree requirements:* For doctorate, comprehensive exam (for some programs), thesis/dissertation (for some programs). *Entrance requirements:* For doctorate, GRE. Additional exam requirements/recommendations for international students: Required—TOEFL (minimum score 550 paper-based; 213 computer-based). *Application deadline:* For fall admission, 7/1 for domestic and international students; for spring admission, 12/1 for international students. Applications are processed on a rolling basis. Application fee: $65. Electronic applications accepted. *Expenses:* Tuition, state resident: full-time $10,048; part-time $558.25 per credit hour. Tuition, nonresident: full-time $19,497; part-time $1083.25 per credit hour. *Required fees:* $405 per semester. Tuition and fees vary according to course load, campus/location and program. *Financial support:* Career-related internships or fieldwork, Federal Work-Study, scholarships/grants, health care benefits, and unspecified assistantships available. Financial award application deadline: 1/15. *Unit head:* Dr. David R. Bevan, Unit Head, 540-231-5040, Fax: 540-231-3010, E-mail: drbevan@vt.edu. *Application contact:* Dennie Munson, Information Contact, 540-231-1928, Fax: 540-231-3010, E-mail: dennie@vt.edu. Web site: http://graduateschool.vt.edu/academics/programs/gbcb/.

Washington University in St. Louis, Graduate School of Arts and Sciences, Division of Biology and Biomedical Sciences, Program in Computational and Systems Biology, St. Louis, MO 63130-4899. Offers PhD. *Degree requirements:* For doctorate, thesis/dissertation. Electronic applications accepted.

Weill Cornell Medical College, Weill Cornell Graduate School of Medical Sciences, Tri-Institutional Training Program in Computational Biology and Medicine, New York, NY 10065. Offers PhD. *Faculty:* 44 full-time (6 women). *Students:* 36 full-time (15 women); includes 15 minority (3 Black or African American, non-Hispanic/Latino; 11 Asian, non-Hispanic/Latino; 1 Native Hawaiian or other Pacific Islander, non-Hispanic/Latino). Average age 23. 144 applicants, 11% accepted, 9 enrolled. In 2011, 4 degrees awarded. Terminal master's awarded for partial completion of doctoral program. *Median time to degree:* Of those who began their doctoral program in fall 2003, 67% received their degree in 8 years or less. *Degree requirements:* For doctorate, comprehensive exam, thesis/dissertation. *Entrance requirements:* For doctorate, GRE General Test, three letters of recommendation. Additional exam requirements/recommendations for international students: Required—TOEFL. *Application deadline:* For winter admission, 1/1 for domestic and international students. Application fee: $70. Electronic applications accepted. *Expenses: Tuition:* Full-time $46,001. *Financial support:* In 2011–12, 36 students received support, including 35 fellowships with full tuition reimbursements available (averaging $39,000 per year), 1 teaching assistantship with full tuition reimbursement available (averaging $18,500 per year). *Faculty research:* Biophysics/structural biology, genomics/bioinformatics, modeling/systems biology, neuroscience, cancer biology. *Unit head:* Kathleen E. Pickering, Executive Director, 212-746-6049, Fax: 212-746-8992, E-mail: cbm@triiprograms.org. *Application contact:* Margie H. Mendoza, Program Administrator, 212-746-5267, Fax: 212-746-8992, E-mail: cbm@triiprograms.org. Web site: http://www.triiprograms.org/cbm/.

Yale University, School of Medicine and Graduate School of Arts and Sciences, Combined Program in Biological and Biomedical Sciences (BBS), Computational Biology and Bioinformatics Track, New Haven, CT 06520. Offers PhD, MD/PhD. *Entrance requirements:* Additional exam requirements/recommendations for international students: Required—TOEFL.

Systems Biology

Dartmouth College, Program in Experimental and Molecular Medicine, Biomedical Physiology Track, Hanover, NH 03755. Offers PhD.

Harvard University, Graduate School of Arts and Sciences, Department of Systems Biology, Cambridge, MA 02138. Offers PhD. *Degree requirements:* For doctorate, thesis/dissertation, lab rotation, qualifying examination. *Entrance requirements:* For doctorate, GRE. Additional exam requirements/recommendations for international students: Required—TOEFL. Electronic applications accepted. *Expenses: Tuition:* Full-time $36,304. *Required fees:* $1186. Full-time tuition and fees vary according to program.

Massachusetts Institute of Technology, School of Engineering and School of Science, Program in Computational and Systems Biology, Cambridge, MA 02139. Offers PhD. *Faculty:* 100 full-time (19 women). *Students:* 39 full-time (14 women); includes 11 minority (2 Black or African American, non-Hispanic/Latino; 1 American Indian or Alaska Native, non-Hispanic/Latino; 7 Asian, non-Hispanic/Latino; 1 Hispanic/Latino), 13 international. Average age 26. 163 applicants, 12% accepted, 7 enrolled. In 2011, 6 doctorates awarded. *Degree requirements:* For doctorate, comprehensive exam, thesis/dissertation. *Entrance requirements:* For doctorate, GRE General Test. Additional exam requirements/recommendations for international students: Required—IELTS (minimum score 6). *Application deadline:* For fall admission, 12/1 for domestic and international students. Application fee: $75. Electronic applications accepted. *Expenses: Tuition:* Full-time $40,460; part-time $630 per credit hour. *Required fees:* $272. *Financial support:* In 2011–12, 38 students received support, including 17 fellowships (averaging $37,900 per year), 22 research assistantships (averaging $32,200 per year); teaching assistantships, Federal Work-Study, institutionally sponsored loans, scholarships/grants, traineeships, health care benefits, and unspecified assistantships also available. *Faculty research:* Computational biology and bioinformatics, biological design and synthetic biology, gene and protein networks, systems biology of cancer, nanobiology and microsystems. *Unit head:* Prof. Douglas A. Lauffenberger, Director, 617-252-1629, E-mail: csbi@mit.edu. *Application contact:* Academic Office, 617-324-0055, Fax: 617-253-8699, E-mail: csbphd@mit.edu. Web site: http://csbi.mit.edu/.

Michigan State University, The Graduate School, College of Natural Science, Quantitative Biology Program, East Lansing, MI 48824. Offers PhD.

Purdue University, College of Pharmacy and Pharmacal Sciences and Graduate School, Graduate Programs in Pharmacy and Pharmacal Sciences, Department of Medicinal Chemistry and Molecular Pharmacology, West Lafayette, IN 47907. Offers biophysical and computational chemistry (PhD); cancer research (PhD); immunology and infectious disease (PhD); medicinal biochemistry and molecular biology (PhD); medicinal chemistry and chemical biology (PhD); molecular pharmacology (PhD); neuropharmacology, neurodegeneration, and neurotoxicity (PhD); systems biology and functional genomics (PhD). *Faculty:* 22 full-time (2 women), 4 part-time/adjunct (1 woman). *Students:* 49 full-time (18 women); includes 3 minority (1 Asian, non-Hispanic/Latino; 2 Hispanic/Latino), 26 international. Average age 27. 250 applicants, 12% accepted, 9 enrolled. In 2011, 10 doctorates awarded. *Degree requirements:* For doctorate, thesis/dissertation. *Entrance requirements:* For doctorate, GRE General Test; GRE Subject Test in biology, biochemistry, and chemistry (recommended), minimum undergraduate GPA of 3.0. Additional exam requirements/recommendations for international students: Required—TOEFL (minimum score 550 paper-based; 77 iBT); Recommended—TWE. *Application deadline:* For fall admission, 2/1 for domestic and international students. Applications are processed on a rolling basis. Application fee: $60 ($75 for international students). Electronic applications accepted. *Financial support:* Fellowships, research assistantships, teaching assistantships, and traineeships available. Support available to part-time students. Financial award applicants required to submit FAFSA. *Faculty research:* Drug design and development, cancer research, drug synthesis and analysis, chemical pharmacology, environmental toxicology. *Unit head:* Dr. Richard F. Borch, Head, 765-494-1403, E-mail: borch@purdue.edu. *Application contact:* Janine C. Mott, Graduate Contact, 765-494-1269, E-mail: jmott@purdue.edu.

Rutgers, The State University of New Jersey, New Brunswick, Graduate School-New Brunswick, BioMaPS Institute for Quantitative Biology, Piscataway, NJ 08854-8097. Offers computational biology and molecular biophysics (PhD). *Degree requirements:* For doctorate, comprehensive exam, thesis/dissertation. *Entrance requirements:* For doctorate, GRE. Additional exam requirements/recommendations for international students: Required—TOEFL. Electronic applications accepted. *Faculty research:* Structural biology, systems biology, bioinformatics, translational medicine, genomics.

Texas A&M Health Science Center, College of Medicine, Department of Systems Biology and Translational Medicine, College Station, TX 77840. Offers PhD. *Degree requirements:* For doctorate, thesis/dissertation. *Entrance requirements:* For doctorate, GRE General Test. *Faculty research:* Cardiovascular physiology, vascular cell and molecular biology.

University of California, Irvine, School of Biological Sciences, Program in Mathematical, Computational and Systems Biology, Irvine, CA 92697. Offers PhD. *Students:* 10 full-time (3 women); includes 4 minority (1 Black or African American, non-Hispanic/Latino; 2 Asian, non-Hispanic/Latino; 1 Hispanic/Latino), 2 international. Average age 24. 93 applicants, 23% accepted, 9 enrolled. Application fee: $80 ($100 for international students). *Unit head:* Prof. Frederic Yui-Ming Wan, Director, 949-824-5529, Fax: 949-824-7993, E-mail: fwan@math.uci.edu. *Application contact:* Prof. R. Michael Mulligan, Associate Dean, 949-824-8433, Fax: 949-824-4709, E-mail: rmmullig@uci.edu. Web site: http://mcsb.bio.uci.edu/.

University of California, Merced, Division of Graduate Studies, School of Natural Sciences, Merced, CA 95343. Offers applied mathematics (MS, PhD); biological engineering and small-scale technologies (MS, PhD); environmental systems (MS,

PhD); mechanical engineering and applied mechanics (MS, PhD); physics and chemistry (PhD); quantitative and systems biology (MS, PhD). *Unit head:* Dr. Samuel J. Traina, Dean, 209-228-4723, Fax: 209-228-6906, E-mail: grad.dean@ucmerced.edu. *Application contact:* Tsu Ya, Graduate Admissions and Academic Services Manager, 209-228-4723, Fax: 209-228-6906, E-mail: tya@ucmerced.edu.

University of California, San Diego, Office of Graduate Studies, Division of Biological Sciences, Program in Plant Systems Biology, La Jolla, CA 92093. Offers PhD.

University of California, San Diego, Office of Graduate Studies, PhD Program in Bioinformatics and Systems Biology, La Jolla, CA 92093. Offers PhD. Offered through the Departments of Bioengineering, Biology, Biomedical Sciences, Chemistry and Biochemistry, Computer Sciences and Engineering, Mathematics, and Physics. *Entrance requirements:* For doctorate, GRE General Test. Electronic applications accepted.

University of Chicago, Division of Biological Sciences, Molecular Biosciences Cluster, Committee on Genetics, Genomics and Systems Biology, Chicago, IL 60637-1513. Offers PhD. *Degree requirements:* For doctorate, thesis/dissertation, ethics class, 2 teaching assistantships. *Entrance requirements:* For doctorate, GRE General Test, minimum GPA of 3.0. Additional exam requirements/recommendations for international students: Required—TOEFL (minimum score 600 paper-based; 250 computer-based; 104 iBT), IELTS (minimum score 7). Electronic applications accepted. *Faculty research:* Molecular genetics, developmental genetics, population genetics, human genetics.

University of Southern California, Keck School of Medicine and Graduate School, Program in Systems Biology and Disease, Los Angeles, CA 90089. Offers PhD. *Faculty:* 224 full-time (56 women). *Students:* 25 full-time (15 women); includes 8 minority (5 Asian, non-Hispanic/Latino; 3 Hispanic/Latino), 7 international. Average age 31. 4 applicants, 75% accepted, 3 enrolled. In 2011, 6 doctorates awarded. *Degree requirements:* For doctorate, comprehensive exam, thesis/dissertation. *Entrance requirements:* For doctorate, GRE, minimum GPA of 3.0. Additional exam requirements/ recommendations for international students: Required—TOEFL (minimum score 600 paper-based; 250 computer-based; 100 iBT). *Application deadline:* For fall admission, 12/1 priority date for domestic students, 12/1 for international students. Application fee: $85. Electronic applications accepted. *Financial support:* In 2011–12, 25 students received support, including 5 fellowships (averaging $29,100 per year), 19 research assistantships with full tuition reimbursements available (averaging $29,100 per year), 1 teaching assistantship with full tuition reimbursement available (averaging $29,100 per year); institutionally sponsored loans, scholarships/grants, traineeships, health care benefits, and unspecified assistantships also available. Financial award application deadline: 5/4; financial award applicants required to submit FAFSA. *Unit head:* Dr. Alicia McDonough, Director, 323-442-1475, Fax: 323-442-1199, E-mail: mcdonoug@usc.edu. *Application contact:* Dawn Burke, Student Program Coordinator, 323-442-1475, Fax: 323-442-1199, E-mail: pibbs@usc.edu. Web site: http://www.usc.edu/intbio.

University of Toronto, School of Graduate Studies, Faculty of Arts and Science, Department of Cell and Systems Biology, Toronto, ON M5S 1A1, Canada. Offers M Sc, PhD. *Degree requirements:* For master's, thesis, thesis defense; for doctorate, thesis/ dissertation, thesis defense, oral thesis examination. *Entrance requirements:* For master's, minimum B+ average in final year, B overall, 3 letters of reference. Additional exam requirements/recommendations for international students: Required—TOEFL (minimum score 580 paper-based; 237 computer-based; 93 iBT), TWE (minimum score 5). Electronic applications accepted.

Virginia Commonwealth University, Graduate School, School of Life Sciences, Doctoral Program in Integrative Life Sciences, Richmond, VA 23284-9005. Offers PhD. *Entrance requirements:* For doctorate, GRE, minimum GPA of 3.0 in last 60 credits of undergraduate work or in graduate degree, 3 letters of recommendation. Additional exam requirements/recommendations for international students: Required—TOEFL (minimum score 600 paper-based; 250 computer-based; 100 iBT). Electronic applications accepted. *Expenses:* Tuition, state resident: full-time $9133; part-time $507 per credit. Tuition, nonresident: full-time $18,777; part-time $1043 per credit. *Required fees:* $77 per credit. Tuition and fees vary according to degree level, campus/location, program and student level.

Washington University in St. Louis, Graduate School of Arts and Sciences, Division of Biology and Biomedical Sciences, Program in Computational and Systems Biology, St. Louis, MO 63130-4899. Offers PhD. *Degree requirements:* For doctorate, thesis/ dissertation. Electronic applications accepted.

Weill Cornell Medical College, Weill Cornell Graduate School of Medical Sciences, Physiology, Biophysics and Systems Biology Program, New York, NY 10065. Offers MS, PhD. *Faculty:* 48 full-time (9 women). *Students:* 48 full-time (15 women); includes 7 minority (1 Black or African American, non-Hispanic/Latino; 4 Asian, non-Hispanic/ Latino; 1 Hispanic/Latino; 1 Native Hawaiian or other Pacific Islander, non-Hispanic/ Latino), 26 international. Average age 23. 37 applicants, 32% accepted, 5 enrolled. In 2011, 12 doctorates awarded. Terminal master's awarded for partial completion of doctoral program. *Degree requirements:* For master's, comprehensive exam; for doctorate, thesis/dissertation, final exam. *Entrance requirements:* For doctorate, GRE General Test, introductory courses in biology, inorganic and organic chemistry, physics, and mathematics. Additional exam requirements/recommendations for international students: Required—TOEFL. *Application deadline:* For fall admission, 12/1 for domestic students. Application fee: $60. *Expenses: Tuition:* Full-time $46,001. *Financial support:* In 2011–12, 4 fellowships (averaging $21,210 per year) were awarded; scholarships/ grants, health care benefits, and stipends (given to all students) also available. *Faculty research:* Receptor-mediated regulation of cell function, molecular properties of channels or receptors, bioinformatics, mathematical modeling. *Unit head:* Dr. Emre Aksay, Co-Director, 212-746-6207, E-mail: ema2004@med.cornell.edu. *Application contact:* Audrey Rivera, Program Coordinator, 212-746-6361, E-mail: ajr2004@ med.cornell.edu. Web site: http://weill.cornell.edu/gradschool/program/physiology.html.

Translational Biology

Baylor College of Medicine, Graduate School of Biomedical Sciences, Program in Translational Biology and Molecular Medicine, Houston, TX 77030-3498. Offers PhD. *Faculty:* 192 full-time (56 women). *Students:* 63 full-time (35 women); includes 24 minority (10 Black or African American, non-Hispanic/Latino; 9 Asian, non-Hispanic/ Latino; 5 Hispanic/Latino), 17 international. Average age 27. 133 applicants, 17% accepted, 12 enrolled. In 2011, 1 doctorate awarded. *Degree requirements:* For doctorate, thesis/dissertation, public defense. *Entrance requirements:* For doctorate, GRE, minimum GPA of 3.0. Additional exam requirements/recommendations for international students: Required—TOEFL. *Application deadline:* For fall admission, 1/1 for domestic students. Application fee: $0. Electronic applications accepted. *Financial support:* In 2011–12, 63 students received support, including 36 fellowships with full tuition reimbursements available (averaging $29,000 per year), 27 research assistantships with full tuition reimbursements available (averaging $29,000 per year); career-related internships or fieldwork, Federal Work-Study, health care benefits, and scholarships (to all students unless there are grant funds available to pay tuition) also available. Financial award applicants required to submit FAFSA. *Faculty research:* Molecular medicine, translational biology, human disease biology and therapy. *Unit head:* Dr. Mary Estes, Director, 713-798-3585, Fax: 713-798-3586, E-mail: tbmm@ bcm.edu. *Application contact:* Wanda Waguespack, Graduate Program Administrator, 713-798-1077, Fax: 713-798-3586, E-mail: wandaw@bcm.edu. Web site: http:// www.bcm.edu/tbmm.

Cedars-Sinai Medical Center, Graduate Program in Biomedical Sciences and Translational Medicine, Los Angeles, CA 90048. Offers PhD. *Degree requirements:* For doctorate, comprehensive exam, thesis/dissertation. *Entrance requirements:* For doctorate, GRE, 3 letters of recommendation. Additional exam requirements/ recommendations for international students: Required—TOEFL (minimum score 560 paper-based; 220 computer-based; 87 iBT). *Faculty research:* Immunology and infection, neuroscience, cardiovascular science, cancer, human genetics.

Texas A&M Health Science Center, College of Medicine, Department of Systems Biology and Translational Medicine, College Station, TX 77840. Offers PhD. *Degree requirements:* For doctorate, thesis/dissertation. *Entrance requirements:* For doctorate, GRE General Test. *Faculty research:* Cardiovascular physiology, vascular cell and molecular biology.

The University of Iowa, Graduate College, Program in Translational Biomedicine, Iowa City, IA 52242-1316. Offers MS, PhD. Terminal master's awarded for partial completion of doctoral program. *Degree requirements:* For master's, comprehensive exam; for doctorate, comprehensive exam, thesis/dissertation. *Entrance requirements:* For master's and doctorate, minimum GPA of 3.0. Additional exam requirements/ recommendations for international students: Required—TOEFL (minimum score 550 paper-based; 213 computer-based; 81 iBT). Electronic applications accepted.

Washington University in St. Louis, School of Medicine, Program in Clinical Investigation, St. Louis, MO 63130-4899. Offers clinical investigation (MS), including genetics/genomics, translational medicine. Part-time programs available. *Faculty:* 64 full-time (17 women), 3 part-time/adjunct (2 women). *Students:* 23 full-time (15 women), 23 part-time (10 women); includes 14 minority (3 Black or African American, non-Hispanic/Latino; 11 Asian, non-Hispanic/Latino). Average age 32. 6 applicants, 83% accepted, 5 enrolled. In 2011, 16 master's awarded. *Degree requirements:* For master's, thesis. *Entrance requirements:* For master's, doctoral-level degree or in process of obtaining doctoral-level degree. Additional exam requirements/recommendations for international students: Required—TOEFL. *Application deadline:* For fall admission, 3/15 for domestic students. Application fee: $0. Electronic applications accepted. *Faculty research:* Anesthesiology, infectious diseases, neurology, obstetrics and gynecology, orthopaedic surgery. *Unit head:* Dr. David Warren, Associate Professor of Medicine, 314-454-8225, Fax: 314-454-5392, E-mail: dwarren@dom.wustl.edu. *Application contact:* Angela B. Wilson, Curriculum and Evaluation Coordinator, 314-454-8936, Fax: 314-454-8279, E-mail: abwilson@dom.wustl.edu. Web site: http://crtc.wustl.edu/.

Section 8
Ecology, Environmental Biology, and Evolutionary Biology

This section contains a directory of institutions offering graduate work in ecology, environmental biology. Additional information about programs listed in the directory but not augmented by an in-depth entry may be obtained by writing directly to the dean of a graduate school or chair of a department at the address given in the directory.

For programs offering related work, see also in this book *Biological and Biomedical Sciences; Botany and Plant Biology; Entomology; Genetics, Developmental Biology, and Reproductive Biology; Microbiological Sciences; Pharmacology and Toxicology; Public Health;* and *Zoology.* In the other guides in this series:

Graduate Programs in the Humanities, Arts & Social Sciences

See *Sociology, Anthropology, and Archaeology*

Graduate Programs in the Physical Sciences, Mathematics, Agricultural Sciences, the Environment & Natural Resources

See *Agricultural and Food Sciences, Geosciences, Marine Sciences and Oceanography,* and *Mathematical Sciences*

Graduate Programs in Engineering & Applied Sciences

See *Civil and Environmental Engineering, Management of Engineering and Technology,* and *Ocean Engineering*

CONTENTS

Program Directories

Conservation Biology

Antioch University New England, Graduate School, Department of Environmental Studies, Program in Conservation Biology, Keene, NH 03431-3552. Offers MS. *Degree requirements:* For master's, thesis or project. *Entrance requirements:* For master's, resume, 3 letters of recommendation.

California State University, Stanislaus, College of Natural Sciences, Program in Ecology and Sustainability (MS), Turlock, CA 95382. Offers ecological conservation (MS); ecological economics (MS). Part-time programs available. *Degree requirements:* For master's, thesis. *Entrance requirements:* For master's, GRE, minimum GPA of 3.0, 3 letters of recommendation, personal statement. Additional exam requirements/recommendations for international students: Required—TOEFL (minimum score 550 paper-based; 213 computer-based). *Application deadline:* For fall admission, 5/1 for domestic students; for spring admission, 1/7 for domestic students. Application fee: $55. Electronic applications accepted. *Expenses: Required fees:* $4616 per year. *Financial support:* Application deadline: 3/1; applicants required to submit FAFSA. *Unit head:* Dr. Matthew Cover, Program Director, 209-667-3153, E-mail: mcover@biology.csustan.edu. *Application contact:* Graduate School, 209-667-3129, Fax: 209-664-7025, E-mail: graduate_school@csustan.edu.

Central Michigan University, College of Graduate Studies, College of Science and Technology, Department of Biology, Mount Pleasant, MI 48859. Offers biology (MS); conservation biology (MS). Part-time programs available. *Degree requirements:* For master's, thesis or alternative. *Entrance requirements:* For master's, GRE, bachelor's degree with a major in biological science, minimum GPA of 3.0. Electronic applications accepted. *Faculty research:* Conservation biology, morphology and taxonomy of aquatic plants, molecular biology and genetics, microbials and invertebrate ecology, vertebrates.

Colorado State University, Graduate School, Warner College of Natural Resources, Department of Fishery and Wildlife Biology, Fort Collins, CO 80523-1474. Offers fish, wildlife and conservation biology (MFWCB); fishery and wildlife biology (MFWB, MS, PhD). *Faculty:* 15 full-time (4 women). *Students:* 11 full-time (3 women), 19 part-time (8 women); includes 2 minority (both Hispanic/Latino). Average age 31. 11 applicants, 55% accepted, 6 enrolled. In 2011, 5 master's, 2 doctorates awarded. Terminal master's awarded for partial completion of doctoral program. *Degree requirements:* For master's, comprehensive exam, thesis (for some programs); for doctorate, comprehensive exam, thesis/dissertation. *Entrance requirements:* For master's, GRE General Test (combined minimum score of 1200 on the Verbal and Quantitative sections), minimum GPA of 3.0, BA or BS in related field, letters of recommendation, resume, transcripts; for doctorate, GRE General Test (minimum score 1000 verbal and quantitative), minimum GPA of 3.0, MS in related field. Additional exam requirements/recommendations for international students: Required—TOEFL (minimum score 550 paper-based; 213 computer-based; 80 iBT). *Application deadline:* For fall admission, 2/15 priority date for domestic students, 2/15 for international students. Applications are processed on a rolling basis. Application fee: $50. Electronic applications accepted. *Expenses:* Tuition, state resident: full-time $7992. Tuition, nonresident: full-time $19,592. *Required fees:* $1735; $58 per credit. *Financial support:* In 2011–12, 4 fellowships with full and partial tuition reimbursements (averaging $25,954 per year), 19 research assistantships with full and partial tuition reimbursements (averaging $14,721 per year), 11 teaching assistantships with full and partial tuition reimbursements (averaging $7,502 per year) were awarded; career-related internships or fieldwork, scholarships/grants, tuition waivers (full and partial), and unspecified assistantships also available. Financial award application deadline: 2/15; financial award applicants required to submit FAFSA. *Faculty research:* Conservation biology, aquatic ecology, animal behavior, population modeling, habitat evaluation and management. *Total annual research expenditures:* $3.2 million. *Unit head:* Dr. Kenneth R. Wilson, Head, 970-491-7755, Fax: 970-491-5091, E-mail: kenneth.wilson@colostate.edu. *Application contact:* Joyce Pratt, Graduate Contact, 970-491-5020, Fax: 970-491-5091, E-mail: joyce.pratt@colostate.edu. Web site: http://warnercnr.colostate.edu/fwcb-home/.

Columbia University, Graduate School of Arts and Sciences, Division of Natural Sciences, Department of Ecology, Evolution and Environmental Biology, New York, NY 10027. Offers conservation biology (MA, Certificate); ecology and evolutionary biology (PhD); environmental policy (Certificate); evolutionary primatology (PhD). *Degree requirements:* For doctorate, one foreign language, thesis/dissertation, teaching experience. *Entrance requirements:* For doctorate, GRE General Test, previous course work in biology. Additional exam requirements/recommendations for international students: Required—TOEFL. Electronic applications accepted. *Faculty research:* Tropical ecology, ethnobotany, global change, systematics.

Columbia University, Graduate School of Arts and Sciences, Program in Conservation Biology, New York, NY 10027. Offers MA. *Degree requirements:* For master's, thesis.

Florida Institute of Technology, Graduate Programs, College of Science, Department of Biological Sciences, Melbourne, FL 32901-6975. Offers biological science (PhD); biotechnology (MS); cell and molecular biology (MS); conservation technology (MS); ecology (MS), including ecology, marine biology. Part-time programs available. *Faculty:* 16 full-time (2 women). *Students:* 84 full-time (52 women), 12 part-time (6 women); includes 6 minority (1 Asian, non-Hispanic/Latino; 3 Hispanic/Latino; 2 Two or more races, non-Hispanic/Latino), 50 international. Average age 26. 241 applicants, 35% accepted, 29 enrolled. In 2011, 21 master's, 3 doctorates awarded. *Degree requirements:* For master's, thesis (for some programs), research, seminar, internship, or summer lab; for doctorate, comprehensive exam, thesis/dissertation, dissertations seminar, publications. *Entrance requirements:* For master's, GRE General Test, 3 letters of recommendation, minimum GPA of 3.0, resume, statement of objectives; for doctorate, GRE General Test, resume, 3 letters of recommendation, minimum GPA of 3.2, statement of objectives. Additional exam requirements/recommendations for international students: Required—TOEFL (minimum score 550 paper-based; 213 computer-based; 79 iBT). *Application deadline:* For fall admission, 3/1 for domestic students, 4/1 for international students; for spring admission, 9/1 for domestic and international students. Applications are processed on a rolling basis. Electronic applications accepted. *Expenses: Tuition:* Full-time $19,620; part-time $1090 per credit hour. Tuition and fees vary according to campus/location. *Financial support:* In 2011–12, 6 fellowships (averaging $20,737 per year), 18 research assistantships with full and partial tuition reimbursements (averaging $10,742 per year), 20 teaching assistantships with full and partial tuition reimbursements (averaging $13,883 per year) were awarded; career-related internships or fieldwork, institutionally sponsored loans, tuition waivers (partial), unspecified assistantships, and tuition remissions also available. Support available to part-time students. Financial award application deadline: 3/1; financial award applicants required to submit FAFSA. *Faculty research:* Initiation of protein synthesis in eukaryotic cells, fixation of radioactive carbon, changes in DNA molecule, endangered or threatened avian and mammalian species, hydroacoustics and feeding preference of the West Indian manatee. *Total annual research expenditures:* $1.9 million. *Unit head:* Dr. Richard B. Aronson, Department Head, 321-674-8034, Fax: 321-674-7238, E-mail: raronson@fit.edu. *Application contact:* Cheryl A. Brown, Associate Director of Graduate Admissions, 321-674-7581, Fax: 321-723-9468, E-mail: cbrown@fit.edu. Web site: http://cos.fit.edu/biology/.

Frostburg State University, Graduate School, College of Liberal Arts and Sciences, Department of Biology, Program in Applied Ecology and Conservation Biology, Frostburg, MD 21532-1099. Offers MS. *Degree requirements:* For master's, thesis. *Entrance requirements:* For master's, GRE General Test, resume. Additional exam requirements/recommendations for international students: Required—TOEFL. Electronic applications accepted. *Faculty research:* Forest ecology, microbiology of man-made wetlands, invertebrate zoology and entomology, wildlife and carnivore ecology, aquatic pollution ecology.

Illinois State University, Graduate School, College of Arts and Sciences, Department of Biological Sciences, Normal, IL 61790-2200. Offers animal behavior (MS); bacteriology (MS); biochemistry (MS); biological sciences (MS); biology (PhD); biophysics (MS); biotechnology (MS); botany (MS, PhD); cell biology (MS); conservation biology (MS); developmental biology (MS); ecology (MS, PhD); entomology (MS); evolutionary biology (MS); genetics (MS, PhD); immunology (MS); microbiology (MS, PhD); molecular biology (MS); molecular genetics (MS); neurobiology (MS); neuroscience (MS); parasitology (MS); physiology (MS, PhD); plant biology (MS); plant molecular biology (MS); plant sciences (MS); structural biology (MS); zoology (MS, PhD). Part-time programs available. *Degree requirements:* For master's, thesis or alternative; for doctorate, variable foreign language requirement, thesis/dissertation, 2 terms of residency. *Entrance requirements:* For master's, GRE General Test, minimum GPA of 2.6 in last 60 hours of course work; for doctorate, GRE General Test. *Faculty research:* Redoc balance and drug development in schistosoma mansoni, control of the growth of listeria monocytogenes at low temperature, regulation of cell expansion and microtubule function by SPRI, CRUI: physiology and fitness consequences of different life history phenotypes.

North Dakota State University, College of Graduate and Interdisciplinary Studies, College of Agriculture, Food Systems, and Natural Resources, Department of Entomology, Fargo, ND 58108. Offers entomology (MS, PhD); environment and conservation science (MS, PhD); natural resource management (MS, PhD). Part-time programs available. *Students:* 7 full-time (4 women), 3 part-time (1 woman), 3 international. Average age 34. 6 applicants, 0% accepted, 0 enrolled. In 2011, 1 master's awarded. *Degree requirements:* For master's, thesis; for doctorate, comprehensive exam, thesis/dissertation. *Entrance requirements:* For master's and doctorate, minimum GPA of 3.0. Additional exam requirements/recommendations for international students: Required—TOEFL (minimum score 550 paper-based; 213 computer-based; 79 iBT). *Application deadline:* For fall admission, 5/1 for international students; for winter admission, 8/1 for international students. Application fee: $35. Electronic applications accepted. *Financial support:* In 2011–12, 11 research assistantships with full tuition reimbursements (averaging $13,800 per year) were awarded; Federal Work-Study, institutionally sponsored loans, and unspecified assistantships also available. Financial award application deadline: 4/15. *Faculty research:* Insect systematics, conservation biology, integrated pest management, insect behavior, insect biology. *Unit head:* Dr. Frank Casey, Chair, 701-231-7582, Fax: 701-231-8557, E-mail: francis.casey@ndsu.edu. *Application contact:* Dr. Jason Harmon, Program Leader, 701-231-7033, Fax: 701-231-8557, E-mail: jason.harmon@ndsu.edu. Web site: http://www.ndsu.nodak.edu/entomology/.

North Dakota State University, College of Graduate and Interdisciplinary Studies, College of Science and Mathematics, Department of Biological Sciences, Fargo, ND 58108. Offers biology (MS); botany (MS, PhD); cellular and molecular biology (PhD); environmental and conservation sciences (MS, PhD); genomics (PhD); natural resources management (MS, PhD); zoology (MS, PhD). *Faculty:* 13 full-time (7 women), 3 part-time/adjunct (1 woman). *Students:* 20 full-time (10 women), 2 part-time (both women); includes 1 minority (American Indian or Alaska Native, non-Hispanic/Latino), 2 international. 12 applicants, 33% accepted, 4 enrolled. In 2011, 3 degrees awarded. *Degree requirements:* For master's, thesis; for doctorate, thesis/dissertation. *Entrance requirements:* For master's and doctorate, GRE General Test. Additional exam requirements/recommendations for international students: Required—TOEFL. *Application deadline:* For fall admission, 1/15 for domestic students. Applications are processed on a rolling basis. Application fee: $35. Electronic applications accepted. *Financial support:* Fellowships with full tuition reimbursements, research assistantships with full tuition reimbursements, teaching assistantships with full tuition reimbursements, career-related internships or fieldwork, Federal Work-Study, institutionally sponsored loans, scholarships/grants, tuition waivers (full), and unspecified assistantships available. Support available to part-time students. Financial award application deadline: 4/15; financial award applicants required to submit FAFSA. *Faculty research:* Comparative endocrinology, physiology, behavioral ecology, plant cell biology, aquatic biology. *Unit head:* Dr. Wendy Reed, Head, 701-231-7087, E-mail: wendy.reed@ndsu.edu. *Application contact:* Sonya Goergen, Marketing, Recruitment, and Public Relations Coordinator, 701-231-7033, Fax: 701-231-6524. Web site: http://biology.ndsu.nodak.edu/.

San Francisco State University, Division of Graduate Studies, College of Science and Engineering, Department of Biology, Program in Conservation Biology, San Francisco, CA 94132-1722. Offers MS. *Application deadline:* Applications are processed on a rolling basis. *Unit head:* Dr. Robert Patterson, Program Coordinator, 415-338-1100, E-mail: patters@sfsu.edu. Web site: http://biology.sfsu.edu/.

State University of New York College of Environmental Science and Forestry, Department of Environmental and Forest Biology, Syracuse, NY 13210-2779. Offers applied ecology (MPS); chemical ecology (MPS, MS, PhD); conservation biology (MPS, MS, PhD); ecology (MPS, MS, PhD); entomology (MPS, MS, PhD); environmental interpretation (MPS, MS, PhD); environmental physiology (MPS, MS, PhD); fish and wildlife biology and management (MPS, MS, PhD); forest pathology and mycology (MPS, MS, PhD); plant biotechnology (MPS); plant science and biotechnology (MPS, MS, PhD). *Degree requirements:* For master's, thesis (for some programs); for doctorate, comprehensive exam, thesis/dissertation. *Entrance requirements:* For master's and doctorate, GRE General Test, GRE Subject Test, minimum GPA of 3.0. Additional exam requirements/recommendations for international students: Required—TOEFL (minimum score 550 paper-based; 213 computer-based; 80 iBT), IELTS (minimum score 6). *Application deadline:* For fall admission, 2/1 priority date for domestic students, 2/1 for international students; for spring admission, 11/1 priority date for domestic students, 11/1 for international students. Applications are processed on a rolling basis. Application fee: $60. *Expenses:* Tuition, state resident: full-time $8870; part-time $370 per credit hour. Tuition, nonresident: full-time $15,160; part-time $632 per credit hour. *Required fees:* $60; $370 per credit hour. $350 per semester. One-time fee: $85. *Financial support:* Fellowships with full and partial tuition reimbursements,

research assistantships with full and partial tuition reimbursements, teaching assistantships with full and partial tuition reimbursements, Federal Work-Study, institutionally sponsored loans, scholarships/grants, health care benefits, and unspecified assistantships available. Financial award application deadline: 6/30. *Faculty research:* Ecology, fish and wildlife biology and management, plant science, entomology. *Total annual research expenditures:* $4.1 million. *Unit head:* Dr. Donald J. Leopold, Chair, 315-470-6760, Fax: 315-470-6934. *Application contact:* Dr. Dudley J. Raynal, Dean, Instruction and Graduate Studies, 315-470-6599, Fax: 315-470-6978, E-mail: esfgrad@esf.edu. Web site: http://www.esf.edu/efb/.

Texas State University–San Marcos, Graduate School, College of Science and Engineering, Department of Biology, Program in Population and Conservation Biology, San Marcos, TX 78666. Offers MS. *Faculty:* 6 full-time (2 women), 1 (woman) part-time/adjunct. *Students:* 12 full-time (8 women), 4 part-time (1 woman); includes 1 minority (Hispanic/Latino), 2 international. Average age 27. 7 applicants, 57% accepted, 3 enrolled. In 2011, 7 master's awarded. *Degree requirements:* For master's, thesis. *Entrance requirements:* For master's, GRE (preferred minimum combined score of 1000 Verbal and Quantitative), bachelor's degree in biology or related discipline, minimum GPA of 3.0 in last 60 hours of undergraduate course work. Additional exam requirements/recommendations for international students: Required—TOEFL (minimum score 550 paper-based; 213 computer-based; 78 iBT). *Application deadline:* For fall admission, 6/15 for domestic students, 6/1 for international students; for spring admission, 10/15 for domestic students, 10/1 for international students. Applications are processed on a rolling basis. Application fee: $40 ($90 for international students). Electronic applications accepted. *Expenses:* Tuition, state resident: full-time $6408; part-time $3204 per semester. Tuition, nonresident: full-time $14,832; part-time $7416 per semester. *Required fees:* $1824; $912 per semester. Tuition and fees vary according to course load. *Financial support:* In 2011–12, 7 students received support, including 12 teaching assistantships (averaging $13,266 per year); research assistantships, Federal Work-Study, institutionally sponsored loans, scholarships/grants, health care benefits, and unspecified assistantships also available. Support available to part-time students. Financial award application deadline: 4/1; financial award applicants required to submit FAFSA. *Unit head:* Dr. Chris Nice, Graduate Advisor, 512-245-2321, E-mail: ccnice@txstate.edu. *Application contact:* Dr. J. Michael Willoughby, Dean of the Graduate School, 512-245-2581, Fax: 512-245-8365, E-mail: jw02@swt.edu. Web site: http://pop.bio.txstate.edu/Masters.html.

Tropical Agriculture Research and Higher Education Center, Graduate School, Turrialba, Costa Rica. Offers agribusiness management (MS); agroforestry systems (PhD); development practices (MS); ecological agriculture (MS); environmental socioeconomics (MS); forestry in tropical and subtropical zones (PhD); integrated watershed management (MS); international sustainable tourism (MS); management and conservation of tropical rainforests and biodiversity (MS); tropical agriculture (PhD); tropical agroforestry (MS). *Entrance requirements:* For master's, GRE, 2 years of related professional experience, letters of recommendation; for doctorate, GRE, 4 letters of recommendation, letter of support from employing organization, master's degree in agronomy, biological sciences, forestry, natural resources or related field. Additional exam requirements/recommendations for international students: Required—TOEFL (minimum score 550 paper-based; 213 computer-based). Electronic applications accepted. *Faculty research:* Biodiversity in fragmented landscapes, ecosystem management, integrated pest management, environmental livestock production, biotechnology carbon balances in diverse land uses.

University at Albany, State University of New York, College of Arts and Sciences, Department of Biological Sciences, Program in Biodiversity, Conservation, and Policy, Albany, NY 12222-0001. Offers MS. *Degree requirements:* For master's, one foreign language. *Entrance requirements:* For master's, GRE General Test. *Faculty research:* Aquatic ecology, plant community ecology, biodiversity and public policy, restoration ecology, coastal and estuarine science.

University of Alberta, Faculty of Graduate Studies and Research, Department of Renewable Resources, Edmonton, AB T6G 2E1, Canada. Offers agroforestry (M Ag, M Sc, MF); conservation biology (M Sc, PhD); forest biology and management (M Sc, PhD); land reclamation and remediation (M Sc, PhD); protected areas and wildlands management (M Sc, PhD); soil science (M Ag, M Sc, PhD); water and land resources (M Ag, M Sc, PhD); wildlife ecology and management (M Sc, PhD); MBA/M Ag; MBA/MF. Part-time programs available. *Degree requirements:* For master's, thesis (for some programs); for doctorate, comprehensive exam, thesis/dissertation. *Entrance requirements:* For master's, minimum 2 years of relevant professional experiences, minimum GPA of 3.0; for doctorate, minimum GPA of 3.0. Additional exam requirements/recommendations for international students: Required—TOEFL (minimum score 550 paper-based; 213 computer-based). Electronic applications accepted. *Faculty research:* Natural and managed landscapes.

University of Central Florida, College of Sciences, Department of Biology, Orlando, FL 32816. Offers biology (MS); conservation biology (PSM, PhD, Certificate). Part-time and evening/weekend programs available. *Faculty:* 21 full-time (5 women), 9 part-time/adjunct (5 women). *Students:* 56 full-time (35 women), 18 part-time (12 women); includes 5 minority (2 Asian, non-Hispanic/Latino; 2 Hispanic/Latino; 1 Two or more races, non-Hispanic/Latino), 4 international. Average age 30. 78 applicants, 37% accepted, 17 enrolled. In 2011, 19 master's, 2 doctorates awarded. *Degree requirements:* For master's, comprehensive exam, thesis or alternative, field exam. *Entrance requirements:* For master's, GRE General Test, minimum GPA of 3.0 in last 60 hours. Additional exam requirements/recommendations for international students: Required—TOEFL. *Application deadline:* For fall admission, 3/1 priority date for domestic students; for spring admission, 10/15 for domestic students. Application fee: $30. Electronic applications accepted. *Expenses:* Tuition, state resident: part-time $277.08 per credit hour. Tuition, nonresident: part-time $277.08 per credit hour. Part-time tuition and fees vary according to degree level and program. *Financial support:* In 2011–12, 50 students received support, including 11 fellowships with partial tuition reimbursements available (averaging $1,500 per year), 14 research assistantships with partial tuition reimbursements available (averaging $9,100 per year), 41 teaching assistantships with partial tuition reimbursements available (averaging $11,600 per year); career-related internships or fieldwork, Federal Work-Study, institutionally sponsored loans, tuition waivers (partial), and unspecified assistantships also available. Financial award application deadline: 3/1; financial award applicants required to submit FAFSA. *Unit head:* Dr. Ross Hinkle, Chair, 407-823-2141, Fax: 407-823-5769, E-mail: rhinkle@ucf.edu. *Application contact:* Barbara Rodriguez, Associate Director, Admissions and Registration, 407-823-2766, Fax: 407-823-6442, E-mail: gradadmissions@ucf.edu. Web site: http://biology.cos.ucf.edu/.

University of Hawaii at Hilo, Program in Tropical Conservation Biology and Environmental Science, Hilo, HI 96720-4091. Offers MS.

University of Hawaii at Manoa, Graduate Division, Interdisciplinary Specialization in Ecology, Evolution and Conservation Biology, Honolulu, HI 96822. Offers MS, PhD. *Degree requirements:* For doctorate, thesis/dissertation. *Faculty research:* Agronomy and soil science, zoology, entomology, genetics and molecular biology, botanical sciences.

University of Illinois at Urbana–Champaign, Graduate College, College of Liberal Arts and Sciences, School of Integrative Biology, Program in Ecology, Evolution and Conservation Biology, Champaign, IL 61820. Offers MS, PhD. *Students:* 20 full-time (15 women), 8 part-time (3 women); includes 5 minority (1 American Indian or Alaska Native, non-Hispanic/Latino; 2 Asian, non-Hispanic/Latino; 1 Hispanic/Latino; 1 Two or more races, non-Hispanic/Latino), 3 international. 33 applicants, 9% accepted, 1 enrolled. In 2011, 2 master's, 4 doctorates awarded. *Entrance requirements:* For master's and doctorate, GRE. Additional exam requirements/recommendations for international students: Required—TOEFL (minimum score 613 paper-based; 257 computer-based; 103 iBT). *Application deadline:* Applications are processed on a rolling basis. Application fee: $75 ($90 for international students). Electronic applications accepted. *Financial support:* In 2011–12, 8 fellowships, 15 research assistantships, 14 teaching assistantships were awarded; tuition waivers (full and partial) also available. *Unit head:* Evan H. DeLucia, Director, 217-333-3044, Fax: 217-244-1224, E-mail: delucia@illinois.edu. *Application contact:* Carol Hall, Secretary, 217-333-8208, Fax: 217-244-1224, E-mail: cahall@illinois.edu. Web site: http://sib.illinois.edu/peec/.

University of Maryland, College Park, Academic Affairs, College of Computer, Mathematical and Natural Sciences, Department of Biology, Program in Sustainable Development and Conservation Biology, College Park, MD 20742. Offers MS. Part-time and evening/weekend programs available. *Students:* 24 full-time (15 women), 6 part-time (3 women); includes 1 minority (Hispanic/Latino), 4 international. 80 applicants, 24% accepted, 10 enrolled. In 2011, 12 master's awarded. *Degree requirements:* For master's, internship, scholarly paper. *Entrance requirements:* For master's, GRE General Test, minimum GPA of 3.0, 3 letters of recommendation. *Application deadline:* For fall admission, 1/15 priority date for domestic students, 1/15 for international students. Applications are processed on a rolling basis. Application fee: $75. Electronic applications accepted. *Expenses:* Tuition, state resident: part-time $525 per credit hour. Tuition, nonresident: part-time $1131 per credit hour. *Required fees:* $386.31 per term. Tuition and fees vary according to program. *Financial support:* In 2011–12, 18 teaching assistantships (averaging $18,831 per year) were awarded. Financial award application deadline: 2/1; financial award applicants required to submit FAFSA. *Faculty research:* Biodiversity, global change, conservation. *Unit head:* Dr. Karen Lips, Director, 301-405-7409, Fax: 301-314-9358, E-mail: klips@umd.edu. *Application contact:* Dr. Charles A. Caramello, Dean of Graduate School, 301-405-0358, Fax: 301-314-9305.

University of Michigan, School of Natural Resources and Environment, Program in Natural Resources and Environment, Ann Arbor, MI 48109. Offers aquatic sciences: research and management (MS); behavior, education and communication (MS); conservation biology (MS); conservation ecology (MS); environmental informatics (MS); environmental justice (MS); environmental policy and planning (MS); natural resources and environment (PhD); sustainable systems (MS); terrestrial ecosystems (MS); MS/JD; MS/MBA; MUP/MS. *Faculty:* 45 full-time, 23 part-time/adjunct. *Students:* 450 full-time (254 women); includes 63 minority (7 Black or African American, non-Hispanic/Latino; 2 American Indian or Alaska Native, non-Hispanic/Latino; 35 Asian, non-Hispanic/Latino; 13 Hispanic/Latino; 6 Two or more races, non-Hispanic/Latino), 70 international. Average age 27. 643 applicants. In 2011, 133 master's, 11 doctorates awarded. Terminal master's awarded for partial completion of doctoral program. *Degree requirements:* For master's, practicum or group project; for doctorate, comprehensive exam, thesis/dissertation, oral defense of dissertation, preliminary exam. *Entrance requirements:* For master's, GRE General Test; for doctorate, GRE General Test, master's degree. Additional exam requirements/recommendations for international students: Required—TOEFL (minimum score 560 paper-based; 220 computer-based; 84 iBT). *Application deadline:* For fall admission, 1/5 priority date for domestic students, 1/5 for international students. Applications are processed on a rolling basis. Application fee: $65 ($75 for international students). Electronic applications accepted. *Financial support:* Fellowships with tuition reimbursements, research assistantships with tuition reimbursements, teaching assistantships with tuition reimbursements, career-related internships or fieldwork, Federal Work-Study, institutionally sponsored loans, scholarships/grants, health care benefits, and unspecified assistantships available. Support available to part-time students. Financial award application deadline: 1/5; financial award applicants required to submit FAFSA. *Faculty research:* Stream ecology, plant-insect interactions, fish biology, resource control and reproductive success, remote sensing, conservation ecology. *Unit head:* Dr. Marie Lynn Miranda, Dean, 734-764-2550, Fax: 734-763-8965, E-mail: mlmirand@umich.edu. *Application contact:* Adam D. Ancira, Graduate Admissions Team, 734-764-6453, Fax: 734-936-2195, E-mail: snre.admissions@umich.edu. Web site: http://www.snre.umich.edu/.

University of Minnesota, Twin Cities Campus, Graduate School, College of Food, Agricultural and Natural Resource Sciences, Program in Conservation Biology, Minneapolis, MN 55455-0213. Offers MS, PhD. Part-time programs available. *Faculty:* 116 full-time (31 women). *Students:* 44 full-time (24 women), 3 part-time (2 women); includes 3 minority (1 Hispanic/Latino; 2 Two or more races, non-Hispanic/Latino), 8 international. Average age 28. 78 applicants, 26% accepted, 15 enrolled. In 2011, 7 master's, 7 doctorates awarded. Terminal master's awarded for partial completion of doctoral program. *Degree requirements:* For master's, comprehensive exam, thesis; for doctorate, comprehensive exam, thesis/dissertation. *Entrance requirements:* For master's and doctorate, GRE, advanced ecology course. Additional exam requirements/recommendations for international students: Required—TOEFL (minimum score 550 paper-based; 213 computer-based; 79 iBT), IELTS (minimum score 6.5), TOEFL preferred. *Application deadline:* For fall admission, 12/15 priority date for domestic students, 12/15 for international students; for spring admission, 10/15 for domestic and international students. Applications are processed on a rolling basis. Application fee: $75 ($95 for international students). Electronic applications accepted. *Financial support:* In 2011–12, fellowships with full tuition reimbursements (averaging $23,500 per year), research assistantships with full and partial tuition reimbursements (averaging $18,000 per year), teaching assistantships with full and partial tuition reimbursements (averaging $18,000 per year) were awarded; scholarships/grants, health care benefits, and unspecified assistantships also available. *Faculty research:* Wildlife conservation, fisheries and aquatic biology, invasive species, human dimensions, GIS, restoration ecology. *Unit head:* Dr. Rob Blair, Director of Graduate Studies, 612-624-2198, E-mail: blairrb@umn.edu. *Application contact:* Anup Joshi, Program Coordinator, 612-524-7751, E-mail: consbio@umn.edu.

University of Missouri, Graduate School, College of Agriculture, Food and Natural Resources, Department of Agricultural Economics, Columbia, MO 65211. Offers agricultural economics (MS, PhD); conservation biology (Graduate Certificate). *Faculty:* 23 full-time (3 women), 3 part-time/adjunct (1 woman). *Students:* 28 full-time (10 women), 15 part-time (5 women); includes 2 minority (1 Asian, non-Hispanic/Latino; 1 Hispanic/Latino), 19 international. Average age 32. 53 applicants, 25% accepted, 7 enrolled. In 2011, 9 master's, 4 doctorates, 2 other advanced degrees awarded. *Degree requirements:* For doctorate, comprehensive exam, thesis/dissertation. *Entrance requirements:* For master's and doctorate, GRE General Test, minimum GPA of 3.0. Additional exam requirements/recommendations for international students: Required—TOEFL (minimum score 550 paper-based; 80 iBT). *Application deadline:* For fall admission, 2/15 priority date for domestic students, 2/15 for international students; for winter admission, 9/15 for domestic and international students. Applications are processed on a rolling basis. Application fee: $55 ($75 for international students).

Electronic applications accepted. *Expenses:* Tuition, state resident: full-time $5881. Tuition, nonresident: full-time $15,183. *Required fees:* $952. Tuition and fees vary according to campus/location and program. *Financial support:* Fellowships, research assistantships with tuition reimbursements, teaching assistantships with tuition reimbursements, Federal Work-Study, institutionally sponsored loans, scholarships/grants, health care benefits, and unspecified assistantships available. Financial award application deadline: 3/1; financial award applicants required to submit FAFSA. *Faculty research:* Agribusiness management, contracting and strategy; collective action and cooperative theory; econometrics and price analysis; entrepreneurship; environmental and natural resource economics; food, biofuel and agricultural policy and regulation; international development; regional economics and rural development policy; science policy and innovation; sustainable agriculture and applied ethics. *Unit head:* Dr. Michael Monson, Department Chair, 573-882-0153, E-mail: monsonm@missouri.edu. *Application contact:* Jody Pestle, Administrative Assistant, 573-882-3747, E-mail: pestlej@missouri.edu. Web site: http://dass.missouri.edu/agecon/grad/.

University of Missouri, Graduate School, School of Natural Resources, Department of Fisheries and Wildlife, Columbia, MO 65211. Offers conservation biology (Certificate); fisheries and wildlife (MS, PhD). *Faculty:* 10 full-time (1 woman). *Students:* 16 full-time (4 women), 15 part-time (9 women); includes 1 minority (Black or African American, non-Hispanic/Latino), 3 international. Average age 30. 14 applicants, 57% accepted, 6 enrolled. In 2011, 8 master's, 3 doctorates, 2 other advanced degrees awarded. *Degree requirements:* For doctorate, thesis/dissertation. *Entrance requirements:* For master's and doctorate, GRE General Test, minimum GPA of 3.0. Additional exam requirements/recommendations for international students: Required—TOEFL (minimum score 550 paper-based; 213 computer-based; 79 iBT). *Application deadline:* Applications are processed on a rolling basis. Application fee: $55 ($75 for international students). *Expenses:* Tuition, state resident: full-time $5881. Tuition, nonresident: full-time $15,183. *Required fees:* $952. Tuition and fees vary according to campus/location and program. *Financial support:* Fellowships, research assistantships, teaching assistantships, institutionally sponsored loans, and scholarships/grants available. *Faculty research:* Limnology; conservation biology; landscape ecology; natural resource policy and management; rare species conservation; Avian ecology; behavior and conservation; large river ecology; native fish ecology and restoration ecology; wildlife disease ecology; behavioral, population and community ecology; conservation biology; mammalian carnivores; fish bioenergetics; compensatory growth; fish population dynamics and aquaculture; endangered species recovery; wildlife stress physiology. *Unit head:* Dr. Jack Jones, Department Chair, 573-882-3543, E-mail: jonesj@missouri.edu. *Application contact:* Janice Faaborg, 573-882-9422, E-mail: faaborgj@missouri.edu. Web site: http://www.snr.missouri.edu/fw/academics/graduate-program.php.

University of Missouri–St. Louis, College of Arts and Sciences, Department of Biology, St. Louis, MO 63121. Offers biotechnology (Certificate); cell and molecular biology (MS, PhD); ecology, evolution and systematics (MS, PhD); tropical biology and conservation (Certificate). Part-time programs available. *Faculty:* 43 full-time (13 women), 4 part-time/adjunct (1 woman). *Students:* 68 full-time (33 women), 64 part-time (28 women); includes 20 minority (9 Black or African American, non-Hispanic/Latino; 7 Asian, non-Hispanic/Latino; 3 Hispanic/Latino; 1 Two or more races, non-Hispanic/Latino), 43 international. Average age 28. 122 applicants, 48% accepted, 36 enrolled. In 2011, 20 master's, 3 doctorates, 11 other advanced degrees awarded. *Degree requirements:* For master's, thesis or alternative; for doctorate, thesis/dissertation, 1 semester of teaching experience. *Entrance requirements:* For master's, 3 letters of recommendation; for doctorate, GRE General Test, 3 letters of recommendation. Additional exam requirements/recommendations for international students: Required—TOEFL. *Application deadline:* For fall admission, 12/15 priority date for domestic students, 12/15 for international students; for spring admission, 12/1 priority date for domestic students, 12/1 for international students. Applications are processed on a rolling basis. Application fee: $35 ($40 for international students). Electronic applications accepted. *Expenses:* Tuition, state resident: full-time $6273; part-time $3866 per year. Tuition, nonresident: full-time $14,969; part-time $9980 per year. *Required fees:* $315 per year. *Financial support:* In 2011–12, 13 research assistantships with full and partial tuition reimbursements (averaging $15,300 per year), 27 teaching assistantships with full and partial tuition reimbursements (averaging $15,300 per year) were awarded; fellowships with full tuition reimbursements, career-related internships or fieldwork, and Federal Work-Study also available. Support available to part-time students. Financial award application deadline: 2/1. *Faculty research:* Molecular biology, microbial genetics, animal behavior, tropical ecology, plant systematics. *Unit head:* Dr. Wendy Olivas, Director of Graduate Studies, 314-516-6200, Fax: 314-516-6233, E-mail: olivasw@umsl.edu. *Application contact:* 314-516-5458, Fax: 314-516-6996, E-mail: gradadm@umsl.edu. Web site: http://www.umsl.edu/divisions/artscience/biology/.

University of Nevada, Reno, Graduate School, Interdisciplinary Program in Ecology, Evolution, and Conservation Biology, Reno, NV 89557. Offers PhD. Offered through the College of Arts and Science, the M. C. Fleischmann College of Agriculture, and the Desert Research Institute. *Degree requirements:* For doctorate, thesis/dissertation. *Entrance requirements:* For doctorate, GRE General Test, GRE Subject Test, minimum GPA of 3.0. Additional exam requirements/recommendations for international students: Required—TOEFL (minimum score 500 paper-based; 173 computer-based; 61 iBT), IELTS (minimum score 6). Electronic applications accepted. *Faculty research:* Population biology, behavioral ecology, plant response to climate change, conservation of endangered species, restoration of natural ecosystems.

University of South Florida, Graduate School, College of Arts and Sciences, Department of Biology, Tampa, FL 33620-9951. Offers cell biology and molecular biology (MS); coastal marine biology (MS); coastal marine biology and ecology (PhD); conservation biology (MS, PhD); molecular and cell biology (PhD). Part-time programs available. *Faculty:* 35 full-time (11 women), 16 part-time/adjunct (5 women). *Students:* 126 full-time (75 women), 24 part-time (17 women); includes 13 minority (1 Black or African American, non-Hispanic/Latino; 4 Asian, non-Hispanic/Latino; 8 Hispanic/Latino), 17 international. Average age 30. 235 applicants, 21% accepted, 30 enrolled. In 2011, 7 master's, 11 doctorates awarded. *Degree requirements:* For master's, comprehensive exam, thesis (for some programs); for doctorate, comprehensive exam, thesis/dissertation. *Entrance requirements:* For master's and doctorate, GRE General Test, minimum GPA of 3.0. Additional exam requirements/recommendations for international students: Required—TOEFL (minimum score 570 paper-based; 213 computer-based). *Application deadline:* For fall admission, 2/15 priority date for domestic students, 1/2 for international students; for spring admission, 8/1 for domestic students, 6/1 for international students. Application fee: $30. Electronic applications accepted. *Financial support:* In 2011–12, 122 students received support, including 46 research assistantships (averaging $24,716 per year), 76 teaching assistantships with tuition reimbursements available (averaging $28,434 per year); unspecified assistantships also available. Financial award application deadline: 6/30; financial award applicants required to submit FAFSA. *Total annual research expenditures:* $5.2 million. *Unit head:* Susan Bell, Co-Chairperson, 813-974-6210, Fax: 813-974-2876, E-mail: sbell@cas.usf.edu. *Application contact:* James Garey, Graduate Advisor, 813-974-8434, Fax: 813-974-3263, E-mail: grarey@cas.usf.edu. Web site: http://www.cas.usf.edu/biology/.

University of Wisconsin–Madison, Graduate School, Gaylord Nelson Institute for Environmental Studies, Conservation Biology and Sustainable Development Program, Madison, WI 53706-1380. Offers MS. Part-time programs available. *Faculty:* 3 full-time (1 woman), 15 part-time/adjunct (4 women). *Students:* 17 full-time, 8 part-time; includes 2 minority (1 Asian, non-Hispanic/Latino; 1 Native Hawaiian or other Pacific Islander, non-Hispanic/Latino), 2 international. Average age 29. 33 applicants, 36% accepted, 4 enrolled. In 2011, 12 master's awarded. *Degree requirements:* For master's, thesis or alternative, exit seminar. *Entrance requirements:* For master's, GRE General Test. Additional exam requirements/recommendations for international students: Required—TOEFL (minimum score 550 paper-based; 213 computer-based; 80 iBT). *Application deadline:* For fall admission, 1/15 for domestic and international students; for spring admission, 10/15 for domestic and international students. Application fee: $56. Electronic applications accepted. *Expenses:* Tuition, state resident: full-time $10,296; part-time $643.51 per credit. Tuition, nonresident: full-time $24,054; part-time $1503.40 per credit. *Required fees:* $70.06 per credit. Tuition and fees vary according to course load, campus/location, program and reciprocity agreements. *Financial support:* In 2011–12, 16 students received support, including 2 fellowships with full tuition reimbursements available (averaging $18,567 per year), 5 research assistantships with full tuition reimbursements available (averaging $20,400 per year), 6 teaching assistantships with full tuition reimbursements available (averaging $9,392 per year); career-related internships or fieldwork, Federal Work-Study, scholarships/grants, health care benefits, unspecified assistantships, and project assistantships also available. Financial award application deadline: 1/2. *Faculty research:* Ornithology, forestry, sociology, rural sociology, plant ecology, biodiversity, sustainability, sustainable development. *Unit head:* Janet M. Silbernagel, Chair, 608-890-2600, Fax: 608-262-2273, E-mail: jmsilber@wisc.edu. *Application contact:* Jim Miller, Student Services Coordinator, 608-263-4373, Fax: 608-262-2273, E-mail: jemiller@wisc.edu. Web site: http://nelson.wisc.edu/graduate_degrees/cbsd.

Ecology

Baylor University, Graduate School, College of Arts and Sciences, The Institute of Ecological, Earth and Environmental Sciences, Waco, TX 76798. Offers PhD. *Students:* 8 full-time (3 women); includes 2 minority (1 Hispanic/Latino; 1 Two or more races, non-Hispanic/Latino), 5 international. *Unit head:* Dr. Joseph D. White, Director, 254-710-2911, E-mail: joseph_d_white@baylor.edu. *Application contact:* Suzanne Keener, Administrative Assistant, 254-710-3588, Fax: 254-710-3870. Web site: http://www.baylor.edu/TIEEES/.

Brown University, Graduate School, Division of Biology and Medicine, Program in Ecology and Evolutionary Biology, Providence, RI 02912. Offers PhD. *Degree requirements:* For doctorate, thesis/dissertation, preliminary exam. *Entrance requirements:* For doctorate, GRE General Test, GRE Subject Test. Additional exam requirements/recommendations for international students: Required—TOEFL. Electronic applications accepted. *Faculty research:* Marine ecology, behavioral ecology, population genetics, evolutionary morphology, plant ecology.

California State University, Stanislaus, College of Natural Sciences, Program in Ecology and Sustainability (MS), Turlock, CA 95382. Offers ecological conservation (MS); ecological economics (MS). Part-time programs available. *Degree requirements:* For master's, thesis. *Entrance requirements:* For master's, GRE, minimum GPA of 3.0, 3 letters of recommendation, personal statement. Additional exam requirements/recommendations for international students: Required—TOEFL (minimum score 550 paper-based; 213 computer-based). *Application deadline:* For fall admission, 5/1 for domestic students; for spring admission, 1/7 for domestic students. Application fee: $55. Electronic applications accepted. *Expenses: Required fees:* $4616 per year. *Financial support:* Application deadline: 3/1; applicants required to submit FAFSA. *Unit head:* Dr. Matthew Cover, Program Director, 209-667-3153, E-mail: mcover@biology.csustan.edu. *Application contact:* Graduate School, 209-667-3129, Fax: 209-664-7025, E-mail: graduate_school@csustan.edu.

Clemson University, Graduate School, College of Agriculture, Forestry and Life Sciences, Department of Biological Sciences, Program in Biological Sciences, Clemson, SC 29634. Offers MS, PhD. *Students:* 38 full-time (24 women), 37 part-time (25 women); includes 6 minority (3 Black or African American, non-Hispanic/Latino; 2 Asian, non-Hispanic/Latino; 1 Hispanic/Latino), 9 international. Average age 34. 72 applicants, 43% accepted, 23 enrolled. In 2011, 6 master's, 2 doctorates awarded. *Degree requirements:* For master's, thesis optional; for doctorate, comprehensive exam, thesis/dissertation. *Entrance requirements:* For master's and doctorate, GRE General Test. Additional exam requirements/recommendations for international students: Required—TOEFL, IELTS. *Application deadline:* For fall admission, 1/15 for domestic students, 4/15 for international students. Applications are processed on a rolling basis. Application fee: $70 ($80 for international students). Electronic applications accepted. *Financial support:* In 2011–12, 29 students received support, including 5 fellowships with full and partial tuition reimbursements available (averaging $7,200 per year), 15 research assistantships with partial tuition reimbursements available (averaging $12,300 per year), 25 teaching assistantships with partial tuition reimbursements available (averaging $13,540 per year); career-related internships or fieldwork, institutionally sponsored loans, scholarships/grants, health care benefits, and unspecified assistantships also available. Support available to part-time students. Financial award application deadline: 3/15; financial award applicants required to submit FAFSA. *Unit head:* Dr. Alfred Wheeler, Department Chair, 864-656-1415, Fax: 864-656-0435, E-mail: wheeler@clemson.edu. *Application contact:* Jay Lyn Martin, Coordinator for Graduate Program, 864-656-3587, Fax: 864-656-0435, E-mail: gradbio@clemson.edu. Web site: http://www.clemson.edu/cafls/departments/biosci/.

Colorado State University, Graduate School, Graduate Degree Program in Ecology, Fort Collins, CO 80523-1401. Offers MS, PhD. Part-time programs available. *Students:* 68 full-time (39 women), 78 part-time (37 women); includes 9 minority (1 Black or African American, non-Hispanic/Latino; 5 Asian, non-Hispanic/Latino; 2 Hispanic/Latino; 1 Two or more races, non-Hispanic/Latino), 10 international. Average age 29. 122 applicants, 26% accepted, 32 enrolled. In 2011, 11 master's, 5 doctorates awarded. Terminal master's awarded for partial completion of doctoral program. *Degree requirements:* For master's, comprehensive exam, thesis; for doctorate, comprehensive exam, thesis/dissertation. *Entrance requirements:* For master's, GRE General Test, minimum GPA of 3.0, BA/BS in agriculture, anthropology, biology, biochemistry, math or physical sciences (preferred), letters of recommendation; for doctorate, GRE General Test, minimum GPA of 3.0, BA/BS in agriculture, anthropology, biology, biochemistry, math or physical sciences (preferred), letters of recommendation, personal statement. Additional exam requirements/recommendations for international students: Required—TOEFL (minimum score 550 paper-based; 213 computer-based; 80 iBT). *Application deadline:* For fall admission, 1/1 priority date for domestic students, 1/1 for international students. Application fee: $50. Electronic applications accepted. *Expenses:* Tuition, state resident: full-time $7992. Tuition, nonresident: full-time $19,592. *Required fees:* $1735; $58 per credit. *Financial support:* Fellowships, research assistantships, and teaching assistantships with full tuition reimbursements available. Financial award application deadline: 1/1; financial award applicants required to submit FAFSA. *Faculty research:* Plant and animal ecology at organismal, population, community, and ecosystem levels. *Unit head:* Dr. N. Leroy Poff, Interim Director, 970-491-2079, Fax: 970-491-2796, E-mail: leroy.poff@colostate.edu. *Application contact:* Jeri Morgan, Program Assistant, 970-491-4373, Fax: 970-491-2796, E-mail: ecology@colostate.edu. Web site: http://www.ecology.colostate.edu/.

Columbia University, Graduate School of Arts and Sciences, Division of Natural Sciences, Department of Ecology, Evolution and Environmental Biology, New York, NY 10027. Offers conservation biology (MA, Certificate); ecology and evolutionary biology (PhD); environmental policy (Certificate); evolutionary primatology (PhD). *Degree requirements:* For doctorate, one foreign language, thesis/dissertation, teaching experience. *Entrance requirements:* For doctorate, GRE General Test, previous course work in biology. Additional exam requirements/recommendations for international students: Required—TOEFL. Electronic applications accepted. *Faculty research:* Tropical ecology, ethnobotany, global change, systematics.

Cornell University, Graduate School, Graduate Fields of Agriculture and Life Sciences, Field of Computational Biology, Ithaca, NY 14853-0001. Offers computational behavioral biology (PhD); computational biology (PhD); computational cell biology (PhD); computational ecology (PhD); computational macromolecular biology (PhD); computational organismal biology (PhD). *Faculty:* 37 full-time (5 women). *Students:* 22 full-time (8 women); includes 4 minority (3 Asian, non-Hispanic/Latino; 1 Native Hawaiian or other Pacific Islander, non-Hispanic/Latino), 9 international. Average age 26. 145 applicants, 7% accepted, 10 enrolled. In 2011, 2 doctorates awarded. *Degree requirements:* For doctorate, comprehensive exam, thesis/dissertation, 2 semesters of teaching experience. *Entrance requirements:* For doctorate, GRE General Test, GRE Subject Test (biology), 2 letters of recommendation. Additional exam requirements/recommendations for international students: Required—TOEFL (minimum score 550 paper-based; 213 computer-based; 77 iBT). *Application deadline:* For fall admission, 2/1 priority date for domestic students. Application fee: $95. Electronic applications accepted. *Financial support:* In 2011–12, 17 fellowships with full tuition reimbursements, 4 research assistantships with full tuition reimbursements, 1 teaching assistantship with full tuition reimbursement were awarded; institutionally sponsored loans, scholarships/grants, health care benefits, tuition waivers (full and partial), and unspecified assistantships also available. Financial award applicants required to submit FAFSA. *Faculty research:* Computational behavioral biology, computational biology, computational cell biology, computational ecology, computational genetics, computational macromolecular biology, computational organismal biology. *Unit head:* Dr. Andrew Clark, Director of Graduate Studies, 607-255-5488, E-mail: ac347@cornell.edu. *Application contact:* Graduate School Application Requests, 607-255-5816, E-mail: gradadmissions@cornell.edu. Web site: http://www.gradschool.cornell.edu/fields.php?id-4A.

Cornell University, Graduate School, Graduate Fields of Agriculture and Life Sciences, Field of Ecology and Evolutionary Biology, Ithaca, NY 14853-0001. Offers ecology (PhD), including animal ecology, applied ecology, biogeochemistry, community and ecosystem ecology, limnology, oceanography, physiological ecology, plant ecology, population ecology, theoretical ecology, vertebrate zoology; evolutionary biology (PhD), including ecological genetics, paleobiology, population biology, systematics. *Faculty:* 51 full-time (14 women). *Students:* 52 full-time (36 women); includes 6 minority (1 Asian, non-Hispanic/Latino; 4 Hispanic/Latino; 1 Two or more races, non-Hispanic/Latino), 10 international. Average age 28. 121 applicants, 9% accepted, 7 enrolled. In 2011, 5 doctorates awarded. *Degree requirements:* For doctorate, comprehensive exam, thesis/dissertation, 2 semesters of teaching experience. *Entrance requirements:* For doctorate, GRE General Test, GRE Subject Test (biology), 2 letters of recommendation. Additional exam requirements/recommendations for international students: Required—TOEFL (minimum score 550 paper-based; 213 computer-based; 77 iBT). *Application deadline:* For fall admission, 12/15 for domestic students. Application fee: $95. Electronic applications accepted. *Financial support:* In 2011–12, 15 fellowships with full tuition reimbursements, 8 research assistantships with full tuition reimbursements, 25 teaching assistantships with full tuition reimbursements were awarded; institutionally sponsored loans, scholarships/grants, health care benefits, tuition waivers (full and partial), and unspecified assistantships also available. Financial award applicants required to submit FAFSA. *Faculty research:* Population and organismal biology, population and evolutionary genetics, systematics and macroevolution, biochemistry, conservation biology. *Unit head:* Director of Graduate Studies, 607-254-4230. *Application contact:* Graduate Field Assistant, 607-254-4230, E-mail: eeb_grad_req@cornell.edu. Web site: http://www.gradschool.cornell.edu/fields.php?id-46&a-2.

Cornell University, Graduate School, Graduate Fields of Agriculture and Life Sciences, Field of Zoology and Wildlife Conservation, Ithaca, NY 14853-0001. Offers animal cytology (MS, PhD); comparative and functional anatomy (MS, PhD); developmental biology (MS, PhD); ecology (MS, PhD); histology (MS, PhD). *Faculty:* 24 full-time (7 women). *Students:* 5 full-time (4 women); includes 1 minority (Two or more races, non-Hispanic/Latino), 2 international. Average age 29. 7 applicants, 14% accepted, 1 enrolled. In 2011, 2 doctorates awarded. *Degree requirements:* For doctorate, comprehensive exam, thesis/dissertation, 2 semesters of teaching experience. *Entrance requirements:* For doctorate, GRE General Test, GRE Subject Test (biology), 2 letters of recommendation. Additional exam requirements/recommendations for international students: Required—TOEFL (minimum score 550 paper-based; 213 computer-based; 77 iBT). *Application deadline:* For fall admission, 2/1 priority date for domestic students. Application fee: $95. Electronic applications accepted. *Financial support:* In 2011–12, 3 research assistantships with full tuition reimbursements, 1 teaching assistantship with full tuition reimbursement were awarded; fellowships with full tuition reimbursements, institutionally sponsored loans, scholarships/grants, health care benefits, tuition waivers (full and partial), and unspecified assistantships also available. Financial award applicants required to submit FAFSA. *Faculty research:* Organismal biology, functional morphology, biomechanics, comparative vertebrate anatomy, comparative invertebrate anatomy, paleontology. *Unit head:* Director of Graduate Studies, 607-253-3276, Fax: 607-253-3756. *Application contact:* Graduate Field Assistant, 607-253-3276, Fax: 607-253-3756, E-mail: graduate_edcvm@cornell.edu. Web site: http://www.gradschool.cornell.edu/fields.php?id-65&a-2.

Dartmouth College, Arts and Sciences Graduate Programs, Program in Ecology and Evolutionary Biology, Hanover, NH 03755. Offers PhD. *Entrance requirements:* For doctorate, GRE General Test, GRE Subject Test in biology (highly recommended). Additional exam requirements/recommendations for international students: Required—TOEFL.

Duke University, Graduate School, Department of Ecology, Durham, NC 27708-0342. Offers PhD, Certificate. *Faculty:* 31 full-time. *Students:* 25 full-time (13 women); includes 3 minority (1 Asian, non-Hispanic/Latino; 2 Hispanic/Latino), 2 international. 54 applicants, 15% accepted, 5 enrolled. In 2011, 9 degrees awarded. *Degree requirements:* For doctorate, thesis/dissertation. *Entrance requirements:* For doctorate, GRE General Test. Additional exam requirements/recommendations for international students: Required—TOEFL (minimum score 550 paper-based; 213 computer-based; 83 iBT), IELTS (minimum score 7). *Application deadline:* For fall admission, 12/8 priority date for domestic students, 12/8 for international students. Application fee: $75. Electronic applications accepted. *Expenses: Tuition:* Full-time $40,720. *Required fees:* $3107. *Financial support:* Fellowships, research assistantships, and teaching assistantships available. Financial award application deadline: 12/8. *Unit head:* Dan Richter, Director of Graduate Studies, 919-613-8002, Fax: 919-613-8061, E-mail: meg.stephens@duke.edu. *Application contact:* Elizabeth Hutton, Director, Graduate Admissions, 919-684-3913, Fax: 919-684-2277, E-mail: grad-admissions@duke.edu. Web site: http://www.ecology.duke.edu/.

Duke University, Graduate School, Department of Environment, Durham, NC 27708. Offers natural resource economics/policy (PhD); natural resource science/ecology (PhD); natural resource systems science (PhD); JD/AM. Part-time programs available. *Faculty:* 28 full-time. *Students:* 53 full-time (32 women); includes 3 minority (1 Black or African American, non-Hispanic/Latino; 2 Asian, non-Hispanic/Latino), 16 international. 87 applicants, 20% accepted, 9 enrolled. In 2011, 10 doctorates awarded. *Degree requirements:* For doctorate, variable foreign language requirement, thesis/dissertation. *Entrance requirements:* For doctorate, GRE General Test. Additional exam requirements/recommendations for international students: Required—TOEFL (minimum score 550 paper-based; 213 computer-based; 83 iBT), IELTS (minimum score 7). *Application deadline:* For fall admission, 12/8 priority date for domestic students, 12/8 for international students. Application fee: $75. Electronic applications accepted. *Expenses: Tuition:* Full-time $40,720. *Required fees:* $3107. *Financial support:* Fellowships, research assistantships, teaching assistantships, and Federal Work-Study available. Financial award application deadline: 12/8. *Unit head:* Gaby Katul, Director of Graduate Studies, 919-613-8002, Fax: 919-613-8061, E-mail: meg.stephens@duke.edu. *Application contact:* Elizabeth Hutton, Director, Graduate Admissions, 919-684-3913, Fax: 919-684-2277, E-mail: grad-admissions@duke.edu. Web site: http://www.env.duke.edu/.

Duke University, Nicholas School of the Environment, Durham, NC 27708-0328. Offers coastal environmental management (MEM); DEL-environmental leadership (MEM); energy and environment (MEM); environmental economics and policy (MEM); environmental health and security (MEM); forest resource management (MF); global environmental change (MEM); resource ecology (MEM); water and air resources (MEM); JD/AM; JD/MEM; JD/MF; MAT/MEM; MBA/MEM; MBA/MF; MEM/MPP; MF/MPP. *Accreditation:* SAF (one or more programs are accredited). Part-time programs available. *Degree requirements:* For master's, thesis. *Entrance requirements:* For master's, GRE General Test, previous course work in biology or ecology, calculus, statistics, and microeconomics; computer familiarity with word processing and data analysis. Additional exam requirements/recommendations for international students: Required—TOEFL (minimum score 550 paper-based; 213 computer-based). Electronic applications accepted. *Expenses:* Contact institution. *Faculty research:* Ecosystem management, conservation ecology, earth systems, risk assessment.

Eastern Kentucky University, The Graduate School, College of Arts and Sciences, Department of Biological Sciences, Richmond, KY 40475-3102. Offers biological sciences (MS); ecology (MS). Part-time programs available. *Degree requirements:* For master's, thesis. *Entrance requirements:* For master's, GRE General Test, minimum GPA of 2.5. *Faculty research:* Systematics, ecology, and biodiversity; animal behavior; protein structure and molecular genetics; biomonitoring and aquatic toxicology; pathogenesis of microbes and parasites.

Eastern Michigan University, Graduate School, College of Arts and Sciences, Department of Biology, Ypsilanti, MI 48197. Offers cell and molecular biology (MS); community college biology teaching (MS); ecology and organismal biology (MS); general biology (MS); water resources (MS). Part-time and evening/weekend programs available. Postbaccalaureate distance learning degree programs offered (minimal on-campus study). *Faculty:* 20 full-time (4 women). *Students:* 12 full-time (7 women), 40 part-time (21 women); includes 3 minority (1 Black or African American, non-Hispanic/Latino; 1 Asian, non-Hispanic/Latino; 1 Two or more races, non-Hispanic/Latino), 12 international. Average age 27. 70 applicants, 43% accepted, 12 enrolled. In 2011, 19 degrees awarded. *Entrance requirements:* For master's, GRE General Test, GRE Subject Test. Additional exam requirements/recommendations for international students: Required—TOEFL. *Application deadline:* Applications are processed on a rolling basis. Application fee: $35. *Expenses:* Tuition, state resident: full-time $10,367; part-time $432 per credit hour. Tuition, nonresident: full-time $20,435; part-time $851 per credit hour. *Required fees:* $39 per credit hour. $46 per semester. One-time fee: $100. Tuition and fees vary according to course level, degree level and reciprocity agreements. *Financial support:* Fellowships, research assistantships with full tuition reimbursements, teaching assistantships with full tuition reimbursements, career-related internships or fieldwork, Federal Work-Study, institutionally sponsored loans, scholarships/grants, tuition waivers (partial), and unspecified assistantships available. Support available to part-time students. Financial award applicants required to submit FAFSA. *Unit head:* Dr. Marianne Laporte, Department Head, 734-487-4242, Fax: 734-487-9235, E-mail: mlaporte@emich.edu. *Application contact:* Graduate Admissions, 734-487-2400, Fax: 734-487-6559, E-mail: graduate.admissions@emich.edu. Web site: http://www.emich.edu/biology.

Eastern New Mexico University, Graduate School, College of Liberal Arts and Sciences, Department of Biology, Portales, NM 88130. Offers applied ecology (MS); cell, molecular biology and biotechnology (MS); education (non-thesis) (MS); microbiology (MS); plant biology (MS); zoology (MS). Part-time programs available. *Faculty:* 7 full-time (0 women). *Students:* 2 full-time (1 woman), 15 part-time (9 women); includes 7 minority (5 Hispanic/Latino; 2 Two or more races, non-Hispanic/Latino), 2 international. Average age 26. 17 applicants, 82% accepted, 3 enrolled. In 2011, 4 master's awarded. *Degree requirements:* For master's, comprehensive exam, thesis optional. *Entrance requirements:* For master's, GRE, minimum GPA of 3.0, 2 letters of recommendation, statement of research interest, bachelor's degree related to field of study or proof of common knowledge. Additional exam requirements/recommendations for international students: Required—TOEFL (minimum score 550 paper-based; 213

computer-based; 79 iBT), IELTS (minimum score 6). *Application deadline:* For fall admission, 7/20 priority date for domestic students, 6/20 for international students; for spring admission, 12/15 priority date for domestic students, 11/15 for international students. Applications are processed on a rolling basis. Application fee: $10. Electronic applications accepted. *Financial support:* In 2011–12, 8 teaching assistantships with partial tuition reimbursements (averaging $8,500 per year) were awarded; scholarships/grants and unspecified assistantships also available. Support available to part-time students. Financial award applicants required to submit FAFSA. *Unit head:* Dr. Zach Jones, Graduate Coordinator, 575-562-2723, Fax: 575-562-2192, E-mail: zach.jones@enmu.edu. *Application contact:* Sharon Potter, Department Secretary, Biology and Physical Sciences, 575-562-2174, Fax: 575-562-2192, E-mail: sharon.potter@enmu.edu. Web site: http://liberal-arts.enmu.edu/biology/graduate.shtml.

Emory University, Laney Graduate School, Division of Biological and Biomedical Sciences, Program in Population Biology, Ecology and Evolution, Atlanta, GA 30322-1100. Offers PhD. *Faculty:* 35 full-time (6 women). *Students:* 30 full-time (18 women); includes 7 minority (1 Black or African American, non-Hispanic/Latino; 2 Asian, non-Hispanic/Latino; 3 Hispanic/Latino; 1 Two or more races, non-Hispanic/Latino), 5 international. Average age 27. 53 applicants, 34% accepted, 6 enrolled. *Degree requirements:* For doctorate, comprehensive exam, thesis/dissertation. *Entrance requirements:* For doctorate, GRE General Test, minimum GPA of 3.0 in science course work (recommended). Additional exam requirements/recommendations for international students: Required—TOEFL. *Application deadline:* For fall admission, 12/1 for domestic and international students. Application fee: $75. Electronic applications accepted. *Expenses: Tuition:* Full-time $34,800. *Required fees:* $1300. *Financial support:* In 2011–12, 11 students received support, including 11 fellowships with full tuition reimbursements available (averaging $26,500 per year); institutionally sponsored loans, scholarships/grants, health care benefits, and tuition waivers (full) also available. *Faculty research:* Evolution of microbes, infectious disease, the immune system, genetic disease in humans, evolution of behavior. *Unit head:* Dr. Michael Zwick, Director, 404-727-9924, Fax: 404-727-3949, E-mail: mzwick@emory.edu. *Application contact:* Kathy Smith, Director of Recruitment and Admissions, 404-727-2547, Fax: 404-727-3322, E-mail: kathy.smith@emory.edu. Web site: http://www.biomed.emory.edu/.

Florida Institute of Technology, Graduate Programs, College of Science, Department of Biological Sciences, Program in Ecology, Melbourne, FL 32901-6975. Offers ecology (MS); marine biology (MS). Part-time programs available. *Faculty:* 16 full-time (2 women). *Students:* 23 full-time (16 women), 2 part-time (both women); includes 5 minority (1 Asian, non-Hispanic/Latino; 2 Hispanic/Latino; 2 Two or more races, non-Hispanic/Latino), 1 international. Average age 24. 49 applicants, 14% accepted, 7 enrolled. In 2011, 8 master's awarded. *Degree requirements:* For master's, thesis, research, seminar, internship or summer lab. *Entrance requirements:* For master's, GRE General Test, minimum GPA of 3.0, 3 letters of recommendation, statement of objectives. Additional exam requirements/recommendations for international students: Required—TOEFL (minimum score 550 paper-based; 213 computer-based; 79 iBT). *Application deadline:* For fall admission, 3/15 for domestic students; for spring admission, 10/1 for domestic students. Applications are processed on a rolling basis. Application fee: $0. Electronic applications accepted. *Expenses: Tuition:* Full-time $19,620; part-time $1090 per credit hour. Tuition and fees vary according to campus/location. *Financial support:* Career-related internships or fieldwork, institutionally sponsored loans, tuition waivers (partial), unspecified assistantships, and tuition remissions available. Support available to part-time students. Financial award application deadline: 3/1; financial award applicants required to submit FAFSA. *Faculty research:* Endangered or threatened avian and mammalian species, hydroacoustics and feeding preference of the West Indian manatee, habitat preference of the Florida scrub jay. *Total annual research expenditures:* $1.9 million. *Unit head:* Dr. Richard B. Aronson, Department Head, 321-674-8034, Fax: 321-674-7238, E-mail: raronson@fit.edu. *Application contact:* Cheryl A. Brown, Associate Director of Graduate Admission, 321-674-7581, Fax: 321-723-9468, E-mail: cbrown@fit.edu. Web site: http://www.cos.fit.edu/biology/.

Florida State University, The Graduate School, College of Arts and Sciences, Department of Biological Science, Specialization in Ecology and Evolutionary Biology, Tallahassee, FL 32306-4295. Offers MS, PhD. *Faculty:* 23 full-time (9 women). *Students:* 51 full-time (25 women); includes 6 minority (1 Asian, non-Hispanic/Latino; 5 Hispanic/Latino), 2 international. 124 applicants, 13% accepted, 8 enrolled. In 2011, 3 master's, 6 doctorates awarded. Terminal master's awarded for partial completion of doctoral program. *Degree requirements:* For master's, comprehensive exam, thesis, teaching experience, seminar presentation; for doctorate, comprehensive exam, thesis/dissertation, teaching experience; seminar presentation. *Entrance requirements:* For master's and doctorate, GRE General Test (minimum combined score 1100, 500 verbal, 500 quantitative in old version; 72% verbal, 67% quantitative in new format), minimum upper-division GPA of 3.0. Additional exam requirements/recommendations for international students: Required—TOEFL (minimum score 600 paper-based; 250 computer-based; 92 iBT). *Application deadline:* For fall admission, 12/15 for domestic and international students. Application fee: $30. Electronic applications accepted. *Expenses:* Tuition, state resident: full-time $9474; part-time $350.88 per credit hour. Tuition, nonresident: full-time $16,236; part-time $601.34 per credit hour. *Required fees:* $630 per semester. One-time fee: $20. Tuition and fees vary according to course load and campus/location. *Financial support:* In 2011–12, 50 students received support, including 5 fellowships (averaging $30,000 per year), 19 research assistantships with full tuition reimbursements available (averaging $21,000 per year), 26 teaching assistantships with full tuition reimbursements available (averaging $21,000 per year). Financial award application deadline: 12/15; financial award applicants required to submit FAFSA. *Faculty research:* Ecology and conservation biology; evolution; marine biology; phylogeny and systematics; theoretical, computational and mathematical biology. *Unit head:* Dr. George W. Bates, Professor and Associate Chairman, 850-644-5749, Fax: 850-644-9829, E-mail: bates@bio.fsu.edu. *Application contact:* Judy Bowers, Coordinator, Graduate Affairs, 850-644-3023, Fax: 850-644-9829, E-mail: gradinfo@bio.fsu.edu. Web site: http://www.bio.fsu.edu/.

Frostburg State University, Graduate School, College of Liberal Arts and Sciences, Department of Biology, Program in Applied Ecology and Conservation Biology, Frostburg, MD 21532-1099. Offers MS. *Degree requirements:* For master's, thesis. *Entrance requirements:* For master's, GRE General Test, resume. Additional exam requirements/recommendations for international students: Required—TOEFL. Electronic applications accepted. *Faculty research:* Forest ecology, microbiology of man-made wetlands, invertebrate zoology and entomology, wildlife and carnivore ecology, aquatic pollution ecology.

Illinois State University, Graduate School, College of Arts and Sciences, Department of Biological Sciences, Normal, IL 61790-2200. Offers animal behavior (MS); bacteriology (MS); biochemistry (MS); biological sciences (MS); biology (PhD); biophysics (MS); biotechnology (MS); botany (MS, PhD); cell biology (MS); conservation biology (MS); developmental biology (MS); ecology (MS, PhD); entomology (MS); evolutionary biology (MS); genetics (MS, PhD); immunology (MS); microbiology (MS, PhD); molecular biology (MS); molecular genetics (MS); neurobiology (MS); neuroscience (MS); parasitology (MS); physiology (MS, PhD); plant biology (MS); plant molecular biology (MS); plant sciences (MS); structural biology (MS); zoology (MS, PhD). Part-time programs available. *Degree requirements:* For master's, thesis or alternative; for doctorate, variable foreign language requirement, thesis/dissertation, 2 terms of residency. *Entrance requirements:* For master's, GRE General Test, minimum GPA of 2.6 in last 60 hours of course work; for doctorate, GRE General Test. *Faculty research:* Redoc balance and drug development in schistosoma mansoni, control of the growth of listeria monocytogenes at low temperature, regulation of cell expansion and microtubule function by SPRI, CRUI: physiology and fitness consequences of different life history phenotypes.

Indiana State University, College of Graduate and Professional Studies, College of Arts and Sciences, Department of Biology, Terre Haute, IN 47809. Offers ecology (PhD); life sciences (MS); microbiology (PhD); physiology (PhD); science education (MS). *Degree requirements:* For master's, thesis (for some programs); for doctorate, comprehensive exam, thesis/dissertation. *Entrance requirements:* For master's and doctorate, GRE General Test. Electronic applications accepted.

Indiana University Bloomington, School of Public and Environmental Affairs, Environmental Science Programs, Bloomington, IN 47405. Offers applied ecology (MSES); energy (MSES); environmental chemistry, toxicology, and risk assessment (MSES); environmental science (PhD); specialized environmental science (MSES); water resources (MSES); JD/MSES; MSES/MPA; MSES/MS. Part-time programs available. *Faculty:* 80 full-time (30 women), 102 part-time/adjunct (43 women). *Students:* 142 full-time, 6 part-time; includes 8 minority (2 Black or African American, non-Hispanic/Latino; 5 Asian, non-Hispanic/Latino; 1 Hispanic/Latino), 18 international. Average age 24. 152 applicants, 57 enrolled. In 2011, 58 master's, 2 doctorates awarded. Terminal master's awarded for partial completion of doctoral program. *Degree requirements:* For master's, core classes; capstone or thesis; internship; for doctorate, comprehensive exam, thesis/dissertation. *Entrance requirements:* For master's, GRE General Test or GMAT, official transcripts, 3 letters of recommendation, resume, personal statement; for doctorate, GRE General Test or LSAT, official transcripts, 3 letters of recommendation, resume or curriculum vitae, statement of purpose. Additional exam requirements/recommendations for international students: Required—TOEFL (minimum score 600 paper-based; 96 iBT); Recommended—IELTS (minimum score 7). *Application deadline:* For fall admission, 2/1 priority date for domestic students, 12/1 for international students. Applications are processed on a rolling basis. Application fee: $55 ($65 for international students). Electronic applications accepted. *Financial support:* Fellowships with partial tuition reimbursements, research assistantships with partial tuition reimbursements, teaching assistantships with partial tuition reimbursements, career-related internships or fieldwork, Federal Work-Study, scholarships/grants, health care benefits, unspecified assistantships, and Service Corps programs available. Financial award application deadline: 2/1; financial award applicants required to submit FAFSA. *Faculty research:* Applied ecology, bio-geo chemistry, toxicology, wetlands ecology, environmental microbiology, forest ecology, environmental chemistry. *Unit head:* Jennifer J. Forney, Director, Graduate Student Services, 812-855-9485, Fax: 812-856-3665, E-mail: speampo@indiana.edu. *Application contact:* Admissions Assistant, 812-855-2840, Fax: 812-856-3665, E-mail: speaapps@indiana.edu. Web site: http://www.indiana.edu/~spea/prospective_students/masters/.

Indiana University Bloomington, University Graduate School, College of Arts and Sciences, Department of Biology, Bloomington, IN 47405. Offers biology teaching (MAT); biotechnology (MA); evolution, ecology, and behavior (MA, PhD); genetics (PhD); microbiology (MA, PhD); molecular, cellular, and developmental biology (PhD); plant sciences (MA, PhD); zoology (MA, PhD). *Faculty:* 58 full-time (15 women), 21 part-time/adjunct (6 women). *Students:* 175 full-time (100 women), 3 part-time (all women); includes 20 minority (5 Black or African American, non-Hispanic/Latino; 8 Asian, non-Hispanic/Latino; 7 Hispanic/Latino), 55 international. Average age 27. 316 applicants, 22% accepted, 31 enrolled. In 2011, 8 master's, 20 doctorates awarded. Terminal master's awarded for partial completion of doctoral program. *Degree requirements:* For master's, thesis, oral defense; for doctorate, thesis/dissertation, oral defense. *Entrance requirements:* For master's and doctorate, GRE General Test. Additional exam requirements/recommendations for international students: Required—TOEFL (minimum score 100 iBT). *Application deadline:* For fall admission, 1/5 priority date for domestic students, 12/1 for international students. Application fee: $55 ($65 for international students). Electronic applications accepted. *Financial support:* In 2011–12, fellowships with tuition reimbursements (averaging $19,484 per year), research assistantships with tuition reimbursements (averaging $20,300 per year), teaching assistantships with tuition reimbursements (averaging $20,521 per year) were awarded; scholarships/grants, traineeships, health care benefits, and unspecified assistantships also available. Financial award application deadline: 1/5. *Faculty research:* Evolution, ecology and behavior; microbiology; molecular biology and genetics; plant biology. *Unit head:* Dr. Roger Innes, Chair, 812-855-2219, Fax: 812-855-6082, E-mail: rinnes@indiana.edu. *Application contact:* Tracey D. Stohr, Graduate Student Recruitment Coordinator, 812-856-6303, Fax: 812-855-6082, E-mail: gradbio@indiana.edu. Web site: http://www.bio.indiana.edu/.

Inter American University of Puerto Rico, Bayamón Campus, Graduate School, Bayamón, PR 00957. Offers biology (MS), including environmental sciences and ecology, molecular biotechnology; human resources (MBA). Part-time and evening/weekend programs available. *Faculty:* 6 full-time (2 women), 2 part-time/adjunct (1 woman). *Students:* 7 full-time (6 women), 120 part-time (83 women); all minorities (1 Asian, non-Hispanic/Latino; 120 Hispanic/Latino; 6 Two or more races, non-Hispanic/Latino). Average age 29. *Degree requirements:* For master's, comprehensive exam, research project. *Entrance requirements:* For master's, EXADEP, GRE General Test, letters of recommendation. *Application deadline:* For fall admission, 7/1 for domestic students, 5/1 for international students; for winter admission, 11/15 priority date for domestic students, 11/15 for international students; for spring admission, 2/15 priority date for domestic students, 2/15 for international students. Application fee: $31. *Unit head:* Prof. Juan F. Martinez, Chancellor, 787-279-1200 Ext. 2295, Fax: 787-279-2205, E-mail: jmartinez@bayamon.inter.edu. *Application contact:* Carlos Alicea, Director of Admission, 787-279-1200 Ext. 2017, Fax: 787-279-2205, E-mail: calicea@bayamon.inter.edu.

Iowa State University of Science and Technology, Program in Ecology and Evolutionary Biology, Ames, IA 50011-1020. Offers MS, PhD. *Degree requirements:* For master's, thesis or alternative; for doctorate, thesis/dissertation. *Entrance requirements:* For master's and doctorate, GRE General Test. Additional exam requirements/recommendations for international students: Required—TOEFL (minimum score 550 paper-based; 79 iBT), IELTS (minimum score 6.5). *Application deadline:* For fall admission, 1/1 priority date for domestic students, 1/1 for international students; for spring admission, 6/1 priority date for domestic students, 6/1 for international students. Application fee: $40 ($90 for international students). Electronic applications accepted. *Faculty research:* Landscape ecology, aquatic and method ecology, physiological ecology, population genetics and evolution, systematics. *Unit head:* Dr. Kirk Moloney, Director of Graduate Education, 515-294-6518, Fax: 515-294-1337, E-mail: eeboffice@iastate.edu. *Application contact:* Charles Sauer, Application Contact, 515-294-6518, Fax: 515-294-1337, E-mail: eeboffice@iastate.edu. Web site: http://www.grad-college.iastate.edu/EEB/homepage.html.

Kent State University, College of Arts and Sciences, Department of Biological Sciences, Program in Ecology, Kent, OH 44242-0001. Offers MS, PhD. *Degree requirements:* For master's, thesis; for doctorate, thesis/dissertation. *Entrance requirements:* For master's, GRE General Test, minimum GPA of 3.0; for doctorate, GRE General Test, minimum GPA of 3.25. Additional exam requirements/recommendations for international students: Required—TOEFL (minimum score 600 paper-based; 287 computer-based). Electronic applications accepted. *Expenses:* Tuition, state resident: full-time $8136; part-time $452 per credit hour. Tuition, nonresident: full-time $14,292; part-time $794 per credit hour.

Laurentian University, School of Graduate Studies and Research, Programme in Biology, Sudbury, ON P3E 2C6, Canada. Offers biology (M Sc); boreal ecology (PhD). Part-time programs available. *Degree requirements:* For master's, thesis. *Entrance requirements:* For master's, honors degree with second class or better. *Faculty research:* Recovery of acid-stressed lakes, effects of climate change, origin and maintenance of biocomplexity, radionuclide dynamics, cytogenetic studies of plants.

Lesley University, Graduate School of Arts and Social Sciences, Cambridge, MA 02138-2790. Offers clinical mental health counseling (MA), including expressive therapies counseling, holistic counseling, school and community counseling; counseling psychology (MA, CAGS), including professional counseling (MA), school counseling (MA); creative arts in learning (CAGS); creative writing (MFA); ecological teaching and learning (MS); environmental education (MS); expressive therapies (MA, PhD, CAGS), including art (MA), dance (MA), expressive therapies, music (MA); independent studies (CAGS); independent study (MA); intercultural relations (MA, CAGS); interdisciplinary studies (MA), including individualized studies, integrative holistic health, women's studies; urban environmental leadership (MA); visual arts (MFA). Part-time and evening/weekend programs available. Postbaccalaureate distance learning degree programs offered (minimal on-campus study). *Faculty:* 45 full-time (36 women), 187 part-time/adjunct (139 women). *Students:* 671 full-time (605 women), 404 part-time (364 women); includes 133 minority (32 Black or African American, non-Hispanic/Latino; 4 American Indian or Alaska Native, non-Hispanic/Latino; 17 Asian, non-Hispanic/Latino; 58 Hispanic/Latino; 4 Native Hawaiian or other Pacific Islander, non-Hispanic/Latino; 18 Two or more races, non-Hispanic/Latino), 65 international. Average age 37. In 2011, 473 master's, 6 doctorates, 9 other advanced degrees awarded. *Degree requirements:* For master's, internship, practicum, thesis (expressive therapies); for doctorate, thesis/dissertation, arts apprenticeship, field placement; for CAGS, thesis, internship (counseling psychology, expressive therapies). *Entrance requirements:* For master's, MAT (counseling psychology), interview, writing samples, art portfolio; for doctorate, GRE or MAT; for CAGS, interview, master's degree. Additional exam requirements/recommendations for international students: Required—TOEFL (minimum score 550 paper-based; 213 computer-based; 80 iBT). *Application deadline:* Applications are processed on a rolling basis. Electronic applications accepted. *Financial support:* In 2011–12, research assistantships (averaging $3,400 per year), 1 teaching assistantship (averaging $7,298 per year) was awarded; career-related internships or fieldwork, Federal Work-Study, scholarships/grants, and unspecified assistantships also available. Support available to part-time students. Financial award applicants required to submit FAFSA. *Faculty research:* Psychotherapy and culture; psychotherapy and psychological trauma; women's issues in art, teaching and psychotherapy; community-based art, psycho-spiritual inquiry. *Unit head:* Dr. Julia Halevy, Dean, 617-349-8317, Fax: 617-349-8366, E-mail: jhalevy@lesley.edu. *Application contact:* Christina Murray, Senior Assistant Director, On-Campus Admissions, 617-349-8827, Fax: 617-349-8313, E-mail: cmurray3@lesley.edu. Web site: http://www.lesley.edu/gsass.html.

Marquette University, Graduate School, College of Arts and Sciences, Department of Biology, Milwaukee, WI 53201-1881. Offers cell biology (MS, PhD); developmental biology (MS, PhD); ecology (MS, PhD); epithelial physiology (MS, PhD); genetics (MS, PhD); microbiology (MS, PhD); molecular biology (MS, PhD); muscle and exercise physiology (MS, PhD); neuroscience (PhD). *Faculty:* 23 full-time (11 women), 1 part-time/adjunct (0 women). *Students:* 33 full-time (14 women), 6 part-time (3 women), 19 international. Average age 25. 78 applicants, 17% accepted, 5 enrolled. In 2011, 6 doctorates awarded. Terminal master's awarded for partial completion of doctoral program. *Degree requirements:* For master's, comprehensive exam, thesis, 1 year of teaching experience or equivalent; for doctorate, thesis/dissertation, 1 year of teaching experience or equivalent, qualifying exam. *Entrance requirements:* For master's and doctorate, GRE General Test, GRE Subject Test, official transcripts from all current and previous colleges/universities except Marquette, statement of professional goals and aspirations, three letters of recommendation. Additional exam requirements/recommendations for international students: Required—TOEFL (minimum score 530 paper-based; 78 computer-based). *Application deadline:* For fall admission, 12/15 for domestic and international students. Application fee: $50. Electronic applications accepted. *Expenses: Tuition:* Full-time $17,010; part-time $945 per credit hour. Tuition and fees vary according to program. *Financial support:* In 2011–12, 39 students received support, including 6 fellowships (averaging $1,208 per year), 4 research assistantships with full tuition reimbursements available (averaging $21,750 per year), 29 teaching assistantships with full tuition reimbursements available (averaging $21,750 per year); scholarships/grants, health care benefits, tuition waivers (full and partial), and unspecified assistantships also available. Support available to part-time students. Financial award application deadline: 2/15. *Faculty research:* Neurobiology, neuroendocrinology, epithelial physiology, neuropeptide interactions, synaptic transmission. *Total annual research expenditures:* $2 million. *Unit head:* Dr. Robert Fitts, Chair, 414-288-1748, Fax: 414-288-7357. *Application contact:* Debbie Weaver, Administrative Assistant, 414-288-7355, Fax: 414-288-7357. Web site: http://www.marquette.edu/biology/.

Michigan State University, The Graduate School, College of Natural Science, Interdepartmental Program in Ecology, Evolutionary Biology and Behavior, East Lansing, MI 48824. Offers PhD. *Entrance requirements:* Additional exam requirements/recommendations for international students: Required—TOEFL. Electronic applications accepted.

Michigan Technological University, Graduate School, School of Forest Resources and Environmental Science, Houghton, MI 49931. Offers applied ecology (MS); forest ecology and management (MS); forest science (PhD); forestry (MF, MS); molecular genetics and biotechnology (MS, PhD). *Accreditation:* SAF. Part-time programs available. *Faculty:* 26 full-time (5 women), 37 part-time/adjunct (13 women). *Students:* 67 full-time (37 women), 18 part-time (8 women), 15 international. Average age 30. 72 applicants, 39% accepted, 24 enrolled. In 2011, 24 degrees awarded. Terminal master's awarded for partial completion of doctoral program. *Degree requirements:* For master's, comprehensive exam (for some programs), thesis (for some programs); for doctorate, comprehensive exam, thesis/dissertation. *Entrance requirements:* For master's and doctorate, GRE (minimum scores: 500 in verbal, 500 quantitative, 3.5 in analytical), statement of purpose, official transcripts, 3 letters of recommendation, resume/curriculum vitae. Additional exam requirements/recommendations for international students: Required—TOEFL (minimum score 79 iBT) or IELTS. *Application deadline:* Applications are processed on a rolling basis. Electronic applications accepted. *Expenses:* Tuition, state resident: full-time $12,636; part-time $702 per credit. Tuition, nonresident: full-time $12,636; part-time $702 per credit. *Required fees:* $226; $226 per year. *Financial support:* In 2011–12, 78 students received support, including 16 fellowships with full tuition reimbursements available (averaging $6,065 per year), 36 research assistantships with full tuition reimbursements available (averaging $6,065 per year), 2 teaching assistantships with full tuition reimbursements available (averaging $6,065 per year); career-related internships or fieldwork, Federal Work-Study, scholarships/grants, health care benefits, tuition waivers (partial), unspecified assistantships, and cooperative program also available. Financial award applicants required to submit FAFSA. *Faculty research:* Forest molecular genetics and biotechnology, forestry, forest ecology and management, applied ecology, wood science. *Total annual research expenditures:* $5.9 million. *Unit head:* Dr. Terry Sharik, Dean, 906-487-2352, Fax: 906-487-2915. *Application contact:* 906-487-2352, Fax: 906-487-2915. Web site: http://www.mtu.edu/forest/.

Montana State University, College of Graduate Studies, College of Letters and Science, Department of Ecology, Bozeman, MT 59717. Offers ecological and environmental statistics (MS); ecology and environmental sciences (PhD); fish and wildlife biology (PhD); fish and wildlife management (MS). Part-time programs available. *Degree requirements:* For master's, comprehensive exam, thesis (for some programs); for doctorate, comprehensive exam, thesis/dissertation. *Entrance requirements:* For master's and doctorate, GRE, minimum GPA of 3.0, letters of recommendation, essay. Additional exam requirements/recommendations for international students: Required—TOEFL (minimum score 550 paper-based; 213 computer-based). Electronic applications accepted. *Faculty research:* Community ecology, population ecology, land-use effects, management and conservation, environmental modeling.

Montclair State University, The Graduate School, College of Science and Mathematics, Department of Biology and Molecular Biology, Montclair, NJ 07043-1624. Offers biology (MS), including biological science education, biology, ecology and evolution, physiology; molecular biology (MS, Certificate). Part-time and evening/weekend programs available. *Students:* 15 full-time (10 women), 33 part-time (23 women); includes 3 minority (all Hispanic/Latino), 1 international. Average age 28. 53 applicants, 47% accepted, 14 enrolled. In 2011, 14 degrees awarded. *Degree requirements:* For master's, comprehensive exam, thesis or alternative. *Entrance requirements:* For master's, GRE General Test, 24 credits of course work in undergraduate biology, 2 letters of recommendation, teaching certificate (biology sciences education concentration); for Certificate, 2 letters of recommendation, essay. Additional exam requirements/recommendations for international students: Required—TOEFL (minimum score 83 iBT) or IELTS. *Application deadline:* For fall admission, 6/1 for international students; for spring admission, 10/1 for international students. Applications are processed on a rolling basis. Application fee: $60. Electronic applications accepted. *Financial support:* In 2011–12, 16 research assistantships with full tuition reimbursements (averaging $7,000 per year), 3 teaching assistantships (averaging $7,000 per year) were awarded; Federal Work-Study, scholarships/grants, and unspecified assistantships also available. Support available to part-time students. Financial award application deadline: 3/1; financial award applicants required to submit FAFSA. *Faculty research:* Ecosystem biology, molecular biology, signal transduction, neuroscience, aquatic and coastal biology. *Total annual research expenditures:* $1.3 million. *Unit head:* Dr. Quinn Vega, Chairperson, 973-655-7178. *Application contact:* Amy Aiello, Director of Graduate Admissions and Operations, 973-655-5147, Fax: 973-655-7869, E-mail: graduate.school@montclair.edu. Web site: http://www.montclair.edu/csam/biology/.

North Dakota State University, College of Graduate and Interdisciplinary Studies, Interdisciplinary Program in Environmental and Conservation Sciences, Fargo, ND 58108. Offers MS, PhD. *Students:* 32 full-time (15 women), 10 part-time (3 women); includes 1 minority (Two or more races, non-Hispanic/Latino), 21 international. 23 applicants, 22% accepted, 5 enrolled. In 2011, 5 master's, 5 doctorates awarded. *Degree requirements:* For master's, comprehensive exam, thesis. *Entrance requirements:* Additional exam requirements/recommendations for international students: Required—TOEFL (minimum score 550 paper-based; 213 computer-based; 79 iBT). *Application deadline:* For fall admission, 5/1 for international students; for spring admission, 8/1 for international students. Application fee: $35. *Unit head:* Dr. Craig Stockwell, Director, 701-231-8449, Fax: 701-231-7149, E-mail: craig.stockwell@ndsu.edu. *Application contact:* Madonna Fitzgerald, Administrative Assistant, 701-231-6456, E-mail: madonna.fitzgerald@ndsu.edu. Web site: http://www.ndsu.nodak.edu/ecs/.

Nova Scotia Agricultural College, Research and Graduate Studies, Truro, NS B2N 5E3, Canada. Offers agriculture (M Sc), including air quality, animal behavior, animal molecular genetics, animal nutrition, animal technology, aquaculture, botany, crop management, crop physiology, ecology, environmental microbiology, food science, horticulture, nutrient management, pest management, physiology, plant biotechnology, plant pathology, soil chemistry, soil fertility, waste management and composting, water quality. Program offered jointly with Dalhousie University. Part-time programs available. *Degree requirements:* For master's, thesis, ATC Exam Teaching Assistantship. *Entrance requirements:* For master's, honors B Sc, minimum GPA of 3.0. Additional exam requirements/recommendations for international students: Required—TOEFL (minimum score 580 paper-based; 237 computer-based; 92 iBT), IELTS, Michigan English Language Assessment Battery, CanTEST, CAEL. *Faculty research:* Bio-product development, organic agriculture, nutrient management, air and water quality, agricultural biotechnology.

The Ohio State University, Graduate School, College of Arts and Sciences, Division of Natural and Mathematical Sciences, Department of Evolution, Ecology, and Organismal Biology, Columbus, OH 43210. Offers MS, PhD. *Faculty:* 29. *Students:* 23 full-time (15 women), 46 part-time (20 women); includes 2 minority (1 Black or African American, non-Hispanic/Latino; 1 Two or more races, non-Hispanic/Latino), 8 international. Average age 28. In 2011, 8 master's, 3 doctorates awarded. *Degree requirements:* For master's, thesis optional; for doctorate, thesis/dissertation. *Entrance requirements:* For master's and doctorate, GRE General Test. Additional exam requirements/recommendations for international students: Required—TOEFL (minimum score 550 paper-based; 250 computer-based; 79 iBT), Michigan English Language Assessment Battery (minimum score 82). *Application deadline:* For fall admission, 8/15 priority date for domestic students, 7/1 for international students; for winter admission, 12/1 priority date for domestic students, 11/1 for international students; for spring admission, 3/1 priority date for domestic students, 2/1 for international students. Applications are processed on a rolling basis. Application fee: $40 ($50 for international students). Electronic applications accepted. *Expenses:* Tuition, state resident: full-time $11,400. Tuition, nonresident: full-time $28,125. Tuition and fees vary according to course load, degree level, campus/location and program. *Financial support:* Fellowships, research assistantships, teaching assistantships, Federal Work-Study, and institutionally sponsored loans available. Support available to part-time students. *Unit head:* Peter S. Curtis, Chair, 614-292-1634, E-mail: curtis.7@osu.edu. *Application contact:* Graduate Admissions, 614-292-6031, Fax: 614-292-3656, E-mail: gradadmissions@osu.edu. Web site: http://eeob.osu.edu/.

Ohio University, Graduate College, College of Arts and Sciences, Department of Biological Sciences, Athens, OH 45701-2979. Offers biological sciences (MS, PhD); cell biology and physiology (MS, PhD); ecology and evolutionary biology (MS, PhD);

exercise physiology and muscle biology (MS, PhD); microbiology (MS, PhD); neuroscience (MS, PhD). *Students:* 35 full-time (12 women), 4 part-time (1 woman), 14 international. 62 applicants, 10% accepted, 5 enrolled. In 2011, 2 master's, 8 doctorates awarded. Terminal master's awarded for partial completion of doctoral program. *Degree requirements:* For master's, comprehensive exam, thesis, 1 quarter of teaching experience; for doctorate, comprehensive exam, thesis/dissertation, 2 quarters of teaching experience. *Entrance requirements:* For master's, GRE General Test, names of three faculty members whose research interests most closely match the applicant's interest; for doctorate, GRE General Test, essay concerning prior training, research interest and career goals, plus names of three faculty members whose research interests most closely match the applicant's interest. Additional exam requirements/recommendations for international students: Required—TOEFL (minimum score 620 paper-based; 105 iBT) or IELTS (minimum score 7.5). *Application deadline:* For fall admission, 1/15 for domestic and international students. Application fee: $50 ($55 for international students). Electronic applications accepted. *Financial support:* In 2011–12, 1 fellowship with full tuition reimbursement (averaging $18,957 per year), 10 research assistantships with full tuition reimbursements (averaging $18,957 per year), 42 teaching assistantships with full tuition reimbursements (averaging $18,957 per year) were awarded; Federal Work-Study and institutionally sponsored loans also available. Financial award application deadline: 1/15. *Faculty research:* Ecology and evolutionary biology, exercise physiology and muscle biology, neurobiology, cell biology, physiology. *Total annual research expenditures:* $2.8 million. *Unit head:* Dr. Ralph DiCaprio, Chair, 740-593-2290, Fax: 740-593-0300, E-mail: dicaprir@ohio.edu. *Application contact:* Dr. Patrick Hassett, Graduate Chair, 740-593-4793, Fax: 740-593-0300, E-mail: hassett@ohio.edu. Web site: http://www.biosci.ohiou.edu/.

Old Dominion University, College of Sciences, Program in Ecological Sciences, Norfolk, VA 23529. Offers PhD. *Faculty:* 13 full-time (3 women), 41 part-time/adjunct (7 women). *Students:* 11 full-time (7 women), 8 part-time (4 women), 4 international. Average age 32. 15 applicants, 40% accepted, 4 enrolled. In 2011, 1 doctorate awarded. *Degree requirements:* For doctorate, one foreign language, comprehensive exam, thesis/dissertation. *Entrance requirements:* For doctorate, GRE General Test, 3 letters of recommendation. Additional exam requirements/recommendations for international students: Required—TOEFL (minimum score 550 paper-based; 213 computer-based; 79 iBT). *Application deadline:* For fall admission, 2/1 priority date for domestic students, 2/1 for international students. Applications are processed on a rolling basis. Application fee: $50. Electronic applications accepted. *Expenses:* Tuition, state resident: full-time $9096; part-time $379 per credit. Tuition, nonresident: full-time $23,064; part-time $961 per credit. *Required fees:* $127 per semester. One-time fee: $50. *Financial support:* In 2011–12, 3 fellowships with full tuition reimbursements (averaging $17,000 per year), 4 research assistantships with full tuition reimbursements (averaging $15,750 per year), 9 teaching assistantships with full tuition reimbursements (averaging $15,000 per year) were awarded; scholarships/grants also available. Financial award application deadline: 2/15; financial award applicants required to submit FAFSA. *Faculty research:* Marine ecology, physiological ecology, systematics and speciation, ecological and evolutionary processes, molecular genetics. *Total annual research expenditures:* $2 million. *Unit head:* Dr. Ian Bartol, Graduate Program Director, 757-683-4737, Fax: 757-683-5283, E-mail: ecolgpd@odu.edu. *Application contact:* William Heffelfinger, Director of Graduate Admissions, 757-683-5554, Fax: 757-683-3255, E-mail: gradadmit@odu.edu. Web site: http://sci.odu.edu/biology/academics/ecologyphd.shtml.

Penn State University Park, Graduate School, Intercollege Graduate Programs, Intercollege Graduate Program in Ecology, State College, University Park, PA 16802-1503. Offers MS, PhD. *Unit head:* Dr. David Eissenstat, Chair, 814-863-3371, Fax: 814-865-9451. *Application contact:* Cynthia E. Nicosia, Director, Graduate Enrollment Services, 814-865-1795, Fax: 814-865-4627, E-mail: cey1@psu.edu. Web site: http://www.ecology.psu.edu/.

Princeton University, Graduate School, Department of Ecology and Evolutionary Biology, Princeton, NJ 08544-1019. Offers PhD. *Degree requirements:* For doctorate, thesis/dissertation. *Entrance requirements:* For doctorate, GRE General Test, GRE Subject Test. Additional exam requirements/recommendations for international students: Required—TOEFL (minimum score 600 paper-based; 250 computer-based). Electronic applications accepted.

Purdue University, Graduate School, College of Agriculture, Department of Forestry and Natural Resources, West Lafayette, IN 47907. Offers fisheries and aquatic sciences (MS, MSF, PhD); forest biology (MS, MSF, PhD); natural resource social science (MS, PhD); natural resources social science (MSF); quantitative ecology (MS, MSF, PhD); wildlife science (MS, MSF, PhD); wood products and wood products manufacturing (MS, MSF, PhD). *Faculty:* 26 full-time (3 women), 9 part-time/adjunct (1 woman). *Students:* 67 full-time (31 women), 8 part-time (3 women); includes 3 minority (2 Hispanic/Latino; 1 Two or more races, non-Hispanic/Latino), 17 international. Average age 29. 58 applicants, 16% accepted, 8 enrolled. In 2011, 9 master's, 11 doctorates awarded. *Degree requirements:* For master's, thesis; for doctorate, thesis/dissertation. *Entrance requirements:* For master's and doctorate, GRE General Test with minimum score required: verbal >=50th percentile; Quantitative >= 50th percentile; Analytical writing = 4.0 or greater, minimum undergraduate GPA of 3.2 or equivalent. Additional exam requirements/recommendations for international students: Required—TOEFL (minimum score 550 paper-based; 77 iBT). *Application deadline:* For fall admission, 1/5 for domestic students, 1/15 for international students; for spring admission, 9/15 for domestic and international students. Applications are processed on a rolling basis. Application fee: $60 ($75 for international students). Electronic applications accepted. *Financial support:* In 2011–12, 10 research assistantships (averaging $15,259 per year) were awarded; fellowships, teaching assistantships, career-related internships or fieldwork, and scholarships/grants also available. Support available to part-time students. Financial award application deadline: 1/5; financial award applicants required to submit FAFSA. *Faculty research:* Wildlife management, forest management, forest ecology, forest soils, limnology. *Unit head:* Dr. Robert K. Swihart, Interim Head, 765-494-3590, Fax: 765-494-9461, E-mail: rswihart@purdue.edu. *Application contact:* Kelly J. Garrett, Graduate Secretary, 765-494-3572, Fax: 765-494-9461, E-mail: kgarrett@purdue.edu. Web site: http://www.fnr.purdue.edu/.

Purdue University, Graduate School, College of Science, Department of Biological Sciences, West Lafayette, IN 47907. Offers biochemistry (PhD); biophysics (PhD); cell and developmental biology (PhD); ecology, evolutionary and population biology (MS, PhD), including ecology, evolutionary biology, population biology; genetics (MS, PhD); microbiology (MS, PhD); molecular biology (PhD); neurobiology (MS, PhD); plant physiology (PhD). *Faculty:* 57 full-time (15 women), 4 part-time/adjunct (1 woman). *Students:* 94 full-time (54 women), 9 part-time (5 women); includes 7 minority (2 Black or African American, non-Hispanic/Latino; 3 Asian, non-Hispanic/Latino; 2 Hispanic/Latino), 51 international. Average age 27. 246 applicants, 11% accepted, 18 enrolled. In 2011, 9 master's, 23 doctorates awarded. Terminal master's awarded for partial completion of doctoral program. *Degree requirements:* For master's, thesis (for some programs); for doctorate, thesis/dissertation, seminars, teaching experience. *Entrance requirements:* For master's, GRE General Test, minimum analytical writing score of 3.5, minimum undergraduate GPA of 3.0; for doctorate, GRE General Test, minimum analytical writing score of 3.5, minimum undergraduate GPA of 3.5. Additional exam requirements/recommendations for international students: Required—TOEFL (minimum score 600 paper-based; 107 iBT) for MS; TOEFL (minimum score 600 paper-based; 80 iBT) for Ph D. *Application deadline:* For fall admission, 12/7 for domestic and international students. Applications are processed on a rolling basis. Application fee: $60 ($75 for international students). Electronic applications accepted. *Financial support:* Fellowships, research assistantships, and teaching assistantships available. Support available to part-time students. Financial award application deadline: 2/15; financial award applicants required to submit FAFSA. *Unit head:* Dr. Richard J. Kuhn, Head, 765-494-4407, E-mail: kuhnr@purdue.edu. *Application contact:* Georgina E. Rupp, Graduate Coordinator, 765-494-8142, Fax: 765-494-0876, E-mail: ruppg@purdue.edu. Web site: http://www.bio.purdue.edu/.

Rice University, Graduate Programs, Wiess School of Natural Sciences, Department of Ecology and Evolutionary Biology, Houston, TX 77251-1892. Offers MA, MS, PhD. Terminal master's awarded for partial completion of doctoral program. *Degree requirements:* For master's, comprehensive exam (for some programs), thesis (for some programs); for doctorate, comprehensive exam, thesis/dissertation. *Entrance requirements:* For master's and doctorate, GRE General Test, GRE Subject Test. Additional exam requirements/recommendations for international students: Required—TOEFL (minimum score 600 paper-based; 250 computer-based; 90 iBT). Electronic applications accepted. *Faculty research:* Trace gas emissions, wetlands, biology, community ecology of forests and grasslands, conservation biology specialization.

Rutgers, The State University of New Jersey, New Brunswick, Graduate School-New Brunswick, Program in Ecology and Evolution, Piscataway, NJ 08854-8097. Offers MS, PhD. Part-time programs available. Terminal master's awarded for partial completion of doctoral program. *Degree requirements:* For master's, comprehensive exam; for doctorate, comprehensive exam, thesis/dissertation. *Entrance requirements:* For master's and doctorate, GRE General Test, minimum GPA of 3.0. Additional exam requirements/recommendations for international students: Required—TOEFL (minimum score 550 paper-based; 213 computer-based). Electronic applications accepted. *Faculty research:* Population and community ecology, population genetics, evolutionary biology, conservation biology, ecosystem ecology.

San Diego State University, Graduate and Research Affairs, College of Sciences, Department of Biology, Program in Ecology, San Diego, CA 92182. Offers MS, PhD. PhD offered jointly with University of California, Davis. *Degree requirements:* For master's, thesis; for doctorate, thesis/dissertation. *Entrance requirements:* For master's, GRE General Test, resumé or curriculum vitae, 2 letters of recommendation.; for doctorate, GRE General Test, GRE Subject Test, resume or curriculum vitae, 3 letters of recommendation. Electronic applications accepted. *Faculty research:* Conservation and restoration ecology, coastal and marine ecology, global change and ecosystem ecology.

San Francisco State University, Division of Graduate Studies, College of Science and Engineering, Department of Biology, Program in Ecology and Systematic Biology, San Francisco, CA 94132-1722. Offers MS. *Application deadline:* Applications are processed on a rolling basis. *Unit head:* Dr. Robert Patterson, Program Coordinator, 415-338-1237, E-mail: patters@sfsu.edu. Web site: http://biology.sfsu.edu/.

San Jose State University, Graduate Studies and Research, College of Science, Department of Biological Sciences, San Jose, CA 95192-0001. Offers biological sciences (MA, MS); molecular biology and microbiology (MS); organismal biology, conservation and ecology (MS); physiology (MS). Part-time programs available. *Entrance requirements:* For master's, GRE. Electronic applications accepted. *Faculty research:* Systemic physiology, molecular genetics, SEM studies, toxicology, large mammal ecology.

State University of New York College of Environmental Science and Forestry, Department of Environmental and Forest Biology, Syracuse, NY 13210-2779. Offers applied ecology (MPS); chemical ecology (MPS, MS, PhD); conservation biology (MPS, MS, PhD); ecology (MPS, MS, PhD); entomology (MPS, MS, PhD); environmental interpretation (MPS, MS, PhD); environmental physiology (MPS, MS, PhD); fish and wildlife biology and management (MPS, MS, PhD); forest pathology and mycology (MPS, MS, PhD); plant biotechnology (MPS); plant science and biotechnology (MPS, MS, PhD). *Degree requirements:* For master's, thesis (for some programs); for doctorate, comprehensive exam, thesis/dissertation. *Entrance requirements:* For master's and doctorate, GRE General Test, GRE Subject Test, minimum GPA of 3.0. Additional exam requirements/recommendations for international students: Required—TOEFL (minimum score 550 paper-based; 213 computer-based; 80 iBT), IELTS (minimum score 6). *Application deadline:* For fall admission, 2/1 priority date for domestic students, 2/1 for international students; for spring admission, 11/1 priority date for domestic students, 11/1 for international students. Applications are processed on a rolling basis. Application fee: $60. *Expenses:* Tuition, state resident: full-time $8870; part-time $370 per credit hour. Tuition, nonresident: full-time $15,160; part-time $632 per credit hour. *Required fees:* $60; $370 per credit hour. $350 per semester. One-time fee: $85. *Financial support:* Fellowships with full and partial tuition reimbursements, research assistantships with full and partial tuition reimbursements, teaching assistantships with full and partial tuition reimbursements, Federal Work-Study, institutionally sponsored loans, scholarships/grants, health care benefits, and unspecified assistantships available. Financial award application deadline: 6/30. *Faculty research:* Ecology, fish and wildlife biology and management, plant science, entomology. *Total annual research expenditures:* $4.1 million. *Unit head:* Dr. Donald J. Leopold, Chair, 315-470-6760, Fax: 315-470-6934. *Application contact:* Dr. Dudley J. Raynal, Dean, Instruction and Graduate Studies, 315-470-6599, Fax: 315-470-6978, E-mail: esfgrad@esf.edu. Web site: http://www.esf.edu/efb/.

State University of New York College of Environmental Science and Forestry, Department of Forest and Natural Resources Management, Syracuse, NY 13210-2779. Offers ecology and ecosystems (MPS, MS, PhD); economics, governance and human dimensions (MPS, MS, PhD); environmental and natural resources policy (MPS, MS); forest and natural resources management (MPS, MS, PhD); monitoring, analysis and modeling (MPS, MS, PhD). *Accreditation:* SAF. *Degree requirements:* For master's, thesis (for some programs); for doctorate, comprehensive exam, thesis/dissertation. *Entrance requirements:* For master's and doctorate, GRE General Test, minimum GPA of 3.0. Additional exam requirements/recommendations for international students: Required—TOEFL (minimum score 550 paper-based; 213 computer-based; 80 iBT), IELTS (minimum score 6). *Application deadline:* For fall admission, 2/1 priority date for domestic students, 2/1 for international students; for spring admission, 11/1 priority date for domestic students, 11/1 for international students. Applications are processed on a rolling basis. Application fee: $60. *Expenses:* Tuition, state resident: full-time $8870; part-time $370 per credit hour. Tuition, nonresident: full-time $15,160; part-time $632 per credit hour. *Required fees:* $60; $370 per credit hour. $350 per semester. One-time fee: $85. *Financial support:* Fellowships with full and partial tuition reimbursements, research assistantships with full and partial tuition reimbursements, teaching assistantships with full and partial tuition reimbursements, career-related internships or fieldwork, Federal Work-Study, institutionally sponsored loans, scholarships/grants, health care benefits, and unspecified assistantships available. Financial award application deadline: 6/30; financial award applicants required to submit FAFSA. *Faculty research:* Silviculture recreation management, tree improvement, operations management, economics. *Total annual research expenditures:* $2.1 million. *Unit head:*

Dr. David Newman, Chair, 315-470-6534, Fax: 315-470-6535. *Application contact:* Dr. Dudley J. Raynal, Dean, Instruction and Graduate Studies, 315-470-6599, Fax: 315-470-6978, E-mail: esfgrad@esf.edu. Web site: http://www.esf.edu/fnrm/.

Stony Brook University, State University of New York, Graduate School, College of Arts and Sciences, Department of Ecology and Evolution, Stony Brook, NY 11794. Offers applied ecology (MA); ecology and evolution (PhD). *Degree requirements:* For doctorate, one foreign language, comprehensive exam, thesis/dissertation, teaching experience. *Entrance requirements:* For doctorate, GRE General Test, GRE Subject Test. Additional exam requirements/recommendations for international students: Required—TOEFL. *Faculty research:* Theoretical and experimental population genetics, numerical taxonomy, biostatistics, population and community ecology, plant ecology.

Tulane University, School of Science and Engineering, Department of Ecology and Evolutionary Biology, New Orleans, LA 70118-5669. Offers MS, PhD. Terminal master's awarded for partial completion of doctoral program. *Degree requirements:* For master's, thesis or alternative; for doctorate, thesis/dissertation. *Entrance requirements:* For master's, GRE General Test, minimum B average in undergraduate course work; for doctorate, GRE General Test. Additional exam requirements/recommendations for international students: Required—TOEFL. Electronic applications accepted. *Faculty research:* Ichthyology, plant systematics, crustacean endocrinology, ecotoxicology, ornithology.

Universidad Nacional Pedro Henriquez Urena, Graduate School, Santo Domingo, Dominican Republic. Offers agricultural diversity (MS), including horticultural/fruit production, tropical animal production; conservation of monuments and cultural assets (M Arch); ecology and environment (MS); environmental engineering (MEE); international relations (MA); natural resource management (MS); political science (MA); project optimization (MPM); project feasibility (MPM); project management (MPM); sanitation engineering (ME); science for teachers (MS); tropical Caribbean architecture (M Arch).

University at Albany, State University of New York, College of Arts and Sciences, Department of Biological Sciences, Specialization in Ecology, Evolution, and Behavior, Albany, NY 12222-0001. Offers MS, PhD. *Degree requirements:* For master's, one foreign language; for doctorate, one foreign language, thesis/dissertation. *Entrance requirements:* For master's and doctorate, GRE General Test.

University at Buffalo, the State University of New York, Graduate School, College of Arts and Sciences, Program in Evolution, Ecology and Behavior, Buffalo, NY 14260. Offers MS, PhD, Certificate. *Faculty:* 18 full-time (8 women). *Students:* 14 full-time (9 women), 3 international. Average age 25. 21 applicants, 43% accepted, 7 enrolled. In 2011, 6 master's, 1 doctorate awarded. Terminal master's awarded for partial completion of doctoral program. *Degree requirements:* For master's, project; for doctorate, comprehensive exam, thesis/dissertation. *Entrance requirements:* For master's, GRE, minimum undergraduate GPA of 3.0; for doctorate, GRE, minimum GPA of 3.0. Additional exam requirements/recommendations for international students: Required—TOEFL (minimum score 550 paper-based; 213 computer-based; 79 iBT). *Application deadline:* For fall admission, 1/15 priority date for domestic students, 1/15 for international students. Applications are processed on a rolling basis. Application fee: $75. Electronic applications accepted. *Financial support:* In 2011–12, 2 fellowships with full tuition reimbursements (averaging $6,000 per year), 6 research assistantships with full tuition reimbursements (averaging $24,000 per year), 4 teaching assistantships with full tuition reimbursements (averaging $17,000 per year) were awarded; Federal Work-Study, scholarships/grants, health care benefits, and unspecified assistantships also available. Financial award application deadline: 1/15; financial award applicants required to submit FAFSA. *Faculty research:* Coral reef ecology, evolution and ecology of aquatic invertebrates, animal communication, paleobiology, primate behavior. *Unit head:* Dr. Howard Lasker, Program Director, 716-645-4870, Fax: 716-645-3999, E-mail: ub-evb@buffalo.edu. *Application contact:* Marty Roth, Secretary, 716-645-3489, Fax: 716-345-3999, E-mail: mlroth@buffalo.edu. Web site: http://www.evolutionecologybehavior.buffalo.edu/.

University of Alberta, Faculty of Graduate Studies and Research, Department of Biological Sciences, Edmonton, AB T6G 2E1, Canada. Offers environmental biology and ecology (M Sc, PhD); microbiology and biotechnology (M Sc, PhD); molecular biology and genetics (M Sc, PhD); physiology and cell biology (M Sc, PhD); plant biology (M Sc, PhD); systematics and evolution (M Sc, PhD). Terminal master's awarded for partial completion of doctoral program. *Degree requirements:* For master's, thesis; for doctorate, thesis/dissertation. *Entrance requirements:* Additional exam requirements/recommendations for international students: Required—TOEFL.

The University of Arizona, College of Science, Department of Ecology and Evolutionary Biology, Tucson, AZ 85721. Offers MS, PhD. *Faculty:* 20 full-time (4 women), 3 part-time/adjunct (0 women). *Students:* 42 full-time (21 women), 13 part-time (4 women); includes 5 minority (1 Black or African American, non-Hispanic/Latino; 1 American Indian or Alaska Native, non-Hispanic/Latino; 1 Hispanic/Latino; 2 Two or more races, non-Hispanic/Latino), 12 international. Average age 30. 87 applicants, 15% accepted, 9 enrolled. In 2011, 6 master's, 2 doctorates awarded. Terminal master's awarded for partial completion of doctoral program. *Degree requirements:* For master's, thesis optional; for doctorate, one foreign language, comprehensive exam, thesis/dissertation. *Entrance requirements:* For master's, GRE General Test, GRE Subject Test, statement of purpose, curriculum vitae, 3 letters of recommendation; for doctorate, GRE General Test, GRE Subject Test, curriculum vitae, 3 letters of recommendation. Additional exam requirements/recommendations for international students: Required—TOEFL (minimum score 550 paper-based; 213 computer-based; 79 iBT). *Application deadline:* For fall admission, 12/1 for domestic students, 12/8 for international students. Application fee: $75. *Expenses:* Tuition, state resident: full-time $10,840. Tuition, nonresident: full-time $25,802. *Financial support:* In 2011–12, 13 research assistantships with full tuition reimbursements (averaging $22,896 per year), 35 teaching assistantships with full tuition reimbursements (averaging $22,896 per year) were awarded; career-related internships or fieldwork, scholarships/grants, health care benefits, and unspecified assistantships also available. *Faculty research:* Biological diversity, evolutionary history, evolutionary mechanisms, community structure. *Total annual research expenditures:* $5.6 million. *Unit head:* Dr. Richard E. Michod, Head, 520-621-7509, Fax: 520-621-9190, E-mail: michod@email.arizona.edu. *Application contact:* Carol Burleson, Administrative Associate, 520-621-1165, Fax: 520-621-9190, E-mail: burleson@email.arizona.edu. Web site: http://eebweb.arizona.edu/.

University of California, Davis, Graduate Studies, Graduate Group in Ecology, Davis, CA 95616. Offers MS, PhD. PhD offered jointly with San Diego State University. *Degree requirements:* For master's, comprehensive exam (for some programs), thesis (for some programs); for doctorate, thesis/dissertation. *Entrance requirements:* For master's and doctorate, GRE General Test. Additional exam requirements/recommendations for international students: Required—TOEFL (minimum score 550 paper-based; 213 computer-based). Electronic applications accepted. *Faculty research:* Agricultural conservation, physiological restoration, environmental policy, ecotoxicology.

University of California, Irvine, School of Biological Sciences, Department of Ecology and Evolutionary Biology, Irvine, CA 92697. Offers biological sciences (MS, PhD). *Students:* 44 full-time (27 women); includes 8 minority (3 Asian, non-Hispanic/Latino; 4

Hispanic/Latino; 1 Two or more races, non-Hispanic/Latino), 5 international. Average age 27. 62 applicants, 27% accepted, 10 enrolled. In 2011, 3 master's, 11 doctorates awarded. *Degree requirements:* For master's, thesis; for doctorate, thesis/dissertation. *Entrance requirements:* For master's and doctorate, GRE General Test, GRE Subject Test, minimum GPA of 3.0. Additional exam requirements/recommendations for international students: Required—TOEFL (minimum score 550 paper-based; 213 computer-based). *Application deadline:* For fall admission, 1/15 priority date for domestic students, 1/15 for international students. Applications are processed on a rolling basis. Application fee: $80 ($100 for international students). Electronic applications accepted. *Financial support:* Fellowships, research assistantships with full tuition reimbursements, teaching assistantships, career-related internships or fieldwork, institutionally sponsored loans, traineeships, health care benefits, and unspecified assistantships available. Financial award application deadline: 3/1; financial award applicants required to submit FAFSA. *Faculty research:* Ecological energetics, quantitative genetics, life history evolution, plant-herbivore and plant-pollinator interactions, molecular evolution. *Unit head:* Peter A. Bowler, Faculty Manager, 949-824-0157, Fax: 949-824-2181, E-mail: pabowler@uci.edu. *Application contact:* Pamela McDonald, 949-824-4743, E-mail: bshipley@uci.edu. Web site: http://ecoevo.bio.uci.edu/.

University of California, Los Angeles, Graduate Division, College of Letters and Science, Department of Ecology and Evolutionary Biology, Los Angeles, CA 90095. Offers MA, PhD. *Faculty:* 23 full-time (5 women). *Students:* 71 full-time (48 women); includes 20 minority (2 Black or African American, non-Hispanic/Latino; 8 Asian, non-Hispanic/Latino; 8 Hispanic/Latino; 2 Two or more races, non-Hispanic/Latino), 9 international. Average age 29. 92 applicants, 26% accepted, 16 enrolled. In 2011, 2 master's, 11 doctorates awarded. Terminal master's awarded for partial completion of doctoral program. *Degree requirements:* For master's, comprehensive exam or thesis; for doctorate, thesis/dissertation, oral and written qualifying exams; teaching experience. *Entrance requirements:* For master's and doctorate, GRE General Test, GRE Subject Test (biology), minimum GPA of 3.0, 3 letters of recommendation. *Application deadline:* For fall admission, 12/1 for domestic and international students. Application fee: $70 ($90 for international students). Electronic applications accepted. *Financial support:* In 2011–12, 64 fellowships with full and partial tuition reimbursements, 20 research assistantships with full and partial tuition reimbursements, 38 teaching assistantships with full and partial tuition reimbursements were awarded; Federal Work-Study, institutionally sponsored loans, scholarships/grants, health care benefits, tuition waivers (full and partial), and unspecified assistantships also available. Financial award application deadline: 3/1; financial award applicants required to submit FAFSA. *Faculty research:* Molecular, cell, and developmental biology; interactive biology; organisms and populations. *Unit head:* Dr. Daniel T. Blumstein, Chair, 310-267-4746, Fax: 310-206-3987, E-mail: marmots@ucla.edu. *Application contact:* Jocelyn Yamadera, Student Affairs Officer, 310-825-1959, Fax: 310-206-5280, E-mail: jocelyny@lifesci.ucla.edu. Web site: http://www.eeb.ucla.edu/.

University of California, Riverside, Graduate Division, Department of Entomology, Riverside, CA 92521-0102. Offers entomology (MS, PhD); evolution and ecology (PhD). Part-time programs available. *Faculty:* 35 full-time (4 women). *Students:* 37 full-time (19 women); includes 8 minority (1 Black or African American, non-Hispanic/Latino; 4 Asian, non-Hispanic/Latino; 3 Hispanic/Latino), 6 international. Average age 28. 27 applicants, 37% accepted, 7 enrolled. In 2011, 2 master's, 8 doctorates awarded. Terminal master's awarded for partial completion of doctoral program. *Degree requirements:* For master's, thesis; for doctorate, thesis/dissertation, qualifying exams. *Entrance requirements:* For master's and doctorate, GRE General Test, minimum GPA of 3.2. Additional exam requirements/recommendations for international students: Required—TOEFL (minimum score 550 paper-based; 213 computer-based; 80 iBT) or IELTS. *Application deadline:* For fall admission, 5/1 for domestic students, 2/1 for international students; for winter admission, 9/1 for domestic students, 7/1 for international students; for spring admission, 12/1 for domestic students, 10/1 for international students. Applications are processed on a rolling basis. Application fee: $80 ($100 for international students). Electronic applications accepted. *Financial support:* In 2011–12, fellowships with tuition reimbursements (averaging $18,000 per year), research assistantships with tuition reimbursements (averaging $19,500 per year), teaching assistantships with tuition reimbursements (averaging $17,310 per year) were awarded; career-related internships or fieldwork, Federal Work-Study, institutionally sponsored loans, and tuition waivers (full and partial) also available. Financial award application deadline: 1/5; financial award applicants required to submit FAFSA. *Faculty research:* Agricultural, urban, medical, and veterinary entomology; biological control; chemical ecology; insect pathogens; novel toxicants. *Unit head:* Dr. Richard Redak, Chair, 951-827-7250, Fax: 951-827-3086, E-mail: richard.redak@ucr.edu. *Application contact:* Melissa L. Gomez, Graduate Student Affairs Officer, 951-827-5913, Fax: 951-827-5517, E-mail: insects@ucr.edu. Web site: http://www.entomology.ucr.edu/.

University of California, San Diego, Office of Graduate Studies, Division of Biological Sciences, Program in Ecology, Behavior, and Evolution, La Jolla, CA 92093. Offers PhD. *Degree requirements:* For doctorate, thesis/dissertation, qualifying exam. Electronic applications accepted.

University of California, Santa Barbara, Graduate Division, College of Letters and Sciences, Division of Mathematics, Life, and Physical Sciences, Department of Ecology, Evolution, and Marine Biology, Santa Barbara, CA 93106-9620. Offers computational science and engineering (MA); computational sciences and engineering (PhD); ecology, evolution, and marine biology (MA, PhD); MA/PhD. *Faculty:* 27 full-time (7 women). *Students:* 58 full-time (39 women); includes 9 minority (1 Black or African American, non-Hispanic/Latino; 5 Asian, non-Hispanic/Latino; 2 Hispanic/Latino; 1 Two or more races, non-Hispanic/Latino), 4 international. Average age 30. 131 applicants, 15% accepted, 8 enrolled. In 2011, 4 master's, 4 doctorates awarded. *Median time to degree:* Of those who began their doctoral program in fall 2003, 100% received their degree in 8 years or less. *Degree requirements:* For master's, comprehensive exam (for some programs), thesis (for some programs); for doctorate, comprehensive exam, thesis/dissertation. *Entrance requirements:* For master's and doctorate, GRE General Test. Additional exam requirements/recommendations for international students: Required—TOEFL (minimum score 550 paper-based; 80 iBT), IELTS. *Application deadline:* For fall admission, 12/15 for domestic and international students. Application fee: $80 ($100 for international students). Electronic applications accepted. *Expenses:* Tuition, state resident: full-time $12,192. Tuition, nonresident: full-time $27,294. *Required fees:* $764.13. *Financial support:* In 2011–12, 54 students received support, including 44 fellowships with full and partial tuition reimbursements available (averaging $10,812 per year), 13 research assistantships with full and partial tuition reimbursements available (averaging $8,441 per year), 22 teaching assistantships with partial tuition reimbursements available (averaging $9,346 per year); Federal Work-Study, scholarships/grants, traineeships, health care benefits, and tuition waivers (full and partial) also available. Financial award application deadline: 12/15; financial award applicants required to submit FAFSA. *Faculty research:* Community ecology, evolution, marine biology, population genetics, stream ecology. *Unit head:* Dr. Cheryl Briggs, Chair, 805-893-2415, Fax: 805-893-5885. *Application contact:* Melanie Fujii, Staff Graduate Advisor, 805-893-2979, Fax: 805-893-5885, E-mail: eemb-info@lifesci.ucsb.edu. Web site: http://www.lifesci.ucsb.edu/EEMB/index.html.

Ecology

University of California, Santa Cruz, Division of Graduate Studies, Division of Physical and Biological Sciences, Department of Ecology and Evolutionary Biology, Santa Cruz, CA 95064. Offers MA, PhD. *Degree requirements:* For master's, thesis; for doctorate, comprehensive exam, thesis/dissertation. *Entrance requirements:* For master's and doctorate, GRE General Test, GRE Subject Test, 3 letters of recommendation. Additional exam requirements/recommendations for international students: Required—TOEFL (minimum score 550 paper-based; 220 computer-based; 83 iBT); Recommended—IELTS (minimum score 8). Electronic applications accepted. *Faculty research:* Population and community ecology, evolutionary biology, physiology and behavior (marine and terrestrial), systematics and biodiversity.

University of Chicago, Division of Biological Sciences, Darwinian Sciences Cluster: Ecological, Integrative and Evolutionary Biology, Department of Ecology and Evolution, Chicago, IL 60637-1513. Offers PhD. *Degree requirements:* For doctorate, thesis/dissertation, ethics class, 2 teaching assistantships. *Entrance requirements:* For doctorate, GRE General Test. Additional exam requirements/recommendations for international students: Required—TOEFL (minimum score 600 paper-based; 250 computer-based; 104 iBT), IELTS (minimum score 7). Electronic applications accepted. *Faculty research:* Population genetics, molecular evolution, behavior.

University of Colorado Boulder, Graduate School, College of Arts and Sciences, Department of Ecology and Evolutionary Biology, Boulder, CO 80309. Offers animal behavior (MA); biology (MA, PhD); environmental biology (MA, PhD); evolutionary biology (MA, PhD); neurobiology (MA); population biology (MA); population genetics (PhD). *Faculty:* 28 full-time (9 women). *Students:* 67 full-time (37 women), 27 part-time (13 women); includes 9 minority (1 Asian, non-Hispanic/Latino; 8 Hispanic/Latino), 5 international. Average age 30. 136 applicants, 13% accepted, 17 enrolled. In 2011, 8 master's, 5 doctorates awarded. Terminal master's awarded for partial completion of doctoral program. *Degree requirements:* For master's, comprehensive exam, thesis or alternative; for doctorate, comprehensive exam, thesis/dissertation. *Entrance requirements:* For master's, GRE General Test, GRE Subject Test, minimum undergraduate GPA of 3.0; for doctorate, GRE General Test, GRE Subject Test. *Application deadline:* For fall admission, 12/30 priority date for domestic students, 12/1 for international students. Application fee: $50 ($60 for international students). Electronic applications accepted. *Financial support:* In 2011–12, 88 students received support, including 35 fellowships (averaging $16,835 per year), 25 research assistantships with full and partial tuition reimbursements available (averaging $22,347 per year), 44 teaching assistantships with full and partial tuition reimbursements available (averaging $21,377 per year); institutionally sponsored loans, scholarships/grants, health care benefits, and unspecified assistantships also available. Financial award applicants required to submit FAFSA. *Faculty research:* Behavior, ecology, genetics, morphology, endocrinology, physiology, systematics. *Total annual research expenditures:* $4.6 million. *Application contact:* E-mail: ebiograd@colorado.edu. Web site: http://ebio.colorado.edu.

University of Colorado Denver, College of Liberal Arts and Sciences, Department of Geography and Environmental Sciences, Denver, CO 80217. Offers environmental sciences (MS), including air quality, ecosystems, environmental health, environmental science education, geo-spatial analysis, hazardous waste, water quality. Part-time and evening/weekend programs available. *Students:* 42 full-time (25 women), 6 part-time (5 women); includes 6 minority (2 Black or African American, non-Hispanic/Latino; 1 Asian, non-Hispanic/Latino; 2 Hispanic/Latino; 1 Two or more races, non-Hispanic/Latino), 10 international. Average age 29. 31 applicants, 68% accepted, 13 enrolled. In 2011, 24 master's awarded. *Degree requirements:* For master's, thesis or alternative, 30 credits including 21 of core requirements and 9 of environmental science electives. *Entrance requirements:* For master's, GRE General Test, BA in one of the natural/physical sciences or engineering (or equivalent background); prerequisite coursework in calculus and physics (one semester each), general chemistry with lab and general biology with lab (two semesters each), three letters of recommendation. Additional exam requirements/recommendations for international students: Required—TOEFL (minimum score 525 paper-based; 197 computer-based). *Application deadline:* For fall admission, 4/1 for domestic and international students; for spring admission, 10/1 for domestic and international students. Application fee: $50 ($75 for international students). Electronic applications accepted. *Financial support:* Research assistantships, teaching assistantships, and Federal Work-Study available. Financial award application deadline: 4/1; financial award applicants required to submit FAFSA. *Faculty research:* Air quality, environmental health, ecosystems, hazardous waste, water quality, geo-spatial analysis and environmental science education. *Unit head:* Dr. Brian K. Page, Department Chair, 303-556-8332, Fax: 303-556-6197, E-mail: john.wyckoff@cudenver.edu. *Application contact:* Sue Eddleman, Program Assistant, 303-556-6197, E-mail: sue.eddleman@ucdenver.edu. Web site: http://www.ucdenver.edu/academics/colleges/CLAS/Departments/ges/Pages/Geography.aspx.

University of Colorado Denver, College of Liberal Arts and Sciences, Department of Integrative Biology, Denver, CO 80217. Offers animal behavior (MS); biology (MS); cell and developmental biology (MS); ecology (MS); evolutionary biology (MS); genetics (MS); microbiology (MS); molecular biology (MS); neurobiology (MS); plant systematics (MS). Part-time programs available. *Faculty:* 16 full-time (8 women). *Students:* 20 full-time (13 women), 5 part-time (4 women); includes 1 minority (Hispanic/Latino), 1 international. Average age 29. 21 applicants, 43% accepted, 5 enrolled. In 2011, 7 master's awarded. *Degree requirements:* For master's, comprehensive exam, thesis or alternative, 30-32 credit hours. *Entrance requirements:* For master's, GRE General Test (minimum score in 50% percentile in each section), BA/BS from accredited institution awarded within the last 10 years; minimum undergraduate GPA of 3.0; prerequisite courses: 1 year each of general biology and general chemistry, and 1 semester each of general genetics, general ecology, cell biology, and a structure/function course. Additional exam requirements/recommendations for international students: Required—TOEFL (minimum score 525 paper-based; 197 computer-based; 71 iBT). *Application deadline:* For fall admission, 2/1 for domestic and international students. Application fee: $50 ($75 for international students). Electronic applications accepted. *Financial support:* Research assistantships, teaching assistantships, Federal Work-Study, scholarships/grants, and unspecified assistantships available. Financial award application deadline: 4/1; financial award applicants required to submit FAFSA. *Faculty research:* Molecular developmental biology; quantitative ecology, biogeography, and population dynamics; environmental signaling and endocrine disruption; speciation, the evolution of reproductive isolation, and hybrid zones; evolutionary, behavioral, and conservation ecology. *Unit head:* Dr. Diana Tomback, Acting Chair, 303-556-2657, E-mail: diana.tomback@ucdenver.edu. *Application contact:* Timberley Roane, Associate Professor/Associate Chair, 303-556-6592, E-mail: timberley.roane@ucdenver.edu. Web site: http://www.ucdenver.edu/academics/colleges/CLAS/Departments/biology/Pages/Biology.aspx.

University of Connecticut, Graduate School, College of Liberal Arts and Sciences, Department of Ecology and Evolutionary Biology, Storrs, CT 06269. Offers botany (MS, PhD); ecology (MS, PhD); entomology (MS, PhD); zoology (MS, PhD). Terminal master's awarded for partial completion of doctoral program. *Degree requirements:* For master's, comprehensive exam; for doctorate, thesis/dissertation. *Entrance requirements:* For master's and doctorate, GRE General Test, GRE Subject Test. Additional exam requirements/recommendations for international students: Required—TOEFL (minimum score 550 paper-based; 213 computer-based). Electronic applications accepted.

University of Connecticut, Graduate School, College of Liberal Arts and Sciences, Department of Psychology, Storrs, CT 06269. Offers behavioral neuroscience (PhD); biopsychology (PhD); clinical psychology (MA, PhD); cognition and instruction (PhD); developmental psychology (MA, PhD); ecological psychology (PhD); experimental psychology (PhD); general psychology (MA, PhD); health psychology (Graduate Certificate); industrial/organizational psychology (PhD); language and cognition (PhD); neuroscience (PhD); occupational health psychology (Graduate Certificate); social psychology (MA, PhD). *Accreditation:* APA. Terminal master's awarded for partial completion of doctoral program. *Degree requirements:* For master's, comprehensive exam; for doctorate, thesis/dissertation. *Entrance requirements:* For master's and doctorate, GRE General Test, GRE Subject Test. Additional exam requirements/recommendations for international students: Required—TOEFL (minimum score 550 paper-based; 213 computer-based). Electronic applications accepted.

University of Delaware, College of Agriculture and Natural Resources, Department of Entomology and Wildlife Ecology, Newark, DE 19716. Offers entomology and applied ecology (MS, PhD), including avian ecology, evolution and taxonomy, insect biological control, insect ecology and behavior (MS), insect genetics, pest management, plant-insect interactions, wildlife ecology and management. Part-time programs available. *Degree requirements:* For master's, comprehensive exam, thesis, oral exam, seminar; for doctorate, comprehensive exam, thesis/dissertation, qualifying exam, seminar. *Entrance requirements:* For master's, GRE General Test, minimum GPA of 3.0 in field, 2.8 overall; for doctorate, GRE General Test, GRE Subject Test (biology), minimum GPA of 3.0 in field, 2.8 overall. Additional exam requirements/recommendations for international students: Required—TOEFL. Electronic applications accepted. *Faculty research:* Ecology and evolution of plant-insect interactions, ecology of wildlife conservation management, habitat restoration, biological control, applied ecosystem management.

University of Delaware, College of Arts and Sciences, Department of Biological Sciences, Newark, DE 19716. Offers biotechnology (MS); cancer biology (MS, PhD); cell and extracellular matrix biology (MS, PhD); cell and systems physiology (MS, PhD); developmental biology (MS, PhD); ecology and evolution (MS, PhD); microbiology (MS, PhD); molecular biology and genetics (MS, PhD). Terminal master's awarded for partial completion of doctoral program. *Degree requirements:* For master's, thesis, preliminary exam; for doctorate, comprehensive exam, thesis/dissertation, preliminary exam. *Entrance requirements:* For master's and doctorate, GRE General Test. Additional exam requirements/recommendations for international students: Required—TOEFL (minimum score 600 paper-based; 250 computer-based); Recommended—TWE. Electronic applications accepted. *Faculty research:* Microorganisms, bone, cancer metastasis, developmental biology, cell biology, DNA.

University of Florida, Graduate School, College of Agricultural and Life Sciences, Department of Wildlife Ecology and Conservation, Gainesville, FL 32611. Offers MS, PhD. *Faculty:* 16 full-time (4 women), 1 part-time/adjunct (0 women). *Students:* 38 full-time (19 women), 12 part-time (6 women); includes 10 minority (4 Black or African American, non-Hispanic/Latino; 1 Asian, non-Hispanic/Latino; 5 Hispanic/Latino), 17 international. Average age 31. 45 applicants, 33% accepted, 12 enrolled. In 2011, 10 master's, 3 doctorates awarded. *Degree requirements:* For master's, comprehensive exam, thesis optional; for doctorate, comprehensive exam, thesis/dissertation. *Entrance requirements:* For master's and doctorate, GRE General Test, minimum GPA of 3.3. Additional exam requirements/recommendations for international students: Required—TOEFL (minimum score 550 paper-based; 213 computer-based; 80 iBT), IELTS (minimum score 6). *Application deadline:* For fall admission, 6/1 priority date for domestic students; for spring admission, 12/1 for domestic students. Applications are processed on a rolling basis. Application fee: $30. Electronic applications accepted. *Financial support:* Fellowships, research assistantships, teaching assistantships, and institutionally sponsored loans available. Financial award applicants required to submit FAFSA. *Faculty research:* Wildlife biology and management, tropical ecology and conservation, conservation biology, landscape ecology and restoration, conservation education. *Unit head:* Dr. John P. Hayes, Department Chair, 352-846-0552, E-mail: hayesj@ufl.edu. *Application contact:* Dr. Wiley Kitchens, Graduate Coordinator, 352-846-0536, Fax: 352-846-0841, E-mail: wiley01@ufl.edu. Web site: http://www.wec.ufl.edu/.

University of Florida, Graduate School, School of Natural Resources and Environment, Gainesville, FL 32611. Offers interdisciplinary ecology (MS, PhD). *Students:* 87 full-time (53 women), 25 part-time (11 women); includes 15 minority (3 Black or African American, non-Hispanic/Latino; 1 American Indian or Alaska Native, non-Hispanic/Latino; 3 Asian, non-Hispanic/Latino; 8 Hispanic/Latino), 39 international. Average age 33. 68 applicants, 19% accepted, 11 enrolled. In 2011, 14 master's, 17 doctorates awarded. *Degree requirements:* For master's, comprehensive exam, thesis; for doctorate, comprehensive exam, thesis/dissertation. *Entrance requirements:* For master's and doctorate, GRE General Test, minimum GPA of 3.0. Additional exam requirements/recommendations for international students: Required—TOEFL (minimum score 550 paper-based; 213 computer-based; 80 iBT), IELTS (minimum score 6). *Application deadline:* For fall admission, 2/1 priority date for domestic students, 2/1 for international students. Applications are processed on a rolling basis. Application fee: $30. Electronic applications accepted. *Financial support:* Fellowships, research assistantships, and teaching assistantships available. Financial award applicants required to submit FAFSA. *Faculty research:* Natural sciences, social sciences, sustainability studies, research design and methods. *Unit head:* Dr. Stephen R. Humphrey, Director and Graduate Coordinator, 352-392-9230, Fax: 352-392-9748, E-mail: humphrey@ufl.edu. *Application contact:* Office of Graduate Admissions, 352-392-1365, E-mail: gradinfo@ufl.edu. Web site: http://www.snre.ufl.edu/.

University of Georgia, School of Ecology, Athens, GA 30602. Offers conservation ecology and sustainable development (MS); ecology (MS, PhD). *Faculty:* 22 full-time (7 women), 6 part-time/adjunct (2 women). *Students:* 66 full-time (43 women), 9 part-time (6 women); includes 6 minority (5 Hispanic/Latino; 1 Two or more races, non-Hispanic/Latino), 2 international. Average age 30. 81 applicants, 25% accepted, 13 enrolled. In 2011, 7 master's, 4 doctorates awarded. *Degree requirements:* For master's, thesis; for doctorate, one foreign language, thesis/dissertation. *Entrance requirements:* For master's and doctorate, GRE General Test. *Application deadline:* For fall admission, 7/1 priority date for domestic students; for spring admission, 11/15 for domestic students. Application fee: $50. Electronic applications accepted. *Financial support:* Fellowships, research assistantships, teaching assistantships, and unspecified assistantships available. *Unit head:* Dr. John L. Gittleman, Dean, 706-542-2968, Fax: 706-542-4819, E-mail: ecohead@uga.edu. *Application contact:* Dr. James Byers, Graduate Coordinator, 706-338-0012, Fax: 706-542-4819, E-mail: jebyers@uga.edu. Web site: http://www.ecology.uga.edu/.

University of Guelph, Graduate Studies, College of Biological Science, Department of Integrative Biology, Botany and Zoology, Guelph, ON N1G 2W1, Canada. Offers botany (M Sc, PhD); zoology (M Sc, PhD). Part-time programs available. *Degree requirements:* For master's, thesis, research proposal; for doctorate, thesis/dissertation, research

proposal, qualifying exam. *Entrance requirements:* For master's, minimum B average during previous 2 years of course work. Additional exam requirements/recommendations for international students: Required—TOEFL (minimum score 550 paper-based; 213 computer-based), IELTS (minimum score 6.5). Electronic applications accepted. *Faculty research:* Aquatic science, environmental physiology, parasitology, wildlife biology, management.

University of Hawaii at Manoa, Graduate Division, Interdisciplinary Specialization in Ecology, Evolution and Conservation Biology, Honolulu, HI 96822. Offers MS, PhD. *Degree requirements:* For doctorate, thesis/dissertation. *Faculty research:* Agronomy and soil science, zoology, entomology, genetics and molecular biology, botanical sciences.

University of Illinois at Urbana–Champaign, Graduate College, College of Liberal Arts and Sciences, School of Integrative Biology, Department of Animal Biology, Champaign, IL 61820. Offers animal biology (ecology, ethology and evolution) (MS, PhD). *Faculty:* 8 full-time (5 women). *Students:* 14 full-time (8 women), 2 part-time (0 women); includes 1 minority (Two or more races, non-Hispanic/Latino), 2 international. 7 applicants, 71% accepted, 4 enrolled. In 2011, 2 master's, 1 doctorate awarded. *Entrance requirements:* For master's and doctorate, GRE. Additional exam requirements/recommendations for international students: Required—TOEFL (minimum score 570 paper-based; 230 computer-based; 88 iBT). *Application deadline:* Applications are processed on a rolling basis. Application fee: $75 ($90 for international students). Electronic applications accepted. *Financial support:* In 2011–12, 3 fellowships, 4 research assistantships, 15 teaching assistantships were awarded; tuition waivers (full and partial) also available. *Unit head:* Ken Paige, Head, 217-244-6606, Fax: 217-244-4565, E-mail: k-paige@illinois.edu. *Application contact:* Lisa Smith, Office Administrator, 217-333-7802, Fax: 217-244-4565, E-mail: ljsmith1@illinois.edu. Web site: http://www.life.illinois.edu/animalbiology.

University of Illinois at Urbana–Champaign, Graduate College, College of Liberal Arts and Sciences, School of Integrative Biology, Program in Ecology, Evolution and Conservation Biology, Champaign, IL 61820. Offers MS, PhD. *Students:* 20 full-time (15 women), 8 part-time (3 women); includes 5 minority (1 American Indian or Alaska Native, non-Hispanic/Latino; 2 Asian, non-Hispanic/Latino; 1 Hispanic/Latino; 1 Two or more races, non-Hispanic/Latino), 3 international. 33 applicants, 9% accepted, 1 enrolled. In 2011, 2 master's, 4 doctorates awarded. *Entrance requirements:* For master's and doctorate, GRE. Additional exam requirements/recommendations for international students: Required—TOEFL (minimum score 613 paper-based; 257 computer-based; 103 iBT). *Application deadline:* Applications are processed on a rolling basis. Application fee: $75 ($90 for international students). Electronic applications accepted. *Financial support:* In 2011–12, 8 fellowships, 15 research assistantships, 14 teaching assistantships were awarded; tuition waivers (full and partial) also available. *Unit head:* Evan H. DeLucia, Director, 217-333-3044, Fax: 217-244-1224, E-mail: delucia@illinois.edu. *Application contact:* Carol Hall, Secretary, 217-333-8208, Fax: 217-244-1224, E-mail: cahall@illinois.edu. Web site: http://sib.illinois.edu/peec/.

The University of Kansas, Graduate Studies, College of Liberal Arts and Sciences, Department of Ecology and Evolutionary Biology, Lawrence, KS 66045. Offers botany (MA, PhD); ecology and evolutionary biology (MA, PhD); entomology (MA, PhD). *Faculty:* 15 full-time (6 women), 25 part-time/adjunct (6 women). *Students:* 64 full-time (31 women), 1 part-time (0 women); includes 4 minority (1 Hispanic/Latino; 3 Two or more races, non-Hispanic/Latino), 20 international. Average age 28. 67 applicants, 34% accepted, 18 enrolled. In 2011, 6 master's, 9 doctorates awarded. Terminal master's awarded for partial completion of doctoral program. *Degree requirements:* For master's, comprehensive exam, thesis (for some programs), 30-36 credits, thesis presentation; for doctorate, comprehensive exam, thesis/dissertation, residency, responsible scholarship and research skills, final exam, dissertation defense. *Entrance requirements:* For master's, GRE General Test, bachelor's degree with minimum undergraduate GPA of 3.0; for doctorate, GRE General Test, bachelor's degree; minimum undergraduate/graduate GPA of 3.0. Additional exam requirements/recommendations for international students: Required—TOEFL or IELTS. *Application deadline:* For fall admission, 12/1 for domestic students, 12/15 for international students; for spring admission, 9/15 for domestic and international students. Application fee: $55 ($65 for international students). Electronic applications accepted. Tuition and fees vary according to course load, campus/location, program and reciprocity agreements. *Financial support:* In 2011–12, 8 fellowships with full and partial tuition reimbursements, 22 research assistantships with full and partial tuition reimbursements, 32 teaching assistantships with full and partial tuition reimbursements were awarded; scholarships/grants, traineeships, health care benefits, and unspecified assistantships also available. Financial award application deadline: 12/1. *Faculty research:* Biodiversity and macroevolution, ecology and global change, evolutionary mechanisms. *Unit head:* Dr. Christopher H. Haufler, Chair, 785-864-3255, Fax: 785-864-5860, E-mail: vulgare@ku.edu. *Application contact:* Jaime Rochelle Keeler, Graduate Coordinator, 785-864-2362, Fax: 785-864-5860, E-mail: jrkeeler@ku.edu. Web site: http://www.ku.edu/~eeb/.

University of Maine, Graduate School, College of Natural Sciences, Forestry, and Agriculture, Department of Biological Sciences, Program in Ecology and Environmental Science, Orono, ME 04469. Offers water resources (PhD). Part-time programs available. *Students:* 40 full-time (31 women), 14 part-time (6 women). Average age 31. 72 applicants, 25% accepted, 12 enrolled. In 2011, 7 master's, 5 doctorates awarded. *Degree requirements:* For doctorate, thesis/dissertation. *Entrance requirements:* For master's and doctorate, GRE General Test. Additional exam requirements/recommendations for international students: Required—TOEFL. *Application deadline:* For fall admission, 2/1 priority date for domestic students. Applications are processed on a rolling basis. Application fee: $65. Electronic applications accepted. *Expenses:* Tuition, state resident: full-time $5016. Tuition, nonresident: full-time $14,424. *Financial support:* Career-related internships or fieldwork, Federal Work-Study, institutionally sponsored loans, and tuition waivers (full) available. Financial award application deadline: 3/1. *Unit head:* Dr. Mark Anderson, Coordinator, 207-581-3198. *Application contact:* Scott G. Delcourt, Associate Dean of the Graduate School, 207-581-3291, Fax: 207-581-3232, E-mail: graduate@maine.edu. Web site: http://www2.umaine.edu/graduate/.

University of Maine, Graduate School, College of Natural Sciences, Forestry, and Agriculture, Department of Plant, Soil, and Environmental Sciences, Orono, ME 04469. Offers biological sciences (PhD); ecology and environmental sciences (MS, PhD); forest resources (PhD); horticulture (MS); plant science (PhD); plant, soil, and environmental sciences (MS); resource utilization (MS). *Faculty:* 9 full-time (3 women), 7 part-time/adjunct (3 women). *Students:* 7 full-time (4 women), 2 part-time (0 women), 2 international. Average age 30. 14 applicants, 50% accepted, 5 enrolled. In 2011, 4 degrees awarded. *Entrance requirements:* For master's and doctorate, GRE General Test. Additional exam requirements/recommendations for international students: Required—TOEFL. *Application deadline:* Applications are processed on a rolling basis. Application fee: $65. Electronic applications accepted. *Expenses:* Tuition, state resident: full-time $5016. Tuition, nonresident: full-time $14,424. *Financial support:* In 2011–12, 16 research assistantships with full tuition reimbursements (averaging $17,336 per year), 1 teaching assistantship with full tuition reimbursement (averaging $13,600 per year) were awarded; scholarships/grants, tuition waivers (full and partial),

and unspecified assistantships also available. *Total annual research expenditures:* $179,065. *Unit head:* Dr. Gregory Porter, Chair, 207-581-2943, Fax: 207-581-3207. *Application contact:* Scott G. Delcourt, Associate Dean of the Graduate School, 207-581-3291, Fax: 207-581-3232, E-mail: graduate@maine.edu. Web site: http://www2.umaine.edu/graduate/.

The University of Manchester, Faculty of Life Sciences, Manchester, United Kingdom. Offers adaptive organismal biology (M Phil, PhD); animal biology (M Phil, PhD); biochemistry (M Phil, PhD); bioinformatics (M Phil, PhD); biomolecular sciences (M Phil, PhD); biotechnology (M Phil, PhD); cell biology (M Phil, PhD); cell matrix research (M Phil, PhD); channels and transporters (M Phil, PhD); developmental biology (M Phil, PhD); Egyptology (M Phil, PhD); environmental biology (M Phil, PhD); evolutionary biology (M Phil, PhD); gene expression (M Phil, PhD); genetics (M Phil, PhD); history of science, technology and medicine (M Phil, PhD); immunology (M Phil, PhD); integrative neurobiology and behavior (M Phil, PhD); membrane trafficking (M Phil, PhD); microbiology (M Phil, PhD); molecular and cellular neuroscience (M Phil, PhD); molecular biology (M Phil, PhD); molecular cancer studies (M Phil, PhD); neuroscience (M Phil, PhD); ophthalmology (M Phil, PhD); optometry (M Phil, PhD); organelle function (M Phil, PhD); pharmacology (M Phil, PhD); physiology (M Phil, PhD); plant sciences (M Phil, PhD); stem cell research (M Phil, PhD); structural biology (M Phil, PhD); systems neuroscience (M Phil, PhD); toxicology (M Phil, PhD).

University of Manitoba, Faculty of Graduate Studies, Faculty of Science, Department of Biological Sciences, Winnipeg, MB R3T 2N2, Canada. Offers botany (M Sc, PhD); ecology (M Sc, PhD); zoology (M Sc, PhD).

University of Maryland, College Park, Academic Affairs, College of Computer, Mathematical and Natural Sciences, Department of Biology, Behavior, Ecology, Evolution, and Systematics Program, College Park, MD 20742. Offers MS, PhD. *Students:* 14 full-time (8 women); includes 2 minority (1 Asian, non-Hispanic/Latino; 1 Two or more races, non-Hispanic/Latino), 2 international. In 2011, 1 master's, 12 doctorates awarded. *Degree requirements:* For master's, thesis, oral defense, seminar; for doctorate, thesis/dissertation, exam, 4 seminars. *Entrance requirements:* For master's and doctorate, GRE General Test, GRE Subject Test (biology); 3 letters of recommendation. Additional exam requirements/recommendations for international students: Required—TOEFL. *Expenses:* Tuition, state resident: part-time $525 per credit hour. Tuition, nonresident: part-time $1131 per credit hour. *Required fees:* $386.31 per term. Tuition and fees vary according to program. *Financial support:* In 2011–12, 4 fellowships with full and partial tuition reimbursements (averaging $17,787 per year), 2 research assistantships (averaging $19,685 per year), 5 teaching assistantships (averaging $19,604 per year) were awarded; Federal Work-Study and scholarships/grants also available. Support available to part-time students. Financial award applicants required to submit FAFSA. *Faculty research:* Animal behavior, biostatistics, ecology, evolution, neurothology. *Unit head:* David Hawthorne, Graduate Director, 301-405-2401, Fax: 301-314-9290, E-mail: djh@umd.edu. *Application contact:* Dr. Charles A. Caramello, Dean of Graduate School, 301-405-0358, Fax: 301-314-9305.

University of Maryland, College Park, Academic Affairs, College of Computer, Mathematical and Natural Sciences, Department of Biology, PhD Program in Biological Sciences, College Park, MD 20742. Offers behavior, ecology, evolution, and systematics (PhD); computational biology, bioinformatics, and genomics (PhD); molecular and cellular biology (PhD); physiological systems (PhD). *Students:* 68 full-time (41 women), 4 part-time (2 women); includes 13 minority (3 Black or African American, non-Hispanic/Latino; 4 Asian, non-Hispanic/Latino; 5 Hispanic/Latino; 1 Two or more races, non-Hispanic/Latino), 21 international. 380 applicants, 15% accepted, 22 enrolled. *Degree requirements:* For doctorate, comprehensive exam, thesis/dissertation, present thesis work in seminar. *Entrance requirements:* For doctorate, GRE General Test; GRE Subject Test in biology (recommended), academic transcripts, statement of purpose/research interests, 3 letters of recommendation. Additional exam requirements/recommendations for international students: Required—TOEFL. *Application deadline:* For fall admission, 12/15 for domestic and international students. Applications are processed on a rolling basis. Application fee: $75. Electronic applications accepted. *Expenses:* Tuition, state resident: part-time $525 per credit hour. Tuition, nonresident: part-time $1131 per credit hour. *Required fees:* $386.31 per term. Tuition and fees vary according to program. *Financial support:* In 2011–12, 11 fellowships with full and partial tuition reimbursements (averaging $14,406 per year), 16 research assistantships (averaging $19,495 per year), 41 teaching assistantships (averaging $18,734 per year) were awarded. *Unit head:* Dr. Barbara Thorne, Director, 301-405-6905, E-mail: bthorne@umd.edu. *Application contact:* Dr. Charles A. Caramello, Dean of Graduate School, 301-405-0358, Fax: 301-314-9305. Web site: http://bisi.umd.edu/biologicalsciencesgraduateprogrambisi.

University of Michigan, Horace H. Rackham School of Graduate Studies, College of Literature, Science, and the Arts, Department of Ecology and Evolutionary Biology, Ann Arbor, MI 48109. Offers ecology and evolutionary biology (MS, PhD); ecology and evolutionary biology-Frontiers (MS). Part-time programs available. *Faculty:* 56 full-time (19 women). *Students:* 75 full-time (42 women); includes 20 minority (6 Black or African American, non-Hispanic/Latino; 2 American Indian or Alaska Native, non-Hispanic/Latino; 4 Asian, non-Hispanic/Latino; 6 Hispanic/Latino; 2 Native Hawaiian or other Pacific Islander, non-Hispanic/Latino), 21 international. Average age 28. 122 applicants, 23% accepted, 9 enrolled. In 2011, 4 master's, 11 doctorates awarded. Terminal master's awarded for partial completion of doctoral program. *Degree requirements:* For master's, thesis (for some programs), two seminars; for doctorate, comprehensive exam, thesis/dissertation, 2 semesters of teaching. *Entrance requirements:* For master's and doctorate, GRE. Additional exam requirements/recommendations for international students: Required—TOEFL (minimum score 560 paper-based; 220 computer-based; 84 iBT). *Application deadline:* For fall admission, 12/1 priority date for domestic students, 12/1 for international students; for winter admission, 10/15 priority date for domestic students, 10/15 for international students. Applications are processed on a rolling basis. Application fee: $65 ($75 for international students). Electronic applications accepted. *Financial support:* In 2011–12, 61 students received support, including 18 fellowships with full tuition reimbursements available (averaging $23,702 per year), 10 research assistantships with full tuition reimbursements available (averaging $23,702 per year), 36 teaching assistantships with full tuition reimbursements available (averaging $23,702 per year); scholarships/grants, traineeships, health care benefits, and unspecified assistantships also available. Financial award applicants required to submit FAFSA. *Faculty research:* Population and community ecology, ecosystem ecology and biogeochemistry, global change biology, biogeography and paleobiology, evolution of behavior, evolutionary genetics, phylogenetic and phylogeography, ecology and evolution of infectious disease. *Total annual research expenditures:* $4 million. *Unit head:* Deborah Goldberg, Chair, 734-615-4912, Fax: 734-763-0544. *Application contact:* Jane Sullivan, Graduate Program Coordinator, 734-615-7338, Fax: 734-763-0544, E-mail: eeb.gradcoord@umich.edu. Web site: http://www.lsa.umich.edu/eeb/.

University of Michigan, School of Natural Resources and Environment, Program in Natural Resources and Environment, Ann Arbor, MI 48109. Offers aquatic sciences: research and management (MS); behavior, education and communication (MS); conservation biology (MS); conservation ecology (MS); environmental informatics (MS); environmental justice (MS); environmental policy and planning (MS); natural resources

and environment (PhD); sustainable systems (MS); terrestrial ecosystems (MS); MS/JD; MS/MBA; MUP/MS. *Faculty:* 45 full-time, 23 part-time/adjunct. *Students:* 450 full-time (254 women); includes 63 minority (7 Black or African American, non-Hispanic/Latino; 2 American Indian or Alaska Native, non-Hispanic/Latino; 35 Asian, non-Hispanic/Latino; 13 Hispanic/Latino; 6 Two or more races, non-Hispanic/Latino), 70 international. Average age 27. 643 applicants. In 2011, 133 master's, 11 doctorates awarded. Terminal master's awarded for partial completion of doctoral program. *Degree requirements:* For master's, practicum or group project; for doctorate, comprehensive exam, thesis/dissertation, oral defense of dissertation, preliminary exam. *Entrance requirements:* For master's, GRE General Test; for doctorate, GRE General Test, master's degree. Additional exam requirements/recommendations for international students: Required—TOEFL (minimum score 560 paper-based; 220 computer-based; 84 iBT). *Application deadline:* For fall admission, 1/5 priority date for domestic students, 1/5 for international students. Applications are processed on a rolling basis. Application fee: $65 ($75 for international students). Electronic applications accepted. *Financial support:* Fellowships with tuition reimbursements, research assistantships with tuition reimbursements, teaching assistantships with tuition reimbursements, career-related internships or fieldwork, Federal Work-Study, institutionally sponsored loans, scholarships/grants, health care benefits, and unspecified assistantships available. Support available to part-time students. Financial award application deadline: 1/5; financial award applicants required to submit FAFSA. *Faculty research:* Stream ecology, plant-insect interactions, fish biology, resource control and reproductive success, remote sensing, conservation ecology. *Unit head:* Dr. Marie Lynn Miranda, Dean, 734-764-2550, Fax: 734-763-8965, E-mail: mlmirand@umich.edu. *Application contact:* Adam D. Ancira, Graduate Admissions Team, 734-764-6453, Fax: 734-936-2195, E-mail: snre.admissions@umich.edu. Web site: http://www.snre.umich.edu/.

University of Minnesota, Twin Cities Campus, Graduate School, College of Biological Sciences, Department of Ecology, Evolution, and Behavior, St. Paul, MN 55418. Offers MS, PhD. Terminal master's awarded for partial completion of doctoral program. *Degree requirements:* For master's, comprehensive exam, thesis or projects; for doctorate, comprehensive exam, thesis/dissertation. *Entrance requirements:* For master's and doctorate, GRE General Test, minimum GPA of 3.0. Additional exam requirements/recommendations for international students: Required—TOEFL (minimum score 550 paper-based; 79 iBT), Michigan English Language Assessment Battery. Electronic applications accepted. *Faculty research:* Behavioral ecology, community ecology, community genetics, ecosystem and global change, evolution and systematics.

University of Missouri, Graduate School, College of Arts and Sciences, Division of Biological Sciences, Program in Evolutionary Biology and Ecology, Columbia, MO 65211. Offers MA, PhD. *Faculty:* 13. *Expenses:* Tuition, state resident: full-time $5881. Tuition, nonresident: full-time $15,183. *Required fees:* $952. Tuition and fees vary according to campus/location and program. *Financial support:* In 2011–12, fellowships (averaging $21,000 per year), teaching assistantships (averaging $16,300 per year) were awarded; research assistantships, scholarships/grants, health care benefits, and tuition waivers (full) also available. *Total annual research expenditures:* $990,000. *Unit head:* Dr. Ray Semlitsch, Director of Graduate Studies, 573-884-6396, E-mail: semlitschr@missouri.edu. *Application contact:* Nila Emerich, Application Contact, 800-553-5698. Web site: http://biology.missouri.edu/research-strengths/evolution/.

University of Missouri–St. Louis, College of Arts and Sciences, Department of Biology, St. Louis, MO 63121. Offers biotechnology (Certificate); cell and molecular biology (MS, PhD); ecology, evolution and systematics (MS, PhD); tropical biology and conservation (Certificate). Part-time programs available. *Faculty:* 43 full-time (13 women), 4 part-time/adjunct (1 woman). *Students:* 68 full-time (33 women), 64 part-time (28 women); includes 20 minority (9 Black or African American, non-Hispanic/Latino; 7 Asian, non-Hispanic/Latino; 3 Hispanic/Latino; 1 Two or more races, non-Hispanic/Latino), 43 international. Average age 28. 122 applicants, 48% accepted, 36 enrolled. In 2011, 20 master's, 3 doctorates, 11 other advanced degrees awarded. *Degree requirements:* For master's, thesis or alternative; for doctorate, thesis/dissertation, 1 semester of teaching experience. *Entrance requirements:* For master's, 3 letters of recommendation; for doctorate, GRE General Test, 3 letters of recommendation. Additional exam requirements/recommendations for international students: Required—TOEFL. *Application deadline:* For fall admission, 12/15 priority date for domestic students, 12/15 for international students; for spring admission, 12/1 priority date for domestic students, 12/1 for international students. Applications are processed on a rolling basis. Application fee: $35 ($40 for international students). Electronic applications accepted. *Expenses:* Tuition, state resident: full-time $6273; part-time $3866 per year. Tuition, nonresident: full-time $14,969; part-time $9980 per year. *Required fees:* $315 per year. *Financial support:* In 2011–12, 13 research assistantships with full and partial tuition reimbursements (averaging $15,300 per year), 27 teaching assistantships with full and partial tuition reimbursements (averaging $15,300 per year) were awarded; fellowships with full tuition reimbursements, career-related internships or fieldwork, and Federal Work-Study also available. Support available to part-time students. Financial award application deadline: 2/1. *Faculty research:* Molecular biology, microbial genetics, animal behavior, tropical ecology, plant systematics. *Unit head:* Dr. Wendy Olivas, Director of Graduate Studies, 314-516-6200, Fax: 314-516-6233, E-mail: olivasw@umsl.edu. *Application contact:* 314-516-5458, Fax: 314-516-6996, E-mail: gradadm@umsl.edu. Web site: http://www.umsl.edu/divisions/artscience/biology/.

The University of Montana, Graduate School, College of Arts and Sciences, Division of Biological Sciences, Program in Ecology of Infectious Disease, Missoula, MT 59812-0002. Offers PhD.

The University of Montana, Graduate School, College of Arts and Sciences, Division of Biological Sciences, Program in Organismal Biology and Ecology, Missoula, MT 59812-0002. Offers MS, PhD. Terminal master's awarded for partial completion of doctoral program. *Degree requirements:* For master's, one foreign language, thesis; for doctorate, 2 foreign languages, thesis/dissertation. *Entrance requirements:* For master's and doctorate, GRE General Test. *Faculty research:* Conservation biology, ecology and behavior, evolutionary genetics, avian biology.

University of Nevada, Reno, Graduate School, Interdisciplinary Program in Ecology, Evolution, and Conservation Biology, Reno, NV 89557. Offers PhD. Offered through the College of Arts and Science, the M. C. Fleischmann College of Agriculture, and the Desert Research Institute. *Degree requirements:* For doctorate, thesis/dissertation. *Entrance requirements:* For doctorate, GRE General Test, GRE Subject Test, minimum GPA of 3.0. Additional exam requirements/recommendations for international students: Required—TOEFL (minimum score 500 paper-based; 173 computer-based; 61 iBT), IELTS (minimum score 6). Electronic applications accepted. *Faculty research:* Population biology, behavioral ecology, plant response to climate change, conservation of endangered species, restoration of natural ecosystems.

The University of North Carolina at Chapel Hill, Graduate School, College of Arts and Sciences, Curriculum in Ecology, Chapel Hill, NC 27599. Offers MA, MS, PhD. *Degree requirements:* For master's, comprehensive exam, thesis (for some programs), oral defense of thesis; for doctorate, comprehensive exam, thesis/dissertation, oral exams, oral defense of dissertation. *Entrance requirements:* For master's and doctorate, GRE General Test. Additional exam requirements/recommendations for international students: Required—TOEFL (minimum score 550 paper-based; 213 computer-based). Electronic applications accepted. *Faculty research:* Community and population ecology and ecosystems, human ecology, landscape ecology, conservation ecology, marine ecology.

The University of North Carolina at Chapel Hill, Graduate School, College of Arts and Sciences, Department of Biology, Chapel Hill, NC 27599. Offers botany (MA, MS, PhD); cell biology, development, and physiology (MA, MS, PhD); cell motility and cytoskeleton (PhD); ecology and behavior (MA, MS, PhD); genetics and molecular biology (MA, MS, PhD); morphology, systematics, and evolution (MA, MS, PhD). Terminal master's awarded for partial completion of doctoral program. *Degree requirements:* For master's, comprehensive exam, thesis (for some programs); for doctorate, comprehensive exam, thesis/dissertation. *Entrance requirements:* For master's, GRE General Test, GRE Subject Test, 2 semesters of calculus or statistics; 2 semesters of physics, organic chemistry; 3 semesters of biology; for doctorate, GRE General Test, GRE Subject Test, 2 semesters calculus or statistics, 2 semesters physics, organic chemistry, 3 semesters of biology. Additional exam requirements/recommendations for international students: Required—TOEFL (minimum score 550 paper-based; 213 computer-based). Electronic applications accepted. *Faculty research:* Gene expression, biomechanics, yeast genetics, plant ecology, plant molecular biology.

University of North Dakota, Graduate School, College of Arts and Sciences, Department of Biology, Grand Forks, ND 58202. Offers botany (MS, PhD); ecology (MS, PhD); entomology (MS, PhD); environmental biology (MS, PhD); fisheries/wildlife (MS, PhD); genetics (MS, PhD); zoology (MS, PhD). Terminal master's awarded for partial completion of doctoral program. *Degree requirements:* For master's, thesis, final exam; for doctorate, comprehensive exam, thesis/dissertation, final exam. *Entrance requirements:* For master's, GRE General Test, GRE Subject Test, minimum GPA of 3.0; for doctorate, GRE General Test, GRE Subject Test, minimum GPA of 3.5. Additional exam requirements/recommendations for international students: Required—TOEFL (minimum score 550 paper-based; 213 computer-based; 79 iBT), IELTS (minimum score 6.5). Electronic applications accepted. *Faculty research:* Population biology, wildlife ecology, RNA processing, hormonal control of behavior.

University of Notre Dame, Graduate School, College of Science, Department of Biological Sciences, Notre Dame, IN 46556. Offers aquatic ecology, evolution and environmental biology (MS, PhD); cellular and molecular biology (MS, PhD); genetics (MS, PhD); physiology (MS, PhD); vector biology and parasitology (MS, PhD). Terminal master's awarded for partial completion of doctoral program. *Degree requirements:* For master's, comprehensive exam, thesis; for doctorate, comprehensive exam, thesis/dissertation, candidacy exam. *Entrance requirements:* For master's and doctorate, GRE General Test. Additional exam requirements/recommendations for international students: Required—TOEFL (minimum score 600 paper-based; 250 computer-based; 80 iBT). Electronic applications accepted. *Faculty research:* Tropical disease, molecular genetics, neurobiology, evolutionary biology, aquatic biology.

University of Oklahoma, College of Arts and Sciences, Department of Microbiology and Plant Biology, Program in Ecology and Evolutionary Biology, Norman, OK 73019. Offers PhD. *Students:* 6 full-time (1 woman), 1 part-time (0 women), 6 international. Average age 29. 7 applicants, 71% accepted, 2 enrolled. *Entrance requirements:* Additional exam requirements/recommendations for international students: Required—TOEFL (minimum score 550 paper-based; 79 iBT). *Application deadline:* For fall admission, 4/1 for domestic students, 3/1 for international students; for spring admission, 9/1 for domestic and international students. Applications are processed on a rolling basis. Application fee: $40 ($90 for international students). Electronic applications accepted. *Expenses:* Tuition, state resident: full-time $4087; part-time $170.30 per credit hour. Tuition, nonresident: full-time $14,875; part-time $619.80 per credit hour. *Required fees:* $2659; $100.25 per credit hour. Tuition and fees vary according to course load and degree level. *Financial support:* In 2011–12, 7 students received support. Scholarships/grants, health care benefits, tuition waivers (partial), and unspecified assistantships available. *Faculty research:* Behavioral ecology, community ecology, evolutionary biology, macroecology, physiological ecology. *Unit head:* Dr. Michael Kaspari, 405-325-4821, Fax: 405-325-7619, E-mail: mkaspari@ou.edu. Web site: http://mpbio.ou.edu/.

University of Oklahoma, College of Arts and Sciences, Department of Zoology, Program in Ecology and Evolutionary Biology, Norman, OK 73019. Offers PhD. *Students:* 17 full-time (9 women), 7 part-time (2 women), 6 international. Average age 28. 10 applicants, 40% accepted, 4 enrolled. In 2011, 2 degrees awarded. *Entrance requirements:* Additional exam requirements/recommendations for international students: Required—TOEFL (minimum score 550 paper-based; 79 iBT). *Application deadline:* For fall admission, 12/15 for domestic and international students. Applications are processed on a rolling basis. Application fee: $40 ($90 for international students). Electronic applications accepted. *Expenses:* Tuition, state resident: full-time $4087; part-time $170.30 per credit hour. Tuition, nonresident: full-time $14,875; part-time $619.80 per credit hour. *Required fees:* $2659; $100.25 per credit hour. Tuition and fees vary according to course load and degree level. *Financial support:* In 2011–12, 23 students received support. Career-related internships or fieldwork, scholarships/grants, health care benefits, tuition waivers (partial), and unspecified assistantships available. Financial award applicants required to submit FAFSA. *Faculty research:* Behavioral ecology, community ecology, evolutionary biology, macroecology, physiological ecology. *Unit head:* Bill Mathhews, Chair, 405-325-4712, Fax: 405-325-6202, E-mail: wmatthews@ou.edu. *Application contact:* Dr. Michael Kaspari, 405-325-4821, E-mail: mkaspari@ou.edu. Web site: http://www.ou.edu/eeb.

University of Oregon, Graduate School, College of Arts and Sciences, Department of Biology, Eugene, OR 97403. Offers ecology and evolution (MA, MS, PhD); marine biology (MA, MS, PhD); molecular, cellular and genetic biology (PhD); neuroscience and development (PhD). Terminal master's awarded for partial completion of doctoral program. *Degree requirements:* For master's, thesis (for some programs); for doctorate, thesis/dissertation. *Entrance requirements:* For master's and doctorate, GRE General Test, minimum GPA of 3.2. Additional exam requirements/recommendations for international students: Required—TOEFL. *Faculty research:* Developmental neurobiology; evolution, population biology, and quantitative genetics; regulation of gene expression; biochemistry of marine organisms.

University of Pittsburgh, Dietrich School of Arts and Sciences, Department of Biological Sciences, Program in Ecology and Evolution, Pittsburgh, PA 15260. Offers PhD. *Faculty:* 9 full-time (2 women). *Students:* 16 full-time (5 women); includes 3 minority (1 American Indian or Alaska Native, non-Hispanic/Latino; 1 Asian, non-Hispanic/Latino; 1 Hispanic/Latino), 2 international. Average age 23. 36 applicants, 25% accepted, 3 enrolled. In 2011, 2 doctorates awarded. *Degree requirements:* For doctorate, comprehensive exam, thesis/dissertation, completion of research integrity module. *Entrance requirements:* For doctorate, GRE General Test, GRE Subject Test. Additional exam requirements/recommendations for international students: Required—TOEFL (minimum score 550 paper-based; 213 computer-based; 80 iBT). *Application deadline:* For fall admission, 1/15 priority date for domestic students, 12/15 for international students. Applications are processed on a rolling basis. Application fee: $0 ($50 for international students). Electronic applications accepted. *Expenses:* Tuition, state resident: full-time $18,774; part-time $760 per credit. Tuition, nonresident: full-time $30,736; part-time $1258 per credit. *Required fees:* $740; $200 per term. Tuition and

fees vary according to program. *Financial support:* In 2011–12, 20 fellowships with full tuition reimbursements (averaging $28,790 per year), 9 research assistantships with full tuition reimbursements (averaging $26,010 per year), 16 teaching assistantships with full tuition reimbursements (averaging $24,601 per year) were awarded; Federal Work-Study, scholarships/grants, traineeships, health care benefits, and tuition waivers (full) also available. *Unit head:* Dr. Jeffrey G. Lawrence, Associate Professor, 412-624-4204, Fax: 412-624-4759, E-mail: jlawrenc@pitt.edu. *Application contact:* Cathleen M. Barr, Graduate Administrator, 412-624-4268, Fax: 412-624-4759, E-mail: cbarr@pitt.edu. Web site: http://www.biology.pitt.edu/.

University of Puerto Rico, Río Piedras, College of Natural Sciences, Department of Biology, San Juan, PR 00931-3300. Offers ecology/systematics (MS, PhD); evolution/genetics (MS, PhD); molecular/cellular biology (MS, PhD); neuroscience (MS, PhD). Part-time programs available. *Degree requirements:* For master's, one foreign language, comprehensive exam, thesis; for doctorate, one foreign language, comprehensive exam, thesis/dissertation. *Entrance requirements:* For master's, GRE Subject Test, interview, minimum GPA of 3.0, letter of recommendation; for doctorate, GRE Subject Test, interview, master's degree, minimum GPA of 3.0, letter of recommendation. *Faculty research:* Environmental, poblational and systematic biology.

University of South Carolina, The Graduate School, College of Arts and Sciences, Department of Biological Sciences, Graduate Training Program in Ecology, Evolution, and Organismal Biology, Columbia, SC 29208. Offers MS, PhD. *Degree requirements:* For master's, one foreign language, comprehensive exam, thesis; for doctorate, one foreign language, comprehensive exam, thesis/dissertation. *Entrance requirements:* For master's and doctorate, GRE General Test, minimum GPA of 3.0 in science. Additional exam requirements/recommendations for international students: Required—TOEFL (minimum score 570 paper-based; 230 computer-based). Electronic applications accepted.

The University of Tennessee, Graduate School, College of Arts and Sciences, Department of Ecology and Evolutionary Biology, Knoxville, TN 37996. Offers behavior (MS, PhD); ecology (MS, PhD); evolutionary biology (MS, PhD). Part-time programs available. *Degree requirements:* For master's, thesis; for doctorate, thesis/dissertation. *Entrance requirements:* For master's and doctorate, GRE General Test, minimum GPA of 2.7. Additional exam requirements/recommendations for international students: Required—TOEFL. Electronic applications accepted. *Expenses:* Tuition, state resident: full-time $8332; part-time $464 per credit hour. Tuition, nonresident: full-time $25,174; part-time $1400 per credit hour. *Required fees:* $1162; $56 per credit hour. Tuition and fees vary according to program.

The University of Tennessee, Graduate School, College of Arts and Sciences, Department of Mathematics, Knoxville, TN 37996. Offers applied mathematics (MS); mathematical ecology (PhD); mathematics (M Math, MS, PhD). Part-time programs available. *Degree requirements:* For master's, thesis or alternative; for doctorate, one foreign language, thesis/dissertation. *Entrance requirements:* For master's and doctorate, minimum GPA of 2.7. Additional exam requirements/recommendations for international students: Required—TOEFL. Electronic applications accepted. *Expenses:* Tuition, state resident: full-time $8332; part-time $464 per credit hour. Tuition, nonresident: full-time $25,174; part-time $1400 per credit hour. *Required fees:* $1162; $56 per credit hour. Tuition and fees vary according to program.

The University of Texas at Austin, Graduate School, College of Natural Sciences, School of Biological Sciences, Program in Ecology, Evolution and Behavior, Austin, TX 78712-1111. Offers PhD. *Entrance requirements:* For doctorate, GRE General Test. Additional exam requirements/recommendations for international students: Required—TOEFL. *Application deadline:* For fall admission, 1/5 for domestic and international students. Applications are processed on a rolling basis. Application fee: $50 ($75 for international students). Electronic applications accepted. *Financial support:* Fellowships, research assistantships, and teaching assistantships available. *Unit head:* Dr. Ulrich Mueller, Graduate Program Chair, 512-471-7619, E-mail: umueller@mail.utexas.edu. *Application contact:* Tamra Rogers, Graduate Coordinator, 512-471-8490, Fax: 512-232-3699, E-mail: tamra@austin.utexas.edu. Web site: http://www.biosci.utexas.edu/graduate/eeb/.

The University of Toledo, College of Graduate Studies, College of Natural Sciences and Mathematics, Department of Environmental Sciences, Toledo, OH 43606-3390. Offers biology (MS, PhD), including ecology. Part-time programs available. *Faculty:* 26. *Students:* 9 full-time (4 women), 2 part-time (1 woman); includes 1 minority (Black or African American, non-Hispanic/Latino), 1 international. Average age 30. 9 applicants, 56% accepted, 5 enrolled. In 2011, 3 master's awarded. *Degree requirements:* For master's, thesis (for some programs). *Entrance requirements:* For master's, GRE General Test, minimum cumulative point-hour ratio of 2.7 for all previous academic work, three letters of recommendation, statement of purpose, transcripts from all prior institutions attended. Additional exam requirements/recommendations for international students: Required—TOEFL (minimum score 550 paper-based; 213 computer-based; 80 iBT), IELTS (minimum score 6.5). *Application deadline:* For fall admission, 1/15 priority date for domestic students, 1/15 for international students. Applications are processed on a rolling basis. Application fee: $45 ($75 for international students). Electronic applications accepted. *Financial support:* In 2011–12, 5 research assistantships with full and partial tuition reimbursements (averaging $18,126 per year), 12 teaching assistantships with full and partial tuition reimbursements (averaging $12,850 per year) were awarded; Federal Work-Study, institutionally sponsored loans, scholarships/grants, tuition waivers (full), and unspecified assistantships also available. Support available to part-time students. *Faculty research:* Environmental geochemistry, geophysics, petrology and mineralogy, paleontology, geohydrology. *Unit head:* Dr. Timothy G. Fisher, Chair, 419-530-2883, E-mail: timothy.fisher@utoledo.edu. *Application contact:* Graduate School Office, 419-530-4723, Fax: 419-530-4724, E-mail: grdsch@utnet.utoledo.edu. Web site: http://www.utoledo.edu/nsm/.

University of Toronto, School of Graduate Studies, Faculty of Arts and Science, Department of Ecology and Evolutionary Biology, Toronto, ON M5S 1A1, Canada. Offers M Sc, PhD. *Degree requirements:* For master's, thesis, thesis defense; for doctorate, thesis/dissertation, thesis defense. *Entrance requirements:* For master's, minimum B average in last 2 years; knowledge of physics, chemistry, and biology. Additional exam requirements/recommendations for international students: Required—TOEFL (minimum score 580 paper-based; 93 iBT), TWE (minimum score 5). Electronic applications accepted.

University of Washington, Graduate School, College of the Environment, School of Environmental and Forest Sciences, Seattle, WA 98195. Offers bioresource science and engineering (MS, PhD); environmental horticulture (MEH); forest ecology (MS, PhD); forest management (MFR); forest soils (MS, PhD); restoration ecology (MS, PhD); restoration ecology and environmental horticulture (MS, PhD); social sciences (MS, PhD); sustainable resource management (MS, PhD); wildlife science (MS, PhD), MFR/MAIS; MPA/MS. *Accreditation:* SAF. Part-time programs available. *Degree requirements:* For master's, thesis; for doctorate, comprehensive exam (for some programs), thesis/dissertation. *Entrance requirements:* For master's and doctorate, GRE, minimum GPA of 3.0. Additional exam requirements/recommendations for international students: Required—TOEFL, GRE. Electronic applications accepted. *Faculty research:* Ecosystem analysis, silviculture and forest protection, paper science and engineering, environmental horticulture and urban forestry, natural resource policy and economics, restoration ecology and environment horticulture, conservation, human dimensions, wildlife, bioresource science and engineering.

University of Wisconsin–Madison, Graduate School, College of Agricultural and Life Sciences, Agroecology Program, Madison, WI 53706-1380. Offers MS. *Degree requirements:* For master's, thesis (for some programs). *Entrance requirements:* For master's, GRE. Additional exam requirements/recommendations for international students: Required—TOEFL (minimum score 580 paper-based; 237 computer-based; 92 iBT), IELTS (minimum score 7). Electronic applications accepted. *Expenses:* Tuition, state resident: full-time $10,296; part-time $643.51 per credit. Tuition, nonresident: full-time $24,054; part-time $1503.40 per credit. *Required fees:* $70.06 per credit. Tuition and fees vary according to course load, campus/location, program and reciprocity agreements. *Faculty research:* Multifunctional landscape, socio-ecological systems, participatory solutions to environmental problems.

University of Wyoming, Program in Ecology, Laramie, WY 82070. Offers MS, PhD. *Entrance requirements:* For master's and doctorate, GRE.

Utah State University, School of Graduate Studies, College of Natural Resources, Department of Environment and Society, Logan, UT 84322. Offers bioregional planning (MS); geography (MA, MS); human dimensions of ecosystem science and management (MS, PhD); recreation resource management (MS, PhD). *Degree requirements:* For master's, comprehensive exam, thesis (for some programs). *Entrance requirements:* For master's and doctorate, GRE General Test, minimum GPA of 3.0. Additional exam requirements/recommendations for international students: Required—TOEFL. Electronic applications accepted. *Faculty research:* Geographic information systems/geographic and environmental education, bioregional planning, natural resource and environmental policy, outdoor recreation and tourism, natural resource and environmental management.

Utah State University, School of Graduate Studies, College of Natural Resources, Department of Watershed Sciences, Logan, UT 84322. Offers ecology (MS, PhD); fisheries biology (MS, PhD); watershed science (MS, PhD). *Degree requirements:* For master's, thesis (for some programs); for doctorate, thesis/dissertation. *Entrance requirements:* For master's and doctorate, GRE General Test, minimum GPA of 3.2. Additional exam requirements/recommendations for international students: Required—TOEFL. Electronic applications accepted. *Faculty research:* Behavior, population ecology, habitat, conservation biology, restoration, aquatic ecology, fisheries management, fluvial geomorphology, remote sensing, conservation biology.

Utah State University, School of Graduate Studies, College of Natural Resources, Department of Wildland Resources, Logan, UT 84322. Offers ecology (MS, PhD); forestry (MS, PhD); range science (MS, PhD); wildlife biology (MS, PhD). Part-time programs available. *Degree requirements:* For master's, thesis; for doctorate, comprehensive exam, thesis/dissertation. *Entrance requirements:* For master's and doctorate, GRE General Test, minimum GPA of 3.0. Additional exam requirements/recommendations for international students: Required—TOEFL. *Faculty research:* Range plant ecophysiology, plant community ecology, ruminant nutrition, population ecology.

Utah State University, School of Graduate Studies, College of Science, Department of Biology, Logan, UT 84322. Offers biology (MS, PhD); ecology (MS, PhD). Part-time programs available. *Degree requirements:* For master's, thesis; for doctorate, thesis/dissertation. *Entrance requirements:* For master's and doctorate, GRE General Test, minimum GPA of 3.0. Additional exam requirements/recommendations for international students: Required—TOEFL (minimum score 575 paper-based). *Faculty research:* Plant, insect, microbial, and animal biology.

Washington University in St. Louis, Graduate School of Arts and Sciences, Division of Biology and Biomedical Sciences, Program in Evolution, Ecology and Population Biology, St. Louis, MO 63130-4899. Offers ecology (PhD); environmental biology (PhD); evolutionary biology (PhD); genetics (PhD). *Degree requirements:* For doctorate, thesis/dissertation. *Entrance requirements:* For doctorate, GRE General Test, GRE Subject Test. Electronic applications accepted.

Wesleyan University, Graduate Programs, Department of Biology, Middletown, CT 06459. Offers animal behavior (PhD); bioformatics/genomics (PhD); cell biology (PhD); developmental biology (PhD); evolution/ecology (PhD); genetics (PhD); neurobiology (PhD); population biology (PhD). *Degree requirements:* For doctorate, variable foreign language requirement, thesis/dissertation. *Entrance requirements:* For doctorate, GRE. Additional exam requirements/recommendations for international students: Required—TOEFL. *Faculty research:* Microbial population genetics, genetic basis of evolutionary adaptation, genetic regulation of differentiation and pattern formation in &ITdrosophila&RO.

Yale University, Graduate School of Arts and Sciences, Department of Ecology and Evolutionary Biology, New Haven, CT 06520. Offers PhD. *Entrance requirements:* For doctorate, GRE General Test, GRE Subject Test (biology).

Environmental Biology

Baylor University, Graduate School, College of Arts and Sciences, Department of Biology, Waco, TX 76798. Offers biology (MA, MS, PhD); environmental biology (MS); limnology (MS). Part-time programs available. *Faculty:* 13 full-time (3 women). *Students:* 37 full-time (19 women), 3 part-time (1 woman); includes 8 minority (3 Asian, non-Hispanic/Latino; 1 Hispanic/Latino; 4 Two or more races, non-Hispanic/Latino), 13 international. In 2011, 5 master's, 3 doctorates awarded. *Degree requirements:* For master's, thesis (for some programs); for doctorate, thesis/dissertation. *Entrance requirements:* For master's and doctorate, GRE General Test. *Application deadline:* For fall admission, 1/31 priority date for domestic students. Applications are processed on a rolling basis. Application fee: $25. *Financial support:* Teaching assistantships, career-

related internships or fieldwork, Federal Work-Study, institutionally sponsored loans, and tuition waivers (full and partial) available. Support available to part-time students. Financial award application deadline: 2/28. *Faculty research:* Terrestrial ecology, aquatic ecology, genetics. *Unit head:* Dr. Myeongwoo Lee, Graduate Program Director, 254-710-2141, Fax: 254-710-2969, E-mail: myeongwoo_lee@baylor.edu. *Application contact:* Tamara Lehmann, Administrative Assistant, 254-710-2911, Fax: 254-710-2969, E-mail: tamara_lehmann@baylor.edu. Web site: http://www.baylor.edu/biology/.

Chatham University, Program in Biology, Pittsburgh, PA 15232-2826. Offers environmental biology-non-thesis track (MS); environmental biology-thesis track (MS); human biology-non-thesis track (MS); human biology-thesis track (MS). Part-time programs available. *Students:* 31 full-time (21 women), 6 part-time (all women); includes 6 minority (1 Black or African American, non-Hispanic/Latino; 1 American Indian or Alaska Native, non-Hispanic/Latino; 2 Asian, non-Hispanic/Latino; 2 Two or more races, non-Hispanic/Latino), 4 international. Average age 26. 71 applicants, 62% accepted, 22 enrolled. In 2011, 8 master's awarded. *Degree requirements:* For master's, thesis optional. *Entrance requirements:* For master's, 3 letters of recommendation. Additional exam requirements/recommendations for international students: Required—TOEFL (minimum score 600 paper-based; 250 computer-based; 100 iBT), IELTS (minimum score 7), TWE. *Application deadline:* For fall admission, 4/1 priority date for domestic students, 4/1 for international students; for spring admission, 11/1 priority date for domestic students, 10/1 for international students. Applications are processed on a rolling basis. Application fee: $45. Electronic applications accepted. Application fee is waived when completed online. *Expenses: Tuition:* Full-time $13,896. Tuition and fees vary according to program. *Financial support:* Applicants required to submit FAFSA. *Faculty research:* Molecular evolution of iron homeostasis, characteristics of soil bacterial communities, gene flow through seed movement, role of gonadotropins in spermatogonial proliferation, phosphatid/linositol metabolism in epithelial cells. *Unit head:* Dr. Lisa Lambert, Director, 412-365-1217, E-mail: lambert@chatham.edu. *Application contact:* Ashlee Bartko, Senior Assistant Director of Graduate Admission, 412-365-1115, Fax: 412-365-1609, E-mail: gradadmissions@chatham.edu. Web site: http://www.chatham.edu/departments/sciences/graduate/biology.

Emporia State University, Graduate School, College of Liberal Arts and Sciences, Department of Biological Sciences, Emporia, KS 66801-5087. Offers botany (MS); environmental biology (MS); general biology (MS); microbial and cellular biology (MS); zoology (MS). Part-time programs available. *Faculty:* 13 full-time (3 women), 1 part-time/adjunct (0 women). *Students:* 8 full-time (5 women), 21 part-time (10 women); includes 3 minority (1 Black or African American, non-Hispanic/Latino; 1 Hispanic/Latino; 1 Two or more races, non-Hispanic/Latino), 6 international. 14 applicants, 86% accepted, 7 enrolled. In 2011, 5 master's awarded. *Degree requirements:* For master's, comprehensive exam or thesis. *Entrance requirements:* For master's, GRE, appropriate undergraduate degree, interview, letters of reference. Additional exam requirements/recommendations for international students: Required—TOEFL (minimum score 520 paper-based; 133 computer-based; 68 iBT). *Application deadline:* For fall admission, 8/15 priority date for domestic students. Applications are processed on a rolling basis. Application fee: $30 ($75 for international students). Electronic applications accepted. *Expenses:* Tuition, state resident: full-time $2342; part-time $195 per credit hour. Tuition, nonresident: full-time $7254; part-time $605 per credit hour. *Required fees:* $66 per credit hour. Tuition and fees vary according to campus/location. *Financial support:* In 2011–12, 8 research assistantships with full tuition reimbursements (averaging $6,589 per year), 10 teaching assistantships with full tuition reimbursements (averaging $7,419 per year) were awarded; career-related internships or fieldwork, Federal Work-Study, institutionally sponsored loans, health care benefits, and unspecified assistantships also available. Financial award application deadline: 3/15; financial award applicants required to submit FAFSA. *Faculty research:* Fisheries, range, and wildlife management; aquatic, plant, grassland, vertebrate, and invertebrate ecology; mammalian and plant systematics, taxonomy, and evolution; immunology, virology, and molecular biology. *Unit head:* Dr. R. Brent Thomas, Chair, 620-341-5311, Fax: 620-341-5608, E-mail: rthomas2@emporia.edu. *Application contact:* Dr. Scott Crupper, Graduate Coordinator, 620-341-5621, Fax: 620-341-5607, E-mail: scrupper@emporia.edu. Web site: http://www.emporia.edu/info/degrees-courses/grad/biology.

Georgia State University, College of Arts and Sciences, Department of Biology, Program in Applied and Environmental Microbiology, Atlanta, GA 30302-3083. Offers MS, PhD. Part-time programs available. Terminal master's awarded for partial completion of doctoral program. *Degree requirements:* For master's, thesis or alternative; for doctorate, thesis/dissertation, exam. *Entrance requirements:* For master's and doctorate, GRE General Test. Additional exam requirements/recommendations for international students: Required—TOEFL. Electronic applications accepted.

Governors State University, College of Arts and Sciences, Program in Environmental Biology, University Park, IL 60484. Offers MS. Part-time and evening/weekend programs available. *Students:* 3 full-time (1 woman), 19 part-time (13 women); includes 7 minority (5 Black or African American, non-Hispanic/Latino; 1 Hispanic/Latino; 1 Two or more races, non-Hispanic/Latino). Average age 32. *Degree requirements:* For master's, thesis or alternative. *Application deadline:* For fall admission, 7/15 priority date for domestic students; for spring admission, 11/10 for domestic students. Applications are processed on a rolling basis. Application fee: $25. *Financial support:* Research assistantships, career-related internships or fieldwork, Federal Work-Study, institutionally sponsored loans, and scholarships/grants available. Support available to part-time students. Financial award application deadline: 5/1. *Faculty research:* Animal physiology, cell biology, animal behavior, plant physiology, plant populations. *Unit head:* Dr. James Howley, Chair, Division of Liberal Arts, 708-534-7893. *Application contact:* Yakeea Daniels, Director of Admission, 708-534-4510, E-mail: ydaniels@govst.edu.

Hampton University, Graduate College, Department of Biological Sciences, Hampton, VA 23668. Offers biology (MS); environmental science (MS); medical science (MS). Part-time and evening/weekend programs available. *Degree requirements:* For master's, thesis optional. *Entrance requirements:* For master's, GRE General Test. *Faculty research:* Marine ecology, microbial and chemical pollution, pesticide problems.

Hood College, Graduate School, Program in Environmental Biology, Frederick, MD 21701-8575. Offers MS. Part-time and evening/weekend programs available. *Degree requirements:* For master's, thesis or alternative. *Entrance requirements:* For master's, minimum GPA of 2.75, 1 year of undergraduate biology and chemistry, 1 semester of mathematics. Additional exam requirements/recommendations for international students: Required—TOEFL (minimum score 575 paper-based; 231 computer-based; 89 iBT). Electronic applications accepted.

Massachusetts Institute of Technology, School of Engineering, Department of Civil and Environmental Engineering, Cambridge, MA 02139. Offers biological oceanography (PhD, Sc D); chemical oceanography (PhD, Sc D); civil and environmental engineering (PhD, Sc D); civil and environmental systems (PhD, Sc D); civil engineering (PhD, Sc D, CE); coastal engineering (PhD, Sc D); construction engineering and management (PhD, Sc D); environmental and water quality engineering (M Eng); environmental biology (PhD, Sc D); environmental chemistry (PhD, Sc D); environmental engineering (PhD, Sc D); environmental fluid mechanics (PhD, Sc D); environmental science and engineering (SM); geotechnical and geoenvironmental engineering (PhD, Sc D); geotechnology (M Eng); high-performance structures (M Eng); hydrology (PhD, Sc D); information technology (PhD, Sc D); mechanics (SM); oceanographic engineering (PhD, Sc D); structures and materials (PhD, Sc D); transportation (M Eng, PhD, Sc D); SM/MBA. *Faculty:* 35 full-time (6 women), 1 part-time/adjunct (0 women). *Students:* 216 full-time (80 women); includes 30 minority (4 Black or African American, non-Hispanic/Latino; 13 Asian, non-Hispanic/Latino; 8 Hispanic/Latino; 5 Two or more races, non-Hispanic/Latino), 110 international. Average age 27. 589 applicants, 26% accepted, 91 enrolled. In 2011, 62 master's, 14 doctorates awarded. *Degree requirements:* For master's and CE, thesis; for doctorate, comprehensive exam, thesis/dissertation. *Entrance requirements:* For master's and doctorate, GRE General Test. Additional exam requirements/recommendations for international students: Required—TOEFL (minimum score 577 paper-based; 233 computer-based; 90 iBT), IELTS (minimum score 7). *Application deadline:* For fall admission, 12/15 for domestic and international students. Application fee: $75. Electronic applications accepted. *Expenses: Tuition:* Full-time $40,460; part-time $630 per credit hour. *Required fees:* $272. *Financial support:* In 2011–12, 180 students received support, including 51 fellowships (averaging $30,800 per year), 110 research assistantships (averaging $29,500 per year), 19 teaching assistantships (averaging $29,500 per year); career-related internships or fieldwork, Federal Work-Study, institutionally sponsored loans, scholarships/grants, health care benefits, and unspecified assistantships also available. *Faculty research:* Environmental chemistry, environmental fluid mechanics and coastal engineering, environmental microbiology, geotechnical engineering and geomechanics, hydrology and hydroclimatology, infrastructure systems, mechanics of materials and structures, transportation systems. *Total annual research expenditures:* $17.7 million. *Unit head:* Prof. Andrew Whittle, Head, 617-253-7101. *Application contact:* Patricia Glidden, Graduate Admissions Coordinator, 617-253-7119, Fax: 617-258-6775, E-mail: cee-admissions@mit.edu. Web site: http://cee.mit.edu/.

Missouri University of Science and Technology, Graduate School, Department of Biological Sciences, Rolla, MO 65409. Offers applied and environmental biology (MS). *Entrance requirements:* For master's, GRE (minimum score 600 quantitative, 4 writing). Additional exam requirements/recommendations for international students: Required—TOEFL (minimum score 570 paper-based; 230 computer-based).

Morgan State University, School of Graduate Studies, School of Computer, Mathematical, and Natural Sciences, Department of Biology, Program in Bioenvironmental Science, Baltimore, MD 21251. Offers PhD. *Degree requirements:* For doctorate, comprehensive exam, thesis/dissertation, oral defense of dissertation. *Entrance requirements:* For doctorate, GRE General Test, GRE Subject Test (biology, chemistry, or related science), bachelor's or master's degree in biology, chemistry, physics or related field; minimum GPA of 3.0. Additional exam requirements/recommendations for international students: Required—TOEFL (minimum score 550 paper-based; 213 computer-based).

Nicholls State University, Graduate Studies, College of Arts and Sciences, Department of Biological Sciences, Thibodaux, LA 70310. Offers marine and environmental biology (MS). Part-time programs available. *Degree requirements:* For master's, comprehensive exam, thesis. *Entrance requirements:* For master's, GRE. Additional exam requirements/recommendations for international students: Required—TOEFL (minimum score 600 paper-based). *Faculty research:* Bioremediation, ecology, public health, biotechnology, physiology.

Nova Scotia Agricultural College, Research and Graduate Studies, Truro, NS B2N 5E3, Canada. Offers agriculture (M Sc), including air quality, animal behavior, animal molecular genetics, animal nutrition, animal technology, aquaculture, botany, crop management, crop physiology, ecology, environmental microbiology, food science, horticulture, nutrient management, pest management, physiology, plant biotechnology, plant pathology, soil chemistry, soil fertility, waste management and composting, water quality. Program offered jointly with Dalhousie University. Part-time programs available. *Degree requirements:* For master's, thesis, ATC Exam Teaching Assistantship. *Entrance requirements:* For master's, honors B Sc, minimum GPA of 3.0. Additional exam requirements/recommendations for international students: Required—TOEFL (minimum score 580 paper-based; 237 computer-based; 92 iBT), IELTS, Michigan English Language Assessment Battery, CanTEST, CAEL. *Faculty research:* Bio-product development, organic agriculture, nutrient management, air and water quality, agricultural biotechnology.

Ohio University, Graduate College, College of Arts and Sciences, Department of Environmental and Plant Biology, Athens, OH 45701-2979. Offers MS, PhD. Part-time programs available. *Students:* 20 full-time (5 women); includes 2 minority (1 Black or African American, non-Hispanic/Latino; 1 Two or more races, non-Hispanic/Latino), 1 international. 21 applicants, 24% accepted, 5 enrolled. In 2011, 5 master's, 1 doctorate awarded. *Degree requirements:* For master's, thesis, 2 quarters of teaching experience; for doctorate, comprehensive exam, thesis/dissertation, 2 quarters of teaching experience. *Entrance requirements:* For master's, GRE General Test, minimum GPA of 3.0; for doctorate, GRE General Test, minimum GPA of 3.2. Additional exam requirements/recommendations for international students: Required—TOEFL (minimum score 620 paper-based; 260 computer-based; 105 iBT) or IELTS (minimum score 7.5). *Application deadline:* For fall admission, 1/15 priority date for domestic students, 1/15 for international students. Applications are processed on a rolling basis. Application fee: $50 ($55 for international students). Electronic applications accepted. *Financial support:* Fellowships with full tuition reimbursements, research assistantships with full tuition reimbursements, teaching assistantships with full tuition reimbursements, Federal Work-Study, institutionally sponsored loans, and scholarships/grants available. Financial award application deadline: 1/15. *Faculty research:* Eastern deciduous forest ecology, evolutionary developmental plant biology, phylogenetic systematics, plant cell wall biotechnology. *Total annual research expenditures:* $859,166. *Unit head:* Dr. Allan C. Showalter, Chair, 740-593-1135, Fax: 740-593-1130, E-mail: showalte@ohio.edu. *Application contact:* Dr. Glenn Matlack, Graduate Chair, 740-593-1131, Fax: 740-593-1130, E-mail: matlack@ohio.edu. Web site: http://www.plantbio.ohiou.edu/.

Rutgers, The State University of New Jersey, New Brunswick, Graduate School-New Brunswick, Department of Environmental Sciences, Piscataway, NJ 08854-8097. Offers air pollution and resources (MS, PhD); aquatic biology (MS, PhD); aquatic chemistry (MS, PhD); atmospheric science (MS, PhD); chemistry and physics of aerosol and hydrosol systems (MS, PhD); environmental chemistry (MS, PhD); environmental microbiology (MS, PhD); environmental toxicology (PhD); exposure assessment (PhD); fate and effects of pollutants (MS, PhD); pollution prevention and control (MS, PhD); water and wastewater treatment (MS, PhD); water resources (MS, PhD). Terminal master's awarded for partial completion of doctoral program. *Degree requirements:* For master's, comprehensive exam, thesis or alternative, oral final exam; for doctorate, comprehensive exam, thesis/dissertation, thesis defense, qualifying exam. *Entrance requirements:* For master's and doctorate, GRE General Test. Additional exam requirements/recommendations for international students: Required—TOEFL. Electronic applications accepted. *Faculty research:* Biological waste treatment; contaminant fate and transport; air, soil and water quality.

Sonoma State University, School of Science and Technology, Department of Biology, Rohnert Park, CA 94928-3609. Offers biochemistry (MA); environmental biology (MA). Part-time programs available. *Faculty:* 10 full-time (2 women). *Students:* 4 full-time (2

women), 14 part-time (9 women); includes 3 minority (1 American Indian or Alaska Native, non-Hispanic/Latino; 1 Asian, non-Hispanic/Latino; 1 Hispanic/Latino), 1 international. Average age 29. 23 applicants, 26% accepted, 3 enrolled. In 2011, 10 master's awarded. *Degree requirements:* For master's, thesis or alternative, oral exam. *Entrance requirements:* For master's, GRE General Test, GRE Subject Test, minimum GPA of 3.0. Additional exam requirements/recommendations for international students: Required—TOEFL (minimum score 500 paper-based; 173 computer-based). *Application deadline:* For fall admission, 11/30 for domestic students. Applications are processed on a rolling basis. Application fee: $55. *Financial support:* In 2011–12, 3 teaching assistantships (averaging $5,343 per year) were awarded; fellowships, research assistantships, career-related internships or fieldwork, Federal Work-Study, and tuition waivers (full) also available. Financial award application deadline: 3/2; financial award applicants required to submit FAFSA. *Faculty research:* Plant physiology, comparative physiology, community ecology, restoration ecology, marine ecology, conservation genetics, primate behavior, behavioral ecology, developmental biology, plant and animal systematics. *Total annual research expenditures:* $238,000. *Unit head:* Chair, 707-664-, E-mail: james.christmann@sonoma.edu. *Application contact:* Dr. Derek Girman, Graduate Adviser, 707-664-3055, E-mail: derek.girman@sonoma.edu. Web site: http://www.sonoma.edu/biology/graduate.

State University of New York College of Environmental Science and Forestry, Department of Environmental and Forest Biology, Syracuse, NY 13210-2779. Offers applied ecology (MPS); chemical ecology (MPS, MS, PhD); conservation biology (MPS, MS, PhD); ecology (MPS, MS, PhD); entomology (MPS, MS, PhD); environmental interpretation (MPS, MS, PhD); environmental physiology (MPS, MS, PhD); fish and wildlife biology and management (MPS, MS, PhD); forest pathology and mycology (MPS, MS, PhD); plant biotechnology (MPS); plant science and biotechnology (MPS, MS, PhD). *Degree requirements:* For master's, thesis (for some programs); for doctorate, comprehensive exam, thesis/dissertation. *Entrance requirements:* For master's and doctorate, GRE General Test, GRE Subject Test, minimum GPA of 3.0. Additional exam requirements/recommendations for international students: Required—TOEFL (minimum score 550 paper-based; 213 computer-based; 80 iBT), IELTS (minimum score 6). *Application deadline:* For fall admission, 2/1 priority date for domestic students, 2/1 for international students; for spring admission, 11/1 priority date for domestic students, 11/1 for international students. Applications are processed on a rolling basis. Application fee: $60. *Expenses:* Tuition, state resident: full-time $8870; part-time $370 per credit hour. Tuition, nonresident: full-time $15,160; part-time $632 per credit hour. *Required fees:* $60; $370 per credit hour. $350 per semester. One-time fee: $85. *Financial support:* Fellowships with full and partial tuition reimbursements, research assistantships with full and partial tuition reimbursements, teaching assistantships with full and partial tuition reimbursements, Federal Work-Study, institutionally sponsored loans, scholarships/grants, health care benefits, and unspecified assistantships available. Financial award application deadline: 6/30. *Faculty research:* Ecology, fish and wildlife biology and management, plant science, entomology. *Total annual research expenditures:* $4.1 million. *Unit head:* Dr. Donald J. Leopold, Chair, 315-470-6760, Fax: 315-470-6934. *Application contact:* Dr. Dudley J. Raynal, Dean, Instruction and Graduate Studies, 315-470-6599, Fax: 315-470-6978, E-mail: esfgrad@esf.edu. Web site: http://www.esf.edu/efb/.

Universidad del Turabo, Graduate Programs, Programs in Science and Technology, Gurabo, PR 00778-3030. Offers environmental analysis (MSE), including environmental chemistry; environmental management (MSE), including pollution management; environmental science (D Sc), including environmental biology. *Students:* 8 full-time (4 women), 101 part-time (68 women); includes 101 minority (all Hispanic/Latino). Average age 39. 58 applicants, 76% accepted, 39 enrolled. In 2011, 16 master's, 3 doctorates awarded. *Entrance requirements:* For master's, GRE, EXADEP, interview. *Application deadline:* For fall admission, 8/5 for domestic students. Application fee: $25. *Unit head:* David Mendez, Head, 787-743-7979. *Application contact:* Virginia Gonzalez, Admissions Officer, 787-746-3009.

University of Alberta, Faculty of Graduate Studies and Research, Department of Biological Sciences, Edmonton, AB T6G 2E1, Canada. Offers environmental biology and ecology (M Sc, PhD); microbiology and biotechnology (M Sc, PhD); molecular biology and genetics (M Sc, PhD); physiology and cell biology (M Sc, PhD); plant biology (M Sc, PhD); systematics and evolution (M Sc, PhD). Terminal master's awarded for partial completion of doctoral program. *Degree requirements:* For master's, thesis; for doctorate, thesis/dissertation. *Entrance requirements:* Additional exam requirements/recommendations for international students: Required—TOEFL.

University of California, Santa Cruz, Division of Graduate Studies, Division of Physical and Biological Sciences, Environmental Toxicology Department, Santa Cruz, CA 95064. Offers MS, PhD. Terminal master's awarded for partial completion of doctoral program. *Degree requirements:* For master's, comprehensive exam, thesis; for doctorate, thesis/dissertation, qualifying exams. *Entrance requirements:* For master's and doctorate, GRE. Additional exam requirements/recommendations for international students: Required—TOEFL (minimum score 550 paper-based; 220 computer-based; 83 iBT); Recommended—IELTS (minimum score 8). Electronic applications accepted. *Faculty research:* Molecular mechanisms of reactive DNA methylation toxicity, anthropogenic perturbations of biogeochemical cycles, anaerobic microbiology and biotransformation of pollutants and toxic metals, organismal responses and therapeutic treatment of toxins, microbiology, molecular genetics, genomics.

University of Guelph, Graduate Studies, Ontario Agricultural College, Department of Environmental Biology, Guelph, ON N1G 2W1, Canada. Offers entomology (M Sc, PhD); environmental microbiology and biotechnology (M Sc, PhD); environmental toxicology (M Sc, PhD); plant and forest systems (M Sc, PhD); plant pathology (M Sc, PhD). Part-time programs available. *Degree requirements:* For master's, thesis; for doctorate, comprehensive exam, thesis/dissertation. *Entrance requirements:* For master's, minimum 75% average during previous 2 years of course work; for doctorate, minimum 75% average. Additional exam requirements/recommendations for international students: Required—TOEFL or IELTS. Electronic applications accepted. *Faculty research:* Entomology, environmental microbiology and biotechnology, environmental toxicology, forest ecology, plant pathology.

University of Louisiana at Lafayette, College of Sciences, Department of Biology, Lafayette, LA 70504. Offers biology (MS); environmental and evolutionary biology (PhD). Terminal master's awarded for partial completion of doctoral program. *Degree requirements:* For master's, thesis; for doctorate, 2 foreign languages, comprehensive exam, thesis/dissertation. *Entrance requirements:* For master's, GRE General Test, minimum GPA of 2.75; for doctorate, GRE General Test, GRE Subject Test, minimum GPA of 3.0. Additional exam requirements/recommendations for international students: Required—TOEFL (minimum score 550 paper-based; 213 computer-based). Electronic applications accepted. *Faculty research:* Structure and ultrastructure, system biology, ecology, processes, environmental physiology.

University of Louisville, Graduate School, College of Arts and Sciences, Department of Biology, Louisville, KY 40292-0001. Offers biology (MS); environmental biology (PhD). *Degree requirements:* For master's, thesis (for some programs); for doctorate, thesis/dissertation. *Entrance requirements:* For master's and doctorate, GRE General Test. *Expenses:* Tuition, state resident: full-time $9692; part-time $539 per credit hour.

Tuition, nonresident: full-time $20,168; part-time $1121 per credit hour. Tuition and fees vary according to program and reciprocity agreements.

The University of Manchester, Faculty of Life Sciences, Manchester, United Kingdom. Offers adaptive organismal biology (M Phil, PhD); animal biology (M Phil, PhD); biochemistry (M Phil, PhD); bioinformatics (M Phil, PhD); biomolecular sciences (M Phil, PhD); biotechnology (M Phil, PhD); cell biology (M Phil, PhD); cell matrix research (M Phil, PhD); channels and transporters (M Phil, PhD); developmental biology (M Phil, PhD); Egyptology (M Phil, PhD); environmental biology (M Phil, PhD); evolutionary biology (M Phil, PhD); gene expression (M Phil, PhD); genetics (M Phil, PhD); history of science, technology and medicine (M Phil, PhD); immunology (M Phil, PhD); integrative neurobiology and behavior (M Phil, PhD); membrane trafficking (M Phil, PhD); microbiology (M Phil, PhD); molecular and cellular neuroscience (M Phil, PhD); molecular biology (M Phil, PhD); molecular cancer studies (M Phil, PhD); neuroscience (M Phil, PhD); ophthalmology (M Phil, PhD); optometry (M Phil, PhD); organelle function (M Phil, PhD); pharmacology (M Phil, PhD); physiology (M Phil, PhD); plant sciences (M Phil, PhD); stem cell research (M Phil, PhD); structural biology (M Phil, PhD); systems neuroscience (M Phil, PhD); toxicology (M Phil, PhD).

University of Massachusetts Amherst, Graduate School, College of Natural Sciences, Department of Environmental Conservation, Amherst, MA 01003. Offers building systems (MS, PhD); environmental policy and human dimensions (MS, PhD); forest resources (MS, PhD); sustainability science (MS); water, wetlands and watersheds (MS, PhD); wildlife and fisheries conservation (MS, PhD). Part-time programs available. *Faculty:* 57 full-time (10 women). *Students:* 61 full-time (26 women), 34 part-time (13 women); includes 4 minority (1 Black or African American, non-Hispanic/Latino; 2 Hispanic/Latino; 1 Two or more races, non-Hispanic/Latino), 12 international. Average age 32. 84 applicants, 40% accepted, 22 enrolled. In 2011, 1 master's, 2 doctorates awarded. Terminal master's awarded for partial completion of doctoral program. *Degree requirements:* For master's, thesis or alternative; for doctorate, comprehensive exam, thesis/dissertation. *Entrance requirements:* For master's and doctorate, GRE General Test. Additional exam requirements/recommendations for international students: Required—TOEFL (minimum score 550 paper-based; 213 computer-based; 80 iBT), IELTS (minimum score 6.5). *Application deadline:* For fall admission, 2/1 for domestic and international students; for spring admission, 10/1 for domestic and international students. Applications are processed on a rolling basis. Application fee: $50 ($65 for international students). Electronic applications accepted. Tuition and fees vary according to course load, campus/location and program. *Financial support:* Fellowships with full and partial tuition reimbursements, research assistantships with full and partial tuition reimbursements, teaching assistantships with full and partial tuition reimbursements, career-related internships or fieldwork, Federal Work-Study, scholarships/grants, traineeships, health care benefits, tuition waivers (full and partial), and unspecified assistantships available. Support available to part-time students. Financial award application deadline: 2/1. *Unit head:* Dr. Kevin McGarigal, Graduate Program Director, 413-545-2257, Fax: 413-545-4358. *Application contact:* Lindsay DeSantis, Interim Supervisor of Admissions, 413-545-0721, Fax: 413-577-0100, E-mail: gradadm@grad.umass.edu. Web site: http://eco.umass.edu/.

University of Massachusetts Boston, Office of Graduate Studies, College of Science and Mathematics, Department of Environmental, Earth and Ocean Sciences, Program in Environmental Biology, Boston, MA 02125-3393. Offers PhD. Part-time and evening/weekend programs available. *Degree requirements:* For doctorate, comprehensive exam, thesis/dissertation, oral exams. *Entrance requirements:* For doctorate, GRE General Test, minimum GPA of 2.75. *Faculty research:* Polychoets biology, predator and prey relationships, population and evolutionary biology, neurobiology, biodiversity.

University of North Dakota, Graduate School, College of Arts and Sciences, Department of Biology, Grand Forks, ND 58202. Offers botany (MS, PhD); ecology (MS, PhD); entomology (MS, PhD); environmental biology (MS, PhD); fisheries/wildlife (MS, PhD); genetics (MS, PhD); zoology (MS, PhD). Terminal master's awarded for partial completion of doctoral program. *Degree requirements:* For master's, thesis, final exam; for doctorate, comprehensive exam, thesis/dissertation, final exam. *Entrance requirements:* For master's, GRE General Test, GRE Subject Test, minimum GPA of 3.0; for doctorate, GRE General Test, GRE Subject Test, minimum GPA of 3.5. Additional exam requirements/recommendations for international students: Required—TOEFL (minimum score 550 paper-based; 213 computer-based; 79 iBT), IELTS (minimum score 6.5). Electronic applications accepted. *Faculty research:* Population biology, wildlife ecology, RNA processing, hormonal control of behavior.

University of Southern California, Graduate School, Dana and David Dornsife College of Letters, Arts and Sciences, Department of Biological Sciences, Program in Marine Biology and Biological Oceanography, Los Angeles, CA 90089. Offers marine and environmental biology (MS); marine biology and biological oceanography (PhD). Terminal master's awarded for partial completion of doctoral program. *Degree requirements:* For master's, research paper; for doctorate, comprehensive exam, thesis/dissertation, qualifying examination, dissertation defense. *Entrance requirements:* For master's and doctorate, GRE, 3 letters of recommendation, personal statement, resume, minimum GPA of 3.0. Additional exam requirements/recommendations for international students: Required—TOEFL (minimum score 600 paper-based; 250 computer-based; 100 iBT). Electronic applications accepted. *Faculty research:* Microbial ecology, biogeochemistry, and geobiology; biodiversity and molecular ecology; integrative organismal biology; conservation biology; marine genomics.

University of Southern Mississippi, Graduate School, College of Science and Technology, Department of Biological Sciences, Hattiesburg, MS 39406-0001. Offers environmental biology (MS, PhD); marine biology (MS, PhD); microbiology (MS, PhD); molecular biology (MS, PhD). *Faculty:* 27 full-time (6 women). *Students:* 57 full-time (28 women), 4 part-time (2 women); includes 5 minority (2 Black or African American, non-Hispanic/Latino; 3 Two or more races, non-Hispanic/Latino), 18 international. Average age 32. 50 applicants, 32% accepted, 12 enrolled. In 2011, 7 master's, 8 doctorates awarded. Terminal master's awarded for partial completion of doctoral program. *Degree requirements:* For master's, comprehensive exam, thesis; for doctorate, comprehensive exam, thesis/dissertation. *Entrance requirements:* For master's, GRE General Test, minimum GPA of 3.0 on last 60 hours; for doctorate, GRE General Test, minimum GPA of 3.5. Additional exam requirements/recommendations for international students: Required—TOEFL, IELTS. *Application deadline:* For fall admission, 3/1 priority date for domestic students, 3/1 for international students; for spring admission, 1/10 priority date for domestic students, 1/10 for international students. Applications are processed on a rolling basis. Application fee: $50. *Financial support:* In 2011–12, 25 research assistantships with full tuition reimbursements (averaging $9,700 per year), 33 teaching assistantships with full tuition reimbursements (averaging $10,600 per year) were awarded; Federal Work-Study, scholarships/grants, health care benefits, and unspecified assistantships also available. Financial award application deadline: 3/15; financial award applicants required to submit FAFSA. *Unit head:* Dr. Glenmore Shearer, Chair, 601-266-4748, Fax: 601-266-5797. *Application contact:* Dr. Jake Schaefer, Director of Graduate Studies, 601-266-4748, Fax: 601-266-5797. Web site: http://www.usm.edu/graduateschool/table.php.

University of West Florida, College of Arts and Sciences: Sciences, School of Allied Health and Life Sciences, Department of Biology, Pensacola, FL 32514-5750. Offers

biological chemistry (MS); biology (MS); biology education (MST); biotechnology (MS); coastal zone studies (MS); environmental biology (MS). *Faculty:* 12 full-time (3 women), 1 part-time/adjunct (0 women). *Students:* 9 full-time (7 women), 30 part-time (16 women); includes 2 minority (both Hispanic/Latino), 3 international. Average age 29. 21 applicants, 48% accepted, 5 enrolled. In 2011, 4 master's awarded. *Degree requirements:* For master's, thesis. *Entrance requirements:* For master's, GRE (minimum score: verbal 450, quantitative 550), official transcripts; BS in biology or related field; letter of interest; relevant past experience; three letters of recommendation from individuals who can evaluate applicant's academic ability. Additional exam requirements/recommendations for international students: Required—TOEFL (minimum score 550 paper-based; 213 computer-based). *Application deadline:* For fall admission, 6/1 for domestic and international students; for spring admission, 10/1 for domestic and international students. Applications are processed on a rolling basis. Application fee: $30. *Expenses:* Tuition, state resident: full-time $5729; part-time $302 per credit hour. Tuition, nonresident: full-time $20,059; part-time $961 per credit hour. *Required fees:* $1509; $63 per credit hour. *Financial support:* In 2011–12, 18 fellowships with partial tuition reimbursements (averaging $126 per year), 14 research assistantships with partial tuition reimbursements (averaging $5,980 per year), 4 teaching assistantships with partial tuition reimbursements (averaging $7,858 per year) were awarded; unspecified assistantships also available. Financial award application deadline: 4/15; financial award applicants required to submit FAFSA. *Unit head:* Dr. George L. Stewart, Chairperson, 850-474-2748. *Application contact:* Terry McCray, Assistant Director of Graduate Admissions, 850-473-7718, Fax: 850-473-7714, E-mail: gradadmissions@uwf.edu.

University of Wisconsin–Madison, School of Medicine and Public Health, Molecular and Environmental Toxicology Center, Madison, WI 53706. Offers MS, PhD. *Faculty:* 77 full-time (25 women), 1 part-time/adjunct (0 women). *Students:* 38 full-time (18 women); includes 10 minority (1 American Indian or Alaska Native, non-Hispanic/Latino; 1 Asian, non-Hispanic/Latino; 6 Hispanic/Latino; 2 Native Hawaiian or other Pacific Islander, non-Hispanic/Latino), 9 international. Average age 28. 53 applicants, 13% accepted, 4 enrolled. In 2011, 4 doctorates awarded. Terminal master's awarded for partial completion of doctoral program. *Degree requirements:* For doctorate, thesis/dissertation. *Entrance requirements:* For master's and doctorate, bachelor's degree in science-related field. Additional exam requirements/recommendations for international students: Required—TOEFL. *Application deadline:* For fall admission, 12/15 priority date for domestic students, 12/15 for international students. Application fee: $56. Electronic applications accepted. *Expenses:* Tuition, state resident: full-time $10,296; part-time $643.51 per credit. Tuition, nonresident: full-time $24,054; part-time $1503.40 per credit. *Required fees:* $70.06 per credit. Tuition and fees vary according to course load, campus/location, program and reciprocity agreements. *Financial support:* In 2011–12, 5 research assistantships with tuition reimbursements (averaging $24,500 per year) were awarded; fellowships with tuition reimbursements, traineeships, health care benefits, and unspecified assistantships also available. *Faculty research:* Toxicology cancer, genetics, cell cycle, xenobotic metabolism. *Unit head:* Dr. Christopher Bradfield, Director, 608-262-2024, E-mail: bradfield@oncology.wisc.edu. *Application contact:* Eileen M. Stevens, Program Administrator, 608-263-4580, Fax: 608-262-5245, E-mail: emstevens@wisc.edu. Web site: http://www.med.wisc.edu/metc/.

Washington University in St. Louis, Graduate School of Arts and Sciences, Division of Biology and Biomedical Sciences, Program in Evolution, Ecology and Population Biology, St. Louis, MO 63130-4899. Offers ecology (PhD); environmental biology (PhD); evolutionary biology (PhD); genetics (PhD). *Degree requirements:* For doctorate, thesis/dissertation. *Entrance requirements:* For doctorate, GRE General Test, GRE Subject Test. Electronic applications accepted.

West Virginia University, Davis College of Agriculture, Forestry and Consumer Sciences, Division of Plant and Soil Sciences, Morgantown, WV 26506. Offers agricultural sciences (PhD), including animal and food sciences, plant and soil sciences; agronomy (MS); entomology (MS); environmental microbiology (MS); horticulture (MS); plant pathology (MS). *Degree requirements:* For master's, thesis. *Entrance requirements:* For master's, GRE, minimum GPA of 2.5. Additional exam requirements/recommendations for international students: Required—TOEFL. *Faculty research:* Water quality, reclamation of disturbed land, crop production, pest control, environmental protection.

West Virginia University, Eberly College of Arts and Sciences, Department of Biology, Morgantown, WV 26506. Offers cell and molecular biology (MS, PhD); environmental and evolutionary biology (MS, PhD); forensic biology (MS, PhD); genomic biology (MS, PhD); neurobiology (MS, PhD). Terminal master's awarded for partial completion of doctoral program. *Degree requirements:* For master's, thesis, final exam; for doctorate, thesis/dissertation, preliminary and final exams. *Entrance requirements:* For master's, GRE General Test, GRE Subject Test, minimum GPA of 3.0; for doctorate, GRE General Test, minimum GPA of 3.0. Additional exam requirements/recommendations for international students: Required—TOEFL. *Faculty research:* Environmental biology, genetic engineering, developmental biology, global change, biodiversity.

Youngstown State University, Graduate School, College of Science, Technology, Engineering and Mathematics, Department of Biological Sciences, Youngstown, OH 44555-0001. Offers environmental biology (MS); molecular biology, microbiology, and genetic (MS); physiology and anatomy (MS). Part-time programs available. *Degree requirements:* For master's, comprehensive exam, thesis, oral review. *Entrance requirements:* For master's, GRE General Test, minimum GPA of 2.7. Additional exam requirements/recommendations for international students: Required—TOEFL. *Faculty research:* Cell biology, neurophysiology, molecular biology, neurobiology, gene regulation.

Evolutionary Biology

Arizona State University, College of Liberal Arts and Sciences, School of Life Sciences, Tempe, AZ 85287-4601. Offers animal behavior (PhD); applied ethics (biomedical and health ethics) (MA); biological design (PhD); biology (MS, PhD); biology (biology and society) (MS, PhD); environmental life sciences (PhD); evolutionary biology (PhD); human and social dimensions of science and technology (PhD); microbiology (PhD); molecular and cellular biology (PhD); neuroscience (PhD); philosophy (history and philosophy of science) (MA); sustainability (PhD). Terminal master's awarded for partial completion of doctoral program. *Degree requirements:* For master's, thesis (for some programs), interactive Program of Study (iPOS) submitted before completing 50 percent of required credit hours; for doctorate, variable foreign language requirement, comprehensive exam, thesis/dissertation, interactive Program of Study (iPOS) submitted before completing 50 percent of required credit hours. *Entrance requirements:* For master's and doctorate, GRE, minimum GPA of 3.0 or equivalent in last 2 years of work leading to bachelor's degree. Additional exam requirements/recommendations for international students: Required—TOEFL (minimum score 600 paper-based; 250 computer-based; 100 iBT). Electronic applications accepted.

Brown University, Graduate School, Division of Biology and Medicine, Program in Ecology and Evolutionary Biology, Providence, RI 02912. Offers PhD. *Degree requirements:* For doctorate, thesis/dissertation, preliminary exam. *Entrance requirements:* For doctorate, GRE General Test, GRE Subject Test. Additional exam requirements/recommendations for international students: Required—TOEFL. Electronic applications accepted. *Faculty research:* Marine ecology, behavioral ecology, population genetics, evolutionary morphology, plant ecology.

Clemson University, Graduate School, College of Agriculture, Forestry and Life Sciences, Department of Biological Sciences, Program in Biological Sciences, Clemson, SC 29634. Offers MS, PhD. *Students:* 38 full-time (24 women), 37 part-time (25 women); includes 6 minority (3 Black or African American, non-Hispanic/Latino; 2 Asian, non-Hispanic/Latino; 1 Hispanic/Latino), 9 international. Average age 34. 72 applicants, 43% accepted, 23 enrolled. In 2011, 6 master's, 2 doctorates awarded. *Degree requirements:* For master's, thesis optional; for doctorate, comprehensive exam, thesis/dissertation. *Entrance requirements:* For master's and doctorate, GRE General Test. Additional exam requirements/recommendations for international students: Required—TOEFL, IELTS. *Application deadline:* For fall admission, 1/15 for domestic students, 4/15 for international students. Applications are processed on a rolling basis. Application fee: $70 ($80 for international students). Electronic applications accepted. *Financial support:* In 2011–12, 29 students received support, including 5 fellowships with full and partial tuition reimbursements available (averaging $7,200 per year), 15 research assistantships with partial tuition reimbursements available (averaging $12,300 per year), 25 teaching assistantships with partial tuition reimbursements available (averaging $13,540 per year); career-related internships or fieldwork, institutionally sponsored loans, scholarships/grants, health care benefits, and unspecified assistantships also available. Support available to part-time students. Financial award application deadline: 3/15; financial award applicants required to submit FAFSA. *Unit head:* Dr. Alfred Wheeler, Department Chair, 864-656-1415, Fax: 864-656-0435, E-mail: wheeler@clemson.edu. *Application contact:* Jay Lyn Martin, Coordinator for Graduate Program, 864-656-3587, Fax: 864-656-0435, E-mail: gradbio@clemson.edu. Web site: http://www.clemson.edu/cafls/departments/biosci/.

Columbia University, Graduate School of Arts and Sciences, Division of Natural Sciences, Department of Ecology, Evolution and Environmental Biology, New York, NY 10027. Offers conservation biology (MA, Certificate); ecology and evolutionary biology (PhD); environmental policy (Certificate); evolutionary primatology (PhD). *Degree requirements:* For doctorate, one foreign language, thesis/dissertation, teaching experience. *Entrance requirements:* For doctorate, GRE General Test, previous course work in biology. Additional exam requirements/recommendations for international students: Required—TOEFL. Electronic applications accepted. *Faculty research:* Tropical ecology, ethnobotany, global change, systematics.

Cornell University, Graduate School, Graduate Fields of Agriculture and Life Sciences, Field of Ecology and Evolutionary Biology, Ithaca, NY 14853-0001. Offers ecology (PhD), including animal ecology, applied ecology, biogeochemistry, community and ecosystem ecology, limnology, oceanography, physiological ecology, plant ecology, population ecology, theoretical ecology, vertebrate zoology; evolutionary biology (PhD), including ecological genetics, paleobiology, population biology, systematics. *Faculty:* 51 full-time (14 women). *Students:* 52 full-time (36 women); includes 6 minority (1 Asian, non-Hispanic/Latino; 4 Hispanic/Latino; 1 Two or more races, non-Hispanic/Latino), 10 international. Average age 28. 121 applicants, 9% accepted, 7 enrolled. In 2011, 5 doctorates awarded. *Degree requirements:* For doctorate, comprehensive exam, thesis/dissertation, 2 semesters of teaching experience. *Entrance requirements:* For doctorate, GRE General Test, GRE Subject Test (biology), 2 letters of recommendation. Additional exam requirements/recommendations for international students: Required—TOEFL (minimum score 550 paper-based; 213 computer-based; 77 iBT). *Application deadline:* For fall admission, 12/15 for domestic students. Application fee: $95. Electronic applications accepted. *Financial support:* In 2011–12, 15 fellowships with full tuition reimbursements, 8 research assistantships with full tuition reimbursements, 25 teaching assistantships with full tuition reimbursements were awarded; institutionally sponsored loans, scholarships/grants, health care benefits, tuition waivers (full and partial), and unspecified assistantships also available. Financial award applicants required to submit FAFSA. *Faculty research:* Population and organismal biology, population and evolutionary genetics, systematics and macroevolution, biochemistry, conservation biology. *Unit head:* Director of Graduate Studies, 607-254-4230. *Application contact:* Graduate Field Assistant, 607-254-4230, E-mail: eeb_grad_req@cornell.edu. Web site: http://www.gradschool.cornell.edu/fields.php?id-46&a-2.

Dartmouth College, Arts and Sciences Graduate Programs, Program in Ecology and Evolutionary Biology, Hanover, NH 03755. Offers PhD. *Entrance requirements:* For doctorate, GRE General Test, GRE Subject Test in biology (highly recommended). Additional exam requirements/recommendations for international students: Required—TOEFL.

Emory University, Laney Graduate School, Division of Biological and Biomedical Sciences, Program in Population Biology, Ecology and Evolution, Atlanta, GA 30322-1100. Offers PhD. *Faculty:* 35 full-time (6 women). *Students:* 30 full-time (18 women); includes 7 minority (1 Black or African American, non-Hispanic/Latino; 2 Asian, non-Hispanic/Latino; 3 Hispanic/Latino; 1 Two or more races, non-Hispanic/Latino), 5 international. Average age 27. 53 applicants, 34% accepted, 6 enrolled. *Degree requirements:* For doctorate, comprehensive exam, thesis/dissertation. *Entrance requirements:* For doctorate, GRE General Test, minimum GPA of 3.0 in science course work (recommended). Additional exam requirements/recommendations for international students: Required—TOEFL. *Application deadline:* For fall admission, 12/1 for domestic and international students. Application fee: $75. Electronic applications accepted. *Expenses: Tuition:* Full-time $34,800. *Required fees:* $1300. *Financial support:* In 2011–12, 11 students received support, including 11 fellowships with full tuition reimbursements available (averaging $26,500 per year); institutionally sponsored loans, scholarships/grants, health care benefits, and tuition waivers (full) also available. *Faculty research:* Evolution of microbes, infectious disease, the immune system, genetic disease in humans, evolution of behavior. *Unit head:* Dr. Michael Zwick, Director, 404-727-9924, Fax: 404-727-3949, E-mail: mzwick@emory.edu. *Application contact:* Kathy

Smith, Director of Recruitment and Admissions, 404-727-2547, Fax: 404-727-3322, E-mail: kathy.smith@emory.edu. Web site: http://www.biomed.emory.edu/.

Florida State University, The Graduate School, College of Arts and Sciences, Department of Biological Science, Specialization in Ecology and Evolutionary Biology, Tallahassee, FL 32306-4295. Offers MS, PhD. *Faculty:* 23 full-time (9 women). *Students:* 51 full-time (25 women); includes 6 minority (1 Asian, non-Hispanic/Latino; 5 Hispanic/Latino), 2 international. 124 applicants, 13% accepted, 8 enrolled. In 2011, 3 master's, 6 doctorates awarded. Terminal master's awarded for partial completion of doctoral program. *Degree requirements:* For master's, comprehensive exam, thesis, teaching experience, seminar presentation; for doctorate, comprehensive exam, thesis/dissertation, teaching experience; seminar presentation. *Entrance requirements:* For master's and doctorate, GRE General Test (minimum combined score 1100, 500 verbal, 500 quantitative in old version; 72% verbal, 67% quantitative in new format), minimum upper-division GPA of 3.0. Additional exam requirements/recommendations for international students: Required—TOEFL (minimum score 600 paper-based; 250 computer-based; 92 iBT). *Application deadline:* For fall admission, 12/15 for domestic and international students. Application fee: $30. Electronic applications accepted. *Expenses:* Tuition, state resident: full-time $9474; part-time $350.88 per credit hour. Tuition, nonresident: full-time $16,236; part-time $601.34 per credit hour. *Required fees:* $630 per semester. One-time fee: $20. Tuition and fees vary according to course load and campus/location. *Financial support:* In 2011–12, 50 students received support, including 5 fellowships (averaging $30,000 per year), 19 research assistantships with full tuition reimbursements available (averaging $21,000 per year), 26 teaching assistantships with full tuition reimbursements available (averaging $21,000 per year). Financial award application deadline: 12/15; financial award applicants required to submit FAFSA. *Faculty research:* Ecology and conservation biology; evolution; marine biology; phylogeny and systematics; theoretical, computational and mathematical biology. *Unit head:* Dr. George W. Bates, Professor and Associate Chairman, 850-644-5749, Fax: 850-644-9829, E-mail: bates@bio.fsu.edu. *Application contact:* Judy Bowers, Coordinator, Graduate Affairs, 850-644-3023, Fax: 850-644-9829, E-mail: gradinfo@bio.fsu.edu. Web site: http://www.bio.fsu.edu/.

Harvard University, Graduate School of Arts and Sciences, Department of Organismic and Evolutionary Biology, Cambridge, MA 02138. Offers biology (PhD). *Degree requirements:* For doctorate, 2 foreign languages, public presentation of thesis research, exam. *Entrance requirements:* For doctorate, GRE General Test, GRE Subject Test (recommended), 7 courses in biology, chemistry, physics, mathematics, computer science, or geology. Additional exam requirements/recommendations for international students: Required—TOEFL. *Expenses: Tuition:* Full-time $36,304. *Required fees:* $1186. Full-time tuition and fees vary according to program.

Illinois State University, Graduate School, College of Arts and Sciences, Department of Biological Sciences, Normal, IL 61790-2200. Offers animal behavior (MS); bacteriology (MS); biochemistry (MS); biological sciences (MS); biology (PhD); biophysics (MS); biotechnology (MS); botany (MS, PhD); cell biology (MS); conservation biology (MS); developmental biology (MS); ecology (MS, PhD); entomology (MS); evolutionary biology (MS); genetics (MS, PhD); immunology (MS); microbiology (MS, PhD); molecular biology (MS); molecular genetics (MS); neurobiology (MS); neuroscience (MS); parasitology (MS); physiology (MS, PhD); plant biology (MS); plant molecular biology (MS); plant sciences (MS); structural biology (MS); zoology (MS, PhD). Part-time programs available. *Degree requirements:* For master's, thesis or alternative; for doctorate, variable foreign language requirement, thesis/dissertation, 2 terms of residency. *Entrance requirements:* For master's, GRE General Test, minimum GPA of 2.6 in last 60 hours of course work; for doctorate, GRE General Test. *Faculty research:* Redoc balance and drug development in schistosoma mansoni, control of the growth of listeria monocytogenes at low temperature, regulation of cell expansion and microtubule function by SPRI, CRUI: physiology and fitness consequences of different life history phenotypes.

Indiana University Bloomington, University Graduate School, College of Arts and Sciences, Department of Biology, Bloomington, IN 47405. Offers biology teaching (MAT); biotechnology (MA); evolution, ecology, and behavior (MA, PhD); genetics (PhD); microbiology (MA, PhD); molecular, cellular, and developmental biology (PhD); plant sciences (MA, PhD); zoology (MA, PhD). *Faculty:* 58 full-time (15 women), 21 part-time/adjunct (6 women). *Students:* 175 full-time (100 women), 3 part-time (all women); includes 20 minority (5 Black or African American, non-Hispanic/Latino; 8 Asian, non-Hispanic/Latino; 7 Hispanic/Latino), 55 international. Average age 27. 316 applicants, 22% accepted, 31 enrolled. In 2011, 8 master's, 20 doctorates awarded. Terminal master's awarded for partial completion of doctoral program. *Degree requirements:* For master's, thesis, oral defense; for doctorate, thesis/dissertation, oral defense. *Entrance requirements:* For master's and doctorate, GRE General Test. Additional exam requirements/recommendations for international students: Required—TOEFL (minimum score 100 iBT). *Application deadline:* For fall admission, 1/5 priority date for domestic students, 12/1 for international students. Application fee: $55 ($65 for international students). Electronic applications accepted. *Financial support:* In 2011–12, fellowships with tuition reimbursements (averaging $19,484 per year), research assistantships with tuition reimbursements (averaging $20,300 per year), teaching assistantships with tuition reimbursements (averaging $20,521 per year) were awarded; scholarships/grants, traineeships, health care benefits, and unspecified assistantships also available. Financial award application deadline: 1/5. *Faculty research:* Evolution, ecology and behavior; microbiology; molecular biology and genetics; plant biology. *Unit head:* Dr. Roger Innes, Chair, 812-855-2219, Fax: 812-855-6082, E-mail: rinnes@indiana.edu. *Application contact:* Tracey D. Stohr, Graduate Student Recruitment Coordinator, 812-856-6303, Fax: 812-855-6082, E-mail: gradbio@indiana.edu. Web site: http://www.bio.indiana.edu/.

Iowa State University of Science and Technology, Program in Ecology and Evolutionary Biology, Ames, IA 50011-1020. Offers MS, PhD. *Degree requirements:* For master's, thesis or alternative; for doctorate, thesis/dissertation. *Entrance requirements:* For master's and doctorate, GRE General Test. Additional exam requirements/recommendations for international students: Required—TOEFL (minimum score 550 paper-based; 79 iBT), IELTS (minimum score 6.5). *Application deadline:* For fall admission, 1/1 priority date for domestic students, 1/1 for international students; for spring admission, 6/1 priority date for domestic students, 6/1 for international students. Application fee: $40 ($90 for international students). Electronic applications accepted. *Faculty research:* Landscape ecology, aquatic and method ecology, physiological ecology, population genetics and evolution, systematics. *Unit head:* Dr. Kirk Moloney, Director of Graduate Education, 515-294-6518, Fax: 515-294-1337, E-mail: eeboffice@iastate.edu. *Application contact:* Charles Sauer, Application Contact, 515-294-6518, Fax: 515-294-1337, E-mail: eeboffice@iastate.edu. Web site: http://www.grad-college.iastate.edu/EEB/homepage.html.

The Johns Hopkins University, School of Medicine, Graduate Programs in Medicine, Center for Functional Anatomy and Evolution, Baltimore, MD 21218-2699. Offers PhD. *Degree requirements:* For doctorate, comprehensive exam, thesis/dissertation, oral exams. *Entrance requirements:* For doctorate, GRE. Additional exam requirements/recommendations for international students: Required—TOEFL. *Faculty research:* Vertebrate evolution, functional anatomy, primate evolution, vertebrate paleobiology, vertebrate morphology.

Michigan State University, The Graduate School, College of Natural Science, Interdepartmental Program in Ecology, Evolutionary Biology and Behavior, East Lansing, MI 48824. Offers PhD. *Entrance requirements:* Additional exam requirements/recommendations for international students: Required—TOEFL. Electronic applications accepted.

Montclair State University, The Graduate School, College of Science and Mathematics, Department of Biology and Molecular Biology, Montclair, NJ 07043-1624. Offers biology (MS), including biological science education, biology, ecology and evolution, physiology; molecular biology (MS, Certificate). Part-time and evening/weekend programs available. *Students:* 15 full-time (10 women), 33 part-time (23 women); includes 3 minority (all Hispanic/Latino), 1 international. Average age 28. 53 applicants, 47% accepted, 14 enrolled. In 2011, 14 degrees awarded. *Degree requirements:* For master's, comprehensive exam, thesis or alternative. *Entrance requirements:* For master's, GRE General Test, 24 credits of course work in undergraduate biology, 2 letters of recommendation, teaching certificate (biology sciences education concentration); for Certificate, 2 letters of recommendation, essay. Additional exam requirements/recommendations for international students: Required—TOEFL (minimum score 83 iBT) or IELTS. *Application deadline:* For fall admission, 6/1 for international students; for spring admission, 10/1 for international students. Applications are processed on a rolling basis. Application fee: $60. Electronic applications accepted. *Financial support:* In 2011–12, 16 research assistantships with full tuition reimbursements (averaging $7,000 per year), 3 teaching assistantships (averaging $7,000 per year) were awarded; Federal Work-Study, scholarships/grants, and unspecified assistantships also available. Support available to part-time students. Financial award application deadline: 3/1; financial award applicants required to submit FAFSA. *Faculty research:* Ecosystem biology, molecular biology, signal transduction, neuroscience, aquatic and coastal biology. *Total annual research expenditures:* $1.3 million. *Unit head:* Dr. Quinn Vega, Chairperson, 973-655-7178. *Application contact:* Amy Aiello, Director of Graduate Admissions and Operations, 973-655-5147, Fax: 973-655-7869, E-mail: graduate.school@montclair.edu. Web site: http://www.montclair.edu/csam/biology/.

Northwestern University, Northwestern University Feinberg School of Medicine and Interdepartmental Programs, Integrated Graduate Programs in the Life Sciences, Chicago, IL 60611. Offers cancer biology (PhD); cell biology (PhD); developmental biology (PhD); evolutionary biology (PhD); immunology and microbial pathogenesis (PhD); molecular biology and genetics (PhD); neurobiology (PhD); pharmacology and toxicology (PhD); structural biology and biochemistry (PhD). *Degree requirements:* For doctorate, comprehensive exam, thesis/dissertation, written and oral qualifying exams. *Entrance requirements:* For doctorate, GRE General Test. Additional exam requirements/recommendations for international students: Required—TOEFL (minimum score 600 paper-based; 250 computer-based). Electronic applications accepted.

The Ohio State University, Graduate School, College of Arts and Sciences, Division of Natural and Mathematical Sciences, Department of Evolution, Ecology, and Organismal Biology, Columbus, OH 43210. Offers MS, PhD. *Faculty:* 29. *Students:* 23 full-time (15 women), 46 part-time (20 women); includes 2 minority (1 Black or African American, non-Hispanic/Latino; 1 Two or more races, non-Hispanic/Latino), 8 international. Average age 28. In 2011, 8 master's, 3 doctorates awarded. *Degree requirements:* For master's, thesis optional; for doctorate, thesis/dissertation. *Entrance requirements:* For master's and doctorate, GRE General Test. Additional exam requirements/recommendations for international students: Required—TOEFL (minimum score 550 paper-based; 250 computer-based; 79 iBT), Michigan English Language Assessment Battery (minimum score 82). *Application deadline:* For fall admission, 8/15 priority date for domestic students, 7/1 for international students; for winter admission, 12/1 priority date for domestic students, 11/1 for international students; for spring admission, 3/1 priority date for domestic students, 2/1 for international students. Applications are processed on a rolling basis. Application fee: $40 ($50 for international students). Electronic applications accepted. *Expenses:* Tuition, state resident: full-time $11,400. Tuition, nonresident: full-time $28,125. Tuition and fees vary according to course load, degree level, campus/location and program. *Financial support:* Fellowships, research assistantships, teaching assistantships, Federal Work-Study, and institutionally sponsored loans available. Support available to part-time students. *Unit head:* Peter S. Curtis, Chair, 614-292-1634, E-mail: curtis.7@osu.edu. *Application contact:* Graduate Admissions, 614-292-6031, Fax: 614-292-3656, E-mail: gradadmissions@osu.edu. Web site: http://eeob.osu.edu/.

Ohio University, Graduate College, College of Arts and Sciences, Department of Biological Sciences, Athens, OH 45701-2979. Offers biological sciences (MS, PhD); cell biology and physiology (MS, PhD); ecology and evolutionary biology (MS, PhD); exercise physiology and muscle biology (MS, PhD); microbiology (MS, PhD); neuroscience (MS, PhD). *Students:* 35 full-time (12 women), 4 part-time (1 woman), 14 international. 62 applicants, 10% accepted, 5 enrolled. In 2011, 2 master's, 8 doctorates awarded. Terminal master's awarded for partial completion of doctoral program. *Degree requirements:* For master's, comprehensive exam, thesis, 1 quarter of teaching experience; for doctorate, comprehensive exam, thesis/dissertation, 2 quarters of teaching experience. *Entrance requirements:* For master's, GRE General Test, names of three faculty members whose research interests most closely match the applicant's interest; for doctorate, GRE General Test, essay concerning prior training, research interest and career goals, plus names of three faculty members whose research interests most closely match the applicant's interest. Additional exam requirements/recommendations for international students: Required—TOEFL (minimum score 620 paper-based; 105 iBT) or IELTS (minimum score 7.5). *Application deadline:* For fall admission, 1/15 for domestic and international students. Application fee: $50 ($55 for international students). Electronic applications accepted. *Financial support:* In 2011–12, 1 fellowship with full tuition reimbursement (averaging $18,957 per year), 10 research assistantships with full tuition reimbursements (averaging $18,957 per year), 42 teaching assistantships with full tuition reimbursements (averaging $18,957 per year) were awarded; Federal Work-Study and institutionally sponsored loans also available. Financial award application deadline: 1/15. *Faculty research:* Ecology and evolutionary biology, exercise physiology and muscle biology, neurobiology, cell biology, physiology. *Total annual research expenditures:* $2.8 million. *Unit head:* Dr. Ralph DiCaprio, Chair, 740-593-2290, Fax: 740-593-0300, E-mail: dicaprir@ohio.edu. *Application contact:* Dr. Patrick Hassett, Graduate Chair, 740-593-4793, Fax: 740-593-0300, E-mail: hassett@ohio.edu. Web site: http://www.biosci.ohiou.edu/.

Princeton University, Graduate School, Department of Ecology and Evolutionary Biology, Princeton, NJ 08544-1019. Offers PhD. *Degree requirements:* For doctorate, thesis/dissertation. *Entrance requirements:* For doctorate, GRE General Test, GRE Subject Test. Additional exam requirements/recommendations for international students: Required—TOEFL (minimum score 600 paper-based; 250 computer-based). Electronic applications accepted.

Purdue University, Graduate School, College of Science, Department of Biological Sciences, West Lafayette, IN 47907. Offers biochemistry (PhD); biophysics (PhD); cell and developmental biology (PhD); ecology, evolutionary and population biology (MS,

PhD), including ecology, evolutionary biology, population biology; genetics (MS, PhD); microbiology (MS, PhD); molecular biology (PhD); neurobiology (MS, PhD); plant physiology (PhD). *Faculty:* 57 full-time (15 women), 4 part-time/adjunct (1 woman). *Students:* 94 full-time (54 women), 9 part-time (5 women); includes 7 minority (2 Black or African American, non-Hispanic/Latino; 3 Asian, non-Hispanic/Latino; 2 Hispanic/Latino), 51 international. Average age 27. 246 applicants, 11% accepted, 18 enrolled. In 2011, 9 master's, 23 doctorates awarded. Terminal master's awarded for partial completion of doctoral program. *Degree requirements:* For master's, thesis (for some programs); for doctorate, thesis/dissertation, seminars, teaching experience. *Entrance requirements:* For master's, GRE General Test, minimum analytical writing score of 3.5, minimum undergraduate GPA of 3.0; for doctorate, GRE General Test, minimum analytical writing score of 3.5, minimum undergraduate GPA of 3.5. Additional exam requirements/recommendations for international students: Required—TOEFL (minimum score 600 paper-based; 107 iBT) for MS; TOEFL (minimum score 600 paper-based; 80 iBT) for Ph D. *Application deadline:* For fall admission, 12/7 for domestic and international students. Applications are processed on a rolling basis. Application fee: $60 ($75 for international students). Electronic applications accepted. *Financial support:* Fellowships, research assistantships, and teaching assistantships available. Support available to part-time students. Financial award application deadline: 2/15; financial award applicants required to submit FAFSA. *Unit head:* Dr. Richard J. Kuhn, Head, 765-494-4407, E-mail: kuhnr@purdue.edu. *Application contact:* Georgina E. Rupp, Graduate Coordinator, 765-494-8142, Fax: 765-494-0876, E-mail: ruppg@purdue.edu. Web site: http://www.bio.purdue.edu/.

Purdue University, Graduate School, PULSe - Purdue University Life Sciences Program, West Lafayette, IN 47907. Offers biomolecular structure and biophysics (PhD); biotechnology (PhD); chemical biology (PhD); chromatin and regulation of gene expression (PhD); integrative neuroscience (PhD); integrative plant sciences (PhD); membrane biology (PhD); microbiology (PhD); molecular evolutionary and cancer biology (PhD); molecular evolutionary genetics (PhD); molecular virology (PhD). *Students:* 90 full-time (45 women); includes 7 minority (3 Black or African American, non-Hispanic/Latino; 1 Asian, non-Hispanic/Latino; 2 Hispanic/Latino; 1 Two or more races, non-Hispanic/Latino), 40 international. Average age 26. 427 applicants, 24% accepted, 35 enrolled. *Entrance requirements:* For doctorate, GRE test required, minimum undergraduate GPA of 3.0. Additional exam requirements/recommendations for international students: Required—TOEFL (minimum score 550 paper-based; 77 iBT). *Application deadline:* For fall admission, 1/15 priority date for domestic students, 1/15 for international students. Applications are processed on a rolling basis. Application fee: $60 ($75 for international students). Electronic applications accepted. *Financial support:* In 2011–12, research assistantships with tuition reimbursements (averaging $22,500 per year), teaching assistantships with tuition reimbursements (averaging $22,500 per year) were awarded. *Unit head:* Dr. Christine A. Hrycyna, Head, 765-494-7322, E-mail: hrycyna@purdue.edu. *Application contact:* Emily E. Bramson, Graduate Contact, 765-494-5865, E-mail: bramson@purdue.edu. Web site: http://www.gradschool.purdue.edu/pulse.

Rice University, Graduate Programs, Wiess School of Natural Sciences, Department of Ecology and Evolutionary Biology, Houston, TX 77251-1892. Offers MA, MS, PhD. Terminal master's awarded for partial completion of doctoral program. *Degree requirements:* For master's, comprehensive exam (for some programs), thesis (for some programs); for doctorate, comprehensive exam, thesis/dissertation. *Entrance requirements:* For master's and doctorate, GRE General Test, GRE Subject Test. Additional exam requirements/recommendations for international students: Required—TOEFL (minimum score 600 paper-based; 250 computer-based; 90 iBT). Electronic applications accepted. *Faculty research:* Trace gas emissions, wetlands, biology, community ecology of forests and grasslands, conservation biology specialization.

Rutgers, The State University of New Jersey, New Brunswick, Graduate School-New Brunswick, Program in Ecology and Evolution, Piscataway, NJ 08854-8097. Offers MS, PhD. Part-time programs available. Terminal master's awarded for partial completion of doctoral program. *Degree requirements:* For master's, comprehensive exam; for doctorate, comprehensive exam, thesis/dissertation. *Entrance requirements:* For master's and doctorate, GRE General Test, minimum GPA of 3.0. Additional exam requirements/recommendations for international students: Required—TOEFL (minimum score 550 paper-based; 213 computer-based). Electronic applications accepted. *Faculty research:* Population and community ecology, population genetics, evolutionary biology, conservation biology, ecosystem ecology.

Rutgers, The State University of New Jersey, New Brunswick, Graduate School-New Brunswick, Program in Plant Biology, Piscataway, NJ 08854-8097. Offers horticulture and plant technology (MS, PhD); molecular and cellular biology (MS, PhD); organismal and population biology (MS, PhD); plant pathology (MS, PhD). Part-time programs available. Terminal master's awarded for partial completion of doctoral program. *Degree requirements:* For master's, comprehensive exam, thesis or alternative; for doctorate, comprehensive exam, thesis/dissertation. *Entrance requirements:* For master's and doctorate, GRE General Test, GRE Subject Test (recommended). Additional exam requirements/recommendations for international students: Required—TOEFL (minimum score 600 paper-based; 250 computer-based). Electronic applications accepted. *Faculty research:* Molecular biology and biochemistry of plants, plant development and genomics, plant protection, plant improvement, plant management of horticultural and field crops.

Stony Brook University, State University of New York, Graduate School, College of Arts and Sciences, Department of Ecology and Evolution, Stony Brook, NY 11794. Offers applied ecology (MA); ecology and evolution (PhD). *Degree requirements:* For doctorate, one foreign language, comprehensive exam, thesis/dissertation, teaching experience. *Entrance requirements:* For doctorate, GRE General Test, GRE Subject Test. Additional exam requirements/recommendations for international students: Required—TOEFL. *Faculty research:* Theoretical and experimental population genetics, numerical taxonomy, biostatistics, population and community ecology, plant ecology.

Tulane University, School of Science and Engineering, Department of Ecology and Evolutionary Biology, New Orleans, LA 70118-5669. Offers MS, PhD. Terminal master's awarded for partial completion of doctoral program. *Degree requirements:* For master's, thesis or alternative; for doctorate, thesis/dissertation. *Entrance requirements:* For master's, GRE General Test, minimum B average in undergraduate course work; for doctorate, GRE General Test. Additional exam requirements/recommendations for international students: Required—TOEFL. Electronic applications accepted. *Faculty research:* Ichthyology, plant systematics, crustacean endocrinology, ecotoxicology, ornithology.

University at Albany, State University of New York, College of Arts and Sciences, Department of Biological Sciences, Specialization in Ecology, Evolution, and Behavior, Albany, NY 12222-0001. Offers MS, PhD. *Degree requirements:* For master's, one foreign language; for doctorate, one foreign language, thesis/dissertation. *Entrance requirements:* For master's and doctorate, GRE General Test.

University at Buffalo, the State University of New York, Graduate School, College of Arts and Sciences, Program in Evolution, Ecology and Behavior, Buffalo, NY 14260. Offers MS, PhD, Certificate. *Faculty:* 18 full-time (8 women). *Students:* 14 full-time (9 women), 3 international. Average age 25. 21 applicants, 43% accepted, 7 enrolled. In 2011, 6 master's, 1 doctorate awarded. Terminal master's awarded for partial completion of doctoral program. *Degree requirements:* For master's, project; for doctorate, comprehensive exam, thesis/dissertation. *Entrance requirements:* For master's, GRE, minimum undergraduate GPA of 3.0; for doctorate, GRE, minimum GPA of 3.0. Additional exam requirements/recommendations for international students: Required—TOEFL (minimum score 550 paper-based; 213 computer-based; 79 iBT). *Application deadline:* For fall admission, 1/15 priority date for domestic students, 1/15 for international students. Applications are processed on a rolling basis. Application fee: $75. Electronic applications accepted. *Financial support:* In 2011–12, 2 fellowships with full tuition reimbursements (averaging $6,000 per year), 6 research assistantships with full tuition reimbursements (averaging $24,000 per year), 4 teaching assistantships with full tuition reimbursements (averaging $17,000 per year) were awarded; Federal Work-Study, scholarships/grants, health care benefits, and unspecified assistantships also available. Financial award application deadline: 1/15; financial award applicants required to submit FAFSA. *Faculty research:* Coral reef ecology, evolution and ecology of aquatic invertebrates, animal communication, paleobiology, primate behavior. *Unit head:* Dr. Howard Lasker, Program Director, 716-645-4870, Fax: 716-645-3999, E-mail: ub-evb@buffalo.edu. *Application contact:* Marty Roth, Secretary, 716-645-3489, Fax: 716-345-3999, E-mail: mlroth@buffalo.edu. Web site: http://www.evolutionecologybehavior.buffalo.edu/.

University of Alberta, Faculty of Graduate Studies and Research, Department of Biological Sciences, Edmonton, AB T6G 2E1, Canada. Offers environmental biology and ecology (M Sc, PhD); microbiology and biotechnology (M Sc, PhD); molecular biology and genetics (M Sc, PhD); physiology and cell biology (M Sc, PhD); plant biology (M Sc, PhD); systematics and evolution (M Sc, PhD). Terminal master's awarded for partial completion of doctoral program. *Degree requirements:* For master's, thesis; for doctorate, thesis/dissertation. *Entrance requirements:* Additional exam requirements/recommendations for international students: Required—TOEFL.

The University of Arizona, College of Science, Department of Ecology and Evolutionary Biology, Tucson, AZ 85721. Offers MS, PhD. *Faculty:* 20 full-time (4 women), 3 part-time/adjunct (0 women). *Students:* 42 full-time (21 women), 13 part-time (4 women); includes 5 minority (1 Black or African American, non-Hispanic/Latino; 1 American Indian or Alaska Native, non-Hispanic/Latino; 1 Hispanic/Latino; 2 Two or more races, non-Hispanic/Latino), 12 international. Average age 30. 87 applicants, 15% accepted, 9 enrolled. In 2011, 6 master's, 2 doctorates awarded. Terminal master's awarded for partial completion of doctoral program. *Degree requirements:* For master's, thesis optional; for doctorate, one foreign language, comprehensive exam, thesis/dissertation. *Entrance requirements:* For master's, GRE General Test, GRE Subject Test, statement of purpose, curriculum vitae, 3 letters of recommendation; for doctorate, GRE General Test, GRE Subject Test, curriculum vitae, 3 letters of recommendation. Additional exam requirements/recommendations for international students: Required—TOEFL (minimum score 550 paper-based; 213 computer-based; 79 iBT). *Application deadline:* For fall admission, 12/1 for domestic students, 12/8 for international students. Application fee: $75. *Expenses:* Tuition, state resident: full-time $10,840. Tuition, nonresident: full-time $25,802. *Financial support:* In 2011–12, 13 research assistantships with full tuition reimbursements (averaging $22,896 per year), 35 teaching assistantships with full tuition reimbursements (averaging $22,896 per year) were awarded; career-related internships or fieldwork, scholarships/grants, health care benefits, and unspecified assistantships also available. *Faculty research:* Biological diversity, evolutionary history, evolutionary mechanisms, community structure. *Total annual research expenditures:* $5.6 million. *Unit head:* Dr. Richard E. Michod, Head, 520-621-7509, Fax: 520-621-9190, E-mail: michod@email.arizona.edu. *Application contact:* Carol Burleson, Administrative Associate, 520-621-1165, Fax: 520-621-9190, E-mail: burleson@email.arizona.edu. Web site: http://eebweb.arizona.edu/.

University of California, Davis, Graduate Studies, Graduate Group in Population Biology, Davis, CA 95616. Offers PhD. *Degree requirements:* For doctorate, thesis/dissertation. *Entrance requirements:* For doctorate, GRE General Test, GRE Subject Test. Additional exam requirements/recommendations for international students: Required—TOEFL (minimum score 550 paper-based; 213 computer-based). Electronic applications accepted. *Faculty research:* Population ecology, population genetics, systematics, evolution, community ecology.

University of California, Irvine, School of Biological Sciences, Department of Ecology and Evolutionary Biology, Irvine, CA 92697. Offers biological sciences (MS, PhD). *Students:* 44 full-time (27 women); includes 8 minority (3 Asian, non-Hispanic/Latino; 4 Hispanic/Latino; 1 Two or more races, non-Hispanic/Latino), 5 international. Average age 27. 62 applicants, 27% accepted, 10 enrolled. In 2011, 3 master's, 11 doctorates awarded. *Degree requirements:* For master's, thesis; for doctorate, thesis/dissertation. *Entrance requirements:* For master's and doctorate, GRE General Test, GRE Subject Test, minimum GPA of 3.0. Additional exam requirements/recommendations for international students: Required—TOEFL (minimum score 550 paper-based; 213 computer-based). *Application deadline:* For fall admission, 1/15 priority date for domestic students, 1/15 for international students. Applications are processed on a rolling basis. Application fee: $80 ($100 for international students). Electronic applications accepted. *Financial support:* Fellowships, research assistantships with full tuition reimbursements, teaching assistantships, career-related internships or fieldwork, institutionally sponsored loans, traineeships, health care benefits, and unspecified assistantships available. Financial award application deadline: 3/1; financial award applicants required to submit FAFSA. *Faculty research:* Ecological energetics, quantitative genetics, life history evolution, plant-herbivore and plant-pollinator interactions, molecular evolution. *Unit head:* Peter A. Bowler, Faculty Manager, 949-824-0157, Fax: 949-824-2181, E-mail: pabowler@uci.edu. *Application contact:* Pamela McDonald, 949-824-4743, E-mail: bshipley@uci.edu. Web site: http://ecoevo.bio.uci.edu/.

University of California, Los Angeles, Graduate Division, College of Letters and Science, Department of Ecology and Evolutionary Biology, Los Angeles, CA 90095. Offers MA, PhD. *Faculty:* 23 full-time (5 women). *Students:* 71 full-time (48 women); includes 20 minority (2 Black or African American, non-Hispanic/Latino; 8 Asian, non-Hispanic/Latino; 8 Hispanic/Latino; 2 Two or more races, non-Hispanic/Latino), 9 international. Average age 29. 92 applicants, 26% accepted, 16 enrolled. In 2011, 2 master's, 11 doctorates awarded. Terminal master's awarded for partial completion of doctoral program. *Degree requirements:* For master's, comprehensive exam or thesis; for doctorate, thesis/dissertation, oral and written qualifying exams; teaching experience. *Entrance requirements:* For master's and doctorate, GRE General Test, GRE Subject Test (biology), minimum GPA of 3.0, 3 letters of recommendation. *Application deadline:* For fall admission, 12/1 for domestic and international students. Application fee: $70 ($90 for international students). Electronic applications accepted. *Financial support:* In 2011–12, 64 fellowships with full and partial tuition reimbursements, 20 research assistantships with full and partial tuition reimbursements, 38 teaching assistantships with full and partial tuition reimbursements were awarded; Federal Work-Study, institutionally sponsored loans, scholarships/grants, health care benefits, tuition waivers (full and partial), and unspecified assistantships also available. Financial award application deadline: 3/1; financial award applicants required to submit FAFSA. *Faculty*

research: Molecular, cell, and developmental biology; interactive biology; organisms and populations. *Unit head:* Dr. Daniel T. Blumstein, Chair, 310-267-4746, Fax: 310-206-3987, E-mail: marmots@ucla.edu. *Application contact:* Jocelyn Yamadera, Student Affairs Officer, 310-825-1959, Fax: 310-206-5280, E-mail: jocelyny@lifesci.ucla.edu. Web site: http://www.eeb.ucla.edu/.

University of California, Riverside, Graduate Division, Department of Biology, Riverside, CA 92521-0102. Offers evolution, ecology and organismal biology (MS, PhD). Terminal master's awarded for partial completion of doctoral program. *Degree requirements:* For master's, thesis, oral defense of thesis; for doctorate, thesis/dissertation, 3 quarters of teaching experience, qualifying exams. *Entrance requirements:* For master's and doctorate, GRE General Test, minimum GPA of 3.2. Additional exam requirements/recommendations for international students: Required—TOEFL (minimum score 550 paper-based, 213 computer-based, 80 iBT) or IELTS. Electronic applications accepted. *Faculty research:* Ecology, evolutionary biology, physiology, quantitative genetics, conservation biology.

University of California, Riverside, Graduate Division, Department of Entomology, Riverside, CA 92521-0102. Offers entomology (MS, PhD); evolution and ecology (PhD). Part-time programs available. *Faculty:* 35 full-time (4 women). *Students:* 37 full-time (19 women); includes 8 minority (1 Black or African American, non-Hispanic/Latino; 4 Asian, non-Hispanic/Latino; 3 Hispanic/Latino), 6 international. Average age 28. 27 applicants, 37% accepted, 7 enrolled. In 2011, 2 master's, 8 doctorates awarded. Terminal master's awarded for partial completion of doctoral program. *Degree requirements:* For master's, thesis; for doctorate, thesis/dissertation, qualifying exams. *Entrance requirements:* For master's and doctorate, GRE General Test, minimum GPA of 3.2. Additional exam requirements/recommendations for international students: Required—TOEFL (minimum score 550 paper-based; 213 computer-based; 80 iBT) or IELTS. *Application deadline:* For fall admission, 5/1 for domestic students, 2/1 for international students; for winter admission, 9/1 for domestic students, 7/1 for international students; for spring admission, 12/1 for domestic students, 10/1 for international students. Applications are processed on a rolling basis. Application fee: $80 ($100 for international students). Electronic applications accepted. *Financial support:* In 2011–12, fellowships with tuition reimbursements (averaging $18,000 per year), research assistantships with tuition reimbursements (averaging $19,500 per year), teaching assistantships with tuition reimbursements (averaging $17,310 per year) were awarded; career-related internships or fieldwork, Federal Work-Study, institutionally sponsored loans, and tuition waivers (full and partial) also available. Financial award application deadline: 1/5; financial award applicants required to submit FAFSA. *Faculty research:* Agricultural, urban, medical, and veterinary entomology; biological control; chemical ecology; insect pathogens; novel toxicants. *Unit head:* Dr. Richard Redak, Chair, 951-827-7250, Fax: 951-827-3086, E-mail: richard.redak@ucr.edu. *Application contact:* Melissa L. Gomez, Graduate Student Affairs Officer, 951-827-5913, Fax: 951-827-5517, E-mail: insects@ucr.edu. Web site: http://www.entomology.ucr.edu/.

University of California, San Diego, Office of Graduate Studies, Division of Biological Sciences, Program in Ecology, Behavior, and Evolution, La Jolla, CA 92093. Offers PhD. *Degree requirements:* For doctorate, thesis/dissertation, qualifying exam. Electronic applications accepted.

University of California, Santa Barbara, Graduate Division, College of Letters and Sciences, Division of Mathematics, Life, and Physical Sciences, Department of Ecology, Evolution, and Marine Biology, Santa Barbara, CA 93106-9620. Offers computational science and engineering (MA); computational sciences and engineering (PhD); ecology, evolution, and marine biology (MA, PhD); MA/PhD. *Faculty:* 27 full-time (7 women). *Students:* 58 full-time (39 women); includes 9 minority (1 Black or African American, non-Hispanic/Latino; 5 Asian, non-Hispanic/Latino; 2 Hispanic/Latino; 1 Two or more races, non-Hispanic/Latino), 4 international. Average age 30. 131 applicants, 15% accepted, 8 enrolled. In 2011, 4 master's, 4 doctorates awarded. *Median time to degree:* Of those who began their doctoral program in fall 2003, 100% received their degree in 8 years or less. *Degree requirements:* For master's, comprehensive exam (for some programs), thesis (for some programs); for doctorate, comprehensive exam, thesis/dissertation. *Entrance requirements:* For master's and doctorate, GRE General Test. Additional exam requirements/recommendations for international students: Required—TOEFL (minimum score 550 paper-based; 80 iBT), IELTS. *Application deadline:* For fall admission, 12/15 for domestic and international students. Application fee: $80 ($100 for international students). Electronic applications accepted. *Expenses:* Tuition, state resident: full-time $12,192. Tuition, nonresident: full-time $27,294. *Required fees:* $764.13. *Financial support:* In 2011–12, 54 students received support, including 44 fellowships with full and partial tuition reimbursements available (averaging $10,812 per year), 13 research assistantships with full and partial tuition reimbursements available (averaging $8,441 per year), 22 teaching assistantships with partial tuition reimbursements available (averaging $9,346 per year); Federal Work-Study, scholarships/grants, traineeships, health care benefits, and tuition waivers (full and partial) also available. Financial award application deadline: 12/15; financial award applicants required to submit FAFSA. *Faculty research:* Community ecology, evolution, marine biology, population genetics, stream ecology. *Unit head:* Dr. Cheryl Briggs, Chair, 805-893-2415, Fax: 805-893-5885. *Application contact:* Melanie Fujii, Staff Graduate Advisor, 805-893-2979, Fax: 805-893-5885, E-mail: eemb-info@lifesci.ucsb.edu. Web site: http://www.lifesci.ucsb.edu/EEMB/index.html.

University of California, Santa Cruz, Division of Graduate Studies, Division of Physical and Biological Sciences, Department of Ecology and Evolutionary Biology, Santa Cruz, CA 95064. Offers MA, PhD. *Degree requirements:* For master's, thesis; for doctorate, comprehensive exam, thesis/dissertation. *Entrance requirements:* For master's and doctorate, GRE General Test, GRE Subject Test, 3 letters of recommendation. Additional exam requirements/recommendations for international students: Required—TOEFL (minimum score 550 paper-based; 220 computer-based; 83 iBT); Recommended—IELTS (minimum score 8). Electronic applications accepted. *Faculty research:* Population and community ecology, evolutionary biology, physiology and behavior (marine and terrestrial), systematics and biodiversity.

University of Chicago, Division of Biological Sciences, Darwinian Sciences Cluster: Ecological, Integrative and Evolutionary Biology, Committee on Evolutionary Biology, Chicago, IL 60637-1513. Offers functional and evolutionary biology (PhD). Terminal master's awarded for partial completion of doctoral program. *Degree requirements:* For doctorate, thesis/dissertation, ethics class, 2 teaching assistantships. *Entrance requirements:* For doctorate, GRE General Test. Additional exam requirements/recommendations for international students: Required—TOEFL (minimum score 600 paper-based; 250 computer-based; 104 iBT), IELTS (minimum score 7). Electronic applications accepted. *Faculty research:* Systematics and evolutionary theory, genetics, functional morphology and physiology, behavior, ecology and biogeography.

University of Colorado Boulder, Graduate School, College of Arts and Sciences, Department of Ecology and Evolutionary Biology, Boulder, CO 80309. Offers animal behavior (MA); biology (MA, PhD); environmental biology (MA, PhD); evolutionary biology (MA, PhD); neurobiology (MA); population biology (MA); population genetics (PhD). *Faculty:* 28 full-time (9 women). *Students:* 67 full-time (37 women), 27 part-time (13 women); includes 9 minority (1 Asian, non-Hispanic/Latino; 8 Hispanic/Latino), 5 international. Average age 30. 136 applicants, 13% accepted, 17 enrolled. In 2011, 8 master's, 5 doctorates awarded. Terminal master's awarded for partial completion of doctoral program. *Degree requirements:* For master's, comprehensive exam, thesis or alternative; for doctorate, comprehensive exam, thesis/dissertation. *Entrance requirements:* For master's, GRE General Test, GRE Subject Test, minimum undergraduate GPA of 3.0; for doctorate, GRE General Test, GRE Subject Test. *Application deadline:* For fall admission, 12/30 priority date for domestic students, 12/1 for international students. Application fee: $50 ($60 for international students). Electronic applications accepted. *Financial support:* In 2011–12, 88 students received support, including 35 fellowships (averaging $16,835 per year), 25 research assistantships with full and partial tuition reimbursements available (averaging $22,347 per year), 44 teaching assistantships with full and partial tuition reimbursements available (averaging $21,377 per year); institutionally sponsored loans, scholarships/grants, health care benefits, and unspecified assistantships also available. Financial award applicants required to submit FAFSA. *Faculty research:* Behavior, ecology, genetics, morphology, endocrinology, physiology, systematics. *Total annual research expenditures:* $4.6 million. *Application contact:* E-mail: ebiograd@colorado.edu. Web site: http://ebio.colorado.edu.

University of Colorado Denver, College of Liberal Arts and Sciences, Department of Integrative Biology, Denver, CO 80217. Offers animal behavior (MS); biology (MS); cell and developmental biology (MS); ecology (MS); evolutionary biology (MS); genetics (MS); microbiology (MS); molecular biology (MS); neurobiology (MS); plant systematics (MS). Part-time programs available. *Faculty:* 16 full-time (8 women). *Students:* 20 full-time (13 women), 5 part-time (4 women); includes 1 minority (Hispanic/Latino), 1 international. Average age 29. 21 applicants, 43% accepted, 5 enrolled. In 2011, 7 master's awarded. *Degree requirements:* For master's, comprehensive exam, thesis or alternative, 30-32 credit hours. *Entrance requirements:* For master's, GRE General Test (minimum score in 50% percentile in each section), BA/BS from accredited institution awarded within the last 10 years; minimum undergraduate GPA of 3.0; prerequisite courses: 1 year each of general biology and general chemistry, and 1 semester each of general genetics, general ecology, cell biology, and a structure/function course. Additional exam requirements/recommendations for international students: Required—TOEFL (minimum score 525 paper-based; 197 computer-based; 71 iBT). *Application deadline:* For fall admission, 2/1 for domestic and international students. Application fee: $50 ($75 for international students). Electronic applications accepted. *Financial support:* Research assistantships, teaching assistantships, Federal Work-Study, scholarships/grants, and unspecified assistantships available. Financial award application deadline: 4/1; financial award applicants required to submit FAFSA. *Faculty research:* Molecular developmental biology; quantitative ecology, biogeography, and population dynamics; environmental signaling and endocrine disruption; speciation, the evolution of reproductive isolation, and hybrid zones; evolutionary, behavioral, and conservation ecology. *Unit head:* Dr. Diana Tomback, Acting Chair, 303-556-2657, E-mail: diana.tomback@ucdenver.edu. *Application contact:* Timberley Roane, Associate Professor/Associate Chair, 303-556-6592, E-mail: timberley.roane@ucdenver.edu. Web site: http://www.ucdenver.edu/academics/colleges/CLAS/Departments/biology/Pages/Biology.aspx.

University of Delaware, College of Arts and Sciences, Department of Biological Sciences, Newark, DE 19716. Offers biotechnology (MS); cancer biology (MS, PhD); cell and extracellular matrix biology (MS, PhD); cell and systems physiology (MS, PhD); developmental biology (MS, PhD); ecology and evolution (MS, PhD); microbiology (MS, PhD); molecular biology and genetics (MS, PhD). Terminal master's awarded for partial completion of doctoral program. *Degree requirements:* For master's, thesis, preliminary exam; for doctorate, comprehensive exam, thesis/dissertation, preliminary exam. *Entrance requirements:* For master's and doctorate, GRE General Test. Additional exam requirements/recommendations for international students: Required—TOEFL (minimum score 600 paper-based; 250 computer-based); Recommended—TWE. Electronic applications accepted. *Faculty research:* Microorganisms, bone, cancer metastasis, developmental biology, cell biology, DNA.

University of Guelph, Graduate Studies, College of Biological Science, Department of Integrative Biology, Botany and Zoology, Guelph, ON N1G 2W1, Canada. Offers botany (M Sc, PhD); zoology (M Sc, PhD). Part-time programs available. *Degree requirements:* For master's, thesis, research proposal; for doctorate, thesis/dissertation, research proposal, qualifying exam. *Entrance requirements:* For master's, minimum B average during previous 2 years of course work. Additional exam requirements/recommendations for international students: Required—TOEFL (minimum score 550 paper-based; 213 computer-based), IELTS (minimum score 6.5). Electronic applications accepted. *Faculty research:* Aquatic science, environmental physiology, parasitology, wildlife biology, management.

University of Hawaii at Manoa, Graduate Division, Interdisciplinary Specialization in Ecology, Evolution and Conservation Biology, Honolulu, HI 96822. Offers MS, PhD. *Degree requirements:* For doctorate, thesis/dissertation. *Faculty research:* Agronomy and soil science, zoology, entomology, genetics and molecular biology, botanical sciences.

University of Illinois at Urbana–Champaign, Graduate College, College of Liberal Arts and Sciences, School of Integrative Biology, Department of Animal Biology, Champaign, IL 61820. Offers animal biology (ecology, ethology and evolution) (MS, PhD). *Faculty:* 8 full-time (5 women). *Students:* 14 full-time (8 women), 2 part-time (0 women); includes 1 minority (Two or more races, non-Hispanic/Latino), 2 international. 7 applicants, 71% accepted, 4 enrolled. In 2011, 2 master's, 1 doctorate awarded. *Entrance requirements:* For master's and doctorate, GRE. Additional exam requirements/recommendations for international students: Required—TOEFL (minimum score 570 paper-based; 230 computer-based; 88 iBT). *Application deadline:* Applications are processed on a rolling basis. Application fee: $75 ($90 for international students). Electronic applications accepted. *Financial support:* In 2011–12, 3 fellowships, 4 research assistantships, 15 teaching assistantships were awarded; tuition waivers (full and partial) also available. *Unit head:* Ken Paige, Head, 217-244-6606, Fax: 217-244-4565, E-mail: k-paige@illinois.edu. *Application contact:* Lisa Smith, Office Administrator, 217-333-7802, Fax: 217-244-4565, E-mail: ljsmith1@illinois.edu. Web site: http://www.life.illinois.edu/animalbiology.

University of Illinois at Urbana–Champaign, Graduate College, College of Liberal Arts and Sciences, School of Integrative Biology, Program in Ecology, Evolution and Conservation Biology, Champaign, IL 61820. Offers MS, PhD. *Students:* 20 full-time (15 women), 8 part-time (3 women); includes 5 minority (1 American Indian or Alaska Native, non-Hispanic/Latino; 2 Asian, non-Hispanic/Latino; 1 Hispanic/Latino; 1 Two or more races, non-Hispanic/Latino), 3 international. 33 applicants, 9% accepted, 1 enrolled. In 2011, 2 master's, 4 doctorates awarded. *Entrance requirements:* For master's and doctorate, GRE. Additional exam requirements/recommendations for international students: Required—TOEFL (minimum score 613 paper-based; 257 computer-based; 103 iBT). *Application deadline:* Applications are processed on a rolling basis. Application fee: $75 ($90 for international students). Electronic applications accepted. *Financial support:* In 2011–12, 8 fellowships, 15 research assistantships, 14 teaching assistantships were awarded; tuition waivers (full and partial) also available. *Unit head:* Evan H. DeLucia, Director, 217-333-3044, Fax: 217-244-1224, E-mail:

delucia@illinois.edu. *Application contact:* Carol Hall, Secretary, 217-333-8208, Fax: 217-244-1224, E-mail: cahall@illinois.edu. Web site: http://sib.illinois.edu/peec/.

The University of Iowa, Graduate College, College of Liberal Arts and Sciences, Department of Biology, Iowa City, IA 52242-1324. Offers biology (MS, PhD); cell and developmental biology (MS, PhD); evolution (MS, PhD); genetics (MS, PhD); neurobiology (MS, PhD). Terminal master's awarded for partial completion of doctoral program. *Degree requirements:* For master's, thesis optional, exam; for doctorate, comprehensive exam, thesis/dissertation. *Entrance requirements:* For master's and doctorate, GRE General Test, minimum GPA of 3.0. Additional exam requirements/recommendations for international students: Required—TOEFL (minimum score 600 paper-based; 250 computer-based; 100 iBT). Electronic applications accepted. *Faculty research:* Neurobiology, evolutionary biology, genetics, cell and developmental biology.

The University of Kansas, Graduate Studies, College of Liberal Arts and Sciences, Department of Ecology and Evolutionary Biology, Lawrence, KS 66045. Offers botany (MA, PhD); ecology and evolutionary biology (MA, PhD); entomology (MA, PhD). *Faculty:* 15 full-time (6 women), 25 part-time/adjunct (6 women). *Students:* 64 full-time (31 women), 1 part-time (0 women); includes 4 minority (1 Hispanic/Latino; 3 Two or more races, non-Hispanic/Latino), 20 international. Average age 28. 67 applicants, 34% accepted, 18 enrolled. In 2011, 6 master's, 9 doctorates awarded. Terminal master's awarded for partial completion of doctoral program. *Degree requirements:* For master's, comprehensive exam, thesis (for some programs), 30-36 credits, thesis presentation; for doctorate, comprehensive exam, thesis/dissertation, residency, responsible scholarship and research skills, final exam, dissertation defense. *Entrance requirements:* For master's, GRE General Test, bachelor's degree with minimum undergraduate GPA of 3.0; for doctorate, GRE General Test, bachelor's degree; minimum undergraduate/graduate GPA of 3.0. Additional exam requirements/recommendations for international students: Required—TOEFL or IELTS. *Application deadline:* For fall admission, 12/1 for domestic students, 12/15 for international students; for spring admission, 9/15 for domestic and international students. Application fee: $55 ($65 for international students). Electronic applications accepted. Tuition and fees vary according to course load, campus/location, program and reciprocity agreements. *Financial support:* In 2011–12, 8 fellowships with full and partial tuition reimbursements, 22 research assistantships with full and partial tuition reimbursements, 32 teaching assistantships with full and partial tuition reimbursements were awarded; scholarships/grants, traineeships, health care benefits, and unspecified assistantships also available. Financial award application deadline: 12/1. *Faculty research:* Biodiversity and macroevolution, ecology and global change, evolutionary mechanisms. *Unit head:* Dr. Christopher H. Haufler, Chair, 785-864-3255, Fax: 785-864-5860, E-mail: vulgare@ku.edu. *Application contact:* Jaime Rochelle Keeler, Graduate Coordinator, 785-864-2362, Fax: 785-864-5860, E-mail: jrkeeler@ku.edu. Web site: http://www.ku.edu/~eeb/.

University of Louisiana at Lafayette, College of Sciences, Department of Biology, Lafayette, LA 70504. Offers biology (MS); environmental and evolutionary biology (PhD). Terminal master's awarded for partial completion of doctoral program. *Degree requirements:* For master's, thesis; for doctorate, 2 foreign languages, comprehensive exam, thesis/dissertation. *Entrance requirements:* For master's, GRE General Test, minimum GPA of 2.75; for doctorate, GRE General Test, GRE Subject Test, minimum GPA of 3.0. Additional exam requirements/recommendations for international students: Required—TOEFL (minimum score 550 paper-based; 213 computer-based). Electronic applications accepted. *Faculty research:* Structure and ultrastructure, system biology, ecology, processes, environmental physiology.

The University of Manchester, Faculty of Life Sciences, Manchester, United Kingdom. Offers adaptive organismal biology (M Phil, PhD); animal biology (M Phil, PhD); biochemistry (M Phil, PhD); bioinformatics (M Phil, PhD); biomolecular sciences (M Phil, PhD); biotechnology (M Phil, PhD); cell biology (M Phil, PhD); cell matrix research (M Phil, PhD); channels and transporters (M Phil, PhD); developmental biology (M Phil, PhD); Egyptology (M Phil, PhD); environmental biology (M Phil, PhD); evolutionary biology (M Phil, PhD); gene expression (M Phil, PhD); genetics (M Phil, PhD); history of science, technology and medicine (M Phil, PhD); immunology (M Phil, PhD); integrative neurobiology and behavior (M Phil, PhD); membrane trafficking (M Phil, PhD); microbiology (M Phil, PhD); molecular and cellular neuroscience (M Phil, PhD); molecular biology (M Phil, PhD); molecular cancer studies (M Phil, PhD); neuroscience (M Phil, PhD); ophthalmology (M Phil, PhD); optometry (M Phil, PhD); organelle function (M Phil, PhD); pharmacology (M Phil, PhD); physiology (M Phil, PhD); plant sciences (M Phil, PhD); stem cell research (M Phil, PhD); structural biology (M Phil, PhD); systems neuroscience (M Phil, PhD); toxicology (M Phil, PhD).

University of Maryland, College Park, Academic Affairs, College of Computer, Mathematical and Natural Sciences, Department of Biology, Behavior, Ecology, Evolution, and Systematics Program, College Park, MD 20742. Offers MS, PhD. *Students:* 14 full-time (8 women); includes 2 minority (1 Asian, non-Hispanic/Latino; 1 Two or more races, non-Hispanic/Latino), 2 international. In 2011, 1 master's, 12 doctorates awarded. *Degree requirements:* For master's, thesis, oral defense, seminar; for doctorate, thesis/dissertation, exam, 4 seminars. *Entrance requirements:* For master's and doctorate, GRE General Test, GRE Subject Test (biology), 3 letters of recommendation. Additional exam requirements/recommendations for international students: Required—TOEFL. *Expenses:* Tuition, state resident: part-time $525 per credit hour. Tuition, nonresident: part-time $1131 per credit hour. *Required fees:* $386.31 per term. Tuition and fees vary according to program. *Financial support:* In 2011–12, 4 fellowships with full and partial tuition reimbursements (averaging $17,787 per year), 2 research assistantships (averaging $19,685 per year), 5 teaching assistantships (averaging $19,604 per year) were awarded; Federal Work-Study and scholarships/grants also available. Support available to part-time students. Financial award applicants required to submit FAFSA. *Faculty research:* Animal behavior, biostatistics, ecology, evolution, neurothology. *Unit head:* David Hawthorne, Graduate Director, 301-405-2401, Fax: 301-314-9290, E-mail: djh@umd.edu. *Application contact:* Dr. Charles A. Caramello, Dean of Graduate School, 301-405-0358, Fax: 301-314-9305.

University of Maryland, College Park, Academic Affairs, College of Computer, Mathematical and Natural Sciences, Department of Biology, PhD Program in Biological Sciences, College Park, MD 20742. Offers behavior, ecology, evolution, and systematics (PhD); computational biology, bioinformatics, and genomics (PhD); molecular and cellular biology (PhD); physiological systems (PhD). *Students:* 68 full-time (41 women), 4 part-time (2 women); includes 13 minority (3 Black or African American, non-Hispanic/Latino; 4 Asian, non-Hispanic/Latino; 5 Hispanic/Latino; 1 Two or more races, non-Hispanic/Latino), 21 international. 380 applicants, 15% accepted, 22 enrolled. *Degree requirements:* For doctorate, comprehensive exam, thesis/dissertation, present thesis work in seminar. *Entrance requirements:* For doctorate, GRE General Test; GRE Subject Test in biology (recommended), academic transcripts, statement of purpose/research interests, 3 letters of recommendation. Additional exam requirements/recommendations for international students: Required—TOEFL. *Application deadline:* For fall admission, 12/15 for domestic and international students. Applications are processed on a rolling basis. Application fee: $75. Electronic applications accepted. *Expenses:* Tuition, state resident: part-time $525 per credit hour. Tuition, nonresident: part-time $1131 per credit hour. *Required fees:* $386.31 per term. Tuition and fees vary according to program. *Financial support:* In 2011–12, 11 fellowships with full and partial tuition reimbursements (averaging $14,406 per year), 16 research assistantships (averaging $19,495 per year), 41 teaching assistantships (averaging $18,734 per year) were awarded. *Unit head:* Dr. Barbara Thorne, Director, 301-405-6905, E-mail: bthorne@umd.edu. *Application contact:* Dr. Charles A. Caramello, Dean of Graduate School, 301-405-0358, Fax: 301-314-9305. Web site: http://bisi.umd.edu/biologicalsciencesgraduateprogrambisi.

University of Massachusetts Amherst, Graduate School, Interdisciplinary Programs, Program in Organismic and Evolutionary Biology, Amherst, MA 01003. Offers MS, PhD. Part-time programs available. *Students:* 32 full-time (12 women), 2 part-time (both women); includes 3 minority (2 Hispanic/Latino; 1 Native Hawaiian or other Pacific Islander, non-Hispanic/Latino), 5 international. Average age 29. 48 applicants, 35% accepted, 9 enrolled. In 2011, 1 master's, 9 doctorates awarded. Terminal master's awarded for partial completion of doctoral program. *Degree requirements:* For master's, thesis or alternative; for doctorate, comprehensive exam, thesis/dissertation. *Entrance requirements:* For master's and doctorate, GRE General Test, 3 letters of recommendation. Additional exam requirements/recommendations for international students: Required—TOEFL (minimum score 550 paper-based; 213 computer-based; 80 iBT), IELTS (minimum score 6.5). *Application deadline:* For fall admission, 12/1 for domestic and international students. Applications are processed on a rolling basis. Application fee: $50 ($65 for international students). Electronic applications accepted. Tuition and fees vary according to course load, campus/location and program. *Financial support:* Fellowships with full and partial tuition reimbursements, research assistantships with full and partial tuition reimbursements, teaching assistantships with full and partial tuition reimbursements, career-related internships or fieldwork, Federal Work-Study, scholarships/grants, traineeships, health care benefits, tuition waivers (full and partial), and unspecified assistantships available. Support available to part-time students. Financial award application deadline: 12/1. *Unit head:* Dr. Elizabeth M. Jakob, Graduate Program Director, 413-545-0928, Fax: 413-545-3243. *Application contact:* Lindsay DeSantis, Interim Supervisor of Admissions, 413-545-0722, Fax: 413-577-0010, E-mail: gradadm@grad.umass.edu. Web site: http://www.bio.umass.edu/oeb/.

University of Massachusetts Amherst, Graduate School, Interdisciplinary Programs, Program in Plant Biology, Amherst, MA 01003. Offers biochemistry and metabolism (MS, PhD); cell biology and physiology (MS, PhD); environmental, ecological and integrative (PhD); environmental, ecological and integrative biology (MS); genetics and evolution (MS, PhD). *Students:* 16 full-time (7 women), 1 (woman) part-time, 7 international. Average age 27. 22 applicants, 50% accepted, 5 enrolled. In 2011, 3 degrees awarded. *Median time to degree:* Of those who began their doctoral program in fall 2003, 100% received their degree in 8 years or less. *Degree requirements:* For master's, thesis; for doctorate, 2 foreign languages, comprehensive exam, thesis/dissertation. *Entrance requirements:* For master's and doctorate, GRE General Test. Additional exam requirements/recommendations for international students: Required—TOEFL (minimum score 550 paper-based; 213 computer-based; 80 iBT), IELTS (minimum score 6.5). *Application deadline:* For fall admission, 12/15 for domestic and international students; for spring admission, 10/1 for domestic and international students. Applications are processed on a rolling basis. Application fee: $50 ($65 for international students). Electronic applications accepted. Tuition and fees vary according to course load, campus/location and program. *Financial support:* Fellowships with full and partial tuition reimbursements, research assistantships with full and partial tuition reimbursements, teaching assistantships with full and partial tuition reimbursements, career-related internships or fieldwork, Federal Work-Study, scholarships/grants, traineeships, health care benefits, tuition waivers (full and partial), and unspecified assistantships available. Support available to part-time students. Financial award application deadline: 12/15. *Unit head:* Dr. Elsbeth L. Walker, Graduate Program Director, 413-577-3217, Fax: 413-545-3243. *Application contact:* Lindsay DeSantis, Interim Supervisor of Admissions, 413-545—0722, Fax: 413-577-0010, E-mail: gradadm@grad.umass.edu. Web site: http://www.bio.umass.edu/plantbio/.

University of Miami, Graduate School, College of Arts and Sciences, Department of Biology, Coral Gables, FL 33124. Offers biology (MS, PhD); genetics and evolution (MS, PhD). Terminal master's awarded for partial completion of doctoral program. *Degree requirements:* For master's, comprehensive exam (for some programs), thesis (for some programs); for doctorate, thesis/dissertation, oral and written qualifying exam. *Entrance requirements:* For master's, GRE General Test, 3 letters of recommendation, research papers; for doctorate, GRE General Test, 3 letters of recommendation, research papers, sponsor letter. Additional exam requirements/recommendations for international students: Required—TOEFL (minimum score 550 paper-based; 213 computer-based; 59 iBT). Electronic applications accepted. *Faculty research:* Neuroscience to ethology; plants, vertebrates and mycorrhizae; phylogenies, life histories and species interactions; molecular biology, gene expression and populations; cells, auditory neurons and vertebrate locomotion.

University of Michigan, Horace H. Rackham School of Graduate Studies, College of Literature, Science, and the Arts, Department of Ecology and Evolutionary Biology, Ann Arbor, MI 48109. Offers ecology and evolutionary biology (MS, PhD); ecology and evolutionary biology-Frontiers (MS). Part-time programs available. *Faculty:* 56 full-time (19 women). *Students:* 75 full-time (42 women); includes 20 minority (6 Black or African American, non-Hispanic/Latino; 2 American Indian or Alaska Native, non-Hispanic/Latino; 4 Asian, non-Hispanic/Latino; 6 Hispanic/Latino; 2 Native Hawaiian or other Pacific Islander, non-Hispanic/Latino), 21 international. Average age 28. 122 applicants, 23% accepted, 9 enrolled. In 2011, 4 master's, 11 doctorates awarded. Terminal master's awarded for partial completion of doctoral program. *Degree requirements:* For master's, thesis (for some programs), two seminars; for doctorate, comprehensive exam, thesis/dissertation, 2 semesters of teaching. *Entrance requirements:* For master's and doctorate, GRE. Additional exam requirements/recommendations for international students: Required—TOEFL (minimum score 560 paper-based; 220 computer-based; 84 iBT). *Application deadline:* For fall admission, 12/1 priority date for domestic students, 12/1 for international students; for winter admission, 10/15 priority date for domestic students, 10/15 for international students. Applications are processed on a rolling basis. Application fee: $65 ($75 for international students). Electronic applications accepted. *Financial support:* In 2011–12, 61 students received support, including 18 fellowships with full tuition reimbursements available (averaging $23,702 per year), 10 research assistantships with full tuition reimbursements available (averaging $23,702 per year), 36 teaching assistantships with full tuition reimbursements available (averaging $23,702 per year); scholarships/grants, traineeships, health care benefits, and unspecified assistantships also available. Financial award applicants required to submit FAFSA. *Faculty research:* Population and community ecology, ecosystem ecology and biogeochemistry, global change biology, biogeography and paleobiology, evolution of behavior, evolutionary genetics, phylogenetic and phylogeography, ecology and evolution of infectious disease. *Total annual research expenditures:* $4 million. *Unit head:* Deborah Goldberg, Chair, 734-615-4912, Fax: 734-763-0544. *Application contact:* Jane Sullivan, Graduate Program Coordinator, 734-615-7338, Fax: 734-763-0544, E-mail: eeb.gradcoord@umich.edu. Web site: http://www.lsa.umich.edu/eeb/.

University of Minnesota, Twin Cities Campus, Graduate School, College of Biological Sciences, Department of Ecology, Evolution, and Behavior, St. Paul, MN 55418. Offers MS, PhD. Terminal master's awarded for partial completion of doctoral program. *Degree*

requirements: For master's, comprehensive exam, thesis or projects; for doctorate, comprehensive exam, thesis/dissertation. *Entrance requirements:* For master's and doctorate, GRE General Test, minimum GPA of 3.0. Additional exam requirements/recommendations for international students: Required—TOEFL (minimum score 550 paper-based; 79 iBT), Michigan English Language Assessment Battery. Electronic applications accepted. *Faculty research:* Behavioral ecology, community ecology, community genetics, ecosystem and global change, evolution and systematics.

University of Missouri, Graduate School, College of Arts and Sciences, Division of Biological Sciences, Program in Evolutionary Biology and Ecology, Columbia, MO 65211. Offers MA, PhD. *Faculty:* 13. *Expenses:* Tuition, state resident: full-time $5881. Tuition, nonresident: full-time $15,183. *Required fees:* $952. Tuition and fees vary according to campus/location and program. *Financial support:* In 2011–12, fellowships (averaging $21,000 per year), teaching assistantships (averaging $16,300 per year) were awarded; research assistantships, scholarships/grants, health care benefits, and tuition waivers (full) also available. *Total annual research expenditures:* $990,000. *Unit head:* Dr. Ray Semlitsch, Director of Graduate Studies, 573-884-6396, E-mail: semlitschr@missouri.edu. *Application contact:* Nila Emerich, Application Contact, 800-553-5698. Web site: http://biology.missouri.edu/research-strengths/evolution/.

University of Missouri–St. Louis, College of Arts and Sciences, Department of Biology, St. Louis, MO 63121. Offers biotechnology (Certificate); cell and molecular biology (MS, PhD); ecology, evolution and systematics (MS, PhD); tropical biology and conservation (Certificate). Part-time programs available. *Faculty:* 43 full-time (13 women), 4 part-time/adjunct (1 woman). *Students:* 68 full-time (33 women), 64 part-time (28 women); includes 20 minority (9 Black or African American, non Hispanic/Latino; 7 Asian, non-Hispanic/Latino; 3 Hispanic/Latino; 1 Two or more races, non-Hispanic/Latino), 43 international. Average age 28. 122 applicants, 48% accepted, 36 enrolled. In 2011, 20 master's, 3 doctorates, 11 other advanced degrees awarded. *Degree requirements:* For master's, thesis or alternative; for doctorate, thesis/dissertation, 1 semester of teaching experience. *Entrance requirements:* For master's, 3 letters of recommendation; for doctorate, GRE General Test, 3 letters of recommendation. Additional exam requirements/recommendations for international students: Required—TOEFL. *Application deadline:* For fall admission, 12/15 priority date for domestic students, 12/15 for international students; for spring admission, 12/1 priority date for domestic students, 12/1 for international students. Applications are processed on a rolling basis. Application fee: $35 ($40 for international students). Electronic applications accepted. *Expenses:* Tuition, state resident: full-time $6273; part-time $3866 per year. Tuition, nonresident: full-time $14,969; part-time $9980 per year. *Required fees:* $315 per year. *Financial support:* In 2011–12, 13 research assistantships with full and partial tuition reimbursements (averaging $15,300 per year), 27 teaching assistantships with full and partial tuition reimbursements (averaging $15,300 per year) were awarded; fellowships with full tuition reimbursements, career-related internships or fieldwork, and Federal Work-Study also available. Support available to part-time students. Financial award application deadline: 2/1. *Faculty research:* Molecular biology, microbial genetics, animal behavior, tropical ecology, plant systematics. *Unit head:* Dr. Wendy Olivas, Director of Graduate Studies, 314-516-6200, Fax: 314-516-6233, E-mail: olivasw@umsl.edu. *Application contact:* 314-516-5458, Fax: 314-516-6996, E-mail: gradadm@umsl.edu. Web site: http://www.umsl.edu/divisions/artscience/biology/.

University of Nevada, Reno, Graduate School, Interdisciplinary Program in Ecology, Evolution, and Conservation Biology, Reno, NV 89557. Offers PhD. Offered through the College of Arts and Science, the M. C. Fleischmann College of Agriculture, and the Desert Research Institute. *Degree requirements:* For doctorate, thesis/dissertation. *Entrance requirements:* For doctorate, GRE General Test, GRE Subject Test, minimum GPA of 3.0. Additional exam requirements/recommendations for international students: Required—TOEFL (minimum score 500 paper-based; 173 computer-based; 61 iBT), IELTS (minimum score 6). Electronic applications accepted. *Faculty research:* Population biology, behavioral ecology, plant response to climate change, conservation of endangered species, restoration of natural ecosystems.

The University of North Carolina at Chapel Hill, Graduate School, College of Arts and Sciences, Department of Biology, Chapel Hill, NC 27599. Offers botany (MA, MS, PhD); cell biology, development, and physiology (MA, MS, PhD); cell motility and cytoskeleton (PhD); ecology and behavior (MA, MS, PhD); genetics and molecular biology (MA, MS, PhD); morphology, systematics, and evolution (MA, MS, PhD). Terminal master's awarded for partial completion of doctoral program. *Degree requirements:* For master's, comprehensive exam, thesis (for some programs); for doctorate, comprehensive exam, thesis/dissertation. *Entrance requirements:* For master's, GRE General Test, GRE Subject Test, 2 semesters of calculus or statistics; 2 semesters of physics, organic chemistry; 3 semesters of biology; for doctorate, GRE General Test, GRE Subject Test, 2 semesters calculus or statistics, 2 semesters physics, organic chemistry, 3 semesters of biology. Additional exam requirements/recommendations for international students: Required—TOEFL (minimum score 550 paper-based; 213 computer-based). Electronic applications accepted. *Faculty research:* Gene expression, biomechanics, yeast genetics, plant ecology, plant molecular biology.

University of Notre Dame, Graduate School, College of Science, Department of Biological Sciences, Notre Dame, IN 46556. Offers aquatic ecology, evolution and environmental biology (MS, PhD); cellular and molecular biology (MS, PhD); genetics (MS, PhD); physiology (MS, PhD); vector biology and parasitology (MS, PhD). Terminal master's awarded for partial completion of doctoral program. *Degree requirements:* For master's, comprehensive exam, thesis; for doctorate, comprehensive exam, thesis/dissertation, candidacy exam. *Entrance requirements:* For master's and doctorate, GRE General Test. Additional exam requirements/recommendations for international students: Required—TOEFL (minimum score 600 paper-based; 250 computer-based; 80 iBT). Electronic applications accepted. *Faculty research:* Tropical disease, molecular genetics, neurobiology, evolutionary biology, aquatic biology.

University of Oklahoma, College of Arts and Sciences, Department of Microbiology and Plant Biology, Program in Ecology and Evolutionary Biology, Norman, OK 73019. Offers PhD. *Students:* 6 full-time (1 woman), 1 part-time (0 women), 6 international. Average age 29. 7 applicants, 71% accepted, 2 enrolled. *Entrance requirements:* Additional exam requirements/recommendations for international students: Required—TOEFL (minimum score 550 paper-based; 79 iBT). *Application deadline:* For fall admission, 4/1 for domestic students, 3/1 for international students; for spring admission, 9/1 for domestic and international students. Applications are processed on a rolling basis. Application fee: $40 ($90 for international students). Electronic applications accepted. *Expenses:* Tuition, state resident: full-time $4087; part-time $170.30 per credit hour. Tuition, nonresident: full-time $14,875; part-time $619.80 per credit hour. *Required fees:* $2659; $100.25 per credit hour. Tuition and fees vary according to course load and degree level. *Financial support:* In 2011–12, 7 students received support. Scholarships/grants, health care benefits, tuition waivers (partial), and unspecified assistantships available. *Faculty research:* Behavioral ecology, community ecology, evolutionary biology, macroecology, physiological ecology. *Unit head:* Dr. Michael Kaspari, 405-325-4821, Fax: 405-325-7619, E-mail: mkaspari@ou.edu. Web site: http://mpbio.ou.edu/.

University of Oklahoma, College of Arts and Sciences, Department of Zoology, Program in Ecology and Evolutionary Biology, Norman, OK 73019. Offers PhD. *Students:* 17 full-time (9 women), 7 part-time (2 women), 6 international. Average age 28. 10 applicants, 40% accepted, 4 enrolled. In 2011, 2 degrees awarded. *Entrance requirements:* Additional exam requirements/recommendations for international students: Required—TOEFL (minimum score 550 paper-based; 79 iBT). *Application deadline:* For fall admission, 12/15 for domestic and international students. Applications are processed on a rolling basis. Application fee: $40 ($90 for international students). Electronic applications accepted. *Expenses:* Tuition, state resident: full-time $4087; part-time $170.30 per credit hour. Tuition, nonresident: full-time $14,875; part-time $619.80 per credit hour. *Required fees:* $2659; $100.25 per credit hour. Tuition and fees vary according to course load and degree level. *Financial support:* In 2011–12, 23 students received support. Career-related internships or fieldwork, scholarships/grants, health care benefits, tuition waivers (partial), and unspecified assistantships available. Financial award applicants required to submit FAFSA. *Faculty research:* Behavioral ecology, community ecology, evolutionary biology, macroecology, physiological ecology. *Unit head:* Bill Mathhews, Chair, 405-325-4712, Fax: 405-325-6202, E-mail: wmatthews@ou.edu. *Application contact:* Dr. Michael Kaspari, 405-325-4821, E-mail: mkaspari@ou.edu. Web site: http://www.ou.edu/eeb.

University of Oregon, Graduate School, College of Arts and Sciences, Department of Biology, Eugene, OR 97403. Offers ecology and evolution (MA, MS, PhD); marine biology (MA, MS, PhD); molecular, cellular and genetic biology (PhD); neuroscience and development (PhD). Terminal master's awarded for partial completion of doctoral program. *Degree requirements:* For master's, thesis (for some programs); for doctorate, thesis/dissertation. *Entrance requirements:* For master's and doctorate, GRE General Test, minimum GPA of 3.2. Additional exam requirements/recommendations for international students: Required—TOEFL. *Faculty research:* Developmental neurobiology; evolution, population biology, and quantitative genetics; regulation of gene expression; biochemistry of marine organisms.

University of Pittsburgh, Dietrich School of Arts and Sciences, Department of Biological Sciences, Program in Ecology and Evolution, Pittsburgh, PA 15260. Offers PhD. *Faculty:* 9 full-time (2 women). *Students:* 16 full-time (5 women); includes 3 minority (1 American Indian or Alaska Native, non-Hispanic/Latino; 1 Asian, non-Hispanic/Latino; 1 Hispanic/Latino), 2 international. Average age 23. 36 applicants, 25% accepted, 3 enrolled. In 2011, 2 doctorates awarded. *Degree requirements:* For doctorate, comprehensive exam, thesis/dissertation, completion of research integrity module. *Entrance requirements:* For doctorate, GRE General Test, GRE Subject Test. Additional exam requirements/recommendations for international students: Required—TOEFL (minimum score 550 paper-based; 213 computer-based; 80 iBT). *Application deadline:* For fall admission, 1/15 priority date for domestic students, 12/15 for international students. Applications are processed on a rolling basis. Application fee: $0 ($50 for international students). Electronic applications accepted. *Expenses:* Tuition, state resident: full-time $18,774; part-time $760 per credit. Tuition, nonresident: full-time $30,736; part-time $1258 per credit. *Required fees:* $740; $200 per term. Tuition and fees vary according to program. *Financial support:* In 2011–12, 20 fellowships with full tuition reimbursements (averaging $28,790 per year), 9 research assistantships with full tuition reimbursements (averaging $26,010 per year), 16 teaching assistantships with full tuition reimbursements (averaging $24,601 per year) were awarded; Federal Work-Study, scholarships/grants, traineeships, health care benefits, and tuition waivers (full) also available. *Unit head:* Dr. Jeffrey G. Lawrence, Associate Professor, 412-624-4204, Fax: 412-624-4759, E-mail: jlawrenc@pitt.edu. *Application contact:* Cathleen M. Barr, Graduate Administrator, 412-624-4268, Fax: 412-624-4759, E-mail: cbarr@pitt.edu. Web site: http://www.biology.pitt.edu/.

University of Puerto Rico, Río Piedras, College of Natural Sciences, Department of Biology, San Juan, PR 00931-3300. Offers ecology/systematics (MS, PhD); evolution/genetics (MS, PhD); molecular/cellular biology (MS, PhD); neuroscience (MS, PhD). Part-time programs available. *Degree requirements:* For master's, one foreign language, comprehensive exam, thesis; for doctorate, one foreign language, comprehensive exam, thesis/dissertation. *Entrance requirements:* For master's, GRE Subject Test, interview, minimum GPA of 3.0, letter of recommendation; for doctorate, GRE Subject Test, interview, master's degree, minimum GPA of 3.0, letter of recommendation. *Faculty research:* Environmental, poblational and systematic biology.

University of South Carolina, The Graduate School, College of Arts and Sciences, Department of Biological Sciences, Graduate Training Program in Ecology, Evolution, and Organismal Biology, Columbia, SC 29208. Offers MS, PhD. *Degree requirements:* For master's, one foreign language, comprehensive exam, thesis; for doctorate, one foreign language, comprehensive exam, thesis/dissertation. *Entrance requirements:* For master's and doctorate, GRE General Test, minimum GPA of 3.0 in science. Additional exam requirements/recommendations for international students: Required—TOEFL (minimum score 570 paper-based; 230 computer-based). Electronic applications accepted.

University of Southern California, Graduate School, Dana and David Dornsife College of Letters, Arts and Sciences, Department of Biological Sciences, Program in Integrative and Evolutionary Biology, Los Angeles, CA 90089. Offers PhD. M.S. in Biology is a terminal degree only. Terminal master's awarded for partial completion of doctoral program. *Degree requirements:* For doctorate, comprehensive exam, thesis/dissertation, qualifying examination, dissertation defense. *Entrance requirements:* For doctorate, GRE, 3 letters of recommendation, personal statement, resume, minimum GPA of 3.0. Additional exam requirements/recommendations for international students: Required—TOEFL (minimum score 600 paper-based; 250 computer-based; 100 iBT). Electronic applications accepted. *Faculty research:* Organisms and their interaction with the environment, evolution and life history, integration of the control and dynamics of physiological processes, biomechanics and rehabilitation engineering, primate behavior and ecology.

The University of Tennessee, Graduate School, College of Arts and Sciences, Department of Ecology and Evolutionary Biology, Knoxville, TN 37996. Offers behavior (MS, PhD); ecology (MS, PhD); evolutionary biology (MS, PhD). Part-time programs available. *Degree requirements:* For master's, thesis; for doctorate, thesis/dissertation. *Entrance requirements:* For master's and doctorate, GRE General Test, minimum GPA of 2.7. Additional exam requirements/recommendations for international students: Required—TOEFL. Electronic applications accepted. *Expenses:* Tuition, state resident: full-time $8332; part-time $464 per credit hour. Tuition, nonresident: full-time $25,174; part-time $1400 per credit hour. *Required fees:* $1162; $56 per credit hour. Tuition and fees vary according to program.

The University of Texas at Austin, Graduate School, College of Natural Sciences, School of Biological Sciences, Program in Ecology, Evolution and Behavior, Austin, TX 78712-1111. Offers PhD. *Entrance requirements:* For doctorate, GRE General Test. Additional exam requirements/recommendations for international students: Required—TOEFL. *Application deadline:* For fall admission, 1/5 for domestic and international students. Applications are processed on a rolling basis. Application fee: $50 ($75 for international students). Electronic applications accepted. *Financial support:* Fellowships, research assistantships, and teaching assistantships available. *Unit head:* Dr. Ulrich Mueller, Graduate Program Chair, 512-471-7619, E-mail: umueller@mail.utexas.edu. *Application contact:* Tamra Rogers, Graduate Coordinator, 512-471-

Evolutionary Biology

8490, Fax: 512-232-3699, E-mail: tamra@austin.utexas.edu. Web site: http://www.biosci.utexas.edu/graduate/eeb/.

University of Toronto, School of Graduate Studies, Faculty of Arts and Science, Department of Ecology and Evolutionary Biology, Toronto, ON M5S 1A1, Canada. Offers M Sc, PhD. *Degree requirements:* For master's, thesis, thesis defense; for doctorate, thesis/dissertation, thesis defense. *Entrance requirements:* For master's, minimum B average in last 2 years; knowledge of physics, chemistry, and biology. Additional exam requirements/recommendations for international students: Required—TOEFL (minimum score 580 paper-based; 93 iBT), TWE (minimum score 5). Electronic applications accepted.

Washington University in St. Louis, Graduate School of Arts and Sciences, Division of Biology and Biomedical Sciences, Program in Evolution, Ecology and Population Biology, St. Louis, MO 63130-4899. Offers ecology (PhD); environmental biology (PhD); evolutionary biology (PhD); genetics (PhD). *Degree requirements:* For doctorate, thesis/dissertation. *Entrance requirements:* For doctorate, GRE General Test, GRE Subject Test. Electronic applications accepted.

Wesleyan University, Graduate Programs, Department of Biology, Middletown, CT 06459. Offers animal behavior (PhD); bioformatics/genomics (PhD); cell biology (PhD); developmental biology (PhD); evolution/ecology (PhD); genetics (PhD); neurobiology (PhD); population biology (PhD). *Degree requirements:* For doctorate, variable foreign language requirement, thesis/dissertation. *Entrance requirements:* For doctorate, GRE. Additional exam requirements/recommendations for international students: Required—TOEFL. *Faculty research:* Microbial population genetics, genetic basis of evolutionary adaptation, genetic regulation of differentiation and pattern formation in &ITdrosophila&RO.

West Virginia University, Eberly College of Arts and Sciences, Department of Biology, Morgantown, WV 26506. Offers cell and molecular biology (MS, PhD); environmental and evolutionary biology (MS, PhD); forensic biology (MS, PhD); genomic biology (MS, PhD); neurobiology (MS, PhD). Terminal master's awarded for partial completion of doctoral program. *Degree requirements:* For master's, thesis, final exam; for doctorate, thesis/dissertation, preliminary and final exams. *Entrance requirements:* For master's, GRE General Test, GRE Subject Test, minimum GPA of 3.0; for doctorate, GRE General Test, minimum GPA of 3.0. Additional exam requirements/recommendations for international students: Required—TOEFL. *Faculty research:* Environmental biology, genetic engineering, developmental biology, global change, biodiversity.

Yale University, Graduate School of Arts and Sciences, Department of Ecology and Evolutionary Biology, New Haven, CT 06520. Offers PhD. *Entrance requirements:* For doctorate, GRE General Test, GRE Subject Test (biology).

Section 9
Entomology

This section contains a directory of institutions offering graduate work in entomology. Additional information about programs listed in the directory may be obtained by writing directly to the dean of a graduate school or chair of a department at the address given in the directory.

For programs offering related work, see also in this book *Biochemistry; Biological and Biomedical Sciences; Botany and Plant Biology; Ecology, Environmental Biology, and Evolutionary Biology; Genetics, Developmental Biology, and Reproductive Biology; Microbiological Sciences; Physiology;* and *Zoology.* In the other guides in this series:

Graduate Programs in the Humanities, Arts & Social Sciences
See *Economics (Agricultural Economics and Agribusiness)*

Graduate Programs in the Physical Sciences, Mathematics, Agricultural Sciences, the Environment & Natural Resources
See *Agricultural and Food Sciences* and *Environmental Sciences and Management*

Graduate Programs in Engineering & Applied Sciences
See *Agricultural Engineering* and *Bioengineering*

CONTENTS

Program Directory

Entomology

Auburn University, Graduate School, College of Agriculture, Department of Entomology and Plant Pathology, Auburn University, AL 36849. Offers entomology (M Ag, MS, PhD); plant pathology (M Ag, MS, PhD). Part-time programs available. *Faculty:* 17 full-time (6 women). *Students:* 25 full-time (9 women), 13 part-time (6 women); includes 1 minority (Black or African American, non-Hispanic/Latino), 18 international. Average age 28. 19 applicants, 63% accepted, 11 enrolled. In 2011, 2 master's, 5 doctorates awarded. *Degree requirements:* For master's, thesis (for some programs); for doctorate, one foreign language, thesis/dissertation. *Entrance requirements:* For master's, GRE General Test; for doctorate, GRE General Test, GRE Subject Test, master's degree with thesis. *Application deadline:* For fall admission, 7/7 for domestic students; for spring admission, 11/24 for domestic students. Applications are processed on a rolling basis. Application fee: $50 ($60 for international students). Electronic applications accepted. *Expenses:* Tuition, state resident: full-time $7290; part-time $405 per credit hour. Tuition, nonresident: full-time $21,870; part-time $1215 per credit hour. *International tuition:* $22,000 full-time. *Required fees:* $1402. *Financial support:* Research assistantships, teaching assistantships, and Federal Work-Study available. Support available to part-time students. Financial award application deadline: 3/15; financial award applicants required to submit FAFSA. *Faculty research:* Pest management, biological control, systematics, medical entomology. *Unit head:* Dr. Arthur Appel, Chair, 334-844-5006. *Application contact:* Dr. George Flowers, Dean of the Graduate School, 334-844-2125.

Clemson University, Graduate School, College of Agriculture, Forestry and Life Sciences, Department of Forestry and Natural Resources, Program in Entomology, Clemson, SC 29634. Offers MS, PhD. Part-time programs available. *Students:* 17 full-time (9 women); includes 2 minority (1 Black or African American, non-Hispanic/Latino; 1 Asian, non-Hispanic/Latino), 4 international. Average age 31. 6 applicants, 17% accepted, 1 enrolled. In 2011, 4 master's, 1 doctorate awarded. *Degree requirements:* For master's, thesis, peer-reviewed manuscript submission; conference presentation; for doctorate, thesis/dissertation, peer-reviewed manuscript submission; conference presentation; one semester of teaching. *Entrance requirements:* For master's, GRE General Test, bachelor's degree in biological science or chemistry (recommended); for doctorate, GRE General Test, master's degree in science and/or independent research experience (recommended). Additional exam requirements/recommendations for international students: Required—TOEFL. *Application deadline:* Applications are processed on a rolling basis. Application fee: $70 ($80 for international students). Electronic applications accepted. *Expenses:* Contact institution. *Financial support:* In 2011–12, 17 students received support, including 5 fellowships with full and partial tuition reimbursements available (averaging $5,640 per year), 11 research assistantships with partial tuition reimbursements available (averaging $15,200 per year), 6 teaching assistantships with partial tuition reimbursements available (averaging $17,333 per year); career-related internships or fieldwork, institutionally sponsored loans, scholarships/grants, health care benefits, and unspecified assistantships also available. Support available to part-time students. Financial award application deadline: 3/1. *Faculty research:* Biodiversity, urban entomology, applied ecology, agricultural entomology. *Unit head:* Dr. Patricia Layton, School Director, 864-656-4829, Fax: 864-656-5065, E-mail: playton@clemson.edu. *Application contact:* Dr. Matthew Turnbull, Entomology Graduate Coordinator, 864-656-5038, Fax: 864-656-5065, E-mail: turnbul@clemson.edu. Web site: http://www.clemson.edu/cafls/departments/entomology_grad/.

Colorado State University, Graduate School, College of Agricultural Sciences, Department of Bioagricultural Sciences and Pest Management, Fort Collins, CO 80523-1177. Offers entomology (MS, PhD); plant pathology and weed science (MS, PhD). Part-time programs available. *Faculty:* 20 full-time (5 women). *Students:* 8 full-time (5 women), 26 part-time (10 women); includes 2 minority (1 American Indian or Alaska Native, non-Hispanic/Latino; 1 Hispanic/Latino), 4 international. Average age 33. 7 applicants, 43% accepted, 1 enrolled. In 2011, 2 master's, 1 doctorate awarded. *Degree requirements:* For master's, comprehensive exam, thesis; for doctorate, comprehensive exam, thesis/dissertation. *Entrance requirements:* For master's, GRE General Test, minimum GPA of 3.0, letters of recommendation; for doctorate, GRE General Test, minimum GPA of 3.0, letters of recommendation, essay. Additional exam requirements/recommendations for international students: Required—TOEFL (minimum score 550 paper-based; 213 computer-based; 80 iBT). *Application deadline:* For fall admission, 1/15 priority date for domestic students, 1/1 for international students; for spring admission, 9/1 priority date for domestic students, 9/1 for international students. Applications are processed on a rolling basis. Application fee: $50. Electronic applications accepted. *Expenses:* Tuition, state resident: full-time $7992. Tuition, nonresident: full-time $19,592. *Required fees:* $1735; $58 per credit. *Financial support:* In 2011–12, 10 fellowships with partial tuition reimbursements (averaging $29,548 per year), 18 research assistantships with full tuition reimbursements (averaging $15,794 per year), 12 teaching assistantships with full tuition reimbursements (averaging $10,933 per year) were awarded; unspecified assistantships also available. Financial award application deadline: 1/15; financial award applicants required to submit FAFSA. *Faculty research:* Entomology specialization, plant pathology specialization, weed science specialization, ecology and biodiversity, integrated pest management. *Total annual research expenditures:* $3 million. *Unit head:* Dr. Thomas O. Holtzer, Head, 970-491-5261, Fax: 970-491-3862, E-mail: tholtzer@lamar.colostate.edu. *Application contact:* Janet Dill, Education Coordinator, 970-491-0402, Fax: 970-491-3862, E-mail: janet.dill@colostate.edu. Web site: http://www.colostate.edu/Depts/bspm/.

Cornell University, Graduate School, Graduate Fields of Agriculture and Life Sciences, Field of Entomology, Ithaca, NY 14853-0001. Offers acarology (MS, PhD); apiculture (MS, PhD); applied entomology (MS, PhD); aquatic entomology (MS, PhD); biological control (MS, PhD); insect behavior (MS, PhD); insect biochemistry (MS, PhD); insect ecology (MS, PhD); insect genetics (MS, PhD); insect morphology (MS, PhD); insect pathology (MS, PhD); insect physiology (MS, PhD); insect systematics (MS, PhD); insect toxicology and insecticide chemistry (MS, PhD); integrated pest management (MS, PhD); medical and veterinary entomology (MS, PhD). *Faculty:* 38 full-time (7 women). *Students:* 30 full-time (14 women); includes 5 minority (1 Black or African American, non-Hispanic/Latino; 1 Asian, non-Hispanic/Latino; 2 Hispanic/Latino; 1 Two or more races, non-Hispanic/Latino), 10 international. Average age 29. 26 applicants, 19% accepted, 5 enrolled. In 2011, 5 degrees awarded. *Degree requirements:* For master's, thesis; for doctorate, comprehensive exam, thesis/dissertation. *Entrance requirements:* For master's and doctorate, GRE General Test, GRE Subject Test (biology), 3 letters of recommendation. Additional exam requirements/recommendations for international students: Required—TOEFL (minimum score 550 paper-based; 213 computer-based; 77 iBT). *Application deadline:* For fall admission, 12/1 for domestic students. Application fee: $95. Electronic applications accepted. *Financial support:* In 2011–12, 3 fellowships with full tuition reimbursements, 13 research assistantships with full tuition reimbursements, 11 teaching assistantships with full tuition reimbursements were awarded; institutionally sponsored loans, scholarships/grants, health care benefits, tuition waivers (full and partial), and unspecified assistantships also available. Financial award applicants required to submit FAFSA. *Faculty research:* Systematics and biodiversity, integrated pest management, pathology and biological control, toxicology and physiology, ecology and behavior. *Unit head:* Director of Graduate Studies, 607-255-6198, Fax: 607-255-0939. *Application contact:* Graduate Field Assistant, 607-255-6198, Fax: 607-255-0939, E-mail: fieldofent2@cornell.edu. Web site: http://www.gradschool.cornell.edu/fields.php?id-47&a-2.

Illinois State University, Graduate School, College of Arts and Sciences, Department of Biological Sciences, Normal, IL 61790-2200. Offers animal behavior (MS); bacteriology (MS); biochemistry (MS); biological sciences (MS); biology (PhD); biophysics (MS); biotechnology (MS); botany (MS, PhD); cell biology (MS); conservation biology (MS); developmental biology (MS); ecology (MS, PhD); entomology (MS); evolutionary biology (MS); genetics (MS, PhD); immunology (MS); microbiology (MS, PhD); molecular biology (MS); molecular genetics (MS); neurobiology (MS); neuroscience (MS); parasitology (MS); physiology (MS, PhD); plant biology (MS); plant molecular biology (MS); plant sciences (MS); structural biology (MS); zoology (MS, PhD). Part-time programs available. *Degree requirements:* For master's, thesis or alternative; for doctorate, variable foreign language requirement, thesis/dissertation, 2 terms of residency. *Entrance requirements:* For master's, GRE General Test, minimum GPA of 2.6 in last 60 hours of course work; for doctorate, GRE General Test. *Faculty research:* Redoc balance and drug development in schistosoma mansoni, control of the growth of listeria monocytogenes at low temperature, regulation of cell expansion and microtubule function by SPRI, CRUI: physiology and fitness consequences of different life history phenotypes.

Iowa State University of Science and Technology, Department of Entomology, Ames, IA 50011-3140. Offers MS, PhD. *Degree requirements:* For master's, thesis; for doctorate, thesis/dissertation. *Entrance requirements:* For master's and doctorate, GRE General Test, GRE Subject Test (biology). Additional exam requirements/recommendations for international students: Required—TOEFL (minimum score 550 paper-based; 79 iBT), IELTS (minimum score 6.5). *Application deadline:* Applications are processed on a rolling basis. Application fee: $40 ($90 for international students). Electronic applications accepted. *Unit head:* Dr. Joel Coats, Director of Graduate Education, 515-294-7400, Fax: 515-294-7406, E-mail: entomology@iastate.edu. *Application contact:* Kelly Kyle, Application Contact, 515-294-7400, Fax: 515-294-7406, E-mail: entomology@iastate.edu. Web site: http://www.ent.iastate.edu/.

Kansas State University, Graduate School, College of Agriculture, Department of Entomology, Manhattan, KS 66506. Offers MS, PhD. *Faculty:* 17 full-time (0 women), 10 part-time/adjunct (1 woman). *Students:* 20 full-time (10 women), 5 part-time (4 women); includes 3 minority (2 American Indian or Alaska Native, non-Hispanic/Latino; 1 Hispanic/Latino), 14 international. Average age 31. 16 applicants, 19% accepted, 2 enrolled. In 2011, 5 master's, 3 doctorates awarded. *Degree requirements:* For master's, thesis, oral exam; for doctorate, thesis/dissertation, written and oral exams. *Application deadline:* For fall admission, 2/1 priority date for domestic students, 2/1 for international students; for spring admission, 8/1 priority date for domestic students, 8/1 for international students. Applications are processed on a rolling basis. Application fee: $40 ($55 for international students). Electronic applications accepted. *Financial support:* In 2011–12, 18 research assistantships (averaging $21,043 per year), 3 teaching assistantships with partial tuition reimbursements (averaging $21,520 per year) were awarded; career-related internships or fieldwork, Federal Work-Study, institutionally sponsored loans, scholarships/grants, and tuition waivers (partial) also available. Support available to part-time students. Financial award application deadline: 3/1; financial award applicants required to submit FAFSA. *Faculty research:* Molecular genetics, biologically-based pest management, host plant resistance, ecological genomics, stored product entomology. *Total annual research expenditures:* $2.2 million. *Unit head:* David C. Margolies, Interim Head, 785-532-6154, Fax: 785-532-6232, E-mail: dmargoli@ksu.edu. *Application contact:* Evelyn Kennedy, Application Contact, 785-532-4702, Fax: 785-532-6232, E-mail: ekennedy@ksu.edu. Web site: http://www.entomology.k-state.edu/DesktopDefault.aspx.

Louisiana State University and Agricultural and Mechanical College, Graduate School, College of Agriculture, Department of Entomology, Baton Rouge, LA 70803. Offers MS, PhD. *Faculty:* 17 full-time (4 women). *Students:* 17 full-time (3 women), 12 part-time (5 women); includes 1 minority (Hispanic/Latino), 12 international. Average age 32. 14 applicants, 29% accepted, 3 enrolled. In 2011, 3 master's, 10 doctorates awarded. *Degree requirements:* For master's, thesis; for doctorate, thesis/dissertation. *Entrance requirements:* For master's and doctorate, GRE General Test, minimum GPA of 3.0. Additional exam requirements/recommendations for international students: Required—TOEFL (minimum score 550 paper-based; 213 computer-based; 79 iBT) or IELTS (minimum score 6.5). *Application deadline:* For fall admission, 1/25 priority date for domestic students, 5/15 for international students; for spring admission, 10/15 for international students. Applications are processed on a rolling basis. Application fee: $50 ($70 for international students). Electronic applications accepted. *Financial support:* In 2011–12, 25 students received support, including 17 research assistantships with partial tuition reimbursements available (averaging $17,406 per year); fellowships, teaching assistantships with partial tuition reimbursements available, Federal Work-Study, institutionally sponsored loans, scholarships/grants, health care benefits, and unspecified assistantships also available. Support available to part-time students. Financial award applicants required to submit FAFSA. *Faculty research:* Conservation biology, insect systematics, insect ecology, urban entomology, agricultural pest management, insect genomics. *Total annual research expenditures:* $10,281. *Unit head:* Dr. Timothy Schowalter, Head, 225-578-1634, Fax: 225-578-2257, E-mail: tschowalter@agcenter.lsu.edu. *Application contact:* James Ottea, Graduate Coordinator, 225-578-1841, E-mail: jottea@lsu.edu. Web site: http://www.entomology.lsu.edu/.

McGill University, Faculty of Graduate and Postdoctoral Studies, Faculty of Agricultural and Environmental Sciences, Department of Natural Resource Sciences, Montréal, QC H3A 2T5, Canada. Offers entomology (M Sc, PhD); environmental assessment (M Sc); forest science (M Sc, PhD); microbiology (M Sc, PhD); micrometeorology (M Sc, PhD); neotropical environment (M Sc, PhD); soil science (M Sc, PhD); wildlife biology (M Sc, PhD).

Michigan State University, The Graduate School, College of Agriculture and Natural Resources and College of Natural Science, Department of Entomology, East Lansing, MI 48824. Offers entomology (MS, PhD); integrated pest management (MS). *Entrance requirements:* Additional exam requirements/recommendations for international students: Required—TOEFL (minimum score 550 paper-based; 213 computer-based), Michigan State University ELT (minimum score 85), Michigan English Language Assessment Battery (minimum score 83). Electronic applications accepted.

Mississippi State University, College of Agriculture and Life Sciences, Department of Biochemistry, Molecular Biology, Entomology and Plant Pathology, Mississippi State, MS 39762. Offers agriculture life sciences (MS), including entomology and plant pathology; molecular biology (PhD). *Faculty:* 25 full-time (1 woman). *Students:* 46 full-time (17 women), 14 part-time (6 women); includes 4 minority (2 Black or African American, non-Hispanic/Latino; 2 Two or more races, non-Hispanic/Latino), 18 international. Average age 30. 43 applicants, 33% accepted, 13 enrolled. In 2011, 7 master's, 5 doctorates awarded. Terminal master's awarded for partial completion of doctoral program. *Degree requirements:* For master's, thesis (for some programs), comprehensive oral or written exam; for doctorate, thesis/dissertation, comprehensive oral and written exam. *Entrance requirements:* For master's, GRE General Test, minimum GPA of 2.75; for doctorate, GRE. Additional exam requirements/recommendations for international students: Required—TOEFL (minimum score 550 paper-based; 213 computer-based; 79 iBT); Recommended—IELTS (minimum score 6.5). *Application deadline:* For fall admission, 7/1 for domestic students, 5/1 for international students; for spring admission, 11/1 for domestic students, 9/1 for international students. Applications are processed on a rolling basis. Application fee: $40. Electronic applications accepted. *Expenses:* Tuition, state resident: full-time $5805; part-time $322.50 per credit hour. Tuition, nonresident: full-time $14,670; part-time $815 per credit hour. *Financial support:* In 2011–12, 41 research assistantships with full tuition reimbursements (averaging $15,714 per year) were awarded; Federal Work-Study, institutionally sponsored loans, and unspecified assistantships also available. Financial award application deadline: 4/1; financial award applicants required to submit FAFSA. *Faculty research:* Fish nutrition, plant and animal molecular biology, plant biochemistry, enzymology, lipid metabolism, chromatin, cell wall synthesis in rice, a model grass bioenergy species and the source of rice stover residues, using reverse genetic and functional genomic and proteomic approaches. *Unit head:* Dr. Scott T. Willard, Professor and Department Head, 662-325-2640, Fax: 662-325-8664, E-mail: swilliard@ads.msstate.edu. *Application contact:* Dr. Din-Pow Ma, Professor/Graduate Coordinator, 662-325-7739, Fax: 662-325-8664, E-mail: dm1@ra.msstate.edu.

New Mexico State University, Graduate School, College of Agricultural, Consumer and Environmental Sciences, Department of Entomology, Plant Pathology and Weed Science, Las Cruces, NM 88003-8001. Offers agricultural biology (MS). Part-time programs available. *Faculty:* 6 full-time (2 women), 2 part-time/adjunct (0 women). *Students:* 11 full-time (3 women), 5 part-time (2 women); includes 5 minority (4 Hispanic/Latino; 1 Two or more races, non-Hispanic/Latino), 3 international. Average age 26. 6 applicants, 67% accepted, 4 enrolled. In 2011, 5 master's awarded. *Degree requirements:* For master's, comprehensive exam, thesis. *Entrance requirements:* For master's, GRE General Test. Additional exam requirements/recommendations for international students: Required—TOEFL (minimum score 550 paper-based; 0 computer-based; 79 iBT), IELTS (minimum score 6.5). *Application deadline:* For fall admission, 7/1 priority date for domestic students; for spring admission, 11/1 priority date for domestic students. Applications are processed on a rolling basis. Application fee: $40 ($50 for international students). Electronic applications accepted. *Expenses:* Tuition, state resident: full-time $5004; part-time $208.50 per credit. Tuition, nonresident: full-time $17,446; part-time $726.90 per credit. *Financial support:* In 2011–12, 9 students received support, including 2 fellowships (averaging $4,304 per year), 9 research assistantships with full tuition reimbursements available (averaging $20,235 per year); teaching assistantships with partial tuition reimbursements available, career-related internships or fieldwork, and health care benefits also available. Financial award application deadline: 3/1. *Faculty research:* Integrated pest management, pesticide application and safety, livestock ectoparasite research, biotechnology, nematology. *Unit head:* Dr. Jill Schroeder, Interim Head, 575-646-3225, Fax: 575-646-8087, E-mail: jischroe@nmsu.edu. *Application contact:* Cindy Bullard, Intermediate Administrative Assistant, 575-646-1145, Fax: 575-646-8087, E-mail: cbullard@nmsu.edu. Web site: http://eppws.nmsu.edu/.

North Carolina State University, Graduate School, College of Agriculture and Life Sciences, Department of Entomology, Raleigh, NC 27695. Offers MS, PhD. Terminal master's awarded for partial completion of doctoral program. *Degree requirements:* For master's, thesis (for some programs); for doctorate, thesis/dissertation. *Entrance requirements:* For master's and doctorate, GRE General Test. Electronic applications accepted. *Faculty research:* Physiology, biocontrol, ecology, forest entomology, apiculture.

North Dakota State University, College of Graduate and Interdisciplinary Studies, College of Agriculture, Food Systems, and Natural Resources, Department of Entomology, Fargo, ND 58108. Offers entomology (MS, PhD); environment and conservation science (MS, PhD); natural resource management (MS, PhD). Part-time programs available. *Students:* 7 full-time (4 women), 3 part-time (1 woman), 3 international. Average age 34. 6 applicants, 0% accepted, 0 enrolled. In 2011, 1 master's awarded. *Degree requirements:* For master's, thesis; for doctorate, comprehensive exam, thesis/dissertation. *Entrance requirements:* For master's and doctorate, minimum GPA of 3.0. Additional exam requirements/recommendations for international students: Required—TOEFL (minimum score 550 paper-based; 213 computer-based; 79 iBT). *Application deadline:* For fall admission, 5/1 for international students; for winter admission, 8/1 for international students. Application fee: $35. Electronic applications accepted. *Financial support:* In 2011–12, 11 research assistantships with full tuition reimbursements (averaging $13,800 per year) were awarded; Federal Work-Study, institutionally sponsored loans, and unspecified assistantships also available. Financial award application deadline: 4/15. *Faculty research:* Insect systematics, conservation biology, integrated pest management, insect behavior, insect biology. *Unit head:* Dr. Frank Casey, Chair, 701-231-7582, Fax: 701-231-8557, E-mail: francis.casey@ndsu.edu. *Application contact:* Dr. Jason Harmon, Program Leader, 701-231-7033, Fax: 701-231-8557, E-mail: jason.harmon@ndsu.edu. Web site: http://www.ndsu.nodak.edu/entomology/.

The Ohio State University, Graduate School, College of Food, Agricultural, and Environmental Sciences, Department of Entomology, Columbus, OH 43210. Offers MS, PhD. *Faculty:* 19. *Students:* 19 full-time (7 women), 9 part-time (4 women), 9 international. Average age 28. In 2011, 4 degrees awarded. *Degree requirements:* For master's, variable foreign language requirement, thesis optional; for doctorate, variable foreign language requirement, thesis/dissertation. *Entrance requirements:* For master's and doctorate, GRE General Test. Additional exam requirements/recommendations for international students: Required—TOEFL (minimum score 600 paper-based; 250 computer-based; 79 iBT), Michigan English Language Assessment Battery (minimum score 82). *Application deadline:* For fall admission, 8/15 priority date for domestic students, 7/1 for international students; for winter admission, 12/1 priority date for domestic students, 11/1 for international students; for spring admission, 3/1 priority date for domestic students, 2/1 for international students. Applications are processed on a rolling basis. Application fee: $40 ($50 for international students). Electronic applications accepted. *Expenses:* Tuition, state resident: full-time $11,400. Tuition, nonresident: full-time $28,125. Tuition and fees vary according to course load, degree level, campus/location and program. *Financial support:* Fellowships, research assistantships, teaching assistantships, Federal Work-Study, and institutionally sponsored loans available. Support available to part-time students. *Faculty research:* Acarology, insect systematics, soil ecology, integrated pest management, chemical ecology. *Unit head:*

Dr. Dan Herms, Chair, 330-202-3506, Fax: 330-263-3686, E-mail: herms.2@osu.edu. *Application contact:* Department of Entomology, 614-292-8209, Fax: 614-292-7162, E-mail: gradadmissions@osu.edu. Web site: http://entomology.osu.edu/.

Oklahoma State University, College of Agricultural Science and Natural Resources, Department of Entomology and Plant Pathology, Stillwater, OK 74078. Offers entomology (PhD); entomology and plant pathology (MS); plant pathology (PhD). *Faculty:* 33 full-time (13 women). *Students:* 4 full-time (1 woman), 24 part-time (11 women); includes 2 minority (1 American Indian or Alaska Native, non-Hispanic/Latino; 1 Asian, non-Hispanic/Latino), 13 international. Average age 29. 21 applicants, 24% accepted, 3 enrolled. In 2011, 4 master's, 2 doctorates awarded. *Degree requirements:* For master's, thesis or alternative; for doctorate, comprehensive exam, thesis/dissertation. *Entrance requirements:* For master's and doctorate, GRE or GMAT. Additional exam requirements/recommendations for international students: Required—TOEFL (minimum score 550 paper-based; 79 iBT). *Application deadline:* For fall admission, 3/1 for international students; for spring admission, 8/1 for international students. Applications are processed on a rolling basis. Application fee: $40 ($75 for international students). Electronic applications accepted. *Expenses:* Tuition, state resident: full-time $4044; part-time $168.50 per credit hour. Tuition, nonresident: full-time $16,008; part-time $667 per credit hour. *Required fees:* $2122; $88.45 per credit hour. One-time fee: $50. Tuition and fees vary according to course load and campus/location. *Financial support:* In 2011–12, 27 research assistantships (averaging $17,665 per year), 1 teaching assistantship (averaging $16,584 per year) were awarded; career-related internships or fieldwork, Federal Work-Study, scholarships/grants, health care benefits, tuition waivers (partial), and unspecified assistantships also available. Support available to part-time students. Financial award application deadline: 3/1; financial award applicants required to submit FAFSA. *Unit head:* Dr. Phil Mulder, Jr., Head, 405-744-5527, Fax: 405-744-6039. *Application contact:* Dr. Brad Kard, Graduate Coordinator, 405-744-2142, Fax: 405-744-6039, E-mail: brad.kard@okstate.edu. Web site: http://www.ento.okstate.edu/.

Penn State University Park, Graduate School, College of Agricultural Sciences, Department of Entomology, State College, University Park, PA 16802-1503. Offers MS, PhD. *Unit head:* Dr. Bruce A. McPheron, Dean, 814-865-2541, Fax: 814-865-3103, E-mail: bam10@psu.edu. *Application contact:* Cynthia E. Nicosia, Director of Graduate Enrollment Services, 814-865-1834, E-mail: cey1@psu.edu. Web site: http://ento.psu.edu/.

Purdue University, Graduate School, College of Agriculture, Department of Entomology, West Lafayette, IN 47907. Offers MS, PhD. Part-time programs available. *Faculty:* 18 full-time (2 women), 7 part-time/adjunct (3 women). *Students:* 28 full-time (12 women), 6 part-time (all women); includes 1 minority (Hispanic/Latino), 12 international. Average age 29. 32 applicants, 22% accepted, 6 enrolled. In 2011, 7 master's, 5 doctorates awarded. *Degree requirements:* For master's, thesis (for some programs), seminar; for doctorate, thesis/dissertation, seminar. *Entrance requirements:* For master's, GRE general test, minimum undergraduate GPA of 3.0 or equivalent; for doctorate, GRE, minimum undergraduate GPA of 3.0 or equivalent; master's degree (highly recommended). Additional exam requirements/recommendations for international students: Required—TOEFL (minimum score 550 paper-based; 77 iBT). *Application deadline:* For fall admission, 7/1 priority date for domestic students, 3/15 for international students; for spring admission, 11/1 for domestic students, 8/15 for international students. Applications are processed on a rolling basis. Application fee: $60 ($75 for international students). Electronic applications accepted. *Financial support:* Fellowships with tuition reimbursements, research assistantships with tuition reimbursements, teaching assistantships with tuition reimbursements, and career-related internships or fieldwork available. Support available to part-time students. Financial award application deadline: 3/1; financial award applicants required to submit FAFSA. *Faculty research:* Insect biochemistry, nematology, aquatic diptera, behavioral ecology, insect physiology. *Unit head:* Dr. J. S. Yaninek, Head, 765-494-4553, Fax: 765-494-0535, E-mail: steve_yaninek@purdue.edu. *Application contact:* Amanda L. Pendleton, Graduate Admissions Office, 765-494-9061, Fax: 765-494-0535, E-mail: apendle@purdue.edu. Web site: http://www.entm.purdue.edu/entomology/entmwww.html.

Rutgers, The State University of New Jersey, New Brunswick, Graduate School-New Brunswick, Program in Entomology, Piscataway, NJ 08854-8097. Offers MS, PhD. *Degree requirements:* For master's, thesis or alternative; for doctorate, thesis/dissertation. *Entrance requirements:* For master's and doctorate, GRE General Test, GRE Subject Test (recommended). Additional exam requirements/recommendations for international students: Required—TOEFL. Electronic applications accepted. *Faculty research:* Insect toxicology, biolorial control, pathology, IPM and ecology, insect systematics.

Simon Fraser University, Graduate Studies, Faculty of Science, Department of Biological Sciences, Burnaby, BC V5A 1S6, Canada. Offers biological sciences (M Sc, PhD); environmental toxicology (MET); pest management (MPM). *Degree requirements:* For master's, thesis; for doctorate, thesis/dissertation. *Entrance requirements:* For master's, minimum GPA of 3.0; for doctorate, minimum GPA of 3.5. Additional exam requirements/recommendations for international students: Required—TOEFL or IELTS. Electronic applications accepted. *Faculty research:* Molecular biology, marine biology, ecology, wildlife biology, endocrinology.

State University of New York College of Environmental Science and Forestry, Department of Environmental and Forest Biology, Syracuse, NY 13210-2779. Offers applied ecology (MPS); chemical ecology (MPS, MS, PhD); conservation biology (MPS, MS, PhD); ecology (MPS, MS, PhD); entomology (MPS, MS, PhD); environmental interpretation (MPS, MS, PhD); environmental physiology (MPS, MS, PhD); fish and wildlife biology and management (MPS, MS, PhD); forest pathology and mycology (MPS, MS, PhD); plant biotechnology (MPS); plant science and biotechnology (MPS, MS, PhD). *Degree requirements:* For master's, thesis (for some programs); for doctorate, comprehensive exam, thesis/dissertation. *Entrance requirements:* For master's and doctorate, GRE General Test, GRE Subject Test, minimum GPA of 3.0. Additional exam requirements/recommendations for international students: Required—TOEFL (minimum score 550 paper-based; 213 computer-based; 80 iBT), IELTS (minimum score 6). *Application deadline:* For fall admission, 2/1 priority date for domestic students, 2/1 for international students; for spring admission, 11/1 priority date for domestic students, 11/1 for international students. Applications are processed on a rolling basis. Application fee: $60. *Expenses:* Tuition, state resident: full-time $8870; part-time $370 per credit hour. Tuition, nonresident: full-time $15,160; part-time $632 per credit hour. *Required fees:* $60; $370 per credit hour. $350 per semester. One-time fee: $85. *Financial support:* Fellowships with full and partial tuition reimbursements, research assistantships with full and partial tuition reimbursements, teaching assistantships with full and partial tuition reimbursements, Federal Work-Study, institutionally sponsored loans, scholarships/grants, health care benefits, and unspecified assistantships available. Financial award application deadline: 6/30. *Faculty research:* Ecology, fish and wildlife biology and management, plant science, entomology. *Total annual research expenditures:* $4.1 million. *Unit head:* Dr. Donald J. Leopold, Chair, 315-470-6760, Fax: 315-470-6934. *Application contact:* Dr. Dudley J.

Entomology

Raynal, Dean, Instruction and Graduate Studies, 315-470-6599, Fax: 315-470-6978, E-mail: esfgrad@esf.edu. Web site: http://www.esf.edu/efb/.

Texas A&M University, College of Agriculture and Life Sciences, Department of Entomology, College Station, TX 77843. Offers M Agr, MS, PhD. *Faculty:* 22. *Students:* 46 full-time (23 women), 8 part-time (2 women); includes 12 minority (1 Black or African American, non-Hispanic/Latino; 2 Asian, non-Hispanic/Latino; 9 Hispanic/Latino), 14 international. Average age 34. In 2011, 2 master's, 3 doctorates awarded. *Degree requirements:* For master's, comprehensive exam, thesis (for some programs); for doctorate, comprehensive exam, thesis/dissertation. *Entrance requirements:* For master's and doctorate, GRE General Test. Additional exam requirements/recommendations for international students: Required—TOEFL. *Application deadline:* For fall admission, 2/1 priority date for domestic students; for spring admission, 10/1 for domestic students. Applications are processed on a rolling basis. Application fee: $50 ($75 for international students). Electronic applications accepted. *Expenses:* Tuition, state resident: full-time $5437; part-time $226.55 per credit hour. Tuition, nonresident: full-time $12,949; part-time $539.55 per credit hour. *Required fees:* $2741. *Financial support:* In 2011–12, research assistantships with partial tuition reimbursements (averaging $16,500 per year), teaching assistantships with partial tuition reimbursements (averaging $16,500 per year) were awarded; fellowships and Federal Work-Study also available. Financial award application deadline: 3/1; financial award applicants required to submit FAFSA. *Faculty research:* Biology, biological control, integrated pest management, systematics, host plant resistance. *Unit head:* David Ragsdale, Head, 979-845-2510, Fax: 979-845-6305, E-mail: dragsdale@tamu.edu. *Application contact:* Graduate Admissions, 979-845-1044, E-mail: admissions@tamu.edu. Web site: http://insects.tamu.edu.

The University of Arizona, Graduate Interdisciplinary Programs, Graduate Interdisciplinary Program in Entomology and Insect Science, Tucson, AZ 85721. Offers MS, PhD. Part-time programs available. *Faculty:* 10 full-time (5 women). *Students:* 27 full-time (11 women); includes 6 minority (2 Asian, non-Hispanic/Latino; 2 Hispanic/Latino; 2 Two or more races, non-Hispanic/Latino), 8 international. Average age 25. 21 applicants, 10% accepted, 1 enrolled. In 2011, 1 master's, 2 doctorates awarded. *Degree requirements:* For master's, thesis; for doctorate, comprehensive exam, thesis/dissertation. *Entrance requirements:* For master's, GRE General Test, GRE Subject Test, minimum GPA of 3.0, 3 letters of recommendation; for doctorate, GRE General Test, GRE Subject Test, minimum GPA of 3.0, 3 letters of recommendation, statement of purpose. Additional exam requirements/recommendations for international students: Required—TOEFL (minimum score 550 paper-based; 213 computer-based). *Application deadline:* For fall admission, 1/1 for domestic students, 12/1 for international students. Applications are processed on a rolling basis. Application fee: $75. *Expenses:* Tuition, state resident: full-time $10,840. Tuition, nonresident: full-time $25,802. *Financial support:* In 2011–12, 1 student received support, including 2 research assistantships with full and partial tuition reimbursements available (averaging $18,554 per year); fellowships, teaching assistantships, Federal Work-Study, institutionally sponsored loans, scholarships/grants, health care benefits, tuition waivers (full and partial), and unspecified assistantships also available. Financial award application deadline: 3/1. *Faculty research:* Toxicology and physiology, plant/insect relations, vector biology, insect pest management, chemical ecology. *Total annual research expenditures:* $2.4 million. *Unit head:* Dr. Bruce E. Tabashnik, Professor and Head, 520-621-1141, Fax: 520-621-1150, E-mail: brucet@ag.arizona.edu. *Application contact:* Patricia L. Baldewiez, Graduate Coordinator, 520-621-1151, Fax: 520-621-1150, E-mail: pbaldewi@ag.arizona.edu. Web site: http://insects.arizona.edu/.

University of Arkansas, Graduate School, Dale Bumpers College of Agricultural, Food and Life Sciences, Department of Entomology, Fayetteville, AR 72701-1201. Offers MS, PhD. *Students:* 3 full-time (0 women), 16 part-time (7 women); includes 4 minority (1 Asian, non-Hispanic/Latino; 1 Hispanic/Latino; 2 Two or more races, non-Hispanic/Latino), 1 international. In 2011, 2 master's, 3 doctorates awarded. *Degree requirements:* For master's, thesis; for doctorate, one foreign language, thesis/dissertation. *Entrance requirements:* For master's, GRE, minimum GPA of 3.0; for doctorate, GRE, minimum GPA of 3.25. *Application deadline:* For fall admission, 4/1 for international students; for spring admission, 10/1 for international students. Applications are processed on a rolling basis. Application fee: $40 ($50 for international students). Electronic applications accepted. *Financial support:* In 2011–12, 19 research assistantships were awarded; fellowships with tuition reimbursements, teaching assistantships, career-related internships or fieldwork, and Federal Work-Study also available. Support available to part-time students. Financial award application deadline: 4/1; financial award applicants required to submit FAFSA. *Faculty research:* Integrated pest management, insect virology, insect taxonomy. *Unit head:* Dr. Robert Wiedenmann, Chair, 479-575-6628, E-mail: rwieden@uark.edu. *Application contact:* Janet Funk, Administrative Assistant I, 479-575-6628, E-mail: jfunk@uark.edu. Web site: http://entomology.uark.edu/.

University of California, Davis, Graduate Studies, Graduate Group in Integrated Pest Management, Davis, CA 95616. Offers MS. *Degree requirements:* For master's, comprehensive exam (for some programs), thesis (for some programs). *Entrance requirements:* For master's, GRE General Test, GRE Subject Test (biology), minimum GPA of 3.0. Additional exam requirements/recommendations for international students: Required—TOEFL (minimum score 550 paper-based; 213 computer-based). Electronic applications accepted.

University of California, Davis, Graduate Studies, Program in Entomology, Davis, CA 95616. Offers MS, PhD. Terminal master's awarded for partial completion of doctoral program. *Degree requirements:* For master's, comprehensive exam (for some programs), thesis (for some programs); for doctorate, thesis/dissertation. *Entrance requirements:* For master's and doctorate, GRE General Test, GRE Subject Test (biology). Additional exam requirements/recommendations for international students: Required—TOEFL (minimum score 550 paper-based; 213 computer-based). Electronic applications accepted. *Faculty research:* Bee biology, biological control, systematics, medical/veterinary entomology, pest management.

University of California, Riverside, Graduate Division, Department of Entomology, Riverside, CA 92521-0102. Offers entomology (MS, PhD); evolution and ecology (PhD). Part-time programs available. *Faculty:* 35 full-time (4 women). *Students:* 37 full-time (19 women); includes 8 minority (1 Black or African American, non-Hispanic/Latino; 4 Asian, non-Hispanic/Latino; 3 Hispanic/Latino), 6 international. Average age 28. 27 applicants, 37% accepted, 7 enrolled. In 2011, 2 master's, 8 doctorates awarded. Terminal master's awarded for partial completion of doctoral program. *Degree requirements:* For master's, thesis; for doctorate, thesis/dissertation, qualifying exams. *Entrance requirements:* For master's and doctorate, GRE General Test, minimum GPA of 3.2. Additional exam requirements/recommendations for international students: Required—TOEFL (minimum score 550 paper-based; 213 computer-based; 80 iBT) or IELTS. *Application deadline:* For fall admission, 5/1 for domestic students, 2/1 for international students; for winter admission, 9/1 for domestic students, 7/1 for international students; for spring admission, 12/1 for domestic students, 10/1 for international students. Applications are processed on a rolling basis. Application fee: $80 ($100 for international students). Electronic applications accepted. *Financial support:* In 2011–12, fellowships with tuition reimbursements (averaging $18,000 per year), research assistantships with tuition

reimbursements (averaging $19,500 per year), teaching assistantships with tuition reimbursements (averaging $17,310 per year) were awarded; career-related internships or fieldwork, Federal Work-Study, institutionally sponsored loans, and tuition waivers (full and partial) also available. Financial award application deadline: 1/5; financial award applicants required to submit FAFSA. *Faculty research:* Agricultural, urban, medical, and veterinary entomology; biological control; chemical ecology; insect pathogens; novel toxicants. *Unit head:* Dr. Richard Redak, Chair, 951-827-7250, Fax: 951-827-3086, E-mail: richard.redak@ucr.edu. *Application contact:* Melissa L. Gomez, Graduate Student Affairs Officer, 951-827-5913, Fax: 951-827-5517, E-mail: insects@ucr.edu. Web site: http://www.entomology.ucr.edu/.

University of Connecticut, Graduate School, College of Liberal Arts and Sciences, Department of Ecology and Evolutionary Biology, Storrs, CT 06269. Offers botany (MS, PhD); ecology (MS, PhD); entomology (MS, PhD); zoology (MS, PhD). Terminal master's awarded for partial completion of doctoral program. *Degree requirements:* For master's, comprehensive exam; for doctorate, thesis/dissertation. *Entrance requirements:* For master's and doctorate, GRE General Test, GRE Subject Test. Additional exam requirements/recommendations for international students: Required—TOEFL (minimum score 550 paper-based; 213 computer-based). Electronic applications accepted.

University of Delaware, College of Agriculture and Natural Resources, Department of Entomology and Wildlife Ecology, Newark, DE 19716. Offers entomology and applied ecology (MS, PhD), including avian ecology, evolution and taxonomy, insect biological control, insect ecology and behavior (MS), insect genetics, pest management, plant-insect interactions, wildlife ecology and management. Part-time programs available. *Degree requirements:* For master's, comprehensive exam, thesis, oral exam, seminar; for doctorate, comprehensive exam, thesis/dissertation, qualifying exam, seminar. *Entrance requirements:* For master's, GRE General Test, minimum GPA of 3.0 in field, 2.8 overall; for doctorate, GRE General Test, GRE Subject Test (biology), minimum GPA of 3.0 in field, 2.8 overall. Additional exam requirements/recommendations for international students: Required—TOEFL. Electronic applications accepted. *Faculty research:* Ecology and evolution of plant-insect interactions, ecology of wildlife conservation management, habitat restoration, biological control, applied ecosystem management.

University of Florida, Graduate School, College of Agricultural and Life Sciences, Department of Entomology and Nematology, Gainesville, FL 32611. Offers MS, PhD. Cooperative PhD program available with Florida A&M University. Part-time and evening/weekend programs available. *Faculty:* 30 full-time (8 women). *Students:* 79 full-time (39 women), 36 part-time (21 women); includes 12 minority (1 Black or African American, non-Hispanic/Latino; 5 Asian, non-Hispanic/Latino; 6 Hispanic/Latino), 36 international. Average age 30. 58 applicants, 57% accepted, 29 enrolled. In 2011, 20 master's, 14 doctorates awarded. *Degree requirements:* For master's, comprehensive exam (for some programs), thesis (for some programs); for doctorate, comprehensive exam, thesis/dissertation. *Entrance requirements:* For master's and doctorate, GRE General Test, GRE Subject Test (biology), minimum GPA of 3.0. Additional exam requirements/recommendations for international students: Required—TOEFL (minimum score 550 paper-based; 213 computer-based; 80 iBT), IELTS (minimum score 6). *Application deadline:* For fall admission, 7/15 priority date for domestic students; for spring admission, 11/15 for domestic students. Applications are processed on a rolling basis. Application fee: $30. Electronic applications accepted. *Financial support:* Fellowships, research assistantships, teaching assistantships, and career-related internships or fieldwork available. Financial award applicants required to submit FAFSA. *Faculty research:* Biological control, pest management, genetics, ecology, physiology, toxicology, systematics and taxonomy, medical and veterinary entomology, urban entomology, nematology. *Total annual research expenditures:* $5 million. *Unit head:* Dr. John L. Capinera, Department Chair, 352-273-3905, Fax: 352-392-0190, E-mail: capinera@ufl.edu. *Application contact:* Dr. Heather J. McAuslane, Graduate Coordinator, 352-273-3923, Fax: 352-392-0190, E-mail: hjmca@ufl.edu. Web site: http://entnemdept.ifas.ufl.edu/.

University of Georgia, College of Agricultural and Environmental Sciences, Department of Entomology, Athens, GA 30602. Offers entomology (MS, PhD); plant protection and pest management (MPPPM). *Faculty:* 27 full-time (3 women), 3 part-time/adjunct (0 women). *Students:* 29 full-time (10 women), 5 part-time (1 woman); includes 3 minority (1 Black or African American, non-Hispanic/Latino; 1 Hispanic/Latino; 1 Two or more races, non-Hispanic/Latino), 10 international. Average age 28. 26 applicants, 38% accepted, 8 enrolled. In 2011, 8 master's, 5 doctorates awarded. *Degree requirements:* For master's, thesis (MS); for doctorate, one foreign language, thesis/dissertation. *Entrance requirements:* For master's and doctorate, GRE General Test. *Application deadline:* For fall admission, 7/1 priority date for domestic students; for spring admission, 11/15 for domestic students. Application fee: $50. Electronic applications accepted. *Financial support:* Unspecified assistantships available. *Faculty research:* Apiculture, acarology, aquatic and soil biology, ecology, systematics. *Unit head:* Dr. Raymond Noblet, Head, 706-542-2816, Fax: 706-542-2279, E-mail: rnoblet@bugs.ent.uga.edu. *Application contact:* Dr. Mark Brown, Graduate Coordinator, 706-542-2317, E-mail: mrbrown@uga.edu. Web site: http://entomology.ent.uga.edu/.

University of Guelph, Graduate Studies, Ontario Agricultural College, Department of Environmental Biology, Guelph, ON N1G 2W1, Canada. Offers entomology (M Sc, PhD); environmental microbiology and biotechnology (M Sc, PhD); environmental toxicology (M Sc, PhD); plant and forest systems (M Sc, PhD); plant pathology (M Sc, PhD). Part-time programs available. *Degree requirements:* For master's, thesis; for doctorate, comprehensive exam, thesis/dissertation. *Entrance requirements:* For master's, minimum 75% average during previous 2 years of course work; for doctorate, minimum 75% average. Additional exam requirements/recommendations for international students: Required—TOEFL or IELTS. Electronic applications accepted. *Faculty research:* Entomology, environmental microbiology and biotechnology, environmental toxicology, forest ecology, plant pathology.

University of Hawaii at Manoa, Graduate Division, College of Tropical Agriculture and Human Resources, Department of Plant and Environmental Protection Sciences, Program in Entomology, Honolulu, HI 96822. Offers MS, PhD. Part-time programs available. *Degree requirements:* For master's, thesis optional; for doctorate, comprehensive exam, thesis/dissertation. *Entrance requirements:* For master's and doctorate, GRE General Test, GRE Subject Test (biology). Additional exam requirements/recommendations for international students: Required—TOEFL (minimum score 500 paper-based; 173 computer-based; 61 iBT), IELTS (minimum score 5). *Faculty research:* Integrated pest management, biological control, urban entomology, medical/forensic entomology resistance.

University of Idaho, College of Graduate Studies, College of Agricultural and Life Sciences, Department of Plant, Soil, and Entomological Sciences, Program in Entomology, Moscow, ID 83844-2282. Offers MS, PhD. *Students:* 13 full-time, 2 part-time. Average age 28. In 2011, 4 master's, 1 doctorate awarded. *Degree requirements:* For master's, thesis (for some programs); for doctorate, one foreign language, thesis/dissertation. *Entrance requirements:* For master's and doctorate, GRE General Test, minimum GPA of 3.0. *Application deadline:* For fall admission, 8/1 for domestic students; for spring admission, 12/15 for domestic students. Applications are processed on a

rolling basis. Application fee: $60. Electronic applications accepted. *Expenses:* Tuition, state resident: full-time $3874; part-time $334 per credit hour. Tuition, nonresident: full-time $16,394; part-time $861 per credit hour. *Required fees:* $2808; $99 per credit hour. Tuition and fees vary according to program. *Financial support:* Applicants required to submit FAFSA. *Faculty research:* Biological control of insect pests/weeds, aquatic entomology-resource management, hop pest management, mosquito reproductive physiology, landscape ecology for sustainability and biological conservation. *Unit head:* Dr. James B. Johnson, Department Head, 208-885-6274, E-mail: nthompson@ uidaho.edu. *Application contact:* Erick Larson, Director of Graduate Admissions, 208-885-4723, E-mail: gadms@uidaho.edu.

University of Illinois at Urbana–Champaign, Graduate College, College of Liberal Arts and Sciences, School of Integrative Biology, Department of Entomology, Champaign, IL 61820. Offers MS, PhD. *Faculty:* 11 full-time (3 women). *Students:* 31 full-time (18 women), 4 part-time (2 women); includes 4 minority (2 Asian, non-Hispanic/Latino; 2 Hispanic/Latino), 9 international. 34 applicants, 29% accepted, 8 enrolled. In 2011, 7 master's, 3 doctorates awarded. Terminal master's awarded for partial completion of doctoral program. *Entrance requirements:* For master's and doctorate, GRE General Test, GRE Subject Test, minimum GPA of 3.0. Additional exam requirements/recommendations for international students: Required—TOEFL (minimum score 550 paper-based). *Application deadline:* Applications are processed on a rolling basis. Application fee: $75 ($90 for international students). Electronic applications accepted. *Financial support:* In 2011–12, 6 fellowships, 30 research assistantships, 19 teaching assistantships were awarded; tuition waivers (full and partial) also available. *Unit head:* Dr. May R. Berenbaum, Head, 217-333-7784, Fax: 217-244-3499, E-mail: maybe@illinois.edu. *Application contact:* Audra Weinstein, Office Administrator, 217-244-2888, Fax: 217-244-3499, E-mail: audra@illinois.edu. Web site: http://www.life.illinois.edu/entomology/.

The University of Kansas, Graduate Studies, College of Liberal Arts and Sciences, Department of Ecology and Evolutionary Biology, Lawrence, KS 66045. Offers botany (MA, PhD); ecology and evolutionary biology (MA, PhD); entomology (MA, PhD). *Faculty:* 15 full-time (6 women), 25 part-time/adjunct (6 women). *Students:* 64 full-time (31 women), 1 part-time (0 women); includes 4 minority (1 Hispanic/Latino; 3 Two or more races, non-Hispanic/Latino), 20 international. Average age 28. 67 applicants, 34% accepted, 18 enrolled. In 2011, 6 master's, 9 doctorates awarded. Terminal master's awarded for partial completion of doctoral program. *Degree requirements:* For master's, comprehensive exam, thesis (for some programs), 30-36 credits, thesis presentation; for doctorate, comprehensive exam, thesis/dissertation, residency, responsible scholarship and research skills, final exam, dissertation defense. *Entrance requirements:* For master's, GRE General Test, bachelor's degree with minimum undergraduate GPA of 3.0; for doctorate, GRE General Test, bachelor's degree; minimum undergraduate/graduate GPA of 3.0. Additional exam requirements/recommendations for international students: Required—TOEFL or IELTS. *Application deadline:* For fall admission, 12/1 for domestic students, 12/15 for international students; for spring admission, 9/15 for domestic and international students. Application fee: $55 ($65 for international students). Electronic applications accepted. Tuition and fees vary according to course load, campus/location, program and reciprocity agreements. *Financial support:* In 2011–12, 8 fellowships with full and partial tuition reimbursements, 22 research assistantships with full and partial tuition reimbursements, 32 teaching assistantships with full and partial tuition reimbursements were awarded; scholarships/grants, traineeships, health care benefits, and unspecified assistantships also available. Financial award application deadline: 12/1. *Faculty research:* Biodiversity and macroevolution, ecology and global change, evolutionary mechanisms. *Unit head:* Dr. Christopher H. Haufler, Chair, 785-864-3255, Fax: 785-864-5860, E-mail: vulgare@ ku.edu. *Application contact:* Jaime Rochelle Keeler, Graduate Coordinator, 785-864-2362, Fax: 785-864-5860, E-mail: jrkeeler@ku.edu. Web site: http://www.ku.edu/~eeb/.

University of Kentucky, Graduate School, College of Agriculture, Program in Entomology, Lexington, KY 40506-0032. Offers MS, PhD. *Degree requirements:* For master's, comprehensive exam, thesis optional; for doctorate, comprehensive exam, thesis/dissertation. *Entrance requirements:* For master's, GRE General Test, minimum undergraduate GPA of 2.75; for doctorate, GRE General Test, minimum graduate GPA of 3.0. Additional exam requirements/recommendations for international students: Required—TOEFL (minimum score 550 paper-based; 213 computer-based). Electronic applications accepted. *Faculty research:* Applied entomology, behavior, insect biology and ecology, biological control, insect physiology and molecular biology.

University of Maine, Graduate School, College of Natural Sciences, Forestry, and Agriculture, Department of Biological Sciences, Program in Entomology, Orono, ME 04469. Offers MS. Part-time programs available. *Students:* 1 (woman) full-time, all international. Average age 23. 3 applicants, 0% accepted, 0 enrolled. *Entrance requirements:* For master's, GRE General Test. Additional exam requirements/recommendations for international students: Required—TOEFL. *Application deadline:* For fall admission, 2/1 priority date for domestic students. Applications are processed on a rolling basis. Application fee: $65. Electronic applications accepted. *Expenses:* Tuition, state resident: full-time $5016. Tuition, nonresident: full-time $14,424. *Financial support:* Career-related internships or fieldwork, Federal Work-Study, institutionally sponsored loans, and tuition waivers (full) available. Financial award application deadline: 3/1. *Unit head:* Dr. Jody Jellison, Coordinator, 207-581-2551. *Application contact:* Scott G. Delcourt, Associate Dean of the Graduate School, 207-581-3291, Fax: 207-581-3232, E-mail: graduate@maine.edu. Web site: http://www2.umaine.edu/graduate/.

University of Manitoba, Faculty of Graduate Studies, Faculty of Agricultural and Food Sciences, Department of Entomology, Winnipeg, MB R3T 2N2, Canada. Offers M Sc, PhD. *Degree requirements:* For master's, thesis; for doctorate, one foreign language, thesis/dissertation.

University of Maryland, College Park, Academic Affairs, College of Computer, Mathematical and Natural Sciences, Department of Entomology, College Park, MD 20742. Offers MS, PhD. Part-time and evening/weekend programs available. *Faculty:* 42 full-time (20 women), 3 part-time/adjunct (all women). *Students:* 19 full-time (7 women); includes 4 minority (1 Black or African American, non-Hispanic/Latino; 1 Asian, non-Hispanic/Latino; 1 Hispanic/Latino; 1 Two or more races, non-Hispanic/Latino), 3 international. 37 applicants, 27% accepted, 8 enrolled. In 2011, 1 master's, 2 doctorates awarded. Terminal master's awarded for partial completion of doctoral program. *Degree requirements:* For master's, thesis; for doctorate, thesis/dissertation, oral qualifying exam. *Entrance requirements:* For master's and doctorate, GRE General Test, minimum GPA of 3.0, 3 letters of recommendation. *Application deadline:* For fall admission, 1/15 for domestic and international students. Applications are processed on a rolling basis. Application fee: $75. Electronic applications accepted. *Expenses:* Tuition, state resident: part-time $525 per credit hour. Tuition, nonresident: part-time $1131 per credit hour. *Required fees:* $386.31 per term. Tuition and fees vary according to program. *Financial support:* In 2011–12, 1 fellowship with full tuition reimbursement (averaging $15,000 per year), 1 research assistantship (averaging $19,685 per year), 19 teaching assistantships (averaging $18,980 per year) were awarded; career-related internships or fieldwork and Federal Work-Study also available. Support available to part-time students. Financial award applicants required to submit FAFSA. *Faculty research:* Pest

management, biosystematics, physiology and morphology, toxicology.. *Total annual research expenditures:* $2.1 million. *Unit head:* Dr. Charles Mitter, Chair, 301-405-3912, Fax: 301-314-9290, E-mail: cmitter@umd.edu. *Application contact:* Dr. Charles A. Caramello, Dean of Graduate School, 301-405-0358, Fax: 301-314-9305.

University of Massachusetts Amherst, Graduate School, College of Natural Sciences, Department of Plant, Soil and Insect Sciences, Program in Entomology, Amherst, MA 01003. Offers MS, PhD. Part-time programs available. *Students:* 3 full-time (1 woman), 2 part-time (both women), 2 international. Average age 29. 12 applicants, 50% accepted, 1 enrolled. Terminal master's awarded for partial completion of doctoral program. *Degree requirements:* For master's, thesis or alternative; for doctorate, comprehensive exam, thesis/dissertation. *Entrance requirements:* For master's and doctorate, GRE General Test. Additional exam requirements/recommendations for international students: Required—TOEFL (minimum score 550 paper-based; 213 computer-based; 80 iBT), IELTS (minimum score 6.5). *Application deadline:* For fall admission, 1/2 for domestic and international students; for spring admission, 10/1 for domestic and international students. Applications are processed on a rolling basis. Application fee: $50 ($65 for international students). Electronic applications accepted. Tuition and fees vary according to course load, campus/location and program. *Financial support:* Fellowships with full and partial tuition reimbursements, research assistantships, teaching assistantships, career-related internships or fieldwork, Federal Work-Study, scholarships/grants, traineeships, health care benefits, tuition waivers (full and partial), and unspecified assistantships available. Support available to part-time students. Financial award application deadline: 1/2. *Unit head:* Dr. Anne Averill, Graduate Program Director, 413-545-2004, Fax: 413-545-2115. *Application contact:* Lindsay DeSantis, Interim Supervisor of Admissions, 413-545-0722, Fax: 413-577-0010, E-mail: gradadm@grad.umass.edu. Web site: http://www.umass.edu/psis/.

University of Minnesota, Twin Cities Campus, Graduate School, College of Food, Agricultural and Natural Resource Sciences, Entomology Graduate Program, Saint Paul, MN 55108. Offers MS, PhD. Part-time programs available. *Faculty:* 28 full-time (8 women). *Students:* 33 full-time (20 women); includes 3 minority (2 Asian, non-Hispanic/Latino; 1 Two or more races, non-Hispanic/Latino), 4 international. Average age 30. 31 applicants, 39% accepted, 11 enrolled. In 2011, 1 degree awarded. *Degree requirements:* For master's, comprehensive exam, thesis; for doctorate, comprehensive exam, thesis/dissertation. *Entrance requirements:* For master's, GRE, minimum undergraduate GPA of 3.0; for doctorate, GRE, minimum undergraduate GPA of 3.0, graduate 3.5. Additional exam requirements/recommendations for international students: Required—TOEFL (minimum score 550 paper-based; 213 computer-based; 79 iBT), IELTS (minimum score 6.5), TOEFL preferred. *Application deadline:* For fall admission, 12/15 priority date for domestic students, 12/15 for international students; for spring admission, 10/15 priority date for domestic students, 12/15 for international students. Applications are processed on a rolling basis. Application fee: $75 ($95 for international students). Electronic applications accepted. *Financial support:* In 2011–12, fellowships with full tuition reimbursements (averaging $23,500 per year), research assistantships with full tuition reimbursements (averaging $18,000 per year), teaching assistantships with full tuition reimbursements (averaging $18,000 per year) were awarded; scholarships/grants, health care benefits, and unspecified assistantships also available. *Faculty research:* Behavior, ecology, molecular genetics, physiology, systematics and taxonomy. *Total annual research expenditures:* $2.2 million. *Unit head:* Dr. George Heimpel, Director of Graduate Studies, 612-624-3480, Fax: 612-625-5299, E-mail: heimp001@umn.edu. *Application contact:* Felicia Christy Horan, Program Coordinator, 612-624-3278, Fax: 612-625-5299, E-mail: christy@umn.edu. Web site: http://www.entomology.umn.edu/.

University of Missouri, Graduate School, College of Agriculture, Food and Natural Resources, Division of Plant Sciences, Program in Entomology, Columbia, MO 65211. Offers MS, PhD. *Degree requirements:* For doctorate, thesis/dissertation. *Application deadline:* Applications are processed on a rolling basis. *Expenses:* Tuition, state resident: full-time $5881. Tuition, nonresident: full-time $15,183. *Required fees:* $952. Tuition and fees vary according to campus/location and program. *Financial support:* Research assistantships, teaching assistantships, and institutionally sponsored loans available. *Unit head:* Dr. Michael Collins, Director, 573-882-1957, E-mail: collinsm@ missouri.edu. *Application contact:* Dr. Jeanne Mihail, Director of Graduate Studies, 573-882-0574, E-mail: mihailj@missouri.edu.

University of Nebraska–Lincoln, Graduate College, College of Agricultural Sciences and Natural Resources, Department of Entomology, Lincoln, NE 68588. Offers MS, PhD. Postbaccalaureate distance learning degree programs offered (no on-campus study). *Degree requirements:* For master's, thesis optional; for doctorate, comprehensive exam, thesis/dissertation. *Entrance requirements:* For master's and doctorate, GRE General Test. Additional exam requirements/recommendations for international students: Required—TOEFL (minimum score 550 paper-based; 213 computer-based). Electronic applications accepted. *Faculty research:* Ecology and behavior, insect-plant interactions, integrated pest management, genetics, urban entomology.

University of North Dakota, Graduate School, College of Arts and Sciences, Department of Biology, Grand Forks, ND 58202. Offers botany (MS, PhD); ecology (MS, PhD); entomology (MS, PhD); environmental biology (MS, PhD); fisheries/wildlife (MS, PhD); genetics (MS, PhD); zoology (MS, PhD). Terminal master's awarded for partial completion of doctoral program. *Degree requirements:* For master's, thesis, final exam; for doctorate, comprehensive exam, thesis/dissertation, final exam. *Entrance requirements:* For master's, GRE General Test, GRE Subject Test, minimum GPA of 3.0; for doctorate, GRE General Test, GRE Subject Test, minimum GPA of 3.5. Additional exam requirements/recommendations for international students: Required—TOEFL (minimum score 550 paper-based; 213 computer-based; 79 iBT), IELTS (minimum score 6.5). Electronic applications accepted. *Faculty research:* Population biology, wildlife ecology, RNA processing, hormonal control of behavior.

University of Rhode Island, Graduate School, College of the Environment and Life Sciences, Department of Plant Sciences, Kingston, RI 02881. Offers entomology (MS, PhD); plant sciences (MS, PhD). Part-time programs available. *Faculty:* 10 full-time (2 women). *Students:* 7 full-time (4 women), 7 part-time (3 women). In 2011, 8 master's awarded. *Degree requirements:* For master's, comprehensive exam (for some programs), thesis optional; for doctorate, comprehensive exam, thesis/dissertation. *Entrance requirements:* For master's and doctorate, GRE, 2 letters of recommendation. Additional exam requirements/recommendations for international students: Required—TOEFL (minimum score 550 paper-based; 213 computer-based). *Application deadline:* For fall admission, 7/15 for domestic students, 2/1 for international students; for spring admission, 11/15 for domestic students, 7/15 for international students. Application fee: $65. Electronic applications accepted. *Expenses:* Tuition, state resident: full-time $10,432; part-time $580 per credit hour. Tuition, nonresident: full-time $23,130; part-time $1285 per credit hour. *Required fees:* $1362; $36 per credit hour. $35 per semester. One-time fee: $130. *Financial support:* In 2011–12, 3 teaching assistantships with full and partial tuition reimbursements (averaging $11,578 per year) were awarded. Financial award application deadline: 7/15; financial award applicants required to submit FAFSA. *Faculty research:* Plant development and management; pest management; tick biology, ecology, and control; identification and replacement of invasive ornamentals.

Entomology

Unit head: Dr. David Bengtson, Interim Chair, 401-874-2668, Fax: 401-874-2494, E-mail: bengtson@uri.edu. *Application contact:* Dr. Thomas Mather, Director of Graduate Studies, 401-874-5616, Fax: 401-874-2494, E-mail: tmather@uri.edu. Web site: http://cels.uri.edu/pls/.

The University of Tennessee, Graduate School, College of Agricultural Sciences and Natural Resources, Department of Entomology and Plant Pathology, Knoxville, TN 37996. Offers entomology (MS, PhD); integrated pest management and bioactive natural products (PhD); plant pathology (MS, PhD). Part-time programs available. *Degree requirements:* For master's, thesis, seminar. *Entrance requirements:* For master's, GRE General Test, minimum GPA of 2.7, 3 reference letters, letter of intent; for doctorate, GRE General Test, minimum GPA of 2.7, 3 reference letters, letter of intent, proposed dissertation research. Additional exam requirements/recommendations for international students: Required—TOEFL. Electronic applications accepted. *Expenses:* Tuition, state resident: full-time $8332; part-time $464 per credit hour. Tuition, nonresident: full-time $25,174; part-time $1400 per credit hour. *Required fees:* $1162; $56 per credit hour. Tuition and fees vary according to program.

University of Wisconsin–Madison, Graduate School, College of Agricultural and Life Sciences, Department of Entomology, Madison, WI 53706-1380. Offers MS, PhD. *Degree requirements:* For master's, thesis; for doctorate, thesis/dissertation. *Entrance requirements:* For master's and doctorate, GRE General Test, minimum GPA of 3.0. Additional exam requirements/recommendations for international students: Required— TOEFL (minimum score 237 computer-based). Electronic applications accepted. *Expenses:* Tuition, state resident: full-time $10,296; part-time $643.51 per credit. Tuition, nonresident: full-time $24,054; part-time $1503.40 per credit. *Required fees:* $70.06 per credit. Tuition and fees vary according to course load, campus/location, program and reciprocity agreements. *Faculty research:* Ecology, biocontrol, molecular.

University of Wyoming, College of Agriculture and Natural Resources, Department of Renewable Resources, Program in Entomology, Laramie, WY 82070. Offers MS, PhD. *Degree requirements:* For master's, thesis; for doctorate, thesis/dissertation. *Entrance requirements:* For master's and doctorate, GRE General Test, minimum GPA of 3.0. Additional exam requirements/recommendations for international students: Required— TOEFL. Electronic applications accepted. *Faculty research:* Insect pest management, taxonomy, biocontrol of weeds, forest insects, insects affecting humans and animals.

Virginia Polytechnic Institute and State University, Graduate School, College of Agriculture and Life Sciences, Department of Entomology, Blacksburg, VA 24061. Offers MSLFS, PhD. *Degree requirements:* For master's, comprehensive exam (for some programs), thesis (for some programs); for doctorate, comprehensive exam (for some programs), thesis/dissertation (for some programs). *Entrance requirements:* For master's and doctorate, GRE. Additional exam requirements/recommendations for international students: Required—TOEFL (minimum score 550 paper-based; 213 computer-based). *Application deadline:* For fall admission, 7/1 for domestic and international students; for spring admission, 12/1 for domestic and international students. Applications are processed on a rolling basis. Application fee: $65. Electronic applications accepted. *Expenses:* Tuition, state resident: full-time $10,048; part-time $558.25 per credit hour. Tuition, nonresident: full-time $19,497; part-time $1083.25 per credit hour. *Required fees:* $405 per semester. Tuition and fees vary according to course load, campus/location and program. *Financial support:* Research assistantships with full tuition reimbursements, teaching assistantships with full tuition reimbursements, career-related internships or fieldwork, Federal Work-Study, scholarships/grants, health care benefits, and unspecified assistantships available. Financial award application deadline: 1/15. *Faculty research:* Physiology, ecology, biocontrol, genetics, taxonomy. *Unit head:* Dr. Loke T. Kok, Unit Head, 540-231-6341, Fax: 540-231-9131, E-mail: ltkok@vt.edu. *Application contact:* J. Reese Voshell, Information Contact, 540-231-5707, Fax: 540-231-9131, E-mail: jvoshell@vt.edu. Web site: http://web.ento.vt.edu/ento/.

Washington State University, Graduate School, College of Agricultural, Human, and Natural Resource Sciences, Department of Entomology, Pullman, WA 99164. Offers MS, PhD. Part-time programs available. *Faculty:* 25. *Students:* 28 full-time (13 women), 4 part-time (2 women); includes 2 minority (1 Hispanic/Latino; 1 Two or more races, non-Hispanic/Latino), 5 international. Average age 28. 12 applicants, 100% accepted, 6 enrolled. In 2011, 4 master's, 2 doctorates awarded. Terminal master's awarded for partial completion of doctoral program. *Degree requirements:* For master's, comprehensive exam (for some programs), thesis (for some programs), oral exam; for doctorate, comprehensive exam, thesis/dissertation, oral exam, written exam. *Entrance requirements:* For master's, GRE General Test, GRE Subject Test in advanced biology (recommended); minimum GPA of 3.0, 3 letters of recommendation; for doctorate, GRE General Test, minimum GPA of 3.0, 3 letters of recommendation. Additional exam requirements/recommendations for international students: Required—TOEFL (minimum score 550 paper-based; 213 computer-based), IELTS. *Application deadline:* For fall admission, 1/10 priority date for domestic students, 1/10 for international students; for spring admission, 7/1 priority date for domestic students, 7/1 for international students. Applications are processed on a rolling basis. Application fee: $75. Electronic applications accepted. *Financial support:* In 2011–12, fellowships (averaging $5,306 per year), research assistantships with full and partial tuition reimbursements (averaging $18,204 per year), teaching assistantships with full and partial tuition reimbursements (averaging $18,204 per year) were awarded; career-related internships or fieldwork, Federal Work-Study, institutionally sponsored loans, tuition waivers (partial), unspecified assistantships, and teaching associateships also available. Financial award application deadline: 2/5; financial award applicants required to submit FAFSA. *Faculty research:* Apiculture, biological control of arthropods, integrated pest management, ecology, physiology and systematics of insects. *Total annual research expenditures:* $4.3 million. *Unit head:* Dr. W. Steve Sheppard, Chair, 509-335-5180, Fax: 509-335-1009, E-mail: shepp@wsu.edu. *Application contact:* Graduate School Admissions, 800-GRADWSU, Fax: 509-335-1949, E-mail: gradsch@wsu.edu. Web site: http://entomology.wsu.edu/.

West Virginia University, Davis College of Agriculture, Forestry and Consumer Sciences, Division of Plant and Soil Sciences, Morgantown, WV 26506. Offers agricultural sciences (PhD), including animal and food sciences, plant and soil sciences; agronomy (MS); entomology (MS); environmental microbiology (MS); horticulture (MS); plant pathology (MS). *Degree requirements:* For master's, thesis. *Entrance requirements:* For master's, GRE, minimum GPA of 2.5. Additional exam requirements/recommendations for international students: Required—TOEFL. *Faculty research:* Water quality, reclamation of disturbed land, crop production, pest control, environmental protection.

Section 10
Genetics, Developmental Biology, and Reproductive Biology

This section contains a directory of institutions offering graduate work in genetics, developmental biology, and reproductive biology, followed by in-depth entries submitted by institutions that chose to prepare detailed program descriptions. Additional information about programs listed in the directory but not augmented by an in-depth entry may be obtained by writing directly to the dean of a graduate school or chair of a department at the address given in the directory.

For programs offering related work, see also all other sections of this book. In the other guides in this series:

Graduate Programs in the Physical Sciences, Mathematics, Agricultural Sciences, the Environment & Natural Resources

See *Agricultural and Food Sciences, Chemistry,* and *Environmental Sciences and Management*

Graduate Programs in Engineering & Applied Sciences

See *Agricultural Engineering and Bioengineering* and *Biomedical Engineering and Biotechnology*

CONTENTS

Developmental Biology

Albert Einstein College of Medicine, Graduate Division of Biomedical Sciences, Department of Anatomy and Structural Biology, Bronx, NY 10461. Offers anatomy (PhD); cell and developmental biology (PhD); MD/PhD. *Degree requirements:* For doctorate, thesis/dissertation. *Entrance requirements:* For doctorate, GRE General Test. Additional exam requirements/recommendations for international students: Required—TOEFL. Electronic applications accepted. *Faculty research:* Cell motility, cell membranes and membrane-cytoskeletal interactions as applied to processing of pancreatic hormones, mechanisms of secretion.

Albert Einstein College of Medicine, Graduate Division of Biomedical Sciences, Division of Biological Sciences, Department of Developmental and Molecular Biology, Bronx, NY 10461. Offers PhD, MD/PhD. *Degree requirements:* For doctorate, thesis/dissertation. *Entrance requirements:* For doctorate, GRE General Test. Additional exam requirements/recommendations for international students: Required—TOEFL. *Faculty research:* DNA, RNA, and protein synthesis in prokaryotes and eukaryotes; chemical and enzymatic alteration of RNA; glycoproteins.

Baylor College of Medicine, Graduate School of Biomedical Sciences, Program in Developmental Biology, Houston, TX 77030-3498. Offers PhD, MD/PhD. *Faculty:* 68 full-time (20 women). *Students:* 55 full-time (28 women); includes 9 minority (7 Asian, non-Hispanic/Latino; 2 Hispanic/Latino), 37 international. Average age 28. 771 applicants, 2% accepted, 10 enrolled. In 2011, 5 degrees awarded. *Median time to degree:* Of those who began their doctoral program in fall 2003, 100% received their degree in 8 years or less. *Degree requirements:* For doctorate, thesis/dissertation, public defense. *Entrance requirements:* For doctorate, GRE General Test, GRE Subject Test (strongly recommended), minimum GPA of 3.0. Additional exam requirements/recommendations for international students: Required—TOEFL. *Application deadline:* For fall admission, 1/1 priority date for domestic students. Application fee: $0. Electronic applications accepted. *Financial support:* In 2011–12, 55 students received support, including 6 fellowships with full tuition reimbursements available (averaging $29,000 per year), 49 research assistantships with full tuition reimbursements available (averaging $29,000 per year); career-related internships or fieldwork, Federal Work-Study, institutionally sponsored loans, health care benefits, tuition waivers (full), and stipends also available. *Faculty research:* Stem cells, cancer, neurobiology, organogenesis, genetics of model organisms. *Unit head:* Dr. Hugo Bellen, Director, 713-798-6410. *Application contact:* Catherine Tasnier, Graduate Program Administrator, 713-798-6410, Fax: 713-798-5386, E-mail: cat@bcm.edu. Web site: http://www.bcm.edu/db/.

See Display on next page and Close-Up on page 311.

Brigham Young University, Graduate Studies, College of Life Sciences, Department of Physiology and Developmental Biology, Provo, UT 84602. Offers neuroscience (MS, PhD); physiology and developmental biology (MS, PhD). Part-time programs available. *Faculty:* 20 full-time (0 women). *Students:* 37 full-time (14 women); includes 9 minority (2 American Indian or Alaska Native, non-Hispanic/Latino; 3 Asian, non-Hispanic/Latino; 4 Hispanic/Latino). Average age 29. 12 applicants, 75% accepted, 8 enrolled. In 2011, 6 master's, 1 doctorate awarded. Terminal master's awarded for partial completion of doctoral program. *Degree requirements:* For master's, thesis; for doctorate, comprehensive exam, thesis/dissertation. *Entrance requirements:* For master's, GRE General Test, minimum GPA of 3.0 during previous 2 years; for doctorate, GRE General Test, minimum GPA of 3.0 overall. Additional exam requirements/recommendations for international students: Required—TOEFL. *Application deadline:* For fall admission, 2/1 priority date for domestic students, 2/1 for international students; for winter admission, 9/10 priority date for domestic students, 9/10 for international students. Application fee: $50. Electronic applications accepted. *Expenses: Tuition:* Full-time $5760; part-time $320 per credit. Tuition and fees vary according to student's religious affiliation. *Financial support:* In 2011–12, 36 students received support, including 1 fellowship with partial tuition reimbursement available (averaging $7,100 per year), 18 research assistantships with full tuition reimbursements available (averaging $15,500 per year), 19 teaching assistantships with partial tuition reimbursements available (averaging $14,900 per year); career-related internships or fieldwork, institutionally sponsored loans, scholarships/grants, tuition waivers (full and partial), unspecified assistantships, and tuition awards also available. Financial award application deadline: 2/1. *Faculty research:* Sex differentiation of the brain, exercise physiology, developmental biology, membrane biophysics, neuroscience. *Total annual research expenditures:* $589,241. *Unit head:* Dr. William W. Winder, Chair, 801-422-3093, Fax: 801-422-0700, E-mail: william_winder@byu.edu. *Application contact:* Dr. Dixon J. Woodbury, Graduate Coordinator, 801-422-7562, Fax: 801-422-0700, E-mail: dixon_woodbury@byu.edu. Web site: http://pdbio.byu.edu.

Brown University, Graduate School, Division of Biology and Medicine, Program in Molecular Biology, Cell Biology, and Biochemistry, Providence, RI 02912. Offers biochemistry (M Med Sc, Sc M, PhD), including biochemistry (Sc M, PhD), biology (Sc M, PhD), medical science (M Med Sc, PhD); biology (MA); cell biology (M Med Sc, Sc M, PhD), including biochemistry (Sc M, PhD), biology (Sc M, PhD), medical science (M Med Sc, PhD); developmental biology (M Med Sc, Sc M, PhD), including biochemistry (Sc M, PhD), biology (Sc M, PhD), medical science (M Med Sc, PhD); immunology (M Med Sc, Sc M, PhD), including biochemistry (Sc M, PhD), biology (Sc M, PhD), medical science (M Med Sc, PhD); molecular microbiology (M Med Sc, Sc M, PhD), including biochemistry (Sc M, PhD), biology (Sc M, PhD), medical science (M Med Sc, PhD); MD/PhD. Part-time programs available. Terminal master's awarded for partial completion of doctoral program. *Degree requirements:* For master's, thesis (for some programs); for doctorate, one foreign language, thesis/dissertation, preliminary exam. *Entrance requirements:* For master's and doctorate, GRE General Test, GRE Subject Test. Additional exam requirements/recommendations for international students: Required—TOEFL. Electronic applications accepted. *Faculty research:* Molecular genetics, gene regulation.

California Institute of Technology, Division of Biology, Program in Developmental Biology, Pasadena, CA 91125-0001. Offers PhD. *Degree requirements:* For doctorate, thesis/dissertation, qualifying exam. *Entrance requirements:* For doctorate, GRE General Test.

Carnegie Mellon University, Mellon College of Science, Department of Biological Sciences, Pittsburgh, PA 15213-3891. Offers biochemistry (PhD); biophysics (PhD); cell biology (PhD); computational biology (MS, PhD); developmental biology (PhD); genetics (PhD); molecular biology (PhD); neuroscience (PhD). *Degree requirements:* For doctorate, comprehensive exam, thesis/dissertation. *Entrance requirements:* For doctorate, GRE General Test, GRE Subject Test, interview. Electronic applications accepted. *Faculty research:* Genetic structure, function, and regulation; protein structure and function; biological membranes; biological spectroscopy.

Columbia University, College of Physicians and Surgeons, Department of Genetics and Development, New York, NY 10032. Offers genetics (M Phil, MA, PhD); MD/PhD. Only candidates for the PhD are admitted. Terminal master's awarded for partial completion of doctoral program. *Degree requirements:* For doctorate, thesis/dissertation. *Entrance requirements:* For master's and doctorate, GRE General Test. Additional exam requirements/recommendations for international students: Required—TOEFL. *Faculty research:* Mammalian cell differentiation and meiosis, developmental genetics, yeast and human genetics, chromosome structure, molecular and cellular biology.

Cornell University, Graduate School, Graduate Fields of Agriculture and Life Sciences, Field of Genetics and Development, Ithaca, NY 14853-0001. Offers developmental biology (PhD); genetics (PhD). *Faculty:* 59 full-time (15 women). *Students:* 57 full-time (35 women); includes 6 minority (1 Black or African American, non-Hispanic/Latino; 3 Asian, non-Hispanic/Latino; 2 Hispanic/Latino), 22 international. Average age 26. 66 applicants, 30% accepted, 8 enrolled. In 2011, 4 doctorates awarded. *Degree requirements:* For doctorate, comprehensive exam, thesis/dissertation, 2 semesters of teaching experience. *Entrance requirements:* For doctorate, GRE General Test, GRE Subject Test in biology or biochemistry (recommended), 2 letters of recommendation. Additional exam requirements/recommendations for international students: Required—TOEFL (minimum score 550 paper-based; 213 computer-based; 77 iBT). *Application deadline:* For fall admission, 1/5 for domestic students. Application fee: $95. Electronic applications accepted. *Financial support:* In 2011–12, 17 fellowships with full tuition reimbursements, 30 research assistantships with full tuition reimbursements, 9 teaching assistantships with full tuition reimbursements were awarded; institutionally sponsored loans, scholarships/grants, health care benefits, tuition waivers (full and partial), and unspecified assistantships also available. Financial award applicants required to submit FAFSA. *Faculty research:* Molecular and general genetics, developmental biology and developmental genetics, evolution and population genetics, plant genetics, microbial genetics. *Unit head:* Director of Graduate Studies, 607-254-2100. *Application contact:* Graduate Field Assistant, 607-254-2100, E-mail: gendev@cornell.edu. Web site: http://www.gradschool.cornell.edu/fields.php?id-51&a-2.

Cornell University, Graduate School, Graduate Fields of Agriculture and Life Sciences, Field of Zoology and Wildlife Conservation, Ithaca, NY 14853-0001. Offers animal cytology (MS, PhD); comparative and functional anatomy (MS, PhD); developmental biology (MS, PhD); ecology (MS, PhD); histology (MS, PhD). *Faculty:* 24 full-time (7 women). *Students:* 5 full-time (4 women); includes 1 minority (Two or more races, non-Hispanic/Latino), 2 international. Average age 29. 7 applicants, 14% accepted, 1 enrolled. In 2011, 2 doctorates awarded. *Degree requirements:* For doctorate, comprehensive exam, thesis/dissertation, 2 semesters of teaching experience. *Entrance requirements:* For doctorate, GRE General Test, GRE Subject Test (biology), 2 letters of recommendation. Additional exam requirements/recommendations for international students: Required—TOEFL (minimum score 550 paper-based; 213 computer-based; 77 iBT). *Application deadline:* For fall admission, 2/1 priority date for domestic students. Application fee: $95. Electronic applications accepted. *Financial support:* In 2011–12, 3 research assistantships with full tuition reimbursements, 1 teaching assistantship with full tuition reimbursement were awarded; fellowships with full tuition reimbursements, institutionally sponsored loans, scholarships/grants, health care benefits, tuition waivers (full and partial), and unspecified assistantships also available. Financial award applicants required to submit FAFSA. *Faculty research:* Organismal biology, functional morphology, biomechanics, comparative vertebrate anatomy, comparative invertebrate anatomy, paleontology. *Unit head:* Director of Graduate Studies, 607-253-3276, Fax: 607-253-3756. *Application contact:* Graduate Field Assistant, 607-253-3276, Fax: 607-253-3756, E-mail: graduate_edcvm@cornell.edu. Web site: http://www.gradschool.cornell.edu/fields.php?id-65&a-2.

Cornell University, Graduate School, Graduate Fields of Comparative Biomedical Sciences, Field of Comparative Biomedical Sciences, Ithaca, NY 14853-0001. Offers cellular and molecular medicine (MS, PhD); developmental and reproductive biology (MS, PhD); infectious diseases (MS, PhD); population medicine and epidemiology (MS, PhD); structural and functional biology (MS, PhD). *Faculty:* 97 full-time (27 women). *Students:* 38 full-time (23 women); includes 5 minority (2 Black or African American, non-Hispanic/Latino; 1 Asian, non-Hispanic/Latino; 2 Hispanic/Latino), 15 international. Average age 30. 45 applicants, 22% accepted, 9 enrolled. In 2011, 2 master's, 7 doctorates awarded. *Degree requirements:* For master's, thesis; for doctorate, comprehensive exam, thesis/dissertation. *Entrance requirements:* For master's and doctorate, GRE General Test, 2 letters of recommendation. Additional exam requirements/recommendations for international students: Required—TOEFL (minimum score 550 paper-based; 213 computer-based; 77 iBT). *Application deadline:* For fall admission, 12/15 for domestic students. Application fee: $95. Electronic applications accepted. *Financial support:* In 2011–12, 12 fellowships with full tuition reimbursements, 25 research assistantships with full tuition reimbursements were awarded; teaching assistantships with full tuition reimbursements, institutionally sponsored loans, scholarships/grants, health care benefits, tuition waivers (full and partial), and unspecified assistantships also available. Financial award applicants required to submit FAFSA. *Faculty research:* Receptors and signal transduction, viral and bacterial infectious diseases, tumor metastasis, clinical sciences/nutritional disease, developmental/neurological disorders. *Unit head:* Director of Graduate Studies, 607-253-3276, Fax: 607-253-3756. *Application contact:* Graduate Field Assistant, 607-253-3276, Fax: 607-253-3756, E-mail: graduate_edcvm@cornell.edu. Web site: http://www.gradschool.cornell.edu/fields.php?id-64&a-2.

Duke University, Graduate School, Program in Developmental Biology, Durham, NC 27710. Offers Certificate. *Faculty:* 45 full-time. *Students:* 14 full-time (6 women); includes 3 minority (1 Black or African American, non-Hispanic/Latino; 1 Asian, non-Hispanic/Latino; 1 Hispanic/Latino), 1 international. 65 applicants, 28% accepted, 11 enrolled. *Entrance requirements:* For degree, GRE General Test. Additional exam requirements/recommendations for international students: Required—TOEFL (minimum score 550 paper-based; 213 computer-based; 83 iBT), IELTS (minimum score 7). *Application deadline:* For fall admission, 12/8 priority date for domestic students, 12/8 for international students. Application fee: $75. *Expenses: Tuition:* Full-time $40,720. *Required fees:* $3107. *Financial support:* Application deadline: 12/8. *Unit head:* John Klingensmith, Head, 919-684-6629, Fax: 919-684-8346, E-mail: leslie.mavengere@duke.edu. *Application contact:* Elizabeth Hutton, Director of Admissions, 919-684-3913, Fax: 919-684-2277, E-mail: grad-admissions@duke.edu. Web site: http://www.cmb.duke.edu/dbp/.

Emory University, Laney Graduate School, Division of Biological and Biomedical Sciences, Program in Biochemistry, Cell and Developmental Biology, Atlanta, GA 30322. Offers PhD. *Faculty:* 52 full-time (10 women). *Students:* 53 full-time (34 women); includes 9 minority (1 Black or African American, non-Hispanic/Latino; 4 Asian, non-Hispanic/Latino; 4 Hispanic/Latino), 10 international. Average age 27. 147 applicants, 11% accepted, 7 enrolled. In 2011, 5 doctorates awarded. *Degree requirements:* For doctorate, comprehensive exam, thesis/dissertation. *Entrance requirements:* For

Program in Developmental Biology
Baylor College of Medicine

If you are interested in obtaining a **Ph.D.**

and doing **top-notch research** on exciting topics

related to **stem cell biology,**

the **development of neurons** and neuronal networks,

human developmental diseases,

genes that cause **cancer,**

reproductive development and disease,

cell death, aging,

as well as many other compelling topics,

join the

Program in Developmental Biology
at Baylor College of Medicine (BCM)

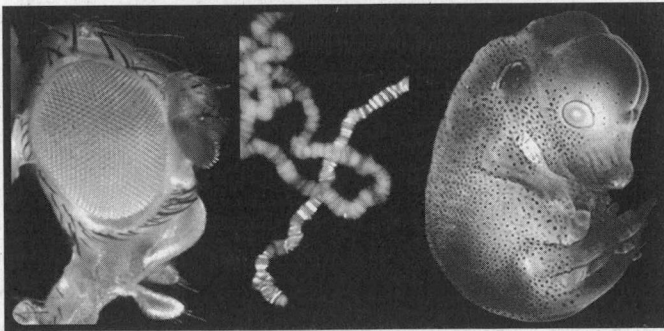

The Program in Developmental Biology at BCM offers a multidisciplinary education in genetics, molecular biology, cell biology, biochemistry, and genomics using different model organisms, including mice, chicken, flies, frogs, worms, and social molds. The Program in Developmental Biology at BCM is interdepartmental and interinstitutional and offers a fun, high quality education to help you pursue a successful career.

Contact Catherine Tasnier
cat@bcm.edu
http://www.bcm.edu/db

We strongly encourage applications from underrepresented minorities, and admit qualified students of any race, sex, sexual orientation, color, national and ethnic origin, disability or age.

doctorate, GRE General Test, minimum GPA of 3.0 in science course work (recommended). Additional exam requirements/recommendations for international students: Required—TOEFL. *Application deadline:* For fall admission, 1/3 for domestic students, 1/1 for international students. Application fee: $75. Electronic applications accepted. *Expenses: Tuition:* Full-time $34,800. *Required fees:* $1300. *Financial support:* In 2011–12, 18 students received support, including 18 fellowships with full tuition reimbursements available (averaging $26,500 per year); institutionally sponsored loans, scholarships/grants, health care benefits, and tuition waivers (full) also available. *Faculty research:* Signal transduction, molecular biology, enzymes and cofactors, receptor and ion channel function, membrane biology. *Unit head:* Dr. Richard Kahn, Program Director, 404-727-3561, Fax: 404-727-3746, E-mail: rkahn@emory.edu. *Application contact:* Kathy Smith, Director of Recruitment and Admissions, 404-727-2547, Fax: 404-727-3322, E-mail: kathy.smith@emory.edu. Web site: http://www.biomed.emory.edu/PROGRAM_SITES/BCDB/.

Illinois State University, Graduate School, College of Arts and Sciences, Department of Biological Sciences, Normal, IL 61790-2200. Offers animal behavior (MS); bacteriology (MS); biochemistry (MS); biological sciences (MS); biology (PhD); biophysics (MS); biotechnology (MS); botany (MS, PhD); cell biology (MS); conservation biology (MS); developmental biology (MS); ecology (MS, PhD); entomology (MS); evolutionary biology (MS); genetics (MS, PhD); immunology (MS); microbiology (MS, PhD); molecular biology (MS); molecular genetics (MS); neurobiology (MS); neuroscience (MS); parasitology (MS); physiology (MS, PhD); plant biology (MS); plant molecular biology (MS); plant sciences (MS); structural biology (MS); zoology (MS, PhD). Part-time programs available. *Degree requirements:* For master's, thesis or alternative; for doctorate, variable foreign language requirement, thesis/dissertation, 2 terms of residency. *Entrance requirements:* For master's, GRE General Test, minimum GPA of 2.6 in last 60 hours of course work; for doctorate, GRE General Test. *Faculty research:* Redoc balance and drug development in schistosoma mansoni, control of the growth of listeria monocytogenes at low temperature, regulation of cell expansion and microtubule function by SPRI, CRUI: physiology and fitness consequences of different life history phenotypes.

Iowa State University of Science and Technology, Program in Molecular, Cellular, and Developmental Biology, Ames, IA 50011. Offers MS, PhD. *Entrance requirements:* For master's and doctorate, GRE General Test. Additional exam requirements/recommendations for international students: Required—TOEFL (minimum score 580 paper-based; 85 iBT), IELTS (minimum score 7). *Application deadline:* For fall admission, 1/15 priority date for domestic students, 1/15 for international students. Application fee: $40 ($90 for international students). Electronic applications accepted. *Unit head:* Dr. Clark Ford, Director of Graduate Education, 515-294-7252, Fax: 515-294-6790, E-mail: idgp@iastate.edu. *Application contact:* Katie Blair, Application Contact, 515-294-7252, Fax: 515-924-6790, E-mail: idgp@iastate.edu. Web site: http://www.mcdb.iastate.edu.

The Johns Hopkins University, National Institutes of Health Sponsored Programs, Baltimore, MD 21218-2699. Offers biology (PhD), including biochemistry, biophysics, cell biology, developmental biology, genetic biology, molecular biology; cell, molecular, and developmental biology and biophysics (PhD). *Degree requirements:* For doctorate, comprehensive exam, thesis/dissertation. *Entrance requirements:* For doctorate, GRE General Test. Additional exam requirements/recommendations for international students: Required—TOEFL (minimum score 600 paper-based; 250 computer-based), TWE. Electronic applications accepted. *Faculty research:* Protein and nucleic acid biochemistry and biophysical chemistry, molecular biology and development.

Louisiana State University Health Sciences Center, School of Graduate Studies in New Orleans, Department of Cell Biology and Anatomy, New Orleans, LA 70112-2223. Offers cell biology and anatomy (MS, PhD), including cell biology, developmental biology, neurobiology and anatomy; MD/PhD. *Degree requirements:* For master's, comprehensive exam, thesis; for doctorate, comprehensive exam, thesis/dissertation. *Entrance requirements:* For master's and doctorate, GRE General Test, GRE Subject Test, minimum undergraduate GPA of 3.0. Additional exam requirements/recommendations for international students: Required—TOEFL. *Faculty research:* Visual system organization, neural development, plasticity of sensory systems, information processing through the nervous system, visuomotor integration.

Marquette University, Graduate School, College of Arts and Sciences, Department of Biology, Milwaukee, WI 53201-1881. Offers cell biology (MS, PhD); developmental biology (MS, PhD); ecology (MS, PhD); epithelial physiology (MS, PhD); genetics (MS, PhD); microbiology (MS, PhD); molecular biology (MS, PhD); muscle and exercise physiology (MS, PhD); neuroscience (PhD). *Faculty:* 23 full-time (11 women), 1 part-time/adjunct (0 women). *Students:* 33 full-time (14 women), 6 part-time (3 women), 19 international. Average age 25. 78 applicants, 17% accepted, 5 enrolled. In 2011, 6 doctorates awarded. Terminal master's awarded for partial completion of doctoral program. *Degree requirements:* For master's, comprehensive exam, thesis, 1 year of teaching experience or equivalent; for doctorate, thesis/dissertation, 1 year of teaching experience or equivalent, qualifying exam. *Entrance requirements:* For master's and doctorate, GRE General Test, GRE Subject Test, official transcripts from all current and previous colleges/universities except Marquette, statement of professional goals and aspirations, three letters of recommendation. Additional exam requirements/recommendations for international students: Required—TOEFL (minimum score 530 paper-based; 78 computer-based). *Application deadline:* For fall admission, 12/15 for domestic and international students. Application fee: $50. Electronic applications accepted. *Expenses: Tuition:* Full-time $17,010; part-time $945 per credit hour. Tuition and fees vary according to program. *Financial support:* In 2011–12, 39 students received support, including 6 fellowships (averaging $1,208 per year), 4 research assistantships with full tuition reimbursements available (averaging $21,750 per year), 29 teaching assistantships with full tuition reimbursements available (averaging $21,750 per year); scholarships/grants, health care benefits, tuition waivers (full and partial), and unspecified assistantships also available. Support available to part-time students. Financial award application deadline: 2/15. *Faculty research:* Neurobiology, neuroendocrinology, epithelial physiology, neuropeptide interactions, synaptic transmission. *Total annual research expenditures:* $2 million. *Unit head:* Dr. Robert Fitts, Chair, 414-288-1748, Fax: 414-288-7357. *Application contact:* Debbie Weaver, Administrative Assistant, 414-288-7355, Fax: 414-288-7357. Web site: http://www.marquette.edu/biology/.

Massachusetts Institute of Technology, School of Science, Department of Biology, Cambridge, MA 02139. Offers biochemistry (PhD); biological oceanography (PhD); biology (PhD); biophysical chemistry and molecular structure (PhD); cell biology (PhD); computational and systems biology (PhD); developmental biology (PhD); genetics (PhD); immunology (PhD); microbiology (PhD); molecular biology (PhD); neurobiology (PhD). *Faculty:* 58 full-time (15 women). *Students:* 248 full-time (129 women); includes 69 minority (5 Black or African American, non-Hispanic/Latino; 1 American Indian or Alaska Native, non-Hispanic/Latino; 25 Asian, non-Hispanic/Latino; 31 Hispanic/Latino; 7 Two or more races, non-Hispanic/Latino), 36 international. Average age 26. 698 applicants, 15% accepted, 44 enrolled. In 2011, 38 doctorates awarded. *Degree requirements:* For doctorate, comprehensive exam, thesis/dissertation. *Entrance requirements:* For doctorate, GRE General Test. Additional exam requirements/

recommendations for international students: Required—TOEFL (minimum score 577 paper-based; 233 computer-based), IELTS (minimum score 6.5). *Application deadline:* For fall admission, 12/1 for domestic and international students. Application fee: $75. Electronic applications accepted. *Expenses: Tuition:* Full-time $40,460; part-time $630 per credit hour. *Required fees:* $272. *Financial support:* In 2011–12, 214 students received support, including 129 fellowships (averaging $33,200 per year), 117 research assistantships (averaging $32,900 per year); teaching assistantships, Federal Work-Study, institutionally sponsored loans, scholarships/grants, traineeships, health care benefits, and unspecified assistantships also available. *Faculty research:* Cellular, developmental and molecular (plant and animal) biology; biochemistry, bioengineering, biophysics and structural biology; classical and molecular genetics; immunology and microbiology; cancer biology, molecular medicine, neurobiology and human disease; computational and systems biology. *Total annual research expenditures:* $53.6 million. *Unit head:* Prof. Tania A. Baker, Head, 617-253-4701, E-mail: mitbio@mit.edu. *Application contact:* Biology Education Office, 617-253-3717, Fax: 617-258-9329, E-mail: gradbio@mit.edu. Web site: https://biology.mit.edu/.

Medical University of South Carolina, College of Graduate Studies, Program in Molecular and Cellular Biology and Pathobiology, Charleston, SC 29425. Offers cancer biology (PhD); cardiovascular biology (PhD); cardiovascular imaging (PhD); cell regulation (PhD); craniofacial biology (PhD); genetics and development (PhD); marine biomedicine (PhD); DMD/PhD; MD/PhD. *Faculty:* 137 full-time (33 women). *Students:* 28 full-time (23 women); includes 5 minority (4 Black or African American, non-Hispanic/Latino; 1 Hispanic/Latino), 5 international. Average age 30. In 2011, 16 doctorates awarded. *Degree requirements:* For doctorate, thesis/dissertation, oral and written exams. *Entrance requirements:* For doctorate, GRE General Test, interview, minimum GPA of 3.0. Additional exam requirements/recommendations for international students: Required—TOEFL (minimum score 600 paper-based; 250 computer-based; 100 iBT). *Application deadline:* For fall admission, 1/15 priority date for domestic students, 1/15 for international students. Applications are processed on a rolling basis. Application fee: $0 ($85 for international students). Electronic applications accepted. *Financial support:* In 2011–12, 39 research assistantships with partial tuition reimbursements (averaging $23,000 per year) were awarded; Federal Work-Study and scholarships/grants also available. Support available to part-time students. Financial award application deadline: 3/10; financial award applicants required to submit FAFSA. *Unit head:* Dr. Donald R. Menick, Director, 843-876-5045, Fax: 843-792-6590, E-mail: menickd@musc.edu. *Application contact:* Dr. Cynthia F. Wright, Associate Dean for Admissions and Career Development, 843-792-2564, Fax: 843-792-6590, E-mail: wrightcf@musc.edu. Web site: http://www.musc.edu/mcbp/.

New York University, Graduate School of Arts and Science, Department of Biology, New York, NY 10012-1019. Offers biology (PhD); biomedical journalism (MS); cancer and molecular biology (PhD); computational biology (PhD); computers in biological research (MS); developmental genetics (PhD); general biology (MS); immunology and microbiology (PhD); molecular genetics (PhD); neurobiology (PhD); oral biology (MS); plant biology (PhD); recombinant DNA technology (MS); MS/MBA. Part-time programs available. *Faculty:* 24 full-time (5 women). *Students:* 146 full-time (90 women), 54 part-time (36 women); includes 49 minority (1 Black or African American, non-Hispanic/Latino; 33 Asian, non-Hispanic/Latino; 12 Hispanic/Latino; 3 Two or more races, non-Hispanic/Latino), 89 international. Average age 27. 394 applicants, 62% accepted, 82 enrolled. In 2011, 68 master's, 6 doctorates awarded. Terminal master's awarded for partial completion of doctoral program. *Degree requirements:* For master's, thesis or alternative, qualifying paper; for doctorate, comprehensive exam, thesis/dissertation. *Entrance requirements:* For master's, GRE General Test; for doctorate, GRE General Test, GRE Subject Test. Additional exam requirements/recommendations for international students: Required—TOEFL. *Application deadline:* For fall admission, 12/1 priority date for domestic students, 12/1 for international students. Application fee: $90. *Financial support:* Fellowships with tuition reimbursements, research assistantships with tuition reimbursements, teaching assistantships with tuition reimbursements, career-related internships or fieldwork, Federal Work-Study, institutionally sponsored loans, scholarships/grants, health care benefits, and unspecified assistantships available. Financial award application deadline: 12/1; financial award applicants required to submit FAFSA. *Faculty research:* Genomics, molecular and cell biology, development and molecular genetics, molecular evolution of plants and animals. *Unit head:* Stephen Small, Chair, 212-998-8200, Fax: 212-995-4015, E-mail: biology@nyu.edu. *Application contact:* Justin Blau, Director of Graduate Studies, 212-998-8200, Fax: 212-995-4015, E-mail: biology@nyu.edu. Web site: http://biology.as.nyu.edu/.

New York University, School of Medicine, New York, NY 10012-1019. Offers biomedical sciences (PhD), including biomedical imaging, cellular and molecular biology, computational biology, developmental genetics, medical and molecular parasitology, microbiology, molecular oncobiology and immunology, neuroscience and physiology, pathobiology, pharmacology, structural biology; clinical investigation (MS); medicine (MD); MD/MA; MD/MPA; MD/MS; MD/PhD. *Accreditation:* LCME/AMA (one or more programs are accredited). *Degree requirements:* For master's, comprehensive exam, thesis; for doctorate, comprehensive exam (for some programs), thesis/dissertation (for some programs). *Entrance requirements:* For doctorate, MCAT (for MD). Additional exam requirements/recommendations for international students: Required—TOEFL. *Expenses:* Contact institution. *Faculty research:* AIDS, cancer, neuroscience, molecular biology, neuroscience, cell biology and molecular genetics, structural biology, microbial pathogenesis and host defense, pharmacology, molecular oncology and immunology.

New York University, School of Medicine and Graduate School of Arts and Science, Sackler Institute of Graduate Biomedical Sciences, Program in Developmental Genetics, New York, NY 10012-1019. Offers PhD. *Students:* 19 full-time (13 women); includes 4 minority (1 American Indian or Alaska Native, non-Hispanic/Latino; 2 Asian, non-Hispanic/Latino; 1 Hispanic/Latino), 4 international. *Unit head:* Dr. Joel D. Oppenheim, Senior Associate Dean for Graduate Studies, 212-263-8001, Fax: 212-263-7600. *Application contact:* Lisabeth Greene, Program Coordinator, 212-263-5648, Fax: 212-263-7600, E-mail: sackler-info@med.nyu.edu. Web site: http://www.med.nyu.edu/dgp/index.html.

New York University, School of Medicine and Graduate School of Arts and Science, Sackler Institute of Graduate Biomedical Sciences, Program in Stem Cell Biology, New York, NY 10012-1019. Offers PhD. *Students:* 4 full-time (2 women); includes 1 minority (Hispanic/Latino), 2 international. *Unit head:* Dr. Joel D. Oppenheim, Senior Associate Dean for Graduate Studies, 212-263-8001, Fax: 212-263-7600. *Application contact:* Lisabeth Greene, Program Coordinator, 212-263-5648, Fax: 212-263-7600, E-mail: sackler-info@med.nyu.edu. Web site: http://sackler.med.nyu.edu/graduate/training-programs/stem-cell-biology.

Northwestern University, The Graduate School, Interdepartmental Biological Sciences Program (IBiS), Evanston, IL 60208. Offers biochemistry, molecular biology, and cell biology (PhD), including biochemistry, cell and molecular biology, molecular biophysics, structural biology; biotechnology (PhD); cell and molecular biology (PhD); developmental biology and genetics (PhD); hormone action and signal transduction (PhD); neuroscience (PhD); structural biology, biochemistry, and biophysics (PhD). Program participants include the Departments of Biochemistry, Molecular Biology, and Cell Biology; Chemistry; Neurobiology and Physiology; Chemical Engineering; Civil Engineering; and Evanston Hospital. *Degree requirements:* For doctorate, thesis/dissertation, qualifying exam. *Entrance requirements:* For doctorate, GRE General Test. Additional exam requirements/recommendations for international students: Required—TOEFL (minimum score 600 paper-based). Electronic applications accepted. *Faculty research:* Developmental genetics, gene regulation, DNA-protein interactions, biological clocks, bioremediation.

Northwestern University, Northwestern University Feinberg School of Medicine and Interdepartmental Programs, Integrated Graduate Programs in the Life Sciences, Chicago, IL 60611. Offers cancer biology (PhD); cell biology (PhD); developmental biology (PhD); evolutionary biology (PhD); immunology and microbial pathogenesis (PhD); molecular biology and genetics (PhD); neurobiology (PhD); pharmacology and toxicology (PhD); structural biology and biochemistry (PhD). *Degree requirements:* For doctorate, comprehensive exam, thesis/dissertation, written and oral qualifying exams. *Entrance requirements:* For doctorate, GRE General Test. Additional exam requirements/recommendations for international students: Required—TOEFL (minimum score 600 paper-based; 250 computer-based). Electronic applications accepted.

The Ohio State University, Graduate School, College of Arts and Sciences, Division of Natural and Mathematical Sciences, Department of Molecular Genetics, Columbus, OH 43210. Offers cell and developmental biology (MS, PhD); genetics (MS, PhD); molecular biology (MS, PhD). *Faculty:* 23. *Students:* 11 full-time (5 women), 23 part-time (11 women); includes 1 minority (Black or African American, non-Hispanic/Latino), 15 international. Average age 26. In 2011, 8 doctorates awarded. *Degree requirements:* For master's, thesis; for doctorate, thesis/dissertation. *Entrance requirements:* For master's and doctorate, GRE General Test, GRE Subject Test in biology or biochemistry (recommended). Additional exam requirements/recommendations for international students: Required—TOEFL (minimum score 550 paper-based; 250 computer-based; 79 iBT), Michigan English Language Assessment Battery (minimum score 82). *Application deadline:* For fall admission, 8/15 priority date for domestic students, 7/1 for international students; for winter admission, 12/1 priority date for domestic students, 11/1 for international students; for spring admission, 3/1 priority date for domestic students, 2/1 for international students. Applications are processed on a rolling basis. Application fee: $40 ($50 for international students). Electronic applications accepted. *Expenses:* Tuition, state resident: full-time $11,400. Tuition, nonresident: full-time $28,125. Tuition and fees vary according to course load, degree level, campus/location and program. *Financial support:* Fellowships, research assistantships, teaching assistantships, Federal Work-Study, and institutionally sponsored loans available. Support available to part-time students. *Unit head:* Dr. Anita Hopper, Chair, 614-688-3306, Fax: 614-292-4466, E-mail: hopper.64@osu.edu. *Application contact:* Graduate Admissions, 614-292-6031, Fax: 614-292-3656, E-mail: gradadmissions@osu.edu. Web site: https://molgen.osu.edu/.

The Ohio State University, Graduate School, College of Arts and Sciences, Division of Natural and Mathematical Sciences, Program in Molecular, Cellular and Developmental Biology, Columbus, OH 43210. Offers MS, PhD. *Faculty:* 169. *Students:* 62 full-time (38 women), 66 part-time (36 women); includes 17 minority (8 Asian, non-Hispanic/Latino; 7 Hispanic/Latino; 2 Two or more races, non-Hispanic/Latino), 70 international. Average age 27. In 2011, 6 master's, 19 doctorates awarded. *Degree requirements:* For master's, thesis; for doctorate, thesis/dissertation. *Entrance requirements:* For master's and doctorate, GRE General Test, GRE Subject Test (biology or biochemistry, cell and molecular biology). Additional exam requirements/recommendations for international students: Required—TOEFL (minimum score 550 paper-based; 250 computer-based; 79 iBT), Michigan English Language Assessment Battery (minimum score 82). *Application deadline:* For fall admission, 8/15 priority date for domestic students, 7/1 for international students; for winter admission, 12/1 priority date for domestic students, 11/1 for international students; for spring admission, 3/1 priority date for domestic students, 2/1 for international students. Applications are processed on a rolling basis. Application fee: $40 ($50 for international students). Electronic applications accepted. *Expenses:* Tuition, state resident: full-time $11,400. Tuition, nonresident: full-time $28,125. Tuition and fees vary according to course load, degree level, campus/location and program. *Unit head:* David M. Bisaro, Director, 614-292-3281, Fax: 614-292-4466, E-mail: bisaro.1@osu.edu. *Application contact:* Graduate Admissions, 614-292-6031, Fax: 614-292-3656, E-mail: gradadmissions@osu.edu. Web site: http://www.biosci.ohio-state.edu/~mcdb/.

Oregon Health & Science University, School of Medicine, Graduate Programs in Medicine, Program in Molecular and Cellular Biosciences, Department of Cell and Developmental Biology, Portland, OR 97239-3098. Offers PhD. *Faculty:* 10 full-time (2 women), 1 part-time/adjunct. *Students:* 27 full-time (12 women); includes 3 minority (1 Asian, non-Hispanic/Latino; 1 Native Hawaiian or other Pacific Islander, non-Hispanic/Latino; 1 Two or more races, non-Hispanic/Latino), 9 international. Average age 30. In 2011, 5 doctorates awarded. *Degree requirements:* For doctorate, comprehensive exam, thesis/dissertation, qualifying exam. *Entrance requirements:* For doctorate, GRE General Test (minimum scores: 153 Verbal/148 Quantitative/4.5 Analytical) or MCAT. Additional exam requirements/recommendations for international students: Required—TOEFL. *Financial support:* Health care benefits, tuition waivers (full), and full tuition and stipends available. *Faculty research:* Developmental mechanisms, molecular biology of cancer, molecular neurobiology, intracellular signaling, growth factors and development. *Unit head:* Dr. Richard Maurer, Program Director, 503-494-7811, E-mail: maurerr@ohsu.edu. *Application contact:* Elaine Offield, Program Coordinator, 503-494-5824, E-mail: offielde@ohsu.edu. Web site: http://www.ohsu.edu/cellbio.

Purdue University, Graduate School, College of Science, Department of Biological Sciences, West Lafayette, IN 47907. Offers biochemistry (PhD); biophysics (PhD); cell and developmental biology (PhD); ecology, evolutionary and population biology (MS, PhD), including ecology, evolutionary biology, population biology; genetics (MS, PhD); microbiology (MS, PhD); molecular biology (PhD); neurobiology (MS, PhD); plant physiology (PhD). *Faculty:* 57 full-time (15 women), 4 part-time/adjunct (1 woman). *Students:* 94 full-time (54 women), 9 part-time (5 women); includes 7 minority (2 Black or African American, non-Hispanic/Latino; 3 Asian, non-Hispanic/Latino; 2 Hispanic/Latino), 51 international. Average age 27. 246 applicants, 11% accepted, 18 enrolled. In 2011, 9 master's, 23 doctorates awarded. Terminal master's awarded for partial completion of doctoral program. *Degree requirements:* For master's, thesis (for some programs); for doctorate, thesis/dissertation, seminars, teaching experience. *Entrance requirements:* For master's, GRE General Test, minimum analytical writing score of 3.5, minimum undergraduate GPA of 3.0; for doctorate, GRE General Test, minimum analytical writing score of 3.5, minimum undergraduate GPA of 3.5. Additional exam requirements/recommendations for international students: Required—TOEFL (minimum score 600 paper-based; 107 iBT) for MS; TOEFL (minimum score 600 paper-based; 80 iBT) for Ph D. *Application deadline:* For fall admission, 12/7 for domestic and international students. Applications are processed on a rolling basis. Application fee: $60 ($75 for international students). Electronic applications accepted. *Financial support:* Fellowships, research assistantships, and teaching assistantships available. Support available to part-time students. Financial award application deadline: 2/15; financial award applicants required to submit FAFSA. *Unit head:* Dr. Richard J. Kuhn, Head, 765-494-4407, E-mail: kuhnr@purdue.edu. *Application contact:* Georgina E. Rupp, Graduate

Coordinator, 765-494-8142, Fax: 765-494-0876, E-mail: ruppg@purdue.edu. Web site: http://www.bio.purdue.edu/.

Rutgers, The State University of New Jersey, New Brunswick, Graduate School-New Brunswick, Programs in the Molecular Biosciences, Program in Cell and Developmental Biology, Piscataway, NJ 08854-8097. Offers MS, PhD. MS, PhD offered jointly with University of Medicine and Dentistry of New Jersey. Part-time programs available. Terminal master's awarded for partial completion of doctoral program. *Degree requirements:* For master's, thesis; for doctorate, thesis/dissertation, written qualifying exam. *Entrance requirements:* For master's, GRE General Test; for doctorate, GRE General Test, GRE Subject Test (recommended), minimum GPA of 3.0. Additional exam requirements/recommendations for international students: Required—TOEFL. Electronic applications accepted. *Faculty research:* Signal transduction and regulation of gene expression, developmental biology, cellular biology, developmental genetics, neurobiology.

San Francisco State University, Division of Graduate Studies, College of Science and Engineering, Department of Biology, Professional Science Master's Program, San Francisco, CA 94132-1722. Offers biotechnology (PSM); stem cell science (PSM). *Unit head:* Dr. Lily Chen, Director, 415-338-6763, E-mail: lilychen@sfsu.edu. *Application contact:* Dr. Linda H. Chen, Program Coordinator, 415-338-1696, E-mail: psm@sfsu.edu. Web site: http://www.sfsu.edu/~psm/.

Stanford University, School of Medicine, Graduate Programs in Medicine, Department of Developmental Biology, Stanford, CA 94305-9991. Offers PhD. *Degree requirements:* For doctorate, thesis/dissertation, qualifying examination. *Entrance requirements:* For doctorate, GRE General Test, GRE Subject Test. Additional exam requirements/recommendations for international students: Required—TOEFL. Electronic applications accepted. *Expenses: Tuition:* Full-time $40,050; part-time $890 per credit. *Faculty research:* Mammalian embryology, developmental genetics with particular emphasis on microbial systems, &ITDictyostelium&RO, &ITDrosophila&RO, the nematode, and the mouse.

Stony Brook University, State University of New York, Graduate School, College of Arts and Sciences, Department of Biochemistry and Cell Biology, Stony Brook, NY 11794. Offers biochemistry and structural biology (PhD); molecular and cellular biology (MA, PhD), including biochemistry and molecular biology (PhD), biological sciences (MA), cellular and developmental biology (PhD), immunology and pathology (PhD), molecular and cellular biology (PhD). *Degree requirements:* For doctorate, comprehensive exam, thesis/dissertation, teaching experience. *Entrance requirements:* For doctorate, GRE General Test, GRE Subject Test. Additional exam requirements/recommendations for international students: Required—TOEFL. *Faculty research:* Genome organization and replication, cell surface dynamics, enzyme structure and mechanism, developmental and regulatory biology.

Stony Brook University, State University of New York, Graduate School, College of Arts and Sciences, Department of Biochemistry and Cell Biology, Molecular and Cellular Biology Program, Specialization in Cellular and Developmental Biology, Stony Brook, NY 11794. Offers PhD. *Degree requirements:* For doctorate, one foreign language, comprehensive exam, thesis/dissertation, teaching experience. *Entrance requirements:* For doctorate, GRE General Test, GRE Subject Test. Additional exam requirements/recommendations for international students: Required—TOEFL.

Thomas Jefferson University, Jefferson College of Graduate Studies, MS Program in Cell and Developmental Biology, Philadelphia, PA 19107. Offers MS. Part-time and evening/weekend programs available. *Faculty:* 22 full-time (7 women), 23 part-time/adjunct (6 women). *Students:* 17 part-time (11 women); includes 2 minority (both Asian, non-Hispanic/Latino), 1 international. 19 applicants, 58% accepted, 10 enrolled. In 2011, 3 master's awarded. *Degree requirements:* For master's, thesis, clerkship. *Entrance requirements:* For master's, GRE General Test or MCAT, minimum GPA of 3.0. Additional exam requirements/recommendations for international students: Required—TOEFL (minimum score 100 iBT) or IELTS (minimum score 7). *Application deadline:* For fall admission, 8/1 priority date for domestic students, 3/1 for international students; for winter admission, 12/1 priority date for domestic students, 6/1 for international students; for spring admission, 4/1 priority date for domestic students. Applications are processed on a rolling basis. Application fee: $50. Electronic applications accepted. *Financial support:* In 2011–12, 7 students received support. Federal Work-Study and institutionally sponsored loans available. Support available to part-time students. Financial award application deadline: 5/1; financial award applicants required to submit FAFSA. *Faculty research:* Developmental biology, cell biology, planning and management, drug development. *Unit head:* Dr. Gerald B. Grunwald, Dean and Program Director, 215-503-4191, Fax: 215-503-6690, E-mail: gerald.grunwald@jefferson.edu. *Application contact:* Eleanor M. Gorman, Assistant Coordinator, Graduate Center Programs, 215-503-5799, Fax: 215-503-3433, E-mail: eleanor.gorman@jefferson.edu. Web site: http://www.jefferson.edu/jcgs/msbs/.

Thomas Jefferson University, Jefferson College of Graduate Studies, PhD Program in Cell and Developmental Biology, Philadelphia, PA 19107. Offers PhD. *Faculty:* 73 full-time (17 women). *Students:* 28 full-time (15 women); includes 4 minority (2 Asian, non-Hispanic/Latino; 2 Hispanic/Latino), 4 international. 58 applicants, 12% accepted, 5 enrolled. In 2011, 3 doctorates awarded. *Degree requirements:* For doctorate, comprehensive exam, thesis/dissertation. *Entrance requirements:* For doctorate, GRE General Test, minimum GPA of 3.2. Additional exam requirements/recommendations for international students: Required—TOEFL (minimum score 250 computer-based; 100 iBT). *Application deadline:* For fall admission, 1/5 priority date for domestic students, 1/5 for international students. Applications are processed on a rolling basis. Application fee: $50. Electronic applications accepted. *Financial support:* In 2011–12, 28 students received support, including 28 fellowships with full tuition reimbursements available (averaging $54,758 per year); Federal Work-Study, institutionally sponsored loans, scholarships/grants, traineeships, and stipends also available. Support available to part-time students. Financial award application deadline: 5/1; financial award applicants required to submit FAFSA. *Total annual research expenditures:* $31.8 million. *Unit head:* Dr. Theodore F. Taraschi, Program Director, 215-503-5020, Fax: 215-503-0206, E-mail: theodore.taraschi@jefferson.edu. *Application contact:* Marc E. Stearns, Director of Admissions, 215-503-0155, Fax: 215-503-9920, E-mail: jcgs-info@jefferson.edu. Web site: http://www.jefferson.edu/jcgs/phd/mcb/.

Tufts University, Sackler School of Graduate Biomedical Sciences, Cell, Molecular and Developmental Biology Program, Medford, MA 02155. Offers PhD. *Faculty:* 39 full-time (15 women). *Students:* 26 full-time (12 women); includes 5 minority (3 Asian, non-Hispanic/Latino; 1 Hispanic/Latino; 1 Two or more races, non-Hispanic/Latino), 4 international. Average age 29. In 2011, 8 doctorates awarded. Terminal master's awarded for partial completion of doctoral program. *Degree requirements:* For doctorate, thesis/dissertation. *Entrance requirements:* For doctorate, GRE General Test, 3 letters of reference. Additional exam requirements/recommendations for international students: Required—TOEFL (minimum score 600 paper-based; 250 computer-based; 100 iBT). *Application deadline:* For fall admission, 12/15 for domestic and international students. Application fee: $70. Electronic applications accepted. *Expenses: Tuition:* Full-time $41,208; part-time $1030 per credit hour. Full-time tuition and fees vary according to degree level, program and student level. Part-time tuition and fees vary according to

course load. *Financial support:* In 2011–12, 25 students received support, including 25 research assistantships with full tuition reimbursements available (averaging $30,000 per year); fellowships and health care benefits also available. *Faculty research:* Reproduction and hormone action, control of gene expression, cell-matrix and cell-cell interactions, growth control and tumorigenesis, cytoskeleton and contractile proteins. *Unit head:* Dr. John Castellot, Program Director, 617-636-0303, Fax: 617-636-0375. *Application contact:* Kellie Johnston, Associate Director of Admissions, 617-636-6767, Fax: 617-636-0375, E-mail: sackler-school@tufts.edu. Web site: http://sackler.tufts.edu/Academics/Degree-Programs/PhD-Programs/Cell-Molecular-and-Developmental-Biology.

University at Albany, State University of New York, College of Arts and Sciences, Department of Biological Sciences, Specialization in Molecular, Cellular, Developmental, and Neural Biology, Albany, NY 12222-0001. Offers MS, PhD. *Degree requirements:* For master's, one foreign language; for doctorate, one foreign language, thesis/dissertation. *Entrance requirements:* For master's and doctorate, GRE General Test.

University of California, Davis, Graduate Studies, Graduate Group in Cell and Developmental Biology, Davis, CA 95616. Offers MS, PhD. *Degree requirements:* For master's, comprehensive exam (for some programs), thesis (for some programs); for doctorate, thesis/dissertation. *Entrance requirements:* For doctorate, GRE General Test, GRE Subject Test. Additional exam requirements/recommendations for international students: Required—TOEFL (minimum score 550 paper-based; 213 computer-based). Electronic applications accepted. *Faculty research:* Molecular basis of cell function and development.

University of California, Irvine, School of Biological Sciences, Department of Developmental and Cell Biology, Irvine, CA 92697. Offers biological sciences (MS, PhD). *Students:* 36 full-time (20 women), 2 part-time (1 woman); includes 22 minority (1 American Indian or Alaska Native, non-Hispanic/Latino; 13 Asian, non-Hispanic/Latino; 8 Hispanic/Latino), 2 international. Average age 28. In 2011, 10 degrees awarded. *Degree requirements:* For doctorate, thesis/dissertation. *Entrance requirements:* For master's and doctorate, GRE General Test, GRE Subject Test, minimum GPA of 3.0. Additional exam requirements/recommendations for international students: Required—TOEFL (minimum score 550 paper-based; 213 computer-based). *Application deadline:* For fall admission, 12/15 priority date for domestic students, 12/15 for international students. Application fee: $80 ($100 for international students). Electronic applications accepted. *Financial support:* Fellowships, research assistantships with full tuition reimbursements, teaching assistantships, institutionally sponsored loans, traineeships, health care benefits, and unspecified assistantships available. Financial award application deadline: 3/1; financial award applicants required to submit FAFSA. *Faculty research:* Genetics and development, oncogene signaling pathways, gene regulation, tissue regeneration and molecular genetics. *Unit head:* Prof. Ken W. Cho, Chair, 949-824-7950, Fax: 949-824-4709, E-mail: kwcho@uci.edu. *Application contact:* Renee Marie Frigo, Program Manager, 949-824-8145, Fax: 949-824-1965, E-mail: rfrigo@uci.edu. Web site: http://devcell.bio.uci.edu/.

University of California, Los Angeles, Graduate Division, College of Letters and Science, Department of Molecular, Cell and Developmental Biology, Los Angeles, CA 90095. Offers PhD. *Faculty:* 23 full-time (8 women). *Students:* 35 full-time (20 women); includes 16 minority (3 Black or African American, non-Hispanic/Latino; 8 Asian, non-Hispanic/Latino; 5 Hispanic/Latino), 8 international. Average age 28. 1 applicant, 100% accepted, 1 enrolled. In 2011, 7 degrees awarded. *Median time to degree:* Of those who began their doctoral program in fall 2003, 67% received their degree in 8 years or less. *Degree requirements:* For doctorate, thesis/dissertation, qualifying exams. *Entrance requirements:* For doctorate, GRE General Test, GRE Subject Test. Additional exam requirements/recommendations for international students: Required—TOEFL. Application fee: $70 ($90 for international students). Electronic applications accepted. *Financial support:* In 2011–12, 28 fellowships, 29 research assistantships, 9 teaching assistantships were awarded; scholarships/grants, traineeships, and unspecified assistantships also available. Financial award application deadline: 3/1. *Unit head:* Dr. Utpal Banerjee, Chair, 310-206-5439, Fax: 310-206-3987, E-mail: banerjee@mbi.ucla.edu. *Application contact:* UCLA ACCESS Coordinator, 310-206-1845, Fax: 310-206-1636, E-mail: uclaaccess@mednet.ucla.edu. Web site: http://www.mcdb.ucla.edu.

University of California, Riverside, Graduate Division, Program in Cell, Molecular, and Developmental Biology, Riverside, CA 92521-0102. Offers MS, PhD. Terminal master's awarded for partial completion of doctoral program. *Degree requirements:* For master's, thesis, oral defense of thesis; for doctorate, thesis/dissertation, oral defense of thesis, qualifying exams, 2 quarters of teaching experience. *Entrance requirements:* For master's and doctorate, GRE General Test, minimum GPA of 3.2. Additional exam requirements/recommendations for international students: Required—TOEFL (minimum score 550 paper-based; 213 computer-based; 80 iBT). Electronic applications accepted.

University of California, San Diego, Office of Graduate Studies, Division of Biological Sciences, Program in Cell and Developmental Biology, La Jolla, CA 92093-0348. Offers PhD. Offered in association with the Salk Institute. *Degree requirements:* For doctorate, thesis/dissertation, qualifying exam. Electronic applications accepted.

University of California, San Diego, School of Medicine and Office of Graduate Studies, Molecular Pathology Program, La Jolla, CA 92093. Offers bioinformatics (PhD); cancer biology/oncology (PhD); cardiovascular sciences and disease (PhD); microbiology (PhD); molecular pathology (PhD); neurological disease (PhD); stem cell and developmental biology (PhD); structural biology/drug design (PhD). *Entrance requirements:* For doctorate, GRE General Test, GRE Subject Test. Additional exam requirements/recommendations for international students: Required—TOEFL. Electronic applications accepted.

University of California, San Francisco, Graduate Division and School of Medicine, Department of Biochemistry and Biophysics, San Francisco, CA 94143. Offers biochemistry and molecular biology (PhD); cell biology (PhD); developmental biology (PhD); genetics (PhD); MD/PhD. *Degree requirements:* For doctorate, thesis/dissertation. *Entrance requirements:* For doctorate, GRE General Test, GRE Subject Test. Additional exam requirements/recommendations for international students: Required—TOEFL. *Expenses:* Contact institution.

University of California, Santa Barbara, Graduate Division, College of Letters and Sciences, Division of Mathematics, Life, and Physical Sciences, Department of Molecular, Cellular, and Developmental Biology, Santa Barbara, CA 93106-9625. Offers MA, PhD, MA/PhD. *Faculty:* 21 full-time (3 women), 7 part-time/adjunct (2 women). *Students:* 52 full-time (29 women); includes 10 minority (1 Black or African American, non-Hispanic/Latino; 8 Asian, non-Hispanic/Latino; 1 Hispanic/Latino), 2 international. Average age 28. 115 applicants, 18% accepted, 9 enrolled. In 2011, 8 master's, 8 doctorates awarded. Terminal master's awarded for partial completion of doctoral program. *Median time to degree:* Of those who began their doctoral program in fall 2003, 100% received their degree in 8 years or less. *Degree requirements:* For master's, comprehensive exam (for some programs), thesis (for some programs); for doctorate, comprehensive exam, thesis/dissertation. *Entrance requirements:* For master's, GRE General Test, 3 letters of recommendation, resume/curriculum vitae; for doctorate, GRE

General Test, 3 letters of recommendation, statement of purpose, personal achievements/contributions statement, resume/curriculum vitae, transcripts for post-secondary institutions attended. Additional exam requirements/recommendations for international students: Required—TOEFL (minimum score 610 paper-based; 102 iBT), IELTS (minimum score 7). *Application deadline:* For fall admission, 12/20 priority date for domestic students, 12/20 for international students. Application fee: $80 ($100 for international students). Electronic applications accepted. *Expenses:* Tuition, state resident: full-time $12,192. Tuition, nonresident: full-time $27,294. *Required fees:* $764.13. *Financial support:* In 2011–12, 14 students received support, including 14 fellowships with full and partial tuition reimbursements available (averaging $6,562 per year), 40 research assistantships with full and partial tuition reimbursements available (averaging $15,250 per year), 46 teaching assistantships with partial tuition reimbursements available (averaging $10,500 per year); career-related internships or fieldwork, Federal Work-Study, institutionally sponsored loans, scholarships/grants, traineeships, health care benefits, and unspecified assistantships also available. Financial award application deadline: 12/20; financial award applicants required to submit FAFSA. *Faculty research:* Microbiology, neurobiology (including stem cell research), developmental, virology, cell biology. *Unit head:* Dr. Joel H. Rothman, Chair, 805-893-7885, E-mail: joel.rothman@lifesci.ucsb.edu. *Application contact:* Nicole McCoy, Graduate Program Advisor, 805-893-8499, E-mail: nicole.mccoy@lifesci.ucsb.edu. Web site: http://www.lifesci.ucsb.edu/mcdb/programs/graduate/graduate.html.

University of California, Santa Cruz, Division of Graduate Studies, Division of Physical and Biological Sciences, Program in Molecular, Cellular, and Developmental Biology, Santa Cruz, CA 95064. Offers MA, PhD. Terminal master's awarded for partial completion of doctoral program. *Degree requirements:* For master's, thesis; for doctorate, thesis/dissertation, qualifying exam. *Entrance requirements:* For master's and doctorate, GRE General Test, 3 letters of recommendation, interview. Additional exam requirements/recommendations for international students: Required—TOEFL (minimum score 550 paper-based; 220 computer-based; 83 iBT); Recommended—IELTS (minimum score 8). Electronic applications accepted. *Faculty research:* RNA biology, chromatin and chromosome biology, neurobiology, stem cell biology and differentiation, cell structure and function.

University of Chicago, Division of Biological Sciences, Molecular Biosciences Cluster, Committee on Development, Regeneration, and Stem Cell Biology, Chicago, IL 60637-1513. Offers cellular differentiation (PhD); developmental endocrinology (PhD); developmental genetics (PhD); developmental neurobiology (PhD); gene expression (PhD). *Degree requirements:* For doctorate, thesis/dissertation, ethics class, 2 teaching assistantships. *Entrance requirements:* For doctorate, GRE General Test. Additional exam requirements/recommendations for international students: Required—TOEFL (minimum score 600 paper-based; 250 computer-based; 104 iBT), IELTS (minimum score 7). Electronic applications accepted. *Faculty research:* Epidermal differentiation, neural lineages, pattern formation.

University of Cincinnati, Graduate School, College of Medicine, Graduate Programs in Biomedical Sciences, Department of Pediatrics, Program in Molecular and Developmental Biology, Cincinnati, OH 45221. Offers PhD. *Degree requirements:* For doctorate, thesis/dissertation, qualifying exam. *Entrance requirements:* For doctorate, GRE General Test, minimum GPA of 3.2. Additional exam requirements/recommendations for international students: Required—TOEFL (minimum score 520 paper-based; 190 computer-based). Electronic applications accepted. *Faculty research:* Cancer biology, cardiovascular biology, developmental biology, human genetics, gene therapy, genomics and bioinformatics, immunobiology, molecular medicine, neuroscience, pulmonary biology, reproductive biology, stem cell biology.

University of Colorado Boulder, Graduate School, College of Arts and Sciences, Department of Molecular, Cellular, and Developmental Biology, Boulder, CO 80309. Offers cellular structure and function (MA, PhD); developmental biology (MA, PhD); molecular biology (MA, PhD). *Faculty:* 16 full-time (6 women). *Students:* 71 full-time (36 women); includes 4 minority (1 American Indian or Alaska Native, non-Hispanic/Latino; 1 Asian, non-Hispanic/Latino; 2 Hispanic/Latino), 13 international. Average age 28. 259 applicants, 13% accepted, 14 enrolled. In 2011, 3 master's, 11 doctorates awarded. Terminal master's awarded for partial completion of doctoral program. *Degree requirements:* For master's, comprehensive exam, thesis or alternative; for doctorate, comprehensive exam, thesis/dissertation. *Entrance requirements:* For master's, GRE General Test, GRE Subject Test, minimum undergraduate GPA of 3.0; for doctorate, GRE General Test, GRE Subject Test. *Application deadline:* For fall admission, 1/1 for domestic students, 12/1 for international students. Application fee: $50 ($60 for international students). *Financial support:* In 2011–12, 86 students received support, including 44 fellowships (averaging $12,916 per year), 48 research assistantships with tuition reimbursements available (averaging $18,648 per year), 15 teaching assistantships with tuition reimbursements available (averaging $19,818 per year); institutionally sponsored loans, scholarships/grants, health care benefits, and unspecified assistantships also available. Financial award application deadline: 2/1; financial award applicants required to submit FAFSA. *Faculty research:* Molecular biology of RNA and DNA, molecular genetics, cell motility and cytoskeleton, cell membranes, developmental genetics, human genetics. *Total annual research expenditures:* $16.2 million. *Application contact:* E-mail: mcdbgrad@colorado.edu. Web site: http://mcdb.colorado.edu/.

University of Colorado Denver, College of Liberal Arts and Sciences, Department of Integrative Biology, Denver, CO 80217. Offers animal behavior (MS); biology (MS); cell and developmental biology (MS); ecology (MS); evolutionary biology (MS); genetics (MS); microbiology (MS); molecular biology (MS); neurobiology (MS); plant systematics (MS). Part-time programs available. *Faculty:* 16 full-time (8 women). *Students:* 20 full-time (13 women), 5 part-time (4 women); includes 1 minority (Hispanic/Latino), 1 international. Average age 29. 21 applicants, 43% accepted, 5 enrolled. In 2011, 7 master's awarded. *Degree requirements:* For master's, comprehensive exam, thesis or alternative, 30-32 credit hours. *Entrance requirements:* For master's, GRE General Test (minimum score in 50% percentile in each section), BA/BS from accredited institution awarded within the last 10 years; minimum undergraduate GPA of 3.0; prerequisite courses: 1 year each of general biology and general chemistry, and 1 semester each of general genetics, general ecology, cell biology, and a structure/function course. Additional exam requirements/recommendations for international students: Required—TOEFL (minimum score 525 paper-based; 197 computer-based; 71 iBT). *Application deadline:* For fall admission, 2/1 for domestic and international students. Application fee: $50 ($75 for international students). Electronic applications accepted. *Financial support:* Research assistantships, teaching assistantships, Federal Work-Study, scholarships/grants, and unspecified assistantships available. Financial award application deadline: 4/1; financial award applicants required to submit FAFSA. *Faculty research:* Molecular developmental biology; quantitative ecology, biogeography, and population dynamics; environmental signaling and endocrine disruption; speciation, the evolution of reproductive isolation, and hybrid zones; evolutionary, behavioral, and conservation ecology. *Unit head:* Dr. Diana Tomback, Acting Chair, 303-556-2657, E-mail: diana.tomback@ucdenver.edu. *Application contact:* Timberley Roane, Associate Professor/Associate Chair, 303-556-6592, E-mail: timberley.roane@ucdenver.edu. Web site: http://www.ucdenver.edu/academics/colleges/CLAS/Departments/biology/Pages/Biology.aspx.

University of Colorado Denver, School of Medicine, Program in Cell Biology, Stem Cells, and Developmental Biology, Aurora, CO 80045. Offers PhD. *Students:* 28 full-time (17 women); includes 2 minority (both Hispanic/Latino), 4 international. Average age 27. 42 applicants, 12% accepted, 5 enrolled. In 2011, 5 doctorates awarded. *Degree requirements:* For doctorate, comprehensive exam, thesis/dissertation, at least 30 credit hours of coursework and 30 credit hours of thesis research; laboratory rotations. *Entrance requirements:* For doctorate, GRE, minimum GPA of 3.0; 3 letters of reference; prerequisite coursework in organic chemistry, biology, biochemistry, physics and calculus; research experience (highly recommended). Additional exam requirements/recommendations for international students: Required—TOEFL (minimum score 550 paper-based; 213 computer-based). *Application deadline:* For fall admission, 12/1 for domestic students, 11/1 for international students. Application fee: $65. Electronic applications accepted. *Expenses:* Contact institution. *Financial support:* Fellowships, research assistantships, teaching assistantships, health care benefits, tuition waivers (full), and stipend available. Financial award application deadline: 3/15; financial award applicants required to submit FAFSA. *Faculty research:* Development and repair of the vertebrate nervous system; molecular, genetic and developmental mechanisms involved in the patterning of the early spinal cord (neural plate) during vertebrate embryogenesis; structural analysis of protein glycosylation using NMR and mass spectrometry; small RNAs and post-transcriptional gene regulation during nematode gametogenesis and early development; diabetes-mediated changes in cardiovascular gene expression and functional exercise capacity. *Total annual research expenditures:* $5.7 million. *Unit head:* Dr. Wendy Macklin, Department Chair, 303-724-3426, E-mail: wendy.macklin@ucdenver.edu. *Application contact:* Jennifer Thurston, Program Manager, 303-724-5902, Fax: 303-724-3420, E-mail: jennifer.thurston@ucdenver.edu. Web site: http://www.ucdenver.edu/academics/colleges/medicalschool/departments/CellDevelopmentalBiology/Pages/CellDevelopmentalBioHome.aspx.

University of Connecticut, Graduate School, College of Liberal Arts and Sciences, Department of Molecular and Cell Biology, Storrs, CT 06269. Offers applied genomics (MS, PSM); biochemistry (MS, PhD); biophysics and structural biology (MS, PhD); cell and developmental biology (MS, PhD); genetics, genomics, and bioinformatics (MS, PhD); microbial systems analysis (MS, PSM); microbiology (MS, PhD); plant cell and molecular biology (MS, PhD). Terminal master's awarded for partial completion of doctoral program. *Degree requirements:* For master's, comprehensive exam; for doctorate, thesis/dissertation. *Entrance requirements:* For master's and doctorate, GRE General Test, GRE Subject Test. Additional exam requirements/recommendations for international students: Required—TOEFL (minimum score 550 paper-based; 213 computer-based). Electronic applications accepted.

University of Connecticut Health Center, Graduate School, Programs in Biomedical Sciences, Program in Genetics and Developmental Biology, Farmington, CT 06030. Offers PhD, DMD/PhD, MD/PhD. *Degree requirements:* For doctorate, comprehensive exam, thesis/dissertation. *Entrance requirements:* For doctorate, GRE General Test, GRE Subject Test. Additional exam requirements/recommendations for international students: Required—TOEFL (minimum score 600 paper-based; 250 computer-based). Electronic applications accepted. *Faculty research:* Developmental biology, genomic imprinting, RNA biology, RNA alternative splicing, human embryonic stem cells.

See Display on page 299 and Close-Up on page 313.

University of Delaware, College of Arts and Sciences, Department of Biological Sciences, Newark, DE 19716. Offers biotechnology (MS); cancer biology (MS, PhD); cell and extracellular matrix biology (MS, PhD); cell and systems physiology (MS, PhD); developmental biology (MS, PhD); ecology and evolution (MS, PhD); microbiology (MS, PhD); molecular biology and genetics (MS, PhD). Terminal master's awarded for partial completion of doctoral program. *Degree requirements:* For master's, thesis, preliminary exam; for doctorate, comprehensive exam, thesis/dissertation, preliminary exam. *Entrance requirements:* For master's and doctorate, GRE General Test. Additional exam requirements/recommendations for international students: Required—TOEFL (minimum score 600 paper-based; 250 computer-based); Recommended—TWE. Electronic applications accepted. *Faculty research:* Microorganisms, bone, cancer metastasis, developmental biology, cell biology, DNA.

University of Hawaii at Manoa, John A. Burns School of Medicine, Program in Developmental and Reproductive Biology, Honolulu, HI 96813. Offers MS, PhD. Part-time programs available. *Degree requirements:* For doctorate, thesis/dissertation. *Entrance requirements:* For doctorate, GRE General Test, GRE Subject Test. Additional exam requirements/recommendations for international students: Recommended—TOEFL (minimum score 560 paper-based; 83 computer-based), IELTS (minimum score 5). *Faculty research:* Biology of gametes and fertilization, reproductive endocrinology.

University of Illinois at Urbana–Champaign, Graduate College, College of Liberal Arts and Sciences, School of Molecular and Cellular Biology, Department of Cell and Developmental Biology, Champaign, IL 61820. Offers PhD. *Faculty:* 14 full-time (5 women), 1 (woman) part-time/adjunct. *Students:* 40 full-time (21 women), 1 part-time (0 women); includes 7 minority (6 Asian, non-Hispanic/Latino; 1 Hispanic/Latino), 24 international. In 2011, 10 doctorates awarded. *Entrance requirements:* For doctorate, GRE, minimum GPA of 3.0. Additional exam requirements/recommendations for international students: Required—TOEFL (minimum score 590 paper-based; 243 computer-based). *Application deadline:* Applications are processed on a rolling basis. Application fee: $75 ($90 for international students). Electronic applications accepted. *Financial support:* In 2011–12, 6 fellowships, 37 research assistantships, 17 teaching assistantships were awarded; tuition waivers (full and partial) also available. *Unit head:* Andrew Belmont, Head, 217-244-2311, Fax: 217-244-1648, E-mail: asbel@illinois.edu. *Application contact:* Delynn Carter, Assistant to the Head, 217-244-8116, Fax: 217-244-1648, E-mail: dmcarter@illinois.edu. Web site: http://mcb.illinois.edu/departments/cdb/.

The University of Kansas, Graduate Studies, College of Liberal Arts and Sciences, Department of Molecular Biosciences, Lawrence, KS 66044. Offers biochemistry and biophysics (MA, PhD); microbiology (MA, PhD); molecular, cellular, and developmental biology (MA, PhD). *Faculty:* 34. *Students:* 57 full-time (29 women), 2 part-time (1 woman); includes 6 minority (2 Asian, non-Hispanic/Latino; 3 Hispanic/Latino; 1 Two or more races, non-Hispanic/Latino), 26 international. Average age 28. 60 applicants, 30% accepted, 10 enrolled. In 2011, 1 master's, 12 doctorates awarded. Terminal master's awarded for partial completion of doctoral program. *Degree requirements:* For master's, comprehensive exam, thesis; for doctorate, comprehensive exam, thesis/dissertation. *Entrance requirements:* For master's and doctorate, GRE General Test. Additional exam requirements/recommendations for international students: Required—TOEFL or IELTS. *Application deadline:* For fall admission, 12/15 for domestic and international students. Application fee: $55 ($65 for international students). Electronic applications accepted. Tuition and fees vary according to course load, campus/location, program and reciprocity agreements. *Financial support:* Fellowships with tuition reimbursements, research assistantships with tuition reimbursements, teaching assistantships with tuition reimbursements, health care benefits, and unspecified assistantships available. Financial award application deadline: 3/1. *Faculty research:* Structure and function of proteins, genetics of organism development, molecular genetics, neurophysiology,

molecular virology and pathogenics, developmental biology, cell biology. *Unit head:* Dr. Mark Richter, Chair, 785-864-3334, Fax: 785-864-5294, E-mail: richter@ku.edu. *Application contact:* John P. Connolly, Graduate Program Assistant, 785-864-4311, Fax: 785-864-5294, E-mail: jconnolly@ku.edu. Web site: http://www.molecularbiosciences.ku.edu/.

The University of Manchester, Faculty of Life Sciences, Manchester, United Kingdom. Offers adaptive organismal biology (M Phil, PhD); animal biology (M Phil, PhD); biochemistry (M Phil, PhD); bioinformatics (M Phil, PhD); biomolecular sciences (M Phil, PhD); biotechnology (M Phil, PhD); cell biology (M Phil, PhD); cell matrix research (M Phil, PhD); channels and transporters (M Phil, PhD); developmental biology (M Phil, PhD); Egyptology (M Phil, PhD); environmental biology (M Phil, PhD); evolutionary biology (M Phil, PhD); gene expression (M Phil, PhD); genetics (M Phil, PhD); history of science, technology and medicine (M Phil, PhD); immunology (M Phil, PhD); integrative neurobiology and behavior (M Phil, PhD); membrane trafficking (M Phil, PhD); microbiology (M Phil, PhD); molecular and cellular neuroscience (M Phil, PhD); molecular biology (M Phil, PhD); molecular cancer studies (M Phil, PhD); neuroscience (M Phil, PhD); ophthalmology (M Phil, PhD); optometry (M Phil, PhD); organelle function (M Phil, PhD); pharmacology (M Phil, PhD); physiology (M Phil, PhD); plant sciences (M Phil, PhD); stem cell research (M Phil, PhD); structural biology (M Phil, PhD); systems neuroscience (M Phil, PhD); toxicology (M Phil, PhD).

The University of Manchester, School of Dentistry, Manchester, United Kingdom. Offers basic dental sciences (cancer studies) (M Phil, PhD); basic dental sciences (molecular genetics) (M Phil, PhD); basic dental sciences (stem cell biology) (M Phil, PhD); biomaterials sciences and dental technology (M Phil, PhD); dental public health/community dentistry (M Phil, PhD); dental science (clinical) (PhD); endodontology (M Phil, PhD); fixed and removable prosthodontics (M Phil, PhD); operative dentistry (M Phil, PhD); oral and maxillofacial surgery (M Phil, PhD); oral radiology (M Phil, PhD); orthodontics (M Phil, PhD); restorative dentistry (M Phil, PhD).

University of Massachusetts Amherst, Graduate School, Interdisciplinary Programs, Program in Molecular and Cellular Biology, Amherst, MA 01003. Offers biological chemistry and molecular biophysics (PhD); biomedicine (PhD); cellular and developmental biology (PhD). Part-time programs available. *Students:* 62 full-time (40 women), 18 part-time (9 women); includes 14 minority (2 Black or African American, non-Hispanic/Latino; 4 Asian, non-Hispanic/Latino; 7 Hispanic/Latino; 1 Two or more races, non-Hispanic/Latino), 28 international. Average age 27. 138 applicants, 36% accepted, 22 enrolled. In 2011, 8 doctorates awarded. Terminal master's awarded for partial completion of doctoral program. *Degree requirements:* For doctorate, comprehensive exam, thesis/dissertation. *Entrance requirements:* For doctorate, GRE General Test. Additional exam requirements/recommendations for international students: Required—TOEFL (minimum score 550 paper-based; 213 computer-based; 80 iBT), IELTS (minimum score 6.5). *Application deadline:* For fall admission, 12/1 for domestic and international students. Applications are processed on a rolling basis. Application fee: $50 ($65 for international students). Electronic applications accepted. Tuition and fees vary according to course load, campus/location and program. *Financial support:* Fellowships with full and partial tuition reimbursements, research assistantships with full and partial tuition reimbursements, teaching assistantships with full and partial tuition reimbursements, career-related internships or fieldwork, Federal Work-Study, scholarships/grants, traineeships, health care benefits, tuition waivers (full and partial), and unspecified assistantships available. Support available to part-time students. Financial award application deadline: 12/1. *Unit head:* Dr. Barbara Osborne, Graduate Program Director, 413-545-3246, Fax: 413-545-1812. *Application contact:* Lindsay DeSantis, Interim Supervisor of Admissions, 413-545-0722, Fax: 413-577-0010, E-mail: gradadm@grad.umass.edu. Web site: http://www.bio.umass.edu/mcb/.

University of Medicine and Dentistry of New Jersey, Graduate School of Biomedical Sciences, Graduate Programs in Biomedical Sciences–Newark, Newark, NJ 07107. Offers biodefense (Certificate); biomedical engineering (PhD); biomedical sciences (multidisciplinary) (PhD); cellular biology, neuroscience and physiology (PhD), including neuroscience, physiology, biophysics, cardiovascular biology, molecular pharmacology, stem cell biology; infection, immunity and inflammation (PhD), including immunology, infectious disease, microbiology, oral biology; molecular biology, genetics and cancer (PhD), including biochemistry, molecular genetics, cancer biology, radiation biology, bioinformatics; neuroscience (Certificate); pharmacological sciences (Certificate); stem cell (Certificate); DMD/PhD; MD/PhD. PhD in biomedical engineering offered jointly with New Jersey Institute of Technology. Part-time and evening/weekend programs available. Terminal master's awarded for partial completion of doctoral program. *Degree requirements:* For doctorate, thesis/dissertation, qualifying exam. *Entrance requirements:* For doctorate, GRE General Test. Additional exam requirements/recommendations for international students: Required—TOEFL. Electronic applications accepted.

University of Miami, Graduate School, Miller School of Medicine, Graduate Programs in Medicine, Department of Cell Biology and Anatomy, Coral Gables, FL 33124. Offers molecular cell and developmental biology (PhD); MD/PhD. *Degree requirements:* For doctorate, thesis/dissertation. *Entrance requirements:* For doctorate, GRE General Test, GRE Subject Test. Additional exam requirements/recommendations for international students: Required—TOEFL. Electronic applications accepted.

University of Michigan, Horace H. Rackham School of Graduate Studies, College of Literature, Science, and the Arts, Department of Molecular, Cellular, and Developmental Biology, Ann Arbor, MI 48109. Offers MS, PhD. Part-time programs available. *Faculty:* 33 full-time (10 women). *Students:* 78 full-time (39 women), 5 part-time (2 women); includes 5 minority (3 Asian, non-Hispanic/Latino; 2 Hispanic/Latino), 40 international. Average age 27. 137 applicants, 17% accepted, 12 enrolled. In 2011, 7 master's, 7 doctorates awarded. Terminal master's awarded for partial completion of doctoral program. *Degree requirements:* For master's, 24 credits with at least 16 in molecular, cellular, and developmental biology and 4 in a cognate field; for doctorate, thesis/dissertation, preliminary exam, oral defense. *Entrance requirements:* For master's and doctorate, GRE General Test. Additional exam requirements/recommendations for international students: Required—TOEFL (minimum score 560 paper-based; 220 computer-based; 83 iBT). *Application deadline:* For fall admission, 1/5 for domestic and international students; for winter admission, 11/1 for domestic and international students; for spring admission, 4/1 for domestic and international students. Applications are processed on a rolling basis. Application fee: $65 ($75 for international students). Electronic applications accepted. *Financial support:* In 2011–12, 55 students received support, including 12 fellowships with full tuition reimbursements available (averaging $26,500 per year), 30 research assistantships with full tuition reimbursements available (averaging $26,500 per year), 13 teaching assistantships with full tuition reimbursements available (averaging $26,500 per year); health care benefits also available. *Faculty research:* Cell biology, microbiology, neurobiology and physiology, developmental biology and plant molecular biology. *Unit head:* Dr. Pamela A. Raymond, Department Chair, 734-764-7476, Fax: 734-615-6337, E-mail: praymond@umich.edu. *Application contact:* Mary Carr, Graduate Coordinator, 734-615-1635, Fax: 734-764-0884, E-mail: carrmm@umich.edu. Web site: http://www.mcdb.lsa.umich.edu.

University of Michigan, Horace H. Rackham School of Graduate Studies, Program in Biomedical Sciences (PIBS), Department of Cell and Developmental Biology, Ann Arbor, MI 48109. Offers PhD. *Faculty:* 29 full-time (10 women). *Students:* 15 full-time (7 women); includes 8 minority (all Asian, non-Hispanic/Latino), 3 international. Average age 30. 28 applicants, 25% accepted, 4 enrolled. In 2011, 6 doctorates awarded. *Degree requirements:* For doctorate, thesis/dissertation, oral defense of dissertation, preliminary exam. *Entrance requirements:* For doctorate, GRE General Test, 3 letters of recommendation, research experience. Additional exam requirements/recommendations for international students: Required—TOEFL (minimum score 84 iBT). *Application deadline:* For fall admission, 12/1 for domestic and international students. Application fee: $60 ($75 for international students). Electronic applications accepted. *Financial support:* In 2011–12, 21 students received support, including 21 fellowships (averaging $26,500 per year); scholarships/grants, health care benefits, tuition waivers (full), and unspecified assistantships also available. Financial award application deadline: 12/1. *Faculty research:* Small stress proteins, cellular stress response, muscle, male reproductive, toxicology, cell cytoskeleton. *Total annual research expenditures:* $3.8 million. *Unit head:* Dr. James Douglas Engel, Chair, 734-615-7509, Fax: 734-763-1166, E-mail: engel@umich.edu. *Application contact:* Michelle S. Melis, Director of Student Life, 734-615-6538, Fax: 734-647-7022, E-mail: msmtegan@umich.edu. Web site: http://www.med.umich.edu/cdb/.

University of Minnesota, Twin Cities Campus, Graduate School, Program in Molecular, Cellular, Developmental Biology and Genetics, Minneapolis, MN 55455-0213. Offers genetic counseling (MS); molecular, cellular, developmental biology and genetics (PhD). Terminal master's awarded for partial completion of doctoral program. *Degree requirements:* For master's, thesis optional; for doctorate, thesis/dissertation. *Entrance requirements:* For master's and doctorate, GRE General Test. Additional exam requirements/recommendations for international students: Required—TOEFL (minimum score 625 paper-based; 263 computer-based; 80 iBT). Electronic applications accepted. *Faculty research:* Membrane receptors and membrane transport, cell interactions, cytoskeleton and cell mobility, regulation of gene expression, plant cell and molecular biology.

University of Minnesota, Twin Cities Campus, Graduate School, Stem Cell Biology Graduate Program, Minneapolis, MN 55455-3007. Offers MS. *Degree requirements:* For master's, thesis. *Entrance requirements:* For master's, GRE, BS, BA, or foreign equivalent in biological sciences or related field; minimum undergraduate GPA of 3.2. Additional exam requirements/recommendations for international students: Required—TOEFL (minimum score 580 paper-based, with a minimum score of 4 in the TWE, or 94 Internet-based, with a minimum score of 22 on each of the reading and listening, 26 on the speaking, and 26 on the writing section. *Faculty research:* Stem cell and developmental biology; embryonic stem cells; iPS cells; muscle satellite cells; hematopoietic stem cells; neuronal stem cells; cardiovascular, kidney and limb development; regenerating systems.

The University of North Carolina at Chapel Hill, Graduate School, College of Arts and Sciences, Department of Biology, Chapel Hill, NC 27599. Offers botany (MA, MS, PhD); cell biology, development, and physiology (MA, MS, PhD); cell motility and cytoskeleton (PhD); ecology and behavior (MA, MS, PhD); genetics and molecular biology (MA, MS, PhD); morphology, systematics, and evolution (MA, MS, PhD). Terminal master's awarded for partial completion of doctoral program. *Degree requirements:* For master's, comprehensive exam, thesis (for some programs); for doctorate, comprehensive exam, thesis/dissertation. *Entrance requirements:* For master's, GRE General Test, GRE Subject Test, 2 semesters of calculus or statistics; 2 semesters of physics, organic chemistry; 3 semesters of biology; for doctorate, GRE General Test, GRE Subject Test, 2 semesters calculus or statistics, 2 semesters physics, organic chemistry, 3 semesters of biology. Additional exam requirements/recommendations for international students: Required—TOEFL (minimum score 550 paper-based; 213 computer-based). Electronic applications accepted. *Faculty research:* Gene expression, biomechanics, yeast genetics, plant ecology, plant molecular biology.

The University of North Carolina at Chapel Hill, School of Medicine and Graduate School, Graduate Programs in Medicine, Department of Cell and Developmental Biology, Chapel Hill, NC 27599. Offers PhD. *Degree requirements:* For doctorate, comprehensive exam, thesis/dissertation. *Entrance requirements:* For doctorate, GRE General Test, GRE Subject Test. Electronic applications accepted. *Faculty research:* Cell adhesion, motility and cytoskeleton; molecular analysis of signal transduction; development biology and toxicology; reproductive biology; cell and molecular imaging.

University of Pennsylvania, Perelman School of Medicine, Biomedical Graduate Studies, Graduate Group in Cell and Molecular Biology, Philadelphia, PA 19104. Offers cancer biology (PhD); cell biology and physiology (PhD); developmental stem cell regenerative biology (PhD); gene therapy and vaccines (PhD); genetics and gene regulation (PhD); microbiology, virology, and parasitology (PhD); MD/PhD; VMD/PhD. *Faculty:* 306. *Students:* 337 full-time (186 women); includes 81 minority (16 Black or African American, non-Hispanic/Latino; 43 Asian, non-Hispanic/Latino; 16 Hispanic/Latino; 6 Two or more races, non-Hispanic/Latino), 41 international. 585 applicants, 21% accepted, 58 enrolled. In 2011, 42 doctorates awarded. *Degree requirements:* For doctorate, thesis/dissertation. *Entrance requirements:* For doctorate, GRE General Test. Additional exam requirements/recommendations for international students: Required—TOEFL. *Application deadline:* For fall admission, 12/1 priority date for domestic students, 12/1 for international students. Applications are processed on a rolling basis. Application fee: $80. Electronic applications accepted. *Expenses: Tuition:* Full-time $26,660; part-time $4944 per course. *Required fees:* $2318; $291 per course. Tuition and fees vary according to course load, degree level and program. *Financial support:* In 2011–12, 337 students received support. Fellowships, research assistantships, scholarships/grants, traineeships, and unspecified assistantships available. *Unit head:* Dr. Daniel Kessler, Graduate Group Chair. *Application contact:* Meagan Schofer, Coordinator. Web site: http://www.med.upenn.edu/camb/.

University of Pittsburgh, Dietrich School of Arts and Sciences, Department of Biological Sciences, Program in Molecular, Cellular, and Developmental Biology, Pittsburgh, PA 15260. Offers PhD. *Faculty:* 22 full-time (4 women). *Students:* 56 full-time (33 women); includes 4 minority (1 Black or African American, non-Hispanic/Latino; 2 Asian, non-Hispanic/Latino; 1 Hispanic/Latino), 17 international. Average age 23. 202 applicants, 10% accepted, 8 enrolled. In 2011, 9 doctorates awarded. *Degree requirements:* For doctorate, comprehensive exam, thesis/dissertation, completion of research integrity module. *Entrance requirements:* For doctorate, GRE General Test, GRE Subject Test. Additional exam requirements/recommendations for international students: Required—TOEFL (minimum score 550 paper-based; 213 computer-based; 80 iBT). *Application deadline:* For fall admission, 1/15 priority date for domestic students, 12/15 for international students. Applications are processed on a rolling basis. Application fee: $0 ($50 for international students). Electronic applications accepted. *Expenses:* Tuition, state resident: full-time $18,774; part-time $760 per credit. Tuition, nonresident: full-time $30,736; part-time $1258 per credit. *Required fees:* $740; $200 per term. Tuition and fees vary according to program. *Financial support:* In 2011–12, 24 fellowships with full tuition reimbursements (averaging $28,790 per year), 111 research assistantships with full tuition reimbursements (averaging $25,793 per year), 24 teaching assistantships with full tuition reimbursements (averaging $24,414 per year) were awarded; Federal Work-Study, scholarships/grants, traineeships, health care benefits, and tuition waivers (full) also available. *Unit head:* Dr. Jeffrey G. Lawrence,

Professor, 412-624-4204, Fax: 412-624-4759, E-mail: jlawrenc@pitt.edu. *Application contact:* Cathleen M. Barr, Graduate Administrator, 412-624-4268, Fax: 412-624-4759, E-mail: cbarr@pitt.edu. Web site: http://www.biology.pitt.edu/.

University of Pittsburgh, School of Medicine, Graduate Programs in Medicine, Molecular Genetics and Developmental Biology Program, Pittsburgh, PA 15260. Offers MS, PhD. *Faculty:* 49 full-time (11 women). *Students:* 14 full-time (7 women); includes 2 minority (1 Asian, non-Hispanic/Latino; 1 Native Hawaiian or other Pacific Islander, non-Hispanic/Latino), 3 international. Average age 27. 514 applicants, 12% accepted, 14 enrolled. In 2011, 4 doctorates awarded. *Degree requirements:* For doctorate, comprehensive exam, thesis/dissertation. *Entrance requirements:* For doctorate, GRE General Test, GRE Subject Test, minimum QPA of 3.0. Additional exam requirements/recommendations for international students: Required—TOEFL (minimum score 600 paper-based; 100 iBT), IELTS (minimum score 7). *Application deadline:* For fall admission, 12/15 priority date for domestic students, 12/15 for international students. Application fee: $50. Electronic applications accepted. *Expenses:* Tuition, state resident: full-time $18,774; part-time $760 per credit. Tuition, nonresident: full-time $30,736; part-time $1258 per credit. *Required fees:* $740; $200 per term. Tuition and fees vary according to program. *Financial support:* In 2011–12, 1 fellowship (averaging $25,500 per year), 13 research assistantships with full tuition reimbursements (averaging $25,500 per year) were awarded; institutionally sponsored loans, scholarships/grants, traineeships, health care benefits, and unspecified assistantships also available. *Faculty research:* Developmental and stem cell biology, DNA replication and repair, gene regulation and signal transduction, oncogenes and tumor suppressor genes, protein structure and molecular dynamics. *Unit head:* Dr. Neil A. Hukriede, Graduate Program Director, 412-648-9918, Fax: 412-624-1401, E-mail: hukriede@pitt.edu. *Application contact:* Graduate Studies Administrator, 412-648-8957, Fax: 412-648-1077, E-mail: gradstudies@medschool.pitt.edu. Web site: http://www.gradbiomed.pitt.edu/.

University of South Carolina, The Graduate School, College of Arts and Sciences, Department of Biological Sciences, Graduate Training Program in Molecular, Cellular, and Developmental Biology, Columbia, SC 29208. Offers MS, PhD. *Degree requirements:* For master's, one foreign language, thesis; for doctorate, one foreign language, thesis/dissertation. *Entrance requirements:* For master's and doctorate, GRE General Test, minimum GPA of 3.0 in science. Electronic applications accepted. *Faculty research:* Marine ecology, population and evolutionary biology, molecular biology and genetics, development.

The University of Texas Health Science Center at Houston, Graduate School of Biomedical Sciences, Program in Genes and Development, Houston, TX 77225-0036. Offers MS, PhD, MD/PhD. Terminal master's awarded for partial completion of doctoral program. *Degree requirements:* For master's, thesis; for doctorate, thesis/dissertation. *Entrance requirements:* For master's and doctorate, GRE General Test. Additional exam requirements/recommendations for international students: Required—TOEFL. Electronic applications accepted. *Faculty research:* Developmental biology, genetics, cell biology, structural biology, cancer.

The University of Texas Southwestern Medical Center, Southwestern Graduate School of Biomedical Sciences, Division of Basic Science, Program in Genetics and Development, Dallas, TX 75390. Offers PhD. *Degree requirements:* For doctorate, thesis/dissertation, qualifying exam. *Entrance requirements:* For doctorate, GRE General Test, minimum GPA of 3.0. Additional exam requirements/recommendations for international students: Required—TOEFL. Electronic applications accepted. *Faculty research:* Human molecular genetics, chromosome structure, gene regulation, molecular biology, gene expression.

Washington University in St. Louis, Graduate School of Arts and Sciences, Division of Biology and Biomedical Sciences, Program in Developmental, Regenerative, and Stem Cell Biology, St. Louis, MO 63130-4899. Offers PhD. *Degree requirements:* For doctorate, thesis/dissertation. *Entrance requirements:* For doctorate, GRE General Test, GRE Subject Test. Electronic applications accepted.

Wesleyan University, Graduate Programs, Department of Biology, Middletown, CT 06459. Offers animal behavior (PhD); bioformatics/genomics (PhD); cell biology (PhD); developmental biology (PhD); evolution/ecology (PhD); genetics (PhD); neurobiology (PhD); population biology (PhD). *Degree requirements:* For doctorate, variable foreign language requirement, thesis/dissertation. *Entrance requirements:* For doctorate, GRE. Additional exam requirements/recommendations for international students: Required—TOEFL. *Faculty research:* Microbial population genetics, genetic basis of evolutionary adaptation, genetic regulation of differentiation and pattern formation in &ITdrosophila&RO.

West Virginia University, Davis College of Agriculture, Forestry and Consumer Sciences, Interdisciplinary Program in Genetics and Developmental Biology, Morgantown, WV 26506. Offers animal breeding (MS, PhD); biochemical and molecular genetics (MS, PhD); cytogenetics (MS, PhD); descriptive embryology (MS, PhD); developmental genetics (MS); experimental morphogenesis/teratology (MS); human genetics (MS, PhD); immunogenetics (MS, PhD); life cycles of animals and plants (MS, PhD); molecular aspects of development (MS, PhD); mutagenesis (MS, PhD); oncology (MS, PhD); plant genetics (MS, PhD); population and quantitative genetics (MS, PhD); regeneration (MS, PhD); teratology (PhD); toxicology (MS, PhD). *Degree requirements:* For master's, thesis; for doctorate, comprehensive exam, thesis/dissertation. *Entrance requirements:* For master's, GRE or MCAT, minimum GPA of 2.75. Additional exam requirements/recommendations for international students: Required—TOEFL.

Yale University, Graduate School of Arts and Sciences, Department of Molecular, Cellular, and Developmental Biology, New Haven, CT 06520. Offers biochemistry, molecular biology and chemical biology (PhD); cellular and developmental biology (PhD); genetics (PhD); neurobiology (PhD); plant sciences (PhD). *Degree requirements:* For doctorate, thesis/dissertation. *Entrance requirements:* For doctorate, GRE General Test, GRE Subject Test.

Genetics

Albert Einstein College of Medicine, Graduate Division of Biomedical Sciences, Division of Biological Sciences, Department of Genetics, Bronx, NY 10461. Offers computational genetics (PhD); molecular genetics (PhD); translational genetics (PhD); MD/PhD. *Degree requirements:* For doctorate, thesis/dissertation. *Entrance requirements:* For doctorate, GRE General Test. Additional exam requirements/recommendations for international students: Required—TOEFL. *Faculty research:* Neurologic genetics in &ITDrosophila&RO, biochemical genetics of yeast, developmental genetics in the mouse.

American University of Beirut, Graduate Programs, Faculty of Medicine, Beirut, Lebanon. Offers anatomy, cell biology and human morphology (MS); biochemistry and medical genetics (MS); biomedical sciences (PhD); experimental pathology, immunology and microbiology (MS); medicine (MD); neuroscience (MS); pharmacology and toxicology (MS). Part-time programs available. *Faculty:* 232 full-time (58 women), 68 part-time/adjunct (7 women). *Students:* 346 full-time (135 women), 69 part-time (57 women). Average age 23. In 2011, 20 master's, 82 doctorates awarded. *Degree requirements:* For master's, one foreign language, comprehensive exam, thesis (for some programs). *Entrance requirements:* For master's, letter of recommendation; for doctorate, MCAT, bachelor's degree. Additional exam requirements/recommendations for international students: Required—TOEFL (minimum score 600 paper-based; 250 computer-based; 100 iBT), IELTS (minimum score 7.5). *Application deadline:* For fall admission, 4/30 for domestic and international students; for spring admission, 11/1 for domestic and international students. Application fee: $50. *Expenses: Tuition:* Full-time $12,780; part-time $710 per credit. Tuition and fees vary according to course load and program. *Financial support:* In 2011–12, 19 students received support. Career-related internships or fieldwork, institutionally sponsored loans, scholarships/grants, health care benefits, and unspecified assistantships available. Financial award application deadline: 2/2. *Faculty research:* Cancer research (targeted therapy, mechanisms of leukemogenesis, tumor cell extravasation and metastasis, cancer stem cells); stem cell research (regenerative medicine, drug discovery); genetic research (neurogenetics, hereditary cardiomyopathy, hemoglobinopathies, pharmacogenomics, proteomics); neuroscience research (pain, neurodegenerative disorder); metabolism (inflammation and metabolism, metabolic disorder, diabetes mellitus); vascular and renal biology, signal transduction. *Total annual research expenditures:* $2.3 million. *Unit head:* Dr. Mohamed Sayegh, Dean, 961-1350000 Ext. 4700, Fax: 961-1744464, E-mail: msayegh@aub.edu.lb. *Application contact:* Dr. Salim Kanaan, Director, Admissions Office, 961-1350000 Ext. 2594, Fax: 961-1750775, E-mail: sk00@aub.edu.lb. Web site: http://www.aub.edu.lb/fm/fm_home/Pages/index.aspx.

Baylor College of Medicine, Graduate School of Biomedical Sciences, Department of Molecular and Human Genetics, Houston, TX 77030-3498. Offers PhD, MD/PhD. *Faculty:* 71 full-time (14 women). *Students:* 77 full-time (45 women); includes 10 minority (2 Black or African American, non-Hispanic/Latino; 5 Asian, non-Hispanic/Latino; 3 Hispanic/Latino), 35 international. Average age 26. 130 applicants, 19% accepted, 10 enrolled. In 2011, 15 doctorates awarded. *Degree requirements:* For doctorate, thesis/dissertation, public defense. *Entrance requirements:* For doctorate, GRE General Test, GRE Subject Test (strongly recommended), minimum GPA of 3.0. Additional exam requirements/recommendations for international students: Required—TOEFL. *Application deadline:* For fall admission, 1/1 priority date for domestic students. Application fee: $0. Electronic applications accepted. *Financial support:* In 2011–12, 25 fellowships with full tuition reimbursements (averaging $29,000 per year), 52 research assistantships with full tuition reimbursements (averaging $29,000 per year) were awarded; career-related internships or fieldwork, Federal Work-Study, institutionally sponsored loans, health care benefits, and scholarships (to all students unless there are grant funds available to pay tuition) also available. Financial award applicants required to submit FAFSA. *Faculty research:* Human genetics, genome biology, epigenetics, gene therapy, model organisms. *Unit head:* Dr. Gad Shaulsky, Director, 713-798-5056. *Application contact:* Judi Coleman, Graduate Program Administrator, 713-798-5056, Fax: 713-798-8597, E-mail: genetics-gradprm@bcm.edu. Web site: http://www.bcm.edu/molgen.

Baylor College of Medicine, Graduate School of Biomedical Sciences, Interdepartmental Program in Cell and Molecular Biology, Houston, TX 77030-3498. Offers biochemistry (PhD); cell and molecular biology (PhD); genetics (PhD); human genetics (PhD); immunology (PhD); microbiology (PhD); virology (PhD); MD/PhD. *Faculty:* 112 full-time (30 women). *Students:* 66 full-time (42 women); includes 21 minority (5 Black or African American, non-Hispanic/Latino; 1 American Indian or Alaska Native, non-Hispanic/Latino; 7 Asian, non-Hispanic/Latino; 8 Hispanic/Latino), 14 international. Average age 27. 126 applicants, 25% accepted, 14 enrolled. In 2011, 7 degrees awarded. *Median time to degree:* Of those who began their doctoral program in fall 2003, 82% received their degree in 8 years or less. *Degree requirements:* For doctorate, thesis/dissertation, public defense. *Entrance requirements:* For doctorate, GRE General Test, GRE Subject Test (strongly recommended), minimum GPA of 3.0. Additional exam requirements/recommendations for international students: Required—TOEFL. *Application deadline:* For fall admission, 1/1 priority date for domestic students. Applications are processed on a rolling basis. Application fee: $0. Electronic applications accepted. *Financial support:* In 2011–12, 66 students received support, including 30 fellowships with full tuition reimbursements available (averaging $29,000 per year), 36 research assistantships with full tuition reimbursements available (averaging $29,000 per year); teaching assistantships, Federal Work-Study, institutionally sponsored loans, health care benefits, and tuition waivers (full) also available. Financial award applicants required to submit FAFSA. *Faculty research:* Molecular and cellular biology; cancer, aging and stem cells; genomics and proteomics; microbiome, molecular microbiology; infectious disease, immunology and translational research. *Unit head:* Dr. Susan Marriott, Director, 713-798-6557. *Application contact:* Lourdes Fernandez, Graduate Program Administrator, 713-798-6557, Fax: 713-798-6325, E-mail: cmbprog@bcm.edu. Web site: http://bcm.edu/cmb/.

Baylor College of Medicine, Graduate School of Biomedical Sciences, Program in Developmental Biology, Houston, TX 77030-3498. Offers PhD, MD/PhD. *Faculty:* 68 full-time (20 women). *Students:* 55 full-time (28 women); includes 9 minority (7 Asian, non-Hispanic/Latino; 2 Hispanic/Latino), 37 international. Average age 28. 771 applicants, 2% accepted, 10 enrolled. In 2011, 5 degrees awarded. *Median time to degree:* Of those who began their doctoral program in fall 2003, 100% received their degree in 8 years or less. *Degree requirements:* For doctorate, thesis/dissertation, public defense. *Entrance requirements:* For doctorate, GRE General Test, GRE Subject Test (strongly recommended), minimum GPA of 3.0. Additional exam requirements/recommendations for international students: Required—TOEFL. *Application deadline:* For fall admission, 1/1 priority date for domestic students. Application fee: $0. Electronic applications accepted. *Financial support:* In 2011–12, 55 students received support, including 6 fellowships with full tuition reimbursements available (averaging $29,000 per year), 49 research assistantships with full tuition reimbursements available (averaging $29,000 per year); career-related internships or fieldwork, Federal Work-Study, institutionally sponsored loans, health care benefits, tuition waivers (full), and stipends

also available. *Faculty research:* Stem cells, cancer, neurobiology, organogenesis, genetics of model organisms. *Unit head:* Dr. Hugo Bellen, Director, 713-798-6410. *Application contact:* Catherine Tasnier, Graduate Program Administrator, 713-798-6410, Fax: 713-798-5386, E-mail: cat@bcm.edu. Web site: http://www.bcm.edu/db/.

See Display on page 287 and Close-Up on page 311.

Baylor College of Medicine, Graduate School of Biomedical Sciences, Program in Translational Biology and Molecular Medicine, Houston, TX 77030-3498. Offers PhD. *Faculty:* 192 full-time (56 women). *Students:* 63 full-time (35 women); includes 24 minority (10 Black or African American, non-Hispanic/Latino; 9 Asian, non-Hispanic/Latino; 5 Hispanic/Latino), 17 international. Average age 27. 133 applicants, 17% accepted, 12 enrolled. In 2011, 1 doctorate awarded. *Degree requirements:* For doctorate, thesis/dissertation, public defense. *Entrance requirements:* For doctorate, GRE, minimum GPA of 3.0. Additional exam requirements/recommendations for international students: Required—TOEFL. *Application deadline:* For fall admission, 1/1 for domestic students. Application fee: $0. Electronic applications accepted. *Financial support:* In 2011–12, 63 students received support, including 36 fellowships with full tuition reimbursements available (averaging $29,000 per year), 27 research assistantships with full tuition reimbursements available (averaging $29,000 per year); career-related internships or fieldwork, Federal Work-Study, health care benefits, and scholarships (to all students unless there are grant funds available to pay tuition) also available. Financial award applicants required to submit FAFSA. *Faculty research:* Molecular medicine, translational biology, human disease biology and therapy. *Unit head:* Dr. Mary Estes, Director, 713-798-3585, Fax: 713-798-3586, E-mail: tbmm@bcm.edu. *Application contact:* Wanda Waguespack, Graduate Program Administrator, 713-798-1077, Fax: 713-798-3586, E-mail: wandaw@bcm.edu. Web site: http://www.bcm.edu/tbmm.

Boston University, School of Medicine, Division of Graduate Medical Sciences, Program in Genetics and Genomics, Boston, MA 02215. Offers PhD. *Faculty:* 18 full-time (3 women). *Students:* 8 full-time (7 women), 2 part-time (both women), 3 international. Average age 27. 20 applicants, 40% accepted, 2 enrolled. In 2011, 5 doctorates awarded. *Degree requirements:* For doctorate, thesis/dissertation. *Entrance requirements:* For doctorate, GRE, letters of recommendation. Additional exam requirements/recommendations for international students: Required—TOEFL. *Application deadline:* For fall admission, 1/15 for domestic students; for spring admission, 10/15 for domestic students. Application fee: $75. Electronic applications accepted. *Expenses: Tuition:* Full-time $40,848; part-time $1276 per credit hour. *Required fees:* $572; $286 per semester. *Financial support:* In 2011–12, 9 research assistantships (averaging $30,500 per year) were awarded. Financial award applicants required to submit FAFSA. *Unit head:* Dr. Shoumita Dasgupta, Associate Professor and Director of Graduate Studies, 617-414-1580, E-mail: dasgupta@bu.edu. Web site: http://www.bumc.bu.edu/gpgg/graduate-program/.

Brandeis University, Graduate School of Arts and Sciences, Program in Molecular and Cell Biology, Waltham, MA 02454-9110. Offers genetics (PhD); microbiology (PhD); molecular and cell biology (MS, PhD); molecular biology (PhD); neurobiology (PhD); quantitative biology (PhD). *Faculty:* 27 full-time (11 women), 4 part-time/adjunct (1 woman). *Students:* 65 full-time (36 women); includes 8 minority (4 Black or African American, non-Hispanic/Latino; 1 American Indian or Alaska Native, non-Hispanic/Latino; 1 Asian, non-Hispanic/Latino; 2 Hispanic/Latino), 14 international. 195 applicants, 26% accepted, 21 enrolled. In 2011, 4 master's, 6 doctorates awarded. Terminal master's awarded for partial completion of doctoral program. *Degree requirements:* For master's, thesis or alternative, research project, research lab, or project lab; for doctorate, comprehensive exam, thesis/dissertation, journal clubs, research seminar; colloquia; teaching requirement; qualifying exam. *Entrance requirements:* For master's, GRE General Test; MCAT may be substituted for the GRE exam for applicants to the M.S. program., official transcript(s), resume, 3 letters of recommendation, statement of purpose; for doctorate, GRE General Test, official transcript(s), resume, 3 letters of recommendation, statement of purpose. Additional exam requirements/recommendations for international students: Required—TOEFL (minimum score 600 paper-based; 250 computer-based; 100 iBT); Recommended—IELTS (minimum score 7). *Application deadline:* For fall admission, 1/15 priority date for domestic students; for spring admission, 11/15 for domestic students. Applications are processed on a rolling basis. Application fee: $75. Electronic applications accepted. *Financial support:* In 2011–12, 17 fellowships with full tuition reimbursements (averaging $29,580 per year), 31 research assistantships with full tuition reimbursements (averaging $29,580 per year), teaching assistantships with partial tuition reimbursements (averaging $3,200 per year) were awarded; scholarships/grants, health care benefits, tuition waivers (full and partial), and unspecified assistantships also available. Financial award application deadline: 4/15; financial award applicants required to submit FAFSA. *Faculty research:* Molecular biology, cell biology, biology, structural biology, immunology, developmental biology, neurobiology, DNA, RNA. *Unit head:* Dr. Bruce Goode, Chair, 781-736-2464, Fax: 781-736-3107, E-mail: goode@brandeis.edu. *Application contact:* Dr. Jessica Maryott, Department Administrator, 781-736-3100, Fax: 781-736-3107, E-mail: jmaryott@brandeis.edu. Web site: http://www.bio.brandeis.edu/grad/mcb/mcb_phd.html.

California Institute of Technology, Division of Biology, Program in Genetics, Pasadena, CA 91125-0001. Offers PhD. *Degree requirements:* For doctorate, thesis/dissertation, qualifying exam. *Entrance requirements:* For doctorate, GRE General Test.

Carnegie Mellon University, Mellon College of Science, Department of Biological Sciences, Pittsburgh, PA 15213-3891. Offers biochemistry (PhD); biophysics (PhD); cell biology (PhD); computational biology (MS, PhD); developmental biology (PhD); genetics (PhD); molecular biology (PhD); neuroscience (PhD). *Degree requirements:* For doctorate, comprehensive exam, thesis/dissertation. *Entrance requirements:* For doctorate, GRE General Test, GRE Subject Test, interview. Electronic applications accepted. *Faculty research:* Genetic structure, function, and regulation; protein structure and function; biological membranes; biological spectroscopy.

Case Western Reserve University, School of Medicine and School of Graduate Studies, Graduate Programs in Medicine, Department of Genetics, Program in Human, Molecular, and Developmental Genetics and Genomics, Cleveland, OH 44106. Offers PhD, MD/PhD. *Degree requirements:* For doctorate, comprehensive exam, thesis/dissertation. *Entrance requirements:* For doctorate, GRE General Test, GRE Subject Test. Additional exam requirements/recommendations for international students: Required—TOEFL. *Faculty research:* Regulation of gene expression, molecular control of development, genomics.

Clemson University, Graduate School, College of Agriculture, Forestry and Life Sciences, Department of Genetics and Biochemistry, Program in Genetics, Clemson, SC 29634. Offers PhD. *Students:* 19 full-time (11 women), 8 international. Average age 29. 19 applicants, 32% accepted, 4 enrolled. In 2011, 3 doctorates awarded. *Degree requirements:* For doctorate, thesis/dissertation. *Entrance requirements:* For doctorate, GRE General Test, minimum GPA of 3.2. Additional exam requirements/recommendations for international students: Required—TOEFL, IELTS. *Application deadline:* For fall admission, 1/1 for domestic students; for spring admission, 9/1 for domestic students. Applications are processed on a rolling basis. Application fee: $70 ($80 for international students). Electronic applications accepted. *Expenses:* Contact institution. *Financial support:* In 2011–12, 19 students received support, including 1 fellowship with full and partial tuition reimbursement available (averaging $7,000 per year), 14 research assistantships with partial tuition reimbursements available (averaging $15,497 per year), 9 teaching assistantships with partial tuition reimbursements available (averaging $17,667 per year). Financial award application deadline: 3/15; financial award applicants required to submit FAFSA. *Faculty research:* Animal, plant, microbial, molecular, and biometrical genetics. *Unit head:* Dr. Keith Murphy, Chair, 864-656-6237, E-mail: kmurph2@clemson.edu. *Application contact:* Sheryl Banks, Administrative Coordinator, 866-656-6878, E-mail: sherylb@clemson.edu. Web site: http://www.clemson.edu/genbiochem.

Clemson University, Graduate School, College of Health, Education, and Human Development, School of Nursing, Clemson, SC 29634. Offers healthcare genetics (PhD); nursing (MS). *Accreditation:* AACN. Part-time programs available. Postbaccalaureate distance learning degree programs offered. *Faculty:* 16 full-time (15 women). *Students:* 53 full-time (48 women), 47 part-time (40 women); includes 11 minority (7 Black or African American, non-Hispanic/Latino; 1 Hispanic/Latino; 3 Two or more races, non-Hispanic/Latino), 3 international. Average age 35. 50 applicants, 62% accepted, 24 enrolled. In 2011, 27 master's awarded. *Degree requirements:* For master's, thesis or alternative; for doctorate, comprehensive exam, thesis/dissertation. *Entrance requirements:* For master's, GRE General Test, RN license; for doctorate, GRE General Test. Additional exam requirements/recommendations for international students: Required—TOEFL. *Application deadline:* For fall admission, 4/1 for domestic students; for spring admission, 10/1 for domestic students. Applications are processed on a rolling basis. Application fee: $70 ($80 for international students). Electronic applications accepted. *Expenses:* Contact institution. *Financial support:* In 2011–12, 25 students received support, including 2 research assistantships with partial tuition reimbursements available (averaging $2,000 per year), teaching assistantships with partial tuition reimbursements available (averaging $5,122 per year); fellowships with full and partial tuition reimbursements available, career-related internships or fieldwork, institutionally sponsored loans, scholarships/grants, health care benefits, and unspecified assistantships also available. Support available to part-time students. Financial award applicants required to submit FAFSA. *Faculty research:* Risk behaviors and chronic risk-taking in early adolescents, stress in older caregivers, home care of elderly, cancer awareness, pain. *Total annual research expenditures:* $175,758. *Unit head:* Dr. Rosanne Pruitt, Director, 864-656-7622, Fax: 864-656-5488, E-mail: prosan@clemson.edu. *Application contact:* Dr. Margaret Ann Wetsel, Graduate Studies Coordinator, 864-656-5527, Fax: 864-656-5488, E-mail: mwetsel@clemson.edu. Web site: http://www.clemson.edu/hehd/departments/nursing/.

Columbia University, College of Physicians and Surgeons, Department of Genetics and Development, New York, NY 10032. Offers genetics (M Phil, MA, PhD); MD/PhD. Only candidates for the PhD are admitted. Terminal master's awarded for partial completion of doctoral program. *Degree requirements:* For doctorate, thesis/dissertation. *Entrance requirements:* For master's and doctorate, GRE General Test. Additional exam requirements/recommendations for international students: Required—TOEFL. *Faculty research:* Mammalian cell differentiation and meiosis, developmental genetics, yeast and human genetics, chromosome structure, molecular and cellular biology.

Columbia University, College of Physicians and Surgeons, Integrated Program in Cellular, Molecular, Structural and Genetic Studies, New York, NY 10032. Offers PhD. Terminal master's awarded for partial completion of doctoral program. *Degree requirements:* For doctorate, thesis/dissertation. *Entrance requirements:* For doctorate, GRE General Test, GRE Subject Test. Additional exam requirements/recommendations for international students: Required—TOEFL. *Expenses:* Contact institution. *Faculty research:* Transcription, macromolecular sorting, gene expression during development, cellular interaction.

Cornell University, Graduate School, Graduate Fields of Agriculture and Life Sciences, Field of Genetics and Development, Ithaca, NY 14853-0001. Offers developmental biology (PhD); genetics (PhD). *Faculty:* 59 full-time (15 women). *Students:* 57 full-time (35 women); includes 6 minority (1 Black or African American, non-Hispanic/Latino; 3 Asian, non-Hispanic/Latino; 2 Hispanic/Latino), 22 international. Average age 26. 66 applicants, 30% accepted, 8 enrolled. In 2011, 4 doctorates awarded. *Degree requirements:* For doctorate, comprehensive exam, thesis/dissertation, 2 semesters of teaching experience. *Entrance requirements:* For doctorate, GRE General Test, GRE Subject Test in biology or biochemistry (recommended), 2 letters of recommendation. Additional exam requirements/recommendations for international students: Required—TOEFL (minimum score 550 paper-based; 213 computer-based; 77 iBT). *Application deadline:* For fall admission, 1/5 for domestic students. Application fee: $95. Electronic applications accepted. *Financial support:* In 2011–12, 17 fellowships with full tuition reimbursements, 30 research assistantships with full tuition reimbursements, 9 teaching assistantships with full tuition reimbursements were awarded; institutionally sponsored loans, scholarships/grants, health care benefits, tuition waivers (full and partial), and unspecified assistantships also available. Financial award applicants required to submit FAFSA. *Faculty research:* Molecular and general genetics, developmental biology and developmental genetics, evolution and population genetics, plant genetics, microbial genetics. *Unit head:* Director of Graduate Studies, 607-254-2100. *Application contact:* Graduate Field Assistant, 607-254-2100, E-mail: gendev@cornell.edu. Web site: http://www.gradschool.cornell.edu/fields.php?id-51&a-2.

Dartmouth College, Graduate Program in Molecular and Cellular Biology, Department of Genetics, Hanover, NH 03755. Offers PhD, MD/PhD. *Entrance requirements:* For doctorate, GRE General Test, letters of recommendation. Additional exam requirements/recommendations for international students: Required—TOEFL (minimum score 450 paper-based; 90 iBT) or IELTS (minimum score 7). Electronic applications accepted.

Drexel University, College of Medicine, Biomedical Graduate Programs, Interdisciplinary Program in Molecular and Cell Biology and Genetics, Philadelphia, PA 19104-2875. Offers MS, PhD, MD/PhD. Terminal master's awarded for partial completion of doctoral program. *Degree requirements:* For master's, comprehensive exam, thesis; for doctorate, thesis/dissertation, qualifying exam. *Entrance requirements:* For master's, GRE General Test, minimum GPA of 2.75; for doctorate, GRE General Test, minimum GPA of 3.0. Additional exam requirements/recommendations for international students: Required—TOEFL. Electronic applications accepted. *Faculty research:* Molecular anatomy, biochemistry, medical biotechnology, molecular pathology, microbiology and immunology.

Duke University, Graduate School, Department of Biochemistry, Durham, NC 27710. Offers crystallography of macromolecules (PhD); enzyme mechanisms (PhD); lipid biochemistry (PhD); membrane structure and function (PhD); molecular genetics (PhD); neurochemistry (PhD); nucleic acid structure and function (PhD); protein structure and function (PhD). *Faculty:* 28 full-time. *Students:* 73 full-time (28 women); includes 6 minority (4 Black or African American, non-Hispanic/Latino; 2 Asian, non-Hispanic/Latino), 29 international. 76 applicants, 17% accepted, 3 enrolled. In 2011, 7 doctorates awarded. *Degree requirements:* For doctorate, thesis/dissertation. *Entrance requirements:* For doctorate, GRE General Test, GRE Subject Test (recommended).

Additional exam requirements/recommendations for international students: Required—TOEFL (minimum score 550 paper-based; 213 computer-based; 83 iBT), IELTS (minimum score 7). *Application deadline:* For fall admission, 12/8 priority date for domestic students, 12/8 for international students. Application fee: $75. Electronic applications accepted. *Expenses: Tuition:* Full-time $40,720. *Required fees:* $3107. *Financial support:* Fellowships, research assistantships, teaching assistantships, and Federal Work-Study available. Financial award application deadline: 12/8. *Unit head:* Leonard Spicer, Director of Graduate Studies, 919-681-8770, Fax: 919-684-8885, E-mail: anorfleet@biochem.duke.edu. *Application contact:* Elizabeth Hutton, Director of Admissions, 919-684-3913, Fax: 919-684-2277, E-mail: grad-admissions@duke.edu. Web site: http://www.biochem.duke.edu/.

Duke University, Graduate School, Program in Genetics and Genomics, Durham, NC 27710. Offers PhD. *Faculty:* 115 full-time. *Students:* 94 full-time (60 women); includes 14 minority (4 Black or African American, non-Hispanic/Latino; 7 Asian, non-Hispanic/Latino; 3 Hispanic/Latino), 12 international. 118 applicants, 27% accepted, 16 enrolled. In 2011, 5 doctorates awarded. *Degree requirements:* For doctorate, variable foreign language requirement, thesis/dissertation. *Entrance requirements:* For doctorate, GRE General Test. Additional exam requirements/recommendations for international students: Required—TOEFL (minimum score 550 paper-based; 213 computer-based; 83 iBT), IELTS (minimum score 7). *Application deadline:* For fall admission, 12/8 priority date for domestic students, 12/8 for international students. Application fee: $75. *Expenses: Tuition:* Full-time $40,720. *Required fees:* $3107. *Financial support:* Fellowships available. Financial award application deadline: 12/8. *Unit head:* Dr. Michael Hauser, Director of Graduate Studies, 919-684-6629, Fax: 919-684-8346, E-mail: leslie.mavengere@duke.edu. *Application contact:* Elizabeth Hutton, Director of Admissions, 919-684-3913, Fax: 919-684-2277, E-mail: grad-admissions@duke.edu. Web site: http://upg.duke.edu/.

Emory University, Laney Graduate School, Division of Biological and Biomedical Sciences, Program in Genetics and Molecular Biology, Atlanta, GA 30322-1100. Offers PhD. *Faculty:* 44 full-time (8 women). *Students:* 51 full-time (29 women); includes 11 minority (5 Black or African American, non-Hispanic/Latino; 3 Asian, non-Hispanic/Latino; 3 Hispanic/Latino), 8 international. Average age 27. 134 applicants, 16% accepted, 8 enrolled. In 2011, 7 degrees awarded. *Median time to degree:* Of those who began their doctoral program in fall 2003, 100% received their degree in 8 years or less. *Degree requirements:* For doctorate, comprehensive exam, thesis/dissertation. *Entrance requirements:* For doctorate, GRE General Test, minimum GPA of 3.0 in science course work (recommended). Additional exam requirements/recommendations for international students: Required—TOEFL. *Application deadline:* For fall admission, 12/1 for domestic and international students. Application fee: $75. Electronic applications accepted. *Expenses: Tuition:* Full-time $34,800. *Required fees:* $1300. *Financial support:* In 2011–12, 18 students received support, including 18 fellowships with full tuition reimbursements available (averaging $26,500 per year); institutionally sponsored loans, scholarships/grants, health care benefits, and tuition waivers (full) also available. *Faculty research:* Gene regulation, genetic combination, developmental regulation. *Unit head:* Dr. Bill Kelly, Director, 404-727-6461, Fax: 404-727-2880, E-mail: william.kelly@emory.edu. *Application contact:* Kathy Smith, Director of Recruitment and Admissions, 404-727-2547, Fax: 404-727-3322, E-mail: kathy.smith@emory.edu. Web site: http://www.biomed.emory.edu/.

Florida State University, The Graduate School, College of Arts and Sciences, Department of Biological Science, Specialization in Cell and Molecular Biology and Genetics, Tallahassee, FL 32306-4295. Offers MS, PhD. *Faculty:* 28 full-time (7 women). *Students:* 44 full-time (19 women); includes 6 minority (all Hispanic/Latino), 15 international. 152 applicants, 16% accepted, 11 enrolled. In 2011, 3 master's, 8 doctorates awarded. Terminal master's awarded for partial completion of doctoral program. *Degree requirements:* For master's, comprehensive exam, thesis, teaching experience, seminar presentation; for doctorate, comprehensive exam, thesis/dissertation, teaching experience; seminar presentation. *Entrance requirements:* For master's and doctorate, GRE General Test (minimum combined score 1100, 500 verbal, 500 quantitative in old version; 72% verbal, 67% quantitative in new format), minimum upper-division GPA of 3.0. Additional exam requirements/recommendations for international students: Required—TOEFL (minimum score 600 paper-based; 250 computer-based; 92 iBT). *Application deadline:* For fall admission, 12/15 for domestic and international students. Application fee: $30. Electronic applications accepted. *Expenses:* Tuition, state resident: full-time $9474; part-time $350.88 per credit hour. Tuition, nonresident: full-time $16,236; part-time $601.34 per credit hour. *Required fees:* $630 per semester. One-time fee: $20. Tuition and fees vary according to course load and campus/location. *Financial support:* In 2011–12, 43 students received support, including 17 research assistantships with full tuition reimbursements available (averaging $21,000 per year), 26 teaching assistantships with full tuition reimbursements available (averaging $21,000 per year); fellowships and unspecified assistantships also available. Financial award application deadline: 12/15; financial award applicants required to submit FAFSA. *Faculty research:* Molecular biology; genetics and genomics; developmental biology and gene expression; cell structure, function, and motility; cellular and organismal physiology; biophysical and structural biology. *Unit head:* Dr. George W. Bates, Professor and Associate Chairman, 850-644-5749, Fax: 850-644-9829, E-mail: bates@bio.fsu.edu. *Application contact:* Judy Bowers, Coordinator, Graduate Affairs, 850-644-3023, Fax: 850-644-9829, E-mail: gradinfo@bio.fsu.edu. Web site: http://www.bio.fsu.edu/.

The George Washington University, Columbian College of Arts and Sciences, Institute for Biomedical Sciences, Program in Biochemistry and Molecular Genetics, Washington, DC 20052. Offers PhD. *Students:* 6 part-time (3 women), 1 international. Average age 28. In 2011, 3 degrees awarded. Terminal master's awarded for partial completion of doctoral program. *Degree requirements:* For doctorate, thesis/dissertation, general exam. *Entrance requirements:* For doctorate, GRE General Test, interview, minimum GPA of 3.0. Additional exam requirements/recommendations for international students: Required—TOEFL (minimum score 600 paper-based; 250 computer-based). *Application deadline:* For fall admission, 12/15 priority date for domestic students, 12/15 for international students; for spring admission, 10/1 priority date for domestic students, 10/1 for international students. Applications are processed on a rolling basis. Application fee: $75. Electronic applications accepted. *Financial support:* In 2011–12, 4 students received support. Fellowships, Federal Work-Study, institutionally sponsored loans, and tuition waivers available. Financial award application deadline: 2/1. *Unit head:* Valerie W. Hu, Director, 202-994-8431, E-mail: valhu@gwu.edu. *Application contact:* Information Contact, 202-994-7120, Fax: 202-994-6100, E-mail: genetics@gwu.edu. Web site: http://www.gwumc.edu/ibs/fields/biochemgenetics.html.

Harvard University, Graduate School of Arts and Sciences, Division of Medical Sciences, Boston, MA 02115. Offers biological chemistry and molecular pharmacology (PhD); cell biology (PhD); genetics (PhD); microbiology and molecular genetics (PhD); pathology (PhD), including experimental pathology. *Degree requirements:* For doctorate, thesis/dissertation. *Entrance requirements:* For doctorate, GRE General Test, GRE Subject Test. Additional exam requirements/recommendations for international students: Required—TOEFL. *Expenses: Tuition:* Full-time $36,304. *Required fees:* $1186. Full-time tuition and fees vary according to program.

Harvard University, Harvard School of Public Health, Department of Genetics and Complex Diseases, Boston, MA 02115-6096. Offers PhD. *Faculty:* 8 full-time (3 women), 1 part-time/adjunct (0 women). *Degree requirements:* For doctorate, thesis/dissertation, qualifying exam. *Entrance requirements:* For doctorate, GRE. Additional exam requirements/recommendations for international students: Required—TOEFL (minimum score 600 paper-based; 240 computer-based; 100 iBT); Recommended—IELTS (minimum score 7). *Application deadline:* For fall admission, 12/8 for domestic and international students. Application fee: $115. Electronic applications accepted. *Expenses: Tuition:* Full-time $36,304. *Required fees:* $1186. Full-time tuition and fees vary according to program. *Financial support:* Fellowships, research assistantships, Federal Work-Study, scholarships/grants, traineeships, and unspecified assistantships available. Financial award application deadline: 2/17; financial award applicants required to submit FAFSA. *Faculty research:* Toxicology, radiation biology. *Unit head:* Dr. Gokhan Hotamisligil, Chair, 617-432-0054, Fax: 617-432-5236, E-mail: ghotamis@hsph.harvard.edu. *Application contact:* Vincent W. James, Director of Admissions, 617-432-1031, Fax: 617-432-7080, E-mail: admissions@hsph.harvard.edu. Web site: http://www.hsph.harvard.edu/departments/genetics-and-complex-diseases/.

Illinois State University, Graduate School, College of Arts and Sciences, Department of Biological Sciences, Normal, IL 61790-2200. Offers animal behavior (MS); bacteriology (MS); biochemistry (MS); biological sciences (MS); biology (PhD); biophysics (MS); biotechnology (MS); botany (MS, PhD); cell biology (MS); conservation biology (MS); developmental biology (MS); ecology (MS, PhD); entomology (MS); evolutionary biology (MS); genetics (MS, PhD); immunology (MS); microbiology (MS, PhD); molecular biology (MS); molecular genetics (MS); neurobiology (MS); neuroscience (MS); parasitology (MS); physiology (MS, PhD); plant biology (MS); plant molecular biology (MS); plant sciences (MS); structural biology (MS); zoology (MS, PhD). Part-time programs available. *Degree requirements:* For master's, thesis or alternative; for doctorate, variable foreign language requirement, thesis/dissertation, 2 terms of residency. *Entrance requirements:* For master's, GRE General Test, minimum GPA of 2.6 in last 60 hours of course work; for doctorate, GRE General Test. *Faculty research:* Redoc balance and drug development in schistosoma mansoni, control of the growth of listeria monocytogenes at low temperature, regulation of cell expansion and microtubule function by SPRI, CRUI: physiology and fitness consequences of different life history phenotypes.

Indiana University Bloomington, University Graduate School, College of Arts and Sciences, Department of Biology, Bloomington, IN 47405. Offers biology teaching (MAT); biotechnology (MA); evolution, ecology, and behavior (MA, PhD); genetics (PhD); microbiology (MA, PhD); molecular, cellular, and developmental biology (PhD); plant sciences (MA, PhD); zoology (MA, PhD). *Faculty:* 58 full-time (15 women), 21 part-time/adjunct (6 women). *Students:* 175 full-time (100 women), 3 part-time (all women); includes 20 minority (5 Black or African American, non-Hispanic/Latino; 8 Asian, non-Hispanic/Latino; 7 Hispanic/Latino), 55 international. Average age 27. 316 applicants, 22% accepted, 31 enrolled. In 2011, 8 master's, 20 doctorates awarded. Terminal master's awarded for partial completion of doctoral program. *Degree requirements:* For master's, thesis, oral defense; for doctorate, thesis/dissertation, oral defense. *Entrance requirements:* For master's and doctorate, GRE General Test. Additional exam requirements/recommendations for international students: Required—TOEFL (minimum score 100 iBT). *Application deadline:* For fall admission, 1/5 priority date for domestic students, 12/1 for international students. Application fee: $55 ($65 for international students). Electronic applications accepted. *Financial support:* In 2011–12, fellowships with tuition reimbursements (averaging $19,484 per year), research assistantships with tuition reimbursements (averaging $20,300 per year), teaching assistantships with tuition reimbursements (averaging $20,521 per year) were awarded; scholarships/grants, traineeships, health care benefits, and unspecified assistantships also available. Financial award application deadline: 1/5. *Faculty research:* Evolution, ecology and behavior; microbiology; molecular biology and genetics; plant biology. *Unit head:* Dr. Roger Innes, Chair, 812-855-2219, Fax: 812-855-6082, E-mail: rinnes@indiana.edu. *Application contact:* Tracey D. Stohr, Graduate Student Recruitment Coordinator, 812-856-6303, Fax: 812-855-6082, E-mail: gradbio@indiana.edu. Web site: http://www.bio.indiana.edu/.

Iowa State University of Science and Technology, Bioinformatics and Computational Biology Program, Ames, IA 50011-3260. Offers MS, PhD. *Degree requirements:* For doctorate, thesis/dissertation. *Entrance requirements:* For master's and doctorate, GRE General Test. Additional exam requirements/recommendations for international students: Recommended—TOEFL, IELTS. *Application deadline:* For fall admission, 1/15 priority date for domestic students, 1/15 for international students; for spring admission, 10/15 for domestic and international students. Application fee: $40 ($90 for international students). Electronic applications accepted. *Faculty research:* Functional and structural genomics, genome evolution, macromolecular structure and function, mathematical biology and biological statistics, metabolic and developmental networks. *Unit head:* Dr. Julie Dickerson, Chair, Supervising Committee, 515-294-5122, Fax: 515-294-6790, E-mail: bcb@iastate.edu. *Application contact:* Information Contact, 515-294-5836, Fax: 515-294-2592, E-mail: grad_admissions@iastate.edu. Web site: http://www.bcb.iastate.edu/.

Iowa State University of Science and Technology, Program in Genetics, Ames, IA 50011-3260. Offers MS, PhD. *Entrance requirements:* For master's and doctorate, GRE General Test. Additional exam requirements/recommendations for international students: Required—TOEFL (minimum score 550 paper-based; 79 iBT), IELTS (minimum score 6.5). *Application deadline:* For fall admission, 2/1 priority date for domestic students, 2/1 for international students; for spring admission, 9/1 priority date for domestic students, 9/1 for international students. Application fee: $40 ($90 for international students). Electronic applications accepted. *Unit head:* Dr. Christopher Tuggle, Director of Graduate Education, 515-294-7697, Fax: 515-294-6669, E-mail: genetics@iastate.edu. *Application contact:* Linda Wild, Program Coordinator, 800-499-7697, Fax: 515-294-6669, E-mail: genetics@iastate.edu. Web site: http://www.genetics.iastate.edu/.

The Johns Hopkins University, Bloomberg School of Public Health, Department of Epidemiology, Baltimore, MD 21205. Offers cancer epidemiology (MHS, Sc M, PhD, Sc D); cardiovascular disease epidemiology (MHS, Sc M, PhD, Sc D); clinical epidemiology (MHS, Sc M, PhD, Sc D); clinical trials (PhD, Sc D); epidemiology (Dr PH); epidemiology (general) (MHS, Sc M, PhD, Sc D); epidemiology of aging (MHS, Sc M, PhD, Sc D); human genetics/genetic epidemiology (MHS, Sc M, PhD, Sc D); infectious disease epidemiology (MHS, Sc M, PhD, Sc D); occupational/environmental epidemiology (MHS, Sc M, PhD, Sc D). Part-time programs available. *Degree requirements:* For master's, comprehensive exam, thesis, 1 year full-time residency; for doctorate, comprehensive exam, thesis/dissertation, 2 years full-time residency, oral and written exams, student teaching. *Entrance requirements:* For master's, GRE General Test or MCAT, 3 letters of recommendation, curriculum vitae; for doctorate, GRE General Test, minimum 1 year of work experience, 3 letters of recommendation, curriculum vitae, academic records from all schools. Additional exam requirements/recommendations for international students: Required—TOEFL (minimum score 600

paper-based; 250 computer-based; 100 iBT); Recommended—IELTS (minimum score 7.5), TWE. Electronic applications accepted. *Faculty research:* Cancer and congenital malformations, nutritional epidemiology, AIDS, tuberculosis, cardiovascular disease, risk assessment.

The Johns Hopkins University, National Institutes of Health Sponsored Programs, Baltimore, MD 21218-2699. Offers biology (PhD), including biochemistry, biophysics, cell biology, developmental biology, genetic biology, molecular biology; cell, molecular, and developmental biology and biophysics (PhD). *Degree requirements:* For doctorate, comprehensive exam, thesis/dissertation. *Entrance requirements:* For doctorate, GRE General Test. Additional exam requirements/recommendations for international students: Required—TOEFL (minimum score 600 paper-based; 250 computer-based), TWE. Electronic applications accepted. *Faculty research:* Protein and nucleic acid biochemistry and biophysical chemistry, molecular biology and development.

Kansas State University, Graduate School, College of Agriculture, Department of Plant Pathology, Manhattan, KS 66506. Offers genetics (MS, PhD); plant pathology (MS, PhD). *Faculty:* 19 full-time (5 women), 2 part-time/adjunct (0 women). *Students:* 33 full-time (13 women), 1 (woman) part-time; includes 3 minority (1 Black or African American, non-Hispanic/Latino; 2 Hispanic/Latino), 18 international. Average age 28. 26 applicants, 23% accepted, 4 enrolled. In 2011, 5 doctorates awarded. Terminal master's awarded for partial completion of doctoral program. *Degree requirements:* For master's, thesis, oral exam; for doctorate, thesis/dissertation, preliminary exams. *Entrance requirements:* For master's and doctorate, minimum undergraduate GPA of 3.0. Additional exam requirements/recommendations for international students: Required—TOEFL (minimum score 550 paper-based; 213 computer-based; 79 iBT). *Application deadline:* For fall admission, 5/15 priority date for domestic students, 12/1 for international students; for spring admission, 10/15 priority date for domestic students, 6/1 for international students. Applications are processed on a rolling basis. Application fee: $40 ($55 for international students). Electronic applications accepted. *Financial support:* In 2011–12, 32 research assistantships (averaging $23,845 per year) were awarded; Federal Work-Study, institutionally sponsored loans, and scholarships/grants also available. Support available to part-time students. Financial award application deadline: 3/1; financial award applicants required to submit FAFSA. *Faculty research:* Applied microbiology, microbial genetics, microbial ecology/epidemiology, integrated pest management, plant genetics/genomics/molecular biology. *Total annual research expenditures:* $6.5 million. *Unit head:* Dr. John Leslie, Head, 785-532-6176, Fax: 785-532-5692, E-mail: jfl@ksu.edu. *Application contact:* Dr. Bill Bockus, Director, 785-532-1378, Fax: 785-532-5692, E-mail: bockus@ksu.edu. Web site: http://www.plantpath.k-state.edu/DesktopDefault.aspx.

Marquette University, Graduate School, College of Arts and Sciences, Department of Biology, Milwaukee, WI 53201-1881. Offers cell biology (MS, PhD); developmental biology (MS, PhD); ecology (MS, PhD); epithelial physiology (MS, PhD); genetics (MS, PhD); microbiology (MS, PhD); molecular biology (MS, PhD); muscle and exercise physiology (MS, PhD); neuroscience (PhD). *Faculty:* 23 full-time (11 women), 1 part-time/adjunct (0 women). *Students:* 33 full-time (14 women), 6 part-time (3 women), 19 international. Average age 25. 78 applicants, 17% accepted, 5 enrolled. In 2011, 6 doctorates awarded. Terminal master's awarded for partial completion of doctoral program. *Degree requirements:* For master's, comprehensive exam, thesis, 1 year of teaching experience or equivalent; for doctorate, thesis/dissertation, 1 year of teaching experience or equivalent, qualifying exam. *Entrance requirements:* For master's and doctorate, GRE General Test, GRE Subject Test, official transcripts from all current and previous colleges/universities except Marquette, statement of professional goals and aspirations, three letters of recommendation. Additional exam requirements/recommendations for international students: Required—TOEFL (minimum score 530 paper-based; 78 computer-based). *Application deadline:* For fall admission, 12/15 for domestic and international students. Application fee: $50. Electronic applications accepted. *Expenses: Tuition:* Full-time $17,010; part-time $945 per credit hour. Tuition and fees vary according to program. *Financial support:* In 2011–12, 39 students received support, including 6 fellowships (averaging $1,208 per year), 4 research assistantships with full tuition reimbursements available (averaging $21,750 per year), 29 teaching assistantships with full tuition reimbursements available (averaging $21,750 per year); scholarships/grants, health care benefits, tuition waivers (full and partial), and unspecified assistantships also available. Support available to part-time students. Financial award application deadline: 2/15. *Faculty research:* Neurobiology, neuroendocrinology, epithelial physiology, neuropeptide interactions, synaptic transmission. *Total annual research expenditures:* $2 million. *Unit head:* Dr. Robert Fitts, Chair, 414-288-1748, Fax: 414-288-7357. *Application contact:* Debbie Weaver, Administrative Assistant, 414-288-7355, Fax: 414-288-7357. Web site: http://www.marquette.edu/biology/.

Massachusetts Institute of Technology, School of Science, Department of Biology, Cambridge, MA 02139. Offers biochemistry (PhD); biological oceanography (PhD); biology (PhD); biophysical chemistry and molecular structure (PhD); cell biology (PhD); computational and systems biology (PhD); developmental biology (PhD); genetics (PhD); immunology (PhD); microbiology (PhD); molecular biology (PhD); neurobiology (PhD). *Faculty:* 58 full-time (15 women). *Students:* 248 full-time (129 women); includes 69 minority (5 Black or African American, non-Hispanic/Latino; 1 American Indian or Alaska Native, non-Hispanic/Latino; 25 Asian, non-Hispanic/Latino; 31 Hispanic/Latino; 7 Two or more races, non-Hispanic/Latino), 36 international. Average age 26. 698 applicants, 15% accepted, 44 enrolled. In 2011, 38 doctorates awarded. *Degree requirements:* For doctorate, comprehensive exam, thesis/dissertation. *Entrance requirements:* For doctorate, GRE General Test. Additional exam requirements/recommendations for international students: Required—TOEFL (minimum score 577 paper-based; 233 computer-based), IELTS (minimum score 6.5). *Application deadline:* For fall admission, 12/1 for domestic and international students. Application fee: $75. Electronic applications accepted. *Expenses: Tuition:* Full-time $40,460; part-time $630 per credit hour. *Required fees:* $272. *Financial support:* In 2011–12, 214 students received support, including 129 fellowships (averaging $33,200 per year), 117 research assistantships (averaging $32,900 per year); teaching assistantships, Federal Work-Study, institutionally sponsored loans, scholarships/grants, traineeships, health care benefits, and unspecified assistantships also available. *Faculty research:* Cellular, developmental and molecular (plant and animal) biology; biochemistry, bioengineering, biophysics and structural biology; classical and molecular genetics; immunology and microbiology; cancer biology, molecular medicine, neurobiology and human disease; computational and systems biology. *Total annual research expenditures:* $53.6 million. *Unit head:* Prof. Tania A. Baker, Head, 617-253-4701, E-mail: mitbio@mit.edu. *Application contact:* Biology Education Office, 617-253-3717, Fax: 617-258-9329, E-mail: gradbio@mit.edu. Web site: https://biology.mit.edu/.

Mayo Graduate School, Graduate Programs in Biomedical Sciences, Program in Virology and Gene Therapy, Rochester, MN 55905. Offers PhD.

Mayo Graduate School, Graduate Programs in Biomedical Sciences, Programs in Biochemistry, Structural Biology, Cell Biology, and Genetics, Rochester, MN 55905. Offers biochemistry and structural biology (PhD); cell biology and genetics (PhD); molecular biology (PhD). *Degree requirements:* For doctorate, oral defense of dissertation, qualifying oral and written exam. *Entrance requirements:* For doctorate,

GRE, 1 year of chemistry, biology, calculus, and physics. Additional exam requirements/recommendations for international students: Required—TOEFL. Electronic applications accepted. *Faculty research:* Gene structure and function, membranes and receptors/cytoskeleton, oncogenes and growth factors, protein structure and function, steroid hormonal action.

McMaster University, Faculty of Health Sciences and School of Graduate Studies, Program in Medical Sciences, Genetics and Cancer Area, Hamilton, ON L8S 4M2, Canada. Offers M Sc, PhD, MD/PhD. *Degree requirements:* For master's, thesis; for doctorate, comprehensive exam, thesis/dissertation. *Entrance requirements:* For master's, honors B Sc, B+ average in related field; for doctorate, M Sc, minimum B+ average, students with proven research experience and an A average may be admitted with a B Sc degree. Additional exam requirements/recommendations for international students: Required—TOEFL (minimum score 580 paper-based; 237 computer-based; 92 iBT).

Medical University of South Carolina, College of Graduate Studies, Program in Molecular and Cellular Biology and Pathobiology, Charleston, SC 29425. Offers cancer biology (PhD); cardiovascular biology (PhD); cardiovascular imaging (PhD); cell regulation (PhD); craniofacial biology (PhD); genetics and development (PhD); marine biomedicine (PhD); DMD/PhD; MD/PhD. *Faculty:* 137 full-time (33 women). *Students:* 28 full-time (23 women); includes 5 minority (4 Black or African American, non-Hispanic/Latino; 1 Hispanic/Latino), 5 international. Average age 30. In 2011, 16 doctorates awarded. *Degree requirements:* For doctorate, thesis/dissertation, oral and written exams. *Entrance requirements:* For doctorate, GRE General Test, interview, minimum GPA of 3.0. Additional exam requirements/recommendations for international students: Required—TOEFL (minimum score 600 paper-based; 250 computer-based; 100 iBT). *Application deadline:* For fall admission, 1/15 priority date for domestic students, 1/15 for international students. Applications are processed on a rolling basis. Application fee: $0 ($85 for international students). Electronic applications accepted. *Financial support:* In 2011–12, 39 research assistantships with partial tuition reimbursements (averaging $23,000 per year) were awarded; Federal Work-Study and scholarships/grants also available. Support available to part-time students. Financial award application deadline: 3/10; financial award applicants required to submit FAFSA. *Unit head:* Dr. Donald R. Menick, Director, 843-876-5045, Fax: 843-792-6590, E-mail: menickd@musc.edu. *Application contact:* Dr. Cynthia F. Wright, Associate Dean for Admissions and Career Development, 843-792-2564, Fax: 843-792-6590, E-mail: wrightcf@musc.edu. Web site: http://www.musc.edu/mcbp/.

Michigan State University, College of Veterinary Medicine and The Graduate School, Graduate Programs in Veterinary Medicine and College of Natural Science and Graduate Programs in Human Medicine, Department of Microbiology and Molecular Genetics, East Lansing, MI 48824. Offers industrial microbiology (MS, PhD); microbiology (MS, PhD); microbiology and molecular genetics (MS, PhD); microbiology–environmental toxicology (PhD). *Entrance requirements:* For master's, GRE General Test. Additional exam requirements/recommendations for international students: Required—TOEFL (minimum score 550 paper-based; 213 computer-based), Michigan State University ELT (minimum score 85), Michigan English Language Assessment Battery (minimum score 83). Electronic applications accepted.

Michigan State University, The Graduate School, College of Agriculture and Natural Resources, MSU-DOE Plant Research Laboratory, East Lansing, MI 48824. Offers biochemistry and molecular biology (PhD); cellular and molecular biology (PhD); crop and soil sciences (PhD); genetics (PhD); microbiology and molecular genetics (PhD); plant biology (PhD); plant physiology (PhD). Offered jointly with the Department of Energy. *Degree requirements:* For doctorate, comprehensive exam, thesis/dissertation, laboratory rotation, defense of dissertation. *Entrance requirements:* For doctorate, GRE General Test, acceptance into one of the affiliated department programs; 3 letters of recommendation; bachelor's degree or equivalent in life sciences, chemistry, biochemistry, or biophysics; research experience. Electronic applications accepted. *Faculty research:* Role of hormones in the regulation of plant development and physiology, molecular mechanisms associated with signal recognition, development and application of genetic methods and materials, protein routing and function.

Michigan State University, The Graduate School, College of Natural Science, Program in Genetics, East Lansing, MI 48824. Offers genetics (MS, PhD); genetics–environmental toxicology (PhD). *Entrance requirements:* Additional exam requirements/recommendations for international students: Required—TOEFL. Electronic applications accepted.

Mississippi State University, College of Agriculture and Life Sciences, Department of Animal Dairy Sciences, Mississippi State, MS 39762. Offers agricultural life sciences (MS), including animal physiology (MS, PhD), genetics (MS, PhD); agricultural science (PhD), including animal dairy sciences, animal nutrition; life sciences (PhD), including animal physiology (MS, PhD), genetics (MS, PhD). *Faculty:* 12 full-time (5 women). *Students:* 22 full-time (14 women), 14 part-time (7 women); includes 4 minority (2 Black or African American, non-Hispanic/Latino; 2 Hispanic/Latino), 7 international. Average age 30. 35 applicants, 20% accepted, 5 enrolled. In 2011, 5 master's, 4 doctorates awarded. *Degree requirements:* For master's, thesis, comprehensive oral or written exam; for doctorate, thesis/dissertation, comprehensive oral or written exam. *Entrance requirements:* For master's, GRE General Test, minimum GPA of 3.0; for doctorate, GRE General Test. Additional exam requirements/recommendations for international students: Required—TOEFL (minimum score 575 paper-based). *Application deadline:* For fall admission, 7/1 for domestic students, 5/1 for international students; for spring admission, 11/1 for domestic students, 9/1 for international students. Applications are processed on a rolling basis. Application fee: $40. Electronic applications accepted. *Expenses:* Tuition, state resident: full-time $5805; part-time $322.50 per credit hour. Tuition, nonresident: full-time $14,670; part-time $815 per credit hour. *Financial support:* In 2011–12, 16 research assistantships (averaging $12,270 per year), 1 teaching assistantship (averaging $10,014 per year) were awarded; Federal Work-Study, institutionally sponsored loans, and unspecified assistantships also available. Financial award application deadline: 4/1; financial award applicants required to submit FAFSA. *Faculty research:* Ecology and population dynamics, physiology, biochemistry and behavior, systematics. *Total annual research expenditures:* $496,000. *Unit head:* Dr. Scott Willard, Professor and Department Head, 662-325-2802, Fax: 662-325-8873, E-mail: swillard@bch.msstate.edu. *Application contact:* Dr. Brian Rude, Professor and Graduate Coordinator, 662-325-2802, Fax: 662-325-8873, E-mail: brude@ads.msstate.edu. Web site: http://www.ads.msstate.edu/.

New York University, Graduate School of Arts and Science, Department of Biology, New York, NY 10012-1019. Offers biology (PhD); biomedical journalism (MS); cancer and molecular biology (PhD); computational biology (PhD); computers in biological research (MS); developmental genetics (PhD); general biology (MS); immunology and microbiology (PhD); molecular genetics (PhD); neurobiology (PhD); oral biology (MS); plant biology (PhD); recombinant DNA technology (MS); MS/MBA. Part-time programs available. *Faculty:* 24 full-time (5 women). *Students:* 146 full-time (90 women), 54 part-time (36 women); includes 49 minority (1 Black or African American, non-Hispanic/Latino; 33 Asian, non-Hispanic/Latino; 12 Hispanic/Latino; 3 Two or more races, non-Hispanic/Latino), 89 international. Average age 27. 394 applicants, 62% accepted, 82 enrolled. In 2011, 68 master's, 6 doctorates awarded. Terminal master's awarded for

partial completion of doctoral program. *Degree requirements:* For master's, thesis or alternative, qualifying paper; for doctorate, comprehensive exam, thesis/dissertation. *Entrance requirements:* For master's, GRE General Test; for doctorate, GRE General Test, GRE Subject Test. Additional exam requirements/recommendations for international students: Required—TOEFL. *Application deadline:* For fall admission, 12/1 priority date for domestic students, 12/1 for international students. Application fee: $90. *Financial support:* Fellowships with tuition reimbursements, research assistantships with tuition reimbursements, teaching assistantships with tuition reimbursements, career-related internships or fieldwork, Federal Work-Study, institutionally sponsored loans, scholarships/grants, health care benefits, and unspecified assistantships available. Financial award application deadline: 12/1; financial award applicants required to submit FAFSA. *Faculty research:* Genomics, molecular and cell biology, development and molecular genetics, molecular evolution of plants and animals. *Unit head:* Stephen Small, Chair, 212-998-8200, Fax: 212-995-4015, E-mail: biology@nyu.edu. *Application contact:* Justin Blau, Director of Graduate Studies, 212-998-8200, Fax: 212-995-4015, E-mail: biology@nyu.edu. Web site: http://biology.as.nyu.edu/.

North Carolina State University, Graduate School, College of Agriculture and Life Sciences, Department of Genetics, Raleigh, NC 27695. Offers MG, MS, PhD. Terminal master's awarded for partial completion of doctoral program. *Degree requirements:* For master's, thesis (for some programs); for doctorate, thesis/dissertation. *Entrance requirements:* For master's and doctorate, GRE General Test, minimum GPA of 3.0. Electronic applications accepted. *Faculty research:* Population and quantitative genetics, plant molecular genetics, developmental genetics.

Northwestern University, The Graduate School, Interdepartmental Biological Sciences Program (IBiS), Evanston, IL 60208. Offers biochemistry, molecular biology, and cell biology (PhD), including biochemistry, cell and molecular biology, molecular biophysics, structural biology; biotechnology (PhD); cell and molecular biology (PhD); developmental biology and genetics (PhD); hormone action and signal transduction (PhD); neuroscience (PhD); structural biology, biochemistry, and biophysics (PhD). Program participants include the Departments of Biochemistry, Molecular Biology, and Cell Biology; Chemistry; Neurobiology and Physiology; Chemical Engineering; Civil Engineering; and Evanston Hospital. *Degree requirements:* For doctorate, thesis/dissertation, qualifying exam. *Entrance requirements:* For doctorate, GRE General Test. Additional exam requirements/recommendations for international students: Required—TOEFL (minimum score 600 paper-based). Electronic applications accepted. *Faculty research:* Developmental genetics, gene regulation, DNA-protein interactions, biological clocks, bioremediation.

Northwestern University, Northwestern University Feinberg School of Medicine and Interdepartmental Programs, Integrated Graduate Programs in the Life Sciences, Chicago, IL 60611. Offers cancer biology (PhD); cell biology (PhD); developmental biology (PhD); evolutionary biology (PhD); immunology and microbial pathogenesis (PhD); molecular biology and genetics (PhD); neurobiology (PhD); pharmacology and toxicology (PhD); structural biology and biochemistry (PhD). *Degree requirements:* For doctorate, comprehensive exam, thesis/dissertation, written and oral qualifying exams. *Entrance requirements:* For doctorate, GRE General Test. Additional exam requirements/recommendations for international students: Required—TOEFL (minimum score 600 paper-based; 250 computer-based). Electronic applications accepted.

The Ohio State University, College of Medicine, School of Biomedical Science, Integrated Biomedical Science Graduate Program, Columbus, OH 43210. Offers immunology (PhD); medical genetics (PhD); molecular virology (PhD); pharmacology (PhD). *Degree requirements:* For doctorate, thesis/dissertation. *Entrance requirements:* For doctorate, GRE, GRE Subject Test in biochemistry, cell and molecular biology (recommended for some). Additional exam requirements/recommendations for international students: Required—TOEFL (minimum score 600 paper-based; 250 computer-based). Electronic applications accepted. *Expenses:* Tuition, state resident: full-time $11,400. Tuition, nonresident: full-time $28,125. Tuition and fees vary according to course load, degree level, campus/location and program.

The Ohio State University, Graduate School, College of Arts and Sciences, Division of Natural and Mathematical Sciences, Department of Molecular Genetics, Columbus, OH 43210. Offers cell and developmental biology (MS, PhD); genetics (MS, PhD); molecular biology (MS, PhD). *Faculty:* 23. *Students:* 11 full-time (5 women), 23 part-time (11 women); includes 1 minority (Black or African American, non-Hispanic/Latino), 15 international. Average age 26. In 2011, 8 doctorates awarded. *Degree requirements:* For master's, thesis; for doctorate, thesis/dissertation. *Entrance requirements:* For master's and doctorate, GRE General Test, GRE Subject Test in biology or biochemistry (recommended). Additional exam requirements/recommendations for international students: Required—TOEFL (minimum score 550 paper-based; 250 computer-based; 79 iBT), Michigan English Language Assessment Battery (minimum score 82). *Application deadline:* For fall admission, 8/15 priority date for domestic students, 7/1 for international students; for winter admission, 12/1 priority date for domestic students, 11/1 for international students; for spring admission, 3/1 priority date for domestic students, 2/1 for international students. Applications are processed on a rolling basis. Application fee: $40 ($50 for international students). Electronic applications accepted. *Expenses:* Tuition, state resident: full-time $11,400. Tuition, nonresident: full-time $28,125. Tuition and fees vary according to course load, degree level, campus/location and program. *Financial support:* Fellowships, research assistantships, teaching assistantships, Federal Work-Study, and institutionally sponsored loans available. Support available to part-time students. *Unit head:* Dr. Anita Hopper, Chair, 614-688-3306, Fax: 614-292-4466, E-mail: hopper.64@osu.edu. *Application contact:* Graduate Admissions, 614-292-6031, Fax: 614-292-3656, E-mail: gradadmissions@osu.edu. Web site: https://molgen.osu.edu/.

Oregon Health & Science University, School of Medicine, Graduate Programs in Medicine, Program in Molecular and Cellular Biosciences, Department of Molecular and Medical Genetics, Portland, OR 97239-3098. Offers PhD. *Faculty:* 15 full-time (9 women). *Students:* 5 full-time (3 women). Average age 30. In 2011, 1 doctorate awarded. Terminal master's awarded for partial completion of doctoral program. *Degree requirements:* For doctorate, comprehensive exam, thesis/dissertation. *Entrance requirements:* For doctorate, GRE General Test (minimum scores: 153 Verbal/148 Quantitative/4.5 Analytical) or MCAT (for some programs). Additional exam requirements/recommendations for international students: Required—TOEFL. Electronic applications accepted. *Financial support:* Health care benefits and full tuition and stipends for PhD students available. *Faculty research:* Biological function and molecular mechanisms of the p53 tumor suppression and c-Myc oncogenic pathways, development of liver- or muscle-directed gene transfer for the treatment of IEM, development of sequence-based testing for rare disorders, development of new rAAV vector-mediated gene and cell therapies to treat various human diseases, cellular signaling pathways involved in the generation of human cancer. *Unit head:* Dr. Susan Olson, Program Director, 503-494-7703, E-mail: olsonsu@oshsu.edu. *Application contact:* Anne Huntzicker, Program Coordinator, 503-494-1771, E-mail: huntzica@ohsu.edu. Web site: http://www.ohsu.edu/ohsuedu/academic/som/basicscience/genetics/.

Oregon State University, Graduate School, College of Agricultural Sciences, Program in Genetics, Corvallis, OR 97331. Offers MA, MAIS, MS, PhD. Part-time programs available. Terminal master's awarded for partial completion of doctoral program. *Degree requirements:* For master's, variable foreign language requirement, thesis or alternative; for doctorate, thesis/dissertation. *Entrance requirements:* For master's and doctorate, GRE General Test, minimum GPA of 3.0 in last 90 hours. Additional exam requirements/recommendations for international students: Required—TOEFL. *Faculty research:* Molecular genetics, cytogenetics, population and quantitative genetics, microbial genetics, plant genetics.

Penn State Hershey Medical Center, College of Medicine, Graduate School Programs in the Biomedical Sciences, Graduate Program in Microbiology and Immunology, Hershey, PA 17033. Offers genetics (PhD); immunology (MS, PhD); microbiology (MS); microbiology/virology (PhD); molecular biology (PhD); MD/PhD. *Students:* 18 full-time (9 women), 6 international. 59 applicants, 5% accepted, 3 enrolled. In 2011, 1 master's, 3 doctorates awarded. Terminal master's awarded for partial completion of doctoral program. *Degree requirements:* For master's, thesis or alternative; for doctorate, comprehensive exam, thesis/dissertation, oral exam. *Entrance requirements:* For doctorate, GRE General Test, minimum GPA of 3.0. Additional exam requirements/recommendations for international students: Required—TOEFL. *Application deadline:* For fall admission, 1/31 priority date for domestic students, 2/1 for international students. Applications are processed on a rolling basis. Application fee: $65. Electronic applications accepted. *Financial support:* In 2011–12, research assistantships with full tuition reimbursements (averaging $23,028 per year) were awarded; fellowships with full tuition reimbursements, scholarships/grants, health care benefits, and unspecified assistantships also available. Financial award applicants required to submit FAFSA. *Faculty research:* Virus replication and assembly, oncogenesis, interactions of viruses with host cells and animal model systems. *Unit head:* Dr. Aron Luckacher, Chair, 717-531-7659, Fax: 717-531-6522, E-mail: micro-grad-hmc@psu.edu. *Application contact:* Billie Burns, Secretary, 717-531-7659, Fax: 717-531-6522, E-mail: micro-grad-hmc@psu.edu. Web site: http://www.pennstatehershey.org/web/microbiology/programs.

Penn State University Park, Graduate School, Intercollege Graduate Programs, Intercollege Graduate Program in Genetics, State College, University Park, PA 16802-1503. Offers MS, PhD. *Unit head:* Dr. Richard Ordway, Chair, 814-863-5693, Fax: 814-865-9131, E-mail: rordway@psu.edu. *Application contact:* Cynthia E. Nicosia, Director, Graduate Enrollment Services, 814-865-1795, Fax: 814-865-4627, E-mail: cey1@psu.edu.

Purdue University, Graduate School, College of Science, Department of Biological Sciences, West Lafayette, IN 47907. Offers biochemistry (PhD); biophysics (PhD); cell and developmental biology (PhD); ecology, evolutionary and population biology (MS, PhD), including ecology, evolutionary biology, population biology; genetics (MS, PhD); microbiology (MS, PhD); molecular biology (PhD); neurobiology (MS, PhD); plant physiology (PhD). *Faculty:* 57 full-time (15 women), 4 part-time/adjunct (1 woman). *Students:* 94 full-time (54 women), 9 part-time (5 women); includes 7 minority (2 Black or African American, non-Hispanic/Latino; 3 Asian, non-Hispanic/Latino; 2 Hispanic/Latino), 51 international. Average age 27. 246 applicants, 11% accepted, 18 enrolled. In 2011, 9 master's, 23 doctorates awarded. Terminal master's awarded for partial completion of doctoral program. *Degree requirements:* For master's, thesis (for some programs); for doctorate, thesis/dissertation, seminars, teaching experience. *Entrance requirements:* For master's, GRE General Test, minimum analytical writing score of 3.5, minimum undergraduate GPA of 3.0; for doctorate, GRE General Test, minimum analytical writing score of 3.5, minimum undergraduate GPA of 3.5. Additional exam requirements/recommendations for international students: Required—TOEFL (minimum score 600 paper-based; 107 iBT) for MS; TOEFL (minimum score 600 paper-based; 80 iBT) for Ph D. *Application deadline:* For fall admission, 12/7 for domestic and international students. Applications are processed on a rolling basis. Application fee: $60 ($75 for international students). Electronic applications accepted. *Financial support:* Fellowships, research assistantships, and teaching assistantships available. Support available to part-time students. Financial award application deadline: 2/15; financial award applicants required to submit FAFSA. *Unit head:* Dr. Richard J. Kuhn, Head, 765-494-4407, E-mail: kuhnr@purdue.edu. *Application contact:* Georgina E. Rupp, Graduate Coordinator, 765-494-8142, Fax: 765-494-0876, E-mail: ruppg@purdue.edu. Web site: http://www.bio.purdue.edu/.

Purdue University, Graduate School, PULSe - Purdue University Life Sciences Program, West Lafayette, IN 47907. Offers biomolecular structure and biophysics (PhD); biotechnology (PhD); chemical biology (PhD); chromatin and regulation of gene expression (PhD); integrative neuroscience (PhD); integrative plant sciences (PhD); membrane biology (PhD); microbiology (PhD); molecular evolutionary and cancer biology (PhD); molecular evolutionary genetics (PhD); molecular virology (PhD). *Students:* 90 full-time (45 women); includes 7 minority (3 Black or African American, non-Hispanic/Latino; 1 Asian, non-Hispanic/Latino; 2 Hispanic/Latino; 1 Two or more races, non-Hispanic/Latino), 40 international. Average age 26. 427 applicants, 24% accepted, 35 enrolled. *Entrance requirements:* For doctorate, GRE test required, minimum undergraduate GPA of 3.0. Additional exam requirements/recommendations for international students: Required—TOEFL (minimum score 550 paper-based; 77 iBT). *Application deadline:* For fall admission, 1/15 priority date for domestic students, 1/15 for international students. Applications are processed on a rolling basis. Application fee: $60 ($75 for international students). Electronic applications accepted. *Financial support:* In 2011–12, research assistantships with tuition reimbursements (averaging $22,500 per year), teaching assistantships with tuition reimbursements (averaging $22,500 per year) were awarded. *Unit head:* Dr. Christine A. Hrycyna, Head, 765-494-7322, E-mail: hrycyna@purdue.edu. *Application contact:* Emily E. Bramson, Graduate Contact, 765-494-5865, E-mail: bramson@purdue.edu. Web site: http://www.gradschool.purdue.edu/pulse.

Rutgers, The State University of New Jersey, New Brunswick, Graduate School-New Brunswick, Programs in the Molecular Biosciences, Program in Microbiology and Molecular Genetics, Piscataway, NJ 08854-8097. Offers applied microbiology (MS, PhD); clinical microbiology (MS, PhD); computational molecular biology (PhD); immunology (MS, PhD); microbial biochemistry (MS, PhD); molecular genetics (MS, PhD); virology (MS, PhD). MS, PhD offered jointly with University of Medicine and Dentistry of New Jersey. Part-time programs available. Terminal master's awarded for partial completion of doctoral program. *Degree requirements:* For master's, comprehensive exam, thesis or alternative; for doctorate, comprehensive exam, thesis/dissertation, written qualifying exam. *Entrance requirements:* For master's, GRE General Test, minimum GPA of 3.0; for doctorate, GRE General Test, GRE Subject Test (recommended), minimum GPA of 3.0. Additional exam requirements/recommendations for international students: Required—TOEFL. Electronic applications accepted. *Faculty research:* Molecular genetics and microbial physiology; virology and pathogenic microbiology; applied, environmental and industrial microbiology; computers in molecular biology.

Stanford University, School of Medicine, Graduate Programs in Medicine, Department of Genetics, Stanford, CA 94305-9991. Offers PhD. *Degree requirements:* For doctorate, thesis/dissertation, qualifying examination. *Entrance requirements:* For doctorate, GRE General Test, GRE Subject Test. Additional exam requirements/recommendations for international students: Required—TOEFL. Electronic applications accepted. *Expenses: Tuition:* Full-time $40,050; part-time $890 per credit. *Faculty*

research: Molecular biology of DNA replication in human cells, analysis of existing and search for new DNA polymorphisms in humans, molecular genetics of prokaryotic and eukaryotic genetic elements, proteins in DNA replication.

Stony Brook University, State University of New York, Graduate School, College of Arts and Sciences, Graduate Program in Genetics, Stony Brook, NY 11794. Offers PhD. *Degree requirements:* For doctorate, comprehensive exam, thesis/dissertation, teaching experience. *Entrance requirements:* For doctorate, GRE General Test, GRE Subject Test. Additional exam requirements/recommendations for international students: Required—TOEFL. *Faculty research:* Gene structure, gene regulation.

Temple University, Health Sciences Center, School of Medicine and Graduate School, Graduate Programs in Medicine, Program in Molecular Biology and Genetics, Philadelphia, PA 19122-6096. Offers MS, PhD, MD/PhD. *Students:* 21 full-time (11 women); includes 1 minority (Asian, non-Hispanic/Latino), 11 international. Average age 27. 7 applicants, 86% accepted, 4 enrolled. In 2011, 2 master's, 2 doctorates awarded. *Degree requirements:* For doctorate, thesis/dissertation, presentation research/literature seminars distinct from area of concentration. *Entrance requirements:* For doctorate, GRE General Test, GRE Subject Test, minimum GPA of 3.0. Additional exam requirements/recommendations for international students: Required—TOEFL (minimum score 620 paper-based; 260 computer-based). *Application deadline:* For fall admission, 1/15 for domestic students, 12/15 for international students. Application fee: $50. Electronic applications accepted. *Expenses:* Tuition, state resident: full-time $12,366; part-time $687 per credit hour. Tuition, nonresident: full-time $17,298; part-time $961 per credit hour. *Required fees:* $590; $213 per year. *Financial support:* Fellowships, research assistantships, Federal Work-Study, institutionally sponsored loans, and tuition waivers (full) available. Financial award application deadline: 1/15; financial award applicants required to submit FAFSA. *Faculty research:* Molecular genetics of normal and malignant cell growth, regulation of gene expression, DNA repair systems and carcinogenesis, hormone-receptor interactions and signal transduction systems, structural biology. *Unit head:* Dr. Scott Shore, Chair, 215-707-3359, Fax: 215-707-2805, E-mail: sks@temple.edu. *Application contact:* Office of Admissions, 215-707-3656, Fax: 215-707-6932, E-mail: medadmissions@temple.edu.

Texas A&M University, College of Veterinary Medicine and Biomedical Sciences, Department of Veterinary Pathobiology, College Station, TX 77843. Offers genetics (MS, PhD); veterinary microbiology (MS, PhD); veterinary parasitology (MS, PhD); veterinary pathology (MS, PhD). Part-time programs available. Postbaccalaureate distance learning degree programs offered. *Faculty:* 25. *Students:* 27 full-time (20 women), 19 part-time (13 women); includes 9 minority (3 Black or African American, non-Hispanic/Latino; 3 Asian, non-Hispanic/Latino; 3 Hispanic/Latino), 9 international. Average age 33. In 2011, 2 degrees awarded. Terminal master's awarded for partial completion of doctoral program. *Degree requirements:* For master's, thesis, seminars; for doctorate, thesis/dissertation, seminars. *Entrance requirements:* For master's and doctorate, GRE General Test, minimum GPA of 3.0 in last 60 hours. Additional exam requirements/recommendations for international students: Required—TOEFL. *Application deadline:* For fall admission, 3/1 priority date for domestic students; for spring admission, 8/1 priority date for domestic students. Applications are processed on a rolling basis. Application fee: $50 ($75 for international students). Electronic applications accepted. *Expenses:* Tuition, state resident: full-time $5437; part-time $226.55 per credit hour. Tuition, nonresident: full-time $12,949; part-time $539.55 per credit hour. *Required fees:* $2741. *Financial support:* In 2011–12, fellowships with partial tuition reimbursements (averaging $16,000 per year), research assistantships with partial tuition reimbursements (averaging $15,400 per year), teaching assistantships with partial tuition reimbursements (averaging $16,000 per year) were awarded; Federal Work-Study, institutionally sponsored loans, scholarships/grants, traineeships, health care benefits, and unspecified assistantships also available. Support available to part-time students. Financial award applicants required to submit FAFSA. *Faculty research:* Infectious and noninfectious diseases of animals and birds, animal genetics, molecular biology, immunology, virology. *Unit head:* Dr. Linda Logan, Head, 979-862-6559, Fax: 979-845-9231, E-mail: llogan@cvm.tamu.edu. *Application contact:* Dr. Patricia Holman, Graduate Advisor, 979-845-4202, Fax: 979-862-1147, E-mail: pholman@cvm.tamu.edu. Web site: http://vetmed.tamu.edu/vtpb.

Thomas Jefferson University, Jefferson College of Graduate Studies, PhD Program in Genetics, Philadelphia, PA 19107. Offers PhD. *Faculty:* 41 full-time (12 women), 3 part-time/adjunct (all women). *Students:* 21 full-time (12 women); includes 4 minority (2 Black or African American, non-Hispanic/Latino; 1 Asian, non-Hispanic/Latino; 1 Hispanic/Latino), 6 international. 35 applicants, 14% accepted, 4 enrolled. In 2011, 8 doctorates awarded. *Degree requirements:* For doctorate, comprehensive exam, thesis/dissertation. *Entrance requirements:* For doctorate, GRE General Test, minimum GPA of 3.2. Additional exam requirements/recommendations for international students: Required—TOEFL (minimum score 250 computer-based; 100 iBT) or IELTS. *Application deadline:* For fall admission, 1/5 priority date for domestic students, 1/5 for international students. Applications are processed on a rolling basis. Application fee: $50. Electronic applications accepted. *Financial support:* In 2011–12, 21 students received support, including 21 fellowships with full tuition reimbursements available (averaging $54,758 per year); Federal Work-Study, institutionally sponsored loans, scholarships/grants, traineeships, and stipends also available. Support available to part-time students. Financial award application deadline: 5/1; financial award applicants required to submit FAFSA. *Faculty research:* Functional genomics, cancer susceptibility, cell cycle, regulation oncogenes and tumor suppressor genes, genetics of neoplastic disease. *Total annual research expenditures:* $21.5 million. *Unit head:* Dr. Linda D. Siracusa, Program Director, 215-503-4536, E-mail: linda.siracusa@jefferson.edu. *Application contact:* Marc E. Stearns, Director of Admissions, 215-503-0155, Fax: 215-503-9920, E-mail: jcgs-info@jefferson.edu. Web site: http://www.jefferson.edu/jcgs/phd/genetics/.

Tufts University, Sackler School of Graduate Biomedical Sciences, Genetics Program, Medford, MA 02155. Offers PhD. *Faculty:* 58 full-time (18 women). *Students:* 29 full-time (21 women); includes 5 minority (3 Asian, non-Hispanic/Latino; 2 Hispanic/Latino), 8 international. Average age 28. 77 applicants, 14% accepted, 5 enrolled. In 2011, 6 doctorates awarded. Terminal master's awarded for partial completion of doctoral program. *Degree requirements:* For doctorate, thesis/dissertation. *Entrance requirements:* For doctorate, GRE General Test, 3 letters of reference. Additional exam requirements/recommendations for international students: Required—TOEFL (minimum score 600 paper-based; 250 computer-based; 100 iBT). *Application deadline:* For fall admission, 12/15 for domestic and international students. Application fee: $70. Electronic applications accepted. *Expenses:* Tuition: Full-time $41,208; part-time $1030 per credit hour. Full-time tuition and fees vary according to degree level, program and student level. Part-time tuition and fees vary according to course load. *Financial support:* In 2011–12, 29 students received support, including 29 research assistantships with full tuition reimbursements available (averaging $30,000 per year); traineeships and health care benefits also available. *Faculty research:* Cancer genetics, developmental and neurogenetics, microbial and yeast genetics, the genetics of bacterial and viral pathogens, Drosophila genetics, human genetics and gene discovery. *Unit head:* Dr. Erik Selsing, Program Director, 617-636-0467. *Application contact:* Kellie Melchin,

Associate Director of Admissions, 617-636-6767, Fax: 617-636-0375. Web site: http://sackler.tufts.edu/Academics/Degree-Programs/PhD-Programs/Genetics.

Université de Montréal, Faculty of Medicine, Program in Medical Genetics, Montréal, QC H3C 3J7, Canada. Offers DESS.

Université du Québec à Chicoutimi, Graduate Programs, Program in Experimental Medicine, Chicoutimi, QC G7H 2B1, Canada. Offers genetics (M Sc). *Degree requirements:* For master's, thesis. *Entrance requirements:* For master's, appropriate bachelor's degree, proficiency in French.

University at Albany, State University of New York, School of Public Health, Department of Biomedical Sciences, Program in Biochemistry, Molecular Biology, and Genetics, Albany, NY 12222-0001. Offers MS, PhD. *Degree requirements:* For master's, thesis; for doctorate, thesis/dissertation. *Entrance requirements:* For master's and doctorate, GRE General Test, GRE Subject Test.

The University of Alabama at Birmingham, Graduate Programs in Joint Health Sciences, Program in Genetics, Birmingham, AL 35294. Offers PhD. *Degree requirements:* For doctorate, thesis/dissertation. *Entrance requirements:* For doctorate, GRE, interview. *Application deadline:* Applications are processed on a rolling basis. Application fee: $35 ($60 for international students). Electronic applications accepted. *Expenses:* Tuition, state resident: full-time $5922; part-time $309 per hour. Tuition, nonresident: full-time $13,428; part-time $726 per hour. Tuition and fees vary according to program. *Financial support:* Fellowships available. *Faculty research:* Clinical cytogenetics, cancer cytogenetics, prenatal diagnosis. *Unit head:* Dr. Bruce R. Korf, Chair, 205-934-9411.

University of Alberta, Faculty of Graduate Studies and Research, Department of Biological Sciences, Edmonton, AB T6G 2E1, Canada. Offers environmental biology and ecology (M Sc, PhD); microbiology and biotechnology (M Sc, PhD); molecular biology and genetics (M Sc, PhD); physiology and cell biology (M Sc, PhD); plant biology (M Sc, PhD); systematics and evolution (M Sc, PhD). Terminal master's awarded for partial completion of doctoral program. *Degree requirements:* For master's, thesis; for doctorate, thesis/dissertation. *Entrance requirements:* Additional exam requirements/recommendations for international students: Required—TOEFL.

University of Alberta, Faculty of Medicine and Dentistry and Faculty of Graduate Studies and Research, Graduate Programs in Medicine, Department of Medical Genetics, Edmonton, AB T6G 2E1, Canada. Offers M Sc, PhD. *Degree requirements:* For master's, comprehensive exam, thesis; for doctorate, comprehensive exam, thesis/dissertation. *Entrance requirements:* For master's and doctorate, minimum GPA of 3.2. *Faculty research:* Clinical and molecular cytogenetics, ocular genetics, Prader-Willi syndrome, genomic instability, developmental genetics.

The University of Arizona, Graduate Interdisciplinary Programs, Graduate Interdisciplinary Program in Genetics, Tucson, AZ 85719. Offers MS, PhD. *Students:* 14 full-time (7 women), 3 international. Average age 28. 15 applicants, 13% accepted, 1 enrolled. In 2011, 1 master's, 2 doctorates awarded. Terminal master's awarded for partial completion of doctoral program. *Degree requirements:* For master's, thesis; for doctorate, one foreign language, comprehensive exam, thesis/dissertation. *Entrance requirements:* For master's, GRE General Test, 3 letters of recommendation; for doctorate, GRE General Test, statement of purpose, 3 letters of recommendation. Additional exam requirements/recommendations for international students: Required—TOEFL (minimum score 550 paper-based; 213 computer-based; 79 iBT). *Application deadline:* For fall admission, 6/1 for domestic students, 12/1 for international students. Applications are processed on a rolling basis. Application fee: $75. Electronic applications accepted. *Expenses:* Tuition, state resident: full-time $10,840. Tuition, nonresident: full-time $25,802. *Financial support:* Career-related internships or fieldwork, scholarships/grants, health care benefits, and unspecified assistantships available. *Faculty research:* Cancer research; DNA repair; plant and animal cytogenetics; molecular, population, and ecological genetics. *Unit head:* Dr. Bosco Giovanni, Chairman, 520-626-3305, Fax: 520-626-5097, E-mail: mhb@peds.arizona.edu. *Application contact:* Lori Taylor, Program Coordinator, 520-626-9821, Fax: 520-626-5097, E-mail: lltaylor@arizona.edu. Web site: http://www.genetics.arizona.edu/.

The University of British Columbia, Faculty of Medicine, Department of Medical Genetics, Medical Genetics Graduate Program, Vancouver, BC V6T 1Z1, Canada. Offers M Sc, PhD. *Degree requirements:* For master's, thesis, 18 credits of coursework; for doctorate, comprehensive exam, thesis/dissertation, 18 credits of coursework. Electronic applications accepted.

The University of British Columbia, Genetics Graduate Program, Vancouver, BC V6T 1Z1, Canada. Offers M Sc, PhD. *Degree requirements:* For master's, comprehensive exam, thesis, thesis defense; for doctorate, comprehensive exam, thesis/dissertation, qualifying exam, oral and written comprehensive exams. *Entrance requirements:* Additional exam requirements/recommendations for international students: Required—TOEFL (minimum score 600 paper-based; 250 computer-based; 100 iBT). *Faculty research:* Prokaryote and eukaryote genetics.

University of California, Davis, Graduate Studies, Graduate Group in Genetics, Davis, CA 95616. Offers MS, PhD. Terminal master's awarded for partial completion of doctoral program. *Degree requirements:* For master's, comprehensive exam (for some programs), thesis (for some programs); for doctorate, thesis/dissertation. *Entrance requirements:* For master's and doctorate, GRE General Test, GRE Subject Test. Additional exam requirements/recommendations for international students: Required—TOEFL (minimum score 550 paper-based; 213 computer-based). Electronic applications accepted. *Faculty research:* Molecular, quantitative, and developmental genetics; cytogenetics; plant breeding.

University of California, Irvine, School of Biological Sciences and School of Medicine, Interdisciplinary Graduate Program in Cellular and Molecular Biosciences, Irvine, CA 92697. Offers PhD. *Faculty:* 138 full-time (35 women). *Students:* 59 full-time (33 women); includes 16 minority (8 Asian, non-Hispanic/Latino; 8 Hispanic/Latino), 6 international. Average age 25. In 2011, 19 doctorates awarded. *Degree requirements:* For doctorate, thesis/dissertation, teaching assignment, preliminary exam. *Entrance requirements:* For doctorate, GRE General Test, minimum GPA of 3.0, research experience. Additional exam requirements/recommendations for international students: Required—TOEFL, IELTS, SPEAK. *Application deadline:* For fall admission, 1/1 for domestic and international students. Application fee: $60 ($80 for international students). Electronic applications accepted. *Expenses:* Contact institution. *Financial support:* In 2011–12, 56 fellowships with full tuition reimbursements (averaging $26,250 per year) were awarded; institutionally sponsored loans, scholarships/grants, tuition waivers (full), unspecified assistantships, and stipends also available. Financial award application deadline: 1/1; financial award applicants required to submit FAFSA. *Faculty research:* Cellular biochemistry; gene structure and expression; protein structure, function, and design; molecular genetics; pathogenesis and inherited disease. *Unit head:* Dr. David Fruman, Director, 949-824-3431, Fax: 949-824-1965, E-mail: gp-mbgb@uci.edu. *Application contact:* Renee Frigo, Administrator, 949-824-8145, Fax: 949-824-1965, E-mail: rfrigo@uci.edu. Web site: http://cmb.uci.edu/.

Genetics

University of California, Riverside, Graduate Division, Graduate Program in Genetics, Genomics, and Bioinformatics, Riverside, CA 92521-0102. Offers genomics and bioinformatics (PhD); molecular genetics (PhD); population and evolutionary genetics (PhD). *Faculty:* 72 full-time (20 women). *Students:* 32 full-time (18 women); includes 2 minority (1 Black or African American, non-Hispanic/Latino; 1 Hispanic/Latino), 15 international. Average age 30. In 2011, 2 doctorates awarded. *Degree requirements:* For doctorate, thesis/dissertation, qualifying exams, teaching experience. *Entrance requirements:* For doctorate, GRE General Test, minimum GPA of 3.2. Additional exam requirements/recommendations for international students: Required—TOEFL (minimum score 550 paper-based; 213 computer-based; 80 iBT). *Application deadline:* For fall admission, 5/1 for domestic students, 2/1 for international students; for winter admission, 9/1 for domestic students, 7/1 for international students; for spring admission, 12/1 for domestic students, 10/1 for international students. Applications are processed on a rolling basis. Application fee: $85 ($100 for international students). Electronic applications accepted. *Financial support:* In 2011–12, fellowships with tuition reimbursements (averaging $12,000 per year), research assistantships with tuition reimbursements (averaging $18,000 per year), teaching assistantships with tuition reimbursements (averaging $16,500 per year) were awarded; career-related internships or fieldwork, Federal Work-Study, institutionally sponsored loans, and tuition waivers (full and partial) also available. *Faculty research:* Molecular genetics, evolution and population genetics, genomics and bioinformatics. *Unit head:* Dr. Shizhong Xu, Director, 951-827-5898. *Application contact:* Deidra Kornfeld, Graduate Program Assistant, 800-735-0717, Fax: 951-827-5517, E-mail: genetics@ucr.edu. Web site: http://ggb.ucr.edu/.

University of California, San Diego, Office of Graduate Studies, Division of Biological Sciences, Program in Genetics and Molecular Biology, La Jolla, CA 92093-0348. Offers PhD. Offered in association with the Salk Institute. *Degree requirements:* For doctorate, thesis/dissertation, qualifying exam. Electronic applications accepted.

University of California, San Francisco, Graduate Division and School of Medicine, Department of Biochemistry and Biophysics, Program in Genetics, San Francisco, CA 94143. Offers PhD, MD/PhD. *Degree requirements:* For doctorate, thesis/dissertation. *Entrance requirements:* For doctorate, GRE General Test, GRE Subject Test. Additional exam requirements/recommendations for international students: Required—TOEFL. *Expenses:* Contact institution. *Faculty research:* Gene expression; chromosome structure and mechanics; medical, somatic cell, and radiation genetics.

University of Chicago, Division of Biological Sciences, Molecular Biosciences Cluster, Committee on Genetics, Genomics and Systems Biology, Chicago, IL 60637-1513. Offers PhD. *Degree requirements:* For doctorate, thesis/dissertation, ethics class, 2 teaching assistantships. *Entrance requirements:* For doctorate, GRE General Test, minimum GPA of 3.0. Additional exam requirements/recommendations for international students: Required—TOEFL (minimum score 600 paper-based; 250 computer-based; 104 iBT), IELTS (minimum score 7). Electronic applications accepted. *Faculty research:* Molecular genetics, developmental genetics, population genetics, human genetics.

University of Colorado Boulder, Graduate School, College of Arts and Sciences, Department of Ecology and Evolutionary Biology, Boulder, CO 80309. Offers animal behavior (MA); biology (MA, PhD); environmental biology (MA, PhD); evolutionary biology (MA, PhD); neurobiology (MA); population biology (MA); population genetics (PhD). *Faculty:* 28 full-time (9 women). *Students:* 67 full-time (37 women), 27 part-time (13 women); includes 9 minority (1 Asian, non-Hispanic/Latino; 8 Hispanic/Latino), 5 international. Average age 30. 136 applicants, 13% accepted, 17 enrolled. In 2011, 8 master's, 5 doctorates awarded. Terminal master's awarded for partial completion of doctoral program. *Degree requirements:* For master's, comprehensive exam, thesis or alternative; for doctorate, comprehensive exam, thesis/dissertation. *Entrance requirements:* For master's, GRE General Test, GRE Subject Test, minimum undergraduate GPA of 3.0; for doctorate, GRE General Test, GRE Subject Test. *Application deadline:* For fall admission, 12/30 priority date for domestic students, 12/1 for international students. Application fee: $50 ($60 for international students). Electronic applications accepted. *Financial support:* In 2011–12, 88 students received support, including 35 fellowships (averaging $16,835 per year), 25 research assistantships with full and partial tuition reimbursements available (averaging $22,347 per year), 44 teaching assistantships with full and partial tuition reimbursements available (averaging $21,377 per year); institutionally sponsored loans, scholarships/grants, health care benefits, and unspecified assistantships also available. Financial award applicants required to submit FAFSA. *Faculty research:* Behavior, ecology, genetics, morphology, endocrinology, physiology, systematics. *Total annual research expenditures:* $4.6 million. *Application contact:* E-mail: ebiograd@colorado.edu. Web site: http://ebio.colorado.edu.

University of Colorado Denver, College of Liberal Arts and Sciences, Department of Integrative Biology, Denver, CO 80217. Offers animal behavior (MS); biology (MS); cell and developmental biology (MS); ecology (MS); evolutionary biology (MS); genetics (MS); microbiology (MS); molecular biology (MS); neurobiology (MS); plant systematics (MS). Part-time programs available. *Faculty:* 16 full-time (8 women). *Students:* 20 full-time (13 women), 5 part-time (4 women); includes 1 minority (Hispanic/Latino), 1 international. Average age 29. 21 applicants, 43% accepted, 5 enrolled. In 2011, 7 master's awarded. *Degree requirements:* For master's, comprehensive exam, thesis or alternative, 30-32 credit hours. *Entrance requirements:* For master's, GRE General Test (minimum score in 50% percentile in each section), BA/BS from accredited institution awarded within the last 10 years; minimum undergraduate GPA of 3.0; prerequisite courses: 1 year each of general biology and general chemistry, and 1 semester each of general genetics, general ecology, cell biology, and a structure/function course. Additional exam requirements/recommendations for international students: Required—TOEFL (minimum score 525 paper-based; 197 computer-based; 71 iBT). *Application deadline:* For fall admission, 2/1 for domestic and international students. Application fee: $50 ($75 for international students). Electronic applications accepted. *Financial support:* Research assistantships, teaching assistantships, Federal Work-Study, scholarships/grants, and unspecified assistantships available. Financial award application deadline: 4/1; financial award applicants required to submit FAFSA. *Faculty research:* Molecular developmental biology; quantitative ecology, biogeography, and population dynamics; environmental signaling and endocrine disruption; speciation, the evolution of reproductive isolation, and hybrid zones; evolutionary, behavioral, and conservation ecology. *Unit head:* Dr. Diana Tomback, Acting Chair, 303-556-2657, E-mail: diana.tomback@ucdenver.edu. *Application contact:* Timberley Roane, Associate Professor/Associate Chair, 303-556-6592, E-mail: timberley.roane@ucdenver.edu. Web site: http://www.ucdenver.edu/academics/colleges/CLAS/Departments/biology/Pages/Biology.aspx.

University of Colorado Denver, School of Medicine, Program in Medical Genetics and Genetic Counseling, Aurora, CO 80045. Offers human medical genetics (PhD). *Students:* 11 full-time (7 women). Average age 27. 18 applicants, 22% accepted, 4 enrolled. *Degree requirements:* For doctorate, comprehensive exam, thesis/dissertation, at least 30 semester hours in course work (rotations and research courses taken prior to the completion of the comprehensive examination) and 30 semester hours of thesis/didactic credits prior to defending. *Entrance requirements:* For doctorate, GRE General Test (minimum combined score of 1205), minimum GPA of 3.0, 4 letters of recommendation; prerequisite courses in biology, chemistry (general and organic),

physics, genetics, calculus, and statistics (recommended). Additional exam requirements/recommendations for international students: Required—TOEFL (minimum score 570 paper-based; 230 computer-based; 80 iBT). *Application deadline:* For fall admission, 1/1 for domestic students. Application fee: $50. Electronic applications accepted. *Expenses:* Contact institution. *Financial support:* Fellowships, research assistantships, teaching assistantships, and Federal Work-Study available. Financial award application deadline: 3/15; financial award applicants required to submit FAFSA. *Faculty research:* Mapping, discovery, and function of disease genes affecting skin and craniofacial development and autoimmunity; genetics of colon cancer; clinical proteomics; biochemical markers of disease, including cancer; modeling human genetic diseases with patient-derived induced pluripotent stem cells; cell cycle control of DNA replication and mutagenesis in yeast and human cancer cells; mechanisms of cancer chemoprevention. *Unit head:* Dr. Richard A. Spritz, Director, 303-724-3107, E-mail: richard.spritz@ucdenver.edu. *Application contact:* M. J. Stewart, Administrator, 303-724-3102, Fax: 303-724-3100, E-mail: mj.stewart@ucdenver.edu. Web site: http://www.ucdenver.edu/academics/colleges/medicalschool/programs/HumanMedicalGenetics/Pages/Genetics.aspx.

University of Connecticut, Graduate School, College of Liberal Arts and Sciences, Department of Molecular and Cell Biology, Field of Genetics, Genomics, and Bioinformatics, Storrs, CT 06269. Offers MS, PhD. Terminal master's awarded for partial completion of doctoral program. *Degree requirements:* For master's, comprehensive exam; for doctorate, thesis/dissertation. *Entrance requirements:* For master's and doctorate, GRE General Test, GRE Subject Test. Additional exam requirements/recommendations for international students: Required—TOEFL (minimum score 550 paper-based; 213 computer-based). Electronic applications accepted.

University of Connecticut Health Center, Graduate School, Programs in Biomedical Sciences, Graduate Program in Molecular Biology and Biochemistry, Farmington, CT 06030. Offers PhD, DMD/PhD, MD/PhD. *Degree requirements:* For doctorate, comprehensive exam, thesis/dissertation. *Entrance requirements:* For doctorate, GRE General Test. Additional exam requirements/recommendations for international students: Required—TOEFL (minimum score 600 paper-based; 250 computer-based). Electronic applications accepted. *Faculty research:* Molecular biology, structural biology, protein biochemistry, microbial physiology and pathogenesis.

See Display on page 219 and Close-Up on page 243.

University of Connecticut Health Center, Graduate School, Programs in Biomedical Sciences, Program in Genetics and Developmental Biology, Farmington, CT 06030. Offers PhD, DMD/PhD, MD/PhD. *Degree requirements:* For doctorate, comprehensive exam, thesis/dissertation. *Entrance requirements:* For doctorate, GRE General Test, GRE Subject Test. Additional exam requirements/recommendations for international students: Required—TOEFL (minimum score 600 paper-based; 250 computer-based). Electronic applications accepted. *Faculty research:* Developmental biology, genomic imprinting, RNA biology, RNA alternative splicing, human embryonic stem cells.

See Display on next page and Close-Up on page 313.

University of Delaware, College of Arts and Sciences, Department of Biological Sciences, Newark, DE 19716. Offers biotechnology (MS); cancer biology (MS, PhD); cell and extracellular matrix biology (MS, PhD); cell and systems physiology (MS, PhD); developmental biology (MS, PhD); ecology and evolution (MS, PhD); microbiology (MS, PhD); molecular biology and genetics (MS, PhD). Terminal master's awarded for partial completion of doctoral program. *Degree requirements:* For master's, thesis, preliminary exam; for doctorate, comprehensive exam, thesis/dissertation, preliminary exam. *Entrance requirements:* For master's and doctorate, GRE General Test. Additional exam requirements/recommendations for international students: Required—TOEFL (minimum score 600 paper-based; 250 computer-based); Recommended—TWE. Electronic applications accepted. *Faculty research:* Microorganisms, bone, cancer metastasis, developmental biology, cell biology, DNA.

University of Florida, College of Medicine and Graduate School, Interdisciplinary Program in Biomedical Sciences, Concentration in Genetics, Gainesville, FL 32611. Offers PhD. *Degree requirements:* For doctorate, thesis/dissertation. *Entrance requirements:* For doctorate, GRE General Test, minimum GPA of 3.0. Additional exam requirements/recommendations for international students: Required—TOEFL. Electronic applications accepted.

University of Georgia, College of Agricultural and Environmental Sciences, Institute of Plant Breeding, Genetics and Genomics, Athens, GA 30602. Offers MS, PhD. *Students:* 19 full-time (6 women), 2 part-time (1 woman), 11 international. Average age 29. 16 applicants, 25% accepted, 1 enrolled. In 2011, 2 master's, 4 doctorates awarded. *Financial support:* Tuition waivers and unspecified assistantships available. *Unit head:* Dr. John H. Dayton, Director, 706-542-5607, Fax: 706-583-8120, E-mail: pbgg@uga.edu. *Application contact:* Dr. Dayton Wilde, Graduate Coordinator, 706-542-5607, E-mail: pbgg@uga.edu. Web site: http://www.plantbreeding.uga.edu/index.html.

University of Georgia, Franklin College of Arts and Sciences, Department of Genetics, Athens, GA 30602. Offers MS, PhD. *Faculty:* 20 full-time (6 women). *Students:* 50 full-time (35 women); includes 6 minority (1 Black or African American, non-Hispanic/Latino; 1 Asian, non-Hispanic/Latino; 4 Hispanic/Latino), 8 international. Average age 28. 62 applicants, 29% accepted, 8 enrolled. In 2011, 11 doctorates awarded. Terminal master's awarded for partial completion of doctoral program. *Degree requirements:* For master's, thesis; for doctorate, comprehensive exam, thesis/dissertation. *Entrance requirements:* For master's and doctorate, GRE General Test. Additional exam requirements/recommendations for international students: Required—TOEFL. *Application deadline:* For fall admission, 1/1 priority date for domestic students, 1/1 for international students; for spring admission, 11/15 for domestic students. Application fee: $50. Electronic applications accepted. *Financial support:* In 2011–12, fellowships with full tuition reimbursements (averaging $19,000 per year), research assistantships with full tuition reimbursements (averaging $19,000 per year), teaching assistantships with full tuition reimbursements (averaging $19,000 per year) were awarded; scholarships/grants and unspecified assistantships also available. *Unit head:* Dr. Allen J. Moore, Head, 706-542-9557, E-mail: ajmoore@uga.edu. *Application contact:* Dr. John P. Wares, Director of Graduate Studies, 706-542-7720, Fax: 706-542-3910, E-mail: jpwares@uga.edu. Web site: http://www.genetics.uga.edu/.

University of Hawaii at Manoa, John A. Burns School of Medicine, Department of Cell and Molecular Biology, Honolulu, HI 96813. Offers MS, PhD. Part-time programs available. Terminal master's awarded for partial completion of doctoral program. *Degree requirements:* For master's, thesis optional; for doctorate, comprehensive exam, thesis/dissertation. *Entrance requirements:* For master's and doctorate, GRE General Test, minimum GPA of 3.0. Additional exam requirements/recommendations for international students: Required—TOEFL (minimum score 500 paper-based; 173 computer-based; 61 iBT), IELTS (minimum score 5).

University of Illinois at Chicago, College of Medicine and Graduate College, Graduate Programs in Medicine, Department of Biochemistry and Molecular Genetics, Chicago, IL 60607-7128. Offers PhD, MD/PhD. Terminal master's awarded for partial completion of doctoral program. *Degree requirements:* For doctorate, thesis/dissertation. *Entrance requirements:* For doctorate, GRE General Test. Additional exam requirements/

recommendations for international students: Required—TOEFL. Electronic applications accepted. *Faculty research:* Nature of cellular components, control of metabolic processes, regulation of gene expression.

The University of Iowa, Graduate College, College of Liberal Arts and Sciences, Department of Biology, Iowa City, IA 52242-1324. Offers biology (MS, PhD); cell and developmental biology (MS, PhD); evolution (MS, PhD); genetics (MS, PhD); neurobiology (MS, PhD). Terminal master's awarded for partial completion of doctoral program. *Degree requirements:* For master's, thesis optional, exam; for doctorate, comprehensive exam, thesis/dissertation. *Entrance requirements:* For master's and doctorate, GRE General Test, minimum GPA of 3.0. Additional exam requirements/recommendations for international students: Required—TOEFL (minimum score 600 paper-based; 250 computer-based; 100 iBT). Electronic applications accepted. *Faculty research:* Neurobiology, evolutionary biology, genetics, cell and developmental biology.

The University of Iowa, Graduate College, Program in Genetics, Iowa City, IA 52242-1316. Offers PhD, MD/PhD. *Degree requirements:* For doctorate, comprehensive exam, thesis/dissertation. *Entrance requirements:* For doctorate, GRE General Test, minimum GPA of 3.0. Additional exam requirements/recommendations for international students: Required—TOEFL (minimum score 600 paper-based; 250 computer-based; 100 iBT). Electronic applications accepted. *Expenses:* Contact institution. *Faculty research:* Developmental genetics, eukaryotic gene expression, human genetics, molecular and biochemical genetics, evolutionary genetics.

The University of Iowa, Roy J. and Lucille A. Carver College of Medicine and Graduate College, Graduate Programs in Medicine, Department of Microbiology, Iowa City, IA 52242-1316. Offers general microbiology and microbial physiology (MS, PhD); immunology (MS, PhD); microbial genetics (MS, PhD); pathogenic bacteriology (MS, PhD); virology (MS, PhD). *Faculty:* 23 full-time (5 women), 12 part-time/adjunct (4 women). *Students:* 37 full-time (24 women); includes 3 minority (2 American Indian or Alaska Native, non-Hispanic/Latino; 1 Hispanic/Latino), 4 international. Average age 25. 56 applicants, 16% accepted, 4 enrolled. In 2011, 1 master's, 6 doctorates awarded. *Degree requirements:* For master's, thesis; for doctorate, comprehensive exam, thesis/dissertation. *Entrance requirements:* For master's and doctorate, GRE General Test. Additional exam requirements/recommendations for international students: Required—TOEFL (minimum score 600 paper-based; 250 computer-based). *Application deadline:* For fall admission, 1/1 for domestic and international students. Application fee: $60 ($85 for international students). Electronic applications accepted. *Financial support:* In 2011–12, 4 fellowships with full tuition reimbursements (averaging $25,500 per year), 33 research assistantships with full tuition reimbursements (averaging $25,500 per year) were awarded; institutionally sponsored loans, scholarships/grants, traineeships, and health care benefits also available. *Faculty research:* Gene regulation, processing and transport of HIV, retroviral pathogenesis, biodegradation, biofilm. *Total annual research expenditures:* $12.6 million. *Unit head:* Dr. Patrick M. Schlievert, Head, 319-335-7810, E-mail: grad-micro-info@uiowa.edu. *Application contact:* Betty Wood, Associate Director of Admissions, 319-335-1525, Fax: 319-335-1535, E-mail: admissions@uiowa.edu. Web site: http://www.uiowa.edu/microbiology/.

The University of Manchester, Faculty of Life Sciences, Manchester, United Kingdom. Offers adaptive organismal biology (M Phil, PhD); animal biology (M Phil, PhD); biochemistry (M Phil, PhD); bioinformatics (M Phil, PhD); biomolecular sciences (M Phil, PhD); biotechnology (M Phil, PhD); cell biology (M Phil, PhD); cell matrix research (M Phil, PhD); channels and transporters (M Phil, PhD); developmental biology (M Phil, PhD); Egyptology (M Phil, PhD); environmental biology (M Phil, PhD); evolutionary biology (M Phil, PhD); gene expression (M Phil, PhD); genetics (M Phil, PhD); history of science, technology and medicine (M Phil, PhD); immunology (M Phil, PhD); integrative neurobiology and behavior (M Phil, PhD); membrane trafficking (M Phil, PhD); microbiology (M Phil, PhD); molecular and cellular neuroscience (M Phil, PhD); molecular biology (M Phil, PhD); molecular cancer studies (M Phil, PhD); neuroscience (M Phil, PhD); ophthalmology (M Phil, PhD); optometry (M Phil, PhD); organelle function (M Phil, PhD); pharmacology (M Phil, PhD); physiology (M Phil, PhD); plant sciences (M Phil, PhD); stem cell research (M Phil, PhD); structural biology (M Phil, PhD); systems neuroscience (M Phil, PhD); toxicology (M Phil, PhD).

University of Massachusetts Amherst, Graduate School, Interdisciplinary Programs, Program in Plant Biology, Amherst, MA 01003. Offers biochemistry and metabolism (MS, PhD); cell biology and physiology (MS, PhD); environmental, ecological and integrative (PhD); environmental, ecological and integrative biology (MS); genetics and evolution (MS, PhD). *Students:* 16 full-time (7 women), 1 (woman) part-time, 7 international. Average age 27. 22 applicants, 50% accepted, 5 enrolled. In 2011, 3 degrees awarded. *Median time to degree:* Of those who began their doctoral program in fall 2003, 100% received their degree in 8 years or less. *Degree requirements:* For master's, thesis; for doctorate, 2 foreign languages, comprehensive exam, thesis/dissertation. *Entrance requirements:* For master's and doctorate, GRE General Test. Additional exam requirements/recommendations for international students: Required—TOEFL (minimum score 550 paper-based; 213 computer-based; 80 iBT), IELTS (minimum score 6.5). *Application deadline:* For fall admission, 12/15 for domestic and international students; for spring admission, 10/1 for domestic and international students. Applications are processed on a rolling basis. Application fee: $50 ($65 for international students). Electronic applications accepted. Tuition and fees vary according to course load, campus/location and program. *Financial support:* Fellowships with full and partial tuition reimbursements, research assistantships with full and partial tuition reimbursements, teaching assistantships with full and partial tuition reimbursements, career-related internships or fieldwork, Federal Work-Study, scholarships/grants, traineeships, health care benefits, tuition waivers (full and partial), and unspecified assistantships available. Support available to part-time students. Financial award application deadline: 12/15. *Unit head:* Dr. Elsbeth L. Walker, Graduate Program Director, 413-577-3217, Fax: 413-545-3243. *Application contact:* Lindsay DeSantis, Interim Supervisor of Admissions, 413-545—0722, Fax: 413-577-0010, E-mail: gradadm@grad.umass.edu. Web site: http://www.bio.umass.edu/plantbio/.

University of Miami, Graduate School, College of Arts and Sciences, Department of Biology, Coral Gables, FL 33124. Offers biology (MS, PhD); genetics and evolution (MS, PhD). Terminal master's awarded for partial completion of doctoral program. *Degree requirements:* For master's, comprehensive exam (for some programs), thesis (for some programs); for doctorate, thesis/dissertation, oral and written qualifying exam. *Entrance requirements:* For master's, GRE General Test, 3 letters of recommendation, research papers; for doctorate, GRE General Test, 3 letters of recommendation, research papers, sponsor letter. Additional exam requirements/recommendations for international students: Required—TOEFL (minimum score 550 paper-based; 213 computer-based; 59 iBT). Electronic applications accepted. *Faculty research:* Neuroscience to ethology; plants, vertebrates and mycorrhizae; phylogenies, life histories and species interactions; molecular biology, gene expression and populations; cells, auditory neurons and vertebrate locomotion.

University of Minnesota, Twin Cities Campus, Graduate School, Program in Molecular, Cellular, Developmental Biology and Genetics, Minneapolis, MN 55455-0213. Offers genetic counseling (MS); molecular, cellular, developmental biology and genetics (PhD). Terminal master's awarded for partial completion of doctoral program. *Degree requirements:* For master's, thesis optional; for doctorate, thesis/dissertation. *Entrance requirements:* For master's and doctorate, GRE General Test. Additional exam requirements/recommendations for international students: Required—TOEFL (minimum score 625 paper-based; 263 computer-based; 80 iBT). Electronic applications accepted. *Faculty research:* Membrane receptors and membrane transport, cell interactions,

University of Connecticut Health Center

UCHC offers you exceptional research opportunities spanning **Cell Analysis and Modeling; Cell Biology; Genetics and Developmental Biology; Immunology; Molecular Biology and Biochemistry; Neuroscience;** and **Skeletal, Craniofacial and Oral Biology**.

Key features of our program include:
- ❖ Integrated admissions with access to more than 100 laboratories.
- ❖ Flexible educational program tailored to the interests of each student.
- ❖ Excellent education in a stimulating, cutting edge research environment.
- ❖ Competitive stipend ($28,000 for 2012–13 year), tuition waiver, and availability of student health plan.
- ❖ State-of-the-art research facilities, including the new Cell and Genome Sciences Building, which houses the UConn Stem Cell Institute, the Center for Cell Analysis and Modeling, and the Department of Genetics and Developmental Biology.

For more information, please contact:
Stephanie Rauch, Biomedical Science Admissions Coordinator
University of Connecticut Health Center
263 Farmington Ave., MC 3906
Farmington, CT 06030
BiomedSciAdmissions@uchc.edu
http://grad.uchc.edu/prospective/programs/phd_biosci/index.html

cytoskeleton and cell mobility, regulation of gene expression, plant cell and molecular biology.

University of Missouri, Graduate School, College of Arts and Sciences, Division of Biological Sciences, Program in Genetic, Cellular and Developmental Biology, Columbia, MO 65211. Offers MA, PhD. *Faculty:* 23. *Expenses:* Tuition, state resident: full-time $5881. Tuition, nonresident: full-time $15,183. *Required fees:* $952. Tuition and fees vary according to campus/location and program. *Financial support:* In 2011–12, fellowships (averaging $21,000 per year), teaching assistantships (averaging $16,300 per year) were awarded; research assistantships, scholarships/grants, health care benefits, and tuition waivers (full) also available. *Total annual research expenditures:* $6.1 million. *Unit head:* Dr. Ray Semlitsch, Director of Graduate Studies, 573-884-6396, E-mail: semlitschr@missouri.edu. *Application contact:* Nila Emerich, Application Contact, 800-553-5698.

University of Missouri, Graduate School, Genetics Area Program, Columbia, MO 65211. Offers PhD. *Students:* 11 full-time (6 women), 4 international. Average age 26. 7 applicants, 57% accepted, 4 enrolled. In 2011, 1 degree awarded. *Degree requirements:* For doctorate, comprehensive exam, thesis/dissertation. *Entrance requirements:* For doctorate, GRE General Test, minimum GPA of 3.0. Additional exam requirements/recommendations for international students: Required—TOEFL (minimum score 580 paper-based; 237 computer-based; 92 iBT). *Application deadline:* For fall admission, 2/1 priority date for domestic students. Applications are processed on a rolling basis. Application fee: $55 ($75 for international students). *Expenses:* Tuition, state resident: full-time $5881. Tuition, nonresident: full-time $15,183. *Required fees:* $952. Tuition and fees vary according to campus/location and program. *Financial support:* Fellowships, research assistantships, teaching assistantships, and institutionally sponsored loans available. *Faculty research:* Aging, cancer, development, disease resistance, evolution, genomics, microbe interactions, plant molecular biology, proteomics, reproductive biology, viral genetics. *Unit head:* Dr. John F. Cannon, Director of Graduate Studies, 573-852-2780, E-mail: cannonj@missouri.edu. *Application contact:* Debbie Allen, 573-882-2816, E-mail: allendebra@missouri.edu. Web site: http://www.gap.missouri.edu/.

University of Nebraska Medical Center, Graduate Studies, Department of Genetics, Cell Biology and Anatomy, Omaha, NE 68198. Offers MS, PhD. Part-time programs available. Terminal master's awarded for partial completion of doctoral program. *Degree requirements:* For master's, comprehensive exam, thesis; for doctorate, comprehensive exam, thesis/dissertation. *Entrance requirements:* For master's and doctorate, GRE General Test. Additional exam requirements/recommendations for international students: Required—TOEFL (minimum score 550 paper-based; 213 computer-based). Electronic applications accepted. *Faculty research:* Hematology, immunology, developmental biology, genetics cancer biology, neuroscience.

University of New Hampshire, Graduate School, College of Life Sciences and Agriculture, Department of Molecular, Cellular and Biomedical Sciences, Program in Genetics, Durham, NH 03824. Offers MS, PhD. Part-time programs available. *Faculty:* 12 full-time. *Students:* 10 full-time (7 women), 7 part-time (4 women); includes 1 minority (Two or more races, non-Hispanic/Latino), 6 international. Average age 32. 28 applicants, 18% accepted, 3 enrolled. In 2011, 1 master's, 1 doctorate awarded. *Degree requirements:* For master's, thesis; for doctorate, thesis/dissertation. *Entrance requirements:* For master's and doctorate, GRE General Test, GRE Subject Test. Additional exam requirements/recommendations for international students: Required—TOEFL (minimum score 550 paper-based; 213 computer-based; 80 iBT). *Application deadline:* For fall admission, 6/1 priority date for domestic students, 4/1 for international students; for spring admission, 12/1 for domestic students. Applications are processed on a rolling basis. Application fee: $65. Electronic applications accepted. *Expenses:* Tuition, state resident: full-time $12,360; part-time $687 per credit hour. Tuition, nonresident: full-time $25,680; part-time $1058 per credit hour. *International tuition:* $29,550 full-time. *Required fees:* $1666; $833 per course. $416.50 per semester. Tuition and fees vary according to course load and degree level. *Financial support:* In 2011–12, 11 students received support, including 4 research assistantships, 7 teaching assistantships; fellowships, career-related internships or fieldwork, Federal Work-Study, and scholarships/grants also available. Support available to part-time students. Financial award application deadline: 2/15. *Unit head:* Dr. Rick Cote, Chair, 603-862-3217. *Application contact:* Flora Joyal, Administrative Assistant, 603-862-2250, E-mail: genetics.dept@unh.edu. Web site: http://genetics.unh.edu/.

University of New Mexico, Health Sciences Center Graduate Programs, Program in Biomedical Sciences, Albuquerque, NM 87131-5196. Offers biochemistry and molecular biology (MS, PhD); cell biology and physiology (MS, PhD); clinical and translational science (Certificate); molecular genetics and microbiology (MS, PhD); neuroscience (MS, PhD); pathology (MS, PhD); toxicology (MS, PhD); university science teaching (Certificate). Part-time programs available. *Faculty:* 64 full-time (26 women), 9 part-time/adjunct (4 women). *Students:* 45 full-time (27 women), 56 part-time (28 women); includes 24 minority (3 Black or African American, non-Hispanic/Latino; 1 American Indian or Alaska Native, non-Hispanic/Latino; 4 Asian, non-Hispanic/Latino; 14 Hispanic/Latino; 1 Native Hawaiian or other Pacific Islander, non-Hispanic/Latino; 1 Two or more races, non-Hispanic/Latino), 18 international. Average age 30. 110 applicants, 18% accepted, 17 enrolled. In 2011, 14 master's, 5 doctorates awarded. Terminal master's awarded for partial completion of doctoral program. *Degree requirements:* For master's, thesis; for doctorate, comprehensive exam, thesis/dissertation. *Entrance requirements:* For master's and doctorate, GRE General Test, minimum undergraduate GPA of 3.0. Additional exam requirements/recommendations for international students: Required—TOEFL. *Application deadline:* For fall admission, 3/1 priority date for domestic students, 3/1 for international students. Applications are processed on a rolling basis. Application fee: $50. Electronic applications accepted. *Financial support:* In 2011–12, 99 students received support, including 28 fellowships with full and partial tuition reimbursements available (averaging $22,000 per year), 73 research assistantships with full tuition reimbursements available (averaging $23,000 per year), 8 teaching assistantships (averaging $2,800 per year); career-related internships or fieldwork, Federal Work-Study, institutionally sponsored loans, scholarships/grants, traineeships, health care benefits, and unspecified assistantships also available. Financial award application deadline: 1/1; financial award applicants required to submit FAFSA. *Faculty research:* Infectious disease/Immunity, cancer biology, cardiovascular and metabolic diseases, brain and behavioral illness, environmental health. *Unit head:* Dr. Helen J. Hathaway, BSGP Program Director, 505-272-1887, Fax: 505-272-2412, E-mail: hhathaway@salud.unm.edu. *Application contact:* Mary Fenton, Admissions Coordinator, 505-272-1887, Fax: 505-272-2412, E-mail: mfenton@salud.unm.edu. Web site: http://hsc.unm.edu/som/research/brep/bsgpabout.shtm.

The University of North Carolina at Chapel Hill, Graduate School, College of Arts and Sciences, Department of Biology, Chapel Hill, NC 27599. Offers botany (MA, MS, PhD); cell biology, development, and physiology (MA, MS, PhD); cell motility and cytoskeleton (PhD); ecology and behavior (MA, MS, PhD); genetics and molecular biology (MA, MS, PhD); morphology, systematics, and evolution (MA, MS, PhD). Terminal master's awarded for partial completion of doctoral program. *Degree requirements:* For master's, comprehensive exam, thesis (for some programs); for doctorate, comprehensive exam, thesis/dissertation. *Entrance requirements:* For master's, GRE General Test, GRE Subject Test, 2 semesters of calculus or statistics; 2 semesters of physics, organic chemistry; 3 semesters of biology; for doctorate, GRE General Test, GRE Subject Test, 2 semesters calculus or statistics, 2 semesters physics, organic chemistry, 3 semesters of biology. Additional exam requirements/recommendations for international students: Required—TOEFL (minimum score 550 paper-based; 213 computer-based). Electronic applications accepted. *Faculty research:* Gene expression, biomechanics, yeast genetics, plant ecology, plant molecular biology.

The University of North Carolina at Chapel Hill, School of Medicine and Graduate School, Graduate Programs in Medicine, Curriculum in Genetics and Molecular Biology, Chapel Hill, NC 27599. Offers MS, PhD. *Degree requirements:* For doctorate, comprehensive exam, thesis/dissertation. *Entrance requirements:* For doctorate, GRE, minimum GPA of 3.0. Additional exam requirements/recommendations for international students: Required—TOEFL. Electronic applications accepted. *Faculty research:* Telomere replication and germline immortality, experimental evolution in microorganisms, genetic vulnerabilities in tumor genomes, genetics of cell cycle control during Drosophila development, mammalian genetics.

University of North Dakota, Graduate School, College of Arts and Sciences, Department of Biology, Grand Forks, ND 58202. Offers botany (MS, PhD); ecology (MS, PhD); entomology (MS, PhD); environmental biology (MS, PhD); fisheries/wildlife (MS, PhD); genetics (MS, PhD); zoology (MS, PhD). Terminal master's awarded for partial completion of doctoral program. *Degree requirements:* For master's, thesis, final exam; for doctorate, comprehensive exam, thesis/dissertation, final exam. *Entrance requirements:* For master's, GRE General Test, GRE Subject Test, minimum GPA of 3.0; for doctorate, GRE General Test, GRE Subject Test, minimum GPA of 3.5. Additional exam requirements/recommendations for international students: Required—TOEFL (minimum score 550 paper-based; 213 computer-based; 79 iBT), IELTS (minimum score 6.5). Electronic applications accepted. *Faculty research:* Population biology, wildlife ecology, RNA processing, hormonal control of behavior.

University of North Texas Health Science Center at Fort Worth, Graduate School of Biomedical Sciences, Fort Worth, TX 76107-2699. Offers anatomy and cell biology (MS, PhD); biochemistry and molecular biology (MS, PhD); biomedical sciences (MS, PhD); biotechnology (MS); forensic genetics (MS); integrative physiology (MS, PhD); medical science (MS); microbiology and immunology (MS, PhD); pharmacology (MS, PhD); science education (MS); DO/MS; DO/PhD. Terminal master's awarded for partial completion of doctoral program. *Degree requirements:* For master's, thesis; for doctorate, thesis/dissertation. *Entrance requirements:* For master's and doctorate, GRE General Test. Additional exam requirements/recommendations for international students: Required—TOEFL. *Expenses:* Contact institution. *Faculty research:* Alzheimer's disease, aging, eye diseases, cancer, cardiovascular disease.

University of Notre Dame, Graduate School, College of Science, Department of Biological Sciences, Notre Dame, IN 46556. Offers aquatic ecology, evolution and environmental biology (MS, PhD); cellular and molecular biology (MS, PhD); genetics (MS, PhD); physiology (MS, PhD); vector biology and parasitology (MS, PhD). Terminal master's awarded for partial completion of doctoral program. *Degree requirements:* For master's, comprehensive exam, thesis; for doctorate, comprehensive exam, thesis/dissertation, candidacy exam. *Entrance requirements:* For master's and doctorate, GRE General Test. Additional exam requirements/recommendations for international students: Required—TOEFL (minimum score 600 paper-based; 250 computer-based; 80 iBT). Electronic applications accepted. *Faculty research:* Tropical disease, molecular genetics, neurobiology, evolutionary biology, aquatic biology.

University of Oregon, Graduate School, College of Arts and Sciences, Department of Biology, Eugene, OR 97403. Offers ecology and evolution (MA, MS, PhD); marine biology (MA, MS, PhD); molecular, cellular and genetic biology (PhD); neuroscience and development (PhD). Terminal master's awarded for partial completion of doctoral program. *Degree requirements:* For master's, thesis (for some programs); for doctorate, thesis/dissertation. *Entrance requirements:* For master's and doctorate, GRE General Test, minimum GPA of 3.2. Additional exam requirements/recommendations for international students: Required—TOEFL. *Faculty research:* Developmental neurobiology; evolution, population biology, and quantitative genetics; regulation of gene expression; biochemistry of marine organisms.

University of Pennsylvania, Perelman School of Medicine, Biomedical Graduate Studies, Graduate Group in Cell and Molecular Biology, Philadelphia, PA 19104. Offers cancer biology (PhD); cell biology and physiology (PhD); developmental stem cell regenerative biology (PhD); gene therapy and vaccines (PhD); genetics and gene regulation (PhD); microbiology, virology, and parasitology (PhD); MD/PhD; VMD/PhD. *Faculty:* 306. *Students:* 337 full-time (186 women); includes 81 minority (16 Black or African American, non-Hispanic/Latino; 43 Asian, non-Hispanic/Latino; 16 Hispanic/Latino; 6 Two or more races, non-Hispanic/Latino), 41 international. 585 applicants, 21% accepted, 58 enrolled. In 2011, 42 doctorates awarded. *Degree requirements:* For doctorate, thesis/dissertation. *Entrance requirements:* For doctorate, GRE General Test. Additional exam requirements/recommendations for international students: Required—TOEFL. *Application deadline:* For fall admission, 12/1 priority date for domestic students, 12/1 for international students. Applications are processed on a rolling basis. Application fee: $80. Electronic applications accepted. *Expenses: Tuition:* Full-time $26,660; part-time $4944 per course. *Required fees:* $2318; $291 per course. Tuition and fees vary according to course load, degree level and program. *Financial support:* In 2011–12, 337 students received support. Fellowships, research assistantships, scholarships/grants, traineeships, and unspecified assistantships available. *Unit head:* Dr. Daniel Kessler, Graduate Group Chair. *Application contact:* Meagan Schofer, Coordinator. Web site: http://www.med.upenn.edu/camb/.

University of Puerto Rico, Río Piedras, College of Natural Sciences, Department of Biology, San Juan, PR 00931-3300. Offers ecology/systematics (MS, PhD); evolution/genetics (MS, PhD); molecular/cellular biology (MS, PhD); neuroscience (MS, PhD). Part-time programs available. *Degree requirements:* For master's, one foreign language, comprehensive exam, thesis; for doctorate, one foreign language, comprehensive exam, thesis/dissertation. *Entrance requirements:* For master's, GRE Subject Test, interview, minimum GPA of 3.0, letter of recommendation; for doctorate, GRE Subject Test, interview, master's degree, minimum GPA of 3.0, letter of recommendation. *Faculty research:* Environmental, poblational and systematic biology.

University of Rochester, School of Medicine and Dentistry, Graduate Programs in Medicine and Dentistry, Department of Biomedical Genetics, Rochester, NY 14627. Offers genetics, genomics and development (PhD). *Degree requirements:* For doctorate, thesis/dissertation, qualifying exam. *Entrance requirements:* For doctorate, GRE General Test. *Expenses: Tuition:* Full-time $41,040.

University of Southern California, Keck School of Medicine and Graduate School, Graduate Programs in Medicine, Department of Preventive Medicine, Division of Biostatistics, Los Angeles, CA 90089. Offers applied biostatistics/epidemiology (MS); biostatistics (MS, PhD); epidemiology (PhD); genetic epidemiology and statistical genetics (PhD); molecular epidemiology (MS, PhD). *Faculty:* 71 full-time (30 women). *Students:* 97 full-time (51 women); includes 24 minority (18 Asian, non-Hispanic/Latino; 3 Hispanic/Latino; 3 Two or more races, non-Hispanic/Latino), 56 international. Average age 29. 68 applicants, 62% accepted, 17 enrolled. In 2011, 7 master's, 8 doctorates

awarded. Terminal master's awarded for partial completion of doctoral program. *Degree requirements:* For master's, thesis; for doctorate, thesis/dissertation. *Entrance requirements:* For master's and doctorate, GRE General Test, GRE Subject Test, minimum GPA of 3.0. Additional exam requirements/recommendations for international students: Required—TOEFL (minimum score 600 paper-based; 300 computer-based; 100 iBT). *Application deadline:* For fall admission, 12/1 priority date for domestic students, 12/1 for international students. Application fee: $85. Electronic applications accepted. *Financial support:* In 2011–12, 3 fellowships with full tuition reimbursements (averaging $29,100 per year), 43 research assistantships with full tuition reimbursements (averaging $29,100 per year), 22 teaching assistantships with full and partial tuition reimbursements (averaging $14,550 per year) were awarded; career-related internships or fieldwork, Federal Work-Study, institutionally sponsored loans, scholarships/grants, traineeships, health care benefits, and unspecified assistantships also available. Financial award application deadline: 5/4; financial award applicants required to submit CSS PROFILE or FAFSA. *Faculty research:* Clinical trials in ophthalmology and cancer research, methods of analysis for epidemiological studies, genetic epidemiology. *Total annual research expenditures:* $1.3 million. *Unit head:* Dr. William Gauderman, Director, 323-442-2633, Fax: 323-442-2993, E-mail: mtrujill@usc.edu. *Application contact:* Mary L. Trujillo, Student Adviser, 323-442-2633, Fax: 323-442-2993, E-mail: mtrujill@usc.edu. Web site: http://keck.usc.edu/Education/Academic_Department_and_Divisions/Department_of_Preventive_Medicine/Divisions/Biostatistics.aspx.

University of Southern California, Keck School of Medicine and Graduate School, Program in Genetic, Molecular and Cellular Biology, Los Angeles, CA 90089. Offers PhD. *Faculty:* 224 full-time (56 women). *Students:* 120 full-time (69 women); includes 29 minority (2 Black or African American, non-Hispanic/Latino; 19 Asian, non-Hispanic/Latino; 6 Hispanic/Latino; 2 Native Hawaiian or other Pacific Islander, non-Hispanic/Latino), 65 international. Average age 29. 360 applicants, 20% accepted, 28 enrolled. In 2011, 11 doctorates awarded. *Degree requirements:* For doctorate, comprehensive exam, thesis/dissertation. *Entrance requirements:* For doctorate, GRE, minimum GPA of 3.0. Additional exam requirements/recommendations for international students: Required—TOEFL (minimum score 600 paper-based; 250 computer-based; 100 iBT). *Application deadline:* For fall admission, 12/1 priority date for domestic students, 12/1 for international students. Application fee: $85. Electronic applications accepted. *Financial support:* In 2011–12, 120 students received support, including 12 fellowships (averaging $29,100 per year), 106 research assistantships with full tuition reimbursements available (averaging $29,100 per year), 2 teaching assistantships with full tuition reimbursements available (averaging $29,100 per year); institutionally sponsored loans, scholarships/grants, traineeships, health care benefits, and unspecified assistantships also available. Financial award application deadline: 5/4; financial award applicants required to submit FAFSA. *Unit head:* Dr. Henry Sucov, Director, 323-442-1475, Fax: 323-442-1199, E-mail: sucov@usc.edu. *Application contact:* Dawn Burke, Student Program Coordinator, 323-442-1475, Fax: 323-442-1199, E-mail: pibbs@usc.edu. Web site: http://www.usc.edu/intbio.

The University of Tennessee, Graduate School, College of Arts and Sciences, Program in Life Sciences, Knoxville, TN 37996. Offers genome science and technology (MS, PhD); plant physiology and genetics (MS, PhD). *Degree requirements:* For doctorate, one foreign language, thesis/dissertation. *Entrance requirements:* For master's and doctorate, GRE General Test, minimum GPA of 2.7. Additional exam requirements/recommendations for international students: Required—TOEFL. Electronic applications accepted. *Expenses:* Tuition, state resident: full-time $8332; part-time $464 per credit hour. Tuition, nonresident: full-time $25,174; part-time $1400 per credit hour. *Required fees:* $1162; $56 per credit hour. Tuition and fees vary according to program.

The University of Texas Health Science Center at Houston, Graduate School of Biomedical Sciences, Program in Genes and Development, Houston, TX 77225-0036. Offers MS, PhD, MD/PhD. Terminal master's awarded for partial completion of doctoral program. *Degree requirements:* For master's, thesis; for doctorate, thesis/dissertation. *Entrance requirements:* For master's and doctorate, GRE General Test. Additional exam requirements/recommendations for international students: Required—TOEFL. Electronic applications accepted. *Faculty research:* Developmental biology, genetics, cell biology, structural biology, cancer.

The University of Texas Medical Branch, Graduate School of Biomedical Sciences, Program in Biochemistry and Molecular Biology, Galveston, TX 77555. Offers biochemistry (PhD); bioinformatics (PhD); biophysics (PhD); cell biology (PhD); computational biology (PhD); structural biology (PhD). *Degree requirements:* For doctorate, thesis/dissertation. *Entrance requirements:* Additional exam requirements/recommendations for international students: Required—TOEFL (minimum score 550 paper-based; 213 computer-based). Electronic applications accepted.

The University of Texas Southwestern Medical Center, Southwestern Graduate School of Biomedical Sciences, Division of Basic Science, Program in Genetics and Development, Dallas, TX 75390. Offers PhD. *Degree requirements:* For doctorate, thesis/dissertation, qualifying exam. *Entrance requirements:* For doctorate, GRE General Test, minimum GPA of 3.0. Additional exam requirements/recommendations for international students: Required—TOEFL. Electronic applications accepted. *Faculty research:* Human molecular genetics, chromosome structure, gene regulation, molecular biology, gene expression.

University of Washington, Graduate School, School of Public Health, Department of Epidemiology, Institute for Public Health Genetics, Seattle, WA 98195. Offers genetic epidemiology (MS); public health genetics (MPH, PhD); MPH/JD. Part-time programs available. *Students:* 20 full-time (17 women), 4 part-time (3 women); includes 5 minority (3 Asian, non-Hispanic/Latino; 2 Hispanic/Latino). Average age 31. 46 applicants, 39% accepted, 5 enrolled. In 2011, 8 degrees awarded. Terminal master's awarded for partial completion of doctoral program. *Degree requirements:* For master's, thesis, practicum (MPH); for doctorate, comprehensive exam, thesis/dissertation. *Entrance requirements:* For master's, GRE General Test, experience in health sciences, bachelor's degree in related field and course in human genetics (preferred); minimum GPA of 3.0; for doctorate, GRE General Test, experience in health sciences and master's degree in related field (preferred); coursework in human genetics, minimum GPA of 3.0. Additional exam requirements/recommendations for international students: Required—TOEFL (minimum score 580 paper-based; 237 computer-based; 92 iBT). *Application deadline:* For fall admission, 12/15 for domestic and international students. Application fee: $75. Electronic applications accepted. *Financial support:* In 2011–12, 4 students received support, including 3 research assistantships with full tuition reimbursements available (averaging $13,725 per year), 1 teaching assistantship with full tuition reimbursement available (averaging $13,725 per year). Financial award application deadline: 2/28; financial award applicants required to submit FAFSA. *Faculty research:* Genetic epidemiology; ethical, legal, social issues of genetics; ecogenetics; health policy. *Unit head:* Dr. Karen L. Edwards, Director, 206-616-9286. *Application contact:* Barb Snyder, Student Services Advisor, 206-616-9286, Fax: 206-685-9651, E-mail: phgen@u.washington.edu. Web site: http://depts.washington.edu/phgen.

University of Wisconsin–Madison, Graduate School, College of Agricultural and Life Sciences and Graduate Programs in Medicine, Department of Genetics, Program in Genetics, Madison, WI 53706-1380. Offers PhD. *Degree requirements:* For doctorate, thesis/dissertation. *Expenses:* Tuition, state resident: full-time $10,296; part-time $643.51 per credit. Tuition, nonresident: full-time $24,054; part-time $1503.40 per credit. *Required fees:* $70.06 per credit. Tuition and fees vary according to course load, campus/location, program and reciprocity agreements.

University of Wisconsin–Madison, School of Medicine and Public Health and Graduate School, Graduate Programs in Medicine, Madison, WI 53705. Offers biomolecular chemistry (MS, PhD); cancer biology (PhD); genetics and medical genetics (MS, PhD), including genetics (PhD); medical genetics (MS); medical physics (MS, PhD), including health physics (MS), medical physics; microbiology (PhD); molecular and cellular pharmacology (PhD); pathology and laboratory medicine (PhD); physiology (PhD); population health sciences (MPH, MS, PhD), including clinical research (MS, PhD), epidemiology (MS, PhD), health services research (MS, PhD), population health sciences (MPH), social and behavioral health sciences (MS, PhD); DPT/MPH; DVM/MPH; MD/MPH; MD/PhD; MPA/MPH; MS/MPH; Pharm D/MPH. Part-time programs available. Postbaccalaureate distance learning degree programs offered (minimal on-campus study). Terminal master's awarded for partial completion of doctoral program. Application fee: $45. Electronic applications accepted. *Expenses:* Contact institution. *Financial support:* Fellowships with full tuition reimbursements, research assistantships with full tuition reimbursements, teaching assistantships with full tuition reimbursements, scholarships/grants, traineeships, and tuition waivers (full) available. *Unit head:* Dr. Richard L. Moss, Senior Associate Dean for Basic Research, Biotechnology and Graduate Studies, 608-265-0523, Fax: 608-265-0522, E-mail: rlmoss@wisc.edu. *Application contact:* Information Contact, 608-262-2433, Fax: 608-262-5134, E-mail: gradadmiss@mail.bascom.wisc.edu. Web site: http://www.med.wisc.edu.

University of Wyoming, Graduate Program in Molecular and Cellular Life Sciences, Laramie, WY 82070. Offers PhD. *Degree requirements:* For doctorate, thesis/dissertation, four eight-week laboratory rotations, comprehensive basic practical exam, two-part qualifying exam, seminars, symposium.

Virginia Commonwealth University, Medical College of Virginia-Professional Programs, School of Medicine, School of Medicine Graduate Programs, Department of Human and Molecular Genetics, Richmond, VA 23284-9005. Offers genetic counseling (MS); human genetics (PhD); molecular biology and genetics (MS, PhD); MD/PhD. *Degree requirements:* For master's, thesis; for doctorate, thesis/dissertation, comprehensive oral and written exams. *Entrance requirements:* For master's, GRE; for doctorate, GRE General Test. Additional exam requirements/recommendations for international students: Required—TOEFL (minimum score 600 paper-based; 250 computer-based; 100 iBT). Electronic applications accepted. *Expenses:* Tuition, state resident: full-time $9133; part-time $507 per credit. Tuition, nonresident: full-time $18,777; part-time $1043 per credit. *Required fees:* $77 per credit. Tuition and fees vary according to degree level, campus/location, program and student level. *Faculty research:* Genetic epidemiology, biochemical genetics, quantitative genetics, human cytogenetics, molecular genetics.

Virginia Polytechnic Institute and State University, Graduate School, Intercollege, Program in Genetics, Bioinformatics and Computational Biology, Blacksburg, VA 24061. Offers PhD. *Degree requirements:* For doctorate, comprehensive exam (for some programs), thesis/dissertation (for some programs). *Entrance requirements:* For doctorate, GRE. Additional exam requirements/recommendations for international students: Required—TOEFL (minimum score 550 paper-based; 213 computer-based). *Application deadline:* For fall admission, 7/1 for domestic and international students; for spring admission, 12/1 for international students. Applications are processed on a rolling basis. Application fee: $65. Electronic applications accepted. *Expenses:* Tuition, state resident: full-time $10,048; part-time $558.25 per credit hour. Tuition, nonresident: full-time $19,497; part-time $1083.25 per credit hour. *Required fees:* $405 per semester. Tuition and fees vary according to course load, campus/location and program. *Financial support:* Career-related internships or fieldwork, Federal Work-Study, scholarships/grants, health care benefits, and unspecified assistantships available. Financial award application deadline: 1/15. *Unit head:* Dr. David R. Bevan, Unit Head, 540-231-5040, Fax: 540-231-3010, E-mail: drbevan@vt.edu. *Application contact:* Dennie Munson, Information Contact, 540-231-1928, Fax: 540-231-3010, E-mail: dennie@vt.edu. Web site: http://graduateschool.vt.edu/academics/programs/gbcb/.

Washington State University, Graduate School, College of Sciences, School of Molecular Biosciences, Program in Genetics and Cell Biology, Pullman, WA 99164. Offers MS, PhD. *Faculty:* 23 full-time (5 women), 21 part-time/adjunct (4 women). *Students:* 9 full-time (6 women); includes 2 minority (1 Hispanic/Latino; 1 Two or more races, non-Hispanic/Latino), 3 international. Average age 29. In 2011, 3 doctorates awarded. Terminal master's awarded for partial completion of doctoral program. *Degree requirements:* For master's, thesis or alternative, oral exam; for doctorate, comprehensive exam, thesis/dissertation, oral exam. *Entrance requirements:* For master's and doctorate, GRE General Test, minimum GPA of 3.0. Additional exam requirements/recommendations for international students: Required—TOEFL (minimum score 550 paper-based; 213 computer-based). *Application deadline:* For fall admission, 12/15 for domestic and international students. Application fee: $75. Electronic applications accepted. *Financial support:* In 2011–12, 1 fellowship with full tuition reimbursement (averaging $18,852 per year), 16 research assistantships with full tuition reimbursements (averaging $18,852 per year), 6 teaching assistantships with full tuition reimbursements (averaging $18,852 per year) were awarded; Federal Work-Study, institutionally sponsored loans, health care benefits, and unspecified assistantships also available. Financial award application deadline: 4/1; financial award applicants required to submit FAFSA. *Faculty research:* Plant molecular biology, growth factors, cancer induction and DNA repair, gene regulation and genetic engineering. *Total annual research expenditures:* $5.8 million. *Unit head:* Dr. John H. Nilson, Director, 509-335-8724, Fax: 509-335-9688, E-mail: jhn@wsu.edu. *Application contact:* Kelly G. McGovern, Academic Coordinator, 509-335-4566, Fax: 509-335-1907, E-mail: smbgrad@wsu.edu. Web site: http://molecular.biosciences.wsu.edu/.

Washington University in St. Louis, Graduate School of Arts and Sciences, Division of Biology and Biomedical Sciences, Program in Evolution, Ecology and Population Biology, St. Louis, MO 63130-4899. Offers ecology (PhD); environmental biology (PhD); evolutionary biology (PhD); genetics (PhD). *Degree requirements:* For doctorate, thesis/dissertation. *Entrance requirements:* For doctorate, GRE General Test, GRE Subject Test. Electronic applications accepted.

Washington University in St. Louis, School of Medicine, Program in Clinical Investigation, St. Louis, MO 63130-4899. Offers clinical investigation (MS), including genetics/genomics, translational medicine. Part-time programs available. *Faculty:* 64 full-time (17 women), 3 part-time/adjunct (2 women). *Students:* 23 full-time (15 women), 23 part-time (10 women); includes 14 minority (3 Black or African American, non-Hispanic/Latino; 11 Asian, non-Hispanic/Latino). Average age 32. 6 applicants, 83% accepted, 5 enrolled. In 2011, 16 master's awarded. *Degree requirements:* For master's, thesis. *Entrance requirements:* For master's, doctoral-level degree or in process of obtaining doctoral-level degree. Additional exam requirements/recommendations for international students: Required—TOEFL. *Application deadline:* For fall admission, 3/15 for domestic students. Application fee: $0. Electronic applications accepted. *Faculty research:* Anesthesiology, infectious diseases, neurology, obstetrics and gynecology,

orthopaedic surgery. *Unit head:* Dr. David Warren, Associate Professor of Medicine, 314-454-8225, Fax: 314-454-5392, E-mail: dwarren@dom.wustl.edu. *Application contact:* Angela B. Wilson, Curriculum and Evaluation Coordinator, 314-454-8936, Fax: 314-454-8279, E-mail: abwilson@dom.wustl.edu. Web site: http://crtc.wustl.edu/.

Wayne State University, Graduate School, Program in Molecular Biology and Genetics, Detroit, MI 48202. Offers MS, PhD, MD/PhD. *Students:* 25 full-time (13 women), 1 part-time (0 women); includes 1 minority (Asian, non-Hispanic/Latino), 7 international. Average age 28. 41 applicants, 17% accepted, 4 enrolled. In 2011, 3 doctorates awarded. Terminal master's awarded for partial completion of doctoral program. *Degree requirements:* For master's, thesis; for doctorate, thesis/dissertation. *Entrance requirements:* For master's and doctorate, GRE General Test, GRE Subject Test (chemistry or biology), minimum GPA of 3.0, strong background in one of the chemical or biological sciences, three letters of recommendation, personal statement, interview. Additional exam requirements/recommendations for international students: Required—TOEFL (minimum score 550 paper-based; 213 computer-based); Recommended—TWE (minimum score 5.5). *Application deadline:* For fall admission, 6/1 priority date for domestic students, 5/1 for international students; for winter admission, 10/1 priority date for domestic students, 9/1 for international students; for spring admission, 2/1 priority date for domestic students, 1/1 for international students. Applications are processed on a rolling basis. Application fee: $50. Electronic applications accepted. *Expenses:* Tuition, state resident: part-time $512.85 per credit. Tuition, nonresident: part-time $1132.65 per credit. *Required fees:* $26.60 per credit. $199.65 per semester. Tuition and fees vary according to course load and program. *Financial support:* In 2011–12, 23 students received support. Fellowships with tuition reimbursements available, research assistantships with tuition reimbursements available, teaching assistantships with tuition reimbursements available, scholarships/grants, and unspecified assistantships available. Financial award application deadline: 2/1. *Faculty research:* Human gene mapping, genome organization and sequencing, gene regulation, molecular evolution. *Unit head:* Dr. Lawrence Grossman, Director, 313-577-5326, E-mail: l.grossman@wayne.edu.

Wesleyan University, Graduate Programs, Department of Biology, Middletown, CT 06459. Offers animal behavior (PhD); bioformatics/genomics (PhD); cell biology (PhD); developmental biology (PhD); evolution/ecology (PhD); genetics (PhD); neurobiology (PhD); population biology (PhD). *Degree requirements:* For doctorate, variable foreign language requirement, thesis/dissertation. *Entrance requirements:* For doctorate, GRE. Additional exam requirements/recommendations for international students: Required—TOEFL. *Faculty research:* Microbial population genetics, genetic basis of evolutionary adaptation, genetic regulation of differentiation and pattern formation in *Drosophila*.

West Virginia University, Davis College of Agriculture, Forestry and Consumer Sciences, Interdisciplinary Program in Genetics and Developmental Biology, Morgantown, WV 26506. Offers animal breeding (MS, PhD); biochemical and molecular genetics (MS, PhD); cytogenetics (MS, PhD); descriptive embryology (MS, PhD); developmental genetics (MS); experimental morphogenesis/teratology (MS); human genetics (MS, PhD); immunogenetics (MS, PhD); life cycles of animals and plants (MS, PhD); molecular aspects of development (MS, PhD); mutagenesis (MS, PhD); oncology (MS, PhD); plant genetics (MS, PhD); population and quantitative genetics (MS, PhD); regeneration (MS, PhD); teratology (PhD); toxicology (MS, PhD). *Degree requirements:* For master's, thesis; for doctorate, comprehensive exam, thesis/dissertation. *Entrance requirements:* For master's, GRE or MCAT, minimum GPA of 2.75. Additional exam requirements/recommendations for international students: Required—TOEFL.

Yale University, Graduate School of Arts and Sciences, Department of Genetics, New Haven, CT 06520. Offers PhD, MD/PhD. *Degree requirements:* For doctorate, thesis/dissertation. *Entrance requirements:* For doctorate, GRE General Test, GRE Subject Test.

Yale University, Graduate School of Arts and Sciences, Department of Molecular, Cellular, and Developmental Biology, Program in Genetics, New Haven, CT 06520. Offers PhD. *Degree requirements:* For doctorate, thesis/dissertation. *Entrance requirements:* For doctorate, GRE General Test, GRE Subject Test.

Yale University, School of Medicine and Graduate School of Arts and Sciences, Combined Program in Biological and Biomedical Sciences (BBS), Molecular Cell Biology, Genetics, and Development Track, New Haven, CT 06520. Offers PhD, MD/PhD. *Entrance requirements:* Additional exam requirements/recommendations for international students: Required—TOEFL.

Genomic Sciences

Albert Einstein College of Medicine, Graduate Division of Biomedical Sciences, Division of Biological Sciences, Department of Genetics, Bronx, NY 10461. Offers computational genetics (PhD); molecular genetics (PhD); translational genetics (PhD); MD/PhD. *Degree requirements:* For doctorate, thesis/dissertation. *Entrance requirements:* For doctorate, GRE General Test. Additional exam requirements/recommendations for international students: Required—TOEFL. *Faculty research:* Neurologic genetics in &ITDrosophila&RO, biochemical genetics of yeast, developmental genetics in the mouse.

Black Hills State University, Graduate Studies, Program in Integrative Genomics, Spearfish, SD 57799. Offers MS. *Entrance requirements:* Additional exam requirements/recommendations for international students: Required—TOEFL (minimum score 500 paper-based; 171 computer-based; 60 iBT).

Boston University, School of Medicine, Division of Graduate Medical Sciences, Program in Genetics and Genomics, Boston, MA 02215. Offers PhD. *Faculty:* 18 full-time (3 women). *Students:* 8 full-time (7 women), 2 part-time (both women), 3 international. Average age 27. 20 applicants, 40% accepted, 2 enrolled. In 2011, 5 doctorates awarded. *Degree requirements:* For doctorate, thesis/dissertation. *Entrance requirements:* For doctorate, GRE, letters of recommendation. Additional exam requirements/recommendations for international students: Required—TOEFL. *Application deadline:* For fall admission, 1/15 for domestic students; for spring admission, 10/15 for domestic students. Application fee: $75. Electronic applications accepted. *Expenses: Tuition:* Full-time $40,848; part-time $1276 per credit hour. *Required fees:* $572; $286 per semester. *Financial support:* In 2011–12, 9 research assistantships (averaging $30,500 per year) were awarded. Financial award applicants required to submit FAFSA. *Unit head:* Dr. Shoumita Dasgupta, Associate Professor and Director of Graduate Studies, 617-414-1580, E-mail: dasgupta@bu.edu. Web site: http://www.bumc.bu.edu/gpgg/graduate-program/.

Case Western Reserve University, School of Medicine and School of Graduate Studies, Graduate Programs in Medicine, Department of Genetics, Program in Human, Molecular, and Developmental Genetics and Genomics, Cleveland, OH 44106. Offers PhD, MD/PhD. *Degree requirements:* For doctorate, comprehensive exam, thesis/dissertation. *Entrance requirements:* For doctorate, GRE General Test, GRE Subject Test. Additional exam requirements/recommendations for international students: Required—TOEFL. *Faculty research:* Regulation of gene expression, molecular control of development, genomics.

Concordia University, School of Graduate Studies, Faculty of Arts and Science, Department of Biology, Montréal, QC H3G 1M8, Canada. Offers biology (M Sc, PhD); biotechnology and genomics (Diploma). *Degree requirements:* For master's, thesis; for doctorate, thesis/dissertation, pedagogical training. *Entrance requirements:* For master's, honors degree in biology; for doctorate, M Sc in life science. *Faculty research:* Cell biology, animal physiology, ecology, microbiology/molecular biology, plant physiology/biochemistry and biotechnology.

Georgia Health Sciences University, College of Graduate Studies, Program in Genomic Medicine, Augusta, GA 30912. Offers MS, PhD. *Faculty:* 9 full-time (1 woman). *Students:* 2 full-time (1 woman), 2 part-time (1 woman); includes 1 minority (Black or African American, non-Hispanic/Latino), 1 international. Average age 29. *Degree requirements:* For doctorate, comprehensive exam, thesis/dissertation. *Entrance requirements:* For doctorate, GRE General Test. Additional exam requirements/recommendations for international students: Required—TOEFL (minimum score 550 paper-based; 213 computer-based; 79 iBT). *Application deadline:* For fall admission, 1/15 for domestic and international students. Application fee: $50. Electronic applications accepted. *Financial support:* In 2011–12, 2 research assistantships with partial tuition reimbursements (averaging $23,000 per year) were awarded; Federal Work-Study, institutionally sponsored loans, and scholarships/grants also available. Support available to part-time students. Financial award application deadline: 5/31; financial award applicants required to submit FAFSA. *Faculty research:* Genetic and genomic basis of diseases (diabetes, cancer, autoimmunity), development of diagnostic markers, bioinformatics, computational biology. *Total annual research expenditures:* $6.4 million. *Unit head:* Dr. Jin-Xiong She, Professor, Chair and Eminent Scholar, 706-721-3540, E-mail: jshe@georgiahealth.edu. *Application contact:* Dr. Patricia L. Cameron, Associate Dean, 706-721-3279, Fax: 706-721-6829, E-mail: pcameron@georgiahealth.edu. Web site: http://www.cbgm.georgiahealth.edu/GraduateProgram/tabid/88/Default.aspx.

Harvard University, Graduate School of Arts and Sciences, Department of Systems Biology, Cambridge, MA 02138. Offers PhD. *Degree requirements:* For doctorate, thesis/dissertation, lab rotation, qualifying examination. *Entrance requirements:* For doctorate, GRE. Additional exam requirements/recommendations for international students: Required—TOEFL. Electronic applications accepted. *Expenses: Tuition:* Full-time $36,304. *Required fees:* $1186. Full-time tuition and fees vary according to program.

North Carolina State University, Graduate School, College of Agriculture and Life Sciences, Graduate Program in Genomic Sciences, Raleigh, NC 27695. Offers MS, PhD.

North Carolina State University, Graduate School, College of Agriculture and Life Sciences, Program in Functional Genomics, Raleigh, NC 27695. Offers MFG, MS, PhD. *Degree requirements:* For master's, thesis (for some programs); for doctorate, thesis/dissertation. *Entrance requirements:* For master's and doctorate, GRE, minimum B average. Additional exam requirements/recommendations for international students: Required—TOEFL. Electronic applications accepted. *Faculty research:* Genome structure, genome expression, molecular evolution, nucleic acid structure/function, proteomics.

North Dakota State University, College of Graduate and Interdisciplinary Studies, College of Science and Mathematics, Department of Biological Sciences, Fargo, ND 58108. Offers biology (MS); botany (MS, PhD); cellular and molecular biology (PhD); environmental and conservation sciences (MS, PhD); genomics (PhD); natural resources management (MS, PhD); zoology (MS, PhD). *Faculty:* 13 full-time (7 women), 3 part-time/adjunct (1 woman). *Students:* 20 full-time (10 women), 2 part-time (both women); includes 1 minority (American Indian or Alaska Native, non-Hispanic/Latino), 2 international. 12 applicants, 33% accepted, 4 enrolled. In 2011, 3 degrees awarded. *Degree requirements:* For master's, thesis; for doctorate, thesis/dissertation. *Entrance requirements:* For master's and doctorate, GRE General Test. Additional exam requirements/recommendations for international students: Required—TOEFL. *Application deadline:* For fall admission, 1/15 for domestic students. Applications are processed on a rolling basis. Application fee: $35. Electronic applications accepted. *Financial support:* Fellowships with full tuition reimbursements, research assistantships with full tuition reimbursements, teaching assistantships with full tuition reimbursements, career-related internships or fieldwork, Federal Work-Study, institutionally sponsored loans, scholarships/grants, tuition waivers (full), and unspecified assistantships available. Support available to part-time students. Financial award application deadline: 4/15; financial award applicants required to submit FAFSA. *Faculty research:* Comparative endocrinology, physiology, behavioral ecology, plant cell biology, aquatic biology. *Unit head:* Dr. Wendy Reed, Head, 701-231-7087, E-mail: wendy.reed@ndsu.edu. *Application contact:* Sonya Goergen, Marketing, Recruitment, and Public Relations Coordinator, 701-231-7033, Fax: 701-231-6524. Web site: http://biology.ndsu.nodak.edu/.

North Dakota State University, College of Graduate and Interdisciplinary Studies, Interdisciplinary Program in Genomics and Bioinformatics, Fargo, ND 58108. Offers MS, PhD. Part-time programs available. *Faculty:* 21 full-time (3 women). *Students:* 3 full-time (2 women), 3 part-time (1 woman), all international. 13 applicants, 8% accepted, 0 enrolled. In 2011, 1 master's, 1 doctorate awarded. *Degree requirements:* For master's, thesis; for doctorate, comprehensive exam, thesis/dissertation. *Entrance requirements:* For master's and doctorate, minimum GPA of 3.0. Additional exam requirements/recommendations for international students: Required—TOEFL (minimum score 525 paper-based; 197 computer-based; 71 iBT). *Application deadline:* For fall admission, 5/1 for international students; for spring admission, 8/1 for international students. Applications are processed on a rolling basis. Application fee: $35. Electronic applications accepted. *Financial support:* In 2011–12, 12 research assistantships with full tuition reimbursements (averaging $15,000 per year) were awarded; unspecified assistantships also available. *Faculty research:* Genome evolution, genome mapping, genome expression, bioinformatics, data mining. *Unit head:* Dr. Phillip E. McClean,

Director, 701-231-8443, Fax: 701-231-8474. *Application contact:* Sonya Goergen, Marketing, Recruitment, and Public Relations Coordinator, 701-231-7033, Fax: 701-231-6524.

Oregon State University, Graduate School, College of Science, Department of Botany and Plant Pathology, Corvallis, OR 97331. Offers applied systematics (MA, MAIS, MS, PhD); ecology (MA, MAIS, MS, PhD); genetics (MA, MAIS, MS, PhD); genomics and computational biology (MA, MAIS, MS, PhD); molecular and cellular biology (MA, MAIS, MS, PhD); mycology (MA, MAIS, MS, PhD); plant pathology (MA, MAIS, MS, PhD); plant physiology (MA, MAIS, MS, PhD); systematics (MA, MAIS, MS, PhD). Part-time programs available. *Degree requirements:* For master's, variable foreign language requirement, thesis optional; for doctorate, thesis/dissertation. *Entrance requirements:* For master's and doctorate, GRE General Test, minimum GPA of 3.0 in last 90 hours. *Faculty research:* Plant ecology, plant molecular biology, systematic botany, epidemiology, host-pathogen interaction.

Purdue University, College of Pharmacy and Pharmacal Sciences and Graduate School, Graduate Programs in Pharmacy and Pharmacal Sciences, Department of Medicinal Chemistry and Molecular Pharmacology, West Lafayette, IN 47907. Offers biophysical and computational chemistry (PhD); cancer research (PhD); immunology and infectious disease (PhD); medicinal biochemistry and molecular biology (PhD); medicinal chemistry and chemical biology (PhD); molecular pharmacology (PhD); neuropharmacology, neurodegeneration, and neurotoxicity (PhD); systems biology and functional genomics (PhD). *Faculty:* 22 full-time (2 women), 4 part-time/adjunct (1 woman). *Students:* 49 full-time (18 women); includes 3 minority (1 Asian, non-Hispanic/Latino; 2 Hispanic/Latino), 26 international. Average age 27. 250 applicants, 12% accepted, 9 enrolled. In 2011, 10 doctorates awarded. *Degree requirements:* For doctorate, thesis/dissertation. *Entrance requirements:* For doctorate, GRE General Test; GRE Subject Test in biology, biochemistry, and chemistry (recommended), minimum undergraduate GPA of 3.0. Additional exam requirements/recommendations for international students: Required—TOEFL (minimum score 550 paper-based; 77 iBT); Recommended—TWE. *Application deadline:* For fall admission, 2/1 for domestic and international students. Applications are processed on a rolling basis. Application fee: $60 ($75 for international students). Electronic applications accepted. *Financial support:* Fellowships, research assistantships, teaching assistantships, and traineeships available. Support available to part-time students. Financial award applicants required to submit FAFSA. *Faculty research:* Drug design and development, cancer research, drug synthesis and analysis, chemical pharmacology, environmental toxicology. *Unit head:* Dr. Richard F. Borch, Head, 765-494-1403, E-mail: borch@purdue.edu. *Application contact:* Janine C. Mott, Graduate Contact, 765-494-1269, E-mail: jmott@purdue.edu.

University of California, Riverside, Graduate Division, Graduate Program in Genetics, Genomics, and Bioinformatics, Riverside, CA 92521-0102. Offers genomics and bioinformatics (PhD); molecular genetics (PhD); population and evolutionary genetics (PhD). *Faculty:* 72 full-time (20 women). *Students:* 32 full-time (18 women); includes 2 minority (1 Black or African American, non-Hispanic/Latino; 1 Hispanic/Latino), 15 international. Average age 30. In 2011, 2 doctorates awarded. *Degree requirements:* For doctorate, thesis/dissertation, qualifying exams, teaching experience. *Entrance requirements:* For doctorate, GRE General Test, minimum GPA of 3.2. Additional exam requirements/recommendations for international students: Required—TOEFL (minimum score 550 paper-based; 213 computer-based; 80 iBT). *Application deadline:* For fall admission, 5/1 for domestic students, 2/1 for international students; for winter admission, 9/1 for domestic students, 7/1 for international students; for spring admission, 12/1 for domestic students, 10/1 for international students. Applications are processed on a rolling basis. Application fee: $85 ($100 for international students). Electronic applications accepted. *Financial support:* In 2011–12, fellowships with tuition reimbursements (averaging $12,000 per year), research assistantships with tuition reimbursements (averaging $18,000 per year), teaching assistantships with tuition reimbursements (averaging $16,500 per year) were awarded; career-related internships or fieldwork, Federal Work-Study, institutionally sponsored loans, and tuition waivers (full and partial) also available. *Faculty research:* Molecular genetics, evolution and population genetics, genomics and bioinformatics. *Unit head:* Dr. Shizhong Xu, Director, 951-827-5898. *Application contact:* Deidra Kornfeld, Graduate Program Assistant, 800-735-0717, Fax: 951-827-5517, E-mail: genetics@ucr.edu. Web site: http://ggb.ucr.edu/.

University of California, San Francisco, School of Pharmacy and Graduate Division, Pharmaceutical Sciences and Pharmacogenomics Graduate Group, San Francisco, CA 94158-0775. Offers PhD. *Faculty:* 52 full-time (14 women). *Students:* 48 full-time (24 women); includes 16 minority (15 Asian, non-Hispanic/Latino; 1 Hispanic/Latino). Average age 23. 92 applicants, 15% accepted, 8 enrolled. In 2011, 7 doctorates awarded. *Degree requirements:* For doctorate, comprehensive exam, thesis/dissertation. *Entrance requirements:* For doctorate, GRE General Test, minimum GPA of 3.0. Additional exam requirements/recommendations for international students: Required—TOEFL. *Application deadline:* For fall admission, 12/1 for domestic and international students. Application fee: $70 ($90 for international students). Electronic applications accepted. *Financial support:* In 2011–12, 6 fellowships with full tuition reimbursements (averaging $28,000 per year), 34 research assistantships with full tuition reimbursements (averaging $28,000 per year), 8 teaching assistantships with full tuition reimbursements (averaging $28,000 per year) were awarded; career-related internships or fieldwork, institutionally sponsored loans, scholarships/grants, traineeships, tuition waivers (full), and unspecified assistantships also available. Financial award application deadline: 4/6. *Faculty research:* Drug development, drug delivery, molecular pharmacology. *Unit head:* Deanna L. Kroetz, Program Director, 415-476-1159, Fax: 415-476-6022, E-mail: deanna.kroetz@ucsf.edu. *Application contact:* Debbie Acoba-Idlebi, Program Coordinator, 415-476-1947, Fax: 415-476-6022, E-mail: debbie.acoba@ucsf.edu. Web site: http://bts.ucsf.edu/pspg/.

University of Chicago, Division of Biological Sciences, Molecular Biosciences Cluster, Committee on Genetics, Genomics and Systems Biology, Chicago, IL 60637-1513. Offers PhD. *Degree requirements:* For doctorate, thesis/dissertation, ethics class, 2 teaching assistantships. *Entrance requirements:* For doctorate, GRE General Test, minimum GPA of 3.0. Additional exam requirements/recommendations for international students: Required—TOEFL (minimum score 600 paper-based; 250 computer-based; 104 iBT), IELTS (minimum score 7). Electronic applications accepted. *Faculty research:* Molecular genetics, developmental genetics, population genetics, human genetics.

University of Cincinnati, Graduate School, College of Medicine, Graduate Programs in Biomedical Sciences, Department of Environmental Health, Programs in Environmental Genetics and Molecular Toxicology, Cincinnati, OH 45221. Offers MS, PhD. *Degree requirements:* For doctorate, thesis/dissertation. *Entrance requirements:* For master's, GRE, minimum GPA of 3.0, 3 letters of recommendation. Additional exam requirements/recommendations for international students: Required—TOEFL (minimum score 520 paper-based; 190 computer-based).

University of Connecticut, Graduate School, College of Liberal Arts and Sciences, Department of Molecular and Cell Biology, Field of Applied Genomics, Storrs, CT 06269. Offers MS, PSM. *Degree requirements:* For master's, comprehensive exam. *Entrance requirements:* For master's, GRE General Test, GRE Subject Test. Additional exam requirements/recommendations for international students: Required—TOEFL (minimum score 550 paper-based; 213 computer-based). Electronic applications accepted.

University of Florida, College of Medicine, Department of Physiology and Functional Genomics, Gainesville, FL 32611. Offers PhD. *Degree requirements:* For doctorate, thesis/dissertation. *Entrance requirements:* For doctorate, GRE General Test, minimum GPA of 3.0. Additional exam requirements/recommendations for international students: Required—TOEFL. Electronic applications accepted. *Faculty research:* Cell and general endocrinology, neuroendocrinology, neurophysiology, respiration, membrane transport and ion channels.

University of Georgia, College of Agricultural and Environmental Sciences, Institute of Plant Breeding, Genetics and Genomics, Athens, GA 30602. Offers MS, PhD. *Students:* 19 full-time (6 women), 2 part-time (1 woman), 11 international. Average age 29. 16 applicants, 25% accepted, 1 enrolled. In 2011, 2 master's, 4 doctorates awarded. *Financial support:* Tuition waivers and unspecified assistantships available. *Unit head:* Dr. John H. Dayton, Director, 706-542-5607, Fax: 706-583-8120, E-mail: pbgg@uga.edu. *Application contact:* Dr. Dayton Wilde, Graduate Coordinator, 706-542-5607, E-mail: pbgg@uga.edu. Web site: http://www.plantbreeding.uga.edu/index.html.

University of Maine, Graduate School, Interdisciplinary Doctoral Program, Orono, ME 04469. Offers communication (PhD); functional genomics (PhD); mass communication (PhD); ocean engineering (PhD). Part-time and evening/weekend programs available. *Students:* 21 full-time (11 women), 22 part-time (16 women); includes 2 minority (both Asian, non-Hispanic/Latino), 3 international. Average age 38. 25 applicants, 32% accepted, 6 enrolled. In 2011, 6 degrees awarded. *Degree requirements:* For doctorate, comprehensive exam, thesis/dissertation. *Entrance requirements:* For doctorate, GRE General Test. Additional exam requirements/recommendations for international students: Required—TOEFL. *Application deadline:* For fall admission, 4/1 for domestic students; for spring admission, 11/1 for domestic students. Applications are processed on a rolling basis. Application fee: $65. Electronic applications accepted. *Expenses:* Tuition, state resident: full-time $5016. Tuition, nonresident: full-time $14,424. *Unit head:* Scott G. Delcourt, Associate Dean of the Graduate School, 207-581-3291, Fax: 207-581-3232, E-mail: graduate@maine.edu. *Application contact:* Scott G. Delcourt, Associate Dean of the Graduate School, 207-581-3291, Fax: 207-581-3232, E-mail: graduate@maine.edu. Web site: http://www2.umaine.edu/graduate/.

University of Maryland, Baltimore, School of Medicine, Department of Epidemiology and Public Health, Baltimore, MD 21201. Offers biostatistics (MS); clinical research (MS); epidemiology and preventative medicine (PhD); epidemiology and preventive medicine (MPH, MS); gerontology (PhD); human genetics and genomic (PhD); human genetics and genomic medicine (MS); molecular epidemiology (MS, PhD); toxicology (MS, PhD); JD/MS; MD/PhD; MS/PhD. *Accreditation:* CEPH. Part-time programs available. *Students:* 94 full-time (68 women), 61 part-time (46 women); includes 51 minority (18 Black or African American, non-Hispanic/Latino; 25 Asian, non-Hispanic/Latino; 7 Hispanic/Latino; 1 Two or more races, non-Hispanic/Latino), 21 international. Average age 32. 109 applicants, 32% accepted, 19 enrolled. In 2011, 13 master's, 9 doctorates awarded. *Degree requirements:* For doctorate, comprehensive exam, thesis/dissertation. *Entrance requirements:* For master's and doctorate, GRE General Test. Additional exam requirements/recommendations for international students: Required—TOEFL (minimum score 550 paper-based; 213 computer-based; 80 iBT); Recommended—IELTS (minimum score 7). *Application deadline:* For fall admission, 2/1 for domestic students, 1/15 for international students. Application fee: $50. Electronic applications accepted. *Expenses:* Contact institution. *Financial support:* In 2011–12, research assistantships with partial tuition reimbursements (averaging $25,000 per year) were awarded; fellowships, Federal Work-Study, scholarships/grants, and unspecified assistantships also available. Financial award application deadline: 3/1; financial award applicants required to submit FAFSA. *Unit head:* Dr. Laura Hungerford, Program Director, 410-706-8492, Fax: 410-706-4225. *Application contact:* Danielle Fitzpatrick, Program Coordinator, 410-706-8492, Fax: 410-706-4225, E-mail: dfitzpatrick@epi.umaryland.edu. Web site: http://epidemiology.umaryland.edu/Pages/Home.aspx.

University of Maryland, College Park, Academic Affairs, College of Computer, Mathematical and Natural Sciences, Department of Biology, PhD Program in Biological Sciences, College Park, MD 20742. Offers behavior, ecology, evolution, and systematics (PhD); computational biology, bioinformatics, and genomics (PhD); molecular and cellular biology (PhD); physiological systems (PhD). *Students:* 68 full-time (41 women), 4 part-time (2 women); includes 13 minority (3 Black or African American, non-Hispanic/Latino; 4 Asian, non-Hispanic/Latino; 5 Hispanic/Latino; 1 Two or more races, non-Hispanic/Latino), 21 international. 380 applicants, 15% accepted, 22 enrolled. *Degree requirements:* For doctorate, comprehensive exam, thesis/dissertation, present thesis work in seminar. *Entrance requirements:* For doctorate, GRE General Test; GRE Subject Test in biology (recommended), academic transcripts, statement of purpose/research interests, 3 letters of recommendation. Additional exam requirements/recommendations for international students: Required—TOEFL. *Application deadline:* For fall admission, 12/15 for domestic and international students. Applications are processed on a rolling basis. Application fee: $75. Electronic applications accepted. *Expenses:* Tuition, state resident: part-time $525 per credit hour. Tuition, nonresident: part-time $1131 per credit hour. *Required fees:* $386.31 per term. Tuition and fees vary according to program. *Financial support:* In 2011–12, 11 fellowships with full and partial tuition reimbursements (averaging $14,406 per year), 16 research assistantships (averaging $19,495 per year), 41 teaching assistantships (averaging $18,734 per year) were awarded. *Unit head:* Dr. Barbara Thorne, Director, 301-405-6905, E-mail: bthorne@umd.edu. *Application contact:* Dr. Charles A. Caramello, Dean of Graduate School, 301-405-0358, Fax: 301-314-9305. Web site: http://bisi.umd.edu/biologicalsciencesgraduateprogrambisi.

University of Pennsylvania, Perelman School of Medicine, Biomedical Graduate Studies, Graduate Group in Genomics and Computational Biology, Philadelphia, PA 19104. Offers PhD, MD/PhD, VMD/PhD. *Faculty:* 60. *Students:* 33 full-time (8 women); includes 13 minority (2 Black or African American, non-Hispanic/Latino; 9 Asian, non-Hispanic/Latino; 2 Hispanic/Latino), 8 international. 69 applicants, 23% accepted, 6 enrolled. In 2011, 2 doctorates awarded. *Degree requirements:* For doctorate, thesis/dissertation optional. *Entrance requirements:* For doctorate, GRE. Additional exam requirements/recommendations for international students: Required—TOEFL. *Application deadline:* For fall admission, 12/1 priority date for domestic students, 12/1 for international students. Applications are processed on a rolling basis. Application fee: $80. Electronic applications accepted. *Expenses: Tuition:* Full-time $26,660; part-time $4944 per course. *Required fees:* $2318; $291 per course. Tuition and fees vary according to course load, degree level and program. *Financial support:* In 2011–12, 33 students received support. Fellowships, research assistantships, scholarships/grants, traineeships, and unspecified assistantships available. *Unit head:* Dr. Maja Bucan, Chairperson, 215-898-0020, E-mail: bucan@pobox.upenn.edu. *Application contact:* Hannah Chervitz, Graduate Coordinator. Web site: http://www.med.upenn.edu/gcb/.

University of Rochester, School of Medicine and Dentistry, Graduate Programs in Medicine and Dentistry, Department of Biomedical Genetics, Rochester, NY 14627. Offers genetics, genomics and development (PhD). *Degree requirements:* For doctorate, thesis/dissertation, qualifying exam. *Entrance requirements:* For doctorate, GRE General Test. *Expenses: Tuition:* Full-time $41,040.

The University of Tennessee, Graduate School, College of Arts and Sciences, Program in Life Sciences, Knoxville, TN 37996. Offers genome science and technology

(MS, PhD); plant physiology and genetics (MS, PhD). *Degree requirements:* For doctorate, one foreign language, thesis/dissertation. *Entrance requirements:* For master's and doctorate, GRE General Test, minimum GPA of 2.7. Additional exam requirements/recommendations for international students: Required—TOEFL. Electronic applications accepted. *Expenses:* Tuition, state resident: full-time $8332; part-time $464 per credit hour. Tuition, nonresident: full-time $25,174; part-time $1400 per credit hour. *Required fees:* $1162; $56 per credit hour. Tuition and fees vary according to program.

The University of Tennessee–Oak Ridge National Laboratory, Graduate Program in Genome Science and Technology, Oak Ridge, TN 37830-8026. Offers life sciences (MS, PhD). *Degree requirements:* For master's, thesis; for doctorate, comprehensive exam, thesis/dissertation. *Entrance requirements:* For master's and doctorate, GRE General Test. Additional exam requirements/recommendations for international students: Required—TOEFL (minimum score 550 paper-based; 213 computer-based). Electronic applications accepted. *Faculty research:* Genetics/genomics, structural biology/proteomics, computational biology/bioinformatics, bioanalytical technologies.

The University of Toledo, College of Graduate Studies, College of Medicine and Life Sciences, Interdepartmental Programs, Toledo, OH 43606-3390. Offers bioinformatics/proteomics/genomics (MSBS, Certificate); human donation sciences (MSBS); medical sciences (MSBS). *Faculty:* 37. *Students:* 66 full-time (26 women), 3 part-time (1 woman); includes 17 minority (2 Black or African American, non-Hispanic/Latino; 12 Asian, non-Hispanic/Latino; 2 Hispanic/Latino; 1 Two or more races, non-Hispanic/Latino), 1 international. Average age 25. 12 applicants, 92% accepted, 10 enrolled. In 2011, 54 master's, 1 Certificate awarded. *Degree requirements:* For master's, thesis or alternative. *Entrance requirements:* For master's, GRE, minimum undergraduate GPA of 3.0, three letters of recommendation, statement of purpose, transcripts from all prior institutions attended, resume; for Certificate, minimum undergraduate GPA of 3.0, three letters of recommendation, statement of purpose, transcripts from all prior institutions attended, resume. Additional exam requirements/recommendations for international students: Required—TOEFL (minimum score 550 paper-based; 213 computer-based; 80 iBT), IELTS (minimum score 6.5). *Application deadline:* For fall admission, 1/15 priority date for domestic students, 1/15 for international students. Application fee: $45 ($75 for international students). Electronic applications accepted. *Financial support:* Tuition scholarships available. *Unit head:* Dr. Randall Ruch, Assistant Dean of Admissions for Biomedical Graduate programs. *Application contact:* Admissions Analyst, 419-383-4116, Fax: 419-383-6140. Web site: http://www.utoledo.edu/med/grad/.

University of Washington, Graduate School, School of Medicine, Graduate Programs in Medicine, Department of Genome Sciences, Seattle, WA 98195. Offers PhD. *Degree requirements:* For doctorate, thesis/dissertation, general exam. *Entrance requirements:* For doctorate, GRE General Test, minimum GPA of 3.0. Additional exam requirements/recommendations for international students: Required—TOEFL. Electronic applications accepted. *Faculty research:* Model organism genetics, human and medical genetics, genomics and proteomics, computational biology.

Wake Forest University, School of Medicine and Graduate School of Arts and Sciences, Graduate Programs in Medicine, Molecular Genetics and Genomics Program, Winston-Salem, NC 27109. Offers PhD, MD/PhD. *Degree requirements:* For doctorate, thesis/dissertation. *Entrance requirements:* For doctorate, GRE General Test. Additional exam requirements/recommendations for international students: Required—TOEFL. Electronic applications accepted. *Faculty research:* Control of gene expression, molecular pathogenesis, protein biosynthesis, cell development, clinical cytogenetics.

Washington University in St. Louis, School of Medicine, Program in Clinical Investigation, St. Louis, MO 63130-4899. Offers clinical investigation (MS), including genetics/genomics, translational medicine. Part-time programs available. *Faculty:* 64 full-time (17 women), 3 part-time/adjunct (2 women). *Students:* 23 full-time (15 women), 23 part-time (10 women); includes 14 minority (3 Black or African American, non-Hispanic/Latino; 11 Asian, non-Hispanic/Latino). Average age 32. 6 applicants, 83% accepted, 5 enrolled. In 2011, 16 master's awarded. *Degree requirements:* For master's, thesis. *Entrance requirements:* For master's, doctoral-level degree or in process of obtaining doctoral-level degree. Additional exam requirements/recommendations for international students: Required—TOEFL. *Application deadline:* For fall admission, 3/15 for domestic students. Application fee: $0. Electronic applications accepted. *Faculty research:* Anesthesiology, infectious diseases, neurology, obstetrics and gynecology, orthopaedic surgery. *Unit head:* Dr. David Warren, Associate Professor of Medicine, 314-454-8225, Fax: 314-454-5392, E-mail: dwarren@dom.wustl.edu. *Application contact:* Angela B. Wilson, Curriculum and Evaluation Coordinator, 314-454-8936, Fax: 314-454-8279, E-mail: abwilson@dom.wustl.edu. Web site: http://crtc.wustl.edu/.

Wesleyan University, Graduate Programs, Department of Biology, Middletown, CT 06459. Offers animal behavior (PhD); bioformatics/genomics (PhD); cell biology (PhD); developmental biology (PhD); evolution/ecology (PhD); genetics (PhD); neurobiology (PhD); population biology (PhD). *Degree requirements:* For doctorate, variable foreign language requirement, thesis/dissertation. *Entrance requirements:* For doctorate, GRE. Additional exam requirements/recommendations for international students: Required—TOEFL. *Faculty research:* Microbial population genetics, genetic basis of evolutionary adaptation, genetic regulation of differentiation and pattern formation in &ITdrosophila&RO.

West Virginia University, Eberly College of Arts and Sciences, Department of Biology, Morgantown, WV 26506. Offers cell and molecular biology (MS, PhD); environmental and evolutionary biology (MS, PhD); forensic biology (MS, PhD); genomic biology (MS, PhD); neurobiology (MS, PhD). Terminal master's awarded for partial completion of doctoral program. *Degree requirements:* For master's, thesis, final exam; for doctorate, thesis/dissertation, preliminary and final exams. *Entrance requirements:* For master's, GRE General Test, GRE Subject Test, minimum GPA of 3.0; for doctorate, GRE General Test, minimum GPA of 3.0. Additional exam requirements/recommendations for international students: Required—TOEFL. *Faculty research:* Environmental biology, genetic engineering, developmental biology, global change, biodiversity.

Yale University, School of Medicine and Graduate School of Arts and Sciences, Combined Program in Biological and Biomedical Sciences (BBS), Computational Biology and Bioinformatics Track, New Haven, CT 06520. Offers PhD, MD/PhD. *Entrance requirements:* Additional exam requirements/recommendations for international students: Required—TOEFL.

Human Genetics

Baylor College of Medicine, Graduate School of Biomedical Sciences, Department of Molecular and Human Genetics, Houston, TX 77030-3498. Offers PhD, MD/PhD. *Faculty:* 71 full-time (14 women). *Students:* 77 full-time (45 women); includes 10 minority (2 Black or African American, non-Hispanic/Latino; 5 Asian, non-Hispanic/Latino; 3 Hispanic/Latino), 35 international. Average age 26. 130 applicants, 19% accepted, 10 enrolled. In 2011, 15 doctorates awarded. *Degree requirements:* For doctorate, thesis/dissertation, public defense. *Entrance requirements:* For doctorate, GRE General Test, GRE Subject Test (strongly recommended), minimum GPA of 3.0. Additional exam requirements/recommendations for international students: Required—TOEFL. *Application deadline:* For fall admission, 1/1 priority date for domestic students. Application fee: $0. Electronic applications accepted. *Financial support:* In 2011–12, 25 fellowships with full tuition reimbursements (averaging $29,000 per year), 52 research assistantships with full tuition reimbursements (averaging $29,000 per year) were awarded; career-related internships or fieldwork, Federal Work-Study, institutionally sponsored loans, health care benefits, and scholarships (to all students unless there are grant funds available to pay tuition) also available. Financial award applicants required to submit FAFSA. *Faculty research:* Human genetics, genome biology, epigenetics, gene therapy, model organisms. *Unit head:* Dr. Gad Shaulsky, Director, 713-798-5056. *Application contact:* Judi Coleman, Graduate Program Administrator, 713-798-5056, Fax: 713-798-8597, E-mail: genetics-gradprm@bcm.edu. Web site: http://www.bcm.edu/molgen.

Baylor College of Medicine, Graduate School of Biomedical Sciences, Interdepartmental Program in Cell and Molecular Biology, Houston, TX 77030-3498. Offers biochemistry (PhD); cell and molecular biology (PhD); genetics (PhD); human genetics (PhD); immunology (PhD); microbiology (PhD); virology (PhD); MD/PhD. *Faculty:* 112 full-time (30 women). *Students:* 66 full-time (42 women); includes 21 minority (5 Black or African American, non-Hispanic/Latino; 1 American Indian or Alaska Native, non-Hispanic/Latino; 7 Asian, non-Hispanic/Latino; 8 Hispanic/Latino), 14 international. Average age 27. 126 applicants, 25% accepted, 14 enrolled. In 2011, 7 degrees awarded. *Median time to degree:* Of those who began their doctoral program in fall 2003, 82% received their degree in 8 years or less. *Degree requirements:* For doctorate, thesis/dissertation, public defense. *Entrance requirements:* For doctorate, GRE General Test, GRE Subject Test (strongly recommended), minimum GPA of 3.0. Additional exam requirements/recommendations for international students: Required—TOEFL. *Application deadline:* For fall admission, 1/1 priority date for domestic students. Applications are processed on a rolling basis. Application fee: $0. Electronic applications accepted. *Financial support:* In 2011–12, 66 students received support, including 30 fellowships with full tuition reimbursements available (averaging $29,000 per year), 36 research assistantships with full tuition reimbursements available (averaging $29,000 per year); teaching assistantships, Federal Work-Study, institutionally sponsored loans, health care benefits, and tuition waivers (full) also available. Financial award applicants required to submit FAFSA. *Faculty research:* Molecular and cellular biology; cancer, aging and stem cells; genomics and proteomics; microbiome, molecular microbiology; infectious disease, immunology and translational research. *Unit head:* Dr. Susan Marriott, Director, 713-798-6557. *Application contact:* Lourdes Fernandez, Graduate Program Administrator, 713-798-6557, Fax: 713-798-6325, E-mail: cmbprog@bcm.edu. Web site: http://bcm.edu/cmb/.

Case Western Reserve University, School of Medicine and School of Graduate Studies, Graduate Programs in Medicine, Department of Genetics, Program in Human, Molecular, and Developmental Genetics and Genomics, Cleveland, OH 44106. Offers PhD, MD/PhD. *Degree requirements:* For doctorate, comprehensive exam, thesis/dissertation. *Entrance requirements:* For doctorate, GRE General Test, GRE Subject Test. Additional exam requirements/recommendations for international students: Required—TOEFL. *Faculty research:* Regulation of gene expression, molecular control of development, genomics.

Emory University, School of Medicine, Programs in Allied Health Professions, Genetic Counseling Training Program, Atlanta, GA 30322. Offers MM Sc. *Faculty:* 1 (woman) full-time, 1 (woman) part-time/adjunct. *Degree requirements:* For master's, thesis or alternative, capstone project. *Entrance requirements:* For master's, GRE General Test. Additional exam requirements/recommendations for international students: Recommended—TOEFL. *Application deadline:* For winter admission, 12/15 for domestic and international students. Application fee: $50. *Expenses: Tuition:* Full-time $34,800. *Required fees:* $1300. *Faculty research:* Cancer genetics. *Unit head:* Dr. Cecelia Bellcross, Program Director, 404-727-3281, E-mail: cecelia.a.bellcross@emory.edu. *Application contact:* Christi Bell, Administrative Assistant, 404-727-5979, E-mail: fcbell@emory.edu. Web site: http://genetics.emory.edu/gc_training/.

The Johns Hopkins University, School of Medicine, Graduate Programs in Medicine, Predoctoral Training Program in Human Genetics, Baltimore, MD 21218-2699. Offers PhD, MD/PhD. Terminal master's awarded for partial completion of doctoral program. *Degree requirements:* For doctorate, comprehensive exam, thesis/dissertation. *Entrance requirements:* For doctorate, GRE General Test, GRE Subject Test. Additional exam requirements/recommendations for international students: Recommended—TOEFL. Electronic applications accepted. *Faculty research:* Human, mammalian, and molecular genetics, bioinformatics, genomics.

Louisiana State University Health Sciences Center, School of Graduate Studies in New Orleans, Department of Human Genetics, New Orleans, LA 70112-2223. Offers MS, PhD, MD/PhD. Part-time programs available. Terminal master's awarded for partial completion of doctoral program. *Degree requirements:* For master's, comprehensive exam, thesis; for doctorate, comprehensive exam, thesis/dissertation. *Entrance requirements:* For master's and doctorate, GRE General Test. Additional exam requirements/recommendations for international students: Required—TOEFL. *Faculty research:* Genetic epidemiology, segregation and linkage analysis, gene mapping.

McGill University, Faculty of Graduate and Postdoctoral Studies, Faculty of Medicine, Department of Human Genetics, Montréal, QC H3A 2T5, Canada. Offers genetic counseling (M Sc); human genetics (M Sc, PhD).

Memorial University of Newfoundland, Faculty of Medicine and School of Graduate Studies, Graduate Programs in Medicine, Division of Human Genetics, St. John's, NL A1C 5S7, Canada. Offers M Sc, PhD, MD/PhD. Part-time programs available. *Degree requirements:* For master's, thesis; for doctorate, comprehensive exam, thesis/dissertation, oral defense of thesis. *Entrance requirements:* For master's, MD or B Sc; for doctorate, MD or M Sc. Additional exam requirements/recommendations for international students: Required—TOEFL. *Faculty research:* Cancer genetics, gene mapping, medical genetics, birth defects, population genetics.

Sarah Lawrence College, Graduate Studies, Joan H. Marks Graduate Program in Human Genetics, Bronxville, NY 10708-5999. Offers MS. Part-time programs available. *Degree requirements:* For master's, thesis, fieldwork. *Entrance requirements:* For master's, previous course work in biology, chemistry, developmental biology, genetics, probability and statistics. *Expenses:* Contact institution.

Tulane University, School of Medicine and School of Liberal Arts, Graduate Programs in Biomedical Sciences, Program in Human Genetics, New Orleans, LA 70118-5669. Offers MBS, PhD, MD/PhD. MS and PhD offered through the Graduate School. *Degree requirements:* For master's, thesis; for doctorate, thesis/dissertation. *Entrance requirements:* For master's, GRE, MCAT; for doctorate, GRE General Test. Additional exam requirements/recommendations for international students: Required—TOEFL. Electronic applications accepted. *Faculty research:* Inborn errors of metabolism, DNA methylation, gene therapy.

University of California, Los Angeles, David Geffen School of Medicine and Graduate Division, Graduate Programs in Medicine, Department of Human Genetics, Los Angeles, CA 90095. Offers MS, PhD. *Faculty:* 14 full-time (6 women). *Students:* 17 full-time (13 women); includes 4 minority (3 Asian, non-Hispanic/Latino; 1 Hispanic/Latino), 6 international. Average age 30. 12 applicants, 8% accepted, 1 enrolled. In 2011, 4 degrees awarded. *Median time to degree:* Of those who began their doctoral program in fall 2003, 71% received their degree in 8 years or less. *Entrance requirements:* For master's and doctorate, GRE General Test. Application fee: $70 ($90 for international students). Electronic applications accepted. *Financial support:* In 2011–12, 14 fellowships, 15 research assistantships, 8 teaching assistantships were awarded. *Unit head:* Dr. Kenneth L. Lange, Chair, 310-206-8076, Fax: 310-825-8685, E-mail: klange@ucla.edu. *Application contact:* Departmental Information Contact for Admission, 310-206-0920, Fax: 310-794-5446, E-mail: humgen@mednet.ucla.edu.

University of California, Los Angeles, Graduate Division, College of Letters and Science and David Geffen School of Medicine, UCLA ACCESS to Programs in the Molecular, Cellular and Integrative Life Sciences, Los Angeles, CA 90095. Offers biochemistry and molecular biology (PhD); biological chemistry (PhD); cellular and molecular pathology (PhD); human genetics (PhD); microbiology, immunology, and molecular genetics (PhD); molecular biology (PhD); molecular toxicology (PhD); molecular, cellular and integrative physiology (PhD); neurobiology (PhD); oral biology (PhD); physiology (PhD). *Students:* 44 full-time (30 women); includes 18 minority (11 Asian, non-Hispanic/Latino; 6 Hispanic/Latino; 1 Two or more races, non-Hispanic/Latino), 9 international. Average age 25. 495 applicants, 18% accepted, 41 enrolled. *Degree requirements:* For doctorate, thesis/dissertation, oral and written qualifying exams. *Entrance requirements:* For doctorate, GRE General Test, minimum undergraduate GPA of 3.0. Additional exam requirements/recommendations for international students: Required—TOEFL. *Application deadline:* For fall admission, 12/15 for domestic and international students. Application fee: $70 ($90 for international students). Electronic applications accepted. *Financial support:* In 2011–12, 51 fellowships with full and partial tuition reimbursements, 9 research assistantships with full and partial tuition reimbursements were awarded; teaching assistantships with full and partial tuition reimbursements, Federal Work-Study, institutionally sponsored loans, scholarships/grants, health care benefits, tuition waivers (full and partial), and unspecified assistantships also available. Financial award application deadline: 3/1; financial award applicants required to submit FAFSA. *Faculty research:* Molecular, cellular, and developmental biology; immunology; microbiology; integrative biology. *Unit head:* Jody Spillane, Project Coordinator, 310-206-1845, E-mail: jspillane@mednet.ucla.edu. *Application contact:* UCLA ACCESS Admissions, 310-206-1845, E-mail: uclaaccess@mednet.ucla.edu. Web site: https://www.uclaaccess.ucla.edu/.

University of Chicago, Division of Biological Sciences, Molecular Biosciences Cluster, Department of Human Genetics, Chicago, IL 60637-1513. Offers PhD. *Degree requirements:* For doctorate, thesis/dissertation, ethics class, 2 teaching assistantships. *Entrance requirements:* For doctorate, GRE General Test. Additional exam requirements/recommendations for international students: Required—TOEFL (minimum score 600 paper-based; 250 computer-based; 104 iBT), IELTS (minimum score 7). Electronic applications accepted.

University of Manitoba, Faculty of Medicine and Faculty of Graduate Studies, Graduate Programs in Medicine, Department of Biochemistry and Medical Genetics, Winnipeg, MB R3T 2N2, Canada. Offers M Sc, PhD. Terminal master's awarded for partial completion of doctoral program. *Degree requirements:* For master's, thesis; for doctorate, thesis/dissertation. *Faculty research:* Cancer, gene expression, membrane lipids, metabolic control, genetic diseases.

University of Maryland, Baltimore, School of Medicine, Department of Epidemiology and Public Health, Baltimore, MD 21201. Offers biostatistics (MS); clinical research (MS); epidemiology and preventative medicine (PhD); epidemiology and preventive medicine (MPH, MS); gerontology (PhD); human genetics and genomic (PhD); human genetics and genomic medicine (MS); molecular epidemiology (MS, PhD); toxicology (MS, PhD); JD/MS; MD/PhD; MS/PhD. *Accreditation:* CEPH. Part-time programs available. *Students:* 94 full-time (68 women), 61 part-time (46 women); includes 51 minority (18 Black or African American, non-Hispanic/Latino; 25 Asian, non-Hispanic/Latino; 7 Hispanic/Latino; 1 Two or more races, non-Hispanic/Latino), 21 international. Average age 32. 109 applicants, 32% accepted, 19 enrolled. In 2011, 13 master's, 9 doctorates awarded. *Degree requirements:* For doctorate, comprehensive exam, thesis/dissertation. *Entrance requirements:* For master's and doctorate, GRE General Test. Additional exam requirements/recommendations for international students: Required—TOEFL (minimum score 550 paper-based; 213 computer-based; 80 iBT); Recommended—IELTS (minimum score 7). *Application deadline:* For fall admission, 2/1 for domestic students, 1/15 for international students. Application fee: $50. Electronic applications accepted. *Expenses:* Contact institution. *Financial support:* In 2011–12, research assistantships with partial tuition reimbursements (averaging $25,000 per year) were awarded; fellowships, Federal Work-Study, scholarships/grants, and unspecified assistantships also available. Financial award application deadline: 3/1; financial award applicants required to submit FAFSA. *Unit head:* Dr. Laura Hungerford, Program Director, 410-706-8492, Fax: 410-706-4225. *Application contact:* Danielle Fitzpatrick, Program Coordinator, 410-706-8492, Fax: 410-706-4225, E-mail: dfitzpatrick@epi.umaryland.edu. Web site: http://epidemiology.umaryland.edu/Pages/Home.aspx.

University of Michigan, Horace H. Rackham School of Graduate Studies, Program in Biomedical Sciences (PIBS), Department of Human Genetics, Ann Arbor, MI 48109. Offers genetic counseling (MS); human genetics (MS, PhD). *Faculty:* 31 full-time (13 women). *Students:* 44 full-time (33 women); includes 9 minority (1 Black or African American, non-Hispanic/Latino; 5 Asian, non-Hispanic/Latino; 3 Two or more races, non-Hispanic/Latino), 5 international. Average age 28. 196 applicants, 15% accepted, 11 enrolled. In 2011, 10 master's, 6 doctorates awarded. Terminal master's awarded for partial completion of doctoral program. *Degree requirements:* For master's, research project; for doctorate, thesis/dissertation, oral preliminary exam, oral defense of dissertation. *Entrance requirements:* For master's, GRE General Test, 3 letters of recommendation, advocacy experience; for doctorate, GRE General Test, 3 letters of recommendation. Additional exam requirements/recommendations for international students: Required—TOEFL (minimum score 84 iBT). *Application deadline:* For fall admission, 12/1 for domestic and international students; for winter admission, 1/15 for

domestic and international students. Application fee: $65 ($75 for international students). Electronic applications accepted. *Financial support:* In 2011–12, 38 students received support, including 22 fellowships with full and partial tuition reimbursements available (averaging $26,500 per year), 14 research assistantships with full tuition reimbursements available (averaging $26,500 per year), 5 teaching assistantships with full tuition reimbursements available (averaging $17,702 per year); Federal Work-Study, institutionally sponsored loans, scholarships/grants, traineeships, health care benefits, and unspecified assistantships also available. Financial award application deadline: 4/30; financial award applicants required to submit FAFSA. *Faculty research:* Molecular genetics, developmental genetics, disease mechanisms, translational clinical research, statistical and population genetics. *Total annual research expenditures:* $8.7 million. *Unit head:* Dr. Sally A. Camper, Chair, 734-763-0682, Fax: 734-763-3784, E-mail: scamper@umich.edu. *Application contact:* Michelle S. Melis, Director of Student Life, 734-615-6538, Fax: 734-647-7022, E-mail: msmtegan@umich.edu. Web site: http://www.hg.med.umich.edu/.

University of Pittsburgh, Graduate School of Public Health, Department of Human Genetics, Pittsburgh, PA 15260. Offers genetic counseling (MS); human genetics (MS, PhD); public health genetics (MPH, Certificate); MD/PhD. *Faculty:* 9 full-time (5 women), 27 part-time/adjunct (8 women). *Students:* 51 full-time (39 women), 16 part-time (15 women); includes 10 minority (2 Black or African American, non-Hispanic/Latino; 4 Asian, non-Hispanic/Latino; 1 Hispanic/Latino; 3 Two or more races, non-Hispanic/Latino), 20 international. Average age 28. 97 applicants, 52% accepted, 20 enrolled. In 2011, 17 master's, 6 doctorates awarded. Terminal master's awarded for partial completion of doctoral program. *Degree requirements:* For master's, thesis (for some programs); for doctorate, thesis/dissertation. *Entrance requirements:* For master's, GRE General Test, previous course work in biochemistry, calculus, and genetics; for doctorate, GRE General Test. Additional exam requirements/recommendations for international students: Required—TOEFL (minimum score 550 paper-based; 80 iBT) or IELTS (minimum score 6.5). *Application deadline:* For fall admission, 4/1 for international students; for winter admission, 9/1 for international students; for spring admission, 2/1 for international students. Applications are processed on a rolling basis. Application fee: $115. Electronic applications accepted. *Expenses:* Tuition, state resident: full-time $18,774; part-time $760 per credit. Tuition, nonresident: full-time $30,736; part-time $1258 per credit. *Required fees:* $740; $200 per term. Tuition and fees vary according to program. *Financial support:* In 2011–12, 21 students received support, including 1 fellowship (averaging $18,394 per year), 20 research assistantships with full tuition reimbursements available (averaging $11,371 per year). *Faculty research:* Genetic mechanisms related to the transition from normal to disease states, how genes and the environment interact to affect the distribution of health and disease in human populations. *Total annual research expenditures:* $4.6 million. *Unit head:* Dr. Mohammad Kamboh, Chairman, 412-624-3066, Fax: 412-624-3020, E-mail: kamboh@pitt.edu. *Application contact:* Jeanette Norbut, Administrative Secretary, 412-624-3018, Fax: 412-624-3020, E-mail: jeanette.norbut@hgen.pitt.edu. Web site: http://www.hgen.pitt.edu.

The University of Texas Health Science Center at Houston, Graduate School of Biomedical Sciences, Program in Human and Molecular Genetics, Houston, TX 77225-0036. Offers MS, PhD, MD/PhD. Terminal master's awarded for partial completion of doctoral program. *Degree requirements:* For master's, thesis; for doctorate, thesis/dissertation. *Entrance requirements:* For master's and doctorate, GRE General Test. Additional exam requirements/recommendations for international students: Required—TOEFL. Electronic applications accepted. *Faculty research:* Computational genomics, cancer genetics, complex disease genetics, medical genetics.

University of Utah, School of Medicine and Graduate School, Graduate Programs in Medicine, Department of Human Genetics, Salt Lake City, UT 84112-1107. Offers MS, PhD. Terminal master's awarded for partial completion of doctoral program. *Degree requirements:* For master's, comprehensive exam, thesis optional; for doctorate, comprehensive exam, thesis/dissertation. Electronic applications accepted. *Faculty research:* RNA metabolism, drosophilia genetics, mouse genetics, protein synthesis.

Vanderbilt University, Graduate School, Program in Human Genetics, Nashville, TN 37240-1001. Offers PhD, MD/PhD. *Students:* 23 full-time (16 women), 2 part-time (0 women); includes 4 minority (2 Black or African American, non-Hispanic/Latino; 1 Hispanic/Latino; 1 Two or more races, non-Hispanic/Latino), 3 international. Average age 29. In 2011, 3 degrees awarded. *Degree requirements:* For doctorate, comprehensive exam, thesis/dissertation. *Entrance requirements:* For doctorate, GRE General Test. Additional exam requirements/recommendations for international students: Required—TOEFL (minimum score 570 paper-based; 230 computer-based; 88 iBT). *Application deadline:* For fall admission, 1/15 for domestic and international students. Application fee: $0. Electronic applications accepted. *Financial support:* Fellowships with full and partial tuition reimbursements, research assistantships with full and partial tuition reimbursements, Federal Work-Study, institutionally sponsored loans, traineeships, and health care benefits available. Financial award application deadline: 1/15; financial award applicants required to submit CSS PROFILE or FAFSA. *Faculty research:* Disease gene discovery, computational genomics, translational genetics. *Unit head:* Dr. Jonathan L. Haines, Director, The Center for Human Genetics Research, 615-343-5851, Fax: 615-322-1453, E-mail: jonathan.haines@vanderbilt.edu. Web site: http://chgr.mc.vanderbilt.edu/page/education.

Virginia Commonwealth University, Medical College of Virginia-Professional Programs, School of Medicine, School of Medicine Graduate Programs, Department of Human and Molecular Genetics, Richmond, VA 23284-9005. Offers genetic counseling (MS); human genetics (PhD); molecular biology and genetics (MS, PhD); MD/PhD. *Degree requirements:* For master's, thesis; for doctorate, thesis/dissertation, comprehensive oral and written exams. *Entrance requirements:* For master's, GRE; for doctorate, GRE General Test. Additional exam requirements/recommendations for international students: Required—TOEFL (minimum score 600 paper-based; 250 computer-based; 100 iBT). Electronic applications accepted. *Expenses:* Tuition, state resident: full-time $9133; part-time $507 per credit. Tuition, nonresident: full-time $18,777; part-time $1043 per credit. *Required fees:* $77 per credit. Tuition and fees vary according to degree level, campus/location, program and student level. *Faculty research:* Genetic epidemiology, biochemical genetics, quantitative genetics, human cytogenetics, molecular genetics.

Virginia Commonwealth University, Program in Pre-Medical Basic Health Sciences, Richmond, VA 23284-9005. Offers anatomy (CBHS); biochemistry (CBHS); human genetics (CBHS); microbiology (CBHS); pharmacology (CBHS); physiology (CBHS). *Entrance requirements:* For degree, GRE, MCAT or DAT, course work in organic chemistry, minimum undergraduate GPA of 2.8. Additional exam requirements/recommendations for international students: Required—TOEFL (minimum score 600 paper-based). Electronic applications accepted. *Expenses:* Tuition, state resident: full-time $9133; part-time $507 per credit. Tuition, nonresident: full-time $18,777; part-time $1043 per credit. *Required fees:* $77 per credit. Tuition and fees vary according to degree level, campus/location, program and student level.

Wake Forest University, School of Medicine and Graduate School of Arts and Sciences, Graduate Programs in Medicine, Molecular Genetics and Genomics Program, Winston-Salem, NC 27109. Offers PhD, MD/PhD. *Degree requirements:* For doctorate,

thesis/dissertation. *Entrance requirements:* For doctorate, GRE General Test. Additional exam requirements/recommendations for international students: Required—TOEFL. Electronic applications accepted. *Faculty research:* Control of gene expression, molecular pathogenesis, protein biosynthesis, cell development, clinical cytogenetics.

Washington University in St. Louis, Graduate School of Arts and Sciences, Division of Biology and Biomedical Sciences, Program in Human and Statistical Genetics, St. Louis, MO 63130-4899. Offers PhD. *Degree requirements:* For doctorate, thesis/dissertation. *Entrance requirements:* For doctorate, GRE General Test, GRE Subject Test. Electronic applications accepted.

West Virginia University, Davis College of Agriculture, Forestry and Consumer Sciences, Interdisciplinary Program in Genetics and Developmental Biology, Morgantown, WV 26506. Offers animal breeding (MS, PhD); biochemical and molecular genetics (MS, PhD); cytogenetics (MS, PhD); descriptive embryology (MS, PhD); developmental genetics (MS); experimental morphogenesis/teratology (MS); human genetics (MS, PhD); immunogenetics (MS, PhD); life cycles of animals and plants (MS, PhD); molecular aspects of development (MS, PhD); mutagenesis (MS, PhD); oncology (MS, PhD); plant genetics (MS, PhD); population and quantitative genetics (MS, PhD); regeneration (MS, PhD); teratology (PhD); toxicology (MS, PhD). *Degree requirements:* For master's, thesis; for doctorate, comprehensive exam, thesis/dissertation. *Entrance requirements:* For master's, GRE or MCAT, minimum GPA of 2.75. Additional exam requirements/recommendations for international students: Required—TOEFL.

Molecular Genetics

Albert Einstein College of Medicine, Graduate Division of Biomedical Sciences, Division of Biological Sciences, Department of Genetics, Bronx, NY 10461. Offers computational genetics (PhD); molecular genetics (PhD); translational genetics (PhD); MD/PhD. *Degree requirements:* For doctorate, thesis/dissertation. *Entrance requirements:* For doctorate, GRE General Test. Additional exam requirements/recommendations for international students: Required—TOEFL. *Faculty research:* Neurologic genetics in &ITDrosophila&RO, biochemical genetics of yeast, developmental genetics in the mouse.

Duke University, Graduate School, Department of Molecular Genetics and Microbiology, Durham, NC 27710. Offers PhD. *Faculty:* 25 full-time. *Students:* 48 full-time (25 women); includes 7 minority (2 Black or African American, non-Hispanic/Latino; 1 American Indian or Alaska Native, non-Hispanic/Latino; 4 Asian, non-Hispanic/Latino), 11 international. 88 applicants, 22% accepted, 9 enrolled. In 2011, 6 degrees awarded. *Degree requirements:* For doctorate, thesis/dissertation. *Entrance requirements:* For doctorate, GRE General Test, GRE Subject Test in biology, chemistry, or biochemistry, cell and molecular biology (recommended). Additional exam requirements/recommendations for international students: Required—TOEFL (minimum score 550 paper-based; 213 computer-based; 83 iBT), IELTS (minimum score 7). *Application deadline:* For fall admission, 12/8 priority date for domestic students, 12/8 for international students. Application fee: $75. Electronic applications accepted. *Expenses: Tuition:* Full-time $40,720. *Required fees:* $3107. *Financial support:* Fellowships with full tuition reimbursements, research assistantships with full tuition reimbursements, and Federal Work-Study available. Financial award application deadline: 12/31. *Unit head:* Dr. Raphael Valdivia, Director of Graduate Studies, 919-684-6629, Fax: 919-684-8346, E-mail: kimberly.kobes@duke.edu. *Application contact:* Elizabeth Hutton, Director of Admissions, 919-684-3913, Fax: 919-684-2277, E-mail: grad-admissions@duke.edu. Web site: http://mgm.duke.edu/graduate/.

Emory University, Laney Graduate School, Division of Biological and Biomedical Sciences, Program in Microbiology and Molecular Genetics, Atlanta, GA 30322-1100. Offers PhD. *Faculty:* 39 full-time (8 women). *Students:* 42 full-time (31 women); includes 7 minority (2 Black or African American, non-Hispanic/Latino; 2 Asian, non-Hispanic/Latino; 3 Hispanic/Latino), 5 international. Average age 27. 129 applicants, 12% accepted, 7 enrolled. In 2011, 7 degrees awarded. *Median time to degree:* Of those who began their doctoral program in fall 2003, 100% received their degree in 8 years or less. *Degree requirements:* For doctorate, comprehensive exam, thesis/dissertation. *Entrance requirements:* For doctorate, GRE General Test, minimum GPA of 3.0 in science course work (recommended). Additional exam requirements/recommendations for international students: Required—TOEFL. *Application deadline:* For fall admission, 12/1 for domestic and international students. Application fee: $75. Electronic applications accepted. *Expenses: Tuition:* Full-time $34,800. *Required fees:* $1300. *Financial support:* In 2011–12, 14 students received support, including 14 fellowships with full tuition reimbursements available (averaging $26,500 per year); institutionally sponsored loans, scholarships/grants, health care benefits, and tuition waivers (full) also available. *Faculty research:* Bacterial genetics and physiology, microbial development, molecular biology of viruses and bacterial pathogens, DNA recombination. *Unit head:* Dr. Phil Rather, Program Director, 404-728-5079, Fax: 404-728-7780, E-mail: prather@emory.edu. *Application contact:* Kathy Smith, Director of Recruitment and Admissions, 404-727-2547, Fax: 404-727-3322, E-mail: kathy.smith@emory.edu. Web site: http://www.biomed.emory.edu/.

The George Washington University, Columbian College of Arts and Sciences, Institute for Biomedical Sciences, Program in Biochemistry and Molecular Genetics, Washington, DC 20052. Offers PhD. *Students:* 6 part-time (3 women), 1 international. Average age 28. In 2011, 3 degrees awarded. Terminal master's awarded for partial completion of doctoral program. *Degree requirements:* For doctorate, thesis/dissertation, general exam. *Entrance requirements:* For doctorate, GRE General Test, interview, minimum GPA of 3.0. Additional exam requirements/recommendations for international students: Required—TOEFL (minimum score 600 paper-based; 250 computer-based). *Application deadline:* For fall admission, 12/15 priority date for domestic students, 12/15 for international students; for spring admission, 10/1 priority date for domestic students, 10/1 for international students. Applications are processed on a rolling basis. Application fee: $75. Electronic applications accepted. *Financial support:* In 2011–12, 4 students received support. Fellowships, Federal Work-Study, institutionally sponsored loans, and tuition waivers available. Financial award application deadline: 2/1. *Unit head:* Valerie W. Hu, Director, 202-994-8431, E-mail: valhu@gwu.edu. *Application contact:* Information Contact, 202-994-7120, Fax: 202-994-6100, E-mail: genetics@gwu.edu. Web site: http://www.gwumc.edu/ibs/fields/biochemgenetics.html.

The George Washington University, School of Medicine and Health Sciences, Department of Biochemistry and Molecular Biology, Washington, DC 20037. Offers biochemistry and molecular biology (MS); biochemistry and molecular genetics (PhD); molecular biochemistry and bioinformatics (MS). *Degree requirements:* For master's, comprehensive exam; for doctorate, thesis/dissertation, general exam. *Entrance requirements:* For master's, GRE General Test, interview, minimum GPA of 3.0; for doctorate, GRE General Test, minimum GPA of 3.0. Additional exam requirements/recommendations for international students: Required—TOEFL (minimum score 550 paper-based; 213 computer-based).

Georgia State University, College of Arts and Sciences, Department of Biology, Program in Molecular Genetics and Biochemistry, Atlanta, GA 30302-3083. Offers MS, PhD. Part-time programs available. Terminal master's awarded for partial completion of doctoral program. *Degree requirements:* For master's, thesis or alternative; for doctorate, thesis/dissertation, exam. *Entrance requirements:* For master's and doctorate, GRE General Test. Additional exam requirements/recommendations for international students: Required—TOEFL. Electronic applications accepted.

Harvard University, Graduate School of Arts and Sciences, Division of Medical Sciences, Boston, MA 02115. Offers biological chemistry and molecular pharmacology (PhD); cell biology (PhD); genetics (PhD); microbiology and molecular genetics (PhD); pathology (PhD), including experimental pathology. *Degree requirements:* For doctorate, thesis/dissertation. *Entrance requirements:* For doctorate, GRE General Test, GRE Subject Test. Additional exam requirements/recommendations for international students: Required—TOEFL. *Expenses: Tuition:* Full-time $36,304. *Required fees:* $1186. Full-time tuition and fees vary according to program.

Illinois State University, Graduate School, College of Arts and Sciences, Department of Biological Sciences, Normal, IL 61790-2200. Offers animal behavior (MS); bacteriology (MS); biochemistry (MS); biological sciences (MS); biology (PhD); biophysics (MS); biotechnology (MS); botany (MS, PhD); cell biology (MS); conservation biology (MS); developmental biology (MS); ecology (MS, PhD); entomology (MS); evolutionary biology (MS); genetics (MS, PhD); immunology (MS); microbiology (MS, PhD); molecular biology (MS); molecular genetics (MS); neurobiology (MS); neuroscience (MS); parasitology (MS); physiology (MS, PhD); plant biology (MS); plant molecular biology (MS); plant sciences (MS); structural biology (MS); zoology (MS, PhD). Part-time programs available. *Degree requirements:* For master's, thesis or alternative; for doctorate, variable foreign language requirement, thesis/dissertation, 2 terms of residency. *Entrance requirements:* For master's, GRE General Test, minimum GPA of 2.6 in last 60 hours of course work; for doctorate, GRE General Test. *Faculty research:* Redoc balance and drug development in schistosoma mansoni, control of the growth of listeria monocytogenes at low temperature, regulation of cell expansion and microtubule function by SPRI, CRUI: physiology and fitness consequences of different life history phenotypes.

Indiana University–Purdue University Indianapolis, Indiana University School of Medicine, Department of Medical and Molecular Genetics, Indianapolis, IN 46202-2896. Offers genetic counseling (MS); medical and molecular genetics (MS, PhD); MD/MS; MD/PhD. Part-time programs available. *Faculty:* 8 full-time (2 women). *Students:* 30 full-time (23 women), 6 part-time (4 women); includes 3 minority (2 Black or African American, non-Hispanic/Latino; 1 Asian, non-Hispanic/Latino), 6 international. Average age 26. 115 applicants, 8% accepted, 6 enrolled. In 2011, 8 master's, 3 doctorates awarded. Terminal master's awarded for partial completion of doctoral program. *Degree requirements:* For master's, thesis optional; for doctorate, thesis/dissertation, research ethics. *Entrance requirements:* For master's and doctorate, GRE General Test, minimum GPA of 3.2. *Application deadline:* For fall admission, 1/15 priority date for domestic students. Application fee: $55 ($65 for international students). *Financial support:* In 2011–12, fellowships with tuition reimbursements (averaging $12,750 per year), teaching assistantships (averaging $22,000 per year) were awarded; research assistantships with tuition reimbursements, Federal Work-Study, and institutionally sponsored loans also available. Support available to part-time students. Financial award application deadline: 1/15. *Faculty research:* Twins, human gene mapping, chromosomes and malignancy, clinical genetics. *Total annual research expenditures:* $2.1 million. *Unit head:* Dr. Joe Christlan, Chairman, 317-274-2241. *Application contact:* Kathleen Wilhelm, Admissions Secretary, 317-274-2241, Fax: 317-274-2387, E-mail: medgen@iupui.edu. Web site: http://medgen.iupui.edu/.

Iowa State University of Science and Technology, Program in Animal Breeding and Genetics, Ames, IA 50011-3150. Offers animal breeding and genetics (MS); immunogenetics (PhD); molecular genetics (PhD); quantitative genetics (PhD). *Entrance requirements:* For master's and doctorate, GRE. Additional exam requirements/recommendations for international students: Required—TOEFL (minimum score 550 paper-based; 80 iBT), IELTS (minimum score 6.5). *Application deadline:* For fall admission, 2/1 for domestic and international students; for spring admission, 9/1 for domestic and international students. Electronic applications accepted. *Unit head:* Joe Sebranek, Director of Graduate Education, 515-294-2160, Fax: 515-294-6994, E-mail: dlnelson@iastate.edu. *Application contact:* Donna Nelson, Application Contact, 515-294-2160, Fax: 515-294-6994, E-mail: dlnelson@iastate.edu. Web site: http://www.ans,iastate.edu/stud/prosp_grad/.

Medical College of Wisconsin, Graduate School of Biomedical Sciences, Department of Microbiology and Molecular Genetics, Milwaukee, WI 53226-0509. Offers MS, PhD, MD/PhD. *Degree requirements:* For doctorate, comprehensive exam, thesis/dissertation. *Entrance requirements:* For master's and doctorate, GRE, official transcripts, three letters of recommendation. Additional exam requirements/recommendations for international students: Required—TOEFL. *Faculty research:* Virology, immunology, bacterial toxins, regulation of gene expression.

Michigan State University, College of Human Medicine and The Graduate School, Graduate Programs in Human Medicine, East Lansing, MI 48824. Offers biochemistry and molecular biology (MS, PhD); epidemiology (MS, PhD); microbiology (MS); microbiology and molecular genetics (PhD); pharmacology and toxicology (MS, PhD); physiology (MS, PhD); public health (MPH). *Entrance requirements:* Additional exam requirements/recommendations for international students: Required—TOEFL.

Michigan State University, College of Osteopathic Medicine and The Graduate School, Graduate Studies in Osteopathic Medicine, East Lansing, MI 48824. Offers biochemistry and molecular biology (MS, PhD); microbiology (MS); microbiology and molecular genetics (PhD); pharmacology and toxicology (MS, PhD), including integrative pharmacology (MS), pharmacology and toxicology, pharmacology and toxicology-environmental toxicology (PhD); physiology (MS, PhD).

New York University, Graduate School of Arts and Science, Department of Biology, New York, NY 10012-1019. Offers biology (PhD); biomedical journalism (MS); cancer and molecular biology (PhD); computational biology (PhD); computers in biological research (MS); developmental genetics (PhD); general biology (MS); immunology and microbiology (PhD); molecular genetics (PhD); neurobiology (PhD); oral biology (MS); plant biology (PhD); recombinant DNA technology (MS); MS/MBA. Part-time programs available. *Faculty:* 24 full-time (5 women). *Students:* 146 full-time (90 women), 54 part-time (36 women); includes 49 minority (1 Black or African American, non-Hispanic/Latino; 33 Asian, non-Hispanic/Latino; 12 Hispanic/Latino; 3 Two or more races, non-Hispanic/Latino), 89 international. Average age 27. 394 applicants, 62% accepted, 82 enrolled. In 2011, 68 master's, 6 doctorates awarded. Terminal master's awarded for partial completion of doctoral program. *Degree requirements:* For master's, thesis or alternative, qualifying paper; for doctorate, comprehensive exam, thesis/dissertation. *Entrance requirements:* For master's, GRE General Test; for doctorate, GRE General Test, GRE Subject Test. Additional exam requirements/recommendations for international students: Required—TOEFL. *Application deadline:* For fall admission, 12/1 priority date for domestic students, 12/1 for international students. Application fee: $90. *Financial support:* Fellowships with tuition reimbursements, research assistantships with tuition reimbursements, teaching assistantships with tuition reimbursements, career-related internships or fieldwork, Federal Work-Study, institutionally sponsored loans, scholarships/grants, health care benefits, and unspecified assistantships available. Financial award application deadline: 12/1; financial award applicants required to submit FAFSA. *Faculty research:* Genomics, molecular and cell biology, development and molecular genetics, molecular evolution of plants and animals. *Unit head:* Stephen Small, Chair, 212-998-8200, Fax: 212-995-4015, E-mail: biology@nyu.edu. *Application contact:* Justin Blau, Director of Graduate Studies, 212-998-8200, Fax: 212-995-4015, E-mail: biology@nyu.edu. Web site: http://biology.as.nyu.edu/.

The Ohio State University, Graduate School, College of Arts and Sciences, Division of Natural and Mathematical Sciences, Department of Molecular Genetics, Columbus, OH 43210. Offers cell and developmental biology (MS, PhD); genetics (MS, PhD); molecular biology (MS, PhD). *Faculty:* 23. *Students:* 11 full-time (5 women), 23 part-time (11 women); includes 1 minority (Black or African American, non-Hispanic/Latino), 15 international. Average age 26. In 2011, 8 doctorates awarded. *Degree requirements:* For master's, thesis; for doctorate, thesis/dissertation. *Entrance requirements:* For master's and doctorate, GRE General Test, GRE Subject Test in biology or biochemistry (recommended). Additional exam requirements/recommendations for international students: Required—TOEFL (minimum score 550 paper-based; 250 computer-based; 79 iBT), Michigan English Language Assessment Battery (minimum score 82). *Application deadline:* For fall admission, 8/15 priority date for domestic students, 7/1 for international students; for winter admission, 12/1 priority date for domestic students, 11/1 for international students; for spring admission, 3/1 priority date for domestic students, 2/1 for international students. Applications are processed on a rolling basis. Application fee: $40 ($50 for international students). Electronic applications accepted. *Expenses:* Tuition, state resident: full-time $11,400. Tuition, nonresident: full-time $28,125. Tuition and fees vary according to course load, degree level, campus/location and program. *Financial support:* Fellowships, research assistantships, teaching assistantships, Federal Work-Study, and institutionally sponsored loans available. Support available to part-time students. *Unit head:* Dr. Anita Hopper, Chair, 614-688-3306, Fax: 614-292-4466, E-mail: hopper.64@osu.edu. *Application contact:* Graduate Admissions, 614-292-6031, Fax: 614-292-3656, E-mail: gradadmissions@osu.edu. Web site: https://molgen.osu.edu.

Oklahoma State University, College of Arts and Sciences, Department of Microbiology and Molecular Genetics, Stillwater, OK 74078. Offers MS, PhD. *Faculty:* 18 full-time (3 women), 1 part-time/adjunct (0 women). *Students:* 10 full-time (4 women), 14 part-time (12 women); includes 1 minority (Asian, non-Hispanic/Latino), 12 international. Average age 29. 113 applicants, 7% accepted, 3 enrolled. In 2011, 2 master's, 3 doctorates awarded. *Degree requirements:* For master's, thesis; for doctorate, comprehensive exam, thesis/dissertation. *Entrance requirements:* For master's, GRE General Test; for doctorate, GRE General Test. Additional exam requirements/recommendations for international students: Required—TOEFL (minimum score 550 paper-based; 79 iBT). *Application deadline:* For fall admission, 3/1 for international students; for spring admission, 8/1 for international students. Applications are processed on a rolling basis. Application fee: $40 ($75 for international students). Electronic applications accepted. *Expenses:* Tuition, state resident: full-time $4044; part-time $168.50 per credit hour. Tuition, nonresident: full-time $16,008; part-time $667 per credit hour. *Required fees:* $2122; $88.45 per credit hour. One-time fee: $50. Tuition and fees vary according to course load and campus/location. *Financial support:* In 2011–12, 16 research assistantships (averaging $19,979 per year), 9 teaching assistantships (averaging $17,567 per year) were awarded; career-related internships or fieldwork, Federal Work-Study, scholarships/grants, health care benefits, tuition waivers (partial), and unspecified assistantships also available. Support available to part-time students. Financial award application deadline: 3/1; financial award applicants required to submit FAFSA. *Faculty research:* Bioinformatics, genomics-genetics, virology, environmental microbiology, development-molecular mechanisms. *Unit head:* Dr. Bill Picking, Head, 405-744-7180, Fax: 405-744-6790. *Application contact:* Dr. Sheryl Tucker, Dean, 405-744-7099, Fax: 405-744-0355, E-mail: grad-i@okstate.edu. Web site: http://microbiology.okstate.edu.

Penn State Hershey Medical Center, College of Medicine, Graduate School Programs in the Biomedical Sciences, Graduate Program in Biomedical Sciences, Hershey, PA 17033. Offers biochemistry and molecular genetics (PhD); biomedical sciences (MS, PhD); translational therapeutics (MS, PhD); virology and immunology (MS, PhD); MD/PhD; PhD/MBA. *Students:* 12 full-time (6 women); includes 2 minority (1 Black or African American, non-Hispanic/Latino; 1 Asian, non-Hispanic/Latino), 1 international. 211 applicants, 16% accepted, 12 enrolled. Terminal master's awarded for partial completion of doctoral program. *Degree requirements:* For master's, thesis (for some programs); for doctorate, comprehensive exam, thesis/dissertation, candidacy exam. *Entrance requirements:* For doctorate, GRE General Test. Additional exam requirements/recommendations for international students: Required—TOEFL (minimum score 550 paper-based; 213 computer-based; 80 iBT). *Application deadline:* For fall admission, 1/1 for domestic students, 2/1 for international students. Applications are processed on a rolling basis. Application fee: $65. Electronic applications accepted. *Financial support:* In 2011–12, research assistantships (averaging $23,028 per year) were awarded; fellowships, scholarships/grants, health care benefits, and unspecified assistantships also available. Financial award applicants required to submit FAFSA. *Unit head:* Dr. Ralph L. Keil, Chair, 717-531-8595, Fax: 717-531-0388, E-mail: rlk9@psu.edu. *Application contact:* Karen Shields, Administrative Support Coordinator, 717-531-1045, Fax: 717-531-0388, E-mail: kpb2@psu.edu. Web site: http://med.psu.edu/web/biomedical-sciences/home.

Rutgers, The State University of New Jersey, New Brunswick, Graduate School-New Brunswick, Programs in the Molecular Biosciences, Program in Microbiology and Molecular Genetics, Piscataway, NJ 08854-8097. Offers applied microbiology (MS, PhD); clinical microbiology (MS, PhD); computational molecular biology (PhD); immunology (MS, PhD); microbial biochemistry (MS, PhD); molecular genetics (MS, PhD); virology (MS, PhD). MS, PhD offered jointly with University of Medicine and Dentistry of New Jersey. Part-time programs available. Terminal master's awarded for partial completion of doctoral program. *Degree requirements:* For master's, comprehensive exam, thesis or alternative; for doctorate, comprehensive exam, thesis/dissertation, written qualifying exam. *Entrance requirements:* For master's, GRE General Test, minimum GPA of 3.0; for doctorate, GRE General Test, GRE Subject Test (recommended), minimum GPA of 3.0. Additional exam requirements/recommendations for international students: Required—TOEFL. Electronic applications accepted. *Faculty research:* Molecular genetics and microbial physiology; virology and pathogenic microbiology; applied, environmental and industrial microbiology; computers in molecular biology.

Stony Brook University, State University of New York, Stony Brook University Medical Center, Health Sciences Center, School of Medicine and Graduate School, Graduate Programs in Medicine, Department of Molecular Genetics and Microbiology, Stony Brook, NY 11794. Offers molecular microbiology (PhD). *Degree requirements:* For doctorate, comprehensive exam, thesis/dissertation. *Entrance requirements:* For doctorate, GRE General Test, GRE Subject Test. Additional exam requirements/recommendations for international students: Required—TOEFL. *Faculty research:* Adenovirus molecular genetics, molecular biology of tumors, virus SV40, mechanism of tumor infection by SAV virus.

Texas Tech University Health Sciences Center, Graduate School of Biomedical Sciences, Department of Cell Biology and Biochemistry, Program in Biochemistry and Molecular Genetics, Lubbock, TX 79430. Offers MS, PhD, MD/PhD, MS/PhD. Terminal master's awarded for partial completion of doctoral program. *Degree requirements:* For master's, comprehensive exam, thesis, preliminary, comprehensive, and final exams; for doctorate, comprehensive exam, thesis/dissertation, preliminary, comprehensive, and final exams. *Entrance requirements:* For master's and doctorate, GRE General Test, minimum GPA of 3.0. Additional exam requirements/recommendations for international students: Required—TOEFL. Electronic applications accepted. *Faculty research:* Reproductive endocrinology, immunology, developmental biochemistry, biochemistry and genetics of cancer, molecular genetics and cell cycle.

The University of Alabama at Birmingham, Graduate Programs in Joint Health Sciences, Program in Biochemistry and Molecular Genetics, Birmingham, AL 35294. Offers PhD. *Degree requirements:* For doctorate, thesis/dissertation. *Entrance requirements:* For doctorate, GRE General Test, interview. *Application deadline:* Applications are processed on a rolling basis. Electronic applications accepted. *Expenses:* Tuition, state resident: full-time $5922; part-time $309 per hour. Tuition, nonresident: full-time $13,428; part-time $726 per hour. Tuition and fees vary according to program. *Financial support:* In 2011–12, 8 fellowships were awarded. *Unit head:* Dr. Tim M. Townes, Chair, 205-934-5294, E-mail: ttownes@uab.edu. *Application contact:* Information Contact, 205-934-6034, Fax: 205-975-2547.

University of California, Irvine, School of Medicine and School of Biological Sciences, Department of Microbiology and Molecular Genetics, Irvine, CA 92697. Offers biological sciences (MS, PhD); MD/PhD. *Students:* 35 full-time (17 women); includes 18 minority (1 Black or African American, non-Hispanic/Latino; 10 Asian, non-Hispanic/Latino; 7 Hispanic/Latino), 1 international. Average age 28. 1 applicant, 100% accepted, 0 enrolled. In 2011, 3 master's, 3 doctorates awarded. *Degree requirements:* For doctorate, thesis/dissertation. *Entrance requirements:* For doctorate, GRE General Test, GRE Subject Test, minimum GPA of 3.0. Additional exam requirements/recommendations for international students: Required—TOEFL (minimum score 550 paper-based; 213 computer-based). *Application deadline:* For fall admission, 12/15 priority date for domestic students, 12/15 for international students. Application fee: $80 ($100 for international students). Electronic applications accepted. *Financial support:* Fellowships, research assistantships with full tuition reimbursements, teaching assistantships, institutionally sponsored loans, traineeships, health care benefits, and unspecified assistantships available. Financial award applicants required to submit FAFSA. *Faculty research:* Molecular biology and genetics of viruses, bacteria, and yeast; immune response; molecular biology of cultured animal cells; genetic basis of cancer; genetics and physiology of infectious agents. *Unit head:* Rozanne M. Sandri-Goldin, Chair, 949-824-7570, Fax: 949-824-8598, E-mail: rmsandri@uci.edu. *Application contact:* Renee Marie Frigo, Program Manager, 949-824-8145, Fax: 949-824-1965, E-mail: rfrigo@uci.edu. Web site: http://www.bio.uci.edu/.

University of California, Los Angeles, David Geffen School of Medicine and Graduate Division, Graduate Programs in Medicine, Department of Microbiology, Immunology and Molecular Genetics, Los Angeles, CA 90095. Offers MS, PhD. *Faculty:* 31 full-time (6 women). *Students:* 55 full-time (25 women); includes 21 minority (1 Black or African American, non-Hispanic/Latino; 8 Asian, non-Hispanic/Latino; 11 Hispanic/Latino; 1 Two or more races, non-Hispanic/Latino), 4 international. Average age 28. 1 applicant, 100% accepted, 1 enrolled. In 2011, 3 master's, 8 doctorates awarded. *Degree requirements:* For doctorate, thesis/dissertation, oral and written qualifying exams. *Entrance requirements:* For doctorate, GRE General Test, GRE Subject Test. Additional exam requirements/recommendations for international students: Required—TOEFL. Application fee: $70 ($90 for international students). Electronic applications accepted. *Financial support:* In 2011–12, 50 fellowships, 50 research assistantships, 20 teaching assistantships were awarded; Federal Work-Study, institutionally sponsored loans, and tuition waivers (full and partial) also available. Financial award application deadline: 3/1. *Unit head:* Dr. Jeff F. Miller, Chair, 310-206-7926, Fax: 310-267-2774, E-mail: jfmiller@ucla.edu. *Application contact:* Bridget Wolfgang, Graduate Student Affairs, 310-825-8482, Fax: 310-206-5231, E-mail: bridgetw@microbio.ucla.edu. Web site: http://www.mimg.ucla.edu/.

University of California, Riverside, Graduate Division, Graduate Program in Genetics, Genomics, and Bioinformatics, Riverside, CA 92521-0102. Offers genomics and bioinformatics (PhD); molecular genetics (PhD); population and evolutionary genetics (PhD). *Faculty:* 72 full-time (20 women). *Students:* 32 full-time (18 women); includes 2 minority (1 Black or African American, non-Hispanic/Latino; 1 Hispanic/Latino), 15 international. Average age 30. In 2011, 2 doctorates awarded. *Degree requirements:* For doctorate, thesis/dissertation, qualifying exams, teaching experience. *Entrance requirements:* For doctorate, GRE General Test, minimum GPA of 3.2. Additional exam requirements/recommendations for international students: Required—TOEFL (minimum score 550 paper-based; 213 computer-based; 80 iBT). *Application deadline:* For fall admission, 5/1 for domestic students, 2/1 for international students; for winter admission, 9/1 for domestic students, 7/1 for international students; for spring admission, 12/1 for domestic students, 10/1 for international students. Applications are processed on a rolling basis. Application fee: $85 ($100 for international students). Electronic applications accepted. *Financial support:* In 2011–12, fellowships with tuition reimbursements (averaging $12,000 per year), research assistantships with tuition reimbursements (averaging $18,000 per year), teaching assistantships with tuition reimbursements (averaging $16,500 per year) were awarded; career-related internships or fieldwork, Federal Work-Study, institutionally sponsored loans, and tuition waivers (full and partial) also available. *Faculty research:* Molecular genetics, evolution and population genetics, genomics and bioinformatics. *Unit head:* Dr. Shizhong Xu, Director, 951-827-5898. *Application contact:* Deidra Kornfeld, Graduate Program Assistant, 800-735-0717, Fax: 951-827-5517, E-mail: genetics@ucr.edu. Web site: http://ggb.ucr.edu/.

Molecular Genetics

University of Cincinnati, Graduate School, College of Medicine, Graduate Programs in Biomedical Sciences, Department of Molecular Genetics, Biochemistry and Microbiology, Cincinnati, OH 45221. Offers MS, PhD. Terminal master's awarded for partial completion of doctoral program. *Degree requirements:* For master's, thesis or alternative; for doctorate, thesis/dissertation, qualifying exam. *Entrance requirements:* For master's and doctorate, GRE General Test. Additional exam requirements/recommendations for international students: Required—TOEFL (minimum score 600 paper-based; 250 computer-based; 100 iBT), TWE. Electronic applications accepted. *Faculty research:* Cancer biology and developmental genetics, gene regulation and chromosome structure, microbiology and pathogenic mechanisms, structural biology, membrane biochemistry and signal transduction.

University of Colorado Denver, School of Medicine, Biochemistry Program, Aurora, CO 80045. Offers biochemistry and molecular genetics (PhD). *Students:* 19 full-time (7 women), 3 international. Average age 30. 28 applicants, 4% accepted, 1 enrolled. In 2011, 6 doctorates awarded. *Degree requirements:* For doctorate, comprehensive exam, thesis/dissertation, 30 credit hours each of coursework and thesis research. *Entrance requirements:* For doctorate, GRE (minimum combined score of 1200 on Verbal and Quantitative portions and at least 4.0 on the Analytical Writing section), minimum of three letters of recommendation from qualified referees. Additional exam requirements/recommendations for international students: Required—TOEFL (minimum score 570 paper-based; 230 computer-based). *Application deadline:* For fall admission, 12/1 for domestic students. Applications are processed on a rolling basis. Application fee: $50. Electronic applications accepted. *Expenses:* Contact institution. *Financial support:* In 2011–12, 6 students received support. Fellowships, health care benefits, tuition waivers (full), and stipend available. Financial award application deadline: 3/15; financial award applicants required to submit FAFSA. *Faculty research:* DNA damage, cancer and neurodegeneration, molecular mechanisms of pro-MRNA splicing, yeast RNA polymerases, DNA replication. *Total annual research expenditures:* $8.6 million. *Unit head:* Dr. Paul Megee, Associate Professor, Department of Biochemistry and Molecular Genetics, 303-724-3270, Fax: 303-724-3215, E-mail: paul.megee@ucdenver.edu. *Application contact:* Jennifer Spaulding, Administrative Assistant, 303-724-3201, Fax: 303-724-3215, E-mail: jennifer.spaulding@ucdenver.edu. Web site: http://www.uchsc.edu/sm/bbgn.

University of Florida, College of Medicine, Department of Molecular Genetics and Microbiology, Gainesville, FL 32611. Offers MS, PhD. Terminal master's awarded for partial completion of doctoral program. *Degree requirements:* For master's, thesis; for doctorate, thesis/dissertation. *Entrance requirements:* For master's and doctorate, GRE General Test, minimum GPA of 3.0. Additional exam requirements/recommendations for international students: Required—TOEFL. Electronic applications accepted.

University of Guelph, Graduate Studies, College of Biological Science, Department of Molecular and Cellular Biology, Guelph, ON N1G 2W1, Canada. Offers biochemistry (M Sc, PhD); biophysics (M Sc, PhD); botany (M Sc, PhD); microbiology (M Sc, PhD); molecular biology and genetics (M Sc, PhD). *Degree requirements:* For master's, thesis, research proposal; for doctorate, comprehensive exam, thesis/dissertation, research proposal. *Entrance requirements:* For master's, minimum B-average during previous 2 years of coursework; for doctorate, minimum A-average. Additional exam requirements/recommendations for international students: Required—TOEFL (minimum score 550 paper-based; 213 computer-based), IELTS (minimum score 6.5). Electronic applications accepted. *Faculty research:* Physiology, structure, genetics, and ecology of microbes; virology and microbial technology.

University of Illinois at Chicago, College of Medicine and Graduate College, Graduate Programs in Medicine, Department of Biochemistry and Molecular Genetics, Chicago, IL 60607-7128. Offers PhD, MD/PhD. Terminal master's awarded for partial completion of doctoral program. *Degree requirements:* For doctorate, thesis/dissertation. *Entrance requirements:* For doctorate, GRE General Test. Additional exam requirements/recommendations for international students: Required—TOEFL. Electronic applications accepted. *Faculty research:* Nature of cellular components, control of metabolic processes, regulation of gene expression.

The University of Manchester, Faculty of Life Sciences, Manchester, United Kingdom. Offers adaptive organismal biology (M Phil, PhD); animal biology (M Phil, PhD); biochemistry (M Phil, PhD); bioinformatics (M Phil, PhD); biomolecular sciences (M Phil, PhD); biotechnology (M Phil, PhD); cell biology (M Phil, PhD); cell matrix research (M Phil, PhD); channels and transporters (M Phil, PhD); developmental biology (M Phil, PhD); Egyptology (M Phil, PhD); environmental biology (M Phil, PhD); evolutionary biology (M Phil, PhD); gene expression (M Phil, PhD); genetics (M Phil, PhD); history of science, technology and medicine (M Phil, PhD); immunology (M Phil, PhD); integrative neurobiology and behavior (M Phil, PhD); membrane trafficking (M Phil, PhD); microbiology (M Phil, PhD); molecular and cellular neuroscience (M Phil, PhD); molecular biology (M Phil, PhD); molecular cancer studies (M Phil, PhD); neuroscience (M Phil, PhD); ophthalmology (M Phil, PhD); optometry (M Phil, PhD); organelle function (M Phil, PhD); pharmacology (M Phil, PhD); physiology (M Phil, PhD); plant sciences (M Phil, PhD); stem cell research (M Phil, PhD); structural biology (M Phil, PhD); systems neuroscience (M Phil, PhD); toxicology (M Phil, PhD).

University of Maryland, College Park, Academic Affairs, College of Computer, Mathematical and Natural Sciences, Department of Cell Biology and Molecular Genetics, Program in Cell Biology and Molecular Genetics, College Park, MD 20742. Offers MS, PhD. *Students:* 42 full-time (20 women), 1 (woman) part-time; includes 4 minority (2 Asian, non-Hispanic/Latino; 2 Hispanic/Latino), 16 international. In 2011, 5 master's, 8 doctorates awarded. *Degree requirements:* For master's, thesis; for doctorate, thesis/dissertation, exams. *Expenses:* Tuition, state resident: part-time $525 per credit hour. Tuition, nonresident: part-time $1131 per credit hour. *Required fees:* $386.31 per term. Tuition and fees vary according to program. *Financial support:* In 2011–12, 5 fellowships with full tuition reimbursements (averaging $28,086 per year), 10 research assistantships (averaging $19,519 per year), 21 teaching assistantships (averaging $19,520 per year) were awarded. Financial award applicants required to submit FAFSA. *Faculty research:* Cytoskeletal activity, membrane biology, cell division, genetics and genomics, virology. *Unit head:* Dr. Barbara Thorne, Director, 301-405-7947, E-mail: bthorne@umd.edu. *Application contact:* Dr. Charles A. Caramello, Dean of Graduate School, 301-405-0358, Fax: 301-314-9305.

University of Massachusetts Worcester, Graduate School of Biomedical Sciences, Worcester, MA 01655-0115. Offers biochemistry and molecular pharmacology (PhD); bioinformatics and computational biology (PhD); cancer biology (PhD); cell biology (PhD); clinical and population health research (PhD); clinical investigation (MS); immunology and virology (PhD); interdisciplinary graduate program (PhD); molecular genetics and microbiology (PhD); neuroscience (PhD); DVM/PhD; MD/PhD. *Faculty:* 1,427 full-time (526 women), 309 part-time/adjunct (196 women). *Students:* 416 full-time (225 women); includes 47 minority (12 Black or African American, non-Hispanic/Latino; 32 Asian, non-Hispanic/Latino; 3 Hispanic/Latino), 144 international. Average age 29. 623 applicants, 17% accepted, 54 enrolled. In 2011, 5 master's, 63 doctorates awarded. Terminal master's awarded for partial completion of doctoral program. *Degree requirements:* For master's, comprehensive exam, thesis; for doctorate, comprehensive exam, thesis/dissertation. *Entrance requirements:* For master's, bachelor's degree; for doctorate, GRE General Test. Additional exam requirements/recommendations for international students: Required—TOEFL (minimum score 600 paper-based; 250 computer-based; 100 iBT) or IELTS (minimum score 7.5). *Application deadline:* For fall admission, 12/15 for domestic and international students; for spring admission, 5/15 for domestic students. Application fee: $50. Electronic applications accepted. *Expenses:* Contact institution. *Financial support:* In 2011–12, 416 students received support, including 416 research assistantships with full tuition reimbursements available (averaging $29,200 per year); scholarships/grants, health care benefits, tuition waivers (full), and unspecified assistantships also available. Financial award application deadline: 4/16. *Faculty research:* RNA interference, cell biology, bioinformatics, clinical research, infectious disease. *Total annual research expenditures:* $262.7 million. *Unit head:* Dr. Anthony Carruthers, Dean, 508-856-4135, E-mail: anthony.carruthers@umassmed.edu. *Application contact:* Dr. Kendall Knight, Associate Dean and Interim Director of Admissions and Recruitment, 508-856-5628, Fax: 508-856-3659, E-mail: kendall.knight@umassmed.edu. Web site: http://www.umassmed.edu/gsbs/.

University of Medicine and Dentistry of New Jersey, Graduate School of Biomedical Sciences, Graduate Programs in Biomedical Sciences–Newark, Department of Microbiology and Molecular Genetics, Newark, NJ 07107. Offers PhD. *Degree requirements:* For doctorate, thesis/dissertation, qualifying exam. *Entrance requirements:* For doctorate, GRE General Test. Additional exam requirements/recommendations for international students: Required—TOEFL. Electronic applications accepted. *Faculty research:* Molecular genetics of yeast, mutagenesis and carcinogenesis of DNA, bacterial protein synthesis, mammalian cell genetics, adenovirus gene expression.

University of Medicine and Dentistry of New Jersey, Graduate School of Biomedical Sciences, Graduate Programs in Biomedical Sciences–Piscataway, Program in Molecular Genetics, Microbiology and Immunology, Piscataway, NJ 08854-5635. Offers MS, PhD, MD/PhD. Terminal master's awarded for partial completion of doctoral program. *Degree requirements:* For master's, thesis, qualifying exam; for doctorate, thesis/dissertation, qualifying exam. *Entrance requirements:* For master's and doctorate, GRE General Test. Additional exam requirements/recommendations for international students: Required—TOEFL. Electronic applications accepted. *Faculty research:* Interferon, receptors, retrovirus evolution, Arbo virus/host cell interactions.

University of Pittsburgh, School of Medicine, Graduate Programs in Medicine, Molecular Genetics and Developmental Biology Program, Pittsburgh, PA 15260. Offers MS, PhD. *Faculty:* 49 full-time (11 women). *Students:* 14 full-time (7 women); includes 2 minority (1 Asian, non-Hispanic/Latino; 1 Native Hawaiian or other Pacific Islander, non-Hispanic/Latino), 3 international. Average age 27. 514 applicants, 12% accepted, 14 enrolled. In 2011, 4 doctorates awarded. *Degree requirements:* For doctorate, comprehensive exam, thesis/dissertation. *Entrance requirements:* For doctorate, GRE General Test, GRE Subject Test, minimum QPA of 3.0. Additional exam requirements/recommendations for international students: Required—TOEFL (minimum score 600 paper-based; 100 iBT), IELTS (minimum score 7). *Application deadline:* For fall admission, 12/15 priority date for domestic students, 12/15 for international students. Application fee: $50. Electronic applications accepted. *Expenses:* Tuition, state resident: full-time $18,774; part-time $760 per credit. Tuition, nonresident: full-time $30,736; part-time $1258 per credit. *Required fees:* $740; $200 per term. Tuition and fees vary according to program. *Financial support:* In 2011–12, 1 fellowship (averaging $25,500 per year), 13 research assistantships with full tuition reimbursements (averaging $25,500 per year) were awarded; institutionally sponsored loans, scholarships/grants, traineeships, health care benefits, and unspecified assistantships also available. *Faculty research:* Developmental and stem cell biology, DNA replication and repair, gene regulation and signal transduction, oncogenes and tumor suppressor genes, protein structure and molecular dynamics. *Unit head:* Dr. Neil A. Hukriede, Graduate Program Director, 412-648-9918, Fax: 412-624-1401, E-mail: hukriede@pitt.edu. *Application contact:* Graduate Studies Administrator, 412-648-8957, Fax: 412-648-1077, E-mail: gradstudies@medschool.pitt.edu. Web site: http://www.gradbiomed.pitt.edu/.

University of Rhode Island, Graduate School, College of the Environment and Life Sciences, Department of Cell and Molecular Biology, Kingston, RI 02881. Offers biochemistry (MS, PhD); clinical laboratory sciences (MS), including biotechnology, clinical laboratory science, cytopathology; microbiology (MS, PhD); molecular genetics (MS, PhD). Part-time programs available. *Faculty:* 14 full-time (5 women), 3 part-time/adjunct (2 women). *Students:* 32 full-time (15 women), 37 part-time (23 women); includes 2 minority (1 Asian, non-Hispanic/Latino; 1 Hispanic/Latino), 1 international. In 2011, 2 master's, 2 doctorates awarded. *Degree requirements:* For master's, comprehensive exam (for some programs); for doctorate, comprehensive exam. *Entrance requirements:* For master's and doctorate, GRE, 2 letters of recommendation. Additional exam requirements/recommendations for international students: Required—TOEFL (minimum score 550 paper-based; 213 computer-based). *Application deadline:* For fall admission, 7/15 for domestic students, 2/1 for international students; for spring admission, 11/15 for domestic students, 7/15 for international students. Application fee: $65. Electronic applications accepted. *Expenses:* Tuition, state resident: full-time $10,432; part-time $580 per credit hour. Tuition, nonresident: full-time $23,130; part-time $1285 per credit hour. *Required fees:* $1362; $36 per credit hour. $35 per semester. One-time fee: $130. *Financial support:* In 2011–12, 2 research assistantships with full and partial tuition reimbursements (averaging $13,894 per year), 6 teaching assistantships with full and partial tuition reimbursements (averaging $12,850 per year) were awarded. Financial award application deadline: 7/15; financial award applicants required to submit FAFSA. *Faculty research:* Genomics and Sequencing Center: an interdisciplinary genomics research and undergraduate and graduate student training program which provides researchers access to cutting-edge technologies in the field of genomics. *Unit head:* Dr. Jay Sperry, Chairperson, 401-874-2201, Fax: 401-874-2202, E-mail: jsperry@mail.uri.edu. *Application contact:* Nasser H. Zawia, Dean of the Graduate School, 401-874-5909, Fax: 401-874-5787, E-mail: nzawia@uri.edu. Web site: http://cels.uri.edu/cmb/.

The University of Texas Health Science Center at Houston, Graduate School of Biomedical Sciences, Program in Human and Molecular Genetics, Houston, TX 77225-0036. Offers MS, PhD, MD/PhD. Terminal master's awarded for partial completion of doctoral program. *Degree requirements:* For master's, thesis; for doctorate, thesis/dissertation. *Entrance requirements:* For master's and doctorate, GRE General Test. Additional exam requirements/recommendations for international students: Required—TOEFL. Electronic applications accepted. *Faculty research:* Computational genomics, cancer genetics, complex disease genetics, medical genetics.

The University of Texas Health Science Center at Houston, Graduate School of Biomedical Sciences, Program in Microbiology and Molecular Genetics, Houston, TX 77225-0036. Offers MS, PhD, MD/PhD. Terminal master's awarded for partial completion of doctoral program. *Degree requirements:* For master's, thesis; for doctorate, thesis/dissertation. *Entrance requirements:* For master's and doctorate, GRE General Test. Additional exam requirements/recommendations for international students: Required—TOEFL. Electronic applications accepted. *Faculty research:* Disease causation, environmental signaling, gene regulation, cell growth and division, cell structure and architecture.

University of Toronto, Faculty of Medicine, Department of Molecular Genetics, Toronto, ON M5S 1A1, Canada. Offers genetic counseling (M Sc); molecular genetics (M Sc, PhD). *Degree requirements:* For master's, thesis; for doctorate, thesis/dissertation. *Entrance requirements:* For master's, B Sc or equivalent; for doctorate, M Sc or equivalent, minimum B+ average. Additional exam requirements/recommendations for international students: Required—TOEFL, IELTS (minimum score 7), Michigan English Language Assessment Battery (minimum score 85) or COPE (minimum score 4). Electronic applications accepted. *Faculty research:* Structural biology, developmental genetics, molecular medicine, genetic counseling.

University of Vermont, College of Medicine and Graduate College, Graduate Programs in Medicine, Department of Microbiology and Molecular Genetics, Burlington, VT 05405. Offers MS, PhD, MD/MS, MD/PhD. *Faculty:* 18 full-time (5 women). *Students:* 24 (14 women); includes 1 minority (Hispanic/Latino), 9 international. 54 applicants, 26% accepted, 2 enrolled. In 2011, 1 master's, 2 doctorates awarded. *Degree requirements:* For master's, thesis; for doctorate, thesis/dissertation. *Entrance requirements:* For master's and doctorate, GRE General Test. Additional exam requirements/recommendations for international students: Required—TOEFL (minimum score 550 paper-based; 213 computer-based; 80 iBT). *Application deadline:* For fall admission, 1/16 priority date for domestic students, 1/16 for international students. Applications are processed on a rolling basis. Application fee: $40. Electronic applications accepted. *Financial support:* Fellowships, research assistantships, and teaching assistantships available. Financial award application deadline: 3/1. *Unit head:* Dr. Susan S. Wallace, Chairperson, 802-656-2164. *Application contact:* Dr. John Burke, Coordinator, 802-656-2164.

University of Virginia, School of Medicine, Department of Biochemistry and Molecular Genetics, Charlottesville, VA 22903. Offers biochemistry (PhD); MD/PhD. *Faculty:* 24 full-time (3 women), 1 (woman) part-time/adjunct. *Students:* 32 full-time (13 women); includes 2 minority (1 Black or African American, non-Hispanic/Latino; 1 Two or more races, non-Hispanic/Latino), 12 international. Average age 26. 150 applicants, 19% accepted, 10 enrolled. In 2011, 7 doctorates awarded. *Degree requirements:* For doctorate, thesis/dissertation, written research proposal and defense. *Entrance requirements:* For doctorate, GRE General Test, 3 letters of recommendation. Additional exam requirements/recommendations for international students: Recommended—TOEFL (minimum score 630 paper-based; 250 computer-based; 90 iBT). Application fee: $60. Electronic applications accepted. *Financial support:* Fellowships, health care benefits, and tuition waivers (full) available. Financial award applicants required to submit FAFSA. *Unit head:* Joel Hockensmith, Faculty Director, 434-924-1230, Fax: 434-924-5069, E-mail: jwh6f@virginia.edu. *Application contact:* Biomedical Sciences Graduate Studies, E-mail: bims@virginia.edu. Web site: http://www.virginia.edu/artsandsciences/.

Wake Forest University, School of Medicine and Graduate School of Arts and Sciences, Graduate Programs in Medicine, Molecular Genetics and Genomics Program, Winston-Salem, NC 27109. Offers PhD, MD/PhD. *Degree requirements:* For doctorate, thesis/dissertation. *Entrance requirements:* For doctorate, GRE General Test. Additional exam requirements/recommendations for international students: Required—TOEFL. Electronic applications accepted. *Faculty research:* Control of gene expression, molecular pathogenesis, protein biosynthesis, cell development, clinical cytogenetics.

Washington University in St. Louis, Graduate School of Arts and Sciences, Division of Biology and Biomedical Sciences, Program in Molecular Genetics and Genomics, St. Louis, MO 63130-4899. Offers PhD. *Degree requirements:* For doctorate, thesis/dissertation. *Entrance requirements:* For doctorate, GRE General Test, GRE Subject Test. Electronic applications accepted.

Reproductive Biology

Cornell University, Graduate School, Graduate Fields of Comparative Biomedical Sciences, Field of Comparative Biomedical Sciences, Ithaca, NY 14853-0001. Offers cellular and molecular medicine (MS, PhD); developmental and reproductive biology (MS, PhD); infectious diseases (MS, PhD); population medicine and epidemiology (MS, PhD); structural and functional biology (MS, PhD). *Faculty:* 97 full-time (27 women). *Students:* 38 full-time (23 women); includes 5 minority (2 Black or African American, non-Hispanic/Latino; 1 Asian, non-Hispanic/Latino; 2 Hispanic/Latino), 15 international. Average age 30. 45 applicants, 22% accepted, 9 enrolled. In 2011, 2 master's, 7 doctorates awarded. *Degree requirements:* For master's, thesis; for doctorate, comprehensive exam, thesis/dissertation. *Entrance requirements:* For master's and doctorate, GRE General Test, 2 letters of recommendation. Additional exam requirements/recommendations for international students: Required—TOEFL (minimum score 550 paper-based; 213 computer-based; 77 iBT). *Application deadline:* For fall admission, 12/15 for domestic students. Application fee: $95. Electronic applications accepted. *Financial support:* In 2011–12, 12 fellowships with full tuition reimbursements, 25 research assistantships with full tuition reimbursements were awarded; teaching assistantships with full tuition reimbursements, institutionally sponsored loans, scholarships/grants, health care benefits, tuition waivers (full and partial), and unspecified assistantships also available. Financial award applicants required to submit FAFSA. *Faculty research:* Receptors and signal transduction, viral and bacterial infectious diseases, tumor metastasis, clinical sciences/nutritional disease, developmental/neurological disorders. *Unit head:* Director of Graduate Studies, 607-253-3276, Fax: 607-253-3756. *Application contact:* Graduate Field Assistant, 607-253-3276, Fax: 607-253-3756, E-mail: graduate_edcvm@cornell.edu. Web site: http://www.gradschool.cornell.edu/fields.php?id=64&a-2.

Eastern Virginia Medical School, Master's Program in Clinical Embryology and Andrology, Norfolk, VA 23501-1980. Offers MS. Postbaccalaureate distance learning degree programs offered (minimal on-campus study). *Faculty:* 12 full-time, 8 part-time/adjunct. *Students:* 66 full-time (44 women); includes 27 minority (5 Black or African American, non-Hispanic/Latino; 13 Asian, non-Hispanic/Latino; 9 Hispanic/Latino). 38 applicants, 76% accepted, 24 enrolled. In 2011, 14 master's awarded. *Entrance requirements:* Additional exam requirements/recommendations for international students: Required—TOEFL (minimum score 550 paper-based; 213 computer-based; 80 iBT). *Application deadline:* For fall admission, 1/14 for domestic and international students. Applications are processed on a rolling basis. Application fee: $60. Electronic applications accepted. *Expenses:* Contact institution. *Unit head:* Dr. Jacob Mayer, Director, 757-446-5049, Fax: 757-446-5905. *Application contact:* Nancy Garcia, Administrator, 757-446-8935, Fax: 757-446-5905, E-mail: garcianw@evms.edu. Web site: http://www.evms.edu/evms-school-of-health-professions/embryology-andrology-ms-distance-learning.html.

Northwestern University, The Graduate School, Interdepartmental Biological Sciences Program (IBiS), Evanston, IL 60208. Offers biochemistry, molecular biology, and cell biology (PhD), including biochemistry, cell and molecular biology, molecular biophysics, structural biology; biotechnology (PhD); cell and molecular biology (PhD); developmental biology and genetics (PhD); hormone action and signal transduction (PhD); neuroscience (PhD); structural biology, biochemistry, and biophysics (PhD). Program participants include the Departments of Biochemistry, Molecular Biology, and Cell Biology; Chemistry; Neurobiology and Physiology; Chemical Engineering; Civil Engineering; and Evanston Hospital. *Degree requirements:* For doctorate, thesis/dissertation, qualifying exam. *Entrance requirements:* For doctorate, GRE General Test. Additional exam requirements/recommendations for international students: Required—TOEFL (minimum score 600 paper-based). Electronic applications accepted. *Faculty research:* Developmental genetics, gene regulation, DNA-protein interactions, biological clocks, bioremediation.

Queen's University at Kingston, School of Graduate Studies and Research, Faculty of Health Sciences, Department of Anatomy and Cell Biology, Kingston, ON K7L 3N6, Canada. Offers biology of reproduction (M Sc, PhD); cancer (M Sc, PhD); cardiovascular pathophysiology (M Sc, PhD); cell and molecular biology (M Sc, PhD); drug metabolism (M Sc, PhD); endocrinology (M Sc, PhD); motor control (M Sc, PhD); neural regeneration (M Sc, PhD); neurophysiology (M Sc, PhD). Part-time programs available. *Degree requirements:* For master's, thesis; for doctorate, one foreign language, comprehensive exam, thesis/dissertation. *Entrance requirements:* Additional exam requirements/recommendations for international students: Required—TOEFL. Electronic applications accepted. *Faculty research:* Human kinetics, neuroscience, reproductive biology, cardiovascular.

Rutgers, The State University of New Jersey, New Brunswick, Graduate School-New Brunswick, Program in Endocrinology and Animal Biosciences, Piscataway, NJ 08854-8097. Offers MS, PhD. Terminal master's awarded for partial completion of doctoral program. *Degree requirements:* For master's, thesis; for doctorate, comprehensive exam, thesis/dissertation. *Entrance requirements:* For master's and doctorate, GRE General Test. Additional exam requirements/recommendations for international students: Required—TOEFL. Electronic applications accepted. *Faculty research:* Comparative and behavioral endocrinology, epigenetic regulation of the endocrine system, exercise physiology and immunology, fetal and neonatal developmental programming, mammary gland biology and breast cancer, neuroendocrinology and alcohol studies, reproductive and developmental toxicology.

Tufts University, Cummings School of Veterinary Medicine, North Grafton, MA 01536. Offers animals and public policy (MS); biomedical sciences (PhD), including digestive diseases, infectious diseases, neuroscience and reproductive biology, pathology; conservation medicine (MS); veterinary medicine (DVM); DVM/MPH; DVM/MS. *Accreditation:* AVMA (one or more programs are accredited). *Faculty:* 93 full-time (42 women), 14 part-time/adjunct (7 women). *Students:* 381 full-time (326 women); includes 47 minority (3 Black or African American, non-Hispanic/Latino; 4 American Indian or Alaska Native, non-Hispanic/Latino; 23 Asian, non-Hispanic/Latino; 16 Hispanic/Latino; 1 Two or more races, non-Hispanic/Latino), 7 international. Average age 25. 762 applicants, 33% accepted, 122 enrolled. In 2011, 8 master's, 80 doctorates awarded. *Degree requirements:* For master's, thesis (for some programs); for doctorate, comprehensive exam, thesis/dissertation (for some programs). *Entrance requirements:* For master's and doctorate, GRE General Test. Additional exam requirements/recommendations for international students: Required—TOEFL or IELTS. *Application deadline:* For fall admission, 11/1 for domestic and international students. Application fee: $70. Electronic applications accepted. *Expenses:* Contact institution. *Financial support:* In 2011–12, 245 students received support, including 6 research assistantships with full tuition reimbursements available (averaging $25,000 per year), 4 teaching assistantships (averaging $5,000 per year); career-related internships or fieldwork, Federal Work-Study, institutionally sponsored loans, scholarships/grants, and institutional aid awards; health care benefits for PhD students also available. Financial award application deadline: 5/15; financial award applicants required to submit FAFSA. *Faculty research:* Oncology, veterinary ethics, international veterinary medicine, veterinary genomics, pathogenesis of Clostridium difficile, wildlife fertility control. *Unit head:* Dr. Deborah T. Kochevar, Dean, 508-839-5302, Fax: 508-839-2953, E-mail: deborah.kochevar@tufts.edu. *Application contact:* Rebecca Russo, Director of Admissions, 508-839-7920, Fax: 508-887-4820, E-mail: vetadmissions@tufts.edu. Web site: http://www.tufts.edu/.

The University of British Columbia, Faculty of Medicine, Department of Obstetrics and Gynecology, Program in Reproductive and Developmental Sciences, Vancouver, BC V6H 3N1, Canada. Offers M Sc, PhD. Part-time programs available. Terminal master's awarded for partial completion of doctoral program. *Degree requirements:* For master's, thesis; for doctorate, thesis/dissertation. *Entrance requirements:* For master's, B Sc or equivalent, MD, DVM, DDS; for doctorate, B Sc with first class honors, M Sc, MD, DVM, DDS. Additional exam requirements/recommendations for international students: Required—TOEFL (minimum score 580 paper-based; 213 computer-based; 80 iBT), IELTS (minimum score 7). Electronic applications accepted. *Faculty research:* Reproductive and placental endocrinology; immunology of reproductive, fertilization, and embryonic development; perinatal metabolism; neonatal development.

University of Hawaii at Manoa, John A. Burns School of Medicine, Program in Developmental and Reproductive Biology, Honolulu, HI 96813. Offers MS, PhD. Part-time programs available. *Degree requirements:* For doctorate, thesis/dissertation. *Entrance requirements:* For doctorate, GRE General Test, GRE Subject Test. Additional exam requirements/recommendations for international students: Recommended—TOEFL (minimum score 560 paper-based; 83 computer-based), IELTS (minimum score 5). *Faculty research:* Biology of gametes and fertilization, reproductive endocrinology.

University of Saskatchewan, College of Medicine, Department of Obstetrics, Gynecology and Reproductive Services, Saskatoon, SK S7N 5A2, Canada. Offers M Sc, PhD. *Degree requirements:* For master's, thesis; for doctorate, thesis/dissertation. *Entrance requirements:* Additional exam requirements/recommendations for international students: Required—TOEFL.

University of Wyoming, College of Agriculture and Natural Resources, Department of Animal Sciences, Program in Reproductive Biology, Laramie, WY 82070. Offers MS, PhD. *Degree requirements:* For master's, thesis; for doctorate, thesis/dissertation. *Entrance requirements:* For master's, GRE General Test, minimum GPA of 3.0; for doctorate, GRE General Test, minimum GPA of 3.0 or MS degree. Additional exam

Reproductive Biology

requirements/recommendations for international students: Required—TOEFL. *Faculty research:* Fetal programming, chemical suppression, ovaria function, genetics.

West Virginia University, Davis College of Agriculture, Forestry and Consumer Sciences, Interdisciplinary Program in Genetics and Developmental Biology, Morgantown, WV 26506. Offers animal breeding (MS, PhD); biochemical and molecular genetics (MS, PhD); cytogenetics (MS, PhD); descriptive embryology (MS, PhD); developmental genetics (MS); experimental morphogenesis/teratology (MS); human genetics (MS, PhD); immunogenetics (MS, PhD); life cycles of animals and plants (MS, PhD); molecular aspects of development (MS, PhD); mutagenesis (MS, PhD); oncology (MS, PhD); plant genetics (MS, PhD); population and quantitative genetics (MS, PhD); regeneration (MS, PhD); teratology (PhD); toxicology (MS, PhD). *Degree requirements:* For master's, GRE or MCAT, minimum GPA of 2.75. Additional exam requirements/recommendations for international students: Required—TOEFL.

Teratology

West Virginia University, Davis College of Agriculture, Forestry and Consumer Sciences, Interdisciplinary Program in Genetics and Developmental Biology, Morgantown, WV 26506. Offers animal breeding (MS, PhD); biochemical and molecular genetics (MS, PhD); cytogenetics (MS, PhD); descriptive embryology (MS, PhD); developmental genetics (MS); experimental morphogenesis/teratology (MS); human genetics (MS, PhD); immunogenetics (MS, PhD); life cycles of animals and plants (MS, PhD); molecular aspects of development (MS, PhD); mutagenesis (MS, PhD); oncology (MS, PhD); plant genetics (MS, PhD); population and quantitative genetics (MS, PhD); regeneration (MS, PhD); teratology (PhD); toxicology (MS, PhD). *Degree requirements:* For master's, thesis; for doctorate, comprehensive exam, thesis/dissertation. *Entrance requirements:* For master's, GRE or MCAT, minimum GPA of 2.75. Additional exam requirements/recommendations for international students: Required—TOEFL.

BAYLOR COLLEGE OF MEDICINE
Graduate Program in Developmental Biology

Program of Study

The Graduate Program in Developmental Biology (DB Program) awards a Ph.D. degree and is designed to prepare students both intellectually and technologically to pursue a successful career in biological and/or biomedical research. The program also participates in the Medical Scientist Training Program, which leads to a combined M.D./Ph.D. degree.

The DB Program provides a wide spectrum of exciting research possibilities and a broad cross-disciplinary training. In order to understand how a single cell develops into a complex organism, the program laboratories use molecular biology, cell biology, biochemistry, imaging, physiology, genetics, and genomics. Studies of organisms as diverse as social molds, worms, flies, frogs, chickens, fish, mice, and humans are conducted using a wide variety of approaches, instruments, and techniques of modern biological research. Members of the DB Program study basic biological mechanisms of direct and fundamental relevance to human development, disease, and stem cell therapy. This allows students to unravel the principles and mechanisms that guide embryonic development, the maintenance and differentiation of stem cells, the differentiation of adult cell types, regeneration of organs and tissues, and the mechanisms underlying aging and neurodegeneration. The major research interests are neurobiology; cancer biology; cell death; aging; neurodegenerative and other human diseases; stem cell biology; gene therapy; reproductive development; oogenesis; skin, muscle, heart, blood, kidney, liver, bone, limb, ear, and eye development; cell lineage specification; and plant differentiation.

During their first year, students take core courses in classical and molecular genetics, cell biology, molecular biology, and biochemistry, as well as several courses and seminars in developmental biology. They also sample several areas of research by doing rotations in the program's laboratories. Before the end of the first year, students take a qualifying exam and select a laboratory in which they carry out their dissertation research. Subsequently, students meet every six months with their thesis committee to evaluate the research accomplished and redefine goals necessary to complete the thesis project. In the final year, students defend their theses in a public seminar. Study for the Ph.D. degree generally requires five years of graduate work, most of which is spent on the dissertation research. The program is supported by a competitive NIH training grant, the local chapter of the March of Dimes, Texas Children's Hospital, and the College.

Research Facilities

DB Program faculty members are well-funded and drawn from eleven departments and four institutions, including Baylor College of Medicine (BCM), the University of Texas M. D. Anderson Cancer Center, the University of Texas Health Science Center-Houston, and Rice University, all within easy walking distance of the Texas Medical Center. They occupy extensive research space with state-of-the-art instrumentation and computing equipment. Cooperative and collaborative interactions among program laboratories and institutions enable students to take full advantage of the facilities of the Texas Medical Center.

Financial Aid

Students enrolled in the program receive a competitive stipend of $29,000 per year plus health insurance at no extra cost. Tuition scholarships are awarded to all students admitted to the program. Separate offices provide assistance to international students and students with financial hardships.

Cost of Study

Tuition is fully covered by the program, the College, or training grants.

Living and Housing Costs

Numerous affordable housing options are available within a few miles of the medical center. Some students rent a nearby house while others rent or buy their own apartment, condo, or townhome. The cost of living in Houston is below that of most large U.S. cities, and there are ample opportunities for employment of spouses in the Texas Medical Center and the greater Houston area.

Student Group

The DB Program currently has 53 full-time graduate students, including 24 women, 34 international students, and 6 MSTP (M.D./Ph.D.) students. Each year, 9–10 students join the program. Because of the program's commitment to excellence, it favors a low student-faculty ratio. In addition to the laboratories in the program, students have contact with students, postdoctoral fellows, and faculty members in other programs and departments throughout the school and the medical center. The BCM graduate school has approximately 550 students, the medical school about 700 students.

Student Outcomes

The Career Resource Center of the graduate school provides career information and counseling for all BCM graduate and postdoctoral students in biomedical sciences. DB students typically graduate with an excellent-to-outstanding publication record and go on to successful careers. The average number of publications per graduate student is above 4.5, with an average of more than 2.5 first-author papers. The average impact factor per graduate student publication is more than 10. The DB graduates have subsequently pursued postdoctoral training in excellent laboratories and high-quality institutions. A substantial number of former graduate students are now faculty members at universities and teaching colleges around the world.

Location

Houston is a dynamic city with an exciting cultural and metropolitan center. Ballet, opera, symphony, theater, and art museums are excellent and accessible to the general population. In addition, there are more than a thousand bars and restaurants, which are moderately priced. Recreation opportunities abound, with facilities for a wide range of professional and amateur sports. The climate offers very pleasant weather from fall through spring and permits participation in a wide variety of outdoor activities. Gulf Coast beaches are a short drive from the city.

The College

Baylor College of Medicine is an independent, private institution dedicated to training in basic and medical sciences. It is located in the heart of the Texas Medical Center, one of the largest medical centers in the world. It has promoted the development of interdisciplinary, interdepartmental, and interinstitutional programs and has consistently identified and encouraged outstanding investigators. Considered one of the top research institutions in the nation, the College continues to develop programs and services that meet new needs and trends, making higher education one of the most exciting and rewarding of human experiences.

Applying

Applicants must have a bachelor's degree, preferably with course work in biology and genetics. GRE General Test scores less than three years old at the time of application must be provided. TOEFL or IELTS scores are required for applicants who did not attend a university where English is the medium of instruction. Applications should be accompanied by transcripts, three letters of recommendation, and a statement of research interest and career goals; they must be complete by December 1. Successful candidates are invited to meet with the participating faculty members and students to have a firsthand look at the DB Program. Expenses for travel and accommodations during the visit are provided for domestic and international students. Admission policies at BCM offer equal opportunity to all, without regard to race, sex, age, religion, country of origin, or handicap. Questions regarding the application process can be directed to cat@bcm.edu.

Correspondence and Information

Graduate Program in Developmental Biology
Baylor College of Medicine
One Baylor Plaza, BCM 225
Houston, Texas 77030
United States
Phone: 713-798-7696
E-mail: cat@bcm.edu
Web site: http://www.bcm.edu/db/

THE FACULTY AND THEIR RESEARCH

Benjamin R. Arenkiel, Assistant Professor of Molecular and Human Genetics and Neuroscience, Neurological Research Institute; Ph.D., Utah, 2004. Molecular genetic studies to investigate mechanisms of neural circuit formation, function, and maintenance during development and adulthood.

Richard R. Behringer, Professor of Genetics, University of Texas M. D. Anderson Cancer Center; Ph.D., South Carolina, 1986. Mammalian embryogenesis; reproductive biology and disease; stem cell biology, evolution, and development.

Hugo J. Bellen, Professor of Molecular and Human Genetics and Neuroscience, Neurological Research Institute; Director, Program in Developmental Biology; and Investigator, Howard Hughes Medical Institute; D.V.M./Ph.D., California, Davis, 1986. Genetic and molecular analysis of nervous system development, neurotransmitter release, and neuronal degeneration in *Drosophila*.

John W. Belmont, Professor of Molecular and Human Genetics, Pathology & Immunology, Stem Cells and Regenerative Medicine Center; M.D./Ph.D., Baylor College of Medicine, 1981. Cardiovascular genetics; vaccine response as a complex trait.

Baylor College of Medicine

Karl-Dimiter Bissig, Assistant Professor of Molecular and Cellular Biology, Center for Cell and Gene Therapy and Stem Cells and Regenerative Medicine Center; M.D./Ph.D., Bern (Switzerland), 2000. Induced pluripotent stem cell technology and cellular programming; cell therapy for liver disease; preclinical animal models for cell therapy.

Janet Braam, Professor and Chair of Biochemistry and Cell Biology, Rice University; Ph.D., Cornell/Sloan-Kettering, 1985. Molecular and developmental responses of plants to environmental stresses.

Rui Chen, Associate Professor of Molecular and Human Genetics, Human Genome Sequencing Center; Ph.D., Baylor College of Medicine, 1999. Functional genomics of visual development and diseases; high throughput technology; bioinformatics.

Thomas A. Cooper, Professor of Pathology & Immunology and Molecular and Cellular Biology; M.D., Temple, 1982. Alternative splicing regulation in development and disease.

Mauro Costa-Mattioli, Assistant Professor of Neuroscience and Molecular and Cellular Biology; Ph.D., Nantes (France), 2002. Cellular and molecular mechanism of memory storage.

Francesco J. DeMayo, Professor of Molecular and Cellular Biology; Ph.D., Michigan, 1983. Molecular and developmental biology of the lung and uterus; cancer; reproductive biology.

Benjamin Deneen, Assistant Professor of Neuroscience, Center for Cell and Gene Therapy and Stem Cells and Regenerative Medicine Center; Ph.D., California, Los Angeles, 2002. Glial cell development and disease.

Mary E. Dickinson, Professor of Molecular Physiology and Biophysics; Ph.D., Columbia, 1996. Vascular remodeling and heart morphogenesis in early vertebrate embryos.

Herman A. Dierick, Assistant Professor of Molecular and Human Genetics and Neuroscience; M.D., Leuven (Belgium), 1991. Genetic and neurobiological mechanism of *Drosophila* aggression.

Michael J. Galko, Assistant Professor of of Biochemistry and Molecular Biology, University of Texas M. D. Anderson Cancer Center; Ph.D., California, San Francisco, 1999. Molecular genetics of tissue repair responses in *Drosophila*.

Ido Golding, Assistant Professor of Biochemistry and Molecular Biology; Ph.D., Tel Aviv (Israel), 2001. Physical principles to understand living systems.

Margaret A. Goodell, Professor of Pediatrics and Molecular and Human Genetics, Center for Cell and Gene Therapy; Director, Stem Cells and Regenerative Medicine Center; Ph.D., Cambridge (United Kingdom), 1991. Murine and human hematopoietic stem cells; genetic and epigenetic regulation and development.

Brett H. Graham, Assistant Professor of Molecular and Human Genetics; M.D./Ph.D., Emory, 1998. Genetics of inborn errors of metabolism; genetic models of mitochondrial disease in *Drosophila* and mice.

Andy K. Groves, Associate Professor of Neuroscience and Molecular and Human Genetics; Co-Director, Program in Developmental Biology; Ph.D., Ludwig Institute for Cancer Research (United Kingdom), 1992. The development, evolution, and regeneration of the inner ear.

Hamed Jafar-Nejad, Assistant Professor of Molecular and Human Genetics; M.D., Tehran (Iran), 1994. Developmental glycobiology; cell biological regulation of developmental signaling pathways.

Milan Jamrich, Professor of Molecular and Human Genetics and Molecular and Cellular Biology; Ph.D., Heidelberg (Germany), 1978. Molecular basis of embryonic pattern formation; ocular development; gene therapy.

Joanna L. Jankowsky, Assistant Professor of Neuroscience; Ph.D., Caltech, 1999. Functional consequences of Aß accumulation in Alzheimer's disease on hippocampal neurogenesis, synaptic plasticity, and cognitive behavior.

Randy L. Johnson, Associate Professor of Biochemistry and Molecular Biology, University of Texas M. D. Anderson Cancer Center; Ph.D., Columbia, 1991. Modeling human disease and development in the mouse.

Monica J. Justice, Professor of Molecular and Human Genetics and Molecular Physiology and Biophysics; Ph.D., Kansas, 1987. Molecular genetic analysis of hematopoiesis; cancer genetics; mouse models of human disease.

Adam Kuspa, Professor of Biochemistry and Molecular Biology, Molecular and Human Genetics, and Pharmacology; Vice President of Research; Ph.D., Stanford, 1989. Genomic studies of cell signaling and development in *Dictyostelium*.

Brendan Lee, Professor of Molecular and Human Genetics and Investigator, Howard Hughes Medical Institute; M.D./Ph.D., SUNY Health Science Center, Brooklyn, 1993. Genetic pathways that specify development and homeostasis: translational studies of skeletal development and urea cycle disorders; therapy for metabolic diseases.

Michael T. Lewis, Associate Professor of Molecular and Cellular Biology, Lester and Sue Smith Breast Center; Ph.D., California, Santa Cruz, 1995. Genetic regulation of mammary gland development and early-stage breast cancer.

Olivier Lichtarge, Professor of Molecular and Human Genetics and Biochemistry and Molecular Biology; Director, Center of Computational and Integrative Biomedical Research; M.D./Ph.D., Stanford, 1990. Evolutionary studies of sequence; structural bioinformatics studies of proteins to study and engineer pathway perturbations.

Hui-Chen Lu, Associate Professor of Pediatrics–Neurology and Neuroscience, Neurological Research Institute; Ph.D., Baylor College of Medicine, 1997. Molecular mechanisms of cortical development.

Peter Y. Lwigale, Assistant Professor of Biochemistry and Cell Biology, Rice University; Ph.D., Kansas, 2001. Eye development; cellular interactions and molecular regulation of neural crest cells during corneal development.

Mirjana Maletic-Savatic, Assistant Professor of Pediatrics, Neurological Research Institute; M.D./Ph.D., Belgrade (Serbia), 1996. Neurogenesis; computational modeling; systems biology of early developmental disorders and autism.

Graeme Mardon, Professor of Pathology & Immunology, Molecular and Human Genetics, and Neuroscience; Ph.D., MIT, 1990. Retinal cell-fate determination, development, and function in *Drosophila* and vertebrates.

James F. Martin, Professor of Molecular Physiology and Biophysics; M.D./Ph.D., Texas Health Sciences Center (Houston), 1995. Molecular mechanisms controlling cell growth and differentiation in the context of vertebrate embryogenesis.

Martin M. Matzuk, Professor of Pathology & Immunology, Molecular and Human Genetics, and Molecular and Cellular Biology; Co-Director, M.D./Ph.D. Medical Scientist Training Program; M.D./Ph.D., Washington (St. Louis), 1989. Mammalian reproduction, oncogenesis, and development.

David D. Moore, Professor of Molecular and Cellular Biology and Molecular and Human Genetics; Ph.D., Wisconsin–Madison, 1979. Nuclear hormone receptors regulate metabolism and cancer.

Daisuke Nakada, Assistant Professor of Molecular and Human Genetics, Center for Cell and Gene Therapy and Stem Cells and Regenerative Medicine Center; Ph.D., Nagoya (Japan), 2005. Molecular and genetics analysis of stem cell function and cancer.

Jeffrey L. Neul, Associate Professor of Pediatrics–Neurology and Molecular Physiology and Biophysics, Neurological Research Institute; M.D./Ph.D., Chicago, 1998. Determination of neuroanatomical, cellular, and molecular pathogenic mechanisms of clinical abnormalities in Rett Syndrome.

Hoang Nguyen, Assistant Professor of Molecular and Cellular Biology, Center for Cell and Gene Therapy and Stem Cells and Regenerative Medicine Center; Ph.D., Cornell/Sloan-Kettering, 2002. Skin epithelial stem cell fate maintenance and lineage determination.

Paul A. Overbeek, Professor of Molecular and Cellular Biology, Molecular and Human Genetics, and Neuroscience; Ph.D., Michigan, 1980. Gene regulation in transgenic mice; ocular development; growth factors; insertional mutagenesis in mice.

Matthew N. Rasband, Associate Professor of Neuroscience; Ph.D., Rochester, 1999. Role of neuronal-glial signaling in brain development, function, injury, and disease.

Antony Rodriguez, Assistant Professor of Molecular and Human Genetics; Ph.D., Texas Southwestern Medical Center at Dallas, 2002. Molecular genetics of mammalian microRNAs.

Jeffrey M. Rosen, Professor of Molecular and Cellular Biology; Ph.D., SUNY at Buffalo, 1971. Mammary gland development, stem cells, and breast cancer.

Marco Sardiello, Assistant Professor of Molecular and Human Genetics, Neurological Research Institute; Ph.D., Bari (Italy), 2003. Lysosomal enhancement as a therapeutic strategy for treating neuronal ceroid lipofuscinoses.

Gad Shaulsky, Professor of Molecular and Human Genetics; Assistant Dean, Graduate School of Biomedical Sciences; Ph.D., Weizmann (Israel), 1991. Developmental genetics in *Dictyostelium;* allorecognition; evolution of sociality; functional genomics.

Joshua M. Shulman, Assistant Professor of Neurology and Molecular and Human Genetics, Neurological Research Institute; M.D., Harvard/MIT, 2005; Ph.D., Cambridge (United Kingdom), 2000. Functional genomics of Alzheimer's disease and Parkinson's disease; integrative genetic analyses in humans and *Drosophila*.

Roy V. Sillitoe, Assistant Professor of Pathology & Immunology, Neuroscience, Neurological Research Institute; Ph.D., Calgary (Canada), 2003. Developmental origins of complex neurological conditions.

Anna Marie Sokac, Assistant Professor of Biochemistry and Molecular Biology; Ph.D., Wisconsin–Madison, 2001. Shaping cells, shaping embryos: coordinated actin and membrane dynamics in flies and frogs.

Kimberly R. Tolias, Assistant Professor of Neuroscience; Ph.D., Harvard, 1998. Molecular signaling pathways in structural development and plasticity of dendrites and synapses.

Ming-Jer Tsai, Professor of Molecular and Cellular Biology; Ph.D., California, Davis, 1971. Pancreas islet and neural development; organogenesis steroid hormone action; prostate cancer.

Sophia Y. Tsai, Professor of Molecular and Cellular Biology; Ph.D., California, Davis, 1969. COUP-TFII and vein identity; angiogenesis; diabetes; obesity; kidney disease.

Kartik Venkatachalam, Assistant Professor of Integrative Biology and Pharmacology, University of Texas Health Sciences Center; Ph.D., Maryland, 2002. Signal transduction in the nervous system.

Meng Wang, Assistant Professor of Molecular and Human Genetics, and Huffington Center on Aging; Ph.D., Rochester, 2005. Systemic studies of endocrine and metabolic signaling in promoting healthy aging.

Thomas F. Westbrook, Assistant Professor of Biochemistry and Molecular Biology and Molecular and Human Genetics; Ph.D., Rochester, 2003. RNAi-based strategies to cancer gene discovery; REST tumor suppressor pathway.

Hui Zheng, Professor of Molecular and Human Genetics, Molecular and Cellular Biology, and Neuroscience; Director, Huffington Center on Aging; Ph.D., Baylor College of Medicine, 1990. Pathophysiological studies of Alzheimer's disease pathways using mouse models.

Zheng Zhou, Associate Professor of Biochemistry and Molecular Biology; Ph.D., Baylor College of Medicine, 1994. Molecular genetic studies of clearance of apoptotic cells in *C. elegans.*

Huda Y. Zoghbi, Professor of Pediatrics, Molecular and Human Genetics, and Neuroscience; Director, Neurological Research Institute; and Investigator, Howard Hughes Medical Institute; M.D., Meharry Medical College, 1979. Pathogenesis of polyglutamine neurodegenerative diseases and Rett syndrome; genes essential for neurodevelopment.

Thomas P. Zwaka, Associate Professor of Molecular and Cellular Biology and Molecular and Human Genetics, Center for Cell and Gene Therapy and Stem Cells and Regenerative Medicine Center; M.D./Ph.D., Ulm (Germany), 2000. The nature of embryonic stem cell pluripotency.

UNIVERSITY OF CONNECTICUT HEALTH CENTER

Graduate Program in Genetics and Developmental Biology

Program of Study

The genetics and developmental biology graduate program provides students with fundamental interdisciplinary training in modern molecular genetics and developmental biology, emphasizing cellular and molecular aspects as well as tissue interactions. The program is intended for students pursuing a Ph.D. degree and prepares students to compete for job opportunities in traditional medical and dental school departments as well as a productive research career in either academia or industry. Combined M.D./Ph.D. and D.M.D/Ph.D. programs are also available. Students are encouraged to obtain in-depth training through research and courses in biochemistry, molecular biology, cell biology, developmental biology, and genetics. Faculty members are from several basic science and clinical departments and study a wide range of organisms including yeast, worms, fruit flies, mice, and humans. Areas of research include the biology of human embryonic stem cells, mapping and cloning of genes responsible for human disease, RNA processing (including RNA editing, alternative splicing, antisense regulation, and RNA interference), the molecular mechanisms of aging, signal transduction pathways, microbial pathogenesis, developmental neurobiology, cell differentiation, musculoskeletal development, morphogenesis and pattern formation, reproductive biology, and endocrinology.

Research Facilities

The Department of Genetics and Developmental Biology is the academic home of the genetics and developmental biology graduate program. The Department of Genetics and Developmental Biology occupies three floors of the state-of-the-art Academic Research Building, which opened in 1999, as well as laboratory space in adjacent buildings. The department houses equipment and facilities for mouse transgenics, ES cell manipulation, DNA microarrays, nucleic acid sequencing, fluorescence microscopy, and digital imaging. Students also have ready access to first-rate flow cytometry and confocal microscopy facilities. Other institutional resources include a computer center and a library containing approximately 200,000 volumes and subscribing to more than 1,400 current periodicals. Students of the program therefore have an excellent opportunity for research and training in cutting-edge areas of genetics and developmental biology.

Financial Aid

Support for doctoral students engaged in full-time degree programs at the Health Center is provided on a competitive basis. Graduate research assistantships for 2012–13 provide a stipend of $28,000 per year, which includes a waiver of tuition/University fees for the fall and spring semesters and a student health insurance plan. While financial aid is offered competitively, the Health Center makes every possible effort to address the financial needs of all students during their period of training.

Cost of Study

For 2012–13, tuition is $10,836 per year for full-time students who are Connecticut residents and $28,116 per year for full-time out-of-state residents. General University fees are added to the cost of tuition for students who do not receive a tuition waiver. These costs are usually met by traineeships or research assistantships for doctoral students.

Living and Housing Costs

There is a wide range of affordable housing options in the greater Hartford area within easy commuting distance of the campus, including an extensive complex that is adjacent to the Health Center. Costs range from $600 to $900 per month for a one-bedroom unit; 2 or more students sharing an apartment usually pay less. University housing is not available at the Health Center.

Student Group

At UCHC, there are about 500 students in the Schools of Medicine and Dental Medicine, 150 Ph.D. students, and 50 postdoctoral fellows. There are no restrictions on the admission of out-of-state graduate students.

Location

The Health Center is located in the historic town of Farmington, Connecticut. Set in the beautiful New England countryside on a hill overlooking the Farmington Valley, it is close to ski areas, hiking trails, and facilities for boating, fishing, and swimming. Connecticut's capital city of Hartford, 7 miles east of Farmington, is the center of an urban region of approximately 800,000 people. The beaches of the Long Island Sound are about 50 minutes away to the south, and the beautiful Berkshires are a short drive to the northwest. New York City and Boston can be reached within 2½ hours by car. Hartford is the home of the acclaimed Hartford Stage Company, TheatreWorks, the Hartford Symphony and Chamber orchestras, two ballet companies, an opera company, the Wadsworth Athenaeum (the oldest public art museum in the nation), the Mark Twain house, the Hartford Civic Center, and many other interesting cultural and recreational facilities. The area is also home to several branches of the University of Connecticut, Trinity College, and the University of Hartford, which includes the Hartt School of Music. Bradley International Airport (about 30 minutes from campus) serves the Hartford/Springfield area with frequent airline connections to major cities in this country and abroad. Frequent bus and rail service is also available from Hartford.

The Health Center

The 200-acre Health Center campus at Farmington houses a division of the University of Connecticut Graduate School, as well as the School of Medicine and Dental Medicine. The campus also includes the John Dempsey Hospital, associated clinics, and extensive medical research facilities, all in a centralized facility with more than 1 million square feet of floor space. The Health Center's newest research addition, the Academic Research Building, was opened in 1999. This impressive eleven-story structure provides 170,000 square feet of state-of-the-art laboratory space. The faculty at the center includes more than 260 full-time members. The institution has a strong commitment to graduate study within an environment that promotes social and intellectual interaction among the various educational programs. Graduate students are represented on various administrative committees concerned with curricular affairs, and the Graduate Student Organization (GSO) represents graduate students' needs and concerns to the faculty and administration, in addition to fostering social contact among graduate students in the Health Center.

Applying

Applications for admission should be submitted via the online application system and should be filed together with transcripts, three letters of recommendation, a personal statement, and recent

University of Connecticut Health Center

results from the General Test of the Graduate Record Examinations. International students must take the Test of English as a Foreign Language (TOEFL) to satisfy Graduate School requirements. The deadline for completed applications and receipt of all supplemental materials is **December 1**. Please note that GRE and TOEFL exams taken after the due date will not be accepted for consideration for admission. In accordance with the laws of the state of Connecticut and of the United States, the University of Connecticut Health Center does not discriminate against any person in its educational and employment activities on the grounds of race, color, creed, national origin, sex, age, or physical disability.

Correspondence and Information

Graduate Admissions Office

Ph.D. in Biomedical Science Program
University of Connecticut Health Center
263 Farmington Ave., MC 3906
Farmington, Connecticut 06030-3906
United States
Phone: 860-679-4509
E-mail: BiomedSciAdmissions@uchc.edu
Web site: http://grad.uchc.edu/prospective/programs/phd_biosci/index.html

THE FACULTY AND THEIR RESEARCH

Hector Leonardo Aguila, Ph.D., Associate Professor of Immunology. Hematopoiesis and bone marrow microenvironment; lymphoid cell development; stem cell biology.

Alexander Amerik, Ph.D., Assistant Professor of Genetics and Developmental Biology. Deubiquitinating enzymes and ubiquitin homeostasis in the yeast *Saccharomyces cerevisiae.*

Andrew Arnold, M.D., Professor of Medicine and Murray-Heilig Chair in Molecular Medicine. Molecular genetic underpinnings of tumors of the endocrine glands; role of the cyclin D1 oncogene.

Peter Benn, Ph.D., Director, Diagnostic Human Genetics Laboratories. Clinical cytogenetics, molecular cytogenetics, and molecular genetics services; prenatal risk evaluation through maternal serum screening.

Michael Blinov, Ph.D., Assistant Professor of Genetics and Developmental Biology, Modeling of signal transcription systems and protein-DNA interactions; bioinformatics: data mining and visualization; developing software tools and mathematical methods for rule-based modeling of signal transduction systems.

Gordon Carmichael, Ph.D., Professor of Genetics and Developmental Biology. Regulation of gene expression in eukaryotes.

Stormy J. Chamberlain, Ph.D., Assistant Professor of Genetics and Developmental Biology. Human induced pluripotent stem (iPS) cell models to study 15q11-q13 imprinting disorders.

Kevin Claffey, Ph.D., Assistant Professor of Cell Biology. Angiogenesis in cancer progression and metastasis; vascular endothelial growth factor (VEGF) expression; hypoxia-mediated gene regulation.

Soheil (Sam) Dadras, M.D., Ph.D., Assistant Professor of Dermatology, and Genetics and Developmental Biology, Discovery of small RNAs (including microRNA) as novel biomarkers in human melanoma progression and metastasis using next generation sequencing.

Asis Das, Ph.D., Professor of Microbiology. Basic genetic and biomechanical mechanisms that govern the elongation-termination and decision in transcription.

Caroline N. Dealy, Ph.D., Assistant Professor of Anatomy. Roles of various growth factors and signaling molecules, particularly IGF-I and insulin, in the regulation of chick limb development.

Paul Epstein, Ph.D., Associate Professor of Pharmacology. Receptor signal transduction, second messengers, and protein phosphorylation in control of cell growth and regulation; purification and regulation of cyclic nucleotide phosphodiesterases; role of calmodulin in mediating Ca^{2+}-dependent cell processes.

Guo-Hua Fong, Ph.D., Assistant Professor of Cell Biology. Developmental biology of the vascular system, VEGF-A receptor signal transduction, embryonic stem cells, and gene knock-out in mice.

Brenton R. Graveley, Ph.D., Associate Professor of Genetics and Developmental Biology. Regulation of alternative splicing in the mammalian nervous system and mechanisms of alternative splicing.

Arthur Günzl, Ph.D., Associate Professor, Center for Microbial Pathogenesis. Transcription and antigenic variation in the mammalian parasite *Trypanosoma brucei.*

Marc Hansen, Ph.D., Professor of Medicine. Molecular genetics of osteosarcoma and related bone diseases.

Laurinda Jaffe, Ph.D., Professor of Cell Biology. Physiology of fertilization.

Barbara Kream, Ph.D., Professor of Medicine. Hormonal regulation of collagen gene expression in bone.

George Kuchel, M.D., Professor of Medicine. Role of hormones and cytokines in geriatric disability. Pathogenesis of impaired detrusor contractility and urinary retention. Molecular mechanisms of bladder muscle survival.

Marc Lalande, Ph.D., Professor of Genetics and Developmental Biology. Genomic imprinting; Angelman syndrome; mechanism of tissue-specific silencing of the Angelman ubiquitin ligase in mouse and human.

James Li, Ph.D., Assistant Professor of Genetics and Developmental Biology. Identifying the molecular mechanisms underlying formation of the mammalian cerebellum.

Alexander Lichtler, Ph.D., Associate Professor of Pediatrics. Regulation of collagen gene transcription; retrovirus vectors; role of homeobox genes in limb development.

Bruce Mayer, Ph.D., Associate Professor of Genetics and Developmental Biology. Biologically relevant Nck-interacting proteins.

Mina Mina, D.M.D., Ph.D., Associate Professor of Pediatric Dentistry. Characterization of genetic and epigenetic influences involved in pattern formation and skeletogenesis of the chick mandible and mouse tooth germ.

William Mohler, Ph.D., Assistant Professor of Genetics and Developmental Biology. Molecular and cellular mechanisms of cell fusion.

D. Kent Morest, M.D., Professor of Neuroscience. Role of cell and tissue interactions in the migration and differentiation of neurons; structure and function of neurons during development and synapse formation.

John Peluso, Ph.D., Professor of Cell Biology. Control of ovarian follicle growth steroidogenesis in vitro; proto-oncogene expression and ovarian follicular growth.

Carol C. Pilbeam, Ph.D., M.D., Professor of Medicine; Mechanisms of regulation of bone formation and resorption.

Justin D. Radolf, M.D., Professor of Medicine and Genetics and Developmental Biology. Molecular pathogenesis and immunobiology of spirochetal infections.

Blanka Rogina, Ph.D., Assistant Professor of Genetics and Developmental Biology. Molecular mechanism underlying aging process in *Drosophila melanogaster.*

Daniel W. Rosenberg, Ph.D., Professor of Medicine. Molecular genetics of colorectal cancer; signaling pathways in the development of tumors; toxicogenomics,

Edward F. Rossomando, D.D.S., Ph.D., Professor of BioStructure and Function. Control of gene expression in tumor and nontumor cell lines in response to stimulation by monokines; coding, transmission, and processing of environmental signals in normal and abnormal development.

Mansoor Sarfarazi, Ph.D., Associate Professor of Surgery. Positional mapping and mutation analysis of human genetic disorders; primary open angle glaucoma; primary congenital glaucoma; synpolydactyly; dyslexia; mitral valve prolapse and ascending aortic aneurysm.

Bruce White, Ph.D., Professor of Physiology. Control of prolactin gene expression at pretranslational level in GH3 cells; control of aromatase gene expression in ovarian and testicular tissues.

Ren-He Xu, Ph.D., Associate Professor of Genetics and Developmental Biology. Biology of human embryonic stem cells.

Ji Yu, Ph.D., Assistant Professor of Genetics and Developmental Biology; Optical imaging technology; regulation mechanisms in dendritic RNA translation; cytoskeletal dynamics.

Section 11
Marine Biology

This section contains a directory of institutions offering graduate work in marine biology. Additional information about programs listed in the directory but not augmented by an in-depth entry may be obtained by writing directly to the dean of a graduate school or chair of a department at the address given in the directory.

For programs offering related work, see also in this book *Biological and Biomedical Sciences* and *Zoology*. In another guide in this series: **Graduate Programs in the Physical Sciences, Mathematics, Agricultural Sciences, the Environment & Natural Resources** See *Marine Sciences and Oceanography*

CONTENTS

Marine Biology

College of Charleston, Graduate School, School of Sciences and Mathematics, Program in Marine Biology, Charleston, SC 29412. Offers MS. *Faculty:* 39 full-time (13 women), 5 part-time/adjunct (4 women). *Students:* 13 full-time (11 women), 32 part-time (22 women); includes 3 minority (2 Asian, non-Hispanic/Latino; 1 Hispanic/Latino). Average age 25. 110 applicants, 15% accepted, 14 enrolled. In 2011, 7 degrees awarded. *Degree requirements:* For master's, comprehensive exam, thesis. *Entrance requirements:* For master's, GRE General Test, 3 letters of recommendation. Additional exam requirements/recommendations for international students: Required—TOEFL (minimum score 81 iBT). *Application deadline:* For fall admission, 2/1 for domestic and international students; for spring admission, 11/1 for domestic and international students. Application fee: $45. Electronic applications accepted. *Expenses:* Tuition, state resident: full-time $5455; part-time $455 per credit. Tuition, nonresident: full-time $13,917; part-time $1160 per credit. *Financial support:* In 2011–12, 4 fellowships (averaging $22,000 per year), 22 research assistantships (averaging $19,000 per year), 19 teaching assistantships (averaging $16,000 per year) were awarded; career-related internships or fieldwork, Federal Work-Study, institutionally sponsored loans, scholarships/grants, and unspecified assistantships also available. Support available to part-time students. Financial award application deadline: 4/1; financial award applicants required to submit FAFSA. *Faculty research:* Ecology, environmental physiology, marine genomics, bioinformatics, toxicology, cell biology, population biology, fisheries science, animal physiology, biodiversity, estuarine ecology, evolution and systematics, microbial processes, plant physiology, immunology. *Unit head:* Dr. Craig J. Plante, Director, 843-953-9187, Fax: 843-953-9199, E-mail: plantec@cofc.edu. *Application contact:* Susan Hallatt, Director of Graduate Admissions, 843-953-5614, Fax: 843-953-1434, E-mail: hallatts@cofc.edu. Web site: http://www.cofc.edu/~marine/.

Florida Institute of Technology, Graduate Programs, College of Science, Department of Biological Sciences, Program in Ecology, Melbourne, FL 32901-6975. Offers ecology (MS); marine biology (MS). Part-time programs available. *Faculty:* 16 full-time (2 women). *Students:* 23 full-time (16 women), 2 part-time (both women); includes 5 minority (1 Asian, non-Hispanic/Latino; 2 Hispanic/Latino; 2 Two or more races, non-Hispanic/Latino), 1 international. Average age 24. 49 applicants, 14% accepted, 7 enrolled. In 2011, 8 master's awarded. *Degree requirements:* For master's, thesis, research, seminar, internship or summer lab. *Entrance requirements:* For master's, GRE General Test, minimum GPA of 3.0, 3 letters of recommendation, statement of objectives. Additional exam requirements/recommendations for international students: Required—TOEFL (minimum score 550 paper-based; 213 computer-based; 79 iBT). *Application deadline:* For fall admission, 3/15 for domestic students; for spring admission, 10/1 for domestic students. Applications are processed on a rolling basis. Application fee: $0. Electronic applications accepted. *Expenses: Tuition:* Full-time $19,620; part-time $1090 per credit hour. Tuition and fees vary according to campus/location. *Financial support:* Career-related internships or fieldwork, institutionally sponsored loans, tuition waivers (partial), unspecified assistantships, and tuition remissions available. Support available to part-time students. Financial award application deadline: 3/1; financial award applicants required to submit FAFSA. *Faculty research:* Endangered or threatened avian and mammalian species, hydroacoustics and feeding preference of the West Indian manatee, habitat preference of the Florida scrub jay. *Total annual research expenditures:* $1.9 million. *Unit head:* Dr. Richard B. Aronson, Department Head, 321-674-8034, Fax: 321-674-7238, E-mail: raronson@fit.edu. *Application contact:* Cheryl A. Brown, Associate Director of Graduate Admission, 321-674-7581, Fax: 321-723-9468, E-mail: cbrown@fit.edu. Web site: http://www.cos.fit.edu/biology/.

Memorial University of Newfoundland, School of Graduate Studies, Department of Biology, St. John's, NL A1C 5S7, Canada. Offers biology (M Sc, PhD); marine biology (M Sc, PhD). Part-time programs available. *Degree requirements:* For master's, thesis; for doctorate, comprehensive exam, thesis/dissertation, oral defense of thesis. *Entrance requirements:* For master's, honors degree (minimum 2nd class standing) in related field. Electronic applications accepted. *Faculty research:* Northern flora and fauna, especially cold ocean and boreal environments.

Nicholls State University, Graduate Studies, College of Arts and Sciences, Department of Biological Sciences, Thibodaux, LA 70310. Offers marine and environmental biology (MS). Part-time programs available. *Degree requirements:* For master's, comprehensive exam, thesis. *Entrance requirements:* For master's, GRE. Additional exam requirements/recommendations for international students: Required—TOEFL (minimum score 600 paper-based). *Faculty research:* Bioremediation, ecology, public health, biotechnology, physiology.

Northeastern University, College of Science, Department of Biology, Boston, MA 02115-5096. Offers bioinformatics (PMS); biology (MS, PhD); biotechnology (MS, PSM); marine biology (MS). Part-time programs available. *Faculty:* 27 full-time, 5 part-time/adjunct. *Students:* 112 full-time, 4 part-time. 255 applicants, 73% accepted. In 2011, 21 master's, 5 doctorates awarded. Terminal master's awarded for partial completion of doctoral program. *Degree requirements:* For master's, thesis (for some programs); for doctorate, thesis/dissertation, qualifying exam. *Entrance requirements:* For master's and doctorate, GRE General Test. Additional exam requirements/recommendations for international students: Required—TOEFL (minimum score 250 computer-based). *Application deadline:* For fall admission, 1/1 priority date for domestic students, 1/1 for international students. Applications are processed on a rolling basis. Application fee: $50. Electronic applications accepted. *Financial support:* In 2011–12, 19 research assistantships with tuition reimbursements (averaging $18,285 per year), 41 teaching assistantships with tuition reimbursements (averaging $18,285 per year) were awarded; fellowships with tuition reimbursements, career-related internships or fieldwork, Federal Work-Study, tuition waivers (full and partial), and unspecified assistantships also available. Financial award application deadline: 3/1; financial award applicants required to submit FAFSA. *Faculty research:* Biochemistry, marine sciences, molecular biology, microbiology and immunology neurobiology, cellular and molecular biology, biochemistry, marine biochemistry and ecology, microbiology, neurobiology, biotechnology. *Unit head:* Dr. Wendy Smith, Graduate Coordinator, 617-373-2260, Fax: 617-373-3724, E-mail: gradbio@neu.edu. *Application contact:* Jo-Anne Dickinson, Admissions Assistant, 617-373-5990, Fax: 617-373-7281, E-mail: gsas@neu.edu. Web site: http://www.biology.neu.edu/.

Nova Southeastern University, Oceanographic Center, Fort Lauderdale, FL 33314-7796. Offers biological sciences (MS); coastal zone management (MS); marine and coastal studies (MA); marine biology (MS); marine biology and oceanography (PhD), including marine biology, oceanography; marine environmental science (MS). Part-time and evening/weekend programs available. *Faculty:* 15 full-time (1 woman), 5 part-time/adjunct (0 women). *Students:* 130 full-time (86 women), 135 part-time (87 women); includes 34 minority (5 Black or African American, non-Hispanic/Latino; 5 Asian, non-Hispanic/Latino; 22 Hispanic/Latino; 2 Two or more races, non-Hispanic/Latino), 7 international. Average age 29. 98 applicants, 82% accepted, 67 enrolled. In 2011, 30 master's, 1 doctorate awarded. *Degree requirements:* For master's, thesis; for doctorate, comprehensive exam, thesis/dissertation, departmental qualifying exam. *Entrance requirements:* For master's, GRE General Test; for doctorate, GRE General Test, master's degree. Additional exam requirements/recommendations for international students: Required—TOEFL (minimum score 550 paper-based). *Application deadline:* Applications are processed on a rolling basis. Application fee: $50. *Expenses:* Contact institution. *Financial support:* In 2011–12, 25 research assistantships (averaging $4,000 per year), 3 teaching assistantships (averaging $3,500 per year) were awarded; career-related internships or fieldwork, Federal Work-Study, scholarships/grants, tuition waivers (partial), and unspecified assistantships also available. Support available to part-time students. Financial award applicants required to submit FAFSA. *Faculty research:* Physical, geological, chemical, and biological oceanography. *Unit head:* Dr. Richard Dodge, Dean, 954-262-3600, Fax: 954-262-4020, E-mail: dodge@nsu.nova.edu. *Application contact:* Dr. Richard Spieler, Director of Academic Programs, 954-262-3600, Fax: 954-262-4020, E-mail: spieler@nova.edu. Web site: http://www.nova.edu/ocean/.

Princeton University, Graduate School, Department of Geosciences, Princeton, NJ 08544-1019. Offers atmospheric and oceanic sciences (PhD); geosciences (PhD); ocean sciences and marine biology (PhD). *Degree requirements:* For doctorate, one foreign language, thesis/dissertation. *Entrance requirements:* For doctorate, GRE General Test. Additional exam requirements/recommendations for international students: Required—TOEFL (minimum score 600 paper-based; 250 computer-based). Electronic applications accepted. *Faculty research:* Biogeochemistry, climate science, earth history, regional geology and tectonics, solid–earth geophysics.

Rutgers, The State University of New Jersey, New Brunswick, Graduate School-New Brunswick, Department of Environmental Sciences, Piscataway, NJ 08854-8097. Offers air pollution and resources (MS, PhD); aquatic biology (MS, PhD); aquatic chemistry (MS, PhD); atmospheric science (MS, PhD); chemistry and physics of aerosol and hydrosol systems (MS, PhD); environmental chemistry (MS, PhD); environmental microbiology (MS, PhD); environmental toxicology (PhD); exposure assessment (PhD); fate and effects of pollutants (MS, PhD); pollution prevention and control (MS, PhD); water and wastewater treatment (MS, PhD); water resources (MS, PhD). Terminal master's awarded for partial completion of doctoral program. *Degree requirements:* For master's, comprehensive exam, thesis or alternative, oral final exam; for doctorate, comprehensive exam, thesis/dissertation, thesis defense, qualifying exam. *Entrance requirements:* For master's and doctorate, GRE General Test. Additional exam requirements/recommendations for international students: Required—TOEFL. Electronic applications accepted. *Faculty research:* Biological waste treatment; contaminant fate and transport; air, soil and water quality.

San Francisco State University, Division of Graduate Studies, College of Science and Engineering, Department of Biology, Program in Marine Biology, San Francisco, CA 94132-1722. Offers MS. *Unit head:* Dr. Frances Wilkerson, Program Coordinator, 415-338-3519, E-mail: fwilkers@sfsu.edu. *Application contact:* Dr. Robert Patterson, Graduate Coordinator, 415-338-1100, E-mail: patters@sfsu.edu. Web site: http://biology.sfsu.edu/graduate/marine_biology.

San Francisco State University, Division of Graduate Studies, College of Science and Engineering, Department of Biology, Program in Marine Science, San Francisco, CA 94132-1722. Offers MS. Program offered through the Moss Landing Marine Laboratories. *Application deadline:* Applications are processed on a rolling basis. *Unit head:* Dr. Kenneth Coale, Director, 831-771- 4400, E-mail: frontdesk@mlml.calstate.edu. *Application contact:* John Machado, Graduate Coordinator, E-mail: jmachado@mlml.calstate.edu. Web site: http://www.sfsu.edu/~bulletin/current/programs/marines.htm#282.

Texas A&M University at Galveston, Department of Marine Biology, Galveston, TX 77553-1675. Offers MS, PhD. *Faculty:* 33 full-time (7 women). *Students:* 20 full-time (15 women), 4 part-time (2 women); includes 1 minority (Hispanic/Latino), 7 international. Average age 24. 13 applicants, 46% accepted, 6 enrolled. In 2011, 2 degrees awarded. Terminal master's awarded for partial completion of doctoral program. *Degree requirements:* For master's, comprehensive exam (for some programs), thesis (for some programs); for doctorate, comprehensive exam, thesis/dissertation. *Entrance requirements:* For master's and doctorate, GRE. Additional exam requirements/recommendations for international students: Required—TOEFL (minimum score 550 paper-based; 213 computer-based; 80 iBT), IELTS (minimum score 6). *Application deadline:* For fall admission, 5/15 for domestic students, 5/1 for international students; for spring admission, 10/15 priority date for domestic students, 10/15 for international students. Application fee: $50 ($90 for international students). Electronic applications accepted. *Expenses:* Tuition, state resident: full-time $2087; part-time $231.85 per contact hour. Tuition, nonresident: full-time $4904; part-time $545 per contact hour. *Required fees:* $65 per contact hour. $110 per semester. One-time fee: $50. *Financial support:* In 2011–12, 20 students received support, including 3 research assistantships, 17 teaching assistantships; scholarships/grants, health care benefits, and unspecified assistantships also available. Financial award applicants required to submit FAFSA. *Faculty research:* Fisheries, coastal and wetland ecologies, phytoplankton, marine mammals, seafood safety, marine invertebrates and marine biospeleology. *Total annual research expenditures:* $2 million. *Unit head:* Dr. Gilbert Rowe, Professor/Chair of Marine Biology Interdisciplinary Program, 409-740-4847, E-mail: roweg@tamug.edu. *Application contact:* Nicole Wilkins, Administrative Coordinator for Graduate Studies, 409-740-4937, Fax: 409-740-4754, E-mail: wilkinsn@tamug.edu.

Texas State University–San Marcos, Graduate School, College of Science and Engineering, Department of Biology, Program in Aquatic Resources, San Marcos, TX 78666. Offers MS, PhD. *Faculty:* 7 full-time, 1 part-time/adjunct. *Students:* 41 full-time (19 women), 15 part-time (10 women); includes 5 minority (4 Hispanic/Latino; 1 Two or more races, non-Hispanic/Latino), 7 international. Average age 32. 27 applicants, 63% accepted, 14 enrolled. In 2011, 3 master's, 5 doctorates awarded. *Degree requirements:* For master's, comprehensive exam, thesis, 3 seminars. *Entrance requirements:* For master's, GRE General Test, previous course work in biology, minimum GPA of 2.75 in last 60 hours of course work. Additional exam requirements/recommendations for international students: Required—TOEFL (minimum score 550 paper-based; 213 computer-based; 78 iBT). *Application deadline:* For fall admission, 6/15 priority date for domestic students, 6/1 for international students; for spring admission, 10/15 priority date for domestic students, 10/1 for international students. Applications are processed on a rolling basis. Application fee: $40 ($90 for international students). Electronic applications accepted. *Expenses:* Tuition, state resident: full-time $6408; part-time $3204 per semester. Tuition, nonresident: full-time $14,832; part-time $7416 per semester. *Required fees:* $1824; $912 per semester. Tuition and fees vary according to course load. *Financial support:* In 2011–12, 10 students received support, including 21 research assistantships (averaging $16,263 per year), 36 teaching assistantships

(averaging $17,606 per year); Federal Work-Study, institutionally sponsored loans, scholarships/grants, health care benefits, and unspecified assistantships also available. Support available to part-time students. Financial award application deadline: 4/1; financial award applicants required to submit FAFSA. *Unit head:* Dr. Tim Bonner, Advisor, 512-245-1616, Fax: 512-245-8713, E-mail: tb14@txstate.edu. *Application contact:* Dr. J. Michael Willoughby, Dean of the Graduate School, 512-245-2581, Fax: 512-245-8365, E-mail: jw02@swt.edu. Web site: http://www.bio.txstate.edu/.

University of Alaska Fairbanks, School of Fisheries and Ocean Sciences, Program in Marine Sciences and Limnology, Fairbanks, AK 99775-7220. Offers marine biology (MS, PhD); oceanography (PhD), including biological oceanography, chemical oceanography, fisheries, geological oceanography, physical oceanography. Part-time programs available. *Faculty:* 6 full-time (4 women). *Students:* 40 full-time (29 women), 17 part-time (12 women); includes 7 minority (3 Asian, non-Hispanic/Latino; 4 Hispanic/Latino), 4 international. Average age 30. 61 applicants, 20% accepted, 12 enrolled. In 2011, 3 master's, 3 doctorates awarded. *Degree requirements:* For master's, comprehensive exam, thesis, oral defense; for doctorate, comprehensive exam, thesis/dissertation, oral defense. *Entrance requirements:* For master's and doctorate, GRE General Test. Additional exam requirements/recommendations for international students: Required—TOEFL (minimum score 550 paper-based; 213 computer-based; 80 iBT). *Application deadline:* For fall admission, 6/1 for domestic students, 3/1 for international students; for spring admission, 10/15 for domestic students, 8/1 for international students. Applications are processed on a rolling basis. Application fee: $60. Electronic applications accepted. *Expenses:* Tuition, state resident: full-time $6696; part-time $372 per credit. Tuition, nonresident: full-time $13,680; part-time $760 per credit. Tuition and fees vary according to course load and reciprocity agreements. *Financial support:* In 2011–12, 26 research assistantships with tuition reimbursements (averaging $11,484 per year), 7 teaching assistantships with tuition reimbursements (averaging $14,772 per year) were awarded; fellowships with tuition reimbursements, career-related internships or fieldwork, Federal Work-Study, scholarships/grants, health care benefits, and unspecified assistantships also available. Support available to part-time students. Financial award application deadline: 7/1; financial award applicants required to submit FAFSA. *Unit head:* Katrin Iken, Co-Chair, 907-474-7289, Fax: 907-474-5863, E-mail: academics@sfos.uaf.edu. *Application contact:* Christina Neumann, Academic Manager, 907-474-7289, Fax: 907-474-5863, E-mail: clneumann@alaska.edu. Web site: http://www.sfos.uaf.edu/academics/prospective/graduate.html.

University of California, San Diego, Office of Graduate Studies, Scripps Institution of Oceanography, La Jolla, CA 92093. Offers earth sciences (PhD); marine biology (PhD); oceanography (PhD). *Degree requirements:* For doctorate, comprehensive exam, thesis/dissertation. *Entrance requirements:* For doctorate, GRE General Test. Additional exam requirements/recommendations for international students: Required—TOEFL (minimum score 550 paper-based; 213 computer-based; 80 iBT). Electronic applications accepted.

University of California, Santa Barbara, Graduate Division, College of Letters and Sciences, Division of Mathematics, Life, and Physical Sciences, Department of Ecology, Evolution, and Marine Biology, Santa Barbara, CA 93106-9620. Offers computational science and engineering (MA); computational sciences and engineering (PhD); ecology, evolution, and marine biology (MA, PhD); MA/PhD. *Faculty:* 27 full-time (7 women). *Students:* 58 full-time (39 women); includes 9 minority (1 Black or African American, non-Hispanic/Latino; 5 Asian, non-Hispanic/Latino; 2 Hispanic/Latino; 1 Two or more races, non-Hispanic/Latino), 4 international. Average age 30. 131 applicants, 15% accepted, 8 enrolled. In 2011, 4 master's, 4 doctorates awarded. *Median time to degree:* Of those who began their doctoral program in fall 2003, 100% received their degree in 8 years or less. *Degree requirements:* For master's, comprehensive exam (for some programs), thesis (for some programs); for doctorate, comprehensive exam, thesis/dissertation. *Entrance requirements:* For master's and doctorate, GRE General Test. Additional exam requirements/recommendations for international students: Required—TOEFL (minimum score 550 paper-based; 80 iBT), IELTS. *Application deadline:* For fall admission, 12/15 for domestic and international students. Application fee: $80 ($100 for international students). Electronic applications accepted. *Expenses:* Tuition, state resident: full-time $12,192. Tuition, nonresident: full-time $27,294. *Required fees:* $764.13. *Financial support:* In 2011–12, 54 students received support, including 44 fellowships with full and partial tuition reimbursements available (averaging $10,812 per year), 13 research assistantships with full and partial tuition reimbursements available (averaging $8,441 per year), 22 teaching assistantships with partial tuition reimbursements available (averaging $9,346 per year); Federal Work-Study, scholarships/grants, traineeships, health care benefits, and tuition waivers (full and partial) also available. Financial award application deadline: 12/15; financial award applicants required to submit FAFSA. *Faculty research:* Community ecology, evolution, marine biology, population genetics, stream ecology. *Unit head:* Dr. Cheryl Briggs, Chair, 805-893-2415, Fax: 805-893-5885. *Application contact:* Melanie Fujii, Staff Graduate Advisor, 805-893-2979, Fax: 805-893-5885, E-mail: eemb-info@lifesci.ucsb.edu. Web site: http://www.lifesci.ucsb.edu/EEMB/index.html.

University of Colorado Boulder, Graduate School, College of Arts and Sciences, Department of Ecology and Evolutionary Biology, Boulder, CO 80309. Offers animal behavior (MA); biology (MA, PhD); environmental biology (MA, PhD); evolutionary biology (MA, PhD); neurobiology (MA); population biology (MA); population genetics (PhD). *Faculty:* 28 full-time (9 women). *Students:* 67 full-time (37 women), 27 part-time (13 women); includes 9 minority (1 Asian, non-Hispanic/Latino; 8 Hispanic/Latino), 5 international. Average age 30. 136 applicants, 13% accepted, 17 enrolled. In 2011, 8 master's, 5 doctorates awarded. Terminal master's awarded for partial completion of doctoral program. *Degree requirements:* For master's, comprehensive exam, thesis or alternative; for doctorate, comprehensive exam, thesis/dissertation. *Entrance requirements:* For master's, GRE General Test, GRE Subject Test, minimum undergraduate GPA of 3.0; for doctorate, GRE General Test, GRE Subject Test. *Application deadline:* For fall admission, 12/30 priority date for domestic students, 12/1 for international students. Application fee: $50 ($60 for international students). Electronic applications accepted. *Financial support:* In 2011–12, 88 students received support, including 35 fellowships (averaging $16,835 per year), 25 research assistantships with full and partial tuition reimbursements available (averaging $22,347 per year), 44 teaching assistantships with full and partial tuition reimbursements available (averaging $21,377 per year); institutionally sponsored loans, scholarships/grants, health care benefits, and unspecified assistantships also available. Financial award applicants required to submit FAFSA. *Faculty research:* Behavior, ecology, genetics, morphology, endocrinology, physiology, systematics. *Total annual research expenditures:* $4.6 million. *Application contact:* E-mail: ebiograd@colorado.edu. Web site: http://ebio.colorado.edu.

University of Guam, Office of Graduate Studies, College of Natural and Applied Sciences, Program in Biology, Mangilao, GU 96923. Offers tropical marine biology (MS). *Degree requirements:* For master's, comprehensive exam, thesis. *Entrance requirements:* For master's, GRE General Test, GRE Subject Test. Additional exam requirements/recommendations for international students: Required—TOEFL. *Faculty research:* Maintenance and ecology of coral reefs.

University of Hawaii at Hilo, Program in Tropical Conservation Biology and Environmental Science, Hilo, HI 96720-4091. Offers MS.

University of Hawaii at Manoa, Graduate Division, School of Ocean and Earth Science and Technology, Interdisciplinary Program in Marine Biology, Honolulu, HI 96822. Offers MS, PhD. *Degree requirements:* For master's, thesis, research project; for doctorate, thesis/dissertation, research project. *Entrance requirements:* For master's and doctorate, GRE. Additional exam requirements/recommendations for international students: Required—TOEFL. *Expenses:* Contact institution. *Faculty research:* Ecology, ichthyology, behavior of marine animals, developmental biology.

University of Maine, Graduate School, College of Natural Sciences, Forestry, and Agriculture, School of Marine Sciences, Program in Marine Biology, Orono, ME 04469. Offers MS, PhD. *Students:* 25 full-time (15 women), 14 part-time (8 women), 3 international. Average age 29. 52 applicants, 8% accepted, 3 enrolled. In 2011, 4 master's, 1 doctorate awarded. *Degree requirements:* For master's, thesis; for doctorate, thesis/dissertation. *Entrance requirements:* For master's and doctorate, GRE General Test. Additional exam requirements/recommendations for international students: Required—TOEFL. *Application deadline:* For fall admission, 2/1 priority date for domestic students. Applications are processed on a rolling basis. Application fee: $65. Electronic applications accepted. *Expenses:* Tuition, state resident: full-time $5016. Tuition, nonresident: full-time $14,424. *Financial support:* Career-related internships or fieldwork, Federal Work-Study, and tuition waivers (full and partial) available. Support available to part-time students. Financial award application deadline: 3/1. *Unit head:* Dr. Susan Brawley, Coordinator, 207-581-2973. *Application contact:* Scott G. Delcourt, Associate Dean of the Graduate School, 207-581-3291, Fax: 207-581-3232, E-mail: graduate@maine.edu. Web site: http://www2.umaine.edu/graduate/.

University of Massachusetts Dartmouth, Graduate School, College of Arts and Sciences, Department of Biology, North Dartmouth, MA 02747-2300. Offers biology (MS); marine biology (MS). Part-time programs available. *Faculty:* 16 full-time (6 women), 4 part-time/adjunct (1 woman). *Students:* 15 full-time (10 women), 9 part-time (7 women); includes 2 minority (1 Asian, non-Hispanic/Latino; 1 Hispanic/Latino). Average age 28. 38 applicants, 50% accepted, 8 enrolled. In 2011, 3 degrees awarded. *Degree requirements:* For master's, thesis. *Entrance requirements:* For master's, GRE General Test, GRE Subject Test, statement of intent, resume, 3 letters of recommendation. Additional exam requirements/recommendations for international students: Required—TOEFL (minimum score 533 paper-based; 200 computer-based; 72 iBT). *Application deadline:* For fall admission, 2/15 for domestic students, 1/15 for international students. Application fee: $40 ($60 for international students). Electronic applications accepted. *Expenses:* Tuition, state resident: full-time $2071; part-time $86.29 per credit. Tuition, nonresident: full-time $8099; part-time $337.46 per credit. *Required fees:* $438.58 per credit. Part-time tuition and fees vary according to class time, course load, degree level and reciprocity agreements. *Financial support:* In 2011–12, 1 research assistantship with full tuition reimbursement (averaging $4,500 per year), 10 teaching assistantships with full tuition reimbursements (averaging $15,000 per year) were awarded; Federal Work-Study and unspecified assistantships also available. Support available to part-time students. Financial award application deadline: 3/1; financial award applicants required to submit FAFSA. *Faculty research:* Fish biology, antibody-mediated protection, bottlenose dolphins, adaptations in fish via genetics, evolutionary biology. *Total annual research expenditures:* $789,879. *Unit head:* Dr. Diego Bernal, Graduate Program Director, 508-999-8307, Fax: 508-999-8196, E-mail: dbernal@umassd.edu. *Application contact:* Elan Turcotte-Shamski, Graduate Admissions Officer, 508-999-8604, Fax: 508-999-8183, E-mail: graduate@umassd.edu. Web site: http://www.umassd.edu/cas/biology/.

University of Miami, Graduate School, Rosenstiel School of Marine and Atmospheric Science, Division of Marine Biology and Fisheries, Coral Gables, FL 33124. Offers MA, MS, PhD. Terminal master's awarded for partial completion of doctoral program. *Degree requirements:* For master's, comprehensive exam, thesis; for doctorate, comprehensive exam, thesis/dissertation. *Entrance requirements:* For master's and doctorate, GRE General Test. Additional exam requirements/recommendations for international students: Required—TOEFL (minimum score 550 paper-based; 213 computer-based). Electronic applications accepted. *Faculty research:* Biochemistry, physiology, plankton, coral, biology.

The University of North Carolina Wilmington, Center for Marine Science, Wilmington, NC 28403-3297. Offers MS. Part-time programs available. *Degree requirements:* For master's, comprehensive exam, thesis. *Entrance requirements:* For master's, GRE, minimum undergraduate B average. Additional exam requirements/recommendations for international students: Required—TOEFL (minimum score 550 paper-based; 217 computer-based; 79 iBT), IELTS (minimum score 6.5).

The University of North Carolina Wilmington, College of Arts and Sciences, Department of Biology and Marine Biology, Wilmington, NC 28403-3297. Offers biology (MS); marine biology (MS, PhD). Part-time programs available. *Degree requirements:* For master's, comprehensive exam, thesis; for doctorate, comprehensive exam, thesis/dissertation. *Entrance requirements:* For master's, GRE General Test, GRE Subject Test, minimum B average in undergraduate major; for doctorate, GRE General Test, minimum B average in undergraduate major and graduate courses. Additional exam requirements/recommendations for international students: Required—TOEFL (minimum score 550 paper-based; 217 computer-based; 79 iBT), IELTS (minimum score 6.5). Electronic applications accepted. *Faculty research:* Ecology, physiology, cell and molecular biology, systematics, biomechanics.

University of Oregon, Graduate School, College of Arts and Sciences, Department of Biology, Eugene, OR 97403. Offers ecology and evolution (MA, MS, PhD); marine biology (MA, MS, PhD); molecular, cellular and genetic biology (PhD); neuroscience and development (PhD). Terminal master's awarded for partial completion of doctoral program. *Degree requirements:* For master's, thesis (for some programs); for doctorate, thesis/dissertation. *Entrance requirements:* For master's and doctorate, GRE General Test, minimum GPA of 3.2. Additional exam requirements/recommendations for international students: Required—TOEFL. *Faculty research:* Developmental neurobiology; evolution, population biology, and quantitative genetics; regulation of gene expression; biochemistry of marine organisms.

University of Southern California, Graduate School, Dana and David Dornsife College of Letters, Arts and Sciences, Department of Biological Sciences, Program in Marine Biology and Biological Oceanography, Los Angeles, CA 90089. Offers marine and environmental biology (MS); marine biology and biological oceanography (PhD). Terminal master's awarded for partial completion of doctoral program. *Degree requirements:* For master's, research paper; for doctorate, comprehensive exam, thesis/dissertation, qualifying examination, dissertation defense. *Entrance requirements:* For master's and doctorate, GRE, 3 letters of recommendation, personal statement, resume, minimum GPA of 3.0. Additional exam requirements/recommendations for international students: Required—TOEFL (minimum score 600 paper-based; 250 computer-based; 100 iBT). Electronic applications accepted. *Faculty research:* Microbial ecology, biogeochemistry, and geobiology; biodiversity and molecular ecology; integrative organismal biology; conservation biology; marine genomics.

Marine Biology

University of Southern Mississippi, Graduate School, College of Science and Technology, Department of Biological Sciences, Hattiesburg, MS 39406-0001. Offers environmental biology (MS, PhD); marine biology (MS, PhD); microbiology (MS, PhD); molecular biology (MS, PhD). *Faculty:* 27 full-time (6 women). *Students:* 57 full-time (28 women), 4 part-time (2 women); includes 5 minority (2 Black or African American, non-Hispanic/Latino; 3 Two or more races, non-Hispanic/Latino), 18 international. Average age 32. 50 applicants, 32% accepted, 12 enrolled. In 2011, 7 master's, 8 doctorates awarded. Terminal master's awarded for partial completion of doctoral program. *Degree requirements:* For master's, comprehensive exam, thesis; for doctorate, comprehensive exam, thesis/dissertation. *Entrance requirements:* For master's, GRE General Test, minimum GPA of 3.0 on last 60 hours; for doctorate, GRE General Test, minimum GPA of 3.5. Additional exam requirements/recommendations for international students: Required—TOEFL, IELTS. *Application deadline:* For fall admission, 3/1 priority date for domestic students, 3/1 for international students; for spring admission, 1/10 priority date for domestic students, 1/10 for international students. Applications are processed on a rolling basis. Application fee: $50. *Financial support:* In 2011–12, 25 research assistantships with full tuition reimbursements (averaging $9,700 per year), 33 teaching assistantships with full tuition reimbursements (averaging $10,600 per year) were awarded; Federal Work-Study, scholarships/grants, health care benefits, and unspecified assistantships also available. Financial award application deadline: 3/15; financial award applicants required to submit FAFSA. *Unit head:* Dr. Glenmore Shearer, Chair, 601-266-4748, Fax: 601-266-5797. *Application contact:* Dr. Jake Schaefer, Director of Graduate Studies, 601-266-4748, Fax: 601-266-5797. Web site: http://www.usm.edu/graduateschool/table.php.

University of South Florida, Graduate School, College of Arts and Sciences, Department of Biology, Tampa, FL 33620-9951. Offers cell biology and molecular biology (MS); coastal marine biology (MS); coastal marine biology and ecology (PhD); conservation biology (MS, PhD); molecular and cell biology (PhD). Part-time programs available. *Faculty:* 35 full-time (11 women), 16 part-time/adjunct (5 women). *Students:* 126 full-time (75 women), 24 part-time (17 women); includes 13 minority (1 Black or African American, non-Hispanic/Latino; 4 Asian, non-Hispanic/Latino; 8 Hispanic/Latino), 17 international. Average age 30. 235 applicants, 21% accepted, 30 enrolled. In 2011, 7 master's, 11 doctorates awarded. *Degree requirements:* For master's, comprehensive exam, thesis (for some programs); for doctorate, comprehensive exam, thesis/dissertation. *Entrance requirements:* For master's and doctorate, GRE General Test, minimum GPA of 3.0. Additional exam requirements/recommendations for international students: Required—TOEFL (minimum score 570 paper-based; 213 computer-based). *Application deadline:* For fall admission, 2/15 priority date for domestic students, 1/2 for international students; for spring admission, 8/1 for domestic students, 6/1 for international students. Application fee: $30. Electronic applications accepted. *Financial support:* In 2011–12, 122 students received support, including 46 research assistantships (averaging $24,716 per year), 76 teaching assistantships with tuition reimbursements available (averaging $28,434 per year); unspecified assistantships also available. Financial award application deadline: 6/30; financial award applicants required to submit FAFSA. *Total annual research expenditures:* $5.2 million. *Unit head:* Susan Bell, Co-Chairperson, 813-974-6210, Fax: 813-974-2876, E-mail: sbell@cas.usf.edu. *Application contact:* James Garey, Graduate Advisor, 813-974-8434, Fax: 813-974-3263, E-mail: grarey@cas.usf.edu. Web site: http://www.cas.usf.edu/biology/.

Western Illinois University, School of Graduate Studies, College of Arts and Sciences, Department of Biological Sciences, Macomb, IL 61455-1390. Offers biological sciences (MS); environmental geographic information systems (Certificate); zoo and aquarium studies (Certificate). Part-time programs available. *Students:* 55 full-time (38 women), 30 part-time (25 women); includes 6 minority (4 Black or African American, non-Hispanic/Latino; 1 Hispanic/Latino; 1 Two or more races, non-Hispanic/Latino), 4 international. Average age 26. 50 applicants, 60% accepted. In 2011, 30 master's, 19 other advanced degrees awarded. *Degree requirements:* For master's, thesis or alternative. *Entrance requirements:* Additional exam requirements/recommendations for international students: Required—TOEFL (minimum score 550 paper-based; 213 computer-based; 80 iBT); Recommended—IELTS. *Application deadline:* Applications are processed on a rolling basis. Application fee: $30. Electronic applications accepted. *Expenses:* Tuition, state resident: part-time $281.16 per credit hour. Tuition, nonresident: part-time $562.32 per credit hour. Part-time tuition and fees vary according to campus/location and reciprocity agreements. *Financial support:* In 2011–12, 28 students received support, including 9 research assistantships with full tuition reimbursements available (averaging $7,360 per year), 19 teaching assistantships with full tuition reimbursements available (averaging $8,480 per year). Financial award applicants required to submit FAFSA. *Unit head:* Dr. Michael Romano, Chairperson, 309-298-1546. *Application contact:* Nancy Parsons, Interim Associate Provost and Director of Graduate Studies, 309-298-1806, Fax: 309-298-2345, E-mail: grad-office@wiu.edu. Web site: http://wiu.edu/biology.

Woods Hole Oceanographic Institution, MIT/WHOI Joint Program in Oceanography/Applied Ocean Science and Engineering, Woods Hole, MA 02543-1541. Offers applied ocean science and engineering (PhD); biological oceanography (PhD); chemical oceanography (PhD); marine geology and geophysics (PhD); physical oceanography (PhD). Program offered jointly with Massachusetts Institute of Technology. *Degree requirements:* For doctorate, thesis/dissertation. *Entrance requirements:* For doctorate, GRE General Test, GRE Subject Test. Additional exam requirements/recommendations for international students: Required—TOEFL. Electronic applications accepted.

Section 12
Microbiological Sciences

This section contains a directory of institutions offering graduate work in microbiological sciences, followed by in-depth entries submitted by institutions that chose to prepare detailed program descriptions. Additional information about programs listed in the directory but not augmented by an in-depth entry may be obtained by writing directly to the dean of a graduate school or chair of a department at the address given in the directory.

For programs offering related work, see also in this book *Allied Health; Biochemistry; Biological and Biomedical Sciences; Botany and Plant Biology; Cell, Molecular, and Structural Biology; Dentistry and Dental Sciences; Ecology, Environmental Biology, and Evolutionary Biology; Entomology; Genetics, Developmental Biology, and Reproductive Biology; Parasitology; Pathology and Pathobiology; Pharmacy and Pharmaceutical Sciences; Public Health; Physiology; Veterinary Medicine and Sciences;* and *Zoology.* In the other guides in this series:

Graduate Programs in the Physical Sciences, Mathematics, Agricultural Sciences, the Environment & Natural Resources

See *Agricultural and Food Sciences* and *Chemistry*

Graduate Programs in Engineering & Applied Sciences

See *Agricultural Engineering and Bioengineering* and *Biomedical Engineering and Biotechnology*

CONTENTS

Bacteriology

Illinois State University, Graduate School, College of Arts and Sciences, Department of Biological Sciences, Normal, IL 61790-2200. Offers animal behavior (MS); bacteriology (MS); biochemistry (MS); biological sciences (MS); biology (PhD); biophysics (MS); biotechnology (MS); botany (MS, PhD); cell biology (MS); conservation biology (MS); developmental biology (MS); ecology (MS, PhD); entomology (MS); evolutionary biology (MS); genetics (MS, PhD); immunology (MS); microbiology (MS, PhD); molecular biology (MS); molecular genetics (MS); neurobiology (MS); neuroscience (MS); parasitology (MS); physiology (MS, PhD); plant biology (MS); plant molecular biology (MS); plant sciences (MS); structural biology (MS); zoology (MS, PhD). Part-time programs available. *Degree requirements:* For master's, thesis or alternative; for doctorate, variable foreign language requirement, thesis/dissertation, 2 terms of residency. *Entrance requirements:* For master's, GRE General Test, minimum GPA of 2.6 in last 60 hours of course work; for doctorate, GRE General Test. *Faculty research:* Redoc balance and drug development in schistosoma mansoni, control of the growth of listeria monocytogenes at low temperature, regulation of cell expansion and microtubule function by SPRI, CRUI: physiology and fitness consequences of different life history phenotypes.

The University of Iowa, Roy J. and Lucille A. Carver College of Medicine and Graduate College, Graduate Programs in Medicine, Department of Microbiology, Iowa City, IA 52242-1316. Offers general microbiology and microbial physiology (MS, PhD); immunology (MS, PhD); microbial genetics (MS, PhD); pathogenic bacteriology (MS, PhD); virology (MS, PhD). *Faculty:* 23 full-time (5 women), 12 part-time/adjunct (4 women). *Students:* 37 full-time (24 women); includes 3 minority (2 American Indian or Alaska Native, non-Hispanic/Latino; 1 Hispanic/Latino), 4 international. Average age 25. 56 applicants, 16% accepted, 4 enrolled. In 2011, 1 master's, 6 doctorates awarded. *Degree requirements:* For master's, thesis; for doctorate, comprehensive exam, thesis/dissertation. *Entrance requirements:* For master's and doctorate, GRE General Test. Additional exam requirements/recommendations for international students: Required—TOEFL (minimum score 600 paper-based; 250 computer-based). *Application deadline:* For fall admission, 1/1 for domestic and international students. Application fee: $60 ($85 for international students). Electronic applications accepted. *Financial support:* In 2011–12, 4 fellowships with full tuition reimbursements (averaging $25,500 per year), 33 research assistantships with full tuition reimbursements (averaging $25,500 per year) were awarded; institutionally sponsored loans, scholarships/grants, traineeships, and health care benefits also available. *Faculty research:* Gene regulation, processing and transport of HIV, retroviral pathogenesis, biodegradation, biofilm. *Total annual research expenditures:* $12.6 million. *Unit head:* Dr. Patrick M. Schlievert, Head, 319-335-7810, E-mail: grad-micro-info@uiowa.edu. *Application contact:* Betty Wood, Associate Director of Admissions, 319-335-1525, Fax: 319-335-1535, E-mail: admissions@uiowa.edu. Web site: http://www.uiowa.edu/microbiology/.

University of Prince Edward Island, Atlantic Veterinary College, Graduate Program in Veterinary Medicine, Charlottetown, PE C1A 4P3, Canada. Offers anatomy (M Sc, PhD); bacteriology (M Sc, PhD); clinical pharmacology (M Sc, PhD); clinical sciences (M Sc, PhD); epidemiology (M Sc, PhD), including reproduction; fish health (M Sc, PhD); food animal nutrition (M Sc, PhD); immunology (M Sc, PhD); microanatomy (M Sc, PhD); parasitology (M Sc, PhD); pathology (M Sc, PhD); pharmacology (M Sc, PhD); physiology (M Sc, PhD); toxicology (M Sc, PhD); veterinary science (M Vet Sc); virology (M Sc, PhD). Part-time programs available. *Degree requirements:* For master's, thesis; for doctorate, thesis/dissertation. *Entrance requirements:* For master's, DVM, B Sc honors degree, or equivalent; for doctorate, M Sc. Additional exam requirements/ recommendations for international students: Required—TOEFL (minimum score 550 paper-based; 213 computer-based; 80 iBT). *Expenses:* Contact institution. *Faculty research:* Animal health management, infectious diseases, fin fish and shellfish health, basic biomedical sciences, ecosystem health.

The University of Texas Medical Branch, Graduate School of Biomedical Sciences, Center for Biodefense and Emerging Infectious Diseases, Galveston, TX 77555. Offers biodefense training (PhD). *Entrance requirements:* For doctorate, GRE, minimum overall GPA of 3.0.

The University of Texas Medical Branch, Graduate School of Biomedical Sciences, Program in Emerging and Tropical Infectious Diseases, Galveston, TX 77555. Offers PhD, MD/PhD. *Degree requirements:* For doctorate, thesis/dissertation. *Entrance requirements:* For doctorate, GRE General Test. *Faculty research:* Emerging diseases, tropical diseases, parasitology, vitology and bacteriology.

University of Washington, Graduate School, School of Public Health, Department of Global Health, Graduate Program in Pathobiology, Seattle, WA 98195. Offers PhD. *Students:* 32 full-time (25 women), 3 part-time (all women); includes 7 minority (2 Black or African American, non-Hispanic/Latino; 3 Asian, non-Hispanic/Latino; 2 Hispanic/Latino), 5 international. Average age 29. 75 applicants, 20% accepted, 5 enrolled. In 2011, 3 doctorates awarded. *Degree requirements:* For doctorate, comprehensive exam, thesis/dissertation, published paper from thesis work. *Entrance requirements:* For doctorate, GRE General Test, minimum GPA of 3.0. Additional exam requirements/ recommendations for international students: Required—TOEFL, IELTS. *Application deadline:* For fall admission, 12/1 for domestic students, 11/1 for international students. Application fee: $75. Electronic applications accepted. *Financial support:* In 2011–12, 34 students received support, including 34 research assistantships with full tuition reimbursements available (averaging $27,348 per year); traineeships and unspecified assistantships also available. *Faculty research:* Malaria, immunological response to mycobacteria infections, HIV-cell interaction and the development of an anti-HIV vaccine, regulation of intercellular communication via gap junctions, genetic and nutritional regulation of proteins involved in lipid transport. *Unit head:* Dr. King Holmes, Chair, 206-744-3620, Fax: 206-744-3694. *Application contact:* Rachel Reichert, Program Manager, 206-543-4338, Fax: 206-543-3873, E-mail: pabio@u.washington.edu.

University of Wisconsin–Madison, Graduate School, College of Agricultural and Life Sciences, Department of Bacteriology, Madison, WI 53706-1380. Offers MS. Part-time programs available. *Entrance requirements:* Additional exam requirements/ recommendations for international students: Required—TOEFL. Electronic applications accepted. *Expenses:* Tuition, state resident: full-time $10,296; part-time $643.51 per credit. Tuition, nonresident: full-time $24,054; part-time $1503.40 per credit. *Required fees:* $70.06 per credit. Tuition and fees vary according to course load, campus/location, program and reciprocity agreements. *Faculty research:* Microbial physiology, gene regulation, microbial ecology, plant-microbe interactions, symbiosis.

Immunology

Albany Medical College, Center for Immunology and Microbial Disease, Albany, NY 12208-3479. Offers MS, PhD. Part-time programs available. Terminal master's awarded for partial completion of doctoral program. *Degree requirements:* For master's, thesis; for doctorate, comprehensive exam, thesis/dissertation, oral qualifying exam, written preliminary exam, 1 published paper-peer review. *Entrance requirements:* For master's, GRE General Test, all transcripts, letters of recommendation; for doctorate, GRE General Test, letters of recommendation. . Additional exam requirements/ recommendations for international students: Required—TOEFL. *Faculty research:* Microbial and viral pathogenesis, cancer development and cell transformation, biochemical and genetic mechanisms responsible for human disease.

Albert Einstein College of Medicine, Graduate Division of Biomedical Sciences, Department of Microbiology and Immunology, Bronx, NY 10461. Offers PhD, MD/PhD. *Degree requirements:* For doctorate, thesis/dissertation. *Entrance requirements:* For doctorate, GRE General Test. Additional exam requirements/recommendations for international students: Required—TOEFL. *Faculty research:* Nature of histocompatibility antigens, lymphoid cell receptors, regulation of immune responses and mechanisms of resistance to infection.

American University of Beirut, Graduate Programs, Faculty of Medicine, Beirut, Lebanon. Offers anatomy, cell biology and human morphology (MS); biochemistry and medical genetics (MS); biomedical sciences (PhD); experimental pathology, immunology and microbiology (MS); medicine (MD); neuroscience (MS); pharmacology and toxicology (MS). Part-time programs available. *Faculty:* 232 full-time (58 women), 68 part-time/adjunct (7 women). *Students:* 346 full-time (135 women), 69 part-time (57 women). Average age 23. In 2011, 20 master's, 82 doctorates awarded. *Degree requirements:* For master's, one foreign language, comprehensive exam, thesis (for some programs). *Entrance requirements:* For master's, letter of recommendation; for doctorate, MCAT, bachelor's degree. Additional exam requirements/recommendations for international students: Required—TOEFL (minimum score 600 paper-based; 250 computer-based; 100 iBT), IELTS (minimum score 7.5). *Application deadline:* For fall admission, 4/30 for domestic and international students; for spring admission, 11/1 for domestic and international students. Application fee: $50. *Expenses:* Tuition: Full-time $12,780; part-time $710 per credit. Tuition and fees vary according to course load and program. *Financial support:* In 2011–12, 19 students received support. Career-related internships or fieldwork, institutionally sponsored loans, scholarships/grants, health care benefits, and unspecified assistantships available. Financial award application deadline: 2/2. *Faculty research:* Cancer research (targeted therapy, mechanisms of leukemogenesis, tumor cell extravasation and metastasis, cancer stem cells); stem cell research (regenerative medicine, drug discovery); genetic research (neurogenetics, hereditary cardiomyopathy, hemoglobinopathies, pharmacogenomics, proteomics); neuroscience research (pain, neurodegenerative disorder); metabolism (inflammation and metabolism, metabolic disorder, diabetes mellitus); vascular and renal biology, signal transduction. *Total annual research expenditures:* $2.3 million. *Unit head:* Dr. Mohamed Sayegh, Dean, 961-1350000 Ext. 4700, Fax: 961-1744464, E-mail: msayegh@aub.edu.lb. *Application contact:* Dr. Salim Kanaan, Director, Admissions Office, 961-1350000 Ext. 2594, Fax: 961-1750775, E-mail: sk00@aub.edu.lb. Web site: http://www.aub.edu.lb/fm/fm_home/Pages/index.aspx.

Baylor College of Medicine, Graduate School of Biomedical Sciences, Department of Immunology, Houston, TX 77030-3498. Offers PhD, MD/PhD. *Faculty:* 50 full-time (15 women). *Students:* 21 full-time (13 women); includes 5 minority (1 Black or African American, non-Hispanic/Latino; 3 Asian, non-Hispanic/Latino; 1 Hispanic/Latino), 14 international. Average age 27. 94 applicants, 6% accepted, 4 enrolled. In 2011, 12 doctorates awarded. *Degree requirements:* For doctorate, thesis/dissertation, public defense. *Entrance requirements:* For doctorate, GRE General Test, GRE Subject Test (strongly recommended), minimum GPA of 3.0. Additional exam requirements/ recommendations for international students: Required—TOEFL. *Application deadline:* For fall admission, 1/1 priority date for domestic students. Application fee: $0. Electronic applications accepted. *Financial support:* In 2011–12, 7 fellowships with full tuition reimbursements (averaging $29,000 per year), 14 research assistantships with full tuition reimbursements (averaging $29,000 per year) were awarded; teaching assistantships, career-related internships or fieldwork, Federal Work-Study, institutionally sponsored loans, health care benefits, and scholarships (to all students unless there are grant funds available to pay tuition) also available. Financial award applicants required to submit FAFSA. *Faculty research:* MHC expression, inflammation and allergy, germinal center biology, HIV pathogenesis, immune responses to gene therapy. *Unit head:* Dr. John Rodgers, Director, 713-798-3903, Fax: 713-798-3700, E-mail: jrodgers@bcm.edu. *Application contact:* Christal Atkins, Graduate Program Administrator, 713-798-3921, Fax: 713-798-3900, E-mail: catkins@bcm.edu. Web site: http://www.bcm.edu/immuno/.

Baylor College of Medicine, Graduate School of Biomedical Sciences, Interdepartmental Program in Cell and Molecular Biology, Houston, TX 77030-3498. Offers biochemistry (PhD); cell and molecular biology (PhD); genetics (PhD); human genetics (PhD); immunology (PhD); microbiology (PhD); virology (PhD); MD/PhD. *Faculty:* 112 full-time (30 women). *Students:* 66 full-time (42 women); includes 21 minority (5 Black or African American, non-Hispanic/Latino; 1 American Indian or Alaska Native, non-Hispanic/Latino; 7 Asian, non-Hispanic/Latino; 8 Hispanic/Latino), 14 international. Average age 27. 126 applicants, 25% accepted, 14 enrolled. In 2011, 7 degrees awarded. *Median time to degree:* Of those who began their doctoral program in fall 2003, 82% received their degree in 8 years or less. *Degree requirements:* For doctorate, thesis/dissertation, public defense. *Entrance requirements:* For doctorate, GRE General Test, GRE Subject Test (strongly recommended), minimum GPA of 3.0. Additional exam requirements/recommendations for international students: Required— TOEFL. *Application deadline:* For fall admission, 1/1 priority date for domestic students.

Applications are processed on a rolling basis. Application fee: $0. Electronic applications accepted. *Financial support:* In 2011–12, 66 students received support, including 30 fellowships with full tuition reimbursements available (averaging $29,000 per year), 36 research assistantships with full tuition reimbursements available (averaging $29,000 per year); teaching assistantships, Federal Work-Study, institutionally sponsored loans, health care benefits, and tuition waivers (full) also available. Financial award applicants required to submit FAFSA. *Faculty research:* Molecular and cellular biology; cancer, aging and stem cells; genomics and proteomics; microbiome, molecular microbiology; infectious disease, immunology and translational research. *Unit head:* Dr. Susan Marriott, Director, 713-798-6557. *Application contact:* Lourdes Fernandez, Graduate Program Administrator, 713-798-6557, Fax: 713-798-6325, E-mail: cmbprog@bcm.edu. Web site: http://bcm.edu/cmb/.

Boston University, School of Medicine, Division of Graduate Medical Sciences, Department of Microbiology, Boston, MA 02118. Offers immunology (PhD); MD/PhD. *Faculty:* 14 full-time (7 women), 2 part-time/adjunct (1 woman). *Students:* 7 full-time (5 women); includes 1 minority (Black or African American, non-Hispanic/Latino). Average age 29. 42 applicants, 17% accepted, 2 enrolled. Terminal master's awarded for partial completion of doctoral program. *Degree requirements:* For doctorate, comprehensive exam, thesis/dissertation. *Entrance requirements:* For doctorate, GRE General Test, GRE Subject Test. Additional exam requirements/recommendations for international students: Required—TOEFL. *Application deadline:* For fall admission, 1/15 priority date for domestic students; for spring admission, 10/15 priority date for domestic students. Application fee: $75. Electronic applications accepted. *Expenses: Tuition:* Full-time $40,848; part-time $1276 per credit hour. *Required fees:* $572; $286 per semester. *Financial support:* In 2011–12, fellowships (averaging $30,500 per year), research assistantships (averaging $30,500 per year) were awarded; Federal Work-Study, scholarships/grants, and traineeships also available. Financial award applicants required to submit FAFSA. *Faculty research:* Eukaryotic cell biology, tumor cell biology, nutrition and cancer, experimental tumor therapy, photobiology. *Unit head:* Dr. Ronald B. Corley, Chairman, 617-638-4284, Fax: 617-638-4286, E-mail: rbcorley@bu.edu. *Application contact:* Dr. Gregory Viglianti, Graduate Director, 617-638-7790, Fax: 617-638-4286, E-mail: gviglian@bu.edu.

Boston University, School of Medicine, Division of Graduate Medical Sciences, Immunology Training Program, Boston, MA 02215. Offers PhD, MD/PhD. *Faculty:* 27 full-time (8 women). *Students:* 14 full-time (9 women); includes 5 minority (1 Black or African American, non-Hispanic/Latino; 2 Asian, non-Hispanic/Latino; 1 Hispanic/Latino; 1 Two or more races, non-Hispanic/Latino), 1 international. Average age 27. 51 applicants, 22% accepted, 2 enrolled. In 2011, 1 doctorate awarded. *Degree requirements:* For doctorate, thesis/dissertation, qualifying exam. *Entrance requirements:* For doctorate, GRE General Test, GRE Subject Test. Additional exam requirements/recommendations for international students: Required—TOEFL. *Application deadline:* For fall admission, 1/15 priority date for domestic students; for spring admission, 10/15 priority date for domestic students. Application fee: $75. Electronic applications accepted. *Expenses: Tuition:* Full-time $40,848; part-time $1276 per credit hour. *Required fees:* $572; $286 per semester. *Financial support:* In 2011–12, fellowships (averaging $30,500 per year), 2 research assistantships (averaging $30,500 per year) were awarded; Federal Work-Study, scholarships/grants, and traineeships also available. Financial award applicants required to submit FAFSA. *Unit head:* Dr. David Sherr, Director, 617-638-6464, E-mail: itp@bu.edu. *Application contact:* Michelle Hall, Assistant Director of Admissions, 617-638-5121, Fax: 617-638-5740, E-mail: natashah@bu.edu. Web site: http://www.bumc.bu.edu/immunology/.

Brown University, Graduate School, Division of Biology and Medicine, Program in Molecular Biology, Cell Biology, and Biochemistry, Providence, RI 02912. Offers biochemistry (M Med Sc, Sc M, PhD), including biochemistry (Sc M, PhD), biology (Sc M, PhD), medical science (M Med Sc, PhD); biology (MA); cell biology (M Med Sc, Sc M, PhD), including biochemistry (Sc M, PhD), biology (Sc M, PhD), medical science (M Med Sc, PhD); developmental biology (M Med Sc, Sc M, PhD), including biochemistry (Sc M, PhD), biology (Sc M, PhD), medical science (M Med Sc, PhD); immunology (M Med Sc, Sc M, PhD), including biochemistry (Sc M, PhD), biology (Sc M, PhD), medical science (M Med Sc, PhD); molecular microbiology (M Med Sc, Sc M, PhD), including biochemistry (Sc M, PhD), biology (Sc M, PhD), medical science (M Med Sc, PhD); MD/PhD. Part-time programs available. Terminal master's awarded for partial completion of doctoral program. *Degree requirements:* For master's, thesis (for some programs); for doctorate, one foreign language, thesis/dissertation, preliminary exam. *Entrance requirements:* For master's and doctorate, GRE General Test, GRE Subject Test. Additional exam requirements/recommendations for international students: Required—TOEFL. Electronic applications accepted. *Faculty research:* Molecular genetics, gene regulation.

Brown University, Graduate School, Division of Biology and Medicine, Program in Pathology and Laboratory Medicine, Providence, RI 02912. Offers biology (PhD); cancer biology (PhD); immunology and infection (PhD); medical science (PhD); pathobiology (Sc M); toxicology and environmental pathology (PhD). Terminal master's awarded for partial completion of doctoral program. *Degree requirements:* For doctorate, thesis/dissertation, preliminary exam. *Entrance requirements:* For master's and doctorate, GRE General Test, GRE Subject Test. Additional exam requirements/recommendations for international students: Required—TOEFL. Electronic applications accepted. *Faculty research:* Environmental pathology, carcinogenesis, immunopathology, signal transduction, innate immunity.

California Institute of Technology, Division of Biology, Program in Immunology, Pasadena, CA 91125-0001. Offers PhD. *Degree requirements:* For doctorate, thesis/dissertation, qualifying exam. *Entrance requirements:* For doctorate, GRE General Test.

Case Western Reserve University, School of Medicine and School of Graduate Studies, Graduate Programs in Medicine, Programs in Molecular and Cellular Basis of Disease/Pathology, Immunology Training Program, Cleveland, OH 44106. Offers MS, PhD, MD/PhD. *Degree requirements:* For doctorate, comprehensive exam, thesis/dissertation. *Entrance requirements:* For doctorate, GRE General Test, GRE Subject Test. Additional exam requirements/recommendations for international students: Required—TOEFL (minimum score 550 paper-based; 213 computer-based). Electronic applications accepted. *Faculty research:* Immunology, immunopathology, immunochemistry, infectious diseases.

Colorado State University, College of Veterinary Medicine and Biomedical Sciences, Department of Microbiology, Immunology and Pathology, Fort Collins, CO 80523-0015. Offers microbiology (MS, PhD); pathology (PhD). *Faculty:* 43 full-time (18 women), 2 part-time/adjunct (0 women). *Students:* 46 full-time (32 women), 38 part-time (28 women); includes 8 minority (2 Asian, non-Hispanic/Latino; 6 Hispanic/Latino), 10 international. Average age 31. 107 applicants, 14% accepted, 14 enrolled. In 2011, 3 master's, 13 doctorates awarded. *Degree requirements:* For master's, thesis; for doctorate, comprehensive exam, thesis/dissertation. *Entrance requirements:* For master's, GRE General Test, minimum GPA of 3.0, BA/BS in biomedical field, reviewer evaluation forms, resume; for doctorate, GRE General Test, minimum GPA of 3.0, BA/BS in biomedical field, reviewer evaluation forms, resume, statement of interest. Additional exam requirements/recommendations for international students: Required—TOEFL (minimum score 550 paper-based). *Application deadline:* For fall admission, 1/1 priority date for domestic students; for spring admission, 10/1 priority date for domestic students. Applications are processed on a rolling basis. Application fee: $50. Electronic applications accepted. *Expenses:* Tuition, state resident: full-time $7992. Tuition, nonresident: full-time $19,592. *Required fees:* $1735; $58 per credit. *Financial support:* In 2011–12, 63 students received support, including 28 fellowships with tuition reimbursements available (averaging $29,347 per year), 30 research assistantships with tuition reimbursements available (averaging $20,869 per year), 5 teaching assistantships with tuition reimbursements available (averaging $14,580 per year); Federal Work-Study, scholarships/grants, traineeships, and unspecified assistantships also available. Financial award applicants required to submit FAFSA. *Faculty research:* Medical and veterinary bacteriology, immunology, microbial physiology, pathology, vector-borne disease. *Total annual research expenditures:* $30.4 million. *Unit head:* Dr. Edward A. Hoover, Head, 970-491-7587, Fax: 970-491-0603, E-mail: edward.hoover@colostate.edu. *Application contact:* Lisa McCann, Academic Programs Coordinator, 970-491-6118, Fax: 970-491-1815, E-mail: lisa.mccann@colostate.edu. Web site: http://www.cvmbs.colostate.edu/mip/.

Cornell University, Graduate School, Graduate Fields of Comparative Biomedical Sciences, Field of Immunology, Ithaca, NY 14853-0001. Offers cellular immunology (MS, PhD); immunochemistry (MS, PhD); immunogenetics (MS, PhD); immunopathology (MS, PhD); infection and immunity (MS, PhD). *Faculty:* 32 full-time (8 women). *Students:* 19 full-time (12 women); includes 3 minority (2 Black or African American, non-Hispanic/Latino; 1 Hispanic/Latino), 6 international. Average age 30. 20 applicants, 20% accepted, 3 enrolled. Terminal master's awarded for partial completion of doctoral program. *Degree requirements:* For master's, thesis; for doctorate, comprehensive exam, thesis/dissertation. *Entrance requirements:* For master's and doctorate, GRE General Test, 2 letters of recommendation. Additional exam requirements/recommendations for international students: Required—TOEFL (minimum score 550 paper-based; 213 computer-based; 77 iBT). *Application deadline:* For fall admission, 12/15 for domestic students. Application fee: $95. Electronic applications accepted. *Financial support:* In 2011–12, 3 fellowships with full tuition reimbursements, 17 research assistantships with full tuition reimbursements were awarded; teaching assistantships with full tuition reimbursements, institutionally sponsored loans, scholarships/grants, health care benefits, tuition waivers (full and partial), and unspecified assistantships also available. Financial award applicants required to submit FAFSA. *Faculty research:* Avian immunology, mucosal immunity, anti-parasite and anti-viral immunity, neutrophil function, reproductive immunology. *Unit head:* Director of Graduate Studies, 607-253-3276, Fax: 607-253-3756. *Application contact:* Graduate Field Assistant, 607-253-3276, Fax: 607-253-3756, E-mail: graduate_edcvm@cornell.edu. Web site: http://www.gradschool.cornell.edu/fields.php?id-52&a-2.

Creighton University, School of Medicine and Graduate School, Graduate Programs in Medicine, Department of Medical Microbiology and Immunology, Omaha, NE 68178-0001. Offers MS, PhD. Terminal master's awarded for partial completion of doctoral program. *Degree requirements:* For master's, comprehensive exam, thesis; for doctorate, thesis/dissertation, preliminary exams. *Entrance requirements:* For master's and doctorate, GRE General Test. Additional exam requirements/recommendations for international students: Required—TOEFL. *Expenses: Tuition:* Full-time $12,672; part-time $704 per credit hour. *Required fees:* $1410; $136 per semester. Tuition and fees vary according to campus/location and reciprocity agreements. *Faculty research:* Infectious diseases, molecular biology, genetics, antimicrobial agents and chemotherapy, virology.

Dalhousie University, Faculty of Medicine, Department of Microbiology and Immunology, Halifax, NS B3H 1X5, Canada. Offers M Sc, PhD. *Degree requirements:* For master's, thesis; for doctorate, comprehensive exam, thesis/dissertation. *Entrance requirements:* For master's, GRE General Test, honors B Sc; for doctorate, GRE General Test, honors B Sc in microbiology, M Sc in discipline or transfer after 1 year in master's program. Additional exam requirements/recommendations for international students: Required—1 of 5 approved tests: TOEFL, IELTS, CANTEST, CAEL, Michigan English Language Assessment Battery. Electronic applications accepted. *Faculty research:* Virology, molecular genetics, pathogenesis, bacteriology, immunology.

Dartmouth College, Graduate Program in Molecular and Cellular Biology, Department of Microbiology and Immunology, Program in Immunology, Hanover, NH 03755. Offers MD/PhD. *Faculty research:* Tumor immunotherapy, cell and molecular biology of connective tissue degradation in rheumatoid arthritis and cancer, immunology and immunotherapy of tumors of the central nervous system, transcriptional regulation of hematopoiesis and leukemia, bacterial pathogenesis.

Drexel University, College of Medicine, Biomedical Graduate Programs, Program in Microbiology and Immunology, Philadelphia, PA 19104-2875. Offers MS, PhD, MD/PhD. Terminal master's awarded for partial completion of doctoral program. *Degree requirements:* For master's, comprehensive exam, thesis; for doctorate, thesis/dissertation, qualifying exam. *Entrance requirements:* For master's, GRE General Test, minimum GPA of 2.75; for doctorate, GRE General Test, minimum GPA of 3.0. Additional exam requirements/recommendations for international students: Required—TOEFL. Electronic applications accepted. *Faculty research:* Immunology of malarial parasites, virology, bacteriology, molecular biology, parasitology.

Duke University, Graduate School, Department of Immunology, Durham, NC 27710. Offers PhD. *Faculty:* 48 full-time. *Students:* 38 full-time (20 women); includes 5 minority (3 Black or African American, non-Hispanic/Latino; 2 Asian, non-Hispanic/Latino), 17 international. 58 applicants, 26% accepted, 7 enrolled. In 2011, 10 doctorates awarded. *Degree requirements:* For doctorate, thesis/dissertation. *Entrance requirements:* For doctorate, GRE General Test, GRE Subject Test in biology or biochemistry, cell and molecular biology (strongly recommended). Additional exam requirements/recommendations for international students: Required—TOEFL (minimum score 550 paper-based; 213 computer-based; 83 iBT), IELTS (minimum score 7). *Application deadline:* For fall admission, 12/8 priority date for domestic students, 12/8 for international students. Application fee: $75. Electronic applications accepted. *Expenses: Tuition:* Full-time $40,720. *Required fees:* $3107. *Financial support:* Fellowships and research assistantships available. Financial award application deadline: 12/8. *Unit head:* Yuan Zhuang, Director of Graduate Studies, 909-613-3578, Fax: 919-684-8982, E-mail: immunologydept@mc.duke.edu. *Application contact:* Elizabeth Hutton, Director of Admissions, 919-684-3913, Fax: 919-684-2277, E-mail: grad-admissions@duke.edu. Web site: http://immunology.mc.duke.edu/.

East Carolina University, Brody School of Medicine, Department of Microbiology and Immunology, Greenville, NC 27858-4353. Offers MS, MD, PhD. *Degree requirements:* For doctorate, comprehensive exam, thesis/dissertation. *Entrance requirements:* For doctorate, GRE General Test. Additional exam requirements/recommendations for international students: Required—TOEFL. *Application deadline:* For fall admission, 4/15 priority date for domestic students. Applications are processed on a rolling basis. Application fee: $50. *Expenses:* Tuition, state resident: full-time $3557; part-time $444.63 per semester hour. Tuition, nonresident: full-time $14,351; part-time $1793.88 per semester hour. *Required fees:* $2016; $252 per semester hour. Part-time tuition and fees vary according to course load, campus/location and program. *Financial support:* Fellowships with tuition reimbursements available. Financial award application deadline: 6/1. *Faculty research:* Molecular virology, genetics of bacteria, yeast and somatic cells,

bacterial physiology and metabolism, bioterrorism. *Unit head:* Dr. Charles J. Smith, Chair, 252-744-2700, Fax: 252-744-3104, E-mail: smithcha@ecu.edu. *Application contact:* Dr. Richard A. Franklin, Director of Graduate Studies, 252-744-2705, Fax: 252-744-3104, E-mail: franklinr@ecu.edu. Web site: http://www.ecu.edu/cs-dhs/microbiology/index.cfm.

Emory University, Laney Graduate School, Division of Biological and Biomedical Sciences, Program in Immunology and Molecular Pathogenesis, Atlanta, GA 30322-1100. Offers PhD. *Faculty:* 49 full-time (6 women). *Students:* 75 full-time (42 women); includes 20 minority (2 Black or African American, non-Hispanic/Latino; 1 American Indian or Alaska Native, non-Hispanic/Latino; 12 Asian, non-Hispanic/Latino; 4 Hispanic/Latino; 1 Two or more races, non-Hispanic/Latino), 5 international. Average age 27. 231 applicants, 15% accepted, 15 enrolled. In 2011, 7 degrees awarded. *Median time to degree:* Of those who began their doctoral program in fall 2003, 100% received their degree in 8 years or less. *Degree requirements:* For doctorate, comprehensive exam, thesis/dissertation. *Entrance requirements:* For doctorate, GRE General Test, minimum GPA of 3.0 in science course work (recommended). Additional exam requirements/recommendations for international students: Required—TOEFL. *Application deadline:* For fall admission, 12/1 for domestic and international students. Application fee: $75. Electronic applications accepted. *Expenses: Tuition:* Full-time $34,800. *Required fees:* $1300. *Financial support:* In 2011–12, 30 students received support, including 30 fellowships with full tuition reimbursements available (averaging $26,500 per year); institutionally sponsored loans, scholarships/grants, health care benefits, and tuition waivers (full) also available. *Faculty research:* Transplantation immunology, autoimmunity, microbial pathogenesis. *Unit head:* Dr. Brian Evavold, Director, 404-727-3393, Fax: 404-727-3659, E-mail: evavold@microbio.emory.edu. *Application contact:* Kathy Smith, Director of Recruitment and Admissions, 404-727-2547, Fax: 404-727-3322, E-mail: kathy.smith@emory.edu. Web site: http://www.biomed.emory.edu/PROGRAM_SITES/IMP/.

Georgetown University, Graduate School of Arts and Sciences, Programs in Biomedical Sciences, Department of Microbiology and Immunology, Washington, DC 20057. Offers biohazardous threat agents and emerging infectious diseases (MS); general microbiology and immunology (MS); global infectious diseases (PhD); microbiology and immunology research (PhD); science policy and advocacy (MS). Part-time programs available. *Degree requirements:* For master's, 30 credit hours of coursework; for doctorate, comprehensive exam, thesis/dissertation. *Entrance requirements:* For master's, GRE General Test, 3 letters of reference, bachelor's degree in related field; for doctorate, GRE General Test, 3 letters of reference, MS/BS in related field. Additional exam requirements/recommendations for international students: Required—TOEFL (minimum score 505 paper-based; 213 computer-based). Electronic applications accepted. *Faculty research:* Pathogenesis and basic biology of the fungus Candida albicans, molecular biology of viral immunopathological mechanisms in Multiple Sclerosis.

The George Washington University, Columbian College of Arts and Sciences, Institute for Biomedical Sciences, Program in Microbiology and Immunology, Washington, DC 20037. Offers PhD. *Students:* 7 full-time (5 women), 15 part-time (10 women); includes 3 minority (1 American Indian or Alaska Native, non-Hispanic/Latino; 1 Asian, non-Hispanic/Latino; 1 Hispanic/Latino), 2 international. Average age 30. In 2011, 6 doctorates awarded. *Degree requirements:* For doctorate, thesis/dissertation. *Entrance requirements:* For doctorate, GRE General Test, minimum GPA of 3.0. Additional exam requirements/recommendations for international students: Required—TOEFL (minimum score 600 paper-based; 250 computer-based). *Application deadline:* For fall admission, 12/15 priority date for domestic students, 12/15 for international students. Applications are processed on a rolling basis. Application fee: $75. Electronic applications accepted. *Financial support:* In 2011–12, 10 students received support. Fellowships with tuition reimbursements available and tuition waivers available. *Unit head:* Dr. David Leitenberg, Director, 202-994-9475, Fax: 202-994-2913, E-mail: dleit@gwu.edu. *Application contact:* Information Contact, 202-994-3532, Fax: 202-994-2913, E-mail: mtmjxl@gwumc.edu. Web site: http://www.gwumc.edu/ibs/fields/microimmuno.html.

Harvard University, Harvard School of Public Health, Department of Immunology and Infectious Diseases, Boston, MA 02115-6096. Offers PhD, SD. Part-time programs available. *Faculty:* 34 full-time (12 women), 6 part-time/adjunct (0 women). *Students:* 8 applicants, 0% accepted. *Degree requirements:* For doctorate, thesis/dissertation, qualifying exam. *Entrance requirements:* For doctorate, GRE. Additional exam requirements/recommendations for international students: Required—TOEFL (minimum score 600 paper-based; 240 computer-based; 100 iBT); Recommended—IELTS (minimum score 7). *Application deadline:* For fall admission, 12/15 for domestic and international students. Application fee: $115. Electronic applications accepted. *Expenses: Tuition:* Full-time $36,304. *Required fees:* $1186. Full-time tuition and fees vary according to program. *Financial support:* Fellowships, research assistantships, Federal Work-Study, scholarships/grants, traineeships, and unspecified assistantships available. Financial award application deadline: 2/17; financial award applicants required to submit FAFSA. *Faculty research:* Infectious disease epidemiology and tropical public health, vector biology, ecology and control, virology. *Unit head:* Dr. Dyann F. Wirth, Chair, 617-432-2234, Fax: 617-739-8348, E-mail: rkenwort@hsph.harvard.edu. *Application contact:* Vincent W. James, Director of Admissions, 617-432-1031, Fax: 617-432-7080, E-mail: admissions@hsph.harvard.edu. Web site: http://www.hsph.harvard.edu/departments/immunology-and-infectious-diseases/.

Hood College, Graduate School, Program in Biomedical Science, Frederick, MD 21701-8575. Offers biomedical science (MS), including biotechnology/molecular biology, microbiology/immunology/virology, regulatory compliance; regulatory compliance (Certificate). Part-time and evening/weekend programs available. *Degree requirements:* For master's, comprehensive exam, thesis or alternative. *Entrance requirements:* For master's, bachelor's degree in biology; minimum GPA of 2.75; undergraduate course work in cell biology, chemistry, organic chemistry, and genetics. Additional exam requirements/recommendations for international students: Required—TOEFL (minimum score 575 paper-based; 231 computer-based; 89 iBT). Electronic applications accepted.

Illinois State University, Graduate School, College of Arts and Sciences, Department of Biological Sciences, Normal, IL 61790-2200. Offers animal behavior (MS); bacteriology (MS); biochemistry (MS); biological sciences (MS); biology (PhD); biophysics (MS); biotechnology (MS); botany (MS, PhD); cell biology (MS); conservation biology (MS); developmental biology (MS); ecology (MS, PhD); entomology (MS); evolutionary biology (MS); genetics (MS, PhD); immunology (MS); microbiology (MS, PhD); molecular biology (MS); molecular genetics (MS); neurobiology (MS); neuroscience (MS); parasitology (MS); physiology (MS, PhD); plant biology (MS); plant molecular biology (MS); plant sciences (MS); structural biology (MS); zoology (MS, PhD). Part-time programs available. *Degree requirements:* For master's, thesis or alternative; for doctorate, variable foreign language requirement, thesis/dissertation, 2 terms of residency. *Entrance requirements:* For master's, GRE General Test, minimum GPA of 2.6 in last 60 hours of course work; for doctorate, GRE General Test. *Faculty research:* Redoc balance and drug development in schistosoma mansoni, control of the growth of listeria monocytogenes at low temperature, regulation of cell expansion and microtubule function by SPRI, CRUI: physiology and fitness consequences of different life history phenotypes.

Indiana University–Purdue University Indianapolis, Indiana University School of Medicine, Department of Microbiology and Immunology, Indianapolis, IN 46202-2896. Offers MS, PhD, MD/MS, MD/PhD. *Faculty:* 20 full-time (2 women). *Students:* 23 full-time (15 women), 9 part-time (5 women); includes 9 minority (2 Black or African American, non-Hispanic/Latino; 4 Asian, non-Hispanic/Latino; 2 Hispanic/Latino; 1 Two or more races, non-Hispanic/Latino), 13 international. Average age 27. 3 applicants, 0% accepted, 0 enrolled. In 2011, 7 degrees awarded. Terminal master's awarded for partial completion of doctoral program. *Degree requirements:* For master's, thesis; for doctorate, thesis/dissertation. *Entrance requirements:* For master's and doctorate, GRE General Test, previous course work in calculus, cell biology, chemistry, genetics, physics, and biochemistry. *Application deadline:* For fall admission, 3/1 for domestic students. Applications are processed on a rolling basis. Application fee: $55 ($65 for international students). *Financial support:* In 2011–12, fellowships with full tuition reimbursements (averaging $8,313 per year), teaching assistantships with full tuition reimbursements (averaging $18,391 per year) were awarded; research assistantships with full tuition reimbursements, Federal Work-Study, institutionally sponsored loans, scholarships/grants, traineeships, and tuition waivers (partial) also available. Financial award application deadline: 2/1. *Faculty research:* Host-parasite interactions, molecular biology, cellular and molecular immunology and hematology, viral and bacterial pathogenesis, cancer research. *Total annual research expenditures:* $4.2 million. *Unit head:* Dr. Hal E. Broxmeyer, Chairman, 317-274-7672, Fax: 317-274-4090, E-mail: hbroxmey@iupui.edu. *Application contact:* 317-274-7671, Fax: 317-274-4090. Web site: http://micro.medicine.iu.edu/.

Iowa State University of Science and Technology, Program in Immunobiology, Ames, IA 50011. Offers MS, PhD. *Entrance requirements:* For master's and doctorate, GRE General Test, resume. Additional exam requirements/recommendations for international students: Required—TOEFL (minimum score 600 paper-based; 85 iBT), IELTS (minimum score 7). *Application deadline:* For fall admission, 1/15 priority date for domestic students, 1/15 for international students. Application fee: $40 ($90 for international students). Electronic applications accepted. *Faculty research:* Immunogenetics, cellular and molecular immunology, infectious disease, neuroimmunology. *Unit head:* Dr. Marian Kohut, Supervisory Committee Chair, 515-294-7252, Fax: 515-294-6790, E-mail: idgp@iastate.edu. *Application contact:* Katie Blair, Application Contact, 515-294-7252, Fax: 515-924-6790, E-mail: idgp@iastate.edu. Web site: http://www.immunobiology.iastate.edu.

The Johns Hopkins University, Bloomberg School of Public Health, W. Harry Feinstone Department of Molecular Microbiology and Immunology, Baltimore, MD 21218-2699. Offers MHS, Sc M, PhD. Terminal master's awarded for partial completion of doctoral program. *Degree requirements:* For master's, comprehensive exam, thesis (for some programs), essay, written exams; for doctorate, comprehensive exam, thesis/dissertation, 1 year full-time residency, oral and written exams. *Entrance requirements:* For master's, GRE General Test or MCAT, 3 letters of recommendation, curriculum vitae; for doctorate, GRE General Test, 3 letters of recommendation, transcripts, curriculum vitae. Additional exam requirements/recommendations for international students: Required—TOEFL (minimum score 600 paper-based; 250 computer-based). Electronic applications accepted. *Faculty research:* Immunology, virology, bacteriology, parasitology, vector biology, disease ecology, pathogenesis of infectious disease, immune responses to infectious agents, vector-borne and tropical diseases, biochemistry and molecular biology of infectious agents, population genetics of insect vectors, genetic regulation and immune responses in insect vectors, vaccine development, hormonal effects on pathogenesis and immune responses.

The Johns Hopkins University, School of Medicine, Graduate Programs in Medicine, Immunology Training Program, Baltimore, MD 21218-2699. Offers PhD. *Degree requirements:* For doctorate, comprehensive exam, thesis/dissertation, oral exam, final thesis seminar. *Entrance requirements:* For doctorate, GRE General Test, 2 letters of recommendation. Additional exam requirements/recommendations for international students: Required—TOEFL (minimum score 550 paper-based). Electronic applications accepted. *Faculty research:* HIV immunity, tumor immunity, major histocompatibility complex, transplantation, genetics of antibodies and T-cell receptors; immune response to infectious agents; antigen recognition; immune regulation; autoimmune diseases; immune cell signaling.

Long Island University–C. W. Post Campus, School of Health Professions and Nursing, Department of Biomedical Sciences, Brookville, NY 11548-1300. Offers cardiovascular perfusion (MS); clinical laboratory management (MS); medical biology (MS), including hematology, immunology, medical biology, medical chemistry, medical microbiology. Part-time and evening/weekend programs available. Postbaccalaureate distance learning degree programs offered. *Degree requirements:* For master's, thesis. *Entrance requirements:* For master's, minimum GPA of 2.75 in major. Electronic applications accepted.

Louisiana State University Health Sciences Center, School of Graduate Studies in New Orleans, Department of Microbiology, Immunology, and Parasitology, New Orleans, LA 70112-1393. Offers microbiology and immunology (MS, PhD); MD/PhD. Terminal master's awarded for partial completion of doctoral program. *Degree requirements:* For master's, comprehensive exam, thesis; for doctorate, comprehensive exam, thesis/dissertation, preliminary exam, qualifying exam. *Entrance requirements:* For master's and doctorate, GRE General Test. Additional exam requirements/recommendations for international students: Required—TOEFL. *Faculty research:* Microbial physiology, animal virology, vaccine development, AIDS drug studies, pathogenic mechanisms, molecular immunology.

Louisiana State University Health Sciences Center at Shreveport, Department of Microbiology and Immunology, Shreveport, LA 71130-3932. Offers MS, PhD, MD/PhD. Terminal master's awarded for partial completion of doctoral program. *Degree requirements:* For master's, thesis; for doctorate, thesis/dissertation. *Entrance requirements:* For master's and doctorate, GRE General Test. Additional exam requirements/recommendations for international students: Required—TOEFL. *Faculty research:* Infectious disease, pathogenesis, molecular virology and biology.

Loyola University Chicago, Graduate School, Department of Microbiology and Immunology, Maywood, IL 60153. Offers immunology (PhD); microbiology (MS); MD/PhD. *Faculty:* 15 full-time (4 women). *Students:* 31 full-time (19 women); includes 4 minority (2 Asian, non-Hispanic/Latino; 2 Hispanic/Latino), 4 international. Average age 27. 94 applicants, 16% accepted, 7 enrolled. In 2011, 2 master's, 7 doctorates awarded. Terminal master's awarded for partial completion of doctoral program. *Degree requirements:* For master's, thesis; for doctorate, comprehensive exam, thesis/dissertation. *Entrance requirements:* For master's and doctorate, GRE General Test. Additional exam requirements/recommendations for international students: Required—TOEFL. *Application deadline:* Applications are processed on a rolling basis. Application fee: $0. Electronic applications accepted. *Expenses: Tuition:* Full-time $15,660; part-time $870 per credit hour. *Required fees:* $125 per semester. Tuition and fees vary according to course load and program. *Financial support:* In 2011–12, 5 fellowships with tuition reimbursements (averaging $25,000 per year), 24 research assistantships with

tuition reimbursements (averaging $25,000 per year) were awarded; institutionally sponsored loans and scholarships/grants also available. Financial award application deadline: 2/15. *Faculty research:* Virology, microbial physiology and genetics, immune system development and regulation, signal transduction and host-pathogen interactions, biofilms. *Total annual research expenditures:* $2.2 million. *Unit head:* Dr. Katherine L. Knight, Chair, 708-216-3385, Fax: 708-216-9574, E-mail: kknight@lumc.edu. *Application contact:* Dr. Karen Visick, Graduate Program Director, 708-216-0869, Fax: 708-216-9574, E-mail: kvisick@lumc.edu.

Loyola University Chicago, Graduate School, Program in Infectious Disease and Immunology, Chicago, IL 60660. Offers MS. *Faculty:* 31 full-time (7 women). *Students:* 9 full-time (8 women); includes 1 minority (Asian, non-Hispanic/Latino). Average age 23. 24 applicants, 38% accepted, 6 enrolled. *Degree requirements:* For master's, thesis. *Entrance requirements:* For master's, GRE. Additional exam requirements/recommendations for international students: Required—TOEFL. *Application deadline:* Applications are processed on a rolling basis. *Expenses: Tuition:* Full-time $15,660; part-time $870 per credit hour. *Required fees:* $125 per semester. Tuition and fees vary according to course load and program. *Faculty research:* Immunological tolerance and memory, molecular analysis of virus assembly and entry, biofilm mediated interactions, molecular analysis of clinical isolates of C. difficile, immune system development and regulation. *Unit head:* Dr. Katherine L. Knight, Co-Director, 708-216-3385, Fax: 708-216-9574, E-mail: kknight@lumc.edu. *Application contact:* Dr. Paul O'Keefe, Director of Admissions Committee, 708-216-6667, Fax: 707-216-9574, E-mail: pokeefe@lumc.edu.

Massachusetts Institute of Technology, School of Science, Department of Biology, Cambridge, MA 02139. Offers biochemistry (PhD); biological oceanography (PhD); biology (PhD); biophysical chemistry and molecular structure (PhD); cell biology (PhD); computational and systems biology (PhD); developmental biology (PhD); genetics (PhD); immunology (PhD); microbiology (PhD); molecular biology (PhD); neurobiology (PhD). *Faculty:* 58 full-time (15 women). *Students:* 248 full-time (129 women); includes 69 minority (5 Black or African American, non-Hispanic/Latino; 1 American Indian or Alaska Native, non-Hispanic/Latino; 25 Asian, non-Hispanic/Latino; 31 Hispanic/Latino; 7 Two or more races, non-Hispanic/Latino), 36 international. Average age 26. 698 applicants, 15% accepted, 44 enrolled. In 2011, 38 doctorates awarded. *Degree requirements:* For doctorate, comprehensive exam, thesis/dissertation. *Entrance requirements:* For doctorate, GRE General Test. Additional exam requirements/recommendations for international students: Required—TOEFL (minimum score 577 paper-based; 233 computer-based), IELTS (minimum score 6.5). *Application deadline:* For fall admission, 12/1 for domestic and international students. Application fee: $75. Electronic applications accepted. *Expenses: Tuition:* Full-time $40,460; part-time $630 per credit hour. *Required fees:* $272. *Financial support:* In 2011–12, 214 students received support, including 129 fellowships (averaging $33,200 per year), 117 research assistantships (averaging $32,900 per year); teaching assistantships, Federal Work-Study, institutionally sponsored loans, scholarships/grants, traineeships, health care benefits, and unspecified assistantships also available. *Faculty research:* Cellular, developmental and molecular (plant and animal) biology; biochemistry, bioengineering, biophysics and structural biology; classical and molecular genetics; immunology and microbiology; cancer biology, molecular medicine, neurobiology and human disease; computational and systems biology. *Total annual research expenditures:* $53.6 million. *Unit head:* Prof. Tania A. Baker, Head, 617-253-4701, E-mail: mitbio@mit.edu. *Application contact:* Biology Education Office, 617-253-3717, Fax: 617-258-9329, E-mail: gradbio@mit.edu. Web site: https://biology.mit.edu/.

Mayo Graduate School, Graduate Programs in Biomedical Sciences, Program in Immunology, Rochester, MN 55905. Offers PhD. *Degree requirements:* For doctorate, oral defense of dissertation, qualifying oral and written exam. *Entrance requirements:* For doctorate, GRE, 1 year of chemistry, biology, calculus, and physics. Additional exam requirements/recommendations for international students: Required—TOEFL. Electronic applications accepted. *Faculty research:* Immunogenetics, autoimmunity, receptor signal transduction, T lymphocyte activation, transplantation.

McGill University, Faculty of Graduate and Postdoctoral Studies, Faculty of Medicine, Department of Microbiology and Immunology, Montréal, QC H3A 2T5, Canada. Offers M Sc, M Sc A, PhD.

McMaster University, Faculty of Health Sciences and School of Graduate Studies, Program in Medical Sciences, Immunity and Infection Area, Hamilton, ON L8S 4M2, Canada. Offers M Sc, PhD, MD/PhD. *Degree requirements:* For master's, thesis; for doctorate, comprehensive exam, thesis/dissertation. *Entrance requirements:* For master's, honors B Sc, B+ average in related field; for doctorate, M Sc, minimum B+ average, students with proven research experience and an A average may be admitted with a B Sc degree. Additional exam requirements/recommendations for international students: Required—TOEFL (minimum score 580 paper-based; 237 computer-based; 92 iBT).

Medical University of South Carolina, College of Graduate Studies, Department of Microbiology and Immunology, Charleston, SC 29425. Offers MS, PhD, DMD/PhD, MD/PhD. *Faculty:* 15 full-time (6 women), 30 part-time/adjunct (9 women). *Students:* 20 full-time (10 women), 1 part-time (0 women); includes 5 minority (2 Black or African American, non-Hispanic/Latino; 1 Asian, non-Hispanic/Latino; 2 Hispanic/Latino), 2 international. Average age 26. 8 applicants, 75% accepted, 4 enrolled. In 2011, 4 master's, 3 doctorates awarded. Terminal master's awarded for partial completion of doctoral program. *Degree requirements:* For master's, thesis; for doctorate, thesis/dissertation, oral and written exams. *Entrance requirements:* For master's, GRE General Test, MCAT, or DAT, minimum GPA of 3.0; for doctorate, GRE General Test, interview, minimum GPA of 3.0, research experience. Additional exam requirements/recommendations for international students: Required—TOEFL (minimum score 600 paper-based; 250 computer-based; 100 iBT). *Application deadline:* For fall admission, 1/15 priority date for domestic students, 1/15 for international students. Applications are processed on a rolling basis. Application fee: $0 ($95 for international students). Electronic applications accepted. *Financial support:* In 2011–12, 10 research assistantships with partial tuition reimbursements (averaging $23,000 per year) were awarded; Federal Work-Study and scholarships/grants also available. Support available to part-time students. Financial award application deadline: 3/10; financial award applicants required to submit FAFSA. *Faculty research:* Inmate and adaptive immunology, gene therapy/vector development, vaccinology, proteomics of biowarfare agents, bacterial and fungal pathogenesis. *Unit head:* Dr. Zihai Li, Chair, 843-792-7915, Fax: 843-792-6590. *Application contact:* Dr. Laura Kasman, Assistant Professor, 843-792-8117, Fax: 843-792-2464, E-mail: kasmanl@musc.edu. Web site: http://academicdepartments.musc.edu/immunology.

Meharry Medical College, School of Graduate Studies, Program in Biomedical Sciences, Microbiology and Immunology Emphasis, Nashville, TN 37208-9989. Offers PhD, MD/PhD. *Degree requirements:* For doctorate, comprehensive exam, thesis/dissertation. *Entrance requirements:* For doctorate, GRE General Test, GRE Subject Test, undergraduate degree in related science. *Faculty research:* Microbial and bacterial pathogenesis, viral transcription, immune response to viruses and parasites.

Memorial University of Newfoundland, Faculty of Medicine and School of Graduate Studies, Graduate Programs in Medicine, Division of Biomedical Sciences, St. John's, NL A1C 5S7, Canada. Offers cancer (M Sc, PhD); cardiovascular (M Sc, PhD); immunology (M Sc, PhD); neuroscience (M Sc, PhD). Part-time programs available. *Degree requirements:* For master's, thesis; for doctorate, comprehensive exam, thesis/dissertation, oral defense of thesis. *Entrance requirements:* For master's, MD or B Sc; for doctorate, MD or M Sc. Additional exam requirements/recommendations for international students: Required—TOEFL. *Faculty research:* Neuroscience, immunology, cardiovascular, and cancer.

Montana State University, College of Graduate Studies, College of Agriculture, Department of Immunology and Infectious Diseases, Bozeman, MT 59717. Offers MS, PhD. Part-time programs available. *Degree requirements:* For master's, comprehensive exam; for doctorate, comprehensive exam, thesis/dissertation. *Entrance requirements:* For master's and doctorate, GRE General Test. Additional exam requirements/recommendations for international students: Required—TOEFL (minimum score 550 paper-based; 213 computer-based). Electronic applications accepted. *Faculty research:* Immunology, mechanisms of infectious disease pathogenesis, mechanisms of host defense, lymphocyte development, host-pathogen interactions.

New York Medical College, Graduate School of Basic Medical Sciences, Microbiology and Immunology Department, Valhalla, NY 10595-1691. Offers MS, PhD, MD/PhD. Part-time and evening/weekend programs available. *Faculty:* 12 full-time (4 women). *Students:* 18 full-time (10 women), 4 part-time (2 women); includes 8 minority (1 Black or African American, non-Hispanic/Latino; 4 Asian, non-Hispanic/Latino; 3 Hispanic/Latino). Average age 27. 15 applicants, 93% accepted, 10 enrolled. In 2011, 4 master's, 4 doctorates awarded. Terminal master's awarded for partial completion of doctoral program. *Median time to degree:* Of those who began their doctoral program in fall 2003, 100% received their degree in 8 years or less. *Degree requirements:* For master's, thesis; for doctorate, comprehensive exam, thesis/dissertation. *Entrance requirements:* For master's and doctorate, GRE General Test. Additional exam requirements/recommendations for international students: Required—TOEFL. *Application deadline:* For fall admission, 7/1 priority date for domestic students, 5/1 for international students; for spring admission, 12/1 priority date for domestic students, 10/1 for international students. Applications are processed on a rolling basis. Application fee: $50 ($75 for international students). Electronic applications accepted. *Financial support:* In 2011–12, 5 fellowships with full tuition reimbursements (averaging $24,000 per year), 6 research assistantships with full tuition reimbursements (averaging $24,000 per year) were awarded; career-related internships or fieldwork, Federal Work-Study, institutionally sponsored loans, scholarships/grants, traineeships, tuition waivers (full), unspecified assistantships, and health benefits (for PhD candidates only) also available. Financial award applicants required to submit FAFSA. *Faculty research:* Tumor cells, cancer vaccines, the role of stem cells in cancer, bacterial genetics pathogenesis of infectious disease and function of influenza virus antigens, molecular virology, and the biochemistry and genetics of emerging pathogens. *Unit head:* Dr. Raj Tiwari, Director, 914-594-4870. *Application contact:* Valerie Romeo-Messana, Admission Coordinator, 914-594-4110, Fax: 914-594-4944, E-mail: v_romeomessana@nymc.edu.

New York University, Graduate School of Arts and Science, Department of Biology, New York, NY 10012-1019. Offers biology (PhD); biomedical journalism (MS); cancer and molecular biology (PhD); computational biology (PhD); computers in biological research (MS); developmental genetics (PhD); general biology (MS); immunology and microbiology (PhD); molecular genetics (PhD); neurobiology (PhD); oral biology (MS); plant biology (PhD); recombinant DNA technology (MS); MS/MBA. Part-time programs available. *Faculty:* 24 full-time (5 women). *Students:* 146 full-time (90 women), 54 part-time (36 women); includes 49 minority (1 Black or African American, non-Hispanic/Latino; 33 Asian, non-Hispanic/Latino; 12 Hispanic/Latino; 3 Two or more races, non-Hispanic/Latino), 89 international. Average age 27. 394 applicants, 62% accepted, 82 enrolled. In 2011, 68 master's, 6 doctorates awarded. Terminal master's awarded for partial completion of doctoral program. *Degree requirements:* For master's, thesis or alternative, qualifying paper; for doctorate, comprehensive exam, thesis/dissertation. *Entrance requirements:* For master's, GRE General Test; for doctorate, GRE General Test, GRE Subject Test. Additional exam requirements/recommendations for international students: Required—TOEFL. *Application deadline:* For fall admission, 12/1 priority date for domestic students, 12/1 for international students. Application fee: $90. *Financial support:* Fellowships with tuition reimbursements, research assistantships with tuition reimbursements, teaching assistantships with tuition reimbursements, career-related internships or fieldwork, Federal Work-Study, institutionally sponsored loans, scholarships/grants, health care benefits, and unspecified assistantships available. Financial award application deadline: 12/1; financial award applicants required to submit FAFSA. *Faculty research:* Genomics, molecular and cell biology, development and molecular genetics, molecular evolution of plants and animals. *Unit head:* Stephen Small, Chair, 212-998-8200, Fax: 212-995-4015, E-mail: biology@nyu.edu. *Application contact:* Justin Blau, Director of Graduate Studies, 212-998-8200, Fax: 212-995-4015, E-mail: biology@nyu.edu. Web site: http://biology.as.nyu.edu/.

New York University, School of Medicine, New York, NY 10012-1019. Offers biomedical sciences (PhD), including biomedical imaging, cellular and molecular biology, computational biology, developmental genetics, medical and molecular parasitology, microbiology, molecular oncobiology and immunology, neuroscience and physiology, pathobiology, pharmacology, structural biology; clinical investigation (MS); medicine (MD); MD/MA; MD/MPA; MD/MS; MD/PhD. *Accreditation:* LCME/AMA (one or more programs are accredited). *Degree requirements:* For master's, comprehensive exam, thesis; for doctorate, comprehensive exam (for some programs), thesis/dissertation (for some programs). *Entrance requirements:* For doctorate, MCAT (for MD). Additional exam requirements/recommendations for international students: Required—TOEFL. *Expenses:* Contact institution. *Faculty research:* AIDS, cancer, neuroscience, molecular biology, neuroscience, cell biology and molecular genetics, structural biology, microbial pathogenesis and host defense, pharmacology, molecular oncology and immunology.

New York University, School of Medicine and Graduate School of Arts and Science, Sackler Institute of Graduate Biomedical Sciences, Program in Immunology and Inflammation, New York, NY 10012-1019. Offers PhD. *Students:* 4 full-time (3 women); includes 1 minority (Hispanic/Latino), 1 international. *Unit head:* Dr. Joel D. Oppenheim, Senior Associate Dean for Graduate Studies, 212-263-8001, Fax: 212-263-7600. *Application contact:* Lisabeth Greene, Program Coordinator, 212-263-5648, Fax: 212-263-7600, E-mail: sackler-info@med.nyu.edu. Web site: http://pathology.med.nyu.edu/education/graduate-programs/immunology-and-inflammation.

New York University, School of Medicine and Graduate School of Arts and Science, Sackler Institute of Graduate Biomedical Sciences, Program in Molecular Oncology and Tumor Immunology, New York, NY 10012-1019. Offers immunology (PhD); molecular oncology (PhD); MD/PhD. *Faculty:* 52 full-time (16 women). *Students:* 29 full-time (17 women); includes 8 minority (3 Black or African American, non-Hispanic/Latino; 2 Asian, non-Hispanic/Latino; 3 Hispanic/Latino), 9 international. Average age 28. In 2011, 2 doctorates awarded. *Degree requirements:* For doctorate, one foreign language, thesis/dissertation, qualifying exam. *Entrance requirements:* For doctorate, GRE General Test, GRE Subject Test. Additional exam requirements/recommendations for international students: Required—TOEFL. *Application deadline:* For fall admission, 2/1 for domestic students. Applications are processed on a rolling basis. Application fee: $85. Electronic

applications accepted. *Financial support:* Tuition waivers (full) available. *Faculty research:* Stem cells, immunology, genome instability, DNA damage checkpoints. *Unit head:* Dr. Joel D. Oppenheim, Senior Associate Dean for Graduate Studies, 212-263-8001, Fax: 212-263-7600. *Application contact:* Dr. David Levy, Graduate Adviser, 212-263-8192, Fax: 212-263-8211, E-mail: david.levy@med.nyu.edu.

North Carolina State University, Graduate School, College of Agriculture and Life Sciences and College of Veterinary Medicine, Program in Immunology, Raleigh, NC 27695. Offers MS, PhD. *Degree requirements:* For master's, thesis; for doctorate, thesis/dissertation. *Entrance requirements:* For master's and doctorate, GRE General Test. Additional exam requirements/recommendations for international students: Required—TOEFL (minimum score 550 paper-based; 213 computer-based). Electronic applications accepted. *Faculty research:* Immunogenetics, immunopathology, immunotoxicology, immunoparasitology, molecular and infectious disease immunology.

Northwestern University, Northwestern University Feinberg School of Medicine and Interdepartmental Programs, Integrated Graduate Programs in the Life Sciences, Chicago, IL 60611. Offers cancer biology (PhD); cell biology (PhD); developmental biology (PhD); evolutionary biology (PhD); immunology and microbial pathogenesis (PhD); molecular biology and genetics (PhD); neurobiology (PhD); pharmacology and toxicology (PhD); structural biology and biochemistry (PhD). *Degree requirements:* For doctorate, comprehensive exam, thesis/dissertation, written and oral qualifying exams. *Entrance requirements:* For doctorate, GRE General Test. Additional exam requirements/recommendations for international students: Required—TOEFL (minimum score 600 paper-based; 250 computer-based). Electronic applications accepted.

The Ohio State University, College of Medicine, School of Biomedical Science, Integrated Biomedical Science Graduate Program, Columbus, OH 43210. Offers immunology (PhD); medical genetics (PhD); molecular virology (PhD); pharmacology (PhD). *Degree requirements:* For doctorate, thesis/dissertation. *Entrance requirements:* For doctorate, GRE, GRE Subject Test in biochemistry, cell and molecular biology (recommended for some). Additional exam requirements/recommendations for international students: Required—TOEFL (minimum score 600 paper-based; 250 computer-based). Electronic applications accepted. *Expenses:* Tuition, state resident: full-time $11,400. Tuition, nonresident: full-time $28,125. Tuition and fees vary according to course load, degree level, campus/location and program.

Oregon Health & Science University, School of Medicine, Graduate Programs in Medicine, Program in Molecular and Cellular Biosciences, Department of Molecular Microbiology and Immunology, Portland, OR 97239-3098. Offers PhD. *Faculty:* 10 full-time (3 women). *Students:* 21 full-time (11 women); includes 6 minority (5 Hispanic/Latino; 1 Two or more races, non-Hispanic/Latino), 3 international. Average age 29. In 2011, 6 doctorates awarded. Terminal master's awarded for partial completion of doctoral program. *Degree requirements:* For doctorate, comprehensive exam, thesis/dissertation, qualifying exam. *Entrance requirements:* For doctorate, GRE General Test (minimum scores: 153 Verbal/148 Quantitative/4.5 Analytical) or MCAT (for some programs). Additional exam requirements/recommendations for international students: Required—TOEFL. Electronic applications accepted. *Financial support:* Health care benefits and full tuition and stipends available. *Faculty research:* Molecular biology of bacterial and viral pathogens, cellular and humoral immunology, molecular biology of microbes. *Unit head:* Dr. Eric Barklis, Program Director, 503-494-7768, E-mail: mmi@ohsu.edu. *Application contact:* Elaine Offield, Program Coordinator, 503-494-5824, E-mail: offielde@ohsu.edu. Web site: http://www.ohsu.edu/microbiology.

Penn State Hershey Medical Center, College of Medicine, Graduate School Programs in the Biomedical Sciences, Graduate Program in Biomedical Sciences, Hershey, PA 17033. Offers biochemistry and molecular genetics (PhD); biomedical sciences (MS, PhD); translational therapeutics (MS, PhD); virology and immunology (MS, PhD); MD/PhD; PhD/MBA. *Students:* 12 full-time (6 women); includes 2 minority (1 Black or African American, non-Hispanic/Latino; 1 Asian, non-Hispanic/Latino), 1 international. 211 applicants, 16% accepted, 12 enrolled. Terminal master's awarded for partial completion of doctoral program. *Degree requirements:* For master's, thesis (for some programs); for doctorate, comprehensive exam, thesis/dissertation, candidacy exam. *Entrance requirements:* For doctorate, GRE General Test. Additional exam requirements/recommendations for international students: Required—TOEFL (minimum score 550 paper-based; 213 computer-based; 80 iBT). *Application deadline:* For fall admission, 1/1 for domestic students, 2/1 for international students. Applications are processed on a rolling basis. Application fee: $65. Electronic applications accepted. *Financial support:* In 2011–12, research assistantships (averaging $23,028 per year) were awarded; fellowships, scholarships/grants, health care benefits, and unspecified assistantships also available. Financial award applicants required to submit FAFSA. *Unit head:* Dr. Ralph L. Keil, Chair, 717-531-8595, Fax: 717-531-0388, E-mail: rlk9@psu.edu. *Application contact:* Karen Shields, Administrative Support Coordinator, 717-531-1045, Fax: 717-531-0388, E-mail: kpb2@psu.edu. Web site: http://med.psu.edu/web/biomedical-sciences/home.

Penn State Hershey Medical Center, College of Medicine, Graduate School Programs in the Biomedical Sciences, Graduate Program in Microbiology and Immunology, Hershey, PA 17033. Offers genetics (PhD); immunology (MS, PhD); microbiology (MS); microbiology/virology (PhD); molecular biology (PhD); MD/PhD. *Students:* 18 full-time (9 women), 6 international. 59 applicants, 5% accepted, 3 enrolled. In 2011, 1 master's, 3 doctorates awarded. Terminal master's awarded for partial completion of doctoral program. *Degree requirements:* For master's, thesis or alternative; for doctorate, comprehensive exam, thesis/dissertation, oral exam. *Entrance requirements:* For doctorate, GRE General Test, minimum GPA of 3.0. Additional exam requirements/recommendations for international students: Required—TOEFL. *Application deadline:* For fall admission, 1/31 priority date for domestic students, 2/1 for international students. Applications are processed on a rolling basis. Application fee: $65. Electronic applications accepted. *Financial support:* In 2011–12, research assistantships with full tuition reimbursements (averaging $23,028 per year) were awarded; fellowships with full tuition reimbursements, scholarships/grants, health care benefits, and unspecified assistantships also available. Financial award applicants required to submit FAFSA. *Faculty research:* Virus replication and assembly, oncogenesis, interactions of viruses with host cells and animal model systems. *Unit head:* Dr. Aron Luckacher, Chair, 717-531-7659, Fax: 717-531-6522, E-mail: micro-grad-hmc@psu.edu. *Application contact:* Billie Burns, Secretary, 717-531-7659, Fax: 717-531-6522, E-mail: micro-grad-hmc@psu.edu. Web site: http://www.pennstatehershey.org/web/microbiology/programs.

Penn State University Park, Graduate School, Intercollege Graduate Programs, Intercollege Graduate Program in Immunology and Infectious Diseases, State College, University Park, PA 16802-1503. Offers MS, PhD. *Unit head:* Dr. Regina Vasilatos-Younken, Senior Associate Dean, 814-865-2516, Fax: 814-863-4627, E-mail: rxv@psu.edu. *Application contact:* Cynthia E. Nicosia, Director, Graduate Enrollment Services, 814-865-1795, Fax: 814-865-4627, E-mail: cey1@psu.edu. Web site: http://www.huck.psu.edu/education/immunology-and-infectious-diseases.

Purdue University, College of Pharmacy and Pharmacal Sciences and Graduate School, Graduate Programs in Pharmacy and Pharmacal Sciences, Department of Medicinal Chemistry and Molecular Pharmacology, West Lafayette, IN 47907. Offers biophysical and computational chemistry (PhD); cancer research (PhD); immunology and infectious disease (PhD); medicinal biochemistry and molecular biology (PhD); medicinal chemistry and chemical biology (PhD); molecular pharmacology (PhD); neuropharmacology, neurodegeneration, and neurotoxicity (PhD); systems biology and functional genomics (PhD). *Faculty:* 22 full-time (2 women), 4 part-time/adjunct (1 woman). *Students:* 49 full-time (18 women); includes 3 minority (1 Asian, non-Hispanic/Latino; 2 Hispanic/Latino), 26 international. Average age 27. 250 applicants, 12% accepted, 9 enrolled. In 2011, 10 doctorates awarded. *Degree requirements:* For doctorate, thesis/dissertation. *Entrance requirements:* For doctorate, GRE General Test; GRE Subject Test in biology, biochemistry, and chemistry (recommended), minimum undergraduate GPA of 3.0. Additional exam requirements/recommendations for international students: Required—TOEFL (minimum score 550 paper-based; 77 iBT); Recommended—TWE. *Application deadline:* For fall admission, 2/1 for domestic and international students. Applications are processed on a rolling basis. Application fee: $60 ($75 for international students). Electronic applications accepted. *Financial support:* Fellowships, research assistantships, teaching assistantships, and traineeships available. Support available to part-time students. Financial award applicants required to submit FAFSA. *Faculty research:* Drug design and development, cancer research, drug synthesis and analysis, chemical pharmacology, environmental toxicology. *Unit head:* Dr. Richard F. Borch, Head, 765-494-1403, E-mail: borch@purdue.edu. *Application contact:* Janine C. Mott, Graduate Contact, 765-494-1269, E-mail: jmott@purdue.edu.

Purdue University, School of Veterinary Medicine and Graduate School, Graduate Programs in Veterinary Medicine, Department of Comparative Pathobiology, West Lafayette, IN 47907-2027. Offers comparative epidemiology and public health (MS); comparative epidemiology and public heath (PhD); comparative microbiology and immunology (MS, PhD); comparative pathobiology (MS, PhD); interdisciplinary studies (PhD), including microbial pathogenesis, molecular signaling and cancer biology, molecular virology; lab animal medicine (MS); veterinary anatomic pathology (MS); veterinary clinical pathology (MS). Terminal master's awarded for partial completion of doctoral program. *Degree requirements:* For master's, thesis (for some programs); for doctorate, thesis/dissertation. *Entrance requirements:* For master's and doctorate, GRE General Test. Additional exam requirements/recommendations for international students: Required—TOEFL (minimum score 575 paper-based; 232 computer-based), IELTS (minimum score 6.5), TWE (minimum score 4). Electronic applications accepted.

Queen's University at Kingston, School of Graduate Studies and Research, Faculty of Health Sciences, Department of Microbiology and Immunology, Kingston, ON K7L 3N6, Canada. Offers M Sc, PhD. Part-time programs available. *Degree requirements:* For master's, thesis; for doctorate, comprehensive exam, thesis/dissertation. *Entrance requirements:* For master's and doctorate, minimum B+ average. Additional exam requirements/recommendations for international students: Required—TOEFL (minimum score 600 paper-based; 250 computer-based). Electronic applications accepted. *Faculty research:* Bacteriology, virology, immunology, education in microbiology and immunology, microbial pathogenesis.

Rosalind Franklin University of Medicine and Science, School of Graduate and Postdoctoral Studies - Interdisciplinary Graduate Program in Biomedical Sciences, Department of Microbiology and Immunology, North Chicago, IL 60064-3095. Offers MS, PhD, MD/PhD. Terminal master's awarded for partial completion of doctoral program. *Degree requirements:* For master's, comprehensive exam, thesis; for doctorate, comprehensive exam, thesis/dissertation. *Entrance requirements:* For master's and doctorate, GRE General Test. Additional exam requirements/recommendations for international students: Required—TOEFL, TWE. *Faculty research:* Molecular biology, parasitology, virology.

Rush University, Graduate College, Division of Immunology and Microbiology, Program in Immunology/Microbiology, Chicago, IL 60612-3832. Offers immunology (MS, PhD); virology (MS, PhD); MD/PhD. Part-time programs available. Terminal master's awarded for partial completion of doctoral program. *Degree requirements:* For master's, thesis; for doctorate, thesis/dissertation, comprehensive preliminary exam. *Entrance requirements:* For master's, GRE General Test; for doctorate, GRE General Test, interview, minimum GPA of 3.0. Additional exam requirements/recommendations for international students: Required—TOEFL. Electronic applications accepted. *Faculty research:* Human genetics, autoimmunity, tumor biology, complement, HIV immunopathology genesis.

Rutgers, The State University of New Jersey, New Brunswick, Graduate School-New Brunswick, Programs in the Molecular Biosciences, Program in Microbiology and Molecular Genetics, Piscataway, NJ 08854-8097. Offers applied microbiology (MS, PhD); clinical microbiology (MS, PhD); computational molecular biology (PhD); immunology (MS, PhD); microbial biochemistry (MS, PhD); molecular genetics (MS, PhD); virology (MS, PhD). MS, PhD offered jointly with University of Medicine and Dentistry of New Jersey. Part-time programs available. Terminal master's awarded for partial completion of doctoral program. *Degree requirements:* For master's, comprehensive exam, thesis or alternative; for doctorate, comprehensive exam, thesis/dissertation, written qualifying exam. *Entrance requirements:* For master's, GRE General Test, minimum GPA of 3.0; for doctorate, GRE General Test, GRE Subject Test (recommended), minimum GPA of 3.0. Additional exam requirements/recommendations for international students: Required—TOEFL. Electronic applications accepted. *Faculty research:* Molecular genetics and microbial physiology; virology and pathogenic microbiology; applied, environmental and industrial microbiology; computers in molecular biology.

Saint Louis University, Graduate Education and School of Medicine, Graduate Program in Biomedical Sciences, Department of Molecular Microbiology and Immunology, St. Louis, MO 63103-2097. Offers PhD. *Degree requirements:* For doctorate, comprehensive exam, thesis/dissertation, qualifying exams. *Entrance requirements:* For doctorate, GRE General Test (GRE Subject Test optional), letters of recommendation, resume, interview. Additional exam requirements/recommendations for international students: Required—TOEFL (minimum score 525 paper-based; 194 computer-based). Electronic applications accepted. *Faculty research:* Pathogenesis of hepatitis C virus, herperviruses, pox viruses, rheumatoid arthritis, antiviral drugs and vaccines in biodefense, cancer gene therapy, virology and immunology.

Stanford University, School of Medicine, Graduate Programs in Medicine, Department of Microbiology and Immunology, Stanford, CA 94305-9991. Offers PhD. *Degree requirements:* For doctorate, comprehensive exam, thesis/dissertation, 2 quarters teaching assistantship. *Entrance requirements:* For doctorate, GRE General Test, GRE Subject Test (biology or biochemistry). Additional exam requirements/recommendations for international students: Required—TOEFL. Electronic applications accepted. *Expenses: Tuition:* Full-time $40,050; part-time $890 per credit. *Faculty research:* Molecular pathogenesis of bacteria viruses and parasites, immune system function, autoimmunity, molecular biology.

Stanford University, School of Medicine, Graduate Programs in Medicine, Program in Immunology, Stanford, CA 94305-9991. Offers PhD. *Degree requirements:* For doctorate, thesis/dissertation, qualifying examination. *Entrance requirements:* For doctorate, GRE General Test, GRE Subject Test. Additional exam requirements/recommendations for international students: Required—TOEFL. Electronic applications accepted. *Expenses: Tuition:* Full-time $40,050; part-time $890 per credit.

State University of New York Upstate Medical University, College of Graduate Studies, Program in Microbiology and Immunology, Syracuse, NY 13210-2334. Offers microbiology (MS); microbiology and immunology (PhD); MD/PhD. Terminal master's awarded for partial completion of doctoral program. *Degree requirements:* For master's, thesis; for doctorate, comprehensive exam, thesis/dissertation. *Entrance requirements:* For master's, GRE General Test, interview; for doctorate, GRE General Test, telephone interview. Additional exam requirements/recommendations for international students: Required—TOEFL. Electronic applications accepted. *Faculty research:* Cancer, disorders of the nervous system, infectious diseases, diabetes/metabolic disorders/cardiovascular diseases.

Stony Brook University, State University of New York, Graduate School, College of Arts and Sciences, Department of Biochemistry and Cell Biology, Molecular and Cellular Biology Program, Stony Brook, NY 11794. Offers biochemistry and molecular biology (PhD); biological sciences (MA); cellular and developmental biology (PhD); immunology and pathology (PhD); molecular and cellular biology (PhD). *Degree requirements:* For doctorate, comprehensive exam, thesis/dissertation, teaching experience. *Entrance requirements:* For doctorate, GRE General Test, GRE Subject Test. Additional exam requirements/recommendations for international students: Required—TOEFL.

Temple University, Health Sciences Center, School of Medicine and Graduate School, Graduate Programs in Medicine, Department of Microbiology and Immunology, Philadelphia, PA 19140. Offers MS, PhD, MD/MS, MD/PhD. *Faculty:* 12 full-time (4 women), 13 part-time/adjunct (1 woman). *Students:* 36 full-time (26 women); includes 8 minority (7 Black or African American, non-Hispanic/Latino; 1 Asian, non-Hispanic/Latino), 13 international. Average age 28. 27 applicants, 30% accepted, 4 enrolled. In 2011, 2 master's, 9 doctorates awarded. *Degree requirements:* For master's, thesis; for doctorate, thesis/dissertation, research seminars. *Entrance requirements:* For master's and doctorate, GRE General Test, GRE Subject Test, minimum GPA of 3.0. Additional exam requirements/recommendations for international students: Required—TOEFL (minimum score 600 paper-based; 250 computer-based). *Application deadline:* For fall admission, 7/1 priority date for domestic students, 12/15 for international students; for spring admission, 11/1 priority date for domestic students, 8/1 for international students. Applications are processed on a rolling basis. Application fee: $60. Electronic applications accepted. *Expenses:* Tuition, state resident: full-time $12,366; part-time $687 per credit hour. Tuition, nonresident: full-time $17,298; part-time $961 per credit hour. *Required fees:* $590; $213 per year. *Financial support:* In 2011–12, 32 students received support, including 15 fellowships with full and partial tuition reimbursements available (averaging $23,000 per year), 17 research assistantships with full tuition reimbursements available (averaging $23,000 per year); Federal Work-Study, institutionally sponsored loans, scholarships/grants, health care benefits, and unspecified assistantships also available. Financial award application deadline: 3/15; financial award applicants required to submit FAFSA. *Faculty research:* Molecular and cellular immunology, molecular and biochemical microbiology, molecular genetics. *Total annual research expenditures:* $2 million. *Unit head:* Dr. Doina Ganea, Chair, 215-707-3207, Fax: 215-707-7788, E-mail: doina.ganea@temple.edu. *Application contact:* Dottie Bathe, Administrative Coordinator, 215-707-6747, Fax: 215-707-7788, E-mail: dbathe@temple.edu. Web site: http://www.temple.edu/medicine/departments_centers/basic_science/microbiology.htm.

Texas A&M Health Science Center, College of Medicine, Department of Microbial and Molecular Pathogenesis, College Station, TX 77840. Offers immunology (PhD); microbiology (PhD); molecular biology (PhD); virology (PhD). *Degree requirements:* For doctorate, thesis/dissertation. *Entrance requirements:* For doctorate, GRE General Test, minimum GPA of 3.0. *Faculty research:* Molecular pathogenesis, microbial therapeutics.

Thomas Jefferson University, Jefferson College of Graduate Studies, PhD Program in Immunology and Microbial Pathogenesis, Philadelphia, PA 19107. Offers PhD. *Faculty:* 33 full-time (5 women), 2 part-time/adjunct (0 women). *Students:* 22 full-time (10 women); includes 3 minority (1 Black or African American, non-Hispanic/Latino; 1 Asian, non-Hispanic/Latino; 1 Hispanic/Latino), 2 international. 58 applicants, 12% accepted, 3 enrolled. In 2011, 4 doctorates awarded. *Degree requirements:* For doctorate, comprehensive exam, thesis/dissertation. *Entrance requirements:* For doctorate, GRE General Test, minimum GPA of 3.2. Additional exam requirements/recommendations for international students: Required—TOEFL (minimum score 250 computer-based; 100 iBT) or IELTS. *Application deadline:* For fall admission, 1/5 priority date for domestic students, 1/5 for international students. Applications are processed on a rolling basis. Application fee: $50. Electronic applications accepted. *Financial support:* In 2011–12, 22 students received support, including 22 fellowships with full tuition reimbursements available (averaging $54,758 per year); Federal Work-Study, institutionally sponsored loans, scholarships/grants, traineeships, and stipends also available. Support available to part-time students. Financial award application deadline: 5/1; financial award applicants required to submit FAFSA. *Total annual research expenditures:* $14.6 million. *Unit head:* Dr. Kishore Alugupalli, Program Director, 215-503-4550, Fax: 215-923-4153, E-mail: kishore.alugupalli@jefferson.edu. *Application contact:* Marc E. Stearns, Director of Admissions, 215-503-0155, Fax: 215-503-9920, E-mail: jcgs-info@jefferson.edu. Web site: http://www.jefferson.edu/jcgs/phd/imp/.

Tufts University, Sackler School of Graduate Biomedical Sciences, Immunology Program, Medford, MA 02155. Offers PhD. *Faculty:* 24 full-time (8 women). *Students:* 24 full-time (11 women); includes 8 minority (2 Black or African American, non-Hispanic/Latino; 2 Asian, non-Hispanic/Latino; 3 Hispanic/Latino; 1 Two or more races, non-Hispanic/Latino), 1 international. Average age 28. 109 applicants, 9% accepted, 4 enrolled. In 2011, 10 doctorates awarded. Terminal master's awarded for partial completion of doctoral program. *Degree requirements:* For doctorate, thesis/dissertation. *Entrance requirements:* For doctorate, GRE General Test, 3 letters of reference. Additional exam requirements/recommendations for international students: Required—TOEFL (minimum score 600 paper-based; 250 computer-based; 100 iBT). *Application deadline:* For fall admission, 12/15 for domestic and international students. Application fee: $70. Electronic applications accepted. *Expenses: Tuition:* Full-time $41,208; part-time $1030 per credit hour. Full-time tuition and fees vary according to degree level, program and student level. Part-time tuition and fees vary according to course load. *Financial support:* In 2011–12, 29 students received support, including 24 research assistantships with full tuition reimbursements available (averaging $30,000 per year). *Faculty research:* Genetic regulation of the ontogeny and activation of lymphocytes, mechanisms of antigen-receptor gene rearrangement, biology and molecular biology of negative selection (tolerance) of B and T cells, activation signal pathways, gene expression and the biochemistry of apoptosis. *Unit head:* Dr. Henry H. Wortis, Director, 617-636-6836, Fax: 617-636-2990. *Application contact:* Kellie JoMelchin, Associate Director of Admissions, 617-636-6767, Fax: 617-636-0375, E-mail: sackler-school@tufts.edu. Web site: http://sackler.tufts.edu/Academics/Degree-Programs/PhD-Programs/Immunology.

Tulane University, School of Medicine and School of Liberal Arts, Graduate Programs in Biomedical Sciences, Department of Microbiology and Immunology, New Orleans, LA 70118-5669. Offers MS, PhD, MD/PhD. MS and PhD offered through the Graduate School. *Degree requirements:* For master's, thesis; for doctorate, 2 foreign languages, thesis/dissertation. *Entrance requirements:* For master's, GRE General Test, minimum B average in undergraduate course work; for doctorate, GRE General Test, GRE Subject Test. Additional exam requirements/recommendations for international students: Required—TOEFL. Electronic applications accepted. *Faculty research:* Vaccine development, viral pathogenesis, molecular virology, bacterial pathogenesis, fungal pathogenesis.

Uniformed Services University of the Health Sciences, School of Medicine, Graduate Programs in the Biomedical Sciences and Public Health, Graduate Program in Emerging Infectious Diseases, Bethesda, MD 20814-4799. Offers PhD. *Faculty:* 35 full-time (5 women), 17 part-time/adjunct (6 women). *Students:* 37 full-time (24 women); includes 5 minority (1 Black or African American, non-Hispanic/Latino; 3 Asian, non-Hispanic/Latino; 1 Hispanic/Latino), 3 international. Average age 26. 43 applicants, 44% accepted, 11 enrolled. In 2011, 7 doctorates awarded. *Degree requirements:* For doctorate, comprehensive exam, thesis/dissertation, qualifying exam. *Entrance requirements:* For doctorate, GRE General Test. Additional exam requirements/recommendations for international students: Required—TOEFL. *Application deadline:* For fall admission, 1/1 priority date for domestic students, 1/1 for international students. Applications are processed on a rolling basis. Application fee: $0. Electronic applications accepted. *Financial support:* In 2011–12, fellowships with full tuition reimbursements (averaging $27,000 per year) were awarded; scholarships/grants, health care benefits, and tuition waivers (full) also available. *Unit head:* Dr. Christopher Broder, Director, 301-295-3401, E-mail: cbroder@usuhs.mil. *Application contact:* Patricia Sinclair, Program Administrative Specialist, 301-295-3400, Fax: 301-295-6772, E-mail: psinclair@usuhs.mil. Web site: http://www.usuhs.mil/eid.

See Display on page 332 and Close-Up on page 353.

Universidad Central del Caribe, School of Medicine, Program in Biomedical Sciences, Bayamón, PR 00960-6032. Offers anatomy and cell biology (MA, MS); biochemistry (MS); biomedical sciences (MA); cellular and molecular biology (PhD); microbiology and immunology (MA, MS); pharmacology (MS); physiology (MS).

Université de Montréal, Faculty of Medicine, Department of Microbiology and Immunology, Montréal, QC H3C 3J7, Canada. Offers M Sc, PhD. Programs offered jointly with Faculty of Veterinary Medicine and Université du Québec, Institut Armand-Frappier. Terminal master's awarded for partial completion of doctoral program. *Degree requirements:* For master's, thesis; for doctorate, thesis/dissertation, general exam. *Entrance requirements:* For master's and doctorate, proficiency in French, knowledge of English. Electronic applications accepted.

Université de Montréal, Faculty of Veterinary Medicine, Program in Virology and Immunology, Montréal, QC H3C 3J7, Canada. Offers PhD. Program offered jointly with Université du Québec, Institut Armand-Frappier. *Degree requirements:* For doctorate, thesis/dissertation, general exam. *Entrance requirements:* For doctorate, proficiency in French, knowledge of English. Electronic applications accepted.

Université de Sherbrooke, Faculty of Medicine and Health Sciences, Graduate Programs in Medicine, Program in Immunology, Sherbrooke, QC J1H 5N4, Canada. Offers M Sc, PhD. Electronic applications accepted. *Faculty research:* Cytokine receptor signal transduction, lipid mediators and inflammation, TGFbeta convertases.

Université du Québec, Institut National de la Recherche Scientifique, Graduate Programs, Research Center - INRS - Institut Armand-Frappier - Human Health, Québec, QC G1K 9A9, Canada. Offers applied microbiology (M Sc); biology (PhD); experimental health sciences (M Sc); virology and immunology (M Sc, PhD). Programs given in French. Part-time programs available. *Faculty:* 41. *Students:* 158 full-time (93 women), 11 part-time (5 women), 52 international. Average age 30. In 2011, 17 master's, 9 doctorates awarded. *Degree requirements:* For master's, thesis optional; for doctorate, thesis/dissertation. *Entrance requirements:* For master's and doctorate, appropriate bachelor's degree, proficiency in French. *Application deadline:* For fall admission, 3/30 for domestic and international students; for winter admission, 11/1 for domestic and international students; for spring admission, 3/1 for domestic and international students. Application fee: $45 Canadian dollars. *Financial support:* In 2011–12, 128 students received support, including fellowships (averaging $16,500 per year); research assistantships also available. *Faculty research:* Immunity, infection and cancer; toxicology and environmental biotechnology; molecular pharmacochemistry. *Unit head:* Charles Dozois, Director, 450-687-5010, Fax: 450-686-5566, E-mail: charles.dozois@iaf.inrs.ca. *Application contact:* Yvonne Boisvert, Registrar, 418-654-3861, Fax: 418-654-3858, E-mail: registrariat@adm.inrs.ca. Web site: http://www.iaf.inrs.ca.

Université Laval, Faculty of Medicine, Graduate Programs in Medicine, Programs in Microbiology-Immunology, Québec, QC G1K 7P4, Canada. Offers M Sc, PhD. Terminal master's awarded for partial completion of doctoral program. *Degree requirements:* For master's, thesis; for doctorate, comprehensive exam, thesis/dissertation. *Entrance requirements:* For master's and doctorate, knowledge of French, comprehension of written English. Electronic applications accepted.

University at Albany, State University of New York, School of Public Health, Department of Biomedical Sciences, Program in Immunobiology and Immunochemistry, Albany, NY 12222-0001. Offers MS, PhD. *Degree requirements:* For master's, thesis; for doctorate, thesis/dissertation. *Entrance requirements:* For master's and doctorate, GRE General Test, GRE Subject Test.

University at Buffalo, the State University of New York, Graduate School, Graduate Programs in Cancer Research and Biomedical Sciences at Roswell Park Cancer Institute, Department of Immunology at Roswell Park Cancer Institute, Buffalo, NY 14260. Offers PhD. *Degree requirements:* For doctorate, comprehensive exam, thesis/dissertation. *Entrance requirements:* For doctorate, GRE. Additional exam requirements/recommendations for international students: Required—TOEFL (minimum score 600 paper-based; 250 computer-based; 100 iBT) or IELTS. Electronic applications accepted. *Faculty research:* Immunochemistry, immunobiology, molecular immunology, hybridoma studies, recombinant DNA studies.

University at Buffalo, the State University of New York, Graduate School, School of Medicine and Biomedical Sciences, Graduate Programs in Medicine and Biomedical Sciences, Department of Microbiology and Immunology, Buffalo, NY 14260. Offers MA, PhD. *Faculty:* 14 full-time (3 women). *Students:* 25 full-time (17 women), 9 international. Average age 28. 26 applicants, 77% accepted, 9 enrolled. In 2011, 1 master's, 4 doctorates awarded. *Degree requirements:* For master's, comprehensive exam; for doctorate, thesis/dissertation, departmental qualifying exam. *Entrance requirements:* For master's and doctorate, GRE General Test, 3 letters of recommendation. Additional exam requirements/recommendations for international students: Required—TOEFL (minimum score 100 iBT). *Application deadline:* For fall admission, 2/1 priority date for domestic students, 2/1 for international students. Applications are processed on a rolling basis. Application fee: $50. Electronic applications accepted. *Financial support:* In 2011–12, 2 students received support, including 3 fellowships with tuition reimbursements available (averaging $21,600 per year), 19 research assistantships with tuition reimbursements available (averaging $24,000 per year); Federal Work-Study, institutionally sponsored loans, traineeships, health care benefits, and unspecified assistantships also available. Financial award application deadline: 2/1; financial award applicants required to submit FAFSA. *Faculty research:* Bacteriology, immunology, parasitology, virology, mycology. *Total annual research expenditures:* $2.6 million. *Unit head:* Dr. John Hay, Interim Chairman, 716-829-2907, Fax: 716-829-2158. *Application*

contact: Dr. Nejat Egilmez, Director of Graduate Studies, 716-829-2176, Fax: 716-829-2158. Web site: http://smbs.buffalo.edu/microb/.

University of Alberta, Faculty of Medicine and Dentistry and Faculty of Graduate Studies and Research, Graduate Programs in Medicine, Department of Medical Microbiology and Immunology, Edmonton, AB T6G 2E1, Canada. Offers M Sc, PhD. Terminal master's awarded for partial completion of doctoral program. *Degree requirements:* For master's, thesis; for doctorate, thesis/dissertation. *Entrance requirements:* For master's and doctorate, minimum GPA of 3.3. Additional exam requirements/recommendations for international students: Required—TOEFL (minimum score 600 paper-based; 232 computer-based; 96 iBT). *Faculty research:* Cellular and reproductive immunology, microbial pathogenesis, mechanisms of antibiotic resistance, molecular biology of mammalian viruses, antiviral chemotherapy.

The University of Arizona, College of Medicine, Department of Immunobiology, Tucson, AZ 85721. Offers MS, PhD. *Faculty:* 8 full-time (2 women). *Students:* 8 full-time (all women); includes 1 minority (Two or more races, non-Hispanic/Latino), 4 international. Average age 27. 91 applicants, 66% accepted. In 2011, 2 master's, 1 doctorate awarded. *Degree requirements:* For master's, thesis; for doctorate, thesis/dissertation. *Entrance requirements:* For master's and doctorate, GRE General Test, minimum GPA of 3.0. *Application deadline:* For fall admission, 3/1 priority date for domestic students; for spring admission, 9/1 for domestic students. Application fee: $75. *Expenses:* Tuition, state resident: full-time $10,840. Tuition, nonresident: full-time $25,802. *Financial support:* In 2011–12, 5 research assistantships with full tuition reimbursements (averaging $25,000 per year) were awarded; fellowships with full tuition reimbursements, teaching assistantships with full tuition reimbursements, institutionally sponsored loans, and tuition waivers (full) also available. Financial award application deadline: 4/30. *Faculty research:* Environmental and pathogenic microbiology, molecular biology. *Total annual research expenditures:* $7.8 million. *Unit head:* Dr. Janko Nikolich-Zugich, Head, 520-626-6065, Fax: 520-626-2100, E-mail: nikolich@email.arizona.edu. *Application contact:* Dr. Richard J. Ablin, Graduate Program Chairman, 520-626-7755, E-mail: ablinrj@email.arizona.edu. Web site: http://immunobiology.arizona.edu/.

University of Arkansas for Medical Sciences, Graduate School, Graduate Programs in Biomedical Sciences, Department of Microbiology and Immunology, Little Rock, AR 72205-7199. Offers MS, PhD, MD/PhD. *Degree requirements:* For master's, thesis; for doctorate, thesis/dissertation. *Entrance requirements:* For master's and doctorate, GRE General Test. Additional exam requirements/recommendations for international students: Required—TOEFL. *Faculty research:* Tumor immunology and immunotherapy, microbial pathogenesis and genetics, allergy, immune response in infectious diseases.

The University of British Columbia, Faculty of Science, Department of Microbiology and Immunology, Vancouver, BC V6T 1Z1, Canada. Offers M Sc, PhD. *Degree requirements:* For master's, thesis; for doctorate, comprehensive exam, thesis/dissertation. *Entrance requirements:* For master's and doctorate, GRE General Test. Additional exam requirements/recommendations for international students: Required—TOEFL (minimum score 590 paper-based; 243 computer-based). Electronic applications accepted. *Faculty research:* Bacterial genetics, metabolism, pathogenic bacteriology, virology.

University of Calgary, Faculty of Medicine and Faculty of Graduate Studies, Department of Medical Science, Calgary, AB T2N 1N4, Canada. Offers cancer biology (M Sc, PhD); immunology (M Sc, PhD); joint injury and arthritis research (M Sc, PhD); medical education (M Sc, PhD); medical science (M Sc, PhD); mountain medicine and high altitude physiology (M Sc). *Degree requirements:* For master's, thesis; for doctorate, thesis/dissertation, candidacy exam. *Entrance requirements:* For master's, minimum undergraduate GPA of 3.2; for doctorate, minimum graduate GPA of 3.2. Additional exam requirements/recommendations for international students: Required—TOEFL (minimum score 600 paper-based; 250 computer-based). Electronic applications accepted. *Faculty research:* Cancer biology, immunology, joint injury and arthritis, medical education, population genomics.

University of California, Berkeley, Graduate Division, School of Public Health, Group in Infectious Diseases and Immunity, Berkeley, CA 94720-1500. Offers PhD. *Entrance requirements:* For doctorate, GRE General Test, minimum GPA of 3.0, 3 letters of recommendation.

University of California, Davis, Graduate Studies, Graduate Group in Immunology, Davis, CA 95616. Offers MS, PhD. Terminal master's awarded for partial completion of doctoral program. *Degree requirements:* For master's, comprehensive exam (for some programs), thesis (for some programs); for doctorate, thesis/dissertation. *Entrance requirements:* For master's and doctorate, GRE General Test. Additional exam requirements/recommendations for international students: Required—TOEFL (minimum score 550 paper-based; 213 computer-based). Electronic applications accepted. *Faculty research:* Immune regulation in autoimmunity, immunopathology, immunotoxicology, tumor immunology, avian immunology.

University of California, Los Angeles, David Geffen School of Medicine and Graduate Division, Graduate Programs in Medicine, Department of Microbiology, Immunology and Molecular Genetics, Los Angeles, CA 90095. Offers MS, PhD. *Faculty:* 31 full-time (6 women). *Students:* 55 full-time (25 women); includes 21 minority (1 Black or African American, non-Hispanic/Latino; 8 Asian, non-Hispanic/Latino; 11 Hispanic/Latino; 1 Two or more races, non-Hispanic/Latino), 4 international. Average age 28. 1 applicant, 100% accepted, 1 enrolled. In 2011, 3 master's, 8 doctorates awarded. *Degree requirements:* For doctorate, thesis/dissertation, oral and written qualifying exams. *Entrance requirements:* For doctorate, GRE General Test, GRE Subject Test. Additional exam requirements/recommendations for international students: Required—TOEFL. Application fee: $70 ($90 for international students). Electronic applications accepted. *Financial support:* In 2011–12, 50 fellowships, 50 research assistantships, 20 teaching assistantships were awarded; Federal Work-Study, institutionally sponsored loans, and tuition waivers (full and partial) also available. Financial award application deadline: 3/1. *Unit head:* Dr. Jeff F. Miller, Chair, 310-206-7926, Fax: 310-267-2774, E-mail: jfmiller@ucla.edu. *Application contact:* Bridget Wolfgang, Graduate Student Affairs, 310-825-8482, Fax: 310-206-5231, E-mail: bridgetw@microbio.ucla.edu. Web site: http://www.mimg.ucla.edu/.

University of California, Los Angeles, Graduate Division, College of Letters and Science and David Geffen School of Medicine, UCLA ACCESS to Programs in the Molecular, Cellular and Integrative Life Sciences, Los Angeles, CA 90095. Offers biochemistry and molecular biology (PhD); biological chemistry (PhD); cellular and molecular pathology (PhD); human genetics (PhD); microbiology, immunology, and molecular genetics (PhD); molecular biology (PhD); molecular toxicology (PhD); molecular, cellular and integrative physiology (PhD); neurobiology (PhD); oral biology (PhD); physiology (PhD). *Students:* 44 full-time (30 women); includes 18 minority (11 Asian, non-Hispanic/Latino; 6 Hispanic/Latino; 1 Two or more races, non-Hispanic/Latino), 9 international. Average age 25. 495 applicants, 18% accepted, 41 enrolled. *Degree requirements:* For doctorate, thesis/dissertation, oral and written qualifying exams. *Entrance requirements:* For doctorate, GRE General Test, minimum undergraduate GPA of 3.0. Additional exam requirements/recommendations for

international students: Required—TOEFL. *Application deadline:* For fall admission, 12/15 for domestic and international students. Application fee: $70 ($90 for international students). Electronic applications accepted. *Financial support:* In 2011–12, 51 fellowships with full and partial tuition reimbursements, 9 research assistantships with full and partial tuition reimbursements were awarded; teaching assistantships with full and partial tuition reimbursements, Federal Work-Study, institutionally sponsored loans, scholarships/grants, health care benefits, tuition waivers (full and partial), and unspecified assistantships also available. Financial award application deadline: 3/1; financial award applicants required to submit FAFSA. *Faculty research:* Molecular, cellular, and developmental biology; immunology; microbiology; integrative biology. *Unit head:* Jody Spillane, Project Coordinator, 310-206-1845, E-mail: jspillane@mednet.ucla.edu. *Application contact:* UCLA ACCESS Admissions, 310-206-1845, E-mail: uclaaccess@mednet.ucla.edu. Web site: https://www.uclaaccess.ucla.edu/.

University of California, San Diego, Office of Graduate Studies, Division of Biological Sciences, Program in Immunology, Virology, and Cancer Biology, La Jolla, CA 92093. Offers PhD. Offered in association with the Salk Institute. *Degree requirements:* For doctorate, thesis/dissertation, qualifying exam. Electronic applications accepted.

University of California, San Francisco, Graduate Division, Department of Microbiology and Immunology, San Francisco, CA 94143. Offers PhD. *Degree requirements:* For doctorate, thesis/dissertation. *Entrance requirements:* For doctorate, GRE General Test.

University of Chicago, Division of Biological Sciences, Biomedical Sciences Cluster: Cancer Biology, Immunology, Molecular Metabolism and Nutrition, Pathology, and Microbiology, Committee on Immunology, Chicago, IL 60637-1513. Offers PhD. *Degree requirements:* For doctorate, thesis/dissertation, ethics class, 2 teaching assistantships. *Entrance requirements:* For doctorate, GRE General Test. Additional exam requirements/recommendations for international students: Required—TOEFL (minimum score 600 paper-based; 250 computer-based; 104 iBT), IELTS (minimum score 7). Electronic applications accepted. *Faculty research:* Molecular immunology, transplantation, autoimmunology, neuroimmunology, tumor immunology.

University of Cincinnati, Graduate School, College of Medicine, Graduate Programs in Biomedical Sciences, Department of Pediatrics, Cincinnati, OH 45221. Offers immunobiology (PhD); molecular and developmental biology (PhD). *Degree requirements:* For doctorate, thesis/dissertation, qualifying exam. *Entrance requirements:* For doctorate, GRE General Test, minimum GPA of 3.0. Additional exam requirements/recommendations for international students: Required—TOEFL (minimum score 600 paper-based; 250 computer-based; 100 iBT). Electronic applications accepted. *Faculty research:* Pulmonary biology, molecular cardiovascular, developmental biology, cancer biology, genetics.

University of Cincinnati, Graduate School, College of Medicine, Graduate Programs in Biomedical Sciences, Immunobiology Training Program, Cincinnati, OH 45221. Offers MS, PhD. *Degree requirements:* For master's, seminar, thesis with oral defense; for doctorate, seminar, dissertation with oral defense, written and oral candidacy exams.

University of Colorado Denver, School of Medicine, Integrated Department of Immunology, Denver, CO 80206. Offers PhD. *Students:* 46 full-time (28 women); includes 5 minority (2 American Indian or Alaska Native, non-Hispanic/Latino; 1 Asian, non-Hispanic/Latino; 2 Hispanic/Latino), 1 international. Average age 28. 32 applicants, 3% accepted, 1 enrolled. In 2011, 8 doctorates awarded. *Degree requirements:* For doctorate, thesis/dissertation, 30 credit hours of formal course work, three laboratory rotations, oral comprehensive examination, 30 credit hours of dissertation research, final defense of the dissertation. *Entrance requirements:* For doctorate, GRE, letters of recommendation, statement of purpose, interview. Additional exam requirements/recommendations for international students: Required—TOEFL (minimum score 550 paper-based; 213 computer-based; 89 iBT). *Application deadline:* For fall admission, 12/1 for domestic students, 11/1 for international students. Application fee: $50 ($75 for international students). Electronic applications accepted. *Expenses:* Contact institution. *Financial support:* Fellowships with full tuition reimbursements, health care benefits, tuition waivers (full), and stipend available. Financial award application deadline: 3/15; financial award applicants required to submit FAFSA. *Faculty research:* Gene regulation, immune signaling, apoptosis, stem cells, vaccines. *Total annual research expenditures:* $5.1 million. *Unit head:* Dr. John C. Cambier, Professor/Chairman, 303-398-1325, E-mail: john.cambier@ucdenver.edu. *Application contact:* Mellodee Phillips, Graduate Program Coordinator, 303-398-1306, Fax: 303-270-2325, E-mail: mellodee.phillips@ucdenver.edu. Web site: http://www.ucdenver.edu/academics/colleges/medicalschool/departments/immunology/immued/immugradprog/Pages/GradHome.aspx.

University of Colorado Denver, School of Medicine, Program in Microbiology, Denver, CO 80217-3364. Offers microbiology (PhD); microbiology and immunology (PhD). *Students:* 17 full-time (7 women); includes 2 minority (1 Asian, non-Hispanic/Latino; 1 Hispanic/Latino). Average age 27. 49 applicants, 6% accepted, 3 enrolled. In 2011, 6 doctorates awarded. *Degree requirements:* For doctorate, comprehensive exam, thesis/dissertation, 3 lab rotations; 30 credit hours coursework. *Entrance requirements:* For doctorate, GRE, three letters of reference, two copies of official transcripts, minimum GPA of 3.0. Additional exam requirements/recommendations for international students: Required—TOEFL (minimum score 550 paper-based; 213 computer-based). *Application deadline:* For fall admission, 12/1 for domestic students, 11/1 for international students. Application fee: $65. Electronic applications accepted. *Expenses:* Contact institution. *Financial support:* In 2011–12, 3 students received support, including 3 fellowships with full tuition reimbursements available (averaging $25,000 per year); health care benefits, tuition waivers (full), and stipend also available. Financial award application deadline: 3/15; financial award applicants required to submit FAFSA. *Faculty research:* Molecular mechanisms of picornavirus replication, mechanisms of papovavirus assembly, human immune response in multiple sclerosis. *Total annual research expenditures:* $5.9 million. *Unit head:* Dr. Randall K. Holmes, Chair, 303-724-4223, E-mail: randall.holmes@ucdenver.edu. *Application contact:* Liz Pruett, Microbiology Graduate Program Administrator, 303-724-3350, E-mail: liz.pruett@ucdenver.edu. Web site: http://www.uchsc.edu/sm/microbio.

University of Connecticut Health Center, Graduate School, Programs in Biomedical Sciences, Graduate Program in Immunology, Farmington, CT 06030. Offers PhD, DMD/PhD, MD/PhD. *Degree requirements:* For doctorate, comprehensive exam, thesis/dissertation. *Entrance requirements:* For doctorate, GRE General Test. Additional exam requirements/recommendations for international students: Required—TOEFL (minimum score 600 paper-based; 250 computer-based). Electronic applications accepted. *Faculty research:* Developmental immunology, T-cell immunity, lymphoid cell development, tolerance and tumor immunity, leukocyte chemotaxis.

See Display on next page and Close-Up on page 355.

University of Florida, College of Medicine, Department of Pathology, Immunology and Laboratory Medicine, Gainesville, FL 32611. Offers immunology and molecular pathology (PhD). *Degree requirements:* For doctorate, thesis/dissertation. *Entrance requirements:* For doctorate, GRE General Test, minimum GPA of 3.0. Additional exam requirements/recommendations for international students: Required—TOEFL.

Electronic applications accepted. *Faculty research:* Molecular immunology, autoimmunity and transplantation, tumor biology, oncogenic viruses, human immunodeficiency viruses.

University of Florida, College of Medicine and Graduate School, Interdisciplinary Program in Biomedical Sciences, Concentration in Immunology and Microbiology, Gainesville, FL 32611. Offers PhD. *Degree requirements:* For doctorate, thesis/dissertation. *Entrance requirements:* For doctorate, GRE General Test, minimum GPA of 3.0. Additional exam requirements/recommendations for international students: Required—TOEFL. Electronic applications accepted.

University of Guelph, Ontario Veterinary College and Graduate Studies, Graduate Programs in Veterinary Sciences, Department of Pathobiology, Guelph, ON N1G 2W1, Canada. Offers anatomic pathology (DV Sc, Diploma); clinical pathology (Diploma); comparative pathology (M Sc, PhD); immunology (M Sc, PhD); laboratory animal science (DV Sc); pathology (M Sc, PhD, Diploma); veterinary infectious diseases (M Sc, PhD); zoo animal/wildlife medicine (DV Sc). *Degree requirements:* For master's, thesis; for doctorate, thesis/dissertation. *Entrance requirements:* For master's, DVM with B average or an honours degree in biological sciences; for doctorate, DVM or MSC degree, minimum B+ average. Additional exam requirements/recommendations for international students: Required—TOEFL (minimum score 550 paper-based; 213 computer-based). *Faculty research:* Pathogenesis; diseases of animals, wildlife, fish, and laboratory animals; parasitology; immunology; veterinary infectious diseases; laboratory animal science.

University of Illinois at Chicago, College of Medicine and Graduate College, Graduate Programs in Medicine, Department of Microbiology and Immunology, Chicago, IL 60607-7128. Offers PhD, MD/PhD. *Degree requirements:* For doctorate, thesis/dissertation. *Entrance requirements:* For doctorate, GRE General Test, minimum GPA of 2.75. Additional exam requirements/recommendations for international students: Required—TOEFL.

The University of Iowa, Graduate College, Program in Immunology, Iowa City, IA 52242-1316. Offers PhD, MD/PhD. *Degree requirements:* For doctorate, comprehensive exam, thesis/dissertation. *Entrance requirements:* For doctorate, GRE General Test, minimum GPA of 3.0. Additional exam requirements/recommendations for international students: Required—TOEFL (minimum score 600 paper-based; 250 computer-based; 100 iBT). Electronic applications accepted.

The University of Iowa, Roy J. and Lucille A. Carver College of Medicine and Graduate College, Graduate Programs in Medicine, Department of Microbiology, Iowa City, IA 52242-1316. Offers general microbiology and microbial physiology (MS, PhD); immunology (MS, PhD); microbial genetics (MS, PhD); pathogenic bacteriology (MS, PhD); virology (MS, PhD). *Faculty:* 23 full-time (5 women), 12 part-time/adjunct (4 women). *Students:* 37 full-time (24 women); includes 3 minority (2 American Indian or Alaska Native, non-Hispanic/Latino; 1 Hispanic/Latino), 4 international. Average age 25. 56 applicants, 16% accepted, 4 enrolled. In 2011, 1 master's, 6 doctorates awarded. *Degree requirements:* For master's, thesis; for doctorate, comprehensive exam, thesis/dissertation. *Entrance requirements:* For master's and doctorate, GRE General Test. Additional exam requirements/recommendations for international students: Required—TOEFL (minimum score 600 paper-based; 250 computer-based). *Application deadline:* For fall admission, 1/1 for domestic and international students. Application fee: $60 ($85 for international students). Electronic applications accepted. *Financial support:* In 2011–12, 4 fellowships with full tuition reimbursements (averaging $25,500 per year), 33 research assistantships with full tuition reimbursements (averaging $25,500 per year) were awarded; institutionally sponsored loans, scholarships/grants, traineeships, and health care benefits also available. *Faculty research:* Gene regulation, processing and transport of HIV, retroviral pathogenesis, biodegradation, biofilm. *Total annual research*

expenditures: $12.6 million. *Unit head:* Dr. Patrick M. Schlievert, Head, 319-335-7810, E-mail: grad-micro-info@uiowa.edu. *Application contact:* Betty Wood, Associate Director of Admissions, 319-335-1525, Fax: 319-335-1535, E-mail: admissions@uiowa.edu. Web site: http://www.uiowa.edu/microbiology/.

University of Louisville, School of Medicine, Department of Microbiology and Immunology, Louisville, KY 40292-0001. Offers MS, PhD, MD/PhD. Terminal master's awarded for partial completion of doctoral program. *Degree requirements:* For master's, thesis; for doctorate, comprehensive exam, thesis/dissertation. *Entrance requirements:* For master's and doctorate, GRE General Test (minimum score of 1000 verbal and quantitative), minimum GPA of 3.0; 1 year of course work in biology, organic chemistry, physics; 1 semester of course work in calculus and quantitative analysis, biochemistry, or molecular biology. Additional exam requirements/recommendations for international students: Required—TOEFL. Electronic applications accepted. *Expenses:* Tuition, state resident: full-time $9692; part-time $539 per credit hour. Tuition, nonresident: full-time $20,168; part-time $1121 per credit hour. Tuition and fees vary according to program and reciprocity agreements. *Faculty research:* Opportunistic and emerging infections; biology and regulation of the immune system; cellular and molecular bases of chronic inflammatory response; role of cytokines and chemokines in cancer, autoimmune and infectious disease; host defense and pathogenesis of viral infections.

The University of Manchester, Faculty of Life Sciences, Manchester, United Kingdom. Offers adaptive organismal biology (M Phil, PhD); animal biology (M Phil, PhD); biochemistry (M Phil, PhD); bioinformatics (M Phil, PhD); biomolecular sciences (M Phil, PhD); biotechnology (M Phil, PhD); cell biology (M Phil, PhD); cell matrix research (M Phil, PhD); channels and transporters (M Phil, PhD); developmental biology (M Phil, PhD); Egyptology (M Phil, PhD); environmental biology (M Phil, PhD); evolutionary biology (M Phil, PhD); gene expression (M Phil, PhD); genetics (M Phil, PhD); history of science, technology and medicine (M Phil, PhD); immunology (M Phil, PhD); integrative neurobiology and behavior (M Phil, PhD); membrane trafficking (M Phil, PhD); microbiology (M Phil, PhD); molecular and cellular neuroscience (M Phil, PhD); molecular biology (M Phil, PhD); molecular cancer studies (M Phil, PhD); neuroscience (M Phil, PhD); ophthalmology (M Phil, PhD); optometry (M Phil, PhD); organelle function (M Phil, PhD); pharmacology (M Phil, PhD); physiology (M Phil, PhD); plant sciences (M Phil, PhD); stem cell research (M Phil, PhD); structural biology (M Phil, PhD); systems neuroscience (M Phil, PhD); toxicology (M Phil, PhD).

University of Manitoba, Faculty of Medicine and Faculty of Graduate Studies, Graduate Programs in Medicine, Department of Immunology, Winnipeg, MB R3T 2N2, Canada. Offers M Sc, PhD. Terminal master's awarded for partial completion of doctoral program. *Degree requirements:* For master's, thesis; for doctorate, one foreign language, thesis/dissertation. *Faculty research:* Immediate hypersensitivity, regulation of the immune response, natural immunity, cytokines, inflammation.

University of Maryland, Baltimore, Graduate School, Graduate Program in Life Sciences, Program in Molecular Microbiology and Immunology, Baltimore, MD 21201. Offers PhD, MD/PhD. *Students:* 42 full-time (24 women); includes 8 minority (3 Black or African American, non-Hispanic/Latino; 3 Asian, non-Hispanic/Latino; 2 Hispanic/Latino), 6 international. Average age 27. 173 applicants, 12% accepted, 1 enrolled. In 2011, 4 doctorates awarded. *Entrance requirements:* For doctorate, GRE. Additional exam requirements/recommendations for international students: Required—TOEFL (minimum score 550 paper-based; 80 iBT); Recommended—IELTS (minimum score 7). *Application deadline:* For fall admission, 1/15 for domestic and international students. Application fee: $50. Electronic applications accepted. *Financial support:* In 2011–12, research assistantships with partial tuition reimbursements (averaging $25,000 per year) were awarded; fellowships also available. Financial award application deadline: 3/1. *Unit head:* Dr. Nicholas Carbonetti, Director, 410-706-7677, E-mail: ncarbone@

University of Connecticut Health Center

UCHC offers you exceptional research opportunities spanning **Cell Analysis and Modeling; Cell Biology; Genetics and Developmental Biology; Immunology; Molecular Biology and Biochemistry; Neuroscience;** and **Skeletal, Craniofacial and Oral Biology**.

Key features of our program include:
- ❖ Integrated admissions with access to more than 100 laboratories.
- ❖ Flexible educational program tailored to the interests of each student.
- ❖ Excellent education in a stimulating, cutting edge research environment.
- ❖ Competitive stipend ($28,000 for 2012–13 year), tuition waiver, and availability of student health plan.
- ❖ State-of-the-art research facilities, including the new Cell and Genome Sciences Building, which houses the UConn Stem Cell Institute, the Center for Cell Analysis and Modeling, and the Department of Genetics and Developmental Biology.

For more information, please contact:
Stephanie Rauch, Biomedical Science Admissions Coordinator
University of Connecticut Health Center
263 Farmington Ave., MC 3906
Farmington, CT 06030
BiomedSciAdmissions@uchc.edu
http://grad.uchc.edu/prospective/programs/phd_biosci/index.html

umaryland.edu. *Application contact:* June Green, Program Coordinator, 410-706-7126, Fax: 410-706-2129, E-mail: jgreen@umaryland.edu. Web site: http://microbiology.umaryland.edu.

University of Massachusetts Worcester, Graduate School of Biomedical Sciences, Worcester, MA 01655-0115. Offers biochemistry and molecular pharmacology (PhD); bioinformatics and computational biology (PhD); cancer biology (PhD); cell biology (PhD); clinical and population health research (PhD); clinical investigation (MS); immunology and virology (PhD); interdisciplinary graduate program (PhD); molecular genetics and microbiology (PhD); neuroscience (PhD); DVM/PhD; MD/PhD. *Faculty:* 1,427 full-time (526 women), 309 part-time/adjunct (196 women). *Students:* 416 full-time (225 women); includes 47 minority (12 Black or African American, non-Hispanic/Latino; 32 Asian, non-Hispanic/Latino; 3 Hispanic/Latino), 144 international. Average age 29. 623 applicants, 17% accepted, 54 enrolled. In 2011, 5 master's, 63 doctorates awarded. Terminal master's awarded for partial completion of doctoral program. *Degree requirements:* For master's, comprehensive exam, thesis; for doctorate, comprehensive exam, thesis/dissertation. *Entrance requirements:* For master's, bachelor's degree; for doctorate, GRE General Test. Additional exam requirements/recommendations for international students: Required—TOEFL (minimum score 600 paper-based; 250 computer-based; 100 iBT) or IELTS (minimum score 7.5). *Application deadline:* For fall admission, 12/15 for domestic and international students; for spring admission, 5/15 for domestic students. Application fee: $50. Electronic applications accepted. *Expenses:* Contact institution. *Financial support:* In 2011–12, 416 students received support, including 416 research assistantships with full tuition reimbursements available (averaging $29,200 per year); scholarships/grants, health care benefits, tuition waivers (full), and unspecified assistantships also available. Financial award application deadline: 4/16. *Faculty research:* RNA interference, cell biology, bioinformatics, clinical research, infectious disease. *Total annual research expenditures:* $262.7 million. *Unit head:* Dr. Anthony Carruthers, Dean, 508-856-4135, E-mail: anthony.carruthers@umassmed.edu. *Application contact:* Dr. Kendall Knight, Associate Dean and Interim Director of Admissions and Recruitment, 508-856-5628, Fax: 508-856-3659, E-mail: kendall.knight@umassmed.edu. Web site: http://www.umassmed.edu/gsbs/.

University of Medicine and Dentistry of New Jersey, Graduate School of Biomedical Sciences, Graduate Programs in Biomedical Sciences–Newark, Program in Molecular Pathology and Immunology, Newark, NJ 07107. Offers PhD. *Entrance requirements:* Additional exam requirements/recommendations for international students: Required—TOEFL. Electronic applications accepted.

University of Medicine and Dentistry of New Jersey, Graduate School of Biomedical Sciences, Graduate Programs in Biomedical Sciences–Piscataway, Program in Molecular Genetics, Microbiology and Immunology, Piscataway, NJ 08854-5635. Offers MS, PhD, MD/PhD. Terminal master's awarded for partial completion of doctoral program. *Degree requirements:* For master's, thesis, qualifying exam; for doctorate, thesis/dissertation, qualifying exam. *Entrance requirements:* For master's and doctorate, GRE General Test. Additional exam requirements/recommendations for international students: Required—TOEFL. Electronic applications accepted. *Faculty research:* Interferon, receptors, retrovirus evolution, Arbo virus/host cell interactions.

University of Medicine and Dentistry of New Jersey, Graduate School of Biomedical Sciences, Graduate Programs in Biomedical Sciences–Stratford, Stratford, NJ 08084-5634. Offers biomedical sciences (MBS, MS); cell and molecular biology (MS, PhD); molecular pathology and immunology (MS); DO/MS; DO/PhD; MBS/MPH; MS/MPH. Part-time and evening/weekend programs available. Terminal master's awarded for partial completion of doctoral program. *Degree requirements:* For master's, thesis (for some programs); for doctorate, thesis/dissertation, qualifying exam. *Entrance requirements:* For master's, GRE General Test, MCAT or DAT; for doctorate, GRE General Test. Additional exam requirements/recommendations for international students: Required—TOEFL. Electronic applications accepted.

University of Miami, Graduate School, Miller School of Medicine, Graduate Programs in Medicine, Department of Microbiology and Immunology, Coral Gables, FL 33124. Offers PhD, MD/PhD. *Degree requirements:* For doctorate, thesis/dissertation, oral and written qualifying exams. *Entrance requirements:* For doctorate, GRE General Test. Additional exam requirements/recommendations for international students: Required—TOEFL. Electronic applications accepted. *Faculty research:* Cellular and molecular immunology, molecular and pathogenic virology, pathogenic bacteriology and gene therapy of cancer.

University of Michigan, Horace H. Rackham School of Graduate Studies, Program in Biomedical Sciences (PIBS), Department of Microbiology and Immunology, Ann Arbor, MI 48109. Offers PhD. *Faculty:* 20 full-time (10 women), 12 part-time/adjunct (4 women). *Students:* 40 full-time (25 women); includes 10 minority (2 Black or African American, non-Hispanic/Latino; 2 American Indian or Alaska Native, non-Hispanic/Latino; 4 Asian, non-Hispanic/Latino; 2 Hispanic/Latino), 4 international. Average age 29. 90 applicants, 14% accepted, 13 enrolled. In 2011, 7 doctorates awarded. *Degree requirements:* For doctorate, thesis/dissertation, oral defense of dissertation, preliminary exam. *Entrance requirements:* For doctorate, GRE General Test. Additional exam requirements/recommendations for international students: Required—TOEFL (minimum score 600 paper-based; 220 computer-based; 84 iBT), TWE. *Application deadline:* For fall admission, 12/1 for domestic and international students. Application fee: $60 ($75 for international students). Electronic applications accepted. *Financial support:* In 2011–12, 15 fellowships with full tuition reimbursements (averaging $24,500 per year), 20 research assistantships with full tuition reimbursements (averaging $24,500 per year) were awarded; health care benefits and tuition waivers (full) also available. Financial award application deadline: 2/1. *Faculty research:* Gene regulation, molecular biology of animal and bacterial viruses, molecular and cellular networks, pathogenesis and microbial genetics. *Total annual research expenditures:* $10.2 million. *Unit head:* Dr. Harry L. T. Mobley, Chair, 734-764-1466, Fax: 734-764-3562, E-mail: hmobley@umich.edu. *Application contact:* Heidi Thompson, Senior Student Administrative Assistant, 734-763-3532, Fax: 734-764-3562, E-mail: heiditho@umich.edu. Web site: http://www.med.umich.edu/microbio/.

University of Michigan, Horace H. Rackham School of Graduate Studies, Program in Biomedical Sciences (PIBS), Program in Immunology, Ann Arbor, MI 48109-0619. Offers PhD. *Faculty:* 55 full-time (14 women). *Students:* 20 full-time (14 women); includes 8 minority (3 Asian, non-Hispanic/Latino; 5 Hispanic/Latino). Average age 27. 15 applicants, 73% accepted, 9 enrolled. In 2011, 2 doctorates awarded. *Degree requirements:* For doctorate, thesis/dissertation, oral defense of dissertation, preliminary exam. *Entrance requirements:* For doctorate, GRE General Test, 3 letters of recommendation, research experience. Additional exam requirements/recommendations for international students: Required—TOEFL (minimum score 84 iBT). *Application deadline:* For fall admission, 12/1 for domestic and international students. Application fee: $65 ($75 for international students). Electronic applications accepted. *Financial support:* In 2011–12, 20 students received support, including 9 fellowships (averaging $26,500 per year), 11 research assistantships with tuition reimbursements available (averaging $26,500 per year); scholarships/grants, health care benefits, tuition waivers, and unspecified assistantships also available. Financial award application deadline: 12/1. *Faculty research:* Cytokine networks, T and B cell activation , autoimmunity, antigen processing/ presentation, cell signaling. *Unit head:* Dr. D. Keith Bishop, Director, 734-763-0326, Fax: 734-936-9715, E-mail: kbishop@umich.edu. *Application contact:* Michelle S. Melis, Director of Student Life, 734-615-6538, Fax: 734-647-7022, E-mail: msmtegan@umich.edu. Web site: http://www.med.umich.edu/immprog/.

University of Minnesota, Duluth, Medical School, Microbiology, Immunology and Molecular Pathobiology Section, Duluth, MN 55812-2496. Offers MS, PhD. MS, PhD offered jointly with University of Minnesota, Twin Cities Campus. Terminal master's awarded for partial completion of doctoral program. *Degree requirements:* For master's, thesis, final oral exam; for doctorate, thesis/dissertation, final exam, oral and written preliminary exams. *Entrance requirements:* For master's and doctorate, GRE General Test. Additional exam requirements/recommendations for international students: Required—TOEFL. *Faculty research:* Immunomodulation, molecular diagnosis of rabies, cytokines, cancer immunology, cytomegalovirus infection.

University of Minnesota, Twin Cities Campus, Graduate School, PhD Program in Microbiology, Immunology and Cancer Biology, Minneapolis, MN 55455-0213. Offers PhD. *Degree requirements:* For doctorate, thesis/dissertation. *Entrance requirements:* For doctorate, GRE General Test. Additional exam requirements/recommendations for international students: Required—TOEFL (minimum score 600 paper-based; 250 computer-based). Electronic applications accepted. *Faculty research:* Virology, microbiology, cancer biology, immunology.

University of Missouri, School of Medicine and Graduate School, Graduate Programs in Medicine, Department of Molecular Microbiology and Immunology, Columbia, MO 65211. Offers MS, PhD. *Faculty:* 20 full-time (4 women), 2 part-time/adjunct (0 women). *Students:* 47 full-time (22 women), 5 part-time (2 women); includes 4 minority (3 Black or African American, non-Hispanic/Latino; 1 American Indian or Alaska Native, non-Hispanic/Latino), 17 international. Average age 28. 42 applicants, 24% accepted, 10 enrolled. In 2011, 1 master's, 6 doctorates awarded. Terminal master's awarded for partial completion of doctoral program. *Degree requirements:* For master's, thesis; for doctorate, thesis/dissertation. *Entrance requirements:* For master's and doctorate, GRE General Test, minimum GPA of 3.0. Additional exam requirements/recommendations for international students: Required—TOEFL (minimum score 580 paper-based; 237 computer-based; 92 iBT). *Application deadline:* For fall admission, 1/31 for domestic students. Application fee: $55 ($75 for international students). *Expenses:* Tuition, state resident: full-time $5881. Tuition, nonresident: full-time $15,183. *Required fees:* $952. Tuition and fees vary according to campus/location and program. *Financial support:* Fellowships, research assistantships, teaching assistantships, and institutionally sponsored loans available. Financial award application deadline: 3/1. *Faculty research:* Molecular biology, host-parasite interactions. *Unit head:* Dr. Mark A. McIntosh, Department Chair, E-mail: mcintoshm@missouri.edu. *Application contact:* Jana Clark, 573-882-3938, E-mail: clarkjl@missouri.edu. Web site: http://mmi.missouri.edu/graduateprogram/programindex.php.

The University of North Carolina at Chapel Hill, School of Medicine and Graduate School, Graduate Programs in Medicine, Department of Microbiology and Immunology, Chapel Hill, NC 27599-7290. Offers immunology (MS, PhD); microbiology (MS, PhD). Terminal master's awarded for partial completion of doctoral program. *Degree requirements:* For master's, comprehensive exam, thesis; for doctorate, comprehensive exam, thesis/dissertation. *Entrance requirements:* For master's and doctorate, GRE General Test, minimum GPA of 3.0. Electronic applications accepted. *Faculty research:* HIV pathogenesis, immune response, t-cell mediated autoimmunity, alpha-viruses, bacterial chemotaxis, francisella tularensis, pertussis, Mycobacterium tuberculosis, Burkholderia, Dengue virus.

University of North Dakota, Graduate School and Graduate School, Graduate Programs in Medicine, Department of Microbiology and Immunology, Grand Forks, ND 58202. Offers MS, PhD. *Degree requirements:* For master's, comprehensive exam, thesis or alternative; for doctorate, comprehensive exam, thesis/dissertation, final examination. *Entrance requirements:* For master's and doctorate, GRE General Test, minimum GPA of 3.0. Additional exam requirements/recommendations for international students: Required—TOEFL (minimum score 550 paper-based; 213 computer-based; 79 iBT), IELTS (minimum score 6.5). Electronic applications accepted. *Faculty research:* Genetic and immunological aspects of a murine model of human multiple sclerosis, termination of DNA replication, cell division in bacteria, yersinia pestis.

University of North Texas Health Science Center at Fort Worth, Graduate School of Biomedical Sciences, Fort Worth, TX 76107-2699. Offers anatomy and cell biology (MS, PhD); biochemistry and molecular biology (MS, PhD); biomedical sciences (MS, PhD); biotechnology (MS); forensic genetics (MS); integrative physiology (MS, PhD); medical science (MS); microbiology and immunology (MS, PhD); pharmacology (MS, PhD); science education (MS); DO/MS; DO/PhD. Terminal master's awarded for partial completion of doctoral program. *Degree requirements:* For master's, thesis; for doctorate, thesis/dissertation. *Entrance requirements:* For master's and doctorate, GRE General Test. Additional exam requirements/recommendations for international students: Required—TOEFL. *Expenses:* Contact institution. *Faculty research:* Alzheimer's disease, aging, eye diseases, cancer, cardiovascular disease.

University of Oklahoma Health Sciences Center, College of Medicine and Graduate College, Graduate Programs in Medicine, Department of Microbiology and Immunology, Oklahoma City, OK 73190. Offers immunology (MS, PhD); microbiology (MS, PhD). Part-time programs available. Terminal master's awarded for partial completion of doctoral program. *Degree requirements:* For master's, thesis or alternative; for doctorate, one foreign language, thesis/dissertation. *Entrance requirements:* For doctorate, GRE General Test, 3 letters of recommendation. Additional exam requirements/recommendations for international students: Required—TOEFL. *Faculty research:* Molecular genetics, pathogenesis, streptococcal infections, gram-positive virulence, monoclonal antibodies.

University of Ottawa, Faculty of Graduate and Postdoctoral Studies, Faculty of Medicine, Department of Biochemistry, Microbiology and Immunology, Ottawa, ON K1N 6N5, Canada. Offers biochemistry (M Sc, PhD); microbiology and immunology (M Sc, PhD). *Degree requirements:* For master's, thesis; for doctorate, comprehensive exam, thesis/dissertation, seminar. *Entrance requirements:* For master's, honors degree or equivalent, minimum B average; for doctorate, master's degree, minimum B+ average. Electronic applications accepted. *Faculty research:* General biochemistry, molecular biology, microbiology, host biology, nutrition and metabolism.

University of Pennsylvania, Perelman School of Medicine, Biomedical Graduate Studies, Graduate Group in Immunology, Philadelphia, PA 19104. Offers PhD, MD/PhD, VMD/PhD. *Faculty:* 109. *Students:* 71 full-time (43 women); includes 17 minority (2 Black or African American, non-Hispanic/Latino; 14 Asian, non-Hispanic/Latino; 1 Hispanic/Latino), 7 international. 109 applicants, 21% accepted, 6 enrolled. In 2011, 7 doctorates awarded. *Degree requirements:* For doctorate, thesis/dissertation, 2 preliminary exams. *Entrance requirements:* For doctorate, GRE General Test, undergraduate major in natural or physical science. Additional exam requirements/recommendations for international students: Required—TOEFL. *Application deadline:* For fall admission, 12/1 priority date for domestic students, 12/1 for international students. Applications are processed on a rolling basis. Application fee: $80. Electronic applications accepted. *Expenses:* *Tuition:* Full-time $26,660; part-time $4944 per

course. *Required fees:* $2318; $291 per course. Tuition and fees vary according to course load, degree level and program. *Financial support:* In 2011–12, 71 students received support. Fellowships, research assistantships, scholarships/grants, traineeships, and unspecified assistantships available. *Faculty research:* Immunoglobulin structure and function, cell surface receptors, lymphocyte functional transplantation immunology, cellular immunology, molecular biology of immunoglobulins. *Unit head:* Dr. E. John Wherry, Chairman. *Application contact:* Timothy Johnson, Graduate Coordinator. Web site: http://www.med.upenn.edu/immun/.

University of Pittsburgh, School of Medicine, Graduate Programs in Medicine, Program in Immunology, Pittsburgh, PA 15260. Offers MS, PhD. *Faculty:* 56 full-time (19 women). *Students:* 42 full-time (23 women); includes 6 minority (2 Black or African American, non-Hispanic/Latino; 3 Asian, non-Hispanic/Latino; 1 Hispanic/Latino), 18 international. Average age 27. 514 applicants, 12% accepted, 28 enrolled. In 2011, 2 doctorates awarded. *Degree requirements:* For doctorate, comprehensive exam, thesis/dissertation. *Entrance requirements:* For doctorate, GRE General Test, GRE Subject Test, minimum QPA of 3.0. Additional exam requirements/recommendations for international students: Required—TOEFL (minimum score 600 paper-based; 100 iBT), IELTS (minimum score 7). *Application deadline:* For fall admission, 12/15 priority date for domestic students, 12/15 for international students. Application fee: $50. Electronic applications accepted. *Expenses:* Tuition, state resident: full-time $18,774; part-time $760 per credit. Tuition, nonresident: full-time $30,736; part-time $1258 per credit. *Required fees:* $740; $200 per term. Tuition and fees vary according to program. *Financial support:* In 2011–12, 42 research assistantships with full tuition reimbursements (averaging $25,500 per year) were awarded; institutionally sponsored loans, scholarships/grants, traineeships, health care benefits, and unspecified assistantships also available. *Faculty research:* Human T-cell biology, opportunistic infections associated with AIDS, autoimmunity, immunoglobin gene expression, tumor immunology. *Unit head:* Dr. Lawrence Kane, Graduate Program Director, 412-648-8947, Fax: 412-383-8096, E-mail: lkane@pitt.edu. *Application contact:* Graduate Studies Administrator, 412-648-8957, Fax: 412-648-1007, E-mail: gradstudies@medschool.pitt.edu. Web site: http://www.gradbiomed.pitt.edu.

University of Prince Edward Island, Atlantic Veterinary College, Graduate Program in Veterinary Medicine, Charlottetown, PE C1A 4P3, Canada. Offers anatomy (M Sc, PhD); bacteriology (M Sc, PhD); clinical pharmacology (M Sc, PhD); clinical sciences (M Sc, PhD); epidemiology (M Sc, PhD), including reproduction; fish health (M Sc, PhD); food animal nutrition (M Sc, PhD); immunology (M Sc, PhD); microanatomy (M Sc, PhD); parasitology (M Sc, PhD); pathology (M Sc, PhD); pharmacology (M Sc, PhD); physiology (M Sc, PhD); toxicology (M Sc, PhD); veterinary science (M Vet Sc); virology (M Sc, PhD). Part-time programs available. *Degree requirements:* For master's, thesis; for doctorate, thesis/dissertation. *Entrance requirements:* For master's, DVM, B Sc honors degree, or equivalent; for doctorate, M Sc. Additional exam requirements/recommendations for international students: Required—TOEFL (minimum score 550 paper-based; 213 computer-based; 80 iBT). *Expenses:* Contact institution. *Faculty research:* Animal health management, infectious diseases, fin fish and shellfish health, basic biomedical sciences, ecosystem health.

University of Rochester, School of Medicine and Dentistry, Graduate Programs in Medicine and Dentistry, Department of Microbiology and Immunology, Program in Microbiology and Immunology, Rochester, NY 14627. Offers MS, PhD. *Expenses:* Tuition: Full-time $41,040.

University of Saskatchewan, College of Medicine, Department of Microbiology and Immunology, Saskatoon, SK S7N 5A2, Canada. Offers M Sc, PhD. *Degree requirements:* For master's, thesis; for doctorate, thesis/dissertation. *Entrance requirements:* Additional exam requirements/recommendations for international students: Required—TOEFL.

The University of South Dakota, Graduate School, School of Medicine and Graduate School, Biomedical Sciences Graduate Program, Molecular Microbiology and Immunology Group, Vermillion, SD 57069-2390. Offers MS, PhD. Terminal master's awarded for partial completion of doctoral program. *Degree requirements:* For master's, thesis; for doctorate, comprehensive exam, thesis/dissertation. *Entrance requirements:* For master's and doctorate, GRE General Test, minimum GPA of 3.0. Additional exam requirements/recommendations for international students: Required—TOEFL (minimum score 550 paper-based; 213 computer-based; 80 iBT), IELTS (minimum score 6). Electronic applications accepted. *Expenses:* Contact institution. *Faculty research:* Structure-function membranes, plasmids, immunology, virology, pathogenesis.

University of Southern California, Keck School of Medicine and Graduate School, Graduate Programs in Medicine, Department of Molecular Microbiology and Immunology, Los Angeles, CA 90089. Offers MS, PhD. Part-time programs available. *Faculty:* 22 full-time (5 women), 1 (woman) part-time/adjunct. *Students:* 27 full-time (17 women); includes 19 minority (all Asian, non-Hispanic/Latino). Average age 24. 43 applicants, 67% accepted, 16 enrolled. In 2011, 10 master's, 1 doctorate awarded. Terminal master's awarded for partial completion of doctoral program. *Degree requirements:* For master's, comprehensive exam (for some programs), thesis optional; for doctorate, comprehensive exam, thesis/dissertation. *Entrance requirements:* For master's, GRE General Test, minimum GPA of 3.0; for doctorate, GRE General Test, GRE Subject Test, minimum GPA of 3.0. Additional exam requirements/recommendations for international students: Required—TOEFL (minimum score 100 iBT). *Application deadline:* For fall admission, 6/1 for domestic students, 5/1 for international students; for spring admission, 11/1 for domestic students, 10/1 for international students. Applications are processed on a rolling basis. Application fee: $85. Electronic applications accepted. *Financial support:* In 2011–12, 2 students received support, including 1 research assistantship with full tuition reimbursement available (averaging $29,100 per year), 1 teaching assistantship with full tuition reimbursement available (averaging $29,100 per year); fellowships, Federal Work-Study, institutionally sponsored loans, scholarships/grants, health care benefits, and unspecified assistantships also available. Financial award application deadline: 5/3; financial award applicants required to submit FAFSA. *Faculty research:* Animal virology, microbial genetics, molecular and cellular immunology, cellular differentiation control of protein synthesis, HIV. *Unit head:* Dr. Jae U. Jung, Professor and Chair, 323-442-1713, Fax: 323-442-1721, E-mail: jaeujung@usc.edu. *Application contact:* Silvina V. Campos, Administrative Assistant II, 323-442-1713, Fax: 323-442-1721, E-mail: scampos@usc.edu. Web site: http://www.usc.edu/schools/medicine/departments/molecularmicrobio_immunology/.

University of Southern Maine, School of Applied Science, Engineering, and Technology, Program in Applied Medical Sciences, Portland, ME 04104-9300. Offers MS. Part-time programs available. *Degree requirements:* For master's, thesis. *Entrance requirements:* For master's, GRE General Test, minimum GPA of 3.0. Additional exam requirements/recommendations for international students: Required—TOEFL. Electronic applications accepted. *Faculty research:* Flow cytometry, cancer, epidemiology, monoclonal antibodies, DNA diagnostics.

The University of Texas Health Science Center at Houston, Graduate School of Biomedical Sciences, Program in Immunology, Houston, TX 77225-0036. Offers MS, PhD, MD/PhD. Terminal master's awarded for partial completion of doctoral program.

Degree requirements: For master's, thesis; for doctorate, thesis/dissertation. *Entrance requirements:* For master's and doctorate, GRE General Test. Additional exam requirements/recommendations for international students: Required—TOEFL. Electronic applications accepted. *Faculty research:* Cancer immunology, molecular immunology, immune cell signaling, immune disease, immune system development.

The University of Texas Health Science Center at San Antonio, Graduate School of Biomedical Sciences, Department of Microbiology and Immunology, San Antonio, TX 78229-3900. Offers PhD. *Degree requirements:* For doctorate, comprehensive exam, thesis/dissertation. *Entrance requirements:* For doctorate, GRE General Test. Additional exam requirements/recommendations for international students: Required—TOEFL (minimum score 560 paper-based; 220 computer-based; 68 iBT). Electronic applications accepted. *Faculty research:* Molecular immunology, mechanisms of microbial pathogenesis, molecular genetics, vaccine and immunodiagnostic development.

The University of Texas Medical Branch, Graduate School of Biomedical Sciences, Program in Microbiology and Immunology, Galveston, TX 77555. Offers MS, PhD. Terminal master's awarded for partial completion of doctoral program. *Degree requirements:* For master's, thesis or alternative; for doctorate, thesis/dissertation. *Entrance requirements:* For doctorate, GRE General Test, minimum GPA of 3.0. Additional exam requirements/recommendations for international students: Required—TOEFL (minimum score 550 paper-based; 213 computer-based). Electronic applications accepted.

The University of Texas Southwestern Medical Center, Southwestern Graduate School of Biomedical Sciences, Division of Basic Science, Program in Immunology, Dallas, TX 75390. Offers PhD. *Degree requirements:* For doctorate, thesis/dissertation, qualifying exam. *Entrance requirements:* For doctorate, GRE General Test, minimum GPA of 3.0. Additional exam requirements/recommendations for international students: Required—TOEFL. Electronic applications accepted. *Faculty research:* Antibody diversity and idiotype, cytotoxic effector mechanisms, natural killer cells, biology of immunoglobulins, oncogenes.

The University of Toledo, College of Graduate Studies, College of Medicine and Life Sciences, Department of Medical Microbiology and Immunology, Toledo, OH 43606-3390. Offers infection, immunity, and transplantation (MSBS, PhD); MD/MSBS; MD/PhD. *Faculty:* 12. *Students:* 19 full-time (9 women), 9 international. Average age 26. 18 applicants, 67% accepted, 7 enrolled. In 2011, 3 degrees awarded. Terminal master's awarded for partial completion of doctoral program. *Degree requirements:* For master's, thesis, qualifying exam; for doctorate, thesis/dissertation, qualifying exam. *Entrance requirements:* For master's and doctorate, GRE, minimum undergraduate GPA of 3.0, three letters of recommendation, statement of purpose, transcripts from all prior institutions attended, resume. Additional exam requirements/recommendations for international students: Required—TOEFL (minimum score 550 paper-based; 213 computer-based; 80 iBT), IELTS (minimum score 6.5). *Application deadline:* For fall admission, 1/15 priority date for domestic students, 1/15 for international students. Application fee: $45 ($75 for international students). Electronic applications accepted. *Financial support:* In 2011–12, 21 research assistantships with full tuition reimbursements (averaging $21,180 per year) were awarded; Federal Work-Study, institutionally sponsored loans, scholarships/grants, tuition waivers (full), and unspecified assistantships also available. *Unit head:* Dr. Akira Takashima, Chair, 419-383-5423, E-mail: akira.takashima@utoledo.edu. *Application contact:* Admissions Analyst, 419-383-4116, Fax: 419-383-6140, E-mail: christine.wile@utoledo.edu. Web site: http://www.utoledo.edu/med/grad/.

University of Toronto, Faculty of Medicine, Department of Immunology, Toronto, ON M5S 1A1, Canada. Offers M Sc, PhD, MD/PhD. *Degree requirements:* For master's, thesis, thesis defense; for doctorate, thesis/dissertation, thesis defense. *Entrance requirements:* For master's, resume, 3 letters of reference. Additional exam requirements/recommendations for international students: Required—TOEFL (minimum score 580 paper-based; 93 iBT), TWE (minimum score 5). Electronic applications accepted.

University of Washington, Graduate School, School of Medicine, Graduate Programs in Medicine, Department of Immunology, Seattle, WA 98195. Offers PhD. *Faculty:* 27 full-time (8 women). *Students:* 38 full-time (20 women); includes 10 minority (3 Black or African American, non-Hispanic/Latino; 3 Asian, non-Hispanic/Latino; 4 Hispanic/Latino), 1 international. Average age 28. 75 applicants, 17% accepted, 6 enrolled. In 2011, 14 doctorates awarded. *Degree requirements:* For doctorate, thesis/dissertation. *Entrance requirements:* For doctorate, GRE General Test, BA or BS in related field. Additional exam requirements/recommendations for international students: Required—TOEFL (minimum score 600 paper-based; 250 computer-based; 100 iBT). *Application deadline:* For fall admission, 12/7 for domestic students, 11/1 for international students. Application fee: $75. Electronic applications accepted. *Financial support:* In 2011–12, 1 student received support, including 15 fellowships with full tuition reimbursements available (averaging $27,348 per year), 24 research assistantships with full tuition reimbursements available (averaging $27,348 per year); scholarships/grants, traineeships, health care benefits, tuition waivers (full), and stipends also available. *Faculty research:* Molecular and cellular immunology, regulation of lymphocyte differentiation and responses, genetics of immune recognition genetics and pathogenesis of autoimmune diseases, signal transduction. *Total annual research expenditures:* $10.8 million. *Unit head:* Dr. Joan M. Goverman, Professor and Interim Chair, 206-543-1010, Fax: 206-543-1013. *Application contact:* Peggy A. McCune, Training Program Manager, 206-685-3955, Fax: 206-543-1013, E-mail: immgrad@u.washington.edu. Web site: http://immunology.washington.edu/.

The University of Western Ontario, Faculty of Graduate Studies, Biosciences Division, Department of Microbiology and Immunology, London, ON N6A 5B8, Canada. Offers M Sc, PhD. *Degree requirements:* For master's, thesis, oral and written exam; for doctorate, thesis/dissertation, oral and written exam. *Entrance requirements:* For master's, honors degree or equivalent in microbiology, immunology, or other biological science; minimum B average; for doctorate, M Sc in microbiology and immunology. Additional exam requirements/recommendations for international students: Required—TOEFL. *Faculty research:* Virology, molecular pathogenesis, cellular immunology, molecular biology.

Vanderbilt University, Graduate School and School of Medicine, Department of Microbiology and Immunology, Nashville, TN 37240-1001. Offers MS, PhD, MD/PhD. *Faculty:* 42 full-time (11 women). *Students:* 42 full-time (23 women); includes 7 minority (3 Black or African American, non-Hispanic/Latino; 3 Asian, non-Hispanic/Latino; 1 Hispanic/Latino), 6 international. Average age 27. In 2011, 7 degrees awarded. Terminal master's awarded for partial completion of doctoral program. *Degree requirements:* For master's, thesis; for doctorate, thesis/dissertation, final and qualifying exams. *Entrance requirements:* For master's and doctorate, GRE General Test, GRE Subject Test (recommended). Additional exam requirements/recommendations for international students: Required—TOEFL (minimum score 570 paper-based; 230 computer-based; 88 iBT). *Application deadline:* For fall admission, 1/15 for domestic and international students. Application fee: $0. Electronic applications accepted. *Financial support:* Fellowships with full tuition reimbursements, research assistantships with full tuition reimbursements, Federal Work-Study, institutionally sponsored loans, scholarships/

grants, traineeships, health care benefits, and tuition waivers (partial) available. Financial award application deadline: 1/15; financial award applicants required to submit CSS PROFILE or FAFSA. *Faculty research:* Cellular and molecular microbiology, viruses, genes, cancer, molecular pathogenesis of microbial diseases, immunobiology. *Unit head:* Dr. Samuel A. Santoro, Chair, 615-322-3234, Fax: 615-322-5551, E-mail: samuel.a.santoro@vanderbilt.edu. *Application contact:* Jean Tidwell, Administrative Assistant/Director of Graduate Studies Assistant, 615-343-3435, Fax: 615-343-7392, E-mail: jean.tidwell@vanderbilt.edu. Web site: http://www.mc.vanderbilt.edu/microbio/.

Virginia Commonwealth University, Medical College of Virginia-Professional Programs, School of Medicine, School of Medicine Graduate Programs, Department of Microbiology and Immunology, Richmond, VA 23284-9005. Offers microbiology and immunology (MS, PhD); MD/PhD. *Degree requirements:* For master's, thesis; for doctorate, thesis/dissertation, comprehensive oral and written exams. *Entrance requirements:* For master's and doctorate, GRE General Test or MCAT. Additional exam requirements/recommendations for international students: Required—TOEFL (minimum score 600 paper-based; 250 computer-based; 100 iBT). Electronic applications accepted. *Expenses:* Tuition, state resident: full-time $9133; part-time $507 per credit. Tuition, nonresident: full-time $18,777; part-time $1043 per credit. *Required fees:* $77 per credit. Tuition and fees vary according to degree level, campus/location, program and student level. *Faculty research:* Microbial physiology and genetics, molecular biology, crystallography of biological molecules, antibiotics and chemotherapy, membrane transport.

Wake Forest University, School of Medicine and Graduate School of Arts and Sciences, Graduate Programs in Medicine, Department of Microbiology and Immunology, Winston-Salem, NC 27109. Offers PhD, MD/PhD. *Degree requirements:* For doctorate, thesis/dissertation. *Entrance requirements:* For doctorate, GRE General Test. Additional exam requirements/recommendations for international students: Required—TOEFL. Electronic applications accepted. *Faculty research:* Molecular immunology, bacterial pathogenesis and molecular genetics, viral pathogenesis, regulation of mRNA metabolism, leukocyte biology.

Washington University in St. Louis, Graduate School of Arts and Sciences, Division of Biology and Biomedical Sciences, Program in Immunology, St. Louis, MO 63130-4899. Offers PhD. *Degree requirements:* For doctorate, thesis/dissertation. *Entrance requirements:* For doctorate, GRE General Test, GRE Subject Test. Electronic applications accepted.

Wayne State University, School of Medicine, Department of Immunology and Microbiology, Detroit, MI 48202. Offers MS, PhD, MD/PhD. *Students:* 13 full-time (5 women); includes 2 minority (1 Black or African American, non-Hispanic/Latino; 1 Hispanic/Latino), 2 international. Average age 27. 17 applicants, 24% accepted, 3 enrolled. In 2011, 4 doctorates awarded. Terminal master's awarded for partial completion of doctoral program. *Degree requirements:* For doctorate, thesis/dissertation. *Entrance requirements:* For doctorate, GRE, minimum GPA of 3.0 in undergraduate degree. Additional exam requirements/recommendations for international students: Required—TOEFL (minimum score 600 paper-based; 250 computer-based; 100 iBT); Recommended—TWE (minimum score 6). *Application deadline:* For fall admission, 6/1 priority date for domestic students, 5/1 for international students. Application fee: $50. Electronic applications accepted. *Expenses:* Tuition, state resident: part-time $512.85 per credit. Tuition, nonresident: part-time $1132.65 per credit. *Required fees:* $26.60 per credit. $199.65 per semester. Tuition and fees vary according to course load and program. *Financial support:* In 2011–12, 2 fellowships with tuition reimbursements (averaging $20,097 per year), 10 research assistantships with tuition reimbursements (averaging $21,487 per year) were awarded; teaching assistantships with tuition reimbursements, career-related internships or fieldwork, Federal Work-Study, scholarships/grants, health care benefits, and unspecified assistantships also available. *Faculty research:* Immune regulation, bacterial pathophysiology, molecular biology/viruses/bacteria, cellular and molecular immunology, microbial pathogenesis. *Unit head:* Dr. Thomas Holland, Graduate Director, 313-577-1298, E-mail: thomas.holland@wayne.edu. Web site: http://www.med.wayne.edu/immunology/Pages/Graduate_Program.html.

Weill Cornell Medical College, Weill Cornell Graduate School of Medical Sciences, Immunology and Microbial Pathogenesis Program, New York, NY 10065. Offers immunology (MS, PhD), including immunology, microbiology, pathology. *Faculty:* 33 full-time (11 women). *Students:* 51 full-time (36 women); includes 7 minority (4 Asian, non-Hispanic/Latino; 2 Hispanic/Latino; 1 Native Hawaiian or other Pacific Islander, non-Hispanic/Latino), 30 international. Average age 23. 133 applicants, 14% accepted, 9 enrolled. In 2011, 1 master's, 7 doctorates awarded. Terminal master's awarded for partial completion of doctoral program. *Degree requirements:* For master's, comprehensive exam; for doctorate, thesis/dissertation, final exam. *Entrance requirements:* For doctorate, GRE General Test, laboratory research experience, course work in biological sciences. Additional exam requirements/recommendations for international students: Required—TOEFL. *Application deadline:* For fall admission, 12/1 for domestic students. Application fee: $60. Electronic applications accepted. *Expenses: Tuition:* Full-time $46,001. *Financial support:* In 2011–12, 7 fellowships (averaging $24,500 per year) were awarded; scholarships/grants, health care benefits, and stipends (given to all students) also available. *Faculty research:* Microbial immunity, tumor immunology, lympholyte and leukocyte biology, auto immunity, stem cell/bone marrow transplantation. *Unit head:* Dr. Ulrich Hammerling, Director, 646-888-2303, E-mail: u-hammerling@ski.mskcc.org. *Application contact:* Stephen Nesbit, Assistant Dean of Admissions, 212-746-6565, Fax: 212-746-8906, E-mail: sjn2001@med.cornell.edu. Web site: http://weill.cornell.edu/gradschool/program/immunology.html.

West Virginia University, Davis College of Agriculture, Forestry and Consumer Sciences, Interdisciplinary Program in Genetics and Developmental Biology, Morgantown, WV 26506. Offers animal breeding (MS, PhD); biochemical and molecular genetics (MS, PhD); cytogenetics (MS, PhD); descriptive embryology (MS, PhD); developmental genetics (MS); experimental morphogenesis/teratology (MS); human genetics (MS, PhD); immunogenetics (MS, PhD); life cycles of animals and plants (MS, PhD); molecular aspects of development (MS, PhD); mutagenesis (MS, PhD); oncology (MS, PhD); plant genetics (MS, PhD); population and quantitative genetics (MS, PhD); regeneration (MS, PhD); teratology (PhD); toxicology (MS, PhD). *Degree requirements:* For master's, thesis; for doctorate, comprehensive exam, thesis/dissertation. *Entrance requirements:* For master's, GRE or MCAT, minimum GPA of 2.75. Additional exam requirements/recommendations for international students: Required—TOEFL.

West Virginia University, School of Medicine, Graduate Programs at the Health Sciences Center, Interdisciplinary Graduate Programs in Biomedical Sciences, Program in Immunology and Microbial Pathogenesis, Morgantown, WV 26506. Offers MS, PhD, MD/PhD. *Degree requirements:* For doctorate, comprehensive exam, thesis/dissertation. *Entrance requirements:* For doctorate, GRE General Test, minimum GPA of 3.0. Additional exam requirements/recommendations for international students: Required—TOEFL. Electronic applications accepted. *Faculty research:* Regulation of signal transduction in immune responses, immune responses in bacterial and viral diseases, peptide and DNA vaccines for contraception, inflammatory bowel disease, physiology of pathogenic microbes.

Wright State University, School of Graduate Studies, College of Science and Mathematics, Program in Microbiology and Immunology, Dayton, OH 45435. Offers MS. Part-time programs available. *Degree requirements:* For master's, thesis. *Entrance requirements:* Additional exam requirements/recommendations for international students: Required—TOEFL. *Faculty research:* Reproductive immunology, viral pathogenesis, virus-host cell interactions.

Yale University, Graduate School of Arts and Sciences, Department of Immunobiology, New Haven, CT 06520. Offers PhD. *Degree requirements:* For doctorate, thesis/dissertation. *Entrance requirements:* For doctorate, GRE General Test.

Yale University, School of Medicine and Graduate School of Arts and Sciences, Combined Program in Biological and Biomedical Sciences (BBS), Immunology Track, New Haven, CT 06520. Offers PhD, MD/PhD. *Degree requirements:* For doctorate, thesis/dissertation. *Entrance requirements:* For doctorate, GRE General Test. Additional exam requirements/recommendations for international students: Required—TOEFL. Electronic applications accepted.

Infectious Diseases

Cornell University, Graduate School, Graduate Fields of Comparative Biomedical Sciences, Field of Comparative Biomedical Sciences, Ithaca, NY 14853-0001. Offers cellular and molecular medicine (MS, PhD); developmental and reproductive biology (MS, PhD); infectious diseases (MS, PhD); population medicine and epidemiology (MS, PhD); structural and functional biology (MS, PhD). *Faculty:* 97 full-time (27 women). *Students:* 38 full-time (23 women); includes 5 minority (2 Black or African American, non-Hispanic/Latino; 1 Asian, non-Hispanic/Latino; 2 Hispanic/Latino), 15 international. Average age 30. 45 applicants, 22% accepted, 9 enrolled. In 2011, 2 master's, 7 doctorates awarded. *Degree requirements:* For master's, thesis; for doctorate, comprehensive exam, thesis/dissertation. *Entrance requirements:* For master's and doctorate, GRE General Test, 2 letters of recommendation. Additional exam requirements/recommendations for international students: Required—TOEFL (minimum score 550 paper-based; 213 computer-based; 77 iBT). *Application deadline:* For fall admission, 12/15 for domestic students. Application fee: $95. Electronic applications accepted. *Financial support:* In 2011–12, 12 fellowships with full tuition reimbursements, 25 research assistantships with full tuition reimbursements were awarded; teaching assistantships with full tuition reimbursements, institutionally sponsored loans, scholarships/grants, health care benefits, tuition waivers (full and partial), and unspecified assistantships also available. Financial award applicants required to submit FAFSA. *Faculty research:* Receptors and signal transduction, viral and bacterial infectious diseases, tumor metastasis, clinical sciences/nutritional disease, developmental/neurological disorders. *Unit head:* Director of Graduate Studies, 607-253-3276, Fax: 607-253-3756. *Application contact:* Graduate Field Assistant, 607-253-3276, Fax: 607-253-3756, E-mail: graduate_edcvm@cornell.edu. Web site: http://www.gradschool.cornell.edu/fields.php?id-64&a-2.

Georgetown University, Graduate School of Arts and Sciences, Programs in Biomedical Sciences, Department of Microbiology and Immunology, Washington, DC 20057. Offers biohazardous threat agents and emerging infectious diseases (MS); general microbiology and immunology (MS); global infectious diseases (PhD); microbiology and immunology research (PhD); science policy and advocacy (MS). Part-time programs available. *Degree requirements:* For master's, 30 credit hours of coursework; for doctorate, comprehensive exam, thesis/dissertation. *Entrance requirements:* For master's, GRE General Test, 3 letters of reference, bachelor's degree in related field; for doctorate, GRE General Test, 3 letters of reference, MS/BS in related field. Additional exam requirements/recommendations for international students: Required—TOEFL (minimum score 505 paper-based; 213 computer-based). Electronic applications accepted. *Faculty research:* Pathogenesis and basic biology of the fungus Candida albicans, molecular biology of viral immunopathological mechanisms in Multiple Sclerosis.

The George Washington University, School of Public Health and Health Services, Department of Epidemiology and Biostatistics, Washington, DC 20052. Offers biostatistics (MPH); epidemiology (MPH); microbiology and emerging infectious diseases (MSPH). *Faculty:* 23 full-time (15 women), 26 part-time/adjunct (15 women). *Students:* 62 full-time (54 women), 41 part-time (30 women); includes 37 minority (16 Black or African American, non-Hispanic/Latino; 16 Asian, non-Hispanic/Latino; 3 Hispanic/Latino; 2 Two or more races, non-Hispanic/Latino), 8 international. Average age 27. 298 applicants, 69% accepted, 35 enrolled. In 2011, 49 master's awarded. *Degree requirements:* For master's, case study or special project. *Entrance requirements:* For master's, GMAT, GRE General Test, or MCAT. Additional exam requirements/recommendations for international students: Required—TOEFL. *Application deadline:* For fall admission, 4/15 priority date for domestic students, 4/15 for international students; for spring admission, 11/1 for domestic and international students. Applications are processed on a rolling basis. Application fee: $75. *Financial support:* In 2011–12, 6 students received support. Tuition waivers available. Financial award application deadline: 2/15. *Unit head:* Dr. Alan E. Greenberg, Chair, 202-994-0612, E-mail: aeg1@gwu.edu. *Application contact:* Jane Smith, Director of Admissions, 202-994-0248, Fax: 202-994-1860, E-mail: sphhsinfo@gwumc.edu.

Harvard University, Harvard School of Public Health, Department of Immunology and Infectious Diseases, Boston, MA 02115-6096. Offers PhD, SD. Part-time programs available. *Faculty:* 34 full-time (12 women), 6 part-time/adjunct (0 women). *Students:* 8 applicants, 0% accepted. *Degree requirements:* For doctorate, thesis/dissertation, qualifying exam. *Entrance requirements:* For doctorate, GRE. Additional exam requirements/recommendations for international students: Required—TOEFL (minimum score 600 paper-based; 240 computer-based; 100 iBT); Recommended—IELTS (minimum score 7). *Application deadline:* For fall admission, 12/15 for domestic and international students. Application fee: $115. Electronic applications accepted. *Expenses: Tuition:* Full-time $36,304. *Required fees:* $1186. Full-time tuition and fees

vary according to program. *Financial support:* Fellowships, research assistantships, Federal Work-Study, scholarships/grants, traineeships, and unspecified assistantships available. Financial award application deadline: 2/17; financial award applicants required to submit FAFSA. *Faculty research:* Infectious disease epidemiology and tropical public health, vector biology, ecology and control, virology. *Unit head:* Dr. Dyann F. Wirth, Chair, 617-432-2234, Fax: 617-739-8348, E-mail: rkenwort@hsph.harvard.edu. *Application contact:* Vincent W. James, Director of Admissions, 617-432-1031, Fax: 617-432-7080, E-mail: admissions@hsph.harvard.edu. Web site: http://www.hsph.harvard.edu/departments/immunology-and-infectious-diseases/.

The Johns Hopkins University, Bloomberg School of Public Health, Department of Epidemiology, Baltimore, MD 21205. Offers cancer epidemiology (MHS, Sc M, PhD, Sc D); cardiovascular disease epidemiology (MHS, Sc M, PhD, Sc D); clinical epidemiology (MHS, Sc M, PhD, Sc D); clinical trials (PhD, Sc D); epidemiology (Dr PH); epidemiology (general) (MHS, Sc M, PhD, Sc D); epidemiology of aging (MHS, Sc M, PhD, Sc D); human genetics/genetic epidemiology (MHS, Sc M, PhD, Sc D); infectious disease epidemiology (MHS, Sc M, PhD, Sc D); occupational/environmental epidemiology (MHS, Sc M, PhD, Sc D). Part-time programs available. *Degree requirements:* For master's, comprehensive exam, thesis, 1 year full-time residency; for doctorate, comprehensive exam, thesis/dissertation, 2 years full-time residency, oral and written exams, student teaching. *Entrance requirements:* For master's, GRE General Test or MCAT, 3 letters of recommendation, curriculum vitae; for doctorate, GRE General Test, minimum 1 year of work experience, 3 letters of recommendation, curriculum vitae, academic records from all schools. Additional exam requirements/recommendations for international students: Required—TOEFL (minimum score 600 paper-based; 250 computer-based; 100 iBT); Recommended—IELTS (minimum score 7.5), TWE. Electronic applications accepted. *Faculty research:* Cancer and congenital malformations, nutritional epidemiology, AIDS, tuberculosis, cardiovascular disease, risk assessment.

Loyola University Chicago, Graduate School, Marcella Niehoff School of Nursing, Population-Based Infection Control and Environmental Safety Program, Chicago, IL 60660. Offers population based infection control (MSN, Certificate). Part-time and evening/weekend programs available. *Students:* 12 part-time (11 women). Average age 37. 3 applicants, 100% accepted, 2 enrolled. In 2011, 6 master's awarded. *Entrance requirements:* For master's, Illinois nursing license, 3 letters of recommendation, minimum nursing GPA of 3.0, 1000 hours experience before starting clinical. Application fee: $50. *Expenses: Tuition:* Full-time $15,660; part-time $870 per credit hour. *Required fees:* $125 per semester. Tuition and fees vary according to course load and program. *Financial support:* Traineeships available. *Unit head:* Dr. Ida Androwich, Professor, 708-216-9276, Fax: 708-216-9555, E-mail: iandrow@luc.edu. *Application contact:* Amy Weatherford, Enrollment Advisor, School of Nursing, 773-508-3249, Fax: 773-508-3241, E-mail: aweatherford@luc.edu. Web site: http://luc.edu/nursing/infectionprevention/.

Loyola University Chicago, Graduate School, Program in Infectious Disease and Immunology, Chicago, IL 60660. Offers MS. *Faculty:* 31 full-time (7 women). *Students:* 9 full-time (8 women); includes 1 minority (Asian, non-Hispanic/Latino). Average age 23. 24 applicants, 38% accepted, 6 enrolled. *Degree requirements:* For master's, thesis. *Entrance requirements:* For master's, GRE. Additional exam requirements/recommendations for international students: Required—TOEFL. *Application deadline:* Applications are processed on a rolling basis. *Expenses: Tuition:* Full-time $15,660; part-time $870 per credit hour. *Required fees:* $125 per semester. Tuition and fees vary according to course load and program. *Faculty research:* Immunological tolerance and memory, molecular analysis of virus assembly and entry, biofilm mediated interactions, molecular analysis of clinical isolates of C. difficile, immune system development and regulation. *Unit head:* Dr. Katherine L. Knight, Co-Director, 708-216-3385, Fax: 708-216-9574, E-mail: kknight@lumc.edu. *Application contact:* Dr. Paul O'Keefe, Director of Admissions Committee, 708-216-6667, Fax: 707-216-9574, E-mail: pokeefe@lumc.edu.

Montana State University, College of Graduate Studies, College of Agriculture, Department of Immunology and Infectious Diseases, Bozeman, MT 59717. Offers MS, PhD. Part-time programs available. *Degree requirements:* For master's, comprehensive exam; for doctorate, comprehensive exam, thesis/dissertation. *Entrance requirements:* For master's and doctorate, GRE General Test. Additional exam requirements/recommendations for international students: Required—TOEFL (minimum score 550 paper-based; 213 computer-based). Electronic applications accepted. *Faculty research:* Immunology, mechanisms of infectious disease pathogenesis, mechanisms of host defense, lymphocyte development, host-pathogen interactions.

North Carolina State University, College of Veterinary Medicine, Program in Comparative Biomedical Sciences, Raleigh, NC 27695. Offers cell biology (MS, PhD); infectious disease (MS, PhD); pathology (MS, PhD); pharmacology (MS, PhD); population medicine (MS, PhD). Part-time programs available. *Degree requirements:* For master's, thesis; for doctorate, thesis/dissertation. *Entrance requirements:* For master's and doctorate, GRE General Test. Additional exam requirements/recommendations for international students: Required—TOEFL (minimum score 550 paper-based; 213 computer-based). Electronic applications accepted. *Expenses:* Contact institution. *Faculty research:* Infectious diseases, cell biology, pharmacology and toxicology, genomics, pathology and population medicine.

Penn State University Park, Graduate School, Intercollege Graduate Programs, Intercollege Graduate Program in Immunology and Infectious Diseases, State College, University Park, PA 16802-1503. Offers MS, PhD. *Unit head:* Dr. Regina Vasilatos-Younken, Senior Associate Dean, 814-865-2516, Fax: 814-863-4627, E-mail: rxv@psu.edu. *Application contact:* Cynthia E. Nicosia, Director, Graduate Enrollment Services, 814-865-1795, Fax: 814-865-4627, E-mail: cey1@psu.edu. Web site: http://www.huck.psu.edu/education/immunology-and-infectious-diseases.

State University of New York Upstate Medical University, College of Graduate Studies, Major Research Areas of the College of Graduate Studies, Syracuse, NY 13210-2334.

Tufts University, Cummings School of Veterinary Medicine, North Grafton, MA 01536. Offers animals and public policy (MS); biomedical sciences (PhD), including digestive diseases, infectious diseases, neuroscience and reproductive biology; pathology; conservation medicine (MS); veterinary medicine (DVM); DVM/MPH; DVM/MS. *Accreditation:* AVMA (one or more programs are accredited). *Faculty:* 93 full-time (42 women), 14 part-time/adjunct (7 women). *Students:* 381 full-time (326 women); includes 47 minority (3 Black or African American, non-Hispanic/Latino; 4 American Indian or Alaska Native, non-Hispanic/Latino; 23 Asian, non-Hispanic/Latino; 16 Hispanic/Latino; 1 Two or more races, non-Hispanic/Latino), 7 international. Average age 25. 762 applicants, 33% accepted, 122 enrolled. In 2011, 8 master's, 80 doctorates awarded. *Degree requirements:* For master's, thesis (for some programs); for doctorate, comprehensive exam, thesis/dissertation (for some programs). *Entrance requirements:* For master's and doctorate, GRE General Test. Additional exam requirements/recommendations for international students: Required—TOEFL or IELTS. *Application deadline:* For fall admission, 11/1 for domestic and international students. Application fee: $70. Electronic applications accepted. *Expenses:* Contact institution. *Financial support:* In 2011–12, 245 students received support, including 6 research assistantships with full tuition reimbursements available (averaging $25,000 per year), 4

teaching assistantships (averaging $5,000 per year); career-related internships or fieldwork, Federal Work-Study, institutionally sponsored loans, scholarships/grants, and institutional aid awards; health care benefits for PhD students also available. Financial award application deadline: 5/15; financial award applicants required to submit FAFSA. *Faculty research:* Oncology, veterinary ethics, international veterinary medicine, veterinary genomics, pathogenesis of Clostridium difficile, wildlife fertility control. *Unit head:* Dr. Deborah T. Kochevar, Dean, 508-839-5302, Fax: 508-839-2953, E-mail: deborah.kochevar@tufts.edu. *Application contact:* Rebecca Russo, Director of Admissions, 508-839-7920, Fax: 508-887-4820, E-mail: vetadmissions@tufts.edu. Web site: http://www.tufts.edu/.

Tulane University, School of Public Health and Tropical Medicine, Department of Tropical Medicine, New Orleans, LA 70118-5669. Offers clinical tropical medicine and travelers health (Diploma); parasitology (MSPH, PhD); public health and tropical medicine (MPHTM); vector borne infectious diseases (MS, PhD); MD/PhD. MS and PhD offered through the Graduate School. *Degree requirements:* For master's, thesis; for doctorate, comprehensive exam, thesis/dissertation. *Entrance requirements:* For master's, GRE General Test, minimum B average in undergraduate course work; for doctorate, GRE General Test. Additional exam requirements/recommendations for international students: Required—TOEFL.

Uniformed Services University of the Health Sciences, School of Medicine, Graduate Programs in the Biomedical Sciences and Public Health, Graduate Program in Emerging Infectious Diseases, Bethesda, MD 20814-4799. Offers PhD. *Faculty:* 35 full-time (5 women), 17 part-time/adjunct (6 women). *Students:* 37 full-time (24 women); includes 5 minority (1 Black or African American, non-Hispanic/Latino; 3 Asian, non-Hispanic/Latino; 1 Hispanic/Latino), 3 international. Average age 26. 43 applicants, 44% accepted, 11 enrolled. In 2011, 7 doctorates awarded. *Degree requirements:* For doctorate, comprehensive exam, thesis/dissertation, qualifying exam. *Entrance requirements:* For doctorate, GRE General Test. Additional exam requirements/recommendations for international students: Required—TOEFL. *Application deadline:* For fall admission, 1/1 priority date for domestic students, 1/1 for international students. Applications are processed on a rolling basis. Application fee: $0. Electronic applications accepted. *Financial support:* In 2011–12, fellowships with full tuition reimbursements (averaging $27,000 per year) were awarded; scholarships/grants, health care benefits, and tuition waivers (full) also available. *Unit head:* Dr. Christopher Broder, Director, 301-295-3401, E-mail: cbroder@usuhs.mil. *Application contact:* Patricia Sinclair, Program Administrative Specialist, 301-295-3400, Fax: 301-295-6772, E-mail: psinclair@usuhs.mil. Web site: http://www.usuhs.mil/eid.

See Display on next page and Close-Up on page 353.

Université Laval, Faculty of Medicine, Post-Professional Programs in Medical Studies, Québec, QC G1K 7P4, Canada. Offers anatomy–pathology (DESS); anesthesiology (DESS); cardiology (DESS); care of older people (Diploma); clinical research (DESS); community health (DESS); dermatology (DESS); diagnostic radiology (DESS); emergency medicine (Diploma); family medicine (DESS); general surgery (DESS); geriatrics (DESS); hematology (DESS); internal medicine (DESS); maternal and fetal medicine (Diploma); medical biochemistry (DESS); medical microbiology and infectious diseases (DESS); medical oncology (DESS); nephrology (DESS); neurology (DESS); neurosurgery (DESS); obstetrics and gynecology (DESS); ophthalmology (DESS); orthopedic surgery (DESS); oto-rhino-laryngology (DESS); palliative medicine (Diploma); pediatrics (DESS); plastic surgery (DESS); psychiatry (DESS); pulmonary medicine (DESS); radiology–oncology (DESS); thoracic surgery (DESS); urology (DESS). *Degree requirements:* For other advanced degree, comprehensive exam. *Entrance requirements:* For degree, knowledge of French. Electronic applications accepted.

University of Calgary, Faculty of Medicine and Faculty of Graduate Studies, Department of Microbiology and Infectious Diseases, Calgary, AB T2N 1N4, Canada. Offers M Sc, PhD. *Degree requirements:* For master's, thesis, oral thesis exam; for doctorate, thesis/dissertation, candidacy exam, oral thesis exam. *Entrance requirements:* For master's and doctorate, minimum GPA of 3.2. Additional exam requirements/recommendations for international students: Required—TOEFL (minimum score 580 paper-based; 237 computer-based). Electronic applications accepted. *Faculty research:* Bacteriology, virology, parasitology, immunology.

University of California, Berkeley, Graduate Division, School of Public Health, Group in Epidemiology, Berkeley, CA 94720-1500. Offers epidemiology (MS, PhD); infectious diseases (MPH, PhD). *Accreditation:* CEPH (one or more programs are accredited). *Degree requirements:* For master's, comprehensive exam; for doctorate, thesis/dissertation, oral and written exam. *Entrance requirements:* For master's, GRE General Test, minimum GPA of 3.0; MD, DDS, DVM, or PhD in biomedical science (MPH); for doctorate, GRE General Test, minimum GPA of 3.0.

University of California, Berkeley, Graduate Division, School of Public Health, Group in Infectious Diseases and Immunity, Berkeley, CA 94720-1500. Offers PhD. *Entrance requirements:* For doctorate, GRE General Test, minimum GPA of 3.0, 3 letters of recommendation.

University of Georgia, College of Veterinary Medicine, Department of Infectious Diseases, Athens, GA 30602. Offers MS, PhD. *Faculty:* 25 full-time (9 women), 2 part-time/adjunct (0 women). *Students:* 47 full-time (28 women), 1 part-time; includes 4 minority (2 Black or African American, non-Hispanic/Latino; 2 Asian, non-Hispanic/Latino), 14 international. Average age 29. 54 applicants, 31% accepted, 7 enrolled. In 2011, 9 doctorates awarded. *Degree requirements:* For master's, thesis; for doctorate, one foreign language, thesis/dissertation. *Entrance requirements:* For master's and doctorate, GRE General Test. *Application deadline:* For fall admission, 7/1 priority date for domestic students; for spring admission, 11/15 for domestic students. Application fee: $50. Electronic applications accepted. *Financial support:* Fellowships, research assistantships, teaching assistantships, and unspecified assistantships available. *Unit head:* Dr. Frederick Quinn, Head, 706-542-5790, Fax: 706-542-5771, E-mail: fquinn@uga.edu. *Application contact:* Dr. David S. Peterson, Graduate Coordinator, 706-542-5242, Fax: 706-542-5771, E-mail: dspete@uga.edu. Web site: http://www.vet.uga.edu/ID/.

University of Guelph, Ontario Veterinary College and Graduate Studies, Graduate Programs in Veterinary Sciences, Department of Pathobiology, Guelph, ON N1G 2W1, Canada. Offers anatomic pathology (DV Sc, Diploma); clinical pathology (Diploma); comparative pathology (M Sc, PhD); immunology (M Sc, PhD); laboratory animal science (DV Sc); pathology (M Sc, PhD, Diploma); veterinary infectious diseases (M Sc, PhD); zoo animal/wildlife medicine (DV Sc). *Degree requirements:* For master's, thesis; for doctorate, thesis/dissertation. *Entrance requirements:* For master's, DVM with B average or an honours degree in biological sciences; for doctorate, DVM or MSC degree, minimum B+ average. Additional exam requirements/recommendations for international students: Required—TOEFL (minimum score 550 paper-based; 213 computer-based). *Faculty research:* Pathogenesis; diseases of animals, wildlife, fish, and laboratory animals; parasitology; immunology; veterinary infectious diseases; laboratory animal science.

Infectious Diseases

University of Medicine and Dentistry of New Jersey, Graduate School of Biomedical Sciences, Graduate Programs in Biomedical Sciences–Newark, Newark, NJ 07107. Offers biodefense (Certificate); biomedical engineering (PhD); biomedical sciences (multidisciplinary) (PhD); cellular biology, neuroscience and physiology (PhD), including neuroscience, physiology, biophysics, cardiovascular biology, molecular pharmacology, stem cell biology; infection, immunity and inflammation (PhD), including immunology, infectious disease, microbiology, oral biology; molecular biology, genetics and cancer (PhD), including biochemistry, molecular genetics, cancer biology, radiation biology, bioinformatics; neuroscience (Certificate); pharmacological sciences (Certificate); stem cell (Certificate); DMD/PhD; MD/PhD. PhD in biomedical engineering offered jointly with New Jersey Institute of Technology. Part-time and evening/weekend programs available. Terminal master's awarded for partial completion of doctoral program. *Degree requirements:* For doctorate, thesis/dissertation, qualifying exam. *Entrance requirements:* For doctorate, GRE General Test. Additional exam requirements/recommendations for international students: Required—TOEFL. Electronic applications accepted.

University of Minnesota, Twin Cities Campus, School of Public Health, Division of Environmental Health Sciences, Area in Environmental Infectious Diseases, Minneapolis, MN 55455-0213. Offers MPH, MS, PhD. *Degree requirements:* For doctorate, thesis/dissertation. *Entrance requirements:* For master's and doctorate, GRE General Test. Electronic applications accepted.

The University of Montana, Graduate School, College of Arts and Sciences, Division of Biological Sciences, Program in Ecology of Infectious Disease, Missoula, MT 59812-0002. Offers PhD.

University of Pittsburgh, Graduate School of Public Health, Department of Infectious Diseases and Microbiology, Pittsburgh, PA 15260. Offers bioscience of infectious diseases (MPH); community and behavioral intervention of infectious diseases (MPH); infectious diseases and microbiology (MS, PhD); LGBT health and wellness (Certificate). Part-time programs available. *Faculty:* 21 full-time (6 women), 24 part-time/adjunct (7 women). *Students:* 57 full-time (44 women), 13 part-time (9 women); includes 15 minority (4 Black or African American, non-Hispanic/Latino; 9 Asian, non-Hispanic/Latino; 2 Hispanic/Latino), 7 international. Average age 27. 157 applicants, 56% accepted, 29 enrolled. In 2011, 13 master's, 3 doctorates awarded. Terminal master's awarded for partial completion of doctoral program. *Degree requirements:* For master's, one foreign language, comprehensive exam (for some programs), thesis; for doctorate, one foreign language, comprehensive exam, thesis/dissertation. *Entrance requirements:* For master's and doctorate, GRE General Test, MCAT, or DAT. Additional exam requirements/recommendations for international students: Required—TOEFL (minimum score 550 paper-based; 80 iBT) or IELTS (minimum score 6.5). *Application deadline:* For fall admission, 1/4 priority date for domestic students, 1/4 for international students. Applications are processed on a rolling basis. Application fee: $115. Electronic applications accepted. *Expenses:* Tuition, state resident: full-time $18,774; part-time $760 per credit. Tuition, nonresident: full-time $30,736; part-time $1258 per credit. *Required fees:* $740; $200 per term. Tuition and fees vary according to program. *Financial support:* In 2011–12, 31 students received support, including 12 fellowships (averaging $7,248 per year), 19 research assistantships with full and partial tuition reimbursements available (averaging $5,448 per year). Financial award applicants required to submit FAFSA. *Faculty research:* HIV, Epstein-Barr virus, virology, immunology, malaria. *Total annual research expenditures:* $15.6 million. *Unit head:* Dr. Charles R. Rinaldo, Jr., Chairman, 412-624-3928, Fax: 412-624-4953, E-mail: rinaldo@pitt.edu. *Application contact:* Dr. Jeremy Martinson, Assistant Professor, 412-624-5646, Fax: 412-383-8926, E-mail: jmartins@pitt.edu. Web site: http://www.idm.pitt.edu/.

The University of Texas Medical Branch, Graduate School of Biomedical Sciences, Center for Biodefense and Emerging Infectious Diseases, Galveston, TX 77555. Offers biodefense training (PhD). *Entrance requirements:* For doctorate, GRE, minimum overall GPA of 3.0.

The University of Texas Medical Branch, Graduate School of Biomedical Sciences, Program in Emerging and Tropical Infectious Diseases, Galveston, TX 77555. Offers PhD, MD/PhD. *Degree requirements:* For doctorate, thesis/dissertation. *Entrance requirements:* For doctorate, GRE General Test. *Faculty research:* Emerging diseases, tropical diseases, parasitology, vitology and bacteriology.

Yale University, School of Medicine and Graduate School of Arts and Sciences, Combined Program in Biological and Biomedical Sciences (BBS), Microbiology Track, New Haven, CT 06520. Offers PhD, MD/PhD. *Degree requirements:* For doctorate, thesis/dissertation. *Entrance requirements:* For doctorate, GRE General Test, GRE Subject Test. Additional exam requirements/recommendations for international students: Required—TOEFL. Electronic applications accepted.

Medical Microbiology

Creighton University, School of Medicine and Graduate School, Graduate Programs in Medicine, Department of Medical Microbiology and Immunology, Omaha, NE 68178-0001. Offers MS, PhD. Terminal master's awarded for partial completion of doctoral program. *Degree requirements:* For master's, comprehensive exam, thesis; for doctorate, thesis/dissertation, preliminary exams. *Entrance requirements:* For master's and doctorate, GRE General Test. Additional exam requirements/recommendations for international students: Required—TOEFL. *Expenses: Tuition:* Full-time $12,672; part-time $704 per credit hour. *Required fees:* $1410; $136 per semester. Tuition and fees vary according to campus/location and reciprocity agreements. *Faculty research:* Infectious diseases, molecular biology, genetics, antimicrobial agents and chemotherapy, virology.

Idaho State University, Office of Graduate Studies, College of Science and Engineering, Department of Biological Sciences, Pocatello, ID 83209-8007. Offers biology (MNS, MS, DA, PhD); clinical laboratory science (MS); microbiology (MS). *Accreditation:* NAACLS. Part-time programs available. *Degree requirements:* For master's, comprehensive exam, thesis; for doctorate, comprehensive exam, thesis/dissertation, 9 credits of internship (for DA). *Entrance requirements:* For master's, GRE General Test, minimum GPA of 3.0 in all upper division classes; for doctorate, GRE

UNIFORMED SERVICES UNIVERSITY

The Uniformed Services University of the Health Sciences is the nation's federal health sciences university and is committed to excellence in military medicine and public health during peace and war.

We provide the nation with health professionals who are dedicated to both civilian and military career service in the Department of Defense and the United States Public Health Service and with scientists who serve the common good.

We serve the uniformed services and the nation as an outstanding academic health sciences center with a worldwide perspective for education, research, service, and consultation. We are unique in relating these activities to military medicine, disaster medicine, and military medical readiness.

For more information, contact:

Uniformed Services University
4301 Jones Bridge Road
Bethesda, Maryland 20814-4799
Phone: 301-295-3913 or 800-772-1747 (toll-free)

http://www.usuhs.mil

General Test, GRE Subject Test (biology), diagnostic exam (DA), minimum GPA of 3.0 in all upper division classes. Additional exam requirements/recommendations for international students: Required—TOEFL (minimum score 550 paper-based; 213 computer-based; 80 iBT). Electronic applications accepted. *Faculty research:* Ecology, plant and animal physiology, plant and animal developmental biology, immunology, molecular biology, bioinfomatics.

Rutgers, The State University of New Jersey, New Brunswick, Graduate School-New Brunswick, Programs in the Molecular Biosciences, Program in Microbiology and Molecular Genetics, Piscataway, NJ 08854-8097. Offers applied microbiology (MS, PhD); clinical microbiology (MS, PhD); computational molecular biology (PhD); immunology (MS, PhD); microbial biochemistry (MS, PhD); molecular genetics (MS, PhD); virology (MS, PhD). MS, PhD offered jointly with University of Medicine and Dentistry of New Jersey. Part-time programs available. Terminal master's awarded for partial completion of doctoral program. *Degree requirements:* For master's, comprehensive exam, thesis or alternative; for doctorate, comprehensive exam, thesis/dissertation, written qualifying exam. *Entrance requirements:* For master's, GRE General Test, minimum GPA of 3.0; for doctorate, GRE General Test, GRE Subject Test (recommended), minimum GPA of 3.0. Additional exam requirements/recommendations for international students: Required—TOEFL. Electronic applications accepted. *Faculty research:* Molecular genetics and microbial physiology; virology and pathogenic microbiology; applied, environmental and industrial microbiology; computers in molecular biology.

Texas Tech University Health Sciences Center, Graduate School of Biomedical Sciences, Department of Microbiology and Immunology, Lubbock, TX 79430. Offers medical microbiology (MS, PhD); MD/PhD; MS/PhD. Terminal master's awarded for partial completion of doctoral program. *Degree requirements:* For master's, thesis; for doctorate, thesis/dissertation. *Entrance requirements:* For master's and doctorate, GRE General Test, minimum GPA of 3.0. Additional exam requirements/recommendations for international students: Required—TOEFL (minimum score 550 paper-based; 213 computer-based). Electronic applications accepted. *Faculty research:* Genetics, pathogenic bacteriology, molecular biology, virology, medical mycology.

Université du Québec, Institut National de la Recherche Scientifique, Graduate Programs, Research Center - INRS - Institut Armand-Frappier - Human Health, Québec, QC G1K 9A9, Canada. Offers applied microbiology (M Sc); biology (PhD); experimental health sciences (M Sc); virology and immunology (M Sc, PhD). Programs given in French. Part-time programs available. *Faculty:* 41. *Students:* 158 full-time (93 women), 11 part-time (5 women), 52 international. Average age 30. In 2011, 17 master's, 9 doctorates awarded. *Degree requirements:* For master's, thesis optional; for doctorate, thesis/dissertation. *Entrance requirements:* For master's and doctorate, appropriate bachelor's degree, proficiency in French. *Application deadline:* For fall admission, 3/30 for domestic and international students; for winter admission, 11/1 for domestic and international students; for spring admission, 3/1 for domestic and international students. Application fee: $45 Canadian dollars. *Financial support:* In 2011–12, 128 students received support, including fellowships (averaging $16,500 per year); research assistantships also available. *Faculty research:* Immunity, infection and cancer; toxicology and environmental biotechnology; molecular pharmacochemistry. *Unit head:* Charles Dozois, Director, 450-687-5010, Fax: 450-686-5566, E-mail: charles.dozois@iaf.inrs.ca. *Application contact:* Yvonne Boisvert, Registrar, 418-654-3861, Fax: 418-654-3858, E-mail: regIstrariat@adm.inrs.ca. Web site: http://www.iaf.inrs.ca.

University of Alberta, Faculty of Medicine and Dentistry and Faculty of Graduate Studies and Research, Graduate Programs in Medicine, Department of Medical Microbiology and Immunology, Edmonton, AB T6G 2E1, Canada. Offers M Sc, PhD. Terminal master's awarded for partial completion of doctoral program. *Degree requirements:* For master's, thesis; for doctorate, thesis/dissertation. *Entrance requirements:* For master's and doctorate, minimum GPA of 3.3. Additional exam requirements/recommendations for international students: Required—TOEFL (minimum score 600 paper-based; 232 computer-based; 96 iBT). *Faculty research:* Cellular and reproductive immunology, microbial pathogenesis, mechanisms of antibiotic resistance, molecular biology of mammalian viruses, antiviral chemotherapy.

University of Hawaii at Manoa, John A. Burns School of Medicine and Graduate Division, Graduate Programs in Biomedical Sciences, Department of Tropical Medicine, Medical Microbiology and Pharmacology, Honolulu, HI 96822. Offers tropical medicine (MS, PhD). Part-time programs available. Terminal master's awarded for partial completion of doctoral program. *Degree requirements:* For master's, thesis optional; for doctorate, comprehensive exam, thesis/dissertation. *Entrance requirements:* For master's and doctorate, GRE General Test. Additional exam requirements/recommendations for international students: Required—TOEFL (minimum score 580 paper-based; 237 computer-based; 92 iBT), IELTS (minimum score 5). *Faculty*

research: Immunological studies of dengue, malaria, Kawasaki's disease, lupus erythematosus, rheumatoid disease.

University of Manitoba, Faculty of Medicine and Faculty of Graduate Studies, Graduate Programs in Medicine, Department of Medical Microbiology, Winnipeg, MB R3T 2N2, Canada. Offers M Sc, PhD. Part-time programs available. Terminal master's awarded for partial completion of doctoral program. *Degree requirements:* For master's, thesis; for doctorate, one foreign language, thesis/dissertation. *Entrance requirements:* For master's and doctorate, minimum GPA of 3.0. Electronic applications accepted. *Faculty research:* HIV, bacterial adhesion, sexually transmitted diseases, virus structure/function and assembly.

University of Minnesota, Duluth, Medical School, Microbiology, Immunology and Molecular Pathobiology Section, Duluth, MN 55812-2496. Offers MS, PhD. MS, PhD offered jointly with University of Minnesota, Twin Cities Campus. Terminal master's awarded for partial completion of doctoral program. *Degree requirements:* For master's, thesis, final oral exam; for doctorate, thesis/dissertation, final exam, oral and written preliminary exams. *Entrance requirements:* For master's and doctorate, GRE General Test. Additional exam requirements/recommendations for international students: Required—TOEFL. *Faculty research:* Immunomodulation, molecular diagnosis of rabies, cytokines, cancer immunology, cytomegalovirus infection.

University of Wisconsin–La Crosse, Office of University Graduate Studies, College of Science and Health, Department of Biology, Program in Clinical Microbiology, La Crosse, WI 54601-3742. Offers MS. Part-time programs available. *Faculty:* 1 (woman) full-time. *Students:* 12 full-time (9 women), 5 part-time (3 women); includes 3 minority (2 Asian, non-Hispanic/Latino; 1 Hispanic/Latino), 1 international. Average age 27. 22 applicants, 41% accepted, 7 enrolled. In 2011, 6 master's awarded. *Degree requirements:* For master's, comprehensive exam, thesis. *Entrance requirements:* For master's, GRE General Test, minimum GPA of 2.85, three letters of recommendation. Additional exam requirements/recommendations for international students: Required—TOEFL (minimum score 550 paper-based; 213 computer-based; 79 iBT). *Application deadline:* For fall admission, 1/20 priority date for domestic students, 1/20 for international students. Applications are processed on a rolling basis. Application fee: $56. Electronic applications accepted. *Expenses:* Tuition, state resident: full-time $8391; part-time $481.17 per credit. Tuition, nonresident: full-time $17,850; part-time $1006.68 per credit. *Required fees:* $2 per credit. $18.25 per semester. Tuition and fees vary according to course load, program, reciprocity agreements and student level. *Financial support:* Federal Work-Study, scholarships/grants, health care benefits, and tuition waivers available. Support available to part-time students. Financial award application deadline: 3/15; financial award applicants required to submit FAFSA. *Faculty research:* Pathogenic bacteriology, mycology, virology, parasitology, immunology. *Unit head:* Dr. Michael Hoffman, Program Director, 608-785-6984, E-mail: hoffman.mic2@uwlax.edu. *Application contact:* Kathryn Kiefer, Director of Admissions, 608-785-8939, E-mail: admissions@uwlax.edu. Web site: http://www.uwlax.edu/microbiology/.

University of Wisconsin–Madison, School of Medicine and Public Health and Graduate School, Graduate Programs in Medicine and College of Agricultural and Life Sciences, Microbiology Doctoral Training Program, Madison, WI 53706. Offers PhD. *Faculty:* 91 full-time (32 women). *Students:* 74 full-time (43 women); includes 11 minority (2 Black or African American, non-Hispanic/Latino; 9 Hispanic/Latino), 4 international. Average age 24. 252 applicants, 18% accepted, 20 enrolled. In 2011, 19 doctorates awarded. *Degree requirements:* For doctorate, thesis/dissertation, preliminary exam, 1semester of teaching, professional development requirement. *Entrance requirements:* For doctorate, GRE. Additional exam requirements/recommendations for international students: Required—TOEFL (minimum score 580 paper-based; 237 computer-based). *Application deadline:* For fall admission, 12/1 for domestic and international students. Application fee: $56. Electronic applications accepted. *Expenses:* Tuition, state resident: full-time $10,296; part-time $643.51 per credit. Tuition, nonresident: full-time $24,054; part-time $1503.40 per credit. *Required fees:* $70.06 per credit. Tuition and fees vary according to course load, campus/location, program and reciprocity agreements. *Financial support:* In 2011–12, 74 students received support, including 28 fellowships with tuition reimbursements available (averaging $24,500 per year), 46 research assistantships with tuition reimbursements available (averaging $24,500 per year); career-related internships or fieldwork, scholarships/grants, traineeships, health care benefits, and tuition waivers (full) also available. Financial award application deadline: 12/1. *Faculty research:* Microbial pathogenesis, gene regulation, immunology, virology, cell biology. *Total annual research expenditures:* $15.1 million. *Unit head:* Dr. John Mansfield, Director, 608-262-2596, Fax: 608-262-8418, E-mail: jmansfield@bact.wisc.edu. *Application contact:* Cathy Davis Gray, Coordinator, 608-265-0689, Fax: 608-262-8418, E-mail: cdg@bact.wisc.edu. Web site: http://www.microbiology.wisc.edu/.

Microbiology

Albany Medical College, Center for Immunology and Microbial Disease, Albany, NY 12208-3479. Offers MS, PhD. Part-time programs available. Terminal master's awarded for partial completion of doctoral program. *Degree requirements:* For master's, thesis; for doctorate, comprehensive exam, thesis/dissertation, oral qualifying exam, written preliminary exam, 1 published paper-peer review. *Entrance requirements:* For master's, GRE General Test, all transcripts, letters of recommendation; for doctorate, GRE General Test, letters of recommendation. Additional exam requirements/recommendations for international students: Required—TOEFL. *Faculty research:* Microbial and viral pathogenesis, cancer development and cell transformation, biochemical and genetic mechanisms responsible for human disease.

Albert Einstein College of Medicine, Graduate Division of Biomedical Sciences, Department of Microbiology and Immunology, Bronx, NY 10461. Offers PhD, MD/PhD. *Degree requirements:* For doctorate, thesis/dissertation. *Entrance requirements:* For doctorate, GRE General Test. Additional exam requirements/recommendations for international students: Required—TOEFL. *Faculty research:* Nature of histocompatibility antigens, lymphoid cell receptors, regulation of immune responses and mechanisms of resistance to infection.

American University of Beirut, Graduate Programs, Faculty of Medicine, Beirut, Lebanon. Offers anatomy, cell biology and human morphology (MS); biochemistry and medical genetics (MS); biomedical sciences (PhD); experimental pathology, immunology and microbiology (MS); medicine (MD); neuroscience (MS); pharmacology and toxicology (MS). Part-time programs available. *Faculty:* 232 full-time (58 women), 68 part-time/adjunct (7 women). *Students:* 346 full-time (135 women), 69 part-time (57 women). Average age 23. In 2011, 20 master's, 82 doctorates awarded. *Degree*

requirements: For master's, one foreign language, comprehensive exam, thesis (for some programs). *Entrance requirements:* For master's, letter of recommendation; for doctorate, MCAT, bachelor's degree. Additional exam requirements/recommendations for international students: Required—TOEFL (minimum score 600 paper-based; 250 computer-based; 100 iBT), IELTS (minimum score 7.5). *Application deadline:* For fall admission, 4/30 for domestic and international students; for spring admission, 11/1 for domestic and international students. Application fee: $50. *Expenses:* Tuition: Full-time $12,780; part-time $710 per credit. Tuition and fees vary according to course load and program. *Financial support:* In 2011–12, 19 students received support. Career-related internships or fieldwork, institutionally sponsored loans, scholarships/grants, health care benefits, and unspecified assistantships available. Financial award application deadline: 2/2. *Faculty research:* Cancer research (targeted therapy, mechanisms of leukemogenesis, tumor cell extravasation and metastasis, cancer stem cells); stem cell research (regenerative medicine, drug discovery); genetic research (neurogenetics, hereditary cardiomyopathy, hemoglobinopathies, pharmacogenomics, proteomics); neuroscience research (pain, neurodegenerative disorder); metabolism (inflammation and metabolism, metabolic disorder, diabetes mellitus); vascular and renal biology, signal transduction. *Total annual research expenditures:* $2.3 million. *Unit head:* Dr. Mohamed Sayegh, Dean, 961-1350000 Ext. 4700, Fax: 961-1744464, E-mail: msayegh@aub.edu.lb. *Application contact:* Dr. Salim Kanaan, Director, Admissions Office, 961-1350000 Ext. 2594, Fax: 961-1750775, E-mail: sk00@aub.edu.lb. Web site: http://www.aub.edu.lb/fm/fm_home/Pages/index.aspx.

Arizona State University, College of Liberal Arts and Sciences, School of Life Sciences, Tempe, AZ 85287-4601. Offers animal behavior (PhD); applied ethics (biomedical and health ethics) (MA); biological design (PhD); biology (MS, PhD); biology

Microbiology

(biology and society) (MS, PhD); environmental life sciences (PhD); evolutionary biology (PhD); human and social dimensions of science and technology (PhD); microbiology (PhD); molecular and cellular biology (PhD); neuroscience (PhD); philosophy (history and philosophy of science) (MA); sustainability (PhD). Terminal master's awarded for partial completion of doctoral program. *Degree requirements:* For master's, thesis (for some programs), interactive Program of Study (iPOS) submitted before completing 50 percent of required credit hours; for doctorate, variable foreign language requirement, comprehensive exam, thesis/dissertation, interactive Program of Study (iPOS) submitted before completing 50 percent of required credit hours. *Entrance requirements:* For master's and doctorate, GRE, minimum GPA of 3.0 or equivalent in last 2 years of work leading to bachelor's degree. Additional exam requirements/recommendations for international students: Required—TOEFL (minimum score 600 paper-based; 250 computer-based; 100 iBT). Electronic applications accepted.

Auburn University, Graduate School, College of Sciences and Mathematics, Department of Biological Sciences, Auburn University, AL 36849. Offers botany (MS, PhD); microbiology (MS, PhD); zoology (MS, PhD). *Faculty:* 35 full-time (11 women). *Students:* 32 full-time (13 women), 73 part-time (33 women); includes 11 minority (3 Black or African American, non-Hispanic/Latino; 1 American Indian or Alaska Native, non-Hispanic/Latino; 5 Asian, non-Hispanic/Latino; 2 Hispanic/Latino), 24 international. Average age 29. 106 applicants, 28% accepted, 19 enrolled. In 2011, 14 master's, 9 doctorates awarded. *Entrance requirements:* For master's and doctorate, GRE General Test. Additional exam requirements/recommendations for international students: Required—TOEFL. *Application deadline:* For fall admission, 7/7 for domestic students; for spring admission, 11/24 for domestic students. Application fee: $50 ($60 for international students). Electronic applications accepted. *Expenses:* Tuition, state resident: full-time $7290; part-time $405 per credit hour. Tuition, nonresident: full-time $21,870; part-time $1215 per credit hour. *International tuition:* $22,000 full-time. *Required fees:* $1402. *Financial support:* Research assistantships and teaching assistantships available. Financial award applicants required to submit FAFSA. *Unit head:* Dr. Jack W. Feminella, Chair, 334-844-3906, Fax: 334-844-1645. *Application contact:* Dr. George Flowers, Dean of the Graduate School, 334-844-2125.

Baylor College of Medicine, Graduate School of Biomedical Sciences, Department of Molecular Virology and Microbiology, Houston, TX 77030-3498. Offers PhD; MD/PhD. *Faculty:* 43 full-time (13 women). *Students:* 35 full-time (16 women); includes 10 minority (1 Black or African American, non-Hispanic/Latino; 5 Asian, non-Hispanic/Latino; 4 Hispanic/Latino), 8 international. Average age 28. 83 applicants, 11% accepted, 3 enrolled. In 2011, 3 doctorates awarded. *Degree requirements:* For doctorate, thesis/dissertation, public defense. *Entrance requirements:* For doctorate, GRE General Test, GRE Subject Test (strongly recommended), minimum GPA of 3.0. Additional exam requirements/recommendations for international students: Required—TOEFL. *Application deadline:* For fall admission, 1/1 priority date for domestic students. Applications are processed on a rolling basis. Application fee: $0. Electronic applications accepted. *Financial support:* In 2011–12, 9 fellowships with full tuition reimbursements (averaging $29,000 per year), 26 research assistantships with full tuition reimbursements (averaging $29,000 per year) were awarded; career-related internships or fieldwork, Federal Work-Study, institutionally sponsored loans, health care benefits, and tuition waivers (full) also available. Financial award applicants required to submit FAFSA. *Faculty research:* Microbiology, viral molecular biology, bacterial molecular biology, microbial pathogenesis, microbial genomics. *Unit head:* Dr. Frank Ramig, Director, 713-798-4830, Fax: 713-798-5075, E-mail: rramig@bcm.edu. *Application contact:* Rosa Banegas, Graduate Program Administrator, 713-798-4472, Fax: 713-798-5075, E-mail: rbanegas@bcm.edu. Web site: http://www.bcm.edu/molvir/.

Baylor College of Medicine, Graduate School of Biomedical Sciences, Interdepartmental Program in Cell and Molecular Biology, Houston, TX 77030-3498. Offers biochemistry (PhD); cell and molecular biology (PhD); genetics (PhD); human genetics (PhD); immunology (PhD); microbiology (PhD); virology (PhD); MD/PhD. *Faculty:* 112 full-time (30 women). *Students:* 66 full-time (42 women); includes 21 minority (5 Black or African American, non-Hispanic/Latino; 1 American Indian or Alaska Native, non-Hispanic/Latino; 7 Asian, non-Hispanic/Latino; 8 Hispanic/Latino), 14 international. Average age 27. 126 applicants, 25% accepted, 14 enrolled. In 2011, 7 degrees awarded. *Median time to degree:* Of those who began their doctoral program in fall 2003, 82% received their degree in 8 years or less. *Degree requirements:* For doctorate, thesis/dissertation, public defense. *Entrance requirements:* For doctorate, GRE General Test, GRE Subject Test (strongly recommended), minimum GPA of 3.0. Additional exam requirements/recommendations for international students: Required—TOEFL. *Application deadline:* For fall admission, 1/1 priority date for domestic students. Applications are processed on a rolling basis. Application fee: $0. Electronic applications accepted. *Financial support:* In 2011–12, 66 students received support, including 30 fellowships with full tuition reimbursements available (averaging $29,000 per year), 36 research assistantships with full tuition reimbursements available (averaging $29,000 per year); teaching assistantships, Federal Work-Study, institutionally sponsored loans, health care benefits, and tuition waivers (full) also available. Financial award applicants required to submit FAFSA. *Faculty research:* Molecular and cellular biology; cancer, aging and stem cells; genomics and proteomics; microbiome, molecular microbiology; infectious disease, immunology and translational research. *Unit head:* Dr. Susan Marriott, Director, 713-798-6557. *Application contact:* Lourdes Fernandez, Graduate Program Administrator, 713-798-6557, Fax: 713-798-6325, E-mail: cmbprog@bcm.edu. Web site: http://bcm.edu/cmb/.

Brandeis University, Graduate School of Arts and Sciences, Program in Molecular and Cell Biology, Waltham, MA 02454-9110. Offers genetics (PhD); microbiology (PhD); molecular and cell biology (MS, PhD); molecular biology (PhD); neurobiology (PhD); quantitative biology (PhD). *Faculty:* 27 full-time (11 women), 4 part-time/adjunct (1 woman). *Students:* 65 full-time (36 women); includes 8 minority (4 Black or African American, non-Hispanic/Latino; 1 American Indian or Alaska Native, non-Hispanic/Latino; 1 Asian, non-Hispanic/Latino; 2 Hispanic/Latino), 14 international. 195 applicants, 26% accepted, 21 enrolled. In 2011, 4 master's, 6 doctorates awarded. Terminal master's awarded for partial completion of doctoral program. *Degree requirements:* For master's, thesis or alternative, research project, research lab, or project lab; for doctorate, comprehensive exam, thesis/dissertation, journal clubs; research seminar; colloquia; teaching requirement; qualifying exam. *Entrance requirements:* For master's, GRE General Test; MCAT may be substituted for the GRE exam for applicants to the M.S. program; official transcript(s), resume, 3 letters of recommendation, statement of purpose; for doctorate, GRE General Test, official transcript(s), resume, 3 letters of recommendation, statement of purpose. Additional exam requirements/recommendations for international students: Required—TOEFL (minimum score 600 paper-based; 250 computer-based; 100 iBT); Recommended—IELTS (minimum score 7). *Application deadline:* For fall admission, 1/15 priority date for domestic students; for spring admission, 11/15 for domestic students. Applications are processed on a rolling basis. Application fee: $75. Electronic applications accepted. *Financial support:* In 2011–12, 17 fellowships with full tuition reimbursements (averaging $29,580 per year), 31 research assistantships with full tuition reimbursements (averaging $29,580 per year), teaching assistantships with partial tuition reimbursements (averaging $3,200 per year) were awarded; scholarships/grants, health care benefits, tuition waivers (full and partial), and unspecified assistantships also

available. Financial award application deadline: 4/15; financial award applicants required to submit FAFSA. *Faculty research:* Molecular biology, cell biology, biology, structural biology, immunology, developmental biology, neurobiology, DNA, RNA. *Unit head:* Dr. Bruce Goode, Chair, 781-736-2464, Fax: 781-736-3107, E-mail: goode@brandeis.edu. *Application contact:* Dr. Jessica Maryott, Department Administrator, 781-736-3100, Fax: 781-736-3107, E-mail: jmaryott@brandeis.edu. Web site: http://www.bio.brandeis.edu/grad/mcb/mcb_phd.html.

Brigham Young University, Graduate Studies, College of Life Sciences, Department of Microbiology and Molecular Biology, Provo, UT 84602-1001. Offers microbiology (MS, PhD); molecular biology (MS, PhD). *Faculty:* 15 full-time (3 women). *Students:* 32 full-time (13 women); includes 4 minority (3 Asian, non-Hispanic/Latino; 1 Hispanic/Latino), 5 international. Average age 28. 25 applicants, 60% accepted, 13 enrolled. In 2011, 1 degree awarded. Terminal master's awarded for partial completion of doctoral program. *Degree requirements:* For master's, comprehensive exam, thesis; for doctorate, comprehensive exam, thesis/dissertation. *Entrance requirements:* For master's, GRE General Test, minimum GPA of 3.0 during previous 2 years; for doctorate, GRE General Test, minimum GPA of 3.0. Additional exam requirements/recommendations for international students: Required—TOEFL (minimum score 580 paper-based; 85 iBT), IELTS (minimum score 7). *Application deadline:* For fall admission, 12/15 priority date for domestic students, 12/15 for international students. Application fee: $50. Electronic applications accepted. *Expenses: Tuition:* Full-time $5760; part-time $320 per credit. Tuition and fees vary according to student's religious affiliation. *Financial support:* In 2011–12, 18 students received support, including 6 research assistantships with full and partial tuition reimbursements available (averaging $18,000 per year), 6 teaching assistantships with full and partial tuition reimbursements available (averaging $18,000 per year); institutionally sponsored loans, scholarships/grants, health care benefits, and unspecified assistantships also available. Financial award application deadline: 2/1. *Faculty research:* Immunobiology, molecular genetics, molecular virology, cancer biology, pathogenic and environmental microbiology. *Total annual research expenditures:* $645,068. *Unit head:* Dr. Laura Bridgewater, Chair, 801-422-2434, Fax: 801-422-0519, E-mail: laura_bridgewater@byu.edu. *Application contact:* Dr. Richard A. Robison, Graduate Coordinator, 801-422-2416, Fax: 801-422-0519, E-mail: richard_robison@byu.edu. Web site: http://mmbio.byu.edu/.

Brown University, Graduate School, Division of Biology and Medicine, Program in Molecular Biology, Cell Biology, and Biochemistry, Providence, RI 02912. Offers biochemistry (M Med Sc, Sc M, PhD), including biochemistry (Sc M, PhD); biology (Sc M, PhD), medical science (M Med Sc, PhD); biology (MA); cell biology (M Med Sc, Sc M, PhD), including biochemistry (Sc M, PhD); biology (Sc M, PhD), medical science (M Med Sc, PhD); developmental biology (M Med Sc, Sc M, PhD), including biochemistry (Sc M, PhD), biology (Sc M, PhD), medical science (M Med Sc, PhD); immunology (M Med Sc, Sc M, PhD), including biochemistry (Sc M, PhD), biology (Sc M, PhD), medical science (M Med Sc, PhD); molecular microbiology (M Med Sc, Sc M, PhD), including biochemistry (Sc M, PhD), biology (Sc M, PhD), medical science (M Med Sc, PhD); MD/PhD. Part-time programs available. Terminal master's awarded for partial completion of doctoral program. *Degree requirements:* For master's, thesis (for some programs); for doctorate, one foreign language, thesis/dissertation, preliminary exam. *Entrance requirements:* For master's and doctorate, GRE General Test, GRE Subject Test. Additional exam requirements/recommendations for international students: Required—TOEFL. Electronic applications accepted. *Faculty research:* Molecular genetics, gene regulation.

California State University, Long Beach, Graduate Studies, College of Natural Sciences and Mathematics, Department of Biological Sciences, Long Beach, CA 90840. Offers biology (MS); microbiology (MS). Part-time programs available. *Faculty:* 23 full-time (8 women). *Students:* 8 full-time (4 women), 56 part-time (31 women); includes 24 minority (1 Black or African American, non-Hispanic/Latino; 8 Asian, non-Hispanic/Latino; 9 Hispanic/Latino; 6 Two or more races, non-Hispanic/Latino), 4 international. Average age 27. 79 applicants, 25% accepted, 13 enrolled. In 2011, 19 master's awarded. *Entrance requirements:* For master's, GRE Subject Test, minimum GPA of 3.0. *Application deadline:* For fall admission, 3/15 for domestic students. Applications are processed on a rolling basis. Application fee: $55. Electronic applications accepted. *Financial support:* Teaching assistantships, Federal Work-Study, institutionally sponsored loans, scholarships/grants, traineeships, and unspecified assistantships available. Financial award application deadline: 3/2. *Unit head:* Dr. Brian Livingston, Chair, 562-985-4807, Fax: 562-985-8878, E-mail: blivings@csulb.edu. *Application contact:* Dr. Christopher Lowe, Graduate Advisor, 562-985-4918, Fax: 562-985-8878, E-mail: clowe@csulb.edu.

Case Western Reserve University, School of Medicine and School of Graduate Studies, Graduate Programs in Medicine, Department of Molecular Biology and Microbiology, Cleveland, OH 44106-4960. Offers cellular biology (PhD); microbiology (PhD); molecular biology (PhD); molecular virology (PhD); MD/PhD. Students are admitted to an integrated Biomedical Sciences Training Program involving 11 basic science programs at Case Western Reserve University. *Degree requirements:* For doctorate, thesis/dissertation. *Entrance requirements:* For doctorate, GRE General Test, GRE Subject Test. Additional exam requirements/recommendations for international students: Required—TOEFL. Electronic applications accepted. *Faculty research:* Gene expression in eukaryotic and prokaryotic systems; microbial physiology; intracellular transport and signaling; mechanisms of oncogenesis; molecular mechanisms of RNA processing, editing, and catalysis.

The Catholic University of America, School of Arts and Sciences, Department of Biology, Washington, DC 20064. Offers cell and microbial biology (MS, PhD), including cell biology, microbiology; clinical laboratory science (MS, PhD); MSLS/MS. Part-time programs available. *Faculty:* 9 full-time (5 women), 3 part-time/adjunct (2 women). *Students:* 19 full-time (16 women), 26 part-time (17 women); includes 10 minority (3 Black or African American, non-Hispanic/Latino; 6 Asian, non-Hispanic/Latino; 1 Hispanic/Latino), 20 international. Average age 29. 53 applicants, 62% accepted, 15 enrolled. In 2011, 1 master's, 2 doctorates awarded. *Degree requirements:* For master's, comprehensive exam, thesis or alternative; for doctorate, comprehensive exam, thesis/dissertation. *Entrance requirements:* For master's and doctorate, GRE General Test, GRE Subject Test, statement of purpose, official copies of academic transcripts, three letters of recommendation. Additional exam requirements/recommendations for international students: Required—TOEFL (minimum score 580 paper-based; 237 computer-based). *Application deadline:* For fall admission, 8/1 priority date for domestic students, 7/15 for international students; for spring admission, 12/1 priority date for domestic students, 10/15 for international students. Applications are processed on a rolling basis. Application fee: $55. Electronic applications accepted. *Expenses: Tuition:* Full-time $35,260; part-time $1380 per credit. *Required fees:* $80; $40 per semester hour. One-time fee: $425. *Financial support:* Fellowships, research assistantships, teaching assistantships, Federal Work-Study, scholarships/grants, tuition waivers (full and partial), and unspecified assistantships available. Financial award application deadline: 2/1; financial award applicants required to submit FAFSA. *Faculty research:* Cell and microbiology, molecular biology of cell proliferation, cellular effects of electromagnetic radiation, biotechnology. *Total annual research expenditures:* $1.4 million. *Unit head:* Dr. Venigalla Rao, Chair, 202-319-5271, Fax: 202-319-5721, E-mail:

rao@cua.edu. *Application contact:* Andrew Woodall, Director of Graduate Admissions, 202-319-5057, Fax: 202-319-6533, E-mail: cua-admissions@cua.edu. Web site: http://biology.cua.edu/.

Clemson University, Graduate School, College of Agriculture, Forestry and Life Sciences, Department of Biological Sciences, Program in Microbiology, Clemson, SC 29634. Offers MS, PhD. *Students:* 18 full-time (8 women), 1 part-time (0 women); includes 1 minority (Black or African American, non-Hispanic/Latino), 9 international. Average age 29. 35 applicants, 17% accepted, 6 enrolled. In 2011, 6 master's, 4 doctorates awarded. *Degree requirements:* For master's, thesis; for doctorate, comprehensive exam, thesis/dissertation. *Entrance requirements:* For master's and doctorate, GRE General Test. Additional exam requirements/recommendations for international students: Required—TOEFL, IELTS. *Application deadline:* For fall admission, 1/15 for domestic students, 4/15 for international students. Application fee: $70 ($80 for international students). Electronic applications accepted. *Expenses:* Contact institution. *Financial support:* In 2011–12, 18 students received support, including 1 fellowship with full and partial tuition reimbursement available (averaging $10,000 per year), 6 research assistantships with partial tuition reimbursements available (averaging $18,500 per year), 13 teaching assistantships with partial tuition reimbursements available (averaging $16,231 per year); career-related internships or fieldwork, institutionally sponsored loans, scholarships/grants, health care benefits, and unspecified assistantships also available. Financial award application deadline: 3/1; financial award applicants required to submit FAFSA. *Faculty research:* Anaerobic microbiology, microbiology and ecology of soil and aquatic systems, microbial genetics, biofilms, nanotechnology. *Unit head:* Dr. Alfred Wheeler, Department Chair, 864-656-1415, Fax: 864-656-0435, E-mail: wheeler@clemson.edu. *Application contact:* Jay Lyn Martin, Coordinator for Graduate Program, 864-656-3587, Fax: 864-656-0435, E-mail: gradbio@clemson.edu. Web site: http://www.clemson.edu/cafls/departments/biosci/index.html.

Colorado State University, College of Veterinary Medicine and Biomedical Sciences, Department of Microbiology, Immunology and Pathology, Fort Collins, CO 80523-0015. Offers microbiology (MS, PhD); pathology (PhD). *Faculty:* 43 full-time (18 women), 2 part-time/adjunct (0 women). *Students:* 46 full-time (32 women), 38 part-time (28 women); includes 8 minority (2 Asian, non-Hispanic/Latino; 6 Hispanic/Latino), 10 international. Average age 31. 107 applicants, 14% accepted, 14 enrolled. In 2011, 3 master's, 13 doctorates awarded. *Degree requirements:* For master's, thesis; for doctorate, comprehensive exam, thesis/dissertation. *Entrance requirements:* For master's, GRE General Test, minimum GPA of 3.0, BA/BS in biomedical field, reviewer evaluation forms, resume; for doctorate, GRE General Test, minimum GPA of 3.0, BA/BS in biomedical field, reviewer evaluation forms, resume, statement of interest. Additional exam requirements/recommendations for international students: Required—TOEFL (minimum score 550 paper-based). *Application deadline:* For fall admission, 1/1 priority date for domestic students; for spring admission, 10/1 priority date for domestic students. Applications are processed on a rolling basis. Application fee: $50. Electronic applications accepted. *Expenses:* Tuition, state resident: full-time $7992. Tuition, nonresident: full-time $19,592. *Required fees:* $1735; $58 per credit. *Financial support:* In 2011–12, 63 students received support, including 28 fellowships with tuition reimbursements available (averaging $29,347 per year), 30 research assistantships with tuition reimbursements available (averaging $20,869 per year), 5 teaching assistantships with tuition reimbursements available (averaging $14,580 per year); Federal Work-Study, scholarships/grants, traineeships, and unspecified assistantships also available. Financial award applicants required to submit FAFSA. *Faculty research:* Medical and veterinary bacteriology, immunology, microbial physiology, pathology, vector-borne disease. *Total annual research expenditures:* $30.4 million. *Unit head:* Dr. Edward A. Hoover, Head, 970-491-7587, Fax: 970-491-0603, E-mail: edward.hoover@colostate.edu. *Application contact:* Lisa McCann, Academic Programs Coordinator, 970-491-6118, Fax: 970-491-1815, E-mail: lisa.mccann@colostate.edu. Web site: http://www.cvmbs.colostate.edu/mip/.

Columbia University, College of Physicians and Surgeons, Department of Microbiology, New York, NY 10032. Offers biomedical sciences (M Phil, MA, PhD); MD/PhD. Only candidates for the PhD are admitted. Terminal master's awarded for partial completion of doctoral program. *Degree requirements:* For doctorate, thesis/dissertation. *Entrance requirements:* For master's, GRE General Test; for doctorate, GRE. Additional exam requirements/recommendations for international students: Required—TOEFL. *Faculty research:* Prokaryotic molecular biology, immunology, virology, yeast molecular genetics, regulation of gene expression.

Cornell University, Graduate School, Graduate Fields of Agriculture and Life Sciences, Field of Microbiology, Ithaca, NY 14853-0001. Offers PhD. *Faculty:* 42 full-time (12 women). *Students:* 33 full-time (19 women); includes 3 minority (1 Black or African American, non-Hispanic/Latino; 1 Asian, non-Hispanic/Latino; 1 Hispanic/Latino), 10 international. Average age 27. 67 applicants, 16% accepted, 5 enrolled. In 2011, 10 doctorates awarded. *Degree requirements:* For doctorate, comprehensive exam, thesis/dissertation, 2 semesters of teaching experience. *Entrance requirements:* For doctorate, GRE General Test, 3 letters of recommendation. Additional exam requirements/recommendations for international students: Required—TOEFL (minimum score 550 paper-based; 213 computer-based; 77 iBT). *Application deadline:* For fall admission, 1/15 for domestic students. Application fee: $95. Electronic applications accepted. *Financial support:* In 2011–12, 4 fellowships with full tuition reimbursements, 19 research assistantships with full tuition reimbursements, 9 teaching assistantships with full tuition reimbursements were awarded; institutionally sponsored loans, scholarships/grants, health care benefits, tuition waivers (full and partial), and unspecified assistantships also available. Financial award applicants required to submit FAFSA. *Faculty research:* Microbial diversity, molecular biology, biotechnology, microbial ecology, phytobacteriology. *Unit head:* Director of Graduate Studies, 607-255-3088. *Application contact:* Graduate Field Assistant, 607-255-3088, E-mail: microfield@cornell.edu. Web site: http://www.gradschool.cornell.edu/fields.php?id-53&a-2.

Dalhousie University, Faculty of Medicine, Department of Microbiology and Immunology, Halifax , NS B3H 1X5, Canada. Offers M Sc, PhD. *Degree requirements:* For master's, thesis; for doctorate, comprehensive exam, thesis/dissertation. *Entrance requirements:* For master's, GRE General Test, honors B Sc; for doctorate, GRE General Test, honors B Sc in microbiology, M Sc in discipline or transfer after 1 year in master's program. Additional exam requirements/recommendations for international students: Required—1 of 5 approved tests: TOEFL, IELTS, CANTEST, CAEL, Michigan English Language Assessment Battery. Electronic applications accepted. *Faculty research:* Virology, molecular genetics, pathogenesis, bacteriology, immunology.

Dartmouth College, Graduate Program in Molecular and Cellular Biology, Department of Microbiology and Immunology, Program in Immunology, Hanover, NH 03755. Offers MD/PhD. *Faculty research:* Tumor immunotherapy, cell and molecular biology of connective tissue degradation in rheumatoid arthritis and cancer, immunology and immunotherapy of tumors of the central nervous system, transcriptional regulation of hematopoiesis and leukemia, bacterial pathogenesis.

Dartmouth College, Graduate Program in Molecular and Cellular Biology, Department of Microbiology and Immunology, Program in Molecular Pathogenesis, Hanover, NH 03755. Offers microbiology and immunology (PhD).

Drexel University, College of Medicine, Biomedical Graduate Programs, Program in Microbiology and Immunology, Philadelphia, PA 19104-2875. Offers MS, PhD, MD/PhD. Terminal master's awarded for partial completion of doctoral program. *Degree requirements:* For master's, comprehensive exam, thesis; for doctorate, thesis/dissertation, qualifying exam. *Entrance requirements:* For master's, GRE General Test, minimum GPA of 2.75; for doctorate, GRE General Test, minimum GPA of 3.0. Additional exam requirements/recommendations for international students: Required—TOEFL. Electronic applications accepted. *Faculty research:* Immunology of malarial parasites, virology, bacteriology, molecular biology, parasitology.

Duke University, Graduate School, Department of Molecular Genetics and Microbiology, Durham, NC 27710. Offers PhD. *Faculty:* 25 full-time. *Students:* 48 full-time (25 women); includes 7 minority (2 Black or African American, non-Hispanic/Latino; 1 American Indian or Alaska Native, non-Hispanic/Latino; 4 Asian, non-Hispanic/Latino), 11 international. 88 applicants, 22% accepted, 9 enrolled. In 2011, 6 degrees awarded. *Degree requirements:* For doctorate, thesis/dissertation. *Entrance requirements:* For doctorate, GRE General Test, GRE Subject Test in biology, chemistry, or biochemistry, cell and molecular biology (recommended). Additional exam requirements/recommendations for international students: Required—TOEFL (minimum score 550 paper-based; 213 computer-based; 83 iBT), IELTS (minimum score 7). *Application deadline:* For fall admission, 12/8 priority date for domestic students, 12/8 for international students. Application fee: $75. Electronic applications accepted. *Expenses:* Tuition: Full-time $40,720. *Required fees:* $3107. *Financial support:* Fellowships with full tuition reimbursements, research assistantships with full tuition reimbursements, and Federal Work-Study available. Financial award application deadline: 12/31. *Unit head:* Dr. Raphael Valdivia, Director of Graduate Studies, 919-684-6629, Fax: 919-684-8346, E-mail: kimberly.kobes@duke.edu. *Application contact:* Elizabeth Hutton, Director of Admissions, 919-684-3913, Fax: 919-684-2277, E-mail: grad-admissions@duke.edu. Web site: http://mgm.duke.edu/graduate/.

East Carolina University, Brody School of Medicine, Department of Microbiology and Immunology, Greenville, NC 27858-4353. Offers MS, MD, PhD. *Degree requirements:* For doctorate, comprehensive exam, thesis/dissertation. *Entrance requirements:* For doctorate, GRE General Test. Additional exam requirements/recommendations for international students: Required—TOEFL. *Application deadline:* For fall admission, 4/15 priority date for domestic students. Applications are processed on a rolling basis. Application fee: $50. *Expenses:* Tuition, state resident: full-time $3557; part-time $444.63 per semester hour. Tuition, nonresident: full-time $14,351; part-time $1793.88 per semester hour. *Required fees:* $2016; $252 per semester hour. Part-time tuition and fees vary according to course load, campus/location and program. *Financial support:* Fellowships with tuition reimbursements available. Financial award application deadline: 6/1. *Faculty research:* Molecular virology, genetics of bacteria, yeast and somatic cells, bacterial physiology and metabolism, bioterrorism. *Unit head:* Dr. Charles J. Smith, Chair, 252-744-2700, Fax: 252-744-3104, E-mail: smithcha@ecu.edu. *Application contact:* Dr. Richard A. Franklin, Director of Graduate Studies, 252-744-2705, Fax: 252-744-3104, E-mail: franklinr@ecu.edu. Web site: http://www.ecu.edu/cs-dhs/microbiology/index.cfm.

Eastern New Mexico University, Graduate School, College of Liberal Arts and Sciences, Department of Biology, Portales, NM 88130. Offers applied ecology (MS); cell, molecular biology and biotechnology (MS); education (non-thesis) (MS); microbiology (MS); plant biology (MS); zoology (MS). Part-time programs available. *Faculty:* 7 full-time (0 women). *Students:* 2 full-time (1 woman), 15 part-time (9 women); includes 7 minority (5 Hispanic/Latino; 2 Two or more races, non-Hispanic/Latino), 2 international. Average age 26. 17 applicants, 82% accepted, 3 enrolled. In 2011, 4 master's awarded. *Degree requirements:* For master's, comprehensive exam, thesis optional. *Entrance requirements:* For master's, GRE, minimum GPA of 3.0, 2 letters of recommendation, statement of research interest, bachelor's degree related to field of study or proof of common knowledge. Additional exam requirements/recommendations for international students: Required—TOEFL (minimum score 550 paper-based; 213 computer-based; 79 iBT), IELTS (minimum score 6). *Application deadline:* For fall admission, 7/20 priority date for domestic students, 6/20 for international students; for spring admission, 12/15 priority date for domestic students, 11/15 for international students. Applications are processed on a rolling basis. Application fee: $10. Electronic applications accepted. *Financial support:* In 2011–12, 8 teaching assistantships with partial tuition reimbursements (averaging $8,500 per year) were awarded; scholarships/grants and unspecified assistantships also available. Support available to part-time students. Financial award applicants required to submit FAFSA. *Unit head:* Dr. Zach Jones, Graduate Coordinator, 575-562-2723, Fax: 575-562-2192, E-mail: zach.jones@enmu.edu. *Application contact:* Sharon Potter, Department Secretary, Biology and Physical Sciences, 575-562-2174, Fax: 575-562-2192, E-mail: sharon.potter@enmu.edu. Web site: http://liberal-arts.enmu.edu/biology/graduate.shtml.

East Tennessee State University, James H. Quillen College of Medicine, Biomedical Science Graduate Program, Johnson City, TN 37614. Offers anatomy and cell biology (PhD); biochemistry and molecular biology (PhD); microbiology (PhD); pharmaceutical sciences (PhD); pharmacology (PhD); physiology (PhD); quantitative biosciences (PhD). *Faculty:* 33 full-time (6 women). *Students:* 29 full-time (15 women), 2 part-time (both women); includes 4 minority (1 Black or African American, non-Hispanic/Latino; 1 Asian, non-Hispanic/Latino; 2 Hispanic/Latino), 6 international. Average age 29. 76 applicants, 12% accepted, 7 enrolled. In 2011, 1 doctorate awarded. *Degree requirements:* For doctorate, thesis/dissertation, comprehensive qualifying exam. *Entrance requirements:* For doctorate, GRE General Test, GRE Subject Test. Additional exam requirements/recommendations for international students: Required—TOEFL (minimum score 550 paper-based; 213 computer-based; 79 iBT). *Application deadline:* For fall admission, 3/15 priority date for domestic students, 3/1 for international students. Application fee: $35 ($45 for international students). Electronic applications accepted. *Expenses:* Contact institution. *Financial support:* In 2011–12, 29 students received support, including 29 research assistantships with full tuition reimbursements available (averaging $19,000 per year); career-related internships or fieldwork, institutionally sponsored loans, scholarships/grants, and unspecified assistantships also available. Financial award application deadline: 7/1; financial award applicants required to submit FAFSA. *Faculty research:* Cardiovascular biology, neuroscience, infectious disease, cancer, inflammatory disease. *Total annual research expenditures:* $3.6 million. *Unit head:* Dr. Mitchell E. Robinson, Associate Dean/Program Director, 423-439-2031, Fax: 423-439-2140, E-mail: robinson@etsu.edu. *Application contact:* Shella Bennett, Graduate Specialist, 423-439-4708, Fax: 423-439-5624, E-mail: bennetsg@etsu.edu.

East Tennessee State University, School of Graduate Studies, College of Arts and Sciences, Department of Biological Sciences, Johnson City, TN 37614. Offers biology (MS); biomedical sciences (MS); microbiology (MS); paleontology (MS). *Faculty:* 14 full-time (2 women), 1 part-time/adjunct (0 women). *Students:* 31 full-time (15 women), 5 part-time (3 women); includes 2 minority (1 Asian, non-Hispanic/Latino; 1 Hispanic/Latino), 12 international. Average age 26. 55 applicants, 35% accepted, 10 enrolled. In 2011, 24 master's awarded. *Degree requirements:* For master's, comprehensive exam, thesis. *Entrance requirements:* For master's, GRE General Test or GRE Subject Test, minimum GPA of 3.0, undergraduate degree in life or physical sciences, two letters of recommendation. Additional exam requirements/recommendations for international

students: Required—TOEFL (minimum score 550 paper-based; 213 computer-based; 79 iBT). *Application deadline:* For fall admission, 4/1 for domestic students, 2/1 for international students; for spring admission, 9/1 for domestic students, 7/1 for international students. Application fee: $35 ($45 for international students). Electronic applications accepted. *Expenses:* Tuition, state resident: full-time $7312; part-time $350 per credit hour. Tuition, nonresident: full-time $18,490; part-time $621 per credit hour. *Required fees:* $63 per credit hour. Tuition and fees vary according to course load and program. *Financial support:* In 2011–12, 29 students received support, including 13 research assistantships with full tuition reimbursements available (averaging $9,000 per year), 14 teaching assistantships with full tuition reimbursements available (averaging $8,500 per year); institutionally sponsored loans, scholarships/grants, and unspecified assistantships also available. Financial award application deadline: 7/1; financial award applicants required to submit FAFSA. *Faculty research:* Genetics, ecology, evolutionary biology, quantitative biology and modeling, plant molecular biology, neurobiology, physiology, biomedical sciences, microbiology, paleobiology. *Total annual research expenditures:* $160,000. *Unit head:* Dr. Darrell Moore, Interim Chair, 423-439-4329, Fax: 423-439-5958, E-mail: zavadam@etsu.edu. *Application contact:* Gail Powers, Graduate Specialist, 423-439-4703, Fax: 423-439-5624, E-mail: powersg@etsu.edu.

Emory University, Laney Graduate School, Division of Biological and Biomedical Sciences, Program in Microbiology and Molecular Genetics, Atlanta, GA 30322-1100. Offers PhD. *Faculty:* 39 full-time (8 women). *Students:* 42 full-time (31 women); includes 7 minority (2 Black or African American, non-Hispanic/Latino; 2 Asian, non-Hispanic/Latino; 3 Hispanic/Latino), 5 international. Average age 27. 129 applicants, 12% accepted, 7 enrolled. In 2011, 7 degrees awarded. *Median time to degree:* Of those who began their doctoral program in fall 2003, 100% received their degree in 8 years or less. *Degree requirements:* For doctorate, comprehensive exam, thesis/dissertation. *Entrance requirements:* For doctorate, GRE General Test, minimum GPA of 3.0 in science course work (recommended). Additional exam requirements/recommendations for international students: Required—TOEFL. *Application deadline:* For fall admission, 12/1 for domestic and international students. Application fee: $75. Electronic applications accepted. *Expenses: Tuition:* Full-time $34,800. *Required fees:* $1300. *Financial support:* In 2011–12, 14 students received support, including 14 fellowships with full tuition reimbursements available (averaging $26,500 per year); institutionally sponsored loans, scholarships/grants, health care benefits, and tuition waivers (full) also available. *Faculty research:* Bacterial genetics and physiology, microbial development, molecular biology of viruses and bacterial pathogens, DNA recombination. *Unit head:* Dr. Phil Rather, Program Director, 404-728-5079, Fax: 404-728-7780, E-mail: prather@emory.edu. *Application contact:* Kathy Smith, Director of Recruitment and Admissions, 404-727-2547, Fax: 404-727-3322, E-mail: kathy.smith@emory.edu. Web site: http://www.biomed.emory.edu/.

Emporia State University, Graduate School, College of Liberal Arts and Sciences, Department of Biological Sciences, Emporia, KS 66801-5087. Offers botany (MS); environmental biology (MS); general biology (MS); microbial and cellular biology (MS); zoology (MS). Part-time programs available. *Faculty:* 13 full-time (3 women), 1 part-time/adjunct (0 women). *Students:* 8 full-time (5 women), 21 part-time (10 women); includes 3 minority (1 Black or African American, non-Hispanic/Latino; 1 Hispanic/Latino; 1 Two or more races, non-Hispanic/Latino), 6 international. 14 applicants, 86% accepted, 7 enrolled. In 2011, 5 master's awarded. *Degree requirements:* For master's, comprehensive exam or thesis. *Entrance requirements:* For master's, GRE, appropriate undergraduate degree, interview, letters of reference. Additional exam requirements/recommendations for international students: Required—TOEFL (minimum score 520 paper-based; 133 computer-based; 68 iBT). *Application deadline:* For fall admission, 8/15 priority date for domestic students. Applications are processed on a rolling basis. Application fee: $30 ($75 for international students). Electronic applications accepted. *Expenses:* Tuition, state resident: full-time $2342; part-time $195 per credit hour. Tuition, nonresident: full-time $7254; part-time $605 per credit hour. *Required fees:* $66 per credit hour. Tuition and fees vary according to campus/location. *Financial support:* In 2011–12, 8 research assistantships with full tuition reimbursements (averaging $6,589 per year), 10 teaching assistantships with full tuition reimbursements (averaging $7,419 per year) were awarded; career-related internships or fieldwork, Federal Work-Study, institutionally sponsored loans, health care benefits, and unspecified assistantships also available. Financial award application deadline: 3/15; financial award applicants required to submit FAFSA. *Faculty research:* Fisheries, range, and wildlife management; aquatic, plant, grassland, vertebrate, and invertebrate ecology; mammalian and plant systematics, taxonomy, and evolution; immunology, virology, and molecular biology. *Unit head:* Dr. R. Brent Thomas, Chair, 620-341-5311, Fax: 620-341-5608, E-mail: rthomas2@emporia.edu. *Application contact:* Dr. Scott Crupper, Graduate Coordinator, 620-341-5621, Fax: 620-341-5607, E-mail: scrupper@emporia.edu. Web site: http://www.emporia.edu/info/degrees-courses/grad/biology.

George Mason University, College of Science, Department of Molecular and Microbiology, Fairfax, VA 22030. Offers biology (MS); biosciences (PhD). *Expenses:* Tuition, state resident: full-time $8750; part-time $364.58 per credit. Tuition, nonresident: full-time $24,092; part-time $1003.83 per credit. *Required fees:* $2514; $104.75 per credit. *Financial support:* Scholarships/grants and unspecified assistantships available. Financial award applicants required to submit FAFSA.

Georgetown University, Graduate School of Arts and Sciences, Programs in Biomedical Sciences, Department of Microbiology and Immunology, Washington, DC 20057. Offers biohazardous threat agents and emerging infectious diseases (MS); general microbiology and immunology (MS); global infectious diseases (PhD); microbiology and immunology research (PhD); science policy and advocacy (MS). Part-time programs available. *Degree requirements:* For master's, 30 credit hours of coursework; for doctorate, comprehensive exam, thesis/dissertation. *Entrance requirements:* For master's, GRE General Test, 3 letters of reference, bachelor's degree in related field; for doctorate, GRE General Test, 3 letters of reference, MS/BS in related field. Additional exam requirements/recommendations for international students: Required—TOEFL (minimum score 505 paper-based; 213 computer-based). Electronic applications accepted. *Faculty research:* Pathogenesis and basic biology of the fungus Candida albicans, molecular biology of viral immunopathological mechanisms in Multiple Sclerosis.

The George Washington University, Columbian College of Arts and Sciences, Institute for Biomedical Sciences, Program in Microbiology and Immunology, Washington, DC 20037. Offers PhD. *Students:* 7 full-time (5 women), 15 part-time (10 women); includes 3 minority (1 American Indian or Alaska Native, non-Hispanic/Latino; 1 Asian, non-Hispanic/Latino; 1 Hispanic/Latino), 2 international. Average age 30. In 2011, 6 doctorates awarded. *Degree requirements:* For doctorate, thesis/dissertation. *Entrance requirements:* For doctorate, GRE General Test, minimum GPA of 3.0. Additional exam requirements/recommendations for international students: Required—TOEFL (minimum score 600 paper-based; 250 computer-based). *Application deadline:* For fall admission, 12/15 priority date for domestic students, 12/15 for international students. Applications are processed on a rolling basis. Application fee: $75. Electronic applications accepted. *Financial support:* In 2011–12, 10 students received support. Fellowships with tuition reimbursements available and tuition waivers available. *Unit head:* Dr. David Leitenberg, Director, 202-994-9475, Fax: 202-994-2913, E-mail: dleit@

gwu.edu. *Application contact:* Information Contact, 202-994-3532, Fax: 202-994-2913, E-mail: mtmjxl@gwumc.edu. Web site: http://www.gwumc.edu/ibs/fields/microimmuno.html.

The George Washington University, School of Medicine and Health Sciences, Health Sciences Programs, Washington, DC 20052. Offers clinical practice management (MSHS); clinical research administration (MSHS); emergency services management (MSHS); end-of-life care (MSHS); immunohematology (MSHS); physical therapy (DPT); physician assistant (MSHS); MSHS/MPH. Postbaccalaureate distance learning degree programs offered (no on-campus study). *Students:* 268 full-time (197 women), 255 part-time (194 women); includes 131 minority (52 Black or African American, non-Hispanic/Latino; 3 American Indian or Alaska Native, non-Hispanic/Latino; 43 Asian, non-Hispanic/Latino; 26 Hispanic/Latino; 7 Native Hawaiian or other Pacific Islander, non-Hispanic/Latino), 24 international. Average age 32. 922 applicants, 32% accepted. In 2011, 140 master's, 29 doctorates awarded. *Entrance requirements:* Additional exam requirements/recommendations for international students: Required—TOEFL (minimum score 550 paper-based; 213 computer-based). *Application deadline:* Applications are processed on a rolling basis. Application fee: $75. *Expenses:* Contact institution. *Unit head:* Jean E. Johnson, Senior Associate Dean, 202-994-3725, E-mail: jejohns@gwu.edu. *Application contact:* Joke Ogundiran, Director of Admission, 202-994-1668, Fax: 202-994-0870, E-mail: jokeogun@gwu.edu.

The George Washington University, School of Public Health and Health Services, Department of Epidemiology and Biostatistics, Washington, DC 20052. Offers biostatistics (MPH); epidemiology (MPH); microbiology and emerging infectious diseases (MSPH). *Faculty:* 23 full-time (15 women), 26 part-time/adjunct (15 women). *Students:* 62 full-time (54 women), 41 part-time (30 women); includes 37 minority (16 Black or African American, non-Hispanic/Latino; 16 Asian, non-Hispanic/Latino; 3 Hispanic/Latino; 2 Two or more races, non-Hispanic/Latino), 8 international. Average age 27. 298 applicants, 69% accepted, 35 enrolled. In 2011, 49 master's awarded. *Degree requirements:* For master's, case study or special project. *Entrance requirements:* For master's, GMAT, GRE General Test, or MCAT. Additional exam requirements/recommendations for international students: Required—TOEFL. *Application deadline:* For fall admission, 4/15 priority date for domestic students, 4/15 for international students; for spring admission, 11/1 for domestic and international students. Applications are processed on a rolling basis. Application fee: $75. *Financial support:* In 2011–12, 6 students received support. Tuition waivers available. Financial award application deadline: 2/15. *Unit head:* Dr. Alan E. Greenberg, Chair, 202-994-0612, E-mail: aeg1@gwu.edu. *Application contact:* Jane Smith, Director of Admissions, 202-994-0248, Fax: 202-994-1860, E-mail: sphhsinfo@gwumc.edu.

Georgia State University, College of Arts and Sciences, Department of Biology, Program in Applied and Environmental Microbiology, Atlanta, GA 30302-3083. Offers MS, PhD. Part-time programs available. Terminal master's awarded for partial completion of doctoral program. *Degree requirements:* For master's, thesis or alternative; for doctorate, thesis/dissertation, exam. *Entrance requirements:* For master's and doctorate, GRE General Test. Additional exam requirements/recommendations for international students: Required—TOEFL. Electronic applications accepted.

Harvard University, Graduate School of Arts and Sciences, Division of Medical Sciences, Boston, MA 02115. Offers biological chemistry and molecular pharmacology (PhD); cell biology (PhD); genetics (PhD); microbiology and molecular genetics (PhD); pathology (PhD), including experimental pathology. *Degree requirements:* For doctorate, thesis/dissertation. *Entrance requirements:* For doctorate, GRE General Test, GRE Subject Test. Additional exam requirements/recommendations for international students: Required—TOEFL. *Expenses: Tuition:* Full-time $36,304. *Required fees:* $1186. Full-time tuition and fees vary according to program.

Hood College, Graduate School, Program in Biomedical Science, Frederick, MD 21701-8575. Offers biomedical science (MS), including biotechnology/molecular biology, microbiology/immunology/virology, regulatory compliance; regulatory compliance (Certificate). Part-time and evening/weekend programs available. *Degree requirements:* For master's, comprehensive exam, thesis or alternative. *Entrance requirements:* For master's, bachelor's degree in biology; minimum GPA of 2.75; undergraduate course work in cell biology, chemistry, organic chemistry, and genetics. Additional exam requirements/recommendations for international students: Required—TOEFL (minimum score 575 paper-based; 231 computer-based; 89 iBT). Electronic applications accepted.

Howard University, College of Medicine, Department of Microbiology, Washington, DC 20059-0002: Offers PhD. *Degree requirements:* For doctorate, one foreign language, comprehensive exam, thesis/dissertation, qualifying exam, teaching experience. *Entrance requirements:* For doctorate, GRE General Test, minimum GPA of 3.0 in sciences. Additional exam requirements/recommendations for international students: Required—TOEFL. *Faculty research:* Immunology, molecular and cellular microbiology, microbial genetics, microbial physiology, pathogenic bacteriology, medical mycology, medical parasitology, virology.

Idaho State University, Office of Graduate Studies, College of Science and Engineering, Department of Biological Sciences, Pocatello, ID 83209-8007. Offers biology (MNS, MS, DA, PhD); clinical laboratory science (MS); microbiology (MS). *Accreditation:* NAACLS. Part-time programs available. *Degree requirements:* For master's, comprehensive exam, thesis; for doctorate, comprehensive exam, thesis/dissertation, 9 credits of internship (for DA). *Entrance requirements:* For master's, GRE General Test, minimum GPA of 3.0 in all upper division classes; for doctorate, GRE General Test, GRE Subject Test (biology), diagnostic exam (DA), minimum GPA of 3.0 in all upper division classes. Additional exam requirements/recommendations for international students: Required—TOEFL (minimum score 550 paper-based; 213 computer-based; 80 iBT). Electronic applications accepted. *Faculty research:* Ecology, plant and animal physiology, plant and animal developmental biology, immunology, molecular biology, bioinfomatics.

Illinois Institute of Technology, Graduate College, College of Science and Letters, Department of Biological, Chemical and Physical Sciences, Biology Division, Chicago, IL 60616. Offers biochemistry (MBS, MS); biology (PhD); biotechnology (MBS, MS); cell and molecular biology (MBS, MS); microbiology (MB, MS); molecular biochemistry and biophysics (PhD); molecular biology and biophysics (MS). Part-time and evening/weekend programs available. Postbaccalaureate distance learning degree programs offered (minimal on-campus study). Terminal master's awarded for partial completion of doctoral program. *Degree requirements:* For master's, comprehensive exam, thesis (for some programs); for doctorate, comprehensive exam, thesis/dissertation. *Entrance requirements:* For master's, GRE General Test (minimum score 1000 Quantitative and Verbal, 2.5 Analytical Writing), minimum undergraduate GPA of 3.0; for doctorate, GRE General Test (minimum score 1200 Quantitative and Verbal, 3.0 Analytical Writing), minimum undergraduate GPA of 3.0. Additional exam requirements/recommendations for international students: Required—TOEFL (minimum score 523 paper-based; 213 computer-based; 70 iBT). Recommended—IELTS (minimum score 5.5). Electronic applications accepted. *Faculty research:* Structure and biophysics of macromolecular systems; efficacy and mechanism of action of chemopreventive agents in experimental

carcinogenesis of breast, colon, lung and prostate; study of fundamental structural biochemistry problems that have direct links to the understanding and treatment of disease; spectroscopic techniques for the study of multi-domain proteins; molecular mechanisms of cancer and cancer gene therapy.

Illinois State University, Graduate School, College of Arts and Sciences, Department of Biological Sciences, Normal, IL 61790-2200. Offers animal behavior (MS); bacteriology (MS); biochemistry (MS); biological sciences (MS); biology (PhD); biophysics (MS); biotechnology (MS); botany (MS, PhD); cell biology (MS); conservation biology (MS); developmental biology (MS); ecology (MS, PhD); entomology (MS); evolutionary biology (MS); genetics (MS, PhD); immunology (MS); microbiology (MS, PhD); molecular biology (MS); molecular genetics (MS); neurobiology (MS); neuroscience (MS); parasitology (MS); physiology (MS, PhD); plant biology (MS); plant molecular biology (MS); plant sciences (MS); structural biology (MS); zoology (MS, PhD). Part-time programs available. *Degree requirements:* For master's, thesis or alternative; for doctorate, variable foreign language requirement, thesis/dissertation, 2 terms of residency. *Entrance requirements:* For master's, GRE General Test, minimum GPA of 2.6 in last 60 hours of course work; for doctorate, GRE General Test. *Faculty research:* Redoc balance and drug development in schistosoma mansoni, control of the growth of listeria monocytogenes at low temperature, regulation of cell expansion and microtubule function by SPRI, CRUI: physiology and fitness consequences of different life history phenotypes.

Indiana State University, College of Graduate and Professional Studies, College of Arts and Sciences, Department of Biology, Terre Haute, IN 47809. Offers ecology (PhD); life sciences (MS); microbiology (PhD); physiology (PhD); science education (MS). *Degree requirements:* For master's, thesis (for some programs); for doctorate, comprehensive exam, thesis/dissertation. *Entrance requirements:* For master's and doctorate, GRE General Test. Electronic applications accepted.

Indiana University Bloomington, University Graduate School, College of Arts and Sciences, Department of Biology, Bloomington, IN 47405. Offers biology teaching (MAT); biotechnology (MA); evolution, ecology, and behavior (MA, PhD); genetics (PhD); microbiology (MA, PhD); molecular, cellular, and developmental biology (PhD); plant sciences (MA, PhD); zoology (MA, PhD). *Faculty:* 58 full-time (15 women), 21 part-time/adjunct (6 women). *Students:* 175 full-time (100 women), 3 part-time (all women); includes 20 minority (5 Black or African American, non-Hispanic/Latino; 8 Asian, non-Hispanic/Latino; 7 Hispanic/Latino), 55 international. Average age 27. 316 applicants, 22% accepted, 31 enrolled. In 2011, 8 master's, 20 doctorates awarded. Terminal master's awarded for partial completion of doctoral program. *Degree requirements:* For master's, thesis, oral defense; for doctorate, thesis/dissertation, oral defense. *Entrance requirements:* For master's and doctorate, GRE General Test. Additional exam requirements/recommendations for international students: Required—TOEFL (minimum score 100 iBT). *Application deadline:* For fall admission, 1/5 priority date for domestic students, 12/1 for international students. Application fee: $55 ($65 for international students). Electronic applications accepted. *Financial support:* In 2011–12, fellowships with tuition reimbursements (averaging $19,484 per year), research assistantships with tuition reimbursements (averaging $20,300 per year), teaching assistantships with tuition reimbursements (averaging $20,521 per year) were awarded; scholarships/grants, traineeships, health care benefits, and unspecified assistantships also available. Financial award application deadline: 1/5. *Faculty research:* Evolution, ecology and behavior; microbiology; molecular biology and genetics; plant biology. *Unit head:* Dr. Roger Innes, Chair, 812-855-2219, Fax: 812-855-6082, E-mail: rinnes@indiana.edu. *Application contact:* Tracey D. Stohr, Graduate Student Recruitment Coordinator, 812-856-6303, Fax: 812-855-6082, E-mail: gradbio@indiana.edu. Web site: http://www.bio.indiana.edu/.

Indiana University–Purdue University Indianapolis, Indiana University School of Medicine, Department of Microbiology and Immunology, Indianapolis, IN 46202-2896. Offers MS, PhD, MD/MS, MD/PhD. *Faculty:* 20 full-time (2 women). *Students:* 23 full-time (15 women), 9 part-time (5 women); includes 9 minority (2 Black or African American, non-Hispanic/Latino; 4 Asian, non-Hispanic/Latino; 2 Hispanic/Latino; 1 Two or more races, non-Hispanic/Latino), 13 international. Average age 27. 3 applicants, 0% accepted, 0 enrolled. In 2011, 7 degrees awarded. Terminal master's awarded for partial completion of doctoral program. *Degree requirements:* For master's, thesis; for doctorate, thesis/dissertation. *Entrance requirements:* For master's and doctorate, GRE General Test, previous course work in calculus, cell biology, chemistry, genetics, physics, and biochemistry. *Application deadline:* For fall admission, 3/1 for domestic students. Applications are processed on a rolling basis. Application fee: $55 ($65 for international students). *Financial support:* In 2011–12, fellowships with full tuition reimbursements (averaging $8,313 per year), teaching assistantships with full tuition reimbursements (averaging $18,391 per year) were awarded; research assistantships with full tuition reimbursements, Federal Work-Study, institutionally sponsored loans, scholarships/grants, traineeships, and tuition waivers (partial) also available. Financial award application deadline: 2/1. *Faculty research:* Host-parasite interactions, molecular biology, cellular and molecular immunology and hematology, viral and bacterial pathogenesis, cancer research. *Total annual research expenditures:* $4.2 million. *Unit head:* Dr. Hal E. Broxmeyer, Chairman, 317-274-7672, Fax: 317-274-4090, E-mail: hbroxmey@iupui.edu. *Application contact:* 317-274-7671, Fax: 317-274-4090. Web site: http://micro.medicine.iu.edu/.

Inter American University of Puerto Rico, Metropolitan Campus, Graduate Programs, Program in Medical Technology, San Juan, PR 00919-1293. Offers administration of clinical laboratories (MS); molecular microbiology (MS). *Accreditation:* NAACLS. Part-time programs available. *Degree requirements:* For master's, comprehensive exam. *Entrance requirements:* For master's, BS in medical technology, minimum GPA of 2.5. Electronic applications accepted.

Iowa State University of Science and Technology, Department of Veterinary Microbiology and Preventive Medicine, Ames, IA 50011-1250. Offers veterinary microbiology (MS, PhD). *Entrance requirements:* For master's and doctorate, GRE General Test. Additional exam requirements/recommendations for international students: Required—TOEFL (minimum score 550 paper-based; 79 iBT), IELTS (minimum score 6.5). *Application deadline:* For fall admission, 2/1 priority date for domestic students, 2/1 for international students. Applications are processed on a rolling basis. Application fee: $40 ($90 for international students). Electronic applications accepted. *Faculty research:* Bacteriology, immunology, virology, public health and food safety. *Unit head:* Dr. Qijing Zhang, Director of Graduate Education, 515-294-5776, Fax: 515-294-8500, E-mail: vetmicro@iastate.edu. *Application contact:* Liz Westberg, Application Contact, 515-294-5776, Fax: 515-294-8500, E-mail: vetmicro@iastate.edu. Web site: http://vetmed.iastate.edu/vmpm.

Iowa State University of Science and Technology, Program in Microbiology, Ames, IA 50011-3211. Offers MS, PhD. *Entrance requirements:* For master's and doctorate, GRE General Test. Additional exam requirements/recommendations for international students: Required—TOEFL (minimum score 550 paper-based; 79 iBT), IELTS (minimum score 6.5). *Application deadline:* For fall admission, 2/1 priority date for domestic students, 2/1 for international students. Application fee: $40 ($90 for international students). Electronic applications accepted. *Unit head:* Dr. Larry Halverson, Director of Graduate Education, 515-294-9052, Fax: 515-294-6019, E-mail: microbiology@iastate.edu. *Application contact:* Dai Nguyen, Information Contact, 515-294-9052, Fax: 515-294-6019, E-mail: microbiology@iastate.edu. Web site: http://www.micrograd.iastate.edu/.

The Johns Hopkins University, Bloomberg School of Public Health, W. Harry Feinstone Department of Molecular Microbiology and Immunology, Baltimore, MD 21218-2699. Offers MHS, Sc M, PhD. Terminal master's awarded for partial completion of doctoral program. *Degree requirements:* For master's, comprehensive exam, thesis (for some programs), essay, written exams; for doctorate, comprehensive exam, thesis/dissertation, 1 year full-time residency, oral and written exams. *Entrance requirements:* For master's, GRE General Test or MCAT, 3 letters of recommendation, curriculum vitae; for doctorate, GRE General Test, 3 letters of recommendation, transcripts, curriculum vitae. Additional exam requirements/recommendations for international students: Required—TOEFL (minimum score 600 paper-based; 250 computer-based). Electronic applications accepted. *Faculty research:* Immunology, virology, bacteriology, parasitology, vector biology, disease ecology, pathogenesis of infectious disease, immune responses to infectious agents, vector-borne and tropical diseases, biochemistry and molecular biology of infectious agents, population genetics of insect vectors, genetic regulation and immune responses in insect vectors, vaccine development, hormonal effects on pathogenesis and immune responses.

Kansas State University, Graduate School, College of Arts and Sciences, Division of Biology, Manhattan, KS 66506. Offers biology (MS, PhD); microbiology (PhD). *Faculty:* 39 full-time (12 women), 10 part-time/adjunct (3 women). *Students:* 55 full-time (29 women), 3 part-time (all women); includes 4 minority (1 Black or African American, non-Hispanic/Latino; 3 Hispanic/Latino), 14 international. Average age 27. 90 applicants, 9% accepted, 8 enrolled. In 2011, 6 master's, 6 doctorates awarded. Terminal master's awarded for partial completion of doctoral program. *Degree requirements:* For master's, thesis; for doctorate, thesis/dissertation. *Entrance requirements:* For master's, GRE General Test, minimum undergraduate GPA of 3.0; for doctorate, GRE General Test, minimum GPA of 3.0. Additional exam requirements/recommendations for international students: Required—TOEFL (minimum score 550 paper-based; 213 computer-based). *Application deadline:* For fall admission, 12/15 priority date for domestic students, 12/15 for international students; for spring admission, 8/1 priority date for domestic students, 8/1 for international students. Applications are processed on a rolling basis. Application fee: $40 ($55 for international students). Electronic applications accepted. *Financial support:* In 2011–12, 2 fellowships with full tuition reimbursements (averaging $30,000 per year), 32 research assistantships with full tuition reimbursements (averaging $21,086 per year), 23 teaching assistantships with full tuition reimbursements (averaging $19,819 per year) were awarded; institutionally sponsored loans and scholarships/grants also available. Support available to part-time students. Financial award application deadline: 3/1; financial award applicants required to submit FAFSA. *Faculty research:* Ecology, genetics, developmental biology, microbiology, cell biology. *Total annual research expenditures:* $8.3 million. *Unit head:* Brian Spooner, Director and University Distinguished Professor, Division of Biology, 785-532-6615, Fax: 785-532-6653, E-mail: biology@ksu.edu. *Application contact:* David Rintoul, Graduate Program Director, 785-532-6795, Fax: 785-532-6653, E-mail: drintoul@ksu.edu. Web site: http://www.k-state.edu/biology/.

Loma Linda University, School of Medicine, Department of Biochemistry/Microbiology, Loma Linda, CA 92350. Offers MS, PhD. Part-time programs available. *Degree requirements:* For master's, thesis or alternative; for doctorate, thesis/dissertation. *Entrance requirements:* For master's and doctorate, GRE General Test. Additional exam requirements/recommendations for international students: Required—TOEFL (minimum score 550 paper-based; 213 computer-based). *Faculty research:* Physical chemistry of macromolecules, biochemistry of endocrine system, biochemical mechanism of bone volume regulation.

Long Island University–C. W. Post Campus, School of Health Professions and Nursing, Department of Biomedical Sciences, Brookville, NY 11548-1300. Offers cardiovascular perfusion (MS); clinical laboratory management (MS); medical biology (MS), including hematology, immunology, medical biology, medical chemistry, medical microbiology. Part-time and evening/weekend programs available. Postbaccalaureate distance learning degree programs offered. *Degree requirements:* For master's, thesis. *Entrance requirements:* For master's, minimum GPA of 2.75 in major. Electronic applications accepted.

Louisiana State University Health Sciences Center, School of Graduate Studies in New Orleans, Department of Microbiology, Immunology, and Parasitology, New Orleans, LA 70112-1393. Offers microbiology and immunology (MS, PhD); MD/PhD. Terminal master's awarded for partial completion of doctoral program. *Degree requirements:* For master's, comprehensive exam, thesis; for doctorate, comprehensive exam, thesis/dissertation, preliminary exam, qualifying exam. *Entrance requirements:* For master's and doctorate, GRE General Test. Additional exam requirements/recommendations for international students: Required—TOEFL. *Faculty research:* Microbial physiology, animal virology, vaccine development, AIDS drug studies, pathogenic mechanisms, molecular immunology.

Louisiana State University Health Sciences Center at Shreveport, Department of Microbiology and Immunology, Shreveport, LA 71130-3932. Offers MS, PhD, MD/PhD. Terminal master's awarded for partial completion of doctoral program. *Degree requirements:* For master's, thesis; for doctorate, thesis/dissertation. *Entrance requirements:* For master's and doctorate, GRE General Test. Additional exam requirements/recommendations for international students: Required—TOEFL. *Faculty research:* Infectious disease, pathogenesis, molecular virology and biology.

Loyola University Chicago, Graduate School, Department of Microbiology and Immunology, Maywood, IL 60153. Offers immunology (PhD); microbiology (MS); MD/PhD. *Faculty:* 15 full-time (4 women). *Students:* 31 full-time (19 women); includes 4 minority (2 Asian, non-Hispanic/Latino; 2 Hispanic/Latino), 4 international. Average age 27. 94 applicants, 16% accepted, 7 enrolled. In 2011, 2 master's, 7 doctorates awarded. Terminal master's awarded for partial completion of doctoral program. *Degree requirements:* For master's, thesis; for doctorate, comprehensive exam, thesis/dissertation. *Entrance requirements:* For master's and doctorate, GRE General Test. Additional exam requirements/recommendations for international students: Required—TOEFL. *Application deadline:* Applications are processed on a rolling basis. Application fee: $0. Electronic applications accepted. *Expenses: Tuition:* Full-time $15,660; part-time $870 per credit hour. *Required fees:* $125 per semester. Tuition and fees vary according to course load and program. *Financial support:* In 2011–12, 5 fellowships with tuition reimbursements (averaging $25,000 per year), 24 research assistantships with tuition reimbursements (averaging $25,000 per year) were awarded; institutionally sponsored loans and scholarships/grants also available. Financial award application deadline: 2/15. *Faculty research:* Virology, microbial physiology and genetics, immune system development and regulation, signal transduction and host-pathogen interactions, biofilms. *Total annual research expenditures:* $2.2 million. *Unit head:* Dr. Katherine L. Knight, Chair, 708-216-3385, Fax: 708-216-9574, E-mail: kknight@lumc.edu. *Application contact:* Dr. Karen Visick, Graduate Program Director, 708-216-0869, Fax: 708-216-9574, E-mail: kvisick@lumc.edu.

Microbiology

Marquette University, Graduate School, College of Arts and Sciences, Department of Biology, Milwaukee, WI 53201-1881. Offers cell biology (MS, PhD); developmental biology (MS, PhD); ecology (MS, PhD); epithelial physiology (MS, PhD); genetics (MS, PhD); microbiology (MS, PhD); molecular biology (MS, PhD); muscle and exercise physiology (MS, PhD); neuroscience (PhD). *Faculty:* 23 full-time (11 women), 1 part-time/adjunct (0 women). *Students:* 33 full-time (14 women), 6 part-time (3 women), 19 international. Average age 25. 78 applicants, 17% accepted, 5 enrolled. In 2011, 6 doctorates awarded. Terminal master's awarded for partial completion of doctoral program. *Degree requirements:* For master's, comprehensive exam, thesis, 1 year of teaching experience or equivalent; for doctorate, thesis/dissertation, 1 year of teaching experience or equivalent, qualifying exam. *Entrance requirements:* For master's and doctorate, GRE General Test, GRE Subject Test, official transcripts from all current and previous colleges/universities except Marquette, statement of professional goals and aspirations, three letters of recommendation. Additional exam requirements/recommendations for international students: Required—TOEFL (minimum score 530 paper-based; 78 computer-based). *Application deadline:* For fall admission, 12/15 for domestic and international students. Application fee: $50. Electronic applications accepted. *Expenses: Tuition:* Full-time $17,010; part-time $945 per credit hour. Tuition and fees vary according to program. *Financial support:* In 2011–12, 39 students received support, including 6 fellowships (averaging $1,208 per year), 4 research assistantships with full tuition reimbursements available (averaging $21,750 per year), 29 teaching assistantships with full tuition reimbursements available (averaging $21,750 per year); scholarships/grants, health care benefits, tuition waivers (full and partial), and unspecified assistantships also available. Support available to part-time students. Financial award application deadline: 2/15. *Faculty research:* Neurobiology, neuroendocrinology, epithelial physiology, neuropeptide interactions, synaptic transmission. *Total annual research expenditures:* $2 million. *Unit head:* Dr. Robert Fitts, Chair, 414-288-1748, Fax: 414-288-7357. *Application contact:* Debbie Weaver, Administrative Assistant, 414-288-7355, Fax: 414-288-7357. Web site: http://www.marquette.edu/biology/.

Massachusetts Institute of Technology, School of Science, Department of Biology, Cambridge, MA 02139. Offers biochemistry (PhD); biological oceanography (PhD); biology (PhD); biophysical chemistry and molecular structure (PhD); cell biology (PhD); computational and systems biology (PhD); developmental biology (PhD); genetics (PhD); immunology (PhD); microbiology (PhD); molecular biology (PhD); neurobiology (PhD). *Faculty:* 58 full-time (15 women). *Students:* 248 full-time (129 women); includes 69 minority (5 Black or African American, non-Hispanic/Latino; 1 American Indian or Alaska Native, non-Hispanic/Latino; 25 Asian, non-Hispanic/Latino; 31 Hispanic/Latino; 7 Two or more races, non-Hispanic/Latino), 36 international. Average age 26. 698 applicants, 15% accepted, 44 enrolled. In 2011, 38 doctorates awarded. *Degree requirements:* For doctorate, comprehensive exam, thesis/dissertation. *Entrance requirements:* For doctorate, GRE General Test. Additional exam requirements/recommendations for international students: Required—TOEFL (minimum score 577 paper-based; 233 computer-based), IELTS (minimum score 6.5). *Application deadline:* For fall admission, 12/1 for domestic and international students. Application fee: $75. Electronic applications accepted. *Expenses: Tuition:* Full-time $40,460; part-time $630 per credit hour. *Required fees:* $272. *Financial support:* In 2011–12, 214 students received support, including 129 fellowships (averaging $33,200 per year), 117 research assistantships (averaging $32,900 per year); teaching assistantships, Federal Work-Study, institutionally sponsored loans, scholarships/grants, traineeships, health care benefits, and unspecified assistantships also available. *Faculty research:* Cellular, developmental and molecular (plant and animal) biology; biochemistry, bioengineering, biophysics and structural biology; classical and molecular genetics; immunology and microbiology; cancer biology, molecular medicine, neurobiology and human disease; computational and systems biology. *Total annual research expenditures:* $53.6 million. *Unit head:* Prof. Tania A. Baker, Head, 617-253-4701, E-mail: mitbio@mit.edu. *Application contact:* Biology Education Office, 617-253-3717, Fax: 617-258-9329, E-mail: gradbio@mit.edu. Web site: https://biology.mit.edu/.

McGill University, Faculty of Graduate and Postdoctoral Studies, Faculty of Agricultural and Environmental Sciences, Department of Natural Resource Sciences, Montréal, QC H3A 2T5, Canada. Offers entomology (M Sc, PhD); environmental assessment (M Sc); forest science (M Sc, PhD); microbiology (M Sc, PhD); micrometeorology (M Sc, PhD); neotropical environment (M Sc, PhD); soil science (M Sc, PhD); wildlife biology (M Sc, PhD).

McGill University, Faculty of Graduate and Postdoctoral Studies, Faculty of Medicine, Department of Microbiology and Immunology, Montréal, QC H3A 2T5, Canada. Offers M Sc, M Sc A, PhD.

Medical College of Wisconsin, Graduate School of Biomedical Sciences, Department of Microbiology and Molecular Genetics, Milwaukee, WI 53226-0509. Offers MS, PhD, MD/PhD. *Degree requirements:* For doctorate, comprehensive exam, thesis/dissertation. *Entrance requirements:* For master's and doctorate, GRE, official transcripts, three letters of recommendation. Additional exam requirements/recommendations for international students: Required—TOEFL. *Faculty research:* Virology, immunology, bacterial toxins, regulation of gene expression.

Medical University of South Carolina, College of Graduate Studies, Department of Microbiology and Immunology, Charleston, SC 29425. Offers MS, PhD, DMD/PhD, MD/PhD. *Faculty:* 15 full-time (6 women), 30 part-time/adjunct (9 women). *Students:* 20 full-time (10 women), 1 part-time (0 women); includes 5 minority (2 Black or African American, non-Hispanic/Latino; 1 Asian, non-Hispanic/Latino; 2 Hispanic/Latino), 2 international. Average age 26. 8 applicants, 75% accepted, 4 enrolled. In 2011, 4 master's, 3 doctorates awarded. Terminal master's awarded for partial completion of doctoral program. *Degree requirements:* For master's, thesis; for doctorate, thesis/dissertation, oral and written exams. *Entrance requirements:* For master's, GRE General Test, MCAT, or DAT, minimum GPA of 3.0; for doctorate, GRE General Test, interview, minimum GPA of 3.0, research experience. Additional exam requirements/recommendations for international students: Required—TOEFL (minimum score 600 paper-based; 250 computer-based; 100 iBT). *Application deadline:* For fall admission, 1/15 priority date for domestic students, 1/15 for international students. Applications are processed on a rolling basis. Application fee: $0 ($95 for international students). Electronic applications accepted. *Financial support:* In 2011–12, 10 research assistantships with partial tuition reimbursements (averaging $23,000 per year) were awarded; Federal Work-Study and scholarships/grants also available. Support available to part-time students. Financial award application deadline: 3/10; financial award applicants required to submit FAFSA. *Faculty research:* Inmate and adaptive immunology, gene therapy/vector development, vaccinology, proteomics of biowarfare agents, bacterial and fungal pathogenesis. *Unit head:* Dr. Zihai Li, Chair, 843-792-7915, Fax: 843-792-6590. *Application contact:* Dr. Laura Kasman, Assistant Professor, 843-792-8117, Fax: 843-792-2464, E-mail: kasmanl@musc.edu. Web site: http://academicdepartments.musc.edu/immunology.

Meharry Medical College, School of Graduate Studies, Program in Biomedical Sciences, Microbiology and Immunology Emphasis, Nashville, TN 37208-9989. Offers PhD, MD/PhD. *Degree requirements:* For doctorate, comprehensive exam, thesis/dissertation. *Entrance requirements:* For doctorate, GRE General Test, GRE Subject Test, undergraduate degree in related science. *Faculty research:* Microbial and bacterial pathogenesis, viral transcription, immune response to viruses and parasites.

Miami University, College of Arts and Science, Department of Microbiology, Oxford, OH 45056. Offers MS, PhD. Part-time programs available. *Students:* 22 full-time (13 women), 1 part-time (0 women); includes 1 minority (Black or African American, non-Hispanic/Latino), 3 international. Average age 27. In 2011, 2 master's, 4 doctorates awarded. *Entrance requirements:* For master's, GRE General Test, minimum undergraduate GPA of 3.0 during previous 2 years or 2.75 overall; for doctorate, GRE General Test, minimum undergraduate GPA of 2.75, 3.0 graduate. Additional exam requirements/recommendations for international students: Required—TOEFL. *Application deadline:* For fall admission, 1/15 for domestic and international students. Application fee: $50. Electronic applications accepted. *Expenses:* Tuition, state resident: full-time $12,023; part-time $501 per credit hour. Tuition, nonresident: full-time $26,554; part-time $1107 per credit hour. *Required fees:* $528. *Financial support:* Fellowships with full tuition reimbursements, research assistantships with full tuition reimbursements, teaching assistantships with full tuition reimbursements, Federal Work-Study, institutionally sponsored loans, scholarships/grants, health care benefits, tuition waivers (full), and unspecified assistantships available. Financial award application deadline: 1/15; financial award applicants required to submit FAFSA. *Unit head:* Dr. Louis A. Actis, Chair, 513-529-5421, Fax: 513-529-2431, E-mail: actisla@muohio.edu. *Application contact:* Dr. Xiao-Wen Cheng, Graduate Admissions Committee Chair, 513-529-5422, E-mail: microbiology@muohio.edu. Web site: http://microbiology.muohio.edu/.

Michigan State University, College of Human Medicine and The Graduate School, Graduate Programs in Human Medicine, East Lansing, MI 48824. Offers biochemistry and molecular biology (MS, PhD); epidemiology (MS, PhD); microbiology (MS); microbiology and molecular genetics (PhD); pharmacology and toxicology (MS, PhD); physiology (MS, PhD); public health (MPH). *Entrance requirements:* Additional exam requirements/recommendations for international students: Required—TOEFL.

Michigan State University, College of Osteopathic Medicine and The Graduate School, Graduate Studies in Osteopathic Medicine, East Lansing, MI 48824. Offers biochemistry and molecular biology (MS, PhD); microbiology (MS); microbiology and molecular genetics (PhD); pharmacology and toxicology (MS, PhD), including integrative pharmacology (MS), pharmacology and toxicology, pharmacology and toxicology-environmental toxicology (PhD); physiology (MS, PhD).

Michigan State University, College of Veterinary Medicine and The Graduate School, Graduate Programs in Veterinary Medicine and College of Natural Science and Graduate Programs in Human Medicine, Department of Microbiology and Molecular Genetics, East Lansing, MI 48824. Offers industrial microbiology (MS, PhD); microbiology (MS, PhD); microbiology and molecular genetics (MS, PhD); microbiology–environmental toxicology (PhD). *Entrance requirements:* For master's, GRE General Test. Additional exam requirements/recommendations for international students: Required—TOEFL (minimum score 550 paper-based; 213 computer-based), Michigan State University ELT (minimum score 85), Michigan English Language Assessment Battery (minimum score 83). Electronic applications accepted.

Michigan State University, The Graduate School, College of Agriculture and Natural Resources, MSU-DOE Plant Research Laboratory, East Lansing, MI 48824. Offers biochemistry and molecular biology (PhD); cellular and molecular biology (PhD); crop and soil sciences (PhD); genetics (PhD); microbiology and molecular genetics (PhD); plant biology (PhD); plant physiology (PhD). Offered jointly with the Department of Energy. *Degree requirements:* For doctorate, comprehensive exam, thesis/dissertation, laboratory rotation, defense of dissertation. *Entrance requirements:* For doctorate, GRE General Test, acceptance into one of the affiliated department programs; 3 letters of recommendation; bachelor's degree or equivalent in life sciences, chemistry, biochemistry, or biophysics; research experience. Electronic applications accepted. *Faculty research:* Role of hormones in the regulation of plant development and physiology, molecular mechanisms associated with signal recognition, development and application of genetic methods and materials, protein routing and function.

Montana State University, College of Graduate Studies, College of Letters and Science, Department of Microbiology, Bozeman, MT 59717. Offers MS, PhD. Part-time programs available. *Degree requirements:* For master's, comprehensive exam; for doctorate, comprehensive exam, thesis/dissertation. *Entrance requirements:* For master's and doctorate, GRE General Test. Additional exam requirements/recommendations for international students: Required—TOEFL (minimum score 550 paper-based; 213 computer-based). Electronic applications accepted. *Faculty research:* Medical microbiology, environmental microbiology, biofilms, immunology, molecular biology and bioinformatics.

New York Medical College, Graduate School of Basic Medical Sciences, Microbiology and Immunology Department, Valhalla, NY 10595-1691. Offers MS, PhD, MD/PhD. Part-time and evening/weekend programs available. *Faculty:* 12 full-time (4 women). *Students:* 18 full-time (10 women), 4 part-time (2 women); includes 8 minority (1 Black or African American, non-Hispanic/Latino; 4 Asian, non-Hispanic/Latino; 3 Hispanic/Latino). Average age 27. 15 applicants, 93% accepted, 10 enrolled. In 2011, 4 master's, 4 doctorates awarded. Terminal master's awarded for partial completion of doctoral program. *Median time to degree:* Of those who began their doctoral program in fall 2003, 100% received their degree in 8 years or less. *Degree requirements:* For master's, thesis; for doctorate, comprehensive exam, thesis/dissertation. *Entrance requirements:* For master's and doctorate, GRE General Test. Additional exam requirements/recommendations for international students: Required—TOEFL. *Application deadline:* For fall admission, 7/1 priority date for domestic students, 5/1 for international students; for spring admission, 12/1 priority date for domestic students, 10/1 for international students. Applications are processed on a rolling basis. Application fee: $50 ($75 for international students). Electronic applications accepted. *Financial support:* In 2011–12, 5 fellowships with full tuition reimbursements (averaging $24,000 per year), 6 research assistantships with full tuition reimbursements (averaging $24,000 per year) were awarded; career-related internships or fieldwork, Federal Work-Study, institutionally sponsored loans, scholarships/grants, traineeships, tuition waivers (full), unspecified assistantships, and health benefits (for PhD candidates only) also available. Financial award applicants required to submit FAFSA. *Faculty research:* Tumor cells, cancer vaccines, the role of stem cells in cancer, bacterial genetics pathogenesis of infectious disease and function of influenza virus antigens, molecular virology, and the biochemistry and genetics of emerging pathogens. *Unit head:* Dr. Raj Tiwari, Director, 914-594-4870. *Application contact:* Valerie Romeo-Messana, Admission Coordinator, 914-594-4110, Fax: 914-594-4944, E-mail: v_romeomessana@nymc.edu.

New York University, Graduate School of Arts and Science, Department of Biology, New York, NY 10012-1019. Offers biology (PhD); biomedical journalism (MS); cancer and molecular biology (PhD); computational biology (PhD); computers in biological research (MS); developmental genetics (PhD); general biology (MS); immunology and microbiology (PhD); molecular genetics (PhD); neurobiology (PhD); oral biology (MS); plant biology (PhD); recombinant DNA technology (MS); MS/MBA. Part-time programs available. *Faculty:* 24 full-time (5 women). *Students:* 146 full-time (90 women), 54 part-time (36 women); includes 49 minority (1 Black or African American, non-Hispanic/

Latino; 33 Asian, non-Hispanic/Latino; 12 Hispanic/Latino; 3 Two or more races, non-Hispanic/Latino), 89 international. Average age 27. 394 applicants, 62% accepted, 82 enrolled. In 2011, 68 master's, 6 doctorates awarded. Terminal master's awarded for partial completion of doctoral program. *Degree requirements:* For master's, thesis or alternative, qualifying paper; for doctorate, comprehensive exam, thesis/dissertation. *Entrance requirements:* For master's, GRE General Test; for doctorate, GRE General Test, GRE Subject Test. Additional exam requirements/recommendations for international students: Required—TOEFL. *Application deadline:* For fall admission, 12/1 priority date for domestic students, 12/1 for international students. Application fee: $90. *Financial support:* Fellowships with tuition reimbursements, research assistantships with tuition reimbursements, teaching assistantships with tuition reimbursements, career-related internships or fieldwork, Federal Work-Study, institutionally sponsored loans, scholarships/grants, health care benefits, and unspecified assistantships available. Financial award application deadline: 12/1; financial award applicants required to submit FAFSA. *Faculty research:* Genomics, molecular and cell biology, development and molecular genetics, molecular evolution of plants and animals. *Unit head:* Stephen Small, Chair, 212-998-8200, Fax: 212-995-4015, E-mail: biology@nyu.edu. *Application contact:* Justin Blau, Director of Graduate Studies, 212-998-8200, Fax: 212-995-4015, E-mail: biology@nyu.edu. Web site: http://biology.as.nyu.edu/.

New York University, School of Medicine, New York, NY 10012-1019. Offers biomedical sciences (PhD), including biomedical imaging, cellular and molecular biology, computational biology, developmental genetics, medical and molecular parasitology, microbiology, molecular oncobiology and immunology, neuroscience and physiology, pathobiology, pharmacology, structural biology; clinical investigation (MS); medicine (MD); MD/MA; MD/MPA; MD/MS; MD/PhD. *Accreditation:* LCME/AMA (one or more programs are accredited). *Degree requirements:* For master's, comprehensive exam, thesis; for doctorate, comprehensive exam (for some programs), thesis/dissertation (for some programs). *Entrance requirements:* For doctorate, MCAT (for MD). Additional exam requirements/recommendations for international students: Required—TOEFL. *Expenses:* Contact institution. *Faculty research:* AIDS, cancer, neuroscience, molecular biology, neuroscience, cell biology and molecular genetics, structural biology, microbial pathogenesis and host defense, pharmacology, molecular oncology and immunology.

New York University, School of Medicine and Graduate School of Arts and Science, Sackler Institute of Graduate Biomedical Sciences, Program in Microbiology, New York, NY 10012-1019. Offers PhD, MD/PhD. *Faculty:* 26 full-time (7 women). *Students:* 28 full-time (16 women); includes 8 minority (2 Black or African American, non-Hispanic/Latino; 3 Asian, non-Hispanic/Latino; 3 Hispanic/Latino), 8 international. Average age 28. In 2011, 4 doctorates awarded. *Degree requirements:* For doctorate, one foreign language, comprehensive exam, thesis/dissertation, qualifying exam. *Entrance requirements:* For doctorate, GRE General Test, GRE Subject Test. Additional exam requirements/recommendations for international students: Required—TOEFL. *Application deadline:* For fall admission, 1/4 priority date for domestic students. Applications are processed on a rolling basis. Application fee: $85. *Financial support:* Fellowships with tuition reimbursements, research assistantships with tuition reimbursements, and teaching assistantships with tuition reimbursements available. *Faculty research:* Aspects of microbiology, parasitology, and genetics; virology. *Unit head:* Dr. Claudio Basilico, Chairman, 212-263-5341, Fax: 212-263-8276. *Application contact:* Dr. Ian Mohr, Graduate Advisor, 212-263-0415, Fax: 212-263-8276, E-mail: mohri01@popmail.med.nyu.edu.

North Carolina State University, Graduate School, College of Agriculture and Life Sciences, Department of Microbiology, Program in Microbiology, Raleigh, NC 27695. Offers MS, PhD. *Degree requirements:* For master's, thesis (for some programs); for doctorate, thesis/dissertation. *Entrance requirements:* For master's and doctorate, GRE. Electronic applications accepted.

North Dakota State University, College of Graduate and Interdisciplinary Studies, College of Agriculture, Food Systems, and Natural Resources, Department of Veterinary and Microbiological Sciences, Fargo, ND 58108. Offers food safety (MS); microbiology (MS); molecular pathogenesis (PhD). Part-time programs available. *Faculty:* 8 full-time (6 women). *Students:* 15 full-time (5 women), 5 part-time (3 women), 9 international. 24 applicants, 46% accepted, 3 enrolled. In 2011, 1 master's, 1 doctorate awarded. *Degree requirements:* For master's, thesis; for doctorate, thesis/dissertation, oral and written preliminary exams. *Entrance requirements:* For master's and doctorate, GRE. Additional exam requirements/recommendations for international students: Required—TOEFL (minimum score 525 paper-based; 197 computer-based; 71 iBT). *Application deadline:* For fall admission, 2/15 priority date for domestic students. Applications are processed on a rolling basis. Application fee: $35. *Financial support:* Fellowships with full tuition reimbursements, research assistantships with full tuition reimbursements, teaching assistantships with full tuition reimbursements, Federal Work-Study, and institutionally sponsored loans available. Financial award application deadline: 4/15. *Faculty research:* Bacterial gene regulation, antibiotic resistance, molecular virology, mechanisms of bacterial pathogenesis, immunology of animals. *Unit head:* Dr. Charlene Wolf-Hall, Head, 701-231-7667, E-mail: charlene.hall@ndsu.edu. *Application contact:* Dr. John McEvoy, Associate Professor, 701-231-8530, Fax: 701-231-7514, E-mail: eugene.berry@ndsu.edu. Web site: http://vetmicro.ndsu.nodak.edu/.

Northwestern University, Northwestern University Feinberg School of Medicine and Interdepartmental Programs, Integrated Graduate Programs in the Life Sciences, Chicago, IL 60611. Offers cancer biology (PhD); cell biology (PhD); developmental biology (PhD); evolutionary biology (PhD); immunology and microbial pathogenesis (PhD); molecular biology and genetics (PhD); neurobiology (PhD); pharmacology and toxicology (PhD); structural biology and biochemistry (PhD). *Degree requirements:* For doctorate, comprehensive exam, thesis/dissertation, written and oral qualifying exams. *Entrance requirements:* For doctorate, GRE General Test. Additional exam requirements/recommendations for international students: Required—TOEFL (minimum score 600 paper-based; 250 computer-based). Electronic applications accepted.

The Ohio State University, Graduate School, College of Arts and Sciences, Division of Natural and Mathematical Sciences, Department of Microbiology, Columbus, OH 43210. Offers MS, PhD. *Faculty:* 16. *Students:* 7 full-time (3 women), 38 part-time (20 women); includes 1 minority (Asian, non-Hispanic/Latino), 18 international. Average age 27. In 2011, 3 master's, 8 doctorates awarded. *Degree requirements:* For master's, thesis optional; for doctorate, thesis/dissertation. *Entrance requirements:* For master's, GRE General Test, GRE Subject Test in biology, biochemistry or chemistry (recommended); for doctorate, GRE General Test; GRE Subject Test in biology, biochemistry or chemistry (recommended). Additional exam requirements/recommendations for international students: Required—TOEFL (minimum score 600 paper-based; 250 computer-based; 79 iBT), Michigan English Language Assessment Battery (minimum score 82). *Application deadline:* For fall admission, 8/15 priority date for domestic students, 7/1 for international students; for winter admission, 12/1 priority date for domestic students, 11/1 for international students; for spring admission, 3/1 priority date for domestic students, 2/1 for international students. Applications are processed on a rolling basis. Application fee: $40 ($50 for international students). Electronic applications accepted. *Expenses:* Tuition, state resident: full-time $11,400. Tuition, nonresident: full-time $28,125. Tuition and fees vary according to course load, degree level, campus/

location and program. *Financial support:* Fellowships, research assistantships, teaching assistantships, Federal Work-Study, and institutionally sponsored loans available. Support available to part-time students. *Unit head:* Dr. Tina M. Henkin, Chair, 614-688-3831, Fax: 614-292-8120, E-mail: henkin.3@osu.edu. *Application contact:* Graduate Admissions, 614-292-6031, Fax: 614-292-3656, E-mail: gradadmissions@osu.edu. Web site: http://microbiology.osu.edu/.

Ohio University, Graduate College, College of Arts and Sciences, Department of Biological Sciences, Athens, OH 45701-2979. Offers biological sciences (MS, PhD); cell biology and physiology (MS, PhD); ecology and evolutionary biology (MS, PhD); exercise physiology and muscle biology (MS, PhD); microbiology (MS, PhD); neuroscience (MS, PhD). *Students:* 35 full-time (12 women), 4 part-time (1 woman), 14 international. 62 applicants, 10% accepted, 5 enrolled. In 2011, 2 master's, 8 doctorates awarded. Terminal master's awarded for partial completion of doctoral program. *Degree requirements:* For master's, comprehensive exam, thesis, 1 quarter of teaching experience; for doctorate, comprehensive exam, thesis/dissertation, 2 quarters of teaching experience. *Entrance requirements:* For master's, GRE General Test, names of three faculty members whose research interests most closely match the applicant's interest; for doctorate, GRE General Test, essay concerning prior training, research interest and career goals, plus names of three faculty members whose research interests most closely match the applicant's interest. Additional exam requirements/recommendations for international students: Required—TOEFL (minimum score 620 paper-based; 105 iBT) or IELTS (minimum score 7.5). *Application deadline:* For fall admission, 1/15 for domestic and international students. Application fee: $50 ($55 for international students). Electronic applications accepted. *Financial support:* In 2011–12, 1 fellowship with full tuition reimbursement (averaging $18,957 per year), 10 research assistantships with full tuition reimbursements (averaging $18,957 per year), 42 teaching assistantships with full tuition reimbursements (averaging $18,957 per year) were awarded; Federal Work-Study and institutionally sponsored loans also available. Financial award application deadline: 1/15. *Faculty research:* Ecology and evolutionary biology, exercise physiology and muscle biology, neurobiology, cell biology, physiology. *Total annual research expenditures:* $2.8 million. *Unit head:* Dr. Ralph DiCaprio, Chair, 740-593-2290, Fax: 740-593-0300, E-mail: dicaprir@ohio.edu. *Application contact:* Dr. Patrick Hassett, Graduate Chair, 740-593-4793, Fax: 740-593-0300, E-mail: hassett@ohio.edu. Web site: http://www.biosci.ohiou.edu/.

Oklahoma State University, College of Arts and Sciences, Department of Microbiology and Molecular Genetics, Stillwater, OK 74078. Offers MS, PhD. *Faculty:* 18 full-time (3 women), 1 part-time/adjunct (0 women). *Students:* 10 full-time (4 women), 14 part-time (12 women); includes 1 minority (Asian, non-Hispanic/Latino), 12 international. Average age 29. 113 applicants, 7% accepted, 3 enrolled. In 2011, 2 master's, 3 doctorates awarded. *Degree requirements:* For master's, thesis; for doctorate, comprehensive exam, thesis/dissertation. *Entrance requirements:* For master's, GRE General Test; for doctorate, GRE General Test. Additional exam requirements/recommendations for international students: Required—TOEFL (minimum score 550 paper-based; 79 iBT). *Application deadline:* For fall admission, 3/1 for international students; for spring admission, 8/1 for international students. Applications are processed on a rolling basis. Application fee: $40 ($75 for international students). Electronic applications accepted. *Expenses:* Tuition, state resident: full-time $4044; part-time $168.50 per credit hour. Tuition, nonresident: full-time $16,008; part-time $667 per credit hour. *Required fees:* $2122; $88.45 per credit hour. One-time fee: $50. Tuition and fees vary according to course load and campus/location. *Financial support:* In 2011–12, 16 research assistantships (averaging $19,979 per year), 9 teaching assistantships (averaging $17,567 per year) were awarded; career-related internships or fieldwork, Federal Work-Study, scholarships/grants, health care benefits, tuition waivers (partial), and unspecified assistantships also available. Support available to part-time students. Financial award application deadline: 3/1; financial award applicants required to submit FAFSA. *Faculty research:* Bioinformatics, genomics-genetics, virology, environmental microbiology, development-molecular mechanisms. *Unit head:* Dr. Bill Picking, Head, 405-744-7180, Fax: 405-744-6790. *Application contact:* Dr. Sheryl Tucker, Dean, 405-744-7099, Fax: 405-744-0355, E-mail: grad-i@okstate.edu. Web site: http://microbiology.okstate.edu.

Oklahoma State University Center for Health Sciences, Graduate Program in Forensic Sciences, Tulsa, OK 74107-1898. Offers forensic DNA/molecular biology (MS); forensic document examination (MS, Graduate Certificate); forensic pathology/microbiology (MS); forensic psychology (MS); forensic science administration (MS); forensic toxicology (MS). Part-time and evening/weekend programs available. Postbaccalaureate distance learning degree programs offered (no on-campus study). *Faculty:* 2 full-time (0 women), 14 part-time/adjunct (5 women). *Students:* 7 full-time (5 women), 22 part-time (12 women); includes 4 minority (3 American Indian or Alaska Native, non-Hispanic/Latino; 1 Hispanic/Latino), 1 international. Average age 34. 12 applicants, 50% accepted, 5 enrolled. In 2011, 7 degrees awarded. *Degree requirements:* For master's, comprehensive exam (for some programs), thesis (for some programs). *Entrance requirements:* For master's, MAT (for MFSA) or GRE General Test, professional experience (MFSA). Additional exam requirements/recommendations for international students: Required—TOEFL (minimum score 600 paper-based; 250 computer-based), TWE (minimum score 5). *Application deadline:* For fall admission, 3/1 for domestic and international students; for spring admission, 10/1 for domestic and international students. Application fee: $40 ($75 for international students). *Financial support:* In 2011–12, 10 students received support, including 2 research assistantships (averaging $12,000 per year); career-related internships or fieldwork, Federal Work-Study, and tuition waivers (partial) also available. Support available to part-time students. Financial award application deadline: 4/1; financial award applicants required to submit FAFSA. *Faculty research:* Studies on the variability in chromosomal DNA; development/enhancement of accessory methods useful for forensic DNA typing; development of universal methods useful for discriminating pathogenic bacteria; forensic dentistry; transmission of microbial diseases by dentures, protective athletic mouth-guards, band wind instruments, and infant pacifiers; changes in ecologies and antibiotic sensitivities of aerobic microorganisms; forensic toxicology and trace chemical method development. *Total annual research expenditures:* $58,000. *Unit head:* Dr. Robert T. Allen, Director, 918-561-1108, Fax: 918-561-8414. *Application contact:* Cathy Newsome, Coordinator, 918-561-1108, Fax: 918-561-8414, E-mail: cathy.newsome@okstate.edu.

Oregon Health & Science University, School of Medicine, Graduate Programs in Medicine, Program in Molecular and Cellular Biosciences, Department of Molecular Microbiology and Immunology, Portland, OR 97239-3098. Offers PhD. *Faculty:* 10 full-time (3 women). *Students:* 21 full-time (11 women); includes 6 minority (5 Hispanic/Latino; 1 Two or more races, non-Hispanic/Latino), 3 international. Average age 29. In 2011, 6 doctorates awarded. Terminal master's awarded for partial completion of doctoral program. *Degree requirements:* For doctorate, comprehensive exam, thesis/dissertation, qualifying exam. *Entrance requirements:* For doctorate, GRE General Test (minimum scores: 153 Verbal/148 Quantitative/4.5 Analytical) or MCAT (for some programs). Additional exam requirements/recommendations for international students: Required—TOEFL. Electronic applications accepted. *Financial support:* Health care benefits and full tuition and stipends available. *Faculty research:* Molecular biology of bacterial and viral pathogens, cellular and humoral immunology, molecular biology of

microbes. *Unit head:* Dr. Eric Barklis, Program Director, 503-494-7768, E-mail: mmi@ohsu.edu. *Application contact:* Elaine Offield, Program Coordinator, 503-494-5824, E-mail: offielde@ohsu.edu. Web site: http://www.ohsu.edu/microbiology.

Oregon State University, Graduate School, College of Science, Department of Microbiology, Corvallis, OR 97331. Offers MA, MAIS, MS, PhD. Part-time programs available. Terminal master's awarded for partial completion of doctoral program. *Degree requirements:* For master's, thesis; for doctorate, one foreign language, thesis/dissertation. *Entrance requirements:* For master's and doctorate, GRE General Test, minimum GPA of 3.0 in last 90 hours. Additional exam requirements/recommendations for international students: Required—TOEFL. *Faculty research:* Genetics, physiology, biotechnology, pathogenic microbiology, plant virology.

Penn State Hershey Medical Center, College of Medicine, Graduate School Programs in the Biomedical Sciences, Graduate Program in Microbiology and Immunology, Hershey, PA 17033. Offers genetics (PhD); immunology (MS, PhD); microbiology (MS); microbiology/virology (PhD); molecular biology (PhD); MD/PhD. *Students:* 18 full-time (9 women), 6 international. 59 applicants, 5% accepted, 3 enrolled. In 2011, 1 master's, 3 doctorates awarded. Terminal master's awarded for partial completion of doctoral program. *Degree requirements:* For master's, thesis or alternative; for doctorate, comprehensive exam, thesis/dissertation, oral exam. *Entrance requirements:* For doctorate, GRE General Test, minimum GPA of 3.0. Additional exam requirements/recommendations for international students: Required—TOEFL. *Application deadline:* For fall admission, 1/31 priority date for domestic students, 2/1 for international students. Applications are processed on a rolling basis. Application fee: $65. Electronic applications accepted. *Financial support:* In 2011–12, research assistantships with full tuition reimbursements (averaging $23,028 per year) were awarded; fellowships with full tuition reimbursements, scholarships/grants, health care benefits, and unspecified assistantships also available. Financial award applicants required to submit FAFSA. *Faculty research:* Virus replication and assembly, oncogenesis, interactions of viruses with host cells and animal model systems. *Unit head:* Dr. Aron Luckacher, Chair, 717-531-7659, Fax: 717-531-6522, E-mail: micro-grad-hmc@psu.edu. *Application contact:* Billie Burns, Secretary, 717-531-7659, Fax: 717-531-6522, E-mail: micro-grad-hmc@psu.edu. Web site: http://www.pennstatehershey.org/web/microbiology/programs.

Penn State University Park, Graduate School, Eberly College of Science, Department of Biochemistry and Molecular Biology, State College, University Park, PA 16802-1503. Offers biochemistry, microbiology, and molecular biology (MS, PhD); biotechnology (MBIOT). *Unit head:* Dr. Richard J. Frisque, Head, 814-863-1851, E-mail: rjf6@psu.edu. *Application contact:* Dr. Ronald Porter, Director of Graduate Studies, 814-863-4903, E-mail: rdp1@psu.edu. Web site: http://bmb.psu.edu.

Purdue University, Graduate School, College of Science, Department of Biological Sciences, West Lafayette, IN 47907. Offers biochemistry (PhD); biophysics (PhD); cell and developmental biology (PhD); ecology, evolutionary and population biology (MS, PhD), including ecology, evolutionary biology, population biology; genetics (MS, PhD); microbiology (MS, PhD); molecular biology (PhD); neurobiology (MS, PhD); plant physiology (PhD). *Faculty:* 57 full-time (15 women), 4 part-time/adjunct (1 woman). *Students:* 94 full-time (54 women), 9 part-time (5 women); includes 7 minority (2 Black or African American, non-Hispanic/Latino; 3 Asian, non-Hispanic/Latino; 2 Hispanic/Latino), 51 international. Average age 27. 246 applicants, 11% accepted, 18 enrolled. In 2011, 9 master's, 23 doctorates awarded. Terminal master's awarded for partial completion of doctoral program. *Degree requirements:* For master's, thesis (for some programs); for doctorate, thesis/dissertation, seminars, teaching experience. *Entrance requirements:* For master's, GRE General Test, minimum analytical writing score of 3.5, minimum undergraduate GPA of 3.0; for doctorate, GRE General Test, minimum analytical writing score of 3.5, minimum undergraduate GPA of 3.5. Additional exam requirements/recommendations for international students: Required—TOEFL (minimum score 600 paper-based; 107 iBT) for MS; TOEFL (minimum score 600 paper-based; 80 iBT) for Ph D. *Application deadline:* For fall admission, 12/7 for domestic and international students. Applications are processed on a rolling basis. Application fee: $60 ($75 for international students). Electronic applications accepted. *Financial support:* Fellowships, research assistantships, and teaching assistantships available. Support available to part-time students. Financial award application deadline: 2/15; financial award applicants required to submit FAFSA. *Unit head:* Dr. Richard J. Kuhn, Head, 765-494-4407, E-mail: kuhnr@purdue.edu. *Application contact:* Georgina E. Rupp, Graduate Coordinator, 765-494-8142, Fax: 765-494-0876, E-mail: ruppg@purdue.edu. Web site: http://www.bio.purdue.edu/.

Purdue University, Graduate School, PULSe - Purdue University Life Sciences Program, West Lafayette, IN 47907. Offers biomolecular structure and biophysics (PhD); biotechnology (PhD); chemical biology (PhD); chromatin and regulation of gene expression (PhD); integrative neuroscience (PhD); integrative plant sciences (PhD); membrane biology (PhD); microbiology (PhD); molecular evolutionary and cancer biology (PhD); molecular evolutionary genetics (PhD); molecular virology (PhD). *Students:* 90 full-time (45 women); includes 7 minority (3 Black or African American, non-Hispanic/Latino; 1 Asian, non-Hispanic/Latino; 2 Hispanic/Latino; 1 Two or more races, non-Hispanic/Latino), 40 international. Average age 26. 427 applicants, 24% accepted, 35 enrolled. *Entrance requirements:* For doctorate, GRE test required, minimum undergraduate GPA of 3.0. Additional exam requirements/recommendations for international students: Required—TOEFL (minimum score 550 paper-based; 77 iBT). *Application deadline:* For fall admission, 1/15 priority date for domestic students, 1/15 for international students. Applications are processed on a rolling basis. Application fee: $60 ($75 for international students). Electronic applications accepted. *Financial support:* In 2011–12, research assistantships with tuition reimbursements (averaging $22,500 per year), teaching assistantships with tuition reimbursements (averaging $22,500 per year) were awarded. *Unit head:* Dr. Christine A. Hrycyna, Head, 765-494-7322, E-mail: hrycyna@purdue.edu. *Application contact:* Emily E. Bramson, Graduate Contact, 765-494-5865, E-mail: bramson@purdue.edu. Web site: http://www.gradschool.purdue.edu/pulse.

Purdue University, School of Veterinary Medicine and Graduate School, Graduate Programs in Veterinary Medicine, Department of Comparative Pathobiology, West Lafayette, IN 47907-2027. Offers comparative epidemiology and public health (MS); comparative epidemiology and public heath (PhD); comparative microbiology and immunology (MS, PhD); comparative pathobiology (MS, PhD); interdisciplinary studies (PhD), including microbial pathogenesis, molecular signaling and cancer biology, molecular virology; lab animal medicine (MS); veterinary anatomic pathology (MS); veterinary clinical pathology (MS). Terminal master's awarded for partial completion of doctoral program. *Degree requirements:* For master's, thesis (for some programs); for doctorate, thesis/dissertation. *Entrance requirements:* For master's and doctorate, GRE General Test. Additional exam requirements/recommendations for international students: Required—TOEFL (minimum score 575 paper-based; 232 computer-based), IELTS (minimum score 6.5), TWE (minimum score 4). Electronic applications accepted.

Queen's University at Kingston, School of Graduate Studies and Research, Faculty of Health Sciences, Department of Microbiology and Immunology, Kingston, ON K7L 3N6, Canada. Offers M Sc, PhD. Part-time programs available. *Degree requirements:* For master's, thesis; for doctorate, comprehensive exam, thesis/dissertation. *Entrance requirements:* For master's and doctorate, minimum B+ average. Additional exam requirements/recommendations for international students: Required—TOEFL (minimum score 600 paper-based; 250 computer-based). Electronic applications accepted. *Faculty research:* Bacteriology, virology, immunology, education in microbiology and immunology, microbial pathogenesis.

Quinnipiac University, School of Health Sciences, Program in Medical Laboratory Sciences, Hamden, CT 06518-1940. Offers biomedical sciences (MHS); laboratory management (MHS); microbiology (MHS). Part-time programs available. *Faculty:* 13 full-time (7 women), 17 part-time/adjunct (7 women). *Students:* 46 full-time (30 women), 31 part-time (13 women); includes 14 minority (8 Black or African American, non-Hispanic/Latino; 4 Asian, non-Hispanic/Latino; 2 Hispanic/Latino), 34 international. 67 applicants, 79% accepted, 46 enrolled. In 2011, 33 master's awarded. *Degree requirements:* For master's, comprehensive exam, thesis optional. *Entrance requirements:* For master's, minimum GPA of 2.75; bachelor's degree in biological, medical, or health sciences. Additional exam requirements/recommendations for international students: Required—TOEFL (minimum score 575 paper-based; 233 computer-based; 90 iBT), IELTS (minimum score 6.5). *Application deadline:* For fall admission, 7/30 priority date for domestic students, 4/30 for international students; for spring admission, 12/15 priority date for domestic students, 9/15 for international students. Applications are processed on a rolling basis. Application fee: $45. Electronic applications accepted. *Expenses: Tuition:* Part-time $855 per credit. *Required fees:* $35 per credit. *Financial support:* In 2011–12, 8 students received support. Federal Work-Study, tuition waivers (partial), and unspecified assistantships available. Support available to part-time students. Financial award application deadline: 4/15; financial award applicants required to submit FAFSA. *Faculty research:* Microbial physiology, fermentation technology. *Unit head:* Dr. Kenneth Kaloustian, Director, 203-582-8676, Fax: 203-582-3443, E-mail: ken.kaloustian@quinnipiac.edu. *Application contact:* Kristin Parent, Assistant Director of Graduate Health Sciences Admissions, 800-462-1944, Fax: 203-582-3443, E-mail: kristin.parent@quinnipiac.edu. Web site: http://www.quinnipiac.edu/gradmedlab.

Rosalind Franklin University of Medicine and Science, School of Graduate and Postdoctoral Studies - Interdisciplinary Graduate Program in Biomedical Sciences, Department of Microbiology and Immunology, North Chicago, IL 60064-3095. Offers MS, PhD, MD/PhD. Terminal master's awarded for partial completion of doctoral program. *Degree requirements:* For master's, comprehensive exam, thesis; for doctorate, comprehensive exam, thesis/dissertation. *Entrance requirements:* For master's and doctorate, GRE General Test. Additional exam requirements/recommendations for international students: Required—TOEFL, TWE. *Faculty research:* Molecular biology, parasitology, virology.

Rush University, Graduate College, Division of Immunology and Microbiology, Chicago, IL 60612-3832. Offers microbiology (PhD); virology (MS, PhD), including immunology, virology; MD/PhD. *Degree requirements:* For doctorate, thesis/dissertation, comprehensive preliminary exam. *Entrance requirements:* For doctorate, GRE General Test, interview, minimum GPA of 3.0. Additional exam requirements/recommendations for international students: Required—TOEFL. *Faculty research:* Immune interactions of cells and membranes, HIV immunopathogenesis, autoimmunity, tumor biology.

Rutgers, The State University of New Jersey, New Brunswick, Graduate School-New Brunswick, Programs in the Molecular Biosciences, Program in Microbiology and Molecular Genetics, Piscataway, NJ 08854-8097. Offers applied microbiology (MS, PhD); clinical microbiology (MS, PhD); computational molecular biology (PhD); immunology (MS, PhD); microbial biochemistry (MS, PhD); molecular genetics (MS, PhD); virology (MS, PhD). MS, PhD offered jointly with University of Medicine and Dentistry of New Jersey. Part-time programs available. Terminal master's awarded for partial completion of doctoral program. *Degree requirements:* For master's, comprehensive exam, thesis or alternative; for doctorate, comprehensive exam, thesis/dissertation, written qualifying exam. *Entrance requirements:* For master's, GRE General Test, minimum GPA of 3.0; for doctorate, GRE General Test, GRE Subject Test (recommended), minimum GPA of 3.0. Additional exam requirements/recommendations for international students: Required—TOEFL. Electronic applications accepted. *Faculty research:* Molecular genetics and microbial physiology; virology and pathogenic microbiology; applied, environmental and industrial microbiology; computers in molecular biology.

Saint Louis University, Graduate Education and School of Medicine, Graduate Program in Biomedical Sciences, Department of Molecular Microbiology and Immunology, St. Louis, MO 63103-2097. Offers PhD. *Degree requirements:* For doctorate, comprehensive exam, thesis/dissertation, qualifying exams. *Entrance requirements:* For doctorate, GRE General Test (GRE Subject Test optional), letters of recommendation, resume, interview. Additional exam requirements/recommendations for international students: Required—TOEFL (minimum score 525 paper-based; 194 computer-based). Electronic applications accepted. *Faculty research:* Pathogenesis of hepatitis C virus, herperviruses, pox viruses, rheumatoid arthritis, antiviral drugs and vaccines in biodefense, cancer gene therapy, virology and immunology.

San Diego State University, Graduate and Research Affairs, College of Sciences, Department of Biology, Program in Microbiology, San Diego, CA 92182. Offers MS. *Degree requirements:* For master's, thesis, oral exam. *Entrance requirements:* For master's, GRE General Test, GRE Subject Test, resume or curriculum vitae, 2 letters of recommendation.. Additional exam requirements/recommendations for international students: Required—TOEFL. Electronic applications accepted.

San Francisco State University, Division of Graduate Studies, College of Science and Engineering, Department of Biology, Program in Microbiology, San Francisco, CA 94132-1722. Offers MS. *Application deadline:* Applications are processed on a rolling basis. *Unit head:* Dr. Diana Chu, Program Coordinator, 415-405-3487, E-mail: chud@sfsu.edu. *Application contact:* Dr. Robert Patterson, Graduate Coordinator, 415-338-1100, E-mail: patters@sfsu.edu. Web site: http://www.sfsu.edu/~biology.

San Jose State University, Graduate Studies and Research, College of Science, Department of Biological Sciences, San Jose, CA 95192-0001. Offers biological sciences (MA, MS); molecular biology and microbiology (MS); organismal biology, conservation and ecology (MS); physiology (MS). Part-time programs available. *Entrance requirements:* For master's, GRE. Electronic applications accepted. *Faculty research:* Systemic physiology, molecular genetics, SEM studies, toxicology, large mammal ecology.

Seton Hall University, College of Arts and Sciences, Department of Biological Sciences, South Orange, NJ 07079-2697. Offers biology (MS); biology/business administration (MS); microbiology (MS); molecular bioscience (PhD); molecular bioscience/neuroscience (PhD). Part-time and evening/weekend programs available. *Degree requirements:* For master's, thesis optional; for doctorate, comprehensive exam, thesis/dissertation. *Entrance requirements:* For master's and doctorate, GRE or MS from accredited university in the U.S.. Additional exam requirements/recommendations for international students: Required—TOEFL. Electronic applications accepted. *Expenses: Tuition:* Part-time $1033 per credit hour. *Required fees:* $85 per semester. *Faculty research:* Neurobiology, genetics, immunology, molecular biology, cellular physiology, toxicology, microbiology, bioinformatics.

South Dakota State University, Graduate School, College of Agriculture and Biological Sciences, Department of Biology and Microbiology, Brookings, SD 57007. Offers

biological sciences (MS, PhD). Part-time programs available. *Degree requirements:* For master's, thesis (for some programs), oral exam; for doctorate, comprehensive exam, thesis/dissertation, oral exam. *Entrance requirements:* For master's and doctorate, GRE General Test. Additional exam requirements/recommendations for international students: Required—TOEFL (minimum score 600 paper-based; 250 computer-based; 100 iBT). *Faculty research:* Ecosystem ecology; plant, animal and microbial genomics; animal infectious disease, microbial bioproducts.

Southern Illinois University Carbondale, Graduate School, College of Science, Program in Molecular Biology, Microbiology, and Biochemistry, Carbondale, IL 62901-4701. Offers MS, PhD. *Faculty:* 16 full-time (2 women). *Students:* 52 full-time (27 women), 42 part-time (25 women); includes 10 minority (5 Black or African American, non-Hispanic/Latino; 5 Asian, non-Hispanic/Latino), 64 international. Average age 25. 139 applicants, 12% accepted, 12 enrolled. In 2011, 14 master's, 8 doctorates awarded. *Degree requirements:* For master's, thesis; for doctorate, thesis/dissertation. *Entrance requirements:* For master's, GRE, minimum GPA of 2.7; for doctorate, GRE, minimum GPA of 3.25. Additional exam requirements/recommendations for international students: Required—TOEFL. *Application deadline:* Applications are processed on a rolling basis. Application fee: $20. *Financial support:* In 2011–12, 40 students received support, including 3 fellowships with full tuition reimbursements available, 24 research assistantships with full tuition reimbursements available, 12 teaching assistantships with full tuition reimbursements available; Federal Work-Study and institutionally sponsored loans also available. Support available to part-time students. Financial award application deadline: 3/1. *Faculty research:* Prokaryotic gene regulation and expression; eukaryotic gene regulation; microbial, phylogenetic, and metabolic diversity; immune responses to tumors, pathogens, and autoantigens; protein folding and structure. *Unit head:* Dr. John Martinko, Director, 618-453-8116, Fax: 618-453-8036, E-mail: martinko.mbmb@science.siu.edu. *Application contact:* Charlotte Keller, Office Systems Specialist, 618-453-7071, Fax: 618-453-8036, E-mail: ckeller@siumed.edu. Web site: http://mbmb.siu.edu/.

Southwestern Oklahoma State University, College of Professional and Graduate Studies, School of Behavioral Sciences and Education, Specialization in Health Sciences and Microbiology, Weatherford, OK 73096-3098. Offers M Ed.

Stanford University, School of Medicine, Graduate Programs in Medicine, Department of Microbiology and Immunology, Stanford, CA 94305-9991. Offers PhD. *Degree requirements:* For doctorate, comprehensive exam, thesis/dissertation, 2 quarters teaching assistantship. *Entrance requirements:* For doctorate, GRE General Test, GRE Subject Test (biology or biochemistry). Additional exam requirements/recommendations for international students: Required—TOEFL. Electronic applications accepted. *Expenses:* Tuition: Full-time $40,050; part-time $890 per credit. *Faculty research:* Molecular pathogenesis of bacteria viruses and parasites, immune system function, autoimmunity, molecular biology.

State University of New York Upstate Medical University, College of Graduate Studies, Program in Microbiology and Immunology, Syracuse, NY 13210-2334. Offers microbiology (MS); microbiology and immunology (PhD); MD/PhD. Terminal master's awarded for partial completion of doctoral program. *Degree requirements:* For master's, thesis; for doctorate, comprehensive exam, thesis/dissertation. *Entrance requirements:* For master's, GRE General Test, interview; for doctorate, GRE General Test, telephone interview. Additional exam requirements/recommendations for international students: Required—TOEFL. Electronic applications accepted. *Faculty research:* Cancer, disorders of the nervous system, infectious diseases, diabetes/metabolic disorders/cardiovascular diseases.

Stony Brook University, State University of New York, Stony Brook University Medical Center, Health Sciences Center, School of Medicine and Graduate School, Graduate Programs in Medicine, Department of Molecular Genetics and Microbiology, Stony Brook, NY 11794. Offers molecular microbiology (PhD). *Degree requirements:* For doctorate, comprehensive exam, thesis/dissertation. *Entrance requirements:* For doctorate, GRE General Test, GRE Subject Test. Additional exam requirements/recommendations for international students: Required—TOEFL. *Faculty research:* Adenovirus molecular genetics, molecular biology of tumors, virus SV40, mechanism of tumor infection by SAV virus.

Temple University, Health Sciences Center, School of Medicine and Graduate School, Graduate Programs in Medicine, Department of Microbiology and Immunology, Philadelphia, PA 19140. Offers MS, PhD, MD/MS, MD/PhD. *Faculty:* 12 full-time (4 women), 13 part-time/adjunct (1 woman). *Students:* 36 full-time (26 women); includes 8 minority (7 Black or African American, non-Hispanic/Latino; 1 Asian, non-Hispanic/Latino), 13 international. Average age 28. 27 applicants, 30% accepted, 4 enrolled. In 2011, 2 master's, 9 doctorates awarded. *Degree requirements:* For master's, thesis; for doctorate, thesis/dissertation, research seminars. *Entrance requirements:* For master's and doctorate, GRE General Test, GRE Subject Test, minimum GPA of 3.0. Additional exam requirements/recommendations for international students: Required—TOEFL (minimum score 600 paper-based; 250 computer-based). *Application deadline:* For fall admission, 7/1 priority date for domestic students, 12/15 for international students; for spring admission, 11/1 priority date for domestic students, 8/1 for international students. Applications are processed on a rolling basis. Application fee: $60. Electronic applications accepted. *Expenses:* Tuition, state resident: full-time $12,366; part-time $687 per credit hour. Tuition, nonresident: full-time $17,298; part-time $961 per credit hour. *Required fees:* $590; $213 per year. *Financial support:* In 2011–12, 32 students received support, including 15 fellowships with full and partial tuition reimbursements available (averaging $23,000 per year), 17 research assistantships with full tuition reimbursements available (averaging $23,000 per year); Federal Work-Study, institutionally sponsored loans, scholarships/grants, health care benefits, and unspecified assistantships also available. Financial award application deadline: 3/15; financial award applicants required to submit FAFSA. *Faculty research:* Molecular and cellular immunology, molecular and biochemical microbiology, molecular genetics. *Total annual research expenditures:* $2 million. *Unit head:* Dr. Doina Ganea, Chair, 215-707-3207, Fax: 215-707-7788, E-mail: doina.ganea@temple.edu. *Application contact:* Dottie Bathe, Administrative Coordinator, 215-707-6747, Fax: 215-707-7788, E-mail: dbathe@temple.edu. Web site: http://www.temple.edu/medicine/departments_centers/basic_science/microbiology.htm.

Texas A&M Health Science Center, College of Medicine, Department of Microbial and Molecular Pathogenesis, College Station, TX 77840. Offers immunology (PhD); microbiology (PhD); molecular biology (PhD); virology (PhD). *Degree requirements:* For doctorate, thesis/dissertation. *Entrance requirements:* For doctorate, GRE General Test, minimum GPA of 3.0. *Faculty research:* Molecular pathogenesis, microbial therapeutics.

Texas A&M University, College of Science, Department of Biology, College Station, TX 77843. Offers biology (MS, PhD); botany (MS, PhD); microbiology (MS, PhD); molecular and cell biology (PhD); neuroscience (MS, PhD); zoology (MS, PhD). *Faculty:* 41. *Students:* 99 full-time (60 women), 8 part-time (4 women); includes 11 minority (1 Black or African American, non-Hispanic/Latino; 5 Asian, non-Hispanic/Latino; 4 Hispanic/Latino; 1 Two or more races, non-Hispanic/Latino), 46 international. Average age 28. In 2011, 5 master's, 7 doctorates awarded. *Degree requirements:* For master's, thesis or alternative; for doctorate, comprehensive exam, thesis/dissertation. *Entrance requirements:* For master's and doctorate, GRE General Test. Additional exam requirements/recommendations for international students: Required—TOEFL. *Application deadline:* For fall admission, 1/15 for domestic students. Applications are processed on a rolling basis. Application fee: $50 ($75 for international students). Electronic applications accepted. *Expenses:* Tuition, state resident: full-time $5437; part-time $226.55 per credit hour. Tuition, nonresident: full-time $12,949; part-time $539.55 per credit hour. *Required fees:* $2741. *Financial support:* Fellowships, research assistantships, and teaching assistantships available. Financial award application deadline: 4/1; financial award applicants required to submit FAFSA. *Unit head:* Dr. Jack McMahan, Department Head, 979-845-2301, E-mail: granster@mail.bio.tamu.edu. *Application contact:* 979-845-7755, Fax: 979-845-2891, E-mail: graduate@bio.tamu.edu. Web site: http://www.bio.tamu.edu/index.html.

Texas A&M University, College of Veterinary Medicine and Biomedical Sciences, Department of Veterinary Pathobiology, College Station, TX 77843. Offers genetics (MS, PhD); veterinary microbiology (MS, PhD); veterinary parasitology (MS, PhD); veterinary pathology (MS, PhD). Part-time programs available. Postbaccalaureate distance learning degree programs offered. *Faculty:* 25. *Students:* 27 full-time (20 women), 19 part-time (13 women); includes 9 minority (3 Black or African American, non-Hispanic/Latino; 3 Asian, non-Hispanic/Latino; 3 Hispanic/Latino), 9 international. Average age 33. In 2011, 2 degrees awarded. Terminal master's awarded for partial completion of doctoral program. *Degree requirements:* For master's, thesis, seminars; for doctorate, thesis/dissertation, seminars. *Entrance requirements:* For master's and doctorate, GRE General Test, minimum GPA of 3.0 in last 60 hours. Additional exam requirements/recommendations for international students: Required—TOEFL. *Application deadline:* For fall admission, 3/1 priority date for domestic students; for spring admission, 8/1 priority date for domestic students. Applications are processed on a rolling basis. Application fee: $50 ($75 for international students). Electronic applications accepted. *Expenses:* Tuition, state resident: full-time $5437; part-time $226.55 per credit hour. Tuition, nonresident: full-time $12,949; part-time $539.55 per credit hour. *Required fees:* $2741. *Financial support:* In 2011–12, fellowships with partial tuition reimbursements (averaging $16,000 per year), research assistantships with partial tuition reimbursements (averaging $15,400 per year), teaching assistantships with partial tuition reimbursements (averaging $16,000 per year) were awarded; Federal Work-Study, institutionally sponsored loans, scholarships/grants, traineeships, health care benefits, and unspecified assistantships also available. Support available to part-time students. Financial award applicants required to submit FAFSA. *Faculty research:* Infectious and noninfectious diseases of animals and birds, animal genetics, molecular biology, immunology, virology. *Unit head:* Dr. Linda Logan, Head, 979-862-6559, Fax: 979-845-9231, E-mail: llogan@cvm.tamu.edu. *Application contact:* Dr. Patricia Holman, Graduate Advisor, 979-845-4202, Fax: 979-862-1147, E-mail: pholman@cvm.tamu.edu. Web site: http://vetmed.tamu.edu/vtpb.

Texas Tech University, Graduate School, College of Arts and Sciences, Department of Biological Sciences, Lubbock, TX 79409-3131. Offers biology (MS, PhD); microbiology (MS); zoology (MS, PhD). Part-time programs available. *Faculty:* 37 full-time (6 women), 2 part-time/adjunct (1 woman). *Students:* 101 full-time (54 women), 11 part-time (7 women); includes 6 minority (1 Asian, non-Hispanic/Latino; 3 Hispanic/Latino; 2 Two or more races, non-Hispanic/Latino), 54 international. Average age 29. 79 applicants, 25% accepted, 11 enrolled. In 2011, 16 master's, 9 doctorates awarded. *Degree requirements:* For master's, thesis or alternative; for doctorate, thesis/dissertation. *Entrance requirements:* For master's and doctorate, GRE General Test. Additional exam requirements/recommendations for international students: Required—TOEFL (minimum score 550 paper-based; 213 computer-based; 79 iBT). *Application deadline:* For fall admission, 6/1 priority date for domestic students, 1/15 for international students; for spring admission, 9/1 priority date for domestic students, 6/15 for international students. Applications are processed on a rolling basis. Application fee: $50 ($75 for international students). Electronic applications accepted. *Expenses:* Tuition, state resident: full-time $5899; part-time $245.80 per credit hour. Tuition, nonresident: full-time $13,411; part-time $558.80 per credit hour. *Required fees:* $2680.60; $86.50 per credit hour. $920.30 per semester. *Financial support:* In 2011–12, 33 students received support. Application deadline: 4/15; applicants required to submit FAFSA. *Faculty research:* Biodiversity and evolution, climate change in arid ecosystems, plant biology and biotechnology, animal communication and behavior, zoonotic and emerging diseases. *Total annual research expenditures:* $2.8 million. *Unit head:* Dr. Llewellyn D. Densmore, Chair, 806-742-2715, Fax: 806-742-2963, E-mail: lou.densmore@ttu.edu. *Application contact:* Dr. Randall M. Jeter, Graduate Adviser, 806-742-2710 Ext. 270, Fax: 806-742-2963, E-mail: randall.jeter@ttu.edu. Web site: http://www.biol.ttu.edu/.

Thomas Jefferson University, Jefferson College of Graduate Studies, MS Program in Microbiology, Philadelphia, PA 19107. Offers MS. Part-time and evening/weekend programs available. *Faculty:* 22 full-time (7 women), 23 part-time/adjunct (6 women). *Students:* 43 part-time (27 women); includes 11 minority (7 Black or African American, non-Hispanic/Latino; 3 Asian, non-Hispanic/Latino; 1 Hispanic/Latino), 2 international. 39 applicants, 69% accepted, 19 enrolled. In 2011, 7 master's awarded. *Degree requirements:* For master's, thesis, clerkship. *Entrance requirements:* For master's, GRE General Test or MCAT, minimum GPA of 3.0. Additional exam requirements/recommendations for international students: Required—TOEFL (minimum score 100 iBT) or IELTS (minimum score 7). *Application deadline:* For fall admission, 8/1 priority date for domestic students, 3/1 for international students; for winter admission, 12/1 priority date for domestic students, 6/1 for international students; for spring admission, 4/1 priority date for domestic students. Applications are processed on a rolling basis. Application fee: $50. Electronic applications accepted. *Expenses:* Contact institution. *Financial support:* In 2011–12, 30 students received support. Federal Work-Study and institutionally sponsored loans available. Support available to part-time students. Financial award application deadline: 5/1; financial award applicants required to submit FAFSA. *Faculty research:* Vaccinology, epidemiology, planning and management, microbiology. *Unit head:* Dr. Jerome G. Buescher, Program Director, 215-503-0159, Fax: 215-503-3433, E-mail: jerome.buescher@jefferson.edu. *Application contact:* Eleanor M. Gorman, Assistant Coordinator, Graduate Center Programs, 215-503-5799, Fax: 215-503-3433, E-mail: eleanor.gorman@jefferson.edu. Web site: http://www.jefferson.edu/jcgs/msbs/.

Thomas Jefferson University, Jefferson College of Graduate Studies, PhD Program in Immunology and Microbial Pathogenesis, Philadelphia, PA 19107. Offers PhD. *Faculty:* 33 full-time (5 women), 2 part-time/adjunct (0 women). *Students:* 22 full-time (10 women); includes 3 minority (1 Black or African American, non-Hispanic/Latino; 1 Asian, non-Hispanic/Latino; 1 Hispanic/Latino), 2 international. 58 applicants, 12% accepted, 3 enrolled. In 2011, 4 doctorates awarded. *Degree requirements:* For doctorate, comprehensive exam, thesis/dissertation. *Entrance requirements:* For doctorate, GRE General Test, minimum GPA of 3.2. Additional exam requirements/recommendations for international students: Required—TOEFL (minimum score 250 computer-based; 100 iBT) or IELTS. *Application deadline:* For fall admission, 1/5 priority date for domestic students, 1/5 for international students. Applications are processed on a rolling basis. Application fee: $50. Electronic applications accepted. *Financial support:* In 2011–12, 22 students received support, including 22 fellowships with full tuition reimbursements available (averaging $54,758 per year); Federal Work-Study, institutionally sponsored loans, scholarships/grants, traineeships, and stipends also available. Support available

to part-time students. Financial award application deadline: 5/1; financial award applicants required to submit FAFSA. *Total annual research expenditures:* $14.6 million. *Unit head:* Dr. Kishore Alugupalli, Program Director, 215-503-4550, Fax: 215-923-4153, E-mail: kishore.alugupalli@jefferson.edu. *Application contact:* Marc E. Stearns, Director of Admissions, 215-503-0155, Fax: 215-503-9920, E-mail: jcgs-info@jefferson.edu. Web site: http://www.jefferson.edu/jcgs/phd/imp/.

Tufts University, Sackler School of Graduate Biomedical Sciences, Molecular Microbiology Program, Medford, MA 02155. Offers PhD. *Faculty:* 15 full-time (6 women). *Students:* 29 full-time (23 women); includes 5 minority (2 Asian, non-Hispanic/Latino; 1 Hispanic/Latino; 2 Two or more races, non-Hispanic/Latino), 1 international. Average age 26. 98 applicants, 15% accepted, 5 enrolled. In 2011, 9 doctorates awarded. Terminal master's awarded for partial completion of doctoral program. *Degree requirements:* For doctorate, thesis/dissertation. *Entrance requirements:* For doctorate, GRE General Test, 3 letters of reference. Additional exam requirements/ recommendations for international students: Required—TOEFL (minimum score 600 paper-based; 250 computer-based; 100 iBT). *Application deadline:* For fall admission, 12/15 for domestic and international students. Application fee: $70. Electronic applications accepted. *Expenses: Tuition:* Full-time $41,208; part-time $1030 per credit hour. Full-time tuition and fees vary according to degree level, program and student level. Part-time tuition and fees vary according to course load. *Financial support:* In 2011–12, 29 students received support, including 29 research assistantships with full tuition reimbursements available (averaging $30,000 per year); traineeships and health care benefits also available. Financial award application deadline: 12/15. *Faculty research:* Mechanisms of gene regulation, interactions of microorganisms and viruses with host cells, infection response. *Unit head:* Dr. Michael Malamy, Director, 617-636-6750, Fax: 617-636-0337, E-mail: michael.malamy@tufts.edu. *Application contact:* Kellie Melchin, Associate Director of Admissions, 617-636-6767, Fax: 617-636-0375, E-mail: sackler-school@tufts.edu. Web site: http://sackler.tufts.edu/Academics/Degree-Programs/PhD-Programs/Molecular-Microbiology.

Tulane University, School of Medicine and School of Liberal Arts, Graduate Programs in Biomedical Sciences, Department of Microbiology and Immunology, New Orleans, LA 70118-5669. Offers MS, PhD, MD/PhD. MS and PhD offered through the Graduate School. *Degree requirements:* For master's, thesis; for doctorate, 2 foreign languages, thesis/dissertation. *Entrance requirements:* For master's, GRE General Test, minimum B average in undergraduate course work; for doctorate, GRE General Test, GRE Subject Test. Additional exam requirements/recommendations for international students: Required—TOEFL. Electronic applications accepted. *Faculty research:* Vaccine development, viral pathogenesis, molecular virology, bacterial pathogenesis, fungal pathogenesis.

Universidad Central del Caribe, School of Medicine, Program in Biomedical Sciences, Bayamón, PR 00960-6032. Offers anatomy and cell biology (MA, MS); biochemistry (MS); biomedical sciences (MA); cellular and molecular biology (PhD); microbiology and immunology (MA, MS); pharmacology (MS); physiology (MS).

Université de Montréal, Faculty of Medicine, Department of Microbiology and Immunology, Montréal, QC H3C 3J7, Canada. Offers M Sc, PhD. Programs offered jointly with Faculty of Veterinary Medicine and Université du Québec, Institut Armand-Frappier. Terminal master's awarded for partial completion of doctoral program. *Degree requirements:* For master's, thesis; for doctorate, thesis/dissertation, general exam. *Entrance requirements:* For master's and doctorate, proficiency in French, knowledge of English. Electronic applications accepted.

Université de Sherbrooke, Faculty of Medicine and Health Sciences, Graduate Programs in Medicine, Program in Microbiology, Sherbrooke, QC J1H 5N4, Canada. Offers M Sc, PhD. Terminal master's awarded for partial completion of doctoral program. *Degree requirements:* For master's, thesis; for doctorate, thesis/dissertation. Electronic applications accepted. *Faculty research:* Oncogenes, alternative splicing mechanisms, genomics, telomerase, DNA repair, Clostridium difficile, Campylobacter jejuni.

Université du Québec, Institut National de la Recherche Scientifique, Graduate Programs, Research Center - INRS - Institut Armand-Frappier - Human Health, Québec, QC G1K 9A9, Canada. Offers applied microbiology (M Sc); biology (PhD); experimental health sciences (M Sc); virology and immunology (M Sc, PhD). Programs given in French. Part-time programs available. *Faculty:* 41. *Students:* 158 full-time (93 women), 11 part-time (5 women), 52 international. Average age 30. In 2011, 17 master's, 9 doctorates awarded. *Degree requirements:* For master's, thesis optional; for doctorate, thesis/dissertation. *Entrance requirements:* For master's and doctorate, appropriate bachelor's degree, proficiency in French. *Application deadline:* For fall admission, 3/30 for domestic and international students; for winter admission, 11/1 for domestic and international students; for spring admission, 3/1 for domestic and international students. Application fee: $45 Canadian dollars. *Financial support:* In 2011–12, 128 students received support, including fellowships (averaging $16,500 per year); research assistantships also available. *Faculty research:* Immunity, infection and cancer; toxicology and environmental biotechnology; molecular pharmacochemistry. *Unit head:* Charles Dozois, Director, 450-687-5010, Fax: 450-686-5566, E-mail: charles.dozois@iaf.inrs.ca. *Application contact:* Yvonne Boisvert, Registrar, 418-654-3861, Fax: 418-654-3858, E-mail: registrariat@adm.inrs.ca. Web site: http://www.iaf.inrs.ca.

Université Laval, Faculty of Agricultural and Food Sciences, Program in Agricultural Microbiology, Québec, QC G1K 7P4, Canada. Offers agricultural microbiology (M Sc); agro-food microbiology (PhD). Terminal master's awarded for partial completion of doctoral program. *Degree requirements:* For master's, thesis; for doctorate, comprehensive exam, thesis/dissertation. *Entrance requirements:* For master's and doctorate, knowledge of French and English. Electronic applications accepted.

Université Laval, Faculty of Medicine, Graduate Programs in Medicine, Programs in Microbiology-Immunology, Québec, QC G1K 7P4, Canada. Offers M Sc, PhD. Terminal master's awarded for partial completion of doctoral program. *Degree requirements:* For master's, thesis; for doctorate, comprehensive exam, thesis/dissertation. *Entrance requirements:* For master's and doctorate, knowledge of French, comprehension of written English. Electronic applications accepted.

Université Laval, Faculty of Sciences and Engineering, Department of Biochemistry and Microbiology, Programs in Microbiology, Québec, QC G1K 7P4, Canada. Offers M Sc, PhD. Terminal master's awarded for partial completion of doctoral program. *Degree requirements:* For master's, thesis; for doctorate, comprehensive exam, thesis/ dissertation. *Entrance requirements:* For master's and doctorate, knowledge of French, comprehension of written English. Electronic applications accepted.

University at Buffalo, the State University of New York, Graduate School, School of Medicine and Biomedical Sciences, Graduate Programs in Medicine and Biomedical Sciences, Department of Microbiology and Immunology, Buffalo, NY 14260. Offers MA, PhD. *Faculty:* 14 full-time (3 women). *Students:* 25 full-time (17 women), 9 international. Average age 28. 26 applicants, 77% accepted, 9 enrolled. In 2011, 1 master's, 4 doctorates awarded. *Degree requirements:* For master's, comprehensive exam; for doctorate, thesis/dissertation, departmental qualifying exam. *Entrance requirements:* For master's and doctorate, GRE General Test, 3 letters of recommendation. Additional exam requirements/recommendations for international students: Required—TOEFL (minimum score 100 iBT). *Application deadline:* For fall admission, 2/1 priority date for domestic students, 2/1 for international students. Applications are processed on a rolling basis. Application fee: $50. Electronic applications accepted. *Financial support:* In 2011–12, 2 students received support, including 3 fellowships with tuition reimbursements available (averaging $21,600 per year), 19 research assistantships with tuition reimbursements available (averaging $24,000 per year); Federal Work-Study, institutionally sponsored loans, traineeships, health care benefits, and unspecified assistantships also available. Financial award application deadline: 2/1; financial award applicants required to submit FAFSA. *Faculty research:* Bacteriology, immunology, parasitology, virology, mycology. *Total annual research expenditures:* $2.6 million. *Unit head:* Dr. John Hay, Interim Chairman, 716-829-2907, Fax: 716-829-2158. *Application contact:* Dr. Nejat Egilmez, Director of Graduate Studies, 716-829-2176, Fax: 716-829-2158. Web site: http://smbs.buffalo.edu/microb/.

The University of Alabama at Birmingham, Graduate Programs in Joint Health Sciences, Program in Microbiology, Birmingham, AL 35294. Offers PhD. *Degree requirements:* For doctorate, thesis/dissertation. *Entrance requirements:* For doctorate, GRE General Test, interview. *Application deadline:* Applications are processed on a rolling basis. Electronic applications accepted. *Expenses:* Tuition, state resident: full-time $5922; part-time $309 per hour. Tuition, nonresident: full-time $13,428; part-time $726 per hour. Tuition and fees vary according to program. *Financial support:* Fellowships available. *Unit head:* Dr. David D. Chaplin, Chair, 205-934-3470, Fax: 205-934-1426. *Application contact:* Information Contact, 205-934-0621, Fax: 205-975-2536.

University of Alberta, Faculty of Graduate Studies and Research, Department of Biological Sciences, Edmonton, AB T6G 2E1, Canada. Offers environmental biology and ecology (M Sc, PhD); microbiology and biotechnology (M Sc, PhD); molecular biology and genetics (M Sc, PhD); physiology and cell biology (M Sc, PhD); plant biology (M Sc, PhD); systematics and evolution (M Sc, PhD). Terminal master's awarded for partial completion of doctoral program. *Degree requirements:* For master's, thesis; for doctorate, thesis/dissertation. *Entrance requirements:* Additional exam requirements/recommendations for international students: Required—TOEFL.

The University of Arizona, College of Agriculture and Life Sciences, Department of Veterinary Science and Microbiology, Program in Microbiology and Pathobiology, Tucson, AZ 85721. Offers MS, PhD. *Students:* 42 full-time (23 women), 43 part-time (22 women); includes 8 minority (2 American Indian or Alaska Native, non-Hispanic/Latino; 2 Asian, non-Hispanic/Latino; 4 Hispanic/Latino), 16 international. Average age 31. Terminal master's awarded for partial completion of doctoral program. *Degree requirements:* For master's, thesis; for doctorate, comprehensive exam, thesis/ dissertation. *Entrance requirements:* For master's and doctorate, GRE, minimum GPA of 3.0, 3 letters of recommendation, letter of intent. Additional exam requirements/ recommendations for international students: Required—TOEFL (minimum score 550 paper-based; 213 computer-based; 80 iBT); Recommended—IELTS (minimum score 7). *Application deadline:* For fall admission, 2/28 for domestic students, 12/1 for international students. Applications are processed on a rolling basis. Application fee: $75. *Expenses:* Tuition, state resident: full-time $10,840. Tuition, nonresident: full-time $25,802. *Financial support:* Research assistantships with tuition reimbursements, teaching assistantships with tuition reimbursements, and scholarships/grants available. Financial award application deadline: 3/22. *Faculty research:* Antibiotic resistance, molecular pathogenesis of bacteria, food safety, diagnosis of animal disease, parasitology. *Unit head:* Dr. Ron Marx, Head, 520-621-1081, E-mail: ronmarx@email.arizona.edu. *Application contact:* Cecilia Carlon, 520-626-1248, E-mail: ccarlon@email.arizona.edu. Web site: http://www.microvet.arizona.edu/.

The University of Arizona, College of Agriculture and Life Sciences, Program in Microbiology, Tucson, AZ 85721. Offers MS, PhD. *Faculty:* 4 full-time (1 woman), 2 part-time/adjunct (1 woman). *Students:* 12 full-time (9 women), 2 part-time (1 woman); includes 7 minority (1 Black or African American, non-Hispanic/Latino; 3 Hispanic/ Latino; 3 Two or more races, non-Hispanic/Latino), 3 international. Average age 29. 31 applicants, 23% accepted, 2 enrolled. In 2011, 4 master's, 3 doctorates awarded. *Degree requirements:* For master's, thesis; for doctorate, comprehensive exam, thesis/ dissertation. *Entrance requirements:* For master's and doctorate, GRE, minimum GPA of 3.0, 3 letters of recommendation, letter of intent. Additional exam requirements/ recommendations for international students: Required—TOEFL (minimum score 550 paper-based; 213 computer-based). *Application deadline:* For fall admission, 2/28 for domestic students, 12/1 for international students. Application fee: $75. *Expenses:* Tuition, state resident: full-time $10,840. Tuition, nonresident: full-time $25,802. *Financial support:* In 2011–12, 5 research assistantships (averaging $17,293 per year), 4 teaching assistantships (averaging $15,210 per year) were awarded. Financial award application deadline: 3/22. *Total annual research expenditures:* $1.9 million. *Unit head:* Dr. Jack Schmitz, Head, 520-626-5482, E-mail: jschmitz@u.arizona.edu. *Application contact:* Elaine Mattes, 520-621-4466, E-mail: emattes@email.arizona.edu.

The University of Arizona, College of Medicine, Department of Immunobiology, Tucson, AZ 85721. Offers MS, PhD. *Faculty:* 8 full-time (2 women). *Students:* 8 full-time (all women); includes 1 minority (Two or more races, non-Hispanic/Latino), 4 international. Average age 27. 91 applicants, 66% accepted. In 2011, 2 master's, 1 doctorate awarded. *Degree requirements:* For master's, thesis; for doctorate, thesis/ dissertation. *Entrance requirements:* For master's and doctorate, GRE General Test, minimum GPA of 3.0. *Application deadline:* For fall admission, 3/1 priority date for domestic students; for spring admission, 9/1 for domestic students. Application fee: $75. *Expenses:* Tuition, state resident: full-time $10,840. Tuition, nonresident: full-time $25,802. *Financial support:* In 2011–12, 5 research assistantships with full tuition reimbursements (averaging $25,000 per year) were awarded; fellowships with full tuition reimbursements, teaching assistantships with full tuition reimbursements, institutionally sponsored loans, and tuition waivers (full) also available. Financial award application deadline: 4/30. *Faculty research:* Environmental and pathogenic microbiology, molecular biology. *Total annual research expenditures:* $7.8 million. *Unit head:* Dr. Janko Nikolich-Zugich, Head, 520-626-6065, Fax: 520-626-2100, E-mail: nikolich@email.arizona.edu. *Application contact:* Dr. Richard J. Ablin, Graduate Program Chairman, 520-626-7755, E-mail: ablinrj@email.arizona.edu. Web site: http://immunobiology.arizona.edu/.

University of Arkansas for Medical Sciences, Graduate School, Graduate Programs in Biomedical Sciences, Department of Microbiology and Immunology, Little Rock, AR 72205-7199. Offers MS, PhD, MD/PhD. *Degree requirements:* For master's, thesis; for doctorate, thesis/dissertation. *Entrance requirements:* For master's and doctorate, GRE General Test. Additional exam requirements/recommendations for international students: Required—TOEFL. *Faculty research:* Tumor immunology and immunotherapy, microbial pathogenesis and genetics, allergy, immune response in infectious diseases.

The University of British Columbia, Faculty of Science, Department of Microbiology and Immunology, Vancouver, BC V6T 1Z1, Canada. Offers M Sc, PhD. *Degree requirements:* For master's, thesis; for doctorate, comprehensive exam, thesis/ dissertation. *Entrance requirements:* For master's and doctorate, GRE General Test. Additional exam requirements/recommendations for international students: Required—TOEFL (minimum score 590 paper-based; 243 computer-based). Electronic applications

accepted. *Faculty research:* Bacterial genetics, metabolism, pathogenic bacteriology, virology.

University of Calgary, Faculty of Medicine and Faculty of Graduate Studies, Department of Microbiology and Infectious Diseases, Calgary, AB T2N 1N4, Canada. Offers M Sc, PhD. *Degree requirements:* For master's, thesis, oral thesis exam; for doctorate, thesis/dissertation, candidacy exam, oral thesis exam. *Entrance requirements:* For master's and doctorate, minimum GPA of 3.2. Additional exam requirements/recommendations for international students: Required—TOEFL (minimum score 580 paper-based; 237 computer-based). Electronic applications accepted. *Faculty research:* Bacteriology, virology, parasitology, immunology.

University of California, Berkeley, Graduate Division, College of Natural Resources, Group in Microbiology, Berkeley, CA 94720-1500. Offers PhD. *Degree requirements:* For doctorate, thesis/dissertation. *Entrance requirements:* For doctorate, GRE General Test, minimum GPA of 3.0, 3 letters of recommendation.

University of California, Davis, Graduate Studies, Graduate Group in Microbiology, Davis, CA 95616. Offers MS, PhD. Terminal master's awarded for partial completion of doctoral program. *Degree requirements:* For master's, thesis; for doctorate, thesis/dissertation. *Entrance requirements:* For master's and doctorate, GRE General Test, minimum GPA of 3.0. Additional exam requirements/recommendations for international students: Required—TOEFL (minimum score 550 paper-based; 213 computer-based). Electronic applications accepted. *Faculty research:* Microbial physiology and genetics, microbial molecular and cellular biology, microbial ecology, microbial pathogenesis and immunology, urology.

University of California, Irvine, School of Medicine and School of Biological Sciences, Department of Microbiology and Molecular Genetics, Irvine, CA 92697. Offers biological sciences (MS, PhD); MD/PhD. *Students:* 35 full-time (17 women); includes 18 minority (1 Black or African American, non-Hispanic/Latino; 10 Asian, non-Hispanic/Latino; 7 Hispanic/Latino), 1 international. Average age 28. 1 applicant, 100% accepted, 0 enrolled. In 2011, 3 master's, 3 doctorates awarded. *Degree requirements:* For doctorate, thesis/dissertation. *Entrance requirements:* For doctorate, GRE General Test, GRE Subject Test, minimum GPA of 3.0. Additional exam requirements/recommendations for international students: Required—TOEFL (minimum score 550 paper-based; 213 computer-based). *Application deadline:* For fall admission, 12/15 priority date for domestic students, 12/15 for international students. Application fee: $80 ($100 for international students). Electronic applications accepted. *Financial support:* Fellowships, research assistantships with full tuition reimbursements, teaching assistantships, institutionally sponsored loans, traineeships, health care benefits, and unspecified assistantships available. Financial award applicants required to submit FAFSA. *Faculty research:* Molecular biology and genetics of viruses, bacteria, and yeast; immune response; molecular biology of cultured animal cells; genetic basis of cancer; genetics and physiology of infectious agents. *Unit head:* Rozanne M. Sandri-Goldin, Chair, 949-824-7570, Fax: 949-824-8598, E-mail: rmsandri@uci.edu. *Application contact:* Renee Marie Frigo, Program Manager, 949-824-8145, Fax: 949-824-1965, E-mail: rfrigo@uci.edu. Web site: http://www.bio.uci.edu/.

University of California, Los Angeles, David Geffen School of Medicine and Graduate Division, Graduate Programs in Medicine, Department of Microbiology, Immunology and Molecular Genetics, Los Angeles, CA 90095. Offers MS, PhD. *Faculty:* 31 full-time (6 women). *Students:* 55 full-time (25 women); includes 21 minority (1 Black or African American, non-Hispanic/Latino; 8 Asian, non-Hispanic/Latino; 11 Hispanic/Latino; 1 Two or more races, non-Hispanic/Latino), 4 international. Average age 28. 1 applicant, 100% accepted, 1 enrolled. In 2011, 3 master's, 8 doctorates awarded. *Degree requirements:* For doctorate, thesis/dissertation, oral and written qualifying exams. *Entrance requirements:* For doctorate, GRE General Test, GRE Subject Test. Additional exam requirements/recommendations for international students: Required—TOEFL. Application fee: $70 ($90 for international students). Electronic applications accepted. *Financial support:* In 2011–12, 50 fellowships, 50 research assistantships, 20 teaching assistantships were awarded; Federal Work-Study, institutionally sponsored loans, and tuition waivers (full and partial) also available. Financial award application deadline: 3/1. *Unit head:* Dr. Jeff F. Miller, Chair, 310-206-7926, Fax: 310-267-2774, E-mail: jfmiller@ucla.edu. *Application contact:* Bridget Wolfgang, Graduate Student Affairs, 310-825-8482, Fax: 310-206-5231, E-mail: bridgetw@microbio.ucla.edu. Web site: http://www.mimg.ucla.edu/.

University of California, Riverside, Graduate Division, Program in Microbiology, Riverside, CA 92521-0102. Offers MS, PhD. Part-time programs available. Terminal master's awarded for partial completion of doctoral program. *Degree requirements:* For master's, thesis; for doctorate, thesis/dissertation, qualifying exams. *Entrance requirements:* For master's and doctorate, GRE General Test, minimum GPA of 3.2. Additional exam requirements/recommendations for international students: Required—TOEFL (minimum score 550 paper-based; 213 computer-based; 80 iBT). Electronic applications accepted. *Faculty research:* Host-pathogen interactions; environmental microbiology; bioremediation; molecular microbiology; microbial genetics, physiology, and pathogenesis.

University of California, San Diego, School of Medicine and Office of Graduate Studies, Molecular Pathology Program, La Jolla, CA 92093. Offers bioinformatics (PhD); cancer biology/oncology (PhD); cardiovascular sciences and disease (PhD); microbiology (PhD); molecular pathology (PhD); neurological disease (PhD); stem cell and developmental biology (PhD); structural biology/drug design (PhD). *Entrance requirements:* For doctorate, GRE General Test, GRE Subject Test. Additional exam requirements/recommendations for international students: Required—TOEFL. Electronic applications accepted.

University of California, San Francisco, Graduate Division, Department of Microbiology and Immunology, San Francisco, CA 94143. Offers PhD. *Degree requirements:* For doctorate, thesis/dissertation. *Entrance requirements:* For doctorate, GRE General Test.

University of Chicago, Division of Biological Sciences, Biomedical Sciences Cluster: Cancer Biology, Immunology, Molecular Metabolism and Nutrition, Pathology, and Microbiology, Committee on Microbiology, Chicago, IL 60637-1513. Offers PhD. *Degree requirements:* For doctorate, thesis/dissertation, ethics class, 2 teaching assistantships. *Entrance requirements:* For doctorate, GRE General Test. Additional exam requirements/recommendations for international students: Required—TOEFL (minimum score 600 paper-based; 250 computer-based; 104 iBT), IELTS (minimum score 7). Electronic applications accepted. *Faculty research:* Molecular genetics, herpes virus, adipoviruses, Picarna viruses, ENS viruses.

University of Cincinnati, Graduate School, College of Medicine, Graduate Programs in Biomedical Sciences, Department of Molecular Genetics, Biochemistry and Microbiology, Cincinnati, OH 45221. Offers MS, PhD. Terminal master's awarded for partial completion of doctoral program. *Degree requirements:* For master's, thesis or alternative; for doctorate, thesis/dissertation, qualifying exam. *Entrance requirements:* For master's and doctorate, GRE General Test. Additional exam requirements/recommendations for international students: Required—TOEFL (minimum score 600 paper-based; 250 computer-based; 100 iBT), TWE. Electronic applications accepted. *Faculty research:* Cancer biology and developmental genetics, gene regulation and

chromosome structure, microbiology and pathogenic mechanisms, structural biology, membrane biochemistry and signal transduction.

University of Colorado Boulder, Graduate School, College of Arts and Sciences, Department of Ecology and Evolutionary Biology, Boulder, CO 80309. Offers animal behavior (MA); biology (MA, PhD); environmental biology (MA, PhD); evolutionary biology (MA, PhD); neurobiology (MA); population biology (MA); population genetics (PhD). *Faculty:* 28 full-time (9 women). *Students:* 67 full-time (37 women), 27 part-time (13 women); includes 9 minority (1 Asian, non-Hispanic/Latino; 8 Hispanic/Latino), 5 international. Average age 30. 136 applicants, 13% accepted, 17 enrolled. In 2011, 8 master's, 5 doctorates awarded. Terminal master's awarded for partial completion of doctoral program. *Degree requirements:* For master's, comprehensive exam, thesis or alternative; for doctorate, comprehensive exam, thesis/dissertation. *Entrance requirements:* For master's, GRE General Test, GRE Subject Test, minimum undergraduate GPA of 3.0; for doctorate, GRE General Test, GRE Subject Test. *Application deadline:* For fall admission, 12/30 priority date for domestic students, 12/1 for international students. Application fee: $50 ($60 for international students). Electronic applications accepted. *Financial support:* In 2011–12, 88 students received support, including 35 fellowships (averaging $16,835 per year), 25 research assistantships with full and partial tuition reimbursements available (averaging $22,347 per year), 44 teaching assistantships with full and partial tuition reimbursements available (averaging $21,377 per year); institutionally sponsored loans, scholarships/grants, health care benefits, and unspecified assistantships also available. Financial award applicants required to submit FAFSA. *Faculty research:* Behavior, ecology, genetics, morphology, endocrinology, physiology, systematics. *Total annual research expenditures:* $4.6 million. *Application contact:* E-mail: ebiograd@colorado.edu. Web site: http://ebio.colorado.edu.

University of Colorado Denver, College of Liberal Arts and Sciences, Department of Integrative Biology, Denver, CO 80217. Offers animal behavior (MS); biology (MS); cell and developmental biology (MS); ecology (MS); evolutionary biology (MS); genetics (MS); microbiology (MS); molecular biology (MS); neurobiology (MS); plant systematics (MS). Part-time programs available. *Faculty:* 16 full-time (8 women). *Students:* 20 full-time (13 women), 5 part-time (4 women); includes 1 minority (Hispanic/Latino), 1 international. Average age 29. 21 applicants, 43% accepted, 5 enrolled. In 2011, 7 master's awarded. *Degree requirements:* For master's, comprehensive exam, thesis or alternative, 30-32 credit hours. *Entrance requirements:* For master's, GRE General Test (minimum score in 50% percentile in each section), BA/BS from accredited institution awarded within the last 10 years; minimum undergraduate GPA of 3.0; prerequisite courses: 1 year each of general biology and general chemistry, and 1 semester each of general genetics, general ecology, cell biology, and a structure/function course. Additional exam requirements/recommendations for international students: Required—TOEFL (minimum score 525 paper-based; 197 computer-based; 71 iBT). *Application deadline:* For fall admission, 2/1 for domestic and international students. Application fee: $50 ($75 for international students). Electronic applications accepted. *Financial support:* Research assistantships, teaching assistantships, Federal Work-Study, scholarships/grants, and unspecified assistantships available. Financial award application deadline: 4/1; financial award applicants required to submit FAFSA. *Faculty research:* Molecular developmental biology; quantitative ecology, biogeography, and population dynamics; environmental signaling and endocrine disruption; speciation, the evolution of reproductive isolation, and hybrid zones; evolutionary, behavioral, and conservation ecology. *Unit head:* Dr. Diana Tomback, Acting Chair, 303-556-2657, E-mail: diana.tomback@ucdenver.edu. *Application contact:* Timberley Roane, Associate Professor/Associate Chair, 303-556-6592, E-mail: timberley.roane@ucdenver.edu. Web site: http://www.ucdenver.edu/academics/colleges/CLAS/Departments/biology/Pages/Biology.aspx.

University of Colorado Denver, School of Medicine, Program in Microbiology, Denver, CO 80217-3364. Offers microbiology (PhD); microbiology and immunology (PhD). *Students:* 17 full-time (7 women); includes 2 minority (1 Asian, non-Hispanic/Latino; 1 Hispanic/Latino). Average age 27. 49 applicants, 6% accepted, 3 enrolled. In 2011, 6 doctorates awarded. *Degree requirements:* For doctorate, comprehensive exam, thesis/dissertation, 3 lab rotations; 30 credit hours coursework. *Entrance requirements:* For doctorate, GRE, three letters of reference, two copies of official transcripts, minimum GPA of 3.0. Additional exam requirements/recommendations for international students: Required—TOEFL (minimum score 550 paper-based; 213 computer-based). *Application deadline:* For fall admission, 12/1 for domestic students, 11/1 for international students. Application fee: $65. Electronic applications accepted. *Expenses:* Contact institution. *Financial support:* In 2011–12, 3 students received support, including 3 fellowships with full tuition reimbursements available (averaging $25,000 per year); health care benefits, tuition waivers (full), and stipend also available. Financial award application deadline: 3/15; financial award applicants required to submit FAFSA. *Faculty research:* Molecular mechanisms of picornavirus replication, mechanisms of papovavirus assembly, human immune response in multiple sclerosis. *Total annual research expenditures:* $5.9 million. *Unit head:* Dr. Randall K. Holmes, Chair, 303-724-4223, E-mail: randall.holmes@ucdenver.edu. *Application contact:* Liz Pruett, Microbiology Graduate Program Administrator, 303-724-3350, E-mail: liz.pruett@ucdenver.edu. Web site: http://www.uchsc.edu/sm/microbio.

University of Connecticut, Graduate School, College of Liberal Arts and Sciences, Department of Molecular and Cell Biology, Field of Microbiology, Storrs, CT 06269. Offers MS, PhD. Terminal master's awarded for partial completion of doctoral program. *Degree requirements:* For master's, comprehensive exam; for doctorate, thesis/dissertation. *Entrance requirements:* For master's and doctorate, GRE General Test, GRE Subject Test. Additional exam requirements/recommendations for international students: Required—TOEFL (minimum score 550 paper-based; 213 computer-based). Electronic applications accepted.

University of Delaware, College of Arts and Sciences, Department of Biological Sciences, Newark, DE 19716. Offers biotechnology (MS); cancer biology (MS, PhD); cell and extracellular matrix biology (MS, PhD); cell and systems physiology (MS, PhD); developmental biology (MS, PhD); ecology and evolution (MS, PhD); microbiology (MS, PhD); molecular biology and genetics (MS, PhD). Terminal master's awarded for partial completion of doctoral program. *Degree requirements:* For master's, thesis, preliminary exam; for doctorate, comprehensive exam, thesis/dissertation, preliminary exam. *Entrance requirements:* For master's and doctorate, GRE General Test. Additional exam requirements/recommendations for international students: Required—TOEFL (minimum score 600 paper-based; 250 computer-based); Recommended—TWE. Electronic applications accepted. *Faculty research:* Microorganisms, bone, cancer metastasis, developmental biology, cell biology, DNA.

University of Florida, College of Medicine, Department of Molecular Genetics and Microbiology, Gainesville, FL 32611. Offers MS, PhD. Terminal master's awarded for partial completion of doctoral program. *Degree requirements:* For master's, thesis; for doctorate, thesis/dissertation. *Entrance requirements:* For master's and doctorate, GRE General Test, minimum GPA of 3.0. Additional exam requirements/recommendations for international students: Required—TOEFL. Electronic applications accepted.

University of Florida, College of Medicine and Graduate School, Interdisciplinary Program in Biomedical Sciences, Concentration in Immunology and Microbiology,

Gainesville, FL 32611. Offers PhD. *Degree requirements:* For doctorate, thesis/dissertation. *Entrance requirements:* For doctorate, GRE General Test, minimum GPA of 3.0. Additional exam requirements/recommendations for international students: Required—TOEFL. Electronic applications accepted.

University of Florida, Graduate School, College of Agricultural and Life Sciences, Department of Microbiology and Cell Science, Gainesville, FL 32611. Offers MS, PhD. *Faculty:* 22 full-time (7 women), 1 part-time/adjunct (0 women). *Students:* 36 full-time (17 women), 1 part-time (0 women); includes 7 minority (4 Asian, non-Hispanic/Latino; 3 Hispanic/Latino), 14 international. Average age 27. 74 applicants, 19% accepted, 9 enrolled. In 2011, 6 master's, 9 doctorates awarded. *Degree requirements:* For master's, comprehensive exam, thesis (for some programs); for doctorate, comprehensive exam, thesis/dissertation. *Entrance requirements:* For master's and doctorate, GRE General Test (minimum score 1000), minimum GPA of 3.0. Additional exam requirements/recommendations for international students: Required—TOEFL (minimum score 550 paper-based; 213 computer-based; 80 iBT), IELTS (minimum score 6). *Application deadline:* For fall admission, 6/1 priority date for domestic students. Applications are processed on a rolling basis. Application fee: $30. Electronic applications accepted. *Financial support:* Fellowships, research assistantships, and teaching assistantships available. Financial award applicants required to submit FAFSA. *Faculty research:* Biomass conversion, membrane and cell wall chemistry, plant biochemistry and genetics. *Unit head:* Dr. Eric Triplett, Chair, 352-392-1906, Fax: 352-392-5922, E-mail: ewt@ufl.edu. *Application contact:* Dr. Tony Romeo, Graduate Coordinator, 352-392-2400, Fax: 352-392-5922, E-mail: tromeo@ufl.edu. Web site: http://microcell.ufl.edu/.

University of Georgia, Franklin College of Arts and Sciences, Department of Microbiology, Athens, GA 30602. Offers MS, PhD. *Faculty:* 17 full-time (4 women). *Students:* 51 full-time (25 women); includes 11 minority (4 Black or African American, non-Hispanic/Latino; 1 Asian, non-Hispanic/Latino; 5 Hispanic/Latino; 1 Two or more races, non-Hispanic/Latino), 5 international. Average age 27. 85 applicants, 22% accepted, 10 enrolled. In 2011, 1 master's, 7 doctorates awarded. *Degree requirements:* For master's, thesis; for doctorate, one foreign language, thesis/dissertation. *Entrance requirements:* For master's and doctorate, GRE General Test. Additional exam requirements/recommendations for international students: Required—TOEFL (minimum score 550 paper-based; 213 computer-based). *Application deadline:* For fall admission, 7/1 priority date for domestic students; for spring admission, 11/15 for domestic students. Application fee: $50. Electronic applications accepted. *Financial support:* In 2011–12, 9 fellowships (averaging $20,000 per year), 20 research assistantships (averaging $18,461 per year), 12 teaching assistantships (averaging $18,461 per year) were awarded; unspecified assistantships also available. Financial award application deadline: 12/15. *Unit head:* Dr. William B. Whitman, Head, 706-542-4219, E-mail: whitman@uga.edu. *Application contact:* Dr. Eric V. Stabb, Graduate Coordinator, 706-542-2414, Fax: 706-542-2674, E-mail: estabb@uga.edu. Web site: http://www.uga.edu/mib/.

University of Guelph, Graduate Studies, College of Biological Science, Department of Molecular and Cellular Biology, Guelph, ON N1G 2W1, Canada. Offers biochemistry (M Sc, PhD); biophysics (M Sc, PhD); botany (M Sc, PhD); microbiology (M Sc, PhD); molecular biology and genetics (M Sc, PhD). *Degree requirements:* For master's, thesis, research proposal; for doctorate, comprehensive exam, thesis/dissertation, research proposal. *Entrance requirements:* For master's, minimum B-average during previous 2 years of coursework; for doctorate, minimum A-average. Additional exam requirements/recommendations for international students: Required—TOEFL (minimum score 550 paper-based; 213 computer-based), IELTS (minimum score 6.5). Electronic applications accepted. *Faculty research:* Physiology, structure, genetics, and ecology of microbes; virology and microbial technology.

University of Hawaii at Manoa, Graduate Division, College of Natural Sciences, Department of Microbiology, Honolulu, HI 96822. Offers MS, PhD. Part-time programs available. *Degree requirements:* For master's, thesis optional; for doctorate, comprehensive exam, thesis/dissertation. *Entrance requirements:* For master's and doctorate, GRE General Test. Additional exam requirements/recommendations for international students: Required—TOEFL (minimum score 580 paper-based; 237 computer-based; 92 iBT), IELTS (minimum score 5). *Faculty research:* Virology, immunology, microbial physiology, medical microbiology, bacterial genetics.

University of Idaho, College of Graduate Studies, College of Science, Department of Biological Sciences, Moscow, ID 83844-3051. Offers biology (MS, PhD); microbiology, molecular biology and biochemistry (MS, PhD). *Faculty:* 12 full-time. *Students:* 29 full-time, 6 part-time. Average age 28. In 2011, 2 master's, 2 doctorates awarded. *Degree requirements:* For doctorate, one foreign language, thesis/dissertation. *Entrance requirements:* For master's, GRE, minimum GPA of 2.8; for doctorate, GRE, minimum undergraduate GPA of 2.8, 3.0 graduate. *Application deadline:* For fall admission, 8/1 for domestic students; for spring admission, 12/15 for domestic students. Applications are processed on a rolling basis. Application fee: $60. Electronic applications accepted. *Expenses:* Tuition, state resident: full-time $3874; part-time $334 per credit hour. Tuition, nonresident: full-time $16,394; part-time $861 per credit hour. *Required fees:* $2808; $99 per credit hour. Tuition and fees vary according to program. *Financial support:* Research assistantships and teaching assistantships available. Financial award applicants required to submit FAFSA. *Faculty research:* Animal behavior development, germ cell development, evolutionary biology, fish reproductive biology, molecular mechanisms. *Unit head:* John Byers, Acting Chair, 208-885-6280. *Application contact:* Erick Larson, Director of Graduate Admissions, 208-885-4723, E-mail: gadms@uidaho.edu. Web site: http://www.uidaho.edu/sci/biology.

University of Illinois at Chicago, College of Medicine and Graduate College, Graduate Programs in Medicine, Department of Microbiology and Immunology, Chicago, IL 60607-7128. Offers PhD, MD/PhD. *Degree requirements:* For doctorate, thesis/dissertation. *Entrance requirements:* For doctorate, GRE General Test, minimum GPA of 2.75. Additional exam requirements/recommendations for international students: Required—TOEFL.

University of Illinois at Urbana–Champaign, Graduate College, College of Liberal Arts and Sciences, School of Molecular and Cellular Biology, Department of Microbiology, Champaign, IL 61820. Offers MS, PhD. *Faculty:* 13 full-time (3 women). *Students:* 61 full-time (39 women); includes 12 minority (1 Black or African American, non-Hispanic/Latino; 1 American Indian or Alaska Native, non-Hispanic/Latino; 3 Asian, non-Hispanic/Latino; 6 Hispanic/Latino; 1 Two or more races, non-Hispanic/Latino), 17 international. In 2011, 8 master's, 13 doctorates awarded. *Entrance requirements:* For master's and doctorate, GRE, minimum GPA of 3.0. Additional exam requirements/recommendations for international students: Required—TOEFL (minimum score 590 paper-based; 243 computer-based; 96 iBT). *Application deadline:* Applications are processed on a rolling basis. Application fee: $75 ($90 for international students). Electronic applications accepted. *Financial support:* In 2011–12, 10 fellowships, 49 research assistantships, 30 teaching assistantships were awarded; tuition waivers (full and partial) also available. *Faculty research:* Bacterial physiology and genetics, bacterial pathogenesis, host-pathogen interaction, molecular immunology. *Unit head:* John E. Cronan, Jr., Head, 217-333-7919, Fax: 217-244-6697, E-mail: jecronan@illinois.edu. *Application contact:* Shawna Smith, Coordinator of Graduate Programs, 217-244-6638, E-mail: smsmith1@illinois.edu. Web site: http://mcb.illinois.edu/departments/microbiology/.

The University of Iowa, Roy J. and Lucille A. Carver College of Medicine and Graduate College, Graduate Programs in Medicine, Department of Microbiology, Iowa City, IA 52242-1316. Offers general microbiology and microbial physiology (MS, PhD); immunology (MS, PhD); microbial genetics (MS, PhD); pathogenic bacteriology (MS, PhD); virology (MS, PhD). *Faculty:* 23 full-time (5 women), 12 part-time/adjunct (4 women). *Students:* 37 full-time (24 women); includes 3 minority (2 American Indian or Alaska Native, non-Hispanic/Latino; 1 Hispanic/Latino), 4 international. Average age 25. 56 applicants, 16% accepted, 4 enrolled. In 2011, 1 master's, 6 doctorates awarded. *Degree requirements:* For master's, thesis; for doctorate, comprehensive exam, thesis/dissertation. *Entrance requirements:* For master's and doctorate, GRE General Test. Additional exam requirements/recommendations for international students: Required—TOEFL (minimum score 600 paper-based; 250 computer-based). *Application deadline:* For fall admission, 1/1 for domestic and international students. Application fee: $60 ($85 for international students). Electronic applications accepted. *Financial support:* In 2011–12, 4 fellowships with full tuition reimbursements (averaging $25,500 per year), 33 research assistantships with full tuition reimbursements (averaging $25,500 per year) were awarded; institutionally sponsored loans, scholarships/grants, traineeships, and health care benefits also available. *Faculty research:* Gene regulation, processing and transport of HIV, retroviral pathogenesis, biodegradation, biofilm. *Total annual research expenditures:* $12.6 million. *Unit head:* Dr. Patrick M. Schlievert, Head, 319-335-7810, E-mail: grad-micro-info@uiowa.edu. *Application contact:* Betty Wood, Associate Director of Admissions, 319-335-1525, Fax: 319-335-1535, E-mail: admissions@uiowa.edu. Web site: http://www.uiowa.edu/microbiology/.

The University of Kansas, Graduate Studies, College of Liberal Arts and Sciences, Department of Molecular Biosciences, Lawrence, KS 66044. Offers biochemistry and biophysics (MA, PhD); microbiology (MA, PhD); molecular, cellular, and developmental biology (MA, PhD). *Faculty:* 34. *Students:* 57 full-time (29 women), 2 part-time (1 woman); includes 6 minority (2 Asian, non-Hispanic/Latino; 3 Hispanic/Latino; 1 Two or more races, non-Hispanic/Latino), 26 international. Average age 28. 60 applicants, 30% accepted, 10 enrolled. In 2011, 1 master's, 12 doctorates awarded. Terminal master's awarded for partial completion of doctoral program. *Degree requirements:* For master's, comprehensive exam, thesis; for doctorate, comprehensive exam, thesis/dissertation. *Entrance requirements:* For master's and doctorate, GRE General Test. Additional exam requirements/recommendations for international students: Required—TOEFL or IELTS. *Application deadline:* For fall admission, 12/15 for domestic and international students. Application fee: $55 ($65 for international students). Electronic applications accepted. Tuition and fees vary according to course load, campus/location, program and reciprocity agreements. *Financial support:* Fellowships with tuition reimbursements, research assistantships with tuition reimbursements, teaching assistantships with tuition reimbursements, health care benefits, and unspecified assistantships available. Financial award application deadline: 3/1. *Faculty research:* Structure and function of proteins, genetics of organism development, molecular genetics, neurophysiology, molecular virology and pathogenics, developmental biology, cell biology. *Unit head:* Dr. Mark Richter, Chair, 785-864-3334, Fax: 785-864-5294, E-mail: richter@ku.edu. *Application contact:* John P. Connolly, Graduate Program Assistant, 785-864-4311, Fax: 785-864-5294, E-mail: jconnolly@ku.edu. Web site: http://www.molecularbiosciences.ku.edu/.

The University of Kansas, University of Kansas Medical Center, School of Medicine, Department of Microbiology, Molecular Genetics and Immunology, Kansas City, KS 66160. Offers microbiology (PhD); MD/PhD. *Faculty:* 14. *Students:* 14 full-time (5 women); includes 1 minority (Two or more races, non-Hispanic/Latino), 8 international. Average age 28. 1 applicant, 100% accepted, 1 enrolled. In 2011, 4 doctorates awarded. *Degree requirements:* For doctorate, comprehensive exam, thesis/dissertation, research skills. *Entrance requirements:* For doctorate, GRE General Test, B Sc. Additional exam requirements/recommendations for international students: Required—TOEFL. *Application deadline:* For fall admission, 1/15 for international students. Tuition and fees vary according to course load, campus/location, program and reciprocity agreements. *Financial support:* Fellowships with tuition reimbursements, research assistantships with partial tuition reimbursements, teaching assistantships with full and partial tuition reimbursements, scholarships/grants, and unspecified assistantships available. Financial award application deadline: 2/15; financial award applicants required to submit FAFSA. *Faculty research:* Immunology, infectious disease, virology, molecular genetics, bacteriology. *Total annual research expenditures:* $4.8 million. *Unit head:* Dr. Michael Parmely, Interim Chair, 913-588-7010, Fax: 913-588-7295, E-mail: mparmely@kumc.edu. *Application contact:* Dr. Indranil Biswas, Microbiology Graduate Studies Director, 913-588-7019, Fax: 913-588-7295, E-mail: ibiswas@kumc.edu. Web site: http://www.kumc.edu/school-of-medicine/microbiology-molecular-genetics-and-immunology.html.

University of Kentucky, Graduate School, Graduate School Programs from the College of Medicine, Program in Microbiology and Immunology, Lexington, KY 40506-0032. Offers microbiology (PhD). *Degree requirements:* For doctorate, comprehensive exam, thesis/dissertation. *Entrance requirements:* For doctorate, GRE General Test, minimum undergraduate GPA of 2.75. Additional exam requirements/recommendations for international students: Required—TOEFL (minimum score 550 paper-based; 213 computer-based). Electronic applications accepted.

University of Louisville, School of Medicine, Department of Microbiology and Immunology, Louisville, KY 40292-0001. Offers MS, PhD, MD/PhD. Terminal master's awarded for partial completion of doctoral program. *Degree requirements:* For master's, thesis; for doctorate, comprehensive exam, thesis/dissertation. *Entrance requirements:* For master's and doctorate, GRE General Test (minimum score of 1000 verbal and quantitative), minimum GPA of 3.0; 1 year of course work in biology, organic chemistry, physics; 1 semester of course work in calculus and quantitative analysis, biochemistry, or molecular biology. Additional exam requirements/recommendations for international students: Required—TOEFL. Electronic applications accepted. *Expenses:* Tuition, state resident: full-time $9692; part-time $539 per credit hour. Tuition, nonresident: full-time $20,168; part-time $1121 per credit hour. Tuition and fees vary according to program and reciprocity agreements. *Faculty research:* Opportunistic and emerging infections; biology and regulation of the immune system; cellular and molecular bases of chronic inflammatory response; role of cytokines and chemokines in cancer, autoimmune and infectious disease; host defense and pathogenesis of viral infections.

University of Maine, Graduate School, College of Natural Sciences, Forestry, and Agriculture, Department of Biochemistry, Molecular Biology, and Microbiology, Orono, ME 04469. Offers biochemistry (MPS, MS); biochemistry and molecular biology (PhD); microbiology (MPS, MS, PhD). *Faculty:* 11 full-time (6 women), 3 part-time/adjunct (2 women). *Students:* 25 full-time (15 women), 35 part-time (23 women); includes 4 minority (2 Asian, non-Hispanic/Latino; 1 Hispanic/Latino; 1 Two or more races, non-Hispanic/Latino), 13 international. Average age 31. 41 applicants, 29% accepted, 11 enrolled. In 2011, 6 master's, 6 doctorates awarded. *Degree requirements:* For doctorate, thesis/dissertation. *Entrance requirements:* For master's and doctorate, GRE General Test. Additional exam requirements/recommendations for international students: Required—TOEFL. *Application deadline:* For fall admission, 2/1 priority date

for domestic students. Applications are processed on a rolling basis. Application fee: $65. Electronic applications accepted. *Expenses:* Tuition, state resident: full-time $5016. Tuition, nonresident: full-time $14,424. *Financial support:* In 2011–12, 5 research assistantships with full tuition reimbursements (averaging $25,368 per year), 12 teaching assistantships with full tuition reimbursements (averaging $20,106 per year) were awarded; tuition waivers (full and partial) also available. Financial award application deadline: 3/1. *Total annual research expenditures:* $242,844. *Unit head:* Dr. Robert Gundersen, Chair, 207-581-2802, Fax: 207-581-2801. *Application contact:* Scott G. Delcourt, Associate Dean of the Graduate School, 207-581-3291, Fax: 207-581-3232, E-mail: graduate@maine.edu. Web site: http://www2.umaine.edu/graduate/.

The University of Manchester, Faculty of Life Sciences, Manchester, United Kingdom. Offers adaptive organismal biology (M Phil, PhD); animal biology (M Phil, PhD); biochemistry (M Phil, PhD); bioinformatics (M Phil, PhD); biomolecular sciences (M Phil, PhD); biotechnology (M Phil, PhD); cell biology (M Phil, PhD); cell matrix research (M Phil, PhD); channels and transporters (M Phil, PhD); developmental biology (M Phil, PhD); Egyptology (M Phil, PhD); environmental biology (M Phil, PhD); evolutionary biology (M Phil, PhD); gene expression (M Phil, PhD); genetics (M Phil, PhD); history of science, technology and medicine (M Phil, PhD); immunology (M Phil, PhD); integrative neurobiology and behavior (M Phil, PhD); membrane trafficking (M Phil, PhD); microbiology (M Phil, PhD); molecular and cellular neuroscience (M Phil, PhD); molecular biology (M Phil, PhD); molecular cancer studies (M Phil, PhD); neuroscience (M Phil, PhD); ophthalmology (M Phil, PhD); optometry (M Phil, PhD); organelle function (M Phil, PhD); pharmacology (M Phil, PhD); physiology (M Phil, PhD); plant sciences (M Phil, PhD); stem cell research (M Phil, PhD); structural biology (M Phil, PhD); systems neuroscience (M Phil, PhD); toxicology (M Phil, PhD).

University of Manitoba, Faculty of Graduate Studies, Faculty of Science, Department of Microbiology, Winnipeg, MB R3T 2N2, Canada. Offers M Sc, PhD. *Degree requirements:* For master's, thesis; for doctorate, one foreign language, thesis/dissertation.

University of Maryland, Baltimore, Graduate School, Graduate Program in Life Sciences, Program in Molecular Microbiology and Immunology, Baltimore, MD 21201. Offers PhD, MD/PhD. *Students:* 42 full-time (24 women); includes 8 minority (3 Black or African American, non-Hispanic/Latino; 3 Asian, non-Hispanic/Latino; 2 Hispanic/Latino), 6 international. Average age 27. 173 applicants, 12% accepted, 1 enrolled. In 2011, 4 doctorates awarded. *Entrance requirements:* For doctorate, GRE. Additional exam requirements/recommendations for international students: Required—TOEFL (minimum score 550 paper-based; 80 iBT); Recommended—IELTS (minimum score 7). *Application deadline:* For fall admission, 1/15 for domestic and international students. Application fee: $50. Electronic applications accepted. *Financial support:* In 2011–12, research assistantships with partial tuition reimbursements (averaging $25,000 per year) were awarded; fellowships also available. Financial award application deadline: 3/1. *Unit head:* Dr. Nicholas Carbonetti, Director, 410-706-7677, E-mail: ncarbone@umaryland.edu. *Application contact:* June Green, Program Coordinator, 410-706-7126, Fax: 410-706-2129, E-mail: jgreen@umaryland.edu. Web site: http://microbiology.umaryland.edu.

University of Massachusetts Amherst, Graduate School, College of Natural Sciences, Department of Microbiology, Amherst, MA 01003. Offers MS, PhD. Part-time programs available. *Faculty:* 16 full-time (3 women). *Students:* 32 full-time (21 women), 3 part-time (0 women); includes 10 minority (2 Black or African American, non-Hispanic/Latino; 4 Asian, non-Hispanic/Latino; 3 Hispanic/Latino; 1 Two or more races, non-Hispanic/Latino), 14 international. Average age 27. 97 applicants, 27% accepted, 14 enrolled. In 2011, 8 master's, 3 doctorates awarded. Terminal master's awarded for partial completion of doctoral program. *Degree requirements:* For master's, thesis or

alternative; for doctorate, comprehensive exam, thesis/dissertation. *Entrance requirements:* For master's and doctorate, GRE General Test. Additional exam requirements/recommendations for international students: Required—TOEFL (minimum score 550 paper-based; 213 computer-based; 80 iBT), IELTS (minimum score 6.5). *Application deadline:* For fall admission, 12/20 for domestic and international students; for spring admission, 10/1 for domestic and international students. Applications are processed on a rolling basis. Application fee: $50 ($65 for international students). Electronic applications accepted. Tuition and fees vary according to course load, campus/location and program. *Financial support:* Fellowships with full and partial tuition reimbursements, research assistantships with full and partial tuition reimbursements, teaching assistantships with full and partial tuition reimbursements, career-related internships or fieldwork, Federal Work-Study, scholarships/grants, traineeships, health care benefits, tuition waivers (full and partial), and unspecified assistantships available. Support available to part-time students. Financial award application deadline: 12/20. *Unit head:* Dr. Klaus Nusslein, Graduate Program Director, 413-545-6675, Fax: 413-545-1578. *Application contact:* Lindsay DeSantis, Interim Supervisor of Admissions, 413-545-0722, Fax: 413-577-0010, E-mail: gradadm@grad.umass.edu. Web site: http://www.bio.umass.edu/micro.

See Display below and Close-Up on page 357.

University of Massachusetts Worcester, Graduate School of Biomedical Sciences, Worcester, MA 01655-0115. Offers biochemistry and molecular pharmacology (PhD); bioinformatics and computational biology (PhD); cancer biology (PhD); cell biology (PhD); clinical and population health research (PhD); clinical investigation (MS); immunology and virology (PhD); interdisciplinary graduate program (PhD); molecular genetics and microbiology (PhD); neuroscience (PhD); DVM/PhD; MD/PhD. *Faculty:* 1,427 full-time (526 women), 309 part-time/adjunct (196 women). *Students:* 416 full-time (225 women); includes 47 minority (12 Black or African American, non-Hispanic/Latino; 32 Asian, non-Hispanic/Latino; 3 Hispanic/Latino), 144 international. Average age 29. 623 applicants, 17% accepted, 54 enrolled. In 2011, 5 master's, 63 doctorates awarded. Terminal master's awarded for partial completion of doctoral program. *Degree requirements:* For master's, comprehensive exam; for doctorate, comprehensive exam, thesis/dissertation. *Entrance requirements:* For master's, bachelor's degree; for doctorate, GRE General Test. Additional exam requirements/recommendations for international students: Required—TOEFL (minimum score 600 paper-based; 250 computer-based; 100 iBT) or IELTS (minimum score 7.5). *Application deadline:* For fall admission, 12/15 for domestic and international students; for spring admission, 5/15 for domestic students. Application fee: $50. Electronic applications accepted. *Expenses:* Contact institution. *Financial support:* In 2011–12, 416 students received support, including 416 research assistantships with full tuition reimbursements available (averaging $29,200 per year); scholarships/grants, health care benefits, tuition waivers (full), and unspecified assistantships also available. Financial award application deadline: 4/16. *Faculty research:* RNA interference, cell biology, bioinformatics, clinical research, infectious disease. *Total annual research expenditures:* $262.7 million. *Unit head:* Dr. Anthony Carruthers, Dean, 508-856-4135, E-mail: anthony.carruthers@umassmed.edu. *Application contact:* Dr. Kendall Knight, Associate Dean and Interim Director of Admissions and Recruitment, 508-856-5628, Fax: 508-856-3659, E-mail: kendall.knight@umassmed.edu. Web site: http://www.umassmed.edu/gsbs/.

University of Medicine and Dentistry of New Jersey, Graduate School of Biomedical Sciences, Graduate Programs in Biomedical Sciences–Newark, Department of Microbiology and Molecular Genetics, Newark, NJ 07107. Offers PhD. *Degree requirements:* For doctorate, thesis/dissertation, qualifying exam. *Entrance requirements:* For doctorate, GRE General Test. Additional exam requirements/recommendations for international students: Required—TOEFL. Electronic applications

State-of-the-art **research** *opportunities for graduate students*

Department of Microbiology at UMass Amherst

The **graduate program in microbiology** offers broad training, which provides our graduates with the **flexibility** and **depth** necessary to compete effectively for research positions in universities, industry, and government.

The following research fields are represented in the department: microbial physiology, genetics, immunology, parasitology, pathogenic bacteriology, molecular biology, microbial ecology, and environmental microbiology.

For more information, contact:

Graduate Program Director
Department of Microbiology
Morrill IV, N203
639 North Pleasant Street
University of Massachusetts Amherst
Amherst, Massachusetts 01003-9298
United States
Phone: 413-545-2051   Fax: 413-545-1578
E-mail: **microbio-dept@microbio.umass.edu**

http://www.micro.umass.edu/

accepted. *Faculty research:* Molecular genetics of yeast, mutagenesis and carcinogenesis of DNA, bacterial protein synthesis, mammalian cell genetics, adenovirus gene expression.

University of Medicine and Dentistry of New Jersey, Graduate School of Biomedical Sciences, Graduate Programs in Biomedical Sciences–Piscataway, Program in Molecular Genetics, Microbiology and Immunology, Piscataway, NJ 08854-5635. Offers MS, PhD, MD/PhD. Terminal master's awarded for partial completion of doctoral program. *Degree requirements:* For master's, thesis, qualifying exam; for doctorate, thesis/dissertation, qualifying exam. *Entrance requirements:* For master's and doctorate, GRE General Test. Additional exam requirements/recommendations for international students: Required—TOEFL. Electronic applications accepted. *Faculty research:* Interferon, receptors, retrovirus evolution, Arbo virus/host cell interactions.

University of Miami, Graduate School, Miller School of Medicine, Graduate Programs in Medicine, Department of Microbiology and Immunology, Coral Gables, FL 33124. Offers PhD, MD/PhD. *Degree requirements:* For doctorate, thesis/dissertation, oral and written qualifying exams. *Entrance requirements:* For doctorate, GRE General Test. Additional exam requirements/recommendations for international students: Required—TOEFL. Electronic applications accepted. *Faculty research:* Cellular and molecular immunology, molecular and pathogenic virology, pathogenic bacteriology and gene therapy of cancer.

University of Michigan, Horace H. Rackham School of Graduate Studies, Program in Biomedical Sciences (PIBS), Department of Microbiology and Immunology, Ann Arbor, MI 48109. Offers PhD. *Faculty:* 20 full-time (10 women), 12 part-time/adjunct (4 women). *Students:* 40 full-time (25 women); includes 10 minority (2 Black or African American, non-Hispanic/Latino; 2 American Indian or Alaska Native, non-Hispanic/Latino; 4 Asian, non-Hispanic/Latino; 2 Hispanic/Latino), 4 international. Average age 29. 90 applicants, 14% accepted, 13 enrolled. In 2011, 7 doctorates awarded. *Degree requirements:* For doctorate, thesis/dissertation, oral defense of dissertation, preliminary exam. *Entrance requirements:* For doctorate, GRE General Test. Additional exam requirements/recommendations for international students: Required—TOEFL (minimum score 600 paper-based; 220 computer-based; 84 iBT), TWE. *Application deadline:* For fall admission, 12/1 for domestic and international students. Application fee: $60 ($75 for international students). Electronic applications accepted. *Financial support:* In 2011–12, 15 fellowships with full tuition reimbursements (averaging $24,500 per year), 20 research assistantships with full tuition reimbursements (averaging $24,500 per year) were awarded; health care benefits and tuition waivers (full) also available. Financial award application deadline: 2/1. *Faculty research:* Gene regulation, molecular biology of animal and bacterial viruses, molecular and cellular networks, pathogenesis and microbial genetics. *Total annual research expenditures:* $10.2 million. *Unit head:* Dr. Harry L. T. Mobley, Chair, 734-764-1466, Fax: 734-764-3562, E-mail: hmobley@umich.edu. *Application contact:* Heidi Thompson, Senior Student Administrative Assistant, 734-763-3532, Fax: 734-764-3562, E-mail: heiditho@umich.edu. Web site: http://www.med.umich.edu/microbio/.

University of Minnesota, Twin Cities Campus, Graduate School, PhD Program in Microbiology, Immunology and Cancer Biology, Minneapolis, MN 55455-0213. Offers PhD. *Degree requirements:* For doctorate, thesis/dissertation. *Entrance requirements:* For doctorate, GRE General Test. Additional exam requirements/recommendations for international students: Required—TOEFL (minimum score 600 paper-based; 250 computer-based). Electronic applications accepted. *Faculty research:* Virology, microbiology, cancer biology, immunology.

University of Mississippi Medical Center, School of Graduate Studies in the Health Sciences, Department of Microbiology, Jackson, MS 39216-4505. Offers MS, PhD, MD/PhD. Terminal master's awarded for partial completion of doctoral program. *Degree requirements:* For master's, thesis; for doctorate, thesis/dissertation, first authored publication. *Entrance requirements:* For master's and doctorate, GRE General Test, minimum GPA of 3.0. Additional exam requirements/recommendations for international students: Recommended—TOEFL. *Faculty research:* Immunology, virology, microbial physiology/genetics, parasitology.

University of Missouri, School of Medicine and Graduate School, Graduate Programs in Medicine, Department of Molecular Microbiology and Immunology, Columbia, MO 65211. Offers MS, PhD. *Faculty:* 20 full-time (4 women), 2 part-time/adjunct (0 women). *Students:* 47 full-time (22 women), 5 part-time (2 women); includes 4 minority (3 Black or African American, non-Hispanic/Latino; 1 American Indian or Alaska Native, non-Hispanic/Latino), 17 international. Average age 28. 42 applicants, 24% accepted, 10 enrolled. In 2011, 1 master's, 6 doctorates awarded. Terminal master's awarded for partial completion of doctoral program. *Degree requirements:* For master's, thesis; for doctorate, thesis/dissertation. *Entrance requirements:* For master's and doctorate, GRE General Test, minimum GPA of 3.0. Additional exam requirements/recommendations for international students: Required—TOEFL (minimum score 580 paper-based; 237 computer-based; 92 iBT). *Application deadline:* For fall admission, 1/31 for domestic students. Application fee: $55 ($75 for international students). *Expenses:* Tuition, state resident: full-time $5881. Tuition, nonresident: full-time $15,183. *Required fees:* $952. Tuition and fees vary according to campus/location and program. *Financial support:* Fellowships, research assistantships, teaching assistantships, and institutionally sponsored loans available. Financial award application deadline: 3/1. *Faculty research:* Molecular biology, host-parasite interactions. *Unit head:* Dr. Mark A. McIntosh, Department Chair, E-mail: mcintoshm@missouri.edu. *Application contact:* Jana Clark, 573-882-3938, E-mail: clarkjl@missouri.edu. Web site: http://mmi.missouri.edu/graduateprogram/programindex.php.

The University of Montana, Graduate School, College of Arts and Sciences, Division of Biological Sciences, Program in Biochemistry and Microbiology, Missoula, MT 59812-0002. Offers biochemistry (MS); integrative microbiology and biochemistry (PhD); microbial ecology (MS, PhD); microbiology (MS). Terminal master's awarded for partial completion of doctoral program. *Degree requirements:* For master's, thesis; for doctorate, variable foreign language requirement, thesis/dissertation. *Entrance requirements:* For master's and doctorate, GRE General Test. *Faculty research:* Ribosome structure, medical microbiology/pathogenesis, microbial ecology/environmental microbiology.

University of Nebraska Medical Center, Graduate Studies, Department of Pathology and Microbiology, Omaha, NE 68198. Offers MS, PhD. Part-time programs available. Terminal master's awarded for partial completion of doctoral program. *Degree requirements:* For master's, comprehensive exam, thesis; for doctorate, comprehensive exam, thesis/dissertation. *Entrance requirements:* For master's, previous course work in biology, chemistry, mathematics, and physics; for doctorate, GRE General Test, previous course work in biology, chemistry, mathematics, and physics. Additional exam requirements/recommendations for international students: Required—TOEFL (minimum score 550 paper-based; 213 computer-based). Electronic applications accepted. *Faculty research:* Carcinogenesis, cancer biology, immunobiology, molecular virology, molecular genetics.

University of New Hampshire, Graduate School, College of Life Sciences and Agriculture, Department of Molecular, Cellular and Biomedical Sciences, Program in Microbiology, Durham, NH 03824. Offers MS, PhD. Part-time programs available. *Faculty:* 7 full-time. *Students:* 12 full-time (7 women), 9 part-time (3 women); includes 6 minority (1 Black or African American, non-Hispanic/Latino; 3 Asian, non-Hispanic/Latino; 2 Hispanic/Latino), 2 international. Average age 27. 30 applicants, 37% accepted, 6 enrolled. In 2011, 5 master's, 1 doctorate awarded. Terminal master's awarded for partial completion of doctoral program. *Degree requirements:* For master's, thesis; for doctorate, thesis/dissertation. *Entrance requirements:* For master's and doctorate, GRE General Test. Additional exam requirements/recommendations for international students: Required—TOEFL (minimum score 550 paper-based; 213 computer-based; 80 iBT). *Application deadline:* For fall admission, 1/15 priority date for domestic students, 1/15 for international students; for spring admission, 11/1 for domestic students. Applications are processed on a rolling basis. Application fee: $65. Electronic applications accepted. *Expenses:* Tuition, state resident: full-time $12,360; part-time $687 per credit hour. Tuition, nonresident: full-time $25,680; part-time $1058 per credit hour. *International tuition:* $29,550 full-time. *Required fees:* $1666; $833 per course. $416.50 per semester. Tuition and fees vary according to course load and degree level. *Financial support:* In 2011–12, 18 students received support, including 1 fellowship, 3 research assistantships, 13 teaching assistantships; career-related internships or fieldwork, Federal Work-Study, scholarships/grants, and tuition waivers (full and partial) also available. Support available to part-time students. Financial award application deadline: 2/15. *Faculty research:* Bacterial host-parasite interactions, immunology, microbial structures, bacterial and bacteriophage genetics, virology. *Unit head:* Dr. Rick Cote, Chairperson, 603-862-0211. *Application contact:* Flora Joyal, Administrative Assistant, 603-862-4095, E-mail: flora.joyal@unh.edu. Web site: http://microbiology.unh.edu/.

University of New Mexico, Health Sciences Center Graduate Programs, Program in Biomedical Sciences, Albuquerque, NM 87131-5196. Offers biochemistry and molecular biology (MS, PhD); cell biology and physiology (MS, PhD); clinical and translational science (Certificate); molecular genetics and microbiology (MS, PhD); neuroscience (MS, PhD); pathology (MS, PhD); toxicology (MS, PhD); university science teaching (Certificate). Part-time programs available. *Faculty:* 64 full-time (26 women), 9 part-time/adjunct (4 women). *Students:* 45 full-time (27 women), 56 part-time (28 women); includes 24 minority (3 Black or African American, non-Hispanic/Latino; 1 American Indian or Alaska Native, non-Hispanic/Latino; 4 Asian, non-Hispanic/Latino; 14 Hispanic/Latino; 1 Native Hawaiian or other Pacific Islander, non-Hispanic/Latino; 1 Two or more races, non-Hispanic/Latino), 18 international. Average age 30. 110 applicants, 18% accepted, 17 enrolled. In 2011, 14 master's, 5 doctorates awarded. Terminal master's awarded for partial completion of doctoral program. *Degree requirements:* For master's, thesis; for doctorate, comprehensive exam, thesis/dissertation. *Entrance requirements:* For master's and doctorate, GRE General Test, minimum undergraduate GPA of 3.0. Additional exam requirements/recommendations for international students: Required—TOEFL. *Application deadline:* For fall admission, 3/1 priority date for domestic students, 3/1 for international students. Applications are processed on a rolling basis. Application fee: $50. Electronic applications accepted. *Financial support:* In 2011–12, 99 students received support, including 28 fellowships with full and partial tuition reimbursements available (averaging $22,000 per year), 73 research assistantships with full tuition reimbursements available (averaging $23,000 per year), 8 teaching assistantships (averaging $2,800 per year); career-related internships or fieldwork, Federal Work-Study, institutionally sponsored loans, scholarships/grants, traineeships, health care benefits, and unspecified assistantships also available. Financial award application deadline: 1/1; financial award applicants required to submit FAFSA. *Faculty research:* Infectious disease/Immunity, cancer biology, cardiovascular and metabolic diseases, brain and behavioral illness, environmental health. *Unit head:* Dr. Helen J. Hathaway, BSGP Program Director, 505-272-1887, Fax: 505-272-2412, E-mail: hhathaway@salud.unm.edu. *Application contact:* Mary Fenton, Admissions Coordinator, 505-272-1887, Fax: 505-272-2412, E-mail: mfenton@salud.unm.edu. Web site: http://hsc.unm.edu/som/research/brep/bsgpabout.shtm.

The University of North Carolina at Chapel Hill, School of Medicine and Graduate School, Graduate Programs in Medicine, Department of Microbiology and Immunology, Chapel Hill, NC 27599-7290. Offers immunology (MS, PhD); microbiology (MS, PhD). Terminal master's awarded for partial completion of doctoral program. *Degree requirements:* For master's, comprehensive exam, thesis; for doctorate, comprehensive exam, thesis/dissertation. *Entrance requirements:* For master's and doctorate, GRE General Test, minimum GPA of 3.0. Electronic applications accepted. *Faculty research:* HIV pathogenesis, immune response, t-cell mediated autoimmunity, alpha-viruses, bacterial chemotaxis, francisella tularensis, pertussis, Mycobacterium tuberculosis, Burkholderia, Dengue virus.

University of North Dakota, Graduate School and Graduate School, Graduate Programs in Medicine, Department of Microbiology and Immunology, Grand Forks, ND 58202. Offers MS, PhD. *Degree requirements:* For master's, comprehensive exam, thesis or alternative; for doctorate, comprehensive exam, thesis/dissertation, final examination. *Entrance requirements:* For master's and doctorate, GRE General Test, minimum GPA of 3.0. Additional exam requirements/recommendations for international students: Required—TOEFL (minimum score 550 paper-based; 213 computer-based; 79 iBT), IELTS (minimum score 6.5). Electronic applications accepted. *Faculty research:* Genetic and immunological aspects of a murine model of human multiple sclerosis, termination of DNA replication, cell division in bacteria, yersinia pestis.

University of North Texas Health Science Center at Fort Worth, Graduate School of Biomedical Sciences, Fort Worth, TX 76107-2699. Offers anatomy and cell biology (MS, PhD); biochemistry and molecular biology (MS, PhD); biomedical sciences (MS, PhD); biotechnology (MS); forensic genetics (MS); integrative physiology (MS, PhD); medical science (MS); microbiology and immunology (MS, PhD); pharmacology (MS, PhD); science education (MS); DO/MS; DO/PhD. Terminal master's awarded for partial completion of doctoral program. *Degree requirements:* For master's, thesis; for doctorate, thesis/dissertation. *Entrance requirements:* For master's and doctorate, GRE General Test. Additional exam requirements/recommendations for international students: Required—TOEFL. *Expenses:* Contact institution. *Faculty research:* Alzheimer's disease, aging, eye diseases, cancer, cardiovascular disease.

University of Oklahoma, College of Arts and Sciences, Department of Microbiology and Plant Biology, Program in Microbiology, Norman, OK 73019. Offers MS, PhD. *Students:* 42 full-time (14 women), 11 part-time (6 women); includes 8 minority (2 Black or African American, non-Hispanic/Latino; 1 American Indian or Alaska Native, non-Hispanic/Latino; 2 Asian, non-Hispanic/Latino; 3 Two or more races, non-Hispanic/Latino), 19 international. Average age 26. 42 applicants, 55% accepted, 17 enrolled. In 2011, 1 master's, 3 doctorates awarded. Terminal master's awarded for partial completion of doctoral program. *Degree requirements:* For master's, thesis, oral exam; for doctorate, one foreign language, thesis/dissertation, general exam. *Entrance requirements:* For master's and doctorate, GRE. Additional exam requirements/recommendations for international students: Required—TOEFL (minimum score 550 paper-based; 79 iBT). *Application deadline:* For fall admission, 4/1 for domestic students, 3/1 for international students; for spring admission, 8/1 for domestic students, 9/1 for international students. Applications are processed on a rolling basis. Application fee: $40 ($90 for international students). Electronic applications accepted. *Expenses:* Tuition, state resident: full-time $4087; part-time $170.30 per credit hour. Tuition,

nonresident: full-time $14,875; part-time $619.80 per credit hour. *Required fees:* $2659; $100.25 per credit hour. Tuition and fees vary according to course load and degree level. *Financial support:* In 2011–12, 53 students received support. Federal Work-Study, institutionally sponsored loans, scholarships/grants, health care benefits, and unspecified assistantships available. Support available to part-time students. Financial award applicants required to submit FAFSA. *Faculty research:* Anaerobic microbiology, microbial ecology, environmental microbiology, molecular biology and genomics, microbial physiology. *Unit head:* Dr. Gordon Uno, Chair, 405-325-4321, Fax: 405-325-7619, E-mail: guno@ou.edu. *Application contact:* Adell Hopper, Staff Assistant, 405-325-4322, Fax: 405-325-7619, E-mail: ahopper@ou.edu. Web site: http://mpbio.ou.edu/.

University of Oklahoma Health Sciences Center, College of Medicine and Graduate College, Graduate Programs in Medicine, Department of Microbiology and Immunology, Oklahoma City, OK 73190. Offers immunology (MS, PhD); microbiology (MS, PhD). Part-time programs available. Terminal master's awarded for partial completion of doctoral program. *Degree requirements:* For master's, thesis or alternative; for doctorate, one foreign language, thesis/dissertation. *Entrance requirements:* For doctorate, GRE General Test, 3 letters of recommendation. Additional exam requirements/recommendations for international students: Required—TOEFL. *Faculty research:* Molecular genetics, pathogenesis, streptococcal infections, gram-positive virulence, monoclonal antibodies.

University of Ottawa, Faculty of Graduate and Postdoctoral Studies, Faculty of Medicine, Department of Biochemistry, Microbiology and Immunology, Ottawa, ON K1N 6N5, Canada. Offers biochemistry (M Sc, PhD); microbiology and immunology (M Sc, PhD). *Degree requirements:* For master's, thesis; for doctorate, comprehensive exam, thesis/dissertation, seminar. *Entrance requirements:* For master's, honors degree or equivalent, minimum B average; for doctorate, master's degree, minimum B+ average. Electronic applications accepted. *Faculty research:* General biochemistry, molecular biology, microbiology, host biology, nutrition and metabolism.

University of Pennsylvania, Perelman School of Medicine, Biomedical Graduate Studies, Graduate Group in Cell and Molecular Biology, Philadelphia, PA 19104. Offers cancer biology (PhD); cell biology and physiology (PhD); developmental stem cell regenerative biology (PhD); gene therapy and vaccines (PhD); genetics and gene regulation (PhD); microbiology, virology, and parasitology (PhD); MD/PhD; VMD/PhD. *Faculty:* 306. *Students:* 337 full-time (186 women); includes 81 minority (16 Black or African American, non-Hispanic/Latino; 43 Asian, non-Hispanic/Latino; 16 Hispanic/Latino; 6 Two or more races, non-Hispanic/Latino), 41 international. 585 applicants, 21% accepted, 58 enrolled. In 2011, 42 doctorates awarded. *Degree requirements:* For doctorate, thesis/dissertation. *Entrance requirements:* For doctorate, GRE General Test. Additional exam requirements/recommendations for international students: Required—TOEFL. *Application deadline:* For fall admission, 12/1 priority date for domestic students, 12/1 for international students. Applications are processed on a rolling basis. Application fee: $80. Electronic applications accepted. *Expenses: Tuition:* Full-time $26,660; part-time $4944 per course. *Required fees:* $2318; $291 per course. Tuition and fees vary according to course load, degree level and program. *Financial support:* In 2011–12, 337 students received support. Fellowships, research assistantships, scholarships/grants, traineeships, and unspecified assistantships available. *Unit head:* Dr. Daniel Kessler, Graduate Group Chair. *Application contact:* Meagan Schofer, Coordinator. Web site: http://www.med.upenn.edu/camb/.

University of Pittsburgh, Graduate School of Public Health, Department of Infectious Diseases and Microbiology, Pittsburgh, PA 15260. Offers bioscience of infectious diseases (MPH); community and behavioral intervention of infectious diseases (MPH); infectious diseases and microbiology (MS, PhD); LGBT health and wellness (Certificate). Part-time programs available. *Faculty:* 21 full-time (6 women), 24 part-time/adjunct (7 women). *Students:* 57 full-time (44 women), 13 part-time (9 women); includes 15 minority (4 Black or African American, non-Hispanic/Latino; 9 Asian, non-Hispanic/Latino; 2 Hispanic/Latino), 7 international. Average age 27. 157 applicants, 56% accepted, 29 enrolled. In 2011, 13 master's, 3 doctorates awarded. Terminal master's awarded for partial completion of doctoral program. *Degree requirements:* For master's, one foreign language, comprehensive exam (for some programs), thesis; for doctorate, one foreign language, comprehensive exam, thesis/dissertation. *Entrance requirements:* For master's and doctorate, GRE General Test, MCAT, or DAT. Additional exam requirements/recommendations for international students: Required—TOEFL (minimum score 550 paper-based; 80 iBT) or IELTS (minimum score 6.5). *Application deadline:* For fall admission, 1/4 priority date for domestic students, 1/4 for international students. Applications are processed on a rolling basis. Application fee: $115. Electronic applications accepted. *Expenses:* Tuition, state resident: full-time $18,774; part-time $760 per credit. Tuition, nonresident: full-time $30,736; part-time $1258 per credit. *Required fees:* $740; $200 per term. Tuition and fees vary according to program. *Financial support:* In 2011–12, 31 students received support, including 12 fellowships (averaging $7,248 per year), 19 research assistantships with full and partial tuition reimbursements available (averaging $5,448 per year). Financial award applicants required to submit FAFSA. *Faculty research:* HIV, Epstein-Barr virus, virology, immunology, malaria. *Total annual research expenditures:* $15.6 million. *Unit head:* Dr. Charles R. Rinaldo, Jr., Chairman, 412-624-3928, Fax: 412-624-4953, E-mail: rinaldo@pitt.edu. *Application contact:* Dr. Jeremy Martinson, Assistant Professor, 412-624-5646, Fax: 412-383-8926, E-mail: jmartins@pitt.edu. Web site: http://www.idm.pitt.edu/.

University of Pittsburgh, School of Medicine, Graduate Programs in Medicine, Program in Molecular Virology and Microbiology, Pittsburgh, PA 15260. Offers MS, PhD. *Faculty:* 46 full-time (11 women). *Students:* 24 full-time (12 women); includes 2 minority (1 Hispanic/Latino; 1 Native Hawaiian or other Pacific Islander, non-Hispanic/Latino), 3 international. Average age 27. 514 applicants, 12% accepted, 24 enrolled. In 2011, 2 doctorates awarded. *Degree requirements:* For doctorate, comprehensive exam, thesis/dissertation. *Entrance requirements:* For doctorate, GRE General Test, GRE Subject Test, minimum QPA of 3.0. Additional exam requirements/recommendations for international students: Required—TOEFL (minimum score 600 paper-based; 100 iBT), IELTS (minimum score 7). *Application deadline:* For fall admission, 12/15 priority date for domestic students, 12/15 for international students. Application fee: $50. Electronic applications accepted. *Expenses:* Tuition, state resident: full-time $18,774; part-time $760 per credit. Tuition, nonresident: full-time $30,736; part-time $1258 per credit. *Required fees:* $740; $200 per term. Tuition and fees vary according to program. *Financial support:* In 2011–12, 1 fellowship (averaging $25,500 per year), 23 research assistantships with full tuition reimbursements (averaging $25,500 per year) were awarded; institutionally sponsored loans, scholarships/grants, traineeships, health care benefits, and unspecified assistantships also available. *Faculty research:* Host-pathogen interactions, persistent microbial infections, microbial genetics and gene expression, microbial pathogenesis, anti-bacterial therapeutics. *Unit head:* Dr. Neal A. DeLuca, Graduate Program Director, 412-648-9947, Fax: 412-624-0298, E-mail: ndeluca@pitt.edu. *Application contact:* Graduate Studies Administrator, 412-648-8957, Fax: 412-648-1077, E-mail: gradstudies@medschool.pitt.edu. Web site: http://www.gradbiomed.pitt.edu.

University of Puerto Rico, Medical Sciences Campus, School of Medicine, Division of Graduate Studies, Department of Microbiology and Medical Zoology, San Juan, PR 00936-5067. Offers MS, PhD. *Degree requirements:* For master's, one foreign language, thesis; for doctorate, one foreign language, comprehensive exam, thesis/dissertation. *Entrance requirements:* For master's and doctorate, GRE General Test, GRE Subject Test, interview, minimum GPA of 3.0, 3 letters of recommendation. *Faculty research:* Molecular and general parasitology, immunology, development of viral vaccines and antiviral agents, antibiotic resistance, bacteriology.

University of Rhode Island, Graduate School, College of the Environment and Life Sciences, Department of Cell and Molecular Biology, Kingston, RI 02881. Offers biochemistry (MS, PhD); clinical laboratory sciences (MS), including biotechnology, clinical laboratory science, cytopathology; microbiology (MS, PhD); molecular genetics (MS, PhD). Part-time programs available. *Faculty:* 14 full-time (5 women), 3 part-time/adjunct (2 women). *Students:* 32 full-time (15 women), 37 part-time (23 women); includes 2 minority (1 Asian, non-Hispanic/Latino; 1 Hispanic/Latino), 1 international. In 2011, 2 master's, 2 doctorates awarded. *Degree requirements:* For master's, comprehensive exam (for some programs); for doctorate, comprehensive exam. *Entrance requirements:* For master's and doctorate, GRE, 2 letters of recommendation. Additional exam requirements/recommendations for international students: Required—TOEFL (minimum score 550 paper-based; 213 computer-based). *Application deadline:* For fall admission, 7/15 for domestic students, 2/1 for international students; for spring admission, 11/15 for domestic students, 7/15 for international students. Application fee: $65. Electronic applications accepted. *Expenses:* Tuition, state resident: full-time $10,432; part-time $580 per credit hour. Tuition, nonresident: full-time $23,130; part-time $1285 per credit hour. *Required fees:* $1362; $36 per credit hour. $35 per semester. One-time fee: $130. *Financial support:* In 2011–12, 2 research assistantships with full and partial tuition reimbursements (averaging $13,894 per year), 6 teaching assistantships with full and partial tuition reimbursements (averaging $12,850 per year) were awarded. Financial award application deadline: 7/15; financial award applicants required to submit FAFSA. *Faculty research:* Genomics and Sequencing Center: an interdisciplinary genomics research and undergraduate and graduate student training program which provides researchers access to cutting-edge technologies in the field of genomics. *Unit head:* Dr. Jay Sperry, Chairperson, 401-874-2201, Fax: 401-874-2202, E-mail: jsperry@mail.uri.edu. *Application contact:* Nasser H. Zawia, Dean of the Graduate School, 401-874-5909, Fax: 401-874-5787, E-mail: nzawia@uri.edu. Web site: http://cels.uri.edu/cmb/.

University of Rochester, School of Medicine and Dentistry, Graduate Programs in Medicine and Dentistry, Department of Microbiology and Immunology, Program in Medical Microbiology, Rochester, NY 14627. Offers MS, PhD. *Expenses: Tuition:* Full-time $41,040.

University of Rochester, School of Medicine and Dentistry, Graduate Programs in Medicine and Dentistry, Department of Microbiology and Immunology, Program in Microbiology and Immunology, Rochester, NY 14627. Offers MS, PhD. *Expenses: Tuition:* Full-time $41,040.

University of Saskatchewan, College of Medicine, Department of Microbiology and Immunology, Saskatoon, SK S7N 5A2, Canada. Offers M Sc, PhD. *Degree requirements:* For master's, thesis; for doctorate, thesis/dissertation. *Entrance requirements:* Additional exam requirements/recommendations for international students: Required—TOEFL.

University of Saskatchewan, Western College of Veterinary Medicine and College of Graduate Studies and Research, Graduate Programs in Veterinary Medicine, Department of Veterinary Microbiology, Saskatoon, SK S7N 5A2, Canada. Offers M Sc, M Vet Sc, PhD. *Degree requirements:* For master's, thesis; for doctorate, comprehensive exam (for some programs), thesis/dissertation. *Entrance requirements:* Additional exam requirements/recommendations for international students: Required—TOEFL (minimum score 80 iBT) or IELTS (minimum score 6.5). Electronic applications accepted. *Faculty research:* Immunology, vaccinology, epidemiology, virology, parasitology.

The University of South Dakota, Graduate School, School of Medicine and Graduate School, Biomedical Sciences Graduate Program, Molecular Microbiology and Immunology Group, Vermillion, SD 57069-2390. Offers MS, PhD. Terminal master's awarded for partial completion of doctoral program. *Degree requirements:* For master's, thesis; for doctorate, comprehensive exam, thesis/dissertation. *Entrance requirements:* For master's and doctorate, GRE General Test, minimum GPA of 3.0. Additional exam requirements/recommendations for international students: Required—TOEFL (minimum score 550 paper-based; 213 computer-based; 80 iBT), IELTS (minimum score 6). Electronic applications accepted. *Expenses:* Contact institution. *Faculty research:* Structure-function membranes, plasmids, immunology, virology, pathogenesis.

University of Southern California, Keck School of Medicine and Graduate School, Graduate Programs in Medicine, Department of Molecular Microbiology and Immunology, Los Angeles, CA 90089. Offers MS, PhD. Part-time programs available. *Faculty:* 22 full-time (5 women), 1 (woman) part-time/adjunct. *Students:* 27 full-time (17 women); includes 19 minority (all Asian, non-Hispanic/Latino). Average age 24. 43 applicants, 67% accepted, 16 enrolled. In 2011, 10 master's, 1 doctorate awarded. Terminal master's awarded for partial completion of doctoral program. *Degree requirements:* For master's, comprehensive exam (for some programs), thesis optional; for doctorate, comprehensive exam, thesis/dissertation. *Entrance requirements:* For master's, GRE General Test, minimum GPA of 3.0; for doctorate, GRE General Test, GRE Subject Test, minimum GPA of 3.0. Additional exam requirements/recommendations for international students: Required—TOEFL (minimum score 100 iBT). *Application deadline:* For fall admission, 6/1 for domestic students, 5/1 for international students; for spring admission, 11/1 for domestic students, 10/1 for international students. Applications are processed on a rolling basis. Application fee: $85. Electronic applications accepted. *Financial support:* In 2011–12, 2 students received support, including 1 research assistantship with full tuition reimbursement available (averaging $29,100 per year), 1 teaching assistantship with full tuition reimbursement available (averaging $29,100 per year); fellowships, Federal Work-Study, institutionally sponsored loans, scholarships/grants, health care benefits, and unspecified assistantships also available. Financial award application deadline: 5/3; financial award applicants required to submit FAFSA. *Faculty research:* Animal virology, microbial genetics, molecular and cellular immunology, cellular differentiation control of protein synthesis, HIV. *Unit head:* Dr. Jae U. Jung, Professor and Chair, 323-442-1713, Fax: 323-442-1721, E-mail: jaeujung@usc.edu. *Application contact:* Silvina V. Campos, Administrative Assistant II, 323-442-1713, Fax: 323-442-1721, E-mail: scampos@usc.edu. Web site: http://www.usc.edu/schools/medicine/departments/molecularmicrobio_immunology/.

University of Southern Mississippi, Graduate School, College of Science and Technology, Department of Biological Sciences, Hattiesburg, MS 39406-0001. Offers environmental biology (MS, PhD); marine biology (MS, PhD); microbiology (MS, PhD); molecular biology (MS, PhD). *Faculty:* 27 full-time (6 women). *Students:* 57 full-time (28 women), 4 part-time (2 women); includes 5 minority (2 Black or African American, non-Hispanic/Latino; 3 Two or more races, non-Hispanic/Latino), 18 international. Average age 32. 50 applicants, 32% accepted, 12 enrolled. In 2011, 7 master's, 8 doctorates awarded. Terminal master's awarded for partial completion of doctoral program. *Degree*

requirements: For master's, comprehensive exam, thesis; for doctorate, comprehensive exam, thesis/dissertation. *Entrance requirements:* For master's, GRE General Test, minimum GPA of 3.0 on last 60 hours; for doctorate, GRE General Test, minimum GPA of 3.5. Additional exam requirements/recommendations for international students: Required—TOEFL, IELTS. *Application deadline:* For fall admission, 3/1 priority date for domestic students, 3/1 for international students; for spring admission, 1/10 priority date for domestic students, 1/10 for international students. Applications are processed on a rolling basis. Application fee: $50. *Financial support:* In 2011–12, 25 research assistantships with full tuition reimbursements (averaging $9,700 per year), 33 teaching assistantships with full tuition reimbursements (averaging $10,600 per year) were awarded; Federal Work-Study, scholarships/grants, health care benefits, and unspecified assistantships also available. Financial award application deadline: 3/15; financial award applicants required to submit FAFSA. *Unit head:* Dr. Glenmore Shearer, Chair, 601-266-4748, Fax: 601-266-5797. *Application contact:* Dr. Jake Schaefer, Director of Graduate Studies, 601-266-4748, Fax: 601-266-5797. Web site: http://www.usm.edu/graduateschool/table.php.

The University of Tennessee, Graduate School, College of Arts and Sciences, Department of Microbiology, Knoxville, TN 37996. Offers MS, PhD. Part-time programs available. *Degree requirements:* For master's, thesis; for doctorate, thesis/dissertation. *Entrance requirements:* For master's and doctorate, GRE General Test, minimum GPA of 2.7. Additional exam requirements/recommendations for international students: Required—TOEFL. Electronic applications accepted. *Expenses:* Tuition, state resident: full-time $8332; part-time $464 per credit hour. Tuition, nonresident: full-time $25,174; part-time $1400 per credit hour. *Required fees:* $1162; $56 per credit hour. Tuition and fees vary according to program.

The University of Texas at Austin, Graduate School, College of Natural Sciences, School of Biological Sciences, Program in Microbiology, Austin, TX 78712-1111. Offers PhD. *Entrance requirements:* For doctorate, GRE General Test. Application fee: $50 ($75 for international students). Electronic applications accepted. *Financial support:* Fellowships with full tuition reimbursements, research assistantships with full and partial tuition reimbursements, and teaching assistantships with full tuition reimbursements available. *Unit head:* Dr. Clarence Chan, Graduate Chair, 512-471-6860, E-mail: clarence_chan@mail.utexas.edu. *Application contact:* Sally Eddleman, Graduate Coordinator, 512-471-4181, E-mail: eddleman@mail.utexas.edu. Web site: http://www.biosci.utexas.edu/graduate/micro/.

The University of Texas Health Science Center at Houston, Graduate School of Biomedical Sciences, Program in Microbiology and Molecular Genetics, Houston, TX 77225-0036. Offers MS, PhD, MD/PhD. Terminal master's awarded for partial completion of doctoral program. *Degree requirements:* For master's, thesis; for doctorate, thesis/dissertation. *Entrance requirements:* For master's and doctorate, GRE General Test. Additional exam requirements/recommendations for international students: Required—TOEFL. Electronic applications accepted. *Faculty research:* Disease causation, environmental signaling, gene regulation, cell growth and division, cell structure and architecture.

The University of Texas Health Science Center at San Antonio, Graduate School of Biomedical Sciences, Department of Microbiology and Immunology, San Antonio, TX 78229-3900. Offers PhD. *Degree requirements:* For doctorate, comprehensive exam, thesis/dissertation. *Entrance requirements:* For doctorate, GRE General Test. Additional exam requirements/recommendations for international students: Required—TOEFL (minimum score 560 paper-based; 220 computer-based; 68 iBT). Electronic applications accepted. *Faculty research:* Molecular immunology, mechanisms of microbial pathogenesis, molecular genetics, vaccine and immunodiagnostic development.

The University of Texas Medical Branch, Graduate School of Biomedical Sciences, Program in Microbiology and Immunology, Galveston, TX 77555. Offers MS, PhD. Terminal master's awarded for partial completion of doctoral program. *Degree requirements:* For master's, thesis or alternative; for doctorate, thesis/dissertation. *Entrance requirements:* For doctorate, GRE General Test, minimum GPA of 3.0. Additional exam requirements/recommendations for international students: Required—TOEFL (minimum score 550 paper-based; 213 computer-based). Electronic applications accepted.

The University of Texas Southwestern Medical Center, Southwestern Graduate School of Biomedical Sciences, Division of Basic Science, Program in Molecular Microbiology, Dallas, TX 75390. Offers PhD. *Degree requirements:* For doctorate, thesis/dissertation, oral and written exams. *Entrance requirements:* For doctorate, GRE General Test, minimum GPA of 3.0. Additional exam requirements/recommendations for international students: Required—TOEFL. Electronic applications accepted. *Faculty research:* Cell and molecular immunology, molecular pathogenesis of infectious disease, virology.

University of Vermont, College of Medicine and Graduate College, Graduate Programs in Medicine, Department of Microbiology and Molecular Genetics, Burlington, VT 05405. Offers MS, PhD, MD/MS, MD/PhD. *Faculty:* 18 full-time (5 women). *Students:* 24 (14 women); includes 1 minority (Hispanic/Latino), 9 international. 54 applicants, 26% accepted, 2 enrolled. In 2011, 1 master's, 2 doctorates awarded. *Degree requirements:* For master's, thesis; for doctorate, thesis/dissertation. *Entrance requirements:* For master's and doctorate, GRE General Test. Additional exam requirements/recommendations for international students: Required—TOEFL (minimum score 550 paper-based; 213 computer-based; 80 iBT). *Application deadline:* For fall admission, 1/16 priority date for domestic students, 1/16 for international students. Applications are processed on a rolling basis. Application fee: $40. Electronic applications accepted. *Financial support:* Fellowships, research assistantships, and teaching assistantships available. Financial award application deadline: 3/1. *Unit head:* Dr. Susan S. Wallace, Chairperson, 802-656-2164. *Application contact:* Dr. John Burke, Coordinator, 802-656-2164.

University of Victoria, Faculty of Graduate Studies, Faculty of Science, Department of Biochemistry and Microbiology, Victoria, BC V8W 2Y2, Canada. Offers biochemistry (M Sc, PhD); microbiology (M Sc, PhD). *Degree requirements:* For master's, thesis, seminar; for doctorate, thesis/dissertation, seminar, candidacy exam. *Entrance requirements:* For master's, GRE General Test, minimum B+ average; for doctorate, GRE General Test, minimum B+ average, M Sc. Additional exam requirements/recommendations for international students: Required—TOEFL (minimum score 600 paper-based; 250 computer-based). Electronic applications accepted. *Faculty research:* Molecular pathogenesis, prokaryotic, eukaryotic, macromolecular interactions, microbial surfaces, virology, molecular genetics.

University of Virginia, School of Medicine, Department of Microbiology, Charlottesville, VA 22903. Offers PhD, MD/PhD. *Faculty:* 34 full-time (14 women), 1 part-time/adjunct (0 women). *Students:* 60 full-time (34 women); includes 11 minority (5 Black or African American, non-Hispanic/Latino; 4 Asian, non-Hispanic/Latino; 2 Hispanic/Latino), 3 international. Average age 28. 154 applicants, 11% accepted, 11 enrolled. In 2011, 17 doctorates awarded. *Degree requirements:* For doctorate, thesis/dissertation. *Entrance requirements:* For doctorate, GRE General Test, 2 or more letters of recommendation. Additional exam requirements/recommendations for international students: Required—TOEFL (minimum score 600 paper-based; 250 computer-based; 90 iBT). *Application deadline:* For fall admission, 2/1 for domestic and international students. Applications are processed on a rolling basis. Application fee: $60. Electronic applications accepted. *Financial support:* Fellowships, traineeships, and unspecified assistantships available. Financial award applicants required to submit FAFSA. *Faculty research:* Virology, membrane biology and molecular genetics. *Unit head:* Kodi S. Ravichandran, Chair, 434-924-1948, Fax: 434-982-1071, E-mail: kr4h@virginia.edu. *Application contact:* Lesley L. Thomas, Director, Admissions Office, 434-924-5571, Fax: 434-982-2586, E-mail: medsch-adm@virginia.edu. Web site: http://records.ureg.virginia.edu/preview_program.php?catoid-18&poid-1401&bc-1.

University of Washington, Graduate School, School of Medicine, Graduate Programs in Medicine, Department of Microbiology, Seattle, WA 98195. Offers PhD. *Degree requirements:* For doctorate, thesis/dissertation. *Entrance requirements:* For doctorate, GRE General Test, GRE Subject Test (recommended). Electronic applications accepted. *Faculty research:* Bacterial genetics and physiology, mechanisms of bacterial and viral pathogenesis, bacterial-plant interaction.

The University of Western Ontario, Faculty of Graduate Studies, Biosciences Division, Department of Microbiology and Immunology, London, ON N6A 5B8, Canada. Offers M Sc, PhD. *Degree requirements:* For master's, thesis, oral and written exam; for doctorate, thesis/dissertation, oral and written exam. *Entrance requirements:* For master's, honors degree or equivalent in microbiology, immunology, or other biological science; minimum B average; for doctorate, M Sc in microbiology and immunology. Additional exam requirements/recommendations for international students: Required—TOEFL. *Faculty research:* Virology, molecular pathogenesis, cellular immunology, molecular biology.

University of Wisconsin–La Crosse, Office of University Graduate Studies, College of Science and Health, Department of Biology, La Crosse, WI 54601-3742. Offers aquatic sciences (MS); biology (MS); cellular and molecular biology (MS); clinical microbiology (MS); microbiology (MS); nurse anesthesia (MS); physiology (MS). Part-time programs available. *Faculty:* 21 full-time (8 women), 3 part-time/adjunct (1 woman). *Students:* 45 full-time (30 women), 47 part-time (22 women); includes 10 minority (1 Black or African American, non-Hispanic/Latino; 5 Asian, non-Hispanic/Latino; 3 Hispanic/Latino; 1 Two or more races, non-Hispanic/Latino), 3 international. Average age 28. 63 applicants, 46% accepted, 24 enrolled. In 2011, 23 master's awarded. *Degree requirements:* For master's, comprehensive exam, thesis. *Entrance requirements:* For master's, GRE General Test, minimum GPA of 2.85. Additional exam requirements/recommendations for international students: Required—TOEFL (minimum score 550 paper-based; 213 computer-based; 79 iBT). *Application deadline:* For fall admission, 2/1 priority date for domestic students, 2/1 for international students; for spring admission, 1/4 priority date for domestic students, 1/4 for international students. Applications are processed on a rolling basis. Application fee: $56. Electronic applications accepted. *Expenses:* Tuition, state resident: full-time $8391; part-time $481.17 per credit. Tuition, nonresident: full-time $17,850; part-time $1006.68 per credit. *Required fees:* $2 per credit. $18.25 per semester. Tuition and fees vary according to course load, program, reciprocity agreements and student level. *Financial support:* In 2011–12, 29 research assistantships with partial tuition reimbursements (averaging $9,712 per year) were awarded; Federal Work-Study, scholarships/grants, health care benefits, and tuition waivers (partial) also available. Support available to part-time students. Financial award application deadline: 3/15; financial award applicants required to submit FAFSA. *Unit head:* Dr. Thomas Volk, Coordinator of Graduate Studies, 608-785-6972, Fax: 608-785-6959, E-mail: volk.thom@uwlax.edu. *Application contact:* Kathryn Kiefer, Director of Admissions, 608-785-8939, E-mail: admissions@uwlax.edu. Web site: http://uwlax.edu/biology/.

University of Wisconsin–Madison, School of Medicine and Public Health and Graduate School, Graduate Programs in Medicine and College of Agricultural and Life Sciences, Microbiology Doctoral Training Program, Madison, WI 53706. Offers PhD. *Faculty:* 91 full-time (32 women). *Students:* 74 full-time (43 women); includes 11 minority (2 Black or African American, non-Hispanic/Latino; 9 Hispanic/Latino), 4 international. Average age 24. 252 applicants, 18% accepted, 20 enrolled. In 2011, 19 doctorates awarded. *Degree requirements:* For doctorate, thesis/dissertation, preliminary exam, 1semester of teaching, professional development requirement. *Entrance requirements:* For doctorate, GRE. Additional exam requirements/recommendations for international students: Required—TOEFL (minimum score 580 paper-based; 237 computer-based). *Application deadline:* For fall admission, 12/1 for domestic and international students. Application fee: $56. Electronic applications accepted. *Expenses:* Tuition, state resident: full-time $10,296; part-time $643.51 per credit. Tuition, nonresident: full-time $24,054; part-time $1503.40 per credit. *Required fees:* $70.06 per credit. Tuition and fees vary according to course load, campus/location, program and reciprocity agreements. *Financial support:* In 2011–12, 74 students received support, including 28 fellowships with tuition reimbursements available (averaging $24,500 per year), 46 research assistantships with tuition reimbursements available (averaging $24,500 per year); career-related internships or fieldwork, scholarships/grants, traineeships, health care benefits, and tuition waivers (full) also available. Financial award application deadline: 12/1. *Faculty research:* Microbial pathogenesis, gene regulation, immunology, virology, cell biology. *Total annual research expenditures:* $15.1 million. *Unit head:* Dr. John Mansfield, Director, 608-262-2596, Fax: 608-262-8418, E-mail: jmansfield@bact.wisc.edu. *Application contact:* Cathy Davis Gray, Coordinator, 608-265-0689, Fax: 608-262-8418, E-mail: cdg@bact.wisc.edu. Web site: http://www.microbiology.wisc.edu/.

University of Wisconsin–Oshkosh, Graduate Studies, College of Letters and Science, Department of Biology and Microbiology, Oshkosh, WI 54901. Offers biology (MS), including botany, microbiology, zoology. *Degree requirements:* For master's, comprehensive exam, thesis. *Entrance requirements:* For master's, GRE General Test, minimum GPA of 3.0, BS in biology. Additional exam requirements/recommendations for international students: Required—TOEFL (minimum score 550 paper-based; 213 computer-based; 79 iBT). Electronic applications accepted.

University of Wyoming, Graduate Program in Molecular and Cellular Life Sciences, Laramie, WY 82070. Offers PhD. *Degree requirements:* For doctorate, thesis/dissertation, four eight-week laboratory rotations, comprehensive basic practical exam, two-part qualifying exam, seminars, symposium.

Vanderbilt University, Graduate School and School of Medicine, Department of Microbiology and Immunology, Nashville, TN 37240-1001. Offers MS, PhD, MD/PhD. *Faculty:* 42 full-time (11 women). *Students:* 42 full-time (23 women); includes 7 minority (3 Black or African American, non-Hispanic/Latino; 3 Asian, non-Hispanic/Latino; 1 Hispanic/Latino), 6 international. Average age 27. In 2011, 7 degrees awarded. Terminal master's awarded for partial completion of doctoral program. *Degree requirements:* For master's, thesis; for doctorate, thesis/dissertation, final and qualifying exams. *Entrance requirements:* For master's and doctorate, GRE General Test, GRE Subject Test (recommended). Additional exam requirements/recommendations for international students: Required—TOEFL (minimum score 570 paper-based; 230 computer-based; 88 iBT). *Application deadline:* For fall admission, 1/15 for domestic and international students. Application fee: $0. Electronic applications accepted. *Financial support:* Fellowships with full tuition reimbursements, research assistantships with full tuition reimbursements, Federal Work-Study, institutionally sponsored loans, scholarships/

grants, traineeships, health care benefits, and tuition waivers (partial) available. Financial award application deadline: 1/15; financial award applicants required to submit CSS PROFILE or FAFSA. *Faculty research:* Cellular and molecular microbiology, viruses, genes, cancer, molecular pathogenesis of microbial diseases, immunobiology. *Unit head:* Dr. Samuel A. Santoro, Chair, 615-322-3234, Fax: 615-322-5551, E-mail: samuel.a.santoro@vanderbilt.edu. *Application contact:* Jean Tidwell, Administrative Assistant/Director of Graduate Studies Assistant, 615-343-3435, Fax: 615-343-7392, E-mail: jean.tidwell@vanderbilt.edu. Web site: http://www.mc.vanderbilt.edu/microbio/.

Virginia Commonwealth University, Medical College of Virginia-Professional Programs, School of Medicine, School of Medicine Graduate Programs, Department of Microbiology and Immunology, Richmond, VA 23284-9005. Offers microbiology and immunology (MS, PhD); MD/PhD. *Degree requirements:* For master's, thesis; for doctorate, thesis/dissertation, comprehensive oral and written exams. *Entrance requirements:* For master's and doctorate, GRE General Test or MCAT. Additional exam requirements/recommendations for international students: Required—TOEFL (minimum score 600 paper-based; 250 computer-based; 100 iBT). Electronic applications accepted. *Expenses:* Tuition, state resident: full-time $9133; part-time $507 per credit. Tuition, nonresident: full-time $18,777; part-time $1043 per credit. *Required fees:* $77 per credit. Tuition and fees vary according to degree level, campus/location, program and student level. *Faculty research:* Microbial physiology and genetics, molecular biology, crystallography of biological molecules, antibiotics and chemotherapy, membrane transport.

Virginia Commonwealth University, Program in Pre-Medical Basic Health Sciences, Richmond, VA 23284-9005. Offers anatomy (CBHS); biochemistry (CBHS); human genetics (CBHS); microbiology (CBHS); pharmacology (CBHS); physiology (CBHS). *Entrance requirements:* For degree, GRE, MCAT or DAT, course work in organic chemistry, minimum undergraduate GPA of 2.8. Additional exam requirements/recommendations for international students: Required—TOEFL (minimum score 600 paper-based). Electronic applications accepted. *Expenses:* Tuition, state resident: full-time $9133; part-time $507 per credit. Tuition, nonresident: full-time $18,777; part-time $1043 per credit. *Required fees:* $77 per credit. Tuition and fees vary according to degree level, campus/location, program and student level.

Virginia Polytechnic Institute and State University, Graduate School, Intercollege, Program in Microbiology, Blacksburg, VA 24061. Offers PhD. *Expenses:* Tuition, state resident: full-time $10,048; part-time $558.25 per credit hour. Tuition, nonresident: full-time $19,497; part-time $1083.25 per credit hour. *Required fees:* $405 per semester. Tuition and fees vary according to course load, campus/location and program. *Unit head:* Dr. Karen P. DePauw, Vice President and Dean for Graduate Education, 540-231-7581, Fax: 540-231-1670, E-mail: kpdepauw@vt.edu. *Application contact:* Jacqueline Nottingham, Director of Graduate Admissions and Academic Progress, 540-231-3092, Fax: 540-231-3750, E-mail: ntnghm@vt.edu.

Wagner College, Division of Graduate Studies, Department of Biological Sciences, Program in Microbiology, Staten Island, NY 10301-4495. Offers MS. Part-time and evening/weekend programs available. *Faculty:* 6 full-time (2 women), 4 part-time/adjunct (3 women). *Students:* 8 full-time (4 women), 3 part-time (0 women); includes 3 minority (2 Asian, non-Hispanic/Latino; 1 Hispanic/Latino). Average age 24. 10 applicants, 90% accepted, 7 enrolled. In 2011, 7 master's awarded. *Degree requirements:* For master's, comprehensive exam or thesis. *Entrance requirements:* For master's, minimum GPA of 2.6, proficiency in statistics, undergraduate major in biological science or chemistry, undergraduate microbiology course, 16 credits of chemistry including organic chemistry with lab. Additional exam requirements/recommendations for international students: Required—TOEFL (minimum score 550 paper-based; 217 computer-based; 79 iBT). *Application deadline:* For fall admission, 5/1 priority date for domestic students, 3/1 for international students; for spring admission, 12/1 for domestic students, 10/1 for international students. Applications are processed on a rolling basis. Application fee: $50 ($85 for international students). *Expenses: Tuition:* Full-time $16,200; part-time $890 per credit. *Financial support:* Career-related internships or fieldwork, unspecified assistantships, and alumni fellowship grant available. Financial award applicants required to submit FAFSA. *Unit head:* Dr. Roy Mosher, Director, 718-420-4072, E-mail: rmosher@wagner.edu. *Application contact:* Patricia Clancy, Administrative Assistant, 718-420-4464, Fax: 718-390-3105, E-mail: patricia.clancy@wagner.edu.

Wake Forest University, School of Medicine and Graduate School of Arts and Sciences, Graduate Programs in Medicine, Department of Microbiology and Immunology, Winston-Salem, NC 27109. Offers PhD, MD/PhD. *Degree requirements:* For doctorate, thesis/dissertation. *Entrance requirements:* For doctorate, GRE General Test. Additional exam requirements/recommendations for international students: Required—TOEFL. Electronic applications accepted. *Faculty research:* Molecular immunology, bacterial pathogenesis and molecular genetics, viral pathogenesis, regulation of mRNA metabolism, leukocyte biology.

Washington State University, Graduate School, College of Sciences, School of Molecular Biosciences, Program in Microbiology, Pullman, WA 99164. Offers MS, PhD. *Faculty:* 23 full-time (5 women), 21 part-time/adjunct (4 women). *Students:* 2 full-time (0 women). Average age 27. Terminal master's awarded for partial completion of doctoral program. *Degree requirements:* For master's, thesis, oral exam; for doctorate, comprehensive exam, thesis/dissertation, oral exam. *Entrance requirements:* For master's and doctorate, GRE General Test, minimum GPA of 3.0. Additional exam requirements/recommendations for international students: Required—TOEFL (minimum score 550 paper-based; 213 computer-based). *Application deadline:* For fall admission, 12/15 for domestic and international students. Application fee: $75. Electronic applications accepted. *Financial support:* In 2011–12, fellowships with full tuition reimbursements (averaging $18,852 per year), 2 research assistantships with full and partial tuition reimbursements (averaging $18,852 per year), 10 teaching assistantships with full and partial tuition reimbursements (averaging $18,852 per year) were awarded; Federal Work-Study, institutionally sponsored loans, health care benefits, and unspecified assistantships also available. Financial award application deadline: 4/1; financial award applicants required to submit FAFSA. *Faculty research:* Viral-host interaction, bacterial-host interaction, microbial medicine, microbial pathogenesis, cancer biology. *Total annual research expenditures:* $5.8 million. *Unit head:* Dr. John H. Nilson, Director, 509-335-8724, Fax: 509-335-9688, E-mail: jhn@wsu.edu. *Application contact:* Kelly G. McGovern, Academic Coordinator, 509-335-4566, Fax: 509-335-1907, E-mail: smbgrad@wsu.edu. Web site: http://molecular.biosciences.wsu.edu/.

Washington University in St. Louis, Graduate School of Arts and Sciences, Division of Biology and Biomedical Sciences, Program in Molecular Microbiology and Microbial Pathogenesis, St. Louis, MO 63130-4899. Offers PhD. *Degree requirements:* For doctorate, thesis/dissertation. *Entrance requirements:* For doctorate, GRE General Test, GRE Subject Test. Electronic applications accepted.

Wayne State University, School of Medicine, Department of Immunology and Microbiology, Detroit, MI 48202. Offers MS, PhD, MD/PhD. *Students:* 13 full-time (5 women); includes 2 minority (1 Black or African American, non-Hispanic/Latino; 1 Hispanic/Latino), 2 international. Average age 27. 17 applicants, 24% accepted, 3 enrolled. In 2011, 4 doctorates awarded. Terminal master's awarded for partial completion of doctoral program. *Degree requirements:* For doctorate, thesis/dissertation. *Entrance requirements:* For doctorate, GRE, minimum GPA of 3.0 in undergraduate degree. Additional exam requirements/recommendations for international students: Required—TOEFL (minimum score 600 paper-based; 250 computer-based; 100 iBT); Recommended—TWE (minimum score 6). *Application deadline:* For fall admission, 6/1 priority date for domestic students, 5/1 for international students. Application fee: $50. Electronic applications accepted. *Expenses:* Tuition, state resident: part-time $512.85 per credit. Tuition, nonresident: part-time $1132.65 per credit. *Required fees:* $26.60 per credit. $199.65 per semester. Tuition and fees vary according to course load and program. *Financial support:* In 2011–12, 2 fellowships with tuition reimbursements (averaging $20,097 per year), 10 research assistantships with tuition reimbursements (averaging $21,487 per year) were awarded; teaching assistantships with tuition reimbursements, career-related internships or fieldwork, Federal Work-Study, scholarships/grants, health care benefits, and unspecified assistantships also available. *Faculty research:* Immune regulation, bacterial pathophysiology, molecular biology/viruses/bacteria, cellular and molecular immunology, microbial pathogenesis. *Unit head:* Dr. Thomas Holland, Graduate Director, 313-577-1298, E-mail: thomas.holland@wayne.edu. Web site: http://www.med.wayne.edu/immunology/Pages/Graduate_Program.html.

West Virginia University, School of Medicine, Graduate Programs at the Health Sciences Center, Interdisciplinary Graduate Programs in Biomedical Sciences, Program in Immunology and Microbial Pathogenesis, Morgantown, WV 26506. Offers MS, PhD, MD/PhD. *Degree requirements:* For doctorate, comprehensive exam, thesis/dissertation. *Entrance requirements:* For doctorate, GRE General Test, minimum GPA of 3.0. Additional exam requirements/recommendations for international students: Required—TOEFL. Electronic applications accepted. *Faculty research:* Regulation of signal transduction in immune responses, immune responses in bacterial and viral diseases, peptide and DNA vaccines for contraception, inflammatory bowel disease, physiology of pathogenic microbes.

Wright State University, School of Graduate Studies, College of Science and Mathematics, Program in Microbiology and Immunology, Dayton, OH 45435. Offers MS. Part-time programs available. *Degree requirements:* For master's, thesis. *Entrance requirements:* Additional exam requirements/recommendations for international students: Required—TOEFL. *Faculty research:* Reproductive immunology, viral pathogenesis, virus-host cell interactions.

Yale University, School of Medicine and Graduate School of Arts and Sciences, Combined Program in Biological and Biomedical Sciences (BBS), Microbiology Track, New Haven, CT 06520. Offers PhD, MD/PhD. *Degree requirements:* For doctorate, thesis/dissertation. *Entrance requirements:* For doctorate, GRE General Test, GRE Subject Test. Additional exam requirements/recommendations for international students: Required—TOEFL. Electronic applications accepted.

Youngstown State University, Graduate School, College of Science, Technology, Engineering and Mathematics, Department of Biological Sciences, Youngstown, OH 44555-0001. Offers environmental biology (MS); molecular biology, microbiology, and genetic (MS); physiology and anatomy (MS). Part-time programs available. *Degree requirements:* For master's, comprehensive exam, thesis, oral review. *Entrance requirements:* For master's, GRE General Test, minimum GPA of 2.7. Additional exam requirements/recommendations for international students: Required—TOEFL. *Faculty research:* Cell biology, neurophysiology, molecular biology, neurobiology, gene regulation.

Virology

Baylor College of Medicine, Graduate School of Biomedical Sciences, Department of Molecular Virology and Microbiology, Houston, TX 77030-3498. Offers PhD, MD/PhD. *Faculty:* 43 full-time (13 women). *Students:* 35 full-time (16 women); includes 10 minority (1 Black or African American, non-Hispanic/Latino; 5 Asian, non-Hispanic/Latino; 4 Hispanic/Latino), 8 international. Average age 28. 83 applicants, 11% accepted, 3 enrolled. In 2011, 3 doctorates awarded. *Degree requirements:* For doctorate, thesis/dissertation, public defense. *Entrance requirements:* For doctorate, GRE General Test, GRE Subject Test (strongly recommended), minimum GPA of 3.0. Additional exam requirements/recommendations for international students: Required—TOEFL. *Application deadline:* For fall admission, 1/1 priority date for domestic students. Applications are processed on a rolling basis. Application fee: $0. Electronic applications accepted. *Financial support:* In 2011–12, 9 fellowships with full tuition reimbursements (averaging $29,000 per year), 26 research assistantships with full tuition reimbursements (averaging $29,000 per year) were awarded; career-related internships or fieldwork, Federal Work-Study, institutionally sponsored loans, health care benefits, and tuition waivers (full) also available. Financial award applicants required to submit FAFSA. *Faculty research:* Microbiology, viral molecular biology, bacterial molecular biology, microbial pathogenesis, microbial genomics. *Unit head:* Dr. Frank Ramig, Director, 713-798-4830, Fax: 713-798-5075, E-mail: rramig@bcm.edu. *Application contact:* Rosa Banegas, Graduate Program Administrator, 713-798-4472, Fax: 713-798-5075, E-mail: rbanegas@bcm.edu. Web site: http://www.bcm.edu/molvir/.

Baylor College of Medicine, Graduate School of Biomedical Sciences, Interdepartmental Program in Cell and Molecular Biology, Houston, TX 77030-3498. Offers biochemistry (PhD); cell and molecular biology (PhD); genetics (PhD); human genetics (PhD); immunology (PhD); microbiology (PhD); virology (PhD); MD/PhD. *Faculty:* 112 full-time (30 women). *Students:* 66 full-time (42 women); includes 21 minority (5 Black or African American, non-Hispanic/Latino; 1 American Indian or Alaska Native, non-Hispanic/Latino; 7 Asian, non-Hispanic/Latino; 8 Hispanic/Latino), 14 international. Average age 27. 126 applicants, 25% accepted, 14 enrolled. In 2011, 7 degrees awarded. *Median time to degree:* Of those who began their doctoral program in fall 2003, 82% received their degree in 8 years or less. *Degree requirements:* For doctorate, thesis/dissertation, public defense. *Entrance requirements:* For doctorate, GRE General Test, GRE Subject Test (strongly recommended), minimum GPA of 3.0.

Virology

Additional exam requirements/recommendations for international students: Required—TOEFL. *Application deadline:* For fall admission, 1/1 priority date for domestic students. Applications are processed on a rolling basis. Application fee: $0. Electronic applications accepted. *Financial support:* In 2011–12, 66 students received support, including 30 fellowships with full tuition reimbursements available (averaging $29,000 per year), 36 research assistantships with full tuition reimbursements available (averaging $29,000 per year); teaching assistantships, Federal Work-Study, institutionally sponsored loans, health care benefits, and tuition waivers (full) also available. Financial award applicants required to submit FAFSA. *Faculty research:* Molecular and cellular biology; cancer, aging and stem cells; genomics and proteomics; microbiome, molecular microbiology; infectious disease, immunology and translational research. *Unit head:* Dr. Susan Marriott, Director, 713-798-6557. *Application contact:* Lourdes Fernandez, Graduate Program Administrator, 713-798-6557, Fax: 713-798-6325, E-mail: cmbprog@bcm.edu. Web site: http://bcm.edu/cmb/.

Case Western Reserve University, School of Medicine and School of Graduate Studies, Graduate Programs in Medicine, Department of Molecular Biology and Microbiology, Program in Molecular Virology, Cleveland, OH 44106. Offers PhD. *Entrance requirements:* Additional exam requirements/recommendations for international students: Required—TOEFL (minimum score 550 paper-based; 213 computer-based).

Mayo Graduate School, Graduate Programs in Biomedical Sciences, Program in Virology and Gene Therapy, Rochester, MN 55905. Offers PhD.

McMaster University, Faculty of Health Sciences and School of Graduate Studies, Program in Medical Sciences, Hamilton, ON L8S 4M2, Canada. Offers blood and vascular (M Sc, PhD); genetics and cancer (M Sc, PhD); immunity and infection (M Sc, PhD); metabolism and nutrition (M Sc, PhD); neurosciences and behavioral sciences (M Sc, PhD); physiology/pharmacology (M Sc, PhD); MD/PhD. *Degree requirements:* For master's, thesis; for doctorate, comprehensive exam, thesis/dissertation. *Entrance requirements:* For master's, honors B Sc, B+ average in related field; for doctorate, M Sc, minimum B+ average. Additional exam requirements/recommendations for international students: Required—TOEFL (minimum score 580 paper-based; 237 computer-based; 92 iBT).

The Ohio State University, College of Medicine, School of Biomedical Science, Integrated Biomedical Science Graduate Program, Columbus, OH 43210. Offers immunology (PhD); medical genetics (PhD); molecular virology (PhD); pharmacology (PhD). *Degree requirements:* For doctorate, thesis/dissertation. *Entrance requirements:* For doctorate, GRE, GRE Subject Test in biochemistry, cell and molecular biology (recommended for some). Additional exam requirements/recommendations for international students: Required—TOEFL (minimum score 600 paper-based; 250 computer-based). Electronic applications accepted. *Expenses:* Tuition, state resident: full-time $11,400. Tuition, nonresident: full-time $28,125. Tuition and fees vary according to course load, degree level, campus/location and program.

Penn State Hershey Medical Center, College of Medicine, Graduate School Programs in the Biomedical Sciences, Graduate Program in Biomedical Sciences, Hershey, PA 17033. Offers biochemistry and molecular genetics (PhD); biomedical sciences (MS, PhD); translational therapeutics (MS, PhD); virology and immunology (MS, PhD); MD/PhD; PhD/MBA. *Students:* 12 full-time (6 women); includes 2 minority (1 Black or African American, non-Hispanic/Latino; 1 Asian, non-Hispanic/Latino), 1 international. 211 applicants, 16% accepted, 12 enrolled. Terminal master's awarded for partial completion of doctoral program. *Degree requirements:* For master's, thesis (for some programs); for doctorate, comprehensive exam, thesis/dissertation, candidacy exam. *Entrance requirements:* For doctorate, GRE General Test. Additional exam requirements/recommendations for international students: Required—TOEFL (minimum score 550 paper-based; 213 computer-based; 80 iBT). *Application deadline:* For fall admission, 1/1 for domestic students, 2/1 for international students. Applications are processed on a rolling basis. Application fee: $65. Electronic applications accepted. *Financial support:* In 2011–12, research assistantships (averaging $23,028 per year) were awarded; fellowships, scholarships/grants, health care benefits, and unspecified assistantships also available. Financial award applicants required to submit FAFSA. *Unit head:* Dr. Ralph L. Keil, Chair, 717-531-8595, Fax: 717-531-0388, E-mail: rlk9@psu.edu. *Application contact:* Karen Shields, Administrative Support Coordinator, 717-531-1045, Fax: 717-531-0388, E-mail: kpb2@psu.edu. Web site: http://med.psu.edu/web/biomedical-sciences/home.

Penn State Hershey Medical Center, College of Medicine, Graduate School Programs in the Biomedical Sciences, Graduate Program in Microbiology and Immunology, Hershey, PA 17033. Offers genetics (PhD); immunology (MS, PhD); microbiology (MS); microbiology/virology (PhD); molecular biology (PhD); MD/PhD. *Students:* 18 full-time (9 women), 6 international. 59 applicants, 5% accepted, 3 enrolled. In 2011, 1 master's, 3 doctorates awarded. Terminal master's awarded for partial completion of doctoral program. *Degree requirements:* For master's, thesis or alternative; for doctorate, comprehensive exam, thesis/dissertation, oral exam. *Entrance requirements:* For doctorate, GRE General Test, minimum GPA of 3.0. Additional exam requirements/recommendations for international students: Required—TOEFL. *Application deadline:* For fall admission, 1/31 priority date for domestic students, 2/1 for international students. Applications are processed on a rolling basis. Application fee: $65. Electronic applications accepted. *Financial support:* In 2011–12, research assistantships with full tuition reimbursements (averaging $23,028 per year) were awarded; fellowships with full tuition reimbursements, scholarships/grants, health care benefits, and unspecified assistantships also available. Financial award applicants required to submit FAFSA. *Faculty research:* Virus replication and assembly, oncogenesis, interactions of viruses with host cells and animal model systems. *Unit head:* Dr. Aron Luckacher, Chair, 717-531-7659, Fax: 717-531-6522, E-mail: micro-grad-hmc@psu.edu. *Application contact:* Billie Burns, Secretary, 717-531-7659, Fax: 717-531-6522, E-mail: micro-grad-hmc@psu.edu. Web site: http://www.pennstatehershey.org/web/microbiology/programs.

Purdue University, Graduate School, PULSe - Purdue University Life Sciences Program, West Lafayette, IN 47907. Offers biomolecular structure and biophysics (PhD); biotechnology (PhD); chemical biology (PhD); chromatin and regulation of gene expression (PhD); integrative neuroscience (PhD); integrative plant sciences (PhD); membrane biology (PhD); microbiology (PhD); molecular evolutionary and cancer biology (PhD); molecular evolutionary genetics (PhD); molecular virology (PhD). *Students:* 90 full-time (45 women); includes 7 minority (3 Black or African American, non-Hispanic/Latino; 1 Asian, non-Hispanic/Latino; 2 Hispanic/Latino; 1 Two or more races, non-Hispanic/Latino), 40 international. Average age 26. 427 applicants, 24% accepted, 35 enrolled. *Entrance requirements:* For doctorate, GRE test required, minimum undergraduate GPA of 3.0. Additional exam requirements/recommendations for international students: Required—TOEFL (minimum score 550 paper-based; 77 iBT). *Application deadline:* For fall admission, 1/15 priority date for domestic students, 1/15 for international students. Applications are processed on a rolling basis. Application fee: $60 ($75 for international students). Electronic applications accepted. *Financial support:* In 2011–12, research assistantships with tuition reimbursements (averaging $22,500 per year), teaching assistantships with tuition reimbursements (averaging $22,500 per year) were awarded. *Unit head:* Dr. Christine A. Hrycyna, Head, 765-494-7322, E-mail: hrycyna@purdue.edu. *Application contact:* Emily E. Bramson, Graduate Contact, 765-494-5865, E-mail: bramson@purdue.edu. Web site: http://www.gradschool.purdue.edu/pulse.

Purdue University, School of Veterinary Medicine and Graduate School, Graduate Programs in Veterinary Medicine, Department of Comparative Pathobiology, West Lafayette, IN 47907-2027. Offers comparative epidemiology and public health (MS); comparative epidemiology and public heath (PhD); comparative microbiology and immunology (MS, PhD); comparative pathobiology (MS, PhD); interdisciplinary studies (PhD), including microbial pathogenesis, molecular signaling and cancer biology, molecular virology; lab animal medicine (MS); veterinary anatomic pathology (MS); veterinary clinical pathology (MS). Terminal master's awarded for partial completion of doctoral program. *Degree requirements:* For master's, thesis (for some programs); for doctorate, thesis/dissertation. *Entrance requirements:* For master's and doctorate, GRE General Test. Additional exam requirements/recommendations for international students: Required—TOEFL (minimum score 575 paper-based; 232 computer-based), IELTS (minimum score 6.5), TWE (minimum score 4). Electronic applications accepted.

Rush University, Graduate College, Division of Immunology and Microbiology, Program in Immunology/Microbiology, Chicago, IL 60612-3832. Offers immunology (MS, PhD); virology (MS, PhD); MD/PhD. Part-time programs available. Terminal master's awarded for partial completion of doctoral program. *Degree requirements:* For master's, thesis; for doctorate, thesis/dissertation, comprehensive preliminary exam. *Entrance requirements:* For master's, GRE General Test; for doctorate, GRE General Test, interview, minimum GPA of 3.0. Additional exam requirements/recommendations for international students: Required—TOEFL. Electronic applications accepted. *Faculty research:* Human genetics, autoimmunity, tumor biology, complement, HIV immunopathology genesis.

Rutgers, The State University of New Jersey, New Brunswick, Graduate School-New Brunswick, Programs in the Molecular Biosciences, Program in Microbiology and Molecular Genetics, Piscataway, NJ 08854-8097. Offers applied microbiology (MS, PhD); clinical microbiology (MS, PhD); computational molecular biology (PhD); immunology (MS, PhD); microbial biochemistry (MS, PhD); molecular genetics (MS, PhD); virology (MS, PhD). MS, PhD offered jointly with University of Medicine and Dentistry of New Jersey. Part-time programs available. Terminal master's awarded for partial completion of doctoral program. *Degree requirements:* For master's, comprehensive exam, thesis or alternative; for doctorate, comprehensive exam, thesis/dissertation, written qualifying exam. *Entrance requirements:* For master's, GRE General Test, minimum GPA of 3.0; for doctorate, GRE General Test, GRE Subject Test (recommended), minimum GPA of 3.0. Additional exam requirements/recommendations for international students: Required—TOEFL. Electronic applications accepted. *Faculty research:* Molecular genetics and microbial physiology; virology and pathogenic microbiology; applied, environmental and industrial microbiology; computers in molecular biology.

Texas A&M Health Science Center, College of Medicine, Department of Microbial and Molecular Pathogenesis, College Station, TX 77840. Offers immunology (PhD); microbiology (PhD); molecular biology (PhD); virology (PhD). *Degree requirements:* For doctorate, thesis/dissertation. *Entrance requirements:* For doctorate, GRE General Test, minimum GPA of 3.0. *Faculty research:* Molecular pathogenesis, microbial therapeutics.

Université de Montréal, Faculty of Veterinary Medicine, Program in Virology and Immunology, Montréal, QC H3C 3J7, Canada. Offers PhD. Program offered jointly with Université du Québec, Institut Armand-Frappier. *Degree requirements:* For doctorate, thesis/dissertation, general exam. *Entrance requirements:* For doctorate, proficiency in French, knowledge of English. Electronic applications accepted.

Université du Québec, Institut National de la Recherche Scientifique, Graduate Programs, Research Center - INRS - Institut Armand-Frappier - Human Health, Québec, QC G1K 9A9, Canada. Offers applied microbiology (M Sc); biology (PhD); experimental health sciences (M Sc); virology and immunology (M Sc, PhD). Programs given in French. Part-time programs available. *Faculty:* 41. *Students:* 158 full-time (93 women), 11 part-time (5 women), 52 international. Average age 30. In 2011, 17 master's, 9 doctorates awarded. *Degree requirements:* For master's, thesis optional; for doctorate, thesis/dissertation. *Entrance requirements:* For master's and doctorate, appropriate bachelor's degree, proficiency in French. *Application deadline:* For fall admission, 3/30 for domestic and international students; for winter admission, 11/1 for domestic and international students; for spring admission, 3/1 for domestic and international students. Application fee: $45 Canadian dollars. *Financial support:* In 2011–12, 128 students received support, including fellowships (averaging $16,500 per year); research assistantships also available. *Faculty research:* Immunity, infection and cancer; toxicology and environmental biotechnology; molecular pharmacochemistry. *Unit head:* Charles Dozois, Director, 450-687-5010, Fax: 450-686-5566, E-mail: charles.dozois@iaf.inrs.ca. *Application contact:* Yvonne Boisvert, Registrar, 418-654-3861, Fax: 418-654-3858, E-mail: registrariat@adm.inrs.ca. Web site: http://www.iaf.inrs.ca.

University of California, San Diego, Office of Graduate Studies, Division of Biological Sciences, Program in Immunology, Virology, and Cancer Biology, La Jolla, CA 92093. Offers PhD. Offered in association with the Salk Institute. *Degree requirements:* For doctorate, thesis/dissertation, qualifying exam. Electronic applications accepted.

The University of Iowa, Roy J. and Lucille A. Carver College of Medicine and Graduate College, Graduate Programs in Medicine, Department of Microbiology, Iowa City, IA 52242-1316. Offers general microbiology and microbial physiology (MS, PhD); immunology (MS, PhD); microbial genetics (MS, PhD); pathogenic bacteriology (MS, PhD); virology (MS, PhD). *Faculty:* 23 full-time (5 women), 12 part-time/adjunct (4 women). *Students:* 37 full-time (24 women); includes 3 minority (2 American Indian or Alaska Native, non-Hispanic/Latino; 1 Hispanic/Latino), 4 international. Average age 25. 56 applicants, 16% accepted, 4 enrolled. In 2011, 1 master's, 6 doctorates awarded. *Degree requirements:* For master's, thesis; for doctorate, comprehensive exam, thesis/dissertation. *Entrance requirements:* For master's and doctorate, GRE General Test. Additional exam requirements/recommendations for international students: Required—TOEFL (minimum score 600 paper-based; 250 computer-based). *Application deadline:* For fall admission, 1/1 for domestic and international students. Application fee: $60 ($85 for international students). Electronic applications accepted. *Financial support:* In 2011–12, 4 fellowships with full tuition reimbursements (averaging $25,500 per year), 33 research assistantships with full tuition reimbursements (averaging $25,500 per year) were awarded; institutionally sponsored loans, scholarships/grants, traineeships, and health care benefits also available. *Faculty research:* Gene regulation, processing and transport of HIV, retroviral pathogenesis, biodegradation, biofilm. *Total annual research expenditures:* $12.6 million. *Unit head:* Dr. Patrick M. Schlievert, Head, 319-335-7810, E-mail: grad-micro-info@uiowa.edu. *Application contact:* Betty Wood, Associate Director of Admissions, 319-335-1525, Fax: 319-335-1535, E-mail: admissions@uiowa.edu. Web site: http://www.uiowa.edu/microbiology/.

University of Massachusetts Worcester, Graduate School of Biomedical Sciences, Worcester, MA 01655-0115. Offers biochemistry and molecular pharmacology (PhD); bioinformatics and computational biology (PhD); cancer biology (PhD); cell biology (PhD); clinical and population health research (PhD); clinical investigation (MS); immunology and virology (PhD); interdisciplinary graduate program (PhD); molecular genetics and microbiology (PhD); neuroscience (PhD); DVM/PhD; MD/PhD. *Faculty:*

1,427 full-time (526 women), 309 part-time/adjunct (196 women). *Students:* 416 full-time (225 women); includes 47 minority (12 Black or African American, non-Hispanic/Latino; 32 Asian, non-Hispanic/Latino; 3 Hispanic/Latino), 144 international. Average age 29. 623 applicants, 17% accepted, 54 enrolled. In 2011, 5 master's, 63 doctorates awarded. Terminal master's awarded for partial completion of doctoral program. *Degree requirements:* For master's, comprehensive exam, thesis; for doctorate, comprehensive exam, thesis/dissertation. *Entrance requirements:* For master's, bachelor's degree; for doctorate, GRE General Test. Additional exam requirements/recommendations for international students: Required—TOEFL (minimum score 600 paper-based; 250 computer-based; 100 iBT) or IELTS (minimum score 7.5). *Application deadline:* For fall admission, 12/15 for domestic and international students; for spring admission, 5/15 for domestic students. Application fee: $50. Electronic applications accepted. *Expenses:* Contact institution. *Financial support:* In 2011–12, 416 students received support, including 416 research assistantships with full tuition reimbursements available (averaging $29,200 per year); scholarships/grants, health care benefits, tuition waivers (full), and unspecified assistantships also available. Financial award application deadline: 4/16. *Faculty research:* RNA interference, cell biology, bioinformatics, clinical research, infectious disease. *Total annual research expenditures:* $262.7 million. *Unit head:* Dr. Anthony Carruthers, Dean, 508-856-4135, E-mail: anthony.carruthers@umassmed.edu. *Application contact:* Dr. Kendall Knight, Associate Dean and Interim Director of Admissions and Recruitment, 508-856-5628, Fax: 508-856-3659, E-mail: kendall.knight@umassmed.edu. Web site: http://www.umassmed.edu/gsbs/.

University of Minnesota, Twin Cities Campus, Graduate School, PhD Program in Microbiology, Immunology and Cancer Biology, Minneapolis, MN 55455-0213. Offers PhD. *Degree requirements:* For doctorate, thesis/dissertation. *Entrance requirements:* For doctorate, GRE General Test. Additional exam requirements/recommendations for international students: Required—TOEFL (minimum score 600 paper-based; 250 computer-based). Electronic applications accepted. *Faculty research:* Virology, microbiology, cancer biology, immunology.

University of Pennsylvania, Perelman School of Medicine, Biomedical Graduate Studies, Graduate Group in Cell and Molecular Biology, Philadelphia, PA 19104. Offers cancer biology (PhD); cell biology and physiology (PhD); developmental stem cell regenerative biology (PhD); gene therapy and vaccines (PhD); genetics and gene regulation (PhD); microbiology, virology, and parasitology (PhD); MD/PhD; VMD/PhD. *Faculty:* 306. *Students:* 337 full-time (186 women); includes 81 minority (16 Black or African American, non-Hispanic/Latino; 43 Asian, non-Hispanic/Latino; 16 Hispanic/Latino; 6 Two or more races, non-Hispanic/Latino), 41 international. 585 applicants, 21% accepted, 58 enrolled. In 2011, 42 doctorates awarded. *Degree requirements:* For doctorate, thesis/dissertation. *Entrance requirements:* For doctorate, GRE General Test. Additional exam requirements/recommendations for international students: Required—TOEFL. *Application deadline:* For fall admission, 12/1 priority date for domestic students, 12/1 for international students. Applications are processed on a rolling basis. Application fee: $80. Electronic applications accepted. *Expenses: Tuition:* Full-time $26,660; part-time $4944 per course. *Required fees:* $2318; $291 per course. Tuition and fees vary according to course load, degree level and program. *Financial support:* In 2011–12, 337 students received support. Fellowships, research assistantships, scholarships/grants, traineeships, and unspecified assistantships available. *Unit head:* Dr. Daniel Kessler, Graduate Group Chair. *Application contact:* Meagan Schofer, Coordinator. Web site: http://www.med.upenn.edu/camb/.

University of Pittsburgh, School of Medicine, Graduate Programs in Medicine, Program in Molecular Virology and Microbiology, Pittsburgh, PA 15260. Offers MS, PhD. *Faculty:* 46 full-time (11 women). *Students:* 24 full-time (12 women); includes 2 minority (1 Hispanic/Latino; 1 Native Hawaiian or other Pacific Islander, non-Hispanic/Latino), 3 international. Average age 27. 514 applicants, 12% accepted, 24 enrolled. In 2011, 2 doctorates awarded. *Degree requirements:* For doctorate, comprehensive exam, thesis/dissertation. *Entrance requirements:* For doctorate, GRE General Test, GRE Subject Test, minimum QPA of 3.0. Additional exam requirements/recommendations for international students: Required—TOEFL (minimum score 600 paper-based; 100 iBT), IELTS (minimum score 7). *Application deadline:* For fall admission, 12/15 priority date for domestic students, 12/15 for international students. Application fee: $50. Electronic applications accepted. *Expenses:* Tuition, state resident: full-time $18,774; part-time $760 per credit. Tuition, nonresident: full-time $30,736; part-time $1258 per credit. *Required fees:* $740; $200 per term. Tuition and fees vary according to program. *Financial support:* In 2011–12, 1 fellowship (averaging $25,500 per year), 23 research assistantships with full tuition reimbursements (averaging $25,500 per year) were awarded; institutionally sponsored loans, scholarships/grants, traineeships, health care benefits, and unspecified assistantships also available. *Faculty research:* Host-pathogen interactions, persistent microbial infections, microbial genetics and gene expression, microbial pathogenesis, anti-bacterial therapeutics. *Unit head:* Dr. Neal A. DeLuca, Graduate Program Director, 412-648-9947, Fax: 412-624-0298, E-mail: ndeluca@pitt.edu. *Application contact:* Graduate Studies Administrator, 412-648-8957, Fax: 412-648-1077, E-mail: gradstudies@medschool.pitt.edu. Web site: http://www.gradbiomed.pitt.edu.

University of Prince Edward Island, Atlantic Veterinary College, Graduate Program in Veterinary Medicine, Charlottetown, PE C1A 4P3, Canada. Offers anatomy (M Sc, PhD); bacteriology (M Sc, PhD); clinical pharmacology (M Sc, PhD); clinical sciences (M Sc, PhD); epidemiology (M Sc, PhD), including reproduction; fish health (M Sc, PhD); food animal nutrition (M Sc, PhD); immunology (M Sc, PhD); microanatomy (M Sc, PhD); parasitology (M Sc, PhD); pathology (M Sc, PhD); pharmacology (M Sc, PhD); physiology (M Sc, PhD); toxicology (M Sc, PhD); veterinary science (M Vet Sc); virology (M Sc, PhD). Part-time programs available. *Degree requirements:* For master's, thesis; for doctorate, thesis/dissertation. *Entrance requirements:* For master's, DVM, B Sc honors degree, or equivalent; for doctorate, M Sc. Additional exam requirements/recommendations for international students: Required—TOEFL (minimum score 550 paper-based; 213 computer-based; 80 iBT). *Expenses:* Contact institution. *Faculty research:* Animal health management, infectious diseases, fin fish and shellfish health, basic biomedical sciences, ecosystem health.

The University of Texas Health Science Center at Houston, Graduate School of Biomedical Sciences, Program in Virology and Gene Therapy, Houston, TX 77225-0036. Offers MS, PhD, MD/PhD. Terminal master's awarded for partial completion of doctoral program. *Degree requirements:* For master's, thesis; for doctorate, thesis/dissertation. *Entrance requirements:* For master's and doctorate, GRE General Test. Additional exam requirements/recommendations for international students: Required—TOEFL. Electronic applications accepted. *Faculty research:* Viruses, infectious diseases, vaccines, gene therapy, cancer.

The University of Texas Medical Branch, Graduate School of Biomedical Sciences, Center for Biodefense and Emerging Infectious Diseases, Galveston, TX 77555. Offers biodefense training (PhD). *Entrance requirements:* For doctorate, GRE, minimum overall GPA of 3.0.

The University of Texas Medical Branch, Graduate School of Biomedical Sciences, Program in Emerging and Tropical Infectious Diseases, Galveston, TX 77555. Offers PhD, MD/PhD. *Degree requirements:* For doctorate, thesis/dissertation. *Entrance requirements:* For doctorate, GRE General Test. *Faculty research:* Emerging diseases, tropical diseases, parasitology, vitology and bacteriology.

Yale University, School of Medicine and Graduate School of Arts and Sciences, Combined Program in Biological and Biomedical Sciences (BBS), Microbiology Track, New Haven, CT 06520. Offers PhD, MD/PhD. *Degree requirements:* For doctorate, thesis/dissertation. *Entrance requirements:* For doctorate, GRE General Test, GRE Subject Test. Additional exam requirements/recommendations for international students: Required—TOEFL. Electronic applications accepted.

UNIFORMED SERVICES UNIVERSITY OF THE HEALTH SCIENCES

F. Edward Hébert School of Medicine
Graduate Program in Emerging Infectious Diseases

Program of Study

One of the missions of the Uniformed Services University (USU) is to provide both civilians and military students with high-quality training leading to advanced degrees in the biomedical sciences. The Graduate Program in Emerging Infectious Diseases (EID) is designed for applicants who wish to pursue an interdisciplinary program of study leading to the Ph.D. degree and was created for students who are primarily interested in the pathogenesis, host response, and epidemiology of infectious diseases. No M.S. degree program is currently offered. A broadly based core program of formal training is combined with an intensive laboratory research experience in the different disciplines encompassed by the field of infectious diseases. Courses are taught by an interdisciplinary EID faculty who hold primary appointments in the Departments of Microbiology and Immunology, Pathology, Preventive Medicine and Biometrics, Pediatrics, and Medicine. Research training emphasizes modern methods in molecular biology and cell biology, as well as interdisciplinary approaches.

During the first two years, all students are required to complete a series of broadly based core courses and laboratory rotations. Students also select one of three academic tracks in which to focus the remainder of their course work. The three tracks are microbiology and immunology, pathology, and preventive medicine/parasitology. Advanced course work is required in each academic track. In addition, each student selects a faculty member with whom he or she would like to carry out a thesis research project. By the end of the second year, the student must complete all requirements for advancement to candidacy for the Ph.D. degree, which includes satisfactory completion of formal course work and passage of the qualifying examination. After advancement to candidacy, the student must complete an original research project and prepare and defend a written dissertation under the supervision of his or her faculty adviser and an advisory committee.

Research Facilities

Each academic department of the University is provided with laboratories for the support of a variety of research projects. Laboratories are available in most areas of study that encompass the interdisciplinary field of emerging infectious diseases, including both basic and medical aspects of bacteriology, bacterial genetics, virology, cellular and molecular immunology, parasitology, pathogenic mechanisms of disease, pathology of infectious disease, and epidemiology of infectious diseases. Resources available to students within the University include real-time PCR, microarray spotters and readers, EPICS, FACSAria and LSRII cell sorters and analyzers, Luminex 100 analyzer, automated oligonucleotide and peptide synthesizers and sequencing, MALDI-TOF Mass Spectrometer, high-resolution electron microscopes, confocal microscopes, a certified central animal facility, and state-of-the-art computer facilities. In addition, a BSL-3 biohazard containment laboratory suite is available. The library/learning resources center houses more than 521,000 bound volumes, subscribes to nearly 3,000 journals (print and online), and maintains 100 IBM and Macintosh personal computers for use by students, faculty members, and staff members. Biostatisticians serve as a resource for students and faculty members.

Financial Aid

Stipends are available for civilian applicants. Awards of stipends are competitive, are for one-year periods, and may be renewed. The 2012–13 stipend level begins at $27,000 per year. Special fellowships are also available.

Cost of Study

Graduate students in the Emerging Infectious Diseases Program are not required to pay tuition or fees. Civilian students do not incur obligations to the United States government for service after completion of their graduate training programs.

Living and Housing Costs

There is a reasonable supply of affordable rental housing in the area. The University does not have housing for graduate students. Living costs in the greater Washington, D.C., area are comparable to those of other East Coast metropolitan areas.

Student Group

The first full-time graduate students were admitted to the EID program in 2000. There are currently 41 full-time students enrolled in the EID graduate program. The University also has Ph.D. programs in departmentally based basic biomedical sciences, as well as interdisciplinary graduate programs in molecular and cell biology and in neurosciences.

Location

The greater Washington metropolitan area has a population of about 3 million that includes the District of Columbia and the surrounding areas of Maryland and Virginia. The region is a center of education and research and is home to five major universities, four medical schools, and numerous other internationally recognized private and government research centers. In addition, multiple cultural advantages exist in the area and include theaters, a major symphony orchestra, major-league sports, and world-famous museums. The Metro subway system has a station adjacent to the campus and provides a convenient connection from the University to cultural attractions and activities in downtown Washington. The international community in Washington is the source of many diverse cuisines and international cultural events. For a wide variety of outdoor activities, the Blue Ridge Mountains, Chesapeake Bay, and Atlantic coast beaches are all within a 1- to 3-hour drive. Many national and local parks serve the area for weekend hikes, bicycling, and picnics.

The University

USU is located just outside Washington, D.C., in Bethesda, Maryland. The campus is situated in an attractive, park-like setting on the grounds of the Walter Reed National Military Medical Center (WRNMMC) and across the street from the National Institutes of Health (NIH). Wooded areas with jogging and biking trails surround the University. NIH and other research institutes in the area provide additional resources to enhance the education experience of graduate students at USU. Students can visit the USUHS Web site at http://www.usuhs.mil/eid.

Applying

The Admissions Committee, in consultation with other faculty members, evaluates applications to the program. Each applicant must submit an application form, complete academic transcripts of postsecondary education, and results of the Graduate Record Examinations. No GRE Subject Test is required. In addition, three letters of recommendation from individuals familiar with the academic achievements and/or research experience of the applicant are required, as well as a personal statement that expresses the applicant's career objectives. USU subscribes fully to the policy of

equal educational opportunity and selects students on a competitive basis without regard to race, color, gender, creed, or national origin. Application forms may be obtained from the University Web site (available at http://ieb.usuhs.mil/gapp/). Completed applications should be received on or before January 1.

Both civilians and military personnel are eligible to apply. Prior to acceptance, each applicant must complete a baccalaureate degree that includes required courses in mathematics, biology, physics, and chemistry (inorganic, organic, and biochemistry). Advanced-level courses in microbiology, molecular biology, genetics, and cell biology are very strongly recommended. All students are expected to have a reasonable level of computer literacy. Active-duty military applicants must obtain the approval and sponsorship of their parent military service, in addition to acceptance into the EID graduate program.

Correspondence and Information

Dr. Eleanor S. Metcalf
Associate Dean for Graduate Education
Uniformed Services University
4301 Jones Bridge Road
Bethesda, Maryland 20814-4755
United States
Phone: 800-772-1747 (toll-free)
Web site: http://www.usuhs.mil

Dr. Christopher C. Broder, Director
Graduate Program in Emerging Infectious Diseases
Uniformed Services University
4301 Jones Bridge Road
Bethesda, Maryland 20814-4755
United States
Phone: 301-295-5749
Fax: 301-295-9861
E-mail: Christopher.broder@usuhs.edu
Web site: http://www.usuhs.mil/eid

THE FACULTY

The interdisciplinary graduate programs at USU are superimposed on the departmental structure. Therefore, all faculty members in the interdisciplinary Graduate Program in Emerging Infectious Diseases (EID) have primary appointments in either a basic science or a clinical department and secondary appointments in EID. The faculty is derived primarily from the Departments of Microbiology and Immunology, Pathology, Preventive Medicine and Biometrics, Pediatrics, and Medicine. Thus, the faculty in EID includes the experts in infectious diseases, regardless of department. For additional information, students should visit the USU Academic Department Web site at http://www.usuhs.mil/academic.html. To address e-mail to specific faculty members at USU, students should use the first letter of their first name plus the last name and @usuhs.mil as the address; for example, to send e-mail to John Doe, the address would be jdoe@usuhs.mil.

Nicole L. Achee, Ph.D.; Research Assistant Professor, Preventive Medicine and Biometrics.

Richard G. Andre, Ph.D.; Professor, Preventive Medicine and Biometrics.

Naomi E. Aronson, M.D.; Professor, Medicine.

Christopher C. Broder, Ph.D.; Professor, Microbiology and Immunology.

Timothy Burgess, M.D., M.P.H.; Assistant Professor, Medicine.

Drusilla L. Burns, Ph.D.; Adjunct Assistant Professor, CBER, FDA.

Richard M. Conran, M.D., Ph.D.; Professor, Pathology.

David F. Cruess, Ph.D.; Professor, Preventive Medicine and Biometrics.

Stephen J. Davies, Ph.D.; Associate Professor, Microbiology and Immunology.

Saibal Dey, Ph.D.; Adjunct Assistant Professor, Biochemistry.

Andre T. Dubois, M.D., Ph.D.; Professor, Medicine.

Michael W. Ellis, M.D.; Assistant Professor, Medicine.

Chou-Zen Giam, Ph.D.; Professor, Microbiology and Immunology.

Scott W. Gordon, Ph.D.; Adjunct Assistant Professor, Preventive Medicine and Biometrics.

John Grieco, Ph.D.; Assistant Professor, Preventive Medicine and Biometrics.

Patricia Guerry, Ph.D.; Assistant Professor, Immunology, NMRC.

Val G. Hemming, M.D.; Professor, Pediatrics.

John W. Huggins, Ph.D.; Adjunct Assistant Professor, Virology, USAMRIID.

Ann E. Jerse, Ph.D.; Professor, Microbiology and Immunology.

Elliott Kagan, M.D.; Professor, Pathology.

Johnan Kaleeba, Ph.D.; Assistant Professor, Microbiology and Immunology.

Barbara Knollman-Ritschel, M.D.; Associate Professor, Pathology.

Tadeusz J. Kochel, Ph.D.; Adjunct Assistant Professor, Immunology, NMRC.

Philip R. Krause, M.D.; Assistant Professor, CBER, FDA.

Larry W. Laughlin, M.D., Ph.D.; Professor, Preventive Medicine and Biometrics.

Radha K. Maheshwari, Ph.D.; Professor, Pathology.

Joseph Mattapallil, Ph.D.; Assistant Professor, Microbiology and Immunology.

Anthony T. Maurelli, Ph.D.; Professor, Microbiology and Immunology.

Ernest L. Maynard, Ph.D.; Assistant Professor, Biochemistry and Molecular Biology.

D. Scotty Merrell, Ph.D.; Associate Professor, Microbiology and Immunology.

Eleanor S. Metcalf, Ph.D.; Professor, Microbiology and Immunology.

Nelson L. Michael, M.D., Ph.D.; Adjunct Assistant Professor, Medicine.

Edward Mitre, M.D.; Assistant Professor, Microbiology and Immunology.

Alison D. O'Brien, Ph.D.; Professor, Microbiology and Immunology.

Christian F. Ockenhouse, M.D., Ph.D.; Adjunct Assistant Professor, Infectious Diseases, WRAIR.

Martin G. Ottolini, M.D.; Associate Professor, Pediatrics.

Gerald V. Quinnan Jr., M.D.; Professor, Preventive Medicine and Biometrics.

Allen L. Richards, Ph.D.; Associate Professor, Preventive Medicine and Biometrics.

Capt. Stephen J. Savarino, MC, USN; Adjunct Assistant Professor, Infectious Diseases, NMRC.

Brian C. Schaefer, Ph.D.; Associate Professor, Microbiology and Immunology.

Connie S. Schmaljohn, Ph.D.; Adjunct Assistant Professor, USAMRIID.

Frank P. Shewmaker, Ph.D.; Assistant Professor, Pharmacology.

Clifford M. Snapper, M.D.; Professor, Pathology.

Andrew L. Snow, Ph.D.; Assistant Professor, Pharmacology.

Shanmuga Sozhamannan, Ph.D.; Adjunct Assistant Professor, Biological Defense Research, NMRC.

V. Ann Stewart, D.V.M., Ph.D.; Assistant Professor, Preventive Medicine and Biometrics.

J. Thomas Stocker, M.D.; Professor, Pathology.

Charles Via, M.D.; Assistant Professor, Pathology.

Shuishu Wang, Ph.D.; Assistant Professor, Biochemistry.

Lt. Col. Glenn W. Wortmann, MC, USA; Adjunct Assistant Professor, Infectious Diseases, WRAIR.

Shuenn-Jue L. Wu, Ph.D.; Adjunct Associate Professor, Immunology, NMRC.

Pengfei Zhang, Ph.D.; Research Associate Professor, Preventive Medicine and Biometrics.

UNIVERSITY OF CONNECTICUT HEALTH CENTER

Graduate Program in Immunology

Program of Study

A Ph.D. in immunology is offered through an interdepartmental program consisting of approximately 15 faculty members. The immunology faculty members also participate in training students in the combined M.D./Ph.D. and D.M.D./Ph.D. programs. The central focus of the program is to train students to become independent investigators who will provide meaningful research and educational contributions to the areas of basic, applied, or clinical immunology. This goal is achieved by lectures, seminars, laboratory rotations, research presentations, and a concentration on laboratory research. In addition to basic and advanced immunology courses, students are given a strong foundation in biomedical sciences through the core curriculum in biochemistry, genetics, molecular biology, and cell biology. Research laboratory training aims to provide a foundation in modern laboratory techniques and concentrates on hypothesis-based analysis of problems. Research in the program is focused on the cellular and molecular aspects of immune system structure and function in animal models and in humans. Areas of emphasis include molecular immunology (mechanisms of antigen presentation, major histocompatibility complex genetics and function, cytokines and cytokine receptors, and tumor antigens), cellular immunology (biochemical mechanisms and biological aspects of signal transduction of lymphocytes and granulocytes; cellular and molecular requirements for thymic T-lymphocyte development, selection, and activation; cytokines in B- and T-cell development; regulation of antitumor immunity; immunoparasitology, including parasite genetics and immune recognition of parasite antigens; and mechanisms of inflammation), organ-based immunology (immune effector mechanisms of the intestine, lymphocyte interactions in the lung, and immune regulation of the eye), immunity to infectious agents (viruses, bacteria, parasites, including vector-borne organisms), and autoimmunity (animal models of autoimmune disease and effector mechanisms in human autoimmunity).

Research Facilities

The Graduate Program in Immunology is interdepartmental, and therefore provides a broad base of training possibilities as well as ample shared facilities. State-of-the-art equipment is available in individual laboratories for analysis of molecular and cellular parameters of immune system structure and function. In addition, Health Center–supported facilities provide equipment and expertise in areas of advanced data acquisition and analysis. These facilities include the Center for Cell Analysis and Modeling, the Fluorescence Flow Cytometry Facility, the Gene Targeting and Transgenic Facility, the Molecular Core Facility, the Microarray Facility, the Gregory P. Mullen Structural Biology Facility, and the Electron Microscopy Facility. The Health Center Library is well equipped with extensive journal and book holdings and rapid electronic access to database searching, the World Wide Web, and library holdings. A computer center is also housed in the library for student use and training.

Financial Aid

Support for doctoral students engaged in full-time degree programs at the Health Center is provided on a competitive basis. Graduate research assistantships for 2012–13 provide a stipend of $28,000 per year, which includes a waiver of tuition/University fees for the fall and spring semesters and a student health insurance plan. While financial aid is offered competitively, the Health Center makes every possible effort to address the financial needs of all students.

Cost of Study

For 2012–13, tuition is $10,836 per year for full-time students who are Connecticut residents and $28,116 per year for full-time out-of-state residents. General University fees are added to the cost of tuition for students who do not receive a tuition waiver. These costs are usually met by traineeships or research assistantships for doctoral students.

Living and Housing Costs

There is a wide range of affordable housing options in the greater Hartford area within easy commuting distance of the campus, including an extensive complex that is adjacent to the Health Center. Costs range from $600 to $900 per month for a one-bedroom unit; 2 or more students sharing an apartment usually pay less. University housing is not available.

Student Group

At present, there are approximately 15 students in the Graduate Program in Immunology. There are 150 students in the various Ph.D. programs on the Health Center campus.

Student Outcomes

Graduates have traditionally been accepted into high-quality laboratories for postdoctoral training. Following their training, graduates have accepted a wide range of positions in research in universities, colleges, research institutes, and industry, including the biotechnology sector.

Location

The Health Center is located in the historic town of Farmington, Connecticut. Set in the beautiful New England countryside on a hill overlooking the Farmington Valley, it is close to ski areas, hiking trails, and facilities for boating, fishing, and swimming. Connecticut's capital city of Hartford, 7 miles east of Farmington, is the center of an urban region of approximately 800,000 people. The beaches of the Long Island Sound are about 50 minutes away to the south, and the beautiful Berkshires are a short drive to the northwest. New York City and Boston can be reached within 2½ hours by car. Hartford is the home of the acclaimed Hartford Stage Company, TheatreWorks, the Hartford Symphony and Chamber orchestras, two ballet companies, an opera company, the Wadsworth Atheneaum (the oldest public art museum in the nation), the Mark Twain house, the Hartford Civic Center, and many other interesting cultural and recreational facilities. The area is also home to several branches of the University of Connecticut, Trinity College, and the University of Hartford, which includes the Hartt School of Music. Bradley International Airport (about 30 minutes from campus) serves the Hartford/Springfield area with frequent airline connections to major cities in this country and abroad. Frequent bus and rail service is also available from Hartford.

The Health Center

The 200-acre Health Center campus at Farmington houses a division of the University of Connecticut Graduate School, as well as the School of Medicine and Dental Medicine. The campus also includes the John Dempsey Hospital, associated clinics, and

extensive medical research facilities, all in a centralized facility with more than 1 million square feet of floor space. The Health Center's newest research addition, the Academic Research Building, was opened in 1999. This impressive eleven-story structure provides 170,000 square feet of state-of-the-art laboratory space. The faculty at the center includes more than 260 full-time members. The institution has a strong commitment to graduate study within an environment that promotes social and intellectual interaction among the various educational programs. Graduate students are represented on various administrative committees concerned with curricular affairs, and the Graduate Student Organization (GSO) represents graduate students' needs and concerns to the faculty and administration, in addition to fostering social contact among graduate students in the Health Center.

Applying

Applications for admission should be submitted via the online application system and should be filed together with transcripts, three letters of recommendation, a personal statement, and recent results from the General Test of the Graduate Record Examinations. International students must take the Test of English as a Foreign Language (TOEFL) to satisfy Graduate School requirements. The deadline for completed applications and receipt of all supplemental materials is **December 1**. Please note that GRE and TOEFL exams taken after the due date will not be accepted for consideration for admission. In accordance with the laws of the state of Connecticut and of the United States, the University of Connecticut Health Center does not discriminate against any person in its educational and employment activities on the grounds of race, color, creed, national origin, sex, age, or physical disability.

Correspondence and Information

Graduate Admissions Office
Ph.D. in Biomedical Science Program
University of Connecticut Health Center
263 Farmington Ave., MC 3906
Farmington, Connecticut 06030-3906
United States
Phone: 860-679-4509
E-mail: BiomedSciAdmissions@uchc.edu
Web site: http://grad.uchc.edu/prospective/programs/phd_biosci/index.html

THE FACULTY AND THEIR RESEARCH

Adam J. Adler, Associate Professor of Immunology; Ph.D., Columbia. Mechanisms of T-cell tolerance induction to peripheral self- and tumor-antigens; immunological properties of prostate cancer.

Hector L. Aguila, Assistant Professor of Immunology; Ph.D., Yeshiva (Einstein). Hematopoiesis and bone marrow microenvironment; lymphoid cell development; stem cell biology.

Linda Cauley, Assistant Professor of Immunology; D.Phil., Oxford. T-cell memory and respiratory virus infections.

Robert B. Clark, Associate Professor of Immunology; M.D., Stanford. Autoimmunity; immune regulation; regulatory T cells.

Chi-Kuang Huang, Associate Professor of Immunology; Ph.D., Connecticut. Signal transduction in stimulated neutrophil and lymphocytes; roles of protein kinase and phosphoproteins in cell activation; chemotaxis.

Kamal Khanna, Assistant Professor of Immunology; Ph.D., Pittsburgh. Identifying the factors and the role they play in controlling the anatomy of a primary and secondary immune response in the hopes of explicating the underlying mechanisms that guide the complex movement of T cells during infection and recall responses in lymphoid and non-lymphoid tissues.

Leo Lefrancois, Professor of Immunology; Ph.D., Wake Forest. T-cell memory; immune response to infection; tolerance; vaccines.

Joseph A. Lorenzo, Professor of Medicine; M.D., SUNY Downstate Medical Center. Relationships between bone-absorbing osteoclasts and immune cells.

Lynn Puddington, Associate Professor of Immunology; Ph.D., Wake Forest. Allergic asthma; neonatal immunity and tolerance; developmental immunology.

Justin D. Radolf, Professor of Medicine and Center for Microbial Pathogenesis; M.D., California, San Francisco. Molecular pathogenesis and immunobiology of spirochetal infections.

Pramod K. Srivastava, Professor of Medicine; Ph.D., Hyderabad (India). Heat shock proteins as peptide chaperones; roles in antigen presentation and applications in immunotherapy of cancer, infectious diseases, and autoimmune disorders.

Roger S. Thrall, Professor of Immunology and Surgery; Ph.D., Marquette. Immune cells; pulmonary inflammation.

Anthony T. Vella, Associate Professor of Immunology; Ph.D., Cornell. T-cell immunity; costimulation; adjuvants and cytokines.

Richard A. Zeff, Associate Professor of Immunology; Ph.D., Rush. Major histocompatibility complex; antigen processing and presentation.

UNIVERSITY OF MASSACHUSETTS AMHERST

Department of Microbiology

Programs of Study

The Department of Microbiology at the University of Massachusetts Amherst (UMass) offers programs of graduate study leading to the M.S. and Ph.D. degrees in microbiology. Postdoctoral training is also available. Courses covering various areas in the field of microbiology are offered by the Departmental faculty members, listed in the Faculty and Their Research section.

In the Ph.D. program, formal course work is completed during the first two years. From the start, a large portion of a student's time is dedicated to research. Students actively participate in ongoing research during two 1-semester rotations and then select dissertation problems from the wide spectrum of research areas pursued by the faculty. The following research fields are represented: microbial physiology, genetics, immunology, parasitology, pathogenic bacteriology, molecular biology, microbial ecology, and environmental microbiology. In the second year, Ph.D. candidates must pass a comprehensive preliminary examination. Degree requirements are completed by submission and defense of a dissertation. There is no foreign language requirement. Completion of the Ph.D. program generally takes four years beyond the bachelor's degree.

Research Facilities

The Department of Microbiology occupies space in the Morrill Science Center. Laboratories are spacious and well equipped for research and teaching. State-of-the-art equipment necessary for investigation into all aspects of microbiology is available within the Department. The Department's facilities include tissue- and cell-culture laboratories, animal quarters, and various instrument rooms containing preparative and analytical ultracentrifuges, scintillation counters, fermentors, anaerobic chambers, equipment for chromatographic and electrophoretic procedures, photography, and other standard laboratory procedures. Centralized facilities provide state-of-the-art equipment and expertise to support research projects, such as the Central Microscopy Facility, Genomics and Bioinformatics Facility, High Field NMR Facility, and Mass Spectrometry Facility.

Financial Aid

Financial aid is available in the form of University fellowships and teaching assistantships. Research assistantships are available for advanced graduate students. All assistantships include a waiver of tuition.

Cost of Study

In academic year 2012–13, annual tuition for in-state residents is $110 per credit; nonresident tuition is $414 per credit. Full-time students register for at least 9 credits per semester. The mandatory fees assessed for full-time graduate students (9 credits) is $5169 per semester for in-state residents and $8100 for nonresidents. Note: These fees include tuition and curriculum fees which are waived with eligible graduate assistantships. Fees are subject to change. More information on fees is available in the Bursar's Office fee schedule online at http://www.umass.edu/bursar/index.html.

Living and Housing Costs

Graduate student housing is available in several twelve-month campus residence halls through University Housing Services. The University owns and manages unfurnished apartments of various sizes for family housing on or near the campus. Off-campus housing is available; rents vary widely and depend on factors such as size and location. A free bus system connects UMass with all neighboring communities.

Student Group

The Department has approximately 40 graduate and 150 undergraduate students as well as 20 postdoctoral fellows. Enrollment at the Amherst campus is about 26,000, including 4,000 graduate students.

Location

The 1,450-acre campus of the University provides a rich cultural environment in a rural setting. Amherst is situated in the picturesque Pioneer Valley in historic western Massachusetts. The area is renowned for its natural beauty. Green open land framed by the outline of the Holyoke Range, clear streams, country roads, forests, grazing cattle, and shade trees are characteristic of the region. A broad spectrum of cultural activities and extensive recreational facilities are available within the University and at four neighboring colleges—Smith, Amherst, Mount Holyoke, and Hampshire. Opportunities for outdoor winter sports are exceptional. Amherst is 90 miles west of Boston and 175 miles north of New York City, and Cape Cod is a 3½-hour drive away.

The University

The University of Massachusetts is the state university of the Commonwealth of Massachusetts and is the flagship campus of the five-campus UMass system. Departments affiliated with the ten colleges and schools of the University offer a variety of graduate degrees through the Graduate School. The Amherst campus consists of approximately 150 buildings, including the twenty-eight-story W. E. B. DuBois Library, which is the largest at a state-supported institution in New England. The library features more than 5.8 million items and is home to a state-of-the-art learning commons equipped with computer workstations and high-speed network access.

Applying

Application forms may be obtained from the Graduate Admissions Office, 530 Goodell Building, University of Massachusetts, 140 Hicks Way, Amherst, Massachusetts 01003-9333, or online at http://www.umass.edu/gradschool. Prospective students are required to take the Graduate Record Examinations. Applications for admission should be received by the Graduate Admissions Office by December 20 for September enrollment and by October 1 for January enrollment. Applications received after these dates are considered only if space is available.

Correspondence and Information

Graduate Program Director
Department of Microbiology
Morrill IV, N203
639 North Pleasant Street
University of Massachusetts Amherst
Amherst, Massachusetts 01003-9298
United States
Phone: 413-545-2051
Fax: 413-545-1578
E-mail: microbio-dept@microbio.umass.edu
Web site: http://www.micro.umass.edu

University of Massachusetts Amherst

THE FACULTY AND THEIR RESEARCH

J. M. Lopes, Professor and Department Head; Ph.D., South Carolina. Regulation of gene expression in eukaryotes. *Mol. Microbiol.* 83:395, 2012; *Eukaryot. Cell* 9:1845, 2010; *Mol. Microbiol.* 70:1529, 2008.

C. L. Baldwin, Adjunct Professor; Ph.D., Cornell. Cellular immunity to intracellular microbial parasites, including *Brucella abortus,* with particular interest in the interaction of the microbe with macrophages and the control of infection by T-cell cytokines; role of gamma delta T cells in host immunity to bacterial pathogens including mycobacteria and leptospira. *J. Infect. Dis.* 206:91, 2012; *J. Infect. Dis.* 203:1136, 2012; *Mol. Immunol.* 48:801, 2011; *BMC Evol. Biol.*10:181, 2010; *Science* 324:522–8, 2009; *BMC Genom.* 10:191, 2009.

J. P. Burand, Professor; Ph.D., Washington State. Biology and molecular biology of insect pathogenic viruses, particularly nonoccluded insect viruses and bee viruses, with emphasis on virus-host interactions that affect the virulence and persistence of these viruses in insects. *Viruses* 4:28–61, 2012; *J. Invertebr. Pathol.* 108:217–9, 2011; *Appl. Environ. Micro.* 75:7862–5, 2009; *Virol. Sin.* 24:428–35, 2009; *Arch. Virol.* 154:909–18, 2009.

P. Chien, Adjunct Assistant Professor; Ph.D., California, San Francisco. Protein degradation during bacterial cell-cycle progression. *Protein Sci.* 19(2):242–54, 2010; *Mol. Microbiol.* 73(4):586–600, 2009; *Structure* 15(10):1296–305, 2007; *Proc. Natl. Acad. Sci. Unit. States Am.* 104(16):6590–5, 2007.

D. R. Cooley, Adjunct Associate Professor; Ph.D., Massachusetts. Ecology of diseases; plant pathogenic fungi and bacteria; plant disease management; integrated pest management; development of sustainable agricultural systems.

S. Goodwin, Dean, College of Natural Sciences; Ph.D., Wisconsin.

K. L. Griffith, Assistant Professor; Ph.D., Maryland. Cell-cell signaling in bacteria; development of tools for studying regulatory networks. *J. Mol. Bio.* 381:261–75, 2008; *Mol. Microbiol.* 70:1012–25, 2008.

J. F. Holden, Associate Professor; Ph.D., Washington (Seattle). Physiology of hyperthermophilic archaea; geomicrobiology of geothermal environments, thermophilic bioenergy. *Proc. Natl. Acad. Sci. Unit. States Am.,* in press; *Oceanography* 25:196–208, 2012; *Appl. Environ. Microbiol.* 77:3169–73, 2011.

M. M. Klingbeil, Associate Professor; Ph.D., Toledo. Molecular and biochemical parasitology, replication and repair of mitochondrial DNA (kinetoplast DNA) and nuclear DNA replication initiation in African trypanosomes. *Eukaryot. Cell* 11:844–55, 2012; *Eukaryot. Cell* 10:734–43, 2011; *Mol. Biochem. Parasitol.* 175:68–75, 2011; *Mol. Microbiol.* 75:1414–25, 2010; *Mol. Cell* 5:398–400, 2009; *Eukaryot. Cell* 7:2141–6, 2008; *Science* 309:409–15, 2005; *Proc. Natl. Acad. Sci. U.S.A.* 101:4333–4, 2004; *J. Biol. Chem.* 278:49095–101, 2003; *Mol. Cell* 10:175–86, 2002; *Protist* 152:255–62, 2001.

D. R. Lovley, Distinguished University Professor; Ph.D., Michigan State. Genome-enabled study of the physiology, ecology, and evolution of novel anaerobic microorganisms; microbe-electrode interactions with a focus on novel bioenergy solutions; direct electron exchange between microorganisms; bioremediation of metal and organic contamination; life in extreme environments. *Nature Nanotechnology* 6:573–9, 2011; *Adv. Microb. Physiol.* 59:1–100, 2011; *Nat. Rev. Microbiol.* 9:39–50, 2011; *Science* 330:1413–5, 2010; *Nature* 435:1098–101, 2005; *Science* 301:934, 2003; *Nature* 416:767–9, 2002; *Science* 295:483–5, 2002; *Nature* 415:312–6, 2002.

L. Ma, Adjunct Assistant Professor; Ph.D., SUNY College of Environmental Science and Forestry. Comparative fungal genomics: A gateway toward understanding genome innovation and adaptation. *Nature* 465:367–73, 2010; *BMC Genom.* 11:208, 2010; *PLoS Genetics* 5(7):e1000549, 2009.

W. J. Manning, Adjunct Professor; Ph.D., Delaware. Effects of ozone on plants and associated mycoflora; plants as bioindicators of ozone; effects of ozone and other air pollutants on plants in urban environments; managing invasive plants with fungal pathogens. *Environ. Pollut.* 126:73–81, 2003.

S. Nugen, Adjunct Assistant Professor; Ph.D., Cornell. Food and water pathogen detection; rapid biosensor technology; microfluidic assay development; nanofabrication; diagnostics for low resource settings. *Microsystem Technologies* 18(6):731–37, 2012; *Biosensors* 2(1):32–42, 2012. *Sensors & Transducers Journal* 13:150–8, 2011; *J. Vet. Sci.* 10(1):35–42, 2009; *Biosens. Bioelectron.* 24(8):2428–33, 2009.

K. Nüsslein, Associate Professor; Ph.D., Michigan State. Microbial ecology of terrestrial and aquatic environments; relating the stress of environmental influences to community structure and function, with emphasis on understanding interactions among bacterial communities. *Front. Extr. Microbiol.* 3:175, 2012; *Appl. Microbiol. Biotechnol.* 2:6, 2012; *Biointerfaces* 87(1):109–15, 2011; *Water Res.* 44:4970–9, 2010; *Curr. Opin. Biotechnol.* 21:339–45, 2010; *Geomicrobiology* 26:9–20, 2009; *Geology* 36:139–42, 2008; *Chemosphere* 70:329–36. 2007; *Appl. Environ. Microbiol.* 73:4171–9, 2007; *FEMS Microb. Ecol.* 60:60–73, 2006; *Microb. Ecol.* 51:441–52, 2006.

S. T. Petsch, Adjunct Associate Professor; Ph.D., Yale. Transport, transformation, and biodegradation of natural organic matter in sediments, soils, and sedimentary rocks. *Geology,* 36:139–42, 2008; *Appl. Environ. Microbiol.* 73:4171–9, 2007; *Geochim. Cosmochim. Acta* 71:4233–50, 2007; *SEPM* 5:5–9, 2007; *Am. J. Sci.* 306:575–615, 2006; *Palaeogeogr. Palaeoclim. Palaeoecol.* 219:157–70, 2005; *Gas Technol. Inst.* GRI-05/0023, 2004; *Am. J. Sci.* 304:234–49, 2004; *Org. Geochem.* 34:731–43, 2003.

S. M. Rich, Associate Professor; Ph.D. California, Irvine. Population genetics and evolution of vectorborne and zoonotic diseases. *Proc. Natl. Acad. Sci. Unit. States Am.* 106:14902–7; *Emerg. Infect. Dis.* 15:585–7; *Gene* 304:65–75; *Proc. Natl. Acad. Sci. Unit. States Am.* 98:15038–43; *J. Clin. Microbiol.* 39:494–7; *Proc. Natl. Acad. Sci. Unit. States Am.* 95:4425–30; *Proc. Natl. Acad. Sci. Unit. States Am.* 94:13040–45; *Insect Mol. Biol.* 6:123–9; *Proc. Natl. Acad. Sci. Unit. States Am.* 92:6284–8.

S. J. Sandler, Professor; Ph.D., Berkeley. Molecular genetics of recombination; DNA replication and DNA repair in bacteria. *Mol. Microbiol.* 57:1074, 2005; *Mol. Microbiol.* 53:1343, 2004.

W. Webley, Associate Professor; Ph.D., Massachusetts. Immunology and pathogenic bacteriology; understanding the role and mechanism of *Chlamydia* involvement in chronic severe asthma; design and development of a novel multi-subunit vaccine display/delivery system for *Chlamydia;* design of a point-of-care diagnostic test for Chlamydia infections in farm animals. *Plos One* 7(4), 2012; *Resp. Res.* 13(1):32, 2012; *Eur. Respir. J.* 38(4)994–5, 2011; *Respirology* 16(7):1081–7, 2011; *Pediatr. Infect. Dis. J.,* 29(12):1093–8, 2010; *Eur. Respir. J.,* 33:1–8, 2009; *Biology of AIDS,* 2nd ed., Dubuque, Iowa: Kendall/Hunt Publishing Company, 2008; *CHEST* 134(suppl.), 2008; *CHEST* 132(4):607, 2007; *J. Clin. Apheresis* 3, 2006; *BMC Infect. Dis.* 6:23, 2006; *Am. J. Respir. Crit. Care Med.* 171(10):1083–8, 2005; *BMC Infect. Dis.* 4(1):23, 2004 (with Stuart and Norkin); *Curr. Microbiol.* 49(1):13–21, 2004; *Am. J. Respir. Crit. Care Med.* 169(7):A586, 2004; *J. Clin. Apheresis* 18(2), 2003; *Exp. Cell Res.* 287(1):67–78, 2003.

H. Xiao, Adjunct Assistant Professor; Ph.D., Wisconsin–Madison. Cancer preventive dietary components, diet-based strategy for cancer prevention, enhancement of biological activity of dietary components by combination regimen, food processing, and nanotechnology.

Section 13
Neuroscience and Neurobiology

This section contains a directory of institutions offering graduate work in neuroscience and neurobiology, followed by in-depth entries submitted by institutions that chose to prepare detailed program descriptions. Additional information about programs listed in the directory but not augmented by an in-depth entry may be obtained by writing directly to the dean of a graduate school or chair of a department at the address given in the directory.

For programs offering related work, see also in this book *Anatomy; Biochemistry; Biological and Biomedical Sciences; Biophysics; Cell, Molecular, and Structural Biology; Genetics, Developmental Biology, and Reproductive Biology; Optometry and Vision Sciences; Pathology and Pathobiology; Pharmacology and Toxicology; Physiology;* and *Zoology.* In another guide in this series:

Graduate Programs in the Humanities, Arts & Social Sciences
See *Psychology and Counseling*

CONTENTS

Biopsychology

Adler School of Professional Psychology, Programs in Psychology, Chicago, IL 60602. Offers advanced Adlerian psychotherapy (Certificate); art therapy (MA); clinical neuropsychology (Certificate); clinical psychology (Psy D); community psychology (MA); counseling and organizational psychology (MA); counseling psychology (MA); forensic psychology (MA); gerontological counseling (MA); marriage and family counseling (MA); marriage and family therapy (Certificate); organizational psychology (MA); police psychology (MA); rehabilitation counseling (MA); sport and health psychology (MA); substance abuse counseling (Certificate); Psy D/Certificate; Psy D/MACAT; Psy D/MACP; Psy D/MAMFC; Psy D/MASAC. *Accreditation:* APA. Part-time and evening/weekend programs available. Postbaccalaureate distance learning degree programs offered (minimal on-campus study). Terminal master's awarded for partial completion of doctoral program. *Degree requirements:* For master's, thesis or alternative, oral exam, practicum; for doctorate, thesis/dissertation, clinical exam, internship, oral exam, practicum, written qualifying exam. *Entrance requirements:* For master's, 12 semester hours in psychology, minimum GPA of 3.0; for doctorate, 18 semester hours in psychology, minimum GPA of 3.25; for Certificate, appropriate master's or doctoral degree. Additional exam requirements/recommendations for international students: Required—TOEFL (minimum score 550 paper-based; 213 computer-based; 79 iBT). Electronic applications accepted.

American University, College of Arts and Sciences, Department of Psychology, Washington, DC 22016-8062. Offers behavior, cognition, and neuroscience (PhD), including psychology; clinical psychology (PhD), including psychology; psychobiology of healing (Certificate); psychology (MA), including experimental/biological psychology, general psychology, personality/social psychology. *Accreditation:* APA. Part-time programs available. *Faculty:* 20 full-time (8 women), 3 part-time/adjunct (2 women). *Students:* 69 full-time (55 women), 51 part-time (38 women); includes 20 minority (4 Black or African American, non-Hispanic/Latino; 6 Asian, non-Hispanic/Latino; 7 Hispanic/Latino; 3 Two or more races, non-Hispanic/Latino), 4 international. Average age 27. 474 applicants, 17% accepted, 39 enrolled. In 2011, 21 master's, 9 doctorates awarded. *Degree requirements:* For master's, comprehensive exam, thesis or alternative; for doctorate, comprehensive exam, thesis/dissertation, tools of research. *Entrance requirements:* For master's, GRE General Test, GRE Subject Test; for doctorate, GRE General Test, GRE Subject Test, 3 letters of recommendation. Additional exam requirements/recommendations for international students: Required—TOEFL. Application fee: $80. *Expenses: Tuition:* Full-time $24,264; part-time $1348 per credit hour. *Required fees:* $430. Tuition and fees vary according to course load and program. *Financial support:* Fellowships, research assistantships, teaching assistantships, career-related internships or fieldwork, Federal Work-Study, institutionally sponsored loans, tuition waivers (full and partial), and unspecified assistantships available. Support available to part-time students. Financial award application deadline: 2/1. *Faculty research:* Anxiety disorders, cognitive assessment, neuropsychology, conditioning and learning, psychopharmacology. *Unit head:* Dr. Anthony Riley, Chair, 202-885-1720, Fax: 202-885-1023, E-mail: alriley@american.edu. *Application contact:* Sara Holland, Senior Administrative Assistant, 202-885-1717, Fax: 202-885-1023, E-mail: holland@american.edu. Web site: http://www.american.edu/CAS/Psychology/.

Argosy University, Atlanta, College of Psychology and Behavioral Sciences, Atlanta, GA 30328. Offers clinical psychology (MA, Psy D, Postdoctoral Respecialization Certificate), including child and family psychology (Psy D), general adult clinical (Psy D), health psychology (Psy D), neuropsychology/geropsychology (Psy D); community counseling (MA), including marriage and family therapy; counselor education and supervision (Ed D); forensic psychology (MA); industrial organizational psychology (MA); marriage and family therapy (Certificate); sport-exercise psychology (MA). *Accreditation:* APA.

Argosy University, Twin Cities, College of Psychology and Behavioral Sciences, Eagan, MN 55121. Offers clinical psychology (MA, Psy D), including child and family psychology (Psy D), forensic psychology (Psy D), health and neuropsychology (Psy D), trauma (Psy D); forensic counseling (Post-Graduate Certificate); forensic psychology (MA); industrial organizational psychology (MA); marriage and family therapy (MA, DMFT), including forensic counseling (MA). *Accreditation:* AAMFT; AAMFT/COAMFTE; APA.

Boston University, School of Medicine, Division of Graduate Medical Sciences, Program in Mental Health Counseling and Behavioral Medicine, Boston, MA 02215. Offers MA. *Faculty:* 8 full-time (4 women), 7 part-time/adjunct (3 women). *Students:* 59 full-time (54 women); includes 11 minority (4 Black or African American, non-Hispanic/Latino; 5 Asian, non-Hispanic/Latino; 2 Hispanic/Latino), 2 international. Average age 24. 53 applicants, 75% accepted, 25 enrolled. In 2011, 29 master's awarded. *Entrance requirements:* For master's, GRE General Test. Additional exam requirements/recommendations for international students: Required—TOEFL. *Application deadline:* Applications are processed on a rolling basis. Application fee: $75. *Expenses: Tuition:* Full-time $40,848; part-time $1276 per credit hour. *Required fees:* $572; $286 per semester. *Financial support:* In 2011–12, 6 students received support. Research assistantships available. Financial award applicants required to submit FAFSA. *Faculty research:* HIV/AIDS, trauma, behavioral medicine (obesity, breast cancer), neurosciences, autism, serious mental illness, sports psychology. *Unit head:* Dr. Stephen Brady, Director, 617-414-2320, Fax: 617-414-2323, E-mail: sbrady@bu.edu. *Application contact:* Bernice Mark, Administrative Assistant, 617-414-2328, E-mail: nicey@bu.edu. Web site: http://www.bumc.bu.edu/mhbm/.

Brown University, Graduate School, Department of Psychology, Providence, RI 02912. Offers behavioral neuroscience (PhD); cognitive processes (PhD); sensation and perception (PhD); social/developmental (PhD); MS/PhD. *Accreditation:* APA. *Degree requirements:* For doctorate, thesis/dissertation. *Entrance requirements:* For doctorate, GRE General Test, GRE Subject Test.

Carnegie Mellon University, College of Humanities and Social Sciences, Department of Psychology, Area of Cognitive Neuroscience, Pittsburgh, PA 15213-3891. Offers PhD. *Degree requirements:* For doctorate, comprehensive exam, thesis/dissertation. *Entrance requirements:* For doctorate, GRE General Test. Additional exam requirements/recommendations for international students: Required—TOEFL.

Columbia University, Graduate School of Arts and Sciences, Division of Natural Sciences, Department of Psychology, New York, NY 10027. Offers experimental psychology (M Phil, MA, PhD); psychobiology (M Phil, MA, PhD); social psychology (M Phil, MA, PhD); JD/MA; JD/PhD; MD/PhD. *Degree requirements:* For master's, thesis; for doctorate, thesis/dissertation. *Entrance requirements:* For master's and doctorate, GRE General Test. Additional exam requirements/recommendations for international students: Required—TOEFL.

Cornell University, Graduate School, Graduate Fields of Arts and Sciences, Field of Psychology, Ithaca, NY 14853-0001. Offers biopsychology (PhD); human experimental psychology (PhD); personality and social psychology (PhD). *Faculty:* 41 full-time (16 women). *Students:* 38 full-time (23 women); includes 7 minority (1 Black or African American, non-Hispanic/Latino; 4 Asian, non-Hispanic/Latino; 1 Hispanic/Latino; 1 Two or more races, non-Hispanic/Latino), 10 international. Average age 28. 266 applicants, 5% accepted, 7 enrolled. In 2011, 3 degrees awarded. *Degree requirements:* For doctorate, comprehensive exam, thesis/dissertation, 2 semesters of teaching experience. *Entrance requirements:* For doctorate, GRE General Test, 3 letters of recommendation. Additional exam requirements/recommendations for international students: Required—TOEFL (minimum score 550 paper-based; 213 computer-based; 77 iBT). *Application deadline:* For fall admission, 12/15 for domestic students. Application fee: $95. Electronic applications accepted. *Financial support:* In 2011–12, 11 fellowships with full tuition reimbursements, 3 research assistantships with full tuition reimbursements, 21 teaching assistantships with full tuition reimbursements were awarded; institutionally sponsored loans, scholarships/grants, health care benefits, tuition waivers (full and partial), and unspecified assistantships also available. Financial award applicants required to submit FAFSA. *Faculty research:* Sensory and perceptual systems, social cognition, cognitive development, quantitative and computational modeling, behavioral neuroscience. *Unit head:* Director of Graduate Studies, 607-255-6364, Fax: 607-255-8433. *Application contact:* Graduate Field Assistant, 607-255-3834, Fax: 607-255-8433, E-mail: psychapp@cornell.edu. Web site: http://www.gradschool.cornell.edu/fields.php?id-62&a-2.

Drexel University, College of Arts and Sciences, Department of Psychology, Philadelphia, PA 19104-2875. Offers clinical psychology (PhD), including clinical psychology, forensic psychology, health psychology, neuropsychology; law-psychology (PhD); psychology (MS); JD/PhD. *Accreditation:* APA (one or more programs are accredited). *Degree requirements:* For doctorate, thesis/dissertation, internship. *Entrance requirements:* For doctorate, GRE General Test. Additional exam requirements/recommendations for international students: Required—TOEFL. Electronic applications accepted. *Expenses:* Contact institution. *Faculty research:* Neurosciences, rehabilitation psychology, cognitive science, neurological assessment.

Duke University, Graduate School, Department of Psychology and Neuroscience, Durham, NC 27708. Offers biological psychology (PhD); clinical psychology (PhD); cognitive psychology (PhD); developmental psychology (PhD); experimental psychology (PhD); health psychology (PhD); human social development (PhD); JD/MA. *Accreditation:* APA (one or more programs are accredited). *Faculty:* 40 full-time. *Students:* 99 full-time (72 women); includes 15 minority (6 Black or African American, non-Hispanic/Latino; 3 Asian, non-Hispanic/Latino; 6 Hispanic/Latino), 12 international. 499 applicants, 4% accepted, 18 enrolled. In 2011, 7 doctorates awarded. *Degree requirements:* For doctorate, thesis/dissertation. *Entrance requirements:* For doctorate, GRE General Test. Additional exam requirements/recommendations for international students: Required—TOEFL (minimum score 550 paper-based; 213 computer-based; 83 iBT), IELTS (minimum score 7). *Application deadline:* For fall admission, 12/8 priority date for domestic students, 12/8 for international students. Application fee: $75. Electronic applications accepted. *Expenses: Tuition:* Full-time $40,720. *Required fees:* $3107. *Financial support:* Fellowships, research assistantships, teaching assistantships, career-related internships or fieldwork, and Federal Work-Study available. Financial award application deadline: 12/8. *Unit head:* Melanie Bonner, Director of Graduate Studies, 919-660-5715, Fax: 919-660-5726, E-mail: morrell@duke.edu. *Application contact:* Elizabeth Hutton, Director of Admissions, 919-684-3913, Fax: 919-684-2277, E-mail: grad-admissions@duke.edu. Web site: http://www.psych.duke.edu/.

Graduate School and University Center of the City University of New York, Graduate Studies, Program in Psychology, New York, NY 10016-4039. Offers basic applied neurocognition (PhD); biopsychology (PhD); clinical psychology (PhD); developmental psychology (PhD); environmental psychology (PhD); experimental psychology (PhD); industrial psychology (PhD); learning processes (PhD); neuropsychology (PhD); psychology (PhD); social personality (PhD). *Degree requirements:* For doctorate, one foreign language, thesis/dissertation. *Entrance requirements:* For doctorate, GRE General Test. Additional exam requirements/recommendations for international students: Required—TOEFL. Electronic applications accepted.

Harvard University, Graduate School of Arts and Sciences, Department of Psychology, Cambridge, MA 02138. Offers psychology (PhD), including behavior and decision analysis, cognition, developmental psychology, experimental psychology, personality, psychobiology, psychopathology, social psychology (PhD). *Accreditation:* APA. *Degree requirements:* For doctorate, thesis/dissertation, general exams. *Entrance requirements:* For doctorate, GRE General Test. Additional exam requirements/recommendations for international students: Required—TOEFL. *Expenses: Tuition:* Full-time $36,304. *Required fees:* $1186. Full-time tuition and fees vary according to program.

Howard University, Graduate School, Department of Psychology, Washington, DC 20059-0002. Offers clinical psychology (PhD); developmental psychology (PhD); experimental psychology (PhD); neuropsychology (PhD); personality psychology (PhD); psychology (MS); social psychology (PhD). *Accreditation:* APA (one or more programs are accredited). Part-time programs available. *Degree requirements:* For master's, thesis; for doctorate, comprehensive exam, thesis/dissertation, qualifying exam. *Entrance requirements:* For master's, GRE General Test, minimum GPA of 2.5, bachelor's degree in psychology or related field; for doctorate, GRE General Test, minimum GPA of 3.0. *Faculty research:* Personality and psychophysiology, educational and social development of African-American children, child and adult psychopathology.

Indiana University–Purdue University Indianapolis, School of Science, Department of Psychology, Psychobiology of Addictions Program, Indianapolis, IN 46202-2896. Offers PhD. *Faculty:* 7 full-time (3 women). *Students:* 12 full-time (10 women), 4 part-time (2 women); includes 3 minority (all Black or African American, non-Hispanic/Latino). Average age 29. 10 applicants, 40% accepted, 4 enrolled. *Application deadline:* For fall admission, 1/1 for domestic students. Application fee: $55 ($65 for international students). *Financial support:* Fellowships with partial tuition reimbursements, research assistantships with partial tuition reimbursements, teaching assistantships with partial tuition reimbursements, career-related internships or fieldwork, and Federal Work-Study available. Financial award application deadline: 3/1; financial award applicants required to submit FAFSA. *Faculty research:* Behavioral genetics, behavior pharmacology, animal models, developmental psychology, neurobehavioral toxicology, neuropsychology of learning and memory, animal models of fetal alcohol syndrome. *Unit head:* Dr. J. Gregor Fetterman, Chairman, 317-274-6945, Fax: 317-274-6756, E-mail: gfetter@iupui.edu. *Application contact:* Dr. Sherry Queener, Director, Graduate Studies and Associate Dean, 317-274-1577, Fax: 317-278-2380. Web site: http://www.psynt.iupui.edu.

Louisiana State University and Agricultural and Mechanical College, Graduate School, College of Humanities and Social Sciences, Department of Psychology, Baton Rouge, LA 70803. Offers biological psychology (MA, PhD); clinical psychology (MA, PhD); cognitive psychology (MA, PhD); developmental psychology (MA, PhD); industrial/organizational psychology (MA, PhD); school psychology (MA, PhD). PhD programs offered jointly with Southeastern Louisiana University. *Accreditation:* APA (one or more programs are accredited). *Faculty:* 23 full-time (10 women). *Students:* 92 full-time (63 women), 18 part-time (13 women); includes 10 minority (4 Black or African American, non-Hispanic/Latino; 1 American Indian or Alaska Native, non-Hispanic/Latino; 1 Asian, non-Hispanic/Latino; 4 Hispanic/Latino), 2 international. Average age 27. 304 applicants, 6% accepted, 18 enrolled. In 2011, 6 master's, 21 doctorates awarded. Terminal master's awarded for partial completion of doctoral program. *Degree requirements:* For master's, thesis; for doctorate, thesis/dissertation, 1-year internship. *Entrance requirements:* For master's and doctorate, GRE General Test, minimum GPA of 3.0. Additional exam requirements/recommendations for international students: Required—TOEFL (minimum score 550 paper-based; 213 computer-based; 79 iBT) or IELTS (minimum score 6.5). *Application deadline:* For fall admission, 1/15 for domestic and international students. Applications are processed on a rolling basis. Application fee: $50 ($70 for international students). Electronic applications accepted. *Financial support:* In 2011–12, 105 students received support, including 3 fellowships (averaging $20,963 per year), 24 research assistantships with partial tuition reimbursements available (averaging $16,932 per year), 44 teaching assistantships with partial tuition reimbursements available (averaging $13,092 per year); career-related internships or fieldwork, Federal Work-Study, institutionally sponsored loans, scholarships/grants, health care benefits, and tuition waivers (full and partial) also available. Financial award applicants required to submit FAFSA. *Faculty research:* Clinical psychology, autism, anxiety, addition, neuropsychology, school psychology, cognitive psychology, experimental psychology. *Total annual research expenditures:* $1.3 million. *Unit head:* Dr. Robert Matthews, Chair, 225-578-8745, Fax: 225-578-4125, E-mail: psmath@lsu.edu. *Application contact:* Dr. Jason Hicks, Coordinator of Graduate Studies, 225-578-4109, Fax: 225-578-4125, E-mail: jhicks@lsu.edu. Web site: http://www.lsu.edu/psychology/graduate.html.

Memorial University of Newfoundland, School of Graduate Studies, Interdisciplinary Program in Cognitive and Behavioral Ecology, St. John's, NL A1C 5S7, Canada. Offers M Sc, PhD. *Degree requirements:* For master's, thesis, public lecture; for doctorate, comprehensive exam, thesis/dissertation, oral defense of dissertation. *Entrance requirements:* For master's, honors degree (minimum 2nd class standing) in related field; for doctorate, master's degree. Electronic applications accepted. *Faculty research:* Seabird feeding ecology, marine mammal and seabird energetics, systems of fish, seabird/seal/fisheries interaction.

Northwestern University, The Graduate School, Judd A. and Marjorie Weinberg College of Arts and Sciences, Department of Psychology, Evanston, IL 60208. Offers brain, behavior and cognition (PhD); clinical psychology (PhD); cognitive psychology (PhD); personality (PhD); social psychology (PhD); JD/PhD. Admissions and degrees offered through The Graduate School. *Accreditation:* APA (one or more programs are accredited). Part-time programs available. *Degree requirements:* For doctorate, thesis/dissertation. *Entrance requirements:* For doctorate, GRE General Test, GRE Subject Test. Additional exam requirements/recommendations for international students: Required—TOEFL. Electronic applications accepted. *Faculty research:* Memory and higher order cognition, anxiety and depression, effectiveness of psychotherapy, social cognition, molecular basis of memory.

Northwestern University, The Graduate School and Northwestern University Feinberg School of Medicine, Program in Clinical Psychology, Evanston, IL 60208. Offers clinical psychology (PhD), including clinical neuropsychology, general clinical. PhD admissions and degree offered through The Graduate School. *Accreditation:* APA. *Degree requirements:* For doctorate, thesis/dissertation, clinical internship. *Entrance requirements:* For doctorate, GRE General Test, GRE Subject Test, minimum GPA of 3.2, course work in psychology. Additional exam requirements/recommendations for international students: Required—TOEFL. *Faculty research:* Cancer and cardiovascular risk reduction, evaluation of mental health services and policy, neuropsychological assessment, outcome of psychotherapy, cognitive therapy, pediatric and clinical child psychology.

Oregon Health & Science University, School of Medicine, Graduate Programs in Medicine, Department of Behavioral Neuroscience, Portland, OR 97239-3098. Offers PhD. *Faculty:* 23 full-time (7 women). *Students:* 32 full-time (20 women); includes 7 minority (1 Black or African American, non-Hispanic/Latino; 1 Asian, non-Hispanic/Latino; 2 Hispanic/Latino; 3 Two or more races, non-Hispanic/Latino). Average age 27. 69 applicants, 10% accepted, 3 enrolled. In 2011, 6 doctorates awarded. Terminal master's awarded for partial completion of doctoral program. *Degree requirements:* For doctorate, comprehensive exam, thesis/dissertation, qualifying exam. *Entrance requirements:* For doctorate, GRE General Test (minimum scores: 153 Verbal/148 Quantitative/4.5 Analytical), undergraduate coursework in biopsychology and other basic science areas. Additional exam requirements/recommendations for international students: Required—TOEFL. *Application deadline:* For fall admission, 12/1 for domestic students. Application fee: $70. Electronic applications accepted. *Financial support:* Fellowships, research assistantships, health care benefits, tuition waivers (full), and stipends for PhD students available. *Faculty research:* Behavioral neuroscience, behavioral genomics, biological basis of drug and alcohol abuse, cognitive neuroscience, neuropharmacology and neuroendocrinology. *Unit head:* Dr. Suzanne Mitchell, Program Director, 503-494-1650, E-mail: mitchesu@ohsu.edu. *Application contact:* Kris Thomason, Graduate Program Manager, 503-494-8464, E-mail: thomason@ohsu.edu. Web site: http://www.ohsu.edu/som-BehNeuro/.

Palo Alto University, PGSP-Stanford Psy D Consortium Program, Palo Alto, CA 94303-4232. Offers Psy D. Program offered jointly with Stanford University. *Accreditation:* APA. *Degree requirements:* For doctorate, thesis/dissertation. *Entrance requirements:* For doctorate, GRE, BA or MA in psychology or related area, minimum undergraduate GPA of 3.0, minimum graduate GPA of 3.3. Additional exam requirements/recommendations for international students: Required—TOEFL. Electronic applications accepted. *Faculty research:* Biopsychosocial research, neurobiology, psychopharmacology.

Penn State University Park, Graduate School, College of Health and Human Development, Department of Biobehavioral Health, State College, University Park, PA 16802-1503. Offers MS, PhD. *Unit head:* Dr. Ann C. Crouter, Dean, 814-865-1428, Fax: 814-865-3282, E-mail: ac1@psu.edu. *Application contact:* Cynthia E. Nicosia, Director, Graduate Enrollment Services, 814-865-1795, Fax: 814-865-4627, E-mail: cey1@psu.edu. Web site: http://bbh.hhdev.psu.edu.

Rutgers, The State University of New Jersey, Newark, Graduate School, Program in Integrative Neuroscience, Newark, NJ 07102. Offers PhD. Part-time programs available. *Degree requirements:* For doctorate, thesis/dissertation. *Entrance requirements:* For doctorate, GRE, minimum GPA of 3.0. Electronic applications accepted. *Faculty research:* Systems neuroscience, cognitive neuroscience, molecular neuroscience, behavioral neuroscience.

Rutgers, The State University of New Jersey, Newark, Graduate School, Program in Psychology, Newark, NJ 07102. Offers cognitive neuroscience (PhD); cognitive science (PhD); perception (PhD); psychobiology (PhD); social cognition (PhD). *Degree requirements:* For doctorate, comprehensive exam, thesis/dissertation. *Entrance requirements:* For doctorate, GRE General Test, GRE Subject Test, minimum undergraduate B average. Electronic applications accepted. *Faculty research:* Visual perception (luminance, motion), neuroendocrine mechanisms in behavior (reproduction, pain), attachment theory, connectionist modeling of cognition.

Rutgers, The State University of New Jersey, New Brunswick, Graduate School-New Brunswick, Program in Psychology, Piscataway, NJ 08854-8097. Offers behavioral neuroscience (PhD); clinical psychology (PhD); cognitive psychology (PhD); interdisciplinary health psychology (PhD); social psychology (PhD). *Accreditation:* APA. *Degree requirements:* For doctorate, comprehensive exam, thesis/dissertation. *Entrance requirements:* For doctorate, GRE General Test, 3 letters of recommendation. Additional exam requirements/recommendations for international students: Required—TOEFL (minimum score 577 paper-based; 233 computer-based). Electronic applications accepted. *Faculty research:* Learning and memory, behavioral ecology, hormones and behavior, psychopharmacology, anxiety disorders.

State University of New York at Binghamton, Graduate School, School of Arts and Sciences, Department of Psychology, Specialization in Behavioral Neuroscience, Binghamton, NY 13902-6000. Offers MA, PhD. *Students:* 18 full-time (10 women), 9 part-time (all women); includes 2 minority (both Hispanic/Latino). Average age 26. 24 applicants, 54% accepted, 6 enrolled. In 2011, 2 master's, 6 doctorates awarded. *Degree requirements:* For master's, thesis; for doctorate, thesis/dissertation, departmental qualifying exam. *Entrance requirements:* For master's and doctorate, GRE General Test, GRE Subject Test. Additional exam requirements/recommendations for international students: Required—TOEFL (minimum score 550 paper-based; 213 computer-based; 80 iBT). *Application deadline:* For fall admission, 1/15 priority date for domestic students, 1/15 for international students. Applications are processed on a rolling basis. Application fee: $60. Electronic applications accepted. *Financial support:* In 2011–12, 23 students received support, including 2 fellowships with full tuition reimbursements available (averaging $17,500 per year), 4 research assistantships with full tuition reimbursements available (averaging $17,500 per year), 15 teaching assistantships with full tuition reimbursements available (averaging $17,500 per year); career-related internships or fieldwork, Federal Work-Study, institutionally sponsored loans, scholarships/grants, health care benefits, tuition waivers (full and partial), and unspecified assistantships also available. Financial award application deadline: 2/15; financial award applicants required to submit FAFSA. *Unit head:* Dr. Lisa Savage, Graduate Coordinator, 607-777-4383, E-mail: lsavage@binghamton.edu. *Application contact:* Catherine Smith, Recruiting and Admissions Coordinator, 607-777-2151, Fax: 607-777-2501, E-mail: cmsmith@binghamton.edu.

Stony Brook University, State University of New York, Graduate School, College of Arts and Sciences, Department of Psychology, Program in Biopsychology, Stony Brook, NY 11794. Offers PhD. *Degree requirements:* For doctorate, thesis/dissertation. *Entrance requirements:* For doctorate, GRE General Test, GRE Subject Test. Additional exam requirements/recommendations for international students: Required—TOEFL.

Texas A&M University, College of Liberal Arts, Department of Psychology, College Station, TX 77843. Offers behavioral and cellular neuroscience (PhD); clinical psychology (PhD); cognitive psychology (PhD); developmental psychology (PhD); industrial/organizational psychology (PhD); social psychology (PhD). *Accreditation:* APA. *Faculty:* 38. *Students:* 90 full-time (56 women), 11 part-time (7 women); includes 27 minority (5 Black or African American, non-Hispanic/Latino; 7 Asian, non-Hispanic/Latino; 15 Hispanic/Latino), 15 international. In 2011, 12 doctorates awarded. *Degree requirements:* For doctorate, comprehensive exam (for some programs), thesis/dissertation. *Entrance requirements:* For doctorate, GRE General Test. Additional exam requirements/recommendations for international students: Required—TOEFL. *Application deadline:* For fall admission, 1/5 for domestic and international students. Application fee: $50 ($75 for international students). Electronic applications accepted. *Expenses:* Tuition, state resident: full-time $5437; part-time $226.55 per credit hour. Tuition, nonresident: full-time $12,949; part-time $539.55 per credit hour. *Required fees:* $2741. *Financial support:* Fellowships with partial tuition reimbursements, research assistantships with partial tuition reimbursements, teaching assistantships with partial tuition reimbursements, career-related internships or fieldwork, institutionally sponsored loans, health care benefits, and unspecified assistantships available. Financial award application deadline: 1/5; financial award applicants required to submit FAFSA. *Unit head:* Ludy T. Benjamin, Jr., Head, 979-845-2540, Fax: 979-845-4727, E-mail: lbenjamin@tamu.edu. *Application contact:* Julie Austin, Graduate Admissions Supervisor, 979-458-1710, Fax: 979-845-4727, E-mail: gradadv@psyc.tamu.edu. Web site: http://psychology.tamu.edu.

University at Albany, State University of New York, College of Arts and Sciences, Department of Psychology, Albany, NY 12222-0001. Offers autism (Certificate); biopsychology (PhD); clinical psychology (PhD); general/experimental psychology (PhD); industrial/organizational psychology (PhD); psychology (MA); social/personality psychology (PhD). *Accreditation:* APA (one or more programs are accredited). *Degree requirements:* For doctorate, thesis/dissertation. *Entrance requirements:* For doctorate, GRE General Test, GRE Subject Test. Additional exam requirements/recommendations for international students: Required—TOEFL (minimum score 550 paper-based; 213 computer-based). Electronic applications accepted.

The University of British Columbia, Faculty of Arts and Faculty of Graduate Studies, Department of Psychology, Vancouver, BC V6T 1Z4, Canada. Offers behavioral neuroscience (MA, PhD); clinical psychology (MA, PhD); cognitive science (MA, PhD); developmental psychology (MA, PhD); health psychology (MA, PhD); quantitative methods (MA, PhD); social/personality psychology (MA, PhD). *Accreditation:* APA (one or more programs are accredited). Terminal master's awarded for partial completion of doctoral program. *Degree requirements:* For master's, thesis; for doctorate, comprehensive exam, thesis/dissertation. *Entrance requirements:* For master's and doctorate, GRE General Test. Additional exam requirements/recommendations for international students: Required—TOEFL (minimum score 550 paper-based; 230 computer-based; 80 iBT). Electronic applications accepted. *Faculty research:* Clinical, developmental, social/personality, cognition, behavioral neuroscience.

University of Connecticut, Graduate School, College of Liberal Arts and Sciences, Department of Psychology, Storrs, CT 06269. Offers behavioral neuroscience (PhD); biopsychology (PhD); clinical psychology (MA, PhD); cognition and instruction (PhD); developmental psychology (MA, PhD); ecological psychology (PhD); experimental psychology (PhD); general psychology (MA, PhD); health psychology (Graduate Certificate); industrial/organizational psychology (PhD); language and cognition (PhD); neuroscience (PhD); occupational health psychology (Graduate Certificate); social psychology (MA, PhD). *Accreditation:* APA. Terminal master's awarded for partial completion of doctoral program. *Degree requirements:* For master's, comprehensive exam; for doctorate, thesis/dissertation. *Entrance requirements:* For master's and doctorate, GRE General Test, GRE Subject Test. Additional exam requirements/recommendations for international students: Required—TOEFL (minimum score 550 paper-based; 213 computer-based). Electronic applications accepted.

Biopsychology

University of Michigan, Horace H. Rackham School of Graduate Studies, College of Literature, Science, and the Arts, Department of Psychology, Ann Arbor, MI 48109. Offers biopsychology (PhD); clinical science (PhD); cognition and cognitive neuroscience (PhD); developmental psychology (PhD); personality and social contexts (PhD); social psychology (PhD). *Accreditation:* APA. *Faculty:* 83 full-time (39 women), 30 part-time/adjunct (14 women). *Students:* 141 full-time (99 women); includes 54 minority (16 Black or African American, non-Hispanic/Latino; 2 American Indian or Alaska Native, non-Hispanic/Latino; 18 Asian, non-Hispanic/Latino; 18 Hispanic/Latino), 15 international. Average age 27. 641 applicants, 6% accepted, 30 enrolled. In 2011, 25 doctorates awarded. *Degree requirements:* For doctorate, comprehensive exam, thesis/dissertation, oral defense of dissertation, preliminary exam. *Entrance requirements:* For doctorate, GRE General Test. Additional exam requirements/recommendations for international students: Required—TOEFL. *Application deadline:* For fall admission, 12/1 for domestic and international students. Application fee: $65 ($75 for international students). Electronic applications accepted. *Financial support:* In 2011–12, 112 students received support, including 56 fellowships with full tuition reimbursements available (averaging $20,900 per year), 30 research assistantships with full tuition reimbursements available (averaging $25,950 per year), 55 teaching assistantships with full tuition reimbursements available (averaging $22,670 per year); career-related internships or fieldwork also available. Financial award application deadline: 4/15. *Total annual research expenditures:* $7.4 million. *Unit head:* Prof. Robert Sellers, Chair, 734-764-7429. *Application contact:* Laurie Brannan, Psychology Student Academic Affairs, 731-764-2580, Fax: 734-615-7584, E-mail: psych.saa@umich.edu. Web site: http://www.lsa.umich.edu/psych/.

University of Minnesota, Twin Cities Campus, Graduate School, College of Liberal Arts, Department of Psychology, Program in Cognitive and Biological Psychology, Minneapolis, MN 55455-0213. Offers PhD. *Degree requirements:* For doctorate, comprehensive exam, thesis/dissertation. *Entrance requirements:* For doctorate, GRE General Test, GRE Subject Test (recommended), 12 credits of upper-level psychology courses, including a course in statistics or psychological measurement. Additional exam requirements/recommendations for international students: Required—TOEFL (minimum score 550 paper-based; 213 computer-based; 79 iBT).

University of Nebraska at Omaha, Graduate Studies, College of Arts and Sciences, Department of Psychology, Omaha, NE 68182. Offers developmental psychology (PhD); industrial/organizational psychology (MS, PhD); psychobiology (PhD); psychology (MA); school psychology (MS, Ed S). Part-time programs available. *Faculty:* 18 full-time (8 women). *Students:* 53 full-time (38 women), 43 part-time (33 women); includes 8 minority (1 Black or African American, non-Hispanic/Latino; 6 Hispanic/Latino; 1 Two or more races, non-Hispanic/Latino), 3 international. Average age 27. 118 applicants, 31% accepted, 35 enrolled. In 2011, 16 master's, 2 doctorates, 6 other advanced degrees awarded. *Degree requirements:* For master's, comprehensive exam, thesis (for some programs); for doctorate, comprehensive exam, thesis/dissertation. *Entrance requirements:* For master's, GRE General Test, GRE Subject Test, previous course work in psychology, including statistics and a laboratory course; minimum GPA of 3.0, 3 letters of recommendation, resume, statement of purpose, writing sample; for doctorate, GRE General Test. Additional exam requirements/recommendations for international students: Required—TOEFL (minimum score 500 paper-based; 173 computer-based; 61 iBT). *Application deadline:* For fall admission, 1/5 for domestic students. Application fee: $45. Electronic applications accepted. *Financial support:* In 2011–12, 53 students received support, including 2 fellowships with tuition reimbursements available, 22 research assistantships with tuition reimbursements available, 24 teaching assistantships with tuition reimbursements available; career-related internships or fieldwork, Federal Work-Study, institutionally sponsored loans, scholarships/grants, tuition waivers (partial), and unspecified assistantships also available. Support available to part-time students. Financial award application deadline: 3/1; financial award applicants required to submit FAFSA. *Unit head:* Dr. Brigette Ryalls, Chairperson, 402-554-2592. *Application contact:* Dr. Joseph Brown, Student Contact, 402-554-2592.

University of Nebraska–Lincoln, Graduate College, College of Arts and Sciences, Department of Psychology, Lincoln, NE 68588. Offers biopsychology (PhD); clinical psychology (PhD); cognitive psychology (PhD); developmental psychology (PhD); psychology (MA); social/personality psychology (PhD); JD/MA; JD/PhD. *Accreditation:* APA (one or more programs are accredited). *Degree requirements:* For master's, thesis optional; for doctorate, comprehensive exam, thesis/dissertation. *Entrance requirements:* For master's and doctorate, GRE General Test. Additional exam requirements/recommendations for international students: Required—TOEFL (minimum score 550 paper-based; 213 computer-based). Electronic applications accepted. *Faculty research:* Law and psychology, rural mental health, chronic mental illness, neuropsychology, child clinical psychology.

University of Oklahoma Health Sciences Center, College of Medicine and Graduate College, Graduate Programs in Medicine, Department of Psychiatry and Behavioral Sciences, Oklahoma City, OK 73190. Offers biological psychology (MS, PhD). *Degree requirements:* For master's, thesis; for doctorate, thesis/dissertation. *Entrance requirements:* For doctorate, GRE General Test, 3 letters of recommendation. Additional exam requirements/recommendations for international students: Required—TOEFL. *Faculty research:* Behavioral neuroscience, human neuropsychology, psychophysiology, behavioral medicine, health psychology.

University of Oregon, Graduate School, College of Arts and Sciences, Department of Psychology, Eugene, OR 97403. Offers clinical psychology (PhD); cognitive psychology (MA, MS, PhD); developmental psychology (MA, MS, PhD); physiological psychology (MA, MS, PhD); psychology (MA, MS, PhD); social/personality psychology (MA, MS, PhD). *Accreditation:* APA (one or more programs are accredited). Terminal master's awarded for partial completion of doctoral program. *Degree requirements:* For doctorate, thesis/dissertation. *Entrance requirements:* For master's, GRE General Test, minimum GPA of 3.0; for doctorate, GRE General Test. Additional exam requirements/recommendations for international students: Required—TOEFL.

The University of Texas at Austin, Graduate School, The Institute for Neuroscience, Austin, TX 78712-1111. Offers PhD, MD/PhD. Terminal master's awarded for partial completion of doctoral program. *Degree requirements:* For doctorate, thesis/dissertation. *Entrance requirements:* For doctorate, GRE. *Application deadline:* For fall admission, 1/15 priority date for domestic students. Application fee: $50 ($75 for international students). Electronic applications accepted. *Financial support:* Fellowships with tuition reimbursements, research assistantships with tuition reimbursements, and teaching assistantships with tuition reimbursements available. Financial award application deadline: 2/1. *Faculty research:* Cellular/molecular biology, neurobiology, pharmacology, behavioral neuroscience. *Unit head:* Dr. Daniel Johnston, Director, 512-232-6564, Fax: 512-471-2181, E-mail: djohnston@mail.clm.utexas.edu. *Application contact:* Dr. John Mihic, Graduate Advisor, 512-212-7174, Fax: 512-471-0390, E-mail: mihic@austin.utexas.edu. Web site: http://www.utexas.edu/neuroscience/.

University of Windsor, Faculty of Graduate Studies, Faculty of Arts and Social Sciences, Department of Psychology, Windsor, ON N9B 3P4, Canada. Offers adult clinical (MA, PhD); applied social psychology (MA, PhD); child clinical (MA, PhD); clinical neuropsychology (MA, PhD). *Accreditation:* APA (one or more programs are accredited). *Degree requirements:* For master's, thesis; for doctorate, comprehensive exam, thesis/dissertation. *Entrance requirements:* For master's, GRE General Test, GRE Subject Test in psychology, minimum B average; for doctorate, GRE General Test, GRE Subject Test in psychology, master's degree. Additional exam requirements/recommendations for international students: Required—TOEFL (minimum score 600 paper-based; 250 computer-based). Electronic applications accepted. *Faculty research:* Gambling, suicidology, emotional competence, psychotherapy and trauma.

University of Wisconsin–Madison, Graduate School, College of Letters and Science, Department of Psychology, Program in Biology of Brain and Behavior, Madison, WI 53706-1380. Offers PhD. *Degree requirements:* For doctorate, comprehensive exam, thesis/dissertation. *Entrance requirements:* For doctorate, GRE General Test, minimum undergraduate GPA of 3.0. Additional exam requirements/recommendations for international students: Required—TOEFL. Electronic applications accepted. *Expenses:* Tuition, state resident: full-time $10,296; part-time $643.51 per credit. Tuition, nonresident: full-time $24,054; part-time $1503.40 per credit. *Required fees:* $70.06 per credit. Tuition and fees vary according to course load, campus/location, program and reciprocity agreements.

Virginia Commonwealth University, Graduate School, College of Humanities and Sciences, Department of Psychology, Program in General Psychology, Richmond, VA 23284-9005. Offers biopsychology (PhD); developmental psychology (PhD); social psychology (PhD). *Students:* 23 full-time (14 women), 6 part-time (5 women); includes 5 minority (4 Black or African American, non-Hispanic/Latino; 1 Hispanic/Latino), 1 international. 84 applicants, 11% accepted, 6 enrolled. In 2011, 5 doctorates awarded. *Degree requirements:* For doctorate, thesis/dissertation. *Entrance requirements:* For doctorate, GRE General Test. Additional exam requirements/recommendations for international students: Required—TOEFL (minimum score 600 paper-based; 250 computer-based; 100 iBT); Recommended—IELTS (minimum score 6.5). *Application deadline:* For fall admission, 12/15 for domestic students. Application fee: $50. Electronic applications accepted. *Expenses:* Tuition, state resident: full-time $9133; part-time $507 per credit. Tuition, nonresident: full-time $18,777; part-time $1043 per credit. *Required fees:* $77 per credit. Tuition and fees vary according to degree level, campus/location, program and student level. *Financial support:* Fellowships, research assistantships, teaching assistantships, Federal Work-Study, institutionally sponsored loans, and scholarships/grants available. Support available to part-time students. *Faculty research:* Biopsychology, developmental and social psychology. *Unit head:* Dr. Michael Southam-Gerow, Director, Graduate Programs in Psychology, 804-828-1193, Fax: 804-828-2237, E-mail: masouthamger@vcu.edu. *Application contact:* Dr. Joseph Porter, Director, Biopsychology Division, 804-828-0096, Fax: 804-828-2237, E-mail: jporter@vcu.edu. Web site: http://www.psychology.vcu.edu/graduate/index.shtml.

Wayne State University, School of Medicine, Department of Psychiatry and Behavioral Neurosciences, Detroit, MI 48202. Offers psychiatry (MS); translational neuroscience (PhD). *Students:* 9 full-time (6 women); includes 1 minority (Asian, non-Hispanic/Latino), 2 international. Average age 28. 13 applicants, 23% accepted, 3 enrolled. *Degree requirements:* For master's, thesis, oral thesis defense. *Entrance requirements:* For master's and doctorate, GRE, minimum undergradute GPA of 3.0, bachelor's degree from accredited institution, coursework in biological sciences and other scientific disciplines, personal statement, three letters of recommendation. Additional exam requirements/recommendations for international students: Required—TOEFL (minimum score 600 paper-based; 250 computer-based; 100 iBT). *Application deadline:* For fall admission, 12/15 for domestic and international students. Application fee: $50. Electronic applications accepted. *Expenses:* Tuition, state resident: part-time $512.85 per credit. Tuition, nonresident: part-time $1132.65 per credit. *Required fees:* $26.60 per credit. $199.65 per semester. Tuition and fees vary according to course load and program. *Financial support:* In 2011–12, 7 students received support. Fellowships with tuition reimbursements available, research assistantships with tuition reimbursements available, scholarships/grants, and unspecified assistantships available. *Faculty research:* Substance abuse, brain imaging, schizophrenia, child psychopathy, child development, neurobiology of monoamine systems. *Unit head:* Dr. David R. Rosenberg, Interim Chair, 313-577-9000, E-mail: drosen@med.wayne.edu. *Application contact:* Dr. Jeffery Stanely, Graduate Program Director, 313-577-9090, E-mail: jstanley@med.wayne.edu. Web site: http://psychiatry.med.wayne.edu/.

Neurobiology

Albert Einstein College of Medicine, Graduate Division of Biomedical Sciences, Department of Neuroscience, Bronx, NY 10461. Offers PhD, MD/PhD. *Degree requirements:* For doctorate, thesis/dissertation. *Entrance requirements:* For doctorate, GRE General Test. Additional exam requirements/recommendations for international students: Required—TOEFL. *Faculty research:* Structure-function relations at chemical and electrical synapses, mechanisms of electrogenesis, analysis of neuronal subsystems.

Boston University, School of Medicine, Division of Graduate Medical Sciences, Department of Anatomy and Neurobiology, Boston, MA 02118. Offers MA, PhD, MD/PhD. Part-time programs available. *Faculty:* 29 full-time (14 women), 16 part-time/adjunct (4 women). *Students:* 33 full-time (15 women), 1 (woman) part-time; includes 4 minority (3 Asian, non-Hispanic/Latino; 1 Hispanic/Latino), 2 international. Average age 27. 38 applicants, 53% accepted, 11 enrolled. In 2011, 4 master's, 10 doctorates awarded. Terminal master's awarded for partial completion of doctoral program. *Degree requirements:* For master's, thesis, qualifying exam; for doctorate, thesis/dissertation, qualifying exam. *Entrance requirements:* For master's and doctorate, GRE General Test, GRE Subject Test. Additional exam requirements/recommendations for international students: Required—TOEFL. *Application deadline:* For fall admission, 1/15 priority date for domestic students; for spring admission, 10/15 priority date for domestic students. Application fee: $75. Electronic applications accepted. *Expenses:* *Tuition:* Full-time $40,848; part-time $1276 per credit hour. *Required fees:* $572; $286 per semester. *Financial support:* In 2011–12, fellowships (averaging $30,500 per year), research

assistantships (averaging $30,500 per year) were awarded; Federal Work-Study, scholarships/grants, and traineeships also available. Financial award applicants required to submit FAFSA. *Faculty research:* Neuroanatomy, development of the nervous system, aging, respiratory system, reproductive system. *Unit head:* Dr. Mark Moss, Chairman, 617-638-4200, Fax: 617-638-4216. *Application contact:* Dr. Jarrett Rushmore, Director of Graduate Program, 617-638-4188, E-mail: rushmore@bu.edu. Web site: http://www.bumc.bu.edu/anatneuro/.

Brandeis University, Graduate School of Arts and Sciences, Program in Molecular and Cell Biology, Waltham, MA 02454-9110. Offers genetics (PhD); microbiology (PhD); molecular and cell biology (MS, PhD); molecular biology (PhD); neurobiology (PhD); quantitative biology (PhD). *Faculty:* 27 full-time (11 women), 4 part-time/adjunct (1 woman). *Students:* 65 full-time (36 women); includes 8 minority (4 Black or African American, non-Hispanic/Latino; 1 American Indian or Alaska Native, non-Hispanic/Latino; 1 Asian, non-Hispanic/Latino; 2 Hispanic/Latino), 14 international. 195 applicants, 26% accepted, 21 enrolled. In 2011, 4 master's, 6 doctorates awarded. Terminal master's awarded for partial completion of doctoral program. *Degree requirements:* For master's, thesis or alternative, research project, research lab, or project lab; for doctorate, comprehensive exam, thesis/dissertation, journal clubs; research seminar; colloquia; teaching requirement; qualifying exam. *Entrance requirements:* For master's, GRE General Test; MCAT may be substituted for the GRE exam for applicants to the M.S. program., official transcript(s), resume, 3 letters of recommendation, statement of purpose; for doctorate, GRE General Test, official transcript(s), resume, 3 letters of recommendation, statement of purpose. Additional exam requirements/recommendations for international students: Required—TOEFL (minimum score 600 paper-based; 250 computer-based; 100 iBT); Recommended—IELTS (minimum score 7). *Application deadline:* For fall admission, 1/15 priority date for domestic students; for spring admission, 11/15 for domestic students. Applications are processed on a rolling basis. Application fee: $75. Electronic applications accepted. *Financial support:* In 2011–12, 17 fellowships with full tuition reimbursements (averaging $29,580 per year), 31 research assistantships with full tuition reimbursements (averaging $29,580 per year), teaching assistantships with partial tuition reimbursements (averaging $3,200 per year) were awarded; scholarships/grants, health care benefits, tuition waivers (full and partial), and unspecified assistantships also available. Financial award application deadline: 4/15; financial award applicants required to submit FAFSA. *Faculty research:* Molecular biology, cell biology, biology, structural biology, immunology, developmental biology, neurobiology, DNA, RNA. *Unit head:* Dr. Bruce Goode, Chair, 781-736-2464, Fax: 781-736-3107, E-mail: goode@brandeis.edu. *Application contact:* Dr. Jessica Maryott, Department Administrator, 781-736-3100, Fax: 781-736-3107, E-mail: jmaryott@brandeis.edu. Web site: http://www.bio.brandeis.edu/grad/mcb/mcb_phd.html.

California Institute of Technology, Division of Biology, Program in Neurobiology, Pasadena, CA 91125-0001. Offers PhD. *Degree requirements:* For doctorate, thesis/dissertation, qualifying exam. *Entrance requirements:* For doctorate, GRE General Test.

Carnegie Mellon University, Mellon College of Science, Department of Biological Sciences, Pittsburgh, PA 15213-3891. Offers biochemistry (PhD); biophysics (PhD); cell biology (PhD); computational biology (MS, PhD); developmental biology (PhD); genetics (PhD); molecular biology (PhD); neuroscience (PhD). *Degree requirements:* For doctorate, comprehensive exam, thesis/dissertation. *Entrance requirements:* For doctorate, GRE General Test, GRE Subject Test, interview. Electronic applications accepted. *Faculty research:* Genetic structure, function, and regulation; protein structure and function; biological membranes; biological spectroscopy.

Case Western Reserve University, School of Medicine and School of Graduate Studies, Graduate Programs in Medicine, Department of Neurosciences, Cleveland, OH 44106. Offers neurobiology (PhD); neuroscience (PhD); MD/PhD. *Degree requirements:* For doctorate, thesis/dissertation. *Entrance requirements:* For doctorate, GRE General Test, 3 letters of recommendation. Additional exam requirements/recommendations for international students: Required—TOEFL. Electronic applications accepted. *Faculty research:* Neurotropic factors, synapse formation, regeneration, determination of cell fate, cellular neuroscience.

Columbia University, College of Physicians and Surgeons, Program in Neurobiology and Behavior, New York, NY 10032. Offers PhD. Only candidates for the PhD are admitted. *Degree requirements:* For doctorate, thesis/dissertation. *Entrance requirements:* For doctorate, GRE General Test. Additional exam requirements/recommendations for international students: Required—TOEFL. *Expenses:* Contact institution. *Faculty research:* Cellular and molecular mechanisms of neural development, neuropathology, neuropharmacology.

Cornell University, Graduate School, Graduate Fields of Agriculture and Life Sciences, Field of Neurobiology and Behavior, Ithaca, NY 14853-0001. Offers behavioral biology (PhD), including behavioral ecology, chemical ecology, ethology, neuroethology, sociobiology; neurobiology (PhD), including cellular and molecular neurobiology, neuroanatomy, neurochemistry, neuropharmacology, neurophysiology, sensory physiology. *Faculty:* 47 full-time (8 women). *Students:* 29 full-time (15 women); includes 4 minority (1 Black or African American, non-Hispanic/Latino; 1 Asian, non-Hispanic/Latino; 2 Hispanic/Latino), 1 international. Average age 28. 57 applicants, 18% accepted, 4 enrolled. In 2011, 6 degrees awarded. *Degree requirements:* For doctorate, comprehensive exam, thesis/dissertation, 1 year of teaching experience, seminar presentation. *Entrance requirements:* For doctorate, GRE General Test, GRE Subject Test (biology), 3 letters of recommendation. Additional exam requirements/recommendations for international students: Required—TOEFL (minimum score 550 paper-based; 213 computer-based; 77 iBT). *Application deadline:* For fall admission, 12/1 for domestic students. Application fee: $95. Electronic applications accepted. *Financial support:* In 2011–12, 14 fellowships with full tuition reimbursements, 7 research assistantships with full tuition reimbursements, 8 teaching assistantships with full tuition reimbursements were awarded; institutionally sponsored loans, scholarships/grants, health care benefits, tuition waivers (full and partial), and unspecified assistantships also available. Financial award applicants required to submit FAFSA. *Faculty research:* Cellular neurobiology and neuropharmacology, integrative neurobiology, social behavior, chemical ecology, neuroethology. *Unit head:* Director of Graduate Studies, 607-254-4340, Fax: 607-254-4340. *Application contact:* Graduate Field Assistant, 607-254-4340, Fax: 607-254-4340, E-mail: nbb_field@cornell.edu. Web site: http://www.gradschool.cornell.edu/fields.php?id-55&a-2.

Dalhousie University, Faculty of Graduate Studies and Faculty of Medicine, Graduate Programs in Medicine, Department of Anatomy and Neurobiology, Halifax, NS B3H 4R2, Canada. Offers M Sc, PhD. *Degree requirements:* For master's, thesis; for doctorate, thesis/dissertation. *Entrance requirements:* For master's and doctorate, GRE (recommended), minimum A- average. Additional exam requirements/recommendations for international students: Required—1 of 5 approved tests: TOEFL, IELTS, CANTEST, CAEL, Michigan English Language Assessment Battery. Electronic applications accepted. *Faculty research:* Neuroscience histology, cell biology, neuroendocrinology, evolutionary biology.

Duke University, Graduate School, Department of Biological Anthropology and Anatomy, Durham, NC 27710. Offers cellular and molecular biology (PhD); gross anatomy and physical anthropology (PhD), including comparative morphology of human and non-human primates, primate social behavior, vertebrate paleontology; neuroanatomy (PhD). *Faculty:* 9 full-time. *Students:* 16 full-time (10 women); includes 3 minority (1 Black or African American, non-Hispanic/Latino; 2 Hispanic/Latino), 1 international. 71 applicants, 7% accepted, 4 enrolled. In 2011, 2 doctorates awarded. *Degree requirements:* For doctorate, one foreign language, thesis/dissertation. *Entrance requirements:* For doctorate, GRE General Test. Additional exam requirements/recommendations for international students: Required—TOEFL (minimum score 550 paper-based; 213 computer-based; 83 iBT), IELTS (minimum score 7). *Application deadline:* For fall admission, 12/8 priority date for domestic students, 12/8 for international students. Application fee: $75. Electronic applications accepted. *Expenses: Tuition:* Full-time $40,720. *Required fees:* $3107. *Financial support:* Fellowships, teaching assistantships, and Federal Work-Study available. Financial award application deadline: 12/31. *Unit head:* Daniel Schmitt, Director of Graduate Studies, 919-684-4124, Fax: 919-684-8542, E-mail: mlsquire@duke.edu. *Application contact:* Elizabeth Hutton, Director of Admissions, 919-684-3913, Fax: 919-684-2277, E-mail: grad-admissions@duke.edu. Web site: http://www.baa.duke.edu/.

Duke University, Graduate School, Department of Neurobiology, Durham, NC 27708-0586. Offers PhD. *Faculty:* 62 full-time. *Students:* 48 full-time (24 women); includes 11 minority (7 Asian, non-Hispanic/Latino; 4 Hispanic/Latino), 15 international. 101 applicants, 14% accepted, 5 enrolled. In 2011, 5 doctorates awarded. *Degree requirements:* For doctorate, variable foreign language requirement, thesis/dissertation. *Entrance requirements:* For doctorate, GRE General Test. Additional exam requirements/recommendations for international students: Required—TOEFL (minimum score 550 paper-based; 213 computer-based; 83 iBT), IELTS (minimum score 7). *Application deadline:* For fall admission, 12/8 priority date for domestic students, 12/8 for international students. Application fee: $75. Electronic applications accepted. *Expenses: Tuition:* Full-time $40,720. *Required fees:* $3107. *Financial support:* Fellowships, research assistantships, teaching assistantships, and Federal Work-Study available. Financial award application deadline: 12/8. *Unit head:* Richard Mooney, Director, 919-681-4243, Fax: 919-684-4431, E-mail: beth.peloquin@duke.edu. *Application contact:* Elizabeth Hutton, Director of Admissions, 919-684-3913, Fax: 919-684-2277, E-mail: grad-admissions@duke.edu. Web site: http://www.neuro.duke.edu/.

Georgia State University, College of Arts and Sciences, Department of Biology, Program in Neurobiology and Behavior, Atlanta, GA 30302-3083. Offers MS, PhD. Part-time programs available. Terminal master's awarded for partial completion of doctoral program. *Degree requirements:* For master's, thesis or alternative; for doctorate, thesis/dissertation, exam. *Entrance requirements:* For master's and doctorate, GRE General Test. Additional exam requirements/recommendations for international students: Required—TOEFL. Electronic applications accepted.

Harvard University, Graduate School of Arts and Sciences, Program in Neuroscience, Boston, MA 02115. Offers neurobiology (PhD). *Degree requirements:* For doctorate, thesis/dissertation, qualifying exam. *Entrance requirements:* For doctorate, GRE General Test, GRE Subject Test. Additional exam requirements/recommendations for international students: Required—TOEFL. *Expenses: Tuition:* Full-time $36,304. *Required fees:* $1186. Full-time tuition and fees vary according to program. *Faculty research:* Relationship between diseases of the nervous system and basic science.

Illinois State University, Graduate School, College of Arts and Sciences, Department of Biological Sciences, Normal, IL 61790-2200. Offers animal behavior (MS); bacteriology (MS); biochemistry (MS); biological sciences (MS); biology (PhD); biophysics (MS); biotechnology (MS); botany (MS, PhD); cell biology (MS); conservation biology (MS); developmental biology (MS); ecology (MS, PhD); entomology (MS); evolutionary biology (MS); genetics (MS, PhD); immunology (MS); microbiology (MS, PhD); molecular biology (MS); molecular genetics (MS); neurobiology (MS); neuroscience (MS); parasitology (MS); physiology (MS, PhD); plant biology (MS); plant molecular biology (MS); plant sciences (MS); structural biology (MS); zoology (MS, PhD). Part-time programs available. *Degree requirements:* For master's, thesis or alternative; for doctorate, variable foreign language requirement, thesis/dissertation, 2 terms of residency. *Entrance requirements:* For master's, GRE General Test, minimum GPA of 2.6 in last 60 hours of course work; for doctorate, GRE General Test. *Faculty research:* Redoc balance and drug development in schistosoma mansoni, control of the growth of listeria monocytogenes at low temperature, regulation of cell expansion and microtubule function by SPRI, CRUI: physiology and fitness consequences of different life history phenotypes.

Louisiana State University Health Sciences Center, School of Graduate Studies in New Orleans, Department of Cell Biology and Anatomy, New Orleans, LA 70112-2223. Offers cell biology and anatomy (MS, PhD), including cell biology, developmental biology, neurobiology and anatomy; MD/PhD. *Degree requirements:* For master's, comprehensive exam, thesis; for doctorate, comprehensive exam, thesis/dissertation. *Entrance requirements:* For master's and doctorate, GRE General Test, GRE Subject Test, minimum undergraduate GPA of 3.0. Additional exam requirements/recommendations for international students: Required—TOEFL. *Faculty research:* Visual system organization, neural development, plasticity of sensory systems, information processing through the nervous system, visuomotor integration.

Loyola University Chicago, Graduate School, Department of Cell Biology, Neurobiology and Anatomy, Chicago, IL 60660. Offers MS, PhD. Part-time programs available. *Faculty:* 16 full-time (6 women), 9 part-time/adjunct (4 women). *Students:* 21 full-time (11 women); includes 4 minority (3 Hispanic/Latino; 1 Two or more races, non-Hispanic/Latino), 1 international. Average age 27. 28 applicants, 29% accepted, 4 enrolled. In 2011, 1 master's, 2 doctorates awarded. Terminal master's awarded for partial completion of doctoral program. *Degree requirements:* For master's, thesis; for doctorate, comprehensive exam, thesis/dissertation. *Entrance requirements:* For master's, GRE General Test, minimum GPA of 3.0; for doctorate, GRE General Test, GRE Subject Test (biology), minimum GPA of 3.0. Additional exam requirements/recommendations for international students: Required—TOEFL (minimum score 600 paper-based; 250 computer-based). *Application deadline:* For fall admission, 5/1 priority date for domestic students, 5/1 for international students. Applications are processed on a rolling basis. Application fee: $50. Electronic applications accepted. *Expenses: Tuition:* Full-time $15,660; part-time $870 per credit hour. *Required fees:* $125 per semester. Tuition and fees vary according to course load and program. *Financial support:* In 2011–12, 5 fellowships with full tuition reimbursements (averaging $23,000 per year), 5 research assistantships with full tuition reimbursements (averaging $23,000 per year) were awarded; Federal Work-Study and unspecified assistantships also available. Financial award application deadline: 5/1; financial award applicants required to submit FAFSA. *Faculty research:* Brain steroids, immunology, neuroregeneration, cytokines. *Total annual research expenditures:* $1 million. *Unit head:* Dr. Phong Le, Head, 708-216-3603, Fax: 708-216-3913, E-mail: ple@lumc.edu. *Application contact:* Ginny Hayes, Graduate Program Secretary, 708-216-3353, Fax: 708-216-3913, E-mail: vhayes@lumc.edu.

Massachusetts Institute of Technology, School of Science, Department of Biology, Cambridge, MA 02139. Offers biochemistry (PhD); biological oceanography (PhD); biology (PhD); biophysical chemistry and molecular structure (PhD); cell biology (PhD); computational and systems biology (PhD); developmental biology (PhD); genetics

(PhD); immunology (PhD); microbiology (PhD); molecular biology (PhD); neurobiology (PhD). *Faculty:* 58 full-time (15 women). *Students:* 248 full-time (129 women); includes 69 minority (5 Black or African American, non-Hispanic/Latino; 1 American Indian or Alaska Native, non-Hispanic/Latino; 25 Asian, non-Hispanic/Latino; 31 Hispanic/Latino; 7 Two or more races, non-Hispanic/Latino), 36 international. Average age 26. 698 applicants, 15% accepted, 44 enrolled. In 2011, 38 doctorates awarded. *Degree requirements:* For doctorate, comprehensive exam, thesis/dissertation. *Entrance requirements:* For doctorate, GRE General Test. Additional exam requirements/recommendations for international students: Required—TOEFL (minimum score 577 paper-based; 233 computer-based), IELTS (minimum score 6.5). *Application deadline:* For fall admission, 12/1 for domestic and international students. Application fee: $75. Electronic applications accepted. *Expenses: Tuition:* Full-time $40,460; part-time $630 per credit hour. *Required fees:* $272. *Financial support:* In 2011–12, 214 students received support, including 129 fellowships (averaging $33,200 per year), 117 research assistantships (averaging $32,900 per year); teaching assistantships, Federal Work-Study, institutionally sponsored loans, scholarships/grants, traineeships, health care benefits, and unspecified assistantships also available. *Faculty research:* Cellular, developmental and molecular (plant and animal) biology; biochemistry, bioengineering, biophysics and structural biology; classical and molecular genetics; immunology and microbiology; cancer biology, molecular medicine, neurobiology and human disease; computational and systems biology. *Total annual research expenditures:* $53.6 million. *Unit head:* Prof. Tania A. Baker, Head, 617-253-4701, E-mail: mitbio@mit.edu. *Application contact:* Biology Education Office, 617-253-3717, Fax: 617-258-9329, E-mail: gradbio@mit.edu. Web site: https://biology.mit.edu/.

New York University, Graduate School of Arts and Science, Department of Biology, New York, NY 10012-1019. Offers biology (PhD); biomedical journalism (MS); cancer and molecular biology (PhD); computational biology (PhD); computers in biological research (MS); developmental genetics (PhD); general biology (MS); immunology and microbiology (PhD); molecular genetics (PhD); neurobiology (PhD); oral biology (MS); plant biology (PhD); recombinant DNA technology (MS); MS/MBA. Part-time programs available. *Faculty:* 24 full-time (5 women). *Students:* 146 full-time (90 women), 54 part-time (36 women); includes 49 minority (1 Black or African American, non-Hispanic/Latino; 33 Asian, non-Hispanic/Latino; 12 Hispanic/Latino; 3 Two or more races, non-Hispanic/Latino), 89 international. Average age 27. 394 applicants, 62% accepted, 82 enrolled. In 2011, 68 master's, 6 doctorates awarded. Terminal master's awarded for partial completion of doctoral program. *Degree requirements:* For master's, thesis or alternative, qualifying paper; for doctorate, comprehensive exam, thesis/dissertation. *Entrance requirements:* For master's, GRE General Test; for doctorate, GRE General Test, GRE Subject Test. Additional exam requirements/recommendations for international students: Required—TOEFL. *Application deadline:* For fall admission, 12/1 priority date for domestic students, 12/1 for international students. Application fee: $90. *Financial support:* Fellowships with tuition reimbursements, research assistantships with tuition reimbursements, teaching assistantships with tuition reimbursements, career-related internships or fieldwork, Federal Work-Study, institutionally sponsored loans, scholarships/grants, health care benefits, and unspecified assistantships available. Financial award application deadline: 12/1; financial award applicants required to submit FAFSA. *Faculty research:* Genomics, molecular and cell biology, development and molecular genetics, molecular evolution of plants and animals. *Unit head:* Stephen Small, Chair, 212-998-8200, Fax: 212-995-4015, E-mail: biology@nyu.edu. *Application contact:* Justin Blau, Director of Graduate Studies, 212-998-8200, Fax: 212-995-4015, E-mail: biology@nyu.edu. Web site: http://biology.as.nyu.edu/.

Northwestern University, The Graduate School, Judd A. and Marjorie Weinberg College of Arts and Sciences, Department of Neurobiology and Physiology, Evanston, IL 60208. Offers MS. Admissions and degrees offered through The Graduate School. Part-time programs available. *Degree requirements:* For master's, thesis. *Entrance requirements:* For master's, GRE General Test and MCAT (strongly recommended). Additional exam requirements/recommendations for international students: Required—TOEFL. Electronic applications accepted. *Expenses:* Contact institution. *Faculty research:* Sensory neurobiology and neuroendocrinology, reproductive biology, vision physiology and psychophysics, cell and developmental biology.

Northwestern University, Northwestern University Feinberg School of Medicine and Interdepartmental Programs, Integrated Graduate Programs in the Life Sciences, Chicago, IL 60611. Offers cancer biology (PhD); cell biology (PhD); developmental biology (PhD); evolutionary biology (PhD); immunology and microbial pathogenesis (PhD); molecular biology and genetics (PhD); neurobiology (PhD); pharmacology and toxicology (PhD); structural biology and biochemistry (PhD). *Degree requirements:* For doctorate, comprehensive exam, thesis/dissertation, written and oral qualifying exams. *Entrance requirements:* For doctorate, GRE General Test. Additional exam requirements/recommendations for international students: Required—TOEFL (minimum score 600 paper-based; 250 computer-based). Electronic applications accepted.

Purdue University, Graduate School, College of Science, Department of Biological Sciences, West Lafayette, IN 47907. Offers biochemistry (PhD); biophysics (PhD); cell and developmental biology (PhD); ecology, evolutionary and population biology (MS, PhD), including ecology, evolutionary biology, population biology; genetics (MS, PhD); microbiology (MS, PhD); molecular biology (PhD); neurobiology (MS, PhD); plant physiology (PhD). *Faculty:* 57 full-time (15 women), 4 part-time/adjunct (1 woman). *Students:* 94 full-time (54 women), 9 part-time (5 women); includes 7 minority (2 Black or African American, non-Hispanic/Latino; 3 Asian, non-Hispanic/Latino; 2 Hispanic/Latino), 51 international. Average age 27. 246 applicants, 11% accepted, 18 enrolled. In 2011, 9 master's, 23 doctorates awarded. Terminal master's awarded for partial completion of doctoral program. *Degree requirements:* For master's, thesis (for some programs); for doctorate, thesis/dissertation, seminars, teaching experience. *Entrance requirements:* For master's, GRE General Test, minimum analytical writing score of 3.5, minimum undergraduate GPA of 3.0; for doctorate, GRE General Test, minimum analytical writing score of 3.5, minimum undergraduate GPA of 3.5. Additional exam requirements/recommendations for international students: Required—TOEFL (minimum score 600 paper-based; 107 iBT) for MS; TOEFL (minimum score 600 paper-based; 80 iBT) for Ph D. *Application deadline:* For fall admission, 12/7 for domestic and international students. Applications are processed on a rolling basis. Application fee: $60 ($75 for international students). Electronic applications accepted. *Financial support:* Fellowships, research assistantships, and teaching assistantships available. Support available to part-time students. Financial award application deadline: 2/15; financial award applicants required to submit FAFSA. *Unit head:* Dr. Richard J. Kuhn, Head, 765-494-4407, E-mail: kuhnr@purdue.edu. *Application contact:* Georgina E. Rupp, Graduate Coordinator, 765-494-8142, Fax: 765-494-0876, E-mail: ruppg@purdue.edu. Web site: http://www.bio.purdue.edu/.

Queen's University at Kingston, School of Graduate Studies and Research, Faculty of Health Sciences, Department of Anatomy and Cell Biology, Kingston, ON K7L 3N6, Canada. Offers biology of reproduction (M Sc, PhD); cancer (M Sc, PhD); cardiovascular pathophysiology (M Sc, PhD); cell and molecular biology (M Sc, PhD); drug metabolism (M Sc, PhD); endocrinology (M Sc, PhD); motor control (M Sc, PhD); neural regeneration (M Sc, PhD); neurophysiology (M Sc, PhD). Part-time programs available. *Degree requirements:* For master's, thesis; for doctorate, one foreign language, comprehensive exam, thesis/dissertation. *Entrance requirements:* Additional exam requirements/recommendations for international students: Required—TOEFL. Electronic applications accepted. *Faculty research:* Human kinetics, neuroscience, reproductive biology, cardiovascular.

Université Laval, Faculty of Medicine, Graduate Programs in Medicine, Programs in Neurobiology, Québec, QC G1K 7P4, Canada. Offers M Sc, PhD. Terminal master's awarded for partial completion of doctoral program. *Degree requirements:* For master's, thesis; for doctorate, comprehensive exam, thesis/dissertation. *Entrance requirements:* For master's and doctorate, knowledge of French and English. Electronic applications accepted.

University at Albany, State University of New York, College of Arts and Sciences, Department of Biological Sciences, Specialization in Molecular, Cellular, Developmental, and Neural Biology, Albany, NY 12222-0001. Offers MS, PhD. *Degree requirements:* For master's, one foreign language; for doctorate, one foreign language, thesis/dissertation. *Entrance requirements:* For master's and doctorate, GRE General Test.

The University of Alabama at Birmingham, Graduate Programs in Joint Health Sciences, Program in Neurobiology, Birmingham, AL 35294. Offers PhD. *Degree requirements:* For doctorate, thesis/dissertation. *Entrance requirements:* For doctorate, GRE, interview. *Application deadline:* Applications are processed on a rolling basis. Electronic applications accepted. *Expenses:* Tuition, state resident: full-time $5922; part-time $309 per hour. Tuition, nonresident: full-time $13,428; part-time $726 per hour. Tuition and fees vary according to program. *Unit head:* Dr. J. David Sweatt, Chair, 205-975-5196, Fax: 205-934-6571. *Application contact:* Information Contact, 205-975-5573, Fax: 205-934-6571. Web site: http://www.neurobiology.uab.edu/grad-program/.

University of Arkansas for Medical Sciences, Graduate School, Graduate Programs in Biomedical Sciences, Department of Neurobiology and Developmental Sciences, Little Rock, AR 72205-7199. Offers MS, PhD, MD/PhD. *Degree requirements:* For master's, thesis; for doctorate, thesis/dissertation. *Entrance requirements:* For master's, GRE General Test; for doctorate, GRE General Test, GRE Subject Test. Additional exam requirements/recommendations for international students: Required—TOEFL. *Faculty research:* Cellular and molecular neuroscience, translation neuroscience.

University of California, Irvine, School of Biological Sciences, Department of Neurobiology and Behavior, Irvine, CA 92697. Offers biological sciences (MS, PhD); MD/PhD. *Students:* 49 full-time (28 women); includes 14 minority (1 American Indian or Alaska Native, non-Hispanic/Latino; 5 Asian, non-Hispanic/Latino; 8 Hispanic/Latino), 1 international. Average age 28. 67 applicants, 10% accepted, 6 enrolled. In 2011, 4 master's, 6 doctorates awarded. *Degree requirements:* For doctorate, thesis/dissertation. *Entrance requirements:* For master's and doctorate, GRE General Test, GRE Subject Test, minimum GPA of 3.0. Additional exam requirements/recommendations for international students: Required—TOEFL (minimum score 550 paper-based; 213 computer-based). *Application deadline:* For fall admission, 1/15 priority date for domestic students, 1/15 for international students. Applications are processed on a rolling basis. Application fee: $80 ($100 for international students). Electronic applications accepted. *Financial support:* Fellowships, research assistantships with full tuition reimbursements, teaching assistantships, institutionally sponsored loans, traineeships, health care benefits, and unspecified assistantships available. Financial award application deadline: 3/1; financial award applicants required to submit FAFSA. *Faculty research:* Synaptic processes, neurophysiology, neuroendocrinology, neuroanatomy, molecular neurobiology. *Unit head:* Prof. Thomas J. Carew, Chair, 949-824-6114, Fax: 949-824-2447, E-mail: tcarew@uci.edu. *Application contact:* Naima Louridi, Student Affairs Officer, 949-824-8519, Fax: 949-824-2447, E-mail: nlouridi@uci.edu. Web site: http://neurobiology.uci.edu/.

University of California, Irvine, School of Medicine and School of Biological Sciences, Department of Anatomy and Neurobiology, Irvine, CA 92697. Offers biological sciences (MS, PhD); MD/PhD. *Students:* 25 full-time (15 women), 4 part-time (all women); includes 11 minority (1 Black or African American, non-Hispanic/Latino; 5 Asian, non-Hispanic/Latino; 5 Hispanic/Latino), 2 international. Average age 28. 1 applicant, 100% accepted, 1 enrolled. In 2011, 1 master's, 6 doctorates awarded. *Degree requirements:* For doctorate, thesis/dissertation. *Entrance requirements:* For master's and doctorate, GRE General Test, GRE Subject Test. Additional exam requirements/recommendations for international students: Required—TOEFL (minimum score 550 paper-based; 213 computer-based). *Application deadline:* For fall admission, 1/15 priority date for domestic students, 1/15 for international students. Applications are processed on a rolling basis. Application fee: $80 ($100 for international students). Electronic applications accepted. *Financial support:* Fellowships, research assistantships with full tuition reimbursements, teaching assistantships, institutionally sponsored loans, traineeships, health care benefits, and unspecified assistantships available. Financial award application deadline: 3/1; financial award applicants required to submit FAFSA. *Faculty research:* Neurotransmitter immunocytochemistry, intracellular physiology, molecular neurobiology, forebrain organization and development, structure and function of sensory and motor systems. *Unit head:* Prof. Ivan Soltesz, Professor and Chair, 949-824-3957, Fax: 949-824-9860, E-mail: isoltesz@uci.edu. *Application contact:* Debra S. Caputo, Chief Administrative Officer, 949-824-6340, Fax: 949-824-8549, E-mail: dscaputo@uci.edu.

University of California, Los Angeles, David Geffen School of Medicine and Graduate Division, Graduate Programs in Medicine, Department of Neurobiology, Los Angeles, CA 90095. Offers PhD. *Faculty:* 21 full-time (0 women). *Students:* 9 full-time (6 women); includes 2 minority (1 Asian, non-Hispanic/Latino; 1 Hispanic/Latino), 1 international. Average age 27. In 2011, 6 degrees awarded. *Median time to degree:* Of those who began their doctoral program in fall 2003, 100% received their degree in 8 years or less. *Degree requirements:* For doctorate, thesis/dissertation, oral and written qualifying exams. *Entrance requirements:* For doctorate, GRE General Test, GRE Subject Test, bachelor's degree in physical or biological science. Application fee: $70 ($90 for international students). Electronic applications accepted. *Financial support:* In 2011–12, 14 fellowships, 12 research assistantships, 3 teaching assistantships were awarded; Federal Work-Study, institutionally sponsored loans, scholarships/grants, and tuition waivers (full and partial) also available. Financial award application deadline: 3/1. *Faculty research:* Neuroendocrinology, neurophysiology. *Unit head:* Dr. Marie-Francoise Chesselet, Chair, 310-267-1781, Fax: 310-267-1786, E-mail: mchesselet@mednet.ucla.edu. *Application contact:* UCLA ACCESS Coordinator, 310-206-1845, Fax: 310-206-1636, E-mail: uclaaccess@mednet.ucla.edu.

University of California, Los Angeles, Graduate Division, College of Letters and Science and David Geffen School of Medicine, UCLA ACCESS to Programs in the Molecular, Cellular and Integrative Life Sciences, Los Angeles, CA 90095. Offers biochemistry and molecular biology (PhD); biological chemistry (PhD); cellular and molecular pathology (PhD); human genetics (PhD); microbiology, immunology, and molecular genetics (PhD); molecular biology (PhD); molecular toxicology (PhD); molecular, cellular and integrative physiology (PhD); neurobiology (PhD); oral biology (PhD); physiology (PhD). *Students:* 44 full-time (30 women); includes 18 minority (11 Asian, non-Hispanic/Latino; 6 Hispanic/Latino; 1 Two or more races, non-Hispanic/Latino), 9 international. Average age 25. 495 applicants, 18% accepted, 41 enrolled.

Degree requirements: For doctorate, thesis/dissertation, oral and written qualifying exams. *Entrance requirements:* For doctorate, GRE General Test, minimum undergraduate GPA of 3.0. Additional exam requirements/recommendations for international students: Required—TOEFL. *Application deadline:* For fall admission, 12/15 for domestic and international students. Application fee: $70 ($90 for international students). Electronic applications accepted. *Financial support:* In 2011–12, 51 fellowships with full and partial tuition reimbursements, 9 research assistantships with full and partial tuition reimbursements were awarded; teaching assistantships with full and partial tuition reimbursements, Federal Work-Study, institutionally sponsored loans, scholarships/grants, health care benefits, tuition waivers (full and partial), and unspecified assistantships also available. Financial award application deadline: 3/1; financial award applicants required to submit FAFSA. *Faculty research:* Molecular, cellular, and developmental biology; immunology; microbiology; integrative biology. *Unit head:* Jody Spillane, Project Coordinator, 310-206-1845, E-mail: jspillane@mednet.ucla.edu. *Application contact:* UCLA ACCESS Admissions, 310-206-1845, E-mail: uclaaccess@mednet.ucla.edu. Web site: https://www.uclaaccess.ucla.edu/.

University of California, San Diego, Office of Graduate Studies, Division of Biological Sciences, Program in Neurobiology, La Jolla, CA 92093. Offers PhD. Offered in association with the Salk Institute. *Degree requirements:* For doctorate, thesis/dissertation, qualifying exam. Electronic applications accepted.

University of Chicago, Division of Biological Sciences, Neuroscience Graduate Programs, Committee on Neurobiology, Chicago, IL 60637-1513. Offers PhD. *Degree requirements:* For doctorate, thesis/dissertation, ethics class, 2 teaching assistantships. *Entrance requirements:* For doctorate, GRE General Test. Additional exam requirements/recommendations for international students: Required—TOEFL (minimum score 600 paper-based; 250 computer-based; 104 iBT), IELTS (minimum score 7). Electronic applications accepted. *Faculty research:* Immunogenetic aspects of neurologic disease.

University of Colorado Boulder, Graduate School, College of Arts and Sciences, Department of Ecology and Evolutionary Biology, Boulder, CO 80309. Offers animal behavior (MA); biology (MA, PhD); environmental biology (MA, PhD); evolutionary biology (MA, PhD); neurobiology (MA); population biology (MA); population genetics (PhD). *Faculty:* 28 full-time (9 women). *Students:* 67 full-time (37 women), 27 part-time (13 women); includes 9 minority (1 Asian, non-Hispanic/Latino; 8 Hispanic/Latino), 5 international. Average age 30. 136 applicants, 13% accepted, 17 enrolled. In 2011, 8 master's, 5 doctorates awarded. Terminal master's awarded for partial completion of doctoral program. *Degree requirements:* For master's, comprehensive exam, thesis or alternative; for doctorate, comprehensive exam, thesis/dissertation. *Entrance requirements:* For master's, GRE General Test, GRE Subject Test, minimum undergraduate GPA of 3.0; for doctorate, GRE General Test, GRE Subject Test. *Application deadline:* For fall admission, 12/30 priority date for domestic students, 12/1 for international students. Application fee: $50 ($60 for international students). Electronic applications accepted. *Financial support:* In 2011–12, 88 students received support, including 35 fellowships (averaging $16,835 per year), 25 research assistantships with full and partial tuition reimbursements available (averaging $22,347 per year), 44 teaching assistantships with full and partial tuition reimbursements available (averaging $21,377 per year); institutionally sponsored loans, scholarships/grants, health care benefits, and unspecified assistantships also available. Financial award applicants required to submit FAFSA. *Faculty research:* Behavior, ecology, genetics, morphology, endocrinology, physiology, systematics. *Total annual research expenditures:* $4.6 million. *Application contact:* E-mail: ebiograd@colorado.edu. Web site: http://ebio.colorado.edu.

University of Colorado Denver, College of Liberal Arts and Sciences, Department of Integrative Biology, Denver, CO 80217. Offers animal behavior (MS); biology (MS); cell and developmental biology (MS); ecology (MS); evolutionary biology (MS); genetics (MS); microbiology (MS); molecular biology (MS); neurobiology (MS); plant systematics (MS). Part-time programs available. *Faculty:* 16 full-time (8 women). *Students:* 20 full-time (13 women), 5 part-time (4 women); includes 1 minority (Hispanic/Latino), 1 international. Average age 29. 21 applicants, 43% accepted, 5 enrolled. In 2011, 7 master's awarded. *Degree requirements:* For master's, comprehensive exam, thesis or alternative, 30-32 credit hours. *Entrance requirements:* For master's, GRE General Test (minimum score in 50% percentile in each section), BA/BS from accredited institution awarded within the last 10 years; minimum undergraduate GPA of 3.0; prerequisite courses: 1 year each of general biology and general chemistry, and 1 semester each of general genetics, general ecology, cell biology, and a structure/function course. Additional exam requirements/recommendations for international students: Required—TOEFL (minimum score 525 paper-based; 197 computer-based; 71 iBT). *Application deadline:* For fall admission, 2/1 for domestic and international students. Application fee: $50 ($75 for international students). Electronic applications accepted. *Financial support:* Research assistantships, teaching assistantships, Federal Work-Study, scholarships/grants, and unspecified assistantships available. Financial award application deadline: 4/1; financial award applicants required to submit FAFSA. *Faculty research:* Molecular developmental biology; quantitative ecology, biogeography, and population dynamics; environmental signaling and endocrine disruption; speciation, the evolution of reproductive isolation, and hybrid zones; evolutionary, behavioral, and conservation ecology. *Unit head:* Dr. Diana Tomback, Acting Chair, 303-556-2657, E-mail: diana.tomback@ucdenver.edu. *Application contact:* Timberley Roane, Associate Professor/Associate Chair, 303-556-6592, E-mail: timberley.roane@ucdenver.edu. Web site: http://www.ucdenver.edu/academics/colleges/CLAS/Departments/biology/Pages/Biology.aspx.

University of Connecticut, Graduate School, College of Liberal Arts and Sciences, Department of Physiology and Neurobiology, Storrs, CT 06269. Offers comparative physiology (MS, PhD); endocrinology (MS, PhD), including comparative physiology (MS); neurobiology (MS); neurobiology (MS, PhD). Terminal master's awarded for partial completion of doctoral program. *Degree requirements:* For master's, comprehensive exam; for doctorate, thesis/dissertation. *Entrance requirements:* For master's and doctorate, GRE General Test, GRE Subject Test. Additional exam requirements/recommendations for international students: Required—TOEFL (minimum score 550 paper-based; 213 computer-based). Electronic applications accepted.

See Display on page 455 and Close-Up on page 463.

University of Illinois at Chicago, Graduate College, Graduate Program in Neuroscience, Chicago, IL 60607-7128. Offers PhD, MD/PhD. Admissions and degrees offered through participating Departments of Anatomy and Cell Biology, Biochemistry, Bioengineering, Biological Sciences, Chemistry, Pathology, Pharmacology, Physiology and Biophysics, and Psychology. *Degree requirements:* For doctorate, thesis/dissertation. *Entrance requirements:* For doctorate, GRE General Test, minimum GPA of 3.75 on a 5.0 scale. Additional exam requirements/recommendations for international students: Required—TOEFL. *Faculty research:* Neurobiology and behavior.

The University of Iowa, Graduate College, College of Liberal Arts and Sciences, Department of Biology, Iowa City, IA 52242-1324. Offers biology (MS, PhD); cell and developmental biology (MS, PhD); evolution (MS, PhD); genetics (MS, PhD); neurobiology (MS, PhD). Terminal master's awarded for partial completion of doctoral program. *Degree requirements:* For master's, thesis optional, exam; for doctorate, comprehensive exam, thesis/dissertation. *Entrance requirements:* For master's and doctorate, GRE General Test, minimum GPA of 3.0. Additional exam requirements/recommendations for international students: Required—TOEFL (minimum score 600 paper-based; 250 computer-based; 100 iBT). Electronic applications accepted. *Faculty research:* Neurobiology, evolutionary biology, genetics, cell and developmental biology.

The University of Iowa, Graduate College, College of Liberal Arts and Sciences, Department of Psychology, Iowa City, IA 52242-1316. Offers neural and behavioral sciences (PhD); psychology (MA, PhD). *Degree requirements:* For master's, thesis optional, exam; for doctorate, comprehensive exam, thesis/dissertation. *Entrance requirements:* For master's and doctorate, GRE General Test, minimum GPA of 3.0. Additional exam requirements/recommendations for international students: Required—TOEFL (minimum score 550 paper-based; 213 computer-based; 81 iBT). Electronic applications accepted.

University of Kentucky, Graduate School, Graduate School Programs from the College of Medicine, Program in Anatomy and Neurobiology, Lexington, KY 40506-0032. Offers anatomy (PhD). *Degree requirements:* For doctorate, comprehensive exam, thesis/dissertation. *Entrance requirements:* For doctorate, GRE General Test, minimum undergraduate GPA of 2.75. Additional exam requirements/recommendations for international students: Required—TOEFL (minimum score 550 paper-based; 213 computer-based). Electronic applications accepted. *Faculty research:* Neuroendocrinology, developmental neurobiology, neurotrophic substances, neural plasticity and trauma, neurobiology of aging.

University of Louisville, School of Medicine, Department of Anatomical Sciences and Neurobiology, Louisville, KY 40292-0001. Offers MS, PhD, MD/PhD. Terminal master's awarded for partial completion of doctoral program. *Degree requirements:* For master's, thesis; for doctorate, comprehensive exam, thesis/dissertation. *Entrance requirements:* For master's and doctorate, GRE General Test (minimum score of 1000 verbal and quantitative), minimum GPA of 3.0. Additional exam requirements/recommendations for international students: Required—TOEFL. Electronic applications accepted. *Expenses:* Tuition, state resident: full-time $9692; part-time $539 per credit hour. Tuition, nonresident: full-time $20,168; part-time $1121 per credit hour. Tuition and fees vary according to program and reciprocity agreements. *Faculty research:* Human adult neural stem cells, development and plasticity of the nervous system, organization of the dorsal thalamus, electrophysiology/neuroanatomy of central neurons mediating control of reproductive and pelvic organs, normal neural mechanisms and plasticity following injury and/or chronic pain, differentiation and regeneration of motor neurons and oligodendrocytes.

The University of Manchester, Faculty of Life Sciences, Manchester, United Kingdom. Offers adaptive organismal biology (M Phil, PhD); animal biology (M Phil, PhD); biochemistry (M Phil, PhD); bioinformatics (M Phil, PhD); biomolecular sciences (M Phil, PhD); biotechnology (M Phil, PhD); cell biology (M Phil, PhD); cell matrix research (M Phil, PhD); channels and transporters (M Phil, PhD); developmental biology (M Phil, PhD); Egyptology (M Phil, PhD); environmental biology (M Phil, PhD); evolutionary biology (M Phil, PhD); gene expression (M Phil, PhD); genetics (M Phil, PhD); history of science, technology and medicine (M Phil, PhD); immunology (M Phil, PhD); integrative neurobiology and behavior (M Phil, PhD); membrane trafficking (M Phil, PhD); microbiology (M Phil, PhD); molecular and cellular neuroscience (M Phil, PhD); molecular biology (M Phil, PhD); molecular cancer studies (M Phil, PhD); neuroscience (M Phil, PhD); ophthalmology (M Phil, PhD); optometry (M Phil, PhD); organelle function (M Phil, PhD); pharmacology (M Phil, PhD); physiology (M Phil, PhD); plant sciences (M Phil, PhD); stem cell research (M Phil, PhD); structural biology (M Phil, PhD); systems neuroscience (M Phil, PhD); toxicology (M Phil, PhD).

University of Maryland, Baltimore, Graduate School, Graduate Program in Life Sciences, Program in Neuroscience, Baltimore, MD 21201. Offers PhD, MD/PhD. Part-time programs available. *Students:* 53 full-time (30 women), 3 part-time (2 women); includes 8 minority (2 Black or African American, non-Hispanic/Latino; 3 Asian, non-Hispanic/Latino; 1 Hispanic/Latino; 2 Two or more races, non-Hispanic/Latino), 6 international. Average age 28. 104 applicants, 22% accepted, 9 enrolled. In 2011, 5 doctorates awarded. *Degree requirements:* For doctorate, comprehensive exam, thesis/dissertation. *Entrance requirements:* For doctorate, GRE General Test, minimum GPA of 3.0. Additional exam requirements/recommendations for international students: Required—TOEFL (minimum score 550 paper-based; 80 iBT); Recommended—IELTS (minimum score 7). *Application deadline:* For fall admission, 1/15 for domestic and international students. Application fee: $50. Electronic applications accepted. *Financial support:* In 2011–12, research assistantships with partial tuition reimbursements (averaging $25,000 per year) were awarded; fellowships, health care benefits, and unspecified assistantships also available. Financial award application deadline: 3/1. *Faculty research:* Molecular, biochemical, and cellular pharmacology; membrane biophysics; synaptology; developmental neurobiology. *Unit head:* Dr. Bruce Krueger, Director, 410-706-5065, E-mail: bkrueger@umaryland.edu. *Application contact:* Jennifer Aumiller, Coordinator, 410-706-4701, Fax: 410-706-4724, E-mail: neurosci@umaryland.edu. Web site: http://neuroscience.umaryland.edu.

University of Minnesota, Twin Cities Campus, Graduate School, Graduate Program in Neuroscience, Minneapolis, MN 55455-0213. Offers MS, PhD. Terminal master's awarded for partial completion of doctoral program. *Degree requirements:* For master's, thesis; for doctorate, thesis/dissertation. *Entrance requirements:* For doctorate, GRE. Additional exam requirements/recommendations for international students: Required—TOEFL. Electronic applications accepted. *Faculty research:* Cellular and molecular neuroscience, behavioral neuroscience, developmental neuroscience, neurodegenerative diseases, pain, addiction, motor control.

University of Missouri, Graduate School, College of Arts and Sciences, Division of Biological Sciences, Program in Neurobiology and Behavior, Columbia, MO 65211. Offers MA, PhD. *Faculty:* 12. *Expenses:* Tuition, state resident: full-time $5881. Tuition, nonresident: full-time $15,183. *Required fees:* $952. Tuition and fees vary according to campus/location and program. *Financial support:* In 2011–12, fellowships (averaging $21,000 per year), teaching assistantships (averaging $16,300 per year) were awarded; research assistantships, scholarships/grants, health care benefits, and tuition waivers (full) also available. *Total annual research expenditures:* $1.8 million. *Unit head:* Dr. Ray Semlitsch, Director of Graduate Studies, 573-884-6396, E-mail: semlitschr@missouri.edu. *Application contact:* Nila Emerich, Application Contact, 800-553-5698. Web site: http://gradschool.missouri.edu/programs/catalog/neuroscience/.

The University of North Carolina at Chapel Hill, School of Medicine and Graduate School, Graduate Programs in Medicine, Curriculum in Neurobiology, Chapel Hill, NC 27599. Offers PhD. *Degree requirements:* For doctorate, comprehensive exam, thesis/dissertation. *Entrance requirements:* For doctorate, GRE General Test, minimum GPA of 3.0. Electronic applications accepted.

University of Oklahoma, College of Arts and Sciences, Department of Chemistry and Biochemistry, Norman, OK 73019. Offers chemistry and biochemistry (MS, PhD), including bioinformatics, cellular and behavioral neurobiology (PhD), chemistry. Part-time programs available. *Faculty:* 27 full-time (6 women). *Students:* 67 full-time (25 women), 22 part-time (9 women); includes 15 minority (5 Black or African American,

non-Hispanic/Latino; 1 American Indian or Alaska Native, non-Hispanic/Latino; 3 Asian, non-Hispanic/Latino; 4 Hispanic/Latino; 2 Two or more races, non-Hispanic/Latino), 40 international. Average age 28. 92 applicants, 17% accepted, 15 enrolled. In 2011, 17 master's, 17 doctorates awarded. Terminal master's awarded for partial completion of doctoral program. *Degree requirements:* For master's, thesis optional; for doctorate, thesis/dissertation. *Entrance requirements:* For master's, GRE, BS in chemistry; for doctorate, GRE. Additional exam requirements/recommendations for international students: Required—TOEFL (minimum score 550 paper-based; 79 iBT). *Application deadline:* For fall admission, 4/1 priority date for domestic students, 3/1 for international students; for spring admission, 9/1 priority date for domestic students, 9/1 for international students. Applications are processed on a rolling basis. Application fee: $40 ($90 for international students). Electronic applications accepted. *Expenses:* Tuition, state resident: full-time $4087; part-time $170.30 per credit hour. Tuition, nonresident: full-time $14,875; part-time $619.80 per credit hour. *Required fees:* $2659; $100.25 per credit hour. Tuition and fees vary according to course load and degree level. *Financial support:* In 2011–12, 89 students received support, including 1 fellowship with full tuition reimbursement available (averaging $5,000 per year), 19 research assistantships with partial tuition reimbursements available (averaging $15,794 per year), 58 teaching assistantships with partial tuition reimbursements available (averaging $16,776 per year); scholarships/grants, tuition waivers (full), and unspecified assistantships also available. Financial award applicants required to submit FAFSA. *Faculty research:* Structural biology, synthesis and catalysis, biomaterials, membrane biochemistry, genomics. *Total annual research expenditures:* $7 million. *Unit head:* Dr. George Richter-Addo, Chair, 405-325-4811, Fax: 405-325-6111, E-mail: grichteraddo@ou.edu. *Application contact:* Angelika Tietz, Graduate Program Assistant, 405-325-4811 Ext. 62946, Fax: 405-325-6111, E-mail: atietz@ou.edu. Web site: http://chem.ou.edu.

University of Oklahoma, College of Arts and Sciences, Department of Zoology and School of Aerospace and Mechanical Engineering and Department of Chemistry and Biochemistry, Program in Cellular and Behavioral Neurobiology, Norman, OK 73019. Offers PhD. *Students:* 2 full-time (1 woman), 2 part-time (1 woman), all international. Average age 27. 1 applicant, 0% accepted, 0 enrolled. *Entrance requirements:* Additional exam requirements/recommendations for international students: Required—TOEFL (minimum score 550 paper-based; 79 iBT). *Application deadline:* For fall admission, 12/1 for domestic and international students. Applications are processed on a rolling basis. Application fee: $40 ($90 for international students). Electronic applications accepted. *Expenses:* Tuition, state resident: full-time $4087; part-time $170.30 per credit hour. Tuition, nonresident: full-time $14,875; part-time $619.80 per credit hour. *Required fees:* $2659; $100.25 per credit hour. Tuition and fees vary according to course load and degree level. *Financial support:* In 2011–12, 4 students received support. Scholarships/grants, health care benefits, and unspecified assistantships available. Financial award applicants required to submit FAFSA. *Faculty research:* Behavioral neurobiology, cellular neurobiology, molecular neurobiology, developmental neurobiology, cell signaling. *Unit head:* Bill Matthews, Academic Chair, 405-325-4712, Fax: 405-325-6202, E-mail: wmatthews@ou.edu. *Application contact:* Dr. Ari Berkowitz, Director, 405-325-3492, Fax: 405-325-6202, E-mail: ari@ou.edu. Web site: http://www.ou.edu/cbn.

University of Rochester, School of Medicine and Dentistry, Graduate Programs in Medicine and Dentistry, Department of Neurobiology and Anatomy, Programs in Neurobiology and Anatomy, Rochester, NY 14627. Offers PhD, MD/MS. *Degree requirements:* For doctorate, thesis/dissertation, qualifying exam. *Entrance requirements:* For doctorate, GRE General Test. *Expenses: Tuition:* Full-time $41,040.

University of Southern California, Graduate School, Dana and David Dornsife College of Letters, Arts and Sciences, Department of Biological Sciences, Program in Neurobiology, Los Angeles, CA 90089. Offers PhD. M.S. is terminal degree only. Terminal master's awarded for partial completion of doctoral program. *Degree requirements:* For doctorate, comprehensive exam, thesis/dissertation, qualifying examination, dissertation defense. *Entrance requirements:* For doctorate, GRE, 3 letters of recommendation, personal statement, resume, minimum GPA of 3.0. Additional exam requirements/recommendations for international students: Required—TOEFL (minimum score 600 paper-based; 250 computer-based; 100 iBT). Electronic applications accepted. *Faculty research:* Neural basis of emotion and motivation, learning and memory, cell biology and physiology of neuronal signaling, sensory processing, development and aging.

University of Southern California, Keck School of Medicine and Graduate School, Graduate Programs in Medicine, Department of Cell and Neurobiology, Los Angeles, CA 90089. Offers MS, PhD. *Faculty:* 32 full-time (10 women). *Students:* 1 (woman) full-time; minority (Asian, non-Hispanic/Latino). In 2011, 1 degree awarded. Terminal master's awarded for partial completion of doctoral program. *Degree requirements:* For master's, thesis or alternative; for doctorate, thesis/dissertation. *Entrance requirements:* For master's, GRE General Test, minimum GPA of 3.0; for doctorate, GRE General Test. Additional exam requirements/recommendations for international students: Recommended—TOEFL (minimum score 600 paper-based; 250 computer-based; 100 iBT). *Application deadline:* For fall admission, 12/1 priority date for domestic students, 12/1 for international students. Application fee: $85. Electronic applications accepted. *Financial support:* In 2011–12, 1 research assistantship (averaging $29,100 per year) was awarded; health care benefits and unspecified assistantships also available. *Faculty research:* Neurobiology and development, gene therapy in vision, lachrymal glands, neuroendocrinology, signal transduction mechanisms. *Total annual research expenditures:* $1.7 million. *Unit head:* Dr. Mikel Henry Snow, Vice-Chair, 323-442-1881, Fax: 323-442-3466. *Application contact:* Janet Stoeckert, Administrative Director, Basic Science Departments, 323-442-3568, Fax: 323-442-1610, E-mail: janet.stoeckert@usc.edu.

The University of Texas at Austin, Graduate School, The Institute for Neuroscience, Austin, TX 78712-1111. Offers PhD, MD/PhD. Terminal master's awarded for partial completion of doctoral program. *Degree requirements:* For doctorate, thesis/dissertation. *Entrance requirements:* For doctorate, GRE. *Application deadline:* For fall admission, 1/15 priority date for domestic students. Application fee: $50 ($75 for international students). Electronic applications accepted. *Financial support:* Fellowships with tuition reimbursements, research assistantships with tuition reimbursements, and teaching assistantships with tuition reimbursements available. Financial award application deadline: 2/1. *Faculty research:* Cellular/molecular biology, neurobiology, pharmacology, behavioral neuroscience. *Unit head:* Dr. Daniel Johnston, Director, 512-232-6564, Fax: 512-471-2181, E-mail: djohnston@mail.clm.utexas.edu. *Application contact:* Dr. John Mihic, Graduate Advisor, 512-212-7174, Fax: 512-471-0390, E-mail: mihic@austin.utexas.edu. Web site: http://www.utexas.edu/neuroscience/.

The University of Texas at San Antonio, College of Sciences, Department of Biology, San Antonio, TX 78249-0617. Offers biology (MS); biotechnology (MS), including bioprocessing technician, biotechnology; cell and molecular biology (PhD); environmental science (MS); neurobiology (PhD). *Faculty:* 34 full-time (6 women), 7 part-time/adjunct (1 woman). *Students:* 117 full-time (62 women), 64 part-time (35 women); includes 63 minority (10 Black or African American, non-Hispanic/Latino; 10 Asian, non-Hispanic/Latino; 36 Hispanic/Latino; 7 Two or more races, non-Hispanic/Latino), 54 international. Average age 27. 239 applicants, 45% accepted, 50 enrolled. In 2011, 62 master's, 3 doctorates awarded. Terminal master's awarded for partial completion of doctoral program. *Degree requirements:* For master's, comprehensive exam, thesis or alternative; for doctorate, thesis/dissertation. *Entrance requirements:* For master's, GRE General Test, bachelor's degree with 18 credit hours in field of study or in another appropriate field of study; for doctorate, GRE General Test, 3 letters of recommendation, statement of purpose, resume. Additional exam requirements/recommendations for international students: Required—TOEFL (minimum score 500 paper-based; 100 iBT), IELTS (minimum score 5). *Application deadline:* For fall admission, 7/1 for domestic students, 4/1 for international students; for spring admission, 11/1 for domestic students, 9/1 for international students. Application fee: $45 ($85 for international students). *Expenses:* Tuition, state resident: full-time $3148; part-time $2176 per semester. Tuition, nonresident: full-time $8782; part-time $5932 per semester. *Required fees:* $719 per semester. *Financial support:* In 2011–12, 66 students received support, including 4 fellowships (averaging $22,350 per year), 34 research assistantships (averaging $22,350 per year), 8 teaching assistantships (averaging $22,350 per year). *Faculty research:* Development of human and veterinary vaccines against a fungal disease, mammalian germ cells and stem cells, dopamine neuron physiology and addiction, plant biochemistry, dendritic computation and synaptic plasticity. *Total annual research expenditures:* $2.8 million. *Unit head:* Dr. Edwin J. Barea-Rodriguez, Chair, 210-458-4511, Fax: 210-458-5658, E-mail: edwin.barea@utsa.edu. *Application contact:* Rene Munguia, Program Coordinator, 210-458-4642, Fax: 210-458-5658, E-mail: rene.munguia@utsa.edu.

University of Utah, School of Medicine and Graduate School, Graduate Programs in Medicine, Department of Neurobiology and Anatomy, Salt Lake City, UT 84112-1107. Offers PhD. Part-time programs available. Terminal master's awarded for partial completion of doctoral program. *Degree requirements:* For doctorate, comprehensive exam, thesis/dissertation. *Entrance requirements:* For doctorate, GRE General Test. Additional exam requirements/recommendations for international students: Required—TOEFL. *Faculty research:* Neuroscience, neuroanatomy, developmental neurobiology, neurogenetics.

University of Washington, Graduate School, School of Medicine, Graduate Programs in Medicine, Graduate Program in Neurobiology and Behavior, Seattle, WA 98195. Offers PhD. *Degree requirements:* For doctorate, thesis/dissertation. *Entrance requirements:* For doctorate, GRE. Additional exam requirements/recommendations for international students: Required—TOEFL. Electronic applications accepted. *Faculty research:* Motor, sensory systems, neuroplasticity, animal behavior, neuroendocrinology, computational neuroscience.

University of Wisconsin–Madison, School of Medicine and Public Health and Graduate School, Graduate Programs in Medicine, Madison, WI 53705. Offers biomolecular chemistry (MS, PhD); cancer biology (PhD); genetics and medical genetics (MS, PhD), including genetics (PhD), medical genetics (MS); medical physics (MS, PhD), including health physics (MS), medical physics; microbiology (PhD); molecular and cellular pharmacology (PhD); pathology and laboratory medicine (PhD); physiology (PhD); population health sciences (MPH, MS, PhD), including clinical research (MS, PhD), epidemiology (MS, PhD), health services research (MS, PhD), population health sciences (MPH), social and behavioral health sciences (MS, PhD); DPT/MPH; DVM/MPH; MD/MPH; MD/PhD; MPA/MPH; MS/MPH; Pharm D/MPH. Part-time programs available. Postbaccalaureate distance learning degree programs offered (minimal on-campus study). Terminal master's awarded for partial completion of doctoral program. Application fee: $45. Electronic applications accepted. *Expenses:* Contact institution. *Financial support:* Fellowships with full tuition reimbursements, research assistantships with full tuition reimbursements, teaching assistantships with full tuition reimbursements, scholarships/grants, traineeships, and tuition waivers (full) available. *Unit head:* Dr. Richard L. Moss, Senior Associate Dean for Basic Research, Biotechnology and Graduate Studies, 608-265-0523, Fax: 608-265-0522, E-mail: rlmoss@wisc.edu. *Application contact:* Information Contact, 608-262-2433, Fax: 608-262-5134, E-mail: gradadmiss@mail.bascom.wisc.edu. Web site: http://www.med.wisc.edu.

Virginia Commonwealth University, Medical College of Virginia-Professional Programs, School of Medicine, School of Medicine Graduate Programs, Department of Anatomy and Neurobiology, Program in Anatomy and Neurobiology, Richmond, VA 23284-9005. Offers PhD. *Accreditation:* APTA. *Degree requirements:* For doctorate, thesis/dissertation. *Entrance requirements:* For doctorate, GRE, MCAT or DAT. Electronic applications accepted. *Expenses:* Tuition, state resident: full-time $9133; part-time $507 per credit. Tuition, nonresident: full-time $18,777; part-time $1043 per credit. *Required fees:* $77 per credit. Tuition and fees vary according to degree level, campus/location, program and student level.

Wake Forest University, School of Medicine and Graduate School of Arts and Sciences, Graduate Programs in Medicine, Department of Neurobiology and Anatomy, Winston-Salem, NC 27109. Offers PhD, MD/PhD. *Degree requirements:* For doctorate, thesis/dissertation. *Entrance requirements:* For doctorate, GRE General Test. Additional exam requirements/recommendations for international students: Required—TOEFL. Electronic applications accepted. *Faculty research:* Sensory neurobiology, reproductive endocrinology, regulatory processes in cell biology.

Wesleyan University, Graduate Programs, Department of Biology, Middletown, CT 06459. Offers animal behavior (PhD); bioformatics/genomics (PhD); cell biology (PhD); developmental biology (PhD); evolution/ecology (PhD); genetics (PhD); neurobiology (PhD); population biology (PhD). *Degree requirements:* For doctorate, variable foreign language requirement, thesis/dissertation. *Entrance requirements:* For doctorate, GRE. Additional exam requirements/recommendations for international students: Required—TOEFL. *Faculty research:* Microbial population genetics, genetic basis of evolutionary adaptation, genetic regulation of differentiation and pattern formation in &ITdrosophila&RO.

West Virginia University, Eberly College of Arts and Sciences, Department of Biology, Morgantown, WV 26506. Offers cell and molecular biology (MS, PhD); environmental and evolutionary biology (MS, PhD); forensic biology (MS, PhD); genomic biology (MS, PhD); neurobiology (MS, PhD). Terminal master's awarded for partial completion of doctoral program. *Degree requirements:* For master's, thesis, final exam; for doctorate, thesis/dissertation, preliminary and final exams. *Entrance requirements:* For master's, GRE General Test, GRE Subject Test, minimum GPA of 3.0; for doctorate, GRE General Test, minimum GPA of 3.0. Additional exam requirements/recommendations for international students: Required—TOEFL. *Faculty research:* Environmental biology, genetic engineering, developmental biology, global change, biodiversity.

Yale University, Graduate School of Arts and Sciences, Department of Molecular, Cellular, and Developmental Biology, Program in Neurobiology, New Haven, CT 06520. Offers PhD. *Degree requirements:* For doctorate, thesis/dissertation. *Entrance requirements:* For doctorate, GRE General Test, GRE Subject Test.

Yale University, School of Medicine and Graduate School of Arts and Sciences, Combined Program in Biological and Biomedical Sciences (BBS), Department of Neurobiology, New Haven, CT 06520. Offers PhD. *Degree requirements:* For doctorate, thesis/dissertation. *Entrance requirements:* For doctorate, GRE General Test, GRE Subject Test.

Neuroscience

Albany Medical College, Center for Neuropharmacology and Neuroscience, Albany, NY 12208-3479. Offers MS, PhD. *Faculty:* 17 full-time (4 women), 11 part-time/adjunct (4 women). *Students:* 15 full-time (4 women); includes 1 minority (Black or African American, non-Hispanic/Latino), 3 international. Average age 24. 20 applicants, 30% accepted, 2 enrolled. In 2011, 1 master's, 3 doctorates awarded. Terminal master's awarded for partial completion of doctoral program. *Median time to degree:* Of those who began their doctoral program in fall 2003, 100% received their degree in 8 years or less. *Degree requirements:* For master's, thesis; for doctorate, comprehensive exam, thesis/dissertation. *Entrance requirements:* For master's, GRE General Test, all transcripts, letters of recommendation; for doctorate, GRE General Test, letters of recommendation. Additional exam requirements/recommendations for international students: Required—TOEFL. *Application deadline:* For fall admission, 3/15 priority date for domestic students, 3/15 for international students. Applications are processed on a rolling basis. Application fee: $0 ($60 for international students). *Financial support:* In 2011–12, 8 research assistantships with full tuition reimbursements (averaging $24,000 per year) were awarded; fellowships with partial tuition reimbursements, Federal Work-Study, scholarships/grants, and tuition waivers (full) also available. Financial award applicants required to submit FAFSA. *Faculty research:* Molecular and cellular neuroscience, neuronal development, addiction. *Unit head:* Dr. Stanley D. Glick, Director, 518-262-5303, Fax: 518-262-5799, E-mail: cnninfo@mail.amc.edu. *Application contact:* Dr. Mark Fleck, Graduate Director, 518-262-6536, Fax: 518-262-5799, E-mail: cnninfo@mail.amc.edu. Web site: http://www.amc.edu/research/cnn.

Alliant International University–San Diego, Shirley M. Hufstedler School of Education, Educational Psychology Programs, San Diego, CA 92131-1799. Offers educational psychology (Psy D); pupil personnel services (Credential); school neuropsychology (Certificate); school psychology (MA); school-based mental health (Certificate). Part-time programs available. *Faculty:* 1 full-time (0 women), 14 part-time/adjunct (9 women). *Students:* 28 full-time (26 women), 31 part-time (25 women); includes 14 minority (5 Black or African American, non-Hispanic/Latino; 9 Hispanic/Latino). Average age 32. In 2011, 10 master's, 2 doctorates awarded. *Degree requirements:* For doctorate, thesis/dissertation, internship. *Entrance requirements:* For master's, minimum GPA of 2.5, letters of recommendation; for doctorate, minimum GPA of 3.0, letters of recommendation. Additional exam requirements/recommendations for international students: Required—TOEFL (minimum score 550 paper-based; 213 computer-based), TWE (minimum score 5). *Application deadline:* For fall admission, 7/1 priority date for domestic students, 7/1 for international students; for spring admission, 12/1 priority date for domestic students, 12/1 for international students. Applications are processed on a rolling basis. Application fee: $55. Electronic applications accepted. Tuition and fees vary according to degree level and program. *Financial support:* Career-related internships or fieldwork, Federal Work-Study, institutionally sponsored loans, and scholarships/grants available. Financial award application deadline: 2/15; financial award applicants required to submit FAFSA. *Faculty research:* School-based mental health, pupil personnel services, childhood mood, school-based assessment. *Unit head:* Dr. Steve Fisher, Program Director, 828-635-4825, Fax: 858-635-4739, E-mail: admissions@alliant.edu. *Application contact:* Alliant International University Central Contact Center, 866-U-ALLIANT, Fax: 858-635-4555, E-mail: admissions@alliant.edu. Web site: http://www.alliant.edu/gsoe.

American University, College of Arts and Sciences, Department of Psychology, Washington, DC 22016-8062. Offers behavior, cognition, and neuroscience (PhD); including psychology; clinical psychology (PhD), including psychology; psychobiology of healing (Certificate); psychology (MA), including experimental/biological psychology, general psychology, personality/social psychology. *Accreditation:* APA. Part-time programs available. *Faculty:* 20 full-time (8 women), 3 part-time/adjunct (2 women). *Students:* 69 full-time (55 women), 51 part-time (38 women); includes 20 minority (4 Black or African American, non-Hispanic/Latino; 6 Asian, non-Hispanic/Latino; 7 Hispanic/Latino; 3 Two or more races, non-Hispanic/Latino), 4 international. Average age 27. 474 applicants, 17% accepted, 39 enrolled. In 2011, 21 master's, 9 doctorates awarded. *Degree requirements:* For master's, comprehensive exam, thesis or alternative; for doctorate, comprehensive exam, thesis/dissertation, tools of research. *Entrance requirements:* For master's, GRE General Test, GRE Subject Test; for doctorate, GRE General Test, GRE Subject Test, 3 letters of recommendation. Additional exam requirements/recommendations for international students: Required—TOEFL. Application fee: $80. *Expenses: Tuition:* Full-time $24,264; part-time $1348 per credit hour. *Required fees:* $430. Tuition and fees vary according to course load and program. *Financial support:* Fellowships, research assistantships, teaching assistantships, career-related internships or fieldwork, Federal Work-Study, institutionally sponsored loans, tuition waivers (full and partial), and unspecified assistantships available. Support available to part-time students. Financial award application deadline: 2/1. *Faculty research:* Anxiety disorders, cognitive assessment, neuropsychology, conditioning and learning, psychopharmacology. *Unit head:* Dr. Anthony Riley, Chair, 202-885-1720, Fax: 202-885-1023, E-mail: alriley@american.edu. *Application contact:* Sara Holland, Senior Administrative Assistant, 202-885-1717, Fax: 202-885-1023, E-mail: holland@american.edu. Web site: http://www.american.edu/CAS/Psychology/.

American University of Beirut, Graduate Programs, Faculty of Medicine, Beirut, Lebanon. Offers anatomy, cell biology and human morphology (MS); biochemistry and medical genetics (MS); biomedical sciences (PhD); experimental pathology, immunology and microbiology (MS); medicine (MD); neuroscience (MS); pharmacology and toxicology (MS). Part-time programs available. *Faculty:* 232 full-time (58 women), 68 part-time/adjunct (7 women). *Students:* 346 full-time (135 women), 69 part-time (57 women). Average age 23. In 2011, 20 master's, 82 doctorates awarded. *Degree requirements:* For master's, one foreign language, comprehensive exam, thesis (for some programs). *Entrance requirements:* For master's, letter of recommendation; for doctorate, MCAT, bachelor's degree. Additional exam requirements/recommendations for international students: Required—TOEFL (minimum score 600 paper-based; 250 computer-based; 100 iBT), IELTS (minimum score 7.5). *Application deadline:* For fall admission, 4/30 for domestic and international students; for spring admission, 11/1 for domestic and international students. Application fee: $50. *Expenses: Tuition:* Full-time $12,780; part-time $710 per credit. Tuition and fees vary according to course load and program. *Financial support:* In 2011–12, 19 students received support. Career-related internships or fieldwork, institutionally sponsored loans, scholarships/grants, health care benefits, and unspecified assistantships available. Financial award application deadline: 2/2. *Faculty research:* Cancer research (targeted therapy, mechanisms of leukemogenesis, tumor cell extravasation and metastasis, cancer stem cells); stem cell research (regenerative medicine, drug discovery); genetic research (neurogenetics, hereditary cardiomyopathy, hemoglobinopathies, pharmacogenomics, proteomics); neuroscience research (pain, neurodegenerative disorder); metabolism (inflammation and metabolism, metabolic disorder, diabetes mellitus); vascular and renal biology, signal transduction. *Total annual research expenditures:* $2.3 million. *Unit head:* Dr. Mohamed Sayegh, Dean, 961-1350000 Ext. 4700, Fax: 961-1744464, E-mail: msayegh@aub.edu.lb. *Application contact:* Dr. Salim Kanaan, Director, Admissions Office, 961-1350000 Ext. 2594, Fax: 961-1750775, E-mail: sk00@aub.edu.lb. Web site: http://www.aub.edu.lb/fm/fm_home/Pages/index.aspx.

Argosy University, Chicago, College of Psychology and Behavioral Sciences, Doctoral Program in Clinical Psychology, Chicago, IL 60601. Offers child and adolescent psychology (Psy D); client-centered and experiential psychotherapies (Psy D); diversity and multicultural psychology (Psy D); family psychology (Psy D); forensic psychology (Psy D); health psychology (Psy D); neuropsychology (Psy D); organizational consulting (Psy D); psychoanalytic psychology (Psy D); psychology and spirituality (Psy D). *Accreditation:* APA.

Argosy University, Phoenix, College of Psychology and Behavioral Sciences, Program in Clinical Psychology, Phoenix, AZ 85021. Offers clinical psychology (MA); neuropsychology (Psy D); sports-exercise psychology (Psy D). *Accreditation:* APA (one or more programs are accredited).

Argosy University, Phoenix, College of Psychology and Behavioral Sciences, Program in Neuropsychology, Phoenix, AZ 85021. Offers Psy D.

Argosy University, Schaumburg, College of Psychology and Behavioral Sciences, Schaumburg, IL 60173-5403. Offers clinical health psychology (Post-Graduate Certificate); clinical psychology (MA, Psy D), including child and family psychology (Psy D), clinical health psychology (Psy D), diversity and multicultural psychology (Psy D), forensic psychology (Psy D), neuropsychology (Psy D); community counseling (MA); counseling psychology (Ed D), including counselor education and supervision; counselor education and supervision (Ed D); forensic psychology (Post-Graduate Certificate); industrial organizational psychology (MA). *Accreditation:* ACA; APA.

Argosy University, Tampa, College of Psychology and Behavioral Sciences, Program in Clinical Psychology, Tampa, FL 33607. Offers clinical psychology (MA, Psy D), including child and adolescent psychology (Psy D), geropsychology (Psy D), marriage/couples and family therapy (Psy D), neuropsychology (Psy D). *Accreditation:* APA.

Arizona State University, College of Liberal Arts and Sciences, Department of Psychology, Tempe, AZ 85287-1104. Offers behavioral neuroscience (PhD); clinical psychology (PhD); cognition, action and perception (PhD); developmental psychology (PhD); quantitative psychology (PhD); social psychology (PhD). *Accreditation:* APA. *Degree requirements:* For doctorate, comprehensive exam, thesis/dissertation, interactive Program of Study (iPOS) submitted before completing 50 percent of required credit hours. *Entrance requirements:* For doctorate, GRE General Test, GRE Subject Test, minimum GPA of 3.0 or equivalent in last 2 years of work leading to bachelor's degree. Additional exam requirements/recommendations for international students: Required—TOEFL (minimum score 80 iBT), TOEFL, IELTS, or Pearson Test of English. Electronic applications accepted.

Arizona State University, College of Liberal Arts and Sciences, School of Life Sciences, Tempe, AZ 85287-4601. Offers animal behavior (PhD); applied ethics (biomedical and health ethics) (MA); biological design (PhD); biology (MS, PhD); biology (biology and society) (MS, PhD); environmental life sciences (PhD); evolutionary biology (PhD); human and social dimensions of science and technology (PhD); microbiology (PhD); molecular and cellular biology (PhD); neuroscience (PhD); philosophy (history and philosophy of science) (MA); sustainability (PhD). Terminal master's awarded for partial completion of doctoral program. *Degree requirements:* For master's, thesis (for some programs), interactive Program of Study (iPOS) submitted before completing 50 percent of required credit hours; for doctorate, variable foreign language requirement, comprehensive exam, thesis/dissertation, interactive Program of Study (iPOS) submitted before completing 50 percent of required credit hours. *Entrance requirements:* For master's and doctorate, GRE, minimum GPA of 3.0 or equivalent in last 2 years of work leading to bachelor's degree. Additional exam requirements/recommendations for international students: Required—TOEFL (minimum score 600 paper-based; 250 computer-based; 100 iBT). Electronic applications accepted.

Arizona State University, Graduate College, Interdisciplinary Graduate Program in Neuroscience, Tempe, AZ 85287-1003. Offers PhD. Terminal master's awarded for partial completion of doctoral program. *Degree requirements:* For doctorate, comprehensive exam, thesis/dissertation, All students must submit an interactive Program of Study (iPOS) before completing 50 percent of the credit hours required for their degree program. A student is not eligible to apply for the Foreign Language Examination (if appl), comprehensive exams, dissertation proposal/prospectus or dissertation defense (if appl) without an approved iPOS.. *Entrance requirements:* For doctorate, GRE, GPA of 3.0 or better in the last 2 years of work leading to the bachelor's degree, 3 letters of recommendation, statement of research interests and goals, CV or resume, and the completed Interdisciplinary Neuroscience Academic Record form. See program web page for additional information.. Additional exam requirements/recommendations for international students: Required—TOEFL (minimum score 550 paper-based; 213 computer-based; 80 iBT), IELTS (minimum score 6.5). Electronic applications accepted.

Baylor College of Medicine, Graduate School of Biomedical Sciences, Department of Neuroscience, Houston, TX 77030-3498. Offers PhD, MD/PhD. *Faculty:* 53 full-time (12 women). *Students:* 53 full-time (28 women); includes 15 minority (2 Black or African American, non-Hispanic/Latino; 5 Asian, non-Hispanic/Latino; 8 Hispanic/Latino), 12 international. Average age 27. 118 applicants, 14% accepted, 8 enrolled. In 2011, 8 doctorates awarded. *Degree requirements:* For doctorate, thesis/dissertation, public defense. *Entrance requirements:* For doctorate, GRE General Test, GRE Subject Test (strongly recommended), minimum GPA of 3.0. Additional exam requirements/recommendations for international students: Required—TOEFL. *Application deadline:* For fall admission, 1/1 priority date for domestic students. Application fee: $0. Electronic applications accepted. *Financial support:* In 2011–12, 13 fellowships with full tuition reimbursements (averaging $29,000 per year), 40 research assistantships with full tuition reimbursements (averaging $29,000 per year) were awarded; Federal Work-Study, institutionally sponsored loans, health care benefits, and scholarships (to all students unless there are grant funds available to pay tuition) also available. Financial award applicants required to submit FAFSA. *Faculty research:* Neurodegenerative, neurodevelopment, neurophysiology, addiction, learning and memory. *Unit head:* Dr. Mariella DeBiasi, Director, 713-798-7270. *Application contact:* Krista Defalco, Graduate Program Administrator, 713-798-7270, Fax: 713-798-3946, E-mail: kdefalco@bcm.edu. Web site: http://neuro.neusc.bcm.edu/.

Baylor College of Medicine, Graduate School of Biomedical Sciences, Program in Developmental Biology, Houston, TX 77030-3498. Offers PhD, MD/PhD. *Faculty:* 68

full-time (20 women). *Students:* 55 full-time (28 women); includes 9 minority (7 Asian, non-Hispanic/Latino; 2 Hispanic/Latino), 37 international. Average age 28. 771 applicants, 2% accepted, 10 enrolled. In 2011, 5 degrees awarded. *Median time to degree:* Of those who began their doctoral program in fall 2003, 100% received their degree in 8 years or less. *Degree requirements:* For doctorate, thesis/dissertation, public defense. *Entrance requirements:* For doctorate, GRE General Test, GRE Subject Test (strongly recommended), minimum GPA of 3.0. Additional exam requirements/recommendations for international students: Required—TOEFL. *Application deadline:* For fall admission, 1/1 priority date for domestic students. Application fee: $0. Electronic applications accepted. *Financial support:* In 2011–12, 55 students received support, including 6 fellowships with full tuition reimbursements available (averaging $29,000 per year), 49 research assistantships with full tuition reimbursements available (averaging $29,000 per year); career-related internships or fieldwork, Federal Work-Study, institutionally sponsored loans, health care benefits, tuition waivers (full), and stipends also available. *Faculty research:* Stem cells, cancer, neurobiology, organogenesis, genetics of model organisms. *Unit head:* Dr. Hugo Bellen, Director, 713-798-6410. *Application contact:* Catherine Tasnier, Graduate Program Administrator, 713-798-6410, Fax: 713-798-5386, E-mail: cat@bcm.edu. Web site: http://www.bcm.edu/db/.

See Display on page 287 and Close-Up on page 311.

Boston University, Graduate School of Arts and Sciences, Department of Cognitive and Neural Systems, Boston, MA 02215. Offers MA, PhD. *Students:* 32 full-time (6 women), 4 part-time (0 women); includes 4 minority (2 Asian, non-Hispanic/Latino; 1 Hispanic/Latino; 1 Two or more races, non-Hispanic/Latino), 9 international. Average age 30. 29 applicants, 7% accepted, 2 enrolled. Terminal master's awarded for partial completion of doctoral program. *Degree requirements:* For master's, one foreign language, comprehensive exam; for doctorate, one foreign language, comprehensive exam, thesis/dissertation. *Entrance requirements:* For master's and doctorate, GRE General Test, GRE Subject Test (recommended), 3 letters of recommendation. Additional exam requirements/recommendations for international students: Required—TOEFL (minimum score 550 paper-based; 213 computer-based). Application fee: $70. Electronic applications accepted. *Expenses: Tuition:* Full-time $40,848; part-time $1276 per credit hour. *Required fees:* $572; $286 per semester. *Financial support:* In 2011–12, 25 research assistantships with full tuition reimbursements (averaging $19,300 per year) were awarded; Federal Work-Study and unspecified assistantships also available. Support available to part-time students. Financial award application deadline: 1/15; financial award applicants required to submit FAFSA. *Unit head:* Ennio Mingolla, Chairman, 617-353-9485, Fax: 617-353-7755, E-mail: ennio@bu.edu. *Application contact:* Carol Y. Jefferson, Administrative Assistant, 617-353-7676, Fax: 617-353-7755, E-mail: caroly@bu.edu. Web site: http://cns-web.bu.edu/.

Boston University, School of Medicine, Division of Graduate Medical Sciences, Graduate Program for Neuroscience, Boston, MA 02215. Offers PhD, MD/PhD. *Faculty:* 57 full-time (17 women). *Students:* 25 full-time (12 women), 1 (woman) part-time; includes 5 minority (1 Black or African American, non-Hispanic/Latino; 3 Asian, non-Hispanic/Latino; 1 Hispanic/Latino), 3 international. Average age 26. 191 applicants, 6% accepted, 10 enrolled. *Degree requirements:* For doctorate, thesis/dissertation. *Entrance requirements:* For doctorate, GRE. Additional exam requirements/recommendations for international students: Required—TOEFL. Application fee: $75. Electronic applications accepted. *Expenses: Tuition:* Full-time $40,848; part-time $1276 per credit hour. *Required fees:* $572; $286 per semester. *Financial support:* In 2011–12, fellowships (averaging $30,500 per year), research assistantships (averaging $30,500 per year), 2 teaching assistantships (averaging $30,500 per year) were awarded. Financial award applicants required to submit FAFSA. *Unit head:* Dr. Shelley Russek, Director, 617-638-4319, E-mail: srussek@bu.edu. *Application contact:* Michelle Hall, Associate Director of Admissions, 617-638-5121, Fax: 617-638-5740, E-mail: natashah@bu.edu. Web site: http://www.bu.edu/neuro/graduate/.

Boston University, School of Medicine, Division of Graduate Medical Sciences, Program in Behavioral Neuroscience, Boston, MA 02215. Offers PhD, MD/PhD. Part-time programs available. *Faculty:* 36 full-time (10 women), 2 part-time/adjunct (both women). *Students:* 8 full-time (4 women), 2 part-time (both women). 37 applicants, 3% accepted, 1 enrolled. In 2011, 1 doctorate awarded. *Degree requirements:* For doctorate, thesis/dissertation. *Entrance requirements:* For doctorate, GRE General Test, GRE Subject Test. Additional exam requirements/recommendations for international students: Required—TOEFL. *Application deadline:* For fall admission, 1/15 priority date for domestic students; for spring admission, 10/15 priority date for domestic students. Application fee: $75. Electronic applications accepted. *Expenses: Tuition:* Full-time $40,848; part-time $1276 per credit hour. *Required fees:* $572; $286 per semester. *Financial support:* In 2011–12, fellowships (averaging $30,500 per year), research assistantships (averaging $30,500 per year) were awarded; Federal Work-Study, scholarships/grants, and traineeships also available. Financial award applicants required to submit FAFSA. *Faculty research:* Human brain dysfunction, language disorders, disorders of purposeful movement, path of learning. *Unit head:* Dr. Marlene Oscar Berman, Director, 617-638-4803, Fax: 617-638-4806, E-mail: oscar@bu.edu. *Application contact:* Michelle Hall, Associate Director of Admissions, 617-638-5121, Fax: 617-638-5740, E-mail: natashah@bu.edu. Web site: http://www.bumc.bu.edu/busm-bns/.

Brandeis University, Graduate School of Arts and Sciences, Department of Psychology, Waltham, MA 02454-9110. Offers brain, body and behavior (PhD); cognitive neuroscience (PhD); general psychology (MA); social/developmental psychology (PhD). Part-time programs available. *Faculty:* 18 full-time (4 women), 2 part-time/adjunct (both women). *Students:* 44 full-time (30 women); includes 4 minority (3 Black or African American, non-Hispanic/Latino; 1 Asian, non-Hispanic/Latino), 12 international. 189 applicants, 15% accepted, 16 enrolled. In 2011, 12 master's, 6 doctorates awarded. Terminal master's awarded for partial completion of doctoral program. *Degree requirements:* For master's, thesis; for doctorate, thesis/dissertation, teaching requirement; research reports. *Entrance requirements:* For master's and doctorate, GRE General Test; GRE Subject Test (recommended), 3 letters of recommendation, statement of purpose, transcript(s), resume. Additional exam requirements/recommendations for international students: Required—TOEFL (minimum score 600 paper-based; 250 computer-based; 100 iBT); Recommended—IELTS (minimum score 7). *Application deadline:* For fall admission, 1/15 priority date for domestic students, 1/15 for international students. Applications are processed on a rolling basis. Application fee: $75. Electronic applications accepted. *Financial support:* In 2011–12, 17 fellowships with full tuition reimbursements (averaging $20,400 per year), 7 research assistantships with full tuition reimbursements (averaging $20,400 per year), 13 teaching assistantships with partial tuition reimbursements (averaging $3,200 per year) were awarded; scholarships/grants, health care benefits, tuition waivers (full and partial), and unspecified assistantships also available. Support available to part-time students. Financial award application deadline: 4/15; financial award applicants required to submit FAFSA. *Unit head:* Prof. Don Katz, Director of Graduate Studies, 781-736-3268, Fax: 781-736-3291, E-mail: dbkatz@brandeis.edu. *Application contact:* Phil Gnatowski, Department Administrator, 781-736-3302, Fax: 781-736-3291, E-mail: gnat@brandeis.edu. Web site: http://www.brandeis.edu/departments/psych/.

Brandeis University, Graduate School of Arts and Sciences, Program in Neuroscience, Waltham, MA 02454-9110. Offers neuroscience (MS, PhD); quantitative biology (PhD). *Faculty:* 23 full-time (9 women). *Students:* 56 full-time (25 women); includes 13 minority (5 Black or African American, non-Hispanic/Latino; 4 Asian, non-Hispanic/Latino; 4 Hispanic/Latino), 4 international. 141 applicants, 22% accepted, 15 enrolled. In 2011, 10 master's, 6 doctorates awarded. Terminal master's awarded for partial completion of doctoral program. *Degree requirements:* For master's, thesis optional, research project; for doctorate, thesis/dissertation, qualifying exams, teaching experience, journal club, research seminars. *Entrance requirements:* For master's and doctorate, GRE General Test, official transcript(s), statement of purpose, resume, 3 letters of recommendation. Additional exam requirements/recommendations for international students: Required—TOEFL (minimum score 600 paper-based; 250 computer-based; 100 iBT); Recommended—IELTS (minimum score 7). *Application deadline:* For fall admission, 1/15 priority date for domestic students. Applications are processed on a rolling basis. Application fee: $75. Electronic applications accepted. *Financial support:* In 2011–12, 5 fellowships with full tuition reimbursements (averaging $29,580 per year), 32 research assistantships with full tuition reimbursements (averaging $29,580 per year), teaching assistantships with partial tuition reimbursements (averaging $3,200 per year) were awarded; scholarships/grants, health care benefits, tuition waivers (full and partial), and unspecified assistantships also available. Support available to part-time students. Financial award application deadline: 4/15; financial award applicants required to submit FAFSA. *Faculty research:* Behavioral neuroscience, cellular and molecular neuroscience, cognitive neuroscience, computational and integrative neuroscience, systems neuroscience. *Unit head:* Dr. Don Katz, Director of Graduate Studies, 781-736-3100, Fax: 781-736-3107, E-mail: dbkatz@brandeis.edu. *Application contact:* Dr. Maryanna Aldrich, Department Administrator, 781-736-3100, Fax: 781-736-3107, E-mail: maldrich@brandeis.edu. Web site: http://www.brandeis.edu/gsas/programs/neuroscience.html.

Brigham Young University, Graduate Studies, College of Family, Home, and Social Sciences, Department of Psychology, Provo, UT 84602. Offers clinical psychology (PhD); general psychology (MS); psychology (PhD), including applied social psychology, behavioral neuroscience. *Accreditation:* APA (one or more programs are accredited). *Faculty:* 31 full-time (5 women), 7 part-time/adjunct (3 women). *Students:* 73 full-time (32 women); includes 12 minority (2 Black or African American, non-Hispanic/Latino; 1 American Indian or Alaska Native, non-Hispanic/Latino; 5 Asian, non-Hispanic/Latino; 4 Hispanic/Latino), 6 international. Average age 26. 118 applicants, 19% accepted, 17 enrolled. In 2011, 12 master's, 18 doctorates awarded. *Degree requirements:* For master's, thesis; for doctorate, comprehensive exam, thesis/dissertation, publishable paper. *Entrance requirements:* For master's and doctorate, GRE General Test, minimum GPA of 3.0 in last 60 hours of upper-division course work. Additional exam requirements/recommendations for international students: Required—TOEFL. *Application deadline:* For fall admission, 1/5 for domestic students. Application fee: $50. Electronic applications accepted. *Expenses: Tuition:* Full-time $5760; part-time $320 per credit. Tuition and fees vary according to student's religious affiliation. *Financial support:* In 2011–12, 17 research assistantships with partial tuition reimbursements (averaging $10,000 per year), 22 teaching assistantships with partial tuition reimbursements (averaging $10,000 per year) were awarded; fellowships, career-related internships or fieldwork, scholarships/grants, tuition waivers (partial), and unspecified assistantships also available. Financial award application deadline: 5/31. *Faculty research:* Psychotherapy process, Alzheimer's disease/dementia, psychology and law, health, psychology, developmental. *Total annual research expenditures:* $1 million. *Unit head:* Dr. Ramona Hopkins, Chair, 801-422-1170, Fax: 801-422-0602, E-mail: ramona_hopkins@byu.edu. *Application contact:* Karen A. Christensen, Coordinator of Student Programs, 801-422-4560, Fax: 801-422-0602, E-mail: karen@byu.edu. Web site: http://psychology.byu.edu/.

Brigham Young University, Graduate Studies, College of Life Sciences, Department of Physiology and Developmental Biology, Provo, UT 84602. Offers neuroscience (MS, PhD); physiology and developmental biology (MS, PhD). Part-time programs available. *Faculty:* 20 full-time (0 women). *Students:* 37 full-time (14 women); includes 9 minority (2 American Indian or Alaska Native, non-Hispanic/Latino; 3 Asian, non-Hispanic/Latino; 4 Hispanic/Latino). Average age 29. 12 applicants, 75% accepted, 8 enrolled. In 2011, 6 master's, 1 doctorate awarded. Terminal master's awarded for partial completion of doctoral program. *Degree requirements:* For master's, thesis; for doctorate, comprehensive exam, thesis/dissertation. *Entrance requirements:* For master's, GRE General Test, minimum GPA of 3.0 during previous 2 years; for doctorate, GRE General Test, minimum GPA of 3.0 overall. Additional exam requirements/recommendations for international students: Required—TOEFL. *Application deadline:* For fall admission, 2/1 priority date for domestic students, 2/1 for international students; for winter admission, 9/10 priority date for domestic students, 9/10 for international students. Application fee: $50. Electronic applications accepted. *Expenses: Tuition:* Full-time $5760; part-time $320 per credit. Tuition and fees vary according to student's religious affiliation. *Financial support:* In 2011–12, 36 students received support, including 1 fellowship with partial tuition reimbursement available (averaging $7,100 per year), 18 research assistantships with full tuition reimbursements available (averaging $15,500 per year), 19 teaching assistantships with partial tuition reimbursements available (averaging $14,900 per year); career-related internships or fieldwork, institutionally sponsored loans, scholarships/grants, tuition waivers (full and partial), unspecified assistantships, and tuition awards also available. Financial award application deadline: 2/1. *Faculty research:* Sex differentiation of the brain, exercise physiology, developmental biology, membrane biophysics, neuroscience. *Total annual research expenditures:* $589,241. *Unit head:* Dr. William W. Winder, Chair, 801-422-3093, Fax: 801-422-0700, E-mail: william_winder@byu.edu. *Application contact:* Dr. Dixon J. Woodbury, Graduate Coordinator, 801-422-7562, Fax: 801-422-0700, E-mail: dixon_woodbury@byu.edu. Web site: http://pdbio.byu.edu.

Brock University, Faculty of Graduate Studies, Faculty of Social Sciences, Program in Psychology, St. Catharines, ON L2S 3A1, Canada. Offers behavioral neuroscience (MA, PhD); life span development (MA, PhD); social personality (MA, PhD). Part-time programs available. *Degree requirements:* For master's, thesis; for doctorate, thesis/dissertation. *Entrance requirements:* For master's, GRE, honors degree; for doctorate, GRE, master's degree. Additional exam requirements/recommendations for international students: Required—TOEFL (minimum score 550 paper-based; 213 computer-based; 80 iBT), IELTS (minimum score 6.5), TWE (minimum score 4). Electronic applications accepted. *Faculty research:* Social personality, behavioral neuroscience, life-span development.

Brown University, Graduate School, Department of Neuroscience, Providence, RI 02912. Offers PhD. *Degree requirements:* For doctorate, comprehensive exam, thesis/dissertation. *Entrance requirements:* For doctorate, GRE.

Brown University, Graduate School, Department of Psychology, Providence, RI 02912. Offers behavioral neuroscience (PhD); cognitive processes (PhD); sensation and perception (PhD); social/developmental (PhD); MS/PhD. *Accreditation:* APA. *Degree requirements:* For doctorate, thesis/dissertation. *Entrance requirements:* For doctorate, GRE General Test, GRE Subject Test.

Brown University, Graduate School, Division of Biology and Medicine, Department of Neuroscience, Providence, RI 02912. Offers PhD. *Degree requirements:* For doctorate, thesis/dissertation, preliminary exam. *Entrance requirements:* For doctorate, GRE General Test, GRE Subject Test. Additional exam requirements/recommendations for international students: Required—TOEFL. Electronic applications accepted. *Faculty research:* Neurophysiology, systems neuroscience, membrane biophysics, neuropharmacology, sensory systems.

Brown University, National Institutes of Health Sponsored Programs, Department of Neuroscience, Providence, RI 02912. Offers PhD. *Degree requirements:* For doctorate, comprehensive exam, thesis/dissertation.

California Institute of Technology, Division of Engineering and Applied Science, Option in Computation and Neural Systems, Pasadena, CA 91125-0001. Offers MS, PhD. Terminal master's awarded for partial completion of doctoral program. *Degree requirements:* For doctorate, thesis/dissertation, qualifying exam. *Entrance requirements:* For doctorate, GRE General Test. *Faculty research:* Biological and artificial computational devices, modeling of sensory processes and learning, theory of collective computation.

Carleton University, Faculty of Graduate Studies, Faculty of Arts and Social Sciences, Department of Psychology, Ottawa, ON K1S 5B6, Canada. Offers neuroscience (M Sc); psychology (MA, PhD). Part-time programs available. *Degree requirements:* For master's, thesis; for doctorate, comprehensive exam, thesis/dissertation. *Entrance requirements:* For master's, honors degree; for doctorate, GRE, master's degree. Additional exam requirements/recommendations for international students: Required—TOEFL. *Faculty research:* Behavioral neuroscience, social and personality psychology, cognitive/perception, developmental psychology, computer user research and evaluation, forensic psychology, health psychology.

Carnegie Mellon University, Center for the Neural Basis of Cognition, Pittsburgh, PA 15213-3891. Offers PhD.

Case Western Reserve University, School of Medicine and School of Graduate Studies, Graduate Programs in Medicine, Department of Neurosciences, Cleveland, OH 44106. Offers neurobiology (PhD); neuroscience (PhD); MD/PhD. *Degree requirements:* For doctorate, thesis/dissertation. *Entrance requirements:* For doctorate, GRE General Test, 3 letters of recommendation. Additional exam requirements/recommendations for international students: Required—TOEFL. Electronic applications accepted. *Faculty research:* Neurotropic factors, synapse formation, regeneration, determination of cell fate, cellular neuroscience.

Central Michigan University, College of Graduate Studies, College of Humanities and Social and Behavioral Sciences, Department of Psychology, Program in Neuroscience, Mount Pleasant, MI 48859. Offers MS, PhD. *Degree requirements:* For master's, comprehensive exam, thesis or alternative; for doctorate, thesis/dissertation. *Entrance requirements:* For master's and doctorate, GRE. Electronic applications accepted.

College of Staten Island of the City University of New York, Graduate Programs, Program in Neuroscience, Mental Retardation and Developmental Disabilities, Staten Island, NY 10314-6600. Offers MS. Part-time and evening/weekend programs available. *Faculty:* 6 full-time (1 woman), 5 part-time/adjunct (2 women). *Students:* 29 (15 women). Average age 29. 26 applicants, 73% accepted, 16 enrolled. Terminal master's awarded for partial completion of doctoral program. *Degree requirements:* For master's, thesis, oral preliminary exam, thesis defense. *Entrance requirements:* For master's, 3 letters of recommendation; minimum GPA of 3.0 in undergraduate biology, mathematics, psychology or other science courses; 2 semesters of course work in biology, chemistry and psychology; 1 semester of course work in calculus and statistics. Additional exam requirements/recommendations for international students: Required—TOEFL (minimum score 550 paper-based; 213 computer-based; 79 iBT), IELTS (minimum score 6.5). *Application deadline:* For fall admission, 4/18 priority date for domestic students, 4/18 for international students; for spring admission, 11/21 priority date for domestic students, 11/21 for international students. Applications are processed on a rolling basis. Application fee: $125. Electronic applications accepted. *Expenses:* Tuition, state resident: full-time $8210; part-time $345 per credit. Tuition, nonresident: part-time $640 per credit. *Required fees:* $128 per semester. *Financial support:* Career-related internships or fieldwork, Federal Work-Study, and scholarships/grants available. Support available to part-time students. Financial award applicants required to submit FAFSA. *Unit head:* Dr. Alejandra Alonso, Coordinator, 718-982-4153, Fax: 718-982-3953, E-mail: alejandra.alonso@csi.cuny.edu. *Application contact:* Sasha Spence, Assistant Director for Graduate Admissions, 718-982-2699, Fax: 718-982-2500, E-mail: sasha.spence@csi.cuny.edu. Web site: http://www.csi.cuny.edu/catalog/graduate/neuro.php3.

Colorado State University, Graduate School, Program in Molecular, Cellular and Integrative Neurosciences, Fort Collins, CO 80523-1617. Offers PhD. *Students:* 4 full-time (3 women); includes 2 minority (1 Asian, non-Hispanic/Latino; 1 Hispanic/Latino). Average age 27. 33 applicants, 12% accepted, 4 enrolled. *Entrance requirements:* For doctorate, GRE, minimum GPA of 3.0, letter of recommendation. Additional exam requirements/recommendations for international students: Required—TOEFL (minimum score 650 paper-based; 267 computer-based; 109 iBT). *Application deadline:* For fall admission, 12/15 priority date for domestic students, 12/15 for international students. Application fee: $50. Electronic applications accepted. *Expenses:* Tuition, state resident: full-time $7992. Tuition, nonresident: full-time $19,592. *Required fees:* $1735; $58 per credit. *Financial support:* In 2011–12, 4 students received support, including 4 research assistantships with partial tuition reimbursements available (averaging $13,375 per year); fellowships, teaching assistantships with partial tuition reimbursements available, scholarships/grants, health care benefits, and unspecified assistantships also available. Financial award application deadline: 1/1; financial award applicants required to submit FAFSA. *Faculty research:* Ion channels, synaptic mechanisms, neuronal circuitry, degeneration and regeneration, artificial neural networks. *Unit head:* Dr. Kathryn Partin, Professor and Director, 970-491-2263, Fax: 970-491-7907, E-mail: kathy.partin@colostate.edu. *Application contact:* Nancy Graham, Administrative Assistant, 970-491-0425, Fax: 970-491-7907, E-mail: njgraham@colostate.edu. Web site: http://mcin.colostate.edu/.

Dalhousie University, Faculty of Graduate Studies, Neuroscience Institute, Halifax, NS B3H 4H7, Canada. Offers M Sc, PhD. *Degree requirements:* For doctorate, thesis/dissertation. *Entrance requirements:* For master's and doctorate, 4 year honors degree or equivalent, minimum A- average. Additional exam requirements/recommendations for international students: Required—1 of 5 approved tests: TOEFL, IELTS, CANTEST, CAEL, Michigan English Language Assessment Battery. Electronic applications accepted. *Faculty research:* Molecular, cellular, systems, behavioral and clinical neuroscience.

Dalhousie University, Faculty of Science, Department of Psychology, Halifax, NS B3H 4R2, Canada. Offers clinical psychology (PhD); psychology (M Sc, PhD); psychology/neuroscience (M Sc, PhD). *Accreditation:* APA (one or more programs are accredited). *Degree requirements:* For master's, thesis; for doctorate, thesis/dissertation. *Entrance requirements:* For doctorate, GRE General Test. Additional exam requirements/recommendations for international students: Required—TOEFL, IELTS, CANTEST, CAEL, or Michigan English Language Assessment Battery. Electronic applications

accepted. *Faculty research:* Physiological psychology, psychology of learning, learning and behavior, forensic clinical health psychology, development perception and cognition.

Dartmouth College, Arts and Sciences Graduate Programs, Department of Psychological and Brain Sciences, Hanover, NH 03755. Offers cognitive neuroscience (PhD); psychology (PhD). *Degree requirements:* For doctorate, thesis/dissertation. *Entrance requirements:* For doctorate, GRE General Test, GRE Subject Test. Additional exam requirements/recommendations for international students: Required—TOEFL. *Faculty research:* Behavioral neuroscience, cognitive neuroscience, cognitive science, social/personality psychology.

Dartmouth College, Arts and Sciences Graduate Programs, Program in Experimental and Molecular Medicine, The Neuroscience Center, Hanover, NH 03755. Offers PhD, MD/PhD. Degrees awarded through participating programs. *Entrance requirements:* Additional exam requirements/recommendations for international students: Required—TOEFL (minimum score 620 paper-based; 260 computer-based; 105 iBT). Electronic applications accepted.

Dartmouth College, Program in Experimental and Molecular Medicine, Neuroscience Track, Hanover, NH 03755. Offers PhD.

Delaware State University, Graduate Programs, Department of Biological Sciences, Dover, DE 19901-2277. Offers biological sciences (MA, MS); biology education (MS); molecular and cellular neuroscience (MS); neuroscience (PhD). Part-time and evening/weekend programs available. *Degree requirements:* For master's, thesis (for some programs). *Entrance requirements:* For master's, GRE, minimum GPA of 3.0 in major, 2.75 overall. Additional exam requirements/recommendations for international students: Required—TOEFL (minimum score 550 paper-based). Electronic applications accepted. *Faculty research:* Cell biology, immunology, microbiology, genetics, ecology.

Drexel University, College of Arts and Sciences, Department of Psychology, Clinical Psychology Program, Philadelphia, PA 19104-2875. Offers clinical psychology (PhD); forensic psychology (PhD); health psychology (PhD); neuropsychology (PhD). *Accreditation:* APA. Terminal master's awarded for partial completion of doctoral program. *Degree requirements:* For doctorate, thesis/dissertation, qualifying exam. *Entrance requirements:* For doctorate, GRE General Test, GRE Subject Test, minimum GPA of 3.0. Electronic applications accepted. *Expenses:* Contact institution. *Faculty research:* Cognitive behavioral therapy, stress and coping, eating disorders, substance abuse, developmental disabilities.

Drexel University, College of Medicine, Biomedical Graduate Programs, Program in Neuroscience, Philadelphia, PA 19104-2875. Offers MS, PhD, MD/PhD. *Degree requirements:* For doctorate, thesis/dissertation, qualifying exam. *Entrance requirements:* For doctorate, GRE General Test, or MCAT, minimum GPA of 2.75. Additional exam requirements/recommendations for international students: Required—TOEFL. Electronic applications accepted. *Faculty research:* Central monoamine systems, drugs of abuse, anatomy/physiology of sensory systems, neurodegenerative disorders and recovery of function, neuromodulation and synaptic plasticity.

Duke University, Graduate School, Department of Cognitive Neuroscience, Durham, NC 27708-0586. Offers PhD, Certificate. *Faculty:* 39 full-time. *Students:* 9 full-time (7 women); includes 2 minority (both Asian, non-Hispanic/Latino), 2 international. 109 applicants, 11% accepted, 4 enrolled. *Degree requirements:* For doctorate, thesis/dissertation. *Entrance requirements:* For doctorate, GRE General Test. Additional exam requirements/recommendations for international students: Required—TOEFL (minimum score 550 paper-based; 213 computer-based; 83 iBT), IELTS (minimum score 7). *Application deadline:* For fall admission, 12/8 priority date for domestic students, 12/8 for international students. Application fee: $75. Electronic applications accepted. *Expenses:* Tuition: Full-time $40,720. *Required fees:* $3107. *Financial support:* Fellowships, research assistantships, and teaching assistantships available. Financial award application deadline: 12/8. *Unit head:* Elizabeth Brannon, Director of Graduate Studies, 919-684-3422, Fax: 919-684-3475, E-mail: emily.clark@duke.edu. *Application contact:* Elizabeth Hutton, Director of Admissions, 919-684-3913, Fax: 919-684-2277, E-mail: grad-admissions@duke.edu. Web site: http://www.mind.duke.edu/.

Emory University, Laney Graduate School, Department of Psychology, Atlanta, GA 30322-1100. Offers clinical psychology (PhD); cognition and development (PhD); neuroscience and animal behavior (PhD). *Accreditation:* APA. *Faculty:* 32 full-time (13 women). *Students:* 71 full-time (53 women); includes 7 minority (4 Black or African American, non-Hispanic/Latino; 2 Asian, non-Hispanic/Latino; 1 Hispanic/Latino), 3 international. Average age 25. 456 applicants, 5% accepted, 15 enrolled. In 2011, 11 doctorates awarded. *Degree requirements:* For doctorate, comprehensive exam, thesis/dissertation. *Entrance requirements:* For doctorate, GRE General Test, minimum GPA of 3.25. Additional exam requirements/recommendations for international students: Required—TOEFL. *Application deadline:* For fall admission, 1/3 for domestic and international students. Application fee: $50. Electronic applications accepted. *Expenses:* Tuition: Full-time $34,800. *Required fees:* $1300. *Financial support:* In 2011–12, 47 students received support, including 52 fellowships with full tuition reimbursements available (averaging $16,796 per year); research assistantships, teaching assistantships, career-related internships or fieldwork, Federal Work-Study, institutionally sponsored loans, scholarships/grants, and tuition waivers also available. Financial award application deadline: 4/15. *Faculty research:* Neuroscience and animal behavior; adult and child psychopathology, cognition development assessment. *Unit head:* Dr. Robyn Fivush, Chair, 404-727-4124, Fax: 404-727-0372. Web site: http://psychology.emory.edu/.

Emory University, Laney Graduate School, Division of Biological and Biomedical Sciences, Program in Neuroscience, Atlanta, GA 30322-1100. Offers PhD. *Faculty:* 107 full-time (25 women). *Students:* 111 full-time (71 women); includes 18 minority (4 Black or African American, non-Hispanic/Latino; 4 Asian, non-Hispanic/Latino; 7 Hispanic/Latino; 3 Two or more races, non-Hispanic/Latino), 8 international. Average age 27. 258 applicants, 15% accepted, 18 enrolled. In 2011, 4 degrees awarded. *Median time to degree:* Of those who began their doctoral program in fall 2003, 94% received their degree in 8 years or less. *Degree requirements:* For doctorate, comprehensive exam, thesis/dissertation. *Entrance requirements:* For doctorate, GRE General Test, minimum GPA of 3.0 in science course work (recommended). Additional exam requirements/recommendations for international students: Required—TOEFL. *Application deadline:* For fall admission, 12/1 for domestic and international students. Application fee: $75. Electronic applications accepted. *Expenses:* Tuition: Full-time $34,800. *Required fees:* $1300. *Financial support:* In 2011–12, 37 students received support, including 37 fellowships with full tuition reimbursements available (averaging $26,500 per year); institutionally sponsored loans, scholarships/grants, health care benefits, and tuition waivers (full) also available. *Faculty research:* Cell and molecular biology, development, behavior, neurodegenerative disease. *Unit head:* Dr. Yoland Smith, Director, 404-727-7519, Fax: 404-727-3278, E-mail: ysmit01@emory.edu. *Application contact:* Kathy Smith, Director of Recruitment and Admissions, 404-727-2547, Fax: 404-727-3322, E-mail: kathy.smith@emory.edu. Web site: http://www.biomed.emory.edu.

Fielding Graduate University, Graduate Programs, School of Psychology, Santa Barbara, CA 93105-3538. Offers clinical psychology (PhD), including forensic psychology, health psychology, neuropsychology, parent-infant mental health, violence

prevention and control; clinical psychology respecialization (Post-Doctoral Certificate); media psychology (PhD), including forensic psychology; media psychology and social change (MA); neuropsychology (Post-Doctoral Certificate). *Accreditation:* APA. Postbaccalaureate distance learning degree programs offered (minimal on-campus study). *Faculty:* 28 full-time (15 women), 9 part-time/adjunct (2 women). *Students:* 514 full-time (379 women), 80 part-time (50 women); includes 156 minority (45 Black or African American, non-Hispanic/Latino; 7 American Indian or Alaska Native, non-Hispanic/Latino; 27 Asian, non-Hispanic/Latino; 57 Hispanic/Latino; 20 Two or more races, non-Hispanic/Latino), 22 international. Average age 42. 242 applicants, 46% accepted, 73 enrolled. In 2011, 14 master's, 47 doctorates, 24 other advanced degrees awarded. Terminal master's awarded for partial completion of doctoral program. *Degree requirements:* For master's, thesis or alternative, capstone project; for doctorate, comprehensive exam, thesis/dissertation. *Entrance requirements:* For doctorate, writing sample, minimum GPA of 3.0, 3 letters of recommendation, resume. *Application deadline:* For fall admission, 2/25 for domestic and international students; for spring admission, 8/25 for domestic and international students. Application fee: $75. Electronic applications accepted. *Expenses:* Contact institution. *Financial support:* In 2011–12, 65 students received support. Scholarships/grants and health care benefits available. Support available to part-time students. *Unit head:* Dr. Gerardo Rodriguez-Menendez, Interim Dean, 805-898-2909, E-mail: grodriguez@fielding.edu. *Application contact:* Admission Counselor, 800-340-1099 Ext. 4098, Fax: 805-687-9793, E-mail: psyadmissions@fielding.edu. Web site: http://www.fielding.edu/programs/psy/default.aspx.

Florida Atlantic University, Charles E. Schmidt College of Science, Center for Complex Systems and Brain Sciences, Boca Raton, FL 33431-0991. Offers PhD. *Faculty:* 6 full-time (3 women). *Students:* 36 full-time (21 women), 13 part-time (9 women); includes 12 minority (2 Black or African American, non-Hispanic/Latino; 3 Asian, non-Hispanic/Latino; 5 Hispanic/Latino; 2 Two or more races, non-Hispanic/Latino), 5 international. Average age 30. 35 applicants, 43% accepted, 8 enrolled. In 2011, 6 doctorates awarded. *Degree requirements:* For doctorate, thesis/dissertation. *Entrance requirements:* For doctorate, GRE General Test, minimum GPA of 3.0 in last 60 hours of undergraduate course work. Additional exam requirements/recommendations for international students: Required—TOEFL. *Application deadline:* For fall admission, 1/15 priority date for domestic students, 1/15 for international students. Application fee: $30. *Expenses: Tuition, area resident:* Part-time $343.02 per credit hour. Tuition, state resident: full-time $8232. Tuition, nonresident: full-time $23,931; part-time $997.14 per credit hour. *Financial support:* Fellowships with full tuition reimbursements, research assistantships with partial tuition reimbursements, teaching assistantships with partial tuition reimbursements, Federal Work-Study, traineeships, and unspecified assistantships available. *Faculty research:* Motor behavior, speech perception, nonlinear dynamics and fractals, behavioral neuroscience, cellular and molecular neuroscience. *Unit head:* Dr. Janet Blanks, Director, 561-297-2229, Fax: 561-297-3634, E-mail: blanks@ccs.fau.edu. *Application contact:* Rhona Frankel, Associate Director, 561-297-2230, E-mail: frankel@fau.edu. Web site: http://www.ccs.fau.edu/.

Florida State University, College of Medicine, Department of Biomedical Sciences, Tallahassee, FL 32306-4300. Offers biomedical sciences (PhD); neuroscience (PhD). *Faculty:* 26 full-time (7 women). *Students:* 29 full-time (13 women); includes 3 minority (1 Black or African American, non-Hispanic/Latino; 2 Hispanic/Latino), 10 international. Average age 27. 63 applicants, 14% accepted, 5 enrolled. In 2011, 3 doctorates awarded. *Degree requirements:* For doctorate, thesis/dissertation. *Entrance requirements:* For doctorate, GRE (minimum score: 1000). Additional exam requirements/recommendations for international students: Required—TOEFL (minimum score 550 paper-based; 80 iBT). *Application deadline:* For fall admission, 2/1 for domestic and international students. Application fee: $30. *Expenses:* Tuition, state resident: full-time $9474; part-time $350.88 per credit hour. Tuition, nonresident: full-time $16,236; part-time $601.34 per credit hour. *Required fees:* $630 per semester. One-time fee: $20. Tuition and fees vary according to course load and campus/location. *Financial support:* In 2011–12, 32 research assistantships with full tuition reimbursements (averaging $21,500 per year) were awarded. Financial award applicants required to submit FAFSA. *Unit head:* Dr. Richard S. Nowakowski, Professor/Chair, 850-644-2013, Fax: 850-645-7153, E-mail: richard.nowakowski@med.fsu.edu. *Application contact:* Lilly Lewis, Academic Program Specialist, 850-645-6420, Fax: 850-645-7153, E-mail: lilly.lewis@med.fsu.edu.

Florida State University, The Graduate School, College of Arts and Sciences, Department of Psychology, Interdisciplinary Program in Neuroscience, Tallahassee, FL 32306. Offers PhD. *Faculty:* 11 full-time (4 women). *Students:* 28 full-time (14 women); includes 6 minority (2 Black or African American, non-Hispanic/Latino; 1 Asian, non-Hispanic/Latino; 3 Hispanic/Latino), 1 international. Average age 26. 54 applicants, 15% accepted, 6 enrolled. In 2011, 4 doctorates awarded. *Degree requirements:* For doctorate, thesis/dissertation, preliminary exam. *Entrance requirements:* For doctorate, GRE General Test (recommended minimum total score of 1100), minimum GPA of 3.0, research experience, letters of recommendation. Additional exam requirements/recommendations for international students: Required—TOEFL (minimum score 550 paper-based; 213 computer-based; 80 iBT). *Application deadline:* For fall admission, 12/14 for domestic and international students. Application fee: $30. Electronic applications accepted. *Expenses:* Tuition, state resident: full-time $9474; part-time $350.88 per credit hour. Tuition, nonresident: full-time $16,236; part-time $601.34 per credit hour. *Required fees:* $630 per semester. One-time fee: $20. Tuition and fees vary according to course load and campus/location. *Financial support:* In 2011–12, 23 students received support, including 5 fellowships with full tuition reimbursements available (averaging $22,000 per year), 8 research assistantships with full tuition reimbursements available (averaging $21,000 per year), 10 teaching assistantships with full tuition reimbursements available (averaging $21,000 per year); Federal Work-Study, institutionally sponsored loans, scholarships/grants, traineeships, health care benefits, and unspecified assistantships also available. Financial award applicants required to submit FAFSA. *Faculty research:* Sensory processes, neural development and plasticity, circadian rhythms, behavioral and molecular genetics, hormonal control of behavior. *Total annual research expenditures:* $3.6 million. *Unit head:* Dr. Richard Hyson, Director, 850-644-3076, Fax: 850-645-0349, E-mail: hyson@psy.fsu.edu. *Application contact:* Cherie P. Miller, Graduate Program Assistant, 850-644-2499, Fax: 850-644-7739, E-mail: grad-info@psy.fsu.edu. Web site: http://www.neuro.fsu.edu.

George Mason University, College of Science, Program in Neuroscience, Fairfax, VA 22030. Offers PhD. *Faculty:* 18 full-time (5 women), 1 part-time/adjunct. *Students:* 19 full-time (9 women), 3 part-time (1 woman); includes 4 minority (all Asian, non-Hispanic/Latino). Average age 32. 26 applicants, 31% accepted, 3 enrolled. In 2011, 1 doctorate awarded. *Degree requirements:* For doctorate, thesis/dissertation, at least one publication in a refereed journal (print or press). *Entrance requirements:* For doctorate, GRE, bachelor's degree in related field with minimum GPA of 3.25; expanded goals statement; 2 copies of official transcripts; 3 letters of recommendation. Additional exam requirements/recommendations for international students: Required—TOEFL (minimum score 570 paper-based; 230 computer-based; 88 iBT), IELTS, Pearson Test of English. *Application deadline:* For fall admission, 4/15 priority date for domestic students. Application fee: $65 ($80 for international students). Electronic applications accepted. *Expenses:* Tuition, state resident: full-time $8750; part-time $364.58 per credit. Tuition, nonresident: full-time $24,092; part-time $1003.83 per credit. *Required fees:* $2514; $104.75 per credit. *Financial support:* In 2011–12, 18 students received support, including 2 fellowships with full tuition reimbursements available (averaging $18,000 per year), 15 research assistantships with full and partial tuition reimbursements available (averaging $22,017 per year), 3 teaching assistantships with full and partial tuition reimbursements available (averaging $12,208 per year); career-related internships or fieldwork, Federal Work-Study, scholarships/grants, unspecified assistantships, and Health care benefits (full-time research or teaching assistantship recipients) also available. Support available to part-time students. Financial award application deadline: 3/1; financial award applicants required to submit FAFSA. *Total annual research expenditures:* $7.4 million. *Unit head:* James L. Olds, Director and Chief Academic Unit Officer, 703-993-4333, Fax: 703-993-4325, E-mail: jolds@gmu.edu. *Application contact:* Kim (Avrama) L. Blackwell, Faculty/Professor, 703-993-4381, Fax: 703-993-4325, E-mail: avrama@gmu.edu. Web site: http://neuroscience.gmu.edu/.

Georgetown University, Graduate School of Arts and Sciences, Programs in Biomedical Sciences, Program in Neuroscience, Washington, DC 20057. Offers PhD, MD/PhD. *Degree requirements:* For doctorate, thesis/dissertation. *Entrance requirements:* For doctorate, GRE General Test. Additional exam requirements/recommendations for international students: Required—TOEFL.

Georgia Health Sciences University, College of Graduate Studies, Program in Neuroscience, Augusta, GA 30912. Offers MS, PhD. *Students:* 18 full-time (10 women); includes 2 minority (1 Asian, non-Hispanic/Latino; 1 Two or more races, non-Hispanic/Latino), 5 international. Average age 29. In 2011, 1 doctorate awarded. *Degree requirements:* For doctorate, comprehensive exam, thesis/dissertation. *Entrance requirements:* For doctorate, GRE General Test. Additional exam requirements/recommendations for international students: Required—TOEFL (minimum score 550 paper-based; 213 computer-based; 79 iBT). *Application deadline:* For fall admission, 1/15 for domestic and international students. Application fee: $50. Electronic applications accepted. *Financial support:* In 2011–12, 2 students received support, including 13 research assistantships with partial tuition reimbursements available (averaging $23,000 per year); Federal Work-Study also available. Support available to part-time students. Financial award application deadline: 5/31. *Faculty research:* Learning and memory, neuronal migration, synapse formation, regeneration, developmental neurobiology, neurodegeneration and neural repair. *Total annual research expenditures:* $1.2 million. *Unit head:* Dr. Lin Mei, Director of Institute of Molecular Medicine and Genetics, 706-721-8775, Fax: 706-721-7915, E-mail: lmei@georgiahealth.edu. *Application contact:* Dr. Patricia L. Cameron, Acting Vice Dean, 706-721-3279, E-mail: pcameron@georgiahealth.edu. Web site: http://www.georgiahealth.edu/neuroscience/.

Graduate School and University Center of the City University of New York, Graduate Studies, Program in Psychology, New York, NY 10016-4039. Offers basic applied neurocognition (PhD); biopsychology (PhD); clinical psychology (PhD); developmental psychology (PhD); environmental psychology (PhD); experimental psychology (PhD); industrial psychology (PhD); learning processes (PhD); neuropsychology (PhD); psychology (PhD); social personality (PhD). *Degree requirements:* For doctorate, one foreign language, thesis/dissertation. *Entrance requirements:* For doctorate, GRE General Test. Additional exam requirements/recommendations for international students: Required—TOEFL. Electronic applications accepted.

Harvard University, Graduate School of Arts and Sciences, Program in Neuroscience, Boston, MA 02115. Offers neurobiology (PhD). *Degree requirements:* For doctorate, thesis/dissertation, qualifying exam. *Entrance requirements:* For doctorate, GRE General Test, GRE Subject Test. Additional exam requirements/recommendations for international students: Required—TOEFL. *Expenses: Tuition:* Full-time $36,304. *Required fees:* $1186. Full-time tuition and fees vary according to program. *Faculty research:* Relationship between diseases of the nervous system and basic science.

Illinois State University, Graduate School, College of Arts and Sciences, Department of Biological Sciences, Normal, IL 61790-2200. Offers animal behavior (MS); bacteriology (MS); biochemistry (MS); biological sciences (MS); biology (PhD); biophysics (MS); biotechnology (MS); botany (MS, PhD); cell biology (MS); conservation biology (MS); developmental biology (MS); ecology (MS, PhD); entomology (MS); evolutionary biology (MS); genetics (MS, PhD); immunology (MS); microbiology (MS, PhD); molecular biology (MS); molecular genetics (MS); neurobiology (MS); neuroscience (MS); parasitology (MS); physiology (MS, PhD); plant biology (MS); plant molecular biology (MS); plant sciences (MS); structural biology (MS); zoology (MS, PhD). Part-time programs available. *Degree requirements:* For master's, thesis or alternative; for doctorate, variable foreign language requirement, thesis/dissertation, 2 terms of residency. *Entrance requirements:* For master's, GRE General Test, minimum GPA of 2.6 in last 60 hours of course work; for doctorate, GRE General Test. *Faculty research:* Redoc balance and drug development in schistosoma mansoni, control of the growth of listeria monocytogenes at low temperature, regulation of cell expansion and microtubule function by SPRI, CRUI: physiology and fitness consequences of different life history phenotypes.

Indiana University Bloomington, University Graduate School, College of Arts and Sciences, Department of Psychological and Brain Sciences, Bloomington, IN 47405-7000. Offers biology and behavior (PhD); clinical science (PhD); cognitive neuroscience (PhD); cognitive psychology (PhD); developmental psychology (PhD); methods of behavior (PhD); molecular systems neuroscience (PhD); psychological and brain sciences (MA); social psychology (PhD). *Accreditation:* APA (one or more programs are accredited). *Faculty:* 49 full-time (12 women). *Students:* 90 full-time (51 women); includes 7 minority (2 Black or African American, non-Hispanic/Latino; 3 Asian, non-Hispanic/Latino; 1 Hispanic/Latino; 1 Two or more races, non-Hispanic/Latino), 17 international. Average age 28. 310 applicants, 8% accepted, 15 enrolled. In 2011, 1 master's, 9 doctorates awarded. *Degree requirements:* For doctorate, comprehensive exam, thesis/dissertation, 2 written projects, 1 semester as an associate instructor, qualifying exam, dissertation defense, course on the teaching of psychology. *Entrance requirements:* For doctorate, GRE. Additional exam requirements/recommendations for international students: Required—TOEFL (minimum score 550 paper-based; 213 computer-based). *Application deadline:* For fall admission, 12/15 for domestic students, 12/1 for international students. Application fee: $55 ($65 for international students). Electronic applications accepted. *Financial support:* In 2011–12, 32 fellowships with full tuition reimbursements (averaging $23,580 per year), 7 research assistantships with full tuition reimbursements (averaging $17,850 per year), 7 teaching assistantships with full tuition reimbursements (averaging $17,850 per year) were awarded; scholarships/grants, health care benefits, and unspecified assistantships also available. *Faculty research:* Clinical science, cognitive neuroscience, cognitive psychology, developmental psychology, mechanisms of behavior, molecular and systems neuroscience, social psychology. *Unit head:* Dr. Linda B. Smith, Chair, 812-855-2012, Fax: 812-855-4691, E-mail: smith4@indiana.edu. *Application contact:* Graduate Admissions, 812-856-2409, Fax: 812-855-4691, E-mail: psychgrd@indiana.edu. Web site: http://www.psych.indiana.edu.

Indiana University Bloomington, University Graduate School, College of Arts and Sciences, Program in Neuroscience, Bloomington, IN 47405-7007. Offers PhD. *Faculty:*

40 full-time (11 women). *Students:* 30 full-time (16 women); includes 1 minority (Black or African American, non-Hispanic/Latino), 8 international. Average age 29. 56 applicants, 4% accepted, 2 enrolled. In 2011, 3 doctorates awarded. *Degree requirements:* For doctorate, comprehensive exam, thesis/dissertation, qualifying exam. *Entrance requirements:* Additional exam requirements/recommendations for international students: Required—TOEFL (minimum score 200 paper-based). *Application deadline:* For fall admission, 1/1 for domestic students, 12/1 for international students. Applications are processed on a rolling basis. Application fee: $55 ($65 for international students). Electronic applications accepted. *Financial support:* In 2011–12, 10 students received support, including 6 fellowships with full and partial tuition reimbursements available (averaging $22,000 per year), 4 teaching assistantships with full and partial tuition reimbursements available (averaging $22,000 per year). Financial award application deadline: 12/1. *Faculty research:* Cellular and molecular neuroscience, cognitive neuroscience, developmental neuroscience, disorders of the nervous system, sensory and motor processes. *Unit head:* Dr. George V. Rebec, Director of Graduate Studies and Director of Program in Neuroscience, 812-855-4832, Fax: 812-855-4520, E-mail: rebec@indiana.edu. *Application contact:* Faye Caylor, Administrative Assistant, 812-855-7756, Fax: 812-855-4520, E-mail: fcaylor@indiana.edu. Web site: http://www.indiana.edu/~neurosci/.

Iowa State University of Science and Technology, Program in Neuroscience, Ames, IA 50011. Offers MS, PhD. *Degree requirements:* For master's, thesis; for doctorate, thesis/dissertation. *Entrance requirements:* For master's and doctorate, GRE General Test, resume. Additional exam requirements/recommendations for international students: Required—TOEFL (minimum score 580 paper-based; 85 iBT), IELTS (minimum score 7). *Application deadline:* For fall admission, 2/1 priority date for domestic students, 2/1 for international students. Application fee: $40 ($90 for international students). Electronic applications accepted. *Faculty research:* Behavioral pharmacology and immunology, developmental neurobiology, neuroendocrinology, neuroregulatory mechanisms at the cellular level, signal transduction in neurons. *Unit head:* Dr. Donald Sakaguchi, Director of Graduate Education, 515-294-7252, Fax: 515-294-6790, E-mail: idgp@iastate.edu. *Application contact:* Katie Blair, Application Contact, 515-294-7252, Fax: 515-924-6790, E-mail: idgp@iastate.edu. Web site: http://www.neuroscience.iastate.edu.

The Johns Hopkins University, School of Medicine, Graduate Programs in Medicine, Neuroscience Training Program, Baltimore, MD 21218-2699. Offers PhD. *Degree requirements:* For doctorate, comprehensive exam, thesis/dissertation, thesis defense. *Entrance requirements:* For doctorate, GRE General Test, bachelor's degree in science or mathematics. Additional exam requirements/recommendations for international students: Required—TOEFL. Electronic applications accepted. *Faculty research:* Neurophysiology, neurochemistry, neuroanatomy, pharmacology, development.

Kent State University, School of Biomedical Sciences, Program in Neuroscience, Kent, OH 44242-0001. Offers MS, PhD. Offered in cooperation with Northeastern Ohio Universities College of Medicine. Terminal master's awarded for partial completion of doctoral program. *Degree requirements:* For master's, thesis; for doctorate, thesis/dissertation. *Entrance requirements:* For master's and doctorate, GRE General Test, minimum GPA of 3.0. Additional exam requirements/recommendations for international students: Required—TOEFL. Electronic applications accepted. *Expenses:* Tuition, state resident: full-time $8136; part-time $452 per credit hour. Tuition, nonresident: full-time $14,292; part-time $794 per credit hour. *Faculty research:* Plasticity of the nervous system, learning and memory processes–neural correlates, neuroendocrinology of cyclic behavior, synaptic neurochemistry.

Lehigh University, College of Arts and Sciences, Department of Biological Sciences, Bethlehem, PA 18015. Offers biochemistry (PhD); integrative biology and neuroscience (PhD); molecular biology (MS, PhD). Part-time programs available. Postbaccalaureate distance learning degree programs offered (no on-campus study). *Faculty:* 16 full-time (7 women). *Students:* 36 full-time (19 women), 22 part-time (15 women); includes 4 minority (2 Black or African American, non-Hispanic/Latino; 2 Asian, non-Hispanic/Latino), 7 international. Average age 30. 70 applicants, 14% accepted, 9 enrolled. In 2011, 11 master's, 3 doctorates awarded. Terminal master's awarded for partial completion of doctoral program. *Degree requirements:* For master's, research report; for doctorate, comprehensive exam, thesis/dissertation. *Entrance requirements:* For doctorate, GRE General Test. Additional exam requirements/recommendations for international students: Required—TOEFL. *Application deadline:* For fall admission, 12/15 for domestic and international students. Applications are processed on a rolling basis. Application fee: $75. Electronic applications accepted. *Financial support:* In 2011–12, 4 fellowships with full tuition reimbursements (averaging $24,500 per year), 6 research assistantships with full tuition reimbursements (averaging $23,750 per year), 16 teaching assistantships with full tuition reimbursements (averaging $23,750 per year) were awarded; scholarships/grants and unspecified assistantships also available. Financial award application deadline: 12/15. *Faculty research:* Gene expression, cytoskeleton and cell structure, cell cycle and growth regulation, neuroscience, animal behavior, microbiology. *Total annual research expenditures:* $2 million. *Unit head:* Dr. Murray Itzkowitz, Chairperson, 610-758-3680, Fax: 610-758-4004, E-mail: mi00@lehigh.edu. *Application contact:* Dr. Jennifer M. Swann, Graduate Coordinator, 610-758-5484, Fax: 610-758-4004, E-mail: jms5@lehigh.edu. Web site: http://www.lehigh.edu/~inbios/.

Louisiana State University Health Sciences Center, School of Graduate Studies in New Orleans, Interdisciplinary Neuroscience Graduate Program, New Orleans, LA 70112-2223. Offers MS, PhD, MD/PhD. *Degree requirements:* For master's, comprehensive exam, thesis; for doctorate, comprehensive exam, thesis/dissertation. *Entrance requirements:* For master's, GRE; for doctorate, GRE General Test, GRE Subject Test, previous course work in chemistry, mathematics, physics, and computer science. Additional exam requirements/recommendations for international students: Required—TOEFL. *Faculty research:* Visual system, second messengers, drugs and behavior, signal transduction, plasticity and development.

Loyola University Chicago, Graduate School, Program in Neuroscience, Maywood, IL 60153. Offers MS, PhD, MD/PhD. *Faculty:* 22 full-time (9 women). *Students:* 8 full-time (5 women), 1 (woman) part-time; includes 1 minority (Asian, non-Hispanic/Latino), 1 international. Average age 27. 29 applicants, 14% accepted, 2 enrolled. In 2011, 1 master's, 5 doctorates awarded. Terminal master's awarded for partial completion of doctoral program. *Degree requirements:* For master's, comprehensive exam, thesis; for doctorate, comprehensive exam, thesis/dissertation. *Entrance requirements:* For master's, GRE or MCAT; for doctorate, GRE General Test. Additional exam requirements/recommendations for international students: Required—TOEFL (minimum score 600 paper-based; 220 computer-based). *Application deadline:* For fall admission, 3/15 priority date for domestic students, 3/15 for international students. Applications are processed on a rolling basis. Application fee: $50. Electronic applications accepted. *Expenses:* Tuition: Full-time $15,660; part-time $870 per credit hour. Required fees: $125 per semester. Tuition and fees vary according to course load and program. *Financial support:* In 2011–12, 3 fellowships with full tuition reimbursements (averaging $25,000 per year) were awarded; Federal Work-Study, scholarships/grants, and health care benefits also available. Financial award application deadline: 3/15; financial award applicants required to submit FAFSA. *Faculty research:* Parkinson's disease, drugs of abuse, neuroendocrinology, neuroimmunology, neurotoxicity. *Total annual research expenditures:* $3.5 million. *Unit head:* Dr. Edward J. Neafsey, Director, 708-216-3355, Fax: 708-216-6823, E-mail: eneafse@lumc.edu. *Application contact:* Kim Stubbs, Administrative Secretary, 708-216-3361, Fax: 708-216-3913, E-mail: kstubbs@lumc.edu.

Marquette University, Graduate School, College of Arts and Sciences, Department of Biology, Milwaukee, WI 53201-1881. Offers cell biology (MS, PhD); developmental biology (MS, PhD); ecology (MS, PhD); epithelial physiology (MS, PhD); genetics (MS, PhD); microbiology (MS, PhD); molecular biology (MS, PhD); muscle and exercise physiology (MS, PhD); neuroscience (PhD). *Faculty:* 23 full-time (11 women), 1 part-time/adjunct (0 women). *Students:* 33 full-time (14 women), 6 part-time (3 women), 19 international. Average age 25. 78 applicants, 17% accepted, 5 enrolled. In 2011, 6 doctorates awarded. Terminal master's awarded for partial completion of doctoral program. *Degree requirements:* For master's, comprehensive exam, thesis, 1 year of teaching experience or equivalent; for doctorate, thesis/dissertation, 1 year of teaching experience or equivalent, qualifying exam. *Entrance requirements:* For master's and doctorate, GRE General Test, GRE Subject Test, official transcripts from all current and previous colleges/universities except Marquette, statement of professional goals and aspirations, three letters of recommendation. Additional exam requirements/recommendations for international students: Required—TOEFL (minimum score 530 paper-based; 78 computer-based). *Application deadline:* For fall admission, 12/15 for domestic and international students. Application fee: $50. Electronic applications accepted. *Expenses: Tuition:* Full-time $17,010; part-time $945 per credit hour. Tuition and fees vary according to program. *Financial support:* In 2011–12, 39 students received support, including 6 fellowships (averaging $1,208 per year), 4 research assistantships with full tuition reimbursements available (averaging $21,750 per year), 29 teaching assistantships with full tuition reimbursements available (averaging $21,750 per year); scholarships/grants, health care benefits, tuition waivers (full and partial), and unspecified assistantships also available. Support available to part-time students. Financial award application deadline: 2/15. *Faculty research:* Neurobiology, neuroendocrinology, epithelial physiology, neuropeptide interactions, synaptic transmission. *Total annual research expenditures:* $2 million. *Unit head:* Dr. Robert Fitts, Chair, 414-288-1748, Fax: 414-288-7357. *Application contact:* Debbie Weaver, Administrative Assistant, 414-288-7355, Fax: 414-288-7357. Web site: http://www.marquette.edu/biology/.

Massachusetts Institute of Technology, School of Science, Department of Brain and Cognitive Sciences, Cambridge, MA 02139. Offers cognitive science (PhD); neuroscience (PhD). *Faculty:* 37 full-time (15 women). *Students:* 94 full-time (29 women); includes 23 minority (2 Black or African American, non-Hispanic/Latino; 1 American Indian or Alaska Native, non-Hispanic/Latino; 8 Asian, non-Hispanic/Latino; 9 Hispanic/Latino; 3 Two or more races, non-Hispanic/Latino), 20 international. Average age 27. 406 applicants, 9% accepted, 18 enrolled. In 2011, 18 doctorates awarded. *Degree requirements:* For doctorate, comprehensive exam, thesis/dissertation. *Entrance requirements:* For doctorate, GRE General Test. Additional exam requirements/recommendations for international students: Required—TOEFL (minimum score 577 paper-based; 233 computer-based; 90 iBT), IELTS (minimum score 7). *Application deadline:* For fall admission, 12/1 for domestic and international students. Application fee: $75. Electronic applications accepted. *Expenses: Tuition:* Full-time $40,460; part-time $630 per credit hour. Required fees: $272. *Financial support:* In 2011–12, 89 students received support, including 69 fellowships (averaging $29,300 per year), 20 research assistantships (averaging $31,700 per year), 5 teaching assistantships (averaging $31,500 per year); Federal Work-Study, institutionally sponsored loans, scholarships/grants, traineeships, health care benefits, and unspecified assistantships also available. *Faculty research:* Vision, audition, and other perceptual systems; physiology and computation; learning, memory, and executive control: molecular and systems approaches; sensorimotor systems: physiology and computation; neural and cognitive development and plasticity; language and high-level cognition: learning, acquisition, and computation. *Total annual research expenditures:* $33.2 million. *Unit head:* Prof. James Dicarlo, Head, 617-258-9344, E-mail: bcs-info@mit.edu. *Application contact:* Academic Office, 617-253-7403, E-mail: bcs-admissions@mit.edu. Web site: http://bcs.mit.edu/.

Mayo Graduate School, Graduate Programs in Biomedical Sciences, Program in Molecular Neuroscience, Rochester, MN 55905. Offers PhD. Program also offered in Jacksonville, FL. *Degree requirements:* For doctorate, oral defense of dissertation, qualifying oral and written exam. *Entrance requirements:* For doctorate, GRE, 1 year of chemistry, biology, calculus, and physics. Additional exam requirements/recommendations for international students: Required—TOEFL. Electronic applications accepted. *Faculty research:* Cholinergic receptor/Alzheimer's; molecular biology, channels, receptors, and mental disease; neuronal cytoskeleton; growth factors; gene regulation.

McGill University, Faculty of Graduate and Postdoctoral Studies, Faculty of Medicine, Department of Neurology and Neurosurgery, Montréal, QC H3A 2T5, Canada. Offers M Sc, PhD.

McMaster University, Faculty of Health Sciences and School of Graduate Studies, Program in Medical Sciences, Neurosciences and Behavioral Sciences Area, Hamilton, ON L8S 4M2, Canada. Offers M Sc, PhD, MD/PhD. *Degree requirements:* For master's, thesis; for doctorate, comprehensive exam, thesis/dissertation. *Entrance requirements:* For master's, honors B Sc, B+ average in related field; for doctorate, M Sc, minimum B+ average, students with proven research experience and an A average may be admitted with a B Sc degree. Additional exam requirements/recommendations for international students: Required—TOEFL (minimum score 580 paper-based; 237 computer-based).

Medical College of Wisconsin, Graduate School of Biomedical Sciences, Neuroscience Doctoral Program, Milwaukee, WI 53226-0509. Offers PhD, MD/PhD. *Degree requirements:* For doctorate, comprehensive exam, thesis/dissertation. *Entrance requirements:* For doctorate, GRE, official transcripts, three letters of recommendation. Additional exam requirements/recommendations for international students: Required—TOEFL. *Faculty research:* Neurobiology, development, neuroscience, teratology.

Medical University of South Carolina, College of Graduate Studies, Department of Neurosciences, Charleston, SC 29425. Offers MS, PhD, DMD/PhD, MD/PhD. *Faculty:* 22 full-time (6 women). *Students:* 26 full-time (12 women), 1 part-time (0 women); includes 2 minority (1 Black or African American, non-Hispanic/Latino; 1 Hispanic/Latino), 3 international. Average age 27. 6 applicants, 0% accepted. Terminal master's awarded for partial completion of doctoral program. *Degree requirements:* For master's, thesis; for doctorate, thesis/dissertation, oral and written exams. *Entrance requirements:* For master's, GRE General Test; for doctorate, GRE General Test, interview, minimum GPA of 3.0. Additional exam requirements/recommendations for international students: Required—TOEFL (minimum score 600 paper-based; 250 computer-based; 100 iBT). *Application deadline:* For fall admission, 1/15 priority date for domestic students, 1/15 for international students. Applications are processed on a rolling basis. Application fee: $0 ($85 for international students). Electronic applications accepted. *Financial support:* In 2011–12, 13 research assistantships with partial tuition reimbursements (averaging $23,000 per year) were awarded; Federal Work-Study and scholarships/grants also

available. Support available to part-time students. Financial award application deadline: 3/10; financial award applicants required to submit FAFSA. *Faculty research:* Addiction, aging, movement disorders, membrane physiology, neurotransmission and behavior. *Unit head:* Dr. Peter Kalivas, Chair, 843-792-4400, Fax: 843-792-6590, E-mail: kalivasp@musc.edu. *Application contact:* Dr. L. Judson Chandler, Associate Professor, 843-792-5224, Fax: 843-792-6590, E-mail: chandj@musc.edu. Web site: http://academicdepartments.musc.edu/neurosciences.

Meharry Medical College, School of Graduate Studies, Program in Biomedical Sciences, Neuroscience Emphasis, Nashville, TN 37208-9989. Offers PhD, MD/PhD. *Degree requirements:* For doctorate, comprehensive exam, thesis/dissertation. *Entrance requirements:* For doctorate, GRE. *Faculty research:* Neurochemistry, pain, smooth muscle tone, HP axis and peptides neural plasticity.

Memorial University of Newfoundland, Faculty of Medicine and School of Graduate Studies, Graduate Programs in Medicine, Division of Biomedical Sciences, St. John's, NL A1C 5S7, Canada. Offers cancer (M Sc, PhD); cardiovascular (M Sc, PhD); immunology (M Sc, PhD); neuroscience (M Sc, PhD). Part-time programs available. *Degree requirements:* For master's, thesis; for doctorate, comprehensive exam, thesis/dissertation, oral defense of thesis. *Entrance requirements:* For master's, MD or B Sc; for doctorate, MD or M Sc. Additional exam requirements/recommendations for international students: Required—TOEFL. *Faculty research:* Neuroscience, immunology, cardiovascular, and cancer.

Michigan State University, The Graduate School, College of Natural Science, Program in Neuroscience, East Lansing, MI 48824. Offers MS, PhD. *Entrance requirements:* Additional exam requirements/recommendations for international students: Required—TOEFL. Electronic applications accepted.

Montana State University, College of Graduate Studies, College of Letters and Science, Department of Cell Biology and Neuroscience, Bozeman, MT 59717. Offers biological sciences (PhD); neuroscience (MS, PhD). Part-time programs available. *Degree requirements:* For master's, comprehensive exam; for doctorate, comprehensive exam, thesis/dissertation. *Entrance requirements:* For master's and doctorate, GRE General Test. Additional exam requirements/recommendations for international students: Required—TOEFL (minimum score 550 paper-based; 213 computer-based). Electronic applications accepted. *Faculty research:* Development of the nervous system, neuronal mechanisms of visual perception, ion channel biophysics, mechanisms of sensory coding, neuroinformatics.

Mount Sinai School of Medicine, Graduate School of Biological Sciences, New York, NY 10029-6504. Offers biomedical sciences (MS, PhD); clinical research education (MS, PhD); community medicine (MPH); genetic counseling (MS); neurosciences (PhD); MD/PhD. Terminal master's awarded for partial completion of doctoral program. *Degree requirements:* For master's, thesis; for doctorate, comprehensive exam, thesis/dissertation. *Entrance requirements:* For master's, GRE General Test; for doctorate, GRE General Test, GRE Subject Test, 3 years of college pre-med course work. Additional exam requirements/recommendations for international students: Required—TOEFL. Electronic applications accepted. *Faculty research:* Cancer, genetics and genomics, immunology, neuroscience, developmental and stem cell biology, translational research.

New York Medical College, Graduate School of Basic Medical Sciences, Department of Cell Biology, Valhalla, NY 10595-1691. Offers cell biology and neuroscience (MS, PhD); MD/PhD. Part-time and evening/weekend programs available. *Faculty:* 16 full-time (2 women), 2 part-time/adjunct (1 woman). *Students:* 4 full-time (3 women); includes 1 minority (Asian, non-Hispanic/Latino). Average age 26. 2 applicants, 50% accepted, 0 enrolled. In 2011, 1 master's awarded. Terminal master's awarded for partial completion of doctoral program. *Degree requirements:* For master's, thesis; for doctorate, comprehensive exam, thesis/dissertation. *Entrance requirements:* For master's, GRE General Test, MCAT, DATGRE General, MCAT, DAT; for doctorate, GRE General Test. Additional exam requirements/recommendations for international students: Required—TOEFL. *Application deadline:* For fall admission, 7/1 priority date for domestic students, 5/1 for international students; for spring admission, 12/1 priority date for domestic students, 10/1 for international students. Applications are processed on a rolling basis. Application fee: $50 ($75 for international students). Electronic applications accepted. *Financial support:* In 2011–12, 4 fellowships (averaging $24,000 per year), 1 research assistantship with full tuition reimbursement (averaging $24,000 per year) were awarded; Federal Work-Study, institutionally sponsored loans, scholarships/grants, traineeships, tuition waivers (full), unspecified assistantships, and health benefits (for PhD candidates only) also available. Financial award applicants required to submit FAFSA. *Faculty research:* Mechanisms of growth control in skeletal muscle, cartilage differentiation, cytoskeletal functions, signal transduction pathways, neuronal development and plasticity. *Unit head:* Dr. Victor Fried, Director, 914-594-4036. *Application contact:* Valerie Romeo-Messana, Admission Coordinator, 914-594-4110, Fax: 914-594-4944, E-mail: v_romeomessana@nymc.edu.

New York University, Graduate School of Arts and Science, Center for Neural Science, New York, NY 10012-1019. Offers PhD. *Faculty:* 15 full-time (3 women). *Students:* 38 full-time (21 women), 2 part-time (1 woman); includes 12 minority (2 Black or African American, non-Hispanic/Latino; 7 Asian, non-Hispanic/Latino; 2 Hispanic/Latino; 1 Two or more races, non-Hispanic/Latino), 9 international. Average age 27. 195 applicants, 13% accepted, 7 enrolled. In 2011, 3 doctorates awarded. *Degree requirements:* For doctorate, one foreign language, thesis/dissertation. *Entrance requirements:* For doctorate, GRE, interview. Additional exam requirements/recommendations for international students: Required—TOEFL. *Application deadline:* For fall admission, 12/12 for domestic students. Application fee: $90. *Financial support:* Fellowships with tuition reimbursements, research assistantships with tuition reimbursements, career-related internships or fieldwork, Federal Work-Study, institutionally sponsored loans, scholarships/grants, health care benefits, and unspecified assistantships available. Financial award application deadline: 12/12; financial award applicants required to submit FAFSA. *Faculty research:* Systems and integrative neuroscience; combining biology, cognition, computation, and theory. *Unit head:* J. Anthony Movshon, Chair, 212-998-7780, Fax: 212-995-4011, E-mail: cns@nyu.edu. *Application contact:* Alex Reyes, Director of Graduate Studies, 212-998-7780, Fax: 212-995-4011, E-mail: cns@nyu.edu. Web site: http://www.cns.nyu.edu/.

New York University, School of Medicine, New York, NY 10012-1019. Offers biomedical sciences (PhD), including biomedical imaging, cellular and molecular biology, computational biology, developmental genetics, medical and molecular parasitology, microbiology, molecular oncobiology and immunology, neuroscience and physiology, pathobiology, pharmacology, structural biology; clinical investigation (MS); medicine (MD); MD/MA; MD/MPA; MD/MS; MD/PhD. *Accreditation:* LCME/AMA (one or more programs are accredited). *Degree requirements:* For master's, comprehensive exam, thesis; for doctorate, comprehensive exam (for some programs), thesis/dissertation (for some programs). *Entrance requirements:* For doctorate, MCAT (for MD). Additional exam requirements/recommendations for international students: Required—TOEFL. *Expenses:* Contact institution. *Faculty research:* AIDS, cancer, neuroscience, molecular biology, neuroscience, cell biology and molecular genetics, structural biology, microbial pathogenesis and host defense, pharmacology, molecular oncology and immunology.

New York University, School of Medicine and Graduate School of Arts and Science, Sackler Institute of Graduate Biomedical Sciences, Program in Neuroscience and Physiology, New York, NY 10012-1019. Offers PhD, MD/PhD. *Faculty:* 52 full-time (8 women). *Students:* 39 full-time (21 women); includes 9 minority (4 Black or African American, non-Hispanic/Latino; 1 Asian, non-Hispanic/Latino; 4 Hispanic/Latino), 11 international. Average age 28. In 2011, 8 doctorates awarded. *Degree requirements:* For doctorate, one foreign language, comprehensive exam, thesis/dissertation, qualifying exam. *Entrance requirements:* For doctorate, GRE General Test. Additional exam requirements/recommendations for international students: Required—TOEFL. *Application deadline:* For fall admission, 1/4 priority date for domestic students. Applications are processed on a rolling basis. Application fee: $85. *Financial support:* Fellowships with tuition reimbursements, research assistantships with tuition reimbursements, and teaching assistantships with tuition reimbursements available. *Faculty research:* Synaptic transmission, retinal physiology, signal transduction, CNS intrinsic properties, cerebellar function. *Unit head:* Dr. Rodolfo R. Llinas, Chairman, 212-263-5415. *Application contact:* Dr. Stewart A. Bloomfield, Graduate Adviser, 212-263-5770, Fax: 212-263-8072, E-mail: blooms01@med.nyu.edu.

Northwestern University, The Graduate School, Institute for Neuroscience, Evanston, IL 60208. Offers PhD. Admissions and degree offered through The Graduate School. *Degree requirements:* For doctorate, thesis/dissertation. *Entrance requirements:* For doctorate, GRE General Test. Additional exam requirements/recommendations for international students: Required—TOEFL. *Faculty research:* Circadian rhythms, synaptic neurotransmissions, cognitive neuroscience, sensory/motor systems, cell biology and structure/function, neurobiology of disease.

Northwestern University, The Graduate School, Interdepartmental Biological Sciences Program (IBiS), Evanston, IL 60208. Offers biochemistry, molecular biology, and cell biology (PhD), including biochemistry, cell and molecular biology, molecular biophysics, structural biology; biotechnology (PhD); cell and molecular biology (PhD); developmental biology and genetics (PhD); hormone action and signal transduction (PhD); neuroscience (PhD); structural biology, biochemistry, and biophysics (PhD). Program participants include the Departments of Biochemistry, Molecular Biology, and Cell Biology; Chemistry; Neurobiology and Physiology; Chemical Engineering; Civil Engineering; and Evanston Hospital. *Degree requirements:* For doctorate, thesis/dissertation, qualifying exam. *Entrance requirements:* For doctorate, GRE General Test. Additional exam requirements/recommendations for international students: Required—TOEFL (minimum score 600 paper-based). Electronic applications accepted. *Faculty research:* Developmental genetics, gene regulation, DNA-protein interactions, biological clocks, bioremediation.

The Ohio State University, Graduate School, College of Arts and Sciences, Division of Natural and Mathematical Sciences, Neuroscience Graduate Studies Program, Columbus, OH 43210. Offers PhD. *Faculty:* 80. *Students:* 16 full-time (10 women), 16 part-time (7 women); includes 2 minority (1 Asian, non-Hispanic/Latino; 1 Two or more races, non-Hispanic/Latino), 4 international. Average age 28. In 2011, 7 doctorates awarded. *Degree requirements:* For doctorate, comprehensive exam, thesis/dissertation. *Entrance requirements:* For doctorate, GRE General Test, GRE Subject Test. Additional exam requirements/recommendations for international students: Required—TOEFL (minimum score 600 paper-based; 250 computer-based), Michigan English Language Assessment Battery (minimum score 82). *Application deadline:* For fall admission, 1/31 for domestic students, 11/30 for international students. Applications are processed on a rolling basis. Application fee: $40 ($50 for international students). Electronic applications accepted. *Expenses:* Tuition, state resident: full-time $11,400. Tuition, nonresident: full-time $28,125. Tuition and fees vary according to course load, degree level, campus/location and program. *Financial support:* In 2011–12, 10 students received support, including 1 fellowship with tuition reimbursement available (averaging $21,000 per year), 9 research assistantships with tuition reimbursements available (averaging $21,000 per year); unspecified assistantships also available. *Faculty research:* Neurotrauma and disease, behavioral neuroscience, systems neuroscience, stress and neuroimmunology, molecular and cellular neuroscience. *Unit head:* Dr. Dana Mctigue, Co-Director, 614-292-5523, Fax: 614-292-7544, E-mail: mctigue.2@osu.edu. *Application contact:* Neuroscience Graduate Studies Program, 614-292-2379, Fax: 614-292-0490, E-mail: ngsp@osu.edu. Web site: http://www.ngsp.osu.edu/.

The Ohio State University, Graduate School, College of Arts and Sciences, Division of Social and Behavioral Sciences, Department of Psychology, Columbus, OH 43210. Offers behavioral neuroscience (PhD); clinical psychology (PhD); cognitive psychology (PhD); developmental psychology (PhD); mental retardation and developmental disabilities (PhD); psychology (MA); quantitative psychology (PhD); social psychology (PhD). *Accreditation:* APA (one or more programs are accredited). *Faculty:* 52. *Students:* 97 full-time (51 women), 42 part-time (34 women); includes 21 minority (5 Black or African American, non-Hispanic/Latino; 4 Asian, non-Hispanic/Latino; 8 Hispanic/Latino; 4 Two or more races, non-Hispanic/Latino), 22 international. Average age 28. In 2011, 25 master's, 23 doctorates awarded. *Degree requirements:* For doctorate, thesis/dissertation. *Entrance requirements:* For master's and doctorate, GRE General Test. Additional exam requirements/recommendations for international students: Required—TOEFL (minimum score 550 paper-based; 250 computer-based; 79 iBT), Michigan English Language Assessment Battery (minimum score 82). *Application deadline:* For fall admission, 12/31 for domestic students, 11/30 for international students. Applications are processed on a rolling basis. Application fee: $40 ($50 for international students). Electronic applications accepted. *Expenses:* Tuition, state resident: full-time $11,400. Tuition, nonresident: full-time $28,125. Tuition and fees vary according to course load, degree level, campus/location and program. *Financial support:* Fellowships, research assistantships, and teaching assistantships available. *Unit head:* Dr. Richard Petty, Chair, 614-292-1640, E-mail: petty.1@osu.edu. *Application contact:* Graduate Admissions, 614-292-6031, Fax: 614-292-3656, E-mail: gradadmissions@osu.edu. Web site: http://www.psy.ohio-state.edu/.

Ohio University, Graduate College, College of Arts and Sciences, Department of Biological Sciences, Athens, OH 45701-2979. Offers biological sciences (MS, PhD); cell biology and physiology (MS, PhD); ecology and evolutionary biology (MS, PhD); exercise physiology and muscle biology (MS, PhD); microbiology (MS, PhD); neuroscience (MS, PhD). *Students:* 35 full-time (12 women), 4 part-time (1 woman), 14 international. 62 applicants, 10% accepted, 5 enrolled. In 2011, 2 master's, 8 doctorates awarded. Terminal master's awarded for partial completion of doctoral program. *Degree requirements:* For master's, comprehensive exam, thesis, 1 quarter of teaching experience; for doctorate, comprehensive exam, thesis/dissertation, 2 quarters of teaching experience. *Entrance requirements:* For master's, GRE General Test, names of three faculty members whose research interests most closely match the applicant's interest; for doctorate, GRE General Test, essay concerning prior training, research interest and career goals, plus names of three faculty members whose research interests most closely match the applicant's interest. Additional exam requirements/recommendations for international students: Required—TOEFL (minimum score 620 paper-based; 105 iBT) or IELTS (minimum score 7.5). *Application deadline:* For fall admission, 1/15 for domestic and international students. Application fee: $50 ($55 for

international students). Electronic applications accepted. *Financial support:* In 2011–12, 1 fellowship with full tuition reimbursement (averaging $18,957 per year), 10 research assistantships with full tuition reimbursements (averaging $18,957 per year), 42 teaching assistantships with full tuition reimbursements (averaging $18,957 per year) were awarded; Federal Work-Study and institutionally sponsored loans also available. Financial award application deadline: 1/15. *Faculty research:* Ecology and evolutionary biology, exercise physiology and muscle biology, neurobiology, cell biology, physiology. *Total annual research expenditures:* $2.8 million. *Unit head:* Dr. Ralph DiCaprio, Chair, 740-593-2290, Fax: 740-593-0300, E-mail: dicaprir@ohio.edu. *Application contact:* Dr. Patrick Hassett, Graduate Chair, 740-593-4793, Fax: 740-593-0300, E-mail: hassett@ohio.edu. Web site: http://www.biosci.ohiou.edu/.

Oregon Health & Science University, School of Medicine, Graduate Programs in Medicine, Department of Behavioral Neuroscience, Portland, OR 97239-3098. Offers PhD. *Faculty:* 23 full-time (7 women). *Students:* 32 full-time (20 women); includes 7 minority (1 Black or African American, non-Hispanic/Latino; 1 Asian, non-Hispanic/Latino; 2 Hispanic/Latino; 3 Two or more races, non-Hispanic/Latino). Average age 27. 69 applicants, 10% accepted, 3 enrolled. In 2011, 6 doctorates awarded. Terminal master's awarded for partial completion of doctoral program. *Degree requirements:* For doctorate, comprehensive exam, thesis/dissertation, qualifying exam. *Entrance requirements:* For doctorate, GRE General Test (minimum scores: 153 Verbal/148 Quantitative/4.5 Analytical), undergraduate coursework in biopsychology and other basic science areas. Additional exam requirements/recommendations for international students: Required—TOEFL. *Application deadline:* For fall admission, 12/1 for domestic students. Application fee: $70. Electronic applications accepted. *Financial support:* Fellowships, research assistantships, health care benefits, tuition waivers (full), and stipends for PhD students available. *Faculty research:* Behavioral neuroscience, behavioral genomics, biological basis of drug and alcohol abuse, cognitive neuroscience, neuropharmacology and neuroendocrinology. *Unit head:* Dr. Suzanne Mitchell, Program Director, 503-494-1650, E-mail: mitchesu@ohsu.edu. *Application contact:* Kris Thomason, Graduate Program Manager, 503-494-8464, E-mail: thomason@ohsu.edu. Web site: http://www.ohsu.edu/som-BehNeuro/.

Oregon Health & Science University, School of Medicine, Graduate Programs in Medicine, Neuroscience Graduate Program, Portland, OR 97239-3098. Offers PhD. *Faculty:* 149 full-time (44 women). *Students:* 52 full-time (28 women); includes 5 minority (4 Asian, non-Hispanic/Latino; 1 Hispanic/Latino), 7 international. Average age 27. 97 applicants, 14% accepted, 6 enrolled. In 2011, 16 doctorates awarded. Terminal master's awarded for partial completion of doctoral program. *Degree requirements:* For doctorate, comprehensive exam, thesis/dissertation, qualifying exam. *Entrance requirements:* For doctorate, GRE General Test (minimum scores: 153 Verbal/148 Quantitative/4.5 Analytical) or MCAT (for some programs). Additional exam requirements/recommendations for international students: Required—TOEFL. *Application deadline:* For fall admission, 12/15 for domestic students. Application fee: $70. Electronic applications accepted. *Financial support:* Health care benefits and full tuition and stipends for PhD Students available. *Faculty research:* Development, neurobiology of disease, molecular, systems, behavioral, cellular, biophysics of channels and transporters, gene regulation, neuronal signaling, synapses and circuits, sensory systems, neuroendocrinology, neurobiology of disease. *Unit head:* Dr. Gary Westbrook, Program Director, 503-494-6932, E-mail: ngp@ohsu.edu. *Application contact:* Liz Lawson-Weber, Program Coordinator, 503-494-6932, E-mail: ngp@ohsu.edu. Web site: http://www.ohsu.edu/xd/education/schools/school-of-medicine/academic-programs/neuroscience-graduate-program/?WT_rank=1.

Penn State Hershey Medical Center, College of Medicine, Graduate School Programs in the Biomedical Sciences, The Huck Institutes of the Life Sciences, Intercollege Graduate Program in Neuroscience, Hershey, PA 17033. Offers MS, PhD, MD/PhD. *Students:* 18 full-time (10 women); includes 5 minority (1 Black or African American, non-Hispanic/Latino; 4 Asian, non-Hispanic/Latino), 2 international. 43 applicants, 21% accepted, 3 enrolled. Terminal master's awarded for partial completion of doctoral program. *Degree requirements:* For master's, thesis or alternative; for doctorate, comprehensive exam, thesis/dissertation, oral exam. *Entrance requirements:* For master's, GRE General Test; for doctorate, GRE General Test, minimum GPA of 3.0. Additional exam requirements/recommendations for international students: Required—TOEFL (minimum score 500 paper-based; 213 computer-based). *Application deadline:* For fall admission, 1/31 priority date for domestic students, 2/1 for international students. Applications are processed on a rolling basis. Application fee: $65. Electronic applications accepted. *Financial support:* In 2011–12, research assistantships with full tuition reimbursements (averaging $23,028 per year) were awarded; fellowships with full tuition reimbursements, career-related internships or fieldwork, institutionally sponsored loans, scholarships/grants, health care benefits, and unspecified assistantships also available. Financial award applicants required to submit FAFSA. *Faculty research:* Behavioral neuroscience, growth factors and neuropeptides, molecular neurobiology and neurogenetics, neuronal aging and brain metabolism, neuronal and glial development. *Unit head:* Dr. Patricia Grigson, Program Director, 717-531-8982, Fax: 717-531-0786, E-mail: neuro-grad-hmc@psu.edu. *Application contact:* Kathy Shuey, Program Assistant, 717-531-8982, Fax: 717-531-0786, E-mail: neuro-grad-hmc@psu.edu. Web site: http://www.huck.psu.edu/education/neuroscience.

Princeton University, Graduate School, Department of Psychology, Princeton, NJ 08544-1019. Offers neuroscience (PhD); psychology (PhD). *Degree requirements:* For doctorate, thesis/dissertation. *Entrance requirements:* For doctorate, GRE General Test, GRE Subject Test. Additional exam requirements/recommendations for international students: Required—TOEFL (minimum score 550 paper-based). Electronic applications accepted.

Princeton University, Princeton Neuroscience Institute, Princeton, NJ 08544-1019. Offers PhD. Electronic applications accepted.

Purdue University, College of Pharmacy and Pharmacal Sciences and Graduate School, Graduate Programs in Pharmacy and Pharmacal Sciences, Department of Medicinal Chemistry and Molecular Pharmacology, West Lafayette, IN 47907. Offers biophysical and computational chemistry (PhD); cancer research (PhD); immunology and infectious disease (PhD); medicinal biochemistry and molecular biology (PhD); medicinal chemistry and chemical biology (PhD); molecular pharmacology (PhD); neuropharmacology, neurodegeneration, and neurotoxicity (PhD); systems biology and functional genomics (PhD). *Faculty:* 22 full-time (2 women), 4 part-time/adjunct (1 woman). *Students:* 49 full-time (18 women); includes 3 minority (1 Asian, non-Hispanic/Latino; 2 Hispanic/Latino), 26 international. Average age 27. 250 applicants, 12% accepted, 9 enrolled. In 2011, 10 doctorates awarded. *Degree requirements:* For doctorate, thesis/dissertation. *Entrance requirements:* For doctorate, GRE General Test; GRE Subject Test in biology, biochemistry, and chemistry (recommended), minimum undergraduate GPA of 3.0. Additional exam requirements/recommendations for international students: Required—TOEFL (minimum score 550 paper-based; 77 iBT); Recommended—TWE. *Application deadline:* For fall admission, 2/1 for domestic and international students. Applications are processed on a rolling basis. Application fee: $60 ($75 for international students). Electronic applications accepted. *Financial support:* Fellowships, research assistantships, teaching assistantships, and traineeships available. Support available to part-time students. Financial award applicants required to submit FAFSA. *Faculty research:* Drug design and development, cancer research, drug synthesis and analysis, chemical pharmacology, environmental toxicology. *Unit head:* Dr. Richard F. Borch, Head, 765-494-1403, E-mail: borch@purdue.edu. *Application contact:* Janine C. Mott, Graduate Contact, 765-494-1269, E-mail: jmott@purdue.edu.

Purdue University, Graduate School, College of Health and Human Sciences, Department of Psychological Sciences, West Lafayette, IN 47907. Offers behavioral neuroscience (PhD); clinical psychology (PhD); cognitive psychology (PhD); industrial/organizational psychology (PhD); mathematical and computational cognitive science (PhD). *Accreditation:* APA. *Faculty:* 43 full-time (14 women), 16 part-time/adjunct (8 women). *Students:* 69 full-time (48 women), 6 part-time (5 women); includes 7 minority (2 Black or African American, non Hispanic/Latino; 1 American Indian or Alaska Native, non-Hispanic/Latino; 1 Asian, non-Hispanic/Latino; 2 Hispanic/Latino; 1 Two or more races, non-Hispanic/Latino), 19 international. Average age 27. 323 applicants, 11% accepted, 21 enrolled. In 2011, 16 doctorates awarded. Terminal master's awarded for partial completion of doctoral program. *Degree requirements:* For doctorate, thesis/dissertation. *Entrance requirements:* For doctorate, GRE General Test, minimum undergraduate GPA of 3.0 or equivalent. Additional exam requirements/recommendations for international students: Required—TOEFL (minimum score 550 paper-based; 77 iBT); Recommended—TWE. *Application deadline:* For fall admission, 12/3 for domestic and international students. Applications are processed on a rolling basis. Application fee: $60 ($75 for international students). Electronic applications accepted. *Financial support:* Fellowships with partial tuition reimbursements, research assistantships with partial tuition reimbursements, teaching assistantships with partial tuition reimbursements, and career-related internships or fieldwork available. Support available to part-time students. Financial award applicants required to submit FAFSA. *Faculty research:* Career development of women in science, development of friendships during childhood and adolescence, social competence, human information processing. *Unit head:* Dr. Christopher R. Agnew, Head, 765-494-6061, Fax: 765-496-1264, E-mail: agnew@psych.purdue.edu. *Application contact:* Nancy A. O'Brien, Graduate Contact, 765-494-6067, Fax: 765-496-1264, E-mail: nobrien@psych.pardue.edu. Web site: http://www.psych.purdue.edu/.

Purdue University, Graduate School, PULSe - Purdue University Life Sciences Program, West Lafayette, IN 47907. Offers biomolecular structure and biophysics (PhD); biotechnology (PhD); chemical biology (PhD); chromatin and regulation of gene expression (PhD); integrative neuroscience (PhD); integrative plant sciences (PhD); membrane biology (PhD); microbiology (PhD); molecular evolutionary and cancer biology (PhD); molecular evolutionary genetics (PhD); molecular virology (PhD). *Students:* 90 full-time (45 women); includes 7 minority (3 Black or African American, non-Hispanic/Latino; 1 Asian, non-Hispanic/Latino; 2 Hispanic/Latino; 1 Two or more races, non-Hispanic/Latino), 40 international. Average age 26. 427 applicants, 24% accepted, 35 enrolled. *Entrance requirements:* For doctorate, GRE test required, minimum undergraduate GPA of 3.0. Additional exam requirements/recommendations for international students: Required—TOEFL (minimum score 550 paper-based; 77 iBT). *Application deadline:* For fall admission, 1/15 priority date for domestic students, 1/15 for international students. Applications are processed on a rolling basis. Application fee: $60 ($75 for international students). Electronic applications accepted. *Financial support:* In 2011–12, research assistantships with tuition reimbursements (averaging $22,500 per year), teaching assistantships with tuition reimbursements (averaging $22,500 per year) were awarded. *Unit head:* Dr. Christine A. Hrycyna, Head, 765-494-7322, E-mail: hrycyna@purdue.edu. *Application contact:* Emily E. Bramson, Graduate Contact, 765-494-5865, E-mail: bramson@purdue.edu. Web site: http://www.gradschool.purdue.edu/pulse.

Queen's University at Kingston, School of Graduate Studies and Research, Faculty of Health Sciences, Department of Anatomy and Cell Biology, Kingston, ON K7L 3N6, Canada. Offers biology of reproduction (M Sc, PhD); cancer (M Sc, PhD); cardiovascular pathophysiology (M Sc, PhD); cell and molecular biology (M Sc, PhD); drug metabolism (M Sc, PhD); endocrinology (M Sc, PhD); motor control (M Sc, PhD); neural regeneration (M Sc, PhD); neurophysiology (M Sc, PhD). Part-time programs available. *Degree requirements:* For master's, thesis; for doctorate, one foreign language, comprehensive exam, thesis/dissertation. *Entrance requirements:* Additional exam requirements/recommendations for international students: Required—TOEFL. Electronic applications accepted. *Faculty research:* Human kinetics, neuroscience, reproductive biology, cardiovascular.

Rosalind Franklin University of Medicine and Science, School of Graduate and Postdoctoral Studies - Interdisciplinary Graduate Program in Biomedical Sciences, Department of Neuroscience, North Chicago, IL 60064-3095. Offers PhD, MD/PhD. *Degree requirements:* For doctorate, comprehensive exam, thesis/dissertation, original research project. *Entrance requirements:* For doctorate, GRE General Test. Additional exam requirements/recommendations for international students: Required—TOEFL, TWE.

Rush University, Graduate College, Division of Neuroscience, Chicago, IL 60612-3832. Offers MS, PhD. Terminal master's awarded for partial completion of doctoral program. *Degree requirements:* For master's, thesis; for doctorate, thesis/dissertation. *Entrance requirements:* For master's and doctorate, GRE General Test. Additional exam requirements/recommendations for international students: Required—TOEFL. Electronic applications accepted. *Faculty research:* Neurodegenerative disorders, neurobiology of memory, aging, pathology and genetics of Alzheimer's disease.

Rutgers, The State University of New Jersey, Newark, Graduate School, Program in Integrative Neuroscience, Newark, NJ 07102. Offers PhD. Part-time programs available. *Degree requirements:* For doctorate, thesis/dissertation. *Entrance requirements:* For doctorate, GRE, minimum GPA of 3.0. Electronic applications accepted. *Faculty research:* Systems neuroscience, cognitive neuroscience, molecular neuroscience, behavioral neuroscience.

Rutgers, The State University of New Jersey, Newark, Graduate School, Program in Psychology, Newark, NJ 07102. Offers cognitive neuroscience (PhD); cognitive science (PhD); perception (PhD); psychobiology (PhD); social cognition (PhD). *Degree requirements:* For doctorate, comprehensive exam, thesis/dissertation. *Entrance requirements:* For doctorate, GRE General Test, GRE Subject Test, minimum undergraduate B average. Electronic applications accepted. *Faculty research:* Visual perception (luminance, motion), neuroendocrine mechanisms in behavior (reproduction, pain), attachment theory, connectionist modeling of cognition.

Rutgers, The State University of New Jersey, New Brunswick, Graduate School-New Brunswick, Program in Endocrinology and Animal Biosciences, Piscataway, NJ 08854-8097. Offers MS, PhD. Terminal master's awarded for partial completion of doctoral program. *Degree requirements:* For master's, thesis; for doctorate, comprehensive exam, thesis/dissertation. *Entrance requirements:* For master's and doctorate, GRE General Test. Additional exam requirements/recommendations for international students: Required—TOEFL. Electronic applications accepted. *Faculty research:* Comparative and behavioral endocrinology, epigenetic regulation of the endocrine system, exercise physiology and immunology, fetal and neonatal developmental programming, mammary gland biology and breast cancer, neuroendocrinology and alcohol studies, reproductive and developmental toxicology.

Neuroscience

Rutgers, The State University of New Jersey, New Brunswick, Graduate School-New Brunswick, Program in Neuroscience, Piscataway, NJ 08854-8097. Offers PhD. Program offered jointly with University of Medicine and Dentistry of New Jersey. *Degree requirements:* For doctorate, thesis/dissertation, qualifying exam, research project. *Entrance requirements:* For doctorate, GRE General Test, 3 letters of recommendation. Additional exam requirements/recommendations for international students: Required—TOEFL. Electronic applications accepted. *Faculty research:* Neural patterning, neurogenesis, neurogenetics, cell population behavior, regeneration.

Seton Hall University, College of Arts and Sciences, Department of Biological Sciences, South Orange, NJ 07079-2697. Offers biology (MS); biology/business administration (MS); microbiology (MS); molecular bioscience (PhD); molecular bioscience/neuroscience (PhD). Part-time and evening/weekend programs available. *Degree requirements:* For master's, thesis optional; for doctorate, comprehensive exam, thesis/dissertation. *Entrance requirements:* For master's and doctorate, GRE or MS from accredited university in the U.S.. Additional exam requirements/recommendations for international students: Required—TOEFL. Electronic applications accepted. *Expenses: Tuition:* Part-time $1033 per credit hour. *Required fees:* $85 per semester. *Faculty research:* Neurobiology, genetics, immunology, molecular biology, cellular physiology, toxicology, microbiology, bioinformatics.

Seton Hall University, College of Arts and Sciences, Department of Psychology, South Orange, NJ 07079-2697. Offers experimental psychology (MS), including behavioral neuroscience. Part-time and evening/weekend programs available. *Entrance requirements:* For master's, GRE. Additional exam requirements/recommendations for international students: Required—TOEFL. Electronic applications accepted. *Expenses: Tuition:* Part-time $1033 per credit hour. *Required fees:* $85 per semester. *Faculty research:* Behavioral neuroscience, cognitive psychology, social psychology, perception/motor skills, memory, depression, anxiety.

Stanford University, School of Medicine, Graduate Programs in Medicine, Neurosciences Program, Stanford, CA 94305-9991. Offers PhD. *Degree requirements:* For doctorate, thesis/dissertation. *Entrance requirements:* For doctorate, GRE General Test, GRE Subject Test. Additional exam requirements/recommendations for international students: Required—TOEFL. Electronic applications accepted. *Expenses: Tuition:* Full-time $40,050; part-time $890 per credit.

State University of New York Downstate Medical Center, School of Graduate Studies, Program in Neural and Behavioral Science, Brooklyn, NY 11203-2098. Offers PhD, MD/PhD. *Degree requirements:* For doctorate, comprehensive exam, thesis/dissertation. *Entrance requirements:* For doctorate, GRE. Additional exam requirements/recommendations for international students: Recommended—TOEFL. *Faculty research:* Molecular neuroscience, cellular neuroscience, systems neuroscience, behavioral neuroscience, behavior.

State University of New York Upstate Medical University, College of Graduate Studies, Program in Neuroscience, Syracuse, NY 13210-2334. Offers PhD. *Degree requirements:* For doctorate, comprehensive exam, thesis/dissertation. *Entrance requirements:* For doctorate, GRE General Test, telephone interview. Additional exam requirements/recommendations for international students: Required—TOEFL. Electronic applications accepted. *Faculty research:* Cancer, disorders of the nervous system, infectious diseases, diabetes/metabolic disorders/cardiovascular diseases.

Stony Brook University, State University of New York, Graduate School, College of Arts and Sciences, Department of Neurobiology and Behavior, Stony Brook, NY 11794. Offers neuroscience (PhD). *Degree requirements:* For doctorate, comprehensive exam, thesis/dissertation, teaching experience. *Entrance requirements:* For doctorate, GRE General Test, GRE Subject Test, minimum GPA of 3.0. Additional exam requirements/recommendations for international students: Required—TOEFL. *Faculty research:* Biophysics; neurochemistry; cellular, developmental, and integrative neurobiology.

Teachers College, Columbia University, Graduate Faculty of Education, Department of Biobehavioral Studies, Program in Neuroscience and Education, New York, NY 10027. Offers MA. *Faculty:* 6 full-time (3 women), 2 part-time/adjunct (1 woman). *Students:* 12 full-time (10 women), 29 part-time (20 women); includes 8 minority (2 Black or African American, non-Hispanic/Latino; 2 Asian, non-Hispanic/Latino; 4 Hispanic/Latino), 7 international. Average age 30. 38 applicants, 82% accepted, 17 enrolled. In 2011, 18 master's awarded. *Degree requirements:* For master's, integrative project, practicum, research experience. *Application deadline:* For fall admission, 1/15 priority date for domestic students. Applications are processed on a rolling basis. Application fee: $65. Electronic applications accepted. *Financial support:* Career-related internships or fieldwork, Federal Work-Study, institutionally sponsored loans, and tuition waivers (full and partial) available. Support available to part-time students. Financial award application deadline: 2/1. *Faculty research:* Neuropsychological diagnosis and intervention. *Unit head:* Prof. Peter Gordon, Program Coordinator, 212-678-8162, E-mail: pgordon@tc.edu. *Application contact:* Debbie Lesperance, Assistant Director of Admission, 212-678-3710, Fax: 212-678-4171. Web site: http://www.tc.edu/bbs/NeuroSci/.

Temple University, Health Sciences Center, School of Medicine and Graduate School, Graduate Programs in Medicine, Department of Neuroscience, Philadelphia, PA 19122-6096. Offers MS, PhD. *Faculty:* 15 full-time (5 women). *Students:* 9 full-time (6 women); includes 2 minority (1 Asian, non-Hispanic/Latino; 1 Hispanic/Latino), 1 international. Average age 28. 23 applicants, 35% accepted, 5 enrolled. In 2011, 1 doctorate awarded. *Entrance requirements:* For master's and doctorate, GRE or MCAT, minimum GPA of 3.0. Additional exam requirements/recommendations for international students: Required—TOEFL. *Application deadline:* For fall admission, 7/15 for domestic students, 12/15 for international students; for spring admission, 1/1 for domestic students, 8/1 for international students. Applications are processed on a rolling basis. Application fee: $50. Electronic applications accepted. *Expenses:* Tuition, state resident: full-time $12,366; part-time $687 per credit hour. Tuition, nonresident: full-time $17,298; part-time $961 per credit hour. *Required fees:* $590; $213 per year. *Financial support:* Application deadline: 1/15; applicants required to submit FAFSA. *Unit head:* Dr. Kamel Khalili, Chair, 215-204-4500, Fax: 215-204-4888, E-mail: kamel.khalili@temple.edu. *Application contact:* Office of Admissions, 215-707-3656, Fax: 215-707-6932, E-mail: medadmissions@temple.edu. Web site: http://www.temple.edu/medicine/departments_centers/basic_science/neuroscience.htm.

Texas A&M Health Science Center, College of Medicine, Department of Neuroscience and Experimental Therapeutics, College Station, TX 77840. Offers PhD.

Texas A&M University, College of Liberal Arts, Department of Psychology, College Station, TX 77843. Offers behavioral and cellular neuroscience (PhD); clinical psychology (PhD); cognitive psychology (PhD); developmental psychology (PhD); industrial/organizational psychology (PhD); social psychology (PhD). *Accreditation:* APA. *Faculty:* 38. *Students:* 90 full-time (56 women), 11 part-time (7 women); includes 27 minority (5 Black or African American, non-Hispanic/Latino; 7 Asian, non-Hispanic/Latino; 15 Hispanic/Latino), 15 international. In 2011, 12 doctorates awarded. *Degree requirements:* For doctorate, comprehensive exam (for some programs), thesis/dissertation. *Entrance requirements:* For doctorate, GRE General Test. Additional exam requirements/recommendations for international students: Required—TOEFL. *Application deadline:* For fall admission, 1/5 for domestic and international students. Application fee: $50 ($75 for international students). Electronic applications accepted. *Expenses:* Tuition, state resident: full-time $5437; part-time $226.55 per credit hour. Tuition, nonresident: full-time $12,949; part-time $539.55 per credit hour. *Required fees:* $2741. *Financial support:* Fellowships with partial tuition reimbursements, research assistantships with partial tuition reimbursements, teaching assistantships with partial tuition reimbursements, career-related internships or fieldwork, institutionally sponsored loans, health care benefits, and unspecified assistantships available. Financial award application deadline: 1/5; financial award applicants required to submit FAFSA. *Unit head:* Ludy T. Benjamin, Jr., Head, 979-845-2540, Fax: 979-845-4727, E-mail: lbenjamin@tamu.edu. *Application contact:* Julie Austin, Graduate Admissions Supervisor, 979-458-1710, Fax: 979-845-4727, E-mail: gradadv@psyc.tamu.edu. Web site: http://psychology.tamu.edu.

Texas A&M University, College of Science, Department of Biology, College Station, TX 77843. Offers biology (MS, PhD); botany (MS, PhD); microbiology (MS, PhD); molecular and cell biology (PhD); neuroscience (MS, PhD); zoology (MS, PhD). *Faculty:* 41. *Students:* 99 full-time (60 women), 8 part-time (4 women); includes 11 minority (1 Black or African American, non-Hispanic/Latino; 5 Asian, non-Hispanic/Latino; 4 Hispanic/Latino; 1 Two or more races, non-Hispanic/Latino), 46 international. Average age 28. In 2011, 5 master's, 7 doctorates awarded. *Degree requirements:* For master's, thesis or alternative; for doctorate, comprehensive exam, thesis/dissertation. *Entrance requirements:* For master's and doctorate, GRE General Test. Additional exam requirements/recommendations for international students: Required—TOEFL. *Application deadline:* For fall admission, 1/15 for domestic students. Applications are processed on a rolling basis. Application fee: $50 ($75 for international students). Electronic applications accepted. *Expenses:* Tuition, state resident: full-time $5437; part-time $226.55 per credit hour. Tuition, nonresident: full-time $12,949; part-time $539.55 per credit hour. *Required fees:* $2741. *Financial support:* Fellowships, research assistantships, and teaching assistantships available. Financial award application deadline: 4/1; financial award applicants required to submit FAFSA. *Unit head:* Dr. Jack McMahan, Department Head, 979-845-2301, E-mail: granster@mail.bio.tamu.edu. *Application contact:* 979-845-7755, Fax: 979-845-2891, E-mail: graduate@bio.tamu.edu. Web site: http://www.bio.tamu.edu/index.html.

Texas Christian University, College of Science and Engineering, Department of Psychology, Fort Worth, TX 76129-0002. Offers experimental psychology (PhD), including cognitive psychology, learning, neuropsychology, social psychology; psychology (MA, MS). *Faculty:* 13 full-time (3 women), 4 part-time/adjunct. *Students:* 14 full-time (8 women), 15 part-time (11 women); includes 1 minority (Two or more races, non-Hispanic/Latino), 5 international. Average age 29. 38 applicants, 42% accepted, 11 enrolled. In 2011, 10 master's, 5 doctorates awarded. Terminal master's awarded for partial completion of doctoral program. *Degree requirements:* For master's, thesis; for doctorate, thesis/dissertation. *Entrance requirements:* For master's and doctorate, GRE General Test. Additional exam requirements/recommendations for international students: Required—TOEFL. *Application deadline:* For fall admission, 3/1 for domestic and international students; for spring admission, 12/1 for domestic students. Applications are processed on a rolling basis. Application fee: $60. Electronic applications accepted. *Expenses: Tuition:* Full-time $20,250; part-time $1125 per credit hour. Part-time tuition and fees vary according to course load and program. *Financial support:* In 2011–12, 20 students received support. Teaching assistantships with full tuition reimbursements available and unspecified assistantships available. Financial award application deadline: 3/1. *Unit head:* Dr. Gary W. Boehm, Coordinator of Graduate Studies, 817-257-7410, Fax: 817-257-7681, E-mail: g.boehm@tcu.edu. *Application contact:* Tami Joyce, Department Manager, 817-257-6437, Fax: 817-257-7681, E-mail: t.joyce@tcu.edu. Web site: http://www.psy.tcu.edu/gradpro.html.

Texas Tech University Health Sciences Center, Graduate School of Biomedical Sciences, Department of Pharmacology and Neuroscience, Lubbock, TX 79430. Offers MS, PhD, MD/PhD, MS/PhD. Terminal master's awarded for partial completion of doctoral program. *Degree requirements:* For master's, thesis; for doctorate, thesis/dissertation. *Entrance requirements:* For master's and doctorate, GRE General Test, minimum GPA of 3.0. Additional exam requirements/recommendations for international students: Required—TOEFL. Electronic applications accepted. *Faculty research:* Neuroscience, neuropsychopharmacology, autonomic pharmacology, cardiovascular pharmacology, molecular pharmacology.

Thomas Jefferson University, Jefferson College of Graduate Studies, PhD Program in Neuroscience, Philadelphia, PA 19107. Offers PhD. Offered jointly with the Farber Institute for Neuroscience. *Faculty:* 36 full-time (12 women). *Students:* 18 full-time (12 women); includes 1 minority (Asian, non-Hispanic/Latino), 3 international. 40 applicants, 23% accepted, 3 enrolled. In 2011, 4 doctorates awarded. *Degree requirements:* For doctorate, comprehensive exam, thesis/dissertation. *Entrance requirements:* For doctorate, GRE General Test, strong background in the sciences, interview, previous research experience. Additional exam requirements/recommendations for international students: Required—TOEFL (minimum score 250 computer-based; 100 iBT) or IELTS. *Application deadline:* For fall admission, 1/5 priority date for domestic students, 1/5 for international students. Application fee: $50. *Financial support:* In 2011–12, 18 students received support, including 18 fellowships with full tuition reimbursements available (averaging $54,758 per year); institutionally sponsored loans, scholarships/grants, and stipends also available. Financial award application deadline: 5/1. *Total annual research expenditures:* $16.5 million. *Unit head:* Dr. Elisabeth J. Van Bockstaele, Program Director, 215-503-1245, Fax: 215-503-9238, E-mail: elisabeth.vanbockstaele@jefferson.edu. *Application contact:* Marc E. Stearns, Director of Admissions and Recruitment, 215-503-4400, Fax: 215-503-9920, E-mail: jcgs-info@jefferson.edu. Web site: http://www.jefferson.edu/jcgs/phd/neuroscience/.

Tufts University, Cummings School of Veterinary Medicine, North Grafton, MA 01536. Offers animals and public policy (MS); biomedical sciences (PhD), including digestive diseases, infectious diseases, neuroscience and reproductive biology, pathology; conservation medicine (MS); veterinary medicine (DVM); DVM/MPH; DVM/MS. *Accreditation:* AVMA (one or more programs are accredited). *Faculty:* 93 full-time (42 women), 14 part-time/adjunct (7 women). *Students:* 381 full-time (326 women); includes 47 minority (3 Black or African American, non-Hispanic/Latino; 4 American Indian or Alaska Native, non-Hispanic/Latino; 23 Asian, non-Hispanic/Latino; 16 Hispanic/Latino; 1 Two or more races, non-Hispanic/Latino), 7 international. Average age 25. 762 applicants, 33% accepted, 122 enrolled. In 2011, 8 master's, 80 doctorates awarded. *Degree requirements:* For master's, thesis (for some programs); for doctorate, comprehensive exam, thesis/dissertation (for some programs). *Entrance requirements:* For master's and doctorate, GRE General Test. Additional exam requirements/recommendations for international students: Required—TOEFL or IELTS. *Application deadline:* For fall admission, 11/1 for domestic and international students. Application fee: $70. Electronic applications accepted. *Expenses:* Contact institution. *Financial support:* In 2011–12, 245 students received support, including 6 research assistantships with full tuition reimbursements available (averaging $25,000 per year), 4 teaching assistantships (averaging $5,000 per year); career-related internships or fieldwork, Federal Work-Study, institutionally sponsored loans, scholarships/grants, and institutional aid awards; health care benefits for PhD students also available. Financial award application deadline: 5/15; financial award applicants required to submit FAFSA.

Faculty research: Oncology, veterinary ethics, international veterinary medicine, veterinary genomics, pathogenesis of Clostridium difficile, wildlife fertility control. *Unit head:* Dr. Deborah T. Kochevar, Dean, 508-839-5302, Fax: 508-839-2953, E-mail: deborah.kochevar@tufts.edu. *Application contact:* Rebecca Russo, Director of Admissions, 508-839-7920, Fax: 508-887-4820, E-mail: vetadmissions@tufts.edu. Web site: http://www.tufts.edu/.

Tufts University, Sackler School of Graduate Biomedical Sciences, Neuroscience Program, Medford, MA 02155. Offers PhD. *Faculty:* 32 full-time (14 women). *Students:* 15 full-time (9 women); includes 5 minority (2 Asian, non-Hispanic/Latino; 1 Hispanic/Latino; 2 Two or more races, non-Hispanic/Latino), 1 international. Average age 28. In 2011, 1 doctorate awarded. *Degree requirements:* For doctorate, thesis/dissertation. *Entrance requirements:* For doctorate, GRE General Test, 3 letters of reference. Additional exam requirements/recommendations for international students: Required—TOEFL (minimum score 600 paper-based; 250 computer-based; 100 iBT). *Application deadline:* For fall admission, 12/15 for domestic and international students. Application fee: $70. Electronic applications accepted. *Expenses: Tuition:* Full-time $41,208; part-time $1030 per credit hour. Full-time tuition and fees vary according to degree level, program and student level. Part-time tuition and fees vary according to course load. *Financial support:* In 2011–12, 12 students received support, including 14 research assistantships with full tuition reimbursements available (averaging $30,000 per year); health care benefits also available. *Faculty research:* Molecular, cellular, and systems analyses of synapses and circuits and their implications for neurological disease. *Unit head:* Dr. Kathleen Dunlap, Director, 617-636-4942. *Application contact:* Kellie Melchin, Associate Director of Admissions, 617-636-6767, Fax: 617-636-0375, E-mail: sackler-school@tufts.edu. Web site: http://sackler.tufts.edu/Academics/Degree-Programs/PhD-Programs/Neuroscience.

Tulane University, School of Medicine and School of Liberal Arts, Graduate Programs in Biomedical Sciences, Program in Neuroscience, New Orleans, LA 70118-5669. Offers MS, PhD, MD/PhD. MS and PhD offered through the Graduate School. *Degree requirements:* For doctorate, thesis/dissertation, qualifying exam. *Entrance requirements:* For doctorate, GRE General Test. Additional exam requirements/recommendations for international students: Required—TOEFL. Electronic applications accepted. *Faculty research:* Neuroendocrinology, ion channels, neuropeptides.

Tulane University, School of Science and Engineering, Neuroscience Program, New Orleans, LA 70118-5669. Offers MS, PhD.

Uniformed Services University of the Health Sciences, School of Medicine, Graduate Programs in the Biomedical Sciences and Public Health, Graduate Program in Neuroscience, Bethesda, MD 20814-4799. Offers PhD. *Faculty:* 35 full-time (13 women), 6 part-time/adjunct (2 women). *Students:* 21 full-time (8 women); includes 2 minority (both Black or African American, non-Hispanic/Latino), 3 international. Average age 26. 22 applicants, 32% accepted, 5 enrolled. In 2011, 6 doctorates awarded. *Degree requirements:* For doctorate, comprehensive exam, thesis/dissertation, qualifying exams. *Entrance requirements:* For doctorate, GRE General Test, minimum GPA of 3.0; course work in biology, general chemistry, organic chemistry. Additional exam requirements/recommendations for international students: Required—TOEFL. *Application deadline:* For fall admission, 1/1 priority date for domestic students, 1/1 for international students. Applications are processed on a rolling basis. Application fee: $0. Electronic applications accepted. *Financial support:* In 2011–12, fellowships with full tuition reimbursements (averaging $27,000 per year) were awarded; scholarships/grants, health care benefits, and tuition waivers (full) also available. *Faculty research:* Neuronal development and plasticity, molecular neurobiology, environmental adaptations, stress and injury. *Unit head:* Dr. Sharon Juliano, Director, 301-295-3673, Fax: 301-295-1996, E-mail: sjuliano@usuhs.mil. *Application contact:* Tina Finley, Administrative Assistant, 301-295-3642, Fax: 301-295-1996, E-mail: nfinley@usuhs.mil. Web site: http://www.usuhs.mil/nes/index.html.

See Display below and Close-Up on page 383.

Universidad de Iberoamerica, Graduate School, San Jose, Costa Rica. Offers clinical neuropsychology (PhD); clinical psychology (M Psych); educational psychology (M Psych); forensic psychology (M Psych); hospital management (MHA); intensive care nursing (MN); medicine (MD).

Université de Montréal, Faculty of Medicine, Department of Physiology, Program in Neurological Sciences, Montréal, QC H3C 3J7, Canada. Offers M Sc, PhD. Terminal master's awarded for partial completion of doctoral program. *Degree requirements:* For master's, thesis; for doctorate, thesis/dissertation, general exam. *Entrance requirements:* For master's and doctorate, proficiency in French, knowledge of English. Electronic applications accepted.

University at Albany, State University of New York, School of Public Health, Department of Biomedical Sciences, Program in Neuroscience, Albany, NY 12222-0001. Offers MS, PhD. *Degree requirements:* For master's, thesis; for doctorate, thesis/dissertation. *Entrance requirements:* For master's and doctorate, GRE General Test, GRE Subject Test.

University at Buffalo, the State University of New York, Graduate School, College of Arts and Sciences, Department of Psychology, Buffalo, NY 14260. Offers behavioral neuroscience (PhD); clinical psychology (PhD); cognitive psychology (PhD); general psychology (MA); social-personality psychology (PhD). *Accreditation:* APA (one or more programs are accredited). *Faculty:* 25 full-time (8 women), 9 part-time/adjunct (5 women). *Students:* 104 full-time (68 women), 4 part-time (1 woman); includes 23 minority (2 Black or African American, non-Hispanic/Latino; 3 American Indian or Alaska Native, non-Hispanic/Latino; 9 Asian, non-Hispanic/Latino; 9 Hispanic/Latino). Average age 27. 330 applicants, 18% accepted, 38 enrolled. In 2011, 18 master's, 9 doctorates awarded. Terminal master's awarded for partial completion of doctoral program. *Degree requirements:* For master's, project; for doctorate, thesis/dissertation. *Entrance requirements:* For master's and doctorate, GRE General Test. Additional exam requirements/recommendations for international students: Required—TOEFL (minimum score 550 paper-based; 213 computer-based; 79 iBT). *Application deadline:* For fall admission, 12/1 for domestic and international students. Application fee: $75. Electronic applications accepted. *Financial support:* In 2011–12, 55 students received support, including 5 fellowships with full tuition reimbursements available (averaging $13,700 per year), 16 research assistantships with full tuition reimbursements available (averaging $13,700 per year), 38 teaching assistantships with full tuition reimbursements available (averaging $13,700 per year); career-related internships or fieldwork, Federal Work-Study, institutionally sponsored loans, scholarships/grants, and tuition waivers (partial) also available. Financial award application deadline: 12/1; financial award applicants required to submit FAFSA. *Faculty research:* Neural, endocrine, and molecular bases of behavior; adult mood and anxiety disorders; relationship dysfunction; attention deficit/hyperactivity disorder; psycho-linguistics. *Total annual research expenditures:* $7.4 million. *Unit head:* Dr. Stephen T. Tiffany, Chair, 716-645-3651, Fax: 716-645-3801, E-mail: chairpsych@buffalo.edu. *Application contact:* Mary Claire Schnepf, Coordinator of Admissions, 716-645-3660, Fax: 716-645-3801, E-mail: psych@abuffalo.edu. Web site: http://www.psychology.buffalo.edu/.

University at Buffalo, the State University of New York, Graduate School, School of Medicine and Biomedical Sciences, Graduate Programs in Medicine and Biomedical Sciences, Program in Neuroscience, Buffalo, NY 14260. Offers MS, PhD. Part-time programs available. *Students:* 24 full-time (10 women), 6 international. Average age 25. 13 applicants, 46% accepted. In 2011, 3 master's, 2 doctorates awarded. Terminal master's awarded for partial completion of doctoral program. *Degree requirements:* For

UNIFORMED SERVICES UNIVERSITY

The Uniformed Services University of the Health Sciences is the nation's federal health sciences university and is committed to excellence in military medicine and public health during peace and war.

We provide the nation with health professionals who are dedicated to both civilian and military career service in the Department of Defense and the United States Public Health Service and with scientists who serve the common good.

We serve the uniformed services and the nation as an outstanding academic health sciences center with a worldwide perspective for education, research, service, and consultation. We are unique in relating these activities to military medicine, disaster medicine, and military medical readiness.

For more information, contact:

Uniformed Services University
4301 Jones Bridge Road
Bethesda, Maryland 20814-4799
Phone: 301-295-3913 or 800-772-1747 (toll-free)

http://www.usuhs.mil

master's, thesis or alternative; for doctorate, comprehensive exam, thesis/dissertation. *Entrance requirements:* For master's, GRE General Test; for doctorate, GRE General Test, 3 letters of recommendation. Additional exam requirements/recommendations for international students: Required—TOEFL (minimum score 79 iBT). *Application deadline:* For fall admission, 2/1 priority date for domestic students, 2/1 for international students. Application fee: $50. *Financial support:* In 2011–12, 17 students received support, including 17 research assistantships with full tuition reimbursements available (averaging $21,000 per year). *Faculty research:* Neural plasticity, development, synapse, neurodisease, genetics of neuropathology. *Total annual research expenditures:* $6 million. *Unit head:* Dr. Malcolm Slaughter, Professor, 716-829-3240, Fax: 716-829-2364, E-mail: mslaught@buffalo.edu. *Application contact:* Kristen Kahi, Program Administrator, 716-829-2419, Fax: 716-829-3849, E-mail: kkms@buffalo.edu.

University of Alberta, Faculty of Medicine and Dentistry and Faculty of Graduate Studies and Research, Graduate Programs in Medicine, Centre for Neuroscience, Edmonton, AB T6G 2E1, Canada. Offers M Sc, PhD. Terminal master's awarded for partial completion of doctoral program. *Degree requirements:* For master's, thesis; for doctorate, thesis/dissertation. *Entrance requirements:* For master's and doctorate, minimum GPA of 3.3. Additional exam requirements/recommendations for international students: Required—TOEFL (minimum score 600 paper-based; 250 computer-based). Electronic applications accepted. *Faculty research:* Sensory and motor mechanisms, neural growth and regeneration, molecular neurobiology, synaptic mechanisms, behavioral and psychiatric neuroscience.

The University of Arizona, Graduate Interdisciplinary Programs, Graduate Interdisciplinary Program in Neuroscience, Tucson, AZ 85719. Offers PhD. *Faculty:* 6 full-time (1 woman). *Students:* 27 full-time (17 women); includes 3 minority (2 Black or African American, non-Hispanic/Latino; 1 Hispanic/Latino), 3 international. Average age 28. 49 applicants, 12% accepted, 4 enrolled. In 2011, 2 doctorates awarded. *Degree requirements:* For doctorate, thesis/dissertation. *Entrance requirements:* For doctorate, GRE (minimum score 1100), minimum GPA of 3.5, 3 letters of recommendation. Additional exam requirements/recommendations for international students: Required—TOEFL (minimum score 550 paper-based; 213 computer-based; 79 iBT). *Application deadline:* For fall admission, 12/1 for domestic and international students. Application fee: $75. Electronic applications accepted. *Expenses:* Tuition, state resident: full-time $10,840. Tuition, nonresident: full-time $25,802. *Financial support:* In 2011–12, 2 research assistantships with full tuition reimbursements (averaging $18,260 per year) were awarded; health care benefits, tuition waivers (full), and unspecified assistantships also available. Financial award application deadline: 12/1. *Faculty research:* Cognitive neuroscience, developmental neurobiology, speech and hearing, motor control, insect neurobiology. *Total annual research expenditures:* $1.4 million. *Unit head:* Dr. Konrad E. Zinsmaier, Chairman, 520-621-1343, Fax: 520-621-8282, E-mail: kez@neurobio.arizona.edu. *Application contact:* Erin Wolfe, Graduate Coordinator, 520-621-8380, Fax: 520-626-2618, E-mail: nrsc@u.arizona.edu. Web site: http://www.neuroscience.arizona.edu/.

The University of British Columbia, Faculty of Arts and Faculty of Graduate Studies, Department of Psychology, Vancouver, BC V6T 1Z4, Canada. Offers behavioral neuroscience (MA, PhD); clinical psychology (MA, PhD); cognitive science (MA, PhD); developmental psychology (MA, PhD); health psychology (MA, PhD); quantitative methods (MA, PhD); social/personality psychology (MA, PhD). *Accreditation:* APA (one or more programs are accredited). Terminal master's awarded for partial completion of doctoral program. *Degree requirements:* For master's, thesis; for doctorate, comprehensive exam, thesis/dissertation. *Entrance requirements:* For master's and doctorate, GRE General Test. Additional exam requirements/recommendations for international students: Required—TOEFL (minimum score 550 paper-based; 230 computer-based; 80 iBT). Electronic applications accepted. *Faculty research:* Clinical, developmental, social/personality, cognition, behavioral neuroscience.

University of Calgary, Faculty of Medicine and Faculty of Graduate Studies, Department of Neuroscience, Calgary, AB T2N 1N4, Canada. Offers M Sc, PhD. *Degree requirements:* For master's, thesis, oral thesis exam; for doctorate, thesis/dissertation, candidacy exam, oral thesis exam. *Entrance requirements:* For master's and doctorate, minimum GPA of 3.2 during previous 2 years. Additional exam requirements/recommendations for international students: Required—TOEFL (minimum score 580 paper-based; 237 computer-based). Electronic applications accepted. *Faculty research:* Cellular pharmacology and neurotoxicology, developmental neurobiology, molecular basis of neurodegenerative diseases, neural systems, ion channels.

University of California, Berkeley, Graduate Division, Neuroscience Graduate Program, Berkeley, CA 94720-3200. Offers PhD. *Degree requirements:* For doctorate, qualifying exam, teaching, research thesis/dissertation. *Entrance requirements:* For doctorate, GRE General Test, minimum GPA of 3.0, 3 letters of recommendation, at least one year of laboratory experience. Additional exam requirements/recommendations for international students: Required—TOEFL or IELTS. Electronic applications accepted. *Faculty research:* Analysis of ion channels, signal transduction mechanisms, and gene regulation; development of neurons, synapses, and circuits; synapse function and plasticity; mechanisms of sensory processing; principles of function of cerebral cortex; neural basis for learning, attention, and sleep; neural basis for human emotion, language, motor control, and other high-level cognitive processes.

University of California, Davis, Graduate Studies, Graduate Group in Neuroscience, Davis, CA 95616. Offers PhD. *Degree requirements:* For doctorate, thesis/dissertation. *Entrance requirements:* For doctorate, GRE General Test, GRE Subject Test. Additional exam requirements/recommendations for international students: Required—TOEFL (minimum score 550 paper-based; 213 computer-based). Electronic applications accepted. *Faculty research:* Neuroethology, cognitive neurosciences, cortical neurophysics, cellular and molecular neurobiology.

University of California, Irvine, School of Biological Sciences, Interdepartmental Neuroscience Program, Irvine, CA 92697. Offers PhD. *Students:* 11 full-time (6 women), 1 (woman) part-time; includes 5 minority (1 Black or African American, non-Hispanic/Latino; 3 Asian, non-Hispanic/Latino; 1 Two or more races, non-Hispanic/Latino), 1 international. Average age 24. 107 applicants, 22% accepted, 11 enrolled. *Application deadline:* For fall admission, 12/2 for domestic students. Application fee: $80 ($100 for international students). Electronic applications accepted. *Unit head:* Prof. Albert F. Bennett, Dean, 949-824-5315, Fax: 949-824-3035, E-mail: abennett@uci.edu. *Application contact:* Gary R. Roman, Program Administrator, 949-824-6226, Fax: 949-824-4150, E-mail: groman@uci.edu. Web site: http://www.inp.uci.edu/.

University of California, Los Angeles, David Geffen School of Medicine and Graduate Division, Graduate Programs in Medicine, Interdepartmental Program in Neuroscience, Los Angeles, CA 90095. Offers PhD. *Students:* 85 full-time (39 women); includes 20 minority (2 Black or African American, non-Hispanic/Latino; 11 Asian, non-Hispanic/Latino; 4 Hispanic/Latino; 3 Two or more races, non-Hispanic/Latino), 4 international. Average age 27. 238 applicants, 13% accepted, 11 enrolled. In 2011, 17 degrees awarded. *Median time to degree:* Of those who began their doctoral program in fall 2003, 79% received their degree in 8 years or less. *Degree requirements:* For doctorate, thesis/dissertation, oral and written qualifying exams. *Entrance requirements:* For doctorate, GRE General Test. *Application deadline:* For fall admission, 12/15 for domestic students. Application fee: $70 ($90 for international students). Electronic applications accepted. *Financial support:* In 2011–12, 84 fellowships, 67 research assistantships, 14 teaching assistantships were awarded; Federal Work-Study, institutionally sponsored loans, scholarships/grants, and tuition waivers (full and partial) also available. Financial award application deadline: 3/1. *Unit head:* Dr. Scott Chandler, Chair, 310-206-6636, E-mail: schandler@physci.ucla.edu. *Application contact:* Program Information, 310-206-2349, E-mail: neurophd@mednet.ucla.edu. Web site: http://www.neuroscience.ucla.edu/.

University of California, Riverside, Graduate Division, Program in Neuroscience, Riverside, CA 92521-0102. Offers PhD. *Degree requirements:* For doctorate, comprehensive exam, thesis/dissertation, 2 quarters of teaching experience, qualifying exams. *Entrance requirements:* For doctorate, GRE General Test, minimum GPA of 3.2. Additional exam requirements/recommendations for international students: Required—TOEFL (minimum score 550 paper-based; 213 computer-based; 80 iBT). Electronic applications accepted. *Faculty research:* Cellular and molecular neuroscience, development and plasticity, systems neuroscience and behavior, computational neuroscience, cognitive neuroscience, medical neuroscience.

University of California, San Diego, Office of Graduate Studies, Interdisciplinary Program in Cognitive Science, La Jolla, CA 92093. Offers cognitive science/anthropology (PhD); cognitive science/communication (PhD); cognitive science/computer science and engineering (PhD); cognitive science/linguistics (PhD); cognitive science/neuroscience (PhD); cognitive science/philosophy (PhD); cognitive science/psychology (PhD); cognitive science/sociology (PhD). Admissions offered through affiliated departments. *Degree requirements:* For doctorate, thesis/dissertation. *Entrance requirements:* For doctorate, GRE General Test, acceptance into one of the eight participating departments. *Faculty research:* Language and cognition, philosophy of mind, visual perception, biological anthropology, sociolinguistics.

University of California, San Diego, School of Medicine and Office of Graduate Studies, Molecular Pathology Program, La Jolla, CA 92093. Offers bioinformatics (PhD); cancer biology/oncology (PhD); cardiovascular sciences and disease (PhD); microbiology (PhD); molecular pathology (PhD); neurological disease (PhD); stem cell and developmental biology (PhD); structural biology/drug design (PhD). *Entrance requirements:* For doctorate, GRE General Test, GRE Subject Test. Additional exam requirements/recommendations for international students: Required—TOEFL. Electronic applications accepted.

University of California, San Diego, School of Medicine and Office of Graduate Studies, Neurosciences Program, La Jolla, CA 92093. Offers PhD. *Degree requirements:* For doctorate, thesis/dissertation, qualifying exam. *Entrance requirements:* For doctorate, GRE General Test, GRE Subject Test. Additional exam requirements/recommendations for international students: Required—TOEFL. Electronic applications accepted. *Faculty research:* Neurophysiology, neuropharmacology, neurochemistry.

University of California, San Francisco, Graduate Division, Program in Neuroscience, San Francisco, CA 94143. Offers PhD. *Degree requirements:* For doctorate, thesis/dissertation. *Entrance requirements:* For doctorate, GRE General Test, GRE Subject Test. *Faculty research:* Molecular neurobiology, synaptic plasticity, mechanisms of motor learning.

University of Chicago, Division of Biological Sciences, Neuroscience Graduate Programs, Committee on Computational Neuroscience, Chicago, IL 60637-1513. Offers PhD. *Degree requirements:* For doctorate, thesis/dissertation, ethics class, 2 teaching assistantships. *Entrance requirements:* For doctorate, GRE General Test. Additional exam requirements/recommendations for international students: Required—TOEFL (minimum score 600 paper-based; 250 computer-based; 104 iBT), IELTS (minimum score 7). Electronic applications accepted.

University of Chicago, Division of Biological Sciences, Neuroscience Graduate Programs, Committee on Integrative Neuroscience, Chicago, IL 60637-1513. Offers cell physiology (PhD); pharmacological and physiological sciences (PhD). *Degree requirements:* For doctorate, thesis/dissertation, preliminary exam. *Entrance requirements:* For doctorate, GRE General Test. Additional exam requirements/recommendations for international students: Required—TOEFL. Electronic applications accepted. *Faculty research:* Psychopharmacology, neuropharmacology.

University of Cincinnati, Graduate School, Interdisciplinary PhD Study Program in Neuroscience, Cincinnati, OH 45221. Offers PhD. *Degree requirements:* For doctorate, thesis/dissertation, qualifying exam. *Entrance requirements:* For doctorate, GRE General Test. Additional exam requirements/recommendations for international students: Required—TOEFL. Electronic applications accepted. *Faculty research:* Developmental neurobiology, membrane and channel biophysics, molecular neurobiology, neuroendocrinology, neuronal cell biology.

University of Colorado Denver, School of Medicine, Program in Neuroscience, Aurora, CO 80045. Offers PhD. *Students:* 30 full-time (16 women), 1 (woman) part-time; includes 3 minority (1 Asian, non-Hispanic/Latino; 1 Hispanic/Latino; 1 Two or more races, non-Hispanic/Latino), 2 international. Average age 29. 39 applicants, 15% accepted, 6 enrolled. In 2011, 8 doctorates awarded. *Degree requirements:* For doctorate, comprehensive exam, thesis/dissertation, structured class schedule each year paired with lab rotations. *Entrance requirements:* For doctorate, GRE, baccalaureate degree in a biological science, chemistry, physics or engineering (recommended); minimum GPA of 3.2. Additional exam requirements/recommendations for international students: Required—TOEFL (minimum score 550 paper-based). *Application deadline:* For fall admission, 12/1 for domestic students, 11/1 for international students. Application fee: $65. Electronic applications accepted. *Expenses:* Contact institution. *Financial support:* In 2011–12, 5 students received support. Fellowships, health care benefits, tuition waivers (full), and stipend available. Financial award application deadline: 3/15; financial award applicants required to submit FAFSA. *Faculty research:* Neurobiology of olfaction, ion channels, schizophrenia, spinal cord regeneration, neurotransplantation. *Unit head:* Dr. Diego Restrepo, Director, 303-724-3405, Fax: 303-724-3420, E-mail: diego.restrepo@ucdenver.edu. *Application contact:* Cammie Kennedy, Program Administrator, 303-724-3120, Fax: 303-724-3121, E-mail: cammie.kennedy@ucdenver.edu. Web site: http://www.ucdenver.edu/academics/colleges/medicalschool/programs/Neuroscience/Pages/Neuroscience.aspx.

University of Connecticut, Graduate School, College of Liberal Arts and Sciences, Department of Psychology, Storrs, CT 06269. Offers behavioral neuroscience (PhD); biopsychology (PhD); clinical psychology (MA, PhD); cognition and instruction (PhD); developmental psychology (MA, PhD); ecological psychology (PhD); experimental psychology (PhD); general psychology (MA, PhD); health psychology (Graduate Certificate); industrial/organizational psychology (PhD); language and cognition (PhD); neuroscience (PhD); occupational health psychology (Graduate Certificate); social psychology (MA, PhD). *Accreditation:* APA. Terminal master's awarded for partial completion of doctoral program. *Degree requirements:* For master's, comprehensive exam; for doctorate, thesis/dissertation. *Entrance requirements:* For master's and doctorate, GRE General Test, GRE Subject Test. Additional exam requirements/recommendations for international students: Required—TOEFL (minimum score 550 paper-based; 213 computer-based). Electronic applications accepted.

University of Connecticut Health Center, Graduate School, Programs in Biomedical Sciences, Program in Neuroscience, Farmington, CT 06030. Offers PhD, DMD/PhD, MD/PhD. *Degree requirements:* For doctorate, comprehensive exam, thesis/dissertation. *Entrance requirements:* For doctorate, GRE General Test, interview (recommended). Additional exam requirements/recommendations for international students: Required—TOEFL (minimum score 600 paper-based; 250 computer-based). Electronic applications accepted. *Faculty research:* Molecular and systems neuroscience, neuroanatomy, neurophysiology, neurochemistry, neuropathology.

See Display below and Close-Up on page 385.

University of Delaware, College of Arts and Sciences, Department of Psychology, Newark, DE 19716. Offers behavioral neuroscience (PhD); clinical psychology (PhD); cognitive psychology (PhD); social psychology (PhD). *Accreditation:* APA. *Degree requirements:* For doctorate, thesis/dissertation. *Entrance requirements:* For doctorate, GRE General Test. Additional exam requirements/recommendations for international students: Required—TOEFL (minimum score 600 paper-based; 250 computer-based). Electronic applications accepted. *Faculty research:* Emotion development, neural and cognitive aspects of memory, neural control of feeding, intergroup relations, social cognition and communication.

University of Denver, Division of Arts, Humanities and Social Sciences, Department of Psychology, Denver, CO 80208. Offers affective/social psychology (PhD); clinical child psychology (PhD); cognitive psychology (PhD); developmental cognitive neuroscience (PhD); developmental psychology (PhD). *Accreditation:* APA. *Faculty:* 19 full-time (8 women), 2 part-time/adjunct (both women). *Students:* 51 full-time (47 women); includes 10 minority (1 Black or African American, non-Hispanic/Latino; 6 Asian, non-Hispanic/Latino; 2 Hispanic/Latino; 1 Two or more races, non-Hispanic/Latino), 2 international. Average age 25. 348 applicants, 3% accepted, 6 enrolled. In 2011, 6 doctorates awarded. Terminal master's awarded for partial completion of doctoral program. *Median time to degree:* Of those who began their doctoral program in fall 2003, 100% received their degree in 8 years or less. *Degree requirements:* For doctorate, variable foreign language requirement, comprehensive exam (for some programs), thesis/dissertation. *Entrance requirements:* For doctorate, GRE General Test, biographical statement, three letters of recommendation. Additional exam requirements/recommendations for international students: Required—TOEFL (minimum score 550 paper-based; 80 iBT). *Application deadline:* For fall admission, 12/1 for domestic students. Application fee: $60. Electronic applications accepted. *Financial support:* In 2011–12, 33 students received support, including 2 fellowships (averaging $20,000 per year), 10 research assistantships with full tuition reimbursements available (averaging $18,000 per year), 22 teaching assistantships with full tuition reimbursements available (averaging $18,000 per year). Financial award application deadline: 2/15; financial award applicants required to submit FAFSA. *Faculty research:* Developmental cognitive neuroscience, social and emotional processes, child and adolescent development, clinical child psychology. *Unit head:* Dr. Daniel N. McIntosh, Chair, 303-871-3712, Fax: 303-871-4747, E-mail: daniel.mcintosh@du.edu. *Application contact:* Paula Plank-Houghtaling, Graduate Program Administrator, 303-871-3803, Fax: 303-871-4747, E-mail: phoughta@du.edu. Web site: http://www.du.edu/psychology/.

University of Florida, College of Medicine, Department of Neuroscience, Gainesville, FL 32611. Offers MS, PhD. Terminal master's awarded for partial completion of doctoral program. *Degree requirements:* For master's, thesis; for doctorate, thesis/dissertation. *Entrance requirements:* For master's and doctorate, GRE General Test, minimum GPA of 3.0. Additional exam requirements/recommendations for international students: Required—TOEFL. Electronic applications accepted. *Faculty research:* Neural injury and repair, neuroimmunology and endocrinology, neurophysiology, neurotoxicology, cellular and molecular neurobiology.

University of Florida, College of Medicine and Graduate School, Interdisciplinary Program in Biomedical Sciences, Concentration in Neuroscience, Gainesville, FL 32611. Offers PhD. *Degree requirements:* For doctorate, thesis/dissertation. *Entrance requirements:* For doctorate, GRE General Test, minimum GPA of 3.0. Additional exam requirements/recommendations for international students: Required—TOEFL. Electronic applications accepted. *Faculty research:* Neural injury and repair, neurophysiology, neurotoxicology, cellular and molecular neurobiology, neuroimmunology and endocrinology.

University of Georgia, Biomedical and Health Sciences Institute, Athens, GA 30602. Offers neuroscience (PhD). *Students:* 21 full-time (13 women), 2 part-time (both women); includes 3 minority (1 Black or African American, non-Hispanic/Latino; 1 Asian, non-Hispanic/Latino; 1 Hispanic/Latino), 5 international. Average age 30. 42 applicants; 29% accepted, 9 enrolled. In 2011, 1 doctorate awarded. *Entrance requirements:* For doctorate, GRE, official transcripts, 3 letters of recommendation, statement of interest. Additional exam requirements/recommendations for international students: Required—TOEFL. *Financial support:* Unspecified assistantships available. Financial award application deadline: 12/31. *Unit head:* Dr. Harry Dailey, Director, 706-542-5922, Fax: 706-542-5285, E-mail: hdailey@uga.edu. *Application contact:* Joy Peterson, Graduate Coordinator, 706-542-2684, E-mail: biomfg@uga.edu. Web site: http://biomed.uga.edu.

University of Guelph, Ontario Veterinary College and Graduate Studies, Graduate Programs in Veterinary Sciences, Department of Biomedical Sciences, Guelph, ON N1G 2W1, Canada. Offers morphology (M Sc, DV Sc, PhD); neuroscience (M Sc, DV Sc, PhD); pharmacology (M Sc, DV Sc, PhD); physiology (M Sc, DV Sc, PhD); toxicology (M Sc, DV Sc, PhD). Part-time programs available. *Degree requirements:* For master's, thesis; for doctorate, comprehensive exam, thesis/dissertation. *Entrance requirements:* For master's, honors B Sc, minimum 75% average in last 20 courses; for doctorate, M Sc with thesis from accredited institution. Additional exam requirements/recommendations for international students: Required—TOEFL (minimum score 550 paper-based; 213 computer-based; 89 iBT). Electronic applications accepted. *Faculty research:* Cellular morphology; endocrine, vascular and reproductive physiology; clinical pharmacology; veterinary toxicology; developmental biology, neuroscience.

University of Guelph, Ontario Veterinary College and Graduate Studies, Graduate Programs in Veterinary Sciences, Department of Clinical Studies, Guelph, ON N1G 2W1, Canada. Offers anesthesiology (M Sc, DV Sc); cardiology (DV Sc, Diploma); clinical studies (Diploma); dermatology (M Sc); diagnostic imaging (M Sc, DV Sc); emergency/critical care (M Sc, DV Sc, Diploma); medicine (M Sc, DV Sc); neurology (M Sc, DV Sc); ophthalmology (M Sc, DV Sc); surgery (M Sc, DV Sc). *Degree requirements:* For master's, thesis; for doctorate, comprehensive exam, thesis/dissertation. *Entrance requirements:* Additional exam requirements/recommendations for international students: Required—TOEFL (minimum score 550 paper-based; 213 computer-based), IELTS (minimum score 6.5). Electronic applications accepted. *Faculty research:* Orthopedics, respirology, oncology, exercise physiology, cardiology.

University of Hartford, College of Arts and Sciences, Department of Biology, Program in Neuroscience, West Hartford, CT 06117-1599. Offers MS. Part-time and evening/weekend programs available. *Degree requirements:* For master's, comprehensive exam, thesis optional, oral exams. *Entrance requirements:* For master's, GRE General Test, GRE Subject Test, MCAT. Additional exam requirements/recommendations for international students: Required—TOEFL (minimum score 550 paper-based; 213 computer-based). Electronic applications accepted. *Faculty research:* Neurobiology of aging, central actions of neural steroids, neuroendocrine control of reproduction, retinopathies in sharks, plasticity in the central nervous system.

University of Idaho, College of Graduate Studies, Program in Neuroscience, Moscow, ID 83844-2282. Offers MS, PhD. *Faculty:* 6 full-time. *Students:* 7 full-time, 1 part-time.

University of Connecticut Health Center

UCHC offers you exceptional research opportunities spanning **Cell Analysis and Modeling; Cell Biology; Genetics and Developmental Biology; Immunology; Molecular Biology and Biochemistry; Neuroscience;** and **Skeletal, Craniofacial and Oral Biology**.

Key features of our program include:
- ❖ Integrated admissions with access to more than 100 laboratories.
- ❖ Flexible educational program tailored to the interests of each student.
- ❖ Excellent education in a stimulating, cutting edge research environment.
- ❖ Competitive stipend ($28,000 for 2012–13 year), tuition waiver, and availability of student health plan.
- ❖ State-of-the-art research facilities, including the new Cell and Genome Sciences Building, which houses the UConn Stem Cell Institute, the Center for Cell Analysis and Modeling, and the Department of Genetics and Developmental Biology.

For more information, please contact:
Stephanie Rauch, Biomedical Science Admissions Coordinator
University of Connecticut Health Center
263 Farmington Ave., MC 3906
Farmington, CT 06030
BiomedSciAdmissions@uchc.edu
http://grad.uchc.edu/prospective/programs/phd_biosci/index.html

Neuroscience

Average age 28. In 2011, 1 doctorate awarded. *Application deadline:* For fall admission, 2/15 for domestic students. Applications are processed on a rolling basis. Application fee: $60. Electronic applications accepted. *Expenses:* Tuition, state resident: full-time $3874; part-time $334 per credit hour. Tuition, nonresident: full-time $16,394; part-time $861 per credit hour. *Required fees:* $2808; $99 per credit hour. Tuition and fees vary according to program. *Financial support:* Applicants required to submit FAFSA. *Unit head:* Dr. Jie Chen, Dean of the College of Graduate Studies, 208-885-6243, Fax: 208-885-6198, E-mail: uigrad@uidaho.edu. *Application contact:* Erick Larson, Director of Graduate Admissions, 208-885-4723, E-mail: gadms@uidaho.edu. Web site: http://www.uidaho.edu/cogs/neuroscience.

University of Illinois at Chicago, College of Medicine and Graduate College, Graduate Programs in Medicine, Department of Anatomy and Cell Biology, Program in Neuroscience, Chicago, IL 60612. Offers cellular and systems neuroscience and cell biology (PhD).

University of Illinois at Urbana–Champaign, Graduate College, College of Liberal Arts and Sciences, School of Molecular and Cellular Biology, Neuroscience Program, Champaign, IL 61820. Offers PhD. *Students:* 67 full-time (36 women), 1 (woman) part-time; includes 23 minority (2 Black or African American, non-Hispanic/Latino; 12 Asian, non-Hispanic/Latino; 7 Hispanic/Latino; 1 Native Hawaiian or other Pacific Islander, non-Hispanic/Latino; 1 Two or more races, non-Hispanic/Latino), 12 international. 125 applicants, 12% accepted, 13 enrolled. In 2011, 4 doctorates awarded. *Entrance requirements:* For doctorate, GRE, minimum GPA of 3.0. Additional exam requirements/recommendations for international students: Required—TOEFL (minimum score 570 paper-based; 230 computer-based). *Application deadline:* Applications are processed on a rolling basis. Application fee: $75 ($90 for international students). Electronic applications accepted. *Financial support:* In 2011–12, 24 fellowships, 34 research assistantships, 30 teaching assistantships were awarded; tuition waivers (full and partial) also available. *Unit head:* Neal J. Cohen, Director, 217-244-4339, Fax: 217-244-4339, E-mail: njc@illinois.edu. *Application contact:* Sam Beshers, Program Coordinator, 217-333-4971, Fax: 217-244-3499, E-mail: beshers@illinois.edu. Web site: http://neuroscience.illinois.edu/.

The University of Iowa, Graduate College, Program in Neuroscience, Iowa City, IA 52242-1316. Offers PhD, MD/PhD. *Degree requirements:* For doctorate, comprehensive exam, thesis/dissertation. *Entrance requirements:* For doctorate, GRE General Test, minimum GPA of 3.0. Additional exam requirements/recommendations for international students: Required—TOEFL (minimum score 600 paper-based; 250 computer-based; 100 iBT). Electronic applications accepted. *Faculty research:* Molecular, cellular, and developmental systems; behavioral neurosciences.

The University of Kansas, Graduate Studies, School of Pharmacy, Program in Neurosciences, Lawrence, KS 66044. Offers MS, PhD. *Faculty:* 64. *Students:* 7 full-time (5 women), 1 part-time (0 women); includes 3 minority (2 Asian, non-Hispanic/Latino; 1 Two or more races, non-Hispanic/Latino), 1 international. Average age 27. 24 applicants, 8% accepted, 1 enrolled. In 2011, 1 degree awarded. *Median time to degree:* Of those who began their doctoral program in fall 2003, 100% received their degree in 8 years or less. *Degree requirements:* For master's, thesis; for doctorate, comprehensive exam, thesis/dissertation. *Entrance requirements:* For master's and doctorate, GRE. Additional exam requirements/recommendations for international students: Required—TOEFL. *Application deadline:* For fall admission, 1/15 priority date for domestic students, 1/15 for international students. Applications are processed on a rolling basis. Application fee: $55 ($65 for international students). Electronic applications accepted. Tuition and fees vary according to course load, campus/location, program and reciprocity agreements. *Financial support:* Fellowships with partial tuition reimbursements, research assistantships with full tuition reimbursements, and teaching assistantships with full tuition reimbursements available. Financial award application deadline: 1/15. *Faculty research:* Neurochemistry, neuropharmacology, neurobiology, behavorial neuroscience, neurology. *Unit head:* Dr. Elias K. Michaelis, Professor/Director, 785-864-4504, Fax: 785-864-5738, E-mail: emichaelis@ku.edu. *Application contact:* Susan D. Wakefield, Program Assistant, 785-864-7339, Fax: 785-864-5738, E-mail: swakefield@ku.edu. Web site: http://www.neuroscience.ku.edu/.

The University of Kansas, University of Kansas Medical Center, School of Medicine, Department of Molecular and Integrative Physiology, Neuroscience Graduate Program, Kansas City, KS 66160. Offers MS, PhD. *Students:* 2 full-time (both women); includes 1 minority (Two or more races, non-Hispanic/Latino). Average age 26. In 2011, 1 doctorate awarded. *Entrance requirements:* Additional exam requirements/recommendations for international students: Required—TOEFL. Tuition and fees vary according to course load, campus/location, program and reciprocity agreements. *Unit head:* Dr. Paul D. Cheney, Chair of Molecular and Integrative Physiology, 913-588-7400, Fax: 913-588-7430, E-mail: pcheney@kumc.edu. *Application contact:* Marcia Jones, Director of Graduate Studies, 913-588-1238, Fax: 913-588-5242, E-mail: mjones@kumc.edu. Web site: http://www.neuroscience.ku.edu/.

University of Lethbridge, School of Graduate Studies, Lethbridge, AB T1K 3M4, Canada. Offers accounting (MScM); addictions counseling (M Sc); agricultural biotechnology (M Sc); agricultural studies (M Sc, MA); anthropology (MA); archaeology (MA); art (MA, MFA); biochemistry (M Sc); biological sciences (M Sc); biomolecular science (PhD); biosystems and biodiversity (PhD); Canadian studies (MA); chemistry (M Sc); computer science (M Sc); computer science and geographical information science (M Sc); counseling psychology (M Ed); dramatic arts (MA); earth, space, and physical science (PhD); economics (MA); educational leadership (M Ed); English (MA); environmental science (M Sc); evolution and behavior (PhD); exercise science (M Sc); finance (MScM); French (MA); French/German (MA); French/Spanish (MA); general education (M Ed); general management (MScM); geography (M Sc, MA); German (MA); health science (M Sc); history (MA); human resource management and labour relations (MScM); individualized multidisciplinary (M Sc, MA); information systems (MScM); international management (MScM); kinesiology (M Sc, MA); management (M Sc, MA); marketing (MScM); mathematics (M Sc); music (M Mus, MA); Native American studies (MA); neuroscience (M Sc, PhD); new media (MA); nursing (M Sc); philosophy (MA); physics (M Sc); policy and strategy (MScM); political science (MA); psychology (M Sc, MA); religious studies (MA); social sciences (MA); sociology (MA); theatre and dramatic arts (MFA); theoretical and computational science (PhD); urban and regional studies (MA); women's studies (MA). Part-time and evening/weekend programs available. *Degree requirements:* For doctorate, comprehensive exam, thesis/dissertation. *Entrance requirements:* For master's, GMAT (M Sc in management), bachelor's degree in related field, minimum GPA of 3.0 during previous 20 graded semester courses, 2 years teaching or related experience (M Ed); for doctorate, master's degree, minimum graduate GPA of 3.5. Additional exam requirements/recommendations for international students: Required—TOEFL. *Faculty research:* Movement and brain plasticity, gibberellin physiology, photosynthesis, carbon cycling, molecular properties of main-group ring components.

University of Maine, Graduate School, Program in Biomedical Sciences, Orono, ME 04469. Offers biomedical engineering (PhD); cell and molecular biology (PhD); neuroscience (PhD); toxicology (PhD). *Students:* 11 full-time (7 women), 19 part-time (11 women), 8 international. Average age 29. 32 applicants, 31% accepted, 8 enrolled. In 2011, 3 degrees awarded. Application fee: $65. *Expenses:* Tuition, state resident: full-time $5016. Tuition, nonresident: full-time $14,424. *Financial support:* In 2011–12, 2 fellowships with full tuition reimbursements (averaging $18,000 per year), 8 research assistantships with full tuition reimbursements (averaging $23,000 per year) were awarded. *Unit head:* Dr. Carol Kim, Unit Head, 207-581-2803. *Application contact:* Scott G. Delcourt, Associate Dean of the Graduate School, 207-581-3291, Fax: 207-581-3232, E-mail: graduate@maine.edu. Web site: http://www2.umaine.edu/graduate.

The University of Manchester, Faculty of Life Sciences, Manchester, United Kingdom. Offers adaptive organismal biology (M Phil, PhD); animal biology (M Phil, PhD); biochemistry (M Phil, PhD); bioinformatics (M Phil, PhD); biomolecular sciences (M Phil, PhD); biotechnology (M Phil, PhD); cell biology (M Phil, PhD); cell matrix research (M Phil, PhD); channels and transporters (M Phil, PhD); developmental biology (M Phil, PhD); Egyptology (M Phil, PhD); environmental biology (M Phil, PhD); evolutionary biology (M Phil, PhD); gene expression (M Phil, PhD); genetics (M Phil, PhD); history of science, technology and medicine (M Phil, PhD); immunology (M Phil, PhD); integrative neurobiology and behavior (M Phil, PhD); membrane trafficking (M Phil, PhD); microbiology (M Phil, PhD); molecular and cellular neuroscience (M Phil, PhD); molecular biology (M Phil, PhD); molecular cancer studies (M Phil, PhD); neuroscience (M Phil, PhD); ophthalmology (M Phil, PhD); optometry (M Phil, PhD); organelle function (M Phil, PhD); pharmacology (M Phil, PhD); physiology (M Phil, PhD); plant sciences (M Phil, PhD); stem cell research (M Phil, PhD); structural biology (M Phil, PhD); systems neuroscience (M Phil, PhD); toxicology (M Phil, PhD).

University of Maryland, Baltimore, Graduate School, Graduate Program in Life Sciences, Program in Neuroscience, Baltimore, MD 21201. Offers PhD, MD/PhD. Part-time programs available. *Students:* 53 full-time (30 women), 3 part-time (2 women); includes 8 minority (2 Black or African American, non-Hispanic/Latino; 3 Asian, non-Hispanic/Latino; 1 Hispanic/Latino; 2 Two or more races, non-Hispanic/Latino), 6 international. Average age 28. 104 applicants, 22% accepted, 9 enrolled. In 2011, 5 doctorates awarded. *Degree requirements:* For doctorate, comprehensive exam, thesis/dissertation. *Entrance requirements:* For doctorate, GRE General Test, minimum GPA of 3.0. Additional exam requirements/recommendations for international students: Required—TOEFL (minimum score 550 paper-based; 80 iBT); Recommended—IELTS (minimum score 7). *Application deadline:* For fall admission, 1/15 for domestic and international students. Application fee: $50. Electronic applications accepted. *Financial support:* In 2011–12, research assistantships with partial tuition reimbursements (averaging $25,000 per year) were awarded; fellowships, health care benefits, and unspecified assistantships also available. Financial award application deadline: 3/1. *Faculty research:* Molecular, biochemical, and cellular pharmacology; membrane biophysics; synaptology; developmental neurobiology. *Unit head:* Dr. Bruce Krueger, Director, 410-706-5065, E-mail: bkrueger@umaryland.edu. *Application contact:* Jennifer Aumiller, Coordinator, 410-706-4701, Fax: 410-706-4724, E-mail: neurosci@umaryland.edu. Web site: http://neuroscience.umaryland.edu.

University of Maryland, Baltimore County, Graduate School, College of Natural and Mathematical Sciences, Department of Biological Sciences, Program in Neuroscience and Cognitive Sciences, Baltimore, MD 21250. Offers PhD. *Faculty:* 4 full-time (3 women). *Students:* 2 full-time (0 women); both minorities (1 Asian, non-Hispanic/Latino; 1 Hispanic/Latino). Average age 30. 9 applicants, 22% accepted, 1 enrolled. *Entrance requirements:* For doctorate, GRE General Test, minimum GPA of 3.0. Additional exam requirements/recommendations for international students: Required—TOEFL. *Application deadline:* For fall admission, 1/15 for domestic students, 12/15 for international students. Applications are processed on a rolling basis. Application fee: $50. Electronic applications accepted. *Financial support:* In 2011–12, 3 research assistantships with full tuition reimbursements (averaging $22,300 per year), 2 teaching assistantships with full tuition reimbursements (averaging $21,300 per year) were awarded. *Unit head:* Dr. Stephen Miller, Graduate Program Director, 410-455-3669, Fax: 410-455-3875, E-mail: biograd@umbc.edu. *Application contact:* Dr. Stephen Miller, Graduate Program Director, 410-455-3669, Fax: 410-455-3875, E-mail: biograd@umbc.edu. Web site: http://www.umbc.edu/biosci/.

University of Maryland, College Park, Academic Affairs, College of Behavioral and Social Sciences, Department of Hearing and Speech Sciences, College Park, MD 20742. Offers audiology (MA, PhD); hearing and speech sciences (Au D); language pathology (MA, PhD); neuroscience (PhD); speech (MA, PhD). *Accreditation:* ASHA (one or more programs are accredited). *Faculty:* 20 full-time (18 women), 15 part-time/adjunct (11 women). *Students:* 68 full-time (61 women), 20 part-time (all women); includes 20 minority (6 Black or African American, non-Hispanic/Latino; 6 Asian, non-Hispanic/Latino; 6 Hispanic/Latino; 2 Two or more races, non-Hispanic/Latino), 2 international. 350 applicants, 26% accepted, 29 enrolled. In 2011, 21 master's, 9 doctorates awarded. *Degree requirements:* For master's, thesis optional; for doctorate, thesis/dissertation, written and oral exams. *Entrance requirements:* For master's, GRE General Test, minimum GPA of 3.5, 3 letters of recommendation; for doctorate, GRE General Test, minimum GPA of 3.5. Additional exam requirements/recommendations for international students: Required—TOEFL. *Application deadline:* For fall admission, 1/15 for domestic and international students. Applications are processed on a rolling basis. Application fee: $75. Electronic applications accepted. *Expenses:* Tuition, state resident: part-time $525 per credit hour. Tuition, nonresident: part-time $1131 per credit hour. *Required fees:* $386.31 per term. Tuition and fees vary according to program. *Financial support:* In 2011–12, 6 fellowships with full and partial tuition reimbursements (averaging $11,324 per year), 14 research assistantships (averaging $15,551 per year), 29 teaching assistantships (averaging $15,714 per year) were awarded; career-related internships or fieldwork, Federal Work-Study, scholarships/grants, and health care benefits also available. Support available to part-time students. Financial award applicants required to submit FAFSA. *Faculty research:* Speech perception, language acquisition, bilingualism, hearing loss. *Total annual research expenditures:* $982,623. *Unit head:* Dr. Nan B. Bernstein-Ratner, Chair, 301-405-4217, Fax: 301-314-2023, E-mail: nratner@umd.edu. *Application contact:* Dr. Charles A. Caramello, Dean of Graduate School, 301-405-0358, Fax: 301-314-9305.

University of Maryland, College Park, Academic Affairs, College of Behavioral and Social Sciences, Program in Neurosciences and Cognitive Sciences, College Park, MD 20742. Offers PhD. *Faculty:* 1 full-time (0 women). *Students:* 54 full-time (29 women); includes 5 minority (2 Black or African American, non-Hispanic/Latino; 2 Asian, non-Hispanic/Latino; 1 Two or more races, non-Hispanic/Latino), 15 international. 101 applicants, 17% accepted, 9 enrolled. In 2011, 3 doctorates awarded. *Degree requirements:* For doctorate, comprehensive exam, thesis/dissertation. *Entrance requirements:* For doctorate, GRE General Test, 3 letters of recommendation. Additional exam requirements/recommendations for international students: Required—TOEFL. *Application deadline:* For fall admission, 12/15 for domestic and international students. Applications are processed on a rolling basis. Application fee: $75. Electronic applications accepted. *Expenses:* Tuition, state resident: part-time $525 per credit hour. Tuition, nonresident: part-time $1131 per credit hour. *Required fees:* $386.31 per term. Tuition and fees vary according to program. *Financial support:* In 2011–12, 12 fellowships with full and partial tuition reimbursements (averaging $16,942 per year), 15 research assistantships (averaging $18,217 per year), 26 teaching assistantships (averaging $17,849 per year) were awarded; Federal Work-Study and scholarships/grants also available. Support available to part-time students. Financial award

applicants required to submit FAFSA. *Faculty research:* Molecular neurobiology, cognition, neural and behavioral systems language, memory, human development. *Total annual research expenditures:* $2.2 million. *Unit head:* Robert Dooling, Director, 301-405-8910, Fax: 301-405-7104, E-mail: rdooling@umd.edu. *Application contact:* Dr. Charles A. Caramello, Dean of Graduate School, 301-405-0358, Fax: 301-314-9305.

University of Massachusetts Amherst, Graduate School, Interdisciplinary Programs, Program in Neuroscience and Behavior, Amherst, MA 01003. Offers animal behavior and learning (PhD); molecular and cellular neuroscience (PhD); neural and behavioral development (PhD); neuroendocrinology (PhD); neuroscience and behavior (MS); sensorimotor, cognitive, and computational neuroscience (PhD). *Students:* 28 full-time (19 women), 1 (woman) part-time; includes 4 minority (2 Asian, non-Hispanic/Latino; 2 Hispanic/Latino), 2 international. Average age 28. 85 applicants, 15% accepted, 4 enrolled. In 2011, 1 master's, 2 doctorates awarded. Terminal master's awarded for partial completion of doctoral program. *Degree requirements:* For master's, thesis or alternative; for doctorate, comprehensive exam, thesis/dissertation. *Entrance requirements:* For master's and doctorate, GRE General Test. Additional exam requirements/recommendations for international students: Required—TOEFL (minimum score 550 paper-based; 213 computer-based; 80 iBT), IELTS (minimum score 6.5). *Application deadline:* For fall admission, 1/2 for domestic and international students. Applications are processed on a rolling basis. Application fee: $50 ($65 for international students). Electronic applications accepted. Tuition and fees vary according to course load, campus/location and program. *Financial support:* Fellowships with full and partial tuition reimbursements, research assistantships with full and partial tuition reimbursements, teaching assistantships with full and partial tuition reimbursements, career-related internships or fieldwork, Federal Work-Study, scholarships/grants, traineeships, health care benefits, tuition waivers (full and partial), and unspecified assistantships available. Support available to part-time students. Financial award application deadline: 1/2. *Unit head:* Dr. Jeffrey D. Blaustein, Graduate Program Director, 413-545-2046, Fax: 413-545-3243. *Application contact:* Lindsay DeSantis, Interim Supervisor of Admissions, 413-545-0722, Fax: 413-577-0010, E-mail: gradadm@grad.umass.edu. Web site: http://www.umass.edu/neuro/.

University of Massachusetts Worcester, Graduate School of Biomedical Sciences, Worcester, MA 01655-0115. Offers biochemistry and molecular pharmacology (PhD); bioinformatics and computational biology (PhD); cancer biology (PhD); cell biology (PhD); clinical and population health research (PhD); clinical investigation (MS); immunology and virology (PhD); interdisciplinary graduate program (PhD); molecular genetics and microbiology (PhD); neuroscience (PhD); DVM/PhD; MD/PhD. *Faculty:* 1,427 full-time (526 women), 309 part-time/adjunct (196 women). *Students:* 416 full-time (225 women); includes 47 minority (12 Black or African American, non-Hispanic/Latino; 32 Asian, non-Hispanic/Latino; 3 Hispanic/Latino), 144 international. Average age 29. 623 applicants, 17% accepted, 54 enrolled. In 2011, 5 master's, 63 doctorates awarded. Terminal master's awarded for partial completion of doctoral program. *Degree requirements:* For master's, comprehensive exam, thesis; for doctorate, comprehensive exam, thesis/dissertation. *Entrance requirements:* For master's, bachelor's degree; for doctorate, GRE General Test. Additional exam requirements/recommendations for international students: Required—TOEFL (minimum score 600 paper-based; 250 computer-based; 100 iBT) or IELTS (minimum score 7.5). *Application deadline:* For fall admission, 12/15 for domestic and international students; for spring admission, 5/15 for domestic students. Application fee: $50. Electronic applications accepted. *Expenses:* Contact institution. *Financial support:* In 2011–12, 416 students received support, including 416 research assistantships with full tuition reimbursements available (averaging $29,200 per year); scholarships/grants, health care benefits, tuition waivers (full), and unspecified assistantships also available. Financial award application deadline: 4/16. *Faculty research:* RNA interference, cell biology, bioinformatics, clinical research, infectious disease. *Total annual research expenditures:* $262.7 million. *Unit head:* Dr. Anthony Carruthers, Dean, 508-856-4135, E-mail: anthony.carruthers@umassmed.edu. *Application contact:* Dr. Kendall Knight, Associate Dean and Interim Director of Admissions and Recruitment, 508-856-5628, Fax: 508-856-3659, E-mail: kendall.knight@umassmed.edu. Web site: http://www.umassmed.edu/gsbs/.

University of Medicine and Dentistry of New Jersey, Graduate School of Biomedical Sciences, Graduate Programs in Biomedical Sciences–Newark, Program in Integrative Neuroscience, Newark, NJ 07107. Offers PhD. Program offered jointly with Rutgers, The State University of New Jersey, New Brunswick. *Degree requirements:* For doctorate, thesis/dissertation, qualifying exam. *Entrance requirements:* For doctorate, GRE General Test, minimum GPA of 3.5. Additional exam requirements/recommendations for international students: Required—TOEFL. Electronic applications accepted.

University of Medicine and Dentistry of New Jersey, Graduate School of Biomedical Sciences, Graduate Programs in Biomedical Sciences–Piscataway, Program in Neuroscience, Piscataway, NJ 08854-5635. Offers MS, PhD, MD/PhD. *Degree requirements:* For master's, thesis, qualifying exam; for doctorate, thesis/dissertation, qualifying exam. *Entrance requirements:* Additional exam requirements/recommendations for international students: Required—TOEFL. Electronic applications accepted.

University of Miami, Graduate School, College of Arts and Sciences, Department of Psychology, Coral Gables, FL 33124. Offers adult clinical (PhD); behavioral neuroscience (PhD); child clinical (PhD); developmental psychology (PhD); health clinical (PhD); psychology (MS). *Accreditation:* APA (one or more programs are accredited). *Degree requirements:* For doctorate, comprehensive exam, thesis/dissertation. *Entrance requirements:* For doctorate, GRE General Test, minimum GPA of 3.5. Additional exam requirements/recommendations for international students: Required—TOEFL. Electronic applications accepted. *Faculty research:* Behavioral factors in cardiovascular disease and cancer adult psychopathology, developmental disabilities, social and emotional development, mechanisms of coping.

University of Miami, Graduate School, Miller School of Medicine, Graduate Programs in Medicine, Neuroscience Program, Coral Gables, FL 33124. Offers PhD, MD/PhD. *Degree requirements:* For doctorate, thesis/dissertation, qualifying exam. *Entrance requirements:* For doctorate, GRE General Test. Additional exam requirements/recommendations for international students: Required—TOEFL (minimum score 550 paper-based; 213 computer-based). Electronic applications accepted. *Faculty research:* Cellular and molecular biology, transduction, nerve regeneration and embryonic development, membrane biophysics.

University of Michigan, Horace H. Rackham School of Graduate Studies, College of Literature, Science, and the Arts, Department of Psychology, Ann Arbor, MI 48109. Offers biopsychology (PhD); clinical science (PhD); cognition and cognitive neuroscience (PhD); developmental psychology (PhD); personality and social contexts (PhD); social psychology (PhD). *Accreditation:* APA. *Faculty:* 83 full-time (39 women), 30 part-time/adjunct (14 women). *Students:* 141 full-time (99 women); includes 54 minority (16 Black or African American, non-Hispanic/Latino; 2 American Indian or Alaska Native, non-Hispanic/Latino; 18 Asian, non-Hispanic/Latino; 18 Hispanic/Latino), 15 international. Average age 27. 641 applicants, 6% accepted, 30 enrolled. In 2011, 25 doctorates awarded. *Degree requirements:* For doctorate, comprehensive exam, thesis/dissertation, oral defense of dissertation, preliminary exam. *Entrance requirements:* For doctorate, GRE General Test. Additional exam requirements/recommendations for international students: Required—TOEFL. *Application deadline:* For fall admission, 12/1 for domestic and international students. Application fee: $65 ($75 for international students). Electronic applications accepted. *Financial support:* In 2011–12, 112 students received support, including 56 fellowships with full tuition reimbursements available (averaging $20,900 per year), 30 research assistantships with full tuition reimbursements available (averaging $25,950 per year), 55 teaching assistantships with full tuition reimbursements available (averaging $22,670 per year); career-related internships or fieldwork also available. Financial award application deadline: 4/15. *Total annual research expenditures:* $7.4 million. *Unit head:* Prof. Robert Sellers, Chair, 734-764-7429. *Application contact:* Laurie Brannan, Psychology Student Academic Affairs, 731-764-2580, Fax: 734-615-7584, E-mail: psych.saa@umich.edu. Web site: http://www.lsa.umich.edu/psych/.

University of Michigan, Horace H. Rackham School of Graduate Studies, Program in Biomedical Sciences (PIBS), Neuroscience Graduate Program, Ann Arbor, MI 48072-2215. Offers PhD. *Faculty:* 122 full-time (35 women). *Students:* 54 full-time (26 women); includes 20 minority (4 Black or African American, non-Hispanic/Latino; 3 Asian, non-Hispanic/Latino; 9 Hispanic/Latino; 4 Two or more races, non-Hispanic/Latino), 3 international. Average age 28. 100 applicants, 10% accepted, 3 enrolled. In 2011, 12 doctorates awarded. *Degree requirements:* For doctorate, thesis/dissertation, oral defense of dissertation, preliminary exam. *Entrance requirements:* For doctorate, GRE General Test, 3 letters of recommendation, research experience. Additional exam requirements/recommendations for international students: Required—TOEFL (minimum score 84 iBT). *Application deadline:* For fall admission, 12/1 for domestic and international students. Application fee: $65 ($75 for international students). Electronic applications accepted. *Financial support:* In 2011–12, 54 students received support, including 54 fellowships with full tuition reimbursements available (averaging $26,500 per year); scholarships/grants, health care benefits, tuition waivers (full), and unspecified assistantships also available. Financial award application deadline: 12/1. *Faculty research:* Developmental neurobiology, cellular and molecular neurobiology, cognitive neuroscience, sensory neuroscience, behavioral neuroscience. *Unit head:* Dr. Edward Stuenkel, Director, 734-763-9638, Fax: 734-647-0717, E-mail: esterm@umich.edu. *Application contact:* Rachel F. Flaten, Student Services Administrator, 734-763-9638, Fax: 734-647-0717, E-mail: rachelfk@umich.edu. Web site: http://www.umich.edu/~neurosci.

University of Minnesota, Twin Cities Campus, Graduate School, Graduate Program in Neuroscience, Minneapolis, MN 55455-0213. Offers MS, PhD. Terminal master's awarded for partial completion of doctoral program. *Degree requirements:* For master's, thesis; for doctorate, thesis/dissertation. *Entrance requirements:* For doctorate, GRE. Additional exam requirements/recommendations for international students: Required—TOEFL. Electronic applications accepted. *Faculty research:* Cellular and molecular neuroscience, behavioral neuroscience, developmental neuroscience, neurodegenerative diseases, pain, addiction, motor control.

University of Missouri, Graduate School, Neuroscience Interdisciplinary Program, Columbia, MO 65211. Offers MS, PhD. *Students:* 11 full-time (3 women), 2 international. Average age 26. 8 applicants, 13% accepted, 1 enrolled. *Entrance requirements:* For master's and doctorate, GRE (minimum score: Verbal and Quantitative 1200), bachelor's degree or its equivalent. Additional exam requirements/recommendations for international students: Required—TOEFL (minimum score 600 paper-based; 250 computer-based; 100 iBT). *Application deadline:* For fall admission, 1/15 for domestic students. *Expenses:* Tuition, state resident: full-time $5881. Tuition, nonresident: full-time $15,183. *Required fees:* $952. Tuition and fees vary according to campus/location and program. *Faculty research:* molecular and cellular organization of the nervous system, structure and function of neural systems (including vision and hearing), behaviors generated by the nervous system, neurological diseases and disorders. *Unit head:* Dr. Pamela Benoit, Vice-Provost for Advanced Studies and Dean of the Graduate School, 573-884-4178, E-mail: benoitp@missouri.edu. *Application contact:* Nila Emerich, 573-882-1847, E-mail: emerichn@missouri.edu. Web site: http://www.neurosci.missouri.edu/program.html.

University of Missouri–St. Louis, College of Arts and Sciences, Department of Psychology, St. Louis, MO 63121. Offers behavioral neuroscience (PhD); clinical community psychology (PhD); clinical psychology respecialization (Certificate); general psychology (MA); industrial/organizational psychology (PhD); trauma studies (Certificate). *Accreditation:* APA (one or more programs are accredited). Evening/weekend programs available. *Faculty:* 19 full-time (9 women), 5 part-time/adjunct (3 women). *Students:* 74 full-time (55 women), 7 part-time (5 women); includes 8 minority (1 Black or African American, non-Hispanic/Latino; 1 American Indian or Alaska Native, non-Hispanic/Latino; 3 Asian, non-Hispanic/Latino; 2 Hispanic/Latino; 1 Two or more races, non-Hispanic/Latino). Average age 28. 230 applicants, 9% accepted, 15 enrolled. In 2011, 15 master's, 9 doctorates awarded. Terminal master's awarded for partial completion of doctoral program. *Degree requirements:* For master's, thesis; for doctorate, thesis/dissertation. *Entrance requirements:* For master's, GRE General Test, 3 letters of recommendation; for doctorate, GRE General Test, GRE Subject Test, 3 letters of recommendation. Additional exam requirements/recommendations for international students: Required—TOEFL (minimum score 550 paper-based; 213 computer-based). *Application deadline:* For fall admission, 12/15 for domestic and international students. Application fee: $35 ($40 for international students). Electronic applications accepted. *Expenses:* Tuition, state resident: full-time $6273; part-time $3866 per year. Tuition, nonresident: full-time $14,969; part-time $9980 per year. *Required fees:* $315 per year. *Financial support:* In 2011–12, 12 research assistantships with full and partial tuition reimbursements (averaging $10,520 per year), 19 teaching assistantships with full and partial tuition reimbursements (averaging $8,780 per year) were awarded; fellowships with full tuition reimbursements also available. Financial award applicants required to submit FAFSA. *Faculty research:* Bereavement and loss, neuroscience, post-traumatic stress disorder, conflict and negotiation, social psychology. *Unit head:* Dr. George Taylor, Chair, 314-516-5391, Fax: 314-516-5392, E-mail: umslpsychology@msx.umsl.edu. *Application contact:* 314-516-5458, Fax: 314-516-6996, E-mail: gradadm@umsl.edu. Web site: http://www.umsl.edu/divisions/artscience/psychology/.

The University of Montana, Graduate School, College of Health Professions and Biomedical Sciences, Skaggs School of Pharmacy, Department of Biomedical and Pharmaceutical Sciences, Missoula, MT 59812-0002. Offers biomedical sciences (PhD); neuroscience (MS, PhD); pharmaceutical sciences (MS); toxicology (MS, PhD). *Accreditation:* ACPE. *Degree requirements:* For master's, oral defense of thesis; for doctorate, research dissertation defense. *Entrance requirements:* For master's and doctorate, GRE General Test. Additional exam requirements/recommendations for international students: Required—TOEFL (minimum score 540 paper-based; 210 computer-based). Electronic applications accepted. *Faculty research:* Cardiovascular pharmacology, medicinal chemistry, neurosciences, environmental toxicology, pharmacogenetics, cancer.

University of Nebraska Medical Center, Graduate Studies, Department of Pharmacology and Experimental Neuroscience, Omaha, NE 68198. Offers neuroscience (MS, PhD); pharmacology (MS, PhD). Terminal master's awarded for partial completion of doctoral program. *Degree requirements:* For master's,

comprehensive exam, thesis; for doctorate, comprehensive exam, thesis/dissertation. *Entrance requirements:* For master's and doctorate, GRE General Test. Additional exam requirements/recommendations for international students: Required—TOEFL (minimum score 600 paper-based; 250 computer-based). Electronic applications accepted. *Faculty research:* Neuropharmacology, molecular pharmacology, toxicology, molecular biology, neuroscience.

University of New Mexico, Health Sciences Center Graduate Programs, Program in Biomedical Sciences, Albuquerque, NM 87131-5196. Offers biochemistry and molecular biology (MS, PhD); cell biology and physiology (MS, PhD); clinical and translational science (Certificate); molecular genetics and microbiology (MS, PhD); neuroscience (MS, PhD); pathology (MS, PhD); toxicology (MS, PhD); university science teaching (Certificate). Part-time programs available. *Faculty:* 64 full-time (26 women), 9 part-time/adjunct (4 women). *Students:* 45 full-time (27 women), 56 part-time (28 women); includes 24 minority (3 Black or African American, non-Hispanic/Latino; 1 American Indian or Alaska Native, non-Hispanic/Latino; 4 Asian, non-Hispanic/Latino; 14 Hispanic/Latino; 1 Native Hawaiian or other Pacific Islander, non-Hispanic/Latino; 1 Two or more races, non-Hispanic/Latino), 18 international. Average age 30. 110 applicants, 18% accepted, 17 enrolled. In 2011, 14 master's, 5 doctorates awarded. Terminal master's awarded for partial completion of doctoral program. *Degree requirements:* For master's, thesis; for doctorate, comprehensive exam, thesis/dissertation. *Entrance requirements:* For master's and doctorate, GRE General Test, minimum undergraduate GPA of 3.0. Additional exam requirements/recommendations for international students: Required—TOEFL. *Application deadline:* For fall admission, 3/1 priority date for domestic students, 3/1 for international students. Applications are processed on a rolling basis. Application fee: $50. Electronic applications accepted. *Financial support:* In 2011–12, 99 students received support, including 28 fellowships with full and partial tuition reimbursements available (averaging $22,000 per year), 73 research assistantships with full tuition reimbursements available (averaging $23,000 per year), 8 teaching assistantships (averaging $2,800 per year); career-related internships or fieldwork, Federal Work-Study, institutionally sponsored loans, scholarships/grants, traineeships, health care benefits, and unspecified assistantships also available. Financial award application deadline: 1/1; financial award applicants required to submit FAFSA. *Faculty research:* Infectious disease/Immunity, cancer biology, cardiovascular and metabolic diseases, brain and behavioral illness, environmental health. *Unit head:* Dr. Helen J. Hathaway, BSGP Program Director, 505-272-1887, Fax: 505-272-2412, E-mail: hhathaway@salud.unm.edu. *Application contact:* Mary Fenton, Admissions Coordinator, 505-272-1887, Fax: 505-272-2412, E-mail: mfenton@salud.unm.edu. Web site: http://hsc.unm.edu/som/research/brep/bsgpabout.shtm.

University of Oklahoma Health Sciences Center, College of Medicine and Graduate College, Graduate Programs in Medicine, Department of Neuroscience, Oklahoma City, OK 73190. Offers MS, PhD. *Degree requirements:* For doctorate, thesis/dissertation. *Entrance requirements:* For master's and doctorate, GRE General Test, 3 letters of recommendation. Additional exam requirements/recommendations for international students: Required—TOEFL.

University of Oregon, Graduate School, College of Arts and Sciences, Department of Biology, Eugene, OR 97403. Offers ecology and evolution (MA, MS, PhD); marine biology (MA, MS, PhD); molecular, cellular and genetic biology (PhD); neuroscience and development (PhD). Terminal master's awarded for partial completion of doctoral program. *Degree requirements:* For master's, thesis (for some programs); for doctorate, thesis/dissertation. *Entrance requirements:* For master's and doctorate, GRE General Test, minimum GPA of 3.2. Additional exam requirements/recommendations for international students: Required—TOEFL. *Faculty research:* Developmental neurobiology; evolution, population biology, and quantitative genetics; regulation of gene expression; biochemistry of marine organisms.

University of Pennsylvania, Perelman School of Medicine, Biomedical Graduate Studies, Graduate Group in Neuroscience, Philadelphia, PA 19104. Offers PhD, MD/PhD, VMD/PhD. *Faculty:* 130. *Students:* 124 full-time (66 women); includes 26 minority (3 Black or African American, non-Hispanic/Latino; 19 Asian, non-Hispanic/Latino; 4 Hispanic/Latino), 9 international. 241 applicants, 17% accepted, 19 enrolled. In 2011, 19 doctorates awarded. *Degree requirements:* For doctorate, thesis/dissertation, research project. *Entrance requirements:* For doctorate, GRE General Test. Additional exam requirements/recommendations for international students: Required—TOEFL. *Application deadline:* For fall admission, 12/1 priority date for domestic students, 12/1 for international students. Applications are processed on a rolling basis. Application fee: $80. Electronic applications accepted. *Expenses: Tuition:* Full-time $26,660; part-time $4944 per course. *Required fees:* $2318; $291 per course. Tuition and fees vary according to course load, degree level and program. *Financial support:* In 2011–12, 124 students received support. Fellowships, research assistantships, teaching assistantships, scholarships/grants, traineeships, and unspecified assistantships available. *Faculty research:* Molecular and cellular neuroscience, behavioral neuroscience, developmental neurobiology, systems neuroscience and neurophysiology, neurochemistry. *Unit head:* Dr. Joshua Gold, Chairperson, 215-746-0028, E-mail: igold@mail.med.upenn.edu. *Application contact:* Jane Hoshi, Coordinator. Web site: http://www.med.upenn.edu/ngg.

University of Pittsburgh, Dietrich School of Arts and Sciences and School of Medicine, Center for Neuroscience, Pittsburgh, PA 15260. Offers neurobiology (PhD); neuroscience (PhD). Program held jointly with School of Medicine. *Faculty:* 100 full-time (30 women). *Students:* 68 full-time (34 women); includes 12 minority (2 Black or African American, non-Hispanic/Latino; 7 Asian, non-Hispanic/Latino; 3 Hispanic/Latino), 16 international. Average age 25. 130 applicants, 28% accepted, 11 enrolled. In 2011, 19 doctorates awarded. *Degree requirements:* For doctorate, comprehensive exam, thesis/dissertation. *Entrance requirements:* For doctorate, GRE, interview. Additional exam requirements/recommendations for international students: Required—TOEFL (minimum score 600 paper-based; 250 computer-based; 100 iBT). *Application deadline:* For fall admission, 12/1 priority date for domestic students, 12/1 for international students. Application fee: $50. Electronic applications accepted. *Expenses:* Contact institution. *Financial support:* In 2011–12, 68 students received support, including 22 fellowships with full tuition reimbursements available (averaging $25,550 per year), 35 research assistantships with full tuition reimbursements available (averaging $25,550 per year), 4 teaching assistantships with full tuition reimbursements available (averaging $25,550 per year). Financial award application deadline: 12/1. *Faculty research:* Behavioral/systems/cognitive, cell and molecular, development/plasticity/repair, neurobiology of disease. *Unit head:* Dr. Alan Sved, Co-Director, 412-624-6996, Fax: 412-624-9188. *Application contact:* Joan M. Blaney, Administrator, 412-624-5043, Fax: 412-624-9198, E-mail: jblaney@pitt.edu. Web site: http://cnup.neurobio.pitt.edu/.

University of Puerto Rico, Río Piedras, College of Natural Sciences, Department of Biology, San Juan, PR 00931-3300. Offers ecology/systematics (MS, PhD); evolution/genetics (MS, PhD); molecular/cellular biology (MS, PhD); neuroscience (MS, PhD). Part-time programs available. *Degree requirements:* For master's, one foreign language, comprehensive exam, thesis; for doctorate, one foreign language, comprehensive exam, thesis/dissertation. *Entrance requirements:* For master's, GRE Subject Test, interview, minimum GPA of 3.0, letter of recommendation; for doctorate, GRE Subject Test, interview, master's degree, minimum GPA of 3.0, letter of recommendation. *Faculty research:* Environmental, poblational and systematic biology.

University of Rochester, School of Medicine and Dentistry, Graduate Programs in Medicine and Dentistry, Department of Neurobiology and Anatomy, Interdepartmental Programs in Neuroscience, Rochester, NY 14627. Offers PhD. Terminal master's awarded for partial completion of doctoral program. *Degree requirements:* For doctorate, one foreign language, thesis/dissertation, qualifying exam. *Entrance requirements:* For doctorate, GRE General Test. *Expenses: Tuition:* Full-time $41,040.

The University of South Dakota, Graduate School, School of Medicine and Graduate School, Biomedical Sciences Graduate Program, Program in Neuroscience, Vermillion, SD 57069-2390. Offers MS, PhD. Terminal master's awarded for partial completion of doctoral program. *Degree requirements:* For master's, thesis; for doctorate, comprehensive exam, thesis/dissertation. *Entrance requirements:* For master's and doctorate, GRE General Test, minimum GPA of 3.0. Additional exam requirements/recommendations for international students: Required—TOEFL (minimum score 550 paper-based; 213 computer-based; 80 iBT), IELTS (minimum score 6). Electronic applications accepted. *Expenses:* Contact institution. *Faculty research:* Central nervous system learning, neural plasticity, respiratory control.

University of Southern California, Graduate School, Dana and David Dornsife College of Letters, Arts and Sciences, Program in Neuroscience, Los Angeles, CA 90089. Offers MS, PhD. M.S. degree is terminal degree only. Terminal master's awarded for partial completion of doctoral program. *Degree requirements:* For master's, research paper; for doctorate, comprehensive exam, thesis/dissertation, qualifying examination, dissertation defense. *Entrance requirements:* For doctorate, GRE, 3 letters of recommendation, personal statement, resume. Additional exam requirements/recommendations for international students: Required—TOEFL (minimum score 600 paper-based; 250 computer-based; 100 iBT). Electronic applications accepted. *Faculty research:* Cellular and molecular neurobiology, behavioral and systems neurobiology, cognitive neuroscience, computation neuroscience and neural engineering, neuroscience of aging.

University of South Florida, Graduate School, College of Arts and Sciences, Department of Psychology, Tampa, FL 33620-9951. Offers clinical psychology (PhD); cognitive and neural sciences (PhD); industrial-organizational psychology (PhD). *Accreditation:* APA. *Faculty:* 32 full-time (12 women), 12 part-time/adjunct (6 women). *Students:* 97 full-time (55 women), 24 part-time (16 women); includes 22 minority (2 Black or African American, non-Hispanic/Latino; 11 Asian, non-Hispanic/Latino; 8 Hispanic/Latino; 1 Two or more races, non-Hispanic/Latino), 16 international. Average age 28. 479 applicants, 6% accepted, 22 enrolled. In 2011, 17 doctorates awarded. *Degree requirements:* For doctorate, comprehensive exam, thesis/dissertation, internship. *Entrance requirements:* For doctorate, GRE, minimum upper-division GPA of 3.4, three letters of recommendation, personal statement. Additional exam requirements/recommendations for international students: Required—TOEFL (minimum score 550 paper-based; 213 computer-based; 79 iBT) or IELTS (minimum score 6.5). *Application deadline:* For fall admission, 12/1 for domestic and international students. Application fee: $30. Electronic applications accepted. *Expenses:* Contact institution. *Financial support:* In 2011–12, 75 students received support, including 18 research assistantships with tuition reimbursements available (averaging $14,727 per year), 57 teaching assistantships with tuition reimbursements available (averaging $14,543 per year); tuition waivers (partial) and unspecified assistantships also available. Financial award applicants required to submit FAFSA. *Faculty research:* Clinical, cognitive, neuroscience, social, industrial/organizational. *Total annual research expenditures:* $2 million. *Unit head:* Michael Brannick, Chairperson, 813-974-0478, Fax: 813-974-4617, E-mail: mbrannick@usf.edu. *Application contact:* Cynthia Cimino, Program Director, 813-974-0385, Fax: 813-974-4617, E-mail: cimino@usf.edu. Web site: http://psychology.usf.edu/.

The University of Texas at Austin, Graduate School, College of Liberal Arts, Department of Psychology, Austin, TX 78712-1111. Offers behavioral neuroscience (PhD); clinical psychology (PhD); cognitive systems (PhD); developmental psychology (PhD); individual differences and evolutionary psychology (PhD); perceptual systems (PhD); social and personality (PhD). *Accreditation:* APA. *Degree requirements:* For doctorate, thesis/dissertation. *Entrance requirements:* For doctorate, GRE General Test. *Application deadline:* For fall admission, 1/15 for domestic students. Application fee: $50 ($75 for international students). Electronic applications accepted. *Financial support:* Fellowships, research assistantships, teaching assistantships, Federal Work-Study, and tuition waivers (partial) available. Financial award application deadline: 1/15. *Faculty research:* Behavioral neuroscience, sensory neuroscience, evolutionary psychology, cognitive processes in psychopathology, cognitive processes and their development. *Unit head:* James W. Pennebaker, Chairman, 512-471-7596, E-mail: pennebaker@mail.utexas.edu. *Application contact:* Graduate Office of Academic Affairs, 512-471-6398, Fax: 512-471-6572, E-mail: gradoffice@psy.utexas.edu. Web site: http://www.psy.utexas.edu/psy/GradProgram/gradhome.html.

The University of Texas at Austin, Graduate School, The Institute for Neuroscience, Austin, TX 78712-1111. Offers PhD, MD/PhD. Terminal master's awarded for partial completion of doctoral program. *Degree requirements:* For doctorate, thesis/dissertation. *Entrance requirements:* For doctorate, GRE. *Application deadline:* For fall admission, 1/15 priority date for domestic students. Application fee: $50 ($75 for international students). Electronic applications accepted. *Financial support:* Fellowships with tuition reimbursements, research assistantships with tuition reimbursements, and teaching assistantships with tuition reimbursements available. Financial award application deadline: 2/1. *Faculty research:* Cellular/molecular biology, neurobiology, pharmacology, behavioral neuroscience. *Unit head:* Dr. Daniel Johnston, Director, 512-232-6564, Fax: 512-471-2181, E-mail: djohnston@mail.clm.utexas.edu. *Application contact:* Dr. John Mihic, Graduate Advisor, 512-212-7174, Fax: 512-471-0390, E-mail: mihic@austin.utexas.edu. Web site: http://www.utexas.edu/neuroscience/.

The University of Texas at Dallas, School of Behavioral and Brain Sciences, Program in Cognition and Neuroscience, Richardson, TX 75080. Offers applied cognition and neuroscience (MS); cognition and neuroscience (PhD). Part-time and evening/weekend programs available. *Faculty:* 25 full-time (9 women), 1 part-time/adjunct (0 women). *Students:* 107 full-time (61 women), 31 part-time (15 women); includes 31 minority (4 Black or African American, non-Hispanic/Latino; 14 Asian, non-Hispanic/Latino; 12 Hispanic/Latino; 1 Two or more races, non-Hispanic/Latino), 16 international. Average age 30. 116 applicants, 51% accepted, 43 enrolled. In 2011, 36 master's, 2 doctorates awarded. *Degree requirements:* For master's, internship; for doctorate, thesis/dissertation. *Entrance requirements:* For master's and doctorate, GRE General Test, minimum GPA of 3.0 in upper-level coursework in field. Additional exam requirements/recommendations for international students: Required—TOEFL (minimum score 550 paper-based; 215 computer-based). *Application deadline:* For fall admission, 7/15 for domestic students, 5/1 for international students; for spring admission, 11/15 for domestic students, 9/1 for international students. Applications are processed on a rolling basis. Application fee: $50 ($100 for international students). Electronic applications accepted. *Expenses:* Tuition, state resident: full-time $11,170; part-time $620.56 per credit hour. Tuition, nonresident: full-time $20,212; part-time $1122.89 per credit hour. *Financial support:* In 2011–12, 79 students received support, including 17 research

assistantships with partial tuition reimbursements available (averaging $23,336 per year), 31 teaching assistantships with partial tuition reimbursements available (averaging $14,850 per year); career-related internships or fieldwork, Federal Work-Study, institutionally sponsored loans, scholarships/grants, and unspecified assistantships also available. Support available to part-time students. Financial award application deadline: 4/30; financial award applicants required to submit FAFSA. *Faculty research:* Neural plasticity, neuroimaging, face recognition, cognitive and neurobiological mechanisms of human memory, treatment interventions for semantic memory retrieval problems. *Unit head:* Dr. James C. Bartlett, Program Head, 972-883-2079, Fax: 972-883-2491, E-mail: jbartlet@utdallas.edu. *Application contact:* Mary Felipe, Program Assistant, 972-883-2358, Fax: 972-883-2491, E-mail: mary.felipe@utdallas.edu. Web site: http://bbs.utdallas.edu/cogneuro/.

The University of Texas Health Science Center at Houston, Graduate School of Biomedical Sciences, Program in Neuroscience, Houston, TX 77225-0036. Offers MS, PhD, MD/PhD. Terminal master's awarded for partial completion of doctoral program. *Degree requirements:* For master's, thesis; for doctorate, thesis/dissertation. *Entrance requirements:* For master's and doctorate, GRE General Test. Additional exam requirements/recommendations for international students: Required—TOEFL. Electronic applications accepted. *Faculty research:* Behavior, cognitive, computational, neuroimaging, substance abuse.

The University of Texas Health Science Center at San Antonio, Graduate School of Biomedical Sciences, Department of Pharmacology, San Antonio, TX 78229-3900. Offers neuroscience (PhD). *Degree requirements:* For doctorate, comprehensive exam, thesis/dissertation. *Entrance requirements:* For doctorate, GRE General Test, minimum GPA of 3.0. Additional exam requirements/recommendations for international students: Required—TOEFL (minimum score 560 paper-based; 220 computer-based; 68 iBT). Electronic applications accepted. *Faculty research:* Neuropharmacology, autonomic and endocrine homeostasis, aging, cancer biology.

The University of Texas Medical Branch, Graduate School of Biomedical Sciences, Program in Neuroscience, Galveston, TX 77555. Offers PhD. *Degree requirements:* For doctorate, thesis/dissertation. *Entrance requirements:* For doctorate, GRE General Test. Additional exam requirements/recommendations for international students: Required—TOEFL (minimum score 550 paper-based; 213 computer-based). Electronic applications accepted.

The University of Texas Southwestern Medical Center, Southwestern Graduate School of Biomedical Sciences, Division of Basic Science, Program in Neuroscience, Dallas, TX 75390. Offers PhD. *Degree requirements:* For doctorate, thesis/dissertation, qualifying exam. *Entrance requirements:* For doctorate, GRE General Test, minimum GPA of 3.0. Additional exam requirements/recommendations for international students: Required—TOEFL. Electronic applications accepted. *Faculty research:* Ion channels, sensory transduction, membrane excitability and biophysics, synaptic transmission, developmental neurogenetics.

The University of Toledo, College of Graduate Studies, College of Medicine and Life Sciences, Department of Neurosciences, Toledo, OH 43606-3390. Offers MSBS, PhD, MD/MSBS, MD/PhD. *Faculty:* 12. *Students:* 7 full-time (1 woman); includes 1 minority (Hispanic/Latino), 3 international. Average age 26. 21 applicants, 38% accepted, 4 enrolled. In 2011, 1 master's, 2 doctorates awarded. Terminal master's awarded for partial completion of doctoral program. *Degree requirements:* For master's, thesis, qualifying exam; for doctorate, thesis/dissertation, qualifying exam. *Entrance requirements:* For master's and doctorate, GRE, minimum undergraduate GPA of 3.0, three letters of recommendation, statement of purpose, transcripts from all prior institutions attended, resume. Additional exam requirements/recommendations for international students: Required—TOEFL (minimum score 550 paper-based; 213 computer-based; 80 iBT), IELTS (minimum score 6.5). *Application deadline:* For fall admission, 1/15 priority date for domestic students, 1/15 for international students. Application fee: $45 ($75 for international students). Electronic applications accepted. *Financial support:* In 2011–12, 8 research assistantships with full tuition reimbursements (averaging $21,180 per year) were awarded; Federal Work-Study, institutionally sponsored loans, scholarships/grants, tuition waivers (full), and unspecified assistantships also available. *Unit head:* Dr. Bryan Yamamoto, Chair, 419-383-8346, E-mail: bryan.yamamoto@utoledo.edu. *Application contact:* Admissions Analyst, 419-383-4116, Fax: 419-383-6140, E-mail: christine.wile@utoledo.edu. Web site: http://www.utoledo.edu/med/grad/.

University of Utah, School of Medicine and Graduate School, Graduate Programs in Medicine, Program in Neuroscience, Salt Lake City, UT 84112-1107. Offers PhD. *Degree requirements:* For doctorate, thesis/dissertation. *Entrance requirements:* For doctorate, GRE General Test, minimum GPA of 3.0. Additional exam requirements/recommendations for international students: Required—TOEFL (minimum score 500 paper-based; 173 computer-based); Recommended—TWE (minimum score 6). Electronic applications accepted. *Faculty research:* Brain and behavioral neuroscience, cellular neuroscience, molecular neuroscience, neurobiology of disease, developmental neuroscience.

University of Vermont, College of Medicine and Graduate College, Graduate Programs in Medicine, Graduate Program in Neuroscience, Burlington, VT 05405. Offers PhD. *Students:* 25 (11 women); includes 5 minority (1 Asian, non-Hispanic/Latino; 4 Hispanic/Latino). 29 applicants, 21% accepted, 3 enrolled. In 2011, 1 degree awarded. *Degree requirements:* For doctorate, thesis/dissertation. *Entrance requirements:* For doctorate, GRE General Test. Additional exam requirements/recommendations for international students: Required—TOEFL (minimum score 550 paper-based; 213 computer-based; 80 iBT). *Application deadline:* For fall admission, 12/15 priority date for domestic students, 12/15 for international students. Application fee: $40. Electronic applications accepted. *Financial support:* Research assistantships and teaching assistantships available. Financial award application deadline: 3/1. *Unit head:* Dr. Rae Nishi, Director, 802-656-2230, E-mail: rae.nishi@uvm.edu. *Application contact:* E-mail: graduate.admissions@uvm.edu.

University of Virginia, School of Medicine, Department of Neuroscience, Charlottesville, VA 22903. Offers PhD, MD/PhD. *Faculty:* 10 full-time (4 women). *Students:* 25 full-time (17 women); includes 6 minority (2 Black or African American, non-Hispanic/Latino; 4 Hispanic/Latino), 2 international. Average age 28. 72 applicants, 32% accepted, 10 enrolled. In 2011, 5 doctorates awarded. *Degree requirements:* For doctorate, thesis/dissertation. *Entrance requirements:* For doctorate, GRE General Test, 2 letters of recommendation. Additional exam requirements/recommendations for international students: Required—TOEFL. *Application deadline:* For fall admission, 4/15 for domestic and international students. Applications are processed on a rolling basis. Application fee: $60. Electronic applications accepted. *Financial support:* Application deadline: 1/15; applicants required to submit FAFSA. *Unit head:* Dr. Kevin Lee, Chair, 434-982-2927, Fax: 434-982-4380, E-mail: neurograd@virginia.edu. *Application contact:* Tracy Mourton, Program Coordinator, 434-982-4285, Fax: 434-982-4380, E-mail: neurograd@virginia.edu. Web site: http://www.healthsystem.virginia.edu/internet/neuroscience/home.cfm.

The University of Western Ontario, Faculty of Graduate Studies, Biosciences Division, Department of Clinical Neurological Sciences, London, ON N6A 5B8, Canada. Offers M Sc, PhD. Terminal master's awarded for partial completion of doctoral program. *Degree requirements:* For master's, thesis; for doctorate, thesis/dissertation. *Entrance requirements:* For master's, honors degree or equivalent, minimum B+ average; for doctorate, master's degree, minimum B+ average. *Faculty research:* Behavioral neuroscience, neural regeneration and degeneration, visual development, human motor function.

University of Wisconsin–Madison, Graduate School, College of Letters and Science, Department of Psychology, Program in Cognitive Neurosciences, Madison, WI 53706-1380. Offers PhD. *Degree requirements:* For doctorate, comprehensive exam, thesis/dissertation. *Entrance requirements:* For doctorate, GRE General Test, minimum undergraduate GPA of 3.0. Additional exam requirements/recommendations for international students: Required—TOEFL. Electronic applications accepted. *Expenses:* Tuition, state resident: full-time $10,296; part-time $643.51 per credit. Tuition, nonresident: full-time $24,054; part-time $1503.40 per credit. *Required fees:* $70.06 per credit. Tuition and fees vary according to course load, campus/location, program and reciprocity agreements.

Virginia Commonwealth University, Medical College of Virginia-Professional Programs, School of Medicine, Graduate Program in Neuroscience, Richmond, VA 23284-9005. Offers PhD. Program offered with Departments of Anatomy, Biochemistry and Molecular Biophysics, Pharmacology and Toxicology, and Physiology. *Entrance requirements:* For doctorate, GRE or MCAT. Additional exam requirements/recommendations for international students: Required—TOEFL (minimum score 600 paper-based; 250 computer-based; 100 iBT). Electronic applications accepted. *Expenses:* Tuition, state resident: full-time $9133; part-time $507 per credit. Tuition, nonresident: full-time $18,777; part-time $1043 per credit. *Required fees:* $77 per credit. Tuition and fees vary according to degree level, campus/location, program and student level.

Virginia Commonwealth University, Medical College of Virginia-Professional Programs, School of Medicine, School of Medicine Graduate Programs, Department of Anatomy and Neurobiology, Richmond, VA 23284-9005. Offers anatomy (MS); anatomy and neurobiology (PhD); neurobiology (MS); neuroscience (MS); MD/PhD. *Degree requirements:* For master's, thesis; for doctorate, thesis/dissertation, comprehensive oral and written exams. *Entrance requirements:* For master's and doctorate, GRE, MCAT or DAT. Electronic applications accepted. *Expenses:* Tuition, state resident: full-time $9133; part-time $507 per credit. Tuition, nonresident: full-time $18,777; part-time $1043 per credit. *Required fees:* $77 per credit. Tuition and fees vary according to degree level, campus/location, program and student level.

Virginia Commonwealth University, Medical College of Virginia-Professional Programs, School of Medicine, School of Medicine Graduate Programs, Department of Pharmacology and Toxicology, Richmond, VA 23284-9005. Offers neuroscience (PhD); pharmacology (Certificate); pharmacology and toxicology (MS, PhD); MD/PhD. Terminal master's awarded for partial completion of doctoral program. *Degree requirements:* For master's, thesis; for doctorate, thesis/dissertation, comprehensive oral and written exams. *Entrance requirements:* For master's and doctorate, GRE or MCAT. Additional exam requirements/recommendations for international students: Required—TOEFL (minimum score 600 paper-based; 250 computer-based; 100 iBT). Electronic applications accepted. *Expenses:* Tuition, state resident: full-time $9133; part-time $507 per credit. Tuition, nonresident: full-time $18,777; part-time $1043 per credit. *Required fees:* $77 per credit. Tuition and fees vary according to degree level, campus/location, program and student level. *Faculty research:* Drug abuse, drug metabolism, pharmacodynamics, peptide synthesis, receptor mechanisms.

Wake Forest University, School of Medicine and Graduate School of Arts and Sciences, Graduate Programs in Medicine, Interdisciplinary Program in Neuroscience, Winston-Salem, NC 27109. Offers PhD, MD/PhD. *Degree requirements:* For doctorate, thesis/dissertation. *Entrance requirements:* For doctorate, GRE General Test. Additional exam requirements/recommendations for international students: Required—TOEFL. Electronic applications accepted. *Faculty research:* Neurobiology of substance abuse, learning and memory, aging, sensory neurobiology, nervous system development.

Washington State University, College of Veterinary Medicine and Graduate School, Graduate Programs in Veterinary Science, Pullman, WA 99164. Offers veterinary and comparative anatomy, pharmacology, and physiology (MS, PhD), including neuroscience, veterinary science; veterinary clinical sciences (MS); veterinary microbiology and pathology (MS, PhD), including veterinary science; DVM/MS; PhD/Certificate. Part-time programs available. *Faculty:* 39 full-time (6 women), 19 part-time/adjunct (6 women). *Students:* 118 full-time (62 women), 1 part-time (0 women); includes 7 minority (2 Black or African American, non-Hispanic/Latino; 2 Asian, non-Hispanic/Latino; 3 Hispanic/Latino), 48 international. Average age 30. 103 applicants, 24% accepted, 21 enrolled. In 2011, 12 master's, 7 doctorates awarded. Terminal master's awarded for partial completion of doctoral program. *Degree requirements:* For master's, thesis, oral exam; for doctorate, thesis/dissertation, oral exam, written exam. *Entrance requirements:* For master's and doctorate, GRE General Test, MCAT, minimum GPA of 3.0. Additional exam requirements/recommendations for international students: Required—TOEFL (minimum score 550 paper-based; 213 computer-based; 80 iBT). *Application deadline:* For fall admission, 12/31 priority date for domestic students, 12/31 for international students; for spring admission, 8/1 for domestic and international students. Applications are processed on a rolling basis. Application fee: $75. Electronic applications accepted. *Expenses:* Contact institution. *Financial support:* In 2011–12, 23 students received support, including 16 fellowships with partial tuition reimbursements available (averaging $28,000 per year), 49 research assistantships with partial tuition reimbursements available (averaging $21,558 per year), 9 teaching assistantships with partial tuition reimbursements available (averaging $21,558 per year); Federal Work-Study, scholarships/grants, health care benefits, and unspecified assistantships also available. Financial award application deadline: 3/1; financial award applicants required to submit FAFSA. *Unit head:* Dr. Bryan K. Slinker, Dean, 509-335-9515, Fax: 509-335-0160, E-mail: vetmed-dean@vetmed.wsu.edu. *Application contact:* Julie K. Smith, Principal Assistant, 509-335-3164, E-mail: jksmith@vetmed.wsu.edu. Web site: http://www.vetmed.wsu.edu/.

Washington State University, College of Veterinary Medicine and Graduate School, Graduate Programs in Veterinary Science, Department of Veterinary and Comparative Anatomy, Pharmacology, and Physiology, Program in Neuroscience, Pullman, WA 99164-6520. Offers MS, PhD. Part-time programs available. *Faculty:* 46 full-time (14 women). *Students:* 33 full-time (14 women); includes 4 minority (2 Asian, non-Hispanic/Latino; 2 Hispanic/Latino), 6 international. Average age 28. 34 applicants, 21% accepted, 5 enrolled. In 2011, 1 master's, 4 doctorates awarded. Terminal master's awarded for partial completion of doctoral program. *Degree requirements:* For master's, thesis, written exam; for doctorate, thesis/dissertation, written exam, oral exam. *Entrance requirements:* For master's and doctorate, GRE General Test, MCAT, minimum GPA of 3.0. Additional exam requirements/recommendations for international students: Required—TOEFL (minimum score 550 paper-based; 213 computer-based; 80 iBT). *Application deadline:* For fall admission, 12/31 for domestic and international students; for spring admission, 8/1 for domestic and international students. Applications are processed on a rolling basis. Application fee: $50. Electronic applications accepted. *Financial support:* In 2011–12, 22 students received support, including 4 fellowships

Neuroscience

with full tuition reimbursements available (averaging $28,000 per year), 14 research assistantships with full tuition reimbursements available (averaging $21,558 per year), 9 teaching assistantships with full tuition reimbursements available (averaging $21,558 per year); scholarships/grants, health care benefits, and unspecified assistantships also available. Financial award application deadline: 4/15. *Faculty research:* Addiction, sleep and performance, body weight and energy balance, emotion and well being, learning and memory, reproduction, vision, movement. *Total annual research expenditures:* $5.5 million. *Unit head:* Dr. Steve Simasko, Chair, 509-335-6624, Fax: 509-335-4650, E-mail: simasko@vetmed.wsu.edu. *Application contact:* Bobbi Sauer, Office Assistant II, 509-335-7675, Fax: 509-335-4650, E-mail: grad.neuro@vetmed.wsu.edu. Web site: http://www.vetmed.wsu.edu/depts-vcapp.

Washington University in St. Louis, Graduate School of Arts and Sciences, Department of Philosophy, Program in Philosophy/Neuroscience/Psychology, St. Louis, MO 63130-4899. Offers PhD. *Degree requirements:* For doctorate, thesis/dissertation. *Entrance requirements:* For doctorate, GRE General Test, sample of written work. Electronic applications accepted.

Washington University in St. Louis, Graduate School of Arts and Sciences, Division of Biology and Biomedical Sciences, Program in Neurosciences, St. Louis, MO 63130-4899. Offers PhD. *Degree requirements:* For doctorate, thesis/dissertation. *Entrance requirements:* For doctorate, GRE General Test, GRE Subject Test. Electronic applications accepted.

Wayne State University, College of Liberal Arts and Sciences, Department of Psychology, Detroit, MI 48202. Offers behavioral and cognitive neuroscience (PhD); clinical psychology (PhD); cognitive, developmental and social psychology (PhD); industrial and organizational psychology (MA, PhD). *Accreditation:* APA (one or more programs are accredited). *Students:* 103 full-time (77 women), 28 part-time (19 women); includes 19 minority (5 Black or African American, non-Hispanic/Latino; 1 American Indian or Alaska Native, non-Hispanic/Latino; 7 Asian, non-Hispanic/Latino; 5 Hispanic/Latino; 1 Two or more races, non-Hispanic/Latino), 8 international. Average age 28. 361 applicants, 14% accepted, 27 enrolled. In 2011, 22 master's, 19 doctorates awarded. *Degree requirements:* For master's, thesis (for some programs); for doctorate, thesis/dissertation, training assignment. *Entrance requirements:* For master's, GRE or GMAT, minimum undergraduate upper-division cumulative GPA of 3.0, courses in introductory psychology and statistics; for doctorate, GRE General Test, at least three letters of recommendation, statement of purpose. Additional exam requirements/recommendations for international students: Required—TOEFL (minimum score 550 paper-based; 213 computer-based); Recommended—TWE (minimum score 5.5). *Application deadline:* For fall admission, 6/15 for domestic students, 5/1 for international students; for winter admission, 10/15 for domestic students, 9/1 for international students; for spring admission, 3/15 for domestic students, 1/1 for international students. Applications are processed on a rolling basis. Application fee: $50. Electronic applications accepted. *Expenses:* Tuition, state resident: part-time $512.85 per credit. Tuition, nonresident: part-time $1132.65 per credit. *Required fees:* $26.60 per credit. $199.65 per semester. Tuition and fees vary according to course load and program. *Financial support:* In 2011–12, 97 students received support, including 11 fellowships with tuition reimbursements available (averaging $19,432 per year), 9 research assistantships with tuition reimbursements available (averaging $15,967 per year), 49 teaching assistantships with tuition reimbursements available (averaging $16,098 per year); career-related internships or fieldwork, scholarships/grants, health care benefits, and unspecified assistantships also available. Financial award application deadline: 2/1. *Faculty research:* Clinical neuropsychology, high risk factors in development, human aging and neuroscience, industrial/organizational psychology, health psychology. *Total annual research expenditures:* $1.2 million. *Unit head:* Douglas Whitman, Chair, 313-577-2803, Fax: 313-577-7636, E-mail: dwhitman@wayne.edu. *Application contact:* Dr. Melissa Kaplan-Estrin, Graduate Director, 313-577-2824, Fax: 313-577-7636, E-mail: mkestrin@sun.science.wayne.edu. Web site: http://www.clas.wayne.edu/psychology/.

Wayne State University, School of Medicine, Department of Psychiatry and Behavioral Neurosciences, Detroit, MI 48202. Offers psychiatry (MS); translational neuroscience (PhD). *Students:* 9 full-time (6 women); includes 1 minority (Asian, non-Hispanic/Latino), 2 international. Average age 28. 13 applicants, 23% accepted, 3 enrolled. *Degree requirements:* For master's, thesis, oral thesis defense. *Entrance requirements:* For master's and doctorate, GRE, minimum undergraduate GPA of 3.0, bachelor's degree from accredited institution, coursework in biological sciences and other scientific disciplines, personal statement, three letters of recommendation. Additional exam requirements/recommendations for international students: Required—TOEFL (minimum score 600 paper-based; 250 computer-based; 100 iBT). *Application deadline:* For fall admission, 12/15 for domestic and international students. Application fee: $50. Electronic applications accepted. *Expenses:* Tuition, state resident: part-time $512.85 per credit. Tuition, nonresident: part-time $1132.65 per credit. *Required fees:* $26.60 per credit. $199.65 per semester. Tuition and fees vary according to course load and program. *Financial support:* In 2011–12, 7 students received support. Fellowships with tuition reimbursements available, research assistantships with tuition reimbursements available, scholarships/grants, and unspecified assistantships available. *Faculty research:* Substance abuse, brain imaging, schizophrenia, child psychopathy, child development, neurobiology of monoamine systems. *Unit head:* Dr. David R. Rosenberg, Interim Chair, 313-577-9000, E-mail: drosen@med.wayne.edu. *Application contact:* Dr. Jeffery Stanely, Graduate Program Director, 313-577-9090, E-mail: jstanley@med.wayne.edu. Web site: http://psychiatry.med.wayne.edu/.

Weill Cornell Medical College, Weill Cornell Graduate School of Medical Sciences, Neuroscience Program, New York, NY 10065. Offers MS, PhD. *Faculty:* 34 full-time (12 women). *Students:* 43 full-time (30 women); includes 7 minority (2 Black or African American, non-Hispanic/Latino; 3 Asian, non-Hispanic/Latino; 2 Native Hawaiian or other Pacific Islander, non-Hispanic/Latino), 10 international. Average age 22. 138 applicants, 11% accepted, 7 enrolled. In 2011, 2 master's, 6 doctorates awarded. Terminal master's awarded for partial completion of doctoral program. *Degree requirements:* For master's, comprehensive exam; for doctorate, thesis/dissertation, final exam. *Entrance requirements:* For doctorate, GRE General Test, undergraduate training in biology, organic chemistry, physics, and mathematics. Additional exam requirements/recommendations for international students: Required—TOEFL. *Application deadline:* For fall admission, 12/1 for domestic students. Application fee: $60. Electronic applications accepted. *Expenses: Tuition:* Full-time $46,001. *Financial support:* Fellowships, scholarships/grants, health care benefits, and stipends (given to all students) available. *Faculty research:* Regulation of neuronal development, neuronal stem cells, information processing, behavior, neuronal plasticity. *Unit head:* Dr. Betty Jo Casey, Director, 212-746-5832, E-mail: bjc2002@med.cornell.edu. *Application contact:* Alime Lukaj, Program Coordinator, 212-746-6582, E-mail: alukaj@med.cornell.edu. Web site: http://weill.cornell.edu/gradschool/program/neuroscience.html.

West Virginia University, School of Medicine, Graduate Programs at the Health Sciences Center, Interdisciplinary Graduate Programs in Biomedical Sciences, Program in Neuroscience, Morgantown, WV 26506. Offers PhD, MD/PhD. *Degree requirements:* For doctorate, comprehensive exam, thesis/dissertation. *Entrance requirements:* For doctorate, GRE General Test, minimum GPA of 3.0. Additional exam requirements/recommendations for international students: Required—TOEFL. Electronic applications accepted. *Faculty research:* Sensory neuroscience, cognitive neuroscience, neural injury, homeostasis, behavioral neuroscience.

Wilfrid Laurier University, Faculty of Graduate and Postdoctoral Studies, Faculty of Science, Department of Psychology, Waterloo, ON N2L 3C5, Canada. Offers behavioral neuroscience (M Sc, PhD); cognitive neuroscience (M Sc, PhD); community psychology (MA, PhD); social and developmental psychology (MA, PhD). Part-time programs available. *Degree requirements:* For master's, thesis; for doctorate, thesis/dissertation. *Entrance requirements:* For master's, GRE General Test, honors BA or the equivalent in psychology, minimum B average in undergraduate course work; for doctorate, GRE General Test, master's degree, minimum A- average. Additional exam requirements/recommendations for international students: Required—TOEFL (minimum score 89 iBT). Electronic applications accepted. *Faculty research:* Brain and cognition, community psychology, social and developmental psychology.

Yale University, Graduate School of Arts and Sciences, Department of Psychology, New Haven, CT 06520. Offers behavioral neuroscience (PhD); clinical psychology (PhD); cognitive psychology (PhD); developmental psychology (PhD); social/personality psychology (PhD). *Accreditation:* APA. *Degree requirements:* For doctorate, thesis/dissertation. *Entrance requirements:* For doctorate, GRE General Test.

Yale University, Graduate School of Arts and Sciences, Interdepartmental Neuroscience Program, New Haven, CT 06520. Offers PhD. *Degree requirements:* For doctorate, thesis/dissertation. *Entrance requirements:* For doctorate, GRE General Test. *Expenses:* Contact institution.

Yale University, School of Medicine and Graduate School of Arts and Sciences, Combined Program in Biological and Biomedical Sciences (BBS), Neuroscience Track, New Haven, CT 06520. Offers PhD, MD/PhD. *Degree requirements:* For doctorate, thesis/dissertation. *Entrance requirements:* For doctorate, GRE General Test. Additional exam requirements/recommendations for international students: Required—TOEFL. Electronic applications accepted.

UNIFORMED SERVICES UNIVERSITY OF THE HEALTH SCIENCES

F. Edward Hébert School of Medicine
Graduate Program in Neuroscience

Program of Study

The Uniformed Services University of the Health Sciences (USUHS) offers the Graduate Program in Neuroscience, a broadly based interdisciplinary program leading to the Ph.D. degree in neuroscience. Courses and research training are provided by the neuroscience faculty members, who hold primary appointments in the Departments of Anatomy, Physiology, and Genetics; Biochemistry; Medical and Clinical Psychology; Microbiology and Immunology; Neurology; Pathology; Pediatrics; Pharmacology; and Psychiatry at the University. The program permits considerable flexibility in the choice of courses and research areas; training programs are tailored to meet the individual requirements of each student. The program is designed for students with strong undergraduate training in the physical sciences, biology, or psychology who wish to pursue a professional career in neuroscience research. Integrated instruction in the development, structure, function, and pathology of the nervous system and its interaction with the environment is provided. Students in the program conduct their research under the direction of neuroscience faculty members in laboratories that are located in the medical school. During the first year of study, students begin formal course work. Each student is required to take laboratory training rotations in the research laboratories of program faculty members. By the end of the first year, students select a research area and a faculty thesis adviser. During the second year, students complete requirements for advancement to candidacy, including required course work and passage of the qualifying examination. After advancement to candidacy, each student develops an original research project and prepares and defends a written dissertation under the guidance of his or her faculty adviser and advisory committee.

Research Facilities

Each academic department at the University is provided with laboratories for the support of a variety of research projects. Neuroscience research laboratories available to students are suitable for research in most areas of neuroscience, including behavioral studies, electrophysiology, molecular and cellular neurobiology, neuroanatomy, neurochemistry, neuropathology, neuropharmacology, and neurophysiology. High-resolution electron microscopes, confocal microscopes, two photon microscopes, deconvolution wide-field fluorescence microscopes, a central resource facility providing custom synthesis of oligonucleotides and peptides and DNA sequencing, centralized animal facilities, computer support, a medical library, and a learning resources center are available within the University.

Financial Aid

Stipends are available on a competitive basis. Awards are made on a yearly basis and are renewable. For the 2012–13 academic year, stipends for entering students begin at $27,000. Outstanding students may be nominated for the Dean's Special Fellowship or other special fellowships, which support a stipend of $32,000.

Cost of Study

Graduate students in the neuroscience program are not required to pay tuition or fees. Civilian students incur no obligation to the United States government for service after completion of their graduate training program. Students are required to carry health insurance.

Living and Housing Costs

There is a reasonable supply of affordable rental housing in the area. The University does not have housing for graduate students. Students are responsible for making their own arrangements for accommodations. Costs in the Washington, D.C., area are comparable to those in other major metropolitan areas.

Student Group

The neuroscience graduate program is an active and growing graduate program; approximately 21 students are enrolled. The Uniformed Services University (USU) also has Ph.D. programs in departmentally based basic biomedical sciences, as well as interdisciplinary graduate programs in molecular and cell biology and in emerging infectious diseases. In addition to the graduate and medical programs in the medical school, the nursing school has graduate programs for nurse practitioners and nurse anesthetists.

Student Outcomes

Graduates hold faculty, research associate, postdoctoral, science policy, and other positions in universities, medical schools, government, and industrial research institutions.

Location

USU is located in Bethesda, Maryland, an immediately adjacent northern suburb of Washington, D.C. The University is located in a parklike setting at the Walter Reed National Military Medical Center, which is across the street from the National Institutes of Health and the National Library of Medicine. A nearby Metro subway and bus station provides convenient access to downtown Washington and surrounding areas. The D.C. metropolitan area has about 3 million people and offers seven major universities (including three other medical schools), numerous colleges, and internationally renowned research facilities. Wooded areas and jogging and biking trails surround the University. Cultural and recreational activities are plentiful, with a major park system, recreation facilities, museums, theaters, symphonies, opera, and major-league sports teams. The Chesapeake Bay, Atlantic Ocean, and Shenandoah Mountains are easily accessible.

The University

The University was established by Congress in 1972 to provide a comprehensive education in medicine to those who demonstrate potential for careers as Medical Corps officers in the uniformed services. Graduate programs in the basic medical sciences are offered to both civilian and military students and are an essential part of the academic environment at the University. The University is located in proximity to major research facilities, including the National Institutes of Health (NIH), the National Library of Medicine, Walter Reed Army Medical Center at the National Naval Medical Center, the Armed Forces Institute of Pathology, the National Institute of Standards and Technology, and numerous biotechnology companies.

Uniformed Services University subscribes fully to the policy of equal educational opportunity and accepts students on a competitive basis without regard to race, color, sex, age, or creed.

Applying

Civilian applicants are accepted as full-time students only. Each applicant must have a bachelor's degree from an accredited academic institution. A strong background in science with courses in several of the following disciplines—biochemistry, biology, chemistry, mathematics, physics, physiology, and psychology—is desirable. Applicants must arrange for official transcripts of all prior college-level courses taken and their GRE scores (taken within the last two years) to be sent to the Office of Graduate Education. Students may elect to submit scores obtained in one or more GRE Subject Tests (from the subject areas listed above) in support of their application. Applicants must also arrange for letters of recommendation from 3 people who are familiar with their academic work to be sent to the University. For full consideration and evaluation for stipend support, completed applications should be received before January 1 for matriculation in late August. Late applications are evaluated on a space-available basis. There is no application fee. Application forms may be obtained from the Web site at http://www.usuhs.mil/nes/progdescription.html#app.

Correspondence and Information

For applications:

Associate Dean for Graduate Education
Uniformed Services University
4301 Jones Bridge Road
Bethesda, Maryland 20814-4799
United States
Phone: 301-295-3913
      800-772-1747 (toll-free)
E-mail: nfinley@usuhs.mil
Web site: http://www.usuhs.mil/graded/

For information about the neuroscience program:

Sharon Juliano, Ph.D.
Director, Graduate Program in Neuroscience
Uniformed Services University
4301 Jones Bridge Road
Bethesda, Maryland 20814-4799
United States
Phone: 301-295-3642
Fax: 301-295-1996
E-mail: netina.finley@usuhs.edu
Web site: http://www.usuhs.mil/nes/index.html

THE FACULTY AND THEIR RESEARCH

Denes V. Agoston, M.D., Ph.D., Associate Professor, Department of Anatomy, Physiology, and Genetics. Molecular and cellular mechanisms of functional recovery after traumatic brain injury.

Juanita Anders, Ph.D., Professor, Department of Anatomy, Physiology, and Genetics. Innovative therapies for neuronal regeneration of injured central and peripheral nervous systems, light-cellular interaction.

Regina Armstrong, Ph.D., Professor, Department of Anatomy, Physiology, and Genetics, and Director, Center for Neuroscience and Regenerative Medicine. Cellular and molecular mechanisms of neural stem/progenitor cell development and regeneration in demyelinating diseases and brain injury models.

Suzanne B. Bausch, Ph.D., Associate Professor, Department of Pharmacology. Synaptic plasticity in traumatic brain injury and epileptogenesis; NMDAR-regulated plasticity in neuronal circuits.

David Benedek, M.D., Professor, Department of Psychiatry.

Rosemary C. Borke, Ph.D., Professor Emerita, Department of Anatomy, Physiology, and Genetics. Neuronal plasticity in development and regeneration.

Diane E. Borst, Ph.D., Research Assistant Professor, Department of Anatomy, Physiology, and Genetics. Molecular mechanisms of retinal gene regulation and function.

Maria F. Braga, D.D.S., Ph.D., Assistant Professor, Department of Anatomy, Physiology, and Genetics. Cellular and molecular mechanisms regulating neuronal excitability in the amygdala; pathophysiology of anxiety disorders and epilepsy.

Howard Bryant, Ph.D., Associate Professor, Department of Anatomy, Physiology, and Genetics. Electrophysiology of vascular smooth muscle.

Kimberly Byrnes, Ph.D., Assistant Professor, Department of Anatomy, Physiology, and Genetics. Microglial and macrophage-based chronic inflammation after traumatic brain and spinal cord injury; noninvasive imaging of post-injury metabolic and inflammatory events.

Col. William W. Campbell, USA, MC; M.D., M.S.H.A.; Professor and Chair, Department of Neurology, and Professor, Department of Neuroscience. Neuromuscular disease and clinical neurophysiology.

Kwang Choi, Ph.D., Research Assistant Professor, Department of Psychiatry. Translational research on psychiatric disorders using genetic, behavioral, and bioinformatic approaches.

Jeffrey Cole, Ph.D., Assistant Professor, Department of Neurology.

De-Maw Chuang, Ph.D., Adjunct Professor, Department of Psychiatry. Molecular and cellular of actions of mood stabilizers: neuroprotection against excitotoxicity-related neurodegeneration.

Thomas Côté, Ph.D., Associate Professor, Department of Pharmacology. Mu opioid receptor interaction with GTP-binding proteins and RGS proteins.

Brian Cox, Ph.D., Professor, Department of Pharmacology. Opiate drugs, endogenous opioids, neuropeptides, and their roles in responses of the brain to pain, stress, and injury.

Clifton Dalgard, Ph.D., Assistant Professor, Department of Anatomy, Physiology, and Genetics. Molecular mechanisms of damage-associated inflammation.

Patricia A. Deuster, Ph.D., M.P.H., Professor, Department of Military and Emergency Medicine. Mechanisms of neuroendocrine and immune activation with stress.

Martin Doughty, Ph.D., Assistant Professor, Department of Anatomy, Physiology, and Genetics.

Ying-Hong Feng, Associate Professor, M.D., Ph.D. Angiotensin receptor and signal transduction.

Zygmunt Galdzicki, Ph.D., Associate Professor, Department of Anatomy, Physiology, and Genetics. Molecular and electrophysiological approach to understand mental retardation in Down syndrome; role of glutamate receptors in neurodegenerative disorders.

Neil Grunberg, Ph.D., Professor, Department of Medical and Clinical Psychology. Nicotine and tobacco; drug abuse; stress; traumatic brain injury; PTSD.

Carl Gunderson, M.D., Professor, Department of Neurology. Education of medical students; history of military neurology.

Harry Holloway, M.D., Professor, Department of Psychiatry. Clinical psychiatry; alcohol and drug misuse; posttraumatic stress; neurobiology of psychiatric disorders; clinical psychopharmacology.

David Jacobowitz, Ph.D., Professor, Department of Anatomy, Physiology, and Genetics. Gene and protein discovery in the diseased and developing brain.

Luke Johnson, Ph.D., Assistant Professor, Department of Psychiatry and Program in Neuroscience. Microanatomy of fear and stress.

Martha Johnson, Ph.D., Associate Professor, Department of Anatomy, Physiology, and Genetics. Education of first-year medical and graduate students in the anatomical and physiological sciences.

Sharon Juliano, Ph.D., Professor, Department of Anatomy, Physiology, and Genetics. Mechanisms of development and plasticity in the cerebral cortex, with particular emphasis on the migration of neurons into the cortical plate and factors maintaining the function and morphology of radial glia and Cajal-Retzius cells.

Fabio Leonessa, M.D., Research Assistant Professor, Department of Neurology. Pathobiology and biomarkers of traumatic brain injury and posttraumatic stress disorder.

He Li, M.D., Ph.D., Associate Professor, Department of Psychiatry. Neurobiological basis of post-traumatic stress disorder: synaptic plasticity and neuronal signaling in the amygdala circuitry.

Geoffrey Ling, M.D., Ph.D., Professor, Departments of Anesthesiology, Neurology, and Surgery. Novel therapeutics and diagnostic tools for traumatic brain injury and hemorrhagic shock; mechanisms of cellular injury and edema formation in traumatic brain injury.

Ann M. Marini, Ph.D., M.D., Professor, Department of Neurology. Molecular and cellular mechanisms of intrinsic survival pathways through glutamate receptors to protect against neurodegenerative disorders.

Joseph McCabe, Ph.D., Professor and Vice Chair, Department of Anatomy, Physiology, and Genetics. Traumatic brain injury, hemorrhagic shock, and gene expression of neuroendocrine-related gene products.

Debra McLaughlin, Ph.D., Research Assistant Professor, Department of Anatomy, Physiology, and Genetics. Sensory processing and cortical neurophysiology.

David Mears, Ph.D., Associate Professor, Department of Anatomy, Physiology, and Genetics. Electrophysiology and calcium signaling in neuroendocrine cells.

Chantal Moratz, Ph.D, Assistant Professor, Department of Medicine. Regulation mechanisms of inflammation; autoimmune diseases, traumatic brain injury, and complement activation.

Gregory Mueller, Ph.D., Professor, Department of Anatomy, Physiology, and Genetics. Neuroendocrine regulation; neuropeptide gene expression; regulation of peptide biosynthesis and the proteomics of neuropeptide secretion.

Aryan Namboodiri, Ph.D., Associate Professor, Department of Anatomy, Physiology, and Genetics. Neurobiology of N-acetylaspartate (NAA), and pathogenesis and treatment of Canavan disease.

Feresh Nugent, Ph.D., Assistant Professor, Department of Pharmacology. Synaptic plasticity and drug addiction.

J. Timothy O'Neill, Ph.D., Assistant Professor, Departments of Pediatrics and Anatomy, Physiology, and Genetics. Mechanisms of control of newborn and developmental cerebral blood and oxygen supply.

Harvey B. Pollard, M.D., Ph.D., Professor and Chair, Department of Anatomy, Physiology, and Genetics. Molecular biology of secretory processes.

Sylvie Poluch, Ph.D., Research Assistant Professor, Department of Anatomy, Physiology, and Genetics. Development of the cerebral cortex.

Brian Schaefer, Ph.D., Associate Professor, Department of Microbiology and Immunology. Biology of lymphocyte activation, particularly the antigen-regulated NF-kappaB pathway; role of inflammation in traumatic brain injury; imaging, biochemical, and cellular approaches to elucidate signal transduction mechanisms.

Aviva Symes, Ph.D., Associate Professor, Department of Pharmacology. Glial response to traumatic brain and spinal cord injury; mechanism of cytokine action in the CNS after injury.

E. Fuller Torrey, M.D., Professor, Department of Psychiatry. Infectious agents as causes of schizophrenia and bipolar disorder.

Jack W. Tsao, M.D., Ph.D., Associate Professor, Department of Neurology and Neuroscience. Clinical studies on phantom limb pain, traumatic brain injury, and low back pain; basic science studies on cellular and developmental mechanisms governing nerve degeneration.

Robert J. Ursano, M.D., Professor and Chairman, Department of Psychiatry, and Director, Center for the Study of Traumatic Stress. Posttraumatic stress disorder.

Maree J. Webster, Ph.D., Assistant Professor, Department of Psychiatry. Neuropathology of severe mental illness; schizophrenia and bipolar disorder.

T. John Wu, Ph.D., Associate Professor, Department of Obstetrics and Gynecology. Neuroendocrine regulation of reproduction and stress.

UNIVERSITY OF CONNECTICUT HEALTH CENTER

Graduate Program in Neuroscience

Program of Study

The neuroscience graduate program at the University of Connecticut Health Center offers an interdisciplinary training environment that is committed to preparing students for research and teaching careers in both academic and industrial settings. The curriculum and research are dedicated to understanding the normal function and disorders of the nervous system.

All course requirements are fulfilled within the first two years of the program. Introductory core courses establish a strong foundation in molecular, cellular, and systems-level neurobiology.

A wide selection of advanced elective courses on such topics as physiology of excitable tissue, computational neuroscience, neuropharmacology, neuroimmunology, neurobiology of disease, microscopy, biochemistry, immunology, genetics, and cell biology allows tailoring of the curriculum to accommodate the specific needs and diverse interests of students. Participation in weekly journal clubs provides a broad perspective of cutting-edge research in the field.

During the first year of the program, three research rotation projects are performed in laboratories of the student's choice and a laboratory is identified for the dissertation research project by the beginning of the second year. Experimental training opportunities ranging from recombinant DNA to human studies are available. The breadth of these opportunities is shown in a survey of the areas of faculty research, which include regulation of gene expression, signal transduction, and intracellular trafficking in neurons and glia; function of voltage-sensitive ion channels and neurotransmitter receptors; biology of neuropeptides; synaptic transmission and neuroplasticity; development of neurons and glia; synaptic organization and stimulus coding; and sensory perception, behavior, and human psychophysics. Research pertaining to specific maladies of the nervous system includes neuroinflammation, autoimmunity, and neurodegeneration; substance abuse; stroke; epilepsy; multiple sclerosis; and deafness. Approaches employed include genetic engineering; cell and brain slice cultures; stem cells; electrophysiology; confocal microscopy and other imaging; neuroanatomical, virtual cell and mathematical modeling; and behavioral and transgenic animal models.

Research Facilities

Because of the interdepartmental format, the students have access to all of the facilities of modern biomedical research at the University of Connecticut Health Center, including those in clinical and basic science departments. Most of the neuroscience faculty members are housed in the same building on adjoining floors, providing for a congenial atmosphere of informal scientific exchange and collaborations between laboratories. The Center for Cell Analysis and Modeling (CCAM) has state-of-the-art facilities for confocal and two-photon microscopy and image analysis and is available to members of the Program in Neuroscience. The Lyman Maynard Stowe Library has an extensive collection of periodicals and monographs as well as subscriptions to journals of current interest in the field of neuroscience.

Financial Aid

Support for doctoral students engaged in full-time degree programs at the Health Center is provided on a competitive basis. Graduate research assistantships for 2012–13 provide a stipend of $28,000 per year, which includes a waiver of tuition/University fees for the fall and spring semesters and a student health insurance plan. While financial aid is offered competitively, the Health Center makes every possible effort to address the financial needs of all students.

Cost of Study

For 2012–13, tuition is $10,836 per year for full-time students who are Connecticut residents and $28,116 per year for full-time students who are out-of-state residents. General University fees are added to the cost of tuition for students who do not receive a tuition waiver. These costs are usually met by traineeships or research assistantships for doctoral students.

Living and Housing Costs

There is a wide range of affordable housing options in the greater Hartford area within easy commuting distance of the campus, including an extensive complex that is adjacent to the Health Center. Costs range from $600 to $900 per month for a one-bedroom unit; 2 or more students sharing an apartment usually pay less. University housing is not available.

Student Group

Seventeen students are registered in the Ph.D. program in the Neuroscience Program (including combined-degree students). The total number of master's and Ph.D. students at the Health Center is approximately 400, and there are about 125 medical and dental students per class.

Location

The Health Center is located in the historic town of Farmington, Connecticut. Set in the beautiful New England countryside on a hill overlooking the Farmington Valley, it is close to ski areas, hiking trails, and facilities for boating, fishing, and swimming. Connecticut's capital city of Hartford, 7 miles east of Farmington, is the center of an urban region of approximately 800,000 people. The beaches of the Long Island Sound are about 50 minutes away to the south, and the beautiful Berkshires are a short drive to the northwest. New York City and Boston can be reached within 2½ hours by car. Hartford is the home of the acclaimed Hartford Stage Company, TheatreWorks, the Hartford Symphony and Chamber orchestras, two ballet companies, an opera company, the Wadsworth Atheneum (the oldest public art museum in the nation), the Mark Twain house, the Hartford Civic Center, and many other interesting cultural and recreational facilities. The area is also home to several branches of the University of Connecticut, Trinity College, and the University of Hartford, which includes the Hartt School of Music. Bradley International Airport (about 30 minutes from campus) serves the Hartford/Springfield area with frequent airline connections to major cities in this country and abroad. Frequent bus and rail service is also available from Hartford.

The Health Center

The 200-acre Health Center campus at Farmington houses a division of the University of Connecticut Graduate School, as well as the School of Medicine and Dental Medicine. The campus also includes the John Dempsey Hospital, associated clinics, and extensive medical research facilities, all in a centralized facility with more than 1 million square feet of floor space. The Health Center's newest research addition, the Academic Research Building, was opened in 1999. This impressive eleven-story structure provides 170,000 square feet of state-of-the-art laboratory space. The faculty at the center includes more than 260 full-time members. The institution has a strong commitment to graduate study within an environment that promotes social and intellectual interaction among the various educational programs. Graduate students are represented on various administrative committees concerned with

University of Connecticut Health Center

curricular affairs, and the Graduate Student Organization (GSO) represents graduate students' needs and concerns to the faculty and administration, in addition to fostering social contact among graduate students in the Health Center.

Applying

Applications for admission should be submitted via the online application system and should be filed together with transcripts, three letters of recommendation, a personal statement, and recent results from the General Test of the Graduate Record Examinations. International students must take the Test of English as a Foreign Language (TOEFL) to satisfy Graduate School requirements. The deadline for completed applications and receipt of all supplemental materials is **December 1**. Please note that GRE and TOEFL exams taken after the due date will not be accepted for consideration for admission. Applicants should have had undergraduate instruction in chemistry and biology. In accordance with the laws of the state of Connecticut and of the United States, the University of Connecticut Health Center does not discriminate against any person in its educational and employment activities on the grounds of race, color, creed, national origin, sex, age, or physical disability.

Correspondence and Information

Graduate Admissions Office
Ph.D. in Biomedical Science Program
University of Connecticut Health Center
263 Farmington Ave., MC 3906
Farmington, Connecticut 06030-3906
United States
Phone: 860-679-4509
E-mail: BiomedSciAdmissions@uchc.edu
Web site: http://grad.uchc.edu/prospective/programs/phd_biosci/index.html

THE FACULTY AND THEIR RESEARCH

Srdjan Antic, Assistant Professor of Neuroscience; M.D., Belgrade. Dendritic integration of synaptic inputs; dopaminergic modulation of dendritic excitability.

Rashmi Bansal, Associate Professor of Neuroscience; Ph.D., Central Drug Research Institute, 1976. Developmental, cellular, and molecular biology of oligodendrocytes; growth-factor regulation of development and function and its relationship to neurodegenerative disease, including multiple sclerosis.

Elisa Barbarese, Professor of Neuroscience and Neurology; Ph.D. McGill, 1978. Molecular and cellular biology of neural cells, with emphasis on RNA trafficking.

Leslie R. Bernstein, Associate Professor of Neuroscience; Ph.D., Illinois, 1984. Behavioral neuroscience: psychoacoustics, binaural hearing.

John H. Carson, Professor of Molecular, Microbial, and Structural Biology; Ph.D., MIT, 1972. Molecular and developmental neurobiology; myelination; intracellular RNA trafficking.

Lisa Conti, Assistant Professor of Psychiatry; Ph.D., Vermont, 1986. Behavioral neuroscience: roles of stress and neuropeptides in animal models of psychiatric disorders.

Jonathan Covault, Associate Professor of Psychiatry; M.D., Ph.D., Iowa, 1982. Genetic correlates of alcohol use disorders; role of neuroactive steroids in the effects of alcohol.

Stephen Crocker, Assistant Professor of Neuroscience; Ph.D., Ottawa. Brain injury and repair in neurodegenerative diseases, with a focus on neuroinflammation; myelin injury; neural stem cell differentiation; signal transduction; glia; matrix metalloproteinases and their tissue inhibitors.

Betty Eipper, Professor of Neuroscience; Ph.D., Harvard, 1973. Cell biology, biochemistry, and physiology of peptide synthesis, storage, and secretion in neurons and endocrine cells.

Marion E. Frank, Professor of BioStructure and Function and Director, Connecticut Chemosensory Clinical Research Center; Ph.D., Brown, 1968. Gustatory neurophysiology, neuroanatomy, behavior, and disorders; chemosensory information processing; clinical testing of oral chemosensory function in humans.

Duck O. Kim, Professor of Neuroscience and Biological Engineering Program; D.Sc., Washington (St. Louis), 1972. Neurobiology and biophysics of the auditory system; computational neuroscience of single neurons and neural systems; experimental otolaryngology; biomedical engineering.

Shigeyuki Kuwada, Professor of Neuroscience; Ph.D., Cincinnati, 1973. Neurophysiology and anatomy of mammalian auditory system; principles of binaural signal processing, electrical audiometry in infants.

Eric S. Levine, Associate Professor of Neuroscience; Ph.D., Princeton, 1992. Synapse plasticity and role of neuromodulators in brain development and learning, focusing on neurotrophins and endocannabinoids.

James Li, Professor of Genetics and Developmental Biology; Ph.D., Texas. Development of the central nervous system, with an emphasis on the cellular and molecular mechanisms underlying formation of the mammalian cerebellum.

Xue-Jun Li, Assistant Professor of Neuroscience; Ph.D., Fudan (China). Stem cell biology: mechanisms and pathways underlying the development and degeneration of human motor neurons, using human stem cells as an experimental system.

Leslie Loew, Professor of Cell Biology; Ph.D., Cornell, 1974. Morphological determinants of cell physiology; image-based computational models of cellular biology; spatial variations of cell membrane electrophysiology; new optical methods for probing living cells.

Xin-Ming Ma, Assistant Professor of Neuroscience; Ph.D., Beijing. Synaptogenesis and spine plasticity in hippocampal neurons; estrogen hormones and synaptic plasticity; stress and neuronal plasticity.

Richard Mains, Professor and Chair of Neuroscience; Ph.D., Harvard, 1973. Pituitary; neuronal tissue culture; peptides, vesicles; enzymes; drug abuse; development.

Louise McCullough, Associate Professor of Neurology and Neuroscience; M.D., Ph.D., Connecticut. Effects of estrogens on stroke.

D. Kent Morest, Professor of Neuroscience and Communication Sciences and Director of the Center for Neurological Sciences; M.D., Yale, 1960. Synaptic organization and fine structure of nervous system: plastic changes following activity changes; noise-induced hearing loss; development of synapses; tissue culture; neuronal transplantation.

Douglas L. Oliver, Professor of Neuroscience and Biomedical Engineering; Ph.D., Duke, 1977. Synaptic organization; parallel information processing in CNS; role of ionic currents, channel expression in information processing; neurocytology, morphology, cellular physiology of CNS sensory systems; biology of hearing and deafness.

Joel S. Pachter, Professor of Cell Biology; Ph.D., NYU, 1983. Mechanisms regulating pathogenesis of CNS infectious/inflammatory disease.

Henry Smilowitz, Professor of Radiology, Ph.D., MIT. Development of novel therapies for experimental advanced, imminently lethal, malignant brain tumors in rats and mice; use of gold nanoparticles to develop a new form of radiation therapy (gold-enhanced radiation therapy) and novel approaches to both tumor and vascular imaging.

David M. Waitzman, Associate Professor of Neurology; M.D./Ph.D., CUNY, Mount Sinai, 1982. Neurophysiology; oculomotor system; gaze control system; modeling of CNS.

Zhaowen Wang, Assistant Professor of Neuroscience; Ph.D., Michigan State, 1993. Molecular mechanisms of synaptic transmission, focusing on neurotransmitter release and mechanisms of potassium channel localization, using *C. elegans* as a model organism.

Ji Yu, Assistant Professor of Genetics and Developmental Biology; Ph.D., Texas, 2002. Optical imaging technology; regulatory mechanisms in dendritic RNA translation; cytoskeletal dynamics.

Nada Zecevic, Assistant Professor of Neuroscience; M.D., 1970, Ph.D., 1978, Belgrade. Cellular and molecular aspects of CNS development; primate cerebral cortex; oligodendrocyte progenitors, stem cells, microglia; multiple sclerosis.

Section 14
Nutrition

This section contains a directory of institutions offering graduate work in nutrition, followed by in-depth entries submitted by institutions that chose to prepare detailed program descriptions. Additional information about programs listed in the directory but not augmented by an in-depth entry may be obtained by writing directly to the dean of a graduate school or chair of a department at the address given in the directory.

For programs offering related work, see also in this book *Allied Health, Biochemistry, Biological and Biomedical Sciences, Botany and Plant Biology, Microbiological Sciences, Pathology and Pathobiology, Pharmacology and Toxicology, Physiology, Public Health,* and *Veterinary Medicine and Sciences.* In the other guides in this series:

Graduate Programs in the Humanities, Arts & Social Sciences
See *Economics (Agricultural Economics and Agribusiness)* and *Family and Consumer Sciences*

Graduate Programs in the Physical Sciences, Mathematics, Agricultural Sciences, the Environment & Natural Resources
See *Agricultural and Food Sciences* and *Chemistry*

Graduate Programs in Engineering & Applied Sciences
See *Agricultural Engineering and Bioengineering* and *Biomedical Engineering and Biotechnology*

CONTENTS

Nutrition

American College of Healthcare Sciences, Graduate Programs, Portland, OR 97239-3719. Offers aromatherapy (Graduate Certificate); complementary alternative medicine (MS, Graduate Certificate); herbal medicine (Graduate Certificate); nutrition (Graduate Certificate). Part-time and evening/weekend programs available. Postbaccalaureate distance learning degree programs offered (no on-campus study). *Degree requirements:* For master's, capstone project. *Entrance requirements:* For master's, interview, letters of recommendation, essay. *Application deadline:* For fall admission, 7/15 for domestic and international students; for spring admission, 11/15 for domestic and international students. Application fee: $0. *Expenses: Tuition:* Full-time $6660; part-time $370 per semester hour. *Required fees:* $2100; $117 per semester hour. *Application contact:* Tracey Abell, Acting Dean of Admissions/Director of Operations, 800-487-8839, Fax: 503-244-0727, E-mail: admissions@achs.edu.

American University of Beirut, Graduate Programs, Faculty of Agricultural and Food Sciences, Beirut, Lebanon. Offers agricultural economics (MS); animal sciences (MS); ecosystem management (MSES); food technology (MS); irrigation (MS); mechanization (MS); nutrition (MS); plant protection (MS); plant science (MS); poultry science (MS); soils (MS). Part-time programs available. *Faculty:* 21 full-time (6 women), 2 part-time/adjunct (0 women). *Students:* 12 full-time (all women), 93 part-time (77 women). Average age 24. 96 applicants, 67% accepted, 21 enrolled. In 2011, 25 master's awarded. *Degree requirements:* For master's, one foreign language, comprehensive exam, thesis (for some programs). *Entrance requirements:* Additional exam requirements/recommendations for international students: Required—TOEFL (minimum score 600 paper-based; 250 computer-based; 100 iBT), IELTS (minimum score 7.5). *Application deadline:* For fall admission, 2/20 for domestic and international students; for spring admission, 11/15 for domestic and international students. Applications are processed on a rolling basis. Application fee: $50. Electronic applications accepted. *Expenses: Tuition:* Full-time $12,780; part-time $710 per credit. Tuition and fees vary according to course load and program. *Financial support:* In 2011–12, 22 research assistantships with partial tuition reimbursements (averaging $15,000 per year), 40 teaching assistantships with full and partial tuition reimbursements (averaging $1,000 per year) were awarded; scholarships/grants, health care benefits, and unspecified assistantships also available. Financial award application deadline: 2/2. *Faculty research:* Nutritional food-based dietary guidelines, community and therapeutic nutrition, food safety and food microbiology, landscape planning, nature and rural heritage conservation, pathology, immunology and control of poultry and animal diseases, agricultural economics and development, production of biodiesel from algae, national study on living conditions of refugees. *Unit head:* Prof. Nahla Hwalla, Dean, 961-1343002 Ext. 4400, Fax: 961-1744460, E-mail: nahla@aub.edu.lb. *Application contact:* Dr. Salim Kanaan, Director, Admissions Office, 961-1350000 Ext. 2594, Fax: 961-1750775, E-mail: sk00@aub.edu.lb. Web site: http://www.aub.edu.lb/fafs/Pages/index.aspx.

Andrews University, School of Graduate Studies, College of Arts and Sciences, Department of Nutrition, Berrien Springs, MI 49104. Offers MS. Part-time programs available. *Faculty:* 2 full-time (0 women), 2 part-time/adjunct (both women). *Students:* 5 full-time (4 women), 12 part-time (all women); includes 7 minority (4 Black or African American, non-Hispanic/Latino; 2 Hispanic/Latino; 1 Two or more races, non-Hispanic/Latino), 2 international. Average age 31. 32 applicants, 53% accepted, 12 enrolled. In 2011, 6 master's awarded. *Entrance requirements:* For master's, GRE. Additional exam requirements/recommendations for international students: Required—TOEFL (minimum score 550 paper-based). *Application deadline:* Applications are processed on a rolling basis. Application fee: $40. *Unit head:* Dr. Winston Craig, Chairperson, 269-471-3370. *Application contact:* Carolyn Hurst, Supervisor of Graduate Admission, 800-253-2874, Fax: 269-471-6321, E-mail: graduate@andrews.edu.

Appalachian State University, Cratis D. Williams Graduate School, Department of Nutrition and Health Care Management, Boone, NC 28608. Offers nutrition (MS). Part-time programs available. *Faculty:* 4 full-time (3 women), 2 part-time/adjunct (both women). *Students:* 19 full-time (17 women), 1 part-time (0 women); includes 2 minority (both Black or African American, non-Hispanic/Latino). 29 applicants, 34% accepted, 10 enrolled. In 2011, 8 master's awarded. *Application deadline:* For fall admission, 3/1 for domestic students, 2/1 for international students; for spring admission, 11/1 for domestic students, 7/1 for international students. Applications are processed on a rolling basis. Application fee: $55. Electronic applications accepted. *Expenses:* Tuition, state resident: full-time $4040; part-time $180 per semester hour. Tuition, nonresident: full-time $15,900; part-time $760 per semester hour. *Required fees:* $2500; $20 per semester hour. Tuition and fees vary according to campus/location. *Financial support:* In 2011–12, 5 research assistantships (averaging $8,000 per year) were awarded; career-related internships or fieldwork, scholarships/grants, and unspecified assistantships also available. Financial award application deadline: 7/1; financial award applicants required to submit FAFSA. *Faculty research:* Food antioxidants and nutrition. *Total annual research expenditures:* $29,000. *Unit head:* Dr. Sarah Jordan, Chair, 828-262-8619, E-mail: jordansr@appstate.edu. *Application contact:* Dr. Martin Root, Graduate Program Director, 828-262-2064, E-mail: rootmm@appstate.edu. Web site: http://nhm.appstate.edu/.

Arizona State University, College of Nursing and Health Innovation, Phoenix, AZ 85004. Offers advanced nursing practice (DNP); child/family mental health nurse practitioner (Graduate Certificate); clinical research management (MS); community and public health practice (Graduate Certificate); community health (MS); exercise and wellness (MS), including exercise and wellness; family nurse practitioner (Graduate Certificate); healthcare innovation (MHI); international health for healthcare (Graduate Certificate); kinesiology (MS, PhD); nursing (MS, Graduate Certificate); nursing and healthcare innovation (PhD); nutrition (MS); physical activity nutrition and wellness (PhD), including physical activity, nutrition and wellness; public health (MPH); regulatory science and health safety (MS). *Accreditation:* AACN. Postbaccalaureate distance learning degree programs offered (minimal on-campus study). *Degree requirements:* For master's, comprehensive exam (for some programs), thesis (for some programs), interactive Program of Study (iPOS) submitted before completing 50 percent of required credit hours; for doctorate, comprehensive exam, thesis/dissertation, interactive Program of Study (iPOS) submitted before completing 50 percent of required credit hours. *Entrance requirements:* For master's and doctorate, GRE, minimum GPA of 3.0 or equivalent in last 2 years of work leading to bachelor's degree. Additional exam requirements/recommendations for international students: Required—TOEFL (minimum score 80 iBT), TOEFL, IELTS, or Pearson Test of English. Electronic applications accepted. *Expenses:* Contact institution.

Auburn University, Graduate School, College of Human Sciences, Department of Nutrition and Food Science, Auburn University, AL 36849. Offers global hospitality and retailing (Graduate Certificate); nutrition (MS, PhD). Part-time programs available. *Faculty:* 13 full-time (5 women). *Students:* 23 full-time (15 women), 25 part-time (16 women); includes 5 minority (4 Black or African American, non-Hispanic/Latino; 1 Asian, non-Hispanic/Latino), 19 international. Average age 29. 56 applicants, 38% accepted, 11 enrolled. In 2011, 4 master's, 2 doctorates awarded. *Degree requirements:* For master's, thesis (for some programs); for doctorate, thesis/dissertation. *Entrance requirements:* For master's and doctorate, GRE General Test. *Application deadline:* For fall admission, 7/7 for domestic students; for spring admission, 11/24 for domestic students. Applications are processed on a rolling basis. Application fee: $50 ($60 for international students). Electronic applications accepted. *Expenses:* Tuition, state resident: full-time $7290; part-time $405 per credit hour. Tuition, nonresident: full-time $21,870; part-time $1215 per credit hour. *International tuition:* $22,000 full-time. *Required fees:* $1402. *Financial support:* Research assistantships, teaching assistantships, career-related internships or fieldwork, and Federal Work-Study available. Support available to part-time students. Financial award application deadline: 3/15; financial award applicants required to submit FAFSA. *Faculty research:* Food quality and safety, diet, food supply, physical activity in maintenance of health, prevention of selected chronic disease states. *Unit head:* Dr. Martin O'Neill, Head, 334-844-3266. *Application contact:* Dr. George Flowers, Dean of the Graduate School, 334-844-2125. Web site: http://www.humsci.auburn.edu/nufs/.

Bastyr University, School of Natural Health Arts and Sciences, Kenmore, WA 98028-4966. Offers counseling psychology (MA); holistic landscape design (Certificate); midwifery (MS); nutrition (MS); nutrition and clinical health psychology (MS). *Accreditation:* AND. Part-time programs available. *Students:* 142 full-time (136 women), 15 part-time (all women); includes 28 minority (3 Black or African American, non-Hispanic/Latino; 5 Asian, non-Hispanic/Latino; 8 Hispanic/Latino; 12 Two or more races, non-Hispanic/Latino), 5 international. Average age 30. In 2011, 36 master's awarded. *Degree requirements:* For master's, thesis optional. *Entrance requirements:* For master's, 1-2 years' basic sciences course work (depending on program). Additional exam requirements/recommendations for international students: Required—TOEFL (minimum score 550 paper-based; 213 computer-based; 79 iBT). *Application deadline:* For fall admission, 3/15 priority date for domestic students, 3/15 for international students. Applications are processed on a rolling basis. Application fee: $75. *Expenses: Tuition:* Full-time $27,653; part-time $6440 per quarter. *Required fees:* $75; $75. One-time fee: $375. Tuition and fees vary according to course load, degree level, program and student level. *Financial support:* In 2011–12, 47 students received support, including 4 teaching assistantships (averaging $2,000 per year); career-related internships or fieldwork, Federal Work-Study, and scholarships/grants also available. Support available to part-time students. Financial award application deadline: 4/15; financial award applicants required to submit FAFSA. *Faculty research:* Whole-food nutrition for type 2 diabetes; meditation in end-of-life care; stress management; Qi Gong, Tai Chi and yoga for older adults; echinacea and immunology. *Unit head:* Dr. Timothy Callahan, Vice President and Provost, 425-602-3110, Fax: 425-823-6222. *Application contact:* Admissions Office, 425-602-3330, Fax: 425-602-3090, E-mail: admissions@bastyr.edu. Web site: http://www.bastyr.edu/academics/schools-departments/school-natural-health-arts-sciences.

Baylor University, Graduate School, Military Programs, Program in Nutrition, Waco, TX 76798. Offers MS. *Students:* 24 full-time (18 women); includes 3 minority (1 Black or African American, non-Hispanic/Latino; 2 Hispanic/Latino). In 2011, 11 master's awarded. *Unit head:* Lt. Col. Lori Sigrist, Graduate Program Director, 210-221-6274, Fax: 210-221-7306, E-mail: lori.sigrist@us.army.mil. *Application contact:* S. Sgt. Janean Ortega, Administrative Assistant, 210-221-6274, E-mail: janean.ortega@us.army.mil. Web site: http://www.baylor.edu/graduate/nutrition/.

Baylor University, Graduate School, School of Education, Department of Health, Human Performance and Recreation, Waco, TX 76798. Offers exercise, nutrition and preventive health (PhD); health, human performance and recreation (MS Ed). *Accreditation:* NCATE. Part-time programs available. *Faculty:* 13 full-time (5 women), 3 part-time/adjunct (1 woman). *Students:* 64 full-time (41 women), 28 part-time (10 women); includes 16 minority (5 Black or African American, non-Hispanic/Latino; 1 Asian, non-Hispanic/Latino; 7 Hispanic/Latino; 3 Two or more races, non-Hispanic/Latino), 8 international. 30 applicants, 87% accepted. In 2011, 42 degrees awarded. *Degree requirements:* For master's, thesis optional. *Entrance requirements:* For master's, GRE General Test. *Application deadline:* For fall admission, 4/1 priority date for domestic students; for spring admission, 10/1 for domestic students. Applications are processed on a rolling basis. Application fee: $25. Electronic applications accepted. *Financial support:* In 2011–12, 35 students received support, including 22 teaching assistantships; career-related internships or fieldwork, Federal Work-Study, institutionally sponsored loans, tuition waivers (partial), and recreation supplements also available. *Faculty research:* Behavior change theory, pedagogy, nutrition and enzyme therapy, exercise testing, health planning. *Unit head:* Dr. Glenn Miller, Graduate Program Director, 254-710-4001, Fax: 254-710-3527, E-mail: glenn_miller@baylor.edu. *Application contact:* Eva Berger-Rhodes, Administrative Assistant, 254-710-4945, Fax: 254-710-3870, E-mail: eva_rhodes@baylor.edu. Web site: http://www.baylor.edu/HHPR/.

Benedictine University, Graduate Programs, Program in Nutrition and Wellness, Lisle, IL 60532-0900. Offers MS. *Students:* 27 full-time (all women), 7 part-time (all women); includes 1 minority (Asian, non-Hispanic/Latino). 43 applicants, 81% accepted, 15 enrolled. In 2011, 15 degrees awarded. *Entrance requirements:* Additional exam requirements/recommendations for international students: Required—TOEFL (minimum score 550 paper-based; 213 computer-based). *Application deadline:* For fall admission, 9/1 for domestic students; for winter admission, 12/1 for domestic students; for spring admission, 2/15 for domestic students. Applications are processed on a rolling basis. Application fee: $40. Electronic applications accepted. *Financial support:* Career-related internships or fieldwork and health care benefits available. Support available to part-time students. *Faculty research:* Community and corporate wellness risk assessment, health behavior change, self-efficacy, evaluation of health program impact and effectiveness. *Total annual research expenditures:* $8,335. *Unit head:* Catherine Arnold, Director, 630-829-6534, E-mail: carnold@ben.edu. *Application contact:* Kari Gibbons, Associate Vice President, Enrollment Center, 630-829-6200, Fax: 630-829-6584, E-mail: kgibbons@ben.edu.

Benedictine University, Graduate Programs, Program in Public Health, Lisle, IL 60532-0900. Offers administration of health care institutions (MPH); dietetics (MPH); disaster management (MPH); health education (MPH); health information systems (MPH); MBA/MPH; MPH/MS. Part-time and evening/weekend programs available. Postbaccalaureate distance learning degree programs offered. *Faculty:* 2 full-time (0 women), 8 part-time/adjunct (3 women). *Students:* 85 full-time (61 women), 437 part-time (333 women); includes 217 minority (133 Black or African American, non-Hispanic/Latino; 1 American Indian or Alaska Native, non-Hispanic/Latino; 65 Asian, non-Hispanic/Latino; 18 Hispanic/Latino), 28 international. Average age 33. 172 applicants, 80% accepted, 113 enrolled. In 2011, 116 master's awarded. *Entrance requirements:* For master's, MAT, GRE, or GMAT. Additional exam requirements/recommendations for

international students: Required—TOEFL (minimum score 550 paper-based; 213 computer-based). *Application deadline:* For fall admission, 9/1 for domestic students; for winter admission, 12/1 for domestic students; for spring admission, 2/15 for domestic students. Application fee: $40. *Financial support:* Career-related internships or fieldwork and health care benefits available. Support available to part-time students. *Unit head:* Dr. Georgeen Polyak, Director, 630-829-6217, E-mail: gpolyak@ben.edu. *Application contact:* Kari Gibbons, Associate Vice President, Enrollment Center, 630-829-6200, Fax: 630-829-6584, E-mail: kgibbons@ben.edu.

Boston University, College of Health and Rehabilitation Sciences: Sargent College, Department of Health Sciences, Program in Nutrition, Boston, MA 02215. Offers MS. *Faculty:* 10 full-time (9 women), 5 part-time/adjunct (3 women). *Students:* 50 full-time (49 women), 5 part-time (all women); includes 4 minority (1 Asian, non-Hispanic/Latino; 3 Hispanic/Latino), 3 international. Average age 25. 131 applicants, 23% accepted, 23 enrolled. In 2011, 27 master's awarded. *Entrance requirements:* For master's, GRE General Test, minimum GPA of 3.0. Additional exam requirements/recommendations for international students: Required—TOEFL (minimum score 550 paper-based; 84 iBT). *Application deadline:* For fall admission, 2/15 priority date for domestic students, 2/15 for international students; for spring admission, 10/1 for domestic and international students. Applications are processed on a rolling basis. Application fee: $70. Electronic applications accepted. *Expenses: Tuition:* Full-time $40,848; part-time $1276 per credit hour. *Required fees:* $572; $286 per semester. *Financial support:* In 2011–12, 39 students received support, including 20 fellowships (averaging $14,250 per year); career-related internships or fieldwork, Federal Work-Study, institutionally sponsored loans, scholarships/grants, and tuition waivers (partial) also available. Support available to part-time students. Financial award application deadline: 4/15; financial award applicants required to submit FAFSA. *Faculty research:* Metabolism, health promotion, obesity, epidemiology. *Unit head:* Dr. Kathleen Morgan, Chair, 617-353-2717, E-mail: kmorgan@bu.edu. *Application contact:* Sharon Sankey, Director, Student Services, 617-353-2713, Fax: 617-353-7500, E-mail: ssankey@bu.edu.

Boston University, School of Medicine, Division of Graduate Medical Sciences, Programs in Medical Nutrition Sciences, Boston, MA 02215. Offers MA, PhD. *Faculty:* 27 full-time (11 women). *Students:* 21 full-time (13 women), 5 part-time (3 women); includes 5 minority (2 Asian, non-Hispanic/Latino; 1 Hispanic/Latino; 1 Native Hawaiian or other Pacific Islander, non-Hispanic/Latino; 1 Two or more races, non-Hispanic/Latino), 7 international. Average age 29. 57 applicants, 47% accepted, 7 enrolled. In 2011, 2 master's, 1 doctorate awarded. *Degree requirements:* For master's, thesis; for doctorate, thesis/dissertation. *Entrance requirements:* For master's and doctorate, GRE or MCAT. Additional exam requirements/recommendations for international students: Required—TOEFL. *Application deadline:* For fall admission, 1/15 priority date for domestic students; for spring admission, 10/15 priority date for domestic students. Applications are processed on a rolling basis. Application fee: $75. Electronic applications accepted. *Expenses: Tuition:* Full-time $40,848; part-time $1276 per credit hour. *Required fees:* $572; $286 per semester. *Financial support:* In 2011–12, 3 students received support, including 2 fellowships (averaging $30,500 per year), 25 research assistantships (averaging $30,500 per year). Financial award applicants required to submit FAFSA. *Unit head:* Dr. Susan K. Fried, Director, 617-638-7110, E-mail: skfried@bu.edu. *Application contact:* Dr. Lynn Moore, Program Director, 617-638-8088, E-mail: llmoore@bu.edu. Web site: http://www.bumc.bu.edu/medicalnutrition/.

Bowling Green State University, Graduate College, College of Education and Human Development, School of Family and Consumer Sciences, Bowling Green, OH 43403. Offers food and nutrition (MFCS); human development and family studies (MFCS). Part-time programs available. *Degree requirements:* For master's, thesis. *Entrance requirements:* For master's, GRE General Test, minimum GPA of 3.0. Additional exam requirements/recommendations for international students: Required—TOEFL. Electronic applications accepted. *Faculty research:* Public health, wellness, social issues and policies, ethnic foods, nutrition and aging.

Brigham Young University, Graduate Studies, College of Life Sciences, Department of Nutrition, Dietetics and Food Science, Provo, UT 84602-1001. Offers food science (MS); nutrition (MS). *Faculty:* 12 full-time (5 women). *Students:* 10 full-time (7 women), 1 (woman) part-time. Average age 24. 3 applicants, 67% accepted, 2 enrolled. In 2011, 3 master's awarded. *Degree requirements:* For master's, comprehensive exam, thesis. *Entrance requirements:* For master's, GRE General Test. Additional exam requirements/recommendations for international students: Required—TOEFL (minimum score 550 paper-based; 213 computer-based). *Application deadline:* For fall admission, 2/1 for domestic and international students; for winter admission, 6/30 for domestic and international students. Application fee: $50. Electronic applications accepted. *Expenses: Tuition:* Full-time $5760; part-time $320 per credit. Tuition and fees vary according to student's religious affiliation. *Financial support:* In 2011–12, 9 students received support, including 4 research assistantships (averaging $20,325 per year), 3 teaching assistantships (averaging $20,325 per year); career-related internships or fieldwork, institutionally sponsored loans, and scholarships/grants also available. Financial award application deadline: 4/1. *Faculty research:* Dairy foods, lipid oxidation, food processes, magnesium and selenium nutrition, nutrient effect on gene expression. *Total annual research expenditures:* $321,576. *Unit head:* Dr. Michael L. Dunn, Chair, 801-422-6670, Fax: 801-422-0258, E-mail: michael_dunn@byu.edu. *Application contact:* Dr. Susan Fullmer, Graduate Coordinator, 801-422-3349, Fax: 801-422-0258, E-mail: susan_fullmer@byu.edu.

Brooklyn College of the City University of New York, Division of Graduate Studies, Department of Health and Nutrition Science, Program in Nutrition, Brooklyn, NY 11210-2889. Offers MS. Part-time programs available. *Degree requirements:* For master's, thesis or alternative. *Entrance requirements:* For master's, 18 credits in health-related areas, 2 letters of recommendation, essay. Additional exam requirements/recommendations for international students: Required—TOEFL. Electronic applications accepted. *Faculty research:* Medical ethics, AIDS, history of public health, diet restriction, palliative care, risk reduction/disease prevention, metabolism, diabetes.

California State University, Chico, Office of Graduate Studies, College of Natural Sciences, Department of Nutrition and Food Science, Chico, CA 95929-0722. Offers general nutritional science (MS); nutrition education (MS). Part-time programs available. *Faculty:* 4 full-time (all women). *Students:* 14 full-time (13 women), 2 part-time (both women); includes 7 minority (1 Black or African American, non-Hispanic/Latino; 4 Asian, non-Hispanic/Latino; 2 Hispanic/Latino), 2 international. Average age 27. 33 applicants, 36% accepted, 9 enrolled. In 2011, 13 master's awarded. *Degree requirements:* For master's, thesis, seminar presentation. *Entrance requirements:* For master's, GRE General Test, two letters of recommendation, statement of purpose, resume. Additional exam requirements/recommendations for international students: Required—TOEFL (minimum score 550 paper-based; 213 computer-based; 80 iBT), IELTS (minimum score 6.5), Pearson Test of English (minimum score 59). *Application deadline:* For fall admission, 3/1 priority date for domestic students, 3/1 for international students; for spring admission, 9/15 priority date for domestic students, 9/15 for international students. Application fee: $55. Electronic applications accepted. Tuition and fees vary according to class time, course load and degree level. *Financial support:* Teaching assistantships, career-related internships or fieldwork, and scholarships/grants available. Financial award application deadline: 3/1; financial award applicants required to submit FAFSA. *Unit head:* Dr. Kathryn Silliman, Graduate Coordinator, 530-898-6805, Fax: 530-898-5586, E-mail: ksilliman@csuchico.edu. *Application contact:* Judy L. Rice, Graduate Admissions Coordinator, 530-898-5416, Fax: 530-898-3342, E-mail: jlrice@csuchico.edu. Web site: http://www.csuchico.edu/nfsc.

California State University, Long Beach, Graduate Studies, College of Health and Human Services, Department of Family and Consumer Sciences, Master of Science in Nutritional Science Program, Long Beach, CA 90840. Offers food science (MS); hospitality foodservice and hotel management (MS); nutritional science (MS). Part-time programs available. *Students:* 32 full-time (29 women), 23 part-time (all women); includes 18 minority (2 Black or African American, non-Hispanic/Latino; 6 Asian, non-Hispanic/Latino; 5 Hispanic/Latino; 5 Two or more races, non-Hispanic/Latino). Average age 27. 108 applicants, 32% accepted, 21 enrolled. In 2011, 11 master's awarded. *Degree requirements:* For master's, thesis, oral presentation of thesis or directed project. *Entrance requirements:* For master's, GRE, minimum GPA of 2.5 in last 60 units. *Application deadline:* For fall admission, 5/1 for domestic students. Applications are processed on a rolling basis. Application fee: $55. Electronic applications accepted. *Financial support:* Federal Work-Study, institutionally sponsored loans, and scholarships/grants available. Financial award application deadline: 3/2. *Faculty research:* Protein and water-soluble vitamins, sensory evaluation of foods, mineral deficiencies in humans, child nutrition, minerals and blood pressure. *Unit head:* Dr. M. Sue Stanley, Chair, 562-985-4484, Fax: 562-985-4414, E-mail: stanleym@csulb.edu. *Application contact:* Dr. Mary Jacob, Graduate Coordinator, 562-985-4484, Fax: 562-985-4414, E-mail: marjacob@csulb.edu.

California State University, Long Beach, Graduate Studies, College of Health and Human Services, Department of Kinesiology, Long Beach, CA 90840. Offers adapted physical education (MA); coaching and student athlete development (MA); exercise physiology and nutrition (MS); exercise science (MS); individualized studies (MA); kinesiology (MA); pedagogical studies (MA); sport and exercise psychology (MS); sport management (MA); sports medicine and injury studies (MS). Part-time programs available. *Faculty:* 9 full-time (5 women), 5 part-time/adjunct (4 women). *Students:* 48 full-time (27 women), 39 part-time (13 women); includes 38 minority (5 Black or African American, non-Hispanic/Latino; 2 American Indian or Alaska Native, non-Hispanic/Latino; 7 Asian, non-Hispanic/Latino; 18 Hispanic/Latino; 6 Two or more races, non-Hispanic/Latino), 2 international. Average age 28. 214 applicants, 50% accepted, 32 enrolled. In 2011, 69 master's awarded. *Degree requirements:* For master's, oral and written comprehensive exams or thesis. *Entrance requirements:* For master's, GRE General Test, minimum GPA of 2.75 during previous 2 years of course work. *Application deadline:* For fall admission, 6/1 for domestic students. Applications are processed on a rolling basis. Application fee: $55. Electronic applications accepted. *Financial support:* Federal Work-Study, institutionally sponsored loans, and scholarships/grants available. Financial award application deadline: 3/2. *Faculty research:* Pulmonary functioning, feedback and practice structure, strength training, history and politics of sports, special population research issues. *Unit head:* Dr. Sharon R. Guthrie, Chair, 562-985-7487, Fax: 562-985-8067, E-mail: guthrie@csulb.edu. *Application contact:* Dr. Grant Hill, Graduate Advisor, 562-985-8856, Fax: 562-985-8067, E-mail: ghill@csulb.edu.

California State University, Los Angeles, Graduate Studies, College of Health and Human Services, Department of Kinesiology and Nutritional Sciences, Los Angeles, CA 90032-8530. Offers nutritional science (MS); physical education and kinesiology (MA, MS). *Accreditation:* AND. Part-time and evening/weekend programs available. *Faculty:* 5 full-time (3 women), 2 part-time/adjunct (1 woman). *Students:* 96 full-time (84 women), 40 part-time (34 women); includes 70 minority (6 Black or African American, non-Hispanic/Latino; 1 American Indian or Alaska Native, non-Hispanic/Latino; 36 Asian, non-Hispanic/Latino; 24 Hispanic/Latino; 3 Two or more races, non-Hispanic/Latino), 12 international. Average age 31. 152 applicants, 51% accepted, 44 enrolled. In 2011, 38 master's awarded. *Degree requirements:* For master's, comprehensive exam, project or thesis. *Entrance requirements:* For master's, minimum GPA of 2.75. Additional exam requirements/recommendations for international students: Required—TOEFL (minimum score 500 paper-based; 173 computer-based). *Application deadline:* For fall admission, 5/1 for domestic and international students. Applications are processed on a rolling basis. Application fee: $55. *Expenses:* Tuition, state resident: full-time $8225. *Financial support:* Federal Work-Study available. Support available to part-time students. Financial award application deadline: 3/1. *Unit head:* Dr. Nazareth Khodiguian, Chair, 323-343-4650, Fax: 323-343-6482, E-mail: nkhodig@calstatela.edu. *Application contact:* Dr. Karin Brown, Acting Associate Dean of Graduate Studies, 323-343-3820, Fax: 323-343-5653, E-mail: kbrown5@calstatela.edu. Web site: http://www.calstatela.edu/dept/pe/.

Canisius College, Graduate Division, Office of Professional Studies, Buffalo, NY 14208-1098. Offers applied nutrition (MS); community and school health (MS). Postbaccalaureate distance learning degree programs offered (no on-campus study). *Faculty:* 9 part-time/adjunct (7 women). *Students:* 17 full-time (15 women), 6 part-time (5 women); includes 3 minority (1 Black or African American, non-Hispanic/Latino; 1 Asian, non-Hispanic/Latino; 1 Two or more races, non-Hispanic/Latino), 2 international. Average age 32. 35 applicants, 74% accepted, 20 enrolled. *Entrance requirements:* Additional exam requirements/recommendations for international students: Required—TOEFL. *Application deadline:* Applications are processed on a rolling basis. Application fee: $25. Electronic applications accepted. *Financial support:* Career-related internships or fieldwork, Federal Work-Study, scholarships/grants, and unspecified assistantships available. Support available to part-time students. Financial award application deadline: 4/30; financial award applicants required to submit FAFSA. *Faculty research:* Nutrition, community and school health. *Unit head:* Dr. Khalid Bibi, Executive Director, 716-888-8296. *Application contact:* Donna Shaffner, Dean of Admissions, 716-888-2200, Fax: 716-888-3230, E-mail: admissions@canisius.edu. Web site: http://www.canisius.edu/professional-studies/.

Case Western Reserve University, School of Medicine and School of Graduate Studies, Graduate Programs in Medicine, Department of Nutrition, Cleveland, OH 44106. Offers dietetics (MS); nutrition (MS, PhD), including molecular nutrition (PhD), nutrition and biochemistry (PhD); public health nutrition (MS). Part-time programs available. Terminal master's awarded for partial completion of doctoral program. *Degree requirements:* For master's, thesis (for some programs); for doctorate, thesis/dissertation. *Entrance requirements:* For master's, GRE General Test; for doctorate, GRE General Test, GRE Subject Test. Additional exam requirements/recommendations for international students: Required—TOEFL. *Faculty research:* Fatty acid metabolism, application of gene therapy to nutritional problems, dietary intake methodology, nutrition and physical fitness, metabolism during infancy and pregnancy.

See Display on next page and Close-Up on page 407.

Central Michigan University, Central Michigan University Global Campus, Program in Health Administration, Mount Pleasant, MI 48859. Offers health administration (DHA); international health (Certificate); nutrition and dietetics (MS). Part-time and evening/weekend programs available. Postbaccalaureate distance learning degree programs offered (minimal on-campus study). Electronic applications accepted. *Financial support:* Scholarships/grants available. Support available to part-time students. Financial award

Nutrition

applicants required to submit FAFSA. *Unit head:* Steven D. Berkshire, Director, 989-774-1640, E-mail: berks1sd@cmich.edu. *Application contact:* Off-Campus Programs Call Center, 877-268-4636, E-mail: cmuoffcampus@cmich.edu.

Central Michigan University, College of Graduate Studies, College of Education and Human Services, Department of Human Environmental Studies, Mount Pleasant, MI 48859. Offers apparel product development and merchandising technology (MS); gerontology (Graduate Certificate); human development and family studies (MA); nutrition and dietetics (MS). Part-time and evening/weekend programs available. *Degree requirements:* For master's, thesis or alternative. Electronic applications accepted. *Faculty research:* Human growth and development, family studies and human sexuality, human nutrition and dietetics, apparel and textile retailing, computer-aided design for apparel.

Central Washington University, Graduate Studies and Research, College of Education and Professional Studies, Department of Nutrition, Exercise and Health Services, Ellensburg, WA 98926. Offers exercise science (MS); nutrition (MS). Part-time programs available. *Faculty:* 19 full-time (7 women). *Students:* 15 full-time (11 women), 1 part-time (0 women). 20 applicants, 55% accepted, 11 enrolled. In 2011, 16 master's awarded. *Degree requirements:* For master's, thesis or alternative. *Entrance requirements:* For master's, GRE, minimum GPA of 3.0; writing sample (for exercise students). Additional exam requirements/recommendations for international students: Required—TOEFL (minimum score 550 paper-based; 213 computer-based; 79 iBT). *Application deadline:* For fall admission, 2/1 priority date for domestic students; for winter admission, 10/1 for domestic students; for spring admission, 1/1 for domestic students. Applications are processed on a rolling basis. Application fee: $50. Electronic applications accepted. *Expenses:* Tuition, state resident: full-time $8112; part-time $270 per credit. Tuition, nonresident: full-time $18,069; part-time $602 per credit. *Required fees:* $924. *Financial support:* In 2011–12, 2 research assistantships (averaging $9,234 per year), 15 teaching assistantships with full and partial tuition reimbursements (averaging $9,234 per year) were awarded; Federal Work-Study and health care benefits also available. Financial award application deadline: 3/1; financial award applicants required to submit FAFSA. *Unit head:* Leo D'Acquisto, Graduate Coordinator, 509-963-1911. *Application contact:* Justine Eason, Admissions Program Coordinator, 509-963-3103, Fax: 509-963-1799, E-mail: masters@cwu.edu. Web site: http://www.cwu.edu/~nehs/.

Chapman University, Schmid College of Science and Technology, Food Science Program, Orange, CA 92866. Offers MS, MBA/MS. Part-time and evening/weekend programs available. *Faculty:* 3 full-time (2 women), 4 part-time/adjunct (all women). *Students:* 24 full-time (20 women), 26 part-time (18 women); includes 22 minority (1 Black or African American, non-Hispanic/Latino; 19 Asian, non-Hispanic/Latino; 1 Hispanic/Latino; 1 Native Hawaiian or other Pacific Islander, non-Hispanic/Latino), 16 international. Average age 27. 40 applicants, 80% accepted, 19 enrolled. In 2011, 14 master's awarded. *Degree requirements:* For master's, comprehensive exam, thesis optional. *Entrance requirements:* For master's, GRE or GMAT, minimum undergraduate GPA of 3.0. Additional exam requirements/recommendations for international students: Required—TOEFL (minimum score 550 paper-based; 213 computer-based; 80 iBT). *Application deadline:* For fall admission, 5/2 priority date for domestic students; for spring admission, 11/1 priority date for domestic students. Application fee: $60. Electronic applications accepted. Tuition and fees vary according to degree level and program. *Financial support:* Fellowships, Federal Work-Study, and scholarships/grants available. Financial award applicants required to submit FAFSA. *Unit head:* Dr. Anuradha Prakash, Program Director, 714-744-7895, E-mail: prakash@chapman.edu. *Application contact:* Gianne Diosomito, Graduate Admission Counselor, 714-997-6711, E-mail: diosomit@chapman.edu.

Clemson University, Graduate School, College of Agriculture, Forestry and Life Sciences, Department of Food, Nutrition and Packaging Sciences, Program in Food, Nutrition, and Culinary Science, Clemson, SC 29634. Offers MS. *Students:* 29 full-time (21 women), 7 part-time (5 women); includes 3 minority (all Hispanic/Latino), 13 international. Average age 28. 82 applicants, 18% accepted, 10 enrolled. In 2011, 7 master's awarded. *Degree requirements:* For master's, thesis. *Entrance requirements:* For master's, GRE General Test. Additional exam requirements/recommendations for international students: Required—TOEFL, IELTS. *Application deadline:* For fall admission, 6/1 for domestic students, 4/15 for international students; for spring admission, 9/15 for international students. Applications are processed on a rolling basis. Application fee: $70 ($80 for international students). Electronic applications accepted. *Expenses:* Contact institution. *Financial support:* In 2011–12, 16 students received support, including 8 research assistantships with partial tuition reimbursements available (averaging $10,189 per year), 10 teaching assistantships with partial tuition reimbursements available (averaging $10,158 per year); fellowships with full and partial tuition reimbursements available, career-related internships or fieldwork, institutionally sponsored loans, scholarships/grants, health care benefits, and unspecified assistantships also available. Support available to part-time students. Financial award applicants required to submit FAFSA. *Unit head:* Dr. Anthony L. Pometto, Chair, 864-656-4382, Fax: 864-656-3131, E-mail: pometto@clemson.edu. *Application contact:* Dr. Paul Dawson, Coordinator, 864-656-1138, Fax: 864-656-3131, E-mail: pdawson@clemson.edu. Web site: http://www.clemson.edu/foodscience

College of Saint Elizabeth, Department of Foods and Nutrition, Morristown, NJ 07960-6989. Offers dietetic internship (Certificate); nutrition (MS). Part-time and evening/weekend programs available. *Faculty:* 2 full-time (both women), 4 part-time/adjunct (all women). *Students:* 8 full-time (7 women), 36 part-time (all women); includes 7 minority (1 Black or African American, non-Hispanic/Latino; 1 American Indian or Alaska Native, non-Hispanic/Latino; 3 Asian, non-Hispanic/Latino; 2 Hispanic/Latino), 3 international. Average age 29. 40 applicants, 60% accepted, 21 enrolled. In 2011, 11 master's, 18 other advanced degrees awarded. *Entrance requirements:* Additional exam requirements/recommendations for international students: Required—TOEFL (minimum score 550 paper-based). *Application deadline:* Applications are processed on a rolling basis. Application fee: $35. Electronic applications accepted. *Expenses: Tuition:* Part-time $899 per credit. *Required fees:* $73 per credit. *Financial support:* Tuition waivers (partial) and unspecified assistantships available. Support available to part-time students. Financial award application deadline: 3/15; financial award applicants required to submit FAFSA. *Faculty research:* Medical nutrition intervention, public policy, obesity, hunger and food security, osteoporosis, nutrition and exercise. *Unit head:* Dr. Jean C. Burge, Director of the Graduate Program in Nutrition, 973-290-4127, Fax: 973-290-4167, E-mail: nutrition@cse.edu. *Application contact:* Donna Tatarka, Dean of Admission, 973-290-4705, Fax: 973-290-4710, E-mail: dtatarka@cse.edu. Web site: http://www.cse.edu/academics/academic-areas/health-wellness/nutrition/?tabID-tabGraduate&divID-progGraduate.

Colorado State University, Graduate School, College of Applied Human Sciences, Department of Food Science and Human Nutrition, Fort Collins, CO 80523-1571. Offers MS, PhD. *Accreditation:* AND. Part-time programs available. *Faculty:* 17 full-time (9 women), 1 (woman) part-time/adjunct. *Students:* 48 full-time (42 women), 39 part-time (28 women); includes 8 minority (1 Black or African American, non-Hispanic/Latino; 2 Asian, non-Hispanic/Latino; 3 Hispanic/Latino; 2 Two or more races, non-Hispanic/Latino), 4 international. Average age 31. 108 applicants, 47% accepted, 23 enrolled. In 2011, 20 master's, 3 doctorates awarded. *Degree requirements:* For master's, thesis; for doctorate, thesis/dissertation. *Entrance requirements:* For master's and doctorate, GRE General Test, minimum GPA of 3.0, resume, 3 letters of recommendation. Additional exam requirements/recommendations for international students: Required—TOEFL

GRADUATE STUDY IN NUTRITION
SCHOOL OF MEDICINE

The Department of Nutrition offers programs that span the breadth of the discipline, from human nutrition and dietetics to basic nutritional sciences.

The Department offers three Master of Science programs: M.S. in Nutrition, M.S. in Public Health Nutrition Internship, and M.S. in coordination with two hospital dietetic internships.

The Ph.D. program builds upon faculty expertise in the Departments of Nutrition, Biochemistry, Molecular Biology, Medicine, Physiology, and Urology. All Ph.D. students are fully supported with a tuition scholarship and a monthly stipend for living expenses.

For additional information, contact the Department at (216)368-2440 or visit our Web site at

www.cwru.edu/med/nutrition/home.html

(minimum score 550 paper-based; 213 computer-based; 80 iBT). *Application deadline:* For fall admission, 2/15 priority date for domestic students, 2/15 for international students; for spring admission, 7/15 priority date for domestic students, 7/15 for international students. Application fee: $50. Electronic applications accepted. *Expenses:* Tuition, state resident: full-time $7992. Tuition, nonresident: full-time $19,592. *Required fees:* $1735; $58 per credit. *Financial support:* In 2011–12, 17 students received support, including 9 research assistantships with full and partial tuition reimbursements available (averaging $10,616 per year), 8 teaching assistantships with full and partial tuition reimbursements available (averaging $9,033 per year); fellowships, Federal Work-Study, scholarships/grants, and unspecified assistantships also available. Financial award application deadline: 3/1; financial award applicants required to submit FAFSA. *Faculty research:* Metabolic regulation, nutrition education, food safety, obesity and diabetes, metabolism. *Total annual research expenditures:* $2.9 million. *Unit head:* Dr. Christopher Melby, Head, 970-491-6736, Fax: 970-491-7252, E-mail: christopher.melby@colostate.edu. *Application contact:* Paula Coleman, Graduate Coordinator, 970-491-3819, Fax: 970-491-3875, E-mail: pcoleman@cahs.colostate.edu. Web site: http://www.fshn.cahs.colostate.edu/.

Colorado State University, Graduate School, College of Applied Human Sciences, Department of Health and Exercise Science, Fort Collins, CO 80523-1582. Offers exercise science and nutrition (MS); health and exercise science (MS); human bioenergetics (PhD). Part-time programs available. *Faculty:* 13 full-time (3 women), 1 part-time/adjunct (0 women). *Students:* 21 full-time (13 women), 13 part-time (6 women); includes 1 minority (Hispanic/Latino), 2 international. Average age 29. 48 applicants, 21% accepted, 7 enrolled. In 2011, 4 master's, 2 doctorates awarded. *Degree requirements:* For master's, thesis; for doctorate, comprehensive exam, thesis/dissertation, mentored teaching. *Entrance requirements:* For master's, GRE General Test, minimum GPA of 3.0; for doctorate, bachelor's or master's degree. Additional exam requirements/recommendations for international students: Required—TOEFL (minimum score 550 paper-based; 213 computer-based; 80 iBT). *Application deadline:* For fall admission, 1/31 priority date for domestic students, 1/31 for international students; for spring admission, 9/30 priority date for domestic students, 9/30 for international students. Application fee: $50. Electronic applications accepted. *Expenses:* Tuition, state resident: full-time $7992. Tuition, nonresident: full-time $19,592. *Required fees:* $1735; $58 per credit. *Financial support:* In 2011–12, 26 students received support, including 10 research assistantships with full tuition reimbursements available (averaging $14,137 per year), 16 teaching assistantships with full tuition reimbursements available (averaging $12,700 per year); fellowships and unspecified assistantships also available. Financial award application deadline: 1/31; financial award applicants required to submit FAFSA. *Faculty research:* Metabolism and metabolic disease, obesity, diabetes, hypertension, physical activity and health across the lifespan, bioenergetics. *Total annual research expenditures:* $2.4 million. *Unit head:* Dr. Richard Gay Israel, Department Head, 970-491-3785, Fax: 970-491-0216, E-mail: richard.israel@colostate.edu. *Application contact:* Robin Noehl, Department Operations, 970-491-7161, Fax: 970-491-0445, E-mail: robin.noehl@colostate.edu. Web site: http://www.hes.cahs.colostate.edu/.

Columbia University, College of Physicians and Surgeons, Institute of Human Nutrition, MS Program in Nutrition, New York, NY 10032. Offers MS, MPH/MS. Part-time and evening/weekend programs available. *Degree requirements:* For master's, thesis. *Entrance requirements:* For master's, GRE General Test, TOEFL, MCAT. Additional exam requirements/recommendations for international students: Required—TOEFL.

Columbia University, College of Physicians and Surgeons, Institute of Human Nutrition and Graduate School of Arts and Sciences at the College of Physicians and Surgeons, PhD Program in Nutrition, New York, NY 10032. Offers PhD. *Degree requirements:* For doctorate, thesis/dissertation. *Entrance requirements:* For doctorate, GRE General Test. Additional exam requirements/recommendations for international students: Required— TOEFL. *Faculty research:* Growth and development, nutrition and metabolism.

Cornell University, Graduate School, Graduate Fields of Agriculture and Life Sciences and Graduate Fields of Human Ecology, Field of Nutrition, Ithaca, NY 14853-0001. Offers animal nutrition (MPS, MS, PhD); community nutrition (MPS, MS, PhD); human nutrition (MPS, MS, PhD); international nutrition (MPS, MS, PhD); nutritional biochemistry (MPS, MS, PhD). *Faculty:* 46 full-time (22 women). *Students:* 62 full-time (51 women); includes 14 minority (3 Black or African American, non-Hispanic/Latino; 3 Asian, non-Hispanic/Latino; 5 Hispanic/Latino; 3 Two or more races, non-Hispanic/Latino), 18 international. Average age 28. 105 applicants, 26% accepted, 24 enrolled. In 2011, 1 master's, 11 doctorates awarded. *Degree requirements:* For master's, thesis (MS), project papers (MPS); for doctorate, comprehensive exam, thesis/dissertation. *Entrance requirements:* For master's and doctorate, GRE General Test, previous course work in organic chemistry (with laboratory) and biochemistry; 2 letters of recommendation. Additional exam requirements/recommendations for international students: Required—TOEFL (minimum score 550 paper-based; 213 computer-based; 77 iBT). *Application deadline:* For fall admission, 1/10 priority date for domestic students; for spring admission, 10/1 for domestic students. Application fee: $95. Electronic applications accepted. *Financial support:* In 2011–12, 17 fellowships with full tuition reimbursements, 16 research assistantships with full tuition reimbursements, 26 teaching assistantships with full tuition reimbursements were awarded; institutionally sponsored loans, scholarships/grants, health care benefits, tuition waivers (full and partial), and unspecified assistantships also available. Financial award applicants required to submit FAFSA. *Faculty research:* Nutritional biochemistry, experimental human and animal nutrition, international nutrition, community nutrition. *Unit head:* Director of Graduate Studies, 607-255-2528, Fax: 607-255-0178. *Application contact:* Graduate Field Assistant, 607-255-2628, Fax: 607-225-0178, E-mail: nutrition_gfr@cornell.edu. Web site: http://www.gradschool.cornell.edu/fields.php?id-56&a-2.

Cornell University, Graduate School, Graduate Fields of Arts and Sciences, Field of International Development, Ithaca, NY 14853-0001. Offers development policy (MPS); international nutrition (MPS); international planning (MPS); international population (MPS); science and technology policy (MPS). *Faculty:* 43 full-time (15 women). *Students:* 8 full-time (4 women); includes 1 minority (Black or African American, non-Hispanic/Latino), 4 international. Average age 29. 37 applicants, 43% accepted, 8 enrolled. In 2011, 6 master's awarded. *Degree requirements:* For master's, project paper. *Entrance requirements:* For master's, GRE General Test (recommended), 2 academic recommendations, 2 years of development experience. Additional exam requirements/recommendations for international students: Required—TOEFL (minimum score 77 iBT). *Application deadline:* Applications are processed on a rolling basis. Application fee: $95. Electronic applications accepted. *Financial support:* In 2011–12, 1 fellowship with full tuition reimbursement was awarded; research assistantships with full tuition reimbursements, teaching assistantships with full tuition reimbursements, institutionally sponsored loans, scholarships/grants, health care benefits, tuition waivers (full and partial), and unspecified assistantships also available. Financial award applicants required to submit FAFSA. *Faculty research:* Development policy, international nutrition, international planning, science and technology policy, international population. *Unit head:* Director of Graduate Studies, 607-255-3037, Fax: 607-255-1005. *Application contact:* Graduate Field Assistant, 607-255-0831, Fax: 607-

255-1005, E-mail: mpsid@cornell.edu. Web site: http://www.gradschool.cornell.edu/fields.php?id-87&a-2.

Drexel University, College of Arts and Sciences, Department of Biology, Program in Human Nutrition, Philadelphia, PA 19104-2875. Offers MS. *Accreditation:* AND. Part-time programs available. Terminal master's awarded for partial completion of doctoral program. *Degree requirements:* For master's, thesis. *Entrance requirements:* For master's, GRE General Test. Additional exam requirements/recommendations for international students: Required—TOEFL. Electronic applications accepted. *Faculty research:* Metabolism of lipids, W-3 fatty acids, obesity, diabetes and heart disease, mineral metabolism.

D'Youville College, Department of Dietetics, Buffalo, NY 14201-1084. Offers MS. Five-year program begins at freshman entry. *Accreditation:* AND. *Faculty:* 2 full-time (1 woman), 3 part-time/adjunct (all women). *Students:* 97 full-time (89 women), 11 part-time (10 women); includes 7 minority (1 Black or African American, non-Hispanic/Latino; 1 American Indian or Alaska Native, non-Hispanic/Latino; 1 Asian, non-Hispanic/Latino; 3 Hispanic/Latino; 1 Two or more races, non-Hispanic/Latino), 10 international. Average age 24. 107 applicants, 80% accepted, 34 enrolled. In 2011, 9 master's awarded. *Degree requirements:* For master's, thesis. *Entrance requirements:* Additional exam requirements/recommendations for international students: Required—TOEFL (minimum score 500 paper-based; 173 computer-based). *Application deadline:* For fall admission, 5/1 for international students; for spring admission, 9/1 for international students. Applications are processed on a rolling basis. Application fee: $25. Electronic applications accepted. *Expenses: Tuition:* Full-time $18,960; part-time $790 per credit hour. *Required fees:* $310. Tuition and fees vary according to degree level and program. *Faculty research:* Nutrition education, clinical nutrition, herbal supplements, obesity. *Unit head:* Dr. Charlotte Baumgart, Chair, 716-829-7752, Fax: 716-829-8137. *Application contact:* Dr. Steven Smith, Director of Admissions, 716-829-7600, Fax: 716-829-7900, E-mail: admiss@dyc.edu.

East Carolina University, Graduate School, College of Human Ecology, Department of Nutrition Science, Greenville, NC 27858-4353. Offers MS. Part-time programs available. *Degree requirements:* For master's, comprehensive exam, thesis optional. *Entrance requirements:* For master's, GRE. Additional exam requirements/recommendations for international students: Required—TOEFL. *Application deadline:* For fall admission, 6/1 priority date for domestic students. Applications are processed on a rolling basis. Application fee: $50. *Expenses:* Tuition, state resident: full-time $3557; part-time $444.63 per semester hour. Tuition, nonresident: full-time $14,351; part-time $1793.88 per semester hour. *Required fees:* $2016; $252 per semester hour. Part-time tuition and fees vary according to course load, campus/location and program. *Financial support:* Fellowships, teaching assistantships with partial tuition reimbursements, Federal Work-Study, institutionally sponsored loans, scholarships/grants, and unspecified assistantships available. Support available to part-time students. Financial award application deadline: 6/1. *Faculty research:* Lifecycle nutrition, nutrition and disease, nutrition for fish species, food service management. *Unit head:* Dr. William A. Forsythe, III, Chair, 252-328-4274, E-mail: forsythew@ecu.edu. *Application contact:* Dean of Graduate School, 252-328-6012, Fax: 252-328-6071, E-mail: gradschool@ecu.edu.

Eastern Illinois University, Graduate School, Lumpkin College of Business and Applied Sciences, School of Family and Consumer Sciences, Charleston, IL 61920-3099. Offers dietetics (MS); family and consumer sciences (MS). Part-time programs available. *Degree requirements:* For master's, comprehensive exam. *Expenses:* Tuition, state resident: part-time $279 per credit hour. Tuition, nonresident: part-time $670 per credit hour. *Required fees:* $179.07 per credit hour. $1253 per semester.

Eastern Kentucky University, The Graduate School, College of Health Sciences, Department of Family and Consumer Sciences, Richmond, KY 40475-3102. Offers community nutrition (MS). Part-time programs available. *Entrance requirements:* For master's, GRE General Test, minimum GPA of 2.5.

Eastern Michigan University, Graduate School, College of Health and Human Services, School of Health Sciences, Programs in Dietetics and Nutrition, Ypsilanti, MI 48197. Offers human nutrition (MS); human nutrition-coordinated track in dietetics (MS). *Accreditation:* AND. Part-time and evening/weekend programs available. Postbaccalaureate distance learning degree programs offered (minimal on-campus study). *Students:* 23 full-time (22 women), 54 part-time (51 women); includes 15 minority (6 Black or African American, non-Hispanic/Latino; 5 Asian, non-Hispanic/Latino; 3 Hispanic/Latino; 1 Native Hawaiian or other Pacific Islander, non-Hispanic/Latino). Average age 35. 57 applicants, 54% accepted, 23 enrolled. In 2011, 30 degrees awarded. *Entrance requirements:* Additional exam requirements/recommendations for international students: Required—TOEFL. *Application deadline:* Applications are processed on a rolling basis. Application fee: $35. *Expenses:* Tuition, state resident: full-time $10,367; part-time $432 per credit hour. Tuition, nonresident: full-time $20,435; part-time $851 per credit hour. *Required fees:* $39 per credit hour. $46 per semester. One-time fee: $100. Tuition and fees vary according to course level, degree level and reciprocity agreements. *Financial support:* Fellowships, research assistantships with full tuition reimbursements, teaching assistantships with full tuition reimbursements, career-related internships or fieldwork, Federal Work-Study, institutionally sponsored loans, scholarships/grants, tuition waivers (partial), and unspecified assistantships available. Support available to part-time students. Financial award applicants required to submit FAFSA. *Unit head:* Lydia Kret, Interim Program Director, 734-487-7862, Fax: 734-487-4095, E-mail: lydia.kret@emich.edu. *Application contact:* Graduate Admissions, 734-487-2400, Fax: 734-487-6559, E-mail: graduate.admissions@emich.edu.

East Tennessee State University, School of Graduate Studies, College of Clinical and Rehabilitative Health Sciences, Department of Allied Health Science, Johnson City, TN 37614. Offers allied health (MSAH); clinical nutrition (MS). Part-time programs available. Postbaccalaureate distance learning degree programs offered (no on-campus study). *Faculty:* 14 full-time (10 women). *Students:* 23 full-time (all women), 30 part-time (27 women); includes 4 minority (3 Black or African American, non-Hispanic/Latino; 1 Two or more races, non-Hispanic/Latino), 1 international. Average age 33. 8 applicants, 25% accepted, 2 enrolled. In 2011, 17 master's awarded. *Degree requirements:* For master's, comprehensive exam, thesis optional, advanced practice seminar (for MSAH non-thesis option); internship (for clinical nutrition). *Entrance requirements:* For master's, GRE General Test, professional license in allied health discipline, minimum GPA of 2.75 (MSAH); bachelor's degree from undergraduate didactic program in dietetics with minimum GPA of 3.0 in DPD coursework (clinical nutrition). Additional exam requirements/recommendations for international students: Required—TOEFL (minimum score 550 paper-based; 213 computer-based; 79 iBT). *Application deadline:* For fall admission, 2/15 for domestic and international students; for spring admission, 11/1 for domestic students, 9/30 for international students. Application fee: $35 ($45 for international students). Electronic applications accepted. *Expenses:* Tuition, state resident: full-time $7312; part-time $350 per credit hour. Tuition, nonresident: full-time $18,490; part-time $621 per credit hour. *Required fees:* $63 per credit hour. Tuition and fees vary according to course load and program. *Financial support:* In 2011–12, 17 students received support, including 4 research assistantships with full tuition reimbursements available (averaging $6,000 per year), 1 teaching assistantship with full tuition reimbursement available (averaging $6,000 per year); career-related internships or fieldwork, institutionally sponsored loans, scholarships/grants, and unspecified

assistantships also available. Financial award application deadline: 7/1; financial award applicants required to submit FAFSA. *Faculty research:* Streptococcus mutans in saliva, oral cavity microbial screening, patient care, occupational stress, rural and urban health administrators. *Unit head:* Dr. Charles Faust, Chair, 423-439-7888, Fax: 423-547-4900, E-mail: faust@etsu.edu. *Application contact:* Mary Duncan, Graduate Specialist, 423-439-4302, Fax: 423-439-5624, E-mail: duncanm@etsu.edu. Web site: http://www.etsu.edu/crhs/alliedhealth/msah/.

Emory University, Laney Graduate School, Division of Biological and Biomedical Sciences, Program in Nutrition and Health Sciences, Atlanta, GA 30322-1100. Offers PhD. *Faculty:* 47 full-time (23 women). *Students:* 31 full-time (30 women); includes 5 minority (3 Asian, non-Hispanic/Latino; 1 Hispanic/Latino; 1 Two or more races, non-Hispanic/Latino), 4 international. Average age 27. 42 applicants, 19% accepted, 5 enrolled. In 2011, 3 degrees awarded. *Median time to degree:* Of those who began their doctoral program in fall 2003, 100% received their degree in 8 years or less. *Degree requirements:* For doctorate, comprehensive exam, thesis/dissertation. *Entrance requirements:* For doctorate, GRE General Test, minimum GPA of 3.0 in science course work (recommended). Additional exam requirements/recommendations for international students: Required—TOEFL. *Application deadline:* For fall admission, 12/1 for domestic and international students. Application fee: $75. Electronic applications accepted. *Expenses: Tuition:* Full-time $34,800. *Required fees:* $1300. *Financial support:* In 2011–12, 9 students received support, including 9 fellowships with full tuition reimbursements available (averaging $26,500 per year); institutionally sponsored loans, scholarships/grants, health care benefits, and tuition waivers (full) also available. *Faculty research:* Biochemistry, molecular and cell biology, clinical nutrition, community and preventive health, nutritional epidemiology. *Unit head:* Dr. Usha Ramakrishnan, Director, 404-727-1092, Fax: 404-727-1278, E-mail: uramakr@sph.emory.edu. *Application contact:* Kathy Smith, Director of Recruitment and Admissions, 404-727-2547, Fax: 404-727-3322, E-mail: kathy.smith@emory.edu. Web site: http://www.biomed.emory.edu/.

Emory University, Rollins School of Public Health, Hubert Department of Global Health, Atlanta, GA 30322-1100. Offers global health (MPH); public nutrition (MSPH). *Accreditation:* CEPH. *Students:* 73 full-time. Average age 27. *Degree requirements:* For master's, thesis, practicum. *Entrance requirements:* For master's, GRE General Test. Additional exam requirements/recommendations for international students: Required—TOEFL (minimum score 550 paper-based; 213 computer-based; 80 iBT). *Application deadline:* For fall admission, 1/5 priority date for domestic students, 1/5 for international students. Application fee: $95. Electronic applications accepted. *Expenses: Tuition:* Full-time $34,800. *Required fees:* $1300. *Financial support:* Fellowships with full and partial tuition reimbursements, career-related internships or fieldwork, Federal Work-Study, institutionally sponsored loans, scholarships/grants, traineeships, health care benefits, and unspecified assistantships available. Support available to part-time students. Financial award application deadline: 1/5; financial award applicants required to submit FAFSA. *Unit head:* Dr. Carlos Del Rio, Chair, 404-727-1557, Fax: 404-727-1278, E-mail: cdelrio@emory.edu. Web site: http://www.sph.emory.edu/gh.

Florida International University, Robert Stempel College of Public Health and Social Work, Department of Dietetics and Nutrition, Miami, FL 33199. Offers MS, PhD. Part-time programs available. *Degree requirements:* For master's, thesis; for doctorate, comprehensive exam, thesis/dissertation. *Entrance requirements:* For master's, minimum GPA of 3.0; for doctorate, GRE General Test, minimum GPA of 3.0, resume, letters of recommendation, faculty sponsor. Additional exam requirements/recommendations for international students: Required—TOEFL (minimum score 550 paper-based; 80 iBT). Electronic applications accepted. *Faculty research:* Clinical nutrition, cultural food habits, pediatric nutrition, diabetes, dietetic education.

Florida State University, The Graduate School, College of Human Sciences, Department of Nutrition, Food and Exercise Sciences, Tallahassee, FL 32306-1493. Offers exercise physiology (PhD); nutrition and food science (MS, PhD), including clinical nutrition (MS), food science, human nutrition (PhD), nutrition education and health promotion (MS), nutrition science (MS), sports nutrition (MS); sports sciences (MS). Part-time programs available. *Faculty:* 18 full-time (10 women). *Students:* 88 full-time (56 women), 15 part-time (5 women); includes 24 minority (9 Black or African American, non-Hispanic/Latino; 4 Asian, non-Hispanic/Latino; 10 Hispanic/Latino; 1 Native Hawaiian or other Pacific Islander, non-Hispanic/Latino), 21 international. Average age 26. 172 applicants, 51% accepted, 32 enrolled. In 2011, 38 master's, 7 doctorates awarded. *Degree requirements:* For master's, comprehensive exam (for some programs), thesis optional; for doctorate, thesis/dissertation. *Entrance requirements:* For master's, GRE General Test, minimum upper-division GPA of 3.0; for doctorate, GRE General Test, minimum upper-division GPA of 3.0, MS. Additional exam requirements/recommendations for international students: Required—TOEFL (minimum score 550 paper-based; 80 iBT). *Application deadline:* For fall admission, 7/1 for domestic students, 3/1 for international students; for spring admission, 11/1 for domestic students, 5/1 for international students. Applications are processed on a rolling basis. Application fee: $30. Electronic applications accepted. *Expenses:* Tuition, state resident: full-time $9474; part-time $350.88 per credit hour. Tuition, nonresident: full-time $16,236; part-time $601.34 per credit hour. *Required fees:* $630 per semester. One-time fee: $20. Tuition and fees vary according to course load and campus/location. *Financial support:* In 2011–12, 59 students received support, including fellowships with partial tuition reimbursements available (averaging $10,000 per year), 17 research assistantships with partial tuition reimbursements available (averaging $8,000 per year), 47 teaching assistantships with partial tuition reimbursements available (averaging $8,000 per year); career-related internships or fieldwork, Federal Work-Study, institutionally sponsored loans, scholarships/grants, and unspecified assistantships also available. Financial award application deadline: 1/15; financial award applicants required to submit FAFSA. *Faculty research:* Body composition, functional food, chronic disease and aging response; food safety, food allergy, and safety/quality detection methods; sports nutrition, energy and human performance; strength training, functional performance, cardiovascular physiology, sarcopenia . *Unit head:* Dr. Bahram H. Arjmandi, Professor/Chair, 850-645-1517, Fax: 850-645-5000, E-mail: barjmandi@fsu.edu. *Application contact:* Joseph J. Carroll, Administrative Support Assistant, 850-644-4800, Fax: 850-645-5000, E-mail: jjcarroll@admin.fsu.edu. Web site: http://www.chs.fsu.edu/.

Framingham State University, Division of Graduate and Continuing Education, Programs in Food and Nutrition, Coordinated Program in Dietetics, Framingham, MA 01701-9101. Offers MS.

Framingham State University, Division of Graduate and Continuing Education, Programs in Food and Nutrition, Food Science and Nutrition Science Program, Framingham, MA 01701-9101. Offers MS. Part-time and evening/weekend programs available. *Entrance requirements:* For master's, GRE General Test.

Framingham State University, Division of Graduate and Continuing Education, Programs in Food and Nutrition, Program in Human Nutrition: Education and Media Technologies, Framingham, MA 01701-9101. Offers MS.

George Mason University, College of Health and Human Services, Department of Global and Community Health, Fairfax, VA 22030. Offers biostatistics (Certificate); epidemiology (Certificate); epidemiology and biostatistics (MS); gerontology (Certificate); global health (MS, Certificate); nutrition (Certificate); public health (MPH, Certificate). *Faculty:* 11 full-time (5 women), 16 part-time/adjunct (12 women). *Students:* 101 full-time (84 women), 114 part-time (92 women); includes 85 minority (43 Black or African American, non-Hispanic/Latino; 30 Asian, non-Hispanic/Latino; 11 Hispanic/Latino; 1 Two or more races, non-Hispanic/Latino), 14 international. Average age 32. 162 applicants, 61% accepted, 53 enrolled. In 2011, 80 master's, 15 other advanced degrees awarded. *Degree requirements:* For master's, comprehensive exam (for some programs), thesis or practicum. *Entrance requirements:* For master's, GRE, 2 official transcripts; expanded goals statement; 3 letters of recommendation; resume; 1 completed course in health science, statistics, natural sciences and social science (for MPH); 6 credits of foreign language if not fluent (for MS in global health); for Certificate, 2 official transcripts; expanded goals statement; 3 letters of recommendation; resume; bachelor's degree from regionally-accredited institution with minimum GPA of 3.0; statistics and college-level algebra with minimum B grade (for Certificate in biostatistics). Additional exam requirements/recommendations for international students: Required—TOEFL (minimum score 575 paper-based; 230 computer-based; 88 iBT), IELTS, Pearson Test of English. *Application deadline:* For fall admission, 4/1 priority date for domestic students; for spring admission, 11/1 priority date for domestic students. Applications are processed on a rolling basis. Application fee: $65 ($80 for international students). Electronic applications accepted. *Expenses:* Tuition, state resident: full-time $8750; part-time $364.58 per credit. Tuition, nonresident: full-time $24,092; part-time $1003.83 per credit. *Required fees:* $2514; $104.75 per credit. *Financial support:* In 2011–12, 14 students received support, including 12 research assistantships with full and partial tuition reimbursements available (averaging $15,000 per year), 2 teaching assistantships with full and partial tuition reimbursements available (averaging $11,781 per year); career-related internships or fieldwork, Federal Work-Study, scholarships/grants, unspecified assistantships, and health care benefits (full-time research and teaching assistantship recipients) also available. Financial award application deadline: 3/1; financial award applicants required to submit FAFSA. *Faculty research:* Providing introductory and advanced degrees in health-related disciplines centered in global and community issues, health issues and the needs of affected populations at the regional and global level. *Total annual research expenditures:* $64,518. *Unit head:* Dr. Carlos Sluzki, Dean, 703-993-1920, Fax: 703-993-1943, E-mail: csluzki@gmu.edu. *Application contact:* Allan Weiss, Office Manager, 703-993-3126, Fax: 703-993-1908, E-mail: aweiss2@gmu.edu. Web site: http://chhs.gmu.edu/gch/index.

Georgia State University, College of Health and Human Sciences, School of Health Professions, Division of Nutrition, Atlanta, GA 30302-3083. Offers MS. *Accreditation:* AND. Part-time and evening/weekend programs available. *Degree requirements:* For master's, thesis optional. *Entrance requirements:* For master's, GRE or MAT. Additional exam requirements/recommendations for international students: Required—TOEFL (minimum score 550 paper-based; 213 computer-based). Electronic applications accepted. *Faculty research:* Food safety, sports nutrition, obesity, food fortification, nutrition interventions.

Harvard University, Harvard School of Public Health, Department of Nutrition, Boston, MA 02115-6096. Offers nutrition (DPH, PhD, SD); nutritional epidemiology (DPH, SD); public health nutrition (DPH, SD). *Faculty:* 22 full-time (4 women), 8 part-time/adjunct (2 women). *Students:* 32 full-time; includes 6 minority (1 Black or African American, non-Hispanic/Latino; 1 American Indian or Alaska Native, non-Hispanic/Latino; 1 Asian, non-Hispanic/Latino; 1 Hispanic/Latino; 2 Two or more races, non-Hispanic/Latino), 17 international. Average age 31. 35 applicants, 17% accepted, 5 enrolled. In 2011, 6 doctorates awarded. *Degree requirements:* For doctorate, thesis/dissertation, qualifying exam. *Entrance requirements:* For doctorate, GRE. Additional exam requirements/recommendations for international students: Required—TOEFL (minimum score 595 paper-based; 240 computer-based; 95 iBT); Recommended—IELTS (minimum score 7). *Application deadline:* For fall admission, 12/15 for domestic and international students. Application fee: $115. Electronic applications accepted. *Expenses: Tuition:* Full-time $36,304. *Required fees:* $1186. Full-time tuition and fees vary according to program. *Financial support:* Fellowships, research assistantships, teaching assistantships, Federal Work-Study, scholarships/grants, traineeships, and unspecified assistantships available. Support available to part-time students. Financial award application deadline: 2/17; financial award applicants required to submit FAFSA. *Faculty research:* Dietary and genetic factors affecting heart diseases in humans; interactions among nutrition, immunity, and infection; role of diet and lifestyle in preventing macrovascular complications in diabetics. *Unit head:* Dr. Walter Willett, Chair, 617-432-1333, Fax: 617-432-2435, E-mail: walter.willett@channing.harvard.edu. *Application contact:* Vincent W. James, Director of Admissions, 617-432-1031, Fax: 617-432-7080, E-mail: admissions@hsph.harvard.edu. Web site: http://www.hsph.harvard.edu/departments/nutrition/.

Howard University, Graduate School, Department of Nutritional Sciences, Washington, DC 20059-0002. Offers nutrition (MS, PhD). Part-time and evening/weekend programs available. *Degree requirements:* For master's, comprehensive exam, thesis; for doctorate, comprehensive exam, thesis/dissertation. *Entrance requirements:* For master's and doctorate, minimum GPA of 3.0, general chemistry, organic chemistry, biochemistry, nutrition. Additional exam requirements/recommendations for international students: Required—TOEFL (minimum score 213 computer-based). Electronic applications accepted. *Faculty research:* Dietary fiber, phytate, trace minerals, cardiovascular diseases, overweight/obesity.

Hunter College of the City University of New York, Graduate School, Schools of the Health Professions, School of Health Sciences, Programs in Urban Public Health, Program in Nutrition and Public Health, New York, NY 10021-5085. Offers MPH. *Accreditation:* AND. Part-time and evening/weekend programs available. *Faculty:* 3 full-time (2 women), 4 part-time/adjunct (all women). *Students:* 5 full-time (all women), 28 part-time (25 women); includes 10 minority (3 Black or African American, non-Hispanic/Latino; 2 Asian, non-Hispanic/Latino; 5 Hispanic/Latino), 2 international. Average age 30. 19 applicants, 68% accepted, 9 enrolled. In 2011, 10 master's awarded. *Degree requirements:* For master's, comprehensive exam, thesis optional, internship. *Entrance requirements:* For master's, GRE General Test, previous course work in calculus and statistics. Additional exam requirements/recommendations for international students: Required—TOEFL. *Application deadline:* For fall admission, 4/1 for domestic students; for spring admission, 11/1 for domestic students. Application fee: $125. *Expenses:* Tuition, state resident: full-time $8210; part-time $345 per credit. Tuition, nonresident: full-time $15,360; part-time $640 per credit. *Required fees:* $280 per semester. One-time fee: $125. Tuition and fees vary according to class time, campus/location and program. *Financial support:* In 2011–12, 6 fellowships were awarded; career-related internships or fieldwork, Federal Work-Study, institutionally sponsored loans, and tuition waivers (partial) also available. Support available to part-time students. *Unit head:* Arlene Spark, Coordinator, 212-481-7950, Fax: 212-481-5260, E-mail: aspark@hunter.cuny.edu. *Application contact:* Milena Solo, Assistant Director for Graduate Admissions, 212-772-4288, Fax: 212-650-3336, E-mail: milena.solo@hunter.cuny.edu. Web site: http://www.hunter.cuny.edu/uph/grad-test/nutrition-food-science.

Huntington College of Health Sciences, Program in Nutrition, Knoxville, TN 37919-7736. Offers MS. Part-time and evening/weekend programs available.

Postbaccalaureate distance learning degree programs offered (no on-campus study). *Faculty:* 1 (woman) full-time, 6 part-time/adjunct (5 women). *Students:* 47 full-time (42 women). Average age 32. *Entrance requirements:* For master's, high school diploma/ bachelor's degree. Additional exam requirements/recommendations for international students: Required—TOEFL (minimum score 500 paper-based; 61 iBT). Application fee: $75. Electronic applications accepted. *Expenses: Tuition:* Full-time $5550; part-time $300 per credit hour. *Unit head:* Jennifer Green, Associate Dean of Academics, 865-524-8079 Ext. 4. *Application contact:* Kim Galyon, Director of Admissions, 865-524-8079 Ext. 1.

Idaho State University, Office of Graduate Studies, Kasiska College of Health Professions, Department of Health and Nutrition Sciences, Pocatello, ID 83209-8109. Offers dietetics (Certificate); health education (MHE); public health (MPH). Part-time programs available. *Degree requirements:* For master's, comprehensive exam, internship, thesis or project. *Entrance requirements:* For master's, GRE General Test or GPA greater than 3.5, minimum GPA of 3.0 for upper division classes, 2 letters of recommendation. Additional exam requirements/recommendations for international students: Required—TOEFL (minimum score 600 paper-based; 213 computer-based). Electronic applications accepted. *Faculty research:* Epidemiology, environmental health, nutrition and aging, dietetics.

Immaculata University, College of Graduate Studies, Program in Nutrition Education, Immaculata, PA 19345. Offers nutrition education (MA); nutrition education/approved pre-professional practice program (MA). Part-time and evening/weekend programs available. *Degree requirements:* For master's, comprehensive exam, thesis optional. *Entrance requirements:* For master's, GRE or MAT, minimum GPA of 3.0. Additional exam requirements/recommendations for international students: Required—TOEFL. Electronic applications accepted. *Faculty research:* Sports nutrition, pediatric nutrition, changes in food consumption patterns in weight loss, nutritional counseling.

Indiana State University, College of Graduate and Professional Studies, College of Arts and Sciences, Department of Family and Consumer Sciences, Terre Haute, IN 47809. Offers dietetics (MS); family and consumer sciences education (MS); inter-area option (MS). *Accreditation:* AND. Part-time programs available. *Degree requirements:* For master's, thesis optional. Electronic applications accepted.

Indiana University Bloomington, School of Health, Physical Education and Recreation, Department of Applied Health Science, Bloomington, IN 47405-7000. Offers biostatistics (MPH); environmental health (MPH, PhD); epidemiology (MPH, PhD); health behavior (PhD); health promotion (MS); human development/family studies (MS); nutrition science (MS); public health administration (MPH); safety management (MS); school and college health programs (MS); social, behavioral and community health (MPH). *Accreditation:* CEPH (one or more programs are accredited). *Faculty:* 24 full-time (12 women). *Students:* 169 full-time (126 women), 25 part-time (17 women); includes 56 minority (39 Black or African American, non-Hispanic/Latino; 2 American Indian or Alaska Native, non-Hispanic/Latino; 4 Asian, non-Hispanic/Latino; 9 Hispanic/ Latino; 2 Two or more races, non-Hispanic/Latino), 29 international. Average age 30. 170 applicants, 74% accepted, 79 enrolled. In 2011, 52 master's, 9 doctorates awarded. *Degree requirements:* For master's, thesis optional; for doctorate, thesis/dissertation. *Entrance requirements:* For master's, GRE (MS in nutrition science), 3 recommendations; for doctorate, GRE, 3 recommendations. Additional exam requirements/recommendations for international students: Required—TOEFL (minimum score 550 paper-based; 213 computer-based; 79 iBT). *Application deadline:* For fall admission, 4/30 priority date for domestic students, 12/1 for international students; for spring admission, 11/15 priority date for domestic students, 9/1 for international students. Application fee: $55 ($65 for international students). *Financial support:* Fellowships, research assistantships with full and partial tuition reimbursements, teaching assistantships with full and partial tuition reimbursements, career-related internships or fieldwork, Federal Work-Study, institutionally sponsored loans, scholarships/grants, tuition waivers (partial), and fee remissions available. Financial award application deadline: 3/1. *Faculty research:* Cancer education, HIV/AIDS and drug education, public health, parent-child interactions, safety education. *Total annual research expenditures:* $2.8 million. *Unit head:* Dr. David K. Lohrmann, Chair, 812-856-5101, Fax: 812-855-3936, E-mail: dlohrman@indiana.edu. *Application contact:* Dr. Susan Middlestadt, Associate Professor and Graduate Coordinator, 812-856-5768, Fax: 812-855-3936, E-mail: semiddle@indiana.edu. Web site: http://www.indiana.edu/ ~aphealth/.

Indiana University of Pennsylvania, School of Graduate Studies and Research, College of Health and Human Services, Department of Food and Nutrition, Program in Food and Nutrition, Indiana, PA 15705-1087. Offers MS. Part-time programs available. *Faculty:* 5 full-time (all women). *Students:* 5 full-time (all women), 15 part-time (all women); includes 1 minority (Asian, non-Hispanic/Latino), 1 international. Average age 26. 35 applicants, 43% accepted, 12 enrolled. In 2011, 9 master's awarded. *Degree requirements:* For master's, thesis optional. *Entrance requirements:* For master's, GRE General Test, 2 letters of recommendation. Additional exam requirements/ recommendations for international students: Required—TOEFL (minimum score 540 paper-based; 207 computer-based). *Application deadline:* Applications are processed on a rolling basis. Application fee: $50. Electronic applications accepted. *Expenses:* Tuition, state resident: full-time $7488; part-time $416 per credit. Tuition, nonresident: full-time $11,232; part-time $624 per credit. *Required fees:* $2070; $192.20 per credit. $90 per semester. *Financial support:* In 2011–12, 5 research assistantships with full and partial tuition reimbursements (averaging $5,112 per year) were awarded. Financial award application deadline: 4/15; financial award applicants required to submit FAFSA. *Unit head:* Dr. Stephanie Taylor-Davis, Graduate Coordinator, 724-357-7733, E-mail: stdavis@iup.edu. Web site: http://www.iup.edu/upper.aspx?id=89259.

Indiana University–Purdue University Indianapolis, School of Health and Rehabilitation Sciences, Indianapolis, IN 46202-2896. Offers health sciences education (MS); nutrition and dietetics (MS); occupational therapy (MS); physical therapy (DPT). Part-time and evening/weekend programs available. *Faculty:* 8 full-time (5 women). *Students:* 197 full-time (162 women), 1 part-time (0 women); includes 13 minority (1 Black or African American, non-Hispanic/Latino; 4 Asian, non-Hispanic/Latino; 2 Hispanic/Latino; 1 Native Hawaiian or other Pacific Islander, non-Hispanic/Latino; 5 Two or more races, non-Hispanic/Latino). Average age 26. 213 applicants, 31% accepted, 62 enrolled. In 2011, 35 master's, 34 doctorates awarded. *Degree requirements:* For master's, thesis (for some programs). *Entrance requirements:* For master's, GRE General Test, minimum GPA of 3.0. Additional exam requirements/recommendations for international students: Required—TOEFL. *Application deadline:* For fall admission, 1/15 priority date for domestic students; for spring admission, 10/15 for domestic students. Application fee: $55 ($65 for international students). *Financial support:* Fellowships, research assistantships, teaching assistantships, Federal Work-Study, institutionally sponsored loans, and scholarships/grants available. Support available to part-time students. Financial award applicants required to submit FAFSA. *Unit head:* Dr. Augustine Agho, Dean, 317-274-4704, E-mail: aagho@iupui.edu. *Application contact:* Dr. Sherry Queener, Director, Graduate Studies and Associate Dean, 317-274-1577, Fax: 317-278-2380. Web site: http://www.shrs.iupui.edu/.

Instituto Tecnologico de Santo Domingo, Graduate School, Area of Health Sciences, Santo Domingo, Dominican Republic. Offers bioethics (M Bioethics); clinical bioethics (Certificate); clinical nutrition (Certificate); comprehensive health and the adolescent (Certificate); comrehensive adloescent health (MS); health and social security (M Mgmt).

Iowa State University of Science and Technology, Program in Diet and Exercise, Ames, IA 50011-1123. Offers MS. *Entrance requirements:* For master's, GRE, minimum GPA of 3.5, 3 letters of recommendation. Additional exam requirements/ recommendations for international students: Required—TOEFL (minimum score 550 paper-based; 79 iBT), IELTS (minimum score 6.5). *Financial support:* Unspecified assistantships available. *Unit head:* Ruth Litchfield, Director of Graduate Education, 515-294-9484, Fax: 515-294-6193, E-mail: litch@iastate.edu. *Application contact:* Ruth Litchfield, Application Contact, 515-294-9484, Fax: 515-294-6193, E-mail: litch@ iastate.edu. Web site: http://www.hs.iastate.edu/dietandexercise/.

Iowa State University of Science and Technology, Program in Nutritional Sciences, Ames, IA 50011-1123. Offers MS, PhD. *Entrance requirements:* For master's and doctorate, GRE General Test. Additional exam requirements/recommendations for international students: Required—TOEFL (minimum score 550 paper-based; 79 iBT), IELTS (minimum score 6.5). *Application deadline:* For fall admission, 1/15 priority date for domestic students, 1/15 for international students. Applications are processed on a rolling basis. Application fee: $40 ($90 for international students). Electronic applications accepted. *Unit head:* Dr. Kevin Schalinske, Director of Graduate Education, 515-294-6442, Fax: 515-294-6193, E-mail: gradsecretary@iastate.edu. *Application contact:* Dr. Wendy White, Application Contact, 515-294-6442, Fax: 515-294-6193, E-mail: gradsecretary@iastate.edu. Web site: http://www.fshn.hs.iastate.edu/graduate-program/nutritional-sciences/.

The Johns Hopkins University, Bloomberg School of Public Health, Department of International Health, Baltimore, MD 21205. Offers global disease epidemiology and control (MHS, PhD); health systems (MHS, PhD); human nutrition (MHS, PhD); international health (Dr PH); social and behavioral interventions (MHS, PhD). *Degree requirements:* For master's, comprehensive exam, thesis (for some programs), 1 year full-time residency, 4-9 month internship; for doctorate, comprehensive exam, thesis/ dissertation or alternative, 1.5 years full-time residency, oral and written exams. *Entrance requirements:* For master's, GRE General Test or MCAT, 3 letters of recommendation, resume; for doctorate, GRE General Test or MCAT, 3 letters of recommendation, resume, transcripts. Additional exam requirements/recommendations for international students: Required—TOEFL (minimum score 600 paper-based; 250 computer-based; 100 iBT); Recommended—IELTS (minimum score 7). Electronic applications accepted. *Faculty research:* Nutrition, infectious diseases, health systems, health economics, humanitarian emergencies.

Kansas State University, Graduate School, College of Human Ecology, Department of Human Nutrition, Manhattan, KS 66506. Offers human nutrition (MS); nutritional sciences (PhD). Part-time programs available. *Faculty:* 15 full-time (7 women), 2 part-time/adjunct (1 woman). *Students:* 17 full-time (11 women), 5 part-time (2 women); includes 3 minority (1 Black or African American, non-Hispanic/Latino; 1 Asian, non-Hispanic/Latino; 1 Hispanic/Latino), 10 international. Average age 32. 31 applicants, 19% accepted, 4 enrolled. In 2011, 1 master's, 8 doctorates awarded. *Degree requirements:* For master's, thesis or alternative, residency; for doctorate, thesis/ dissertation, residency. *Entrance requirements:* For master's, GRE General Test, minimum undergraduate GPA of 3.0; for doctorate, GRE General Test, minimum graduate GPA of 3.5, course work in biochemistry and statistics. Additional exam requirements/recommendations for international students: Required—TOEFL (minimum score 600 paper-based; 250 computer-based). *Application deadline:* For fall admission, 2/1 priority date for domestic students, 2/1 for international students; for spring admission, 8/1 priority date for domestic students, 8/1 for international students. Applications are processed on a rolling basis. Application fee: $40 ($55 for international students). Electronic applications accepted. *Financial support:* In 2011–12, 18 research assistantships (averaging $24,063 per year), 4 teaching assistantships with tuition reimbursements (averaging $14,300 per year) were awarded; career-related internships or fieldwork, Federal Work-Study, institutionally sponsored loans, scholarships/grants, and tuition waivers (full) also available. Support available to part-time students. Financial award application deadline: 3/1; financial award applicants required to submit FAFSA. *Faculty research:* Sensory analysis and consumer behavior, nutrition education and communication, human metabolism and performance, molecular and biochemical nutrition, public health nutrition and obesity. *Total annual research expenditures:* $1.1 million. *Unit head:* Mark Haub, Interim Head, 785-532-5508, Fax: 785-532-3132, E-mail: haub@ksu.edu. *Application contact:* Janet Finney, Senior Administrative Specialist, 785-532-5508, Fax: 785-532-3132, E-mail: janetkay@ksu.edu. Web site: http:// www.he.k-state.edu/hn/.

Kent State University, Graduate School of Education, Health, and Human Services, School of Health Sciences, Program in Nutrition, Kent, OH 44242-0001. Offers dietetic (MS). *Faculty:* 6 full-time (all women), 1 (woman) part-time/adjunct. *Students:* 32 full-time (28 women), 8 part-time (all women); includes 1 minority (Asian, non-Hispanic/ Latino). 45 applicants, 62% accepted. In 2011, 12 master's awarded. *Degree requirements:* For master's, thesis optional. *Entrance requirements:* For master's, 3 letters of reference, goals statement, minimum GPA of 3.0. Additional exam requirements/recommendations for international students: Required—TOEFL (minimum score 550 paper-based; 213 computer-based; 80 iBT). Application fee: $30 ($60 for international students). *Expenses:* Tuition, state resident: full-time $8136; part-time $452 per credit hour. Tuition, nonresident: full-time $14,292; part-time $794 per credit hour. *Financial support:* In 2011–12, 3 research assistantships (averaging $8,500 per year) were awarded; Federal Work-Study also available. *Unit head:* Karen Gordon, Coordinator, 330-672-2248, E-mail: klowry@kent.edu. *Application contact:* Nancy Miller, Academic Program Coordinator, Office of Graduate Student Services, 330-672-2576, Fax: 330-672-9162.

Lehman College of the City University of New York, Division of Natural and Social Sciences, Department of Health Sciences, Program in Nutrition, Bronx, NY 10468-1589. Offers clinical nutrition (MS); community nutrition (MS); dietetic internship (MS). *Degree requirements:* For master's, thesis or alternative.

Lipscomb University, Program in Exercise and Nutrition Science, Nashville, TN 37204-3951. Offers MS. Part-time and evening/weekend programs available. *Faculty:* 5 full-time (4 women), 1 part-time/adjunct (0 women). *Students:* 31 full-time (27 women), 24 part-time (15 women); includes 5 minority (3 Black or African American, non-Hispanic/ Latino; 1 Asian, non-Hispanic/Latino; 1 Hispanic/Latino), 1 international. Average age 26. 44 applicants, 57% accepted, 19 enrolled. In 2011, 15 master's awarded. *Degree requirements:* For master's, comprehensive exam (for some programs), thesis (for some programs). *Entrance requirements:* For master's, GRE (minimum score of 800), minimum GPA of 2.75 on all undergraduate work; 2 letters of recommendation; resume. Additional exam requirements/recommendations for international students: Required—TOEFL (minimum score 570 paper-based; 230 computer-based). *Application deadline:* For fall admission, 6/1 for domestic students; for spring admission, 12/1 for domestic students. Applications are processed on a rolling basis. Application fee: $50 ($75 for international students). Electronic applications accepted. *Expenses: Tuition:* Full-time $16,830; part-time $935 per credit hour. Tuition and fees vary according to degree level and program. *Financial support:* Applicants required to submit FAFSA. *Unit head:* Dr.

Nutrition

Karen Robichaud, Director, 615-966-5602, E-mail: karen.robichaud@lipscomb.edu. Web site: http://exns.lipscomb.edu/.

Logan University–College of Chiropractic, University Programs, Chesterfield, MO 63006-1065. Offers nutrition and human performance (MS); sports science and rehabilitation (MS). *Faculty:* 10 full-time (6 women), 16 part-time/adjunct (6 women). *Students:* 27 full-time (12 women), 39 part-time (10 women); includes 12 minority (7 Black or African American, non-Hispanic/Latino; 4 Asian, non-Hispanic/Latino; 1 Hispanic/Latino). Average age 26. 45 applicants, 98% accepted, 34 enrolled. In 2011, 51 master's awarded. *Degree requirements:* For master's, comprehensive exam. *Entrance requirements:* For master's, GRE or National Board of Chiropractic Examiners test, minimum GPA of 2.5. Additional exam requirements/recommendations for international students: Required—TOEFL (minimum score 79 iBT). *Application deadline:* For fall admission, 7/15 priority date for domestic students, 7/15 for international students; for winter admission, 11/15 priority date for domestic students, 11/15 for international students; for spring admission, 3/15 priority date for domestic students, 3/15 for international students. Application fee: $50. *Expenses:* Contact institution. *Financial support:* In 2011–12, 35 students received support. Federal Work-Study and scholarships/grants available. Support available to part-time students. Financial award applicants required to submit FAFSA. *Faculty research:* Ankle injury prevention in high school athletes, low back pain in college football players, short arc banding and low back pain, the effects of enzymes on inflammatory blood markers, gait analysis in high school and college athletes. *Unit head:* Dr. Elizabeth A. Goodman, Dean, 636-227-2100, Fax: 636-207-2431, E-mail: elizabeth.goodman@logan.edu. *Application contact:* Steve Held, Director of Admissions, 636-227-2100 Ext. 1754, Fax: 636-207-2425, E-mail: loganadm@logan.edu.

Loma Linda University, School of Public Health, Department of Nutrition, Loma Linda, CA 92350. Offers public health nutrition (MPH, Dr PH). *Accreditation:* AND. *Degree requirements:* For doctorate, thesis/dissertation. *Entrance requirements:* For doctorate, GRE General Test. Additional exam requirements/recommendations for international students: Required—Michigan English Language Assessment Battery or TOEFL. *Faculty research:* Sports nutrition in minorities, dietary determinance of chronic disease, protein adequacy in vegetarian diets, relationship of dietary intake to hormone level.

Long Island University–C. W. Post Campus, School of Health Professions and Nursing, Department of Nutrition, Brookville, NY 11548-1300. Offers dietetic internship (Certificate); nutrition (MS). Part-time and evening/weekend programs available. *Degree requirements:* For master's, thesis. *Entrance requirements:* For master's, minimum GPA of 2.75 in major. Electronic applications accepted. *Faculty research:* Hematopoiesis, interleukins in allergy, growth factors effect in metastasis affecting behavioral change for nutrition.

Louisiana Tech University, Graduate School, College of Applied and Natural Sciences, School for Human Ecology, Ruston, LA 71272. Offers dietetics (MS); human ecology (MS). Part-time programs available. *Degree requirements:* For master's, thesis or alternative, Registered Dietician Exam eligibility. *Entrance requirements:* For master's, GRE General Test.

Loyola University Chicago, Graduate School, Marcella Niehoff School of Nursing, Dietetics Program, Chicago, IL 60660. Offers MS, Certificate. *Students:* 19 full-time (16 women), 11 part-time (all women); includes 2 minority (both Hispanic/Latino). Average age 26. 12 applicants, 92% accepted, 10 enrolled. *Expenses: Tuition:* Full-time $15,660; part-time $870 per credit hour. *Required fees:* $125 per semester. Tuition and fees vary according to course load and program. *Unit head:* Dr. Joanna Kouba, Director, 708-216-4132, E-mail: jkouba@luc.edu. *Application contact:* Amy Weatherford, Enrollment Advisor, School of Nursing, 773-508-3249, Fax: 773-508-3241, E-mail: aweatherford@luc.edu.

Marshall University, Academic Affairs Division, College of Health Professions, Department of Dietetics, Huntington, WV 25755. Offers MS. *Faculty:* 2 full-time (both women). *Students:* 6 full-time (all women), 2 part-time (both women); includes 1 minority (Black or African American, non-Hispanic/Latino). Average age 26. In 2011, 12 master's awarded. *Unit head:* Dr. Kelli Williams, Chairperson, 304-696-4336, E-mail: williamsk@marshall.edu. *Application contact:* Information Contact, 304-746-1900, Fax: 304-746-1902, E-mail: services@marshall.edu.

Marywood University, Academic Affairs, College of Health and Human Services, Department of Nutrition and Dietetics, Program in Dietetic Internship, Scranton, PA 18509-1598. Offers Certificate. *Entrance requirements:* Additional exam requirements/recommendations for international students: Required—TOEFL (minimum score 550 paper-based; 213 computer-based; 79 iBT). Application fee: $35. Electronic applications accepted. *Financial support:* Research assistantships, career-related internships or fieldwork, scholarships/grants, and unspecified assistantships available. Support available to part-time students. Financial award application deadline: 6/30; financial award applicants required to submit FAFSA. *Unit head:* Maureen Dunne-Touhey, 570-961-4751. Web site: http://www.marywood.edu/nutrition/internship/.

Marywood University, Academic Affairs, College of Health and Human Services, Department of Nutrition and Dietetics, Program in Nutrition, Scranton, PA 18509-1598. Offers MS. *Entrance requirements:* Additional exam requirements/recommendations for international students: Required—TOEFL (minimum score 550 paper-based; 213 computer-based; 79 iBT). *Application deadline:* For fall admission, 4/1 priority date for domestic students, 3/31 for international students; for spring admission, 11/1 priority date for domestic students, 8/31 for international students. Applications are processed on a rolling basis. Application fee: $35. Electronic applications accepted. *Financial support:* Career-related internships or fieldwork, scholarships/grants, and unspecified assistantships available. Support available to part-time students. Financial award application deadline: 6/30; financial award applicants required to submit FAFSA. *Faculty research:* Obesity and childhood nutrition, dietary supplements (Resveratrol). *Unit head:* Dr. Lee Harrison, Chair, 570-348-6211 Ext. 2303, E-mail: harrisonl@marywood.edu. Web site: http://www.marywood.edu/nutrition/graduate-programs/nutrition/.

Marywood University, Academic Affairs, College of Health and Human Services, Department of Nutrition and Dietetics, Program in Sports Nutrition and Exercise Science, Scranton, PA 18509-1598. Offers MS. *Entrance requirements:* Additional exam requirements/recommendations for international students: Required—TOEFL (minimum score 550 paper-based; 213 computer-based; 79 iBT). *Application deadline:* For fall admission, 4/1 priority date for domestic students, 3/31 for international students; for spring admission, 11/1 priority date for domestic students, 8/31 for international students. Applications are processed on a rolling basis. Application fee: $35. Electronic applications accepted. *Financial support:* Career-related internships or fieldwork, scholarships/grants, and unspecified assistantships available. Support available to part-time students. Financial award application deadline: 6/30; financial award applicants required to submit FAFSA. *Faculty research:* Lung function studies (pulmonary diffusing capacity of nitric oxide). *Unit head:* Dr. Lee Harrison, Chair, 570-348-6211 Ext. 2303, E-mail: harrisonl@marywood.edu. Web site: http://www.marywood.edu/nutrition/graduate-programs/sports-nutrition/.

McGill University, Faculty of Graduate and Postdoctoral Studies, Faculty of Agricultural and Environmental Sciences, School of Dietetics and Human Nutrition, Montréal, QC H3A 2T5, Canada. Offers dietetics (M Sc A, Graduate Diploma); human nutrition (M Sc, M Sc A, PhD).

McMaster University, Faculty of Health Sciences and School of Graduate Studies, Program in Medical Sciences, Metabolism and Nutrition Area, Hamilton, ON L8S 4M2, Canada. Offers M Sc, PhD, MD/PhD. *Degree requirements:* For master's, thesis; for doctorate, comprehensive exam, thesis/dissertation. *Entrance requirements:* For master's, honors B Sc, B+ average in related field; for doctorate, M Sc, minimum B+ average, students with proven research experience and an A average may be admitted with a B Sc degree. Additional exam requirements/recommendations for international students: Required—TOEFL (minimum score 580 paper-based; 237 computer-based; 92 iBT).

McNeese State University, Doré School of Graduate Studies, Burton College of Education, Department of Health and Human Performance, Lake Charles, LA 70609. Offers exercise physiology (MS); health promotion (MS); nutrition and wellness (MS). *Accreditation:* NCATE. Evening/weekend programs available. *Faculty:* 5 full-time (2 women). *Students:* 42 full-time (28 women), 11 part-time (8 women); includes 14 minority (11 Black or African American, non-Hispanic/Latino; 1 Asian, non-Hispanic/Latino; 1 Hispanic/Latino; 1 Two or more races, non-Hispanic/Latino), 5 international. In 2011, 23 master's awarded. *Entrance requirements:* For master's, GRE, undergraduate major or minor in health and human performance or related field of study. *Application deadline:* For fall admission, 5/15 priority date for domestic students, 5/15 for international students; for spring admission, 10/15 priority date for domestic students, 10/15 for international students. Applications are processed on a rolling basis. Application fee: $20 ($30 for international students). *Expenses:* Tuition, state resident: part-time $519 per credit hour. Tuition and fees vary according to course load. *Financial support:* Application deadline: 5/1. *Unit head:* Dr. Michael Soileau, Head, 337-475-5374, Fax: 337-475-5947, E-mail: msoileau@mcneese.edu. *Application contact:* Dr. George F. Mead, Jr., Interim Dean of Dore' School of Graduate Studies, 337-475-5396, Fax: 337-475-5397, E-mail: admissions@mcneese.edu.

Meredith College, John E. Weems Graduate School, Department of Human Environmental Sciences, Raleigh, NC 27607-5298. Offers dietetic internship (Postbaccalaureate Certificate); nutrition (MS). *Faculty:* 4 full-time (3 women), 2 part-time/adjunct (both women). *Students:* 28 full-time (all women), 34 part-time (33 women); includes 7 minority (2 Black or African American, non-Hispanic/Latino; 1 American Indian or Alaska Native, non-Hispanic/Latino; 1 Hispanic/Latino; 3 Two or more races, non-Hispanic/Latino). Average age 29. 128 applicants, 29% accepted, 26 enrolled. In 2011, 13 master's, 13 other advanced degrees awarded. *Degree requirements:* For master's, thesis optional. *Entrance requirements:* For master's, GRE, recommendations, interview. Additional exam requirements/recommendations for international students: Required—TOEFL. *Application deadline:* For fall admission, 7/1 priority date for domestic students, 7/1 for international students; for spring admission, 11/1 priority date for domestic students, 11/1 for international students. Applications are processed on a rolling basis. Application fee: $50. Electronic applications accepted. *Expenses:* Contact institution. *Financial support:* Application deadline: 2/15; applicants required to submit FAFSA. *Unit head:* Dr. Deborah Tippett, Head, 919-760-2355, Fax: 919-760-2819, E-mail: tipettd@meredith.edu. *Application contact:* Dr. William H. Landis, Director, 919-760-2355, Fax: 919-760-2819, E-mail: landisb@meredith.edu.

Michigan State University, The Graduate School, College of Agriculture and Natural Resources and College of Natural Science, Department of Food Science and Human Nutrition, East Lansing, MI 48824. Offers food science (MS, PhD); food science - environmental toxicology (PhD); human nutrition (MS, PhD); human nutrition-environmental toxicology (PhD). *Entrance requirements:* Additional exam requirements/recommendations for international students: Required—TOEFL (minimum score 550 paper-based; 213 computer-based), Michigan State University ELT (minimum score 85), Michigan English Language Assessment Battery (minimum score 83). Electronic applications accepted.

Mississippi State University, College of Agriculture and Life Sciences, Department of Food Science, Nutrition and Health Promotion, Mississippi State, MS 39762. Offers food science and technology (MS, PhD); health promotion (MS); nutrition (MS, PhD). Postbaccalaureate distance learning degree programs offered (no on-campus study). *Faculty:* 9 full-time (3 women), 3 part-time/adjunct (1 woman). *Students:* 45 full-time (33 women), 38 part-time (31 women); includes 15 minority (8 Black or African American, non-Hispanic/Latino; 2 American Indian or Alaska Native, non-Hispanic/Latino; 1 Asian, non-Hispanic/Latino; 2 Hispanic/Latino; 1 Native Hawaiian or other Pacific Islander, non-Hispanic/Latino; 1 Two or more races, non-Hispanic/Latino), 18 international. Average age 30. 132 applicants, 28% accepted, 26 enrolled. In 2011, 27 master's, 3 doctorates awarded. *Degree requirements:* For master's, comprehensive exam, thesis; for doctorate, comprehensive exam, thesis/dissertation. *Entrance requirements:* For master's, GRE General Test, minimum GPA of 2.8; for doctorate, GRE General Test, minimum GPA of 3.0. Additional exam requirements/recommendations for international students: Required—TOEFL (minimum score 475 paper-based; 153 computer-based; 53 iBT); Recommended—IELTS (minimum score 4.5). *Application deadline:* For fall admission, 7/1 for domestic students, 5/1 for international students; for spring admission, 11/1 for domestic students, 9/1 for international students. Applications are processed on a rolling basis. Application fee: $40. Electronic applications accepted. *Expenses:* Tuition, state resident: full-time $5805; part-time $322.50 per credit hour. Tuition, nonresident: full-time $14,670; part-time $815 per credit hour. *Financial support:* In 2011–12, 8 research assistantships with full tuition reimbursements (averaging $13,126 per year), 4 teaching assistantships with full tuition reimbursements (averaging $12,741 per year) were awarded; Federal Work-Study, institutionally sponsored loans, scholarships/grants, and unspecified assistantships also available. Financial award application deadline: 4/1; financial award applicants required to submit FAFSA. *Faculty research:* Food preservation, food chemistry, food safety, food processing, product development. *Unit head:* Dr. Juan Silva, Professor and Interim Head, 662-325-3200, Fax: 662-325-8728, E-mail: jls@ra.msstate.edu. Web site: http://www.fsnhp.msstate.edu.

Montclair State University, The Graduate School, College of Education and Human Services, Department of Exercise Science and Physical Education, Nutrition and Exercise Science Certificate Program, Montclair, NJ 07043-1624. Offers Certificate. *Students:* 2 full-time (both women), 7 part-time (6 women); includes 2 minority (both Hispanic/Latino), 1 international. Average age 31. 7 applicants, 100% accepted, 6 enrolled. In 2011, 3 degrees awarded. *Application deadline:* Applications are processed on a rolling basis. Application fee: $60. Electronic applications accepted. *Financial support:* Federal Work-Study and scholarships/grants available. Support available to part-time students. *Unit head:* Dr. Susana Juniu, Chairperson, 973-655-7093. *Application contact:* Amy Aliello, Executive Director of The Graduate School, 973-655-5147, Fax: 973-655-7869, E-mail: graduate.school@montclair.edu. Web site: http://cehs.montclair.edu/academic/es/programs/nutritionexercert.shtml.

Montclair State University, The Graduate School, College of Education and Human Services, Department of Health and Nutrition Sciences, Post Baccalaureate Didactic Program in Dietetics Certificate, Montclair, NJ 07043-1624. Offers Postbaccalaureate Certificate. Part-time and evening/weekend programs available. *Students:* 10 full-time (all women), 5 part-time (all women); includes 2 minority (1 Black or African American, non-

Hispanic/Latino; 1 Asian, non-Hispanic/Latino), 4 international. Average age 31. 17 applicants, 65% accepted, 3 enrolled. In 2011, 10 Postbaccalaureate Certificates awarded. *Entrance requirements:* Additional exam requirements/recommendations for international students: Required—TOEFL (minimum score 83 computer-based; 65 iBT), IELTS. *Application deadline:* Applications are processed on a rolling basis. Application fee: $60. Electronic applications accepted. *Financial support:* Federal Work-Study, scholarships/grants, and unspecified assistantships available. Support available to part-time students. Financial award application deadline: 3/1; financial award applicants required to submit FAFSA. *Unit head:* Dr. Eva Goldfarb, Chairperson, 973-655-4154. *Application contact:* Amy Aiello, Director of Graduate Admissions and Operations, 973-655-5147, Fax: 973-655-7869, E-mail: graduate.school@montclair.edu. Web site: http://cehs.montclair.edu/academic/hns/programs/certificate.shtml#adaprogram.

Montclair State University, The Graduate School, College of Education and Human Services, Department of Health and Nutrition Sciences, Program in Nutrition and Food Science, Montclair, NJ 07043-1624. Offers MS. Part-time and evening/weekend programs available. *Students:* 33 full-time (25 women), 39 part-time (31 women); includes 19 minority (7 Black or African American, non-Hispanic/Latino; 5 Asian, non-Hispanic/Latino; 7 Hispanic/Latino), 4 international. Average age 31. 62 applicants, 65% accepted, 33 enrolled. In 2011, 21 master's awarded. *Degree requirements:* For master's, comprehensive exam, thesis or alternative. *Entrance requirements:* For master's, GRE General Test, essay, 2 letters of recommendation. Additional exam requirements/recommendations for international students: Required—TOEFL (minimum score 83 iBT), IELTS (minimum score 6.5). *Application deadline:* Applications are processed on a rolling basis. Application fee: $60. Electronic applications accepted. *Financial support:* In 2011–12, 8 research assistantships with full tuition reimbursements (averaging $7,000 per year), 1 teaching assistantship with partial tuition reimbursement (averaging $7,000 per year) were awarded; Federal Work-Study, scholarships/grants, and unspecified assistantships also available. Support available to part-time students. Financial award application deadline: 3/1; financial award applicants required to submit FAFSA. *Unit head:* Dr. Eva Goldfarb, Chairperson, 973-655-4154. *Application contact:* Amy Aiello, Executive Director of The Graduate School, 973-655-5147, Fax: 973-655-7869, E-mail: graduate.school@montclair.edu. Web site: http://cehs.montclair.edu/academic/hns/programs/ms_nutrition_food.shtml.

Mount Mary College, Graduate Programs, Program in Dietetics, Milwaukee, WI 53222-4597. Offers administrative dietetics (MS); clinical dietetics (MS); nutrition education (MS). Part-time and evening/weekend programs available. *Faculty:* 1 (woman) full-time, 5 part-time/adjunct (4 women). *Students:* 12 full-time (all women), 21 part-time (all women), 1 international. Average age 28. 102 applicants, 12% accepted, 12 enrolled. In 2011, 1 master's awarded. *Degree requirements:* For master's, thesis. *Entrance requirements:* For master's, minimum GPA of 2.75, completion of ADA and DPD requirements. Additional exam requirements/recommendations for international students: Required—TOEFL (minimum score 500 paper-based; 173 computer-based). *Application deadline:* For fall admission, 2/15 priority date for domestic students. Application fee: $45 ($100 for international students). *Financial support:* In 2011–12, 1 student received support. Career-related internships or fieldwork and Federal Work-Study available. Support available to part-time students. Financial award application deadline: 5/1; financial award applicants required to submit FAFSA. *Unit head:* Lisa Stark, Director, 414-258-4810 Ext. 398, E-mail: starkl@mtmary.edu. *Application contact:* Dr. Douglas J. Mickelson, Associate Dean for Graduate and Continuing Education, 414-256-1252, Fax: 414-256-0167, E-mail: mickelsd@mtmary.edu.

Mount Saint Vincent University, Graduate Programs, Department of Applied Human Nutrition, Halifax, NS B3M 2J6, Canada. Offers M Sc AHN, MAHN. Part-time and evening/weekend programs available. *Degree requirements:* For master's, thesis (for some programs). *Entrance requirements:* For master's, bachelor's degree in related field, minimum GPA of 3.0, professional experience. Electronic applications accepted.

New Mexico State University, Graduate School, College of Agricultural, Consumer and Environmental Sciences, Department of Family and Consumer Sciences, Las Cruces, NM 88003-8001. Offers family and child science (MS); family and consumer science education (MS); food science and technology (MS); marriage and family therapy (MS); nutrition and dietetic science (MS). Part-time programs available. *Faculty:* 11 full-time (9 women), 1 (woman) part-time/adjunct. *Students:* 30 full-time (29 women), 18 part-time (15 women); includes 22 minority (1 American Indian or Alaska Native, non-Hispanic/Latino; 1 Asian, non-Hispanic/Latino; 20 Hispanic/Latino), 5 international. Average age 31. 21 applicants, 67% accepted, 12 enrolled. In 2011, 21 master's awarded. *Degree requirements:* For master's, comprehensive exam (for some programs), thesis (for some programs), oral exam. *Entrance requirements:* For master's, GRE, 3 letters of reference, resume. Additional exam requirements/recommendations for international students: Required—TOEFL (minimum score 550 paper-based; 0 computer-based; 79 iBT), IELTS (minimum score 6.5). *Application deadline:* For fall admission, 6/30 priority date for domestic students, 3/1 for international students; for spring admission, 11/30 for domestic and international students. Applications are processed on a rolling basis. Application fee: $40 ($50 for international students). Electronic applications accepted. *Expenses:* Tuition, state resident: full-time $5004; part-time $208.50 per credit. Tuition, nonresident: full-time $17,446; part-time $726.90 per credit. *Financial support:* In 2011–12, 1 fellowship (averaging $3,754 per year), 3 research assistantships (averaging $21,281 per year), 10 teaching assistantships (averaging $11,851 per year) were awarded; career-related internships or fieldwork, Federal Work-Study, scholarships/grants, health care benefits, and unspecified assistantships also available. Support available to part-time students. Financial award application deadline: 3/1; financial award applicants required to submit FAFSA. *Faculty research:* Work, stress, and family functioning; food product analysis; childhood obesity; relationship education. *Total annual research expenditures:* $750,000. *Unit head:* Dr. Esther Devall, Head, 575-646-3936, Fax: 575-646-1889, E-mail: edevall@nmsu.edu. *Application contact:* Dr. Roselyn Smitley, Coordinator, 575-646-1183, Fax: 575-646-1889, E-mail: rosmile@nmsu.edu. Web site: http://fcs.nmsu.edu.

New York Chiropractic College, Program in Applied Clinical Nutrition, Seneca Falls, NY 13148-0800. Offers MS. Part-time and evening/weekend programs available. *Entrance requirements:* For master's, minimum GPA of 2.5, transcripts, writing sample. Additional exam requirements/recommendations for international students: Recommended—TOEFL. Electronic applications accepted.

New York Institute of Technology, Graduate Division, School of Health Professions, Program in Clinical Nutrition, Old Westbury, NY 11568-8000. Offers MS, DO/MS. Part-time and evening/weekend programs available. *Students:* 7 full-time (all women), 39 part-time (36 women); includes 14 minority (4 Black or African American, non-Hispanic/Latino; 5 Asian, non-Hispanic/Latino; 5 Hispanic/Latino), 1 international. Average age 33. In 2011, 10 master's awarded. *Degree requirements:* For master's, comprehensive exam, thesis (for some programs). *Entrance requirements:* For master's, minimum QPA of 2.85. Additional exam requirements/recommendations for international students: Required—TOEFL (minimum score 550 paper-based; 213 computer-based). *Application deadline:* For fall admission, 7/1 priority date for domestic students; for spring admission, 12/1 priority date for domestic students. Applications are processed on a rolling basis. Application fee: $50. Electronic applications accepted. *Expenses:* *Tuition:* Part-time $930 per credit hour. *Financial support:* Fellowships, research assistantships with partial tuition reimbursements, career-related internships or fieldwork, institutionally sponsored loans, tuition waivers (full and partial), and unspecified assistantships available. Support available to part-time students. Financial award applicants required to submit FAFSA. *Faculty research:* Medical nutrition training. *Unit head:* Mindy Haar, Director, 516-686-3818, Fax: 516-686-3795, E-mail: mhaar@nyit.edu. *Application contact:* Dr. Jacquelyn Nealon, Vice President for Enrollment Services, 516-686-7925, Fax: 516-686-7597, E-mail: jnealon@nyit.edu.

New York University, Steinhardt School of Culture, Education, and Human Development, Department of Nutrition, Food Studies, and Public Health, Program in Nutrition and Dietetics, New York, NY 10012-1019. Offers nutrition and dietetics (MS), including clinical nutrition, food and nutrition. Part-time programs available. *Degree requirements:* For master's, thesis (for some programs); for doctorate, thesis/dissertation. *Entrance requirements:* For doctorate, GRE General Test, interview. Additional exam requirements/recommendations for international students: Required—TOEFL. Electronic applications accepted. *Faculty research:* Nutrition and race, childhood obesity and other eating disorders, nutritional epidemiology, nutrition policy, nutrition and health promotion.

North Carolina Agricultural and Technical State University, School of Graduate Studies, School of Agriculture and Environmental Sciences, Department of Family and Consumer Sciences, Greensboro, NC 27411. Offers child development early education and family studies (MAT); family and consumer sciences (MAT); food and nutrition (MS). Part-time and evening/weekend programs available. *Degree requirements:* For master's, comprehensive exam, thesis or alternative, qualifying exam. *Entrance requirements:* For master's, GRE General Test, minimum GPA of 2.6.

North Carolina State University, Graduate School, College of Agriculture and Life Sciences and College of Veterinary Medicine, Program in Nutrition, Raleigh, NC 27695. Offers MN, MS, PhD. Part-time programs available. *Degree requirements:* For master's, thesis (for some programs); for doctorate, thesis/dissertation. *Entrance requirements:* For master's and doctorate, GRE General Test. Additional exam requirements/recommendations for international students: Required—TOEFL (minimum score 550 paper-based; 213 computer-based). Electronic applications accepted. *Faculty research:* Effects of food/feed ingredients and components on health and growth, community nutrition, waste management and reduction, experimental animal nutrition.

North Dakota State University, College of Graduate and Interdisciplinary Studies, College of Human Development and Education, Department of Health, Nutrition, and Exercise Sciences, Fargo, ND 58108. Offers dietetics (MS); entry level athletic training (MS); exercise science (MS); nutrition science (MS); public health (MS); sport pedagogy (MS); sports recreation management (MS). Part-time and evening/weekend programs available. Postbaccalaureate distance learning degree programs offered (no on-campus study). *Faculty:* 15 full-time (8 women). *Students:* 10 full-time (4 women). 37 applicants, 84% accepted, 10 enrolled. In 2011, 15 master's awarded. *Degree requirements:* For master's, thesis (for some programs). *Entrance requirements:* For master's, minimum GPA of 3.0. Additional exam requirements/recommendations for international students: Required—TOEFL (minimum score 525 paper-based; 197 computer-based; 71 iBT). *Application deadline:* For fall admission, 3/1 priority date for domestic students, 3/1 for international students. Applications are processed on a rolling basis. Application fee: $35. Electronic applications accepted. *Financial support:* In 2011–12, 18 teaching assistantships with full tuition reimbursements (averaging $6,500 per year) were awarded. Financial award application deadline: 3/31. *Faculty research:* Biomechanics, sport specialization, recreation, nutrition, athletic training. *Unit head:* Dr. Margaret Fitzgerald, Head, 701-231-7474, Fax: 701-231-8872, E-mail: margaret.fitzgerald@ndsu.edu. *Application contact:* Dr. Gary Liguori, Graduate Coordinator, 701-231-7474, Fax: 701-231-6524. Web site: http://www.ndsu.edu/hnes/.

Northern Illinois University, Graduate School, College of Health and Human Sciences, School of Family, Consumer and Nutrition Sciences, De Kalb, IL 60115-2854. Offers applied family and child studies (MS); nutrition and dietetics (MS). *Accreditation:* AAMFT/COAMFTE. Part-time programs available. *Faculty:* 16 full-time (14 women), 2 part-time/adjunct (1 woman). *Students:* 65 full-time (54 women), 17 part-time (14 women); includes 14 minority (4 Black or African American, non-Hispanic/Latino; 4 Asian, non-Hispanic/Latino; 5 Hispanic/Latino; 1 Two or more races, non-Hispanic/Latino), 6 international. Average age 26. 97 applicants, 44% accepted, 21 enrolled. In 2011, 39 master's awarded. *Degree requirements:* For master's, comprehensive exam, internship, thesis (nutrition and dietetics). *Entrance requirements:* For master's, GRE General Test, minimum GPA of 2.75. Additional exam requirements/recommendations for international students: Required—TOEFL (minimum score 550 paper-based; 213 computer-based). *Application deadline:* For fall admission, 6/1 for domestic students, 5/1 for international students; for spring admission, 11/1 for domestic students, 10/1 for international students. Applications are processed on a rolling basis. Application fee: $40. Electronic applications accepted. *Financial support:* In 2011–12, 12 research assistantships with full tuition reimbursements, 23 teaching assistantships with full tuition reimbursements were awarded; fellowships with full tuition reimbursements, career-related internships or fieldwork, Federal Work-Study, scholarships/grants, tuition waivers (full), and staff assistantships also available. Support available to part-time students. Financial award applicants required to submit FAFSA. *Faculty research:* Preliminary child development, hospitality administration in Asia, sports nutrition, eating disorders. *Unit head:* Dr. Laura Smart, Chair, 815-753-6342, Fax: 815-753-1321, E-mail: lsmart@niu.edu. *Application contact:* Graduate School Office, 815-753-0395, E-mail: gradsch@niu.edu. Web site: http://www.fcns.niu.edu/.

Northwestern Health Sciences University, College of Graduate Health Sciences, Bloomington, MN 55431-1599. Offers clinical chiropractic orthopedics (MHS); clinical nutrition (MHS); diagnostic imaging (MHS).

The Ohio State University, Graduate School, College of Education and Human Ecology, Department of Human Nutrition, Nutrition Program, Columbus, OH 43210. Offers PhD. Offered jointly with College of Food, Agricultural, and Environmental Sciences, College of Medicine, and College of Veterinary Medicine. *Faculty:* 14. *Students:* 12 full-time (8 women), 9 part-time (6 women), 13 international. Average age 30. In 2011, 8 doctorates awarded. *Degree requirements:* For doctorate, thesis/dissertation. *Entrance requirements:* For doctorate, GRE. Additional exam requirements/recommendations for international students: Required—TOEFL (minimum score 550 paper-based; 79 iBT), Michigan English Language Assessment Battery (minimum score 82). *Application deadline:* Applications are processed on a rolling basis. Application fee: $40 ($50 for international students). Electronic applications accepted. *Expenses:* Tuition, state resident: full-time $11,400. Tuition, nonresident: full-time $28,125. Tuition and fees vary according to course load, degree level, campus/location and program. *Financial support:* Applicants required to submit FAFSA. *Unit head:* Dr. Jeff Firkins, Director, 614-292-9957, E-mail: osun@osu.edu. *Application contact:* Graduate Admissions, 614-292-6031, Fax: 614-292-3656, E-mail: gradadmissions@osu.edu. Web site: http://ehe.osu.edu/osun/.

The Ohio State University, Graduate School, College of Food, Agricultural, and Environmental Sciences, Department of Food Science and Nutrition, Columbus, OH 43210. Offers food science (MS, PhD). *Accreditation:* AND. *Faculty:* 15. *Students:* 48 full-time (31 women), 15 part-time (7 women); includes 11 minority (5 Black or African

American, non-Hispanic/Latino; 4 Asian, non-Hispanic/Latino; 2 Hispanic/Latino), 29 international. Average age 28. In 2011, 10 master's, 10 doctorates awarded. *Degree requirements:* For master's, thesis optional; for doctorate, thesis/dissertation. *Entrance requirements:* For master's and doctorate, GRE General Test. Additional exam requirements/recommendations for international students: Required—TOEFL (minimum score 550 paper-based; 213 computer-based), IELTS (minimum score 6.5), or Michigan English Language Assessment Battery (minimum score 82). *Application deadline:* For fall admission, 8/15 priority date for domestic students, 7/1 for international students; for winter admission, 12/1 priority date for domestic students, 11/1 for international students; for spring admission, 3/1 priority date for domestic students, 2/1 for international students. Applications are processed on a rolling basis. Application fee: $40 ($50 for international students). Electronic applications accepted. *Expenses:* Tuition, state resident: full-time $11,400. Tuition, nonresident: full-time $28,125. Tuition and fees vary according to course load, degree level, campus/location and program. *Financial support:* Fellowships, research assistantships, Federal Work-Study, and institutionally sponsored loans available. Support available to part-time students. *Unit head:* Richard Linton, Chair, 614-247-7881, E-mail: linton.60@osu.edu. *Application contact:* Graduate Admissions, 614-292-6031, Fax: 614-292-3656, E-mail: gradadmissions@osu.edu. Web site: http://fst.osu.edu/.

Ohio University, Graduate College, College of Health Sciences and Professions, School of Applied Health Sciences and Wellness, Program in Food and Nutrition, Athens, OH 45701-2979. Offers human and consumer sciences (MS). *Students:* 15 full-time (12 women), 1 (woman) part-time; includes 1 minority (Hispanic/Latino), 8 international. 28 applicants, 32% accepted, 5 enrolled. In 2011, 3 master's awarded. *Unit head:* Dr. Robert G. Brannan, Director, 740-593-2879, Fax: 740-593-0289, E-mail: brannan@ohio.edu. *Application contact:* Marnie Miller, Student Services Coordinator, 740-593-2800, Fax: 740-593-4625, E-mail: graduate@ohio.edu. Web site: http://www.ouchsp.org/foods-and-nutrition.

Oklahoma State University, College of Human Environmental Sciences, Department of Nutritional Sciences, Stillwater, OK 74078. Offers MS, PhD. Postbaccalaureate distance learning degree programs offered. *Faculty:* 19 full-time (16 women), 1 (woman) part-time/adjunct. *Students:* 48 full-time (44 women), 22 part-time (19 women); includes 9 minority (4 Black or African American, non-Hispanic/Latino; 2 American Indian or Alaska Native, non-Hispanic/Latino; 1 Asian, non-Hispanic/Latino; 1 Hispanic/Latino; 1 Two or more races, non-Hispanic/Latino), 14 international. Average age 29. 45 applicants, 53% accepted, 19 enrolled. In 2011, 15 master's, 4 doctorates awarded. *Degree requirements:* For master's, thesis (for some programs); for doctorate, comprehensive exam, thesis/dissertation. *Entrance requirements:* For master's and doctorate, GRE or GMAT. Additional exam requirements/recommendations for international students: Required—TOEFL (minimum score 550 paper-based; 79 iBT). *Application deadline:* For fall admission, 3/1 for international students; for spring admission, 8/1 for international students. Applications are processed on a rolling basis. Application fee: $40 ($75 for international students). Electronic applications accepted. *Expenses:* Tuition, state resident: full-time $4044; part-time $168.50 per credit hour. Tuition, nonresident: full-time $16,008; part-time $667 per credit hour. *Required fees:* $2122; $88.45 per credit hour. One-time fee: $50. Tuition and fees vary according to course load and campus/location. *Financial support:* In 2011–12, 32 research assistantships (averaging $8,951 per year), 16 teaching assistantships (averaging $8,369 per year) were awarded; career-related internships or fieldwork, Federal Work-Study, scholarships/grants, health care benefits, tuition waivers (partial), and unspecified assistantships also available. Support available to part-time students. Financial award application deadline: 3/1; financial award applicants required to submit FAFSA. *Faculty research:* Nutritional sciences, micronutrients and chronic disease, phytochemicals, nutrition education, osteoporosis, food service administration. *Unit head:* Dr. Nancy M. Betts, Head, 405-744-5040, Fax: 405-744-1357. *Application contact:* Dr. Sheryl Tucker, Dean, 405-744-7099, Fax: 405-744-0355, E-mail: grad-i@okstate.edu. Web site: http://humansciences.okstate.edu/nsci/.

Oregon Health & Science University, School of Medicine, Graduate Programs in Medicine, Program in Clinical Nutrition, Portland, OR 97239-3098. Offers MS, Certificate. Part-time programs available. *Faculty:* 1 (woman) full-time, 3 part-time/adjunct (all women). *Students:* 30 full-time (27 women), 2 part-time (both women); includes 1 minority (Asian, non-Hispanic/Latino). Average age 25. 83 applicants, 31% accepted, 23 enrolled. In 2011, 6 master's, 22 other advanced degrees awarded. *Degree requirements:* For master's, thesis optional. *Entrance requirements:* For master's, GRE General Test (minimum scores: 153 Verbal/148 Quantitative/4.5 Analytical). *Application deadline:* For fall admission, 1/1 for domestic students. Application fee: $120. *Financial support:* Health care benefits available. *Unit head:* Dr. Diane Stadler, Program Director. *Application contact:* Chandra Nautiyal, Administrative Coordinator, 503-494-7596, E-mail: nautiyal@ohsu.edu.

Penn State University Park, Graduate School, College of Health and Human Development, Department of Nutritional Sciences, State College, University Park, PA 16802-1503. Offers MS, PhD. *Unit head:* Dr. Ann C. Crouter, Dean, 814-865-1428, Fax: 814-865-3282, E-mail: ac1@psu.edu. *Application contact:* Cynthia E. Nicosia, Director, Graduate Enrollment Services, 814-865-1795, Fax: 814-865-4627, E-mail: cey1@psu.edu. Web site: http://nutrition.hhdev.psu.edu/.

Purdue University, Graduate School, College of Health and Human Sciences, Department of Nutrition Science, West Lafayette, IN 47907. Offers animal health (MS, PhD); biochemical and molecular nutrition (MS, PhD); growth and development (MS, PhD); human and clinical nutrition (MS, PhD); public health and education (MS, PhD). *Faculty:* 17 full-time (10 women), 14 part-time/adjunct (12 women). *Students:* 35 full-time (33 women), 2 part-time (both women); includes 3 minority (1 Black or African American, non-Hispanic/Latino; 2 Asian, non-Hispanic/Latino), 17 international. Average age 28. 120 applicants, 18% accepted, 11 enrolled. In 2011, 5 master's, 8 doctorates awarded. *Degree requirements:* For master's, thesis; for doctorate, thesis/dissertation. *Entrance requirements:* For master's and doctorate, GRE General Test, scores in verbal and quantitative areas must be greater than 1000 or 300 if the GRE was taken August 1, 2011 or after, minimum undergraduate GPA of 3.0 or equivalent. Additional exam requirements/recommendations for international students: Required—TOEFL (minimum score 600 paper-based; 77 iBT). *Application deadline:* For fall admission, 1/15 for domestic and international students. Applications are processed on a rolling basis. Application fee: $60 ($75 for international students). Electronic applications accepted. *Financial support:* Fellowships, research assistantships, and teaching assistantships available. Support available to part-time students. Financial award applicants required to submit FAFSA. *Faculty research:* Nutrient requirements, nutrient metabolism, nutrition and disease prevention. *Unit head:* Dr. Connie M. Weaver, Head, 765-494-8237, Fax: 765-494-0674, E-mail: weavercm@purdue.edu. *Application contact:* Marilyn McCammack, Graduate Secretary, 765-476-7492, E-mail: mccammac@purdue.edu. Web site: http://www.cfs.purdue.edu/fn/.

Rosalind Franklin University of Medicine and Science, College of Health Professions, Department of Nutrition, North Chicago, IL 60064-3095. Offers clinical nutrition (MS); nutrition education (MS). Part-time and evening/weekend programs available. Postbaccalaureate distance learning degree programs offered (no on-campus study). *Degree requirements:* For master's, thesis optional, portfolio. *Entrance requirements:* For master's, minimum GPA of 2.75, registered dietitian (RD), professional certificate or license. Additional exam requirements/recommendations for international students: Required—TOEFL. *Expenses:* Contact institution. *Faculty research:* Nutrition education, distance learning, computer-based graduate education, childhood obesity, nutrition medical education.

Rush University, College of Health Sciences, Department of Clinical Nutrition, Chicago, IL 60612. Offers MS. Part-time programs available. *Degree requirements:* For master's, thesis. *Entrance requirements:* For master's, GRE General Test, minimum GPA of 3.0, course work in statistics, undergraduate didactic program approved by the American Dietetic Association. Additional exam requirements/recommendations for international students: Required—TOEFL. *Faculty research:* Food service management, chronic disease prevention/treatment, obesity, Alzheimer's.

Rutgers, The State University of New Jersey, New Brunswick, Graduate School-New Brunswick, Program in Nutritional Sciences, Piscataway, NJ 08854-8097. Offers MS, PhD. Part-time programs available. Terminal master's awarded for partial completion of doctoral program. *Degree requirements:* For master's, thesis; for doctorate, thesis/dissertation, written qualifying exam. *Entrance requirements:* For master's and doctorate, GRE General Test, 3 letters of recommendation. Additional exam requirements/recommendations for international students: Required—TOEFL (minimum score 560 paper-based; 220 computer-based; 83 iBT). Electronic applications accepted. *Faculty research:* Nutrition and gene expression, nutrition and disease (obesity, diabetes, cancer, osteoporosis, alcohol), community nutrition and nutrition education, cellular lipid transport and metabolism.

Sage Graduate School, School of Health Sciences, Program in Nutrition, Troy, NY 12180-4115. Offers applied nutrition (MS); dietetic internship (Certificate). Part-time and evening/weekend programs available. *Faculty:* 3 full-time (all women), 2 part-time/adjunct (both women). *Students:* 43 full-time (40 women), 14 part-time (12 women); includes 1 minority (Asian, non-Hispanic/Latino), 2 international. Average age 28. 104 applicants, 52% accepted, 25 enrolled. In 2011, 12 master's, 11 other advanced degrees awarded. *Entrance requirements:* For master's, minimum GPA of 2.75, resume, 2 letters of recommendation, interview with director. Additional exam requirements/recommendations for international students: Required—TOEFL (minimum score 550 paper-based; 213 computer-based). *Application deadline:* Applications are processed on a rolling basis. Application fee: $40. *Expenses: Tuition:* Full-time $11,880; part-time $660 per credit hour. Tuition and fees vary according to program. *Financial support:* Fellowships, research assistantships, Federal Work-Study, scholarships/grants, and unspecified assistantships available. Support available to part-time students. *Unit head:* Dr. Esther Haskevitz, Interim Dean, School of Health Sciences, 518-244-2296, Fax: 518-244-4571, E-mail: haskve@sage.edu. *Application contact:* Rayane AbuSabha, Director of Didactic Program in Dietetics, 518-244-2396, Fax: 518-244-4586, E-mail: abusar@sage.edu.

Sage Graduate School, School of Management, Program in Health Services Administration, Troy, NY 12180-4115. Offers dietetic internship (Certificate); gerontology (MS). Part-time and evening/weekend programs available. *Faculty:* 2 full-time (both women), 8 part-time/adjunct (1 woman). *Students:* 5 full-time (4 women), 24 part-time (17 women); includes 5 minority (4 Black or African American, non-Hispanic/Latino; 1 Hispanic/Latino). Average age 30. 33 applicants, 48% accepted, 11 enrolled. In 2011, 12 master's awarded. *Entrance requirements:* For master's, minimum GPA of 2.75, resume, 2 letters of recommendation. Additional exam requirements/recommendations for international students: Required—TOEFL (minimum score 550 paper-based; 213 computer-based). Application fee: $40. *Expenses: Tuition:* Full-time $11,880; part-time $660 per credit hour. Tuition and fees vary according to program. *Financial support:* Fellowships, research assistantships, Federal Work-Study, scholarships/grants, and unspecified assistantships available. Support available to part-time students. Financial award application deadline: 3/1; financial award applicants required to submit FAFSA. *Unit head:* Dr. Kimberly Fredricks, Program Director, 518-292-1782, Fax: 518-292-1964, E-mail: fredek1@sage.edu. *Application contact:* Wendy D. Diefendorf, Director of Graduate and Adult Admission, 518-244-2443, Fax: 518-244-6880, E-mail: diefew@sage.edu.

Saint Louis University, Graduate Education, Doisy College of Health Sciences and Graduate Education, Department of Nutrition and Dietetics, St. Louis, MO 63103-2097. Offers medical dietetics (MS); nutrition and physical performance (MS). Part-time programs available. *Degree requirements:* For master's, comprehensive exam (for some programs). *Entrance requirements:* For master's, GRE General Test, letters of recommendation, resume, interview. Additional exam requirements/recommendations for international students: Required—TOEFL (minimum score 525 paper-based; 194 computer-based). Electronic applications accepted. *Faculty research:* Sustainable food systems, nutrition education, public health nutrition, culinary nutrition and physical performance.

Sam Houston State University, College of Humanities and Social Sciences, Department of Family and Consumer Sciences, Huntsville, TX 77341. Offers dietetics (MS); family and consumer sciences (MS). Part-time and evening/weekend programs available. *Faculty:* 5 full-time (4 women). *Students:* 19 full-time (17 women), 2 part-time (both women); includes 4 minority (1 American Indian or Alaska Native, non-Hispanic/Latino; 2 Hispanic/Latino; 1 Native Hawaiian or other Pacific Islander, non-Hispanic/Latino). Average age 24. 27 applicants, 41% accepted, 10 enrolled. In 2011, 12 master's awarded. *Entrance requirements:* For master's, GRE General Test, minimum GPA of 2.5. Additional exam requirements/recommendations for international students: Required—TOEFL (minimum score 550 paper-based; 213 computer-based; 79 iBT). *Application deadline:* For fall admission, 8/1 for domestic students, 6/25 for international students; for spring admission, 12/1 for domestic students, 11/12 for international students. Applications are processed on a rolling basis. Application fee: $45 ($75 for international students). Electronic applications accepted. *Expenses:* Tuition, state resident: full-time $4420; part-time $221 per credit hour. Tuition, nonresident: full-time $10,680; part-time $534 per credit hour. *Required fees:* $329 per credit hour. *Financial support:* Teaching assistantships available. Financial award application deadline: 5/31; financial award applicants required to submit FAFSA. *Unit head:* Dr. Janis White, Chair, 936-294-1242, Fax: 936-294-4204, E-mail: jwhite@shsu.edu. *Application contact:* Dr. Claudia Sealey-Potts, Advisor, 936-294-1250, E-mail: clapotts@shsu.edu. Web site: http://www.shsu.edu/~hec_www/.

San Diego State University, Graduate and Research Affairs, College of Health and Human Services, School of Exercise and Nutritional Sciences, Program in Nutritional Sciences, San Diego, CA 92182. Offers MS, MS/MS. *Degree requirements:* For master's, thesis. *Entrance requirements:* For master's, GRE General Test, 2 letters of reference. Additional exam requirements/recommendations for international students: Required—TOEFL. Electronic applications accepted.

San Jose State University, Graduate Studies and Research, College of Applied Sciences and Arts, Department of Nutrition, Food Science, and Packaging, San Jose, CA 95192-0001. Offers nutritional science (MS). Electronic applications accepted.

Saybrook University, Graduate College of Mind-Body Medicine, San Francisco, CA 94111-1920. Offers MS, PhD, Certificate. *Faculty:* 95 part-time/adjunct (53 women). *Students:* 55 full-time (52 women). *Entrance requirements:* Additional exam

requirements/recommendations for international students: Required—TOEFL (minimum score 580 paper-based; 237 computer-based; 93 iBT). *Application deadline:* For fall admission, 5/1 priority date for domestic students, 5/1 for international students; for spring admission, 10/1 priority date for domestic students, 10/1 for international students. Applications are processed on a rolling basis. Electronic applications accepted. *Application contact:* Admissions Specialist, 800-825-4480, Fax: 415-433-9271, E-mail: admissions@saybrook.edu. Web site: http://www.saybrook.edu/mbm.

Simmons College, School of Nursing and Health Sciences, Boston, MA 02115. Offers didactic dietetics (Certificate); health professions education (CAGS); nursing (MS); nursing administration (MS); nursing practice (DNP); nutrition (MS, Certificate); physical therapy (DPT); sports nutrition (Certificate); sports nutrition/didactic dietetics (Certificate); MS/Certificate. *Unit head:* Dr. Judy Beal, Dean, 617-521-2139, Fax: 617-521-3137, E-mail: judy.beal@simmons.edu. *Application contact:* Carmen Fortin, Assistant Dean/Director of Admission, 617-521-2651, Fax: 617-521-3137, E-mail: gshsadm@simmons.edu. Web site: http://www.simmons.edu/snhs/.

South Carolina State University, School of Graduate Studies, Department of Family and Consumer Sciences, Orangeburg, SC 29117-0001. Offers individual and family development (MS); nutritional sciences (MS). Part-time and evening/weekend programs available. *Faculty:* 2 full-time (both women). *Students:* 13 full-time (all women), 15 part-time (13 women); includes 27 minority (all Black or African American, non-Hispanic/Latino). Average age 33. 8 applicants, 88% accepted, 7 enrolled. In 2011, 12 master's awarded. *Degree requirements:* For master's, comprehensive exam, thesis optional, departmental qualifying exam. *Entrance requirements:* For master's, GRE, MAT, or NTE, minimum GPA of 2.7. *Application deadline:* For fall admission, 6/15 priority date for domestic students, 6/15 for international students; for spring admission, 11/1 for domestic and international students. Applications are processed on a rolling basis. Application fee: $25. Electronic applications accepted. *Expenses:* Tuition, state resident: full-time $8688; part-time $514 per credit hour. Tuition, nonresident: full-time $17,600; part-time $1009 per credit hour. *Required fees:* $570. *Financial support:* In 2011–12, 3 fellowships (averaging $6,319 per year) were awarded; institutionally sponsored loans also available. Financial award application deadline: 6/1. *Faculty research:* Societal competence, relationship of parent-child interaction to adult, quality of well-being of rural elders. *Unit head:* Dr. Ethel G. Jones, Chair, 803-536-8958, Fax: 803-533-3268, E-mail: egjones@scsu.edu. *Application contact:* Annette Hazzard-Jones, Program Coordinator II, 803-536-8809, Fax: 803-536-8812, E-mail: zs_ahazzard@scsu.edu.

South Dakota State University, Graduate School, College of Education and Human Sciences, Department of Nutrition, Food Science and Hospitality, Brookings, SD 57007. Offers dietetics (MS); nutrition, food science and hospitality (MFCS); nutritional sciences (MS, PhD). Part-time programs available. *Degree requirements:* For master's, comprehensive exam (for some programs), thesis (for some programs), oral exam. *Entrance requirements:* Additional exam requirements/recommendations for international students: Required—TOEFL (minimum score 525 paper-based). *Faculty research:* Food chemistry, bone density, functional food, nutrition education, nutrition biochemistry.

Southeast Missouri State University, School of Graduate Studies, Department of Health, Human Performance and Recreation, Cape Girardeau, MO 63701-4799. Offers nutrition and exercise science (MS). Part-time and evening/weekend programs available. *Faculty:* 7 full-time (1 woman), 2 part-time/adjunct (1 woman). *Students:* 17 full-time (6 women), 7 part-time (4 women), 10 international. Average age 26. 20 applicants, 95% accepted, 8 enrolled. In 2011, 4 master's awarded. *Degree requirements:* For master's, comprehensive exam, thesis optional, internship. *Entrance requirements:* For master's, GRE General Test (minimum combined score of 950), minimum undergraduate GPA of 3.0, minimum B grade in prerequisite courses. Additional exam requirements/recommendations for international students: Required—TOEFL (minimum score 550 paper-based; 213 computer-based; 79 iBT); Recommended—IELTS (minimum score 6). *Application deadline:* For fall admission, 8/1 for domestic students, 7/1 for international students; for spring admission, 11/21 for domestic students, 11/1 for international students. Applications are processed on a rolling basis. Application fee: $30 ($40 for international students). Electronic applications accepted. *Expenses:* Tuition, state resident: full-time $4896; part-time $272 per credit hour. Tuition, nonresident: full-time $8649; part-time $480.50 per credit hour. *Financial support:* In 2011–12, 16 students received support, including 4 teaching assistantships with full tuition reimbursements available (averaging $7,600 per year); career-related internships or fieldwork, Federal Work-Study, scholarships/grants, tuition waivers (full), and unspecified assistantships also available. Financial award application deadline: 6/30; financial award applicants required to submit FAFSA. *Faculty research:* Health issues of athletes, body composition assessment, exercise testing, exercise training, perceptual responses to physical activity. *Unit head:* Dr. Joe Pujol, Chairperson, 573-651-2664, Fax: 573-651-5150, E-mail: jpujol@semo.edu. *Application contact:* Alisa Aleen McFerron, Assistant Director of Admissions for Operations, 573-651-5937, Fax: 573-651-5936, E-mail: amcferron@semo.edu. Web site: http://www.semo.edu/health/.

Southern Illinois University Carbondale, Graduate School, College of Agriculture, Department of Animal Science, Food and Nutrition, Program in Food and Nutrition, Carbondale, IL 62901-4701. Offers MS. *Faculty:* 15 full-time (6 women). *Students:* 9 full-time (8 women), 8 part-time (all women). Average age 29. 18 applicants, 50% accepted, 5 enrolled. In 2011, 7 master's awarded. *Degree requirements:* For master's, thesis or alternative. *Entrance requirements:* For master's, minimum GPA of 2.7. Additional exam requirements/recommendations for international students: Required—TOEFL. *Application deadline:* Applications are processed on a rolling basis. Application fee: $0. *Financial support:* In 2011–12, 12 students received support. Fellowships, research assistantships, teaching assistantships, career-related internships or fieldwork, Federal Work-Study, institutionally sponsored loans, and tuition waivers (full) available. Support available to part-time students. *Faculty research:* Public health nutrition, nutrition physiology, soybean utilization, nutrition education. *Total annual research expenditures:* $100,000. *Unit head:* Dr. Todd A. Winters, Interim Chair, 618-453-1760, Fax: 618-453-5231, E-mail: tw3a@siu.edu. *Application contact:* Dr. Carol Boushey, Director, Dietetic Internship Program, 618-453-7514, Fax: 618-453-7517. Web site: http://www.coas.siu.edu/default2.asp?active_page_id=112.

State University of New York College at Oneonta, Graduate Education, Department of Human Ecology, Oneonta, NY 13820-4015. Offers nutrition and dietetics (MS). Postbaccalaureate distance learning degree programs offered (no on-campus study).

Syracuse University, Falk College of Sport and Human Dynamics, Program in Nutrition Science, Syracuse, NY 13244. Offers MA, MS. *Accreditation:* AND. Part-time programs available. *Students:* 20 full-time (19 women), 2 part-time (both women); includes 3 minority (all Asian, non-Hispanic/Latino), 7 international. Average age 25. 46 applicants, 43% accepted, 13 enrolled. In 2011, 13 degrees awarded. *Degree requirements:* For master's, thesis (for some programs). *Entrance requirements:* For master's, GRE General Test. Additional exam requirements/recommendations for international students: Required—TOEFL (minimum score 100 iBT). *Application deadline:* For fall admission, 3/15 priority date for domestic students, 3/15 for international students; for spring admission, 11/1 priority date for domestic students, 11/1 for international students. Applications are processed on a rolling basis. Application fee: $75. Electronic applications accepted. *Expenses: Tuition:* Part-time $1206 per credit. *Financial support:* Fellowships with full tuition reimbursements, research assistantships with full and partial tuition reimbursements, teaching assistantships with full and partial tuition reimbursements, and tuition waivers (partial) available. Financial award application deadline: 1/1; financial award applicants required to submit FAFSA. *Unit head:* Dr. Kay Bruening, Program Director, 315-443-9326, Fax: 315-443-2562, E-mail: inquire@hshp.syr.edu. *Application contact:* Kathy Pitts, Information Contact, 315-443-5555, E-mail: inquire@hshp.syr.edu. Web site: http://falk.syr.edu/NutritionScienceDietetics/Default.aspx.

Teachers College, Columbia University, Graduate Faculty of Education, Department of Health and Behavior Studies, Program in Nutrition and Education, New York, NY 10027. Offers nutrition education (Ed M, MS, Ed D); nutrition education and public health nutrition (Ed M, MS, Ed D), including community nutrition education (Ed M), nutrition and public health (MS, Ed D), nutrition education (MS, Ed D). Part-time and evening/weekend programs available. *Faculty:* 4 full-time (all women), 9 part-time/adjunct (7 women). *Students:* 41 full-time (40 women), 103 part-time (97 women); includes 34 minority (9 Black or African American, non-Hispanic/Latino; 1 American Indian or Alaska Native, non-Hispanic/Latino; 15 Asian, non-Hispanic/Latino; 6 Hispanic/Latino; 3 Two or more races, non-Hispanic/Latino), 13 international. Average age 29. 88 applicants, 74% accepted, 35 enrolled. In 2011, 38 master's, 3 doctorates awarded. Terminal master's awarded for partial completion of doctoral program. *Degree requirements:* For master's, thesis optional, integrative project; for doctorate, thesis/dissertation. *Entrance requirements:* For master's, GRE General Test; for doctorate, GRE General Test, sample of written work. *Application deadline:* For fall admission, 1/15 for domestic students; for spring admission, 11/1 for domestic students. Applications are processed on a rolling basis. Application fee: $65. Electronic applications accepted. *Financial support:* Fellowships, research assistantships, career-related internships or fieldwork, Federal Work-Study, institutionally sponsored loans, and tuition waivers (full and partial) available. Support available to part-time students. Financial award application deadline: 2/1; financial award applicants required to submit FAFSA. *Faculty research:* Psychosocial determinants of eating behavior, food supply and environmental education, development and evaluation of nutrition education. *Unit head:* Prof. Isobel R. Contento, Program Coordinator, 212-678-3950, E-mail: nutrition-tc@columbia.edu. *Application contact:* Peter Shon, Assistant Director of Admission, 212-678-3305, Fax: 212-678-4171, E-mail: shon@exchange.tc.columbia.edu. Web site: http://www.tc.columbia.edu/hbs/Nutrition.

Teachers College, Columbia University, Graduate Faculty of Education, Department of Health and Behavior Studies, Program in Nutrition and Public Health, New York, NY 10027-6696. Offers MS, Ed D. *Unit head:* Prof. Isobel R. Contento, Program Coordinator, 212-678-3950. *Application contact:* Elizabeth Puleio, Admissions Contact, 212-678-3710.

Texas A&M University, College of Agriculture and Life Sciences, Department of Nutrition and Food Science, College Station, TX 77843. Offers food science and technology (M Agr); nutrition (MS, PhD). *Faculty:* 15. *Students:* 56 full-time (40 women), 5 part-time (2 women); includes 8 minority (2 Black or African American, non-Hispanic/Latino; 3 Asian, non-Hispanic/Latino; 3 Hispanic/Latino), 25 international. *Degree requirements:* For master's, thesis; for doctorate, thesis/dissertation. *Entrance requirements:* For master's and doctorate, GRE General Test. Additional exam requirements/recommendations for international students: Required—TOEFL. *Application deadline:* For fall admission, 2/1 priority date for domestic students; for spring admission, 10/1 priority date for domestic students. Applications are processed on a rolling basis. Application fee: $50 ($75 for international students). *Expenses:* Tuition, state resident: full-time $5437; part-time $226.55 per credit hour. Tuition, nonresident: full-time $12,949; part-time $539.55 per credit hour. *Required fees:* $2741. *Financial support:* Fellowships, research assistantships, teaching assistantships, career-related internships or fieldwork, and scholarships/grants available. *Faculty research:* Food safety, microbiology, product development. *Unit head:* Dr. Jimmy T. Keeton, Department Head, 979-458-3428, E-mail: jkeeton@tamu.edu. *Application contact:* Graduate Admissions, 979-845-1044, E-mail: admissions@tamu.edu. Web site: http://nfs.tamu.edu.

Texas State University–San Marcos, Graduate School, College of Applied Arts, Department of Family and Consumer Science, San Marcos, TX 78666. Offers family and child studies (MS); human nutrition (MS). Part-time programs available. *Faculty:* 10 full-time (9 women), 2 part-time/adjunct (both women). *Students:* 50 full-time (48 women), 27 part-time (all women); includes 16 minority (4 Black or African American, non-Hispanic/Latino; 1 American Indian or Alaska Native, non-Hispanic/Latino; 3 Asian, non-Hispanic/Latino; 7 Hispanic/Latino; 1 Two or more races, non-Hispanic/Latino), 3 international. Average age 27. 68 applicants, 56% accepted, 24 enrolled. In 2011, 20 master's awarded. *Degree requirements:* For master's, comprehensive exam, thesis (for some programs). *Entrance requirements:* For master's, GRE General Test (preferred), minimum GPA of 3.0 in last 60 hours of course work. Additional exam requirements/recommendations for international students: Required—TOEFL (minimum score 550 paper-based; 213 computer-based; 78 iBT). *Application deadline:* For fall admission, 6/15 priority date for domestic students, 6/1 for international students; for spring admission, 10/15 priority date for domestic students, 10/1 for international students. Applications are processed on a rolling basis. Application fee: $40 ($90 for international students). Electronic applications accepted. *Expenses:* Tuition, state resident: full-time $6408; part-time $3204 per semester. Tuition, nonresident: full-time $14,832; part-time $7416 per semester. *Required fees:* $1824; $912 per semester. Tuition and fees vary according to course load. *Financial support:* In 2011–12, 38 students received support, including 7 research assistantships (averaging $10,090 per year), 20 teaching assistantships (averaging $8,728 per year). Financial award application deadline: 4/1. *Faculty research:* Healthy marriages, best food fits, hair fiber products, retinol and cancer met, light/color assessment, interactive VIT A, testing of ALKA-V6, dietary herbs. *Total annual research expenditures:* $836,723. *Unit head:* Dr. Maria E. Canabal, Chair, 512-245-2155, Fax: 512-245-3829, E-mail: mc57@txstate.edu. *Application contact:* Dr. Elizabeth Russell, Graduate Adviser, 512-245-2155, Fax: 512-245-3829, E-mail: er15@txstate.edu. Web site: http://www.fcs.txstate.edu/.

Texas Tech University, Graduate School, College of Human Sciences, Department of Nutrition, Hospitality, and Retailing, Program in Nutritional Sciences, Lubbock, TX 79409. Offers MS, PhD. Part-time programs available. *Students:* 42 full-time (40 women), 15 part-time (all women); includes 4 minority (1 Black or African American, non-Hispanic/Latino; 1 Asian, non-Hispanic/Latino; 2 Hispanic/Latino), 19 international. Average age 26. 41 applicants, 68% accepted, 20 enrolled. In 2011, 18 master's, 1 doctorate awarded. *Degree requirements:* For master's, thesis or alternative; for doctorate, thesis/dissertation. *Entrance requirements:* For master's and doctorate, GRE General Test. Additional exam requirements/recommendations for international students: Required—TOEFL (minimum score 550 paper-based; 213 computer-based; 79 iBT). *Application deadline:* For fall admission, 6/1 priority date for domestic students, 1/15 for international students; for spring admission, 9/1 priority date for domestic students, 6/15 for international students. Applications are processed on a rolling basis. Application fee: $50 ($75 for international students). Electronic applications accepted. *Expenses:* Tuition, state resident: full-time $5899; part-time $245.80 per credit hour.

Tuition, nonresident: full-time $13,411; part-time $558.80 per credit hour. *Required fees:* $2680.60; $86.50 per credit hour. $920.30 per semester. *Financial support:* Application deadline: 4/15; applicants required to submit FAFSA. *Faculty research:* Obesity prevention, fat metabolism, nutrition education for underserved populations, nanonutrition and chronic diseases, health effects of selenium. *Unit head:* Dr. Debra Reed, Graduate Advisor, 806-742-3068 Ext. 251, Fax: 806-742-3042, E-mail: debra.reed@ttu.edu. *Application contact:* Dr. Debra Reed, Graduate Advisor, 806-742-3068 Ext. 251, Fax: 806-742-3042, E-mail: debra.reed@ttu.edu. Web site: http://www.depts.ttu.edu/hs/nhr/ns.

Texas Woman's University, Graduate School, College of Health Sciences, Department of Nutrition and Food Sciences, Denton, TX 76201. Offers exercise and sports nutrition (MS); food science (MS); food systems administration (MS); nutrition (MS, PhD). Part-time and evening/weekend programs available. *Faculty:* 14 full-time (7 women). *Students:* 94 full-time (88 women), 79 part-time (73 women); includes 42 minority (10 Black or African American, non-Hispanic/Latino; 15 Asian, non-Hispanic/Latino; 17 Hispanic/Latino), 13 international. Average age 28. 103 applicants, 85% accepted, 51 enrolled. In 2011, 58 master's, 2 doctorates awarded. *Degree requirements:* For master's, comprehensive exam, thesis or alternative; for doctorate, comprehensive exam, thesis/dissertation, qualifying exam. *Entrance requirements:* For master's, GRE General Test (preferred minimum score 143 [350 old version] Verbal, 141 [450 old version] Quantitative), minimum GPA of 3.25, resume; for doctorate, GRE General Test (preferred minimum score 150 [450 old version] Verbal, 141 [550 old version] Quantitative), minimum GPA of 3.5 on last 60 undergraduate hours and graduate course work, 2 letters of reference, resume. Additional exam requirements/recommendations for international students: Required—TOEFL (minimum score 550 paper-based; 213 computer-based; 79 iBT). *Application deadline:* For fall admission, 7/1 priority date for domestic students, 3/1 for international students; for spring admission, 12/1 priority date for domestic students, 7/1 for international students. Applications are processed on a rolling basis. Application fee: $50 ($75 for international students). Electronic applications accepted. *Expenses:* Tuition, state resident: full-time $3834; part-time $213 per credit hour. Tuition, nonresident: full-time $9468; part-time $526 per credit hour. *Required fees:* $213 per credit hour. Tuition and fees vary according to course load. *Financial support:* In 2011–12, 138 students received support, including 23 research assistantships (averaging $12,942 per year), teaching assistantships (averaging $12,942 per year); career-related internships or fieldwork, Federal Work-Study, institutionally sponsored loans, scholarships/grants, traineeships, health care benefits, and unspecified assistantships also available. Support available to part-time students. Financial award application deadline: 3/1; financial award applicants required to submit FAFSA. *Faculty research:* Bioactive food components and cancer, nutraceuticals and functional foods in diabetes, obesity and bone health, food safety, dietary modulation of dyslipidemia, childhood obesity prevention. *Total annual research expenditures:* $612,544. *Unit head:* Dr. Chandan Prasad, Chair, 940-898-2636, Fax: 940-898-2634, E-mail: cprasad@twu.edu. *Application contact:* Dr. Samuel Wheeler, Assistant Director of Admissions, 940-898-3188, Fax: 940-898-3081, E-mail: wheelersr@twu.edu. Web site: http://www.twu.edu/nutrition-food-sciences/.

Tufts University, The Gerald J. and Dorothy R. Friedman School of Nutrition Science and Policy, Medford, MA 02155. Offers humanitarian assistance (MAHA); nutrition (MS, PhD). Part-time programs available. *Degree requirements:* For doctorate, comprehensive exam, thesis/dissertation. *Entrance requirements:* For master's and doctorate, GRE General Test. Additional exam requirements/recommendations for international students: Required—TOEFL. Electronic applications accepted. *Expenses:* Contact institution. *Faculty research:* Nutritional biochemistry and metabolism, cell and molecular biochemistry, epidemiology, policy/planning, applied nutrition.

Tulane University, School of Public Health and Tropical Medicine, Department of Community Health Sciences, Program in Nutrition, New Orleans, LA 70118-5669. Offers MPH. *Degree requirements:* For master's, comprehensive exam. *Entrance requirements:* For master's, GRE General Test. Additional exam requirements/recommendations for international students: Required—TOEFL.

Tuskegee University, Graduate Programs, College of Agricultural, Environmental and Natural Sciences, Department of Food and Nutritional Sciences, Tuskegee, AL 36088. Offers MS. *Faculty:* 4 full-time (3 women). *Students:* 8 full-time (7 women); includes 6 minority (all Black or African American, non-Hispanic/Latino), 2 international. Average age 28. In 2011, 7 master's awarded. *Degree requirements:* For master's, thesis. *Entrance requirements:* For master's, GRE General Test. Additional exam requirements/recommendations for international students: Required—TOEFL (minimum score 500 paper-based; 69 computer-based). *Application deadline:* For fall admission, 7/15 for domestic students. Applications are processed on a rolling basis. Application fee: $25 ($35 for international students). *Expenses: Tuition:* Full-time $17,070; part-time $705 per credit hour. *Financial support:* Application deadline: 4/15. *Unit head:* Dr. Ralphenia Pace, Head, 334-727-8162. *Application contact:* Dr. Robert L. Laney, Jr., Vice President/Director of Admissions and Enrollment Management, 334-727-8580, Fax: 334-727-5750, E-mail: planey@tuskegee.edu.

Université de Moncton, School of Food Science, Nutrition and Family Studies, Moncton, NB E1A 3E9, Canada. Offers foods/nutrition (M Sc). Part-time programs available. *Degree requirements:* For master's, one foreign language, thesis. *Entrance requirements:* For master's, previous course work in statistics. Electronic applications accepted. *Faculty research:* Clinic nutrition (anemia, elderly, osteoporosis), applied nutrition, metabolic activities of lactic bacteria, solubility of low density lipoproteins, bile acids.

Université de Montréal, Faculty of Medicine, Department of Nutrition, Montréal, QC H3C 3J7, Canada. Offers M Sc, PhD, DESS. Terminal master's awarded for partial completion of doctoral program. *Degree requirements:* For master's, thesis; for doctorate, thesis/dissertation, general exam. *Entrance requirements:* For master's, MD, B Sc in nutrition or equivalent, proficiency in French; for doctorate, M Sc in nutrition or equivalent, proficiency in French. Electronic applications accepted. *Faculty research:* Nutritional aspects of diabetes, obesity, anorexia nervosa, lipid metabolism, hepatic function.

Université Laval, Faculty of Agricultural and Food Sciences, Department of Food Sciences and Nutrition, Programs in Nutrition, Québec, QC G1K 7P4, Canada. Offers M Sc, PhD. Terminal master's awarded for partial completion of doctoral program. *Degree requirements:* For master's, thesis; for doctorate, comprehensive exam, thesis/dissertation. *Entrance requirements:* For master's and doctorate, knowledge of French and English. Electronic applications accepted.

University at Buffalo, the State University of New York, Graduate School, School of Public Health and Health Professions, Department of Exercise and Nutrition Sciences, Buffalo, NY 14260. Offers exercise science (MS, PhD); nutrition (MS, Advanced Certificate). Part-time programs available. *Faculty:* 11 full-time (2 women). *Students:* 87 full-time (54 women), 1 part-time (0 women); includes 11 minority (1 Black or African American, non-Hispanic/Latino; 1 American Indian or Alaska Native, non-Hispanic/Latino; 9 Asian, non-Hispanic/Latino), 22 international. Average age 24. 131 applicants, 48% accepted, 37 enrolled. In 2011, 28 master's, 3 doctorates, 13 other advanced degrees awarded. *Degree requirements:* For master's, comprehensive exam or thesis; for doctorate, comprehensive exam, thesis/dissertation. *Entrance requirements:* For master's, GRE General Test (exercise science and nutrition), minimum GPA of 3.0; for doctorate, GRE General Test, minimum GPA of 3.0 (PhD). Additional exam requirements/recommendations for international students: Required—TOEFL (minimum score 550 paper-based; 213 computer-based; 79 iBT), IELTS (minimum score 6.5). *Application deadline:* For fall admission, 4/1 for domestic students, 2/1 for international students; for spring admission, 8/15 for international students. Applications are processed on a rolling basis. Application fee: $50. Electronic applications accepted. *Financial support:* In 2011–12, 10 students received support, including 1 research assistantship with tuition reimbursement available (averaging $18,000 per year), 9 teaching assistantships with full and partial tuition reimbursements available (averaging $11,000 per year); career-related internships or fieldwork, Federal Work-Study, institutionally sponsored loans, scholarships/grants, health care benefits, tuition waivers (full and partial), unspecified assistantships, and stipends also available. Financial award application deadline: 3/15; financial award applicants required to submit FAFSA. *Faculty research:* Cardiovascular disease-diet and exercise, respiratory control and muscle function, plasticity of connective and neural tissue, exercise nutrition, diet and cancer. *Unit head:* Dr. David Pendergast, Chair, 716-829-6795, Fax: 716-829-2979, E-mail: dpenderg@buffalo.edu. *Application contact:* Dr. Gaspar Farkas, Director of Graduate Studies, 716-829-6756, Fax: 716-829-2428, E-mail: farkas@buffalo.edu. Web site: http://phhp.buffalo.edu/ens/.

The University of Akron, Graduate School, College of Health Sciences and Human Services, School of Family and Consumer Sciences, Program in Nutrition and Dietetics, Akron, OH 44325. Offers MS. *Students:* 3 full-time (2 women), 2 part-time (1 woman). Average age 27. 9 applicants, 11% accepted, 1 enrolled. In 2011, 1 master's awarded. *Degree requirements:* For master's, comprehensive exam, thesis or project. *Entrance requirements:* For master's, GRE, minimum GPA of 2.75, three letters of recommendation, statement of purpose, resume. Additional exam requirements/recommendations for international students: Required—TOEFL (minimum score 550 paper-based; 213 computer-based; 79 iBT). *Application deadline:* For fall admission, 3/1 for domestic and international students; for spring admission, 10/1 for domestic and international students. Application fee: $30 ($40 for international students). Electronic applications accepted. *Expenses:* Tuition, state resident: full-time $7038; part-time $391 per credit hour. Tuition, nonresident: full-time $12,051; part-time $670 per credit hour. *Required fees:* $1274; $34 per credit hour. *Unit head:* Dr. Deborah Marino, Associate Professor, 330-972-6322, E-mail: debora7@uakron.edu. *Application contact:* Dr. Pamela Schulze, Graduate Director, 330-972-7725, E-mail: schulze@uakron.edu.

The University of Alabama, Graduate School, College of Human Environmental Sciences, Department of Human Nutrition and Hospitality Management, Tuscaloosa, AL 35487. Offers MSHES. Part-time programs available. Postbaccalaureate distance learning degree programs offered (no on-campus study). *Faculty:* 7 full-time (5 women). *Students:* 11 full-time (9 women), 77 part-time (all women); includes 12 minority (7 Black or African American, non-Hispanic/Latino; 2 Asian, non-Hispanic/Latino; 3 Hispanic/Latino). Average age 30. 54 applicants, 59% accepted, 25 enrolled. In 2011, 34 degrees awarded. *Degree requirements:* For master's, comprehensive exam, thesis optional. *Entrance requirements:* For master's, minimum GPA of 3.0. Additional exam requirements/recommendations for international students: Required—TOEFL. *Application deadline:* For fall admission, 7/6 for domestic students. Applications are processed on a rolling basis. Application fee: $50 ($60 for international students). Electronic applications accepted. *Expenses:* Tuition, state resident: full-time $8600. Tuition, nonresident: full-time $21,900. *Financial support:* In 2011–12, 4 students received support, including 2 research assistantships (averaging $8,100 per year), 4 teaching assistantships (averaging $8,100 per year); career-related internships or fieldwork also available. Financial award application deadline: 3/15. *Faculty research:* Maternal and child nutrition, childhood obesity, community nutrition interventions, geriatric nutrition, family eating patterns, food chemistry, phytochemicals, dietary antioxidants. *Total annual research expenditures:* $60,305. *Unit head:* Dr. Mary K. Meyer, Chair/Professor, 205-348-6150, Fax: 205-348-3789, E-mail: mkmeyer@ches.ua.edu. *Application contact:* Patrick D. Fuller, Admissions Officer, 205-348-5923, Fax: 205-348-0400, E-mail: patrick.d.fuller@ua.edu. Web site: http://www.ches.ua.edu/.

The University of Alabama at Birmingham, School of Health Professions, Program in Nutrition Sciences, Birmingham, AL 35294. Offers PhD. *Degree requirements:* For doctorate, thesis/dissertation. *Entrance requirements:* For doctorate, GRE General Test. *Expenses:* Tuition, state resident: full-time $5922; part-time $309 per hour. Tuition, nonresident: full-time $13,428; part-time $726 per hour. Tuition and fees vary according to program. *Financial support:* Fellowships with tuition reimbursements, research assistantships with tuition reimbursements, and career-related internships or fieldwork available. *Faculty research:* Energy metabolism, obesity, body composition, cancer prevention, bone metabolism. *Unit head:* Dr. Timothy R. Garvey, Interim Chair, 205-934-6103. *Application contact:* Julie Bryant, Director of Graduate Admissions, 205-934-8227, Fax: 205-934-8413, E-mail: jbryant@uab.edu.

University of Alaska Fairbanks, School of Fisheries and Ocean Sciences, Fairbanks, AK 99775-7220. Offers fisheries (MS, PhD); marine sciences and limnology (MS, PhD), including marine biology, oceanography (PhD); seafood science and nutrition (MS, PhD). Part-time programs available. *Faculty:* 61 full-time (24 women), 5 part-time/adjunct (3 women). *Students:* 94 full-time (55 women), 52 part-time (28 women); includes 15 minority (1 American Indian or Alaska Native, non-Hispanic/Latino; 4 Asian, non-Hispanic/Latino; 8 Hispanic/Latino; 2 Two or more races, non-Hispanic/Latino), 10 international. Average age 30. 105 applicants, 27% accepted, 27 enrolled. In 2011, 11 master's, 7 doctorates awarded. Terminal master's awarded for partial completion of doctoral program. *Degree requirements:* For master's, comprehensive exam, thesis or alternative; for doctorate, comprehensive exam, thesis/dissertation, oral defense. *Entrance requirements:* For master's and doctorate, GRE General Test. Additional exam requirements/recommendations for international students: Required—TOEFL (minimum score 550 paper-based; 213 computer-based; 80 iBT). *Application deadline:* For fall admission, 6/1 for domestic students, 3/1 for international students; for spring admission, 10/15 for domestic students, 9/1 for international students. Applications are processed on a rolling basis. Application fee: $60. Electronic applications accepted. *Expenses:* Tuition, state resident: full-time $6696; part-time $372 per credit. Tuition, nonresident: full-time $13,680; part-time $760 per credit. Tuition and fees vary according to course load and reciprocity agreements. *Financial support:* In 2011–12, 58 research assistantships with tuition reimbursements (averaging $11,946 per year), 13 teaching assistantships with tuition reimbursements (averaging $11,840 per year) were awarded; fellowships with tuition reimbursements, career-related internships or fieldwork, Federal Work-Study, scholarships/grants, health care benefits, and unspecified assistantships also available. Support available to part-time students. Financial award application deadline: 2/15; financial award applicants required to submit FAFSA. *Faculty research:* Marine mammals, hydrology, sea ice, harmful algal blooms, polar ecology. *Total annual research expenditures:* $18 million. *Unit head:* Michael Castellini, Dean, 907-474-7824, Fax: 907-474-7204, E-mail: info@sfos.uaf.edu. *Application contact:* Christina Neumann, Academic Manager, 907-474-7289, Fax: 907-474-5863, E-mail: clneumann@alaska.edu. Web site: http://www.sfos.uaf.edu/.

The University of Arizona, College of Agriculture and Life Sciences, Department of Nutritional Sciences, Tucson, AZ 85721. Offers MS, PhD. *Faculty:* 8 full-time (4 women), 1 (woman) part-time/adjunct. *Students:* 17 full-time (14 women), 2 part-time (both women); includes 3 minority (2 Hispanic/Latino; 1 Two or more races, non-Hispanic/ Latino), 2 international. Average age 29. 26 applicants, 23% accepted, 5 enrolled. In 2011, 3 master's, 3 doctorates awarded. *Entrance requirements:* For master's, GRE, minimum GPA of 3.0, 2 letters of recommendation; for doctorate, GRE, minimum GPA of 3.0, 2 letters of recommendation, statement of purpose. Additional exam requirements/ recommendations for international students: Required—TOEFL. *Application deadline:* Applications are processed on a rolling basis. Application fee: $75. Electronic applications accepted. *Expenses:* Tuition, state resident: full-time $10,840. Tuition, nonresident: full-time $25,802. *Financial support:* In 2011–12, 5 research assistantships with full and partial tuition reimbursements (averaging $22,500 per year), 6 teaching assistantships with full and partial tuition reimbursements (averaging $20,010 per year) were awarded; fellowships, scholarships/grants, health care benefits, tuition waivers (full and partial), and unspecified assistantships also available. *Faculty research:* Bioactive compounds, nutrients and lifestyle: relationships to cancer; metabolic and behavior factors Influencing body composition; diabetes, obesity, musculoskeletal and cardiovascular diseases. *Total annual research expenditures:* $7.7 million. *Unit head:* Dr. Joy Winzerling, Head, 520-621-3096, E-mail: jwinzerl@ag.arizona.edu. *Application contact:* Nancy Driscoll, Information Contact, 520-626-0970, Fax: 520-621-9446, E-mail: nancya@email.arizona.edu.

University of Arkansas for Medical Sciences, Graduate School, Program in Clinical Nutrition, Little Rock, AR 72205-7199. Offers MS. Part-time programs available. *Degree requirements:* For master's, thesis. *Entrance requirements:* For master's, GRE. Additional exam requirements/recommendations for international students: Required—TOEFL. *Faculty research:* Geriatric nutrition, pediatric nutrition, nutrition and health promotion wellness emphasis, community nutrition.

University of Bridgeport, Nutrition Institute, Bridgeport, CT 06604. Offers human nutrition (MS). Part-time and evening/weekend programs available. Postbaccalaureate distance learning degree programs offered (no on-campus study). *Faculty:* 2 full-time (0 women), 12 part-time/adjunct (6 women). *Students:* 4 full-time (all women), 238 part-time (189 women); includes 53 minority (15 Black or African American, non-Hispanic/ Latino; 12 Asian, non-Hispanic/Latino; 14 Hispanic/Latino; 12 Two or more races, non-Hispanic/Latino), 5 international. Average age 37. 281 applicants, 56% accepted, 39 enrolled. In 2011, 88 master's awarded. *Degree requirements:* For master's, thesis, research project. *Entrance requirements:* For master's, previous course work in anatomy, biochemistry, organic chemistry, or physiology. Additional exam requirements/ recommendations for international students: Recommended—TOEFL (minimum score 550 paper-based; 213 computer-based; 80 iBT), IELTS (minimum score 6.5). *Application deadline:* For fall admission, 8/1 priority date for domestic students, 8/1 for international students; for spring admission, 12/1 priority date for domestic students, 12/ 1 for international students. Applications are processed on a rolling basis. Application fee: $50. Electronic applications accepted. *Expenses:* Contact institution. *Financial support:* In 2011–12, 33 students received support. Available to part-time students. Application deadline: 6/1; applicants required to submit FAFSA. *Unit head:* Dr. David M. Brady, Director, 203-576-4667, Fax: 203-576-4591, E-mail: dbrady@bridgeport.edu. *Application contact:* Leanne Proctor, Director of Health Science Admission, 203-576-4352, Fax: 203-576-4941, E-mail: nutrition@bridgeport.edu.

The University of British Columbia, Faculty of Land and Food Systems, Human Nutrition Program, Vancouver, BC V6T 1Z1, Canada. Offers M Sc, PhD. Part-time programs available. Terminal master's awarded for partial completion of doctoral program. *Degree requirements:* For master's, thesis; for doctorate, comprehensive exam, thesis/dissertation. *Entrance requirements:* Additional exam requirements/ recommendations for international students: Required—TOEFL (minimum score 577 paper-based; 233 computer-based; 90 iBT), IELTS (minimum score 6.5). Electronic applications accepted. *Faculty research:* Basic nutrition, clinical nutrition, community nutrition, women's health, pediatric nutrition.

University of California, Berkeley, Graduate Division, College of Natural Resources, Group in Molecular and Biochemical Nutrition, Berkeley, CA 94720-1500. Offers PhD. *Degree requirements:* For doctorate, thesis/dissertation, qualifying exam. *Entrance requirements:* For doctorate, GRE General Test, minimum GPA of 3.0, 3 letters of recommendation. Additional exam requirements/recommendations for international students: Required—TOEFL. Electronic applications accepted. *Faculty research:* Regulation of metabolism; nutritional genomics and nutrient-gene interactions; transport, metabolism and function of minerals; carcinogenesis and dietary anti-carcinogens.

University of California, Davis, Graduate Studies, Graduate Group in Nutritional Biology, Davis, CA 95616. Offers MS, PhD. *Degree requirements:* For master's, thesis; for doctorate, thesis/dissertation. *Entrance requirements:* For master's and doctorate, GRE General Test, minimum GPA of 3.0. Additional exam requirements/ recommendations for international students: Required—TOEFL (minimum score 550 paper-based; 213 computer-based). Electronic applications accepted. *Faculty research:* Human/animal nutrition.

University of California, Davis, Graduate Studies, Program in Maternal and Child Nutrition, Davis, CA 95616. Offers MAS. *Degree requirements:* For master's, comprehensive exam. *Entrance requirements:* Additional exam requirements/ recommendations for international students: Required—TOEFL (minimum score 550 paper-based; 213 computer-based).

University of Central Oklahoma, College of Graduate Studies and Research, College of Education and Professional Studies, Department of Human Environmental Sciences, Edmond, OK 73034-5209. Offers family and child studies (MS); family and consumer science education (MS); interior design (MS); nutrition-food management (MS). Part-time programs available. *Faculty:* 8 full-time (7 women), 8 part time/adjunct (6 women). *Students:* 52 full-time (49 women), 75 part-time (71 women); includes 40 minority (32 Black or African American, non-Hispanic/Latino; 5 Hispanic/Latino; 3 Two or more races, non-Hispanic/Latino), 6 international. Average age 30. In 2011, 45 master's awarded. *Entrance requirements:* Additional exam requirements/recommendations for international students: Required—TOEFL (minimum score 550 paper-based; 213 computer-based). *Application deadline:* Applications are processed on a rolling basis. Application fee: $50. Electronic applications accepted. *Expenses:* Tuition, state resident: full-time $3901; part-time $218.30 per credit hour. Tuition, nonresident: full-time $9198; part-time $511.20 per credit hour. Tuition and fees vary according to program. *Financial support:* Career-related internships or fieldwork and unspecified assistantships available. Financial award application deadline: 3/31; financial award applicants required to submit FAFSA. *Faculty research:* Dietetics and food science. *Unit head:* Dr. Kaye Sears, Chairperson, 405-974-5786, E-mail: ksears@uco.edu. *Application contact:* Dr. Richard Bernard, Dean, Graduate College, 405-974-3493, Fax: 405-974-3852, E-mail: gradcoll@uco.edu.

University of Chicago, Division of Biological Sciences, Biomedical Sciences Cluster: Cancer Biology, Immunology, Molecular Metabolism and Nutrition, Pathology, and Microbiology, Committee on Molecular Metabolism and Nutrition, Chicago, IL 60637-1513. Offers PhD. *Degree requirements:* For doctorate, thesis/dissertation, ethics class, 2 teaching assistantships. *Entrance requirements:* For doctorate, GRE General Test. Additional exam requirements/recommendations for international students: Required—TOEFL (minimum score 600 paper-based; 250 computer-based; 104 iBT), IELTS (minimum score 7). Electronic applications accepted. *Faculty research:* Regulation of lipoprotein metabolism, cellular vitamin metabolism, obesity and body composition, adipocyte differentiation.

University of Cincinnati, Graduate School, College of Allied Health Sciences, Department of Nutritional Sciences, Cincinnati, OH 45221. Offers MS. Part-time programs available. *Degree requirements:* For master's, thesis. *Entrance requirements:* For master's, GRE General Test. Additional exam requirements/recommendations for international students: Required—TOEFL (minimum score 550 paper-based; 230 computer-based). Electronic applications accepted. *Faculty research:* Phytochemicals-osteoarthritis, pediatric hypertension and hypercholesterol, cancer prevention/Type II diabetes.

University of Colorado at Colorado Springs, College of Letters, Arts and Sciences, Master of Sciences Program, Colorado Springs, CO 80933-7150. Offers applied science - bioscience (M Sc); applied science - physics (M Sc); biology (M Sc); chemistry (M Sc); health promotion (M Sc); mathematics (M Sc); physics (M Sc); sports medicine (M Sc); sports nutrition (M Sc). Part-time programs available. *Students:* 13 full-time (5 women), 11 part-time (6 women); includes 3 minority (2 Asian, non-Hispanic/Latino; 1 Hispanic/ Latino). Average age 33. 15 applicants, 53% accepted, 3 enrolled. In 2011, 39 degrees awarded. *Degree requirements:* For master's, thesis or alternative. *Entrance requirements:* For master's, minimum GPA of 2.75. Additional exam requirements/ recommendations for international students: Recommended—TOEFL. *Application deadline:* For fall admission, 6/1 priority date for domestic students; for spring admission, 12/1 for domestic students. Application fee: $60 ($75 for international students). *Expenses:* Contact institution. *Financial support:* In 2011–12, 5 students received support. Fellowships, research assistantships, teaching assistantships, career-related internships or fieldwork, Federal Work-Study, and scholarships/grants available. Support available to part-time students. Financial award application deadline: 3/1; financial award applicants required to submit FAFSA. *Faculty research:* Biomechanics and physiology of elite athletic training, genetic engineering in yeast and bacteria including phage display and DNA repair, immunology and cell biology, synthetic organic chemistry. *Unit head:* Dr. Tom Christensen, Dean, 719-255-4550, Fax: 719-255-4200, E-mail: tchriste@uccs.edu. *Application contact:* Taryn Bailey, Information Contact, 719-255-3702, Fax: 719-255-3037, E-mail: gradinfo@uccs.edu.

University of Connecticut, Graduate School, College of Agriculture and Natural Resources, Department of Nutritional Sciences, Storrs, CT 06269. Offers MS, PhD. Terminal master's awarded for partial completion of doctoral program. *Degree requirements:* For master's, comprehensive exam, thesis; for doctorate, thesis/ dissertation. *Entrance requirements:* For master's and doctorate, GRE General Test. Additional exam requirements/recommendations for international students: Required—TOEFL (minimum score 550 paper-based; 213 computer-based). Electronic applications accepted.

University of Delaware, College of Health Sciences, Department of Behavioral Health and Nutrition, Newark, DE 19716. Offers health promotion (MS); human nutrition (MS). Part-time programs available. *Degree requirements:* For master's, thesis. *Entrance requirements:* For master's, GRE General Test, interview, minimum GPA of 3.0. Additional exam requirements/recommendations for international students: Required—TOEFL (minimum score 550 paper-based; 213 computer-based). Electronic applications accepted. *Faculty research:* Sport biomechanics, rehabilitation biomechanics, vascular dynamics.

University of Georgia, College of Family and Consumer Sciences, Department of Foods and Nutrition, Athens, GA 30602. Offers MFCS, MS, PhD. *Faculty:* 14 full-time (10 women). *Students:* 29 full-time (26 women), 22 part-time (18 women); includes 7 minority (6 Black or African American, non-Hispanic/Latino; 1 Asian, non-Hispanic/ Latino), 2 international. Average age 32. 74 applicants, 47% accepted, 15 enrolled. In 2011, 11 master's, 3 doctorates awarded. *Degree requirements:* For master's, thesis (MS); for doctorate, thesis/dissertation. *Entrance requirements:* For master's, GRE General Test, minimum GPA of 3.0, course work in biochemistry and physiology; for doctorate, GRE General Test, master's degree, minimum GPA of 3.0. *Application deadline:* For fall admission, 7/1 priority date for domestic students; for spring admission, 11/15 for domestic students. Application fee: $50. Electronic applications accepted. *Financial support:* Fellowships, research assistantships, teaching assistantships, and unspecified assistantships available. *Unit head:* Dr. Rebecca Lynn Bailey, Head, 706-542-4875, Fax: 706-542-5059, E-mail: rlb@uga.edu. *Application contact:* Dr. Mary Ann Johnson, Graduate Coordinator, 706-542-2292, E-mail: mjohnson@fcs.uga.edu. Web site: http://www.fcs.uga.edu/fdn/.

University of Guelph, Graduate Studies, College of Biological Science, Department of Human Health and Nutritional Sciences, Guelph, ON N1G 2W1, Canada. Offers nutritional sciences (M Sc, PhD). Part-time programs available. *Degree requirements:* For master's, thesis (for some programs); for doctorate, comprehensive exam, thesis/ dissertation. *Entrance requirements:* For master's, minimum B-average during previous 2 years of coursework; for doctorate, minimum A-average. Additional exam requirements/recommendations for international students: Required—TOEFL (minimum score 550 paper-based; 213 computer-based). Electronic applications accepted. *Faculty research:* Nutrition and biochemistry, exercise metabolism and physiology, toxicology, gene expression, biomechanics and ergonomics.

University of Guelph, Graduate Studies, College of Social and Applied Human Sciences, Department of Family Relations and Applied Nutrition, Guelph, ON N1G 2W1, Canada. Offers applied nutrition (MAN); family relations and human development (M Sc, PhD), including applied human nutrition, couple and family therapy (M Sc), family relations and human development. *Accreditation:* AAMFT/COAMFTE (one or more programs are accredited). Part-time programs available. *Degree requirements:* For master's, thesis (for some programs); for doctorate, comprehensive exam, thesis/ dissertation. *Entrance requirements:* For master's, minimum B+ average; for doctorate, master's degree in family relations and human development or related field with a minimum B+ average or master's degree in applied human nutrition. Additional exam requirements/recommendations for international students: Required—TOEFL (minimum score 600 paper-based; 250 computer-based). Electronic applications accepted. *Faculty research:* Child and adolescent development, social gerontology, family roles and relations, couple and family therapy, applied human nutrition.

University of Hawaii at Manoa, Graduate Division, College of Tropical Agriculture and Human Resources, Department of Human Nutrition, Food and Animal Sciences, Program in Nutrition, Honolulu, HI 96822. Offers PhD. Part-time programs available. *Degree requirements:* For doctorate, comprehensive exam, thesis/dissertation. *Entrance requirements:* For doctorate, GRE General Test. Additional exam requirements/recommendations for international students: Required—TOEFL (minimum score 580 paper-based; 237 computer-based; 92 iBT), IELTS (minimum score 5).

University of Hawaii at Manoa, Graduate Division, College of Tropical Agriculture and Human Resources, Department of Human Nutrition, Food and Animal Sciences, Program in Nutritional Sciences, Honolulu, HI 96822. Offers MS, PhD. Part-time

programs available. *Degree requirements:* For master's, thesis optional; for doctorate, comprehensive exam, thesis/dissertation. *Entrance requirements:* For master's and doctorate, GRE General Test. Additional exam requirements/recommendations for international students: Required—TOEFL (minimum score 580 paper-based; 237 computer-based; 92 iBT), IELTS (minimum score 5). *Faculty research:* Nutritional biochemistry, human nutrition, nutrition education, international nutrition, nutritional epidemiology.

University of Houston, College of Liberal Arts and Social Sciences, Department of Health and Human Performance, Houston, TX 77204. Offers exercise science (MS); human nutrition (MS); human space exploration sciences (MS); kinesiology (PhD); physical education (M Ed). *Accreditation:* NCATE (one or more programs are accredited). Part-time and evening/weekend programs available. *Degree requirements:* For master's, comprehensive exam (for some programs), thesis (for some programs); for doctorate, comprehensive exam, thesis/dissertation, qualifying exam, candidacy paper. *Entrance requirements:* For master's, GRE (minimum 35th percentile on each section), minimum cumulative GPA of 3.0; for doctorate, GRE (minimum 35th percentile on each section), minimum cumulative GPA of 3.3. Additional exam requirements/ recommendations for international students: Required—TOEFL (minimum score 550 paper-based; 79 iBT). Electronic applications accepted. *Faculty research:* Biomechanics, exercise physiology, obesity, nutrition, space exploration science.

University of Illinois at Chicago, Graduate College, College of Applied Health Sciences, Program in Nutrition, Chicago, IL 60607-7128. Offers MS, PhD. *Accreditation:* AND. *Degree requirements:* For master's, thesis; for doctorate, thesis/dissertation. *Entrance requirements:* For master's and doctorate, GRE General Test, minimum GPA of 2.75. Additional exam requirements/recommendations for international students: Required—TOEFL. Electronic applications accepted. *Faculty research:* Nutrition for the elderly, inborn errors of metabolism, nutrition and cancer, lipid metabolism, dietary fat markers.

University of Illinois at Urbana–Champaign, Graduate College, College of Agricultural, Consumer and Environmental Sciences, Department of Food Science and Human Nutrition, Champaign, IL 61820. Offers food science (MS); food science and human nutrition (MS, PhD), including professional science (MS); human nutrition (MS). Part-time programs available. Postbaccalaureate distance learning degree programs offered (minimal on-campus study). *Faculty:* 25 full-time (11 women), 1 (woman) part-time/adjunct. *Students:* 72 full-time (51 women), 28 part-time (20 women); includes 13 minority (2 Black or African American, non-Hispanic/Latino; 9 Asian, non-Hispanic/ Latino; 1 Hispanic/Latino; 1 Two or more races, non-Hispanic/Latino), 42 international. 175 applicants, 27% accepted, 37 enrolled. In 2011, 30 master's, 3 doctorates awarded. *Entrance requirements:* For master's and doctorate, GRE, minimum GPA of 3.0. Additional exam requirements/recommendations for international students: Required—TOEFL (minimum score 550 paper-based; 213 computer-based; 79 iBT) or IELTS (minimum score 6.5). *Application deadline:* Applications are processed on a rolling basis. Application fee: $75 ($90 for international students). Electronic applications accepted. *Financial support:* In 2011–12, 14 fellowships, 44 research assistantships, 16 teaching assistantships were awarded; tuition waivers (full and partial) also available. *Unit head:* Faye L. Dong, Head, 217-244-4498, Fax: 217-265-0925, E-mail: fayedong@ illinois.edu. *Application contact:* Terri Cummings, Director of Student Services, 217-244-4405, Fax: 217-265-0925, E-mail: tcumming@illinois.edu. Web site: http:// fshn.illinois.edu/.

University of Illinois at Urbana–Champaign, Graduate College, College of Agricultural, Consumer and Environmental Sciences, Division of Nutritional Sciences, Champaign, IL 61820. Offers MS, PhD. *Students:* 48 full-time (33 women), 3 part-time (all women); includes 11 minority (2 Black or African American, non-Hispanic/Latino; 7 Asian, non-Hispanic/Latino; 2 Hispanic/Latino), 9 international. 67 applicants, 10% accepted, 5 enrolled. In 2011, 6 master's, 8 doctorates awarded. *Entrance requirements:* For master's and doctorate, GRE, minimum GPA of 3.0. Additional exam requirements/recommendations for international students: Required—TOEFL (minimum score 560 paper-based; 220 computer-based; 83 iBT) or IELTS (minimum score 6.5). *Application deadline:* Applications are processed on a rolling basis. Application fee: $75 ($90 for international students). Electronic applications accepted. *Financial support:* In 2011–12, 14 fellowships, 31 research assistantships, 13 teaching assistantships were awarded; tuition waivers (full and partial) also available. *Unit head:* Rodney W. Johnson, Director, 217-333-2118, Fax: 217-333-9368, E-mail: rwjohn@illinois.edu. *Application contact:* Jessica L. Hartke, Program Coordinator, 217-333-4177, Fax: 217-333-9368, E-mail: jessh@illinois.edu. Web site: http://www.nutrsci.illinois.edu/.

The University of Kansas, University of Kansas Medical Center, School of Health Professions, Department of Dietetics and Nutrition, Lawrence, KS 66045. Offers dietetic internship (Certificate); dietetics and nutrition (MS); medical nutrition science (PhD). Part-time programs available. Postbaccalaureate distance learning degree programs offered (no on-campus study). *Faculty:* 16. *Students:* 43 full-time (41 women), 20 part-time (19 women); includes 3 minority (1 American Indian or Alaska Native, non-Hispanic/Latino; 1 Asian, non-Hispanic/Latino; 1 Two or more races, non-Hispanic/ Latino), 5 international. Average age 26. 60 applicants, 37% accepted, 22 enrolled. In 2011, 18 master's, 15 other advanced degrees awarded. *Degree requirements:* For master's, thesis optional, oral exam; for doctorate, comprehensive exam, thesis/ dissertation, oral exam. *Entrance requirements:* For master's, GRE, prerequisite courses in nutrition, biochemistry, and physiology; for doctorate and Certificate, GRE. Additional exam requirements/recommendations for international students: Required—TOEFL (minimum score 228 computer-based; 92 iBT). *Application deadline:* For fall admission, 8/1 for domestic students, 7/1 for international students; for winter admission, 12/1 for domestic students, 11/1 for international students; for spring admission, 5/1 for domestic students, 4/1 for international students. Applications are processed on a rolling basis. Application fee: $60. Electronic applications accepted. Tuition and fees vary according to course load, campus/location, program and reciprocity agreements. *Financial support:* Fellowships, research assistantships with full tuition reimbursements, teaching assistantships with full tuition reimbursements, career-related internships or fieldwork, Federal Work-Study, institutionally sponsored loans, scholarships/grants, traineeships, tuition waivers, and unspecified assistantships available. Support available to part-time students. Financial award application deadline: 2/14; financial award applicants required to submit FAFSA. *Faculty research:* Obesity prevention and treatment, omega-3 fatty acids impact on infant development and immunity, vitamin D and bone metabolism in osteosarcoma cells, cancer prevention and recovery maternal diet intake and weight gain impact on infant body composition and development. *Total annual research expenditures:* $919,029. *Unit head:* Dr. Debra Kay Sullivan, Chairperson, 913-588-5357, Fax: 913-588-8946, E-mail: dsulliva@kumc.edu. *Application contact:* Dr. Linda Dianne Griffith, Graduate Director, 913-588-7652, Fax: 913-588-8946, E-mail: lgriffith@kumc.edu. Web site: http://dietetics.kumc.edu/.

University of Kentucky, Graduate School, College of Agriculture, Program in Hospitality and Dietetic Administration, Lexington, KY 40506-0032. Offers MS. *Degree requirements:* For master's, comprehensive exam, thesis optional. *Entrance requirements:* For master's, GRE General Test, minimum undergraduate GPA of 2.75. Additional exam requirements/recommendations for international students: Required—TOEFL (minimum score 550 paper-based; 213 computer-based). Electronic applications accepted.

University of Kentucky, Graduate School, Program in Nutritional Sciences, Lexington, KY 40506-0032. Offers MSNS, PhD. *Degree requirements:* For doctorate, comprehensive exam, thesis/dissertation. *Entrance requirements:* For master's, GRE General Test, minimum undergraduate GPA of 2.75; for doctorate, GRE General Test, minimum graduate GPA of 3.0. Additional exam requirements/recommendations for international students: Required—TOEFL (minimum score 550 paper-based; 213 computer-based). Electronic applications accepted. *Faculty research:* Nutrition and AIDS, nutrition and alcoholism, nutrition and cardiovascular disease, nutrition and cancer, nutrition and diabetes.

University of Maine, Graduate School, College of Natural Sciences, Forestry, and Agriculture, Department of Food Science and Human Nutrition, Orono, ME 04469. Offers food and nutritional sciences (PhD); food science and human nutrition (MS). Part-time programs available. *Faculty:* 7 full-time (6 women), 5 part-time/adjunct (2 women). *Students:* 33 full-time (26 women), 7 part-time (6 women); includes 5 minority (3 American Indian or Alaska Native, non-Hispanic/Latino; 2 Asian, non-Hispanic/Latino), 5 international. Average age 27. 22 applicants, 59% accepted, 9 enrolled. In 2011, 9 master's, 1 doctorate awarded. *Degree requirements:* For master's, thesis; for doctorate, thesis/dissertation. *Entrance requirements:* For master's, GRE General Test, minimum GPA of 3.0; for doctorate, GRE General Test. Additional exam requirements/ recommendations for international students: Required—TOEFL. *Application deadline:* For fall admission, 2/1 priority date for domestic students. Applications are processed on a rolling basis. Application fee: $65. Electronic applications accepted. *Expenses:* Tuition, state resident: full-time $5016. Tuition, nonresident: full-time $14,424. *Financial support:* In 2011–12, 4 research assistantships with full tuition reimbursements (averaging $18,596 per year), 3 teaching assistantships with full tuition reimbursements (averaging $13,600 per year) were awarded; scholarships/grants and tuition waivers (full and partial) also available. Financial award application deadline: 3/1. *Faculty research:* Product development of fruit and vegetables, lipid oxidation in fish and meat, analytical methods development, metabolism of potato glycoalkaloids, seafood quality. *Unit head:* Dr. Rodney Bush, 207-581-1621. *Application contact:* Scott G. Delcourt, Associate Dean of the Graduate School, 207-581-3291, Fax: 207-581-3232, E-mail: graduate@ maine.edu. Web site: http://www2.umaine.edu/graduate/.

University of Manitoba, Faculty of Graduate Studies, Faculty of Agricultural and Food Sciences, Department of Food Science, Winnipeg, MB R3T 2N2, Canada. Offers food and nutritional sciences (PhD); food science (M Sc); foods and nutrition (M Sc). *Degree requirements:* For master's, thesis.

University of Manitoba, Faculty of Graduate Studies, Faculty of Human Ecology, Department of Human Nutritional Sciences, Winnipeg, MB R3T 2N2, Canada. Offers M Sc. *Degree requirements:* For master's, thesis.

University of Maryland, College Park, Academic Affairs, College of Agriculture and Natural Resources, Department of Nutrition and Food Science, Program in Nutrition, College Park, MD 20742. Offers MS, PhD. *Students:* 17 full-time (15 women), 6 part-time (all women); includes 9 minority (2 Black or African American, non-Hispanic/Latino; 5 Asian, non-Hispanic/Latino; 1 Hispanic/Latino; 1 Two or more races, non-Hispanic/ Latino), 8 international. 44 applicants, 9% accepted, 4 enrolled. In 2011, 2 master's, 2 doctorates awarded. *Degree requirements:* For master's, thesis; for doctorate, comprehensive exam, thesis/dissertation, candidacy exam. *Entrance requirements:* For master's, GRE General Test, minimum GPA of 3.0, 3 letters of recommendation; for doctorate, GRE General Test, minimum GPA of 3.0. Additional exam requirements/ recommendations for international students: Required—TOEFL. *Application deadline:* For fall admission, 12/15 for domestic and international students; for spring admission, 6/1 for domestic and international students. Applications are processed on a rolling basis. Application fee: $75. Electronic applications accepted. *Expenses:* Tuition, state resident: part-time $525 per credit hour. Tuition, nonresident: part-time $1131 per credit hour. *Required fees:* $386.31 per term. Tuition and fees vary according to program. *Financial support:* In 2011–12, 3 research assistantships (averaging $15,367 per year), 7 teaching assistantships with tuition reimbursements (averaging $15,443 per year) were awarded; fellowships with tuition reimbursements also available. Financial award applicants required to submit FAFSA. *Faculty research:* Nutrition education, carbohydrates and physical activity. *Unit head:* Lucy Yu, Acting Chair, 301-405-0773, E-mail: lyu5@umd.edu. *Application contact:* Dr. Charles A. Caramello, Dean of Graduate School, 301-405-0358, Fax: 301-314-9305, E-mail: ccaramel@umd.edu.

University of Massachusetts Amherst, Graduate School, School of Public Health and Health Sciences, Department of Nutrition, Amherst, MA 01003. Offers community nutrition (MS); nutrition science (MS). Part-time and evening/weekend programs available. Postbaccalaureate distance learning degree programs offered (no on-campus study). *Faculty:* 13 full-time (8 women). *Students:* 9 full-time (all women), 1 (woman) part-time; includes 2 minority (1 Asian, non-Hispanic/Latino; 1 Two or more races, non-Hispanic/Latino). Average age 31. 42 applicants, 19% accepted, 2 enrolled. In 2011, 6 degrees awarded. Terminal master's awarded for partial completion of doctoral program. *Degree requirements:* For master's, thesis or alternative. *Entrance requirements:* For master's, GRE General Test. Additional exam requirements/ recommendations for international students: Required—TOEFL (minimum score 550 paper-based; 213 computer-based; 80 iBT), IELTS (minimum score 6.5). *Application deadline:* For fall admission, 2/1 for domestic and international students; for spring admission, 10/1 for domestic and international students. Applications are processed on a rolling basis. Application fee: $50 ($65 for international students). Electronic applications accepted. Tuition and fees vary according to course load, campus/location and program. *Financial support:* Fellowships with full and partial tuition reimbursements, research assistantships with full and partial tuition reimbursements, teaching assistantships with full and partial tuition reimbursements, career-related internships or fieldwork, Federal Work-Study, scholarships/grants, traineeships, health care benefits, tuition waivers (full), and unspecified assistantships available. Support available to part-time students. Financial award application deadline: 2/1. *Unit head:* Dr. Elena T. Carbone, Graduate Program Director, 413-545-0740, Fax: 413-545-1074. *Application contact:* Lindsay DeSantis, Interim Supervisor of Admissions, 413-545-0722, Fax: 413-577-0010, E-mail: gradadm@grad.umass.edu. Web site: http://www.umass.edu/sphhs/ nutrition/.

University of Massachusetts Amherst, Graduate School, School of Public Health and Health Sciences, Department of Public Health, Amherst, MA 01003. Offers biostatistics (MPH, MS, PhD); community health education (MPH, MS, PhD); environmental health sciences (MPH, MS, PhD); epidemiology (MPH, MS, PhD); health policy and management (MPH, MS, PhD); nutrition (MPH, PhD); public health practice (MPH); MPH/MPPA. *Accreditation:* CEPH (one or more programs are accredited). Part-time and evening/weekend programs available. Postbaccalaureate distance learning degree programs offered (no on-campus study). *Faculty:* 46 full-time (26 women). *Students:* 118 full-time (88 women), 249 part-time (183 women); includes 75 minority (28 Black or African American, non-Hispanic/Latino; 21 Asian, non-Hispanic/Latino; 20 Hispanic/ Latino; 6 Two or more races, non-Hispanic/Latino), 55 international. Average age 36. 377 applicants, 67% accepted, 91 enrolled. In 2011, 83 master's, 4 doctorates awarded. Terminal master's awarded for partial completion of doctoral program. *Degree*

requirements: For master's, thesis (for some programs); for doctorate, comprehensive exam, thesis/dissertation. *Entrance requirements:* For master's and doctorate, GRE General Test. Additional exam requirements/recommendations for international students: Required—TOEFL (minimum score 550 paper-based; 213 computer-based; 80 iBT), IELTS (minimum score 6.5). *Application deadline:* For fall admission, 2/1 for domestic and international students. Applications are processed on a rolling basis. Application fee: $40 ($65 for international students). Electronic applications accepted. Tuition and fees vary according to course load, campus/location and program. *Financial support:* Fellowships with full and partial tuition reimbursements, research assistantships with full and partial tuition reimbursements, teaching assistantships with full and partial tuition reimbursements, career-related internships or fieldwork, Federal Work-Study, scholarships/grants, traineeships, health care benefits, tuition waivers (full and partial), and unspecified assistantships available. Support available to part-time students. Financial award application deadline: 2/1. *Unit head:* Dr. Paula Stamps, Graduate Program Director, 413-545-2861, Fax: 413-545-1645. *Application contact:* Lindsay DeSantis, Interim Supervisor of Admissions, 413-545-0722, Fax: 413-577-0010, E-mail: gradadm@grad.umass.edu. Web site: http://www.umass.edu/sphhs/public_health/.

University of Massachusetts Lowell, School of Health and Environment, Department of Clinical Laboratory and Nutritional Sciences, Lowell, MA 01854-2881. Offers clinical laboratory sciences (MS); clinical pathology (Graduate Certificate); nutritional sciences (Graduate Certificate); public health laboratory sciences (Graduate Certificate). *Accreditation:* NAACLS. Part-time programs available. Postbaccalaureate distance learning degree programs offered. *Degree requirements:* For master's, thesis optional. *Entrance requirements:* For master's, GRE General Test, minimum GPA of 3.0, letters of recommendation. *Faculty research:* Cardiovascular disease, lipoprotein metabolism, micronutrient evaluation, alcohol metabolism, mycobacterial drug resistance.

University of Medicine and Dentistry of New Jersey, School of Health Related Professions, Department of Interdisciplinary Studies, Program in Health Sciences, Newark, NJ 07107-1709. Offers cardiopulmonary sciences (PhD); clinical laboratory sciences (PhD); health sciences (MS); interdisciplinary studies (PhD); nutrition (PhD); physical therapy/movement science (PhD). Part-time and evening/weekend programs available. Postbaccalaureate distance learning degree programs offered (no on-campus study). *Faculty:* 4 full-time (all women), 10 part-time/adjunct (7 women). *Students:* 3 full-time, 130 part-time; includes 32 minority (10 Black or African American, non-Hispanic/Latino; 10 Asian, non-Hispanic/Latino; 11 Hispanic/Latino; 1 Native Hawaiian or other Pacific Islander, non-Hispanic/Latino). Average age 41. 132 applicants, 51% accepted, 51 enrolled. In 2011, 17 master's, 4 doctorates awarded. *Degree requirements:* For doctorate, thesis/dissertation. *Entrance requirements:* For master's, BS, 2 reference letters, statement of career goals, curriculum vitae; for doctorate, GRE, interview, writing sample, 3 reference letters, curriculum vitae. Additional exam requirements/recommendations for international students: Required—TOEFL. *Application deadline:* For fall admission, 3/1 for domestic students. Applications are processed on a rolling basis. Application fee: $75. Electronic applications accepted. *Unit head:* Dr. Bob Denmark, Director, 973-972-5410, Fax: 973-972-7403, E-mail: ms-phd-hs@umdnj.edu. *Application contact:* Diane Hanrahan, Manager of Admissions, 973-972-5336, Fax: 973-972-7463, E-mail: shrpadm@umdnj.edu.

University of Medicine and Dentistry of New Jersey, School of Health Related Professions, Department of Nutritional Sciences, Dietetic Internship Program, Newark, NJ 07107-1709. Offers Certificate. Postbaccalaureate distance learning degree programs offered (minimal on-campus study). *Faculty:* 1 (woman) full-time, 1 (woman) part-time/adjunct. *Students:* 16 full-time (14 women); includes 2 minority (1 Asian, non-Hispanic/Latino; 1 Hispanic/Latino). Average age 23. 85 applicants, 19% accepted, 15 enrolled. In 2011, 17 degrees awarded. *Entrance requirements:* For degree, bachelor's degree in dietetics, nutrition, or related field; interview; minimum GPA of 2.9. Additional exam requirements/recommendations for international students: Required—TOEFL (minimum score 500 paper-based; 79 iBT). *Application deadline:* For fall admission, 2/15 for domestic and international students. Applications are processed on a rolling basis. Application fee: $75. Electronic applications accepted. *Unit head:* Geri Mckay, Director, 908-889-2488, Fax: 908-889-2487, E-mail: langevdd@umdnj.edu. *Application contact:* Diane Hanrahan, Manager of Admissions, 973-972-5336, Fax: 973-972-7463, E-mail: shrpadm@umdnj.edu.

University of Medicine and Dentistry of New Jersey, School of Health Related Professions, Department of Nutritional Sciences, Program in Clinical Nutrition, Newark, NJ 07107-1709. Offers MS, DCN. Part-time and evening/weekend programs available. Postbaccalaureate distance learning degree programs offered (minimal on-campus study). *Faculty:* 7 full-time (6 women), 18 part-time/adjunct (all women). *Students:* 77 part-time; includes 9 minority (1 Black or African American, non-Hispanic/Latino; 6 Asian, non-Hispanic/Latino; 2 Hispanic/Latino). Average age 37. 47 applicants, 72% accepted, 24 enrolled. In 2011, 17 master's, 8 doctorates awarded. *Entrance requirements:* For master's, statement of career goals, minimum GPA of 3.2, proof of registered dietician status, interview, transcript of highest degree, bachelor's degree, 1 reference letter; for doctorate, minimum GPA of 3.4, transcript of highest degree, statement of career goals, interview, master's degree, 1 reference letter. Additional exam requirements/recommendations for international students: Required—TOEFL (minimum score 500 paper-based; 79 iBT). *Application deadline:* For fall admission, 4/1 for domestic students, 3/1 for international students; for spring admission, 10/15 for domestic students, 7/1 for international students. Applications are processed on a rolling basis. Application fee: $75. Electronic applications accepted. *Unit head:* Dr. Riva Touger-Decker, Chair, 973-972-6596, Fax: 973-972-7403, E-mail: decker@umdnj.edu. *Application contact:* Diane Hanrahan, Manager of Admissions, 973-972-5336, Fax: 973-972-7463, E-mail: shrpadm@umdnj.edu.

University of Memphis, Graduate School, College of Education, Department of Health and Sport Sciences, Memphis, TN 38152. Offers clinical nutrition (MS); exercise and sport science (MS); health promotion (MS); physical education teacher education (MS), including teacher education; sport and leisure commerce (MS). Part-time and evening/weekend programs available. *Degree requirements:* For master's, comprehensive exam, thesis. *Entrance requirements:* For master's, GRE General Test or GMAT (sport and leisure commerce). *Faculty research:* Sport marketing and consumer analysis, health psychology, smoking cessation, psychosocial aspects of cardiovascular disease, global health promotion.

University of Michigan, School of Public Health, Department of Environmental Health Sciences, Ann Arbor, MI 48109. Offers environmental health sciences (MS, PhD); environmental quality and health (MPH); human nutrition (MPH); industrial hygiene (MPH, MS); nutritional sciences (MS); occupational and environmental epidemiology (MPH); toxicology (MPH, MS, PhD). *Accreditation:* CEPH (one or more programs are accredited). Part-time programs available. Terminal master's awarded for partial completion of doctoral program. *Degree requirements:* For master's, thesis (for some programs); for doctorate, thesis/dissertation, preliminary exam, oral defense of dissertation. *Entrance requirements:* For master's and doctorate, GRE General Test and/or MCAT. Additional exam requirements/recommendations for international students: Required—TOEFL (minimum score 560 paper-based; 220 computer-based; 100 iBT). Electronic applications accepted. *Faculty research:* Toxicology, occupational hygiene, nutrition, environmental exposure sciences, environmental epidemiology.

University of Minnesota, Twin Cities Campus, Graduate School, College of Food, Agricultural and Natural Resource Sciences, Program in Nutrition, Minneapolis, MN 55455-0213. Offers MS, PhD. Part-time programs available. *Faculty:* 30 full-time (all women). *Students:* 46 full-time (36 women), 4 part-time (all women); includes 7 minority (3 Asian, non-Hispanic/Latino; 2 Hispanic/Latino; 2 Two or more races, non-Hispanic/Latino), 17 international. Average age 30. 62 applicants, 66% accepted, 16 enrolled. In 2011, 5 master's, 10 doctorates awarded. Terminal master's awarded for partial completion of doctoral program. *Degree requirements:* For master's, comprehensive exam, thesis; for doctorate, comprehensive exam, thesis/dissertation. *Entrance requirements:* For master's, GRE General Test, previous course work in general chemistry, organic chemistry, physiology, biology, biochemistry, statistics; minimum GPA of 3.0 (preferred); for doctorate, GRE General Test, previous course work in general chemistry, organic chemistry, calculus, biology, physics, physiology, biochemistry, statistics; minimum GPA of 3.0 (preferred). Additional exam requirements/recommendations for international students: Required—TOEFL (minimum score 550 paper-based; 213 computer-based; 79 iBT), IELTS (minimum score 6.5), TOEFL preferred. *Application deadline:* For fall admission, 12/15 for domestic and international students; for spring admission, 10/15 for domestic and international students. Applications are processed on a rolling basis. Application fee: $75 ($95 for international students). Electronic applications accepted. *Financial support:* In 2011–12, fellowships with full tuition reimbursements (averaging $23,500 per year), research assistantships with partial tuition reimbursements (averaging $17,500 per year), teaching assistantships with partial tuition reimbursements (averaging $17,500 per year) were awarded; career-related internships or fieldwork, scholarships/grants, traineeships, health care benefits, and unspecified assistantships also available. Support available to part-time students. *Faculty research:* Diet and chronic disease: from basic biological and molecular biology approaches to a public health/intervention/epidemiology perspective. *Total annual research expenditures:* $2.1 million. *Unit head:* Dr. Marla Reicks, Director of Graduate Studies, 612-624-4735, Fax: 612-625-5272, E-mail: mreicks@umn.edu. *Application contact:* Nancy L. Toedt, Program Coordinator, 612-624-6753, Fax: 612-625-5272, E-mail: sviker@umn.edu. Web site: http://fscn.cfans.umn.edu/education/nutritiongraduate/.

University of Minnesota, Twin Cities Campus, School of Public Health, Major in Public Health Nutrition, Minneapolis, MN 55455-0213. Offers MPH. *Accreditation:* AND. Part-time programs available. *Degree requirements:* For master's, fieldwork, project. *Entrance requirements:* For master's, GRE General Test. Additional exam requirements/recommendations for international students: Required—TOEFL. Electronic applications accepted. *Expenses:* Contact institution. *Faculty research:* Nutrition and pregnancy outcomes, nutrition and women's health, child growth and nutrition, child and adolescent nutrition and eating behaviors, obesity and eating disorder prevention.

University of Missouri, Graduate School, College of Agriculture, Food and Natural Resources, Department of Food Science, Columbia, MO 65211. Offers food science (MS, PhD); foods and food systems management (MS); human nutrition (MS). *Faculty:* 12 full-time (4 women), 2 part-time/adjunct (0 women). *Students:* 37 full-time (23 women), 11 part-time (3 women); includes 1 minority (Hispanic/Latino), 31 international. Average age 26. 67 applicants, 37% accepted, 16 enrolled. In 2011, 7 degrees awarded. Terminal master's awarded for partial completion of doctoral program. *Degree requirements:* For doctorate, comprehensive exam, thesis/dissertation. *Entrance requirements:* For master's, GRE General Test (minimum score: Verbal and Quantitative 1000 with neither section below 400, Analytical 3.5), minimum GPA of 3.0; BS in food science from accredited university; for doctorate, GRE General Test (minimum score: Verbal and Quantitative 1000 with neither section below 400, Analytical 3.5), minimum GPA of 3.0; BS and MS in food science from accredited university. Additional exam requirements/recommendations for international students: Required—TOEFL (minimum score 550 paper-based; 79 iBT). *Application deadline:* For fall admission, 4/1 priority date for domestic students; for winter admission, 10/1 priority date for domestic students. Applications are processed on a rolling basis. Application fee: $55 ($75 for international students). Electronic applications accepted. *Expenses:* Tuition, state resident: full-time $5881. Tuition, nonresident: full-time $15,183. *Required fees:* $952. Tuition and fees vary according to campus/location and program. *Financial support:* Fellowships, research assistantships with tuition reimbursements, teaching assistantships with tuition reimbursements, institutionally sponsored loans, scholarships/grants, health care benefits, and unspecified assistantships available. Support available to part-time students. *Faculty research:* Food chemistry, food analysis, food microbiology, food engineering and process control, functional foods, meat science and processing technology. *Unit head:* Dr. Jinglu Tan, Department Chair, 573-882-2369, E-mail: tanj@missouri.edu. *Application contact:* JoAnn Lewis, 573-882-4113, E-mail: lewisj@missouri.edu. Web site: http://foodscience.missouri.edu/graduate/.

University of Missouri, Graduate School, College of Human Environmental Sciences, Department of Nutritional Sciences, Columbia, MO 65211. Offers exercise physiology (MA, PhD); nutritional sciences (MS, PhD). *Faculty:* 10 full-time (7 women). *Students:* 7 full-time (5 women), 8 part-time (4 women), 2 international. Average age 26. 27 applicants, 15% accepted, 4 enrolled. In 2011, 3 master's, 4 doctorates awarded. *Degree requirements:* For doctorate, thesis/dissertation. *Entrance requirements:* For master's and doctorate, GRE General Test, minimum GPA of 3.0. Additional exam requirements/recommendations for international students: Required—TOEFL (minimum score 500 paper-based; 173 computer-based; 61 iBT). *Application deadline:* Applications are processed on a rolling basis. Application fee: $55 ($75 for international students). *Expenses:* Tuition, state resident: full-time $5881. Tuition, nonresident: full-time $15,183. *Required fees:* $952. Tuition and fees vary according to campus/location and program. *Financial support:* Fellowships, research assistantships, teaching assistantships, and institutionally sponsored loans available. *Faculty research:* Fitness and wellness; body composition research; child care provider workforce development; childhood overweight: etiology and outcomes; development during infancy and early childhood; regulation and organization of glycolysis; metabolomics; diabetes and smooth muscle metabolism; lipid metabolism and lipotoxicity - mitochondrial dysfunction in diabetes, atherosclerosis, and cell phenotype transformation; magnetic resonance measures of cellular metabolism; smooth muscle physiology/pathophysiology. *Application contact:* Twila J. Stokes, 573-882-4136, E-mail: stokest@missouri.edu. Web site: http://ns.missouri.edu/.

University of Nebraska–Lincoln, Graduate College, College of Agricultural Sciences and Natural Resources, Interdepartmental Area of Nutrition, Lincoln, NE 68588. Offers MS, PhD. *Degree requirements:* For master's, thesis optional; for doctorate, comprehensive exam, thesis/dissertation. *Entrance requirements:* For master's and doctorate, GRE General Test. Additional exam requirements/recommendations for international students: Required—TOEFL (minimum score 550 paper-based; 213 computer-based). Electronic applications accepted. *Faculty research:* Human nutrition and metabolism, animal nutrition and metabolism, biochemistry, community and clinical nutrition.

University of Nebraska–Lincoln, Graduate College, College of Education and Human Sciences, Department of Nutrition and Health Sciences, Lincoln, NE 68588. Offers

community nutrition and health promotion (MS); nutrition (MS, PhD); nutrition and exercise (MS); nutrition and health sciences (MS, PhD). *Degree requirements:* For master's, thesis optional. *Entrance requirements:* For master's, GRE General Test. Additional exam requirements/recommendations for international students: Required—TOEFL (minimum score 550 paper-based; 213 computer-based). Electronic applications accepted. *Faculty research:* Foods/food service administration, community nutrition science, diet-health relationships.

University of Nebraska Medical Center, School of Allied Health Professions and College of Medicine, UNMC Dietetic Internship Program (Medical Nutrition Education Division), Omaha, NE 68198. Offers Certificate. *Entrance requirements:* Additional exam requirements/recommendations for international students: Required—TOEFL. *Faculty research:* Nutrition intervention outcomes.

University of Nevada, Reno, Graduate School, College of Agriculture, Biotechnology and Natural Resources, Department of Nutrition, Reno, NV 89557. Offers MS. *Degree requirements:* For master's, thesis optional. *Entrance requirements:* For master's, GRE, minimum GPA of 2.75. Additional exam requirements/recommendations for international students: Required—TOEFL (minimum score 500 paper-based; 173 computer-based; 61 iBT), IELTS (minimum score 6). Electronic applications accepted. *Faculty research:* Nutritional education, food technology, therapeutic human nutrition, human nutritional requirements, diet and disease.

University of New Hampshire, Graduate School, College of Life Sciences and Agriculture, Department of Molecular, Cellular and Biomedical Sciences, Program in Animal and Nutritional Sciences, Durham, NH 03824. Offers PhD. Part-time programs available. *Faculty:* 23 full-time. *Students:* 3 full-time (2 women), 3 part-time (all women); includes 1 minority (Hispanic/Latino). Average age 39. 5 applicants, 40% accepted, 1 enrolled. *Entrance requirements:* For doctorate, GRE. Additional exam requirements/recommendations for international students: Required—TOEFL (minimum score 550 paper-based; 213 computer-based; 80 iBT). *Application deadline:* For fall admission, 6/1 priority date for domestic students, 4/1 for international students; for spring admission, 12/1 for domestic students. Application fee: $65. Electronic applications accepted. *Expenses:* Tuition, state resident: full-time $12,360; part-time $687 per credit hour. Tuition, nonresident: full-time $25,680; part-time $1058 per credit hour. *International tuition:* $29,550 full-time. *Required fees:* $1666; $833 per course. $416.50 per semester. Tuition and fees vary according to course load and degree level. *Financial support:* In 2011–12, 4 students received support, including 1 research assistantship, 3 teaching assistantships; fellowships, scholarships/grants, traineeships, and unspecified assistantships also available. Support available to part-time students. *Unit head:* Dr. Rick Cote, Chairperson, 603-862-2458. *Application contact:* Flora Joyal, Administrative Assistant, 603-862-4095, E-mail: ansc.grad.program.info@unh.edu. Web site: http://www.biolsci.unh.edu/.

University of New Hampshire, Graduate School, College of Life Sciences and Agriculture, Department of Molecular, Cellular and Biomedical Sciences, Program in Nutritional Sciences, Durham, NH 03824. Offers MS. Part-time programs available. *Faculty:* 23 full-time. *Students:* 1 (woman) part-time. Average age 24. 16 applicants, 6% accepted, 0 enrolled. In 2011, 2 master's awarded. *Degree requirements:* For master's, thesis. *Entrance requirements:* Additional exam requirements/recommendations for international students: Required—TOEFL (minimum score 550 paper-based; 213 computer-based; 80 iBT). *Application deadline:* For fall admission, 4/1 priority date for domestic students, 4/1 for international students; for spring admission, 12/1 for domestic students. Applications are processed on a rolling basis. Application fee: $65. Electronic applications accepted. *Expenses:* Tuition, state resident: full-time $12,360; part-time $687 per credit hour. Tuition, nonresident: full-time $25,680; part-time $1058 per credit hour. *International tuition:* $29,550 full-time. *Required fees:* $1666; $833 per course. $416.50 per semester. Tuition and fees vary according to course load and degree level. *Financial support:* In 2011–12, 1 student received support, including 1 teaching assistantship; fellowships, research assistantships, career-related internships or fieldwork, Federal Work-Study, and scholarships/grants also available. Support available to part-time students. Financial award application deadline: 2/15. *Unit head:* Dr. Rick Cote, Chair, 603-862-2458. *Application contact:* Flora Joyal, Administrative Assistant, 603-862-4095. Web site: http://www.msnutrition.unh.edu/.

University of New Haven, Graduate School, College of Arts and Sciences, Program in Human Nutrition, West Haven, CT 06516-1916. Offers MS. *Students:* 14 full-time (11 women), 18 part-time (15 women); includes 3 minority (1 Asian, non-Hispanic/Latino; 2 Hispanic/Latino), 9 international. 12 applicants, 100% accepted, 9 enrolled. In 2011, 4 master's awarded. *Entrance requirements:* Additional exam requirements/recommendations for international students: Required—TOEFL (minimum score 520 paper-based; 190 computer-based; 70 iBT); Recommended—IELTS (minimum score 5.5). *Application deadline:* For fall admission, 5/31 for international students; for winter admission, 10/15 for international students; for spring admission, 1/15 for international students. Applications are processed on a rolling basis. Application fee: $50. Electronic applications accepted. *Expenses: Tuition:* Part-time $750 per credit. *Financial support:* Research assistantships with partial tuition reimbursements, teaching assistantships with partial tuition reimbursements, career-related internships or fieldwork, Federal Work-Study, scholarships/grants, tuition waivers, and unspecified assistantships available. Support available to part-time students. Financial award applicants required to submit FAFSA. *Unit head:* Dr. Rosa A. Mo, Director, 203-932-7352. *Application contact:* Eloise Gormley, Director of Graduate Admissions, 203-932-7449, Fax: 203-932-7137, E-mail: gradinfo@newhaven.edu. Web site: http://www.newhaven.edu/4729/.

University of New Mexico, Graduate School, College of Education, Department of Individual, Family and Community Education, Program in Nutrition, Albuquerque, NM 87131-2039. Offers MS. Part-time programs available. *Students:* 8 full-time (all women), 10 part-time (all women); includes 3 minority (1 Asian, non-Hispanic/Latino; 2 Hispanic/Latino). Average age 31. 16 applicants, 75% accepted, 9 enrolled. In 2011, 3 degrees awarded. *Degree requirements:* For master's, comprehensive exam or thesis. *Entrance requirements:* For master's, GRE. *Application deadline:* For fall admission, 2/1 priority date for domestic students; for spring admission, 11/1 priority date for domestic students. Application fee: $50. Electronic applications accepted. *Financial support:* In 2011–12, 12 students received support, including 2 fellowships (averaging $2,290 per year). Financial award application deadline: 3/1; financial award applicants required to submit FAFSA. *Faculty research:* Nutritional needs of children, obesity prevention, phytochemicals, international nutrition. *Unit head:* Dr. Carole Conn, Graduate Coordinator, 505-277-8185, Fax: 505-277-8361, E-mail: cconn@unm.edu. *Application contact:* Cynthia Salas, Program Office, 505-277-4535, Fax: 505-277-8361, E-mail: casalas@unm.edu. Web site: http://coe.unm.edu/departments/ifce/nutrition-and-dietetics/nutrition-ms.html.

The University of North Carolina at Chapel Hill, Graduate School, School of Public Health, Department of Nutrition, Chapel Hill, NC 27599. Offers nutrition (MPH, Dr PH, PhD); nutritional biochemistry (MS); professional practice program (MPH). *Accreditation:* AND. *Degree requirements:* For master's, comprehensive exam, thesis, major paper; for doctorate, comprehensive exam, thesis/dissertation. *Entrance requirements:* For master's and doctorate, GRE General Test, minimum GPA of 3.0. Additional exam requirements/recommendations for international students: Required—TOEFL. Electronic applications accepted. *Faculty research:* Nutrition policy, management and leadership development, lipid and carbohydrate metabolism, dietary trends and determinants, transmembrane signal transduction and carcinogenesis, maternal and child nutrition.

The University of North Carolina at Greensboro, Graduate School, School of Human Environmental Sciences, Department of Nutrition, Greensboro, NC 27412-5001. Offers MS, PhD. *Degree requirements:* For master's, thesis; for doctorate, thesis/dissertation. *Entrance requirements:* For master's and doctorate, GRE General Test. Additional exam requirements/recommendations for international students: Required—TOEFL. Electronic applications accepted.

University of North Florida, Brooks College of Health, Department of Nutrition and Dietetics, Jacksonville, FL 32224. Offers MSH. Part-time programs available. *Faculty:* 6 full-time (all women). *Students:* 29 full-time (27 women), 2 part-time (both women); includes 4 minority (3 Black or African American, non-Hispanic/Latino; 1 Two or more races, non-Hispanic/Latino). Average age 24. 45 applicants, 36% accepted, 13 enrolled. In 2011, 14 master's awarded. *Entrance requirements:* For master's, GRE General Test, minimum GPA of 3.0 in last 60 hours. Additional exam requirements/recommendations for international students: Required—TOEFL (minimum score 500 paper-based; 173 computer-based; 61 iBT). *Application deadline:* For fall admission, 7/1 for domestic students, 5/1 for international students; for spring admission, 11/1 for domestic students, 10/1 for international students. Applications are processed on a rolling basis. Application fee: $30. Electronic applications accepted. *Expenses:* Tuition, state resident: full-time $8793; part-time $366.38 per credit hour. Tuition, nonresident: full-time $23,502; part-time $979.24 per credit hour. *Required fees:* $1384; $57.66 per credit hour. Tuition and fees vary according to course load and program. *Financial support:* In 2011–12, 14 students received support, including 1 research assistantship; career-related internships or fieldwork, Federal Work-Study, scholarships/grants, and tuition waivers (partial) also available. Financial award application deadline: 4/1; financial award applicants required to submit FAFSA. *Total annual research expenditures:* $45,591. *Unit head:* Dr. Pamela Chally, Dean, 904-620-2810, Fax: 904-620-1030, E-mail: pchally@unf.edu. *Application contact:* Dr. Catherine Christie, Program Director, 904-620-1423, Fax: 904-620-1942, E-mail: c.christie@unf.edu. Web site: http://www.unf.edu/brooks/nutrition.

University of Oklahoma Health Sciences Center, Graduate College, College of Allied Health, Department of Nutritional Sciences, Oklahoma City, OK 73190. Offers MS. *Accreditation:* AND. *Degree requirements:* For master's, comprehensive exam, thesis optional. *Entrance requirements:* For master's, GRE General Test, interview, 3 letters of reference. Additional exam requirements/recommendations for international students: Required—TOEFL (minimum score 550 paper-based).

University of Pittsburgh, School of Health and Rehabilitation Sciences, Coordinated Master's in Dietetics Program, Pittsburgh, PA 15260. Offers MS. *Accreditation:* AND. Part-time and evening/weekend programs available. *Faculty:* 3 full-time (all women). *Students:* 34 full-time (30 women); includes 2 minority (1 Asian, non-Hispanic/Latino; 1 Hispanic/Latino), 1 international. Average age 26. 28 applicants, 68% accepted, 17 enrolled. In 2011, 17 master's awarded. *Entrance requirements:* For master's, GRE. Additional exam requirements/recommendations for international students: Required—TOEFL (minimum score 550 paper-based; 213 computer-based; 80 iBT), IELTS (minimum score 6.5). *Application deadline:* For fall admission, 3/15 for domestic students, 3/1 for international students. Application fee: $50. Electronic applications accepted. *Expenses:* Contact institution. *Faculty research:* Targeted approaches to weight control, pediatric obesity treatment, effect of tart cherry juice on muscles. *Total annual research expenditures:* $40,979. *Unit head:* Dr. Scott Lephart, Department Chair and Associate Professor, 412-383-6530, Fax: 412-383-6527, E-mail: lephart@pitt.edu. *Application contact:* Shameem Gangjee, Director of Admissions, 412-383-6558, Fax: 412-383-6535, E-mail: admissions@shrs.pitt.edu. Web site: http://www.shrs.pitt.edu/cmd/.

University of Pittsburgh, School of Health and Rehabilitation Sciences, Master's Programs in Health and Rehabilitation Sciences, Pittsburgh, PA 15260. Offers health and rehabilitation sciences (MS), including clinical dietetics and nutrition, health care supervision and management, health information systems, occupational therapy, physical therapy, rehabilitation counseling, rehabilitation science and technology, sports medicine, wellness and human performance. *Accreditation:* APTA. Part-time and evening/weekend programs available. *Faculty:* 22 full-time (16 women), 4 part-time/adjunct (2 women). *Students:* 144 full-time (91 women), 35 part-time (23 women); includes 23 minority (8 Black or African American, non-Hispanic/Latino; 8 Asian, non-Hispanic/Latino; 3 Hispanic/Latino; 4 Two or more races, non-Hispanic/Latino), 74 international. Average age 28. 399 applicants, 61% accepted, 121 enrolled. In 2011, 86 master's awarded. *Degree requirements:* For master's, comprehensive exam (for some programs), thesis optional. *Entrance requirements:* For master's, minimum GPA of 3.0. Additional exam requirements/recommendations for international students: Required—TOEFL (minimum score 550 paper-based; 213 computer-based; 80 iBT), IELTS (minimum score 6.5). *Application deadline:* For fall admission, 3/1 for international students; for spring admission, 7/31 for international students. Applications are processed on a rolling basis. Application fee: $50. Electronic applications accepted. *Expenses:* Contact institution. *Financial support:* Research assistantships, teaching assistantships, Federal Work-Study, institutionally sponsored loans, traineeships, and unspecified assistantships available. Financial award applicants required to submit FAFSA. *Faculty research:* Assistive technology, seating and wheeled mobility, cellular neurophysiology, low back syndrome, augmentative communication. *Total annual research expenditures:* $7.8 million. *Unit head:* Dr. Clifford E. Brubaker, Dean, 412-383-6560, Fax: 412-383-6535, E-mail: cliffb@pitt.edu. *Application contact:* Shameem Gangjee, Director of Admissions, 412-383-6558, Fax: 412-383-6535, E-mail: admissions@shrs.pitt.edu. Web site: http://www.shrs.pitt.edu/.

University of Puerto Rico, Medical Sciences Campus, Graduate School of Public Health, Department of Human Development, Program in Nutrition, San Juan, PR 00936-5067. Offers MS. Part-time programs available. *Degree requirements:* For master's, thesis. *Entrance requirements:* For master's, GRE, previous course work in algebra, biochemistry, biology, chemistry, and social sciences.

University of Puerto Rico, Medical Sciences Campus, School of Health Professions, Program in Dietetics Internship, San Juan, PR 00936-5067. Offers Certificate. *Degree requirements:* For Certificate, one foreign language, clinical practice. *Entrance requirements:* For degree, minimum GPA of 2.5, interview, participation in the computer matching process by the American Dietetic Association.

University of Puerto Rico, Medical Sciences Campus, School of Medicine, Division of Graduate Studies, Department of Biochemistry, San Juan, PR 00936-5067. Offers MS, PhD. *Degree requirements:* For master's, thesis; for doctorate, comprehensive exam, thesis/dissertation. *Entrance requirements:* For master's and doctorate, GRE General Test, GRE Subject Test, interview, minimum GPA of 3.0. Electronic applications accepted. *Faculty research:* Genetics, cell and molecular biology, cancer biology, protein structure/function, glycosilation of proteins.

University of Puerto Rico, Río Piedras, College of Education, Program in Family Ecology and Nutrition, San Juan, PR 00931-3300. Offers M Ed. Part-time programs available. *Degree requirements:* For master's, thesis. *Entrance requirements:* For master's, PAEG or GRE, minimum GPA of 3.0, letter of recommendation.

University of Rhode Island, Graduate School, College of the Environment and Life Sciences, Department of Nutrition and Food Sciences, Kingston, RI 02881. Offers food science (MS, PhD); nutrition (MS, PhD). Part-time programs available. *Faculty:* 7 full-time (5 women), 1 (woman) part-time/adjunct. *Students:* 15 full-time (14 women), 13 part-time (10 women); includes 1 minority (Asian, non-Hispanic/Latino), 1 international. In 2011, 9 master's awarded. *Degree requirements:* For master's, comprehensive exam (for some programs), thesis optional; for doctorate, thesis/dissertation. *Entrance requirements:* For master's and doctorate, GRE, 2 letters of recommendation. Additional exam requirements/recommendations for international students: Required—TOEFL (minimum score 550 paper-based; 213 computer-based). *Application deadline:* For fall admission, 7/15 for domestic students, 2/1 for international students; for spring admission, 11/15 for domestic students, 7/15 for international students. Application fee: $65. Electronic applications accepted. *Expenses:* Tuition, state resident: full-time $10,432; part-time $580 per credit hour. Tuition, nonresident: full-time $23,130; part-time $1285 per credit hour. *Required fees:* $1362; $36 per credit hour. $35 per semester. One-time fee: $130. *Financial support:* In 2011–12, 1 research assistantship with full and partial tuition reimbursement (averaging $8,471 per year), 4 teaching assistantships with full and partial tuition reimbursements (averaging $11,298 per year) were awarded. Financial award application deadline: 7/15; financial award applicants required to submit FAFSA. *Faculty research:* Food safety and quality, marine resource utilization, nutrition in underserved populations, eating behavior, lipid metabolism. *Unit head:* Dr. Geoffrey Greene, Chair, 401-874-4028, Fax: 401-874-5974, E-mail: gwg@uri.edu. *Application contact:* Dr. Geoffrey Greene, Director of Graduate Studies, 401-874-4028, E-mail: gwg@uri.edu. Web site: http://cels.uri.edu/nfs/.

University of Saint Joseph, Department of Nutrition, West Hartford, CT 06117-2700. Offers MS. Part-time and evening/weekend programs available. Postbaccalaureate distance learning degree programs offered. *Students:* 11 full-time (all women), 63 part-time (58 women); includes 3 minority (2 Black or African American, non-Hispanic/Latino; 1 Hispanic/Latino). Average age 34. *Entrance requirements:* For master's, 2 letters of recommendation. *Application deadline:* Applications are processed on a rolling basis. Application fee: $50. Electronic applications accepted. Application fee is waived when completed online. *Expenses: Tuition:* Part-time $670 per credit. *Required fees:* $40 per credit. Tuition and fees vary according to course load, degree level, campus/location and program. *Financial support:* Career-related internships or fieldwork and unspecified assistantships available. Support available to part-time students. Financial award applicants required to submit FAFSA. *Application contact:* Graduate Admissions Office, 860-231-5261, E-mail: graduate@usj.edu.

University of Southern Mississippi, Graduate School, College of Health, Department of Community Health Sciences, Hattiesburg, MS 39406-0001. Offers epidemiology and biostatistics (MPH); health education (MPH); health policy/administration (MPH); occupational/environmental health (MPH); public health nutrition (MPH). *Accreditation:* CEPH. Part-time and evening/weekend programs available. *Faculty:* 8 full-time (4 women), 1 part-time/adjunct (0 women). *Students:* 81 full-time (66 women), 17 part-time (13 women); includes 49 minority (43 Black or African American, non-Hispanic/Latino; 1 Asian, non-Hispanic/Latino; 2 Hispanic/Latino; 3 Two or more races, non-Hispanic/Latino), 7 international. Average age 32. 70 applicants, 94% accepted, 43 enrolled. In 2011, 45 degrees awarded. *Degree requirements:* For master's, comprehensive exam, thesis (for some programs). *Entrance requirements:* For master's, GRE General Test, minimum GPA of 2.75 in last 60 hours. Additional exam requirements/recommendations for international students: Required—TOEFL, IELTS. *Application deadline:* For fall admission, 3/1 priority date for domestic students, 3/1 for international students; for spring admission, 1/10 priority date for domestic students, 1/10 for international students. Applications are processed on a rolling basis. Application fee: $50. Electronic applications accepted. *Financial support:* In 2011–12, 5 research assistantships with full tuition reimbursements (averaging $7,000 per year), 1 teaching assistantship with full tuition reimbursement (averaging $8,263 per year) were awarded; career-related internships or fieldwork, Federal Work-Study, institutionally sponsored loans, scholarships/grants, health care benefits, and unspecified assistantships also available. Financial award application deadline: 3/15; financial award applicants required to submit FAFSA. *Faculty research:* Rural health care delivery, school health, nutrition of pregnant teens, risk factor reduction, sexually transmitted diseases. *Unit head:* Dr. Emanual Ahua, Interim Chair, 601-266-5437, Fax: 601-266-5043. *Application contact:* Shonna Breland, Manager of Graduate Admissions, 601-266-6563, Fax: 601-266-5138. Web site: http://www.usm.edu/chs.

University of Southern Mississippi, Graduate School, College of Health, Department of Nutrition and Food Systems, Hattiesburg, MS 39406-0001. Offers nutrition (MS, PhD). Part-time programs available. *Faculty:* 6 full-time (5 women). *Students:* 18 full-time (17 women), 35 part-time (31 women); includes 8 minority (4 Black or African American, non-Hispanic/Latino; 1 Asian, non-Hispanic/Latino; 1 Hispanic/Latino; 2 Two or more races, non-Hispanic/Latino), 1 international. Average age 30. 21 applicants, 57% accepted, 4 enrolled. In 2011, 18 master's, 1 doctorate awarded. *Degree requirements:* For master's, comprehensive exam, thesis (for some programs); for doctorate, comprehensive exam, thesis/dissertation. *Entrance requirements:* For master's, GRE General Test, minimum GPA of 2.75 on last 60 hours; for doctorate, GRE General Test, minimum GPA of 3.5. Additional exam requirements/recommendations for international students: Required—TOEFL, IELTS. *Application deadline:* For fall admission, 3/1 for domestic and international students; for spring admission, 1/10 priority date for domestic students, 1/10 for international students. Application fee: $50. *Financial support:* In 2011–12, 2 research assistantships with full tuition reimbursements (averaging $12,069 per year), 6 teaching assistantships with full tuition reimbursements (averaging $7,676 per year) were awarded; career-related internships or fieldwork, Federal Work-Study, institutionally sponsored loans, scholarships/grants, traineeships, health care benefits, and unspecified assistantships also available. Financial award applicants required to submit FAFSA. *Unit head:* Dr. Kathleen Yadrick, Chair, 601-266-5377, Fax: 601-266-6343. *Application contact:* Belynda Brock, Graduate Admission Secretary, 601-266-5377, Fax: 601-266-5138. Web site: http://www.usm.edu/graduateschool/table.php.

The University of Tennessee, Graduate School, College of Education, Health and Human Sciences, Department of Nutrition, Knoxville, TN 37996. Offers nutrition (MS), including nutrition science, public health nutrition; MS/MPH. Part-time programs available. *Degree requirements:* For master's, thesis or alternative. *Entrance requirements:* For master's, GRE General Test, minimum GPA of 2.7. Additional exam requirements/recommendations for international students: Required—TOEFL. Electronic applications accepted. *Expenses:* Tuition, state resident: full-time $8332; part-time $464 per credit hour. Tuition, nonresident: full-time $25,174; part-time $1400 per credit hour. *Required fees:* $1162; $56 per credit hour. Tuition and fees vary according to program.

The University of Tennessee at Martin, Graduate Programs, College of Agriculture and Applied Sciences, Department of Family and Consumer Sciences, Martin, TN 38238-1000. Offers dietetics (MSFCS); general family and consumer sciences (MSFCS). Part-time programs available. Postbaccalaureate distance learning degree programs offered (minimal on-campus study). *Faculty:* 8. *Students:* 36 (34 women); includes 11 minority (6 Black or African American, non-Hispanic/Latino; 4 Hispanic/Latino; 1 Two or more races, non-Hispanic/Latino), 1 international. 28 applicants, 71% accepted, 15 enrolled. In 2011, 15 master's awarded. *Degree requirements:* For master's, comprehensive exam, thesis optional. *Entrance requirements:* For master's, GRE General Test, minimum GPA of 2.5. Additional exam requirements/recommendations for international students: Required—TOEFL (minimum score 525 paper-based; 197 computer-based; 71 iBT). *Application deadline:* For fall admission, 8/1 priority date for domestic students, 6/15 for international students; for spring admission, 12/15 priority date for domestic students, 12/1 for international students. Applications are processed on a rolling basis. Application fee: $30 ($130 for international students). Electronic applications accepted. *Expenses:* Tuition, state resident: full-time $6726; part-time $374 per credit hour. Tuition, nonresident: full-time $19,136; part-time $1064 per credit hour. *Required fees:* $61 per credit hour. *Financial support:* In 2011–12, 2 students received support, including 2 research assistantships with full tuition reimbursements available (averaging $6,283 per year); scholarships/grants and unspecified assistantships also available. Support available to part-time students. Financial award application deadline: 2/15; financial award applicants required to submit FAFSA. *Faculty research:* Children with developmental disabilities, regional food product development and marketing, parent education. *Unit head:* Dr. Lisa LeBleu, Coordinator, 731-881-7116, Fax: 731-881-7106, E-mail: llebleu@utm.edu. *Application contact:* Linda S. Arant, Student Services Specialist, 731-881-7012, Fax: 731-881-7499, E-mail: larant@utm.edu. Web site: http://www.utm.edu/departments/caas/fcs/index.php.

The University of Texas at Austin, Graduate School, College of Natural Sciences, School of Human Ecology, Program in Nutritional Sciences, Austin, TX 78712-1111. Offers nutrition (MA); nutritional sciences (PhD). *Degree requirements:* For master's, thesis; for doctorate, thesis/dissertation. *Entrance requirements:* For master's and doctorate, GRE General Test. Additional exam requirements/recommendations for international students: Required—TOEFL. *Application deadline:* For fall admission, 1/1 priority date for domestic students; for spring admission, 10/1 for domestic students. Application fee: $50 ($75 for international students). Electronic applications accepted. *Financial support:* Fellowships, research assistantships, and teaching assistantships with tuition reimbursements available. Financial award application deadline: 1/1. *Faculty research:* Nutritional biochemistry, nutrient health assessment, obesity, nutrition education, molecular/cellular aspects of nutrient functions. *Unit head:* Kathy McWilliams, Graduate Coordinator, 512-471-0337, Fax: 512-471-5844, E-mail: kathymcw@mail.utexas.edu. Web site: http://he.utexas.edu/ntr/graduate-program.

The University of Texas Southwestern Medical Center, Southwestern School of Health Professions, Clinical Nutrition Program, Dallas, TX 75390. Offers MCN. *Accreditation:* AND.

University of the District of Columbia, College of Arts and Sciences, Department of Biological and Environmental Sciences, Program in Nutrition and Dietetics, Washington, DC 20008-1175. Offers MS. *Degree requirements:* For master's, thesis. *Entrance requirements:* For master's, GRE, 3 letters of recommendation, personal interview. *Expenses: Tuition, area resident:* Full-time $7580; part-time $421 per credit hour. Tuition, state resident: full-time $8580; part-time $477 per credit hour. Tuition, nonresident: full-time $14,580; part-time $810 per credit hour. *Required fees:* $620; $30 per credit hour. $310 per semester.

University of the Incarnate Word, School of Graduate Studies and Research, H-E-B School of Business and Administration, Programs in Administration, San Antonio, TX 78209-6397. Offers adult education (MAA); applied administration (MAA); communication arts (MAA); healthcare administration (MAA); instructional technology (MAA); international business (Certificate); nutrition (MAA); organizational development (MAA, Certificate); project management (Certificate); sports management (MAA). Part-time and evening/weekend programs available. Postbaccalaureate distance learning degree programs offered (no on-campus study). *Faculty:* 23 full-time (10 women), 26 part-time/adjunct (12 women). *Students:* 25 full-time (18 women), 54 part-time (33 women); includes 50 minority (10 Black or African American, non-Hispanic/Latino; 40 Hispanic/Latino), 5 international. Average age 34. 35 applicants, 94% accepted, 19 enrolled. In 2011, 38 master's awarded. *Degree requirements:* For master's, capstone. *Entrance requirements:* For master's, GRE, GMAT, undergraduate degree, minimum GPA of 2.5. Additional exam requirements/recommendations for international students: Required—TOEFL (minimum score 560 paper-based; 220 computer-based; 83 iBT). *Application deadline:* Applications are processed on a rolling basis. Application fee: $20. Electronic applications accepted. *Expenses: Tuition:* Part-time $725 per credit hour. Tuition and fees vary according to degree level. *Financial support:* Federal Work-Study and scholarships/grants available. Financial award applicants required to submit FAFSA. *Unit head:* Dr. Mark Teachout, MAA Programs Director, 210-829-3177, Fax: 210-805-3564, E-mail: teachout@uiwtx.edu. *Application contact:* Andrea Cyterski-Acosta, Dean of Enrollment, 210-829-6005, Fax: 210-829-3921, E-mail: admis@uiwtx.edu. Web site: http://www.uiw.edu/maa/index.htm and http://www.uiw.edu/maa/admissions.html.

University of the Incarnate Word, School of Graduate Studies and Research, School of Mathematics, Science, and Engineering, Program in Nutrition, San Antonio, TX 78209-6397. Offers administration (MS); medical nutrition therapy (MS); nutrition education and health promotion (MS); nutrition services administration (MS). Part-time and evening/weekend programs available. *Faculty:* 3 full-time (2 women), 1 (woman) part-time/adjunct. *Students:* 7 full-time (all women), 16 part-time (15 women); includes 8 minority (1 Black or African American, non-Hispanic/Latino; 2 Asian, non-Hispanic/Latino; 5 Hispanic/Latino), 1 international. Average age 25. 26 applicants, 92% accepted, 9 enrolled. In 2011, 5 master's awarded. *Degree requirements:* For master's, comprehensive exam, thesis or alternative. *Entrance requirements:* For master's, two letters of recommendation. Additional exam requirements/recommendations for international students: Required—TOEFL (minimum score 560 paper-based; 220 computer-based; 83 iBT). *Application deadline:* Applications are processed on a rolling basis. Application fee: $20. Electronic applications accepted. *Expenses: Tuition:* Part-time $725 per credit hour. Tuition and fees vary according to degree level. *Financial support:* In 2011–12, research assistantships (averaging $5,000 per year) were awarded; Federal Work-Study and scholarships/grants also available. Financial award applicants required to submit FAFSA. *Faculty research:* Nutrition. *Total annual research expenditures:* $109,000. *Unit head:* Dr. Beth Senne-Duff, Associate Professor, 210-829-3165, Fax: 210-829-3153, E-mail: beths@uiwtx.edu. *Application contact:* Andrea Cyterski-Acosta, Dean of Enrollment, 210-829-6005, Fax: 210-829-3921, E-mail: admis@uiwtx.edu. Web site: http://www.uiw.edu/nutrition/nutrition3.htm.

The University of Toledo, College of Graduate Studies, College of Medicine and Life Sciences, Department of Public Health and Preventative Medicine, Toledo, OH 43606-3390. Offers biostatistics and epidemiology (Certificate); contemporary gerontological practice (Certificate); environmental and occupational health and safety (MPH); epidemiology (MPH, Certificate); global public health (Certificate); health administration (MPH); health promotion (MPH); medical health and science education (Certificate); nutrition (MPH); occupational health (MSOH, Certificate); public health and emergency response (Certificate); MD/MPH. Part-time and evening/weekend programs available. *Faculty:* 6. *Students:* 95 full-time (74 women), 66 part-time (45 women); includes 37 minority (21 Black or African American, non-Hispanic/Latino; 11 Asian, non-Hispanic/Latino; 3 Hispanic/Latino; 2 Two or more races, non-Hispanic/Latino), 6 international.

Nutrition

Average age 29. 132 applicants, 75% accepted, 70 enrolled. In 2011, 60 master's, 26 other advanced degrees awarded. *Degree requirements:* For master's, thesis or alternative. *Entrance requirements:* For master's, GRE, minimum undergraduate GPA of 3.0, three letters of recommendation, statement of purpose, transcripts from all prior institutions attended, resume; for Certificate, minimum undergraduate GPA of 3.0, three letters of recommendation, statement of purpose, transcripts from all prior institutions attended, resume. Additional exam requirements/recommendations for international students: Required—TOEFL (minimum score 550 paper-based; 213 computer-based; 80 iBT), IELTS (minimum score 6.5). *Application deadline:* For fall admission, 3/15 for domestic and international students. Applications are processed on a rolling basis. Application fee: $45 ($75 for international students). Electronic applications accepted. *Financial support:* In 2011–12, 15 research assistantships with full tuition reimbursements (averaging $10,000 per year) were awarded; Federal Work-Study, institutionally sponsored loans, scholarships/grants, tuition waivers (full and partial), and unspecified assistantships also available. *Unit head:* Dr. Sheryl A. Milz, Chair, 419-383-3976, Fax: 419-383-6140, E-mail: sheryl.milz@utoledo.edu. *Application contact:* Joan Mulligan, Admissions Analyst, 419-383-4186, Fax: 419-383-6140, E-mail: joan.mulligan@utoledo.edu. Web site: http://nocphmph.org/.

University of Toronto, Faculty of Medicine, Department of Nutritional Sciences, Toronto, ON M5S 1A1, Canada. Offers M Sc, PhD. Part-time programs available. *Degree requirements:* For master's, thesis, oral thesis defense; for doctorate, comprehensive exam, thesis/dissertation, departmental examination, oral examination. *Entrance requirements:* For master's, minimum B average, background in nutrition or an area of biological or health sciences, 2 letters of reference; for doctorate, minimum B+ average in final 2 years, background in nutrition or an area of biological or health sciences, 2 letters of reference. Additional exam requirements/recommendations for international students: Required—TOEFL (580 paper-based; 237 computer-based), TWE (5), IELTS (7), Michigan English Language Assessment Battery (85), or COPE (4). Electronic applications accepted.

University of Utah, Graduate School, College of Health, Division of Nutrition, Salt Lake City, UT 84112. Offers MS. *Accreditation:* AND. *Faculty:* 5 full-time (3 women), 3 part-time/adjunct (all women). *Students:* 28 full-time (26 women), 1 part-time (0 women); includes 1 minority (Asian, non-Hispanic/Latino), 2 international. Average age 28. 71 applicants, 24% accepted, 14 enrolled. In 2011, 14 degrees awarded. *Degree requirements:* For master's, comprehensive exam, thesis. *Entrance requirements:* For master's, GRE General Test, minimum undergraduate GPA of 3.0. Additional exam requirements/recommendations for international students: Required—TOEFL (minimum score 500 paper-based; 173 computer-based). *Application deadline:* For fall admission, 2/15 for domestic and international students. Application fee: $55 ($65 for international students). Electronic applications accepted. *Expenses:* Contact institution. *Financial support:* In 2011–12, 21 students received support, including 1 research assistantship with partial tuition reimbursement available (averaging $6,000 per year), 11 teaching assistantships with partial tuition reimbursements available (averaging $6,000 per year); fellowships, career-related internships or fieldwork, Federal Work-Study, and institutionally sponsored loans also available. Financial award application deadline: 2/15; financial award applicants required to submit FAFSA. *Faculty research:* Cholesterol metabolism, sport nutrition education, metabolic and critical care, cardiovascular nutrition, wilderness nutrition, pediatric nutrition. *Total annual research expenditures:* $25,520. *Unit head:* Dr. E. Wayne Askew, Director, 801-581-8240, Fax: 801-585-3874, E-mail: wayne.askew@health.utah.edu. *Application contact:* Jean Zancanella, Academic Adviser, 801-581-5280, Fax: 801-585-3874, E-mail: jean.zancanella@health.utah.edu. Web site: http://www.health.utah.edu/fdnu/.

University of Vermont, Graduate College, College of Agriculture and Life Sciences, Department of Nutrition and Food Sciences, Program in Dietetics, Burlington, VT 05405. Offers MSD. *Students:* 14 (all women); includes 1 minority (Hispanic/Latino). 19 applicants, 32% accepted, 5 enrolled. In 2011, 4 master's awarded. *Entrance requirements:* For master's, GRE General Test. Additional exam requirements/recommendations for international students: Required—TOEFL (minimum score 550 paper-based; 213 computer-based; 80 iBT). *Application deadline:* For fall admission, 12/15 priority date for domestic students, 12/15 for international students. Application fee: $40. Electronic applications accepted. *Unit head:* Dr. Jane Ross, Director, 802-656-3374. *Application contact:* Amy Nickerson, Coordinator, 802-656-3374.

University of Vermont, Graduate College, College of Agriculture and Life Sciences, Program in Animal, Nutrition and Food Sciences, Burlington, VT 05405. Offers PhD. *Students:* 18 (7 women); includes 2 minority (both Asian, non-Hispanic/Latino), 10 international. 10 applicants, 20% accepted, 1 enrolled. In 2011, 2 doctorates awarded. *Degree requirements:* For doctorate, one foreign language, thesis/dissertation. *Entrance requirements:* For doctorate, GRE General Test. Additional exam requirements/recommendations for international students: Required—TOEFL (minimum score 550 paper-based; 213 computer-based; 80 iBT). *Application deadline:* For fall admission, 4/1 priority date for domestic students, 4/1 for international students. Applications are processed on a rolling basis. Application fee: $40. Electronic applications accepted. *Financial support:* Application deadline: 3/1. *Unit head:* Dr. Andre-Denis Wright, Chairperson, 802-656-2070. *Application contact:* Dr. David Kerr, Coordinator, 802-656-2070.

University of Washington, Graduate School, School of Public Health, Department of Epidemiology, Interdisciplinary Graduate Program in Nutritional Sciences, Seattle, WA 98195. Offers MPH, MS, PhD. *Accreditation:* AND. Part-time programs available. *Students:* 34 full-time (29 women), 14 part-time (11 women); includes 9 minority (8 Asian, non-Hispanic/Latino; 1 Hispanic/Latino), 2 international. Average age 29. 127 applicants, 41% accepted, 23 enrolled. In 2011, 17 master's, 1 doctorate awarded. Terminal master's awarded for partial completion of doctoral program. *Degree requirements:* For master's, thesis, practicum (MPH); for doctorate, thesis/dissertation. *Entrance requirements:* For master's, GRE General Test, experience in health sciences (preferred), minimum GPA of 3.0; for doctorate, GRE General Test, master's degree, experience in health sciences (preferred), minimum GPA of 3.0. Additional exam requirements/recommendations for international students: Required—TOEFL (minimum score 500 paper-based; 173 computer-based; 61 iBT), IELTS (minimum score 6). *Application deadline:* For fall admission, 2/1 for domestic students, 11/1 for international students. Application fee: $75. Electronic applications accepted. *Financial support:* In 2011–12, 2 teaching assistantships with partial tuition reimbursements were awarded; scholarships/grants also available. *Faculty research:* Dietary behavior, dietary supplements, obesity, clinical nutrition, addictive behaviors. *Unit head:* Dr. Adam Drewnowski, Chair, 206-543-1065. *Application contact:* Carey Purnell, Graduate Program Assistant, 206-543-1730, Fax: 206-685-1696, E-mail: nutr@u.washington.edu. Web site: http://depts.washington.edu/nutr/.

University of Wisconsin–Madison, Graduate School, College of Agricultural and Life Sciences, Department of Nutritional Sciences, Madison, WI 53706. Offers MS, PhD. Terminal master's awarded for partial completion of doctoral program. *Degree requirements:* For master's, thesis or research report; for doctorate, comprehensive exam, thesis/dissertation. *Entrance requirements:* For master's and doctorate, GRE General Test. Additional exam requirements/recommendations for international students: Required—TOEFL (minimum score 550 paper-based; 213 computer-based;

80 iBT). Electronic applications accepted. *Expenses:* Tuition, state resident: full-time $10,296; part-time $643.51 per credit. Tuition, nonresident: full-time $24,054; part-time $1503.40 per credit. *Required fees:* $70.06 per credit. Tuition and fees vary according to course load, campus/location, program and reciprocity agreements. *Faculty research:* Human and animal nutrition, nutrition epidemiology, nutrition education, biochemical and molecular nutrition.

University of Wisconsin–Stevens Point, College of Professional Studies, School of Health Promotion and Human Development, Program in Nutritional Sciences, Stevens Point, WI 54481-3897. Offers MS. Part-time programs available. *Degree requirements:* For master's, thesis or alternative. *Entrance requirements:* For master's, minimum GPA of 2.75.

University of Wisconsin–Stout, Graduate School, College of Human Development, Program in Food and Nutritional Sciences, Menomonie , WI 54751. Offers MS. Part-time programs available. *Degree requirements:* For master's, thesis. *Entrance requirements:* For master's, minimum GPA of 3.0. Additional exam requirements/recommendations for international students: Required—TOEFL (minimum score 500 paper-based; 173 computer-based; 61 iBT). Electronic applications accepted. *Faculty research:* Disease states and nutrition, childhood obesity, nutraceuticals, food safety, nanotechnology.

University of Wyoming, College of Agriculture and Natural Resources, Department of Animal Sciences, Program in Food Science and Human Nutrition, Laramie, WY 82070. Offers MS. *Degree requirements:* For master's, thesis. *Entrance requirements:* For master's, GRE General Test, minimum GPA of 3.0. Additional exam requirements/recommendations for international students: Required—TOEFL (minimum score 525 paper-based). Electronic applications accepted. *Faculty research:* Protein and lipid metabolism, food microbiology, food safety, meat science.

Utah State University, School of Graduate Studies, College of Agriculture, Department of Nutrition, Dietetics, and Food Sciences, Logan, UT 84322. Offers dietetic administration (MDA); nutrition and food sciences (MS, PhD). Postbaccalaureate distance learning degree programs offered. *Degree requirements:* For master's, thesis; for doctorate, comprehensive exam, thesis/dissertation, teaching experience. *Entrance requirements:* For master's, GRE General Test, minimum GPA of 3.0, course work in chemistry, biochemistry, physics, math, bacteriology, physiology; for doctorate, GRE General Test, minimum GPA of 3.2, course work in chemistry, MS or manuscript in referred journal. Additional exam requirements/recommendations for international students: Required—TOEFL (minimum score 550 paper-based). Electronic applications accepted. *Faculty research:* Mineral balance, meat microbiology and nitrate interactions, milk ultrafiltration, lactic culture, milk coagulation.

Virginia Polytechnic Institute and State University, Graduate School, College of Agriculture and Life Sciences, Department of Human Nutrition, Foods and Exercise, Blacksburg, VA 24061. Offers behavioral and community science (MS, PhD); clinical physiology and metabolism (MS, PhD); molecular and cellular science (MS, PhD). *Degree requirements:* For master's, comprehensive exam (for some programs), thesis (for some programs); for doctorate, comprehensive exam (for some programs), thesis/dissertation (for some programs). *Entrance requirements:* For master's and doctorate, GRE. Additional exam requirements/recommendations for international students: Required—TOEFL (minimum score 550 paper-based; 213 computer-based). *Application deadline:* For fall admission, 7/1 for domestic and international students; for spring admission, 12/1 for domestic and international students. Applications are processed on a rolling basis. Application fee: $65. Electronic applications accepted. *Expenses:* Tuition, state resident: full-time $10,048; part-time $558.25 per credit hour. Tuition, nonresident: full-time $19,497; part-time $1083.25 per credit hour. *Required fees:* $405 per semester. Tuition and fees vary according to course load, campus/location and program. *Financial support:* Fellowships with full tuition reimbursements, research assistantships with full tuition reimbursements, teaching assistantships with full tuition reimbursements, career-related internships or fieldwork, Federal Work-Study, scholarships/grants, health care benefits, and unspecified assistantships available. Financial award application deadline: 1/15. *Faculty research:* Nutrition and food science research. *Unit head:* Dr. Susan M. Hutson, Unit Head, 540-231-8766, Fax: 540-231-3916, E-mail: susanh5@vt.edu. *Application contact:* Robert Grange, Information Contact, 540-231-2725, Fax: 540-231-3916, E-mail: rgrange@vt.edu. Web site: http://www.hnfe.vt.edu/.

Washington State University, Graduate School, College of Pharmacy, Department of Nutrition and Physiology, Program in Human Nutrition, Pullman, WA 99164. Offers MS. *Faculty:* 13. *Degree requirements:* For master's, comprehensive exam (for some programs), thesis (for some programs), oral exam, written exam. *Entrance requirements:* For master's, GRE General Test, minimum GPA of 3.0, resume, 3 letters of recommendation, letter of interest. Additional exam requirements/recommendations for international students: Required—TOEFL (minimum score 550 paper-based; 213 computer-based). *Application deadline:* For fall admission, 2/1 priority date for domestic students, 2/1 for international students; for spring admission, 8/1 priority date for domestic students, 7/1 for international students. Applications are processed on a rolling basis. Application fee: $75. Electronic applications accepted. *Financial support:* In 2011–12, 3 students received support, including 1 research assistantship with full and partial tuition reimbursement available (averaging $13,917 per year), 2 teaching assistantships with full and partial tuition reimbursements available (averaging $13,056 per year); career-related internships or fieldwork, Federal Work-Study, scholarships/grants, tuition waivers (partial), and unspecified assistantships also available. Financial award application deadline: 2/1; financial award applicants required to submit FAFSA. *Faculty research:* Nutrition education programs, cultural issues in community nutrition programs. *Unit head:* Dr. Kathryn E. Meier, Chair, 509-335-3573, Fax: 509-335-5902, E-mail: kmeier@wsu.edu. *Application contact:* Graduate School Admissions, 800-GRADWSU, Fax: 509-335-1949, E-mail: gradsch@wsu.edu. Web site: http://www.pharmacy.wsu.edu/nep/index.html.

Washington State University, Graduate School, College of Pharmacy, Department of Nutrition and Physiology, Program in Nutrition, Pullman, WA 99164. Offers PhD. *Faculty:* 10. *Degree requirements:* For doctorate, comprehensive exam, thesis/dissertation, oral exam, written exam. *Entrance requirements:* For doctorate, GRE, minimum GPA of 3.0, resume, 3 letters of recommendation. Additional exam requirements/recommendations for international students: Required—TOEFL (minimum score 550 paper-based; 213 computer-based). *Application deadline:* For fall admission, 2/1 priority date for domestic students, 2/1 for international students; for spring admission, 8/1 priority date for domestic students, 7/1 for international students. Applications are processed on a rolling basis. Application fee: $75. Electronic applications accepted. *Financial support:* In 2011–12, 2 students received support, including 1 fellowship (averaging $3,250 per year), 1 research assistantship with full and partial tuition reimbursement available (averaging $13,917 per year), teaching assistantships with full and partial tuition reimbursements available (averaging $13,056 per year); career-related internships or fieldwork, Federal Work-Study, institutionally sponsored loans, scholarships/grants, health care benefits, tuition waivers (partial), and unspecified assistantships also available. Financial award application deadline: 2/1; financial award applicants required to submit FAFSA. *Faculty research:* Breastfeeding and lactation influence on maternal child wellbeing, sports anemia preschool nutrition. *Unit head:* Dr. Kathryn E. Meier, Chair, 509-335-3573, Fax: 509-335-5902, E-mail:

kmeier@wsu.edu. *Application contact:* Graduate School Admissions, 800-GRADWSU, Fax: 509-335-1949, E-mail: gradsch@wsu.edu.

Wayne State University, College of Liberal Arts and Sciences, Department of Nutrition and Food Science, Detroit, MI 48202. Offers MA, MS, PhD. *Students:* 45 full-time (37 women), 18 part-time (17 women); includes 11 minority (3 Black or African American, non-Hispanic/Latino; 7 Asian, non-Hispanic/Latino; 1 Two or more races, non-Hispanic/Latino), 19 international. Average age 30. 91 applicants, 43% accepted, 22 enrolled. In 2011, 8 master's, 4 doctorates awarded. Terminal master's awarded for partial completion of doctoral program. *Degree requirements:* For master's, thesis (for some programs), essay (for MA); for doctorate, thesis/dissertation. *Entrance requirements:* For master's, GRE General Test, minimum GPA of 3.0, basic courses in nutrition and food science; for doctorate, GRE General Test, minimum GPA of 3.0; two letters of recommendation; personal statement. Additional exam requirements/recommendations for international students: Required—TOEFL (minimum score 550 paper-based; 213 computer-based); Recommended—TWE (minimum score 5.5). *Application deadline:* For fall admission, 12/31 for domestic students, 12/1 for international students; for winter admission, 10/1 priority date for domestic students, 9/1 for international students; for spring admission, 2/1 priority date for domestic students, 1/1 for international students. Applications are processed on a rolling basis. Application fee: $50. Electronic applications accepted. *Expenses:* Tuition, state resident: part-time $512.85 per credit. Tuition, nonresident: part-time $1132.65 per credit. *Required fees:* $26.60 per credit. $199.65 per semester. Tuition and fees vary according to course load and program. *Financial support:* In 2011–12, 22 students received support, including 1 fellowship with tuition reimbursement available (averaging $15,750 per year), 3 research assistantships with tuition reimbursements available (averaging $19,332 per year), 8 teaching assistantships with tuition reimbursements available (averaging $17,467 per year); career-related internships or fieldwork, Federal Work-Study, scholarships/grants, health care benefits, and unspecified assistantships also available. Financial award application deadline: 4/1. *Faculty research:* Nutrition, cancer and gene expression, food microbiology and food safety, lipids, lipoprotein and cholesterol metabolism, obesity and diabetes, metabolomics. *Total annual research expenditures:* $261,392. *Unit head:* Dr. K. L. Catherine Jen, Chair, 313-577-2500, E-mail: ac1578@wayne.edu. *Application contact:* Debra Zebrari, Academic Services Officer II, E-mail: ab8207@wayne.edu. Web site: http://www.science.wayne.edu/~nfs/.

West Virginia University, Davis College of Agriculture, Forestry and Consumer Sciences, Division of Animal and Nutritional Sciences, Program in Animal and Nutritional Sciences, Morgantown, WV 26506. Offers breeding (MS); food sciences (MS); nutrition (MS); physiology (MS); production management (MS); reproduction (MS). Part-time programs available. *Degree requirements:* For master's, thesis, oral and written exams. *Entrance requirements:* For master's, GRE, minimum GPA of 2.5. Additional exam requirements/recommendations for international students: Required—TOEFL. *Faculty research:* Animal nutrition, reproductive physiology, food science.

Winthrop University, College of Arts and Sciences, Department of Human Nutrition, Rock Hill, SC 29733. Offers MS. Part-time programs available. *Degree requirements:* For master's, thesis optional. *Entrance requirements:* For master's, GRE General Test, PRAXIS, or MAT, interview, minimum GPA of 3.0. Electronic applications accepted.

CASE WESTERN RESERVE UNIVERSITY

Case School of Medicine
Department of Nutrition

Programs of Study

The Department of Nutrition offers programs that span the breadth of the discipline, from applied nutrition and dietetics to basic nutritional sciences. These include the Master of Science in Nutrition program; the Master of Science in Public Health Nutrition Internship program, with fieldwork experiences in public health and community-based agencies; and the Coordinated Dietetic Internship/Master's program, with University Hospitals Case Medical Center and Veterans Affairs Medical Center. The Doctor of Philosophy degree is also offered.

The master's degree programs require from one to two years of course work, depending upon the student's undergraduate preparation and the specific program. A thesis or nonthesis option may be selected.

The Ph.D. program emphasizes nutritional biochemistry/metabolism, molecular nutrition, and human nutrition. It builds upon faculty expertise in the Departments of Nutrition, Biochemistry, Molecular Biology, Medicine, and Pediatrics. In recent years, investigators in nutritional biochemistry have used molecular biology techniques to enhance understanding of human metabolism. In the first year, nutrition students join graduate students from the other basic science departments in an integrated course that provides a broad introduction to cellular and molecular biology. The subsequent graduate program includes formal courses in human nutrition and nutritional biochemistry, seminars, and, most importantly, the performance of original research.

Research Facilities

Several well-equipped laboratories are housed in the Case School of Medicine Building. The Department has access to clinical research units at University Hospitals Case Medical Center and Cleveland Clinic Lerner College of Medicine for the conduct of human clinical nutrition and whole-body metabolism studies. The Department has all general equipment necessary for conducting studies in nutritional biochemistry, including three gas chromatographs and mass spectrometers used for human investigation with stable isotopes. Facilities for isolated organ perfusion and a comprehensive organic chemistry laboratory for synthesis of new nutrients are also available.

Financial Aid

The University sponsors a federally funded work-study program as well as loan assistance. Students in the Coordinated Dietetic Internship/Master's Program are paid a stipend by the hospital for the first twelve months of the program. Ph.D. students in nutritional biochemistry or molecular nutrition receive an annual stipend of $25,000 in 2012–13.

Cost of Study

Tuition for 2012–13 is $1546 per credit hour. It is $18,560 per semester for 12 or more credit hours. Partial-tuition scholarships are available for some master's students. Full-tuition scholarships are provided by the Department for students in the Ph.D. nutritional biochemistry or molecular nutrition program.

Living and Housing Costs

Most graduate students find privately owned apartments near the campus. Costs are below average for large urban areas.

Student Group

The University has 9,228 students, of whom about 5,360 are enrolled in graduate and professional schools. About 305 students attend adjacent institutes of music and art. Approximately 85 graduate students are in residence in the Department.

Location

Cleveland is an industrial and financial center. The city is richly endowed with cultural facilities, nearly all of them located in a single area known as the University Circle. In this area are the University, the Cleveland Orchestra, the Museum of Art, the Museum of Natural History, and several excellent repertory theaters. The city is also the home of the Cleveland Indians and Cavaliers and the Rock and Roll Hall of Fame. The camping, sailing, and skiing areas of Ohio, western Pennsylvania, and western New York are readily accessible.

The University and The Department

The strength of its combined science departments places the University in the top rank of institutions in this country. The Department of Nutrition has a number of associate members in several departments in the Case School of Medicine and in the University and has strong ties with the Departments of Chemistry, Biology, and Biomedical Engineering. A major emphasis is on interdisciplinary training programs in biological and chemical sciences.

Applying

Prerequisites for entrance into the Ph.D. program are organic chemistry, biology, and mathematics through calculus. Applications should be submitted in late autumn or early winter for an anticipated entrance in the following autumn semester. Application forms may be obtained from the Department or online at http://www.applyweb.com/apply/cwrug/menu.html. Ph.D. applicants are required to take the Graduate Record Examinations, including the General Test and one Subject Test.

Information concerning application and prerequisites for specific master's programs should be obtained directly from the Department.

Correspondence and Information

Graduate Admissions Committee
Department of Nutrition (M.S. or Ph.D.)
Case Western Reserve University
10900 Euclid Avenue
Cleveland, Ohio 44106-4954
United States
Phone: 216-368-2440
E-mail: paw5@cwru.edu
Web site: http://www.cwru.edu/med/nutrition/home.html

Coordinator
Biomedical Science Training Program (Ph.D. only)
Case School of Medicine
WG1
Case Western Reserve University
Cleveland, Ohio 44106-4935
United States
Phone: 216-368-3347

THE FACULTY AND THEIR RESEARCH

Hope Barkoukis, Associate Professor; Ph.D., Case Western Reserve, 1997. Clinical nutrition, diet and liver cirrhosis.

Henri Brunengraber, Professor and Chairman; M.D., 1968, Ph.D., 1976, Brussels. Metabolic regulation; control of flux through metabolic pathways; design and testing of artificial nutrients; noninvasive probes of liver metabolism; markers of alcoholism; mass spectrometry.

Colleen Croniger, Associate Professor; Ph.D., Case Western Reserve, 1990. Metabolic regulation of carbohydrate and lipid metabolism using genetically altered animal models.

Paul Ernsberger, Associate Professor; Ph.D., Northwestern, 1984. Genetic obesity and the role of nutrition in cardiovascular disease; novel signaling pathways.

Stephanie Harris, Assistant Professor, Ph.D., Case Western Reserve, 2011. The application of metabolomics in the discovery of new metabolites, metabolic pathways, and the characterization of metabolic perturbations induced by drugs and/or specific diseases; mass spectrometry.

Maria Hatzoglou, Professor; Ph.D., Athens, 1985. Identification of retroviral receptors and their use in gene therapy.

Mary Beth Kavanagh, Senior Instructor; M.S., Case Western Reserve, 1992; RD, LD. Nutritional education for nursing and dentistry; nutrition and the media.

Jane Korsberg, Senior Instructor and Private Practice; M.S., Case Western Reserve, 1977; RD, LD.

Edith Lerner, Associate Professor Emeritus; Ph.D., Wisconsin, 1971. Assessment of nutritional status during pregnancy; trace-mineral metabolism during pregnancy; nutritional requirements for the preterm infant.

Danny Manor, Associate Professor; Ph.D., Yeshiva (Einstein), 1989. Molecular-level treatment and prevention of cancer.

Isabel Parraga, Associate Professor and Director, M.S. in Public Health Nutrition Internship Program; Ph.D., Case Western Reserve, 1992. Nutritional anthropology; maternal and child nutrition; public health nutrition; child growth and schistosomiasis.

Kay Sisk, Visiting Instructor; M.S., Case Western Reserve, 2011; RD, LD.

James Swain, Associate Professor and Director, Didactic Program in Dietetics; Ph.D., Iowa State, 2000; RD. Food chemistry; nutrition in management of chronic disease; absorption and efficacy in humans of different forms of iron used in food fortification.

Case Western Reserve University

Guofang Zhang, Assistant Professor, Metabolimics Center; Ph.D., Nanjing (China), 2001; Lipid metabolism in the heart.

Secondary Appointments

Elaine Borawski, A. B. Williamson Professor, Epidemiology and Biostatistics; Ph.D., Case Western Reserve, 1992.

Catherine Demko, Assistant Professor in Dentistry; Ph.D., Case Western Reserve, 2002.

Saul Genuth, Professor in Medicine; M.D., Western Reserve, 1957. Diabetes mellitus; blood glucose control and complications.

Sharon Groh-Wargo, Assistant Professor in Pediatrics and Neonatal Nutritionist, MetroHealth Medical Center, Cleveland, Ohio; Ph.D.; Case Western Reserve, 2002. Tolerance of a nutrient-enriched post-discharge formula for preterm infants.

Sanjay Gupta, Associate Professor in Urology; Ph.D., Avadh (India), 1992. Mechanisms of prostate carcinogenesis, treatment and prevention of prostate cancer.

Richard Hanson, Professor in Biochemistry; Ph.D., Brown, 1963. Hormonal control of gene expression.

Janos Kerner, Assistant Professor; Ph.D., Hungarian Academy, 1986. Mitochondrial fatty acid oxidation and the regulation of the pathway by a malonyl-CoA.

Douglas Kerr, Associate Professor in Pediatrics; M.D./Ph.D., Western Reserve, 1965. Metabolic disorders in infants.

John Kirwan, Associate Professor in Reproductive Biology; Ph.D., Ball State, 1987. Aging; metabolism; endocrinology.

Laura Nagy, Professor in Pathobiology, Cleveland Clinic, Lerner College of Medicine; Ph.D., Berkeley, 1986. Effects of environmental factors such as diet and drugs on cellular signal transduction mechanisms.

Noa Noy, Professor in Pharmacology; Ph.D., Tel Aviv, 1981. Transcriptional regulations by nuclear hormone receptors.

Juan Sanabria, Assistant Professor in Department of Surgery, University Hospitals Case Medical Center; M.D., 1985, Universidad del Rosario (Columbia). Metabolomics in human liver in health and disease.

Adjunct Faculty

Adjunct faculty members provide students with specialized clinical, research, and/or public health fieldwork experiences. Their current job position is listed directly after their name.

Victoria Adeleke, Wake County Human Services WIC Program, Raleigh, North Carolina; M.P.H., North Carolina at Chapel Hill, 1992; RD, LDN.

Phyllis Allen, Office of Public Health, Columbia, South Carolina; M.S., Case Western Reserve, 1989; RD.

Janet Anselmo, Diabetes Self Management Program, Louis Stokes VA Medical Center, Cleveland, Ohio; M.S., Case Western Reserve, 1988; RD, LD.

Karen S. Bakies, American Dairy Association, Columbus, Ohio; B.S., Miami (Ohio), 1984; RD, LD.

Cynthia Bayerl, Massachusetts Department of Public Health; M.S., Boston University, 1976; RD, LDN.

Gina Bayless, Transplant Institute, University Hospitals Case Medical Center, M.S., Case Western Reserve, 2005; RD, LD.

Jennifer Bier, MetroHealth Center for Community Health; M.S., Case Western Reserve, 2002; RD, LD.

Mark Bindus, Twinsburg City School District; B.S., Akron, 1993, RD, LD.

Josephine Anne Cialone, North Carolina Division of Maternal and Child Health; M.S., Case Western Reserve, 1980; RD.

Rachel Colchamiro, Massachusetts WIC Nutrition Program; M.S., Berkeley, 1999; RD, LDN.

Cheri Collier, Clement Center, MetroHealth Center for Community Health, Cleveland, Ohio; M.S. Case Western Reserve, 1998; RD, LD.

Janice Davis, Western Reserve Area on Aging, Cleveland, Ohio; M.S., Case Western Reserve, 1986; RD.

Helen Dumski, Diabetes Association of Greater Cleveland; B.S., Ohio State; RD, LD.

Maureen Faron, Hudson City School District, Hudson, Ohio; B.S., Case Western Reserve; RD, LD.

Marcie Fenton, Los Angeles County Department of Public Health, Los Angeles, California; M.S., Case Western Reserve, 1982; RD.

Denise Ferris, West Virginia Office of Nutrition Services; Ph.D., Pittsburgh, 1989; RD.

Karen Fiedler, Adjunct Associate Professor; Ph.D., Tennessee, Knoxville, 1977.

Cynthia Finohr, Orange City School District; B.S., Kent State, 1981; RD, LD.

Michelle Lundon Fox, Abbott Nutrition, Cleveland, Ohio; M.Ed., Vanderbilt; RD, LD.

Lorna Fuller, Sodexho Marriott Services, Huron Hospital; M.S., Kent State, 1995; RD, LD.

Diana Garrison, Regency Hospitals–Cleveland West, Cleveland, Ohio; B.S. Michigan State, 2001; RD, LD.

Brenda Garritson, Baylor University Medical Center, Dallas, Texas; M.S., Texas Woman's, 1993; RD, LD.

Martha Halko, Cuyahoga County Board of Health; M.S., Akron, 2000; RD, LD.

Samia Hamdan, USDA, Food and Nutrition Service, Chicago; M.P.H., Minnesota, Twin Cities, 2003; RD.

Brigette Hires, Ohio Department of Education; Ph.D., Kentucky, 2005; RD.

Karen Horvath, UH Bedford Medical Center; B.S., Akron, 1986; RD, LD.

Claire Hughes, Hawaii State Department of Health; Dr.P.H., Hawaii, 1998; RD.

Deborah Hutsler, Children's Hospital Medical Center of Akron; Kent State, M.S., 1991; RD, LD.

Rima Itani Al-Nimr, Adjunct Instructor; M.S., Case Western Reserve, 2004; RD, LD.

Natalia Kliszczuk-Smolio, Mt. Alverna Home, Inc., Parma, Ohio; B.S., Cincinnati, 1982; RD, LD.

Katherine Koch, MetroHealth Center for Community Health, Cleveland, Ohio; M.S., Case Western Reserve, 1988; RD, LD.

Richard Koletsky, Adjunct Assistant Clinical Professor; M.D., Case Western Reserve, 1975.

Jennifer Kravec, MetroHealth Medical Center; B.S., Ohio State, 1997; RD, LD.

Lois Lenard, Nutrition and Food Service, Louis Stokes Cleveland VA Medical Center, Cleveland, Ohio; B.S., Kent State, 1974; RD, LD.

Janelle L'Heureux, AIDS Project Los Angeles, Los Angeles, California; M.S., New Haven, Connecticut, 1998; RD.

Patricia Liang-Tong, Native Hawaiian Health Care System; B.S., Hawaii at Manoa, 1998; RD, CDE, CDM, CFPP.

Lauren Melnick, Expanded Food and Nutrition Education Program, OSU Extension, Cleveland, Ohio; M.S., Case Western Reserve, 2007; RD, LD.

Lisa Ogg, Nutrition Health Professional, Cuyahoga County WIC Program; B.S., Kent State, 1996; RD, LD.

Alison Patrick, Cuyahoga County Board of Health; M.P.H., Ohio State, 2006; RD, LD.

Lisa M. Plungas, Adjunct Instructor; M.S., Case Western Reserve, 2012.

Valerie M. Poirier, Cuyahoga County Board of Health, Cleveland, Ohio; B.S., Kent State, 1983; RD, LD.

Stephen Previs, Ph.D., Merck Research Laboratories, Case Western Reserve, 1997.

Barbara Pryor, Ohio Department of Health; M.S., Ohio State, 1994; RD, LD.

Jacqueline Rohr, Parma City School District; B.S., Case Western Reserve, 1973; RD, LD.

Anna Rostafinski, MetroHealth Medical Center (WIC); M.S., Case Western Reserve, 1988; RD, LD.

Maryanne Salsbury, Cuyahoga County WIC Program, Cleveland, Ohio; B.S., Seton Hill; RD, LD.

Joanne Samuels, Solon City School District; B.S., SUNY, 1992; RD, LD.

Sharon Sass, Arizona Department of Health Services, Bureau of Nutrition and Physical Activity; B.S., Nebraska–Lincoln, 1975; RD.

Najeeba Shine, Cuyahoga County Board of Health; M.S., Case Western Reserve, 1992; RD, LD.

Barbara Sipe, Summit County Health District, Ohio; M.A., Kent State, 1979.

Gil Sisneros, California Department of Health Services, Sacramento, California; M.P.H., California State, 1990.

Donna Skoda, Summit County General Health District, Stow, Ohio; M.S., Case Western Reserve, 1980; RD.

Mary Kay Solera, Centers for Disease Control and Prevention, Atlanta, Georgia; M.S., Whitworth, 1988; CHES.

Lura Elizabeth Spinks, Berea City Schools; M.S., Ohio State; RD.

Ann Stahlheber, Cuyahoga County Board of Health, Ohio; M.A., Simmons, 2004; RD, LD, CSN.

Alison Steiber, Adjunct Associate Professor; Ph.D., Michigan State, 2005; RD. General nutrition assessment of patients, with emphasis in chronic renal failure.

Denise Tabar, Olmsted Falls City School District, Ohio; M.S., Kent State, 1982; RD, LD.

Felicia Vatakis, UHCMS Department of Nutrition Services; M.S., NYIT; RD, LD.

Sarah Walden, DaVita Dialysis; M.S., Case Western Reserve, 2002; RD, LD.

Diane Ohama Yates, Medical Nutritional Representative, Ross Products Division, Abbott Laboratories, Cleveland, Ohio; B.S., Hawaii, 1978; RD, LD.

Wendy Youmans, Davita Dialysis; M.S., Case Western Reserve, 1996; RD, LD.

Sharon Zwick-Hamilton, Harborside Health Care; M.S., Case Western Reserve, 1988; RD, LD, CDE, CSG.

Section 15
Parasitology

This section contains a directory of institutions offering graduate work in parasitology. Additional information about programs listed in the directory but not augmented by an in-depth entry may be obtained by writing directly to the dean of a graduate school or chair of a department at the address given in the directory.

For programs offering related work, see also in this book *Allied Health, Biological and Biomedical Sciences, Microbiological Sciences,* and *Public Health.*

CONTENTS

Program Directory

Parasitology

Illinois State University, Graduate School, College of Arts and Sciences, Department of Biological Sciences, Normal, IL 61790-2200. Offers animal behavior (MS); bacteriology (MS); biochemistry (MS); biological sciences (MS); biology (PhD); biophysics (MS); biotechnology (MS); botany (MS, PhD); cell biology (MS); conservation biology (MS); developmental biology (MS); ecology (MS, PhD); entomology (MS); evolutionary biology (MS); genetics (MS, PhD); immunology (MS); microbiology (MS, PhD); molecular biology (MS); molecular genetics (MS); neurobiology (MS); neuroscience (MS); parasitology (MS); physiology (MS, PhD); plant biology (MS); plant molecular biology (MS); plant sciences (MS); structural biology (MS); zoology (MS, PhD). Part-time programs available. *Degree requirements:* For master's, thesis or alternative; for doctorate, variable foreign language requirement, thesis/dissertation, 2 terms of residency. *Entrance requirements:* For master's, GRE General Test, minimum GPA of 2.6 in last 60 hours of course work; for doctorate, GRE General Test. *Faculty research:* Redoc balance and drug development in schistosoma mansoni, control of the growth of listeria monocytogenes at low temperature, regulation of cell expansion and microtubule function by SPRI, CRUI: physiology and fitness consequences of different life history phenotypes.

Louisiana State University Health Sciences Center, School of Graduate Studies in New Orleans, Department of Microbiology, Immunology, and Parasitology, New Orleans, LA 70112-1393. Offers microbiology and immunology (MS, PhD); MD/PhD. Terminal master's awarded for partial completion of doctoral program. *Degree requirements:* For master's, comprehensive exam, thesis; for doctorate, comprehensive exam, thesis/dissertation, preliminary exam, qualifying exam. *Entrance requirements:* For master's and doctorate, GRE General Test. Additional exam requirements/recommendations for international students: Required—TOEFL. *Faculty research:* Microbial physiology, animal virology, vaccine development, AIDS drug studies, pathogenic mechanisms, molecular immunology.

McGill University, Faculty of Graduate and Postdoctoral Studies, Faculty of Agricultural and Environmental Sciences, Institute of Parasitology, Montréal, QC H3A 2T5, Canada. Offers biotechnology (M Sc A, Certificate); parasitology (M Sc, PhD).

New York University, School of Medicine, New York, NY 10012-1019. Offers biomedical sciences (PhD), including biomedical imaging, cellular and molecular biology, computational biology, developmental genetics, medical and molecular parasitology, microbiology, molecular oncobiology and immunology, neuroscience and physiology, pathobiology, pharmacology, structural biology; clinical investigation (MS); medicine (MD); MD/MA; MD/MPA; MD/MS; MD/PhD. *Accreditation:* LCME/AMA (one or more programs are accredited). *Degree requirements:* For master's, comprehensive exam, thesis; for doctorate, comprehensive exam (for some programs), thesis/dissertation (for some programs). *Entrance requirements:* For doctorate, MCAT (for MD). Additional exam requirements/recommendations for international students: Required—TOEFL. *Expenses:* Contact institution. *Faculty research:* AIDS, cancer, neuroscience, molecular biology, neuroscience, cell biology and molecular genetics, structural biology, microbial pathogenesis and host defense, pharmacology, molecular oncology and immunology.

Texas A&M University, College of Veterinary Medicine and Biomedical Sciences, Department of Veterinary Pathobiology, College Station, TX 77843. Offers genetics (MS, PhD); veterinary microbiology (MS, PhD); veterinary parasitology (MS, PhD); veterinary pathology (MS, PhD). Part-time programs available. Postbaccalaureate distance learning degree programs offered. *Faculty:* 25. *Students:* 27 full-time (20 women), 19 part-time (13 women); includes 9 minority (3 Black or African American, non-Hispanic/Latino; 3 Asian, non-Hispanic/Latino; 3 Hispanic/Latino), 9 international. Average age 33. In 2011, 2 degrees awarded. Terminal master's awarded for partial completion of doctoral program. *Degree requirements:* For master's, thesis, seminars; for doctorate, thesis/dissertation, seminars. *Entrance requirements:* For master's and doctorate, GRE General Test, minimum GPA of 3.0 in last 60 hours. Additional exam requirements/recommendations for international students: Required—TOEFL. *Application deadline:* For fall admission, 3/1 priority date for domestic students; for spring admission, 8/1 priority date for domestic students. Applications are processed on a rolling basis. Application fee: $50 ($75 for international students). Electronic applications accepted. *Expenses:* Tuition, state resident: full-time $5437; part-time $226.55 per credit hour. Tuition, nonresident: full-time $12,949; part-time $539.55 per credit hour. *Required fees:* $2741. *Financial support:* In 2011–12, fellowships with partial tuition reimbursements (averaging $16,000 per year), research assistantships with partial tuition reimbursements (averaging $15,400 per year), teaching assistantships with partial tuition reimbursements (averaging $16,000 per year) were awarded; Federal Work-Study, institutionally sponsored loans, scholarships/grants, traineeships, health care benefits, and unspecified assistantships also available. Support available to part-time students. Financial award applicants required to submit FAFSA. *Faculty research:* Infectious and noninfectious diseases of animals and birds, animal genetics, molecular biology, immunology, virology. *Unit head:* Dr. Linda Logan, Head, 979-862-6559, Fax: 979-845-9231, E-mail: llogan@cvm.tamu.edu. *Application contact:* Dr. Patricia Holman, Graduate Advisor, 979-845-4202, Fax: 979-862-1147, E-mail: pholman@cvm.tamu.edu. Web site: http://vetmed.tamu.edu/vtpb.

Tulane University, School of Public Health and Tropical Medicine, Department of Tropical Medicine, New Orleans, LA 70118-5669. Offers clinical tropical medicine and travelers health (Diploma); parasitology (MSPH, PhD); public health and tropical medicine (MPHTM); vector borne infectious diseases (MS, PhD); MD/PhD. MS and PhD offered through the Graduate School. *Degree requirements:* For master's, thesis; for doctorate, comprehensive exam, thesis/dissertation. *Entrance requirements:* For master's, GRE General Test, minimum B average in undergraduate course work; for doctorate, GRE General Test. Additional exam requirements/recommendations for international students: Required—TOEFL.

University of Notre Dame, Graduate School, College of Science, Department of Biological Sciences, Notre Dame, IN 46556. Offers aquatic ecology, evolution and environmental biology (MS, PhD); cellular and molecular biology (MS, PhD); genetics (MS, PhD); physiology (MS, PhD); vector biology and parasitology (MS, PhD). Terminal master's awarded for partial completion of doctoral program. *Degree requirements:* For master's, comprehensive exam, thesis; for doctorate, comprehensive exam, thesis/dissertation, candidacy exam. *Entrance requirements:* For master's and doctorate, GRE General Test. Additional exam requirements/recommendations for international students: Required—TOEFL (minimum score 600 paper-based; 250 computer-based; 80 iBT). Electronic applications accepted. *Faculty research:* Tropical disease, molecular genetics, neurobiology, evolutionary biology, aquatic biology.

University of Prince Edward Island, Atlantic Veterinary College, Graduate Program in Veterinary Medicine, Charlottetown, PE C1A 4P3, Canada. Offers anatomy (M Sc, PhD); bacteriology (M Sc, PhD); clinical pharmacology (M Sc, PhD); clinical sciences (M Sc, PhD); epidemiology (M Sc, PhD), including reproduction; fish health (M Sc, PhD); food animal nutrition (M Sc, PhD); immunology (M Sc, PhD); microanatomy (M Sc, PhD); parasitology (M Sc, PhD); pathology (M Sc, PhD); pharmacology (M Sc, PhD); physiology (M Sc, PhD); toxicology (M Sc, PhD); veterinary science (M Vet Sc); virology (M Sc, PhD). Part-time programs available. *Degree requirements:* For master's, thesis; for doctorate, thesis/dissertation. *Entrance requirements:* For master's, DVM, B Sc honors degree, or equivalent; for doctorate, M Sc. Additional exam requirements/recommendations for international students: Required—TOEFL (minimum score 550 paper-based; 213 computer-based; 80 iBT). *Expenses:* Contact institution. *Faculty research:* Animal health management, infectious diseases, fin fish and shellfish health, basic biomedical sciences, ecosystem health.

University of Washington, Graduate School, School of Public Health, Department of Global Health, Graduate Program in Pathobiology, Seattle, WA 98195. Offers PhD. *Students:* 32 full-time (25 women), 3 part-time (all women); includes 7 minority (2 Black or African American, non-Hispanic/Latino; 3 Asian, non-Hispanic/Latino; 2 Hispanic/Latino), 5 international. Average age 29. 75 applicants, 20% accepted, 5 enrolled. In 2011, 3 doctorates awarded. *Degree requirements:* For doctorate, comprehensive exam, thesis/dissertation, published paper from thesis work. *Entrance requirements:* For doctorate, GRE General Test, minimum GPA of 3.0. Additional exam requirements/recommendations for international students: Required—TOEFL, IELTS. *Application deadline:* For fall admission, 12/1 for domestic students, 11/1 for international students. Application fee: $75. Electronic applications accepted. *Financial support:* In 2011–12, 34 students received support, including 34 research assistantships with full tuition reimbursements available (averaging $27,348 per year); traineeships and unspecified assistantships also available. *Faculty research:* Malaria, immunological response to mycobacteria infections, HIV-cell interaction and the development of an anti-HIV vaccine, regulation of intercellular communication via gap junctions, genetic and nutritional regulation of proteins involved in lipid transport. *Unit head:* Dr. King Holmes, Chair, 206-744-3620, Fax: 206-744-3694. *Application contact:* Rachel Reichert, Program Manager, 206-543-4338, Fax: 206-543-3873, E-mail: pabio@u.washington.edu.

Section 16
Pathology and Pathobiology

This section contains a directory of institutions offering graduate work in pathology and pathobiology, followed by an in-depth entry submitted by an institution that chose to submit a detailed program description. Additional information about programs listed in the directory but not augmented by an in-depth entry may be obtained by writing directly to the dean of a graduate school or chair of a department at the address given in the directory.

For programs offering related work, see also in this book *Allied Health; Anatomy; Biochemistry; Biological and Biomedical Sciences; Cell, Molecular, and Structural Biology; Genetics, Developmental Biology, and Reproductive Biology; Microbiological Sciences; Pharmacology and Toxicology; Physiology, Public Health,* and *Veterinary Medicine and Sciences.*

CONTENTS

Molecular Pathogenesis

Dartmouth College, Graduate Program in Molecular and Cellular Biology, Department of Microbiology and Immunology, Program in Molecular Pathogenesis, Hanover, NH 03755. Offers microbiology and immunology (PhD).

Emory University, Laney Graduate School, Division of Biological and Biomedical Sciences, Program in Immunology and Molecular Pathogenesis, Atlanta, GA 30322-1100. Offers PhD. *Faculty:* 49 full-time (6 women). *Students:* 75 full-time (42 women); includes 20 minority (2 Black or African American, non-Hispanic/Latino; 1 American Indian or Alaska Native, non-Hispanic/Latino; 12 Asian, non-Hispanic/Latino; 4 Hispanic/Latino; 1 Two or more races, non-Hispanic/Latino), 5 international. Average age 27. 231 applicants, 15% accepted, 15 enrolled. In 2011, 7 degrees awarded. *Median time to degree:* Of those who began their doctoral program in fall 2003, 100% received their degree in 8 years or less. *Degree requirements:* For doctorate, comprehensive exam, thesis/dissertation. *Entrance requirements:* For doctorate, GRE General Test, minimum GPA of 3.0 in science course work (recommended). Additional exam requirements/recommendations for international students: Required—TOEFL. *Application deadline:* For fall admission, 12/1 for domestic and international students. Application fee: $75. Electronic applications accepted. *Expenses: Tuition:* Full-time $34,800. *Required fees:* $1300. *Financial support:* In 2011–12, 30 students received support, including 30 fellowships with full tuition reimbursements available (averaging $26,500 per year); institutionally sponsored loans, scholarships/grants, health care benefits, and tuition waivers (full) also available. *Faculty research:* Transplantation immunology, autoimmunity, microbial pathogenesis. *Unit head:* Dr. Brian Evavold, Director, 404-727-3393, Fax: 404-727-3659, E-mail: evavold@microbio.emory.edu. *Application contact:* Kathy Smith, Director of Recruitment and Admissions, 404-727-2547, Fax: 404-727-3322, E-mail: kathy.smith@emory.edu. Web site: http://www.biomed.emory.edu/PROGRAM_SITES/IMP/.

North Dakota State University, College of Graduate and Interdisciplinary Studies, College of Agriculture, Food Systems, and Natural Resources, Department of Veterinary and Microbiological Sciences, Fargo, ND 58108. Offers food safety (MS); microbiology (MS); molecular pathogenesis (PhD). Part-time programs available. *Faculty:* 8 full-time (6 women). *Students:* 15 full-time (5 women), 5 part-time (3 women), 9 international. 24 applicants, 46% accepted, 3 enrolled. In 2011, 1 master's, 1 doctorate awarded. *Degree requirements:* For master's, thesis; for doctorate, thesis/dissertation, oral and written preliminary exams. *Entrance requirements:* For master's and doctorate, GRE. Additional exam requirements/recommendations for international students: Required—TOEFL (minimum score 525 paper-based; 197 computer-based; 71 iBT). *Application deadline:* For fall admission, 2/15 priority date for domestic students. Applications are processed on a rolling basis. Application fee: $35. *Financial support:* Fellowships with full tuition reimbursements, research assistantships with full tuition reimbursements, teaching assistantships with full tuition reimbursements, Federal Work-Study, and institutionally sponsored loans available. Financial award application deadline: 4/15. *Faculty research:* Bacterial gene regulation, antibiotic resistance, molecular virology, mechanisms of bacterial pathogenesis, immunology of animals. *Unit head:* Dr. Charlene Wolf-Hall, Head, 701-231-7667, E-mail: charlene.hall@ndsu.edu. *Application contact:* Dr. John McEvoy, Associate Professor, 701-231-8530, Fax: 701-231-7514, E-mail: eugene.berry@ndsu.edu. Web site: http://vetmicro.ndsu.nodak.edu/.

Texas A&M Health Science Center, College of Medicine, Department of Microbial and Molecular Pathogenesis, College Station, TX 77840. Offers immunology (PhD); microbiology (PhD); molecular biology (PhD); virology (PhD). *Degree requirements:* For doctorate, thesis/dissertation. *Entrance requirements:* For doctorate, GRE General Test, minimum GPA of 3.0. *Faculty research:* Molecular pathogenesis, microbial therapeutics.

University at Albany, State University of New York, School of Public Health, Department of Biomedical Sciences, Program in Molecular Pathogenesis, Albany, NY 12222-0001. Offers MS, PhD. *Degree requirements:* For master's, thesis; for doctorate, thesis/dissertation. *Entrance requirements:* For master's and doctorate, GRE General Test, GRE Subject Test.

University of Chicago, Division of Biological Sciences, Biomedical Sciences Cluster: Cancer Biology, Immunology, Molecular Metabolism and Nutrition, Pathology, and Microbiology, Department of Pathology, Chicago, IL 60637-1513. Offers molecular pathogenesis and molecular medicine (PhD). *Degree requirements:* For doctorate, thesis/dissertation, ethics class, 2 teaching assistantships. *Entrance requirements:* For doctorate, GRE General Test. Additional exam requirements/recommendations for international students: Required—IELTS (minimum score 7); Recommended—TOEFL (minimum score 600 paper-based; 250 computer-based; 104 iBT). Electronic applications accepted. *Faculty research:* Vascular biology, apolipoproteins, cardiovascular disease, immunopathology.

Washington University in St. Louis, Graduate School of Arts and Sciences, Division of Biology and Biomedical Sciences, Program in Molecular Microbiology and Microbial Pathogenesis, St. Louis, MO 63130-4899. Offers PhD. *Degree requirements:* For doctorate, thesis/dissertation. *Entrance requirements:* For doctorate, GRE General Test, GRE Subject Test. Electronic applications accepted.

Molecular Pathology

Texas Tech University Health Sciences Center, School of Allied Health Sciences, Program in Molecular Pathology, Lubbock, TX 79430. Offers MS. *Faculty:* 10 full-time (8 women). *Students:* 18 full-time (5 women); includes 7 minority (4 Asian, non-Hispanic/Latino; 3 Hispanic/Latino). Average age 29. 36 applicants, 53% accepted, 18 enrolled. In 2011, 20 master's awarded. *Entrance requirements:* Additional exam requirements/recommendations for international students: Required—TOEFL, IELTS. *Application deadline:* For spring admission, 3/1 priority date for domestic students. Application fee: $35. Electronic applications accepted. *Financial support:* Career-related internships or fieldwork, institutionally sponsored loans, and scholarships/grants available. Financial award applicants required to submit FAFSA. *Unit head:* Dr. Hal Larsen, Chair, 806-743-3223, E-mail: hal.larsen@ttuhsc.edu. *Application contact:* Jeri Moravcik, Assistant Director of Admissions and Student Affairs, 806-743-3220, Fax: 806-743-2994, E-mail: jeri.moravcik@ttuhsc.edu.

University of California, San Diego, School of Medicine and Office of Graduate Studies, Molecular Pathology Program, La Jolla, CA 92093. Offers bioinformatics (PhD); cancer biology/oncology (PhD); cardiovascular sciences and disease (PhD); microbiology (PhD); molecular pathology (PhD); neurological disease (PhD); stem cell and developmental biology (PhD); structural biology/drug design (PhD). *Entrance requirements:* For doctorate, GRE General Test, GRE Subject Test. Additional exam requirements/recommendations for international students: Required—TOEFL. Electronic applications accepted.

University of Medicine and Dentistry of New Jersey, Graduate School of Biomedical Sciences, Graduate Programs in Biomedical Sciences–Newark, Program in Molecular Pathology and Immunology, Newark, NJ 07107. Offers PhD. *Entrance requirements:* Additional exam requirements/recommendations for international students: Required—TOEFL. Electronic applications accepted.

University of Medicine and Dentistry of New Jersey, Graduate School of Biomedical Sciences, Graduate Programs in Biomedical Sciences–Stratford, Stratford, NJ 08084-5634. Offers biomedical sciences (MBS, MS); cell and molecular biology (MS, PhD); molecular pathology and immunology (MS); DO/MS; DO/PhD; MBS/MPH; MS/MPH. Part-time and evening/weekend programs available. Terminal master's awarded for partial completion of doctoral program. *Degree requirements:* For master's, thesis (for some programs); for doctorate, thesis/dissertation, qualifying exam. *Entrance requirements:* For master's, GRE General Test, MCAT or DAT; for doctorate, GRE General Test. Additional exam requirements/recommendations for international students: Required—TOEFL. Electronic applications accepted.

University of Michigan, Horace H. Rackham School of Graduate Studies, Program in Biomedical Sciences (PIBS), Program in Molecular and Cellular Pathology, Ann Arbor, MI 48109-2200. Offers PhD. *Faculty:* 39 full-time (10 women). *Students:* 23 full-time (11 women); includes 10 minority (1 Black or African American, non-Hispanic/Latino; 9 Asian, non-Hispanic/Latino). Average age 29. 62 applicants, 13% accepted, 5 enrolled. In 2011, 3 doctorates awarded. *Degree requirements:* For doctorate, comprehensive exam, thesis/dissertation. *Entrance requirements:* For doctorate, GRE General Test, 3 letters of recommendation, research experience. Additional exam requirements/recommendations for international students: Required—TOEFL (minimum score 84 iBT). *Application deadline:* For fall admission, 12/1 for domestic and international students. Application fee: $60 ($75 for international students). Electronic applications accepted. *Financial support:* In 2011–12, research assistantships with full tuition reimbursements (averaging $26,500 per year) were awarded; scholarships/grants, traineeships, health care benefits, and unspecified assistantships also available. *Faculty research:* Cancer biology, stem cell and developmental biology, immunopathology and inflammatory disease, epigenetics and gene regulation, cell death and regulation. *Unit head:* Dr. Nicholas W. Lukacs, Professor of Pathology/Director, 734-763-6454, Fax: 734-615-2331, E-mail: pathgradprog@med.umich.edu. *Application contact:* Laura A. Labut, Administrative Specialist, 734-763-6454, Fax: 734-615-2331, E-mail: laszczem@med.umich.edu. Web site: http://www.pathology.med.umich.edu/.

University of Pittsburgh, School of Medicine, Graduate Programs in Medicine, Program in Cellular and Molecular Pathology, Pittsburgh, PA 15260. Offers MS, PhD. *Faculty:* 66 full-time (17 women). *Students:* 35 full-time (20 women); includes 9 minority (3 Black or African American, non-Hispanic/Latino; 4 Asian, non-Hispanic/Latino; 2 Hispanic/Latino), 8 international. Average age 27. 514 applicants, 12% accepted, 28 enrolled. In 2011, 8 doctorates awarded. *Degree requirements:* For doctorate, comprehensive exam, thesis/dissertation. *Entrance requirements:* For doctorate, GRE General Test, GRE Subject Test, minimum QPA of 3.0. Additional exam requirements/recommendations for international students: Required—TOEFL (minimum score 600 paper-based; 100 iBT), IELTS (minimum score 7). *Application deadline:* For fall admission, 12/15 priority date for domestic students, 12/15 for international students. Application fee: $50. Electronic applications accepted. *Expenses:* Tuition, state resident: full-time $18,774; part-time $760 per credit. Tuition, nonresident: full-time $30,736; part-time $1258 per credit. *Required fees:* $740; $200 per term. Tuition and fees vary according to program. *Financial support:* In 2011–12, 11 fellowships with full tuition reimbursements (averaging $25,500 per year), 24 research assistantships with full tuition reimbursements (averaging $25,500 per year) were awarded; teaching assistantships with full tuition reimbursements, institutionally sponsored loans, scholarships/grants, traineeships, health care benefits, and unspecified assistantships also available. *Faculty research:* Liver growth and differentiation, pathogenesis of neurodegeneration, cancer research. *Unit head:* Dr. Wendy Mars, Graduate Program Director, 412-648-9690, Fax: 412-648-9846, E-mail: wmars@pitt.edu. *Application contact:* Graduate Studies Administrator, 412-648-8957, Fax: 412-648-1077, E-mail: gradstudies@medschool.pitt.edu. Web site: http://www.gradbiomed.pitt.edu.

The University of Texas Health Science Center at Houston, Graduate School of Biomedical Sciences, Program in Molecular Pathology, Houston, TX 77225-0036. Offers MS, PhD, MD/PhD. Terminal master's awarded for partial completion of doctoral program. *Degree requirements:* For master's, thesis; for doctorate, thesis/dissertation. *Entrance requirements:* For master's and doctorate, GRE General Test. Additional exam requirements/recommendations for international students: Required—TOEFL. Electronic applications accepted. *Faculty research:* Infectious disease, carcinogenesis, structural biology, cell biology.

Yale University, School of Medicine and Graduate School of Arts and Sciences, Combined Program in Biological and Biomedical Sciences (BBS), Pharmacological Sciences and Molecular Medicine Track, New Haven, CT 06520. Offers PhD, MD/PhD. *Degree requirements:* For doctorate, thesis/dissertation. *Entrance requirements:* For doctorate, GRE General Test. Additional exam requirements/recommendations for international students: Required—TOEFL. Electronic applications accepted.

Pathobiology

Auburn University, College of Veterinary Medicine and Graduate School, Graduate Programs in Veterinary Medicine, Auburn University, AL 36849. Offers biomedical sciences (MS, PhD), including anatomy, physiology and pharmacology (MS), biomedical sciences (PhD), clinical sciences (MS), large animal surgery and medicine (MS), pathobiology (MS), radiology (MS), small animal surgery and medicine (MS); DVM/MS. Part-time programs available. *Faculty:* 100 full-time (40 women), 5 part-time/adjunct (1 woman). *Students:* 17 full-time (13 women), 59 part-time (33 women); includes 6 minority (1 Black or African American, non-Hispanic/Latino; 3 Asian, non-Hispanic/Latino; 2 Hispanic/Latino), 30 international. Average age 30. 36 applicants, 69% accepted, 11 enrolled. In 2011, 19 master's awarded. *Degree requirements:* For doctorate, thesis/dissertation. *Entrance requirements:* For master's, GRE General Test; for doctorate, GRE General Test, GRE Subject Test. *Application deadline:* For fall admission, 7/7 for domestic students; for spring admission, 11/24 for domestic students. Applications are processed on a rolling basis. Application fee: $50 ($60 for international students). Electronic applications accepted. *Expenses:* Tuition, state resident: full-time $7290; part-time $405 per credit hour. Tuition, nonresident: full-time $21,870; part-time $1215 per credit hour. *International tuition:* $22,000 full-time. *Required fees:* $1402. *Financial support:* Research assistantships, teaching assistantships, and Federal Work-Study available. Support available to part-time students. Financial award application deadline: 3/15; financial award applicants required to submit FAFSA. *Unit head:* Dr. Calvin Johnson, Acting Dean, 334-844-2650. *Application contact:* Dr. George Flowers, Dean of the Graduate School, 334-844-2125.

Brown University, Graduate School, Division of Biology and Medicine, Program in Pathology and Laboratory Medicine, Providence, RI 02912. Offers biology (PhD); cancer biology (PhD); immunology and infection (PhD); medical science (PhD); pathobiology (Sc M); toxicology and environmental pathology (PhD). Terminal master's awarded for partial completion of doctoral program. *Degree requirements:* For doctorate, thesis/dissertation, preliminary exam. *Entrance requirements:* For master's and doctorate, GRE General Test, GRE Subject Test. Additional exam requirements/recommendations for international students: Required—TOEFL. Electronic applications accepted. *Faculty research:* Environmental pathology, carcinogenesis, immunopathology, signal transduction, innate immunity.

Columbia University, College of Physicians and Surgeons, Department of Pathology, New York, NY 10032. Offers pathobiology (M Phil, MA, PhD); MD/PhD. Only candidates for the PhD are admitted. Terminal master's awarded for partial completion of doctoral program. *Degree requirements:* For doctorate, thesis/dissertation. *Entrance requirements:* For master's and doctorate, GRE General Test. Additional exam requirements/recommendations for international students: Required—TOEFL. *Faculty research:* Virology, molecular biology, cell biology, neurobiology, immunology.

Drexel University, College of Medicine, Biomedical Graduate Programs, Interdisciplinary Program in Molecular Pathobiology, Philadelphia, PA 19104-2875. Offers MS, PhD, MD/PhD. *Degree requirements:* For doctorate, comprehensive exam, thesis/dissertation, qualifying exams. *Entrance requirements:* For doctorate, GRE General Test, minimum GPA of 3.0. Additional exam requirements/recommendations for international students: Required—TOEFL. Electronic applications accepted. *Faculty research:* Cell and molecular immunology, tumor immunology, molecular genetics, immunopathology, immunology of aging.

The Johns Hopkins University, School of Medicine, Graduate Programs in Medicine, Department of Pathology, Baltimore, MD 21218-2699. Offers pathobiology (PhD). *Degree requirements:* For doctorate, thesis/dissertation, qualifying oral exam. *Entrance requirements:* For doctorate, GRE General Test, previous course work with laboratory in organic and inorganic chemistry, general biology, calculus; interview. Additional exam requirements/recommendations for international students: Required—TOEFL. Electronic applications accepted. *Faculty research:* Role of mutant proteins in Alzheimer's disease, nuclear protein function in breast and prostate cancer, medically important fungi, glycoproteins in HIV pathogenesis.

Kansas State University, College of Veterinary Medicine, Department of Diagnostic Medicine/Pathobiology, Manhattan, KS 66506. Offers biomedical science (MS); diagnostic medicine/pathobiology (PhD). *Faculty:* 24 full-time (7 women), 4 part-time/adjunct (2 women). *Students:* 30 full-time (16 women), 23 part-time (15 women); includes 6 minority (1 Black or African American, non-Hispanic/Latino; 1 Asian, non-Hispanic/Latino; 3 Hispanic/Latino; 1 Native Hawaiian or other Pacific Islander, non-Hispanic/Latino), 15 international. Average age 29. 8 applicants, 50% accepted, 1 enrolled. In 2011, 16 master's, 11 doctorates awarded. Terminal master's awarded for partial completion of doctoral program. *Degree requirements:* For doctorate, thesis/dissertation. *Entrance requirements:* For master's and doctorate, interviews. Additional exam requirements/recommendations for international students: Required—TOEFL (minimum score 550 paper-based; 213 computer-based). *Application deadline:* For fall admission, 2/1 priority date for domestic students, 2/1 for international students; for spring admission, 8/1 priority date for domestic students, 8/1 for international students. Applications are processed on a rolling basis. Application fee: $40 ($55 for international students). Electronic applications accepted. *Financial support:* In 2011–12, 22 research assistantships (averaging $21,849 per year) were awarded; Federal Work-Study, institutionally sponsored loans, and scholarships/grants also available. Financial award application deadline: 3/1; financial award applicants required to submit FAFSA. *Faculty research:* Infectious disease of animals, food safety and security, epidemiology and public health, toxicology, and pathology. *Total annual research expenditures:* $6.8 million. *Unit head:* M. M. Chengappa, Head, 785-532-4403, E-mail: chengap@ksu.edu. *Application contact:* T. G. Nagaraja, Director, 785-532-1214, E-mail: tnagaraj@ksu.edu. Web site: http://www.vet.k-state.edu/depts/dmp/.

Medical University of South Carolina, College of Graduate Studies, Program in Molecular and Cellular Biology and Pathobiology, Charleston, SC 29425. Offers cancer biology (PhD); cardiovascular biology (PhD); cardiovascular imaging (PhD); cell regulation (PhD); craniofacial biology (PhD); genetics and development (PhD); marine biomedicine (PhD); DMD/PhD; MD/PhD. *Faculty:* 137 full-time (33 women). *Students:* 28 full-time (23 women); includes 5 minority (4 Black or African American, non-Hispanic/Latino; 1 Hispanic/Latino), 5 international. Average age 30. In 2011, 16 doctorates awarded. *Degree requirements:* For doctorate, thesis/dissertation, oral and written exams. *Entrance requirements:* For doctorate, GRE General Test, interview, minimum GPA of 3.0. Additional exam requirements/recommendations for international students: Required—TOEFL (minimum score 600 paper-based; 250 computer-based; 100 iBT). *Application deadline:* For fall admission, 1/15 priority date for domestic students, 1/15 for international students. Applications are processed on a rolling basis. Application fee: $0 ($85 for international students). Electronic applications accepted. *Financial support:* In 2011–12, 39 research assistantships with partial tuition reimbursements (averaging $23,000 per year) were awarded; Federal Work-Study and scholarships/grants also available. Support available to part-time students. Financial award application deadline: 3/10; financial award applicants required to submit FAFSA. *Unit head:* Dr. Donald R. Menick, Director, 843-876-5045, Fax: 843-792-6590, E-mail: menickd@musc.edu. *Application contact:* Dr. Cynthia F. Wright, Associate Dean for Admissions and Career Development, 843-792-2564, Fax: 843-792-6590, E-mail: wrightcf@musc.edu. Web site: http://www.musc.edu/mcbp/.

Michigan State University, College of Veterinary Medicine and The Graduate School, Graduate Programs in Veterinary Medicine, Department of Pathobiology and Diagnostic Investigation, East Lansing, MI 48824. Offers pathology (MS, PhD); pathology–environmental toxicology (PhD). *Entrance requirements:* Additional exam requirements/recommendations for international students: Required—TOEFL. Electronic applications accepted.

New York University, School of Medicine, New York, NY 10012-1019. Offers biomedical sciences (PhD), including biomedical imaging, cellular and molecular biology, computational biology, developmental genetics, medical and molecular parasitology, microbiology, molecular oncobiology and immunology, neuroscience and physiology, pathobiology, pharmacology, structural biology; clinical investigation (MS); medicine (MD); MD/MA; MD/MPA; MD/MS; MD/PhD. *Accreditation:* LCME/AMA (one or more programs are accredited). *Degree requirements:* For master's, comprehensive exam, thesis; for doctorate, comprehensive exam (for some programs), thesis/dissertation (for some programs). *Entrance requirements:* For doctorate, MCAT (for MD). Additional exam requirements/recommendations for international students: Required—TOEFL. *Expenses:* Contact institution. *Faculty research:* AIDS, cancer, neuroscience, molecular biology, neuroscience, cell biology and molecular genetics, structural biology, microbial pathogenesis and host defense, pharmacology, molecular oncology and immunology.

New York University, School of Medicine and Graduate School of Arts and Science, Sackler Institute of Graduate Biomedical Sciences, Program in Pathobiology, New York, NY 10012-1019. Offers PhD. *Faculty:* 19 full-time (4 women). *Students:* 20 full-time (14 women); includes 6 minority (2 Black or African American, non-Hispanic/Latino; 4 Hispanic/Latino), 2 international. Average age 26. *Unit head:* Dr. Joel D. Oppenheim, Senior Associate Dean for Graduate Studies, 212-263-8001, Fax: 212-263-7600. *Application contact:* Lisabeth Greene, Program Coordinator, 212-263-5648, Fax: 212-263-7600, E-mail: sackler-info@med.nyu.edu.

The Ohio State University, College of Medicine, Department of Pathology, Columbus, OH 43210. Offers experimental pathobiology (MS); pathology assistant (MS); MD/PhD. *Accreditation:* NAACLS. *Degree requirements:* For master's, comprehensive exam (for some programs), thesis. *Entrance requirements:* For master's, GRE General Test. Additional exam requirements/recommendations for international students: Required—TOEFL (minimum score 550 paper-based; 213 computer-based). Electronic applications accepted. *Expenses:* Tuition, state resident: full-time $11,400. Tuition, nonresident: full-time $28,125. Tuition and fees vary according to course load, degree level, campus/location and program. *Faculty research:* Clinical pathology, transplantation pathology, cancer research, neuropathology, vascular pathology.

Penn State University Park, Graduate School, College of Agricultural Sciences, Department of Veterinary and Biomedical Sciences, State College, University Park, PA 16802-1503. Offers pathobiology (MS, PhD). *Unit head:* Dr. Bruce A. McPheron, Dean, 814-865-2541, Fax: 814-865-3103, E-mail: bam10@psu.edu. *Application contact:* Cynthia E. Nicosia, Director of Graduate Enrollment Services, 814-865-1834, E-mail: cey1@psu.edu. Web site: http://vbs.psu.edu/.

Purdue University, School of Veterinary Medicine and Graduate School, Graduate Programs in Veterinary Medicine, Department of Comparative Pathobiology, West Lafayette, IN 47907-2027. Offers comparative epidemiology and public health (MS); comparative epidemiology and public heath (PhD); comparative microbiology and immunology (MS, PhD); comparative pathobiology (MS, PhD); interdisciplinary studies (PhD), including microbial pathogenesis, molecular signaling and cancer biology, molecular virology; lab animal medicine (MS); veterinary anatomic pathology (MS); veterinary clinical pathology (MS). Terminal master's awarded for partial completion of doctoral program. *Degree requirements:* For master's, thesis (for some programs); for doctorate, thesis/dissertation. *Entrance requirements:* For master's and doctorate, GRE General Test. Additional exam requirements/recommendations for international students: Required—TOEFL (minimum score 575 paper-based; 232 computer-based), IELTS (minimum score 6.5), TWE (minimum score 4). Electronic applications accepted.

Texas A&M University, College of Veterinary Medicine and Biomedical Sciences, Department of Veterinary Pathobiology, College Station, TX 77843. Offers genetics (MS, PhD); veterinary microbiology (MS, PhD); veterinary parasitology (MS, PhD); veterinary pathology (MS, PhD). Part-time programs available. Postbaccalaureate distance learning degree programs offered. *Faculty:* 25. *Students:* 27 full-time (20 women), 19 part-time (13 women); includes 9 minority (3 Black or African American, non-Hispanic/Latino; 3 Asian, non-Hispanic/Latino; 3 Hispanic/Latino), 9 international. Average age 33. In 2011, 2 degrees awarded. Terminal master's awarded for partial completion of doctoral program. *Degree requirements:* For master's, thesis, seminars; for doctorate, thesis/dissertation, seminars. *Entrance requirements:* For master's and doctorate, GRE General Test, minimum GPA of 3.0 in last 60 hours. Additional exam requirements/recommendations for international students: Required—TOEFL. *Application deadline:* For fall admission, 3/1 priority date for domestic students; for spring admission, 8/1 priority date for domestic students. Applications are processed on a rolling basis. Application fee: $50 ($75 for international students). Electronic applications accepted. *Expenses:* Tuition, state resident: full-time $5437; part-time $226.55 per credit hour. Tuition, nonresident: full-time $12,949; part-time $539.55 per credit hour. *Required fees:* $2741. *Financial support:* In 2011–12, fellowships with partial tuition reimbursements (averaging $16,000 per year), research assistantships with partial tuition reimbursements (averaging $15,400 per year), teaching assistantships with partial tuition reimbursements (averaging $16,000 per year) were awarded; Federal Work-Study, institutionally sponsored loans, scholarships/grants, traineeships, health care benefits, and unspecified assistantships also available. Support available to part-time students. Financial award applicants required to submit FAFSA. *Faculty research:* Infectious and noninfectious diseases of animals and birds, animal genetics, molecular biology, immunology, virology. *Unit head:* Dr. Linda Logan, Head, 979-862-6559, Fax: 979-845-9231, E-mail: llogan@cvm.tamu.edu. *Application contact:* Dr. Patricia Holman, Graduate Advisor, 979-845-4202, Fax: 979-862-1147, E-mail: pholman@cvm.tamu.edu. Web site: http://vetmed.tamu.edu/vtpb.

The University of Arizona, College of Agriculture and Life Sciences, Department of Veterinary Science and Microbiology, Program in Microbiology and Pathobiology, Tucson, AZ 85721. Offers MS, PhD. *Students:* 42 full-time (23 women), 43 part-time (22 women); includes 8 minority (2 American Indian or Alaska Native, non-Hispanic/Latino; 2

Pathobiology

Asian, non-Hispanic/Latino; 4 Hispanic/Latino), 16 international. Average age 31. Terminal master's awarded for partial completion of doctoral program. *Degree requirements:* For master's, thesis; for doctorate, comprehensive exam, thesis/dissertation. *Entrance requirements:* For master's and doctorate, GRE, minimum GPA of 3.0, 3 letters of recommendation, letter of intent. Additional exam requirements/recommendations for international students: Required—TOEFL (minimum score 550 paper-based; 213 computer-based; 80 iBT); Recommended—IELTS (minimum score 7). *Application deadline:* For fall admission, 2/28 for domestic students, 12/1 for international students. Applications are processed on a rolling basis. Application fee: $75. *Expenses:* Tuition, state resident: full-time $10,840. Tuition, nonresident: full-time $25,802. *Financial support:* Research assistantships with tuition reimbursements, teaching assistantships with tuition reimbursements, and scholarships/grants available. Financial award application deadline: 3/22. *Faculty research:* Antibiotic resistance, molecular pathogenesis of bacteria, food safety, diagnosis of animal disease, parasitology. *Unit head:* Dr. Ron Marx, Head, 520-621-1081, E-mail: ronmarx@email.arizona.edu. *Application contact:* Cecilia Carlon, 520-626-1248, E-mail: ccarlon@email.arizona.edu. Web site: http://www.microvet.arizona.edu/.

University of Cincinnati, Graduate School, College of Medicine, Graduate Programs in Biomedical Sciences, Program in Pathobiology and Molecular Medicine, Cincinnati, OH 45221. Offers pathology (PhD), including anatomic pathology, laboratory medicine, pathobiology and molecular medicine. *Degree requirements:* For doctorate, thesis/dissertation, qualifying exam. *Entrance requirements:* For doctorate, GRE General Test. Additional exam requirements/recommendations for international students: Required—TOEFL (minimum score 620 paper-based; 260 computer-based). Electronic applications accepted. *Faculty research:* Cardiovascular and lipid disorders, digestive and kidney disease, endocrine and metabolic disorders, hematologic and oncogenic, immunology and infectious disease.

University of Connecticut, Graduate School, College of Agriculture and Natural Resources, Department of Pathobiology and Veterinary Science, Storrs, CT 06269. Offers pathobiology (MS, PhD). Terminal master's awarded for partial completion of doctoral program. *Degree requirements:* For master's, comprehensive exam; for doctorate, thesis/dissertation. *Entrance requirements:* For master's and doctorate, GRE General Test, GRE Subject Test. Additional exam requirements/recommendations for international students: Required—TOEFL (minimum score 550 paper-based; 213 computer-based). Electronic applications accepted.

University of Illinois at Urbana–Champaign, College of Veterinary Medicine, Department of Pathobiology, Urbana, IL 61802. Offers MS, PhD, DVM/PhD. Part-time programs available. *Faculty:* 18 full-time (6 women). *Students:* 8 full-time (5 women), 7 part-time (1 woman); includes 1 minority (Asian, non-Hispanic/Latino), 7 international. 17 applicants, 6% accepted, 1 enrolled. In 2011, 1 degree awarded. Terminal master's awarded for partial completion of doctoral program. *Degree requirements:* For doctorate, thesis/dissertation. *Entrance requirements:* For master's and doctorate, GRE, minimum GPA of 3.0. Additional exam requirements/recommendations for international students: Required—TOEFL (minimum score 590 paper-based; 243 computer-based). *Application deadline:* Applications are processed on a rolling basis. Application fee: $75 ($90 for international students). Electronic applications accepted. *Financial support:* In 2011–12, 2 fellowships, 7 research assistantships, 5 teaching assistantships were awarded; tuition waivers (full and partial) also available. *Faculty research:* Epidemiology, immunology, microbiology, parasitology, clinical pathology. *Unit head:* Mark S. Kuhlenschmidt, Head, 217-333-9039, Fax: 217-244-7421, E-mail: kuhlensc@illinois.edu. *Application contact:* Paula Moxley, Administrative Aide, 217-244-8924, Fax: 217-244-7421, E-mail: pkm@illinois.edu. Web site: http://vetmed.illinois.edu/path/.

University of Missouri, College of Veterinary Medicine and Graduate School, Graduate Programs in Veterinary Medicine, Department of Veterinary Pathobiology, Columbia, MO 65211. Offers comparative medicine (MS); pathobiology (MS, PhD). *Faculty:* 41 full-time (14 women), 5 part-time/adjunct (2 women). *Students:* 25 full-time (13 women), 16 part-time (11 women); includes 4 minority (1 Asian, non-Hispanic/Latino; 3 Hispanic/Latino), 7 international. Average age 31. 32 applicants, 44% accepted, 11 enrolled. In 2011, 2 master's, 3 doctorates awarded. *Degree requirements:* For master's, thesis; for doctorate, 2 foreign languages, thesis/dissertation. *Entrance requirements:* For master's and doctorate, GRE General Test, minimum GPA of 3.0. Additional exam requirements/recommendations for international students: Required—TOEFL (minimum score 500 paper-based; 61 iBT). *Application deadline:* For fall admission, 5/1 for domestic students. Application fee: $55 ($75 for international students). Electronic applications accepted. *Expenses:* Tuition, state resident: full-time $5881. Tuition, nonresident: full-time $15,183. *Required fees:* $952. Tuition and fees vary according to campus/location and program. *Financial support:* Research assistantships with full tuition reimbursements, teaching assistantships with full tuition reimbursements, and institutionally sponsored loans available. *Unit head:* Dr. George C. Stewart, Department Chair, 573-884-2866, E-mail: stewartgc@missouri.edu. *Application contact:* Anne Chegwidden, Grants and Contracts Specialist, 573-884-2444, E-mail: chegwiddena@missouri.edu. Web site: http://www.cvm.missouri.edu/vpbio/.

University of Southern California, Keck School of Medicine and Graduate School, Graduate Programs in Medicine, Department of Pathology, Los Angeles, CA 90089-9092. Offers experimental and molecular pathology (MS); pathobiology (PhD). *Faculty:* 34 full-time (6 women), 4 part-time/adjunct (1 woman). *Students:* 29 full-time (16 women); includes 12 minority (9 Asian, non-Hispanic/Latino; 3 Hispanic/Latino), 10 international. Average age 26. 6 applicants, 83% accepted, 4 enrolled. In 2011, 6 master's, 4 doctorates awarded. *Degree requirements:* For master's, thesis; for doctorate, thesis/dissertation. *Entrance requirements:* For master's, GRE General Test, minimum GPA of 3.0; for doctorate, GRE General Test, minimum GPA of 3.0, BS in natural sciences. Additional exam requirements/recommendations for international students: Required—TOEFL (minimum score 600 paper-based; 250 computer-based; 100 iBT). *Application deadline:* For fall admission, 12/1 priority date for domestic students, 12/1 for international students. Application fee: $85. Electronic applications accepted. *Financial support:* In 2011–12, 17 students received support, including 1 fellowship with full and partial tuition reimbursement available (averaging $29,100 per year), 16 research assistantships with full and partial tuition reimbursements available (averaging $29,100 per year); Federal Work-Study, institutionally sponsored loans, scholarships/grants, health care benefits, and unspecified assistantships also available. Financial award application deadline: 5/4; financial award applicants required to submit CSS PROFILE or FAFSA. *Faculty research:* Cellular and molecular biology of cancer; chemical carcinogenesis; virology; stem cell and developmental pathology; liver and pulmonary diseases; environmental pathology; circulatory, endocrine, and neurodegenerative diseases. *Total annual research expenditures:* $961.5 million. *Unit head:* Dr. Michael E. Selsted, Chair, 323-442-1179, Fax: 323-442-3049, E-mail: selsted@usc.edu. *Application contact:* Lisa A. Doumak, Student Services Assistant, 323-442-1168, Fax: 323-442-3049, E-mail: doumak@usc.edu. Web site: http://www.usc.edu/hsc/medicine/pathology/.

University of Toronto, Faculty of Medicine, Department of Laboratory Medicine and Pathobiology, Toronto, ON M5S 1A1, Canada. Offers M Sc, PhD. *Degree requirements:* For master's, thesis; for doctorate, thesis/dissertation, oral defense of thesis. *Entrance requirements:* For master's, minimum B+ average in final 2 years, research experience, 2 letters of recommendation, resume, interview; for doctorate, minimum A- average, 2 letters of recommendation, research experience, resume, interview. Additional exam requirements/recommendations for international students: Required—TOEFL (600 paper-based, 250 computer-based), TWE (5) or IELTS (7). Electronic applications accepted.

University of Washington, Graduate School, School of Public Health, Department of Global Health, Graduate Program in Pathobiology, Seattle, WA 98195. Offers PhD. *Students:* 32 full-time (25 women), 3 part-time (all women); includes 7 minority (2 Black or African American, non-Hispanic/Latino; 3 Asian, non-Hispanic/Latino; 2 Hispanic/Latino), 5 international. Average age 29. 75 applicants, 20% accepted, 5 enrolled. In 2011, 3 doctorates awarded. *Degree requirements:* For doctorate, comprehensive exam, thesis/dissertation, published paper from thesis work. *Entrance requirements:* For doctorate, GRE General Test, minimum GPA of 3.0. Additional exam requirements/recommendations for international students: Required—TOEFL, IELTS. *Application deadline:* For fall admission, 12/1 for domestic students, 11/1 for international students. Application fee: $75. Electronic applications accepted. *Financial support:* In 2011–12, 34 students received support, including 34 research assistantships with full tuition reimbursements available (averaging $27,348 per year); traineeships and unspecified assistantships also available. *Faculty research:* Malaria, immunological response to mycobacteria infections, HIV-cell interaction and the development of an anti-HIV vaccine, regulation of intercellular communication via gap junctions, genetic and nutritional regulation of proteins involved in lipid transport. *Unit head:* Dr. King Holmes, Chair, 206-744-3620, Fax: 206-744-3694. *Application contact:* Rachel Reichert, Program Manager, 206-543-4338, Fax: 206-543-3873, E-mail: pabio@u.washington.edu.

University of Wyoming, College of Agriculture and Natural Resources, Department of Veterinary Sciences, Laramie, WY 82070. Offers pathobiology (MS). *Degree requirements:* For master's, thesis. *Entrance requirements:* For master's, GRE General Test, minimum GPA of 3.0. Additional exam requirements/recommendations for international students: Required—TOEFL. *Faculty research:* Infectious diseases, pathology, toxicology, immunology, microbiology.

Wake Forest University, School of Medicine and Graduate School of Arts and Sciences, Graduate Programs in Medicine, Program in Molecular and Cellular Pathobiology, Winston-Salem, NC 27109. Offers MS, PhD, MD/PhD. *Degree requirements:* For master's, thesis; for doctorate, thesis/dissertation. *Entrance requirements:* For master's and doctorate, GRE General Test. Additional exam requirements/recommendations for international students: Required—TOEFL. Electronic applications accepted. *Faculty research:* Atherosclerosis, lipoproteins, arterial wall metabolism.

Yale University, School of Medicine and Graduate School of Arts and Sciences, Combined Program in Biological and Biomedical Sciences (BBS), Pharmacological Sciences and Molecular Medicine Track, New Haven, CT 06520. Offers PhD, MD/PhD. *Degree requirements:* For doctorate, thesis/dissertation. *Entrance requirements:* For doctorate, GRE General Test. Additional exam requirements/recommendations for international students: Required—TOEFL. Electronic applications accepted.

Pathology

Albert Einstein College of Medicine, Graduate Division of Biomedical Sciences, Department of Pathology, Bronx, NY 10467. Offers PhD, MD/PhD. *Degree requirements:* For doctorate, thesis/dissertation. *Entrance requirements:* For doctorate, GRE General Test. Additional exam requirements/recommendations for international students: Required—TOEFL. *Faculty research:* Clinical and disease-related research at tissue, cellular, and subcellular levels; biochemistry and morphology of enzyme and lysosome disorders.

Baylor College of Medicine, Graduate School of Biomedical Sciences, Program in Developmental Biology, Houston, TX 77030-3498. Offers PhD, MD/PhD. *Faculty:* 68 full-time (20 women). *Students:* 55 full-time (28 women); includes 9 minority (7 Asian, non-Hispanic/Latino; 2 Hispanic/Latino), 37 international. Average age 28. 771 applicants, 2% accepted, 10 enrolled. In 2011, 5 degrees awarded. *Median time to degree:* Of those who began their doctoral program in fall 2003, 100% received their degree in 8 years or less. *Degree requirements:* For doctorate, thesis/dissertation, public defense. *Entrance requirements:* For doctorate, GRE General Test, GRE Subject Test (strongly recommended), minimum GPA of 3.0. Additional exam requirements/recommendations for international students: Required—TOEFL. *Application deadline:* For fall admission, 1/1 priority date for domestic students. Application fee: $0. Electronic applications accepted. *Financial support:* In 2011–12, 55 students received support, including 6 fellowships with full tuition reimbursements available (averaging $29,000 per year), 49 research assistantships with full tuition reimbursements available (averaging $29,000 per year); career-related internships or fieldwork, Federal Work-Study, institutionally sponsored loans, health care benefits, tuition waivers (full), and stipends also available. *Faculty research:* Stem cells, cancer, neurobiology, organogenesis, genetics of model organisms. *Unit head:* Dr. Hugo Bellen, Director, 713-798-6410. *Application contact:* Catherine Tasnier, Graduate Program Administrator, 713-798-6410, Fax: 713-798-5386, E-mail: cat@bcm.edu. Web site: http://www.bcm.edu/db/.

See Display on page 287 and Close-Up on page 311.

Boston University, School of Medicine, Division of Graduate Medical Sciences, Department of Pathology and Laboratory Medicine, Boston, MA 02118. Offers PhD, MD/PhD. Part-time programs available. *Faculty:* 17 full-time (10 women), 9 part-time/adjunct (1 woman). *Students:* 17 full-time (9 women); includes 1 minority (Asian, non-Hispanic/Latino), 6 international. Average age 28. 27 applicants, 41% accepted, 6 enrolled. In 2011, 2 doctorates awarded. *Degree requirements:* For doctorate, thesis/dissertation, qualifying exam. *Entrance requirements:* For doctorate, GRE General Test, GRE Subject Test. Additional exam requirements/recommendations for international students: Required—TOEFL. *Application deadline:* For fall admission, 1/15 priority date

for domestic students; for spring admission, 10/15 priority date for domestic students. Application fee: $75. Electronic applications accepted. *Expenses: Tuition:* Full-time $40,848; part-time $1276 per credit hour. *Required fees:* $572; $286 per semester. *Financial support:* In 2011–12, fellowships (averaging $30,500 per year), 4 research assistantships (averaging $30,500 per year) were awarded; Federal Work-Study, scholarships/grants, and traineeships also available. Financial award applicants required to submit FAFSA. *Faculty research:* Toxicology, carcinogenesis, endocytosis, cytogenetics. *Unit head:* Dr. Daniel G. Remick, Chairman, E-mail: remickd@bu.edu. *Application contact:* Dr. Adrianne Rogers, Associate Chairman, 617-638-4500, Fax: 617-638-4085, E-mail: aerogers@bu.edu. Web site: http://www.bumc.bu.edu/busm pathology/.

Brown University, Graduate School, Division of Biology and Medicine, Program in Pathology and Laboratory Medicine, Providence, RI 02912. Offers biology (PhD); cancer biology (PhD); immunology and infection (PhD); medical science (PhD); pathobiology (Sc M); toxicology and environmental pathology (PhD). Terminal master's awarded for partial completion of doctoral program. *Degree requirements:* For doctorate, thesis/dissertation, preliminary exam. *Entrance requirements:* For master's and doctorate, GRE General Test, GRE Subject Test. Additional exam requirements/recommendations for international students: Required—TOEFL. Electronic applications accepted. *Faculty research:* Environmental pathology, carcinogenesis, immunopathology, signal transduction, innate immunity.

Case Western Reserve University, School of Medicine and School of Graduate Studies, Graduate Programs in Medicine, Programs in Molecular and Cellular Basis of Disease/Pathology, Cleveland, OH 44106. Offers cancer biology (PhD); cell biology (MS, PhD); immunology (MS, PhD); pathology (MS, PhD); MD/PhD. Terminal master's awarded for partial completion of doctoral program. *Degree requirements:* For master's, thesis; for doctorate, thesis/dissertation. *Entrance requirements:* For master's and doctorate, GRE General Test, GRE Subject Test. Additional exam requirements/recommendations for international students: Required—TOEFL (minimum score 550 paper-based; 213 computer-based). Electronic applications accepted. *Faculty research:* Neurobiology, molecular biology, cancer biology, biomaterials, biocompatibility.

Colorado State University, College of Veterinary Medicine and Biomedical Sciences, Department of Microbiology, Immunology and Pathology, Fort Collins, CO 80523-0015. Offers microbiology (MS, PhD); pathology (PhD). *Faculty:* 43 full-time (18 women), 2 part-time/adjunct (0 women). *Students:* 46 full-time (32 women), 38 part-time (28 women); includes 8 minority (2 Asian, non-Hispanic/Latino; 6 Hispanic/Latino), 10 international. Average age 31. 107 applicants, 14% accepted, 14 enrolled. In 2011, 3 master's, 13 doctorates awarded. *Degree requirements:* For master's, thesis; for doctorate, comprehensive exam, thesis/dissertation. *Entrance requirements:* For master's, GRE General Test, minimum GPA of 3.0, BA/BS in biomedical field, reviewer evaluation forms, resume; for doctorate, GRE General Test, minimum GPA of 3.0, BA/BS in biomedical field, reviewer evaluation forms, resume, statement of interest. Additional exam requirements/recommendations for international students: Required—TOEFL (minimum score 550 paper-based). *Application deadline:* For fall admission, 1/1 priority date for domestic students; for spring admission, 10/1 priority date for domestic students. Applications are processed on a rolling basis. Application fee: $50. Electronic applications accepted. *Expenses:* Tuition, state resident: full-time $7992. Tuition, nonresident: full-time $19,592. *Required fees:* $1735; $58 per credit. *Financial support:* In 2011–12, 63 students received support, including 28 fellowships with tuition reimbursements available (averaging $29,347 per year), 30 research assistantships with tuition reimbursements available (averaging $20,869 per year), 5 teaching assistantships with tuition reimbursements available (averaging $14,580 per year); Federal Work-Study, scholarships/grants, traineeships, and unspecified assistantships also available. Financial award applicants required to submit FAFSA. *Faculty research:* Medical and veterinary bacteriology, immunology, microbial physiology, pathology, vector-borne disease. *Total annual research expenditures:* $30.4 million. *Unit head:* Dr. Edward A. Hoover, Head, 970-491-7587, Fax: 970-491-0603, E-mail: edward.hoover@colostate.edu. *Application contact:* Lisa McCann, Academic Programs Coordinator, 970-491-6118, Fax: 970-491-1815, E-mail: lisa.mccann@colostate.edu. Web site: http://www.cvmbs.colostate.edu/mip/.

Columbia University, College of Physicians and Surgeons, Department of Pathology, New York, NY 10032. Offers pathobiology (M Phil, MA, PhD); MD/PhD. Only candidates for the PhD are admitted. Terminal master's awarded for partial completion of doctoral program. *Degree requirements:* For doctorate, thesis/dissertation. *Entrance requirements:* For master's and doctorate, GRE General Test. Additional exam requirements/recommendations for international students: Required—TOEFL. *Faculty research:* Virology, molecular biology, cell biology, neurobiology, immunology.

Dalhousie University, Faculty of Graduate Studies and Faculty of Medicine, Graduate Programs in Medicine, Department of Pathology, Halifax, NS B3H 4R2, Canada. Offers M Sc, PhD. *Degree requirements:* For master's, oral defense of thesis. *Entrance requirements:* Additional exam requirements/recommendations for international students: Required—1 of 5 approved tests: TOEFL, IELTS, CANTEST, CAEL, Michigan English Language Assessment Battery. Electronic applications accepted. *Faculty research:* Tumor immunology, molecular oncology, clinical chemistry, hematology, molecular genetics/oncology.

Duke University, Graduate School, Department of Pathology, Durham, NC 27710. Offers PhD. *Accreditation:* NAACLS. *Faculty:* 31 full-time. *Students:* 33 full-time (19 women); includes 5 minority (2 Black or African American, non-Hispanic/Latino; 2 Asian, non-Hispanic/Latino; 1 Hispanic/Latino), 11 international. 28 applicants, 11% accepted, 2 enrolled. In 2011, 7 doctorates awarded. *Degree requirements:* For doctorate, thesis/dissertation. *Entrance requirements:* For doctorate, GRE General Test, GRE Subject Test (recommended). Additional exam requirements/recommendations for international students: Required—TOEFL (minimum score 550 paper-based; 213 computer-based; 73 iBT), IELTS (minimum score 7). *Application deadline:* For fall admission, 12/8 priority date for domestic students, 12/8 for international students. Application fee: $75. Electronic applications accepted. *Expenses: Tuition:* Full-time $40,720. *Required fees:* $3107. *Financial support:* Fellowships, research assistantships, and Federal Work-Study available. Financial award application deadline: 12/8. *Unit head:* Soman Abraham, Director of Graduate Studies, 919-684-9929, Fax: 919-681-8868, E-mail: pamela.harris@duke.edu. *Application contact:* Elizabeth Hutton, Director of Admissions, 919-684-3913, Fax: 919-684-2277, E-mail: grad-admissions@duke.edu. Web site: http://www.pathology.mc.duke.edu/.

Duke University, School of Medicine, Pathologists' Assistant Program, Durham, NC 27708-0586. Offers MHS. *Accreditation:* NAACLS. *Faculty:* 1 (woman) full-time, 45 part-time/adjunct (23 women). *Students:* 16 full-time (13 women); includes 6 minority (1 Black or African American, non-Hispanic/Latino; 5 Asian, non-Hispanic/Latino). Average age 26. 48 applicants, 17% accepted, 8 enrolled. In 2011, 8 master's awarded. *Degree requirements:* For master's, comprehensive exam. *Entrance requirements:* For master's, GRE. Additional exam requirements/recommendations for international students: Required—TOEFL, IELTS. *Application deadline:* For fall admission, 1/31 priority date for domestic students. Application fee: $55. *Expenses:* Contact institution. *Financial support:* In 2011–12, 15 students received support. Fellowships, research assistantships, teaching assistantships, and scholarships/grants available. Financial award application deadline: 5/1; financial award applicants required to submit FAFSA. *Unit head:* Dr. Rex C. Bentley, Program Director, 919-684-6423, Fax: 919-681-7799, E-mail: bentl003@mc.duke.edu. *Application contact:* Pamela Vollmer, Associate Director, 919-684-2159, E-mail: vollm003@mc.duke.edu. Web site: http://pathology.mc.duke.edu/.

East Carolina University, Brody School of Medicine, Department of Pathology and Laboratory Medicine, Greenville, NC 27858-4353. Offers PhD. *Degree requirements:* For doctorate, comprehensive exam, thesis/dissertation. *Entrance requirements:* For doctorate, GRE General Test, bachelor's degree in biological chemistry or physical science. *Application deadline:* For fall admission, 6/1 priority date for domestic students. Application fee: $50. *Expenses:* Tuition, state resident: full-time $3557; part-time $444.63 per semester hour. Tuition, nonresident: full-time $14,351; part-time $1793.88 per semester hour. *Required fees:* $2016; $252 per semester hour. Part-time tuition and fees vary according to course load, campus/location and program. *Financial support:* Fellowships available. Financial award application deadline: 6/1. *Unit head:* Dr. Peter J. Kragel, Chair, 252-744-2803, E-mail: kragelp@ecu.edu. Web site: http://www.pathology.ecu.edu/Public/graduate/phdinfo_new.htm.

Georgetown University, Graduate School of Arts and Sciences, Programs in Biomedical Sciences, Department of Pathology, Washington, DC 20057. Offers MS, PhD, MD/PhD, MS/PhD. *Degree requirements:* For master's, thesis; for doctorate, comprehensive exam, thesis/dissertation. *Entrance requirements:* For master's and doctorate, GRE General Test. Additional exam requirements/recommendations for international students: Required—TOEFL. *Faculty research:* Virus-induced diabetes, viral oncology, renal pathophysiology.

Harvard University, Graduate School of Arts and Sciences, Division of Medical Sciences, Boston, MA 02115. Offers biological chemistry and molecular pharmacology (PhD); cell biology (PhD); genetics (PhD); microbiology and molecular genetics (PhD); pathology (PhD), including experimental pathology. *Degree requirements:* For doctorate, thesis/dissertation. *Entrance requirements:* For doctorate, GRE General Test, GRE Subject Test. Additional exam requirements/recommendations for international students: Required—TOEFL. *Expenses: Tuition:* Full-time $36,304. *Required fees:* $1186. Full-time tuition and fees vary according to program.

Indiana University–Purdue University Indianapolis, Indiana University School of Medicine, Department of Pathology and Laboratory Medicine, Indianapolis, IN 46202-2896. Offers MS, PhD, MD/PhD. *Faculty:* 27 full-time (4 women). *Students:* 5 full-time (3 women), 4 part-time (all women); includes 2 minority (both Hispanic/Latino), 1 international. Average age 26. 36 applicants, 17% accepted, 4 enrolled. In 2011, 5 master's awarded. *Degree requirements:* For master's, thesis; for doctorate, thesis/dissertation. *Entrance requirements:* For master's and doctorate, GRE General Test. Additional exam requirements/recommendations for international students: Required—TOEFL. *Application deadline:* For fall admission, 1/15 priority date for domestic students. Applications are processed on a rolling basis. Application fee: $55 ($65 for international students). *Financial support:* In 2011–12, teaching assistantships with full tuition reimbursements (averaging $10,711 per year) were awarded; fellowships, research assistantships with full tuition reimbursements, and institutionally sponsored loans also available. Financial award application deadline: 2/1. *Faculty research:* Intestinal microecology and anaerobes, molecular pathogenesis of infectious diseases, AIDS pneumocystis, sports medicine toxicology, neuropathology of aging. *Unit head:* Dr. John Eble, Chairman, 317-274-4806. *Application contact:* Dr. Diane S. Leland, Graduate Adviser, 317-274-0148. Web site: http://www.pathology.iupui.edu.

Iowa State University of Science and Technology, Department of Veterinary Pathology, Ames, IA 50011-1250. Offers MS, PhD. *Entrance requirements:* For master's and doctorate, GRE General Test. Additional exam requirements/recommendations for international students: Recommended—TOEFL (minimum score 550 paper-based; 79 iBT), IELTS (minimum score 6.5). *Application deadline:* Applications are processed on a rolling basis. Application fee: $40 ($90 for international students). Electronic applications accepted. *Unit head:* Dr. Jesse M. Hostetter, Director of Graduate Education, 515-294-0953, E-mail: jesseh@iastate.edu. *Application contact:* Jesse M. Hostetter, Application Contact, 515-294-0953, E-mail: grad_admissions@iastate.edu. Web site: http://vetmed.iastate.edu/vpath/academics/graduate-program.

The Johns Hopkins University, School of Medicine, Graduate Programs in Medicine, Department of Pathology, Baltimore, MD 21218-2699. Offers pathobiology (PhD). *Degree requirements:* For doctorate, thesis/dissertation, qualifying oral exam. *Entrance requirements:* For doctorate, GRE General Test, previous course work with laboratory in organic and inorganic chemistry, general biology, calculus; interview. Additional exam requirements/recommendations for international students: Required—TOEFL. Electronic applications accepted. *Faculty research:* Role of mutant proteins in Alzheimer's disease, nuclear protein function in breast and prostate cancer, medically important fungi, glycoproteins in HIV pathogenesis.

Loma Linda University, School of Medicine, Department of Pathology and Human Anatomy, Loma Linda, CA 92350. Offers MS, PhD. Part-time programs available. Terminal master's awarded for partial completion of doctoral program. *Degree requirements:* For master's, thesis; for doctorate, 2 foreign languages, thesis/dissertation. *Entrance requirements:* For master's and doctorate, GRE General Test. Additional exam requirements/recommendations for international students: Required—TOEFL (minimum score 550 paper-based; 213 computer-based). *Faculty research:* Neuroendocrine system, histochemistry and image analysis, effect of age and diabetes on PNS, electron microscopy, histology.

McGill University, Faculty of Graduate and Postdoctoral Studies, Faculty of Medicine, Department of Pathology, Montréal, QC H3A 2T5, Canada. Offers M Sc, PhD.

Medical University of South Carolina, College of Graduate Studies, Department of Pathology and Laboratory Medicine, Charleston, SC 29425. Offers MS, PhD, DMD/PhD, MD/PhD. *Faculty:* 11 full-time (5 women). *Students:* 7 full-time (4 women); includes 2 minority (1 Black or African American, non-Hispanic/Latino; 1 Asian, non-Hispanic/Latino). Average age 26. 7 applicants, 29% accepted, 1 enrolled. In 2011, 1 doctorate awarded. Terminal master's awarded for partial completion of doctoral program. *Degree requirements:* For master's, thesis; for doctorate, thesis/dissertation, oral and written exams. *Entrance requirements:* For master's, GRE General Test; for doctorate, GRE General Test, interview, minimum GPA of 3.0. Additional exam requirements/recommendations for international students: Required—TOEFL (minimum score 600 paper-based; 250 computer-based; 100 iBT). *Application deadline:* For fall admission, 1/15 priority date for domestic students, 1/15 for international students. Applications are processed on a rolling basis. Application fee: $0 ($85 for international students). Electronic applications accepted. *Financial support:* In 2011–12, 3 fellowships with full and partial tuition reimbursements (averaging $28,000 per year) were awarded; Federal Work-Study and scholarships/grants also available. Support available to part-time students. Financial award application deadline: 3/10; financial award applicants required to submit FAFSA. *Faculty research:* Neurobiology of hearing loss; inner ear ion homeostasis; cancer biology, genetics and stem cell biology; cellular defense mechanisms. *Unit head:* Dr. Janice M. Lage, Chair, 843-792-3121, Fax: 843-792-6590, E-mail: lagejm@musc.edu. *Application contact:* Dr. Victoria Jane Findlay, Assistant

Professor and Coordinator of Graduate Studies, 843-792-1889, Fax: 843-792-6590, E-mail: findlay@musc.edu. Web site: http://www.musc.edu/pathology/.

Michigan State University, College of Veterinary Medicine and The Graduate School, Graduate Programs in Veterinary Medicine, Department of Pathobiology and Diagnostic Investigation, East Lansing, MI 48824. Offers pathology (MS, PhD); pathology–environmental toxicology (PhD). *Entrance requirements:* Additional exam requirements/recommendations for international students: Required—TOEFL. Electronic applications accepted.

New York Medical College, Graduate School of Basic Medical Sciences, Program in Pathology, Valhalla, NY 10595-1691. Offers MS, PhD, MD/PhD. Part-time and evening/weekend programs available. *Faculty:* 19 full-time (2 women). *Students:* 7 full-time (3 women); includes 6 minority (2 Black or African American, non-Hispanic/Latino; 3 Asian, non-Hispanic/Latino; 1 Hispanic/Latino). Average age 27. 6 applicants, 83% accepted, 2 enrolled. In 2011, 7 master's awarded. Terminal master's awarded for partial completion of doctoral program. *Median time to degree:* Of those who began their doctoral program in fall 2003, 50% received their degree in 8 years or less. *Degree requirements:* For master's, thesis; for doctorate, comprehensive exam, thesis/dissertation. *Entrance requirements:* For master's and doctorate, GRE General Test. Additional exam requirements/recommendations for international students: Required—TOEFL. *Application deadline:* For fall admission, 7/1 priority date for domestic students, 5/1 for international students; for spring admission, 12/1 priority date for domestic students, 10/1 for international students. Applications are processed on a rolling basis. Application fee: $50 ($75 for international students). Electronic applications accepted. *Financial support:* In 2011–12, 1 fellowship with full tuition reimbursement (averaging $24,000 per year) was awarded; Federal Work-Study, institutionally sponsored loans, scholarships/grants, traineeships, tuition waivers (full), unspecified assistantships, and health benefits (for PhD candidates only) also available. Financial award applicants required to submit FAFSA. *Faculty research:* Examination of the underlying mechanisms involved in biochemical toxicology, cancer cell biology, cell-cycle regulation and apoptosis, chemical carcinogenesis and tissue engineering. *Unit head:* Dr. Fred Moy, Director, 914-594-4174, Fax: 914-594-4944. *Application contact:* Valerie Romeo-Messana, Admission Coordinator, 914-594-4110, Fax: 914-594-4944, E-mail: v_romeomessana@nymc.edu.

North Carolina State University, College of Veterinary Medicine, Program in Comparative Biomedical Sciences, Raleigh, NC 27695. Offers cell biology (MS, PhD); infectious disease (MS, PhD); pathology (MS, PhD); pharmacology (MS, PhD); population medicine (MS, PhD). Part-time programs available. *Degree requirements:* For master's, thesis; for doctorate, thesis/dissertation. *Entrance requirements:* For master's and doctorate, GRE General Test. Additional exam requirements/recommendations for international students: Required—TOEFL (minimum score 550 paper-based; 213 computer-based). Electronic applications accepted. *Expenses:* Contact institution. *Faculty research:* Infectious diseases, cell biology, pharmacology and toxicology, genomics, pathology and population medicine.

North Dakota State University, College of Graduate and Interdisciplinary Studies, College of Agriculture, Food Systems, and Natural Resources, Department of Veterinary and Microbiological Sciences, Fargo, ND 58108. Offers food safety (MS); microbiology (MS); molecular pathogenesis (PhD). Part-time programs available. *Faculty:* 8 full-time (6 women). *Students:* 15 full-time (5 women), 5 part-time (3 women), 9 international. 24 applicants, 46% accepted, 3 enrolled. In 2011, 1 master's, 1 doctorate awarded. *Degree requirements:* For master's, thesis; for doctorate, thesis/dissertation, oral and written preliminary exams. *Entrance requirements:* For master's and doctorate, GRE. Additional exam requirements/recommendations for international students: Required—TOEFL (minimum score 525 paper-based; 197 computer-based; 71 iBT). *Application deadline:* For fall admission, 2/15 priority date for domestic students. Applications are processed on a rolling basis. Application fee: $35. *Financial support:* Fellowships with full tuition reimbursements, research assistantships with full tuition reimbursements, teaching assistantships with full tuition reimbursements, Federal Work-Study, and institutionally sponsored loans available. Financial award application deadline: 4/15. *Faculty research:* Bacterial gene regulation, antibiotic resistance, molecular virology, mechanisms of bacterial pathogenesis, immunology of animals. *Unit head:* Dr. Charlene Wolf-Hall, Head, 701-231-7667, E-mail: charlene.hall@ndsu.edu. *Application contact:* Dr. John McEvoy, Associate Professor, 701-231-8530, Fax: 701-231-7514, E-mail: eugene.berry@ndsu.edu. Web site: http://vetmicro.ndsu.nodak.edu/.

The Ohio State University, College of Medicine, Department of Pathology, Columbus, OH 43210. Offers experimental pathobiology (MS); pathology assistant (MS); MD/PhD. *Accreditation:* NAACLS. *Degree requirements:* For master's, comprehensive exam (for some programs), thesis. *Entrance requirements:* For master's, GRE General Test. Additional exam requirements/recommendations for international students: Required—TOEFL (minimum score 550 paper-based; 213 computer-based). Electronic applications accepted. *Expenses:* Tuition, state resident: full-time $11,400. Tuition, nonresident: full-time $28,125. Tuition and fees vary according to course load, degree level, campus/location and program. *Faculty research:* Clinical pathology, transplantation pathology, cancer research, neuropathology, vascular pathology.

Oklahoma State University Center for Health Sciences, Graduate Program in Forensic Sciences, Tulsa, OK 74107-1898. Offers forensic DNA/molecular biology (MS); forensic document examination (MS, Graduate Certificate); forensic pathology/microbiology (MS); forensic psychology (MS); forensic science administration (MS); forensic toxicology (MS). Part-time and evening/weekend programs available. Postbaccalaureate distance learning degree programs offered (no on-campus study). *Faculty:* 2 full-time (0 women), 14 part-time/adjunct (5 women). *Students:* 7 full-time (5 women), 22 part-time (12 women); includes 4 minority (3 American Indian or Alaska Native, non-Hispanic/Latino; 1 Hispanic/Latino), 1 international. Average age 34. 12 applicants, 50% accepted, 5 enrolled. In 2011, 7 degrees awarded. *Degree requirements:* For master's, comprehensive exam (for some programs), thesis (for some programs). *Entrance requirements:* For master's, MAT (for MFSA) or GRE General Test, professional experience (MFSA). Additional exam requirements/recommendations for international students: Required—TOEFL (minimum score 600 paper-based; 250 computer-based), TWE (minimum score 5). *Application deadline:* For fall admission, 3/1 for domestic and international students; for spring admission, 10/1 for domestic and international students. Application fee: $40 ($75 for international students). *Financial support:* In 2011–12, 10 students received support, including 2 research assistantships (averaging $12,000 per year); career-related internships or fieldwork, Federal Work-Study, and tuition waivers (partial) also available. Support available to part-time students. Financial award application deadline: 4/1; financial award applicants required to submit FAFSA. *Faculty research:* Studies on the variability in chromosomal DNA; development/enhancement of accessory methods useful for forensic DNA typing; development of universal methods useful for discriminating pathogenic bacteria; forensic dentistry; transmission of microbial diseases by dentures, protective athletic mouth-guards, band wind instruments, and infant pacifiers; changes in ecologies and antibiotic sensitivities of aerobic microorganisms; forensic toxicology and trace chemical method development. *Total annual research expenditures:* $58,000. *Unit head:* Dr. Robert T. Allen, Director, 918-561-1108, Fax: 918-561-8414. *Application contact:* Cathy Newsome, Coordinator, 918-561-1108, Fax: 918-561-8414, E-mail: cathy.newsome@okstate.edu.

Purdue University, School of Veterinary Medicine and Graduate School, Graduate Programs in Veterinary Medicine, Department of Comparative Pathobiology, West Lafayette, IN 47907-2027. Offers comparative epidemiology and public health (MS); comparative epidemiology and public heath (PhD); comparative microbiology and immunology (MS, PhD); comparative pathobiology (MS, PhD); interdisciplinary studies (PhD), including microbial pathogenesis, molecular signaling and cancer biology, molecular virology; lab animal medicine (MS); veterinary anatomic pathology (MS); veterinary clinical pathology (MS). Terminal master's awarded for partial completion of doctoral program. *Degree requirements:* For master's, thesis (for some programs); for doctorate, thesis/dissertation. *Entrance requirements:* For master's and doctorate, GRE General Test. Additional exam requirements/recommendations for international students: Required—TOEFL (minimum score 575 paper-based; 232 computer-based), IELTS (minimum score 6.5), TWE (minimum score 4). Electronic applications accepted.

Queen's University at Kingston, School of Graduate Studies and Research, Faculty of Health Sciences, Department of Pathology and Molecular Medicine, Kingston, ON K7L 3N6, Canada. Offers M Sc, PhD. Part-time programs available. *Degree requirements:* For master's, thesis; for doctorate, comprehensive exam, thesis/dissertation. *Entrance requirements:* Additional exam requirements/recommendations for international students: Required—TOEFL. *Faculty research:* Immunopathology, cancer biology, immunology and metastases, cell differentiation, blood coagulation.

Quinnipiac University, School of Health Sciences, Program for Pathologists' Assistant, Hamden, CT 06518-1940. Offers MHS. *Accreditation:* NAACLS. *Faculty:* 2 full-time (1 woman), 6 part-time/adjunct (3 women). *Students:* 36 full-time (26 women); includes 4 minority (1 Black or African American, non-Hispanic/Latino; 3 Asian, non-Hispanic/Latino). Average age 27. 130 applicants, 14% accepted, 18 enrolled. In 2011, 18 master's awarded. *Degree requirements:* For master's, residency. *Entrance requirements:* For master's, interview, coursework in biological and health sciences, minimum GPA of 2.8. Additional exam requirements/recommendations for international students: Required—TOEFL (minimum score 575 paper-based; 233 computer-based; 90 iBT), IELTS (minimum score 6.5). *Application deadline:* For fall admission, 12/15 for domestic students. Applications are processed on a rolling basis. Application fee: $45. Electronic applications accepted. *Expenses:* *Tuition:* Part-time $855 per credit. *Required fees:* $35 per credit. *Financial support:* In 2011–12, 8 students received support. Career-related internships or fieldwork, tuition waivers (partial), and unspecified assistantships available. Financial award application deadline: 4/15; financial award applicants required to submit FAFSA. *Unit head:* Dr. Kenneth Kaloustian, Director, 203-582-8676, Fax: 203-582-3443, E-mail: ken.kaloustian@quinnipiac.edu. *Application contact:* Kristin Parent, Assistant Director of Graduate Health Sciences Admissions, 800-462-1944, Fax: 203-582-3443, E-mail: kristin.parent@quinnipiac.edu. Web site: http://www.quinnipiac.edu/gradpathologists.

Rosalind Franklin University of Medicine and Science, College of Health Professions, Pathologists' Assistant Department, North Chicago, IL 60064-3095. Offers MS. *Entrance requirements:* For master's, bachelor's degree from an accredited college or university, minimum cumulative GPA of 3.0. Additional exam requirements/recommendations for international students: Required—TOEFL. *Faculty research:* Adaptation of ACGME/ADASP pathology resident training competencies to pathologists' assistant clinical education, utilization of structural portfolios in pathologists' assistant clinical education.

Saint Louis University, Graduate Education and School of Medicine, Graduate Program in Biomedical Sciences and Graduate Education, Department of Pathology, St. Louis, MO 63103-2097. Offers PhD. *Degree requirements:* For doctorate, comprehensive exam, thesis/dissertation, oral and written preliminary exams, oral defense of dissertation. *Entrance requirements:* For doctorate, GRE General Test (GRE Subject Test optional), letters of recommendation, resume, interview. Additional exam requirements/recommendations for international students: Required—TOEFL (minimum score 525 paper-based; 194 computer-based). Electronic applications accepted. *Faculty research:* Cancer research, hepatitis C virology, cell imaging, liver disease.

Stony Brook University, State University of New York, Graduate School, College of Arts and Sciences, Department of Biochemistry and Cell Biology, Molecular and Cellular Biology Program, Stony Brook, NY 11794. Offers biochemistry and molecular biology (PhD); biological sciences (MA); cellular and developmental biology (PhD); immunology and pathology (PhD); molecular and cellular biology (PhD). *Degree requirements:* For doctorate, comprehensive exam, thesis/dissertation, teaching experience. *Entrance requirements:* For doctorate, GRE General Test, GRE Subject Test. Additional exam requirements/recommendations for international students: Required—TOEFL.

Temple University, Health Sciences Center, School of Medicine and Graduate School, Graduate Programs in Medicine, Department of Pathology and Laboratory Medicine, Philadelphia, PA 19122-6096. Offers PhD. *Faculty:* 5 full-time (1 woman). *Students:* 3 full-time (2 women), 1 international. Average age 29. 7 applicants, 43% accepted, 1 enrolled. *Degree requirements:* For doctorate, one foreign language, thesis/dissertation, research seminars. *Entrance requirements:* For doctorate, GRE General Test, GRE Subject Test, minimum GPA of 3.0. Additional exam requirements/recommendations for international students: Required—TOEFL (minimum score 550 paper-based; 213 computer-based; 79 iBT). *Application deadline:* For fall admission, 1/15 priority date for domestic students, 12/15 for international students; for spring admission, 11/1 priority date for domestic students, 8/1 for international students. Applications are processed on a rolling basis. Application fee: $50. Electronic applications accepted. *Expenses:* Tuition, state resident: full-time $12,366; part-time $687 per credit hour. Tuition, nonresident: full-time $17,298; part-time $961 per credit hour. *Required fees:* $590; $213 per year. *Financial support:* Fellowships and research assistantships available. Financial award application deadline: 1/15; financial award applicants required to submit FAFSA. *Faculty research:* Molecular cloning, cell proliferation, cell cycle regulation, DNA repair, cytogenetics. *Unit head:* Dr. Yuri Persidsky, Chair, 215-707-4353, Fax: 215-707-2781, E-mail: yuri.persidsky@temple.edu. *Application contact:* Office of Admissions, 215-707-3656, Fax: 215-707-6932, E-mail: medadmissions@temple.edu. Web site: http://www.temple.edu/medicine/departments_centers/clinical_departments/pathology_laboratory.htm.

Texas A&M University, College of Veterinary Medicine and Biomedical Sciences, Department of Veterinary Pathobiology, College Station, TX 77843. Offers genetics (MS, PhD); veterinary microbiology (MS, PhD); veterinary parasitology (MS, PhD); veterinary pathology (MS, PhD). Part-time programs available. Postbaccalaureate distance learning degree programs offered. *Faculty:* 25. *Students:* 27 full-time (20 women), 19 part-time (13 women); includes 9 minority (3 Black or African American, non-Hispanic/Latino; 3 Asian, non-Hispanic/Latino; 3 Hispanic/Latino), 9 international. Average age 33. In 2011, 2 degrees awarded. Terminal master's awarded for partial completion of doctoral program. *Degree requirements:* For master's, thesis, seminars; for doctorate, thesis/dissertation, seminars. *Entrance requirements:* For master's and doctorate, GRE General Test, minimum GPA of 3.0 in last 60 hours. Additional exam requirements/recommendations for international students: Required—TOEFL. *Application deadline:* For fall admission, 3/1 priority date for domestic students; for spring admission, 8/1 priority date for domestic students. Applications are processed on a rolling basis. Application fee: $50 ($75 for international students). Electronic applications accepted. *Expenses:* Tuition, state resident: full-time $5437; part-time

$226.55 per credit hour. Tuition, nonresident: full-time $12,949; part-time $539.55 per credit hour. *Required fees:* $2741. *Financial support:* In 2011–12, fellowships with partial tuition reimbursements (averaging $16,000 per year), research assistantships with partial tuition reimbursements (averaging $15,400 per year), teaching assistantships with partial tuition reimbursements (averaging $16,000 per year) were awarded; Federal Work-Study, institutionally sponsored loans, scholarships/grants, traineeships, health care benefits, and unspecified assistantships also available. Support available to part-time students. Financial award applicants required to submit FAFSA. *Faculty research:* Infectious and noninfectious diseases of animals and birds, animal genetics, molecular biology, immunology, virology. *Unit head:* Dr. Linda Logan, Head, 979-862-6559, Fax: 979-845-9231, E-mail: llogan@cvm.tamu.edu. *Application contact:* Dr. Patricia Holman, Graduate Advisor, 979-845-4202, Fax: 979-862-1147, E-mail: pholman@cvm.tamu.edu. Web site: http://vetmed.tamu.edu/vtpb.

Tufts University, Cummings School of Veterinary Medicine, North Grafton, MA 01536. Offers animals and public policy (MS); biomedical sciences (PhD), including digestive diseases, infectious diseases, neuroscience and reproductive biology, pathology; conservation medicine (MS); veterinary medicine (DVM); DVM/MPH; DVM/MS. *Accreditation:* AVMA (one or more programs are accredited). *Faculty:* 93 full-time (42 women), 14 part-time/adjunct (7 women). *Students:* 381 full-time (326 women); includes 47 minority (3 Black or African American, non-Hispanic/Latino; 4 American Indian or Alaska Native, non-Hispanic/Latino; 23 Asian, non-Hispanic/Latino; 16 Hispanic/Latino; 1 Two or more races, non-Hispanic/Latino), 7 international. Average age 25. 762 applicants, 33% accepted, 122 enrolled. In 2011, 8 master's, 80 doctorates awarded. *Degree requirements:* For master's, thesis (for some programs); for doctorate, comprehensive exam, thesis/dissertation (for some programs). *Entrance requirements:* For master's and doctorate, GRE General Test. Additional exam requirements/recommendations for international students: Required—TOEFL or IELTS. *Application deadline:* For fall admission, 11/1 for domestic and international students. Application fee: $70. Electronic applications accepted. *Expenses:* Contact institution. *Financial support:* In 2011–12, 245 students received support, including 6 research assistantships with full tuition reimbursements available (averaging $25,000 per year), 4 teaching assistantships (averaging $5,000 per year); career-related internships or fieldwork, Federal Work-Study, institutionally sponsored loans, scholarships/grants, and institutional aid awards; health care benefits for PhD students also available. Financial award application deadline: 5/15; financial award applicants required to submit FAFSA. *Faculty research:* Oncology, veterinary ethics, international veterinary medicine, veterinary genomics, pathogenesis of Clostridium difficile, wildlife fertility control. *Unit head:* Dr. Deborah T. Kochevar, Dean, 508-839-5302, Fax: 508-839-2953, E-mail: deborah.kochevar@tufts.edu. *Application contact:* Rebecca Russo, Director of Admissions, 508-839-7920, Fax: 508-887-4820, E-mail: vetadmissions@tufts.edu. Web site: http://www.tufts.edu/.

Université de Montréal, Faculty of Medicine, Department of Pathology and Cellular Biology, Montréal, QC H3C 3J7, Canada. Offers M Sc, PhD. Terminal master's awarded for partial completion of doctoral program. *Degree requirements:* For master's, thesis; for doctorate, thesis/dissertation, general exam. *Entrance requirements:* For master's and doctorate, proficiency in French, knowledge of English. Electronic applications accepted. *Faculty research:* Immunopathology, cardiovascular pathology, oncogenetics, cellular neurocytology, muscular dystrophy.

Université Laval, Faculty of Medicine, Post-Professional Programs in Medical Studies, Québec, QC G1K 7P4, Canada. Offers anatomy–pathology (DESS); anesthesiology (DESS); cardiology (DESS); care of older people (Diploma); clinical research (DESS); community health (DESS); dermatology (DESS); diagnostic radiology (DESS); emergency medicine (Diploma); family medicine (DESS); general surgery (DESS); geriatrics (DESS); hematology (DESS); internal medicine (DESS); maternal and fetal medicine (Diploma); medical biochemistry (DESS); medical microbiology and infectious diseases (DESS); medical oncology (DESS); nephrology (DESS); neurology (DESS); neurosurgery (DESS); obstetrics and gynecology (DESS); ophthalmology (DESS); orthopedic surgery (DESS); oto-rhino-laryngology (DESS); palliative medicine (Diploma); pediatrics (DESS); plastic surgery (DESS); psychiatry (DESS); pulmonary medicine (DESS); radiology–oncology (DESS); thoracic surgery (DESS); urology (DESS). *Degree requirements:* For other advanced degree, comprehensive exam. *Entrance requirements:* For degree, knowledge of French. Electronic applications accepted.

University at Buffalo, the State University of New York, Graduate School, Graduate Programs in Cancer Research and Biomedical Sciences at Roswell Park Cancer Institute, Department of Cancer Pathology and Prevention at Roswell Park Cancer Institute, Buffalo, NY 14263-0001. Offers PhD. *Degree requirements:* For doctorate, comprehensive exam, thesis/dissertation, dissertation defense, project. *Entrance requirements:* For doctorate, GRE, minimum GPA of 3.0, 3 letters of recommendation. Additional exam requirements/recommendations for international students: Required—TOEFL (minimum score paper-based 600, computer 250, iBT 100) or IELTS (minimum score 7). Electronic applications accepted. *Faculty research:* Molecular pathology of cancer, chemoprevention of cancer, genomic instability, molecular diagnosis and prognosis of cancer, molecular epidemiology.

University at Buffalo, the State University of New York, Graduate School, School of Medicine and Biomedical Sciences, Graduate Programs in Medicine and Biomedical Sciences, Department of Pathology and Anatomical Sciences, Buffalo, NY 14260. Offers anatomical sciences (MA, PhD); pathology (MA, PhD). Part-time programs available. *Faculty:* 14 full-time (3 women). *Students:* 7 full-time (2 women); includes 2 minority (both Asian, non-Hispanic/Latino), 2 international. Average age 29. 11 applicants, 27% accepted, 1 enrolled. In 2011, 3 doctorates awarded. *Degree requirements:* For master's, thesis; for doctorate, comprehensive exam, thesis/dissertation. *Entrance requirements:* For master's, GRE, MCAT, or DAT, 3 letters of recommendation; for doctorate, GRE, 3 letters of recommendation. Additional exam requirements/recommendations for international students: Required—TOEFL (minimum score 600 paper-based; 250 computer-based; 100 iBT). *Application deadline:* For fall admission, 3/1 priority date for domestic students, 3/1 for international students. Application fee: $50. *Financial support:* In 2011–12, 2 students received support, including 1 fellowship with full tuition reimbursement available (averaging $24,000 per year), 1 research assistantship with full tuition reimbursement available (averaging $22,000 per year); health care benefits also available. Financial award application deadline: 2/1; financial award applicants required to submit FAFSA. *Faculty research:* Immunopathology-immunobiology, experimental hypertension, neuromuscular disease, molecular pathology, cell motility and cytoskeleton. *Unit head:* Dr. John E. Tomaszewski, Chairman, 716-829-2847, Fax: 716-829-2086, E-mail: johntoma@buffalo.edu. *Application contact:* Patricia Simons, Graduate Program Secretary, 716-829-2846, Fax: 716-829-2086, E-mail: pesimons@buffalo.edu. Web site: http://wings.buffalo.edu/smbs/path/.

The University of Alabama at Birmingham, Graduate Programs in Joint Health Sciences, Program in Pathology, Birmingham, AL 35294. Offers PhD. *Degree requirements:* For doctorate, thesis/dissertation. *Entrance requirements:* For doctorate, GRE General Test, interview. *Application deadline:* Applications are processed on a rolling basis. Application fee: $35 ($60 for international students). Electronic applications

accepted. *Expenses:* Tuition, state resident: full-time $5922; part-time $309 per hour. Tuition, nonresident: full-time $13,428; part-time $726 per hour. Tuition and fees vary according to program. *Financial support:* Fellowships and career-related internships or fieldwork available. *Unit head:* Dr. Kevin Roth, Chairman, 205-934-5802, Fax: 205-934-5499.

University of Alberta, Faculty of Medicine and Dentistry and Faculty of Graduate Studies and Research, Graduate Programs in Medicine, Department of Laboratory Medicine and Pathology, Edmonton, AB T6G 2E1, Canada. Offers medical sciences (M Sc, PhD). Part-time programs available. Terminal master's awarded for partial completion of doctoral program. *Degree requirements:* For master's, thesis; for doctorate, thesis/dissertation, candidacy exam. *Entrance requirements:* For master's and doctorate, 3 letters of recommendation, minimum GPA of 3.0. Additional exam requirements/recommendations for international students: Required—TOEFL. *Faculty research:* Transplantation, renal pathology, molecular mechanisms of diseases, cryobiology, immunodiagnostics, informatics/cyber medicine, neuroimmunology, microbiology.

University of Arkansas for Medical Sciences, Graduate School, Graduate Programs in Biomedical Sciences, Department of Pathology, Little Rock, AR 72205-7199. Offers MS. *Degree requirements:* For master's, thesis. *Entrance requirements:* For master's, GRE General Test. Additional exam requirements/recommendations for international students: Required—TOEFL. *Faculty research:* Metastasis of cancer pediatric cancers, oxidative damage of DNA.

The University of British Columbia, Faculty of Medicine, Department of Pathology and Laboratory Medicine, Vancouver, BC V5Z 1M9, Canada. Offers experimental pathology (M Sc, PhD). *Degree requirements:* For master's, thesis; for doctorate, comprehensive exam, thesis/dissertation, internal oral defense. *Entrance requirements:* For master's, GRE, upper-level course work in biochemistry and physiology; for doctorate, GRE. Additional exam requirements/recommendations for international students: Required—TOEFL (minimum score 550 paper-based; 80 computer-based), IELTS (minimum score 6.5). Electronic applications accepted. *Faculty research:* Molecular biology of disease processes, cancer, hematopathology, atherosclerosis, pulmonary and cardiovascular pathophysiology.

University of California, Davis, Graduate Studies, Graduate Group in Comparative Pathology, Davis, CA 95616. Offers MS, PhD. *Accreditation:* NAACLS. Terminal master's awarded for partial completion of doctoral program. *Degree requirements:* For master's, comprehensive exam (for some programs), thesis (for some programs); for doctorate, thesis/dissertation. *Entrance requirements:* For master's and doctorate, GRE General Test. Additional exam requirements/recommendations for international students: Required—TOEFL (minimum score 550 paper-based; 213 computer-based). Electronic applications accepted. *Faculty research:* Immunopathology, toxicological and environmental pathology, reproductive pathology, pathology of infectious diseases.

University of California, Irvine, School of Medicine, Department of Pathology and Laboratory Medicine, Irvine, CA 92697. Offers experimental pathology (PhD). *Students:* 8 full-time (4 women); includes 5 minority (2 Asian, non-Hispanic/Latino; 3 Hispanic/Latino), 1 international. Average age 29. In 2011, 2 doctorates awarded. *Unit head:* Dr. Fritz Lin, Interim Chairman, 714-456-6141, Fax: 714-456-5873, E-mail: flin@uci.edu. *Application contact:* Dr. Edwin Monuki, Director of Graduate Program, 949-824-6574, Fax: 949-824-2160, E-mail: emonuki@uci.edu. Web site: http://www.pathology.uci.edu/gradProg.html.

University of California, Los Angeles, David Geffen School of Medicine and Graduate Division, Graduate Programs in Medicine, Program in Cellular and Molecular Pathology, Los Angeles, CA 90095. Offers MS, PhD. *Students:* 23 full-time (15 women); includes 11 minority (8 Asian, non-Hispanic/Latino; 2 Hispanic/Latino; 1 Two or more races, non-Hispanic/Latino), 3 international. Average age 29. 3 applicants, 100% accepted, 3 enrolled. In 2011, 6 doctorates awarded. Application fee: $70 ($90 for international students). Electronic applications accepted. *Financial support:* In 2011–12, 16 fellowships, 16 research assistantships, 4 teaching assistantships were awarded. *Unit head:* Dr. Kenneth I. Dorshkind, Program Director, 310-206-9535, E-mail: kdorshki@mednet.ucla.edu. *Application contact:* UCLA ACCESS Information, 310-206-6051, E-mail: uclaaccess@mednet.ucla.edu. Web site: http://www.pathnet.medsch.ucla.edu/educ/CMP/home.php.

University of California, Los Angeles, David Geffen School of Medicine and Graduate Division, Graduate Programs in Medicine, Program in Experimental Pathology, Los Angeles, CA 90095. Offers MS, PhD. In 2011, 2 master's, 3 doctorates awarded. *Degree requirements:* For doctorate, thesis/dissertation, oral and written qualifying exams. *Entrance requirements:* For master's, GRE General Test; for doctorate, GRE General Test, previous course work in physical chemistry and physics. Application fee: $70 ($90 for international students). *Financial support:* In 2011–12, 4 teaching assistantships were awarded; fellowships, research assistantships, Federal Work-Study, institutionally sponsored loans, scholarships/grants, and tuition waivers (full and partial) also available. Financial award application deadline: 3/1. *Unit head:* Dr. Jonathan Braun, Chair, 310-825-5719. *Application contact:* UCLA ACCESS Coordinator, 800-284-8252, Fax: 310-206-5280, E-mail: uclaaccess@lbes.medsch.ucla.edu.

University of California, Los Angeles, Graduate Division, College of Letters and Science and David Geffen School of Medicine, UCLA ACCESS to Programs in the Molecular, Cellular and Integrative Life Sciences, Los Angeles, CA 90095. Offers biochemistry and molecular biology (PhD); biological chemistry (PhD); cellular and molecular pathology (PhD); human genetics (PhD); microbiology, immunology, and molecular genetics (PhD); molecular biology (PhD); molecular toxicology (PhD); molecular, cellular and integrative physiology (PhD); neurobiology (PhD); oral biology (PhD); physiology (PhD). *Students:* 44 full-time (30 women); includes 18 minority (11 Asian, non-Hispanic/Latino; 6 Hispanic/Latino; 1 Two or more races, non-Hispanic/Latino), 9 international. Average age 25. 495 applicants, 18% accepted, 41 enrolled. *Degree requirements:* For doctorate, thesis/dissertation, oral and written qualifying exams. *Entrance requirements:* For doctorate, GRE General Test, minimum undergraduate GPA of 3.0. Additional exam requirements/recommendations for international students: Required—TOEFL. *Application deadline:* For fall admission, 12/15 for domestic and international students. Application fee: $70 ($90 for international students). Electronic applications accepted. *Financial support:* In 2011–12, 51 fellowships with full and partial tuition reimbursements, 9 research assistantships with full and partial tuition reimbursements were awarded; teaching assistantships with full and partial tuition reimbursements, Federal Work-Study, institutionally sponsored loans, scholarships/grants, health care benefits, tuition waivers (full and partial), and unspecified assistantships also available. Financial award application deadline: 3/1; financial award applicants required to submit FAFSA. *Faculty research:* Molecular, cellular, and developmental biology; immunology; microbiology; integrative biology. *Unit head:* Jody Spillane, Project Coordinator, 310-206-1845, E-mail: jspillane@mednet.ucla.edu. *Application contact:* UCLA ACCESS Admissions, 310-206-1845, E-mail: uclaaccess@mednet.ucla.edu. Web site: https://www.uclaaccess.ucla.edu/.

University of California, San Francisco, Graduate Division, Biomedical Sciences Graduate Group, San Francisco, CA 94143. Offers anatomy (PhD); endocrinology

(PhD); experimental pathology (PhD); physiology (PhD). *Degree requirements:* For doctorate, thesis/dissertation. *Entrance requirements:* For doctorate, GRE General Test.

University of Chicago, Division of Biological Sciences, Biomedical Sciences Cluster: Cancer Biology, Immunology, Molecular Metabolism and Nutrition, Pathology, and Microbiology, Department of Pathology, Chicago, IL 60637-1513. Offers molecular pathogenesis and molecular medicine (PhD). *Degree requirements:* For doctorate, thesis/dissertation, ethics class, 2 teaching assistantships. *Entrance requirements:* For doctorate, GRE General Test. Additional exam requirements/recommendations for international students: Required—IELTS (minimum score 7); Recommended—TOEFL (minimum score 600 paper-based; 250 computer-based; 104 iBT). Electronic applications accepted. *Faculty research:* Vascular biology, apolipoproteins, cardiovascular disease, immunopathology.

University of Cincinnati, Graduate School, College of Medicine, Graduate Programs in Biomedical Sciences, Program in Pathobiology and Molecular Medicine, Cincinnati, OH 45221. Offers pathology (PhD), including anatomic pathology, laboratory medicine, pathobiology and molecular medicine. *Degree requirements:* For doctorate, thesis/dissertation, qualifying exam. *Entrance requirements:* For doctorate, GRE General Test. Additional exam requirements/recommendations for international students: Required—TOEFL (minimum score 620 paper-based; 260 computer-based). Electronic applications accepted. *Faculty research:* Cardiovascular and lipid disorders, digestive and kidney disease, endocrine and metabolic disorders, hematologic and oncogenic, immunology and infectious disease.

University of Florida, College of Medicine, Department of Pathology, Immunology and Laboratory Medicine, Gainesville, FL 32611. Offers immunology and molecular pathology (PhD). *Degree requirements:* For doctorate, thesis/dissertation. *Entrance requirements:* For doctorate, GRE General Test, minimum GPA of 3.0. Additional exam requirements/recommendations for international students: Required—TOEFL. Electronic applications accepted. *Faculty research:* Molecular immunology, autoimmunity and transplantation, tumor biology, oncogenic viruses, human immunodeficiency viruses.

University of Georgia, College of Veterinary Medicine, Department of Pathology, Athens, GA 30602. Offers MS, PhD. *Faculty:* 19 full-time (12 women), 6 part-time/adjunct (2 women). *Students:* 18 full-time (12 women), 2 part-time (1 woman); includes 1 minority (Hispanic/Latino), 8 international. Average age 33. 26 applicants, 23% accepted, 3 enrolled. In 2011, 4 doctorates awarded. *Degree requirements:* For master's, thesis; for doctorate, one foreign language, thesis/dissertation. *Entrance requirements:* For master's and doctorate, GRE General Test. *Application deadline:* For fall admission, 7/1 priority date for domestic students; for spring admission, 11/15 for domestic students. Application fee: $50. Electronic applications accepted. *Financial support:* Fellowships, research assistantships, teaching assistantships, and unspecified assistantships available. *Unit head:* Dr. R. Keith Harris, Acting Head, 706-542-5831, Fax: 706-542-5828, E-mail: rkharris@uga.edu. *Application contact:* Dr. Jaroslava Halper, Graduate Coordinator, 706-542-5830, Fax: 706-542-5828, E-mail: jhalper@uga.edu. Web site: http://www.vet.uga.edu/VPP/.

University of Guelph, Ontario Veterinary College and Graduate Studies, Graduate Programs in Veterinary Sciences, Department of Pathobiology, Guelph, ON N1G 2W1, Canada. Offers anatomic pathology (DV Sc, Diploma); clinical pathology (Diploma); comparative pathology (M Sc, PhD); immunology (M Sc, PhD); laboratory animal science (DV Sc); pathology (M Sc, PhD, Diploma); veterinary infectious diseases (M Sc, PhD); zoo animal/wildlife medicine (DV Sc). *Degree requirements:* For master's, thesis; for doctorate, thesis/dissertation. *Entrance requirements:* For master's, DVM with B average or an honours degree in biological sciences; for doctorate, DVM or MSC degree, minimum B+ average. Additional exam requirements/recommendations for international students: Required—TOEFL (minimum score 550 paper-based; 213 computer-based). *Faculty research:* Pathogenesis; diseases of animals, wildlife, fish, and laboratory animals; parasitology; immunology; veterinary infectious diseases; laboratory animal science.

The University of Iowa, Roy J. and Lucille A. Carver College of Medicine and Graduate College, Graduate Programs in Medicine, Department of Pathology, Iowa City, IA 52242-1316. Offers MS. *Faculty:* 24 full-time (6 women). *Students:* 5 full-time (3 women); includes 1 minority (Two or more races, non-Hispanic/Latino), 1 international. Average age 25. 8 applicants, 25% accepted, 2 enrolled. In 2011, 1 master's awarded. *Degree requirements:* For master's, thesis. *Entrance requirements:* For master's, GRE, minimum GPA of 3.0. Additional exam requirements/recommendations for international students: Required—TOEFL. *Application deadline:* For fall admission, 2/15 priority date for domestic students, 1/15 for international students. Applications are processed on a rolling basis. Application fee: $60 ($100 for international students). Electronic applications accepted. *Financial support:* In 2011–12, 5 students received support, including 5 research assistantships with full tuition reimbursements available (averaging $25,500 per year); health care benefits also available. *Faculty research:* Oncology, microbiology, vascular biology, immunology, neuroscience, stem cells, virology, signaling and cell death. *Total annual research expenditures:* $3 million. *Unit head:* Dr. Barry DeYoung, Head, 319-335-8232, Fax: 319-335-8348, E-mail: barry-deyoung@uiowa.edu. *Application contact:* Dr. Thomas J. Waldschmidt, Graduate Program Director, 319-335-8223, Fax: 319-335-8453, E-mail: thomas-waldschmidt@uiowa.edu. Web site: http://www.medicine.uiowa.edu/pathology/.

The University of Kansas, University of Kansas Medical Center, School of Medicine, Department of Pathology and Laboratory Medicine, Kansas City, KS 66160. Offers MA, PhD, MD/PhD. *Faculty:* 30. *Students:* 14 full-time (8 women); includes 1 minority (Hispanic/Latino), 8 international. Average age 28. 15 applicants, 100% accepted, 2 enrolled. In 2011, 5 doctorates awarded. Terminal master's awarded for partial completion of doctoral program. *Degree requirements:* For master's, comprehensive exam (for some programs), thesis; for doctorate, comprehensive exam, thesis/dissertation. *Entrance requirements:* For master's, GRE, curriculum vitae, 3 reference letters; for doctorate, GRE, curriculum vitae, statement of research and career interests, official transcripts for all undergraduate and graduate coursework, 3 reference letters. Additional exam requirements/recommendations for international students: Required—TOEFL (preferred) or IELTS. *Application deadline:* For fall admission, 1/15 priority date for domestic students, 1/15 for international students. Applications are processed on a rolling basis. Application fee: $60. Tuition and fees vary according to course load, campus/location, program and reciprocity agreements. *Financial support:* In 2011–12, 11 research assistantships with full tuition reimbursements (averaging $24,000 per year), 4 teaching assistantships with full and partial tuition reimbursements (averaging $24,000 per year) were awarded; Federal Work-Study, scholarships/grants, traineeships, tuition waivers (full), and unspecified assistantships also available. Financial award application deadline: 2/14; financial award applicants required to submit FAFSA. *Faculty research:* Cancer biology, developmental biology and cell differentiation, stem cell biology, microbial and viral pathogenesis. *Total annual research expenditures:* $5.1 million. *Unit head:* Dr. Soumen Paul, Director, Pathology Graduate Program, 913-588-7236, Fax: 913-588-5242, E-mail: spaul2@kumc.edu. *Application contact:* Graduate Studies, 785-864-8040, Fax: 785-864-7209, E-mail: graduate@ku.edu. Web site: http://www2.kumc.edu/dcdb/gradprog.html.

University of Manitoba, Faculty of Medicine and Faculty of Graduate Studies, Graduate Programs in Medicine, Department of Pathology, Winnipeg, MB R3E 3P5, Canada. Offers M Sc. *Degree requirements:* For master's, thesis. *Entrance requirements:* For master's, B Sc honours degree. Additional exam requirements/recommendations for international students: Required—TOEFL (minimum score 550 paper-based; 213 computer-based; 80 iBT), IELTS (minimum score 6.5). *Faculty research:* Experimental hydrocephalus; brain development; stroke; developmental neurobiology; myelination in Rett Syndrome; glial migration during cortical development; growth factors and breast cancer; transgenic models of breast cancer; molecular genetics and cancer diagnosis; graft-vs-host disease; biology of natural killer cells; transplantation immunology.

University of Maryland, Baltimore, School of Medicine, Department of Pathology, Baltimore, MD 21201. Offers pathologists' assistant (MS). *Accreditation:* NAACLS. *Students:* 20 full-time (18 women), 1 (woman) part-time; includes 2 minority (both Asian, non-Hispanic/Latino), 2 international. Average age 27. 54 applicants, 22% accepted, 11 enrolled. In 2011, 7 master's awarded. *Entrance requirements:* For master's, GRE General Test. Additional exam requirements/recommendations for international students: Required—TOEFL (minimum score 600 paper-based; 250 computer-based; 100 iBT); Recommended—IELTS (minimum score 7). *Application deadline:* For fall admission, 2/1 for domestic and international students. Application fee: $50. Electronic applications accepted. *Expenses:* Contact institution. *Financial support:* Application deadline: 3/1; applicants required to submit FAFSA. *Unit head:* Dr. Rudy Castellani, Program Director, 410-328-5555, Fax: 410-706-8414, E-mail: rcastellani@som.umaryland.edu. *Application contact:* Carlen Miller, Associate Director, 410-328-5555, Fax: 410-706-8414, E-mail: cmiller@som.umaryland.edu. Web site: http://medschool.umaryland.edu/pathology/.

University of Massachusetts Lowell, School of Health and Environment, Department of Clinical Laboratory and Nutritional Sciences, Lowell, MA 01854-2881. Offers clinical laboratory sciences (MS); clinical pathology (Graduate Certificate); nutritional sciences (Graduate Certificate); public health laboratory sciences (Graduate Certificate). *Accreditation:* NAACLS. Part-time programs available. Postbaccalaureate distance learning degree programs offered. *Degree requirements:* For master's, thesis optional. *Entrance requirements:* For master's, GRE General Test, minimum GPA of 3.0, letters of recommendation. *Faculty research:* Cardiovascular disease, lipoprotein metabolism, micronutrient evaluation, alcohol metabolism, mycobacterial drug resistance.

University of Medicine and Dentistry of New Jersey, Graduate School of Biomedical Sciences, Graduate Programs in Biomedical Sciences–Newark, Program in Molecular Pathology and Immunology, Newark, NJ 07107. Offers PhD. *Entrance requirements:* Additional exam requirements/recommendations for international students: Required—TOEFL. Electronic applications accepted.

University of Michigan, Horace H. Rackham School of Graduate Studies, Program in Biomedical Sciences (PIBS), Program in Molecular and Cellular Pathology, Ann Arbor, MI 48109-2200. Offers PhD. *Faculty:* 39 full-time (10 women). *Students:* 23 full-time (11 women); includes 10 minority (1 Black or African American, non-Hispanic/Latino; 9 Asian, non-Hispanic/Latino). Average age 29. 62 applicants, 13% accepted, 5 enrolled. In 2011, 3 doctorates awarded. *Degree requirements:* For doctorate, comprehensive exam, thesis/dissertation. *Entrance requirements:* For doctorate, GRE General Test, 3 letters of recommendation, research experience. Additional exam requirements/recommendations for international students: Required—TOEFL (minimum score 84 iBT). *Application deadline:* For fall admission, 12/1 for domestic and international students. Application fee: $60 ($75 for international students). Electronic applications accepted. *Financial support:* In 2011–12, research assistantships with full tuition reimbursements (averaging $26,500 per year) were awarded; scholarships/grants, traineeships, health care benefits, and unspecified assistantships also available. *Faculty research:* Cancer biology, stem cell and developmental biology, immunopathology and inflammatory disease, epigenetics and gene regulation, cell death and regulation. *Unit head:* Dr. Nicholas W. Lukacs, Professor of Pathology/Director, 734-763-6454, Fax: 734-615-2331, E-mail: pathgradprog@med.umich.edu. *Application contact:* Laura A. Labut, Administrative Specialist, 734-763-6454, Fax: 734-615-2331, E-mail: laszczem@med.umich.edu. Web site: http://www.pathology.med.umich.edu/.

University of Mississippi Medical Center, School of Graduate Studies in the Health Sciences, Department of Pathology, Jackson, MS 39216-4505. Offers MS, PhD, MD/PhD. Terminal master's awarded for partial completion of doctoral program. *Degree requirements:* For master's, thesis; for doctorate, thesis/dissertation, first authored publication in peer-reviewed journal. *Entrance requirements:* For master's, GRE General Test, minimum GPA of 3.0; for doctorate, GRE General Test, GRE Subject Test, minimum GPA of 3.0. *Faculty research:* Effects of rehabilitation therapy on immune system/hypothalamic/pituitary adrenal axis interaction; HLA, GC, CM, KM, and/or genetic factors in the pathogenesis of AIDS; stem cell research; renal disease.

University of Missouri, School of Medicine and Graduate School, Graduate Programs in Medicine, Department of Pathology and Anatomical Sciences, Columbia, MO 65211. Offers MS. *Faculty:* 22 full-time (8 women), 7 part-time/adjunct (3 women). *Students:* 3 full-time (1 woman), 1 part-time (0 women), 1 international. Average age 28. 4 applicants, 50% accepted, 2 enrolled. In 2011, 3 degrees awarded. *Entrance requirements:* For master's, GRE (minimum Verbal and Analytical score of 1250), letters of recommendation, minimum GPA of 3.5. Additional exam requirements/recommendations for international students: Required—TOEFL. *Expenses:* Tuition, state resident: full-time $5881. Tuition, nonresident: full-time $15,183. *Required fees:* $952. Tuition and fees vary according to campus/location and program. *Faculty research:* Anatomic pathology, cancer biology, diabetes, integrative anatomy, laboratory medicine, neurobiology, tissue procurement core. *Unit head:* Dr. Douglas Anthony, Chair, 573-882-1205, E-mail: anthonydc@missouri.edu. *Application contact:* Dr. Carol V. Ward, Director of Graduate Studies, 573-884-7303, E-mail: wardcv@missouri.edu. Web site: http://pathology-anatomy.missouri.edu/.

University of Nebraska Medical Center, Graduate Studies, Department of Pathology and Microbiology, Omaha, NE 68198. Offers MS, PhD. Part-time programs available. Terminal master's awarded for partial completion of doctoral program. *Degree requirements:* For master's, comprehensive exam, thesis; for doctorate, comprehensive exam, thesis/dissertation. *Entrance requirements:* For master's, previous course work in biology, chemistry, mathematics, and physics; for doctorate, GRE General Test, previous course work in biology, chemistry, mathematics, and physics. Additional exam requirements/recommendations for international students: Required—TOEFL (minimum score 550 paper-based; 213 computer-based). Electronic applications accepted. *Faculty research:* Carcinogenesis, cancer biology, immunobiology, molecular virology, molecular genetics.

University of New Mexico, Health Sciences Center Graduate Programs, Program in Biomedical Sciences, Albuquerque, NM 87131-5196. Offers biochemistry and molecular biology (MS, PhD); cell biology and physiology (MS, PhD); clinical and translational science (Certificate); molecular genetics and microbiology (MS, PhD); neuroscience (MS, PhD); pathology (MS, PhD); toxicology (MS, PhD); university science teaching (Certificate). Part-time programs available. *Faculty:* 64 full-time (26 women), 9 part-time/

adjunct (4 women). *Students:* 45 full-time (27 women), 56 part-time (28 women); includes 24 minority (3 Black or African American, non-Hispanic/Latino; 1 American Indian or Alaska Native, non-Hispanic/Latino; 4 Asian, non-Hispanic/Latino; 14 Hispanic/Latino; 1 Native Hawaiian or other Pacific Islander, non-Hispanic/Latino; 1 Two or more races, non-Hispanic/Latino), 18 international. Average age 30. 110 applicants, 18% accepted, 17 enrolled. In 2011, 14 master's, 5 doctorates awarded. Terminal master's awarded for partial completion of doctoral program. *Degree requirements:* For master's, thesis; for doctorate, comprehensive exam, thesis/dissertation. *Entrance requirements:* For master's and doctorate, GRE General Test, minimum undergraduate GPA of 3.0. Additional exam requirements/recommendations for international students: Required—TOEFL. *Application deadline:* For fall admission, 3/1 priority date for domestic students, 3/1 for international students. Applications are processed on a rolling basis. Application fee: $50. Electronic applications accepted. *Financial support:* In 2011–12, 99 students received support, including 28 fellowships with full and partial tuition reimbursements available (averaging $22,000 per year), 73 research assistantships with full tuition reimbursements available (averaging $23,000 per year), 8 teaching assistantships (averaging $2,800 per year); career-related internships or fieldwork, Federal Work-Study, institutionally sponsored loans, scholarships/grants, traineeships, health care benefits, and unspecified assistantships also available. Financial award application deadline: 1/1; financial award applicants required to submit FAFSA. *Faculty research:* Infectious disease/Immunity, cancer biology, cardiovascular and metabolic diseases, brain and behavioral illness, environmental health. *Unit head:* Dr. Helen J. Hathaway, BSGP Program Director, 505-272-1887, Fax: 505-272-2412, E-mail: hhathaway@salud.unm.edu. *Application contact:* Mary Fenton, Admissions Coordinator, 505-272-1887, Fax: 505-272-2412, E-mail: mfenton@salud.unm.edu. Web site: http://hsc.unm.edu/som/research/brep/bsgpabout.shtm.

The University of North Carolina at Chapel Hill, School of Medicine and Graduate School, Graduate Programs in Medicine, Department of Pathology and Laboratory Medicine, Chapel Hill, NC 27599-7525. Offers experimental pathology (PhD). *Accreditation:* NAACLS. *Degree requirements:* For doctorate, comprehensive exam, thesis/dissertation, oral exam, proposal defense. *Entrance requirements:* For doctorate, GRE General Test. Additional exam requirements/recommendations for international students: Required—TOEFL (minimum score 550 paper-based; 213 computer-based). Electronic applications accepted. *Faculty research:* Carcinogenesis, mutagenesis and cancer biology; molecular biology, genetics and animal models of human disease; cardiovascular biology, hemostasis, and thrombosis; immunology and infectious disease; progenitor cell research.

University of Oklahoma Health Sciences Center, College of Medicine and Graduate College, Graduate Programs in Medicine, Department of Pathology, Oklahoma City, OK 73190. Offers PhD. *Degree requirements:* For doctorate, thesis/dissertation. *Entrance requirements:* For doctorate, GRE General Test, 3 letters of recommendation. Additional exam requirements/recommendations for international students: Required—TOEFL. *Faculty research:* Molecular pathology, tissue response in disease, anatomic pathology, immunopathology, histocytochemistry.

University of Pittsburgh, School of Medicine, Graduate Programs in Medicine, Program in Cellular and Molecular Pathology, Pittsburgh, PA 15260. Offers MS, PhD. *Faculty:* 66 full-time (17 women). *Students:* 35 full-time (20 women); includes 9 minority (3 Black or African American, non-Hispanic/Latino; 4 Asian, non-Hispanic/Latino; 2 Hispanic/Latino), 8 international. Average age 27. 514 applicants, 12% accepted, 28 enrolled. In 2011, 8 doctorates awarded. *Degree requirements:* For doctorate, comprehensive exam, thesis/dissertation. *Entrance requirements:* For doctorate, GRE General Test, GRE Subject Test, minimum QPA of 3.0. Additional exam requirements/recommendations for international students: Required—TOEFL (minimum score 600 paper-based; 100 iBT), IELTS (minimum score 7). *Application deadline:* For fall admission, 12/15 priority date for domestic students, 12/15 for international students. Application fee: $50. Electronic applications accepted. *Expenses:* Tuition, state resident: full-time $18,774; part-time $760 per credit. Tuition, nonresident: full-time $30,736; part-time $1258 per credit. *Required fees:* $740; $200 per term. Tuition and fees vary according to program. *Financial support:* In 2011–12, 11 fellowships with full tuition reimbursements (averaging $25,500 per year), 24 research assistantships with full tuition reimbursements (averaging $25,500 per year) were awarded; teaching assistantships with full tuition reimbursements, institutionally sponsored loans, scholarships/grants, traineeships, health care benefits, and unspecified assistantships also available. *Faculty research:* Liver growth and differentiation, pathogenesis of neurodegeneration, cancer research. *Unit head:* Dr. Wendy Mars, Graduate Program Director, 412-648-9690, Fax: 412-648-9846, E-mail: wmars@pitt.edu. *Application contact:* Graduate Studies Administrator, 412-648-8957, Fax: 412-648-1077, E-mail: gradstudies@medschool.pitt.edu. Web site: http://www.gradbiomed.pitt.edu.

University of Prince Edward Island, Atlantic Veterinary College, Graduate Program in Veterinary Medicine, Charlottetown, PE C1A 4P3, Canada. Offers anatomy (M Sc, PhD); bacteriology (M Sc, PhD); clinical pharmacology (M Sc, PhD); clinical sciences (M Sc, PhD); epidemiology (M Sc, PhD), including reproduction; fish health (M Sc, PhD); food animal nutrition (M Sc, PhD); immunology (M Sc, PhD); microanatomy (M Sc, PhD); parasitology (M Sc, PhD); pathology (M Sc, PhD); pharmacology (M Sc, PhD); physiology (M Sc, PhD); toxicology (M Sc, PhD); veterinary science (M Vet Sc); virology (M Sc, PhD). Part-time programs available. *Degree requirements:* For master's, thesis; for doctorate, thesis/dissertation. *Entrance requirements:* For master's, DVM, B Sc honors degree, or equivalent; for doctorate, M Sc. Additional exam requirements/recommendations for international students: Required—TOEFL (minimum score 550 paper-based; 213 computer-based; 80 iBT). *Expenses:* Contact institution. *Faculty research:* Animal health management, infectious diseases, fin fish and shellfish health, basic biomedical sciences, ecosystem health.

University of Rochester, School of Medicine and Dentistry, Graduate Programs in Medicine and Dentistry, Department of Pathology and Laboratory Medicine, Rochester, NY 14627. Offers pathology (PhD). *Degree requirements:* For doctorate, variable foreign language requirement, thesis/dissertation, qualifying exam. *Entrance requirements:* For doctorate, GRE General Test, GRE Subject Test. *Expenses:* Tuition: Full-time $41,040.

University of Saskatchewan, College of Medicine, Department of Pathology, Saskatoon, SK S7N 5A2, Canada. Offers M Sc, PhD. *Degree requirements:* For master's, thesis; for doctorate, thesis/dissertation. *Entrance requirements:* Additional exam requirements/recommendations for international students: Required—TOEFL.

University of Saskatchewan, Western College of Veterinary Medicine and College of Graduate Studies and Research, Graduate Programs in Veterinary Medicine, Department of Veterinary Pathology, Saskatoon, SK S7N 5A2, Canada. Offers M Sc, M Vet Sc, PhD. *Degree requirements:* For master's, thesis; for doctorate, comprehensive exam (for some programs), thesis/dissertation. *Entrance requirements:* Additional exam requirements/recommendations for international students: Required—TOEFL or IELTS (minimum score 6.5). Electronic applications accepted. *Faculty research:* Thyroid, oncology, immunology/infectious diseases, vaccinology.

University of Southern California, Keck School of Medicine and Graduate School, Graduate Programs in Medicine, Department of Pathology, Los Angeles, CA 90089-9092. Offers experimental and molecular pathology (MS); pathobiology (PhD). *Faculty:* 34 full-time (6 women), 4 part-time/adjunct (1 woman). *Students:* 29 full-time (16 women); includes 12 minority (9 Asian, non-Hispanic/Latino; 3 Hispanic/Latino), 10 international. Average age 26. 6 applicants, 83% accepted, 4 enrolled. In 2011, 6 master's, 4 doctorates awarded. *Degree requirements:* For master's, thesis; for doctorate, thesis/dissertation. *Entrance requirements:* For master's, GRE General Test, minimum GPA of 3.0; for doctorate, GRE General Test, minimum GPA of 3.0, BS in natural sciences. Additional exam requirements/recommendations for international students: Required—TOEFL (minimum score 600 paper-based; 250 computer-based; 100 iBT). *Application deadline:* For fall admission, 12/1 priority date for domestic students, 12/1 for international students. Application fee: $85. Electronic applications accepted. *Financial support:* In 2011–12, 17 students received support, including 1 fellowship with full and partial tuition reimbursement available (averaging $29,100 per year), 16 research assistantships with full and partial tuition reimbursements available (averaging $29,100 per year); Federal Work-Study, institutionally sponsored loans, scholarships/grants, health care benefits, and unspecified assistantships also available. Financial award application deadline: 5/4; financial award applicants required to submit CSS PROFILE or FAFSA. *Faculty research:* Cellular and molecular biology of cancer; chemical carcinogenesis; virology; stem cell and developmental pathology; liver and pulmonary diseases; environmental pathology; circulatory, endocrine, and neurodegenerative diseases. *Total annual research expenditures:* $961.5 million. *Unit head:* Dr. Michael E. Selsted, Chair, 323-442-1179, Fax: 323-442-3049, E-mail: selsted@usc.edu. *Application contact:* Lisa A. Doumak, Student Services Assistant, 323-442-1168, Fax: 323-442-3049, E-mail: doumak@usc.edu. Web site: http://www.usc.edu/hsc/medicine/pathology/.

The University of Texas Medical Branch, Graduate School of Biomedical Sciences, Program in Experimental Pathology, Galveston, TX 77555. Offers PhD. *Degree requirements:* For doctorate, thesis/dissertation. *Entrance requirements:* For doctorate, GRE General Test. Additional exam requirements/recommendations for international students: Required—TOEFL (minimum score 550 paper-based; 213 computer-based). Electronic applications accepted.

The University of Toledo, College of Graduate Studies, College of Medicine and Life Sciences, Department of Pathology, Toledo, OH 43606-3390. Offers Certificate. *Faculty:* 4. *Students:* 3 part-time (2 women). Average age 24. 3 applicants, 100% accepted, 3 enrolled. In 2011, 3 Certificates awarded. *Entrance requirements:* For degree, second-year medical student in good academic standing with recommendation by UT Medical School. Application fee: $45 ($75 for international students). Electronic applications accepted. *Financial support:* In 2011–12, 3 fellowships with full tuition reimbursements were awarded; tuition waivers (full and partial) also available. *Unit head:* Dr. Robert Mrak, Professor/Chairman, 419-383-3469, E-mail: robert.mrak@utoledo.edu. *Application contact:* Cathie Harman, Assistant to the Chair, 419-383-3469, E-mail: cathie.harman@utoledo.edu. Web site: http://www.utoledo.edu/med/grad/.

University of Utah, School of Medicine and Graduate School, Graduate Programs in Medicine, Department of Pathology, Salt Lake City, UT 84112-1107. Offers experimental pathology (PhD); laboratory medicine and biomedical science (MS). PhD offered after acceptance into the combined Program in Molecular Biology. *Degree requirements:* For doctorate, comprehensive exam, thesis/dissertation. *Entrance requirements:* For doctorate, GRE, minimum GPA of 3.0. *Faculty research:* Immunology, cell biology, signal transduction, gene regulation, receptor biology.

University of Vermont, College of Medicine and Graduate College, Graduate Programs in Medicine, Department of Pathology, Burlington, VT 05405. Offers MS, MD/MS. *Students:* 3 (1 woman); includes 2 minority (1 Asian, non-Hispanic/Latino; 1 Hispanic/Latino). 7 applicants, 14% accepted, 1 enrolled. *Degree requirements:* For master's, thesis. *Entrance requirements:* For master's, GRE General Test. Additional exam requirements/recommendations for international students: Required—TOEFL (minimum score 550 paper-based; 213 computer-based; 80 iBT). *Application deadline:* For fall admission, 3/1 priority date for domestic students, 3/1 for international students. Applications are processed on a rolling basis. Application fee: $40. Electronic applications accepted. *Financial support:* Fellowships, research assistantships, and traineeships available. Financial award application deadline: 3/1. *Unit head:* Dr. E. Bovill, Chairperson, 802-656-0397. *Application contact:* Dr. David Yandell, Coordinator, 802-656-2210.

University of Virginia, School of Medicine, Program in Experimental Pathology, Charlottesville, VA 22903. Offers PhD. *Students:* 13 full-time (8 women); includes 3 minority (2 Black or African American, non-Hispanic/Latino; 1 Asian, non-Hispanic/Latino), 3 international. Average age 27. *Degree requirements:* For doctorate, thesis/dissertation, oral defense of thesis. *Entrance requirements:* For doctorate, GRE General Test; GRE Subject Test (recommended), 2 letters of recommendation. Additional exam requirements/recommendations for international students: Required—TOEFL. *Application deadline:* For fall admission, 1/15 for domestic and international students. *Financial support:* Application deadline: 1/15. *Unit head:* Janet V. Cross, Program Director, 434-924-7185, E-mail: molmed@virginia.edu. *Application contact:* Lesley L. Thomas, Director, Admissions Office, 434-924-5571, Fax: 434-982-2586, E-mail: medsch-adm@virginia.edu. Web site: http://www.healthsystem.virginia.edu/internet/bims-molmed/training/phd_path.cfm.

University of Washington, Graduate School, School of Medicine, Graduate Programs in Medicine, Department of Pathology, Seattle, WA 98195. Offers experimental and molecular pathology (PhD). *Degree requirements:* For doctorate, thesis/dissertation. *Entrance requirements:* For doctorate, GRE General Test. *Faculty research:* Viral oncogenesis, aging, mutagenesis and repair, extracellular matrix biology, vascular biology.

The University of Western Ontario, Faculty of Graduate Studies, Biosciences Division, Department of Pathology, London, ON N6A 5B8, Canada. Offers M Sc, PhD. *Degree requirements:* For master's, thesis; for doctorate, comprehensive exam, thesis/dissertation. *Entrance requirements:* For master's and doctorate, minimum B+ average, honors degree. Additional exam requirements/recommendations for international students: Required—TOEFL. *Faculty research:* Heavy metal toxicology, transplant pathology, immunopathology, immunological cancers, neurochemistry, aging and dementia, cancer pathology.

University of Wisconsin–Madison, School of Medicine and Public Health and Graduate School, Graduate Programs in Medicine, Department of Pathology and Laboratory Medicine, Madison, WI 53706-1380. Offers PhD. *Accreditation:* NAACLS. *Faculty:* 72 full-time (19 women). *Students:* 39 full-time (21 women); includes 10 minority (2 Black or African American, non-Hispanic/Latino; 1 American Indian or Alaska Native, non-Hispanic/Latino; 3 Asian, non-Hispanic/Latino; 4 Hispanic/Latino), 7 international. Average age 25. 162 applicants, 14% accepted, 11 enrolled. In 2011, 1 doctorate awarded. *Degree requirements:* For doctorate, thesis/dissertation. *Entrance requirements:* For doctorate, GRE, minimum GPA of 3.0. Additional exam requirements/recommendations for international students: Required—TOEFL (minimum score 580 paper-based; 237 computer-based; 92 iBT). *Application deadline:* For fall admission, 12/1 priority date for domestic students, 12/1 for international students. Applications are processed on a rolling basis. Application fee: $66. Electronic applications accepted. *Expenses:* Tuition, state resident: full-time $10,296; part-time $643.51 per credit.

Pathology

Tuition, nonresident: full-time $24,054; part-time $1503.40 per credit. *Required fees:* $70.06 per credit. Tuition and fees vary according to course load, campus/location, program and reciprocity agreements. *Financial support:* In 2011–12, 39 students received support, including 12 fellowships with full tuition reimbursements available (averaging $24,000 per year), 27 research assistantships with full tuition reimbursements available (averaging $24,000 per year); health care benefits also available. Financial award application deadline: 12/1. *Faculty research:* Cellular and molecular pathology: immunology/immunopathology, cancer biology, neuroscience/neuropathology, growth factor/matrix biology, developmental pathology. *Unit head:* Dr. Andreas Friedl, Chair, 608-265-4262, Fax: 608-265-3301, E-mail: krasmusson@wisc.edu. *Application contact:* Joanne Thornton, Student Services Coordinator, 608-262-2665, Fax: 608-265-3301, E-mail: gradinfo@pathology.wisc.edu. Web site: http://www.pathology.wisc.edu/.

See Close-Up on page 421.

Vanderbilt University, Graduate School and School of Medicine, Department of Pathology, Nashville, TN 37240-1001. Offers PhD, MD/PhD. *Faculty:* 42 full-time (11 women). *Students:* 21 full-time (12 women); includes 9 minority (4 Black or African American, non-Hispanic/Latino; 1 Asian, non-Hispanic/Latino; 4 Hispanic/Latino), 3 international. Average age 28. In 2011, 3 doctorates awarded. *Degree requirements:* For doctorate, thesis/dissertation, qualifying and final exams. *Entrance requirements:* For doctorate, GRE General Test. Additional exam requirements/recommendations for international students: Required—TOEFL (minimum score 570 paper-based; 230 computer-based; 88 iBT). *Application deadline:* For fall admission, 1/15 for domestic and international students. Application fee: $0. Electronic applications accepted. *Financial support:* Fellowships with full tuition reimbursements, research assistantships with full tuition reimbursements, Federal Work-Study, institutionally sponsored loans, traineeships, health care benefits, and tuition waivers (partial) available. Financial award application deadline: 1/15; financial award applicants required to submit CSS PROFILE or FAFSA. *Faculty research:* Vascular biology and biochemistry, tumor pathology, the immune response, inflammation and repair, the biology of the extracellular matrix in response to disease processes, the pathogenesis of infectious agents, the regulation of gene expression in disease. *Unit head:* Dr. Samuel A. Santoro, Chair, 615-322-3234, Fax: 615-322-5551, E-mail: samuel.a.santoro@vanderbilt.edu. *Application contact:* Lorie Franklin, Administrative Assistant/Director of Graduate Studies Assistant, 615-343-4882, Fax: 615-322-0576, E-mail: lorie.franklin@vanderbilt.edu. Web site: http://www.mc.vanderbilt.edu/pathology/.

Virginia Commonwealth University, Medical College of Virginia-Professional Programs, School of Medicine, School of Medicine Graduate Programs, Department of Pathology, Richmond, VA 23284-9005. Offers PhD, MD/PhD. Part-time programs available. Terminal master's awarded for partial completion of doctoral program. *Degree requirements:* For doctorate, thesis/dissertation, comprehensive oral and written exams. *Entrance requirements:* For doctorate, GRE General Test, MCAT. *Expenses:* Tuition, state resident: full-time $9133; part-time $507 per credit. Tuition, nonresident: full-time $18,777; part-time $1043 per credit. *Required fees:* $77 per credit. Tuition and fees vary according to degree level, campus/location, program and student level. *Faculty research:* Biochemical and clinical applications of enzyme and protein immobilization, clinical enzymology.

Wayne State University, School of Medicine, Department of Pathology, Detroit, MI 48202. Offers PhD. *Accreditation:* NAACLS. *Students:* 13 full-time (7 women), 1 (woman) part-time; includes 2 minority (1 Asian, non-Hispanic/Latino; 1 Two or more races, non-Hispanic/Latino), 6 international. Average age 29. 17 applicants, 6% accepted, 1 enrolled. *Degree requirements:* For doctorate, thesis/dissertation. *Entrance requirements:* For doctorate, GRE General Test. Additional exam requirements/recommendations for international students: Required—TOEFL (minimum score 550 paper-based; 213 computer-based; 100 iBT); Recommended—TWE (minimum score 5.5). *Application deadline:* For fall admission, 6/1 for domestic students, 5/1 for international students. Application fee: $50. Electronic applications accepted. *Expenses:* Tuition, state resident: part-time $512.85 per credit. Tuition, nonresident: part-time $1132.65 per credit. *Required fees:* $26.60 per credit. $199.65 per semester. Tuition and fees vary according to course load and program. *Financial support:* In 2011–12, 10 students received support, including 5 fellowships with tuition reimbursements available (averaging $29,289 per year), 6 research assistantships with tuition reimbursements available (averaging $21,287 per year); teaching assistantships with tuition reimbursements available, career-related internships or fieldwork, Federal Work-Study, scholarships/grants, health care benefits, and unspecified assistantships also available. Financial award application deadline: 2/1. *Faculty research:* Cardiovascular physiology, cancer biology, cellular and tissue proteases, cancer chemoprevention, lung development, diabetes. *Unit head:* Dr. Todd Leff, Program Director, 313-577-3006, E-mail: tleff@med.wayne.edu. Web site: http://www.pathology.med.wayne.edu/.

Yale University, Graduate School of Arts and Sciences, Department of Experimental Pathology, New Haven, CT 06520. Offers MS, PhD. *Degree requirements:* For doctorate, thesis/dissertation, qualifying exam. *Entrance requirements:* For doctorate, GRE General Test.

Yale University, School of Medicine and Graduate School of Arts and Sciences, Combined Program in Biological and Biomedical Sciences (BBS), Pharmacological Sciences and Molecular Medicine Track, New Haven, CT 06520. Offers PhD, MD/PhD. *Degree requirements:* For doctorate, thesis/dissertation. *Entrance requirements:* For doctorate, GRE General Test. Additional exam requirements/recommendations for international students: Required—TOEFL. Electronic applications accepted.

UNIVERSITY OF WISCONSIN–MADISON

Department of Pathology and Laboratory Medicine

Program of Study

The Cellular and Molecular Pathology (CMP) graduate training program originated more than fifty years ago as a program focused on general pathology research and education. Through the years, much of the training involved examination of pathological specimens, and graduates were highly valued for their skills by health institutions and industry. Seven years ago, the graduate program was restructured to emphasize the pathogenesis of human disease, and the program faculty was expanded. Today, the faculty of the CMP program includes 60 National Institutes of Health/National Science Foundation or similarly funded investigators focusing on research programs in immunology, cancer biology, neuropathology, and signal transduction. These investigators come from twenty different basic science, preclinical, and clinical departments. Of these trainers, 31 hold Ph.D. degrees and 29 hold M.D. or M.D./Ph.D. degrees, and carry out both patient care and basic research. The Department of Pathology serves as a core for the CMP graduate program, integrating these faculty and trainers from across campus into a unified, multidisciplinary graduate training program focused on the pathogenesis of human diseases.

The primary objective of the CMP program is to prepare graduates for productive careers in scientific research and education and to position them to make significant contributions toward the nation's health-related research needs.

The CMP program focuses on the integration of medical knowledge into graduate education, and the Department of Pathology offers a translational bridge between basic and clinical sciences by offering an interdisciplinary curriculum focused on the concepts of human disease pathogenesis and translational research.

Research Facilities

The Department is housed in the Medical School complex at the center of the Madison campus and at the Clinical Sciences Center on the west side of campus. The Department has modern research facilities including centralized support facilities. In addition, the Integrated Microscopy Resource on the Madison campus is a national microscopy center that provides equipment and support for scanning and transmission of electron microscopy and video-enhanced fluorescence microscopy. Extensive library facilities, including Departmental collections, the Medical School Library, and extensive holdings at other science libraries on the Madison campus, are available.

Financial Aid

It is the intention of the program that students receive stipend support during the duration of their graduate study. Support for students is offered through a variety of sources, including Department teaching and research assistantships, research assistantships from individual faculty research grants, project assistantships, fellowships, the thesis adviser's research funds, or other campus sources. In addition, students compete for University fellowships and research assistantships on several training grants on the Madison campus. For the 2012–13 school year, the stipend rate for graduate students in the Department of Pathology and Laboratory Medicine is $24,500, with an increase of approximately 4 percent annually. In addition, assistantship recipients qualify for full remission of nonresident and resident tuition and subsidized enrollment in the Graduate Assistant Health Insurance program.

Cost of Study

As discussed in the Financial Aid section, students receive stipend support throughout their graduate study. In the fall of 2012, tuition and fees are $6475.28 per semester for Wisconsin residents and $13,138.48 per semester for nonresidents.

Living and Housing Costs

For single graduate students, the University maintains graduate student apartments that offer one- and two-bedroom units; rents range from $812 to $1036 per month in 2012–13. University Student Apartments, better known as Eagle Heights, offers one- to three-bedroom unfurnished apartments; rents range from $694 to $1036 per month in 2012–13. There may be a waiting list for the Eagle Heights units, and priority is given to students with dependent children. For more details, students should visit the Division of University Housing Web site at http://www.housing.wisc.edu. Most students live off campus; costs for off-campus housing vary depending on size and location. Additional information about off-campus housing is available at the UW–Madison Campus Information, Assistance, and Orientation Web site at http://www.wisc.edu/cac/housing/.

Student Group

The Madison campus is the flagship of the University of Wisconsin, with an enrollment of more than 40,000 students, including 9,000 graduate students. In the sciences, the graduate students belong to individual department graduate programs or are members of interdepartmental training programs, such as the CMP program.

Student Outcomes

Students in this program have successfully pursued a number of options after obtaining their Ph.D. degrees. They have received postdoctoral training and obtained faculty positions in academic institutions, taken research positions in industry, or continued on to medical school and secured faculty positions in medical institutions.

Location

Madison, recently ranked as one of the top American cities to live in, is the capital of the state, with a metropolitan population of approximately 215,000. The city, situated on four picturesque lakes, is approximately 150 miles northwest of Chicago. The city and the University offer a wide variety of educational, cultural, and recreational opportunities. Superb facilities are available for summer and winter sports, such as sailing, camping, hiking, ice skating, skiing, and bicycling.

The University

The University, founded in 1848, is one of the Big Ten schools and has a rich tradition of excellence in research. The University System includes the main campus in Madison plus twelve other comprehensive universities, thirteen freshman/sophomore campuses (UW Colleges), and the UW–Extension Program.

Applying

Applicants should have a bachelor's degree and an undergraduate minimum grade point average of 3.0 (on a 4.0 scale). Applicants should have a strong background in organic and physical chemistry, biochemistry, biology (including genetics), and mathematics through calculus. Completed application forms, Graduate Record Examinations (GRE) scores, transcripts, a resume, statement of purpose, and a minimum of three letters of recommendation are required for an admission decision. The application submission deadline for fall admission is December 1.

Correspondence and Information

CMP Program Coordinator
Department of Pathology
3170-10K/L Medical Foundation Centennial Building
University of Wisconsin
1685 Highland Avenue
Madison, Wisconsin 53705
United States
Phone: 608-262-2665
Fax: 608-265-3301
E-mail: gradinfo@pathology.wisc.edu
Web site: http://www.cmp.wisc.edu

THE FACULTY AND THEIR RESEARCH

Nihal Ahmad, Associate Professor, Dermatology. Cancer biology; prevention and experimental therapeutics of cancer.

Caroline Alexander, Associate Professor, Oncology. Role of breast stem cells in tumor induction; multiple functions of Wnt signaling in the regulation of mammary epithelial cell growth; changes in tumor susceptibility that are effected by alterations of normal development.

B. Lynn Allen-Hoffmann, Professor, Pathology. Keratinocytes; cancer biology; extracellular matrices.

David Andes, Associate Professor, Medicine. Identification of strategies to combat antimicrobial (especially antifungal) drug resistance.

Fotis Asimakopoulos, Assistant Professor, Medicine. Myeloma research; phase I experimental therapeutics.

Alan Attie, Professor, Biochemistry. Identify genes and pathways involved in obesity-induced type 2 diabetes.

University of Wisconsin–Madison

Barbara Bendlin, Assistant Professor, Medicine. Aging; Alzheimer's disease, neurobiology of disease, behavior, and cognition.

Craig S. Atwood, Associate Professor, Medicine. Hormonal regulation of aging and neurodegenerative diseases.

Emery H. Bresnick, Professor, Pharmacology. Regulation of transcription, hematopoiesis, and leukemogenesis.

William J. Burlingham, Professor, Surgery. Mechanisms of transplant tolerance and rejection.

Michael Carrithers, Associate Professor, Neurology. Novel immune-mediated repair mechanisms relevant to the pathogenesis of multiple sclerosis and other inflammatory diseases.

Herbert Chen, Professor, Surgery. Development, progression, and treatment of endocrine tumors including gastrointestinal carcinoids, thyroid cancer, adrenal cancer, and pancreatic islet cell tumors.

Clifford Cho, Assistant Professor, Surgery. Influence of cancer on the integrity of the immune system.

Joshua Coon, Assistant Professor, Chemistry. Bioanalytical chemistry; mass spectrometry.

Cameron Currie, Associate Professor, Bacteriology. Evolution of symbiotic associations between animals and microbes.

Loren Denlinger, Assistant Professor, Medicine. Host-pathogen interactions; the role of macrophages in immunity to intracellular pathogens.

Arjang Djamali, Assistant Professor, Medicine. The mechanisms of disease progression in kidney disease.

Marina Emborg, Assistant Professor, Medical Physics. Solutions for neurodegenerative disorders, in particular Parkinson's disease.

Zsuzsa Fabry, Professor, Pathology. Immunopathology; neuroimmunology; multiple sclerosis.

John Fleming, Professor, Neurology. Multiple sclerosis.

Andreas Friedl, Professor, Pathology. Heparan sulfate proteoglycans as modulators of growth factors in human disease; tumor angiogenesis.

Thomas Friedrich, Assistant Professor, Pathobiological Sciences. Viral immunity; pathogenesis.

Ying Ge, Assistant Professor, Cell and Regenerative Biology. Ultra high-resolution mass spectrometry-based proteomics and metabolomics technology for biomedical research.

James Gern, Professor, Pediatrics. Interactions between host and viral factors.

Daniel Greenspan, Professor, Pathology. Extracellular controls of cell behavior.

Jenny Gumperz, Associate Professor, Medical Microbiology and Immunology. Autoreactivity.

Jeff Hardin, Professor, Zoology. Morphogenesis and pattern formation during early development.

Peiman Hematti, Assistant Professor, Medicine. Characterization and study of mesenchymal stromal cells derived from human embryonic stem cells; development of a preclinical rhesus macaque model.

Anna Huttenlocher, Associate Professor, Medical Microbiology and Immunology. Cell migration and chemotaxis; adhesive mechanisms that regulate cell migration; the role of integrin signaling.

Nizar Jarjour, Professor, Medicine. Asthma; circadian rhythm; investigative bronchoscopy.

Juan Jaume, Assistant Professor, Medicine. Endocrine autoimmunity, type 1 diabetes, and thyroid diseases.

Shannon Kenney, Professor, Medicine. Epstein-Barr virus pathogenesis and treatment.

K C. Kent, Professor, Surgery. Molecular and cellular mechanisms underlying vascular disease

Michelle Kimple, Assistant Professor. How beta cells of the pancreas respond to nutrient and hormonal stimulation to affect biological changes.

Bruce Klein, Professor, Pediatrics. Microbial immunology and pathogenesis.

Kevin Kozak, Assistant Professor, Oncology. Identifying molecular, cellular and organ-level barriers to effective anti-neoplastic therapy.

John Kuo, Assistant Professor, Neurosurgery. Brain tumor stem cells; molecular mechanisms of tumorigenesis.

Aparna Lakkaraju, Assistant Professor, Ophthalmology and Visual Services. Cellular basis of retinal degenerative diseases.

Youngsook Lee, Associate Professor, Anatomy. Transcriptional control of cardiovascular development and mechanisms of cardiac-specific gene regulation.

Bo Liu, Associate Professor, Surgery. Vascular diseases, cell apoptosis, inflammation, signaling, adult progenitor cells, gene therapy.

Riccardo Lloyd, Professor, Department of Pathology and Laboratory Medicine.

Dan Loeb, Professor, Department of Oncology. Molecular biology of the hepatitis B viruses.

Gary E. Lyons, Associate Professor, Anatomy. Developmental biology of the mammalian cardiovascular system.

Albee Messing, Professor, Pathobiological Sciences. Transgenic mice; developmental neuropathology; molecular neurobiology.

Joshua Mezrich, Assistant Professor, Surgery. Transplant tolerance.

Deane F. Mosher, Professor, Medicine. Extracellular matrix and cell adhesion.

Robert Nickells, Professor, Ophthalmology and Visual Sciences. Glaucoma; neurodegeneration; complex genetics; neuronal apoptosis.

David O'Connor, Assistant Professor, Pathology. HIV/AIDS pathogenesis.

Shelby O'Connor, Assistant Professor, Pathology and Laboratory Medicine. Host and vaccine-elicited immune responses to SIV/HIV.

Julie Olson, Assistant Professor, Neurological Surgery. Role of resident immune cells and infiltrating peripheral immune cells in the response to virus infection in the CNS.

Caitlin Pepperell, Assistant Professor, Medicine. Bacterial pathogenesis.

Donna P. Peters, Professor, Pathology. Cell-matrix signaling in the human eye; glaucoma.

Luigi Puglielli, Associate Professor, Medicine. Aging of the brain; Alzheimer's disease; neurodegeneration; lipid signaling; protein signaling; post-translational modification; membrane transport; translational research.

Alan Rapraeger, Professor, Pathology. Mechanisms by which the syndecan family of cell-surface receptors regulate cell growth, adhesion, and migration.

Matyas Sandor, Professor, Pathology. Immune responses to infectious disease.

Christine M. Seroogy, Assistant Professor, Pediatrics. Biological role of a novel E3 ubiquitin ligase called GRAIL in T-cell function and hematopoietic tissue development.

John Sheehan, Associate Professor, Medicine. Blood coagulation; intrinsic tenase regulation; coagulation factor IX.

Nader Sheibani, Associate Professor, Ophthalmology and Visual Sciences. Cell adhesion and signaling in vascular cells; diabetic retinopathy.

Igor Slukvin, Assistant Professor, Pathology. Hematopoietic differentiation of human embryonic stem cells; immune-privileged properties of embryonic and fetal tissues.

Judy Smith, Assistant Professor, Pediatrics, Regulation of type I IFN production in macrophages.

Paul M. Sondel, Professor, Pediatrics. Immune-mediated recognition and destruction of neoplasms.

Rupa Sridharan, Assistant Professor, Cell and Regenerative Biology. Epigenetics of cell fate change.

M. Suresh, Associate Professor, Pathobiological Sciences. Molecular and cellular basis of T-cell memory; CD8+ T-cell responses in chronic viral infections.

Masatoshi Suzuki, Assistant Professor, Comparative Biosciences. Application of stem cells to developmental modeling and cell-based therapy.

John Svaren, Associate Professor, Comparative Biosciences. Role of EGR and NAB proteins in peripheral nerve myelination; genomic analysis of physiological regulation; role of chromatin structure in gene regulation.

Adel Talaat, Assistant Professor, Pathobiological Sciences. Genomic and functional analyses of tuberculosis and paratuberculosis to understand pathogenesis and develop novel vaccines.

Robert Thorne, Assistant Professor, Pharmacy. Using biopharmaceuticals to treat neurological disorders (e.g., Alzheimer's disease, Parkinson's disease, and stroke); intranasal targeting of drugs to the brain, spinal cord, and cervical lymph nodes.

Raghu Vemuganti, Associate Professor, Neurosurgery. Traumatic brain injury.

Deric Wheeler, Assistant Professor, Human Oncology. Mechanisms of resistance to targeted therapies.

Jon P. Woods, Associate Professor, Medical Microbiology and Immunology. *Histoplasma capsulatum* molecular pathogenesis and host interactions.

Timothy Yoshino, Professor, Pathobiological Sciences. Physiological interactions between parasites and their invertebrate hosts.

Xinyu Zhao, Neuroscience. Using molecular mechanisms that regulate neural stem cells and neurodevelopment to treat neurological disorders and injuries.

Weixiong Zhong, Assistant Professor, Pathology. Redox effects of selenium in human prostate cancer chemoprevention.

Section 17
Pharmacology and Toxicology

This section contains a directory of institutions offering graduate work in pharmacology and toxicology. Additional information about programs listed in the directory but not augmented by an in-depth entry may be obtained by writing directly to the dean of a graduate school or chair of a department at the address given in the directory.

For programs offering related work, see also in this book *Biochemistry; Biological and Biomedical Sciences; Cell, Molecular, and Structural Biology; Ecology, Environmental Biology, and Evolutionary Biology; Genetics, Developmental Biology, and Reproductive Biology; Neuroscience and Neurobiology; Nutrition; Pathology and Pathobiology; Pharmacy and Pharmaceutical Sciences; Physiology; Public Health;* and *Veterinary Medicine and Sciences.* In the other guides in this series:

Graduate Programs in the Humanities, Arts & Social Sciences
See *Psychology and Counseling*
Graduate Programs in the Physical Sciences, Mathematics, Agricultural Sciences, the Environment & Natural Resources
See *Chemistry* and *Environmental Sciences and Management*
Graduate Programs in Engineering & Applied Sciences
See *Chemical Engineering* and *Civil and Environmental Engineering*

CONTENTS

Program Directories

Display and Close-Up

Molecular Pharmacology

Albert Einstein College of Medicine, Graduate Division of Biomedical Sciences, Division of Biological Sciences, Department of Molecular Pharmacology, Bronx, NY 10461. Offers PhD, MD/PhD. *Degree requirements:* For doctorate, thesis/dissertation. *Entrance requirements:* For doctorate, GRE General Test. Additional exam requirements/recommendations for international students: Required—TOEFL. *Faculty research:* Effects of drugs on macromolecules, enzyme systems, cell morphology and function.

Brown University, Graduate School, Division of Biology and Medicine, Program in Molecular Pharmacology and Physiology, Providence, RI 02912. Offers MA, Sc M, PhD, MD/PhD. *Degree requirements:* For doctorate, thesis/dissertation, preliminary exam. *Entrance requirements:* For master's and doctorate, GRE General Test, GRE Subject Test. Additional exam requirements/recommendations for international students: Required—TOEFL. Electronic applications accepted. *Faculty research:* Structural biology, antiplatelet drugs, nicotinic receptor structure/function.

Dartmouth College, Program in Experimental and Molecular Medicine, Molecular Pharmacology, Toxicology and Experimental Therapeutics Track, Hanover, NH 03755. Offers PhD.

Harvard University, Graduate School of Arts and Sciences, Division of Medical Sciences, Boston, MA 02115. Offers biological chemistry and molecular pharmacology (PhD); cell biology (PhD); genetics (PhD); microbiology and molecular genetics (PhD); pathology (PhD), including experimental pathology. *Degree requirements:* For doctorate, thesis/dissertation. *Entrance requirements:* For doctorate, GRE General Test, GRE Subject Test. Additional exam requirements/recommendations for international students: Required—TOEFL. *Expenses: Tuition:* Full-time $36,304. *Required fees:* $1186. Full-time tuition and fees vary according to program.

Mayo Graduate School, Graduate Programs in Biomedical Sciences, Program in Molecular Pharmacology and Experimental Therapeutics, Rochester, MN 55905. Offers PhD. *Degree requirements:* For doctorate, oral defense of dissertation, qualifying oral and written exam. *Entrance requirements:* For doctorate, GRE, 1 year of chemistry, biology, calculus, and physics. Additional exam requirements/recommendations for international students: Required—TOEFL. Electronic applications accepted. *Faculty research:* Patch clamping, G-proteins, pharmacogenetics, receptor-induced transcriptional events, cholinesterase biology.

Medical University of South Carolina, College of Graduate Studies, Program in Cell and Molecular Pharmacology and Experimental Therapeutics, Charleston, SC 29425. Offers MS, PhD, DMD/PhD, MD/PhD. *Faculty:* 16 full-time (3 women). *Students:* 4 full-time (3 women). Average age 24. 5 applicants, 0% accepted. In 2011, 2 doctorates awarded. Terminal master's awarded for partial completion of doctoral program. *Degree requirements:* For master's, thesis; for doctorate, comprehensive exam, thesis/dissertation, oral and written exams. *Entrance requirements:* For master's, GRE General Test; for doctorate, GRE General Test, interview, minimum GPA of 3.0. Additional exam requirements/recommendations for international students: Required—TOEFL (minimum score 600 paper-based; 250 computer-based; 100 iBT). *Application deadline:* For fall admission, 1/15 priority date for domestic students, 1/15 for international students. Applications are processed on a rolling basis. Application fee: $0 ($85 for international students). Electronic applications accepted. *Financial support:* In 2011–12, fellowships with partial tuition reimbursements (averaging $23,000 per year) were awarded; Federal Work-Study and scholarships/grants also available. Support available to part-time students. Financial award application deadline: 3/10; financial award applicants required to submit FAFSA. *Faculty research:* Cancer drug discovery and development, growth factor receptor signaling, regulation of G-protein signaling, redox signal transduction, proteomics and mass spectrometry. *Unit head:* Dr. Kenneth D. Tew, Chair, 843-792-2514, Fax: 843-792-9588, E-mail: tewk@musc.edu. *Application contact:* Dr. Lauren Ball, Assistant Professor and Co-Director of the Graduate Training Program, 843-792-4513, Fax: 843-792-6590, E-mail: ballle@musc.edu. Web site: http://www.musc.edu/pharm.

New York University, School of Medicine and Graduate School of Arts and Science, Sackler Institute of Graduate Biomedical Sciences, Program in Molecular Pharmacology, New York, NY 10012-1019. Offers PhD, MD/PhD. *Faculty:* 31 full-time (4 women). *Students:* 13 full-time (9 women); includes 2 minority (both Asian, non-Hispanic/Latino), 6 international. Average age 28. In 2011, 4 doctorates awarded. *Degree requirements:* For doctorate, comprehensive exam, thesis/dissertation, qualifying exam. *Entrance requirements:* For doctorate, GRE General Test. Additional exam requirements/recommendations for international students: Required—TOEFL. *Application deadline:* For fall admission, 1/4 priority date for domestic students. Applications are processed on a rolling basis. Application fee: $85. *Financial support:* Fellowships with tuition reimbursements, research assistantships with tuition reimbursements, teaching assistantships with tuition reimbursements, and tuition waivers (full) available. *Faculty research:* Pharmacology and neurobiology, neuropeptides, receptor biochemistry, cytoskeleton, endocrinology. *Unit head:* Dr. Erika Bach, Chair, 212-263-5963, E-mail: bache02@popmail.nyu.edu. *Application contact:* Dr. Jan Sap, Graduate Student Adviser, 212-263-7120, E-mail: sapj01@popmail.med.nyu.edu.

Penn State University Park, Graduate School, Intercollege Graduate Programs, Intercollege Graduate Program in Integrative Biosciences, State College, University Park, PA 16802-1503. Offers integrative biosciences (MS, PhD), including biomolecular transport dynamics (PhD), integrative biosciences (MS). *Unit head:* Dr. Peter J. Hudson, Director, 814-865-6057, Fax: 814-863-1357. *Application contact:* Cynthia E. Nicosia, Director, Graduate Enrollment Services, 814-865-1795, Fax: 814-865-4627, E-mail: cey1@psu.edu.

Purdue University, College of Pharmacy and Pharmacal Sciences and Graduate School, Graduate Programs in Pharmacy and Pharmacal Sciences, West Lafayette, IN 47907. Offers industrial and physical pharmacy (MS, PhD, Certificate), including pharmaceutics (PhD), regulatory quality compliance (MS, Certificate); medicinal chemistry and molecular pharmacology (MS, PhD), including analytical medicinal chemistry (PhD), biophysical and computational chemistry (PhD), cancer research (PhD), immunology and infectious disease (PhD), medicinal and bioorganic chemistry (PhD), medicinal biochemistry and molecular biology (PhD), medicinal chemistry and chemical biology (PhD), molecular pharmacology (PhD), natural products and pharmacognosy (PhD), neuropharmacology, neurodegeneration, and neurotoxicology (PhD), nuclear pharmacy (MS), radiopharmaceutical chemistry and nuclear pharmacy (PhD), systems biology and functional genomics (PhD); pharmacy practice (MS, PhD), including clinical pharmacy, pharmacy administration. Part-time programs available. *Faculty:* 47 full-time (9 women), 46 part-time/adjunct (10 women). *Students:* 89 full-time (43 women), 29 part-time (18 women); includes 18 minority (3 Black or African American, non-Hispanic/Latino; 10 Asian, non-Hispanic/Latino; 5 Hispanic/Latino), 51 international. Average age 31. 371 applicants, 15% accepted, 25 enrolled. In 2011, 12 master's, 15 doctorates, 13 other advanced degrees awarded. Terminal master's awarded for partial completion of doctoral program. *Degree requirements:* For doctorate, thesis/dissertation. *Entrance requirements:* For master's and doctorate, GRE General Test, minimum undergraduate GPA of 3.0. Additional exam requirements/recommendations for international students: Required—TOEFL. *Application deadline:* Applications are processed on a rolling basis. Application fee: $60 ($75 for international students). Electronic applications accepted. *Financial support:* Fellowships, research assistantships, teaching assistantships, career-related internships or fieldwork, and traineeships available. Support available to part-time students. Financial award applicants required to submit FAFSA. *Faculty research:* Medicinal chemistry and pharmaceutics, cancer research, monoclonal antibodies. *Unit head:* Dr. C. K. Svensson, Dean, 765-494-1368, E-mail: svensson@purdue.edu. *Application contact:* Dr. G. Marc Loudon, Associate Dean for Graduate Programs, 765-494-1362.

Rosalind Franklin University of Medicine and Science, School of Graduate and Postdoctoral Studies - Interdisciplinary Graduate Program in Biomedical Sciences, Department of Cellular and Molecular Pharmacology, North Chicago, IL 60064-3095. Offers MS, PhD, MD/PhD. Terminal master's awarded for partial completion of doctoral program. *Degree requirements:* For master's, comprehensive exam, thesis; for doctorate, comprehensive exam, thesis/dissertation. *Entrance requirements:* For master's and doctorate, GRE General Test. Additional exam requirements/recommendations for international students: Required—TOEFL, TWE. Electronic applications accepted. *Faculty research:* Control of gene expression in higher organisms, molecular mechanism of action of growth factors and hormones, hormonal regulation in brain neuropsychopharmacology.

Rutgers, The State University of New Jersey, New Brunswick, Graduate School-New Brunswick, Program in Cellular and Molecular Pharmacology, Piscataway, NJ 08854-8097. Offers PhD. Program offered jointly with University of Medicine and Dentistry of New Jersey. *Degree requirements:* For doctorate, thesis/dissertation, qualifying exam. *Entrance requirements:* For doctorate, GRE General Test, GRE Subject Test. Additional exam requirements/recommendations for international students: Required—TOEFL. *Faculty research:* Molecular, cellular, and neuropharmacology; drug metabolism; intracellular signaling systems; protein synthesis and processing; carcinogenesis.

Stanford University, School of Medicine, Graduate Programs in Medicine, Department of Molecular Pharmacology, Stanford, CA 94305-9991. Offers PhD. *Degree requirements:* For doctorate, thesis/dissertation, qualifying examination. *Entrance requirements:* For doctorate, GRE General Test, GRE Subject Test. Additional exam requirements/recommendations for international students: Required—TOEFL. Electronic applications accepted. *Expenses: Tuition:* Full-time $40,050; part-time $890 per credit. *Faculty research:* Action of such drugs as epinephrine, cell differentiation and development, microsomal enzymes, neuropeptide gene expression.

Thomas Jefferson University, Jefferson College of Graduate Studies, PhD Program in Molecular Pharmacology and Structural Biology, Philadelphia, PA 19107. Offers PhD. *Faculty:* 39 full-time (8 women). *Students:* 18 full-time (9 women); includes 5 minority (all Asian, non-Hispanic/Latino), 5 international. 34 applicants, 18% accepted, 3 enrolled. In 2011, 1 doctorate awarded. *Degree requirements:* For doctorate, comprehensive exam, thesis/dissertation. *Entrance requirements:* For doctorate, GRE General Test, minimum GPA of 3.2. Additional exam requirements/recommendations for international students: Required—TOEFL (minimum score 250 computer-based; 100 iBT) or IELTS. *Application deadline:* For fall admission, 1/2 priority date for domestic students, 1/2 for international students. Applications are processed on a rolling basis. Application fee: $50. Electronic applications accepted. *Financial support:* In 2011–12, 18 students received support, including 18 fellowships with full tuition reimbursements available (averaging $54,758 per year); Federal Work-Study, institutionally sponsored loans, scholarships/grants, traineeships, and stipends also available. Support available to part-time students. Financial award application deadline: 5/1; financial award applicants required to submit FAFSA. *Faculty research:* Biochemistry and cell, molecular and structural biology of cell-surface and intracellular receptors; molecular modeling; signal transduction. *Total annual research expenditures:* $22.7 million. *Unit head:* Dr. Philip Wedegaertner, Program Director, 215-503-3137, Fax: 215-923-2117, E-mail: philip.wedegaertner@mail.tju.edu. *Application contact:* Marc E. Stearns, Director of Admissions, 215-503-0155, Fax: 215-503-9920, E-mail: jcgs-info@jefferson.edu. Web site: http://www.jefferson.edu/jcgs/phd/mpsb/.

University of Massachusetts Worcester, Graduate School of Biomedical Sciences, Worcester, MA 01655-0115. Offers biochemistry and molecular pharmacology (PhD); bioinformatics and computational biology (PhD); cancer biology (PhD); cell biology (PhD); clinical and population health research (PhD); clinical investigation (MS); immunology and virology (PhD); interdisciplinary graduate program (PhD); molecular genetics and microbiology (PhD); neuroscience (PhD); DVM/PhD; MD/PhD. *Faculty:* 1,427 full-time (526 women), 309 part-time/adjunct (196 women). *Students:* 416 full-time (225 women); includes 47 minority (12 Black or African American, non-Hispanic/Latino; 32 Asian, non-Hispanic/Latino; 3 Hispanic/Latino), 144 international. Average age 29. 623 applicants, 17% accepted, 54 enrolled. In 2011, 5 master's, 63 doctorates awarded. Terminal master's awarded for partial completion of doctoral program. *Degree requirements:* For master's, comprehensive exam, thesis; for doctorate, comprehensive exam, thesis/dissertation. *Entrance requirements:* For master's, bachelor's degree; for doctorate, GRE General Test. Additional exam requirements/recommendations for international students: Required—TOEFL (minimum score 600 paper-based; 250 computer-based; 100 iBT) or IELTS (minimum score 7.5). *Application deadline:* For fall admission, 12/15 for domestic and international students; for spring admission, 5/15 for domestic students. Application fee: $50. Electronic applications accepted. *Expenses:* Contact institution. *Financial support:* In 2011–12, 416 students received support, including 416 research assistantships with full tuition reimbursements available (averaging $29,200 per year); scholarships/grants, health care benefits, tuition waivers (full), and unspecified assistantships also available. Financial award application deadline: 4/16. *Faculty research:* RNA interference, cell biology, bioinformatics, clinical research, infectious disease. *Total annual research expenditures:* $262.7 million. *Unit head:* Dr. Anthony Carruthers, Dean, 508-856-4135, E-mail: anthony.carruthers@umassmed.edu. *Application contact:* Dr. Kendall Knight, Associate Dean and Interim Director of Admissions and Recruitment, 508-856-5628, Fax: 508-856-3659, E-mail: kendall.knight@umassmed.edu. Web site: http://www.umassmed.edu/gsbs/.

University of Medicine and Dentistry of New Jersey, Graduate School of Biomedical Sciences, Graduate Programs in Biomedical Sciences–Piscataway, Program in Cellular and Molecular Pharmacology, Piscataway, NJ 08854-5635. Offers MS, PhD, MD/PhD.

Degree requirements: For master's, thesis, qualifying exam; for doctorate, thesis/dissertation, qualifying exam. *Entrance requirements:* Additional exam requirements/recommendations for international students: Required—TOEFL. Electronic applications accepted.

University of Nevada, Reno, Graduate School, Interdisciplinary Program in Cellular and Molecular Pharmacology and Physiology, Reno, NV 89557. Offers PhD. *Degree requirements:* For doctorate, one foreign language, thesis/dissertation. *Entrance requirements:* For doctorate, GRE General Test or MCAT, minimum GPA of 3.0. Additional exam requirements/recommendations for international students: Required—TOEFL (minimum score 500 paper-based; 173 computer-based; 61 iBT), IELTS (minimum score 6). Electronic applications accepted. *Faculty research:* Neuropharmacology, toxicology, cardiovascular pharmacology, neuromuscular pharmacology.

University of Pittsburgh, School of Medicine, Graduate Programs in Medicine, Program in Molecular Pharmacology, Pittsburgh, PA 15260. Offers MS, PhD. *Faculty:* 60 full-time (10 women). *Students:* 24 full-time (16 women); includes 2 minority (1 Black or African American, non-Hispanic/Latino; 1 Asian, non-Hispanic/Latino), 4 international. Average age 27. 514 applicants, 12% accepted, 24 enrolled. In 2011, 5 doctorates awarded. *Degree requirements:* For doctorate, comprehensive exam, thesis/dissertation. *Entrance requirements:* For doctorate, GRE General Test, GRE Subject Test, minimum QPA of 3.0. Additional exam requirements/recommendations for international students: Required—TOEFL (minimum score 600 paper-based; 100 iBT), IELTS (minimum score 7). *Application deadline:* For fall admission, 12/15 priority date for domestic students, 12/15 for international students. Application fee: $50. Electronic applications accepted. *Expenses:* Tuition, state resident: full-time $18,774; part-time $760 per credit. Tuition, nonresident: full-time $30,736; part-time $1258 per credit. *Required fees:* $740; $200 per term. Tuition and fees vary according to program. *Financial support:* In 2011–12, 5 fellowships with full tuition reimbursements (averaging $25,500 per year), 19 research assistantships with full tuition reimbursements (averaging $25,500 per year) were awarded; institutionally sponsored loans, scholarships/grants, traineeships, health care benefits, tuition waivers (full), and unspecified assistantships also available. *Faculty research:* Drug discovery, signal transduction, cancer therapeutics, neuropharmacology, cardiovascular and renal pharmacology. *Unit head:* Dr. Patrick Pagano, Graduate Program Director, 412-383-6505, Fax: 412-648-9009, E-mail: pagano@pitt.edu. *Application contact:* Graduate Studies Administrator, 412-648-8957, Fax: 412-648-1007, E-mail: gradstudies@medschool.pitt.edu. Web site: http://www.gradbiomed.pitt.edu/.

University of Southern California, Graduate School, School of Pharmacy, Graduate Programs in Molecular Pharmacology and Toxicology, Los Angeles, CA 90033. Offers pharmacology and pharmaceutical sciences (MS, PhD). Terminal master's awarded for partial completion of doctoral program. *Degree requirements:* For master's, comprehensive exam, thesis, 24 units of formal course work, excluding research and seminar courses; for doctorate, comprehensive exam, thesis/dissertation, 24 units of formal course work, excluding research and seminar courses. *Entrance requirements:* For master's and doctorate, GRE. Additional exam requirements/recommendations for international students: Required—TOEFL (minimum score 603 paper-based; 250 computer-based; 100 iBT). Electronic applications accepted. *Expenses:* Contact institution. *Faculty research:* Degenerative diseases, toxicology of drugs.

Molecular Toxicology

Massachusetts Institute of Technology, School of Science, Department of Biology, Cambridge, MA 02139. Offers biochemistry (PhD); biological oceanography (PhD); biology (PhD); biophysical chemistry and molecular structure (PhD); cell biology (PhD); computational and systems biology (PhD); developmental biology (PhD); genetics (PhD); immunology (PhD); microbiology (PhD); molecular biology (PhD); neurobiology (PhD). *Faculty:* 58 full-time (15 women). *Students:* 248 full-time (129 women); includes 69 minority (5 Black or African American, non-Hispanic/Latino; 1 American Indian or Alaska Native, non-Hispanic/Latino; 25 Asian, non-Hispanic/Latino; 31 Hispanic/Latino; 7 Two or more races, non-Hispanic/Latino), 36 international. Average age 26. 698 applicants, 15% accepted, 44 enrolled. In 2011, 38 doctorates awarded. *Degree requirements:* For doctorate, comprehensive exam, thesis/dissertation. *Entrance requirements:* For doctorate, GRE General Test. Additional exam requirements/recommendations for international students: Required—TOEFL (minimum score 577 paper-based; 233 computer-based), IELTS (minimum score 6.5). *Application deadline:* For fall admission, 12/1 for domestic and international students. Application fee: $75. Electronic applications accepted. *Expenses: Tuition:* Full-time $40,460; part-time $630 per credit hour. *Required fees:* $272. *Financial support:* In 2011–12, 214 students received support, including 129 fellowships (averaging $33,200 per year), 117 research assistantships (averaging $32,900 per year); teaching assistantships, Federal Work-Study, institutionally sponsored loans, scholarships/grants, traineeships, health care benefits, and unspecified assistantships also available. *Faculty research:* Cellular, developmental and molecular (plant and animal) biology; biochemistry, bioengineering, biophysics and structural biology; classical and molecular genetics; immunology and microbiology; cancer biology, molecular medicine, neurobiology and human disease; computational and systems biology. *Total annual research expenditures:* $53.6 million. *Unit head:* Prof. Tania A. Baker, Head, 617-253-4701, E-mail: mitbio@mit.edu. *Application contact:* Biology Education Office, 617-253-3717, Fax: 617-258-9329, E-mail: gradbio@mit.edu. Web site: https://biology.mit.edu/.

New York University, Graduate School of Arts and Science, Department of Environmental Medicine, New York, NY 10012-1019. Offers environmental health sciences (MS, PhD), including biostatistics (PhD), environmental hygiene (MS), epidemiology (PhD), ergonomics and biomechanics (PhD), exposure assessment and health effects (PhD), molecular toxicology/carcinogenesis (PhD), toxicology. Part-time programs available. *Faculty:* 26 full-time (7 women). *Students:* 62 full-time (43 women), 9 part-time (4 women); includes 12 minority (2 Black or African American, non-Hispanic/Latino; 3 Asian, non-Hispanic/Latino; 7 Hispanic/Latino), 27 international. Average age 30. 70 applicants, 56% accepted, 26 enrolled. In 2011, 9 master's, 8 doctorates awarded. Terminal master's awarded for partial completion of doctoral program. *Degree requirements:* For master's, thesis or alternative; for doctorate, one foreign language, thesis/dissertation, oral and written exams. *Entrance requirements:* For master's and doctorate, GRE General Test, GRE Subject Test, minimum GPA of 3.0; bachelor's degree in biological, physical, or engineering science. Additional exam requirements/recommendations for international students: Required—TOEFL. *Application deadline:* For fall admission, 12/12 for domestic and international students. Application fee: $90. *Financial support:* Fellowships with tuition reimbursements, teaching assistantships with tuition reimbursements, career-related internships or fieldwork, Federal Work-Study, institutionally sponsored loans, and health care benefits available. Financial award application deadline: 12/12; financial award applicants required to submit FAFSA. *Unit head:* Dr. Max Costa, Chair, 845-731-3661, Fax: 845-351-4510, E-mail: ehs@env.med.nyu.edu. *Application contact:* Dr. Jerome J. Solomon, Director of Graduate Studies, 845-731-3661, Fax: 845-351-4510, E-mail: ehs@env.med.nyu.edu. Web site: http://environmental-medicine.med.nyu.edu/.

North Carolina State University, Graduate School, College of Agriculture and Life Sciences and College of Veterinary Medicine, Department of Environmental and Molecular Toxicology, Raleigh, NC 27695. Offers M Tox, MS, PhD. Terminal master's awarded for partial completion of doctoral program. *Degree requirements:* For master's, thesis (for some programs); for doctorate, thesis/dissertation. *Entrance requirements:* For master's and doctorate, GRE General Test, minimum GPA of 3.0. Electronic applications accepted. *Faculty research:* Chemical fate, carcinogenesis, developmental and endocrine toxicity, xenobiotic metabolism, signal transduction.

Oregon State University, Graduate School, College of Agricultural Sciences, Department of Environmental and Molecular Toxicology, Corvallis, OR 97331. Offers toxicology (MS, PhD).

Penn State Hershey Medical Center, College of Medicine, Graduate School Programs in the Biomedical Sciences, The Huck Institutes of the Life Sciences, Intercollege Graduate Program in Molecular Toxicology, Hershey, PA 17033. Offers MS, PhD, MD/PhD. *Students:* 5 full-time (2 women), 4 international. 4 applicants, 75% accepted, 2 enrolled. *Degree requirements:* For doctorate, comprehensive exam, thesis/dissertation. *Entrance requirements:* For doctorate, GRE. Additional exam requirements/recommendations for international students: Required—TOEFL (minimum score 550 paper-based). *Application deadline:* For fall admission, 3/1 priority date for domestic students, 2/1 for international students. Applications are processed on a rolling basis. Application fee: $65. Electronic applications accepted. *Financial support:* In 2011–12, research assistantships with full tuition reimbursements (averaging $23,028 per year) were awarded; fellowships with full tuition reimbursements, career-related internships or fieldwork, scholarships/grants, and unspecified assistantships also available. *Unit head:* Dr. Jong Yun, Head, 717-531-8982, E-mail: grad-hmc@psu.edu. *Application contact:* Kathy Shuey, Administrative Assistant, 717-531-8982, Fax: 717-531-0786, E-mail: grad-hmc@psu.edu. Web site: http://www.huck.psu.edu/education/molecular-toxicology.

University of California, Berkeley, Graduate Division, College of Natural Resources, Group in Molecular Toxicology, Berkeley, CA 94720-1500. Offers PhD. *Entrance requirements:* For doctorate, GRE General Test, 3 letters of recommendation.

University of California, Los Angeles, Graduate Division, School of Public Health, Department of Environmental Health Sciences, Interdepartmental Program in Molecular Toxicology, Los Angeles, CA 90095. Offers PhD. *Degree requirements:* For doctorate, thesis/dissertation, oral and written qualifying exams. *Entrance requirements:* For doctorate, GRE General Test. Electronic applications accepted.

University of Cincinnati, Graduate School, College of Medicine, Graduate Programs in Biomedical Sciences, Department of Environmental Health, Programs in Environmental Genetics and Molecular Toxicology, Cincinnati, OH 45221. Offers MS, PhD. *Degree requirements:* For doctorate, thesis/dissertation. *Entrance requirements:* For master's, GRE, minimum GPA of 3.0, 3 letters of recommendation. Additional exam requirements/recommendations for international students: Required—TOEFL (minimum score 520 paper-based; 190 computer-based).

Pharmacology

Albany College of Pharmacy and Health Sciences, School of Pharmacy and Pharmaceutical Sciences, Albany, NY 12208. Offers pharmaceutical sciences (MS), including pharmaceutics, pharmacology; pharmacy (Pharm D). *Accreditation:* ACPE. *Faculty:* 66 full-time (30 women), 11 part-time/adjunct (6 women). *Students:* 510 full-time (313 women), 3 part-time (2 women); includes 114 minority (21 Black or African American, non-Hispanic/Latino; 1 American Indian or Alaska Native, non-Hispanic/Latino; 69 Asian, non-Hispanic/Latino; 12 Hispanic/Latino; 11 Two or more races, non-Hispanic/Latino), 47 international. Average age 23. 1,477 applicants, 14% accepted, 106 enrolled. In 2011, 3 master's, 230 doctorates awarded. *Degree requirements:* For master's, thesis; for doctorate, practice experience. *Entrance requirements:* For master's, GRE, minimum GPA of 3.0; for doctorate, PCAT, minimum GPA of 2.5. Additional exam requirements/recommendations for international students: Required—TOEFL (minimum score 474 paper-based; 84 iBT). *Application deadline:* For fall admission, 3/1 for domestic and international students. Applications are processed on a rolling basis. Application fee: $100. Electronic applications accepted. *Expenses: Tuition:* Full-time $29,100; part-time $855 per credit hour. *Required fees:* $1230; $680. Tuition and fees vary according to degree level. *Financial support:* In 2011–12, 20 students received support. Federal Work-Study and scholarships/grants available. Support

available to part-time students. Financial award application deadline: 3/1; financial award applicants required to submit FAFSA. *Faculty research:* Therapeutic use of drugs, pharmacokinetics, drug delivery and design. *Unit head:* Dr. Mehdi Boroujerdi, Provost, 518-694-7212, Fax: 518-694-7063. *Application contact:* Donna Myers, Director of Pharmacy and Graduate Admissions, 518-694-7186, Fax: 518-694-7929, E-mail: graduate@acphs.edu. Web site: http://www.acphs.edu.

See Display on page 927 and Close-Up on page 935.

Albany Medical College, Center for Neuropharmacology and Neuroscience, Albany, NY 12208-3479. Offers MS, PhD. *Faculty:* 17 full-time (4 women), 11 part-time/adjunct (4 women). *Students:* 15 full-time (4 women); includes 1 minority (Black or African American, non-Hispanic/Latino), 3 international. Average age 24. 20 applicants, 30% accepted, 2 enrolled. In 2011, 1 master's, 3 doctorates awarded. Terminal master's awarded for partial completion of doctoral program. *Median time to degree:* Of those who began their doctoral program in fall 2003, 100% received their degree in 8 years or less. *Degree requirements:* For master's, thesis; for doctorate, comprehensive exam, thesis/dissertation. *Entrance requirements:* For master's, GRE General Test, all transcripts, letters of recommendation; for doctorate, GRE General Test, letters of recommendation. Additional exam requirements/recommendations for international students: Required—TOEFL. *Application deadline:* For fall admission, 3/15 priority date for domestic students, 3/15 for international students. Applications are processed on a rolling basis. Application fee: $0 ($60 for international students). *Financial support:* In 2011–12, 8 research assistantships with full tuition reimbursements (averaging $24,000 per year) were awarded; fellowships with partial tuition reimbursements, Federal Work-Study, scholarships/grants, and tuition waivers (full) also available. Financial award applicants required to submit FAFSA. *Faculty research:* Molecular and cellular neuroscience, neuronal development, addiction. *Unit head:* Dr. Stanley D. Glick, Director, 518-262-5303, Fax: 518-262-5799, E-mail: cnninfo@mail.amc.edu. *Application contact:* Dr. Mark Fleck, Graduate Director, 518-262-6536, Fax: 518-262-5799, E-mail: cnninfo@mail.amc.edu. Web site: http://www.amc.edu/research/cnn.

Alliant International University–San Francisco, California School of Professional Psychology, Program in Psychopharmacology, San Francisco, CA 94133-1221. Offers Post-Doctoral MS. Part-time programs available. Postbaccalaureate distance learning degree programs offered. *Faculty:* 1 full-time (0 women), 9 part-time/adjunct (1 woman). *Students:* 71 part-time (43 women). Average age 43. In 2011, 19 master's awarded. *Entrance requirements:* For master's, doctorate in clinical psychology. Additional exam requirements/recommendations for international students: Required—TOEFL (minimum score 550 paper-based; 213 computer-based; 80 iBT), TWE (minimum score 5). *Application deadline:* For fall admission, 4/1 priority date for domestic students, 4/1 for international students. Applications are processed on a rolling basis. Application fee: $65. Electronic applications accepted. *Financial support:* Federal Work-Study available. Financial award application deadline: 2/15; financial award applicants required to submit FAFSA. *Unit head:* Dr. Steven R. Tulkin, Director, 415-955-2073, Fax: 415-955-2179, E-mail: stulkin@alliant.edu. *Application contact:* Alliant International University Central Contact Center, 866-U-ALLIANT, Fax: 858-635-4555, E-mail: admissions@alliant.edu.

American University of Beirut, Graduate Programs, Faculty of Medicine, Beirut, Lebanon. Offers anatomy, cell biology and human morphology (MS); biochemistry and medical genetics (MS); biomedical sciences (PhD); experimental pathology, immunology and microbiology (MS); medicine (MD); neuroscience (MS); pharmacology and toxicology (MS). Part-time programs available. *Faculty:* 232 full-time (58 women), 68 part-time/adjunct (7 women). *Students:* 346 full-time (135 women), 69 part-time (57 women). Average age 23. In 2011, 20 master's, 82 doctorates awarded. *Degree requirements:* For master's, one foreign language, comprehensive exam, thesis (for some programs). *Entrance requirements:* For master's, letter of recommendation; for doctorate, MCAT, bachelor's degree. Additional exam requirements/recommendations for international students: Required—TOEFL (minimum score 600 paper-based; 250 computer-based; 100 iBT), IELTS (minimum score 7.5). *Application deadline:* For fall admission, 4/30 for domestic and international students; for spring admission, 11/1 for domestic and international students. Application fee: $50. *Expenses: Tuition:* Full-time $12,780; part-time $710 per credit. Tuition and fees vary according to course load and program. *Financial support:* In 2011–12, 19 students received support. Career-related internships or fieldwork, institutionally sponsored loans, scholarships/grants, health care benefits, and unspecified assistantships available. Financial award application deadline: 2/2. *Faculty research:* Cancer research (targeted therapy, mechanisms of leukemogenesis, tumor cell extravasation and metastasis, cancer stem cells); stem cell research (regenerative medicine, drug discovery); genetic research (neurogenetics, hereditary cardiomyopathy, hemoglobinopathies, pharmacogenomics, proteomics); neuroscience research (pain, neurodegenerative disorder); metabolism (inflammation and metabolism, metabolic disorder, diabetes mellitus); vascular and renal biology, signal transduction. *Total annual research expenditures:* $2.3 million. *Unit head:* Dr. Mohamed Sayegh, Dean, 961-1350000 Ext. 4700, Fax: 961-1744464, E-mail: msayegh@aub.edu.lb. *Application contact:* Dr. Salim Kanaan, Director, Admissions Office, 961-1350000 Ext. 2594, Fax: 961-1750775, E-mail: sk00@aub.edu.lb. Web site: http://www.aub.edu.lb/fm/fm_home/Pages/index.aspx.

Argosy University, Hawai`i, College of Psychology and Behavioral Sciences, Program in Psychopharmacology, Honolulu, HI 96813. Offers MS, Certificate.

Auburn University, College of Veterinary Medicine and Graduate School, Graduate Programs in Veterinary Medicine, Auburn University, AL 36849. Offers biomedical sciences (MS, PhD), including anatomy, physiology and pharmacology (MS); biomedical sciences (PhD); clinical sciences (MS); large animal surgery and medicine (MS); pathobiology (MS); radiology (MS); small animal surgery and medicine (MS); DVM/MS. Part-time programs available. *Faculty:* 100 full-time (40 women), 5 part-time/adjunct (1 woman). *Students:* 17 full-time (13 women), 59 part-time (33 women); includes 6 minority (1 Black or African American, non-Hispanic/Latino; 3 Asian, non-Hispanic/Latino; 2 Hispanic/Latino), 30 international. Average age 30. 36 applicants, 69% accepted, 11 enrolled. In 2011, 19 master's awarded. *Degree requirements:* For doctorate, thesis/dissertation. *Entrance requirements:* For master's, GRE General Test; for doctorate, GRE General Test, GRE Subject Test. *Application deadline:* For fall admission, 7/7 for domestic students; for spring admission, 11/24 for domestic students. Applications are processed on a rolling basis. Application fee: $50 ($60 for international students). Electronic applications accepted. *Expenses: Tuition:* state resident: full-time $7290; part-time $405 per credit hour. Tuition, nonresident: full-time $21,870; part-time $1215 per credit hour. *International tuition:* $22,000 full-time. *Required fees:* $1402. *Financial support:* Research assistantships, teaching assistantships, and Federal Work-Study available. Support available to part-time students. Financial award application deadline: 3/15; financial award applicants required to submit FAFSA. *Unit head:* Dr. Calvin Johnson, Acting Dean, 334-844-2650. *Application contact:* Dr. George Flowers, Dean of the Graduate School, 334-844-2125.

Baylor College of Medicine, Graduate School of Biomedical Sciences, Department of Pharmacology, Houston, TX 77030-3498. Offers PhD, MD/PhD. *Faculty:* 18 full-time (1 woman). *Students:* 6 full-time (2 women); includes 2 minority (1 Black or African American, non-Hispanic/Latino; 1 Asian, non-Hispanic/Latino), 3 international. Average age 24. 38 applicants, 11% accepted, 2 enrolled. *Degree requirements:* For doctorate, thesis/dissertation, public defense. *Entrance requirements:* For doctorate, GRE General Test, GRE Subject Test (strongly recommended), minimum GPA of 3.0. Additional exam requirements/recommendations for international students: Required—TOEFL. *Application deadline:* For fall admission, 1/1 priority date for domestic students. Application fee: $0. Electronic applications accepted. *Financial support:* In 2011–12, 6 students received support, including 2 fellowships with full tuition reimbursements available (averaging $29,000 per year), 4 research assistantships with full tuition reimbursements available (averaging $29,000 per year); career-related internships or fieldwork, Federal Work-Study, institutionally sponsored loans, health care benefits, and scholarships (to all students unless there are grant funds available to pay tuition) also available. Financial award applicants required to submit FAFSA. *Faculty research:* Drug discovery, antibiotics, antitumor, computational drug design, signal transduction complex. *Unit head:* Dr. P. K. Chan, Director, 713-798-7915, E-mail: pchan@bcm.edu. *Application contact:* Kim Tran, Graduate Program Administrator, 713-798-4457, E-mail: kimt@bcm.edu.

Boston University, School of Medicine, Division of Graduate Medical Sciences, Department of Pharmacology and Experimental Therapeutics, Boston, MA 02118. Offers MA, PhD, MD/PhD. *Faculty:* 11 full-time (4 women), 16 part-time/adjunct (4 women). *Students:* 9 full-time (8 women), 5 part-time (4 women); includes 4 minority (1 Black or African American, non-Hispanic/Latino; 2 Asian, non-Hispanic/Latino; 1 Hispanic/Latino). Average age 30. 46 applicants, 17% accepted, 2 enrolled. In 2011, 3 doctorates awarded. Terminal master's awarded for partial completion of doctoral program. *Degree requirements:* For master's, thesis; for doctorate, thesis/dissertation. *Entrance requirements:* For master's and doctorate, GRE General Test, GRE Subject Test. Additional exam requirements/recommendations for international students: Required—TOEFL. *Application deadline:* For fall admission, 1/15 priority date for domestic students; for spring admission, 10/15 priority date for domestic students. Application fee: $75. Electronic applications accepted. *Expenses: Tuition:* Full-time $40,848; part-time $1276 per credit hour. *Required fees:* $572; $286 per semester. *Financial support:* In 2011–12, 1 fellowship (averaging $30,500 per year), research assistantships (averaging $30,500 per year) were awarded; Federal Work-Study, scholarships/grants, traineeships, tuition waivers, and research stipends also available. Financial award applicants required to submit FAFSA. *Faculty research:* Molecular pharmacology, neuropharmacology, peptide receptors, psychopharmacology. *Unit head:* Dr. David H. Farb, Chairman, 617-638-4300, Fax: 617-638-4329, E-mail: dfarb@bu.edu. *Application contact:* Dr. Carol T. Walsh, Graduate Director, 617-638-4326, Fax: 617-638-4329, E-mail: ctwalsh@bu.edu. Web site: http://www.bumc.bu.edu/.

Boston University, School of Medicine, Division of Graduate Medical Sciences, Program in Clinical Investigation, Boston, MA 02215. Offers MA. *Faculty:* 10 full-time (8 women). *Students:* 7 full-time (6 women), 14 part-time (10 women), 7 international. Average age 29. 12 applicants, 83% accepted, 4 enrolled. In 2011, 7 master's awarded. *Degree requirements:* For master's, thesis. *Entrance requirements:* For master's, GRE. Additional exam requirements/recommendations for international students: Required—TOEFL. *Application deadline:* For spring admission, 10/15 priority date for domestic students. Application fee: $75. *Expenses: Tuition:* Full-time $40,848; part-time $1276 per credit hour. *Required fees:* $572; $286 per semester. *Financial support:* Applicants required to submit FAFSA. *Unit head:* Dr. Susan S. Fish, Director, 617-638-7715, E-mail: sfish@bu.edu. *Application contact:* Stacey Hess Pino, Assistant Director, 617-638-5211, Fax: 617-638-5740, E-mail: sahess@bu.edu. Web site: http://www.bumc.bu.edu/maci/.

Case Western Reserve University, School of Medicine and School of Graduate Studies, Graduate Programs in Medicine, Department of Pharmacology, Cleveland, OH 44106. Offers PhD, MD/PhD. Terminal master's awarded for partial completion of doctoral program. *Degree requirements:* For doctorate, comprehensive exam, thesis/dissertation. *Entrance requirements:* For doctorate, GRE General Test, GRE Subject Test, or MCAT. Additional exam requirements/recommendations for international students: Required—TOEFL. Electronic applications accepted. *Faculty research:* Aspects of cellular, molecular, and clinical pharmacology; neuroendocrine pharmacology; drug metabolism.

Columbia University, College of Physicians and Surgeons, Department of Pharmacology, New York, NY 10032. Offers pharmacology (M Phil, MA, PhD); pharmacology-toxicology (M Phil, MA, PhD); MD/PhD. Only candidates for the PhD are admitted. Terminal master's awarded for partial completion of doctoral program. *Degree requirements:* For doctorate, thesis/dissertation. *Entrance requirements:* For master's and doctorate, GRE General Test. Additional exam requirements/recommendations for international students: Required—TOEFL. *Faculty research:* Cardiovascular pharmacology, receptor pharmacology, neuropharmacology, membrane biophysics, eicosanoids.

Cornell University, Graduate School, Graduate Fields of Comparative Biomedical Sciences, Field of Pharmacology, Ithaca, NY 14853-0001. Offers MS, PhD. *Faculty:* 33 full-time (9 women). *Students:* 14 full-time (9 women); includes 4 minority (1 Black or African American, non-Hispanic/Latino; 2 Hispanic/Latino; 1 Native Hawaiian or other Pacific Islander, non-Hispanic/Latino), 3 international. Average age 27. 24 applicants, 8% accepted, 2 enrolled. In 2011, 2 doctorates awarded. *Degree requirements:* For master's, thesis; for doctorate, comprehensive exam, thesis/dissertation. *Entrance requirements:* For master's and doctorate, GRE General Test, 3 letters of recommendation. Additional exam requirements/recommendations for international students: Required—TOEFL (minimum score 550 paper-based; 213 computer-based; 77 iBT). *Application deadline:* For fall admission, 12/5 for domestic students. Application fee: $95. Electronic applications accepted. *Financial support:* In 2011–12, 9 students received support, including 3 fellowships with full tuition reimbursements available, 7 research assistantships with full tuition reimbursements available, 3 teaching assistantships with full tuition reimbursements available; institutionally sponsored loans, scholarships/grants, health care benefits, tuition waivers (full and partial), and unspecified assistantships also available. Financial award applicants required to submit FAFSA. *Faculty research:* Signal transduction, ion channels, calcium signaling, G proteins, cancer cell biology. *Unit head:* Director of Graduate Studies, 607-253-3276, Fax: 607-253-3756. *Application contact:* Graduate Field Assistant, 607-253-3276, Fax: 607-253-3756, E-mail: graduate_edcvm@cornell.edu. Web site: http://www.gradschool.cornell.edu/fields.php?id-66&a-2.

Creighton University, School of Medicine and Graduate School, Graduate Programs in Medicine, Department of Pharmacology, Omaha, NE 68178-0001. Offers pharmaceutical sciences (MS); pharmacology (MS, PhD); Pharm D/MS. Terminal master's awarded for partial completion of doctoral program. *Degree requirements:* For master's, comprehensive exam, thesis; for doctorate, comprehensive exam, thesis/dissertation, oral and written preliminary exams. *Entrance requirements:* For master's and doctorate, GRE General Test, minimum GPA of 3.0, undergraduate degree in sciences. Additional exam requirements/recommendations for international students: Required—TOEFL. Electronic applications accepted. *Expenses: Tuition:* Full-time $12,672; part-time $704 per credit hour. *Required fees:* $1410; $136 per semester.

Tuition and fees vary according to campus/location and reciprocity agreements. *Faculty research:* Pharmacology secretion, cardiovascular-renal pharmacology, adrenergic receptors, signal transduction, genetic regulation of receptors.

Dalhousie University, Faculty of Graduate Studies and Faculty of Medicine, Graduate Programs in Medicine, Department of Pharmacology, Halifax, NS B3H 4R2, Canada. Offers M Sc, PhD. *Degree requirements:* For master's, thesis; for doctorate, comprehensive exam, thesis/dissertation. *Entrance requirements:* Additional exam requirements/recommendations for international students: Required—1 of 5 approved tests: TOEFL, IELTS, CANTEST, CAEL, Michigan English Language Assessment Battery. Electronic applications accepted. *Faculty research:* Electrophysiology and neurochemistry; endocrinology, immunology and cancer research; molecular biology; cardiovascular and autonomic; drug biotransformation and metabolism; ocular pharmacology.

Dartmouth College, Arts and Sciences Graduate Programs, Department of Pharmacology and Toxicology, Hanover, NH 03755. Offers PhD, MD/PhD. *Degree requirements:* For doctorate, thesis/dissertation. *Entrance requirements:* For doctorate, GRE General Test, GRE Subject Test, bachelor's degree in biological, chemical, or physical science. Additional exam requirements/recommendations for international students: Required—TOEFL. Electronic applications accepted. *Faculty research:* Molecular biology of carcinogenesis, DNA repair and gene expression, biochemical and environmental toxicology, protein receptor ligand interactions.

Drexel University, College of Medicine, Biomedical Graduate Programs, Pharmacology and Physiology Program, Philadelphia, PA 19104-2875. Offers MS, PhD, MD/PhD. Part-time programs available. Terminal master's awarded for partial completion of doctoral program. *Degree requirements:* For master's, comprehensive exam; for doctorate, thesis/dissertation, qualifying exam. *Entrance requirements:* For master's, GRE General Test, minimum GPA of 2.75; for doctorate, GRE General Test, minimum GPA of 3.0. Additional exam requirements/recommendations for international students: Required—TOEFL. Electronic applications accepted. *Faculty research:* Cardiovascular pharmacology, drugs of abuse, neurotransmitter mechanisms.

Duke University, Graduate School, Department of Pharmacology and Cancer Biology, Durham, NC 27710. Offers pharmacology (PhD). *Faculty:* 39 full-time. *Students:* 58 full-time (36 women). Average age 23. 76 applicants, 16% accepted, 6 enrolled. In 2011, 14 doctorates awarded. *Degree requirements:* For doctorate, thesis/dissertation. *Entrance requirements:* For doctorate, GRE General Test, minimum GPA of 3.0. Additional exam requirements/recommendations for international students: Required—TOEFL or IELTS (preferred). *Application deadline:* For fall admission, 12/8 priority date for domestic students, 12/8 for international students. Application fee: $75. Electronic applications accepted. *Expenses: Tuition:* Full-time $40,720. *Required fees:* $3107. *Financial support:* In 2011–12, 11 fellowships with tuition reimbursements (averaging $28,000 per year), 8 research assistantships with tuition reimbursements (averaging $28,000 per year), 2 teaching assistantships with tuition reimbursements (averaging $28,000 per year) were awarded; scholarships/grants, traineeships, health care benefits, and unspecified assistantships also available. Financial award application deadline: 12/31. *Faculty research:* Developmental pharmacology, neuropharmacology, molecular pharmacology, toxicology, cell growth and metabolism. *Unit head:* Dr. Jeffrey Rathmell, Director of Graduate Studies, 919-681-1084, Fax: 919-684-8922, E-mail: jeff.rathmell@duke.edu. *Application contact:* Jamie Baize-Smith, Assistant Director of Graduate Studies, 919-613-8600, Fax: 919-681-7139, E-mail: baize@duke.edu. Web site: http://pharmacology.mc.duke.edu/.

Duquesne University, Mylan School of Pharmacy, Graduate School of Pharmaceutical Sciences, Program in Pharmacology, Pittsburgh, PA 15282-0001. Offers MS, PhD. *Faculty:* 6 full-time (4 women). *Students:* 13 full-time (10 women); includes 1 minority (Black or African American, non-Hispanic/Latino), 4 international. Average age 28. 61 applicants, 10% accepted, 2 enrolled. In 2011, 1 master's, 3 doctorates awarded. *Degree requirements:* For master's, thesis; for doctorate, comprehensive exam, thesis/dissertation. *Entrance requirements:* For master's and doctorate, GRE General Test. Additional exam requirements/recommendations for international students: Required—TOEFL. *Application deadline:* For fall admission, 2/1 priority date for domestic students, 2/1 for international students; for spring admission, 10/1 priority date for domestic students, 10/1 for international students. Applications are processed on a rolling basis. Application fee: $50. Electronic applications accepted. *Expenses: Tuition:* Full-time $16,596; part-time $922 per credit. *Required fees:* $1584; $88 per credit. Tuition and fees vary according to program. *Financial support:* In 2011–12, 11 students received support, including 1 research assistantship with full tuition reimbursement available, 10 teaching assistantships with full tuition reimbursements available. *Unit head:* Dr. Christopher K. Surratt, Head, 412-396-5007. *Application contact:* Information Contact, 412-396-1172, E-mail: gsps-adm@duq.edu. Web site: http://www.duq.edu/pharmacy/graduate.cfm.

East Carolina University, Brody School of Medicine, Department of Pharmacology and Toxicology, Greenville, NC 27858-4353. Offers PhD, MD/PhD. *Degree requirements:* For doctorate, comprehensive exam, thesis/dissertation. *Entrance requirements:* For doctorate, GRE General Test, GRE Subject Test. Additional exam requirements/recommendations for international students: Required—TOEFL. *Application deadline:* For fall admission, 6/15 priority date for domestic students. Applications are processed on a rolling basis. Application fee: $50. *Expenses: Tuition:* state resident: full-time $3557; part-time $444.63 per semester hour. Tuition, nonresident: full-time $14,351; part-time $1793.88 per semester hour. *Required fees:* $2016; $252 per semester hour. Part-time tuition and fees vary according to course load, campus/location and program. *Financial support:* In 2011–12, fellowships with full tuition reimbursements (averaging $21,500 per year) were awarded. Financial award application deadline: 6/1. *Faculty research:* GNS/behavioral pharmacology, cardiovascular pharmacology, cell signaling and second messenger, effects of calcium channel blockers. *Unit head:* Dr. David A. Taylor, Chairman, 252-744-2734, Fax: 252-744-3203, E-mail: taylorda@ecu.edu. Web site: http://www.ecu.edu/cs-dhs/pharmacology/Graduate-Program09.cfm.

East Tennessee State University, James H. Quillen College of Medicine, Biomedical Science Graduate Program, Johnson City, TN 37614. Offers anatomy and cell biology (PhD); biochemistry and molecular biology (PhD); microbiology (PhD); pharmaceutical sciences (PhD); pharmacology (PhD); physiology (PhD); quantitative biosciences (PhD). *Faculty:* 33 full-time (6 women). *Students:* 29 full-time (15 women), 2 part-time (both women); includes 4 minority (1 Black or African American, non-Hispanic/Latino; 1 Asian, non-Hispanic/Latino; 2 Hispanic/Latino), 6 international. Average age 29. 76 applicants, 12% accepted, 7 enrolled. In 2011, 1 doctorate awarded. *Degree requirements:* For doctorate, thesis/dissertation, comprehensive qualifying exam. *Entrance requirements:* For doctorate, GRE General Test, GRE Subject Test. Additional exam requirements/recommendations for international students: Required—TOEFL (minimum score 550 paper-based; 213 computer-based; 79 iBT). *Application deadline:* For fall admission, 3/15 priority date for domestic students, 3/1 for international students. Application fee: $35 ($45 for international students). Electronic applications accepted. *Expenses:* Contact institution. *Financial support:* In 2011–12, 29 students received support, including 29

research assistantships with full tuition reimbursements available (averaging $19,000 per year); career-related internships or fieldwork, institutionally sponsored loans, scholarships/grants, and unspecified assistantships also available. Financial award application deadline: 7/1; financial award applicants required to submit FAFSA. *Faculty research:* Cardiovascular biology, neuroscience, infectious disease, cancer, inflammatory disease. *Total annual research expenditures:* $3.6 million. *Unit head:* Dr. Mitchell E. Robinson, Associate Dean/Program Director, 423-439-2031, Fax: 423-439-2140, E-mail: robinson@etsu.edu. *Application contact:* Shella Bennett, Graduate Specialist, 423-439-4708, Fax: 423-439-5624, E-mail: bennetsg@etsu.edu.

Emory University, Laney Graduate School, Division of Biological and Biomedical Sciences, Program in Molecular and Systems Pharmacology, Atlanta, GA 30322-1100. Offers PhD. *Faculty:* 49 full-time (10 women). *Students:* 45 full-time (22 women); includes 10 minority (6 Black or African American, non-Hispanic/Latino; 1 Asian, non-Hispanic/Latino; 1 Hispanic/Latino; 1 Native Hawaiian or other Pacific Islander, non-Hispanic/Latino; 1 Two or more races, non-Hispanic/Latino), 3 international. Average age 27. 98 applicants, 11% accepted, 6 enrolled. In 2011, 4 doctorates awarded. *Degree requirements:* For doctorate, comprehensive exam, thesis/dissertation. *Entrance requirements:* For doctorate, GRE General Test, minimum GPA of 3.0 in science course work (recommended). Additional exam requirements/recommendations for international students: Required—TOEFL. *Application deadline:* For fall admission, 12/1 for domestic and international students. Application fee: $75. Electronic applications accepted. *Expenses: Tuition:* Full-time $34,800. *Required fees:* $1300. *Financial support:* In 2011–12, 16 students received support, including 16 fellowships with full tuition reimbursements available (averaging $26,500 per year); institutionally sponsored loans, scholarships/grants, health care benefits, and tuition waivers (full) also available. *Faculty research:* Transmembrane signaling, neuropharmacology, neurophysiology and neurodegeneration, metabolism and molecular toxicology, cell and developmental biology. *Unit head:* Dr. Randy Hall, Program Director, 404-727-3699, Fax: 404-727-0365, E-mail: rhall3@emory.edu. *Application contact:* Kathy Smith, Director of Recruitment and Admissions, 404-727-2547, Fax: 404-727-3322, E-mail: kathy.smith@emory.edu. Web site: http://www.biomed.emory.edu/.

Fairleigh Dickinson University, College at Florham, Silberman College of Business, Program in Pharmaceutical Studies, Madison, NJ 07940-1099. Offers MBA, Certificate.

Florida Agricultural and Mechanical University, Division of Graduate Studies, Research, and Continuing Education, College of Pharmacy and Pharmaceutical Sciences, Graduate Programs in Pharmaceutical Sciences, Tallahassee, FL 32307-3200. Offers environmental toxicology (PhD); medicinal chemistry (MS, PhD); pharmaceutics (MS, PhD); pharmacology/toxicology (MS, PhD); pharmacy administration (MS). *Accreditation:* CEPH. *Degree requirements:* For master's, comprehensive exam, thesis, publishable paper; for doctorate, comprehensive exam, thesis/dissertation, publishable paper. *Entrance requirements:* For master's and doctorate, GRE General Test, minimum GPA of 3.0 in last 60 hours. Additional exam requirements/recommendations for international students: Required—TOEFL. *Faculty research:* Anticancer agents, anti-inflammatory drugs, chronopharmacology, neuroendocrinology, microbiology.

Georgetown University, Graduate School of Arts and Sciences, Programs in Biomedical Sciences, Department of Pharmacology, Washington, DC 20057. Offers MS, PhD, MD/PhD, MS/PhD. *Degree requirements:* For doctorate, comprehensive exam, thesis/dissertation. *Entrance requirements:* For doctorate, GRE General Test, previous course work in biology and chemistry. Additional exam requirements/recommendations for international students: Required—TOEFL. *Faculty research:* Neuropharmacology, techniques in biochemistry and tissue culture.

Georgia Health Sciences University, College of Graduate Studies, Program in Pharmacology, Augusta, GA 30912. Offers MS, PhD. *Faculty:* 13 full-time (2 women), 1 (woman) part-time/adjunct. *Students:* 6 full-time (3 women); includes 2 minority (1 Black or African American, non-Hispanic/Latino; 1 Asian, non-Hispanic/Latino), 1 international. Average age 29. In 2011, 1 doctorate awarded. *Degree requirements:* For doctorate, comprehensive exam, thesis/dissertation. *Entrance requirements:* For doctorate, GRE General Test. Additional exam requirements/recommendations for international students: Required—TOEFL (minimum score 550 paper-based; 213 computer-based; 79 iBT). *Application deadline:* For fall admission, 1/15 for domestic and international students. Application fee: $50. Electronic applications accepted. *Financial support:* In 2011–12, 3 students received support, including 8 research assistantships with partial tuition reimbursements available (averaging $23,000 per year); fellowships with partial tuition reimbursements available, Federal Work-Study, institutionally sponsored loans, and scholarships/grants also available. Support available to part-time students. Financial award application deadline: 5/31; financial award applicants required to submit FAFSA. *Faculty research:* Protein signaling, neural development, cardiovascular pharmacology, endothelial cell function, neuropharmacology. *Total annual research expenditures:* $3.5 million. *Unit head:* Dr. R. William Caldwell, Chair, 706-721-3383, Fax: 706-721-6059, E-mail: wcaldwell@georgiahealth.edu. *Application contact:* Dr. Patricia L. Cameron, Acting Vice Dean, 706-721-3279, E-mail: pcameron@georgiahealth.edu. Web site: http://www.georgiahealth.edu/medicine/phmtox/.

Howard University, College of Medicine, Department of Pharmacology, Washington, DC 20059-0002. Offers MS, PhD, MD/PhD. Part-time programs available. *Degree requirements:* For master's, comprehensive exam, thesis; for doctorate, one foreign language, comprehensive exam, thesis/dissertation, qualifying exam. *Entrance requirements:* For master's, GRE General Test, minimum GPA of 3.2, BS in chemistry, biology, pharmacy, psychology or related field; for doctorate, GRE General Test, minimum graduate GPA of 3.2. Additional exam requirements/recommendations for international students: Recommended—TOEFL. *Faculty research:* Biochemical pharmacology, molecular pharmacology, neuropharmacology, drug metabolism, cancer research.

Idaho State University, Office of Graduate Studies, College of Pharmacy, Department of Biomedical and Pharmaceutical Sciences, Pocatello, ID 83209-8334. Offers biopharmaceutical analysis (PhD); drug delivery (PhD); medicinal chemistry (PhD); pharmaceutical sciences (MS); pharmacology (PhD). Part-time programs available. *Degree requirements:* For master's, one foreign language, comprehensive exam, thesis, thesis research, classes in speech and technical writing; for doctorate, comprehensive exam, thesis/dissertation, written and oral exams, classes in speech and technical writing. *Entrance requirements:* For master's, GRE General Test, minimum GPA of 3.0, 3 letters of recommendation; for doctorate, GRE General Test, BS in pharmacy or related field, minimum GPA of 3.0, 3 letters of recommendation. Additional exam requirements/recommendations for international students: Required—TOEFL (minimum score 550 paper-based; 213 computer-based; 80 iBT). Electronic applications accepted. *Expenses:* Contact institution. *Faculty research:* Metabolic toxicity of heavy metals, neuroendocrine pharmacology, cardiovascular pharmacology, cancer biology, immunopharmacology.

Indiana University–Purdue University Indianapolis, Indiana University School of Medicine, Department of Pharmacology and Toxicology, Indianapolis, IN 46202-2896.

Pharmacology

Offers pharmacology (MS, PhD); toxicology (MS, PhD); MD/PhD. *Faculty:* 11 full-time (2 women). *Students:* 12 full-time (10 women), 13 part-time (7 women); includes 3 minority (1 Asian, non-Hispanic/Latino; 2 Hispanic/Latino), 10 international. Average age 27. 5 applicants, 0% accepted, 0 enrolled. In 2011, 4 master's, 3 doctorates awarded. Terminal master's awarded for partial completion of doctoral program. *Degree requirements:* For master's, thesis; for doctorate, thesis/dissertation. *Entrance requirements:* For master's and doctorate, GRE General Test, GRE Subject Test, minimum GPA of 3.0. *Application deadline:* For fall admission, 1/15 priority date for domestic students. Applications are processed on a rolling basis. Application fee: $55 ($65 for international students). *Financial support:* In 2011–12, teaching assistantships (averaging $20,940 per year) were awarded; fellowships with partial tuition reimbursements, research assistantships with partial tuition reimbursements, Federal Work-Study, institutionally sponsored loans, and tuition waivers (partial) also available. Financial award application deadline: 1/15. *Faculty research:* Neuropharmacology, cardiovascular biopharmacology, chemotherapy, oncogenesis. *Unit head:* Dr. Michael Vasko, Jr., Chairman, 317-274-7844, Fax: 317-274-7714. *Application contact:* Director of Graduate Studies, 317-274-1564, Fax: 317-274-7714. Web site: http://pharmtox.iusm.iu.edu/.

The Johns Hopkins University, School of Medicine, Graduate Programs in Medicine, Department of Pharmacology and Molecular Sciences, Baltimore, MD 21205. Offers PhD. *Degree requirements:* For doctorate, comprehensive exam, thesis/dissertation, departmental seminar. *Entrance requirements:* For doctorate, GRE General Test. Additional exam requirements/recommendations for international students: Required—TOEFL. Electronic applications accepted.

Kent State University, School of Biomedical Sciences, Program in Pharmacology, Kent, OH 44242-0001. Offers MS, PhD. Offered in cooperation with Northeastern Ohio Universities College of Medicine. Terminal master's awarded for partial completion of doctoral program. *Degree requirements:* For master's, thesis; for doctorate, thesis/dissertation. *Entrance requirements:* For master's and doctorate, GRE General Test, minimum GPA of 3.0, 3 letters of recommendation. Additional exam requirements/recommendations for international students: Required—TOEFL. Electronic applications accepted. *Expenses:* Tuition, state resident: full-time $8136; part-time $452 per credit hour. Tuition, nonresident: full-time $14,292; part-time $794 per credit hour. *Faculty research:* Neuropharmacology, psychotherapeutics and substance abuse, molecular biology of substance abuse, toxicology.

Loma Linda University, School of Medicine, Department of Physiology/Pharmacology, Loma Linda, CA 92350. Offers MS, PhD. Part-time programs available. *Degree requirements:* For master's, thesis or alternative; for doctorate, 2 foreign languages, thesis/dissertation. *Entrance requirements:* For master's and doctorate, GRE General Test. *Faculty research:* Drug metabolism, biochemical pharmacology, structure and function of cell membranes, neuropharmacology.

Long Island University–Brooklyn Campus, Arnold and Marie Schwartz College of Pharmacy and Health Sciences, Graduate Programs in Pharmacy, Division of Pharmaceutical Sciences, Brooklyn, NY 11201-8423. Offers cosmetic science (MS); industrial pharmacy (MS); pharmaceutics (PhD); pharmacology/toxicology (MS). Part-time and evening/weekend programs available. Terminal master's awarded for partial completion of doctoral program. *Degree requirements:* For master's, thesis optional; for doctorate, thesis/dissertation, candidacy exam. *Entrance requirements:* For master's and doctorate, minimum GPA of 3.0.

Louisiana State University Health Sciences Center, School of Graduate Studies in New Orleans, Department of Pharmacology and Experimental Therapeutics, New Orleans, LA 70112-2223. Offers MS, PhD, MD/PhD. Terminal master's awarded for partial completion of doctoral program. *Degree requirements:* For master's, comprehensive exam, thesis; for doctorate, comprehensive exam, thesis/dissertation. *Entrance requirements:* For master's, GRE; for doctorate, GRE General Test. Additional exam requirements/recommendations for international students: Required—TOEFL. *Faculty research:* Neuropharmacology, gastrointestinal pharmacology, drug metabolism, behavioral pharmacology, cardiovascular pharmacology.

Louisiana State University Health Sciences Center at Shreveport, Department of Pharmacology, Toxicology and Neuroscience, Shreveport, LA 71130-3932. Offers pharmacology (PhD); MD/PhD. Terminal master's awarded for partial completion of doctoral program. *Degree requirements:* For doctorate, thesis/dissertation. *Entrance requirements:* For doctorate, GRE General Test, minimum GPA of 3.0. Additional exam requirements/recommendations for international students: Required—TOEFL. *Faculty research:* Behavioral, cardiovascular, clinical, and gastrointestinal pharmacology; neuropharmacology; psychopharmacology; drug abuse; pharmacokinetics; neuroendocrinology, psychoneuroimmunology, and stress; toxicology.

Loyola University Chicago, Graduate School, Department of Molecular Pharmacology and Therapeutics, Chicago, IL 60626. Offers MS, PhD, MD/PhD, MS/MBA. *Faculty:* 18 full-time (4 women), 11 part-time/adjunct (2 women). *Students:* 17 full-time (10 women), 6 international. Average age 26. 37 applicants, 24% accepted, 6 enrolled. In 2011, 1 degree awarded. Terminal master's awarded for partial completion of doctoral program. *Degree requirements:* For master's, comprehensive exam, thesis; for doctorate, comprehensive exam, thesis/dissertation. *Entrance requirements:* For master's and doctorate, GRE General Test, minimum GPA of 3.0. Additional exam requirements/recommendations for international students: Required—TOEFL. *Application deadline:* For fall admission, 2/1 for domestic and international students. Application fee: $50. Electronic applications accepted. *Expenses: Tuition:* Full-time $15,660; part-time $870 per credit hour. *Required fees:* $125 per semester. Tuition and fees vary according to course load and program. *Financial support:* In 2011–12, 2 fellowships with full tuition reimbursements (averaging $32,165 per year), 7 research assistantships with full tuition reimbursements (averaging $25,000 per year), 1 teaching assistantship with full tuition reimbursement (averaging $36,000 per year) were awarded; career-related internships or fieldwork and Federal Work-Study also available. Financial award application deadline: 2/1; financial award applicants required to submit FAFSA. *Faculty research:* Neuropharmacology, molecular pharmacology, neuroendocrinology, hematopharmacology, neurodegeneration. *Unit head:* Dr. Tarun Patel, Chair, 708-216-5773, Fax: 708-216-6956. *Application contact:* Dr. Kenneth L. Byron, Graduate Program Director, 708-327-2819, Fax: 708-216-6596, E-mail: kbyron@luc.edu. Web site: http://www.stritch.luc.edu/depts/pharmacology/index.cfm.

Massachusetts College of Pharmacy and Health Sciences, Graduate Studies, Program in Pharmacology, Boston, MA 02115-5896. Offers MS, PhD. *Accreditation:* ACPE (one or more programs are accredited). *Students:* 20 full-time (7 women); includes 1 minority (Asian, non-Hispanic/Latino), 18 international. Average age 31. 85 applicants, 24% accepted, 17 enrolled. In 2011, 1 degree awarded. Terminal master's awarded for partial completion of doctoral program. *Degree requirements:* For master's, oral defense of thesis; for doctorate, one foreign language, oral defense of dissertation, qualifying exam. *Entrance requirements:* For master's and doctorate, GRE General Test, minimum QPA of 3.0. Additional exam requirements/recommendations for international students: Required—TOEFL (minimum score 550 paper-based; 213 computer-based; 79 iBT). *Application deadline:* For fall admission, 2/1 priority date for domestic students, 1/1 for international students. Application fee: $70. *Expenses: Tuition:* Full-time $30,200; part-time $945 per credit hour. *Financial support:* Fellowships with partial tuition reimbursements, research assistantships with partial tuition reimbursements, teaching assistantships with full tuition reimbursements, tuition waivers (partial), and library assistantships available. Financial award application deadline: 3/15. *Faculty research:* Neuropharmacology, cardiovascular pharmacology, nutritional pharmacology, pulmonary physiology, drug metabolism. *Unit head:* Dr. Dan Kiel, Assistant Professor, 617-732-2975, E-mail: dan.kiel@mcphs.edu. *Application contact:* Brian Barilone, Associate Director of Transfer and Graduate Admission, 617-879-5032, E-mail: admissions@mcphs.edu.

McGill University, Faculty of Graduate and Postdoctoral Studies, Faculty of Medicine, Department of Pharmacology and Therapeutics, Montréal, QC H3A 2T5, Canada. Offers M Sc, PhD.

McMaster University, Faculty of Health Sciences and School of Graduate Studies, Program in Medical Sciences, Physiology/Pharmacology Area, Hamilton, ON L8S 4M2, Canada. Offers M Sc, PhD, MD/PhD. *Degree requirements:* For master's, thesis; for doctorate, comprehensive exam, thesis/dissertation. *Entrance requirements:* For master's, honors B Sc, B+ average in related field; for doctorate, M Sc, minimum B+ average, students with proven research experience and an A average may be admitted with a B Sc degree. Additional exam requirements/recommendations for international students: Required—TOEFL (minimum score 580 paper-based; 237 computer-based; 92 iBT).

Medical College of Wisconsin, Graduate School of Biomedical Sciences, Department of Pharmacology and Toxicology, Milwaukee, WI 53226-0509. Offers PhD, MD/PhD. *Degree requirements:* For doctorate, comprehensive exam, thesis/dissertation, oral and written qualifying exams. *Entrance requirements:* For doctorate, GRE, official transcripts, three letters of recommendation. Additional exam requirements/recommendations for international students: Required—TOEFL. *Faculty research:* Cardiovascular physiology and pharmacology, drugs of abuse, environmental and aquatic toxicology, central nervous system and biochemical pharmacology, signal transduction.

Meharry Medical College, School of Graduate Studies, Program in Biomedical Sciences, Pharmacology Emphasis, Nashville, TN 37208-9989. Offers PhD, MD/PhD. *Degree requirements:* For doctorate, comprehensive exam, thesis/dissertation. *Entrance requirements:* For doctorate, GRE. *Faculty research:* Neuropharmacology, cardiovascular pharmacology, behavioral pharmacology, molecular pharmacology, drug metabolism, anticancer.

Michigan State University, College of Human Medicine and The Graduate School, Graduate Programs in Human Medicine, East Lansing, MI 48824. Offers biochemistry and molecular biology (MS, PhD); epidemiology (MS, PhD); microbiology (MS); microbiology and molecular genetics (PhD); pharmacology and toxicology (MS, PhD); physiology (MS, PhD); public health (MPH). *Entrance requirements:* Additional exam requirements/recommendations for international students: Required—TOEFL.

Michigan State University, College of Osteopathic Medicine and The Graduate School, Graduate Studies in Osteopathic Medicine and Graduate Programs in Human Medicine and Graduate Programs in Veterinary Medicine, Department of Pharmacology and Toxicology, East Lansing, MI 48824. Offers integrative pharmacology (MS); pharmacology and toxicology (MS, PhD); pharmacology and toxicology-environmental toxicology (PhD). *Entrance requirements:* Additional exam requirements/recommendations for international students: Required—TOEFL (minimum score 600 paper-based; 220 computer-based). Electronic applications accepted.

Michigan State University, College of Veterinary Medicine and The Graduate School, Graduate Programs in Veterinary Medicine, East Lansing, MI 48824. Offers comparative medicine and integrative biology (MS, PhD), including comparative medicine and integrative biology, comparative medicine and integrative biology–environmental toxicology (PhD); food safety and toxicology (MS), including food safety; integrative toxicology (PhD), including animal science–environmental toxicology, biochemistry and molecular biology–environmental toxicology, chemistry–environmental toxicology, crop and soil sciences–environmental toxicology, environmental engineering–environmental toxicology, environmental geosciences–environmental toxicology, fisheries and wildlife–environmental toxicology, food science–environmental toxicology, forestry–environmental toxicology, genetics–environmental toxicology, human nutrition–environmental toxicology, microbiology–environmental toxicology, pharmacology and toxicology–environmental toxicology, zoology–environmental toxicology; large animal clinical sciences (MS, PhD); microbiology and molecular genetics (MS, PhD), including industrial microbiology, microbiology, microbiology and molecular genetics, microbiology–environmental toxicology (PhD); pathobiology and diagnostic investigation (MS, PhD), including pathology, pathology–environmental toxicology (PhD); pharmacology and toxicology (MS, PhD); pharmacology and toxicology–environmental toxicology (PhD); physiology (MS, PhD); small animal clinical sciences (MS). Electronic applications accepted. *Faculty research:* Molecular genetics, food safety/toxicology, comparative orthopedics, airway disease, population medicine.

Montclair State University, The Graduate School, College of Science and Mathematics, Department of Chemistry and Biochemistry, Program in Pharmaceutical Biochemistry, Montclair, NJ 07043-1624. Offers MS. Part-time and evening/weekend programs available. *Students:* 6 full-time (4 women), 3 part-time (2 women); includes 3 minority (2 Asian, non-Hispanic/Latino; 1 Hispanic/Latino), 2 international. Average age 28. 14 applicants, 43% accepted, 4 enrolled. *Entrance requirements:* For master's, GRE General Test, 24 undergraduate credits in chemistry, 2 letters of recommendation, essay. *Application deadline:* Applications are processed on a rolling basis. Application fee: $60. Electronic applications accepted. *Financial support:* Federal Work-Study, scholarships/grants, and unspecified assistantships available. Support available to part-time students. Financial award application deadline: 3/1. *Faculty research:* Enzyme kinetics, enzyme expression, pharmaceutical biochemistry, medicinal chemistry, biophysical chemistry. *Unit head:* Dr. Marc Kasner, Chair, 973-655-6864. *Application contact:* Amy Aiello, Executive Director of The Graduate School, 973-655-5147, E-mail: graduate.school@montclair.edu. Web site: http://www.montclair.edu/csam/chemistry-biochemistry/graduate-programs/ms-pharmaceutical-biochemistry/.

New Jersey Institute of Technology, Office of Graduate Studies, Newark College of Engineering, Department of Chemical Engineering, Program in Pharmaceutical Bioprocessing, Newark, NJ 07102. Offers MS. *Students:* 3 full-time (all women), 2 part-time (0 women), 3 international. Average age 26. 11 applicants, 64% accepted, 4 enrolled. *Entrance requirements:* Additional exam requirements/recommendations for international students: Required—TOEFL (minimum score 550 paper-based; 213 computer-based; 79 iBT). *Application deadline:* For fall admission, 6/1 priority date for domestic students, 5/1 for international students; for spring admission, 11/15 priority date for domestic students, 11/15 for international students. Applications are processed on a rolling basis. Application fee: $65. Electronic applications accepted. *Expenses:*

Tuition, state resident: full-time $7980; part-time $867 per credit. Tuition, nonresident: full-time $11,336; part-time $1196 per credit. *Required fees:* $230 per credit. *Financial support:* Application deadline: 1/15. *Unit head:* Dr. Norman Loney, Chair, 973-596-6598, E-mail: norman.loney@njit.edu. *Application contact:* Kathryn Kelly, Director of Admissions, 973-596-3300, Fax: 973-596-3461, E-mail: admissions@njit.edu. Web site: http://chemicaleng.njit.edu/academics/graduate/masters/pharmbioprocessing/index.php.

New York Medical College, Graduate School of Basic Medical Sciences, Program in Pharmacology, Valhalla, NY 10595-1691. Offers MS, PhD, MD/PhD. Part-time and evening/weekend programs available. *Faculty:* 13 full-time (2 women). *Students:* 10 full-time (6 women), 2 part-time (both women); includes 5 minority (1 Black or African American, non-Hispanic/Latino; 4 Asian, non-Hispanic/Latino). Average age 27. 19 applicants, 53% accepted, 3 enrolled. In 2011, 2 degrees awarded. Terminal master's awarded for partial completion of doctoral program. *Degree requirements:* For master's, thesis; for doctorate, comprehensive exam, thesis/dissertation. *Entrance requirements:* For master's and doctorate, GRE General Test. Additional exam requirements/recommendations for international students: Required—TOEFL. *Application deadline:* For fall admission, 7/1 priority date for domestic students, 5/1 for international students; for spring admission, 12/1 priority date for domestic students, 10/1 for international students. Applications are processed on a rolling basis. Application fee: $50 ($75 for international students). Electronic applications accepted. *Financial support:* In 2011–12, 3 research assistantships with full tuition reimbursements (averaging $24,000 per year) were awarded; Federal Work-Study, institutionally sponsored loans, scholarships/grants, traineeships, health care benefits, tuition waivers, unspecified assistantships, and health benefits (for PhD applicants only) also available. Financial award applicants required to submit FAFSA. *Faculty research:* Investigation into the therapeutic and pathophysiologic role of bioactive lipids (eicosanoids) in cancer, ophthalmology, and cardiovascular diseases including hypertension, kidney disease, stroke, diabetes, atherosclerosis and inflammatory conditions, cytochrome P-450 function and control, patch-clamp analysis of ion transport, and the roles of vasoactive hormones and inflammatory cytokines in hypertension and end-organ damage and cardiovascular function. *Unit head:* Dr. Charles Steir, Program Director, 914-594-4138, Fax: 914-594-4944, E-mail: charles_stier@nymc.edu. *Application contact:* Valerie Romeo-Messana, Admission Coordinator, 914-594-4110, Fax: 914-594-4944, E-mail: v_romeomessana@nymc.edu.

New York University, School of Medicine, New York, NY 10012-1019. Offers biomedical sciences (PhD), including biomedical imaging, cellular and molecular biology, computational biology, developmental genetics, medical and molecular parasitology, microbiology, molecular oncobiology and immunology, neuroscience and physiology, pathobiology, pharmacology, structural biology; clinical investigation (MS); medicine (MD); MD/MA; MD/MPA; MD/MS; MD/PhD. *Accreditation:* LCME/AMA (one or more programs are accredited). *Degree requirements:* For master's, comprehensive exam, thesis; for doctorate, comprehensive exam (for some programs), thesis/dissertation (for some programs). *Entrance requirements:* For doctorate, MCAT (for MD). Additional exam requirements/recommendations for international students: Required—TOEFL. *Expenses:* Contact institution. *Faculty research:* AIDS, cancer, neuroscience, molecular biology, neuroscience, cell biology and molecular genetics, structural biology, microbial pathogenesis and host defense, pharmacology, molecular oncology and immunology.

North Carolina State University, College of Veterinary Medicine, Program in Comparative Biomedical Sciences, Raleigh, NC 27695. Offers cell biology (MS, PhD); infectious disease (MS, PhD); pathology (MS, PhD); pharmacology (MS, PhD); population medicine (MS, PhD). Part-time programs available. *Degree requirements:* For master's, thesis; for doctorate, thesis/dissertation. *Entrance requirements:* For master's and doctorate, GRE General Test. Additional exam requirements/recommendations for international students: Required—TOEFL (minimum score 550 paper-based; 213 computer-based). Electronic applications accepted. *Expenses:* Contact institution. *Faculty research:* Infectious diseases, cell biology, pharmacology and toxicology, genomics, pathology and population medicine.

Northwestern University, Northwestern University Feinberg School of Medicine and Interdepartmental Programs, Integrated Graduate Programs in the Life Sciences, Chicago, IL 60611. Offers cancer biology (PhD); cell biology (PhD); developmental biology (PhD); evolutionary biology (PhD); immunology and microbial pathogenesis (PhD); molecular biology and genetics (PhD); neurobiology (PhD); pharmacology and toxicology (PhD); structural biology and biochemistry (PhD). *Degree requirements:* For doctorate, comprehensive exam, thesis/dissertation, written and oral qualifying exams. *Entrance requirements:* For doctorate, GRE General Test. Additional exam requirements/recommendations for international students: Required—TOEFL (minimum score 600 paper-based; 250 computer-based). Electronic applications accepted.

Nova Southeastern University, Center for Psychological Studies, Fort Lauderdale, FL 33314-7796. Offers clinical psychology (PhD, Psy D); clinical psychopharmacology (MS); counseling (MS); general psychology (MS); mental health counseling (MS); school counseling (MS); school psychology (Psy D, Psy S). *Accreditation:* APA (one or more programs are accredited). Postbaccalaureate distance learning degree programs offered. *Faculty:* 34 full-time (11 women), 68 part-time/adjunct (32 women). *Students:* 943 full-time (804 women), 787 part-time (703 women); includes 756 minority (265 Black or African American, non-Hispanic/Latino; 2 American Indian or Alaska Native, non-Hispanic/Latino; 39 Asian, non-Hispanic/Latino; 421 Hispanic/Latino; 1 Native Hawaiian or other Pacific Islander, non-Hispanic/Latino; 28 Two or more races, non-Hispanic/Latino), 31 international. Average age 30. 1,433 applicants, 49% accepted, 520 enrolled. In 2011, 339 master's, 102 doctorates, 23 other advanced degrees awarded. Terminal master's awarded for partial completion of doctoral program. *Degree requirements:* For master's, comprehensive exam, 3 practica; for doctorate, thesis/dissertation, clinical internship, competency exam; for Psy S, comprehensive exam, internship. *Entrance requirements:* For doctorate, GRE General Test, GRE Subject Test (recommended), minimum undergraduate GPA of 3.0; for Psy S, GRE General Test. Additional exam requirements/recommendations for international students: Required—TOEFL (minimum score 550 paper-based; 213 computer-based). *Application deadline:* Applications are processed on a rolling basis. Application fee: $50. Electronic applications accepted. *Expenses:* Contact institution. *Financial support:* In 2011–12, 5 research assistantships, 34 teaching assistantships (averaging $1,000 per year) were awarded; career-related internships or fieldwork, Federal Work-Study, institutionally sponsored loans, scholarships/grants, and unspecified assistantships also available. Support available to part-time students. Financial award application deadline: 4/1. *Faculty research:* Clinical and child clinical psychology, geriatrics, interpersonal violence. *Unit head:* Karen Grosby, Dean, 954-262-5701, Fax: 954-262-3859, E-mail: grosby@nova.edu. *Application contact:* Carlos Perez, Enrollment Management, 954-262-5790, Fax: 954-262-3893, E-mail: cpsinfo@cps.nova.edu. Web site: http://www.cps.nova.edu/.

The Ohio State University, College of Medicine, School of Biomedical Science, Integrated Biomedical Science Graduate Program, Columbus, OH 43210. Offers immunology (PhD); medical genetics (PhD); molecular virology (PhD); pharmacology (PhD). *Degree requirements:* For doctorate, thesis/dissertation. *Entrance requirements:* For doctorate, GRE, GRE Subject Test in biochemistry, cell and molecular biology (recommended for some). Additional exam requirements/recommendations for international students: Required—TOEFL (minimum score 600 paper-based; 250 computer-based). Electronic applications accepted. *Expenses:* Tuition, state resident: full-time $11,400. Tuition, nonresident: full-time $28,125. Tuition and fees vary according to course load, degree level, campus/location and program.

The Ohio State University, College of Pharmacy, Columbus, OH 43210. Offers MS, PhD, Pharm D. *Accreditation:* ACPE (one or more programs are accredited). Part-time programs available. *Faculty:* 47. *Students:* 567 full-time (329 women), 29 part-time (15 women); includes 141 minority (18 Black or African American, non-Hispanic/Latino; 1 American Indian or Alaska Native, non-Hispanic/Latino; 104 Asian, non-Hispanic/Latino; 12 Hispanic/Latino; 6 Two or more races, non-Hispanic/Latino), 58 international. Average age 27. In 2011; 5 master's, 135 doctorates awarded. *Degree requirements:* For doctorate, thesis/dissertation (for some programs). *Entrance requirements:* For master's, GRE General Test, minimum GPA of 3.0; for doctorate, GRE General Test; PCAT (for Pharm D), minimum GPA of 3.0. Additional exam requirements/recommendations for international students: Required—TOEFL, Michigan English Language Assessment Battery (minimum score 82). *Application deadline:* For fall admission, 1/1 priority date for domestic students. Application fee: $40 ($50 for international students). Electronic applications accepted. *Expenses:* Contact institution. *Financial support:* Fellowships with full tuition reimbursements, research assistantships with full tuition reimbursements, teaching assistantships with full tuition reimbursements, career-related internships or fieldwork, Federal Work-Study, institutionally sponsored loans, scholarships/grants, and traineeships available. *Unit head:* Dr. Robert W. Brueggemeier, Dean, 614-292-5711, Fax: 614-292-2588, E-mail: odmail@pharmacy.ohio-state.edu. *Application contact:* Graduate Program Coordinator, 614-292-6822, Fax: 614-292-2588, E-mail: gradprogram@pharmacy.ohio-state.edu. Web site: http://www.pharmacy.ohio-state.edu.

Oregon Health & Science University, School of Medicine, Graduate Programs in Medicine, Program in Molecular and Cellular Biosciences, Department of Physiology and Pharmacology, Portland, OR 97239-3098. Offers PhD. *Faculty:* 16 full-time (4 women), 2 part-time/adjunct. *Students:* 11 full-time (9 women); includes 1 minority (Asian, non-Hispanic/Latino), 1 international. Average age 28. In 2011, 1 doctorate awarded. *Degree requirements:* For doctorate, comprehensive exam, thesis/dissertation. *Entrance requirements:* For doctorate, GRE General Test (minimum scores: 153 Verbal/148 Quantitative/4.5 Analytical) or MCAT (for some programs). Additional exam requirements/recommendations for international students: Required—TOEFL. Electronic applications accepted. *Financial support:* Full tuition and stipends available. *Faculty research:* Ion conduction and gating in k+ channels, autonomic neuron plasticity, neurotransmitter/receptor expression, fetal/neonatal pharmacology, molecular pharmacology. *Unit head:* Dr. Beth Habecker, Program Director, 503-494-6252, E-mail: habecker@ohsu.edu. *Application contact:* Julie Walvatne, Program Coordinator, 503-494-6252.

Penn State Hershey Medical Center, College of Medicine, Graduate School Programs in the Biomedical Sciences, Graduate Program in Pharmacology, Hershey, PA 17033. Offers MS, PhD, MD/PhD, PhD/MBA. PhD/MBA offered jointly with Penn State Harrisburg. *Students:* 11 full-time (6 women), 5 international. 2 applicants, 100% accepted, 2 enrolled. In 2011, 1 master's awarded. Terminal master's awarded for partial completion of doctoral program. *Degree requirements:* For master's, thesis or alternative; for doctorate, comprehensive exam, thesis/dissertation, oral exam. *Entrance requirements:* For master's, GRE General Test; for doctorate, GRE General Test, minimum GPA of 3.0. Additional exam requirements/recommendations for international students: Required—TOEFL (minimum score 550 paper-based; 213 computer-based). *Application deadline:* For fall admission, 1/31 priority date for domestic students, 2/1 for international students. Applications are processed on a rolling basis. Application fee: $65. Electronic applications accepted. *Financial support:* In 2011–12, research assistantships with full tuition reimbursements (averaging $23,028 per year) were awarded; fellowships with full tuition reimbursements, institutionally sponsored loans, scholarships/grants, health care benefits, and unspecified assistantships also available. Financial award applicants required to submit FAFSA. *Faculty research:* Ion pump structure and function, drug development and targeting, mechanisms of drug resistance, neuropharmacology and toxicology, breast cancer, identification of molecular targets for drug development in cancer and cardiovascular and neurological diseases. *Unit head:* Dr. Kent Vrana, Chair, 717-531-8285, Fax: 717-531-5013, E-mail: pharm-grad-hmc@psu.edu. *Application contact:* Elaine Neldigh, Program Secretary, 717-531-8285, Fax: 717-531-5013, E-mail: pharm-grad-hmc@psu.edu. Web site: http://www.pennstatehershey.org/web/pharmacology/programs.

Purdue University, College of Pharmacy and Pharmacal Sciences and Graduate School, Graduate Programs in Pharmacy and Pharmacal Sciences, Department of Medicinal Chemistry and Molecular Pharmacology, West Lafayette, IN 47907. Offers biophysical and computational chemistry (PhD); cancer research (PhD); immunology and infectious disease (PhD); medicinal biochemistry and molecular biology (PhD); medicinal chemistry and chemical biology (PhD); molecular pharmacology (PhD); neuropharmacology, neurodegeneration, and neurotoxicity (PhD); systems biology and functional genomics (PhD). *Faculty:* 22 full-time (2 women), 4 part-time/adjunct (1 woman). *Students:* 49 full-time (18 women); includes 3 minority (1 Asian, non-Hispanic/Latino; 2 Hispanic/Latino), 26 international. Average age 27. 250 applicants, 12% accepted, 9 enrolled. In 2011, 10 doctorates awarded. *Degree requirements:* For doctorate, thesis/dissertation. *Entrance requirements:* For doctorate, GRE General Test; GRE Subject Test in biology, biochemistry, and chemistry (recommended), minimum undergraduate GPA of 3.0. Additional exam requirements/recommendations for international students: Required—TOEFL (minimum score 550 paper-based; 77 iBT); Recommended—TWE. *Application deadline:* For fall admission, 2/1 for domestic and international students. Applications are processed on a rolling basis. Application fee: $60 ($75 for international students). Electronic applications accepted. *Financial support:* Fellowships, research assistantships, teaching assistantships, and traineeships available. Support available to part-time students. Financial award applicants required to submit FAFSA. *Faculty research:* Drug design and development, cancer research, drug synthesis and analysis, chemical pharmacology, environmental toxicology. *Unit head:* Dr. Richard F. Borch, Head, 765-494-1403, E-mail: borch@purdue.edu. *Application contact:* Janine C. Mott, Graduate Contact, 765-494-1269, E-mail: jmott@purdue.edu.

Purdue University, School of Veterinary Medicine and Graduate School, Graduate Programs in Veterinary Medicine, Department of Basic Medical Sciences, West Lafayette, IN 47907. Offers anatomy (MS, PhD); pharmacology (MS, PhD); physiology (MS, PhD). Part-time programs available. Terminal master's awarded for partial completion of doctoral program. *Degree requirements:* For master's, thesis; for doctorate, thesis/dissertation. *Entrance requirements:* For master's and doctorate, GRE General Test. Additional exam requirements/recommendations for international students: Required—TOEFL. Electronic applications accepted. *Faculty research:* Development and regeneration, tissue injury and shock, biomedical engineering, ovarian function, bone and cartilage biology, cell and molecular biology.

Pharmacology

Queen's University at Kingston, School of Graduate Studies and Research, Faculty of Health Sciences, Department of Pharmacology and Toxicology, Kingston, ON K7L 3N6, Canada. Offers M Sc, PhD. *Degree requirements:* For master's, thesis; for doctorate, comprehensive exam, thesis/dissertation. *Entrance requirements:* For master's, minimum 2nd class standing, honors bachelor of science degree (life sciences, health sciences, or equivalent); for doctorate, masters of science degree or outstanding performance in honors bachelor of science program. Additional exam requirements/recommendations for international students: Required—TOEFL (minimum score 600 paper-based; 250 computer-based). Electronic applications accepted. *Faculty research:* Biochemical toxicology, cardiovascular pharmacology and neuropharmacology.

Rush University, Graduate College, Division of Pharmacology, Chicago, IL 60612-3832. Offers clinical research (MS); pharmacology (MS, PhD); MD/PhD. Terminal master's awarded for partial completion of doctoral program. *Degree requirements:* For master's, thesis; for doctorate, thesis/dissertation. *Entrance requirements:* For master's and doctorate, GRE General Test, interview. Additional exam requirements/recommendations for international students: Required—TOEFL (minimum score 550 paper-based; 213 computer-based). *Faculty research:* Dopamine neurobiology and Parkinson's disease; cardiac electrophysiology and clinical pharmacology; neutrophil motility, apoptosis, and adhesion; angiogenesis; pulmonary vascular physiology.

Saint Louis University, Graduate Education and School of Medicine, Graduate Program in Biomedical Sciences and Graduate Education, Department of Pharmacological and Physiological Science, St. Louis, MO 63103-2097. Offers PhD. *Degree requirements:* For doctorate, comprehensive exam, thesis/dissertation, departmental qualifying exams. *Entrance requirements:* For doctorate, GRE General Test (GRE Subject Test optional), letters of recommendation, resume, interview. Additional exam requirements/recommendations for international students: Required—TOEFL (minimum score 525 paper-based; 194 computer-based). Electronic applications accepted. *Faculty research:* Molecular endocrinology, neuropharmacology, cardiovascular science, drug abuse, neurotransmitter and hormonal signaling mechanisms.

Southern Illinois University Carbondale, Graduate School, Graduate Program in Medicine, Program in Pharmacology, Springfield, IL 62794-9629. Offers MS, PhD. *Faculty:* 13 full-time (1 woman). *Students:* 20 full-time (9 women), 1 (woman) part-time; includes 1 minority (Asian, non-Hispanic/Latino), 14 international. Average age 30. 28 applicants, 18% accepted, 5 enrolled. *Degree requirements:* For master's, thesis; for doctorate, thesis/dissertation. *Entrance requirements:* For master's, minimum GPA of 3.0; for doctorate, minimum GPA of 3.25. Additional exam requirements/recommendations for international students: Required—TOEFL. *Application deadline:* For fall admission, 2/15 for domestic students; for spring admission, 12/31 for domestic students. Applications are processed on a rolling basis. Application fee: $0. *Financial support:* Fellowships with full tuition reimbursements and tuition waivers (full) available. *Faculty research:* Autonomic nervous system pharmacology, biochemical pharmacology, neuropharmacology, toxicology, cardiovascular pharmacology. *Unit head:* Dr. Carl L. Faingold, Chairman, 217-545-2185, Fax: 217-524-0145, E-mail: cfaingold@siumed.edu. *Application contact:* Linda Moss, Secretary, 217-545-2875, E-mail: lmoss@siumed.edu. Web site: http://www.siumed.edu/pharm/home.html.

State University of New York Upstate Medical University, College of Graduate Studies, Program in Pharmacology, Syracuse, NY 13210-2334. Offers PhD, MD/PhD. Terminal master's awarded for partial completion of doctoral program. *Degree requirements:* For doctorate, comprehensive exam, thesis/dissertation. *Entrance requirements:* For doctorate, GRE General Test, telephone interview. Additional exam requirements/recommendations for international students: Required—TOEFL. Electronic applications accepted. *Faculty research:* Cancer, disorders of the nervous system, infectious diseases, diabetes/metabolic disorders/cardiovascular diseases.

Stony Brook University, State University of New York, Stony Brook University Medical Center, Health Sciences Center, School of Medicine and Graduate School, Graduate Programs in Medicine, Department of Pharmacological Sciences, Graduate Program in Molecular and Cellular Pharmacology, Stony Brook, NY 11794. Offers PhD. *Degree requirements:* For doctorate, thesis/dissertation, departmental qualifying exam. *Entrance requirements:* For doctorate, GRE General Test. Additional exam requirements/recommendations for international students: Required—TOEFL. Electronic applications accepted. *Faculty research:* Toxicology, molecular and cellular biochemistry.

Temple University, Health Sciences Center, School of Medicine and Graduate School, Graduate Programs in Medicine, Department of Pharmacology, Philadelphia, PA 19122-6096. Offers PhD, MD/PhD. *Faculty:* 12 full-time (3 women). *Students:* 19 full-time (11 women), 2 part-time (1 woman); includes 5 minority (4 Asian, non-Hispanic/Latino; 1 Two or more races, non-Hispanic/Latino), 9 international. Average age 28. 17 applicants, 41% accepted, 5 enrolled. In 2011, 3 doctorates awarded. Terminal master's awarded for partial completion of doctoral program. *Degree requirements:* For doctorate, one foreign language, thesis/dissertation, research seminars. *Entrance requirements:* For doctorate, GRE General Test, minimum GPA of 3.0. Additional exam requirements/recommendations for international students: Required—TOEFL (minimum score 620 paper-based; 260 computer-based). *Application deadline:* For fall admission, 1/15 priority date for domestic students, 12/15 for international students. Applications are processed on a rolling basis. Application fee: $50. Electronic applications accepted. *Expenses:* Tuition, state resident: full-time $12,366; part-time $687 per credit hour. Tuition, nonresident: full-time $17,298; part-time $961 per credit hour. *Required fees:* $590; $213 per year. *Financial support:* Fellowships, research assistantships, and Federal Work-Study available. Financial award application deadline: 1/15; financial award applicants required to submit FAFSA. *Faculty research:* Cardiovascular and central nervous systems, biochemical pharmacology. *Unit head:* Dr. Walter Koch, Chair, 215-707-9820, Fax: 215-707-9890, E-mail: walter.koch@temple.edu. *Application contact:* Office of Admissions, 215-707-3656, Fax: 215-707-6932, E-mail: medadmissions@temple.edu. Web site: http://www.temple.edu/medicine/departments_centers/basic_science/pharmacology.htm.

Texas Tech University Health Sciences Center, Graduate School of Biomedical Sciences, Department of Pharmacology and Neuroscience, Lubbock, TX 79430. Offers MS, PhD, MD/PhD, MS/PhD. Terminal master's awarded for partial completion of doctoral program. *Degree requirements:* For master's, thesis; for doctorate, thesis/dissertation. *Entrance requirements:* For master's and doctorate, GRE General Test, minimum GPA of 3.0. Additional exam requirements/recommendations for international students: Required—TOEFL. Electronic applications accepted. *Faculty research:* Neuroscience, neuropsychopharmacology, autonomic pharmacology, cardiovascular pharmacology, molecular pharmacology.

Thomas Jefferson University, Jefferson College of Graduate Studies, MS Program in Pharmacology, Philadelphia, PA 19107. Offers MS. Part-time and evening/weekend programs available. *Faculty:* 18 full-time (5 women), 11 part-time/adjunct (4 women). *Students:* 34 part-time (20 women); includes 14 minority (5 Black or African American, non-Hispanic/Latino; 9 Asian, non-Hispanic/Latino), 4 international. 25 applicants, 72%

accepted, 18 enrolled. In 2011, 12 master's awarded. *Degree requirements:* For master's, thesis, clerkship. *Entrance requirements:* For master's, GRE General Test or MCAT, minimum GPA of 3.0. Additional exam requirements/recommendations for international students: Required—TOEFL (minimum score 100 iBT) or IELTS (minimum score 7). *Application deadline:* For fall admission, 8/1 priority date for domestic students, 3/1 for international students; for winter admission, 12/1 priority date for domestic students, 6/1 for international students; for spring admission, 4/1 priority date for domestic students. Applications are processed on a rolling basis. Application fee: $50. Electronic applications accepted. *Expenses:* Contact institution. *Financial support:* In 2011–12, 9 students received support. Federal Work-Study and institutionally sponsored loans available. Support available to part-time students. Financial award application deadline: 5/1; financial award applicants required to submit FAFSA. *Faculty research:* Pharmacology, drug development, planning and management, biostatistics. *Unit head:* Dr. Carol L. Beck, Assistant Dean/Director, 215-503-6539, Fax: 215-503-3433, E-mail: carol.beck@jefferson.edu. *Application contact:* Eleanor M. Gorman, Assistant Coordinator, Graduate Center Programs, 215-503-5799, Fax: 215-503-3433, E-mail: eleanor.gorman@jefferson.edu. Web site: http://www.jefferson.edu/jcgs/msbs/.

Tufts University, Sackler School of Graduate Biomedical Sciences, Pharmacology and Experimental Therapeutics Program, Medford, MA 02155. Offers PhD. *Faculty:* 21 full-time (4 women). *Students:* 13 full-time (9 women); includes 5 minority (4 Black or African American, non-Hispanic/Latino; 1 Asian, non-Hispanic/Latino), 6 international. Average age 31. 51 applicants, 6% accepted, 2 enrolled. In 2011, 4 doctorates awarded. *Degree requirements:* For doctorate, thesis/dissertation. *Entrance requirements:* For doctorate, GRE General Test, 3 letters of reference. Additional exam requirements/recommendations for international students: Required—TOEFL (minimum score 600 paper-based; 250 computer-based; 100 iBT). *Application deadline:* For fall admission, 12/15 for domestic and international students. Application fee: $70. Electronic applications accepted. *Expenses:* Tuition: Full-time $41,208; part-time $1030 per credit hour. Full-time tuition and fees vary according to degree level, program and student level. Part-time tuition and fees vary according to course load. *Financial support:* In 2011–12, 7 research assistantships with full tuition reimbursements (averaging $30,000 per year) were awarded; health care benefits also available. Financial award application deadline: 1/15. *Faculty research:* Biochemical mechanisms of narcotic addiction, clinical psychopharmacology, pharmacokinetics, neurotransmitter receptors, neuropeptides. *Unit head:* Dr. Michael Court, Director, 617-636-2741. *Application contact:* Kellie Melchin, Associate Director of Admissions, 617-636-6767, Fax: 617-636-0375, E-mail: sackler-school@tufts.edu. Web site: http://sackler.tufts.edu/Academics/Degree-Programs/PhD-Programs/Pharmacology-and-Experimental-Therapeutics.

Tulane University, School of Medicine and School of Liberal Arts, Graduate Programs in Biomedical Sciences, Department of Pharmacology, New Orleans, LA 70118-5669. Offers MS, PhD, MD/MS, MD/PhD. MS and PhD offered through the Graduate School. *Degree requirements:* For master's, one foreign language, thesis; for doctorate, 2 foreign languages, thesis/dissertation. *Entrance requirements:* For master's, GRE General Test, minimum B average in undergraduate course work; for doctorate, GRE General Test. Additional exam requirements/recommendations for international students: Required—TOEFL. Electronic applications accepted.

Universidad Central del Caribe, School of Medicine, Program in Biomedical Sciences, Bayamón, PR 00960-6032. Offers anatomy and cell biology (MA, MS); biochemistry (MS); biomedical sciences (MA); cellular and molecular biology (PhD); microbiology and immunology (MA, MS); pharmacology (MS); physiology (MS).

Université de Montréal, Faculty of Medicine, Department of Pharmacology, Montréal, QC H3C 3J7, Canada. Offers M Sc, PhD. Terminal master's awarded for partial completion of doctoral program. *Degree requirements:* For master's, thesis; for doctorate, thesis/dissertation, general exam. *Entrance requirements:* For master's, proficiency in French, knowledge of English; for doctorate, master's degree, proficiency in French. Electronic applications accepted. *Faculty research:* Molecular, clinical, and cardiovascular pharmacology; pharmacokinetics; mechanisms of drug interactions and toxicity; neuropharmacology and receptology.

Université de Sherbrooke, Faculty of Medicine and Health Sciences, Graduate Programs in Medicine, Department of Pharmacology, Sherbrooke, QC J1H 5N4, Canada. Offers M Sc, PhD. Terminal master's awarded for partial completion of doctoral program. *Degree requirements:* For master's, thesis; for doctorate, thesis/dissertation. Electronic applications accepted. *Faculty research:* Pharmacology of peptide hormones, pharmacology of lipid mediators, protein-protein interactions, medicinal pharmacology.

University at Buffalo, the State University of New York, Graduate School, School of Medicine and Biomedical Sciences, Graduate Programs in Medicine and Biomedical Sciences, Department of Pharmacology and Toxicology, Buffalo, NY 14260. Offers biochemical pharmacology (MS); pharmacology (MA, PhD); MD/PhD. *Faculty:* 21 full-time (3 women), 1 part-time/adjunct (0 women). *Students:* 27 full-time (14 women); includes 6 minority (5 Black or African American, non-Hispanic/Latino; 1 Asian, non-Hispanic/Latino), 5 international. Average age 25. 32 applicants, 34% accepted, 11 enrolled. In 2011, 3 master's, 2 doctorates awarded. Terminal master's awarded for partial completion of doctoral program. *Degree requirements:* For master's, thesis; for doctorate, thesis/dissertation. *Entrance requirements:* For master's and doctorate, GRE General Test, 3 letters of recommendation. Additional exam requirements/recommendations for international students: Required—TOEFL (minimum score 100 iBT). *Application deadline:* For fall admission, 2/14 priority date for domestic students, 2/14 for international students. Applications are processed on a rolling basis. Application fee: $50. Electronic applications accepted. *Financial support:* In 2011–12, 3 fellowships with full tuition reimbursements (averaging $30,000 per year), 13 research assistantships with full tuition reimbursements (averaging $24,000 per year) were awarded; teaching assistantships, Federal Work-Study, scholarships/grants, health care benefits, and unspecified assistantships also available. Financial award application deadline: 2/14; financial award applicants required to submit FAFSA. *Faculty research:* Neuropharmacology, toxicology, signal transduction, molecular pharmacology, behavioral pharmacology. Total annual research expenditures: $1.6 million. *Unit head:* Dr. Margarita Dubocovich, Chairman, 716-829-3048, Fax: 716-829-2801, E-mail: mdubo@buffalo.edu. *Application contact:* Linda LeRoy, Admissions Assistant, 716-829-2800, Fax: 716-829-2801, E-mail: lleroy@buffalo.edu. Web site: http://medicine.buffalo.edu/pharmtox.

The University of Alabama at Birmingham, Graduate Programs in Joint Health Sciences, Program in Pharmacology and Toxicology, Birmingham, AL 35294. Offers PhD. *Degree requirements:* For doctorate, thesis/dissertation. *Entrance requirements:* For doctorate, GRE General Test, interview. *Application deadline:* Applications are processed on a rolling basis. Application fee: $35 ($60 for international students). Electronic applications accepted. *Expenses:* Contact institution. *Financial support:* Fellowships available. *Faculty research:* Biochemical pharmacology, neuropharmacology, endocrine pharmacology. *Unit head:* Dr. Mary-Ann Bjornsti, Interim Chair, 205-934-4579. *Application contact:* Graduate Coordinator, 205-934-4584, Fax: 205-934-4209.

University of Alberta, Faculty of Graduate Studies and Research, Department of Pharmacology, Edmonton, AB T6G 2E1, Canada. Offers M Sc, PhD. Terminal master's awarded for partial completion of doctoral program. *Degree requirements:* For master's, thesis; for doctorate, thesis/dissertation. *Entrance requirements:* For master's, B Sc, minimum GPA of 3.3; for doctorate, M Sc in pharmacology or closely related field, honors B Sc in pharmacology. *Faculty research:* Cardiovascular pharmacology, neuropharmacology, cancer pharmacology, molecular pharmacology, toxicology.

The University of Arizona, College of Pharmacy, Department of Pharmacology and Toxicology, Graduate Program in Medical Pharmacology, Tucson, AZ 85721. Offers medical pharmacology (PhD); perfusion science (MS). *Faculty:* 11 full-time (3 women). *Students:* 32 full-time (22 women), 2 part-time (1 woman); includes 10 minority (1 Black or African American, non-Hispanic/Latino; 3 Asian, non-Hispanic/Latino; 4 Hispanic/Latino; 2 Two or more races, non-Hispanic/Latino), 8 international. Average age 28. 40 applicants, 13% accepted, 5 enrolled. In 2011, 4 master's, 2 doctorates awarded. *Degree requirements:* For master's, thesis; for doctorate, comprehensive exam, thesis/dissertation. *Entrance requirements:* For master's, GRE General Test, 3 letters of recommendation; for doctorate, GRE General Test, personal statement, 3 letters of recommendation. Additional exam requirements/recommendations for international students: Required—TOEFL (minimum score 550 paper-based; 213 computer-based; 79 iBT). *Application deadline:* For fall admission, 1/1 for domestic and international students. Applications are processed on a rolling basis. Application fee: $75. Electronic applications accepted. *Expenses:* Tuition, state resident: full-time $10,840. Tuition, nonresident: full-time $25,802. *Financial support:* In 2011–12, 17 research assistantships with full tuition reimbursements (averaging $23,929 per year) were awarded; institutionally sponsored loans and tuition waivers (partial) also available. Financial award applicants required to submit FAFSA. *Faculty research:* Immunopharmacology, pharmacogenetics, pharmacogenomics, clinical pharmacology, ocularpharmacology and neuropharmacology. *Unit head:* Dr. I. Glenn Sipes, Head, 520-626-7123, Fax: 520-626-2204, E-mail: sipes@email.arizona.edu. *Application contact:* Trisha Stanley, Coordinator, 520-626-7218, Fax: 520-626-2204, E-mail: stanley@email.arizona.edu. Web site: http://www.pharmacology.arizona.edu/.

University of Arkansas for Medical Sciences, Graduate School, Graduate Programs in Biomedical Sciences, Pharmacology Program, Little Rock, AR 72205-7199. Offers MS, PhD, MD/PhD. *Degree requirements:* For master's, thesis; for doctorate, thesis/dissertation. *Entrance requirements:* For master's and doctorate, GRE General Test. Additional exam requirements/recommendations for international students: Required—TOEFL. *Faculty research:* Neuroscience, behavior, pharmacokinetics, metabolism.

The University of British Columbia, Faculty of Medicine, Department of Anesthesiology, Pharmacology and Therapeutics, Vancouver, BC V6T 1Z3, Canada. Offers M Sc, PhD. Terminal master's awarded for partial completion of doctoral program. *Degree requirements:* For master's, thesis; for doctorate, comprehensive exam, thesis/dissertation. *Entrance requirements:* For master's, MD or appropriate bachelor's degree; for doctorate, MD or M Sc. Additional exam requirements/recommendations for international students: Required—TOEFL (minimum score 600 paper-based; 250 computer-based; 100 iBT). Electronic applications accepted. *Faculty research:* Cellular, biochemical, autonomic, cardiovascular pharmacology; neuropharmacology and pulmonary pharmacology.

University of California, Davis, Graduate Studies, Graduate Group in Pharmacology and Toxicology, Davis, CA 95616. Offers MS, PhD. Terminal master's awarded for partial completion of doctoral program. *Degree requirements:* For master's, comprehensive exam or thesis; for doctorate, thesis/dissertation, qualifying exam. *Entrance requirements:* For master's and doctorate, GRE General Test, minimum GPA of 3.0, course work in biochemistry and/or physiology. Additional exam requirements/recommendations for international students: Required—TOEFL (minimum score 550 paper-based; 213 computer-based). Electronic applications accepted. *Faculty research:* Respiratory, neurochemical, molecular, genetic, and ecological toxicology.

University of California, Irvine, School of Medicine, Department of Pharmacology, Irvine, CA 92697. Offers pharmacology and toxicology (MS, PhD); MD/PhD. *Students:* 27 full-time (11 women), 1 part-time (0 women); includes 11 minority (2 Black or African American, non-Hispanic/Latino; 7 Asian, non-Hispanic/Latino; 1 Hispanic/Latino; 1 Two or more races, non-Hispanic/Latino), 6 international. Average age 29. 40 applicants, 20% accepted, 5 enrolled. In 2011, 6 master's, 2 doctorates awarded. *Degree requirements:* For doctorate, thesis/dissertation. *Entrance requirements:* For master's, GRE, minimum GPA of 3.0; for doctorate, GRE General Test, GRE Subject Test, minimum GPA of 3.0. Additional exam requirements/recommendations for international students: Required—TOEFL (minimum score 550 paper-based; 213 computer-based). *Application deadline:* For fall admission, 1/15 priority date for domestic students, 1/15 for international students. Applications are processed on a rolling basis. Application fee: $80 ($100 for international students). Electronic applications accepted. *Financial support:* Fellowships, research assistantships with full tuition reimbursements, teaching assistantships, institutionally sponsored loans, traineeships, health care benefits, and unspecified assistantships available. Financial award application deadline: 3/1; financial award applicants required to submit FAFSA. *Faculty research:* Mechanisms of action and effects of drugs on the nervous system, behavior, skeletal muscle, heart, and blood vessels; basic processes in the nervous system, skeletal muscle, heart, and blood vessels. *Unit head:* Prof. Olivier Civelli, Chair and Professor, 949-824-2522, Fax: 949-824-4855, E-mail: ocivelli@uci.edu. *Application contact:* Pamela J. Bhalla, Chief Administrative Officer, 949-824-6772, Fax: 949-824-4855, E-mail: pamela.bhalla@uci.edu.

University of California, Los Angeles, David Geffen School of Medicine and Graduate Division, Graduate Programs in Medicine, Department of Molecular and Medical Pharmacology, Los Angeles, CA 90095. Offers PhD. *Faculty:* 26 full-time (7 women). *Students:* 64 full-time (33 women); includes 18 minority (2 Black or African American, non-Hispanic/Latino; 12 Asian, non-Hispanic/Latino; 3 Hispanic/Latino; 1 Two or more races, non-Hispanic/Latino), 21 international. Average age 27. 80 applicants, 20% accepted, 8 enrolled. In 2011, 11 doctorates awarded. *Degree requirements:* For doctorate, thesis/dissertation, qualifying exams. *Entrance requirements:* For doctorate, GRE General Test. Application fee: $70 ($90 for international students). Electronic applications accepted. *Financial support:* In 2011–12, 57 fellowships, 49 research assistantships, 7 teaching assistantships were awarded; scholarships/grants also available. Financial award application deadline: 3/1. *Faculty research:* Cardiovascular pharmacology, chemical pharmacology, neuropharmacology, clinical pharmacology, molecular pharmacology. *Unit head:* Dr. Michael Phelps, Chair, 310-825-6539, E-mail: mphelps@mednet.ucla.edu. *Application contact:* Sarah Starrett, Student Affairs Office, 310-825-0390, Fax: 310-794-1819, E-mail: sstarrett@mednet.ucla.edu. Web site: http://www.pharmacology.ucla.edu/.

University of California, San Diego, School of Medicine and Office of Graduate Studies, Graduate Studies in Biomedical Sciences, Department of Pharmacology, La Jolla, CA 92093-0685. Offers PhD. *Degree requirements:* For doctorate, thesis/dissertation, qualifying exam. *Entrance requirements:* For doctorate, GRE General Test.

Additional exam requirements/recommendations for international students: Required—TOEFL. Electronic applications accepted. *Faculty research:* Molecular and cellular pharmacology, cell and organ physiology, cellular and molecular biology.

University of California, San Francisco, School of Pharmacy and Graduate Division, Pharmaceutical Sciences and Pharmacogenomics Graduate Group, San Francisco, CA 94158-0775. Offers PhD. *Faculty:* 52 full-time (14 women). *Students:* 48 full-time (24 women); includes 16 minority (15 Asian, non-Hispanic/Latino; 1 Hispanic/Latino). Average age 23. 92 applicants, 15% accepted, 8 enrolled. In 2011, 7 doctorates awarded. *Degree requirements:* For doctorate, comprehensive exam, thesis/dissertation. *Entrance requirements:* For doctorate, GRE General Test, minimum GPA of 3.0. Additional exam requirements/recommendations for international students: Required—TOEFL. *Application deadline:* For fall admission, 12/1 for domestic and international students. Application fee: $70 ($90 for international students). Electronic applications accepted. *Financial support:* In 2011–12, 6 fellowships with full tuition reimbursements (averaging $28,000 per year), 34 research assistantships with full tuition reimbursements (averaging $28,000 per year), 8 teaching assistantships with full tuition reimbursements (averaging $28,000 per year) were awarded; career-related internships or fieldwork, institutionally sponsored loans, scholarships/grants, traineeships, tuition waivers (full), and unspecified assistantships also available. Financial award application deadline: 4/6. *Faculty research:* Drug development, drug delivery, molecular pharmacology. *Unit head:* Deanna L. Kroetz, Program Director, 415-476-1159, Fax: 415-476-6022, E-mail: deanna.kroetz@ucsf.edu. *Application contact:* Debbie Acoba-Idlebi, Program Coordinator, 415-476-1947, Fax: 415-476-6022, E-mail: debbie.acoba@ucsf.edu. Web site: http://bts.ucsf.edu/pspg/.

University of Chicago, Division of Biological Sciences, Neuroscience Graduate Programs, Committee on Integrative Neuroscience, Chicago, IL 60637-1513. Offers cell physiology (PhD); pharmacological and physiological sciences (PhD). *Degree requirements:* For doctorate, thesis/dissertation, preliminary exam. *Entrance requirements:* For doctorate, GRE General Test. Additional exam requirements/recommendations for international students: Required—TOEFL. Electronic applications accepted. *Faculty research:* Psychopharmacology, neuropharmacology.

University of Cincinnati, Graduate School, College of Medicine, Graduate Programs in Biomedical Sciences, Department of Pharmacology and Cell Biophysics, Cincinnati, OH 45221. Offers cell biophysics (PhD); pharmacology (PhD). *Degree requirements:* For doctorate, thesis/dissertation, qualifying exam. *Entrance requirements:* For doctorate, GRE General Test. Additional exam requirements/recommendations for international students: Required—TOEFL. Electronic applications accepted. *Faculty research:* Lipoprotein research, enzyme regulation, electrophysiology, gene actuation.

University of Colorado Denver, School of Medicine, Program in Pharmacology, Aurora, CO 80045. Offers bioinformatics (PhD); biomolecular structure (PhD); pharmacology (PhD). *Students:* 24 full-time (15 women); includes 4 minority (1 Black or African American, non-Hispanic/Latino; 2 Asian, non-Hispanic/Latino; 1 Hispanic/Latino). Average age 28. 18 applicants, 17% accepted, 3 enrolled. In 2011, 4 doctorates awarded. *Degree requirements:* For doctorate, comprehensive exam, thesis/dissertation, major seminar, 3 research rotations in the first year, 30 hours each of course work and thesis. *Entrance requirements:* For doctorate, GRE General Test. Additional exam requirements/recommendations for international students: Required—TOEFL (minimum score 550 paper-based; 213 computer-based; 80 iBT). *Application deadline:* For fall admission, 12/15 for domestic students, 11/15 for international students. Application fee: $50 ($75 for international students). Electronic applications accepted. *Expenses:* Contact institution. *Financial support:* Fellowships, research assistantships, teaching assistantships, health care benefits, tuition waivers (full), and stipend available. Financial award application deadline: 3/15; financial award applicants required to submit FAFSA. *Faculty research:* Cancer biology, drugs of abuse, neuroscience, signal transduction, structural biology. *Total annual research expenditures:* $16.7 million. *Unit head:* Dr. Andrew Thorburn, Interim Chair, 303-724-3290, Fax: 303-724-3663, E-mail: andrew.thorburn@ucdenver.edu. *Application contact:* Elizabeth Bowen, Graduate Training Coordinator, 303-724-3565, E-mail: elizabeth.bowen@ucdenver.edu. Web site: http://pharmacology.ucdenver.edu/.

University of Connecticut, Graduate School, School of Pharmacy, Department of Pharmaceutical Sciences, Graduate Program in Pharmacology and Toxicology, Storrs, CT 06269. Offers pharmacology (MS, PhD); toxicology (MS, PhD). Terminal master's awarded for partial completion of doctoral program. *Degree requirements:* For master's, comprehensive exam, thesis; for doctorate, thesis/dissertation. *Entrance requirements:* For master's and doctorate, GRE General Test. Additional exam requirements/recommendations for international students: Required—TOEFL (minimum score 550 paper-based; 213 computer-based). Electronic applications accepted.

University of Florida, College of Medicine, Department of Pharmacology and Therapeutics, Gainesville, FL 32611. Offers PhD. *Degree requirements:* For doctorate, thesis/dissertation. *Entrance requirements:* For doctorate, GRE General Test, minimum GPA of 3.0. Additional exam requirements/recommendations for international students: Required—TOEFL. Electronic applications accepted. *Faculty research:* Receptor and membrane pharmacology, autonomics, tetralogy, enzymes, opioid peptides.

University of Florida, College of Medicine and Graduate School, Interdisciplinary Program in Biomedical Sciences, Concentration in Physiology and Pharmacology, Gainesville, FL 32611. Offers PhD. *Degree requirements:* For doctorate, thesis/dissertation. *Entrance requirements:* For doctorate, GRE General Test, minimum GPA of 3.0. Electronic applications accepted.

University of Florida, Graduate School, College of Pharmacy and Graduate School, Graduate Programs in Pharmacy, Department of Pharmacodynamics, Gainesville, FL 32611. Offers MSP, PhD, Pharm D/PhD. *Faculty:* 8 full-time (4 women). *Students:* 12 full-time (7 women), 9 international. Average age 28. 11 applicants, 18% accepted, 2 enrolled. In 2011, 3 doctorates awarded. *Degree requirements:* For doctorate, comprehensive exam, thesis/dissertation. *Entrance requirements:* For doctorate, GRE General Test, minimum GPA of 3.0. Additional exam requirements/recommendations for international students: Required—TOEFL (minimum score 550 paper-based; 213 computer-based; 80 iBT), IELTS (minimum score 6). *Application deadline:* For fall admission, 2/15 priority date for domestic students, 2/15 for international students. Applications are processed on a rolling basis. Application fee: $30. Electronic applications accepted. *Financial support:* In 2011–12, 7 students received support, including 1 fellowship, 2 research assistantships, 4 teaching assistantships; institutionally sponsored loans and unspecified assistantships also available. Support available to part-time students. Financial award application deadline: 2/15; financial award applicants required to submit FAFSA. *Faculty research:* Neurochemistry and neurologic pathways involved in addiction and stress; cellular and molecular neurobiology of epilepsy, dementia and Parkinson's; hypertension and cardiac hypertrophy; stress hormone effects on fetal and neonatal development; cellular mechanism of glaucoma. *Total annual research expenditures:* $1.1 million. *Unit head:* Dr. Maureen Keller-Wood, Chair, 352-273-7687, Fax: 352-392-9187, E-mail: kellerwd@cop.ufl.edu. *Application contact:* Michael J. Katovich, Graduate Coordinator, 352-273-

7690, Fax: 352-392-9187, E-mail: katovich@cop.ufl.edu. Web site: http://www.cop.ufl.edu/research/pharmacodynamics/.

University of Georgia, College of Veterinary Medicine, Department of Physiology and Pharmacology, Athens, GA 30602. Offers pharmacology (MS, PhD); physiology (MS, PhD). *Faculty:* 12 full-time (4 women), 1 part-time/adjunct (0 women). *Students:* 19 full-time (8 women); includes 2 minority (1 Asian, non-Hispanic/Latino; 1 Hispanic/Latino), 12 international. Average age 28. 11 applicants, 27% accepted, 3 enrolled. In 2011, 1 doctorate awarded. *Degree requirements:* For master's, thesis; for doctorate, one foreign language, thesis/dissertation. *Entrance requirements:* For master's and doctorate, GRE General Test. *Application deadline:* For fall admission, 7/1 priority date for domestic students; for spring admission, 11/15 for domestic students. Application fee: $50. Electronic applications accepted. *Financial support:* Fellowships, research assistantships, teaching assistantships, and unspecified assistantships available. *Unit head:* Dr. Gaylen L. Edwards, Acting Head, 706-542-3014, Fax: 706-542-3015, E-mail: gedwards@uga.edu. *Application contact:* Dr. John Wagner, Graduate Coordinator, 706-542-6428, Fax: 706-542-3015, E-mail: jwagner@uga.edu. Web site: http://www.vet.uga.edu/vph/.

University of Guelph, Ontario Veterinary College and Graduate Studies, Graduate Programs in Veterinary Sciences, Department of Biomedical Sciences, Guelph, ON N1G 2W1, Canada. Offers morphology (M Sc, DV Sc, PhD); neuroscience (M Sc, DV Sc, PhD); pharmacology (M Sc, DV Sc, PhD); physiology (M Sc, DV Sc, PhD); toxicology (M Sc, DV Sc, PhD). Part-time programs available. *Degree requirements:* For master's, thesis; for doctorate, comprehensive exam, thesis/dissertation. *Entrance requirements:* For master's, honors B Sc, minimum 75% average in last 20 courses; for doctorate, M Sc with thesis from accredited institution. Additional exam requirements/recommendations for international students: Required—TOEFL (minimum score 550 paper-based; 213 computer-based; 89 iBT). Electronic applications accepted. *Faculty research:* Cellular morphology; endocrine, vascular and reproductive physiology; clinical pharmacology; veterinary toxicology; developmental biology, neuroscience.

University of Houston, College of Pharmacy, Houston, TX 77204. Offers pharmaceutics (MSPHR, PhD); pharmacology (MSPHR, PhD); pharmacy (Pharm D); pharmacy administration (MSPHR, PhD). *Accreditation:* ACPE. Part-time programs available. Terminal master's awarded for partial completion of doctoral program. *Entrance requirements:* For doctorate, PCAT (for Pharm D). Additional exam requirements/recommendations for international students: Required—TOEFL. Electronic applications accepted. *Faculty research:* Drug screening and design, cardiovascular pharmacology, infectious disease, asthma research, herbal medicine.

University of Illinois at Chicago, College of Medicine and Graduate College, Graduate Programs in Medicine, Department of Pharmacology, Chicago, IL 60612. Offers PhD, MD/PhD. *Degree requirements:* For doctorate, thesis/dissertation. *Entrance requirements:* For doctorate, GRE General Test. Additional exam requirements/recommendations for international students: Required—TOEFL. *Faculty research:* Cardiovascular and lung biology, cell signaling, molecular pharmacology of G-proteins, immunopharmcology, molecular and cellular basis of inflammation, neuroscience.

The University of Iowa, Roy J. and Lucille A. Carver College of Medicine and Graduate College, Graduate Programs in Medicine, Department of Pharmacology, Iowa City, IA 52242-1316. Offers MS, PhD. *Faculty:* 11 full-time (1 woman), 10 part-time/adjunct (4 women). *Students:* 23 full-time (9 women); includes 2 minority (1 Black or African American, non-Hispanic/Latino; 1 Hispanic/Latino), 7 international. Average age 28. 33 applicants, 12% accepted, 2 enrolled. In 2011, 1 master's, 5 doctorates awarded. Terminal master's awarded for partial completion of doctoral program. *Degree requirements:* For master's, thesis; for doctorate, comprehensive exam, thesis/dissertation. *Entrance requirements:* For master's, GRE General Test; for doctorate, GRE General Test, minimum GPA of 3.0, undergraduate course work in biochemistry. Additional exam requirements/recommendations for international students: Required—TOEFL (minimum score 600 paper-based; 250 computer-based). *Application deadline:* For fall admission, 2/1 priority date for domestic students, 2/1 for international students. Applications are processed on a rolling basis. Application fee: $60 ($85 for international students). Electronic applications accepted. *Financial support:* In 2011–12, 23 research assistantships with full tuition reimbursements (averaging $25,500 per year) were awarded; scholarships/grants, traineeships, and unspecified assistantships also available. *Faculty research:* Cancer and cell cycle, hormones and growth factors, nervous system function and dysfunction, receptors and signal transduction, stroke and hypertension. *Total annual research expenditures:* $2.7 million. *Unit head:* Dr. Curt Sigmund, Head, 319-335-7946, Fax: 319-335-8930, E-mail: curt-sigmund@uiowa.edu. *Application contact:* Dr. Stefan Strack, Director, Graduate Admissions, 319-384-4439, Fax: 319-335-8930, E-mail: pharmacology-admissions@uiowa.edu. Web site: http://www.medicine.uiowa.edu/pharmacology/.

The University of Kansas, Graduate Studies, School of Pharmacy, Department of Pharmacology and Toxicology, Program in Pharmacology and Toxicology, Lawrence, KS 66045. Offers MS, PhD. *Faculty:* 11 full-time (3 women). *Students:* 16 full-time (all women); includes 1 minority (Hispanic/Latino), 9 international. Average age 25. 50 applicants, 8% accepted, 4 enrolled. Terminal master's awarded for partial completion of doctoral program. *Degree requirements:* For master's, comprehensive exam, thesis; for doctorate, comprehensive exam, thesis/dissertation. *Entrance requirements:* For master's, GRE; for doctorate, GRE (minimum score: 600 verbal, 600 quantitative, 4.5 analytical). Additional exam requirements/recommendations for international students: Required—TOEFL (minimum score 600 paper-based; 250 computer-based; 100 iBT). *Application deadline:* For fall admission, 1/15 priority date for domestic students, 2/1 for international students. Applications are processed on a rolling basis. Application fee: $55 ($65 for international students). Electronic applications accepted. Tuition and fees vary according to course load, campus/location, program and reciprocity agreements. *Financial support:* Fellowships with full tuition reimbursements and research assistantships with full tuition reimbursements available. *Faculty research:* Neuropharmacology, neurodegeneration. *Unit head:* Dr. Nancy Muma, Chair, 785-864-4001, Fax: 785-864-5219, E-mail: nmuma@ku.edu. *Application contact:* Dr. R. Alexandar Moise, Assistant Professor/Director, 785-864-1010, Fax: 785-864-5219, E-mail: alexmoise@ku.edu. Web site: http://www.pharmtox.pharm.ku.edu.

The University of Kansas, University of Kansas Medical Center, School of Medicine, Department of Pharmacology, Toxicology and Therapeutics, Kansas City, KS 66160. Offers pharmacology (MA, MS, PhD); toxicology (MS, PhD); MD/MS; MD/PhD. *Faculty:* 27. *Students:* 24 full-time (14 women), 1 part-time (0 women); includes 1 minority (Hispanic/Latino), 11 international. Average age 28. 1 applicant, 100% accepted, 1 enrolled. In 2011, 10 doctorates awarded. Terminal master's awarded for partial completion of doctoral program. *Degree requirements:* For master's, comprehensive exam, thesis; for doctorate, one foreign language, comprehensive exam, thesis/dissertation. *Entrance requirements:* For master's and doctorate, GRE General Test. Additional exam requirements/recommendations for international students: Required—TOEFL. *Application deadline:* For fall admission, 1/15 priority date for domestic students. Applications are processed on a rolling basis. Application fee: $0. Electronic applications accepted. Tuition and fees vary according to course load, campus/location, program and reciprocity agreements. *Financial support:* Fellowships with full tuition reimbursements, research assistantships with full tuition reimbursements, teaching assistantships with full tuition reimbursements, Federal Work-Study, scholarships/grants, traineeships, and unspecified assistantships available. Support available to part-time students. Financial award application deadline: 2/14; financial award applicants required to submit FAFSA. *Faculty research:* Liver nuclear receptors, hepatobiliary transporters, pharmacogenomics, estrogen-induced carcinogenesis, neuropharmacology of pain and depression. *Total annual research expenditures:* $9.1 million. *Unit head:* Dr. Hartmut Jaeschke, Professor and Chair, 913-588-7969, Fax: 913-588-7501, E-mail: hjaeschke@kumc.edu. *Application contact:* Dr. Bruno Hagenbuch, Chair, Departmental Graduate Committee, 913-588-0028, Fax: 913-588-7501, E-mail: bhagenbuch@kumc.edu. Web site: http://www.kumc.edu/pharmacology.

University of Kentucky, Graduate School, Graduate School Programs from the College of Medicine, Program in Molecular and Biomedical Pharmacology, Lexington, KY 40506-0032. Offers pharmacology (PhD); MD/PhD. *Degree requirements:* For doctorate, comprehensive exam, thesis/dissertation. *Entrance requirements:* For doctorate, GRE General Test, minimum undergraduate GPA of 2.75, graduate 3.0. Additional exam requirements/recommendations for international students: Required—TOEFL (minimum score 550 paper-based; 213 computer-based). Electronic applications accepted.

University of Louisville, School of Medicine, Department of Pharmacology and Toxicology, Louisville, KY 40292-0001. Offers MS, PhD, MD/PhD. Terminal master's awarded for partial completion of doctoral program. *Degree requirements:* For master's, thesis; for doctorate, comprehensive exam, thesis/dissertation. *Entrance requirements:* For master's and doctorate, GRE General Test (minimum score of 1000 verbal and quantitative), minimum GPA of 3.0. Additional exam requirements/recommendations for international students: Required—TOEFL. Electronic applications accepted. *Expenses:* Tuition, state resident: full-time $9692; part-time $539 per credit hour. Tuition, nonresident: full-time $20,168; part-time $1121 per credit hour. Tuition and fees vary according to program and reciprocity agreements. *Faculty research:* Molecular pharmacogenetics; epidemiology; functional genomics; genetic predisposition to chemical carcinogenesis and drug toxicity; mechanisms of oxidative stress; alcohol-induced hepatitis, pancreatitis, and hepatocellular carcinoma; molecular and cardiac toxicology; molecular biology and genetics of DNA damage and repair in humans; mechanisms of chemoresistance; arsenic toxicity and cell cycle disruption; molecular pharmacology of novel G protein-coupled receptors.

The University of Manchester, Faculty of Life Sciences, Manchester, United Kingdom. Offers adaptive organismal biology (M Phil, PhD); animal biology (M Phil, PhD); biochemistry (M Phil, PhD); bioinformatics (M Phil, PhD); biomolecular sciences (M Phil, PhD); biotechnology (M Phil, PhD); cell biology (M Phil, PhD); cell matrix research (M Phil, PhD); channels and transporters (M Phil, PhD); developmental biology (M Phil, PhD); Egyptology (M Phil, PhD); environmental biology (M Phil, PhD); evolutionary biology (M Phil, PhD); gene expression (M Phil, PhD); genetics (M Phil, PhD); history of science, technology and medicine (M Phil, PhD); immunology (M Phil, PhD); integrative neurobiology and behavior (M Phil, PhD); membrane trafficking (M Phil, PhD); microbiology (M Phil, PhD); molecular and cellular neuroscience (M Phil, PhD); molecular biology (M Phil, PhD); molecular cancer studies (M Phil, PhD); neuroscience (M Phil, PhD); ophthalmology (M Phil, PhD); optometry (M Phil, PhD); organelle function (M Phil, PhD); pharmacology (M Phil, PhD); physiology (M Phil, PhD); plant sciences (M Phil, PhD); stem cell research (M Phil, PhD); structural biology (M Phil, PhD); systems neuroscience (M Phil, PhD); toxicology (M Phil, PhD).

University of Manitoba, Faculty of Medicine and Faculty of Graduate Studies, Graduate Programs in Medicine, Department of Pharmacology and Therapeutics, Winnipeg, MB R3T 2N2, Canada. Offers M Sc, PhD. Part-time programs available. Terminal master's awarded for partial completion of doctoral program. *Degree requirements:* For master's, thesis; for doctorate, thesis/dissertation. *Entrance requirements:* For master's and doctorate, GRE. Additional exam requirements/recommendations for international students: Required—TOEFL. *Faculty research:* Clinical pharmacology; neuropharmacology; cardiac, hepatic, and renal pharmacology.

University of Maryland, Baltimore, Graduate School, Graduate Program in Life Sciences, Program in Molecular Medicine, Baltimore, MD 21201. Offers cancer biology (PhD); cell and molecular physiology (PhD); human genetics and genomic medicine (PhD); molecular medicine (MS); molecular toxicology and pharmacology (PhD); MD/PhD. *Students:* 80 full-time (53 women), 11 part-time (4 women); includes 21 minority (8 Black or African American, non-Hispanic/Latino; 6 Asian, non-Hispanic/Latino; 4 Hispanic/Latino; 3 Two or more races, non-Hispanic/Latino), 13 international. Average age 27. 207 applicants, 24% accepted, 15 enrolled. In 2011, 3 master's, 5 doctorates awarded. *Entrance requirements:* Additional exam requirements/recommendations for international students: Required—TOEFL (minimum score 600 paper-based; 100 iBT); Recommended—IELTS (minimum score 7). *Application deadline:* For fall admission, 1/15 for domestic and international students. Application fee: $50. Electronic applications accepted. *Financial support:* In 2011–12, research assistantships with partial tuition reimbursements (averaging $25,000 per year) were awarded; fellowships also available. Financial award application deadline: 3/1. *Unit head:* Dr. Toni Antalis, Director, 410-706-8222, E-mail: tantalis@som.umaryland.edu. *Application contact:* Sharron Graves, Program Coordinator, 410-706-6044, Fax: 410-706-6040, E-mail: sgraves@som.umaryland.edu. Web site: http://molecularmedicine.umaryland.edu.

University of Medicine and Dentistry of New Jersey, Graduate School of Biomedical Sciences, Graduate Programs in Biomedical Sciences–Newark, Department of Pharmacology and Physiology, Newark, NJ 07107. Offers PhD. *Degree requirements:* For doctorate, thesis/dissertation, qualifying exam. *Entrance requirements:* For doctorate, GRE General Test. Additional exam requirements/recommendations for international students: Required—TOEFL. Electronic applications accepted.

University of Miami, Graduate School, Miller School of Medicine, Graduate Programs in Medicine, Department of Molecular and Cellular Pharmacology, Coral Gables, FL 33124. Offers PhD, MD/PhD. *Degree requirements:* For doctorate, thesis/dissertation, dissertation defense, laboratory rotations, qualifying exam. *Entrance requirements:* For doctorate, GRE General Test. Additional exam requirements/recommendations for international students: Required—TOEFL (minimum score 550 paper-based; 213 computer-based). *Faculty research:* Membrane and cardiovascular pharmacology, muscle contraction, hormone action signal transduction, nuclear transport.

University of Michigan, Horace H. Rackham School of Graduate Studies, Program in Biomedical Sciences (PIBS), Department of Pharmacology, Ann Arbor, MI 48109-5632. Offers MS, PhD. *Faculty:* 21 full-time (5 women), 4 part-time/adjunct (0 women). *Students:* 24 full-time (14 women); includes 6 minority (3 Black or African American, non-Hispanic/Latino; 2 Asian, non-Hispanic/Latino; 1 Hispanic/Latino), 2 international. Average age 26. 39 applicants, 26% accepted, 7 enrolled. In 2011, 4 doctorates awarded. *Degree requirements:* For master's, written thesis; for doctorate, thesis/dissertation, oral preliminary exam, oral defense of dissertation. *Entrance requirements:*

For master's and doctorate, GRE General Test, 3 letters of recommendation, research experience, all undergraduate transcripts. Additional exam requirements/recommendations for international students: Required—TOEFL (minimum score 84 iBT). *Application deadline:* For fall admission, 12/1 for domestic students. Application fee: $65 ($75 for international students). Electronic applications accepted. *Financial support:* In 2011–12, 24 students received support, including 16 fellowships with full tuition reimbursements available (averaging $26,500 per year), 8 research assistantships with full tuition reimbursements available (averaging $26,500 per year); scholarships/grants, traineeships, health care benefits, and unspecified assistantships also available. Financial award application deadline: 12/1. *Faculty research:* Signal transduction, addiction research, cancer pharmacology, drug metabolism and pharmacogenetics. *Total annual research expenditures:* $7.2 million. *Unit head:* Dr. Paul F. Hollenberg, Professor/Chair, 734-764-8166, Fax: 734-763-5387, E-mail: phollen@umich.edu. *Application contact:* Michelle S. Melis, Director of Student Life, 734-615-6538, Fax: 734-647-7022, E-mail: msmtegan@umich.edu. Web site: http://www.pharmacology.med.umich.edu/Pharmacology/Home.html.

University of Minnesota, Duluth, Medical School, Program in Pharmacology, Duluth, MN 55812-2496. Offers MS, PhD. MS, PhD offered jointly with University of Minnesota, Twin Cities Campus. Terminal master's awarded for partial completion of doctoral program. *Degree requirements:* For master's, thesis, final oral exam; for doctorate, thesis/dissertation, final oral exam, oral and written preliminary exams. *Entrance requirements:* For master's and doctorate, GRE General Test. Additional exam requirements/recommendations for international students: Required—TOEFL. *Faculty research:* Drug addiction, alcohol and hypertension, neurotransmission, allergic airway disease, auditory neuroscience.

University of Minnesota, Twin Cities Campus, College of Pharmacy and Graduate School, Graduate Programs in Pharmacy, Graduate Program in Experimental and Clinical Pharmacology, Minneapolis, MN 55455-0213. Offers MS, PhD. *Degree requirements:* For doctorate, thesis/dissertation.

University of Minnesota, Twin Cities Campus, Medical School, Department of Pharmacology, Minneapolis, MN 55455. Offers MS, PhD. *Faculty:* 46 full-time (9 women). *Students:* 38 full-time (22 women), 1 (woman) part-time; includes 5 minority (4 Asian, non-Hispanic/Latino; 1 Two or more races, non-Hispanic/Latino), 13 international. Average age 27. 65 applicants, 17% accepted, 8 enrolled. In 2011, 3 master's, 8 doctorates awarded. Terminal master's awarded for partial completion of doctoral program. *Degree requirements:* For master's, thesis (for some programs); for doctorate, thesis/dissertation. *Entrance requirements:* For master's and doctorate, GRE General Test. Additional exam requirements/recommendations for international students: Required—TOEFL (minimum score 603 paper-based; 250 computer-based; 100 iBT). *Application deadline:* For fall admission, 12/15 for domestic and international students. Applications are processed on a rolling basis. Application fee: $75 ($95 for international students). Electronic applications accepted. *Financial support:* In 2011–12, 39 students received support, including 16 fellowships with full tuition reimbursements available (averaging $24,500 per year), 31 research assistantships with full tuition reimbursements, available (averaging $24,500 per year); scholarships/grants, traineeships, and unspecified assistantships also available. Financial award application deadline: 4/15. *Faculty research:* Molecular pharmacology, cancer chemotherapy, neuropharmacology, biochemical pharmacology, behavioral pharmacology. *Total annual research expenditures:* $6.9 million. *Unit head:* Dr. Horace Loh, Head, 612-625-9997, Fax: 612-625-8408, E-mail: lohxx001@umn.edu. *Application contact:* Graduate Program Assistant, 612-625-9997, Fax: 612-625-8408, E-mail: phclgrad@umn.edu. Web site: http://www.pharmacology.med.umn.edu/.

University of Mississippi, Graduate School, School of Pharmacy, Graduate Programs in Pharmacy, Oxford, University, MS 38677. Offers medicinal chemistry (PhD); pharmaceutical sciences (MS); pharmaceutics (PhD); pharmacognosy (PhD); pharmacology (PhD); pharmacy administration (PhD). *Students:* 96 full-time (33 women), 11 part-time (3 women); includes 11 minority (4 Black or African American, non-Hispanic/Latino; 5 Asian, non-Hispanic/Latino; 1 Hispanic/Latino; 1 Two or more races, non-Hispanic/Latino), 68 international. In 2011, 8 master's, 10 doctorates awarded. *Unit head:* Dr. Barbara G. Wells, Dean, 662-915-7265, Fax: 662-915-5704, E-mail: pharmacy@olemiss.edu. *Application contact:* Dr. Christy M. Wyandt, Associate Dean, 662-915-7474, Fax: 662-915-7577, E-mail: cwyandt@olemiss.edu.

University of Mississippi Medical Center, School of Graduate Studies in the Health Sciences, Department of Pharmacology and Toxicology, Jackson, MS 39216-4505. Offers pharmacology (MS, PhD); toxicology (MS, PhD); MD/PhD. Terminal master's awarded for partial completion of doctoral program. *Degree requirements:* For master's, thesis; for doctorate, thesis/dissertation, first authored publication. *Entrance requirements:* For master's and doctorate, GRE General Test, minimum GPA of 3.0. *Faculty research:* Neuropharmacology, environmental toxicology, aging, immunopharmacology, cardiovascular pharmacology.

University of Missouri, School of Medicine and Graduate School, Graduate Programs in Medicine, Department of Medical Pharmacology and Physiology, Columbia, MO 65211. Offers pharmacology (MS, PhD); physiology (MS, PhD). *Faculty:* 29 full-time (4 women), 3 part-time/adjunct (1 woman). *Students:* 17 full-time (10 women), 3 part-time (2 women); includes 2 minority (both Black or African American, non-Hispanic/Latino), 13 international. Average age 27. 34 applicants, 24% accepted, 7 enrolled. In 2011, 1 master's, 1 doctorate awarded. *Degree requirements:* For master's, thesis; for doctorate, thesis/dissertation. *Entrance requirements:* For master's and doctorate, GRE General Test, minimum GPA of 3.0. Additional exam requirements/recommendations for international students: Required—TOEFL (minimum score 500 paper-based; 173 computer-based; 61 iBT). *Application deadline:* For fall admission, 2/1 for domestic students. Application fee: $55 ($75 for international students). *Expenses:* Tuition, state resident: full-time $5881. Tuition, nonresident: full-time $15,183. *Required fees:* $952. Tuition and fees vary according to campus/location and program. *Financial support:* Fellowships, research assistantships, teaching assistantships, and institutionally sponsored loans available. *Faculty research:* Endocrine and metabolic pharmacology, biochemical pharmacology, neuropharmacology, receptors and transmembrane signaling. *Unit head:* Dr. Ron Korthuis, Department Chair, E-mail: korthuisr@missouri.edu. *Application contact:* Monica Elliott, 573-882-4957, E-mail: elliottm@missouri.edu. Web site: http://mpp.missouri.edu/.

University of Missouri–Kansas City, School of Pharmacy, Kansas City, MO 64110-2499. Offers pharmaceutical sciences (PhD); pharmacology and toxicology (PhD); pharmacy (Pharm D). PhD offered through School of Graduate Studies. *Accreditation:* ACPE (one or more programs are accredited). Postbaccalaureate distance learning degree programs offered (minimal on-campus study). *Faculty:* 54 full-time (22 women), 6 part-time/adjunct (3 women). *Students:* 364 full-time (233 women); includes 39 minority (10 Black or African American, non-Hispanic/Latino; 1 American Indian or Alaska Native, non-Hispanic/Latino; 24 Asian, non-Hispanic/Latino; 2 Hispanic/Latino; 2 Two or more races, non-Hispanic/Latino), 4 international. Average age 25. 419 applicants, 40% accepted, 162 enrolled. In 2011, 113 doctorates awarded. *Degree*

requirements: For doctorate, comprehensive exam (for some programs), thesis/dissertation (for some programs). *Entrance requirements:* For doctorate, PCAT (for Pharm D). Additional exam requirements/recommendations for international students: Required—TOEFL (minimum score 550 paper-based; 213 computer-based; 80 iBT). *Application deadline:* For fall admission, 3/1 for domestic and international students. Applications are processed on a rolling basis. Application fee: $45 ($50 for international students). Electronic applications accepted. *Expenses:* Contact institution. *Financial support:* In 2011–12, 31 research assistantships with full and partial tuition reimbursements (averaging $9,797 per year), 23 teaching assistantships with full tuition reimbursements (averaging $11,995 per year) were awarded; career-related internships or fieldwork, Federal Work-Study, Institutionally sponsored loans, tuition waivers (full and partial), and unspecified assistantships also available. Financial award application deadline: 3/1; financial award applicants required to submit FAFSA. *Faculty research:* Bio-organic and medicinal chemistry, drug delivery, pharmaceutics, molecular neurobiology, neurology. *Unit head:* Dr. Russell B. Melchert, Dean, 816-235-1609, Fax: 816-235-5190, E-mail: melchertr@umkc.edu. *Application contact:* Shelly M. Janasz, Director, Student Services, 816-235-2400, Fax: 816-235-5190, E-mail: janaszs@umkc.edu. Web site: http://pharmacy.umkc.edu/.

University of Nebraska Medical Center, Graduate Studies, Department of Pharmacology and Experimental Neuroscience, Omaha, NE 68198. Offers neuroscience (MS, PhD); pharmacology (MS, PhD). Terminal master's awarded for partial completion of doctoral program. *Degree requirements:* For master's, comprehensive exam, thesis; for doctorate, comprehensive exam, thesis/dissertation. *Entrance requirements:* For master's and doctorate, GRE General Test. Additional exam requirements/recommendations for international students: Required—TOEFL (minimum score 600 paper-based; 250 computer-based). Electronic applications accepted. *Faculty research:* Neuropharmacology, molecular pharmacology, toxicology, molecular biology, neuroscience.

The University of North Carolina at Chapel Hill, School of Medicine and Graduate School, Graduate Programs in Medicine, Department of Pharmacology, Chapel Hill, NC 27599-7365. Offers PhD. *Degree requirements:* For doctorate, comprehensive exam, thesis/dissertation. *Entrance requirements:* For doctorate, GRE General Test, minimum GPA of 3.0. Additional exam requirements/recommendations for international students: Required—TOEFL. Electronic applications accepted. *Faculty research:* Signal transduction, cell adhesion, receptors, ion channels.

University of North Dakota, Graduate School and Graduate School, Graduate Programs in Medicine, Department of Pharmacology, Physiology, and Therapeutics, Grand Forks, ND 58202. Offers pharmacology (MS, PhD); physiology (MS, PhD). *Degree requirements:* For master's, comprehensive exam, thesis; for doctorate, thesis/dissertation, written and oral exams. *Entrance requirements:* For master's, GRE General Test or MCAT, minimum GPA of 3.0; for doctorate, GRE General Test, minimum GPA of 3.5. Additional exam requirements/recommendations for international students: Required—TOEFL (minimum score 550 paper-based; 213 computer-based; 79 iBT), IELTS (minimum score 6.5). Electronic applications accepted.

University of North Texas Health Science Center at Fort Worth, Graduate School of Biomedical Sciences, Fort Worth, TX 76107-2699. Offers anatomy and cell biology (MS, PhD); biochemistry and molecular biology (MS, PhD); biomedical sciences (MS, PhD); biotechnology (MS); forensic genetics (MS); integrative physiology (MS, PhD); medical science (MS); microbiology and immunology (MS, PhD); pharmacology (MS, PhD); science education (MS); DO/MS; DO/PhD. Terminal master's awarded for partial completion of doctoral program. *Degree requirements:* For master's, thesis; for doctorate, thesis/dissertation. *Entrance requirements:* For master's and doctorate, GRE General Test. Additional exam requirements/recommendations for international students: Required—TOEFL. *Expenses:* Contact institution. *Faculty research:* Alzheimer's disease, aging, eye diseases, cancer, cardiovascular disease.

University of Pennsylvania, Perelman School of Medicine, Biomedical Graduate Studies, Graduate Group in Pharmacology, Philadelphia, PA 19104. Offers pharmacology (PhD); MD/PhD; VMD/PhD. *Faculty:* 93. *Students:* 62 full-time (33 women); includes 15 minority (1 Black or African American, non-Hispanic/Latino; 11 Asian, non-Hispanic/Latino; 3 Hispanic/Latino), 6 international. 90 applicants, 20% accepted, 9 enrolled. In 2011, 12 doctorates awarded. *Degree requirements:* For doctorate, thesis/dissertation. *Entrance requirements:* For doctorate, GRE General Test, previous course work in physical or natural science. Additional exam requirements/recommendations for international students: Required—TOEFL. *Application deadline:* For fall admission, 12/1 priority date for domestic students, 12/1 for international students. Applications are processed on a rolling basis. Application fee: $80. Electronic applications accepted. *Expenses: Tuition:* Full-time $26,660; part-time $4944 per course. *Required fees:* $2318; $291 per course. Tuition and fees vary according to course load, degree level and program. *Financial support:* In 2011–12, 62 students received support. Fellowships, research assistantships, scholarships/grants, traineeships, and unspecified assistantships available. *Faculty research:* Properties and regulation of receptors for biogenic amines, molecular aspects of transduction, mechanisms of biosynthesis, biological mechanisms of depression, developmental events in the nervous system. *Unit head:* Dr. Vladimir Muzykantov, Chair. *Application contact:* Sarah Squire, Coordinator. Web site: http://www.med.upenn.edu/ggps.

University of Prince Edward Island, Atlantic Veterinary College, Graduate Program in Veterinary Medicine, Charlottetown, PE C1A 4P3, Canada. Offers anatomy (M Sc, PhD); bacteriology (M Sc, PhD); clinical pharmacology (M Sc, PhD); clinical sciences (M Sc, PhD); epidemiology (M Sc, PhD), including reproduction; fish health (M Sc, PhD); food animal nutrition (M Sc, PhD); immunology (M Sc, PhD); microanatomy (M Sc, PhD); parasitology (M Sc, PhD); pathology (M Sc, PhD); pharmacology (M Sc, PhD); physiology (M Sc, PhD); toxicology (M Sc, PhD); veterinary science (M Vet Sc); virology (M Sc, PhD). Part-time programs available. *Degree requirements:* For master's, thesis; for doctorate, thesis/dissertation. *Entrance requirements:* For master's, DVM, B Sc honors degree, or equivalent; for doctorate, M Sc. Additional exam requirements/recommendations for international students: Required—TOEFL (minimum score 550 paper-based; 213 computer-based; 80 iBT). *Expenses:* Contact institution. *Faculty research:* Animal health management, infectious diseases, fin fish and shellfish health, basic biomedical sciences, ecosystem health.

University of Puerto Rico, Medical Sciences Campus, School of Medicine, Division of Graduate Studies, Department of Pharmacology and Toxicology, San Juan, PR 00936-5067. Offers MS, PhD. *Degree requirements:* For master's, one foreign language, thesis; for doctorate, one foreign language, comprehensive exam, thesis/dissertation. *Entrance requirements:* For master's and doctorate, GRE General Test, GRE Subject Test, interview, minimum GPA of 3.0, 3 letters of recommendation. Electronic applications accepted. *Faculty research:* Cardiovascular, central nervous system, and endocrine pharmacology; anti-cancer drugs; sodium pump; mitochondrial DNA repair; Huntington's disease.

University of Rhode Island, Graduate School, College of Pharmacy, Department of Biomedical and Pharmaceutical Sciences, Kingston, RI 02881. Offers medicinal

chemistry and pharmacognosy (MS, PhD); pharmaceutics and pharmacokinetics (MS, PhD); pharmacology and toxicology (MS, PhD). Part-time programs available. *Faculty:* 20 full-time (6 women), 2 part-time/adjunct (1 woman). *Students:* 41 full-time (21 women), 16 part-time (7 women); includes 8 minority (1 Black or African American, non-Hispanic/Latino; 6 Asian, non-Hispanic/Latino; 1 Two or more races, non-Hispanic/Latino), 24 international. In 2011, 4 master's, 3 doctorates awarded. *Entrance requirements:* For master's and doctorate, GRE, 2 letters of recommendation. Additional exam requirements/recommendations for international students: Required—TOEFL (minimum score 550 paper-based; 213 computer-based). Application fee: $65. Electronic applications accepted. *Expenses:* Tuition, state resident: full-time $10,432; part-time $580 per credit hour. Tuition, nonresident: full-time $23,130; part-time $1285 per credit hour. *Required fees:* $1362; $36 per credit hour. $35 per semester. One-time fee: $130. *Financial support:* In 2011–12, 8 research assistantships with partial tuition reimbursements (averaging $9,529 per year), 11 teaching assistantships with full and partial tuition reimbursements (averaging $9,807 per year) were awarded. Financial award applicants required to submit FAFSA. *Faculty research:* Chemical carcinogenesis with a major emphasis on the structural and synthetic aspects of DNA-adduct formation, drug-drug/herb interaction, drug-genetic interaction, signaling of nuclear receptors, transcriptional regulation, oncogenesis. *Unit head:* Dr. Clinton O. Chichester, Chair, 401-874-5034, Fax: 401-874-5787, E-mail: chichester@uri.edu. *Application contact:* Dr. David C. Rowley, Graduate Coordinator, 401-874-9228, Fax: 401-874-2516, E-mail: drowley@uri.edu. Web site: http://www.uri.edu/pharmacy/departments/bps/index.shtml.

University of Rochester, School of Medicine and Dentistry, Graduate Programs in Medicine and Dentistry, Department of Pharmacology and Physiology, Programs in Pharmacology, Rochester, NY 14627. Offers MS, PhD. Terminal master's awarded for partial completion of doctoral program. *Degree requirements:* For master's, thesis; for doctorate, thesis/dissertation, qualifying exam. *Entrance requirements:* For master's and doctorate, GRE General Test. *Expenses:* Tuition: Full-time $41,040.

University of Saskatchewan, College of Medicine, Department of Pharmacology, Saskatoon, SK S7N 5A2, Canada. Offers M Sc, PhD. *Degree requirements:* For master's, thesis; for doctorate, thesis/dissertation. *Entrance requirements:* Additional exam requirements/recommendations for international students: Required—TOEFL. *Faculty research:* Neuropharmacology, mechanisms of action of anticancer drugs, clinical pharmacology, cardiovascular pharmacology, toxicology: alcohol-related changes in fetal brain development.

The University of South Dakota, Graduate School, School of Medicine and Graduate School, Biomedical Sciences Graduate Program, Physiology and Pharmacology Group, Vermillion, SD 57069-2390. Offers MS, PhD. Terminal master's awarded for partial completion of doctoral program. *Degree requirements:* For master's, thesis; for doctorate, comprehensive exam, thesis/dissertation. *Entrance requirements:* For master's and doctorate, GRE General Test, minimum GPA of 3.0. Additional exam requirements/recommendations for international students: Required—TOEFL (minimum score 550 paper-based; 213 computer-based; 80 iBT), IELTS (minimum score 6). Electronic applications accepted. *Expenses:* Contact institution. *Faculty research:* Pulmonary physiology and pharmacology, drug abuse, reproduction, signal transduction, cardiovascular physiology and pharmacology.

The University of Texas at Austin, Graduate School, College of Pharmacy, Graduate Programs in Pharmacy, Austin, TX 78712-1111. Offers health outcomes and pharmacy practice (PhD); health outcomes and pharmacy practice (MS); medicinal chemistry (PhD); pharmaceutics (PhD); pharmacology and toxicology (PhD); pharmacotherapy (MS, PhD); translational science (PhD). PhD in translational science offered jointly with The University of Texas Health Science Center at San Antonio and The University of Texas at San Antonio. *Degree requirements:* For master's, thesis; for doctorate, thesis/dissertation. *Entrance requirements:* For master's and doctorate, GRE General Test. *Application deadline:* For fall admission, 1/15 priority date for domestic students, 1/15 for international students; for spring admission, 10/1 for domestic students. Applications are processed on a rolling basis. Application fee: $50 ($75 for international students). Electronic applications accepted. *Financial support:* Fellowships, research assistantships, teaching assistantships with partial tuition reimbursements, Federal Work-Study, scholarships/grants, health care benefits, and unspecified assistantships available. Financial award application deadline: 2/1; financial award applicants required to submit FAFSA. *Faculty research:* Synthetic medical chemistry, synthetic molecular biology, bio-organic chemistry, pharmacoeconomics, pharmacy practice. *Unit head:* Dr. M. Lynn Crismon, Dean, 512-471-3718, E-mail: lynn.crismon@austin.utexas.edu.

The University of Texas Health Science Center at San Antonio, Graduate School of Biomedical Sciences, Department of Pharmacology, San Antonio, TX 78229-3900. Offers neuroscience (PhD). *Degree requirements:* For doctorate, comprehensive exam, thesis/dissertation. *Entrance requirements:* For doctorate, GRE General Test, minimum GPA of 3.0. Additional exam requirements/recommendations for international students: Required—TOEFL (minimum score 560 paper-based; 220 computer-based; 68 iBT). Electronic applications accepted. *Faculty research:* Neuropharmacology, autonomic and endocrine homeostasis, aging, cancer biology.

The University of Texas Medical Branch, Graduate School of Biomedical Sciences, Program in Pharmacology and Toxicology, Galveston, TX 77555. Offers pharmacology (MS); pharmacology and toxicology (PhD). *Degree requirements:* For master's, thesis or alternative; for doctorate, thesis/dissertation. *Entrance requirements:* For master's and doctorate, GRE General Test. Additional exam requirements/recommendations for international students: Required—TOEFL (minimum score 550 paper-based; 213 computer-based).

University of the Sciences in Philadelphia, College of Graduate Studies, Program in Chemistry, Biochemistry and Pharmacognosy, Philadelphia, PA 19104-4495. Offers biochemistry (MS, PhD); chemistry (MS, PhD); pharmacognosy (MS, PhD). Part-time programs available. *Degree requirements:* For master's, thesis, qualifying exams; for doctorate, comprehensive exam, thesis/dissertation, qualifying exams. *Entrance requirements:* For master's and doctorate, GRE General Test, GRE Subject Test. Additional exam requirements/recommendations for international students: Required—TOEFL, TWE. *Expenses:* Contact institution. *Faculty research:* Organic and medicinal synthesis, mass spectroscopy use in protein analysis, study of analogues of taxol, cholesteryl esters.

University of the Sciences in Philadelphia, College of Graduate Studies, Program in Pharmacology and Toxicology, Philadelphia, PA 19104-4495. Offers pharmacology (MS, PhD); toxicology (MS, PhD). Terminal master's awarded for partial completion of doctoral program. *Degree requirements:* For master's, thesis; for doctorate, comprehensive exam, thesis/dissertation. *Entrance requirements:* For master's and doctorate, GRE General Test. Additional exam requirements/recommendations for international students: Required—TOEFL, TWE. *Expenses:* Contact institution. *Faculty research:* Autonomic, cardiovascular, cellular, and molecular pharmacology; mechanisms of carcinogenesis; drug metabolism.

The University of Toledo, College of Graduate Studies, College of Pharmacy and Pharmaceutical Sciences, Program in Pharmaceutical Sciences, Toledo, OH 43606-3390. Offers administrative pharmacy (MSPS); industrial pharmacy (MSPS); pharmacology toxicology (MSPS). *Degree requirements:* For master's, thesis. *Entrance requirements:* For master's, GRE General Test. Additional exam requirements/recommendations for international students: Required—TOEFL (minimum score 550 paper-based; 213 computer-based; 80 iBT). Electronic applications accepted.

University of Toronto, Faculty of Medicine, Department of Pharmacology and Toxicology, Toronto, ON M5S 1A1, Canada. Offers pharmacology (M Sc, PhD). Part-time programs available. *Degree requirements:* For master's, thesis; for doctorate, thesis/dissertation. *Entrance requirements:* For master's, B Sc or equivalent; background in pharmacology, biochemistry, and physiology; minimum B+ earned in at least 4 senior level classes; for doctorate, minimum B+ average. Additional exam requirements/recommendations for international students: Required—TOEFL (minimum score 580 paper-based; 93 iBT), TWE (minimum score 5). Electronic applications accepted.

University of Utah, Graduate School, College of Pharmacy, Department of Pharmacology and Toxicology, Salt Lake City, UT 84112. Offers PhD. *Faculty:* 15 full-time (4 women), 2 part-time/adjunct (0 women). *Students:* 13 full-time (7 women), 1 part-time (0 women); includes 1 minority (Hispanic/Latino), 4 international. Average age 28. 64 applicants, 13% accepted, 3 enrolled. In 2011, 6 degrees awarded. Terminal master's awarded for partial completion of doctoral program. *Median time to degree:* Of those who began their doctoral program in fall 2003, 95% received their degree in 8 years or less. *Degree requirements:* For doctorate, comprehensive exam, thesis/dissertation, final exam. *Entrance requirements:* For doctorate, GRE General Test, BS in biology, chemistry, neuroscience. Additional exam requirements/recommendations for international students: Required—TOEFL (minimum score 600 paper-based; 250 computer-based; 100 iBT). *Application deadline:* For fall admission, 1/15 for domestic and international students. Application fee: $55 ($65 for international students). *Financial support:* In 2011–12, 13 students received support, including 13 research assistantships with full tuition reimbursements available (averaging $26,000 per year); fellowships with tuition reimbursements available also available. Financial award application deadline: 1/15. *Faculty research:* Neuropharmacology, neurochemistry, biochemistry, molecular pharmacology, analytical chemistry. *Total annual research expenditures:* $5.4 million. *Unit head:* Dr. William R. Crowley, Chairman, 801-581-6287, Fax: 801-585-5111, E-mail: william.crowley@deans.pharm.utah.edu. *Application contact:* Sandy Hiskey, Program Assistant, 801-581-6287, Fax: 801-585-5111, E-mail: sandy.hiskey@utah.edu. Web site: http://www.pharmacy.utah.edu/pharmtox/.

University of Vermont, College of Medicine and Graduate College, Graduate Programs in Medicine, Department of Pharmacology, Burlington, VT 05405. Offers MS, PhD, MD/MS, MD/PhD. *Faculty:* 12 full-time (1 woman). *Students:* 5 (2 women); includes 1 minority (Hispanic/Latino), 2 international. 36 applicants, 0% accepted, 0 enrolled. In 2011, 1 degree awarded. *Degree requirements:* For master's, thesis; for doctorate, thesis/dissertation. *Entrance requirements:* For master's and doctorate, GRE General Test. Additional exam requirements/recommendations for international students: Required—TOEFL (minimum score 550 paper-based; 213 computer-based; 80 iBT). *Application deadline:* For fall admission, 1/15 priority date for domestic students, 1/15 for international students. Applications are processed on a rolling basis. Application fee: $40. Electronic applications accepted. *Financial support:* Fellowships, research assistantships, and teaching assistantships available. Financial award application deadline: 3/1. *Faculty research:* Cardiovascular drugs, anticancer drugs. *Unit head:* Dr. M. Nelson, Chairperson, 802-656-2500. *Application contact:* Dr. Anthony Morielli, Director of Graduate Studies, 802-656-2500.

University of Virginia, School of Medicine, Department of Pharmacology, Charlottesville, VA 22903. Offers PhD, MD/PhD. *Faculty:* 25 full-time (7 women), 1 part-time/adjunct (0 women). *Students:* 10 full-time (8 women), 1 international. Average age 26. In 2011, 6 doctorates awarded. *Degree requirements:* For doctorate, thesis/dissertation. *Entrance requirements:* For doctorate, GRE General Test, GRE Subject Test (recommended), 2 letters of recommendation. Additional exam requirements/recommendations for international students: Required—TOEFL. *Application deadline:* For fall admission, 1/15 for domestic and international students. Applications are processed on a rolling basis. Application fee: $60. Electronic applications accepted. *Financial support:* Fellowships, research assistantships, and teaching assistantships available. Financial award applicants required to submit FAFSA. *Unit head:* Dr. Douglas A. Bayliss, Chairman, 434-924-1919, Fax: 434-982-3878, E-mail: dab3y@virginia.edu. *Application contact:* Lesley L. Thomas, Director, Admissions Office, 434-924-5571, Fax: 434-982-2586, E-mail: medsch-adm@virginia.edu. Web site: http://www.healthsystem.virginia.edu/internet/pharmacology/.

University of Washington, Graduate School, School of Medicine, Graduate Programs in Medicine, Department of Pharmacology, Seattle, WA 98195. Offers PhD. *Degree requirements:* For doctorate, thesis/dissertation. *Entrance requirements:* For doctorate, GRE General Test, minimum GPA of 3.0. *Faculty research:* Neuroscience, cell physiology, molecular biology, regulation of metabolism, signal transduction.

University of Wisconsin–Madison, School of Medicine and Public Health and Graduate School, Graduate Programs in Medicine, Molecular and Cellular Pharmacology Program, Madison, WI 53706. Offers PhD. *Faculty:* 55 full-time (12 women). *Students:* 41 full-time (22 women); includes 10 minority (2 Black or African American, non-Hispanic/Latino; 5 Asian, non-Hispanic/Latino; 2 Hispanic/Latino; 1 Native Hawaiian or other Pacific Islander, non-Hispanic/Latino), 5 international. Average age 26. 69 applicants, 20% accepted, 5 enrolled. In 2011, 12 doctorates awarded. *Degree requirements:* For doctorate, comprehensive exam, thesis/dissertation. *Entrance requirements:* For doctorate, GRE. Additional exam requirements/recommendations for international students: Required—TOEFL (minimum score 550 paper-based; 213 computer-based). *Application deadline:* For fall admission, 12/1 priority date for domestic students, 12/1 for international students. Applications are processed on a rolling basis. Application fee: $56. Electronic applications accepted. *Expenses:* Tuition, state resident: full-time $10,296; part-time $643.51 per credit. Tuition, nonresident: full-time $24,054; part-time $1503.40 per credit. *Required fees:* $70.06 per credit. Tuition and fees vary according to course load, campus/location, program and reciprocity agreements. *Financial support:* In 2011–12, 41 students received support, including 11 fellowships with full tuition reimbursements available (averaging $24,000 per year), 30 research assistantships with full tuition reimbursements available (averaging $24,000 per year), teaching assistantships with full tuition reimbursements available (averaging $24,000 per year); scholarships/grants, traineeships, health care benefits, and unspecified assistantships also available. *Faculty research:* Protein kinases, signaling pathways, neurotransmitters, molecular recognition, receptors and transporters. *Unit head:* Dr. Patricia J. Keely, Director, 608-213-6820, E-mail: pjkeely@wisc.edu. *Application contact:* Lynn Louise Squire, Student Services Coordinator, 608-262-9826, E-mail: lsquire@wisc.edu. Web site: http://molpharm.wisc.edu/.

Vanderbilt University, Graduate School and School of Medicine, Department of Pharmacology, Nashville, TN 37240-1001. Offers PhD, MD/PhD. *Faculty:* 23 full-time (6 women). *Students:* 51 full-time (22 women); includes 9 minority (4 Black or African American, non-Hispanic/Latino; 3 Asian, non-Hispanic/Latino; 2 Two or more races, non-Hispanic/Latino), 7 international. Average age 28. In 2011, 9 doctorates awarded. *Degree requirements:* For doctorate, comprehensive exam, thesis/dissertation, preliminary, qualifying, and final exams. *Entrance requirements:* For doctorate, GRE General Test, GRE Subject Test (recommended). Additional exam requirements/recommendations for international students: Required—TOEFL (minimum score 570 paper-based; 230 computer-based; 88 iBT). *Application deadline:* For fall admission, 1/15 for domestic and international students. Application fee: $0. Electronic applications accepted. *Financial support:* Fellowships with full tuition reimbursements, research assistantships with full tuition reimbursements, Federal Work-Study, institutionally sponsored loans, scholarships/grants, traineeships, health care benefits, and tuition waivers (partial) available. Financial award application deadline: 1/15; financial award applicants required to submit CSS PROFILE or FAFSA. *Faculty research:* Molecular pharmacology, neuropharmacology, drug disposition and toxicology, genetic mechanics, cell regulation. *Unit head:* Dr. Heidi E. Hamm, Chair, 615-343-3533, Fax: 615-343-1084, E-mail: heidi.hamm@vanderbilt.edu. *Application contact:* Dr. Karen Gieg, Director of Graduate Studies/Educational Programs Coordinator, 615-322-1182, Fax: 615-936-3910, E-mail: karen.gieg@vanderbilt.edu. Web site: http://www.mc.vanderbilt.edu/pharmacology/.

Virginia Commonwealth University, Medical College of Virginia-Professional Programs, School of Medicine, School of Medicine Graduate Programs, Department of Pharmacology and Toxicology, Richmond, VA 23284-9005. Offers neuroscience (PhD); pharmacology (Certificate); pharmacology and toxicology (MS, PhD); MD/PhD. Terminal master's awarded for partial completion of doctoral program. *Degree requirements:* For master's, thesis; for doctorate, thesis/dissertation, comprehensive oral and written exams. *Entrance requirements:* For master's and doctorate, GRE or MCAT. Additional exam requirements/recommendations for international students: Required—TOEFL (minimum score 600 paper-based; 250 computer-based; 100 iBT). Electronic applications accepted. *Expenses:* Tuition, state resident: full-time $9133; part-time $507 per credit. Tuition, nonresident: full-time $18,777; part-time $1043 per credit. *Required fees:* $77 per credit. Tuition and fees vary according to degree level, campus/location, program and student level. *Faculty research:* Drug abuse, drug metabolism, pharmacodynamics, peptide synthesis, receptor mechanisms.

Virginia Commonwealth University, Program in Pre-Medical Basic Health Sciences, Richmond, VA 23284-9005. Offers anatomy (CBHS); biochemistry (CBHS); human genetics (CBHS); microbiology (CBHS); pharmacology (CBHS); physiology (CBHS). *Entrance requirements:* For degree, GRE, MCAT or DAT, course work in organic chemistry, minimum undergraduate GPA of 2.8. Additional exam requirements/recommendations for international students: Required—TOEFL (minimum score 600 paper-based). Electronic applications accepted. *Expenses:* Tuition, state resident: full-time $9133; part-time $507 per credit. Tuition, nonresident: full-time $18,777; part-time $1043 per credit. *Required fees:* $77 per credit. Tuition and fees vary according to degree level, campus/location, program and student level.

Wake Forest University, School of Medicine and Graduate School of Arts and Sciences, Graduate Programs in Medicine, Program in Physiology and Pharmacology, Winston-Salem, NC 27109. Offers pharmacology (PhD); physiology (PhD); MD/PhD. *Degree requirements:* For doctorate, thesis/dissertation. *Entrance requirements:* For doctorate, GRE General Test. Additional exam requirements/recommendations for international students: Required—TOEFL. Electronic applications accepted. *Faculty research:* Aging, substance abuse, cardiovascular control, endocrine systems, toxicology.

Wayne State University, Eugene Applebaum College of Pharmacy and Health Sciences, Department of Pharmaceutical Sciences, Detroit, MI 48202. Offers medicinal chemistry (MS, PhD); pharmaceutics (MS, PhD); pharmacology/toxicology (MS, PhD). *Accreditation:* ACPE (one or more programs are accredited). Part-time programs available. *Students:* 15 full-time (6 women), 4 part-time (3 women); includes 2 minority (1 Black or African American, non-Hispanic/Latino; 1 Asian, non-Hispanic/Latino), 11 international. Average age 27. 234 applicants, 3% accepted, 7 enrolled. In 2011, 1 degree awarded. *Degree requirements:* For master's, thesis; for doctorate, thesis/dissertation. *Entrance requirements:* For master's, GRE General Test, bachelor's degree with minimum GPA of 3.0, three letters of recommendation, personal statement; for doctorate, GRE General Test, bachelor's degree with minimum GPA of 3.0, three letters of recommendation. Additional exam requirements/recommendations for international students: Required—TOEFL (minimum score 550 paper-based; 213 computer-based); Recommended—TWE (minimum score 6). *Application deadline:* For fall admission, 3/1 for domestic and international students. Application fee: $50. Electronic applications accepted. *Expenses:* Tuition, state resident: part-time $512.85 per credit. Tuition, nonresident: part-time $1132.65 per credit. *Required fees:* $26.60 per credit. $199.65 per semester. Tuition and fees vary according to course load and program. *Financial support:* In 2011–12, 1 fellowship with tuition reimbursement (averaging $1,800 per year), 11 research assistantships with full tuition reimbursements (averaging $23,682 per year) were awarded; career-related internships or fieldwork, scholarships/grants, health care benefits, and unspecified assistantships also available. Support available to part-time students. *Faculty research:* Mechanisms of resistance of bacteria to anti-microbial agents, drug metabolism and disposition in children, treatment strategies for stroke/neurovascular disease, prevalence and treatment of diabetes in Arab-Americans, ethnic variability in development of osteoporosis. *Unit head:* Dr. George B. Corcoran, Chair, 313-577-1737, Fax: 313-577-2033, E-mail: corcoran@wayne.edu. *Application contact:* 313-577-1047, E-mail: pscgrad@wayne.edu. Web site: http://www.cphs.wayne.edu/psc/index.php.

Wayne State University, School of Medicine, Department of Pharmacology, Detroit, MI 48202. Offers MS, PhD, MD/PhD. *Students:* 7 full-time (6 women); includes 2 minority (1 Asian, non-Hispanic/Latino; 1 Hispanic/Latino), 2 international. Average age 27. 54 applicants, 6% accepted, 2 enrolled. In 2011, 7 degrees awarded. *Degree requirements:* For doctorate, thesis/dissertation. *Entrance requirements:* For doctorate, GRE General Test, minimum undergraduate GPA of 3.0 for upper-division course work, personal statement, three letters of recommendation. Additional exam requirements/recommendations for international students: Required—TOEFL (minimum score 600 paper-based; 250 computer-based; 100 iBT); Recommended—TWE (minimum score 6). *Application deadline:* For fall admission, 4/15 for domestic and international students. Electronic applications accepted. *Expenses:* Tuition, state resident: part-time $512.85 per credit. Tuition, nonresident: part-time $1132.65 per credit. *Required fees:* $26.60 per credit. $199.65 per semester. Tuition and fees vary according to course load and program. *Financial support:* In 2011–12, 1 fellowship with tuition reimbursement (averaging $21,787 per year), 7 research assistantships with tuition reimbursements (averaging $21,946 per year) were awarded; teaching assistantships, health care benefits, and All students accepted in the program are given full stipend support ($20,000 per year) with tuition and full medical also available. *Faculty research:* Molecular and cellular biology of cancer and anti-cancer therapies; molecular and cellular biology of protein trafficking, signal transduction and aging; environmental toxicology and drug metabolism; functional cellular and in vivo imaging; neuroscience. *Unit head:* Dr. Bonnie Sloane, Chair, 313-577-1580, Fax: 313-577-6739, E-mail: bsloane@med.wayne.edu. *Application contact:* Dr. Hai-Young Wu, Chairman, Graduate Admissions Committee, 313-577-6737, E-mail: haiwu@med.wayne.edu. Web site: http://www.med.wayne.edu/pharmacology/.

Weill Cornell Medical College, Weill Cornell Graduate School of Medical Sciences, Pharmacology Program, New York, NY 10065. Offers MS, PhD. *Faculty:* 30 full-time (7 women). *Students:* 66 full-time (38 women); includes 15 minority (3 Black or African American, non-Hispanic/Latino; 8 Asian, non-Hispanic/Latino; 1 Hispanic/Latino; 3 Native Hawaiian or other Pacific Islander, non-Hispanic/Latino), 18 international. 75 applicants, 29% accepted, 11 enrolled. In 2011, 3 master's, 11 doctorates awarded. Terminal master's awarded for partial completion of doctoral program. *Degree requirements:* For master's, comprehensive exam; for doctorate, thesis/dissertation, final exam. *Entrance requirements:* For doctorate, GRE General Test, previous course work in natural and/or health sciences. Additional exam requirements/recommendations for international students: Required—TOEFL. *Application deadline:* For fall admission, 12/1 for domestic students. Application fee: $60. *Expenses: Tuition:* Full-time $46,001. *Financial support:* In 2011–12, 7 fellowships (averaging $21,210 per year) were awarded; scholarships/grants, health care benefits, and stipends (given to all students) also available. *Faculty research:* Modulation of gene expression by drugs, signal transduction, nitric oxide signaling RNA trafficking, neuropharmacology of opiates. *Unit head:* Dr. Yueming Li, Director, 646-888-2194, E-mail: liy@mskcc.org. *Application contact:* Aileen Ibagon, Program Coordinator, 212-746-6250, E-mail: aii@med.cornell.edu. Web site: http://weill.cornell.edu/gradschool/program/pharmacology.html.

West Virginia University, School of Medicine, Graduate Programs at the Health Sciences Center, Interdisciplinary Graduate Programs in Biomedical Sciences, Program in Pharmaceutical and Pharmacological Sciences, Morgantown, WV 26506. Offers MS, PhD, MD/PhD. *Degree requirements:* For doctorate, comprehensive exam, thesis/dissertation. *Entrance requirements:* For doctorate, GRE General Test, minimum GPA of 3.0. Additional exam requirements/recommendations for international students: Required—TOEFL. Electronic applications accepted. *Faculty research:* Medicinal chemistry, pharmacokinetics, nano-pharmaceutics, polymer-based drug delivery, molecular therapeutics.

Wright State University, School of Medicine, Program in Pharmacology and Toxicology, Dayton, OH 45435. Offers MS. *Degree requirements:* For master's, thesis optional.

Yale University, School of Medicine and Graduate School of Arts and Sciences, Combined Program in Biological and Biomedical Sciences (BBS), Department of Pharmacology, New Haven, CT 06520. Offers PhD. *Degree requirements:* For doctorate, thesis/dissertation. *Entrance requirements:* For doctorate, GRE General Test. Additional exam requirements/recommendations for international students: Required—TOEFL. *Expenses:* Contact institution.

Yale University, School of Medicine and Graduate School of Arts and Sciences, Combined Program in Biological and Biomedical Sciences (BBS), Pharmacological Sciences and Molecular Medicine Track, New Haven, CT 06520. Offers PhD, MD/PhD. *Degree requirements:* For doctorate, thesis/dissertation. *Entrance requirements:* For doctorate, GRE General Test. Additional exam requirements/recommendations for international students: Required—TOEFL. Electronic applications accepted.

Toxicology

American University of Beirut, Graduate Programs, Faculty of Medicine, Beirut, Lebanon. Offers anatomy, cell biology and human morphology (MS); biochemistry and medical genetics (MS); biomedical sciences (PhD); experimental pathology, immunology and microbiology (MS); medicine (MD); neuroscience (MS); pharmacology and toxicology (MS). Part-time programs available. *Faculty:* 232 full-time (58 women), 68 part-time/adjunct (7 women). *Students:* 346 full-time (135 women), 69 part-time (57 women). Average age 23. In 2011, 20 master's, 82 doctorates awarded. *Degree requirements:* For master's, one foreign language, comprehensive exam, thesis (for some programs). *Entrance requirements:* For master's, letter of recommendation; for doctorate, MCAT, bachelor's degree. Additional exam requirements/recommendations for international students: Required—TOEFL (minimum score 600 paper-based; 250 computer-based; 100 iBT), IELTS (minimum score 7.5). *Application deadline:* For fall admission, 4/30 for domestic and international students; for spring admission, 11/1 for domestic and international students. Application fee: $50. *Expenses: Tuition:* Full-time $12,780; part-time $710 per credit. Tuition and fees vary according to course load and program. *Financial support:* In 2011–12, 19 students received support. Career-related internships or fieldwork, institutionally sponsored loans, scholarships/grants, health care benefits, and unspecified assistantships available. Financial award application deadline: 2/2. *Faculty research:* Cancer research (targeted therapy, mechanisms of leukemogenesis, tumor cell extravasation and metastasis, cancer stem cells); stem cell research (regenerative medicine, drug discovery); genetic research (neurogenetics, hereditary cardiomyopathy, hemoglobinopathies, pharmacogenomics, proteomics); neuroscience research (pain, neurodegenerative disorder); metabolism (inflammation and metabolism, metabolic disorder, diabetes mellitus); vascular and renal biology, signal transduction. *Total annual research expenditures:* $2.3 million. *Unit head:* Dr. Mohamed Sayegh, Dean, 961-1350000 Ext. 4700, Fax: 961-1744464, E-mail: msayegh@aub.edu.lb. *Application contact:* Dr. Salim Kanaan, Director, Admissions Office, 961-1350000 Ext. 2594, Fax: 961-1750775, E-mail: sk00@aub.edu.lb. Web site: http://www.aub.edu.lb/fm/fm_home/Pages/index.aspx.

Toxicology

Brown University, Graduate School, Division of Biology and Medicine, Program in Pathology and Laboratory Medicine, Providence, RI 02912. Offers biology (PhD); cancer biology (PhD); immunology and infection (PhD); medical science (PhD); pathobiology (Sc M); toxicology and environmental pathology (PhD). Terminal master's awarded for partial completion of doctoral program. *Degree requirements:* For doctorate, thesis/dissertation, preliminary exam. *Entrance requirements:* For master's and doctorate, GRE General Test, GRE Subject Test. Additional exam requirements/recommendations for international students: Required—TOEFL. Electronic applications accepted. *Faculty research:* Environmental pathology, carcinogenesis, immunopathology, signal transduction, innate immunity.

Columbia University, College of Physicians and Surgeons, Department of Pharmacology, New York, NY 10032. Offers pharmacology (M Phil, MA, PhD); pharmacology-toxicology (M Phil, MA, PhD); MD/PhD. Only candidates for the PhD are admitted. Terminal master's awarded for partial completion of doctoral program. *Degree requirements:* For doctorate, thesis/dissertation. *Entrance requirements:* For master's and doctorate, GRE General Test. Additional exam requirements/recommendations for international students: Required—TOEFL. *Faculty research:* Cardiovascular pharmacology, receptor pharmacology, neuropharmacology, membrane biophysics, eicosanoids.

Cornell University, Graduate School, Graduate Fields of Agriculture and Life Sciences, Field of Environmental Toxicology, Ithaca, NY 14853-0001. Offers cellular and molecular toxicology (MS, PhD); ecotoxicology and environmental chemistry (MS, PhD); nutritional and food toxicology (MS, PhD); risk assessment, management and public policy (MS, PhD). *Faculty:* 38 full-time (11 women). *Students:* 8 full-time (3 women), 3 international. Average age 27. 28 applicants, 4% accepted, 1 enrolled. In 2011, 3 degrees awarded. *Degree requirements:* For master's, thesis; for doctorate, comprehensive exam, thesis/dissertation. *Entrance requirements:* For master's and doctorate, GRE General Test, GRE Subject Test (biology or chemistry recommended), 2 letters of recommendation. Additional exam requirements/recommendations for international students: Required—TOEFL (minimum score 600 paper-based; 250 computer-based; 77 iBT). *Application deadline:* For fall admission, 1/15 for domestic students. Application fee: $95. Electronic applications accepted. *Financial support:* In 2011–12, 7 research assistantships with full tuition reimbursements, 1 teaching assistantship with full tuition reimbursement were awarded; fellowships with full tuition reimbursements, institutionally sponsored loans, scholarships/grants, health care benefits, tuition waivers (full and partial), and unspecified assistantships also available. Financial award applicants required to submit FAFSA. *Faculty research:* Cellular and molecular toxicology, cancer toxicology, bioremediation, ecotoxicology, nutritional and food toxicology, reproductive toxicology. *Unit head:* Director of Graduate Studies, 607-255-8008, Fax: 607-755-0238. *Application contact:* Graduate Field Assistant, 607-255-8008, Fax: 607-255-0238, E-mail: envtox@cornell.edu. Web site: http://www.gradschool.cornell.edu/fields.php?id-48&a-2.

Dartmouth College, Arts and Sciences Graduate Programs, Department of Pharmacology and Toxicology, Hanover, NH 03755. Offers PhD, MD/PhD. *Degree requirements:* For doctorate, thesis/dissertation. *Entrance requirements:* For doctorate, GRE General Test, GRE Subject Test, bachelor's degree in biological, chemical, or physical science. Additional exam requirements/recommendations for international students: Required—TOEFL. Electronic applications accepted. *Faculty research:* Molecular biology of carcinogenesis, DNA repair and gene expression, biochemical and environmental toxicology, protein receptor ligand interactions.

Dartmouth College, Program in Experimental and Molecular Medicine, Molecular Pharmacology, Toxicology and Experimental Therapeutics Track, Hanover, NH 03755. Offers PhD.

Duke University, Graduate School, Integrated Toxicology and Environmental Health Program, Durham, NC 27708. Offers PhD, Certificate. *Faculty:* 36 full-time. *Students:* 4 full-time (0 women). 21 applicants, 14% accepted, 2 enrolled. *Entrance requirements:* For doctorate, GRE General Test. Additional exam requirements/recommendations for international students: Required—TOEFL (minimum score 550 paper-based; 213 computer-based; 83 iBT), IELTS (minimum score 7). *Application deadline:* For fall admission, 12/8 priority date for domestic students, 12/8 for international students. Application fee: $75. Electronic applications accepted. *Expenses: Tuition:* Full-time $40,720. *Required fees:* $3107. *Financial support:* Fellowships available. Financial award application deadline: 12/8. *Unit head:* Cynthia Kuhn, Director, 919-613-8078, Fax: 919-668-1799. *Application contact:* Elizabeth Hutton, Director of Admissions, 919-684-3913, Fax: 919-684-2277, E-mail: grad-admissions@duke.edu. Web site: http://toxicology.geneimprint.com/graduate/.

Florida Agricultural and Mechanical University, Division of Graduate Studies, Research, and Continuing Education, College of Pharmacy and Pharmaceutical Sciences, Graduate Programs in Pharmaceutical Sciences, Tallahassee, FL 32307-3200. Offers environmental toxicology (PhD); medicinal chemistry (MS, PhD); pharmaceutics (MS, PhD); pharmacology/toxicology (MS, PhD); pharmacy administration (MS). *Accreditation:* CEPH. *Degree requirements:* For master's, comprehensive exam, thesis, publishable paper; for doctorate, comprehensive exam, thesis/dissertation, publishable paper. *Entrance requirements:* For master's and doctorate, GRE General Test, minimum GPA of 3.0 in last 60 hours. Additional exam requirements/recommendations for international students: Required—TOEFL. *Faculty research:* Anticancer agents, anti-inflammatory drugs, chronopharmacology, neuroendocrinology, microbiology.

The George Washington University, Columbian College of Arts and Sciences, Department of Forensic Sciences, Washington, DC 20052. Offers crime scene investigation (MFS); forensic chemistry (MFS); forensic molecular biology (MFS); forensic toxicology (MFS); high-technology crime investigation (MFS); security management (MFS). High-technology crime investigation and security management programs offered in Arlington, VA. Part-time and evening/weekend programs available. *Faculty:* 6 full-time (1 woman), 24 part-time/adjunct (4 women). *Students:* 89 full-time (70 women), 68 part-time (37 women); includes 41 minority (15 Black or African American, non-Hispanic/Latino; 1 American Indian or Alaska Native, non-Hispanic/Latino; 10 Asian, non-Hispanic/Latino; 10 Hispanic/Latino; 1 Native Hawaiian or other Pacific Islander, non-Hispanic/Latino; 4 Two or more races, non-Hispanic/Latino), 7 international. Average age 27. 155 applicants, 82% accepted, 63 enrolled. In 2011, 67 master's awarded. *Degree requirements:* For master's, comprehensive exam. *Entrance requirements:* For master's, GRE General Test, minimum GPA of 3.0. Additional exam requirements/recommendations for international students: Required—TOEFL (minimum score 550 paper-based; 213 computer-based; 80 iBT). *Application deadline:* For fall admission, 1/16 for international students; for spring admission, 10/1 priority date for domestic students, 9/1 for international students. Applications are processed on a rolling basis. Application fee: $75. Electronic applications accepted. *Financial support:* In 2011–12, 19 students received support. Fellowships with partial tuition reimbursements available, Federal Work-Study, and tuition waivers available. *Unit head:* Dr. Walter F. Rowe, Chair, 202-994-1469, E-mail: wfrowe@gwu.edu. *Application contact:* 202-994-6210, Fax: 202-994-6213, E-mail: askccas@gwu.edu. Web site: http://www.gwu.edu/~forensic/.

Indiana University Bloomington, School of Public and Environmental Affairs, Environmental Science Programs, Bloomington, IN 47405. Offers applied ecology (MSES); energy (MSES); environmental chemistry, toxicology, and risk assessment (MSES); environmental science (PhD); specialized environmental science (MSES); water resources (MSES); JD/MSES; MSES/MPA; MSES/MS. Part-time programs available. *Faculty:* 80 full-time (30 women), 102 part-time/adjunct (43 women). *Students:* 142 full-time, 6 part-time; includes 8 minority (2 Black or African American, non-Hispanic/Latino; 5 Asian, non-Hispanic/Latino; 1 Hispanic/Latino), 18 international. Average age 24. 152 applicants, 57 enrolled. In 2011, 58 master's, 2 doctorates awarded. Terminal master's awarded for partial completion of doctoral program. *Degree requirements:* For master's, core classes; capstone or thesis; internship; for doctorate, comprehensive exam, thesis/dissertation. *Entrance requirements:* For master's, GRE General Test or GMAT, official transcripts, 3 letters of recommendation, resume, personal statement; for doctorate, GRE General Test or LSAT, official transcripts, 3 letters of recommendation, resume or curriculum vitae, statement of purpose. Additional exam requirements/recommendations for international students: Required—TOEFL (minimum score 600 paper-based; 96 iBT); Recommended—IELTS (minimum score 7). *Application deadline:* For fall admission, 2/1 priority date for domestic students, 12/1 for international students. Applications are processed on a rolling basis. Application fee: $55 ($65 for international students). Electronic applications accepted. *Financial support:* Fellowships with partial tuition reimbursements, research assistantships with partial tuition reimbursements, teaching assistantships with partial tuition reimbursements, career-related internships or fieldwork, Federal Work-Study, scholarships/grants, health care benefits, unspecified assistantships, and Service Corps programs available. Financial award application deadline: 2/1; financial award applicants required to submit FAFSA. *Faculty research:* Applied ecology, bio-geo chemistry, toxicology, wetlands ecology, environmental microbiology, forest ecology, environmental chemistry. *Unit head:* Jennifer J. Forney, Director, Graduate Student Services, 812-855-9485, Fax: 812-856-3665, E-mail: speampo@indiana.edu. *Application contact:* Admissions Assistant, 812-855-2840, Fax: 812-856-3665, E-mail: speaapps@indiana.edu. Web site: http://www.indiana.edu/~spea/prospective_students/masters/.

Indiana University–Purdue University Indianapolis, Indiana University School of Medicine, Department of Pharmacology and Toxicology, Indianapolis, IN 46202-2896. Offers pharmacology (MS, PhD); toxicology (MS, PhD); MD/PhD. *Faculty:* 11 full-time (2 women). *Students:* 12 full-time (10 women), 13 part-time (7 women); includes 3 minority (1 Asian, non-Hispanic/Latino; 2 Hispanic/Latino), 10 international. Average age 27. 5 applicants, 0% accepted, 0 enrolled. In 2011, 4 master's, 3 doctorates awarded. Terminal master's awarded for partial completion of doctoral program. *Degree requirements:* For master's, thesis; for doctorate, thesis/dissertation. *Entrance requirements:* For master's and doctorate, GRE General Test, GRE Subject Test, minimum GPA of 3.0. *Application deadline:* For fall admission, 1/15 priority date for domestic students. Applications are processed on a rolling basis. Application fee: $55 ($65 for international students). *Financial support:* In 2011–12, teaching assistantships (averaging $20,940 per year) were awarded; fellowships with partial tuition reimbursements, research assistantships with partial tuition reimbursements, Federal Work-Study, institutionally sponsored loans, and tuition waivers (partial) also available. Financial award application deadline: 1/15. *Faculty research:* Neuropharmacology, cardiovascular biopharmacology, chemotherapy, oncogenesis. *Unit head:* Dr. Michael Vasko, Jr., Chairman, 317-274-7844, Fax: 317-274-7714. *Application contact:* Director of Graduate Studies, 317-274-1564, Fax: 317-274-7714. Web site: http://pharmtox.iusm.iu.edu/.

Iowa State University of Science and Technology, Department of Biochemistry, Biophysics, and Molecular Biology, Ames, IA 50011. Offers biochemistry (MS, PhD); biophysics (MS, PhD); genetics (MS, PhD); molecular, cellular, and developmental biology (MS, PhD); toxicology (MS, PhD). *Degree requirements:* For master's, thesis; for doctorate, thesis/dissertation. *Entrance requirements:* For master's and doctorate, GRE General Test. Additional exam requirements/recommendations for international students: Required—TOEFL (minimum score 550 paper-based; 79 iBT), IELTS (minimum score 6.5). *Application deadline:* For fall admission, 1/1 priority date for domestic students, 1/1 for international students. Application fee: $40 ($90 for international students). Electronic applications accepted. *Unit head:* Dr. Reuben Peters, Director of Graduate Education, 515-294-6116, Fax: 515-294-0453, E-mail: biochem@iastate.edu. *Application contact:* Connie Garnett, Application Contact, 515-294-6116, Fax: 515-294-0453, E-mail: biochem@iastate.edu. Web site: http://www.bbmb.iastate.edu/index.php?.

Iowa State University of Science and Technology, Program in Toxicology, Ames, IA 50011-3260. Offers MS, PhD. *Entrance requirements:* For master's and doctorate, GRE General Test. Additional exam requirements/recommendations for international students: Required—TOEFL (minimum score 550 paper-based; 79 iBT), IELTS (minimum score 6.5). *Application deadline:* For fall admission, 2/1 priority date for domestic students, 2/1 for international students. Applications are processed on a rolling basis. Application fee: $40 ($90 for international students). Electronic applications accepted. *Unit head:* Dr. Richard Martin, Director of Graduate Education, 515-294-7697, Fax: 515-294-6669, E-mail: toxmajor@iastate.edu. *Application contact:* Linda Wild, Application Contact, 800-499-7697, Fax: 515-294-6669, E-mail: toxmajor@iastate.edu. Web site: http://www.toxicology.iastate.edu/.

The Johns Hopkins University, Bloomberg School of Public Health, Department of Environmental Health Sciences, Baltimore, MD 21218-2699. Offers environmental health engineering (PhD); environmental health sciences (MHS, Dr PH); occupational and environmental health (PhD); occupational and environmental hygiene (MHS, MHS); physiology (PhD); toxicology (PhD). Postbaccalaureate distance learning degree programs offered (minimal on-campus study). *Degree requirements:* For master's, essay, presentation; for doctorate, comprehensive exam, thesis/dissertation, 1 year full-time residency, oral and written exams. *Entrance requirements:* For master's, GRE General Test or MCAT, 3 letters of recommendation, transcripts; for doctorate, GRE General Test or MCAT, 3 letters of recommendation. Additional exam requirements/recommendations for international students: Required—TOEFL (minimum score 600 paper-based; 250 computer-based). Electronic applications accepted. *Faculty research:* Chemical carcinogenesis/toxicology, lung disease, occupational and environmental health, nuclear imaging, molecular epidemiology.

Long Island University–Brooklyn Campus, Arnold and Marie Schwartz College of Pharmacy and Health Sciences, Graduate Programs in Pharmacy, Division of Pharmaceutical Sciences, Brooklyn, NY 11201-8423. Offers cosmetic science (MS); industrial pharmacy (MS); pharmaceutics (PhD); pharmacology/toxicology (MS). Part-time and evening/weekend programs available. Terminal master's awarded for partial completion of doctoral program. *Degree requirements:* For master's, thesis optional; for doctorate, thesis/dissertation, candidacy exam. *Entrance requirements:* For master's and doctorate, minimum GPA of 3.0.

Louisiana State University and Agricultural and Mechanical College, Graduate School, School of the Coast and Environment, Department of Environmental Sciences, Baton Rouge, LA 70803. Offers environmental planning and management (MS); environmental toxicology (MS). *Faculty:* 9 full-time (3 women). *Students:* 24 full-time (16 women), 9 part-time (4 women); includes 6 minority (3 Black or African American, non-Hispanic/Latino; 2 Asian, non-Hispanic/Latino; 1 Hispanic/Latino), 6 international. Average age 27. 19 applicants, 74% accepted, 7 enrolled. In 2011, 14 master's awarded. *Degree requirements:* For master's, thesis (for some programs). *Entrance requirements:* For master's, GRE General Test, minimum GPA of 3.0. Additional exam requirements/recommendations for international students: Required—TOEFL (minimum score 550 paper-based; 213 computer-based; 79 iBT) or IELTS (minimum score 6.5). *Application deadline:* For fall admission, 1/25 priority date for domestic students, 5/15 for international students; for spring admission, 10/15 for international students. Applications are processed on a rolling basis. Application fee: $50 ($70 for international students). Electronic applications accepted. *Financial support:* In 2011–12, 30 students received support, including 1 fellowship with full and partial tuition reimbursement available (averaging $17,831 per year), 15 research assistantships with full and partial tuition reimbursements available (averaging $15,467 per year), 6 teaching assistantships with full and partial tuition reimbursements available (averaging $10,333 per year); career-related internships or fieldwork, Federal Work-Study, institutionally sponsored loans, scholarships/grants, health care benefits, and unspecified assistantships also available. Support available to part-time students. Financial award applicants required to submit FAFSA. *Faculty research:* Environmental toxicology, environmental policy and law, microbial ecology, bioremediation, genetic toxicology. *Total annual research expenditures:* $1.9 million. *Unit head:* Dr. Ed Laws, Chair, 225-578-8521, Fax: 225-578-4286, E-mail: edlaws@lsu.edu. *Application contact:* Charlotte G. St. Romain, Academic Coordinator, 225-578-8522, Fax: 225-578-4286, E-mail: cstrom4@lsu.edu. Web site: http://info.envs.lsu.edu/.

Massachusetts Institute of Technology, School of Engineering, Department of Biological Engineering, Cambridge, MA 02139. Offers applied biosciences (PhD, Sc D); bioengineering (PhD, Sc D); biological engineering (PhD, Sc D); biomedical engineering (M Eng); toxicology (SM); SM/MBA. *Faculty:* 33 full-time (7 women). *Students:* 124 full-time (55 women); includes 36 minority (3 Black or African American, non-Hispanic/Latino; 22 Asian, non-Hispanic/Latino; 7 Hispanic/Latino; 4 Two or more races, non-Hispanic/Latino), 38 international. Average age 26. 483 applicants, 10% accepted, 30 enrolled. In 2011, 3 master's, 13 doctorates awarded. Terminal master's awarded for partial completion of doctoral program. *Degree requirements:* For master's, thesis; for doctorate, comprehensive exam, thesis/dissertation. *Entrance requirements:* For master's and doctorate, GRE General Test. Additional exam requirements/recommendations for international students: Required—IELTS (minimum score 7). *Application deadline:* For fall admission, 12/15 for domestic and international students. Application fee: $75. Electronic applications accepted. *Expenses: Tuition:* Full-time $40,460; part-time $630 per credit hour. *Required fees:* $272. *Financial support:* In 2011–12, 113 students received support, including 67 fellowships (averaging $36,300 per year), 53 research assistantships (averaging $34,000 per year), 1 teaching assistantship (averaging $33,100 per year); Federal Work-Study, institutionally sponsored loans, scholarships/grants, traineeships, health care benefits, and unspecified assistantships also available. *Faculty research:* Bioinformatics, computational, systems, and synthetic biology; biological materials, imaging, and transport phenomena; biomolecular and cell engineering; cancer initiation, progression, and therapeutics; genomics, proteomics, and glycomics; nanoscale engineering of biological systems; neurobiological systems; systems biology; macromolecular biochemistry and biophysics. *Total annual research expenditures:* $36.7 million. *Unit head:* Prof. Douglas A. Lauffenburger, Head, 617-253-1712, E-mail: be-acad@mit.edu. Web site: http://web.mit.edu/be/.

Medical College of Wisconsin, Graduate School of Biomedical Sciences, Department of Pharmacology and Toxicology, Milwaukee, WI 53226-0509. Offers PhD, MD/PhD. *Degree requirements:* For doctorate, comprehensive exam, thesis/dissertation, oral and written qualifying exams. *Entrance requirements:* For doctorate, GRE, official transcripts, three letters of recommendation. Additional exam requirements/recommendations for international students: Required—TOEFL. *Faculty research:* Cardiovascular physiology and pharmacology, drugs of abuse, environmental and aquatic toxicology, central nervous system and biochemical pharmacology, signal transduction.

Medical University of South Carolina, College of Graduate Studies, Department of Pharmaceutical and Biomedical Sciences, Charleston, SC 29425. Offers cell injury and repair (PhD); drug discovery (PhD); medicinal chemistry (PhD); toxicology (PhD); DMD/PhD; MD/PhD; Pharm D/PhD. *Faculty:* 8 full-time (1 woman), 1 part-time/adjunct (0 women). *Students:* 26 full-time (12 women), 7 international. Average age 29. In 2011, 3 doctorates awarded. *Degree requirements:* For doctorate, thesis/dissertation, oral and written exams, teaching and research seminar. *Entrance requirements:* For doctorate, GRE General Test, interview, minimum GPA of 3.0. Additional exam requirements/recommendations for international students: Required—TOEFL (minimum score 600 paper-based; 250 computer-based; 100 iBT). *Application deadline:* For fall admission, 1/15 priority date for domestic students, 1/15 for international students. Applications are processed on a rolling basis. Application fee: $0 ($85 for international students). Electronic applications accepted. *Financial support:* In 2011–12, 7 students received support, including 17 research assistantships with partial tuition reimbursements available (averaging $23,000 per year); Federal Work-Study, scholarships/grants, and traineeships also available. Support available to part-time students. Financial award application deadline: 3/10; financial award applicants required to submit FAFSA. *Faculty research:* Drug discovery, toxicology, metabolomics, cell stress and injury. *Unit head:* Dr. Rick Schnellmann, Eminent Scholar, Professor and Chair, 843-792-3754, Fax: 843-792-6590, E-mail: schnell@musc.edu. *Application contact:* Dr. Craig C. Beeson, Associate Professor, 843-876-5091, Fax: 843-792-6590, E-mail: beesonc@musc.edu. Web site: http://www.musc.edu/psci/index.html.

Michigan State University, College of Human Medicine and The Graduate School, Graduate Programs in Human Medicine, East Lansing, MI 48824. Offers biochemistry and molecular biology (MS, PhD); epidemiology (MS, PhD); microbiology (MS); microbiology and molecular genetics (PhD); pharmacology and toxicology (MS, PhD); physiology (MS, PhD); public health (MPH). *Entrance requirements:* Additional exam requirements/recommendations for international students: Required—TOEFL.

Michigan State University, College of Osteopathic Medicine and The Graduate School, Graduate Studies in Osteopathic Medicine and Graduate Programs in Human Medicine and Graduate Programs in Veterinary Medicine, Department of Pharmacology and Toxicology, East Lansing, MI 48824. Offers integrative pharmacology (MS); pharmacology and toxicology (MS, PhD); pharmacology and toxicology-environmental toxicology (PhD). *Entrance requirements:* Additional exam requirements/recommendations for international students: Required—TOEFL (minimum score 600 paper-based; 220 computer-based). Electronic applications accepted.

Michigan State University, College of Veterinary Medicine and The Graduate School, Graduate Programs in Veterinary Medicine, Center for Integrative Toxicology, East Lansing, MI 48824. Offers animal science–environmental toxicology (PhD); biochemistry and molecular biology–environmental toxicology (PhD); chemistry–environmental toxicology (PhD); crop and soil sciences–environmental toxicology (PhD); environmental engineering–environmental toxicology (PhD); environmental geosciences–environmental toxicology (PhD); fisheries and wildlife–environmental toxicology (PhD); food science–environmental toxicology (PhD); forestry–environmental toxicology (PhD); genetics–environmental toxicology (PhD); human nutrition–environmental toxicology (PhD); microbiology–environmental toxicology (PhD); pharmacology and toxicology–environmental toxicology (PhD); zoology–environmental toxicology (PhD). *Entrance requirements:* Additional exam requirements/recommendations for international students: Required—TOEFL (minimum score 550 paper-based; 213 computer-based), Michigan State University ELT (minimum score 85), Michigan English Language Assessment Battery (minimum score 83). Electronic applications accepted. *Faculty research:* Environmental risk assessment, toxicogenomics, phytoremediation, storage and disposal of hazardous waste, environmental regulation.

Michigan State University, College of Veterinary Medicine and The Graduate School, Graduate Programs in Veterinary Medicine and College of Natural Science and Graduate Programs in Human Medicine, Department of Microbiology and Molecular Genetics, East Lansing, MI 48824. Offers industrial microbiology (MS, PhD); microbiology (MS, PhD); microbiology and molecular genetics (MS, PhD); microbiology–environmental toxicology (PhD). *Entrance requirements:* For master's, GRE General Test. Additional exam requirements/recommendations for international students: Required—TOEFL (minimum score 550 paper-based; 213 computer-based), Michigan State University ELT (minimum score 85), Michigan English Language Assessment Battery (minimum score 83). Electronic applications accepted.

Michigan State University, The Graduate School, College of Agriculture and Natural Resources, Department of Animal Science, East Lansing, MI 48824. Offers animal science (MS, PhD); animal science-environmental toxicology (PhD). *Entrance requirements:* Additional exam requirements/recommendations for international students: Required—TOEFL (minimum score 550 paper-based; 213 computer-based), Michigan State University ELT (minimum score 85), Michigan English Language Assessment Battery (minimum score 83). Electronic applications accepted.

Michigan State University, The Graduate School, College of Agriculture and Natural Resources, Department of Crop and Soil Sciences, East Lansing, MI 48824. Offers crop and soil sciences (MS, PhD); crop and soil sciences-environmental toxicology (PhD); plant breeding and genetics-crop and soil sciences (MS); plant breeding, genetics and biotechnology-crop and soil sciences (PhD). *Entrance requirements:* Additional exam requirements/recommendations for international students: Required—TOEFL (minimum score 550 paper-based; 213 computer-based), Michigan State University ELT (minimum score 85), Michigan Michigan English Language Assessment Battery (minimum score 83). Electronic applications accepted.

Michigan State University, The Graduate School, College of Agriculture and Natural Resources and College of Natural Science, Department of Food Science and Human Nutrition, East Lansing, MI 48824. Offers food science (MS, PhD); food science - environmental toxicology (PhD); human nutrition (MS, PhD); human nutrition-environmental toxicology (PhD). *Entrance requirements:* Additional exam requirements/recommendations for international students: Required—TOEFL (minimum score 550 paper-based; 213 computer-based), Michigan State University ELT (minimum score 85), Michigan English Language Assessment Battery (minimum score 83). Electronic applications accepted.

Michigan State University, The Graduate School, College of Engineering, Department of Civil and Environmental Engineering, East Lansing, MI 48824. Offers civil engineering (MS, PhD); environmental engineering (MS, PhD); environmental engineering-environmental toxicology (PhD). Part-time programs available. *Entrance requirements:* Additional exam requirements/recommendations for international students: Required—TOEFL. Electronic applications accepted.

Michigan State University, The Graduate School, College of Natural Science and Graduate Programs in Human Medicine and Graduate Studies in Osteopathic Medicine, Department of Biochemistry and Molecular Biology, East Lansing, MI 48824. Offers biochemistry and molecular biology (MS, PhD); biochemistry and molecular biology/environmental toxicology (PhD). *Entrance requirements:* Additional exam requirements/recommendations for international students: Required—TOEFL. Electronic applications accepted.

Michigan State University, The Graduate School, College of Natural Science, Department of Chemistry, East Lansing, MI 48824. Offers chemical physics (PhD); chemistry (MS, PhD); chemistry-environmental toxicology (PhD); computational chemistry (MS). *Entrance requirements:* Additional exam requirements/recommendations for international students: Required—TOEFL. Electronic applications accepted. *Faculty research:* Analytical chemistry, inorganic and organic chemistry, nuclear chemistry, physical chemistry, theoretical and computational chemistry.

Michigan State University, The Graduate School, College of Natural Science, Department of Geological Sciences, East Lansing, MI 48824. Offers environmental geosciences (MS, PhD); environmental geosciences-environmental toxicology (PhD); geological sciences (MS, PhD). *Degree requirements:* For master's, thesis (for those without prior thesis work); for doctorate, thesis/dissertation. *Entrance requirements:* For master's, GRE General Test, minimum GPA of 3.0, course work in geoscience, 3 letters of recommendation; for doctorate, GRE General Test, 3 letters of recommendation. Additional exam requirements/recommendations for international students: Required—TOEFL (minimum score 550 paper-based; 213 computer-based), Michigan State University ELT (minimum score 85), Michigan English Language Assessment Battery (minimum score 83). Electronic applications accepted. *Faculty research:* Water in the environment, global and biological change, crystal dynamics.

Michigan State University, The Graduate School, College of Natural Science, Program in Genetics, East Lansing, MI 48824. Offers genetics (MS, PhD); genetics–environmental toxicology (PhD). *Entrance requirements:* Additional exam requirements/recommendations for international students: Required—TOEFL. Electronic applications accepted.

New York University, Graduate School of Arts and Science, Department of Environmental Medicine, New York, NY 10012-1019. Offers environmental health sciences (MS, PhD), including biostatistics (PhD), environmental hygiene (MS), epidemiology (PhD), ergonomics and biomechanics (PhD), exposure assessment and health effects (PhD), molecular toxicology/carcinogenesis (PhD), toxicology. Part-time programs available. *Faculty:* 26 full-time (7 women). *Students:* 62 full-time (43 women), 9 part-time (4 women); includes 12 minority (2 Black or African American, non-Hispanic/Latino; 3 Asian, non-Hispanic/Latino; 7 Hispanic/Latino), 27 international. Average age 30. 70 applicants, 56% accepted, 26 enrolled. In 2011, 9 master's, 8 doctorates awarded. Terminal master's awarded for partial completion of doctoral program. *Degree*

requirements: For master's, thesis or alternative; for doctorate, one foreign language, thesis/dissertation, oral and written exams. *Entrance requirements:* For master's and doctorate, GRE General Test, GRE Subject Test, minimum GPA of 3.0; bachelor's degree in biological, physical, or engineering science. Additional exam requirements/ recommendations for international students: Required—TOEFL. *Application deadline:* For fall admission, 12/12 for domestic and international students. Application fee: $90. *Financial support:* Fellowships with tuition reimbursements, teaching assistantships with tuition reimbursements, career-related internships or fieldwork, Federal Work-Study, institutionally sponsored loans, and health care benefits available. Financial award application deadline: 12/12; financial award applicants required to submit FAFSA. *Unit head:* Dr. Max Costa, Chair, 845-731-3661, Fax: 845-351-4510, E-mail: ehs@env.med.nyu.edu. *Application contact:* Dr. Jerome J. Solomon, Director of Graduate Studies, 845-731-3661, Fax: 845-351-4510, E-mail: ehs@env.med.nyu.edu. Web site: http://environmental-medicine.med.nyu.edu/.

North Carolina State University, Graduate School, College of Agriculture and Life Sciences and College of Veterinary Medicine, Department of Environmental and Molecular Toxicology, Raleigh, NC 27695. Offers M Tox, MS, PhD. Terminal master's awarded for partial completion of doctoral program. *Degree requirements:* For master's, thesis (for some programs); for doctorate, thesis/dissertation. *Entrance requirements:* For master's and doctorate, GRE General Test, minimum GPA of 3.0. Electronic applications accepted. *Faculty research:* Chemical fate, carcinogenesis, developmental and endocrine toxicity, xenobiotic metabolism, signal transduction.

Northwestern University, Northwestern University Feinberg School of Medicine and Interdepartmental Programs, Integrated Graduate Programs in the Life Sciences, Chicago, IL 60611. Offers cancer biology (PhD); cell biology (PhD); developmental biology (PhD); evolutionary biology (PhD); immunology and microbial pathogenesis (PhD); molecular biology and genetics (PhD); neurobiology (PhD); pharmacology and toxicology (PhD); structural biology and biochemistry (PhD). *Degree requirements:* For doctorate, comprehensive exam, thesis/dissertation, written and oral qualifying exams. *Entrance requirements:* For doctorate, GRE General Test. Additional exam requirements/recommendations for international students: Required—TOEFL (minimum score 600 paper-based; 250 computer-based). Electronic applications accepted.

Oklahoma State University Center for Health Sciences, Graduate Program in Forensic Sciences, Tulsa, OK 74107-1898. Offers forensic DNA/molecular biology (MS); forensic document examination (MS, Graduate Certificate); forensic pathology/ microbiology (MS); forensic psychology (MS); forensic science administration (MS); forensic toxicology (MS). Part-time and evening/weekend programs available. Postbaccalaureate distance learning degree programs offered (no on-campus study). *Faculty:* 2 full-time (0 women), 14 part-time/adjunct (5 women). *Students:* 7 full-time (5 women), 22 part-time (12 women); includes 4 minority (3 American Indian or Alaska Native, non-Hispanic/Latino; 1 Hispanic/Latino), 1 international. Average age 34. 12 applicants, 50% accepted, 5 enrolled. In 2011, 7 degrees awarded. *Degree requirements:* For master's, comprehensive exam (for some programs), thesis (for some programs). *Entrance requirements:* For master's, MAT (for MFSA) or GRE General Test, professional experience (MFSA). Additional exam requirements/recommendations for international students: Required—TOEFL (minimum score 600 paper-based; 250 computer-based), TWE (minimum score 5). *Application deadline:* For fall admission, 3/1 for domestic and international students; for spring admission, 10/1 for domestic and international students. Application fee: $40 ($75 for international students). *Financial support:* In 2011–12, 10 students received support, including 2 research assistantships (averaging $12,000 per year); career-related internships or fieldwork, Federal Work-Study, and tuition waivers (partial) also available. Support available to part-time students. Financial award application deadline: 4/1; financial award applicants required to submit FAFSA. *Faculty research:* Studies on the variability in chromosomal DNA; development/enhancement of accessory methods useful for forensic DNA typing; development of universal methods useful for discriminating pathogenic bacteria; forensic dentistry; transmission of microbial diseases by dentures, protective athletic mouth-guards, band wind instruments, and infant pacifiers; changes in ecologies and antibiotic sensitivities of aerobic microorganisms; forensic toxicology and trace chemical method development. *Total annual research expenditures:* $58,000. *Unit head:* Dr. Robert T. Allen, Director, 918-561-1108, Fax: 918-561-8414. *Application contact:* Cathy Newsome, Coordinator, 918-561-1108, Fax: 918-561-8414, E-mail: cathy.newsome@okstate.edu.

Oregon State University, Graduate School, College of Agricultural Sciences, Department of Environmental and Molecular Toxicology, Program in Toxicology, Corvallis, OR 97331. Offers MS, PhD. *Degree requirements:* For master's, thesis; for doctorate, thesis/dissertation. *Entrance requirements:* For master's and doctorate, GRE, bachelor's degree in chemistry or biological sciences, minimum GPA of 3.0 in last 90 hours of course work. Additional exam requirements/recommendations for international students: Required—TOEFL. *Faculty research:* Biochemical mechanisms for toxicology; analytical, comparative, aquatic, and food toxicology; aquaculture of salmonids; immunotoxicology; fish toxicology.

Prairie View A&M University, College of Arts and Sciences, Department of Biology, Prairie View, TX 77446-0519. Offers bio- environmental toxicology (MS); biology (MS). Part-time and evening/weekend programs available. *Degree requirements:* For master's, comprehensive exam, thesis optional. *Entrance requirements:* For master's, GRE General Test. Additional exam requirements/recommendations for international students: Required—TOEFL. *Faculty research:* Geonomics, hypertension, control of gene express, proteins, kigands that interact with hormone receptors, prostate cancer, renin-angiotensin yeast metabolism.

Purdue University, Graduate School, College of Health and Human Sciences, School of Health Sciences, West Lafayette, IN 47907. Offers health physics (MS, PhD); medical physics (MS, PhD); occupational and environmental health science (MS, PhD), including aerosol deposition and lung disease , ergonomics, exposure and risk assessment, indoor air quality and bioaerosols (PhD), liver/lung toxicology; occupational and environmental health science` (PhD), including indoor air quality and bioaerosols; radiation biology (PhD); toxicology (PhD); MS/PhD. Part-time programs available. *Faculty:* 10 full-time (3 women), 24 part-time/adjunct (3 women). *Students:* 24 full-time (9 women), 7 part-time (2 women); includes 2 minority (both Asian, non-Hispanic/ Latino), 13 international. Average age 30. 49 applicants, 37% accepted, 7 enrolled. In 2011, 18 master's, 5 doctorates awarded. *Degree requirements:* For master's, thesis optional; for doctorate, one foreign language, thesis/dissertation. *Entrance requirements:* For master's and doctorate, GRE General Test, minimum undergraduate GPA of 3.0 or equivalent. Additional exam requirements/recommendations for international students: Required—TOEFL (minimum score 550 computer-based; 77 iBT); Recommended—TWE. *Application deadline:* For fall admission, 5/15 for domestic and international students; for spring admission, 10/15 for domestic and international students. Applications are processed on a rolling basis. Application fee: $60 ($75 for international students). Electronic applications accepted. *Financial support:* In 2011–12, fellowships with tuition reimbursements (averaging $14,400 per year), research assistantships with tuition reimbursements (averaging $12,000 per year), teaching assistantships with tuition reimbursements (averaging $12,000 per year) were awarded; career-related internships or fieldwork and traineeships also available. Support available to part-time students. Financial award applicants required to submit FAFSA. *Faculty research:* Environmental toxicology, industrial hygiene, radiation dosimetry. *Unit head:* Dr. Wei Zheng, Head, 765-494-1419, E-mail: wz18@purdue.edu. *Application contact:* Jennifer S. Franklin, Graduate Contact, 765-494-0248, E-mail: jfranklin@purdue.edu. Web site: http://www.healthsciences.purdue.edu/.

Queen's University at Kingston, School of Graduate Studies and Research, Faculty of Health Sciences, Department of Pharmacology and Toxicology, Kingston, ON K7L 3N6, Canada. Offers M Sc, PhD. *Degree requirements:* For master's, thesis; for doctorate, comprehensive exam, thesis/dissertation. *Entrance requirements:* For master's, minimum 2nd class standing, honors bachelor of science degree (life sciences, health sciences, or equivalent); for doctorate, masters of science degree or outstanding performance in honors bachelor of science program. Additional exam requirements/ recommendations for international students: Required—TOEFL (minimum score 600 paper-based; 250 computer-based). Electronic applications accepted. *Faculty research:* Biochemical toxicology, cardiovascular pharmacology and neuropharmacology.

Rutgers, The State University of New Jersey, New Brunswick, Graduate School-New Brunswick, Department of Environmental Sciences, Piscataway, NJ 08854-8097. Offers air pollution and resources (MS, PhD); aquatic biology (MS, PhD); aquatic chemistry (MS, PhD); atmospheric science (MS, PhD); chemistry and physics of aerosol and hydrosol systems (MS, PhD); environmental chemistry (MS, PhD); environmental microbiology (MS, PhD); environmental toxicology (PhD); exposure assessment (PhD); fate and effects of pollutants (MS, PhD); pollution prevention and control (MS, PhD); water and wastewater treatment (MS, PhD); water resources (MS, PhD). Terminal master's awarded for partial completion of doctoral program. *Degree requirements:* For master's, comprehensive exam, thesis or alternative, oral final exam; for doctorate, comprehensive exam, thesis/dissertation, thesis defense, qualifying exam. *Entrance requirements:* For master's and doctorate, GRE General Test. Additional exam requirements/recommendations for international students: Required—TOEFL. Electronic applications accepted. *Faculty research:* Biological waste treatment; contaminant fate and transport; air, soil and water quality.

Rutgers, The State University of New Jersey, New Brunswick, Graduate School-New Brunswick, Joint Program in Toxicology, Piscataway, NJ 08854-8097. Offers environmental toxicology (MS, PhD); industrial-occupational toxicology (MS, PhD); nutritional toxicology (MS, PhD); pharmaceutical toxicology (MS, PhD). MS, PhD offered jointly with University of Medicine and Dentistry of New Jersey. *Degree requirements:* For master's, thesis; for doctorate, comprehensive exam, thesis/dissertation, qualifying exams (written and oral). *Entrance requirements:* For master's and doctorate, GRE General Test. Additional exam requirements/recommendations for international students: Required—TOEFL. Electronic applications accepted. *Faculty research:* Neurotoxicants, immunotoxicology, carcinogenesis and chemoprevention, molecular toxicology, xenobiotic metabolism.

St. John's University, College of Pharmacy and Health Sciences, Graduate Programs in Pharmacy, Program in Toxicology, Queens, NY 11439. Offers MS, PhD. Part-time and evening/weekend programs available. *Students:* 7 full-time (4 women), 16 part-time (9 women); includes 12 minority (2 Black or African American, non-Hispanic/Latino; 5 Asian, non-Hispanic/Latino; 5 Hispanic/Latino), 5 international. Average age 26. 16 applicants, 56% accepted, 6 enrolled. In 2011, 9 master's awarded. *Degree requirements:* For master's, comprehensive exam, thesis optional, one-year residency. *Entrance requirements:* For master's, GRE General Test, minimum GPA of 3.0; 2 letters of recommendation, bachelor's degree in related area. Additional exam requirements/ recommendations for international students: Required—TOEFL (minimum score 600 paper-based; 250 computer-based; 100 iBT), IELTS (minimum score 5.5). *Application deadline:* For fall admission, 3/1 priority date for domestic students, 5/1 for international students; for spring admission, 11/1 priority date for domestic students, 11/1 for international students. Applications are processed on a rolling basis. Application fee: $70. Electronic applications accepted. *Expenses:* Contact institution. *Financial support:* Fellowships, research assistantships, career-related internships or fieldwork, and scholarships/grants available. Support available to part-time students. Financial award application deadline: 3/1; financial award applicants required to submit FAFSA. *Faculty research:* Neurotoxicology, renal toxicology, toxicity of metals, regulatory toxicology. *Unit head:* Dr. Louis Trombetta, Chair, 718-990-6025, E-mail: trombetl@stjohns.edu. *Application contact:* Robert Medrano, Director of Graduate Admission, 718-990-1601, Fax: 718-990-5686, E-mail: gradhelp@stjohns.edu.

San Diego State University, Graduate and Research Affairs, College of Health and Human Services, Graduate School of Public Health, San Diego, CA 92182. Offers environmental health (MPH); epidemiology (MPH, PhD), including biostatistics (MPH); global emergency preparedness and response (MS); global health (PhD); health behavior (PhD); health promotion (MPH); health services administration (MPH); toxicology (MS); MPH/MA; MSW/MPH. *Accreditation:* ABET (one or more programs are accredited); CAHME (one or more programs are accredited); CEPH (one or more programs are accredited). Part-time programs available. *Degree requirements:* For master's, comprehensive exam (for some programs), thesis (for some programs); for doctorate, thesis/dissertation. *Entrance requirements:* For master's, GMAT (MPH in health services administration), GRE General Test; for doctorate, GRE General Test. Additional exam requirements/recommendations for international students: Required—TOEFL. *Faculty research:* Evaluation of tobacco, AIDS prevalence and prevention, mammography, infant death project, Alzheimer's in elderly Chinese.

Simon Fraser University, Graduate Studies, Faculty of Science, Department of Biological Sciences, Burnaby, BC V5A 1S6, Canada. Offers biological sciences (M Sc, PhD); environmental toxicology (MET); pest management (MPM). *Degree requirements:* For master's, thesis; for doctorate, thesis/dissertation. *Entrance requirements:* For master's, minimum GPA of 3.0; for doctorate, minimum GPA of 3.5. Additional exam requirements/recommendations for international students: Required—TOEFL or IELTS. Electronic applications accepted. *Faculty research:* Molecular biology, marine biology, ecology, wildlife biology, endocrinology.

Texas A&M University, College of Veterinary Medicine and Biomedical Sciences, Department of Veterinary Integrative Biosciences, College Station, TX 77843. Offers epidemiology (MS); food safety/toxicology/environmental health (MS); science and technology journalism (MS); veterinary public health (MS). *Faculty:* 23. *Students:* 34 full-time (18 women), 12 part-time (9 women); includes 10 minority (2 Black or African American, non-Hispanic/Latino; 5 Asian, non-Hispanic/Latino; 3 Hispanic/Latino), 19 international. Average age 30. Terminal master's awarded for partial completion of doctoral program. *Degree requirements:* For master's, comprehensive exam, thesis. *Entrance requirements:* For master's, GRE General Test, minimum undergraduate GPA of 3.0. Additional exam requirements/recommendations for international students: Required—TOEFL. *Application deadline:* For fall admission, 7/15 priority date for domestic students, 4/1 for international students; for spring admission, 10/1 priority date for domestic students, 9/15 for international students. Applications are processed on a

rolling basis. Application fee: $50 ($75 for international students). Electronic applications accepted. *Expenses:* Tuition, state resident: full-time $5437; part-time $226.55 per credit hour. Tuition, nonresident: full-time $12,949; part-time $539.55 per credit hour. *Required fees:* $2741. *Financial support:* In 2011–12, fellowships (averaging $18,000 per year), research assistantships (averaging $15,600 per year), teaching assistantships (averaging $15,600 per year) were awarded; institutionally sponsored loans, unspecified assistantships, and clinical associateships also available. Financial award application deadline: 7/15; financial award applicants required to submit FAFSA. *Faculty research:* Metal toxicology, reproductive biology, genetics of neural development, developmental biology, environmental toxicology. *Unit head:* Dr. Evelyn Tiffany-Castiglioni, Head, 979-458-1077, E-mail: c-tiffany@tamu.edu. *Application contact:* Graduate Admissions, 979-845-1044, E-mail: admissions@tamu.edu. Web site: http://vetmed.tamu.edu/vibs.

Texas A&M University, College of Veterinary Medicine and Biomedical Sciences, Department of Veterinary Physiology and Pharmacology, College Station, TX 77843. Offers biomedical science (MS, PhD); toxicology (PhD). *Faculty:* 14. *Students:* 27 full-time (17 women), 2 part-time (1 woman); includes 3 minority (1 Black or African American, non-Hispanic/Latino; 2 Asian, non-Hispanic/Latino), 9 international. Average age 30. *Entrance requirements:* For master's and doctorate, GRE General Test. Additional exam requirements/recommendations for international students: Required—TOEFL. Application fee: $50 ($75 for international students). *Expenses:* Tuition, state resident: full-time $5437; part-time $226.55 per credit hour. Tuition, nonresident: full-time $12,949; part-time $539.55 per credit hour. *Required fees:* $2741. *Financial support:* Fellowships, research assistantships, and teaching assistantships available. Financial award application deadline: 4/1; financial award applicants required to submit FAFSA. *Faculty research:* Gamete and embryo physiology, endocrinology, equine laminitis. *Unit head:* Glen Laine, Head, 979-845-7261, E-mail: glaine@tamu.edu. *Application contact:* Graduate Admissions, 979-845-1044, E-mail: admissions@tamu.edu. Web site: http://vetmed.tamu.edu/vtpp.

Texas Southern University, School of Science and Technology, Program in Environmental Toxicology, Houston, TX 77004-4584. Offers MS, PhD. Part-time programs available. *Degree requirements:* For master's, thesis; for doctorate, thesis/dissertation. *Entrance requirements:* For master's, minimum GPA of 2.75; for doctorate, GRE, minimum GPA of 2.75. Electronic applications accepted. *Expenses:* Contact institution. *Faculty research:* Air quality, water quality, soil remediation, computer modeling.

Texas Tech University, Graduate School, College of Arts and Sciences, Department of Environmental Toxicology, Lubbock, TX 79409. Offers MS, PhD, JD/MS, MBA/MS, MS/MPA. Part-time programs available. *Faculty:* 13 full-time (2 women), 2 part-time/adjunct (0 women). *Students:* 47 full-time (26 women), 1 (woman) part-time; includes 5 minority (1 Black or African American, non-Hispanic/Latino; 3 Hispanic/Latino; 1 Two or more races, non-Hispanic/Latino), 17 international. Average age 27. 40 applicants, 48% accepted, 8 enrolled. In 2011, 8 master's, 4 doctorates awarded. *Degree requirements:* For master's, thesis; for doctorate, thesis/dissertation. *Entrance requirements:* For master's and doctorate, GRE General Test. Additional exam requirements/recommendations for international students: Required—TOEFL (minimum score 550 paper-based; 213 computer-based; 79 iBT). *Application deadline:* For fall admission, 6/1 priority date for domestic students, 1/15 for international students; for spring admission, 9/1 priority date for domestic students, 6/15 for international students. Applications are processed on a rolling basis. Application fee: $50 ($75 for international students). Electronic applications accepted. *Expenses:* Tuition, state resident: full-time $5899; part-time $245.80 per credit hour. Tuition, nonresident: full-time $13,411; part-time $558.80 per credit hour. *Required fees:* $2680.60; $86.50 per credit hour. $920.30 per semester. *Financial support:* In 2011–12, 25 students received support. Application deadline: 4/15; applicants required to submit FAFSA. *Faculty research:* Terrestrial and aquatic toxicology, biochemical and developmental toxicology, advanced materials, countermeasures to biologic and chemical threats, molecular epidemiology and modeling. *Total annual research expenditures:* $2.1 million. *Unit head:* Dr. Ronald J. Kendall, Director and Chairman, 806-885-4567, Fax: 806-885-2132, E-mail: ron.kendall@tiehh.ttu.edu. *Application contact:* Ryan Bounds, Assistant Managing Director, 806-885-4567, Fax: 806-885-2132, E-mail: ryan.bounds@ttu.edu. Web site: http://www.tiehh.ttu.edu/.

Université de Montréal, Faculty of Medicine, Program in Toxicology and Risk Analysis, Montréal, QC H3C 3J7, Canada. Offers DESS. Electronic applications accepted.

University at Albany, State University of New York, School of Public Health, Department of Environmental Health Sciences, Albany, NY 12222-0001. Offers environmental and analytical chemistry (MS, PhD); environmental and occupational health (MS, PhD); toxicology (MS, PhD). *Degree requirements:* For master's, thesis; for doctorate, comprehensive exam, thesis/dissertation. *Entrance requirements:* For master's and doctorate, GRE General Test, GRE Subject Test, 3 letters of reference. Additional exam requirements/recommendations for international students: Required—TOEFL (minimum score 600 paper-based; 213 computer-based). Electronic applications accepted. *Faculty research:* Xenobiotic metabolism, neurotoxicity of halogenated hydrocarbons, pharmac/toxicogenomics, environmental analytical chemistry.

University at Buffalo, the State University of New York, Graduate School, School of Medicine and Biomedical Sciences, Graduate Programs in Medicine and Biomedical Sciences, Department of Pharmacology and Toxicology, Buffalo, NY 14260. Offers biochemical pharmacology (MS); pharmacology (MA, PhD); MD/PhD. *Faculty:* 21 full-time (3 women), 1 part-time/adjunct (0 women). *Students:* 27 full-time (14 women); includes 6 minority (5 Black or African American, non-Hispanic/Latino; 1 Asian, non-Hispanic/Latino), 5 international. Average age 25. 32 applicants, 34% accepted, 11 enrolled. In 2011, 3 master's, 2 doctorates awarded. Terminal master's awarded for partial completion of doctoral program. *Degree requirements:* For master's, thesis; for doctorate, thesis/dissertation. *Entrance requirements:* For master's and doctorate, GRE General Test, 3 letters of recommendation. Additional exam requirements/recommendations for international students: Required—TOEFL (minimum score 100 iBT). *Application deadline:* For fall admission, 2/14 priority date for domestic students, 2/14 for international students. Applications are processed on a rolling basis. Application fee: $50. Electronic applications accepted. *Financial support:* In 2011–12, 3 fellowships with full tuition reimbursements (averaging $30,000 per year), 13 research assistantships with full tuition reimbursements (averaging $24,000 per year) were awarded; teaching assistantships, Federal Work-Study, scholarships/grants, health care benefits, and unspecified assistantships also available. Financial award application deadline: 2/14; financial award applicants required to submit FAFSA. *Faculty research:* Neuropharmacology, toxicology, signal transduction, molecular pharmacology, behavioral pharmacology. *Total annual research expenditures:* $1.6 million. *Unit head:* Dr. Margarita Dubocovich, Chairman, 716-829-3048, Fax: 716-829-2801, E-mail: mdubo@buffalo.edu. *Application contact:* Linda LeRoy, Admissions Assistant, 716-829-2800, Fax: 716-829-2801, E-mail: lleroy@buffalo.edu. Web site: http://medicine.buffalo.edu/pharmtox.

The University of Alabama at Birmingham, Graduate Programs in Joint Health Sciences, Program in Pharmacology and Toxicology, Birmingham, AL 35294. Offers PhD. *Degree requirements:* For doctorate, thesis/dissertation. *Entrance requirements:* For doctorate, GRE General Test, interview. *Application deadline:* Applications are processed on a rolling basis. Application fee: $35 ($60 for international students). Electronic applications accepted. *Expenses:* Contact institution. *Financial support:* Fellowships available. *Faculty research:* Biochemical pharmacology, neuropharmacology, endocrine pharmacology. *Unit head:* Dr. Mary-Ann Bjornsti, Interim Chair, 205-934-4579. *Application contact:* Graduate Coordinator, 205-934-4584, Fax: 205-934-4209.

University of Arkansas for Medical Sciences, Graduate School, Graduate Programs in Biomedical Sciences, Interdisciplinary Toxicology Program, Little Rock, AR 72205-7199. Offers MS, PhD, MD/PhD. *Degree requirements:* For master's, thesis; for doctorate, thesis/dissertation. *Entrance requirements:* For master's and doctorate, GRE General Test. Additional exam requirements/recommendations for international students: Required—TOEFL.

University of California, Davis, Graduate Studies, Graduate Group in Pharmacology and Toxicology, Davis, CA 95616. Offers MS, PhD. Terminal master's awarded for partial completion of doctoral program. *Degree requirements:* For master's, comprehensive exam or thesis; for doctorate, thesis/dissertation, qualifying exam. *Entrance requirements:* For master's and doctorate, GRE General Test, minimum GPA of 3.0, course work in biochemistry and/or physiology. Additional exam requirements/recommendations for international students: Required—TOEFL (minimum score 550 paper-based; 213 computer-based). Electronic applications accepted. *Faculty research:* Respiratory, neurochemical, molecular, genetic, and ecological toxicology.

University of California, Irvine, School of Medicine, Department of Pharmacology, Program in Pharmacology and Toxicology, Irvine, CA 92697. Offers MS, PhD, MD/PhD. *Students:* 27 full-time (11 women), 1 part-time (0 women); includes 11 minority (2 Black or African American, non-Hispanic/Latino; 7 Asian, non-Hispanic/Latino; 1 Hispanic/Latino; 1 Two or more races, non-Hispanic/Latino), 6 international. Average age 29. 40 applicants, 20% accepted, 5 enrolled. In 2011, 6 master's, 2 doctorates awarded. *Degree requirements:* For doctorate, thesis/dissertation. *Entrance requirements:* For master's, GRE, minimum GPA of 3.0; for doctorate, GRE General Test, GRE Subject Test, minimum GPA of 3.0. Additional exam requirements/recommendations for international students: Required—TOEFL (minimum score 550 paper-based; 213 computer-based). *Application deadline:* For fall admission, 1/15 priority date for domestic students, 1/15 for international students. Applications are processed on a rolling basis. Application fee: $80 ($100 for international students). Electronic applications accepted. *Financial support:* Fellowships, research assistantships, teaching assistantships, institutionally sponsored loans, traineeships, and unspecified assistantships available. Financial award application deadline: 3/1; financial award applicants required to submit FAFSA. *Unit head:* Dr. Olivier Civelli, Chair, 949-924-2522, Fax: 949-824-4855, E-mail: ocivelli@uci.edu. *Application contact:* Pamela J. Bhalla, Chief Administrative Officer, 949-824-6772, Fax: 949-824-4855, E-mail: pamela.bhalla@uci.edu.

University of California, Los Angeles, Graduate Division, College of Letters and Science and David Geffen School of Medicine, UCLA ACCESS to Programs in the Molecular, Cellular and Integrative Life Sciences, Los Angeles, CA 90095. Offers biochemistry and molecular biology (PhD); biological chemistry (PhD); cellular and molecular pathology (PhD); human genetics (PhD); microbiology, immunology, and molecular genetics (PhD); molecular biology (PhD); molecular toxicology (PhD); molecular, cellular and integrative physiology (PhD); neurobiology (PhD); oral biology (PhD); physiology (PhD). *Students:* 44 full-time (30 women); includes 18 minority (11 Asian, non-Hispanic/Latino; 6 Hispanic/Latino; 1 Two or more races, non-Hispanic/Latino), 9 international. Average age 25. 495 applicants, 18% accepted, 41 enrolled. *Degree requirements:* For doctorate, thesis/dissertation, oral and written qualifying exams. *Entrance requirements:* For doctorate, GRE General Test, minimum undergraduate GPA of 3.0. Additional exam requirements/recommendations for international students: Required—TOEFL. *Application deadline:* For fall admission, 12/15 for domestic and international students. Application fee: $70 ($90 for international students). Electronic applications accepted. *Financial support:* In 2011–12, 51 fellowships with full and partial tuition reimbursements, 9 research assistantships with full and partial tuition reimbursements were awarded; teaching assistantships with full and partial tuition reimbursements, Federal Work-Study, institutionally sponsored loans, scholarships/grants, health care benefits, tuition waivers (full and partial), and unspecified assistantships also available. Financial award application deadline: 3/1; financial award applicants required to submit FAFSA. *Faculty research:* Molecular, cellular, and developmental biology; immunology; microbiology; integrative biology. *Unit head:* Jody Spillane, Project Coordinator, 310-206-1845, E-mail: jspillane@mednet.ucla.edu. *Application contact:* UCLA ACCESS Admissions, 310-206-1845, E-mail: uclaaccess@mednet.ucla.edu. Web site: https://www.uclaaccess.ucla.edu/.

University of California, Riverside, Graduate Division, Program in Environmental Toxicology, Riverside, CA 92521-0102. Offers MS, PhD. Terminal master's awarded for partial completion of doctoral program. *Degree requirements:* For master's, thesis; for doctorate, comprehensive exam, thesis/dissertation, qualifying exams. *Entrance requirements:* For master's and doctorate, GRE General Test, minimum GPA of 3.25. Additional exam requirements/recommendations for international students: Required—TOEFL (minimum score 550 paper-based; 213 computer-based; 80 iBT). Electronic applications accepted. *Faculty research:* Cellular/molecular toxicology, atmospheric chemistry, bioremediation, carcinogenesis, mechanism of toxicity.

University of California, Santa Cruz, Division of Graduate Studies, Division of Physical and Biological Sciences, Environmental Toxicology Department, Santa Cruz, CA 95064. Offers MS, PhD. Terminal master's awarded for partial completion of doctoral program. *Degree requirements:* For master's, comprehensive exam, thesis; for doctorate, thesis/dissertation, qualifying exams. *Entrance requirements:* For master's and doctorate, GRE. Additional exam requirements/recommendations for international students: Required—TOEFL (minimum score 550 paper-based; 220 computer-based; 83 iBT); Recommended—IELTS (minimum score 8). Electronic applications accepted. *Faculty research:* Molecular mechanisms of reactive DNA methylation toxicity, anthropogenic perturbations of biogeochemical cycles, anaerobic microbiology and biotransformation of pollutants and toxic metals, organismal responses and therapeutic treatment of toxins, microbiology, molecular genetics, genomics.

University of Colorado Denver, School of Pharmacy, Program in Toxicology, Aurora, CO 80045. Offers PhD. *Students:* 25 full-time (16 women); includes 2 minority (both Hispanic/Latino), 10 international. Average age 27. 17 applicants, 41% accepted, 6 enrolled. In 2011, 6 doctorates awarded. *Degree requirements:* For doctorate, comprehensive exam, thesis/dissertation, 60 credit hours (30 in upper-level course work and 30 in thesis research hours). *Entrance requirements:* For doctorate, GRE, minimum undergraduate GPA of 3.0; prior coursework in general chemistry, organic chemistry, calculus, biology, and physics. Additional exam requirements/recommendations for

international students: Required—TOEFL (minimum score 550 paper-based; 213 computer-based). Application fee: $50 ($75 for international students). Electronic applications accepted. *Expenses:* Contact institution. *Financial support:* Fellowships, research assistantships, teaching assistantships, Federal Work-Study, scholarships/grants, and unspecified assistantships available. Financial award application deadline: 3/15; financial award applicants required to submit FAFSA. *Faculty research:* Regulation of apoptotic cell death; cancer chemoprevention; innate immunity and hepatotoxicity; role of chronic inflammation in cancer; Parkinson's disease, epilepsy and oxidative stress. *Unit head:* Dr. David Ross, Chair/Professor of Toxicology, 303-724-7265, Fax: 303-724-7266, E-mail: david.ross@ucdenver.edu. *Application contact:* Jackie Milowski, Information Contact, 303-724-7263, E-mail: jackie.milowski@ucdenver.edu. Web site: http://www.ucdenver.edu/academics/colleges/pharmacy/Pages/SchoolofPharmacy.aspx.

University of Connecticut, Graduate School, School of Pharmacy, Department of Pharmaceutical Sciences, Graduate Program in Pharmacology and Toxicology, Storrs, CT 06269. Offers pharmacology (MS, PhD); toxicology (MS, PhD). Terminal master's awarded for partial completion of doctoral program. *Degree requirements:* For master's, comprehensive exam, thesis; for doctorate, thesis/dissertation. *Entrance requirements:* For master's and doctorate, GRE General Test. Additional exam requirements/recommendations for international students: Required—TOEFL (minimum score 550 paper-based; 213 computer-based). Electronic applications accepted.

University of Florida, College of Veterinary Medicine, Graduate Program in Veterinary Medical Sciences, Gainesville, FL 32611. Offers forensic toxicology (Certificate); veterinary medical sciences (MS, PhD), including forensic toxicology (MS). Postbaccalaureate distance learning degree programs offered (no on-campus study). Terminal master's awarded for partial completion of doctoral program. *Degree requirements:* For master's, thesis; for doctorate, thesis/dissertation. *Entrance requirements:* For master's and doctorate, GRE General Test, minimum GPA of 3.0. Additional exam requirements/recommendations for international students: Required—TOEFL (minimum score 550 paper-based; 213 computer-based). Electronic applications accepted. *Expenses:* Contact institution.

University of Florida, Graduate School, College of Pharmacy, Programs in Forensic Science, Gainesville, FL 32611. Offers clinical toxicology (Certificate); drug chemistry (Certificate); environmental forensics (Certificate); forensic death investigation (Certificate); forensic DNA and serology (MSP, Certificate); forensic drug chemistry (MSP); forensic science (MSP); forensic toxicology (Certificate). Postbaccalaureate distance learning degree programs offered (no on-campus study). *Degree requirements:* For master's, comprehensive exam. *Entrance requirements:* For master's, GRE General Test (minimum score 1000), minimum GPA of 3.0. Additional exam requirements/recommendations for international students: Required—TOEFL (minimum score 550 paper-based; 213 computer-based; 80 iBT), IELTS (minimum score 6).

University of Guelph, Graduate Studies, Ontario Agricultural College, Department of Environmental Biology, Guelph, ON N1G 2W1, Canada. Offers entomology (M Sc, PhD); environmental microbiology and biotechnology (M Sc, PhD); environmental toxicology (M Sc, PhD); plant and forest systems (M Sc, PhD); plant pathology (M Sc, PhD). Part-time programs available. *Degree requirements:* For master's, thesis; for doctorate, comprehensive exam, thesis/dissertation. *Entrance requirements:* For master's, minimum 75% average during previous 2 years of course work; for doctorate, minimum 75% average. Additional exam requirements/recommendations for international students: Required—TOEFL or IELTS. Electronic applications accepted. *Faculty research:* Entomology, environmental microbiology and biotechnology, environmental toxicology, forest ecology, plant pathology.

University of Guelph, Ontario Veterinary College and Graduate Studies, Graduate Programs in Veterinary Sciences, Department of Biomedical Sciences, Guelph, ON N1G 2W1, Canada. Offers morphology (M Sc, DV Sc, PhD); neuroscience (M Sc, DV Sc, PhD); pharmacology (M Sc, DV Sc, PhD); physiology (M Sc, DV Sc, PhD); toxicology (M Sc, DV Sc, PhD). Part-time programs available. *Degree requirements:* For master's, thesis; for doctorate, comprehensive exam, thesis/dissertation. *Entrance requirements:* For master's, honors B Sc, minimum 75% average in last 20 courses; for doctorate, M Sc with thesis from accredited institution. Additional exam requirements/recommendations for international students: Required—TOEFL (minimum score 550 paper-based; 213 computer-based; 89 iBT). Electronic applications accepted. *Faculty research:* Cellular morphology; endocrine, vascular and reproductive physiology; clinical pharmacology; veterinary toxicology; developmental biology, neuroscience.

University of Guelph, Ontario Veterinary College, Interdepartmental Program in Toxicology, Guelph, ON N1G 2W1, Canada. Offers M Sc, PhD. Part-time programs available. *Degree requirements:* For master's, thesis (for some programs); for doctorate, comprehensive exam, thesis/dissertation. *Entrance requirements:* For master's, B Sc; for doctorate, M Sc. Additional exam requirements/recommendations for international students: Required—TOEFL (minimum score 550 paper-based; 213 computer-based; 89 iBT).

The University of Iowa, Graduate College, Program in Human Toxicology, Iowa City, IA 52242-1316. Offers MS, PhD. *Degree requirements:* For master's, thesis; for doctorate, comprehensive exam, thesis/dissertation. *Entrance requirements:* For master's and doctorate, GRE General Test, minimum GPA of 3.0. Additional exam requirements/recommendations for international students: Required—TOEFL (minimum score 600 paper-based; 250 computer-based; 100 iBT). Electronic applications accepted.

The University of Kansas, Graduate Studies, School of Pharmacy, Department of Pharmacology and Toxicology, Program in Pharmacology and Toxicology, Lawrence, KS 66045. Offers MS, PhD. *Faculty:* 11 full-time (3 women). *Students:* 16 full-time (all women); includes 1 minority (Hispanic/Latino), 9 international. Average age 25. 50 applicants, 8% accepted, 4 enrolled. Terminal master's awarded for partial completion of doctoral program. *Degree requirements:* For master's, comprehensive exam, thesis; for doctorate, comprehensive exam, thesis/dissertation. *Entrance requirements:* For master's, GRE; for doctorate, GRE (minimum score: 600 verbal, 600 quantitative, 4.5 analytical). Additional exam requirements/recommendations for international students: Required—TOEFL (minimum score 600 paper-based; 250 computer-based; 100 iBT). *Application deadline:* For fall admission, 1/15 priority date for domestic students, 2/1 for international students. Applications are processed on a rolling basis. Application fee: $55 ($65 for international students). Electronic applications accepted. Tuition and fees vary according to course load, campus/location, program and reciprocity agreements. *Financial support:* Fellowships with full tuition reimbursements and research assistantships with full tuition reimbursements available. *Faculty research:* Neuropharmacology, neurodegeneration. *Unit head:* Dr. Nancy Muma, Chair, 785-864-4001, Fax: 785-864-5219, E-mail: nmuma@ku.edu. *Application contact:* Dr. R. Alexandar Moise, Assistant Professor/Director, 785-864-1010, Fax: 785-864-5219, E-mail: alexmoise@ku.edu. Web site: http://www.pharmtox.pharm.ku.edu.

The University of Kansas, University of Kansas Medical Center, School of Medicine, Department of Pharmacology, Toxicology and Therapeutics, Kansas City, KS 66160. Offers pharmacology (MA, MS, PhD); toxicology (MS, PhD); MD/MS; MD/PhD. *Faculty:* 27. *Students:* 24 full-time (14 women), 1 part-time (0 women); includes 1 minority (Hispanic/Latino), 11 international. Average age 28. 1 applicant, 100% accepted, 1 enrolled. In 2011, 10 doctorates awarded. Terminal master's awarded for partial completion of doctoral program. *Degree requirements:* For master's, comprehensive exam, thesis; for doctorate, one foreign language, comprehensive exam, thesis/dissertation. *Entrance requirements:* For master's and doctorate, GRE General Test. Additional exam requirements/recommendations for international students: Required—TOEFL. *Application deadline:* For fall admission, 1/15 priority date for domestic students. Applications are processed on a rolling basis. Application fee: $0. Electronic applications accepted. Tuition and fees vary according to course load, campus/location, program and reciprocity agreements. *Financial support:* Fellowships with full tuition reimbursements, research assistantships with full tuition reimbursements, teaching assistantships with full tuition reimbursements, Federal Work-Study, scholarships/grants, traineeships, and unspecified assistantships available. Support available to part-time students. Financial award application deadline: 2/14; financial award applicants required to submit FAFSA. *Faculty research:* Liver nuclear receptors, hepatobiliary transporters, pharmacogenomics, estrogen-induced carcinogenesis, neuropharmacology of pain and depression. *Total annual research expenditures:* $9.1 million. *Unit head:* Dr. Hartmut Jaeschke, Professor and Chair, 913-588-7969, Fax: 913-588-7501, E-mail: hjaeschke@kumc.edu. *Application contact:* Dr. Bruno Hagenbuch, Chair, Departmental Graduate Committee, 913-588-0028, Fax: 913-588-7501, E-mail: bhagenbuch@kumc.edu. Web site: http://www.kumc.edu/pharmacology.

University of Kentucky, Graduate School, Graduate School Programs from the College of Medicine, Program in Toxicology, Lexington, KY 40506-0032. Offers MS, PhD. Terminal master's awarded for partial completion of doctoral program. *Degree requirements:* For master's, comprehensive exam, thesis optional; for doctorate, comprehensive exam, thesis/dissertation. *Entrance requirements:* For master's, GRE General Test, minimum undergraduate GPA of 2.75; for doctorate, GRE General Test, minimum graduate GPA of 3.0. Additional exam requirements/recommendations for international students: Required—TOEFL (minimum score 550 paper-based; 213 computer-based). Electronic applications accepted. *Faculty research:* Chemical carcinogenesis, immunotoxicology, neurotoxicology, metabolism and disposition, gene regulation.

University of Louisville, School of Medicine, Department of Pharmacology and Toxicology, Louisville, KY 40292-0001. Offers MS, PhD, MD/PhD. Terminal master's awarded for partial completion of doctoral program. *Degree requirements:* For master's, thesis; for doctorate, comprehensive exam, thesis/dissertation. *Entrance requirements:* For master's and doctorate, GRE General Test (minimum score of 1000 verbal and quantitative), minimum GPA of 3.0. Additional exam requirements/recommendations for international students: Required—TOEFL. Electronic applications accepted. *Expenses:* Tuition, state resident: full-time $9692; part-time $539 per credit hour. Tuition, nonresident: full-time $20,168; part-time $1121 per credit hour. Tuition and fees vary according to program and reciprocity agreements. *Faculty research:* Molecular pharmacogenetics; epidemiology; functional genomics; genetic predisposition to chemical carcinogenesis and drug toxicity; mechanisms of oxidative stress; alcohol-induced hepatitis, pancreatitis, and hepatocellular carcinoma; molecular and cardiac toxicology; molecular biology and genetics of DNA damage and repair in humans; mechanisms of chemoresistance; arsenic toxicity and cell cycle disruption; molecular pharmacology of novel G protein-coupled receptors.

University of Maine, Graduate School, Program in Biomedical Sciences, Orono, ME 04469. Offers biomedical engineering (PhD); cell and molecular biology (PhD); neuroscience (PhD); toxicology (PhD). *Students:* 11 full-time (7 women), 19 part-time (11 women), 8 international. Average age 29. 32 applicants, 31% accepted, 8 enrolled. In 2011, 3 degrees awarded. Application fee: $65. *Expenses:* Tuition, state resident: full-time $5016. Tuition, nonresident: full-time $14,424. *Financial support:* In 2011–12, 2 fellowships with full tuition reimbursements (averaging $18,000 per year), 8 research assistantships with full tuition reimbursements (averaging $23,000 per year) were awarded. *Unit head:* Dr. Carol Kim, Unit Head, 207-581-2803. *Application contact:* Scott G. Delcourt, Associate Dean of the Graduate School, 207-581-3291, Fax: 207-581-3232, E-mail: graduate@maine.edu. Web site: http://www2.umaine.edu/graduate.

The University of Manchester, Faculty of Life Sciences, Manchester, United Kingdom. Offers adaptive organismal biology (M Phil, PhD); animal biology (M Phil, PhD); biochemistry (M Phil, PhD); bioinformatics (M Phil, PhD); biomolecular sciences (M Phil, PhD); biotechnology (M Phil, PhD); cell biology (M Phil, PhD); cell matrix research (M Phil, PhD); channels and transporters (M Phil, PhD); developmental biology (M Phil, PhD); Egyptology (M Phil, PhD); environmental biology (M Phil, PhD); evolutionary biology (M Phil, PhD); gene expression (M Phil, PhD); genetics (M Phil, PhD); history of science, technology and medicine (M Phil, PhD); immunology (M Phil, PhD); integrative neurobiology and behavior (M Phil, PhD); membrane trafficking (M Phil, PhD); microbiology (M Phil, PhD); molecular and cellular neuroscience (M Phil, PhD); molecular biology (M Phil, PhD); molecular cancer studies (M Phil, PhD); neuroscience (M Phil, PhD); ophthalmology (M Phil, PhD); optometry (M Phil, PhD); organelle function (M Phil, PhD); pharmacology (M Phil, PhD); physiology (M Phil, PhD); plant sciences (M Phil, PhD); stem cell research (M Phil, PhD); structural biology (M Phil, PhD); systems neuroscience (M Phil, PhD); toxicology (M Phil, PhD).

University of Maryland, Baltimore, Graduate School, Graduate Program in Life Sciences, Program in Toxicology, Baltimore, MD 21201. Offers MS, PhD, MD/MS, MD/PhD. Part-time programs available. *Students:* 20 full-time (12 women), 10 part-time (5 women); includes 5 minority (1 Black or African American, non-Hispanic/Latino; 3 Asian, non-Hispanic/Latino; 1 Hispanic/Latino), 9 international. Average age 31. 62 applicants, 16% accepted, 3 enrolled. In 2011, 4 degrees awarded. *Degree requirements:* For doctorate, comprehensive exam, thesis/dissertation. *Entrance requirements:* For master's and doctorate, GRE General Test, GRE Subject Test, minimum GPA of 3.0. Additional exam requirements/recommendations for international students: Required—TOEFL (minimum score 550 paper-based; 80 iBT); Recommended—IELTS (minimum score 7). *Application deadline:* For fall admission, 2/1 for domestic students, 1/15 for international students. Application fee: $50. Electronic applications accepted. *Financial support:* In 2011–12, research assistantships with partial tuition reimbursements (averaging $25,000 per year) were awarded; fellowships also available. Financial award application deadline: 3/1. *Unit head:* Dr. Katherine S. Squibb, Director, 410-706-8196, E-mail: ksquibb@umaryland.edu. *Application contact:* Linda Horne, Program Coordinator, E-mail: lhorne@som.umaryland.edu. Web site: http://toxicology.umaryland.edu.

University of Maryland, Baltimore, School of Medicine, Department of Epidemiology and Public Health, Baltimore, MD 21201. Offers biostatistics (MS); clinical research (MS); epidemiology and preventative medicine (PhD); epidemiology and preventive medicine (MPH, MS); gerontology (PhD); human genetics and genomic (PhD); human genetics and genomic medicine (MS); molecular epidemiology (MS, PhD); toxicology

(MS, PhD); JD/MS; MD/PhD; MS/PhD. *Accreditation:* CEPH. Part-time programs available. *Students:* 94 full-time (68 women), 61 part-time (46 women); includes 51 minority (18 Black or African American, non-Hispanic/Latino; 25 Asian, non-Hispanic/Latino; 7 Hispanic/Latino; 1 Two or more races, non-Hispanic/Latino), 21 international. Average age 32. 109 applicants, 32% accepted, 19 enrolled. In 2011, 13 master's, 9 doctorates awarded. *Degree requirements:* For doctorate, comprehensive exam, thesis/ dissertation. *Entrance requirements:* For master's and doctorate, GRE General Test. Additional exam requirements/recommendations for international students: Required— TOEFL (minimum score 550 paper-based; 213 computer-based; 80 iBT); Recommended—IELTS (minimum score 7). *Application deadline:* For fall admission, 2/1 for domestic students, 1/15 for international students. Application fee: $50. Electronic applications accepted. *Expenses:* Contact institution. *Financial support:* In 2011–12, research assistantships with partial tuition reimbursements (averaging $25,000 per year) were awarded; fellowships, Federal Work-Study, scholarships/grants, and unspecified assistantships also available. Financial award application deadline: 3/1; financial award applicants required to submit FAFSA. *Unit head:* Dr. Laura Hungerford, Program Director, 410-706-8492, Fax: 410-706-4225. *Application contact:* Danielle Fitzpatrick, Program Coordinator, 410-706-8492, Fax: 410-706-4225, E-mail: dfitzpatrick@ epi.umaryland.edu. Web site: http://epidemiology.umaryland.edu/Pages/Home.aspx.

University of Maryland Eastern Shore, Graduate Programs, Department of Natural Sciences, Program in Toxicology, Princess Anne, MD 21853-1299. Offers MS, PhD.

University of Medicine and Dentistry of New Jersey, Graduate School of Biomedical Sciences, Graduate Programs in Biomedical Sciences–Piscataway, Piscataway, NJ 08854-5635. Offers biochemistry and molecular biology (MS, PhD); biomedical engineering (MS, PhD); biomedical science (MS); cellular and molecular pharmacology (MS, PhD); clinical and translational science (MS); environmental sciences/exposure assessment (PhD); molecular genetics, microbiology and immunology (MS, PhD); neuroscience (MS, PhD); physiology and integrative biology (MS, PhD); toxicology (PhD); MD/PhD. Terminal master's awarded for partial completion of doctoral program. *Degree requirements:* For master's, thesis (for some programs), ethics training; for doctorate, comprehensive exam, thesis/dissertation, ethics training. *Entrance requirements:* For master's, GRE General Test, MCAT, DAT; for doctorate, GRE General Test. Additional exam requirements/recommendations for international students: Required—TOEFL. Electronic applications accepted.

University of Michigan, School of Public Health, Department of Environmental Health Sciences, Ann Arbor, MI 48109. Offers environmental health sciences (MS, PhD); environmental quality and health (MPH); human nutrition (MPH); industrial hygiene (MPH, MS); nutritional sciences (MS); occupational and environmental epidemiology (MPH); toxicology (MPH, MS, PhD). *Accreditation:* CEPH (one or more programs are accredited). Part-time programs available. Terminal master's awarded for partial completion of doctoral program. *Degree requirements:* For master's, thesis (for some programs); for doctorate, thesis/dissertation, preliminary exam, oral defense of dissertation. *Entrance requirements:* For master's and doctorate, GRE General Test and/or MCAT. Additional exam requirements/recommendations for international students: Required—TOEFL (minimum score 560 paper-based; 220 computer-based; 100 iBT). Electronic applications accepted. *Faculty research:* Toxicology, occupational hygiene, nutrition, environmental exposure sciences, environmental epidemiology.

University of Minnesota, Duluth, Graduate School, Program in Toxicology, Duluth, MN 55812-2496. Offers MS, PhD. MS, PhD offered jointly with University of Minnesota, Twin Cities Campus. Terminal master's awarded for partial completion of doctoral program. *Degree requirements:* For master's, thesis; for doctorate, comprehensive exam, thesis/dissertation, written and oral preliminary and final exams. *Entrance requirements:* For master's and doctorate, GRE General Test, BS in basic science; full year each of biology, chemistry, and physics; mathematics coursework through calculus. Additional exam requirements/recommendations for international students: Required— TOEFL (minimum score 550 paper-based; 79 iBT). Electronic applications accepted. *Faculty research:* Structure activity correlations, neurotoxicity, aquatic toxicology, biochemical mechanisms, immunotoxicology.

University of Minnesota, Duluth, Medical School, Department of Biochemistry, Molecular Biology and Biophysics, Duluth, MN 55812-2496. Offers biochemistry, molecular biology and biophysics (MS); biology and biophysics (PhD); social, administrative, and clinical pharmacy (MS, PhD); toxicology (MS, PhD). Terminal master's awarded for partial completion of doctoral program. *Degree requirements:* For master's, comprehensive exam, thesis; for doctorate, comprehensive exam, thesis/ dissertation. *Entrance requirements:* For master's and doctorate, GRE General Test. Additional exam requirements/recommendations for international students: Required— TOEFL. Electronic applications accepted. *Faculty research:* Intestinal cancer biology; hepatotoxins and mitochondriopathies; toxicology; cell cycle regulation in stem cells; neurobiology of brain development, trace metal function and blood-brain barrier; hibernation biology.

University of Minnesota, Twin Cities Campus, School of Public Health, Division of Environmental Health Sciences, Area in Environmental Toxicology, Minneapolis, MN 55455-0213. Offers MPH, MS, PhD. *Degree requirements:* For doctorate, thesis/ dissertation. *Entrance requirements:* For master's and doctorate, GRE General Test. Electronic applications accepted.

University of Mississippi Medical Center, School of Graduate Studies in the Health Sciences, Department of Pharmacology and Toxicology, Jackson, MS 39216-4505. Offers pharmacology (MS, PhD); toxicology (MS, PhD); MD/PhD. Terminal master's awarded for partial completion of doctoral program. *Degree requirements:* For master's, thesis; for doctorate, thesis/dissertation, first authored publication. *Entrance requirements:* For master's and doctorate, GRE General Test, minimum GPA of 3.0. *Faculty research:* Neuropharmacology, environmental toxicology, aging, immunopharmacology, cardiovascular pharmacology.

University of Missouri–Kansas City, School of Pharmacy, Kansas City, MO 64110-2499. Offers pharmaceutical sciences (PhD); pharmacology and toxicology (PhD); pharmacy (Pharm D). PhD offered through School of Graduate Studies. *Accreditation:* ACPE (one or more programs are accredited). Postbaccalaureate distance learning degree programs offered (minimal on-campus study). *Faculty:* 54 full-time (22 women), 6 part-time/adjunct (3 women). *Students:* 364 full-time (233 women); includes 39 minority (10 Black or African American, non-Hispanic/Latino; 1 American Indian or Alaska Native, non-Hispanic/Latino; 24 Asian, non-Hispanic/Latino; 2 Hispanic/Latino; 2 Two or more races, non-Hispanic/Latino), 4 international. Average age 25. 419 applicants, 40% accepted, 162 enrolled. In 2011, 113 doctorates awarded. *Degree requirements:* For doctorate, comprehensive exam (for some programs), thesis/ dissertation (for some programs). *Entrance requirements:* For doctorate, PCAT (for Pharm D). Additional exam requirements/recommendations for international students: Required—TOEFL (minimum score 550 paper-based; 213 computer-based; 80 iBT). *Application deadline:* For fall admission, 3/1 for domestic and international students. Applications are processed on a rolling basis. Application fee: $45 ($50 for international students). Electronic applications accepted. *Expenses:* Contact institution. *Financial

support: In 2011–12, 31 research assistantships with full and partial tuition reimbursements (averaging $9,797 per year), 23 teaching assistantships with full tuition reimbursements (averaging $11,995 per year) were awarded; career-related internships or fieldwork, Federal Work-Study, institutionally sponsored loans, tuition waivers (full and partial), and unspecified assistantships also available. Financial award application deadline: 3/1; financial award applicants required to submit FAFSA. *Faculty research:* Bio-organic and medicinal chemistry, drug delivery, pharmaceutics, molecular neurobiology, neurology. *Unit head:* Dr. Russell B. Melchert, Dean, 816-235-1609, Fax: 816-235-5190, E-mail: melchertr@umkc.edu. *Application contact:* Shelly M. Janasz, Director, Student Services, 816-235-2400, Fax: 816-235-5190, E-mail: janaszs@ umkc.edu. Web site: http://pharmacy.umkc.edu/.

The University of Montana, Graduate School, College of Health Professions and Biomedical Sciences, Skaggs School of Pharmacy, Department of Biomedical and Pharmaceutical Sciences, Missoula, MT 59812-0002. Offers biomedical sciences (PhD); neuroscience (MS, PhD); pharmaceutical sciences (MS); toxicology (MS, PhD). *Accreditation:* ACPE. *Degree requirements:* For master's, oral defense of thesis; for doctorate, research dissertation defense. *Entrance requirements:* For master's and doctorate, GRE General Test. Additional exam requirements/recommendations for international students: Required—TOEFL (minimum score 540 paper-based; 210 computer-based). Electronic applications accepted. *Faculty research:* Cardiovascular pharmacology, medicinal chemistry, neurosciences, environmental toxicology, pharmacogenetics, cancer.

University of Nebraska–Lincoln, Graduate College, Interdepartmental Area of Environmental Health, Occupational Health and Toxicology, Lincoln, NE 68588. Offers MS, PhD. MS, PhD offered jointly with University of Nebraska Medical Center. *Entrance requirements:* Additional exam requirements/recommendations for international students: Required—TOEFL (minimum score 550 paper-based; 213 computer-based). Electronic applications accepted.

University of Nebraska Medical Center, Graduate Studies, Program in Environmental Health, Occupational Health and Toxicology, Omaha, NE 68198. Offers MS, PhD. Terminal master's awarded for partial completion of doctoral program. *Degree requirements:* For master's, comprehensive exam (for some programs), thesis; for doctorate, comprehensive exam (for some programs), thesis/dissertation. *Entrance requirements:* For master's, GRE General Test, bachelor's degree in chemistry, biology, biochemistry or related area; for doctorate, GRE General Test, BS in chemistry, biology, biochemistry or related area. Additional exam requirements/recommendations for international students: Required—TOEFL (minimum score 550 paper-based; 213 computer-based). Electronic applications accepted. *Faculty research:* Mechanisms of carcinogenesis, alcohol and metal toxicity, DNA damage, human molecular genetics, agrochemicals in soil and water.

University of New Mexico, Health Sciences Center Graduate Programs, Program in Biomedical Sciences, Albuquerque, NM 87131-5196. Offers biochemistry and molecular biology (MS, PhD); cell biology and physiology (MS, PhD); clinical and translational science (Certificate); molecular genetics and microbiology (MS, PhD); neuroscience (MS, PhD); pathology (MS, PhD); toxicology (MS, PhD); university science teaching (Certificate). Part-time programs available. *Faculty:* 64 full-time (26 women), 9 part-time/ adjunct (4 women). *Students:* 45 full-time (27 women), 56 part-time (28 women); includes 24 minority (3 Black or African American, non-Hispanic/Latino; 1 American Indian or Alaska Native, non-Hispanic/Latino; 4 Asian, non-Hispanic/Latino; 14 Hispanic/ Latino; 1 Native Hawaiian or other Pacific Islander, non-Hispanic/Latino; 1 Two or more races, non-Hispanic/Latino), 18 international. Average age 30. 110 applicants, 18% accepted, 17 enrolled. In 2011, 14 master's, 5 doctorates awarded. Terminal master's awarded for partial completion of doctoral program. *Degree requirements:* For master's, thesis; for doctorate, comprehensive exam, thesis/dissertation. *Entrance requirements:* For master's and doctorate, GRE General Test, minimum undergraduate GPA of 3.0. Additional exam requirements/recommendations for international students: Required— TOEFL. *Application deadline:* For fall admission, 3/1 priority date for domestic students, 3/1 for international students. Applications are processed on a rolling basis. Application fee: $50. Electronic applications accepted. *Financial support:* In 2011–12, 99 students received support, including 28 fellowships with full and partial tuition reimbursements available (averaging $22,000 per year), 73 research assistantships with full tuition reimbursements available (averaging $23,000 per year), 8 teaching assistantships (averaging $2,800 per year); career-related internships or fieldwork, Federal Work-Study, institutionally sponsored loans, scholarships/grants, traineeships, health care benefits, and unspecified assistantships also available. Financial award application deadline: 1/1; financial award applicants required to submit FAFSA. *Faculty research:* Infectious disease/Immunity, cancer biology, cardiovascular and metabolic diseases, brain and behavioral illness, environmental health. *Unit head:* Dr. Helen J. Hathaway, BSGP Program Director, 505-272-1887, Fax: 505-272-2412, E-mail: hhathaway@ salud.unm.edu. *Application contact:* Mary Fenton, Admissions Coordinator, 505-272-1887, Fax: 505-272-2412, E-mail: mfenton@salud.unm.edu. Web site: http:// hsc.unm.edu/som/research/brep/bsgpabout.shtm.

The University of North Carolina at Chapel Hill, School of Medicine, Curriculum in Toxicology, Chapel Hill, NC 27599. Offers MS, PhD. Terminal master's awarded for partial completion of doctoral program. *Degree requirements:* For master's, comprehensive exam, thesis; for doctorate, comprehensive exam, thesis/dissertation. *Entrance requirements:* For doctorate, GRE General Test. Electronic applications accepted. *Faculty research:* Molecular and cellular toxicology, carcinogenesis, neurotoxicology, pulmonary toxicology, developmental toxicology.

University of Prince Edward Island, Atlantic Veterinary College, Graduate Program in Veterinary Medicine, Charlottetown, PE C1A 4P3, Canada. Offers anatomy (M Sc, PhD); bacteriology (M Sc, PhD); clinical pharmacology (M Sc, PhD); clinical sciences (M Sc, PhD); epidemiology (M Sc, PhD), including reproduction, fish health (M Sc, PhD); food animal nutrition (M Sc, PhD); immunology (M Sc, PhD); microanatomy (M Sc, PhD); parasitology (M Sc, PhD); pathology (M Sc, PhD); pharmacology (M Sc, PhD); physiology (M Sc, PhD); toxicology (M Sc, PhD); veterinary science (M Vet Sc); virology (M Sc, PhD). Part-time programs available. *Degree requirements:* For master's, thesis; for doctorate, thesis/dissertation. *Entrance requirements:* For master's, DVM, B Sc honors degree, or equivalent; for doctorate, M Sc. Additional exam requirements/ recommendations for international students: Required—TOEFL (minimum score 550 paper-based; 213 computer-based; 80 iBT). *Expenses:* Contact institution. *Faculty research:* Animal health management, infectious diseases, fin fish and shellfish health, basic biomedical sciences, ecosystem health.

University of Puerto Rico, Medical Sciences Campus, School of Medicine, Division of Graduate Studies, Department of Pharmacology and Toxicology, San Juan, PR 00936-5067. Offers MS, PhD. *Degree requirements:* For master's, one foreign language, thesis; for doctorate, one foreign language, comprehensive exam, thesis/ dissertation. *Entrance requirements:* For master's and doctorate, GRE General Test, GRE Subject Test, interview, minimum GPA of 3.0, 3 letters of recommendation. Electronic applications accepted. *Faculty research:* Cardiovascular, central nervous

system, and endocrine pharmacology; anti-cancer drugs; sodium pump; mitochondrial DNA repair; Huntington's disease.

University of Rhode Island, Graduate School, College of Pharmacy, Department of Biomedical and Pharmaceutical Sciences, Kingston, RI 02881. Offers medicinal chemistry and pharmacognosy (MS, PhD); pharmaceutics and pharmacokinetics (MS, PhD); pharmacology and toxicology (MS, PhD). Part-time programs available. *Faculty:* 20 full-time (6 women), 2 part-time/adjunct (1 woman). *Students:* 41 full-time (21 women), 16 part-time (7 women); includes 8 minority (1 Black or African American, non-Hispanic/Latino; 6 Asian, non-Hispanic/Latino; 1 Two or more races, non-Hispanic/Latino), 24 international. In 2011, 4 master's, 3 doctorates awarded. *Entrance requirements:* For master's and doctorate, GRE, 2 letters of recommendation. Additional exam requirements/recommendations for international students: Required—TOEFL (minimum score 550 paper-based; 213 computer-based). Application fee: $65. Electronic applications accepted. *Expenses:* Tuition, state resident: full-time $10,432; part-time $580 per credit hour. Tuition, nonresident: full-time $23,130; part-time $1285 per credit hour. *Required fees:* $1362; $36 per credit hour. $35 per semester. One-time fee: $130. *Financial support:* In 2011–12, 8 research assistantships with partial tuition reimbursements (averaging $9,529 per year), 11 teaching assistantships with full and partial tuition reimbursements (averaging $9,807 per year) were awarded. Financial award applicants required to submit FAFSA. *Faculty research:* Chemical carcinogenesis with a major emphasis on the structural and synthetic aspects of DNA-adduct formation, drug-drug/herb interaction, drug-genetic interaction, signaling of nuclear receptors, transcriptional regulation, oncogenesis. *Unit head:* Dr. Clinton O. Chichester, Chair, 401-874-5034, Fax: 401-874-5787, E-mail: chichester@uri.edu. *Application contact:* Dr. David C. Rowley, Graduate Coordinator, 401-874-9228, Fax: 401-874-2516, E-mail: drowley@uri.edu. Web site: http://www.uri.edu/pharmacy/departments/bps/index.shtml.

University of Rochester, School of Medicine and Dentistry, Graduate Programs in Medicine and Dentistry, Department of Environmental Medicine, Programs in Toxicology, Rochester, NY 14627. Offers PhD. *Degree requirements:* For doctorate, thesis/dissertation, qualifying exam. *Entrance requirements:* For doctorate, GRE General Test. *Expenses: Tuition:* Full-time $41,040.

University of Saskatchewan, College of Graduate Studies and Research, Toxicology Centre, Saskatoon, SK S7N 5A2, Canada. Offers M Sc, PhD, Diploma. *Degree requirements:* For master's, thesis; for doctorate, thesis/dissertation. *Entrance requirements:* Additional exam requirements/recommendations for international students: Required—TOEFL.

University of South Alabama, Graduate School, Program in Environmental Toxicology, Mobile, AL 36688-0002. Offers MS. *Students:* 11 full-time (5 women), 2 part-time (1 woman), 4 international. 11 applicants, 45% accepted, 3 enrolled. In 2011, 4 master's awarded. *Degree requirements:* For master's, thesis. *Entrance requirements:* For master's, GRE. *Application deadline:* For fall admission, 7/15 for domestic students, 6/15 for international students; for spring admission, 12/1 for domestic students, 11/1 for international students. Application fee: $35. *Expenses:* Tuition, state resident: full-time $7968; part-time $332 per credit hour. Tuition, nonresident: full-time $15,936; part-time $664 per credit hour. *Unit head:* Dr. Julio F. Turrens, Director of Graduate Studies, 251-380-2714. *Application contact:* Dr. B. Keith Harrison, Dean of the Graduate School, 251-460-6310, Fax: 251-461-1513, E-mail: kharriso@usouthal.edu.

University of Southern California, Graduate School, School of Pharmacy, Graduate Programs in Molecular Pharmacology and Toxicology, Los Angeles, CA 90033. Offers pharmacology and pharmaceutical sciences (MS, PhD). Terminal master's awarded for partial completion of doctoral program. *Degree requirements:* For master's, comprehensive exam, thesis, 24 units of formal course work, excluding research and seminar courses; for doctorate, comprehensive exam, thesis/dissertation, 24 units of formal course work, excluding research and seminar courses. *Entrance requirements:* For master's and doctorate, GRE. Additional exam requirements/recommendations for international students: Required—TOEFL (minimum score 603 paper-based; 250 computer-based; 100 iBT). Electronic applications accepted. *Expenses:* Contact institution. *Faculty research:* Degenerative diseases, toxicology of drugs.

The University of Texas at Austin, Graduate School, College of Pharmacy, Graduate Programs in Pharmacy, Austin, TX 78712-1111. Offers health outcomes and pharmacy practice (PhD); health outcomes and pharmacy practice (MS); medicinal chemistry (PhD); pharmaceutics (PhD); pharmacology and toxicology (PhD); pharmacotherapy (MS, PhD); translational science (PhD). PhD in translational science offered jointly with The University of Texas Health Science Center at San Antonio and The University of Texas at San Antonio. *Degree requirements:* For master's, thesis; for doctorate, thesis/dissertation. *Entrance requirements:* For master's and doctorate, GRE General Test. *Application deadline:* For fall admission, 1/15 priority date for domestic students, 1/15 for international students; for spring admission, 10/1 for domestic students. Applications are processed on a rolling basis. Application fee: $50 ($75 for international students). Electronic applications accepted. *Financial support:* Fellowships, research assistantships, teaching assistantships with partial tuition reimbursements, Federal Work-Study, scholarships/grants, health care benefits, and unspecified assistantships available. Financial award application deadline: 2/1; financial award applicants required to submit FAFSA. *Faculty research:* Synthetic medical chemistry, synthetic molecular biology, bio-organic chemistry, pharmacoeconomics, pharmacy practice. *Unit head:* Dr. M. Lynn Crismon, Dean, 512-471-3718, E-mail: lynn.crismon@austin.utexas.edu.

The University of Texas Medical Branch, Graduate School of Biomedical Sciences, Program in Pharmacology and Toxicology, Galveston, TX 77555. Offers pharmacology (MS); pharmacology and toxicology (PhD). *Degree requirements:* For master's, thesis or alternative; for doctorate, thesis/dissertation. *Entrance requirements:* For master's and doctorate, GRE General Test. Additional exam requirements/recommendations for international students: Required—TOEFL (minimum score 550 paper-based; 213 computer-based).

University of the Sciences in Philadelphia, College of Graduate Studies, Program in Pharmacology and Toxicology, Philadelphia, PA 19104-4495. Offers pharmacology (MS, PhD); toxicology (MS, PhD). Terminal master's awarded for partial completion of doctoral program. *Degree requirements:* For master's, thesis; for doctorate, comprehensive exam, thesis/dissertation. *Entrance requirements:* For master's and doctorate, GRE General Test. Additional exam requirements/recommendations for international students: Required—TOEFL, TWE. *Expenses:* Contact institution. *Faculty research:* Autonomic, cardiovascular, cellular, and molecular pharmacology; mechanisms of carcinogenesis; drug metabolism.

University of Utah, Graduate School, College of Pharmacy, Department of Pharmacology and Toxicology, Salt Lake City, UT 84112. Offers PhD. *Faculty:* 15 full-time (4 women), 2 part-time/adjunct (0 women). *Students:* 13 full-time (7 women), 1 part-time (0 women); includes 1 minority (Hispanic/Latino), 4 international. Average age 28. 64 applicants, 13% accepted, 3 enrolled. In 2011, 6 degrees awarded. Terminal master's awarded for partial completion of doctoral program. *Median time to degree:* Of those who began their doctoral program in fall 2003, 95% received their degree in 8 years or less. *Degree requirements:* For doctorate, comprehensive exam, thesis/dissertation, final exam. *Entrance requirements:* For doctorate, GRE General Test, BS in biology, chemistry, neuroscience. Additional exam requirements/recommendations for international students: Required—TOEFL (minimum score 600 paper-based; 250 computer-based; 100 iBT). *Application deadline:* For fall admission, 1/15 for domestic and international students. Application fee: $55 ($65 for international students). *Financial support:* In 2011–12, 13 students received support, including 13 research assistantships with full tuition reimbursements available (averaging $26,000 per year); fellowships with tuition reimbursements available also available. Financial award application deadline: 1/15. *Faculty research:* Neuropharmacology, neurochemistry, biochemistry, molecular pharmacology, analytical chemistry. *Total annual research expenditures:* $5.4 million. *Unit head:* Dr. William R. Crowley, Chairman, 801-581-6287, Fax: 801-585-5111, E-mail: william.crowley@deans.pharm.utah.edu. *Application contact:* Sandy Hiskey, Program Assistant, 801-581-6287, Fax: 801-585-5111, E-mail: sandy.hiskey@utah.edu. Web site: http://www.pharmacy.utah.edu/pharmtox/.

University of Washington, Graduate School, School of Public Health, Department of Environmental and Occupational Health Sciences, Seattle, WA 98195. Offers environmental and occupational health (MPH); environmental and occupational hygiene (PhD); environmental health (MS); occupational and environmental exposure sciences (MS); occupational and environmental medicine (MPH); toxicology (MS, PhD); MPH/MPA; MS/MPA. Part-time programs available. *Faculty:* 31 full-time (4 women), 7 part-time/adjunct (2 women). *Students:* 66 full-time (40 women), 10 part-time (6 women); includes 18 minority (1 Black or African American, non-Hispanic/Latino; 2 American Indian or Alaska Native, non-Hispanic/Latino; 10 Asian, non-Hispanic/Latino; 5 Hispanic/Latino), 4 international. Average age 29. 127 applicants, 36% accepted, 27 enrolled. In 2011, 21 degrees awarded. Terminal master's awarded for partial completion of doctoral program. *Degree requirements:* For master's, comprehensive exam, thesis (for some programs), project or thesis; for doctorate, comprehensive exam, thesis/dissertation. *Entrance requirements:* For master's, GRE General Test, one year each of physics, general chemistry, and biology; two quarters of organic chemistry; one quarter of calculus; for doctorate, GRE General Test, minimum GPA of 3.0, prerequisite course work in biology, chemistry, physics, calculus. Additional exam requirements/recommendations for international students: Required—TOEFL (minimum score 580 paper-based; 237 computer-based; 92 iBT). *Application deadline:* For fall admission, 1/1 for domestic students, 11/1 for international students. Application fee: $75. Electronic applications accepted. *Financial support:* In 2011–12, 72 fellowships with full tuition reimbursements (averaging $42,000 per year), 89 research assistantships with full tuition reimbursements (averaging $42,000 per year), 11 teaching assistantships with full tuition reimbursements (averaging $42,000 per year) were awarded; career-related internships or fieldwork, institutionally sponsored loans, traineeships, health care benefits, and unspecified assistantships also available. Financial award application deadline: 1/1. *Faculty research:* Developmental and behavioral toxicology, biochemical toxicology, exposure assessment, hazardous waste, industrial chemistry. *Unit head:* Dr. David Kalman, Chair, 206-543-6991, Fax: 206-543-0477. *Application contact:* Rory A. Murphy, Manager, Student Services, 206-543-6991, Fax: 206-543-0477, E-mail: ehgrad@u.washington.edu. Web site: http://depts.washington.edu/envhlth/.

University of Wisconsin–Madison, School of Medicine and Public Health, Molecular and Environmental Toxicology Center, Madison, WI 53706. Offers MS, PhD. *Faculty:* 77 full-time (25 women), 1 part-time/adjunct (0 women). *Students:* 38 full-time (18 women); includes 10 minority (1 American Indian or Alaska Native, non-Hispanic/Latino; 1 Asian, non-Hispanic/Latino; 6 Hispanic/Latino; 2 Native Hawaiian or other Pacific Islander, non-Hispanic/Latino), 9 international. Average age 28. 53 applicants, 13% accepted, 4 enrolled. In 2011, 4 doctorates awarded. Terminal master's awarded for partial completion of doctoral program. *Degree requirements:* For doctorate, thesis/dissertation. *Entrance requirements:* For master's and doctorate, bachelor's degree in science-related field. Additional exam requirements/recommendations for international students: Required—TOEFL. *Application deadline:* For fall admission, 12/15 priority date for domestic students, 12/15 for international students. Application fee: $56. Electronic applications accepted. *Expenses:* Tuition, state resident: full-time $10,296; part-time $643.51 per credit. Tuition, nonresident: full-time $24,054; part-time $1503.40 per credit. *Required fees:* $70.06 per credit. Tuition and fees vary according to course load, campus/location, program and reciprocity agreements. *Financial support:* In 2011–12, 5 research assistantships with tuition reimbursements (averaging $24,500 per year) were awarded; fellowships with tuition reimbursements, traineeships, health care benefits, and unspecified assistantships also available. *Faculty research:* Toxicology cancer, genetics, cell cycle, xenobotic metabolism. *Unit head:* Dr. Christopher Bradfield, Director, 608-262-2024, E-mail: bradfield@oncology.wisc.edu. *Application contact:* Eileen M. Stevens, Program Administrator, 608-263-4580, Fax: 608-262-5245, E-mail: emstevens@wisc.edu. Web site: http://www.med.wisc.edu/metc/.

Utah State University, School of Graduate Studies, College of Agriculture, Program in Toxicology, Logan, UT 84322. Offers MS, PhD. Terminal master's awarded for partial completion of doctoral program. *Degree requirements:* For master's, thesis; for doctorate, thesis/dissertation. *Entrance requirements:* For master's and doctorate, GRE General Test, minimum GPA of 3.0. Additional exam requirements/recommendations for international students: Required—TOEFL. *Faculty research:* Free-radical mechanisms, toxicity of iron, carcinogenesis of natural compounds, molecular mechanisms of retinoid toxicity, aflatoxins.

Virginia Commonwealth University, Graduate School, College of Humanities and Sciences, Department of Forensic Science, Richmond, VA 23284-9005. Offers forensic biology (MS); forensic chemistry/drugs and toxicology (MS); forensic chemistry/trace (MS); forensic physical evidence (MS). Part-time programs available. *Students:* 42 full-time (28 women), 1 (woman) part-time; includes 9 minority (1 Black or African American, non-Hispanic/Latino; 5 Asian, non-Hispanic/Latino; 2 Hispanic/Latino; 1 Two or more races, non-Hispanic/Latino), 3 international. 123 applicants, 37% accepted, 24 enrolled. In 2011, 22 master's awarded. *Entrance requirements:* For master's, GRE General Test, bachelor's degree in a natural science discipline, including forensic science, or a degree with equivalent work. Additional exam requirements/recommendations for international students: Required—TOEFL (minimum score 600 paper-based; 250 computer-based; 100 iBT) or IELTS (minimum score 6.5). *Application deadline:* For fall admission, 3/1 for domestic students. Application fee: $50. Electronic applications accepted. *Expenses:* Tuition, state resident: full-time $9133; part-time $507 per credit. Tuition, nonresident: full-time $18,777; part-time $1043 per credit. *Required fees:* $77 per credit. Tuition and fees vary according to degree level, campus/location, program and student level. *Financial support:* Federal Work-Study, institutionally sponsored loans, and tuition waivers (full and partial) available. Support available to part-time students. Financial award applicants required to submit FAFSA. *Unit head:* Dr. Michelle R. Peace, Interim Chair, 804-828-8420, E-mail: mrpeace@vcu.edu. *Application contact:* Dr. Tracey Dawson Cruz, Graduate Director, 804-828-0642, E-mail: tcdawson@vcu.edu. Web site: http://www.has.vcu.edu/forensics/.

Virginia Commonwealth University, Medical College of Virginia-Professional Programs, School of Medicine, School of Medicine Graduate Programs, Department of Pharmacology and Toxicology, Richmond, VA 23284-9005. Offers neuroscience (PhD);

pharmacology (Certificate); pharmacology and toxicology (MS, PhD); MD/PhD. Terminal master's awarded for partial completion of doctoral program. *Degree requirements:* For master's, thesis; for doctorate, thesis/dissertation, comprehensive oral and written exams. *Entrance requirements:* For master's and doctorate, GRE or MCAT. Additional exam requirements/recommendations for international students: Required—TOEFL (minimum score 600 paper-based; 250 computer-based; 100 iBT). Electronic applications accepted. *Expenses:* Tuition, state resident: full-time $9133; part-time $507 per credit. Tuition, nonresident: full-time $18,777; part-time $1043 per credit. *Required fees:* $77 per credit. Tuition and fees vary according to degree level, campus/location, program and student level. *Faculty research:* Drug abuse, drug metabolism, pharmacodynamics, peptide synthesis, receptor mechanisms.

Wayne State University, Eugene Applebaum College of Pharmacy and Health Sciences, Department of Pharmaceutical Sciences, Detroit, MI 48202. Offers medicinal chemistry (MS, PhD); pharmaceutics (MS, PhD); pharmacology/toxicology (MS, PhD). *Accreditation:* ACPE (one or more programs are accredited). Part-time programs available. *Students:* 15 full-time (6 women), 4 part-time (3 women); includes 2 minority (1 Black or African American, non-Hispanic/Latino; 1 Asian, non-Hispanic/Latino), 11 international. Average age 27. 234 applicants, 3% accepted, 7 enrolled. In 2011, 1 degree awarded. *Degree requirements:* For master's, thesis; for doctorate, thesis/dissertation. *Entrance requirements:* For master's, GRE General Test, bachelor's degree with minimum GPA of 3.0, three letters of recommendation, personal statement; for doctorate, GRE General Test, bachelor's degree with minimum GPA of 3.0, three letters of recommendation. Additional exam requirements/recommendations for international students: Required—TOEFL (minimum score 550 paper-based; 213 computer-based); Recommended—TWE (minimum score 6). *Application deadline:* For fall admission, 3/1 for domestic and international students. Application fee: $50. Electronic applications accepted. *Expenses:* Tuition, state resident: part-time $512.85 per credit. Tuition, nonresident: part-time $1132.65 per credit. *Required fees:* $26.60 per credit. $199.65 per semester. Tuition and fees vary according to course load and program. *Financial support:* In 2011–12, 1 fellowship with tuition reimbursement (averaging $1,800 per year), 11 research assistantships with full tuition reimbursements (averaging $23,682 per year) were awarded; career-related internships or fieldwork, scholarships/grants, health care benefits, and unspecified assistantships also available. Support available to part-time students. *Faculty research:* Mechanisms of resistance of bacteria to anti-microbial agents, drug metabolism and disposition in children, treatment strategies for stroke/neurovascular disease, prevalence and treatment of diabetes in Arab-Americans, ethnic variability in development of osteoporosis. *Unit head:* Dr. George B. Corcoran, Chair, 313-577-1737, Fax: 313-577-2033, E-mail: corcoran@wayne.edu. *Application contact:* 313-577-1047, E-mail: pscgrad@wayne.edu. Web site: http://www.cphs.wayne.edu/psc/index.php.

Wayne State University, Graduate School, Interdisciplinary Program in Molecular and Cellular Toxicology, Detroit, MI 48201-2427. Offers MS, PhD. *Students:* 5 full-time (3 women), 4 international. Average age 26. 17 applicants, 12% accepted, 2 enrolled. *Degree requirements:* For doctorate, thesis/dissertation. *Entrance requirements:* For master's, recommendation by thesis adviser or graduate program director; for doctorate, GRE, bachelor's degree from accredited college, preferably with a background in the basic sciences; minimum undergraduate GPA of 3.0. Additional exam requirements/recommendations for international students: Required—TOEFL (minimum score 550 paper-based; 213 computer-based); Recommended—TWE (minimum score 6). *Application deadline:* For fall admission, 6/1 priority date for domestic students, 5/1 for international students; for winter admission, 10/1 priority date for domestic students, 9/1 for international students; for spring admission, 2/1 priority date for domestic students, 1/1 for international students. Applications are processed on a rolling basis. Application fee: $50. Electronic applications accepted. *Expenses:* Tuition, state resident: part-time $512.85 per credit. Tuition, nonresident: part-time $1132.65 per credit. *Required fees:* $26.60 per credit. $199.65 per semester. Tuition and fees vary according to course load and program. *Financial support:* Fellowships with tuition reimbursements, research assistantships with tuition reimbursements, teaching assistantships, with tuition reimbursements, Institutionally sponsored loans, scholarships/grants, and unspecified assistantships available. Financial award application deadline: 2/1. *Faculty research:* Molecular and cellular mechanisms of chemically-induced cell injury and death; effect of xenobiotics on cell growth, proliferation, transformation and differentiation; regulation of gene expression; cell signaling; global gene expression profiling. *Unit head:* Dr. Melissa Runge-Morris, Professor and Director, Institute of Environmental Health Sciences, 313-577-5598, E-mail: m.runge-morris@wayne.edu. Web site: http://www.iehs.wayne.edu/graduate/program.php.

West Virginia University, Davis College of Agriculture, Forestry and Consumer Sciences, Interdisciplinary Program in Genetics and Developmental Biology, Morgantown, WV 26506. Offers animal breeding (MS, PhD); biochemical and molecular genetics (MS, PhD); cytogenetics (MS, PhD); descriptive embryology (MS, PhD); developmental genetics (MS); experimental morphogenesis/teratology (MS); human genetics (MS, PhD); immunogenetics (MS, PhD); life cycles of animals and plants (MS, PhD); molecular aspects of development (MS, PhD); mutagenesis (MS, PhD); oncology (MS, PhD); plant genetics (MS, PhD); population and quantitative genetics (MS, PhD); regeneration (MS, PhD); teratology (PhD); toxicology (MS, PhD). *Degree requirements:* For master's, thesis; for doctorate, comprehensive exam, thesis/dissertation. *Entrance requirements:* For master's, GRE or MCAT, minimum GPA of 2.75. Additional exam requirements/recommendations for international students: Required—TOEFL.

West Virginia University, School of Pharmacy, Program in Pharmaceutical and Pharmacological Sciences, Morgantown, WV 26506. Offers administrative pharmacy (PhD); behavioral pharmacy (MS, PhD); biopharmaceutics/pharmacokinetics (MS, PhD); industrial pharmacy (MS); medicinal chemistry (MS, PhD); pharmaceutical chemistry (MS, PhD); pharmaceutics (MS, PhD); pharmacology and toxicology (MS); pharmacy (MS); pharmacy administration (MS). Part-time programs available. Terminal master's awarded for partial completion of doctoral program. *Degree requirements:* For master's, thesis; for doctorate, one foreign language, comprehensive exam, thesis/dissertation. *Entrance requirements:* For master's and doctorate, GRE General Test, minimum GPA of 2.75. Additional exam requirements/recommendations for international students: Required—TOEFL; Recommended—TWE. Electronic applications accepted. *Expenses:* Contact institution. *Faculty research:* Pharmaceutics, medicinal chemistry, biopharmaceutics/pharmacokinetics, health outcomes research.

Wright State University, School of Medicine, Program in Pharmacology and Toxicology, Dayton, OH 45435. Offers MS. *Degree requirements:* For master's, thesis optional.

Section 18
Physiology

This section contains a directory of institutions offering graduate work in physiology, followed by in-depth entries submitted by institutions that chose to prepare detailed program descriptions. Additional information about programs listed in the directory but not augmented by an in-depth entry may be obtained by writing directly to the dean of a graduate school or chair of a department at the address given in the directory.

For programs offering related work, see also all other sections in this book. In the other guides in this series:

Graduate Programs in the Physical Sciences, Mathematics, Agricultural Sciences, the Environment & Natural Resources

See *Agricultural and Food Sciences, Chemistry,* and *Marine Sciences and Oceanography*

Graduate Programs in Engineering & Applied Sciences

See *Agricultural Engineering and Bioengineering, Biomedical Engineering and Biotechnology, Electrical and Computer Engineering,* and *Mechanical Engineering and Mechanics*

CONTENTS

Cardiovascular Sciences

Albany Medical College, Center for Cardiovascular Sciences, Albany, NY 12208-3479. Offers MS, PhD. Part-time programs available. Terminal master's awarded for partial completion of doctoral program. *Degree requirements:* For master's, thesis; for doctorate, comprehensive exam, thesis/dissertation, candidacy exam, written preliminary exam, 1 published paper-peer review. *Entrance requirements:* For master's, GRE General Test, letters of recommendation; for doctorate, GRE General Test, all transcripts, letters of recommendation. Additional exam requirements/recommendations for international students: Required—TOEFL. *Faculty research:* Vascular smooth muscle, endothelial cell biology, molecular and genetic bases underlying cardiac disease, reactive oxygen and nitrogen species biology, fatty acid trafficking and fatty acid mediated transcription control.

Baylor College of Medicine, Graduate School of Biomedical Sciences, Department of Molecular Physiology and Biophysics, Houston, TX 77030-3498. Offers cardiovascular sciences (PhD); molecular physiology and biophysics (PhD); MD/PhD. *Faculty:* 110 full-time (23 women). *Students:* 30 full-time (12 women); includes 7 minority (4 Black or African American, non-Hispanic/Latino; 2 Asian, non-Hispanic/Latino; 1 Hispanic/Latino), 9 international. Average age 27. 39 applicants, 26% accepted, 4 enrolled. In 2011, 3 doctorates awarded. *Degree requirements:* For doctorate, thesis/dissertation, public defense. *Entrance requirements:* For doctorate, GRE General Test, GRE Subject Test (strongly recommended), minimum GPA of 3.0. Additional exam requirements/recommendations for international students: Required—TOEFL. *Application deadline:* For fall admission, 1/1 priority date for domestic students. Electronic applications accepted. *Financial support:* In 2011–12, 10 fellowships with full tuition reimbursements (averaging $29,000 per year), 20 research assistantships with full tuition reimbursements (averaging $29,000 per year) were awarded; career-related internships or fieldwork, Federal Work-Study, institutionally sponsored loans, health care benefits, and scholarships (to all students unless there are grant funds available to pay tuition) also available. Financial award applicants required to submit FAFSA. *Faculty research:* Cardiovascular disease; skeletal muscle disease (myasthenia gravis, muscular dystrophy, malignant hyperthermia, central core disease); cancer; Alzheimer's disease; developmental diseases of the nervous system, eye and heart; diabetes; motor neuron disease (amyotrophic lateral sclerosis and spinal muscular atrophy); asthma; autoimmune diseases. *Unit head:* Dr. Robia Pautler, Co-Director, 713-798-3892, E-mail: rpautler@bcm.edu. *Application contact:* Dr. Steen Pedersen, Co-Director, 713-798-3888, E-mail: pedersen@bcm.edu. Web site: http://www.bcm.edu/physio/.

Dartmouth College, Program in Experimental and Molecular Medicine, Cardiovascular Diseases Track, Hanover, NH 03755. Offers PhD.

Geneva College, Master of Science in Cardiovascular Science Program, Beaver Falls, PA 15010-3599. Offers MS. *Faculty:* 1 full-time (0 women), 9 part-time/adjunct (3 women). *Students:* 3 full-time (0 women); includes 1 minority (Two or more races, non-Hispanic/Latino). Average age 23. 2 applicants, 100% accepted, 2 enrolled. In 2011, 2 master's awarded. *Degree requirements:* For master's, six semesters (includes 2 summers), RCIS and RCES registry exams. *Entrance requirements:* For master's, GRE, BS in biology or related field, minimum undergraduate GPA of 3.0, two letters of reference, one-day orientation at the cardiac catheterization labs at INOVA Heart and Vascular Institute campus. Additional exam requirements/recommendations for international students: Required—TOEFL. *Application deadline:* For fall admission, 5/30 for domestic students. Applications are processed on a rolling basis. Electronic applications accepted. *Expenses: Tuition:* Part-time $625 per credit hour. Tuition and fees vary according to program. *Financial support:* Application deadline: 8/1; applicants required to submit FAFSA. *Unit head:* Dr. David A. Essig, Program Coordinator, 724-847-6900, E-mail: dessig@geneva.edu. *Application contact:* Dr. David A. Essig, Program Coordinator, 724-846-6900, E-mail: dessig@geneva.edu. Web site: http://www.geneva.edu/object/cvt.

Georgia Health Sciences University, College of Graduate Studies, Program in Vascular Biology, Augusta, GA 30912. Offers MS, PhD. *Faculty:* 20 full-time (4 women), 1 (woman) part-time/adjunct. *Students:* 11 full-time (8 women); includes 2 minority (both Black or African American, non-Hispanic/Latino), 6 international. Average age 28. In 2011, 3 doctorates awarded. *Degree requirements:* For doctorate, comprehensive exam, thesis/dissertation. *Entrance requirements:* For doctorate, GRE General Test. Additional exam requirements/recommendations for international students: Required—TOEFL (minimum score 550 paper-based; 213 computer-based; 79 iBT). *Application deadline:* For fall admission, 1/15 for domestic and international students. Application fee: $50. Electronic applications accepted. *Financial support:* In 2011–12, 5 fellowships with partial tuition reimbursements (averaging $26,000 per year), 19 research assistantships with partial tuition reimbursements (averaging $23,000 per year) were awarded; Federal Work-Study, institutionally sponsored loans, scholarships/grants, and traineeships also available. Support available to part-time students. Financial award application deadline: 5/31. *Faculty research:* Hypertension and renal disease, diabetes and obesity, peripheral vascular disease, acute lung injury, signal transduction. *Total annual research expenditures:* $8.3 million. *Unit head:* Dr. John D. Catravas, Professor/Director of Vascular Biology Center, 706-721-6338, Fax: 706-721-8545, E-mail: jcatrava@mail.mcg.edu. *Application contact:* Dr. Patricia L. Cameron, Acting Vice Dean, 706-721-3279, E-mail: pcameron@georgiahealth.edu. Web site: http://www.georgiahealth.edu/centers/vbc/grad_prog.html.

Long Island University–C. W. Post Campus, School of Health Professions and Nursing, Department of Biomedical Sciences, Brookville, NY 11548-1300. Offers cardiovascular perfusion (MS); clinical laboratory management (MS); medical biology (MS), including hematology, immunology, medical biology, medical chemistry, medical microbiology. Part-time and evening/weekend programs available. Postbaccalaureate distance learning degree programs offered. *Degree requirements:* For master's, thesis. *Entrance requirements:* For master's, minimum GPA of 2.75 in major. Electronic applications accepted.

Loyola University Chicago, Graduate School, Marcella Niehoff School of Nursing, Adult Nurse Practitioner Program, Chicago, IL 60660. Offers adult clinical nurse practitioner (MSN), including cardiovascular ; adult health (Certificate); adult nurse practitioner (MSN); cardiovascular (MSN); cardiovascular nursing (Certificate). *Accreditation:* AACN. Part-time and evening/weekend programs available. *Students:* 1 (woman) full-time, 55 part-time (53 women); includes 9 minority (1 Black or African American, non-Hispanic/Latino; 6 Asian, non-Hispanic/Latino; 2 Hispanic/Latino). Average age 34. 23 applicants, 48% accepted, 8 enrolled. In 2011, 23 master's awarded. *Degree requirements:* For master's, comprehensive exam or oral thesis defense. *Entrance requirements:* For master's, BSN, minimum nursing GPA of 3.0, Illinois nursing license, 3 letters of recommendation, 1000 hours experience before starting clinical. *Application deadline:* Applications are processed on a rolling basis. Application fee: $50. Electronic applications accepted. *Expenses: Tuition:* Full-time $15,660; part-time $870 per credit hour. *Required fees:* $125 per semester. Tuition and

fees vary according to course load and program. *Financial support:* Traineeships available. *Faculty research:* Menopause. *Unit head:* Dr. Marijo Letizia, Associate Professor, 708-216-9325, Fax: 708-216-9555, E-mail: mletizi@luc.edu. *Application contact:* Amy Weatherford, Enrollment Advisor, School of Nursing, 773-508-3249, Fax: 773-508-3241, E-mail: aweatherford@luc.edu. Web site: http://www.luc.edu/nursing/np/

Marquette University, Graduate School, Program in Transfusion Medicine, Milwaukee, WI 53201-1881. Offers MSTM. Program is an ongoing collaboration with BloodCenter of Wisconsin. Part-time programs available. *Students:* 2 part-time (1 woman), 1 international. Average age 47. 6 applicants, 17% accepted, 1 enrolled. In 2011, 2 master's awarded. *Entrance requirements:* For master's, official transcripts from all current and previous colleges, three letters of recommendation. Additional exam requirements/recommendations for international students: Required—TOEFL. *Application deadline:* For fall admission, 4/1 for domestic and international students. Application fee: $50. *Expenses: Tuition:* Full-time $17,010; part-time $945 per credit hour. Tuition and fees vary according to program. *Unit head:* Dr. Jeanne Hossenlopp, Vice Provost for Research/Dean, 414-288-1532, Fax: 414-288-1578. *Application contact:* Craig Pierce, Assistant Dean of the Graduate School, 414-288-5740, Fax: 414-288-1902, E-mail: craig.pierce@marquette.edu. Web site: http://www.bcw.edu/bcw/education/sbbprogram/mstm/index.htm.

McMaster University, Faculty of Health Sciences and School of Graduate Studies, Program in Medical Sciences, Blood and Vascular Area, Hamilton, ON L8S 4M2, Canada. Offers M Sc, PhD, MD/PhD. *Degree requirements:* For master's, thesis; for doctorate, comprehensive exam, thesis/dissertation. *Entrance requirements:* For master's, honors B Sc, B+ average in related field; for doctorate, M Sc, minimum B+ average, students with proven research experience and an A average may be admitted with a B Sc degree. Additional exam requirements/recommendations for international students: Required—TOEFL (minimum score 580 paper-based; 237 computer-based; 92 iBT).

Medical University of South Carolina, College of Graduate Studies, Program in Molecular and Cellular Biology and Pathobiology, Charleston, SC 29425. Offers cancer biology (PhD); cardiovascular biology (PhD); cardiovascular imaging (PhD); cell regulation (PhD); craniofacial biology (PhD); genetics and development (PhD); marine biomedicine (PhD); DMD/PhD; MD/PhD. *Faculty:* 137 full-time (33 women). *Students:* 28 full-time (23 women); includes 5 minority (4 Black or African American, non-Hispanic/Latino; 1 Hispanic/Latino), 5 international. Average age 30. In 2011, 16 doctorates awarded. *Degree requirements:* For doctorate, thesis/dissertation, oral and written exams. *Entrance requirements:* For doctorate, GRE General Test, interview, minimum GPA of 3.0. Additional exam requirements/recommendations for international students: Required—TOEFL (minimum score 600 paper-based; 250 computer-based; 100 iBT). *Application deadline:* For fall admission, 1/15 priority date for domestic students, 1/15 for international students. Applications are processed on a rolling basis. Application fee: $0 ($85 for international students). Electronic applications accepted. *Financial support:* In 2011–12, 39 research assistantships with partial tuition reimbursements (averaging $23,000 per year) were awarded; Federal Work-Study and scholarships/grants also available. Support available to part-time students. Financial award application deadline: 3/10; financial award applicants required to submit FAFSA. *Unit head:* Dr. Donald R. Menick, Director, 843-876-5045, Fax: 843-792-6590, E-mail: menickd@musc.edu. *Application contact:* Dr. Cynthia F. Wright, Associate Dean for Admissions and Career Development, 843-792-2564, Fax: 843-792-6590, E-mail: wrightcf@musc.edu. Web site: http://www.musc.edu/mcbp/.

Memorial University of Newfoundland, Faculty of Medicine and School of Graduate Studies, Graduate Programs in Medicine, Division of Biomedical Sciences, St. John's, NL A1C 5S7, Canada. Offers cancer (M Sc, PhD); cardiovascular (M Sc, PhD); immunology (M Sc, PhD); neuroscience (M Sc, PhD). Part-time programs available. *Degree requirements:* For master's, thesis; for doctorate, comprehensive exam, thesis/dissertation, oral defense of thesis. *Entrance requirements:* For master's, MD or B Sc; for doctorate, MD or M Sc. Additional exam requirements/recommendations for international students: Required—TOEFL. *Faculty research:* Neuroscience, immunology, cardiovascular, and cancer.

Midwestern University, Glendale Campus, College of Health Sciences, Arizona Campus, Program in Cardiovascular Science, Glendale, AZ 85308. Offers MCVS. *Faculty:* 4 full-time (1 woman). *Students:* 54 full-time (23 women), 1 part-time (0 women); includes 16 minority (4 Black or African American, non-Hispanic/Latino; 3 Asian, non-Hispanic/Latino; 8 Hispanic/Latino; 1 Two or more races, non-Hispanic/Latino), 1 international. Average age 28. 98 applicants, 37% accepted, 29 enrolled. In 2011, 10 master's awarded. *Application fee:* $50. *Expenses:* Contact institution. *Unit head:* Dr. Jon Austin, Dean, 623-572-3616. *Application contact:* James Walter, Director of Admissions, 888-247-9277, Fax: 623-572-3229, E-mail: admissaz@midwestern.edu.

Milwaukee School of Engineering, Department of Electrical Engineering and Computer Science, Program in Cardiovascular Studies, Milwaukee, WI 53202-3109. Offers MS. Part-time and evening/weekend programs available. *Faculty:* 1 full-time (0 women), 1 part-time/adjunct (0 women). *Students:* 4 part-time (1 woman). Average age 29. 4 applicants, 100% accepted, 1 enrolled. *Degree requirements:* For master's, thesis. *Entrance requirements:* For master's, GRE General Test or GMAT, 2 letters of recommendation. Additional exam requirements/recommendations for international students: Required—TOEFL (minimum score 79 iBT) or IELTS. *Application deadline:* Applications are processed on a rolling basis. Electronic applications accepted. Application fee is waived when completed online. *Expenses: Tuition:* Full-time $17,550; part-time $650 per credit hour. *Financial support:* In 2011–12, 2 students received support. *Unit head:* Dr. Ronald Gerrits, Director, 414-277-7561, Fax: 414-277-7494, E-mail: gerrits@msoe.edu. *Application contact:* Katie Gassenhuber, Graduate Program Associate, 800-321-6763, Fax: 414-277-7208, E-mail: gassenhuber@msoe.edu.

Milwaukee School of Engineering, Department of Electrical Engineering and Computer Science, Program in Perfusion, Milwaukee, WI 53202-3109. Offers MS. Part-time and evening/weekend programs available. *Faculty:* 1 full-time (0 women), 3 part-time/adjunct (1 woman). *Students:* 11 full-time (3 women); includes 1 minority (Black or African American, non-Hispanic/Latino). Average age 33. 19 applicants, 42% accepted, 5 enrolled. *Degree requirements:* For master's, comprehensive exam, thesis, exam. *Entrance requirements:* For master's, GRE General Test or GMAT, BS in appropriate discipline, undergraduate work in human physiology or anatomy, 3 letters of recommendation, interview, observation of 2 perfusion cases. Additional exam requirements/recommendations for international students: Required—TOEFL (minimum score 79 iBT). *Application deadline:* Applications are processed on a rolling basis. Electronic applications accepted. Application fee is waived when completed online. *Expenses: Tuition:* Full-time $17,550; part-time $650 per credit hour. *Financial support:* In 2011–12, 10 students received support. Career-related internships or fieldwork

available. Support available to part-time students. Financial award applicants required to submit FAFSA. *Faculty research:* Heart medicine. *Unit head:* Dr. Ronald Gerrits, Director, 414-277-7561, Fax: 414-277-7494, E-mail: gerrits@msoe.edu. *Application contact:* Katie Gassenhuber, Graduate Program Associate, 800-321-6763, Fax: 414-277-7208, E-mail: gassenhuber@msoe.edu. Web site: http://www.msoe.edu/academics/academic_departments/eecs/msp/.

Queen's University at Kingston, School of Graduate Studies and Research, Faculty of Health Sciences, Department of Anatomy and Cell Biology, Kingston, ON K7L 3N6, Canada. Offers biology of reproduction (M Sc, PhD); cancer (M Sc, PhD); cardiovascular pathophysiology (M Sc, PhD); cell and molecular biology (M Sc, PhD); drug metabolism (M Sc, PhD); endocrinology (M Sc, PhD); motor control (M Sc, PhD); neural regeneration (M Sc, PhD); neurophysiology (M Sc, PhD). Part-time programs available. *Degree requirements:* For master's, thesis; for doctorate, one foreign language, comprehensive exam, thesis/dissertation. *Entrance requirements:* Additional exam requirements/recommendations for international students: Required—TOEFL. Electronic applications accepted. *Faculty research:* Human kinetics, neuroscience, reproductive biology, cardiovascular.

Quinnipiac University, School of Health Sciences, Program in Cardiovascular Perfusion, Hamden, CT 06518-1940. Offers MHS. *Faculty:* 1 full-time (0 women), 3 part-time/adjunct (0 women). *Students:* 7 full-time (4 women), 7 part-time (2 women). 27 applicants, 44% accepted, 7 enrolled. In 2011, 13 master's awarded. *Entrance requirements:* For master's, bachelor's degree in science or health-related discipline from an accredited American or Canadian college or university; 2 years health care work experience; interview. Additional exam requirements/recommendations for international students: Required—TOEFL (minimum score 575 paper-based; 233 computer-based; 90 iBT), IELTS (minimum score 6.5). *Application deadline:* For fall admission, 7/30 priority date for domestic students, 4/30 for international students. Applications are processed on a rolling basis. Application fee: $45. Electronic applications accepted. *Expenses: Tuition:* Part-time $855 per credit. *Required fees:* $35 per credit. *Financial support:* In 2011–12, 5 students received support. Career-related internships or fieldwork, tuition waivers, and unspecified assistantships available. Financial award application deadline: 4/15; financial award applicants required to submit FAFSA. *Unit head:* Michael Smith, Director, 203-582-3427, Fax: 203-582-8706, E-mail: michael.smith@quinnipiac.edu. *Application contact:* Kristin Parent, Assistant Director of Graduate Health Sciences Admissions, 800-462-1944, Fax: 208-582-3443, E-mail: kristin.parent@quinnipiac.edu. Web site: http://www.quinnipiac.edu/gradperfusion.

State University of New York Upstate Medical University, College of Graduate Studies, Major Research Areas of the College of Graduate Studies, Syracuse, NY 13210-2334.

Université Laval, Faculty of Medicine, Post-Professional Programs in Medical Studies, Québec, QC G1K 7P4, Canada. Offers anatomy–pathology (DESS); anesthesiology (DESS); cardiology (DESS); care of older people (Diploma); clinical research (DESS); community health (DESS); dermatology (DESS); diagnostic radiology (DESS); emergency medicine (Diploma); family medicine (DESS); general surgery (DESS); geriatrics (DESS); hematology (DESS); internal medicine (DESS); maternal and fetal medicine (Diploma); medical biochemistry (DESS); medical microbiology and infectious diseases (DESS); medical oncology (DESS); nephrology (DESS); neurology (DESS); neurosurgery (DESS); obstetrics and gynecology (DESS); ophthalmology (DESS); orthopedic surgery (DESS); oto-rhino-laryngology (DESS); palliative medicine (Diploma); pediatrics (DESS); plastic surgery (DESS); psychiatry (DESS); pulmonary medicine (DESS); radiology–oncology (DESS); thoracic surgery (DESS); urology (DESS). *Degree requirements:* For other advanced degree, comprehensive exam. *Entrance requirements:* For degree, knowledge of French. Electronic applications accepted.

University of Calgary, Faculty of Medicine and Faculty of Graduate Studies, Department of Cardiovascular and Respiratory Sciences, Calgary, AB T2N 1N4, Canada. Offers M Sc, PhD. *Degree requirements:* For master's, thesis; for doctorate, thesis/dissertation, candidacy exam. *Entrance requirements:* For master's and doctorate, minimum GPA of 3.2. Additional exam requirements/recommendations for international students: Required—TOEFL (minimum score 600 paper-based; 250 computer-based). Electronic applications accepted. *Faculty research:* Cardiac mechanics, physiology and pharmacology; lung mechanics, physiology and pathophysiology; smooth muscle biochemistry; physiology and pharmacology.

University of California, San Diego, School of Medicine and Office of Graduate Studies, Molecular Pathology Program, La Jolla, CA 92093. Offers bioinformatics (PhD); cancer biology/oncology (PhD); cardiovascular sciences and disease (PhD); microbiology (PhD); molecular pathology (PhD); neurological disease (PhD); stem cell and developmental biology (PhD); structural biology/drug design (PhD). *Entrance requirements:* For doctorate, GRE General Test, GRE Subject Test. Additional exam requirements/recommendations for international students: Required—TOEFL. Electronic applications accepted.

University of Guelph, Ontario Veterinary College and Graduate Studies, Graduate Programs in Veterinary Sciences, Department of Clinical Studies, Guelph, ON N1G 2W1, Canada. Offers anesthesiology (M Sc, DV Sc); cardiology (DV Sc, Diploma); clinical studies (Diploma); dermatology (M Sc); diagnostic imaging (M Sc, DV Sc); emergency/critical care (M Sc, DV Sc, Diploma); medicine (M Sc, DV Sc); neurology (M Sc, DV Sc); ophthalmology (M Sc, DV Sc); surgery (M Sc, DV Sc). *Degree requirements:* For master's, thesis; for doctorate, comprehensive exam, thesis/dissertation. *Entrance requirements:* Additional exam requirements/recommendations for international students: Required—TOEFL (minimum score 550 paper-based; 213 computer-based), IELTS (minimum score 6.5). Electronic applications accepted. *Faculty research:* Orthopedics, respirology, oncology, exercise physiology, cardiology.

University of Mary, School of Health Sciences, Program in Respiratory Therapy, Bismarck, ND 58504-9652. Offers MS. *Faculty:* 4 full-time (2 women). *Students:* 3 part-time (2 women). Average age 23. 2 applicants, 100% accepted, 2 enrolled. *Entrance requirements:* For master's, minimum GPA of 3.0, 3 letters of reference, interview. Additional exam requirements/recommendations for international students: Required—TOEFL (minimum score 500 paper-based; 197 computer-based; 71 iBT). *Application deadline:* For fall admission, 2/15 priority date for domestic students. Application fee: $40. Electronic applications accepted. *Financial support:* Career-related internships or fieldwork available. Financial award application deadline: 8/1; financial award applicants required to submit FAFSA. *Unit head:* Dr. Will Beachey, Director, 701-530-7757, Fax: 701-255-7387, E-mail: wbeachey@primecare.org. *Application contact:* Dr. Kathy Perrin, Director of Graduate Studies, 701-355-8119, Fax: 701-255-7687, E-mail: kperrin@umary.edu.

University of Medicine and Dentistry of New Jersey, School of Health Related Professions, Department of Interdisciplinary Studies, Program in Health Sciences, Newark, NJ 07107-1709. Offers cardiopulmonary sciences (PhD); clinical laboratory sciences (PhD); health sciences (MS); interdisciplinary studies (PhD); nutrition (PhD); physical therapy/movement science (PhD). Part-time and evening/weekend programs available. Postbaccalaureate distance learning degree programs offered (no on-campus study). *Faculty:* 4 full-time (all women), 10 part-time/adjunct (7 women). *Students:* 3 full-time, 130 part-time; includes 32 minority (10 Black or African American, non-Hispanic/Latino; 10 Asian, non-Hispanic/Latino; 11 Hispanic/Latino; 1 Native Hawaiian or other Pacific Islander, non-Hispanic/Latino). Average age 41. 132 applicants, 51% accepted, 51 enrolled. In 2011, 17 master's, 4 doctorates awarded. *Degree requirements:* For doctorate, thesis/dissertation. *Entrance requirements:* For master's, BS, 2 reference letters, statement of career goals, curriculum vitae; for doctorate, GRE, interview, writing sample, 3 reference letters, curriculum vitae. Additional exam requirements/recommendations for international students: Required—TOEFL. *Application deadline:* For fall admission, 3/1 for domestic students. Applications are processed on a rolling basis. Application fee: $75. Electronic applications accepted. *Unit head:* Dr. Bob Denmark, Director, 973-972-5410, Fax: 973-972-7403, E-mail: ms-phd-hs@umdnj.edu. *Application contact:* Diane Hanrahan, Manager of Admissions, 973-972-5336, Fax: 973-972-7463, E-mail: shrpadm@umdnj.edu.

The University of South Dakota, Graduate School, School of Medicine and Graduate School, Biomedical Sciences Graduate Program, Cardiovascular Research Program, Vermillion, SD 57069-2390. Offers MS, PhD. Terminal master's awarded for partial completion of doctoral program. *Degree requirements:* For master's, thesis; for doctorate, comprehensive exam, thesis/dissertation. *Entrance requirements:* For master's and doctorate, GRE General Test, minimum GPA of 3.0. Additional exam requirements/recommendations for international students: Required—TOEFL (minimum score 550 paper-based; 213 computer-based; 80 iBT), IELTS (minimum score 6). Electronic applications accepted. *Expenses:* Contact institution. *Faculty research:* Cardiovascular disease.

The University of Toledo, College of Graduate Studies, College of Medicine and Life Sciences, Department of Physiology and Pharmacology, Toledo, OH 43606-3390. Offers cardiovascular and metabolic diseases (MSBS, PhD); MD/MSBS; MD/PhD. *Faculty:* 20. *Students:* 27 full-time (12 women), 3 part-time (1 woman); includes 5 minority (2 Black or African American, non-Hispanic/Latino; 3 Asian, non-Hispanic/Latino), 19 international. Average age 28. 26 applicants, 38% accepted, 6 enrolled. In 2011, 1 master's, 4 doctorates awarded. Terminal master's awarded for partial completion of doctoral program. *Degree requirements:* For master's, thesis, qualifying exam; for doctorate, thesis/dissertation, qualifying exam. *Entrance requirements:* For master's and doctorate, GRE, minimum undergraduate GPA of 3.0, three letters of recommendation, statement of purpose, transcripts from all prior institutions attended, resume. Additional exam requirements/recommendations for international students: Required—TOEFL (minimum score 550 paper-based; 213 computer-based; 80 iBT), IELTS (minimum score 6.5). *Application deadline:* For fall admission, 1/15 priority date for domestic students, 1/15 for international students. Application fee: $45 ($75 for international students). Electronic applications accepted. *Financial support:* In 2011–12, 36 research assistantships with full tuition reimbursements (averaging $21,180 per year) were awarded; Federal Work-Study, institutionally sponsored loans, scholarships/grants, tuition waivers (full), and unspecified assistantships also available. *Unit head:* Dr. Nader Abraham, Chair, 419-383-4425, E-mail: nader.abraham@utoledo.edu. *Application contact:* Admissions Analyst, 419-383-4116, Fax: 419-383-6140. Web site: http://www.utoledo.edu/med/grad/.

Molecular Physiology

Baylor College of Medicine, Graduate School of Biomedical Sciences, Department of Molecular Physiology and Biophysics, Houston, TX 77030-3498. Offers cardiovascular sciences (PhD); molecular physiology and biophysics (PhD); MD/PhD. *Faculty:* 110 full-time (23 women). *Students:* 30 full-time (12 women); includes 7 minority (4 Black or African American, non-Hispanic/Latino; 2 Asian, non-Hispanic/Latino; 1 Hispanic/Latino), 9 international. Average age 27. 39 applicants, 26% accepted, 4 enrolled. In 2011, 3 doctorates awarded. *Degree requirements:* For doctorate, thesis/dissertation, public defense. *Entrance requirements:* For doctorate, GRE General Test, GRE Subject Test (strongly recommended), minimum GPA of 3.0. Additional exam requirements/recommendations for international students: Required—TOEFL. *Application deadline:* For fall admission, 1/1 priority date for domestic students. Electronic applications accepted. *Financial support:* In 2011–12, 10 fellowships with full tuition reimbursements (averaging $29,000 per year), 20 research assistantships with full tuition reimbursements (averaging $29,000 per year) were awarded; career-related internships or fieldwork, Federal Work-Study, institutionally sponsored loans, health care benefits, and scholarships (to all students unless there are grant funds available to pay tuition) also available. Financial award applicants required to submit FAFSA. *Faculty research:* Cardiovascular disease; skeletal muscle disease (myasthenia gravis, muscular dystrophy, malignant hyperthermia, central core disease); cancer; Alzheimer's disease; developmental diseases of the nervous system, eye and heart; diabetes; motor neuron disease (amyotrophic lateral sclerosis and spinal muscular atrophy); asthma; autoimmune diseases. *Unit head:* Dr. Robia Pautler, Co-Director, 713-798-3892, E-mail: rpautler@bcm.edu. *Application contact:* Dr. Steen Pedersen, Co-Director, 713-798-3888, E-mail: pedersen@bcm.edu. Web site: http://www.bcm.edu/physio/.

Case Western Reserve University, School of Medicine and School of Graduate Studies, Graduate Programs in Medicine, Department of Physiology and Biophysics, Cleveland, OH 44106. Offers cell and molecular physiology (MS); cell physiology (PhD); molecular/cellular biophysics (PhD); physiology and biophysics (PhD); systems physiology (PhD); MD/PhD. Terminal master's awarded for partial completion of doctoral program. *Degree requirements:* For master's, thesis; for doctorate, thesis/dissertation. *Entrance requirements:* For master's, GRE General Test, minimum GPA of 3.28; for doctorate, GRE General Test, minimum GPA of 3.6. Additional exam requirements/recommendations for international students: Required—TOEFL. Electronic applications accepted. *Faculty research:* Cardiovascular physiology, calcium metabolism, epithelial cell biology.

See Display on page 450 and Close-Up on page 461.

Molecular Physiology

Loyola University Chicago, Graduate School, Programs in Cell and Molecular Physiology, Chicago, IL 60660. Offers MS, PhD. *Faculty:* 17 full-time (4 women), 5 part-time/adjunct (1 woman). *Students:* 22 full-time (5 women); includes 7 minority (1 Black or African American, non-Hispanic/Latino; 5 Asian, non-Hispanic/Latino; 1 Two or more races, non-Hispanic/Latino), 3 international. Average age 25. 75 applicants, 48% accepted, 16 enrolled. In 2011, 1 master's, 2 doctorates awarded. *Degree requirements:* For master's, thesis; for doctorate, comprehensive exam, thesis/dissertation. *Entrance requirements:* For master's, GRE General Test or MCAT; for doctorate, GRE General Test. Additional exam requirements/recommendations for international students: Required—TOEFL. *Application deadline:* For fall admission, 5/15 for domestic and international students. Application fee: $0. Electronic applications accepted. *Expenses: Tuition:* Full-time $15,660; part-time $870 per credit hour. *Required fees:* $125 per semester. Tuition and fees vary according to course load and program. *Financial support:* In 2011–12, 5 fellowships with tuition reimbursements (averaging $23,000 per year), 9 research assistantships with tuition reimbursements (averaging $23,000 per year) were awarded. *Faculty research:* Cardiovascular system-emphasis in neural and metabolic control of circulation, ion channels, excitation contraction coupling, molecular cloning. *Unit head:* Dr. Pieter deTombe, Chair, 708-216-6305, Fax: 708-216-6308, E-mail: pdetombe@lumc.edu. *Application contact:* Dr. Ruben Mestril, Graduate Program Director, 708-327-2395, Fax: 708-216-6308, E-mail: rmestri@lumc.edu.

Rutgers, The State University of New Jersey, New Brunswick, Graduate School-New Brunswick, Program in Endocrinology and Animal Biosciences, Piscataway, NJ 08854-8097. Offers MS, PhD. Terminal master's awarded for partial completion of doctoral program. *Degree requirements:* For master's, thesis; for doctorate, comprehensive exam, thesis/dissertation. *Entrance requirements:* For master's and doctorate, GRE General Test. Additional exam requirements/recommendations for international students: Required—TOEFL. Electronic applications accepted. *Faculty research:* Comparative and behavioral endocrinology, epigenetic regulation of the endocrine system, exercise physiology and immunology, fetal and neonatal developmental programming, mammary gland biology and breast cancer, neuroendocrinology and alcohol studies, reproductive and developmental toxicology.

Stony Brook University, State University of New York, Stony Brook University Medical Center, Health Sciences Center, School of Medicine and Graduate School, Graduate Programs in Medicine, Department of Physiology and Biophysics, Stony Brook, NY 11794. Offers PhD. *Degree requirements:* For doctorate, comprehensive exam, thesis/dissertation. *Entrance requirements:* For doctorate, GRE General Test, GRE Subject Test, BS in related field, minimum GPA of 3.0. Additional exam requirements/recommendations for international students: Required—TOEFL. *Faculty research:* Cellular electrophysiology, membrane permeation and transport, metabolic endocrinology.

Texas Tech University Health Sciences Center, Graduate School of Biomedical Sciences, Department of Cell Physiology and Molecular Biophysics, Lubbock, TX 79430. Offers MS, PhD, MD/PhD. Terminal master's awarded for partial completion of doctoral program. *Degree requirements:* For master's, thesis; for doctorate, thesis/dissertation. *Entrance requirements:* For master's and doctorate, GRE General Test, minimum GPA of 3.4. Additional exam requirements/recommendations for international students: Required—TOEFL. Electronic applications accepted. *Faculty research:* Cardiovascular physiology, neurophysiology, renal physiology, respiratory physiology.

Thomas Jefferson University, Jefferson College of Graduate Studies, Program in Molecular Physiology and Biophysics, Philadelphia, PA 19107. Offers PhD. *Faculty:* 10 full-time (5 women). *Students:* 1 full-time (0 women). *Degree requirements:* For doctorate, comprehensive exam, thesis/dissertation. *Entrance requirements:* For doctorate, GRE General Test, minimum GPA of 3.2. Additional exam requirements/recommendations for international students: Required—TOEFL (minimum score 250 computer-based; 100 iBT). *Application deadline:* For fall admission, 1/15 priority date for domestic students, 1/15 for international students. Applications are processed on a rolling basis. Application fee: $50. Electronic applications accepted. *Financial support:* In 2011–12, 1 student received support, including 1 fellowship with full tuition reimbursement available (averaging $54,758 per year); Federal Work-Study, institutionally sponsored loans, scholarships/grants, traineeships, and stipends also available. Support available to part-time students. Financial award application deadline: 5/1; financial award applicants required to submit FAFSA. *Faculty research:* Cardiovascular physiology, smooth muscle physiology, pathophysiology of myocardial ischemia, endothelial cell physiology, molecular biology of ion channel physiology. *Total annual research expenditures:* $893,526. *Unit head:* Dr. Thomas M. Butler, Program Director, 215-503-6583, E-mail: thomas.butler@jefferson.edu. *Application contact:* Marc E. Stearns, Director of Admissions, 215-503-0155, Fax: 215-503-9920, E-mail: jcgs-info@jefferson.edu. Web site: http://www.jefferson.edu/physiology/.

Tufts University, Sackler School of Graduate Biomedical Sciences, Cellular and Molecular Physiology Program, Medford, MA 02155. Offers MS, PhD. *Faculty:* 18 full-time (6 women). *Students:* 13 full-time (6 women); includes 2 minority (1 Hispanic/Latino; 1 Two or more races, non-Hispanic/Latino), 5 international. Average age 28. In 2011, 3 doctorates awarded. *Degree requirements:* For doctorate, thesis/dissertation. *Entrance requirements:* For doctorate, GRE General Test, 3 letters of reference. Additional exam requirements/recommendations for international students: Required—TOEFL (minimum score 600 paper-based; 250 computer-based; 100 iBT). *Application deadline:* For fall admission, 12/15 for domestic and international students. Application fee: $70. Electronic applications accepted. *Expenses: Tuition:* Full-time $41,208; part-time $1030 per credit hour. Full-time tuition and fees vary according to degree level, program and student level. Part-time tuition and fees vary according to course load. *Financial support:* In 2011–12, 13 students received support, including 13 research assistantships with full tuition reimbursements available (averaging $28,250 per year); health care benefits also available. *Faculty research:* Molecular signaling networks controlling cell growth and motility, molecular and cellular dissection of protein- and lipid-based trafficking pathways, signaling within and among neurons and glia. *Unit head:* Dr. Ira Herman, Director, 617-636-02991. *Application contact:* Kellie Melchin, Associate Director of Admissions, 617-636-6767, Fax: 617-636-0375, E-mail: sackler-school@tufts.edu. Web site: http://sackler.tufts.edu/Acádemics/Degree-Programs/PhD-Programs/Cellular-and-Molecular-Physiology.

The University of Alabama at Birmingham, Graduate Programs in Joint Health Sciences, Program in Cellular and Molecular Physiology, Birmingham, AL 35294. Offers PhD. Application fee: $35 ($60 for international students). *Expenses:* Tuition, state resident: full-time $5922; part-time $309 per hour. Tuition, nonresident: full-time $13,428; part-time $726 per hour. Tuition and fees vary according to program. *Unit head:* Dr. Etty Benvenister, Chair, 205-934-7667, Fax: 205-975-6748, E-mail: tika@uab.edu.

University of Chicago, Division of Biological Sciences, Neuroscience Graduate Programs, Chicago, IL 60637-1513. Offers cellular and molecular physiology (PhD); computational neuroscience (PhD); integrative neuroscience (PhD), including cell physiology, pharmacological and physiological sciences; neurobiology (PhD). *Degree requirements:* For doctorate, thesis/dissertation, ethics class, 2 teaching assistantships. *Entrance requirements:* For doctorate, GRE General Test. Additional exam requirements/recommendations for international students: Required—TOEFL (minimum score 600 paper-based; 250 computer-based; 104 iBT), IELTS (minimum score 7). Electronic applications accepted.

University of Chicago, Division of Biological Sciences, Program in Cellular and Molecular Physiology, Chicago, IL 60637-1513. Offers PhD. *Degree requirements:* For doctorate, thesis/dissertation, ethics class, 2 teaching assistantships. *Entrance requirements:* For doctorate, GRE General Test. Additional exam requirements/recommendations for international students: Required—TOEFL (minimum score 600 paper-based; 250 computer-based; 104 iBT), IELTS (minimum score 7). Electronic applications accepted. *Faculty research:* Molecular genetics, biochemical biological and physical approaches to cell physiology.

University of Illinois at Urbana–Champaign, Graduate College, College of Liberal Arts and Sciences, School of Molecular and Cellular Biology, Department of Molecular and Integrative Physiology, Champaign, IL 61820. Offers MS, PhD. *Faculty:* 12 full-time (4 women). *Students:* 31 full-time (16 women), 2 part-time (0 women); includes 5 minority (1 Black or African American, non-Hispanic/Latino; 2 Asian, non-Hispanic/Latino; 2 Hispanic/Latino), 11 international. In 2011, 4 master's, 6 doctorates awarded. *Entrance requirements:* For master's and doctorate, GRE, minimum GPA of 3.0. Additional exam requirements/recommendations for international students: Required—TOEFL (minimum score 590 paper-based; 243 computer-based). *Application deadline:* Applications are processed on a rolling basis. Application fee: $75 ($90 for international students). Electronic applications accepted. *Financial support:* In 2011–12, 8 fellowships, 23 research assistantships, 10 teaching assistantships were awarded; tuition waivers (full and partial) also available. *Unit head:* Byron Kemper, Head, 217-333-1146, Fax: 217-333-1133, E-mail: byronkem@illinois.edu. *Application contact:* Shawn Smith, Office Manager, 217-244-6638, Fax: 217-333-1133, E-mail: smsmith1@illinois.edu. Web site: http://mcb.illinois.edu/departments/mip/.

The University of North Carolina at Chapel Hill, School of Medicine and Graduate School, Graduate Programs in Medicine, Department of Cell and Molecular Physiology, Chapel Hill, NC 27599. Offers PhD. Terminal master's awarded for partial completion of doctoral program. *Degree requirements:* For doctorate, comprehensive exam, thesis/dissertation, ethics training. *Entrance requirements:* For doctorate, GRE General Test. Electronic applications accepted. *Faculty research:* Signal transduction; growth factors; cardiovascular diseases; neurobiology; hormones, receptors, ion channels.

University of Pittsburgh, School of Medicine, Graduate Programs in Medicine, Program in Cell Biology and Molecular Physiology, Pittsburgh, PA 15260. Offers MS, PhD. *Faculty:* 45 full-time (12 women). *Students:* 8 full-time (6 women); includes 1 minority (Asian, non-Hispanic/Latino), 3 international. Average age 27. 514 applicants, 12% accepted, 8 enrolled. In 2011, 4 doctorates awarded. *Degree requirements:* For doctorate, comprehensive exam, thesis/dissertation. *Entrance requirements:* For doctorate, GRE General Test, GRE Subject Test, minimum QPA of 3.0. Additional exam requirements/recommendations for international students: Required—TOEFL (minimum score 600 paper-based; 100 iBT), IELTS (minimum score 7). *Application deadline:* For fall admission, 12/15 priority date for domestic students, 12/15 for international students. Application fee: $50. Electronic applications accepted. *Expenses:* Tuition, state resident: full-time $18,774; part-time $760 per credit. Tuition, nonresident: full-time $30,736; part-time $1258 per credit. *Required fees:* $740; $200 per term. Tuition and fees vary according to program. *Financial support:* In 2011–12, 3 research assistantships with full tuition reimbursements (averaging $25,500 per year), 5 teaching assistantships with full tuition reimbursements (averaging $25,500 per year) were awarded; institutionally sponsored loans, scholarships/grants, traineeships, health care benefits, and unspecified assistantships also available. *Faculty research:* Genetic disorders of ion channels, regulation of gene expression/development, membrane traffic of proteins and lipids, reproductive biology, signal transduction in diabetes and metabolism. *Unit head:* Dr. William H. Walker, Graduate Program Director, 412-641-7672, Fax: 412-641-7676, E-mail: walkerw@pitt.edu. *Application contact:* Graduate Studies Administrator, 412-648-8957, Fax: 412-648-1077, E-mail: gradstudies@medschool.pitt.edu. Web site: http://www.gradbiomed.pitt.edu.

University of Vermont, College of Medicine and Graduate College, Graduate Programs in Medicine, Department of Molecular Physiology and Biophysics, Burlington, VT 05405. Offers MS, PhD, MD/MS, MD/PhD. *Students:* 5 (2 women), 1 international. 4 applicants, 25% accepted, 1 enrolled. *Degree requirements:* For master's, thesis; for doctorate, thesis/dissertation. *Entrance requirements:* For master's and doctorate, GRE General Test. Additional exam requirements/recommendations for international students: Required—TOEFL (minimum score 550 paper-based; 213 computer-based; 80 iBT). *Application deadline:* For fall admission, 2/15 priority date for domestic students, 2/15 for international students. Applications are processed on a rolling basis. Application fee: $40. Electronic applications accepted. *Financial support:* Fellowships, research assistantships, and teaching assistantships available. Financial award application deadline: 3/1. *Unit head:* Dr. D. Warshaw, Chairperson, 802-656-2540. *Application contact:* Dr. Terese Ruiz, Coordinator, 802-656-2540.

University of Virginia, School of Medicine, Department of Molecular Physiology and Biological Physics, Charlottesville, VA 22903. Offers biological and physical sciences (MS); physiology (PhD); MD/PhD. *Faculty:* 29 full-time (5 women), 2 part-time/adjunct (0 women). *Students:* 19 full-time (10 women); includes 2 minority (both Black or African American, non-Hispanic/Latino). Average age 28. In 2011, 14 master's, 2 doctorates awarded. *Entrance requirements:* For doctorate, GRE General Test, GRE Subject Test. Additional exam requirements/recommendations for international students: Required—TOEFL. *Application deadline:* For fall admission, 2/15 for domestic and international students. Applications are processed on a rolling basis. Application fee: $60. Electronic applications accepted. *Financial support:* Fellowships, research assistantships, and teaching assistantships available. Financial award applicants required to submit FAFSA. *Unit head:* Dr. Mark Yeager, Chair, 434-924-5108, Fax: 434-982-1616, E-mail: my3r@virginia.edu. *Application contact:* Lesley L. Thomas, Director, Admissions Office, 434-924-5571, Fax: 434-982-2586, E-mail: medsch-adm@virginia.edu. Web site: http://www.healthsystem.virginia.edu/internet/physio/.

Vanderbilt University, Graduate School and School of Medicine, Department of Molecular Physiology and Biophysics, Nashville, TN 37240-1001. Offers MS, PhD, MD/PhD. *Faculty:* 37 full-time (8 women). *Students:* 39 full-time (25 women); includes 10 minority (4 Black or African American, non-Hispanic/Latino; 1 American Indian or Alaska Native, non-Hispanic/Latino; 3 Hispanic/Latino; 2 Two or more races, non-Hispanic/Latino), 4 international. Average age 28. In 2011, 3 doctorates awarded. *Degree requirements:* For doctorate, comprehensive exam, thesis/dissertation, preliminary, qualifying, and final exams. *Entrance requirements:* For doctorate, GRE General Test, GRE Subject Test (recommended). Additional exam requirements/recommendations for international students: Required—TOEFL (minimum score 570 paper-based; 230 computer-based; 88 iBT). *Application deadline:* For fall admission, 1/15 for domestic and international students. Application fee: $0. Electronic applications accepted. *Financial support:* Fellowships with full tuition reimbursements, research assistantships with full tuition reimbursements, Federal Work-Study, institutionally sponsored loans, scholarships/grants, traineeships, health care benefits, and tuition waivers (partial) available. Financial award application deadline: 1/15; financial award applicants required to submit CSS PROFILE or FAFSA. *Faculty research:* Biophysics, cell signaling and gene regulation, human genetics, diabetes and obesity, neuroscience. *Unit head:* Dr.

Roger Cone, Chair, 615-936-7085, Fax: 615-343-4075, E-mail: roger.cone@vanderbilt.edu. *Application contact:* Angie Pernell, Administrative Assistant/Director of Graduate Studies Assistant, 615-322-7001, Fax: 615-343-0490, E-mail: angie.pernell@vanderbilt.edu. Web site: http://www.mc.vanderbilt.edu/medschool/mpb/.

Yale University, Graduate School of Arts and Sciences, Department of Cellular and Molecular Physiology, New Haven, CT 06520. Offers PhD. *Degree requirements:* For doctorate, thesis/dissertation. *Entrance requirements:* For doctorate, GRE General Test, GRE Subject Test.

Physiology

Albert Einstein College of Medicine, Graduate Division of Biomedical Sciences, Department of Physiology and Biophysics, Bronx, NY 10461. Offers PhD, MD/PhD. *Degree requirements:* For doctorate, thesis/dissertation. *Entrance requirements:* For doctorate, GRE General Test. Additional exam requirements/recommendations for international students: Required—TOEFL. *Faculty research:* Biophysical and biochemical basis of body function at the subcellular, cellular, organ, and whole-body level.

Ball State University, Graduate School, College of Sciences and Humanities, Department of Physiology and Health Science, Program in Physiology, Muncie, IN 47306-1099. Offers MA, MS. *Faculty:* 16. *Students:* 34 full-time (13 women), 4 part-time (2 women); includes 3 minority (1 Black or African American, non-Hispanic/Latino; 1 Asian, non-Hispanic/Latino; 1 Two or more races, non-Hispanic/Latino), 9 international. Average age 22. 37 applicants, 73% accepted, 19 enrolled. In 2011, 12 master's awarded. Application fee: $50. Tuition and fees vary according to program and reciprocity agreements. *Financial support:* In 2011–12, 10 students received support, including 10 teaching assistantships with full tuition reimbursements available (averaging $9,226 per year). Financial award application deadline: 3/1. *Unit head:* Dr. Jeffrey K. Clark, Director, 765-285-8360, Fax: 765-285-3210. *Application contact:* Dr. Marianna Tucker, Director of Graduate Programs, 765-285-5961, Fax: 765-285-3210, E-mail: jclark@bsu.edu. Web site: http://www.bsu.edu/chs/phs/.

Boston University, College of Health and Rehabilitation Sciences: Sargent College, Department of Health Sciences, Programs in Applied Anatomy and Physiology, Boston, MA 02215. Offers MS, PhD. *Faculty:* 10 full-time (9 women), 5 part-time/adjunct (2 women). *Students:* 4 full-time (2 women), 4 part-time (all women), 1 international. Average age 27. 37 applicants, 41% accepted. In 2011, 11 degrees awarded. Terminal master's awarded for partial completion of doctoral program. *Degree requirements:* For master's, thesis or alternative; for doctorate, comprehensive exam, thesis/dissertation. *Entrance requirements:* For master's, GRE General Test, minimum GPA of 3.0; for doctorate, GRE General Test. Additional exam requirements/recommendations for international students: Required—TOEFL (minimum score 550 paper-based; 84 iBT). *Application deadline:* For fall admission, 1/15 priority date for domestic students, 1/15 for international students; for spring admission, 10/1 for domestic and international students. Applications are processed on a rolling basis. Application fee: $70. Electronic applications accepted. *Expenses: Tuition:* Full-time $40,848; part-time $1276 per credit hour. *Required fees:* $572; $286 per semester. *Financial support:* In 2011–12, 2 fellowships (averaging $21,000 per year), 1 research assistantship with full tuition reimbursement (averaging $18,000 per year), 3 teaching assistantships with full and partial tuition reimbursements were awarded; career-related internships or fieldwork, Federal Work-Study, institutionally sponsored loans, scholarships/grants, and tuition waivers (partial) also available. Support available to part-time students. Financial award application deadline: 4/15; financial award applicants required to submit FAFSA. *Faculty research:* Skeletal muscle, neural systems, smooth muscle, muscular dystrophy. *Total annual research expenditures:* $3 million. *Unit head:* Dr. Kathleen Morgan, Chair, 617-353-2717, E-mail: kmorgan@bu.edu. *Application contact:* Sharon Sankey, Director, Student Services, 617-353-2713, Fax: 617-353-7500, E-mail: ssankey@bu.edu.

Boston University, School of Medicine, Division of Graduate Medical Sciences, Department of Physiology and Biophysics, Boston, MA 02118. Offers MA, PhD, MD/PhD. Part-time programs available. *Faculty:* 21 full-time (6 women), 1 part-time/adjunct. *Students:* 14 full-time (7 women), 3 part-time (1 woman); includes 3 minority (2 Asian, non-Hispanic/Latino; 1 Hispanic/Latino), 5 international. Average age 26. 18 applicants, 44% accepted, 4 enrolled. In 2011, 1 master's, 4 doctorates awarded. Terminal master's awarded for partial completion of doctoral program. *Degree requirements:* For master's, thesis, qualifying exam; for doctorate, thesis/dissertation, qualifying exam. *Entrance requirements:* For master's and doctorate, GRE General Test, GRE Subject Test (strongly recommended). Additional exam requirements/recommendations for international students: Required—TOEFL. *Application deadline:* For fall admission, 1/15 priority date for domestic students; for spring admission, 10/15 priority date for domestic students. Application fee: $75. Electronic applications accepted. *Expenses: Tuition:* Full-time $40,848; part-time $1276 per credit hour. *Required fees:* $572; $286 per semester. *Financial support:* In 2011–12, 5 research assistantships (averaging $30,500 per year) were awarded; fellowships, scholarships/grants, and traineeships also available. *Faculty research:* X-ray scattering, NMR spectroscopy, protein crystallography, structural electron microscopy, molecular modeling. *Unit head:* Dr. David Atkinson, Chairman, 617-638-4015, Fax: 617-638-4041, E-mail: atkinson@bu.edu. *Application contact:* Dr. Esther Bullitt, 617-638-5037, E-mail: bullitt@bu.edu. Web site: http://www.bumc.bu.edu/phys-biophys/.

Brigham Young University, Graduate Studies, College of Life Sciences, Department of Physiology and Developmental Biology, Provo, UT 84602. Offers neuroscience (MS, PhD); physiology and developmental biology (MS, PhD). Part-time programs available. *Faculty:* 20 full-time (0 women). *Students:* 37 full-time (14 women); includes 9 minority (2 American Indian or Alaska Native, non-Hispanic/Latino; 3 Asian, non Hispanic/Latino; 4 Hispanic/Latino). Average age 29. 12 applicants, 75% accepted, 8 enrolled. In 2011, 6 master's, 1 doctorate awarded. Terminal master's awarded for partial completion of doctoral program. *Degree requirements:* For master's, thesis; for doctorate, comprehensive exam, thesis/dissertation. *Entrance requirements:* For master's, GRE General Test, minimum GPA of 3.0 during previous 2 years; for doctorate, GRE General Test, minimum GPA of 3.0 overall. Additional exam requirements/recommendations for international students: Required—TOEFL. *Application deadline:* For fall admission, 2/1 priority date for domestic students, 2/1 for international students; for winter admission, 9/10 priority date for domestic students, 9/10 for international students. Application fee: $50. Electronic applications accepted. *Expenses: Tuition:* Full-time $5760; part-time $320 per credit. Tuition and fees vary according to student's religious affiliation. *Financial support:* In 2011–12, 36 students received support, including 1 fellowship with partial tuition reimbursement available (averaging $7,100 per year), 18 research assistantships with full tuition reimbursements available (averaging $15,500 per year), 19 teaching assistantships with partial tuition reimbursements available (averaging $14,900 per year); career-related internships or fieldwork, institutionally sponsored loans, scholarships/grants, tuition waivers (full and partial), unspecified assistantships, and tuition awards also available. Financial award application deadline: 2/1. *Faculty*

research: Sex differentiation of the brain, exercise physiology, developmental biology, membrane biophysics, neuroscience. *Total annual research expenditures:* $589,241. *Unit head:* Dr. William W. Winder, Chair, 801-422-3093, Fax: 801-422-0700, E-mail: william_winder@byu.edu. *Application contact:* Dr. Dixon J. Woodbury, Graduate Coordinator, 801-422-7562, Fax: 801-422-0700, E-mail: dixon_woodbury@byu.edu. Web site: http://pdbio.byu.edu.

Brown University, Graduate School, Division of Biology and Medicine, Program in Molecular Pharmacology and Physiology, Providence, RI 02912. Offers MA, Sc M, PhD, MD/PhD. *Degree requirements:* For doctorate, thesis/dissertation, preliminary exam. *Entrance requirements:* For master's and doctorate, GRE General Test, GRE Subject Test. Additional exam requirements/recommendations for international students: Required—TOEFL. Electronic applications accepted. *Faculty research:* Structural biology, antiplatelet drugs, nicotinic receptor structure/function.

Case Western Reserve University, School of Medicine and School of Graduate Studies, Graduate Programs in Medicine, Department of Physiology and Biophysics, Cleveland, OH 44106. Offers cell and molecular physiology (MS); cell physiology (PhD); molecular/cellular biophysics (PhD); physiology and biophysics (PhD); systems physiology (PhD); MD/PhD. Terminal master's awarded for partial completion of doctoral program. *Degree requirements:* For master's, thesis; for doctorate, thesis/dissertation. *Entrance requirements:* For master's, GRE General Test, minimum GPA of 3.28; for doctorate, GRE General Test, minimum GPA of 3.6. Additional exam requirements/recommendations for international students: Required—TOEFL. Electronic applications accepted. *Faculty research:* Cardiovascular physiology, calcium metabolism, epithelial cell biology.

See Display on next page and Close-Up on page 461.

Columbia University, College of Physicians and Surgeons, Department of Physiology and Cellular Biophysics, New York, NY 10032. Offers M Phil, MA, PhD, MD/PhD. Only candidates for the PhD are admitted. Terminal master's awarded for partial completion of doctoral program. *Degree requirements:* For doctorate, thesis/dissertation. *Entrance requirements:* For master's and doctorate, GRE General Test. Additional exam requirements/recommendations for international students: Required—TOEFL. *Faculty research:* Membrane physiology, cellular biology, cardiovascular physiology, neurophysiology.

Cornell University, Graduate School, Graduate Fields of Comparative Biomedical Sciences, Field of Molecular and Integrative Physiology, Ithaca, NY 14853-0001. Offers behavioral physiology (MS, PhD); cardiovascular and respiratory physiology (MS, PhD); endocrinology (MS, PhD); environmental and comparative physiology (MS, PhD); gastrointestinal and metabolic physiology (MS, PhD); membrane and epithelial physiology (MS, PhD); molecular and cellular physiology (MS, PhD); neural and sensory physiology (MS, PhD); physiological genomics (MS, PhD); reproductive physiology (MS, PhD). *Faculty:* 40 full-time (15 women). *Students:* 15 full-time (10 women); includes 1 minority (Asian, non-Hispanic/Latino), 8 international. Average age 30. 8 applicants, 13% accepted, 1 enrolled. In 2011, 1 degree awarded. *Degree requirements:* For master's, thesis; for doctorate, comprehensive exam, thesis/dissertation, 1 semester of teaching experience, seminar presentation. *Entrance requirements:* For master's and doctorate, GRE General Test, GRE Subject Test (biochemistry, cell and molecular biology, biology, or chemistry), 2 letters of recommendation. Additional exam requirements/recommendations for international students: Required—TOEFL (minimum score 550 paper-based; 213 computer-based; 77 iBT). *Application deadline:* For fall admission, 12/15 for domestic students. Application fee: $95. Electronic applications accepted. *Financial support:* In 2011–12, 2 fellowships with full tuition reimbursements, 11 research assistantships with full tuition reimbursements, 2 teaching assistantships with full tuition reimbursements were awarded; institutionally sponsored loans, scholarships/grants, health care benefits, tuition waivers (full and partial), and unspecified assistantships also available. Financial award applicants required to submit FAFSA. *Faculty research:* Endocrinology and reproductive physiology, cardiovascular and respiratory physiology, gastrointestinal and metabolic physiology, molecular and cellular physiology, physiological genomics. *Unit head:* Director of Graduate Studies, 607-253-3276, Fax: 607-253-3756. *Application contact:* Graduate Field Assistant, 607-253-3276, Fax: 607-253-3756, E-mail: graduate_edcvm@cornell.edu. Web site: http://www.gradschool.cornell.edu/fields.php?id-57&a-2.

Dalhousie University, Faculty of Medicine, Department of Physiology and Biophysics, Halifax, NS B3H 1X5, Canada. Offers M Sc, PhD, M Sc/PhD. *Degree requirements:* For master's, thesis; for doctorate, thesis/dissertation. *Entrance requirements:* For master's and doctorate, GRE Subject Test (for international students). Additional exam requirements/recommendations for international students: Required—1 of 5 approved tests: TOEFL, IELTS, CANTEST, CAEL, Michigan English Language Assessment Battery. Electronic applications accepted. *Faculty research:* Computer modeling, reproductive and endocrine physiology, cardiovascular physiology, neurophysiology, membrane biophysics.

Dartmouth College, Arts and Sciences Graduate Programs, Department of Physiology, Lebanon, NH 03756. Offers PhD, MD/PhD. *Degree requirements:* For doctorate, thesis/dissertation. *Entrance requirements:* For doctorate, GRE General Test, GRE Subject Test. Additional exam requirements/recommendations for international students: Required—TOEFL. *Faculty research:* Respiratory control, endocrinology of reproduction and immunology, regulation of receptors and channels, electrophysiology of membranes, renal function.

East Carolina University, Brody School of Medicine, Department of Physiology, Greenville, NC 27858-4353. Offers PhD. *Degree requirements:* For doctorate, comprehensive exam, thesis/dissertation. *Entrance requirements:* For doctorate, GRE General Test. Additional exam requirements/recommendations for international students: Required—TOEFL. *Application deadline:* For fall admission, 6/1 priority date for domestic students. Applications are processed on a rolling basis. Application fee: $50. *Expenses:* Tuition, state resident: full-time $3557; part-time $444.63 per semester hour. Tuition, nonresident: full-time $14,351; part-time $1793.88 per semester hour. *Required fees:* $2016; $252 per semester hour. Part-time tuition and fees vary according to course load, campus/location and program. *Financial support:* Fellowships with full and partial tuition reimbursements available. Financial award application

Physiology

deadline: 6/1. *Faculty research:* Cell and nerve biophysics; neurophysiology; cardiovascular, renal, endocrine, and gastrointestinal physiology; pulmonary/asthma. *Unit head:* Dr. Robert Lust, Chairman, 252-744-2762, Fax: 252-744-3460, E-mail: lustr@ecu.edu. *Application contact:* Dr. Mike Van Scott, Graduate Director, 252-744-3654, Fax: 252-744-3460, E-mail: vanscottmi@ecu.edu. Web site: http://www.ecu.edu/physiology/.

Eastern Michigan University, Graduate School, College of Health and Human Services, School of Health Promotion and Human Performance, Programs in Exercise Physiology, Ypsilanti, MI 48197. Offers exercise physiology (MS); sports medicine-biomechanics (MS); sports medicine-corporate adult fitness (MS); sports medicine-exercise physiology (MS). Part-time and evening/weekend programs available. *Students:* 22 full-time (16 women), 42 part-time (18 women); includes 8 minority (4 Black or African American, non-Hispanic/Latino; 2 American Indian or Alaska Native, non-Hispanic/Latino; 1 Hispanic/Latino; 1 Two or more races, non-Hispanic/Latino), 4 international. Average age 30. 59 applicants, 68% accepted, 22 enrolled. In 2011, 20 degrees awarded. *Degree requirements:* For master's, comprehensive exam, thesis or 450-hour internship. *Entrance requirements:* Additional exam requirements/recommendations for international students: Required—TOEFL. *Application deadline:* For fall admission, 8/1 for domestic students, 5/1 for international students; for winter admission, 12/1 for domestic students, 10/1 for international students; for spring admission, 3/15 for domestic students, 3/1 for international students. Application fee: $35. *Expenses:* Tuition, state resident: full-time $10,367; part-time $432 per credit hour. Tuition, nonresident: full-time $20,435; part-time $851 per credit hour. *Required fees:* $39 per credit hour. $46 per semester. One-time fee: $100. Tuition and fees vary according to course level, degree level and reciprocity agreements. *Unit head:* Dr. Steve McGregor, Program Coordinator, 734-487-0090, Fax: 734-487-2024, E-mail: stephen.mcgregor@emich.edu. *Application contact:* Dr. Brenda Riemer, Chair, Graduate Programs, 734-487-0090 Ext. 2745, Fax: 734-487-2024, E-mail: briemer@emich.edu.

East Tennessee State University, James H. Quillen College of Medicine, Biomedical Science Graduate Program, Johnson City, TN 37614. Offers anatomy and cell biology (PhD); biochemistry and molecular biology (PhD); microbiology (PhD); pharmaceutical sciences (PhD); pharmacology (PhD); physiology (PhD); quantitative biosciences (PhD). *Faculty:* 33 full-time (6 women). *Students:* 29 full-time (15 women), 2 part-time (both women); includes 4 minority (1 Black or African American, non-Hispanic/Latino; 1 Asian, non-Hispanic/Latino; 2 Hispanic/Latino), 6 international. Average age 29. 76 applicants, 12% accepted, 7 enrolled. In 2011, 1 doctorate awarded. *Degree requirements:* For doctorate, thesis/dissertation, comprehensive qualifying exam. *Entrance requirements:* For doctorate, GRE General Test, GRE Subject Test. Additional exam requirements/recommendations for international students: Required—TOEFL (minimum score 550 paper-based; 213 computer-based; 79 iBT). *Application deadline:* For fall admission, 3/15 priority date for domestic students, 3/1 for international students. Application fee: $35 ($45 for international students). Electronic applications accepted. *Expenses:* Contact institution. *Financial support:* In 2011–12, 29 students received support, including 29 research assistantships with full tuition reimbursements available (averaging $19,000 per year); career-related internships or fieldwork, institutionally sponsored loans, scholarships/grants, and unspecified assistantships also available. Financial award application deadline: 7/1; financial award applicants required to submit FAFSA. *Faculty research:* Cardiovascular biology, neuroscience, infectious disease, cancer, inflammatory disease. *Total annual research expenditures:* $3.6 million. *Unit head:* Dr. Mitchell E. Robinson, Associate Dean/Program Director, 423-439-2031, Fax: 423-439-2140, E-mail: robinson@etsu.edu. *Application contact:* Shella Bennett, Graduate Specialist, 423-439-4708, Fax: 423-439-5624, E-mail: bennetsg@etsu.edu.

Georgetown University, Graduate School of Arts and Sciences, Programs in Biomedical Sciences, Department of Physiology and Biophysics, Washington, DC 20057. Offers MS, PhD, MD/PhD. *Degree requirements:* For doctorate, thesis/dissertation. *Entrance requirements:* For master's, GRE General Test, MCAT; for doctorate, GRE General Test. Additional exam requirements/recommendations for international students: Required—TOEFL.

Georgia Health Sciences University, College of Graduate Studies, Program in Physiology, Augusta, GA 30912. Offers MS, PhD. *Faculty:* 10 full-time (4 women), 2 part-time/adjunct (both women). *Students:* 19 full-time (16 women), 1 part-time (0 women); includes 2 minority (both Black or African American, non-Hispanic/Latino), 11 international. Average age 28. In 2011, 5 doctorates awarded. *Degree requirements:* For doctorate, comprehensive exam, thesis/dissertation. *Entrance requirements:* For doctorate, GRE General Test. Additional exam requirements/recommendations for international students: Required—TOEFL (minimum score 550 paper-based; 213 computer-based; 79 iBT). *Application deadline:* For fall admission, 1/15 for domestic and international students. Application fee: $50. Electronic applications accepted. *Financial support:* In 2011–12, 1 student received support, including 4 fellowships with partial tuition reimbursements available (averaging $26,000 per year), 7 research assistantships with partial tuition reimbursements available (averaging $23,000 per year); Federal Work-Study, institutionally sponsored loans, scholarships/grants, and traineeships also available. Support available to part-time students. Financial award application deadline: 5/31; financial award applicants required to submit FAFSA. *Faculty research:* Cardiovascular and renal physiology, behavioral neuroscience and genetics, neurophysiology, adrenal steroid endocrinology and genetics, inflammatory mediators and cardiovascular disease, hypertension, diabetes and stroke. *Total annual research expenditures:* $4.8 million. *Unit head:* Dr. Clinton Webb, Chair and Professor, 706-721-7742, Fax: 706-721-7299, E-mail: cwebb@georgiahealth.edu. *Application contact:* Dr. Patricia L. Cameron, Acting Vice Dean, 706-721-3279, E-mail: pcameron@georgiahealth.edu. Web site: http://www.georgiahealth.edu/medicine/phy/.

Georgia Institute of Technology, Graduate Studies and Research, College of Sciences, School of Applied Physiology, Program in Prosthetics and Orthotics, Atlanta, GA 30332-0001. Offers MS.

Georgia State University, College of Arts and Sciences, Department of Biology, Program in Cellular and Molecular Biology and Physiology, Atlanta, GA 30302-3083. Offers MS, PhD. Part-time programs available. Terminal master's awarded for partial completion of doctoral program. *Degree requirements:* For master's, thesis or alternative; for doctorate, thesis/dissertation, exam. *Entrance requirements:* For master's and doctorate, GRE General Test. Additional exam requirements/recommendations for international students: Required—TOEFL.

Harvard University, Graduate School of Arts and Sciences, Department of Systems Biology, Cambridge, MA 02138. Offers PhD. *Degree requirements:* For doctorate, thesis/dissertation, lab rotation, qualifying examination. *Entrance requirements:* For doctorate, GRE. Additional exam requirements/recommendations for international students: Required—TOEFL. Electronic applications accepted. *Expenses: Tuition:* Full-time $36,304. *Required fees:* $1186. Full-time tuition and fees vary according to program.

Harvard University, Harvard School of Public Health, Department of Environmental Health, Boston, MA 02115-6096. Offers environmental health (MOH, SM, DPH, PhD, SD); occupational health (MOH, SM, DPH, SD); physiology (PhD, SD). Part-time programs available. *Faculty:* 43 full-time (8 women), 23 part-time/adjunct (7 women). *Students:* 74 full-time, 3 part-time; includes 14 minority (4 Black or African American, non-Hispanic/Latino; 8 Asian, non-Hispanic/Latino; 2 Hispanic/Latino), 38 international. Average age 29. 88 applicants, 39% accepted, 26 enrolled. In 2011, 15 master's, 12

CASE WESTERN RESERVE UNIVERSITY
EST. 1826

Department of Physiology and Biophysics

Research training is focused on answering questions of biomedical relevance in the following areas of faculty interest and expertise:

- Structural Biology
- Molecular Neurobiology
- Ion Transport and Metabolism
- Endothelial and Epithelial Function

- Cell Signaling
- Inflammatory Signal Transduction
- Neural Degenerative Diseases

- Brain Blood Flow and Metabolism
- Neuronal Control of the Stress Response
- Muscle Contractility

- Cardiovascular Physiology and Metabolism
- Control of Kidney Function
- Acid-Base Balance

- Oxidative Stress
- Sleep Disorders
- Cystic Fibrosis
- Diabetes

For more information, please contact:
Coordinator, Educational Programs
Department of Physiology and Biophysics
Case Western Reserve University
School of Medicine
Cleveland, Ohio 44106-4970
Phone: 216.368.2084   *E-mail:* jean.davis@case.edu

For application information:
http://physiology.case.edu/edu_apply_grad.php   http://physiology.case.edu/home_noflash.php

doctorates awarded. *Degree requirements:* For doctorate, thesis/dissertation, qualifying exam. *Entrance requirements:* For master's and doctorate, GRE. Additional exam requirements/recommendations for international students: Required—TOEFL (minimum score 595 paper-based; 240 computer-based; 95 iBT); Recommended—IELTS (minimum score 7). *Application deadline:* For fall admission, 12/15 for domestic and international students. *Application fee:* $115. Electronic applications accepted. *Expenses: Tuition:* Full-time $36,304. *Required fees:* $1186. Full-time tuition and fees vary according to program. *Financial support:* Fellowships, research assistantships, teaching assistantships, career-related internships or fieldwork, Federal Work-Study, scholarships/grants, traineeships, and unspecified assistantships available. Support available to part-time students. Financial award application deadline: 2/17; financial award applicants required to submit FAFSA. *Faculty research:* Industrial hygiene and occupational safety, population genetics, indoor and outdoor air pollution, cell and molecular biology of the lungs, infectious diseases. *Unit head:* Dr. Douglas Dockery, Chairman, 617-432-1270, Fax: 617-432-6913. *Application contact:* Vincent W. James, Director of Admissions, 617-432-1031, Fax: 617-432-7080, E-mail: admissions@hsph.harvard.edu. Web site: http://www.hsph.harvard.edu/departments/environmental-health/.

Howard University, Graduate School, Department of Physiology and Biophysics, Washington, DC 20059-0002. Offers biophysics (PhD); physiology (PhD). *Degree requirements:* For doctorate, comprehensive exam, thesis/dissertation. *Entrance requirements:* For doctorate, GRE General Test, minimum B average in field. *Faculty research:* Cardiovascular physiology, pulmonary physiology, renal physiology, neurophysiology, endocrinology.

Illinois State University, Graduate School, College of Arts and Sciences, Department of Biological Sciences, Normal, IL 61790-2200. Offers animal behavior (MS); bacteriology (MS); biochemistry (MS); biological sciences (MS); biology (PhD); biophysics (MS); biotechnology (MS); botany (MS, PhD); cell biology (MS); conservation biology (MS); developmental biology (MS); ecology (MS, PhD); entomology (MS); evolutionary biology (MS); genetics (MS, PhD); immunology (MS); microbiology (MS, PhD); molecular biology (MS); molecular genetics (MS); neurobiology (MS); neuroscience (MS); parasitology (MS); physiology (MS, PhD); plant biology (MS); plant molecular biology (MS); plant sciences (MS); structural biology (MS); zoology (MS, PhD). Part-time programs available. *Degree requirements:* For master's, thesis or alternative; for doctorate, variable foreign language requirement, thesis/dissertation, 2 terms of residency. *Entrance requirements:* For master's, GRE General Test, minimum GPA of 2.6 in last 60 hours of course work; for doctorate, GRE General Test. *Faculty research:* Redoc balance and drug development in schistosoma mansoni, control of the growth of listeria monocytogenes at low temperature, regulation of cell expansion and microtubule function by SPRI, CRUI: physiology and fitness consequences of different life history phenotypes.

Indiana State University, College of Graduate and Professional Studies, College of Arts and Sciences, Department of Biology, Terre Haute, IN 47809. Offers ecology (PhD); life sciences (MS); microbiology (PhD); physiology (PhD); science education (MS). *Degree requirements:* For master's, thesis (for some programs); for doctorate, comprehensive exam, thesis/dissertation. *Entrance requirements:* For master's and doctorate, GRE General Test. Electronic applications accepted.

The Johns Hopkins University, Bloomberg School of Public Health, Department of Environmental Health Sciences, Baltimore, MD 21218-2699. Offers environmental health engineering (PhD); environmental health sciences (MHS, Dr PH); occupational and environmental health (PhD); occupational and environmental hygiene (MHS, MHS); physiology (PhD); toxicology (PhD). Postbaccalaureate distance learning degree programs offered (minimal on-campus study). *Degree requirements:* For master's, essay, presentation; for doctorate, comprehensive exam, thesis/dissertation, 1 year full-time residency, oral and written exams. *Entrance requirements:* For master's, GRE General Test or MCAT, 3 letters of recommendation, transcripts; for doctorate, GRE General Test or MCAT, 3 letters of recommendation. Additional exam requirements/recommendations for international students: Required—TOEFL (minimum score 600 paper-based; 250 computer-based). Electronic applications accepted. *Faculty research:* Chemical carcinogenesis/toxicology, lung disease, occupational and environmental health, nuclear imaging, molecular epidemiology.

The Johns Hopkins University, School of Medicine, Graduate Programs in Medicine, Department of Physiology, Baltimore, MD 21205. Offers cellular and molecular physiology (PhD); physiology (PhD). *Degree requirements:* For doctorate, thesis/dissertation, oral and qualifying exams. *Entrance requirements:* For doctorate, GRE General Test, previous course work in biology, calculus, chemistry, and physics. Additional exam requirements/recommendations for international students: Required—TOEFL. Electronic applications accepted. *Faculty research:* Membrane biochemistry and biophysics; signal transduction; developmental genetics and physiology; physiology and biochemistry; transporters, carriers, and ion channels.

Kansas State University, College of Veterinary Medicine, Department of Anatomy and Physiology, Manhattan, KS 66506. Offers physiology (PhD). *Faculty:* 19 full-time (6 women), 9 part-time/adjunct (3 women). *Students:* 12 full-time (5 women), 1 part-time, 8 international. Average age 28. 2 applicants, 50% accepted, 1 enrolled. Terminal master's awarded for partial completion of doctoral program. *Entrance requirements:* For doctorate, GRE. Additional exam requirements/recommendations for international students: Required—TOEFL. *Application deadline:* For fall admission, 2/1 for international students; for spring admission, 8/1 for international students. Applications are processed on a rolling basis. *Application fee:* $40 ($55 for international students). Electronic applications accepted. *Financial support:* In 2011–12, 46 research assistantships (averaging $23,772 per year) were awarded; fellowships, teaching assistantships with partial tuition reimbursements, Federal Work-Study, institutionally sponsored loans, and scholarships/grants also available. Financial award application deadline: 3/1. *Faculty research:* Cardiovascular and pulmonary, immunophysiology, neuroscience, pharmacology, epithelial. *Total annual research expenditures:* $3.7 million. *Unit head:* Michael J. Kenney, Head, 785-532-2741, Fax: 785-532-4557, E-mail: mkenny@vet.ksu.edu. *Application contact:* Jishu Shi, Director, 785-532-4506, Fax: 785-532-4557, E-mail: jshi@vet.k-state.edu. Web site: http://www.vet.k-state.edu/depts/ap/.

Kent State University, College of Arts and Sciences, Department of Biological Sciences, Program in Physiology, Kent, OH 44242-0001. Offers MS, PhD. *Degree requirements:* For master's, thesis; for doctorate, thesis/dissertation. *Entrance requirements:* For master's, GRE General Test, minimum GPA of 3.0; for doctorate, GRE General Test, minimum GPA of 3.25. Additional exam requirements/recommendations for international students: Required—TOEFL (minimum score 600 paper-based; 257 computer-based). *Expenses:* Tuition, state resident: full-time $8136; part-time $452 per credit hour. Tuition, nonresident: full-time $14,292; part-time $794 per credit hour.

Kent State University, School of Biomedical Sciences, Program in Physiology, Kent, OH 44242-0001. Offers MS, PhD. *Degree requirements:* For master's, thesis; for doctorate, thesis/dissertation. *Entrance requirements:* For master's and doctorate, GRE General Test, minimum GPA of 3.0, 3 letters of recommendation. Additional exam requirements/recommendations for international students: Required—TOEFL (minimum

score 600 paper-based; 287 computer-based). Electronic applications accepted. *Expenses:* Tuition, state resident: full-time $8136; part-time $452 per credit hour. Tuition, nonresident: full-time $14,292; part-time $794 per credit hour.

Loma Linda University, School of Medicine, Department of Physiology/Pharmacology, Loma Linda, CA 92350. Offers MS, PhD. Part-time programs available. *Degree requirements:* For master's, thesis or alternative; for doctorate, 2 foreign languages, thesis/dissertation. *Entrance requirements:* For master's and doctorate, GRE General Test. *Faculty research:* Drug metabolism, biochemical pharmacology, structure and function of cell membranes, neuropharmacology.

Louisiana State University Health Sciences Center, School of Graduate Studies in New Orleans, Department of Physiology, New Orleans, LA 70112-2223. Offers MS, PhD, MD/PhD. Terminal master's awarded for partial completion of doctoral program. *Degree requirements:* For master's, comprehensive exam, thesis; for doctorate, comprehensive exam, thesis/dissertation. *Entrance requirements:* For master's and doctorate, GRE General Test. Additional exam requirements/recommendations for international students: Required—TOEFL. *Faculty research:* Host defense, lipoprotein metabolism, regulation of cardiopulmonary function, alcohol and drug abuse, cell to cell communication, cytokinesis, physiologic functions of nitric oxide.

Louisiana State University Health Sciences Center at Shreveport, Department of Molecular and Cellular Physiology, Shreveport, LA 71130-3932. Offers physiology (MS, PhD); MD/PhD. *Degree requirements:* For master's, thesis; for doctorate, thesis/dissertation. *Entrance requirements:* For master's and doctorate, GRE General Test. Additional exam requirements/recommendations for international students: Required—TOEFL. *Faculty research:* Cardiovascular, gastrointestinal, renal, and neutrophil function; cellular detoxification systems; hypoxia and mitochondria function.

Loyola University Chicago, Graduate School, Programs in Cell and Molecular Physiology, Chicago, IL 60660. Offers MS, PhD. *Faculty:* 17 full-time (4 women), 5 part-time/adjunct (1 woman). *Students:* 22 full-time (5 women); includes 7 minority (1 Black or African American, non-Hispanic/Latino; 5 Asian, non-Hispanic/Latino; 1 Two or more races, non-Hispanic/Latino), 3 international. Average age 25. 75 applicants, 48% accepted, 16 enrolled. In 2011, 1 master's, 2 doctorates awarded. *Degree requirements:* For master's, thesis; for doctorate, comprehensive exam, thesis/dissertation. *Entrance requirements:* For master's, GRE General Test or MCAT; for doctorate, GRE General Test. Additional exam requirements/recommendations for international students: Required—TOEFL. *Application deadline:* For fall admission, 5/15 for domestic and international students. Application fee: $0. Electronic applications accepted. *Expenses: Tuition:* Full-time $15,660; part-time $870 per credit hour. *Required fees:* $125 per semester. Tuition and fees vary according to course load and program. *Financial support:* In 2011–12, 5 fellowships with tuition reimbursements (averaging $23,000 per year), 9 research assistantships with tuition reimbursements (averaging $23,000 per year) were awarded. *Faculty research:* Cardiovascular system-emphasis in neural and metabolic control of circulation, ion channels, excitation contraction coupling, molecular cloning. *Unit head:* Dr. Pieter deTombe, Chair, 708-216-6305, Fax: 708-216-6308, E-mail: pdetombe@lumc.edu. *Application contact:* Dr. Ruben Mestril, Graduate Program Director, 708-327-2395, Fax: 708-216-6308, E-mail: rmestri@lumc.edu.

Marquette University, Graduate School, College of Arts and Sciences, Department of Biology, Milwaukee, WI 53201-1881. Offers cell biology (MS, PhD); developmental biology (MS, PhD); ecology (MS, PhD); epithelial physiology (MS, PhD); genetics (MS, PhD); microbiology (MS, PhD); molecular biology (MS, PhD); muscle and exercise physiology (MS, PhD); neuroscience (PhD). *Faculty:* 23 full-time (11 women), 1 part-time/adjunct (0 women). *Students:* 33 full-time (14 women), 6 part-time (3 women), 19 international. Average age 25. 78 applicants, 17% accepted, 5 enrolled. In 2011, 6 doctorates awarded. Terminal master's awarded for partial completion of doctoral program. *Degree requirements:* For master's, comprehensive exam, thesis, 1 year of teaching experience or equivalent; for doctorate, thesis/dissertation, 1 year of teaching experience or equivalent, qualifying exam. *Entrance requirements:* For master's and doctorate, GRE General Test, GRE Subject Test, official transcripts from all current and previous colleges/universities except Marquette, statement of professional goals and aspirations, three letters of recommendation. Additional exam requirements/recommendations for international students: Required—TOEFL (minimum score 530 paper-based; 78 computer-based). *Application deadline:* For fall admission, 12/15 for domestic and international students. Application fee: $50. Electronic applications accepted. *Expenses: Tuition:* Full-time $17,010; part-time $945 per credit hour. Tuition and fees vary according to program. *Financial support:* In 2011–12, 39 students received support, including 6 fellowships (averaging $1,208 per year), 4 research assistantships with full tuition reimbursements available (averaging $21,750 per year), 29 teaching assistantships with full tuition reimbursements available (averaging $21,750 per year); scholarships/grants, health care benefits, tuition waivers (full and partial), and unspecified assistantships also available. Support available to part-time students. Financial award application deadline: 2/15. *Faculty research:* Neurobiology, neuroendocrinology, epithelial physiology, neuropeptide interactions, synaptic transmission. *Total annual research expenditures:* $2 million. *Unit head:* Dr. Robert Fitts, Chair, 414-288-1748, Fax: 414-288-7357. *Application contact:* Debbie Weaver, Administrative Assistant, 414-288-7355, Fax: 414-288-7357. Web site: http://www.marquette.edu/biology/.

McGill University, Faculty of Graduate and Postdoctoral Studies, Faculty of Medicine, Department of Physiology, Montréal, QC H3A 2T5, Canada. Offers M Sc, PhD.

McMaster University, Faculty of Health Sciences and School of Graduate Studies, Program in Medical Sciences, Physiology/Pharmacology Area, Hamilton, ON L8S 4M2, Canada. Offers M Sc, PhD, MD/PhD. *Degree requirements:* For master's, thesis; for doctorate, comprehensive exam, thesis/dissertation. *Entrance requirements:* For master's, honors B Sc, B+ average in related field; for doctorate, M Sc, minimum B+ average, students with proven research experience and an A average may be admitted with a B Sc degree. Additional exam requirements/recommendations for international students: Required—TOEFL (minimum score 580 paper-based; 237 computer-based; 92 iBT).

Medical College of Wisconsin, Graduate School of Biomedical Sciences, Interdisciplinary Physiology Program, Milwaukee, WI 53226-0509. Offers PhD, MD/PhD. *Degree requirements:* For doctorate, comprehensive exam, thesis/dissertation. *Entrance requirements:* For doctorate, GRE, official transcripts, three letters of recommendation. Additional exam requirements/recommendations for international students: Required—TOEFL. *Faculty research:* Cardiovascular, respiratory, renal, and exercise physiology; mathematical modeling; molecular and cellular biology.

Michigan State University, College of Human Medicine and The Graduate School, Graduate Programs in Human Medicine, East Lansing, MI 48824. Offers biochemistry and molecular biology (MS, PhD); epidemiology (MS, PhD); microbiology (MS); microbiology and molecular genetics (PhD); pharmacology and toxicology (MS, PhD); physiology (MS, PhD); public health (MPH). *Entrance requirements:* Additional exam requirements/recommendations for international students: Required—TOEFL.

Michigan State University, College of Osteopathic Medicine and The Graduate School, Graduate Studies in Osteopathic Medicine, East Lansing, MI 48824. Offers biochemistry and molecular biology (MS, PhD); microbiology (MS); microbiology and

molecular genetics (PhD); pharmacology and toxicology (MS, PhD), including integrative pharmacology (MS), pharmacology and toxicology, pharmacology and toxicology-environmental toxicology (PhD); physiology (MS, PhD).

Michigan State University, College of Veterinary Medicine and The Graduate School, Graduate Programs in Veterinary Medicine, East Lansing, MI 48824. Offers comparative medicine and integrative biology (MS, PhD), including comparative medicine and integrative biology, comparative medicine and integrative biology–environmental toxicology (PhD); food safety and toxicology (MS), including food safety; integrative toxicology (PhD), including animal science–environmental toxicology, biochemistry and molecular biology–environmental toxicology, chemistry–environmental toxicology, crop and soil sciences–environmental toxicology, environmental engineering–environmental toxicology, environmental geosciences–environmental toxicology, fisheries and wildlife–environmental toxicology, food science–environmental toxicology, forestry–environmental toxicology, genetics–environmental toxicology, human nutrition–environmental toxicology, microbiology–environmental toxicology, pharmacology and toxicology–environmental toxicology, zoology–environmental toxicology; large animal clinical sciences (MS, PhD); microbiology and molecular genetics (MS, PhD), including industrial microbiology, microbiology, microbiology and molecular genetics, microbiology–environmental toxicology (PhD); pathobiology and diagnostic investigation (MS, PhD), including pathology, pathology–environmental toxicology (PhD); pharmacology and toxicology (MS, PhD); pharmacology and toxicology–environmental toxicology (PhD); physiology (MS, PhD); small animal clinical sciences (MS). Electronic applications accepted. *Faculty research:* Molecular genetics, food safety/toxicology, comparative orthopedics, airway disease, population medicine.

Michigan State University, The Graduate School, College of Natural Science and Graduate Programs in Human Medicine and Graduate Studies in Osteopathic Medicine, Department of Physiology, East Lansing, MI 48824. Offers MS, PhD. *Entrance requirements:* Additional exam requirements/recommendations for international students: Required—TOEFL (minimum score 600 paper-based; 220 computer-based). Electronic applications accepted.

Montclair State University, The Graduate School, College of Science and Mathematics, Department of Biology and Molecular Biology, Montclair, NJ 07043-1624. Offers biology (MS), including biological science education, biology, ecology and evolution, physiology; molecular biology (MS, Certificate). Part-time and evening/weekend programs available. *Students:* 15 full-time (10 women), 33 part-time (23 women); includes 3 minority (all Hispanic/Latino), 1 international. Average age 28. 53 applicants, 47% accepted, 14 enrolled. In 2011, 14 degrees awarded. *Degree requirements:* For master's, comprehensive exam, thesis or alternative. *Entrance requirements:* For master's, GRE General Test, 24 credits of course work in undergraduate biology, 2 letters of recommendation, teaching certificate (biology sciences education concentration); for Certificate, 2 letters of recommendation, essay. Additional exam requirements/recommendations for international students: Required—TOEFL (minimum score 83 iBT) or IELTS. *Application deadline:* For fall admission, 6/1 for international students; for spring admission, 10/1 for international students. Applications are processed on a rolling basis. Application fee: $60. Electronic applications accepted. *Financial support:* In 2011–12, 16 research assistantships with full tuition reimbursements (averaging $7,000 per year), 3 teaching assistantships (averaging $7,000 per year) were awarded; Federal Work-Study, scholarships/grants, and unspecified assistantships also available. Support available to part-time students. Financial award application deadline: 3/1; financial award applicants required to submit FAFSA. *Faculty research:* Ecosystem biology, molecular biology, signal transduction, neuroscience, aquatic and coastal biology. *Total annual research expenditures:* $1.3 million. *Unit head:* Dr. Quinn Vega, Chairperson, 973-655-7178. *Application contact:* Amy Aiello, Director of Graduate Admissions and Operations, 973-655-5147, Fax: 973-655-7869, E-mail: graduate.school@montclair.edu. Web site: http://www.montclair.edu/csam/biology/.

New York Medical College, Graduate School of Basic Medical Sciences, Program in Physiology, Valhalla, NY 10595-1691. Offers MS, PhD, MD/PhD. Part-time and evening/weekend programs available. *Faculty:* 22 full-time (2 women), 1 (woman) part-time/adjunct. *Students:* 7 full-time (4 women), 1 (woman) part-time; includes 2 minority (both Asian, non-Hispanic/Latino). Average age 27. 10 applicants, 70% accepted, 4 enrolled. In 2011, 3 degrees awarded. Terminal master's awarded for partial completion of doctoral program. *Degree requirements:* For master's, thesis; for doctorate, comprehensive exam, thesis/dissertation. *Entrance requirements:* For master's and doctorate, GRE General Test. Additional exam requirements/recommendations for international students: Required—TOEFL. *Application deadline:* For fall admission, 7/1 priority date for domestic students, 5/1 for international students; for spring admission, 12/1 priority date for domestic students, 10/1 for international students. Applications are processed on a rolling basis. Application fee: $50 ($75 for international students). Electronic applications accepted. *Financial support:* In 2011–12, 2 fellowships with full tuition reimbursements (averaging $24,000 per year), 8 research assistantships with full tuition reimbursements (averaging $24,000 per year) were awarded; Federal Work-Study, institutionally sponsored loans, scholarships/grants, traineeships, health care benefits, tuition waivers, unspecified assistantships, and health benefits (for PhD candidates only) also available. Financial award applicants required to submit FAFSA. *Faculty research:* Cellular neurophysiology, regulation of sleep and awake states, neural and endocrine control of the heart and circulation microcirculation, the physiology of gene expression, heart failure and the physiological effects of oxygen metabolites. *Unit head:* Dr. Carl I. Thompson, Director, 914-594-4106, Fax: 914-594-4966, E-mail: carl_thompson@nymc.edu. *Application contact:* Valerie Romeo-Messana, Admission Coordinator, 914-594-4110, Fax: 914-594-4944, E-mail: v_romeomessana@nymc.edu.

New York University, School of Medicine, New York, NY 10012-1019. Offers biomedical sciences (PhD), including biomedical imaging, cellular and molecular biology, computational biology, developmental genetics, medical and molecular parasitology, microbiology, molecular oncobiology and immunology, neuroscience and physiology, pathobiology, pharmacology, structural biology; clinical investigation (MS); medicine (MD); MD/MA; MD/MPA; MD/MS; MD/PhD. *Accreditation:* LCME/AMA (one or more programs are accredited). *Degree requirements:* For master's, comprehensive exam, thesis; for doctorate, comprehensive exam (for some programs), thesis/dissertation (for some programs). *Entrance requirements:* For doctorate, MCAT (for MD). Additional exam requirements/recommendations for international students: Required—TOEFL. *Expenses:* Contact institution. *Faculty research:* AIDS, cancer, neuroscience, molecular biology, neuroscience, cell biology and molecular genetics, structural biology, microbial pathogenesis and host defense, pharmacology, molecular oncology and immunology.

New York University, School of Medicine and Graduate School of Arts and Science, Sackler Institute of Graduate Biomedical Sciences, Program in Neuroscience and Physiology, New York, NY 10012-1019. Offers PhD, MD/PhD. *Faculty:* 52 full-time (8 women). *Students:* 39 full-time (21 women); includes 9 minority (4 Black or African American, non-Hispanic/Latino; 1 Asian, non-Hispanic/Latino; 4 Hispanic/Latino), 11 international. Average age 28. In 2011, 8 doctorates awarded. *Degree requirements:* For doctorate, one foreign language, comprehensive exam, thesis/dissertation, qualifying exam. *Entrance requirements:* For doctorate, GRE General Test. Additional exam requirements/recommendations for international students: Required—TOEFL. *Application deadline:* For fall admission, 1/4 priority date for domestic students. Applications are processed on a rolling basis. Application fee: $85. *Financial support:* Fellowships with tuition reimbursements, research assistantships with tuition reimbursements, and teaching assistantships with tuition reimbursements available. *Faculty research:* Synaptic transmission, retinal physiology, signal transduction, CNS intrinsic properties, cerebellar function. *Unit head:* Dr. Rodolfo R. Llinas, Chairman, 212-263-5415. *Application contact:* Dr. Stewart A. Bloomfield, Graduate Adviser, 212-263-5770, Fax: 212-263-8072, E-mail: blooms01@med.nyu.edu.

North Carolina State University, Graduate School, College of Agriculture and Life Sciences and College of Veterinary Medicine, Program in Physiology, Raleigh, NC 27695. Offers MP, MS, PhD. *Degree requirements:* For master's, thesis (for some programs); for doctorate, thesis/dissertation. *Entrance requirements:* For master's and doctorate, GRE General Test. Electronic applications accepted. *Faculty research:* Neurophysiology, gastrointestinal physiology, reproductive physiology, environmental/stress physiology, cardiovascular physiology.

Northwestern University, The Graduate School, Judd A. and Marjorie Weinberg College of Arts and Sciences, Department of Neurobiology and Physiology, Evanston, IL 60208. Offers MS. Admissions and degrees offered through The Graduate School. Part-time programs available. *Degree requirements:* For master's, thesis. *Entrance requirements:* For master's, GRE General Test and MCAT (strongly recommended). Additional exam requirements/recommendations for international students: Required—TOEFL. Electronic applications accepted. *Expenses:* Contact institution. *Faculty research:* Sensory neurobiology and neuroendocrinology, reproductive biology, vision physiology and psychophysics, cell and developmental biology.

Nova Scotia Agricultural College, Research and Graduate Studies, Truro, NS B2N 5E3, Canada. Offers agriculture (M Sc), including air quality, animal behavior, animal molecular genetics, animal nutrition, animal technology, aquaculture, botany, crop management, crop physiology, ecology, environmental microbiology, food science, horticulture, nutrient management, pest management, physiology, plant biotechnology, plant pathology, soil chemistry, soil fertility, waste management and composting, water quality. Program offered jointly with Dalhousie University. Part-time programs available. *Degree requirements:* For master's, thesis, ATC Exam Teaching Assistantship. *Entrance requirements:* For master's, honors B Sc, minimum GPA of 3.0. Additional exam requirements/recommendations for international students: Required—TOEFL (minimum score 580 paper-based; 237 computer-based; 92 iBT), IELTS, Michigan English Language Assessment Battery, CanTEST, CAEL. *Faculty research:* Bio-product development, organic agriculture, nutrient management, air and water quality, agricultural biotechnology.

Ohio University, Graduate College, College of Arts and Sciences, Department of Biological Sciences, Athens, OH 45701-2979. Offers biological sciences (MS, PhD); cell biology and physiology (MS, PhD); ecology and evolutionary biology (MS, PhD); exercise physiology and muscle biology (MS, PhD); microbiology (MS, PhD); neuroscience (MS, PhD). *Students:* 35 full-time (12 women), 4 part-time (1 woman), 14 international. 62 applicants, 10% accepted, 5 enrolled. In 2011, 2 master's, 8 doctorates awarded. Terminal master's awarded for partial completion of doctoral program. *Degree requirements:* For master's, comprehensive exam, thesis, 1 quarter of teaching experience; for doctorate, comprehensive exam, thesis/dissertation, 2 quarters of teaching experience. *Entrance requirements:* For master's, GRE General Test, names of three faculty members whose research interests most closely match the applicant's interest; for doctorate, GRE General Test, essay concerning prior training, research interest and career goals, plus names of three faculty members whose research interests most closely match the applicant's interest. Additional exam requirements/recommendations for international students: Required—TOEFL (minimum score 620 paper-based; 105 iBT) or IELTS (minimum score 7.5). *Application deadline:* For fall admission, 1/15 for domestic and international students. Application fee: $50 ($55 for international students). Electronic applications accepted. *Financial support:* In 2011–12, 1 fellowship with full tuition reimbursement (averaging $18,957 per year), 10 research assistantships with full tuition reimbursements (averaging $18,957 per year), 42 teaching assistantships with full tuition reimbursements (averaging $18,957 per year) were awarded; Federal Work-Study and institutionally sponsored loans also available. Financial award application deadline: 1/15. *Faculty research:* Ecology and evolutionary biology, exercise physiology and muscle biology, neurobiology, cell biology, physiology. *Total annual research expenditures:* $2.8 million. *Unit head:* Dr. Ralph DiCaprio, Chair, 740-593-2290, Fax: 740-593-0300, E-mail: dicaprir@ohio.edu. *Application contact:* Dr. Patrick Hassett, Graduate Chair, 740-593-4793, Fax: 740-593-0300, E-mail: hassett@ohio.edu. Web site: http://www.biosci.ohiou.edu/.

Oregon Health & Science University, School of Medicine, Graduate Programs in Medicine, Program in Molecular and Cellular Biosciences, Department of Physiology and Pharmacology, Portland, OR 97239-3098. Offers PhD. *Faculty:* 16 full-time (4 women), 2 part-time/adjunct. *Students:* 11 full-time (9 women); includes 1 minority (Asian, non-Hispanic/Latino), 1 international. Average age 28. In 2011, 1 doctorate awarded. *Degree requirements:* For doctorate, comprehensive exam, thesis/dissertation. *Entrance requirements:* For doctorate, GRE General Test (minimum scores: 153 Verbal/148 Quantitative/4.5 Analytical) or MCAT (for some programs). Additional exam requirements/recommendations for international students: Required—TOEFL. Electronic applications accepted. *Financial support:* Full tuition and stipends available. *Faculty research:* Ion conduction and gating in k+ channels, autonomic neuron plasticity, neurotransmitter/receptor expression, fetal/neonatal pharmacology, molecular pharmacology. *Unit head:* Dr. Beth Habecker, Program Director, 503-494-6252, E-mail: habecker@ohsu.edu. *Application contact:* Julie Walvatne, Program Coordinator, 503-494-6252.

Penn State Hershey Medical Center, College of Medicine, Graduate School Programs in the Biomedical Sciences, The Huck Institutes of the Life Sciences, Intercollege Graduate Program in Physiology, Hershey, PA 17033. Offers MS, PhD, MD/PhD. *Students:* 8 full-time (1 woman); includes 1 minority (Hispanic/Latino), 3 international. 14 applicants, 57% accepted, 3 enrolled. In 2011, 2 doctorates awarded. Terminal master's awarded for partial completion of doctoral program. *Degree requirements:* For master's, thesis or alternative; for doctorate, comprehensive exam, thesis/dissertation, oral exam. *Entrance requirements:* For master's, GRE General Test or MCAT; for doctorate, GRE General Test or MCAT, minimum GPA of 3.0. Additional exam requirements/recommendations for international students: Required—TOEFL (minimum score 500 paper-based; 213 computer-based). *Application deadline:* For fall admission, 1/31 priority date for domestic students, 2/1 for international students. Applications are processed on a rolling basis. Application fee: $65. Electronic applications accepted. *Financial support:* In 2011–12, research assistantships with full tuition reimbursements (averaging $23,028 per year) were awarded; fellowships with full tuition reimbursements, career-related internships or fieldwork, scholarships/grants, traineeships, health care benefits, and unspecified assistantships also available. Financial award applicants required to submit FAFSA. *Faculty research:* Gene expression, diabetes obesity and insulin resistance, DNA repair and carcinogenesis, telomerase cell senescence and cancer, ion channels and cardiovascular function. *Unit head:* Dr. Chester Ray, Chair, 717-531-8566, Fax: 717-531-7667, E-mail: physio-grad-

hmc@psu.edu. *Application contact:* Lisa Harman, Secretary, 717-531-8566, Fax: 717-531-7667, E-mail: physio-grad-hmc@psu.edu. Web site: http://www.pennstatehershey.org/web/physiology/programs.

Penn State University Park, Graduate School, Intercollege Graduate Programs, Intercollege Graduate Program in Physiology, State College, University Park, PA 16802-1503. Offers MS, PhD. *Unit head:* Dr. Leonard Jefferson, Jr., Chair, 717-531-8567, Fax: 814-865-9451. *Application contact:* Cynthia E. Nicosia, Director, Graduate Enrollment Services, 814-865-1795, Fax: 814-865-4627, E-mail: cey1@psu.edu. Web site: http://www.physiology.psu.edu/.

Purdue University, School of Veterinary Medicine and Graduate School, Graduate Programs in Veterinary Medicine, Department of Basic Medical Sciences, West Lafayette, IN 47907. Offers anatomy (MS, PhD); pharmacology (MS, PhD); physiology (MS, PhD). Part-time programs available. Terminal master's awarded for partial completion of doctoral program. *Degree requirements:* For master's, thesis; for doctorate, thesis/dissertation. *Entrance requirements:* For master's and doctorate, GRE General Test. Additional exam requirements/recommendations for international students: Required—TOEFL. Electronic applications accepted. *Faculty research:* Development and regeneration, tissue injury and shock, biomedical engineering, ovarian function, bone and cartilage biology, cell and molecular biology.

Queen's University at Kingston, School of Graduate Studies and Research, Faculty of Health Sciences, Department of Physiology, Kingston, ON K7L 3N6, Canada. Offers M Sc, PhD. *Degree requirements:* For master's, thesis; for doctorate, comprehensive exam, thesis/dissertation. *Entrance requirements:* For master's, minimum upper B average. Additional exam requirements/recommendations for international students: Required—TOEFL. *Faculty research:* Cardiovascular and respiratory physiology, exercise, gastrointestinal physiology, neuroscience.

Rocky Mountain University of Health Professions, Doctor of Science Program in Clinical Electrophysiology, Provo, UT 84606. Offers D Sc. *Degree requirements:* For doctorate, thesis/dissertation. *Entrance requirements:* For doctorate, clinical entry-level master's or doctorate degree; professional licensure as a chiropractor, nurse practitioner, occupational therapist, physical therapist, physician or physician assistant; minimum of 100 hours experience in electroneuromyography.

Rosalind Franklin University of Medicine and Science, School of Graduate and Postdoctoral Studies - Interdisciplinary Graduate Program in Biomedical Sciences, Department of Physiology and Biophysics, North Chicago, IL 60064-3095. Offers MS, PhD, MD/PhD. Terminal master's awarded for partial completion of doctoral program. *Degree requirements:* For master's, comprehensive exam, thesis; for doctorate, comprehensive exam, thesis/dissertation. *Entrance requirements:* For master's and doctorate, GRE General Test. Additional exam requirements/recommendations for international students: Required—TOEFL, TWE. *Faculty research:* Membrane transport, mechanisms of cellular regulation, brain metabolism, peptide metabolism.

Rush University, Graduate College, Department of Molecular Biophysics and Physiology, Chicago, IL 60612-3832. Offers physiology (PhD); MD/PhD. *Degree requirements:* For doctorate, thesis/dissertation. *Entrance requirements:* For doctorate, GRE General Test. Additional exam requirements/recommendations for international students: Required—TOEFL. *Faculty research:* Physiological exocytosis, raft formation and growth, voltage-gated proton channels, molecular biophysics and physiology.

Rutgers, The State University of New Jersey, New Brunswick, Graduate School-New Brunswick, Program in Endocrinology and Animal Biosciences, Piscataway, NJ 08854-8097. Offers MS, PhD. Terminal master's awarded for partial completion of doctoral program. *Degree requirements:* For master's, thesis; for doctorate, comprehensive exam, thesis/dissertation. *Entrance requirements:* For master's and doctorate, GRE General Test. Additional exam requirements/recommendations for international students: Required—TOEFL. Electronic applications accepted. *Faculty research:* Comparative and behavioral endocrinology, epigenetic regulation of the endocrine system, exercise physiology and immunology, fetal and neonatal developmental programming, mammary gland biology and breast cancer, neuroendocrinology and alcohol studies, reproductive and developmental toxicology.

Saint Louis University, Graduate Education and School of Medicine, Graduate Program in Biomedical Sciences and Graduate Education, Department of Pharmacological and Physiological Science, St. Louis, MO 63103-2097. Offers PhD. *Degree requirements:* For doctorate, comprehensive exam, thesis/dissertation, departmental qualifying exams. *Entrance requirements:* For doctorate, GRE General Test (GRE Subject Test optional), letters of recommendation, resume, interview. Additional exam requirements/recommendations for international students: Required—TOEFL (minimum score 525 paper-based; 194 computer-based). Electronic applications accepted. *Faculty research:* Molecular endocrinology, neuropharmacology, cardiovascular science, drug abuse, neurotransmitter and hormonal signaling mechanisms.

Salisbury University, Graduate Division, Program in Applied Health Physiology, Salisbury, MD 21801-6837. Offers MS. Part-time and evening/weekend programs available. *Faculty:* 5 full-time (0 women), 1 part-time/adjunct (0 women). *Students:* 29 full-time (18 women), 22 part-time (12 women); includes 12 minority (8 Black or African American, non-Hispanic/Latino; 1 American Indian or Alaska Native, non-Hispanic/Latino; 3 Hispanic/Latino). Average age 26. 21 applicants, 81% accepted, 17 enrolled. In 2011, 22 master's awarded. *Degree requirements:* For master's, internship. *Entrance requirements:* For master's, minimum GPA of 2.75, 2 recommendations, personal statement, undergraduate course work in anatomy and physiology. Additional exam requirements/recommendations for international students: Required—TOEFL (minimum score 550 paper-based; 79 iBT). *Application deadline:* Applications are processed on a rolling basis. Application fee: $45. Electronic applications accepted. *Expenses: Tuition, area resident:* Part-time $306 per credit hour. Tuition, state resident: part-time $306 per credit hour. Tuition, nonresident: part-time $595 per credit hour. *Required fees:* $68 per credit hour. *Financial support:* In 2011–12, 26 students received support, including 6 teaching assistantships with full tuition reimbursements available (averaging $4,075 per year); career-related internships or fieldwork, institutionally sponsored loans, and unspecified assistantships also available. Support available to part-time students. Financial award application deadline: 3/1; financial award applicants required to submit FAFSA. *Unit head:* Dr. Sidney R. Schneider, Director, 410-543-6409, Fax: 410-548-9185, E-mail: srschneider@salisbury.edu. *Application contact:* Sue Harman, Program Management Specialist, 410-543-6365, E-mail: admissions@salisbury.edu. Web site: http://www.salisbury.edu/ahph.

San Francisco State University, Division of Graduate Studies, College of Science and Engineering, Department of Biology, Program in Physiology and Behavioral Biology, San Francisco, CA 94132-1722. Offers MS. *Application deadline:* Applications are processed on a rolling basis. *Unit head:* Dr. Megumi Fuse, Coordinator, 415-405-0728, E-mail: fuse@sfsu.edu. *Application contact:* Dr. Robert Patterson, Graduate Coordinator, 415-338-1100, E-mail: patters@sfsu.edu. Web site: http://www.sfsu.edu/~biology.

San Jose State University, Graduate Studies and Research, College of Science, Department of Biological Sciences, San Jose, CA 95192-0001. Offers biological sciences (MA, MS); molecular biology and microbiology (MS); organismal biology, conservation and ecology (MS); physiology (MS). Part-time programs available. *Entrance requirements:* For master's, GRE. Electronic applications accepted. *Faculty research:* Systemic physiology, molecular genetics, SEM studies, toxicology, large mammal ecology.

Southern Illinois University Carbondale, Graduate School, Graduate Program in Medicine, Department of Physiology, Carbondale, IL 62901-4701. Offers MS, PhD. *Faculty:* 18 full-time (4 women). Terminal master's awarded for partial completion of doctoral program. *Degree requirements:* For master's, thesis; for doctorate, thesis/dissertation. *Entrance requirements:* For master's, GRE General Test, minimum GPA of 3.0; for doctorate, GRE General Test, minimum GPA of 3.25. Additional exam requirements/recommendations for international students: Required—TOEFL. *Application deadline:* For fall admission, 6/1 priority date for domestic students. Applications are processed on a rolling basis. Application fee: $0. *Financial support:* In 2011–12, 3 fellowships with full tuition reimbursements, 1 research assistantship with full tuition reimbursement, 10 teaching assistantships with full tuition reimbursements were awarded; institutionally sponsored loans and tuition waivers (full) also available. *Faculty research:* Hormones, neurotransmitters, cell biology, membrane protein, membranes transport. *Unit head:* Richard Steger, Chair, 618-453-1512, Fax: 618-453-1517, E-mail: rsteger@siumed.edu. *Application contact:* Graduate Program Committee, 618-453-1544, Fax: 618-453-1517.

Southern Illinois University Carbondale, Graduate School, Graduate Program in Medicine, Program in Molecular, Cellular and Systemic Physiology, Carbondale, IL 62901-4701. Offers MS. *Students:* 7 full-time (5 women), 16 part-time (8 women); includes 2 minority (1 Black or African American, non-Hispanic/Latino; 1 American Indian or Alaska Native, non-Hispanic/Latino), 10 international. 24 applicants, 8% accepted, 1 enrolled. In 2011, 3 master's awarded. *Unit head:* Richard Steger, Chair, 618-453-1512, Fax: 618-453-1517, E-mail: rsteger@siumed.edu. *Application contact:* Graduate Program Committee, 618-453-1544, Fax: 618-453-1517.

Stanford University, School of Medicine, Graduate Programs in Medicine, Department of Molecular and Cellular Physiology, Stanford, CA 94305-9991. Offers PhD. *Degree requirements:* For doctorate, thesis/dissertation, qualifying exams. *Entrance requirements:* For doctorate, GRE General Test, GRE Subject Test. Additional exam requirements/recommendations for international students: Required—TOEFL. Electronic applications accepted. *Expenses: Tuition:* Full-time $40,050; part-time $890 per credit. *Faculty research:* Signal transduction, ion channels, intracellular calcium, synaptic transmission.

State University of New York Upstate Medical University, College of Graduate Studies, Program in Physiology, Syracuse, NY 13210-2334. Offers MS, PhD, MD/PhD. Terminal master's awarded for partial completion of doctoral program. *Degree requirements:* For master's, thesis; for doctorate, comprehensive exam, thesis/dissertation. *Entrance requirements:* For master's, GRE General Test, interview; for doctorate, GRE General Test, telephone interview. Additional exam requirements/recommendations for international students: Required—TOEFL. Electronic applications accepted.

Stony Brook University, State University of New York, Stony Brook University Medical Center, Health Sciences Center, School of Medicine and Graduate School, Graduate Programs in Medicine, Department of Physiology and Biophysics, Stony Brook, NY 11794. Offers PhD. *Degree requirements:* For doctorate, comprehensive exam, thesis/dissertation. *Entrance requirements:* For doctorate, GRE General Test, GRE Subject Test, BS in related field, minimum GPA of 3.0. Additional exam requirements/recommendations for international students: Required—TOEFL. *Faculty research:* Cellular electrophysiology, membrane permeation and transport, metabolic endocrinology.

Teachers College, Columbia University, Graduate Faculty of Education, Department of Biobehavioral Studies, Program in Applied Physiology, New York, NY 10027. Offers Ed M, MA, Ed D. *Faculty:* 5 full-time (2 women), 2 part-time/adjunct (1 woman). *Students:* 9 full-time (3 women), 28 part-time (11 women); includes 9 minority (4 Black or African American, non-Hispanic/Latino; 1 Asian, non-Hispanic/Latino; 4 Hispanic/Latino), 5 international. Average age 28. In 2011, 11 master's awarded. *Degree requirements:* For master's, final project; for doctorate, comprehensive exam (for some programs), thesis/dissertation. *Application deadline:* For fall admission, 1/15 for domestic students. Applications are processed on a rolling basis. Application fee: $65. *Faculty research:* Modulators of autonomic outflow, the effects of aerobic improvements on autonomic and blood pressure regulation, the role of physical activity in the prevention and treatment of chronic diseases, rehabilitation and cerebral palsy. *Unit head:* Prof. Carol Ewing Garber, Program Coordinator, 212-678-3891, E-mail: ceg2140@columbia.edu. *Application contact:* Morgan Oakes, Admissions Counselor, 212-678-6613, E-mail: meo2142@columbia.edu. Web site: http://www.tc.edu/bbs/Movement/.

Temple University, Health Sciences Center, School of Medicine and Graduate School, Graduate Programs in Medicine, Department of Physiology, Philadelphia, PA 19122-6096. Offers PhD, MD/PhD. *Faculty:* 6 full-time (0 women). *Students:* 11 full-time (7 women); includes 3 minority (1 Black or African American, non-Hispanic/Latino; 1 Asian, non-Hispanic/Latino; 1 Hispanic/Latino), 4 international. Average age 30. 22 applicants, 59% accepted, 9 enrolled. In 2011, 2 doctorates awarded. *Degree requirements:* For doctorate, thesis/dissertation, research seminars. *Entrance requirements:* For doctorate, GRE General Test, minimum GPA of 3.0. Additional exam requirements/recommendations for international students: Required—TOEFL (minimum score 550 paper-based; 213 computer-based; 79 iBT). *Application deadline:* For fall admission, 12/15 for international students. Applications are processed on a rolling basis. Application fee: $50. Electronic applications accepted. *Expenses:* Tuition, state resident: full-time $12,366; part-time $687 per credit hour. Tuition, nonresident: full-time $17,298; part-time $961 per credit hour. *Required fees:* $590; $213 per year. *Financial support:* Fellowships available. Financial award application deadline: 1/15; financial award applicants required to submit FAFSA. *Faculty research:* Pulmonary, microvascular, and molecular physiology; cardiac electrophysiology. *Unit head:* Dr. Steven Houser, Chair, 215-707-4045, Fax: 215-707-0170, E-mail: srhouser@temple.edu. *Application contact:* Office of Admissions, 215-707-3656, Fax: 215-707-6932, E-mail: medadmissions@temple.edu. Web site: http://www.temple.edu/medicine/departments_centers/basic_science/physiology.htm.

Texas A&M University, College of Veterinary Medicine and Biomedical Sciences, Department of Veterinary Physiology and Pharmacology, College Station, TX 77843. Offers biomedical science (MS, PhD); toxicology (PhD). *Faculty:* 14. *Students:* 27 full-time (17 women), 2 part-time (1 woman); includes 3 minority (1 Black or African American, non-Hispanic/Latino; 2 Asian, non-Hispanic/Latino), 9 international. Average age 30. *Entrance requirements:* For master's and doctorate, GRE General Test. Additional exam requirements/recommendations for international students: Required—TOEFL. Application fee: $50 ($75 for international students). *Expenses:* Tuition, state resident: full-time $5437; part-time $226.55 per credit hour. Tuition, nonresident: full-time $12,949; part-time $539.55 per credit hour. *Required fees:* $2741. *Financial support:* Fellowships, research assistantships, and teaching assistantships available.

Financial award application deadline: 4/1; financial award applicants required to submit FAFSA. *Faculty research:* Gamete and embryo physiology, endocrinology, equine laminitis. *Unit head:* Glen Laine, Head, 979-845-7261, E-mail: glaine@tamu.edu. *Application contact:* Graduate Admissions, 979-845-1044, E-mail: admissions@tamu.edu. Web site: http://vetmed.tamu.edu/vtpp.

Tulane University, School of Medicine and School of Liberal Arts, Graduate Programs in Biomedical Sciences, Department of Physiology, New Orleans, LA 70118-5669. Offers MS, PhD, MD/PhD. MS and PhD offered through the Graduate School. *Degree requirements:* For master's, one foreign language, thesis; for doctorate, 2 foreign languages, thesis/dissertation. *Entrance requirements:* For master's, GRE General Test, minimum B average in undergraduate course work; for doctorate, GRE General Test. Additional exam requirements/recommendations for international students: Required—TOEFL. Electronic applications accepted. *Faculty research:* Renal microcirculation, neurophysiology, NA+ transport, renin/angio tensin system, cell and molecular endocrinology.

Universidad Central del Caribe, School of Medicine, Program in Biomedical Sciences, Bayamón, PR 00960-6032. Offers anatomy and cell biology (MA, MS); biochemistry (MS); biomedical sciences (MA); cellular and molecular biology (PhD); microbiology and immunology (MA, MS); pharmacology (MS); physiology (MS).

Université de Montréal, Faculty of Medicine, Department of Physiology, Montréal, QC H3C 3J7, Canada. Offers neurological sciences (M Sc, PhD); physiology (M Sc, PhD). Terminal master's awarded for partial completion of doctoral program. *Degree requirements:* For master's, thesis; for doctorate, thesis/dissertation, general exam. *Entrance requirements:* For master's and doctorate, proficiency in French, knowledge of English. Electronic applications accepted. *Faculty research:* Cardiovascular, neuropeptides, membrane transport and biophysics, signaling pathways.

Université de Sherbrooke, Faculty of Medicine and Health Sciences, Graduate Programs in Medicine, Department of Physiology and Biophysics, Sherbrooke, QC J1H 5N4, Canada. Offers M Sc, PhD. Terminal master's awarded for partial completion of doctoral program. *Degree requirements:* For master's, thesis; for doctorate, thesis/dissertation. Electronic applications accepted. *Faculty research:* Ion channels, neurological basis of pain, insulin resistance, obesity.

Université Laval, Faculty of Medicine, Graduate Programs in Medicine, Programs in Physiology-Endocrinology, Québec, QC G1K 7P4, Canada. Offers M Sc, PhD. Terminal master's awarded for partial completion of doctoral program. *Degree requirements:* For master's, thesis; for doctorate, comprehensive exam, thesis/dissertation. Electronic applications accepted.

University at Buffalo, the State University of New York, Graduate School, School of Medicine and Biomedical Sciences, Graduate Programs in Medicine and Biomedical Sciences, Department of Physiology and Biophysics, Buffalo, NY 14260. Offers biophysics (MS, PhD); physiology (MA, PhD). *Faculty:* 19 full-time (4 women). *Students:* 30 full-time (11 women); includes 1 minority (Asian, non-Hispanic/Latino), 14 international. Average age 29. 38 applicants, 21% accepted, 4 enrolled. In 2011, 2 master's, 2 doctorates awarded. Terminal master's awarded for partial completion of doctoral program. *Degree requirements:* For master's, thesis, oral exam, project; for doctorate, thesis/dissertation, oral and written qualifying exam or 2 research proposals. *Entrance requirements:* For master's and doctorate, GRE General Test. Additional exam requirements/recommendations for international students: Required—TOEFL (minimum score 600 paper-based; 250 computer-based; 100 iBT). *Application deadline:* For fall admission, 2/1 priority date for domestic students, 2/1 for international students. Applications are processed on a rolling basis. Application fee: $50. Electronic applications accepted. *Financial support:* In 2011–12, fellowships with tuition reimbursements (averaging $21,000 per year), 17 research assistantships with tuition reimbursements (averaging $21,000 per year) were awarded; Federal Work-Study, institutionally sponsored loans, health care benefits, and unspecified assistantships also available. Financial award application deadline: 2/1; financial award applicants required to submit FAFSA. *Faculty research:* Neurosciences, ion channels, cardiac physiology, renal/epithelial transport, cardiopulmonary exercise. *Total annual research expenditures:* $5.4 million. *Unit head:* Dr. Perry M. Hogan, Chair, 716-829-2738, Fax: 716-829-2344, E-mail: phogan@buffalo.edu. *Application contact:* Shaun C. Hoppel, Academic Coordinator, 716-829-2417, Fax: 716-829-2344, E-mail: schoppel@buffalo.edu.

University of Alberta, Faculty of Graduate Studies and Research, Department of Biological Sciences, Edmonton, AB T6G 2E1, Canada. Offers environmental biology and ecology (M Sc, PhD); microbiology and biotechnology (M Sc, PhD); molecular biology and genetics (M Sc, PhD); physiology and cell biology (M Sc, PhD); plant biology (M Sc, PhD); systematics and evolution (M Sc, PhD). Terminal master's awarded for partial completion of doctoral program. *Degree requirements:* For master's, thesis; for doctorate, thesis/dissertation. *Entrance requirements:* Additional exam requirements/recommendations for international students: Required—TOEFL.

University of Alberta, Faculty of Medicine and Dentistry and Faculty of Graduate Studies and Research, Graduate Programs in Medicine, Department of Physiology, Edmonton, AB T6G 2E1, Canada. Offers M Sc, PhD. Terminal master's awarded for partial completion of doctoral program. *Degree requirements:* For master's, thesis; for doctorate, thesis/dissertation. *Entrance requirements:* For master's and doctorate, minimum GPA of 3.0. Additional exam requirements/recommendations for international students: Required—TOEFL (minimum score 580 paper-based; 237 computer-based). Electronic applications accepted. *Faculty research:* Membrane transport, cell biology, perinatal endocrinology, neurophysiology, cardiovascular.

The University of Arizona, Graduate Interdisciplinary Programs, Graduate Interdisciplinary Program in Physiological Sciences, Tucson, AZ 85721. Offers MS, PhD. *Faculty:* 14 full-time (6 women), 1 part-time/adjunct. *Students:* 43 full-time (22 women), 5 part-time (3 women); includes 10 minority (1 Black or African American, non-Hispanic/Latino; 3 Hispanic/Latino; 6 Two or more races, non-Hispanic/Latino), 6 international. Average age 26. 37 applicants, 57% accepted, 19 enrolled. In 2011, 12 master's, 5 doctorates awarded. *Degree requirements:* For doctorate, thesis/dissertation. *Entrance requirements:* For master's, GRE General Test, 3 letters of recommendation, statement of purpose; for doctorate, GRE General Test, 3 letters of recommendation. Additional exam requirements/recommendations for international students: Required—TOEFL (minimum score 600 paper-based). *Application deadline:* For fall admission, 3/15 for domestic and international students. Applications are processed on a rolling basis. Application fee: $75. Electronic applications accepted. *Expenses:* Tuition, state resident: full-time $10,840. Tuition, nonresident: full-time $25,802. *Financial support:* In 2011–12, 12 research assistantships with full tuition reimbursements (averaging $20,867 per year), 13 teaching assistantships with full tuition reimbursements (averaging $27,699 per year) were awarded; health care benefits and unspecified assistantships also available. *Faculty research:* Cellular transport and signaling, receptor and messenger modulation, neural interaction and biomechanics, fluid network regulation, environmental adaptation. *Total annual research expenditures:* $8.3 million. *Unit head:* Dr. Ronald Lynch, Department Chair, 520-626-2472, E-mail: rlynch@u.arizona.edu. *Application contact:* Holly Lopez, Information Contact, 520-626-2898, Fax: 520-626-2382, E-mail: idp@ccit.arizona.edu. Web site: http://physiosc.web.arizona.edu/.

University of Arkansas for Medical Sciences, Graduate School, Graduate Programs in Biomedical Sciences, Department of Physiology and Biophysics, Little Rock, AR 72205-7199. Offers MS, PhD, MD/PhD. *Degree requirements:* For master's, thesis; for doctorate, thesis/dissertation. *Entrance requirements:* For master's and doctorate, GRE General Test. Additional exam requirements/recommendations for international students: Required—TOEFL. *Faculty research:* Gene transcription, protein targeting, membrane biology, cell-cell communication.

The University of British Columbia, Faculty of Medicine, Department of Cellular and Physiological Sciences, Division of Physiology, Vancouver, BC V6T 1Z1, Canada. Offers M Sc, PhD. Terminal master's awarded for partial completion of doctoral program. *Degree requirements:* For master's, thesis, oral defense; for doctorate, comprehensive exam, thesis/dissertation, oral defense. *Entrance requirements:* Additional exam requirements/recommendations for international students: Required—TOEFL (minimum score 550 paper-based; 213 computer-based), IELTS (minimum score 6.2). Electronic applications accepted. *Faculty research:* Neurophysiology, gastroenterology, endocrinology, cardiovascular physiology.

University of California, Berkeley, Graduate Division, College of Letters and Science, Group in Endocrinology, Berkeley, CA 94720-1500. Offers MA, PhD. *Degree requirements:* For doctorate, thesis/dissertation, oral qualifying exam. *Entrance requirements:* For master's, GRE General Test or the equivalent (MCAT), minimum GPA of 3.0, 3 letters of recommendation; for doctorate, GRE General Test or the equivalent (MCAT), minimum GPA of 3.4, 3 letters of recommendation. Additional exam requirements/recommendations for international students: Required—TOEFL.

University of California, Davis, Graduate Studies, Molecular, Cellular and Integrative Physiology Graduate Group, Davis, CA 95616. Offers MS, PhD. *Degree requirements:* For master's, comprehensive exam (for some programs), thesis (for some programs); for doctorate, thesis/dissertation. *Entrance requirements:* For master's and doctorate, GRE General Test. Additional exam requirements/recommendations for international students: Required—TOEFL (minimum score 550 paper-based; 213 computer-based). Electronic applications accepted. *Faculty research:* Systemic physiology, cellular physiology, neurophysiology, cardiovascular physiology, endocrinology.

University of California, Irvine, School of Medicine and School of Biological Sciences, Department of Physiology and Biophysics, Irvine, CA 92697. Offers biological sciences (PhD); MD/PhD. *Students:* 12 full-time (6 women); includes 5 minority (1 American Indian or Alaska Native, non-Hispanic/Latino; 3 Asian, non-Hispanic/Latino; 1 Hispanic/Latino), 1 international. Average age 28. 1 applicant, 100% accepted, 1 enrolled. In 2011, 1 degree awarded. *Degree requirements:* For doctorate, thesis/dissertation. *Entrance requirements:* For doctorate, GRE General Test, GRE Subject Test, minimum GPA of 3.0. Additional exam requirements/recommendations for international students: Required—TOEFL (minimum score 550 paper-based; 213 computer-based). *Application deadline:* For fall admission, 1/15 priority date for domestic students, 1/15 for international students. Application fee: $80 ($100 for international students). Electronic applications accepted. *Financial support:* Fellowships, research assistantships with full tuition reimbursements, teaching assistantships, institutionally sponsored loans, traineeships, health care benefits, and unspecified assistantships available. Financial award application deadline: 3/1; financial award applicants required to submit FAFSA. *Faculty research:* Membrane physiology, exercise physiology, regulation of hormone biosynthesis and action, endocrinology, ion channels and signal transduction. *Unit head:* Prof. Michael Cahalan, Chairman, 949-824-7776, Fax: 949-824-3143, E-mail: mcahalan@uci.edu. *Application contact:* Vicki C. Ledray, Chief Administrative Officer, 949-824-5865, Fax: 949-824-0019, E-mail: ledray@uci.edu. Web site: http://www.physiology.uci.edu/.

University of California, Los Angeles, David Geffen School of Medicine and Graduate Division, Graduate Programs in Medicine, Department of Physiology, Los Angeles, CA 90095. Offers PhD. *Degree requirements:* For doctorate, thesis/dissertation, oral and written qualifying exams. *Entrance requirements:* For doctorate, GRE General Test, GRE Subject Test. *Faculty research:* Membrane physiology, cell physiology, muscle physiology, neurophysiology, cardiopulmonary physiology.

University of California, Los Angeles, Graduate Division, College of Letters and Science, Department of Physiological Science, Los Angeles, CA 90095. Offers physiological science (MS). *Faculty:* 18 full-time (4 women). *Students:* 22 full-time (8 women); includes 14 minority (2 Black or African American, non-Hispanic/Latino; 9 Asian, non-Hispanic/Latino; 3 Two or more races, non-Hispanic/Latino), 1 international. Average age 26. 24 applicants, 38% accepted, 9 enrolled. In 2011, 11 master's awarded. *Degree requirements:* For master's, thesis. *Entrance requirements:* For master's, GRE General Test or MCAT, minimum GPA of 3.0, bachelor's degree in biological or physical sciences. *Application deadline:* For fall admission, 6/30 for domestic and international students. Application fee: $70 ($90 for international students). Electronic applications accepted. *Financial support:* In 2011–12, 19 fellowships with full and partial tuition reimbursements, 10 research assistantships with full and partial tuition reimbursements, 22 teaching assistantships with full and partial tuition reimbursements were awarded; Federal Work-Study, institutionally sponsored loans, scholarships/grants, health care benefits, tuition waivers (full and partial), and unspecified assistantships also available. Financial award applicants required to submit FAFSA. *Faculty research:* Diet and exercise in the prevention and management of degenerative diseases, neuromuscular physiology and plasticity, neural control of movement and homeostasis. *Unit head:* Dr. Barney Schlinger, Chair, 310-825-5716, E-mail: schlinge@lifesci.ucla.edu. *Application contact:* Michael Carr, Departmental Office, 310-825-3891, E-mail: mcarr@physci.ucla.edu. Web site: http://www.physci.ucla.edu/.

University of California, Los Angeles, Graduate Division, College of Letters and Science and David Geffen School of Medicine, UCLA ACCESS to Programs in the Molecular, Cellular and Integrative Life Sciences, Los Angeles, CA 90095. Offers biochemistry and molecular biology (PhD); biological chemistry (PhD); cellular and molecular pathology (PhD); human genetics (PhD); microbiology, immunology, and molecular genetics (PhD); molecular biology (PhD); molecular toxicology (PhD); molecular, cellular and integrative physiology (PhD); neurobiology (PhD); oral biology (PhD); physiology (PhD). *Students:* 44 full-time (30 women); includes 18 minority (11 Asian, non-Hispanic/Latino; 6 Hispanic/Latino; 1 Two or more races, non-Hispanic/Latino), 9 international. Average age 25. 495 applicants, 18% accepted, 41 enrolled. *Degree requirements:* For doctorate, thesis/dissertation, oral and written qualifying exams. *Entrance requirements:* For doctorate, GRE General Test, minimum undergraduate GPA of 3.0. Additional exam requirements/recommendations for international students: Required—TOEFL. *Application deadline:* For fall admission, 12/15 for domestic and international students. Application fee: $70 ($90 for international students). Electronic applications accepted. *Financial support:* In 2011–12, 51 fellowships with full and partial tuition reimbursements, 9 research assistantships with full and partial tuition reimbursements were awarded; teaching assistantships with full and partial tuition reimbursements, Federal Work-Study, institutionally sponsored loans, scholarships/grants, health care benefits, tuition waivers (full and partial), and

unspecified assistantships also available. Financial award application deadline: 3/1; financial award applicants required to submit FAFSA. *Faculty research:* Molecular, cellular, and developmental biology; immunology; microbiology; integrative biology. *Unit head:* Jody Spillane, Project Coordinator, 310-206-1845, E-mail: jspillane@mednet.ucla.edu. *Application contact:* UCLA ACCESS Admissions, 310-206-1845, E-mail: uclaaccess@mednet.ucla.edu. Web site: https://www.uclaaccess.ucla.edu/.

University of California, San Diego, School of Medicine and Office of Graduate Studies, Graduate Studies in Biomedical Sciences, Physiology Program, La Jolla, CA 92093. Offers PhD. *Degree requirements:* For doctorate, thesis/dissertation, qualifying exam. *Entrance requirements:* For doctorate, GRE General Test. Additional exam requirements/recommendations for international students: Required—TOEFL. Electronic applications accepted. *Faculty research:* Cell and organ physiology, eukaryotic regulatory and molecular biology, molecular and cellular pharmacology.

University of California, San Francisco, Graduate Division, Biomedical Sciences Graduate Group, San Francisco, CA 94143. Offers anatomy (PhD); endocrinology (PhD); experimental pathology (PhD); physiology (PhD). *Degree requirements:* For doctorate, thesis/dissertation. *Entrance requirements:* For doctorate, GRE General Test.

University of Chicago, Division of Biological Sciences, Neuroscience Graduate Programs, Committee on Integrative Neuroscience, Chicago, IL 60637-1513. Offers cell physiology (PhD); pharmacological and physiological sciences (PhD). *Degree requirements:* For doctorate, thesis/dissertation, preliminary exam. *Entrance requirements:* For doctorate, GRE General Test. Additional exam requirements/recommendations for international students: Required—TOEFL. Electronic applications accepted. *Faculty research:* Psychopharmacology, neuropharmacology.

University of Cincinnati, Graduate School, College of Medicine, Graduate Programs in Biomedical Sciences, Department of Molecular and Cellular Physiology, Cincinnati, OH 45221. Offers physiology (PhD). *Degree requirements:* For doctorate, comprehensive exam, thesis/dissertation, publication. *Entrance requirements:* For doctorate, GRE General Test, GRE Subject Test. Additional exam requirements/recommendations for international students: Required—TOEFL (minimum score 560 paper-based; 220 computer-based). Electronic applications accepted. *Faculty research:* Endocrinology, cardiovascular physiology, muscle physiology, neurophysiology, transgenic mouse physiology.

University of Colorado Boulder, Graduate School, College of Arts and Sciences, Department of Integrative Physiology, Boulder, CO 80309. Offers MS, PhD. *Faculty:* 21 full-time (7 women). *Students:* 66 full-time (24 women), 7 part-time (2 women); includes 8 minority (1 American Indian or Alaska Native, non-Hispanic/Latino; 3 Asian, non-Hispanic/Latino; 3 Hispanic/Latino; 1 Two or more races, non-Hispanic/Latino), 3 international. Average age 27. 83 applicants, 25% accepted, 17 enrolled. In 2011, 20 master's, 3 doctorates awarded. Terminal master's awarded for partial completion of doctoral program. *Median time to degree:* Of those who began their doctoral program in fall 2003, 67% received their degree in 8 years or less. *Degree requirements:* For master's, comprehensive exam, thesis or alternative; for doctorate, thesis/dissertation. *Entrance requirements:* For master's, GRE General Test, minimum undergraduate GPA of 2.75. *Application deadline:* For fall admission, 1/15 for domestic students, 12/15 for international students. Applications are processed on a rolling basis. Application fee: $50 ($60 for international students). Electronic applications accepted. *Financial support:* In 2011–12, 106 students received support, including 28 fellowships (averaging $7,566 per year), 37 research assistantships with full and partial tuition reimbursements available (averaging $15,350 per year), 41 teaching assistantships with full and partial tuition reimbursements available (averaging $16,968 per year); institutionally sponsored loans, scholarships/grants, health care benefits, and unspecified assistantships also available. Financial award application deadline: 2/1; financial award applicants required

to submit FAFSA. *Faculty research:* Integrative or cellular kinesiology. *Total annual research expenditures:* $9.2 million. *Application contact:* E-mail: iphygrad@colorado.edu. Web site: http://www.colorado.edu/intphys/.

University of Colorado Denver, School of Medicine, Program in Physiology, Aurora, CO 80045. Offers PhD. *Students:* 8 full-time (0 women), 3 international. Average age 28. 3 applicants, 0% accepted, 0 enrolled. *Degree requirements:* For doctorate, comprehensive exam, 30 semester credit hours each of coursework and thesis, 3 lab rotations within 1st year. *Entrance requirements:* For doctorate, GRE General Test, 2 transcripts, 4 letters of recommendation; minimum GPA of 3.2; completion of college-level mathematics through calculus; one year each of organic chemistry, physical chemistry, and physics; two years of biology. Additional exam requirements/recommendations for international students: Required—TOEFL (minimum score 550 paper-based; 213 computer-based). *Application deadline:* For fall admission, 1/1 for domestic students, 12/1 for international students. Application fee: $50 ($75 for international students). Electronic applications accepted. *Expenses:* Contact institution. *Financial support:* In 2011–12, 1 fellowship with full tuition reimbursement (averaging $25,000 per year) was awarded; health care benefits, tuition waivers (full), and stipend also available. Financial award application deadline: 3/15; financial award applicants required to submit FAFSA. *Faculty research:* Nicotonic receptors, immunity, molecular structure, function and regulation of ion channels, calcium influx in the function of cytotoxic T lymphocytes. *Unit head:* Dr. Sukumar Vijayaraghavan, Director, 303-724-4531, E-mail: sukumar.v@ucdenver.edu. *Application contact:* Shelly Sutherland, Office of Admissions, 303-724-4500, Fax: 303-724-4501, E-mail: rachelle.sutherland@ucdenver.edu. Web site: http://www.ucdenver.edu/academics/colleges/medicalschool/departments/physiology/Pages/home.aspx.

University of Connecticut, Graduate School, College of Liberal Arts and Sciences, Department of Physiology and Neurobiology, Storrs, CT 06269. Offers comparative physiology (MS, PhD); endocrinology (MS, PhD), including comparative physiology (MS), neurobiology (MS); neurobiology (MS, PhD). Terminal master's awarded for partial completion of doctoral program. *Degree requirements:* For master's, comprehensive exam; for doctorate, thesis/dissertation. *Entrance requirements:* For master's and doctorate, GRE General Test, GRE Subject Test. Additional exam requirements/recommendations for international students: Required—TOEFL (minimum score 550 paper-based; 213 computer-based). Electronic applications accepted.

See Display below and Close-Up on page 463.

University of Delaware, College of Arts and Sciences, Department of Biological Sciences, Newark, DE 19716. Offers biotechnology (MS); cancer biology (MS, PhD); cell and extracellular matrix biology (MS, PhD); cell and systems physiology (MS, PhD); developmental biology (MS, PhD); ecology and evolution (MS, PhD); microbiology (MS, PhD); molecular biology and genetics (MS, PhD). Terminal master's awarded for partial completion of doctoral program. *Degree requirements:* For master's, thesis, preliminary exam; for doctorate, comprehensive exam, thesis/dissertation, preliminary exam. *Entrance requirements:* For master's and doctorate, GRE General Test. Additional exam requirements/recommendations for international students: Required—TOEFL (minimum score 600 paper-based; 250 computer-based); Recommended—TWE. Electronic applications accepted. *Faculty research:* Microorganisms, bone, cancer metastasis, developmental biology, cell biology, DNA.

University of Delaware, College of Health Sciences, Department of Kinesiology and Applied Physiology, Newark, DE 19716. Offers MS, PhD.

University of Florida, College of Medicine, Department of Physiology and Functional Genomics, Gainesville, FL 32611. Offers PhD. *Degree requirements:* For doctorate, thesis/dissertation. *Entrance requirements:* For doctorate, GRE General Test, minimum GPA of 3.0. Additional exam requirements/recommendations for international students:

UCONN

Graduate Studies in Physiology & Neurobiology

The Department of Physiology and Neurobiology offers a program of graduate study leading to both M.S. and Ph.D. degrees. The Program prepares students for successful research careers in academia or industry by providing a structured yet flexible plan of coursework and research.

See: http://www.pnb.uconn.edu/PNB_Base/grad/pdfs/PNB%20brochure1.pdf

Ph.D. candidates can expect financial assistance, including full tuition waiver, health insurance, and stipend (academic year and summer).

Health-related research areas include:

- Adult Stem Cells and Brain Repair (Dr. J. Conover)
- Neural Development and Brain Disorders (Dr. J. LoTurco)
- Autism (Dr. R. Walikonis)
- Epilepsy and Stroke (Dr. A. Tzingounis)
- Mental and Neurological Disorders (Dr. A. de Blas)
- Multiple Sclerosis (Dr. A. Nishiyama)
- Obstructive Sleep Apnea (Dr. D. Mulkey)

For more information, please contact:

Kathy Dobson, Graduate Coordinator
Graduate Studies in Physiology & Neurobiology
University of Connecticut
75 North Eagleville Road, U-3156
Storrs, CT 06269-3156
kathleen.kelleher@uconn.edu

http://www.pnb.uconn.edu/PNB_Base/grad/index.html

Physiology

Required—TOEFL. Electronic applications accepted. *Faculty research:* Cell and general endocrinology, neuroendocrinology, neurophysiology, respiration, membrane transport and ion channels.

University of Florida, College of Medicine and Graduate School, Interdisciplinary Program in Biomedical Sciences, Concentration in Physiology and Pharmacology, Gainesville, FL 32611. Offers PhD. *Degree requirements:* For doctorate, thesis/dissertation. *Entrance requirements:* For doctorate, GRE General Test, minimum GPA of 3.0. Electronic applications accepted.

University of Florida, Graduate School, College of Health and Human Performance, Department of Applied Physiology and Kinesiology, Gainesville, FL 32611. Offers athletic training/sport medicine (MS); biobehavioral science (MS, PhD); clinical exercise physiology (MS); exercise physiology (MS, PhD); health and human performance (PhD); human performance (MS). *Degree requirements:* For master's, comprehensive exam, thesis (for some programs); for doctorate, comprehensive exam, thesis/dissertation. *Entrance requirements:* For doctorate, GRE General Test. Additional exam requirements/recommendations for international students: Required—TOEFL (minimum score 550 paper-based; 213 computer-based; 80 iBT), IELTS (minimum score 6). Electronic applications accepted. *Faculty research:* Cardiovascular disease; basic mechanisms that underlie exercise-induced changes in the body at the organ, tissue, cellular and molecular level; development of rehabilitation techniques for regaining motor control after stroke or as a consequence of Parkinson's disease; maintaining optimal health and delaying age-related declines in physiological function; psychomotor mechanisms impacting health and performance across the life span.

University of Georgia, College of Veterinary Medicine, Department of Physiology and Pharmacology, Athens, GA 30602. Offers pharmacology (MS, PhD); physiology (MS, PhD). *Faculty:* 12 full-time (4 women), 1 part-time/adjunct (0 women). *Students:* 19 full-time (8 women); includes 2 minority (1 Asian, non-Hispanic/Latino; 1 Hispanic/Latino), 12 international. Average age 28. 11 applicants, 27% accepted, 3 enrolled. In 2011, 1 doctorate awarded. *Degree requirements:* For master's, thesis; for doctorate, one foreign language, thesis/dissertation. *Entrance requirements:* For master's and doctorate, GRE General Test. *Application deadline:* For fall admission, 7/1 priority date for domestic students; for spring admission, 11/15 for domestic students. Application fee: $50. Electronic applications accepted. *Financial support:* Fellowships, research assistantships, teaching assistantships, and unspecified assistantships available. *Unit head:* Dr. Gaylen L. Edwards, Acting Head, 706-542-3014, Fax: 706-542-3015, E-mail: gedwards@uga.edu. *Application contact:* Dr. John Wagner, Graduate Coordinator, 706-542-6428, Fax: 706-542-3015, E-mail: jwagner@uga.edu. Web site: http://www.vet.uga.edu/vph/.

University of Guelph, Ontario Veterinary College and Graduate Studies, Graduate Programs in Veterinary Sciences, Department of Biomedical Sciences, Guelph, ON N1G 2W1, Canada. Offers morphology (M Sc, DV Sc, PhD); neuroscience (M Sc, DV Sc, PhD); pharmacology (M Sc, DV Sc, PhD); physiology (M Sc, DV Sc, PhD); toxicology (M Sc, DV Sc, PhD). Part-time programs available. *Degree requirements:* For master's, thesis; for doctorate, comprehensive exam, thesis/dissertation. *Entrance requirements:* For master's, honors B Sc, minimum 75% average in last 20 courses; for doctorate, M Sc with thesis from accredited institution. Additional exam requirements/recommendations for international students: Required—TOEFL (minimum score 550 paper-based; 213 computer-based; 89 iBT). Electronic applications accepted. *Faculty research:* Cellular morphology; endocrine, vascular and reproductive physiology; clinical pharmacology; veterinary toxicology; developmental biology, neuroscience.

University of Hawaii at Manoa, John A. Burns School of Medicine, Program in Developmental and Reproductive Biology, Honolulu, HI 96813. Offers MS, PhD. Part-time programs available. *Degree requirements:* For doctorate, thesis/dissertation. *Entrance requirements:* For doctorate, GRE General Test, GRE Subject Test. Additional exam requirements/recommendations for international students: Recommended—TOEFL (minimum score 560 paper-based; 83 computer-based), IELTS (minimum score 5). *Faculty research:* Biology of gametes and fertilization, reproductive endocrinology.

University of Illinois at Chicago, College of Medicine and Graduate College, Graduate Programs in Medicine, Department of Physiology and Biophysics, Chicago, IL 60607-7128. Offers MS, PhD. Terminal master's awarded for partial completion of doctoral program. *Degree requirements:* For master's, thesis; for doctorate, thesis/dissertation. *Entrance requirements:* For master's and doctorate, GRE General Test. Additional exam requirements/recommendations for international students: Required—TOEFL. Electronic applications accepted. *Faculty research:* Neuroscience, endocrinology and reproduction, cell physiology, exercise physiology, NMR.

University of Illinois at Urbana–Champaign, Graduate College, College of Liberal Arts and Sciences, School of Integrative Biology, Program in Physiological and Molecular Plant Biology, Champaign, IL 61820. Offers PhD. *Students:* 3 full-time (1 woman), 2 international. In 2011, 6 doctorates awarded. *Entrance requirements:* For doctorate, GRE, minimum GPA of 3.0. Additional exam requirements/recommendations for international students: Required—TOEFL (minimum score 570 paper-based; 230 computer-based; 89 iBT). *Application deadline:* Applications are processed on a rolling basis. Application fee: $75 ($90 for international students). Electronic applications accepted. *Financial support:* In 2011–12, 2 research assistantships, 2 teaching assistantships were awarded; fellowships and tuition waivers (full and partial) also available. *Unit head:* Stephen Moose, Director, 217-244-6308, Fax: 217-244-1224, E-mail: smoose@illinois.edu. *Application contact:* Carol Hall, Office Manager, 217-333-8208, Fax: 217-244-1224, E-mail: cahall@illinois.edu. Web site: http://www.life.illinois.edu/plantbio/pmpb/.

University of Illinois at Urbana–Champaign, Graduate College, College of Liberal Arts and Sciences, School of Molecular and Cellular Biology, Department of Molecular and Integrative Physiology, Champaign, IL 61820. Offers MS, PhD. *Faculty:* 12 full-time (4 women). *Students:* 31 full-time (16 women), 2 part-time (0 women); includes 5 minority (1 Black or African American, non-Hispanic/Latino; 2 Asian, non-Hispanic/Latino; 2 Hispanic/Latino), 11 international. In 2011, 4 master's, 6 doctorates awarded. *Entrance requirements:* For master's and doctorate, GRE, minimum GPA of 3.0. Additional exam requirements/recommendations for international students: Required—TOEFL (minimum score 590 paper-based; 243 computer-based). *Application deadline:* Applications are processed on a rolling basis. Application fee: $75 ($90 for international students). Electronic applications accepted. *Financial support:* In 2011–12, 8 fellowships, 23 research assistantships, 10 teaching assistantships were awarded; tuition waivers (full and partial) also available. *Unit head:* Byron Kemper, Head, 217-333-1146, Fax: 217-333-1133, E-mail: byronkem@illinois.edu. *Application contact:* Shawn Smith, Office Manager, 217-244-6638, Fax: 217-333-1133, E-mail: smsmith1@illinois.edu. Web site: http://mcb.illinois.edu/departments/mip/.

The University of Iowa, Roy J. and Lucille A. Carver College of Medicine and Graduate College, Graduate Programs in Medicine, Department of Molecular Physiology and Biophysics, Iowa City, IA 52242-1316. Offers MS, PhD. *Faculty:* 16 full-time (2 women), 17 part-time/adjunct (2 women). *Students:* 22 full-time (5 women); includes 8 minority (1 American Indian or Alaska Native, non-Hispanic/Latino; 7 Asian, non-Hispanic/Latino). Average age 25. In 2011, 4 degrees awarded. Terminal master's awarded for partial completion of doctoral program. *Median time to degree:* Of those who began their

doctoral program in fall 2003, 100% received their degree in 8 years or less. *Degree requirements:* For master's, comprehensive exam; for doctorate, comprehensive exam, thesis/dissertation, teaching experience. *Entrance requirements:* For master's, GRE General Test; for doctorate, GRE General Test, minimum GPA of 3.0. Additional exam requirements/recommendations for international students: Required—TOEFL. *Application deadline:* For fall admission, 4/1 for domestic students, 3/1 for international students; for spring admission, 10/1 for domestic students, 9/1 for international students. Applications are processed on a rolling basis. Application fee: $60 ($80 for international students). Electronic applications accepted. *Financial support:* In 2011–12, 2 fellowships with full tuition reimbursements (averaging $25,500 per year), 20 research assistantships with full tuition reimbursements (averaging $25,500 per year) were awarded; traineeships also available. Financial award application deadline: 4/1. *Faculty research:* Cellular and molecular endocrinology, membrane structure and function, cardiac cell electrophysiology, regulation of gene expression, neurophysiology. *Unit head:* Dr. Kevin P. Campbell, Head, 319-335-7800, Fax: 319-335-7330, E-mail: kevin-campbell@uiowa.edu. *Application contact:* Dr. Michael Anderson, Director of Graduate Studies, 319-335-7839, Fax: 319-335-7330, E-mail: michael-g-anderson@uiowa.edu. Web site: http://www.physiology.uiowa.edu/.

The University of Kansas, University of Kansas Medical Center, School of Medicine, Department of Molecular and Integrative Physiology, Kansas City, KS 66160. Offers molecular and integrative physiology (MS, PhD); neuroscience (MS, PhD); MD/PhD. *Faculty:* 45. *Students:* 30 full-time (13 women); includes 2 minority (1 Black or African American, non-Hispanic/Latino; 1 Hispanic/Latino), 17 international. Average age 28. 6 applicants, 100% accepted, 6 enrolled. In 2011, 4 doctorates awarded. Terminal master's awarded for partial completion of doctoral program. *Degree requirements:* For master's, thesis; for doctorate, comprehensive exam, thesis/dissertation. *Entrance requirements:* For doctorate, GRE. Additional exam requirements/recommendations for international students: Required—TOEFL. *Application deadline:* For fall admission, 1/15 priority date for domestic students, 1/15 for international students. Applications are processed on a rolling basis. Application fee: $10. Electronic applications accepted. Tuition and fees vary according to course load, campus/location, program and reciprocity agreements. *Financial support:* Scholarships/grants and unspecified assistantships available. Financial award application deadline: 2/14; financial award applicants required to submit FAFSA. *Faculty research:* Male reproductive physiology and contraception, ovarian development and regulation by pituitary and hypothalamus, neural control of movement and stroke recovery, pulmonary physiology and hypoxia, plasticity of the autonomic nervous system. *Total annual research expenditures:* $9 million. *Unit head:* Dr. Paul D. Cheney, Chairman, 913-588-7400, Fax: 913-588-7430, E-mail: pcheney@kumc.edu. *Application contact:* Dr. Michael W. Wolfe, Director of Graduate Studies, 913-588-7418, Fax: 913-588-7430, E-mail: mwolfe2@kumc.edu. Web site: http://www.kumc.edu/physiology/index.html.

University of Kentucky, Graduate School, Graduate School Programs from the College of Medicine, Program in Physiology, Lexington, KY 40506-0032. Offers MS, PhD. *Degree requirements:* For doctorate, comprehensive exam, thesis/dissertation. *Entrance requirements:* For master's, GRE General Test, minimum undergraduate GPA of 2.75; for doctorate, GRE General Test, minimum undergraduate GPA of 2.75, graduate 3.0. Additional exam requirements/recommendations for international students: Required—TOEFL (minimum score 550 paper-based; 213 computer-based). Electronic applications accepted.

University of Louisville, School of Medicine, Department of Physiology and Biophysics, Louisville, KY 40292-0001. Offers MS, PhD, MD/PhD. Terminal master's awarded for partial completion of doctoral program. *Degree requirements:* For master's, thesis; for doctorate, comprehensive exam, thesis/dissertation. *Entrance requirements:* For master's and doctorate, GRE General Test (minimum score of 1000 verbal and quantitative), minimum GPA of 3.0. Additional exam requirements/recommendations for international students: Required—TOEFL. Electronic applications accepted. *Expenses:* Tuition, state resident: full-time $9692; part-time $539 per credit hour. Tuition, nonresident: full-time $20,168; part-time $1121 per credit hour. Tuition and fees vary according to program and reciprocity agreements. *Faculty research:* Control of microvascular function during normal and disease states; mechanisms of cellular adhesive interactions on endothelial cells lining blood vessels; changes in blood rheological properties and mechanisms associated with increased blood fibrinogen content; role of nutrition in microvascular control mechanisms; mechanism of cardiovascular-renal remodeling in hypertension, diabetes, and heart failure.

The University of Manchester, Faculty of Life Sciences, Manchester, United Kingdom. Offers adaptive organismal biology (M Phil, PhD); animal biology (M Phil, PhD); biochemistry (M Phil, PhD); bioinformatics (M Phil, PhD); biomolecular sciences (M Phil, PhD); biotechnology (M Phil, PhD); cell biology (M Phil, PhD); cell matrix research (M Phil, PhD); channels and transporters (M Phil, PhD); developmental biology (M Phil, PhD); Egyptology (M Phil, PhD); environmental biology (M Phil, PhD); evolutionary biology (M Phil, PhD); gene expression (M Phil, PhD); genetics (M Phil, PhD); history of science, technology and medicine (M Phil, PhD); immunology (M Phil, PhD); integrative neurobiology and behavior (M Phil, PhD); membrane trafficking (M Phil, PhD); microbiology (M Phil, PhD); molecular and cellular neuroscience (M Phil, PhD); molecular biology (M Phil, PhD); molecular cancer studies (M Phil, PhD); neuroscience (M Phil, PhD); ophthalmology (M Phil, PhD); optometry (M Phil, PhD); organelle function (M Phil, PhD); pharmacology (M Phil, PhD); physiology (M Phil, PhD); plant sciences (M Phil, PhD); stem cell research (M Phil, PhD); structural biology (M Phil, PhD); systems neuroscience (M Phil, PhD); toxicology (M Phil, PhD).

University of Manitoba, Faculty of Medicine and Faculty of Graduate Studies, Graduate Programs in Medicine, Department of Physiology, Winnipeg, MB R3T 2N2, Canada. Offers M Sc, PhD, MD/PhD. Terminal master's awarded for partial completion of doctoral program. *Degree requirements:* For master's, one foreign language, thesis; for doctorate, one foreign language, thesis/dissertation. *Entrance requirements:* For master's, minimum GPA of 3.5; for doctorate, minimum GPA of 3.5, M Sc. *Faculty research:* Cardiovascular research, gene technology, cell biology, neuroscience, respiration.

University of Massachusetts Amherst, Graduate School, Interdisciplinary Programs, Program in Plant Biology, Amherst, MA 01003. Offers biochemistry and metabolism (MS, PhD); cell biology and physiology (MS, PhD); environmental, ecological and integrative (PhD); environmental, ecological and integrative biology (MS); genetics and evolution (MS, PhD). *Students:* 16 full-time (7 women), 1 (woman) part-time, 7 international. Average age 27. 22 applicants, 50% accepted, 5 enrolled. In 2011, 3 degrees awarded. *Median time to degree:* Of those who began their doctoral program in fall 2003, 100% received their degree in 8 years or less. *Degree requirements:* For master's, thesis; for doctorate, 2 foreign languages, comprehensive exam, thesis/dissertation. *Entrance requirements:* For master's and doctorate, GRE General Test. Additional exam requirements/recommendations for international students: Required—TOEFL (minimum score 550 paper-based; 213 computer-based; 80 iBT), IELTS (minimum score 6.5). *Application deadline:* For fall admission, 12/15 for domestic and international students; for spring admission, 10/1 for domestic and international students. Applications are processed on a rolling basis. Application fee: $50 ($65 for international students). Electronic applications accepted. Tuition and fees vary

according to course load, campus/location and program. *Financial support:* Fellowships with full and partial tuition reimbursements, research assistantships with full and partial tuition reimbursements, teaching assistantships with full and partial tuition reimbursements, career-related internships or fieldwork, Federal Work-Study, scholarships/grants, traineeships, health care benefits, tuition waivers (full and partial), and unspecified assistantships available. Support available to part-time students. Financial award application deadline: 12/15. *Unit head:* Dr. Elsbeth L. Walker, Graduate Program Director, 413-577-3217, Fax: 413-545-3243. *Application contact:* Lindsay DeSantis, Interim Supervisor of Admissions, 413-545—0722, Fax: 413-577-0010, E-mail: gradadm@grad.umass.edu. Web site: http://www.bio.umass.edu/plantbio/.

University of Medicine and Dentistry of New Jersey, Graduate School of Biomedical Sciences, Graduate Programs in Biomedical Sciences–Newark, Department of Pharmacology and Physiology, Newark, NJ 07107. Offers PhD. *Degree requirements:* For doctorate, thesis/dissertation, qualifying exam. *Entrance requirements:* For doctorate, GRE General Test. Additional exam requirements/recommendations for international students: Required—TOEFL. Electronic applications accepted.

University of Medicine and Dentistry of New Jersey, Graduate School of Biomedical Sciences, Graduate Programs in Biomedical Sciences–Piscataway, Program in Physiology and Integrative Biology, Piscataway, NJ 08854-5635. Offers MS, PhD, MD/PhD. *Entrance requirements:* Additional exam requirements/recommendations for international students: Required—TOEFL. Electronic applications accepted.

University of Miami, Graduate School, Miller School of Medicine, Graduate Programs in Medicine, Department of Physiology and Biophysics, Coral Gables, FL 33124. Offers PhD, MD/PhD. *Degree requirements:* For doctorate, thesis/dissertation, qualifying exam. *Entrance requirements:* For doctorate, GRE General Test, minimum GPA of 3.0 in sciences. Additional exam requirements/recommendations for international students: Required—TOEFL. *Faculty research:* Cell and membrane physiology, cell-to-cell communication, molecular neurobiology, neuroimmunology, neural development.

University of Michigan, Horace H. Rackham School of Graduate Studies, Program in Biomedical Sciences (PIBS), Department of Molecular and Integrative Physiology, Ann Arbor, MI 48109. Offers PhD. *Faculty:* 35 full-time (13 women), 1 part-time/adjunct (0 women). *Students:* 33 full-time (16 women); includes 10 minority (2 Black or African American, non-Hispanic/Latino; 7 Asian, non-Hispanic/Latino; 1 Two or more races, non-Hispanic/Latino). Average age 27. 29 applicants, 34% accepted, 5 enrolled. In 2011, 3 doctorates awarded. *Degree requirements:* For doctorate, thesis/dissertation, oral defense of dissertation, preliminary exam. *Entrance requirements:* For doctorate, GRE General Test, 3 letters of recommendation, research experience. Additional exam requirements/recommendations for international students: Required—TOEFL (minimum score 84 iBT) or Michigan English Language Assessment Battery. *Application deadline:* For fall admission, 12/1 for domestic and international students. Application fee: $60 ($75 for international students). Electronic applications accepted. *Financial support:* In 2011–12, 33 students received support, including 24 fellowships with full tuition reimbursements available (averaging $26,500 per year); scholarships/grants, health care benefits, tuition waivers (full), and unspecified assistantships also available. Financial award application deadline: 12/1. *Faculty research:* Ion transport, cardiovascular physiology, gene expression, hormone action, gastrointestinal physiology, endocrinology, muscle, signal transduction. *Total annual research expenditures:* $8.4 million. *Unit head:* Dr. Bishr Omary, Chair, 734-764-4376, Fax: 734-936-8813, E-mail: mbishr@umich.edu. *Application contact:* Michelle S. Melis, Director of Student Life, 734-615-6538, Fax: 734-647-7022, E-mail: msmtegan@umich.edu. Web site: http://www.physiology.med.umich.edu/.

University of Minnesota, Duluth, Medical School, Graduate Program in Physiology, Duluth, MN 55812-2496. Offers MS, PhD. MS, PhD offered jointly with University of Minnesota, Twin Cities Campus. Terminal master's awarded for partial completion of doctoral program. *Degree requirements:* For master's, thesis; for doctorate, thesis/dissertation. *Entrance requirements:* For master's, GRE or MCAT; for doctorate, GRE or MCAT, 1 year of course work in each calculus, physics, and biology; 2 years of course work in chemistry; minimum GPA of 3.0 in science. Additional exam requirements/recommendations for international students: Required—TOEFL. *Faculty research:* Neural control of posture and locomotion, transport and metabolic phenomena in biological systems, control of organ blood flow, intracellular means of communication.

University of Minnesota, Twin Cities Campus, Graduate School, Department of Integrative Biology and Physiology, Minneapolis, MN 55455-0213. Offers PhD. Part-time programs available. *Degree requirements:* For doctorate, comprehensive exam, thesis/dissertation. *Entrance requirements:* For doctorate, GRE General Test. Electronic applications accepted. *Faculty research:* Cardiovascular physiology.

University of Mississippi Medical Center, School of Graduate Studies in the Health Sciences, Department of Physiology and Biophysics, Jackson, MS 39216-4505. Offers MS, PhD, MD/PhD. *Degree requirements:* For master's, thesis; for doctorate, thesis/dissertation, first authored publication. *Entrance requirements:* For master's and doctorate, GRE General Test, minimum GPA of 3.0. *Faculty research:* Cardiovascular, renal, endocrine, and cellular neurophysiology; molecular physiology.

University of Missouri, School of Medicine and Graduate School, Graduate Programs in Medicine, Department of Medical Pharmacology and Physiology, Columbia, MO 65211. Offers pharmacology (MS, PhD); physiology (MS, PhD). *Faculty:* 29 full-time (4 women), 3 part-time/adjunct (1 woman). *Students:* 17 full-time (10 women), 3 part-time (2 women); includes 2 minority (both Black or African American, non-Hispanic/Latino), 13 international. Average age 27. 34 applicants, 24% accepted, 7 enrolled. In 2011, 1 master's, 1 doctorate awarded. *Degree requirements:* For master's, thesis; for doctorate, thesis/dissertation. *Entrance requirements:* For master's and doctorate, GRE General Test, minimum GPA of 3.0. Additional exam requirements/recommendations for international students: Required—TOEFL (minimum score 500 paper-based; 173 computer-based; 61 iBT). *Application deadline:* For fall admission, 2/1 for domestic students. Application fee: $55 ($75 for international students). *Expenses:* Tuition, state resident: full-time $5881. Tuition, nonresident: full-time $15,183. *Required fees:* $952. Tuition and fees vary according to campus/location and program. *Financial support:* Fellowships, research assistantships, teaching assistantships, and institutionally sponsored loans available. *Faculty research:* Endocrine and metabolic pharmacology, biochemical pharmacology, neuropharmacology, receptors and transmembrane signaling. *Unit head:* Dr. Ron Korthuis, Department Chair, E-mail: korthuisr@missouri.edu. *Application contact:* Monica Elliott, 573-882-4957, E-mail: elliottm@missouri.edu. Web site: http://mpp.missouri.edu/.

University of Nebraska Medical Center, Graduate Studies, Department of Cellular and Integrative Physiology, Omaha, NE 68198. Offers physiology (MS, PhD). Terminal master's awarded for partial completion of doctoral program. *Degree requirements:* For master's, comprehensive exam, thesis optional; for doctorate, comprehensive exam, thesis/dissertation, at least one first-author research publication. *Entrance requirements:* For master's and doctorate, GRE General Test or MCAT, course work in biology, chemistry, mathematics, and physics. Additional exam requirements/recommendations for international students: Required—TOEFL (minimum score 600 paper-based; 250 computer-based; 100 iBT). Electronic applications accepted. *Faculty research:* Cardiovascular, renal and visual physiology, neuroscience, reproductive endocrinology.

University of Nevada, Reno, Graduate School, Interdisciplinary Program in Cellular and Molecular Pharmacology and Physiology, Reno, NV 89557. Offers PhD. *Degree requirements:* For doctorate, one foreign language, thesis/dissertation. *Entrance requirements:* For doctorate, GRE General Test or MCAT, minimum GPA of 3.0. Additional exam requirements/recommendations for international students: Required—TOEFL (minimum score 500 paper-based; 173 computer-based; 61 iBT), IELTS (minimum score 6). Electronic applications accepted. *Faculty research:* Neuropharmacology, toxicology, cardiovascular pharmacology, neuromuscular pharmacology.

University of New Mexico, Health Sciences Center Graduate Programs, Program in Biomedical Sciences, Albuquerque, NM 87131-5196. Offers biochemistry and molecular biology (MS, PhD); cell biology and physiology (MS, PhD); clinical and translational science (Certificate); molecular genetics and microbiology (MS, PhD); neuroscience (MS, PhD); pathology (MS, PhD); toxicology (MS, PhD); university science teaching (Certificate). Part-time programs available. *Faculty:* 64 full-time (26 women), 9 part-time/adjunct (4 women). *Students:* 45 full-time (27 women), 56 part-time (28 women); includes 24 minority (3 Black or African American, non-Hispanic/Latino; 1 American Indian or Alaska Native, non-Hispanic/Latino; 4 Asian, non-Hispanic/Latino; 14 Hispanic/Latino; 1 Native Hawaiian or other Pacific Islander, non-Hispanic/Latino; 1 Two or more races, non-Hispanic/Latino), 18 international. Average age 30. 110 applicants, 18% accepted, 17 enrolled. In 2011, 14 master's, 5 doctorates awarded. Terminal master's awarded for partial completion of doctoral program. *Degree requirements:* For master's, thesis; for doctorate, comprehensive exam, thesis/dissertation. *Entrance requirements:* For master's and doctorate, GRE General Test, minimum undergraduate GPA of 3.0. Additional exam requirements/recommendations for international students: Required—TOEFL. *Application deadline:* For fall admission, 3/1 priority date for domestic students, 3/1 for international students. Applications are processed on a rolling basis. Application fee: $50. Electronic applications accepted. *Financial support:* In 2011–12, 99 students received support, including 28 fellowships with full and partial tuition reimbursements available (averaging $22,000 per year), 73 research assistantships with full tuition reimbursements available (averaging $23,000 per year), 8 teaching assistantships (averaging $2,800 per year); career-related internships or fieldwork, Federal Work-Study, institutionally sponsored loans, scholarships/grants, traineeships, health care benefits, and unspecified assistantships also available. Financial award application deadline: 1/1; financial award applicants required to submit FAFSA. *Faculty research:* Infectious disease/Immunity, cancer biology, cardiovascular and metabolic diseases, brain and behavioral illness, environmental health. *Unit head:* Dr. Helen J. Hathaway, BSGP Program Director, 505-272-1887, Fax: 505-272-2412, E-mail: hhathaway@salud.unm.edu. *Application contact:* Mary Fenton, Admissions Coordinator, 505-272-1887, Fax: 505-272-2412, E-mail: mfenton@salud.unm.edu. Web site: http://hsc.unm.edu/som/research/brep/bsgpabout.shtm.

University of North Dakota, Graduate School and Graduate School, Graduate Programs in Medicine, Department of Pharmacology, Physiology, and Therapeutics, Grand Forks, ND 58202. Offers pharmacology (MS, PhD); physiology (MS, PhD). *Degree requirements:* For master's, comprehensive exam, thesis; for doctorate, thesis/dissertation, written and oral exams. *Entrance requirements:* For master's, GRE General Test or MCAT, minimum GPA of 3.0; for doctorate, GRE General Test, minimum GPA of 3.5. Additional exam requirements/recommendations for international students: Required—TOEFL (minimum score 550 paper-based; 213 computer-based; 79 iBT), IELTS (minimum score 6.5). Electronic applications accepted.

University of North Texas Health Science Center at Fort Worth, Graduate School of Biomedical Sciences, Fort Worth, TX 76107-2699. Offers anatomy and cell biology (MS, PhD); biochemistry and molecular biology (MS, PhD); biomedical sciences (MS, PhD); biotechnology (MS); forensic genetics (MS); integrative physiology (MS, PhD); medical science (MS); microbiology and immunology (MS, PhD); pharmacology (MS, PhD); science education (MS); DO/MS; DO/PhD. Terminal master's awarded for partial completion of doctoral program. *Degree requirements:* For master's, thesis; for doctorate, thesis/dissertation. *Entrance requirements:* For master's and doctorate, GRE General Test. Additional exam requirements/recommendations for international students: Required—TOEFL. *Expenses:* Contact institution. *Faculty research:* Alzheimer's disease, aging, eye diseases, cancer, cardiovascular disease.

University of Notre Dame, Graduate School, College of Science, Department of Biological Sciences, Notre Dame, IN 46556. Offers aquatic ecology, evolution and environmental biology (MS, PhD); cellular and molecular biology (MS, PhD); genetics (MS, PhD); physiology (MS, PhD); vector biology and parasitology (MS, PhD). Terminal master's awarded for partial completion of doctoral program. *Degree requirements:* For master's, comprehensive exam, thesis; for doctorate, comprehensive exam, thesis/dissertation, candidacy exam. *Entrance requirements:* For master's and doctorate, GRE General Test. Additional exam requirements/recommendations for international students: Required—TOEFL (minimum score 600 paper-based; 250 computer-based; 80 iBT). Electronic applications accepted. *Faculty research:* Tropical disease, molecular genetics, neurobiology, evolutionary biology, aquatic biology.

University of Oklahoma Health Sciences Center, College of Medicine and Graduate College, Graduate Programs in Medicine, Department of Physiology, Oklahoma City, OK 73190. Offers MS, PhD. Part-time programs available. Terminal master's awarded for partial completion of doctoral program. *Degree requirements:* For master's, thesis (for some programs); for doctorate, thesis/dissertation. *Entrance requirements:* For master's, GRE General Test, statement of career goals, 3 letters of recommendation; for doctorate, GRE General Test, 3 letters of recommendation. Additional exam requirements/recommendations for international students: Required—TOEFL. *Faculty research:* Cardiopulmonary physiology, neurophysiology, exercise physiology, cell and molecular physiology.

University of Oregon, Graduate School, College of Arts and Sciences, Department of Human Physiology, Eugene, OR 97403. Offers MS, PhD. *Degree requirements:* For master's, thesis optional; for doctorate, one foreign language, thesis/dissertation. *Entrance requirements:* For master's, GRE General Test, minimum GPA of 2.75 in undergraduate course work; for doctorate, GRE General Test. *Faculty research:* Balance control, muscle fatigue, lower extremity function, knee control.

University of Pennsylvania, Perelman School of Medicine, Biomedical Graduate Studies, Graduate Group in Cell and Molecular Biology, Philadelphia, PA 19104. Offers cancer biology (PhD); cell biology and physiology (PhD); developmental stem cell regenerative biology (PhD); gene therapy and vaccines (PhD); genetics and gene regulation (PhD); microbiology, virology, and parasitology (PhD); MD/PhD; VMD/PhD. *Faculty:* 306. *Students:* 337 full-time (186 women); includes 81 minority (16 Black or African American, non-Hispanic/Latino; 43 Asian, non-Hispanic/Latino; 16 Hispanic/Latino; 6 Two or more races, non-Hispanic/Latino), 41 international. 585 applicants, 21% accepted, 58 enrolled. In 2011, 42 doctorates awarded. *Degree requirements:* For doctorate, thesis/dissertation. *Entrance requirements:* For doctorate, GRE General Test. Additional exam requirements/recommendations for international students: Required—TOEFL. *Application deadline:* For fall admission, 12/1 priority date for domestic students, 12/1 for international students. Applications are processed on a rolling basis. Application fee: $80. Electronic applications accepted. *Expenses:* Tuition: Full-time $26,660; part-time $4944 per course. *Required fees:* $2318; $291 per course. Tuition

and fees vary according to course load, degree level and program. *Financial support:* In 2011–12, 337 students received support. Fellowships, research assistantships, scholarships/grants, traineeships, and unspecified assistantships available. *Unit head:* Dr. Daniel Kessler, Graduate Group Chair. *Application contact:* Meagan Schofer, Coordinator. Web site: http://www.med.upenn.edu/camb/.

University of Prince Edward Island, Atlantic Veterinary College, Graduate Program in Veterinary Medicine, Charlottetown, PE C1A 4P3, Canada. Offers anatomy (M Sc, PhD); bacteriology (M Sc, PhD); clinical pharmacology (M Sc, PhD); clinical sciences (M Sc, PhD); epidemiology (M Sc, PhD), including reproduction; fish health (M Sc, PhD); food animal nutrition (M Sc, PhD); immunology (M Sc, PhD); microanatomy (M Sc, PhD); parasitology (M Sc, PhD); pathology (M Sc, PhD); pharmacology (M Sc, PhD); physiology (M Sc, PhD); toxicology (M Sc, PhD); veterinary science (M Vet Sc); virology (M Sc, PhD). Part-time programs available. *Degree requirements:* For master's, thesis; for doctorate, thesis/dissertation. *Entrance requirements:* For master's, DVM, B Sc honors degree, or equivalent; for doctorate, M Sc. Additional exam requirements/recommendations for international students: Required—TOEFL (minimum score 550 paper-based; 213 computer-based; 80 iBT). *Expenses:* Contact institution. *Faculty research:* Animal health management, infectious diseases, fin fish and shellfish health, basic biomedical sciences, ecosystem health.

University of Puerto Rico, Medical Sciences Campus, School of Medicine, Division of Graduate Studies, Department of Physiology, San Juan, PR 00936-5067. Offers MS, PhD. Terminal master's awarded for partial completion of doctoral program. *Degree requirements:* For master's, one foreign language, thesis; for doctorate, one foreign language, comprehensive exam, thesis/dissertation. *Entrance requirements:* For master's and doctorate, GRE General Test, GRE Subject Test, interview; course work in biology, chemistry and physics; minimum GPA of 3.0; 3 letters of recommendation. Electronic applications accepted. *Faculty research:* Respiration, neuroendocrinology, cellular and molecular physiology, cardiovascular, exercise physiology and neurobiology.

University of Rochester, School of Medicine and Dentistry, Graduate Programs in Medicine and Dentistry, Department of Pharmacology and Physiology, Programs in Physiology, Rochester, NY 14627. Offers MS, PhD. Terminal master's awarded for partial completion of doctoral program. *Degree requirements:* For master's, thesis; for doctorate, thesis/dissertation, qualifying exam. *Entrance requirements:* For master's and doctorate, GRE General Test. *Expenses: Tuition:* Full-time $41,040.

University of Saskatchewan, College of Medicine, Department of Physiology, Saskatoon, SK S7N 5A2, Canada. Offers M Sc, PhD. *Degree requirements:* For master's, thesis; for doctorate, thesis/dissertation. *Entrance requirements:* Additional exam requirements/recommendations for international students: Required—TOEFL.

University of Saskatchewan, Western College of Veterinary Medicine and College of Graduate Studies and Research, Graduate Programs in Veterinary Medicine, Department of Veterinary Biomedical Sciences, Saskatoon, SK S7N 5A2, Canada. Offers veterinary anatomy (M Sc); veterinary biomedical sciences (M Vet Sc); veterinary physiological sciences (M Sc, PhD). *Degree requirements:* For master's, thesis; for doctorate, comprehensive exam (for some programs), thesis/dissertation. *Entrance requirements:* Additional exam requirements/recommendations for international students: Required—TOEFL (minimum score 80 iBT); Recommended—IELTS (minimum score 6.5). Electronic applications accepted. *Faculty research:* Toxicology, animal reproduction, pharmacology, chloride channels, pulmonary pathobiology.

The University of South Dakota, Graduate School, School of Medicine and Graduate School, Biomedical Sciences Graduate Program, Physiology and Pharmacology Group, Vermillion, SD 57069-2390. Offers MS, PhD. Terminal master's awarded for partial completion of doctoral program. *Degree requirements:* For master's, thesis; for doctorate, comprehensive exam, thesis/dissertation. *Entrance requirements:* For master's and doctorate, GRE General Test, minimum GPA of 3.0. Additional exam requirements/recommendations for international students: Required—TOEFL (minimum score 550 paper-based; 213 computer-based; 80 iBT), IELTS (minimum score 6). Electronic applications accepted. *Expenses:* Contact institution. *Faculty research:* Pulmonary physiology and pharmacology, drug abuse, reproduction, signal transduction, cardiovascular physiology and pharmacology.

University of Southern California, Keck School of Medicine and Graduate School, Graduate Programs in Medicine, Department of Physiology and Biophysics, Los Angeles, CA 90089. Offers MS, PhD, MD/PhD. *Faculty:* 9 full-time (1 woman). *Students:* 8 full-time (4 women), 5 international. Average age 29. 1 applicant, 100% accepted, 1 enrolled. Terminal master's awarded for partial completion of doctoral program. *Degree requirements:* For master's, thesis optional; for doctorate, comprehensive exam, thesis/dissertation. *Entrance requirements:* For master's and doctorate, GRE General Test, minimum GPA of 3.0. Additional exam requirements/recommendations for international students: Required—TOEFL (minimum score 600 paper-based; 250 computer-based; 100 iBT). *Application deadline:* For fall admission, 12/1 priority date for domestic students, 12/1 for international students. Application fee: $85. Electronic applications accepted. *Financial support:* In 2011–12, 5 research assistantships with full tuition reimbursements (averaging $29,100 per year) were awarded; Federal Work-Study, institutionally sponsored loans, scholarships/grants, traineeships, health care benefits, and unspecified assistantships also available. Financial award application deadline: 5/4. *Faculty research:* Endocrinology and metabolism, neurophysiology, mathematical modeling, cell transport, autoimmunity and cancer immunotherapy. *Total annual research expenditures:* $2.1 million. *Unit head:* Dr. Berislav Zlokavic, Chair, 323-442-2566, Fax: 323-442-2230, E-mail: zlokovic@usc.edu. *Application contact:* Janet Stoeckert, Administrative Director, Basic Sciences Departments, 323-442-3568, Fax: 323-442-1610, E-mail: janet.stoeckert@usc.edu.

The University of Tennessee, Graduate School, College of Agricultural Sciences and Natural Resources, Department of Animal Science, Knoxville, TN 37996. Offers animal anatomy (PhD); breeding (MS, PhD); management (MS, PhD); nutrition (MS, PhD); physiology (MS, PhD). Part-time programs available. *Degree requirements:* For master's, thesis; for doctorate, thesis/dissertation. *Entrance requirements:* For master's and doctorate, GRE General Test, minimum GPA of 2.7. Additional exam requirements/recommendations for international students: Required—TOEFL. Electronic applications accepted. *Expenses:* Tuition, state resident: full-time $8332; part-time $464 per credit hour. Tuition, nonresident: full-time $25,174; part-time $1400 per credit hour. *Required fees:* $1162; $56 per credit hour. Tuition and fees vary according to program.

The University of Texas Health Science Center at San Antonio, Graduate School of Biomedical Sciences, Department of Physiology, San Antonio, TX 78229-3900. Offers MS, PhD. *Degree requirements:* For master's, thesis; for doctorate, comprehensive exam, thesis/dissertation. *Entrance requirements:* For master's, GRE General Test, MAT; for doctorate, GRE General Test. Additional exam requirements/recommendations for international students: Required—TOEFL (minimum score 560 paper-based; 220 computer-based; 68 iBT). Electronic applications accepted. *Faculty research:* Ion channels, cardiovascular function, neuroscience and aging.

The University of Texas Medical Branch, Graduate School of Biomedical Sciences, Program in Cellular Physiology and Molecular Biophysics, Galveston, TX 77555. Offers MS, PhD. *Degree requirements:* For master's, thesis or alternative; for doctorate, thesis/dissertation. *Entrance requirements:* For master's and doctorate, GRE General Test. Additional exam requirements/recommendations for international students: Required—TOEFL (minimum score 550 paper-based; 213 computer-based). Electronic applications accepted.

University of Toronto, Faculty of Medicine, Department of Physiology, Toronto, ON M5S 1A1, Canada. Offers M Sc, PhD, MD/PhD. *Degree requirements:* For master's, thesis; for doctorate, thesis/dissertation. *Entrance requirements:* For master's and doctorate, minimum B+ average in final year, 2 letters of reference. Additional exam requirements/recommendations for international students: Required—TOEFL (600 paper-based, 250 computer-based), Michigan English Language Assessment Battery (95), IELTS (8) or COPE (5). Electronic applications accepted.

University of Utah, School of Medicine and Graduate School, Graduate Programs in Medicine, Department of Physiology, Salt Lake City, UT 84112-1107. Offers PhD. *Degree requirements:* For doctorate, thesis/dissertation, comprehensive qualifying exam, preliminary exam. *Entrance requirements:* For doctorate, GRE General Test, GRE Subject Test, minimum GPA of 3.0. Additional exam requirements/recommendations for international students: Required—TOEFL (minimum score 650 paper-based; 250 computer-based; 100 iBT); Recommended—TWE (minimum score 6). Electronic applications accepted. *Faculty research:* Cell neurobiology, chemosensory systems, cardiovascular and kidney physiology, endocrinology.

University of Virginia, School of Medicine, Department of Molecular Physiology and Biological Physics, Program in Physiology, Charlottesville, VA 22903. Offers PhD, MD/PhD. *Students:* 12 full-time (5 women); includes 2 minority (both Black or African American, non-Hispanic/Latino). Average age 28. In 2011, 2 doctorates awarded. *Entrance requirements:* For doctorate, GRE General Test, 2 letters of recommendation. Additional exam requirements/recommendations for international students: Required—TOEFL. *Application deadline:* For fall admission, 1/15 for domestic and international students. Applications are processed on a rolling basis. Application fee: $60. Electronic applications accepted. *Financial support:* Fellowships, research assistantships, and teaching assistantships available. Financial award applicants required to submit FAFSA. *Unit head:* Dr. Mark Yeager, Chair, 434-924-5108, Fax: 434-982-1616, E-mail: my3r@virginia.edu. *Application contact:* Lesley L. Thomas, Director, Admissions Office, 434-924-5571, Fax: 434-982-2586, E-mail: medsch-adm@virginia.edu. Web site: http://www.healthsystem.virginia.edu/internet/physio/.

University of Washington, Graduate School, School of Medicine, Graduate Programs in Medicine, Department of Physiology and Biophysics, Seattle, WA 98195. Offers PhD. *Degree requirements:* For doctorate, thesis/dissertation. *Entrance requirements:* For doctorate, GRE General Test. Additional exam requirements/recommendations for international students: Required—TOEFL (minimum score 580 paper-based; 237 computer-based; 70 iBT). *Faculty research:* Membrane and cell biophysics, neuroendocrinology, cardiovascular and respiratory physiology, systems neurophysiology and behavior, molecular physiology.

The University of Western Ontario, Faculty of Graduate Studies, Biosciences Division, Department of Physiology and Pharmacology, London, ON N6A 5B8, Canada. Offers M Sc, PhD. *Degree requirements:* For master's, thesis, seminar course; for doctorate, comprehensive exam, thesis/dissertation. *Entrance requirements:* For master's, minimum B average, honors degree; for doctorate, minimum B average, honors degree, M Sc. *Faculty research:* Reproductive and endocrine physiology, neurophysiology, cardiovascular and renal physiology, cell physiology, gastrointestinal and metabolic physiology.

University of Wisconsin–La Crosse, Office of University Graduate Studies, College of Science and Health, Department of Biology, La Crosse, WI 54601-3742. Offers aquatic sciences (MS); biology (MS); cellular and molecular biology (MS); clinical microbiology (MS); microbiology (MS); nurse anesthesia (MS); physiology (MS). Part-time programs available. *Faculty:* 21 full-time (8 women), 3 part-time/adjunct (1 woman). *Students:* 45 full-time (30 women), 47 part-time (22 women); includes 10 minority (1 Black or African American, non-Hispanic/Latino; 5 Asian, non-Hispanic/Latino; 3 Hispanic/Latino; 1 Two or more races, non-Hispanic/Latino), 3 international. Average age 28. 63 applicants, 46% accepted, 24 enrolled. In 2011, 23 master's awarded. *Degree requirements:* For master's, comprehensive exam, thesis. *Entrance requirements:* For master's, GRE General Test, minimum GPA of 2.85. Additional exam requirements/recommendations for international students: Required—TOEFL (minimum score 550 paper-based; 213 computer-based; 79 iBT). *Application deadline:* For fall admission, 2/1 priority date for domestic students, 2/1 for international students; for spring admission, 1/4 priority date for domestic students, 1/4 for international students. Applications are processed on a rolling basis. Application fee: $56. Electronic applications accepted. *Expenses:* Tuition, state resident: full-time $8391; part-time $481.17 per credit. Tuition, nonresident: full-time $17,850; part-time $1006.68 per credit. *Required fees:* $2 per credit. $18.25 per semester. Tuition and fees vary according to course load, program, reciprocity agreements and student level. *Financial support:* In 2011–12, 29 research assistantships with partial tuition reimbursements (averaging $9,712 per year) were awarded; Federal Work-Study, scholarships/grants, health care benefits, and tuition waivers (partial) also available. Support available to part-time students. Financial award application deadline: 3/15; financial award applicants required to submit FAFSA. *Unit head:* Dr. Thomas Volk, Coordinator of Graduate Studies, 608-785-6972, Fax: 608-785-6959, E-mail: volk.thom@uwlax.edu. *Application contact:* Kathryn Kiefer, Director of Admissions, 608-785-8939, E-mail: admissions@uwlax.edu. Web site: http://uwlax.edu/biology/.

University of Wisconsin–Madison, School of Medicine and Public Health, Endocrinology-Reproductive Physiology Program, Madison, WI 53706-1380. Offers MS, PhD. Terminal master's awarded for partial completion of doctoral program. *Degree requirements:* For master's, comprehensive exam, thesis, oral defense of thesis; for doctorate, comprehensive exam, thesis/dissertation, oral defense of dissertation. *Entrance requirements:* For master's, GRE, resume, 3 letters of recommendation; for doctorate, GRE, resumé, 3 letters of recommendation. Additional exam requirements/recommendations for international students: Required—TOEFL (minimum score 550 paper-based; 213 computer-based). Electronic applications accepted. *Expenses:* Tuition, state resident: full-time $10,296; part-time $643.51 per credit. Tuition, nonresident: full-time $24,054; part-time $1503.40 per credit. *Required fees:* $70.06 per credit. Tuition and fees vary according to course load, campus/location, program and reciprocity agreements. *Faculty research:* Ovarian physiology and endocrinology, fertilization and gamete biology, hormone action and cell signaling, placental function and pregnancy, embryo and fetal development.

University of Wisconsin–Madison, School of Medicine and Public Health and Graduate School, Graduate Programs in Medicine, Madison, WI 53705. Offers biomolecular chemistry (MS, PhD); cancer biology (PhD); genetics and medical genetics (MS, PhD), including genetics (PhD), medical genetics (MS); medical physics (MS, PhD), including health physics (MS), medical physics; microbiology (PhD); molecular and cellular pharmacology (PhD); pathology and laboratory medicine (PhD); physiology (PhD); population health sciences (MPH, MS, PhD), including clinical research (MS, PhD), epidemiology (MS, PhD), health services research (MS, PhD), population health sciences (MPH), social and behavioral health sciences (MS, PhD); DPT/MPH; DVM/

MPH; MD/MPH; MD/PhD; MPA/MPH; MS/MPH; Pharm D/MPH. Part-time programs available. Postbaccalaureate distance learning degree programs offered (minimal on-campus study). Terminal master's awarded for partial completion of doctoral program. Application fee: $45. Electronic applications accepted. *Expenses:* Contact institution. *Financial support:* Fellowships with full tuition reimbursements, research assistantships with full tuition reimbursements, teaching assistantships with full tuition reimbursements, scholarships/grants, traineeships, and tuition waivers (full) available. *Unit head:* Dr. Richard L. Moss, Senior Associate Dean for Basic Research, Biotechnology and Graduate Studies, 608-265-0523, Fax: 608-265-0522, E-mail: rlmoss@wisc.edu. *Application contact:* Information Contact, 608-262-2433, Fax: 608-262-5134, E-mail: gradadmiss@mail.bascom.wisc.edu. Web site: http://www.med.wisc.edu.

University of Wyoming, College of Arts and Sciences, Department of Zoology and Physiology, Laramie, WY 82070. Offers MS, PhD. Part-time programs available. *Degree requirements:* For master's, comprehensive exam (for some programs), thesis; for doctorate, comprehensive exam (for some programs), thesis/dissertation. *Entrance requirements:* For master's and doctorate, GRE General Test, minimum GPA of 3.0. Additional exam requirements/recommendations for international students: Required—TOEFL. Electronic applications accepted. *Faculty research:* Cell biology, ecology/wildlife, organismal physiology, zoology.

Virginia Commonwealth University, Graduate School, School of Allied Health Professions, Department of Physical Therapy, Richmond, VA 23284-9005. Offers advanced physical therapy (DPT); entry-level physical therapy (DPT); health related sciences (PhD); physiology/physical therapy (PhD). *Accreditation:* APTA (one or more programs are accredited). *Students:* 168 full-time (105 women), 17 part-time (12 women); includes 21 minority (6 Black or African American, non-Hispanic/Latino; 10 Asian, non-Hispanic/Latino; 4 Hispanic/Latino; 1 Two or more races, non-Hispanic/Latino), 2 international. In 2011, 85 degrees awarded. *Degree requirements:* For doctorate, thesis/dissertation. *Entrance requirements:* For doctorate, GRE General Test, Physical Therapist Centralized Application Service (PTCAS). Additional exam requirements/recommendations for international students: Required—TOEFL (minimum score 600 paper-based; 250 computer-based; 100 iBT). *Application deadline:* For fall admission, 11/2 for domestic students. Electronic applications accepted. *Expenses:* Tuition, state resident: full-time $9133; part-time $507 per credit. Tuition, nonresident: full-time $18,777; part-time $1043 per credit. *Required fees:* $77 per credit. Tuition and fees vary according to degree level, campus/location, program and student level. *Financial support:* Fellowships available. *Faculty research:* Eye movement, bilabyrinthectomy on ferret muscle fiber typing, neck disability index, cost-effective care, training effect on muscle. *Unit head:* Dr. Thomas P. Mayhew, Chair, 804-828-0234, Fax: 804-828-8111, E-mail: tpmayhew@vcu.edu. *Application contact:* Judy Kendrick, Student Coordinator, 804-828-0234, Fax: 804-828-8111, E-mail: jkendric@vcu.edu. Web site: http://www.sahp.vcu.edu/pt/.

Virginia Commonwealth University, Medical College of Virginia-Professional Programs, School of Medicine, School of Medicine Graduate Programs, Department of Physiology and Biophysics, Richmond, VA 23284-9005. Offers physical therapy (PhD); physiology (MS, PhD); MD/PhD. Terminal master's awarded for partial completion of doctoral program. *Degree requirements:* For master's, thesis; for doctorate, thesis/dissertation, comprehensive oral and written exams. *Entrance requirements:* For master's, GRE General Test, MCAT, or DAT; for doctorate, GRE, MCAT or DAT. Additional exam requirements/recommendations for international students: Required—TOEFL (minimum score 600 paper-based; 250 computer-based; 100 iBT). Electronic applications accepted. *Expenses:* Tuition, state resident: full-time $9133; part-time $507 per credit. Tuition, nonresident: full-time $18,777; part-time $1043 per credit. *Required fees:* $77 per credit. Tuition and fees vary according to degree level, campus/location, program and student level.

Virginia Commonwealth University, Program in Pre-Medical Basic Health Sciences, Richmond, VA 23284-9005. Offers anatomy (CBHS); biochemistry (CBHS); human genetics (CBHS); microbiology (CBHS); pharmacology (CBHS); physiology (CBHS). *Entrance requirements:* For degree, GRE, MCAT or DAT, course work in organic chemistry, minimum undergraduate GPA of 2.8. Additional exam requirements/recommendations for international students: Required—TOEFL (minimum score 600 paper-based). Electronic applications accepted. *Expenses:* Tuition, state resident: full-time $9133; part-time $507 per credit. Tuition, nonresident: full-time $18,777; part-time $1043 per credit. *Required fees:* $77 per credit. Tuition and fees vary according to degree level, campus/location, program and student level.

Virginia Polytechnic Institute and State University, Graduate School, College of Agriculture and Life Sciences, Department of Human Nutrition, Foods and Exercise, Blacksburg, VA 24061. Offers behavioral and community science (MS, PhD); clinical physiology and metabolism (MS, PhD); molecular and cellular science (MS, PhD). *Degree requirements:* For master's, comprehensive exam (for some programs), thesis (for some programs); for doctorate, comprehensive exam (for some programs), thesis/dissertation (for some programs). *Entrance requirements:* For master's and doctorate, GRE. Additional exam requirements/recommendations for international students: Required—TOEFL (minimum score 550 paper-based; 213 computer-based). *Application deadline:* For fall admission, 7/1 for domestic and international students; for spring admission, 12/1 for domestic and international students. Applications are processed on a rolling basis. Application fee: $65. Electronic applications accepted. *Expenses:* Tuition, state resident: full-time $10,048; part-time $558.25 per credit hour. Tuition, nonresident: full-time $19,497; part-time $1083.25 per credit hour. *Required fees:* $405 per semester. Tuition and fees vary according to course load, campus/location and program. *Financial support:* Fellowships with full tuition reimbursements, research assistantships with full tuition reimbursements, teaching assistantships with full tuition reimbursements, career-related internships or fieldwork, Federal Work-Study, scholarships/grants, health care benefits, and unspecified assistantships available. Financial award application deadline: 1/15. *Faculty research:* Nutrition and food science research. *Unit head:* Dr. Susan M. Hutson, Unit Head, 540-231-8766, Fax: 540-231-3916, E-mail: susanh5@vt.edu. *Application contact:* Robert Grange, Information Contact, 540-231-2725, Fax: 540-231-3916, E-mail: rgrange@vt.edu. Web site: http://www.hnfe.vt.edu/.

Wake Forest University, School of Medicine and Graduate School of Arts and Sciences, Graduate Programs in Medicine, Program in Physiology and Pharmacology, Winston-Salem, NC 27109. Offers pharmacology (PhD); physiology (PhD); MD/PhD. *Degree requirements:* For doctorate, thesis/dissertation. *Entrance requirements:* For doctorate, GRE General Test. Additional exam requirements/recommendations for international students: Required—TOEFL. Electronic applications accepted. *Faculty research:* Aging, substance abuse, cardiovascular control, endocrine systems, toxicology.

Wayne State University, School of Medicine, Department of Physiology, Detroit, MI 48202. Offers MS, PhD, MD/PhD. *Students:* 31 full-time (20 women), 7 part-time (3 women); includes 10 minority (3 Black or African American, non-Hispanic/Latino; 5 Asian, non-Hispanic/Latino; 1 Hispanic/Latino; 1 Two or more races, non-Hispanic/Latino), 7 international. Average age 30. 56 applicants, 11% accepted, 3 enrolled. In 2011, 7 degrees awarded. *Degree requirements:* For master's, thesis; for doctorate, thesis/dissertation. *Entrance requirements:* For master's, GRE General Test, GRE Subject Test, minimum GPA of 2.75, personal statement, resume, three letters of recommendation; for doctorate, GRE General Test, GRE Subject Test, minimum GPA of 3.0, personal statement, resume, three letters of recommendation. Additional exam requirements/recommendations for international students: Recommended—TOEFL (minimum score 600 paper-based; 250 computer-based; 100 iBT). *Application deadline:* For fall admission, 6/1 priority date for domestic students, 5/1 for international students; for winter admission, 10/1 priority date for domestic students, 9/1 for international students; for spring admission, 2/1 priority date for domestic students, 1/1 for international students. Applications are processed on a rolling basis. Application fee: $50. Electronic applications accepted. *Expenses:* Tuition, state resident: part-time $512.85 per credit. Tuition, nonresident: part-time $1132.65 per credit. *Required fees:* $26.60 per credit. $199.65 per semester. Tuition and fees vary according to course load and program. *Financial support:* In 2011–12, 23 students received support, including 7 fellowships with tuition reimbursements available (averaging $27,268 per year), 17 research assistantships with tuition reimbursements available (averaging $22,730 per year); teaching assistantships, scholarships/grants, and unspecified assistantships also available. Support available to part-time students. Financial award application deadline: 2/15. *Faculty research:* Regulation of brain blood flow, mechanism of hormone action, regulation of pituitary hormone secretion, regulation of cellular membranes, nano biotechnology. *Unit head:* Dr. Jian-Ping Jin, Chair, 313-577-1520, E-mail: jjin@med.wayne.edu. Web site: http://physiology.med.wayne.edu/.

Weill Cornell Medical College, Weill Cornell Graduate School of Medical Sciences, Physiology, Biophysics and Systems Biology Program, New York, NY 10065. Offers MS, PhD. *Faculty:* 36 full-time (9 women). *Students:* 48 full-time (15 women); includes 7 minority (1 Black or African American, non-Hispanic/Latino; 4 Asian, non-Hispanic/Latino; 1 Hispanic/Latino; 1 Native Hawaiian or other Pacific Islander, non-Hispanic/Latino), 26 international. Average age 23. 37 applicants, 32% accepted, 5 enrolled. In 2011, 12 doctorates awarded. Terminal master's awarded for partial completion of doctoral program. *Degree requirements:* For master's, comprehensive exam; for doctorate, thesis/dissertation, final exam. *Entrance requirements:* For doctorate, GRE General Test, introductory courses in biology, inorganic and organic chemistry, physics, and mathematics. Additional exam requirements/recommendations for international students: Required—TOEFL. *Application deadline:* For fall admission, 12/1 for domestic students. Application fee: $60. *Expenses: Tuition:* Full-time $46,001. *Financial support:* In 2011–12, 4 fellowships (averaging $21,210 per year) were awarded; scholarships/grants, health care benefits, and stipends (given to all students) also available. *Faculty research:* Receptor-mediated regulation of cell function, molecular properties of channels or receptors, bioinformatics, mathematical modeling. *Unit head:* Dr. Emre Aksay, Co-Director, 212-746-6207, E-mail: ema2004@med.cornell.edu. *Application contact:* Audrey Rivera, Program Coordinator, 212-746-6361, E-mail: ajr2004@med.cornell.edu. Web site: http://weill.cornell.edu/gradschool/program/physiology.html.

Western Michigan University, Graduate College, College of Education and Human Development, Department of Health, Physical Education and Recreation, Kalamazoo, MI 49008. Offers exercise and sports medicine (MS), including athletic training, exercise physiology; physical education (MA), including coaching sport performance, pedagogy, special physical education, sport management.

West Virginia University, Davis College of Agriculture, Forestry and Consumer Sciences, Division of Animal and Nutritional Sciences, Program in Animal and Nutritional Sciences, Morgantown, WV 26506. Offers breeding (MS); food sciences (MS); nutrition (MS); physiology (MS); production management (MS); reproduction (MS). Part-time programs available. *Degree requirements:* For master's, thesis, oral and written exams. *Entrance requirements:* For master's, GRE, minimum GPA of 2.5. Additional exam requirements/recommendations for international students: Required—TOEFL. *Faculty research:* Animal nutrition, reproductive physiology, food science.

West Virginia University, Davis College of Agriculture, Forestry and Consumer Sciences, Interdisciplinary Program in Reproductive Physiology, Morgantown, WV 26506. Offers MS, PhD. Part-time programs available. Terminal master's awarded for partial completion of doctoral program. *Degree requirements:* For master's, thesis; for doctorate, comprehensive exam, thesis/dissertation. *Entrance requirements:* For master's, minimum GPA of 2.75; for doctorate, minimum GPA of 3.0. Additional exam requirements/recommendations for international students: Required—TOEFL. Electronic applications accepted. *Faculty research:* Uterine prostaglandins, luteal function, neural control of luteinizing hormone and follicle-stimulating hormone, follicular development, embryonic and fetal loss.

West Virginia University, School of Medicine, Graduate Programs at the Health Sciences Center, Interdisciplinary Graduate Programs in Biomedical Sciences, Program in Cellular and Integrative Physiology, Morgantown, WV 26506. Offers MS, PhD, MD/PhD. *Degree requirements:* For doctorate, comprehensive exam, thesis/dissertation. *Entrance requirements:* For doctorate, GRE General Test, minimum GPA of 3.0. Additional exam requirements/recommendations for international students: Required—TOEFL. Electronic applications accepted. *Faculty research:* Cell signaling and development of the microvasculature, neural control of reproduction, learning and memory, airway responsiveness and remodeling.

Wright State University, School of Graduate Studies, College of Science and Mathematics, Department of Neuroscience, Cell Biology, and Physiology, Dayton, OH 45435. Offers anatomy (MS); physiology and biophysics (MS). *Degree requirements:* For master's, thesis optional. *Entrance requirements:* Additional exam requirements/recommendations for international students: Required—TOEFL. *Faculty research:* Reproductive cell biology, neurobiology of pain, neurohistochemistry.

Yale University, School of Medicine and Graduate School of Arts and Sciences, Combined Program in Biological and Biomedical Sciences (BBS), Physiology and Integrative Medical Biology Track, New Haven, CT 06520. Offers PhD, MD/PhD. *Entrance requirements:* Additional exam requirements/recommendations for international students: Required—TOEFL.

Youngstown State University, Graduate School, College of Science, Technology, Engineering and Mathematics, Department of Biological Sciences, Youngstown, OH 44555-0001. Offers environmental biology (MS); molecular biology, microbiology, and genetic (MS); physiology and anatomy (MS). Part-time programs available. *Degree requirements:* For master's, comprehensive exam, thesis, oral review. *Entrance requirements:* For master's, GRE General Test, minimum GPA of 2.7. Additional exam requirements/recommendations for international students: Required—TOEFL. *Faculty research:* Cell biology, neurophysiology, molecular biology, neurobiology, gene regulation.

CASE WESTERN RESERVE UNIVERSITY

Case School of Medicine
Department of Physiology and Biophysics

Programs of Study

The Department's Ph.D. training programs in biomedical physiology and structural biology and biophysics are tailored to prepare students for successful careers in biomedical, pharmaceutical, and/or industrial research. The Department of Physiology and Biophysics ranks among the best physiology departments in the country. The Ph.D. programs feature individual attention from committed faculty members, are tuition-free, carry a stipend, and provide health insurance. The training programs are designed to provide a mentored training environment that maximizes faculty-student interaction and emphasizes the use of state-of-the art experimental approaches. Prospective students should visit the Department's Web sites (http://physiology.cwru.edu or http://biophysics.cwru.edu) for additional information on the Department, individual investigators, and graduate programs.

The Ph.D. program in biomedical physiology embraces investigation that seeks to understand the fundamental organizational and physiological functions of cells, organs, and whole organisms utilizing state-of-the-art scientific methodology and conceptual approaches. The Ph.D. program in structural biology and biophysics emphasizes biophysics and bioengineering concepts and technologies and seeks to develop the students' quantitative skills. The M.D./Ph.D. program consists of core medical training plus advanced graduate research training, in any of the disciplines outlined above, thereby leading to a combined degree. The Ph.D. for M.D.'s program is specifically designed for individuals who already have an M.D. degree. It can be linked to research-oriented residency programs, such as the clinical investigator pathway, approved by the American Board of Internal Medicine, and other similar programs.

The Master of Science in Medical Physiology program is a 1–3 year post-baccalaureate program designed to prepare students for admission to medical or dental school or careers in the biomedical industry. The Master of Science in Physiology and Biophysics program (Tech Master's program) is designed for research assistants working at the University, area hospitals, or biotechnology companies that want to expand their critical research knowledge and skills. This program provides an excellent foundation for careers in biomedical professions including academia or industrial research.

Research Facilities

The Department is housed in recently renovated, state-of-the-art laboratory and office space on the fifth and sixth floors of the School of Medicine. These areas were specifically designed to facilitate faculty-student interaction. They are fully equipped with modern research instruments for sophisticated spectroscopic studies, video-enhanced light microscopy with image processing, molecular biology, structural biology, and extensive computer facilities. Interdisciplinary programs with other departments enable students to have access to additional specialized equipment.

Financial Aid

As long as the students in the Ph.D. programs are in good standing, they receive full tuition, a $25,000-per-year cost-of-living stipend, and health insurance. Tuition for the M.S. in Physiology and Biophysics program (Tech Master's program) is usually paid by the students' employer. Students in the M.S. in Medical Physiology program should contact the University's Office of Financial Aid to identify appropriate financial assistance programs.

Cost of Study

Tuition for a full time student (12 credit hours) at Case Western Reserve University's Graduate School is approximately $37,000 per year.

Living and Housing Costs

A large variety of off-campus housing is available within 2 miles for married and single graduate students. The cost of living in Cleveland is among the lowest in the United States.

Location

Case Western Reserve University is located 4 miles from downtown Cleveland in University Circle, a 500-acre area referred to as Ohio's most spectacular square mile. It contains more than thirty educational, scientific, medical, cultural, and religious institutions. The park-like setting of University Circle contains the world-renowned Cleveland Museum of Art and Severance Hall, home of the famous Cleveland Orchestra. Metropolitan Cleveland has a population of approximately 2 million people and offers a wide array of recreational and cultural activities, including national sports events, theater, ballet, and cinema.

The University and The School

Case Western Reserve University is a private, nonprofit institution created in 1967 by the federation of the adjacent Western Reserve University (founded in 1826) and Case Institute of Technology (founded in 1880). The Case School of Medicine ranks among the top twenty-five medical schools nationally. It is part of the dynamic and innovative consortium of biomedical research centers that include University Hospitals Case Medical Center, the MetroHealth Medical Center, the Cleveland Veterans Administration Medical Center, and the Cleveland Clinic Foundation. This consortium creates an exceptional array of research and learning opportunities.

Applying

Requirements for admission are an undergraduate degree with a strong background in the natural sciences from an accredited college or university, GRE General Test scores or MCAT scores, a personal statement, and three letters of recommendation. Competitive candidates are invited to visit the Department to view the facility and meet the faculty members. For the Ph.D. and Tech Master's programs, applications should be submitted by January 1, but late applications are also considered. The deadline for application to the M.S. in Medical Physiology program is June 1.

Correspondence and Information

Coordinator, Graduate Degree Programs
Department of Physiology and Biophysics
Case School of Medicine
Case Western Reserve University
Cleveland, Ohio 44106-4970
United States
Phone: 216-368-2084
Fax: 216-368-5586
E-mail: PHOL-INFO@case.edu
Web site: http://physiology.cwru.edu
http://biophysics.cwru.edu

THE FACULTY AND THEIR RESEARCH

Mary Barkley, Professor; Ph.D., California, San Diego, 1964. Structure and function of reverse transcriptase.

Venkaiah Betapudi, Assistant Professor; Ph.D., Devi Ahilya University, Indore (India), 1995. Cell cytoskeleton and cancer development; myosin II ubiquitination from basic mechanism to disease development.

Walter Boron, Professor and Chairman; M.D./Ph.D., Washington (St. Louis), 1977. Regulation of intracellular pH; molecular physiology and structural biology of HCO_3 transporters; control of

renal proximal-tubule HCO_3 transport; CO_2/HCO_3 receptors; gas channels.

Matthias Buck, Associate Professor; D.Phil., Oxford, 1996. Protein structure and dynamics in transmission of signals in cells.

Cathleen Carlin, Professor; Ph.D., North Carolina at Chapel Hill, 1979. Regulation of ErbB receptor tyrosine kinase membrane protein sorting.

Sudha Chakrapani, Assistant Professor; Ph.D., SUNY at Buffalo, 2004. Understanding atomic level details of ion channel functioning.

Margaret Chandler, Assistant Professor; Ph.D., Kent State, 1998. Myocardial energy metabolism in the pathophysiology of heart failure and diabetes.

Calvin Cotton, Associate Professor; Ph.D., North Carolina at Chapel Hill, 1984. Regulation of ion transport in cells of respiratory, gastrointestinal, and renal epithelia.

Isabelle Deschenes, Assistant Professor; Ph.D., Laval, 1999. Cellular and molecular mechanisms of cardiac arrhythmias.

Paul DiCorleto, Professor; Ph.D., Cornell, 1978. Regulation of growth factor and leukocyte adhesion molecule genes by the endothelium.

Anthony F. DiMarco, Professor; M.D., Tufts, 1974. Restoration of respiratory muscle function in spinal cord injury.

J. Kevin Donahue, Professor; M.D., Washington (St. Louis), 1992. Cardiac electrophysiology; cardiac arrhythmias.

George Dubyak, Professor; Ph.D., Pennsylvania, 1979. Extracellular ATP release and metabolism in inflammation.

Mark Dunlap, Associate Professor; M.D., Tennessee Health Sciences, 1982. Nicotinic acetylcholine receptors; autonomic nervous system; heart failure; parasympathetic/sympathetic physiology; baroreceptors; reflexes; neurohumoral abnormalities.

Dominique Durand, Professor; Ph.D., Toronto, 1982. Electrical stimulation of neural tissue and biomagnetism.

Thomas Egelhoff, Professor; Ph.D., Stanford, 1987. Signaling pathways that control actin/myosin motility during cell migration in wound healing and cancer.

Christopher Ford, Assistant Professor; Ph.D., Alberta, 2003. Regulation of synaptic transmission in the dopamine system of the VTA.

Joan E. B. Fox, Professor; Ph.D., McMaster, 1979; D.Sc., Southampton (UK), 1993. Molecular basis of integrin-mediated migration in the cardiovascular system.

Anne Hamik, M.D., Assistant Professor, Oklahoma, 1999. Cardiovascular effects of the transcription factor KLF4.

Brian Hoit, Professor; M.D., Illinois, 1979. Cardiac function; noninvasive cardiology; phenotypic analysis of transgenic mice; transesophageal echocardiography; pericardial disease.

Ulrich Hopfer, Professor Emeritus; M.D., Göttingen (Germany), 1966; Ph.D., Johns Hopkins, 1970. Cell biology, physiology, and pathology of epithelial transport.

Arie Horowitz, Assistant Professor; Ph.D., Technion (Israel), 1988. Enodothelial cell signaling and motility in angiogenesis; molecular mechanisms of blood vessel sprouting; membrane trafficking.

Mukesh K. Jain, Ellery Sedgwick Jr. Professor and Director, Case Cardiovascular Research Institute; M.D., Buffalo, SUNY, 1991. Transcriptional regulation of cardiovascular cell function.

Stephen Jones, Professor; Ph.D., Cornell, 1980. Voltage-dependent ion channels; mechanisms of channel gating, permeation, and modulation.

John P. Kirwan, Professor; Ph.D., Ball State, 1987. Insulin signaling; glucose transport; protein expression, activity, and phosphorylation; intramyocellular lipid content; exercise; low-glycemic diet; body composition.

Joseph LaManna, Professor; Ph.D., Duke, 1975. Control of adaptation to hypoxia and the pathophysiology of stroke; CNS function in cardiac arrest.

Carole Liedtke, Professor; Ph.D., Case Western Reserve, 1980. Regulation of Na-K-2Cl cotransport during fluid and electrolyte balance in epithelia.

Richard Martin, Professor; M.B.B.S., Sydney (Australia), 1970. Respiratory control; lung injury/maturation; airway reactivity;

nitric oxide; apnea of prematurity; developmental pulmonology; airway maturation; desaturation; hyperoxia; lung parenchyma; cardiorespiratory monitoring; pulmonary function monitoring; pulse oximetry; multiple intraluminal impedance monitoring; RTPCR; Western blotting; immunohistochemistry; in vivo physiological recording; assays; patch clamping.

Sam Mesiano, Assistant Professor; Ph.D., Monash (Australia), 1988. Hormonal control of human parturition and the interaction of estrogen and progesterone receptors in the control of reproduction.

Robert H. Miller, Professor and Vice Dean for Research; Ph.D., UCL, London, 1981. Biology of neural diseases; cellular and molecular control of nervous system glial specification.

Saurav Misra, Assistant Professor; Ph.D., Illinois, 1997. Molecular basis of protein quality control.

Vera Moiseenkova-Bell, Assistant Professor; Ph.D., Texas Medical Branch, 2004. Structural and functional analysis of TRP ion channels.

Tingwei Mu, Assistant Professor; Ph.D., Caltech, 2005. Understanding ion channel protein homeostasis in the cell.

Thomas M. Nosek, Professor; Ph.D., Ohio State, 1973. Control of muscle contraction; cellular basis of muscle fatigue.

Mark Parker, Instructor; Ph.D., Bristol (UK), 2000. Causes and consequences of structural and functional diversity among Na^+-coupled HCO_3-transporters.

Xin Qi, Assistant Professor; Ph.D., Hokkaido (Japan), 2005. Mitochondrial dysfunction in disease.

Rajesh Ramachandran, Assistant Professor; Ph.D., Texas A&M, 2004. Molecular biophysics of membrane remodeling in membrane fusion and fission.

Andrea Romani, Associate Professor; M.D., Siena (Italy), 1984; Ph.D., Turin, 1990. Regulation of transmembrane Mg^{2+} transport and the role of Mg^{2+} transport in metabolism.

William Schilling, Professor; Ph.D., Medical University of South Carolina, 1981. Mammalian TRP channel function; role of Ca^{2+} channels in cell death.

John Sedor, Professor; M.D., Virginia, 1978. Clinical, cellular, and genetic basis of kidney disease.

Daniel I. Simon, Professor; M.D., Harvard, 1987. Inflammation in vascular injury.

Corey Smith, Associate Professor; Ph.D., Colorado Health Sciences Center, 1996. Release of transmitter molecules from adrenal chromaffin cells and the sympathetic stress response.

Julian E. Stelzer, Assistant Professor; Ph.D., Oregon State, 2002. Cellular and molecular mechanisms of cardiac muscle contraction in health and disease.

Kingman P. Strohl, Professor; M.D., Northwestern, 1974. Respiratory physiology and sleep disorders.

Ben W. Strowbridge, Professor; Ph.D., Yale, 1991. Synaptic physiology; hippocampus; modeling; computational neuroscience; olfactory bulb.

Witold Surewicz, Professor; Ph.D., Lodz (Poland), 1982. Structure and function of prion proteins.

Richard Walsh, Professor; M.D., Georgetown, 1972. The heart and cardiovascular disease.

Christopher Wilson, Associate Professor; Ph.D., California, Davis, 1996. Neural control of autonomic function which incorporates cardio-respiratory integration at the level of the brain stem.

M. Michael Wolfe, M.D., Ohio State, 1976. Gastroenterology including acid-peptic and esophageal disorders; neuroendocrine tumors.

Sichun Yang, Assistant Professor; Ph.D., Chicago, 2006. Structure, dynamics, and function of nuclear hormone receptors; computational biophysics and small-angle X-ray scattering (SAXS).

Xin Yu, Associate Professor; Sc.D., Harvard/MIT, 1996. Magnetic resonance imaging and spectroscopy; cardiac biomechanics of genetically manipulated mice using MRI tagging; systems biology of metabolism; cardiovascular physiology; myocardial structural characterization in diseased hearts using diffusion tensor MRI; cardiac metabolism in diabetic hearts using MRI spectroscopy and systems biology.

UNIVERSITY OF CONNECTICUT

College of Liberal Arts and Sciences
Department of Physiology and Neurobiology

Programs of Study

The Department offers course work and research programs leading to M.S. and Ph.D. degrees in physiology and neurobiology with concentrations in the areas of neurobiology, endocrinology, and comparative physiology. In addition, the Department of Molecular and Cell Biology, the Department of Ecology and Evolutionary Biology, and the Biotechnology Center provide the opportunity for students to obtain a comprehensive background in biological sciences and offer the possibility of collaborative research.

Graduate programs are designed to fit the individual student's background and scientific interests. In the first year, students take two courses on the foundations of physiology and neurobiology. Through the first two years, and occasionally into the third year of training, students select from a number of additional seminars and courses in their area of major interest and related areas. By the end of the first year, the student selects the area of dissertation research, and a committee consisting of a major adviser and 3 associate advisers is formed. Students may begin dissertation research during the first year.

Research Facilities

The Department of Physiology and Neurobiology is located primarily in the new state-of-the-art Pharmacy/Biology Building. The Department houses both shared and individual laboratories for behavioral, cellular, electrophysiological, and molecular research in physiology. The Department also houses the University's electron microscopy facility, which contains equipment for scanning and transmission EM as well as electron probe analysis. Departmental faculty members also utilize the Marine Research Laboratories at Noank and Avery Point, Connecticut.

Financial Aid

Several types of financial support are available to graduate students. Most students are supported either on teaching assistantships or research assistantships from faculty grants. In 2012–13, full-time assistantships (nine months) pay $19,384 for beginning graduate students, $20,396 for those with an M.S. or the equivalent, and $22,676 for those who have passed the Ph.D. general examination. Both half and full graduate assistantships come with a tuition waiver, and students may purchase excellent health-care coverage, heavily subsidized by the University of Connecticut. In addition, the Graduate School provides the Outstanding Scholar Award to as many as 10 incoming Ph.D. candidates during the first year of study. Several additional research fellowships and University fellowships are awarded on a competitive basis. Many labs also provide additional funding for summer research (up to $4000).

Cost of Study

In 2012–13, tuition is $5112 per semester for legal residents of Connecticut and $13,266 per semester for nonresidents, plus fees. Tuition is waived for graduate assistants; however, they pay the full-time University fees of $953 per semester. Tuition is prorated for students registering for fewer than 9 credits per semester. University fees are subject to change without notice.

Living and Housing Costs

Dormitory rooms are available for unmarried graduate students. University-owned and privately owned apartments are available near the campus at moderate rents. Houses and apartments for rent may also be found in the surrounding communities. In 2012–13, the fee for accommodations in graduate residence halls range upward from $3886 per semester; meal plans are separate. Yearly expenses, including books and travel, for a single student living off campus are upward from $19,000.

Student Group

Approximately 17,345 undergraduates and 8,153 graduate students are enrolled at the main campus at Storrs. Eighty percent of the undergraduate students and 73 percent of the graduate students are from Connecticut. The rest of the students come from many other states and more than 100 countries. The Department of Physiology and Neurobiology has about 40 graduate students.

Location

The University is located in a scenic countryside setting of small villages, streams, and rolling hills. There is easy access by car and bus to major urban and cultural centers, including Hartford, New Haven, Boston, and New York, and to other educational institutions, such as Yale, Harvard, and MIT. Recreational opportunities include skiing, fishing, sailing, hiking, ice-skating, and athletic events. Cultural opportunities available at the Storrs campus include film series, plays, symphony and chamber music series, public lectures, and art exhibits. A small shopping center is within walking distance of the campus, and several large shopping centers are nearby.

The University

Perennially ranked the top public university in New England, the University of Connecticut now stands among the best public institutions in the nation. The University was founded in 1881 and is a state-supported institution. The 1,800-acre main campus at Storrs is the site of vigorous undergraduate and graduate programs in agriculture, liberal arts and sciences, fine arts, engineering, education, business administration, human development and family relations, physical education, pharmacy, nursing, and physical therapy. Extensive cultural and recreational programs and athletic facilities are available.

Applying

For admission to the fall semester, it is suggested that applications be submitted by January 15. To be considered for financial support, students must submit applications by March 15 for admission the following September. U.S. applicants must submit scores on the General Test of the Graduate Record Examinations and must have maintained at least a 3.0 quality point ratio (QPR) for admission as graduate students with regular status. Applications and credentials from international students must be received by March 1 for admission in the fall semester or by October 1 for the spring semester and must include TOEFL scores. The University does not discriminate in admission on the basis of race, gender, age, or national origin. Students can apply online at http://www.grad.uconn.edu/applications.html.

Correspondence and Information

Graduate Admissions Committee
Department of Physiology and Neurobiology
University of Connecticut
Box U-3156
Storrs, Connecticut 06269-3156
United States
Phone: 860-486-3304
Fax: 860-486-3303
E-mail: kathleen.kelleher@uconn.edu
Web site: http://www.pnb.uconn.edu

THE FACULTY AND THEIR RESEARCH

Lawrence E. Armstrong, Professor (primary appointment in Kinesiology); Ph.D., Ball State. Research focuses on human physiological responses to exercise, dietary intervention (i.e., caffeine, low-salt diet, glucose-electrolyte solutions, amino acid supplementation), pharmacological agents, heat tolerance, and acclimatization to heat. Laboratory measurements of local sweat production; skin blood flow; and metabolic, ventilatory, cardiovascular, fluid-electrolyte, and strength perturbations are complemented by field observations. This research includes illnesses that arise in association with exercise in hot environments.

Marie E. Cantino, Associate Professor; Ph.D., Washington (Seattle). Research in this laboratory is directed toward understanding the mechanisms of contraction in striated muscle. In particular, the lab is using electron microscopy and biochemical and mechanical assays

to study the structure and organization of proteins in the contractile filaments and the mechanisms by which calcium regulates the interactions of these proteins.

William D. Chapple, Professor; Ph.D., Stanford. The interests of the laboratory center on the cellular mechanisms by which arthropods generate and control movement despite varying external forces. The model system is the hermit crab abdomen, which is used to support the animal's shell. To understand the interactions between local and global mechanisms that produce this control, identified motoneurons and interneurons are studied electrophysiologically and their properties are incorporated into a control systems model.

Thomas T. Chen, Professor (primary appointment in Molecular and Cell Biology); Ph.D., Alberta; postdoctoral study at Queen's. Structure, evolution, regulation, and molecular actions of growth hormone and insulin-like growth factor genes; regulation of foreign genes in transgenic fish; development of model transgenic fish.

Joanne Conover, Assistant Professor; Ph.D., Bath (England). Research in the laboratory focuses on neurogenesis and neuronal migration in the adult mouse brain. A combination of techniques including cell culture of neural stem cells, RT-PCR-based gene expression analysis, and examination of mouse genetic models for neurodegenerative diseases aid us in understanding neuronal proliferation, differentiation, and migration in the adult brain.

Joseph F. Crivello, Professor (joint appointment in Marine Sciences); Ph.D., Wisconsin. Research is centered in two areas. One area examines the impact of pollution on marine organisms at a biochemical and genetic level. The other area examines pollution as a selective pressure altering the genetic diversity of marine organisms.

Angel L. de Blas, Professor; Ph.D., Indiana. Research mainly focuses on the brain receptors for the inhibitory transmitter GABA. Studies are being conducted on elucidating the molecular structure of the receptors and the molecular interactions with other proteins that determine the synaptic localization of the GABA receptors. Effects of drugs and aging on GABAergic synaptic transmission are also studied. Techniques include recombinant DNA, monoclonal antibodies, cell culture, and light, electron, and laser confocal microscopy.

Robert V. Gallo, Professor; Ph.D., Purdue. The objective of the research program is to understand the neuroendocrine mechanisms regulating luteinizing hormone release during different physiological conditions. In particular, the research examines the involvement of CNS neurotransmitters and endogenous opioid peptides in this process.

Rahul N. Kanadia, Assistant Professor, Ph.D., Florida. Research is focused on deciphering the role of alternative splicing in neural development. The neural mouse retina is employed as a model system to investigate this question. Various techniques such as in situ hybridizations and molecular biology techniques are used to detect different forms of RNA. Since this is studied in development, live imaging is also used to document changes in splice pattern and its impact on cell fate determination and differentiation.

William J. Kraemer, Professor (primary appointment in Kinesiology); Ph.D., Wyoming. Research focus is directed at the neuroendocrine responses and adaptations with exercise as it relates to target tissues of muscle, bone, and immune cells. Current studies utilize receptor techniques and hormonal immunoassays and bioassays to better understand androgen, adrenal, and pituitary hormone interactions with target cells and their relationship to outcome variables of physiological function and physical performance.

Joseph J. LoTurco, Professor; Ph.D., Stanford. Research in the laboratory focuses on understanding mechanisms that direct development of the neocortex. Currently, a combination of molecular genetics, patch clamp electrophysiology, and cell culture are being used to study the mechanisms that regulate neurogenesis in the cerebral cortex.

Carl M. Maresh, Professor and Director, Human Performance Laboratory (primary appointment in Kinesiology, Department Head); Ph.D., Wyoming. Research focus is directed at the neuroendocrine, body fluid, and substrate responses and adaptations to environmental stress and training in humans. Current projects examine the efficacy of different methods of rehydration, muscle and bone adaptations to physical training in women, and exercise interventions in children at risk for obesity and diabetes.

Andrew Moiseff, Professor; Ph.D., Cornell. The laboratory is interested in the extraction and processing of sensory information by the nervous system. At present, research is concentrated on how the nervous system of the barn owl analyzes interaural time and intensity differences to obtain spatial information. Another line of research is the behavioral analysis of synchronous flashing by fireflies with an aim toward the understanding of the neural mechanisms controlling this communication behavior.

Daniel K. Mulkey, Assistant Professor; Ph.D., Wright State. Research focuses on the cellular and molecular mechanisms by which the brain controls breathing, in particular, understanding the molecular mechanism by which respiratory chemoreceptors sense changes in pH to drive breathing and the cellular mechanisms that modulate activity of these cells. Another interest is the role of nitric oxide on state-dependent modulation of respiratory motor neurons for a better understanding of the mechanisms underlying respiratory control, leading to new therapeutic approaches for the treatment of disorders such as sudden infant death syndrome and sleep apnea. Techniques include cellular electrophysiology in brain slices, cell culture, and single-cell RT-PCR.

Akiko Nishiyama, Professor; M.D., Nippon Medical School; Ph.D., Niigata (Japan). Research focuses on the biology of glial progenitor cells identified by the NG2 proteoglycan in normal and mutant mice and in demyelinating and excitotoxic lesions. Current studies employ immunohistochemical, tissue culture, biochemical, and molecular biological techniques to understand the mechanisms that regulate proliferation and differentiation of these glial cells and to explore their function.

Linda S. Pescatello, Associate Professor and Director, Center for Health Promotion (primary appointment in School of Allied Health); Ph.D., Connecticut. Research focus is on the interaction between the environment, neurohormones, and genetics on the exercise response in order to determine for whom exercise works best as a therapeutic modality. Current projects examine humoral, nutritional, and genetic explanations for postexercise hypotension, the exercise dose response for postexercise hypotension, and the influence of genetics on the muscle strength and hypertrophy response to resistance exercise training.

J. Larry Renfro, Professor and Department Head; Ph.D., Oklahoma. The research program is concerned with the mechanisms and regulation of epithelial transport. Current research deals with transepithelial transport and excretion of sulfate, and phosphate and environmental pollutants in tissues isolated from the urinary systems of a variety of vertebrates, including rats, birds, and fishes. Work has concentrated on ion secretion and its regulation in primary monolayer cultures of renal epithelium and choroid plexus. The laboratory also studies transport by renal tubule brush border and basolateral membrane vesicles.

Daniel Schwartz, Assistant Professor; Ph.D., Harvard. Research is focused on computational and experimental techniques to discover, catalog, and functionally understand short linear protein motifs. Specific projects include: (1) the continued improvement of the motif-x and scan-x web-tools, (2) the development of experimental methodologies to uncover kinase motifs, and (3) the analysis of motif signatures on viral protein primary structure toward the goal of elucidating mechanisms of viral propagation and developing therapeutic agents.

Anastasios Tzingounis, Assistant Professor; Ph.D., Oregon Health & Science. Research in the laboratory concentrates on the cellular and molecular mechanisms that control neuronal excitability in the mammalian brain. To study the molecules and signaling networks that tune the brain's innate ability to prevent epilepsy, a multidisciplinary approach is used that combines molecular and genetic techniques with optical imaging and electrophysiology.

Randall S. Walikonis, Associate Professor; Ph.D., Mayo. Research is directed at studying the postsynaptic signal transduction systems of excitatory synapses. The laboratory uses biochemical and molecular biological techniques to identify proteins associated with NMDA receptors and to determine their specific roles in the function of excitatory synapses. The lab also studies the role of growth factors in modifying excitatory synapses.

Steven A. Zinn, Associate Professor (primary appointment in Animal Science); Ph.D., Michigan State. The laboratory is interested in the somatotropic axis and its influence on growth and lactation. Specifically, the laboratory is investigating the influence of exogenous somatotropin on insulin-like growth factor I and the insulin-like growth factor binding proteins and their role in growth.

Adam Zweifach, Professor (primary appointment in Molecular and Cell Biology); Ph.D., Yale. Research focuses on the physiology of cytotoxic T lymphocytes (CTLs) and natural killer cells (NKs), cells that kill virus-infected cells, tumor cells, and transplanted tissues. The long-term goal is to understand signal transduction in these cells, which play critical roles in the immune response to viruses and cancers, and which are also involved in transplant rejection and the etiology of many autoimmune diseases.

Section 19
Zoology

This section contains a directory of institutions offering graduate work in zoology. Additional information about programs listed in the directory but not augmented by an in-depth entry may be obtained by writing directly to the dean of a graduate school or chair of a department at the address given in the directory.

For programs offering related work, see also in this book *Anatomy; Biochemistry; Biological and Biomedical Sciences; Cell, Molecular, and Structural Biology; Ecology, Environmental Biology, and Evolutionary Biology; Entomology; Genetics, Developmental Biology, and Reproductive Biology; Microbiological Sciences; Neuroscience and Neurobiology; Neurobiology; Physiology;* and *Veterinary Medicine and Sciences.* In the other guides in this series:

Graduate Programs in the Physical Sciences, Mathematics, Agricultural Sciences, the Environment & Natural Resources

See *Agricultural and Food Sciences, Environmental Sciences and Management,* and *Marine Sciences and Oceanography*

Graduate Programs in Engineering & Applied Sciences

See *Agricultural Engineering and Bioengineering* and *Ocean Engineering*

CONTENTS

Program Directories

Animal Behavior

Arizona State University, College of Liberal Arts and Sciences, School of Life Sciences, Tempe, AZ 85287-4601. Offers animal behavior (PhD); applied ethics (biomedical and health ethics) (MA); biological design (PhD); biology (MS, PhD); biology (biology and society) (MS, PhD); environmental life sciences (PhD); evolutionary biology (PhD); human and social dimensions of science and technology (PhD); microbiology (PhD); molecular and cellular biology (PhD); neuroscience (PhD); philosophy (history and philosophy of science) (MA); sustainability (PhD). Terminal master's awarded for partial completion of doctoral program. *Degree requirements:* For master's, thesis (for some programs), interactive Program of Study (iPOS) submitted before completing 50 percent of required credit hours; for doctorate, variable foreign language requirement, comprehensive exam, thesis/dissertation, interactive Program of Study (iPOS) submitted before completing 50 percent of required credit hours. *Entrance requirements:* For master's and doctorate, GRE, minimum GPA of 3.0 or equivalent in last 2 years of work leading to bachelor's degree. Additional exam requirements/recommendations for international students: Required—TOEFL (minimum score 600 paper-based; 250 computer-based; 100 iBT). Electronic applications accepted.

Bucknell University, Graduate Studies, College of Arts and Sciences, Department of Animal Behavior, Lewisburg, PA 17837. Offers MS. *Students:* 2 full-time (both women). In 2011, 1 master's awarded. *Degree requirements:* For master's, thesis. *Entrance requirements:* For master's, GRE General Test, GRE Subject Test, minimum GPA of 3.0. Additional exam requirements/recommendations for international students: Required—TOEFL (minimum score 600 paper-based). *Application deadline:* For fall admission, 2/1 priority date for domestic students, 1/1 for international students. Applications are processed on a rolling basis. Application fee: $25. *Financial support:* In 2011–12, 2 students received support, including 2 research assistantships with full tuition reimbursements available (averaging $20,000 per year); unspecified assistantships also available. Financial award application deadline: 2/1. *Unit head:* Dr. Peter Judge, Acting Head, 570-577-1200. *Application contact:* Gretchen H. Fegley, Coordinator, 570-577-3655, Fax: 570-577-3760, E-mail: gfegley@bucknell.edu. Web site: http://www.bucknell.edu/.

Cornell University, Graduate School, Graduate Fields of Agriculture and Life Sciences, Field of Neurobiology and Behavior, Ithaca, NY 14853-0001. Offers behavioral biology (PhD), including behavioral ecology, chemical ecology, ethology, neuroethology, sociobiology; neurobiology (PhD), including cellular and molecular neurobiology, neuroanatomy, neurochemistry, neuropharmacology, neurophysiology, sensory physiology. *Faculty:* 47 full-time (8 women). *Students:* 29 full-time (15 women); includes 4 minority (1 Black or African American, non-Hispanic/Latino; 1 Asian, non-Hispanic/Latino; 2 Hispanic/Latino), 1 international. Average age 28. 57 applicants, 18% accepted, 4 enrolled. In 2011, 6 degrees awarded. *Degree requirements:* For doctorate, comprehensive exam, thesis/dissertation, 1 year of teaching experience, seminar presentation. *Entrance requirements:* For doctorate, GRE General Test, GRE Subject Test (biology), 3 letters of recommendation. Additional exam requirements/recommendations for international students: Required—TOEFL (minimum score 550 paper-based; 213 computer-based; 77 iBT). *Application deadline:* For fall admission, 12/1 for domestic students. Application fee: $95. Electronic applications accepted. *Financial support:* In 2011–12, 14 fellowships with full tuition reimbursements, 7 research assistantships with full tuition reimbursements, 8 teaching assistantships with full tuition reimbursements were awarded; institutionally sponsored loans, scholarships/grants, health care benefits, tuition waivers (full and partial), and unspecified assistantships also available. Financial award applicants required to submit FAFSA. *Faculty research:* Cellular neurobiology and neuropharmacology, integrative neurobiology, social behavior, chemical ecology, neuroethology. *Unit head:* Director of Graduate Studies, 607-254-4340, Fax: 607-254-4340. *Application contact:* Graduate Field Assistant, 607-254-4340, Fax: 607-254-4340, E-mail: nbb_field@cornell.edu. Web site: http://www.gradschool.cornell.edu/fields.php?id-55&a-2.

Emory University, Laney Graduate School, Department of Psychology, Atlanta, GA 30322-1100. Offers clinical psychology (PhD); cognition and development (PhD); neuroscience and animal behavior (PhD). *Accreditation:* APA. *Faculty:* 32 full-time (13 women). *Students:* 71 full-time (53 women); includes 7 minority (4 Black or African American, non-Hispanic/Latino; 2 Asian, non-Hispanic/Latino; 1 Hispanic/Latino), 3 international. Average age 25. 456 applicants, 5% accepted, 15 enrolled. In 2011, 11 doctorates awarded. *Degree requirements:* For doctorate, comprehensive exam, thesis/dissertation. *Entrance requirements:* For doctorate, GRE General Test, minimum GPA of 3.25. Additional exam requirements/recommendations for international students: Required—TOEFL. *Application deadline:* For fall admission, 1/3 for domestic and international students. Application fee: $50. Electronic applications accepted. *Expenses: Tuition:* Full-time $34,800. *Required fees:* $1300. *Financial support:* In 2011–12, 47 students received support, including 52 fellowships with full tuition reimbursements available (averaging $16,796 per year); research assistantships, teaching assistantships, career-related internships or fieldwork, Federal Work-Study, institutionally sponsored loans, scholarships/grants, and tuition waivers also available. Financial award application deadline: 4/15. *Faculty research:* Neuroscience and animal behavior; adult and child psychopathology, cognition development assessment. *Unit head:* Dr. Robyn Fivush, Chair, 404-727-4124, Fax: 404-727-0372. Web site: http://psychology.emory.edu/.

Illinois State University, Graduate School, College of Arts and Sciences, Department of Biological Sciences, Normal, IL 61790-2200. Offers animal behavior (MS); bacteriology (MS); biochemistry (MS); biological sciences (MS); biology (PhD); biophysics (MS); biotechnology (MS); botany (MS, PhD); cell biology (MS); conservation biology (MS); developmental biology (MS); ecology (MS, PhD); entomology (MS); evolutionary biology (MS); genetics (MS, PhD); immunology (MS); microbiology (MS, PhD); molecular biology (MS); molecular genetics (MS); neurobiology (MS); neuroscience (MS); parasitology (MS); physiology (MS, PhD); plant biology (MS); plant molecular biology (MS); plant sciences (MS); structural biology (MS); zoology (MS, PhD). Part-time programs available. *Degree requirements:* For master's, thesis or alternative; for doctorate, variable foreign language requirement, thesis/dissertation, 2 terms of residency. *Entrance requirements:* For master's, GRE General Test, minimum GPA of 2.6 in last 60 hours of course work; for doctorate, GRE General Test. *Faculty research:* Redoc balance and drug development in schistosoma mansoni, control of the growth of listeria monocytogenes at low temperature, regulation of cell expansion and microtubule function by SPRI, CRUI: physiology and fitness consequences of different life history phenotypes.

University of California, Davis, Graduate Studies, Graduate Group in Animal Behavior, Davis, CA 95616. Offers PhD. *Degree requirements:* For doctorate, thesis/dissertation. *Entrance requirements:* For doctorate, GRE General Test. Additional exam requirements/recommendations for international students: Required—TOEFL (minimum score 550 paper-based; 213 computer-based), IELTS (minimum score 7). Electronic applications accepted. *Faculty research:* Wildlife behavior, conservation biology, companion animal behavior, behavioral endocrinology, animal communication.

University of Colorado Boulder, Graduate School, College of Arts and Sciences, Department of Ecology and Evolutionary Biology, Boulder, CO 80309. Offers animal behavior (MA); biology (MA, PhD); environmental biology (MA, PhD); evolutionary biology (MA, PhD); neurobiology (MA); population biology (MA); population genetics (PhD). *Faculty:* 28 full-time (9 women). *Students:* 67 full-time (37 women), 27 part-time (13 women); includes 9 minority (1 Asian, non-Hispanic/Latino; 8 Hispanic/Latino), 5 international. Average age 30. 136 applicants, 13% accepted, 17 enrolled. In 2011, 8 master's, 5 doctorates awarded. Terminal master's awarded for partial completion of doctoral program. *Degree requirements:* For master's, comprehensive exam, thesis or alternative; for doctorate, comprehensive exam, thesis/dissertation. *Entrance requirements:* For master's, GRE General Test, GRE Subject Test, minimum undergraduate GPA of 3.0; for doctorate, GRE General Test, GRE Subject Test. *Application deadline:* For fall admission, 12/30 priority date for domestic students, 12/1 for international students. Application fee: $50 ($60 for international students). Electronic applications accepted. *Financial support:* In 2011–12, 88 students received support, including 35 fellowships (averaging $16,835 per year), 25 research assistantships with full and partial tuition reimbursements available (averaging $22,347 per year), 44 teaching assistantships with full and partial tuition reimbursements available (averaging $21,377 per year); institutionally sponsored loans, scholarships/grants, health care benefits, and unspecified assistantships also available. Financial award applicants required to submit FAFSA. *Faculty research:* Behavior, ecology, genetics, morphology, endocrinology, physiology, systematics. *Total annual research expenditures:* $4.6 million. *Application contact:* E-mail: ebiograd@colorado.edu. Web site: http://ebio.colorado.edu.

University of Colorado Denver, College of Liberal Arts and Sciences, Department of Integrative Biology, Denver, CO 80217. Offers animal behavior (MS); biology (MS); cell and developmental biology (MS); ecology (MS); evolutionary biology (MS); genetics (MS); microbiology (MS); molecular biology (MS); neurobiology (MS); plant systematics (MS). Part-time programs available. *Faculty:* 16 full-time (8 women). *Students:* 20 full-time (13 women), 5 part-time (4 women); includes 1 minority (Hispanic/Latino), 1 international. Average age 29. 21 applicants, 43% accepted, 5 enrolled. In 2011, 7 master's awarded. *Degree requirements:* For master's, comprehensive exam, thesis or alternative, 30-32 credit hours. *Entrance requirements:* For master's, GRE General Test (minimum score in 50% percentile in each section), BA/BS from accredited institution awarded within the last 10 years; minimum undergraduate GPA of 3.0; prerequisite courses: 1 year each of general biology and general chemistry, and 1 semester each of general genetics, general ecology, cell biology, and a structure/function course. Additional exam requirements/recommendations for international students: Required—TOEFL (minimum score 525 paper-based; 197 computer-based; 71 iBT). *Application deadline:* For fall admission, 2/1 for domestic and international students. Application fee: $50 ($75 for international students). Electronic applications accepted. *Financial support:* Research assistantships, teaching assistantships, Federal Work-Study, scholarships/grants, and unspecified assistantships available. Financial award application deadline: 4/1; financial award applicants required to submit FAFSA. *Faculty research:* Molecular developmental biology; quantitative ecology, biogeography, and population dynamics; environmental signaling and endocrine disruption; speciation, the evolution of reproductive isolation, and hybrid zones; evolutionary, behavioral, and conservation ecology. *Unit head:* Dr. Diana Tomback, Acting Chair, 303-556-2657, E-mail: diana.tomback@ucdenver.edu. *Application contact:* Timberley Roane, Associate Professor/Associate Chair, 303-556-6592, E-mail: timberley.roane@ucdenver.edu. Web site: http://www.ucdenver.edu/academics/colleges/CLAS/Departments/biology/Pages/Biology.aspx.

University of Massachusetts Amherst, Graduate School, Interdisciplinary Programs, Program in Neuroscience and Behavior, Amherst, MA 01003. Offers animal behavior and learning (PhD); molecular and cellular neuroscience (PhD); neural and behavioral development (PhD); neuroendocrinology (PhD); neuroscience and behavior (MS); sensorimotor, cognitive, and computational neuroscience (PhD). *Students:* 28 full-time (19 women), 1 (woman) part-time; includes 4 minority (2 Asian, non-Hispanic/Latino; 2 Hispanic/Latino), 2 international. Average age 28. 85 applicants, 15% accepted, 4 enrolled. In 2011, 1 master's, 2 doctorates awarded. Terminal master's awarded for partial completion of doctoral program. *Degree requirements:* For master's, thesis or alternative; for doctorate, comprehensive exam, thesis/dissertation. *Entrance requirements:* For master's and doctorate, GRE General Test. Additional exam requirements/recommendations for international students: Required—TOEFL (minimum score 550 paper-based; 213 computer-based; 80 iBT), IELTS (minimum score 6.5). *Application deadline:* For fall admission, 1/2 for domestic and international students. Applications are processed on a rolling basis. Application fee: $50 ($65 for international students). Electronic applications accepted. Tuition and fees vary according to course load, campus/location and program. *Financial support:* Fellowships with full and partial tuition reimbursements, research assistantships with full and partial tuition reimbursements, teaching assistantships with full and partial tuition reimbursements, career-related internships or fieldwork, Federal Work-Study, scholarships/grants, traineeships, health care benefits, tuition waivers (full and partial), and unspecified assistantships available. Support available to part-time students. Financial award application deadline: 1/2. *Unit head:* Dr. Jeffrey D. Blaustein, Graduate Program Director, 413-545-2046, Fax: 413-545-3243. *Application contact:* Lindsay DeSantis, Interim Supervisor of Admissions, 413-545-0722, Fax: 413-577-0010, E-mail: gradadm@grad.umass.edu. Web site: http://www.umass.edu/neuro/.

University of Minnesota, Twin Cities Campus, Graduate School, College of Biological Sciences, Department of Ecology, Evolution, and Behavior, St. Paul, MN 55418. Offers MS, PhD. Terminal master's awarded for partial completion of doctoral program. *Degree requirements:* For master's, comprehensive exam, thesis or projects; for doctorate, comprehensive exam, thesis/dissertation. *Entrance requirements:* For master's and doctorate, GRE General Test, minimum GPA of 3.0. Additional exam requirements/recommendations for international students: Required—TOEFL (minimum score 550 paper-based; 79 iBT), Michigan English Language Assessment Battery. Electronic applications accepted. *Faculty research:* Behavioral ecology, community ecology, community genetics, ecosystem and global change, evolution and systematics.

The University of Montana, Graduate School, College of Arts and Sciences, Department of Psychology, Missoula, MT 59812-0002. Offers clinical psychology (PhD); experimental psychology (PhD), including animal behavior psychology, developmental psychology; school psychology (MA, PhD, Ed S). *Accreditation:* APA (one or more programs are accredited). Terminal master's awarded for partial completion of doctoral program. *Degree requirements:* For master's, thesis; for doctorate, thesis/dissertation. *Entrance requirements:* For master's, doctorate, and Ed S, GRE General Test.

Additional exam requirements/recommendations for international students: Required—TOEFL.

The University of Tennessee, Graduate School, College of Arts and Sciences, Department of Ecology and Evolutionary Biology, Knoxville, TN 37996. Offers behavior (MS, PhD); ecology (MS, PhD); evolutionary biology (MS, PhD). Part-time programs available. *Degree requirements:* For master's, thesis; for doctorate, thesis/dissertation. *Entrance requirements:* For master's and doctorate, GRE General Test, minimum GPA of 2.7. Additional exam requirements/recommendations for international students: Required—TOEFL. Electronic applications accepted. *Expenses:* Tuition, state resident: full-time $8332; part-time $464 per credit hour. Tuition, nonresident: full-time $25,174; part-time $1400 per credit hour. *Required fees:* $1162; $56 per credit hour. Tuition and fees vary according to program.

The University of Texas at Austin, Graduate School, College of Natural Sciences, School of Biological Sciences, Program in Ecology, Evolution and Behavior, Austin, TX 78712-1111. Offers PhD. *Entrance requirements:* For doctorate, GRE General Test. Additional exam requirements/recommendations for international students: Required—TOEFL. *Application deadline:* For fall admission, 1/5 for domestic and international students. Applications are processed on a rolling basis. Application fee: $50 ($75 for international students). Electronic applications accepted. *Financial support:* Fellowships, research assistantships, and teaching assistantships available. *Unit head:* Dr. Ulrich Mueller, Graduate Program Chair, 512-471-7619, E-mail: umueller@mail.utexas.edu. *Application contact:* Tamra Rogers, Graduate Coordinator, 512-471-8490, Fax: 512-232-3699, E-mail: tamra@austin.utexas.edu. Web site: http://www.biosci.utexas.edu/graduate/eeb/.

University of Washington, Graduate School, College of Arts and Sciences, Department of Psychology, Seattle, WA 98195. Offers animal behavior (PhD); child psychology (PhD); clinical psychology (PhD); cognition and perception (PhD); developmental psychology (PhD); quantitative psychology (PhD); social psychology and personality (PhD). *Accreditation:* APA. *Degree requirements:* For doctorate, thesis/dissertation. *Entrance requirements:* For doctorate, GRE General Test, minimum GPA of 3.0. Electronic applications accepted. *Faculty research:* Addictive behaviors, artificial intelligence, child psychopathology, mechanisms and development of vision, physiology of ingestive behaviors.

Wesleyan University, Graduate Programs, Department of Biology, Middletown, CT 06459. Offers animal behavior (PhD); bioformatics/genomics (PhD); cell biology (PhD); developmental biology (PhD); evolution/ecology (PhD); genetics (PhD); neurobiology (PhD); population biology (PhD). *Degree requirements:* For doctorate, variable foreign language requirement, thesis/dissertation. *Entrance requirements:* For doctorate, GRE. Additional exam requirements/recommendations for international students: Required—TOEFL. *Faculty research:* Microbial population genetics, genetic basis of evolutionary adaptation, genetic regulation of differentiation and pattern formation in &ITdrosophila&RO.

Zoology

Auburn University, Graduate School, College of Sciences and Mathematics, Department of Biological Sciences, Auburn University, AL 36849. Offers botany (MS, PhD); microbiology (MS, PhD); zoology (MS, PhD). *Faculty:* 35 full-time (11 women). *Students:* 32 full-time (13 women), 73 part-time (33 women); includes 11 minority (3 Black or African American, non-Hispanic/Latino; 1 American Indian or Alaska Native, non-Hispanic/Latino; 5 Asian, non-Hispanic/Latino; 2 Hispanic/Latino), 24 international. Average age 29. 106 applicants, 28% accepted, 19 enrolled. In 2011, 14 master's, 9 doctorates awarded. *Entrance requirements:* For master's and doctorate, GRE General Test. Additional exam requirements/recommendations for international students: Required—TOEFL. *Application deadline:* For fall admission, 7/7 for domestic students; for spring admission, 11/24 for domestic students. Application fee: $50 ($60 for international students). Electronic applications accepted. *Expenses:* Tuition, state resident: full-time $7290; part-time $405 per credit hour. Tuition, nonresident: full-time $21,870; part-time $1215 per credit hour. *International tuition:* $22,000 full-time. *Required fees:* $1402. *Financial support:* Research assistantships and teaching assistantships available. Financial award applicants required to submit FAFSA. *Unit head:* Dr. Jack W. Feminella, Chair, 334-844-3906, Fax: 334-844-1645. *Application contact:* Dr. George Flowers, Dean of the Graduate School, 334-844-2125.

Canisius College, Graduate Division, College of Arts and Sciences, Department of Animal Behavior, Ecology and Conservation, Buffalo, NY 14208-1098. Offers anthrozoology (MS). Fall entry only. Part-time programs available. Postbaccalaureate distance learning degree programs offered (minimal on-campus study). *Faculty:* 3 full-time (1 woman), 2 part-time/adjunct (both women). *Students:* 25 full-time (19 women), 11 part-time (all women); includes 3 minority (2 Hispanic/Latino; 1 Two or more races, non-Hispanic/Latino). Average age 32. 47 applicants, 83% accepted, 36 enrolled. *Entrance requirements:* Additional exam requirements/recommendations for international students: Required—TOEFL. *Application deadline:* For fall admission, 3/1 for domestic and international students. Applications are processed on a rolling basis. Application fee: $25. Electronic applications accepted. *Financial support:* Scholarships/grants available. Financial award application deadline: 4/30; financial award applicants required to submit FAFSA. *Unit head:* Dr. Michael Noonan, Program Director, 716-888-2770, E-mail: noonan@canisius.edu. *Application contact:* Jim Bagwell, Director, Graduate Admissions, 716-888-2545, Fax: 716-888-3290, E-mail: bagwellj@canisius.edu. Web site: http://www.canisius.edu/masters-degree-in-anthrozoology/.

Colorado State University, Graduate School, College of Natural Sciences, Department of Biology, Fort Collins, CO 80523-1878. Offers botany (MS, PhD); zoology (MS, PhD). Postbaccalaureate distance learning degree programs offered (no on-campus study). *Faculty:* 26 full-time (11 women). *Students:* 17 full-time (10 women), 32 part-time (19 women); includes 8 minority (3 Asian, non-Hispanic/Latino; 4 Hispanic/Latino; 1 Two or more races, non-Hispanic/Latino), 6 international. Average age 29. 61 applicants, 15% accepted, 7 enrolled. In 2011, 6 master's, 4 doctorates awarded. Terminal master's awarded for partial completion of doctoral program. *Degree requirements:* For master's, comprehensive exam (for some programs), thesis (for some programs); for doctorate, comprehensive exam, thesis/dissertation. *Entrance requirements:* For master's, GRE General Test, minimum GPA of 3.0; 3 letters of recommendation; for doctorate, GRE General Test, minimum GPA of 3.0; statement of purpose; 2 transcripts; 3 letters of recommendation. Additional exam requirements/recommendations for international students: Required—TOEFL (minimum score 550 paper-based; 213 computer-based; 80 iBT). *Application deadline:* For fall admission, 1/15 priority date for domestic students, 1/15 for international students; for spring admission, 11/1 priority date for domestic students, 11/1 for international students. Applications are processed on a rolling basis. Application fee: $50. Electronic applications accepted. *Expenses:* Tuition, state resident: full-time $7992. Tuition, nonresident: full-time $19,592. *Required fees:* $1735; $58 per credit. *Financial support:* In 2011–12, 20 fellowships (averaging $34,499 per year), 32 research assistantships with full tuition reimbursements (averaging $12,041 per year), 59 teaching assistantships with full tuition reimbursements (averaging $12,668 per year) were awarded; health care benefits also available. Financial award application deadline: 1/15; financial award applicants required to submit FAFSA. *Faculty research:* Aquatic and terrestrial ecology, cell biology and genetics, plant/animal physiology, developmental biology, evolutionary biology. *Total annual research expenditures:* $6.1 million. *Unit head:* Dr. Daniel R. Bush, Chair, 970-491-7013, Fax: 970-491-0649, E-mail: dbush@colostate.edu. *Application contact:* Dorothy Ramirez, Graduate Coordinator, 970-491-1923, Fax: 970-491-0649, E-mail: dorothy.ramirez@colostate.edu. Web site: http://www.biology.colostate.edu/.

Cornell University, Graduate School, Graduate Fields of Agriculture and Life Sciences, Field of Zoology and Wildlife Conservation, Ithaca, NY 14853-0001. Offers animal cytology (MS, PhD); comparative and functional anatomy (MS, PhD); developmental biology (MS, PhD); ecology (MS, PhD); histology (MS, PhD). *Faculty:* 24 full-time (7 women). *Students:* 5 full-time (4 women); includes 1 minority (Two or more races, non-Hispanic/Latino), 2 international. Average age 29. 7 applicants, 14% accepted, 1 enrolled. In 2011, 2 doctorates awarded. *Degree requirements:* For doctorate, comprehensive exam, thesis/dissertation, 2 semesters of teaching experience. *Entrance requirements:* For doctorate, GRE General Test, GRE Subject Test (biology), 2 letters of recommendation. Additional exam requirements/recommendations for international students: Required—TOEFL (minimum score 550 paper-based; 213 computer-based; 77 iBT). *Application deadline:* For fall admission, 2/1 priority date for domestic students. Application fee: $95. Electronic applications accepted. *Financial support:* In 2011–12, 3 research assistantships with full tuition reimbursements, 1 teaching assistantship with full tuition reimbursement were awarded; fellowships with full tuition reimbursements, institutionally sponsored loans, scholarships/grants, health care benefits, tuition waivers (full and partial), and unspecified assistantships also available. Financial award applicants required to submit FAFSA. *Faculty research:* Organismal biology, functional morphology, biomechanics, comparative vertebrate anatomy, comparative invertebrate anatomy, paleontology. *Unit head:* Director of Graduate Studies, 607-253-3276, Fax: 607-253-3756. *Application contact:* Graduate Field Assistant, 607-253-3276, Fax: 607-253-3756, E-mail: graduate_edcvm@cornell.edu. Web site: http://www.gradschool.cornell.edu/fields.php?id-65&a-2.

Eastern New Mexico University, Graduate School, College of Liberal Arts and Sciences, Department of Biology, Portales, NM 88130. Offers applied ecology (MS); cell, molecular biology and biotechnology (MS); education (non-thesis) (MS); microbiology (MS); plant biology (MS); zoology (MS). Part-time programs available. *Faculty:* 7 full-time (0 women). *Students:* 2 full-time (1 woman), 15 part-time (9 women); includes 7 minority (5 Hispanic/Latino; 2 Two or more races, non-Hispanic/Latino), 2 international. Average age 26. 17 applicants, 82% accepted, 3 enrolled. In 2011, 4 master's awarded. *Degree requirements:* For master's, comprehensive exam, thesis optional. *Entrance requirements:* For master's, GRE, minimum GPA of 3.0, 2 letters of recommendation, statement of research interest, bachelor's degree related to field of study or proof of common knowledge. Additional exam requirements/recommendations for international students: Required—TOEFL (minimum score 550 paper-based; 213 computer-based; 79 iBT), IELTS (minimum score 6). *Application deadline:* For fall admission, 7/20 priority date for domestic students, 6/20 for international students; for spring admission, 12/15 priority date for domestic students, 11/15 for international students. Applications are processed on a rolling basis. Application fee: $10. Electronic applications accepted. *Financial support:* In 2011–12, 8 teaching assistantships with partial tuition reimbursements (averaging $8,500 per year) were awarded; scholarships/grants and unspecified assistantships also available. Support available to part-time students. Financial award applicants required to submit FAFSA. *Unit head:* Dr. Zach Jones, Graduate Coordinator, 575-562-2723, Fax: 575-562-2192, E-mail: zach.jones@enmu.edu. *Application contact:* Sharon Potter, Department Secretary, Biology and Physical Sciences, 575-562-2174, Fax: 575-562-2192, E-mail: sharon.potter@enmu.edu. Web site: http://liberal-arts.enmu.edu/biology/graduate.shtml.

Emporia State University, Graduate School, College of Liberal Arts and Sciences, Department of Biological Sciences, Emporia, KS 66801-5087. Offers botany (MS); environmental biology (MS); general biology (MS); microbial and cellular biology (MS); zoology (MS). Part-time programs available. *Faculty:* 13 full-time (3 women), 1 part-time/adjunct (0 women). *Students:* 8 full-time (5 women), 21 part-time (10 women); includes 3 minority (1 Black or African American, non-Hispanic/Latino; 1 Hispanic/Latino; 1 Two or more races, non-Hispanic/Latino), 6 international. 14 applicants, 86% accepted, 7 enrolled. In 2011, 5 master's awarded. *Degree requirements:* For master's, comprehensive exam or thesis. *Entrance requirements:* For master's, GRE, appropriate undergraduate degree, interview, letters of reference. Additional exam requirements/recommendations for international students: Required—TOEFL (minimum score 520 paper-based; 133 computer-based; 68 iBT). *Application deadline:* For fall admission, 8/15 priority date for domestic students. Applications are processed on a rolling basis. Application fee: $30 ($75 for international students). Electronic applications accepted. *Expenses:* Tuition, state resident: full-time $2342; part-time $195 per credit hour. Tuition, nonresident: full-time $7254; part-time $605 per credit hour. *Required fees:* $66 per credit hour. Tuition and fees vary according to campus/location. *Financial support:* In 2011–12, 8 research assistantships with full tuition reimbursements (averaging $6,589 per year), 10 teaching assistantships with full tuition reimbursements (averaging $7,419 per year) were awarded; career-related internships or fieldwork, Federal Work-Study, institutionally sponsored loans, health care benefits, and unspecified assistantships also available. Financial award application deadline: 3/15; financial award applicants required to submit FAFSA. *Faculty research:* Fisheries, range, and wildlife management; aquatic, plant, grassland, vertebrate, and invertebrate ecology; mammalian and plant systematics, taxonomy, and evolution; immunology, virology, and molecular biology. *Unit head:* Dr. R. Brent Thomas, Chair, 620-341-5311, Fax: 620-341-5608, E-mail: rthomas2@emporia.edu. *Application contact:* Dr. Scott Crupper, Graduate Coordinator, 620-341-5621, Fax: 620-341-5607, E-mail: scrupper@emporia.edu. Web site: http://www.emporia.edu/info/degrees-courses/grad/biology.

Illinois State University, Graduate School, College of Arts and Sciences, Department of Biological Sciences, Normal, IL 61790-2200. Offers animal behavior (MS); bacteriology (MS); biochemistry (MS); biological sciences (MS); biology (PhD); biophysics (MS); biotechnology (MS); botany (MS, PhD); cell biology (MS); conservation

Zoology

biology (MS); developmental biology (MS); ecology (MS, PhD); entomology (MS); evolutionary biology (MS); genetics (MS, PhD); immunology (MS); microbiology (MS, PhD); molecular biology (MS); molecular genetics (MS); neurobiology (MS); neuroscience (MS); parasitology (MS); physiology (MS, PhD); plant biology (MS); plant molecular biology (MS); plant sciences (MS); structural biology (MS); zoology (MS, PhD). Part-time programs available. *Degree requirements:* For master's, thesis or alternative; for doctorate, variable foreign language requirement, thesis/dissertation, 2 terms of residency. *Entrance requirements:* For master's, GRE General Test, minimum GPA of 2.6 in last 60 hours of course work; for doctorate, GRE General Test. *Faculty research:* Redoc balance and drug development in schistosoma mansoni, control of the growth of listeria monocytogenes at low temperature, regulation of cell expansion and microtubule function by SPRI, CRUI: physiology and fitness consequences of different life history phenotypes.

Indiana University Bloomington, University Graduate School, College of Arts and Sciences, Department of Biology, Bloomington, IN 47405. Offers biology teaching (MAT); biotechnology (MA); evolution, ecology, and behavior (MA, PhD); genetics (PhD); microbiology (MA, PhD); molecular, cellular, and developmental biology (PhD); plant sciences (MA, PhD); zoology (MA, PhD). *Faculty:* 58 full-time (15 women), 21 part-time/adjunct (6 women). *Students:* 175 full-time (100 women), 3 part-time (all women); includes 20 minority (5 Black or African American, non-Hispanic/Latino; 8 Asian, non-Hispanic/Latino; 7 Hispanic/Latino), 55 international. Average age 27. 316 applicants, 22% accepted, 31 enrolled. In 2011, 8 master's, 20 doctorates awarded. Terminal master's awarded for partial completion of doctoral program. *Degree requirements:* For master's, thesis, oral defense; for doctorate, thesis/dissertation, oral defense. *Entrance requirements:* For master's and doctorate, GRE General Test. Additional exam requirements/recommendations for international students: Required—TOEFL (minimum score 100 iBT). *Application deadline:* For fall admission, 1/5 priority date for domestic students, 12/1 for international students. Application fee: $55 ($65 for international students). Electronic applications accepted. *Financial support:* In 2011–12, fellowships with tuition reimbursements (averaging $19,484 per year), research assistantships with tuition reimbursements (averaging $20,300 per year), teaching assistantships with tuition reimbursements (averaging $20,521 per year) were awarded; scholarships/grants, traineeships, health care benefits, and unspecified assistantships also available. Financial award application deadline: 1/5. *Faculty research:* Evolution, ecology and behavior; microbiology; molecular biology and genetics; plant biology. *Unit head:* Dr. Roger Innes, Chair, 812-855-2219, Fax: 812-855-6082, E-mail: rinnes@indiana.edu. *Application contact:* Tracey D. Stohr, Graduate Student Recruitment Coordinator, 812-856-6303, Fax: 812-855-6082, E-mail: gradbio@indiana.edu. Web site: http://www.bio.indiana.edu/.

Miami University, College of Arts and Science, Department of Zoology, Oxford, OH 45056. Offers biological sciences (MAT); zoology (MS, PhD). Part-time programs available. *Students:* 46 full-time (28 women), 231 part-time (184 women); includes 24 minority (3 Black or African American, non-Hispanic/Latino; 1 American Indian or Alaska Native, non-Hispanic/Latino; 7 Asian, non-Hispanic/Latino; 9 Hispanic/Latino; 1 Native Hawaiian or other Pacific Islander, non-Hispanic/Latino; 3 Two or more races, non-Hispanic/Latino), 18 international. Average age 33. In 2011, 5 master's, 4 doctorates awarded. *Entrance requirements:* For master's, GRE General Test, minimum undergraduate GPA of 3.0 during previous 2 years or 2.75 overall; for doctorate, minimum undergraduate GPA of 2.75, 3.0 graduate. Additional exam requirements/recommendations for international students: Required—TOEFL. *Application deadline:* For fall admission, 1/15 for domestic and international students. Application fee: $50. Electronic applications accepted. *Expenses:* Tuition, state resident: full-time $12,023; part-time $501 per credit hour. Tuition, nonresident: full-time $26,554; part-time $1107 per credit hour. *Required fees:* $528. *Financial support:* Fellowships with full tuition reimbursements, research assistantships with full tuition reimbursements, teaching assistantships with full tuition reimbursements, Federal Work-Study, health care benefits, tuition waivers (full), and unspecified assistantships available. Financial award application deadline: 1/15; financial award applicants required to submit FAFSA. *Unit head:* Dr. Douglas Meikle, Chair, 513-529-3103, E-mail: meikled@muohio.edu. *Application contact:* Dr. Paul F. James, Director of Graduate Program, 513-529-3129, E-mail: jamespf@muohio.edu. Web site: http://zoology.muohio.edu/.

Michigan State University, The Graduate School, College of Natural Science, Department of Zoology, East Lansing, MI 48824. Offers zoo and aquarium management (MS); zoology (MS, PhD); zoology-environmental toxicology (PhD). *Entrance requirements:* Additional exam requirements/recommendations for international students: Required—TOEFL. Electronic applications accepted.

North Carolina State University, Graduate School, College of Agriculture and Life Sciences, Department of Zoology, Raleigh, NC 27695. Offers MS, MZS, PhD. Terminal master's awarded for partial completion of doctoral program. *Degree requirements:* For master's, thesis (for some programs), oral exam; for doctorate, thesis/dissertation, oral and written exams. *Entrance requirements:* For master's and doctorate, GRE General Test, minimum GPA of 3.0. Additional exam requirements/recommendations for international students: Required—TOEFL. Electronic applications accepted. *Faculty research:* Acquatic and terrestrial ecology, herpetology, behavioral biology, neurobiology, avian ecology.

North Dakota State University, College of Graduate and Interdisciplinary Studies, College of Science and Mathematics, Department of Biological Sciences, Fargo, ND 58108. Offers biology (MS); botany (MS, PhD); cellular and molecular biology (PhD); environmental and conservation sciences (MS, PhD); genomics (PhD); natural resources management (MS, PhD); zoology (MS, PhD). *Faculty:* 13 full-time (7 women), 3 part-time/adjunct (1 woman). *Students:* 20 full-time (10 women), 2 part-time (both women); includes 1 minority (American Indian or Alaska Native, non-Hispanic/Latino), 2 international. 12 applicants, 33% accepted, 4 enrolled. In 2011, 3 degrees awarded. *Degree requirements:* For master's, thesis; for doctorate, thesis/dissertation. *Entrance requirements:* For master's and doctorate, GRE General Test. Additional exam requirements/recommendations for international students: Required—TOEFL. *Application deadline:* For fall admission, 1/15 for domestic students. Applications are processed on a rolling basis. Application fee: $35. Electronic applications accepted. *Financial support:* Fellowships with full tuition reimbursements, research assistantships with full tuition reimbursements, teaching assistantships with full tuition reimbursements, career-related internships or fieldwork, Federal Work-Study, institutionally sponsored loans, scholarships/grants, tuition waivers (full), and unspecified assistantships available. Support available to part-time students. Financial award application deadline: 4/15; financial award applicants required to submit FAFSA. *Faculty research:* Comparative endocrinology, physiology, behavioral ecology, plant cell biology, aquatic biology. *Unit head:* Dr. Wendy Reed, Head, 701-231-7087, E-mail: wendy.reed@ndsu.edu. *Application contact:* Sonya Goergen, Marketing, Recruitment, and Public Relations Coordinator, 701-231-7033, Fax: 701-231-6524. Web site: http://biology.ndsu.nodak.edu/.

Oklahoma State University, College of Arts and Sciences, Department of Zoology, Stillwater, OK 74078. Offers MS, PhD. *Faculty:* 19 full-time (7 women). *Students:* 5 full-time (2 women), 54 part-time (31 women); includes 13 minority (3 Black or African American, non-Hispanic/Latino; 2 American Indian or Alaska Native, non-Hispanic/Latino; 3 Asian, non-Hispanic/Latino; 2 Hispanic/Latino; 3 Two or more races, non-Hispanic/Latino), 6 international. Average age 28. 41 applicants, 44% accepted, 11 enrolled. In 2011, 8 master's, 2 doctorates awarded. *Degree requirements:* For master's, thesis; for doctorate, comprehensive exam, thesis/dissertation. *Entrance requirements:* For master's and doctorate, GRE General Test. Additional exam requirements/recommendations for international students: Required—TOEFL (minimum score 550 paper-based; 79 iBT). *Application deadline:* For fall admission, 3/1 for international students; for spring admission, 8/1 for international students. Applications are processed on a rolling basis. Application fee: $40 ($75 for international students). Electronic applications accepted. *Expenses:* Tuition, state resident: full-time $4044; part-time $168.50 per credit hour. Tuition, nonresident: full-time $16,008; part-time $667 per credit hour. *Required fees:* $2122; $88.45 per credit hour. One-time fee: $50. Tuition and fees vary according to course load and campus/location. *Financial support:* In 2011–12, 10 research assistantships (averaging $18,766 per year), 44 teaching assistantships (averaging $16,602 per year) were awarded; career-related internships or fieldwork, Federal Work-Study, scholarships/grants, health care benefits, tuition waivers (partial), and unspecified assistantships also available. Support available to part-time students. Financial award application deadline: 3/1; financial award applicants required to submit FAFSA. *Unit head:* Dr. Loren Smith, Head, 405-744-5555, Fax: 405-744-7824. *Application contact:* Dr. Sheryl Tucker, Dean, 405-744-7099, Fax: 405-744-0355, E-mail: grad-i@okstate.edu. Web site: http://zoology.okstate.edu.

Oregon State University, Graduate School, College of Science, Department of Zoology, Corvallis, OR 97331. Offers MA, MAIS, MS, PhD. Terminal master's awarded for partial completion of doctoral program. *Degree requirements:* For doctorate, thesis/dissertation. *Entrance requirements:* For master's and doctorate, GRE General Test, GRE Subject Test, minimum GPA of 3.0 in last 90 hours. Additional exam requirements/recommendations for international students: Required—TOEFL. *Faculty research:* Cell and developmental biology, population biology and marine community ecology, behavioral physiology, comparative immunology, plant-herbivore interaction.

Southern Illinois University Carbondale, Graduate School, College of Science, Department of Zoology, Carbondale, IL 62901-4701. Offers MS, PhD. *Faculty:* 25 full-time (1 woman). *Students:* 17 full-time (6 women), 71 part-time (39 women); includes 5 minority (2 Black or African American, non-Hispanic/Latino; 1 Asian, non-Hispanic/Latino; 2 Hispanic/Latino), 5 international. Average age 25. 35 applicants, 40% accepted, 14 enrolled. In 2011, 16 master's, 5 doctorates awarded. *Degree requirements:* For master's, thesis; for doctorate, thesis/dissertation. *Entrance requirements:* For master's, GRE, minimum GPA of 2.7; for doctorate, GRE, minimum GPA of 3.25. Additional exam requirements/recommendations for international students: Required—TOEFL. *Application deadline:* Applications are processed on a rolling basis. Application fee: $20. *Financial support:* In 2011–12, 5 fellowships with full tuition reimbursements, 45 research assistantships with full tuition reimbursements, 20 teaching assistantships with full tuition reimbursements were awarded; Federal Work-Study, institutionally sponsored loans, and tuition waivers (full) also available. Support available to part-time students. *Faculty research:* Ecology, fisheries and wildlife, systematics, behavior, vertebrate and invertebrate biology. *Unit head:* William Muhlach, Chairperson, 618-536-2314, E-mail: muhlach@zoology.siu.edu. *Application contact:* Carey Krajewski, Director of Graduate Studies, 618-453-4132, Fax: 618-453-2806, E-mail: careyk@siu.edu.

Texas A&M University, College of Science, Department of Biology, College Station, TX 77843. Offers biology (MS, PhD); botany (MS, PhD); microbiology (MS, PhD); molecular and cell biology (PhD); neuroscience (MS, PhD); zoology (MS, PhD). *Faculty:* 41. *Students:* 99 full-time (60 women), 8 part-time (4 women); includes 11 minority (1 Black or African American, non-Hispanic/Latino; 5 Asian, non-Hispanic/Latino; 4 Hispanic/Latino; 1 Two or more races, non-Hispanic/Latino), 46 international. Average age 28. In 2011, 5 master's, 7 doctorates awarded. *Degree requirements:* For master's, thesis or alternative; for doctorate, comprehensive exam, thesis/dissertation. *Entrance requirements:* For master's and doctorate, GRE General Test. Additional exam requirements/recommendations for international students: Required—TOEFL. *Application deadline:* For fall admission, 1/15 for domestic students. Applications are processed on a rolling basis. Application fee: $50 ($75 for international students). Electronic applications accepted. *Expenses:* Tuition, state resident: full-time $5437; part-time $226.55 per credit hour. Tuition, nonresident: full-time $12,949; part-time $539.55 per credit hour. *Required fees:* $2741. *Financial support:* Fellowships, research assistantships, and teaching assistantships available. Financial award application deadline: 4/1; financial award applicants required to submit FAFSA. *Unit head:* Dr. Jack McMahan, Department Head, 979-845-2301, E-mail: granster@mail.bio.tamu.edu. *Application contact:* 979-845-7755, Fax: 979-845-2891, E-mail: graduate@bio.tamu.edu. Web site: http://www.bio.tamu.edu/index.html.

Texas Tech University, Graduate School, College of Arts and Sciences, Department of Biological Sciences, Lubbock, TX 79409-3131. Offers biology (MS, PhD); microbiology (MS); zoology (MS, PhD). Part-time programs available. *Faculty:* 37 full-time (6 women), 2 part-time/adjunct (1 woman). *Students:* 101 full-time (54 women), 11 part-time (7 women); includes 6 minority (1 Asian, non-Hispanic/Latino; 3 Hispanic/Latino; 2 Two or more races, non-Hispanic/Latino), 54 international. Average age 29. 79 applicants, 25% accepted, 11 enrolled. In 2011, 16 master's, 9 doctorates awarded. *Degree requirements:* For master's, thesis or alternative; for doctorate, thesis/dissertation. *Entrance requirements:* For master's and doctorate, GRE General Test. Additional exam requirements/recommendations for international students: Required—TOEFL (minimum score 550 paper-based; 213 computer-based; 79 iBT). *Application deadline:* For fall admission, 6/1 priority date for domestic students, 1/15 for international students; for spring admission, 9/1 priority date for domestic students, 6/15 for international students. Applications are processed on a rolling basis. Application fee: $50 ($75 for international students). Electronic applications accepted. *Expenses:* Tuition, state resident: full-time $5899; part-time $245.80 per credit hour. Tuition, nonresident: full-time $13,411; part-time $558.80 per credit hour. *Required fees:* $2680.60; $86.50 per credit hour. $920.30 per semester. *Financial support:* In 2011–12, 33 students received support. Application deadline: 4/15; applicants required to submit FAFSA. *Faculty research:* Biodiversity and evolution, climate change in arid ecosystems, plant biology and biotechnology, animal communication and behavior, zoonotic and emerging diseases. *Total annual research expenditures:* $2.8 million. *Unit head:* Dr. Llewellyn D. Densmore, Chair, 806-742-2715, Fax: 806-742-2963, E-mail: lou.densmore@ttu.edu. *Application contact:* Dr. Randall M. Jeter, Graduate Adviser, 806-742-2710 Ext. 270, Fax: 806-742-2963, E-mail: randall.jeter@ttu.edu. Web site: http://www.biol.ttu.edu/.

Uniformed Services University of the Health Sciences, School of Medicine, Graduate Programs in the Biomedical Sciences and Public Health, Bethesda, MD 20814. Offers emerging infectious diseases (PhD); medical and clinical psychology (PhD), including clinical psychology, medical and clinical psychology, medical psychology; molecular and cell biology (MS, PhD); neuroscience (PhD); preventive medicine and biometrics (MPH, MS, MSPH, MTMH, Dr PH, PhD), including environmental health sciences (PhD), healthcare administration and policy (MS), medical zoology (PhD), public health (MPH, MSPH, Dr PH), tropical medicine and hygiene (MTMH). *Faculty:* 372 full-time (119 women), 4,044 part-time/adjunct (908 women). *Students:* 176 full-time (96 women); includes 31 minority (6 Black or African

American, non-Hispanic/Latino; 4 American Indian or Alaska Native, non-Hispanic/Latino; 14 Asian, non-Hispanic/Latino; 7 Hispanic/Latino), 11 international. Average age 28. 278 applicants, 20% accepted, 47 enrolled. In 2011, 36 master's, 17 doctorates awarded. Terminal master's awarded for partial completion of doctoral program. *Degree requirements:* For master's, comprehensive exam, thesis or alternative; for doctorate, comprehensive exam, thesis/dissertation, qualifying exam. *Entrance requirements:* For master's, GRE General Test; for doctorate, GRE General Test, minimum GPA of 3.0. Additional exam requirements/recommendations for international students: Required—TOEFL. *Application deadline:* For fall admission, 1/1 priority date for domestic students, 1/1 for international students. Applications are processed on a rolling basis. Application fee: $0. Electronic applications accepted. *Financial support:* In 2011–12, fellowships with full tuition reimbursements (averaging $26,000 per year), research assistantships with full tuition reimbursements (averaging $26,000 per year) were awarded; career-related internships or fieldwork, scholarships/grants, health care benefits, and tuition waivers (full) also available. *Unit head:* Dr. Eleanor S. Metcalf, Associate Dean, 301-295-1104, E-mail: emetcalf@usuhs.edu. *Application contact:* Elena Marina Sherman, Program Administrative Specialist, 301-295-3913, Fax: 301-295-6772, E-mail: elena.sherman@usuhs.mil. Web site: http://www.usuhs.mil/graded.

Uniformed Services University of the Health Sciences, School of Medicine, Graduate Programs in the Biomedical Sciences and Public Health, Department of Preventive Medicine and Biometrics, Program in Medical Zoology, Bethesda, MD 20814-4799. Offers PhD. *Faculty:* 43 full-time (14 women), 143 part-time/adjunct (25 women). *Students:* 1 (woman) full-time. Average age 33. 5 applicants, 0% accepted. *Degree requirements:* For doctorate, comprehensive exam, thesis/dissertation, qualifying exam. *Entrance requirements:* For doctorate, GRE General Test, GRE Subject Test, minimum GPA of 3.0, U.S. citizenship. Additional exam requirements/recommendations for international students: Required—TOEFL. *Application deadline:* For fall admission, 1/1 priority date for domestic students. Applications are processed on a rolling basis. Application fee: $0. *Financial support:* In 2011–12, fellowships with full tuition reimbursements (averaging $26,000 per year) were awarded; scholarships/grants, health care benefits, and tuition waivers (full) also available. *Faculty research:* Epidemiology, biostatistics, tropical public health, parasitology, vector biology. *Unit head:* Dr. David Cruess, Director, 301-295-3465, Fax: 301-295-1933, E-mail: dcruess@usuhs.mil. *Application contact:* Elena Marina Sherman, Program Administrative Specialist, 301-295-3913, Fax: 301-295-6772, E-mail: elena.sherman@usuhs.mil. Web site: http://www.usuhs.mil/pmb.

University of Alaska Fairbanks, College of Natural Sciences and Mathematics, Department of Biology and Wildlife, Fairbanks, AK 99775-6100. Offers biological sciences (MS, PhD), including biology, botany, wildlife biology (PhD), zoology; biology (MAT, MS); wildlife biology (MS). Part-time programs available. *Faculty:* 20 full-time (10 women). *Students:* 74 full-time (43 women), 29 part-time (18 women); includes 12 minority (1 Asian, non-Hispanic/Latino; 6 Hispanic/Latino; 5 Two or more races, non-Hispanic/Latino), 4 international. Average age 29. 45 applicants, 40% accepted, 15 enrolled. In 2011, 12 master's, 11 doctorates awarded. *Degree requirements:* For master's, comprehensive exam, thesis, oral exam, oral defense; for doctorate, comprehensive exam, thesis/dissertation, oral exam, oral defense. *Entrance requirements:* For master's and doctorate, GRE General Test, GRE Subject Test (biology). Additional exam requirements/recommendations for international students: Required—TOEFL (minimum score 550 paper-based; 213 computer-based; 80 iBT), TWE. *Application deadline:* For fall admission, 6/1 for domestic students, 3/1 for international students; for spring admission, 10/15 for domestic students, 9/1 for international students. Applications are processed on a rolling basis. Application fee: $60. Electronic applications accepted. *Expenses:* Tuition, state resident: full-time $6696; part-time $372 per credit. Tuition, nonresident: full-time $13,680; part-time $760 per credit. Tuition and fees vary according to course load and reciprocity agreements. *Financial support:* In 2011–12, 26 research assistantships with tuition reimbursements (averaging $13,976 per year), 26 teaching assistantships with tuition reimbursements (averaging $14,955 per year) were awarded; fellowships with tuition reimbursements, career-related internships or fieldwork, Federal Work-Study, scholarships/grants, health care benefits, and unspecified assistantships also available. Support available to part-time students. Financial award application deadline: 7/1; financial award applicants required to submit FAFSA. *Faculty research:* Plant-herbivore interactions, plant metabolic defenses, insect manufacture of glycerol, ice nucleators, structure and functions of arctic and subarctic freshwater ecosystems. *Unit head:* Christa Mulder, Department Chair, 907-474-7671, Fax: 907-474-6716, E-mail: fybio@uaf.edu. *Application contact:* Mike Earnest, Director of Admissions, 907-474-7500, Fax: 907-474-5379, E-mail: admissions@uaf.edu. Web site: http://www.bw.uaf.edu.

The University of British Columbia, Faculty of Science, Department of Zoology, Vancouver, BC V6T 1Z1, Canada. Offers M Sc, PhD. *Degree requirements:* For master's, thesis, final defense; for doctorate, comprehensive exam, thesis/dissertation, final defense. *Entrance requirements:* For master's and doctorate, faculty support. Additional exam requirements/recommendations for international students: Required—TOEFL. Electronic applications accepted. *Faculty research:* Cell and developmental biology; community, environmental, and population biology; comparative physiology and biochemistry; fisheries; ecology and evolutionary biology.

University of California, Davis, Graduate Studies, Graduate Group in Avian Sciences, Davis, CA 95616. Offers MS. *Degree requirements:* For master's, comprehensive exam (for some programs), thesis (for some programs). *Entrance requirements:* For master's, GRE General Test, minimum GPA of 3.0. Additional exam requirements/recommendations for international students: Required—TOEFL (minimum score 550 paper-based; 213 computer-based). Electronic applications accepted. *Faculty research:* Reproduction, nutrition, toxicology, food products, ecology of avian species.

University of Chicago, Division of Biological Sciences, Darwinian Sciences Cluster: Ecological, Integrative and Evolutionary Biology, Department of Organismal Biology and Anatomy, Chicago, IL 60637-1513. Offers integrative biology (PhD). *Degree requirements:* For doctorate, thesis/dissertation, ethics class, 2 teaching assistantships. *Entrance requirements:* For doctorate, GRE General Test. Additional exam requirements/recommendations for international students: Required—TOEFL (minimum score 600 paper-based; 250 computer-based; 104 iBT), IELTS (minimum score 7). Electronic applications accepted. *Faculty research:* Ecological physiology, evolution of fossil reptiles, vertebrate paleontology.

University of Connecticut, Graduate School, College of Liberal Arts and Sciences, Department of Ecology and Evolutionary Biology, Storrs, CT 06269. Offers botany (MS, PhD); ecology (MS, PhD); entomology (MS, PhD); zoology (MS, PhD). Terminal master's awarded for partial completion of doctoral program. *Degree requirements:* For master's, comprehensive exam; for doctorate, thesis/dissertation. *Entrance requirements:* For master's and doctorate, GRE General Test, GRE Subject Test. Additional exam requirements/recommendations for international students: Required—TOEFL (minimum score 550 paper-based; 213 computer-based). Electronic applications accepted.

University of Florida, Graduate School, College of Liberal Arts and Sciences, Department of Zoology, Gainesville, FL 32611. Offers MS, MST, PhD. In 2011, 8 master's, 11 doctorates awarded. *Degree requirements:* For master's, comprehensive exam (for some programs), thesis; for doctorate, comprehensive exam, thesis/dissertation. *Entrance requirements:* Additional exam requirements/recommendations for international students: Required—TOEFL (minimum score 550 paper-based; 213 computer-based; 80 iBT). *Application deadline:* For fall admission, 12/1 for domestic and international students. Applications are processed on a rolling basis. Electronic applications accepted. *Financial support:* In 2011–12, 95 students received support, including 39 fellowships, 14 research assistantships (averaging $23,199 per year), 42 teaching assistantships (averaging $22,469 per year); unspecified assistantships also available. Financial award application deadline: 12/15; financial award applicants required to submit FAFSA. *Faculty research:* Ecology, evolution, genetics, molecular and cellular biology, physiology. *Total annual research expenditures:* $4.8 million. *Unit head:* Dr. Alice Harmon, Chair, 352-273-0127, E-mail: harmon@ufl.edu. *Application contact:* Dr. Rebecca T. Kimball, Graduate Coordinator, 352-846-3737, Fax: 352-392-3704, E-mail: rkimball@ufl.edu. Web site: http://www.zoo.ufl.edu/.

University of Guelph, Graduate Studies, College of Biological Science, Department of Integrative Biology, Botany and Zoology, Guelph, ON N1G 2W1, Canada. Offers botany (M Sc, PhD); zoology (M Sc, PhD). Part-time programs available. *Degree requirements:* For master's, thesis, research proposal; for doctorate, thesis/dissertation, research proposal, qualifying exam. *Entrance requirements:* For master's, minimum B average during previous 2 years of course work. Additional exam requirements/recommendations for international students: Required—TOEFL (minimum score 550 paper-based; 213 computer-based), IELTS (minimum score 6.5). Electronic applications accepted. *Faculty research:* Aquatic science, environmental physiology, parasitology, wildlife biology, management.

University of Hawaii at Manoa, Graduate Division, College of Natural Sciences, Department of Zoology, Honolulu, HI 96822. Offers MS, PhD. Part-time programs available. *Degree requirements:* For master's, one foreign language, thesis optional; for doctorate, one foreign language, comprehensive exam, thesis/dissertation, seminar. *Entrance requirements:* For master's and doctorate, GRE General Test, GRE Subject Test. Additional exam requirements/recommendations for international students: Required—TOEFL (minimum score 600 paper-based; 250 computer-based; 100 iBT), IELTS (minimum score 7). *Faculty research:* Molecular evolution, reproductive biology, animal behavior, conservation biology, avian biology.

University of Illinois at Urbana–Champaign, Graduate College, College of Liberal Arts and Sciences, School of Integrative Biology, Department of Animal Biology, Champaign, IL 61820. Offers animal biology (ecology, ethology and evolution) (MS, PhD). *Faculty:* 8 full-time (5 women). *Students:* 14 full-time (8 women), 2 part-time (0 women); includes 1 minority (Two or more races, non-Hispanic/Latino), 2 international. 7 applicants, 71% accepted, 4 enrolled. In 2011, 2 master's, 1 doctorate awarded. *Entrance requirements:* For master's and doctorate, GRE. Additional exam requirements/recommendations for international students: Required—TOEFL (minimum score 570 paper-based; 230 computer-based; 88 iBT). *Application deadline:* Applications are processed on a rolling basis. Application fee: $75 ($90 for international students). Electronic applications accepted. *Financial support:* In 2011–12, 3 fellowships, 4 research assistantships, 15 teaching assistantships were awarded; tuition waivers (full and partial) also available. *Unit head:* Ken Paige, Head, 217-244-6606, Fax: 217-244-4565, E-mail: k-paige@illinois.edu. *Application contact:* Lisa Smith, Office Administrator, 217-333-7802, Fax: 217-244-4565, E-mail: ljsmith1@illinois.edu. Web site: http://www.life.illinois.edu/animalbiology.

University of Maine, Graduate School, College of Natural Sciences, Forestry, and Agriculture, Department of Biological Sciences, Program in Zoology, Orono, ME 04469. Offers MS, PhD. *Students:* 1 (woman) full-time, 2 part-time (both women). Average age 24. 5 applicants, 20% accepted, 1 enrolled. In 2011, 1 master's awarded. Terminal master's awarded for partial completion of doctoral program. *Degree requirements:* For master's, variable foreign language requirement, thesis; for doctorate, one foreign language, thesis/dissertation. *Entrance requirements:* For master's and doctorate, GRE General Test. Additional exam requirements/recommendations for international students: Required—TOEFL. *Application deadline:* For fall admission, 2/1 priority date for domestic students. Applications are processed on a rolling basis. Application fee: $65. Electronic applications accepted. *Expenses:* Tuition, state resident: full-time $5016. Tuition, nonresident: full-time $14,424. *Financial support:* Career-related internships or fieldwork available. Financial award application deadline: 3/1. *Unit head:* Dr. Jody Jellison, Coordinator, 207-581-2551. *Application contact:* Scott G. Delcourt, Associate Dean of the Graduate School, 207-581-3291, Fax: 207-581-3232, E-mail: graduate@maine.edu. Web site: http://www2.umaine.edu/graduate/.

University of Manitoba, Faculty of Graduate Studies, Faculty of Science, Department of Biological Sciences, Winnipeg, MB R3T 2N2, Canada. Offers botany (M Sc, PhD); ecology (M Sc, PhD); zoology (M Sc, PhD).

The University of Montana, Graduate School, College of Arts and Sciences, Division of Biological Sciences, Program in Organismal Biology and Ecology, Missoula, MT 59812-0002. Offers MS, PhD. Terminal master's awarded for partial completion of doctoral program. *Degree requirements:* For master's, one foreign language, thesis; for doctorate, 2 foreign languages, thesis/dissertation. *Entrance requirements:* For master's and doctorate, GRE General Test. *Faculty research:* Conservation biology, ecology and behavior, evolutionary genetics, avian biology.

University of New Hampshire, Graduate School, College of Life Sciences and Agriculture, Department of Biological Sciences, Program in Zoology, Durham, NH 03824. Offers MS, PhD. Part-time programs available. *Faculty:* 25 full-time. *Students:* 19 full-time (8 women), 17 part-time (12 women); includes 1 minority (Asian, non-Hispanic/Latino), 2 international. Average age 31. 29 applicants, 28% accepted, 8 enrolled. In 2011, 1 master's awarded. Terminal master's awarded for partial completion of doctoral program. *Degree requirements:* For master's, thesis; for doctorate, one foreign language, thesis/dissertation. *Entrance requirements:* For master's and doctorate, GRE General Test, GRE Subject Test. Additional exam requirements/recommendations for international students: Required—TOEFL (minimum score 550 paper-based; 213 computer-based; 80 iBT). *Application deadline:* For fall admission, 6/1 priority date for domestic students, 4/1 for international students; for spring admission, 12/1 for domestic students. Applications are processed on a rolling basis. Application fee: $65. Electronic applications accepted. *Expenses:* Tuition, state resident: full-time $12,360; part-time $687 per credit hour. Tuition, nonresident: full-time $25,680; part-time $1058 per credit hour. *International tuition:* $29,550 full-time. *Required fees:* $1666; $833 per course. $416.50 per semester. Tuition and fees vary according to course load and degree level. *Financial support:* In 2011–12, 22 students received support, including 2 fellowships, 6 research assistantships, 11 teaching assistantships; career-related internships or fieldwork, Federal Work-Study, scholarships/grants, and tuition waivers (full and partial) also available. Support available to part-time students. Financial award application deadline: 2/15. *Faculty research:* Behavior development, ecology, endocrinology, fisheries, invertebrates. *Unit head:* Dr. Larry Harris, Chairperson, 603-862-3897. *Application contact:* Diane Lavalliere, Administrative Assistant, 603-862-2100, E-mail: zoology.dept@unh.edu. Web site: http://zoology.unh.edu/.

University of North Dakota, Graduate School, College of Arts and Sciences, Department of Biology, Grand Forks, ND 58202. Offers botany (MS, PhD); ecology (MS,

Zoology

PhD); entomology (MS, PhD); environmental biology (MS, PhD); fisheries/wildlife (MS, PhD); genetics (MS, PhD); zoology (MS, PhD). Terminal master's awarded for partial completion of doctoral program. *Degree requirements:* For master's, thesis, final exam; for doctorate, comprehensive exam, thesis/dissertation, final exam. *Entrance requirements:* For master's, GRE General Test, GRE Subject Test, minimum GPA of 3.0; for doctorate, GRE General Test, GRE Subject Test, minimum GPA of 3.5. Additional exam requirements/recommendations for international students: Required—TOEFL (minimum score 550 paper-based; 213 computer-based; 79 iBT), IELTS (minimum score 6.5). Electronic applications accepted. *Faculty research:* Population biology, wildlife ecology, RNA processing, hormonal control of behavior.

University of Oklahoma, College of Arts and Sciences, Department of Zoology, Norman, OK 73019. Offers cellular and behavioral neurobiology (PhD); ecology and evolutionary biology (PhD); zoology (M Nat Sci, MS, PhD), including natural science (M Nat Sci), zoology (MS, PhD). Part-time programs available. *Faculty:* 42 full-time (11 women), 1 part-time/adjunct (0 women). *Students:* 32 full-time (14 women), 22 part-time (14 women); includes 3 minority (2 Asian, non-Hispanic/Latino; 1 Hispanic/Latino), 17 international. Average age 28. 34 applicants, 41% accepted, 12 enrolled. In 2011, 8 master's, 6 doctorates awarded. Terminal master's awarded for partial completion of doctoral program. *Degree requirements:* For master's, thesis defense; for doctorate, dissertation defense, general exam. *Entrance requirements:* For master's and doctorate, GRE General Test, GRE Subject Test, 3 letters of recommendation. Additional exam requirements/recommendations for international students: Required—TOEFL (minimum score 550 paper-based; 79 iBT). *Application deadline:* For fall admission, 12/15 for domestic and international students. Applications are processed on a rolling basis. Application fee: $40 ($90 for international students). *Expenses:* Tuition, state resident: full-time $4087; part-time $170.30 per credit hour. Tuition, nonresident: full-time $14,875; part-time $619.80 per credit hour. *Required fees:* $2659; $100.25 per credit hour. Tuition and fees vary according to course load and degree level. *Financial support:* In 2011–12, 54 students received support, including 6 fellowships with full tuition reimbursements available (averaging $4,667 per year), 11 research assistantships with partial tuition reimbursements available (averaging $16,358 per year), 31 teaching assistantships with partial tuition reimbursements available (averaging $15,069 per year); institutionally sponsored loans, scholarships/grants, health care benefits, and unspecified assistantships also available. Financial award applicants required to submit FAFSA. *Faculty research:* Cell signaling, ecology and evolution biology, neurobiology, animal behavior, development. *Total annual research expenditures:* $1.4 million. *Unit head:* Bill Matthews, Chair, 405-325-4821, Fax: 405-325-6202, E-mail: wmatthews@ou.edu. *Application contact:* Dr. Rosemary Knapp, Associate Professor and Director of Graduate Studies, 405-325-4389, Fax: 405-325-6202, E-mail: rknapp@ou.edu. Web site: http://zoology.ou.edu.

The University of Western Ontario, Faculty of Graduate Studies, Biosciences Division, Department of Zoology, London, ON N6A 5B8, Canada. Offers M Sc, PhD. *Degree requirements:* For master's, thesis; for doctorate, thesis/dissertation.

University of Wisconsin–Madison, Graduate School, College of Letters and Science, Department of Zoology, Madison, WI 53706-1380. Offers MA, MS, PhD. Part-time programs available. *Degree requirements:* For master's, thesis; for doctorate, one foreign language, thesis/dissertation. *Entrance requirements:* For master's and doctorate, GRE General Test. Additional exam requirements/recommendations for international students: Required—TOEFL. Electronic applications accepted. *Expenses:* Tuition, state resident: full-time $10,296; part-time $643.51 per credit. Tuition, nonresident: full-time $24,054; part-time $1503.40 per credit. *Required fees:* $70.06 per credit. Tuition and fees vary according to course load, campus/location, program and reciprocity agreements. *Faculty research:* Developmental biology, ecology, neurobiology, aquatic ecology, animal behavior.

University of Wisconsin–Oshkosh, Graduate Studies, College of Letters and Science, Department of Biology and Microbiology, Oshkosh, WI 54901. Offers biology (MS), including botany, microbiology, zoology. *Degree requirements:* For master's,

comprehensive exam, thesis. *Entrance requirements:* For master's, GRE General Test, minimum GPA of 3.0, BS in biology. Additional exam requirements/recommendations for international students: Required—TOEFL (minimum score 550 paper-based; 213 computer-based; 79 iBT). Electronic applications accepted.

University of Wyoming, College of Arts and Sciences, Department of Zoology and Physiology, Laramie, WY 82070. Offers MS, PhD. Part-time programs available. *Degree requirements:* For master's, comprehensive exam (for some programs), thesis; for doctorate, comprehensive exam (for some programs), thesis/dissertation. *Entrance requirements:* For master's and doctorate, GRE General Test, minimum GPA of 3.0. Additional exam requirements/recommendations for international students: Required—TOEFL. Electronic applications accepted. *Faculty research:* Cell biology, ecology/wildlife, organismal physiology, zoology.

Washington State University, Graduate School, College of Sciences, School of Biological Sciences, Department of Zoology, Pullman, WA 99164. Offers MS, PhD. *Faculty:* 33. *Students:* 20 full-time (10 women), 1 international. Average age 30. 29 applicants, 24% accepted, 7 enrolled. In 2011, 2 master's, 4 doctorates awarded. *Degree requirements:* For master's, comprehensive exam (for some programs), thesis (for some programs), oral exam; for doctorate, comprehensive exam, thesis/dissertation, oral exam, written exam. *Entrance requirements:* For master's and doctorate, GRE General Test, GRE Subject Test, three letters of recommendation, official transcripts from each university-level school attended, minimum GPA of 3.0. Additional exam requirements/recommendations for international students: Required—TOEFL, IELTS. *Application deadline:* For fall admission, 1/10 priority date for domestic students, 1/10 for international students; for spring admission, 7/1 for domestic and international students. Applications are processed on a rolling basis. Application fee: $75. *Financial support:* In 2011–12, 4 fellowships (averaging $4,500 per year), 3 research assistantships with full and partial tuition reimbursements (averaging $13,917 per year), 21 teaching assistantships with full and partial tuition reimbursements (averaging $13,056 per year) were awarded; Federal Work-Study, institutionally sponsored loans, and tuition waivers (partial) also available. Financial award application deadline: 4/1; financial award applicants required to submit FAFSA. *Unit head:* Dr. Gary H. Thorgaard, Director, 509-335-7438, Fax: 509-335-3184, E-mail: thorglab@wsu.edu. *Application contact:* Graduate School Admissions, 800-GRADWSU, Fax: 509-335-1949, E-mail: gradsch@wsu.edu.

Western Illinois University, School of Graduate Studies, College of Arts and Sciences, Department of Biological Sciences, Macomb, IL 61455-1390. Offers biological sciences (MS); environmental geographic information systems (Certificate); zoo and aquarium studies (Certificate). Part-time programs available. *Students:* 55 full-time (38 women), 30 part-time (25 women); includes 6 minority (4 Black or African American, non-Hispanic/Latino; 1 Hispanic/Latino; 1 Two or more races, non-Hispanic/Latino), 4 international. Average age 26. 50 applicants, 60% accepted. In 2011, 30 master's, 19 other advanced degrees awarded. *Degree requirements:* For master's, thesis or alternative. *Entrance requirements:* Additional exam requirements/recommendations for international students: Required—TOEFL (minimum score 550 paper-based; 213 computer-based; 80 iBT); Recommended—IELTS. *Application deadline:* Applications are processed on a rolling basis. Application fee: $30. Electronic applications accepted. *Expenses:* Tuition, state resident: part-time $281.16 per credit hour. Tuition, nonresident: part-time $562.32 per credit hour. Part-time tuition and fees vary according to campus/location and reciprocity agreements. *Financial support:* In 2011–12, 28 students received support, including 9 research assistantships with full tuition reimbursements available (averaging $7,360 per year), 19 teaching assistantships with full tuition reimbursements available (averaging $8,480 per year). Financial award applicants required to submit FAFSA. *Unit head:* Dr. Michael Romano, Chairperson, 309-298-1546. *Application contact:* Nancy Parsons, Interim Associate Provost and Director of Graduate Studies, 309-298-1806, Fax: 309-298-2345, E-mail: grad-office@wiu.edu. Web site: http://wiu.edu/biology.

ACADEMIC AND PROFESSIONAL PROGRAMS IN HEALTH-RELATED PROFESSIONS

Section 20
Allied Health

This section contains a directory of institutions offering graduate work in allied health, followed by in-depth entries submitted by institutions that chose to prepare detailed program descriptions. Additional information about programs listed in the directory but not augmented by an in-depth entry may be obtained by writing directly to the dean of a graduate school or chair of a department at the address given in the directory.

For programs offering related work, see also in this book *Anatomy, Biophysics, Dentistry and Dental Sciences, Health Services, Microbiological Sciences, Pathology and Pathobiology, Physiology,* and *Public Health.* In the other guides in this series:

Graduate Programs in the Humanities, Arts & Social Sciences
See *Art and Art History (Art Therapy), Family and Consumer Sciences (Gerontology), Performing Arts (Therapies),* and *Psychology and Counseling*

Graduate Programs in the Physical Sciences, Mathematics, Agricultural Sciences, the Environment & Natural Resources
See *Physics (Acoustics)*

Graduate Programs in Engineering & Applied Sciences
See *Agricultural Engineering and Bioengineering (Bioengineering), Biomedical Engineering and Biotechnology,* and *Energy and Power Engineering (Nuclear Engineering)*

Graduate Programs in Business, Education, Information Studies, Law & Social Work
See *Administration, Instruction, and Theory (Educational Psychology); Special Focus (Education of the Multiply Handicapped); Social Work;* and *Subject Areas (Counselor Education)*

CONTENTS

Allied Health—General

Alabama State University, College of Health Sciences, Montgomery, AL 36101-0271. Offers DPT. *Faculty:* 7 full-time (5 women). *Students:* 115 full-time (82 women), 16 part-time (13 women); includes 83 minority (80 Black or African American, non-Hispanic/Latino; 2 Asian, non-Hispanic/Latino; 1 Hispanic/Latino), 2 international. Average age 28. 166 applicants, 25% accepted, 22 enrolled. In 2011, 1 doctorate awarded. *Entrance requirements:* Additional exam requirements/recommendations for international students: Required—TOEFL (minimum score 500 paper-based; 173 computer-based). *Application deadline:* For fall admission, 7/15 for domestic students; for spring admission, 12/15 for domestic students. Applications are processed on a rolling basis. Application fee: $10. *Financial support:* In 2011–12, 4 research assistantships (averaging $9,450 per year) were awarded. *Unit head:* Dr. Denise Chapman, Dean, 334-229-4707, Fax: 334-229-4964, E-mail: dchapman@alasu.edu. *Application contact:* Dr. Doris Screws, Dean of Graduate Studies, 334-229-4274, Fax: 334-229-4928, E-mail: dscrews@alasu.edu. Web site: http://www.alasu.edu/academics/colleges—departments/health-sciences/index.aspx.

American College of Healthcare Sciences, Graduate Programs, Portland, OR 97239-3719. Offers aromatherapy (Graduate Certificate); complementary alternative medicine (MS, Graduate Certificate); herbal medicine (Graduate Certificate); nutrition (Graduate Certificate). Part-time and evening/weekend programs available. Postbaccalaureate distance learning degree programs offered (no on-campus study). *Degree requirements:* For master's, capstone project. *Entrance requirements:* For master's, interview, letters of recommendation, essay. *Application deadline:* For fall admission, 7/15 for domestic and international students; for spring admission, 11/15 for domestic and international students. Application fee: $0. *Expenses: Tuition:* Full-time $6660; part-time $370 per semester hour. *Required fees:* $2100; $117 per semester hour. *Application contact:* Tracey Abell, Acting Dean of Admissions/Director of Operations, 800-487-8839, Fax: 503-244-0727, E-mail: admissions@achs.edu.

Andrews University, School of Graduate Studies, College of Arts and Sciences, Department of Medical Laboratory Sciences, Berrien Springs, MI 49104. Offers MSMLS. *Accreditation:* APTA. *Faculty:* 4 full-time (2 women). *Students:* 8 applicants, 0% accepted, 0 enrolled. *Entrance requirements:* For master's, GRE. Additional exam requirements/recommendations for international students: Required—TOEFL (minimum score 550 paper-based). *Application deadline:* Applications are processed on a rolling basis. Application fee: $40. *Unit head:* Dr. Marcia A. Kilsby, Chair, 269-471-3336. *Application contact:* Carolyn Hurst, Supervisor of Graduate Admission, 800-253-2874, Fax: 269-471-6321, E-mail: graduate@andrews.edu.

Athabasca University, Centre for Nursing and Health Studies, Athabasca, AB T9S 3A3, Canada. Offers advanced nursing practice (MN, Advanced Diploma); generalist (MN); health studies-leadership (MHS). Part-time programs available. Postbaccalaureate distance learning degree programs offered. *Degree requirements:* For master's, comprehensive exam (for some programs). *Entrance requirements:* For master's, bachelor's degree in health-related field, 2 years professional health service experience (MHS), bachelor's degree in nursing, 2 years nursing experience (MN), minimum GPA of 3.0 in final 30 credits; for Advanced Diploma, RN license, 2 years health care experience. Electronic applications accepted. *Expenses:* Contact institution.

A.T. Still University of Health Sciences, Arizona School of Health Sciences, Mesa, AZ 85206. Offers advanced occupational therapy (MS); advanced physician assistant (MS); athletic training (MS); audiology (Au D); health sciences (DHSc); human movement (MS); occupational therapy (MS); physical therapy (DPT); physician assistant (MS); transitional audiology (Au D); transitional physical therapy (DPT). *Accreditation:* AOTA (one or more programs are accredited); ASHA. Part-time and evening/weekend programs available. Postbaccalaureate distance learning degree programs offered (minimal on-campus study). *Faculty:* 44 full-time (27 women), 235 part-time/adjunct (141 women). *Students:* 410 full-time (275 women), 1,010 part-time (675 women); includes 320 minority (73 Black or African American, non-Hispanic/Latino; 18 American Indian or Alaska Native, non-Hispanic/Latino; 158 Asian, non-Hispanic/Latino; 62 Hispanic/Latino; 9 Two or more races, non-Hispanic/Latino), 6 international. Average age 35. 4,395 applicants, 18% accepted, 694 enrolled. In 2011, 221 master's, 406 doctorates awarded. *Median time to degree:* Of those who began their doctoral program in fall 2003, 98% received their degree in 8 years or less. *Degree requirements:* For master's, thesis (for some programs); for doctorate, thesis/dissertation (for some programs). *Entrance requirements:* For master's, GRE General Test; for doctorate, GRE, Evaluation of Practicing Audiologists Capabilities (Au D), Physical Therapist Evaluation Tool (DPT), current state licensure, master's degree or equivalent (Au D). Additional exam requirements/recommendations for international students: Required—TOEFL (minimum score 550 paper-based; 213 computer-based; 80 iBT). *Application deadline:* For fall admission, 8/1 priority date for domestic students, 8/1 for international students. Applications are processed on a rolling basis. Application fee: $60. *Expenses:* Contact institution. *Financial support:* In 2011–12, 272 students received support, including 14 fellowships (averaging $16,000 per year); Federal Work-Study and scholarships/grants also available. Financial award application deadline: 5/1; financial award applicants required to submit FAFSA. *Faculty research:* Physical therapy: metabolism during exercise and activity; neuromuscular function after injury, prevention of lifestyle diseases, prevention and treatment of overuse injuries; athletic training: pediatric sport-related concussion, adolescent athlete health-related quality of life; occupational therapy: spirituality and health disparities, geriatric and pediatric well-being, pain management for participation. *Total annual research expenditures:* $75,682. *Unit head:* Dr. Randy Danielsen, Dean, 480-219-6000, Fax: 480-219-6110, E-mail: rdanielsen@atsu.edu. *Application contact:* Donna Sparks, Associate Director, Admissions Processing, 660-626-2117, Fax: 660-626-2969, E-mail: admissions@atsu.edu. Web site: http://www.atsu.edu/ashs.

Baylor University, Graduate School, Military Programs, Waco, TX 76798. Offers MHA, MPT, MS, D Sc, D Sc PA, DPT. *Accreditation:* APTA (one or more programs are accredited). *Students:* 213 full-time (91 women); includes 24 minority (8 Black or African American, non-Hispanic/Latino; 1 American Indian or Alaska Native, non-Hispanic/Latino; 2 Asian, non-Hispanic/Latino; 8 Hispanic/Latino; 1 Native Hawaiian or other Pacific Islander, non-Hispanic/Latino; 4 Two or more races, non-Hispanic/Latino). In 2011, 45 master's, 44 doctorates awarded. *Entrance requirements:* For master's, GRE General Test. *Application deadline:* Applications are processed on a rolling basis. Application fee: $25. *Expenses:* Contact institution. *Unit head:* Col. Darwin L. Fretwell, Dean, 210-221-8715, Fax: 210-221-7306. *Application contact:* Suzanne Keener, Administrative Assistant, 254-710-3588, Fax: 254-710-3870.

Belmont University, College of Health Sciences, Nashville, TN 37212-3757. Offers MSN, MSOT, DPT, OTD. Part-time programs available. Postbaccalaureate distance learning degree programs offered (minimal on-campus study). *Faculty:* 19 full-time (14 women), 28 part-time/adjunct (21 women). *Students:* 254 full-time (220 women), 46 part-time (43 women); includes 27 minority (15 Black or African American, non-Hispanic/Latino; 1 American Indian or Alaska Native, non-Hispanic/Latino; 4 Asian, non-Hispanic/Latino; 6 Hispanic/Latino; 1 Two or more races, non-Hispanic/Latino), 1 international. Average age 26. 874 applicants, 22% accepted, 131 enrolled. In 2011, 56 master's, 58 doctorates awarded. *Degree requirements:* For master's, comprehensive exam, thesis; for doctorate, comprehensive exam. *Entrance requirements:* For master's, GRE, BSN, minimum GPA of 3.0. Additional exam requirements/recommendations for international students: Required—TOEFL (minimum score 550 paper-based; 213 computer-based). *Application deadline:* Applications are processed on a rolling basis. Application fee: $50. Electronic applications accepted. *Expenses:* Contact institution. *Financial support:* In 2011–12, 204 students received support, including teaching assistantships with full tuition reimbursements available (averaging $7,020 per year); career-related internships or fieldwork, scholarships/grants, and traineeships also available. Financial award application deadline: 3/1; financial award applicants required to submit FAFSA. *Unit head:* Dean, 615-460-6916, Fax: 615-460-6750. *Application contact:* David Mee, Dean of Enrollment Services, 615-460-6785, Fax: 615-460-5434, E-mail: david.mee@belmont.edu. Web site: http://www.belmont.edu/.

Bennington College, Graduate Programs, Postbaccalaureate Premedical Program, Bennington, VT 05201. Offers allied and health sciences (Certificate). *Faculty:* 9 full-time (3 women), 1 (woman) part-time/adjunct. *Students:* 11 full-time (6 women); includes 1 minority (Two or more races, non-Hispanic/Latino). Average age 25. 54 applicants, 61% accepted, 11 enrolled. In 2011, 7 Certificates awarded. *Application deadline:* For fall admission, 2/15 priority date for domestic students. Applications are processed on a rolling basis. Application fee: $60. *Expenses:* Contact institution. *Financial support:* Scholarships/grants available. Financial award application deadline: 4/1; financial award applicants required to submit FAFSA. *Faculty research:* Cellular functions of Hsp90, foundations of quantum mechanics, history and philosophy of physics, cytosolic quality control, forest ecology, plate tectonics of rift systems, amphibian evolutionary physiology, photochemistry of gold complexes. *Unit head:* Dr. Janet Foley, Chief Health Professions Adviser, 802-440-4463, Fax: 802-440-4461, E-mail: jfoley@bennington.edu. *Application contact:* Ferrilyn Sourdiffe, Graduate Admissions Counselor, 802-440-4885, Fax: 802-440-4320, E-mail: fsourdiffe@bennington.edu. Web site: http://www.bennington.edu/Academics/GraduateCertificatePrograms/Postbac.aspx.

Boston University, College of Health and Rehabilitation Sciences: Sargent College, Boston, MA 02215. Offers MS, MSOT, D Sc, DPT, OTD, PhD, CAGS. *Accreditation:* APTA (one or more programs are accredited). Postbaccalaureate distance learning degree programs offered (minimal on-campus study). *Faculty:* 54 full-time (42 women), 44 part-time/adjunct (28 women). *Students:* 408 full-time (354 women), 77 part-time (52 women); includes 61 minority (5 Black or African American, non-Hispanic/Latino; 2 American Indian or Alaska Native, non-Hispanic/Latino; 33 Asian, non-Hispanic/Latino; 12 Hispanic/Latino; 2 Native Hawaiian or other Pacific Islander, non-Hispanic/Latino; 7 Two or more races, non-Hispanic/Latino), 26 international. Average age 27. 763 applicants, 42% accepted, 110 enrolled. In 2011, 116 master's, 102 doctorates awarded. Terminal master's awarded for partial completion of doctoral program. *Degree requirements:* For master's, comprehensive exam (for some programs), thesis optional; for doctorate, variable foreign language requirement, comprehensive exam (for some programs), thesis/dissertation (for some programs). *Entrance requirements:* For master's, doctorate, and CAGS, GRE General Test. Additional exam requirements/recommendations for international students: Required—TOEFL (minimum score 550 paper-based; 84 computer-based). *Application deadline:* For fall admission, 2/1 priority date for domestic students, 2/1 for international students. Applications are processed on a rolling basis. Application fee: $70. Electronic applications accepted. *Expenses: Tuition:* Full-time $40,848; part-time $1276 per credit hour. *Required fees:* $572; $286 per semester. *Financial support:* In 2011–12, 300 students received support, including 119 fellowships with full and partial tuition reimbursements available (averaging $15,000 per year), 9 research assistantships with partial tuition reimbursements available (averaging $18,000 per year), 15 teaching assistantships with partial tuition reimbursements available (averaging $6,000 per year); career-related internships or fieldwork, Federal Work-Study, institutionally sponsored loans, scholarships/grants, and health care benefits also available. Support available to part-time students. Financial award application deadline: 4/15; financial award applicants required to submit FAFSA. *Faculty research:* Outcome measurement, gerontology, neuroanatomy, aphasia, autism, Parkinson's Disease, psychiatric rehabilitation, obesity prevention, speech production and imaging. *Total annual research expenditures:* $10.4 million. *Unit head:* Dr. Gloria S. Waters, Dean, 617-353-2704, Fax: 617-353-7500, E-mail: gwaters@bu.edu. *Application contact:* Sharon Sankey, Director, Student Services, 617-353-2713, Fax: 617-353-7500, E-mail: ssankey@bu.edu. Web site: http://www.bu.edu/sargent/.

Brock University, Faculty of Graduate Studies, Faculty of Applied Health Sciences, St. Catharines, ON L2S 3A1, Canada. Offers M Sc, MA, PhD. *Degree requirements:* For master's, thesis. *Entrance requirements:* For master's, honors degree, BA and/or B Sc. Additional exam requirements/recommendations for international students: Required—TOEFL (minimum score 550 paper-based; 213 computer-based; 80 iBT), IELTS (minimum score 6.5), TWE (minimum score 4). Electronic applications accepted. *Faculty research:* Health and physical activity, aging and health, health advocacy, exercise psychology, community development.

Canisius College, Graduate Division, Office of Professional Studies, Buffalo, NY 14208-1098. Offers applied nutrition (MS); community and school health (MS). Postbaccalaureate distance learning degree programs offered (no on-campus study). *Faculty:* 9 part-time/adjunct (7 women). *Students:* 17 full-time (15 women), 6 part-time (5 women); includes 3 minority (1 Black or African American, non-Hispanic/Latino; 1 Asian, non-Hispanic/Latino; 1 Two or more races, non-Hispanic/Latino), 2 international. Average age 32. 35 applicants, 74% accepted, 20 enrolled. *Entrance requirements:* Additional exam requirements/recommendations for international students: Required—TOEFL. *Application deadline:* Applications are processed on a rolling basis. Application fee: $25. Electronic applications accepted. *Financial support:* Career-related internships or fieldwork, Federal Work-Study, scholarships/grants, and unspecified assistantships available. Support available to part-time students. Financial award application deadline: 4/30; financial award applicants required to submit FAFSA. *Faculty research:* Nutrition, community and school health. *Unit head:* Dr. Khalid Bibi, Executive Director, 716-888-8296. *Application contact:* Donna Shaffner, Dean of Admissions, 716-888-2200, Fax: 716-888-3230, E-mail: admissions@canisius.edu. Web site: http://www.canisius.edu/professional-studies/.

Cleveland State University, College of Graduate Studies, College of Sciences and Health Professions, School of Health Sciences, Program in Health Sciences, Cleveland, OH 44115. Offers health sciences (MS); online health sciences (MS). Part-time and evening/weekend programs available. Postbaccalaureate distance learning degree programs offered (no on-campus study). *Faculty:* 20 full-time (14 women), 16 part-time/adjunct (11 women). *Students:* 75 full-time (51 women), 36 part-time (31 women);

includes 23 minority (13 Black or African American, non-Hispanic/Latino; 5 Asian, non-Hispanic/Latino; 3 Hispanic/Latino; 2 Two or more races, non-Hispanic/Latino), 4 international. Average age 30. 85 applicants, 73% accepted, 50 enrolled. In 2011, 64 master's awarded. *Degree requirements:* For master's, thesis. *Application deadline:* For fall admission, 5/15 for international students; for winter admission, 4/1 for international students; for spring admission, 11/1 for international students. *Expenses:* Tuition, state resident: full-time $6416; part-time $494 per credit hour. Tuition, nonresident: full-time $12,074; part-time $929 per credit hour. *Financial support:* Research assistantships available. *Faculty research:* Assisted technologies, biomechanics, clinical administration, cultural health, gerontology. *Unit head:* Dr. Myrita Sipp Wilhite, Director, 216-687-3808, E-mail: m.wilhite@csuohio.edu. *Application contact:* Karen Armstrong, Secretary, 216-687-3567, Fax: 216-687-9316, E-mail: k.bradley@csuohio.edu. Web site: http://www.csuohio.edu/sciences/dept/healthsciences/graduate/index.html.

Creighton University, School of Pharmacy and Health Professions, Omaha, NE 68178-0001. Offers MS, DPT, OTD, Pharm D, Pharm D/MS. *Accreditation:* ACPE (one or more programs are accredited). Postbaccalaureate distance learning degree programs offered (minimal on-campus study). *Entrance requirements:* For doctorate, PCAT (for Pharm D). Electronic applications accepted. *Expenses:* Contact institution. *Faculty research:* Patient safety in health services research, health information technology and health services research, interdisciplinary educational research in the health professions, outcomes research in the health professions, cross-cultural care in the health professions.

Dominican College, Division of Allied Health, Orangeburg, NY 10962-1210. Offers MS, DPT. Part-time and evening/weekend programs available. Postbaccalaureate distance learning degree programs offered (minimal on-campus study).

Drexel University, College of Nursing and Health Professions, Philadelphia, PA 19104-2875. Offers MA, MFT, MHS, MS, MSN, DPT, Dr NP, PPDPT, PhD, Certificate, PMC. *Accreditation:* NLN. Part-time and evening/weekend programs available. Terminal master's awarded for partial completion of doctoral program. *Degree requirements:* For master's, comprehensive exam, thesis (for some programs); for doctorate, thesis/dissertation, qualifying exam. *Entrance requirements:* For doctorate, GRE General Test. Electronic applications accepted.

Duquesne University, John G. Rangos, Sr. School of Health Sciences, Pittsburgh, PA 15282-0001. Offers health management systems (MHMS); occupational therapy (MS); physical therapy (DPT); physician assistant studies (MPAS); rehabilitation science (MS, PhD); speech-language pathology (MS); MBA/MHMS. *Accreditation:* AOTA (one or more programs are accredited); APTA (one or more programs are accredited); ASHA. *Faculty:* 34 full-time (23 women), 20 part-time/adjunct (11 women). *Students:* 227 full-time (180 women), 12 part-time (7 women); includes 8 minority (4 Black or African American, non-Hispanic/Latino; 1 Asian, non-Hispanic/Latino; 1 Hispanic/Latino; 1 Native Hawaiian or other Pacific Islander, non-Hispanic/Latino; 1 Two or more races, non-Hispanic/Latino), 3 international. Average age 24. 537 applicants, 12% accepted, 17 enrolled. In 2011, 43 master's, 31 doctorates awarded. *Degree requirements:* For doctorate, comprehensive exam (for some programs), thesis/dissertation (for some programs). *Entrance requirements:* For master's, GRE General Test (speech-language pathology), 3 letters of recommendation; minimum GPA of 2.75 (health management systems), 3.0 (speech-language pathology and health sciences); for doctorate, GRE General Test (for physical therapy and rehabilitation science), 3 letters of recommendation, minimum GPA of 3.0, personal interview. Additional exam requirements/recommendations for international students: Required—TOEFL (minimum score 550 paper-based; 233 computer-based; 90 iBT). *Application deadline:* Applications are processed on a rolling basis. Electronic applications accepted. *Expenses:* Contact institution. *Financial support:* Federal Work-Study available. Financial award applicants required to submit FAFSA. *Faculty research:* Neuronal processing, electrical stimulation on peripheral neuropathy, CNS stimulatory and inhibitory signals, behavioral genetic methodologies to development disorders of speech, neurogenic communication disorders. *Total annual research expenditures:* $83,650. *Unit head:* Dr. Gregory H. Frazer, Dean, 412-396-5303, Fax: 412-396-5554, E-mail: frazer@duq.edu. *Application contact:* Christopher R. Hilf, Recruiter/Academic Advisor, 412-396-5653, Fax: 412-396-5554, E-mail: hilfc@duq.edu. Web site: http://www.duq.edu/healthsciences/health.html.

East Carolina University, Graduate School, School of Allied Health Sciences, Greenville, NC 27858-4353. Offers MS, MSOT, DPT, PhD, Certificate, Au D/PhD. Part-time and evening/weekend programs available. Postbaccalaureate distance learning degree programs offered (no on-campus study). *Degree requirements:* For master's, comprehensive exam. *Entrance requirements:* For master's, GRE General Test. Additional exam requirements/recommendations for international students: Required—TOEFL. *Application fee:* $50. *Expenses:* Tuition, state resident: full-time $3557; part-time $444.63 per semester hour. Tuition, nonresident: full-time $14,351; part-time $1793.88 per semester hour. *Required fees:* $2016; $252 per semester hour. Part-time tuition and fees vary according to course load, campus/location and program. *Financial support:* Research assistantships with partial tuition reimbursements, teaching assistantships with partial tuition reimbursements, career-related internships or fieldwork, Federal Work-Study, and scholarships/grants available. Support available to part-time students. Financial award application deadline: 6/1; financial award applicants required to submit FAFSA. *Faculty research:* Hearing, stuttering, therapeutic activities, ACL injury. *Unit head:* Dr. Stephen Thomas, Dean, 252-744-6010, E-mail: thomass@ecu.edu. *Application contact:* Dean of Graduate School, 252-328-6012, Fax: 252-328-6071, E-mail: gradschool@ecu.edu.

Eastern Kentucky University, The Graduate School, College of Health Sciences, Richmond, KY 40475-3102. Offers MPH, MS, MSN. Part-time programs available. *Entrance requirements:* For master's, GRE General Test, minimum GPA of 2.75.

East Tennessee State University, School of Graduate Studies, College of Clinical and Rehabilitative Health Sciences, Department of Allied Health Science, Johnson City, TN 37614. Offers allied health (MSAH); clinical nutrition (MS). Part-time programs available. Postbaccalaureate distance learning degree programs offered (no on-campus study). *Faculty:* 14 full-time (10 women). *Students:* 23 full-time (all women), 30 part-time (27 women); includes 4 minority (3 Black or African American, non-Hispanic/Latino; 1 Two or more races, non-Hispanic/Latino), 1 international. Average age 33. 8 applicants, 25% accepted, 2 enrolled. In 2011, 17 master's awarded. *Degree requirements:* For master's, comprehensive exam, thesis optional, advanced practice seminar (for MSAH non-thesis option); internship (for clinical nutrition). *Entrance requirements:* For master's, GRE General Test, professional license in allied health discipline, minimum GPA of 2.75 (MSAH); bachelor's degree from undergraduate didactic program in dietetics with minimum GPA of 3.0 in DPD coursework (clinical nutrition). Additional exam requirements/recommendations for international students: Required—TOEFL (minimum score 550 paper-based; 213 computer-based; 79 iBT). *Application deadline:* For fall admission, 2/15 for domestic and international students; for spring admission, 11/1 for domestic students, 9/30 for international students. Application fee: $35 ($45 for international students). Electronic applications accepted. *Expenses:* Tuition, state resident: full-time $7312; part-time $350 per credit hour. Tuition, nonresident: full-time $18,490; part-time $621 per credit hour. *Required fees:* $63 per credit hour. Tuition and fees vary according to course load and program. *Financial support:* In 2011–12, 17

students received support, including 4 research assistantships with full tuition reimbursements available (averaging $6,000 per year), 1 teaching assistantship with full tuition reimbursement available (averaging $6,000 per year); career-related internships or fieldwork, institutionally sponsored loans, scholarships/grants, and unspecified assistantships also available. Financial award application deadline: 7/1; financial award applicants required to submit FAFSA. *Faculty research:* Streptococcus mutans in saliva, oral cavity microbial screening, patient care, occupational stress, rural and urban health administrators. *Unit head:* Dr. Charles Faust, Chair, 423-439-7888, Fax: 423-547-4900, E-mail: faust@etsu.edu. *Application contact:* Mary Duncan, Graduate Specialist, 423-439-4302, Fax: 423-439-5624, E-mail: duncanm@etsu.edu. Web site: http://www.etsu.edu/crhs/alliedhealth/msah/.

East Tennessee State University, School of Graduate Studies, College of Public Health, Johnson City, TN 37614. Offers MPH, MSEH, DPH, PhD, Postbaccalaureate Certificate. Part-time and evening/weekend programs available. *Faculty:* 28 full-time (5 women), 1 (woman) part-time/adjunct. *Students:* 65 full-time (44 women), 48 part-time (30 women); includes 24 minority (15 Black or African American, non-Hispanic/Latino; 6 Asian, non-Hispanic/Latino; 2 Hispanic/Latino; 1 Two or more races, non-Hispanic/Latino), 16 international. Average age 32. In 2011, 25 master's, 1 doctorate, 7 other advanced degrees awarded. *Expenses:* Tuition, state resident: full-time $7312; part-time $350 per credit hour. Tuition, nonresident: full-time $18,490; part-time $621 per credit hour. *Required fees:* $63 per credit hour. Tuition and fees vary according to course load and program. *Financial support:* In 2011–12, 52 students received support, including 33 research assistantships with full tuition reimbursements available (averaging $9,000 per year), 3 teaching assistantships with full tuition reimbursements available (averaging $10,000 per year). Financial award application deadline: 7/1; financial award applicants required to submit FAFSA. *Unit head:* Dr. Randy Wykoff, Dean, 423-439-4243, Fax: 423-439-5238, E-mail: wykoff@etsu.edu. *Application contact:* Graduate Specialist, 423-439-4221, Fax: 423-439-5624, E-mail: gradsch@etsu.edu.

Emory University, School of Medicine, Programs in Allied Health Professions, Atlanta, GA 30322-1100. Offers MM Sc, DPT. *Faculty:* 24 full-time (17 women), 26 part-time/adjunct (17 women). *Students:* 418 full-time (274 women); includes 99 minority (41 Black or African American, non-Hispanic/Latino; 32 Asian, non-Hispanic/Latino; 16 Hispanic/Latino; 1 Native Hawaiian or other Pacific Islander, non-Hispanic/Latino; 9 Two or more races, non-Hispanic/Latino), 3 international. Average age 28. 1,765 applicants, 14% accepted, 162 enrolled. In 2011, 86 master's, 41 doctorates awarded. *Entrance requirements:* For master's, GRE or MCAT; for doctorate, GRE. *Application deadline:* Applications are processed on a rolling basis. Electronic applications accepted. *Expenses:* Contact institution. *Financial support:* In 2011–12, 293 students received support. Institutionally sponsored loans and scholarships/grants available. Financial award application deadline: 3/1; financial award applicants required to submit FAFSA. *Unit head:* Dr. John William Eley, Executive Associate Dean, Office of Medical Education and Student Affairs, 404-727-5655, Fax: 404-727-0045, E-mail: jeley@emory.edu. *Application contact:* Mary Kaye Garcia, Associate Director of Registration and Student Affairs, 404-712-9921, Fax: 404-727-0045, E-mail: mkgarci@emory.edu.

Ferris State University, College of Allied Health Sciences, Big Rapids, MI 49307. Offers MSN. Part-time and evening/weekend programs available. Postbaccalaureate distance learning degree programs offered (no on-campus study). *Faculty:* 5 full-time (all women), 1 (woman) part-time/adjunct. *Students:* 7 full-time (all women), 80 part-time (70 women); includes 3 minority (1 Black or African American, non-Hispanic/Latino; 2 Two or more races, non-Hispanic/Latino). Average age 42. 34 applicants, 85% accepted, 24 enrolled. In 2011, 16 master's awarded. *Degree requirements:* For master's, comprehensive exam, practicum, scholarly project. *Entrance requirements:* For master's, BS in nursing or bachelor's degree in related field with registered nurse license; minimum GPA of 3.0; writing sample; 3 professional references. Additional exam requirements/recommendations for international students: Required—TOEFL (minimum score 500 paper-based; 173 computer-based; 61 iBT). *Application deadline:* For fall admission, 4/15 priority date for domestic students; for spring admission, 10/5 for domestic students. Applications are processed on a rolling basis. Application fee: $30. Electronic applications accepted. Application fee is waived when completed online. *Financial support:* In 2011–12, 3 students received support. Career-related internships or fieldwork and scholarships/grants available. Financial award application deadline: 4/15; financial award applicants required to submit FAFSA. *Unit head:* Dr. Marrietta Bell-Scriber, Interim MSN Program Coordinator, 231-591-2288, Fax: 231-591-3788, E-mail: bellscm@ferris.edu. *Application contact:* Debby Buck, Off-Campus Student Support, 231-591-2094, Fax: 231-591-3788, E-mail: buckd@ferris.edu. Web site: http://www.ferris.edu/htmls/colleges/alliedhe/.

Florida Agricultural and Mechanical University, Division of Graduate Studies, Research, and Continuing Education, School of Allied Health Sciences, Tallahassee, FL 32307-3200. Offers health administration (MS); occupational therapy (MOT); physical therapy (MPT). *Degree requirements:* For master's, thesis (for some programs). *Entrance requirements:* For master's, GRE General Test or GMAT, minimum GPA of 3.0. Additional exam requirements/recommendations for international students: Required—TOEFL (minimum score 550 paper-based).

Florida Gulf Coast University, College of Health Professions, Fort Myers, FL 33965-6565. Offers MS, MSN, DPT. *Accreditation:* AOTA. Part-time and evening/weekend programs available. Postbaccalaureate distance learning degree programs offered (minimal on-campus study). *Faculty:* 45 full-time (32 women), 22 part-time/adjunct (14 women). *Students:* 110 full-time (91 women), 57 part-time (51 women); includes 40 minority (13 Black or African American, non-Hispanic/Latino; 7 Asian, non-Hispanic/Latino; 17 Hispanic/Latino; 3 Two or more races, non-Hispanic/Latino), 1 international. Average age 31. 211 applicants, 47% accepted, 83 enrolled. In 2011, 65 master's awarded. *Degree requirements:* For master's, thesis or alternative. *Entrance requirements:* For master's, GRE General Test or MAT, minimum GPA of 3.0. Additional exam requirements/recommendations for international students: Required—TOEFL (minimum score 550 paper-based; 213 computer-based). *Application deadline:* Applications are processed on a rolling basis. Application fee: $30. Electronic applications accepted. *Expenses:* Tuition, state resident: full-time $8289. Tuition, nonresident: full-time $28,895. *Required fees:* $1831. One-time fee: $30 full-time. *Financial support:* Career-related internships or fieldwork, Federal Work-Study, and institutionally sponsored loans available. *Faculty research:* Gerontology, health care policy, health administration, community-based services. *Unit head:* Dr. Mitchell Cordova, Dean, 239-590-7451, Fax: 239-590-7474. *Application contact:* Lynn O'Hare, Administrative Assistant, 239-590-7451, Fax: 239-590-7474, E-mail: lohare@fgcu.edu.

Georgia Health Sciences University, College of Graduate Studies, Program in Allied Health Sciences, Augusta, GA 30912. Offers dental hygiene (MS). Part-time programs available. Postbaccalaureate distance learning degree programs offered (no on-campus study). *Students:* 5 full-time (4 women); includes 3 minority (2 Black or African American, non-Hispanic/Latino; 1 Two or more races, non-Hispanic/Latino), 1 international. Average age 31. 4 applicants, 0% accepted. *Degree requirements:* For master's, thesis. *Entrance requirements:* For master's, GRE General Test. Additional exam requirements/recommendations for international students: Required—TOEFL (minimum score 550 paper-based; 213 computer-based; 79 iBT). *Application deadline:* For fall admission, 5/1 for domestic students, 3/1 for international students. Application fee: $50. Electronic

applications accepted. *Financial support:* Federal Work-Study, institutionally sponsored loans, tuition waivers, and unspecified assistantships available. Support available to part-time students. Financial award application deadline: 5/31; financial award applicants required to submit FAFSA. *Faculty research:* Patient- and family-centered care, public health informatics, vascular health promotion through physical activity, improving air quality for school children, movement therapies for Parkinson's Disease. *Total annual research expenditures:* $545,444. *Unit head:* Dr. Douglas Keskula, Acting Dean, 706-721-2621, Fax: 706-721-7312, E-mail: dkeskula@georgiahealth.edu. *Application contact:* Dr. Marie Collins, Acting Associate Dean for Student, Faculty and Community Affairs, 706-721-3436, Fax: 706-721-6067, E-mail: mcollins@georgiahealth.edu. Web site: http://www.mcg.edu/GradStudies/.

Georgia Southern University, Jack N. Averitt College of Graduate Studies, College of Health and Human Sciences, Statesboro, GA 30460. Offers MS, MSN, DNP, Certificate. Part-time and evening/weekend programs available. Postbaccalaureate distance learning degree programs offered (no on-campus study). *Faculty:* 56 full-time (38 women). *Students:* 67 full-time (37 women), 157 part-time (92 women); includes 44 minority (32 Black or African American, non-Hispanic/Latino; 2 Asian, non-Hispanic/Latino; 6 Hispanic/Latino; 1 Native Hawaiian or other Pacific Islander, non-Hispanic/Latino; 3 Two or more races, non-Hispanic/Latino), 4 international. Average age 31. 165 applicants, 61% accepted, 72 enrolled. In 2011, 101 master's, 11 doctorates awarded. *Degree requirements:* For master's, comprehensive exam (for some programs), thesis (for some programs), exams; for doctorate, comprehensive exam, practicum. *Entrance requirements:* For master's, GRE General Test, MAT or GMAT; for doctorate, GRE or MAT. Additional exam requirements/recommendations for international students: Required—TOEFL (minimum score 550 paper-based; 213 computer-based; 80 iBT). *Application deadline:* For fall admission, 3/1 priority date for domestic students, 3/1 for international students; for spring admission, 10/1 priority date for domestic students, 10/1 for international students. Applications are processed on a rolling basis. Application fee: $50. Electronic applications accepted. *Expenses:* Tuition, state resident: full-time $6300; part-time $263 per semester hour. Tuition, nonresident: full-time $25,174; part-time $1049 per semester hour. *Required fees:* $1872. *Financial support:* In 2011–12, 105 students received support, including 57 research assistantships with partial tuition reimbursements available (averaging $7,200 per year), teaching assistantships with partial tuition reimbursements available (averaging $7,200 per year); career-related internships or fieldwork, Federal Work-Study, scholarships/grants, traineeships, tuition waivers (partial), and unspecified assistantships also available. Support available to part-time students. Financial award application deadline: 4/15; financial award applicants required to submit FAFSA. *Unit head:* Dr. Jjean Bartels, Dean, 912-478-5322, Fax: 912-478-5349, E-mail: jbartels@georgiasouthern.edu. *Application contact:* Amanda Gilliland, Coordinator for Graduate Student Recruitment, 912-478-5384, Fax: 912-478-0740, E-mail: gradadmissions@georgiasouthern.edu. Web site: http://chhs.georgiasouthern.edu/.

Georgia State University, College of Health and Human Sciences, Atlanta, GA 30302-3083. Offers MPH, MS, MSW, DPT, PhD, Certificate. *Accreditation:* CSWE. Part-time and evening/weekend programs available. *Degree requirements:* For master's, thesis (for some programs); for doctorate, comprehensive exam, thesis/dissertation. *Entrance requirements:* For master's, GRE (some programs accept MAT, GMAT); for doctorate, GRE General Test, RN license, interview. Additional exam requirements/recommendations for international students: Required—TOEFL (minimum score 550 paper-based; 213 computer-based). Electronic applications accepted. *Faculty research:* Public health issues, obesity, life-cycle health, substance abuse prevention, women's health.

Georgia State University, College of Health and Human Sciences, School of Health Professions, Division of Respiratory Therapy, Atlanta, GA 30302-3083. Offers MS. Part-time programs available. *Degree requirements:* For master's, project-P. *Entrance requirements:* For master's, GRE. *Faculty research:* Aerosol drug delivery, tuberculosis education, respiratory therapy pharmacology.

Grand Valley State University, College of Health Professions, Allendale, MI 49401-9403. Offers MPAS, MS, DPT. *Entrance requirements:* For master's, volunteer work, interview, minimum GPA of 3.0, writing sample; for doctorate, GRE, 50 hours of volunteer work, interview, minimum GPA of 3.0 in last 60 hours and in prerequisites, writing sample. Additional exam requirements/recommendations for international students: Required—TOEFL (minimum score 610 paper-based; 253 computer-based). Electronic applications accepted. *Faculty research:* Skeletal muscle structure, blood platelets, thrombospondin activity, FES exercise for quadriplegics, balance.

Idaho State University, Office of Graduate Studies, Kasiska College of Health Professions, Pocatello, ID 83209-8090. Offers M Coun, MHE, MOT, MPAS, MPH, MS, Au D, DPT, PhD, Certificate, Ed S, Post-Doctoral Certificate, Post-Master's Certificate, Postbaccalaureate Certificate. *Accreditation:* APTA (one or more programs are accredited). Part-time programs available. *Degree requirements:* For master's, comprehensive exam, thesis (for some programs), 8-week externship; for doctorate, comprehensive exam, thesis/dissertation, clinical rotation (for some programs); for other advanced degree, comprehensive exam, thesis, case study, oral exam. *Entrance requirements:* For master's, GRE General Test or MAT, minimum GPA of 3.0, 3 letters of recommendation; for doctorate, GRE General Test or MAT, minimum GPA of 3.0, counseling license, professional research, interview, work experience, 3 letters of recommendation; for other advanced degree, GRE General Test or MAT, master's degree in similar field of study, 3 letters of recommendation, 2 years of work experience. Additional exam requirements/recommendations for international students: Required—TOEFL (minimum score 600 paper-based; 250 computer-based; 80 iBT). Electronic applications accepted. *Expenses:* Contact institution. *Faculty research:* Mental health, information technology, dental health, nursing.

Ithaca College, Division of Graduate and Professional Studies, School of Health Sciences and Human Performance, Ithaca, NY 14850. Offers MS, DPT. Part-time programs available. *Faculty:* 57 full-time (38 women), 1 (woman) part-time/adjunct. *Students:* 312 full-time (236 women), 25 part-time (15 women); includes 27 minority (3 Black or African American, non-Hispanic/Latino; 1 American Indian or Alaska Native, non-Hispanic/Latino; 10 Asian, non-Hispanic/Latino; 6 Hispanic/Latino; 7 Two or more races, non-Hispanic/Latino), 12 international. Average age 23. In 2011, 192 master's, 88 doctorates awarded. Terminal master's awarded for partial completion of doctoral program. *Degree requirements:* For master's, comprehensive exam (for some programs), thesis optional; for doctorate, thesis/dissertation optional. *Entrance requirements:* Additional exam requirements/recommendations for international students: Required—TOEFL (minimum score 550 paper-based; 213 computer-based; 80 iBT). *Application deadline:* Applications are processed on a rolling basis. Application fee: $40. Electronic applications accepted. *Expenses:* Contact institution. *Financial support:* In 2011–12, 201 students received support, including 75 teaching assistantships (averaging $9,233 per year); career-related internships or fieldwork, Federal Work-Study, scholarships/grants, and unspecified assistantships also available. Support available to part-time students. Financial award applicants required to submit CSS PROFILE or FAFSA. *Unit head:* Dr. John Sigg, Acting Dean, 607-274-3143, Fax: 607-274-1263, E-mail: gps@ithaca.edu. *Application contact:* Gerard Turbide, Director, Office of Admission, 607-274-3143, Fax: 607-274-1263, E-mail: gps@ithaca.edu. Web site: http://www.ithaca.edu/hshp.

Loma Linda University, School of Allied Health Professions, Loma Linda, CA 92350. Offers MHIS, MOT, MPT, MS, D Sc, DPT, DPTSc, OTD. *Accreditation:* AOTA; APTA. *Entrance requirements:* For master's, minimum GPA of 2.0; for doctorate, minimum 2.0 GPA, associate degree in physical therapy. Additional exam requirements/recommendations for international students: Required—TOEFL (minimum score 550 paper-based; 213 computer-based). Electronic applications accepted.

Long Island University–C. W. Post Campus, School of Health Professions and Nursing, Brookville, NY 11548-1300. Offers MS, MSW, Certificate. Part-time and evening/weekend programs available. Postbaccalaureate distance learning degree programs offered. *Degree requirements:* For master's, thesis. Electronic applications accepted. *Faculty research:* PCR techniques, breast CA-mammography compliance, smoking patterns.

Marymount University, School of Health Professions, Arlington, VA 22207-4299. Offers MS, MSN, DNP, DPT, Certificate. Part-time and evening/weekend programs available. *Faculty:* 17 full-time (15 women), 17 part-time/adjunct (11 women). *Students:* 123 full-time (89 women), 85 part-time (81 women); includes 63 minority (34 Black or African American, non-Hispanic/Latino; 2 American Indian or Alaska Native, non-Hispanic/Latino; 17 Asian, non-Hispanic/Latino; 10 Hispanic/Latino), 11 international. Average age 32. 466 applicants, 40% accepted, 69 enrolled. In 2011, 40 master's, 24 doctorates, 2 other advanced degrees awarded. *Degree requirements:* For master's, thesis or alternative. *Entrance requirements:* For master's, GRE, MAT, 2 letters of recommendation, interview, resume; for doctorate, GRE, 2 letters of recommendation, resume; for Certificate, interview. Additional exam requirements/recommendations for international students: Required—TOEFL (minimum score 600 paper-based; 250 computer-based; 96 iBT), IELTS (minimum score 6.5). *Application deadline:* For fall admission, 7/1 for international students; for spring admission, 9/15 for international students. Applications are processed on a rolling basis. Application fee: $40. Electronic applications accepted. *Expenses: Tuition:* Part-time $770 per credit hour. *Required fees:* $8 per credit hour. One-time fee: $180 full-time. *Financial support:* In 2011–12, 16 students received support. Research assistantships with full and partial tuition reimbursements available, career-related internships or fieldwork, Federal Work-Study, scholarships/grants, and unspecified assistantships available. Support available to part-time students. Financial award applicants required to submit FAFSA. *Unit head:* Dr. Tess Cappello, Dean, 703-284-1580, Fax: 703-284-3819, E-mail: tess.cappello@marymount.edu. *Application contact:* Francesca Reed, Director, Graduate Admissions, 703-284-5901, Fax: 703-527-3815, E-mail: grad.admissions@marymount.edu. Web site: http://www.marymount.edu/academics/schools/shp.

Maryville University of Saint Louis, School of Health Professions, St. Louis, MO 63141-7299. Offers MARC, MMT, MOT, MSN, DNP, DPT, CAGS. *Accreditation:* CORE. Part-time and evening/weekend programs available. *Faculty:* 25 full-time (19 women), 12 part-time/adjunct (10 women). *Students:* 120 full-time (97 women), 233 part-time (208 women); includes 18 minority (12 Black or African American, non-Hispanic/Latino; 4 Asian, non-Hispanic/Latino; 1 Hispanic/Latino; 1 Two or more races, non-Hispanic/Latino), 1 international. Average age 30. In 2011, 67 master's awarded. *Entrance requirements:* Additional exam requirements/recommendations for international students: Required—TOEFL (minimum score 550 paper-based). *Application deadline:* Applications are processed on a rolling basis. Application fee: $40 ($60 for international students). Electronic applications accepted. *Expenses: Tuition:* Full-time $21,922; part-time $675 per credit hour. *Required fees:* $233.75 per semester. *Financial support:* Career-related internships or fieldwork, Federal Work-Study, and campus employment available. Financial award application deadline: 3/1; financial award applicants required to submit FAFSA. *Faculty research:* Disability work transition, assessment, reducing work-related musculoskeletal injuries, women's health-AIDS. *Unit head:* Dr. Charles Gulas, Dean, 314-529-9625, Fax: 314-529-9495, E-mail: hlthprofessions@maryville.edu. *Application contact:* Dr. Donna Payne, Assistant Vice President, Adult and Continuing Education, 314-529-9676, Fax: 314-529-9927, E-mail: dpayne@maryville.edu. Web site: http://www.maryville.edu/academics-hp.

Medical University of South Carolina, College of Health Professions, Charleston, SC 29425. Offers MHA, MRA, MS, MSNA, MSRS, DHA, DPT, PhD. *Accreditation:* CAHME (one or more programs are accredited). Part-time programs available. *Faculty:* 39 full-time (17 women), 6 part-time/adjunct (4 women). *Students:* 664 full-time (485 women), 28 part-time (18 women); includes 90 minority (57 Black or African American, non-Hispanic/Latino; 3 American Indian or Alaska Native, non-Hispanic/Latino; 11 Asian, non-Hispanic/Latino; 19 Hispanic/Latino), 2 international. Average age 28. 1,158 applicants, 33% accepted, 292 enrolled. In 2011, 209 master's, 70 doctorates awarded. *Degree requirements:* For doctorate, comprehensive exam, thesis/dissertation. *Entrance requirements:* For master's, GRE. Additional exam requirements/recommendations for international students: Required—TOEFL (minimum score 600 paper-based; 250 computer-based). Application fee: $85. Electronic applications accepted. *Expenses:* Contact institution. *Financial support:* In 2011–12, 20 students received support. Career-related internships or fieldwork, Federal Work-Study, scholarships/grants, and tuition waivers (partial) available. Support available to part-time students. Financial award application deadline: 3/10; financial award applicants required to submit FAFSA. *Faculty research:* Spinal cord injury, geriatrics, health economics, health psychology, behavioral medicine. *Total annual research expenditures:* $2.7 million. *Unit head:* Dr. Lisa Saladin, Interim Dean, 843-792-3328, Fax: 843-792-3322, E-mail: sothmann@musc.edu. *Application contact:* Melissa Freeland, Recruitment and Student Affairs Coordinator, 843-792-8510, Fax: 843-792-3327, E-mail: freelan@musc.edu. Web site: http://www.musc.edu/chp.

Mercy College, School of Health and Natural Sciences, Dobbs Ferry, NY 10522-1189. Offers communication disorders (MS); nursing (MS, Certificate), including nursing administration, nursing education; nursing education (Certificate), including nursing administration (MS, Certificate), nursing education (MS, Certificate); occupational therapy (MS); physical therapy (DPT); physician assistant (MS), including physician assistant studies. Part-time and evening/weekend programs available. Postbaccalaureate distance learning degree programs offered (minimal on-campus study). *Degree requirements:* For master's, comprehensive exam (for some programs), thesis (for some programs). *Entrance requirements:* For master's, interview, resume, essay, letters of recommendation; for doctorate, 2 references, typewritten essay, work experience, minimum GPA of 3.0. Additional exam requirements/recommendations for international students: Required—TOEFL (minimum score 600 paper-based; 250 computer-based; 100 iBT), IELTS (minimum score 8). Electronic applications accepted.

Midwestern University, Downers Grove Campus, College of Health Sciences, Illinois Campus, Doctor of Health Science Program, Downers Grove, IL 60515-1235. Offers DHS. Part-time programs available. *Students:* 10 full-time (8 women). 10 applicants, 90% accepted, 9 enrolled. *Entrance requirements:* For doctorate, master's or bachelor's degree, minimum cumulative GPA of 3.0. *Unit head:* Dr. Jacquelyn J. Smith, Dean, 630-515-6388. *Application contact:* Michael Laken, Director of Admissions, 630-515-6171, Fax: 630-971-6086, E-mail: admissil@midwestern.edu. Web site: http://www.midwestern.edu/Programs_and_Admission/IL_Doctor_of_Health_Science_Degree.html.

Midwestern University, Glendale Campus, College of Health Sciences, Arizona Campus, Glendale, AZ 85308. Offers MA, MBS, MCVS, MMS, MOT, MS, DPM, DPT, Psy D. Part-time programs available. *Faculty:* 44 full-time (21 women), 4 part-time/ adjunct (3 women). *Students:* 750 full-time (444 women), 6 part-time (0 women); includes 153 minority (15 Black or African American, non-Hispanic/Latino; 2 American Indian or Alaska Native, non-Hispanic/Latino; 56 Asian, non-Hispanic/Latino; 54 Hispanic/Latino; 5 Native Hawaiian or other Pacific Islander, non-Hispanic/Latino; 21 Two or more races, non-Hispanic/Latino), 10 international. Average age 27. 1,349 applicants, 31% accepted, 230 enrolled. In 2011, 107 master's awarded. *Application deadline:* For fall admission, 6/4 for domestic students. Applications are processed on a rolling basis. Application fee: $50. *Expenses:* Contact institution. *Financial support:* Federal Work-Study available. *Unit head:* Dr. Jacquelyn Smith, Dean, 623-572-3601, Fax: 623-572-3601. *Application contact:* James Walter, Director of Admissions, 888-247-9277, Fax: 623-572-3229, E-mail: admissaz@midwestern.edu.

Minnesota State University Mankato, College of Graduate Studies, College of Allied Health and Nursing, Mankato, MN 56001. Offers MA, MS, MSN, DNP, Postbaccalaureate Certificate. Part-time programs available. *Students:* 132 full-time (97 women), 336 part-time (284 women). *Degree requirements:* For master's, comprehensive exam; for Postbaccalaureate Certificate, thesis. *Entrance requirements:* For master's, GRE (for some programs), minimum GPA of 3.0 during previous 2 years; for Postbaccalaureate Certificate, GRE General Test, minimum GPA of 3.0. *Application deadline:* Applications are processed on a rolling basis. Application fee: $40. Electronic applications accepted. *Financial support:* Research assistantships with full tuition reimbursements, teaching assistantships with full tuition reimbursements, career-related internships or fieldwork, Federal Work-Study, institutionally sponsored loans, and unspecified assistantships available. Support available to part-time students. Financial award application deadline: 3/15; financial award applicants required to submit FAFSA. *Unit head:* Dr. Harry Krampf, Interim Dean, 507-389-6315. *Application contact:* 507-389-2321, E-mail: grad@mnsu.edu. Web site: http://ahn.mnsu.edu/.

Misericordia University, College of Health Sciences, Dallas, PA 18612-1098. Offers MSN, MSOT, MSPT, MSSLP, DPT, OTD. Part-time and evening/weekend programs available. *Faculty:* 24 full-time (17 women), 21 part-time/adjunct (17 women). *Students:* 121 full-time (97 women), 125 part-time (106 women); includes 12 minority (2 Black or African American, non-Hispanic/Latino; 2 American Indian or Alaska Native, non-Hispanic/Latino; 1 Asian, non-Hispanic/Latino; 5 Hispanic/Latino; 2 Two or more races, non-Hispanic/Latino). Average age 28. In 2011, 107 master's, 23 doctorates awarded. *Entrance requirements:* For doctorate, interview, references. Additional exam requirements/recommendations for international students: Required—TOEFL. *Application deadline:* Applications are processed on a rolling basis. Application fee: $25. Electronic applications accepted. *Expenses: Tuition:* Full-time $25,700; part-time $575 per credit. *Financial support:* In 2011–12, 155 students received support. Teaching assistantships, career-related internships or fieldwork, Federal Work-Study, scholarships/grants, traineeships, and tuition waivers (partial) available. Support available to part-time students. Financial award application deadline: 6/30; financial award applicants required to submit FAFSA. *Unit head:* Dr. Jean A. Dyer, Dean, 570-674-8152, E-mail: jdyer@misericordia.edu. *Application contact:* Larree Brown, Assistant Director of Admissions, Part-Time Undergraduate and Graduate Programs, 570-674-6451, Fax: 570-674-6232, E-mail: lbrown@misericordia.edu.

Moravian College, Moravian College Comenius Center, Business and Management Programs, Bethlehem, PA 18018-6650. Offers accounting (MBA); general management (MBA); health care management (MBA); human resource management (MBA); leadership (MSHRM); learning and performance management (MSHRM); supply chain management (MBA). Part-time and evening/weekend programs available. *Entrance requirements:* For master's, GMAT. Additional exam requirements/recommendations for international students: Required—TOEFL (minimum score 550 paper-based; 260 computer-based; 90 iBT). *Expenses:* Contact institution. *Faculty research:* Leadership, change management, human resources.

Mountain State University, School of Graduate Studies, Program in Health Science, Beckley, WV 25802-9003. Offers MHS. Part-time and evening/weekend programs available. Postbaccalaureate distance learning degree programs offered (no on-campus study). *Faculty:* 2 part-time/adjunct (0 women). *Students:* 3 full-time (2 women), 1 (woman) part-time; includes 3 minority (all Black or African American, non-Hispanic/ Latino). Average age 45. 18 applicants, 6% accepted, 1 enrolled. In 2011, 3 master's awarded. *Degree requirements:* For master's, thesis or alternative. *Entrance requirements:* Additional exam requirements/recommendations for international students: Required—TOEFL (minimum score 550 paper-based; 213 computer-based); Recommended—IELTS (minimum score 6.5). *Application deadline:* For fall admission, 5/31 priority date for domestic students, 5/31 for international students. Applications are processed on a rolling basis. Application fee: $25 ($50 for international students). Electronic applications accepted. *Financial support:* Federal Work-Study, scholarships/ grants, and unspecified assistantships available. Support available to part-time students. Financial award applicants required to submit FAFSA. *Unit head:* Dr. William White, Interim Dean, School of Graduate Studies/Dean, School of Leadership and Professional Development, 304-929-1658, Fax: 304-929-1637, E-mail: wwhite@mountainstate.edu.

New Jersey City University, Graduate Studies and Continuing Education, College of Professional Studies, Department of Health Sciences, Jersey City, NJ 07305-1597. Offers community health education (MS); health administration (MS); school health education (MS). Part-time and evening/weekend programs available. *Students:* 6 full-time (5 women), 45 part-time (37 women); includes 19 minority (13 Black or African American, non-Hispanic/Latino; 4 Asian, non-Hispanic/Latino; 2 Hispanic/Latino), 2 international. Average age 41. In 2011, 16 master's awarded. *Degree requirements:* For master's, thesis or alternative, internship. *Entrance requirements:* Additional exam requirements/recommendations for international students: Required—TOEFL. *Application deadline:* For fall admission, 8/1 priority date for domestic students; for spring admission, 12/1 for domestic students. Applications are processed on a rolling basis. Application fee: $0. *Expenses:* Tuition, state resident: part-time $494 per credit. Tuition, nonresident: part-time $911.30 per credit. *Required fees:* $95.90 per year. *Financial support:* Career-related internships or fieldwork and unspecified assistantships available. *Unit head:* Dr. Lilliam Rosado, Chairperson, 201-200-3431, E-mail: lrosado@njcu.edu. *Application contact:* Dr. William Bajor, Dean of Graduate Studies, 201-200-3409, Fax: 201-200-3411, E-mail: wbajor@njcu.edu.

Northeastern University, Bouvé College of Health Sciences, Boston, MA 02115-5096. Offers MPH, MS, Au D, DPT, PhD, CAGS, CAS, MS/MBA. *Accreditation:* ACPE (one or more programs are accredited). Part-time and evening/weekend programs available. *Faculty:* 162 full-time (100 women), 117 part-time/adjunct (86 women). *Students:* 1,132 full-time (834 women), 213 part-time (172 women). 1,778 applicants, 36% accepted, 259 enrolled. In 2011, 418 master's, 125 doctorates awarded. *Degree requirements:* For doctorate, thesis/dissertation (for some programs); for other advanced degree, comprehensive exam. *Entrance requirements:* For master's and other advanced degree, GRE General Test or MAT; for doctorate, GRE General Test, prior admission to undergraduate pharmacy program (for Pharm D). Additional exam requirements/ recommendations for international students: Required—TOEFL. Application fee: $50. Electronic applications accepted. *Financial support:* Fellowships, research

assistantships with full tuition reimbursements, teaching assistantships with full tuition reimbursements, career-related internships or fieldwork, Federal Work-Study, institutionally sponsored loans, scholarships/grants, traineeships, tuition waivers (full and partial), and administrative assistantships available. Support available to part-time students. Financial award application deadline: 3/1; financial award applicants required to submit FAFSA. *Faculty research:* Counseling, physical therapy, biomedical sciences, cardiopulmonary sciences, nursing. *Unit head:* Suzanne B. Greenberg, Director, 617-373-3195, E-mail: s.greenberg@neu.edu. *Application contact:* Margaret Schnabel, Director of Graduate Admissions, 617-373-2708, E-mail: bouvegrad@neu.edu. Web site: http://www.northeastern.edu/bouve.

Northern Arizona University, Graduate College, College of Health and Human Services, Flagstaff, AZ 86011. Offers M Ad, MPAS, MPH, MS, MSN, DNP, DPT, Certificate. *Accreditation:* APTA (one or more programs are accredited). Part-time programs available. *Faculty:* 93 full-time (70 women). *Students:* 227 full-time (158 women), 151 part-time (136 women); includes 66 minority (4 Black or African American, non-Hispanic/Latino; 3 American Indian or Alaska Native, non-Hispanic/Latino; 9 Asian, non-Hispanic/Latino; 42 Hispanic/Latino; 1 Native Hawaiian or other Pacific Islander, non-Hispanic/Latino; 7 Two or more races, non-Hispanic/Latino). Average age 31. 1,112 applicants, 8% accepted, 74 enrolled. In 2011, 82 master's, 52 doctorates awarded. Application fee: $65. *Expenses:* Tuition, state resident: full-time $7190; part-time $355 per credit hour. Tuition, nonresident: full-time $18,092; part-time $1005 per credit hour. *Required fees:* $818; $328 per semester. *Financial support:* Tuition waivers (full and partial) available. Financial award applicants required to submit FAFSA. *Unit head:* Leslie Schulz, Executive Dean, 928-523-4331, E-mail: leslie.schulz@nau.edu. *Application contact:* April Sandoval, Coordinator, 928-523-4348, Fax: 928-523-8950, E-mail: april.sandoval@nau.edu. Web site: http://nau.edu/chhs/.

Nova Southeastern University, Health Professions Division, College of Health Care Sciences, Fort Lauderdale, FL 33314-7796. Offers audiology (Au D); health science (MH Sc, DHSc, PhD); occupational therapy (MOT, OTD, PhD); physical therapy (DPT, PhD); physical therapy (transitional) (TDPT). Postbaccalaureate distance learning degree programs offered (minimal on-campus study). *Faculty:* 85 full-time (57 women), 52 part-time/adjunct (27 women). *Students:* 993 full-time (702 women), 514 part-time (356 women); includes 465 minority (160 Black or African American, non-Hispanic/ Latino; 6 American Indian or Alaska Native, non-Hispanic/Latino; 96 Asian, non-Hispanic/Latino; 177 Hispanic/Latino; 3 Native Hawaiian or other Pacific Islander, non-Hispanic/Latino; 23 Two or more races, non-Hispanic/Latino), 13 international. Average age 31. 3,837 applicants, 18% accepted, 446 enrolled. In 2011, 293 master's, 147 doctorates awarded. *Degree requirements:* For master's, thesis; for doctorate, comprehensive exam, thesis/dissertation. *Entrance requirements:* For master's and doctorate, GRE General Test. *Application deadline:* Applications are processed on a rolling basis. Application fee: $50. Electronic applications accepted. *Expenses:* Contact institution. *Financial support:* In 2011–12, 12 students received support, including 1 fellowship (averaging $10,000 per year), 4 teaching assistantships (averaging $10,200 per year); institutionally sponsored loans and unspecified assistantships also available. *Unit head:* Dr. Richard Davis, Dean, 954-262-1203, E-mail: redavis@nova.edu. *Application contact:* Joey Jankie, Admissions Counselor, 954-262-7249, E-mail: joey@ nova.edu. Web site: http://www.nova.edu/chcs/.

Oakland University, Graduate Study and Lifelong Learning, School of Health Sciences, Rochester, MI 48309-4401. Offers MS, MSPT, DPT, Dr Sc PT, Certificate. *Accreditation:* APTA (one or more programs are accredited). *Entrance requirements:* For master's, minimum GPA of 3.0 for unconditional admission; for doctorate, GRE General Test. Additional exam requirements/recommendations for international students: Required— TOEFL (minimum score 550 paper-based; 213 computer-based). Electronic applications accepted. *Expenses:* Contact institution. *Faculty research:* Community emergency response team preparedness; appropriateness, comprehensiveness, sensitivity, and practicality of outcome measures; assessing effectiveness of innovative intervention program for spinal cord injuries.

The Ohio State University, College of Medicine, School of Allied Medical Professions, Columbus, OH 43210. Offers allied health (MS); health and rehabilitation sciences (PhD); occupational therapy (MOT); physical therapy (DPT). *Accreditation:* AOTA; APTA. Part-time programs available. *Degree requirements:* For master's, thesis or alternative. *Entrance requirements:* Additional exam requirements/recommendations for international students: Required—TOEFL (paper-based 550; computer-based 213) or Michigan English Language Assessment Battery (82). Electronic applications accepted. *Expenses:* Tuition, state resident: full-time $11,400. Tuition, nonresident: full-time $28,125. Tuition and fees vary according to course load, degree level, campus/location and program. *Faculty research:* Geriatrics, quality assurance, nutrition, interdisciplinary health care.

Old Dominion University, College of Health Sciences, Norfolk, VA 23529. Offers MPH, MS, MSN, DNP, DPT, PhD. Part-time and evening/weekend programs available. Postbaccalaureate distance learning degree programs offered (minimal on-campus study). *Faculty:* 55 full-time (36 women), 56 part-time/adjunct (43 women). *Students:* 212 full-time (188 women), 296 part-time (261 women); includes 135 minority (76 Black or African American, non-Hispanic/Latino; 1 American Indian or Alaska Native, non-Hispanic/Latino; 19 Asian, non-Hispanic/Latino; 25 Hispanic/Latino; 5 Native Hawaiian or other Pacific Islander, non-Hispanic/Latino; 9 Two or more races, non-Hispanic/ Latino), 14 international. Average age 33. 1,263 applicants, 30% accepted, 296 enrolled. In 2011, 187 master's, 72 doctorates awarded. *Degree requirements:* For master's and doctorate, comprehensive exam. *Entrance requirements:* Additional exam requirements/recommendations for international students: Required—TOEFL. *Application deadline:* Applications are processed on a rolling basis. Application fee: $50. Electronic applications accepted. *Expenses:* Tuition, state resident: full-time $9096; part-time $379 per credit. Tuition, nonresident: full-time $23,064; part-time $961 per credit. *Required fees:* $127 per semester. One-time fee: $50. *Financial support:* In 2011–12, 210 students received support, including 9 fellowships with full tuition reimbursements available (averaging $15,000 per year), 6 research assistantships with tuition reimbursements available (averaging $10,000 per year), 10 teaching assistantships with tuition reimbursements available (averaging $11,000 per year); career-related internships or fieldwork, institutionally sponsored loans, scholarships/ grants, traineeships, tuition waivers (partial), and unspecified assistantships also available. Support available to part-time students. Financial award application deadline: 2/15; financial award applicants required to submit FAFSA. *Faculty research:* Health promotion and wellness, health care ethics, health policy, health services, cultural competency. *Total annual research expenditures:* $2.7 million. *Unit head:* Dr. Shelley Mishoe, Dean, 757-683-4960, Fax: 757-683-3674, E-mail: smishoe@odu.edu. *Application contact:* William Heffelfinger, Director of Graduate Admissions, 757-683-5554, Fax: 757-683-3255, E-mail: gradadmit@odu.edu. Web site: http://hs.odu.edu/.

Purdue University, Graduate School, College of Health and Human Sciences, School of Health Sciences, West Lafayette, IN 47907. Offers health physics (MS, PhD); medical physics (MS, PhD); occupational and environmental health science (MS, PhD), including aerosol deposition and lung disease , ergonomics, exposure and risk assessment, indoor air quality and bioaerosols (PhD), liver/lung toxicology; occupational and environmental health science (PhD), including indoor air quality and bioaerosols;

radiation biology (PhD); toxicology (PhD); MS/PhD. Part-time programs available. *Faculty:* 10 full-time (3 women), 24 part-time/adjunct (3 women). *Students:* 24 full-time (9 women), 7 part-time (2 women); includes 2 minority (both Asian, non-Hispanic/Latino), 13 international. Average age 30. 49 applicants, 37% accepted, 7 enrolled. In 2011, 18 master's, 5 doctorates awarded. *Degree requirements:* For master's, thesis optional; for doctorate, one foreign language, thesis/dissertation. *Entrance requirements:* For master's and doctorate, GRE General Test, minimum undergraduate GPA of 3.0 or equivalent. Additional exam requirements/recommendations for international students: Required—TOEFL (minimum score 550 computer-based; 77 iBT); Recommended—TWE. *Application deadline:* For fall admission, 5/15 for domestic and international students; for spring admission, 10/15 for domestic and international students. Applications are processed on a rolling basis. Application fee: $60 ($75 for international students). Electronic applications accepted. *Financial support:* In 2011–12, fellowships with tuition reimbursements (averaging $14,400 per year), research assistantships with tuition reimbursements (averaging $12,000 per year), teaching assistantships with tuition reimbursements (averaging $12,000 per year) were awarded; career-related internships or fieldwork and traineeships also available. Support available to part-time students. Financial award applicants required to submit FAFSA. *Faculty research:* Environmental toxicology, industrial hygiene, radiation dosimetry. *Unit head:* Dr. Wei Zheng, Head, 765-494-1419, E-mail: wz18@purdue.edu. *Application contact:* Jennifer S. Franklin, Graduate Contact, 765-494-0248, E-mail: jfranklin@purdue.edu. Web site: http://www.healthsciences.purdue.edu/.

Quinnipiac University, School of Health Sciences, Hamden, CT 06518-1940. Offers MHS, MHS, MOT, MPT, MS, MSN, DPT. *Accreditation:* AOTA. *Faculty:* 116 full-time (61 women), 164 part-time/adjunct (79 women). *Students:* 513 full-time (412 women), 107 part-time (71 women); includes 87 minority (29 Black or African American, non-Hispanic/Latino; 1 American Indian or Alaska Native, non-Hispanic/Latino; 31 Asian, non-Hispanic/Latino; 26 Hispanic/Latino), 39 international. 1,621 applicants, 40% accepted, 521 enrolled. In 2011, 511 master's, 98 doctorates awarded. *Entrance requirements:* Additional exam requirements/recommendations for international students: Required—TOEFL (minimum score 575 paper-based; 233 computer-based; 90 iBT), IELTS (minimum score 6.5). *Application deadline:* For fall admission, 4/30 for international students; for spring admission, 9/15 for international students. Applications are processed on a rolling basis. Application fee: $45. Electronic applications accepted. *Expenses: Tuition:* Part-time $855 per credit. *Required fees:* $35 per credit. *Financial support:* In 2011–12, 383 students received support. Career-related internships or fieldwork, traineeships, tuition waivers (partial), and unspecified assistantships available. Support available to part-time students. Financial award application deadline: 4/15; financial award applicants required to submit FAFSA. *Unit head:* Dr. Edward O'Connor, Dean, 203-582-8710, Fax: 203-582-8706. *Application contact:* Kristin Parent, Assistant Director of Graduate Health Sciences Admissions, 800-462-1944, Fax: 203-582-3443, E-mail: kristin.parent@quinnipiac.edu. Web site: http://www.quinnipiac.edu/gradstudies.

Regis University, Rueckert-Hartman College for Health Professions, Denver, CO 80221-1099. Offers family nurse practitioner (MSN); health informatics (Postbaccalaureate Certificate); health services administration (MS); leadership in healthcare systems (MSN); neonatal nurse practitioner (MSN); nursing (MSN); pharmacy (Pharm D); physical therapy (DPT, TDPT). *Entrance requirements:* Additional exam requirements/recommendations for international students: Required—TOEFL (minimum score 550 paper-based; 213 computer-based; 82 iBT). Electronic applications accepted. *Expenses:* Contact institution. *Faculty research:* Normal and pathological balance and gait research, normal/pathological upper limb motor control/biomechanics, exercise energy/metabolism research, optical treatment protocols for therapeutic modalities.

Rosalind Franklin University of Medicine and Science, College of Health Professions, North Chicago, IL 60064-3095. Offers MS, D Sc, DPT, PhD, TDPT, Certificate. Part-time programs available. Postbaccalaureate distance learning degree programs offered (minimal on-campus study). Terminal master's awarded for partial completion of doctoral program.

Saint Louis University, Graduate Education, Doisy College of Health Sciences, St. Louis, MO 63103-2097. Offers MAT, MMS, MOT, MS, MSN, DNP, DPT, PhD, Certificate. Part-time programs available. *Degree requirements:* For master's, comprehensive exam. *Entrance requirements:* Additional exam requirements/recommendations for international students: Required—TOEFL (minimum score 525 paper-based; 194 computer-based).

Seton Hall University, School of Health and Medical Sciences, Program in Health Sciences, South Orange, NJ 07079-2697. Offers PhD. Part-time and evening/weekend programs available. *Degree requirements:* For doctorate, comprehensive exam (for some programs), thesis/dissertation, candidacy exam, practicum, research projects. *Entrance requirements:* For doctorate, GRE (preferred), interview, minimum GPA of 3.0, letters of recommendation. Additional exam requirements/recommendations for international students: Required—TOEFL. Electronic applications accepted. *Expenses: Tuition:* Part-time $1033 per credit hour. *Required fees:* $85 per semester. *Faculty research:* Movement science, motor learning, dual tasks, clinical decision making, online education, teaching strategies.

Shenandoah University, School of Health Professions, Winchester, VA 22601-5195. Offers MS, MSN, DNP, DPT, Certificate. Part-time programs available. Postbaccalaureate distance learning degree programs offered. *Faculty:* 29 full-time (23 women), 9 part-time/adjunct (6 women). *Students:* 326 full-time (257 women), 246 part-time (214 women); includes 88 minority (40 Black or African American, non-Hispanic/Latino; 1 American Indian or Alaska Native, non-Hispanic/Latino; 27 Asian, non-Hispanic/Latino; 19 Hispanic/Latino; 1 Two or more races, non-Hispanic/Latino), 13 international. Average age 32. 1,374 applicants, 26% accepted, 214 enrolled. In 2011, 90 master's, 102 doctorates, 17 other advanced degrees awarded. *Entrance requirements:* For master's, GRE; for doctorate, GRE, PCAT. Additional exam requirements/recommendations for international students: Required—TOEFL (minimum score 550 paper-based; 213 computer-based; 79 iBT), IELTS (minimum score 6.5), Sakae Institute of Study Abroad (minimum score 550). *Application deadline:* Applications are processed on a rolling basis. Application fee: $30. Electronic applications accepted. *Expenses: Tuition:* Full-time $17,952; part-time $748 per credit. *Required fees:* $500 per term. Tuition and fees vary according to course level, course load and program. *Financial support:* In 2011–12, 48 students received support, including 3 teaching assistantships with partial tuition reimbursements available (averaging $4,224 per year); career-related internships or fieldwork, institutionally sponsored loans, scholarships/grants, unspecified assistantships, and federal loans, alternative loans also available. Support available to part-time students. Financial award application deadline: 3/15; financial award applicants required to submit FAFSA. *Application contact:* David Anthony, Dean of Admissions, 540-665-4581, Fax: 540-665-4627, E-mail: admit@su.edu.

South Carolina State University, School of Graduate Studies, Department of Health Sciences, Orangeburg, SC 29117-0001. Offers speech pathology and audiology (MA). *Accreditation:* ASHA. Part-time and evening/weekend programs available. *Faculty:* 7 full-time (6 women), 2 part-time/adjunct (0 women). *Students:* 34 full-time (33 women), 33 part-time (all women); includes 54 minority (53 Black or African American, non-Hispanic/Latino; 1 Hispanic/Latino), 1 international. Average age 30. 40 applicants, 95% accepted, 28 enrolled. In 2011, 13 master's awarded. *Degree requirements:* For master's, thesis optional, departmental qualifying exam. *Entrance requirements:* For master's, GRE or NTE, minimum GPA of 3.0. *Application deadline:* For fall admission, 6/15 for domestic and international students; for spring admission, 11/1 for domestic and international students. Application fee: $25. Electronic applications accepted. *Expenses:* Tuition, state resident: full-time $8688; part-time $514 per credit hour. Tuition, nonresident: full-time $17,600; part-time $1009 per credit hour. *Required fees:* $570. *Financial support:* In 2011–12, 7 fellowships (averaging $4,143 per year) were awarded; career-related internships or fieldwork, Federal Work-Study, and institutionally sponsored loans also available. Financial award application deadline: 6/1. *Unit head:* Dr. Gwendolyn D. Wilson, Chair, 803-536-7063, Fax: 803-536-8593, E-mail: gdwilson@scsu.edu. *Application contact:* Annette Hazzard-Jones, Program Coordinator II, 803-536-8809, Fax: 803-536-8812, E-mail: zs_ahazzard@scsu.edu.

Southwestern Oklahoma State University, College of Professional and Graduate Studies, School of Behavioral Sciences and Education, Specialization in Health Sciences and Microbiology, Weatherford, OK 73096-3098. Offers M Ed.

Temple University, Health Sciences Center, College of Health Professions and Social Work, Philadelphia, PA 19122-6096. Offers Ed M, MA, MOT, MPH, MS, MSN, MSW, DOT, DPT, PhD. *Accreditation:* APTA (one or more programs are accredited). Part-time and evening/weekend programs available. Postbaccalaureate distance learning degree programs offered (minimal on-campus study). *Faculty:* 55 full-time (28 women). *Students:* 429 full-time (330 women), 261 part-time (203 women); includes 113 minority (52 Black or African American, non-Hispanic/Latino; 37 Asian, non-Hispanic/Latino; 18 Hispanic/Latino; 2 Native Hawaiian or other Pacific Islander, non-Hispanic/Latino; 4 Two or more races, non-Hispanic/Latino), 31 international. Average age 30. 383 applicants, 81% accepted, 197 enrolled. In 2011, 107 master's, 157 doctorates awarded. *Degree requirements:* For doctorate, thesis/dissertation. Application fee: $50. *Expenses:* Tuition, state resident: full-time $12,366; part-time $687 per credit hour. Tuition, nonresident: full-time $17,298; part-time $961 per credit hour. *Required fees:* $590; $213 per year. *Financial support:* Fellowships, research assistantships, teaching assistantships with full tuition reimbursements, career-related internships or fieldwork, Federal Work-Study, institutionally sponsored loans, traineeships, and tuition waivers (partial) available. Support available to part-time students. Financial award application deadline: 1/15. *Faculty research:* Balance dysfunction, repetitive stress injury, neurobehavioral disorders, bilingual speech-language therapy, smoking cessation. *Unit head:* Dr. Michael Sitler, Interim Dean, 215-707-4800, Fax: 215-707-7819, E-mail: sitler@temple.edu. *Application contact:* Tara Schumacher, Coordinator of Outreach, 215-204-6575, Fax: 215-204-8781, E-mail: tara.schumacher@temple.edu. Web site: http://chpsw.temple.edu/.

Tennessee State University, The School of Graduate Studies and Research, College of Health Sciences, Nashville, TN 37209-1561. Offers MPT, MS, DPT. *Accreditation:* ASHA (one or more programs are accredited). Part-time and evening/weekend programs available. *Entrance requirements:* For master's, GRE General Test, MAT, minimum GPA of 3.5. Electronic applications accepted. *Faculty research:* Community problems of the elderly, language disorders in children, aphasia, sickle cell disturbances, regional and foreign dialects.

Texas Christian University, Harris College of Nursing and Health Sciences, Fort Worth, TX 76129-0002. Offers MS, MSN, DNP, DNP-A. Postbaccalaureate distance learning degree programs offered. *Faculty:* 37 full-time (28 women), 5 part-time/adjunct (3 women). *Students:* 93 full-time (61 women), 237 part-time (166 women); includes 56 minority (14 Black or African American, non-Hispanic/Latino; 2 American Indian or Alaska Native, non-Hispanic/Latino; 13 Asian, non-Hispanic/Latino; 22 Hispanic/Latino; 1 Native Hawaiian or other Pacific Islander, non-Hispanic/Latino; 4 Two or more races, non-Hispanic/Latino), 1 international. Average age 34. 279 applicants, 47% accepted, 102 enrolled. In 2011, 91 master's, 21 doctorates awarded. *Degree requirements:* For master's and doctorate, professional project. *Entrance requirements:* For master's, GRE General Test or MAT, 3 letters of reference; for doctorate, APRN recognition (national certification) or master's and experience in nursing administration. Additional exam requirements/recommendations for international students: Required—TOEFL, Spoken English Test. *Expenses: Tuition:* Full-time $20,250; part-time $1125 per credit hour. Part-time tuition and fees vary according to course load and program. *Financial support:* Teaching assistantships available. Financial award applicants required to submit FAFSA. *Unit head:* Dr. Paulette Burns, Dean, 817-257-6742, Fax: 817-257-6751, E-mail: p.burns@tcu.edu. *Application contact:* Sybil J. White, Assistant to the Dean of Graduate Studies, 817-257-6750, Fax: 817-257-6751, E-mail: s.white@tcu.edu. Web site: http://www.harriscollege.tcu.edu/graduate.htm.

Texas State University–San Marcos, Graduate School, College of Health Professions, San Marcos, TX 78666. Offers MA, MHA, MS, MSCD, DPT. Part-time and evening/weekend programs available. *Faculty:* 32 full-time (16 women), 5 part-time/adjunct (1 woman). *Students:* 187 full-time (126 women), 70 part-time (49 women); includes 83 minority (11 Black or African American, non-Hispanic/Latino; 6 Asian, non-Hispanic/Latino; 61 Hispanic/Latino; 5 Two or more races, non-Hispanic/Latino), 3 international. Average age 27. 452 applicants, 14% accepted, 39 enrolled. In 2011, 60 master's awarded. *Degree requirements:* For master's, comprehensive exam. *Entrance requirements:* For master's, GRE General Test (for some programs); for doctorate, GRE (minimum score of 1000 Verbal and Quantitative), bachelor's degree in physical therapy. Additional exam requirements/recommendations for international students: Required—TOEFL (minimum score 550 paper-based; 213 computer-based; 78 iBT). *Application deadline:* For fall admission, 6/15 for domestic students, 6/1 for international students; for spring admission, 10/15 priority date for domestic students, 10/1 for international students. Applications are processed on a rolling basis. Application fee: $40 ($90 for international students). Electronic applications accepted. *Expenses:* Tuition, state resident: full-time $6408; part-time $3204 per semester. Tuition, nonresident: full-time $14,832; part-time $7416 per semester. *Required fees:* $1824; $912 per semester. Tuition and fees vary according to course load. *Financial support:* In 2011–12, 169 students received support, including 7 research assistantships (averaging $5,697 per year), 28 teaching assistantships (averaging $7,560 per year); fellowships, career-related internships or fieldwork, Federal Work-Study, institutionally sponsored loans, scholarships/grants, unspecified assistantships, and stipends also available. Support available to part-time students. Financial award application deadline: 4/1; financial award applicants required to submit FAFSA. *Faculty research:* ARRA: health information, health information technology, cognitive impairment, hand-held cell phone use. *Total annual research expenditures:* $1.7 million. *Unit head:* Dr. Ruth Welborn, Dean, 512-245-3300, Fax: 512-245-3791, E-mail: mw01@txstate.edu. *Application contact:* Dr. J. Michael Willoughby, Dean of Graduate School, 512-245-2581, Fax: 512-245-8365, E-mail: gradcollege@txstate.edu. Web site: http://www.health.txstate.edu/.

Texas Tech University Health Sciences Center, School of Allied Health Sciences, Lubbock, TX 79430. Offers MAT, MOT, MPAS, MRC, MS, Au D, DPT, PhD, Sc D. *Accreditation:* APTA (one or more programs are accredited). *Faculty:* 75 full-time (38 women). *Students:* 656 full-time (473 women), 329 part-time (210 women); includes 262 minority (63 Black or African American, non-Hispanic/Latino; 5 American Indian or

Alaska Native, non-Hispanic/Latino; 60 Asian, non-Hispanic/Latino; 127 Hispanic/Latino; 3 Native Hawaiian or other Pacific Islander, non-Hispanic/Latino; 4 Two or more races, non-Hispanic/Latino), 2 international. Average age 30. 2,255 applicants, 19% accepted, 436 enrolled. In 2011, 208 master's, 97 doctorates awarded. *Entrance requirements:* Additional exam requirements/recommendations for international students: Required—TOEFL, IELTS. Application fee: $35. Electronic applications accepted. *Financial support:* Fellowships, research assistantships, teaching assistantships, career-related internships or fieldwork, institutionally sponsored loans, scholarships/grants, and tuition waivers (full) available. Financial award application deadline: 9/1; financial award applicants required to submit FAFSA. *Unit head:* Lindsay R. Johnson, Associate Dean for Admissions and Student Affairs, 806-743-3220, Fax: 806-743-2994, E-mail: lindsay.johnson@ttuhsc.edu. *Application contact:* Jeri Moravcik, Assistant Director of Admissions and Student Affairs, 806-743-3220, Fax: 806-743-2994, E-mail: jeri.moravcik@ttuhsc.edu. Web site: http://www.ttuhsc.edu/sah/.

Texas Woman's University, Graduate School, College of Health Sciences, Denton, TX 76201. Offers MA, MHA, MOT, MS, DPT, Ed D, PhD. Part-time and evening/weekend programs available. Postbaccalaureate distance learning degree programs offered. *Faculty:* 119 full-time (87 women), 3 part-time/adjunct (1 woman). *Students:* 962 full-time (841 women), 510 part-time (422 women); includes 471 minority (150 Black or African American, non-Hispanic/Latino; 8 American Indian or Alaska Native, non-Hispanic/Latino; 106 Asian, non-Hispanic/Latino; 204 Hispanic/Latino; 3 Native Hawaiian or other Pacific Islander, non-Hispanic/Latino), 56 international. Average age 30. 1,341 applicants, 38% accepted, 347 enrolled. In 2011, 399 master's, 130 doctorates awarded. Terminal master's awarded for partial completion of doctoral program. *Degree requirements:* For master's, comprehensive exam (for some programs), thesis (for some programs); for doctorate, comprehensive exam, thesis/dissertation, qualifying exam. *Entrance requirements:* For master's and doctorate, minimum GPA of 3.0. Additional exam requirements/recommendations for international students: Required—TOEFL (minimum score 550 paper-based; 213 computer-based; 79 iBT). *Application deadline:* For fall admission, 7/1 priority date for domestic students, 3/1 for international students; for spring admission, 12/1 priority date for domestic students, 7/1 for international students. Applications are processed on a rolling basis. Application fee: $50 ($75 for international students). Electronic applications accepted. *Expenses:* Tuition, state resident: full-time $3834; part-time $213 per credit hour. Tuition, nonresident: full-time $9468; part-time $526 per credit hour. *Required fees:* $213 per credit hour. Tuition and fees vary according to course load. *Financial support:* In 2011–12, 747 students received support, including 59 research assistantships (averaging $11,499 per year), 15 teaching assistantships (averaging $11,499 per year); career-related internships or fieldwork, Federal Work-Study, institutionally sponsored loans, scholarships/grants, traineeships, health care benefits, and unspecified assistantships also available. Support available to part-time students. Financial award application deadline: 3/1; financial award applicants required to submit FAFSA. *Total annual research expenditures:* $690,244. *Unit head:* Dr. Jimmy Ishee, Dean, 940-898-2852, Fax: 940-898-2853, E-mail: jishee@twu.edu. *Application contact:* Dr. Samuel Wheeler, Assistant Director of Admissions, 940-898-3188, Fax: 940-898-3081, E-mail: wheelersr@twu.edu. Web site: http://www.twu.edu/college-health-sciences/.

Towson University, Program in Health Science, Towson, MD 21252-0001. Offers MS. Part-time and evening/weekend programs available. *Students:* 14 full-time (13 women), 120 part-time (102 women); includes 47 minority (41 Black or African American, non-Hispanic/Latino; 1 American Indian or Alaska Native, non-Hispanic/Latino; 2 Asian, non-Hispanic/Latino; 2 Hispanic/Latino; 1 Two or more races, non-Hispanic/Latino), 8 international. *Degree requirements:* For master's, thesis optional. *Entrance requirements:* For master's, previous course work in health sciences, minimum GPA of 2.75. *Application deadline:* Applications are processed on a rolling basis. Application fee: $50. Electronic applications accepted. *Expenses:* Tuition, state resident: part-time $337 per credit. Tuition, nonresident: part-time $709 per credit. *Required fees:* $99 per credit. *Financial support:* Application deadline: 4/1; applicants required to submit FAFSA. *Unit head:* Dr. Susan Radius, Director, 410-704-4216, Fax: 410-704-4670, E-mail: sradius@towson.edu.

University at Buffalo, the State University of New York, Graduate School, School of Public Health and Health Professions, Buffalo, NY 14260. Offers MA, MPH, MS, DPT, PhD, Advanced Certificate, Certificate. Part-time programs available. *Faculty:* 60 full-time (27 women), 12 part-time/adjunct (5 women). *Students:* 370 full-time (232 women), 28 part-time (15 women); includes 55 minority (13 Black or African American, non-Hispanic/Latino; 1 American Indian or Alaska Native, non-Hispanic/Latino; 35 Asian, non-Hispanic/Latino; 5 Hispanic/Latino; 1 Native Hawaiian or other Pacific Islander, non-Hispanic/Latino), 61 international. Average age 27. 468 applicants, 52% accepted, 123 enrolled. In 2011, 110 master's, 50 doctorates, 15 other advanced degrees awarded. Terminal master's awarded for partial completion of doctoral program. *Degree requirements:* For master's, comprehensive exam (for some programs), thesis (for some programs); for doctorate, comprehensive exam, thesis/dissertation. *Entrance requirements:* For master's and doctorate, GRE General Test. Additional exam requirements/recommendations for international students: Required—TOEFL (minimum score 250 computer-based; 79 iBT). *Application deadline:* For fall admission, 2/1 priority date for domestic students, 2/1 for international students. Application fee: $50. Electronic applications accepted. *Financial support:* In 2011–12, 47 students received support, including 9 fellowships with full tuition reimbursements available (averaging $2,500 per year), 16 research assistantships with full tuition reimbursements available (averaging $15,000 per year), 14 teaching assistantships with full tuition reimbursements available (averaging $8,500 per year); career-related internships or fieldwork, Federal Work-Study, institutionally sponsored loans, scholarships/grants, tuition waivers (full and partial), and unspecified assistantships also available. Financial award application deadline: 3/15; financial award applicants required to submit FAFSA. *Faculty research:* Public health, epidemiology, rehabilitation, assistive technology, exercise and nutrition science. *Total annual research expenditures:* $6.7 million. *Unit head:* Dr. Lynn Kozlowski, Dean, 716-829-6951, Fax: 716-829-6040, E-mail: lk22@buffalo.edu. *Application contact:* Cassandra Walker-Whiteside, Project Director, Office of Academic and Student Affairs, 716-829-6769, Fax: 716-829-2034, E-mail: phhpadv@buffalo.edu. Web site: http://sphhp.buffalo.edu/.

The University of Alabama at Birmingham, School of Health Professions, Birmingham, AL 35294. Offers MS, MSHA, MSHI, MSPAS, D Sc, DPT, PhD. *Accreditation:* AANA/CANAEP (one or more programs are accredited); APTA (one or more programs are accredited); CAHME (one or more programs are accredited). Part-time programs available. *Degree requirements:* For doctorate, thesis/dissertation. Electronic applications accepted. *Expenses:* Contact institution. *Financial support:* Fellowships, research assistantships, teaching assistantships, career-related internships or fieldwork, Federal Work-Study, institutionally sponsored loans, scholarships/grants, traineeships, and unspecified assistantships available. Support available to part-time students. *Unit head:* Dr. Harold P. Jones, Dean, 205-934-5149, Fax: 205-934-2412, E-mail: jonesh@uab.edu. Web site: http://www.uab.edu/shp/.

University of Arkansas at Little Rock, Graduate School, College of Professional Studies, Department of Health Sciences, Little Rock, AR 72204-1099. Offers MS. Part-time and evening/weekend programs available. *Degree requirements:* For master's, directed study or residency. *Entrance requirements:* For master's, GMAT or GRE General Test, interview, minimum GPA of 2.75.

University of Connecticut, Graduate School, College of Agriculture and Natural Resources, Department of Allied Health Sciences, Storrs, CT 06269. Offers MS. *Accreditation:* APTA. *Degree requirements:* For master's, comprehensive exam. *Entrance requirements:* For master's, GRE General Test. Additional exam requirements/recommendations for international students: Required—TOEFL (minimum score 550 paper-based; 213 computer-based). Electronic applications accepted.

University of Detroit Mercy, College of Health Professions, Detroit, MI 48221. Offers MHSA, MS, MSN, Certificate. *Entrance requirements:* For master's, GRE General Test, minimum GPA of 3.0. *Faculty research:* Research design, respiratory physiology, AIDS prevention, adolescent health, community, low income health education.

University of Florida, Graduate School, College of Public Health and Health Professions, Gainesville, FL 32611. Offers MA, MHA, MHS, MOT, MPH, Au D, DPT, PhD. *Accreditation:* CAHME (one or more programs are accredited). Part-time programs available. *Faculty:* 76 full-time (36 women), 19 part-time/adjunct (10 women). *Students:* 613 full-time (458 women), 137 part-time (105 women); includes 186 minority (67 Black or African American, non-Hispanic/Latino; 3 American Indian or Alaska Native, non-Hispanic/Latino; 51 Asian, non-Hispanic/Latino; 65 Hispanic/Latino), 82 international. Average age 32. 1,343 applicants, 29% accepted, 202 enrolled. In 2011, 175 master's, 87 doctorates awarded. Terminal master's awarded for partial completion of doctoral program. *Degree requirements:* For master's, thesis (for some programs); for doctorate, comprehensive exam, thesis/dissertation. *Entrance requirements:* For master's and doctorate, GRE General Test, minimum GPA of 3.0. Additional exam requirements/recommendations for international students: Required—TOEFL (minimum score 550 paper-based; 213 computer-based; 80 iBT), IELTS (minimum score 6). *Application deadline:* Applications are processed on a rolling basis. Application fee: $30. Electronic applications accepted. *Financial support:* In 2011–12, 87 students received support, including 17 fellowships, 56 research assistantships, 14 teaching assistantships; career-related internships or fieldwork, Federal Work-Study, institutionally sponsored loans, and unspecified assistantships also available. Support available to part-time students. Financial award applicants required to submit FAFSA. *Unit head:* Dr. Michael G. Perri, Dean, 352-273-6214, Fax: 352-273-6199, E-mail: mperri@phhp.ufl.edu. Web site: http://www.phhp.ufl.edu/.

University of Illinois at Chicago, Graduate College, College of Applied Health Sciences, Chicago, IL 60607-7128. Offers MS, DPT, OTD, PhD. *Accreditation:* AOTA. Part-time programs available. *Degree requirements:* For doctorate, thesis/dissertation. *Entrance requirements:* For master's, GRE General Test, minimum GPA of 2.75. Additional exam requirements/recommendations for international students: Required—TOEFL. Electronic applications accepted. *Faculty research:* Care of the elderly, nutritional status for various diseases, immunohematology, computer-aided graphics.

The University of Kansas, University of Kansas Medical Center, School of Health Professions, Kansas City, KS 66160. Offers MA, MOT, MS, Au D, DPT, OTD, PhD, Certificate. *Faculty:* 112. *Students:* 323 full-time (248 women), 80 part-time (67 women); includes 33 minority (9 Black or African American, non-Hispanic/Latino; 4 American Indian or Alaska Native, non-Hispanic/Latino; 12 Asian, non-Hispanic/Latino; 4 Hispanic/Latino; 4 Two or more races, non-Hispanic/Latino), 21 international. Average age 28. 446 applicants, 36% accepted, 139 enrolled. In 2011, 64 master's, 63 doctorates, 15 other advanced degrees awarded. *Entrance requirements:* Additional exam requirements/recommendations for international students: Required—TOEFL. Tuition and fees vary according to course load, campus/location, program and reciprocity agreements. *Total annual research expenditures:* $2.2 million. *Unit head:* Dr. Karen L. Miller, Dean, 913-588-5235, Fax: 913-588-5254, E-mail: kmiller@kumc.edu. *Application contact:* Moffett Ferguson, Student Affairs Coordinator, 913-588-5275, Fax: 913-588-5254, E-mail: mfergus1@kumc.edu. Web site: http://healthprofessions.kumc.edu/.

University of Kentucky, Graduate School, College of Health Sciences, Lexington, KY 40506-0032. Offers MS, MSCD, MSHP, MSPAS, MSPT, MSRMP, DS, PhD. Part-time programs available. *Degree requirements:* For master's, comprehensive exam, thesis (for some programs). *Entrance requirements:* For master's, GRE General Test, minimum undergraduate GPA of 2.75; for doctorate, GRE General Test, minimum undergraduate GPA of 3.0. Additional exam requirements/recommendations for international students: Required—TOEFL (minimum score 550 paper-based; 213 computer-based). Electronic applications accepted.

University of Massachusetts Lowell, School of Health and Environment, Lowell, MA 01854-2881. Offers MS, DPT, PhD, Sc D, Certificate, Graduate Certificate. *Accreditation:* APTA (one or more programs are accredited). Part-time programs available. *Degree requirements:* For master's, thesis optional; for doctorate, thesis/dissertation. *Entrance requirements:* For master's and doctorate, GRE General Test.

University of Medicine and Dentistry of New Jersey, School of Health Related Professions, Newark, NJ 07107-1709. Offers MS, DCN, DPT, PhD, Certificate, DMD/MS, MD/MS. *Accreditation:* APTA (one or more programs are accredited); NAACLS. Part-time programs available. *Students:* 442 full-time, 425 part-time; includes 280 minority (80 Black or African American, non-Hispanic/Latino; 1 American Indian or Alaska Native, non-Hispanic/Latino; 135 Asian, non-Hispanic/Latino; 64 Hispanic/Latino). Average age 32. *Degree requirements:* For master's, thesis (for some programs). *Entrance requirements:* Additional exam requirements/recommendations for international students: Required—TOEFL. *Application deadline:* Applications are processed on a rolling basis. Application fee: $75. Electronic applications accepted. *Expenses:* Contact institution. *Financial support:* Fellowships, research assistantships, teaching assistantships, Federal Work-Study, and institutionally sponsored loans available. Financial award application deadline: 5/1. *Faculty research:* Clinical outcomes. *Unit head:* Dr. Julie O'Sullivan Maillet, Interim Dean, 973-972-4276, Fax: 973-972-7028, E-mail: maillet@umdnj.edu. *Application contact:* Diane Hanrahan, Manager of Admissions, 973-972-5336, Fax: 973-972-7463, E-mail: shrpadm@umdnj.edu. Web site: http://www.shrp.umdnj.edu/.

University of Mississippi Medical Center, School of Health Related Professions, Jackson, MS 39216-4505. Offers MOT, MPT. *Accreditation:* AOTA; NAACLS. Part-time programs available.

University of Nebraska Medical Center, School of Allied Health Professions, Omaha, NE 68198-4000. Offers MPAS, MPS, DPT, Certificate. *Accreditation:* APTA (one or more programs are accredited). *Entrance requirements:* For master's and doctorate, GRE. Additional exam requirements/recommendations for international students: Required—TOEFL.

University of Nevada, Las Vegas, Graduate College, School of Allied Health Sciences, Las Vegas, NV 89154-3018. Offers MS, DPT. Part-time programs available. *Faculty:* 21 full-time (7 women), 6 part-time/adjunct (0 women). *Students:* 105 full-time (63 women), 29 part-time (10 women); includes 29 minority (1 Black or African American, non-Hispanic/Latino; 1 American Indian or Alaska Native, non-Hispanic/Latino; 9 Asian, non-Hispanic/Latino; 12 Hispanic/Latino; 6 Two or more races, non-Hispanic/Latino), 2 international. Average age 27. 41 applicants, 80% accepted, 13 enrolled. In 2011, 13 master's, 30 doctorates awarded. *Degree requirements:* For master's, thesis optional.

Allied Health—General

Entrance requirements: Additional exam requirements/recommendations for international students: Required—TOEFL (minimum score 550 paper-based; 213 computer-based; 80 iBT), IELTS (minimum score 7). *Application deadline:* For fall admission, 5/1 for international students; for spring admission, 10/1 for international students. Application fee: $60 ($95 for international students). Electronic applications accepted. *Financial support:* In 2011–12, 33 students received support, including 13 research assistantships with partial tuition reimbursements available (averaging $10,657 per year), 20 teaching assistantships with partial tuition reimbursements available (averaging $9,113 per year); institutionally sponsored loans, scholarships/grants, health care benefits, and unspecified assistantships also available. Financial award application deadline: 3/1. *Total annual research expenditures:* $604,481. *Unit head:* Dr. Carolyn Yucha, Interim Dean, 702-895-3906, Fax: 702-895-5050, E-mail: carolyn.yucha@unlv.edu. *Application contact:* Graduate College Admissions Evaluator, 702-895-3320, Fax: 702-895-4180, E-mail: gradcollege@unlv.edu. Web site: http://healthsciences.unlv.edu/.

The University of North Carolina at Chapel Hill, School of Medicine and Graduate School, Graduate Programs in Medicine, Department of Allied Health Sciences, Chapel Hill, NC 27599. Offers human movement science (PhD); occupational science (MS, PhD), including occupational science; physical therapy (DPT), including physical therapy - off campus, physical therapy - on campus; rehabilitation counseling and psychology (MS); speech and hearing sciences (MS, Au D, PhD), including audiology (Au D); speech and hearing sciences (MS, PhD). *Accreditation:* APTA (one or more programs are accredited). Postbaccalaureate distance learning degree programs offered. *Entrance requirements:* For master's, GRE General Test; for doctorate, GRE General Test, minimum GPA of 3.0. Additional exam requirements/recommendations for international students: Required—TOEFL (minimum score 550 paper-based; 79 computer-based), TWE. Electronic applications accepted.

University of North Florida, Brooks College of Health, Jacksonville, FL 32224. Offers MHA, MPH, MS, MSH, MSN, DNP, DPT, Certificate. Part-time and evening/weekend programs available. *Faculty:* 63 full-time (47 women), 9 part-time/adjunct (6 women). *Students:* 320 full-time (226 women), 130 part-time (101 women); includes 86 minority (34 Black or African American, non-Hispanic/Latino; 4 American Indian or Alaska Native, non-Hispanic/Latino; 20 Asian, non-Hispanic/Latino; 21 Hispanic/Latino; 7 Two or more races, non-Hispanic/Latino), 9 international. Average age 30. 774 applicants, 26% accepted, 125 enrolled. In 2011, 137 master's, 28 doctorates awarded. *Entrance requirements:* For master's, GRE General Test, minimum GPA of 3.0 in last 60 hours. Additional exam requirements/recommendations for international students: Required—TOEFL (minimum score 500 paper-based; 173 computer-based; 61 iBT). *Application deadline:* For fall admission, 7/1 priority date for domestic students, 5/1 for international students; for spring admission, 11/1 priority date for domestic students, 10/1 for international students. Applications are processed on a rolling basis. Application fee: $30. Electronic applications accepted. *Expenses:* Contact institution. *Financial support:* In 2011–12, 168 students received support. Research assistantships, teaching assistantships, career-related internships or fieldwork, Federal Work-Study, scholarships/grants, and tuition waivers (partial) available. Support available to part-time students. Financial award application deadline: 4/1; financial award applicants required to submit FAFSA. *Faculty research:* Adolescent substance abuse, detection of bacterial agents, spirituality and health, non-vitamin and non-mineral supplements, analyzing ticks and their ability to transfer diseases to humans. *Total annual research expenditures:* $902,143. *Unit head:* Dr. Pamela Chally, Dean, 904-620-2810, Fax: 904-620-1030, E-mail: pchally@unf.edu. *Application contact:* Heather Kenney, Director of Advising, 904-620-2810, Fax: 904-620-1030, E-mail: heather.kenney@unf.edu. Web site: http://www.unf.edu/brooks.

University of Oklahoma Health Sciences Center, College of Medicine, Program in Physician Associate, Oklahoma City, OK 73190. Offers MHS.

University of Oklahoma Health Sciences Center, Graduate College, College of Allied Health, Oklahoma City, OK 73190. Offers MOT, MPT, MS, Au D, PhD, Certificate. *Accreditation:* AOTA; APTA. Part-time programs available. Terminal master's awarded for partial completion of doctoral program. *Degree requirements:* For master's, comprehensive exam, thesis optional; for doctorate, one foreign language, comprehensive exam, thesis/dissertation. *Entrance requirements:* For master's and doctorate, GRE General Test, 3 letters of recommendation. Additional exam requirements/recommendations for international students: Required—TOEFL.

University of Phoenix–Las Vegas Campus, College of Human Services, Las Vegas, NV 89128. Offers marriage, family, and child therapy (MSC); mental health counseling (MSC); school counseling (MSC). Postbaccalaureate distance learning degree programs offered. *Entrance requirements:* For master's, minimum undergraduate GPA of 2.5, 3 years of work experience. Additional exam requirements/recommendations for international students: Required—TOEFL (minimum score 550 paper-based; 213 computer-based; 79 iBT). Electronic applications accepted.

University of Puerto Rico, Medical Sciences Campus, School of Health Professions, San Juan, PR 00936-5067. Offers MS, Au D, Certificate. *Degree requirements:* For master's, one foreign language, thesis (for some programs). *Entrance requirements:* For master's, GRE or EXADEP, interview; for doctorate, EXADEP; for Certificate, Allied Health Professions Admissions Test, minimum GPA of 2.5, interview. Electronic applications accepted. *Faculty research:* Infantile autism, aphasia, language problems, toxicology, immunohematology, medical record documentation and quality.

University of Saint Francis, Graduate School, Department of Allied Health, Fort Wayne, IN 46808-3994. Offers nursing (MSN); physician assistant studies (MS). *Accreditation:* ARC-PA. Part-time programs available. Postbaccalaureate distance learning degree programs offered (minimal on-campus study). *Students:* 99 full-time (86 women), 97 part-time (88 women); includes 15 minority (11 Black or African American, non-Hispanic/Latino; 2 Asian, non-Hispanic/Latino; 2 Hispanic/Latino). In 2011, 57 master's awarded. *Entrance requirements:* For master's, GRE or MCAT, previous courses in biology, chemistry, and psychology, previous direct patient care. Additional exam requirements/recommendations for international students: Required—TOEFL. *Application deadline:* Applications are processed on a rolling basis. Application fee: $20. Application fee is waived when completed online. *Financial support:* Career-related internships or fieldwork, scholarships/grants, tuition waivers (full and partial), and unspecified assistantships available. Support available to part-time students. Financial award applicants required to submit FAFSA. *Unit head:* Dr. Nancy Gillespie, Dean, 260-399-7700 Ext. 8504, Fax: 260-399-8167, E-mail: ngillespie@sf.edu. *Application contact:* James Cashdollar, Admissions Counselor, 260-399-7700 Ext. 6302, E-mail: jcashdollar@sf.edu.

University of South Alabama, Graduate School, College of Allied Health Professions, Mobile, AL 36688-0002. Offers MHS, MS, Au D, DPT, PhD. *Faculty:* 26 full-time (12 women). *Students:* 330 full-time (265 women), 2 part-time (both women); includes 22 minority (13 Black or African American, non-Hispanic/Latino; 5 Asian, non-Hispanic/Latino; 3 Hispanic/Latino; 1 Native Hawaiian or other Pacific Islander, non-Hispanic/Latino), 2 international. 143 applicants, 99% accepted, 92 enrolled. In 2011, 83 master's, 67 doctorates awarded. *Degree requirements:* For master's, thesis optional, externship; for doctorate, thesis/dissertation, clinical internship. *Entrance requirements:*

For master's, GRE General Test; for doctorate, GRE (for Au D). Additional exam requirements/recommendations for international students: Required—TOEFL (minimum score 525 paper-based; 197 computer-based). *Application deadline:* For fall admission, 7/15 priority date for domestic students, 6/15 for international students; for spring admission, 12/1 for domestic students, 11/1 for international students. Applications are processed on a rolling basis. Application fee: $35. *Expenses:* Tuition, state resident: full-time $7968; part-time $332 per credit hour. Tuition, nonresident: full-time $15,936; part-time $664 per credit hour. *Financial support:* Fellowships, research assistantships, and career-related internships or fieldwork available. Support available to part-time students. Financial award application deadline: 4/1. *Unit head:* Dr. Richard Talbott, Dean, 251-445-9250. *Application contact:* Dr. Julio Turrens, Director of Graduate Studies, 251-445-9250. Web site: http://www.southalabama.edu/alliedhealth.

The University of South Dakota, Graduate School, School of Health Sciences, Vermillion, SD 57069-2390. Offers occupational therapy (MS); physical therapy (DPT); physician assistant studies (MS). Part-time programs available. *Entrance requirements:* For master's, GRE General Test, GRE Subject Test. *Expenses:* Tuition, state resident: full-time $3118.50; part-time $173.25 per credit hour. Tuition, nonresident: full-time $6601; part-time $366.70 per credit hour. *Required fees:* $2268; $126 per credit hour. Tuition and fees vary according to program. *Faculty research:* Occupational therapy, physical therapy, vision, pediatrics, geriatrics.

The University of Tennessee Health Science Center, College of Allied Health Sciences, Memphis, TN 38163-0002. Offers MCP, MDH, MHIIM, MOT, MSCLS, MSPT, DPT, ScDPT, TDPT. *Accreditation:* AOTA; APTA. Part-time and evening/weekend programs available. Postbaccalaureate distance learning degree programs offered (minimal on-campus study). Terminal master's awarded for partial completion of doctoral program. *Degree requirements:* For master's, comprehensive exam, thesis; for doctorate, comprehensive exam, residency. *Entrance requirements:* For master's, GRE (MOT, MSCLS), minimum GPA of 3.0, 3 letters of reference, state license (MDH), national accreditation (MSCLS), GRE if GPA is less than 3.0 (MCP); for doctorate, GRE. Additional exam requirements/recommendations for international students: Required—TOEFL (minimum score 550 paper-based; 213 computer-based; 80 iBT). Electronic applications accepted. *Expenses:* Contact institution. *Faculty research:* Gait deviation, muscular dystrophy and strength, hemophilia and exercise, pediatric neurology, self-efficacy.

The University of Tennessee Health Science Center, College of Graduate Health Sciences, Memphis, TN 38163-0002. Offers MS, PhD, Pharm D/PhD. Part-time programs available. Terminal master's awarded for partial completion of doctoral program. *Degree requirements:* For master's, comprehensive exam, thesis; for doctorate, thesis/dissertation, oral and written preliminary and comprehensive exams. *Entrance requirements:* For master's and doctorate, GRE General Test, minimum GPA of 3.0. Additional exam requirements/recommendations for international students: Required—TOEFL. Electronic applications accepted.

The University of Texas at El Paso, Graduate School, College of Health Sciences, Program in Interdisciplinary Health Sciences, El Paso, TX 79968-0001. Offers PhD. *Students:* 34 (26 women); includes 16 minority (3 Black or African American, non-Hispanic/Latino; 1 American Indian or Alaska Native, non-Hispanic/Latino; 1 Asian, non-Hispanic/Latino; 11 Hispanic/Latino), 8 international. In 2011, 3 doctorates awarded. *Degree requirements:* For doctorate, thesis/dissertation. *Entrance requirements:* For doctorate, GRE, letters of reference, relevant personal/professional experience, master's degree in health. Additional exam requirements/recommendations for international students: Required—TOEFL; Recommended—IELTS. *Application deadline:* For fall admission, 8/1 for domestic students, 3/1 for international students; for spring admission, 11/1 for domestic students, 9/3 for international students. Applications are processed on a rolling basis. Application fee: $45 ($80 for international students). Electronic applications accepted. *Financial support:* Fellowships with partial tuition reimbursements, research assistantships with partial tuition reimbursements, teaching assistantships with partial tuition reimbursements, institutionally sponsored loans, scholarships/grants, health care benefits, tuition waivers (partial), and unspecified assistantships available. Support available to part-time students. Financial award application deadline: 3/15; financial award applicants required to submit FAFSA. *Unit head:* Dr. Gloria McKee Lopez, Director, 915-747-7234, Fax: 915-747-7207, E-mail: gmckee@utep.edu. *Application contact:* Dr. Benjamin Flores, Interim Dean of the Graduate School, 915-747-5491, Fax: 915-747-5788, E-mail: bflores@utep.edu.

The University of Texas Medical Branch, School of Health Professions, Galveston, TX 77555. Offers MOT, MPAS, MPT, DPT. *Degree requirements:* For master's, thesis or alternative; for doctorate, thesis/dissertation or alternative. *Entrance requirements:* For master's, GRE, experience in field, minimum GPA of 3.0; for doctorate, GRE, documentation of 40 hours experience. Additional exam requirements/recommendations for international students: Required—TOEFL (minimum score 550 paper-based; 212 computer-based). Electronic applications accepted.

University of Vermont, Graduate College, College of Nursing and Health Sciences, Burlington, VT 05405. Offers MS, DPT. Part-time programs available. *Students:* 221 (190 women); includes 11 minority (1 American Indian or Alaska Native, non-Hispanic/Latino; 5 Asian, non-Hispanic/Latino; 5 Hispanic/Latino), 1 international. 475 applicants, 33% accepted, 43 enrolled. In 2011, 33 master's, 39 doctorates awarded. *Degree requirements:* For master's, thesis. *Entrance requirements:* For master's, GRE General Test. Additional exam requirements/recommendations for international students: Required—TOEFL (minimum score 550 paper-based; 213 computer-based; 80 iBT). *Application deadline:* For fall admission, 4/1 priority date for domestic students. Applications are processed on a rolling basis. Application fee: $40. Electronic applications accepted. *Financial support:* Fellowships, research assistantships, teaching assistantships, and Federal Work-Study available. Financial award application deadline: 3/1. *Unit head:* Dr. Patricia Prelock, Dean, 802-656-3830.

University of Wisconsin–Milwaukee, Graduate School, College of Health Sciences, Milwaukee, WI 53211. Offers MS, DPT, PhD, Certificate. Part-time programs available. *Faculty:* 42 full-time (24 women), 4 part-time/adjunct (2 women). *Students:* 210 full-time (160 women), 34 part-time (19 women); includes 14 minority (2 Black or African American, non-Hispanic/Latino; 7 Asian, non-Hispanic/Latino; 1 Hispanic/Latino; 4 Two or more races, non-Hispanic/Latino), 19 international. Average age 28. 321 applicants, 22% accepted, 44 enrolled. In 2011, 66 master's, 3 doctorates awarded. *Degree requirements:* For master's, thesis; for doctorate, comprehensive exam, thesis/dissertation. *Entrance requirements:* For doctorate, GRE General Test, master's degree. Additional exam requirements/recommendations for international students: Required—TOEFL (minimum score 600 paper-based; 250 computer-based), IELTS (minimum score 6.5). *Application deadline:* For fall admission, 1/1 priority date for domestic students; for spring admission, 9/1 for domestic students. Applications are processed on a rolling basis. Application fee: $56 ($96 for international students). *Expenses:* Contact institution. *Financial support:* In 2011–12, 6 research assistantships, 12 teaching assistantships were awarded; career-related internships or fieldwork, Federal Work-Study, and unspecified assistantships also available. Support available to part-time students. Financial award application deadline: 4/15. *Total annual research expenditures:* $2.5 million. *Unit head:* Chukuka S. Enwemeka, Dean, 414-229-4712, E-mail: enwemeka@uwm.edu. *Application contact:* Roger O. Smith, General

Information Contact, 414-229-6697, Fax: 414-229-6697, E-mail: smithro@uwm.edu. Web site: http://www4.uwm.edu/chs/.

Virginia Commonwealth University, Graduate School, School of Allied Health Professions, Doctoral Program in Health Related Sciences, Richmond, VA 23284-9005. Offers clinical laboratory sciences (PhD); gerontology (PhD); health administration (PhD); nurse anesthesia (PhD); occupational therapy (PhD); physical therapy (PhD); radiation sciences (PhD); rehabilitation leadership (PhD). *Faculty:* 2 full-time (1 woman). *Students:* 23 full-time (15 women), 34 part-time (23 women); includes 7 minority (4 Black or African American, non-Hispanic/Latino; 1 Asian, non-Hispanic/Latino; 1 Hispanic/Latino; 1 Two or more races, non-Hispanic/Latino), 2 international. 37 applicants, 38% accepted, 11 enrolled. In 2011, 11 doctorates awarded. *Entrance requirements:* For doctorate, GRE General Test or MAT, minimum GPA of 3.3 in master's degree. Additional exam requirements/recommendations for international students: Required—TOEFL (minimum score 600 paper-based; 250 computer-based; 100 iBT); Recommended—IELTS (minimum score 6.5). *Application deadline:* For fall admission, 3/15 for domestic students. Application fee: $50. Electronic applications accepted. *Expenses:* Tuition, state resident: full-time $9133; part-time $507 per credit. Tuition, nonresident: full-time $18,777; part-time $1043 per credit. *Required fees:* $77 per credit. Tuition and fees vary according to degree level, campus/location, program and student level. *Unit head:* Dr. Paula K. Kupstas, Director, Health Related Sciences Program, 804-828-7247, E-mail: pkupstas@vcu.edu. *Application contact:* Monica L. White, Director of Student Services, 804-828-3273, Fax: 804-828-8656, E-mail: mlwhite1@vcu.edu. Web site: http://www.pubapps.vcu.edu/BULLETINS/prog_search/?did=20005.

Washington University in St. Louis, School of Medicine, Graduate Programs in Medicine, St. Louis, MO 63130-4899. Offers movement science (PhD); occupational therapy (MSOT, OTD); physical therapy (DPT, PPDPT, PhD); rehabilitation and participation science (PhD). *Degree requirements:* For doctorate, thesis/dissertation. *Expenses:* Contact institution.

Western University of Health Sciences, College of Allied Health Professions, Pomona, CA 91766-1854. Offers MS, DPT. *Accreditation:* APTA (one or more programs are accredited). *Faculty:* 23 full-time (20 women), 2 part-time/adjunct (both women). *Students:* 355 full-time (254 women), 34 part-time (27 women); includes 169 minority (12 Black or African American, non-Hispanic/Latino; 111 Asian, non-Hispanic/Latino; 26 Hispanic/Latino; 2 Native Hawaiian or other Pacific Islander, non-Hispanic/Latino; 18 Two or more races, non-Hispanic/Latino), 4 international. Average age 29. 2,275 applicants, 13% accepted, 163 enrolled. In 2011, 104 master's, 38 doctorates awarded. *Entrance requirements:* For doctorate, GRE General Test, minimum GPA of 2.8, letters of recommendation, interview, bachelor's degree. *Application deadline:* For fall admission, 12/1 for domestic students. Electronic applications accepted. *Expenses:* Contact institution. *Financial support:* Institutionally sponsored loans and scholarships/grants available. Financial award application deadline: 3/2; financial award applicants required to submit FAFSA. *Unit head:* Dr. Stephanie Bowlin, Dean, 909-469-5383. *Application contact:* Karen Hutton-Lopez, Director of Admissions, 909-469-5650, Fax: 909-469-5570, E-mail: admissions@westernu.edu. Web site: http://www.westernu.edu/xp/edu/cahp/welcome.xml.

Wichita State University, Graduate School, College of Health Professions, Wichita, KS 67260. Offers MA, MPA, MSN, Au D, DNP, DPT, PhD, MSN/MBA. *Accreditation:* APTA (one or more programs are accredited). Part-time programs available. *Expenses:* Tuition, state resident: full-time $4746; part-time $263.65 per credit. Tuition, nonresident: full-time $11,669; part-time $648.30 per credit. *Unit head:* Dr. Peter A. Cohen, Dean, 316-978-3600, Fax: 316-978-3025, E-mail: peter.cohon@wichita.edu. *Application contact:* Carrie C. Henderson, Admissions Coordinator, 316-978-3095, Fax: 316-978-3253, E-mail: carrie.henderson@wichita.edu. Web site: http://www.wichita.edu/.

Anesthesiologist Assistant Studies

Case Western Reserve University, School of Medicine and School of Graduate Studies, Graduate Programs in Medicine, Department of Anesthesiology, Cleveland, OH 44106. Offers MS. *Accreditation:* AANA/CANAEP. *Degree requirements:* For master's, thesis. *Entrance requirements:* For master's, MCAT. Additional exam requirements/recommendations for international students: Required—TOEFL. Electronic applications accepted. *Faculty research:* Metabolism of bioamines, cerebral metabolism, cardiovascular hemodynamics, genetics.

Emory University, School of Medicine, Programs in Allied Health Professions, Anesthesiology Assistant Program, Atlanta, GA 30329. Offers MM Sc. *Faculty:* 10 part-time/adjunct (5 women). *Students:* 79 full-time (37 women); includes 18 minority (6 Black or African American, non-Hispanic/Latino; 8 Asian, non-Hispanic/Latino; 2 Hispanic/Latino; 1 Native Hawaiian or other Pacific Islander, non-Hispanic/Latino; 1 Two or more races, non-Hispanic/Latino). Average age 29. 232 applicants, 18% accepted, 40 enrolled. In 2011, 37 master's awarded. *Entrance requirements:* For master's, GRE General Test or MCAT. Additional exam requirements/recommendations for international students: Required—TOEFL (minimum score 600 paper-based; 250 computer-based; 100 iBT). *Application deadline:* For fall admission, 12/15 for domestic and international students. Applications are processed on a rolling basis. Application fee: $60. Electronic applications accepted. *Expenses:* Contact institution. *Financial support:* In 2011–12, 61 students received support. Institutionally sponsored loans and scholarships/grants available. Financial award application deadline: 3/1; financial award applicants required to submit FAFSA. *Unit head:* Dr. Richard G. Brouillard, Director of Academic Affairs, 404-727-5910, Fax: 404-727-3021. *Application contact:* Jerri J. Elder, Associate Director of Admissions, 404-727-7125, Fax: 404-727-3021. Web site: http://www.anesthesiology.emory.edu/.

South University, Graduate Programs, College of Health Professions, Program in Anesthesiologist Assistant, Savannah, GA 31406. Offers MM Sc.

See Close-Up on page 555.

Université Laval, Faculty of Medicine, Post-Professional Programs in Medical Studies, Québec, QC G1K 7P4, Canada. Offers anatomy–pathology (DESS); anesthesiology (DESS); cardiology (DESS); care of older people (Diploma); clinical research (DESS); community health (DESS); dermatology (DESS); diagnostic radiology (DESS); emergency medicine (Diploma); family medicine (DESS); general surgery (DESS); geriatrics (DESS); hematology (DESS); internal medicine (DESS); maternal and fetal medicine (Diploma); medical biochemistry (DESS); medical microbiology and infectious diseases (DESS); medical oncology (DESS); nephrology (DESS); neurology (DESS); neurosurgery (DESS); obstetrics and gynecology (DESS); ophthalmology (DESS); orthopedic surgery (DESS); oto-rhino-laryngology (DESS); palliative medicine (Diploma); pediatrics (DESS); plastic surgery (DESS); psychiatry (DESS); pulmonary medicine (DESS); radiology–oncology (DESS); thoracic surgery (DESS); urology (DESS). *Degree requirements:* For other advanced degree, comprehensive exam. *Entrance requirements:* For degree, knowledge of French. Electronic applications accepted.

University of Guelph, Ontario Veterinary College and Graduate Studies, Graduate Programs in Veterinary Sciences, Department of Clinical Studies, Guelph, ON N1G 2W1, Canada. Offers anesthesiology (M Sc, DV Sc); cardiology (DV Sc, Diploma); clinical studies (Diploma); dermatology (M Sc); diagnostic imaging (M Sc, DV Sc); emergency/critical care (M Sc, DV Sc, Diploma); medicine (M Sc, DV Sc); neurology (M Sc, DV Sc); ophthalmology (M Sc, DV Sc); surgery (M Sc, DV Sc). *Degree requirements:* For master's, thesis; for doctorate, comprehensive exam, thesis/dissertation. *Entrance requirements:* Additional exam requirements/recommendations for international students: Required—TOEFL (minimum score 550 paper-based; 213 computer-based), IELTS (minimum score 6.5). Electronic applications accepted. *Faculty research:* Orthopedics, respirology, oncology, exercise physiology, cardiology.

University of Missouri–Kansas City, School of Medicine, Kansas City, MO 64110-2499. Offers anesthesia (MS); bioinformatics (MS); medicine (MD); MD/PhD. *Accreditation:* LCME/AMA. *Faculty:* 38 full-time (13 women), 15 part-time/adjunct (4 women). *Students:* 424 full-time (224 women), 11 part-time (7 women); includes 230 minority (25 Black or African American, non-Hispanic/Latino; 1 American Indian or Alaska Native, non-Hispanic/Latino; 190 Asian, non-Hispanic/Latino; 12 Hispanic/Latino; 2 Two or more races, non-Hispanic/Latino), 2 international. Average age 23. 821 applicants, 15% accepted, 107 enrolled. In 2011, 4 master's, 101 doctorates awarded. *Degree requirements:* For doctorate, one foreign language, United States Medical Licensing Exam Step 1 and 2. *Entrance requirements:* For doctorate, interview. *Application deadline:* For fall admission, 11/15 for domestic and international students. Application fee: $50. *Expenses:* Contact institution. *Financial support:* Career-related internships or fieldwork, Federal Work-Study, institutionally sponsored loans, scholarships/grants, and tuition waivers (partial) available. Financial award application deadline: 3/1; financial award applicants required to submit FAFSA. *Faculty research:* Cardiovascular disease, women's and children's health, trauma and infectious diseases, neurological, metabolic disease. *Unit head:* Dr. Betty Drees, Dean, 816-235-1808, E-mail: dreesb@umkc.edu. *Application contact:* Kelly Kasper-Cushman, Interim Admissions Coordinator, 816-235-1870, Fax: 816-235-6579, E-mail: kasperkm@umkc.edu. Web site: http://www.med.umkc.edu/.

Clinical Laboratory Sciences/Medical Technology

Austin Peay State University, College of Graduate Studies, College of Science and Mathematics, Department of Biology, Clarksville, TN 37044. Offers clinical laboratory science (MS); radiologic science (MS). Part-time programs available. *Faculty:* 8 full-time (3 women), 1 part-time/adjunct (0 women). *Students:* 6 full-time (2 women), 19 part-time (12 women); includes 3 minority (2 Black or African American, non-Hispanic/Latino; 1 Hispanic/Latino), 1 international. Average age 28. 13 applicants, 92% accepted, 9 enrolled. In 2011, 9 master's awarded. *Degree requirements:* For master's, comprehensive exam, thesis optional. *Entrance requirements:* For master's, GRE General Test, 3 letters of recommendation, minimum undergraduate GPA of 2.5. Additional exam requirements/recommendations for international students: Required—TOEFL (minimum score 500 paper-based; 173 computer-based). *Application deadline:* For fall admission, 8/1 priority date for domestic students. Applications are processed on a rolling basis. Application fee: $25. Electronic applications accepted. *Expenses:* Tuition, state resident: part-time $350 per credit hour. Tuition, nonresident: full-time $20,644; part-time $971 per credit hour. *Required fees:* $1224; $61.20 per credit hour. *Financial support:* In 2011–12, research assistantships with full tuition reimbursements (averaging $5,184 per year) were awarded; career-related internships or fieldwork, Federal Work-Study, institutionally sponsored loans, scholarships/grants, and unspecified assistantships also available. Support available to part-time students. Financial award application deadline: 3/1. *Faculty research:* Non-paint source pollution, amphibian biomonitoring, aquatic toxicology, biological indicators of water quality, taxonomy. *Unit head:* Dr. Don Dailey, Chair, 931-221-7781, Fax: 931-221-6323, E-mail: daileyd@apsu.edu. *Application contact:* Kendra Bryant, Graduate Admissions, 800-844-2778, Fax: 931-221-6188, E-mail: admissionsweb@apsu.edu. Web site: http://www.apsu.edu/biology.

Baylor College of Medicine, Graduate School of Biomedical Sciences, Program in Clinical Scientist Training, Houston, TX 77030-3498. Offers MS, PhD. *Faculty:* 76 full-time (22 women). *Students:* 37 full-time (17 women); includes 18 minority (15 Asian, non-Hispanic/Latino; 3 Hispanic/Latino), 9 international. Average age 36. 13 applicants, 62% accepted, 8 enrolled. In 2011, 7 master's, 4 doctorates awarded. Terminal master's awarded for partial completion of doctoral program. *Degree requirements:* For master's, thesis; for doctorate, thesis/dissertation, public defense. *Application deadline:* For fall admission, 1/1 priority date for domestic students. Application fee: $0. Electronic applications accepted. *Financial support:* In 2011–12, 37 students received support,

including 9 fellowships with full tuition reimbursements available, 37 research assistantships with full tuition reimbursements available; career-related internships or fieldwork, Federal Work-Study, institutionally sponsored loans, health care benefits, and scholarships (to all students unless there are grant funds available to pay tuition) also available. *Faculty research:* Cardiology, pulmonary, HIV, rheumatology, cancer. *Unit head:* Dr. Morey Haymond, Director, 713-798-6776, Fax: 713-798-7119, E-mail: mhaymond@bcm.edu. *Application contact:* Dr. Olga Watkins, Graduate Program Administrator/Co-Director, 713-798-7132, Fax: 713-798-7119, E-mail: owatkins@bcm.edu. Web site: http://www.bcm.edu/cstp.

The Catholic University of America, School of Arts and Sciences, Department of Biology, Washington, DC 20064. Offers cell and microbial biology (MS, PhD), including cell biology, microbiology; clinical laboratory science (MS, PhD); MSLS/MS. Part-time programs available. *Faculty:* 9 full-time (5 women), 3 part-time/adjunct (2 women). *Students:* 19 full-time (16 women), 26 part-time (17 women); includes 10 minority (3 Black or African American, non-Hispanic/Latino; 6 Asian, non-Hispanic/Latino; 1 Hispanic/Latino), 20 international. Average age 29. 53 applicants, 62% accepted, 15 enrolled. In 2011, 1 master's, 2 doctorates awarded. *Degree requirements:* For master's, comprehensive exam, thesis or alternative; for doctorate, comprehensive exam, thesis/dissertation. *Entrance requirements:* For master's and doctorate, GRE General Test, GRE Subject Test, statement of purpose, official copies of academic transcripts, three letters of recommendation. Additional exam requirements/recommendations for international students: Required—TOEFL (minimum score 580 paper-based; 237 computer-based). *Application deadline:* For fall admission, 8/1 priority date for domestic students, 7/15 for international students; for spring admission, 12/1 priority date for domestic students, 10/15 for international students. Applications are processed on a rolling basis. Application fee: $55. Electronic applications accepted. *Expenses: Tuition:* Full-time $35,260; part-time $1380 per credit. *Required fees:* $80; $40 per semester hour. One-time fee: $425. *Financial support:* Fellowships, research assistantships, teaching assistantships, Federal Work-Study, scholarships/grants, tuition waivers (full and partial), and unspecified assistantships available. Financial award application deadline: 2/1; financial award applicants required to submit FAFSA. *Faculty research:* Cell and microbiology, molecular biology of cell proliferation, cellular effects of electromagnetic radiation, biotechnology. *Total annual research expenditures:* $1.4 million. *Unit head:* Dr. Venigalla Rao, Chair, 202-319-5271, Fax: 202-319-5721, E-mail: rao@cua.edu. *Application contact:* Andrew Woodall, Director of Graduate Admissions, 202-319-5057, Fax: 202-319-6533, E-mail: cua-admissions@cua.edu. Web site: http://biology.cua.edu/.

Duke University, School of Medicine, Clinical Leadership Program, Durham, NC 27701. Offers MHS. *Faculty:* 9 part-time/adjunct (4 women). *Students:* 9 part-time (5 women); includes 5 minority (2 Black or African American, non-Hispanic/Latino; 1 American Indian or Alaska Native, non-Hispanic/Latino; 1 Asian, non-Hispanic/Latino; 1 Hispanic/Latino). 9 applicants, 100% accepted, 9 enrolled. In 2011, 1 master's awarded. *Degree requirements:* For master's, project. *Entrance requirements:* For master's, GRE. *Application deadline:* For fall admission, 5/1 priority date for domestic students; for spring admission, 9/1 priority date for domestic students. Applications are processed on a rolling basis. Application fee: $100. *Expenses: Tuition:* Full-time $40,720. *Required fees:* $3107. *Financial support:* Fellowships, research assistantships, and teaching assistantships available. Financial award application deadline: 5/1; financial award applicants required to submit FAFSA. *Unit head:* Dr. Anh N. Tran, Assistant Professor, 919-681-5724, Fax: 919-613-6899, E-mail: anh.tran@duke.edu. *Application contact:* Claudia Graham, MBA, MPH, Project Coordinator, 919-681-5724, Fax: 919-681-6899, E-mail: claudia.graham@duke.edu.

Fairleigh Dickinson University, Metropolitan Campus, University College: Arts, Sciences, and Professional Studies, Henry P. Becton School of Nursing and Allied Health, Program in Medical Technology, Teaneck, NJ 07666-1914. Offers MS.

Inter American University of Puerto Rico, Metropolitan Campus, Graduate Programs, Program in Medical Technology, San Juan, PR 00919-1293. Offers administration of clinical laboratories (MS); molecular microbiology (MS). *Accreditation:* NAACLS. Part-time programs available. *Degree requirements:* For master's, comprehensive exam. *Entrance requirements:* For master's, BS in medical technology, minimum GPA of 2.5. Electronic applications accepted.

Long Island University–C. W. Post Campus, School of Health Professions and Nursing, Department of Biomedical Sciences, Brookville, NY 11548-1300. Offers cardiovascular perfusion (MS); clinical laboratory management (MS); medical biology (MS), including hematology, immunology, medical biology, medical chemistry, medical microbiology. Part-time and evening/weekend programs available. Postbaccalaureate distance learning degree programs offered. *Degree requirements:* For master's, thesis. *Entrance requirements:* For master's, minimum GPA of 2.75 in major. Electronic applications accepted.

Medical College of Wisconsin, Graduate School of Biomedical Sciences, Program in Basic and Translational Science, Milwaukee, WI 53226-0509. Offers PhD. *Entrance requirements:* For doctorate, GRE, official transcripts, three letters of recommendation. Additional exam requirements/recommendations for international students: Required—TOEFL.

Medical College of Wisconsin, Graduate School of Biomedical Sciences, Program in Clinical and Translational Science, Milwaukee, WI 53226-0509. Offers MS. Program offered in collaboration with the Clinical and Translational Science Institute (CTSI) of Southeast Wisconsin. *Entrance requirements:* For master's, GRE, official transcripts, three letters of recommendation. Additional exam requirements/recommendations for international students: Required—TOEFL.

Medical College of Wisconsin, Graduate School of Biomedical Sciences, Program in Health Care Technologies Management, Milwaukee, WI 53226-0509. Offers MS. *Entrance requirements:* For master's, GRE, official transcripts, three letters of recommendation. Additional exam requirements/recommendations for international students: Required—TOEFL.

Michigan State University, The Graduate School, College of Natural Science, Biomedical Laboratory Diagnostics Program, East Lansing, MI 48824. Offers biomedical laboratory operations (MS); clinical laboratory sciences (MS). *Entrance requirements:* Additional exam requirements/recommendations for international students: Required—TOEFL. Electronic applications accepted.

Milwaukee School of Engineering, Department of Electrical Engineering and Computer Science, Program in Perfusion, Milwaukee, WI 53202-3109. Offers MS. Part-time and evening/weekend programs available. *Faculty:* 1 full-time (0 women), 3 part-time/adjunct (1 woman). *Students:* 11 full-time (3 women); includes 1 minority (Black or African American, non-Hispanic/Latino). Average age 33. 19 applicants, 42% accepted, 5 enrolled. *Degree requirements:* For master's, comprehensive exam, thesis, exam. *Entrance requirements:* For master's, GRE General Test or GMAT, BS in appropriate discipline, undergraduate work in human physiology or anatomy, 3 letters of recommendation, interview, observation of 2 perfusion cases. Additional exam requirements/recommendations for international students: Required—TOEFL (minimum score 79 iBT). *Application deadline:* Applications are processed on a rolling basis. Electronic applications accepted. Application fee is waived when completed online. *Expenses: Tuition:* Full-time $17,550; part-time $650 per credit hour. *Financial support:* In 2011–12, 10 students received support. Career-related internships or fieldwork available. Support available to part-time students. Financial award applicants required to submit FAFSA. *Faculty research:* Heart medicine. *Unit head:* Dr. Ronald Gerrits, Director, 414-277-7561, Fax: 414-277-7494, E-mail: gerrits@msoe.edu. *Application contact:* Katie Gassenhuber, Graduate Program Associate, 800-321-6763, Fax: 414-277-7208, E-mail: gassenhuber@msoe.edu. Web site: http://www.msoe.edu/academics/academic_departments/eecs/msp/.

Northwestern University, School of Continuing Studies, Program in Regulatory Compliance, Evanston, IL 60208. Offers MS. Offered in partnership with Northwestern University's Clinical and Translational Sciences Institute.

Pontifical Catholic University of Puerto Rico, College of Sciences, School of Medical Technology, Ponce, PR 00717-0777. Offers Certificate. *Entrance requirements:* For degree, letters of recommendation, interview, minimum GPA of 2.75.

Quinnipiac University, School of Health Sciences, Program for Pathologists' Assistant, Hamden, CT 06518-1940. Offers MHS. *Accreditation:* NAACLS. *Faculty:* 2 full-time (1 woman), 6 part-time/adjunct (3 women). *Students:* 36 full-time (26 women); includes 4 minority (1 Black or African American, non-Hispanic/Latino; 3 Asian, non-Hispanic/Latino). Average age 27. 130 applicants, 14% accepted, 18 enrolled. In 2011, 18 master's awarded. *Degree requirements:* For master's, residency. *Entrance requirements:* For master's, interview, coursework in biological and health sciences, minimum GPA of 2.8. Additional exam requirements/recommendations for international students: Required—TOEFL (minimum score 575 paper-based; 233 computer-based; 90 iBT), IELTS (minimum score 6.5). *Application deadline:* For fall admission, 12/15 for domestic students. Applications are processed on a rolling basis. Application fee: $45. Electronic applications accepted. *Expenses: Tuition:* Part-time $855 per credit. *Required fees:* $35 per credit. *Financial support:* In 2011–12, 8 students received support. Career-related internships or fieldwork, tuition waivers (partial), and unspecified assistantships available. Financial award application deadline: 4/15; financial award applicants required to submit FAFSA. *Unit head:* Dr. Kenneth Kaloustian, Director, 203-582-8676, Fax: 203-582-3443, E-mail: ken.kaloustian@quinnipiac.edu. *Application contact:* Kristin Parent, Assistant Director of Graduate Health Sciences Admissions, 800-462-1944, Fax: 203-582-3443, E-mail: kristin.parent@quinnipiac.edu. Web site: http://www.quinnipiac.edu/gradpathologists.

Quinnipiac University, School of Health Sciences, Program in Medical Laboratory Sciences, Hamden, CT 06518-1940. Offers biomedical sciences (MHS); laboratory management (MHS); microbiology (MHS). Part-time programs available. *Faculty:* 13 full-time (7 women), 17 part-time/adjunct (7 women). *Students:* 46 full-time (30 women), 31 part-time (13 women); includes 14 minority (8 Black or African American, non-Hispanic/Latino; 4 Asian, non-Hispanic/Latino; 2 Hispanic/Latino), 34 international. 67 applicants, 79% accepted, 46 enrolled. In 2011, 33 master's awarded. *Degree requirements:* For master's, comprehensive exam, thesis optional. *Entrance requirements:* For master's, minimum GPA of 2.75; bachelor's degree in biological, medical, or health sciences. Additional exam requirements/recommendations for international students: Required—TOEFL (minimum score 575 paper-based; 233 computer-based; 90 iBT), IELTS (minimum score 6.5). *Application deadline:* For fall admission, 7/30 priority date for domestic students, 4/30 for international students; for spring admission, 12/15 priority date for domestic students, 9/15 for international students. Applications are processed on a rolling basis. Application fee: $45. Electronic applications accepted. *Expenses: Tuition:* Part-time $855 per credit. *Required fees:* $35 per credit. *Financial support:* In 2011–12, 8 students received support. Federal Work-Study, tuition waivers (partial), and unspecified assistantships available. Support available to part-time students. Financial award application deadline: 4/15; financial award applicants required to submit FAFSA. *Faculty research:* Microbial physiology, fermentation technology. *Unit head:* Dr. Kenneth Kaloustian, Director, 203-582-8676, Fax: 203-582-3443, E-mail: ken.kaloustian@quinnipiac.edu. *Application contact:* Kristin Parent, Assistant Director of Graduate Health Sciences Admissions, 800-462-1944, Fax: 203-582-3443, E-mail: kristin.parent@quinnipiac.edu. Web site: http://www.quinnipiac.edu/gradmedlab.

Rush University, College of Health Sciences, Department of Clinical Laboratory Sciences, Chicago, IL 60612-3832. Offers clinical laboratory management (MS); clinical laboratory science (MS). *Accreditation:* NAACLS. Part-time programs available. *Degree requirements:* For master's, comprehensive exam, graduate project. *Entrance requirements:* For master's, 16 semester hours of chemistry, 12 semester hours of biology, 3 semester hours of mathematics, interview. Additional exam requirements/recommendations for international students: Required—TOEFL. Electronic applications accepted. *Faculty research:* Hematopoietic disorders, molecular techniques, biochemistry, microbial susceptibility, immunology.

State University of New York Upstate Medical University, Program in Medical Technology, Syracuse, NY 13210-2334. Offers MS. *Accreditation:* NAACLS. *Degree requirements:* For master's, thesis. *Entrance requirements:* For master's, GRE General Test, GRE Subject Test, 2 years of medical technology experience.

Thomas Jefferson University, Jefferson School of Health Professions, Department of Bioscience Technologies, Philadelphia, PA 19107. Offers MS. Part-time and evening/weekend programs available. *Entrance requirements:* For master's, GRE General Test or MAT. Additional exam requirements/recommendations for international students: Required—TOEFL (minimum score 213 computer-based). Electronic applications accepted. *Faculty research:* Molecular biology of BCR-ABL in chronic myeloid leukemia, diagnostic cytogenetics, ATP binding cassette (ABC), gene family, education outcome studies.

Universidad de las Américas–Puebla, Division of Graduate Studies, School of Sciences, Program in Clinical Analysis (Biomedicine), Puebla, Mexico. Offers MS. Part-time and evening/weekend programs available. *Degree requirements:* For master's, one foreign language, thesis. *Faculty research:* Clinical techniques, clinical research.

Université de Sherbrooke, Faculty of Medicine and Health Sciences, Graduate Programs in Medicine, Program in Clinical Sciences, Sherbrooke, QC J1H 5N4, Canada. Offers M Sc, PhD. Part-time programs available. Terminal master's awarded for partial completion of doctoral program. *Degree requirements:* For master's, thesis; for doctorate, thesis/dissertation. Electronic applications accepted. *Faculty research:* Population health, health services, ethics, clinical research.

University at Buffalo, the State University of New York, Graduate School, School of Medicine and Biomedical Sciences, Graduate Programs in Medicine and Biomedical Sciences, Department of Biotechnical and Clinical Laboratory Sciences, Buffalo, NY 14214. Offers biotechnology (MS). *Accreditation:* NAACLS. Part-time programs available. *Faculty:* 8 full-time (3 women). *Students:* 15 full-time (9 women), 1 (woman) part-time; includes 1 minority (Asian, non-Hispanic/Latino), 11 international. 128 applicants, 9% accepted, 11 enrolled. In 2011, 9 master's awarded. *Degree requirements:* For master's, thesis. *Entrance requirements:* For master's, GRE General Test, minimum GPA of 3.0 or equivalent, 4-year U.S. bachelor's degree or equivalent. Additional exam requirements/recommendations for international students: Required—TOEFL (minimum score 213 computer-based; 79 iBT), IELTS (minimum score 6). *Application deadline:* For fall admission, 3/1 priority date for domestic students, 2/1 for international students. Applications are processed on a rolling basis. Application fee:

$50. Electronic applications accepted. *Financial support:* In 2011–12, 5 teaching assistantships with full tuition reimbursements (averaging $9,000 per year) were awarded; health care benefits and unspecified assistantships also available. *Faculty research:* Tumor immunology, oxidative stress, breast cancer, erythropoiesis, toxicology. *Total annual research expenditures:* $756,762. *Unit head:* Dr. Stephen Thomas Koury, Director of Graduate Studies, 716-829-5188, Fax: 716-829-3601, E-mail: stvkoury@buffalo.edu. *Application contact:* Elizabeth A. White, Administrative Director, 716-829-3399, Fax: 716-829-2437, E-mail: bethw@buffalo.edu. Web site: http://www.smbs.buffalo.edu/cls/biotech-ms.html.

The University of Alabama at Birmingham, School of Health Professions, Program in Clinical Laboratory Science, Birmingham, AL 35294. Offers MS. *Accreditation:* NAACLS. *Degree requirements:* For master's, thesis optional. *Entrance requirements:* For master's, GRE General Test, interview. *Application deadline:* Applications are processed on a rolling basis. Electronic applications accepted. *Expenses:* Tuition, state resident: full-time $5922; part-time $309 per hour. Tuition, nonresident: full-time $13,428; part-time $726 per hour. Tuition and fees vary according to program. *Financial support:* Application deadline: 4/15. *Faculty research:* Computer-enhanced instruction, antiphospholipid antibodies, alternate site testing, technology assessment. *Unit head:* Dr. Janelle Chiasera, Director, 205-934-5994. *Application contact:* Julie Bryant, Director of Graduate Admissions, 205-934-8227, Fax: 205-934-8413, E-mail: jbryant@uab.edu. Web site: http://www.uab.edu/cds/academic/graduate/cls.

University of Alberta, Faculty of Medicine and Dentistry and Faculty of Graduate Studies and Research, Graduate Programs in Medicine, Department of Laboratory Medicine and Pathology, Edmonton, AB T6G 2E1, Canada. Offers medical sciences (M Sc, PhD). Part-time programs available. Terminal master's awarded for partial completion of doctoral program. *Degree requirements:* For master's, thesis; for doctorate, thesis/dissertation, candidacy exam. *Entrance requirements:* For master's and doctorate, 3 letters of recommendation, minimum GPA of 3.0. Additional exam requirements/recommendations for international students: Required—TOEFL. *Faculty research:* Transplantation, renal pathology, molecular mechanisms of diseases, cryobiology, immunodiagnostics, informatics/cyber medicine, neuroimmunology, microbiology.

University of Colorado Denver, College of Engineering and Applied Science, Department of Bioengineering, Aurora, CO 80045-2560. Offers bioengineering (PhD); clinical application (PhD); clinical imaging (MS); commercialization of medical technologies (MS, PhD); device design and entrepreneurship (MS); research (MS). Part-time programs available. *Faculty:* 3 full-time (1 woman). *Students:* 38 full-time (13 women), 1 part-time; includes 7 minority (3 Black or African American, non-Hispanic/Latino; 2 Asian, non-Hispanic/Latino; 1 Hispanic/Latino; 1 Two or more races, non-Hispanic/Latino), 2 international. Average age 27. 56 applicants, 48% accepted, 24 enrolled. Terminal master's awarded for partial completion of doctoral program. *Degree requirements:* For master's, thesis or alternative, 30 credit hours; for doctorate, comprehensive exam, thesis/dissertation, 36 credit hours of classwork (18 core, 18 elective), additional 30 hours of thesis work, three formal examinations, approval of dissertations. *Entrance requirements:* For master's and doctorate, GRE, transcripts, three letters of recommendation, resume, statement of purpose. Additional exam requirements/recommendations for international students: Required—TOEFL (minimum score 550 paper-based; 213 computer-based; 79 iBT), TOEFL (minimum score 600 paper-based; 250 computer-based; 100 iBT) for Ph D. *Application deadline:* For fall admission, 2/15 for domestic students. Application fee: $50. Electronic applications accepted. *Expenses:* Contact institution. *Financial support:* Fellowships, research assistantships, teaching assistantships, and Federal Work-Study available. Financial award application deadline: 4/1; financial award applicants required to submit FAFSA. *Faculty research:* Imaging and biophotonics, cardiovascular biomechanics and hemodynamics, orthopedic biomechanics, ophthalmology, neuroscience engineering, diabetes, surgery and urological sciences. *Unit head:* Dr. Robin Shandas, Chair, 303-724-4196, E-mail: robin.shandas@ucdenver.edu. *Application contact:* Graduate School Admissions, 303-556-2704, E-mail: admissions@ucdenver.edu. Web site: http://bioengineering.ucdenver.edu/.

University of Colorado Denver, School of Medicine, Clinical Science Graduate Program, Aurora, CO 80045. Offers clinical investigation (PhD); clinical sciences (MS); health information technology (PhD); health services research (PhD). *Students:* 24 full-time (15 women), 18 part-time (10 women); includes 6 minority (2 Black or African American, non-Hispanic/Latino; 2 American Indian or Alaska Native, non-Hispanic/Latino; 2 Asian, non-Hispanic/Latino), 1 international. Average age 38. 15 applicants, 53% accepted, 8 enrolled. In 2011, 3 master's, 6 doctorates awarded. *Degree requirements:* For master's, thesis, minimum of 30 credit hours, defense/final exam of thesis or publishable paper; for doctorate, comprehensive exam, thesis/dissertation, at least 30 credit hours of thesis work. *Entrance requirements:* For master's, GRE General Test or MCAT (waived if candidate has earned MS/MA or PhD from accredited U.S. school), minimum undergraduate GPA of 3.0; for doctorate, GRE General Test or MCAT (waived if candidate has earned MS/MA or PhD from accredited U.S. school), health care graduate, professional degree, or graduate degree related to health sciences; minimum GPA of 3.0. Additional exam requirements/recommendations for international students: Required—TOEFL (minimum score 550 paper-based; 213 computer-based). *Application deadline:* For fall admission, 2/1 for domestic students; for spring admission, 10/1 for domestic students. Application fee: $50 ($75 for international students). Electronic applications accepted. *Expenses:* Contact institution. *Financial support:* Fellowships, research assistantships, and teaching assistantships available. Financial award application deadline: 3/15; financial award applicants required to submit FAFSA. *Unit head:* Dr. Lisa Cicutto, Program Director, 303-398-1538, E-mail: cicuttol@njc.org. *Application contact:* Galit Mankin, Program Administrator, 720-848-6249, Fax: 303-848-7381, E-mail: galit.mankin@ucdenver.edu. Web site: http://cctsi.ucdenver.edu/training-and-education/CLSC/Pages/default.aspx.

University of Florida, Graduate School, College of Public Health and Health Professions, Department of Clinical and Health Psychology, Gainesville, FL 32611. Offers clinical and health psychology (PhD); clinical and translational science (PhD). *Accreditation:* APA. *Faculty:* 21 full-time (8 women), 2 part-time/adjunct (1 woman). *Students:* 80 full-time (58 women), 17 part-time (15 women); includes 23 minority (8 Black or African American, non-Hispanic/Latino; 1 American Indian or Alaska Native, non-Hispanic/Latino; 6 Asian, non-Hispanic/Latino; 8 Hispanic/Latino), 2 international. Average age 27. 314 applicants, 6% accepted, 16 enrolled. In 2011, 2 doctorates awarded. *Degree requirements:* For doctorate, comprehensive exam, thesis/dissertation, pre-doctoral internship. *Entrance requirements:* For doctorate, GRE General Test (minimum score 1000), minimum GPA of 3.0. Additional exam requirements/recommendations for international students: Required—TOEFL (minimum score 550 paper-based; 213 computer-based; 80 iBT), IELTS (minimum score 6). *Application deadline:* For fall admission, 12/1 for domestic and international students. Application fee: $30. Electronic applications accepted. *Financial support:* In 2011–12, 18 students received support, including 3 fellowships with partial tuition reimbursements available, 15 research assistantships with partial tuition reimbursements available; career-related internships or fieldwork, Federal Work-Study, institutionally sponsored loans, scholarships/grants, and unspecified assistantships also available. Financial

award application deadline: 12/1; financial award applicants required to submit FAFSA. *Faculty research:* Clinical child and pediatric psychology, medical psychology, neuropsychology, health promotion and aging. *Total annual research expenditures:* $3.6 million. *Unit head:* Dr. Russell M. Bauer, Chair, 352-273-6140, Fax: 352-273-6156, E-mail: rbauer@phhp.ufl.edu. *Application contact:* Dr. Stephen R. Boggs, Program Director, 352-273-6146, Fax: 352-273-6156, E-mail: sboggs@phhp.ufl.edu. Web site: http://www.phhp.ufl.edu/chp/.

University of Kentucky, Graduate School, College of Health Sciences, Program in Clinical Sciences, Lexington, KY 40506-0032. Offers MS, DS. *Accreditation:* NAACLS. *Degree requirements:* For master's, comprehensive exam; for doctorate, comprehensive exam, thesis/dissertation. *Entrance requirements:* For master's, GRE General Test, minimum undergraduate GPA of 2.75; for doctorate, GRE General Test, minimum undergraduate GPA of 3.0. Additional exam requirements/recommendations for international students: Required—TOEFL (minimum score 550 paper-based; 213 computer-based). Electronic applications accepted.

University of Maryland, Baltimore, Graduate School, Department of Medical and Research Technology, Baltimore, MD 21201. Offers MS. *Accreditation:* NAACLS. Part-time programs available. *Students:* 2 full-time (1 woman), 10 part-time (7 women); includes 8 minority (5 Black or African American, non-Hispanic/Latino; 1 Asian, non-Hispanic/Latino; 1 Hispanic/Latino; 1 Two or more races, non-Hispanic/Latino), 2 international. Average age 34. 6 applicants, 50% accepted, 1 enrolled. In 2011, 2 master's awarded. *Degree requirements:* For master's, thesis or management project. *Entrance requirements:* For master's, GRE General Test, minimum GPA of 3.0. Additional exam requirements/recommendations for international students: Required—TOEFL (minimum score 550 paper-based; 80. iBT) or IELTS (minimum score 7). *Application deadline:* For fall admission, 5/1 priority date for domestic students, 1/15 for international students; for spring admission, 11/30 priority date for domestic students. Application fee: $50. Electronic applications accepted. *Financial support:* Fellowships and research assistantships available. Financial award application deadline: 3/1; financial award applicants required to submit FAFSA. *Faculty research:* Clinical microbiology, immunology, immunohematology, hematology, clinical chemistry, molecular biology. *Unit head:* Dr. Sanford Stass, Chair, 410-328-1237. *Application contact:* Dr. Ivana Vucenik; Graduate Program Director, 410-706-1832, E-mail: ivucenik@som.umaryland.edu.

University of Massachusetts Lowell, School of Health and Environment, Department of Clinical Laboratory and Nutritional Sciences, Lowell, MA 01854-2881. Offers clinical laboratory sciences (MS); clinical pathology (Graduate Certificate); nutritional sciences (Graduate Certificate); public health laboratory sciences (Graduate Certificate). *Accreditation:* NAACLS. Part-time programs available. Postbaccalaureate distance learning degree programs offered. *Degree requirements:* For master's, thesis optional. *Entrance requirements:* For master's, GRE General Test, minimum GPA of 3.0, letters of recommendation. *Faculty research:* Cardiovascular disease, lipoprotein metabolism, micronutrient evaluation, alcohol metabolism, mycobacterial drug resistance.

University of Medicine and Dentistry of New Jersey, Graduate School of Biomedical Sciences, Graduate Programs in Biomedical Sciences–Piscataway, Piscataway, NJ 08854-5635. Offers biochemistry and molecular biology (MS, PhD); biomedical engineering (MS, PhD); biomedical science (MS); cellular and molecular pharmacology (MS, PhD); clinical and translational science (MS); environmental sciences/exposure assessment (PhD); molecular genetics, microbiology and immunology (MS, PhD); neuroscience (MS, PhD); physiology and integrative biology (MS, PhD); toxicology (PhD); MD/PhD. Terminal master's awarded for partial completion of doctoral program. *Degree requirements:* For master's, thesis (for some programs), ethics training; for doctorate, comprehensive exam, thesis/dissertation, ethics training. *Entrance requirements:* For master's, GRE General Test, MCAT, DAT; for doctorate, GRE General Test. Additional exam requirements/recommendations for international students: Required—TOEFL. Electronic applications accepted.

University of Medicine and Dentistry of New Jersey, School of Health Related Professions, Department of Interdisciplinary Studies, Program in Health Sciences, Newark, NJ 07107-1709. Offers cardiopulmonary sciences (PhD); clinical laboratory sciences (PhD); health sciences (MS); interdisciplinary studies (PhD); nutrition (PhD); physical therapy/movement science (PhD). Part-time and evening/weekend programs available. Postbaccalaureate distance learning degree programs offered (no on-campus study). *Faculty:* 4 full-time (all women), 10 part-time/adjunct (7 women). *Students:* 3 full-time, 130 part-time; includes 32 minority (10 Black or African American, non-Hispanic/Latino; 10 Asian, non-Hispanic/Latino; 11 Hispanic/Latino; 1 Native Hawaiian or other Pacific Islander, non-Hispanic/Latino). Average age 41. 132 applicants, 51% accepted, 51 enrolled. In 2011, 17 master's, 4 doctorates awarded. *Degree requirements:* For doctorate, thesis/dissertation. *Entrance requirements:* For master's, BS, 2 reference letters, statement of career goals, curriculum vitae; for doctorate, GRE, interview, writing sample, 3 reference letters, curriculum vitae. Additional exam requirements/recommendations for international students: Required—TOEFL. *Application deadline:* For fall admission, 3/1 for domestic students. Applications are processed on a rolling basis. Application fee: $75. Electronic applications accepted. *Unit head:* Dr. Bob Denmark, Director, 973-972-5410, Fax: 973-972-7403, E-mail: ms-phd-hs@umdnj.edu. *Application contact:* Diane Hanrahan, Manager of Admissions, 973-972-5336, Fax: 973-972-7463, E-mail: shrpadm@umdnj.edu.

University of Mississippi Medical Center, School of Graduate Studies in the Health Sciences, Program in Clinical Health Sciences, Jackson, MS 39216-4505. Offers MS, PhD. Part-time programs available. Terminal master's awarded for partial completion of doctoral program. *Degree requirements:* For master's, thesis; for doctorate, thesis/dissertation. *Entrance requirements:* For master's and doctorate, GRE, 1 year of clinical experience. Additional exam requirements/recommendations for international students: Required—TOEFL. *Faculty research:* Clinical outcomes assessment via qualitative measures, health information systems; experimental laboratory evaluation of materials, drugs, hormones, and techniques used in clinical practice.

University of Nebraska Medical Center, School of Allied Health Professions, Program in Clinical Perfusion Education, Omaha, NE 68198-4144. Offers distance education perfusion education (MPS); perfusion science (MPS). *Accreditation:* NAACLS. Postbaccalaureate distance learning degree programs offered. *Degree requirements:* For master's, comprehensive exam, thesis. *Entrance requirements:* For master's, GRE. Electronic applications accepted. *Faculty research:* Platelet gel, hemoconcentrators.

University of Nebraska Medical Center, School of Allied Health Professions, Program in Cytotechnology, Omaha, NE 68198. Offers Certificate. *Accreditation:* NAACLS. Postbaccalaureate distance learning degree programs offered (minimal on-campus study). Electronic applications accepted. *Faculty research:* HPV vaccine.

University of New Mexico, Health Sciences Center Graduate Programs, Masters in Clinical Laboratory Science Program, Albuquerque, NM 87131-0001. Offers education (MS); laboratory management (MS); research and development (MS). Part-time and evening/weekend programs available. *Faculty:* 2 full-time (1 woman), 1 (woman) part-time/adjunct. *Students:* 2 part-time (both women). Average age 34. 8 applicants, 13% accepted, 0 enrolled. *Degree requirements:* For master's, project thesis; presentation at national meeting. *Application deadline:* For fall admission, 7/15 priority date for domestic

students, 6/15 for international students. Electronic applications accepted. *Financial support:* In 2011–12, 1 student received support. Career-related internships or fieldwork available. Financial award application deadline: 7/15; financial award applicants required to submit FAFSA. *Faculty research:* Prostate cancer, educational techniques, online training, molecular diagnostics, laboratory medicine, laboratory management, laboratory test assessment. *Unit head:* Dr. Paul B. Roth, Dean, 505-272-8273, Fax: 505-272-6857. *Application contact:* Dr. Roberto Gomez, Associate Dean of Students, 505-272-3414, Fax: 505-272-6857, E-mail: rgomez@unm.edu. Web site: http://pathology.unm.edu/medical-laboratory-sciences/program/graduate-m.s.-degree-program.html.

University of New Mexico, Health Sciences Center Graduate Programs, Program in Biomedical Sciences, Program in Clinical and Translational Science, Albuquerque, NM 87131-2039. Offers Certificate. *Unit head:* Dr. Helen Hathaway, Program Director, 505-272-1469, E-mail: hhathaway@salud.unm.edu. *Application contact:* Angel Cooke-Jackson, Coordinator, 505-272-1887, Fax: 505-272-8738, E-mail: acooke-jackson@salud.unm.edu.

University of North Dakota, Graduate School and Graduate School, Graduate Programs in Medicine, Department of Clinical Laboratory Science, Grand Forks, ND 58202. Offers MS. *Accreditation:* NAACLS. Postbaccalaureate distance learning degree programs offered (minimal on-campus study). *Degree requirements:* For master's, comprehensive exam, thesis or alternative. *Entrance requirements:* For master's, minimum GPA of 3.0. Additional exam requirements/recommendations for international students: Required—TOEFL (minimum score 550 paper-based; 213 computer-based; 79 iBT), IELTS (minimum score 5.5). Electronic applications accepted.

University of Pennsylvania, Perelman School of Medicine, Master's Program in Translational Research, Philadelphia, PA 19104-4283. Offers translational therapeutics (MTR); MD/MTR. *Faculty:* 22 full-time (4 women), 29 part-time/adjunct (9 women). *Students:* 36 full-time (18 women); includes 16 minority (1 Black or African American, non-Hispanic/Latino; 12 Asian, non-Hispanic/Latino; 1 Hispanic/Latino; 2 Two or more races, non-Hispanic/Latino). Average age 32. 20 applicants, 75% accepted, 13 enrolled. In 2011, 13 degrees awarded. *Degree requirements:* For master's, thesis. *Entrance requirements:* For master's, curriculum vitae; personal statement; research plan; primary mentor's NIH biosketch; 3 recommendations including one from department chair or division chief and one from primary mentor. *Application deadline:* For fall admission, 4/1 priority date for domestic students, 4/1 for international students. Applications are processed on a rolling basis. Application fee: $45. Electronic applications accepted. *Expenses:* Contact institution. *Financial support:* In 2011–12, 13 students received support, including 13 fellowships with full tuition reimbursements available. Financial award application deadline: 10/15. *Faculty research:* Neurobiology of schizophrenia, development of long-term drug delivery systems, insulin sensitivity and insulin release, genetic and inflammatory factors of cardiovascular metabolism and disorders, biology and structure of PF4 (Platelet factor 4). *Unit head:* Dr. Emma A. Meagher, Director, 215-662-2174, Fax: 215-614-0378, E-mail: mtrpor@mail.med.upenn.edu. *Application contact:* Marti Dandridge, Admissions Coordinator, 215-349-8627, Fax: 215-614-0378, E-mail: mtrpor@mail.med.upenn.edu. Web site: http://www.itmat.upenn.edu/ctsa/mtr/index.shtml.

University of Pittsburgh, School of Medicine, Programs in Clinical Research, Program in Clinical and Translational Science, Pittsburgh, PA 15260. Offers PhD. Part-time programs available. *Faculty:* 48 full-time (18 women). *Students:* 5 part-time (1 woman); includes 1 minority (Black or African American, non-Hispanic/Latino), 1 international. Average age 32. 4 applicants, 75% accepted, 3 enrolled. *Degree requirements:* For doctorate, comprehensive exam, thesis/dissertation. *Entrance requirements:* For doctorate, MCAT, GRE, GMAT or PCAT. Additional exam requirements/recommendations for international students: Required—TOEFL (minimum score 600 paper-based; 250 computer-based; 100 iBT). *Application deadline:* For spring admission, 4/15 priority date for domestic students, 4/15 for international students. Electronic applications accepted. *Expenses:* Tuition, state resident: full-time $18,774; part-time $760 per credit. Tuition, nonresident: full-time $30,736; part-time $1258 per credit. *Required fees:* $740; $200 per term. Tuition and fees vary according to program. *Faculty research:* Research design and methodology, healthcare outcomes and process assessment, organ and tissue donation and transplantation, measuring and improving function in patients with chronic kidney disease. *Unit head:* Dr. Wishwa Kapoor, Program Director, 412-586-9670, Fax: 412-586-9672, E-mail: kapoorwn@upmc.edu. *Application contact:* Jennifer Holliman, Program Coordinator, 412-586-9673, Fax: 412-586-9672, E-mail: hollimanjm@upmc.edu. Web site: http://www.icre.pitt.edu/phd/index.html.

University of Puerto Rico, Medical Sciences Campus, School of Health Professions, Program in Clinical Laboratory Science, San Juan, PR 00936-5067. Offers MS. *Accreditation:* NAACLS. Part-time and evening/weekend programs available. *Degree requirements:* For master's, one foreign language, thesis or alternative. *Entrance requirements:* For master's, EXADEP or GRE General Test, minimum GPA of 2.75, bachelor's degree in medical technology, 1 year lab experience, interview. *Faculty research:* Toxicology, virology, biochemistry, immunohematology, nervous system regeneration.

University of Puerto Rico, Medical Sciences Campus, School of Health Professions, Program in Cytotechnology, San Juan, PR 00936-5067. Offers Certificate. *Degree requirements:* For Certificate, one foreign language, research project. *Entrance requirements:* For degree, minimum GPA of 2.5, interview.

University of Puerto Rico, Medical Sciences Campus, School of Health Professions, Program in Medical Technology, San Juan, PR 00936-5067. Offers Certificate. Part-time programs available. *Degree requirements:* For Certificate, one foreign language, clinical practice. *Entrance requirements:* For degree, bachelor's degree in science, minimum GPA of 2.5.

University of Rhode Island, Graduate School, College of the Environment and Life Sciences, Department of Cell and Molecular Biology, Kingston, RI 02881. Offers biochemistry (MS, PhD); clinical laboratory sciences (MS), including biotechnology, clinical laboratory science, cytopathology; microbiology (MS, PhD); molecular genetics (MS, PhD). Part-time programs available. *Faculty:* 14 full-time (5 women), 3 part-time/adjunct (2 women). *Students:* 32 full-time (15 women), 37 part-time (23 women); includes 2 minority (1 Asian, non-Hispanic/Latino; 1 Hispanic/Latino), 1 international. In 2011, 2 master's, 2 doctorates awarded. *Degree requirements:* For master's, comprehensive exam (for some programs); for doctorate, comprehensive exam. *Entrance requirements:* For master's and doctorate, GRE, 2 letters of recommendation. Additional exam requirements/recommendations for international students: Required—TOEFL (minimum score 550 paper-based; 213 computer-based). *Application deadline:* For fall admission, 7/15 for domestic students, 2/1 for international students; for spring admission, 11/15 for domestic students, 7/15 for international students. Application fee: $65. Electronic applications accepted. *Expenses:* Tuition, state resident: full-time $10,432; part-time $580 per credit hour. Tuition, nonresident: full-time $23,130; part-time $1285 per credit hour. *Required fees:* $1362; $36 per credit hour. $35 per semester. One-time fee: $130. *Financial support:* In 2011–12, 2 research assistantships with full and partial tuition reimbursements (averaging $13,894 per year), 6 teaching assistantships with full and partial tuition reimbursements (averaging $12,850 per year)

were awarded. Financial award application deadline: 7/15; financial award applicants required to submit FAFSA. *Faculty research:* Genomics and Sequencing Center: an interdisciplinary genomics research and undergraduate and graduate student training program which provides researchers access to cutting-edge technologies in the field of genomics. *Unit head:* Dr. Jay Sperry, Chairperson, 401-874-2201, Fax: 401-874-2202, E-mail: jsperry@mail.uri.edu. *Application contact:* Nasser H. Zawia, Dean of the Graduate School, 401-874-5909, Fax: 401-874-5787, E-mail: nzawia@uri.edu. Web site: http://cels.uri.edu/cmb/.

University of Southern Mississippi, Graduate School, College of Health, Department of Medical Technology, Hattiesburg, MS 39406-0001. Offers MS. *Accreditation:* NAACLS. Part-time programs available. Postbaccalaureate distance learning degree programs offered. *Faculty:* 5 full-time (all women). *Students:* 17 full-time (12 women), 9 part-time (7 women); includes 8 minority (5 Black or African American, non-Hispanic/Latino; 2 Asian, non-Hispanic/Latino; 1 Hispanic/Latino), 1 international. Average age 28. 15 applicants, 73% accepted, 9 enrolled. In 2011, 2 degrees awarded. *Degree requirements:* For master's, comprehensive exam, thesis (for some programs). *Entrance requirements:* For master's, GRE General Test, minimum GPA of 2.75. Additional exam requirements/recommendations for international students: Required—TOEFL, IELTS. *Application deadline:* For fall admission, 3/1 priority date for domestic students, 3/1 for international students; for spring admission, 1/10 priority date for domestic students, 1/10 for international students. Application fee: $50. Electronic applications accepted. *Financial support:* In 2011–12, 3 teaching assistantships with full tuition reimbursements (averaging $7,200 per year) were awarded; research assistantships, career-related internships or fieldwork, Federal Work-Study, institutionally sponsored loans, scholarships/grants, health care benefits, and unspecified assistantships also available. Financial award application deadline: 3/15; financial award applicants required to submit FAFSA. *Faculty research:* Clinical chemistry, clinical microbiology, hematology, clinical management and education, immunohematology. *Unit head:* Dr. Mary Lux, Chair, 601-266-4908. *Application contact:* Dr. Mary Lux, Chair, 601-266-4908. Web site: http://www.usm.edu/graduateschool/table.php.

The University of Texas at Austin, Graduate School, College of Pharmacy, Graduate Programs in Pharmacy, Austin, TX 78712-1111. Offers health outcomes and pharmacy practice (PhD); health outcomes and pharmacy practice (MS); medicinal chemistry (PhD); pharmaceutics (PhD); pharmacology and toxicology (PhD); pharmacotherapy (MS, PhD); translational science (PhD). PhD in translational science offered jointly with The University of Texas Health Science Center at San Antonio and The University of Texas at San Antonio. *Degree requirements:* For master's, thesis; for doctorate, thesis/dissertation. *Entrance requirements:* For master's and doctorate, GRE General Test. *Application deadline:* For fall admission, 1/15 priority date for domestic students, 1/15 for international students; for spring admission, 10/1 for domestic students. Applications are processed on a rolling basis. Application fee: $50 ($75 for international students). Electronic applications accepted. *Financial support:* Fellowships, research assistantships, teaching assistantships with partial tuition reimbursements, Federal Work-Study, scholarships/grants, health care benefits, and unspecified assistantships available. Financial award application deadline: 2/1; financial award applicants required to submit FAFSA. *Faculty research:* Synthetic medical chemistry, synthetic molecular biology, bio-organic chemistry, pharmacoeconomics, pharmacy practice. *Unit head:* Dr. M. Lynn Crismon, Dean, 512-471-3718, E-mail: lynn.crismon@austin.utexas.edu.

The University of Texas Health Science Center at San Antonio, School of Health Professions, San Antonio, TX 78229-3900. Offers clinical laboratory sciences (MS); deaf education and hearing science (MED); dental hygiene (MS); occupational therapy (MOT); physical therapy (MPT); physician assistant studies (MS). *Accreditation:* AOTA; APTA; ARC-PA. *Degree requirements:* For master's, thesis. *Entrance requirements:* Additional exam requirements/recommendations for international students: Required—TOEFL (minimum score 560 paper-based; 280 computer-based; 68 iBT). Electronic applications accepted.

The University of Texas Medical Branch, Graduate School of Biomedical Sciences, Program in Clinical Science, Galveston, TX 77555. Offers MS, PhD.

University of Utah, School of Medicine and Graduate School, Graduate Programs in Medicine, Department of Pathology, Program in Laboratory Medicine and Biomedical Science, Salt Lake City, UT 84112-1107. Offers MS. Part-time programs available. *Degree requirements:* For master's, comprehensive exam, thesis, thesis research. *Entrance requirements:* For master's, minimum GPA of 3.0 during last 2 years of undergraduate course work, BS in medical laboratory science or related field. Additional exam requirements/recommendations for international students: Required—TOEFL (minimum score 550 paper-based). *Faculty research:* Clinical chemistry, hematology, diagnostic microbiology, immunohematology, cell biology, immunology.

University of Vermont, College of Medicine and Graduate College, Graduate Programs in Medicine, Program in Clinical and Translational Science, Burlington, VT 05405. Offers MS, PhD. *Students:* 11 (8 women), 1 international. 7 applicants, 14% accepted, 1 enrolled. In 2011, 1 master's awarded. *Entrance requirements:* For master's and doctorate, GRE. Additional exam requirements/recommendations for international students: Recommended—TOEFL (minimum score 550 paper-based; 213 computer-based; 80 iBT). *Application deadline:* For fall admission, 3/1 for domestic and international students. Applications are processed on a rolling basis. Application fee: $40. Electronic applications accepted. *Financial support:* Teaching assistantships available. *Unit head:* Dr. Alan Rubin, Director, 802-847-8268, E-mail: alan.rubin@uvm.edu.

University of Washington, Graduate School, School of Medicine, Graduate Programs in Medicine, Department of Laboratory Medicine, Seattle, WA 98195. Offers MS. *Accreditation:* NAACLS. Part-time programs available. *Degree requirements:* For master's, thesis. *Entrance requirements:* For master's, GRE General Test, medical technology certification or specialist in an area of laboratory medicine.

Virginia Commonwealth University, Graduate School, School of Allied Health Professions, Department of Clinical Laboratory Sciences, Richmond, VA 23284-9005. Offers MS. *Accreditation:* NAACLS. *Students:* 9 full-time (7 women), 10 part-time (6 women); includes 2 minority (both Black or African American, non-Hispanic/Latino). 22 applicants, 27% accepted, 4 enrolled. In 2011, 10 master's awarded. *Degree requirements:* For master's, one foreign language, thesis. *Entrance requirements:* For master's, GRE General Test, major in clinical laboratory sciences, biology, or chemistry; minimum GPA of 2.7. Additional exam requirements/recommendations for international students: Required—TOEFL (minimum score 600 paper-based; 250 computer-based; 100 iBT); Recommended—IELTS (minimum score 6.5). *Application deadline:* For fall admission, 6/1 for domestic students; for spring admission, 11/1 for domestic students. Application fee: $50. Electronic applications accepted. *Expenses:* Tuition, state resident: full-time $9133; part-time $507 per credit. Tuition, nonresident: full-time $18,777; part-time $1043 per credit. *Required fees:* $77 per credit. Tuition and fees vary according to degree level, campus/location, program and student level. *Faculty research:* Educational outcomes assessment, virtual instrumentation development, cost-effective treatment of bacteremia using third generation cephalosporins. *Unit head:* Dr. Theresa Nadder, Chair, 804-828-9470, E-mail: tsnadder@vcu.edu. *Application contact:*

Monica L. White, Director of Student Services, 804-828-7247, Fax: 804-828-8656, E-mail: mlwhite1@vcu.edu. Web site: http://griffin.vcu.edu.views/sahp/cls/.

Virginia Commonwealth University, Graduate School, School of Allied Health Professions, Doctoral Program in Health Related Sciences, Richmond, VA 23284-9005. Offers clinical laboratory sciences (PhD); gerontology (PhD); health administration (PhD); nurse anesthesia (PhD); occupational therapy (PhD); physical therapy (PhD); radiation sciences (PhD); rehabilitation leadership (PhD). *Faculty:* 2 full-time (1 woman). *Students:* 23 full-time (15 women), 34 part-time (23 women); includes 7 minority (4 Black or African American, non-Hispanic/Latino; 1 Asian, non-Hispanic/Latino; 1 Hispanic/Latino; 1 Two or more races, non-Hispanic/Latino), 2 international. 37 applicants, 38% accepted, 11 enrolled. In 2011, 11 doctorates awarded. *Entrance requirements:* For doctorate, GRE General Test or MAT, minimum GPA of 3.3 in master's degree.

Additional exam requirements/recommendations for international students: Required—TOEFL (minimum score 600 paper-based; 250 computer-based; 100 iBT); Recommended—IELTS (minimum score 6.5). *Application deadline:* For fall admission, 3/15 for domestic students. Application fee: $50. Electronic applications accepted. *Expenses:* Tuition, state resident: full-time $9133; part-time $507 per credit. Tuition, nonresident: full-time $18,777; part-time $1043 per credit. *Required fees:* $77 per credit. Tuition and fees vary according to degree level, campus/location, program and student level. *Unit head:* Dr. Paula K. Kupstas, Director, Health Related Sciences Program, 804-828-7247, E-mail: pkupstas@vcu.edu. *Application contact:* Monica L. White, Director of Student Services, 804-828-3273, Fax: 804-828-8656, E-mail: mlwhite1@vcu.edu. Web site: http://www.pubapps.vcu.edu/BULLETINS/prog_search/?did=20005.

Clinical Research

Boston University, School of Medicine, Division of Graduate Medical Sciences, Program in Clinical Investigation, Boston, MA 02215. Offers MA. *Faculty:* 10 full-time (8 women). *Students:* 7 full-time (6 women), 14 part-time (10 women), 7 international. Average age 29. 12 applicants, 83% accepted, 4 enrolled. In 2011, 7 master's awarded. *Degree requirements:* For master's, thesis. *Entrance requirements:* For master's, GRE. Additional exam requirements/recommendations for international students: Required—TOEFL. *Application deadline:* For spring admission, 10/15 priority date for domestic students. Application fee: $75. *Expenses: Tuition:* Full-time $40,848; part-time $1276 per credit hour. *Required fees:* $572; $286 per semester. *Financial support:* Applicants required to submit FAFSA. *Unit head:* Dr. Susan S. Fish, Director, 617-638-7715, E-mail: sfish@bu.edu. *Application contact:* Stacey Hess Pino, Assistant Director, 617-638-5211, Fax: 617-638-5740, E-mail: sahess@bu.edu. Web site: http://www.bumc.bu.edu/maci/.

Case Western Reserve University, School of Medicine, Clinical Research Scholars Program, Cleveland, OH 44106. Offers MS.

Duke University, School of Medicine, Clinical Research Program, Durham, NC 27708-0586. Offers MHS. Part-time programs available. *Faculty:* 23 part-time/adjunct (4 women). *Students:* 22 full-time (10 women), 83 part-time (47 women); includes 42 minority (8 Black or African American, non-Hispanic/Latino; 31 Asian, non-Hispanic/Latino; 3 Hispanic/Latino). 87 applicants, 97% accepted, 84 enrolled. In 2011, 25 master's awarded. *Degree requirements:* For master's, research project. *Entrance requirements:* For master's, GRE. *Application deadline:* For fall admission, 5/15 for domestic students. *Expenses:* Contact institution. *Financial support:* In 2011–12, 2 students received support. Fellowships, research assistantships, teaching assistantships, and scholarships/grants available. Financial award application deadline: 5/1; financial award applicants required to submit FAFSA. *Unit head:* Dr. Steven C. Grambow, Director, 919-286-0411, Fax: 919-681-4569, E-mail: steven.grambow@duke.edu. *Application contact:* Gail Ladd, Program Coordinator, 919-681-4560, Fax: 919-681-4569, E-mail: ladd0002@mc.duke.edu. Web site: http://crtp.mc.duke.edu/.

Eastern Michigan University, Graduate School, College of Health and Human Services, School of Health Sciences, Program in Clinical Research Administration, Ypsilanti, MI 48197. Offers MS, Graduate Certificate. Part-time and evening/weekend programs available. Postbaccalaureate distance learning degree programs offered (minimal on-campus study). *Students:* 19 full-time (9 women), 60 part-time (41 women); includes 8 minority (3 Black or African American, non-Hispanic/Latino; 2 Asian, non-Hispanic/Latino; 2 Hispanic/Latino; 1 Native Hawaiian or other Pacific Islander, non-Hispanic/Latino), 49 international. Average age 29. 174 applicants, 44% accepted, 25 enrolled. In 2011, 15 master's, 8 other advanced degrees awarded. *Entrance requirements:* Additional exam requirements/recommendations for international students: Required—TOEFL. *Application deadline:* Applications are processed on a rolling basis. Application fee: $35. *Expenses:* Tuition, state resident: full-time $10,367; part-time $432 per credit hour. Tuition, nonresident: full-time $20,435; part-time $851 per credit hour. *Required fees:* $39 per credit hour. $46 per semester. One-time fee: $100. Tuition and fees vary according to course level, degree level and reciprocity agreements. *Financial support:* Fellowships, research assistantships with full tuition reimbursements, teaching assistantships with full tuition reimbursements, career-related internships or fieldwork, Federal Work-Study, institutionally sponsored loans, scholarships/grants, tuition waivers (partial), and unspecified assistantships available. Support available to part-time students. Financial award applicants required to submit FAFSA. *Unit head:* Dr. Stephen Sonstein, Program Coordinator, 734-487-1238, Fax: 734-487-4095, E-mail: stephen.sonstein@emich.edu. *Application contact:* Graduate Admissions, 734-487-2400, Fax: 734-487-6559, E-mail: graduate.admissions@emich.edu.

Emory University, Laney Graduate School, Program in Clinical Research, Atlanta, GA 30322-1100. Offers MS. Part-time programs available. *Faculty:* 35 part-time/adjunct (15 women). *Students:* 22 full-time (11 women), 3 part-time (0 women); includes 7 minority (2 Black or African American, non-Hispanic/Latino; 5 Asian, non-Hispanic/Latino), 2 international. Average age 34. 19 applicants, 95% accepted, 17 enrolled. In 2011, 10 master's awarded. *Degree requirements:* For master's, thesis. *Application deadline:* For fall admission, 5/31 for domestic students. Applications are processed on a rolling basis. Application fee: $45. *Expenses: Tuition:* Full-time $34,800. *Required fees:* $1300. *Financial support:* Scholarships/grants available. *Unit head:* Cheryl Sroka, Graduate Program Administrator, 404-727-5096, Fax: 404-727-8768, E-mail: csroka@emory.edu. *Application contact:* Kharen Fulton, Director of Admissions, 404-727-0184, Fax: 404-727-4990, E-mail: gradkef@emory.edu. Web site: http://www.actsi.org/areas/retcd/mscr1/mscr_emory/.

Georgia Health Sciences University, College of Graduate Studies, Program in Clinical and Translational Science, Augusta, GA 30912. Offers MCTS, CCTS. *Faculty:* 12 full-time (5 women), 2 part-time/adjunct (1 woman). *Students:* 2 part-time (0 women); includes 1 minority (Asian, non-Hispanic/Latino). Average age 39. 10 applicants, 90% accepted. In 2011, 3 master's awarded. Application fee: $50. *Unit head:* Dr. Varghese George, Chair, 706-721-3785, E-mail: vgeorge@georgiahealth.edu. *Application contact:* Dr. Jennifer Waller, Co-Director of Training Programs, 706-721-0814, E-mail: jwaller@georgiahealth.edu. Web site: http://biostat.mcg.edu/CTS.html.

The Johns Hopkins University, Bloomberg School of Public Health, Graduate Training Program in Clinical Investigation, Baltimore, MD 21287. Offers MHS, ScM, PhD. *Degree requirements:* For master's, comprehensive exam, thesis; for doctorate, comprehensive exam, thesis/dissertation. *Entrance requirements:* For master's, GRE or MCAT; United States Medical Licensing Exam, 2 letters of recommendation, curriculum vitae, transcripts, statement of purpose; for doctorate, GRE or MCAT; United States

Medical Licensing Exam, 2 letters of recommendation, curriculum vitae. Additional exam requirements/recommendations for international students: Required—TOEFL (minimum score 600 paper-based; 250 computer-based). Electronic applications accepted. *Faculty research:* Ethical issues, biomedical writing, grant writing, epidemiology, biostatistics.

Loyola University Chicago, Graduate School, Program in Clinical Research Methods, Chicago, IL 60660. Offers MS. *Students:* 1 (woman) full-time, 9 part-time (7 women); includes 2 minority (1 Black or African American, non-Hispanic/Latino; 1 Asian, non-Hispanic/Latino), 1 international. Average age 31. 11 applicants, 45% accepted, 5 enrolled. In 2011, 4 master's awarded. *Degree requirements:* For master's, research project. *Expenses: Tuition:* Full-time $15,660; part-time $870 per credit hour. *Required fees:* $125 per semester. Tuition and fees vary according to course load and program. *Unit head:* Dr. Samuel Attoh, Dean, 773-508-3459, Fax: 773-508-2460, E-mail: sattoh@luc.edu. *Application contact:* Ron Martin, Assistant Director of Enrollment Management, 312-915-8950, Fax: 312-915-8905, E-mail: gradapp@luc.edu.

Medical College of Wisconsin, Graduate School of Biomedical Sciences, Medical Scientist Training Program, Milwaukee, WI 53226-0509. Offers MD/PhD. *Entrance requirements:* Additional exam requirements/recommendations for international students: Required—TOEFL.

Medical University of South Carolina, South Carolina Clinical and Translational Research Institute, Charleston, SC 29425. Offers MS. Postbaccalaureate distance learning degree programs offered (no on-campus study). *Faculty:* 7 full-time (2 women), 1 part-time/adjunct (0 women). *Students:* 79 full-time (42 women), 16 part-time (9 women); includes 6 minority (4 Black or African American, non-Hispanic/Latino; 2 Asian, non-Hispanic/Latino), 74 international. Average age 32. 18 applicants, 83% accepted, 13 enrolled. In 2011, 15 master's awarded. *Entrance requirements:* Additional exam requirements/recommendations for international students: Required—TOEFL (minimum score 600 paper-based; 250 computer-based; 100 iBT). *Application deadline:* For fall admission, 5/19 priority date for domestic students, 12/31 for international students. Applications are processed on a rolling basis. Application fee: $95. Electronic applications accepted. *Financial support:* In 2011–12, 9 students received support. Federal Work-Study, scholarships/grants, and unspecified assistantships available. Support available to part-time students. Financial award application deadline: 3/10; financial award applicants required to submit FAFSA. *Unit head:* Dr. Thomas C. Hulsey, Director, 843-792-9907, Fax: 843-792-0227, E-mail: hulseytc@musc.edu. *Application contact:* Lisa E. Frawley, Program Coordinator, 843-792-8449, Fax: 843-792-0227, E-mail: frawleyl@musc.edu. Web site: https://sctr.musc.edu/.

Memorial University of Newfoundland, Faculty of Medicine and School of Graduate Studies, Graduate Programs in Medicine, Division of Applied Health Services Research, St. John's, NL A1C 5S7, Canada. Offers M Sc.

Morehouse School of Medicine, Master of Science in Clinical Research Program, Atlanta, GA 30310-1495. Offers MS. Part-time programs available. *Degree requirements:* For master's, thesis. Electronic applications accepted.

Mount Sinai School of Medicine, Graduate School of Biological Sciences, New York, NY 10029-6504. Offers biomedical sciences (MS, PhD); clinical research education (MS, PhD); community medicine (MPH); genetic counseling (MS); neurosciences (PhD); MD/PhD. Terminal master's awarded for partial completion of doctoral program. *Degree requirements:* For master's, thesis; for doctorate, comprehensive exam, thesis/dissertation. *Entrance requirements:* For master's, GRE General Test; for doctorate, GRE General Test, GRE Subject Test, 3 years of college pre-med course work. Additional exam requirements/recommendations for international students: Required—TOEFL. Electronic applications accepted. *Faculty research:* Cancer, genetics and genomics, immunology, neuroscience, developmental and stem cell biology, translational research.

New York University, College of Dentistry, Program in Clinical Research, New York, NY 10010. Offers MS. Part-time programs available. *Faculty:* 242 full-time (85 women), 689 part-time/adjunct (186 women). *Students:* 14 full-time (7 women); includes 3 minority (all Asian, non-Hispanic/Latino). Average age 29. 14 applicants, 100% accepted, 14 enrolled. In 2011, 7 master's awarded. *Entrance requirements:* For master's, GRE. Additional exam requirements/recommendations for international students: Required—TOEFL (minimum score 570 paper-based; 230 computer-based; 90 iBT). *Application deadline:* For fall admission, 2/28 for domestic and international students. Application fee: $100. Electronic applications accepted. *Financial support:* Application deadline: 3/1. *Unit head:* Dr. Ralph V. Katz, Chair, 212-998-9550, Fax: 212-995-4436, E-mail: ralph.katz@nyu.edu. *Application contact:* Dr. Anthony M. Palatta, Assistant Dean for Student Affairs and Admissions, 212-998-9918, Fax: 212-995-4240, E-mail: ap16@nyu.edu.

New York University, School of Medicine, New York, NY 10012-1019. Offers biomedical sciences (PhD), including biomedical imaging, cellular and molecular biology, computational biology, developmental genetics, medical and molecular parasitology, microbiology, molecular oncobiology and immunology, neuroscience and physiology, pathobiology, pharmacology, structural biology; clinical investigation (MS); medicine (MD); MD/MA; MD/MPA; MD/MS; MD/PhD. *Accreditation:* LCME/AMA (one or more programs are accredited). *Degree requirements:* For master's, comprehensive exam, thesis; for doctorate, comprehensive exam (for some programs), thesis/dissertation (for some programs). *Entrance requirements:* For doctorate, MCAT (for MD). Additional exam requirements/recommendations for international students: Required—TOEFL. *Expenses:* Contact institution. *Faculty research:* AIDS, cancer, neuroscience, molecular biology, neuroscience, cell biology and molecular genetics, structural biology, microbial pathogenesis and host defense, pharmacology, molecular oncology and immunology.

Northwestern University, The Graduate School, Program in Clinical Investigation, Evanston, IL 60208. Offers MSCI, Certificate. Part-time and evening/weekend programs available. *Faculty research:* Wide range of epidemiologic, clinical and bench research across all medical school departments.

Northwestern University, Northwestern University Feinberg School of Medicine, Department of Clinical Investigation, Evanston, IL 60208. Offers MSCI. Part-time and evening/weekend programs available. *Entrance requirements:* For master's, GRE or MCAT, doctoral degree in healthcare-related field. Additional exam requirements/recommendations for international students: Required—TOEFL. Electronic applications accepted. *Faculty research:* Clinical research.

Oregon Health & Science University, School of Medicine, Graduate Programs in Medicine, Human Investigations Program, Portland, OR 97239-3098. Offers clinical research (MCR, Certificate). Master of Clinical Research program only open to those currently in the Human Investigations Certificate program. Part-time programs available. *Faculty:* 37. *Students:* 2 full-time (1 woman), 80 part-time (51 women); includes 17 minority (4 Black or African American, non-Hispanic/Latino; 1 American Indian or Alaska Native, non-Hispanic/Latino; 9 Asian, non-Hispanic/Latino; 1 Hispanic/Latino; 2 Two or more races, non-Hispanic/Latino), 5 international. Average age 36. 123 applicants, 47% accepted, 40 enrolled. In 2011, 14 master's, 13 Certificates awarded. *Entrance requirements:* For master's and Certificate, MD, MD/PhD, DO, DDS, DMD, DC, Pharm D, OD, ND or PhD with clinical responsibilities or patient-oriented research; faculty or staff member, clinical or post-doctoral fellows and graduate students at OHSU, Kaiser Permanente, Portland VA Medical Center or other health care facilities in Oregon or the Northwest. *Application deadline:* For fall admission, 7/15 for domestic students; for winter admission, 12/15 for domestic students; for spring admission, 3/15 for domestic students. Applications are processed on a rolling basis. Electronic applications accepted. *Unit head:* Dr. Cynthia Morris, Director, 503-494-3095, Fax: 503-494-5128, E-mail: morrisc@ohsu.edu. *Application contact:* Karen McCracken, Education Program Coordinator, 503-494-3095, Fax: 503-494-5128, E-mail: hip@ohsu.edu. Web site: http://www.ohsu.edu/hip.

Palmer College of Chiropractic, Division of Graduate Studies, Davenport, IA 52803-5287. Offers clinical research (MS). *Degree requirements:* For master's, 2 mentored practicum projects. *Entrance requirements:* For master's, GRE General Test, minimum GPA of 2.5, bachelor's and doctoral-level health professions degrees. Additional exam requirements/recommendations for international students: Required—TOEFL. Electronic applications accepted. *Expenses:* Contact institution. *Faculty research:* Chiropractic clinical research.

Thomas Jefferson University, Jefferson College of Graduate Studies, Certificate Programs in Clinical Research, Human Clinical Investigation, and Infectious Diseases, Philadelphia, PA 19107. Offers Certificate. *Faculty:* 22 full-time (7 women), 23 part-time/adjunct (6 women). *Students:* 14 part-time (10 women); includes 7 minority (2 Black or African American, non-Hispanic/Latino; 4 Asian, non-Hispanic/Latino; 1 Hispanic/Latino), 3 international. 20 applicants, 75% accepted, 11 enrolled. In 2011, 6 Certificates awarded. *Entrance requirements:* For degree, GRE General Test (recommended). Additional exam requirements/recommendations for international students: Required—TOEFL (minimum score 100 iBT) or IELTS (minimum score 7). *Application deadline:* For fall admission, 8/1 priority date for domestic students, 3/1 for international students; for winter admission, 12/1 priority date for domestic students, 6/1 for international students; for spring admission, 4/1 priority date for domestic students. Applications are processed on a rolling basis. Application fee: $50. Electronic applications accepted. *Financial support:* In 2011–12, 5 students received support. Federal Work-Study and institutionally sponsored loans available. Support available to part-time students. Financial award application deadline: 5/1; financial award applicants required to submit FAFSA. *Faculty research:* Epidemiology, clinical research, statistics, planning and management, disease control. *Unit head:* Dr. Dennis M. Gross, Associate Dean, 215-503-0156, Fax: 215-503-3433, E-mail: dennis.gross@jefferson.edu. *Application contact:* Eleanor M. Gorman, Assistant Coordinator, Graduate Center Programs, 215-503-5799, Fax: 215-503-3433, E-mail: eleanor.gorman@jefferson.edu. Web site: http://www.jefferson.edu/jcgs/cert/.

Trident University International, College of Health Sciences, Program in Health Sciences, Cypress, CA 90630. Offers clinical research administration (MS, Certificate); emergency and disaster management (MS, Certificate); environmental health science (Certificate); health care administration (PhD); health care management (MS), including health informatics; health education (MS, Certificate); health informatics (Certificate); health sciences (PhD); international health (MS); international health: educator or researcher option (PhD); international health: practitioner option (PhD); law and expert witness studies (MS, Certificate); public health (MS); quality assurance (Certificate). Part-time and evening/weekend programs available. Postbaccalaureate distance learning degree programs offered (no on-campus study). *Degree requirements:* For doctorate, comprehensive exam, thesis/dissertation, defense of dissertation. *Entrance requirements:* For master's, minimum GPA of 2.5 (students with GPA 3.0 or greater may transfer up to 30% of graduate level credits); for doctorate, minimum GPA of 3.4, curriculum vitae, course work in research methods or statistics. Additional exam requirements/recommendations for international students: Required—TOEFL. Electronic applications accepted.

Tufts University, Sackler School of Graduate Biomedical Sciences, Clinical and Translational Science Program, Medford, MA 02155. Offers MS, PhD. *Faculty:* 33 full-time (9 women). *Students:* 31 full-time (16 women); includes 6 minority (4 Asian, non-Hispanic/Latino; 1 Hispanic/Latino; 1 Two or more races, non-Hispanic/Latino), 13 international. Average age 33. In 2011, 11 degrees awarded. Terminal master's awarded for partial completion of doctoral program. *Degree requirements:* For master's, thesis; for doctorate, thesis/dissertation. *Entrance requirements:* For master's and doctorate, MD or PhD, strong clinical research background. Additional exam requirements/recommendations for international students: Required—TOEFL (minimum score 600 paper-based; 250 computer-based; 100 iBT). *Application deadline:* For fall admission, 12/15 for domestic and international students. Application fee: $70. Electronic applications accepted. *Expenses:* Tuition: Full-time $41,208; part-time $1030 per credit hour. Full-time tuition and fees vary according to degree level, program and student level. Part-time tuition and fees vary according to course load. *Financial support:* Application deadline: 12/15. *Faculty research:* Clinical study design, mathematical modeling, meta analysis, epidemiologic research, coronary heart disease. *Unit head:* Dr. David Kent, Program Director, 617-636-3234, Fax: 617-636-8023, E-mail: dkent@tuftsmedicalcenter.edu. *Application contact:* Kellie Melchin, Associate Director of Admissions, 617-636-6767, Fax: 617-636-0375, E-mail: sackler-school@tufts.edu. Web site: http://sackler.tufts.edu/Academics/Degree-Programs/PhD-Programs/Clinical-and-Translational-Science.

University of California, Berkeley, UC Berkeley Extension, Certificate Programs in Sciences, Biotechnology and Mathematics, Berkeley, CA 94720-1500. Offers clinical research conduct and management (Certificate). Postbaccalaureate distance learning degree programs offered.

University of California, Davis, Graduate Studies, Graduate Group in Clinical Research, Davis, CA 95616. Offers MAS. *Degree requirements:* For master's,

comprehensive exam. *Entrance requirements:* Additional exam requirements/recommendations for international students: Required—TOEFL (minimum score 550 paper-based; 213 computer-based)

University of California, Los Angeles, David Geffen School of Medicine and Graduate Division, Graduate Programs in Medicine, Department of Biomathematics, Program in Clinical Research, Los Angeles, CA 90095. Offers MS. *Faculty:* 230 full-time (46 women). *Students:* 16 full-time (9 women); includes 7 minority (6 Asian, non-Hispanic/Latino; 1 Hispanic/Latino). Average age 34. 11 applicants, 91% accepted, 10 enrolled. In 2011, 9 master's awarded. Application fee: $70 ($90 for international students). Electronic applications accepted. *Financial support:* In 2011–12, 7 fellowships were awarded; research assistantships and teaching assistantships also available. *Unit head:* Dr. Elliot Landaw, Chair, 310-825-6743, Fax: 310-825-8685, E-mail: elandaw@biomath.ucla.edu. *Application contact:* Departmental Office, 310-825-5554, Fax: 310-825-8685, E-mail: gradprog@biomath.ucla.edu. Web site: http://www.biomath.ucla.edu/grad/.

University of California, San Diego, School of Medicine, Program in Clinical Research, La Jolla, CA 92093. Offers MAS.

University of Colorado Denver, School of Medicine, Clinical Science Graduate Program, Aurora, CO 80045. Offers clinical investigation (PhD); clinical sciences (MS); health information technology (PhD); health services research (PhD). *Students:* 24 full-time (15 women), 18 part-time (10 women); includes 6 minority (2 Black or African American, non-Hispanic/Latino; 2 American Indian or Alaska Native, non-Hispanic/Latino; 2 Asian, non-Hispanic/Latino), 1 international. Average age 38. 15 applicants, 53% accepted, 8 enrolled. In 2011, 3 master's, 6 doctorates awarded. *Degree requirements:* For master's, thesis, minimum of 30 credit hours, defense/final exam of thesis or publishable paper; for doctorate, comprehensive exam, thesis/dissertation, at least 30 credit hours of thesis work. *Entrance requirements:* For master's, GRE General Test or MCAT (waived if candidate has earned MS/MA or PhD from accredited U.S. school), minimum undergraduate GPA of 3.0; for doctorate, GRE General Test or MCAT (waived if candidate has earned MS/MA or PhD from accredited U.S. school), health care graduate, professional degree, or graduate degree related to health sciences; minimum GPA of 3.0. Additional exam requirements/recommendations for international students: Required—TOEFL (minimum score 550 paper-based; 213 computer-based). *Application deadline:* For fall admission, 2/1 for domestic students; for spring admission, 10/1 for domestic students. Application fee: $50 ($75 for international students). Electronic applications accepted. *Expenses:* Contact institution. *Financial support:* Fellowships, research assistantships, and teaching assistantships available. Financial award application deadline: 3/15; financial award applicants required to submit FAFSA. *Unit head:* Dr. Lisa Cicutto, Program Director, 303-398-1538, E-mail: cicuttol@njc.org. *Application contact:* Galit Mankin, Program Administrator, 720-848-6249, Fax: 303-848-7381, E-mail: galit.mankin@ucdenver.edu. Web site: http://cctsi.ucdenver.edu/training-and-education/CLSC/Pages/default.aspx.

University of Connecticut, Graduate School, University of Connecticut Health Center, Field of Clinical and Translational Research, Storrs, CT 06269. Offers MS. *Degree requirements:* For master's, comprehensive exam. *Entrance requirements:* Additional exam requirements/recommendations for international students: Required—TOEFL (minimum score 550 paper-based; 213 computer-based). Electronic applications accepted.

University of Connecticut Health Center, Graduate School, Program in Clinical and Translational Research, Farmington, CT 06030. Offers MS. Part-time programs available. *Entrance requirements:* For master's, GRE. Additional exam requirements/recommendations for international students: Required—TOEFL (minimum score 600 paper-based; 250 computer-based).

University of Florida, College of Medicine, Program in Clinical Investigation, Gainesville, FL 32611. Offers clinical investigation (MS); epidemiology (MS); public health (MPH). Part-time programs available. *Entrance requirements:* For master's, GRE, MD, PhD, DMD/DDS or Pharm D.

The University of Iowa, Graduate College, College of Public Health, Department of Epidemiology, Iowa City, IA 52242-1316. Offers clinical investigation (MS); epidemiology (MS, PhD). *Accreditation:* CEPH. *Degree requirements:* For master's, thesis optional, exam; for doctorate, comprehensive exam, thesis/dissertation. *Entrance requirements:* For master's and doctorate, GRE General Test, minimum GPA of 3.0. Additional exam requirements/recommendations for international students: Required—TOEFL (minimum score 600 paper-based; 250 computer-based; 100 iBT). Electronic applications accepted.

The University of Kansas, University of Kansas Medical Center, School of Medicine, Department of Preventive Medicine and Public Health, Kansas City, KS 66160. Offers biostatistics (MPH); clinical research (MS); environmental health sciences (MPH); epidemiology (MPH); public health management (MPH); social and behavioral health (MPH); MD/MPH; MPH/MSN; PhD/MPH. Part-time programs available. *Faculty:* 76. *Students:* 51 full-time (32 women), 74 part-time (53 women); includes 35 minority (10 Black or African American, non-Hispanic/Latino; 4 American Indian or Alaska Native, non-Hispanic/Latino; 9 Asian, non-Hispanic/Latino; 8 Hispanic/Latino; 4 Two or more races, non-Hispanic/Latino), 6 international. Average age 33. 77 applicants, 69% accepted, 45 enrolled. In 2011, 25 master's awarded. *Degree requirements:* For master's, thesis, capstone practicum defense. *Entrance requirements:* For master's, GRE, MCAT, LSAT, GMAT or other equivalent graduate professional exam. Additional exam requirements/recommendations for international students: Required—TOEFL. *Application deadline:* For fall admission, 3/1 for domestic and international students. Applications are processed on a rolling basis. Application fee: $60. Tuition and fees vary according to course load, campus/location, program and reciprocity agreements. *Financial support:* In 2011–12, 21 research assistantships (averaging $10,200 per year) were awarded; career-related internships or fieldwork, Federal Work-Study, scholarships/grants, and unspecified assistantships also available. Financial award application deadline: 2/14; financial award applicants required to submit FAFSA. *Faculty research:* Cancer screening and prevention, smoking cessation, obesity and physical activity, health services/outcomes research. *Total annual research expenditures:* $8 million. *Unit head:* Dr. Edward F. Ellerbeck, Chairman, 913-588-2774, Fax: 913-588-2780, E-mail: eellerbe@kumc.edu. *Application contact:* Tanya Honderick, Assistant Director, KU-MPH, 913-588-2720, Fax: 913-588-8505, E-mail: thonderick@kumc.edu. Web site: http://ph.kumc.edu/.

University of Louisville, Graduate School, School of Public Health and Information Sciences, Louisville, KY 40292-0001. Offers bioinformatics and biostatistics (MS, PhD), including biostatistics (MPH, MS, PhD), decision science (MS); clinical investigation sciences (M Sc, Certificate); environmental and occupational health sciences (PhD), including public health; epidemiology and population health (MS), including epidemiology (MPH, MS, PhD); epidemiology and public health (MPH, PhD), including biostatistics (MPH, MS, PhD), environmental and occupational health sciences (MPH), epidemiology (MPH, MS, PhD), health management, health promotion and behavior (MPH); health management and systems sciences (PhD), including public health sciences - health management; health promotion and behavioral sciences (PhD), including health promotion; public health sciences (PhD), including environmental

health, epidemiology (MPH, MS, PhD), health management (MPH, PhD), health promotion. Part-time and evening/weekend programs available. *Degree requirements:* For master's, thesis; for doctorate, comprehensive exam, thesis/dissertation. *Entrance requirements:* For master's, GRE General Test, GMAT, DAT, MCAT, official transcripts, statement of purpose, resume/curriculum vitae, letters of recommendation; for doctorate, GRE General Test, official transcripts, statement of purpose, resume/curriculum vitae, letters of recommendation. Additional exam requirements/recommendations for international students: Required—TOEFL (minimum score 600 paper-based; 250 computer-based; 100 iBT). Electronic applications accepted. *Expenses:* Tuition, state resident: full-time $9692; part-time $539 per credit hour. Tuition, nonresident: full-time $20,168; part-time $1121 per credit hour. Tuition and fees vary according to program and reciprocity agreements. *Faculty research:* Clinical research training, cancer and environmental exposure, health effects of air pollution, occupational injuries and illness, network science applications in health.

University of Maryland, Baltimore, School of Medicine, Department of Epidemiology and Public Health, Baltimore, MD 21201. Offers biostatistics (MS); clinical research (MS); epidemiology and preventative medicine (PhD); epidemiology and preventive medicine (MPH, MS); gerontology (PhD); human genetics and genomic (PhD); human genetics and genomic medicine (MS); molecular epidemiology (MS, PhD); toxicology (MS, PhD); JD/MS; MD/PhD; MS/PhD. *Accreditation:* CEPH. Part-time programs available. *Students:* 94 full-time (68 women), 61 part-time (46 women); includes 51 minority (18 Black or African American, non-Hispanic/Latino; 25 Asian, non-Hispanic/Latino; 7 Hispanic/Latino; 1 Two or more races, non-Hispanic/Latino), 21 international. Average age 32. 109 applicants, 32% accepted, 19 enrolled. In 2011, 13 master's, 9 doctorates awarded. *Degree requirements:* For doctorate, comprehensive exam, thesis/dissertation. *Entrance requirements:* For master's and doctorate, GRE General Test. Additional exam requirements/recommendations for international students: Required—TOEFL (minimum score 550 paper-based; 213 computer-based; 80 iBT); Recommended—IELTS (minimum score 7). *Application deadline:* For fall admission, 2/1 for domestic students, 1/15 for international students. Application fee: $50. Electronic applications accepted. *Expenses:* Contact institution. *Financial support:* In 2011–12, research assistantships with partial tuition reimbursements (averaging $25,000 per year) were awarded; fellowships, Federal Work-Study, scholarships/grants, and unspecified assistantships also available. Financial award application deadline: 3/1; financial award applicants required to submit FAFSA. *Unit head:* Dr. Laura Hungerford, Program Director, 410-706-8492, Fax: 410-706-4225. *Application contact:* Danielle Fitzpatrick, Program Coordinator, 410-706-8492, Fax: 410-706-4225, E-mail: dfitzpatrick@epi.umaryland.edu. Web site: http://epidemiology.umaryland.edu/Pages/Home.aspx.

University of Massachusetts Worcester, Graduate School of Biomedical Sciences, Worcester, MA 01655-0115. Offers biochemistry and molecular pharmacology (PhD); bioinformatics and computational biology (PhD); cancer biology (PhD); cell biology (PhD); clinical and population health research (PhD); clinical investigation (MS); immunology and virology (PhD); interdisciplinary graduate program (PhD); molecular genetics and microbiology (PhD); neuroscience (PhD); DVM/PhD; MD/PhD. *Faculty:* 1,427 full-time (526 women), 309 part-time/adjunct (196 women). *Students:* 416 full-time (225 women); includes 47 minority (12 Black or African American, non-Hispanic/Latino; 32 Asian, non-Hispanic/Latino; 3 Hispanic/Latino), 144 international. Average age 29. 623 applicants, 17% accepted, 54 enrolled. In 2011, 5 master's, 63 doctorates awarded. Terminal master's awarded for partial completion of doctoral program. *Degree requirements:* For master's, comprehensive exam, thesis; for doctorate, comprehensive exam, thesis/dissertation. *Entrance requirements:* For master's, bachelor's degree; for doctorate, GRE General Test. Additional exam requirements/recommendations for international students: Required—TOEFL (minimum score 600 paper-based; 250 computer-based; 100 iBT) or IELTS (minimum score 7.5). *Application deadline:* For fall admission, 12/15 for domestic and international students; for spring admission, 5/15 for domestic students. Application fee: $50. Electronic applications accepted. *Expenses:* Contact institution. *Financial support:* In 2011–12, 416 students received support, including 416 research assistantships with full tuition reimbursements available (averaging $29,200 per year); scholarships/grants, health care benefits, tuition waivers (full), and unspecified assistantships also available. Financial award application deadline: 4/16. *Faculty research:* RNA interference, cell biology, bioinformatics, clinical research, infectious disease. *Total annual research expenditures:* $262.7 million. *Unit head:* Dr. Anthony Carruthers, Dean, 508-856-4135, E-mail: anthony.carruthers@umassmed.edu. *Application contact:* Dr. Kendall Knight, Associate Dean and Interim Director of Admissions and Recruitment, 508-856-5628, Fax: 508-856-3659, E-mail: kendall.knight@umassmed.edu. Web site: http://www.umassmed.edu/gsbs/.

University of Michigan, School of Public Health, Program in Clinical Research Design and Statistical Analysis, Ann Arbor, MI 48109. Offers MS. Offered through the Horace H. Rackham School of Graduate Studies; program admits applicants in odd-numbered calendar years only. Evening/weekend programs available. *Degree requirements:* For master's, comprehensive exam. *Entrance requirements:* For master's, GRE General Test or MCAT. Additional exam requirements/recommendations for international students: Recommended—TOEFL (minimum score 560 paper-based; 220 computer-based; 100 iBT). Electronic applications accepted. *Expenses:* Contact institution. *Faculty research:* Survival analysis, missing data, Bayesian inference, health economics, quality of life.

University of Minnesota, Twin Cities Campus, School of Public Health, Major in Clinical Research, Minneapolis, MN 55455-0213. Offers MS. Part-time programs available. *Degree requirements:* For master's, thesis. *Entrance requirements:* For master's, advanced health professional degree. Additional exam requirements/recommendations for international students: Required—TOEFL. Electronic applications accepted. *Faculty research:* Osteoporosis prevention; heart disease prevention; role of inflammatory dental disease in the genesis of atherosclerosis; interventional research into AIDS and cancer.

University of Pittsburgh, School of Medicine, Programs in Clinical Research, Pittsburgh, PA 15260. Offers clinical and translational science (PhD); clinical research (MS, Certificate). Part-time programs available. *Faculty:* 48 full-time (18 women). *Students:* 97 part-time (44 women); includes 21 minority (4 Black or African American, non-Hispanic/Latino; 1 American Indian or Alaska Native, non-Hispanic/Latino; 13 Asian, non-Hispanic/Latino; 1 Hispanic/Latino; 2 Two or more races, non-Hispanic/Latino), 24 international. Average age 35. 33 applicants, 91% accepted, 30 enrolled. In 2011, 12 master's, 11 other advanced degrees awarded. *Degree requirements:* For master's, thesis. *Entrance requirements:* For master's, MCAT, GRE, GMAT, or PCAT. Additional exam requirements/recommendations for international students: Required—TOEFL (minimum score 600 paper-based; 250 computer-based; 100 iBT). *Application deadline:* For fall admission, 10/31 priority date for domestic students, 10/31 for international students; for spring admission, 4/15 priority date for domestic students, 4/15 for international students. Applications are processed on a rolling basis. Electronic applications accepted. *Expenses:* Tuition, state resident: full-time $18,774; part-time $760 per credit. Tuition, nonresident: full-time $30,736; part-time $1258 per credit. *Required fees:* $740; $200 per term. Tuition and fees vary according to program. *Financial support:* Tuition waivers (partial) available. *Faculty research:* Quality of life, mood disorders in children, pediatric palliative care, female pelvic medicines, antibiotic

use and racial variations, medication use. *Unit head:* Dr. Wishwa Kapoor, Program Director, 412-692-2686, Fax: 412-586-9672, E-mail: kapoorwn@upmc.edu. *Application contact:* Jennifer Holliman, Program Coordinator, 412-586-9673, Fax: 412-586-9672, E-mail: hollimanjm@upmc.edu. Web site: http://www.icre.pitt.edu/degrees/degrees.html.

University of Puerto Rico, Medical Sciences Campus, School of Health Professions, Program in Clinical Research, San Juan, PR 00936-5067. Offers MS, Graduate Certificate.

University of Rochester, School of Medicine and Dentistry, Graduate Programs in Medicine and Dentistry, Department of Community and Preventive Medicine, Programs in Public Health and Clinical Investigation, Rochester, NY 14627. Offers clinical investigation (MS); public health (MPH); MBA/MPH; MD/MPH; MPH/MS; MPH/PhD. *Accreditation:* CEPH. *Entrance requirements:* For master's, GRE General Test. *Expenses: Tuition:* Full-time $41,040.

University of Rochester, School of Medicine and Dentistry, Graduate Programs in Medicine and Dentistry, Interdepartmental Program in Clinical Translational Research, Rochester, NY 14627. Offers MS. *Expenses: Tuition:* Full-time $41,040.

University of Rochester, School of Nursing, Rochester, NY 14642. Offers acute care nurse practitioner (MS); adult nurse practitioner (MS); adult/geriatric nurse practitioner (MS); care of children and families/pediatric nurse practitioner (MS); care of children and families/pediatric nurse practitioner/neonatal nurse practitioner (MS); clinical nurse leader (MS); clinical research coordinator (MS); family nurse practitioner (MS); family psychiatric mental health nurse practitioner (MS); health care organization management and leadership (MS); health practice research (PhD); nursing (DNP). *Accreditation:* AACN; NLN (one or more programs are accredited). Part-time programs available. Postbaccalaureate distance learning degree programs offered (minimal on-campus study). *Faculty:* 49 full-time (42 women), 72 part-time/adjunct (60 women). *Students:* 38 full-time (32 women), 196 part-time (181 women); includes 37 minority (20 Black or African American, non-Hispanic/Latino; 9 Asian, non-Hispanic/Latino; 8 Hispanic/Latino), 5 international. Average age 36. 68 applicants, 56% accepted, 26 enrolled. In 2011, 49 master's, 7 doctorates awarded. Terminal master's awarded for partial completion of doctoral program. *Median time to degree:* Of those who began their doctoral program in fall 2003, 40% received their degree in 8 years or less. *Degree requirements:* For doctorate, thesis/dissertation. *Entrance requirements:* For master's, BS in nursing, minimum GPA of 3.0, course work in statistics; for doctorate, GRE General Test, MS in nursing, minimum GPA of 3.5. Additional exam requirements/recommendations for international students: Required—or IELTS (minimum score 6.5); Recommended—TOEFL (minimum score 560 paper-based; 230 computer-based; 88 iBT). *Application deadline:* For fall admission, 4/1 priority date for domestic students, 4/1 for international students; for spring admission, 9/1 for domestic and international students. Application fee: $50. Electronic applications accepted. *Expenses: Tuition:* Full-time $41,040. *Financial support:* In 2011–12, 49 students received support, including 1 fellowship with full and partial tuition reimbursement available (averaging $18,700 per year); scholarships/grants, traineeships, health care benefits, tuition waivers (partial), and unspecified assistantships also available. Support available to part-time students. Financial award application deadline: 6/30. *Faculty research:* Clinical research in aging, managing asthma in children, interventions to improve outcomes in critically ill children and their mothers, nurse home visitation studies, medical device evaluation, critical care clinical studies, high risk behavior and prevention, palliative care, pregnancy-related weight gain. *Total annual research expenditures:* $4.3 million. *Unit head:* Dr. Kathy H. Rideout, Interim Dean, 585-273-8902, Fax: 585-273-1268, E-mail: kathy_rideout@urmc.rochester.edu. *Application contact:* Elaine Andolina, Director of Admissions, 585-275-2375, Fax: 585-756-8299, E-mail: elaine_andolina@urmc.rochester.edu. Web site: http://www.son.rochester.edu.

University of Southern California, Graduate School, School of Pharmacy, Regulatory Science Programs, Los Angeles, CA 90089. Offers clinical research design and management (Graduate Certificate); food safety (Graduate Certificate); patient and product safety (Graduate Certificate); preclinical drug development (Graduate Certificate); regulatory and clinical affairs (Graduate Certificate); regulatory science (MS, DRSc). Part-time and evening/weekend programs available. Postbaccalaureate distance learning degree programs offered (minimal on-campus study). Terminal master's awarded for partial completion of doctoral program. *Degree requirements:* For master's, thesis optional; for doctorate, comprehensive exam, thesis/dissertation. *Entrance requirements:* For master's, GRE. Additional exam requirements/recommendations for international students: Required—TOEFL (minimum score 603 paper-based; 250 computer-based; 100 iBT). Electronic applications accepted.

The University of Texas Health Science Center at San Antonio, Graduate School of Biomedical Sciences, Program in Clinical Investigation, San Antonio, TX 78229-3900. Offers MS. Part-time programs available. *Degree requirements:* For master's, comprehensive exam, submission of one full-length research manuscript to peer-reviewed scientific or medical journal. *Entrance requirements:* Additional exam requirements/recommendations for international students: Required—TOEFL. Electronic applications accepted. *Faculty research:* Evaluation and medical management of elders; inflammation in tissue injury, regeneration, and disease; mammalian TOR in aging and cancer; psychometrics; Type 2 diabetes; metabolic studies.

University of Virginia, School of Medicine, Department of Public Health Sciences, Program in Clinical Research, Charlottesville, VA 22903. Offers clinical investigation and patient-oriented research (MS); informatics in medicine (MS). Part-time programs available. *Students:* 5 full-time (2 women), 13 part-time (7 women); includes 5 minority (3 Asian, non-Hispanic/Latino; 2 Hispanic/Latino), 1 international. Average age 37. 11 applicants, 73% accepted, 8 enrolled. In 2011, 16 master's awarded. *Degree requirements:* For master's, thesis (for some programs). *Entrance requirements:* For master's, 2 letters of recommendation. Additional exam requirements/recommendations for international students: Required—TOEFL (minimum score 600 paper-based; 250 computer-based; 90 iBT). *Application deadline:* For fall admission, 3/1 priority date for domestic students, 3/1 for international students. Application fee: $60. Electronic applications accepted. *Financial support:* Career-related internships or fieldwork available. Financial award applicants required to submit FAFSA. *Unit head:* Dr. Ruth Gaare Bernheim, Chair, 434-924-8430, Fax: 434-924-8437. *Application contact:* Tracey L. Brookman, Academic Programs Administrator, 434-924-8430, Fax: 434-924-8437, E-mail: ms-hes@virginia.edu. Web site: http://www.healthsystem.virginia.edu/internet/phs/ms/mshome.cfm.

University of Washington, Graduate School, School of Public Health, Department of Biostatistics, Seattle, WA 98195. Offers biostatistics (MPH, MS, PhD); clinical research (MS), including biostatistics; statistical genetics (PhD). Part-time programs available. *Faculty:* 39 full-time (18 women), 6 part-time/adjunct (2 women). *Students:* 73 full-time (36 women), 7 part-time (2 women); includes 12 minority (10 Asian, non-Hispanic/Latino; 2 Hispanic/Latino), 23 international. Average age 28. 251 applicants, 14% accepted, 17 enrolled. In 2011, 9 master's, 7 doctorates awarded. Terminal master's awarded for partial completion of doctoral program. *Degree requirements:* For master's, comprehensive exam, thesis, practicum (MPH); for doctorate, comprehensive exam,

thesis/dissertation. *Entrance requirements:* For master's and doctorate, GRE General Test, coursework on multivariate calculus, linear algebra and probability; minimum GPA of 3.0. Additional exam requirements/recommendations for international students: Required—TOEFL. *Application deadline:* For fall admission, 1/2 for domestic students. Application fee: $75. Electronic applications accepted. *Financial support:* In 2011–12, 73 research assistantships with full tuition reimbursements (averaging $21,000 per year), 19 teaching assistantships with full tuition reimbursements (averaging $21,000 per year) were awarded; scholarships/grants, traineeships, health care benefits, and tuition waivers (partial) also available. *Faculty research:* Statistical methods for survival data analysis, clinical trials, epidemiological case control and cohort studies, statistical genetics. *Unit head:* Dr. Bruce Weir, Department Chair, 206-543-1044. *Application contact:* Alex MacKenzie, Counseling Services Coordinator, 206-543-1044, Fax: 206-543-3286, E-mail: alexam@u.washington.edu. Web site: http://www.biostat.washington.edu/.

University of Washington, Graduate School, School of Public Health, Department of Epidemiology, Seattle, WA 98195. Offers clinical research (MS); epidemiology (MPH, MS, PhD); global health (MPH); maternal/child health (MPH); nutritional sciences (MPH, MS, PhD); public health genetics (MPH, MS, PhD), including genetic epidemiology (MS); public health genetics (MPH, PhD); MPH/JD; MPH/MPA; MS/MPA. *Accreditation:* CEPH (one or more programs are accredited). *Faculty:* 62 full-time (35 women), 45 part-time/adjunct (22 women). *Students:* 135 full-time (93 women), 37 part-time (23 women); includes 37 minority (6 Black or African American, non-Hispanic/Latino; 1 American Indian or Alaska Native, non-Hispanic/Latino; 23 Asian, non-Hispanic/Latino; 7 Hispanic/Latino), 17 international. Average age 32. 291 applicants, 35% accepted, 58 enrolled. In 2011, 45 master's, 16 doctorates awarded. *Degree requirements:* For master's, comprehensive exam (for some programs), thesis; for doctorate, comprehensive exam, thesis/dissertation. *Entrance requirements:* For master's, GRE General Test (except for those holding PhD, MD, DDS, DVM, DO or equivalent from U.S. schools); for doctorate, GRE. Additional exam requirements/recommendations for international students: Required—TOEFL (minimum score 580 paper-based; 237 computer-based; 92 iBT) or IELTS (minimum score 7). *Application deadline:* For fall admission, 12/1 for domestic students, 11/1 for international students. Application fee: $75. Electronic applications accepted. *Expenses:* Contact institution. *Financial support:* In 2011–12, 152 students received support, including 75 fellowships with partial tuition reimbursements available, 49 research assistantships with partial tuition reimbursements available, 4 teaching assistantships with partial tuition reimbursements available; career-related internships or fieldwork, Federal Work-Study, traineeships, health care benefits, and unspecified assistantships also available. Support available to part-time students. Financial award applicants required to submit FAFSA. *Faculty research:* Chronic disease, health disparities and social determinants of health, aging and neuroepidemiology, maternal and child health, molecular and genetic epidemiology. *Unit head:* Dr. Scott Davis, Chair, 206-543-1065, Fax: 206-543-8525. *Application contact:* Kate O'Brien, Student Services Manager, 206-543-1065, Fax: 206-543-8525, E-mail: epi@u.washington.edu. Web site: http://depts.washington.edu/epidem/.

University of Washington, Graduate School, School of Public Health, Department of Health Services, Seattle, WA 98195. Offers bioinformatics (PhD); cancer prevention and control (PhD); clinical research (MS); community-oriented public health practice (MPH); economics or finance (PhD); evaluation sciences (PhD); health behavior and health promotion (PhD); health policy research (PhD); health services (MS, PhD); health services administration (EMHA, MHA); health systems policy (MPH); maternal and child health (MPH, PhD); occupational health (PhD); population health and social determinants (PhD); social and behavioral sciences (MPH); sociology and demography (PhD); JD/MHA; MHA/MBA; MHA/MD; MHA/MPA; MPH/JD; MPH/MD; MPH/MN; MPH/MPA; MPH/MS; MPH/MSD; MPH/MSW; MPH/PhD. Part-time and evening/weekend programs available. Postbaccalaureate distance learning degree programs offered (minimal on-campus study). *Faculty:* 40 full-time (23 women), 62 part-time/adjunct (25 women). *Students:* 98 full-time (78 women), 86 part-time (64 women); includes 49 minority (7 Black or African American, non-Hispanic/Latino; 3 American Indian or Alaska Native, non-Hispanic/Latino; 28 Asian, non-Hispanic/Latino; 11 Hispanic/Latino), 3 international. Average age 32. 374 applicants, 49% accepted, 104 enrolled. In 2011, 43 master's, 5 doctorates awarded. Terminal master's awarded for partial completion of doctoral program. *Degree requirements:* For master's, thesis (for some programs), practicum (MPH); for doctorate, comprehensive exam, thesis/dissertation. *Entrance requirements:* For master's and doctorate, GRE General Test, minimum GPA of 3.0. Additional exam requirements/recommendations for international students: Required—TOEFL (minimum score 580 paper-based; 237 computer-based; 92 iBT), IELTS (minimum score 7). *Application deadline:* For fall admission, 1/1 for domestic students, 11/1 for international students. Application fee: 75 Albanian leks. Electronic applications accepted. *Financial support:* In 2011–12, 47 students received support, including 10 fellowships with full and partial tuition reimbursements available (averaging $22,000 per year), 10 research assistantships with full and partial tuition reimbursements available (averaging $18,700 per year), 3 teaching assistantships with full and partial tuition reimbursements available (averaging $4,575 per year); institutionally sponsored loans, traineeships, and health care benefits also available. Financial award application deadline: 2/28; financial award applicants required to submit FAFSA. *Faculty research:* Public health practice, health promotion and disease prevention, maternal and child health, organizational behavior and culture, health policy. *Unit head:* Dr. Larry Kessler, Chair, 206-543-2930. *Application contact:* Kitty A. Andert, MPH/MS/PhD Programs Manager, 206-616-2926, Fax: 206-543-3964, E-mail: kitander@u.washington.edu. Web site: http://depts.washington.edu/hserv/.

University of Wisconsin–Madison, School of Medicine and Public Health and Graduate School, Graduate Programs in Medicine, Department of Population Health Sciences, Madison, WI 53726. Offers epidemiology (MS, PhD); population health (MS, PhD), including clinical research, epidemiology, health services research, social and behavioral health sciences; public health (MPH); DPT/MPH; DVM/MPH; JD/MPH; MD/MPH; MPA/MPH; MS/MPH; Pharm D/MPH. *Accreditation:* CEPH. Part-time programs available. *Faculty:* 104 full-time (54 women), 2 part-time/adjunct (0 women). *Students:* 69 full-time (50 women), 13 part-time (9 women); includes 19 minority (8 Black or African American, non-Hispanic/Latino; 8 Asian, non-Hispanic/Latino; 3 Hispanic/Latino), 15 international. Average age 31. 96 applicants, 41% accepted, 26 enrolled. In 2011, 5 master's, 6 doctorates awarded. Terminal master's awarded for partial completion of doctoral program. *Degree requirements:* For master's, thesis, defense; for doctorate, comprehensive exam, thesis/dissertation, qualifying exam, preliminary exam, dissertation defense. *Entrance requirements:* For master's and doctorate, GRE (MCAT or LSAT acceptable for those with doctoral degrees) taken within the last 5 years, minimum GPA of 3.0, quantitative preparation (calculus, statistics, or other) with minimum B average. Additional exam requirements/recommendations for international students: Required—TOEFL (minimum score 580 paper-based; 237 computer-based; 92 iBT). *Application deadline:* For fall admission, 1/15 for domestic and international students. Application fee: $56. Electronic applications accepted. *Expenses:* Tuition, state resident: full-time $10,296; part-time $643.51 per credit. Tuition, nonresident: full-time $24,054; part-time $1503.40 per credit. *Required fees:* $70.06 per credit. Tuition and fees vary according to course load, campus/location, program and reciprocity agreements. *Financial support:* Fellowships with full tuition reimbursements, research assistantships with full tuition reimbursements, teaching assistantships with full tuition reimbursements, scholarships/grants, traineeships, health care benefits, and unspecified assistantships available. Support available to part-time students. *Faculty research:* Epidemiology (cancer, environmental, aging, infectious and genetic disease), determinants of population health, health services research, social and behavioral health sciences, biostatistics. *Total annual research expenditures:* $11.4 million. *Unit head:* Kathy Rutlin, MS/PhD Programs Coordinator, 608-265-8108, Fax: 608-263-2820, E-mail: karutlin@wisc.edu. *Application contact:* Quinn H. Fullenkamp, MS/PhD Assistant Programs Coordinator, 608-263-6583, Fax: 608-263-2820, E-mail: qhfullen@wisc.edu. Web site: http://www.pophealth.wisc.edu.

Vanderbilt University, School of Medicine, Clinical Investigation Program, Nashville, TN 37240-1001. Offers MS. *Entrance requirements:* Additional exam requirements/recommendations for international students: Required—TOEFL.

Walden University, Graduate Programs, School of Health Sciences, Minneapolis, MN 55401. Offers clinical research administration (MS, Postbaccalaureate Certificate); health informatics (MS); health services (PhD), including community health education and advocacy, general program, healthcare administration, leadership, public health policy, self-designed; healthcare administration (MHA); public health (MPH, PhD), including community health and education (PhD), epidemiology (PhD). Part-time and evening/weekend programs available. Postbaccalaureate distance learning degree programs offered (minimal on-campus study). *Faculty:* 20 full-time (13 women), 175 part-time/adjunct (81 women). *Students:* 2,777 full-time (2,158 women), 1,350 part-time (1,038 women); includes 2,379 minority (1,935 Black or African American, non-Hispanic/Latino; 33 American Indian or Alaska Native, non-Hispanic/Latino; 173 Asian, non-Hispanic/Latino; 180 Hispanic/Latino; 9 Native Hawaiian or other Pacific Islander, non-Hispanic/Latino; 49 Two or more races, non-Hispanic/Latino), 247 international. Average age 40. In 2011, 528 master's, 79 doctorates, 1 other advanced degree awarded. *Degree requirements:* For doctorate, thesis/dissertation, residency. *Entrance requirements:* For master's, bachelor's degree or equivalent in related field, minimum GPA of 2.5; for doctorate, master's degree or equivalent in related field; minimum GPA of 3.0; official transcripts; three years of related professional/academic experience (preferred); access to computer and Internet. Additional exam requirements/recommendations for international students: Required—TOEFL (minimum score 550 paper-based; 213 computer-based), IELTS (minimum score 6.5), or Michigan English Language Assessment Battery (minimum score 82). *Application deadline:* Applications are processed on a rolling basis. Application fee: $50. Electronic applications accepted. *Financial support:* Federal Work-Study, scholarships/grants, unspecified assistantships, and family tuition reduction, active duty/veteran tuition reduction, group tuition reduction, interest-free payment plans, employee tuition reduction available. Support available to part-time students. Financial award applicants required to submit FAFSA. *Unit head:* Dr. Jorg Westermann, Associate Dean, 800-925-3368. *Application contact:* Jennifer Hall, Vice President of Enrollment Management, 866-4-WALDEN, E-mail: info@waldenu.edu. Web site: http://www.waldenu.edu/Colleges-and-Schools/College-of-Health-Sciences/School-of-Health-Sciences.htm.

Washington University in St. Louis, School of Medicine, Program in Clinical Investigation, St. Louis, MO 63130-4899. Offers clinical investigation (MS), including genetics/genomics, translational medicine. Part-time programs available. *Faculty:* 64 full-time (17 women), 3 part-time/adjunct (2 women). *Students:* 23 full-time (15 women), 23 part-time (10 women); includes 14 minority (3 Black or African American, non-Hispanic/Latino; 11 Asian, non-Hispanic/Latino). Average age 32. 6 applicants, 83% accepted, 5 enrolled. In 2011, 16 master's awarded. *Degree requirements:* For master's, thesis. *Entrance requirements:* For master's, doctoral-level degree or in process of obtaining doctoral-level degree. Additional exam requirements/recommendations for international students: Required—TOEFL. *Application deadline:* For fall admission, 3/15 for domestic students. Application fee: $0. Electronic applications accepted. *Faculty research:* Anesthesiology, infectious diseases, neurology, obstetrics and gynecology, orthopaedic surgery. *Unit head:* Dr. David Warren, Associate Professor of Medicine, 314-454-8225, Fax: 314-454-5392, E-mail: dwarren@dom.wustl.edu. *Application contact:* Angela B. Wilson, Curriculum and Evaluation Coordinator, 314-454-8936, Fax: 314-454-8279, E-mail: abwilson@dom.wustl.edu. Web site: http://crtc.wustl.edu/.

Communication Disorders

Abilene Christian University, Graduate School, College of Education and Human Services, Department of Communication Sciences and Disorders, Abilene, TX 79699-9100. Offers MS. *Accreditation:* ASHA. *Faculty:* 5 part-time/adjunct (4 women). *Students:* 33 full-time (32 women), 1 (woman) part-time; includes 8 minority (2 Black or African American, non-Hispanic/Latino; 5 Hispanic/Latino; 1 Two or more races, non-Hispanic/Latino). 75 applicants, 55% accepted, 18 enrolled. In 2011, 12 master's awarded. *Degree requirements:* For master's, one foreign language, comprehensive exam. *Entrance requirements:* For master's, GRE General Test. Additional exam requirements/recommendations for international students: Required—TOEFL (minimum score 550 paper-based; 213 computer-based; 80 iBT), IELTS (minimum score 6). *Application deadline:* For fall admission, 2/1 priority date for domestic students. Applications are processed on a rolling basis. Application fee: $50. Electronic applications accepted. *Expenses:* Tuition: Full-time $14,168; part-time $787 per hour. *Required fees:* $82 per hour. $10 per term. *Financial support:* In 2011–12, 15 students received support. Research assistantships and scholarships/grants available. Financial award application deadline: 4/1; financial award applicants required to submit FAFSA. *Unit head:* Dr. Terry Baggs, Graduate Director, 325-674-4819, Fax: 325-674-2552, E-mail: terry.baggs@acu.edu. *Application contact:* David Pittman, Graduate Admissions Counselor, 325-674-2656, Fax: 325-674-6717, E-mail: gradinfo@acu.edu.

Adelphi University, Ruth S. Ammon School of Education, Program in Communication Sciences and Disorders, Garden City, NY 11530-0701. Offers audiology (MS, DA); speech-language pathology (MS, DA). *Accreditation:* ASHA. Part-time programs available. *Students:* 202 full-time (197 women), 46 part-time (42 women); includes 39

minority (5 Black or African American, non-Hispanic/Latino; 7 Asian, non-Hispanic/Latino; 24 Hispanic/Latino; 1 Native Hawaiian or other Pacific Islander, non-Hispanic/Latino; 2 Two or more races, non-Hispanic/Latino). Average age 26. In 2011, 108 master's, 4 doctorates awarded. *Degree requirements:* For master's, comprehensive exam, clinical practice; for doctorate, one foreign language, comprehensive exam, thesis/dissertation. *Entrance requirements:* For master's, GRE General Test, writing exam, 3 letters of recommendation, interview, resume, 19 credits of prerequisite course work or communications disorders training; for doctorate, GRE General Test, 3 letters of recommendation, interview. Additional exam requirements/recommendations for international students: Required—TOEFL (minimum score 550 paper-based; 213 computer-based; 80 iBT). *Application deadline:* For fall admission, 3/1 priority date for domestic students, 3/1 for international students; for spring admission, 10/1 priority date for domestic students, 10/1 for international students. Applications are processed on a rolling basis. Application fee: $50. Electronic applications accepted. *Expenses: Tuition:* Full-time $29,600; part-time $930 per credit. *Required fees:* $1100. *Financial support:* Fellowships, research assistantships with partial tuition reimbursements, teaching assistantships, career-related internships or fieldwork, Federal Work-Study, institutionally sponsored loans, tuition waivers (full), and unspecified assistantships available. Support available to part-time students. Financial award application deadline: 2/15; financial award applicants required to submit FAFSA. *Faculty research:* Pediatric audiology, child speech perception with hearing loss, auditory deprivation, fluency, cultural diversity. *Unit head:* Dr. Robert Goldfarb, Chairperson, 516-877-4785, E-mail: goldfarb2@adelphi.edu. *Application contact:* Christine Murphy, Director of Admissions, 516-877-3050, Fax: 516-877-3039, E-mail: graduateadmissions@adelphi.edu.

Alabama Agricultural and Mechanical University, School of Graduate Studies, School of Education, Department of Counseling and Special Education, Area in Communicative Disorders, Huntsville, AL 35811. Offers M Ed, MS. *Accreditation:* ASHA. Part-time programs available. *Degree requirements:* For master's, comprehensive exam. *Entrance requirements:* For master's, GRE General Test, minimum GPA of 2.5. Additional exam requirements/recommendations for international students: Required—TOEFL (minimum score 500 paper-based; 173 computer-based; 61 iBT). Electronic applications accepted. *Faculty research:* Alternative methods of teaching speech and language to handicapped individuals.

Appalachian State University, Cratis D. Williams Graduate School, Department of Communication Sciences and Disorders, Boone, NC 28608. Offers speech-language pathology (MS). Part-time programs available. *Faculty:* 9 full-time (6 women), 8 part-time/adjunct (all women). *Students:* 82 full-time (78 women), 1 (woman) part-time; includes 3 minority (2 American Indian or Alaska Native, non-Hispanic/Latino; 1 Hispanic/Latino). 310 applicants, 36% accepted, 34 enrolled. In 2011, 45 master's awarded. *Degree requirements:* For master's, comprehensive exam, thesis optional. *Entrance requirements:* For master's, GRE General Test, 3 letters of recommendation. Additional exam requirements/recommendations for international students: Required—TOEFL (minimum score 570 paper-based; 230 computer-based), IELTS (minimum score 6.5). *Application deadline:* For fall admission, 3/1 for domestic students, 2/1 for international students; for spring admission, 10/1 for domestic students, 7/1 for international students. Applications are processed on a rolling basis. Application fee: $55. Electronic applications accepted. *Expenses:* Tuition, state resident: full-time $4040; part-time $180 per semester hour. Tuition, nonresident: full-time $15,900; part-time $760 per semester hour. *Required fees:* $2500; $20 per semester hour. Tuition and fees vary according to campus/location. *Financial support:* In 2011–12, 16 research assistantships (averaging $4,000 per year) were awarded; teaching assistantships, career-related internships or fieldwork, Federal Work-Study, scholarships/grants, and unspecified assistantships also available. Financial award application deadline: 7/1; financial award applicants required to submit FAFSA. *Faculty research:* Clinical service delivery, voice disorders, language disorders, fluency disorders, neurogenic disorders. *Total annual research expenditures:* $133,000. *Unit head:* Dr. Angela Losardo, Chair, 828-262-7182, Fax: 828-262-3153, E-mail: losardoas@appstate.edu. *Application contact:* Eveline Watts, Administrative Assistant, 828-262-2182, E-mail: wattsem@appstate.edu. Web site: http://comdis.appstate.edu/.

Arizona State University, College of Liberal Arts and Sciences, Department of Speech and Hearing Science, Tempe, AZ 85287-0102. Offers audiology (Au D); communication disorders (MS); speech and hearing science (PhD). *Accreditation:* ASHA (one or more programs are accredited). *Degree requirements:* For master's, comprehensive exam (for some programs), thesis optional, interactive Program of Study (iPOS) submitted before completing 50 percent of required credit hours; for doctorate, comprehensive exam, thesis/dissertation (for some programs), academic/practicum components (Au D); interactive Program of Study (iPOS) submitted before completing 50 percent of required credit hours. *Entrance requirements:* For master's and doctorate, GRE, minimum GPA of 3.0 or equivalent in last 2 years of work leading to bachelor's degree. Additional exam requirements/recommendations for international students: Required—TOEFL (minimum score 80 iBT), TOEFL, IELTS, or Pearson Test of English. *Expenses:* Contact institution.

Arkansas State University, Graduate School, College of Nursing and Health Professions, Department of Communication Disorders, Jonesboro, State University, AR 72467. Offers MCD. *Accreditation:* ASHA. Part-time programs available. *Faculty:* 5 full-time (3 women). *Students:* 49 full-time (48 women); includes 3 minority (2 Black or African American, non-Hispanic/Latino; 1 Native Hawaiian or other Pacific Islander, non-Hispanic/Latino). Average age 25. 46 applicants, 50% accepted, 23 enrolled. In 2011, 20 master's awarded. *Degree requirements:* For master's, comprehensive exam, thesis or alternative. *Entrance requirements:* For master's, GRE General Test, appropriate bachelor's degree, letters of recommendation, official transcripts, immunization records. Additional exam requirements/recommendations for international students: Required—TOEFL (minimum score 550 paper-based; 213 computer-based; 79 iBT), IELTS (minimum score 6), Pearson Test of English Academic (minimum score 56). *Application deadline:* For fall admission, 2/15 for domestic and international students. Applications are processed on a rolling basis. Application fee: $30 ($40 for international students). Electronic applications accepted. *Expenses:* Contact institution. *Financial support:* In 2011–12, 6 students received support. Career-related internships or fieldwork, scholarships/grants, and unspecified assistantships available. Financial award application deadline: 7/1; financial award applicants required to submit FAFSA. *Unit head:* Dr. Richard Neeley, Director, 870-972-3106, Fax: 870-972-3788, E-mail: rneeley@astate.edu. *Application contact:* Dr. Andrew Sustich, Dean of the Graduate School, 870-972-3029, Fax: 870-972-3857, E-mail: sustich@astate.edu. Web site: http://www.astate.edu/a/conhp/communication-disorders/index.dot.

Armstrong Atlantic State University, School of Graduate Studies, Program in Education, Savannah, GA 31419-1997. Offers adult education (M Ed); curriculum and instruction (M Ed); early childhood education (M Ed); education (M Ed); elementary education (M Ed); middle grades education (M Ed); secondary education (M Ed), including business education, English education, mathematics education, science education, social science education; special education (M Ed), including behavioral disorders, learning disabilities, speech-language pathology. *Accreditation:* NCATE. Part-time and evening/weekend programs available. Postbaccalaureate distance learning degree programs offered (minimal on-campus study). *Faculty:* 33 full-time (23 women), 3 part-time/adjunct (2 women). *Students:* 97 full-time (91 women), 262 part-time (227 women); includes 83 minority (70 Black or African American, non-Hispanic/Latino; 3 Asian, non-Hispanic/Latino; 8 Hispanic/Latino; 2 Two or more races, non-Hispanic/Latino), 5 international. Average age 34. 169 applicants, 69% accepted, 102 enrolled. In 2011, 227 master's awarded. *Degree requirements:* For master's, comprehensive exam, portfolio. *Entrance requirements:* For master's, GRE General Test or MAT, minimum GPA of 2.5, letters of recommendation. Additional exam requirements/recommendations for international students: Required—TOEFL (minimum score 523 paper-based; 193 computer-based). *Application deadline:* For fall admission, 7/1 priority date for domestic students, 5/1 for international students; for spring admission, 11/15 priority date for domestic students, 9/15 for international students. Applications are processed on a rolling basis. Application fee: $30. Electronic applications accepted. *Expenses:* Tuition, state resident: full-time $3402. Tuition, nonresident: full-time $12,636. *Financial support:* In 2011–12, research assistantships with full tuition reimbursements (averaging $5,000 per year) were awarded; career-related internships or fieldwork, Federal Work-Study, scholarships/grants, and unspecified assistantships also available. Support available to part-time students. Financial award applicants required to submit FAFSA. *Unit head:* Dr. Patricia Wachholz, Dean, College of Education, 912-344-2797, E-mail: patricia.wachholz@armstrong.edu. *Application contact:* Jill Bell, Director, Graduate Enrollment Services, 912-344-2798, Fax: 912-344-3488, E-mail: graduate@armstrong.edu. Web site: http://www.armstrong.edu/Education/coe_deans_office/coe_education_welcome.

A.T. Still University of Health Sciences, Arizona School of Health Sciences, Mesa, AZ 85206. Offers advanced occupational therapy (MS); advanced physician assistant (MS); athletic training (MS); audiology (Au D); health sciences (DHSc); human movement (MS); occupational therapy (MS); physical therapy (DPT); physician assistant (MS); transitional audiology (Au D); transitional physical therapy (DPT). *Accreditation:* AOTA (one or more programs are accredited); ASHA. Part-time and evening/weekend programs available. Postbaccalaureate distance learning degree programs offered (minimal on-campus study). *Faculty:* 44 full-time (27 women), 235 part-time/adjunct (141 women). *Students:* 410 full-time (275 women), 1,010 part-time (675 women); includes 320 minority (73 Black or African American, non-Hispanic/Latino; 18 American Indian or Alaska Native, non-Hispanic/Latino; 158 Asian, non-Hispanic/Latino; 62 Hispanic/Latino; 9 Two or more races, non-Hispanic/Latino), 6 international. Average age 35. 4,395 applicants, 18% accepted, 694 enrolled. In 2011, 221 master's, 406 doctorates awarded. *Median time to degree:* Of those who began their doctoral program in fall 2003, 98% received their degree in 8 years or less. *Degree requirements:* For master's, thesis (for some programs); for doctorate, thesis/dissertation (for some programs). *Entrance requirements:* For master's, GRE General Test; for doctorate, GRE, Evaluation of Practicing Audiologists Capabilities (Au D), Physical Therapist Evaluation Tool (DPT), current state licensure, master's degree or equivalent (Au D). Additional exam requirements/recommendations for international students: Required—TOEFL (minimum score 550 paper-based; 213 computer-based; 80 iBT). *Application deadline:* For fall admission, 8/1 priority date for domestic students, 8/1 for international students. Applications are processed on a rolling basis. Application fee: $60. *Expenses:* Contact institution. *Financial support:* In 2011–12, 272 students received support, including 14 fellowships (averaging $16,000 per year); Federal Work-Study and scholarships/grants also available. Financial award application deadline: 5/1; financial award applicants required to submit FAFSA. *Faculty research:* Physical therapy: metabolism during exercise and activity; neuromuscular function after injury, prevention of lifestyle diseases, prevention and treatment of overuse injuries; athletic training: pediatric sport-related concussion, adolescent athlete health-related quality of life; occupational therapy: spirituality and health disparities, geriatric and pediatric well-being, pain management for participation. *Total annual research expenditures:* $75,682. *Unit head:* Dr. Randy Danielsen, Dean, 480-219-6000, Fax: 480-219-6110, E-mail: rdanielsen@atsu.edu. *Application contact:* Donna Sparks, Associate Director, Admissions Processing, 660-626-2117, Fax: 660-626-2969, E-mail: admissions@atsu.edu. Web site: http://www.atsu.edu/ashs.

Auburn University, Graduate School, College of Liberal Arts, Department of Communication Disorders, Auburn University, AL 36849. Offers audiology (MCD, MS, Au D); speech pathology (MCD, MS). *Accreditation:* ASHA (one or more programs are accredited). Part-time programs available. *Faculty:* 17 full-time (13 women), 2 part-time/adjunct (both women). *Students:* 71 full-time (67 women), 8 part-time (7 women); includes 3 minority (2 Black or African American, non-Hispanic/Latino; 1 Asian, non-Hispanic/Latino). Average age 23. 206 applicants, 22% accepted, 34 enrolled. In 2011, 23 master's, 7 doctorates awarded. *Degree requirements:* For master's, comprehensive exam (MCD), thesis (MS). *Entrance requirements:* For master's, GRE General Test. *Application deadline:* For fall admission, 7/7 for domestic students; for spring admission, 11/24 for domestic students. Applications are processed on a rolling basis. Application fee: $50 ($60 for international students). Electronic applications accepted. *Expenses:* Tuition, state resident: full-time $7290; part-time $405 per credit hour. Tuition, nonresident: full-time $21,870; part-time $1215 per credit hour. *International tuition:* $22,000 full-time. *Required fees:* $1402. *Financial support:* Research assistantships, teaching assistantships, and Federal Work-Study available. Support available to part-time students. Financial award application deadline: 3/15; financial award applicants required to submit FAFSA. *Unit head:* Dr. Rebekah H. Pindzola, Chair, 334-844-7916. *Application contact:* Dr. George Flowers, Dean of the Graduate School, 334-844-2125. Web site: http://www.cla.auburn.edu/communicationdisorders/.

Ball State University, Graduate School, College of Sciences and Humanities, Department of Speech Pathology and Audiology, Muncie, IN 47306-1099. Offers MA, Au D. *Accreditation:* ASHA. *Faculty:* 13 full-time (10 women), 2 part-time/adjunct (both women). *Students:* 99 full-time (90 women), 35 part-time (33 women); includes 10 minority (2 Black or African American, non-Hispanic/Latino; 3 Hispanic/Latino; 1 Native Hawaiian or other Pacific Islander, non-Hispanic/Latino; 4 Two or more races, non-Hispanic/Latino), 2 international. Average age 25. 247 applicants, 20% accepted, 28 enrolled. In 2011, 36 master's, 5 doctorates awarded. *Entrance requirements:* For master's, GRE General Test; for doctorate, GRE General Test, interview. Application fee: $50. Tuition and fees vary according to program and reciprocity agreements. *Financial support:* In 2011–12, 51 students received support, including 48 teaching assistantships with full and partial tuition reimbursements available (averaging $7,513 per year); research assistantships with full tuition reimbursements available and career-related internships or fieldwork also available. Financial award application deadline: 3/1. *Faculty research:* Adult neurological disorders, stuttering, tinnitus masking, brain stem responses. *Unit head:* Dr. Mary Jo Germani, Chairman, 765-285-8162, Fax: 765-285-5623, E-mail: mgermani@gw.bsu.edu. *Application contact:* Dr. Robert Morris, Associate Provost for Research and Dean of the Graduate School, 765-285-1300, E-mail: rmorris@bsu.edu. Web site: http://www.bsu.edu/csh/spa/.

Barry University, School of Education, Program in Education for Teachers of Students with Hearing Impairments, Miami Shores, FL 33161-6695. Offers MS.

Baylor University, Graduate School, College of Arts and Sciences, Department of Communication Sciences and Disorders, Waco, TX 76798. Offers MA, MSCSD. *Accreditation:* ASHA (one or more programs are accredited). *Faculty:* 9 full-time (6 women), 1 (woman) part-time/adjunct. *Students:* 44 full-time (43 women); includes 4 minority (all Hispanic/Latino), 1 international. In 2011, 31 master's awarded. *Entrance*

requirements: For master's, GRE General Test. *Application deadline:* Applications are processed on a rolling basis. Application fee: $25. *Expenses:* Contact institution. *Financial support:* In 2011–12, 25 students received support, including 20 fellowships; Federal Work-Study, institutionally sponsored loans, and tuition waivers (partial) also available. Financial award application deadline: 5/1. *Faculty research:* Nasality, language impairment, stuttering, Spanish speech perception. *Unit head:* Dr. David Garrett, Program Director, 254-710-2567, Fax: 254-710-2590. *Application contact:* Kathryn Williams, Administrative Assistant, 254-710-3588, Fax: 254-710-3870, E-mail: kathryn_williams@baylor.edu. Web site: http://www.baylor.edu/communication_disorders/.

Bloomsburg University of Pennsylvania, School of Graduate Studies, College of Education, Department of Exceptionality Programs, Program in Education of the Deaf/Hard of Hearing, Bloomsburg, PA 17815-1301. Offers MS. *Entrance requirements:* For master's, PRAXIS, minimum QPA of 3.0. Additional exam requirements/recommendations for international students: Required—TOEFL (minimum score 550 paper-based; 213 computer-based; 79 iBT). Electronic applications accepted. *Faculty research:* Teaching sign language and speech reading through videodisc technology, oral communication skills, sign language.

Bloomsburg University of Pennsylvania, School of Graduate Studies, College of Science and Technology, Department of Audiology and Speech Pathology, Program in Audiology, Bloomsburg, PA 17815-1301. Offers Au D. *Accreditation:* ASHA. *Entrance requirements:* For doctorate, GRE, 3 letters of recommendation. Additional exam requirements/recommendations for international students: Required—TOEFL. Electronic applications accepted. *Faculty research:* Electrophysiological, industrial, and clinical audiology; hearing aid education; pediatric audiology; auditory processing.

Bloomsburg University of Pennsylvania, School of Graduate Studies, College of Science and Technology, Department of Audiology and Speech Pathology, Program in Speech-Language Pathology, Bloomsburg, PA 17815-1301. Offers MS. *Accreditation:* ASHA. *Entrance requirements:* For master's, GRE General Test, minimum QPA of 3.0, 3 letters of recommendation. Additional exam requirements/recommendations for international students: Required—TOEFL (minimum score 550 paper-based; 213 computer-based; 79 iBT). Electronic applications accepted. *Faculty research:* Language disorders in children, augmentative communication, neurogenic disorders of speech and language, stuttering, speech science.

Boston University, College of Health and Rehabilitation Sciences: Sargent College, Department of Speech, Language and Hearing Sciences, Boston, MA 02215. Offers audiology (PhD); speech-language pathology (MS, PhD, CAGS). *Accreditation:* ASHA. *Faculty:* 12 full-time (10 women), 12 part-time/adjunct (5 women). *Students:* 72 full-time (69 women); includes 7 minority (1 Black or African American, non-Hispanic/Latino; 3 Asian, non-Hispanic/Latino; 2 Hispanic/Latino; 1 Two or more races, non-Hispanic/Latino), 2 international. Average age 24. 535 applicants, 31% accepted, 38 enrolled. In 2011, 33 master's awarded. *Degree requirements:* For master's, comprehensive exam, thesis optional; for doctorate, comprehensive exam, thesis/dissertation. *Entrance requirements:* For master's, doctorate, and CAGS, GRE General Test. Additional exam requirements/recommendations for international students: Required—TOEFL (minimum score 550 paper-based; 84 computer-based). *Application deadline:* For fall admission, 1/15 priority date for domestic students, 1/15 for international students. Applications are processed on a rolling basis. Application fee: $100. Electronic applications accepted. *Expenses: Tuition:* Full-time $40,848; part-time $1276 per credit hour. *Required fees:* $572; $286 per semester. *Financial support:* In 2011–12, 54 students received support, including 5 fellowships (averaging $14,400 per year), 2 research assistantships with full tuition reimbursements available (averaging $18,000 per year), 11 teaching assistantships (averaging $2,400 per year); career-related internships or fieldwork, Federal Work-Study, institutionally sponsored loans, scholarships/grants, and tuition waivers (partial) also available. Financial award application deadline: 4/15; financial award applicants required to submit FAFSA. *Faculty research:* Child language, fluency, autism, speech science, perception of complex sounds. *Total annual research expenditures:* $1.6 million. *Unit head:* Dr. Melanie Matthies, Chair, 617-353-3188, E-mail: slhs@bu.edu. *Application contact:* Sharon Sankey, Director, Student Services, 617-353-2713, Fax: 617-353-7500, E-mail: ssankey@bu.edu. Web site: http://www.bu.edu/sargent/.

Bowling Green State University, Graduate College, College of Education and Human Development, School of Education and Intervention Services, Intervention Services Division, Program in Special Education, Bowling Green, OH 43403. Offers assistive technology (M Ed); early childhood intervention (M Ed); gifted education (M Ed); hearing impaired intervention (M Ed); mild/moderate intervention (M Ed); moderate/intensive intervention (M Ed). *Accreditation:* NCATE. Part-time programs available. *Degree requirements:* For master's, thesis or alternative. *Entrance requirements:* For master's, GRE General Test. Additional exam requirements/recommendations for international students: Required—TOEFL. Electronic applications accepted. *Faculty research:* Reading and special populations, deafness, early childhood, gifted and talented, behavior disorders.

Bowling Green State University, Graduate College, College of Health and Human Services, Department of Communication Disorders, Bowling Green, OH 43403. Offers communication disorders (PhD); speech-language pathology (MS). *Accreditation:* ASHA (one or more programs are accredited). *Degree requirements:* For master's, thesis or alternative; for doctorate, comprehensive exam, thesis/dissertation, foreign language or research tool. *Entrance requirements:* For master's, GRE General Test, minimum GPA of 3.0; for doctorate, GRE General Test, minimum GPA of 3.2. Additional exam requirements/recommendations for international students: Required—TOEFL. Electronic applications accepted. *Faculty research:* Rehabilitation and mental disorders, forensic rehabilitation, rehabilitation and substance abuse, private rehabilitation and disability management, adjustment to disability.

Brigham Young University, Graduate Studies, David O. McKay School of Education, Department of Communication Disorders, Provo, UT 84602-1001. Offers MS. *Accreditation:* ASHA. *Faculty:* 10 full-time (4 women), 3 part-time/adjunct (all women). *Students:* 21 full-time (20 women), 19 part-time (14 women); includes 1 minority (Hispanic/Latino). Average age 25. 70 applicants, 39% accepted, 21 enrolled. In 2011, 8 master's awarded. *Degree requirements:* For master's, comprehensive exam, thesis, exit interview, PRAXIS. *Entrance requirements:* For master's, GRE General Test, 3 letters of recommendation, statement of intent. Additional exam requirements/recommendations for international students: Required—TOEFL (minimum score 580 paper-based; 237 computer-based; 85 iBT). *Application deadline:* For fall admission, 2/1 for domestic and international students. Application fee: $50. Electronic applications accepted. *Expenses: Tuition:* Full-time $5760; part-time $320 per credit. Tuition and fees vary according to student's religious affiliation. *Financial support:* In 2011–12, 24 students received support, including 20 research assistantships (averaging $1,701 per year), 18 teaching assistantships (averaging $2,786 per year); fellowships, institutionally sponsored loans, and scholarships/grants also available. Financial award application deadline: 2/1. *Faculty research:* Foreign language speech audiometry materials; language sample analysis, language measurement; speech motor control physiology; aerodynamic and kinematic analysis of speech production; social skills and outcomes of children with language impairment. *Unit head:* Dr. Christopher Dromey, Chair, 801-422-

6461, Fax: 801-422-0197, E-mail: christopher_dromey@byu.edu. *Application contact:* Sandy Alger, Department Secretary, 801-422-5117, Fax: 801-422-0197, E-mail: sandy_alger@byu.edu. Web site: http://education.byu.edu/comd/.

Brooklyn College of the City University of New York, Division of Graduate Studies, Department of Speech Communication Arts and Sciences, Brooklyn, NY 11210-2889. Offers audiology (Au D); speech (MA), including public communication; speech and hearing sciences (PhD); speech pathology (MS). Au D offered jointly with Hunter College of the City University of New York. *Accreditation:* ASHA (one or more programs are accredited). Part-time programs available. Terminal master's awarded for partial completion of doctoral program. *Degree requirements:* For master's, comprehensive exam, NTE. *Entrance requirements:* For master's, GRE, minimum GPA of 3.0, interview, essay. Additional exam requirements/recommendations for international students: Required—TOEFL (minimum score 500 paper-based; 173 computer-based; 61 iBT). Electronic applications accepted. *Faculty research:* Language and learning disorders, aphasia, auditory disorders, public and business communication, voice and fluency disorders.

Buffalo State College, State University of New York, The Graduate School, Faculty of Applied Science and Education, Department of Speech-Language Pathology, Buffalo, NY 14222-1095. Offers MS Ed. *Accreditation:* ASHA. Part-time and evening/weekend programs available. *Degree requirements:* For master's, thesis or alternative, project. *Entrance requirements:* For master's, minimum GPA of 3.0 in last 60 hours, 22 hours in communication disorders. Additional exam requirements/recommendations for international students: Required—TOEFL (minimum score 550 paper-based; 213 computer-based).

California State University, Chico, Office of Graduate Studies, College of Communication and Education, Department of Communication Arts and Sciences, Program in Communication Sciences and Disorders, Chico, CA 95929-0722. Offers MA. *Accreditation:* ASHA. *Faculty:* 3 full-time (all women), 7 part-time/adjunct (6 women). *Students:* 42 full-time (40 women), 2 part-time (both women); includes 4 minority (all Hispanic/Latino). Average age 27. 120 applicants, 20% accepted, 21 enrolled. In 2011, 46 master's awarded. *Degree requirements:* For master's, thesis or alternative. *Entrance requirements:* For master's, GRE General Test, 3 letters of recommendation, statement of purpose, resume. Additional exam requirements/recommendations for international students: Required—TOEFL (minimum score 550 paper-based; 213 computer-based; 80 iBT), IELTS (minimum score 6.5), Pearson Test of English (minimum score 59). *Application deadline:* For fall admission, 3/1 for domestic and international students. Application fee: $55. Electronic applications accepted. Tuition and fees vary according to class time, course load and degree level. *Financial support:* Teaching assistantships, career-related internships or fieldwork, scholarships/grants, traineeships, and unspecified assistantships available. *Unit head:* Dr. Suzanne B. Miller, Department Chair, 530-898-5751, Fax: 530-898-4096, E-mail: cmas@csuchico.edu. *Application contact:* Judy L. Rice, Graduate Admissions Coordinator, 530-898-5416, Fax: 530-898-3342.

California State University, East Bay, Office of Academic Programs and Graduate Studies, College of Letters, Arts, and Social Sciences, Department of Communicative Sciences and Disorders, Hayward, CA 94542-3000. Offers speech-language pathology (MS). *Accreditation:* ASHA. Part-time programs available. *Faculty:* 2 full-time (1 woman), 3 part-time/adjunct (all women). *Students:* 83 full-time (78 women), 21 part-time (19 women); includes 27 minority (2 Black or African American, non-Hispanic/Latino; 15 Asian, non-Hispanic/Latino; 8 Hispanic/Latino; 1 Native Hawaiian or other Pacific Islander, non-Hispanic/Latino; 1 Two or more races, non-Hispanic/Latino), 2 international. Average age 29. 322 applicants, 12% accepted, 36 enrolled. In 2011, 33 master's awarded. *Degree requirements:* For master's, comprehensive exam, internship or thesis. *Entrance requirements:* For master's, minimum GPA of 3.0 in last 2 years of course work; baccalaureate degree in speech pathology and audiology; minimum of 60 hours supervised clinical practice. Additional exam requirements/recommendations for international students: Required—TOEFL (minimum score 550 paper-based; 213 computer-based). *Application deadline:* For fall admission, 6/30 for domestic and international students. Application fee: $55. Electronic applications accepted. *Expenses:* Tuition, state resident: full-time $6738; part-time $1302 per quarter. Tuition, nonresident: full-time $12,690; part-time $2294 per quarter. *Required fees:* $449 per quarter. Tuition and fees vary according to degree level, program and reciprocity agreements. *Financial support:* Fellowships, teaching assistantships, career-related internships or fieldwork, Federal Work-Study, institutionally sponsored loans, and scholarships/grants available. Support available to part-time students. Financial award application deadline: 3/2. *Faculty research:* Aphasia, autism, dementia, diversity, voice. *Unit head:* Dr. Marilyn Silva, Interim Chair, 510-885-3233, Fax: 510-885-2186, E-mail: marilyn.silva@csueastbay.edu. *Application contact:* Prof. Robert Peppard, Graduate Admissions Coordinator, 510-885-4310, Fax: 510-885-2186, E-mail: robert.peppard@csueastbay.edu. Web site: http://www20.csueastbay.edu/class/departments/commsci/index.html.

California State University, Fresno, Division of Graduate Studies, College of Health and Human Services, Department of Communicative Disorders, Fresno, CA 93740-8027. Offers communicative disorders (MA), including deaf education, speech/language pathology. *Accreditation:* ASHA. Part-time programs available. *Degree requirements:* For master's, thesis or alternative. *Entrance requirements:* For master's, GRE General Test, minimum GPA of 3.0. Additional exam requirements/recommendations for international students: Required—TOEFL. Electronic applications accepted. *Faculty research:* Disabilities education, technology, writing skills at multiple levels, stuttering treatment.

California State University, Fullerton, Graduate Studies, College of Communications, Department of Human Communications, Fullerton, CA 92834-9480. Offers communicative disorders (MA); speech communication (MA). *Accreditation:* ASHA. Part-time programs available. *Students:* 75 full-time (65 women), 26 part-time (17 women); includes 47 minority (7 Black or African American, non-Hispanic/Latino; 15 Asian, non-Hispanic/Latino; 24 Hispanic/Latino; 1 Two or more races, non-Hispanic/Latino), 6 international. Average age 30. 436 applicants, 10% accepted, 32 enrolled. In 2011, 48 master's awarded. *Degree requirements:* For master's, comprehensive exam, thesis or alternative. *Entrance requirements:* For master's, minimum GPA of 3.0 in major. Application fee: $55. *Financial support:* Teaching assistantships, career-related internships or fieldwork, Federal Work-Study, institutionally sponsored loans, and scholarships/grants available. Support available to part-time students. Financial award application deadline: 3/1; financial award applicants required to submit FAFSA. *Faculty research:* Speech therapy. *Unit head:* Dr. John Reinard, Chair, 657-278-3617. *Application contact:* Admissions/Applications, 657-278-2371.

California State University, Fullerton, Graduate Studies, College of Humanities and Social Sciences, Program in Linguistics, Fullerton, CA 92834-9480. Offers analysis of specific language structures (MA); anthropological linguistics (MA); applied linguistics (MA); communication and semantics (MA); disorders of communication (MA); experimental phonetics (MA). Part-time programs available. *Students:* 11 full-time (8 women), 8 part-time (4 women); includes 5 minority (3 Asian, non-Hispanic/Latino; 2 Hispanic/Latino), 6 international. Average age 31. 43 applicants, 56% accepted, 9 enrolled. In 2011, 10 master's awarded. *Degree requirements:* For master's, one foreign

language, thesis or alternative, project. *Entrance requirements:* For master's, minimum GPA of 3.0, undergraduate major in linguistics or related field. Application fee: $55. *Financial support:* Career-related internships or fieldwork, Federal Work-Study, institutionally sponsored loans, and scholarships/grants available. Support available to part-time students. Financial award application deadline: 3/1; financial award applicants required to submit FAFSA. *Unit head:* Dr. Franz Muller-Gotama, Adviser, 657-278-2441. *Application contact:* Admissions/Applications, 657-278-2371.

California State University, Long Beach, Graduate Studies, College of Health and Human Services, Department of Communicative Disorders, Long Beach, CA 90840. Offers MA. *Accreditation:* ASHA. Part-time programs available. *Faculty:* 7 full-time (all women), 1 (woman) part-time/adjunct. *Students:* 23 full-time (22 women), 36 part-time (34 women); includes 25 minority (3 Black or African American, non-Hispanic/Latino; 1 American Indian or Alaska Native, non-Hispanic/Latino; 7 Asian, non-Hispanic/Latino; 10 Hispanic/Latino; 4 Two or more races, non-Hispanic/Latino), 1 international. Average age 31. 302 applicants, 8% accepted, 14 enrolled. In 2011, 27 master's awarded. *Degree requirements:* For master's, comprehensive exam or thesis. *Entrance requirements:* For master's, GRE, minimum GPA of 3.0 in last 60 units. *Application deadline:* For fall admission, 2/1 for domestic students. Applications are processed on a rolling basis. Application fee: $55. Electronic applications accepted. *Financial support:* Federal Work-Study, institutionally sponsored loans, and scholarships/grants available. Financial award application deadline: 3/2. *Unit head:* Dr. Carolyn Conway Madding, Chair, 562-985-5283, Fax: 562-985-4584, E-mail: madding@csulb.edu. *Application contact:* Dr. Jennifer Ostergren, Graduate Advisor, 562-985-8843, Fax: 562-985-4584, E-mail: ostergren@msn.com.

California State University, Los Angeles, Graduate Studies, College of Health and Human Services, Department of Communication Disorders, Los Angeles, CA 90032-8530. Offers speech and hearing (MA); speech-language pathology (MA). *Accreditation:* ASHA. Part-time and evening/weekend programs available. *Faculty:* 5 full-time (3 women), 8 part-time/adjunct (5 women). *Students:* 75 full-time (68 women), 93 part-time (80 women); includes 95 minority (2 Black or African American, non-Hispanic/Latino; 42 Asian, non-Hispanic/Latino; 47 Hispanic/Latino; 4 Two or more races, non-Hispanic/Latino), 2 international. Average age 29. 410 applicants, 32% accepted, 74 enrolled. In 2011, 22 master's awarded. *Degree requirements:* For master's, comprehensive exam. *Entrance requirements:* For master's, undergraduate major in communication disorders or related area, minimum GPA of 2.75 in last 90 units. Additional exam requirements/recommendations for international students: Required—TOEFL (minimum score 500 paper-based; 173 computer-based). *Application deadline:* For fall admission, 5/1 for domestic and international students. Applications are processed on a rolling basis. Application fee: $55. *Expenses:* Tuition, state resident: full-time $8225. *Financial support:* Career-related internships or fieldwork and Federal Work-Study available. Support available to part-time students. Financial award application deadline: 3/1. *Faculty research:* Language disabilities, minority child language learning. *Unit head:* Dr. Edward Klein, Chair, 323-343-4690, Fax: 323-343-4698, E-mail: eklein@cslanet.calstatela.edu. *Application contact:* Dr. Karin Brown, Acting Associate Dean of Graduate Studies, 323-343-3820, Fax: 323-343-5653, E-mail: kbrown5@calstatela.edu. Web site: http://www.calstatela.edu/dept/com_dis/.

California State University, Northridge, Graduate Studies, College of Health and Human Development, Department of Communication Disorders and Sciences, Northridge, CA 91330. Offers audiology (MS); speech language pathology (MS). *Accreditation:* ASHA. *Degree requirements:* For master's, PRAXIS. *Entrance requirements:* For master's, GRE or minimum GPA of 3.5. Additional exam requirements/recommendations for international students: Required—TOEFL. *Faculty research:* Infant stimulation, early intervention program.

California State University, Sacramento, Office of Graduate Studies, College of Health and Human Services, Department of Speech Pathology and Audiology, Sacramento, CA 95819-6071. Offers audiology (MS); speech pathology (MS). *Accreditation:* ASHA. *Faculty:* 5 full-time (4 women), 18 part-time/adjunct (13 women). *Students:* 75 full-time, 20 part-time; includes 13 minority (3 Asian, non-Hispanic/Latino; 7 Hispanic/Latino; 1 Native Hawaiian or other Pacific Islander, non-Hispanic/Latino; 2 Two or more races, non-Hispanic/Latino), 1 international. Average age 28. 208 applicants, 26% accepted, 42 enrolled. In 2011, 26 master's awarded. *Degree requirements:* For master's, thesis, project, or comprehensive exam; writing proficiency exam. *Entrance requirements:* For master's, GRE General Test, appropriate bachelor's degree, minimum GPA of 3.0 in last 2 years of course work. Additional exam requirements/recommendations for international students: Required—TOEFL. *Application deadline:* For fall admission, 2/15 for domestic students, 3/1 for international students; for spring admission, 9/30 for international students. Applications are processed on a rolling basis. Application fee: $55. Electronic applications accepted. *Financial support:* Career-related internships or fieldwork and Federal Work-Study available. Support available to part-time students. Financial award application deadline: 3/1; financial award applicants required to submit FAFSA. *Unit head:* Laureen O'Hanlon, Chair, 916-278-6601, Fax: 916-278-7730, E-mail: ohanlon@csus.edu. *Application contact:* Jose Martinez, Outreach and Graduate Diversity Coordinator, 916-278-6470, Fax: 916-278-5669, E-mail: martinj@skymail.csus.edu. Web site: http://www.csus.edu/hhs/spa.

California University of Pennsylvania, School of Graduate Studies and Research, College of Education and Human Services, Department of Communication Disorders, California, PA 15419-1394. Offers MS. *Accreditation:* ASHA. Part-time and evening/weekend programs available. *Degree requirements:* For master's, comprehensive exam, thesis optional. *Entrance requirements:* For master's, GRE General Test, minimum GPA of 3.0, references. Additional exam requirements/recommendations for international students: Required—TOEFL (minimum score 550 paper-based; 213 computer-based; 80 iBT). Electronic applications accepted. *Faculty research:* Normative voice database, communication disorders and health.

Canisius College, Graduate Division, School of Education and Human Services, Department of Graduate Education and Leadership, Buffalo, NY 14208-1098. Offers college student personnel (MS Ed); deaf education (MS Ed); deaf/adolescent education, grades 7-12 (MS Ed); deaf/childhood education, grades 1-6 (MS Ed); differential instruction (MS Ed); education administration (MS Ed); gifted education extention (Certificate); literacy (MS Ed); reading (Certificate); school building leadership (MS Ed, Certificate); school district leadership (Certificate). *Accreditation:* NCATE. Part-time and evening/weekend programs available. Postbaccalaureate distance learning degree programs offered (minimal on-campus study). *Faculty:* 7 full-time (6 women), 36 part-time/adjunct (22 women). *Students:* 149 full-time (114 women), 242 part-time (177 women); includes 42 minority (29 Black or African American, non-Hispanic/Latino; 2 American Indian or Alaska Native, non-Hispanic/Latino; 3 Asian, non-Hispanic/Latino; 6 Hispanic/Latino; 2 Two or more races, non-Hispanic/Latino), 3 international. Average age 30. 250 applicants, 84% accepted, 124 enrolled. In 2011, 135 degrees awarded. *Entrance requirements:* For master's, GRE if cumulative GPA less than 2.7, transcripts, two letters of recommendation. Additional exam requirements/recommendations for international students: Required—TOEFL. *Application deadline:* Applications are processed on a rolling basis. Application fee: $25. Electronic applications accepted. *Financial support:* Career-related internships or fieldwork, Federal Work-Study, scholarships/grants, tuition waivers (partial), and unspecified assistantships available.

Support available to part-time students. Financial award application deadline: 4/30; financial award applicants required to submit FAFSA. *Faculty research:* Asperger's disease, autism, private higher education, reading strategies. *Unit head:* Dr. Rosemary K. Murray, Chair/Associate Professor of Graduate Education and Leadership, 716-888-3723, E-mail: murray1@canisius.edu. *Application contact:* Jim Bagwell, Director of Graduate Recruitment and Admissions, 716-888-2544, Fax: 716-888-3290, E-mail: bagwellj@canisius.edu. Web site: http://www.canisius.edu/education/graduate.asp.

Carlos Albizu University, Graduate Programs, San Juan, PR 00901. Offers clinical psychology (MS, PhD, Psy D); general psychology (PhD); industrial/organizational psychology (MS, PhD); speech and language pathology (MS). *Accreditation:* APA (one or more programs are accredited). Part-time and evening/weekend programs available. Terminal master's awarded for partial completion of doctoral program. *Degree requirements:* For master's, one foreign language, comprehensive exam, thesis; for doctorate, one foreign language, comprehensive exam, thesis/dissertation, written qualifying exams. *Entrance requirements:* For master's, GRE General Test or EXADEP, interview; minimum GPA of 3.0 (industrial/organizational psychology), 3.25 (speech and language pathology); for doctorate, GRE General Test or EXADEP, interview; minimum GPA of 3.0 (industrial/organizational psychology), 3.25 (PhD and Psy D in clinical psychology). *Faculty research:* Psychotherapeutic techniques for Hispanics, psychology of the aged, school dropouts, stress, violence.

Case Western Reserve University, School of Graduate Studies, Psychological Sciences Department, Program in Communication Sciences, Cleveland, OH 44106. Offers speech-language pathology (MA, PhD). *Accreditation:* ASHA (one or more programs are accredited). Part-time programs available. *Faculty:* 5 full-time (all women), 4 part-time/adjunct (2 women). *Students:* 9 full-time (all women), 3 part-time (all women), 1 international. Average age 23. 80 applicants, 11% accepted, 8 enrolled. In 2011, 6 master's awarded. Terminal master's awarded for partial completion of doctoral program. *Degree requirements:* For master's, comprehensive exam, thesis optional; for doctorate, thesis/dissertation. *Entrance requirements:* For master's and doctorate, GRE General Test, 3 letters of recommendation. Additional exam requirements/recommendations for international students: Required—TOEFL (minimum score 577 paper-based; 213 computer-based; 90 iBT); Recommended—IELTS (minimum score 7). *Application deadline:* For fall admission, 2/15 for domestic students. Applications are processed on a rolling basis. Application fee: $50. Electronic applications accepted. *Financial support:* Research assistantships, tuition waivers (partial), and unspecified assistantships available. Financial award application deadline: 2/15; financial award applicants required to submit FAFSA. *Faculty research:* Traumatic brain injury, phonological disorders, child language disorders, communication problems in the aged and Alzheimer's patients, cleft palate, voice disorders. *Unit head:* Prof. Lee Thompson, Interim Chair, 216-368-6477, Fax: 216-368-6078, E-mail: lee.thompson@case.edu. *Application contact:* Patricia Maar, Assistant, 216-368-2470, Fax: 216-368-6078, E-mail: cosgrad@case.edu. Web site: http://www.case.edu/artsci/cosi/.

Central Michigan University, College of Graduate Studies, The Herbert H. and Grace A. Dow College of Health Professions, Department of Communication Disorders, Doctor of Audiology Program, Mount Pleasant, MI 48859. Offers Au D. *Accreditation:* ASHA. *Degree requirements:* For doctorate, comprehensive exam, thesis/dissertation or alternative. *Entrance requirements:* For doctorate, GRE, interview. Electronic applications accepted. *Faculty research:* Auditory electrophysiology, auditory process disorders, neuroanatomy, pediatric audiology, rehabilitative audiology.

Central Michigan University, College of Graduate Studies, The Herbert H. and Grace A. Dow College of Health Professions, Department of Communication Disorders, Program in Speech-Language Pathology, Mount Pleasant, MI 48859. Offers MA. *Accreditation:* ASHA. *Degree requirements:* For master's, thesis or alternative. Electronic applications accepted. *Expenses:* Contact institution. *Faculty research:* Traumatic brain injury, neuro-linguistics, multidisciplinary and transdisciplinary therapy, speech audiometry, phonological disorders.

Chapman University, College of Educational Studies, Orange, CA 92866. Offers communication sciences and disorders (MS); counseling (MA), including school counseling (MA, Credential); education (MA, PhD), including cultural and curricular studies (PhD), disability studies (PhD), school psychology (PhD, Credential); educational psychology (MA); professional clear (Credential); pupil personnel services (Credential), including school counseling (MA, Credential), school psychology (PhD, Credential); school psychology (Ed S); single subject (Credential); special education (MA); special education (level ii) (Credential), including mild/moderate, moderate/severe; special education (preliminary) (Credential), including mild/moderate, moderate/severe; speech language pathology (Credential); teaching (MA), including elementary education, secondary education. *Accreditation:* Teacher Education Accreditation Council. Part-time and evening/weekend programs available. *Faculty:* 27 full-time (18 women), 35 part-time/adjunct (24 women). *Students:* 220 full-time (188 women), 164 part-time (128 women); includes 140 minority (12 Black or African American, non-Hispanic/Latino; 1 American Indian or Alaska Native, non-Hispanic/Latino; 44 Asian, non-Hispanic/Latino; 73 Hispanic/Latino; 4 Native Hawaiian or other Pacific Islander, non-Hispanic/Latino; 6 Two or more races, non-Hispanic/Latino), 1 international. Average age 29. 436 applicants, 38% accepted, 126 enrolled. In 2011, 130 master's, 5 doctorates awarded. *Entrance requirements:* Additional exam requirements/recommendations for international students: Required—TOEFL (minimum score 550 paper-based; 213 computer-based; 80 iBT). *Application deadline:* Applications are processed on a rolling basis. Application fee: $60. Electronic applications accepted. Tuition and fees vary according to degree level and program. *Financial support:* Fellowships and scholarships/grants available. Financial award application deadline: 6/30; financial award applicants required to submit FAFSA. *Unit head:* Dr. Don Cardinal, Dean, 714-997-6781, E-mail: cardinal@chapman.edu. *Application contact:* Admissions Coordinator, 714-997-6714. Web site: http://www.chapman.edu/CES/.

Clarion University of Pennsylvania, Office of Graduate Programs, Master of Science in Speech Language Pathology Program, Clarion, PA 16214. Offers MS. *Accreditation:* ASHA. Part-time programs available. *Students:* 85 full-time (78 women), 14 part-time (12 women); includes 2 minority (1 Asian, non-Hispanic/Latino; 1 Hispanic/Latino). Average age 24. In 2011, 43 master's awarded. *Degree requirements:* For master's, thesis or alternative. *Entrance requirements:* For master's, minimum QPA of 3.0. Additional exam requirements/recommendations for international students: Required—TOEFL (minimum score 573 paper-based; 230 computer-based; 89 iBT). *Application deadline:* For fall admission, 1/31 for domestic and international students. Application fee: $30. Electronic applications accepted. *Expenses:* Tuition, state resident: part-time $429 per credit. Tuition, nonresident: part-time $644 per credit. *Financial support:* Research assistantships with partial tuition reimbursements and career-related internships or fieldwork available. Support available to part-time students. Financial award application deadline: 3/1. *Unit head:* Dr. Colleen McAleer, Chair, 814-393-2581, Fax: 814-393-2206, E-mail: cmcaleer@clarion.edu. *Application contact:* Dr. Janis Jarecki-Liu, Graduate Coordinator, 814-393-2445, Fax: 814-393-2206, E-mail: jjareckiliu@clarion.edu. Web site: http://www.clarion.edu/26317/.

Cleveland State University, College of Graduate Studies, College of Sciences and Health Professions, School of Health Sciences, Program in Speech Pathology and Audiology, Cleveland, OH 44115. Offers MA. *Accreditation:* ASHA. *Faculty:* 7 full-time (6

women), 5 part-time/adjunct (all women). *Students:* 50 full-time (49 women), 3 part-time (all women); includes 2 minority (both Asian, non-Hispanic/Latino). Average age 27. 265 applicants, 24% accepted, 26 enrolled. In 2011, 13 master's awarded. *Degree requirements:* For master's, comprehensive exam, thesis optional. *Entrance requirements:* For master's, GRE. Additional exam requirements/recommendations for international students: Required—TOEFL. *Application deadline:* For fall admission, 2/1 priority date for domestic students, 2/1 for international students. Application fee: $30. Electronic applications accepted. *Expenses:* Tuition, state resident: full-time $6416; part-time $494 per credit hour. Tuition, nonresident: full-time $12,074; part-time $929 per credit hour. *Financial support:* In 2011–12, 9 students received support, including 9 teaching assistantships with partial tuition reimbursements available; career-related internships or fieldwork, Federal Work-Study, and unspecified assistantships also available. Financial award application deadline: 2/1; financial award applicants required to submit FAFSA. *Faculty research:* Child language and literacy development, cultural diversity, variant dialects, voice disorders, neurogenic communication disorders. *Unit head:* Dr. Monica Gordon Pershey, Program Director, 216-687-4534, Fax: 216-687-6993, E-mail: m.pershey@csuohio.edu. *Application contact:* Donna Helwig, Administrative Coordinator to the Chairperson, 216-687-3807, Fax: 216-687-6993, E-mail: d.helwig@csuohio.edu. Web site: http://www.csuohio.edu/sciences/dept/healthsciences/graduate/SPH/index.html.

The College of Saint Rose, Graduate Studies, School of Education, Department of Communication Disorders, Albany, NY 12203-1419. Offers MS Ed. *Accreditation:* ASHA. Part-time and evening/weekend programs available. *Degree requirements:* For master's, comprehensive exam or thesis. *Entrance requirements:* For master's, minimum undergraduate GPA of 3.0, on-campus interview, 32 undergraduate credits if undergraduate degree is not in communication disorders. Additional exam requirements/recommendations for international students: Required—TOEFL (minimum score 550 paper-based; 213 computer-based). Electronic applications accepted.

Dalhousie University, Faculty of Health Professions, School of Human Communication Disorders, Halifax, NS B3H 1R2, Canada. Offers audiology (M Sc); speech-language pathology (M Sc). *Degree requirements:* For master's, thesis or alternative. *Entrance requirements:* Additional exam requirements/recommendations for international students: Required—TOEFL, IELTS, CANTEST, CAEL; or Michigan English Language Assessment Battery. Electronic applications accepted. *Expenses:* Contact institution. *Faculty research:* Audiology, hearing aids, speech and voice disorders, language development and disorders, treatment efficacy.

Duquesne University, John G. Rangos, Sr. School of Health Sciences, Pittsburgh, PA 15282-0001. Offers health management systems (MHMS); occupational therapy (MS); physical therapy (DPT); physician assistant studies (MPAS); rehabilitation science (MS, PhD); speech-language pathology (MS); MBA/MHMS. *Accreditation:* AOTA (one or more programs are accredited); APTA (one or more programs are accredited); ASHA. *Faculty:* 34 full-time (23 women), 20 part-time/adjunct (11 women). *Students:* 227 full-time (180 women), 12 part-time (7 women); includes 8 minority (4 Black or African American, non-Hispanic/Latino; 1 Asian, non-Hispanic/Latino; 1 Hispanic/Latino; 1 Native Hawaiian or other Pacific Islander, non-Hispanic/Latino; 1 Two or more races, non-Hispanic/Latino), 3 international. Average age 24. 537 applicants, 12% accepted, 17 enrolled. In 2011, 43 master's, 31 doctorates awarded. *Degree requirements:* For doctorate, comprehensive exam (for some programs), thesis/dissertation (for some programs). *Entrance requirements:* For master's, GRE General Test (speech-language pathology), 3 letters of recommendation; minimum GPA of 2.75 (health management systems), 3.0 (speech-language pathology and health sciences); for doctorate, GRE General Test (for physical therapy and rehabilitation science), 3 letters of recommendation, minimum GPA of 3.0, personal interview. Additional exam requirements/recommendations for international students: Required—TOEFL (minimum score 550 paper-based; 233 computer-based; 90 iBT). *Application deadline:* Applications are processed on a rolling basis. Electronic applications accepted. *Expenses:* Contact institution. *Financial support:* Federal Work-Study available. Financial award applicants required to submit FAFSA. *Faculty research:* Neuronal processing, electrical stimulation on peripheral neuropathy, CNS stimulatory and inhibitory signals, behavioral genetic methodologies to development disorders of speech, neurogenic communication disorders. *Total annual research expenditures:* $83,650. *Unit head:* Dr. Gregory H. Frazer, Dean, 412-396-5303, Fax: 412-396-5554, E-mail: frazer@duq.edu. *Application contact:* Christopher R. Hilf, Recruiter/Academic Advisor, 412-396-5653, Fax: 412-396-5554, E-mail: hilfc@duq.edu. Web site: http://www.duq.edu/healthsciences/health.html.

East Carolina University, Graduate School, College of Education, Department of Curriculum and Instruction, Greenville, NC 27858-4353. Offers assistive technology (Certificate); autism (Certificate); deaf/blindness (Certificate); elementary education (MA Ed); English education (MA Ed); history (MA Ed); middle grade education (MA Ed); reading education (MA Ed); special education (MA Ed); teaching (MAT). Part-time programs available. Postbaccalaureate distance learning degree programs offered. *Degree requirements:* For master's, comprehensive exam, thesis optional. *Entrance requirements:* For master's, GRE General Test or MAT, interview, bachelor's degree in related field, minimum GPA of 2.5, teaching license. Additional exam requirements/recommendations for international students: Required—TOEFL. *Application deadline:* For fall admission, 6/1 priority date for domestic students. Applications are processed on a rolling basis. Application fee: $50. *Expenses:* Tuition, state resident: full-time $3557; part-time $444.63 per semester hour. Tuition, nonresident: full-time $14,351; part-time $1793.88 per semester hour. *Required fees:* $2016; $252 per semester hour. Part-time tuition and fees vary according to course load, campus/location and program. *Financial support:* Research assistantships, teaching assistantships, and Federal Work-Study available. Support available to part-time students. Financial award application deadline: 6/1; financial award applicants required to submit FAFSA. *Unit head:* Carolyn C. Ledford, Interim Chair, 252-328-1100, E-mail: ledfordc@ecu.edu. *Application contact:* Dean of Graduate School, 252-328-6012, Fax: 252-328-6071, E-mail: gradschool@ecu.edu. Web site: http://www.ecu.edu/cs-educ/ci/Graduate.cfm.

East Carolina University, Graduate School, School of Allied Health Sciences, Department of Communication Sciences and Disorders, Greenville, NC 27858-4353. Offers communication sciences and disorders (PhD); speech, language and auditory pathology (MS); Au D/PhD. *Accreditation:* ASHA (one or more programs are accredited). Postbaccalaureate distance learning degree programs offered (no on-campus study). *Degree requirements:* For master's, comprehensive exam, thesis or alternative; for doctorate, comprehensive exam, thesis/dissertation. *Entrance requirements:* For master's and doctorate, GRE General Test. Additional exam requirements/recommendations for international students: Required—TOEFL. *Application deadline:* For fall admission, 4/1 for domestic students. Application fee: $50. *Expenses:* Tuition, state resident: full-time $3557; part-time $444.63 per semester hour. Tuition, nonresident: full-time $14,351; part-time $1793.88 per semester hour. *Required fees:* $2016; $252 per semester hour. Part-time tuition and fees vary according to course load, campus/location and program. *Financial support:* Research assistantships with partial tuition reimbursements, teaching assistantships with partial tuition reimbursements, and unspecified assistantships available. Financial award application deadline: 6/1. *Faculty research:* Hearing, language disorders, stuttering, reading

disorder, *Unit head:* Dr. Gregg Givens, Chair, 252-744-6080, Fax: 252-744-6081, E-mail: givensg@ecu.edu. *Application contact:* Dean of Graduate School, 252-328-6012, Fax: 252-328-6071, E-mail: gradschool@ecu.edu. Web site: http://www.ecu.edu/cs-dhs/csd/index.cfm.

Eastern Illinois University, Graduate School, College of Sciences, Department of Communication Disorders and Sciences, Charleston, IL 61920-3099. Offers MS. *Accreditation:* ASHA. *Degree requirements:* For master's, comprehensive exam. *Expenses:* Tuition, state resident: part-time $279 per credit hour. Tuition, nonresident: part-time $670 per credit hour. *Required fees:* $179.07 per credit hour. $1253 per semester.

Eastern Kentucky University, The Graduate School, College of Education, Department of Special Education, Program in Communication Disorders, Richmond, KY 40475-3102. Offers MA Ed. *Accreditation:* ASHA. *Degree requirements:* For master's, comprehensive exam, thesis optional, 375 clinical clock hours. *Entrance requirements:* For master's, GRE General Test, minimum GPA of 3.0. *Faculty research:* Distance learning, fluency, phonemic awareness, technology, autism.

Eastern Michigan University, Graduate School, College of Education, Department of Special Education, Program in Hearing Impairment, Ypsilanti, MI 48197. Offers MA. *Students:* 1 (woman) full-time; minority (Black or African American, non-Hispanic/Latino). Average age 28. 1 applicant, 0% accepted, 0 enrolled. In 2011, 1 master's awarded. Application fee: $35. *Expenses:* Tuition, state resident: full-time $10,367; part-time $432 per credit hour. Tuition, nonresident: full-time $20,435; part-time $851 per credit hour. *Required fees:* $39 per credit hour. $46 per semester. One-time fee: $100. Tuition and fees vary according to course level, degree level and reciprocity agreements. *Unit head:* Linda Polter, Coordinator, 734-487-3300, Fax: 734-487-2473, E-mail: lpolter1@emich.edu. *Application contact:* Graduate Admissions, 734-487-2400, Fax: 734-487-6559, E-mail: graduate.admissions@emich.edu.

Eastern Michigan University, Graduate School, College of Education, Department of Special Education, Program in Speech and Language Pathology, Ypsilanti, MI 48197. Offers MA. *Accreditation:* ASHA. Part-time and evening/weekend programs available. Postbaccalaureate distance learning degree programs offered (minimal on-campus study). *Students:* 61 full-time (55 women), 28 part-time (27 women); includes 5 minority (3 Asian, non-Hispanic/Latino; 1 Hispanic/Latino; 1 Two or more races, non-Hispanic/Latino), 2 international. Average age 28. 246 applicants, 12% accepted, 25 enrolled. In 2011, 29 degrees awarded. *Entrance requirements:* For master's, GRE General Test. Additional exam requirements/recommendations for international students: Required—TOEFL. *Application deadline:* Applications are processed on a rolling basis. Application fee: $35. *Expenses:* Tuition, state resident: full-time $10,367; part-time $432 per credit hour. Tuition, nonresident: full-time $20,435; part-time $851 per credit hour. *Required fees:* $39 per credit hour. $46 per semester. One-time fee: $100. Tuition and fees vary according to course level, degree level and reciprocity agreements. *Financial support:* Fellowships, research assistantships with full tuition reimbursements, teaching assistantships with full tuition reimbursements, career-related internships or fieldwork, Federal Work-Study, institutionally sponsored loans, scholarships/grants, tuition waivers (partial), and unspecified assistantships available. Support available to part-time students. Financial award applicants required to submit FAFSA. *Unit head:* Dr. Lizbeth Stevens, Coordinator, 734-487-3300, Fax: 734-487-2473, E-mail: lstevens@emich.edu. *Application contact:* Dr. Sarah Ginsberg, Advisor, 734-487-3300, Fax: 734-487-2473, E-mail: sginsberg@emich.edu.

Eastern New Mexico University, Graduate School, College of Liberal Arts and Sciences, Department of Health and Human Services, Portales, NM 88130. Offers speech pathology and audiology (MS). *Accreditation:* ASHA. Part-time programs available. Postbaccalaureate distance learning degree programs offered (minimal on-campus study). *Faculty:* 4 full-time (2 women), 1 (woman) part-time/adjunct. *Students:* 22 full-time (20 women), 71 part-time (66 women); includes 41 minority (5 Black or African American, non-Hispanic/Latino; 1 Asian, non-Hispanic/Latino; 34 Hispanic/Latino; 1 Two or more races, non-Hispanic/Latino), 1 international. Average age 29. 49 applicants, 96% accepted, 28 enrolled. In 2011, 14 master's awarded. *Degree requirements:* For master's, thesis optional, oral and written comprehensive exam, oral presentation of professional portfolio. *Entrance requirements:* For master's, GRE, three letters of recommendation, resume, two essays. Additional exam requirements/recommendations for international students: Required—TOEFL (minimum score 550 paper-based; 213 computer-based; 79 iBT), IELTS (minimum score 6). *Application deadline:* For fall admission, 3/1 priority date for domestic students, 3/1 for international students. Applications are processed on a rolling basis. Application fee: $10. Electronic applications accepted. *Financial support:* In 2011–12, 11 research assistantships with partial tuition reimbursements (averaging $4,250 per year) were awarded; scholarships/grants and unspecified assistantships also available. Support available to part-time students. Financial award applicants required to submit FAFSA. *Unit head:* Dr. Suzanne Swift, Chair/Interim Graduate Coordinator, 575-562-2724, Fax: 575-562-2380, E-mail: suzanne.swift@enmu.edu. *Application contact:* Wendy Turner, Department Secretary, 575-562-2156, Fax: 575-562-2380, E-mail: wendy.turner@enmu.edu. Web site: http://liberal-arts.enmu.edu/health/cdis/graduate-cdis.shtml.

Eastern Washington University, Graduate Studies, College of Science, Health and Engineering, Department of Communication Disorders, Cheney, WA 99004-2431. Offers MS. *Accreditation:* ASHA. *Faculty:* 12 full-time (9 women). *Students:* 46 full-time (43 women); includes 2 minority (1 American Indian or Alaska Native, non-Hispanic/Latino; 1 Hispanic/Latino). Average age 30. 151 applicants, 17% accepted, 25 enrolled. In 2011, 26 master's awarded. *Degree requirements:* For master's, comprehensive exam, thesis or alternative. *Entrance requirements:* For master's, GRE General Test, minimum GPA of 3.0. *Application deadline:* For fall admission, 3/1 for domestic students. Applications are processed on a rolling basis. Application fee: $60. *Financial support:* In 2011–12, 12 teaching assistantships with partial tuition reimbursements (averaging $7,000 per year) were awarded; career-related internships or fieldwork, Federal Work-Study, institutionally sponsored loans, scholarships/grants, health care benefits, tuition waivers (partial), and unspecified assistantships also available. Support available to part-time students. Financial award application deadline: 2/1; financial award applicants required to submit FAFSA. *Unit head:* Dr. Judd A. Case, Dean, 509-359-2532, E-mail: jcase@mail.ewu.edu. *Application contact:* Dr. Roberta Jackson, Advisor, 509-359-6622, Fax: 509-359-6802. Web site: http://www.ewu.edu/CSHE/Programs/Communication-Disorders/ComD-Degrees/MSCD.xml.

East Stroudsburg University of Pennsylvania, Graduate School, College of Health Sciences, Department of Speech Pathology and Audiology, East Stroudsburg, PA 18301-2999. Offers MS. *Accreditation:* ASHA. Part-time and evening/weekend programs available. *Degree requirements:* For master's, comprehensive exam, portfolio. *Entrance requirements:* For master's, GRE General Test, minimum undergraduate QPA of 3.0 overall and in major, 3 letters of recommendation. Additional exam requirements/recommendations for international students: Required—TOEFL (minimum score 560 paper-based; 220 computer-based; 83 iBT). *Faculty research:* Computer-assisted classroom instruction.

East Tennessee State University, School of Graduate Studies, College of Clinical and Rehabilitative Health Sciences, Department of Audiology and Speech-Language

Pathology, Johnson City, TN 37614-1710. Offers audiology (Au D); communicative disorders (MS), including speech pathology. *Accreditation:* ASHA (one or more programs are accredited). *Faculty:* 8 full-time (5 women), 7 part-time/adjunct (4 women). *Students:* 74 full-time (70 women), 11 part-time (8 women); includes 4 minority (2 Black or African American, non-Hispanic/Latino; 1 Asian, non-Hispanic/Latino; 1 Hispanic/Latino), 1 international. Average age 27. 256 applicants, 35% accepted, 39 enrolled. In 2011, 18 master's, 7 doctorates awarded. *Degree requirements:* For master's, comprehensive exam, thesis optional, case study (for non-thesis option); for doctorate, comprehensive exam, externship. *Entrance requirements:* For master's, GRE General Test, minimum GPA of 3.0, three letters of recommendation, resume; for doctorate, GRE General Test, minimum GPA of 3.0, three letters of recommendation. Additional exam requirements/recommendations for international students: Required—TOEFL (minimum score 550 paper-based; 213 computer-based; 79 iBT). *Application deadline:* For fall admission, 2/1 for domestic and international students. Application fee: $35 ($45 for international students). Electronic applications accepted. *Expenses:* Tuition, state resident: full-time $7312; part-time $350 per credit hour. Tuition, nonresident: full-time $18,490; part-time $621 per credit hour. *Required fees:* $63 per credit hour. Tuition and fees vary according to course load and program. *Financial support:* In 2011–12, 57 students received support, including 28 research assistantships with full and partial tuition reimbursements available (averaging $3,200 per year), 3 teaching assistantships with full tuition reimbursements available (averaging $6,000 per year); career-related internships or fieldwork, institutionally sponsored loans, scholarships/grants, and unspecified assistantships also available. Financial award application deadline: 7/1; financial award applicants required to submit FAFSA. *Faculty research:* Treatment efficacy, hearing aid trials, language development of cleft palate children, phonological processes, neurogenic disorders. *Total annual research expenditures:* $280,000. *Unit head:* Dr. Brenda Louw, Chair, 423-439-4272, Fax: 423-439-4350, E-mail: louwb1@etsu.edu. *Application contact:* Shella Bennett, Graduate Specialist, 423-439-4708, Fax: 423-439-5624, E-mail: bennetsg@etsu.edu. Web site: http://www.etsu.edu/crhs/aslp/.

Edinboro University of Pennsylvania, College of Arts and Sciences, Department of Speech, Language and Hearing, Edinboro, PA 16444. Offers speech language pathology (MA). *Accreditation:* ASHA. Part-time and evening/weekend programs available. *Faculty:* 3 full-time (1 woman). *Students:* 40 full-time (36 women), 1 (woman) part-time; includes 1 minority (Asian, non-Hispanic/Latino). Average age 27. In 2011, 20 master's awarded. *Degree requirements:* For master's, thesis or alternative, competency exam. *Entrance requirements:* For master's, GRE or MAT, minimum QPA of 2.5. *Application deadline:* Applications are processed on a rolling basis. Application fee: $30. Electronic applications accepted. *Financial support:* In 2011–12, 12 research assistantships with full and partial tuition reimbursements (averaging $4,050 per year) were awarded; career-related internships or fieldwork, Federal Work-Study, scholarships/grants, and unspecified assistantships also available. Support available to part-time students. Financial award application deadline: 2/15; financial award applicants required to submit FAFSA. *Unit head:* Dr. Charlotte Molrine, Coordinator, 814-732-2432, Fax: 814-732-2629, E-mail: cmolrine@edinboro.edu. *Application contact:* Dr. Alan Biel, Dean, 814-732-2752, Fax: 814-732-2268, E-mail: abiel@edinboro.edu.

Elms College, Division of Communication Sciences and Disorders, Chicopee, MA 01013-2839. Offers autism spectrum disorders (MS, CAGS); autism spectrum disorders with practicum (MS, CAGS); communication sciences and disorders (CAGS). Part-time programs available. *Entrance requirements:* For degree, minimum GPA of 3.0. Additional exam requirements/recommendations for international students: Required—TOEFL.

Emerson College, Graduate Studies, School of Communication, Department of Communication Sciences and Disorders, Program in Communication Disorders, Boston, MA 02116-4624. Offers MS. *Accreditation:* ASHA. *Degree requirements:* For master's, comprehensive exam, thesis or alternative. *Entrance requirements:* For master's, GRE General Test. Additional exam requirements/recommendations for international students: Required—TOEFL (minimum score 550 paper-based; 213 computer-based; 80 iBT), IELTS (minimum score 6.5). Electronic applications accepted.

Florida Atlantic University, College of Education, Department of Communication Sciences and Disorders, Boca Raton, FL 33431-0991. Offers speech-language pathology (MS). *Accreditation:* ASHA. *Faculty:* 5 full-time (3 women), 8 part-time/adjunct (5 women). *Students:* 44 full-time (41 women), 11 part-time (10 women); includes 10 minority (2 Black or African American, non-Hispanic/Latino; 2 Asian, non-Hispanic/Latino; 6 Hispanic/Latino). Average age 27. 224 applicants, 21% accepted, 11 enrolled. In 2011, 21 master's awarded. *Degree requirements:* For master's, thesis optional. *Entrance requirements:* For master's, GRE General Test, minimum undergraduate GPA of 3.0 in last 60 hours of course work or graduate 3.5. *Application deadline:* For fall admission, 2/1 for domestic and international students. Application fee: $30. *Expenses: Tuition, area resident:* Part-time $343.02 per credit hour. Tuition, state resident: full-time $8232. Tuition, nonresident: full-time $23,931; part-time $997.14 per credit hour. *Financial support:* Career-related internships or fieldwork available. *Faculty research:* Fluency disorders, auditory processing, child language, adult language and cognition, multicultural speech and language issues. *Unit head:* Dr. Deena Louise Wener, Chair, 561-297-2258, Fax: 561-297-2268, E-mail: wener@fau.edu. *Application contact:* Dr. Eliah Watlington, Associate Dean, 561-296-8520, Fax: 261-297-2991, E-mail: ewatling@fau.edu. Web site: http://www.coe.fau.edu/academicdepartments/csd/.

Florida International University, College of Nursing and Health Sciences, Department of Communication Sciences and Disorders, Miami, FL 33199. Offers speech-language pathology (MS). *Accreditation:* ASHA. Part-time and evening/weekend programs available. *Degree requirements:* For master's, thesis optional. *Entrance requirements:* For master's, minimum undergraduate GPA of 3.0 in upper-level coursework; letter of intent; 2 letters of recommendation. Additional exam requirements/recommendations for international students: Required—TOEFL (minimum score 550 paper-based; 80 iBT). Electronic applications accepted.

Florida State University, The Graduate School, College of Communication and Information, School of Communication Science and Disorders, Tallahassee, FL 32306-1200. Offers Adv M, MS, PhD. *Accreditation:* ASHA (one or more programs are accredited). Part-time programs available. Postbaccalaureate distance learning degree programs offered (minimal on-campus study). *Faculty:* 17 full-time (13 women), 13 part-time/adjunct (all women). *Students:* 84 full-time (79 women), 72 part-time (all women); includes 33 minority (15 Black or African American, non-Hispanic/Latino; 1 American Indian or Alaska Native, non-Hispanic/Latino; 1 Asian, non-Hispanic/Latino; 16 Hispanic/Latino). Average age 26. 234 applicants, 44% accepted, 60 enrolled. In 2011, 36 master's, 7 doctorates awarded. *Degree requirements:* For master's, thesis optional; for doctorate, thesis/dissertation. *Entrance requirements:* For master's, GRE General Test, minimum GPA of 3.0; for doctorate, GRE General Test, minimum GPA of 3.0 (undergraduate), 3.5 (graduate). Additional exam requirements/recommendations for international students: Required—TOEFL (minimum score 550 paper-based; 213 computer-based; 80 iBT). *Application deadline:* For fall admission, 1/15 for domestic and international students. Application fee: $30. Electronic applications accepted. *Expenses:* Tuition, state resident: full-time $9474; part-time $350.88 per credit hour. Tuition, nonresident: full-time $16,236; part-time $601.34 per credit hour. *Required fees:* $630 per semester. One-time fee: $20. Tuition and fees vary according to course load and campus/location. *Financial support:* In 2011–12, 50 students received support, including 1 fellowship with full tuition reimbursement available (averaging $11,000 per year), 28 research assistantships with full and partial tuition reimbursements available (averaging $5,300 per year), 34 teaching assistantships with full and partial tuition reimbursements available (averaging $5,000 per year); career-related internships or fieldwork, Federal Work-Study, institutionally sponsored loans, scholarships/grants, tuition waivers (partial), and unspecified assistantships also available. Financial award application deadline: 1/1; financial award applicants required to submit FAFSA. *Faculty research:* Autism, neurogenic disorders, early intervention, child language disorders, literacy development and disorders, augmentative communication, dialectal influences on language development, speech development. *Unit head:* Dr. Kenn Apel, Director, 850-645-6566, Fax: 850-645-8994, E-mail: kenn.apel@cci.fsu.edu. *Application contact:* Erica Lee Heasley, Academic Coordinator, 850-644-2253, Fax: 850-644-8994, E-mail: erica.lee@cci.fsu.edu. Web site: http://www.commdisorders.cci.fsu.edu/.

Fontbonne University, Graduate Programs, Department of Communication Disorders and Deaf Education, Studies in Early Intervention in Deaf Education, St. Louis, MO 63105-3098. Offers MA. *Entrance requirements:* For master's, minimum GPA of 3.0.

Fontbonne University, Graduate Programs, Department of Communication Disorders and Deaf Education, Studies in Speech-Language Pathology, St. Louis, MO 63105-3098. Offers MS. *Entrance requirements:* For master's, minimum GPA of 3.0.

Fort Hays State University, Graduate School, College of Health and Life Sciences, Department of Communication Disorders, Hays, KS 67601-4099. Offers speech-language pathology (MS). *Accreditation:* ASHA. Part-time programs available. *Degree requirements:* For master's, comprehensive exam, thesis optional. *Entrance requirements:* For master's, GRE General Test. Additional exam requirements/recommendations for international students: Required—TOEFL (minimum score 550 paper-based; 213 computer-based). Electronic applications accepted. *Faculty research:* Aural rehabilitation, phonological and articulation skills, middle ear diseases, output capability of stereo cassette units, language development.

Gallaudet University, The Graduate School, Washington, DC 20002-3625. Offers audiology (Au D); clinical psychology (PhD); critical studies in the education of deaf learners (PhD); deaf and hard of hearing infants, toddlers, and their families (Certificate); deaf education (Ed S); deaf education: advanced studies (MA); deaf education: special programs in deaf education (MA); deaf history (Certificate); deaf studies (MA, Certificate); education deaf students with disabilities (Certificate); education: teacher preparation (MA), including deaf education, early childhood education and deaf education, elementary education and deaf education, secondary education and deaf education; hearing, speech and language sciences (MS, PhD); international development (MA); interpretation (MA, PhD); linguistics (MA, PhD); mental health counseling (MA); public administration (MA); school counseling (MA); school psychology (Psy S); sign language teaching (MA); social work (MSW); speech-language pathology (MS). Part-time programs available. *Faculty:* 62 full-time (44 women). *Students:* 300 full-time (246 women), 110 part-time (82 women); includes 80 minority (27 Black or African American, non-Hispanic/Latino; 1 American Indian or Alaska Native, non-Hispanic/Latino; 11 Asian, non-Hispanic/Latino; 25 Hispanic/Latino; 1 Native Hawaiian or other Pacific Islander, non-Hispanic/Latino; 15 Two or more races, non-Hispanic/Latino), 24 international. Average age 30. 498 applicants, 45% accepted, 168 enrolled. In 2011, 129 master's, 24 doctorates, 19 other advanced degrees awarded. Terminal master's awarded for partial completion of doctoral program. *Degree requirements:* For master's, comprehensive exam (for some programs), thesis optional; for doctorate, comprehensive exam, thesis/dissertation. *Entrance requirements:* For master's and doctorate, GRE General Test or MAT, letters of recommendation, interviews, goals statement, ASL proficiency interview, written English competency. Additional exam requirements/recommendations for international students: Required—TOEFL. *Application deadline:* For fall admission, 2/15 for domestic students. Applications are processed on a rolling basis. Application fee: $50. Electronic applications accepted. *Expenses: Tuition:* Full-time $12,770; part-time $710 per credit. *Required fees:* $376. *Financial support:* In 2011–12, 287 students received support. Fellowships, research assistantships, teaching assistantships, career-related internships or fieldwork, Federal Work-Study, scholarships/grants, tuition waivers (partial), and unspecified assistantships available. Support available to part-time students. Financial award applicants required to submit FAFSA. *Faculty research:* Bimodal bilingualism development, audiology, telecommunications access, early childhood education, linguistics, visual language and visual learning, rehabilitation and hearing enhancement. *Unit head:* Dr. Carol J. Erting, Dean, 202-651-5520, Fax: 202-651-5027, E-mail: carol.erting@gallaudet.edu. *Application contact:* Wednesday Luria, Coordinator of Prospective Graduate Student Services, 202-651-5400, Fax: 202-651-5295, E-mail: graduate.school@gallaudet.edu. Web site: http://www.gallaudet.edu/x26696.xml.

The George Washington University, Columbian College of Arts and Sciences, Department of Speech and Hearing Sciences, Washington, DC 20052. Offers speech-language pathology (MA). *Accreditation:* ASHA. *Faculty:* 9 full-time (6 women), 6 part-time/adjunct (5 women). *Students:* 53 full-time (50 women), 16 part-time (all women); includes 11 minority (3 Asian, non-Hispanic/Latino; 7 Hispanic/Latino; 1 Two or more races, non-Hispanic/Latino). Average age 25. 310 applicants, 20% accepted, 30 enrolled. In 2011, 28 master's awarded. *Degree requirements:* For master's, comprehensive exam, thesis or alternative. *Entrance requirements:* For master's, GRE General Test, interview, minimum GPA of 3.0. Additional exam requirements/recommendations for international students: Required—TOEFL (minimum score 550 paper-based; 213 computer-based; 80 iBT). *Application deadline:* For fall admission, 2/1 priority date for domestic students, 1/15 for international students. Applications are processed on a rolling basis. Application fee: $75. Electronic applications accepted. *Financial support:* In 2011–12, 16 students received support. Fellowships with tuition reimbursements available, teaching assistantships with tuition reimbursements available, career-related internships or fieldwork, Federal Work-Study, and tuition waivers available. Financial award application deadline: 1/15. *Unit head:* Geralyn M. Schulz, Chair, 202-994-6130, E-mail: schulz@gwu.edu. *Application contact:* Information Contact, 202-994-7362, Fax: 202-994-2589, E-mail: gwusphr@gwu.edu. Web site: http://www.gwu.edu/~sphr/.

Georgia State University, College of Education, Department of Educational Psychology and Special Education, Program in Communication Disorders, Atlanta, GA 30302-3083. Offers M Ed. *Accreditation:* ASHA; NCATE. *Degree requirements:* For master's, portfolio. *Entrance requirements:* For master's, GRE General Test, minimum GPA of 2.5, 2 letters of recommendation. *Faculty research:* Language development, adult language disorders, voice disorders.

Governors State University, College of Health Professions, Program in Communication Disorders, University Park, IL 60484. Offers MHS. *Accreditation:* ASHA. Part-time and evening/weekend programs available. *Students:* 48 full-time (45 women), 62 part-time (57 women); includes 26 minority (9 Black or African American, non-Hispanic/Latino; 1 Asian, non-Hispanic/Latino; 14 Hispanic/Latino; 1 Native Hawaiian or other Pacific Islander, non-Hispanic/Latino; 1 Two or more races, non-Hispanic/Latino). Average age 29. *Degree requirements:* For master's, comprehensive exam, thesis or alternative, practicum. *Entrance requirements:* For master's, minimum GPA of 3.3.

Application deadline: For fall admission, 3/1 priority date for domestic students. Applications are processed on a rolling basis. Application fee: $25. *Financial support:* Research assistantships, career-related internships or fieldwork, Federal Work-Study, institutionally sponsored loans, scholarships/grants, and tuition waivers (full and partial) available. Support available to part-time students. Financial award application deadline: 5/1. *Faculty research:* Speech perception of hearing-impaired, effects of binaural listening, communication assessment of infants, voice characteristics of head-neck cancer patients. *Unit head:* Dr. Elizabeth Cada, Dean, 708-534-7295. *Application contact:* Interim Director of Admission.

Graduate School and University Center of the City University of New York, Graduate Studies, Program in Audiology, New York, NY 10016-4039. Offers Au D. *Entrance requirements:* For doctorate, GRE General Test. Additional exam requirements/recommendations for international students: Required—TOEFL. Electronic applications accepted.

Graduate School and University Center of the City University of New York, Graduate Studies, Program in Speech and Hearing Sciences, New York, NY 10016-4039. Offers PhD. *Accreditation:* ASHA. *Degree requirements:* For doctorate, one foreign language, thesis/dissertation. *Entrance requirements:* For doctorate, GRE General Test. Additional exam requirements/recommendations for international students: Required—TOEFL. Electronic applications accepted.

Hampton University, Graduate College, Department of Communicative Sciences and Disorders, Hampton, VA 23668. Offers speech-language pathology (MA). *Accreditation:* ASHA. Part-time and evening/weekend programs available. *Entrance requirements:* For master's, GRE General Test. *Faculty research:* Language development, language pathology.

Harding University, College of Communication, Searcy, AR 72149-0001. Offers speech-language pathology (MS). *Accreditation:* ASHA. *Faculty:* 8 full-time (6 women), 2 part-time/adjunct (both women). *Students:* 32 full-time (30 women); includes 2 minority (1 Black or African American, non-Hispanic/Latino; 1 American Indian or Alaska Native, non-Hispanic/Latino). Average age 24. 64 applicants, 30% accepted, 13 enrolled. In 2011, 13 master's awarded. *Degree requirements:* For master's, comprehensive exam, thesis, 400 clinical hours, minimum GPA of 3.0, no grade below C. *Entrance requirements:* For master's, GRE (minimum score 900), minimum undergraduate GPA of 3.0, 3 letters of recommendation. Additional exam requirements/recommendations for international students: Required—TOEFL (minimum score 550 paper-based; 79 computer-based). *Application deadline:* For fall admission, 3/1 for domestic students. Application fee: $40. *Expenses: Tuition:* Full-time $10,512; part-time $584 per credit hour. *Required fees:* $500; $25 per credit hour. Tuition and fees vary according to course load, degree level and program. *Financial support:* In 2011–12, 11 students received support. Unspecified assistantships available. Financial award applicants required to submit FAFSA. *Unit head:* Dr. Daniel C. Tullos, Department Chairman, 501-279-4633, Fax: 501-279-4325, E-mail: tullos@harding.edu. *Application contact:* Martha Vendetti, Administrative Assistant, 501-279-4648, E-mail: mvendett@harding.edu.

Harvard University, Harvard Medical School and Graduate School of Arts and Sciences, Division of Health Sciences and Technology, Speech and Hearing Bioscience and Technology Program, Cambridge, MA 02138. Offers PhD, Sc D. Program offered jointly with Massachusetts Institute of Technology. *Accreditation:* ASHA. *Faculty:* 66 full-time (18 women). *Students:* 42 full-time (17 women); includes 11 minority (8 Asian, non-Hispanic/Latino; 3 Two or more races, non-Hispanic/Latino), 3 international. Average age 28. 35 applicants, 20% accepted, 6 enrolled. In 2011, 6 doctorates awarded. *Degree requirements:* For doctorate, thesis/dissertation. *Entrance requirements:* For doctorate, bachelor's degree in engineering or science, previous coursework in differential equations. Additional exam requirements/recommendations for international students: Required—TOEFL. *Application deadline:* For fall admission, 12/15 for domestic and international students. Application fee: $75. Electronic applications accepted. *Expenses:* Contact institution. *Financial support:* In 2011–12, 42 students received support, including 26 fellowships with full and partial tuition reimbursements available (averaging $54,672 per year), 17 research assistantships with full and partial tuition reimbursements available (averaging $46,451 per year), 5 teaching assistantships with full and partial tuition reimbursements available (averaging $25,431 per year); career-related internships or fieldwork, scholarships/grants, traineeships, health care benefits, and unspecified assistantships also available. Financial award application deadline: 12/15; financial award applicants required to submit FAFSA. *Faculty research:* Neuroscience audition, physiology, hearing science psychoacoustics, speech communications. *Unit head:* Dr. Louis D. Braida, Director, 617-253-2575, E-mail: braida@mit.edu. *Application contact:* Dr. Christopher Shera, Co-Chair, Admissions Committee, 617-573-4235, Fax: 617-720-4408, E-mail: shera@mit.edu.

Hofstra University, College of Liberal Arts and Sciences, Department of Speech Language-Hearing Sciences, Hempstead, NY 11549. Offers audiology (Au D); speech-language pathology (MA). *Accreditation:* ASHA (one or more programs are accredited). *Faculty:* 8 full-time (4 women), 10 part-time/adjunct (8 women). *Students:* 87 full-time (84 women), 3 part-time (2 women); includes 9 minority (3 Black or African American, non-Hispanic/Latino; 1 American Indian or Alaska Native, non-Hispanic/Latino; 4 Hispanic/Latino; 1 Two or more races, non-Hispanic/Latino). Average age 24. 273 applicants, 43% accepted, 45 enrolled. In 2011, 31 master's awarded. *Degree requirements:* For master's, comprehensive exam, thesis optional, minimum GPA of 3.0; for doctorate, comprehensive exam, thesis/dissertation, minimum GPA of 3.0. *Entrance requirements:* For master's, GRE, 3 letters of recommendation; essay; for doctorate, GRE or master's degree, 3 letters of recommendation; essay. Additional exam requirements/recommendations for international students: Required—TOEFL (minimum score 550 paper-based; 213 computer-based; 80 iBT). *Application deadline:* For fall admission, 1/15 for domestic and international students. Application fee: $70 ($75 for international students). Electronic applications accepted. *Expenses: Tuition:* Full-time $18,990; part-time $1055 per credit hour. *Required fees:* $970. Tuition and fees vary according to program. *Financial support:* In 2011–12, 31 students received support, including 25 fellowships with full and partial tuition reimbursements available (averaging $2,887 per year), 2 research assistantships with full and partial tuition reimbursements available (averaging $9,120 per year); Federal Work-Study, institutionally sponsored loans, scholarships/grants, tuition waivers (full and partial), and unspecified assistantships also available. Support available to part-time students. Financial award applicants required to submit FAFSA. *Faculty research:* Efficacy of storytelling strategies in aphasia, language and literacy development in internationally adopted children, aerodynamic aspects of speech in people who stutter, second language acquisition and first language attrition, acoustic aspects of normal and disordered speech production. *Unit head:* Dr. Carole T. Ferrand, Program Director, 516-463-5511, Fax: 516-463-5260, E-mail: sphctf@hofstra.edu. *Application contact:* Carol Drummer, Dean of Graduate Admissions, 516-463-4876, Fax: 516-463-4664, E-mail: gradstudent@hofstra.edu. Web site: http://www.hofstra.edu/hclas.

Howard University, School of Communications, Department of Communication Sciences and Disorders, Washington, DC 20059-0002. Offers communication sciences (PhD); speech pathology (MS). Offered through the Graduate School of Arts and Sciences. *Accreditation:* ASHA (one or more programs are accredited). Part-time programs available. *Degree requirements:* For master's, comprehensive exam, thesis or alternative; for doctorate, one foreign language, comprehensive exam, thesis/dissertation. *Entrance requirements:* For master's, GRE General Test, minimum GPA of 3.2; for doctorate, GRE General Test, minimum GPA of 3.5. Additional exam requirements/recommendations for international students: Required—TOEFL. Electronic applications accepted. *Faculty research:* Multiculturalism, augmentative communication, adult neurological disorders, child language disorders.

Hunter College of the City University of New York, Graduate School, Schools of the Health Professions, School of Health Sciences, Communication Sciences Program, New York, NY 10021-5085. Offers speech-language pathology (MS). *Accreditation:* ASHA. Part-time programs available. *Faculty:* 7 full-time (5 women), 9 part-time/adjunct (all women). *Students:* 11 full-time (all women), 1 (woman) part-time; includes 3 minority (1 Black or African American, non-Hispanic/Latino; 1 American Indian or Alaska Native, non-Hispanic/Latino; 1 Hispanic/Latino). Average age 27. 264 applicants, 5% accepted, 6 enrolled. In 2011, 5 master's awarded. *Degree requirements:* For master's, comprehensive exam (for some programs), NTE, research project. *Entrance requirements:* For master's, GRE, letters of reference. Additional exam requirements/recommendations for international students: Required—TOEFL. *Application deadline:* For fall admission, 4/1 for domestic students, 2/1 for international students; for spring admission, 11/1 for domestic students, 9/1 for international students. Application fee: $125. *Expenses:* Tuition, state resident: full-time $8210; part-time $345 per credit. Tuition, nonresident: full-time $15,360; part-time $640 per credit. *Required fees:* $280 per semester. One-time fee: $125. Tuition and fees vary according to class time, campus/location and program. *Financial support:* In 2011–12, 11 students received support, including 3 fellowships with partial tuition reimbursements available (averaging $1,000 per year), 6 research assistantships; career-related internships or fieldwork, Federal Work-Study, institutionally sponsored loans, scholarships/grants, and tuition waivers (full and partial) also available. Support available to part-time students. Financial award application deadline: 3/1. *Faculty research:* Aging and communication disorders, fluency, speech science, diagnostic audiology, amplification. *Total annual research expenditures:* $600,000. *Unit head:* Dr. Dava Waltzman, Program Director, 212-481-4339, Fax: 212-481-4467, E-mail: dwaltzma@hejira.hunter.cuny.edu. *Application contact:* William Zlata, Director for Graduate Admissions, 212-772-4482, Fax: 212-650-3336, E-mail: admissions@hunter.cuny.edu. Web site: http://www.hunter.cuny.edu/schoolhp/comsc/index.htm.

Idaho State University, Office of Graduate Studies, Kasiska College of Health Professions, Department of Communication Sciences and Disorders and Education of the Deaf, Pocatello, ID 83209-8116. Offers audiology (MS, Au D); communication sciences and disorders (Postbaccalaureate Certificate); communication sciences and disorders and education of the deaf (Certificate); deaf education (MS); speech language pathology (MS). *Accreditation:* ASHA (one or more programs are accredited). Part-time programs available. *Degree requirements:* For master's, thesis optional, written and oral comprehensive exams; for doctorate, comprehensive exam, thesis/dissertation optional, externship, 1 year full time clinical practicum, 3rd year spent in Boise. *Entrance requirements:* For master's, GRE General Test, minimum GPA of 3.0, 3 letters of recommendation; for doctorate, GRE General Test (at least 2 scores minimum 40th percentile), minimum GPA of 3.0, 3 letters of recommendation, bachelor's degree. Additional exam requirements/recommendations for international students: Required—TOEFL (minimum score 600 paper-based; 250 computer-based; 80 iBT). Electronic applications accepted. *Faculty research:* Neurogenic disorders, central auditory processing disorders, vestibular disorders, cochlear implants, language disorders, professional burnout, swallowing disorders.

Illinois State University, Graduate School, College of Arts and Sciences, Department of Communication Sciences and Disorders, Normal, IL 61790-2200. Offers MA, MS. *Accreditation:* ASHA. *Degree requirements:* For master's, thesis or alternative, 1 term of residency, 2 practica. *Entrance requirements:* For master's, GRE General Test, minimum GPA of 3.0 in last 60 hours.

Indiana University Bloomington, University Graduate School, College of Arts and Sciences, Department of Speech and Hearing Sciences, Clinical Program in Audiology, Bloomington, IN 47405-7000. Offers Au D. *Students:* 24 full-time (21 women); includes 7 minority (5 Black or African American, non-Hispanic/Latino; 2 Two or more races, non-Hispanic/Latino), 1 international. Average age 27. 62 applicants, 56% accepted, 7 enrolled. In 2011, 12 doctorates awarded. Application fee: $55 ($65 for international students). *Unit head:* Karen Forrest, Chairperson, 812-855-2602, E-mail: kforrest@indiana.edu. *Application contact:* Jennifer J. Lentz, Graduate Advisor, 812-855-8945, E-mail: jjlentz@indiana.edu. Web site: http://www.indiana.edu/~sphs/academics/aud/.

Indiana University Bloomington, University Graduate School, College of Arts and Sciences, Department of Speech and Hearing Sciences, Program in Speech and Hearing Sciences, Bloomington, IN 47405-7000. Offers auditory sciences (Au D, PhD); language sciences (PhD); speech and voice sciences (PhD); speech-language pathology (MA). *Faculty:* 34 full-time (25 women), 11 part-time/adjunct (8 women). *Students:* 85 full-time (82 women), 5 part-time (all women); includes 11 minority (2 Asian, non-Hispanic/Latino; 9 Hispanic/Latino), 9 international. Average age 26. 268 applicants, 35% accepted, 38 enrolled. In 2011, 34 degrees awarded. *Application deadline:* For fall admission, 1/15 priority date for domestic students, 12/1 for international students. Application fee: $55 ($65 for international students). *Financial support:* In 2011–12, 4 fellowships (averaging $19,530 per year), 5 teaching assistantships (averaging $14,475 per year) were awarded. *Unit head:* Karen Forrest, Chairperson, 812-855-2602, E-mail: kforrest@indiana.edu. *Application contact:* Kimberly Elkins, Graduate Secretary, 812-855-4202, E-mail: kelkins@indiana.edu. Web site: http://www.indiana.edu/~sphs/home/.

Indiana University of Pennsylvania, School of Graduate Studies and Research, College of Education and Educational Technology, Department of Special Education and Clinical Services, Program in Speech-Language Pathology, Indiana, PA 15705-1087. Offers MS. *Accreditation:* ASHA. *Faculty:* 8 full-time (7 women), 3 part-time/adjunct (2 women). *Students:* 43 full-time (42 women). Average age 24. 237 applicants, 9% accepted, 21 enrolled. In 2011, 24 master's awarded. *Degree requirements:* For master's, comprehensive exam, thesis optional. *Entrance requirements:* For master's, 2 letters of recommendation. Additional exam requirements/recommendations for international students: Required—TOEFL (minimum score 540 paper-based; 207 computer-based). *Application deadline:* For fall admission, 2/15 priority date for domestic students. Application fee: $50. Electronic applications accepted. *Expenses:* Tuition, state resident: full-time $7488; part-time $416 per credit. Tuition, nonresident: full-time $11,232; part-time $624 per credit. *Required fees:* $2070; $192.20 per credit. $90 per semester. *Financial support:* In 2011–12, 1 fellowship (averaging $500 per year), 12 research assistantships with full and partial tuition reimbursements (averaging $3,173 per year) were awarded; career-related internships or fieldwork and Federal Work-Study also available. Support available to part-time students. Financial award application deadline: 4/15; financial award applicants required to submit FAFSA. *Unit head:* Dr. David Stein, Graduate Coordinator, 724-357-7841, E-mail: david.stein@iup.edu. *Application contact:* Dr. Edward Nardi, Associate Dean, 724-357-2480, Fax: 724-357-5595, E-mail: ewnardi@iup.edu. Web site: http://www.iup.edu/grad/speechlanguage/default.aspx.

Indiana University–Purdue University Fort Wayne, College of Arts and Sciences, Department of Communication Sciences and Disorders, Fort Wayne, IN 46805-1499. Offers speech and language pathology (MA). *Unit head:* Dr. Jonathan Dalby, Interim Chair and Associate Professor, 260-481-6409, Fax: 260-481-6985, E-mail: dalbyj@ipfw.edu. *Application contact:* Susan Humphrey, Graduate Applications Coordinator, 260-481-6145, Fax: 260-481-6880, E-mail: ask@ipfw.edu.

Ithaca College, Division of Graduate and Professional Studies, School of Health Sciences and Human Performance, Program in Speech-Language Pathology and Audiology and TSSL, Ithaca, NY 14850. Offers speech pathology (MS); teacher of students with speech and language disabilities (MS). *Accreditation:* ASHA. *Faculty:* 9 full-time (6 women). *Students:* 56 full-time (55 women); includes 2 minority (1 Hispanic/Latino; 1 Two or more races, non-Hispanic/Latino). Average age 24. 180 applicants, 32% accepted, 24 enrolled. In 2011, 24 master's awarded. *Degree requirements:* For master's, comprehensive exam, thesis optional. *Entrance requirements:* For master's, GRE General Test, minimum GPA of 3.0. Additional exam requirements/recommendations for international students: Required—TOEFL (minimum score 550 paper-based; 213 computer-based; 80 iBT). *Application deadline:* For fall admission, 2/1 priority date for domestic students, 2/1 for international students. Applications are processed on a rolling basis. Application fee: $40. Electronic applications accepted. *Expenses: Tuition:* Part-time $663 per credit hour. *Required fees:* $663 per credit hour. *Financial support:* In 2011–12, 27 students received support, including 27 teaching assistantships (averaging $8,703 per year); career-related internships or fieldwork, Federal Work-Study, scholarships/grants, and unspecified assistantships also available. Support available to part-time students. Financial award application deadline: 2/1; financial award applicants required to submit CSS PROFILE or FAFSA. *Faculty research:* Learning enhancement in higher education, augmentative/alternative communication, cultural and linguistic variables in communication, language and literacy acquisition. *Unit head:* Dr. Richard Schissel, Graduate Chair, 607-274-3143, Fax: 607-274-1263, E-mail: gps@ithaca.edu. *Application contact:* Gerard Turbide, Director, Office of Admission, 607-274-3143, Fax: 607-274-1263, E-mail: gps@ithaca.edu. Web site: http://www.ithaca.edu/gps/gradprograms/programsites/slpa.

Jackson State University, Graduate School, College of Public Service, Department of Communicative Disorders, Jackson, MS 39217. Offers MS. *Accreditation:* ASHA. *Degree requirements:* For master's, comprehensive exam. *Entrance requirements:* For master's, GRE General Test. Additional exam requirements/recommendations for international students: Required—TOEFL (minimum score 520 paper-based; 195 computer-based; 67 iBT).

James Madison University, The Graduate School, College of Integrated Science and Technology, Department of Communication Sciences and Disorders, Program in Audiology, Harrisonburg, VA 22807. Offers Au D. *Accreditation:* ASHA. Part-time programs available. *Students:* 21 full-time (19 women); includes 2 minority (1 Black or African American, non-Hispanic/Latino; 1 Native Hawaiian or other Pacific Islander, non-Hispanic/Latino). Average age 27. In 2011, 3 doctorates awarded. *Entrance requirements:* For doctorate, 3 letters of recommendation, interview. Additional exam requirements/recommendations for international students: Required—TOEFL. *Application deadline:* For fall admission, 2/1 for domestic students. Applications are processed on a rolling basis. Application fee: $55. Electronic applications accepted. *Expenses:* Tuition, state resident: full-time $8016; part-time $334 per credit hour. Tuition, nonresident: full-time $22,656; part-time $944 per credit hour. *Financial support:* In 2011–12, 16 students received support, including teaching assistantships with full tuition reimbursements available (averaging $8,664 per year); 3 graduate assistantships ($7382), 13 doctoral assistantships ($14,500) also available. Financial award application deadline: 3/1. *Unit head:* Dr. Cynthia R. O'Donoghue, Interim Department Head, 540-568-6440, E-mail: odonogcr@jmu.edu. *Application contact:* Lynette M. Bible, Director of Graduate Admissions, 540-568-6395, Fax: 540-568-7860, E-mail: biblem@jmu.edu.

James Madison University, The Graduate School, College of Integrated Science and Technology, Department of Communication Sciences and Disorders, Program in Speech-Language Pathology, Harrisonburg, VA 22807. Offers audiology (PhD); clinical audiology (PhD); speech-language pathology (MS, PhD). *Accreditation:* ASHA. Part-time programs available. *Students:* 72 full-time (71 women), 17 part-time (all women); includes 6 minority (2 Asian, non-Hispanic/Latino; 1 Hispanic/Latino; 3 Two or more races, non-Hispanic/Latino), 1 international. Average age 27. In 2011, 32 degrees awarded. *Degree requirements:* For master's, thesis. *Entrance requirements:* For master's, GRE General Test, 2 letters of recommendation; for doctorate, GRE, 3 letters of recommendation, interview. Additional exam requirements/recommendations for international students: Required—TOEFL. *Application deadline:* For fall admission, 5/1 priority date for domestic students. Applications are processed on a rolling basis. Application fee: $55. Electronic applications accepted. *Expenses:* Tuition, state resident: full-time $8016; part-time $334 per credit hour. Tuition, nonresident: full-time $22,656; part-time $944 per credit hour. *Financial support:* In 2011–12, 37 students received support. Federal Work-Study and 33 graduate assistantships ($7382), 4 doctoral assistantships ($14,500) available. Financial award application deadline: 3/1; financial award applicants required to submit FAFSA. *Unit head:* Dr. Cynthia R. O'Donoghue, Interim Academic Unit Head, 540-568-6440, E-mail: odonogcr@jmu.edu. *Application contact:* Lynette M. Bible, Director of Graduate Admissions, 540-568-6395, Fax: 540-568-7860, E-mail: biblem@jmu.edu.

Kansas State University, Graduate School, College of Human Ecology, School of Family Studies and Human Services, Manhattan, KS 66506. Offers communication sciences and disorders (MS); early childhood education (MS); family studies (MS); life span human development (MS); marriage and family therapy (MS). *Accreditation:* AAMFT/COAMFTE; ASHA. Part-time programs available. *Faculty:* 28 full-time (18 women), 4 part-time/adjunct (3 women). *Students:* 56 full-time (47 women), 158 part-time (100 women); includes 34 minority (19 Black or African American, non-Hispanic/Latino; 3 American Indian or Alaska Native, non-Hispanic/Latino; 4 Asian, non-Hispanic/Latino; 7 Hispanic/Latino; 1 Two or more races, non-Hispanic/Latino), 2 international. Average age 32. 195 applicants, 41% accepted, 46 enrolled. In 2011, 56 master's awarded. *Degree requirements:* For master's, thesis or alternative, oral exam, residency. *Entrance requirements:* For master's, GRE, minimum GPA of 3.0 in last 2 years of undergraduate study. Additional exam requirements/recommendations for international students: Required—TOEFL (minimum score 600 paper-based; 250 computer-based). *Application deadline:* For fall admission, 2/1 priority date for domestic students, 2/1 for international students; for spring admission, 8/1 priority date for domestic students, 8/1 for international students. Applications are processed on a rolling basis. Application fee: $40 ($55 for international students). Electronic applications accepted. *Financial support:* In 2011–12, 27 research assistantships (averaging $12,839 per year), 17 teaching assistantships with full and partial tuition reimbursements (averaging $12,771 per year) were awarded; Federal Work-Study, institutionally sponsored loans, scholarships/grants, and unspecified assistantships also available. Support available to part-time students. Financial award application deadline: 3/1; financial award applicants required to submit FAFSA. *Faculty research:* Health and security of military families, personal and family risk assessment and evaluation, disorders of communication and swallowing, families and health. *Total annual research expenditures:* $13.5 million. *Unit head:* Dr. Maurice McDonald, Head, 785-532-5510,

Fax: 785-532-5505, E-mail: morey@ksu.edu. *Application contact:* Connie Fechter, Administrative Specialist, 785-532-5510, Fax: 785-532-5505, E-mail: fechter@ksu.edu. Web site: http://www.he.k-state.edu/fshs/.

Kean University, College of Education, Program in Speech Language Pathology, Union, NJ 07083. Offers MA. *Accreditation:* ASHA. *Faculty:* 8 full-time (6 women). *Students:* 130 full-time (125 women), 36 part-time (32 women); includes 34 minority (4 Black or African American, non-Hispanic/Latino; 8 Asian, non-Hispanic/Latino; 20 Hispanic/Latino; 2 Two or more races, non-Hispanic/Latino), 2 international. Average age 27. 369 applicants, 29% accepted, 68 enrolled. In 2011, 43 master's awarded. *Degree requirements:* For master's, comprehensive exam, thesis, practicum, clinical. *Entrance requirements:* For master's, GRE General Test, minimum GPA of 3.2, 3 letters of recommendation, interview, transcripts, resume. Additional exam requirements/recommendations for international students: Required—TOEFL (minimum score 79 iBT). *Application deadline:* For fall admission, 2/1 for domestic and international students. Application fee: $75 ($150 for international students). Electronic applications accepted. *Expenses: Tuition,* state resident: full-time $11,302; part-time $550 per credit. Tuition, nonresident: full-time $15,318; part-time $674 per credit. *Required fees:* $2849; $130 per credit. Tuition and fees vary according to degree level. *Financial support:* In 2011–12, 16 research assistantships with full tuition reimbursements (averaging $3,263 per year) were awarded; unspecified assistantships also available. Financial award applicants required to submit FAFSA. *Unit head:* Dr. Barbara D. Glazewski, Program Coordinator, 908-737-5807, E-mail: bglazews@kean.edu. *Application contact:* Steven Koch, Admissions Counselor, 908-737-5924, Fax: 908-737-5925, E-mail: skoch@kean.edu. Web site: http://www.kean.edu/KU/Speech-Language-Pathology.

Kent State University, Graduate School of Education, Health, and Human Services, School of Health Sciences, Program in Audiology, Kent, OH 44242-0001. Offers Au D, PhD. *Faculty:* 3 full-time (1 woman), 7 part-time/adjunct (6 women). *Students:* 40 full-time (37 women); includes 5 minority (1 Black or African American, non-Hispanic/Latino; 3 Asian, non-Hispanic/Latino; 1 Hispanic/Latino). 44 applicants, 20% accepted. *Entrance requirements:* For doctorate, GRE, 3 letters of reference, goals statement. Additional exam requirements/recommendations for international students: Required—TOEFL (minimum score 550 paper-based; 213 computer-based; 80 iBT). Application fee: $30 ($60 for international students). *Expenses:* Tuition, state resident: full-time $8136; part-time $452 per credit hour. Tuition, nonresident: full-time $14,292; part-time $794 per credit hour. *Financial support:* In 2011–12, 1 research assistantship (averaging $8,500 per year) was awarded; fellowships, Federal Work-Study, scholarships/grants, and unspecified assistantships also available. *Unit head:* John Hawks, Coordinator, 330-672-0251, Fax: 330-672-2643, E-mail: jhawks@kent.edu. *Application contact:* Nancy Miller, Academic Program Coordinator, 330-672-2576, Fax: 330-672-9162, E-mail: ogs@kent.edu.

Kent State University, Graduate School of Education, Health, and Human Services, School of Health Sciences, Program in Speech Language Pathology, Kent, OH 44242-0001. Offers MA, PhD. *Accreditation:* ASHA. *Faculty:* 12 full-time (all women), 1 (woman) part-time/adjunct. *Students:* 78 full-time (77 women), 1 (woman) part-time; includes 3 minority (1 Black or African American, non-Hispanic/Latino; 2 Asian, non-Hispanic/Latino). 317 applicants, 23% accepted. In 2011, 32 degrees awarded. *Degree requirements:* For doctorate, comprehensive exam, thesis/dissertation. *Entrance requirements:* For master's and doctorate, GRE, 3 letters of reference, goals statement. Additional exam requirements/recommendations for international students: Required—TOEFL (minimum score 550 paper-based; 213 computer-based; 80 iBT). Application fee: $30 ($60 for international students). *Expenses:* Tuition, state resident: full-time $8136; part-time $452 per credit hour. Tuition, nonresident: full-time $14,292; part-time $794 per credit hour. *Financial support:* In 2011–12, 2 fellowships (averaging $8,500 per year), 6 research assistantships (averaging $8,500 per year) were awarded; Federal Work-Study, institutionally sponsored loans, and unspecified assistantships also available. *Unit head:* John Hawks, Coordinator, 330-672-0251, E-mail: jhawks@kent.edu. *Application contact:* Nancy Miller, Academic Program Coordinator, Office of Graduate Student Services, 330-672-2576, Fax: 330-672-9162, E-mail: ogs@kent.edu.

Kent State University, Graduate School of Education, Health, and Human Services, School of Lifespan Development and Educational Sciences, Program in Special Education, Kent, OH 44242-0001. Offers deaf education (M Ed); general special education (M Ed); gifted education (M Ed); mild/moderate intervention (M Ed); moderate/intensive intervention (M Ed); special education (PhD, Ed S). *Accreditation:* NCATE. *Faculty:* 24 full-time (18 women), 21 part-time/adjunct (20 women). *Students:* 96 full-time (76 women), 81 part-time (64 women); includes 8 minority (5 Black or African American, non-Hispanic/Latino; 2 Asian, non-Hispanic/Latino; 1 Hispanic/Latino). 66 applicants, 56% accepted. In 2011, 48 master's, 3 doctorates awarded. *Degree requirements:* For doctorate, comprehensive exam, thesis/dissertation. *Entrance requirements:* For master's, minimum undergraduate GPA of 2.75, moral character form, 2 letters of reference, goals statement; for doctorate and Ed S, GRE General Test, goals statement, 2 letter of reference, interview, resume. Additional exam requirements/recommendations for international students: Required—TOEFL (minimum score 550 paper-based; 213 computer-based; 80 iBT). *Application deadline:* Applications are processed on a rolling basis. Application fee: $30 ($60 for international students). Electronic applications accepted. *Expenses:* Tuition, state resident: full-time $8136; part-time $452 per credit hour. Tuition, nonresident: full-time $14,292; part-time $794 per credit hour. *Financial support:* In 2011–12, 1 fellowship with full tuition reimbursement (averaging $12,000 per year), 4 research assistantships with full tuition reimbursements (averaging $9,375 per year) were awarded; teaching assistantships with full tuition reimbursements, career-related internships or fieldwork, Federal Work-Study, institutionally sponsored loans, scholarships/grants, health care benefits, unspecified assistantships, and 5 administrative assistantships (averaging $10,600 per year) also available. Support available to part-time students. Financial award application deadline: 4/1; financial award applicants required to submit FAFSA. *Faculty research:* Social/emotional needs of gifted, inclusion transition services, early intervention/ecobehavioral assessments, applied behavioral analysis. *Unit head:* Lyle Barton, Coordinator, 330-672-0578, E-mail: lbarton@kent.edu. *Application contact:* Nancy Miller, Academic Program Coordinator, Office of Graduate Student Services, 330-672-2576, Fax: 330-672-9162, E-mail: ogs@kent.edu. Web site: http://www.kent.edu/ehhs/sped/.

Lamar University, College of Graduate Studies, College of Fine Arts and Communication, Department of Speech and Hearing Science, Beaumont, TX 77710. Offers audiology (MS, Au D); speech language pathology (MS). *Faculty:* 7 full-time (4 women), 1 part-time/adjunct (0 women). *Students:* 72 full-time (64 women), 11 part-time (9 women); includes 28 minority (15 Black or African American, non-Hispanic/Latino; 4 Asian, non-Hispanic/Latino; 9 Hispanic/Latino). Average age 27. 129 applicants, 36% accepted, 10 enrolled. In 2011, 23 master's, 1 doctorate awarded. *Degree requirements:* For master's, thesis optional; for doctorate, thesis/dissertation. *Entrance requirements:* For master's, GRE General Test, performance IQ score of 115 (for deaf students), minimum GPA of 2.5; for doctorate, GRE General Test, performance IQ score of 115 (for deaf students). Additional exam requirements/recommendations for international students: Required—TOEFL. *Application deadline:* For fall admission, 8/1 priority date for domestic students; for spring admission, 12/1 for domestic students. Applications are

processed on a rolling basis. Application fee: $25 ($50 for international students). *Expenses:* Tuition, state resident: full-time $5430; part-time $272 per credit hour. Tuition, nonresident: full-time $11,540; part-time $577 per credit hour. *Required fees:* $1916. *Financial support:* Fellowships with tuition reimbursements, teaching assistantships, and institutionally sponsored loans available. Support available to part-time students. Financial award application deadline: 4/1. *Unit head:* Dr. Russ A. Schultz, Dean, 409-880-8137, Fax: 409-880-2286, E-mail: russ.schultz@lamar.edu. *Application contact:* Debbie Piper, Coordinator of Graduate Admissions, 409-880-8356, Fax: 409-880-8414, E-mail: gradmissions@hal.lamar.edu.

La Salle University, School of Nursing and Health Sciences, Program in Speech-Language-Hearing Science, Philadelphia, PA 19141-1199. Offers MS. *Accreditation:* ASHA.

Lehman College of the City University of New York, Division of Arts and Humanities, Department of Speech–Language–Hearing Sciences, Bronx, NY 10468-1589. Offers speech-language pathology and audiology (MA). *Accreditation:* ASHA. Part-time and evening/weekend programs available. *Degree requirements:* For master's, thesis or alternative.

Lewis & Clark College, Graduate School of Education and Counseling, Department of Teacher Education, Program in Special Education, Portland, OR 97219-7899. Offers M Ed. *Accreditation:* NCATE. Part-time and evening/weekend programs available. *Faculty:* 1 (woman) full-time, 2 part-time/adjunct (both women). *Students:* 3 full-time (all women), 21 part-time (17 women); includes 2 minority (both Two or more races, non-Hispanic/Latino). Average age 37. 11 applicants, 82% accepted, 8 enrolled. In 2011, 5 master's awarded. *Entrance requirements:* For master's, minimum GPA of 2.75. Additional exam requirements/recommendations for international students: Required—TOEFL (minimum score 575 paper-based; 233 computer-based). *Application deadline:* Applications are processed on a rolling basis. Application fee: $50. Electronic applications accepted. *Expenses: Tuition:* Part-time $738 per semester hour. Tuition and fees vary according to course level and campus/location. *Financial support:* In 2011–12, 1 student received support. Career-related internships or fieldwork, Federal Work-Study, institutionally sponsored loans, scholarships/grants, health care benefits, and tuition waivers (partial) available. Support available to part-time students. Financial award application deadline: 3/1; financial award applicants required to submit FAFSA. *Unit head:* Christine Moore, Program Coordinator, 503-768-6128, E-mail: cmoore@lclark.edu. *Application contact:* Becky Haas, Director of Admissions, 503-768-6200, Fax: 503-768-6205, E-mail: gseadmit@lclark.edu. Web site: http://graduate.lclark.edu/departments/teacher_education/current_teachers/masters_special_education/.

Loma Linda University, School of Allied Health Professions, Department of Speech-Language Pathology and Audiology, Loma Linda, CA 92350. Offers MS. *Accreditation:* ASHA. Part-time programs available. *Degree requirements:* For master's, thesis or alternative. *Entrance requirements:* For master's, GRE General Test. Additional exam requirements/recommendations for international students: Required—TOEFL (minimum score 550 paper-based; 213 computer-based). Electronic applications accepted.

Long Island University–Brooklyn Campus, Richard L. Conolly College of Liberal Arts and Sciences, Department of Communication Sciences and Disorders, Brooklyn, NY 11201-8423. Offers speech-language pathology (MS). *Accreditation:* ASHA. *Entrance requirements:* For master's, 2 letters of recommendation. Additional exam requirements/recommendations for international students: Required—TOEFL (minimum score 500 paper-based; 173 computer-based). Electronic applications accepted.

Long Island University–C. W. Post Campus, School of Education, Department of Communication Sciences and Disorders, Brookville, NY 11548-1300. Offers speech language pathology (MA). *Accreditation:* ASHA. Part-time and evening/weekend programs available. *Degree requirements:* For master's, comprehensive exam or thesis. *Entrance requirements:* For master's, minimum GPA of 3.0, bachelor's degree in communication sciences and disorders. Electronic applications accepted. *Faculty research:* Aural rehabilitation, spouses' perceptions of speech therapy with their ephasic partners, establish norms associated with swallowing.

Longwood University, Office of Graduate Studies, College of Education and Human Services, Program in Communication Sciences and Disorders, Farmville, VA 23909. Offers MS. *Accreditation:* ASHA.

Louisiana State University and Agricultural and Mechanical College, Graduate School, College of Humanities and Social Sciences, Department of Communication Sciences and Disorders, Baton Rouge, LA 70803. Offers MA, PhD. *Accreditation:* ASHA (one or more programs are accredited). *Faculty:* 12 full-time (11 women). *Students:* 63 full-time (60 women), 5 part-time (all women); includes 12 minority (11 Black or African American, non-Hispanic/Latino; 1 Hispanic/Latino), 3 international. Average age 26. 114 applicants, 26% accepted, 27 enrolled. In 2011, 16 master's, 3 doctorates awarded. *Degree requirements:* For doctorate, thesis/dissertation. *Entrance requirements:* For master's and doctorate, GRE General Test, minimum GPA of 3.0. Additional exam requirements/recommendations for international students: Required—TOEFL (minimum score 550 paper-based; 213 computer-based; 79 iBT) or IELTS (minimum score 6.5). *Application deadline:* For fall admission, 1/25 priority date for domestic students, 5/15 for international students; for spring admission, 10/15 for international students. Application fee: $25. Electronic applications accepted. *Financial support:* In 2011–12, 53 students received support, including 1 fellowship with full tuition reimbursement available (averaging $22,978 per year), 11 research assistantships with partial tuition reimbursements available (averaging $12,309 per year), 13 teaching assistantships with partial tuition reimbursements available (averaging $11,026 per year); Federal Work-Study, institutionally sponsored loans, health care benefits, and unspecified assistantships also available. Financial award application deadline: 4/1; financial award applicants required to submit FAFSA. *Faculty research:* Language development, language intervention, aphasia, language of the deaf. *Total annual research expenditures:* $511,240. *Unit head:* Dr. Paul R. Hoffman, Chair, 225-578-2545, Fax: 225-578-2995, E-mail: cdhoff@lsu.edu. *Application contact:* Dr. Janna Oetting, Graduate Adviser, 225-578-6682, Fax: 225-578-2995, E-mail: cdjana@lsu.edu. Web site: http://appl003.lsu.edu/artsci/comd.nsf/index.

Louisiana State University Health Sciences Center, School of Allied Health Professions, Department of Communication Disorders, New Orleans, LA 70112-2223. Offers audiology (Au D); speech pathology (MCD). *Accreditation:* ASHA (one or more programs are accredited). *Degree requirements:* For master's, comprehensive exam or thesis. *Entrance requirements:* For master's, GRE General Test, minimum undergraduate GPA of 3.0, 3 letters of recommendation; for doctorate, GRE General Test (minimum 900 combined score), 3 letters of recommendation, minimum undergraduate GPA of 3.0. *Faculty research:* Hearing aids, clinical audiology, swallowing respiration, language acquisition, speech science.

Louisiana Tech University, Graduate School, College of Liberal Arts, Department of Speech, Ruston, LA 71272. Offers speech (MA); speech pathology and audiology (MA). *Accreditation:* ASHA. *Degree requirements:* For master's, thesis or alternative. *Entrance requirements:* For master's, GRE General Test.

Loyola University Maryland, Graduate Programs, College of Arts and Sciences, Department of Speech-Language Pathology and Audiology, Baltimore, MD 21210-2699. Offers speech language pathology (MS). *Accreditation:* ASHA. *Faculty:* 31 full-time (30 women), 16 part-time/adjunct (all women). *Students:* 104 full-time (102 women); includes 13 minority (5 Black or African American, non-Hispanic/Latino; 5 Asian, non-Hispanic/Latino; 3 Two or more races, non-Hispanic/Latino). Average age 24. In 2011, 64 master's awarded. *Degree requirements:* For master's, comprehensive exam, thesis, PRAXIS. *Entrance requirements:* For master's, GRE General Test, GRE Subject Test (recommended). Additional exam requirements/recommendations for international students: Required—TOEFL (minimum score 550 paper-based; 213 computer-based). *Application deadline:* For fall admission, 2/1 for domestic students. Application fee: $50. Electronic applications accepted. *Financial support:* Research assistantships and unspecified assistantships available. Financial award application deadline: 4/15; financial award applicants required to submit FAFSA. *Unit head:* Dr. Janet Preis, Director of Graduate Programs, 410-617-2578, E-mail: jpreis1@loyola.edu. *Application contact:* Maureen Faux, Executive Director, Graduate Admissions, 410-617-5020, Fax: 410-617-2002, E-mail: graduate@loyola.edu. Web site: http://www.loyola.edu/speechpathology/.

Marquette University, Graduate School, College of Health Sciences, Department of Speech Pathology and Audiology, Milwaukee, WI 53201-1881. Offers bilingual English/Spanish (Certificate); speech-language pathology (MS). *Accreditation:* ASHA (one or more programs are accredited). Part-time programs available. *Faculty:* 11 full-time (7 women), 3 part-time/adjunct (all women). *Students:* 39 full-time (38 women), 11 part-time (all women); includes 10 minority (1 Black or African American, non-Hispanic/Latino; 1 Asian, non-Hispanic/Latino; 7 Hispanic/Latino; 1 Two or more races, non-Hispanic/Latino), 1 international. Average age 24. 229 applicants, 32% accepted, 25 enrolled. In 2011, 26 master's, 4 other advanced degrees awarded. *Degree requirements:* For master's, comprehensive exam, thesis (for some programs). *Entrance requirements:* For master's, GRE General Test, official transcripts from all current and previous colleges/universities except Marquette, three letters of recommendation, personal statement. Additional exam requirements/recommendations for international students: Required—TOEFL (minimum score 530 paper-based; 78 computer-based). *Application deadline:* For fall admission, 1/15 for domestic students. Application fee: $50. Electronic applications accepted. *Expenses: Tuition:* Full-time $17,010; part-time $945 per credit hour. Tuition and fees vary according to program. *Financial support:* In 2011–12, 30 students received support, including 1 fellowship with full tuition reimbursement available (averaging $20,000 per year), 4 research assistantships with full tuition reimbursements available (averaging $13,285 per year); career-related internships or fieldwork, scholarships/grants, health care benefits, tuition waivers (partial), and unspecified assistantships also available. Support available to part-time students. Financial award application deadline: 2/15. *Faculty research:* Language processing in the brain, vocal aging, early language development, birth-to-three intervention, computer applications. *Total annual research expenditures:* $1.1 million. *Unit head:* Dr. Edward Korabic, Chair, 414-288-5665, Fax: 414-288-3980, E-mail: edward.korabic@marquette.edu. *Application contact:* Craig Pierce, Assistant Dean of the Graduate School, 414-288-5740, Fax: 414-288-1902, E-mail: craig.pierce@marquette.edu. Web site: http://www.marquette.edu/chs/speech/graduate.shtml.

Marshall University, Academic Affairs Division, College of Health Professions, Department of Communication Disorders, Huntington, WV 25755. Offers MS. *Accreditation:* ASHA. *Faculty:* 8 full-time (all women), 1 (woman) part-time/adjunct. *Students:* 58 full-time (55 women), 5 part-time (all women); includes 3 minority (1 Black or African American, non-Hispanic/Latino; 1 Asian, non-Hispanic/Latino; 1 Hispanic/Latino), 2 international. Average age 25. In 2011, 11 master's awarded. *Degree requirements:* For master's, thesis optional. *Entrance requirements:* For master's, GRE General Test. Application fee: $40. *Financial support:* Fellowships available. *Unit head:* Karen McNealy, Chairperson, 304-696-3634, E-mail: mcnealy@marshall.edu. *Application contact:* Information Contact, 304-746-1900, Fax: 304-746-1902, E-mail: services@marshall.edu.

Marywood University, Academic Affairs, Reap College of Education and Human Development, Department of Communication Sciences and Disorders, Program in Speech-Language Pathology, Scranton, PA 18509-1598. Offers MS. *Entrance requirements:* Additional exam requirements/recommendations for international students: Required—TOEFL (minimum score 550 paper-based; 213 computer-based; 79 iBT). *Application deadline:* For fall admission, 2/16 priority date for domestic students, 2/16 for international students. Application fee: $35. Electronic applications accepted. *Financial support:* Career-related internships or fieldwork, scholarships/grants, and unspecified assistantships available. Support available to part-time students. Financial award application deadline: 6/30; financial award applicants required to submit FAFSA. *Unit head:* Dr. Mona Griffer, Chairperson, 570-348-6211 Ext. 2363, E-mail: griffer@marywood.edu. *Application contact:* Tammy Manka, 570-348-6211 Ext. 2322, E-mail: tmanka@marywood.edu.

Massachusetts Institute of Technology, Harvard-MIT Division of Health Sciences and Technology, Speech and Hearing Bioscience and Technology Program, Cambridge, MA 02139-4307. Offers PhD, Sc D. PhD and Sc D offered jointly with Harvard University. *Accreditation:* ASHA. *Faculty:* 66 full-time (18 women). *Students:* 42 full-time (17 women); includes 11 minority (8 Asian, non-Hispanic/Latino; 3 Two or more races, non-Hispanic/Latino), 3 international. Average age 28. 35 applicants, 20% accepted, 6 enrolled. In 2011, 6 doctorates awarded. *Degree requirements:* For doctorate, thesis/dissertation. *Entrance requirements:* For doctorate, BS in engineering or science, previous course work in differential equations. Additional exam requirements/recommendations for international students: Required—TOEFL. *Application deadline:* For fall admission, 12/15 for domestic and international students. Application fee: $75. Electronic applications accepted. *Expenses:* Contact institution. *Financial support:* In 2011–12, 42 students received support, including 26 fellowships with full and partial tuition reimbursements available (averaging $54,672 per year), 17 research assistantships with full and partial tuition reimbursements available (averaging $46,451 per year), 5 teaching assistantships with full and partial tuition reimbursements available (averaging $25,431 per year); career-related internships or fieldwork, scholarships/grants, traineeships, health care benefits, and unspecified assistantships also available. Financial award application deadline: 12/15; financial award applicants required to submit FAFSA. *Faculty research:* Neuroscience, auditory physiology, hearing science, psychoacoustics, speech communications. *Unit head:* Dr. Louis D. Braida, Director, 617-253-2575, Fax: 617-258-7354, E-mail: braida@cbgrle.mit.edu. *Application contact:* Dr. Christopher Shera, Co-Chair, Admissions Committee, 617-573-4235, Fax: 617-720-4408, E-mail: shera@mit.edu. Web site: http://hst.mit.edu/academics/shbt.

McGill University, Faculty of Graduate and Postdoctoral Studies, Faculty of Medicine, School of Communication Sciences and Disorders, Montréal, QC H3A 2T5, Canada. Offers communication science and disorders (M Sc); communication sciences and disorders (PhD); speech-language pathology (M Sc A). *Accreditation:* ASHA.

Mercy College, School of Health and Natural Sciences, Program in Communication Disorders, Dobbs Ferry, NY 10522-1189. Offers MS. *Accreditation:* ASHA. Part-time and evening/weekend programs available. *Entrance requirements:* For master's, interview, resume, 2 letters of recommendation. Additional exam requirements/recommendations for international students: Required—TOEFL (minimum score 600 paper-based; 250 computer-based; 100 iBT), IELTS (minimum score 8). Electronic

applications accepted. *Expenses:* Contact institution. *Faculty research:* Phonology, articulation, hearing deficits, fluency, attention.

MGH Institute of Health Professions, School of Health and Rehabilitation Sciences, Department of Communication Sciences and Disorders, Boston, MA 02129. Offers reading (Certificate); speech-language pathology (MS). *Accreditation:* ASHA (one or more programs are accredited). Part-time programs available. *Faculty:* 12 full-time (9 women), 2 part-time/adjunct (1 woman). *Students:* 111 full-time (104 women), 28 part-time (all women); includes 19 minority (4 Black or African American, non-Hispanic/Latino; 15 Asian, non-Hispanic/Latino). Average age 28. 367 applicants, 31% accepted, 69 enrolled. In 2011, 55 master's, 26 other advanced degrees awarded. *Degree requirements:* For master's, thesis or alternative, research proposal. *Entrance requirements:* For master's, GRE General Test, bachelor's degree from regionally-accredited college or university. Additional exam requirements/recommendations for international students: Required—TOEFL (minimum score 550 paper-based; 213 computer-based; 80 iBT). *Application deadline:* For fall admission, 1/15 for domestic and international students. Application fee: $65. Electronic applications accepted. *Expenses: Tuition:* Full-time $12,720; part-time $1060 per credit. Required fees: $1725; $430 per semester. One-time fee: $350. *Financial support:* In 2011–12, 45 students received support, including 8 research assistantships (averaging $1,200 per year), 4 teaching assistantships (averaging $1,200 per year); career-related internships or fieldwork, scholarships/grants, and unspecified assistantships also available. Support available to part-time students. Financial award application deadline: 4/1; financial award applicants required to submit FAFSA. *Faculty research:* Children's language disorders, reading, speech disorders, voice disorders, augmentative communication, autism. *Unit head:* Dr. Gregory L. Lof, Department Chair, 617-724-6313, E-mail: glof@mghihp.edu. *Application contact:* Maureen Rika Judd, Director of Admissions, 617-726-6069, Fax: 617-726-8010, E-mail: admissions@mghihp.edu. Web site: http://www.mghihp.edu/academics/communication-sciences-and-disorders/.

Miami University, College of Arts and Science, Department of Speech Pathology and Audiology, Oxford, OH 45056. Offers MA, MS. *Accreditation:* ASHA. Part-time programs available. *Students:* 46 full-time (all women), 1 (woman) part-time; includes 3 minority (1 Black or African American, non-Hispanic/Latino; 1 Hispanic/Latino; 1 Two or more races, non-Hispanic/Latino). Average age 24. In 2011, 17 master's awarded. *Entrance requirements:* For master's, GRE, minimum undergraduate GPA of 3.0 during previous 2 years or 2.75 overall. Additional exam requirements/recommendations for international students: Required—TOEFL. *Application deadline:* For fall admission, 1/1 for domestic and international students. Application fee: $50. *Expenses:* Tuition, state resident: full-time $12,023; part-time $501 per credit hour. Tuition, nonresident: full-time $26,554; part-time $1107 per credit hour. Required fees: $528. *Financial support:* Fellowships with full tuition reimbursements, research assistantships, teaching assistantships, career-related internships or fieldwork, Federal Work-Study, health care benefits, and unspecified assistantships available. Financial award application deadline: 2/15; financial award applicants required to submit FAFSA. *Unit head:* Dr. Kathleen Hutchinson, Chair, 513-529-2500, E-mail: spa@muohio.edu. *Application contact:* Dr. Laura J. Kelly, Graduate Program Coordinator, 513-529-2500, E-mail: spa@muohio.edu. Web site: http://www.units.muohio.edu/spa/.

Michigan State University, The Graduate School, College of Communication Arts and Sciences, Department of Communicative Sciences and Disorders, East Lansing, MI 48824. Offers MA, PhD. *Accreditation:* ASHA (one or more programs are accredited). *Entrance requirements:* Additional exam requirements/recommendations for international students: Required—TOEFL. Electronic applications accepted.

Minnesota State University Mankato, College of Graduate Studies, College of Allied Health and Nursing, Program in Communication Disorders, Mankato, MN 56001. Offers MS. *Accreditation:* ASHA. Part-time programs available. *Students:* 41 full-time (all women), 2 part-time (both women). *Degree requirements:* For master's, comprehensive exam, thesis or alternative. *Entrance requirements:* For master's, GRE General Test, minimum GPA of 3.0 during previous 2 years, references, writing sample. Additional exam requirements/recommendations for international students: Required—TOEFL. *Application deadline:* For fall admission, 2/1 priority date for domestic students, 2/1 for international students. Applications are processed on a rolling basis. Application fee: $40. *Financial support:* Research assistantships with full tuition reimbursements, teaching assistantships with full tuition reimbursements, career-related internships or fieldwork, Federal Work-Study, and institutionally sponsored loans available. Support available to part-time students. Financial award application deadline: 3/15; financial award applicants required to submit FAFSA. *Faculty research:* Internet/technology issues related to speech-language pathology. *Unit head:* Dr. Renee Shellum, Graduate Coordinator, 507-389-5842. *Application contact:* 507-389-2321, E-mail: grad@mnsu.edu. Web site: http://ahn.mnsu.edu/cd/graduate/.

Minnesota State University Moorhead, Graduate Studies, College of Education and Human Services, Program in Speech-Language Pathology, Moorhead, MN 56563-0002. Offers MS. *Accreditation:* ASHA. *Degree requirements:* For master's, comprehensive exam, final oral exam, project or thesis. *Entrance requirements:* For master's, GRE General Test, minimum GPA of 2.75, undergraduate major in speech/language/hearing sciences, 3 letters of recommendation. Additional exam requirements/recommendations for international students: Required—TOEFL (minimum score 550 paper-based; 213 computer-based). Electronic applications accepted.

Minot State University, Graduate School, Department of Communication Disorders, Minot, ND 58707-0002. Offers audiology (MS); speech-language pathology (MS). *Accreditation:* ASHA. *Degree requirements:* For master's, comprehensive exam (for some programs), thesis (for some programs). *Entrance requirements:* For master's, GRE General Test, minimum GPA of 3.0. Additional exam requirements/recommendations for international students: Required—TOEFL. *Faculty research:* Auditory evoked potentials, pathologies of auditory system, newborn hearing screening, cleft palate research, intervention, the diagnostic process, early language, the pedagogy of clinical teaching, phonology, geriatric communication problems, dysphagia, and brain functioning after injury.

Misericordia University, College of Health Sciences, Department of Speech-Language Pathology, Dallas, PA 18612-1098. Offers MSSLP. *Accreditation:* ASHA. *Faculty:* 5 full-time (3 women), 5 part-time/adjunct (4 women). *Students:* 27 full-time (26 women). Average age 25. In 2011, 31 master's awarded. *Entrance requirements:* For master's, GRE, minimum undergraduate GPA of 3.3. *Application deadline:* For fall admission, 2/1 priority date for domestic students. Application fee: $25. *Expenses: Tuition:* Full-time $25,700; part-time $575 per credit. *Financial support:* In 2011–12, 27 students received support. Scholarships/grants available. Support available to part-time students. Financial award application deadline: 6/30; financial award applicants required to submit FAFSA. *Unit head:* Dr. Glen Tellis, Chair, 570-674-6471, E-mail: gtellis@misericordia.edu. *Application contact:* David Pasquini, Assistant Director of Admissions, 570-674-6255, Fax: 570-674-6232, E-mail: dpasquin@misericordia.edu. Web site: http://www.misericordia.edu/slp.

Mississippi University for Women, Graduate School, College of Nursing and Speech Language Pathology, Columbus, MS 39701-9998. Offers nursing (MSN, PMC); speech-language pathology (MS). *Accreditation:* AACN. Part-time programs available. *Degree requirements:* For master's, comprehensive exam, thesis. *Entrance requirements:* For master's, GRE General Test, bachelor's degree in nursing, previous course work in statistics, proficiency in English.

Missouri State University, Graduate College, College of Health and Human Services, Department of Communication Sciences and Disorders, Springfield, MO 65897. Offers audiology (Au D); communication sciences and disorders (MS), including education of deaf/hard of hearing, speech-language pathology. *Accreditation:* ASHA (one or more programs are accredited). *Faculty:* 18 full-time (13 women), 5 part-time/adjunct (1 woman). *Students:* 112 full-time (100 women), 1 (woman) part-time; includes 6 minority (1 American Indian or Alaska Native, non-Hispanic/Latino; 2 Asian, non-Hispanic/Latino; 2 Hispanic/Latino; 1 Two or more races, non-Hispanic/Latino), 5 international. Average age 25. 39 applicants, 36% accepted, 14 enrolled. In 2011, 35 master's, 6 doctorates awarded. *Degree requirements:* For master's, comprehensive exam, thesis or alternative; for doctorate, comprehensive exam, thesis/dissertation or alternative, clinical externship. *Entrance requirements:* For master's and doctorate, GRE, minimum GPA of 3.0. Additional exam requirements/recommendations for international students: Required—TOEFL (minimum score 550 paper-based; 213 computer-based; 79 iBT). *Application deadline:* For fall admission, 2/1 for domestic and international students. Application fee: $35 ($50 for international students). Electronic applications accepted. *Expenses:* Tuition, state resident: full-time $4086; part-time $227 per credit hour. Tuition, nonresident: full-time $8172; part-time $454 per credit hour. Required fees: $275 per semester. Tuition and fees vary according to course load, campus/location and program. *Financial support:* Career-related internships or fieldwork, Federal Work-Study, scholarships/grants, and unspecified assistantships available. Support available to part-time students. Financial award application deadline: 3/31; financial award applicants required to submit FAFSA. *Faculty research:* Dysphagia, phonological intervention, elderly adult aural rehabilitation, vestibular disorders. *Unit head:* Dr. Neil DiSarno, Head, 417-836-5368, Fax: 417-836-4242, E-mail: neildisarno@missouristate.edu. *Application contact:* Misty Stewart, Coordinator of Graduate Recruitment, 417-836-6079, Fax: 417-836-6200, E-mail: mistystewart@missouristate.edu. Web site: http://www.missouristate.edu/CSD/.

Molloy College, Program in Speech Language Pathology, Rockville Centre, NY 11571-5002. Offers MS. *Faculty:* 5 full-time (all women). *Students:* 7 full-time (all women). Average age 23. 33 applicants, 67% accepted, 7 enrolled. *Faculty research:* Dysphagia; neurophysiology and language; hearing science; reading, cognition and learning; motor speech. *Unit head:* Dr. Barbara Schmidt, Associate Dean and Director, 516-678-5000, Fax: 516-256-2253. *Application contact:* Alina Haitz, Assistant Director of Graduate Admissions, 516-678-5000 Ext. 6399, Fax: 516-256-2247, E-mail: ahaitz@molloy.edu.

Montclair State University, The Graduate School, College of Humanities and Social Sciences, Department of Communication Sciences and Disorders, Doctoral Program in Audiology, Montclair, NJ 07043-1624. Offers Sc D. Part-time and evening/weekend programs available. *Students:* 8 full-time (6 women), 3 part-time (all women); includes 2 minority (1 Asian, non-Hispanic/Latino; 1 Hispanic/Latino). Average age 31. 3 applicants, 0% accepted, 0 enrolled. In 2011, 4 degrees awarded. *Degree requirements:* For doctorate, comprehensive exam (for some programs), thesis/dissertation (for some programs). *Entrance requirements:* For doctorate, GRE General Test, essay, 2 letters of recommendation. Additional exam requirements/recommendations for international students: Required—TOEFL (minimum score 83 iBT), IELTS (minimum score 6.5). *Application deadline:* For fall admission, 2/1 for domestic students. Applications are processed on a rolling basis. Application fee: $60. Electronic applications accepted. *Financial support:* In 2011–12, 12 research assistantships with partial tuition reimbursements (averaging $7,500 per year) were awarded; Federal Work-Study, scholarships/grants, and unspecified assistantships also available. Support available to part-time students. Financial award application deadline: 3/1; financial award applicants required to submit FAFSA. *Faculty research:* Child language development and disorders, word finding in discourse of aphasica and non-aphasics, phonological assessment and remediation, behavioral and electrophysiological measures of aging and spatial hearing, behavioral and electrophysiological measures of bilingual speech perception. *Unit head:* Dr. Janet Koehnke, Chairperson, 973-655-3305. *Application contact:* Amy Aiello, Director of Graduate Admissions and Operations, 973-655-5147, Fax: 973-655-7869, E-mail: graduate.school@montclair.edu.

Montclair State University, The Graduate School, College of Humanities and Social Sciences, Department of Communication Sciences and Disorders, Program in Audiology, Montclair, NJ 07043-1624. Offers Au D. Part-time and evening/weekend programs available. *Students:* 27 full-time (24 women), 8 part-time (all women); includes 3 minority (1 Asian, non-Hispanic/Latino; 2 Hispanic/Latino). Average age 31. 68 applicants, 29% accepted, 15 enrolled. In 2011, 4 doctorates awarded. *Degree requirements:* For doctorate, comprehensive exam (for some programs), thesis/dissertation (for some programs). *Entrance requirements:* For doctorate, GRE General Test, 3 letters of recommendation, essay. Additional exam requirements/recommendations for international students: Required—TOEFL (minimum score 83 iBT), IELTS (minimum score 6.5). *Application deadline:* For fall admission, 2/1 for domestic students. Applications are processed on a rolling basis. Application fee: $60. Electronic applications accepted. *Financial support:* Federal Work-Study, scholarships/grants, and unspecified assistantships available. Support available to part-time students. Financial award application deadline: 3/1; financial award applicants required to submit FAFSA. *Faculty research:* Child language development and disorders, word finding in discourse of aphasica and non-aphasics, phonological assessment and remediation, behavioral and electrophysiological measures of aging and spatial hearing, behavioral and electrophysiological measures of bilingual speech perception. *Unit head:* Dr. Janet Koehnke, Chairperson, 973-655-3305. *Application contact:* Amy Aiello, Executive Director of The Graduate School, 973-655-5147, Fax: 973-655-7869, E-mail: graduate.school@montclair.edu. Web site: http://chss.montclair.edu/csd/programs/audiologyaud.html.

Montclair State University, The Graduate School, College of Humanities and Social Sciences, Department of Communication Sciences and Disorders, Program in Communication Sciences and Disorders, Montclair, NJ 07043-1624. Offers MA. Part-time and evening/weekend programs available. *Students:* 78 full-time (74 women), 21 part-time (all women); includes 7 minority (1 Black or African American, non-Hispanic/Latino; 2 Asian, non-Hispanic/Latino; 4 Hispanic/Latino), 2 international. Average age 31. 531 applicants, 10% accepted, 34 enrolled. In 2011, 21 degrees awarded. *Degree requirements:* For master's, comprehensive exam, thesis (for some programs). *Entrance requirements:* For master's, GRE General Test, 2 letters of recommendation, essay. Additional exam requirements/recommendations for international students: Required—TOEFL (minimum score 83 iBT), IELTS (minimum score 6.5). *Application deadline:* For fall admission, 3/1 for domestic students. Applications are processed on a rolling basis. Application fee: $60. Electronic applications accepted. *Financial support:* In 2011–12, 7 research assistantships with full tuition reimbursements (averaging $7,000 per year) were awarded; Federal Work-Study, scholarships/grants, and unspecified assistantships also available. Support available to part-time students. Financial award application deadline: 3/1; financial award applicants required to submit FAFSA. *Faculty research:* Child language development and disorders, word-finding in discourse of aphasica and non-aphasics, phonological assessment and remediation, behavioral and

electrophysiological measures of aging and spatial hearing, behavioral and electrophysiological measures of bilingual speech perception. *Unit head:* Dr. Janet Koehnke, Chairperson, 973-655-3305. *Application contact:* Amy Aiello, Director of Graduate Admissions and Operations, 973-655-5147, Fax: 973-655-7869, E-mail: graduate.school@montclair.edu. Web site: http://chss.montclair.edu/csd/programs/speechlanguage.html.

Murray State University, College of Health Sciences and Human Services, Department of Wellness and Therapeutic Sciences, Program in Speech-Language Pathology, Murray, KY 42071. Offers MS. *Accreditation:* ASHA. Part-time programs available. *Degree requirements:* For master's, comprehensive exam, thesis optional. *Entrance requirements:* For master's, GRE General Test or MAT, minimum GPA of 3.0. Additional exam requirements/recommendations for international students: Required—TOEFL.

National University, Academic Affairs, School of Education, Department of Special Education, La Jolla, CA 92037-1011. Offers autism (Certificate); deaf and hard-of-hearing education (MS); generalist in special education (MS); juvenile justice special education (MS); special education (MS). Part-time and evening/weekend programs available. Postbaccalaureate distance learning degree programs offered (no on-campus study). *Degree requirements:* For master's, thesis (for some programs). *Entrance requirements:* For master's, interview, minimum GPA of 2.5. Additional exam requirements/recommendations for international students: Required—TOEFL (minimum score 550 paper-based; 213 computer-based; 79 iBT), IELTS (minimum score 6). *Application deadline:* Applications are processed on a rolling basis. Application fee: $60 ($65 for international students). Electronic applications accepted. *Financial support:* Career-related internships or fieldwork, institutionally sponsored loans, scholarships/grants, and tuition waivers (partial) available. Support available to part-time students. Financial award application deadline: 6/30; financial award applicants required to submit FAFSA. *Unit head:* Dr. Denise Hexom, Associate Professor, 858-642-8320, Fax: 858-642-8729, E-mail: dhexom@nu.edu. *Application contact:* Dominick Giovanniello, Associate Regional Dean, 800-NAT-UNIV, Fax: 858-541-779, E-mail: dgiovann@nu.edu. Web site: http://www.nu.edu/OurPrograms/SchoolOfEducation/SpecialEducation.html.

Nazareth College of Rochester, Graduate Studies, Department of Speech-Language Pathology, Communication Sciences and Disorders Program, Rochester, NY 14618-3790. Offers MS. *Accreditation:* ASHA. Part-time programs available. Postbaccalaureate distance learning degree programs offered. *Degree requirements:* For master's, comprehensive exam. *Entrance requirements:* For master's, GRE General Test, minimum GPA of 3.0.

New Mexico State University, Graduate School, College of Education, Department of Special Education and Communication Disorders, Las Cruces, NM 88003-8001. Offers bilingual/multicultural special education (Ed D, PhD); communication disorders (MA); special education (MA, Ed D, PhD). *Accreditation:* ASHA (one or more programs are accredited); NCATE. Part-time and evening/weekend programs available. Postbaccalaureate distance learning degree programs offered. *Faculty:* 13 full-time (11 women), 1 part-time/adjunct (0 women). *Students:* 69 full-time (65 women), 56 part-time (41 women); includes 55 minority (2 American Indian or Alaska Native, non-Hispanic/Latino; 1 Asian, non-Hispanic/Latino; 51 Hispanic/Latino; 1 Two or more races, non-Hispanic/Latino), 4 international. Average age 37. 111 applicants, 32% accepted, 30 enrolled. In 2011, 41 master's, 3 doctorates awarded. *Degree requirements:* For master's, comprehensive exam, thesis optional; for doctorate, comprehensive exam, thesis/dissertation. *Entrance requirements:* For master's, GRE General Test or MAT. Additional exam requirements/recommendations for international students: Required—TOEFL (minimum score 550 paper-based; 79 iBT), IELTS (minimum score 6.5). *Application deadline:* For fall admission, 2/1 priority date for domestic students. Applications are processed on a rolling basis. Application fee: $40 ($50 for international students). Electronic applications accepted. *Expenses:* Tuition, state resident: full-time $5004; part-time $208.50 per credit. Tuition, nonresident: full-time $17,446; part-time $726.90 per credit. *Financial support:* In 2011–12, 1 research assistantship (averaging $1,975 per year), 16 teaching assistantships (averaging $10,248 per year) were awarded; fellowships, career-related internships or fieldwork, Federal Work-Study, and health care benefits also available. Support available to part-time students. Financial award application deadline: 3/1; financial award applicants required to submit FAFSA. *Faculty research:* Multicultural special education, multicultural communication disorders, mild disability, multicultural assessment, deaf education, early childhood, bilingual special education. *Unit head:* Dr. Eric Joseph Lopez, Interim Department Head, 575-646-2402, Fax: 575-646-7712, E-mail: leric@nmsu.edu. *Application contact:* Coordinator, 575-646-2736, Fax: 575-646-7721, E-mail: gradinfo@nmsu.edu. Web site: http://education.nmsu.edu/spedcd/.

New York Medical College, School of Health Sciences and Practice, Department of Speech-Language Pathology, Valhalla, NY 10595-1691. Offers MS. *Accreditation:* ASHA. *Faculty:* 5 full-time, 15 part-time/adjunct. *Students:* 75 full-time. Average age 27. 125 applicants, 28% accepted, 25 enrolled. In 2011, 25 master's awarded. *Degree requirements:* For master's, comprehensive exam. *Entrance requirements:* For master's, GRE, minimum GPA of 3.5. Additional exam requirements/recommendations for international students: Required—TOEFL (minimum score 637 paper-based; 250 computer-based; 117 iBT), IELTS (minimum score 7). *Application deadline:* For fall admission, 3/1 priority date for domestic students, 3/30 for international students. Applications are processed on a rolling basis. Application fee: $75 ($100 for international students). Electronic applications accepted. *Financial support:* Applicants required to submit FAFSA. *Unit head:* Dr. Ben C. Watson, Chair, 914-594-4239, Fax: 914-594-4853, E-mail: shsp_admissions@nymc.edu. *Application contact:* Pamela Suett, Director of Recruitment, 914-594-4510, Fax: 914-594-4292, E-mail: shsp_admissions@nymc.edu. Web site: http://nymc.edu./slp.

New York University, Steinhardt School of Culture, Education, and Human Development, Department of Communication Sciences and Disorders, New York, NY 10003-6860. Offers MS, PhD. *Accreditation:* ASHA. Part-time programs available. *Faculty:* 10 full-time (9 women), 23 part-time/adjunct (20 women). *Students:* 157 full-time (151 women), 32 part-time (30 women); includes 30 minority (3 Black or African American, non-Hispanic/Latino; 10 Asian, non-Hispanic/Latino; 13 Hispanic/Latino; 4 Two or more races, non-Hispanic/Latino), 7 international. Average age 31. 411 applicants, 42% accepted, 60 enrolled. In 2011, 68 master's awarded. *Degree requirements:* For master's, thesis (for some programs); for doctorate, thesis/dissertation. *Entrance requirements:* For master's, GRE General Test; for doctorate, GRE General Test, interview. Additional exam requirements/recommendations for international students: Required—TOEFL. *Application deadline:* For fall admission, 12/1 priority date for domestic students, 12/1 for international students. Applications are processed on a rolling basis. Application fee: $75. Electronic applications accepted. *Financial support:* Fellowships with full and partial tuition reimbursements, research assistantships with full and partial tuition reimbursements, career-related internships or fieldwork, Federal Work-Study, institutionally sponsored loans, scholarships/grants, tuition waivers (partial), and unspecified assistantships available. Support available to part-time students. Financial award application deadline: 2/1; financial award applicants required to submit FAFSA. *Faculty research:* Evidence-based practice, phonological acquisition, dysphagia, child language acquisition and disorders, neuromotor disorders. *Unit head:* Dr. Celia Stewart, Chairperson, 212-998-5230, Fax: 212-995-4356. *Application contact:* 212-998-5030, Fax: 212-995-4328, E-mail: steinhardt.gradadmissions@nyu.edu. Web site: http://steinhardt.nyu.edu/csd.

North Carolina Central University, Division of Academic Affairs, School of Education, Department of Communication Disorders, Durham, NC 27707-3129. Offers M Ed. *Accreditation:* ASHA. Part-time and evening/weekend programs available. *Degree requirements:* For master's, comprehensive exam, thesis or alternative. *Entrance requirements:* For master's, GRE, minimum GPA of 3.0 in major, 2.5 overall. Additional exam requirements/recommendations for international students: Required—TOEFL. *Faculty research:* Vocational programs for special needs learners.

Northeastern State University, Graduate College, College of Science and Health Professions, Department of Speech-Language Pathology, Tahlequah, OK 74464-2399. Offers MS. *Accreditation:* ASHA. Part-time and evening/weekend programs available. *Students:* 58 full-time (55 women); includes 12 minority (1 Black or African American, non-Hispanic/Latino; 11 American Indian or Alaska Native, non-Hispanic/Latino), 3 international. In 2011, 21 master's awarded. *Degree requirements:* For master's, thesis, capstone experience. *Entrance requirements:* For master's, GRE, minimum GPA of 2.75. Additional exam requirements/recommendations for international students: Required—TOEFL (minimum score 213 computer-based). *Application deadline:* For fall admission, 6/1 priority date for domestic students. Applications are processed on a rolling basis. Application fee: $25. Electronic applications accepted. *Financial support:* Teaching assistantships, career-related internships or fieldwork, and Federal Work-Study available. Financial award application deadline: 3/1. *Unit head:* Dr. Karen Patterson, Chair, 918-456-5111 Ext. 3778, Fax: 918-458-2351. *Application contact:* Margie Railey, Administrative Assistant, 918-456-5511 Ext. 2093, Fax: 918-458-2061, E-mail: railey@nsouk.edu.

Northeastern University, Bouvé College of Health Sciences, Department of Speech-Language Pathology and Audiology, Boston, MA 02115-5096. Offers audiology (Au D); speech-language pathology (MS). *Accreditation:* ASHA. *Faculty:* 12 full-time, 6 part-time/adjunct. *Students:* 91. 442 applicants, 35% accepted, 43 enrolled. In 2011, 32 master's, 9 doctorates awarded. *Degree requirements:* For master's, comprehensive exam, thesis optional. *Entrance requirements:* For master's, GRE General Test or MAT. Additional exam requirements/recommendations for international students: Required—TOEFL (minimum score 100 iBT). *Application deadline:* For fall admission, 2/15 for domestic students. Applications are processed on a rolling basis. Application fee: $50. Electronic applications accepted. *Financial support:* Research assistantships with full tuition reimbursements, teaching assistantships with full tuition reimbursements, career-related internships or fieldwork, Federal Work-Study, scholarships/grants, tuition waivers (partial), and unspecified assistantships available. Support available to part-time students. Financial award application deadline: 3/1; financial award applicants required to submit FAFSA. *Faculty research:* Psychoacoustics, applied and theoretical aspects of aphasia, developmentally delayed children, hearing impairments. *Unit head:* Dr. Therese O'Neil-Pirozzi, Director, 617-373-5750, Fax: 617-373-8756, E-mail: t.oneil-pirozzi@neu.edu. *Application contact:* Margaret Schnabel, Director of Graduate Admissions, 617-373-2708, E-mail: bouvegrad@neu.edu.

Northern Arizona University, Graduate College, College of Health and Human Services, Department of Communication Sciences and Disorders, Flagstaff, AZ 86011. Offers clinical speech pathology (MS). *Accreditation:* ASHA. Part-time programs available. *Faculty:* 10 full-time (9 women). *Students:* 60 full-time (52 women), 83 part-time (79 women); includes 28 minority (1 Black or African American, non-Hispanic/Latino; 2 Asian, non-Hispanic/Latino; 24 Hispanic/Latino; 1 Two or more races, non-Hispanic/Latino). Average age 28. 245 applicants, 11% accepted, 19 enrolled. In 2011, 63 degrees awarded. *Entrance requirements:* For master's, GRE General Test, minimum GPA of 3.0. Additional exam requirements/recommendations for international students: Required—TOEFL (minimum score 550 paper-based; 213 computer-based; 80 iBT), IELTS (minimum score 7). *Application deadline:* For fall admission, 1/31 priority date for domestic students, 1/31 for international students. Application fee: $65. Electronic applications accepted. *Expenses:* Tuition, state resident: full-time $7190; part-time $355 per credit hour. Tuition, nonresident: full-time $18,092; part-time $1005 per credit hour. *Required fees:* $818; $328 per semester. *Financial support:* Career-related internships or fieldwork, Federal Work-Study, scholarships/grants, health care benefits, tuition waivers (full and partial), and unspecified assistantships available. Financial award applicants required to submit FAFSA. *Faculty research:* Meta-analysis of language, laryngeal speech, aphasia. *Unit head:* Dr. Elise Lindstedt, Chair, 928-523-2969, E-mail: elise.lindstedt@nau.edu. *Application contact:* Joan Brakefield, Program Coordinator, 928-523-7444, Fax: 928-523-0034, E-mail: speech@nau.edu. Web site: http://nau.edu/chhs/csd/.

Northern Illinois University, Graduate School, College of Health and Human Sciences, School of Allied Health and Communicative Disorders, Program in Communicative Disorders, De Kalb, IL 60115-2854. Offers MA, Au D. *Accreditation:* ASHA (one or more programs are accredited); CORE. *Faculty:* 9 full-time (6 women), 2 part-time/adjunct (1 woman). *Students:* 119 full-time (106 women), 10 part-time (8 women); includes 23 minority (3 Black or African American, non-Hispanic/Latino; 4 Asian, non-Hispanic/Latino; 12 Hispanic/Latino; 4 Two or more races, non-Hispanic/Latino), 3 international. Average age 26. In 2011, 30 master's, 7 doctorates awarded. *Degree requirements:* For master's, comprehensive exam, thesis optional, practicum; for doctorate, practicum, research project. *Entrance requirements:* For master's, GRE General Test, minimum undergraduate GPA of 3.0; for doctorate, GRE General Test, minimum undergraduate GPA of 3.2. Additional exam requirements/recommendations for international students: Required—TOEFL (minimum score 550 paper-based; 213 computer-based). *Application deadline:* For fall admission, 2/1 priority date for domestic students, 5/1 for international students; for spring admission, 9/1 priority date for domestic students, 10/1 for international students. Applications are processed on a rolling basis. Application fee: $40. Electronic applications accepted. *Financial support:* Fellowships with full tuition reimbursements, research assistantships with full tuition reimbursements, teaching assistantships with full tuition reimbursements, career-related internships or fieldwork, Federal Work-Study, scholarships/grants, tuition waivers (full), and unspecified assistantships available. Support available to part-time students. Financial award applicants required to submit FAFSA. *Faculty research:* Impact of disability employment, deaf education, American Sign Language, autism, bilingualism. *Unit head:* Dr. Sue Ouellette, Chair, 815-753-1484, Fax: 815-753-9123, E-mail: souellette@niu.edu. *Application contact:* Graduate School Office, 815-753-0395, E-mail: gradsch@niu.edu. Web site: http://www.chhs.niu.edu/ahcd/about/index.shtml.

Northwestern University, The Graduate School, School of Communication, The Roxelyn and Richard Pepper Department of Communication Sciences and Disorders, Evanston, IL 60208. Offers audiology (Au D); communication sciences and disorders (PhD); speech, language, and learning (MS). Admissions and degrees offered through The Graduate School. *Accreditation:* ASHA (one or more programs are accredited). Terminal master's awarded for partial completion of doctoral program. *Degree requirements:* For master's, seminar paper; for doctorate, thesis/dissertation, pre-dissertation research project, qualifying exam. *Entrance requirements:* For master's and doctorate, GRE General Test, letters of recommendation. Additional exam requirements/recommendations for international students: Required—TOEFL. *Faculty*

research: Swallow behavior, verb structure in aphasia, language decline in dementia, cognitive processing in children, word-finding defects in children.

Nova Southeastern University, Abraham S. Fischler School of Education, Fort Lauderdale, FL 33314-7796. Offers education (MS, Ed D, Ed S); instructional design and diversity education (MS); instructional technology and distance education (MS); speech language pathology (MS, SLPD); teaching and learning (MA). Part-time and evening/weekend programs available. *Students:* 3,832 full-time (3,039 women), 4,222 part-time (3,452 women); includes 4,795 minority (3,209 Black or African American, non-Hispanic/Latino; 27 American Indian or Alaska Native, non-Hispanic/Latino; 97 Asian, non-Hispanic/Latino; 1,394 Hispanic/Latino; 16 Native Hawaiian or other Pacific Islander, non-Hispanic/Latino; 52 Two or more races, non-Hispanic/Latino), 54 international. Average age 40. In 2011, 1,669 master's, 383 doctorates, 402 other advanced degrees awarded. *Degree requirements:* For master's, practicum, internship; for doctorate, thesis/dissertation; for Ed S, thesis, practicum, internship. *Entrance requirements:* For master's, MAT or GRE (for some programs), CLAST, PRAXIS I, CBEST, General Knowledge Test, teaching certification, minimum GPA of 2.5, verification of teaching, BS; for doctorate, MAT or GRE, master's degree, minimum cumulative GPA of 3.0; for Ed S, MAT or GRE, master's degree, teaching certificate, minimum GPA of 3.0. Additional exam requirements/recommendations for international students: Recommended—TOEFL (minimum score 550 paper-based; 213 computer-based; 80 iBT), IELTS (minimum score 6). *Application deadline:* Applications are processed on a rolling basis. Application fee: $50. Electronic applications accepted. *Financial support:* In 2011–12, 2 fellowships with full tuition reimbursements (averaging $30,000 per year) were awarded; career-related internships or fieldwork, Federal Work-Study, and tuition waivers (full) also available. Support available to part-time students. Financial award application deadline: 4/15; financial award applicants required to submit FAFSA. *Unit head:* Dr. H. Wells Singleton, Provost/Dean, 954-262-8730, Fax: 954-262-3894, E-mail: singlew@nova.edu. *Application contact:* Dr. Jennifer Quinones Nottingham, Dean of Student Affairs, 800-986-3223 Ext. 8500, E-mail: jlquinon@nova.edu. Web site: http://www.fischlerschool.nova.edu/.

Nova Southeastern University, Health Professions Division, College of Health Care Sciences, Audiology Department, Fort Lauderdale, FL 33314-7796. Offers Au D. *Accreditation:* ASHA. *Faculty:* 5 full-time (all women), 5 part-time/adjunct (0 women). *Students:* 54 full-time (47 women); includes 22 minority (5 Black or African American, non-Hispanic/Latino; 2 Asian, non-Hispanic/Latino; 11 Hispanic/Latino; 1 Native Hawaiian or other Pacific Islander, non-Hispanic/Latino; 3 Two or more races, non-Hispanic/Latino), 8 international. Average age 26. 108 applicants, 22% accepted, 18 enrolled. In 2011, 14 doctorates awarded. *Degree requirements:* For doctorate, didactic and clinical competencies. *Entrance requirements:* For doctorate, GRE, three letters of recommendation, essays, transcripts. *Application deadline:* For winter admission, 2/15 priority date for domestic students, 2/15 for international students. Applications are processed on a rolling basis. Application fee: $50. Electronic applications accepted. *Financial support:* In 2011–12, 8 students received support, including 4 teaching assistantships (averaging $10,200 per year); scholarships/grants also available. Financial award application deadline: 5/30; financial award applicants required to submit FAFSA. *Faculty research:* Amplification, ethics, professionalism, auditory processing, tinnitus. *Unit head:* Dr. Erica Friedland, AuD, Chair and Associate Professor, 954-262-7765, Fax: 954-262-2908, E-mail: ericaf@nova.edu. *Application contact:* Monica Sanchez, Admissions Counselor, 954-262-1100, E-mail: mh1156@nova.edu. Web site: http://www.nova.edu/aud/.

The Ohio State University, Graduate School, College of Arts and Sciences, Division of Social and Behavioral Sciences, Department of Speech and Hearing Science, Columbus, OH 43210. Offers audiology (Au D, PhD); hearing science (PhD); speech hearing science (MA); speech-language pathology (MA, PhD); speech-language science (PhD). *Accreditation:* ASHA (one or more programs are accredited). *Faculty:* 13. *Students:* 85 full-time (79 women), 29 part-time (25 women); includes 13 minority (4 Black or African American, non-Hispanic/Latino; 4 Asian, non-Hispanic/Latino; 1 Hispanic/Latino; 4 Two or more races, non-Hispanic/Latino), 4 international. Average age 28. In 2011, 23 master's, 12 doctorates awarded. *Degree requirements:* For master's, thesis optional; for doctorate, thesis/dissertation. *Entrance requirements:* For master's and doctorate, GRE General Test. Additional exam requirements/recommendations for international students: Required—TOEFL (minimum score 620 paper-based; 260 computer-based), Michigan English Language Assessment Battery (minimum score 82). *Application deadline:* For fall admission, 8/15 priority date for domestic students, 7/1 for international students; for winter admission, 12/1 priority date for domestic students, 11/1 for international students; for spring admission, 3/1 priority date for domestic students, 2/1 for international students. Applications are processed on a rolling basis. Application fee: $40 ($50 for international students). Electronic applications accepted. *Expenses:* Tuition, state resident: full-time $11,400. Tuition, nonresident: full-time $28,125. Tuition and fees vary according to course load, degree level, campus/location and program. *Financial support:* Fellowships, research assistantships, teaching assistantships, Federal Work-Study, and institutionally sponsored loans available. Support available to part-time students. *Unit head:* Robert A. Fox, Chair, 614-292-1628, E-mail: fox.2@osu.edu. *Application contact:* Vikki Back, Graduate Program Coordinator, 614-292-4673, Fax: 614-292-7504, E-mail: back.3@osu.edu. Web site: http://sphs.osu.edu/.

Ohio University, Graduate College, College of Health Sciences and Professions, School of Rehabilitation and Communication Sciences, Division of Communication Sciences and Disorders, Athens, OH 45701-2979. Offers clinical audiology (Au D); hearing science (PhD); speech language pathology (MA); speech language science (PhD). *Students:* 70 full-time (64 women), 26 part-time (23 women); includes 4 minority (1 Black or African American, non-Hispanic/Latino; 2 Hispanic/Latino; 1 Two or more races, non-Hispanic/Latino), 11 international. 204 applicants, 19% accepted, 35 enrolled. In 2011, 30 master's, 5 doctorates awarded. *Unit head:* Dr. Jeffrey DiGiovanni, Director, 740-593-1260, Fax: 740-593-0287, E-mail: digiovan@ohio.edu. *Application contact:* Teresa M. Tyson-Drummer, Administrative Associate, 740-593-0309, Fax: 740-593-0287, E-mail: tyson-dr@ohio.edu. Web site: http://www.ouchsp.org/csd.

Oklahoma State University, College of Arts and Sciences, Department of Communications Sciences and Disorders, Stillwater, OK 74078. Offers MS. *Accreditation:* ASHA. *Faculty:* 8 full-time (6 women), 18 part-time/adjunct (17 women). *Students:* 52 full-time (all women), 3 part-time (1 woman); includes 7 minority (3 American Indian or Alaska Native, non-Hispanic/Latino; 1 Asian, non-Hispanic/Latino; 1 Hispanic/Latino; 2 Two or more races, non-Hispanic/Latino), 3 international. Average age 25. 92 applicants, 29% accepted, 23 enrolled. In 2011, 14 degrees awarded. *Degree requirements:* For master's, thesis or creative research project, clinical practicum experience. *Entrance requirements:* For master's, GRE, minimum GPA of 3.0 in undergraduate major. Additional exam requirements/recommendations for international students: Required—TOEFL (minimum score 550 paper-based; 79 iBT). *Application deadline:* For fall admission, 3/1 for international students; for spring admission, 8/1 for international students. Applications are processed on a rolling basis. Application fee: $40 ($75 for international students). Electronic applications accepted. *Expenses:* Tuition, state resident: full-time $4044; part-time $168.50 per credit hour. Tuition, nonresident: full-time $16,008; part-time $667 per credit hour. *Required fees:*

$2122; $88.45 per credit hour. One-time fee: $50. Tuition and fees vary according to course load and campus/location. *Financial support:* In 2011–12, 16 teaching assistantships (averaging $5,514 per year) were awarded; career-related internships or fieldwork, Federal Work-Study, scholarships/grants, health care benefits, tuition waivers (partial), and unspecified assistantships also available. Support available to part-time students. Financial award application deadline: 3/1; financial award applicants required to submit FAFSA. *Faculty research:* Speech communications. *Unit head:* Dr. Larry Mullins, Interim Head, 405-744-8938, Fax: 405-744-8070. *Application contact:* Dr. Sheryl Tucker, Dean, 405-744-7099, Fax: 405-744-0355, E-mail: grad-i@okstate.edu. Web site: http://cdis.okstate.edu/.

Old Dominion University, Darden College of Education, Program in Speech-Language Pathology, Norfolk, VA 23529. Offers MS Ed. *Accreditation:* ASHA. *Faculty:* 8 full-time (6 women), 5 part-time/adjunct (all women). *Students:* 36 full-time (all women), 15 part-time (14 women); includes 3 minority (1 Asian, non-Hispanic/Latino; 1 Native Hawaiian or other Pacific Islander, non-Hispanic/Latino; 1 Two or more races, non-Hispanic/Latino). Average age 26. 112 applicants, 21% accepted, 24 enrolled. In 2011, 18 master's awarded. *Degree requirements:* For master's, comprehensive exam, thesis, written exams, practica. *Entrance requirements:* For master's, GRE General Test, minimum GPA of 3.0 in major, 2.8 overall. *Application deadline:* For fall admission, 3/15 for domestic students; for spring admission, 11/1 for domestic students. Applications are processed on a rolling basis. Application fee: $50. Electronic applications accepted. *Expenses:* Tuition, state resident: full-time $9096; part-time $379 per credit. Tuition, nonresident: full-time $23,064; part-time $961 per credit. *Required fees:* $127 per semester. One-time fee: $50. *Financial support:* In 2011–12, 14 students received support, including 10 fellowships (averaging $5,000 per year), 1 research assistantship, 3 teaching assistantships with tuition reimbursements available (averaging $6,000 per year); career-related internships or fieldwork, scholarships/grants, and tuition waivers (partial) also available. Financial award application deadline: 2/15; financial award applicants required to submit CSS PROFILE or FAFSA. *Faculty research:* Childhood language disorders, phonological disorders, stuttering, social dialects, aphasia. *Total annual research expenditures:* $255,000. *Unit head:* Dr. Nicholas G. Bountress, Graduate Program Director, 757-683-4117, Fax: 757-683-5593, E-mail: nbountre@odu.edu. *Application contact:* William Heffelfinger, Director of Graduate Admissions, 757-683-5554, Fax: 757-683-3255, E-mail: gradadmit@odu.edu. Web site: http://education.odu.edu/esse/academics/spath/gradsp.shtml.

Our Lady of the Lake University of San Antonio, School of Professional Studies, Program in Communication and Learning Disorders, San Antonio, TX 78207-4689. Offers MA. *Accreditation:* ASHA. Part-time and evening/weekend programs available. *Degree requirements:* For master's, thesis optional, comprehensive clinical practicum. *Entrance requirements:* For master's, GRE General Test or MAT, interview. Additional exam requirements/recommendations for international students: Required—TOEFL. Electronic applications accepted. *Faculty research:* Multicultural issues, neurogenic disorders, neural networks, equivalence learning.

Penn State University Park, Graduate School, College of Health and Human Development, Department of Communication Sciences and Disorders, State College, University Park, PA 16802-1503. Offers MS, PhD, Certificate. *Accreditation:* ASHA (one or more programs are accredited). *Unit head:* Dr. Ann C. Crouter, Dean, 814-865-1428, Fax: 814-865-3282, E-mail: ac1@psu.edu. *Application contact:* Cynthia E. Nicosia, Director, Graduate Enrollment Services, 814-865-1795, Fax: 814-865-4627, E-mail: cey1@psu.edu. Web site: http://csd.hhdev.psu.edu/.

Portland State University, Graduate Studies, College of Liberal Arts and Sciences, Department of Speech and Hearing Sciences, Portland, OR 97207-0751. Offers speech-language pathology (MA, MS). *Accreditation:* ASHA (one or more programs are accredited). *Degree requirements:* For master's, variable foreign language requirement, thesis or alternative, oral exam. *Entrance requirements:* For master's, GRE General Test, minimum GPA of 3.0 in upper-division course work or 2.75 overall, BA/BS in speech and hearing sciences. Additional exam requirements/recommendations for international students: Required—TOEFL (minimum score 550 paper-based; 213 computer-based). *Faculty research:* Adolescents with clefts, spectral analysis of stuttering, communication in late talkers, speech intelligibility, brainstem response in fitting hearing aids.

Purdue University, Graduate School, College of Health and Human Sciences, Department of Speech, Language, and Hearing Sciences, West Lafayette, IN 47907. Offers audiology clinic (MS, Au D, PhD); linguistics (MS, PhD); speech and hearing science (MS, PhD); speech-language pathology (MS, PhD). *Accreditation:* ASHA. *Faculty:* 22 full-time (11 women), 3 part-time/adjunct (0 women). *Students:* 96 full-time (92 women), 5 part-time (3 women); includes 3 minority (1 Asian, non-Hispanic/Latino; 1 Hispanic/Latino; 1 Two or more races, non-Hispanic/Latino), 8 international. Average age 26. 269 applicants, 37% accepted, 38 enrolled. In 2011, 29 master's, 7 doctorates awarded. *Degree requirements:* For master's, comprehensive exam (for some programs), thesis optional; for doctorate, comprehensive exam, thesis/dissertation. *Entrance requirements:* For master's and doctorate, GRE General Test, minimum undergraduate GPA of 3.0 or equivalent. Additional exam requirements/recommendations for international students: Required—TOEFL (minimum score 77 iBT). *Application deadline:* For fall admission, 1/1 priority date for domestic students, 1/1 for international students; for spring admission, 8/1 priority date for domestic students, 8/1 for international students. Applications are processed on a rolling basis. Application fee: $60 ($75 for international students). Electronic applications accepted. *Financial support:* Fellowships with full tuition reimbursements, research assistantships with full tuition reimbursements, teaching assistantships with full tuition reimbursements, career-related internships or fieldwork, and scholarships/grants available. Support available to part-time students. Financial award application deadline: 2/1; financial award applicants required to submit FAFSA. *Faculty research:* Psychoacoustics, speech perception, speech physiology, stuttering, child language. *Unit head:* Dr. Keith R. Kluender, Head, 765-494-3788, Fax: 765-494-0771, E-mail: kkluender@purdue.edu. *Application contact:* Vickie L. Parker-Black, Graduate Contact, 765-494-3786, Fax: 765-494-0771, E-mail: vpblack@purdue.edu. Web site: http://www.purdue.edu/hhs/slhs/.

Queens College of the City University of New York, Division of Graduate Studies, Arts and Humanities Division, Department of Linguistics and Communication Disorders, Program in Speech Pathology, Flushing, NY 11367-1597. Offers MA. *Accreditation:* ASHA. *Faculty:* 9 full-time (6 women). *Students:* 30 full-time (28 women); includes 3 minority (2 Asian, non-Hispanic/Latino; 1 Hispanic/Latino). 274 applicants, 7% accepted, 16 enrolled. In 2011, 16 master's awarded. *Degree requirements:* For master's, thesis optional, clinical internships. *Entrance requirements:* For master's, GRE General Test, minimum GPA of 3.0. Additional exam requirements/recommendations for international students: Required—TOEFL. *Application deadline:* For fall admission, 2/1 for domestic students. Applications are processed on a rolling basis. Application fee: $125. *Expenses:* Tuition, state resident: part-time $345 per credit. Tuition, nonresident: part-time $640 per credit. *Required fees:* $145.25 per semester. *Financial support:* Career-related internships or fieldwork, Federal Work-Study, institutionally sponsored loans, and tuition waivers (partial) available. Support available to part-time students. Financial award application deadline: 4/1; financial award applicants required to submit FAFSA. *Unit head:* Dr. Sima Gerber, Graduate Adviser, 718-520-2934, E-mail: sima_gerber@

qc.edu. *Application contact:* Mario Caruso, Director of Graduate Admissions, 718-997-5200, Fax: 718-997-5193, E-mail: graduate_admissions@qc.edu.

Radford University, College of Graduate and Professional Studies, Waldron College of Health and Human Services, Department of Communication Sciences and Disorders, Radford, VA 24142. Offers speech-language pathology (MS). *Accreditation:* ASHA (one or more programs are accredited). Part-time programs available. *Faculty:* 7 full-time (all women), 7 part-time/adjunct (4 women). *Students:* 60 full-time (59 women), 3 part-time (all women); includes 6 minority (4 Black or African American, non-Hispanic/Latino; 1 Asian, non-Hispanic/Latino; 1 Hispanic/Latino). Average age 24. 157 applicants, 46% accepted, 34 enrolled. In 2011, 25 master's awarded. *Degree requirements:* For master's, comprehensive exam, thesis (for some programs). *Entrance requirements:* For master's, GRE, minimum GPA of 3.0; 3 letters of reference; personal essay, resume, official transcripts. Additional exam requirements/recommendations for international students: Required—TOEFL (minimum score 550 paper-based; 213 computer-based; 79 iBT). *Application deadline:* For fall admission, 2/15 priority date for domestic students, 12/1 for international students; for spring admission, 7/1 for international students. Applications are processed on a rolling basis. Application fee: $50. Electronic applications accepted. *Expenses:* Tuition, state resident: full-time $6262; part-time $261 per credit hour. Tuition, nonresident: full-time $14,540; part-time $606 per credit hour. *Required fees:* $2812; $117 per credit hour. Tuition and fees vary according to program. *Financial support:* In 2011–12, 26 students received support, including 24 research assistantships with partial tuition reimbursements available (averaging $4,406 per year), 3 teaching assistantships with partial tuition reimbursements available (averaging $5,939 per year); career-related internships or fieldwork, Federal Work-Study, institutionally sponsored loans, scholarships/grants, and unspecified assistantships also available. Financial award application deadline: 3/1; financial award applicants required to submit FAFSA. *Unit head:* Dr. Kenneth M. Cox, Chair, 540-831-7600, Fax: 540-831-7699, E-mail: kcox3@radford.edu. *Application contact:* Rebecca Conner, Graduate Admissions, 540-831-5431, Fax: 540-831-6061, E-mail: gradcollege@radford.edu. Web site: http://cosd-web.asp.radford.edu/.

The Richard Stockton College of New Jersey, School of Graduate and Continuing Studies, Program in Communication Disorders, Pomona, NJ 08240-0195. Offers MS. Fall enrollment only. *Accreditation:* ASHA. *Faculty:* 3 full-time (all women), 5 part-time/adjunct (4 women). *Students:* 40 full-time (35 women), 9 part-time (all women); includes 7 minority (2 Black or African American, non-Hispanic/Latino; 4 Hispanic/Latino; 1 Two or more races, non-Hispanic/Latino). Average age 27. 174 applicants, 32% accepted, 45 enrolled. *Degree requirements:* For master's, thesis optional. *Entrance requirements:* For master's, GRE, 3 letters of recommendation, official transcripts from all colleges/universities attended. *Application deadline:* For fall admission, 2/1 for domestic students. *Expenses:* Tuition, state resident: full-time $13,035; part-time $543 per credit. Tuition, nonresident: full-time $20,065; part-time $836 per credit. *Required fees:* $3920; $163 per credit. Tuition and fees vary according to degree level. *Financial support:* In 2011–12, 7 research assistantships with partial tuition reimbursements were awarded; fellowships also available. *Unit head:* Dr. Amy Hadley, Program Director, 609-626-3640, E-mail: graduatestudies@stockton.edu. *Application contact:* Tara Williams, Assistant Director of Enrollment Management, 609-626-3640, Fax: 609-626-6050, E-mail: gradschool@stockton.edu.

Rockhurst University, School of Graduate and Professional Studies, Program in Communication Sciences and Disorders, Kansas City, MO 64110-2561. Offers MS. *Accreditation:* ASHA. Part-time and evening/weekend programs available. *Faculty:* 5 full-time (all women), 1 part-time/adjunct (0 women). *Students:* 56 full-time (54 women), 17 part-time (all women); includes 5 minority (1 Black or African American, non-Hispanic/Latino; 4 Hispanic/Latino). Average age 25. 130 applicants, 43% accepted, 23 enrolled. In 2011, 36 master's awarded. *Entrance requirements:* For master's, GRE General Test, interview, minimum GPA of 3.0, letters of recommendation. Additional exam requirements/recommendations for international students: Required—TOEFL (minimum score 550 paper-based; 213 computer-based; 79 iBT). *Application deadline:* Applications are processed on a rolling basis. Application fee: $25. Electronic applications accepted. Application fee is waived when completed online. *Financial support:* Career-related internships or fieldwork, institutionally sponsored loans, and unspecified assistantships available. Financial award applicants required to submit FAFSA. *Faculty research:* Bioacoustics, physiology, applied speech science, pediatric nutrition/dysphagia, communication/cognition. *Unit head:* Dr. Carol Koch, Chair, 816-501-4518, Fax: 816-501-4169, E-mail: carol.koch@rockhurst.edu. *Application contact:* Cheryl Hooper, Director of Graduate Admission, 816-501-4097, Fax: 816-501-4241, E-mail: cherly.hooper@rockhurst.edu. Web site: http://www.rockhurst.edu/academic/csd/index.asp.

Rush University, College of Health Sciences, Department of Communication Disorders and Sciences, Chicago, IL 60612-3832. Offers audiology (Au D); speech-language pathology (MS). *Accreditation:* ASHA (one or more programs are accredited). Part-time programs available. *Degree requirements:* For master's, comprehensive exam, thesis optional; for doctorate, comprehensive exam, investigative project. *Entrance requirements:* For master's and doctorate, GRE General Test, minimum GPA of 3.0. Additional exam requirements/recommendations for international students: Required—TOEFL. Electronic applications accepted. *Expenses:* Contact institution. *Faculty research:* Electrostimulation of subthalamic nucleus, sensory feedback in speech modulation, sentence complexity in children's writing, velopharyngeal function, adult neurology.

St. Ambrose University, College of Education and Health Sciences, Program in Speech-Language Pathology, Davenport, IA 52803-2898. Offers MSLP. Part-time and evening/weekend programs available. *Faculty:* 6 full-time (5 women), 1 (woman) part-time/adjunct. *Students:* 25 full-time (all women), 21 part-time (18 women); includes 3 minority (1 Asian, non-Hispanic/Latino; 1 Hispanic/Latino; 1 Two or more races, non-Hispanic/Latino). Average age 25. 143 applicants, 27% accepted, 22 enrolled. In 2011, 22 master's awarded. *Entrance requirements:* Additional exam requirements/recommendations for international students: Required—TOEFL. *Application deadline:* For fall admission, 8/1 for domestic students; for winter admission, 12/15 for domestic students; for spring admission, 1/1 for domestic students. Applications are processed on a rolling basis. Application fee: $25. Electronic applications accepted. *Expenses: Tuition:* Full-time $13,770; part-time $765 per credit hour. *Required fees:* $60 per semester. Tuition and fees vary according to degree level, program and reciprocity agreements. *Financial support:* Career-related internships or fieldwork, scholarships/grants, tuition waivers (partial), and unspecified assistantships available. Financial award applicants required to submit FAFSA. *Unit head:* Dr. Elisa Huff, Director, 563-333-3922, E-mail: huffelisag@sau.edu. *Application contact:* Elizabeth Loveless, Director of Graduate Student Recruitment, 563-333-6271, Fax: 563-333-6268, E-mail: lovelesselizabethb@sau.edu. Web site: http://www.sau.edu/Academic_Programs/Master_of_Speech-Language_Pathology.html.

St. Cloud State University, School of Graduate Studies, College of Liberal Arts, Department of Communication Sciences and Disorders, St. Cloud, MN 56301-4498. Offers MS. *Accreditation:* ASHA. *Degree requirements:* For master's, comprehensive exam (for some programs), thesis or alternative. *Entrance requirements:* For master's, GRE General Test, minimum GPA of 2.75. Additional exam requirements/

recommendations for international students: Required—Michigan English Language Assessment Battery; Recommended—TOEFL (minimum score 550 paper-based; 213 computer-based), IELTS (minimum score 6.5). Electronic applications accepted.

St. John's University, St. John's College of Liberal Arts and Sciences, Department of Communication Sciences and Disorders, Queens, NY 11439. Offers MA, Au D. *Accreditation:* ASHA. Evening/weekend programs available. *Students:* 89 full-time (87 women), 67 part-time (61 women); includes 36 minority (9 Black or African American, non-Hispanic/Latino; 7 Asian, non-Hispanic/Latino; 15 Hispanic/Latino; 2 Native Hawaiian or other Pacific Islander, non-Hispanic/Latino; 3 Two or more races, non-Hispanic/Latino). Average age 25. 481 applicants, 28% accepted, 33 enrolled. In 2011, 57 master's, 5 doctorates awarded. *Degree requirements:* For master's, comprehensive exam, thesis, practicum; for doctorate, practicum. *Entrance requirements:* For master's, GRE, minimum GPA of 3.0, 3 letters of recommendation, statement of goals. Additional exam requirements/recommendations for international students: Required—TOEFL (minimum score 600 paper-based; 250 computer-based; 100 iBT), IELTS (minimum score 5.5). *Application deadline:* For fall admission, 2/1 for domestic and international students; for spring admission, 10/1 for domestic and international students. Applications are processed on a rolling basis. Application fee: $70. Electronic applications accepted. *Expenses:* Contact institution. *Financial support:* Research assistantships, career-related internships or fieldwork, and scholarships/grants available. Support available to part-time students. Financial award application deadline: 3/1; financial award applicants required to submit FAFSA. *Faculty research:* Bilingualism and adult and child language disorders, neural processing of speech, dysphagia, speech motor control, electrophysiological measurement of hearing, central auditory processing disorders, scholarship of teaching and learning, evidence-based education, developmental dyslexia. *Total annual research expenditures:* $24,000. *Unit head:* Dr. Jose G. Centeno, Chair, 718-990-2629, E-mail: centenoj@stjohns.edu. *Application contact:* Robert Medrano, Director of Graduate Admission, 718-990-1601, Fax: 718-990-5686, E-mail: gradhelp@stjohns.edu.

Saint Joseph's University, College of Arts and Sciences, Department of Education, Philadelphia, PA 19131-1395. Offers curriculum supervisor of instruction (Certificate); educational leadership (MS, Ed D); elementary education (MS, Certificate); elementary/middle years (Certificate); English second language specialist online (Certificate); hearing impaired: N-12th grade (Certificate); instructional technology (MS, Certificate); principal certification (Certificate); professional education (MS); reading specialist (MS, Certificate); reading supervisory (Certificate); secondary education (MS, Certificate); special education (MS, Certificate); superintendent's letter of eligibility (Certificate); supervisor of special education (Certificate); Wilson reading certificate online (Certificate). Part-time and evening/weekend programs available. Postbaccalaureate distance learning degree programs offered (no on-campus study). *Faculty:* 26 full-time (24 women), 83 part-time/adjunct (52 women). *Students:* 112 full-time (92 women), 923 part-time (709 women); includes 147 minority (92 Black or African American, non-Hispanic/Latino; 4 American Indian or Alaska Native, non-Hispanic/Latino; 19 Asian, non-Hispanic/Latino; 28 Hispanic/Latino; 4 Two or more races, non-Hispanic/Latino), 8 international. Average age 31. 285 applicants, 77% accepted, 176 enrolled. In 2011, 276 master's, 13 doctorates, 2 other advanced degrees awarded. *Entrance requirements:* For master's, 2 letters of recommendation, minimum GPA of 3.0, official transcripts, personal statement; for doctorate, GRE, master's degree from accredited institution, minimum graduate GPA of 3.5, computer competence, commitment to participate in cohort, interview with program director. Additional exam requirements/recommendations for international students: Required—TOEFL (minimum score 550 paper-based; 213 computer-based; 79 iBT). *Application deadline:* For fall admission, 7/15 priority date for domestic students, 4/15 for international students; for winter admission, 11/15 for domestic students, 1/15 for international students; for spring admission, 11/15 priority date for domestic students, 10/15 for international students. Applications are processed on a rolling basis. Application fee: $35. Electronic applications accepted. *Expenses:* Contact institution. *Financial support:* Unspecified assistantships available. Financial award applicants required to submit FAFSA. *Faculty research:* Public education professional development, factors predicting early mathematics skills for low income children. *Total annual research expenditures:* $92,975. *Unit head:* Dr. Jeanne Brady, Associate Dean, Education, 610-660-1580, E-mail: jebrady@sju.edu. *Application contact:* Kate McConnell, Director, Graduate College of Arts and Sciences Admissions and Retention, 610-660-3184, Fax: 610-660-3230, E-mail: kate.mcconnell@sju.edu.

Saint Louis University, Graduate Education, College of Arts and Sciences and Graduate Education, Department of Communication Sciences and Disorders, St. Louis, MO 63103-2097. Offers MA, MA-R. *Accreditation:* ASHA (one or more programs are accredited). *Degree requirements:* For master's, thesis optional, comprehensive oral and written exams. *Entrance requirements:* For master's, GRE General Test, letters of recommendation, resume. Additional exam requirements/recommendations for international students: Required—TOEFL (minimum score 525 paper-based; 194 computer-based). Electronic applications accepted. *Faculty research:* Communication disorders in culturally and linguistically diverse populations, disability study-specific to World Health Organization classifications, early intervention in communication disorders and literacy skills, communication difficulties in internationally adopted children, voice and swallowing disorders secondary to cancer treatments.

Saint Xavier University, Graduate Studies, College of Arts and Sciences, Department of Communication Sciences and Disorders, Chicago, IL 60655-3105. Offers speech-language pathology (MS). *Accreditation:* ASHA. *Entrance requirements:* For master's, GRE General Test, minimum GPA of 3.0, undergraduate course work in speech. *Application deadline:* For fall admission, 3/1 for domestic students. Application fee: $35. *Expenses:* Contact institution. *Financial support:* Career-related internships or fieldwork available. Support available to part-time students. Financial award applicants required to submit FAFSA. *Unit head:* Prof. Michael Flahive, Graduate Director, 773-298-3566, Fax: 773-298-3007, E-mail: flahive@sxu.edu. *Application contact:* Beth Gierach, Managing Director of Admission, 773-298-3053, Fax: 773-298-3076, E-mail: gierach@sxu.edu.

Salus University, George S. Osborne College of Audiology, Elkins Park, PA 19027-1598. Offers Au D. *Accreditation:* ASHA. *Entrance requirements:* Additional exam requirements/recommendations for international students: Required—TOEFL. Electronic applications accepted.

San Diego State University, Graduate and Research Affairs, College of Health and Human Services, School of Speech, Language, and Hearing Sciences, San Diego, CA 92182. Offers audiology (Au D); communicative disorders (MA); language and communicative disorders (PhD). PhD offered jointly with University of California, San Diego. *Accreditation:* ASHA (one or more programs are accredited). Part-time programs available. *Degree requirements:* For master's, comprehensive exam (for some programs), thesis (for some programs); for doctorate, thesis/dissertation. *Entrance requirements:* For master's and doctorate, GRE General Test. Additional exam requirements/recommendations for international students: Required—TOEFL. Electronic applications accepted. *Faculty research:* Brain/behavior relationships in language development, grammatical processing and language disorders, interdisciplinary training of bilingual speech pathologists.

San Francisco State University, Division of Graduate Studies, College of Education, Department of Special Education, Program in Communicative Disorders, San Francisco,

CA 94132-1722. Offers MS. *Accreditation:* ASHA. *Unit head:* Dr. Nicholas J. Certo, Department Chair, 415-338-1161, E-mail: ncerto@sfsu.edu. *Application contact:* Nancy Robinson, Office Coordinator, 415-338-1161, E-mail: nancyr@sfsu.edu. Web site: http://coe.sfsu.edu/sped.

San Jose State University, Graduate Studies and Research, Connie L. Lurie College of Education, Department of Communicative Disorders and Sciences, San Jose, CA 95192-0001. Offers speech-language pathology (MA). *Accreditation:* ASHA. Evening/weekend programs available. *Entrance requirements:* For master's, MAT. Electronic applications accepted.

Seton Hall University, School of Health and Medical Sciences, Program in Speech-Language Pathology, South Orange, NJ 07079-2697. Offers MS. *Accreditation:* ASHA. *Entrance requirements:* For master's, GRE, bachelor's degree, clinical experience; minimum GPA of 3.0, undergraduate preprofessional coursework in communication sciences and disorders. Additional exam requirements/recommendations for international students: Recommended—TOEFL. Electronic applications accepted. *Expenses: Tuition:* Part-time $1033 per credit hour. *Required fees:* $85 per semester. *Faculty research:* Child language disorders, motor speech control, voice disorders, dysphagia, early intervention/teaming.

South Carolina State University, School of Graduate Studies, Department of Health Sciences, Orangeburg, SC 29117-0001. Offers speech pathology and audiology (MA). *Accreditation:* ASHA. Part-time and evening/weekend programs available. *Faculty:* 7 full-time (6 women), 2 part-time/adjunct (0 women). *Students:* 34 full-time (33 women), 33 part-time (all women); includes 54 minority (53 Black or African American, non-Hispanic/Latino; 1 Hispanic/Latino), 1 International. Average age 30. 40 applicants, 95% accepted, 28 enrolled. In 2011, 13 master's awarded. *Degree requirements:* For master's, thesis optional, departmental qualifying exam. *Entrance requirements:* For master's, GRE or NTE, minimum GPA of 3.0. *Application deadline:* For fall admission, 6/15 for domestic and international students; for spring admission, 11/1 for domestic and international students. Application fee: $25. Electronic applications accepted. *Expenses:* Tuition, state resident: full-time $8688; part-time $514 per credit hour. Tuition, nonresident: full-time $17,600; part-time $1009 per credit hour. *Required fees:* $570. *Financial support:* In 2011–12, 7 fellowships (averaging $4,143 per year) were awarded; career-related internships or fieldwork, Federal Work-Study, and institutionally sponsored loans also available. Financial award application deadline: 6/1. *Unit head:* Dr. Gwendolyn D. Wilson, Chair, 803-536-7063, Fax: 803-536-8593, E-mail: gdwilson@scsu.edu. *Application contact:* Annette Hazzard-Jones, Program Coordinator II, 803-536-8809, Fax: 803-536-8812, E-mail: zs_ahazzard@scsu.edu.

Southeastern Louisiana University, College of Nursing and Health Sciences, Department of Communication Sciences and Disorders, Hammond, LA 70402. Offers MS. *Accreditation:* ASHA; NCATE. *Faculty:* 10 full-time (9 women), 1 (woman) part-time/adjunct. *Students:* 44 full-time (39 women), 17 part-time (15 women); includes 9 minority (3 Black or African American, non-Hispanic/Latino; 1 Asian, non-Hispanic/Latino; 3 Hispanic/Latino; 2 Two or more races, non-Hispanic/Latino), 1 international. Average age 26. 92 applicants, 100% accepted, 18 enrolled. In 2011, 20 degrees awarded. *Degree requirements:* For master's, comprehensive exam, thesis optional, 25 clock hours of clinical observation. *Entrance requirements:* For master's, GRE (verbal and quantitative), minimum GPA of 2.75; undergraduate degree; three letters of reference; favorable criminal background check. Additional exam requirements/recommendations for international students: Required—TOEFL (minimum score 500 paper-based; 173 computer-based; 61 iBT). *Application deadline:* For fall admission, 3/1 priority date for domestic students, 6/1 for international students; for spring admission, 10/1 priority date for domestic students, 10/1 for international students. Applications are processed on a rolling basis. Application fee: $20 ($30 for international students). Electronic applications accepted. *Expenses:* Tuition, state resident: full-time $3977; part-time $283 per semester hour. Tuition, nonresident: full-time $13,482; part-time $811 per semester hour. *Financial support:* Career-related internships or fieldwork, Federal Work-Study, institutionally sponsored loans, scholarships/grants, and unspecified assistantships available. Support available to part-time students. Financial award application deadline: 5/1; financial award applicants required to submit FAFSA. *Faculty research:* Aphasia, autism spectrum disorders, child language and literacy, language and dementia, clinical supervision. *Total annual research expenditures:* $19,424. *Unit head:* Dr. Rebecca Davis, Interim Department Head, 985-549-2214, Fax: 985-549-5030, E-mail: rdavis@selu.edu. *Application contact:* Sandra Meyers, Graduate Admissions Analyst, 985-549-5620, Fax: 985-549-5632, E-mail: admissions@selu.edu. Web site: http://www.selu.edu/acad_research/depts/csd.

Southeast Missouri State University, School of Graduate Studies, Department of Communication Disorders, Cape Girardeau, MO 63701-4799. Offers MA. Fall admission only. *Accreditation:* ASHA. *Faculty:* 7 full-time (5 women), 1 (woman) part-time/adjunct. *Students:* 32 full-time (31 women), 2 part-time (both women); includes 1 minority (Asian, non-Hispanic/Latino). Average age 24. 117 applicants, 16% accepted, 18 enrolled. In 2011, 15 master's awarded. *Degree requirements:* For master's, comprehensive exam (for some programs), thesis (for some programs), clinic/externship. *Entrance requirements:* For master's, GRE General Test, minimum undergraduate GPA of 3.0; departmental letter of application; 2 letters of recommendation; undergraduate degree in field or prerequisite coursework. Additional exam requirements/recommendations for international students: Required—TOEFL (minimum score 550 paper-based; 213 computer-based; 79 iBT); Recommended—IELTS (minimum score 6). *Application deadline:* For fall admission, 2/1 for domestic and international students. Applications are processed on a rolling basis. Application fee: $30 ($40 for international students). Electronic applications accepted. *Expenses:* Tuition, state resident: full-time $4896; part-time $272 per credit hour. Tuition, nonresident: full-time $8649; part-time $480.50 per credit hour. *Financial support:* In 2011–12, 9 students received support, including 4 teaching assistantships with full tuition reimbursements available (averaging $7,600 per year); career-related internships or fieldwork, Federal Work-Study, scholarships/grants, tuition waivers (full), and unspecified assistantships also available. Financial award application deadline: 6/30; financial award applicants required to submit FAFSA. *Faculty research:* Autism, SLP-assistants/implementers, lateral dominance, brain injury, dysphagia. *Unit head:* Dr. Thomas Linares, Chairperson and Graduate Program Coordinator, 573-651-2488, E-mail: tlinares@semo.edu. *Application contact:* Alisa Aleen McFerron, Assistant Director of Admissions for Operations, 573-651-5937, Fax: 573-651-5936, E-mail: amcferron@semo.edu. Web site: http://www5.semo.edu/commdisorders/.

Southern Connecticut State University, School of Graduate Studies, School of Health and Human Services, Department of Communication Disorders, New Haven, CT 06515-1355. Offers speech pathology (MS). *Accreditation:* ASHA. Part-time programs available. *Faculty:* 9 full-time (6 women), 5 part-time/adjunct (4 women). *Students:* 91 full-time (85 women), 4 part-time (3 women); includes 8 minority (1 Black or African American, non-Hispanic/Latino; 2 Asian, non-Hispanic/Latino; 3 Hispanic/Latino; 2 Two or more races, non-Hispanic/Latino), 1 international. 276 applicants, 14% accepted, 35 enrolled. In 2011, 34 master's awarded. *Degree requirements:* For master's, thesis or alternative, clinical experience. *Entrance requirements:* For master's, GRE, interview, minimum QPA of 3.0. *Application deadline:* For fall admission, 3/1 for domestic students. Application fee: $50. Electronic applications accepted. *Expenses:* Tuition, state

resident: full-time $5137; part-time $413 per credit. *Required fees:* $4008; $55 per term. *Financial support:* Career-related internships or fieldwork available. Financial award application deadline: 4/15; financial award applicants required to submit FAFSA. *Unit head:* Dr. James Dempsey, Chairperson, 203-392-5962, Fax: 203-392-5968, E-mail: dempsey@southernct.edu. *Application contact:* Dr. Deborah Weiss, Graduate Coordinator, 203-392-6615, Fax: 203-392-5968, E-mail: weissd1@southernct.edu.

Southern Illinois University Carbondale, Graduate School, College of Education and Human Services, Rehabilitation Institute, Department of Communication Disorders and Sciences, Carbondale, IL 62901-4701. Offers MS. *Accreditation:* ASHA. *Faculty:* 4 full-time (2 women). *Students:* 47 full-time (45 women), 7 part-time (6 women); includes 8 minority (6 Black or African American, non-Hispanic/Latino; 1 Asian, non-Hispanic/Latino; 1 Hispanic/Latino). Average age 29. 150 applicants, 8% accepted, 12 enrolled. In 2011, 27 master's awarded. *Degree requirements:* For master's, thesis. *Entrance requirements:* For master's, GRE, minimum GPA of 3.0. Additional exam requirements/recommendations for international students: Required—TOEFL. *Application deadline:* For fall admission, 2/1 for domestic students. Application fee: $20. *Financial support:* In 2011–12, 17 students received support, including 1 fellowship with full tuition reimbursement available, 7 research assistantships with full tuition reimbursements available; teaching assistantships with full tuition reimbursements available, career-related internships or fieldwork, Federal Work-Study, institutionally sponsored loans, tuition waivers (full), and unspecified assistantships also available. *Faculty research:* Neurolinguistics, language processing, child language, fluency, phonology. *Unit head:* Dr. John Benshoff, Director, 618-453-8281, E-mail: jbenshof@siu.edu. *Application contact:* Mary Falaster, Administrative Clerk, 618-453-8274, E-mail: mfalast@siu.edu.

Southern Illinois University Edwardsville, Graduate School, School of Education, Department of Special Education and Communication Disorders, Program in Speech-Language Pathology, Edwardsville, IL 62026. Offers MS. *Accreditation:* ASHA. Part-time and evening/weekend programs available. *Students:* 40 full-time (all women), 20 part-time (all women); includes 3 minority (1 Black or African American, non-Hispanic/Latino; 1 Hispanic/Latino; 1 Two or more races, non-Hispanic/Latino). 174 applicants, 3% accepted. In 2011, 29 master's awarded. *Degree requirements:* For master's, thesis (for some programs), final exam. *Entrance requirements:* For master's, GRE, minimum GPA of 3.0. Additional exam requirements/recommendations for international students: Required—TOEFL (minimum score 550 paper-based; 213 computer-based; 79 iBT), IELTS (minimum score 6.5). *Application deadline:* For fall admission, 2/1 for domestic and international students. Application fee: $30. Electronic applications accepted. Tuition and fees vary according to course load and program. *Financial support:* In 2011–12, 2 fellowships with full tuition reimbursements (averaging $8,370 per year), 3 research assistantships with full tuition reimbursements (averaging $9,927 per year), 9 teaching assistantships with full tuition reimbursements (averaging $9,927 per year) were awarded; institutionally sponsored loans, scholarships/grants, and unspecified assistantships also available. Financial award application deadline: 3/1; financial award applicants required to submit FAFSA. *Unit head:* Dr. T. K. Parthasarathy, Chair, 618-650-5423, E-mail: tpartha@siue.edu. *Application contact:* Michelle Robinson, Coordinator of Graduate Recruitment, 618-650-2811, Fax: 618-650-3523, E-mail: michero@siue.edu. Web site: http://www.siue.edu/education/secd/.

State University of New York at Fredonia, Graduate Studies, Department of Speech Pathology and Audiology, Fredonia, NY 14063-1136. Offers MS, MS Ed. *Accreditation:* ASHA. Part-time and evening/weekend programs available. *Degree requirements:* For master's, thesis optional, clinical practice. *Expenses:* Tuition, state resident: full-time $6666; part-time $370 per credit hour. Tuition, nonresident: full-time $11,376; part-time $632 per credit hour. *Required fees:* $1059.30; $58.85 per credit hour. Tuition and fees vary according to course load.

State University of New York at New Paltz, Graduate School, School of Liberal Arts and Sciences, Department of Communication Disorders, New Paltz, NY 12561. Offers communication disorders (MS), including speech-language disabilities, speech-language pathology. *Accreditation:* ASHA. Part-time and evening/weekend programs available. *Faculty:* 8 full-time (all women), 4 part-time/adjunct (3 women). *Students:* 49 full-time (48 women), 5 part-time (all women); includes 7 minority (1 Black or African American, non-Hispanic/Latino; 1 American Indian or Alaska Native, non-Hispanic/Latino; 4 Hispanic/Latino; 1 Two or more races, non-Hispanic/Latino). Average age 28. 195 applicants, 22% accepted, 23 enrolled. In 2011, 13 master's awarded. *Degree requirements:* For master's, comprehensive exam, thesis. *Entrance requirements:* For master's, GRE General Test or MAT, minimum GPA of 3.0. Additional exam requirements/recommendations for international students: Required—TOEFL (minimum score 550 paper-based; 213 computer-based; 80 iBT), IELTS (minimum score 6.5). *Application deadline:* For fall admission, 3/1 for domestic and international students. Application fee: $50. Electronic applications accepted. *Expenses:* Tuition, state resident: full-time $8870; part-time $370 per credit. Tuition, nonresident: full-time $15,160; part-time $632 per credit. *Required fees:* $1188; $34 per credit. $184 per semester. *Financial support:* In 2011–12, 5 students received support, including 1 fellowship (averaging $3,500 per year), 4 teaching assistantships with partial tuition reimbursements available (averaging $5,000 per year); Federal Work-Study, institutionally sponsored loans, scholarships/grants, health care benefits, and unspecified assistantships also available. Financial award application deadline: 8/1; financial award applicants required to submit FAFSA. *Unit head:* Dr. Stella Turk, Chairman, 845-257-3603, E-mail: turks@newpaltz.edu. *Application contact:* Dr. Anne Balant, Graduate Coordinator, 845-257-3453, E-mail: balanta@newpaltz.edu. Web site: http://www.newpaltz.edu/commdis/.

State University of New York at Plattsburgh, Division of Education, Health, and Human Services, Department of Communication Disorders, Plattsburgh, NY 12901-2681. Offers speech-language pathology (MA). *Accreditation:* ASHA. Part-time programs available. *Students:* 34 full-time (33 women); includes 4 minority (2 Black or African American, non-Hispanic/Latino; 2 Two or more races, non-Hispanic/Latino), 4 international. Average age 24. *Entrance requirements:* For master's, GRE General Test, minimum GPA of 3.0. Additional exam requirements/recommendations for international students: Required—TOEFL. *Application deadline:* For fall admission, 2/15 priority date for domestic students. Applications are processed on a rolling basis. Application fee: $75. *Financial support:* Career-related internships or fieldwork and Federal Work-Study available. Support available to part-time students. Financial award application deadline: 4/15; financial award applicants required to submit FAFSA. *Faculty research:* Ototoxins and noise effects on hearing, language impairment in Alzheimer's disease, attitudes on stuttering, diagnostic audiology. *Unit head:* Dr. Raymond Domenico, Chair, 518-564-3154, E-mail: domenira@plattsburgh.edu. *Application contact:* Marguerite Adelman, Assistant Director, Graduate Admissions, 518-564-4723, Fax: 518-564-4722, E-mail: adelmaml@plattsburgh.edu.

Stephen F. Austin State University, Graduate School, College of Education, Department of Human Services, Nacogdoches, TX 75962. Offers counseling (MA); school psychology (MA); special education (M Ed); speech pathology (MS). *Accreditation:* ACA (one or more programs are accredited); ASHA (one or more programs are accredited); CORE; NCATE. *Degree requirements:* For master's, comprehensive exam, thesis (for some programs). *Entrance requirements:* For master's,

GRE General Test, minimum GPA of 2.8. Additional exam requirements/recommendations for international students: Required—TOEFL.

Syracuse University, College of Arts and Sciences, Program in Audiology, Syracuse, NY 13244. Offers Au D, PhD. *Accreditation:* ASHA. Part-time programs available. *Students:* 21 full-time (20 women), 2 part-time (both women); includes 1 minority (Black or African American, non-Hispanic/Latino), 4 international. Average age 25. 46 applicants, 70% accepted, 10 enrolled. In 2011, 5 doctorates awarded. *Degree requirements:* For doctorate, thesis/dissertation. *Entrance requirements:* For doctorate, GRE General Test. Additional exam requirements/recommendations for international students: Required—TOEFL (minimum score 100 iBT). *Application deadline:* For fall admission, 2/1 priority date for domestic students, 2/1 for international students. Application fee: $75. Electronic applications accepted. *Expenses: Tuition:* Part-time $1206 per credit. *Financial support:* Fellowships with tuition reimbursements, research assistantships with tuition reimbursements, and teaching assistantships with tuition reimbursements available. Financial award application deadline: 1/1. *Unit head:* Dr. Linda Milosky, Department Chair, 315-443-9637. *Application contact:* Jennifer Steigerwald, Information Contact, 315-443-9615, E-mail: jssteige@syr.edu. Web site: http://csd.syr.edu/.

Syracuse University, College of Arts and Sciences, Program in Speech Language Pathology, Syracuse, NY 13244. Offers MS, PhD. *Accreditation:* ASHA. Part-time programs available. *Students:* 69 full-time (68 women), 1 (woman) part-time; includes 10 minority (3 Black or African American, non-Hispanic/Latino; 2 Asian, non-Hispanic/Latino; 3 Hispanic/Latino; 2 Two or more races, non-Hispanic/Latino), 6 international. Average age 24. 150 applicants, 54% accepted, 32 enrolled. In 2011, 23 master's, 1 doctorate awarded. *Degree requirements:* For master's, thesis or alternative; for doctorate, thesis/dissertation. *Entrance requirements:* For master's and doctorate, GRE. Additional exam requirements/recommendations for international students: Required—TOEFL (minimum score 100 iBT). *Application deadline:* For fall admission, 2/1 priority date for domestic students, 2/1 for international students. Application fee: $75. Electronic applications accepted. *Expenses: Tuition:* Part-time $1206 per credit. *Financial support:* Fellowships with full tuition reimbursements, research assistantships with full and partial tuition reimbursements, and teaching assistantships with full and partial tuition reimbursements available. Financial award application deadline: 1/1; financial award applicants required to submit FAFSA. *Unit head:* Dr. Linda Milosky, Chair, 315-443-9637, E-mail: csd@syr.edu. *Application contact:* Jennifer Steigerwald, Information Contact, 315-443-9615. Web site: http://csd.syr.edu/.

Teachers College, Columbia University, Graduate Faculty of Education, Department of Biobehavioral Studies, Program in Speech-Language Pathology, New York, NY 10027-6696. Offers Ed M, MS, Ed D, PhD. *Accreditation:* ASHA. *Faculty:* 6 full-time (4 women), 8 part-time/adjunct (6 women). *Students:* 105 full-time (101 women), 80 part-time (78 women); includes 62 minority (12 Black or African American, non-Hispanic/Latino; 22 Asian, non-Hispanic/Latino; 28 Hispanic/Latino), 22 international. Average age 27. 751 applicants, 15% accepted, 53 enrolled. In 2011, 48 degrees awarded. Terminal master's awarded for partial completion of doctoral program. *Degree requirements:* For doctorate, thesis/dissertation. *Entrance requirements:* For doctorate, professional master's degree in communication sciences and disorders. *Application deadline:* For fall admission, 1/2 priority date for domestic students. Applications are processed on a rolling basis. Application fee: $75. *Financial support:* Fellowships, teaching assistantships, career-related internships or fieldwork, Federal Work-Study, institutionally sponsored loans, and tuition waivers (full and partial) available. Support available to part-time students. Financial award application deadline: 2/1. *Faculty research:* Neuropathology of speech, stuttering, language disorders in children and adults, motor speech. *Unit head:* Prof. John Saxman, Program Coordinator, 212-678-3895, E-mail: saxman@tc.edu. *Application contact:* Morgan Oakes, Admission Counselor, 212-678-6613, E-mail: meo2142@columbia.edu.

Teachers College, Columbia University, Graduate Faculty of Education, Department of Health and Behavior Studies, Program in Hearing Impairment, New York, NY 10027-6696. Offers MA, Ed D. *Faculty:* 7 full-time (4 women), 11 part-time/adjunct (10 women). *Students:* 12 full-time (11 women), 14 part-time (all women); includes 8 minority (4 Black or African American, non-Hispanic/Latino; 2 Asian, non-Hispanic/Latino; 2 Hispanic/Latino), 1 international. Average age 24. 23 applicants, 78% accepted, 10 enrolled. In 2011, 16 master's awarded. *Degree requirements:* For master's, comprehensive exam (for some programs), project; for doctorate, thesis/dissertation. *Application deadline:* For fall admission, 1/2 priority date for domestic students; for spring admission, 11/1 for domestic students. Applications are processed on a rolling basis. Application fee: $65. Electronic applications accepted. *Financial support:* Fellowships, career-related internships or fieldwork, Federal Work-Study, institutionally sponsored loans, and tuition waivers (full and partial) available. Support available to part-time students. Financial award application deadline: 2/1; financial award applicants required to submit FAFSA. *Faculty research:* Language development, reading/writing, cognitive abilities, text analysis, auditory streaming. *Unit head:* Prof. Robert Kretschmer, Program Coordinator, 212-678-3867, E-mail: kretschmer@tc.edu. *Application contact:* Elizabeth Puleio, Assistant Director of Admission, 212-678-3710, Fax: 212-678-4171, E-mail: tcinfo@tc.edu.

Teachers College, Columbia University, Graduate Faculty of Education, Department of Health and Behavior Studies, Program in Teaching of Sign Language, New York, NY 10027-6696. Offers MA. *Accreditation:* NCATE. *Faculty:* 2 full-time (0 women). *Students:* 1 full-time (0 women), 11 part-time (8 women); includes 3 minority (2 Hispanic/Latino; 1 Two or more races, non-Hispanic/Latino). Average age 26. 7 applicants, 100% accepted, 6 enrolled. In 2011, 7 master's awarded. *Degree requirements:* For master's, comprehensive exam, project. *Entrance requirements:* For master's, demonstrated proficiency in American Sign Language. *Application deadline:* For fall admission, 1/15 priority date for domestic students; for spring admission, 11/1 for domestic students. Applications are processed on a rolling basis. Application fee: $65. Electronic applications accepted. *Financial support:* Applicants required to submit FAFSA. *Faculty research:* Teaching of the deaf and hard of hearing; linguistics of English and ASL; literacy development; text structure; school psychology; auditory streaming; sociology, anthropology, and history of deaf community and culture; American Sign Language; second language acquisition, curriculum, and instruction; disability studies. *Unit head:* Prof. Russell S. Rosen, Program Coordinator, 212-678-3813, E-mail: rrosen@tc.edu. *Application contact:* Elizabeth Puleio, Assistant Director of Admission, 212-678-3710, Fax: 212-678-4171, E-mail: eap2136@tc.columbia.edu.

Temple University, Health Sciences Center, College of Health Professions and Social Work, Department of Communication Sciences and Disorders, Philadelphia, PA 19122-6096. Offers communication sciences (PhD); linguistics (MA); speech-language-hearing (MA). *Accreditation:* ASHA. Part-time and evening/weekend programs available. *Faculty:* 7 full-time (3 women). *Students:* 65 full-time (63 women), 6 part-time (all women); includes 8 minority (4 Asian, non-Hispanic/Latino; 2 Hispanic/Latino; 2 Two or more races, non-Hispanic/Latino), 1 international. Average age 26. 383 applicants, 18% accepted, 26 enrolled. In 2011, 10 master's, 1 doctorate awarded. *Degree requirements:* For doctorate, thesis/dissertation. *Entrance requirements:* For master's and doctorate, GRE General Test, minimum GPA of 3.0. Additional exam requirements/recommendations for international students: Required—TOEFL (minimum score 550 paper-based; 213 computer-based; 79 iBT). Application fee: $50. Electronic applications accepted. *Expenses:* Tuition, state resident: full-time $12,366; part-time $687 per credit hour. Tuition, nonresident: full-time $17,298; part-time $961 per credit hour. *Required fees:* $590; $213 per year. *Financial support:* Fellowships, research assistantships, teaching assistantships with full tuition reimbursements, career-related internships or fieldwork, Federal Work-Study, institutionally sponsored loans, and tuition waivers (partial) available. Financial award application deadline: 1/15. *Faculty research:* Fluency, infants and families, multilingual/multicultural communication, geriatrics, conflict process, language, health communication. *Unit head:* Dr. Carol Scheffner Hammer, Interim Chair, 215-204-7543, E-mail: cjhammer@temple.edu. *Application contact:* Tara Schumacher, Coordinator of Outreach, 215-204-6575, Fax: 215-204-8781, E-mail: tara.schumacher@temple.edu. Web site: http://chpsw.temple.edu/commsci/.

Tennessee State University, The School of Graduate Studies and Research, College of Health Sciences, Department of Speech Pathology and Audiology, Nashville, TN 37209-1561. Offers speech and hearing science (MS). Part-time programs available. Postbaccalaureate distance learning degree programs offered (minimal on-campus study). *Degree requirements:* For master's, comprehensive exam, thesis optional. *Entrance requirements:* For master's, GRE General Test, MAT, minimum GPA of 3.5. Additional exam requirements/recommendations for international students: Required—TOEFL. *Faculty research:* Auditory dunction to sickle cell disease, assessment and management of dysphagia, early intervention language disorders, multicultural diversity.

Texas A&M University–Kingsville, College of Graduate Studies, College of Arts and Sciences, Department of Communication, Kingsville, TX 78363. Offers MS. *Accreditation:* ASHA. *Degree requirements:* For master's, comprehensive exam, thesis or alternative. *Entrance requirements:* For master's, GRE General Test. Additional exam requirements/recommendations for international students: Required—TOEFL.

Texas Christian University, Harris College of Nursing and Health Sciences, Department of Communication Sciences and Disorders, Fort Worth, TX 76129-0002. Offers speech-language pathology (MS). *Accreditation:* ASHA. *Faculty:* 6 full-time (4 women). *Students:* 23 full-time (20 women), 3 part-time (all women); includes 9 minority (1 Black or African American, non-Hispanic/Latino; 1 American Indian or Alaska Native, non-Hispanic/Latino; 7 Hispanic/Latino). Average age 24. 157 applicants, 9% accepted, 13 enrolled. In 2011, 15 master's awarded. *Degree requirements:* For master's, comprehensive exam, thesis optional. *Entrance requirements:* For master's, GRE General Test, previous course work in speech-language pathology. Additional exam requirements/recommendations for international students: Required—TOEFL. *Application deadline:* For fall admission, 2/1 for domestic students. Application fee: $60. *Expenses: Tuition:* Full-time $20,250; part-time $1125 per credit hour. Part-time tuition and fees vary according to course load and program. *Financial support:* In 2011–12, 26 students received support, including 26 teaching assistantships; unspecified assistantships also available. Financial award application deadline: 2/1; financial award applicants required to submit FAFSA. *Unit head:* Dr. Christopher Watts, Chairperson, 817-257-7621, E-mail: c.watts@tcu.edu. *Application contact:* Admissions, TCU Graduate Studies Office, 817-257-7515, Fax: 817-257-7484, E-mail: frogmail@tcu.edu. Web site: http://www.csd.tcu.edu/graduate.asp.

Texas State University–San Marcos, Graduate School, College of Health Professions, Department of Communication Disorders, San Marcos, TX 78666. Offers MA, MSCD. *Accreditation:* ASHA (one or more programs are accredited). Part-time programs available. *Faculty:* 9 full-time (7 women). *Students:* 55 full-time (53 women); includes 28 minority (1 Black or African American, non-Hispanic/Latino; 27 Hispanic/Latino). Average age 25. 350 applicants, 8% accepted, 17 enrolled. In 2011, 23 master's awarded. *Degree requirements:* For master's, comprehensive exam, thesis (for some programs), practicum. *Entrance requirements:* For master's, minimum GPA of 3.0 in communications disorders and in last 60 hours of course work; 25 hours of observation; 2 letters of recommendation from professors in previous major; resume on form provided by department. Additional exam requirements/recommendations for international students: Required—TOEFL (minimum score 550 paper-based; 213 computer-based; 78 iBT). *Application deadline:* For fall admission, 2/1 for domestic and international students. Applications are processed on a rolling basis. Application fee: $40 ($90 for international students). Electronic applications accepted. *Expenses:* Tuition, state resident: full-time $6408; part-time $3204 per semester. Tuition, nonresident: full-time $14,832; part-time $7416 per semester. *Required fees:* $1824; $912 per semester. Tuition and fees vary according to course load. *Financial support:* In 2011–12, 42 students received support, including 6 research assistantships (averaging $5,004 per year), 6 teaching assistantships (averaging $5,076 per year); fellowships, career-related internships or fieldwork, Federal Work-Study, institutionally sponsored loans, scholarships/grants, and unspecified assistantships also available. Support available to part-time students. Financial award application deadline: 4/1; financial award applicants required to submit FAFSA. *Faculty research:* Cognitive Impairment. *Total annual research expenditures:* $41,623. *Unit head:* Dr. Maria Dianna Gonzales, Chair, 512-245-2330, Fax: 512-245-2029, E-mail: mg29@txstate.edu. *Application contact:* Dr. J. Michael Willoughby, Dean of Graduate School, 512-245-2581, Fax: 512-245-8365, E-mail: gradcollege@txstate.edu. Web site: http://www.health.txstate.edu/CDIS/.

Texas Tech University Health Sciences Center, School of Allied Health Sciences, Program in Speech, Language and Hearing Sciences, Lubbock, TX 79430. Offers MS, Au D, PhD. *Accreditation:* ASHA (one or more programs are accredited). *Faculty:* 22 full-time (17 women). *Students:* 117 full-time (113 women), 12 part-time (8 women); includes 20 minority (1 Black or African American, non-Hispanic/Latino; 1 American Indian or Alaska Native, non-Hispanic/Latino; 3 Asian, non-Hispanic/Latino; 13 Hispanic/Latino; 1 Native Hawaiian or other Pacific Islander, non-Hispanic/Latino; 1 Two or more races, non-Hispanic/Latino). Average age 26. 188 applicants, 26% accepted, 49 enrolled. In 2011, 29 master's, 9 doctorates awarded. *Degree requirements:* For master's, comprehensive exam, thesis optional; for doctorate, comprehensive exam, thesis/dissertation. *Entrance requirements:* For master's, GRE General Test, GRE Writing Test; for doctorate, GRE. Additional exam requirements/recommendations for international students: Required—TOEFL, IELTS. *Application deadline:* For fall admission, 11/1 for domestic students; for spring admission, 2/1 for domestic students. Application fee: $35. Electronic applications accepted. *Financial support:* In 2011–12, 15 students received support, including 6 research assistantships, 5 teaching assistantships; career-related internships or fieldwork, institutionally sponsored loans, and scholarships/grants also available. Financial award application deadline: 9/1; financial award applicants required to submit FAFSA. *Faculty research:* Craniofacial anomalies, evoked potentials, neurolinguistics, language simulations, vocal fold burns. *Total annual research expenditures:* $150,000. *Unit head:* Dr. Rajinder Koul, Chairperson, 806-743-5660 Ext. 227, Fax: 806-742-0907, E-mail: rajinder.koul@ttuhsc.edu. *Application contact:* Jeri Moravcik, Assistant Director, 806-743-3220, Fax: 806-742-2994, E-mail: jeri.moravcik@ttuhsc.edu. Web site: http://www.ttuhsc.edu/sah/cdu/.

Texas Woman's University, Graduate School, College of Health Sciences, Department of Communication Sciences and Disorders, Denton, TX 76201. Offers education of the deaf (MS); speech/language pathology (MS). *Accreditation:* ASHA. Part-time programs available. Postbaccalaureate distance learning degree programs offered (no on-campus

study). *Faculty:* 17 full-time (15 women). *Students:* 171 full-time (160 women), 38 part-time (35 women); includes 76 minority (10 Black or African American, non-Hispanic/Latino; 1 American Indian or Alaska Native, non-Hispanic/Latino; 11 Asian, non-Hispanic/Latino; 54 Hispanic/Latino). Average age 32. 139 applicants, 10% accepted, 12 enrolled. In 2011, 148 master's awarded. *Degree requirements:* For master's, comprehensive exam, thesis (for some programs). *Entrance requirements:* For master's, GRE General Test (preferred minimum score 156 [550 old version] Verbal, 140 [400 old version] Quantitative), 2 letters of reference (3 for speech/language pathology), personal essay. Additional exam requirements/recommendations for international students: Required—TOEFL (minimum score 550 paper-based; 213 computer-based; 79 iBT). *Application deadline:* For fall admission, 2/1 priority date for domestic students, 2/1 for international students. Applications are processed on a rolling basis. Application fee: $50 ($75 for international students). Electronic applications accepted. *Expenses:* Tuition, state resident: full-time $3834; part-time $213 per credit hour. Tuition, nonresident: full-time $9468; part-time $526 per credit hour. *Required fees:* $213 per credit hour. Tuition and fees vary according to course load. *Financial support:* In 2011–12, 94 students received support, including 9 research assistantships (averaging $9,684 per year); career-related internships or fieldwork, Federal Work-Study, institutionally sponsored loans, scholarships/grants, traineeships, health care benefits, and unspecified assistantships also available. Support available to part-time students. Financial award application deadline: 3/1; financial award applicants required to submit FAFSA. *Faculty research:* Stroke, language assessment auditory processing and relationship between speech and language, effectiveness of distance education learning, neuromodulation of recovery of aphasia. *Total annual research expenditures:* $11,160. *Unit head:* Dr. Gay James, Interim Chair, 940-898-2025, Fax: 940-898-2070, E-mail: coms@twu.edu. *Application contact:* Dr. Samuel Wheeler, Assistant Director of Admissions, 940-898-3188, Fax: 940-898-3081, E-mail: wheelersr@twu.edu. Web site: http://www.twu.edu/communication-sciences/.

Touro College, School of Health Sciences, Bay Shore, NY 11706. Offers occupational therapy (MS); Oriental medicine (MSOM); physical therapy (DPT); public health (MPH); speech-language pathology (MS). *Faculty:* 20 full-time, 94 part-time/adjunct. *Students:* 136. *Expenses:* Contact institution. *Financial support:* Fellowships available. *Unit head:* Dr. Louis Primavera, Dean, 516-673-3200. *Application contact:* Dean, School of Health Sciences, 516-673-3200.

Towson University, Program in Audiology, Towson, MD 21252-0001. Offers Au D. *Accreditation:* ASHA. *Students:* 39 full-time (36 women), 6 part-time (all women); includes 7 minority (4 Black or African American, non-Hispanic/Latino; 1 Asian, non-Hispanic/Latino; 2 Hispanic/Latino). *Entrance requirements:* For doctorate, GRE, 3 letters of recommendation, minimum GPA of 3.0. Additional exam requirements/recommendations for international students: Required—TOEFL (minimum score 600 paper-based). *Application deadline:* For fall admission, 2/1 for domestic students. Application fee: $50. Electronic applications accepted. *Expenses:* Tuition, state resident: part-time $337 per credit. Tuition, nonresident: part-time $709 per credit. *Required fees:* $99 per credit. *Financial support:* Tuition waivers (partial) available. Financial award application deadline: 4/1; financial award applicants required to submit FAFSA. *Faculty research:* Auditory processing, cortical potentials, otoacoustic emissions, electrophysiology, cochlear implants. *Unit head:* Dr. Diana Emanuel, Graduate Program Director, 410-704-2417, Fax: 410-704-4131, E-mail: demanuel@towson.edu. Web site: http://www.towson.edu/csd/.

Towson University, Program in Speech-Language Pathology, Towson, MD 21252-0001. Offers MS. *Accreditation:* ASHA. *Students:* 91 full-time (88 women), 1 (woman) part-time; includes 5 minority (all Black or African American, non-Hispanic/Latino), 1 international. *Degree requirements:* For master's, thesis (for some programs), exam. *Entrance requirements:* For master's, GRE, minimum GPA of 3.0 in major, undergraduate coursework in speech-language pathology with 42 hours clinical observation or 33 units in pathology. Additional exam requirements/recommendations for international students: Required—TOEFL (minimum score 600 paper-based). *Application deadline:* For fall admission, 1/15 for domestic students. Application fee: $50. Electronic applications accepted. *Expenses:* Tuition, state resident: part-time $337 per credit. Tuition, nonresident: part-time $709 per credit. *Required fees:* $99 per credit. *Financial support:* In 2011–12, 7 students received support. Application deadline: 4/1; applicants required to submit FAFSA. *Unit head:* Dr. Celia Bassich, Graduate Program Director, 410-704-2449, Fax: 410-704-4131, E-mail: cbassich@towson.edu. Web site: http://www.towson.edu/csd/index.htm.

Truman State University, Graduate School, School of Health Sciences and Education, Program in Communication Disorders, Kirksville, MO 63501-4221. Offers MA. *Accreditation:* ASHA. *Degree requirements:* For master's, comprehensive exam, thesis optional. *Entrance requirements:* For master's, GRE General Test, minimum GPA of 3.0. Additional exam requirements/recommendations for international students: Required—TOEFL (minimum score 550 paper-based; 213 computer-based). Electronic applications accepted.

Universidad del Turabo, Graduate Programs, School of Health Sciences, Program in Speech and Language Pathology, Gurabo, PR 00778-3030. Offers MS. *Students:* 37 full-time (34 women), 16 part-time (15 women); includes 50 minority (all Hispanic/Latino). Average age 29. 71 applicants, 61% accepted, 19 enrolled. In 2011, 16 master's awarded. *Unit head:* David Mendez, Head, 787-743-7979. *Application contact:* Virginia Gonzalez, Admissions Officer, 787-746-3009.

Université de Montréal, Faculty of Medicine, School of Speech Therapy and Audiology, Montréal, QC H3C 3J7, Canada. Offers audiology (PMS); speech therapy (PMS, DESS). *Degree requirements:* For master's, thesis. *Entrance requirements:* For master's, B Sc in speech-language pathology and audiology, proficiency in French. Electronic applications accepted. *Faculty research:* Aphasia in adults, dysarthria, speech and hearing-impaired children, noise-induced hearing impairment, computerized audiometry.

Université Laval, Faculty of Medicine, Graduate Programs in Medicine, Program in Speech Therapy, Québec, QC G1K 7P4, Canada. Offers M Sc. *Entrance requirements:* For master's, knowledge of French, interview. Electronic applications accepted.

University at Buffalo, the State University of New York, Graduate School, College of Arts and Sciences, Department of Communicative Disorders and Sciences, Buffalo, NY 14260. Offers audiology (Au D); communicative disorders and sciences (MA, PhD). *Accreditation:* ASHA (one or more programs are accredited). *Faculty:* 20 full-time (15 women), 2 part-time/adjunct (1 woman). *Students:* 108 full-time (103 women); includes 9 minority (1 Black or African American, non-Hispanic/Latino; 7 Asian, non-Hispanic/Latino; 1 Hispanic/Latino), 40 international. 168 applicants, 43% accepted, 45 enrolled. In 2011, 24 master's, 9 doctorates awarded. *Degree requirements:* For master's, thesis or alternative, exam; for doctorate, thesis/dissertation, exams. *Entrance requirements:* For master's and doctorate, GRE General Test, minimum GPA of 3.0. Additional exam requirements/recommendations for international students: Required—TOEFL (minimum score 550 paper-based; 213 computer-based; 79 iBT). *Application deadline:* For fall admission, 1/1 priority date for domestic students, 1/1 for international students. Application fee: $75. Electronic applications accepted. *Financial support:* In 2011–12, 20 students received support, including 2 fellowships with full tuition reimbursements available (averaging $3,000 per year), 4 research assistantships with full and partial tuition reimbursements available (averaging $13,500 per year), 18 teaching assistantships with full and partial tuition reimbursements available (averaging $8,400 per year); career-related internships or fieldwork, Federal Work-Study, institutionally sponsored loans, scholarships/grants, health care benefits, tuition waivers (partial), and unspecified assistantships also available. Financial award applicants required to submit FAFSA. *Faculty research:* Hearing and speech science, child and adult language disorders, augmentative communication, cochlear implants, tinnitis. *Total annual research expenditures:* $2.3 million. *Unit head:* Dr. Joan Sussman, Chairperson, 716-829-5551, Fax: 716-829-3979, E-mail: jsussman@buffalo.edu. *Application contact:* Linda L. Mehnert, Graduate Admissions Coordinator, 716-829-5570, Fax: 716-829-3979, E-mail: lmehnert@buffalo.edu. Web site: http://cdswebserver.med.buffalo.edu/drupal/.

The University of Akron, Graduate School, College of Health Sciences and Human Services, School of Speech-Language Pathology and Audiology, Program in Audiology, Akron, OH 44325. Offers Au D. *Accreditation:* ASHA. *Students:* 40 full-time (34 women), 1 international. Average age 25. 54 applicants, 30% accepted, 10 enrolled. In 2011, 9 doctorates awarded. *Degree requirements:* For doctorate, 2000 clock hours of clinical experience, academic and clinical competency-based exams. *Entrance requirements:* For doctorate, GRE, minimum GPA of 3.0, letters of recommendation. Additional exam requirements/recommendations for international students: Required—TOEFL (minimum score 550 paper-based; 213 computer-based; 79 iBT). *Application deadline:* For fall admission, 2/1 for domestic and international students. Application fee: $30 ($40 for international students). Electronic applications accepted. *Expenses:* Tuition, state resident: full-time $7038; part-time $391 per credit hour. Tuition, nonresident: full-time $12,051; part-time $670 per credit hour. *Required fees:* $1274; $34 per credit hour. *Unit head:* Dr. Sharon Lesner, Coordinator, 330-972-6118, E-mail: lesner@uakron.edu. *Application contact:* Dr. Mark Tausig, Associate Dean, 330-972-6266, Fax: 330-972-6475, E-mail: mtausig@uakron.edu.

The University of Akron, Graduate School, College of Health Sciences and Human Services, School of Speech-Language Pathology and Audiology, Program in Speech-Language Pathology, Akron, OH 44325. Offers MA. *Accreditation:* ASHA. *Students:* 83 full-time (81 women), 38 part-time (36 women); includes 8 minority (5 Black or African American, non-Hispanic/Latino; 1 Asian, non-Hispanic/Latino; 2 Hispanic/Latino). Average age 27. 289 applicants, 15% accepted, 40 enrolled. In 2011, 55 master's awarded. *Degree requirements:* For master's, thesis optional. *Entrance requirements:* For master's, GRE, baccalaureate degree in speech-language pathology, minimum GPA of 2.75, three letters of recommendation, statement of purpose, resume. Additional exam requirements/recommendations for international students: Required—TOEFL (minimum score 550 paper-based; 213 computer-based; 79 iBT). *Application deadline:* For fall admission, 1/1 for domestic and international students. Application fee: $30 ($40 for international students). Electronic applications accepted. *Expenses:* Tuition, state resident: full-time $7038; part-time $391 per credit hour. Tuition, nonresident: full-time $12,051; part-time $670 per credit hour. *Required fees:* $1274; $34 per credit hour. *Unit head:* Dr. Roberta DePompei, Director, 330-972-6114, E-mail: rdepom1@uakron.edu. *Application contact:* Dr. Mark Tausig, Associate Dean, 330-972-6266, Fax: 330-972-6475, E-mail: mtausig@uakron.edu.

The University of Alabama, Graduate School, College of Arts and Sciences, Department of Communicative Disorders, Tuscaloosa, AL 35487-0242. Offers speech language pathology (MS). *Accreditation:* ASHA. *Faculty:* 11 full-time (8 women), 1 (woman) part-time/adjunct. *Students:* 50 full-time (49 women), 7 part-time (all women); includes 12 minority (7 Black or African American, non-Hispanic/Latino; 5 Hispanic/Latino). Average age 24. 148 applicants, 36% accepted, 25 enrolled. In 2011, 25 degrees awarded. *Degree requirements:* For master's, comprehensive exam, thesis optional. *Entrance requirements:* For master's, GRE or MAT, minimum GPA of 3.0. Additional exam requirements/recommendations for international students: Required—TOEFL. *Application deadline:* For fall and spring admission, 2/1 for domestic and international students. Applications are processed on a rolling basis. Application fee: $50 ($60 for international students). Electronic applications accepted. *Expenses:* Tuition, state resident: full-time $8600. Tuition, nonresident: full-time $21,900. *Financial support:* In 2011–12, 12 students received support, including 3 fellowships with full tuition reimbursements available (averaging $15,000 per year), 16 teaching assistantships with partial tuition reimbursements available (averaging $6,003 per year); career-related internships or fieldwork, Federal Work-Study, scholarships/grants, traineeships, health care benefits, and unspecified assistantships also available. Financial award application deadline: 2/10. *Faculty research:* Aphasia, cochlear implants, autism, voice, balance, multicultural, fluency. *Total annual research expenditures:* $496,510. *Unit head:* Dr. Marcia Jean Hay-McCutcheon, Associate Professor and Chair, 205-348-7131, Fax: 205-348-1845, E-mail: mhaymccu@as.ua.edu. Web site: http://www.as.ua.edu/cd/.

University of Alberta, Faculty of Graduate Studies and Research, Department of Speech Pathology and Audiology, Edmonton, AB T6G 2E1, Canada. Offers speech pathology and audiology (PhD); speech-language pathology (M Sc). *Degree requirements:* For master's, thesis (for some programs), clinical practicum (MSLP). *Entrance requirements:* For master's, GRE, minimum GPA of 6.5 on a 9.0 scale. Additional exam requirements/recommendations for international students: Required—TOEFL. *Faculty research:* Clinical education, hearing conservation, motor speech disorders, child language, voice resonance.

The University of Arizona, College of Science, Department of Speech, Language, and Hearing Sciences, Tucson, AZ 85721. Offers MS, Au D, PhD. *Accreditation:* ASHA (one or more programs are accredited). *Faculty:* 13 full-time (8 women). *Students:* 58 full-time (53 women); includes 8 minority (1 Black or African American, non-Hispanic/Latino; 2 Asian, non-Hispanic/Latino; 4 Hispanic/Latino; 1 Two or more races, non-Hispanic/Latino), 1 international. Average age 29. 205 applicants, 17% accepted, 27 enrolled. In 2011, 26 master's, 2 doctorates awarded. *Degree requirements:* For master's, thesis optional; for doctorate, thesis/dissertation. *Entrance requirements:* For master's, GRE General Test, 3 letters of recommendation; for doctorate, GRE General Test, 3 letters of recommendation, personal statement, writing sample. Additional exam requirements/recommendations for international students: Required—TOEFL (minimum score 550 paper-based; 213 computer-based; 79 iBT). *Application deadline:* Applications are processed on a rolling basis. Application fee: $75. Electronic applications accepted. *Expenses:* Tuition, state resident: full-time $10,840. Tuition, nonresident: full-time $25,802. *Financial support:* In 2011–12, 13 research assistantships with full tuition reimbursements (averaging $21,933 per year), 16 teaching assistantships with full tuition reimbursements (averaging $15,058 per year) were awarded; career-related internships or fieldwork, Federal Work-Study, institutionally sponsored loans, scholarships/grants, health care benefits, tuition waivers (full and partial), and unspecified assistantships also available. Financial award application deadline: 2/1. *Faculty research:* Alzheimer's disease, speech motor control, auditory-evoked potentials, analyzing pathological speech. *Total annual research expenditures:* $3.8 million. *Unit head:* Dr. Pelagie Beeson, Head, 520-621-9879, Fax: 520-621-9901, E-mail: pelagie@email.arizona.edu. *Application contact:* Pamela Adams, Information

Contact, 520-621-1644, Fax: 520-621-9901, E-mail: adamsp@email.arizona.edu. Web site: http://slhs.arizona.edu/.

University of Arkansas, Graduate School, College of Education and Health Professions, Department of Rehabilitation, Human Resources and Communication Disorders, Program in Communication Disorders, Fayetteville, AR 72701-1201. Offers MS. *Accreditation:* ASHA. Part-time programs available. *Students:* 45 full-time (44 women), 1 (woman) part-time; includes 4 minority (1 Black or African American, non-Hispanic/Latino; 1 American Indian or Alaska Native, non-Hispanic/Latino; 1 Hispanic/Latino; 1 Two or more races, non-Hispanic/Latino), 1 international. In 2011, 20 master's awarded. *Degree requirements:* For master's, thesis optional, 8-week externship. *Entrance requirements:* For master's, GRE General Test. *Application deadline:* For fall admission, 4/1 for international students; for spring admission, 10/1 for international students. Applications are processed on a rolling basis. Application fee: $40 ($50 for international students). Electronic applications accepted. *Financial support:* In 2011–12, 5 research assistantships were awarded; fellowships, teaching assistantships, career-related internships or fieldwork, and Federal Work-Study also available. Support available to part-time students. Financial award application deadline: 4/1; financial award applicants required to submit FAFSA. *Unit head:* Dr. Fran Hagstrom, Head, 479-575-4758, E-mail: fhagstr@uark.edu. *Application contact:* Dr. Brent Williams, Program Coordinator, 479-575-4758, E-mail: btwilli@uark.edu. Web site: http://cdis.uark.edu.

University of Arkansas for Medical Sciences, Graduate School, Program in Communicative Disorders, Little Rock, AR 72205-7199. Offers MS, PhD. MS offered jointly with University of Arkansas at Little Rock. Part-time programs available. *Degree requirements:* For master's, thesis or alternative. *Entrance requirements:* For master's, GRE General Test. Additional exam requirements/recommendations for international students: Required—TOEFL.

The University of British Columbia, Faculty of Medicine, School of Audiology and Speech Sciences, Vancouver, BC V6T 1Z3, Canada. Offers M Sc, PhD. *Accreditation:* ASHA. *Degree requirements:* For master's, thesis or alternative, externship; for doctorate, comprehensive exam, thesis/dissertation. *Entrance requirements:* Additional exam requirements/recommendations for international students: Required—TOEFL (minimum score 600 paper-based; 250 computer-based; 100 iBT), IELTS (minimum score 7). Electronic applications accepted. *Faculty research:* Language development, experimental phonetics, linguistic aphasiology, amplification, auditory physiology.

University of California, San Diego, Office of Graduate Studies, Interdisciplinary Program in Language and Communicative Disorders, La Jolla, CA 92093. Offers PhD. Program offered jointly with San Diego State University. *Accreditation:* ASHA. Electronic applications accepted.

University of California, San Diego, School of Medicine, Program in Audiology, La Jolla, CA 92093. Offers Au D.

University of Central Arkansas, Graduate School, College of Health and Behavioral Sciences, Department of Communication Sciences and Disorders, Conway, AR 72035-0001. Offers communication sciences and disorders (PhD); speech-language pathology (MS). *Accreditation:* ASHA (one or more programs are accredited). *Faculty:* 8 full-time (5 women), 3 part-time/adjunct (2 women). *Students:* 103 full-time (99 women), 7 part-time (all women); includes 11 minority (6 Black or African American, non-Hispanic/Latino; 1 Asian, non-Hispanic/Latino; 4 Hispanic/Latino). Average age 24. 80 applicants, 35% accepted, 27 enrolled. In 2011, 48 master's awarded. *Degree requirements:* For master's, comprehensive exam, thesis optional, portfolio, internship. *Entrance requirements:* For master's, GRE General Test, NTE, minimum GPA of 2.7. Additional exam requirements/recommendations for international students: Required—TOEFL (minimum score 550 paper-based; 213 computer-based). *Application deadline:* For fall admission, 3/1 priority date for domestic students; for spring admission, 10/1 for domestic students. Applications are processed on a rolling basis. Application fee: $25 ($50 for international students). *Expenses:* Contact institution. *Financial support:* In 2011–12, 3 research assistantships with full and partial tuition reimbursements (averaging $4,000 per year), 3 teaching assistantships (averaging $3,000 per year) were awarded; career-related internships or fieldwork, Federal Work-Study, scholarships/grants, traineeships, and unspecified assistantships also available. Financial award application deadline: 2/15; financial award applicants required to submit FAFSA. *Unit head:* Dr. Kathryn Bayles, Chairperson, 501-852-0696, Fax: 501-450-5474, E-mail: kbayles@uca.edu. *Application contact:* Susan Wood, Administrative Specialist, 501-450-3124, Fax: 501-450-5678, E-mail: swood@uca.edu. Web site: http://www.uca.edu/divisions/academic/slp/.

University of Central Florida, College of Education, Education Doctoral Programs, Orlando, FL 32816. Offers communication sciences and disorders (PhD); counselor education (PhD); education (Ed D); elementary education (PhD); exceptional education (PhD); exercise physiology (PhD); higher education (PhD); hospitality education (PhD); instructional technology (PhD); mathematics education (PhD); reading education (PhD); science education (PhD); social science education (PhD); TESOL (PhD). *Students:* 135 full-time (87 women), 73 part-time (51 women); includes 49 minority (21 Black or African American, non-Hispanic/Latino; 4 Asian, non-Hispanic/Latino; 20 Hispanic/Latino; 4 Two or more races, non-Hispanic/Latino), 18 international. Average age 39. 125 applicants, 46% accepted, 46 enrolled. In 2011, 43 doctorates awarded. Application fee: $30. Electronic applications accepted. *Expenses:* Tuition, state resident: part-time $277.08 per credit hour. Tuition, nonresident: part-time $277.08 per credit hour. Part-time tuition and fees vary according to degree level and program. *Financial support:* In 2011–12, 85 students received support, including 48 fellowships with partial tuition reimbursements available (averaging $5,900 per year), 36 research assistantships with partial tuition reimbursements available (averaging $6,900 per year), 59 teaching assistantships with partial tuition reimbursements available (averaging $6,900 per year). *Unit head:* Dr. Rex Culp, Associate Dean, 407-823-5391, E-mail: rex.culp@ucf.edu. *Application contact:* Barbara Rodriguez, Associate Director, Admissions and Registration, 407-823-2766, Fax: 407-823-6442, E-mail: gradadmissions@ucf.edu. Web site: http://education.ucf.edu/departments.cfm.

University of Central Florida, College of Health and Public Affairs, Department of Communication Sciences and Disorders, Orlando, FL 32816. Offers child language disorders (Certificate); communication sciences and disorders (MA); medical speech-language pathology (Certificate). *Accreditation:* ASHA (one or more programs are accredited). Part-time and evening/weekend programs available. *Faculty:* 25 full-time (16 women), 15 part-time/adjunct (12 women). *Students:* 190 full-time (178 women), 9 part-time (8 women); includes 38 minority (7 Black or African American, non-Hispanic/Latino; 2 American Indian or Alaska Native, non-Hispanic/Latino; 7 Asian, non-Hispanic/Latino; 21 Hispanic/Latino; 1 Two or more races, non-Hispanic/Latino), 1 international. Average age 26. 289 applicants, 71% accepted, 34 enrolled. In 2011, 101 master's awarded. *Degree requirements:* For master's, comprehensive exam, thesis or alternative. *Entrance requirements:* For master's, GRE General Test, minimum GPA of 3.0 in last 60 hours. Additional exam requirements/recommendations for international students: Required—TOEFL. *Application deadline:* For fall admission, 4/1 for domestic students; for spring admission, 11/1 for domestic students. Electronic applications accepted. *Expenses:* Tuition, state resident: part-time $277.08 per credit hour. Tuition, nonresident: part-time $277.08 per credit hour. Part-time tuition and fees vary according to degree level and program. *Financial support:* In 2011–12, 22 students received support, including 15 fellowships with partial tuition reimbursements available (averaging $7,500 per year), 2 research assistantships with partial tuition reimbursements available (averaging $5,400 per year), 8 teaching assistantships with partial tuition reimbursements available (averaging $4,000 per year); career-related internships or fieldwork, Federal Work-Study, institutionally sponsored loans, and unspecified assistantships also available. Financial award application deadline: 3/1; financial award applicants required to submit FAFSA. *Unit head:* Dr. Thomas Mullin, Interim Chair, 407-823-0346, E-mail: thomas.mullin@ucf.edu. *Application contact:* Barbara Rodriguez, Director, Admissions and Registration, 407-823-2766, Fax: 407-823-6442, E-mail: gradadmissions@ucf.edu. Web site: http://www.cohpa.ucf.edu/comdis/.

University of Central Missouri, The Graduate School, College of Health and Human Services, Warrensburg, MO 64093. Offers criminal justice (MS); industrial hygiene (MS); occupational safety management (MS); physical education/exercise and sport science (MS); rural family nursing (MS); social gerontology (MS); sociology (MA); speech language pathology and audiology (MS). *Accreditation:* NCATE. Part-time programs available. Postbaccalaureate distance learning degree programs offered. *Entrance requirements:* Additional exam requirements/recommendations for international students: Required—TOEFL (minimum score 550 paper-based; 79 computer-based). Electronic applications accepted.

University of Central Oklahoma, College of Graduate Studies and Research, College of Education and Professional Studies, Department of Advanced Professional and Special Services, Program in Speech-Language Pathology, Edmond, OK 73034-5209. Offers MS. *Accreditation:* ASHA. Part-time programs available. *Entrance requirements:* For master's, GRE General Test. Additional exam requirements/recommendations for international students: Required—TOEFL (minimum score 550 paper-based; 213 computer-based). *Application deadline:* For fall admission, 7/1 for international students; for spring admission, 11/1 for international students. Applications are processed on a rolling basis. Application fee: $25. Electronic applications accepted. *Expenses:* Tuition, state resident: full-time $3901; part-time $218.30 per credit hour. Tuition, nonresident: full-time $9198; part-time $511.20 per credit hour. Tuition and fees vary according to program. *Financial support:* Unspecified assistantships available. Financial award application deadline: 3/31; financial award applicants required to submit FAFSA. *Unit head:* Dr. Barbara Green, Director, 405-974-5283, Fax: 405-974-3822, E-mail: smclaughlin@uco.edu. *Application contact:* Dr. Richard Bernard, Dean, Jackson College of Graduate Studies, 405-974-3493, Fax: 405-974-3852, E-mail: gradcoll@uco.edu. Web site: http://www.uco.edu/ceps/dept/apss/slp/slp-ms.asp.

University of Cincinnati, Graduate School, College of Allied Health Sciences, Department of Communication Sciences and Disorders, Cincinnati, OH 45221. Offers MA, Au D, PhD. *Accreditation:* ASHA (one or more programs are accredited). *Degree requirements:* For master's, thesis optional; for doctorate, comprehensive exam, thesis/dissertation. *Entrance requirements:* For master's and doctorate, GRE General Test, minimum GPA of 3.0. Additional exam requirements/recommendations for international students: Required—TOEFL (minimum score 600 paper-based; 250 computer-based). Electronic applications accepted. *Faculty research:* Neurogenic speech and language disorders, speech science, linguistics, swallowing disorders, speech-language pathology.

University of Cincinnati, Graduate School, College of Education, Criminal Justice, and Human Services, Division of Teacher Education, Cincinnati, OH 45221. Offers curriculum and instruction (M Ed, Ed D); deaf studies (Certificate); early childhood education (M Ed); middle childhood education (M Ed); postsecondary literacy instruction (Certificate); reading/literacy (M Ed, Ed D); secondary education (M Ed); special education (M Ed, Ed D); teaching English as a second language (M Ed, Ed D, Certificate); teaching science (MS). Part-time programs available. *Degree requirements:* For doctorate, thesis/dissertation. *Entrance requirements:* For master's, GRE General Test. Additional exam requirements/recommendations for international students: Required—TOEFL (minimum score 550 paper-based). Electronic applications accepted.

University of Colorado Boulder, Graduate School, College of Arts and Sciences, Department of Speech, Language and Hearing Sciences, Boulder, CO 80309. Offers audiology (Au D, PhD); clinical research and practice in audiology (PhD); speech, language and hearing science (MA); speech-language pathology (MA, PhD); speech-language-hearing sciences (PhD). *Accreditation:* ASHA (one or more programs are accredited). *Faculty:* 11 full-time (8 women). *Students:* 123 full-time (101 women), 7 part-time (all women); includes 18 minority (1 Black or African American, non-Hispanic/Latino; 6 Asian, non-Hispanic/Latino; 9 Hispanic/Latino; 2 Two or more races, non-Hispanic/Latino), 2 international. Average age 30. 455 applicants, 14% accepted, 57 enrolled. In 2011, 29 master's, 5 doctorates awarded. Terminal master's awarded for partial completion of doctoral program. *Degree requirements:* For master's, comprehensive exam, thesis or alternative; for doctorate, one foreign language, thesis/dissertation. *Entrance requirements:* For master's, GRE General Test, minimum undergraduate GPA of 3.25; for doctorate, GRE General Test. *Application deadline:* For fall admission, 2/1 priority date for domestic students, 2/1 for international students. Applications are processed on a rolling basis. Application fee: $50 ($60 for international students). Electronic applications accepted. *Financial support:* In 2011–12, 106 students received support, including 61 fellowships (averaging $4,855 per year), 1 research assistantship with full and partial tuition reimbursement available (averaging $21,053 per year), 11 teaching assistantships with full and partial tuition reimbursements available (averaging $21,355 per year); institutionally sponsored loans, scholarships/grants, health care benefits, and unspecified assistantships also available. Financial award application deadline: 2/1; financial award applicants required to submit FAFSA. *Faculty research:* Speech-language pathology. *Total annual research expenditures:* $1.5 million. *Application contact:* E-mail: slhsgrad@colorado.edu. Web site: http://www.colorado.edu/slhs/.

University of Connecticut, Graduate School, College of Liberal Arts and Sciences, Department of Communication Sciences, Program in Audiology, Storrs, CT 06269. Offers Au D, PhD, Au D/PhD. *Accreditation:* ASHA. *Degree requirements:* For doctorate, thesis/dissertation. *Entrance requirements:* For doctorate, GRE General Test. Additional exam requirements/recommendations for international students: Required—TOEFL (minimum score 550 paper-based; 213 computer-based). Electronic applications accepted.

University of Connecticut, Graduate School, College of Liberal Arts and Sciences, Department of Communication Sciences, Program in Speech-Language Pathology, Storrs, CT 06269. Offers MA, PhD. *Accreditation:* ASHA. Terminal master's awarded for partial completion of doctoral program. *Degree requirements:* For master's, comprehensive exam, thesis optional; for doctorate, thesis/dissertation. *Entrance requirements:* For master's and doctorate, GRE General Test. Additional exam requirements/recommendations for international students: Required—TOEFL (minimum score 550 paper-based; 213 computer-based). Electronic applications accepted.

University of Florida, Graduate School, College of Public Health and Health Professions, Department of Speech, Language and Hearing Sciences, Gainesville, FL 32611. Offers MA, Au D, PhD. *Accreditation:* ASHA (one or more programs are accredited). *Faculty:* 8 full-time (4 women), 9 part-time/adjunct (4 women). *Students:*

141 full-time (121 women), 16 part-time (13 women); includes 33 minority (10 Black or African American, non-Hispanic/Latino; 1 American Indian or Alaska Native, non-Hispanic/Latino; 8 Asian, non-Hispanic/Latino; 14 Hispanic/Latino), 12 international. Average age 30. 265 applicants, 24% accepted, 31 enrolled. In 2011, 32 master's, 67 doctorates awarded. *Degree requirements:* For master's, thesis optional; for doctorate, comprehensive exam, thesis/dissertation. *Entrance requirements:* For master's and doctorate, GRE General Test, minimum GPA of 3.0. Additional exam requirements/recommendations for international students: Required—TOEFL (minimum score 550 paper-based; 213 computer-based; 80 iBT), IELTS (minimum score 6). *Application deadline:* For fall admission, 1/15 priority date for domestic students. Applications are processed on a rolling basis. Application fee: $30. Electronic applications accepted. *Financial support:* In 2011–12, 15 students received support, including 3 fellowships, 12 research assistantships; career-related internships or fieldwork and unspecified assistantships also available. Financial award application deadline: 1/15; financial award applicants required to submit FAFSA. *Faculty research:* Phonetic science, cochlear implant, dyslexia, auditory development, voice. *Unit head:* Dr. Christine M. Sapienza, Chair, 352-273-3712, E-mail: sapienza@ufl.edu. *Application contact:* Betsy P. Vinson, Graduate Coordinator, 352-273-3736 Ext. 258, Fax: 352-846-0243, E-mail: bvinson@ufl.edu. Web site: http://slhs.phhp.ufl.edu/.

University of Georgia, College of Education, Department of Communication Sciences and Special Education, Athens, GA 30602. Offers communication science and disorders (M Ed, MA, PhD, Ed S); special education (M Ed, Ed D, PhD, Ed S). *Accreditation:* ASHA (one or more programs are accredited). *Faculty:* 15 full-time (9 women). *Students:* 86 full-time (82 women), 125 part-time (107 women); includes 51 minority (41 Black or African American, non-Hispanic/Latino; 1 American Indian or Alaska Native, non-Hispanic/Latino; 3 Asian, non-Hispanic/Latino; 3 Hispanic/Latino; 3 Two or more races, non-Hispanic/Latino), 1 international. Average age 34. 224 applicants, 30% accepted, 32 enrolled. In 2011, 33 master's, 4 doctorates, 3 other advanced degrees awarded. Terminal master's awarded for partial completion of doctoral program. *Degree requirements:* For master's, comprehensive exam (for some programs), thesis (for some programs); for doctorate, thesis/dissertation. *Entrance requirements:* For master's, doctorate, and Ed S, GRE General Test. Additional exam requirements/recommendations for international students: Required—TOEFL. *Application deadline:* For fall admission, 7/1 priority date for domestic students; for spring admission, 11/15 for domestic students. Application fee: $50. Electronic applications accepted. *Financial support:* Fellowships, research assistantships, teaching assistantships, and unspecified assistantships available. *Unit head:* Dr. Albert De Chicchis, Interim Head, 706-542-4582, Fax: 706-542-5348, E-mail: alde@.uga.edu. *Application contact:* Dr. Rebecca S. Marshall, Interim Graduate Coordinator, 706-542-0737, E-mail: rshisler@.uga.edu. Web site: http://www.coe.uga.edu/csse/.

University of Hawaii at Manoa, John A. Burns School of Medicine, Department of Communication Sciences and Disorders, Honolulu, HI 96822. Offers MS. *Accreditation:* ASHA. Part-time programs available. *Degree requirements:* For master's, thesis optional. *Entrance requirements:* For master's, GRE General Test, minimum GPA of 3.0. Additional exam requirements/recommendations for international students: Required—TOEFL (minimum score 580 paper-based; 237 computer-based; 92 iBT), IELTS (minimum score 5). *Faculty research:* Emerging language (child phonology and special populations), central auditory function, developmental phonology, processing in the aging.

University of Houston, College of Liberal Arts and Social Sciences, Department of Communication Sciences and Disorders, Houston, TX 77204. Offers MA. *Accreditation:* ASHA. Part-time programs available. *Degree requirements:* For master's, comprehensive exam, thesis optional. *Entrance requirements:* For master's, GRE General Test, minimum GPA of 3.0 in last 60 hours. Additional exam requirements/recommendations for international students: Required—TOEFL (minimum score 550 paper-based; 79 computer-based; 79 iBT). *Faculty research:* Stuttering, voice disorders, language disorders, phonological processing, cognition.

University of Illinois at Urbana–Champaign, Graduate College, College of Applied Health Sciences, Department of Speech and Hearing Science, Champaign, IL 61820. Offers audiology (Au D); speech and hearing science (MA, PhD). *Accreditation:* ASHA (one or more programs are accredited). *Faculty:* 18 full-time (10 women), 1 part-time/adjunct (0 women). *Students:* 77 full-time (69 women), 3 part-time (all women); includes 5 minority (1 Black or African American, non-Hispanic/Latino; 2 Asian, non-Hispanic/Latino; 2 Two or more races, non-Hispanic/Latino), 3 international. 232 applicants, 13% accepted, 25 enrolled. In 2011, 18 master's, 9 doctorates awarded. *Entrance requirements:* For master's, GRE General Test, minimum GPA of 3.0. Additional exam requirements/recommendations for international students: Required—TOEFL (minimum score 550 paper-based; 213 computer-based; 79 iBT). *Application deadline:* Applications are processed on a rolling basis. Application fee: $75 ($90 for international students). Electronic applications accepted. *Financial support:* In 2011–12, 4 fellowships, 17 research assistantships, 26 teaching assistantships were awarded; tuition waivers (full and partial) also available. *Unit head:* Adrienne L. Perlman, Head, 217-244-2545, Fax: 217-244-2235, E-mail: aperlman@illinois.edu. *Application contact:* Carey Ann Cash, Office Administrator, 217-244-2537, Fax: 217-244-2235, E-mail: careyann@illinois.edu. Web site: http://www.shs.illinois.edu/.

The University of Iowa, Graduate College, College of Liberal Arts and Sciences, Department of Communication Sciences and Disorders, Program in Professional Speech Pathology and Audiology, Iowa City, IA 52242-1316. Offers MA, Au D, Au D/PhD. *Accreditation:* ASHA. *Degree requirements:* For master's, thesis optional, exam; for doctorate, practicum. *Entrance requirements:* For master's and doctorate, GRE General Test, minimum GPA of 3.0. Additional exam requirements/recommendations for international students: Required—TOEFL (minimum score 550 paper-based; 213 computer-based; 81 iBT). Electronic applications accepted.

The University of Iowa, Graduate College, College of Liberal Arts and Sciences, Department of Communication Sciences and Disorders, Program in Speech and Hearing Science, Iowa City, IA 52242-1316. Offers PhD, Au D/PhD. *Degree requirements:* For doctorate, comprehensive exam, thesis/dissertation. *Entrance requirements:* For doctorate, GRE General Test, minimum GPA of 3.0. Additional exam requirements/recommendations for international students: Required—TOEFL (minimum score 600 paper-based; 250 computer-based; 100 iBT). Electronic applications accepted.

The University of Kansas, Graduate Studies, College of Liberal Arts and Sciences, Department of Speech-Language-Hearing: Sciences and Disorders, Lawrence, KS 66045. Offers audiology (PhD); speech-language pathology (MA, PhD). Offered jointly with the Department of Hearing and Speech at the Kansas City campus. *Accreditation:* ASHA. Part-time programs available. *Faculty:* 13 full-time (9 women). *Students:* 76 full-time (69 women), 5 part-time (all women); includes 6 minority (1 American Indian or Alaska Native, non-Hispanic/Latino; 5 Hispanic/Latino), 5 international. Average age 27. 161 applicants, 41% accepted, 33 enrolled. In 2011, 30 master's, 2 doctorates awarded. *Degree requirements:* For master's, comprehensive exam, thesis optional; for doctorate, comprehensive exam, thesis/dissertation. *Entrance requirements:* For master's and doctorate, GRE General Test, MAT, minimum GPA of 3.0. Additional exam requirements/recommendations for international students: Required—TOEFL.

Application deadline: For fall admission, 1/15 for domestic and international students; for spring admission, 10/1 for domestic and international students. Application fee: $55 ($65 for international students). Electronic applications accepted. Tuition and fees vary according to course load, campus/location, program and reciprocity agreements. *Financial support:* Fellowships with full tuition reimbursements, research assistantships, teaching assistantships with full and partial tuition reimbursements, career-related internships or fieldwork, Federal Work-Study, institutionally sponsored loans, and unspecified assistantships available. Support available to part-time students. Financial award application deadline: 3/1; financial award applicants required to submit FAFSA. *Faculty research:* Reading disorders, language acquisition, auditory electrophysiology, genetics of language, phonological development. *Unit head:* Hugh W. Catts, Chair, 785-864-0630, Fax: 785-864-3974, E-mail: catts@ku.edu. *Application contact:* Diane Wright-Cook, Coordinator, 913-588-5935, E-mail: dswright@kumc.edu. Web site: http://www.ku.edu/~splh/.

The University of Kansas, University of Kansas Medical Center, School of Health Professions, Intercampus Program in Communicative Disorders, Lawrence, KS 66045. Offers audiology (MA, Au D). *Faculty:* 43. *Students:* 20 full-time (19 women), 11 part-time (9 women); includes 2 minority (1 Black or African American, non-Hispanic/Latino; 1 Two or more races, non-Hispanic/Latino). Average age 26. 29 applicants, 59% accepted, 8 enrolled. In 2011, 6 doctorates awarded. Terminal master's awarded for partial completion of doctoral program. *Degree requirements:* For master's, thesis optional, formative and summative exams; for doctorate, comprehensive exam, thesis/dissertation. *Entrance requirements:* For master's and doctorate, GRE, bachelor's degree. Additional exam requirements/recommendations for international students: Required—TOEFL. *Application deadline:* For fall admission, 1/15 for domestic and international students. Application fee: $60. Electronic applications accepted. Tuition and fees vary according to course load, campus/location, program and reciprocity agreements. *Financial support:* Research assistantships with partial tuition reimbursements, teaching assistantships with partial tuition reimbursements, institutionally sponsored loans, scholarships/grants, traineeships, and unspecified assistantships available. Financial award application deadline: 2/14; financial award applicants required to submit FAFSA. *Faculty research:* Child language development, diagnosis and treatment of language disorders; newborn/pediatric hearing testing and treatment of hearing loss in children; voice disorders; auditory physiology and applied electrophysiology; diagnosis and treatment for adult speech and language disorders. *Total annual research expenditures:* $524,940. *Unit head:* Dr. John A. Ferraro, Chair, Department of Hearing and Speech/Co-Director, 913-588-5937, Fax: 913-588-5923, E-mail: jferraro@kumc.edu. *Application contact:* Diane Wright-Cook, Coordinator, 913-588-5937, Fax: 913-588-5923, E-mail: hearingspeech@kumc.edu. Web site: http://ku.edu/~splh/ipcd.

University of Kentucky, Graduate School, College of Health Sciences, Program in Communication Disorders, Lexington, KY 40506-0032. Offers MSCD. *Accreditation:* ASHA. *Degree requirements:* For master's, comprehensive exam. *Entrance requirements:* For master's, GRE General Test, minimum undergraduate GPA of 2.75. Additional exam requirements/recommendations for international students: Required—TOEFL (minimum score 550 paper-based; 213 computer-based). Electronic applications accepted. *Faculty research:* Swallowing disorders, infant speech development, child language intervention, augmentative communication.

University of Louisiana at Lafayette, College of Liberal Arts, Department of Communicative Disorders, Lafayette, LA 70504. Offers MS, PhD. *Accreditation:* ASHA (one or more programs are accredited). *Degree requirements:* For master's, thesis or alternative. *Entrance requirements:* For master's, GRE General Test, minimum GPA of 2.75. Additional exam requirements/recommendations for international students: Required—TOEFL (minimum score 550 paper-based; 213 computer-based).

University of Louisiana at Monroe, Graduate School, College of Health Sciences, Department of Speech-Language Pathology, Monroe, LA 71209-0001. Offers MS. *Accreditation:* ASHA. *Faculty:* 6 full-time (all women), 3 part-time/adjunct (all women). *Students:* 38 full-time (all women), 5 part-time (all women); includes 5 minority (2 Black or African American, non-Hispanic/Latino; 2 Hispanic/Latino; 1 Two or more races, non-Hispanic/Latino), 1 international. Average age 25. 53 applicants, 49% accepted, 23 enrolled. In 2011, 18 master's awarded. *Degree requirements:* For master's, thesis. *Entrance requirements:* For master's, GRE, minimum GPA of 2.5. Additional exam requirements/recommendations for international students: Required—TOEFL (minimum score 500 paper-based; 173 computer-based; 61 iBT). *Application deadline:* For fall admission, 8/24 priority date for domestic students, 7/1 for international students; for winter admission, 12/14 priority date for domestic students; for spring admission, 1/19 for domestic students, 11/1 for international students. Applications are processed on a rolling basis. Application fee: $20 ($30 for international students). Electronic applications accepted. *Expenses:* Tuition, state resident: full-time $3436; part-time $240 per credit hour. Tuition, nonresident: full-time $3436; part-time $240 per credit hour. *International tuition:* $10,733 full-time. *Required fees:* $1460.90. *Financial support:* In 2011–12, 26 research assistantships with full tuition reimbursements (averaging $6,032 per year) were awarded; career-related internships or fieldwork, Federal Work-Study, and unspecified assistantships also available. Financial award application deadline: 4/1; financial award applicants required to submit FAFSA. *Faculty research:* Child language, stuttering, multicultural issues, ethics. *Unit head:* Dr. Johanna Rose Boult, Department Head, 318-342-1390, Fax: 318-342-1687, E-mail: boult@ulm.edu. *Application contact:* Dr. Paxton E. Oliver, Associate Dean, 318-342-1622, Fax: 318-342-1606, E-mail: poliver@ulm.edu. Web site: http://www.ulm.edu/slp/.

University of Louisville, School of Medicine, Department of Surgery, Louisville, KY 40292-0001. Offers audiology (Au D); communicative disorders (MS). *Expenses:* Tuition, state resident: full-time $9692; part-time $539 per credit hour. Tuition, nonresident: full-time $20,168; part-time $1121 per credit hour. Tuition and fees vary according to program and reciprocity agreements.

University of Maine, Graduate School, College of Liberal Arts and Sciences, Department of Communication Sciences and Disorders, Orono, ME 04469. Offers MA. *Accreditation:* ASHA. *Faculty:* 6 full-time (4 women), 6 part-time/adjunct (5 women). *Students:* 40 full-time (38 women), 2 part-time (both women), 3 international. Average age 26. 77 applicants, 44% accepted, 26 enrolled. In 2011, 14 master's awarded. *Entrance requirements:* For master's, GRE General Test. Additional exam requirements/recommendations for international students: Required—TOEFL. *Application deadline:* For fall admission, 2/1 priority date for domestic students. Applications are processed on a rolling basis. Application fee: $65. Electronic applications accepted. *Expenses:* Tuition, state resident: full-time $5016. Tuition, nonresident: full-time $14,424. *Financial support:* In 2011–12, 6 teaching assistantships with partial tuition reimbursements (averaging $5,500 per year) were awarded; career-related internships or fieldwork, Federal Work-Study, institutionally sponsored loans, and tuition waivers (full and partial) also available. Support available to part-time students. Financial award application deadline: 3/1. *Faculty research:* Interpersonal communication between supervisor and supervised, clinicians and clients; language and voice impairments; children's pragmatics. *Total annual research expenditures:* $719. *Unit head:* Dr. Judy Walker, Chair, 207-581-2006, Fax: 207-581-1953. *Application contact:* Scott G. Delcourt,

Associate Dean of the Graduate School, 207-581-3291, Fax: 207-581-3232, E-mail: graduate@maine.edu. Web site: http://www2.edu/graduate/.

The University of Manchester, School of Psychological Sciences, Manchester, United Kingdom. Offers audiology (M Phil, PhD); clinical psychology (M Phil, PhD, Psy D); psychology (M Phil, PhD).

University of Maryland, College Park, Academic Affairs, College of Behavioral and Social Sciences, Department of Hearing and Speech Sciences, College Park, MD 20742. Offers audiology (MA, PhD); hearing and speech sciences (Au D); language pathology (MA, PhD); neuroscience (PhD); speech (MA, PhD). *Accreditation:* ASHA (one or more programs are accredited). *Faculty:* 20 full-time (18 women), 15 part-time/adjunct (11 women). *Students:* 68 full-time (61 women), 20 part-time (all women); includes 20 minority (6 Black or African American, non-Hispanic/Latino; 6 Asian, non-Hispanic/Latino; 6 Hispanic/Latino; 2 Two or more races, non-Hispanic/Latino), 2 international. 350 applicants, 26% accepted, 29 enrolled. In 2011, 21 master's, 9 doctorates awarded. *Degree requirements:* For master's, thesis optional; for doctorate, thesis/dissertation, written and oral exams. *Entrance requirements:* For master's, GRE General Test, minimum GPA of 3.5, 3 letters of recommendation; for doctorate, GRE General Test, minimum GPA of 3.5. Additional exam requirements/recommendations for international students: Required—TOEFL. *Application deadline:* For fall admission, 1/15 for domestic and international students. Applications are processed on a rolling basis. Application fee: $75. Electronic applications accepted. *Expenses:* Tuition, state resident: part-time $525 per credit hour. Tuition, nonresident: part-time $1131 per credit hour. *Required fees:* $386.31 per term. Tuition and fees vary according to program. *Financial support:* In 2011–12, 6 fellowships with full and partial tuition reimbursements (averaging $11,324 per year), 14 research assistantships (averaging $15,551 per year), 29 teaching assistantships (averaging $15,714 per year) were awarded; career-related internships or fieldwork, Federal Work-Study, scholarships/grants, and health care benefits also available. Support available to part-time students. Financial award applicants required to submit FAFSA. *Faculty research:* Speech perception, language acquisition, bilingualism, hearing loss. *Total annual research expenditures:* $982,623. *Unit head:* Dr. Nan B. Bernstein-Ratner, Chair, 301-405-4217, Fax: 301-314-2023, E-mail: nratner@umd.edu. *Application contact:* Dr. Charles A. Caramello, Dean of Graduate School, 301-405-0358, Fax: 301-314-9305.

University of Massachusetts Amherst, Graduate School, School of Public Health and Health Sciences, Department of Communication Disorders, Amherst, MA 01003. Offers audiology (Au D, PhD); clinical audiology (PhD); speech-language pathology (MA, PhD). *Accreditation:* ASHA (one or more programs are accredited). Part-time programs available. *Faculty:* 15 full-time (13 women). *Students:* 92 full-time (87 women), 5 part-time (all women); includes 5 minority (1 Black or African American, non-Hispanic/Latino; 2 Asian, non-Hispanic/Latino; 1 Hispanic/Latino; 1 Two or more races, non-Hispanic/Latino). Average age 28. 280 applicants, 26% accepted, 32 enrolled. In 2011, 22 master's, 3 doctorates awarded. Terminal master's awarded for partial completion of doctoral program. *Degree requirements:* For master's, thesis optional; for doctorate, comprehensive exam, thesis/dissertation. *Entrance requirements:* For master's and doctorate, GRE General Test. Additional exam requirements/recommendations for international students: Required—TOEFL (minimum score 550 paper-based; 213 computer-based; 80 iBT), IELTS (minimum score 6.5). *Application deadline:* For fall admission, 2/1 for domestic and international students; for spring admission, 10/1 for domestic and international students. Applications are processed on a rolling basis. Application fee: $50 ($65 for international students). Electronic applications accepted. Tuition and fees vary according to course load, campus/location and program. *Financial support:* Fellowships with full and partial tuition reimbursements, research assistantships with full and partial tuition reimbursements, teaching assistantships with full and partial tuition reimbursements, career-related internships or fieldwork, Federal Work-Study, scholarships/grants, traineeships, health care benefits, tuition waivers (full), and unspecified assistantships available. Support available to part-time students. Financial award application deadline: 2/1; financial award applicants required to submit FAFSA. *Unit head:* Dr. Karen S. Helfer, Graduate Program Director, 413-545-0131, Fax: 413-545-0803. *Application contact:* Lindsay DeSantis, Interim Supervisor of Admissions, 413-545-0722, Fax: 413-577-0010, E-mail: gradadm@grad.umass.edu. Web site: http://www.umass.edu/sphhs/comdis/.

University of Memphis, Graduate School, School of Audiology and Speech-Language Pathology, Memphis, TN 38152. Offers MA, Au D, PhD. *Accreditation:* ASHA. Part-time programs available. Terminal master's awarded for partial completion of doctoral program. *Degree requirements:* For master's, comprehensive exam, thesis or alternative; for doctorate, thesis/dissertation, qualifying exam. *Entrance requirements:* For master's, GRE General Test or MAT, minimum GPA of 3.0, ASHA certification; for doctorate, GRE General Test, minimum GPA of 3.5, letters of recommendation. *Faculty research:* Hearing aid characteristic selection, language acquisition, speech disorders, characteristics of the aging voice, hearing science.

University of Minnesota, Duluth, Graduate School, College of Education and Human Service Professions, Department of Communication Sciences and Disorders, Duluth, MN 55812-2496. Offers MA. *Accreditation:* ASHA. Part-time programs available. *Degree requirements:* For master's, research project, oral exam. *Entrance requirements:* For master's, minimum GPA of 3.0, undergraduate degree in communication sciences and disorders. Additional exam requirements/recommendations for international students: Required—TOEFL (minimum score 550 paper-based; 213 computer-based). *Faculty research:* Clinical supervision, augmentative communication, speech understanding, fluency, developmental apraxia of speech.

University of Minnesota, Twin Cities Campus, Graduate School, College of Liberal Arts, Department of Speech-Language-Hearing Sciences, Minneapolis, MN 55455. Offers audiology (Au D); speech-language pathology (MA); speech-language-hearing sciences (PhD). *Accreditation:* ASHA (one or more programs are accredited). Terminal master's awarded for partial completion of doctoral program. *Degree requirements:* For master's, thesis, 375 client contact hours; for doctorate, comprehensive exam, thesis/dissertation. *Entrance requirements:* For master's and doctorate, GRE General Test, minimum GPA of 3.0. Additional exam requirements/recommendations for international students: Required—TOEFL. Electronic applications accepted. *Faculty research:* Normal and disordered child phonology, specific language impairment, bilingual and multicultural aspects of language, TBI, AAC.

University of Mississippi, Graduate School, School of Applied Sciences, Department of Communicative Disorders, Oxford, University, MS 38677. Offers MS. *Accreditation:* ASHA. *Students:* 47 full-time (all women), 3 part-time (2 women); includes 8 minority (7 Black or African American, non-Hispanic/Latino; 1 Two or more races, non-Hispanic/Latino). In 2011, 20 master's awarded. *Entrance requirements:* For master's, GRE General Test, minimum GPA of 3.0. Additional exam requirements/recommendations for international students: Required—TOEFL. *Application deadline:* For fall admission, 2/1 for domestic students; for spring admission, 10/1 for domestic students. Applications are processed on a rolling basis. Application fee: $25. Electronic applications accepted. *Financial support:* Scholarships/grants available. Financial award application deadline: 3/1; financial award applicants required to submit FAFSA. *Unit head:* Dr. Lennette J. Ivy, Interim Chair, 662-915-7652, Fax: 662-915-5717, E-mail: livy@olemiss.edu. *Application contact:* Dr. Christy M. Wyandt, Associate Dean, 662-915-7474, Fax: 662-915-7577, E-mail: cwyandt@olemiss.edu.

University of Missouri, School of Health Professions, Program in Communication Science and Disorders, Columbia, MO 65211. Offers MHS. *Accreditation:* ASHA. *Faculty:* 8 full-time (7 women), 2 part-time/adjunct (1 woman). *Students:* 36 full-time (34 women), 2 part-time (both women); includes 3 minority (all Black or African American, non-Hispanic/Latino). Average age 25. 51 applicants, 25% accepted, 13 enrolled. In 2011, 11 degrees awarded. *Entrance requirements:* For master's, GRE General Test, minimum GPA of 3.0. Additional exam requirements/recommendations for international students: Required—TOEFL (minimum score 600 paper-based; 250 computer-based; 100 iBT). *Application deadline:* For fall admission, 2/15 priority date for domestic students. Applications are processed on a rolling basis. Application fee: $55 ($75 for international students). *Expenses:* Tuition, state resident: full-time $5881. Tuition, nonresident: full-time $15,183. *Required fees:* $952. Tuition and fees vary according to campus/location and program. *Financial support:* Research assistantships, teaching assistantships, and institutionally sponsored loans available. *Unit head:* Dr. Judith Goodman, Department Chair, 573-882-8407, E-mail: goodmanjc@health.missouri.edu. *Application contact:* Dr. Barbara McLay, Director of Graduate Studies, 573-882-8409, E-mail: mclayb@missouri.edu. Web site: http://shp.missouri.edu/csd/.

University of Montevallo, College of Arts and Sciences, Department of Communication Science and Disorders, Montevallo, AL 35115. Offers speech-language pathology (MS). *Accreditation:* ASHA. *Students:* 47 full-time (46 women); includes 1 minority (Two or more races, non-Hispanic/Latino). In 2011, 19 master's awarded. *Degree requirements:* For master's, comprehensive exam. *Entrance requirements:* For master's, GRE General Test, MAT. Additional exam requirements/recommendations for international students: Required—TOEFL (minimum score 550 paper-based). *Application deadline:* For fall admission, 7/15 for domestic students; for spring admission, 11/15 for domestic students. Application fee: $25. *Financial support:* Federal Work-Study, scholarships/grants, and unspecified assistantships available. *Unit head:* Dr. Marlene Salas-Provance, Chair, 205-665-6725, E-mail: provancem@montevallo.edu. *Application contact:* Dr. Margaret L. Johnson, Graduate Program Coordinator, 205-665-6717, E-mail: johnsonm@montevallo.edu. Web site: http://www.montevallo.edu/csd/.

University of Nebraska at Kearney, Graduate Studies, College of Education, Department of Communication Disorders, Kearney, NE 68849-0001. Offers speech pathology (MS Ed). *Accreditation:* ASHA. Part-time programs available. *Entrance requirements:* For master's, GRE General Test. Electronic applications accepted. *Faculty research:* Neurogenic, communication disorders in adults, phonological development and disorders, orofacial anomalies, audiologic rehabilitation of the elderly.

University of Nebraska at Omaha, Graduate Studies, College of Education, Department of Special Education and Communication Disorders, Omaha, NE 68182. Offers special education (MS); speech-language pathology (MA, MS). *Accreditation:* ASHA (one or more programs are accredited); NCATE. Part-time and evening/weekend programs available. *Faculty:* 10 full-time (6 women). *Students:* 27 full-time (25 women), 58 part-time (47 women); includes 4 minority (1 American Indian or Alaska Native, non-Hispanic/Latino; 2 Asian, non-Hispanic/Latino; 1 Hispanic/Latino). Average age 29. 108 applicants, 31% accepted, 15 enrolled. In 2011, 45 master's awarded. *Degree requirements:* For master's, comprehensive exam, thesis (for some programs). *Entrance requirements:* For master's, GRE General Test or MAT, minimum GPA of 3.0, statement of purpose, letters of recommendation. Additional exam requirements/recommendations for international students: Required—TOEFL (minimum score 500 paper-based; 173 computer-based; 61 iBT). *Application deadline:* For fall admission, 2/1 for domestic students; for spring admission, 9/1 for domestic students. Applications are processed on a rolling basis. Application fee: $45. Electronic applications accepted. *Financial support:* In 2011–12, 4 students received support, including 2 research assistantships with tuition reimbursements available; fellowships, career-related internships or fieldwork, Federal Work-Study, institutionally sponsored loans, scholarships/grants, tuition waivers (partial), and unspecified assistantships also available. Support available to part-time students. Financial award application deadline: 3/1; financial award applicants required to submit FAFSA. *Unit head:* Dr. Kristine Swain, Chairperson, 402-554-2201. *Application contact:* Dr. Thomas Lorsbach, 402-554-2201.

University of Nebraska–Lincoln, Graduate College, College of Education and Human Sciences, Department of Special Education and Communication Disorders, Program in Speech-Language Pathology and Audiology, Lincoln, NE 68588. Offers audiology and hearing science (Au D); speech-language pathology and audiology (MS). *Accreditation:* ASHA. *Degree requirements:* For master's, thesis optional. *Entrance requirements:* For master's, GRE. Additional exam requirements/recommendations for international students: Required—TOEFL (minimum score 500 paper-based; 173 computer-based). Electronic applications accepted.

University of Nevada, Reno, Graduate School, Division of Health Sciences, Department of Speech Pathology and Audiology, Reno, NV 89557. Offers speech pathology (PhD); speech pathology and audiology (MS). *Accreditation:* ASHA (one or more programs are accredited). Terminal master's awarded for partial completion of doctoral program. *Degree requirements:* For master's, thesis optional; for doctorate, thesis/dissertation. *Entrance requirements:* For master's, GRE General Test, minimum GPA of 2.75; for doctorate, GRE General Test, minimum GPA of 3.0. Additional exam requirements/recommendations for international students: Required—TOEFL (minimum score 500 paper-based; 173 computer-based; 61 iBT), IELTS (minimum score 6). Electronic applications accepted. *Faculty research:* Language impairment in children, voice disorders, stuttering.

University of New Hampshire, Graduate School, School of Health and Human Services, Department of Communication Sciences and Disorders, Durham, NH 03824. Offers communication sciences and disorders (MS); early childhood intervention (MS); language and literature disabilities (MS). Program offered in fall only. *Accreditation:* ASHA. Part-time programs available. *Faculty:* 7 full-time (3 women). *Students:* 36 full-time (all women), 4 part-time (all women); includes 1 minority (Asian, non-Hispanic/Latino), 1 international. Average age 26. 160 applicants, 19% accepted, 18 enrolled. In 2011, 16 master's awarded. *Degree requirements:* For master's, thesis or alternative. *Entrance requirements:* For master's, GRE General Test or MAT. Additional exam requirements/recommendations for international students: Required—TOEFL (minimum score 550 paper-based; 213 computer-based; 80 iBT). *Application deadline:* For fall admission, 1/15 priority date for domestic students, 4/1 for international students. Applications are processed on a rolling basis. Application fee: $65. Electronic applications accepted. *Expenses:* Tuition, state resident: full-time $12,360; part-time $687 per credit hour. Tuition, nonresident: full-time $25,680; part-time $1058 per credit hour. *International tuition:* $29,550 full-time. *Required fees:* $1666; $833 per course. $416.50 per semester. Tuition and fees vary according to course load and degree level. *Financial support:* In 2011–12, 9 students received support, including 5 teaching assistantships; fellowships, research assistantships, career-related internships or fieldwork, Federal Work-Study, scholarships/grants, and tuition waivers (full and partial) also available. Support available to part-time students. Financial award application deadline: 2/15. *Faculty research:* Speech pathology. *Unit head:* Penelope Webster, Chairperson, 603-862-2125. *Application contact:* Maria Russell, Administrative

Assistant, 603-862-0144, E-mail: communication.disorders@unh.edu. Web site: http://chhs.unh.edu/csd/index.

University of New Mexico, Graduate School, College of Arts and Sciences, Department of Speech and Hearing Sciences, Albuquerque, NM 87131-2039. Offers speech-language pathology (MS). *Accreditation:* ASHA. *Faculty:* 6 full-time (4 women), 3 part-time/adjunct (all women). *Students:* 36 full-time (33 women), 3 part-time (all women); includes 15 minority (1 Black or African American, non-Hispanic/Latino; 1 American Indian or Alaska Native, non-Hispanic/Latino; 11 Hispanic/Latino; 2 Two or more races, non-Hispanic/Latino). Average age 31. 88 applicants, 18% accepted, 15 enrolled. In 2011, 13 degrees awarded. *Degree requirements:* For master's, comprehensive exam, thesis optional. *Entrance requirements:* For master's, GRE General Test, minimum GPA of 3.2 in speech and hearing sciences coursework. Additional exam requirements/recommendations for international students: Required—TOEFL (minimum score 550 paper-based; 213 computer-based; 80 iBT). *Application deadline:* For fall admission, 2/1 for domestic students, 1/1 for international students. Application fee: $50. Electronic applications accepted. *Financial support:* In 2011–12, 33 students received support, including 1 fellowship (averaging $7,200 per year); career-related internships or fieldwork, Federal Work-Study, scholarships/grants, health care benefits, and unspecified assistantships also available. Financial award application deadline: 3/1; financial award applicants required to submit FAFSA. *Faculty research:* AAC (Augmentative and Alternative Communication), behavioral genetic studies of language, child language assessment, bilingual language acquisition, bilingual phonology, speech perception, swallowing disorders, transition from oral language to literacy. *Total annual research expenditures:* $10,935. *Unit head:* Dr. Philip S. Dale, Chair, 505-277-5338, Fax: 505-277-0968, E-mail: dalep@unm.edu. *Application contact:* Tracy Wenzl, Department Administrator, 505-277-4453, Fax: 505-277-0968, E-mail: twenzl@unm.edu. Web site: http://www.unm.edu/~sphrsci.

The University of North Carolina at Chapel Hill, School of Medicine and Graduate School, Graduate Programs in Medicine, Chapel Hill, NC 27599. Offers allied health sciences (MPT, MS, Au D, DPT, PhD), including human movement science (MS, PhD), occupational science (MS, PhD), physical therapy (MPT, MS, DPT), rehabilitation counseling and psychology (MS), speech and hearing sciences (MS, Au D, PhD); biochemistry and biophysics (MS, PhD); bioinformatics and computational biology (PhD); biomedical engineering (MS, PhD); cell and developmental biology (PhD); cell and molecular physiology (PhD); genetics and molecular biology (PhD); microbiology and immunology (MS, PhD), including immunology, microbiology; neurobiology (PhD); pathology and laboratory medicine (PhD), including experimental pathology; pharmacology (PhD); MD/PhD. Postbaccalaureate distance learning degree programs offered. Terminal master's awarded for partial completion of doctoral program. *Degree requirements:* For master's, comprehensive exam; for doctorate, thesis/dissertation. Electronic applications accepted. *Expenses:* Contact institution.

The University of North Carolina at Chapel Hill, School of Medicine and Graduate School, Graduate Programs in Medicine, Department of Allied Health Sciences, Division of Speech and Hearing Sciences, Chapel Hill, NC 27599. Offers audiology (Au D); speech and hearing sciences (MS, PhD). *Accreditation:* ASHA (one or more programs are accredited). Postbaccalaureate distance learning degree programs offered (no on-campus study). *Degree requirements:* For master's, comprehensive exam, thesis optional; for doctorate, comprehensive exam, thesis/dissertation. *Entrance requirements:* For master's, GRE General Test, minimum GPA of 3.0; for doctorate, GRE, minimum GPA of 3.0. Additional exam requirements/recommendations for international students: Required—TOEFL (minimum score 550 paper-based; 79 computer-based). Electronic applications accepted. *Faculty research:* Child language and literacy, family participation in early intervention, child and adult hearing loss and treatment, vocal characteristics of African-American speakers and aging populations, adult apraxia of speech.

The University of North Carolina at Greensboro, Graduate School, School of Health and Human Performance, Department of Communication Sciences and Disorders, Greensboro, NC 27412-5001. Offers speech language pathology (PhD); speech pathology and audiology (MA). *Accreditation:* ASHA. *Degree requirements:* For master's, thesis or alternative. *Entrance requirements:* For master's, GRE General Test. Additional exam requirements/recommendations for international students: Required—TOEFL. Electronic applications accepted.

University of North Dakota, Graduate School, College of Arts and Sciences, Department of Communication Sciences and Disorders, Grand Forks, ND 58202. Offers communication sciences and disorders (PhD); speech-language pathology (MS). *Accreditation:* ASHA (one or more programs are accredited). Part-time programs available. *Degree requirements:* For master's, comprehensive exam, thesis or alternative; for doctorate, comprehensive exam, thesis/dissertation, final exam. *Entrance requirements:* For master's and doctorate, GRE General Test, minimum GPA of 3.0. Additional exam requirements/recommendations for international students: Required—TOEFL (minimum score 550 paper-based; 213 computer-based; 79 iBT), IELTS (minimum score 6.5). Electronic applications accepted. *Faculty research:* Mass communications, journalism, community law, international communications, cultural studies.

University of Northern Colorado, Graduate School, College of Natural and Health Sciences, School of Human Sciences, Program in Audiology and Speech Language Sciences, Greeley, CO 80639. Offers audiology (Au D); speech language pathology (MA). *Accreditation:* ASHA (one or more programs are accredited). Part-time and evening/weekend programs available. Postbaccalaureate distance learning degree programs offered (no on-campus study). *Degree requirements:* For master's, comprehensive exam, thesis or alternative; for doctorate, comprehensive exam, thesis/dissertation. *Entrance requirements:* For master's and doctorate, GRE General Test. Electronic applications accepted.

University of Northern Iowa, Graduate College, College of Humanities, Arts and Sciences, Department of Communicative Sciences and Disorders, Cedar Falls, IA 50614. Offers speech-language pathology (MA). *Accreditation:* ASHA. Part-time and evening/weekend programs available. *Students:* 69 full-time (65 women), 3 part-time (all women); includes 4 minority (1 Asian, non-Hispanic/Latino; 3 Hispanic/Latino), 1 international. 142 applicants, 16% accepted, 23 enrolled. In 2011, 31 master's awarded. *Degree requirements:* For master's, comprehensive exam, thesis or alternative. *Entrance requirements:* For master's, GRE, minimum GPA of 3.0. Additional exam requirements/recommendations for international students: Required—TOEFL (minimum score 500 paper-based; 180 computer-based; 61 iBT). *Application deadline:* For fall admission, 8/1 priority date for domestic students. Applications are processed on a rolling basis. Application fee: $50 ($70 for international students). *Expenses:* Tuition, state resident: full-time $7476. Tuition, nonresident: full-time $16,410. *Required fees:* $942. *Financial support:* Career-related internships or fieldwork, Federal Work-Study, scholarships/grants, and tuition waivers (full and partial) available. Financial award application deadline: 2/1. *Unit head:* Dr. Carlin Hageman, Department Head/Professor, 319-273-2497, Fax: 319-273-6384, E-mail: carlin.hageman@uni.edu. *Application contact:* Laurie S. Russell, Record Analyst, 319-273-2623, Fax: 319-273-2885, E-mail: laurie.russell@uni.edu. Web site: http://www.uni.edu/comdis/.

University of North Florida, College of Education and Human Services, Department of Exceptional Student and Deaf Education, Jacksonville, FL 32224. Offers American sign language/English interpreting (M Ed); applied behavior analysis (M Ed); autism (M Ed); deaf education (M Ed); disability services (M Ed); exceptional student education (M Ed). *Accreditation:* NCATE. Part-time and evening/weekend programs available. *Faculty:* 7 full-time (5 women), 2 part-time/adjunct (both women). *Students:* 51 full-time (48 women), 48 part-time (45 women); includes 20 minority (9 Black or African American, non-Hispanic/Latino; 2 Asian, non-Hispanic/Latino; 7 Hispanic/Latino; 2 Two or more races, non-Hispanic/Latino), 2 international. Average age 31. 53 applicants, 66% accepted, 25 enrolled. In 2011, 34 master's awarded. *Entrance requirements:* For master's, GRE General Test, minimum GPA of 3.0 in last 60 hours, interview, 3 letters of recommendation. Additional exam requirements/recommendations for international students: Required—TOEFL (minimum score 500 paper-based; 173 computer-based). *Application deadline:* For fall admission, 7/1 priority date for domestic students, 5/1 for international students; for spring admission, 11/1 priority date for domestic students, 10/1 for international students. Applications are processed on a rolling basis. Application fee: $30. Electronic applications accepted. *Expenses:* Tuition, state resident: full-time $8793; part-time $366.38 per credit hour. Tuition, nonresident: full-time $23,502; part-time $979.24 per credit hour. *Required fees:* $1384; $57.66 per credit hour. Tuition and fees vary according to course load and program. *Financial support:* In 2011–12, 44 students received support, including 2 research assistantships (averaging $4,800 per year); teaching assistantships, career-related internships or fieldwork, Federal Work-Study, scholarships/grants, tuition waivers (partial), and unspecified assistantships also available. Support available to part-time students. Financial award application deadline: 4/1; financial award applicants required to submit FAFSA. *Faculty research:* Transition, integrating technology into teacher education, written language development, professional school development, learning strategies. *Total annual research expenditures:* $855,653. *Unit head:* Dr. Karen Patterson, Chair, 904-620-2930, Fax: 904-620-3895, E-mail: karen.patterson@unf.edu. *Application contact:* Lillith Richardson, Assistant Director, The Graduate School, 904-620-1360, Fax: 904-620-1362, E-mail: graduateschool@unf.edu. Web site: http://www.unf.edu/coehs/edie/.

University of North Texas, Toulouse Graduate School, College of Arts and Sciences, Department of Speech and Hearing Sciences, Denton, TX 76203. Offers audiology (Au D); speech-language pathology (MA, MS). *Accreditation:* ASHA. Part-time programs available. *Degree requirements:* For master's, comprehensive exam, thesis optional, internship; for doctorate, comprehensive exam, thesis/dissertation, internship/externship. *Entrance requirements:* For master's, GRE General Test, minimum GPA of 3.0 in major, 2.8 overall; 15 hours of course work in communication disorders; for doctorate, GRE General Test. Additional exam requirements/recommendations for international students: Recommended—TOEFL (minimum score 550 paper-based; 213 computer-based; 79 iBT). Electronic applications accepted. *Expenses:* Tuition, state resident: part-time $100 per credit hour. Tuition, nonresident: part-time $413 per credit hour. *Faculty research:* Cognition and hearing aids, assessment of noise technology, meta analysis on adaptive testing and binaural listening in cochlear implant language literacy for school aged children, tissue specificity in culture using corticle and non-corticle neuronal networks growing on microelectrode arrays.

University of Oklahoma Health Sciences Center, Graduate College, College of Allied Health, Department of Communication Sciences and Disorders, Oklahoma City, OK 73190. Offers audiology (MS, Au D, PhD); communication sciences and disorders (Certificate), including reading, speech-language pathology; education of the deaf (MS); speech-language pathology (MS, PhD). *Accreditation:* ASHA (one or more programs are accredited). Part-time programs available. Terminal master's awarded for partial completion of doctoral program. *Degree requirements:* For master's, comprehensive exam, thesis optional; for doctorate, one foreign language, comprehensive exam, thesis/dissertation. *Entrance requirements:* For master's and doctorate, GRE General Test, 3 letters of recommendation. Additional exam requirements/recommendations for international students: Required—TOEFL (minimum score 550 paper-based). *Faculty research:* Event-related potentials, cleft palate, fluency disorders, language disorders, hearing and speech science.

University of Ottawa, Faculty of Graduate and Postdoctoral Studies, Faculty of Health Sciences, School of Rehabilitation Sciences, Ottawa, ON K1N 6N5, Canada. Offers audiology (M Sc); orthophony (M Sc). Part-time and evening/weekend programs available. *Entrance requirements:* For master's, honors degree or equivalent, minimum B average. Electronic applications accepted.

University of Pittsburgh, School of Health and Rehabilitation Sciences, Department of Communication Science and Disorders, Pittsburgh, PA 15260. Offers MA, MS, Au D, CScD, PhD. *Accreditation:* ASHA (one or more programs are accredited). *Faculty:* 17 full-time (13 women), 9 part-time/adjunct (5 women). *Students:* 138 full-time (124 women), 18 part-time (16 women); includes 15 minority (4 Black or African American, non-Hispanic/Latino; 7 Asian, non-Hispanic/Latino; 4 Hispanic/Latino), 12 international. Average age 28. 378 applicants, 42% accepted, 63 enrolled. In 2011, 39 master's, 14 doctorates awarded. *Degree requirements:* For master's, comprehensive exam, thesis (for some programs); for doctorate, comprehensive exam, thesis/dissertation. *Entrance requirements:* For master's and doctorate, GRE General Test. Additional exam requirements/recommendations for international students: Required—TOEFL (minimum score 550 paper-based; 213 computer-based; 80 iBT), IELTS (minimum score 6.5). *Application deadline:* For fall admission, 1/15 for domestic and international students. Applications are processed on a rolling basis. Application fee: $100. Electronic applications accepted. *Expenses:* Contact institution. *Financial support:* In 2011–12, 18 students received support, including 15 research assistantships with full tuition reimbursements available (averaging $14,716 per year), 3 teaching assistantships with full tuition reimbursements available (averaging $17,013 per year); fellowships, career-related internships or fieldwork, Federal Work-Study, scholarships/grants, and traineeships also available. Financial award applicants required to submit FAFSA. *Faculty research:* Pediatric and geriatric neurogenic speech and language, pediatric hearing disorders, hearing aids, language development, speech motor control. *Unit head:* Dr. Malcolm R. McNeil, Chairman, 412-383-6541, Fax: 412-383-6555, E-mail: mcneil@pitt.edu. *Application contact:* Theresa Niecgorski, Administrator, 412-383-6540, Fax: 412-383-6555, E-mail: thn49@pitt.edu. Web site: http://www.shrs.pitt.edu/csd/.

University of Puerto Rico, Medical Sciences Campus, School of Health Professions, Program in Audiology, San Juan, PR 00936-5067. Offers Au D. *Faculty research:* Hearing, auditory brainstem responses, otoacoustic emissions.

University of Puerto Rico, Medical Sciences Campus, School of Health Professions, Program in Speech-Language Pathology, San Juan, PR 00936-5067. Offers MS. *Accreditation:* ASHA. *Degree requirements:* For master's, one foreign language, comprehensive exam, thesis or alternative. *Entrance requirements:* For master's, EXADEP, interview; previous course work in linguistics, statistics, human development, and basic concepts in speech-language pathology; minimum GPA of 2.5. *Faculty research:* Aphasia, autism, language, aphasia, assistive technology.

University of Redlands, College of Arts and Sciences, Department of Communicative Disorders, Redlands, CA 92373-0999. Offers MS. *Accreditation:* ASHA. *Degree requirements:* For master's, final exam. *Entrance requirements:* For master's, GMAT or GRE, minimum GPA of 3.0, 3 letters of recommendation. Additional exam requirements/

recommendations for international students: Required—TOEFL (minimum score 550 paper-based; 213 computer-based). Electronic applications accepted. *Expenses:* Contact institution. *Faculty research:* Neuropathy.

University of Rhode Island, Graduate School, College of Human Science and Services, Department of Communicative Disorders, Kingston, RI 02881. Offers speech-language pathology (MS). *Accreditation:* ASHA. Part-time programs available. *Faculty:* 8 full-time (6 women). *Students:* 37 full-time (36 women), 12 part-time (11 women); includes 3 minority (1 Asian, non-Hispanic/Latino; 2 Hispanic/Latino). In 2011, 15 master's awarded. *Degree requirements:* For master's, comprehensive exam (for some programs), thesis optional. *Entrance requirements:* For master's, GRE or MAT, 2 letters of recommendation. Additional exam requirements/recommendations for international students: Required—TOEFL (minimum score 550 paper-based; 213 computer-based). *Application deadline:* For fall admission, 3/1 for domestic students, 2/1 for international students; for spring admission, 10/15 for domestic students, 7/15 for international students. Application fee: $65. Electronic applications accepted. *Expenses:* Tuition, state resident: full-time $10,432; part-time $580 per credit hour. Tuition, nonresident: full-time $23,130; part-time $1285 per credit hour. *Required fees:* $1362; $36 per credit hour. $35 per semester. One-time fee: $130. *Financial support:* In 2011–12, 3 teaching assistantships with full and partial tuition reimbursements (averaging $6,947 per year) were awarded. Financial award application deadline: 3/1; financial award applicants required to submit FAFSA. *Faculty research:* Efficacy of treatment for acquired alexia in individuals with aphasia, application of principles of neuroplasticity to individuals with motor speech disorders secondary to neurological deficits, study of the conversation factors that promote fluency or exacerbate stuttering in young children. *Unit head:* Dr. Dana Kovarsky, Chair, 401-874-2735, Fax: 401-874-4404, E-mail: dana@uri.edu. *Application contact:* Nasser H. Zawia, Dean of the Graduate School, 401-874-5909, Fax: 401-874-5787, E-mail: nzawia@uri.edu. Web site: http://www.uri.edu/hss/cmd/.

University of San Diego, School of Leadership and Education Sciences, Department of Learning and Teaching, San Diego, CA 92110-2492. Offers curriculum and instruction (M Ed); special education (M Ed); special education with deaf and hard of hearing (M Ed); teaching (MAT); TESOL, literacy and culture (M Ed). Part-time and evening/weekend programs available. *Faculty:* 11 full-time (8 women), 41 part-time/adjunct (32 women). *Students:* 86 full-time (69 women), 73 part-time (62 women); includes 54 minority (7 Black or African American, non-Hispanic/Latino; 1 American Indian or Alaska Native, non-Hispanic/Latino; 7 Asian, non-Hispanic/Latino; 27 Hispanic/Latino; 1 Native Hawaiian or other Pacific Islander, non-Hispanic/Latino; 11 Two or more races, non-Hispanic/Latino), 12 international. Average age 28. 177 applicants, 60% accepted, 61 enrolled. In 2011, 57 master's awarded. *Degree requirements:* For master's, thesis (for some programs). *Entrance requirements:* For master's, minimum GPA of 3.0. Additional exam requirements/recommendations for international students: Required—TOEFL (minimum score 580 paper-based; 237 computer-based; 83 iBT), TWE. *Application deadline:* For fall admission, 3/1 priority date for domestic students, 3/1 for international students; for spring admission, 10/15 priority date for domestic students, 10/15 for international students. Application fee: $45. Electronic applications accepted. *Expenses: Tuition:* Full-time $22,482; part-time $1249 per unit. *Required fees:* $224. Full-time tuition and fees vary according to course load and degree level. *Financial support:* In 2011–12, 77 students received support. Career-related internships or fieldwork, Federal Work-Study, institutionally sponsored loans, and stipends available. Support available to part-time students. Financial award application deadline: 4/1; financial award applicants required to submit FAFSA. *Faculty research:* Action research methodology, cultural studies, instructional theories and practices, second language acquisition, school reform. *Unit head:* Dr. Heather Lattimer, Director, 619-260-7616, Fax: 619-260-8159, E-mail: hlattimer@sandiego.edu. *Application contact:* Monica Mahon, Associate Director of Graduate Admissions, 619-260-4524, Fax: 619-260-4158, E-mail: grads@sandiego.edu. Web site: http://www.sandiego.edu/soles/programs/learning_and_teaching/.

University of South Alabama, Graduate School, College of Allied Health Professions, Department of Speech Pathology and Audiology, Mobile, AL 36688-0002. Offers audiology (Au D); communication sciences and disorders (PhD); speech and hearing sciences (MS). *Accreditation:* ASHA. *Faculty:* 8 full-time (5 women). *Students:* 77 full-time (72 women), 2 part-time (both women); includes 3 minority (all Black or African American, non-Hispanic/Latino). 55 applicants, 100% accepted, 23 enrolled. In 2011, 23 master's, 11 doctorates awarded. *Degree requirements:* For master's, thesis optional, externship; for doctorate, thesis/dissertation, clinical internship; minimum of 11 full-time semesters of academic study. *Entrance requirements:* For master's, GRE, bachelor's degree in communication sciences and disorders; for doctorate, GRE, minimum GPA of 3.0. Additional exam requirements/recommendations for international students: Required—TOEFL. *Application deadline:* For fall admission, 2/1 priority date for domestic students. Applications are processed on a rolling basis. Application fee: $35. *Expenses:* Tuition, state resident: full-time $7968; part-time $332 per credit hour. Tuition, nonresident: full-time $15,936; part-time $664 per credit hour. *Financial support:* Fellowships, research assistantships, and career-related internships or fieldwork available. Support available to part-time students. Financial award application deadline: 4/1. *Faculty research:* Computer applications to speech and hearing science, telecommunications and clinical research in articulation and languages. *Unit head:* Dr. Robert Moore, Chair, 251-445-9378, E-mail: rmoore@usouthal.edu. *Application contact:* Dr. Julio Turrens, Director of Graduate Studies, 251-445-9250. Web site: http://www.southalabama.edu/alliedhealth/speechandhearing.

University of South Carolina, The Graduate School, Arnold School of Public Health, Department of Communication Sciences and Disorders, Columbia, SC 29208. Offers MCD, MSP, PhD. *Accreditation:* ASHA (one or more programs are accredited). Postbaccalaureate distance learning degree programs offered. *Degree requirements:* For master's, thesis optional; for doctorate, comprehensive exam, thesis/dissertation. *Entrance requirements:* For master's, GRE General Test, minimum GPA of 3.0; for doctorate, GRE General Test. Electronic applications accepted. *Faculty research:* Noise-induced hearing loss, recurrent laryngeal nerve regeneration, cleft palate, child language-phonology, epidemiology of craniofacial anomalies.

The University of South Dakota, Graduate School, College of Arts and Sciences, Department of Communication Disorders, Vermillion, SD 57069-2390. Offers audiology (Au D); communications disorders (MA); speech-language pathology (MA). *Accreditation:* ASHA (one or more programs are accredited). Part-time programs available. *Degree requirements:* For master's, comprehensive exam; for doctorate, comprehensive exam, thesis/dissertation. *Entrance requirements:* For master's, GRE General Test, minimum GPA of 3.0. Additional exam requirements/recommendations for international students: Required—TOEFL (minimum score 550 paper-based; 213 computer-based; 79 iBT). Electronic applications accepted. *Expenses:* Tuition, state resident: full-time $3118.50; part-time $173.25 per credit hour. Tuition, nonresident: full-time $6601; part-time $366.70 per credit hour. *Required fees:* $2268; $126 per credit hour. Tuition and fees vary according to program. *Faculty research:* Craniofacial anomalies, central auditory processing, phonological disorders.

University of Southern Mississippi, Graduate School, College of Health, Department of Speech and Hearing Sciences, Hattiesburg, MS 39406-0001. Offers audiology (Au D); speech language pathology (MA, MS), including deaf education (MS). *Accreditation:* ASHA (one or more programs are accredited). *Faculty:* 10 full-time (4 women). *Students:* 74 full-time (69 women), 5 part-time (all women); includes 8 minority (6 Black or African American, non-Hispanic/Latino; 1 Asian, non-Hispanic/Latino; 1 Hispanic/Latino), 2 international. Average age 27. 87 applicants, 39% accepted, 19 enrolled. In 2011, 17 master's, 9 doctorates awarded. *Degree requirements:* For master's, comprehensive exam, thesis or alternative; for doctorate, comprehensive exam, thesis/dissertation. *Entrance requirements:* For master's, GRE General Test, minimum GPA of 3.0 in field of study, 2.75 in last 60 hours; for doctorate, GRE General Test, minimum GPA of 3.5. Additional exam requirements/recommendations for international students: Required—TOEFL, IELTS. *Application deadline:* For fall admission, 3/1 for domestic and international students; for spring admission, 1/10 priority date for domestic students, 1/10 for international students. Application fee: $50. Electronic applications accepted. *Financial support:* In 2011–12, 9 research assistantships with full and partial tuition reimbursements (averaging $7,200 per year), teaching assistantships with full and partial tuition reimbursements (averaging $7,200 per year) were awarded; career-related internships or fieldwork, Federal Work-Study, institutionally sponsored loans, scholarships/grants, health care benefits, and unspecified assistantships also available. Financial award application deadline: 3/15; financial award applicants required to submit FAFSA. *Faculty research:* Voice disorders, auditory-evoked responses, acoustic analysis of speech, child language, parent-child interaction. *Unit head:* Dr. Steve Cloud, Interim Chair, 601-266-5217. *Application contact:* Dr. Steve Cloud, Interim Chair, 601-266-5217, Fax: 601-266-5138. Web site: http://www.usm.edu/graduateschool/table.php.

University of South Florida, Graduate School, College of Behavioral and Community Sciences, Department of Communication Sciences and Disorders, Tampa, FL 33620. Offers audiology (Au D); hearing science (PhD); language and speech science (PhD); neurocommunicative science (PhD); speech-language pathology (MS). *Accreditation:* ASHA (one or more programs are accredited). Part-time and evening/weekend programs available. Postbaccalaureate distance learning degree programs offered (minimal on-campus study). *Faculty:* 30 full-time (23 women), 14 part-time/adjunct (10 women). *Students:* 169 full-time (153 women), 54 part-time (50 women); includes 45 minority (13 Black or African American, non-Hispanic/Latino; 5 Asian, non-Hispanic/Latino; 27 Hispanic/Latino), 4 international. Average age 27. 484 applicants, 23% accepted, 92 enrolled. In 2011, 61 master's, 11 doctorates awarded. *Degree requirements:* For doctorate, comprehensive exam, thesis/dissertation. *Entrance requirements:* For master's, GRE (minimum scores: 52nd percentile Verbal, 32nd percentile Quantitative), minimum GPA of 3.2 in last 60 hours, three letters of recommendation, letter of intent, resume; for doctorate, GRE (minimum score in 33rd percentile or above in all sections), minimum GPA of 3.0, three letters of recommendation, letter of intent. Additional exam requirements/recommendations for international students: Required—TOEFL (minimum score 550 paper-based; 213 computer-based; 79 iBT) or IELTS (minimum score 6.5). *Application deadline:* For fall admission, 12/1 for domestic and international students; for spring admission, 2/1 for domestic and international students. Application fee: $30. Electronic applications accepted. *Financial support:* In 2011–12, 25 students received support, including 1 research assistantship with tuition reimbursement available (averaging $10,920 per year), 15 teaching assistantships with full and partial tuition reimbursements available (averaging $10,881 per year); career-related internships or fieldwork, traineeships, health care benefits, and unspecified assistantships also available. Financial award application deadline: 2/1; financial award applicants required to submit FAFSA. *Faculty research:* Speech perception, motor speech, neurogenic communication disorder, oncology, speech acoustics. *Total annual research expenditures:* $439,878. *Unit head:* Dr. Theresa Chisolm, Chair, 813-974-9826, E-mail: tchisolm@bcs.usf.edu. *Application contact:* Dr. Jean Krause, 813-974-9798, Fax: 813-974-0822, E-mail: jeankrause@usf.edu. Web site: http://csd.bcs.usf.edu/.

The University of Tennessee, Graduate School, College of Arts and Sciences, Department of Audiology and Speech Pathology, Program in Audiology, Knoxville, TN 37996. Offers MA. *Accreditation:* ASHA. *Degree requirements:* For master's, thesis or alternative. *Entrance requirements:* For master's, GRE General Test, minimum GPA of 2.7. Additional exam requirements/recommendations for international students: Required—TOEFL. Electronic applications accepted. *Expenses:* Tuition, state resident: full-time $8332; part-time $464 per credit hour. Tuition, nonresident: full-time $25,174; part-time $1400 per credit hour. *Required fees:* $1162; $56 per credit hour. Tuition and fees vary according to program.

The University of Tennessee, Graduate School, College of Arts and Sciences, Department of Audiology and Speech Pathology, Program in Speech and Hearing Science, Knoxville, TN 37996. Offers audiology (PhD); hearing science (PhD); speech and language pathology (PhD); speech and language science (PhD). *Accreditation:* ASHA. *Degree requirements:* For doctorate, thesis/dissertation. *Entrance requirements:* For doctorate, GRE General Test, minimum GPA of 2.7. Additional exam requirements/recommendations for international students: Required—TOEFL. Electronic applications accepted. *Expenses:* Tuition, state resident: full-time $8332; part-time $464 per credit hour. Tuition, nonresident: full-time $25,174; part-time $1400 per credit hour. *Required fees:* $1162; $56 per credit hour. Tuition and fees vary according to program.

The University of Tennessee, Graduate School, College of Arts and Sciences, Department of Audiology and Speech Pathology, Program in Speech Pathology, Knoxville, TN 37996. Offers MA. *Accreditation:* ASHA. *Degree requirements:* For master's, thesis or alternative. *Entrance requirements:* For master's, GRE General Test, minimum GPA of 2.7. Additional exam requirements/recommendations for international students: Required—TOEFL. Electronic applications accepted. *Expenses:* Tuition, state resident: full-time $8332; part-time $464 per credit hour. Tuition, nonresident: full-time $25,174; part-time $1400 per credit hour. *Required fees:* $1162; $56 per credit hour. Tuition and fees vary according to program.

The University of Tennessee, Graduate School, College of Education, Health and Human Sciences, Program in Education, Knoxville, TN 37996. Offers art education (MS); counseling education (PhD); cultural studies in education (PhD); curriculum (MS, Ed S); curriculum, educational research and evaluation (Ed D, PhD); early childhood education (PhD); early childhood special education (MS); education of deaf and hard of hearing (MS); educational administration and policy studies (Ed D, PhD); educational administration and supervision (Ed S); educational psychology (Ed D, PhD); elementary education (MS, Ed S); elementary teaching (MS); English education (MS, Ed S); exercise science (PhD); foreign language/ESL education (MS, Ed S); instructional technology (MS, Ed D, PhD, Ed S); literacy, language and ESL education (PhD); literacy, language education, and ESL education (Ed D); mathematics education (MS, Ed S); modified and comprehensive special education (MS); reading education (MS, Ed S); school counseling (Ed S); school psychology (PhD, Ed S); science education (MS, Ed S); secondary teaching (MS); social foundations (MS); social science education (MS, Ed S); socio-cultural foundations of sports and education (PhD); special education (Ed S); teacher education (Ed D, PhD). *Accreditation:* NCATE. Part-time and evening/weekend programs available. *Degree requirements:* For master's and Ed S, thesis optional; for doctorate, variable foreign language requirement, thesis/dissertation. *Entrance requirements:* For master's, minimum GPA of 2.7; for doctorate and Ed S, GRE General Test, minimum GPA of 2.7. Additional exam requirements/

recommendations for international students: Required—TOEFL. Electronic applications accepted. *Expenses:* Tuition, state resident: full-time $8332; part-time $464 per credit hour. Tuition, nonresident: full-time $25,174; part-time $1400 per credit hour. *Required fees:* $1162; $56 per credit hour. Tuition and fees vary according to program.

The University of Texas at Austin, Graduate School, College of Communication, Department of Communication Sciences and Disorders, Austin, TX 78712-1111. Offers audiology (Au D); communication sciences and disorders (PhD); speech language pathology (MA). *Accreditation:* ASHA (one or more programs are accredited). *Entrance requirements:* For master's and doctorate, GRE General Test. Application fee: $50 ($75 for international students). *Financial support:* Application deadline: 2/1. *Unit head:* Dr. Craig Champlin, Chair, 512-471-6345, E-mail: champlin@mail.utexas.edu. *Application contact:* Dr. Mark Bernstein, Associate Dean, 512-471-1553, E-mail: mark.bernstein@austin.utexas.edu. Web site: http://csd.utexas.edu/graduate.

The University of Texas at Dallas, School of Behavioral and Brain Sciences, Program in Audiology, Dallas, TX 75235. Offers Au D. *Accreditation:* ASHA. *Faculty:* 6 full-time (2 women), 3 part-time/adjunct (2 women). *Students:* 33 full-time (27 women), 7 part-time (6 women); includes 7 minority (4 Asian, non-Hispanic/Latino; 1 Hispanic/Latino; 2 Two or more races, non-Hispanic/Latino), 3 international. Average age 28. 72 applicants, 25% accepted, 11 enrolled. In 2011, 6 doctorates awarded. *Entrance requirements:* Additional exam requirements/recommendations for international students: Required—TOEFL (minimum score 550 paper-based; 215 computer-based). *Application deadline:* For fall admission, 7/15 for domestic students, 5/1 for international students; for spring admission, 11/15 for domestic students, 9/1 for international students. Applications are processed on a rolling basis. Application fee: $50 ($100 for international students). Electronic applications accepted. *Expenses:* Tuition, state resident: full-time $11,170; part-time $620.56 per credit hour. Tuition, nonresident: full-time $20,212; part-time $1122.89 per credit hour. *Financial support:* In 2011–12, 38 students received support. Research assistantships with partial tuition reimbursements available, teaching assistantships with partial tuition reimbursements available, career-related internships or fieldwork, Federal Work-Study, institutionally sponsored loans, scholarships/grants, and unspecified assistantships available. Support available to part-time students. Financial award application deadline: 4/30; financial award applicants required to submit FAFSA. *Faculty research:* Hearing disorders, amplification of hearing aids, cochlear implants and aural habilitation. *Unit head:* Dr. Ross Roeser, Program Head, 214-905-3002, E-mail: roeser@callier.utdallas.edu. *Application contact:* Cathie Bittner, Program Assistant, 214-905-3034, E-mail: audiology@utdallas.edu. Web site: http://bbs.utdallas.edu/aud.

The University of Texas at Dallas, School of Behavioral and Brain Sciences, Program in Communication Sciences and Disorders, Richardson, TX 75080. Offers communication disorders (MS); communication science and disorders (PhD). Part-time and evening/weekend programs available. *Faculty:* 15 full-time (8 women), 7 part-time/adjunct (5 women). *Students:* 232 full-time (225 women), 18 part-time (16 women); includes 44 minority (2 Black or African American, non-Hispanic/Latino; 14 Asian, non-Hispanic/Latino; 22 Hispanic/Latino; 6 Two or more races, non-Hispanic/Latino), 8 international. Average age 26. 413 applicants, 21% accepted, 60 enrolled. In 2011, 125 master's, 2 doctorates awarded. *Degree requirements:* For doctorate, thesis/dissertation. *Entrance requirements:* For master's and doctorate, GRE General Test, minimum GPA of 3.0 in upper-level course work in field. Additional exam requirements/recommendations for international students: Required—TOEFL (minimum score 550 paper-based; 215 computer-based). *Application deadline:* For fall admission, 7/15 for domestic students, 5/1 for international students; for spring admission, 11/15 for domestic students, 9/1 for international students. Applications are processed on a rolling basis. Application fee: $50 ($100 for international students). Electronic applications accepted. *Expenses:* Tuition, state resident: full-time $11,170; part-time $620.56 per credit hour. Tuition, nonresident: full-time $20,212; part-time $1122.89 per credit hour. *Financial support:* In 2011–12, 147 students received support, including 3 research assistantships with partial tuition reimbursements available (averaging $29,957 per year), 10 teaching assistantships with partial tuition reimbursements available (averaging $14,850 per year); fellowships, Federal Work-Study, institutionally sponsored loans, scholarships/grants, and unspecified assistantships also available. Support available to part-time students. Financial award application deadline: 4/30; financial award applicants required to submit FAFSA. *Faculty research:* Developmental neurolinguistics, brain plasticity and biofeedback treatment, autism spectrum disorders, speech production, neurogenic speech and language disorders. *Unit head:* Dr. Robert D. Stillman, Program Head, 214-905-3106, Fax: 972-883-3022, E-mail: stillman@utdallas.edu. *Application contact:* Maria Felipe, Program Assistant, 972-883-2358, E-mail: maria.felipe@utdallas.edu. Web site: http://bbs.utdallas.edu/csd/.

The University of Texas at El Paso, Graduate School, College of Health Sciences, Department of Speech-Language Pathology, El Paso, TX 79968-0001. Offers MS. *Accreditation:* ASHA. *Students:* 39 (33 women); includes 30 minority (1 Black or African American, non-Hispanic/Latino; 1 American Indian or Alaska Native, non-Hispanic/Latino; 28 Hispanic/Latino), 1 international. Average age 34. In 2011, 15 master's awarded. *Degree requirements:* For master's, thesis optional. *Entrance requirements:* For master's, GRE, minimum GPA of 3.0, resume, letters of recommendation. Additional exam requirements/recommendations for international students: Required—TOEFL; Recommended—IELTS. *Application deadline:* For fall admission, 8/1 for domestic students, 3/1 for international students; for spring admission, 11/1 for domestic students, 9/3 for international students. Applications are processed on a rolling basis. Application fee: $45 ($80 for international students). Electronic applications accepted. *Financial support:* In 2011–12, research assistantships with partial tuition reimbursements (averaging $18,825 per year), teaching assistantships with partial tuition reimbursements (averaging $18,000 per year) were awarded; fellowships with partial tuition reimbursements, institutionally sponsored loans, scholarships/grants, health care benefits, tuition waivers (partial), and unspecified assistantships also available. Support available to part-time students. Financial award application deadline: 3/15; financial award applicants required to submit FAFSA. *Faculty research:* Cleft palate, bilingual language disorders, clinical supervision, hearing loss. *Unit head:* Dr. Anthony Salvatore, Chair, 915-747-7250, Fax: 915-747-7207, E-mail: asalvatore@utep.edu. *Application contact:* Dr. Benjamin Flores, Interim Dean of the Graduate School, 915-747-5491, Fax: 915-747-5788, E-mail: bflores@utep.edu.

The University of Texas Health Science Center at San Antonio, School of Health Professions, San Antonio, TX 78229-3900. Offers clinical laboratory sciences (MS); deaf education and hearing science (MED); dental hygiene (MS); occupational therapy (MOT); physical therapy (MPT); physician assistant studies (MS). *Accreditation:* AOTA; APTA; ARC-PA. *Degree requirements:* For master's, thesis. *Entrance requirements:* Additional exam requirements/recommendations for international students: Required—TOEFL (minimum score 560 paper-based; 280 computer-based; 68 iBT). Electronic applications accepted.

The University of Texas–Pan American, College of Health Sciences and Human Services, Department of Communication Sciences and Disorders, Edinburg, TX 78539. Offers MS. *Accreditation:* ASHA. *Degree requirements:* For master's, comprehensive exam, thesis optional, NESPA exam. *Entrance requirements:* For master's, GRE General Test, minimum GPA of 3.0 in major, 3 letters of recommendation, resume. Additional exam requirements/recommendations for international students: Required—

TOEFL (minimum score 550 paper-based). *Application deadline:* For fall admission, 2/7 for domestic and international students. Application fee: $35. Electronic applications accepted. Tuition and fees vary according to course load, program and student level. *Financial support:* Research assistantships, teaching assistantships, career-related internships or fieldwork, Federal Work-Study, institutionally sponsored loans, and scholarships/grants available. Financial award application deadline: 9/1; financial award applicants required to submit FAFSA. *Faculty research:* Bilingual/bicultural language development/disorders, elementary-age language disorders, voice disorders. *Unit head:* Dr. Teri Mata-Pistokache, Graduate Coordinator, 956-665-3582, E-mail: tmpistok@utpa.edu. Web site: http://portal.utpa.edu/utpa_main/daa_home/hshs_home/comm_home.

University of the District of Columbia, College of Arts and Sciences, Department of Language and Communication Disorders, Program in Speech and Language Pathology, Washington, DC 20008-1175. Offers MS. *Accreditation:* ASHA. Part-time programs available. *Degree requirements:* For master's, comprehensive exam, thesis optional. *Entrance requirements:* For master's, GRE General Test, writing proficiency exam. *Expenses: Tuition, area resident:* Full-time $7580; part-time $421 per credit hour. Tuition, state resident: full-time $8580; part-time $477 per credit hour. Tuition, nonresident: full-time $14,580; part-time $810 per credit hour. *Required fees:* $620; $30 per credit hour. $310 per semester. *Faculty research:* Child language, dialect variation, English as a second language.

University of the Pacific, Thomas J. Long School of Pharmacy and Health Sciences, Department of Speech-Language Pathology, Stockton, CA 95211-0197. Offers MS. *Accreditation:* ASHA. *Faculty:* 9 full-time (5 women), 14 part-time/adjunct (13 women). *Students:* 77 full-time (70 women), 1 (woman) part-time; includes 20 minority (1 American Indian or Alaska Native, non-Hispanic/Latino; 10 Asian, non-Hispanic/Latino; 9 Hispanic/Latino). Average age 28. 157 applicants, 27% accepted, 29 enrolled. In 2011, 27 master's awarded. *Entrance requirements:* For master's, GRE General Test. Additional exam requirements/recommendations for international students: Required—TOEFL (minimum score 475 paper-based; 150 computer-based). *Application deadline:* For fall admission, 2/1 for domestic students. Application fee: $75. *Expenses: Tuition:* Full-time $18,900; part-time $1181 per unit. *Required fees:* $949. *Financial support:* Institutionally sponsored loans available. Support available to part-time students. Financial award application deadline: 2/1; financial award applicants required to submit FAFSA. *Unit head:* Dr. Robert Hanyak, Chairman, 209-946-3223, E-mail: rhanyak@pacific.edu. *Application contact:* Cyndi Porter, Outreach Officer, 209-946-3957, Fax: 209-946-2410, E-mail: cporter@pacific.edu.

The University of Toledo, College of Graduate Studies, Judith Herb College of Education, Health Science and Human Service, Department of Rehabilitation Sciences, Toledo, OH 43606-3390. Offers occupational therapy (OTD); physical therapy (DPT); speech-language pathology (MA). *Faculty:* 18. *Students:* 163 full-time (128 women), 24 part-time (20 women); includes 13 minority (4 Black or African American, non-Hispanic/Latino; 1 American Indian or Alaska Native, non-Hispanic/Latino; 5 Asian, non-Hispanic/Latino; 2 Hispanic/Latino; 1 Two or more races, non-Hispanic/Latino). Average age 25. 488 applicants, 23% accepted, 73 enrolled. In 2011, 29 master's, 46 doctorates awarded. *Degree requirements:* For master's, comprehensive exam, thesis; for doctorate, thesis/dissertation or alternative. *Entrance requirements:* For master's, GRE, minimum cumulative GPA of 2.7 for all previous academic work, letters of recommendation; for doctorate, GRE, minimum cumulative GPA of 3.0 for all previous academic work, letters of recommendation; OTCAS or PTCAS application and UT supplemental application (for OTD and DPT). Additional exam requirements/recommendations for international students: Required—TOEFL (minimum score 550 paper-based; 213 computer-based; 80 iBT), IELTS (minimum score 6.5). *Application deadline:* For fall admission, 11/1 for domestic and international students. Application fee: $45 ($75 for international students). Electronic applications accepted. *Financial support:* In 2011–12, 5 research assistantships with full and partial tuition reimbursements (averaging $10,705 per year), 11 teaching assistantships with full and partial tuition reimbursements (averaging $6,182 per year) were awarded; Federal Work-Study, scholarships/grants, tuition waivers (full and partial), and unspecified assistantships also available. *Unit head:* Dr. Michelle Masterson, Chair, 419-530-6671, Fax: 419-530-4780, E-mail: michelle.masterson@utoledo.edu. *Application contact:* College of Graduate Studies - HSC, 419-383-4112, Fax: 419-383-6140, E-mail: grdsch@utnet.utoledo.edu. Web site: http://www.utoledo.edu/eduhshs/.

University of Toronto, Faculty of Medicine, Department of Speech-Language Pathology, Toronto, ON M5S 1A1, Canada. Offers M Sc, MH Sc, PhD. Part-time programs available. *Degree requirements:* For master's, thesis (for some programs), clinical internship (MH Sc), oral thesis defense (M Sc); for doctorate, comprehensive exam, thesis/dissertation, oral thesis defense. *Entrance requirements:* For master's, minimum B+ average in last 2 years (MH Sc), B average in final year (M Sc); volunteer/work experience in a clinical setting (MH Sc); for doctorate, previous research experience or thesis, resume, 3 writing samples, 3 letters of recommendation. Electronic applications accepted.

University of Tulsa, Graduate School, College of Arts and Sciences, Program in Speech-Language Pathology, Tulsa, OK 74104-3189. Offers MS. *Accreditation:* ASHA. Part-time programs available. *Faculty:* 8 full-time (all women). *Students:* 33 full-time (all women), 1 (woman) part-time; includes 3 minority (1 Asian, non-Hispanic/Latino; 2 Hispanic/Latino). Average age 24. 61 applicants, 62% accepted, 22 enrolled. In 2011, 14 master's awarded. *Degree requirements:* For master's, thesis optional. *Entrance requirements:* For master's, GRE General Test. Additional exam requirements/recommendations for international students: Required—TOEFL (minimum score 577 paper-based; 233 computer-based; 90 iBT), IELTS (minimum score 6.5). *Application deadline:* For fall admission, 2/1 priority date for domestic students. Application fee: $40. Electronic applications accepted. *Expenses: Tuition:* Full-time $17,748; part-time $986 per hour. *Required fees:* $5 per contact hour. $75 per semester. Tuition and fees vary according to program. *Financial support:* In 2011–12, 13 students received support, including 1 fellowship with full and partial tuition reimbursement available (averaging $14,584 per year), 12 teaching assistantships with full and partial tuition reimbursements available (averaging $8,361 per year); career-related internships or fieldwork, Federal Work-Study, scholarships/grants, traineeships, health care benefits, tuition waivers (full and partial), and unspecified assistantships also available. Support available to part-time students. Financial award application deadline: 2/1; financial award applicants required to submit FAFSA. *Faculty research:* Disorders of fluency, delayed language and literacy, aphasia, voice, speech articulation, swallowing, cognition. *Unit head:* Dr. Paula Cadogan, Chairperson, 918-631-2897, Fax: 918-631-3668, E-mail: paula-cadogan@utulsa.edu. *Application contact:* Dr. Paula Cadogan, Adviser, 918-631-2897, Fax: 918-631-3668, E-mail: paula-cadogan@utulsa.edu. Web site: http://www.cas.utulsa.edu/commdis/.

University of Utah, Graduate School, College of Education, Department of Special Education, Salt Lake City, UT 84112. Offers early childhood hearing impairments (M Ed, MS); early childhood special education (M Ed, PhD); early childhood vision impairments (M Ed, MS); hearing impairments (M Ed, MS); mild/moderate disabilities (M Ed, MS, PhD); professional practice (M Ed); research in special education (MS); severe disabilities (M Ed, MS, PhD); vision impairments (M Ed). Part-time and evening/

weekend programs available. Postbaccalaureate distance learning degree programs offered (no on-campus study). *Faculty:* 16 full-time (11 women). *Students:* 34 full-time (26 women), 25 part-time (22 women); includes 11 minority (1 Black or African American, non-Hispanic/Latino; 3 American Indian or Alaska Native, non-Hispanic/Latino; 4 Hispanic/Latino; 1 Native Hawaiian or other Pacific Islander, non-Hispanic/Latino; 2 Two or more races, non-Hispanic/Latino), 1 international. Average age 35. 37 applicants, 54% accepted, 16 enrolled. In 2011, 26 degrees awarded. Terminal master's awarded for partial completion of doctoral program. *Degree requirements:* For master's, comprehensive exam, thesis (for some programs), qualifying exam; for doctorate, thesis/dissertation, qualifying exam. *Entrance requirements:* For master's, GRE or Analytical/Writing portion of GRE plus PRAXIS I, minimum GPA of 3.0; for doctorate, GRE General Test (minimum scores: Verbal 600; Quantitative 600; Analytical/Writing 4), minimum GPA of 3.0, 3.5 (recommended). Additional exam requirements/recommendations for international students: Required—TOEFL (minimum score 600 paper-based; 250 computer-based; 100 iBT); Recommended—IELTS (minimum score 7). *Application deadline:* For fall admission, 3/1 for domestic and international students; for spring admission, 11/1 for domestic and international students. Applications are processed on a rolling basis. Application fee: $55 ($65 for international students). Electronic applications accepted. *Expenses:* Contact institution. *Financial support:* In 2011–12, 25 students received support, including 25 fellowships with full tuition reimbursements available (averaging $7,124 per year), 3 teaching assistantships with full tuition reimbursements available (averaging $10,750 per year); research assistantships and career-related internships or fieldwork also available. Support available to part-time students. Financial award application deadline: 3/1; financial award applicants required to submit FAFSA. *Faculty research:* Inclusive education, positive behavior support, reading, instruction and intervention strategies. *Total annual research expenditures:* $5,926. *Unit head:* Dr. Robert E. O'Neill, Chair, 801-581-8121, Fax: 801-585-6476, E-mail: rob.oneill@utah.edu. *Application contact:* Patty Davis, Academic Advisor, 801-581-4764, Fax: 801-585-6476, E-mail: patty.davis@utah.edu. Web site: http://www.ed.utah.edu/sped/.

University of Utah, Graduate School, College of Health, Department of Communication Sciences and Disorders, Salt Lake City, UT 84112. Offers audiology (Au D, PhD); speech-language pathology (MA, MS, PhD). *Accreditation:* ASHA (one or more programs are accredited). *Faculty:* 11 full-time (6 women). *Students:* 103 full-time (86 women), 8 part-time (5 women); includes 10 minority (1 American Indian or Alaska Native, non-Hispanic/Latino; 1 Asian, non-Hispanic/Latino; 7 Hispanic/Latino; 1 Two or more races, non-Hispanic/Latino), 4 international. Average age 27. 200 applicants, 52% accepted, 48 enrolled. In 2011, 32 master's, 5 doctorates awarded. Terminal master's awarded for partial completion of doctoral program. *Degree requirements:* For master's, thesis optional, written exam; for doctorate, thesis/dissertation, written and oral exams. *Entrance requirements:* For master's and doctorate, GRE General Test, minimum GPA of 3.0. Additional exam requirements/recommendations for international students: Required—TOEFL (minimum score 600 paper-based; 250 computer-based; 100 iBT). *Application deadline:* For fall admission, 2/1 priority date for domestic students, 2/1 for international students. Application fee: $55 ($65 for international students). Electronic applications accepted. *Expenses:* Contact institution. *Financial support:* In 2011–12, 19 students received support, including 18 research assistantships with partial tuition reimbursements available (averaging $8,000 per year), 1 teaching assistantship with partial tuition reimbursement available (averaging $16,000 per year); career-related internships or fieldwork, Federal Work-Study, scholarships/grants, tuition waivers (partial), and unspecified assistantships also available. Financial award application deadline: 2/15; financial award applicants required to submit FAFSA. *Faculty research:* Motor speech disorders, fluency disorders, language disorders, voice disorders, cochlear implants and speech perception. *Total annual research expenditures:* $97,244. *Unit head:* Dr. Michael Blomgren, Department Chair, 801-581-6725, Fax: 801-581-7955, E-mail: michael.blomgren@hsc.utah.edu. *Application contact:* Dr. Kathy Chapman, Director of Graduate Studies, 801-581-6725, Fax: 801-581-7955, E-mail: kathy.chapman@hsc.utah.edu. Web site: http://www.health.utah.edu/csd.

University of Virginia, Curry School of Education, Department of Human Services, Program in Communication Disorders, Charlottesville, VA 22903. Offers M Ed. *Accreditation:* ASHA. *Students:* 70 full-time (69 women); includes 8 minority (4 Black or African American, non-Hispanic/Latino; 2 Asian, non-Hispanic/Latino; 2 Hispanic/Latino). Average age 24. 197 applicants, 37% accepted, 28 enrolled. In 2011, 19 master's awarded. *Entrance requirements:* For master's, GRE General Test, 2 letters of recommendation. Additional exam requirements/recommendations for international students: Required—TOEFL (minimum score 600 paper-based; 250 computer-based; 90 iBT), IELTS (minimum score 7). *Application deadline:* Applications are processed on a rolling basis. Application fee: $60. Electronic applications accepted. *Financial support:* Applicants required to submit FAFSA. *Unit head:* Randall R. Robey, Director, 434-924-6351, E-mail: robey@virginia.edu. *Application contact:* Lynn Renfroe, Information Contact, 434-924-6254, E-mail: ldr9t@virginia.edu. Web site: http://www.curry.edschool.virginia.edu/curry/dept/.

University of Washington, Graduate School, College of Arts and Sciences, Department of Speech and Hearing Sciences, Seattle, WA 98195. Offers audiology (Au D); speech and hearing sciences (PhD); speech-language pathology (MS). *Accreditation:* ASHA (one or more programs are accredited). *Degree requirements:* For master's, comprehensive exam, thesis or alternative; for doctorate, thesis/dissertation. *Entrance requirements:* For master's and doctorate, GRE, minimum GPA of 3.0. Additional exam requirements/recommendations for international students: Required—TOEFL. Electronic applications accepted. *Faculty research:* Treatment of communication disorders across the life span, speech physiology, auditory perception, behavioral and physiologic audiology.

The University of Western Ontario, Faculty of Graduate Studies, Health Sciences Division, School of Communication Sciences and Disorders, London, ON N6A 5B8, Canada. Offers audiology (M Cl Sc, M Sc); speech-language pathology (M Cl Sc, M Sc). *Degree requirements:* For master's, thesis (for some programs), supervised clinical practicum. *Entrance requirements:* For master's, 14 hours volunteer experience in field of study, minimum B average during last 2 years, previous course work in developmental psychology and statistics, 4 year honors degree. Additional exam requirements/recommendations for international students: Required—TOEFL (minimum score 620 paper-based; 260 computer-based). *Faculty research:* Child language, voice, neurogenics; auditory function, stuttering.

University of West Georgia, College of Education, Department of Collaborative Support and Intervention, Carrollton, GA 30118. Offers English to speakers of other languages (Ed S); guidance and counseling (M Ed, Ed S); professional counseling (M Ed, Ed S); professional counseling and supervision (Ed D, Ed S); reading education (M Ed, Ed S); reading endorsement (Ed S); special education-general (M Ed, Ed S); speech-language pathology (M Ed). Part-time and evening/weekend programs available. *Faculty:* 22 full-time (13 women), 6 part-time/adjunct (4 women). *Students:* 174 full-time (140 women), 253 part-time (228 women); includes 155 minority (127 Black or African American, non-Hispanic/Latino; 3 Asian, non-Hispanic/Latino; 14 Hispanic/Latino; 11 Two or more races, non-Hispanic/Latino), 2 international. Average age 33. 282 applicants, 49% accepted, 50 enrolled. In 2011, 98 master's, 27 other advanced degrees awarded. *Degree requirements:* For master's, comprehensive exam; for Ed S, research project. *Entrance requirements:* For master's, minimum GPA of 2.7; for Ed S, master's degree, minimum graduate GPA of 2.7. Additional exam requirements/recommendations for international students: Required—TOEFL (minimum score 523 paper-based; 193 computer-based; 69 iBT); Recommended—IELTS (minimum score 6). *Application deadline:* For fall admission, 6/3 for domestic students, 6/1 for international students; for spring admission, 10/7 for domestic students, 10/15 for international students. Applications are processed on a rolling basis. Application fee: $30. Electronic applications accepted. *Expenses:* Tuition, state resident: full-time $4336; part-time $181 per credit hour. Tuition, nonresident: full-time $17,362; part-time $724 per credit hour. Tuition and fees vary according to course load, degree level, campus/location and program. *Financial support:* In 2011–12, 5 research assistantships with full tuition reimbursements (averaging $3,000 per year) were awarded; career-related internships or fieldwork and scholarships/grants also available. Support available to part-time students. Financial award applicants required to submit FAFSA. *Unit head:* Dr. Michael Garrett, Chair, 678-839-6567, Fax: 678-839-6162, E-mail: mgarrett@westga.edu. *Application contact:* Deanna Richards, Coordinator, Graduate Studies, 678-839-5946, E-mail: drichard@westga.edu. Web site: http://www.westga.edu/coecsi.

University of Wisconsin–Eau Claire, College of Education and Human Sciences, Program in Communication Sciences and Disorders, Eau Claire, WI 54702-4004. Offers MS. *Accreditation:* ASHA. *Faculty:* 4 full-time (all women). *Students:* 34 full-time (30 women), 3 part-time (all women); includes 1 minority (Asian, non-Hispanic/Latino). Average age 26. 188 applicants, 11% accepted, 20 enrolled. In 2011, 14 master's awarded. *Degree requirements:* For master's, comprehensive exam, written or oral exam with thesis, externship. *Entrance requirements:* For master's, GRE, Wisconsin residency; minimum GPA of 3.0 in communication disorders, 2.75 overall. Additional exam requirements/recommendations for international students: Required—TOEFL (minimum score 550 paper-based; 213 computer-based; 79 iBT); Recommended—IELTS (minimum score 7). *Application deadline:* For fall admission, 2/1 priority date for domestic students, 2/1 for international students. Applications are processed on a rolling basis. Application fee: $56. *Expenses:* Tuition, state resident: full-time $7312; part-time $406 per credit. Tuition, nonresident: full-time $16,771; part-time $932 per credit. *Required fees:* $1101; $61 per credit. *Financial support:* In 2011–12, 12 students received support. Federal Work-Study and unspecified assistantships available. Financial award application deadline: 3/1; financial award applicants required to submit FAFSA. *Unit head:* Dr. Kristine Retherford, Chair, 715-836-4186, Fax: 715-836-4846, E-mail: retherk@uwec.edu. *Application contact:* Dr. Marie Stadler, Coordinator, 715-836-4861, E-mail: stadlema@uwec.edu. Web site: http://www.uwec.edu/csd/.

University of Wisconsin–Madison, Graduate School, College of Letters and Science, Department of Communicative Disorders, Madison, WI 53706-1380. Offers normal aspects of speech, language and hearing (MS, PhD); speech-language pathology (MS, PhD); MS/PhD. *Accreditation:* ASHA (one or more programs are accredited). *Degree requirements:* For doctorate, thesis/dissertation. *Entrance requirements:* For master's and doctorate, GRE. Electronic applications accepted. *Expenses:* Tuition, state resident: full-time $10,296; part-time $643.51 per credit. Tuition, nonresident: full-time $24,054; part-time $1503.40 per credit. *Required fees:* $70.06 per credit. Tuition and fees vary according to course load, campus/location, program and reciprocity agreements. *Faculty research:* Language disorders in children and adults, disorders of speech production, intelligibility, fluency, hearing impairment, deafness.

University of Wisconsin–Milwaukee, Graduate School, College of Health Sciences, Department of Communication Sciences and Disorders, Milwaukee, WI 53211. Offers MS, Certificate. *Accreditation:* ASHA (one or more programs are accredited). Part-time programs available. *Faculty:* 6 full-time (5 women), 1 (woman) part-time/adjunct. *Students:* 50 full-time (48 women), 1 (woman) part-time; includes 3 minority (2 Asian, non-Hispanic/Latino; 1 Two or more races, non-Hispanic/Latino), 1 international. Average age 31. 200 applicants, 13% accepted, 25 enrolled. In 2011, 25 master's awarded. *Degree requirements:* For master's, comprehensive exam, thesis optional. *Entrance requirements:* For master's, GRE General Test, minimum GPA of 3.0. Additional exam requirements/recommendations for international students: Required—TOEFL (minimum score 550 paper-based; 79 iBT), IELTS (minimum score 6.5). *Application deadline:* For fall admission, 1/1 priority date for domestic students; for spring admission, 9/1 for domestic students. Applications are processed on a rolling basis. Application fee: $56 ($96 for international students). One-time fee: $506.10 full-time. Tuition and fees vary according to course load and reciprocity agreements. *Financial support:* In 2011–12, 1 teaching assistantship was awarded; fellowships, research assistantships, career-related internships or fieldwork, unspecified assistantships, and project assistantships also available. Support available to part-time students. Financial award application deadline: 4/15. *Total annual research expenditures:* $725,363. *Unit head:* Marylou Gelfer, Department Chair, 414-229-6465, E-mail: gelfer@uwm.edu. *Application contact:* General Information Contact, 414-229-4982, Fax: 414-229-6967, E-mail: gradschool@uwm.edu. Web site: http://www4.uwm.edu/chs/academics/comm_sci_disorders/.

University of Wisconsin–River Falls, Outreach and Graduate Studies, College of Education and Professional Studies, Department of Communicative Disorders, River Falls, WI 54022. Offers communicative disorders (MS); secondary education-communicative disorders (MSE). *Accreditation:* ASHA (one or more programs are accredited). Part-time programs available. *Degree requirements:* For master's, comprehensive exam. *Entrance requirements:* For master's, minimum GPA of 2.75, 3 letters of reference. Additional exam requirements/recommendations for international students: Required—TOEFL (minimum score 500 paper-based; 65 iBT), IELTS (minimum score 5.5). *Faculty research:* SHRG, voice, language, audiology.

University of Wisconsin–Stevens Point, College of Professional Studies, School of Communicative Disorders, Stevens Point, WI 54481-3897. Offers audiology (Au D); speech-language pathology (MS). *Accreditation:* ASHA (one or more programs are accredited). *Degree requirements:* For master's, thesis optional, clinical semester and capstone project; for doctorate, capstone project, full-time clinical externship. *Entrance requirements:* For master's, completion of specific course contents and practicum experiences at the undergraduate level.

University of Wisconsin–Whitewater, School of Graduate Studies, College of Education and Professional Studies, Program in Communication Sciences and Disorders, Whitewater, WI 53190-1790. Offers MS. *Accreditation:* ASHA. Part-time and evening/weekend programs available. Postbaccalaureate distance learning degree programs offered (no on-campus study). *Students:* 27 full-time (all women); includes 1 minority (Asian, non-Hispanic/Latino). Average age 26. 165 applicants, 7% accepted, 8 enrolled. In 2011, 16 master's awarded. *Degree requirements:* For master's, comprehensive exam. *Entrance requirements:* For master's, 2 letters of recommendation, departmental application. Additional exam requirements/recommendations for international students: Required—TOEFL (minimum score 550 paper-based; 213 computer-based; 80 iBT), IELTS (minimum score 6). *Application deadline:* For fall admission, 2/1 for domestic and international students. Applications are processed on a rolling basis. Application fee: $56. Electronic applications accepted. *Expenses:* Tuition, state resident: full-time $4088. Tuition, nonresident: full-time $8817. Tuition and fees vary according to program. *Financial support:* In 2011–12, research

assistantships with tuition reimbursements (averaging $5,175 per year) were awarded; Federal Work-Study, unspecified assistantships, and out-of-state fee waivers also available. Support available to part-time students. Financial award application deadline: 3/15; financial award applicants required to submit FAFSA. *Faculty research:* Occupational hearing conservation. *Unit head:* Dr. Scott Bradley, Coordinator, 262-472-5202, Fax: 262-472-5027, E-mail: bradleys@uww.edu. *Application contact:* Sally A. Lange, School of Graduate Studies, 262-472-1006, Fax: 262-472-5027, E-mail: gradschl@uww.edu.

University of Wyoming, College of Health Sciences, Division of Communication Disorders, Laramie, WY 82070. Offers speech-language pathology (MS). *Accreditation:* ASHA. Part-time programs available. Postbaccalaureate distance learning degree programs offered (minimal on-campus study). *Entrance requirements:* For master's, GRE General Test, minimum GPA of 3.0. Additional exam requirements/recommendations for international students: Required—TOEFL. Electronic applications accepted. *Faculty research:* Child language, visual reinforcement audiometry, voice, auditory brain response, TBI.

Utah State University, School of Graduate Studies, Emma Eccles Jones College of Education and Human Services, Department of Communicative Disorders and Deaf Education, Logan, UT 84322. Offers audiology (Au D, Ed S); communication disorders and deaf education (M Ed); communicative disorders and deaf education (MA, MS). *Accreditation:* ASHA (one or more programs are accredited). Evening/weekend programs available. Postbaccalaureate distance learning degree programs offered (minimal on-campus study). *Degree requirements:* For master's, thesis optional; for Ed S, thesis or alternative. *Entrance requirements:* For master's, GRE General Test, minimum GPA of 3.0, 3 recommendations; for doctorate, GRE General Test, interview, minimum GPA of 3.25. Additional exam requirements/recommendations for international students: Required—TOEFL. *Expenses:* Contact institution. *Faculty research:* Parent-infant intervention with hearing-impaired infants, voice disorders, language development and disorders, oto-accoustic emissions, deaf or hard-of-hearing infants.

Vanderbilt University, School of Medicine, Department of Hearing and Speech Sciences, Nashville, TN 37240-1001. Offers audiology (Au D, PhD); deaf education (MED); speech-language pathology (MS). *Degree requirements:* For master's, thesis optional; for doctorate, thesis/dissertation, final and qualifying exams. *Entrance requirements:* For master's and doctorate, GRE General Test. Additional exam requirements/recommendations for international students: Required—TOEFL. Electronic applications accepted. *Faculty research:* Child language.

Washington State University Spokane, Graduate Programs, Program in Speech and Hearing Sciences, Spokane, WA 99210. Offers MA. *Faculty:* 10. *Students:* 49 full-time (45 women), 2 part-time (both women); includes 5 minority (3 Asian, non-Hispanic/Latino; 1 Hispanic/Latino; 1 Two or more races, non-Hispanic/Latino), 1 international. Average age 25. 99 applicants, 29% accepted, 29 enrolled. In 2011, 19 master's awarded. *Degree requirements:* For master's, comprehensive exam, thesis (for some programs). *Entrance requirements:* For master's, GRE, minimum GPA of 3.0, 3 letters of recommendation. Additional exam requirements/recommendations for international students: Required—TOEFL (minimum score 550 paper-based; 213 computer-based). *Application deadline:* For fall admission, 1/10 priority date for domestic students, 1/10 for international students; for spring admission, 9/1 priority date for domestic students, 7/1 for international students. Application fee: $75. *Financial support:* In 2011–12, research assistantships with full and partial tuition reimbursements (averaging $14,634 per year), teaching assistantships with full and partial tuition reimbursements (averaging $13,383 per year) were awarded; Federal Work-Study, scholarships/grants, health care benefits, tuition waivers (partial), and unspecified assistantships also available. Financial award application deadline: 2/15. *Faculty research:* Central auditory processing disorders, articulation, cleft palate. *Total annual research expenditures:* $1.6 million. *Unit head:* Dr. Chuck Madison, Professor/Coordinator, 509-358-7602, E-mail: madisonc@wsu.edu. *Application contact:* Graduate School Admissions, 800-GRADWSU, Fax: 509-335-1949, E-mail: gradsch@wsu.edu. Web site: http://spokane.wsu.edu/academics/Health_Sciences/SHS/.

Washington University in St. Louis, School of Medicine, Program in Audiology and Communication Sciences, Saint Louis, MO 63110. Offers audiology (Au D); deaf education (MS); speech and hearing sciences (PhD). *Accreditation:* ASHA (one or more programs are accredited). *Faculty:* 22 full-time (12 women), 18 part-time/adjunct (12 women). *Students:* 72 full-time (69 women). Average age 24. 130 applicants, 17% accepted, 22 enrolled. In 2011, 11 master's, 16 doctorates awarded. *Median time to degree:* Of those who began their doctoral program in fall 2003, 100% received their degree in 8 years or less. *Degree requirements:* For master's, comprehensive exam, thesis, independent study project, oral exam; for doctorate, comprehensive exam, thesis/dissertation, capstone project. *Entrance requirements:* For master's, GRE General Test, minimum B average in undergraduate course work; for doctorate, GRE General Test, minimum B average. Additional exam requirements/recommendations for international students: Required—TOEFL (minimum score 600 paper-based; 250 computer-based; 100 iBT). *Application deadline:* For fall admission, 2/15 for domestic and international students. Application fee: $60 ($80 for international students). Electronic applications accepted. *Expenses:* Contact institution. *Financial support:* In 2011–12, 72 students received support, including 72 fellowships with full and partial tuition reimbursements available (averaging $15,000 per year), 5 teaching assistantships with partial tuition reimbursements available (averaging $1,000 per year); career-related internships or fieldwork, Federal Work-Study, institutionally sponsored loans, scholarships/grants, traineeships, health care benefits, tuition waivers (partial), and unspecified assistantships also available. Financial award application deadline: 2/15; financial award applicants required to submit FAFSA. *Faculty research:* Audiology, deaf education, speech and hearing sciences, sensory neuroscience. *Unit head:* Dr. William W. Clark, Program Director, 314-747-0104, Fax: 314-747-0105. *Application contact:* Elizabeth A. Elliott, Manager, Financial Operations and Admissions, 314-747-0104, Fax: 314-747-0105, E-mail: elliottb@wustl.edu. Web site: http://pacs.wustl.edu/.

Wayne State University, College of Liberal Arts and Sciences, Department of Communication Sciences and Disorders, Detroit, MI 48202. Offers audiology (Au D); communication disorders and science (PhD); speech-language pathology (MA). *Accreditation:* ASHA (one or more programs are accredited). *Students:* 121 full-time (109 women), 7 part-time (all women); includes 11 minority (2 Black or African American, non-Hispanic/Latino; 1 American Indian or Alaska Native, non-Hispanic/Latino; 2 Asian, non-Hispanic/Latino; 3 Hispanic/Latino; 3 Two or more races, non-Hispanic/Latino), 15 international. Average age 29. 302 applicants, 18% accepted, 48 enrolled. In 2011, 33 master's, 8 doctorates awarded. *Degree requirements:* For master's, comprehensive exam (for some programs), thesis (for some programs); for doctorate, thesis/dissertation. *Entrance requirements:* For master's and doctorate, GRE, letters of recommendation, minimum GPA of 3.0, three letters of recommendation, written statement of intent, official transcripts. Additional exam requirements/recommendations for international students: Required—TOEFL (minimum score 550 paper-based; 213 computer-based); Recommended—TWE (minimum score 5.5). *Application deadline:* For fall admission, 1/15 for domestic and international students. Application fee: $50. Electronic applications accepted. *Expenses:* Tuition, state resident: part-time $512.85 per credit. Tuition, nonresident: part-time $1132.65 per credit. *Required fees:* $26.60 per credit. $199.65 per semester. Tuition and fees vary according to course load and program. *Financial support:* In 2011–12, 45 students received support. Fellowships with tuition reimbursements available, research assistantships with tuition reimbursements available, teaching assistantships, career-related internships or fieldwork, scholarships/grants, health care benefits, and unspecified assistantships available. Support available to part-time students. *Faculty research:* Language disorders in children and adults, speech perception and production, neuroimaging of speech and language, tinnitus and electrophysiology, acquired brain damage. *Total annual research expenditures:* $110,512. *Unit head:* Dr. Jean Andruski, Chair, 313-577-3339, E-mail: aa3925@wayne.edu. *Application contact:* E-mail: csdadmissions@wayne.edu. Web site: http://www.clas.wayne.edu/csd/.

West Chester University of Pennsylvania, College of Health Sciences, Department of Communicative Disorders, West Chester, PA 19383. Offers communicative disorders (MA); speech correction (Teaching Certificate). *Accreditation:* ASHA (one or more programs are accredited). Part-time and evening/weekend programs available. *Faculty:* 1 (woman) full-time, 12 part-time/adjunct (all women). *Students:* 50 full-time (49 women), 8 part-time (all women); includes 3 minority (2 Hispanic/Latino; 1 Two or more races, non-Hispanic/Latino), 1 international. Average age 28. 253 applicants, 11% accepted, 27 enrolled. In 2011, 19 degrees awarded. *Degree requirements:* For master's, comprehensive exam, thesis optional, 62 semester credit hours. *Entrance requirements:* For master's, GRE, two letters of recommendation, personal statement of academic and professional goals, logs of clinical observation and practicum hours, minimum cumulative and major GPA of 3.0; for Teaching Certificate, bachelor's degree in speech language pathology. Additional exam requirements/recommendations for international students: Required—TOEFL (minimum score 550 paper-based; 213 computer-based; 80 iBT). *Application deadline:* For fall admission, 4/15 priority date for domestic students, 3/15 for international students; for spring admission, 10/15 priority date for domestic students, 9/1 for international students. Applications are processed on a rolling basis. Application fee: $45. Electronic applications accepted. *Expenses:* Tuition, state resident: full-time $7488; part-time $416 per credit. Tuition, nonresident: full-time $11,232; part-time $624 per credit. *Required fees:* $1784.64; $67.59 per credit. Tuition and fees vary according to program. *Financial support:* Unspecified assistantships available. Support available to part-time students. Financial award application deadline: 2/15; financial award applicants required to submit FAFSA. *Faculty research:* Identification/interaction with students with communicative disorders, voice therapy, autism, bilingual assessment and intervention, critical thinking, literacy development, fluency. *Unit head:* Dr. Michael Weiss, Chair, 610-436-3401, Fax: 610-436-3388, E-mail: mweiss@wcupa.edu. *Application contact:* Dr. Mareile Koenig, Graduate Coordinator, 610-436-3218, Fax: 610-436-3388, E-mail: mkoenig@wcupa.edu. Web site: http://www.wcupa.edu/_academics/sch_shs.spp/.

Western Carolina University, Graduate School, College of Health and Human Sciences, Department of Communication Sciences and Disorders, Cullowhee, NC 28723. Offers MS. *Accreditation:* ASHA. Part-time programs available. *Students:* 62 full-time (58 women), 1 (woman) part-time; includes 7 minority (1 Black or African American, non-Hispanic/Latino; 1 American Indian or Alaska Native, non-Hispanic/Latino; 2 Asian, non-Hispanic/Latino; 3 Hispanic/Latino). Average age 28. 182 applicants, 21% accepted, 28 enrolled. In 2011, 24 master's awarded. *Degree requirements:* For master's, comprehensive exam, thesis or alternative. *Entrance requirements:* For master's, GRE, appropriate undergraduate degree with minimum GPA of 3.0, 3 letters of recommendation. Additional exam requirements/recommendations for international students: Required—TOEFL (minimum score 550 paper-based; 270 computer-based; 79 iBT). *Application deadline:* For fall admission, 2/15 for domestic students. Application fee: $50. *Expenses:* Tuition, state resident: full-time $3348. Tuition, nonresident: full-time $12,933. *Required fees:* $3155. *Financial support:* Fellowships, research assistantships, teaching assistantships, institutionally sponsored loans, traineeships, and unspecified assistantships available. Financial award application deadline: 3/31; financial award applicants required to submit FAFSA. *Faculty research:* Early assessment and intervention in language, stuttering, school-family partnerships, voice and organic disorders, accent reduction. *Unit head:* Dr. Bill Ogletree, Head, 828-227-3379, Fax: 828-227-3312, E-mail: ogletree@email.wcu.edu. *Application contact:* Admissions Specialist for Communication Sciences and Disorders, 828-227-7398, Fax: 828-227-7480, E-mail: gradsch@email.wcu.edu. Web site: http://www.wcu.edu/8389.asp.

Western Illinois University, School of Graduate Studies, College of Fine Arts and Communication, Department of Communication Sciences and Disorders, Macomb, IL 61455-1390. Offers MS. *Accreditation:* ASHA. Part-time programs available. *Students:* 34 full-time (33 women), 3 international. Average age 24. 114 applicants, 18% accepted. In 2011, 16 master's awarded. *Degree requirements:* For master's, comprehensive exam, thesis or alternative. *Entrance requirements:* For master's, GRE, minimum GPA of 3.0. Additional exam requirements/recommendations for international students: Required—TOEFL (minimum score 550 paper-based; 213 computer-based; 80 iBT). *Application deadline:* For fall admission, 2/1 priority date for domestic students. Applications are processed on a rolling basis. Application fee: $30. Electronic applications accepted. *Expenses:* Tuition, state resident: part-time $281.16 per credit hour. Tuition, nonresident: part-time $562.32 per credit hour. Part-time tuition and fees vary according to campus/location and reciprocity agreements. *Financial support:* In 2011–12, 12 students received support, including 12 research assistantships with full tuition reimbursements available (averaging $7,360 per year). Financial award applicants required to submit FAFSA. *Unit head:* Dr. Stacy Betz, Chairperson, 309-298-1955. *Application contact:* Dr. Nancy Parsons, Interim Associate Provost and Director of Graduate Studies, 309-298-1806, Fax: 309-298-2345, E-mail: grad-office@wiu.edu. Web site: http://wiu.edu/csd.

Western Kentucky University, Graduate Studies, College of Health and Human Services, Department of Communication Disorders, Bowling Green, KY 42101. Offers MS. *Accreditation:* ASHA. Part-time and evening/weekend programs available. Postbaccalaureate distance learning degree programs offered (no on-campus study). *Degree requirements:* For master's, comprehensive exam, written exam. *Entrance requirements:* For master's, GRE General Test, 3 letters of recommendation. Additional exam requirements/recommendations for international students: Required—TOEFL (minimum score 555 paper-based; 213 computer-based; 79 iBT).

Western Michigan University, Graduate College, College of Health and Human Services, Department of Speech Pathology and Audiology, Kalamazoo, MI 49008. Offers audiology (Au D); speech-language pathology (MA). *Accreditation:* ASHA. *Degree requirements:* For master's, thesis optional, clinical practicum. *Entrance requirements:* For master's, GRE General Test.

Western Washington University, Graduate School, College of Humanities and Social Sciences, Department of Communication Sciences and Disorders, Bellingham, WA 98225-5996. Offers MA. *Accreditation:* ASHA. Part-time programs available. *Degree requirements:* For master's, comprehensive exam, thesis optional. *Entrance requirements:* For master's, GRE General Test, minimum GPA of 3.0 in last 60 semester hours or last 90 quarter hours. Additional exam requirements/recommendations for international students: Required—TOEFL (minimum score 567 paper-based; 227 computer-based). Electronic applications accepted. *Faculty research:* Autism, stroke

and stroke perception, aural rehabilitation and cochlear implants, auditory processing, speech in individuals with Parkinson's disease.

West Texas A&M University, College of Nursing and Health Sciences, Department of Communication Disorders, Canyon, TX 79016-0001. Offers MS. *Accreditation:* ASHA. Part-time programs available. *Degree requirements:* For master's, comprehensive exam, thesis optional. *Entrance requirements:* For master's, GRE General Test, minimum B average in all clinical courses, liability insurance, first aid card, immunizations. Additional exam requirements/recommendations for international students: Required—TOEFL (minimum score 550 paper-based).

West Virginia University, College of Human Resources and Education, Department of Speech Pathology and Audiology, Morgantown, WV 26506. Offers audiology (Au D); speech-language pathology (MS). *Accreditation:* ASHA. *Degree requirements:* For master's, thesis optional, PRAXIS; for doctorate, thesis/dissertation or alternative, PRAXIS. *Entrance requirements:* For master's, GRE General Test, minimum GPA of 3.0, letter of recommendation; for doctorate, GRE General Test, letters of recommendation, minimum GPA of 3.0. Additional exam requirements/recommendations for international students: Required—TOEFL. Electronic applications accepted. *Faculty research:* Speech perception, language disorders in children, auditory skills, fluency disorders, phonological disorders in children.

Wichita State University, Graduate School, College of Health Professions, Department of Communication Sciences and Disorders, Wichita, KS 67260. Offers MA, Au D, PhD. *Accreditation:* ASHA (one or more programs are accredited). *Expenses:* Tuition, state resident: full-time $4746; part-time $263.65 per credit. Tuition, nonresident: full-time $11,669; part-time $648.30 per credit. *Financial support:* Teaching assistantships available. *Unit head:* Dr. Kathy Coufal, Chairperson, 316-978-3240, Fax: 316-978-3302, E-mail: kathy.coufal@wichita.edu. *Application contact:* Carrie C. Henderson, Admissions Coordinator, 316-978-3095, Fax: 316-978-3253, E-mail: carrie.henderson@wichita.edu. Web site: http://www.wichita.edu/.

William Paterson University of New Jersey, College of Science and Health, Wayne, NJ 07470-8420. Offers biotechnology (MS); communication disorders (MS); general biology (MS); nursing (MSN). Part-time and evening/weekend programs available. *Entrance requirements:* For master's, GRE General Test, minimum GPA of 2.75. Electronic applications accepted. *Faculty research:* Plant tissue culture, DNA cloning, cellular structure, language development, speech and hearing science.

Worcester State University, Graduate Studies, Program in Speech-Language Pathology, Worcester, MA 01602-2597. Offers MS. *Accreditation:* ASHA. Part-time and evening/weekend programs available. *Faculty:* 5 full-time (3 women), 4 part-time/adjunct (all women). *Students:* 54 full-time (52 women), 36 part-time (33 women); includes 2 minority (1 Hispanic/Latino; 1 Two or more races, non-Hispanic/Latino). Average age 26. 273 applicants, 19% accepted, 33 enrolled. In 2011, 28 master's awarded. *Degree requirements:* For master's, comprehensive exam, thesis, national licensing exam. *Entrance requirements:* For master's, GRE General Test or MAT, 15 credits of course work in human communication. Additional exam requirements/recommendations for international students: Required—TOEFL (minimum score 500 paper-based; 61 iBT). *Application deadline:* For fall admission, 2/1 for domestic and international students. Applications are processed on a rolling basis. Application fee: $40. Electronic applications accepted. *Expenses:* Contact institution. *Financial support:* In 2011–12, 10 students received support, including 10 research assistantships with full and partial tuition reimbursements available (averaging $4,640 per year); career-related internships or fieldwork, scholarships/grants, and unspecified assistantships also available. Financial award application deadline: 3/1; financial award applicants required to submit FAFSA. *Faculty research:* Hearing threshold norms, language learning disabilities. *Unit head:* Dr. Maryann Power, Coordinator, 508-929-8629, Fax: 508-929-8475, E-mail: mpower@worcester.edu. *Application contact:* Sara Grady, Assistant Dean of Graduate and Continuing Education, 508-929-8787, Fax: 508-929-8100, E-mail: sara.grady@worcester.edu.

Dental Hygiene

Boston University, Henry M. Goldman School of Dental Medicine, Boston, MA 02118. Offers advanced general dentistry (CAGS); dental public health (MS, MSD, D Sc D, CAGS); dentistry (DMD); endodontics (MSD, D Sc D, CAGS); operative dentistry (MSD, D Sc D, CAGS); oral and maxillofacial surgery (MSD, D Sc D, CAGS); oral biology (MSD, D Sc, D Sc D, PhD); orthodontics (MSD, D Sc D, CAGS); pediatric dentistry (MSD, D Sc D, CAGS); periodontology (MSD, D Sc D, CAGS); prosthodontics (MSD, D Sc D, CAGS). *Accreditation:* ADA (one or more programs are accredited). *Faculty:* 119 full-time (53 women), 83 part-time/adjunct (24 women). *Students:* 802 full-time (386 women); includes 155 minority (6 Black or African American, non-Hispanic/Latino; 2 American Indian or Alaska Native, non-Hispanic/Latino; 110 Asian, non-Hispanic/Latino; 35 Hispanic/Latino; 2 Native Hawaiian or other Pacific Islander, non-Hispanic/Latino), 329 international. Average age 27. In 2011, 17 master's, 173 doctorates, 61 other advanced degrees awarded. *Degree requirements:* For master's and CAGS, thesis; for doctorate, thesis/dissertation (for some programs). *Entrance requirements:* For doctorate, DAT (for DMD), minimum recommended GPA of 3.0 (for DMD); for CAGS, dental degree. Additional exam requirements/recommendations for international students: Required—TOEFL. *Application deadline:* Applications are processed on a rolling basis. Application fee: $75 ($105 for international students). Electronic applications accepted. *Expenses:* Contact institution. *Financial support:* In 2011–12, 480 students received support. Career-related internships or fieldwork, institutionally sponsored loans, and scholarships/grants available. Financial award application deadline: 4/15; financial award applicants required to submit FAFSA. *Faculty research:* Defense mechanisms, bone-cell regulation, protein biochemistry, molecular biology, biomaterials. *Unit head:* Dr. Jeffrey W. Hutter, Dean, 617-638-4780. *Application contact:* Admissions Representative, 617-638-4787, Fax: 617-638-4798, E-mail: sdmadmis@bu.edu. Web site: http://www.bu.edu/dental.

Eastern Washington University, Graduate Studies, College of Science, Health and Engineering, Department of Dental Hygiene, Cheney, WA 99004-2431. Offers MS. *Students:* 15 full-time (11 women), 6 part-time (all women); includes 3 minority (all Asian, non-Hispanic/Latino). 18 applicants, 67% accepted, 11 enrolled. Application fee: $50. *Financial support:* In 2011–12, 3 teaching assistantships (averaging $7,000 per year) were awarded. *Unit head:* Rebecca Stolberg, Chair, 509-368-6528, Fax: 509-368-6514, E-mail: rstolberg@mail.ewu.edu. *Application contact:* Julie Marr, Advisor/Recruiter for Graduate Studies, 509-359-6297, Fax: 509-359-6044, E-mail: gradprograms@ewu.edu. Web site: http://www.ewu.edu/cshe/programs/dental-hygiene.xml.

Georgia Health Sciences University, College of Graduate Studies, Program in Allied Health Sciences, Augusta, GA 30912. Offers dental hygiene (MS). Part-time programs available. Postbaccalaureate distance learning degree programs offered (no on-campus study). *Students:* 5 full-time (4 women); includes 3 minority (2 Black or African American, non-Hispanic/Latino; 1 Two or more races, non-Hispanic/Latino), 1 international. Average age 31. 4 applicants, 0% accepted. *Degree requirements:* For master's, thesis. *Entrance requirements:* For master's, GRE General Test. Additional exam requirements/recommendations for international students: Required—TOEFL (minimum score 550 paper-based; 213 computer-based; 79 iBT). *Application deadline:* For fall admission, 5/1 for domestic students, 3/1 for international students. Application fee: $50. Electronic applications accepted. *Financial support:* Federal Work-Study, institutionally sponsored loans, tuition waivers, and unspecified assistantships available. Support available to part-time students. Financial award application deadline: 5/31; financial award applicants required to submit FAFSA. *Faculty research:* Patient- and family-centered care, public health informatics, vascular health promotion through physical activity, improving air quality for school children, movement therapies for Parkinson's Disease. *Total annual research expenditures:* $545,444. *Unit head:* Dr. Douglas Keskula, Acting Dean, 706-721-2621, Fax: 706-721-7312, E-mail: dkeskula@georgiahealth.edu. *Application contact:* Dr. Marie Collins, Acting Associate Dean for Student, Faculty and Community Affairs, 706-721-3436, Fax: 706-721-6067, E-mail: mcollins@georgiahealth.edu. Web site: http://www.mcg.edu/GradStudies/.

Idaho State University, Office of Graduate Studies, Kasiska College of Health Professions, Department of Dental Hygiene, Pocatello, ID 83209-8048. Offers MS. Part-time programs available. *Degree requirements:* For master's, comprehensive exam, thesis, thesis defense, practicum experience, oral exam. *Entrance requirements:* For master's, GRE, MAT, baccalaureate degree in dental hygiene, minimum GPA of 3.0 in upper-division and dental hygiene coursework, current dental hygiene licensure in good standing. Additional exam requirements/recommendations for international students:

Required—TOEFL (minimum score 600 paper-based; 213 computer-based; 80 iBT). Electronic applications accepted.

Missouri Southern State University, Program in Dental Hygiene, Joplin, MO 64801-1595. Offers MS. Program offered jointly with University of Missouri–Kansas City. Part-time programs available. *Degree requirements:* For master's, project. *Entrance requirements:* For master's, copy of current dental hygiene license. Electronic applications accepted.

Old Dominion University, College of Health Sciences, School of Dental Hygiene, Norfolk, VA 23529. Offers MS. Part-time and evening/weekend programs available. Postbaccalaureate distance learning degree programs offered (no on-campus study). *Faculty:* 9 full-time (8 women). *Students:* 6 full-time (3 women), 14 part-time (all women); includes 2 minority (1 Black or African American, non-Hispanic/Latino; 1 Two or more races, non-Hispanic/Latino), 5 international. Average age 32. 16 applicants, 69% accepted, 7 enrolled. In 2011, 4 master's awarded. *Degree requirements:* For master's, comprehensive exam, thesis optional, writing proficiency exam. *Entrance requirements:* For master's, Dental Hygiene National Board Examination, BS or certificate in dental hygiene or related area, minimum GPA of 2.8 (3.0 in major), letters of recommendation. Additional exam requirements/recommendations for international students: Required—TOEFL (minimum score 550 paper-based; 213 computer-based; 79 iBT). *Application deadline:* For fall admission, 7/1 for domestic students, 4/15 for international students; for spring admission, 12/1 for domestic students, 10/1 for international students. Applications are processed on a rolling basis. Application fee: $50. Electronic applications accepted. *Expenses:* Tuition, state resident: full-time $9096; part-time $379 per credit. Tuition, nonresident: full-time $23,064; part-time $961 per credit. *Required fees:* $127 per semester. One-time fee: $50. *Financial support:* In 2011–12, 4 students received support, including 4 teaching assistantships with partial tuition reimbursements available (averaging $10,000 per year); fellowships, research assistantships, career-related internships or fieldwork, scholarships/grants, tuition waivers, and unspecified assistantships also available. Support available to part-time students. Financial award application deadline: 2/15; financial award applicants required to submit CSS PROFILE or FAFSA. *Faculty research:* Clinical dental hygiene, dental hygiene client health behaviors, dental hygiene education interventions, oral product testing, cold plasma. *Total annual research expenditures:* $48,237. *Unit head:* Prof. Gayle B. McCombs, Graduate Program Director, 757-683-3338, Fax: 757-683-5329, E-mail: gmccombs@odu.edu. *Application contact:* William Heffelfinger, Director of Graduate Admissions, 757-683-5554, Fax: 757-683-3255, E-mail: gradadmit@odu.edu. Web site: http://hs.odu.edu/dental/academics/ms/about.shtml.

Texas A&M Health Science Center, Baylor College of Dentistry, Caruth School of Dental Hygiene, College Station, TX 77840. Offers MS. Part-time programs available. *Degree requirements:* For master's, thesis (for some programs). *Entrance requirements:* For master's, GRE General Test, National Dental Hygiene Board Examination, minimum GPA of 3.0 in dental hygiene course work, 2.7 overall. *Faculty research:* Assessment of outcomes, dental materials, educational research, HIV patients, underserved patient populations, handicapped patients.

Université de Montréal, Faculty of Dental Medicine, Program in Stomatology Residency, Montréal, QC H3C 3J7, Canada. Offers Certificate.

University of Alberta, Faculty of Medicine and Dentistry, Department of Dentistry, Program in Dental Hygiene, Edmonton, AB T6G 2E1, Canada. Offers Diploma. Electronic applications accepted.

University of Bridgeport, Fones School of Dental Hygiene, Bridgeport, CT 06604. Offers MS. Part-time and evening/weekend programs available. Postbaccalaureate distance learning degree programs offered (no on-campus study). *Faculty:* 3 full-time (all women), 3 part-time/adjunct (all women). *Students:* 1 (woman) full-time, 30 part-time (all women); includes 5 minority (1 Black or African American, non-Hispanic/Latino; 1 Asian, non-Hispanic/Latino; 1 Hispanic/Latino; 2 Two or more races, non-Hispanic/Latino). Average age 36. 29 applicants, 0% accepted, 0 enrolled. In 2011, 1 master's awarded. *Degree requirements:* For master's, thesis. *Entrance requirements:* For master's, Dental Hygiene National Board Examination. Additional exam requirements/recommendations for international students: Recommended—TOEFL (minimum score 550 paper-based; 213 computer-based; 80 iBT), IELTS (minimum score 6.5). *Application deadline:* For fall admission, 8/1 priority date for domestic students, 8/1 for international students; for spring admission, 12/1 priority date for domestic students, 12/1 for international students. Application fee: $50. *Expenses:* Tuition: Full-time $22,880; part-time $700 per credit. *Required fees:* $1870; $95 per semester. Tuition and fees vary according to

course load and program. *Unit head:* Dr. Margaret H. Zayan, Dean, 203-576-4138, Fax: 203-576-4220, E-mail: mzayan@bridgeport.edu. *Application contact:* Leanne Proctor, Director of Health Science Admissions, 203-576-4352, Fax: 203-576-4941, E-mail: fones@bridgeport.edu.

University of Maryland, Baltimore, Graduate School, Graduate Programs in Dentistry, Department of Dental Hygiene, Baltimore, MD 21201. Offers MS. *Students:* 4 full-time (3 women), 9 part-time (all women); includes 3 minority (1 Asian, non-Hispanic/Latino; 1 Hispanic/Latino; 1 Two or more races, non-Hispanic/Latino), 1 international. Average age 36. 14 applicants, 36% accepted, 3 enrolled. In 2011, 2 master's awarded. *Degree requirements:* For master's, thesis or alternative. *Entrance requirements:* For master's, minimum GPA of 3.0. Additional exam requirements/recommendations for international students: Required—TOEFL (minimum score 550 paper-based; 80 iBT) or IELTS (minimum score 7). *Application deadline:* For fall admission, 6/30 for domestic students, 1/15 for international students; for spring admission, 11/30 for domestic students. Application fee: $50. Electronic applications accepted. *Financial support:* Fellowships available. Support available to part-time students. Financial award application deadline: 2/15. *Faculty research:* Dental hygiene education, health care management, health system theory and policy development, hospital dental hygiene, clinical practice. *Unit head:* Jacqueline Fried, Chairperson, 410-706-7773, Fax: 410-706-0349. *Application contact:* Kathryn Battani, Graduate Program Director, 410-706-7773, E-mail: kbattani@umaryland.edu.

University of Michigan, School of Dentistry and Horace H. Rackham School of Graduate Studies, Graduate Programs in Dentistry, Dental Hygiene Program, Ann Arbor, MI 48109-1078. Offers MS. Part-time and evening/weekend programs available. Postbaccalaureate distance learning degree programs offered (minimal on-campus study). *Students:* 2 full-time (both women). 3 applicants, 67% accepted, 2 enrolled. Terminal master's awarded for partial completion of doctoral program. *Degree requirements:* For master's, thesis. *Entrance requirements:* For master's, bachelor's degree in dental hygiene. Additional exam requirements/recommendations for international students: Required—TOEFL (minimum score 84 iBT). *Application deadline:* Applications are processed on a rolling basis. Application fee: $65 ($75 for international students). Electronic applications accepted. *Unit head:* Karen Ridley, Director, 734-763-1068, E-mail: kjr@umich.edu. *Application contact:* Patricia Katcher, Associate Admissions Director, 734-763-1068, Fax: 734-764-1922, E-mail: graddentinquiry@umich.edu. Web site: http://www.dent.umich.edu/dentalhygiene/education/MShome.

University of Missouri–Kansas City, School of Dentistry, Kansas City, MO 64110-2499. Offers advanced education in dentistry (Graduate Dental Certificate); dental hygiene education (MS); dentistry (DDS); endodontics (Graduate Dental Certificate); oral and maxillofacial surgery (Graduate Dental Certificate); oral biology (MS, PhD); orthodontics and dentofacial orthopedics (Graduate Dental Certificate); pediatric dentistry (Graduate Dental Certificate); periodontics (Graduate Dental Certificate). PhD (interdisciplinary) offered through the School of Graduate Studies. *Accreditation:* ADA (one or more programs are accredited). *Faculty:* 95 full-time (41 women), 62 part-time/adjunct (18 women). *Students:* 420 full-time (182 women), 44 part-time (26 women); includes 67 minority (7 Black or African American, non-Hispanic/Latino; 2 American Indian or Alaska Native, non-Hispanic/Latino; 45 Asian, non-Hispanic/Latino; 11 Hispanic/Latino; 2 Two or more races, non-Hispanic/Latino), 2 international. Average age 27. 511 applicants, 23% accepted, 115 enrolled. In 2011, 9 master's, 98 doctorates, 17 other advanced degrees awarded. *Degree requirements:* For master's, thesis; for doctorate, thesis/dissertation (for some programs). *Entrance requirements:* For master's, DAT, letters of evaluation, personal interview; for doctorate, DAT (for DDS); for Graduate Dental Certificate, DDS. Additional exam requirements/recommendations for international students: Required—TOEFL (minimum score 550 paper-based; 213 computer-based; 80 iBT). *Application deadline:* For fall admission, 2/1 for domestic and international students. Application fee: $45 ($50 for international students). *Expenses:* Contact institution. *Financial support:* In 2011–12, 3 fellowships (averaging $59,417 per year), 3 research assistantships (averaging $19,471 per year) were awarded; career-related internships or fieldwork, Federal Work-Study, institutionally sponsored loans, and tuition waivers (full and partial) also available. Support available to part-time students. Financial award application deadline: 3/1; financial award applicants required to submit FAFSA. *Faculty research:* Biomaterials, dental use of lasers, effectiveness of periodontal treatments, temporomandibular joint dysfunction. *Unit head:* Dr. Marsha Pyle, Dean, 816-235-2010. *Application contact:* Dr. John Killip, Associate Dean for Student Programs, 816-235-2080. Web site: http://dentistry.umkc.edu/.

University of New Mexico, Health Sciences Center Graduate Programs, Division of Dental Hygiene, Albuquerque, NM 87131-2039. Offers MS. Part-time and evening/weekend programs available. Postbaccalaureate distance learning degree programs offered (no on-campus study). *Faculty:* 5 full-time (all women). *Students:* 4 full-time (all women), 10 part-time (8 women); includes 11 minority (1 Black or African American, non-Hispanic/Latino; 1 Asian, non-Hispanic/Latino; 8 Hispanic/Latino; 1 Two or more races, non-Hispanic/Latino). Average age 32. 12 applicants, 58% accepted, 5 enrolled. In 2011, 2 degrees awarded. *Application deadline:* For fall admission, 4/15 for domestic and international students; for winter admission, 1/31 priority date for domestic students, 1/31 for international students. Application fee: $50. *Financial support:* In 2011–12, 7 students received support. *Unit head:* Prof. Christine N. Nathe, Director, 505-272-8147, Fax: 505-272-5584, E-mail: cnathe@unm.edu. *Application contact:* Prof. Demetra D. Logothetis, Graduate Program Director, 505-272-6687, Fax: 505-272-5584, E-mail: dlogothetis@salud.unm.edu. Web site: http://dentalmedicine.unm.edu/dentalhy/index.html.

The University of North Carolina at Chapel Hill, School of Dentistry and Graduate School, Graduate Programs in Dentistry, Chapel Hill , NC 27599. Offers dental hygiene (MS); endodontics (MS); epidemiology (PhD); operative dentistry (MS); oral and maxillofacial pathology (MS); oral and maxillofacial radiology (MS); oral biology (PhD); orthodontics (MS); pediatric dentistry (MS); periodontology (MS); prosthodontics (MS). *Faculty:* 82 full-time (28 women). *Students:* 90 full-time (46 women); includes 20 minority (7 Black or African American, non-Hispanic/Latino; 10 Asian, non-Hispanic/Latino; 3 Hispanic/Latino), 30 international. Average age 28. 475 applicants, 7% accepted, 31 enrolled. In 2011, 20 master's, 2 doctorates awarded. *Degree requirements:* For master's, thesis; for doctorate, thesis/dissertation. *Entrance requirements:* For master's, GRE General Test (for orthodontics and oral biology only); National Dental Board Part I (Part II if available), dental degree (for all except dental hygiene); for doctorate, GRE General Test. Additional exam requirements/recommendations for international students: Required—TOEFL (minimum score 550 paper-based; 213 computer-based; 79 iBT). Application fee: $78. Electronic applications accepted. *Expenses:* Contact institution. *Financial support:* In 2011–12, research assistantships with partial tuition reimbursements (averaging $22,000 per year), teaching assistantships with partial tuition reimbursements (averaging $6,420 per year) were awarded; fellowships also available. Financial award application deadline: 3/1; financial award applicants required to submit FAFSA. *Faculty research:* Clinical research, inflammation, immunology, neuroscience, molecular biology. *Total annual research expenditures:* $6 million. *Unit head:* Dr. Ceib Phillips, Assistant Dean for Advanced Education and Graduate Studies, 919-966-2763, Fax: 919-843-8864, E-mail: ceib_phillips@dentistry.unc.edu. *Application contact:* Koyah Rivera, Graduate Registrar, 919-537-3347, Fax: 919-966-5795, E-mail: koyah_rivera@dentistry.unc.edu. Web site: http://www.dentistry.unc.edu/.

The University of Texas Health Science Center at San Antonio, School of Health Professions, San Antonio, TX 78229-3900. Offers clinical laboratory sciences (MS); deaf education and hearing science (MED); dental hygiene (MS); occupational therapy (MOT); physical therapy (MPT); physician assistant studies (MS). *Accreditation:* AOTA; APTA; ARC-PA. *Degree requirements:* For master's, thesis. *Entrance requirements:* Additional exam requirements/recommendations for international students: Required—TOEFL (minimum score 560 paper-based; 280 computer-based; 68 iBT). Electronic applications accepted.

Emergency Medical Services

Baylor University, Graduate School, Military Programs, Program in Emergency Medicine, Waco, TX 76798. Offers D Sc PA. *Students:* 14 full-time (0 women); includes 1 minority (Black or African American, non-Hispanic/Latino). In 2011, 6 doctorates awarded. *Unit head:* Maj. Larry Lindsay, Graduate Program Director, 210-916-4542, Fax: 210-221-7306, E-mail: larry.lindsay1@us.army.mil. *Application contact:* Maj. Sue Love, 210-916-4542, Fax: 254-710-3870, E-mail: sue.love@us.army.mil.

Drexel University, College of Nursing and Health Professions, Emergency and Public Safety Services Program, Philadelphia, PA 19104-2875. Offers MS. Part-time and evening/weekend programs available. *Degree requirements:* For master's, comprehensive exam. *Entrance requirements:* For master's, GRE General Test, minimum GPA of 2.75.

San Diego State University, Graduate and Research Affairs, College of Health and Human Services, Graduate School of Public Health, San Diego, CA 92182. Offers environmental health (MPH); epidemiology (MPH, PhD), including biostatistics (MPH); global emergency preparedness and response (MS); global health (PhD); health behavior (PhD); health promotion (MPH); health services administration (MPH); toxicology (MS); MPH/MA; MSW/MPH. *Accreditation:* ABET (one or more programs are accredited); CAHME (one or more programs are accredited); CEPH (one or more programs are accredited). Part-time programs available. *Degree requirements:* For master's, comprehensive exam (for some programs), thesis (for some programs); for doctorate, thesis/dissertation. *Entrance requirements:* For master's, GMAT (MPH in health services administration), GRE General Test; for doctorate, GRE General Test. Additional exam requirements/recommendations for international students: Required—TOEFL. *Faculty research:* Evaluation of tobacco, AIDS prevalence and prevention, mammography, infant death project, Alzheimer's in elderly Chinese.

Université Laval, Faculty of Medicine, Post-Professional Programs in Medical Studies, Québec, QC G1K 7P4, Canada. Offers anatomy–pathology (DESS); anesthesiology (DESS); cardiology (DESS); care of older people (Diploma); clinical research (DESS); community health (DESS); dermatology (DESS); diagnostic radiology (DESS); emergency medicine (Diploma); family medicine (DESS); general surgery (DESS); geriatrics (DESS); hematology (DESS); internal medicine (DESS); maternal and fetal medicine (Diploma); medical biochemistry (DESS); medical microbiology and infectious diseases (DESS); medical oncology (DESS); nephrology (DESS); neurology (DESS); neurosurgery (DESS); obstetrics and gynecology (DESS); ophthalmology (DESS); orthopedic surgery (DESS); oto-rhino-laryngology (DESS); palliative medicine (Diploma); pediatrics (DESS); plastic surgery (DESS); psychiatry (DESS); pulmonary medicine (DESS); radiology–oncology (DESS); thoracic surgery (DESS); urology (DESS). *Degree requirements:* For other advanced degree, comprehensive exam. *Entrance requirements:* For degree, knowledge of French. Electronic applications accepted.

University of Guelph, Ontario Veterinary College and Graduate Studies, Graduate Programs in Veterinary Sciences, Department of Clinical Studies, Guelph, ON N1G 2W1, Canada. Offers anesthesiology (M Sc, DV Sc); cardiology (DV Sc, Diploma); clinical studies (Diploma); dermatology (M Sc); diagnostic imaging (M Sc, DV Sc); emergency/critical care (M Sc, DV Sc, Diploma); medicine (M Sc, DV Sc); neurology (M Sc, DV Sc); ophthalmology (M Sc, DV Sc); surgery (M Sc, DV Sc). *Degree requirements:* For master's, thesis; for doctorate, comprehensive exam, thesis/dissertation. *Entrance requirements:* Additional exam requirements/recommendations for international students: Required—TOEFL (minimum score 550 paper-based; 213 computer-based), IELTS (minimum score 6.5). Electronic applications accepted. *Faculty research:* Orthopedics, respirology, oncology, exercise physiology, cardiology.

Occupational Therapy

Alvernia University, Graduate Studies, Program in Occupational Therapy, Reading, PA 19607-1799. Offers MSOT. *Accreditation:* AOTA. Part-time and evening/weekend programs available. *Degree requirements:* For master's, thesis optional. Electronic applications accepted.

American International College, School of Health Sciences, Program in Occupational Therapy, Springfield, MA 01109-3189. Offers MSOT. *Accreditation:* AOTA. *Degree requirements:* For master's, comprehensive exam, thesis (for some programs), clinical observation. *Entrance requirements:* Additional exam requirements/recommendations for international students: Required—TOEFL. Electronic applications accepted. *Expenses:* Contact institution.

A.T. Still University of Health Sciences, Arizona School of Health Sciences, Mesa, AZ 85206. Offers advanced occupational therapy (MS); advanced physician assistant (MS); athletic training (MS); audiology (Au D); health sciences (DHSc); human movement (MS); occupational therapy (MS); physical therapy (DPT); physician assistant (MS); transitional audiology (Au D); transitional physical therapy (DPT). *Accreditation:* AOTA (one or more programs are accredited); ASHA. Part-time and evening/weekend programs available. Postbaccalaureate distance learning degree programs offered (minimal on-campus study). *Faculty:* 44 full-time (27 women), 235 part-time/adjunct (141 women). *Students:* 410 full-time (275 women), 1,010 part-time (675 women); includes 320 minority (73 Black or African American, non-Hispanic/Latino; 18 American Indian or Alaska Native, non-Hispanic/Latino; 158 Asian, non-Hispanic/Latino; 62 Hispanic/Latino; 9 Two or more races, non-Hispanic/Latino), 6 international. Average age 35. 4,395 applicants, 18% accepted, 694 enrolled. In 2011, 221 master's, 406 doctorates awarded. *Median time to degree:* Of those who began their doctoral program in fall 2003, 98% received their degree in 8 years or less. *Degree requirements:* For master's, thesis (for some programs); for doctorate, thesis/dissertation (for some programs). *Entrance requirements:* For master's, GRE General Test; for doctorate, GRE, Evaluation of Practicing Audiologists Capabilities (Au D), Physical Therapist Evaluation Tool (DPT), current state licensure, master's degree or equivalent (Au D). Additional exam requirements/recommendations for international students: Required—TOEFL (minimum score 550 paper-based; 213 computer-based; 80 iBT). *Application deadline:* For fall admission, 8/1 priority date for domestic students, 8/1 for international students. Applications are processed on a rolling basis. *Application fee:* $60. *Expenses:* Contact institution. *Financial support:* In 2011–12, 272 students received support, including 14 fellowships (averaging $16,000 per year); Federal Work-Study and scholarships/grants also available. Financial award application deadline: 5/1; financial award applicants required to submit FAFSA. *Faculty research:* Physical therapy: metabolism during exercise and activity; neuromuscular function after injury, prevention of lifestyle diseases, prevention and treatment of overuse injuries; athletic training: pediatric sport-related concussion, adolescent athlete health-related quality of life; occupational therapy: spirituality and health disparities, geriatric and pediatric well-being, pain management for participation. *Total annual research expenditures:* $75,682. *Unit head:* Dr. Randy Danielsen, Dean, 480-219-6000, Fax: 480-219-6110, E-mail: rdanielsen@atsu.edu. *Application contact:* Donna Sparks, Associate Director, Admissions Processing, 660-626-2117, Fax: 660-626-2969, E-mail: admissions@atsu.edu. Web site: http://www.atsu.edu/ashs.

Barry University, College of Health Sciences, Program in Occupational Therapy, Miami Shores, FL 33161-6695. Offers MS. *Accreditation:* AOTA. Electronic applications accepted.

Bay Path College, Program in Occupational Therapy, Longmeadow, MA 01106-2292. Offers MOT, MS. *Accreditation:* AOTA. Part-time programs available. *Students:* 109 full-time (95 women), 4 part-time (all women); includes 20 minority (10 Black or African American, non-Hispanic/Latino; 5 Asian, non-Hispanic/Latino; 5 Hispanic/Latino). Average age 27. 59 applicants, 64% accepted, 29 enrolled. In 2011, 36 master's awarded. *Application deadline:* For fall admission, 3/1 priority date for domestic students. Applications are processed on a rolling basis. Application fee: $45. Electronic applications accepted. Application fee is waived when completed online. *Expenses:* Tuition: Part-time $665 per credit. Tuition and fees vary according to program. *Financial support:* In 2011–12, 77 students received support. Scholarships/grants available. Financial award applicants required to submit FAFSA. *Application contact:* Lisa Adams, Director of Graduate Admissions, 413-565-1317, Fax: 413-565-1250, E-mail: ladams@baypath.edu.

Belmont University, College of Health Sciences, School of Occupational Therapy, Nashville, TN 37212-3757. Offers MSOT, OTD. *Accreditation:* AOTA. Evening/weekend programs available. *Faculty:* 9 full-time (8 women), 12 part-time/adjunct (9 women). *Students:* 133 full-time (117 women); includes 17 minority (9 Black or African American, non-Hispanic/Latino; 1 American Indian or Alaska Native, non-Hispanic/Latino; 3 Asian, non-Hispanic/Latino; 4 Hispanic/Latino). Average age 27. 271 applicants, 24% accepted, 64 enrolled. In 2011, 31 master's, 25 doctorates awarded. *Degree requirements:* For master's, thesis, 6 months of supervised clinical work; for doctorate, comprehensive exam, thesis/dissertation, 6 months of supervised clinical work, 3-month residency. *Entrance requirements:* For master's, GRE General Test, 50 observation hours, 1 year experience as licensed healthcare professional; for doctorate, GRE General Test, 50 observation hours, baccalaureate degree. Additional exam requirements/recommendations for international students: Required—TOEFL (minimum score 500 paper-based; 173 computer-based). *Application deadline:* For fall admission, 3/1 priority date for domestic students. Application fee: $50. Electronic applications accepted. *Expenses:* Contact institution. *Financial support:* Fellowships, research assistantships, and teaching assistantships available. Financial award applicants required to submit FAFSA. *Faculty research:* Rehabilitation outcomes, pediatrics, low vision, assistive technology, elder care, driving evaluation, wheelchair management-pressure mapping. *Unit head:* Dr. Scott D. McPhee, Associate Dean, 615-460-6700, Fax: 615-460-6475, E-mail: scott.mcphee@belmont.edu. *Application contact:* Christina Harness, Admissions Assistant, 615-460-6798, Fax: 615-460-6475, E-mail: otd@belmont.edu. Web site: http://www.belmont.edu/ot/.

Boston University, College of Health and Rehabilitation Sciences: Sargent College, Department of Occupational Therapy, Boston, MA 02215. Offers occupational therapy (MSOT, OTD); rehabilitation sciences (D Sc). *Accreditation:* AOTA (one or more programs are accredited). Postbaccalaureate distance learning degree programs offered (minimal on-campus study). *Faculty:* 13 full-time (all women), 2 part-time/adjunct (both women). *Students:* 109 full-time (104 women), 19 part-time (16 women); includes 16 minority (10 Asian, non-Hispanic/Latino; 2 Hispanic/Latino; 1 Native Hawaiian or other Pacific Islander, non-Hispanic/Latino; 3 Two or more races, non-Hispanic/Latino), 6 international. Average age 27. 131 applicants, 44% accepted, 24 enrolled. In 2011, 50 master's, 5 doctorates awarded. *Degree requirements:* For master's, thesis optional, full-time internship; for doctorate, comprehensive exam, thesis/dissertation. *Entrance*

requirements: For master's, minimum GPA of 3.0; BS in area related to occupational therapy; for doctorate, GRE General Test. Additional exam requirements/recommendations for international students: Required—TOEFL (minimum score 550 paper-based; 84 computer-based), TWE (minimum score 5). *Application deadline:* For fall admission, 1/15 priority date for domestic students, 1/15 for international students. Applications are processed on a rolling basis. Application fee: $125. Electronic applications accepted. *Expenses:* Tuition: Full-time $40,848; part-time $1276 per credit hour. *Required fees:* $572; $286 per semester. *Financial support:* In 2011–12, 64 students received support, including 14 fellowships (averaging $17,000 per year); career-related internships or fieldwork, Federal Work-Study, institutionally sponsored loans, scholarships/grants, and tuition waivers (partial) also available. Financial award application deadline: 4/15; financial award applicants required to submit FAFSA. *Faculty research:* Sensory integration, outcomes measurement, impact of Parkinson's disease, families of people with autism. *Total annual research expenditures:* $620,356. *Unit head:* Dr. Wendy J. Coster, Department Chair, 617-353-2727, Fax: 617-353-2926, E-mail: wjcoster@bu.edu. *Application contact:* Sharon Sankey, Director, Student Services, 617-353-2713, Fax: 617-353-7500, E-mail: ssankey@bu.edu. Web site: http://www.bu.edu/sargent/.

Brenau University, Sydney O. Smith Graduate School, College of Health and Science, Gainesville, GA 30501. Offers family nurse practitioner (MSN); nurse educator (MSN); nursing management (MSN); occupational therapy (MS); psychology (MS). *Accreditation:* AOTA; NLN. Part-time and evening/weekend programs available. *Degree requirements:* For master's, comprehensive exam (for some programs), thesis (for some programs), clinical practicum hours. *Entrance requirements:* For master's, GRE General Test or MAT (for some programs), interview, writing sample, references (for some programs). Additional exam requirements/recommendations for international students: Required—TOEFL (minimum score 500 paper-based; 173 computer-based; 61 iBT); Recommended—IELTS (minimum score 5). Electronic applications accepted. *Expenses:* Contact institution.

California State University, Dominguez Hills, College of Professional Studies, School of Health and Human Services, Program in Occupational Therapy, Carson, CA 90747-0001. Offers MS. *Accreditation:* AOTA. *Faculty:* 5 full-time (4 women), 4 part-time/adjunct (all women). *Students:* 135 full-time (116 women); includes 67 minority (1 Black or African American, non-Hispanic/Latino; 43 Asian, non-Hispanic/Latino; 22 Hispanic/Latino; 1 Two or more races, non-Hispanic/Latino), 2 international. Average age 29. 3 applicants, 0% accepted, 0 enrolled. In 2011, 65 master's awarded. *Degree requirements:* For master's, comprehensive exam. *Entrance requirements:* For master's, GRE. Additional exam requirements/recommendations for international students: Required—TOEFL, TWE. *Application deadline:* For fall admission, 9/15 priority date for domestic students. Electronic applications accepted. *Faculty research:* Child school functioning, assessment, lifespan occupational development, low vision occupational therapy intervention. *Unit head:* Dr. Terry Peralta-Catipon, Program Director, 310-243-2812, E-mail: tperalta@csudh.edu. *Application contact:* Brandy McLelland, Interim Director, Student Information Services, 310-243-3645, E-mail: bmclelland@csudh.edu. Web site: http://www.csudh.edu/cps/hhs/ot/.

Chatham University, Program in Occupational Therapy, Pittsburgh, PA 15232-2826. Offers MOT, OTD. *Accreditation:* AOTA. *Students:* 104 full-time (94 women), 13 part-time (12 women); includes 10 minority (6 Black or African American, non-Hispanic/Latino; 1 American Indian or Alaska Native, non-Hispanic/Latino; 3 Asian, non-Hispanic/Latino). Average age 30. 204 applicants, 42% accepted, 74 enrolled. *Entrance requirements:* For master's, recommendation letter, community service, volunteer service. Additional exam requirements/recommendations for international students: Required—TOEFL (minimum score 600 paper-based; 250 computer-based; 100 iBT), IELTS (minimum score 7), TWE. *Application deadline:* For fall admission, 12/5 priority date for domestic students, 12/5 for international students. Applications are processed on a rolling basis. Application fee: $45. Electronic applications accepted. Application fee is waived when completed online. *Expenses:* Contact institution. *Financial support:* Applicants required to submit FAFSA. *Unit head:* Dr. Joyce Salls, Director, 412-365-1177, E-mail: salls@chatham.edu. *Application contact:* Ashlee Bartko, Senior Assistant Director of Graduate Admission, 412-365-1115, Fax: 412-365-1609, E-mail: gradadmissions@chatham.edu. Web site: http://www.chatham.edu/ot.

Cleveland State University, College of Graduate Studies, College of Sciences and Health Professions, School of Health Sciences, Program in Occupational Therapy, Cleveland, OH 44115. Offers MOT. *Accreditation:* AOTA. *Faculty:* 7 full-time (5 women), 2 part-time/adjunct (both women). *Students:* 65 full-time (56 women), 32 part-time (27 women); includes 8 minority (3 Black or African American, non-Hispanic/Latino; 2 Asian, non-Hispanic/Latino; 2 Hispanic/Latino; 1 Two or more races, non-Hispanic/Latino). Average age 28. 181 applicants, 21% accepted, 33 enrolled. In 2011, 30 master's awarded. *Degree requirements:* For master's, fieldwork, capstone research project. *Entrance requirements:* For master's, GRE (if overall GPA less than 3.0). Additional exam requirements/recommendations for international students: Recommended—TOEFL (minimum score 525 paper-based; 197 computer-based; 14 iBT), IELTS (minimum score 6). *Application deadline:* For fall admission, 1/5 priority date for domestic students, 1/15 for international students. Application fee: $55. Electronic applications accepted. *Expenses:* Tuition, state resident: full-time $6416; part-time $494 per credit hour. Tuition, nonresident: full-time $12,074; part-time $929 per credit hour. *Financial support:* In 2011–12, 8 students received support, including 8 teaching assistantships (averaging $11,000 per year); unspecified assistantships also available. Financial award application deadline: 3/15; financial award applicants required to submit FAFSA. *Faculty research:* Pediatrics, psychology, daily living, exercise physiology, neuromuscular disorders. *Unit head:* Dr. Glenn D. Goodman, Director, 216-687-2493, Fax: 216-687-9316, E-mail: g.goodman@csuohio.edu. *Application contact:* Karen J. Armstrong, Administrative Assistant, 216-687-3567, Fax: 216-687-9316, E-mail: k.bradley@csuohio.edu. Web site: http://www.csuohio.edu/sciences/dept/healthsciences/graduate/MOT/index.html.

College of Saint Mary, Program in Occupational Therapy, Omaha, NE 68106. Offers MOT. *Accreditation:* AOTA.

The College of St. Scholastica, Graduate Studies, Department of Occupational Therapy, Duluth, MN 55811-4199. Offers MA. *Accreditation:* AOTA. Part-time programs available. *Faculty:* 5 full-time (4 women). *Students:* 71 full-time (67 women), 2 part-time (both women); includes 3 minority (1 American Indian or Alaska Native, non-Hispanic/Latino; 1 Asian, non-Hispanic/Latino; 1 Hispanic/Latino). Average age 24. 12 applicants, 67% accepted, 8 enrolled. In 2011, 26 master's awarded. *Degree requirements:* For master's, thesis. *Entrance requirements:* For master's, interview, minimum GPA of 2.7. Additional exam requirements/recommendations for international students: Required—TOEFL (minimum score 550 paper-based; 213 computer-based; 79 iBT). *Application*

deadline: For fall admission, 11/15 for domestic and international students. Applications are processed on a rolling basis. Application fee: $50. Electronic applications accepted. *Financial support:* In 2011–12, 32 students received support, including 1 teaching assistantship (averaging $1,192 per year); Federal Work-Study and scholarships/grants also available. Support available to part-time students. Financial award applicants required to submit FAFSA. *Faculty research:* Gerontology, occupational therapy administration, neurorehabilitation, occupational therapy in nontraditional settings, clinical fieldwork issues. *Unit head:* Diane Anderson, Director, 218-723-5915, Fax: 218-723-6290, E-mail: danders4@css.edu. *Application contact:* Lindsay Lahti, Director of Graduate and Extended Studies Recruitment, 218-733-2240, Fax: 218-733-2275, E-mail: gradstudies@css.edu. Web site: http://www.css.edu/Academics/School-of-Health-Sciences/Occupational-Therapy.html.

Colorado State University, Graduate School, College of Applied Human Sciences, Department of Occupational Therapy, Fort Collins, CO 80523-1573. Offers MOT, MS. *Accreditation:* AOTA. *Faculty:* 7 full-time (4 women). *Students:* 119 full-time (114 women), 2 part-time (both women); includes 10 minority (2 Black or African American, non-Hispanic/Latino; 1 Asian, non-Hispanic/Latino; 2 Hispanic/Latino; 1 Native Hawaiian or other Pacific Islander, non-Hispanic/Latino; 4 Two or more races, non-Hispanic/Latino). Average age 27. 271 applicants, 18% accepted, 42 enrolled. In 2011, 40 master's awarded. *Degree requirements:* For master's, thesis optional. *Entrance requirements:* For master's, GRE Analytical Writing Test (minimum score 4.0), minimum GPA of 3.0, 3 letters of reference, resume, experience with people who have disabilities. Additional exam requirements/recommendations for international students: Required—TOEFL (minimum score 240 computer-based; 94 iBT). *Application deadline:* For fall admission, 1/15 for domestic and international students; for spring admission, 10/15 for domestic and international students. Application fee: $50. Electronic applications accepted. *Expenses:* Tuition, state resident: full-time $7992. Tuition, nonresident: full-time $19,592. *Required fees:* $1735; $58 per credit. *Financial support:* In 2011–12, 4 students received support, including 1 research assistantship with partial tuition reimbursement available (averaging $2,771 per year), 3 teaching assistantships with partial tuition reimbursements available (averaging $9,554 per year); fellowships also available. Financial award application deadline: 3/1; financial award applicants required to submit FAFSA. *Faculty research:* Geriatrics, school-based service, traumatic brain injury, neurorehabilitation, neurobehavioral development. *Total annual research expenditures:* $711,803. *Unit head:* Dr. Wendy Wood, Department Head, 970-491-1882, Fax: 970-491-6920, E-mail: wwood@cahs.colostate.edu. *Application contact:* Linda McDowell, Admissions Coordinator, 970-491-6243, Fax: 970-491-6290, E-mail: mcdowell@cahs.colostate.edu. Web site: http://www.ot.cahs.colostate.edu/.

Columbia University, College of Physicians and Surgeons, Programs in Occupational Therapy, New York, NY 10032. Offers movement science (Ed D), including occupational therapy; occupational therapy (professional) (MS); occupational therapy administration or education (post-professional) (MS); MPH/MS. *Accreditation:* AOTA. *Degree requirements:* For master's, project, 6 months of fieldwork, thesis (for post-professional students); for doctorate, comprehensive exam, thesis/dissertation. *Entrance requirements:* For master's, undergraduate course work in anatomy, physiology, statistics, psychology, social sciences, humanities, English composition; NBCOT eligibility; for doctorate, NBCOT certification, MS. Additional exam requirements/recommendations for international students: Required—TOEFL (minimum score 250 computer-based; 100 iBT), TWE (minimum score 4). Electronic applications accepted. *Expenses:* Contact institution. *Faculty research:* Community mental health, developmental tasks of late life, infant play, cognition, obesity, motor learning.

Concordia University Wisconsin, Graduate Programs, School of Human Services, Program in Occupational Therapy, Mequon, WI 53097-2402. Offers MOT. *Accreditation:* AOTA. *Faculty:* 6 full-time (4 women), 2 part-time/adjunct (1 woman). *Students:* 77 full-time (67 women), 3 part-time (2 women); includes 2 minority (1 Black or African American, non-Hispanic/Latino; 1 Hispanic/Latino). Average age 31. In 2011, 5 master's awarded. *Degree requirements:* For master's, comprehensive exam, thesis or alternative. *Entrance requirements:* Additional exam requirements/recommendations for international students: Required—TOEFL. Application fee: $35 ($125 for international students). *Financial support:* Application deadline: 8/1. *Unit head:* Dr. Linda Samuel, Interim Director, 262-243-4469, E-mail: linda.samuel@cuw.edu. *Application contact:* Graduate Admissions, 262-243-4248, Fax: 262-243-4428. Web site: http://www.cuw.edu/.

Creighton University, School of Pharmacy and Health Professions, Program in Occupational Therapy, Omaha, NE 68178-0001. Offers OTD. *Accreditation:* AOTA. Postbaccalaureate distance learning degree programs offered (minimal on-campus study). Electronic applications accepted. *Expenses: Tuition:* Full-time $12,672; part-time $704 per credit hour. *Required fees:* $1410; $136 per semester. Tuition and fees vary according to campus/location and reciprocity agreements. *Faculty research:* Patient safety in health services research, health information technology and health services research, health care services in minority and underserved populations, occupational therapy in school-based programs, educational technology use in the classroom.

Dalhousie University, Faculty of Health Professions, School of Occupational Therapy, Halifax, NS B3H3J5, Canada. Offers occupational therapy (entry to profession) (M Sc); occupational therapy (post-professional) (M Sc). Part-time and evening/weekend programs available. Postbaccalaureate distance learning degree programs offered (no on-campus study). *Degree requirements:* For master's, thesis. *Entrance requirements:* Additional exam requirements/recommendations for international students: Required—TOEFL, IELTS, CANTEST, CAEL, or Michigan English Language Assessment Battery. Electronic applications accepted. *Faculty research:* Gender, health systems, design, geriatrics power and empowerment.

Dominican College, Division of Allied Health, Department of Occupational Therapy, Orangeburg, NY 10962-1210. Offers MS. Students enter program as undergraduates. *Accreditation:* AOTA. Part-time and evening/weekend programs available. *Degree requirements:* For master's, 2 clinical affiliations. *Entrance requirements:* For master's, minimum GPA of 3.0, writing sample, 3 letters of recommendation. Additional exam requirements/recommendations for international students: Required—TOEFL (minimum score 550 paper-based; 213 computer-based).

Dominican University of California, Graduate Programs, School of Health and Natural Sciences, Program in Occupational Therapy, San Rafael, CA 94901-2298. Offers MS. *Accreditation:* AOTA. Part-time programs available. *Students:* 59 full-time (48 women), 19 part-time (17 women); includes 32 minority (2 Black or African American, non-Hispanic/Latino; 13 Asian, non-Hispanic/Latino; 15 Hispanic/Latino; 1 Native Hawaiian or other Pacific Islander, non-Hispanic/Latino; 1 Two or more races, non-Hispanic/Latino). Average age 29. 160 applicants, 32% accepted, 32 enrolled. In 2011, 21 master's awarded. *Degree requirements:* For master's, thesis. *Entrance requirements:* For master's, GRE, minimum GPA of 3.0, minimum of 40 hours of experience, medical terminology. Additional exam requirements/recommendations for international students: Required—TOEFL (minimum score 550 paper-based; 213 computer-based; 80 iBT), IELTS (minimum score 7). *Application deadline:* For fall admission, 3/1 priority date for domestic students. Applications are processed on a rolling basis. Application fee: $40. Electronic applications accepted. *Expenses: Tuition:* Full-time $15,660. *Required fees:* $300. Tuition and fees vary according to program. *Financial support:* In 2011–12, 58 students received support. Scholarships/grants available. Support available to part-time students. Financial award application deadline: 3/2; financial award applicants required to submit FAFSA. *Unit head:* Dr. Ruth Ramsey, Department Chair and Program Director, 415-257-1393, E-mail: rramsey@dominican.edu. *Application contact:* Shannon Lovelace-White, Assistant Vice President, 415-485-3287, Fax: 415-485-3214, E-mail: shannon.lovelace-white@dominican.edu. Web site: http://www.dominican.edu/.

Duquesne University, John G. Rangos, Sr. School of Health Sciences, Pittsburgh, PA 15282-0001. Offers health management systems (MHMS); occupational therapy (MS); physical therapy (DPT); physician assistant studies (MPAS); rehabilitation science (MS, PhD); speech-language pathology (MS); MBA/MHMS. *Accreditation:* AOTA (one or more programs are accredited); APTA (one or more programs are accredited); ASHA. *Faculty:* 34 full-time (23 women), 20 part-time/adjunct (11 women). *Students:* 227 full-time (180 women), 12 part-time (7 women); includes 8 minority (4 Black or African American, non-Hispanic/Latino; 1 Asian, non-Hispanic/Latino; 1 Hispanic/Latino; 1 Native Hawaiian or other Pacific Islander, non-Hispanic/Latino; 1 Two or more races, non-Hispanic/Latino), 3 international. Average age 24. 537 applicants, 12% accepted, 17 enrolled. In 2011, 43 master's, 31 doctorates awarded. *Degree requirements:* For doctorate, comprehensive exam (for some programs), thesis/dissertation (for some programs). *Entrance requirements:* For master's, GRE General Test (speech-language pathology), 3 letters of recommendation; minimum GPA of 2.75 (health management systems), 3.0 (speech-language pathology and health sciences); for doctorate, GRE General Test (for physical therapy and rehabilitation science), 3 letters of recommendation, minimum GPA of 3.0, personal interview. Additional exam requirements/recommendations for international students: Required—TOEFL (minimum score 550 paper-based; 233 computer-based; 90 iBT). *Application deadline:* Applications are processed on a rolling basis. Electronic applications accepted. *Expenses:* Contact institution. *Financial support:* Federal Work-Study available. Financial award applicants required to submit FAFSA. *Faculty research:* Neuronal processing, electrical stimulation on peripheral neuropathy, CNS stimulatory and inhibitory signals, behavioral genetic methodologies to development disorders of speech, neurogenic communication disorders. *Total annual research expenditures:* $83,650. *Unit head:* Dr. Gregory H. Frazer, Dean, 412-396-5303, Fax: 412-396-5554, E-mail: frazer@duq.edu. *Application contact:* Christopher R. Hilf, Recruiter/Academic Advisor, 412-396-5653, Fax: 412-396-5554, E-mail: hilfc@duq.edu. Web site: http://www.duq.edu/healthsciences/health.html.

D'Youville College, Occupational Therapy Department, Buffalo, NY 14201-1084. Offers MS. *Accreditation:* AOTA. *Faculty:* 8 full-time (all women), 2 part-time/adjunct (both women). *Students:* 188 full-time (168 women), 12 part-time (10 women); includes 25 minority (10 Black or African American, non-Hispanic/Latino; 2 American Indian or Alaska Native, non-Hispanic/Latino; 7 Asian, non-Hispanic/Latino; 5 Hispanic/Latino; 1 Two or more races, non-Hispanic/Latino), 24 international. Average age 24. 260 applicants, 61% accepted, 82 enrolled. In 2011, 17 master's awarded. *Degree requirements:* For master's, research project. *Entrance requirements:* For master's, minimum undergraduate GPA of 3.0. Additional exam requirements/recommendations for international students: Required—TOEFL (minimum score 500 paper-based; 173 computer-based). *Application deadline:* For fall admission, 5/1 for international students; for spring admission, 9/1 for international students. Applications are processed on a rolling basis. Application fee: $25. Electronic applications accepted. *Expenses: Tuition:* Full-time $18,960; part-time $790 per credit hour. *Required fees:* $310. Tuition and fees vary according to degree level and program. *Financial support:* In 2011–12, 1 research assistantship with partial tuition reimbursement (averaging $3,000 per year) was awarded; scholarships/grants, tuition waivers (partial), and unspecified assistantships also available. *Faculty research:* Learning styles, range of motion in the elderly, hospice care, culture, health, differences in education and performance of Afro-American children, autistic spectrum disorder and social stories, autistic disorders and listening programs. *Unit head:* Dr. Amy Nwora, Chair, 716-829-7707, Fax: 716-829-8137. *Application contact:* Linda Fisher, Graduate Admissions Director, 716-829-8400, Fax: 716-829-7900, E-mail: graduateadmissions@dyc.edu.

East Carolina University, Graduate School, School of Allied Health Sciences, Department of Addictions and Rehabilitation Studies, Greenville, NC 27858-4353. Offers rehabilitation counseling (MS); rehabilitation counseling and administration (PhD); substance abuse and clinical counseling (MS); vocational evaluation (Certificate). *Accreditation:* CORE. Part-time and evening/weekend programs available. *Degree requirements:* For master's, comprehensive exam, thesis or alternative, internship. *Entrance requirements:* For master's, GRE General Test or MAT. Additional exam requirements/recommendations for international students: Required—TOEFL. *Application deadline:* For fall admission, 3/1 priority date for domestic students; for spring admission, 10/1 priority date for domestic students. Applications are processed on a rolling basis. Application fee: $50. *Expenses:* Tuition, state resident: full-time $3557; part-time $444.63 per semester hour. Tuition, nonresident: full-time $14,351; part-time $1793.88 per semester hour. *Required fees:* $2016; $252 per semester hour. Part-time tuition and fees vary according to course load, campus/location and program. *Financial support:* Research assistantships with partial tuition reimbursements, teaching assistantships with partial tuition reimbursements, Federal Work-Study, and scholarships/grants available. Support available to part-time students. Financial award application deadline: 3/1. *Unit head:* Dr. Lloyd Goodwin, Interim Chair, 252-744-6292, E-mail: goodwinl@ecu.edu. *Application contact:* Dean of Graduate School, 252-328-6012, Fax: 252-328-6071, E-mail: gradschool@ecu.edu. Web site: http://www.ecu.edu/rehb/.

East Carolina University, Graduate School, School of Allied Health Sciences, Department of Occupational Therapy, Greenville, NC 27858-4353. Offers MSOT. *Accreditation:* AOTA. Part-time programs available. Postbaccalaureate distance learning degree programs offered (minimal on-campus study). *Degree requirements:* For master's, comprehensive exam, thesis or research project. *Entrance requirements:* For master's, GRE General Test. Additional exam requirements/recommendations for international students: Required—TOEFL. *Application deadline:* For fall admission, 6/1 for domestic students. Applications are processed on a rolling basis. Application fee: $50. Electronic applications accepted. *Expenses:* Tuition, state resident: full-time $3557; part-time $444.63 per semester hour. Tuition, nonresident: full-time $14,351; part-time $1793.88 per semester hour. *Required fees:* $2016; $252 per semester hour. Part-time tuition and fees vary according to course load, campus/location and program. *Financial support:* Research assistantships, career-related internships or fieldwork, and Federal Work-Study available. Financial award application deadline: 6/1; financial award applicants required to submit FAFSA. *Faculty research:* Quality of life, assistive technology, environmental contributions, modifications of occupation to health, therapeutic activities. *Unit head:* Dr. Walter L. Jenkins, Chair, 252-744-6234, E-mail: jenkinsw@ecu.edu. *Application contact:* Dean of Graduate School, 252-328-6012, Fax: 252-328-6071, E-mail: gradschool@ecu.edu. Web site: http://www.ecu.edu/ot/.

Eastern Kentucky University, The Graduate School, College of Health Sciences, Department of Occupational Therapy, Richmond, KY 40475-3102. Offers MS. *Accreditation:* AOTA. Part-time programs available. *Degree requirements:* For master's, thesis optional. *Entrance requirements:* For master's, GRE General Test, minimum GPA of 3.0. *Faculty research:* Rehabilitation, pediatrics, leadership issues.

Occupational Therapy

Eastern Michigan University, Graduate School, College of Health and Human Services, School of Health Sciences, Program in Occupational Therapy, Ypsilanti, MI 48197. Offers MOT, MS. Part-time and evening/weekend programs available. Postbaccalaureate distance learning degree programs offered (minimal on-campus study). *Students:* 52 full-time (46 women), 24 part-time (22 women); includes 6 minority (3 Black or African American, non-Hispanic/Latino; 3 Asian, non-Hispanic/Latino). Average age 27. 48 applicants, 65% accepted, 26 enrolled. In 2011, 19 degrees awarded. *Entrance requirements:* Additional exam requirements/recommendations for international students: Required—TOEFL. *Application deadline:* Applications are processed on a rolling basis. Application fee: $35. *Expenses:* Tuition, state resident: full-time $10,367; part-time $432 per credit hour. Tuition, nonresident: full-time $20,435; part-time $851 per credit hour. *Required fees:* $39 per credit hour. $46 per semester. One-time fee: $100. Tuition and fees vary according to course level, degree level and reciprocity agreements. *Financial support:* Fellowships, research assistantships with full tuition reimbursements, teaching assistantships with full tuition reimbursements, career-related internships or fieldwork, Federal Work-Study, institutionally sponsored loans, scholarships/grants, tuition waivers (partial), and unspecified assistantships available. Support available to part-time students. Financial award applicants required to submit FAFSA. *Unit head:* Dr. Valerie Howells, Program Director, 734-487-3227, Fax: 734-487-4095, E-mail: valerie.howells@emich.edu. *Application contact:* Graduate Admissions, 734-487-2400, Fax: 734-487-6559, E-mail: graduate.admissions@emich.edu.

Eastern Washington University, Graduate Studies, College of Science, Health and Engineering, Department of Occupational Therapy, Cheney, WA 99004-2431. Offers MOT. *Accreditation:* AOTA. *Faculty:* 6 full-time (5 women). *Students:* 71 full-time (56 women); includes 5 minority (1 Black or African American, non-Hispanic/Latino; 2 Asian, non-Hispanic/Latino; 2 Hispanic/Latino), 1 international. 15 applicants, 80% accepted, 1 enrolled. In 2011, 29 master's awarded. *Degree requirements:* For master's, comprehensive exam. *Financial support:* Career-related internships or fieldwork, Federal Work-Study, institutionally sponsored loans, scholarships/grants, tuition waivers (partial), and unspecified assistantships available. Support available to part-time students. Financial award applicants required to submit FAFSA. *Unit head:* Dr. Gregory Wintz, Chair, 509-368-6562, Fax: 509-368-6561. *Application contact:* Julie Marr, Associate Dean for Graduate Studies, 509-359-6297, Fax: 509-359-6044, E-mail: gradprograms@ewu.edu. Web site: http://www.ewu.edu/cshe/programs/occupational-therapy.xml.

Elizabethtown College, Department of Occupational Therapy, Elizabethtown, PA 17022-2298. Offers MS. *Accreditation:* AOTA.

Florida Agricultural and Mechanical University, Division of Graduate Studies, Research, and Continuing Education, School of Allied Health Sciences, Division of Occupational Therapy, Tallahassee, FL 32307-3200. Offers MOT. *Accreditation:* AOTA.

Florida Gulf Coast University, College of Health Professions, Department of Occupational Therapy, Fort Myers, FL 33965-6565. Offers MS. *Faculty:* 45 full-time (32 women), 22 part-time/adjunct (14 women). *Students:* 26 full-time (23 women), 29 part-time (26 women); includes 5 minority (3 Asian, non-Hispanic/Latino; 2 Hispanic/Latino), 1 international. Average age 27. 96 applicants, 33% accepted, 28 enrolled. In 2011, 1 master's awarded. *Entrance requirements:* For master's, GRE General Test, MAT, minimum GPA of 3.0. Additional exam requirements/recommendations for international students: Required—TOEFL (minimum score 550 paper-based; 213 computer-based). *Application deadline:* For fall admission, 2/1 for domestic students. Applications are processed on a rolling basis. Application fee: $30. Electronic applications accepted. *Expenses:* Tuition, state resident: full-time $8289. Tuition, nonresident: full-time $28,895. *Required fees:* $1831. One-time fee: $30 full-time. *Unit head:* Dr. Linda Martin, Head, 239-590-7556, Fax: 239-590-7474, E-mail: lmartin@fgcu.edu. *Application contact:* Wanda Smith, Office Manager, 239-590-7550, Fax: 239-590-7474, E-mail: wsmith@fgcu.edu.

Florida International University, College of Nursing and Health Sciences, Department of Occupational Therapy, Miami, FL 33199. Offers entry level professional (MS). *Accreditation:* AOTA. Part-time programs available. *Degree requirements:* For master's, thesis or alternative. *Entrance requirements:* For master's, minimum undergraduate GPA of 3.0 in upper-level course work, letter of intent, 3 letters of recommendation, resume. Additional exam requirements/recommendations for international students: Required—TOEFL (minimum score 550 paper-based; 80 iBT). Electronic applications accepted. *Expenses:* Contact institution. *Faculty research:* Senior transportation and driving, foster care, adolescent transitions, independent living skills development, family and patient-centered care, aging, quality of life, social justice, cognition.

Gannon University, School of Graduate Studies, Morosky College of Health Professions and Sciences, School of Health Professions, Program in Occupational Therapy, Erie, PA 16541-0001. Offers MS. Program requires five years to complete. *Accreditation:* AOTA. *Students:* 55 full-time (50 women); includes 1 minority (Black or African American, non-Hispanic/Latino). Average age 23. 48 applicants, 60% accepted, 11 enrolled. In 2011, 31 master's awarded. *Degree requirements:* For master's, thesis, research project. *Entrance requirements:* For master's, letters of recommendation, interview, minimum GPA of 3.0. Additional exam requirements/recommendations for international students: Required—TOEFL (minimum score 79 iBT). *Application deadline:* For fall admission, 1/15 for domestic students. Application fee: $25. Electronic applications accepted. *Expenses:* Contact institution. *Financial support:* Scholarships/grants and unspecified assistantships available. Financial award application deadline: 7/1; financial award applicants required to submit FAFSA. *Faculty research:* The effect of chronic disease on occupational function and purpose, therapist preparedness when addressing sensitive subjects like sexuality and spirituality, the effect of disease/injury/illness on the caregiver/family. *Unit head:* Dr. Bernadette Hattjar, Director, 814-871-5332, E-mail: hattjar001@gannon.edu. *Application contact:* Kara Morgan, Director of Graduate Admissions, 814-871-5831, Fax: 814-871-5827, E-mail: graduate@gannon.edu.

Governors State University, College of Health Professions, Program in Occupational Therapy, University Park, IL 60484. Offers MOT. *Accreditation:* AOTA. *Students:* 91 full-time (74 women), 8 part-time (7 women); includes 32 minority (22 Black or African American, non-Hispanic/Latino; 5 Asian, non-Hispanic/Latino; 5 Hispanic/Latino). Average age 30. *Degree requirements:* For master's, thesis or alternative. *Entrance requirements:* For master's, minimum GPA of 3.0 in field, 2.75 overall. *Application deadline:* For fall admission, 4/30 priority date for domestic students. Application fee: $25. *Financial support:* Application deadline: 5/1. *Unit head:* Dr. Elizabeth Cada, Dean, 708-534-7295.

Grand Valley State University, College of Health Professions, Occupational Therapy Program, Allendale, MI 49401-9403. Offers MS. *Accreditation:* AOTA. *Degree requirements:* For master's, thesis or alternative, fieldwork, project. *Entrance requirements:* For master's, interview, volunteer work, writing sample. Additional exam requirements/recommendations for international students: Required—TOEFL (minimum score 610 paper-based; 253 computer-based). Electronic applications accepted. *Faculty research:* Teaching/learning methods, continuing professional education, clinical reasoning, geriatrics, performing artists.

Husson University, School of Graduate and Professional Studies, Masters in Occupational Therapy Program, Bangor, ME 04401-2999. Offers MSOT. *Accreditation:* AOTA. *Faculty:* 4 full-time (all women), 7 part-time/adjunct (6 women). *Students:* 43 full-time (37 women), 11 part-time (all women). Average age 23. 50 applicants, 76% accepted, 38 enrolled. In 2011, 33 master's awarded. *Degree requirements:* For master's, research project, paper and presentation. *Entrance requirements:* For master's, GRE, BS with minimum GPA of 3.0. Additional exam requirements/recommendations for international students: Required—TOEFL (minimum score 550 paper-based). *Application deadline:* Applications are processed on a rolling basis. Application fee: $40. *Expenses:* Contact institution. *Financial support:* Federal Work-Study, scholarships/grants, and unspecified assistantships available. Financial award application deadline: 4/15; financial award applicants required to submit FAFSA. *Unit head:* Dr. Laurie Mouradian, Program Director, 207-404-5630, E-mail: mouradianl@husson.edu. *Application contact:* Kristen Card, Director of Graduate Admissions, 207-404-5660, E-mail: cardk@husson.edu. Web site: http://www.husson.edu/occupational-therapy.

Idaho State University, Office of Graduate Studies, Kasiska College of Health Professions, Department of Physical and Occupational Therapy, Program in Occupational Therapy, Pocatello, ID 83209-8045. Offers MOT. *Accreditation:* AOTA. *Degree requirements:* For master's, comprehensive exam, thesis, oral and written exam. *Entrance requirements:* For master's, GRE General Test, minimum GPA of 3.0, 80 hours in 2 practice settings of occupational therapy. Additional exam requirements/recommendations for international students: Required—TOEFL (minimum score 600 paper-based; 213 computer-based). Electronic applications accepted. *Expenses:* Contact institution. *Faculty research:* Human movement, health care.

Indiana University–Purdue University Indianapolis, School of Health and Rehabilitation Sciences, Indianapolis, IN 46202-2896. Offers health sciences education (MS); nutrition and dietetics (MS); occupational therapy (MS); physical therapy (DPT). Part-time and evening/weekend programs available. *Faculty:* 8 full-time (5 women). *Students:* 197 full-time (162 women), 1 part-time (0 women); includes 13 minority (1 Black or African American, non-Hispanic/Latino; 4 Asian, non-Hispanic/Latino; 2 Hispanic/Latino; 1 Native Hawaiian or other Pacific Islander, non-Hispanic/Latino; 5 Two or more races, non-Hispanic/Latino). Average age 26. 213 applicants, 31% accepted, 62 enrolled. In 2011, 35 master's, 34 doctorates awarded. *Degree requirements:* For master's, thesis (for some programs). *Entrance requirements:* For master's, GRE General Test, minimum GPA of 3.0. Additional exam requirements/recommendations for international students: Required—TOEFL. *Application deadline:* For fall admission, 1/15 priority date for domestic students; for spring admission, 10/15 for domestic students. Application fee: $55 ($65 for international students). *Financial support:* Fellowships, research assistantships, teaching assistantships, Federal Work-Study, institutionally sponsored loans, and scholarships/grants available. Support available to part-time students. Financial award applicants required to submit FAFSA. *Unit head:* Dr. Augustine Agho, Dean, 317-274-4704, E-mail: aagho@iupui.edu. *Application contact:* Dr. Sherry Queener, Director, Graduate Studies and Associate Dean, 317-274-1577, Fax: 317-278-2380. Web site: http://www.shrs.iupui.edu/.

Ithaca College, Division of Graduate and Professional Studies, School of Health Sciences and Human Performance, Program in Occupational Therapy, Ithaca, NY 14850. Offers MS. Students enter the program as freshmen. *Accreditation:* AOTA. *Faculty:* 8 full-time (all women), 1 (woman) part-time/adjunct. *Students:* 53 full-time (48 women), 4 part-time (all women); includes 3 minority (1 Asian, non-Hispanic/Latino; 1 Hispanic/Latino; 1 Two or more races, non-Hispanic/Latino). Average age 24. In 2011, 27 master's awarded. *Degree requirements:* For master's, thesis optional, clinical fieldwork. *Entrance requirements:* Additional exam requirements/recommendations for international students: Required—TOEFL (minimum score 550 paper-based; 213 computer-based; 80 iBT). *Expenses:* Tuition: Part-time $663 per credit hour. *Required fees:* $663 per credit hour. *Financial support:* In 2011–12, 22 students received support. Career-related internships or fieldwork, Federal Work-Study, and scholarships/grants available. Support available to part-time students. Financial award application deadline: 3/1; financial award applicants required to submit CSS PROFILE or FAFSA. *Faculty research:* Sensory integration intervention, therapeutic listening, motor control intervention for pediatrics and adults, adult neuromuscular facilitation for individuals with neurological impairments, school-aged handwriting assessment, psychosocial community, intervention and assessment, virtual reality and robotic training for children with neurological and or sensory disorders, clinical reasoning, aging and human occupations. *Unit head:* Dr. Melinda Cozzolino, Chairperson, 607-274-3143, Fax: 607-274-1263, E-mail: gps@ithaca.edu. *Application contact:* Gerard Turbide, Director, Office of Admission, 607-274-3143, Fax: 607-274-1263, E-mail: gps@ithaca.edu. Web site: http://www.ithaca.edu/gps/gradprograms/programsites/ot.

James Madison University, The Graduate School, College of Integrated Science and Technology, Department of Health Sciences, Program in Occupational Therapy, Harrisonburg, VA 22807. Offers MOT. *Accreditation:* AOTA. Part-time programs available. *Students:* 56 full-time (54 women); includes 5 minority (1 Black or African American, non-Hispanic/Latino; 3 Hispanic/Latino; 1 Two or more races, non-Hispanic/Latino), 1 international. Average age 27. In 2011, 20 master's awarded. *Entrance requirements:* For master's, GRE General Test, GRE Subject Test, 3 reference forms, evidence of one instructional experience, documentation of competency in computer technology and information seeking skills. *Application deadline:* For fall admission, 2/1 priority date for domestic students. Application fee: $55. *Expenses:* Tuition, state resident: full-time $8016; part-time $334 per credit hour. Tuition, nonresident: full-time $22,656; part-time $944 per credit hour. *Financial support:* In 2011–12, 3 students received support. 3 graduate assistantships ($7382) available. Financial award application deadline: 3/1; financial award applicants required to submit FAFSA. *Unit head:* Dr. Jeff Loveland, Director, 540-568-2399, E-mail: lovelajd@jmu.edu. *Application contact:* Lynette M. Bible, Director of Graduate Admissions, 540-568-6395, Fax: 540-568-7860, E-mail: biblelm@jmu.edu.

Jefferson College of Health Sciences, Program in Occupational Therapy, Roanoke, VA 24031-3186. Offers MS. *Accreditation:* AOTA. Part-time programs available. *Entrance requirements:* For master's, GRE. Additional exam requirements/recommendations for international students: Required—TOEFL (minimum score 550 paper-based; 213 computer-based; 80 iBT). Electronic applications accepted.

Kean University, Nathan Weiss Graduate College, Program in Occupational Therapy, Union, NJ 07083. Offers MS. *Accreditation:* AOTA. Part-time and evening/weekend programs available. *Faculty:* 5 full-time (all women). *Students:* 57 full-time (48 women), 29 part-time (26 women); includes 17 minority (2 Black or African American, non-Hispanic/Latino; 5 Asian, non-Hispanic/Latino; 9 Hispanic/Latino; 1 Two or more races, non-Hispanic/Latino). Average age 26. 234 applicants, 17% accepted, 29 enrolled. In 2011, 31 master's awarded. *Degree requirements:* For master's, 6 months of field work, final project. *Entrance requirements:* For master's, minimum GPA of 3.0, 3 letters of recommendation, interview, documented observation of occupational therapy service in 2 or more settings of a total of 40 hours, transcripts. Additional exam requirements/recommendations for international students: Required—TOEFL (minimum score 79 iBT). *Application deadline:* For fall admission, 2/1 for domestic and international students. Applications are processed on a rolling basis. Application fee: $75 ($150 for

international students). Electronic applications accepted. *Expenses:* Tuition, state resident: full-time $11,302; part-time $550 per credit. Tuition, nonresident: full-time $15,318; part-time $674 per credit. *Required fees:* $2849; $130 per credit. Tuition and fees vary according to degree level. *Financial support:* In 2011–12, 7 research assistantships with full tuition reimbursements (averaging $3,263 per year) were awarded; unspecified assistantships also available. Financial award applicants required to submit FAFSA. *Unit head:* Dr. Laurie Knis-Matthews, Program Coordinator, 908-737-5850, Fax: 908-737-3377, E-mail: ot@kean.edu. *Application contact:* Reenat Hasan, Admissions Counselor, 908-737-5923, Fax: 908-737-5925, E-mail: hasanr@kean.edu. Web site: http://www.kean.edu/KU/Occupational-Therapy.

Keuka College, Program in Occupational Therapy, Keuka Park, NY 14478-0098. Offers MS. *Accreditation:* AOTA. *Degree requirements:* For master's, thesis or alternative, clinical internships. *Entrance requirements:* For master's, minimum GPA of 3.0, BS in occupational therapy at Keuka College. Additional exam requirements/recommendations for international students: Required—TOEFL (minimum score 550 paper-based; 213 computer-based). *Expenses:* Contact institution.

Lenoir-Rhyne University, Graduate Programs, School of Occupational Therapy, Hickory, NC 28601. Offers MS. *Accreditation:* AOTA. *Entrance requirements:* For master's, GRE or MAT, minimum GPA of 2.7.

Loma Linda University, School of Allied Health Professions, Department of Occupational Therapy, Loma Linda, CA 92350. Offers MOT, OTD.

Louisiana State University Health Sciences Center, School of Allied Health Professions, Department of Occupational Therapy, New Orleans, LA 70112-2223. Offers MOT. *Accreditation:* AOTA. *Entrance requirements:* For master's, GRE (minimum combined score 900), bachelor's degree, 40 hours of observation in occupational therapy, 3 recommendation letters.

Maryville University of Saint Louis, School of Health Professions, Occupational Therapy Program, St. Louis, MO 63141-7299. Offers MOT. *Accreditation:* AOTA. *Students:* 26 part-time (all women); includes 1 minority (Asian, non-Hispanic/Latino). Average age 24. In 2011, 25 master's awarded. *Entrance requirements:* For master's, ACT (minimum composite score of 21) or SAT-I (minimum combined score of 990) unless applicant has completed more than 30 college credits, minimum cumulative GPA of 3.0, resume, interview, writing sample. Additional exam requirements/recommendations for international students: Required—TOEFL (minimum score 550 paper-based). *Application deadline:* Applications are processed on a rolling basis. Application fee: $40 ($60 for international students). Electronic applications accepted. *Expenses:* Contact institution. *Financial support:* Career-related internships or fieldwork, Federal Work-Study, and campus employment available. Financial award application deadline: 3/1; financial award applicants required to submit FAFSA. *Faculty research:* Older driver safety rehabilitation options, adaptive equipment and training remediation, injured workers disability interventions. *Unit head:* Dr. Paula Bohr, Director, 314-529-9682, Fax: 314-529-9191, E-mail: pbohr@maryville.edu. *Application contact:* Dr. Donna Payne, 314-529-9676, Fax: 314-529-9927, E-mail: dpayne@maryville.edu. Web site: http://www.maryville.edu/academics-hp-occtherapy.

McMaster University, Faculty of Health Sciences, Professional Program in Occupational Therapy, Hamilton, ON L8S 4M2, Canada. Offers M Sc. *Degree requirements:* For master's, fieldwork and independent research project. *Entrance requirements:* For master's, minimum B average over last 60 undergraduate units. Additional exam requirements/recommendations for international students: Required—TOEFL (minimum score 600 paper-based; 250 computer-based).

Medical University of South Carolina, College of Health Professions, Department of Health Professions, Program in Occupational Therapy, Charleston, SC 29425. Offers MSRS. *Accreditation:* AOTA. *Faculty:* 5 full-time (3 women), 4 part-time/adjunct (all women). *Students:* 83 full-time (79 women); includes 7 minority (3 Black or African American, non-Hispanic/Latino; 2 Asian, non-Hispanic/Latino; 2 Hispanic/Latino). Average age 25. 99 applicants, 55% accepted, 39 enrolled. In 2011, 33 master's awarded. *Degree requirements:* For master's, thesis or alternative, research project. *Entrance requirements:* For master's, GRE General Test, interview, minimum GPA of 3.0, references. Additional exam requirements/recommendations for international students: Required—TOEFL (minimum score 600 paper-based; 250 computer-based). *Application deadline:* For fall admission, 1/15 priority date for domestic students, 1/15 for international students; for spring admission, 11/1 for international students. Application fee: $85. Electronic applications accepted. *Financial support:* Federal Work-Study and scholarships/grants available. Support available to part-time students. Financial award application deadline: 3/10; financial award applicants required to submit FAFSA. *Faculty research:* Therapeutic interventions for children with cerebral palsy; function, well being, quality of life for adults with chronic conditions and health disparities; driving interventions for adults with head and neck cancer; oral health for adults with tetraplegia; interprofessional education. *Total annual research expenditures:* $458,634. *Unit head:* Dr. Maralynne Mitcham, Director, 843-792-9734, Fax: 843-792-0710, E-mail: mitchamm@musc.edu. *Application contact:* Susan Johnson, Student Services Program Coordinator, 843-792-5377, Fax: 843-792-0710, E-mail: johnsoss@musc.edu. Web site: http://www.musc.edu/chp/ot/index.htm.

Mercy College, School of Health and Natural Sciences, Program in Occupational Therapy, Dobbs Ferry, NY 10522-1189. Offers MS. *Accreditation:* AOTA. Evening/weekend programs available. *Degree requirements:* For master's, thesis, fieldwork. *Entrance requirements:* For master's, minimum GPA of 3.0, 3 references, resume. Additional exam requirements/recommendations for international students: Required—TOEFL (minimum score 600 paper-based; 250 computer-based; 100 iBT), IELTS (minimum score 8). Electronic applications accepted. *Expenses:* Contact institution.

Midwestern University, Downers Grove Campus, College of Health Sciences, Illinois Campus, Program in Occupational Therapy, Downers Grove, IL 60515-1235. Offers MOT. *Accreditation:* AOTA. *Faculty:* 8 full-time (all women). *Students:* 113 full-time (103 women); includes 17 minority (2 Black or African American, non-Hispanic/Latino; 7 Asian, non-Hispanic/Latino; 6 Hispanic/Latino; 1 Native Hawaiian or other Pacific Islander, non-Hispanic/Latino; 1 Two or more races, non-Hispanic/Latino). Average age 26. 498 applicants, 15% accepted, 38 enrolled. In 2011, 14 master's awarded. *Entrance requirements:* For master's, GRE General Test. *Application deadline:* Applications are processed on a rolling basis. Application fee: $50. *Expenses:* Contact institution. *Financial support:* Federal Work-Study and scholarships/grants available. Financial award applicants required to submit FAFSA. *Unit head:* Kimberly A. Bryze, Director, 630-515-7226, E-mail: kbryze@midwestern.edu. *Application contact:* Michael Laken, Director of Admissions, 630-515-6171, Fax: 630-971-6086, E-mail: admissil@midwestern.edu.

Midwestern University, Glendale Campus, College of Health Sciences, Arizona Campus, Program in Occupational Therapy, Glendale, AZ 85308. Offers MOT. *Accreditation:* AOTA. *Faculty:* 5 full-time (all women). *Students:* 89 full-time (80 women); includes 13 minority (1 Black or African American, non-Hispanic/Latino; 4 Asian, non-Hispanic/Latino; 7 Hispanic/Latino; 1 Two or more races, non-Hispanic/Latino). Average age 26. 351 applicants, 13% accepted, 31 enrolled. In 2011, 8 master's awarded. *Entrance requirements:* For master's, GRE. *Application deadline:* Applications are processed on a rolling basis. Application fee: $50. *Expenses:* Contact institution. *Unit head:* Christine R. Merchant, Director, 623-572-3638, E-mail: cmerch@midwestern.edu. *Application contact:* James Walter, Director of Admissions, 888-247-9277, Fax: 623-572-3229, E-mail: admissaz@midwestern.edu.

Milligan College, Program in Occupational Therapy, Milligan College, TN 37682. Offers MSOT. *Accreditation:* AOTA. *Faculty:* 6 full-time (4 women), 5 part-time/adjunct (4 women). *Students:* 75 full-time (66 women), 3 part-time (all women). Average age 28. 150 applicants, 22% accepted, 31 enrolled. In 2011, 29 degrees awarded. *Degree requirements:* For master's, thesis. *Entrance requirements:* For master's, GRE. Additional exam requirements/recommendations for international students: Required—TOEFL (minimum score 550 paper-based; 213 computer-based; 80 iBT). *Application deadline:* For spring admission, 1/15 priority date for domestic students, 4/1 for international students. Application fee: $30. Electronic applications accepted. *Expenses:* Contact institution. *Financial support:* Career-related internships or fieldwork and institutionally sponsored loans available. Financial award application deadline: 4/15; financial award applicants required to submit FAFSA. *Faculty research:* Handwriting, creativity, leadership in health care and rehabilitation, prevention and rehabilitation of work-related musculoskeletal disorders, parent-child interaction therapy, community-based occupational therapy programs. *Unit head:* Dr. Jeff Snodgrass, Program Director and Associate Professor, 423-975-8010, Fax: 423-975-8019, E-mail: jsnodgrass@milligan.edu. *Application contact:* Kristia Brown, Office Manager and Admissions Representative, 423-975-8010, Fax: 423-975-8019, E-mail: kngarland@milligan.edu. Web site: http://www.milligan.edu/msot/.

Misericordia University, College of Health Sciences, Program in Occupational Therapy, Dallas, PA 18612-1098. Offers MSOT, OTD. *Accreditation:* AOTA. *Faculty:* 6 full-time (4 women), 11 part-time/adjunct (8 women). *Students:* 24 full-time (all women), 21 part-time (18 women); includes 2 minority (1 Black or African American, non-Hispanic/Latino; 1 Two or more races, non-Hispanic/Latino). Average age 31. In 2011, 34 master's, 6 doctorates awarded. *Entrance requirements:* For master's, minimum undergraduate GPA of 2.8, 2 letters of reference; for doctorate, minimum graduate GPA of 3.0, interview, 3 letters of reference. *Application deadline:* Applications are processed on a rolling basis. Application fee: $25. Electronic applications accepted. *Expenses: Tuition:* Full-time $25,700; part-time $575 per credit. *Financial support:* In 2011–12, 30 students received support. Teaching assistantships, career-related internships or fieldwork, and scholarships/grants available. Support available to part-time students. Financial award application deadline: 6/30; financial award applicants required to submit FAFSA. *Unit head:* Dr. Grace Fisher, Chair, 570-674-8015, E-mail: gfisher@misericordia.edu. *Application contact:* Larree Brown, Assistant Director of Admissions, Part-Time Undergraduate and Graduate Programs, 570-674-6451, E-mail: lbrown@misericordia.edu. Web site: http://www.misericordia.edu/ot.

Mount Mary College, Graduate Programs, Program in Occupational Therapy, Milwaukee, WI 53222-4597. Offers MS. *Accreditation:* AOTA. Part-time and evening/weekend programs available. *Faculty:* 4 full-time (all women), 13 part-time/adjunct (11 women). *Students:* 107 full-time (103 women), 13 part-time (11 women); includes 11 minority (3 Black or African American, non-Hispanic/Latino; 4 Asian, non-Hispanic/Latino; 1 Hispanic/Latino; 3 Two or more races, non-Hispanic/Latino). Average age 31. 115 applicants, 37% accepted, 36 enrolled. In 2011, 18 master's awarded. *Degree requirements:* For master's, comprehensive exam, thesis or alternative, professional development portfolio. *Entrance requirements:* For master's, minimum GPA of 2.75, occupational therapy license, 1 year of work experience. Additional exam requirements/recommendations for international students: Required—TOEFL (minimum score 500 paper-based; 173 computer-based). *Application deadline:* For fall admission, 10/15 priority date for domestic students, 10/15 for international students; for spring admission, 3/15 for domestic and international students. Application fee: $45 ($100 for international students). *Financial support:* In 2011–12, 11 students received support. Career-related internships or fieldwork and Federal Work-Study available. Support available to part-time students. Financial award application deadline: 5/1; financial award applicants required to submit FAFSA. *Faculty research:* Clinical reasoning, occupational science, sensory integration. *Unit head:* Dr. Jane Olson, Director, 414-258-4810 Ext. 348, E-mail: olsonj@mtmary.edu. *Application contact:* Dr. Douglas J. Mickelson, Associate Dean for Graduate and Continuing Education, 414-256-1252, Fax: 414-256-0167, E-mail: mickelsd@mtmary.edu.

New England Institute of Technology, Program in Occupational Therapy, Warwick, RI 02886-2244. Offers MS. *Degree requirements:* For master's, fieldwork.

New York Institute of Technology, Graduate Division, School of Health Professions, Program in Occupational Therapy, Old Westbury, NY 11568-8000. Offers MS. *Accreditation:* AOTA. *Students:* 98 full-time (70 women), 2 part-time (both women); includes 38 minority (6 Black or African American, non-Hispanic/Latino; 1 American Indian or Alaska Native, non-Hispanic/Latino; 28 Asian, non-Hispanic/Latino; 1 Hispanic/Latino; 1 Native Hawaiian or other Pacific Islander, non-Hispanic/Latino; 1 Two or more races, non-Hispanic/Latino), 1 international. Average age 25. In 2011, 15 master's awarded. *Degree requirements:* For master's, thesis. *Entrance requirements:* For master's, minimum GPA of 2.0 in science or mathematics, 2.5 overall; 100 hours of supervised volunteer work; interview; 2 professional letters of recommendation. Additional exam requirements/recommendations for international students: Required—TOEFL (minimum score 550 paper-based; 213 computer-based). *Application deadline:* For fall admission, 7/1 priority date for domestic students; for spring admission, 12/1 priority date for domestic students. Applications are processed on a rolling basis. Application fee: $50. Electronic applications accepted. *Expenses: Tuition:* Part-time $930 per credit hour. *Financial support:* Research assistantships with partial tuition reimbursements available. Financial award applicants required to submit FAFSA. *Unit head:* Dr. Ellen Greer, Department Chair, 516-686-3862, E-mail: egreer@nyit.edu. *Application contact:* Dr. Jacquelyn Nealon, Vice President for Enrollment Services, 516-686-7925, Fax: 516-686-7597, E-mail: jnealon@nyit.edu.

New York University, Steinhardt School of Culture, Education, and Human Development, Department of Occupational Therapy, New York, NY 10012. Offers advanced occupational therapy (MA); occupational therapy (MS, DPS); research in occupational therapy (PhD). *Accreditation:* AOTA (one or more programs are accredited). Part-time programs available. *Faculty:* 10 full-time (7 women), 16 part-time/adjunct (11 women). *Students:* 169 full-time (162 women), 23 part-time (20 women); includes 59 minority (9 Black or African American, non-Hispanic/Latino; 26 Asian, non-Hispanic/Latino; 20 Hispanic/Latino; 1 Native Hawaiian or other Pacific Islander, non-Hispanic/Latino; 3 Two or more races, non-Hispanic/Latino), 15 international. Average age 26. 491 applicants, 37% accepted, 66 enrolled. In 2011, 55 master's, 4 doctorates awarded. *Degree requirements:* For master's, thesis (for some programs), terminal project; fieldwork; for doctorate, thesis/dissertation, terminal project. *Entrance requirements:* For doctorate, GRE General Test, interview. Additional exam requirements/recommendations for international students: Required—TOEFL. *Application deadline:* For fall admission, 12/1 priority date for domestic students, 12/1 for international students. Applications are processed on a rolling basis. Application fee: $75. Electronic applications accepted. *Financial support:* Fellowships with full and partial tuition reimbursements, teaching assistantships with full and partial tuition reimbursements, career-related internships or fieldwork, Federal Work-Study, institutionally sponsored loans, scholarships/grants, traineeships, tuition waivers

(partial), and unspecified assistantships available. Support available to part-time students. Financial award application deadline: 2/1; financial award applicants required to submit FAFSA. *Faculty research:* Pediatrics, assistive rehabilitation technology, adaptive computer technology for children with disabilities, cognitive bases of adult disablement, upper limb rehabilitation. *Unit head:* Dr. Jane Bear-Lehman, Chairperson, 212-998-5846, Fax: 212-995-4044, E-mail: occupational.therapy@nyu.edu. *Application contact:* 212-998-5030, Fax: 212-995-4328, E-mail: steinhardt.gradadmissions@nyu.edu. Web site: http://steinhardt.nyu.edu/ot.

Nova Southeastern University, Health Professions Division, College of Health Care Sciences, Fort Lauderdale, FL 33314-7796. Offers audiology (Au D); health science (MH Sc, DHSc, PhD); occupational therapy (MOT, OTD, PhD); physical therapy (DPT, PhD); physical therapy (transitional) (TDPT). Postbaccalaureate distance learning degree programs offered (minimal on-campus study). *Faculty:* 85 full-time (57 women), 52 part-time/adjunct (27 women). *Students:* 993 full-time (702 women), 514 part-time (356 women); includes 465 minority (160 Black or African American, non-Hispanic/Latino; 6 American Indian or Alaska Native, non-Hispanic/Latino; 96 Asian, non-Hispanic/Latino; 177 Hispanic/Latino; 3 Native Hawaiian or other Pacific Islander, non-Hispanic/Latino; 23 Two or more races, non-Hispanic/Latino), 13 international. Average age 31. 3,837 applicants, 18% accepted, 446 enrolled. In 2011, 293 master's, 147 doctorates awarded. *Degree requirements:* For master's, thesis; for doctorate, comprehensive exam, thesis/dissertation. *Entrance requirements:* For master's and doctorate, GRE General Test. *Application deadline:* Applications are processed on a rolling basis. Application fee: $50. Electronic applications accepted. *Expenses:* Contact institution. *Financial support:* In 2011–12, 12 students received support, including 1 fellowship (averaging $10,000 per year), 4 teaching assistantships (averaging $10,200 per year); institutionally sponsored loans and unspecified assistantships also available. *Unit head:* Dr. Richard Davis, Dean, 954-262-1203, E-mail: redavis@nova.edu. *Application contact:* Joey Jankie, Admissions Counselor, 954-262-7249, E-mail: joey@nova.edu. Web site: http://www.nova.edu/chcs/.

The Ohio State University, College of Medicine, School of Allied Medical Professions, Program in Occupational Therapy, Columbus, OH 43210. Offers MOT. *Accreditation:* AOTA. *Entrance requirements:* For master's, GRE General Test. Additional exam requirements/recommendations for international students: Required—TOEFL (paper-based 550; computer-based 213) or Michigan English Language Assessment Battery (82). Electronic applications accepted. *Expenses:* Tuition, state resident: full-time $11,400. Tuition, nonresident: full-time $28,125. Tuition and fees vary according to course load, degree level, campus/location and program.

Pacific University, School of Occupational Therapy, Forest Grove, OR 97116-1797. Offers MOT. *Accreditation:* AOTA. *Degree requirements:* For master's, research project, professional project. Electronic applications accepted. *Expenses:* Contact institution. *Faculty research:* Cultural competency development, disability policy, scholarship of teaching and learning, driver rehabilitation and older adult visual perception, neurorehabilitation and motor learning.

Philadelphia University, College of Science, Health and the Liberal Arts, Program in Occupational Therapy, Philadelphia, PA 19144. Offers MS. *Accreditation:* AOTA. Evening/weekend programs available. *Degree requirements:* For master's, practicum. *Entrance requirements:* For master's, GRE or MAT. Additional exam requirements/recommendations for international students: Required—TOEFL (minimum score 550 paper-based; 213 computer-based; 79 iBT). Electronic applications accepted.

Queen's University at Kingston, School of Graduate Studies and Research, Faculty of Health Sciences, School of Rehabilitation Therapy, Kingston, ON K7L 3N6, Canada. Offers occupational therapy (M Sc OT); physical therapy (M Sc PT); rehabilitation science (M Sc, PhD). Part-time programs available. *Degree requirements:* For master's, thesis; for doctorate, comprehensive exam, thesis/dissertation. *Entrance requirements:* Additional exam requirements/recommendations for international students: Required—TOEFL. *Faculty research:* Disability, community, motor performance, rehabilitation, treatment efficiency.

Quinnipiac University, School of Health Sciences, Program in Occupational Therapy, Hamden, CT 06518-1940. Offers MOT. Students are admitted to the program as undergraduates. *Faculty:* 5 part-time/adjunct (all women). *Students:* 106 full-time (101 women), 28 part-time (all women); includes 17 minority (6 Black or African American, non-Hispanic/Latino; 5 Asian, non-Hispanic/Latino; 6 Hispanic/Latino). Average age 24. 68 applicants, 100% accepted, 67 enrolled. In 2011, 8 master's awarded. *Entrance requirements:* Additional exam requirements/recommendations for international students: Required—TOEFL (minimum score 575 paper-based; 233 computer-based; 90 iBT). *Expenses: Tuition:* Part-time $855 per credit. *Required fees:* $35 per credit. *Financial support:* In 2011–12, 41 students received support. Scholarships/grants and unspecified assistantships available. Financial award application deadline: 4/15; financial award applicants required to submit FAFSA. *Unit head:* Kimberly Hartmann, Chairperson, 203-582-8679, E-mail: kim.hartmann@quinnipiac.edu. *Application contact:* 800-462-1944, E-mail: admissions@quinnipiac.edu. Web site: http://www.quinnipiac.edu/x758.xml.

Radford University, College of Graduate and Professional Studies, Waldron College of Health and Human Services, Department of Occupational Therapy, Radford , VA 24142. Offers MOT. *Accreditation:* AOTA. Part-time and evening/weekend programs available. *Faculty:* 5 full-time (4 women), 1 (woman) part-time/adjunct. *Students:* 42 full-time (36 women), 1 part-time (0 women); includes 2 minority (1 Black or African American, non-Hispanic/Latino; 1 Two or more races, non-Hispanic/Latino). Average age 28. 30 applicants, 77% accepted, 16 enrolled. *Degree requirements:* For master's, comprehensive exam. *Entrance requirements:* For master's, GRE, minimum GPA of 3.25, minimum C grade in prerequisite courses, 2 letters of recommendation, professional resume, 40 hours of observation, official transcripts. Additional exam requirements/recommendations for international students: Required—TOEFL (minimum score 550 paper-based; 213 computer-based; 79 iBT). *Application deadline:* For fall admission, 2/15 priority date for domestic students, 12/1 for international students; for spring admission, 7/1 for international students. Applications are processed on a rolling basis. Application fee: $50. Electronic applications accepted. *Expenses:* Contact institution. *Financial support:* In 2011–12, 12 students received support, including 13 research assistantships (averaging $4,500 per year); career-related internships or fieldwork, Federal Work-Study, institutionally sponsored loans, scholarships/grants, and unspecified assistantships also available. Financial award application deadline: 3/1; financial award applicants required to submit FAFSA. *Unit head:* Dr. Douglas Mitchell, Chair, 540-831-7643, E-mail: dmmitchell@radford.edu. *Application contact:* Rebecca Conner, Graduate Admissions Office, 540-831-5431, Fax: 540-831-6061, E-mail: gradcollege@radford.edu. Web site: http://www.radford.edu/content/wchs/home/occupational-therapy.html/.

The Richard Stockton College of New Jersey, School of Graduate and Continuing Studies, Program in Occupational Therapy, Pomona, NJ 08240-0195. Offers MSOT. *Accreditation:* AOTA. *Faculty:* 5 full-time (4 women), 2 part-time/adjunct (1 woman). *Students:* 42 full-time (35 women), 23 part-time (22 women); includes 6 minority (3 Asian, non-Hispanic/Latino; 3 Hispanic/Latino). Average age 28. 171 applicants, 17% accepted, 21 enrolled. In 2011, 20 master's awarded. *Degree requirements:* For master's, fieldwork, research project. *Entrance requirements:* For master's, minimum GPA of 3.0, 120 hours of work, volunteer or community service. Additional exam requirements/recommendations for international students: Required—TOEFL. *Application deadline:* For fall admission, 1/15 for domestic and international students. Application fee: $50. Electronic applications accepted. *Expenses:* Tuition, state resident: full-time $13,035; part-time $543 per credit. Tuition, nonresident: full-time $20,065; part-time $836 per credit. *Required fees:* $3920; $163 per credit. Tuition and fees vary according to degree level. *Financial support:* In 2011–12, 16 students received support, including 2 fellowships, 28 research assistantships with partial tuition reimbursements available; career-related internships or fieldwork, scholarships/grants, and unspecified assistantships also available. Support available to part-time students. Financial award application deadline: 3/1; financial award applicants required to submit FAFSA. *Faculty research:* Home health-based occupational therapy for women with HIV/AIDS. *Unit head:* Dr. Kim Furphy, Program Director, 609-626-3640, E-mail: msot@stockton.edu. *Application contact:* Tara Williams, Assistant Director of Graduate Enrollment Management, 609-626-3640, Fax: 609-626-6050, E-mail: gradschool@stockton.edu.

Rockhurst University, School of Graduate and Professional Studies, Program in Occupational Therapy, Kansas City, MO 64110-2561. Offers MOT. *Accreditation:* AOTA. Part-time programs available. *Faculty:* 5 full-time (all women), 5 part-time/adjunct (3 women). *Students:* 72 full-time (64 women), 2 part-time (both women); includes 7 minority (5 Asian, non-Hispanic/Latino; 1 Hispanic/Latino; 1 Native Hawaiian or other Pacific Islander, non-Hispanic/Latino). Average age 26. 147 applicants, 36% accepted, 38 enrolled. In 2011, 33 master's awarded. *Entrance requirements:* For master's, minimum GPA of 3.0. Additional exam requirements/recommendations for international students: Required—TOEFL (minimum score 550 paper-based; 213 computer-based; 79 iBT). *Application deadline:* Applications are processed on a rolling basis. Application fee: $25. Electronic applications accepted. Application fee is waived when completed online. *Financial support:* Career-related internships or fieldwork, institutionally sponsored loans, and unspecified assistantships available. Financial award applicants required to submit FAFSA. *Faculty research:* Problem-based learning, cognitive rehabilitation behavioral state in infants and children, adult neurological defects and prosthetics. *Unit head:* Dr. Kris Vacek, Chair, 816-501-4635, Fax: 816-501-4643, E-mail: kris.vacek@rockhurst.edu. *Application contact:* Cheryl Hooper, Director of Graduate Recruitment and Admission, 816-501-4097, Fax: 816-501-4241, E-mail: cheryl.hooper@rockhurst.edu. Web site: http://www.rockhurst.edu/academic/ot/index.asp.

Rocky Mountain University of Health Professions, Program in Occupational Therapy, Provo, UT 84606. Offers OTD.

Rush University, College of Health Sciences, Department of Occupational Therapy, Chicago, IL 60612-3832. Offers MS. *Accreditation:* AOTA. *Degree requirements:* For master's, thesis optional. *Entrance requirements:* For master's, GRE General Test. Electronic applications accepted. *Faculty research:* Intervention and practice strategies in the stroke population and the impact of evidenced based interventions.

Sacred Heart University, Graduate Programs, College of Health Professions, Program in Occupational Therapy, Fairfield, CT 06825-1000. Offers MSOT. *Accreditation:* AOTA. *Entrance requirements:* For master's, minimum GPA of 3.0. Additional exam requirements/recommendations for international students: Required—TOEFL (minimum score 550 paper-based; 213 computer-based). Electronic applications accepted. *Expenses:* Contact institution.

Sage Graduate School, School of Health Sciences, Program in Occupational Therapy, Troy, NY 12180-4115. Offers MS. *Accreditation:* AOTA. Part-time and evening/weekend programs available. *Faculty:* 7 full-time (all women), 3 part-time/adjunct (all women). *Students:* 59 full-time (55 women), 32 part-time (all women); includes 4 minority (2 Asian, non-Hispanic/Latino; 1 Hispanic/Latino; 1 Two or more races, non-Hispanic/Latino). Average age 27. 111 applicants, 39% accepted, 35 enrolled. In 2011, 27 master's awarded. *Entrance requirements:* For master's, baccalaureate degree, minimum undergraduate GPA of 3.0, completion of program prerequisites with minimum C grade, completion of 20 hours of clinical observation. Additional exam requirements/recommendations for international students: Required—TOEFL (minimum score 550 paper-based; 213 computer-based). *Application deadline:* For fall admission, 2/1 for domestic students. Applications are processed on a rolling basis. Application fee: $40. *Expenses: Tuition:* Full-time $11,880; part-time $660 per credit hour. Tuition and fees vary according to program. *Financial support:* Fellowships, research assistantships, Federal Work-Study, scholarships/grants, and unspecified assistantships available. Support available to part-time students. *Unit head:* Dr. Esther Haskevitz, Interim Dean, School of Health Sciences, 518-244-2296, Fax: 518-244-4571, E-mail: haskve@sage.edu. *Application contact:* Theresa Hand, Chair and Program Director, 518-244-2056, Fax: 518-244-4524, E-mail: handt@sage.edu.

Saginaw Valley State University, Crystal M. Lange College of Nursing and Health Sciences, Program in Occupational Therapy, University Center, MI 48710. Offers MSOT. *Accreditation:* AOTA. *Students:* 85 full-time (73 women), 61 part-time (51 women); includes 5 minority (1 Black or African American, non-Hispanic/Latino; 2 Asian, non-Hispanic/Latino; 2 Hispanic/Latino), 3 international. Average age 25. 1 applicant, 100% accepted, 1 enrolled. In 2011, 22 master's awarded. *Entrance requirements:* Additional exam requirements/recommendations for international students: Required—TOEFL (minimum score 525 paper-based; 197 computer-based; 71 iBT). *Expenses:* Tuition, state resident: full-time $8300; part-time $5333 per year. Tuition, nonresident: full-time $15,613; part-time $10,209 per year. *International tuition:* $15,631 full-time. *Financial support:* Federal Work-Study and scholarships/grants available. Support available to part-time students. *Unit head:* Dr. Donald Earley, Associate Professor, 989-964-4689, E-mail: dwe@svsu.edu. *Application contact:* P. Laine Blasch, Graduate Recruitment Coordinator, 989-964-2182, Fax: 989-790-0180, E-mail: blasch@svsu.edu.

St. Ambrose University, College of Education and Health Sciences, Program in Occupational Therapy, Davenport, IA 52803-2898. Offers MOT. *Accreditation:* AOTA. *Faculty:* 9 full-time (8 women), 2 part-time/adjunct (1 woman). *Students:* 73 full-time (69 women), 1 (woman) part-time; includes 1 minority (Asian, non-Hispanic/Latino), 1 international. Average age 24. 91 applicants, 53% accepted, 48 enrolled. In 2011, 28 master's awarded. *Degree requirements:* For master's, board exams. *Entrance requirements:* For master's, 50 hours of volunteer experience in 2 occupational therapy settings, minimum GPA of 2.7, essay or interview on campus, 3 letters of reference. Additional exam requirements/recommendations for international students: Required—TOEFL. *Application deadline:* For fall admission, 1/31 for domestic students. Application fee: $25. Electronic applications accepted. *Expenses: Tuition:* Full-time $13,770; part-time $765 per credit hour. *Required fees:* $60 per semester. Tuition and fees vary according to degree level, program and reciprocity agreements. *Financial support:* In 2011–12, 57 students received support, including 10 research assistantships with partial tuition reimbursements available (averaging $3,500 per year); career-related internships or fieldwork, scholarships/grants, tuition waivers (partial), and unspecified assistantships also available. Financial award application deadline: 8/15; financial award applicants required to submit FAFSA. *Unit head:* Dr. Lynn Frank, Director, 563-333-6407, Fax: 563-333-6243, E-mail: franklynnm@sau.edu. *Application contact:* Lori J. Parker, Administrative Assistant, 563-333-6413, Fax: 563-333-6243, E-mail: parkerlorij@

sau.edu. Web site: http://www.sau.edu/Academic_Programs/Master_of_Occupational_Therapy.html.

St. Catherine University, Graduate Programs, Program in Occupational Therapy, St. Paul, MN 55105. Offers MA. *Accreditation:* AOTA. Part-time and evening/weekend programs available. *Degree requirements:* For master's, thesis. *Entrance requirements:* For master's, GRE, minimum GPA of 3.0. Additional exam requirements/recommendations for international students: Required—Michigan English Language Assessment Battery or TOEFL. *Expenses: Required fees:* $30 per semester. Tuition and fees vary according to program.

Saint Francis University, Department of Occupational Therapy, Loretto, PA 15940-0600. Offers MOT. *Accreditation:* AOTA. *Faculty:* 6 full-time (4 women), 1 (woman) part-time/adjunct. *Students:* 36 full-time (30 women). Average age 22. 36 applicants, 100% accepted, 36 enrolled. In 2011, 23 master's awarded. *Degree requirements:* For master's, one foreign language, thesis. *Expenses: Tuition:* Part-time $815 per credit. *Required fees:* $504 per semester. One-time fee: $40 part-time. Tuition and fees vary according to degree level, program and reciprocity agreements. *Faculty research:* Retention, technology, work injury, distance learning. *Unit head:* Dr. Edward Mihelcic, Chair, 814-472-2760, Fax: 814-472-3950, E-mail: emihelcic@francis.edu. *Application contact:* Dr. Peter Raymond Skoner, Associate Vice President for Academic Affairs, 814-472-3085, Fax: 814-472-3365, E-mail: pskoner@francis.edu. Web site: http://www.francis.edu/ot.

Saint Louis University, Graduate Education, Doisy College of Health Sciences, Department of Occupational Science and Occupational Therapy, St. Louis, MO 63103-2097. Offers MOT. *Accreditation:* AOTA. *Degree requirements:* For master's, project. *Entrance requirements:* For master's, minimum GPA of 2.8. Additional exam requirements/recommendations for international students: Required—TOEFL (minimum score 525 paper-based; 194 computer-based; 55 iBT). Electronic applications accepted. *Faculty research:* Autism spectrum and Asperger's disease, early intervention with children of homeless families, disability awareness program development of developing countries, environmental adaptations and universal design for persons who are disabled and/or aging, physical activity models for persons with dementia.

Salem State University, School of Graduate Studies, Program in Occupational Therapy, Salem, MA 01970-5353. Offers MS. *Accreditation:* AOTA. Part-time and evening/weekend programs available. *Entrance requirements:* For master's, GRE or MAT. Additional exam requirements/recommendations for international students: Required—TOEFL (minimum score 550 paper-based; 80 iBT), IELTS (minimum score 5.5).

Samuel Merritt University, Department of Occupational Therapy, Oakland, CA 94609-3108. Offers MOT. *Accreditation:* AOTA. *Degree requirements:* For master's, project. *Entrance requirements:* For master's, GRE General Test, minimum GPA of 2.6 in science, 2.8 overall; 40-70 hours of volunteer or professional occupational therapy experience; interview. Additional exam requirements/recommendations for international students: Required—TOEFL. *Expenses:* Contact institution.

San Jose State University, Graduate Studies and Research, College of Applied Sciences and Arts, Department of Occupational Therapy, San Jose, CA 95192-0001. Offers MS. *Accreditation:* AOTA. *Degree requirements:* For master's, thesis or alternative. *Entrance requirements:* For master's, GRE, minimum GPA of 3.0. Electronic applications accepted. *Faculty research:* Generic occupational therapy, psychosocial rehabilitation, physical rehabilitation, organizational development, occupational performance.

Seton Hall University, School of Health and Medical Sciences, Program in Occupational Therapy, South Orange, NJ 07079-2697. Offers MS. *Accreditation:* AOTA. *Entrance requirements:* For master's, health care experience, minimum GPA of 3.0, 50 hours of occupational therapy volunteer work, pre-requisite courses. Additional exam requirements/recommendations for international students: Required—TOEFL. Electronic applications accepted. *Expenses: Tuition:* Part-time $1033 per credit hour. *Required fees:* $85 per semester. *Faculty research:* Occupational genesis, occupational technology, pediatric OT, community practice, families of children with special needs; family routines; complementary medicine and wellness.

Shawnee State University, Program in Occupational Therapy, Portsmouth, OH 45662-4344. Offers MOT. *Accreditation:* AOTA.

Shenandoah University, School of Health Professions, Division of Occupational Therapy, Winchester, VA 22601-5195. Offers MS. *Accreditation:* AOTA. *Faculty:* 4 full-time (3 women), 1 (woman) part-time/adjunct. *Students:* 49 full-time (43 women), 26 part-time (25 women); includes 7 minority (3 Black or African American, non-Hispanic/Latino; 2 Asian, non-Hispanic/Latino; 2 Hispanic/Latino). Average age 29. 137 applicants, 28% accepted, 25 enrolled. In 2011, 25 master's awarded. *Degree requirements:* For master's, comprehensive exam, thesis, fieldwork. *Entrance requirements:* For master's, GRE (minimum score 480 quantitative), 24 hours of clinical exposure, 2 references, writing sample, minimum GPA of 3.0. Additional exam requirements/recommendations for international students: Required—TOEFL (minimum score 550 paper-based; 213 computer-based; 79 iBT), IELTS (minimum score 6.5), Sakae Institute of Study Abroad (minimum score 550). *Application deadline:* For fall admission, 7/1 for domestic students. Applications are processed on a rolling basis. Application fee: $30. Electronic applications accepted. *Expenses:* Contact institution. *Financial support:* In 2011–12, 11 students received support. Career-related internships or fieldwork, institutionally sponsored loans, scholarships/grants, and federal loans, alternative loans available. Support available to part-time students. Financial award application deadline: 3/15; financial award applicants required to submit FAFSA. *Application contact:* David Anthony, Dean of Admissions, 540-665-4581, Fax: 540-665-4627, E-mail: admit@su.edu.

Spalding University, Graduate Studies, College of Health and Natural Sciences, Auerbach School of Occupational Therapy, Louisville, KY 40203-2188. Offers occupational therapy (advanced-level) (MS); occupational therapy (entry-level) (MS). *Accreditation:* AOTA. *Faculty:* 5 full-time (3 women), 5 part-time/adjunct (3 women). *Students:* 100 full-time (85 women), 40 part-time (36 women); includes 13 minority (9 Black or African American, non-Hispanic/Latino; 1 Asian, non-Hispanic/Latino; 3 Two or more races, non-Hispanic/Latino), 1 international. Average age 28. 106 applicants, 51% accepted, 46 enrolled. In 2011, 36 degrees awarded. *Degree requirements:* For master's, project. *Entrance requirements:* For master's, interview, letters of recommendation. Additional exam requirements/recommendations for international students: Required—TOEFL (minimum score 535 paper-based; 203 computer-based). *Application deadline:* Applications are processed on a rolling basis. Application fee: $30 ($400 for international students). Electronic applications accepted. *Expenses: Tuition:* Full-time $12,438. Tuition and fees vary according to course load, degree level and program. *Financial support:* In 2011–12, 48 students received support, including 3 research assistantships with partial tuition reimbursements available (averaging $5,207 per year); unspecified assistantships also available. Financial award applicants required to submit FAFSA. *Faculty research:* High-risk youth, community-dwelling older adults, assistive technology, mother-infant relationships, community accessibility. *Unit head:* Dr. Laura Schluter Strickland, Associate Professor/Chairperson, 502-873-4219, E-mail: lstrickland@spalding.edu. *Application contact:* Arlisa Spaulding, Administrative Office Coordinator, 502-873-7196, E-mail: aspaulding@spalding.edu.

Springfield College, Graduate Programs, Program in Occupational Therapy, Springfield, MA 01109-3797. Offers M Ed, MS, CAGS. *Accreditation:* AOTA (one or more programs are accredited). Part-time programs available. *Degree requirements:* For master's, comprehensive exam. *Entrance requirements:* For master's, prerequisite courses for accreditation. Additional exam requirements/recommendations for international students: Required—TOEFL (minimum score 550 paper-based; 213 computer-based). Electronic applications accepted.

Stony Brook University, State University of New York, Stony Brook University Medical Center, Health Sciences Center, School of Health Technology and Management, Stony Brook, NY 11794. Offers health care management (Advanced Certificate); health care policy and management (MS); occupational therapy (MS); physical therapy (DPT); physician assistant (MS). *Accreditation:* APTA. Part-time programs available. *Degree requirements:* For master's, thesis. *Entrance requirements:* For master's, GRE General Test, minimum GPA of 3.0, work experience in field. *Faculty research:* Health promotion and disease prevention.

Temple University, Health Sciences Center, College of Health Professions and Social Work, Program in Occupational Therapy, Philadelphia, PA 19122-6096. Offers MOT, DOT. *Accreditation:* AOTA. Part-time programs available. *Faculty:* 4 full-time (3 women). *Students:* 78 full-time (69 women), 9 part-time (7 women); includes 9 minority (2 Black or African American, non-Hispanic/Latino; 3 Asian, non-Hispanic/Latino; 3 Hispanic/Latino; 1 Two or more races, non-Hispanic/Latino). Average age 27. 81 applicants, 83% accepted, 51 enrolled. In 2011, 30 master's, 9 doctorates awarded. *Degree requirements:* For master's, comprehensive exam (for some programs), thesis. *Entrance requirements:* For master's, GRE General Test or MAT, minimum GPA of 3.0, interview. Additional exam requirements/recommendations for international students: Required—TOEFL (minimum score 550 paper-based; 213 computer-based; 79 iBT). *Application deadline:* For fall admission, 8/1 for domestic students, 12/15 for international students; for spring admission, 12/1 for domestic students, 8/1 for international students. Applications are processed on a rolling basis. Application fee: $50. Electronic applications accepted. *Expenses:* Contact institution. *Financial support:* Research assistantships, teaching assistantships with full tuition reimbursements, career-related internships or fieldwork, Federal Work-Study, and institutionally sponsored loans available. Financial award application deadline: 1/15; financial award applicants required to submit FAFSA. *Faculty research:* Pediatrics, elderly, sensory integration, education, participation. *Unit head:* Dr. Mark Salzer, Chair, 215-204-7879, Fax: 215-707-7656, E-mail: otchpsw@temple.edu. *Application contact:* Tara Schumacher, Coordinator of Outreach, 215-204-6575, Fax: 215-204-8781, E-mail: tara.schumacher@temple.edu. Web site: http://chpsw.temple.edu/rs/occupational-therapy.

Texas Tech University Health Sciences Center, School of Allied Health Sciences, Program in Occupational Therapy, Lubbock, TX 79430. Offers MOT. *Accreditation:* AOTA. *Faculty:* 5 full-time (3 women). *Students:* 106 full-time (94 women); includes 18 minority (3 Black or African American, non-Hispanic/Latino; 3 Asian, non-Hispanic/Latino; 11 Hispanic/Latino; 1 Two or more races, non-Hispanic/Latino). Average age 29. 258 applicants, 14% accepted, 36 enrolled. In 2011, 34 master's awarded. *Entrance requirements:* Additional exam requirements/recommendations for international students: Required—TOEFL, IELTS. *Application deadline:* For fall admission, 10/1 priority date for domestic students; for spring admission, 12/15 priority date for domestic students. Application fee: $35. Electronic applications accepted. *Financial support:* Career-related internships or fieldwork, institutionally sponsored loans, and scholarships/grants available. Financial award application deadline: 9/1; financial award applicants required to submit FAFSA. *Unit head:* Dr. Steve Sawyer, Chair, 806-743-3226, Fax: 806-743-3249, E-mail: steve.sawyer@ttuhsc.edu. *Application contact:* Jeri Moravcik, Assistant Director of Admissions and Student Affairs, 806-743-3220, Fax: 806-743-2994, E-mail: jeri.moravcik@ttuhsc.edu. Web site: http://www.ttuhsc.edu/sah/mot/.

Texas Woman's University, Graduate School, College of Health Sciences, School of Occupational Therapy, Denton, TX 76201. Offers MA, MOT, PhD. *Accreditation:* AOTA (one or more programs are accredited). Part-time and evening/weekend programs available. Postbaccalaureate distance learning degree programs offered. *Faculty:* 33 full-time (30 women), 1 (woman) part-time/adjunct. *Students:* 310 full-time (292 women), 88 part-time (76 women); includes 132 minority (31 Black or African American, non-Hispanic/Latino; 4 American Indian or Alaska Native, non-Hispanic/Latino; 30 Asian, non-Hispanic/Latino; 67 Hispanic/Latino), 2 international. Average age 31. 469 applicants, 27% accepted, 104 enrolled. In 2011, 117 master's, 2 doctorates awarded. *Degree requirements:* For master's, thesis or alternative; for doctorate, comprehensive exam, thesis/dissertation. *Entrance requirements:* For master's, minimum GPA of 3.0 on prerequisites, interview, recommendation based on 20 hours of observation with one supervising OTR; for doctorate, GRE General Test, essay, interview, 3 letters of reference, certification and master's degree in occupational therapy or related field. Additional exam requirements/recommendations for international students: Required—TOEFL (minimum score 550 paper-based; 213 computer-based; 79 iBT). *Application deadline:* For fall admission, 9/15 priority date for domestic students, 9/15 for international students. Applications are processed on a rolling basis. Application fee: $50 ($75 for international students). Electronic applications accepted. *Expenses:* Tuition, state resident: full-time $3834; part-time $213 per credit hour. Tuition, nonresident: full-time $9468; part-time $526 per credit hour. *Required fees:* $213 per credit hour. Tuition and fees vary according to course load. *Financial support:* In 2011–12, 204 students received support, including 4 research assistantships (averaging $10,746 per year); career-related internships or fieldwork, Federal Work-Study, institutionally sponsored loans, scholarships/grants, traineeships, health care benefits, and unspecified assistantships also available. Support available to part-time students. Financial award application deadline: 3/1; financial award applicants required to submit FAFSA. *Faculty research:* Quality of life/wellness, Alzheimer's disease, hand rehabilitation, psychosocial dysfunction, adaptation/chronic disability, long term care. *Total annual research expenditures:* $3,866. *Unit head:* Dr. Catherine Candler, Director, 940-898-2350, Fax: 940-898-2806, E-mail: ot@twu.edu. *Application contact:* Dr. Samuel Wheeler, Assistant Director of Admissions, 940-898-3188, Fax: 940-898-3081, E-mail: wheelersr@twu.edu. Web site: http://www.twu.edu/occupational-therapy/.

Thomas Jefferson University, Jefferson School of Health Professions, Department of Occupational Therapy, Philadelphia, PA 19107. Offers MS, OTD. *Accreditation:* AOTA. Part-time programs available. *Degree requirements:* For master's, thesis (for some programs). *Entrance requirements:* For master's, GRE General Test or MAT. Additional exam requirements/recommendations for international students: Required—TOEFL (minimum score 213 computer-based). Electronic applications accepted. *Expenses:* Contact institution. *Faculty research:* Functional outcomes in traumatic brain injury, clinical reasoning in therapist/patient interactions, gerontology, sensory integration in pediatrics, effective intervention for homeless.

Touro College, School of Health Sciences, Bay Shore, NY 11706. Offers occupational therapy (MS); Oriental medicine (MSOM); physical therapy (DPT); public health (MPH); speech-language pathology (MS). *Faculty:* 20 full-time, 94 part-time/adjunct. *Students:* 136. *Expenses:* Contact institution. *Financial support:* Fellowships available. *Unit head:*

Occupational Therapy

Dr. Louis Primavera, Dean, 516-673-3200. *Application contact:* Dean, School of Health Sciences, 516-673-3200.

Towson University, Program in Occupational Therapy, Towson, MD 21252-0001. Offers MS. *Accreditation:* AOTA. Part-time and evening/weekend programs available. *Students:* 141 full-time (131 women), 10 part-time (all women); includes 19 minority (12 Black or African American, non-Hispanic/Latino; 3 Asian, non-Hispanic/Latino; 3 Hispanic/Latino; 1 Two or more races, non-Hispanic/Latino), 1 international. *Degree requirements:* For master's, thesis optional, exam. *Entrance requirements:* For master's, minimum GPA of 3.0, 3 letters of recommendation, 30 hours of human service activity. *Application deadline:* For spring admission, 8/1 for domestic students. Applications are processed on a rolling basis. Application fee: $50. *Expenses:* Tuition, state resident: part-time $337 per credit. Tuition, nonresident: part-time $709 per credit. *Required fees:* $99 per credit. *Financial support:* Application deadline: 4/1; applicants required to submit FAFSA. *Unit head:* Sonia Lawson, Graduate Program Director, 410-704-2313, Fax: 410-704-2322, E-mail: slawson@towson.edu. *Application contact:* Lynne Murphy, The Graduate School, 410-704-4439, Fax: 410-704-2322, E-mail: lmurphy@towson.edu.

Tufts University, Graduate School of Arts and Sciences, Department of Occupational Therapy, Medford, MA 02155. Offers MA, MS, OTD. *Accreditation:* AOTA. *Faculty:* 6 full-time, 9 part-time/adjunct. *Students:* 116 full-time (107 women); includes 16 minority (2 Black or African American, non-Hispanic/Latino; 1 American Indian or Alaska Native, non-Hispanic/Latino; 6 Asian, non-Hispanic/Latino; 7 Hispanic/Latino), 12 international. Average age 27. 175 applicants, 43% accepted, 34 enrolled. In 2011, 38 master's, 2 doctorates awarded. *Degree requirements:* For master's, thesis (for some programs); for doctorate, leadership project. *Entrance requirements:* For master's and doctorate, GRE General Test. Additional exam requirements/recommendations for international students: Required—TOEFL (minimum score 550 paper-based; 213 computer-based; 80 iBT). *Application deadline:* For fall admission, 2/15 for domestic students, 12/15 for international students; for spring admission, 10/15 for domestic students, 9/15 for international students. Applications are processed on a rolling basis. Application fee: $75. Electronic applications accepted. *Expenses:* Contact institution. *Financial support:* Teaching assistantships with partial tuition reimbursements, Federal Work-Study, scholarships/grants, and tuition waivers (partial) available. Support available to part-time students. Financial award application deadline: 2/15; financial award applicants required to submit FAFSA. *Unit head:* Linda Tickle-Degnen, 617-627-5720. *Application contact:* Elizabeth Owen, Staff Assistant, 617-627-5720. Web site: http://ase.tufts.edu/bsot/.

Tufts University, Graduate School of Arts and Sciences, Graduate Certificate Programs, Advanced Professional Study in Occupational Therapy Program, Medford, MA 02155. Offers Certificate. Part-time and evening/weekend programs available. Electronic applications accepted. *Expenses:* Contact institution.

Université de Montréal, Faculty of Medicine, Programs in Ergonomics, Montréal, QC H3C 3J7, Canada. Offers occupational therapy (DESS). Program offered jointly with École Polytechnique de Montréal.

University at Buffalo, the State University of New York, Graduate School, School of Public Health and Health Professions, Department of Rehabilitation Science, Program in Occupational Therapy, Buffalo, NY 14260. Offers physical disabilities/developmental disabilities (MS); school-based therapy/early intervention (MS). *Accreditation:* AOTA. *Faculty:* 6 full-time (5 women), 2 part-time/adjunct (1 woman). *Students:* 40 full-time (34 women); includes 2 minority (1 Black or African American, non-Hispanic/Latino; 1 Asian, non-Hispanic/Latino). Average age 25. 44 applicants, 68% accepted, 18 enrolled. In 2011, 47 master's awarded. *Degree requirements:* For master's, thesis, project. *Entrance requirements:* For master's, GRE, BS in occupational therapy. Additional exam requirements/recommendations for international students: Required—TOEFL (minimum score 550 paper-based; 213 computer-based; 79 iBT). *Application deadline:* For fall admission, 6/1 priority date for domestic students, 4/1 for international students; for spring admission, 11/1 priority date for domestic students, 9/1 for international students. Application fee: $50. Electronic applications accepted. *Financial support:* In 2011–12, 2 students received support, including 5 teaching assistantships with partial tuition reimbursements available (averaging $2,500 per year); unspecified assistantships also available. Financial award application deadline: 2/1; financial award applicants required to submit FAFSA. *Faculty research:* Sensory integration, assistive technology, aging and technology, transition for students with emotional/behavioral problems. *Total annual research expenditures:* $479,000. *Unit head:* Dr. Susan Nochajski, Graduate Program Director, 716-829-6942, Fax: 716-829-3217, E-mail: phhpadv@buffalo.edu. *Application contact:* MaryAnn Venezia, Program Coordinator, 716-829-6942, Fax: 716-829-3217, E-mail: venezia3@buffalo.edu. Web site: http://www.sphhp.buffalo.edu/rs/ot/bsms/.

The University of Alabama at Birmingham, School of Health Professions, Program in Occupational Therapy, Birmingham, AL 35294. Offers MS. *Accreditation:* AOTA. *Expenses:* Tuition, state resident: full-time $5922; part-time $309 per hour. Tuition, nonresident: full-time $13,428; part-time $726 per hour. Tuition and fees vary according to program. *Unit head:* Dr. Jan Rowe, Chair, 205-934-5982, Fax: 205-934-0402. *Application contact:* Julie Bryant, Director of Graduate Admissions, 205-934-8227, Fax: 205-934-8413, E-mail: jbryant@uab.edu. Web site: http://www.uab.edu/ot/otel.

University of Alberta, Faculty of Graduate Studies and Research, Department of Occupational Therapy, Edmonton, AB T6G 2E1, Canada. Offers M Sc, PhD. Part-time programs available. *Degree requirements:* For master's, thesis. *Entrance requirements:* For master's, bachelor's degree in occupational therapy, minimum GPA of 6.9 on a 9.0 scale. Additional exam requirements/recommendations for international students: Required—TOEFL. Electronic applications accepted. *Faculty research:* Work evaluation, pediatrics, geriatrics, program evaluation, community-based rehabilitation.

The University of British Columbia, Faculty of Medicine, Department of Occupational Science and Occupational Therapy, Vancouver, BC V6T 1Z1, Canada. Offers MOT. *Entrance requirements:* Additional exam requirements/recommendations for international students: Required—TOEFL (minimum score 600 paper-based; 250 computer-based; 100 iBT), IELTS (minimum score 6.5). Electronic applications accepted.

University of Central Arkansas, Graduate School, College of Health and Behavioral Sciences, Department of Occupational Therapy, Conway, AR 72035-0001. Offers MS. *Accreditation:* AOTA. *Faculty:* 7 full-time (6 women). *Students:* 46 full-time (41 women), 1 (woman) part-time; includes 7 minority (3 Black or African American, non-Hispanic/Latino; 1 American Indian or Alaska Native, non-Hispanic/Latino; 1 Asian, non-Hispanic/Latino; 2 Hispanic/Latino). Average age 24. In 2011, 46 master's awarded. *Degree requirements:* For master's, thesis optional, internship. *Entrance requirements:* For master's, GRE General Test, minimum GPA of 2.7. Additional exam requirements/recommendations for international students: Required—TOEFL (minimum score 550 paper-based; 213 computer-based). *Application deadline:* For fall admission, 3/1 priority date for domestic students; for spring admission, 10/1 for domestic students. Applications are processed on a rolling basis. Application fee: $25 ($50 for international students). *Expenses:* Contact institution. *Financial support:* In 2011–12, 6 research assistantships (averaging $2,200 per year) were awarded; Federal Work-Study, scholarships/grants, and unspecified assistantships also available. Financial award application deadline: 2/15; financial award applicants required to submit FAFSA. *Unit*

head: Dr. Linda Musselman, Chair, 501-450-3192, Fax: 501-450-5503, E-mail: lindam@uca.edu. *Application contact:* Susan Wood, Administrative Assistant, 501-450-3124, Fax: 501-450-5678, E-mail: swood@uca.edu. Web site: http://uca.edu/ot/.

The University of Findlay, Graduate and Professional Studies, College of Health Professions, Master of Occupational Therapy Program, Findlay, OH 45840-3653. Offers MOT. *Accreditation:* AOTA. Evening/weekend programs available. *Faculty:* 10 full-time (9 women), 2 part-time/adjunct (both women). *Students:* 47 full-time (40 women), 23 part-time (22 women); includes 1 minority (Hispanic/Latino). Average age 35. 40 applicants, 70% accepted, 28 enrolled. In 2011, 40 master's awarded. *Entrance requirements:* For master's, bachelor's degree from accredited institution, 50 hours of observation, 3 letters of recommendation, minimum GPA of 3.0. Additional exam requirements/recommendations for international students: Required—TOEFL (minimum score 550 paper-based; 213 computer-based; 80 iBT). *Application deadline:* For fall admission, 2/1 for domestic and international students. Applications are processed on a rolling basis. Application fee: $25. Electronic applications accepted. *Expenses: Tuition:* Full-time $6300; part-time $700 per semester hour. *Required fees:* $35 per semester hour. One-time fee: $25. Tuition and fees vary according to course load, degree level and program. *Financial support:* In 2011–12, 2 teaching assistantships with full tuition reimbursements (averaging $3,600 per year) were awarded; Federal Work-Study, health care benefits, and unspecified assistantships also available. Financial award application deadline: 4/1; financial award applicants required to submit FAFSA. *Unit head:* Cynthia Goodwin, Director, 419-434-6936, Fax: 419-434-4822. *Application contact:* Heather Riffle, Assistant Director, Graduate and Professional Studies, 419-434-4640, Fax: 419-434-5517, E-mail: riffle@findlay.edu.

University of Florida, Graduate School, College of Public Health and Health Professions, Department of Occupational Therapy, Gainesville, FL 32611. Offers MHS, MOT. *Accreditation:* AOTA. *Degree requirements:* For master's, clinical rotations. *Entrance requirements:* For master's, GRE General Test (minimum score 1000), minimum GPA of 3.0. Additional exam requirements/recommendations for international students: Required—TOEFL (minimum score 550 paper-based; 213 computer-based; 80 iBT), IELTS (minimum score 6). Electronic applications accepted. *Faculty research:* Rehabilitation intervention outcomes assessment, safe driving and community participation - assessment of driving skills and impact on participation, stroke and upper extremity rehabilitation - effective rehabilitation outcomes, community participation in families and children with muscular dystrophy - assessment of the impact of MD on community participation, assistive technology - AT effectiveness and availability.

University of Illinois at Chicago, Graduate College, College of Applied Health Sciences, Department of Occupational Therapy, Chicago, IL 60607-7128. Offers MS, OTD. *Accreditation:* AOTA. Part-time programs available. *Degree requirements:* For master's, thesis. *Entrance requirements:* For master's, GRE General Test, minimum GPA of 2.75, previous course work in statistics. Additional exam requirements/recommendations for international students: Required—TOEFL. Electronic applications accepted. *Faculty research:* Sensory integration, perception, play, treatment efficacy, instrument development.

University of Indianapolis, Graduate Programs, School of Occupational Therapy, Indianapolis, IN 46227-3697. Offers MHS, MOT, DHS. *Accreditation:* AOTA. Part-time and evening/weekend programs available. *Faculty:* 4 full-time (all women), 2 part-time/adjunct (1 woman). *Students:* 98 full-time (88 women), 83 part-time (73 women); includes 12 minority (5 Black or African American, non-Hispanic/Latino; 4 Asian, non-Hispanic/Latino; 3 Hispanic/Latino), 5 international. Average age 27. In 2011, 64 master's, 1 doctorate awarded. *Degree requirements:* For master's, thesis. *Entrance requirements:* For master's, minimum GPA of 3.0, interview; for doctorate, minimum GPA of 3.3, BA/BS or MA/MS from occupational therapy program, current state license, currently in practice as occupational therapist or have 1000 hours of practice in last 5 years. Additional exam requirements/recommendations for international students: Required—TOEFL (minimum score 550 paper-based; 237 computer-based; 92 iBT), TWE (minimum score 5). *Application deadline:* For fall admission, 11/1 for domestic students, 2/1 for international students. Application fee: $55. *Expenses:* Contact institution. *Financial support:* Career-related internships or fieldwork, Federal Work-Study, tuition waivers (full and partial), and unspecified assistantships available. Financial award application deadline: 5/1; financial award applicants required to submit FAFSA. *Unit head:* Dr. Stephanie Kelly, Dean, College of Health Sciences, 317-788-3500, Fax: 317-788-3542, E-mail: spkelly@uindy.edu. *Application contact:* Anne Hardwick, Director, Marketing and Admissions, 317-788-3495, Fax: 317-788-3542, E-mail: ahardwick@uindy.edu. Web site: http://ot.uindy.edu/.

The University of Kansas, University of Kansas Medical Center, School of Health Professions, Department of Occupational Therapy Education, Kansas City, KS 66160. Offers occupational therapy (MOT, MS, OTD); therapeutic science (PhD). *Accreditation:* AOTA. Part-time programs available. *Faculty:* 11. *Students:* 66 full-time (55 women), 17 part-time (16 women); includes 8 minority (2 Black or African American, non-Hispanic/Latino; 1 American Indian or Alaska Native, non-Hispanic/Latino; 4 Asian, non-Hispanic/Latino; 1 Hispanic/Latino), 2 international. Average age 28. 105 applicants, 34% accepted, 34 enrolled. In 2011, 27 master's, 2 doctorates awarded. *Degree requirements:* For doctorate, comprehensive exam, thesis/dissertation, oral defense. *Entrance requirements:* For master's, 40 hours of paid work or volunteer experience working directly with people with special needs, 3 letters of recommendation, personal statement and program statement of interest, 90 hours of elective course work with 40 hours of prerequisite work, minimum GPA of 3.0; for doctorate, 24 hours of master's-level research. Additional exam requirements/recommendations for international students: Required—TOEFL. *Application deadline:* For fall admission, 12/31 for domestic students, 4/1 for international students. Applications are processed on a rolling basis. Application fee: $60. Electronic applications accepted. Tuition and fees vary according to course load, campus/location, program and reciprocity agreements. *Financial support:* Research assistantships with partial tuition reimbursements, teaching assistantships with full and partial tuition reimbursements, traineeships, and unspecified assistantships available. Financial award application deadline: 2/14; financial award applicants required to submit FAFSA. *Faculty research:* Impact of sensory processing in everyday life; improving balance, motor skills, and independence with community nonprofit organizations serving people with special needs; improving self-confidence and self-sufficiency with poverty-based services in community; working with autism population in a community-wide aquatics program. *Total annual research expenditures:* $42,046. *Unit head:* Dr. Winifred W. Dunn, Professor/Chair, 913-588-7195, Fax: 913-588-4568, E-mail: wdunn@kumc.edu. *Application contact:* Wendy Hildenbrand, Admissions Representative, 913-588-7174, Fax: 913-588-4568, E-mail: whildenb@kumc.edu. Web site: http://ot.kumc.edu.

University of Manitoba, Faculty of Graduate Studies, School of Medical Rehabilitation, Winnipeg, MB R3T 2N2, Canada. Offers applied health sciences (PhD); occupational therapy (MOT); physical therapy (MPT); rehabilitation (M Sc).

University of Mary, School of Health Sciences, Program in Occupational Therapy, Bismarck, ND 58504-9652. Offers MSOT. *Accreditation:* AOTA. Part-time programs available. Postbaccalaureate distance learning degree programs offered (minimal on-campus study). *Faculty:* 7 full-time (5 women). *Students:* 26 full-time (22 women), 30 part-time (24 women); includes 2 minority (1 American Indian or Alaska Native, non-

Hispanic/Latino; 1 Asian, non-Hispanic/Latino), 2 international. Average age 25. 59 applicants, 0% accepted, 0 enrolled. In 2011, 22 master's awarded. *Degree requirements:* For master's, thesis or alternative, practicum. *Entrance requirements:* For master's, ACT or equivalent, minimum GPA of 2.75, 48 hours of volunteer experience. Additional exam requirements/recommendations for international students: Required—TOEFL (minimum score 550 paper-based). *Application deadline:* For spring admission, 3/15 priority date for domestic students, 3/15 for international students. Applications are processed on a rolling basis. Application fee: $40. Electronic applications accepted. *Expenses:* Contact institution. *Financial support:* In 2011–12, 2 teaching assistantships with full tuition reimbursements (averaging $2,500 per year) were awarded. Financial award application deadline: 8/1; financial award applicants required to submit FAFSA. *Faculty research:* Safe homes for well elderly, occupation and spirituality, professional development in the spiritual domain, case method instruction, ergonomics, assistive technology. *Total annual research expenditures:* $4,000. *Unit head:* Dr. Janeene Sibla, Program Director, 701-255-7500, Fax: 701-255-7687. *Application contact:* Dr. Wanda Berg, Occupational Therapy Admissions Director, 701-355-8022, E-mail: wberg@umary.edu.

University of Mississippi Medical Center, School of Health Related Professions, Department of Occupational Therapy, Jackson, MS 39216-4505. Offers MOT. *Accreditation:* AOTA.

University of Missouri, School of Health Professions, Program in Occupational Therapy, Columbia, MO 65211. Offers MOT. *Accreditation:* AOTA. *Faculty:* 8 full-time (all women). *Students:* 31 full-time (29 women); includes 3 minority (2 Asian, non-Hispanic/Latino; 1 Hispanic/Latino). Average age 24. 5 applicants, 0% accepted. In 2011, 22 degrees awarded. *Entrance requirements:* Additional exam requirements/recommendations for international students: Required—TOEFL (minimum score 500 paper-based; 173 computer-based; 61 iBT). *Application deadline:* For spring admission, 12/31 for domestic students. Application fee: $55 ($75 for international students). *Expenses:* Tuition, state resident: full-time $5881. Tuition, nonresident: full-time $15,183. Required fees: $952. Tuition and fees vary according to campus/location and program. *Faculty research:* Health literacy, disability advocacy, nontraditional students in health professions educational programs, faculty teaching styles vs. student learning style preferences, brain plasticity in health and disease, neurorehabilitation, autism, gender, aging, HIV/AIDS, sub-Saharan Africa, integrating qualitative and quantitative methods. *Unit head:* Dr. Guy L. McCormack, Department Chair, 573-882-3988, E-mail: muot@health.missouri.edu. *Application contact:* Leanna Garrison, Department Administrator, 573-884-2113, E-mail: garrisonl@missouri.edu. Web site: http://gradschool.missouri.edu/programs/catalog/occupational-therapy/.

University of New England, Westbrook College of Health Professions, Program in Occupational Therapy, Biddeford, ME 04005-9526. Offers occupational therapy (MS). *Accreditation:* AOTA. *Faculty:* 7 full-time, 1 part-time/adjunct. *Students:* 95 full-time (89 women). In 2011, 1 master's awarded. *Degree requirements:* For master's, research project. *Entrance requirements:* For master's, minimum undergraduate GPA of 3.0, 1 level II clinical. *Application deadline:* Applications are processed on a rolling basis. Application fee: $40. *Expenses:* Contact institution. *Financial support:* Application deadline: 5/1; applicants required to submit FAFSA. *Faculty research:* Aging and cognition, neurobehavioral basis of motor control, post-breast surgery syndrome, sensory modulation, ergonomics. *Unit head:* Jane O'Brien, Director, 207-221-4107, Fax: 207-602-5963, E-mail: jobrien@une.edu. *Application contact:* Stacy Gato, Assistant Director of Graduate Admissions, 207-221-4225, Fax: 207-221-4898, E-mail: gradadmissions@une.edu.

University of New Hampshire, Graduate School, School of Health and Human Services, Department of Occupational Therapy, Durham, NH 03824. Offers MS, Postbaccalaureate Certificate. *Accreditation:* AOTA. Part-time programs available. *Faculty:* 6 full-time (5 women). *Students:* 73 full-time (69 women), 2 part-time (both women); includes 4 minority (2 Asian, non-Hispanic/Latino; 2 Hispanic/Latino). Average age 24. 129 applicants, 34% accepted, 33 enrolled. In 2011, 57 master's, 1 other advanced degree awarded. *Degree requirements:* For master's, thesis or alternative. *Entrance requirements:* For master's, GRE General Test, current certification as an OTR from the American Occupational Therapy Board or World Federation of Occupational Therapy. Additional exam requirements/recommendations for international students: Required—TOEFL (minimum score 550 paper-based; 213 computer-based; 80 iBT). *Application deadline:* For fall admission, 4/1 for domestic and international students. Applications are processed on a rolling basis. Application fee: $65. Electronic applications accepted. *Expenses:* Tuition, state resident: full-time $12,360; part-time $687 per credit hour. Tuition, nonresident: full-time $25,680; part-time $1058 per credit hour. *International tuition:* $29,550 full-time. *Required fees:* $1666; $833 per course. $416.50 per semester. Tuition and fees vary according to course load and degree level. *Financial support:* Fellowships, research assistantships, teaching assistantships, career-related internships or fieldwork, Federal Work-Study, and scholarships/grants available. Support available to part-time students. Financial award application deadline: 2/15. *Unit head:* Dr. Shelly Mulligan, Chairperson, 603-862-3528. *Application contact:* Janice Mutschler, Administrative Assistant, 603-862-2110, E-mail: ot.dept@unh.edu. Web site: http://www.chhs.unh.edu/ot/index.

University of New Mexico, Health Sciences Center Graduate Programs, Program in Occupational Therapy, Albuquerque, NM 87131-0001. Offers MOT. *Accreditation:* AOTA. Part-time programs available. *Faculty:* 6 full-time (all women), 1 (woman) part-time/adjunct. *Students:* 71 full-time (64 women), 2 part-time (both women); includes 28 minority (3 Asian, non-Hispanic/Latino; 25 Hispanic/Latino). Average age 33. 133 applicants, 17% accepted, 20 enrolled. In 2011, 22 degrees awarded. *Degree requirements:* For master's, thesis, clinical fieldwork. *Entrance requirements:* For master's, interview, writing sample, volunteer experience. *Application deadline:* For fall admission, 1/15 priority date for domestic students. Applications are processed on a rolling basis. Application fee: $50. Electronic applications accepted. *Financial support:* In 2011–12, 29 students received support. Research assistantships, Federal Work-Study, institutionally sponsored loans, scholarships/grants, traineeships, and unspecified assistantships available. Financial award application deadline: 3/1; financial award applicants required to submit FAFSA. *Faculty research:* Sensory processing, scleroderma treatment, use of therapy dogs, educational scholarship. *Unit head:* Dr. Betsy VanLeit, Director, 505-272-1753, Fax: 505-272-3583, E-mail: bvanleit@salud.unm.edu. *Application contact:* Janet Werner, Coordinator, 505-272-1753, Fax: 505-272-3583, E-mail: werner@salud.unm.edu. Web site: http://hsc.unm.edu/som/ot/.

The University of North Carolina at Chapel Hill, School of Medicine and Graduate School, Graduate Programs in Medicine, Chapel Hill, NC 27599. Offers allied health sciences (MPT, MS, Au D, DPT, PhD), including human movement science (MS, PhD), occupational science (MS, PhD), physical therapy (MPT, MS, DPT), rehabilitation counseling and psychology (MS), speech and hearing sciences (MS, Au D, PhD); biochemistry and biophysics (MS, PhD); bioinformatics and computational biology (PhD); biomedical engineering (MS, PhD); cell and developmental biology (PhD); cell and molecular physiology (PhD); genetics and molecular biology (PhD); microbiology and immunology (MS, PhD), including immunology, microbiology; neurobiology (PhD); pathology and laboratory medicine (PhD), including experimental pathology; pharmacology (PhD); MD/PhD. Postbaccalaureate distance learning degree programs offered. Terminal master's awarded for partial completion of doctoral program. *Degree requirements:* For master's, comprehensive exam; for doctorate, thesis/dissertation. Electronic applications accepted. *Expenses:* Contact institution.

The University of North Carolina at Chapel Hill, School of Medicine and Graduate School, Graduate Programs in Medicine, Department of Allied Health Sciences, Division of Occupational Science and Occupational Therapy, Chapel Hill, NC 27599. Offers occupational science (PhD); occupational therapy (MS). *Accreditation:* AOTA. *Degree requirements:* For master's, comprehensive exam, thesis optional, collaborative research project; for doctorate, thesis/dissertation. *Entrance requirements:* For master's, GRE General Test; for doctorate, GRE, master's degree in occupational therapy, relevant social behavioral sciences or health field. Additional exam requirements/recommendations for international students: Required—TOEFL (minimum score 550 paper-based; 79 computer-based). Electronic applications accepted. *Faculty research:* Parents and infants in co-occupations, psychosocial dysfunction, predictors of autism, factors influencing the occupation of primates, factors influencing occupations of people with dementia, occupational development of young children.

University of North Dakota, Graduate School and Graduate School, Graduate Programs in Medicine, Department of Occupational Therapy, Grand Forks, ND 58202. Offers MOT. *Accreditation:* AOTA. Part-time programs available. *Entrance requirements:* For master's, letter of reference; volunteer or work experience, preferably from health-related field; interview; minimum GPA of 2.7. Additional exam requirements/recommendations for international students: Required—TOEFL (minimum score 550 paper-based; 213 computer-based; 79 iBT), IELTS (minimum score 6.5). Electronic applications accepted.

University of Oklahoma Health Sciences Center, Graduate College, College of Allied Health, Department of Occupational Therapy, Oklahoma City, OK 73190. Offers MOT. *Accreditation:* AOTA.

University of Pittsburgh, School of Health and Rehabilitation Sciences, Master of Occupational Therapy Program, Pittsburgh, PA 15260. Offers MOT. *Accreditation:* AOTA. *Faculty:* 4 full-time (all women), 2 part-time/adjunct (both women). *Students:* 92 full-time (82 women), 9 part-time (7 women); includes 5 minority (2 Black or African American, non-Hispanic/Latino; 1 Asian, non-Hispanic/Latino; 2 Hispanic/Latino). Average age 27. 300 applicants, 30% accepted, 48 enrolled. In 2011, 44 master's awarded. *Entrance requirements:* For master's, GRE General Test, volunteer experience. Additional exam requirements/recommendations for international students: Required—TOEFL (minimum score 550 paper-based; 213 computer-based; 80 iBT), IELTS (minimum score 6.5). *Application deadline:* Applications are processed on a rolling basis. Application fee: $125. Electronic applications accepted. *Expenses:* Contact institution. *Financial support:* Fellowships, research assistantships, teaching assistantships, and Federal Work-Study available. *Faculty research:* Expertise in evidence-based practice, measuring occupational performance, ergonomics, geriatrics, mental health, neurorehabilitation, research. *Total annual research expenditures:* $524,243. *Unit head:* Dr. Joan Rogers, Associate Dean of Graduate Studies, 412-383-6620, Fax: 412-383-6613, E-mail: jcr@pitt.edu. *Application contact:* Joyce Broadwick, Administrator, 412-383-6620, Fax: 412-383-6613, E-mail: otpitt@shrs.pitt.edu. Web site: http://www.shrs.pitt.edu/mot/.

University of Pittsburgh, School of Health and Rehabilitation Sciences, Master's Programs in Health and Rehabilitation Sciences, Pittsburgh, PA 15260. Offers health and rehabilitation sciences (MS), including clinical dietetics and nutrition, health care supervision and management, health information systems, occupational therapy, physical therapy, rehabilitation counseling, rehabilitation science and technology, sports medicine, wellness and human performance. *Accreditation:* APTA. Part-time and evening/weekend programs available. *Faculty:* 22 full-time (16 women), 4 part-time/adjunct (2 women). *Students:* 144 full-time (91 women), 35 part-time (23 women); includes 23 minority (8 Black or African American, non-Hispanic/Latino; 8 Asian, non-Hispanic/Latino; 3 Hispanic/Latino; 4 Two or more races, non-Hispanic/Latino), 74 international. Average age 28. 399 applicants, 61% accepted, 121 enrolled. In 2011, 86 master's awarded. *Degree requirements:* For master's, comprehensive exam (for some programs), thesis optional. *Entrance requirements:* For master's, minimum GPA of 3.0. Additional exam requirements/recommendations for international students: Required—TOEFL (minimum score 550 paper-based; 213 computer-based; 80 iBT), IELTS (minimum score 6.5). *Application deadline:* For fall admission, 3/1 for international students; for spring admission, 7/31 for international students. Applications are processed on a rolling basis. Application fee: $50. Electronic applications accepted. *Expenses:* Contact institution. *Financial support:* Research assistantships, teaching assistantships, Federal Work-Study, institutionally sponsored loans, traineeships, and unspecified assistantships available. Financial award applicants required to submit FAFSA. *Faculty research:* Assistive technology, seating and wheeled mobility, cellular neurophysiology, low back syndrome, augmentative communication. *Total annual research expenditures:* $7.8 million. *Unit head:* Dr. Clifford E. Brubaker, Dean, 412-383-6560, Fax: 412-383-6535, E-mail: cliffb@pitt.edu. *Application contact:* Shameem Gangjee, Director of Admissions, 412-383-6558, Fax: 412-383-6535, E-mail: admissions@shrs.pitt.edu. Web site: http://www.shrs.pitt.edu/.

University of Puerto Rico, Medical Sciences Campus, School of Health Professions, Program in Occupational Therapy, San Juan, PR 00936-5067. Offers MS. *Accreditation:* AOTA.

University of Puget Sound, Graduate Studies, School of Occupational Therapy, Tacoma, WA 98416. Offers MOT, MSOT. *Accreditation:* AOTA. *Faculty:* 8 full-time (6 women), 1 (woman) part-time/adjunct. *Students:* 61 full-time (57 women), 42 part-time (39 women); includes 20 minority (2 Black or African American, non-Hispanic/Latino; 1 American Indian or Alaska Native, non-Hispanic/Latino; 8 Asian, non-Hispanic/Latino; 2 Hispanic/Latino; 1 Native Hawaiian or other Pacific Islander, non-Hispanic/Latino; 6 Two or more races, non-Hispanic/Latino), 1 international. Average age 28. 107 applicants, 57% accepted, 31 enrolled. In 2011, 33 master's awarded. *Degree requirements:* For master's, thesis, publishable paper or program development project. *Entrance requirements:* For master's, GRE General Test, minimum GPA of 3.0. Additional exam requirements/recommendations for international students: Required—TOEFL (minimum score 550 paper-based; 213 computer-based; 80 iBT). *Application deadline:* For fall admission, 1/15 priority date for domestic students, 1/15 for international students. Application fee: $75. Electronic applications accepted. *Financial support:* In 2011–12, 26 students received support, including 15 fellowships (averaging $9,600 per year); career-related internships or fieldwork and scholarships/grants also available. Financial award application deadline: 3/31; financial award applicants required to submit FAFSA. *Faculty research:* Scope of practice for school-based occupational therapy, family occupational adaptation to autism, clinical decision-making, low vision adaptation, assistive technology. *Unit head:* Dr. George S. Tomlin, Professor and Program Director, 253-879-3522, Fax: 253-879-2933, E-mail: tomlin@pugetsound.edu. *Application contact:* Dr. George H. Mills, Jr., Vice President for Enrollment, 253-879-3211, Fax: 253-879-3993, E-mail: admission@pugetsound.edu. Web site: http://www.pugetsound.edu/academics/departments-and-programs/graduate/school-of-occupational-therapy/.

Occupational Therapy

University of St. Augustine for Health Sciences, Graduate Programs, Division of Occupational Therapy, St. Augustine, FL 32086. Offers MOT, OTD. *Accreditation:* AOTA. *Entrance requirements:* For master's, GRE General Test.

The University of Scranton, College of Graduate and Continuing Education, Program in Occupational Therapy, Scranton, PA 18510. Offers MS. *Accreditation:* AOTA. *Faculty:* 6 full-time (5 women). *Students:* 34 full-time (all women); includes 1 minority (Hispanic/ Latino). Average age 22. In 2011, 34 master's awarded. *Degree requirements:* For master's, thesis, capstone experience. *Entrance requirements:* For master's, minimum GPA of 2.75. Additional exam requirements/recommendations for international students: Required—TOEFL (minimum score 500 paper-based; 173 computer-based), IELTS (minimum score 5.5). *Application deadline:* Applications are processed on a rolling basis. Application fee: $0. *Financial support:* In 2011–12, 5 students received support, including 5 teaching assistantships with full tuition reimbursements available (averaging $4,400 per year); career-related internships or fieldwork, Federal Work-Study, and unspecified assistantships also available. Support available to part-time students. Financial award application deadline: 3/1. *Unit head:* Dr. Marlene Joy Morgan, Director, 570-941-5789, Fax: 570-941-4380. *Application contact:* Joseph M. Roback, Director of Admissions, 570-941-4385, Fax: 570-941-5928, E-mail: robackj2@scranton.edu.

University of South Alabama, Graduate School, College of Allied Health Professions, Department of Occupational Therapy, Mobile, AL 36688-0002. Offers MS. *Accreditation:* AOTA. *Faculty:* 3 full-time (all women). *Students:* 75 full-time (67 women); includes 9 minority (6 Black or African American, non-Hispanic/Latino; 1 Asian, non-Hispanic/ Latino; 2 Hispanic/Latino). 27 applicants, 96% accepted, 23 enrolled. In 2011, 25 master's awarded. *Degree requirements:* For master's, clinical externship. *Entrance requirements:* For master's, GRE, minimum GPA of 3.0; bachelor's degree or 96 semester hours of prerequisites and electives. Additional exam requirements/ recommendations for international students: Required—TOEFL (minimum score 525 paper-based; 197 computer-based). *Application deadline:* For fall admission, 1/2 for domestic and international students. Application fee: $75. *Expenses:* Tuition, state resident: full-time $7968; part-time $332 per credit hour. Tuition, nonresident: full-time $15,936; part-time $664 per credit hour. *Unit head:* Dr. Majorie Scaffa, Chair, 251-445-9222, Fax: 251-4459211, E-mail: otdept@usouthal.edu. *Application contact:* Dr. Julio Turrens, Director of Graduate Studies, 251-445-9250. Web site: http://www.southalabama.edu/alliedhealth/ot/.

The University of South Dakota, Graduate School, School of Health Sciences, Department of Occupational Therapy, Vermillion, SD 57069-2390. Offers MS. *Accreditation:* AOTA. Part-time programs available. *Degree requirements:* For master's, thesis optional, 6 months of supervised fieldwork. *Entrance requirements:* For master's, courses in human anatomy, human physiology, general psychology, abnormal psychology, lifespan development, statistics. Additional exam requirements/ recommendations for international students: Required—TOEFL (minimum score 550 paper-based; 213 computer-based). *Expenses:* Contact institution. *Faculty research:* Low vision in youth and adults, agricultural/rural, health, childhood obesity, adolescent mental health, elder health and well being.

University of Southern California, Graduate School, Herman Ostrow School of Dentistry, Division of Occupational Science and Occupational Therapy, Graduate Program in Occupational Science, Los Angeles, CA 90089. Offers PhD. *Degree requirements:* For doctorate, thesis/dissertation, qualifying exam. *Entrance requirements:* For doctorate, GRE (minimum combined score of 1100), minimum GPA of 3.0. Additional exam requirements/recommendations for international students: Required—TOEFL (minimum score 600 paper-based; 250 computer-based; 100 iBT). Electronic applications accepted. *Faculty research:* Health and well-being; health disparities and cultural influences on health and recovery; family life; community re-integration and social participation; engagement, activity and neuroscience; rehabilitation science and ethics; society and social justice; autism and sensory integration; interventions; health disparities in autism diagnosis.

University of Southern California, Graduate School, Herman Ostrow School of Dentistry, Division of Occupational Science and Occupational Therapy, Graduate Programs in Occupational Therapy, Los Angeles, CA 90089. Offers MA, OTD. *Accreditation:* AOTA. Part-time programs available. *Degree requirements:* For master's, comprehensive exam (for some programs), thesis or alternative; for doctorate, residency, portfolio. *Entrance requirements:* For master's and doctorate, GRE (minimum score 1000), minimum cumulative GPA of 3.0. Additional exam requirements/ recommendations for international students: Required—TOEFL (minimum score 600 paper-based; 250 computer-based; 100 iBT). Electronic applications accepted. *Faculty research:* Health and well-being; health disparities and cultural influences on health and recovery; family life; community re-integration and social participation; engagement, activity and neuroscience; rehabilitation science and ethics; society and social justice; autism and sensory integration; interventions; health disparities in autism diagnosis.

University of Southern Indiana, Graduate Studies, College of Nursing and Health Professions, Program in Occupational Therapy, Evansville, IN 47712-3590. Offers MSOT. *Accreditation:* AOTA. Part-time programs available. Postbaccalaureate distance learning degree programs offered (minimal on-campus study). *Faculty:* 5 full-time (4 women). *Students:* 24 full-time (21 women), 1 (woman) part-time. Average age 23. In 2011, 29 master's awarded. *Entrance requirements:* Additional exam requirements/ recommendations for international students: Required—TOEFL (minimum score 550 paper-based; 213 computer-based; 79 iBT), IELTS (minimum score 6). *Application deadline:* For fall admission, 8/15 priority date for domestic students, 3/1 for international students. Applications are processed on a rolling basis. Application fee: $35. Electronic applications accepted. *Expenses:* Tuition, state resident: full-time $5044; part-time $280.21 per credit hour. Tuition, nonresident: full-time $9949; part-time $552.71 per credit hour. *Required fees:* $240; $22.75 per term. Tuition and fees vary according to course load and reciprocity agreements. *Financial support:* In 2011–12, 3 students received support. Federal Work-Study, scholarships/grants, tuition waivers (full and partial), and unspecified assistantships available. Financial award application deadline: 3/1; financial award applicants required to submit FAFSA. *Unit head:* Dr. Barbara Williams, Director, 812-461-5396, E-mail: bjwilliams4@usi.edu. *Application contact:* Dr. Wes Durham, Interim Director, Graduate Studies, 812-465-7015, Fax: 812-464-1956, E-mail: wdurham@usi.edu. Web site: http://health.usi.edu/acadprog/ot/default.asp.

University of Southern Maine, Program in Occupational Therapy, Lewiston, ME 04240. Offers MOT. *Accreditation:* AOTA. *Degree requirements:* For master's, fieldwork, original research. *Entrance requirements:* For master's, minimum GPA of 3.0, writing sample, interview, reference letters, job shadow observation. Electronic applications accepted. *Faculty research:* Multicultural curricula, cultural competence, parents responses to fussy infants, chronic pain, early childhood eating disorders.

The University of Texas at El Paso, Graduate School, College of Health Sciences, Program in Occupational Therapy, El Paso, TX 79968-0001. Offers MOT. *Accreditation:* AOTA. *Students:* 52 (42 women); includes 37 minority (1 Black or African American, non-Hispanic/Latino; 1 American Indian or Alaska Native, non-Hispanic/Latino; 2 Asian, non-Hispanic/Latino; 32 Hispanic/Latino; 1 Two or more races, non-Hispanic/Latino), 1 international. Average age 34. In 2011, 1 master's awarded. *Degree requirements:* For master's, thesis optional. *Entrance requirements:* For master's, GRE. Additional exam requirements/recommendations for international students: Required—TOEFL; Recommended—IELTS. *Application deadline:* For fall admission, 8/1 for domestic students, 3/1 for international students; for spring admission, 11/1 for domestic students, 9/3 for international students. Application fee: $45 ($80 for international students). *Financial support:* Fellowships with partial tuition reimbursements, research assistantships with partial tuition reimbursements, teaching assistantships with partial tuition reimbursements, institutionally sponsored loans, scholarships/grants, health care benefits, tuition waivers (partial), and unspecified assistantships available. Support available to part-time students. Financial award application deadline: 3/15; financial award applicants required to submit FAFSA. *Unit head:* Dr. Stephanie Capshaw, Chair, 915-747-8207, Fax: 915-747-8211, E-mail: scapshaw@utep.edu. *Application contact:* Dr. Benjamin Flores, Interim Dean of the Graduate School, 915-747-5491, Fax: 915-747-5788, E-mail: bflores@utep.edu.

The University of Texas Health Science Center at San Antonio, School of Health Professions, San Antonio, TX 78229-3900. Offers clinical laboratory sciences (MS); deaf education and hearing science (MED); dental hygiene (MS); occupational therapy (MOT); physical therapy (MPT); physician assistant studies (MS). *Accreditation:* AOTA; APTA; ARC-PA. *Degree requirements:* For master's, thesis. *Entrance requirements:* Additional exam requirements/recommendations for international students: Required—TOEFL (minimum score 560 paper-based; 280 computer-based; 68 iBT). Electronic applications accepted.

The University of Texas Medical Branch, School of Health Professions, Department of Occupational Therapy, Galveston, TX 77555. Offers MOT. *Accreditation:* AOTA. *Entrance requirements:* For master's, MAT, 20 volunteer hours, telephone interview, 2 references.

The University of Texas–Pan American, College of Health Sciences and Human Services, Department of Occupational Therapy, Edinburg, TX 78539. Offers MS. *Accreditation:* AOTA. Evening/weekend programs available. *Entrance requirements:* For master's, Health Occupations Aptitude Examination. *Application deadline:* For fall admission, 5/31 for domestic students; for winter admission, 11/1 priority date for domestic students. Application fee: $35. Tuition and fees vary according to course load, program and student level. *Financial support:* Fellowships, research assistantships, teaching assistantships, career-related internships or fieldwork, Federal Work-Study, institutionally sponsored loans, scholarships/grants, traineeships, and unspecified assistantships available. *Faculty research:* Parenting of children with disabilities, effects of healing touch on student stress, impact of RGV culture on women's roles. *Unit head:* Dr. Shirley A. Wells, Chair, 956-665-2475, E-mail: wellssa@utpa.edu. Web site: http://www.panam.edu/dept/occtherapy/.

The University of Toledo, College of Graduate Studies, Judith Herb College of Education, Health Science and Human Service, Department of Rehabilitation Sciences, Toledo, OH 43606-3390. Offers occupational therapy (OTD); physical therapy (DPT); speech-language pathology (MA). *Faculty:* 18. *Students:* 163 full-time (128 women), 24 part-time (20 women); includes 13 minority (4 Black or African American, non-Hispanic/ Latino; 1 American Indian or Alaska Native, non-Hispanic/Latino; 5 Asian, non-Hispanic/ Latino; 2 Hispanic/Latino; 1 Two or more races, non-Hispanic/Latino). Average age 25. 488 applicants, 23% accepted, 73 enrolled. In 2011, 29 master's, 46 doctorates awarded. *Degree requirements:* For master's, comprehensive exam, thesis; for doctorate, thesis/dissertation or alternative. *Entrance requirements:* For master's, GRE, minimum cumulative GPA of 2.7 for all previous academic work, letters of recommendation; for doctorate, GRE, minimum cumulative GPA of 3.0 for all previous academic work, letters of recommendation; OTCAS or PTCAS application and UT supplemental application (for OTD and DPT). Additional exam requirements/ recommendations for international students: Required—TOEFL (minimum score 550 paper-based; 213 computer-based; 80 iBT), IELTS (minimum score 6.5). *Application deadline:* For fall admission, 11/1 for domestic and international students. Application fee: $45 ($75 for international students). Electronic applications accepted. *Financial support:* In 2011–12, 5 research assistantships with full and partial tuition reimbursements (averaging $10,705 per year), 11 teaching assistantships with full and partial tuition reimbursements (averaging $6,182 per year) were awarded; Federal Work-Study, scholarships/grants, tuition waivers (full and partial), and unspecified assistantships also available. *Unit head:* Dr. Michelle Masterson, Chair, 419-530-6671, Fax: 419-530-4780, E-mail: michelle.masterson@utoledo.edu. *Application contact:* College of Graduate Studies - HSC, 419-383-4112, Fax: 419-383-6140, E-mail: grdsch@utnet.utoledo.edu. Web site: http://www.utoledo.edu/eduhshs/.

University of Toronto, Faculty of Medicine, Department of Occupational Science and Occupational Therapy, Toronto, ON M5S 1A1, Canada. Offers occupational therapy (M Sc OT). *Entrance requirements:* For master's, bachelor's degree with high academic standing from recognized university with minimum B average in final year, personal statement. Additional exam requirements/recommendations for international students: Required—TOEFL (minimum score 600 paper-based; 100 iBT), TWE (minimum score 5). Electronic applications accepted.

University of Utah, Graduate School, College of Health, Division of Occupational Therapy, Salt Lake City, UT 84108. Offers MOT, OTD. *Accreditation:* AOTA. Part-time and evening/weekend programs available. Postbaccalaureate distance learning degree programs offered (no on-campus study). *Faculty:* 10 full-time (9 women). *Students:* 80 full-time (54 women), 5 part-time (3 women); includes 7 minority (1 Black or African American, non-Hispanic/Latino; 2 Asian, non-Hispanic/Latino; 3 Hispanic/Latino; 1 Two or more races, non-Hispanic/Latino). Average age 30. 86 applicants, 43% accepted, 32 enrolled. In 2011, 33 degrees awarded. *Degree requirements:* For master's, thesis or alternative, project; for doctorate, thesis/dissertation or alternative, capstone. *Entrance requirements:* For master's, GRE General Test. Additional exam requirements/ recommendations for international students: Required—TOEFL (minimum score 575 paper-based; 233 computer-based). *Application deadline:* For fall admission, 12/1 for domestic and international students. Application fee: $0. *Expenses:* Contact institution. *Financial support:* In 2011–12, 10 students received support. Career-related internships or fieldwork, Federal Work-Study, institutionally sponsored loans, scholarships/grants, and unspecified assistantships available. Financial award application deadline: 2/15; financial award applicants required to submit FAFSA. *Faculty research:* Community-based practice, occupational science, obesity, refugees, resilience, low vision, traumatic brain injury. *Total annual research expenditures:* $13,409. *Unit head:* Dr. Lorie Richards, Chairperson, 801-585-1069, Fax: 801-585-1001, E-mail: lorie.richards@hsc.utah.edu. *Application contact:* Kelly C. Brown, Academic Advisor, 801-585-0555, Fax: 801-585-1001, E-mail: kelly.brown@hsc.utah.edu. Web site: http://www.health.utah.edu/ot/.

University of Washington, Graduate School, School of Medicine, Graduate Programs in Medicine, Department of Rehabilitation Medicine, Seattle, WA 98195-6490. Offers occupational therapy (MOT); physical therapy (DPT); prosthetics and orthotics (MPO); rehabilitation science (PhD). *Faculty:* 65. *Students:* 200. Average age 25. In 2011, 25 master's, 30 doctorates awarded. *Degree requirements:* For doctorate, comprehensive exam (for some programs), thesis/dissertation (for some programs). *Entrance requirements:* For master's and doctorate, GRE. Additional exam requirements/ recommendations for international students: Required—TOEFL. Application fee: $75. *Financial support:* In 2011–12, 1 fellowship (averaging $5,000 per year) was awarded. Financial award applicants required to submit FAFSA. *Faculty research:* Biomechanics,

balance, brain injury, spinal cord injury, pain, degenerative diseases. *Unit head:* Dr. Peter C. Esselman, Professor and Chair, 206-744-3167, E-mail: esselman@u.washington.edu. *Application contact:* Dr. Deborah Kartin, Graduate Program Coordinator, 206-598-5338, Fax: 206-685-3244, E-mail: kartin@u.washington.edu. Web site: http://rehab.washington.edu/education/degree/.

The University of Western Ontario, Faculty of Graduate Studies, Health Sciences Division, School of Occupational Therapy, London, ON N6A 5B8, Canada. Offers M Sc. Part-time programs available. *Degree requirements:* For master's, thesis. *Entrance requirements:* For master's, Canadian BA in occupational therapy or equivalent, minimum B+ average in last 2 years of 4 year degree. Additional exam requirements/recommendations for international students: Required—TOEFL (minimum score 570 paper-based; 250 computer-based). *Faculty research:* Human occupation, clumsy children, biomechanics, learning disabilities, ergonomics.

University of Wisconsin–La Crosse, Office of University Graduate Studies, College of Science and Health, Department of Health Professions, Program in Occupational Therapy, La Crosse, WI 54601-3742. Offers MS. *Accreditation:* AOTA. *Faculty:* 6 full-time (all women). *Students:* 51 full-time (47 women), 23 part-time (all women); includes 5 minority (3 Asian, non-Hispanic/Latino; 1 Hispanic/Latino; 1 Two or more races, non-Hispanic/Latino), 1 international. Average age 25. 85 applicants, 31% accepted, 26 enrolled. In 2011, 23 master's awarded. *Degree requirements:* For master's, 6-month clinical internship. *Entrance requirements:* For master's, minimum GPA of 3.0, 20 job shadowing hours. Additional exam requirements/recommendations for international students: Required—TOEFL (minimum score 550 paper-based; 213 computer-based; 79 iBT). *Application deadline:* For fall admission, 1/4 for domestic students. Application fee: $66. Electronic applications accepted. *Expenses:* Contact institution. *Financial support:* Federal Work-Study, scholarships/grants, and health care benefits available. Support available to part-time students. Financial award application deadline: 3/15; financial award applicants required to submit FAFSA. *Unit head:* Dr. Peggy Denton, Director, 608-785-8470, E-mail: pdenton@uwlax.edu. *Application contact:* Kathy Keifer, Director of Admissions, 608-785-8939, E-mail: admissions@uwlax.edu. Web site: http://www.uwlax.edu/ot/.

University of Wisconsin–Madison, Graduate School, School of Education, Department of Kinesiology, Occupational Therapy Program, Madison, WI 53706-1380. Offers MS, PhD. *Degree requirements:* For doctorate, thesis/dissertation. Application fee: $56. *Expenses:* Tuition, state resident: full-time $10,296; part-time $643.51 per credit. Tuition, nonresident: full-time $24,054; part-time $1503.40 per credit. *Required fees:* $70.06 per credit. Tuition and fees vary according to course load, campus/location, program and reciprocity agreements. *Financial support:* Fellowships with full tuition reimbursements, research assistantships with full tuition reimbursements, teaching assistantships with full tuition reimbursements, traineeships, and project assistantships available. *Unit head:* Dr. Mary Schneider, Coordinator, 608-262-2936, E-mail: schneider@education.wisc.edu. *Application contact:* Admissions Coordinator. Web site: http://www.education.wisc.edu/kinesiology/OT.

University of Wisconsin–Milwaukee, Graduate School, College of Health Sciences, Department of Occupational Science and Technology, Milwaukee, WI 53201-0413. Offers ergonomics (Certificate); occupational therapy (MS); therapeutic recreation (Certificate). *Accreditation:* AOTA. *Faculty:* 11 full-time (6 women), 1 (woman) part-time/adjunct. *Students:* 36 full-time (30 women), 11 part-time (7 women), 3 international. Average age 30. 16 applicants, 31% accepted, 0 enrolled. In 2011, 29 degrees awarded. *Degree requirements:* For master's, thesis or alternative. *Entrance requirements:* Additional exam requirements/recommendations for international students: Required—TOEFL (minimum score 550 paper-based; 79 iBT), IELTS (minimum score 6.5). *Application deadline:* For fall admission, 1/1 priority date for domestic students; for spring admission, 9/1 for domestic students. Applications are processed on a rolling basis. Application fee: $45 ($75 for international students). One-time fee: $506.10 full-time. Tuition and fees vary according to course load and reciprocity agreements. *Financial support:* Fellowships, research assistantships, teaching assistantships, and unspecified assistantships available. Support available to part-time students. Financial award application deadline: 4/15. *Total annual research expenditures:* $21,103. *Unit head:* Carol Haertlein Sells, Department Chair, 414-229-6933, E-mail: chaert@uwm.edu. *Application contact:* Roger O. Smith, General Information Contact, 414-229-6697, Fax: 414-229-6697, E-mail: smithro@uwm.edu. Web site: http://www4.uwm.edu/chs/academics/occupational_therapy/.

Utica College, Program in Occupational Therapy, Utica, NY 13502-4892. Offers MS. *Accreditation:* AOTA. Part-time and evening/weekend programs available. *Degree requirements:* For master's, thesis. *Entrance requirements:* For master's, physical health exam, CPR certification, 60 hours of volunteer experience, minimum GPA of 3.0. Additional exam requirements/recommendations for international students: Required—TOEFL (minimum score 525 paper-based; 195 computer-based). Electronic applications accepted. *Expenses:* Contact institution.

Virginia Commonwealth University, Graduate School, School of Allied Health Professions, Department of Occupational Therapy, Richmond, VA 23284-9005. Offers MS, MSOT, OTD. *Accreditation:* AOTA (one or more programs are accredited). *Students:* 130 full-time (119 women), 12 part-time (all women); includes 17 minority (5 Black or African American, non-Hispanic/Latino; 3 Asian, non-Hispanic/Latino; 6 Hispanic/Latino; 3 Two or more races, non-Hispanic/Latino), 1 international. In 2011, 44 master's, 1 doctorate awarded. *Degree requirements:* For master's, fieldwork. *Entrance requirements:* For master's, GRE General Test. Additional exam requirements/recommendations for international students: Required—TOEFL (minimum score 600 paper-based; 250 computer-based; 100 iBT); Recommended—IELTS (minimum score 6.5). *Application deadline:* For fall admission, 12/1 for domestic students. Application fee: $50. Electronic applications accepted. *Expenses:* Tuition, state resident: full-time $9133; part-time $507 per credit. Tuition, nonresident: full-time $18,777; part-time $1043 per credit. *Required fees:* $77 per credit. Tuition and fees vary according to degree level, campus/location, program and student level. *Financial support:* Applicants required to submit FAFSA. *Faculty research:* Children with complex care needs, instrument development, carpal tunnel syndrome, development of oral-motor feeding programs, school system practice. *Unit head:* Dr. Dianne Simons, Director, Entry-Level Occupational Therapy Program, 804-828-2230, Fax: 804-828-0782, E-mail: dfsimons@vcu.edu. *Application contact:* Lawrencine Smith, Program Manager, 804-828-2219, Fax: 804-828-0782, E-mail: lsmith@vcu.edu. Web site: http://www.sahp.vcu.edu/occu/.

Virginia Commonwealth University, Graduate School, School of Allied Health Professions, Doctoral Program in Health Related Sciences, Richmond, VA 23284-9005. Offers clinical laboratory sciences (PhD); gerontology (PhD); health administration (PhD); nurse anesthesia (PhD); occupational therapy (PhD); physical therapy (PhD); radiation sciences (PhD); rehabilitation leadership (PhD). *Faculty:* 2 full-time (1 woman). *Students:* 23 full-time (15 women), 34 part-time (23 women); includes 7 minority (4 Black or African American, non-Hispanic/Latino; 1 Asian, non-Hispanic/Latino; 1 Hispanic/Latino; 1 Two or more races, non-Hispanic/Latino), 2 international. 37 applicants, 38% accepted, 11 enrolled. In 2011, 11 doctorates awarded. *Entrance requirements:* For doctorate, GRE General Test or MAT, minimum GPA of 3.3 in master's degree. Additional exam requirements/recommendations for international students: Required—TOEFL (minimum score 600 paper-based; 250 computer-based; 100 iBT); Recommended—IELTS (minimum score 6.5). *Application deadline:* For fall admission, 3/15 for domestic students. Application fee: $50. Electronic applications accepted. *Expenses:* Tuition, state resident: full-time $9133; part-time $507 per credit. Tuition, nonresident: full-time $18,777; part-time $1043 per credit. *Required fees:* $77 per credit. Tuition and fees vary according to degree level, campus/location, program and student level. *Unit head:* Dr. Paula K. Kupstas, Director, Health Related Sciences Program, 804-828-7247, E-mail: pkupstas@vcu.edu. *Application contact:* Monica L. White, Director of Student Services, 804-828-3273, Fax: 804-828-8656, E-mail: mlwhite1@vcu.edu. Web site: http://www.pubapps.vcu.edu/BULLETINS/prog_search/?did=20005.

Washington University in St. Louis, School of Medicine, Graduate Programs in Medicine, Program in Occupational Therapy, Saint Louis, MO 63108. Offers MSOT, OTD. *Accreditation:* AOTA. *Faculty:* 19 full-time (13 women), 10 part-time/adjunct (7 women). *Students:* 265 full-time (250 women); includes 41 minority (10 Black or African American, non-Hispanic/Latino; 2 American Indian or Alaska Native, non-Hispanic/Latino; 23 Asian, non-Hispanic/Latino; 6 Hispanic/Latino), 1 international. Average age 23. 361 applicants, 41% accepted, 92 enrolled. In 2011, 52 master's, 12 doctorates awarded. Terminal master's awarded for partial completion of doctoral program. *Degree requirements:* For master's, fieldwork experiences; for doctorate, fieldwork and apprenticeship experiences. *Entrance requirements:* For master's, GRE General Test, bachelor's degree in another field or enrollment in an affiliated 3/2 institution; for doctorate, GRE General Test, bachelor's degree in another field or enrollment in an affiliated institution. Additional exam requirements/recommendations for international students: Required—TOEFL (minimum score 250 computer-based), TWE (minimum score 5). *Application deadline:* For fall admission, 1/31 priority date for domestic students, 1/31 for international students. Applications are processed on a rolling basis. Application fee: $0. Electronic applications accepted. *Financial support:* In 2011–12, 16 research assistantships with partial tuition reimbursements (averaging $4,000 per year), 23 teaching assistantships with partial tuition reimbursements (averaging $3,750 per year) were awarded; Federal Work-Study, scholarships/grants, and health care benefits also available. Support available to part-time students. Financial award application deadline: 1/31; financial award applicants required to submit FAFSA. *Faculty research:* Brain injury, ergonomics, work performance, care giving, quality of life, rehabilitation. *Total annual research expenditures:* $1.8 million. *Unit head:* Dr. Carolyn Baum, Director, 314-286-1600 Ext. 1619, Fax: 314-286-1601, E-mail: baumc@wustl.edu. *Application contact:* Rebecca Molen, Recruitment Manager, 314-286-1600 Ext. 1613, Fax: 314-286-1601, E-mail: molenr@wusm.wustl.edu. Web site: http://ot.wustl.edu/.

Wayne State University, Eugene Applebaum College of Pharmacy and Health Sciences, Department of Health Care Sciences, Program in Occupational Therapy, Detroit, MI 48202. Offers MOT, MS. MOT program begins at the undergraduate level. *Accreditation:* AOTA. Part-time programs available. *Students:* 27 full-time (22 women); includes 5 minority (1 Black or African American, non-Hispanic/Latino; 2 Asian, non-Hispanic/Latino; 1 Hispanic/Latino; 1 Two or more races, non-Hispanic/Latino), 2 international. Average age 27. 48 applicants, 0% accepted, 0 enrolled. In 2011, 27 master's awarded. *Entrance requirements:* For master's, personal resume; 20 contact hours under supervision of an OTR; two professional recommendations; interview. Additional exam requirements/recommendations for international students: Required—TOEFL (minimum score 550 paper-based; 213 computer-based); Recommended—TWE (minimum score 6). *Application deadline:* For fall admission, 2/28 for domestic and international students. Application fee: $50. Electronic applications accepted. *Expenses:* Tuition, state resident: part-time $512.85 per credit. Tuition, nonresident: part-time $1132.65 per credit. *Required fees:* $26.60 per credit. $199.65 per semester. Tuition and fees vary according to course load and program. *Financial support:* Research assistantships with tuition reimbursements, teaching assistantships, career-related internships or fieldwork, and scholarships/grants available. Support available to part-time students. *Faculty research:* Assistive technology, education and fieldwork innovation, gerontology, motor control, rehabilitation outcomes. *Unit head:* Dr. Doreen Head, Program Director, 313-577-5884, E-mail: doreenh@wayne.edu. *Application contact:* Dr. Regina Parnell, Graduate Coordinator for the Master of Occupational Therapy Program, 313-577-1435, E-mail: ad9049@wayne.edu. Web site: http://www.cphs.wayne.edu/ot/.

Western Michigan University, Graduate College, College of Health and Human Services, Department of Occupational Therapy, Kalamazoo, MI 49008. Offers MS. *Accreditation:* AOTA. *Entrance requirements:* For master's, GRE General Test.

Western New Mexico University, Graduate Division, Program in Occupational Therapy, Silver City, NM 88062-0680. Offers MOT. *Accreditation:* AOTA. Part-time programs available. Postbaccalaureate distance learning degree programs offered.

West Virginia University, School of Medicine, Graduate Programs in Human Performance, Division of Occupational Therapy, Morgantown, WV 26506. Offers MOT. Students enter program as undergraduates. *Accreditation:* AOTA. Postbaccalaureate distance learning degree programs offered. *Degree requirements:* For master's, clinical rotation. *Entrance requirements:* For master's, interview, 2 reference forms, minimum GPA of 3.0, 60 hours of volunteer experience with people with disabilities. *Expenses:* Contact institution.

Winston-Salem State University, Department of Occupational Therapy, Winston-Salem, NC 27110-0003. Offers MS. *Accreditation:* AOTA. *Entrance requirements:* For master's, GRE, 3 letters of recommendation (one from a licensed occupational therapist where volunteer or work experiences were performed; the other two from former professors or persons acquainted with academic potential); writing sample. Additional exam requirements/recommendations for international students: Required—TOEFL. Electronic applications accepted. *Faculty research:* Assistive technology, environmental adaptations, comprehensive performance evaluations.

Worcester State University, Graduate Studies, Program in Occupational Therapy, Worcester, MA 01602-2597. Offers MOT. *Accreditation:* AOTA. *Faculty:* 5 full-time (all women). *Students:* 47 full-time (38 women), 15 part-time (all women); includes 2 minority (1 Asian, non-Hispanic/Latino; 1 Hispanic/Latino). Average age 35. 98 applicants, 37% accepted, 21 enrolled. In 2011, 11 master's awarded. *Degree requirements:* For master's, comprehensive exam (for some programs), thesis optional, fieldwork. *Entrance requirements:* For master's, GRE General Test or MAT, minimum undergraduate GPA of 3.2. Additional exam requirements/recommendations for international students: Required—TOEFL (minimum score 500 paper-based; 61 iBT). *Application deadline:* For fall admission, 3/1 priority date for domestic students, 3/1 for international students. Applications are processed on a rolling basis. Application fee: $40. Electronic applications accepted. *Expenses:* Contact institution. *Financial support:* In 2011–12, 6 students received support, including 6 research assistantships with full tuition reimbursements available (averaging $4,800 per year); career-related internships or fieldwork, scholarships/grants, and unspecified assistantships also available. Financial award application deadline: 3/1; financial award applicants required to submit FAFSA. *Unit head:* Dr. Margaret Hart, Coordinator, 508-929-8785, Fax: 508-929-8178, E-mail: mhart@worcester.edu. *Application contact:* Sara Grady, Assistant Dean of Continuing Education, 508-929-8787, Fax: 508-929-8100, E-mail: sara.grady@worcester.edu.

Occupational Therapy

Xavier University, College of Social Sciences, Health and Education, Occupational Therapy Program, Cincinnati, OH 45207. Offers MOT. *Accreditation:* AOTA. *Faculty:* 5 full-time (all women), 1 (woman) part-time/adjunct. *Students:* 28 full-time (26 women), 28 part-time (27 women); includes 1 minority (Black or African American, non-Hispanic/Latino). Average age 26. 38 applicants, 84% accepted, 25 enrolled. In 2011, 29 master's awarded. *Degree requirements:* For master's, one foreign language, group research project. *Entrance requirements:* For master's, GRE (minimum of 33% average across all GRE sections - verbal, quantitative, analytical writing), minimum GPA of 3.0, completion of 40 volunteer hours, completion of all prerequisite courses with no more than 2 grades of C or lower. Additional exam requirements/recommendations for international students: Required—TOEFL or IELTS. *Application deadline:* For winter admission, 6/1 priority date for domestic students, 6/1 for international students. Application fee: $35. Electronic applications accepted. *Expenses:* Contact institution. *Financial support:* In 2011–12, 22 students received support. Scholarships/grants and tuition waivers (partial) available. Financial award application deadline: 5/23; financial award applicants required to submit FAFSA. *Faculty research:* Occupation, ethics, pediatric, occupational therapy interventions, pediatric occupational therapy assessment. *Unit head:* Dr. Carol Scheerer, Chair, 513-745-3310, Fax: 513-745-3261, E-mail: scheerer@xavier.edu. *Application contact:* Georganna Miller, Academic Advisor, 513-745-3104, Fax: 513-745-3261, E-mail: millerg@xavier.edu. Web site: http://www.xavier.edu/OT/.

Perfusion

Long Island University–C. W. Post Campus, School of Health Professions and Nursing, Department of Biomedical Sciences, Brookville, NY 11548-1300. Offers cardiovascular perfusion (MS); clinical laboratory management (MS); medical biology (MS), including hematology, immunology, medical biology, medical chemistry, medical microbiology. Part-time and evening/weekend programs available. Postbaccalaureate distance learning degree programs offered. *Degree requirements:* For master's, thesis. *Entrance requirements:* For master's, minimum GPA of 2.75 in major. Electronic applications accepted.

Milwaukee School of Engineering, Department of Electrical Engineering and Computer Science, Program in Perfusion, Milwaukee, WI 53202-3109. Offers MS. Part-time and evening/weekend programs available. *Faculty:* 1 full-time (0 women), 3 part-time/adjunct (1 woman). *Students:* 11 full-time (3 women); includes 1 minority (Black or African American, non-Hispanic/Latino). Average age 33. 19 applicants, 42% accepted, 5 enrolled. *Degree requirements:* For master's, comprehensive exam, thesis, exam. *Entrance requirements:* For master's, GRE General Test or GMAT, BS in appropriate discipline, undergraduate work in human physiology or anatomy, 3 letters of recommendation, interview, observation of 2 perfusion cases. Additional exam requirements/recommendations for international students: Required—TOEFL (minimum score 79 iBT). *Application deadline:* Applications are processed on a rolling basis. Electronic applications accepted. Application fee is waived when completed online. *Expenses: Tuition:* Full-time $17,550; part-time $650 per credit hour. *Financial support:* In 2011–12, 10 students received support. Career-related internships or fieldwork available. Support available to part-time students. Financial award applicants required to submit FAFSA. *Faculty research:* Heart medicine. *Unit head:* Dr. Ronald Gerrits, Director, 414-277-7561, Fax: 414-277-7494, E-mail: gerrits@msoe.edu. *Application contact:* Katie Gassenhuber, Graduate Program Associate, 800-321-6763, Fax: 414-277-7208, E-mail: gassenhuber@msoe.edu. Web site: http://www.msoe.edu/academics/academic_departments/eecs/msp/.

Quinnipiac University, School of Health Sciences, Program in Cardiovascular Perfusion, Hamden, CT 06518-1940. Offers MHS. *Faculty:* 1 full-time (0 women), 3 part-time/adjunct (0 women). *Students:* 7 full-time (4 women), 7 part-time (2 women). 27 applicants, 44% accepted, 7 enrolled. In 2011, 13 master's awarded. *Entrance requirements:* For master's, bachelor's degree in science or health-related discipline from an accredited American or Canadian college or university; 2 years health care work experience; interview. Additional exam requirements/recommendations for international students: Required—TOEFL (minimum score 575 paper-based; 233 computer-based; 90 iBT), IELTS (minimum score 6.5). *Application deadline:* For fall admission, 7/30 priority date for domestic students, 4/30 for international students. Applications are processed on a rolling basis. Application fee: $45. Electronic applications accepted.

Expenses: Tuition: Part-time $855 per credit. *Required fees:* $35 per credit. *Financial support:* In 2011–12, 5 students received support. Career-related internships or fieldwork, tuition waivers, and unspecified assistantships available. Financial award application deadline: 4/15; financial award applicants required to submit FAFSA. *Unit head:* Michael Smith, Director, 203-582-3427, Fax: 203-582-8706, E-mail: michael.smith@quinnipiac.edu. *Application contact:* Kristin Parent, Assistant Director of Graduate Health Sciences Admissions, 800-462-1944, Fax: 208-582-3443, E-mail: kristin.parent@quinnipiac.edu. Web site: http://www.quinnipiac.edu/gradperfusion.

The University of Arizona, College of Pharmacy, Department of Pharmacology and Toxicology, Graduate Program in Medical Pharmacology, Tucson, AZ 85721. Offers medical pharmacology (PhD); perfusion science (MS). *Faculty:* 11 full-time (3 women). *Students:* 32 full-time (22 women), 2 part-time (1 woman); includes 10 minority (1 Black or African American, non-Hispanic/Latino; 3 Asian, non-Hispanic/Latino; 4 Hispanic/Latino; 2 Two or more races, non-Hispanic/Latino), 8 international. Average age 28. 40 applicants, 13% accepted, 5 enrolled. In 2011, 4 master's, 2 doctorates awarded. *Degree requirements:* For master's, thesis; for doctorate, comprehensive exam, thesis/dissertation. *Entrance requirements:* For master's, GRE General Test, 3 letters of recommendation; for doctorate, GRE General Test, personal statement, 3 letters of recommendation. Additional exam requirements/recommendations for international students: Required—TOEFL (minimum score 550 paper-based; 213 computer-based; 79 iBT). *Application deadline:* For fall admission, 1/1 for domestic and international students. Applications are processed on a rolling basis. Application fee: $75. Electronic applications accepted. *Expenses:* Tuition, state resident: full-time $10,840. Tuition, nonresident: full-time $25,802. *Financial support:* In 2011–12, 17 research assistantships with full tuition reimbursements (averaging $23,929 per year) were awarded; institutionally sponsored loans and tuition waivers (partial) also available. Financial award applicants required to submit FAFSA. *Faculty research:* Immunopharmacology, pharmacogenetics, pharmacogenomics, clinical pharmacology, ocularpharmacology and neuropharmacology. *Unit head:* Dr. I. Glenn Sipes, Head, 520-626-7123, Fax: 520-626-2204, E-mail: sipes@email.arizona.edu. *Application contact:* Trisha Stanley, Coordinator, 520-626-7218, Fax: 520-626-2204, E-mail: stanley@email.arizona.edu. Web site: http://www.pharmacology.arizona.edu/.

University of Nebraska Medical Center, School of Allied Health Professions, Program in Clinical Perfusion Education, Omaha, NE 68198-4144. Offers distance education perfusion education (MPS); perfusion science (MPS). *Accreditation:* NAACLS. Postbaccalaureate distance learning degree programs offered. *Degree requirements:* For master's, comprehensive exam, thesis. *Entrance requirements:* For master's, GRE. Electronic applications accepted. *Faculty research:* Platelet gel, hemoconcentrators.

Physical Therapy

Alabama State University, College of Health Sciences, Department of Physical Therapy, Montgomery, AL 36101-0271. Offers DPT. *Accreditation:* APTA. *Faculty:* 7 full-time (5 women). *Students:* 57 full-time (34 women), 15 part-time (12 women); includes 39 minority (38 Black or African American, non-Hispanic/Latino; 1 Hispanic/Latino), 2 international. Average age 29. In 2011, 1 degree awarded. Terminal master's awarded for partial completion of doctoral program. *Entrance requirements:* Additional exam requirements/recommendations for international students: Required—TOEFL (minimum score 500 paper-based; 173 computer-based). *Application deadline:* For fall admission, 7/15 for domestic students; for spring admission, 12/15 for domestic students. Applications are processed on a rolling basis. Application fee: $10. *Financial support:* In 2011–12, 4 research assistantships (averaging $9,450 per year) were awarded. *Unit head:* Dr. Denise Chapman, Dean, 334-229-4707, Fax: 334-229-4964, E-mail: dchapman@alasu.edu. *Application contact:* Dr. Doris Screws, Dean of Graduate Studies, 334-229-4274, Fax: 334-229-4928, E-mail: dscrews@alasu.edu. Web site: http://www.alasu.edu/academics/colleges—departments/health-sciences/physical-therapy/index.aspx.

American International College, School of Health Sciences, Program in Physical Therapy, Springfield, MA 01109-3189. Offers DPT. *Accreditation:* APTA. *Entrance requirements:* For doctorate, minimum GPA of 3.2. Additional exam requirements/recommendations for international students: Required—TOEFL. Electronic applications accepted. *Expenses:* Contact institution.

Andrews University, School of Graduate Studies, College of Arts and Sciences, Department of Physical Therapy, Postprofessional Physical Therapy Program, Berrien Springs, MI 49104. Offers Dr Sc PT, TDPT. *Accreditation:* APTA. *Students:* 109 full-time (60 women), 40 part-time (22 women); includes 45 minority (10 Black or African American, non-Hispanic/Latino; 2 American Indian or Alaska Native, non-Hispanic/Latino; 21 Asian, non-Hispanic/Latino; 9 Hispanic/Latino; 3 Two or more races, non-Hispanic/Latino), 9 international. Average age 29. 241 applicants, 22% accepted, 33 enrolled. *Application deadline:* For fall admission, 12/1 priority date for domestic students. Applications are processed on a rolling basis. Application fee: $40. *Expenses:* Contact institution. *Financial support:* Federal Work-Study, institutionally sponsored loans, and scholarships/grants available. Financial award application deadline: 9/1; financial award applicants required to submit FAFSA. *Faculty research:* Home health patient profile, clinical education, breeding success of marine birds, trends in home

health care for physical therapy, patient motivation in acute rehabilitation. *Unit head:* Kathy Berglund, Director of Professional Programs, 269-471-6076, Fax: 269-471-2866, E-mail: berglund@andrews.edu. *Application contact:* Dixie Scott, Director of Admissions, 800-827-2878, Fax: 269-471-2867, E-mail: pt-info@andrews.edu. Web site: http://www.andrews.edu/PHTH/.

Angelo State University, College of Graduate Studies, College of Health and Human Services, Department of Physical Therapy, San Angelo, TX 76909. Offers DPT. *Accreditation:* APTA. *Faculty:* 7 full-time (4 women), 1 part-time/adjunct (0 women). *Students:* 62 full-time (40 women); includes 7 minority (1 Black or African American, non-Hispanic/Latino; 2 Asian, non-Hispanic/Latino; 4 Hispanic/Latino). Average age 25. 20 applicants, 100% accepted, 20 enrolled. *Entrance requirements:* Additional exam requirements/recommendations for international students: Required—TOEFL or IELTS. *Application deadline:* For fall admission, 2/1 for domestic students, 3/10 for international students. Application fee: $40 ($50 for international students). Electronic applications accepted. *Financial support:* In 2011–12, 50 students received support. Scholarships/grants available. Financial award application deadline: 3/1; financial award applicants required to submit FAFSA. *Faculty research:* Women and lipoproteins, international distance education, quadriceps femoris and the VMO, ergonomics, children and obesity. *Unit head:* Dr. Scott Hasson, Department Head, 325-942-2581 Ext. 278, Fax: 325-942-2548, E-mail: ptdept@angelo.edu. *Application contact:* Dr. Scott Hasson, Department Head, 325-942-2581 Ext. 278, Fax: 325-942-2548, E-mail: ptdept@angelo.edu. Web site: http://www.angelo.edu/dept/physical_therapy/.

Arcadia University, Graduate Studies, Department of Physical Therapy, Glenside, PA 19038-3295. Offers DPT. *Accreditation:* APTA. *Faculty:* 6 full-time (4 women), 20 part-time/adjunct (15 women). *Students:* 112 full-time (82 women), 117 part-time (86 women); includes 31 minority (5 Black or African American, non-Hispanic/Latino; 1 American Indian or Alaska Native, non-Hispanic/Latino; 10 Asian, non-Hispanic/Latino; 1 Native Hawaiian or other Pacific Islander, non-Hispanic/Latino; 14 Two or more races, non-Hispanic/Latino), 3 international. Average age 29. In 2011, 91 doctorates awarded. *Application deadline:* For fall admission, 1/31 for domestic students. Application fee: $50. *Expenses:* Contact institution. *Financial support:* In 2011–12, 15 students received support. Career-related internships or fieldwork, tuition waivers (partial), and unspecified assistantships available. *Unit head:* Dr. Rebecca L. Craik, Chair, 215-572-2143. *Application contact:* 215-572-2910, Fax: 215-572-4049, E-mail: admiss@arcadia.edu.

Arkansas State University, Graduate School, College of Nursing and Health Professions, Department of Physical Therapy, Jonesboro, State University, AR 72467. Offers DPT. *Accreditation:* APTA. Part-time programs available. *Faculty:* 8 full-time (4 women). *Students:* 84 full-time (51 women), 1 (woman) part-time; includes 8 minority (4 Black or African American, non-Hispanic/Latino; 2 Asian, non-Hispanic/Latino; 1 Native Hawaiian or other Pacific Islander, non-Hispanic/Latino; 1 Two or more races, non-Hispanic/Latino). Average age 25. 189 applicants, 17% accepted, 30 enrolled. *Degree requirements:* For doctorate, comprehensive exam, thesis/dissertation. *Entrance requirements:* For doctorate, GRE, Allied Health Professions Admissions Test, appropriate bachelor's or master's degree, letters of reference, resume, official transcript, volunteer experience, criminal background check, immunization records, writing sample. Additional exam requirements/recommendations for international students: Required—TOEFL (minimum score 550 paper-based; 213 computer-based; 79 iBT), IELTS (minimum score 6), Pearson Test of English Academic (minimum score 56). *Application deadline:* For fall admission, 2/1 for domestic and international students. Applications are processed on a rolling basis. Application fee: $50. Electronic applications accepted. *Expenses:* Contact institution. *Financial support:* In 2011–12, 10 students received support. Fellowships, career-related internships or fieldwork, scholarships/grants, and unspecified assistantships available. Financial award application deadline: 7/1; financial award applicants required to submit FAFSA. *Unit head:* Shawn Drake, Interim Chair, 870-972-3591, Fax: 870-972-3652, E-mail: sdrake@ astate.edu. *Application contact:* Dr. Andrew Sustich, Dean of the Graduate School, 870-972-3029, Fax: 870-972-3857, E-mail: sustich@astate.edu. Web site: http://www.astate.edu/a/conhp/pt/index.dot.

Armstrong Atlantic State University, School of Graduate Studies, Program in Physical Therapy, Savannah, GA 31419-1997. Offers DPT. *Accreditation:* APTA. *Faculty:* 6 full-time (3 women). *Students:* 56 full-time (39 women); includes 2 minority (both Black or African American, non-Hispanic/Latino). Average age 25. In 2011, 20 doctorates awarded. *Degree requirements:* For doctorate, thesis/dissertation, licensure exam. *Entrance requirements:* For doctorate, GRE General Test, course work in general chemistry, physics, anatomy, physiology, statistics; letters of recommendation, bachelor's degree. Additional exam requirements/recommendations for international students: Required—TOEFL (minimum score 523 paper-based; 193 computer-based). *Application deadline:* For fall admission, 1/15 for domestic students. Applications are processed on a rolling basis. Application fee: $30. Electronic applications accepted. *Expenses:* Tuition, state resident: full-time $3402. Tuition, nonresident: full-time $12,636. *Financial support:* In 2011–12, research assistantships with full tuition reimbursements (averaging $5,000 per year) were awarded; career-related internships or fieldwork, scholarships/grants, and unspecified assistantships also available. Financial award applicants required to submit FAFSA. *Faculty research:* Exercise modalities, physical agents, magnetic therapy, leadership development, perception of physical therapists. *Unit head:* Dr. David Lake, Interim Department Head, 912-344-2580, Fax: 912-344-3469. *Application contact:* Jill Bell, Director, Graduate Enrollment Services, 912-344-2798, Fax: 912-344-3488, E-mail: graduate@armstrong.edu. Web site: http://www.pt.armstrong.edu/.

A.T. Still University of Health Sciences, Arizona School of Health Sciences, Mesa, AZ 85206. Offers advanced occupational therapy (MS); advanced physician assistant (MS); athletic training (MS); audiology (Au D); health sciences (DHSc); human movement (MS); occupational therapy (MS); physical therapy (DPT); physician assistant (MS); transitional audiology (Au D); transitional physical therapy (DPT). *Accreditation:* AOTA (one or more programs are accredited); ASHA. Part-time and evening/weekend programs available. Postbaccalaureate distance learning degree programs offered (minimal on-campus study). *Faculty:* 44 full-time (27 women), 235 part-time/adjunct (141 women). *Students:* 410 full-time (275 women), 1,010 part-time (675 women); includes 320 minority (73 Black or African American, non-Hispanic/Latino; 18 American Indian or Alaska Native, non-Hispanic/Latino; 158 Asian, non-Hispanic/Latino; 62 Hispanic/Latino; 9 Two or more races, non-Hispanic/Latino), 6 international. Average age 35. 4,395 applicants, 18% accepted, 694 enrolled. In 2011, 221 master's, 406 doctorates awarded. *Median time to degree:* Of those who began their doctoral program in fall 2003, 98% received their degree in 8 years or less. *Degree requirements:* For master's, thesis (for some programs); for doctorate, thesis/dissertation (for some programs). *Entrance requirements:* For master's, GRE General Test; for doctorate, GRE, Evaluation of Practicing Audiologists Capabilities (Au D), Physical Therapist Evaluation Tool (DPT), current state licensure, master's degree or equivalent (Au D). Additional exam requirements/recommendations for international students: Required—TOEFL (minimum score 550 paper-based; 213 computer-based; 80 iBT). *Application deadline:* For fall admission, 8/1 priority date for domestic students, 8/1 for international students. Applications are processed on a rolling basis. Application fee: $60. *Expenses:* Contact institution. *Financial support:* In 2011–12, 272 students received support, including 14 fellowships (averaging $16,000 per year); Federal Work-Study and scholarships/grants also available. Financial award application deadline: 5/1; financial award applicants required to submit FAFSA. *Faculty research:* Physical therapy: metabolism during exercise and activity; neuromuscular function after injury, prevention of lifestyle diseases, prevention and treatment of overuse injuries; athletic training: pediatric sport-related concussion, adolescent athlete health-related quality of life; occupational therapy: spirituality and health disparities, geriatric and pediatric well-being, pain management for participation. *Total annual research expenditures:* $75,682. *Unit head:* Dr. Randy Danielsen, Dean, 480-219-6000, Fax: 480-219-6110, E-mail: rdanielsen@ atsu.edu. *Application contact:* Donna Sparks, Associate Director, Admissions Processing, 660-626-2117, Fax: 660-626-2969, E-mail: admissions@atsu.edu. Web site: http://www.atsu.edu/ashs.

Azusa Pacific University, School of Behavioral and Applied Sciences, Department of Physical Therapy, Azusa, CA 91702-7000. Offers DPT. *Accreditation:* APTA. *Faculty:* 7 full-time (4 women). *Students:* 119 full-time (80 women); includes 35 minority (2 Black or African American, non-Hispanic/Latino; 1 American Indian or Alaska Native, non-Hispanic/Latino; 19 Asian, non-Hispanic/Latino; 9 Hispanic/Latino; 4 Native Hawaiian or other Pacific Islander, non-Hispanic/Latino). 40 applicants, 100% accepted, 39 enrolled. In 2011, 39 degrees awarded. *Degree requirements:* For doctorate, thesis/dissertation. *Entrance requirements:* For doctorate, GRE General Test. Additional exam requirements/recommendations for international students: Required—TOEFL (minimum score 600 paper-based; 250 computer-based). *Application deadline:* For fall admission, 10/1 for domestic and international students. Applications are processed on a rolling basis. Application fee: $0. Electronic applications accepted. *Expenses:* Contact institution. *Financial support:* Career-related internships or fieldwork available. Financial award applicants required to submit FAFSA. *Faculty research:* Antioxidants and endothelial function, EEG and pain, imaging ultrasound for MSK, metabolic function in obesity. *Total annual research expenditures:* $250,000. *Unit head:* Dr. Michael Laymon, Chair, 626-815-5020, Fax: 626-815-5017, E-mail: mlaymon@apu.edu. *Application contact:* Anel Herrera, Administrative Manager, 626-815-5014, Fax: 626-815-5017, E-mail: aherrera@apu.edu. Web site: http://www.apu.edu/bas/physicaltherapy/.

Baylor University, Graduate School, Military Programs, Program in Orthopedics, Waco, TX 76798. Offers D Sc. *Students:* 30 full-time (11 women); includes 1 minority (Hispanic/Latino). In 2011, 15 doctorates awarded. *Unit head:* Maj. Craig Paige, Graduate Program Director, 915-443-4215, Fax: 210-221-7306, E-mail: craig.v.paige@

us.army.mil. *Application contact:* Lori McNamara, Administrative Assistant, 254-710-3588, Fax: 254-710-3870.

Baylor University, Graduate School, Military Programs, Program in Physical Therapy, Waco, TX 76798. Offers MPT, DPT. Program offered jointly with the U.S. Army. *Accreditation:* APTA. *Students:* 48 full-time (19 women); includes 5 minority (2 Black or African American, non-Hispanic/Latino; 1 Asian, non-Hispanic/Latino; 2 Two or more races, non-Hispanic/Latino). In 2011, 23 doctorates awarded. *Degree requirements:* For master's, comprehensive exam, research paper. *Entrance requirements:* For master's, GRE General Test. *Application deadline:* For fall admission, 2/1 for domestic students. Applications are processed on a rolling basis. Application fee: $25. *Faculty research:* Effect of electrical stimulation on normal and immobilized muscle, effects of inversion traction. *Unit head:* Col. Josef Moore, Graduate Program Director, 210-221-8410, Fax: 210-221-7585, E-mail: josef.moore@cen.amedd.army.mil. *Application contact:* Cindy Quiroz, Training Technician, 210-221-8410, E-mail: cynthia.quiroz@ cen.amedd.army.mil. Web site: http://www.cs.amedd.army.mil/baylorpt/.

Bellarmine University, Donna and Allan Lansing School of Nursing and Health Sciences, Louisville, KY 40205-0671. Offers family nurse practitioner (MSN); nursing administration (MSN); nursing education (MSN); nursing practice (DNP); physical therapy (DPT). *Accreditation:* AACN; APTA. Part-time and evening/weekend programs available. *Faculty:* 21 full-time (16 women), 7 part-time/adjunct (2 women). *Students:* 128 full-time (82 women), 116 part-time (111 women); includes 13 minority (5 Black or African American, non-Hispanic/Latino; 1 American Indian or Alaska Native, non-Hispanic/Latino; 2 Asian, non-Hispanic/Latino; 3 Hispanic/Latino; 2 Two or more races, non-Hispanic/Latino). Average age 31. In 2011, 19 master's, 50 doctorates awarded. *Degree requirements:* For doctorate, comprehensive exam, thesis/dissertation. *Entrance requirements:* For master's, GRE General Test, RN license; for doctorate, GRE General Test, Physical Therapist Centralized Application Service (for DPT). Additional exam requirements/recommendations for international students: Required—TOEFL (minimum score 550 paper-based; 213 computer-based; 80 iBT). Application fee: $25. Electronic applications accepted. *Expenses:* Contact institution. *Financial support:* Career-related internships or fieldwork and scholarships/grants available. *Faculty research:* Nursing: pain, empathy, leadership styles, control; physical therapy: service-learning; exercise in chronic and pre-operative conditions, athletes; women's health; aging. *Unit head:* Dr. Susan H. Davis, Dean, 800-274-4723 Ext. 8217, E-mail: sdavis@bellarmine.edu. *Application contact:* Julie Armstrong-Binnix, Health Science Recruiter, 800-274-4723 Ext. 8364, E-mail: julieab@bellarmine.edu. Web site: http://www.bellarmine.edu/lansing.

Belmont University, College of Health Sciences, School of Physical Therapy, Nashville, TN 37212-3757. Offers DPT. *Accreditation:* APTA. *Faculty:* 9 full-time (5 women), 13 part-time/adjunct (9 women). *Students:* 99 full-time (81 women); includes 3 minority (1 Black or African American, non-Hispanic/Latino; 1 Asian, non-Hispanic/Latino; 1 Two or more races, non-Hispanic/Latino). Average age 24. 538 applicants, 16% accepted, 34 enrolled. In 2011, 33 doctorates awarded. *Degree requirements:* For doctorate, comprehensive exam. *Entrance requirements:* For doctorate, GRE General Test, minimum GPA of 3.0, 50 observation hours, 2 recommendations (1 from licensed physical therapist), undergraduate degree in any discipline. Additional exam requirements/recommendations for international students: Required—TOEFL (minimum score 550 paper-based; 213 computer-based; 80 iBT). *Application deadline:* For fall admission, 8/15 priority date for domestic students, 8/15 for international students; for spring admission, 5/15 for domestic students, 5/16 for international students. Applications are processed on a rolling basis. Application fee: $50. Electronic applications accepted. *Expenses:* Contact institution. *Financial support:* In 2011–12, 38 students received support. Scholarships/grants available. Financial award applicants required to submit FAFSA. *Faculty research:* Electrophysiology, orthopedic neuromuscular functions, assessment of whole body vibration, pediatric balance scale, motion analysis. *Unit head:* Dr. John S. Halle, Associate Dean, 615-460-6727, Fax: 615-460-6729, E-mail: john.halle@belmont.edu. *Application contact:* Christina Harness, Program Assistant, 615-460-6722, Fax: 615-460-6729, E-mail: pt@belmont.edu. Web site: http://www.belmont.edu/pt/.

Boston University, College of Health and Rehabilitation Sciences: Sargent College, Department of Physical Therapy and Athletic Training, Boston, MA 02215. Offers physical therapy (DPT); rehabilitation sciences (D Sc). *Accreditation:* APTA (one or more programs are accredited). Postbaccalaureate distance learning degree programs offered (minimal on-campus study). *Faculty:* 13 full-time (10 women), 26 part-time/adjunct (12 women). *Students:* 142 full-time (107 women), 53 part-time (33 women); includes 28 minority (2 Black or African American, non-Hispanic/Latino; 2 American Indian or Alaska Native, non-Hispanic/Latino; 16 Asian, non-Hispanic/Latino; 5 Hispanic/Latino; 1 Native Hawaiian or other Pacific Islander, non-Hispanic/Latino; 2 Two or more races, non-Hispanic/Latino), 6 international. Average age 28. 542 applicants, 26% accepted, 38 enrolled. In 2011, 97 doctorates awarded. *Degree requirements:* For doctorate, comprehensive exam, thesis/dissertation. *Entrance requirements:* For doctorate, GRE General Test, master's degree (for Sc D), bachelor's degree (for DPT). Additional exam requirements/recommendations for international students: Required—TOEFL (minimum score 550 paper-based; 84 computer-based). *Application deadline:* For fall admission, 1/7 priority date for domestic students, 1/7 for international students. Applications are processed on a rolling basis. Application fee: $120. Electronic applications accepted. *Expenses:* Tuition: Full-time $40,848; part-time $1276 per credit hour. *Required fees:* $572; $286 per semester. *Financial support:* In 2011–12, 125 students received support, including 14 fellowships (averaging $16,000 per year), 10 teaching assistantships with partial tuition reimbursements available (averaging $3,000 per year); career-related internships or fieldwork, Federal Work-Study, institutionally sponsored loans, scholarships/grants, and tuition waivers (partial) also available. Financial award application deadline: 4/15; financial award applicants required to submit FAFSA. *Faculty research:* Gait, balance, motor control, dynamic systems analysis, spinal cord injury. *Total annual research expenditures:* $1.3 million. *Unit head:* Dr. Melanie Matthies, Chairman, 617-353-2724, E-mail: pt@bu.edu. *Application contact:* Sharon Sankey, Director, Student Services, 617-353-2713, Fax: 617-353-7500, E-mail: ssankey@bu.edu. Web site: http://www.bu.edu/sargent/.

Bradley University, Graduate School, College of Education and Health Sciences, Department of Physical Therapy and Health Science, Peoria, IL 61625-0002. Offers physical therapy (DPT). *Accreditation:* APTA. *Entrance requirements:* For doctorate, GRE, 2 letters of recommendation. Additional exam requirements/recommendations for international students: Required—TOEFL (minimum score 600 paper-based; 250 computer-based; 100 iBT). *Expenses:* Contact institution.

California State University, Fresno, Division of Graduate Studies, College of Health and Human Services, Department of Physical Therapy, Fresno, CA 93740-8027. Offers MPT, DPT. *Accreditation:* APTA. *Degree requirements:* For master's, comprehensive exam. *Entrance requirements:* For master's, GRE General Test, minimum GPA of 3.0. Additional exam requirements/recommendations for international students: Required—TOEFL. Electronic applications accepted. *Faculty research:* Dance, occupational health, ethics.

California State University, Long Beach, Graduate Studies, College of Health and Human Services, Department of Physical Therapy, Long Beach, CA 90840. Offers MPT.

Physical Therapy

Accreditation: APTA. *Faculty:* 5 full-time (4 women), 10 part-time/adjunct (7 women). *Students:* 76 full-time (41 women), 24 part-time (17 women); includes 43 minority (3 Black or African American, non-Hispanic/Latino; 2 American Indian or Alaska Native, non-Hispanic/Latino; 27 Asian, non-Hispanic/Latino; 7 Hispanic/Latino; 4 Two or more races, non-Hispanic/Latino), 1 international. Average age 28. 369 applicants, 11% accepted, 17 enrolled. In 2011, 35 master's awarded. *Degree requirements:* For master's, comprehensive exam, thesis, project or directive studies. *Entrance requirements:* For master's, GRE General Test, minimum GPA of 3.0 in upper-division prerequisites. Additional exam requirements/recommendations for international students: Required—TOEFL. *Application deadline:* For fall admission, 1/15 for domestic students. Applications are processed on a rolling basis. Application fee: $55. Electronic applications accepted. *Financial support:* Federal Work-Study, institutionally sponsored loans, and scholarships/grants available. Financial award application deadline: 3/2; financial award applicants required to submit FAFSA. *Unit head:* Dr. Kay Cerny, Chair, 562-985-4072, Fax: 562-985-4069, E-mail: kcerny@csulb.edu. *Application contact:* Rachel Brophy, Student Programs Coordinator, 562-985-4546, Fax: 562-985-7786, E-mail: rpbrophy@csulb.edu.

California State University, Northridge, Graduate Studies, College of Health and Human Development, Department of Physical Therapy, Northridge, CA 91330. Offers MPT. *Accreditation:* APTA. *Entrance requirements:* For master's, GRE General Test or minimum GPA of 3.0. Additional exam requirements/recommendations for international students: Required—TOEFL.

Carroll University, Program in Physical Therapy, Waukesha, WI 53186-5593. Offers MPT, DPT. *Accreditation:* APTA. *Degree requirements:* For master's, thesis (for some programs). *Entrance requirements:* For master's, GRE General Test, recommendations, clinical observation. Additional exam requirements/recommendations for international students: Required—TOEFL. *Expenses:* Contact institution. *Faculty research:* Physical therapy education, geriatrics, neural control of movement, wellness and prevention in apparently healthy individuals with disease and disability.

Central Michigan University, College of Graduate Studies, The Herbert H. and Grace A. Dow College of Health Professions, School of Rehabilitation and Medical Sciences, Mount Pleasant, MI 48859. Offers physical therapy (DPT); physician assistant (MS). *Accreditation:* APTA; ARC-PA. *Degree requirements:* For master's, thesis or alternative; for doctorate, thesis/dissertation or alternative. *Entrance requirements:* For master's and doctorate, GRE. Electronic applications accepted.

Chapman University, Schmid College of Science and Technology, Department of Physical Therapy, Orange, CA 92866. Offers DPT. *Accreditation:* APTA. *Faculty:* 9 full-time (6 women), 3 part-time/adjunct (1 woman). *Students:* 92 full-time (51 women), 51 part-time (34 women); includes 47 minority (1 Black or African American, non-Hispanic/Latino; 30 Asian, non-Hispanic/Latino; 10 Hispanic/Latino; 6 Two or more races, non-Hispanic/Latino), 1 international. Average age 26. 956 applicants, 26% accepted, 47 enrolled. In 2011, 38 doctorates awarded. *Degree requirements:* For doctorate, 1440 hours of clinical experience. *Entrance requirements:* For doctorate, GRE, minimum undergraduate GPA of 3.0; 40 hours of physical therapy observation (or paid work). Additional exam requirements/recommendations for international students: Required—TOEFL (minimum score 550 paper-based; 213 computer-based; 80 iBT). *Application deadline:* For fall admission, 11/15 for domestic students. Application fee: $65. Electronic applications accepted. *Expenses:* Contact institution. *Financial support:* Fellowships, Federal Work-Study, and scholarships/grants available. Financial award applicants required to submit FAFSA. *Unit head:* Dr. Jacki Brechter, Chair, 714-744-7649, E-mail: brechter@chapman.edu. *Application contact:* Gianne Diosomito, Admission Counselor, 714-997-6711, E-mail: diosomito@chapman.edu. Web site: http://www.chapman.edu/dpt/.

Chatham University, Program in Physical Therapy, Pittsburgh, PA 15232-2826. Offers DPT, TDPT. *Accreditation:* APTA. *Students:* 93 full-time (67 women), 40 part-time (28 women); includes 15 minority (3 Black or African American, non-Hispanic/Latino; 1 American Indian or Alaska Native, non-Hispanic/Latino; 4 Asian, non-Hispanic/Latino; 4 Hispanic/Latino; 3 Two or more races, non-Hispanic/Latino), 1 international. Average age 30. 421 applicants, 21% accepted, 46 enrolled. In 2011, 28 doctorates awarded. *Entrance requirements:* For doctorate, GRE, community service, interview, minimum GPA of 3.0, writing sample, volunteer/work experience, 3 references. Additional exam requirements/recommendations for international students: Required—TOEFL (minimum score 600 paper-based; 250 computer-based; 100 iBT), IELTS (minimum score 7), TWE. *Application deadline:* For fall admission, 12/1 priority date for domestic students, 12/1 for international students. Application fee: $0. *Expenses:* Contact institution. *Financial support:* Career-related internships or fieldwork available. Financial award applicants required to submit FAFSA. *Faculty research:* Stroke rehabilitation, osteoporosis and fall prevention, physical therapy for children with disabilities, evidence-based practice and decision-making, low back pain in children and adolescents. *Unit head:* Dr. Patricia Downey, Director, 412-365-1199, Fax: 412-365-1505, E-mail: downey@chatham.edu. *Application contact:* Ashlee Bartko, Senior Assistant Director of Graduate Admission, 412-365-2988, Fax: 412-365-1609, E-mail: gradadmissions@chatham.edu. Web site: http://www.chatham.edu/departments/healthmgmt/graduate/pt.

Clarke University, Physical Therapy Program, Dubuque, IA 52001-3198. Offers DPT. *Accreditation:* APTA. *Faculty:* 6 full-time (3 women), 2 part-time/adjunct (both women). *Students:* 82 full-time (56 women); includes 3 minority (1 Asian, non-Hispanic/Latino; 1 Hispanic/Latino; 1 Native Hawaiian or other Pacific Islander, non-Hispanic/Latino). Average age 22. In 2011, 19 doctorates awarded. *Entrance requirements:* For doctorate, minimum GPA of 3.0, 16-24 hours of clinical experience in 3 different areas. *Application deadline:* For spring admission, 3/31 for domestic students. Application fee: $0. *Expenses:* Tuition: Part-time $690 per credit hour. *Required fees:* $35 per credit hour. Tuition and fees vary according to program and student level. *Financial support:* In 2011–12, 4 students received support. Career-related internships or fieldwork available. Support available to part-time students. Financial award applicants required to submit FAFSA. *Faculty research:* Qualitative research, occupational health, discontinuous anaerobic studies, low back dysfunction. *Unit head:* Dr. Andrew Priest, Chair, 319-588-6382, Fax: 319-588-8684. *Application contact:* Joan Coates, Information Contact, 563-588-6354, Fax: 563-588-6789, E-mail: graduate@clarke.edu. Web site: http://www.clarke.edu/.

Clarkson University, Graduate School, School of Arts and Sciences, Department of Physical Therapy, Potsdam, NY 13699. Offers DPT. *Accreditation:* APTA. *Faculty:* 8 full-time (4 women), 6 part-time/adjunct (3 women). *Students:* 60 full-time (48 women); includes 13 minority (2 Black or African American, non-Hispanic/Latino; 3 Asian, non-Hispanic/Latino; 4 Hispanic/Latino; 4 Two or more races, non-Hispanic/Latino), 1 international. Average age 23. 219 applicants, 13% accepted, 23 enrolled. In 2011, 13 doctorates awarded. *Entrance requirements:* For doctorate, GRE, Physical Therapy Centralized Application Service (PTCAS) application, including transcripts of all college coursework, two personal essays, and three letters of recommendation. Additional exam requirements/recommendations for international students: Required—TOEFL. *Application deadline:* Applications are processed on a rolling basis. Application fee: $125. Electronic applications accepted. *Expenses:* Tuition: Full-time $14,376; part-time $1198 per credit hour. *Required fees:* $295 per semester. *Financial support:* In 2011–12, 60 students received support. Scholarships/grants and tuition waivers (partial) available. *Faculty research:* Smart prosthetics research integration, psychophysical models, telemedicine device. Total annual research expenditures: $113,985. *Unit head:* Dr. George Fulk, Chair, 315-268-3786, Fax: 315-268-1539, E-mail: gfulk@clarkson.edu. *Application contact:* Jennifer Reed, Graduate School Coordinator, School of Arts and Sciences, 315-268-3802, Fax: 315-268-3989, E-mail: sciencegrad@clarkson.edu. Web site: http://www.clarkson.edu/pt/.

Cleveland State University, College of Graduate Studies, College of Sciences and Health Professions, School of Health Sciences, Program in Physical Therapy, Cleveland, OH 44115. Offers DPT. *Accreditation:* APTA. *Faculty:* 7 full-time (6 women), 7 part-time/adjunct (5 women). *Students:* 91 full-time (64 women); includes 5 minority (1 Black or African American, non-Hispanic/Latino; 3 Asian, non-Hispanic/Latino; 1 Hispanic/Latino), 2 international. Average age 26. 27 applicants. In 2011, 31 doctorates awarded. *Degree requirements:* For doctorate, comprehensive exam. *Entrance requirements:* For doctorate, GRE (minimum scores: 400-450 Verbal; 500-550 quantitative; 4.0 analytical writing). Additional exam requirements/recommendations for international students: Required—TOEFL (minimum score 550 paper-based; 220 computer-based). *Application deadline:* For spring admission, 2/15 priority date for domestic students, 2/15 for international students. Electronic applications accepted. Application fee is waived when completed online. *Expenses:* Contact institution. *Financial support:* In 2011–12, 13 teaching assistantships with partial tuition reimbursements (averaging $9,122 per year) were awarded; scholarships/grants also available. *Faculty research:* Biomechanics, exercise physiology, motor control, physical dysfunctions, health disparities/urban health. *Unit head:* Dr. Karen Ann O'Loughlin, Director, 216-687-3581, Fax: 216-687-9316, E-mail: k.oloughlin@@csuohio.edu. *Application contact:* Lisa Pistone, Administrative Secretary, 216-687-3566, Fax: 216-687-9316, E-mail: l.pistone@csuohio.edu.

College of Mount St. Joseph, Physical Therapy Program, Cincinnati, OH 45233-1670. Offers DPT. *Accreditation:* APTA. *Faculty:* 13 full-time (6 women), 8 part-time/adjunct (5 women). *Students:* 65 full-time (39 women), 34 part-time (24 women); includes 6 minority (1 Black or African American, non-Hispanic/Latino; 2 Asian, non-Hispanic/Latino; 2 Hispanic/Latino; 1 Two or more races, non-Hispanic/Latino). Average age 24. 264 applicants, 21% accepted, 31 enrolled. In 2011, 27 doctorates awarded. *Degree requirements:* For doctorate, clinical internship; integrative project. *Entrance requirements:* For doctorate, GRE, minimum GPA of 3.0, prerequisite coursework in sciences, humanities, social sciences and statistics, 80 observation hours. Additional exam requirements/recommendations for international students: Required—TOEFL (minimum score 560 paper-based; 220 computer-based; 83 iBT). *Application deadline:* For fall admission, 11/1 for domestic students. Application fee: $50. Electronic applications accepted. *Expenses:* Contact institution. *Financial support:* In 2011–12, 7 students received support. Applicants required to submit FAFSA. *Faculty research:* Utilizing technology in learning, neurobiology, assessment of student learning, critical thinking, effectiveness of distance education methods. *Unit head:* Dr. Karen Holtgrefe, Chair, 513-244-3299, Fax: 513-451-2547, E-mail: karen_holtgrefe@mail.msj.edu. *Application contact:* Marilyn Hoskins, Assistant Director of Graduate Recruitment, 513-244-4723, Fax: 513-244-4629, E-mail: marilyn_hoskins@mail.msj.edu. Web site: http://www.msj.edu/view/academics/graduate-programs/physical-therapy.aspx.

The College of St. Scholastica, Graduate Studies, Department of Physical Therapy, Duluth, MN 55811-4199. Offers DPT. *Accreditation:* APTA. *Faculty:* 9 full-time (7 women), 3 part-time/adjunct (1 woman). *Students:* 90 full-time (61 women), 102 part-time (37 women); includes 29 minority (4 Black or African American, non-Hispanic/Latino; 18 Asian, non-Hispanic/Latino; 3 Hispanic/Latino; 4 Two or more races, non-Hispanic/Latino). Average age 34. 149 applicants, 58% accepted, 70 enrolled. In 2011, 79 doctorates awarded. *Entrance requirements:* For doctorate, GRE, minimum GPA of 3.0, interview. Additional exam requirements/recommendations for international students: Required—TOEFL (minimum score 550 paper-based; 213 computer-based; 79 iBT). *Application deadline:* For fall admission, 10/1 for domestic and international students. Applications are processed on a rolling basis. Application fee: $50. Electronic applications accepted. *Financial support:* In 2011–12, 81 students received support, including 4 teaching assistantships (averaging $1,042 per year); Federal Work-Study and scholarships/grants also available. Support available to part-time students. Financial award applicants required to submit FAFSA. *Faculty research:* Postural control, reliability and validity of spinal assessment tools, biomechanics of golf swing and low back pain, gait assessment and treatment, ethical issues. *Unit head:* Dr. Denise Wise, Director, 218-723-6523, E-mail: dwise@css.edu. *Application contact:* Lindsay Lahti, Director of Graduate and Extended Studies Recruitment, 218-733-2240, Fax: 218-733-2275, E-mail: gradstudies@css.edu. Web site: http://www.css.edu/Academics/School-of-Health-Sciences/Physical-Therapy.html.

Columbia University, College of Physicians and Surgeons, Program in Physical Therapy, New York, NY 10032. Offers DPT. *Accreditation:* APTA. *Faculty:* 12 full-time (8 women), 15 part-time/adjunct (6 women). *Students:* 160 full-time (135 women); includes 32 minority (2 Black or African American, non-Hispanic/Latino; 20 Asian, non-Hispanic/Latino; 6 Hispanic/Latino; 2 Native Hawaiian or other Pacific Islander, non-Hispanic/Latino; 2 Two or more races, non-Hispanic/Latino). Average age 24. 394 applicants, 20% accepted, 68 enrolled. In 2011, 54 doctorates awarded. *Degree requirements:* For doctorate, fieldwork, capstone project. *Entrance requirements:* For doctorate, GRE General Test, undergraduate course work in biology, chemistry, physics, psychology, statistics and humanities. Additional exam requirements/recommendations for international students: Required—TOEFL. *Application deadline:* For fall admission, 12/3 priority date for domestic students, 12/3 for international students. Applications are processed on a rolling basis. Application fee: $0. Electronic applications accepted. *Expenses:* Contact institution. *Financial support:* In 2011–12, 90 students received support. Career-related internships or fieldwork, Federal Work-Study, institutionally sponsored loans, and scholarships/grants available. Financial award application deadline: 4/15; financial award applicants required to submit FAFSA. *Faculty research:* Motor control, motion analysis, back assessment, recovery of function following neurological injury, women's health, disability awareness, pediatrics, orthopedics. Total annual research expenditures: $2.5 million. *Unit head:* Dr. Risa Granick, Director, 212-305-6907, Fax: 212-305-4569, E-mail: rg2135@columbia.edu. *Application contact:* Cynthia Worthington, Admissions Coordinator, 212-305-0470, Fax: 212-305-4569, E-mail: cw75@columbia.edu. Web site: http://www.columbiaphysicaltherapy.org.

Concordia University Wisconsin, Graduate Programs, School of Human Services, Program in Physical Therapy, Mequon, WI 53097-2402. Offers MSPT, DPT. *Accreditation:* APTA. *Faculty:* 5 part-time/adjunct (2 women). *Students:* 72 full-time (42 women), 5 part-time (3 women); includes 5 minority (2 Black or African American, non-Hispanic/Latino; 2 Asian, non-Hispanic/Latino; 1 Two or more races, non-Hispanic/Latino). Average age 26. In 2011, 2 master's, 20 doctorates awarded. *Degree requirements:* For master's, comprehensive exam, thesis or alternative. *Entrance requirements:* Additional exam requirements/recommendations for international students: Required—TOEFL. *Application deadline:* For fall admission, 3/1 for domestic students. Application fee: $50 ($125 for international students). *Expenses:* Contact institution. *Financial support:* Application deadline: 8/1. *Unit head:* Dr. Teresa Steffen, Director, 262-243-4280, E-mail: teresa.steffen@cuw.edu. *Application contact:* Mary

Eberhardt, Graduate Admissions, 262-243-4551, Fax: 262-243-4428, E-mail: mary.eberhardt@cuw.edu.

Creighton University, School of Pharmacy and Health Professions, Program in Physical Therapy, Omaha, NE 68178-0001. Offers DPT. *Accreditation:* APTA. *Entrance requirements:* For doctorate, GRE. Electronic applications accepted. *Expenses: Tuition:* Full-time $12,672; part-time $704 per credit hour. *Required fees:* $1410; $136 per semester. Tuition and fees vary according to campus/location and reciprocity agreements. *Faculty research:* Patient safety in health services research, health information technology and health services research, Parkinson's rigidity and rehabilitation sciences, prion disease transmission, outcomes research in the rehabilitation sciences.

Daemen College, Department of Physical Therapy, Amherst, NY 14226-3592. Offers orthopedic manual physical therapy (Advanced Certificate); physical therapy-direct entry (DPT); transitional (DPT). *Accreditation:* APTA. Part-time programs available. *Degree requirements:* For doctorate, minimum C grade in all coursework; for Advanced Certificate, minimum GPA of 3.0; degree completion in maximum of 3 years. *Entrance requirements:* For doctorate, baccalaureate degree with minimum GPA of 2.8 in science coursework; letter of intent; resume; 2 letters of reference; 120 hours of PT exposure; transcripts; for Advanced Certificate, BS/BA; license to practice physical therapy; current registration; 2 recommendations; letter of intent; 2 years of physical therapy experience. Additional exam requirements/recommendations for international students: Required—TOEFL (minimum score 500 paper-based; 173 computer-based; 63 iBT), IELTS (minimum score 5.5). Electronic applications accepted. *Faculty research:* Athletic injuries, myofacial pain syndrome, electrical stimulation and tissue healing, lumbar spine dysfunction, temporomandibular joint syndrome.

Dalhousie University, Faculty of Health Professions, School of Physiotherapy, Halifax, NS B3H 3J5, Canada. Offers physiotherapy (entry to profession) (M Sc); physiotherapy (rehabilitation research) (M Sc). *Entrance requirements:* Additional exam requirements/recommendations for international students: Required—TOEFL, IELTS, CANTEST, CAEL, or Michigan English Language Assessment Battery. Electronic applications accepted.

Des Moines University, College of Health Sciences, Program in Physical Therapy, Des Moines, IA 50312-4104. Offers DPT. *Accreditation:* APTA. *Entrance requirements:* For doctorate, GRE. Additional exam requirements/recommendations for international students: Required—TOEFL. Electronic applications accepted. *Expenses:* Contact institution.

Dominican College, Division of Allied Health, Department of Physical Therapy, Orangeburg, NY 10962-1210. Offers MS, DPT. *Accreditation:* APTA. Part-time and evening/weekend programs available. *Degree requirements:* For master's, 3 clinical affiliations. *Entrance requirements:* For master's, minimum GPA of 3.0. Additional exam requirements/recommendations for international students: Required—TOEFL (minimum score 550 paper-based; 213 computer-based).

Drexel University, College of Nursing and Health Professions, Department of Physical Therapy and Rehabilitation Sciences, Philadelphia, PA 19102. Offers clinical biomechanics and orthopedics (PhD); hand and upper quarter rehabilitation (Certificate); hand therapy (MHS, PPDPT); orthopedics (MHS, PPDPT); pediatric rehabilitation (Certificate); pediatrics (MHS, PPDPT, PhD); physical therapy (DPT). *Accreditation:* APTA. Part-time programs available. Terminal master's awarded for partial completion of doctoral program. *Degree requirements:* For master's, comprehensive exam; for doctorate, thesis/dissertation, qualifying exam. *Entrance requirements:* For master's and doctorate, GRE General Test. Additional exam requirements/recommendations for international students: Required—TOEFL. Electronic applications accepted. *Faculty research:* Cerebral palsy, chronic low back pain, shoulder dysfunction, early intervention/community programs.

Duke University, School of Medicine, Physical Therapy Division, Durham, NC 27708. Offers DPT. *Accreditation:* APTA. *Faculty:* 17 full-time (9 women), 22 part-time/adjunct (14 women). *Students:* 199 full-time (163 women); includes 25 minority (4 Black or African American, non-Hispanic/Latino; 12 Asian, non-Hispanic/Latino; 9 Hispanic/Latino). 501 applicants, 24% accepted, 66 enrolled. In 2011, 54 doctorates awarded. *Degree requirements:* For doctorate, comprehensive exam, scholarly project. *Entrance requirements:* For doctorate, GRE, previous course work in anatomy, physiology, biological sciences, chemistry, physics, psychology, and statistics. Additional exam requirements/recommendations for international students: Required—TOEFL. *Application deadline:* For fall admission, 12/1 priority date for domestic students, 12/1 for international students. Applications are processed on a rolling basis. Application fee: $0. Electronic applications accepted. *Expenses:* Contact institution. *Financial support:* Fellowships, research assistantships, teaching assistantships, and Federal Work-Study available. Financial award application deadline: 5/1; financial award applicants required to submit FAFSA. *Faculty research:* Geriatrics, visual plasticity, educational outcomes, orthopaedics, neurology. *Unit head:* Dr. Michel D. Landry, Chief, 919-613-4520, Fax: 919-684-1846, E-mail: mike.landry@duke.edu. *Application contact:* Anita Aiken, Admissions Coordinator, 919-668-5206, Fax: 919-688-3024, E-mail: anita.aiken@duke.edu. Web site: http://ptot.duhs.duke.edu/modules/ptot_mission/index.php?id=1.

Duquesne University, John G. Rangos, Sr. School of Health Sciences, Pittsburgh, PA 15282-0001. Offers health management systems (MHMS); occupational therapy (MS); physical therapy (DPT); physician assistant studies (MPAS); rehabilitation science (MS, PhD); speech-language pathology (MS); MBA/MHMS. *Accreditation:* AOTA (one or more programs are accredited); APTA (one or more programs are accredited); ASHA. *Faculty:* 34 full-time (23 women), 20 part-time/adjunct (11 women). *Students:* 227 full-time (180 women), 12 part-time (7 women); includes 8 minority (4 Black or African American, non-Hispanic/Latino; 1 Asian, non-Hispanic/Latino; 1 Hispanic/Latino; 1 Native Hawaiian or other Pacific Islander, non-Hispanic/Latino; 1 Two or more races, non-Hispanic/Latino), 3 international. Average age 24. 537 applicants, 12% accepted, 17 enrolled. In 2011, 43 master's, 31 doctorates awarded. *Degree requirements:* For doctorate, comprehensive exam (for some programs), thesis/dissertation (for some programs). *Entrance requirements:* For master's, GRE General Test (speech-language pathology), 3 letters of recommendation; minimum GPA of 2.75 (health management systems), 3.0 (speech-language pathology and health sciences); for doctorate, GRE General Test (for physical therapy and rehabilitation science), 3 letters of recommendation, minimum GPA of 3.0, personal interview. Additional exam requirements/recommendations for international students: Required—TOEFL (minimum score 550 paper-based; 233 computer-based; 90 iBT). *Application deadline:* Applications are processed on a rolling basis. Electronic applications accepted. *Expenses:* Contact institution. *Financial support:* Federal Work-Study available. Financial award applicants required to submit FAFSA. *Faculty research:* Neuronal processing, electrical stimulation on peripheral neuropathy, CNS stimulatory and inhibitory signals, behavioral genetic methodologies to development disorders of speech, neurogenic communication disorders. *Total annual research expenditures:* $83,650. *Unit head:* Dr. Gregory H. Frazer, Dean, 412-396-5303, Fax: 412-396-5554, E-mail: frazer@duq.edu. *Application contact:* Christopher R. Hilf, Recruiter/Academic Advisor, 412-396-5653, Fax: 412-396-5554, E-mail: hilfc@duq.edu. Web site: http://www.duq.edu/healthsciences/health.html.

D'Youville College, Department of Physical Therapy, Buffalo, NY 14201-1084. Offers advanced orthopedic physical therapy (Certificate); manual physical therapy (Certificate); physical therapy (MPT, MS, DPT). *Accreditation:* APTA. Part-time programs available. Postbaccalaureate distance learning degree programs offered (minimal on-campus study). *Faculty:* 7 full-time (4 women), 4 part-time/adjunct (3 women). *Students:* 144 full-time (69 women), 21 part-time (7 women); includes 15 minority (7 Black or African American, non-Hispanic/Latino; 5 Asian, non-Hispanic/Latino; 2 Hispanic/Latino; 1 Two or more races, non-Hispanic/Latino), 49 international. Average age 25. 209 applicants, 42% accepted, 55 enrolled. In 2011, 42 doctorates awarded. *Degree requirements:* For master's and doctorate, comprehensive exam, project or thesis. *Entrance requirements:* For doctorate, bachelor's degree, minimum GPA of 3.0. Additional exam requirements/recommendations for international students: Required—TOEFL (minimum score 500 paper-based; 173 computer-based). *Application deadline:* For fall admission, 5/1 for international students; for spring admission, 9/1 for international students. Applications are processed on a rolling basis. Application fee: $25. Electronic applications accepted. *Expenses: Tuition:* Full-time $18,960; part-time $790 per credit hour. *Required fees:* $310. Tuition and fees vary according to degree level and program. *Financial support:* In 2011–12, 3 research assistantships with partial tuition reimbursements were awarded; Federal Work-Study and scholarships/grants also available. Financial award application deadline: 3/1; financial award applicants required to submit FAFSA. *Faculty research:* Therapeutic effects of Tai Chi, selected topics in orthopedics, health promotion in Type 2 diabetes, athletic performance in youth and college sports, behavioral determinants in childhood obesity. *Total annual research expenditures:* $4,000. *Unit head:* Dr. Lynn Rivers, Chair, 716-829-7708 Ext. 7708, Fax: 716-829-8137, E-mail: riversl@dyc.edu. *Application contact:* Linda Fisher, Graduate Admissions Director, 716-829-8400, Fax: 716-829-7900, E-mail: graduateadmissions@dyc.edu.

East Carolina University, Graduate School, School of Allied Health Sciences, Department of Physical Therapy, Greenville, NC 27858-4353. Offers DPT. *Accreditation:* APTA. *Entrance requirements:* Additional exam requirements/recommendations for international students: Required—TOEFL. *Application deadline:* For fall admission, 1/15 for domestic students. Application fee: $50. *Expenses:* Tuition, state resident: full-time $3557; part-time $444.63 per semester hour. Tuition, nonresident: full-time $14,351; part-time $1793.88 per semester hour. *Required fees:* $2016; $252 per semester hour. Part-time tuition and fees vary according to course load, campus/location and program. *Financial support:* Application deadline: 6/1. *Faculty research:* Diabetes and obesity, diabetic foot, ACL injury. *Unit head:* Dr. Walter L. Jenkins, Chair, 252-744-6234, E-mail: jenkinsw@ecu.edu. *Application contact:* Dean of Graduate School, 252-328-6012, Fax: 252-328-6071, E-mail: gradschool@ecu.edu.

Eastern Washington University, Graduate Studies, College of Science, Health and Engineering, Department of Physical Therapy, Cheney, WA 99004-2431. Offers DPT. *Accreditation:* APTA. *Faculty:* 5 full-time (2 women). *Students:* 117 full-time (71 women), 1 (woman) part-time; includes 5 minority (1 American Indian or Alaska Native, non-Hispanic/Latino; 1 Asian, non-Hispanic/Latino; 3 Hispanic/Latino). Average age 26. 369 applicants, 10% accepted, 38 enrolled. In 2011, 37 doctorates awarded. *Degree requirements:* For doctorate, comprehensive exam, thesis/dissertation or final project. *Entrance requirements:* For doctorate, GRE General Test, minimum GPA of 3.0, 75 hours of experience, 3 letters of recommendation. Application fee: $75. *Financial support:* In 2011–12, 6 teaching assistantships were awarded; career-related internships or fieldwork, Federal Work-Study, institutionally sponsored loans, scholarships/grants, health care benefits, tuition waivers (partial), and unspecified assistantships also available. Support available to part-time students. Financial award application deadline: 2/1; financial award applicants required to submit FAFSA. *Unit head:* Dr. Byron Russell, Chair, 509-368-6608, Fax: 509-623-4321. *Application contact:* Prof. Meryl Gersh, Director of Admissions, 509-623-4302.

East Tennessee State University, School of Graduate Studies, College of Clinical and Rehabilitative Health Sciences, Department of Physical Therapy, Johnson City, TN 37614. Offers DPT. Program begins in spring semesters only. *Accreditation:* APTA. *Faculty:* 7 full-time (4 women). *Students:* 94 full-time (55 women); includes 3 minority (2 Black or African American, non-Hispanic/Latino; 1 Hispanic/Latino). Average age 26. In 2011, 29 doctorates awarded. *Degree requirements:* For doctorate, comprehensive exam, internship. *Entrance requirements:* For doctorate, GRE General Test, minimum GPA of 3.0. Additional exam requirements/recommendations for international students: Required—TOEFL (minimum score 550 paper-based; 213 computer-based; 79 iBT). *Application deadline:* For spring admission, 7/1 for domestic and international students. Application fee: $35 ($45 for international students). Electronic applications accepted. *Expenses:* Tuition, state resident: full-time $7312; part-time $350 per credit hour. Tuition, nonresident: full-time $18,490; part-time $621 per credit hour. *Required fees:* $63 per credit hour. Tuition and fees vary according to course load and program. *Financial support:* In 2011–12, 10 students received support, including 2 research assistantships with partial tuition reimbursements available (averaging $3,000 per year); career-related internships or fieldwork, institutionally sponsored loans, scholarships/grants, and unspecified assistantships also available. Financial award application deadline: 7/1; financial award applicants required to submit FAFSA. *Faculty research:* Diabetes, pulmonary disease, wound care, adult developmental delay, vestibular dysfunction, musculoskeletal dysfunction, educational technology. *Unit head:* Dr. David Arnall, Chair, 423-439-8793, Fax: 423-439-8077, E-mail: arnall@etsu.edu. *Application contact:* Mary Duncan, Graduate Specialist, 423-439-4302, Fax: 423-439-5624, E-mail: duncanm@etsu.edu.

Elon University, Program in Physical Therapy, Elon, NC 27244-2010. Offers DPT. *Accreditation:* APTA. *Faculty:* 13 full-time (9 women), 7 part-time/adjunct (4 women). *Students:* 115 full-time (80 women); includes 6 minority (1 Black or African American, non-Hispanic/Latino; 2 American Indian or Alaska Native, non-Hispanic/Latino; 1 Asian, non-Hispanic/Latino; 2 Hispanic/Latino). Average age 25. 655 applicants, 18% accepted, 50 enrolled. In 2011, 33 doctorates awarded. *Entrance requirements:* For doctorate, GRE General Test. Additional exam requirements/recommendations for international students: Required—TOEFL (minimum score 550 paper-based; 213 computer-based; 79 iBT). *Application deadline:* For winter admission, 12/1 priority date for domestic students. Applications are processed on a rolling basis. Application fee: $50. Electronic applications accepted. *Expenses:* Contact institution. *Financial support:* In 2011–12, 20 students received support. Federal Work-Study and scholarships/grants available. Financial award application deadline: 10/1; financial award applicants required to submit FAFSA. *Faculty research:* Exercise readiness in female survivors of domestic violence, animal-assisted therapy, locomotor training for multiple sclerosis patients, effect of infant positioning on the attainment of gross motor skills, physical activity levels for methadone maintenance treatment patients. *Unit head:* Dr. Elizabeth A. Rogers, Chair, 336-278-6400, Fax: 336-278-6414, E-mail: rogers@elon.edu. *Application contact:* Art Fadde, Director of Graduate Admissions, 800-334-8448 Ext. 3, Fax: 336-278-7699, E-mail: afadde@elon.edu. Web site: http://www.elon.edu/dpt/.

Emory University, School of Medicine, Programs in Allied Health Professions, Physical Therapy Program, Atlanta, GA 30322-1100. Offers DPT. *Accreditation:* APTA. *Faculty:* 15 full-time (10 women), 9 part-time/adjunct (7 women). *Students:* 179 full-time (126 women); includes 42 minority (20 Black or African American, non-Hispanic/Latino; 12

Asian, non-Hispanic/Latino; 5 Hispanic/Latino; 5 Two or more races, non-Hispanic/Latino), 3 international. Average age 25. 473 applicants, 28% accepted, 66 enrolled. In 2011, 41 doctorates awarded. *Entrance requirements:* For doctorate, GRE General Test. Additional exam requirements/recommendations for international students: Recommended—TOEFL. *Application deadline:* For fall admission, 10/1 priority date for domestic students, 10/1 for international students. Applications are processed on a rolling basis. Application fee: $60. Electronic applications accepted. *Expenses:* Contact institution. *Financial support:* In 2011–12, 140 students received support. Institutionally sponsored loans and scholarships/grants available. Financial award application deadline: 3/1; financial award applicants required to submit FAFSA. *Faculty research:* Sensorimotor plasticity, biomechanics of walking, qualitative distinctions of moral practice. *Unit head:* Dr. Zoher F. Kapasi, Director, 404-712-5683, Fax: 404-712-4130, E-mail: pt_admissions@learnlink.emory.edu. *Application contact:* Monica George-Komi, Admission Coordinator, 404-712-5657, Fax: 404-712-4130, E-mail: mgeorg2@emory.edu. Web site: http://www.rehabmed.emory.edu/pt/.

Florida Agricultural and Mechanical University, Division of Graduate Studies, Research, and Continuing Education, School of Allied Health Sciences, Division of Physical Therapy, Tallahassee, FL 32307-3200. Offers MPT. *Accreditation:* APTA. *Entrance requirements:* For master's, GRE General Test or GMAT, minimum GPA of 3.0. Additional exam requirements/recommendations for international students: Required—TOEFL.

Florida Gulf Coast University, College of Health Professions, Department of Physical Therapy, Fort Myers, FL 33965-6565. Offers MS, DPT. *Accreditation:* APTA. Part-time programs available. Postbaccalaureate distance learning degree programs offered (minimal on-campus study). *Faculty:* 45 full-time (32 women), 22 part-time/adjunct (14 women). *Students:* 49 full-time (34 women), 25 part-time (14 women); includes 11 minority (1 Black or African American, non-Hispanic/Latino; 2 Asian, non-Hispanic/Latino; 6 Hispanic/Latino; 2 Two or more races, non-Hispanic/Latino). Average age 26. 41 applicants, 68% accepted, 25 enrolled. In 2011, 19 master's awarded. *Degree requirements:* For master's, thesis or alternative. *Entrance requirements:* For master's, GRE General Test or MAT, minimum GPA of 3.0. Additional exam requirements/recommendations for international students: Required—TOEFL (minimum score 550 paper-based; 213 computer-based). *Application deadline:* For fall admission, 1/15 priority date for domestic students. Applications are processed on a rolling basis. Application fee: $30. Electronic applications accepted. *Expenses:* Tuition, state resident: full-time $8289. Tuition, nonresident: full-time $28,895. *Required fees:* $1831. One-time fee: $30 full-time. *Financial support:* Career-related internships or fieldwork, Federal Work-Study, and institutionally sponsored loans available. *Faculty research:* Physical therapy practice and education. *Unit head:* Sharon Bevins, Chair, 239-590-7533, Fax: 239-590-7474, E-mail: sbevins@fgcu.edu. *Application contact:* Lynn O'Hare, Administrative Assistant, 239-590-7451, Fax: 239-590-7474, E-mail: lohare@fgcu.edu.

Florida International University, College of Nursing and Health Sciences, Department of Physical Therapy, Miami, FL 33199. Offers DPT. *Accreditation:* APTA. Part-time programs available. *Degree requirements:* For doctorate, comprehensive exam. *Entrance requirements:* For doctorate, minimum undergraduate GPA of 3.0 in upper-level coursework; letter of intent; resume; at least 40 hours of observation within physical therapy clinic or facility. Additional exam requirements/recommendations for international students: Required—TOEFL (minimum score 550 paper-based; 80 iBT). Electronic applications accepted. *Faculty research:* Isokinetic test results and gait abnormalities after knee arthroscopy.

Franklin Pierce University, Graduate Studies, Rindge, NH 03461-0060. Offers curriculum and instruction (M Ed); emerging network technologies (Graduate Certificate); energy and sustainability studies (MBA); health administration (MBA, Graduate Certificate); human resource management (MBA, Graduate Certificate); information technology (MBA); information technology management (MS); leadership (MBA, DA); nursing (MS); physical therapy (DPT); physician assistant studies (MPAS); special education (M Ed); sports management (MBA). *Accreditation:* APTA. Part-time programs available. Postbaccalaureate distance learning degree programs offered (no on-campus study). *Degree requirements:* For master's, concentrated original research projects; student teaching; fieldwork and/or internship; leadership project; PRAXIS I and II (for M Ed); for doctorate, concentrated original research projects, clinical fieldwork and/or internship, leadership project. *Entrance requirements:* For master's, minimum GPA of 2.5, 3 letters of recommendation; competencies in accounting, economics, statistics, and computer skills through life experience or undergraduate coursework (for MBA); certification/e-portfolio, minimum C grade in all education courses (for M Ed); license to practice as RN (for MS in nursing); for doctorate, GRE, BA/BS, 3 letters of recommendation, personal mission statement, interview, writing sample, minimum cumulative GPA of 2.8, master's degree (for DA); 80 hours of observation/work in PT settings, completion of anatomy, chemistry, physics, and statistics, minimum GPA of 3.0 (for DPT). Additional exam requirements/recommendations for international students: Required—TOEFL (minimum score 550 paper-based; 195 computer-based; 61 iBT). Electronic applications accepted. *Faculty research:* Evidence-based practice in sports physical therapy, human resource management in economic crisis, leadership in nursing, innovation in sports facility management, differentiated learning and understanding by design.

Gannon University, School of Graduate Studies, Morosky College of Health Professions and Sciences, School of Health Professions, Program in Physical Therapy, Erie, PA 16541-0001. Offers DPT. *Accreditation:* APTA. *Students:* 122 full-time (80 women); includes 7 minority (2 Black or African American, non-Hispanic/Latino; 3 Asian, non-Hispanic/Latino; 2 Hispanic/Latino), 3 international. Average age 24. 151 applicants, 60% accepted, 43 enrolled. In 2011, 40 doctorates awarded. *Degree requirements:* For doctorate, thesis/dissertation or alternative, research project. *Entrance requirements:* For doctorate, interview, minimum QPA of 3.0, letters of recommendation. Additional exam requirements/recommendations for international students: Required—TOEFL (minimum score 79 iBT). *Application deadline:* For fall admission, 1/15 for domestic students. Application fee: $50. Electronic applications accepted. *Expenses:* Contact institution. *Financial support:* Federal Work-Study, scholarships/grants, and unspecified assistantships available. Financial award application deadline: 7/1; financial award applicants required to submit FAFSA. *Faculty research:* Service-learning, interprofessional education, physical therapy education, spinal dysfunction, fear of falling. *Unit head:* Dr. Kristine Legters, Chair, 814-871-5641, E-mail: legters001@gannon.edu. *Application contact:* Kara Morgan, Director of Graduate Admissions, 814-871-5831, Fax: 814-871-5827, E-mail: graduate@gannon.edu.

George Fox University, Department of Physical Therapy, Newberg, OR 97132-2697. Offers DPT. *Entrance requirements:* For doctorate, bachelor's degree from regionally-accredited university or college, minimum GPA of 3.0. Additional exam requirements/recommendations for international students: Required—TOEFL, IELTS. *Application deadline:* For fall admission, 12/1 for domestic and international students. Application fee: $40. Electronic applications accepted. *Financial support:* Applicants required to submit FAFSA. *Unit head:* Dr. Tyler Cuddeford, Director/Assistant Professor, 503-554-2452, E-mail: tcuddeford@georgefox.edu. *Application contact:* Patrick Kelley, Admissions Counselor, 503-554-2223, Fax: 503-554-3110, E-mail: dpt@georgefox.edu. Web site: http://www.georgefox.edu/physical-therapy/index.html.

The George Washington University, School of Medicine and Health Sciences, Health Sciences Programs, Program in Physical Therapy, Washington, DC 20052. Offers DPT. *Accreditation:* APTA. *Students:* 103 full-time (75 women); includes 24 minority (4 Black or African American, non-Hispanic/Latino; 1 American Indian or Alaska Native, non-Hispanic/Latino; 10 Asian, non-Hispanic/Latino; 8 Hispanic/Latino; 1 Native Hawaiian or other Pacific Islander, non-Hispanic/Latino), 2 international. Average age 26. 274 applicants, 44% accepted, 36 enrolled. In 2011, 29 doctorates awarded. *Entrance requirements:* Additional exam requirements/recommendations for international students: Required—TOEFL (minimum score 550 paper-based; 213 computer-based). *Application deadline:* For spring admission, 7/31 priority date for domestic students. Applications are processed on a rolling basis. Application fee: $75. *Unit head:* Dr. Margaret Plack, Director, 202-994-7763, E-mail: hspmxp@gwumc.edu. *Application contact:* Marsha White, Information Contact, 202-994-8184, E-mail: hspmkw@gwumc.edu.

Georgia State University, College of Health and Human Sciences, School of Health Professions, Division of Physical Therapy, Atlanta, GA 30302-3083. Offers DPT. *Accreditation:* APTA. *Entrance requirements:* Additional exam requirements/recommendations for international students: Required—TOEFL (minimum score 550 paper-based; 213 computer-based). Electronic applications accepted. *Expenses:* Contact institution. *Faculty research:* Myofacial trigger points, myofacial pain, muscle injury, wellness programs.

Governors State University, College of Health Professions, Program in Physical Therapy, University Park, IL 60484. Offers MPT, DPT. *Accreditation:* APTA. *Students:* 87 full-time (62 women), 9 part-time (6 women); includes 19 minority (6 Black or African American, non-Hispanic/Latino; 2 Asian, non-Hispanic/Latino; 8 Hispanic/Latino; 3 Two or more races, non-Hispanic/Latino), 1 international. Average age 29. *Degree requirements:* For master's, thesis or alternative. *Entrance requirements:* For master's, minimum GPA of 3.0 in field, 2.75 overall. *Application deadline:* For fall admission, 1/31 priority date for domestic students. Application fee: $25. *Financial support:* Application deadline: 5/1. *Unit head:* Dr. Elizabeth Cada, Dean, 708-534-7295.

Graduate School and University Center of the City University of New York, Graduate Studies, Program in Physical Therapy, New York, NY 10016-4039. Offers DPT. Program offered jointly with College of Staten Island of the City University of New York and Hunter College of the City University of New York. *Accreditation:* APTA. *Degree requirements:* For doctorate, exams, publishable research project. *Entrance requirements:* For doctorate, GRE, CPR certification, 100 hours clinical experience, minimum undergraduate GPA of 3.0. Additional exam requirements/recommendations for international students: Required—TOEFL.

Grand Valley State University, College of Health Professions, Physical Therapy Program, Allendale, MI 49401-9403. Offers DPT. *Accreditation:* APTA. *Entrance requirements:* For doctorate, GRE, minimum GPA of 3.0 in most recent 60 hours and in prerequisites, 50 hours of volunteer work, interview, writing sample. Additional exam requirements/recommendations for international students: Required—TOEFL (minimum score 610 paper-based; 253 computer-based). Electronic applications accepted. *Faculty research:* Balance deficits, motion analysis, nutritional knowledge of female athletes, trust in athletic performance, spinal functions dysfunction.

Hampton University, Graduate College, Department of Physical Therapy, Hampton, VA 23668. Offers DPT. *Accreditation:* APTA. *Degree requirements:* For doctorate, thesis/dissertation, oral defense, qualifying exam. *Entrance requirements:* For doctorate, GRE General Test, minimum GPA of 3.0 or master's degree in physics or related field.

Hardin-Simmons University, Graduate School, Holland School of Sciences and Mathematics, Doctoral Program in Physical Therapy, Abilene, TX 79698. Offers DPT. *Accreditation:* APTA. *Faculty:* 8 full-time (4 women), 1 part-time/adjunct (0 women). *Students:* 82 full-time (62 women); includes 7 minority (2 Black or African American, non-Hispanic/Latino; 2 Asian, non-Hispanic/Latino; 3 Hispanic/Latino). Average age 23. 168 applicants, 27% accepted, 28 enrolled. In 2011, 26 doctorates awarded. *Degree requirements:* For doctorate, comprehensive exam, thesis/dissertation or alternative. *Entrance requirements:* For doctorate, GRE, letters of recommendation, interview, writing sample. Additional exam requirements/recommendations for international students: Required—TOEFL (minimum score 550 paper-based; 213 computer-based; 75 iBT). *Application deadline:* For fall admission, 10/1 priority date for domestic students, 10/1 for international students. Application fee: $50 ($100 for international students). *Expenses:* Contact institution. *Financial support:* In 2011–12, 82 students received support. Scholarships/grants available. Financial award application deadline: 3/1; financial award applicants required to submit FAFSA. *Faculty research:* Gait parameters, health promotion for seniors/disabled populations, sports injuries and recovery, spirituality, vibration platforms, sensory integration, postural stability. *Unit head:* Dr. Janelle K. O'Connell, Department Head and Professor, 325-670-5860, Fax: 325-670-5868, E-mail: ptoffice@hsutx.edu. *Application contact:* Dr. Janelle K. O'Connell, Department Head, 325-670-5860, Fax: 325-670-5868, E-mail: ptoffice@hsutx.edu. Web site: http://www.hsutx.edu/academics/holland/graduate/physicaltherapy.

Humboldt State University, Academic Programs, College of Professional Studies, Department of Kinesiology and Recreation Administration, Arcata, CA 95521-8299. Offers athletic training education (MS); exercise science/wellness management (MS); pre-physical therapy (MS); teaching/coaching (MS). *Students:* 11 full-time (7 women), 10 part-time (6 women); includes 4 minority (1 American Indian or Alaska Native, non-Hispanic/Latino; 2 Hispanic/Latino; 1 Two or more races, non-Hispanic/Latino). Average age 28. 9 applicants, 100% accepted, 6 enrolled. In 2011, 7 master's awarded. *Degree requirements:* For master's, thesis or alternative. *Entrance requirements:* For master's, GMAT, minimum GPA of 2.5. Additional exam requirements/recommendations for international students: Required—TOEFL. *Application deadline:* For fall admission, 6/1 for domestic students; for spring admission, 12/2 for domestic students. Applications are processed on a rolling basis. Application fee: $55. *Expenses:* Tuition, state resident: full-time $6734. Tuition, nonresident: full-time $15,662; part-time $372 per credit. *Required fees:* $903. Tuition and fees vary according to program. *Financial support:* Teaching assistantships, career-related internships or fieldwork, Federal Work-Study, and institutionally sponsored loans available. Financial award application deadline: 3/1; financial award applicants required to submit FAFSA. *Faculty research:* Human performance, adapted physical education, physical therapy. *Unit head:* Dr. Chris Hooper, Chair, 707-826-3853, Fax: 707-826-5451, E-mail: cah3@humboldt.edu. *Application contact:* Dr. Rock Braithwaite, Coordinator, 707-826-4543, Fax: 707-826-5451, E-mail: reb22@humboldt.edu. Web site: http://www.humboldt.edu/kra/.

Husson University, School of Graduate and Professional Studies, Doctorate in Physical Therapy Program, Bangor, ME 04401-2999. Offers DPT. *Accreditation:* APTA. *Faculty:* 8 full-time (4 women), 7 part-time/adjunct (4 women). *Students:* 73 full-time (49 women), 11 part-time (6 women); includes 1 minority (Asian, non-Hispanic/Latino). Average age 23. 76 applicants, 58% accepted, 37 enrolled. In 2011, 55 doctorates awarded. *Entrance requirements:* For doctorate, GRE (minimum score of 1500), essay, minimum GPA of 3.0. Additional exam requirements/recommendations for international

students: Required—TOEFL (minimum score 550 paper-based). *Application deadline:* For fall admission, 4/15 for domestic and international students. Application fee: $40. Electronic applications accepted. *Expenses: Tuition:* Full-time $4500; part-time $500 per credit hour. One-time fee: $100. Tuition and fees vary according to class time, degree level and program. *Financial support:* Federal Work-Study and unspecified assistantships available. Financial award application deadline: 4/15; financial award applicants required to submit FAFSA. *Unit head:* Dr. Suzanne Gordon, Director, 207-941-7797, E-mail: gordons@husson.edu. *Application contact:* Cecile Ferguson, Administrative Assistant, 207-941-7101, E-mail: pt@fc.husson.edu.

Idaho State University, Office of Graduate Studies, Kasiska College of Health Professions, Department of Physical and Occupational Therapy, Program in Physical Therapy, Pocatello, ID 83209-8045. Offers DPT. *Accreditation:* APTA. *Degree requirements:* For doctorate, comprehensive exam, thesis/dissertation, oral and written exam. *Entrance requirements:* For doctorate, GRE General Test, minimum GPA of 3.0, 80 hours in 2 practice settings of physical therapy. Additional exam requirements/recommendations for international students: Required—TOEFL (minimum score 600 paper-based; 213 computer-based). Electronic applications accepted. *Expenses:* Contact institution. *Faculty research:* Cardiovascular/pulmonary balance, neural plasticity, orthopedics, geriatrics, hypertension.

Indiana University–Purdue University Indianapolis, School of Health and Rehabilitation Sciences, Indianapolis, IN 46202-2896. Offers health sciences education (MS); nutrition and dietetics (MS); occupational therapy (MS); physical therapy (DPT). Part-time and evening/weekend programs available. *Faculty:* 8 full-time (5 women). *Students:* 197 full-time (162 women), 1 part-time (0 women); includes 13 minority (1 Black or African American, non-Hispanic/Latino; 4 Asian, non-Hispanic/Latino; 2 Hispanic/Latino; 1 Native Hawaiian or other Pacific Islander, non-Hispanic/Latino; 5 Two or more races, non-Hispanic/Latino). Average age 26. 213 applicants, 31% accepted, 62 enrolled. In 2011, 35 master's, 34 doctorates awarded. *Degree requirements:* For master's, thesis (for some programs). *Entrance requirements:* For master's, GRE General Test, minimum GPA of 3.0. Additional exam requirements/recommendations for international students: Required—TOEFL. *Application deadline:* For fall admission, 1/15 priority date for domestic students; for spring admission, 10/15 for domestic students. Application fee: $55 ($65 for international students). *Financial support:* Fellowships, research assistantships, teaching assistantships, Federal Work-Study, institutionally sponsored loans, and scholarships/grants available. Support available to part-time students. Financial award applicants required to submit FAFSA. *Unit head:* Dr. Augustine Agho, Dean, 317-274-4704, E-mail: aagho@iupui.edu. *Application contact:* Dr. Sherry Queener, Director, Graduate Studies and Associate Dean, 317-274-1577, Fax: 317-278-2380. Web site: http://www.shrs.iupui.edu/.

Ithaca College, Division of Graduate and Professional Studies, School of Health Sciences and Human Performance, Program in Physical Therapy, Ithaca, NY 14850. Offers MS, DPT. Students enter the program as freshmen. *Accreditation:* APTA. *Faculty:* 19 full-time (11 women). *Students:* 144 full-time (104 women); includes 14 minority (1 American Indian or Alaska Native, non-Hispanic/Latino; 8 Asian, non-Hispanic/Latino; 2 Hispanic/Latino; 3 Two or more races, non-Hispanic/Latino). Average age 22. In 2011, 92 master's, 88 doctorates awarded. *Degree requirements:* For doctorate, thesis/dissertation optional, clinical internships. *Entrance requirements:* Additional exam requirements/recommendations for international students: Required—TOEFL (minimum score 550 paper-based; 213 computer-based; 80 iBT). *Expenses: Tuition:* Part-time $663 per credit hour. *Required fees:* $663 per credit hour. *Financial support:* In 2011–12, 95 students received support. Career-related internships or fieldwork, Federal Work-Study, and scholarships/grants available. Support available to part-time students. Financial award applicants required to submit CSS PROFILE or FAFSA. *Faculty research:* Expertise and evaluation in clinical education, problem-based learning, needs assessment and faculty development for new faculty in part-time education programs, student's perceptions of professional behavior, pediatric PT. *Unit head:* Dr. Kathy Buccieri, Graduate Chair, 607-274-3143, Fax: 607-274-1263, E-mail: gps@ithaca.edu. *Application contact:* Gerard Turbide, Director, Office of Admission, 607-274-3143, Fax: 607-274-1263, E-mail: gps@ithaca.edu. Web site: http://www.ithaca.edu/gps/gradprograms/programsites/pt.

Langston University, School of Physical Therapy, Langston, OK 73050. Offers DPT. *Accreditation:* APTA.

Lebanon Valley College, Physical Therapy Department, Annville, PA 17003-1400. Offers DPT. *Accreditation:* APTA. *Faculty:* 8 full-time (3 women). *Students:* 59 full-time (16 women). In 2011, 28 doctorates awarded. Application fee: $30. Electronic applications accepted. *Expenses: Tuition:* Full-time $35,720; part-time $465 per credit. *Required fees:* $610. Part-time tuition and fees vary according to program. *Financial support:* Scholarships/grants available. Financial award application deadline: 5/1; financial award applicants required to submit FAFSA. *Unit head:* Dr. Stan M. Dacko, Chairperson/Associate Professor, 717-867-6843, Fax: 717-867-6849, E-mail: dacko@lvc.edu. *Application contact:* E. J. Smith, Admission Counselor, 866-582-4236, Fax: 717-867-6026, E-mail: ejsmith@lvc.edu. Web site: http://www.lvc.edu/physical-therapy/index.aspx?bhiw-952.

Loma Linda University, School of Allied Health Professions, Department of Physical Therapy, Loma Linda, CA 92350. Offers MPT, D Sc, DPT, DPTSc. *Accreditation:* APTA. *Entrance requirements:* Additional exam requirements/recommendations for international students: Required—TOEFL (minimum score 550 paper-based; 213 computer-based). Electronic applications accepted.

Long Island University–Brooklyn Campus, School of Health Professions, Division of Physical Therapy, Brooklyn, NY 11201-8423. Offers DPT, TDPT. *Accreditation:* APTA. Part-time and evening/weekend programs available. *Entrance requirements:* Additional exam requirements/recommendations for international students: Required—TOEFL (minimum score 500 paper-based; 173 computer-based). Electronic applications accepted.

Louisiana State University Health Sciences Center, School of Allied Health Professions, Department of Physical Therapy, New Orleans, LA 70112-2223. Offers DPT. *Accreditation:* APTA. *Degree requirements:* For doctorate, thesis/dissertation optional. *Entrance requirements:* For doctorate, GRE General Test (minimum combined score: 900), 60 hours of experience in physical therapy, minimum GPA of 3.0 in bachelor's degree, 3 recommendation letters. *Faculty research:* Wound healing, spinal cord injury, pain management, geriatrics, muscle physiology, muscle damage, motor control, balance.

Lynchburg College, Graduate Studies, School of Health Sciences and Human Performance, Doctor of Physical Therapy Program, Lynchburg, VA 24501-3199. Offers DPT. *Faculty:* 9 full-time (5 women), 2 part-time/adjunct (1 woman). *Students:* 102 full-time (72 women); includes 9 minority (5 Black or African American, non-Hispanic/Latino; 2 Asian, non-Hispanic/Latino; 1 Hispanic/Latino; 1 Two or more races, non-Hispanic/Latino). Average age 25. 556 applicants, 17% accepted, 31 enrolled. *Degree requirements:* For doctorate, comprehensive exam. *Entrance requirements:* For doctorate, GRE, graduation from a 4-year program, observation hours, references, bachelor's degree. Additional exam requirements/recommendations for international students: Required—TOEFL (minimum score 89 computer-based). *Application deadline:* For spring admission, 2/1 priority date for domestic students, 2/1 for international students. Applications are processed on a rolling basis. Application fee: $135. Electronic applications accepted. *Expenses:* Contact institution. *Financial support:* Scholarships/grants, tuition waivers (partial), and unspecified assistantships available. Financial award application deadline: 7/31; financial award applicants required to submit FAFSA. *Unit head:* Dr. A. Russell Smith, Jr., Associate Professor/Director of DPT Program, 434-544-8880, E-mail: smith.ar@lynchburg.edu. *Application contact:* Savannah G. Cook, Admissions Coordinator, 434-544-8885, Fax: 434-544-8887, E-mail: cook.s@lynchburg.edu. Web site: http://www.lynchburg.edu/dpt.xml.

Marquette University, Graduate School, College of Health Sciences, Department of Physical Therapy, Milwaukee, WI 53201-1881. Offers clinical and translational rehabilitation science (MS, PhD); physical therapy (DPT). *Accreditation:* APTA. *Faculty:* 12 full-time (6 women), 31 part-time/adjunct (23 women). *Students:* 98 full-time (80 women), 2 part-time (1 woman); includes 14 minority (1 Black or African American, non-Hispanic/Latino; 5 Asian, non-Hispanic/Latino; 7 Hispanic/Latino; 1 Two or more races, non-Hispanic/Latino). Average age 24. 99 applicants, 34% accepted, 18 enrolled. In 2011, 56 doctorates awarded. *Degree requirements:* For doctorate, clinical rotations. *Entrance requirements:* For doctorate, GRE General Test. Additional exam requirements/recommendations for international students: Required—TOEFL. Application fee: $50. Electronic applications accepted. *Expenses:* Contact institution. *Financial support:* In 2011–12, 2 students received support, including 2 research assistantships with full tuition reimbursements available (averaging $21,750 per year); health care benefits and unspecified assistantships also available. Financial award application deadline: 2/15. *Faculty research:* Urban health issues, mechanisms and management of pain, kinesiologic principles, brain and spinal cord control of human locomotion, mechanisms of motor impairment. *Total annual research expenditures:* $377,810. *Unit head:* Dr. Lawrence Pan, Dean, 414-288-7161, Fax: 414-288-5987, E-mail: lawrence.pan@marquette.edu. *Application contact:* Craig Pierce, Assistant Dean of the Graduate School, 414-288-5740, Fax: 414-288-1902, E-mail: craig.pierce@marquette.edu. Web site: http://www.marquette.edu/chs/pt/.

Marshall University, Academic Affairs Division, College of Health Professions, School of Physical Therapy, Huntington, WV 25755. Offers DPT.

Marymount University, School of Health Professions, Program in Physical Therapy, Arlington, VA 22207-4299. Offers DPT. *Accreditation:* APTA. *Faculty:* 7 full-time (6 women), 13 part-time/adjunct (8 women). *Students:* 98 full-time (65 women); includes 18 minority (5 Black or African American, non-Hispanic/Latino; 8 Asian, non-Hispanic/Latino; 5 Hispanic/Latino), 4 international. Average age 26. 400 applicants, 36% accepted, 35 enrolled. In 2011, 24 doctorates awarded. *Degree requirements:* For doctorate, comprehensive exam, thesis/dissertation. *Entrance requirements:* For doctorate, GRE, 2 letters of recommendation, interview, resume, 40 hours of clinical work experience, essay, minimum GPA of 3.0 from previous university coursework. Additional exam requirements/recommendations for international students: Required—TOEFL (minimum score 600 paper-based; 250 computer-based; 96 iBT), IELTS (minimum score 6.5). *Application deadline:* For fall admission, 12/13 priority date for domestic students, 12/15 for international students. Application fee: $180. Electronic applications accepted. *Expenses:* Contact institution. *Financial support:* In 2011–12, 11 students received support. Research assistantships with full tuition reimbursements available, career-related internships or fieldwork, Federal Work-Study, scholarships/grants, and unspecified assistantships available. Financial award applicants required to submit FAFSA. *Unit head:* Dr. Rita Wong, Chair, 703-284-5982, Fax: 703-284-5981, E-mail: rita.wong@marymount.edu. *Application contact:* Francesca Reed, Director, Graduate Admissions, 703-284-5901, Fax: 703-527-3815, E-mail: grad.admissions@marymount.edu. Web site: http://www.marymount.edu/academics/programs/physicalTherapy.

Maryville University of Saint Louis, School of Health Professions, Physical Therapy Program, St. Louis, MO 63141-7299. Offers DPT. *Accreditation:* APTA. *Students:* 73 full-time (60 women), 40 part-time (28 women); includes 2 minority (1 Black or African American, non-Hispanic/Latino; 1 Hispanic/Latino). Average age 24. *Degree requirements:* For doctorate, clinical rotations. *Entrance requirements:* For doctorate, minimum cumulative GPA of 3.0, 2 letters of recommendation, interview. Additional exam requirements/recommendations for international students: Required—TOEFL (minimum score 560 paper-based). *Application deadline:* Applications are processed on a rolling basis. Application fee: $40 ($60 for international students). Electronic applications accepted. *Expenses: Tuition:* Full-time $21,922; part-time $675 per credit hour. *Required fees:* $233.75 per semester. *Financial support:* Career-related internships or fieldwork, Federal Work-Study, and campus employment available. Financial award application deadline: 3/1; financial award applicants required to submit FAFSA. *Faculty research:* Memory and exercise. *Unit head:* Dr. Michelle Unterberg, Director, 314-529-9590, Fax: 314-529-9946, E-mail: munterberg@maryville.edu. *Application contact:* Dr. Donna Payne, 314-529-9676, Fax: 314-529-9927, E-mail: dpayne@maryville.edu. Web site: http://www.maryville.edu/hp/physical-therapy/.

Mayo School of Health Sciences, Program in Physical Therapy, Rochester, MN 55905. Offers DPT. *Accreditation:* APTA. *Faculty:* 5 full-time (0 women), 3 part-time/adjunct (all women). *Students:* 86 full-time (65 women); includes 7 minority (2 Black or African American, non-Hispanic/Latino; 1 American Indian or Alaska Native, non-Hispanic/Latino; 3 Asian, non-Hispanic/Latino; 1 Hispanic/Latino). Average age 25. 560 applicants, 8% accepted, 28 enrolled. In 2011, 26 degrees awarded. *Median time to degree:* Of those who began their doctoral program in fall 2003, 100% received their degree in 8 years or less. *Degree requirements:* For doctorate, comprehensive exam. *Entrance requirements:* For doctorate, GRE. Additional exam requirements/recommendations for international students: Required—TOEFL. *Application deadline:* For fall admission, 11/1 for domestic and international students. Applications are processed on a rolling basis. Electronic applications accepted. *Expenses: Tuition:* Full-time $20,485. Full-time tuition and fees vary according to degree level and program. *Financial support:* In 2011–12, 74 students received support. Scholarships/grants available. Financial award applicants required to submit FAFSA. *Faculty research:* Biomechanics, gait analysis, growth factor-mediated plasticity in muscle, musculoskeletal clinical tests and measures, Parkinson's disease, coordination testing. *Unit head:* Dr. John Hollman, Director, 507-284-9547, Fax: 507-284-0656, E-mail: hollman.john@mayo.edu. *Application contact:* Carol Cooper, Secretary, 507-284-2054, Fax: 507-284-0656, E-mail: cooper.carol@mayo.edu. Web site: http://www.mayo.edu/mshs/pt-ptmp-rch.html.

McMaster University, Faculty of Health Sciences, Professional Program in Physiotherapy, Hamilton, ON L8S 4M2, Canada. Offers M Sc. *Degree requirements:* For master's, clinical placements, independent research project. *Entrance requirements:* For master's, minimum B average over last 60 undergraduate units. Additional exam requirements/recommendations for international students: Required—TOEFL (minimum score 600 paper-based; 250 computer-based).

Medical University of South Carolina, College of Health Professions, Department of Health Professions, Program in Physical Therapy, Charleston, SC 29425. Offers DPT. *Accreditation:* APTA. Postbaccalaureate distance learning degree programs offered (minimal on-campus study). *Faculty:* 7 full-time (4 women), 4 part-time/adjunct (3 women). *Students:* 189 full-time (141 women); includes 12 minority (4 Black or African

American, non-Hispanic/Latino; 2 American Indian or Alaska Native, non-Hispanic/Latino; 4 Asian, non-Hispanic/Latino; 2 Hispanic/Latino), 1 international. Average age 25. 309 applicants, 37% accepted, 65 enrolled. In 2011, 55 doctorates awarded. *Entrance requirements:* For doctorate, GRE, references, minimum GPA of 3.0, volunteer hours. Additional exam requirements/recommendations for international students: Required—TOEFL (minimum score 600 paper-based; 250 computer-based). *Application deadline:* For fall admission, 1/15 priority date for domestic students, 1/15 for international students. Application fee: $85. Electronic applications accepted. *Financial support:* Federal Work-Study and scholarships/grants available. Support available to part-time students. Financial award application deadline: 3/10; financial award applicants required to submit FAFSA. *Faculty research:* Low back pain, spinal cord injury. *Total annual research expenditures:* $58,231. *Unit head:* Dr. David Morrisette, Interim Program Director, 843-792-2940, Fax: 843-792-0710, E-mail: morrisdc@musc.edu. *Application contact:* Susan Johnson, Student Services Program Coordinator, 843-792-5377, Fax: 843-792-0710, E-mail: johnsoss@musc.edu. Web site: http://www.musc.edu/chp/pt/index.htm.

Mercy College, School of Health and Natural Sciences, Program in Physical Therapy, Dobbs Ferry, NY 10522-1189. Offers DPT. *Accreditation:* APTA. Evening/weekend programs available. *Entrance requirements:* For doctorate, interview, two letters of reference, official college transcripts, minimum GPA of 3.0, two-page typewritten essay on reasons for pursuing career in physical therapy, volunteer/work experience forms demonstrating at least eighty hours of volunteer work or work-related experience. Additional exam requirements/recommendations for international students: Required—TOEFL (minimum score 600 paper-based; 250 computer-based; 100 iBT), IELTS (minimum score 8). Electronic applications accepted. *Expenses:* Contact institution.

MGH Institute of Health Professions, School of Health and Rehabilitation Sciences, Post-Professional Graduate Program in Physical Therapy, Boston, MA 02129. Offers MS, DPT, Certificate. Part-time and evening/weekend programs available. *Faculty:* 14 full-time (11 women), 6 part-time/adjunct (all women). *Students:* 16 full-time (14 women), 82 part-time (64 women); includes 45 minority (2 Black or African American, non-Hispanic/Latino; 41 Asian, non-Hispanic/Latino; 2 Hispanic/Latino). Average age 35. 144 applicants, 81% accepted, 53 enrolled. In 2011, 42 master's, 58 doctorates, 5 other advanced degrees awarded. *Degree requirements:* For master's, thesis, clinical preceptorship. *Entrance requirements:* For master's, GRE General Test, graduation from an approved program in physical therapy. Additional exam requirements/recommendations for international students: Required—TOEFL (minimum score 550 paper-based; 213 computer-based; 80 iBT). *Application deadline:* For fall admission, 3/1 priority date for domestic students, 3/1 for international students; for winter admission, 7/1 priority date for domestic students, 7/1 for international students; for spring admission, 11/1 priority date for domestic students, 11/1 for international students. Applications are processed on a rolling basis. Application fee: $65. Electronic applications accepted. *Expenses: Tuition:* Full-time $12,720; part-time $1060 per credit. *Required fees:* $1725; $430 per semester. One-time fee: $350. *Financial support:* In 2011–12, 4 students received support. Career-related internships or fieldwork, scholarships/grants, and unspecified assistantships available. Support available to part-time students. Financial award application deadline: 4/1; financial award applicants required to submit FAFSA. *Faculty research:* Disability in the elderly; gait, balance and posture; cardiac rehabilitation; relationship of impairment to disability; effect of muscle strengthening in the elderly. *Unit head:* Dr. Leslie G. Portney, Interim Dean/Department Chair, 617-726-3170, Fax: 617-724-6321, E-mail: lportney@mghihp.edu. *Application contact:* Maureen Rika Judd, Director of Admissions, 617-726-6069, Fax: 617-726-8010, E-mail: admissions@mghihp.edu. Web site: http://www.mghihp.edu/academics/school-of-health-and-rehabilitation-sciences/.

MGH Institute of Health Professions, School of Health and Rehabilitation Sciences, Professional Graduate Program in Physical Therapy, Boston, MA 02129. Offers DPT. *Accreditation:* APTA. *Faculty:* 14 full-time (11 women), 6 part-time/adjunct (all women). *Students:* 108 full-time (81 women), 58 part-time (45 women); includes 23 minority (2 Black or African American, non-Hispanic/Latino; 1 American Indian or Alaska Native, non-Hispanic/Latino; 17 Asian, non-Hispanic/Latino; 2 Hispanic/Latino; 1 Native Hawaiian or other Pacific Islander, non-Hispanic/Latino). Average age 26. 450 applicants, 23% accepted, 59 enrolled. In 2011, 95 degrees awarded. *Degree requirements:* For doctorate, thesis/dissertation or alternative, research project. *Entrance requirements:* For doctorate, GRE General Test, interview, minimum of 10 physical therapy observation hours, bachelor's degree from regionally-accredited college or university. Additional exam requirements/recommendations for international students: Required—TOEFL (minimum score 550 paper-based; 213 computer-based; 80 iBT). *Application deadline:* For spring admission, 10/15 for domestic students, 11/15 for international students. Application fee: $0. Electronic applications accepted. *Expenses: Tuition:* Full-time $12,720; part-time $1060 per credit. *Required fees:* $1725; $430 per semester. One-time fee: $350. *Financial support:* In 2011–12, 36 students received support, including 4 research assistantships, 9 teaching assistantships; career-related internships or fieldwork, scholarships/grants, and unspecified assistantships also available. Support available to part-time students. Financial award application deadline: 4/1; financial award applicants required to submit FAFSA. *Faculty research:* Disability in the elderly; gait, balance, and posture; cardiac rehabilitation: relationship of impairment to disability. *Unit head:* Dr. Leslie G. Portney, Director, 617-726-3170, Fax: 617-724-6321, E-mail: lportney@mghihp.edu. *Application contact:* Maureen Rika Judd, Director of Admissions, 617-726-6069, Fax: 617-726-8010, E-mail: admissions@mghihp.edu. Web site: http://www.mghihp.edu/academics/school-of-health-and-rehabilitation-sciences/.

Midwestern University, Downers Grove Campus, College of Health Sciences, Illinois Campus, Program in Physical Therapy, Downers Grove, IL 60515-1235. Offers DPT. *Accreditation:* APTA. *Faculty:* 10 full-time (7 women). *Students:* 138 full-time (93 women); includes 13 minority (1 American Indian or Alaska Native, non-Hispanic/Latino; 4 Asian, non-Hispanic/Latino; 2 Hispanic/Latino; 1 Native Hawaiian or other Pacific Islander, non-Hispanic/Latino; 5 Two or more races, non-Hispanic/Latino). Average age 25. 1,024 applicants, 14% accepted, 48 enrolled. In 2011, 28 doctorates awarded. *Entrance requirements:* For doctorate, GRE General Test. *Application deadline:* Applications are processed on a rolling basis. Application fee: $50. *Expenses:* Contact institution. *Financial support:* In 2011–12, 87 students received support. Federal Work-Study available. *Unit head:* Donna Cech, Director, 630-515-7221, E-mail: dcechx@midwestern.edu. *Application contact:* Michael Laken, Director of Admissions, 630-515-6171, Fax: 630-971-6086, E-mail: admissil@midwestern.edu. Web site: http://www.midwestern.edu/.

Midwestern University, Glendale Campus, College of Health Sciences, Arizona Campus, Program in Physical Therapy, Glendale, AZ 85308. Offers DPT. *Students:* 95 full-time (53 women), 1 part-time (0 women); includes 16 minority (2 Black or African American, non-Hispanic/Latino; 2 Asian, non-Hispanic/Latino; 8 Hispanic/Latino; 1 Native Hawaiian or other Pacific Islander, non-Hispanic/Latino; 3 Two or more races, non-Hispanic/Latino), 1 international. Average age 25. 639 applicants, 16% accepted, 50 enrolled. *Entrance requirements:* For doctorate, GRE General Test, bachelor's degree, minimum cumulative GPA of 2.75. *Application deadline:* For fall admission, 12/15 for domestic students. Applications are processed on a rolling basis. *Unit head:* Dr. Jacquelyn Smith, Dean, 623-572-3601, Fax: 623-572-3601. *Application contact:* James Walter, Director of Admissions, 888-247-9277, Fax: 623-572-3229, E-mail: admissaz@midwestern.edu.

Misericordia University, College of Health Sciences, Program in Physical Therapy, Dallas, PA 18612-1098. Offers MSPT, DPT. *Accreditation:* APTA. *Faculty:* 8 full-time (5 women). *Students:* 70 full-time (47 women), 52 part-time (37 women); includes 8 minority (1 Black or African American, non-Hispanic/Latino; 1 American Indian or Alaska Native, non-Hispanic/Latino; 1 Asian, non-Hispanic/Latino; 4 Hispanic/Latino; 1 Two or more races, non-Hispanic/Latino). Average age 25. In 2011, 37 master's, 17 doctorates awarded. *Degree requirements:* For master's, thesis optional. *Entrance requirements:* For doctorate, GRE General Test, minimum undergraduate GPA of 3.0, volunteer experience. *Application deadline:* For fall admission, 12/15 priority date for domestic students. Applications are processed on a rolling basis. Application fee: $25. Electronic applications accepted. *Expenses: Tuition:* Full-time $25,700; part-time $575 per credit. *Financial support:* In 2011–12, 69 students received support. Teaching assistantships, career-related internships or fieldwork, scholarships/grants, and tuition waivers (partial) available. Support available to part-time students. Financial award application deadline: 6/30; financial award applicants required to submit FAFSA. *Faculty research:* Wound care, computer-assisted instruction, instruction in applied physiology, isokinetics, prosthetics. *Unit head:* Dr. Susan Barker, Chair, 570-674-6422, E-mail: sbarker@misericordia.edu. *Application contact:* David Pasquini, Assistant Director of Admissions, 570-674-6255, Fax: 570-674-6232, E-mail: dpasquin@misericordia.edu. Web site: http://www.misericordia.edu/pt.

Missouri State University, Graduate College, College of Health and Human Services, Department of Physical Therapy, Springfield, MO 65897. Offers DPT. *Accreditation:* APTA. *Faculty:* 8 full-time (4 women), 1 part-time/adjunct (0 women). *Students:* 86 full-time (52 women), 11 part-time (8 women); includes 4 minority (1 American Indian or Alaska Native, non-Hispanic/Latino; 2 Asian, non-Hispanic/Latino; 1 Hispanic/Latino), 1 international. Average age 26. 33 applicants, 94% accepted, 31 enrolled. In 2011, 24 doctorates awarded. *Degree requirements:* For doctorate, comprehensive exam, thesis/dissertation or alternative. *Entrance requirements:* For doctorate, GRE, minimum GPA of 3.0. Additional exam requirements/recommendations for international students: Required—TOEFL (minimum score 550 paper-based; 213 computer-based; 79 iBT). *Application deadline:* For fall admission, 12/15 for domestic and international students. Application fee: $35 ($50 for international students). Electronic applications accepted. *Expenses:* Tuition, state resident: full-time $4086; part-time $227 per credit hour. Tuition, nonresident: full-time $8172; part-time $454 per credit hour. *Required fees:* $275 per semester. Tuition and fees vary according to course load, campus/location and program. *Financial support:* Federal Work-Study, institutionally sponsored loans, and unspecified assistantships available. Financial award application deadline: 3/31; financial award applicants required to submit FAFSA. *Faculty research:* Complex regional pain syndrome (CRPS), posture and the temporomandibular joint, clinical orthopedics, aging of the motor system. *Unit head:* Dr. Akinniran Oladehin, Head, 417-836-8728, E-mail: physicaltherapy@missouristate.edu. *Application contact:* Misty Stewart, Coordinator of Graduate Recruitment, 417-836-6079, Fax: 417-836-6200, E-mail: mistystewart@missouristate.edu. Web site: http://www.missouristate.edu/physicaltherapy/.

Mount St. Mary's College, Graduate Division, Department of Physical Therapy, Los Angeles, CA 90007. Offers DPT. *Accreditation:* APTA. *Entrance requirements:* For doctorate, GRE General Test, minimum GPA of 3.0. Additional exam requirements/recommendations for international students: Required—TOEFL (minimum score 550 paper-based). *Application deadline:* For fall admission, 12/1 priority date for domestic students, 12/1 for international students. *Expenses:* Contact institution. *Financial support:* Application deadline: 3/15; applicants required to submit FAFSA. *Unit head:* Dr. Deborah Lynn Lowe, Chair, 213-477-2601, Fax: 213-477-2609, E-mail: dlowe@msmc.la.edu. Web site: http://www.msmc.la.edu/graduate-programs/physical-therapy.asp.

Nazareth College of Rochester, Graduate Studies, Department of Physical Therapy, Doctoral Program in Physical Therapy, Rochester, NY 14618-3790. Offers DPT. *Entrance requirements:* For doctorate, minimum GPA of 3.0.

Nazareth College of Rochester, Graduate Studies, Department of Physical Therapy, Master's Program in Physical Therapy, Rochester, NY 14618-3790. Offers MS. *Accreditation:* APTA. *Entrance requirements:* For master's, minimum GPA of 3.0.

Neumann University, Program in Physical Therapy, Aston, PA 19014-1298. Offers DPT. *Accreditation:* APTA. Evening/weekend programs available. *Entrance requirements:* Additional exam requirements/recommendations for international students: Required—TOEFL. Electronic applications accepted. *Expenses:* Contact institution.

New York Institute of Technology, Graduate Division, School of Health Professions, Program in Physical Therapy, Old Westbury, NY 11568-8000. Offers DPT. *Accreditation:* APTA. *Students:* 97 full-time (53 women), 3 part-time (2 women); includes 23 minority (4 Black or African American, non-Hispanic/Latino; 15 Asian, non-Hispanic/Latino; 4 Hispanic/Latino). Average age 24. In 2011, 46 doctorates awarded. *Entrance requirements:* Additional exam requirements/recommendations for international students: Required—TOEFL (minimum score 550 paper-based; 213 computer-based). *Application deadline:* For fall admission, 7/1 priority date for domestic students; for spring admission, 12/1 priority date for domestic students. Application fee: $50. *Expenses: Tuition:* Part-time $930 per credit hour. *Financial support:* Research assistantships with partial tuition reimbursements available. Financial award applicants required to submit FAFSA. *Unit head:* Dr. Karen Friel, Department Chair, 516-686-7651, Fax: 516-686-7699, E-mail: kfriel@nyit.edu. *Application contact:* Dr. Jacquelyn Nealon, Vice President for Enrollment Services, 516-686-7925, Fax: 516-686-7597, E-mail: jnealon@nyit.edu.

New York Medical College, School of Health Sciences and Practice, Department of Physical Therapy, Valhalla, NY 10595-1691. Offers DPT. *Accreditation:* APTA. *Faculty:* 6 full-time, 15 part-time/adjunct. *Students:* 85 full-time. Average age 27. 450 applicants, 8% accepted, 30 enrolled. In 2011, 26 doctorates awarded. *Degree requirements:* For doctorate, comprehensive exam, final project. *Entrance requirements:* For doctorate, GRE, minimum GPA of 3.2. Additional exam requirements/recommendations for international students: Required—TOEFL (minimum score 637 paper-based; 250 computer-based; 117 iBT), IELTS (minimum score 7). *Application deadline:* For winter admission, 3/1 priority date for domestic students, 1/30 for international students. Applications are processed on a rolling basis. Application fee: $75 ($100 for international students). Electronic applications accepted. *Expenses:* Contact institution. *Financial support:* Applicants required to submit FAFSA. *Unit head:* Dr. Michael Majsak, Chair, 914-594-4916, Fax: 914-594-4292, E-mail: michael_majsak@nymc.edu. *Application contact:* Pamela Suett, Director of Recruitment, 914-594-4510, Fax: 914-594-4292, E-mail: shsp_admissions@nymc.edu. Web site: http://www.nymc.edu/pt.

New York University, Steinhardt School of Culture, Education, and Human Development, Department of Physical Therapy, New York, NY 10010-5615. Offers orthopedic physical therapy (Advanced Certificate); physical therapy (MA, DPT), including pathokinesiology (MA); physical therapy for practicing physical therapists

(DPT); research in physical therapy (PhD). *Accreditation:* APTA (one or more programs are accredited). Part-time programs available. *Faculty:* 10 full-time (6 women), 9 part-time/adjunct (4 women). *Students:* 96 full-time (72 women), 19 part-time (13 women); includes 34 minority (4 Black or African American, non-Hispanic/Latino; 22 Asian, non-Hispanic/Latino; 6 Hispanic/Latino; 1 Native Hawaiian or other Pacific Islander, non-Hispanic/Latino; 1 Two or more races, non-Hispanic/Latino), 12 international. Average age 26. 391 applicants, 27% accepted, 42 enrolled. In 2011, 5 master's, 42 doctorates awarded. *Degree requirements:* For master's, thesis (for some programs); for doctorate, thesis/dissertation. *Entrance requirements:* For master's, physical therapy certificate; for doctorate, GRE General Test, interview, physical therapy certificate. Additional exam requirements/recommendations for International students: Required—TOEFL. *Application deadline:* For fall admission, 12/1 priority date for domestic students, 12/1 for international students; for spring admission, 11/1 for domestic and international students. Applications are processed on a rolling basis. Application fee: $75. Electronic applications accepted. *Financial support:* Fellowships with full and partial tuition reimbursements, research assistantships with full and partial tuition reimbursements, career-related internships or fieldwork, Federal Work-Study, scholarships/grants, tuition waivers (partial), and unspecified assistantships available. Support available to part-time students. Financial award application deadline: 2/1; financial award applicants required to submit FAFSA. *Faculty research:* Motor learning and control, neuromuscular disorders, biomechanics and ergonomics, movement analysis, exercise physiology, neurocognitive function in joint instability, pathomechanics. *Unit head:* Dr. Wen K. Ling, Chairperson, 212-998-9400, Fax: 212-995-4190. *Application contact:* 212-998-5030, Fax: 212-995-4328, E-mail: steinhardt.gradadmissions@nyu.edu. Web site: http://steinhardt.nyu.edu/pt.

Northeastern University, Bouvé College of Health Sciences, Program in Physical Therapy (Post Baccalaureate), Boston, MA 02115-5096. Offers DPT. *Accreditation:* APTA. *Faculty:* 21 full-time, 16 part-time/adjunct. *Students:* 152 full-time, 2 part-time. 112 applicants, 41% accepted, 29 enrolled. *Entrance requirements:* Additional exam requirements/recommendations for international students: Required—TOEFL (minimum score 100 iBT). *Application deadline:* For fall admission, 12/1 for domestic students, 3/1 for international students. Applications are processed on a rolling basis. Application fee: $50. Electronic applications accepted. *Financial support:* Scholarships/grants available. *Unit head:* Suzanne B. Greenberg, Director, 617-373-3195, E-mail: s.greenberg@neu.edu. *Application contact:* Dr. Maura Iverson, Director, 617-373-2708. Web site: http://www.northeastern.edu/bouve/pt/programs/pbdpt.html.

Northern Arizona University, Graduate College, College of Health and Human Services, Department of Physical Therapy, Flagstaff, AZ 86011. Offers DPT. *Accreditation:* APTA. *Faculty:* 13 full-time (7 women). *Students:* 142 full-time (84 women); includes 21 minority (2 Black or African American, non-Hispanic/Latino; 2 American Indian or Alaska Native, non-Hispanic/Latino; 4 Asian, non-Hispanic/Latino; 8 Hispanic/Latino; 5 Two or more races, non-Hispanic/Latino). Average age 30. 796 applicants, 6% accepted, 47 enrolled. In 2011, 52 degrees awarded. *Entrance requirements:* For doctorate, GRE General Test, minimum GPA of 3.0. Additional exam requirements/recommendations for international students: Required—TOEFL (minimum score 550 paper-based; 213 computer-based; 80 iBT), IELTS (minimum score 7). *Application deadline:* For fall admission, 11/1 priority date for domestic students, 11/1 for international students. Applications are processed on a rolling basis. Application fee: $65. Electronic applications accepted. *Expenses:* Contact institution. *Financial support:* Career-related internships or fieldwork, Federal Work-Study, scholarships/grants, health care benefits, tuition waivers (full and partial), and unspecified assistantships available. Financial award applicants required to submit FAFSA. *Unit head:* Dr. Mark Cornwall, Chair, 928-523-1606, Fax: 928-523-0148, E-mail: mark.cornwall@nau.edu. *Application contact:* Alicia Beekman, Program Coordinator, 928-523-4270, Fax: 928-523-9289, E-mail: physical.therapy@nau.edu. Web site: http://nau.edu/chhs/physical-therapy/.

Northern Illinois University, Graduate School, College of Health and Human Sciences, School of Allied Health and Communicative Disorders, Program in Physical Therapy, De Kalb, IL 60115-2854. Offers physical therapy (MPT). *Accreditation:* APTA; CEPH. Part-time programs available. *Faculty:* 9 full-time (6 women). *Students:* 106 full-time (57 women), 7 part-time (5 women); includes 19 minority (2 Black or African American, non-Hispanic/Latino; 7 Asian, non-Hispanic/Latino; 8 Hispanic/Latino; 2 Two or more races, non-Hispanic/Latino). Average age 24. In 2011, 38 master's awarded. *Degree requirements:* For master's, comprehensive exam, thesis optional, internship, research paper in public health. *Entrance requirements:* For master's, GRE General Test, minimum GPA of 2.75. Additional exam requirements/recommendations for international students: Required—TOEFL (minimum score 550 paper-based; 213 computer-based). *Application deadline:* For fall admission, 6/1 for domestic students, 5/1 for international students; for spring admission, 11/1 for domestic students, 10/1 for international students. Applications are processed on a rolling basis. Application fee: $40. Electronic applications accepted. *Financial support:* Fellowships with full tuition reimbursements, research assistantships with full tuition reimbursements, teaching assistantships with full tuition reimbursements, career-related internships or fieldwork, Federal Work-Study, scholarships/grants, tuition waivers (full), and unspecified assistantships available. Support available to part-time students. Financial award applicants required to submit FAFSA. *Faculty research:* Stroke rehabilitation, radon exposure prevention, environmental causes of cancer, body image in young girls. *Unit head:* Dr. Sue Ouellette, Interim Chair, 815-753-1486, Fax: 815-753-0720, E-mail: soupllette@niu.edu. *Application contact:* Graduate School Office, 815-753-0395, E-mail: gradsch@niu.edu. Web site: http://catalog.niu.edu/preview_program.php?catoid=19&poid=3262&returnto=581.

North Georgia College & State University, Department of Physical Therapy, Dahlonega, GA 30597. Offers DPT. *Accreditation:* APTA. *Faculty:* 10 full-time (7 women), 1 part-time/adjunct. *Students:* 85 full-time (52 women); includes 4 minority (1 Black or African American, non-Hispanic/Latino; 2 Asian, non-Hispanic/Latino; 1 Two or more races, non-Hispanic/Latino), 1 international. Average age 25. 260 applicants, 12% accepted, 30 enrolled. In 2011, 23 doctorates awarded. *Entrance requirements:* For doctorate, GRE, interview, recommendations, physical therapy observations hours. Additional exam requirements/recommendations for international students: Required—TOEFL (minimum score 550 paper-based; 213 computer-based; 79 iBT), IELTS (minimum score 6.5). Application fee: $50. Electronic applications accepted. *Expenses:* Tuition, state resident: full-time $3528; part-time $196 per credit hour. Tuition, nonresident: full-time $14,094; part-time $783 per credit hour. *Required fees:* $1718; $859 per semester. Tuition and fees vary according to course load, campus/location and program. *Financial support:* Unspecified assistantships available. Financial award application deadline: 5/1; financial award applicants required to submit CSS PROFILE or FAFSA. *Faculty research:* Ergonomics, spinal mobility measurements, electrophysiology, orthopedic physical therapy. *Unit head:* Dr. Stefanie D. Palma, Department Chair, 706-864-1422, Fax: 706-864-1493, E-mail: sdpalma@northgeorgia.edu. *Application contact:* Susan L. Perry, Graduate Admissions Coordinator, 706-864-1543, Fax: 706-867-2795, E-mail: slperry@northgeorgia.edu. Web site: http://www.northgeorgia.edu/PT/Admissions/.

Northwestern University, Northwestern University Feinberg School of Medicine, Department of Physical Therapy and Human Movement Sciences, Chicago, IL 60611-2814. Offers movement and rehabilitation science (PhD); physical therapy (DPT). *Accreditation:* APTA. *Faculty:* 24 full-time (14 women), 4 part-time/adjunct (3 women). *Students:* 211 full-time (170 women); includes 27 minority (4 Black or African American, non-Hispanic/Latino; 8 Asian, non-Hispanic/Latino; 11 Hispanic/Latino; 1 Native Hawaiian or other Pacific Islander, non-Hispanic/Latino; 3 Two or more races, non-Hispanic/Latino). Average age 24. 486 applicants, 44% accepted, 81 enrolled. *Degree requirements:* For doctorate, synthesis research project. *Entrance requirements:* For doctorate, GRE General Test (DPT), baccalaureate degree with minimum GPA of 3.0 in required course work (DPT). Additional exam requirements/recommendations for international students: Required—TOEFL (minimum score 265 computer-based). *Application deadline:* For fall admission, 10/1 for domestic and international students. Applications are processed on a rolling basis. Application fee: $40. Electronic applications accepted. *Expenses:* Contact institution. *Financial support:* In 2011–12, 184 students received support. Federal Work-Study, institutionally sponsored loans, and scholarships/grants available. Financial award application deadline: 2/15; financial award applicants required to submit FAFSA. *Faculty research:* Motor control, robotics, neuromuscular imaging, student performance (academic/professional), clinical outcomes. *Total annual research expenditures:* $3.8 million. *Unit head:* Dr. Julius P. A. Dewald, Professor and Chair, 312-908-6788, Fax: 312-908-0741, E-mail: j-dewald@northwestern.edu. *Application contact:* Dr. Jane Sullivan, Associate Professor and Assistant Chair for Recruitment and Admissions, 312-908-6789, Fax: 312-908-0741, E-mail: j-sullivan@northwestern.edu.

Nova Southeastern University, Health Professions Division, College of Health Care Sciences, Fort Lauderdale, FL 33314-7796. Offers audiology (Au D); health science (MH Sc, DHSc, PhD); occupational therapy (MOT, OTD, PhD); physical therapy (DPT, PhD); physical therapy (transitional) (TDPT). Postbaccalaureate distance learning degree programs offered (minimal on-campus study). *Faculty:* 85 full-time (57 women), 52 part-time/adjunct (27 women). *Students:* 993 full-time (702 women), 514 part-time (356 women); includes 465 minority (160 Black or African American, non-Hispanic/Latino; 6 American Indian or Alaska Native, non-Hispanic/Latino; 96 Asian, non-Hispanic/Latino; 177 Hispanic/Latino; 3 Native Hawaiian or other Pacific Islander, non-Hispanic/Latino; 23 Two or more races, non-Hispanic/Latino), 13 international. Average age 31. 3,837 applicants, 18% accepted, 446 enrolled. In 2011, 293 master's, 147 doctorates awarded. *Degree requirements:* For master's, thesis; for doctorate, comprehensive exam, thesis/dissertation. *Entrance requirements:* For master's and doctorate, GRE General Test. *Application deadline:* Applications are processed on a rolling basis. Application fee: $50. Electronic applications accepted. *Expenses:* Contact institution. *Financial support:* In 2011–12, 12 students received support, including 1 fellowship (averaging $10,000 per year), 4 teaching assistantships (averaging $10,200 per year); institutionally sponsored loans and unspecified assistantships also available. *Unit head:* Dr. Richard Davis, Dean, 954-262-1203, E-mail: redavis@nova.edu. *Application contact:* Joey Jankie, Admissions Counselor, 954-262-7249, E-mail: joey@nova.edu. Web site: http://www.nova.edu/chcs/.

Oakland University, Graduate Study and Lifelong Learning, School of Health Sciences, Program in Physical Therapy, Rochester, MI 48309-4401. Offers neurological rehabilitation (Certificate); orthopedic manual physical therapy (Certificate); orthopedic physical therapy (Certificate); pediatric rehabilitation (Certificate); physical therapy (MSPT, DPT, Dr Sc PT); teaching and learning for rehabilitation professionals (Certificate). *Accreditation:* APTA. *Degree requirements:* For master's, thesis (for some programs). *Entrance requirements:* For master's, acceptance in the 2-year preparatory post-baccalaureate program, minimum GPA of 3.0; for doctorate, GRE General Test. Additional exam requirements/recommendations for international students: Required—TOEFL (minimum score 550 paper-based; 213 computer-based). *Expenses:* Contact institution.

The Ohio State University, College of Medicine, School of Allied Medical Professions, Program in Physical Therapy, Columbus, OH 43210. Offers DPT. *Accreditation:* APTA. *Entrance requirements:* Additional exam requirements/recommendations for international students: Required—TOEFL (paper-based 550; computer-based 213) or Michigan English Language Assessment Battery (82). Electronic applications accepted. *Expenses:* Tuition, state resident: full-time $11,400. Tuition, nonresident: full-time $28,125. Tuition and fees vary according to course load, degree level, campus/location and program.

Ohio University, Graduate College, College of Health Sciences and Professions, School of Rehabilitation and Communication Sciences, Division of Physical Therapy, Athens, OH 45701-2979. Offers DPT. Applications accepted for summer term only. *Accreditation:* APTA. *Students:* 121 full-time (84 women); includes 5 minority (2 Black or African American, non-Hispanic/Latino; 1 Hispanic/Latino; 2 Two or more races, non-Hispanic/Latino), 1 international. 4 applicants, 0% accepted, 0 enrolled. In 2011, 40 doctorates awarded. *Entrance requirements:* For doctorate, GRE. Additional exam requirements/recommendations for international students: Required—TOEFL (minimum score 550 paper-based; 80 iBT) or IELTS (minimum score 6.5). Application fee: $50 ($55 for international students). Electronic applications accepted. *Financial support:* In 2011–12, 26 students received support. Research assistantships with full tuition reimbursements available, teaching assistantships with full tuition reimbursements available, Federal Work-Study, institutionally sponsored loans, scholarships/grants, tuition waivers (full), and unspecified assistantships available. *Faculty research:* Motor control, muscle architecture, postural control, morphonetrics, sensory integration. *Unit head:* Dr. Gary Chleboun, Director, 740-593-1214, Fax: 740-593-0293, E-mail: chleboun@ohio.edu. *Application contact:* Janice Carnahan, Administrative Associate, 740-593-1224, Fax: 740-593-0292, E-mail: carnahan@ohio.edu. Web site: http://www.ohio.edu/chsp/rcs/pt/academics/dptinfo.cfm.

Old Dominion University, College of Health Sciences, School of Physical Therapy, Norfolk, VA 23529. Offers DPT. *Accreditation:* APTA. *Faculty:* 10 full-time (6 women), 5 part-time/adjunct (3 women). *Students:* 126 full-time (89 women), 1 (woman) part-time; includes 23 minority (10 Black or African American, non-Hispanic/Latino; 3 Asian, non-Hispanic/Latino; 5 Hispanic/Latino; 1 Native Hawaiian or other Pacific Islander, non-Hispanic/Latino; 4 Two or more races, non-Hispanic/Latino), 1 international. Average age 25. 475 applicants, 17% accepted, 45 enrolled. In 2011, 43 doctorates awarded. *Degree requirements:* For doctorate, comprehensive exam, clinical internships. *Entrance requirements:* For doctorate, GRE, 3 letters of recommendation (1 of which is from a physical therapist); 80 hours of volunteer experience. Additional exam requirements/recommendations for international students: Required—TOEFL. *Application deadline:* For fall admission, 11/1 for domestic and international students. Application fee: $50. Electronic applications accepted. *Expenses:* Contact institution. *Financial support:* In 2011–12, 4 students received support, including 1 fellowship (averaging $15,000 per year), 4 teaching assistantships with partial tuition reimbursements available (averaging $7,500 per year); career-related internships or fieldwork and unspecified assistantships also available. Financial award applicants required to submit FAFSA. *Faculty research:* Virtual reality and rehabilitation, rehabilitation for amputees, electromyography, biomechanics, gait and balance. *Total annual research expenditures:* $103,022. *Unit head:* Dr. Martha Walker, Graduate Program Director, 757-683-4519, Fax: 757-683-4410, E-mail: ptgpd@odu.edu. *Application contact:* William Heffelfinger, Director of Graduate Admissions, 757-683-

5554, Fax: 757-683-3255, E-mail: gradadmit@odu.edu. Web site: http://hs.odu.edu/physther/.

Pacific University, School of Physical Therapy, Forest Grove, OR 97116-1797. Offers entry level (DPT); post-professional (DPT). *Accreditation:* APTA. *Degree requirements:* For doctorate, evidence-based capstone project thesis. *Entrance requirements:* For doctorate, 100 hours of volunteer/observational hours, minimum cumulative GPA of 3.0, prerequisite courses with a C grade or better, minimum GPA of 2.5 in science/statistics. Additional exam requirements/recommendations for international students: Required—TOEFL (minimum score 600 paper-based; 250 computer-based). Electronic applications accepted. *Expenses:* Contact institution. *Faculty research:* Balance disorders, geriatrics, orthopedic treatment outcomes, obesity, women's health.

Queen's University at Kingston, School of Graduate Studies and Research, Faculty of Health Sciences, School of Rehabilitation Therapy, Kingston, ON K7L 3N6, Canada. Offers occupational therapy (M Sc OT); physical therapy (M Sc PT); rehabilitation science (M Sc, PhD). Part-time programs available. *Degree requirements:* For master's, thesis; for doctorate, comprehensive exam, thesis/dissertation. *Entrance requirements:* Additional exam requirements/recommendations for international students: Required—TOEFL. *Faculty research:* Disability, community, motor performance, rehabilitation, treatment efficiency.

Quinnipiac University, School of Health Sciences, Program in Physical Therapy, Hamden, CT 06518-1940. Offers MPT, DPT. Students are admitted to the program as undergraduates. *Accreditation:* APTA. *Faculty:* 10 full-time (8 women), 7 part-time/adjunct (3 women). *Students:* 194 full-time (159 women); includes 13 minority (1 Black or African American, non-Hispanic/Latino; 5 Asian, non-Hispanic/Latino; 7 Hispanic/Latino). 68 applicants, 100% accepted, 68 enrolled. In 2011, 43 degrees awarded. *Degree requirements:* For doctorate, capstone research project. *Entrance requirements:* For doctorate, BS in health science studies with minor in biology. *Expenses: Tuition:* Part-time $855 per credit. *Required fees:* $35 per credit. *Financial support:* In 2011–12, 194 students received support. Scholarships/grants, tuition waivers (partial), and unspecified assistantships available. Financial award application deadline: 4/15; financial award applicants required to submit FAFSA. *Unit head:* Donald Kowalsky, Chairperson, 203-582-8681, E-mail: donald.kowalsky@quinnipiac.edu. *Application contact:* 800-462-1944, Fax: 203-582-8901, E-mail: admission@quinnipiac.edu. Web site: http://www.quinnipiac.edu/x760.xml.

Radford University, College of Graduate and Professional Studies, Waldron College of Health and Human Services, Department of Physical Therapy, Roanoke, VA 24013. Offers DPT. *Faculty:* 8 full-time (3 women). *Students:* 14 full-time (8 women). Average age 26. 33 applicants, 55% accepted, 14 enrolled. *Degree requirements:* For doctorate, comprehensive exam, capstone research project suitable for publication. *Entrance requirements:* For doctorate, GRE, 40 hours clinical experience; minimum overall GPA of 3.25, 3.0 in math and science prerequisites; essay; 3 references; CPR certification; criminal background check; verification of immunizations; resume; official transcripts. Additional exam requirements/recommendations for international students: Required—TOEFL (minimum score 575 paper-based; 88 iBT), IELTS (minimum score 6.5). *Application deadline:* Applications are processed on a rolling basis. Application fee: $50. Electronic applications accepted. *Expenses:* Tuition, state resident: full-time $6262; part-time $261 per credit hour. Tuition, nonresident: full-time $14,540; part-time $606 per credit hour. *Required fees:* $2812; $117 per credit hour. Tuition and fees vary according to program. *Financial support:* In 2011–12, 3 students received support. Application deadline: 3/1; applicants required to submit FAFSA. *Unit head:* Dr. Edward C. Swanson, Chair, 540-224-6675, Fax: 540-224-6660, E-mail: eswanson3@radford.edu. *Application contact:* Rebecca Conner, Graduate Admissions Office, 540-831-5431, Fax: 540-831-6061, E-mail: gradcollege@radford.edu. Web site: http://www.radford.edu/content/wchs/home/pt/about.html.

Regis University, Rueckert-Hartman College for Health Professions, Denver, CO 80221-1099. Offers family nurse practitioner (MSN); health informatics (Postbaccalaureate Certificate); health services administration (MS); leadership in healthcare systems (MSN); neonatal nurse practitioner (MSN); nursing (MSN); pharmacy (Pharm D); physical therapy (DPT, TDPT). *Entrance requirements:* Additional exam requirements/recommendations for international students: Required—TOEFL (minimum score 550 paper-based; 213 computer-based; 82 iBT). Electronic applications accepted. *Expenses:* Contact institution. *Faculty research:* Normal and pathological balance and gait research, normal/pathological upper limb motor control/biomechanics, exercise energy/metabolism research, optical treatment protocols for therapeutic modalities.

The Richard Stockton College of New Jersey, School of Graduate and Continuing Studies, Program in Physical Therapy, Pomona, NJ 08240-0195. Offers DPT. *Accreditation:* APTA. *Faculty:* 9 full-time (7 women). *Students:* 49 full-time (32 women), 46 part-time (35 women); includes 26 minority (5 Black or African American, non-Hispanic/Latino; 14 Asian, non-Hispanic/Latino; 3 Hispanic/Latino; 1 Native Hawaiian or other Pacific Islander, non-Hispanic/Latino; 3 Two or more races, non-Hispanic/Latino). Average age 34. 159 applicants, 29% accepted, 33 enrolled. In 2011, 50 doctorates awarded. *Entrance requirements:* Additional exam requirements/recommendations for international students: Required—TOEFL. *Application deadline:* For fall admission, 12/1 priority date for domestic students, 12/1 for international students. Applications are processed on a rolling basis. Application fee: $50. Electronic applications accepted. *Expenses:* Tuition, state resident: full-time $13,035; part-time $543 per credit. Tuition, nonresident: full-time $20,065; part-time $836 per credit. *Required fees:* $3920; $163 per credit. Tuition and fees vary according to degree level. *Financial support:* In 2011–12, 33 students received support, including 8 fellowships, 35 research assistantships with partial tuition reimbursements available; career-related internships or fieldwork, Federal Work-Study, scholarships/grants, and unspecified assistantships also available. Support available to part-time students. Financial award application deadline: 3/1; financial award applicants required to submit FAFSA. *Faculty research:* Spinal flexibility in the well elderly, use of traditional Chinese medicine concepts in physical therapy, computerized vs. traditional study in human gross anatomy. *Unit head:* Dr. Elaine Bukowski, Program Director, 609-626-3640, E-mail: gradschool@stockton.edu. *Application contact:* Tara Williams, Assistant Director of Graduate Enrollment Management, 609-626-3640, Fax: 609-626-6050, E-mail: gradschool@stockton.edu.

Rockhurst University, School of Graduate and Professional Studies, Program in Physical Therapy, Kansas City, MO 64110-2561. Offers DPT. *Accreditation:* APTA. *Faculty:* 9 full-time (5 women), 7 part-time/adjunct (6 women). *Students:* 134 full-time (90 women), 1 (woman) part-time; includes 18 minority (1 Black or African American, non-Hispanic/Latino; 7 Asian, non-Hispanic/Latino; 7 Hispanic/Latino; 3 Two or more races, non-Hispanic/Latino). Average age 25. 497 applicants, 33% accepted, 44 enrolled. In 2011, 43 doctorates awarded. *Entrance requirements:* For doctorate, 3 letters of recommendation, interview, minimum GPA of 3.0, physical therapy experience. Additional exam requirements/recommendations for international students: Required—TOEFL (minimum score 550 paper-based; 213 computer-based; 79 iBT). *Application deadline:* Applications are processed on a rolling basis. Application fee: $25. Electronic applications accepted. Application fee is waived when completed online. *Financial support:* In 2011–12, 5 research assistantships, 10 teaching assistantships were awarded; career-related internships or fieldwork, institutionally sponsored loans, and unspecified assistantships also available. Financial award application deadline: 4/1; financial award applicants required to submit FAFSA. *Faculty research:* Clinical decision-making, geriatrics, balance in persons with neurological disorders, physical rehabilitation following total joint replacement, clinical education. *Unit head:* Dr. Brian McKiernan, Chair, 816-501-4059, Fax: 816-501-4169, E-mail: brian.mckiernan@rockhurst.edu. *Application contact:* Cheryl Hooper, Director of Graduate Admission, 816-501-4097, Fax: 816-501-4241, E-mail: cheryl.hooper@rockhurst.edu. Web site: http://www.rockhurst.edu/academic/pt/index.asp.

Rocky Mountain University of Health Professions, Program in Orthopaedic and Sports Science, Provo, UT 84606. Offers PhD. *Degree requirements:* For doctorate, thesis/dissertation.

Rocky Mountain University of Health Professions, Programs in Physical Therapy, Provo, UT 84606. Offers DPT, TDPT. *Entrance requirements:* For doctorate, GRE, bachelor's degree; two courses each of general chemistry and general physics with lab (for science majors); one course each in biology, human anatomy (with lab), and physiology (with lab); three semester hours of statistics; six semester hours in the behavioral sciences (life span development preferred); minimum cumulative GPA of 3.0.

Rosalind Franklin University of Medicine and Science, College of Health Professions, Department of Physical Therapy, North Chicago, IL 60064-3095. Offers MS, DPT, TDPT. *Accreditation:* APTA. Postbaccalaureate distance learning degree programs offered (minimal on-campus study). *Degree requirements:* For master's, thesis. *Entrance requirements:* For master's, physical therapy license. Additional exam requirements/recommendations for international students: Required—TOEFL. *Faculty research:* Clinical research, development/analysis of tests, measures, education.

Rutgers, The State University of New Jersey, Camden, Graduate School of Arts and Sciences, Program in Physical Therapy, Stratford, NJ 08084. Offers DPT. Program offered jointly with University of Medicine and Dentistry of New Jersey. *Accreditation:* APTA. *Entrance requirements:* For doctorate, GRE, physical therapy experience, 3 letters of recommendation, statement of personal, professional and academic goals, resume. Additional exam requirements/recommendations for international students: Required—TOEFL, IELTS. Electronic applications accepted. *Faculty research:* Clinical education, migrant workers, biomechanical constraints on motor control, high intensity strength training and the elderly, posture and ergonomics.

Sacred Heart University, Graduate Programs, College of Health Professions, Department of Physical Therapy, Fairfield, CT 06825-1000. Offers DPT. *Accreditation:* APTA. *Entrance requirements:* Additional exam requirements/recommendations for international students: Required—TOEFL (minimum score 550 paper-based; 213 computer-based). Electronic applications accepted. *Expenses:* Contact institution.

Sage Graduate School, School of Health Sciences, Program in Physical Therapy, Troy, NY 12180-4115. Offers DPT. *Accreditation:* APTA. *Faculty:* 11 full-time (10 women), 4 part-time/adjunct (3 women). *Students:* 110 full-time (79 women), 19 part-time (18 women); includes 12 minority (1 Black or African American, non-Hispanic/Latino; 7 Asian, non-Hispanic/Latino; 2 Hispanic/Latino; 2 Two or more races, non-Hispanic/Latino), 2 international. Average age 28. 151 applicants, 38% accepted, 35 enrolled. In 2011, 39 doctorates awarded. *Entrance requirements:* For doctorate, current resume; 2 letters of recommendation; minimum GPA of 3.0 overall and in science prerequisites; completion of 40 hours of physical therapy observation. Additional exam requirements/recommendations for international students: Required—TOEFL (minimum score 550 paper-based; 213 computer-based). *Application deadline:* Applications are processed on a rolling basis. Application fee: $40. *Expenses: Tuition:* Full-time $11,880; part-time $660 per credit hour. Tuition and fees vary according to program. *Financial support:* Federal Work-Study, scholarships/grants, and unspecified assistantships available. Support available to part-time students. Financial award application deadline: 3/1; financial award applicants required to submit FAFSA. *Unit head:* Dr. Esther Haskevitz, Interim Dean, School of Health Sciences, 518-244-2296, Fax: 518-244-4571, E-mail: haskve@sage.edu. *Application contact:* Dr. Patricia Pohl, Professor and Chair, 518-244-2056, Fax: 518-244-4524, E-mail: pohlp@sage.edu.

St. Ambrose University, College of Education and Health Sciences, Department of Physical Therapy, Davenport, IA 52803-2898. Offers DPT. *Accreditation:* APTA. *Faculty:* 9 full-time (4 women), 2 part-time/adjunct (both women). *Students:* 83 full-time (66 women), 2 part-time (1 woman); includes 2 minority (both Hispanic/Latino). Average age 24. 352 applicants, 12% accepted, 37 enrolled. In 2011, 38 doctorates awarded. *Degree requirements:* For doctorate, board exams. *Entrance requirements:* For doctorate, GRE, interview. Additional exam requirements/recommendations for international students: Required—TOEFL. *Application deadline:* For fall admission, 1/15 priority date for domestic students. Application fee: $25. *Expenses: Tuition:* Full-time $13,770; part-time $765 per credit hour. *Required fees:* $60 per semester. Tuition and fees vary according to degree level, program and reciprocity agreements. *Financial support:* In 2011–12, 69 students received support, including 8 research assistantships with partial tuition reimbursements available (averaging $3,600 per year); career-related internships or fieldwork, scholarships/grants, tuition waivers (partial), and unspecified assistantships also available. Financial award application deadline: 3/15; financial award applicants required to submit FAFSA. *Faculty research:* Human motor control, orthopedic physical therapy, cardiopulmonary physical therapy, kinesiology/biomechanics. *Unit head:* Dr. Sandra L. Cassady, Director, 563-333-6409, Fax: 563-333-6410, E-mail: cassadysandral@sau.edu. *Application contact:* Carrie Meador-Bliss, Office Administrator, 563-333-6401, Fax: 563-333-6410, E-mail: meador-blisscarrie@sau.edu. Web site: http://web.sau.edu/pt/.

St. Catherine University, Graduate Programs, Program in Physical Therapy, St. Paul, MN 55105. Offers DPT. Offered on the Minneapolis campus only. *Accreditation:* APTA. *Degree requirements:* For doctorate, research project. *Entrance requirements:* For doctorate, GRE, minimum GPA of 3.0, coursework in biology/zoology, anatomy, physiology, chemistry, physics, psychology, statistics, mathematics and medical terminology. Additional exam requirements/recommendations for international students: Required—Michigan English Language Assessment Battery or TOEFL (minimum score 600 paper-based; 250 computer-based; 100 iBT). *Expenses:* Contact institution.

Saint Francis University, Department of Physical Therapy, Loretto, PA 15940-0600. Offers DPT. *Accreditation:* APTA. *Faculty:* 8 full-time (3 women), 13 part-time/adjunct (8 women). *Students:* 119 full-time (78 women); includes 4 minority (2 Black or African American, non-Hispanic/Latino; 2 Asian, non-Hispanic/Latino). Average age 23. 58 applicants, 57% accepted, 18 enrolled. In 2011, 37 doctorates awarded. *Entrance requirements:* Additional exam requirements/recommendations for international students: Required—TOEFL. *Application deadline:* For winter admission, 1/15 for domestic and international students. Application fee: $30. Electronic applications accepted. *Expenses: Tuition:* Part-time $815 per credit. *Required fees:* $504 per semester. One-time fee: $40 part-time. Tuition and fees vary according to degree level, program and reciprocity agreements. *Financial support:* In 2011–12, 8 students received support, including 8 teaching assistantships with partial tuition reimbursements available; unspecified assistantships also available. *Faculty research:* Childhood asthma, athletic performance, energy expenditure, sports injuries, balance and falls. *Unit head:* Dr. Kay Malek, Chair/Associate Professor, 814-472-3123, Fax: 814-472-

3140, E-mail: kmalek@francis.edu. *Application contact:* Dr. Peter Raymond Skoner, Associate Provost, 814-472-3085, Fax: 814-472-3365, E-mail: pskoner@francis.edu.

Saint Louis University, Graduate Education, Doisy College of Health Sciences, Department of Physical Therapy, St. Louis, MO 63103-2097. Offers athletic training (MAT); physical therapy (DPT). *Accreditation:* APTA. Part-time programs available. *Entrance requirements:* Additional exam requirements/recommendations for international students: Required—TOEFL (minimum score 525 paper-based; 194 computer-based; 55 iBT). Electronic applications accepted. *Faculty research:* Patellofemoral pain and associated risk factors; prevalence of disordered eating in physical therapy students; effects of selected interventions for children with cerebral palsy on gait and posture; hippotherapy, ankle strengthening, supported treadmill training, spirituality in physical therapy/patient care, risk factors for exercise-related leg pain in running athletes.

Samuel Merritt University, Department of Physical Therapy, Oakland, CA 94609-3108. Offers DPT. *Accreditation:* APTA. *Entrance requirements:* Additional exam requirements/recommendations for international students: Required—TOEFL. *Expenses:* Contact institution. *Faculty research:* Human movement, motor control, falls prevention in the elderly.

San Francisco State University, Division of Graduate Studies, College of Health and Human Services, Program in Physical Therapy, San Francisco, CA 94132-1722. Offers DPT, Dr Sc PT. MS, Dr Sc PT, and DPT offered jointly with University of California, San Francisco. *Accreditation:* APTA. *Financial support:* Career-related internships or fieldwork and institutionally sponsored loans available. *Unit head:* Dr. Linda Wanek, Director, 415-338-2001, E-mail: lwanek@sfsu.edu. *Application contact:* Jill Lienau, Academic Office Coordinator, 415-338-2001, E-mail: jlineau@sfsu.edu. Web site: http://ptrehab.medschool.ucsf.edu/Education.

Seton Hall University, School of Health and Medical Sciences, Program in Physical Therapy, South Orange, NJ 07079-2697. Offers professional physical therapy (DPT). *Accreditation:* APTA. *Degree requirements:* For doctorate, research project. *Entrance requirements:* Additional exam requirements/recommendations for international students: Required—TOEFL. Electronic applications accepted. *Expenses: Tuition:* Part-time $1033 per credit hour. *Required fees:* $85 per semester. *Faculty research:* Electrical stimulation, motor learning, backpacks, gait and balance, orthopedic injury, women's health, pediatric obesity.

Shenandoah University, School of Health Professions, Division of Physical Therapy, Winchester, VA 22601-5195. Offers physical therapy and non-traditional physical therapy (DPT). *Accreditation:* APTA. Part-time programs available. Postbaccalaureate distance learning degree programs offered. *Faculty:* 6 full-time (4 women), 4 part-time/adjunct (1 woman). *Students:* 109 full-time (75 women), 111 part-time (86 women); includes 27 minority (9 Black or African American, non-Hispanic/Latino; 13 Asian, non-Hispanic/Latino; 5 Hispanic/Latino), 9 international. Average age 32. 550 applicants, 28% accepted, 81 enrolled. In 2011, 100 doctorates awarded. *Degree requirements:* For doctorate, internship. *Entrance requirements:* For doctorate, GRE General Test, minimum GPA of 2.8, 2 letters of recommendation, 100 hours of clinical experience (2 places). Additional exam requirements/recommendations for international students: Required—TOEFL (minimum score 550 paper-based; 213 computer-based; 79 iBT), IELTS (minimum score 6.5), Sakae Institute of Study Abroad (minimum score 550). *Application deadline:* For fall admission, 10/17 for domestic and international students. Applications are processed on a rolling basis. Application fee: $30. Electronic applications accepted. *Expenses:* Contact institution. *Financial support:* In 2011–12, 12 students received support. Career-related internships or fieldwork, institutionally sponsored loans, scholarships/grants, and federal loans, alternative loans available. Support available to part-time students. Financial award application deadline: 3/15; financial award applicants required to submit FAFSA. *Total annual research expenditures:* $4,050. *Unit head:* Dr. Karen Abraham-Justice, Director, 540-665-5520, Fax: 540-545-7387, E-mail: kabraham@su.edu. *Application contact:* David Anthony, Dean of Admissions, 540-665-4581, Fax: 540-665-4627, E-mail: admit@su.edu. Web site: http://www.su.edu/pt.

Simmons College, School of Nursing and Health Sciences, Boston, MA 02115. Offers didactic dietetics (Certificate); health professions education (CAGS); nursing (MS); nursing administration (MS); nursing practice (DNP); nutrition (MS, Certificate); physical therapy (DPT); sports nutrition (Certificate); sports nutrition/didactic dietetics (Certificate); MS/Certificate. *Unit head:* Dr. Judy Beal, Dean, 617-521-2139, Fax: 617-521-3137, E-mail: judy.beal@simmons.edu. *Application contact:* Carmen Fortin, Assistant Dean/Director of Admission, 617-521-2651, Fax: 617-521-3137, E-mail: gshsadm@simmons.edu. Web site: http://www.simmons.edu/snhs/.

Slippery Rock University of Pennsylvania, Graduate Studies (Recruitment), College of Health, Environment, and Science, School of Physical Therapy, Slippery Rock, PA 16057-1383. Offers DPT. *Accreditation:* APTA. *Faculty:* 9 full-time (7 women), 1 (woman) part-time/adjunct. *Students:* 131 full-time (97 women); includes 1 minority (Hispanic/Latino), 1 international. Average age 23. 251 applicants, 30% accepted, 32 enrolled. In 2011, 51 degrees awarded. *Median time to degree:* Of those who began their doctoral program in fall 2003, 93% received their degree in 8 years or less. *Degree requirements:* For doctorate, clinical residency. *Entrance requirements:* For doctorate, GRE General Test, minimum GPA of 3.0, three letters of recommendation, essay, 100 hours of PT experience with a licensed physical therapist, CPR certification. Additional exam requirements/recommendations for international students: Required—TOEFL (minimum score 550 paper-based; 213 computer-based; 80 iBT). *Application deadline:* For fall admission, 11/1 priority date for domestic students, 11/1 for international students. Application fee: $35. Electronic applications accepted. *Expenses:* Contact institution. *Financial support:* Career-related internships or fieldwork, Federal Work-Study, institutionally sponsored loans, scholarships/grants, tuition waivers (partial), and unspecified assistantships available. Financial award application deadline: 5/1; financial award applicants required to submit FAFSA. *Unit head:* Dr. Carol Martin-Elkins, Graduate Coordinator, 724-738-2916, Fax: 724-738-2113, E-mail: carol.martin-elkins@sru.edu. *Application contact:* Angela Barrett, Director of Graduate Admissions, 724-738-2051, Fax: 724-738-2146, E-mail: graduate.admissions@sru.edu.

Southwest Baptist University, Program in Physical Therapy, Bolivar, MO 65613-2597. Offers DPT. *Accreditation:* APTA. *Degree requirements:* For doctorate, comprehensive exam, 3-4 clinical education experiences. *Entrance requirements:* Additional exam requirements/recommendations for international students: Required—TOEFL (minimum score 550 paper-based; 213 computer-based). *Expenses:* Contact institution. *Faculty research:* Balance and falls prevention, distance and web based learning, foot and ankle intervention, pediatrics, musculoskeletal management.

Springfield College, Graduate Programs, Program in Physical Therapy, Springfield, MA 01109-3797. Offers DPT. *Accreditation:* APTA. Part-time programs available. *Degree requirements:* For doctorate, comprehensive exam, thesis/dissertation, research project. *Entrance requirements:* For doctorate, GRE General Test, prerequisite courses. Additional exam requirements/recommendations for international students: Required—TOEFL (minimum score 550 paper-based; 213 computer-based). Electronic applications accepted.

State University of New York Upstate Medical University, Department of Physical Therapy, Syracuse, NY 13210-2334. Offers DPT. *Accreditation:* APTA. Part-time and evening/weekend programs available. Postbaccalaureate distance learning degree programs offered (minimal on-campus study). Electronic applications accepted.

Stony Brook University, State University of New York, Stony Brook University Medical Center, Health Sciences Center, School of Health Technology and Management, Stony Brook, NY 11794. Offers health care management (Advanced Certificate); health care policy and management (MS); occupational therapy (MS); physical therapy (DPT); physician assistant (MS). *Accreditation:* APTA. Part-time programs available. *Degree requirements:* For master's, thesis. *Entrance requirements:* For master's, GRE General Test, minimum GPA of 3.0, work experience in field. *Faculty research:* Health promotion and disease prevention.

Temple University, Health Sciences Center, College of Health Professions and Social Work, Department of Physical Therapy, Philadelphia, PA 19122-6096. Offers DPT, PhD. *Accreditation:* APTA (one or more programs are accredited). Part-time and evening/weekend programs available. *Faculty:* 4 full-time (2 women). *Students:* 149 full-time (97 women), 103 part-time (76 women); includes 24 minority (4 Black or African American, non-Hispanic/Latino; 13 Asian, non-Hispanic/Latino; 4 Hispanic/Latino; 2 Native Hawaiian or other Pacific Islander, non-Hispanic/Latino; 1 Two or more races, non-Hispanic/Latino), 3 international. Average age 29. 29 applicants, 100% accepted, 26 enrolled. In 2011, 140 doctorates awarded. *Degree requirements:* For doctorate, thesis/dissertation. *Entrance requirements:* For doctorate, GRE General Test, interview. Additional exam requirements/recommendations for international students: Required—TOEFL (minimum score 550 paper-based; 213 computer-based; 79 iBT). *Application deadline:* For fall admission, 4/1 for domestic students, 12/15 for international students. Application fee: $50. Electronic applications accepted. *Expenses:* Tuition, state resident: full-time $12,366; part-time $687 per credit hour. Tuition, nonresident: full-time $17,298; part-time $961 per credit hour. *Required fees:* $590; $213 per year. *Financial support:* Career-related internships or fieldwork and institutionally sponsored loans available. Support available to part-time students. Financial award application deadline: 1/15; financial award applicants required to submit FAFSA. *Faculty research:* Balance dysfunction, biomechanics, development, qualitative research, developmental neuroscience, health services. *Unit head:* Dr. Emily A. Keshner, Chair, 215-707-4815, Fax: 215-707-7500, E-mail: deptpt@temple.edu. *Application contact:* Tara Schumacher, Coordinator of Outreach, 215-204-6575, Fax: 215-204-8781, E-mail: tara.schumacher@temple.edu. Web site: http://www.temple.edu/chp/departments/PT/.

Tennessee State University, The School of Graduate Studies and Research, College of Health Sciences, Department of Physical Therapy, Nashville, TN 37209-1561. Offers MPT, DPT. *Accreditation:* APTA. Part-time programs available. Postbaccalaureate distance learning degree programs offered (minimal on-campus study). *Degree requirements:* For master's, comprehensive exam, thesis optional. *Entrance requirements:* For master's, GRE General Test, MAT. Electronic applications accepted. *Faculty research:* Evidence-based research clinical research case studies/reports qualitative research education assessment total knee anthroplasty; ergonomics; childhood obesity.

Texas State University–San Marcos, Graduate School, College of Health Professions, Department of Physical Therapy, San Marcos, TX 78666. Offers DPT. Applicants accepted in summer only. *Accreditation:* APTA. *Faculty:* 8 full-time (5 women), 3 part-time/adjunct (1 woman). *Students:* 81 full-time (47 women), 38 part-time (22 women); includes 30 minority (2 Black or African American, non-Hispanic/Latino; 2 American Indian or Alaska Native, non-Hispanic/Latino; 3 Asian, non-Hispanic/Latino; 23 Hispanic/Latino), 1 international. Average age 27. 636 applicants, 9% accepted, 40 enrolled. *Degree requirements:* For doctorate, comprehensive exam. *Entrance requirements:* For doctorate, GRE General Test (minimum combined score of 1000 Verbal and Quantitative), bachelor's degree in physical therapy; minimum GPA of 3.0 on last 60 hours of undergraduate and science courses. Additional exam requirements/recommendations for international students: Required—TOEFL (minimum score 550 paper-based; 213 computer-based; 78 iBT). *Application deadline:* For spring admission, 10/15 for domestic and international students. Applications are processed on a rolling basis. Application fee: $65 ($115 for international students). Electronic applications accepted. *Expenses:* Tuition, state resident: full-time $6408; part-time $3204 per semester. Tuition, nonresident: full-time $14,832; part-time $7416 per semester. *Required fees:* $1824; $912 per semester. Tuition and fees vary according to course load. *Financial support:* In 2011–12, 78 students received support, including 10 teaching assistantships (averaging $6,957 per year); research assistantships, career-related internships or fieldwork, Federal Work-Study, institutionally sponsored loans, scholarships/grants, and unspecified assistantships also available. Support available to part-time students. Financial award application deadline: 4/1; financial award applicants required to submit FAFSA. *Faculty research:* Effect of a cultural competence education module on the cultural competence of student physical therapists. *Total annual research expenditures:* $2,199. *Unit head:* Dr. Barbara Sanders, Chair, 512-245-8351, Fax: 512-245-8736, E-mail: bs04@txstate.edu. *Application contact:* Dr. J. Michael Willoughby, Dean of Graduate School, 512-245-2581, Fax: 512-245-8365, E-mail: gradcollege@txstate.edu. Web site: http://www.health.txstate.edu/pt/.

Texas Tech University Health Sciences Center, School of Allied Health Sciences, Program in Physical Therapy, Lubbock, TX 79430. Offers DPT, Sc D. *Accreditation:* APTA. *Faculty:* 21 full-time (6 women). *Students:* 194 full-time (113 women), 117 part-time (57 women); includes 97 minority (12 Black or African American, non-Hispanic/Latino; 2 American Indian or Alaska Native, non-Hispanic/Latino; 32 Asian, non-Hispanic/Latino; 50 Hispanic/Latino; 1 Native Hawaiian or other Pacific Islander, non-Hispanic/Latino), 1 international. Average age 29. 463 applicants, 21% accepted, 96 enrolled. In 2011, 88 doctorates awarded. *Entrance requirements:* Additional exam requirements/recommendations for international students: Required—TOEFL, IELTS. *Application deadline:* For fall admission, 9/15 priority date for domestic students; for winter admission, 1/15 priority date for domestic students. Application fee: $35. Electronic applications accepted. *Financial support:* Career-related internships or fieldwork, institutionally sponsored loans, and scholarships/grants available. Financial award application deadline: 9/1; financial award applicants required to submit FAFSA. *Faculty research:* Closed chain proprioception; effects of unloading; retrospective studies including ACL, hippotherapy, orthopedic/sports medicine injuries. *Unit head:* Dr. Steve Sawyer, Chair, 806-743-3226, Fax: 806-743-3249, E-mail: steve.sawyer@ttuhsc.edu. *Application contact:* Jeri Moravcik, Assistant Director of Admissions and Student Affairs, 806-743-3220, Fax: 806-743-2994, E-mail: jeri.moravcik@ttuhsc.edu. Web site: http://www.ttuhsc.edu/sah/mpt/pt.aspx.

Texas Woman's University, Graduate School, College of Health Sciences, School of Physical Therapy, Denton, TX 76201. Offers DPT, PhD. *Accreditation:* APTA (one or more programs are accredited). Part-time programs available. *Faculty:* 23 full-time (17 women), 1 (woman) part-time/adjunct. *Students:* 286 full-time (222 women), 51 part-time (41 women); includes 78 minority (12 Black or African American, non-Hispanic/Latino; 30 Asian, non-Hispanic/Latino; 36 Hispanic/Latino), 10 international. Average age 28. 478 applicants, 33% accepted, 107 enrolled. In 2011, 116 doctorates awarded. *Degree requirements:* For doctorate, comprehensive exam, thesis/dissertation. *Entrance requirements:* For doctorate, interview, resume, essay; eligibility for licensure and 2

letters of recommendation (PhD); 3 letters of recommendation on department form (DPT). Additional exam requirements/recommendations for international students: Required—TOEFL (minimum score 550 paper-based; 213 computer-based; 79 iBT). *Application deadline:* For fall admission, 11/1 priority date for domestic students, 11/1 for international students. Applications are processed on a rolling basis. Application fee: $50 ($75 for international students). Electronic applications accepted. *Expenses:* Tuition, state resident: full-time $3834; part-time $213 per credit hour. Tuition, nonresident: full-time $9468; part-time $526 per credit hour. *Required fees:* $213 per credit hour. Tuition and fees vary according to course load. *Financial support:* In 2011–12, 228 students received support, including 4 research assistantships (averaging $12,942 per year); career-related internships or fieldwork, Federal Work-Study, institutionally sponsored loans, scholarships/grants, traineeships, health care benefits, and unspecified assistantships also available. Support available to part-time students. Financial award application deadline: 3/1; financial award applicants required to submit FAFSA. *Faculty research:* Gait training in stroke survivors, physical activity to promote health in youth and adults, exercise training for individuals with amputation, treatment of balance and gait deficits in persons with multiple sclerosis. *Total annual research expenditures:* $43,129. *Unit head:* Dr. Sharon Olson, Director, 940-898-2460, Fax: 713-794-2361, E-mail: pt@twu.edu. *Application contact:* Dr. Samuel Wheeler, Assistant Director of Admissions, 940-898-3188, Fax: 940-898-3081, E-mail: wheelersr@twu.edu. Web site: http://www.twu.edu/physical-therapy/.

Thomas Jefferson University, Jefferson School of Health Professions, Department of Physical Therapy, Philadelphia, PA 19107. Offers DPT. *Accreditation:* APTA. *Entrance requirements:* Additional exam requirements/recommendations for international students: Required—TOEFL (minimum score 213 computer-based). Electronic applications accepted. *Expenses:* Contact institution. *Faculty research:* Gait and motion analysis, motor control and learning, single motor unit discharge in human muscle, musculoskeletal injuries, cancer rehabilitation.

Touro College, School of Health Sciences, Bay Shore, NY 11706. Offers occupational therapy (MS); Oriental medicine (MSOM); physical therapy (DPT); public health (MPH); speech-language pathology (MS). *Faculty:* 20 full-time, 94 part-time/adjunct. *Students:* 136. *Expenses:* Contact institution. *Financial support:* Fellowships available. *Unit head:* Dr. Louis Primavera, Dean, 516-673-3200. *Application contact:* Dean, School of Health Sciences, 516-673-3200.

University at Buffalo, the State University of New York, Graduate School, School of Public Health and Health Professions, Department of Rehabilitation Science, Program in Physical Therapy, Buffalo, NY 14214. Offers DPT. *Accreditation:* APTA. *Faculty:* 9 full-time (5 women), 3 part-time/adjunct (1 woman). *Students:* 136 full-time (73 women); includes 18 minority (14 Asian, non-Hispanic/Latino; 4 Hispanic/Latino). Average age 22. 101 applicants, 45% accepted, 45 enrolled. In 2011, 41 doctorates awarded. *Entrance requirements:* For doctorate, GRE. Additional exam requirements/recommendations for international students: Required—TOEFL (minimum score 79 iBT). *Application deadline:* For fall admission, 11/1 for domestic and international students. Application fee: $50. Electronic applications accepted. *Financial support:* Career-related internships or fieldwork and Federal Work-Study available. Financial award application deadline: 2/1; financial award applicants required to submit FAFSA. *Faculty research:* Functional limitations and rehabilitation for individuals with osteoporosis, multiple sclerosis, juvenile arthritis and aging; neuroscience concepts as they relate to rehabilitation in stroke and cerebral palsy; neural mechanisms associated with development, aging and neuromuscular disorders; sleep apnea and episodic hypoxia as it relates to muscles in the upper airway and cardiovascular system, neurobiological changes in ventilator control. *Total annual research expenditures:* $240,810. *Unit head:* Dr. Kirkwood Personious, Program Director, 716-829-6742, Fax: 716-829-3217, E-mail: kep7@buffalo.edu. *Application contact:* MaryAnne Venezia, Program Coordinator, 716-829-6742, Fax: 716-829-3217, E-mail: venezia3@buffalo.edu. Web site: http://sphhp.buffalo.edu/rs/dpt/.

The University of Alabama at Birmingham, School of Health Professions, Program in Physical Therapy, Birmingham, AL 35294. Offers DPT. *Accreditation:* APTA. *Expenses:* Tuition, state resident: full-time $5922; part-time $309 per hour. Tuition, nonresident: full-time $13,428; part-time $726 per hour. Tuition and fees vary according to program. *Financial support:* Fellowships with tuition reimbursements, research assistantships, career-related internships or fieldwork, Federal Work-Study, and institutionally sponsored loans available. Financial award application deadline: 11/15. *Faculty research:* Geriatrics, exercise physiology, aquatic therapy, industrial rehabilitation, outcome measurement. *Total annual research expenditures:* $44,538. *Unit head:* Dr. Sharon E. Shaw, Chair, 205-934-3566, Fax: 205-934-3566, E-mail: sshaw@uab.edu. Web site: http://www.uab.edu/dopt/.

University of Alberta, Faculty of Graduate Studies and Research, Department of Physical Therapy, Edmonton, AB T6G 2E1, Canada. Offers M Sc, PhD. Part-time programs available. *Degree requirements:* For master's, thesis. *Entrance requirements:* For master's, bachelor's degree in physical therapy, minimum GPA of 6.5 on a 9.0 scale. Additional exam requirements/recommendations for international students: Required—TOEFL. Electronic applications accepted. *Faculty research:* Spinal disorders, musculoskeletal disorders, ergonomics, sports therapy, motor development, cardiac rehabilitation/therapeutic exercise.

University of California, San Francisco, Graduate Division, Program in Physical Therapy, San Francisco, CA 94143. Offers MS, DPT, DPTSc. MS, DPT, DPTSc offered jointly with San Francisco State University. *Accreditation:* APTA. *Entrance requirements:* For master's, GRE General Test.

University of Central Arkansas, Graduate School, College of Health and Behavioral Sciences, Department of Physical Therapy, Conway, AR 72035-0001. Offers DPT, PhD. *Accreditation:* APTA. *Faculty:* 17 full-time (10 women). *Students:* 164 full-time (99 women), 8 part-time (all women); includes 12 minority (4 Black or African American, non-Hispanic/Latino; 3 American Indian or Alaska Native, non-Hispanic/Latino; 2 Asian, non-Hispanic/Latino; 3 Hispanic/Latino), 2 international. Average age 24. 59 applicants, 100% accepted, 59 enrolled. In 2011, 44 doctorates awarded. *Degree requirements:* For doctorate, comprehensive exam, thesis/dissertation. *Entrance requirements:* Additional exam requirements/recommendations for international students: Required—TOEFL (minimum score 550 paper-based; 213 computer-based). *Application deadline:* For fall admission, 3/1 priority date for domestic students; for spring admission, 10/1 for domestic students. Applications are processed on a rolling basis. Application fee: $25 ($50 for international students). *Expenses:* Contact institution. *Financial support:* In 2011–12, 4 research assistantships with partial tuition reimbursements (averaging $6,000 per year) were awarded; Federal Work-Study, scholarships/grants, and unspecified assistantships also available. Financial award application deadline: 2/15; financial award applicants required to submit FAFSA. *Unit head:* Dr. Nancy Reese, Chairperson, 501-450-3611, Fax: 501-450-5822, E-mail: nancyr@uca.edu. *Application contact:* Sandy Burks, Administrative Assistant, 501-450-3124, Fax: 501-450-5678, E-mail: slburks@uca.edu. Web site: http://uca.edu/pt/.

University of Central Florida, College of Health and Public Affairs, Department of Health Professions, Program in Physical Therapy, Orlando, FL 32816. Offers DPT. *Accreditation:* APTA. *Students:* 69 full-time (43 women), 1 (woman) part-time; includes 9 minority (2 Black or African American, non-Hispanic/Latino; 1 American Indian or Alaska Native, non-Hispanic/Latino; 1 Asian, non-Hispanic/Latino; 5 Hispanic/Latino). Average age 25. 255 applicants, 25% accepted, 34 enrolled. In 2011, 28 doctorates awarded. Application fee: $30. Electronic applications accepted. *Expenses:* Contact institution. *Financial support:* In 2011–12, 1 student received support, including 1 fellowship (averaging $10,000 per year); research assistantships, teaching assistantships, career-related internships or fieldwork, institutionally sponsored loans, scholarships/grants, tuition waivers (partial), and unspecified assistantships also available. *Unit head:* Dr. Patrick Pabian, Interim Director, 407-823-3457, E-mail: patrick.pabian@ucf.edu. *Application contact:* Barbara Rodriguez, Director, Admissions and Registration, 407-823-2766, Fax: 407-823-6442, E-mail: gradadmissions@ucf.edu.

University of Colorado Denver, School of Medicine, Program in Physical Therapy, Denver, CO 80217-3364. Offers DPT. *Accreditation:* APTA. Part-time programs available. *Students:* 179 full-time (148 women), 32 part-time (24 women); includes 5 minority (3 Asian, non-Hispanic/Latino; 2 Hispanic/Latino). Average age 29. 286 applicants, 20% accepted, 57 enrolled. In 2011, 59 doctorates awarded. *Degree requirements:* For doctorate, thesis/dissertation or alternative, 116 credit hours, 44 weeks of clinical experiences, capstone project at end of year 3. *Entrance requirements:* For doctorate, GRE, minimum GPA of 3.0; prerequisite coursework in anatomy, physiology, chemistry, physics, psychology, English composition or writing, college-level math, statistics, and upper-level science, 45 hours of observation. Additional exam requirements/recommendations for international students: Required—TOEFL (minimum score 550 paper-based; 213 computer-based). *Application deadline:* For fall admission, 10/1 for domestic students, 8/8 for international students. Application fee: $120. Electronic applications accepted. *Expenses:* Contact institution. *Financial support:* Research assistantships, teaching assistantships, Federal Work-Study, and scholarships/grants available. Financial award application deadline: 3/15; financial award applicants required to submit FAFSA. *Faculty research:* Interventions for early and mid-stages of Parkinson's disease, physical therapy for individuals with recurrent lower back pain. *Unit head:* Margaret Schenkman, Program Director, 303-724-9375, E-mail: margaret.schenkman@ucdenver.edu. *Application contact:* Betti Krapfl, Admissions Advisor, 303-724-9133, E-mail: betti.krapfl@ucdenver.edu. Web site: http://www.uchsc.edu/pt/.

University of Connecticut, Graduate School, Neag School of Education, Department of Physical Therapy, Storrs, CT 06269. Offers DPT. *Accreditation:* APTA. *Entrance requirements:* Additional exam requirements/recommendations for international students: Required—TOEFL (minimum score 550 paper-based; 213 computer-based). Electronic applications accepted.

University of Dayton, Department of Health and Sport Science, Dayton, OH 45469-1300. Offers exercise science (MS Ed); physical therapy (DPT). Part-time programs available. *Faculty:* 16 full-time (7 women). *Students:* 113 full-time (70 women), 4 part-time (1 woman); includes 4 minority (all Black or African American, non-Hispanic/Latino), 5 international. Average age 36. 195 applicants, 43% accepted, 41 enrolled. In 2011, 3 master's, 34 doctorates awarded. *Degree requirements:* For master's, thesis; for doctorate, thesis/dissertation. *Entrance requirements:* For master's, GRE General Test, MAT, minimum GPA of 2.75; for doctorate, GRE General Test, minimum GPA of 3.0, 80 observation hours. Additional exam requirements/recommendations for international students: Required—TOEFL (minimum score 550 paper-based; 213 computer-based; 80 iBT). *Application deadline:* For fall admission, 2/15 priority date for domestic students, 3/1 for international students; for winter admission, 7/1 for international students; for spring admission, 1/1 for international students. Applications are processed on a rolling basis. Application fee: $0 ($50 for international students). Electronic applications accepted. *Expenses: Tuition:* Full-time $8400; part-time $700 per credit hour. *Required fees:* $25 per semester. Tuition and fees vary according to degree level. *Financial support:* In 2011–12, 4 students received support, including 8 research assistantships with partial tuition reimbursements available (averaging $4,800 per year), 5 teaching assistantships with full tuition reimbursements available (averaging $8,550 per year); career-related internships or fieldwork, institutionally sponsored loans, health care benefits, and unspecified assistantships also available. Financial award applicants required to submit FAFSA. *Faculty research:* Energy expenditure, strength, training, teaching nutrition and calcium intake for children and families in Head-Start. *Unit head:* Dr. Lloyd Laubach, Interim Chair, 937-229-4240, Fax: 937-229-4244, E-mail: llaubach1@udayton.edu. *Application contact:* Laura Greger, Administrative Assistant, 937-229-4225, E-mail: lgreger1@udayton.edu.

University of Delaware, College of Health Sciences, Department of Physical Therapy, Newark, DE 19716. Offers DPT. *Accreditation:* APTA. *Entrance requirements:* For doctorate, GRE, 100 hours clinical experience, 3 letters of recommendation. Additional exam requirements/recommendations for international students: Required—TOEFL (minimum score 550 paper-based; 213 computer-based). Electronic applications accepted. *Faculty research:* Movement sciences, applied physiology, physical rehabilitation.

University of Evansville, College of Education and Health Sciences, Department of Physical Therapy, Evansville, IN 47722. Offers DPT. *Accreditation:* APTA. *Degree requirements:* For doctorate, 30 weeks of full-time clinical internships (20 credit hours). *Entrance requirements:* For doctorate, bachelor's degree, science and math prerequisite courses, minimum GPA of 2.75, interview, recommendations. Additional exam requirements/recommendations for international students: Required—TOEFL (minimum score 570 paper-based; 88 iBT). *Expenses:* Contact institution. *Faculty research:* Cultural awareness, selective functional movement screening, concussion management, pretend play in children with and without disabilities, quality of life of individuals with developmental disabilities and their families.

The University of Findlay, Graduate and Professional Studies, College of Health Professions, Doctor of Physical Therapy Program, Findlay, OH 45840-3653. Offers DPT. *Accreditation:* APTA. Evening/weekend programs available. *Faculty:* 12 full-time (8 women), 4 part-time/adjunct (1 woman). *Students:* 114 full-time (71 women), 25 part-time (15 women); includes 4 minority (3 Black or African American, non-Hispanic/Latino; 1 Hispanic/Latino). Average age 35. 103 applicants, 69% accepted, 32 enrolled. In 2011, 49 doctorates awarded. *Entrance requirements:* For doctorate, GRE, Physical Therapy Central Application Service (PTCAS), 100 hours of observation, minimum GPA of 3.0, bachelor's degree, one year of experience (for the weekend program). Additional exam requirements/recommendations for international students: Required—TOEFL (minimum score 550 paper-based; 213 computer-based; 80 iBT). *Application deadline:* For fall admission, 11/15 for domestic and international students; for winter admission, 5/1 for domestic and international students. Applications are processed on a rolling basis. Application fee: $25. Electronic applications accepted. *Expenses: Tuition:* Full-time $6300; part-time $700 per semester hour. *Required fees:* $35 per semester hour. One-time fee: $25. Tuition and fees vary according to course load, degree level and program. *Financial support:* In 2011–12, 2 teaching assistantships with full and partial tuition reimbursements (averaging $3,600 per year) were awarded; Federal Work-Study, health care benefits, tuition waivers (full and partial), and unspecified assistantships also available. Financial award application deadline: 4/1; financial award applicants required to submit FAFSA. *Unit head:* Dr. Robert Frampton, Chair, 419-434-6752, Fax: 419-434-

4822. *Application contact:* Heather Riffle, Assistant Director, Graduate and Professional Studies, 419-434-4640, Fax: 419-434-5517, E-mail: riffle@findlay.edu.

University of Florida, Graduate School, College of Public Health and Health Professions, Department of Physical Therapy, Gainesville, FL 32611. Offers DPT. *Accreditation:* APTA. *Faculty:* 10 full-time (5 women), 1 (woman) part-time/adjunct. *Students:* Average age 34. In 2011, 11 doctorates awarded. *Entrance requirements:* For doctorate, GRE General Test, minimum GPA of 3.0. Additional exam requirements/recommendations for international students: Required—TOEFL (minimum score 515 paper-based; 213 computer-based; 80 iBT), IELTS (minimum score 6). *Application deadline:* For fall admission, 6/1 priority date for domestic students; for spring admission, 2/15 priority date for domestic students. Applications are processed on a rolling basis. Application fee: $30. Electronic applications accepted. *Financial support:* In 2011–12, 21 students received support, including 8 fellowships, 13 research assistantships (averaging $19,365 per year); career-related internships or fieldwork also available. Financial award applicants required to submit FAFSA. *Faculty research:* Exercise physiology, motor control, rehabilitation, geriatrics. *Unit head:* Dr. Krista Vandenborne, Department Chair and Associate Dean for Research and Planning, 352-273-6085, Fax: 352-273-6109, E-mail: kvandenb@phhp.ufl.edu. *Application contact:* Dr. Jane Day, Associate Chair, 352-273-6433, Fax: 352-273-6109, E-mail: jday@phhp.ufl.edu. Web site: http://ot.phhp.ufl.edu/.

University of Hartford, College of Education, Nursing, and Health Professions, Program in Physical Therapy, West Hartford, CT 06117-1599. Offers MSPT, DPT. *Accreditation:* APTA. *Entrance requirements:* For master's, GRE, 3 letters of recommendation. Additional exam requirements/recommendations for international students: Required—TOEFL (minimum score 550 paper-based; 213 computer-based).

University of Illinois at Chicago, Graduate College, College of Applied Health Sciences, Department of Physical Therapy, Chicago, IL 60607-7128. Offers MS, DPT. *Accreditation:* APTA. *Degree requirements:* For master's, thesis. *Entrance requirements:* For master's, GRE General Test, minimum GPA of 2.75. Additional exam requirements/recommendations for international students: Required—TOEFL. Electronic applications accepted.

University of Indianapolis, Graduate Programs, Krannert School of Physical Therapy, Indianapolis, IN 46227-3697. Offers MHS, DHS, DPT, TDPT. *Accreditation:* APTA (one or more programs are accredited). Part-time and evening/weekend programs available. *Faculty:* 10 full-time (5 women), 6 part-time/adjunct (5 women). *Students:* 125 full-time (87 women), 95 part-time (74 women); includes 4 minority (2 Asian, non-Hispanic/Latino; 2 Hispanic/Latino), 66 international. Average age 26. In 2011, 13 master's, 57 doctorates awarded. *Entrance requirements:* For doctorate, GRE General Test (for DPT), minimum GPA of 3.0 (for DPT), 3 letters of recommendation. Additional exam requirements/recommendations for international students: Required—TOEFL (minimum score 250 computer-based; 100 iBT), TWE (minimum score 5). *Application deadline:* For fall admission, 10/10 for domestic students. Application fee: $50. Electronic applications accepted. *Expenses:* Contact institution. *Financial support:* Teaching assistantships, career-related internships or fieldwork, Federal Work-Study, scholarships/grants, tuition waivers (full and partial), and unspecified assistantships available. Support available to part-time students. Financial award application deadline: 5/1; financial award applicants required to submit FAFSA. *Faculty research:* Patella positioning, reaction time, allocation of physical therapy resources. *Unit head:* Dr. Stephanie Kelly, Dean, College of Health Sciences, 317-788-3500, Fax: 317-788-3542, E-mail: huerm@uindy.edu. *Application contact:* Anne Hardwick, Director, Marketing and Admissions, 317-788-3495, Fax: 317-788-3542, E-mail: ahardwick@uindy.edu. Web site: http://pt.uindy.edu/.

The University of Iowa, Roy J. and Lucille A. Carver College of Medicine and Graduate College, Biosciences Program, Iowa City, IA 52242-1316. Offers anatomy and biology (PhD); biochemistry (PhD); biology (PhD); biomedical engineering (PhD); chemistry (PhD); free radical and radiation biology (PhD); genetics (PhD); human toxicology (PhD); immunology (PhD); microbiology (PhD); molecular and cellular biology (PhD); molecular physiology and biophysics (PhD); neuroscience (PhD); pharmacology (PhD); physical therapy and rehabilitation science (PhD); speech and hearing (PhD). *Faculty:* 310 full-time. *Students:* 9 full-time (5 women); includes 4 minority (1 Black or African American, non-Hispanic/Latino; 2 Asian, non-Hispanic/Latino; 1 Hispanic/Latino). 225 applicants. *Degree requirements:* For doctorate, thesis/dissertation. *Entrance requirements:* For doctorate, GRE General Test, minimum GPA of 3.0. Additional exam requirements/recommendations for international students: Required—TOEFL (minimum score 600 paper-based; 250 computer-based; 100 iBT). *Application deadline:* For fall admission, 1/15 priority date for domestic students, 1/15 for international students. Applications are processed on a rolling basis. Application fee: $60 ($100 for international students). Electronic applications accepted. *Expenses:* Contact institution. *Financial support:* In 2011–12, 9 students received support, including 9 research assistantships with full tuition reimbursements available (averaging $25,000 per year); fellowships, teaching assistantships, and health care benefits also available. *Unit head:* Dr. Douglas Spitz, Director, 319-335-8001, Fax: 319-335-7656, E-mail: andrew-russo@uiowa.edu. *Application contact:* Jodi M. Graff, Program Associate, 319-335-8305, Fax: 319-335-7656, E-mail: biosciences-admissions@uiowa.edu. Web site: http://www.biology.uiowa.edu/graduate.php.

The University of Iowa, Roy J. and Lucille A. Carver College of Medicine and Graduate College, Graduate Programs in Medicine, Graduate Program in Physical Therapy and Rehabilitation Science, Iowa City, IA 52242-1316. Offers physical therapy (DPT); rehabilitation science (PhD). *Accreditation:* APTA (one or more programs are accredited). *Faculty:* 7 full-time (3 women), 47 part-time/adjunct (28 women). *Students:* 116 full-time (85 women), 4 part-time (1 woman); includes 4 minority (1 Black or African American, non-Hispanic/Latino; 2 Asian, non-Hispanic/Latino; 1 Hispanic/Latino), 3 international. Average age 24. 352 applicants, 14% accepted, 36 enrolled. In 2011, 3 doctorates awarded. Terminal master's awarded for partial completion of doctoral program. *Degree requirements:* For doctorate, thesis/dissertation (for some programs). *Entrance requirements:* For doctorate, GRE. Additional exam requirements/recommendations for international students: Required—TOEFL. *Application deadline:* For fall admission, 12/1 priority date for domestic students, 5/15 for international students; for winter admission, 10/15 for international students; for spring admission, 3/15 for international students. Application fee: $60 ($85 for international students). Electronic applications accepted. *Expenses:* Contact institution. *Financial support:* In 2011–12, 94 students received support, including 1 fellowship with partial tuition reimbursement available (averaging $9,000 per year), 6 research assistantships with partial tuition reimbursements available (averaging $10,129 per year), teaching assistantships with partial tuition reimbursements available (averaging $10,129 per year); Federal Work-Study, institutionally sponsored loans, scholarships/grants, health care benefits, and unspecified assistantships also available. Support available to part-time students. Financial award application deadline: 6/30; financial award applicants required to submit FAFSA. *Faculty research:* Muscle fatigue, motor control, pain mechanisms, body composition, sports medicine, occupational safety, neuromuscular physiology, neural control of movement. *Total annual research expenditures:* $1.4 million. *Unit head:* Dr. Richard K. Shields, Director, 319-335-9791, Fax: 319-335-9707, E-mail: physical-therapy@uiowa.edu. *Application contact:* Carol Leigh, Project Assistant, 319-335-9792, Fax: 319-335-9707, E-mail: carol-leigh@uiowa.edu. Web site: http://www.healthcare.uiowa.edu/physicaltherapy/index.html.

The University of Kansas, University of Kansas Medical Center, School of Health Professions, Department of Physical Therapy and Rehabilitation Science, Kansas City, KS 66160. Offers physical therapy (DPT); rehabilitation science (PhD). *Accreditation:* APTA. *Faculty:* 30. *Students:* 123 full-time (86 women), 29 part-time (22 women); includes 9 minority (2 Black or African American, non-Hispanic/Latino; 1 American Indian or Alaska Native, non-Hispanic/Latino; 5 Asian, non-Hispanic/Latino; 1 Hispanic/Latino), 10 international. Average age 29. 150 applicants, 31% accepted, 46 enrolled. In 2011, 55 doctorates awarded. *Degree requirements:* For doctorate, comprehensive exam, research project with paper. *Entrance requirements:* For doctorate, GRE General Test, minimum GPA of 3.0. Additional exam requirements/recommendations for international students: Required—TOEFL. *Application deadline:* For fall admission, 11/1 for domestic students. Applications are processed on a rolling basis. Application fee: $60. Electronic applications accepted. *Expenses:* Contact institution. *Financial support:* Research assistantships with tuition reimbursements, teaching assistantships with full and partial tuition reimbursements, career-related internships or fieldwork, Federal Work-Study, institutionally sponsored loans, scholarships/grants, traineeships, and unspecified assistantships available. Financial award application deadline: 2/14; financial award applicants required to submit FAFSA. *Faculty research:* Stroke rehabilitation and the effects on balance and coordination; deep brain stimulation and Parkinson's Disease; peripheral neuropathies, pain and the effects of exercise; islet transplants for Type 1 diabetes; cardiac disease associated with diabetes. *Total annual research expenditures:* $615,660. *Unit head:* Dr. Lisa Stehno-Bittel, Chair, 913-588-6733, Fax: 913-588-4568, E-mail: lbittel@kumc.edu. *Application contact:* Robert Bagley, Admission Coordinator, 913-588-6799, Fax: 913-588-4568, E-mail: rbagley@kumc.edu. Web site: http://ptrs.kumc.edu.

University of Kentucky, Graduate School, College of Health Sciences, Program in Physical Therapy, Lexington, KY 40506-0032. Offers MSPT. *Accreditation:* APTA. *Degree requirements:* For master's, comprehensive exam, thesis optional. *Entrance requirements:* For master's, GRE General Test, minimum undergraduate GPA of 2.75, U.S. physical therapist license. Additional exam requirements/recommendations for international students: Required—TOEFL (minimum score 550 paper-based; 213 computer-based). Electronic applications accepted. *Faculty research:* Orthopedics, biomechanics, electrophysiological stimulation, neural plasticity, brain damage and mechanism.

University of Manitoba, Faculty of Graduate Studies, School of Medical Rehabilitation, Winnipeg, MB R3T 2N2, Canada. Offers applied health sciences (PhD); occupational therapy (MOT); physical therapy (MPT); rehabilitation (M Sc).

University of Mary, School of Health Sciences, Program in Physical Therapy, Bismarck, ND 58504-9652. Offers DPT. *Accreditation:* APTA. *Faculty:* 7 full-time (4 women), 5 part-time/adjunct (3 women). *Students:* 70 full-time (49 women); includes 5 minority (1 Black or African American, non-Hispanic/Latino; 1 American Indian or Alaska Native, non-Hispanic/Latino; 2 Asian, non-Hispanic/Latino; 1 Hispanic/Latino). Average age 25. 237 applicants, 17% accepted, 36 enrolled. In 2011, 30 doctorates awarded. *Degree requirements:* For doctorate, comprehensive exam, professional paper. *Entrance requirements:* For doctorate, minimum GPA of 3.0 in core requirements, 40 hours of paid/volunteer experience, interview. Additional exam requirements/recommendations for international students: Required—TOEFL (minimum score 500 paper-based; 197 computer-based; 71 iBT). *Application deadline:* Applications are processed on a rolling basis. Application fee: $40. Electronic applications accepted. *Expenses:* Contact institution. *Financial support:* In 2011–12, teaching assistantships with partial tuition reimbursements (averaging $2,500 per year) were awarded; career-related internships or fieldwork also available. Financial award application deadline: 8/1; financial award applicants required to submit FAFSA. *Faculty research:* Proprioception, falls and elderly, clinical biomechanics, admission predictors, electromyography and muscle performance, wellness. *Unit head:* Dr. Mary Kay Dockter, Program Director, 701-355-8045, Fax: 701-255-7687, E-mail: mcdoc@umary.edu. *Application contact:* Dr. Kathy Perrin, Director of Graduate Studies, 701-355-8119, Fax: 701-255-7687, E-mail: kperrin@umary.edu.

University of Maryland, Baltimore, School of Medicine, Department of Physical Therapy and Rehabilitation Science, Baltimore, MD 21201. Offers physical rehabilitation science (PhD); physical therapy and rehabilitation science (DPT). *Accreditation:* APTA. *Students:* 120 full-time (76 women), 48 part-time (33 women); includes 34 minority (12 Black or African American, non-Hispanic/Latino; 12 Asian, non-Hispanic/Latino; 6 Hispanic/Latino; 4 Two or more races, non-Hispanic/Latino), 5 international. Average age 25. In 2011, 80 doctorates awarded. *Entrance requirements:* For doctorate, GRE General Test, BS, science coursework. Additional exam requirements/recommendations for international students: Required—TOEFL (minimum score 213 computer-based; 80 iBT). Electronic applications accepted. *Expenses:* Contact institution. *Financial support:* Career-related internships or fieldwork, Federal Work-Study, scholarships/grants, traineeships, health care benefits, and unspecified assistantships available. Financial award application deadline: 3/1; financial award applicants required to submit FAFSA. *Unit head:* Dr. Mary Rodgers, Chair, 410-706-5216, Fax: 410-706-4903, E-mail: mrodgers@som.umaryland.edu. *Application contact:* Terry Heron, Program Coordinator, 410-706-5215, Fax: 410-706-6387, E-mail: theron@som.umaryland.edu. Web site: http://pt.umaryland.edu/pros.asp.

University of Maryland Eastern Shore, Graduate Programs, Department of Physical Therapy, Princess Anne, MD 21853-1299. Offers DPT. *Accreditation:* APTA. *Degree requirements:* For doctorate, thesis/dissertation, clinical practicum, research project. *Entrance requirements:* For doctorate, minimum GPA of 3.0, course work in science and mathematics, interview, knowledge of the physical therapy field. Additional exam requirements/recommendations for international students: Required—TOEFL (minimum score 213 computer-based; 80 iBT). Electronic applications accepted. *Faculty research:* Allied health projects.

University of Massachusetts Lowell, School of Health and Environment, Department of Physical Therapy, Lowell, MA 01854-2881. Offers DPT. *Accreditation:* APTA. *Entrance requirements:* For doctorate, GRE General Test, minimum GPA of 3.0, 3 letters of recommendation. Additional exam requirements/recommendations for international students: Required—TOEFL (minimum score 560 paper-based; 220 computer-based). *Faculty research:* Orthopedics, pediatrics, electrophysiology, cardiopulmonary, neurology.

University of Medicine and Dentistry of New Jersey, School of Health Related Professions, Department of Interdisciplinary Studies, Program in Health Sciences, Newark, NJ 07107-1709. Offers cardiopulmonary sciences (PhD); clinical laboratory sciences (PhD); health sciences (MS); interdisciplinary studies (PhD); nutrition (PhD); physical therapy/movement science (PhD). Part-time and evening/weekend programs available. Postbaccalaureate distance learning degree programs offered (no on-campus study). *Faculty:* 4 full-time (all women), 10 part-time/adjunct (7 women). *Students:* 3 full-time, 130 part-time; includes 32 minority (10 Black or African American, non-Hispanic/Latino; 10 Asian, non-Hispanic/Latino; 11 Hispanic/Latino; 1 Native Hawaiian or other Pacific Islander, non-Hispanic/Latino). Average age 41. 132 applicants, 51% accepted,

51 enrolled. In 2011, 17 master's, 4 doctorates awarded. *Degree requirements:* For doctorate, thesis/dissertation. *Entrance requirements:* For master's, BS, 2 reference letters, statement of career goals, curriculum vitae; for doctorate, GRE, interview, writing sample, 3 reference letters, curriculum vitae. Additional exam requirements/recommendations for international students: Required—TOEFL. *Application deadline:* For fall admission, 3/1 for domestic students. Applications are processed on a rolling basis. Application fee: $75. Electronic applications accepted. *Unit head:* Dr. Bob Denmark, Director, 973-972-5410, Fax: 973-972-7403, E-mail: ms-phd-hs@umdnj.edu. *Application contact:* Diane Hanrahan, Manager of Admissions, 973-972-5336, Fax: 973-972-7463, E-mail: shrpadm@umdnj.edu.

University of Medicine and Dentistry of New Jersey, School of Health Related Professions, Department of Rehabilitation and Movement Sciences, Program in Physical Therapy (Entry Level) –Newark, Newark, NJ 07107-1709. Offers DPT. *Accreditation:* APTA. *Faculty:* 16 full-time (14 women), 55 part-time/adjunct (35 women). *Students:* 163 full-time (108 women); includes 43 minority (4 Black or African American, non-Hispanic/Latino; 24 Asian, non-Hispanic/Latino; 15 Hispanic/Latino). Average age 25. 272 applicants, 39% accepted, 59 enrolled. In 2011, 42 degrees awarded. *Entrance requirements:* For doctorate, GRE, chemistry, physics, calculus, psychology, statistics, interview, 3 reference letters. Additional exam requirements/recommendations for international students: Required—TOEFL (minimum score 500 paper-based; 79 iBT). *Application deadline:* For fall admission, 11/15 priority date for domestic students, 3/1 for international students. Applications are processed on a rolling basis. Application fee: $50. Electronic applications accepted. *Unit head:* Dr. Alma S. Merians, Director, 973-972-7820, Fax: 973-972-3717, E-mail: merians@umdnj.edu. *Application contact:* Diane Hanrahan, Assistant Dean, 973-972-5336, Fax: 973-972-7463, E-mail: shrpadm@umdnj.edu.

University of Medicine and Dentistry of New Jersey, School of Health Related Professions, Department of Rehabilitation and Movement Sciences, Program in Physical Therapy–Stratford, Newark, NJ 07107-1709. Offers DPT. *Accreditation:* APTA. *Faculty:* 8 full-time (4 women), 20 part-time/adjunct (8 women). *Students:* 88 full-time (59 women); includes 16 minority (3 Black or African American, non-Hispanic/Latino; 12 Asian, non-Hispanic/Latino; 1 Hispanic/Latino). Average age 25. 138 applicants, 30% accepted, 33 enrolled. In 2011, 26 degrees awarded. *Entrance requirements:* For doctorate, GRE, BS, 3 reference letters, interview. Additional exam requirements/recommendations for international students: Required—TOEFL (minimum score 500 paper-based; 79 iBT). *Application deadline:* For fall admission, 11/15 priority date for domestic students, 3/1 for international students. Applications are processed on a rolling basis. Application fee: $75. Electronic applications accepted. *Unit head:* Marie Koval Nardone, Director, 856-566-6456, Fax: 856-566-6458, E-mail: mptgradm@umdnj.edu. *Application contact:* Diane Hanrahan, Assistant Dean, 973-972-5336, Fax: 973-972-7463, E-mail: shrpadm@umdnj.edu.

University of Miami, Graduate School, Miller School of Medicine, Graduate Programs in Medicine, Department of Physical Therapy, Coral Gables, FL 33124. Offers DPT, PhD. *Accreditation:* APTA (one or more programs are accredited). *Degree requirements:* For doctorate, comprehensive exam, thesis/dissertation. *Entrance requirements:* For doctorate, GRE General Test. Additional exam requirements/recommendations for international students: Required—TOEFL. Electronic applications accepted. *Expenses:* Contact institution. *Faculty research:* Central pattern generators in SCI balance and vestibular function in children, amputee rehabilitation.

University of Michigan–Flint, School of Health Professions and Studies, Program in Physical Therapy, Flint, MI 48502-1950. Offers online transitional (DPT); traditional entry-level (DPT). *Accreditation:* APTA. Part-time programs available. Postbaccalaureate distance learning degree programs offered. *Degree requirements:* For doctorate, comprehensive exam, thesis/dissertation or alternative. *Entrance requirements:* For doctorate, GRE (Verbal score between 340-480; Quantitative 370-710), minimum GPA of 3.16. Additional exam requirements/recommendations for international students: Required—TOEFL (minimum score 560 paper-based; 220 computer-based; 84 iBT), IELTS (minimum score 6.5). Electronic applications accepted. *Expenses:* Contact institution. *Faculty research:* Cumulative trauma disorders, oncology rehabilitation, neurological rehabilitation, musculoskeletal rehabilitation, cardiopulmonary rehabilitation.

University of Minnesota, Twin Cities Campus, Medical School, Program in Physical Therapy, Minneapolis, MN 55455. Offers DPT. *Accreditation:* APTA. *Degree requirements:* For doctorate, research project. *Entrance requirements:* For doctorate, GRE. Additional exam requirements/recommendations for international students: Required—TOEFL (minimum score 79 iBT). Electronic applications accepted. *Expenses:* Contact institution. *Faculty research:* Aging, stroke, muscle, balance, spine, Parkinson's disease, dystonia, biomechanics, ergonomics.

University of Mississippi Medical Center, School of Health Related Professions, Department of Physical Therapy, Jackson, MS 39216-4505. Offers MPT. *Accreditation:* APTA. *Faculty research:* Pain, acupressure, seating, patient satisfaction, physical therapy educational issues.

University of Missouri, School of Health Professions, Program in Physical Therapy, Columbia, MO 65211. Offers MPT. *Accreditation:* APTA. *Faculty:* 8 full-time (6 women), 1 (woman) part-time/adjunct. *Students:* 117 full-time (89 women); includes 1 minority (Black or African American, non-Hispanic/Latino). Average age 24. 186 applicants, 31% accepted, 55 enrolled. *Entrance requirements:* For master's, GRE General Test, minimum GPA of 3.0. Additional exam requirements/recommendations for international students: Required—TOEFL (minimum score 600 paper-based; 250 computer-based; 100 iBT). *Application deadline:* For spring admission, 1/10 for domestic students. Applications are processed on a rolling basis. Application fee: $55 ($75 for international students). *Expenses:* Tuition, state resident: full-time $5881. Tuition, nonresident: full-time $15,183. *Required fees:* $952. Tuition and fees vary according to campus/location and program. *Financial support:* Research assistantships, teaching assistantships, and institutionally sponsored loans available. *Faculty research:* Fall prevention; early identification of motor impairments in high risk infants, the impact of treadmill training on gait in children with motor impairments, the clinical use of motion analysis to assess functional changes in movement in the pediatric population; injuries common in endurance athletes, patellofemoral dysfunction; manual therapy for the treatment of spinal disorders, estrogen action in skeletal muscle, biopsychosocial factors, exercise in an older adult population. *Unit head:* Dr. Marian Minor, Director of Graduate Studies, 573-882-1579, E-mail: minorm@missouri.edu. *Application contact:* Beverly Denbigh, 573-882-7103, E-mail: denbighb@missouri.edu. Web site: http://shp.missouri.edu/pt/index.php.

The University of Montana, Graduate School, College of Health Professions and Biomedical Sciences, School of Physical Therapy and Rehabilitation Science, Missoula, MT 59812-0002. Offers physical therapy (DPT). *Accreditation:* APTA. *Degree requirements:* For doctorate, professional paper. *Entrance requirements:* For doctorate, GRE General Test. Additional exam requirements/recommendations for international students: Required—TOEFL. Electronic applications accepted. *Expenses:* Contact institution. *Faculty research:* Muscle stiffness, fitness with a disability, psychosocial aspects of disability, clinical learning, motion analysis.

University of Nebraska Medical Center, School of Allied Health Professions, Division of Physical Therapy Education, Omaha, NE 68198. Offers DPT. *Accreditation:* APTA.

University of Nevada, Las Vegas, Graduate College, School of Allied Health Sciences, Department of Physical Therapy, Las Vegas, NV 89154-3029. Offers DPT. *Accreditation:* APTA. *Faculty:* 7 full-time (3 women), 1 part-time/adjunct (0 women). *Students:* 83 full-time (53 women), 1 part-time (0 women); includes 15 minority (1 American Indian or Alaska Native, non-Hispanic/Latino; 4 Asian, non-Hispanic/Latino; 6 Hispanic/Latino; 4 Two or more races, non-Hispanic/Latino). Average age 27. In 2011, 29 doctorates awarded. *Entrance requirements:* Additional exam requirements/recommendations for international students: Required—TOEFL (minimum score 550 paper-based; 213 computer-based; 80 iBT), IELTS (minimum score 7). *Application deadline:* For fall admission, 5/1 for international students; for spring admission, 10/1 for international students. Applications are processed on a rolling basis. Application fee: $60 ($95 for international students). Electronic applications accepted. *Financial support:* In 2011–12, 6 students received support, including 2 research assistantships with partial tuition reimbursements available (averaging $7,000 per year), 4 teaching assistantships with partial tuition reimbursements available (averaging $12,000 per year); institutionally sponsored loans, scholarships/grants, health care benefits, and unspecified assistantships also available. Financial award application deadline: 3/1. *Faculty research:* Spinal manipulation, balance assessment and impairment, falls and fall avoidance behavior, wound care and acute care delivery services, pediatric physical therapy, pain reduction and pain science education. *Total annual research expenditures:* $3,713. *Unit head:* Dr. Merrill Landers, Chair/Associate Professor, 702-895-1377, Fax: 702-895-4883, E-mail: merrill.landers@unlv.edu. *Application contact:* Graduate College Admissions Evaluator, 702-895-3320, Fax: 702-895-4180, E-mail: gradcollege@unlv.edu. Web site: http://pt.unlv.edu/.

University of New England, Westbrook College of Health Professions, Program in Physical Therapy, Biddeford, ME 04005-9526. Offers physical therapy (DPT); post professional physical therapy (DPT). *Accreditation:* APTA. *Faculty:* 8 full-time, 5 part-time/adjunct. *Students:* 164 full-time (117 women). In 2011, 48 doctorates awarded. *Entrance requirements:* Additional exam requirements/recommendations for international students: Required—TOEFL. *Application deadline:* For fall admission, 2/1 for domestic students. Applications are processed on a rolling basis. Application fee: $40. Electronic applications accepted. *Expenses:* Contact institution. *Financial support:* Scholarships/grants available. Financial award application deadline: 5/1; financial award applicants required to submit FAFSA. *Faculty research:* Biomechanics, motor control, clinical education, functional outcomes, health policy. *Unit head:* Michael Sheldon, Director, 207-221-4591, E-mail: msheldon@une.edu. *Application contact:* Stacy Gato, Director of Graduate Admissions, 207-221-4225, Fax: 207-221-4898, E-mail: gradadmissions@une.edu.

University of New Mexico, Health Sciences Center Graduate Programs, Physical Therapy Doctoral Program, Albuquerque, NM 87131-0001. Offers DPT. *Accreditation:* APTA. *Faculty:* 10 full-time (5 women). *Students:* 81 full-time (60 women); includes 33 minority (3 American Indian or Alaska Native, non-Hispanic/Latino; 1 Asian, non-Hispanic/Latino; 29 Hispanic/Latino). Average age 30. 33 applicants, 100% accepted, 30 enrolled. In 2011, 21 doctorates awarded. *Degree requirements:* For doctorate, comprehensive exam, thesis/dissertation. *Entrance requirements:* Additional exam requirements/recommendations for international students: Required—TOEFL (minimum score 580 paper-based; 237 computer-based). *Application deadline:* For fall admission, 12/15 priority date for domestic students. Applications are processed on a rolling basis. Application fee: $50. *Financial support:* In 2011–12, 69 students received support, including 1 fellowship (averaging $3,600 per year); Federal Work-Study, institutionally sponsored loans, and scholarships/grants also available. Financial award application deadline: 3/1; financial award applicants required to submit FAFSA. *Faculty research:* Gait analysis, motion analysis, balance, articular cartilage, quality of life. *Total annual research expenditures:* $7,800. *Unit head:* Dr. Susan A. Queen, Director, 505-272-5756, Fax: 505-272-8079, E-mail: squeen@salud.unm.edu. *Application contact:* Rosalia Loya Vejar, Administrative Assistant, 505-272-6956, Fax: 505-272-8079, E-mail: rloyavejar@salud.unm.edu. Web site: http://hsc.unm.edu/som/physther/.

The University of North Carolina at Chapel Hill, School of Medicine and Graduate School, Graduate Programs in Medicine, Chapel Hill, NC 27599. Offers allied health sciences (MPT, MS, Au D, DPT, PhD), including human movement science (MS, PhD), occupational science (MS, PhD), physical therapy (MPT, MS, DPT), rehabilitation counseling and psychology (MS), speech and hearing sciences (MS, Au D, PhD); biochemistry and biophysics (MS, PhD); bioinformatics and computational biology (PhD); biomedical engineering (MS, PhD); cell and developmental biology (PhD); cell and molecular physiology (PhD); genetics and molecular biology (PhD); microbiology and immunology (MS, PhD), including immunology, microbiology; neurobiology (PhD); pathology and laboratory medicine (PhD), including experimental pathology; pharmacology (PhD); MD/PhD. Postbaccalaureate distance learning degree programs offered. Terminal master's awarded for partial completion of doctoral program. *Degree requirements:* For master's, comprehensive exam; for doctorate, thesis/dissertation. Electronic applications accepted. *Expenses:* Contact institution.

The University of North Carolina at Chapel Hill, School of Medicine and Graduate School, Graduate Programs in Medicine, Department of Allied Health Sciences, Program in Physical Therapy, Chapel Hill, NC 27599. Offers physical therapy - off campus (DPT); physical therapy - on campus (DPT). *Accreditation:* APTA. Part-time and evening/weekend programs available. Postbaccalaureate distance learning degree programs offered (no on-campus study). *Degree requirements:* For doctorate, thesis/dissertation or alternative. *Entrance requirements:* For doctorate, physical therapy license. Additional exam requirements/recommendations for international students: Required—TOEFL (minimum score 550 paper-based; 79 computer-based). Electronic applications accepted. *Faculty research:* Traumatic brain injury, quality of life after heart and/or lung transplant, cultural diversity, life care planning, rehabilitation education and supervision.

University of North Dakota, Graduate School and Graduate School, Graduate Programs in Medicine, Department of Physical Therapy, Grand Forks, ND 58202. Offers MPT, DPT. *Accreditation:* APTA. *Degree requirements:* For master's, comprehensive exam, thesis or alternative. *Entrance requirements:* For master's and doctorate, minimum GPA of 3.0, pre-physical therapy program. Additional exam requirements/recommendations for international students: Required—TOEFL (minimum score 550 paper-based; 213 computer-based; 79 iBT), IELTS (minimum score 6.5). *Faculty research:* Practice-based program.

University of North Florida, Brooks College of Health, Department of Clinical and Applied Movement Sciences, Jacksonville, FL 32224. Offers exercise science and chronic disease (MSH); physical therapy (DPT). *Accreditation:* APTA. Part-time and evening/weekend programs available. *Faculty:* 14 full-time (9 women), 2 part-time/adjunct (0 women). *Students:* 87 full-time (52 women); includes 10 minority (2 Black or African American, non-Hispanic/Latino; 1 Asian, non-Hispanic/Latino; 5 Hispanic/Latino; 2 Two or more races, non-Hispanic/Latino), 2 international. Average age 25. 303 applicants, 17% accepted, 27 enrolled. In 2011, 24 doctorates awarded. *Degree requirements:* For master's, internship. *Entrance requirements:* For master's, GRE General Test, minimum GPA of 3.0 in last 60 hours, volunteer/observation experience.

Additional exam requirements/recommendations for international students: Required—TOEFL (minimum score 500 paper-based; 173 computer-based). *Application deadline:* For fall admission, 2/15 for domestic students, 1/15 for international students. Application fee: $30. Electronic applications accepted. *Expenses:* Tuition, state resident: full-time $8793; part-time $366.38 per credit hour. Tuition, nonresident: full-time $23,502; part-time $979.24 per credit hour. *Required fees:* $1384; $57.66 per credit hour. Tuition and fees vary according to course load and program. *Financial support:* In 2011–12, 35 students received support. Teaching assistantships, career-related internships or fieldwork, Federal Work-Study, scholarships/grants, and tuition waivers (partial) available. Support available to part-time students. Financial award application deadline: 4/1; financial award applicants required to submit FAFSA. *Faculty research:* Clinical outcomes related to orthopedic physical therapy interventions, instructional multimedia in physical therapy education, effect of functional electrical stimulation orthostatic hypotension in acute complete spinal cord injury individuals. *Total annual research expenditures:* $72,169. *Unit head:* Dr. Lillia Loriz, Chair, 904-620-2841, E-mail: lloriz@unf.edu. *Application contact:* Beth Dibble, Program Director, 904-620-2418, E-mail: ptadmissions@unf.edu. Web site: http://www.unf.edu/brooks/movement_science/.

University of Oklahoma Health Sciences Center, Graduate College, College of Allied Health, Department of Physical Therapy, Oklahoma City, OK 73190. Offers MPT. *Accreditation:* APTA.

University of Pittsburgh, School of Health and Rehabilitation Sciences, Doctor of Physical Therapy Program, Pittsburgh, PA 15260. Offers DPT. *Accreditation:* APTA. *Faculty:* 11 full-time (7 women), 1 (woman) part-time/adjunct. *Students:* 171 full-time (121 women), 1 part-time (0 women); includes 8 minority (5 Black or African American, non-Hispanic/Latino; 3 Asian, non-Hispanic/Latino), 1 international. Average age 26. 747 applicants, 19% accepted, 53 enrolled. In 2011, 62 doctorates awarded. *Degree requirements:* For doctorate, clinical practice. *Entrance requirements:* For doctorate, GRE, volunteer work in physical therapy. Additional exam requirements/recommendations for international students: Required—TOEFL (minimum score 550 paper-based; 213 computer-based; 80 iBT), IELTS (minimum score 6.5). *Application deadline:* For fall admission, 12/15 for domestic students. Applications are processed on a rolling basis. Application fee: $125. Electronic applications accepted. *Expenses:* Contact institution. *Financial support:* Federal Work-Study, scholarships/grants, and traineeships available. Support available to part-time students. Financial award applicants required to submit FAFSA. *Faculty research:* Biomechanics, neuromuscular system, sports medicine, movement analysis, validity/outcomes of clinical procedures. *Total annual research expenditures:* $748,362. *Unit head:* Dr. Anthony Delitto, Chairman, 412-383-6630, Fax: 412-383-6629, E-mail: delitto@pitt.edu. *Application contact:* Corinne Grubb, Administrator, PT Student Services, 412-383-8169, Fax: 412-648-5970, E-mail: cgrubb@pitt.edu. Web site: http://www.shrs.pitt.edu/dpt/.

University of Pittsburgh, School of Health and Rehabilitation Sciences, Master's Programs in Health and Rehabilitation Sciences, Pittsburgh, PA 15260. Offers health and rehabilitation sciences (MS), including clinical dietetics and nutrition, health care supervision and management, health information systems, occupational therapy, physical therapy, rehabilitation counseling, rehabilitation science and technology, sports medicine, wellness and human performance. *Accreditation:* APTA. Part-time and evening/weekend programs available. *Faculty:* 22 full-time (16 women), 4 part-time/adjunct (2 women). *Students:* 144 full-time (91 women), 35 part-time (23 women); includes 23 minority (8 Black or African American, non-Hispanic/Latino; 8 Asian, non-Hispanic/Latino; 3 Hispanic/Latino; 4 Two or more races, non-Hispanic/Latino), 74 international. Average age 28. 399 applicants, 61% accepted, 121 enrolled. In 2011, 86 master's awarded. *Degree requirements:* For master's, comprehensive exam (for some programs), thesis optional. *Entrance requirements:* For master's, minimum GPA of 3.0. Additional exam requirements/recommendations for international students: Required—TOEFL (minimum score 550 paper-based; 213 computer-based; 80 iBT), IELTS (minimum score 6.5). *Application deadline:* For fall admission, 3/1 for international students; for spring admission, 7/31 for international students. Applications are processed on a rolling basis. Application fee: $50. Electronic applications accepted. *Expenses:* Contact institution. *Financial support:* Research assistantships, teaching assistantships, Federal Work-Study, institutionally sponsored loans, traineeships, and unspecified assistantships available. Financial award applicants required to submit FAFSA. *Faculty research:* Assistive technology, seating and wheeled mobility, cellular neurophysiology, low back syndrome, augmentative communication. *Total annual research expenditures:* $7.8 million. *Unit head:* Dr. Clifford E. Brubaker, Dean, 412-383-6560, Fax: 412-383-6535, E-mail: cliffb@pitt.edu. *Application contact:* Shameem Gangjee, Director of Admissions, 412-383-6558, Fax: 412-383-6535, E-mail: admissions@shrs.pitt.edu. Web site: http://www.shrs.pitt.edu/.

University of Puerto Rico, Medical Sciences Campus, School of Health Professions, Program in Physical Therapy, San Juan, PR 00936-5067. Offers MS. *Accreditation:* APTA. Part-time and evening/weekend programs available. *Degree requirements:* For master's, one foreign language, thesis. *Entrance requirements:* For master's, EXADEP, minimum GPA of 2.8, interview, first aid training and CPR certification.

University of Puget Sound, Graduate Studies, School of Physical Therapy, Tacoma, WA 98416. Offers DPT. *Accreditation:* APTA. *Faculty:* 7 full-time (4 women), 9 part-time/adjunct (6 women). *Students:* 108 full-time (67 women), 2 part-time (both women); includes 15 minority (9 Asian, non-Hispanic/Latino; 4 Hispanic/Latino; 1 Native Hawaiian or other Pacific Islander, non-Hispanic/Latino; 1 Two or more races, non-Hispanic/Latino), 1 international. Average age 25. 484 applicants, 26% accepted, 36 enrolled. In 2011, 34 doctorates awarded. *Entrance requirements:* Additional exam requirements/recommendations for international students: Required—TOEFL (minimum score 550 paper-based; 213 computer-based; 80 iBT). *Application deadline:* For fall admission, 12/15 priority date for domestic students, 12/15 for international students. Application fee: $145. Electronic applications accepted. *Financial support:* In 2011–12, 19 students received support, including 11 fellowships (averaging $14,100 per year); career-related internships or fieldwork and scholarships/grants also available. Financial award application deadline: 3/31; financial award applicants required to submit FAFSA. *Faculty research:* Manual therapy, assessment of chronic pain, movement assessment of children, pediatric gait. *Unit head:* Dr. Kathleen Hummel-Berry, Director, 253-879-3531, Fax: 253-879-2933, E-mail: hummel@pugetsound.edu. *Application contact:* Dr. George H. Mills, Jr., Vice President for Enrollment, 253-879-3211, Fax: 253-879-3993, E-mail: admission@pugetsound.edu. Web site: http://www.pugetsound.edu/academics/departments-and-programs/graduate/school-of-physical-therapy/.

University of Rhode Island, Graduate School, College of Human Science and Services, Physical Therapy Department, Kingston, RI 02881. Offers DPT. *Accreditation:* APTA. Part-time programs available. *Faculty:* 10 full-time (7 women). *Students:* 53 full-time (31 women), 34 part-time (26 women); includes 5 minority (1 Black or African American, non-Hispanic/Latino; 1 American Indian or Alaska Native, non-Hispanic/Latino; 1 Asian, non-Hispanic/Latino; 2 Hispanic/Latino), 2 international. In 2011, 26 doctorates awarded. *Degree requirements:* For doctorate, comprehensive exam. *Entrance requirements:* For doctorate, GRE, 2 letters of recommendation. Additional exam requirements/recommendations for international students: Required—TOEFL (minimum score 550 paper-based; 213 computer-based). *Application deadline:* For fall admission, 12/15 for domestic and international students. Application fee: $65. Electronic applications accepted. *Expenses:* Tuition, state resident: full-time $10,432; part-time $580 per credit hour. Tuition, nonresident: full-time $23,130; part-time $1285 per credit hour. *Required fees:* $1362; $36 per credit hour. $35 per semester. One-time fee: $130. *Financial support:* In 2011–12, 2 teaching assistantships with partial tuition reimbursements (averaging $3,474 per year) were awarded. Financial award application deadline: 12/15; financial award applicants required to submit FAFSA. *Unit head:* Dr. Beth Marcoux, Chair, 401-574-5001, E-mail: bmarcoux@mail.uri.edu. *Application contact:* Dr. Susan E. Roush, Admissions Committee Chair, 401-874-5626, E-mail: roush@uri.edu. Web site: http://www.uri.edu/hss/pt/.

University of St. Augustine for Health Sciences, Graduate Programs, Division of Advanced Studies, St. Augustine, FL 32086. Offers MH Sc, DH Sc, TDPT. Part-time programs available. Postbaccalaureate distance learning degree programs offered (minimal on-campus study). *Entrance requirements:* For master's, GRE General Test, BS in physical therapy or equivalent; for doctorate, GRE General Test, master's degree in related field. Additional exam requirements/recommendations for international students: Required—TOEFL.

University of St. Augustine for Health Sciences, Graduate Programs, Division of Entry-Level Physical Therapy, St. Augustine, FL 32086. Offers DPT. *Accreditation:* APTA.

University of St. Augustine for Health Sciences, Graduate Programs, Division of Physical Therapy, St. Augustine, FL 32086. Offers DPT, Certificate. *Accreditation:* APTA. *Entrance requirements:* Additional exam requirements/recommendations for international students: Required—TOEFL.

The University of Scranton, College of Graduate and Continuing Education, Department of Physical Therapy, Scranton, PA 18510. Offers MPT, DPT. *Accreditation:* APTA. Part-time programs available. Postbaccalaureate distance learning degree programs offered (no on-campus study). *Faculty:* 7 full-time (3 women). *Students:* 118 full-time (80 women), 46 part-time (30 women); includes 4 minority (3 Asian, non-Hispanic/Latino; 1 Hispanic/Latino). Average age 27. 682 applicants, 15% accepted. In 2011, 46 degrees awarded. *Degree requirements:* For master's, thesis (for some programs), capstone experience. *Entrance requirements:* For master's, minimum GPA of 3.0; for doctorate, physical therapist license. Additional exam requirements/recommendations for international students: Required—TOEFL (minimum score 500 paper-based; 173 computer-based), IELTS (minimum score 5.5). *Application deadline:* Applications are processed on a rolling basis. Application fee: $0. *Financial support:* In 2011–12, 14 students received support, including 14 teaching assistantships (averaging $4,400 per year); career-related internships or fieldwork, Federal Work-Study, and unspecified assistantships also available. Support available to part-time students. Financial award application deadline: 3/1. *Unit head:* Dr. John P. Sanko, Chair, 570-941-7934, Fax: 570-941-7940, E-mail: sankoi1@scranton.edu. *Application contact:* Joseph M. Roback, Director of Admissions, 570-941-4385, Fax: 570-941-5928, E-mail: robackj2@scranton.edu.

University of South Alabama, Graduate School, College of Allied Health Professions, Department of Physical Therapy, Mobile, AL 36688-0002. Offers DPT. *Accreditation:* APTA. *Faculty:* 5 full-time (2 women). *Students:* 101 full-time (69 women); includes 4 minority (2 Black or African American, non-Hispanic/Latino; 1 Asian, non-Hispanic/Latino; 1 Hispanic/Latino), 1 international. 35 applicants, 100% accepted, 34 enrolled. In 2011, 56 doctorates awarded. *Entrance requirements:* For doctorate, GRE, minimum GPA of 3.0. Additional exam requirements/recommendations for international students: Required—TOEFL (minimum score 600 paper-based; 250 computer-based). *Application deadline:* For fall admission, 12/15 priority date for domestic students. Applications are processed on a rolling basis. Application fee: $75. *Expenses:* Tuition, state resident: full-time $7968; part-time $332 per credit hour. Tuition, nonresident: full-time $15,936; part-time $664 per credit hour. *Financial support:* Application deadline: 4/1. *Unit head:* Dr. Dennis Fell, Chair, 251-445-9330, E-mail: ptdept@jaguar1.usouthal.edu. *Application contact:* Dr. Julio Turrens, Director of Graduate Studies, 251-445-9250. Web site: http://www.southalabama.edu/alliedhealth/pt/.

The University of South Dakota, Graduate School, School of Health Sciences, Department of Physical Therapy, Vermillion, SD 57069-2390. Offers DPT. *Accreditation:* APTA. *Entrance requirements:* For doctorate, GRE General Test. Additional exam requirements/recommendations for international students: Required—TOEFL. *Expenses:* Contact institution. *Faculty research:* Physical therapy, knee rehabilitation, pediatric intervention, wound care, motion analysis.

University of Southern California, Graduate School, Herman Ostrow School of Dentistry, Division of Biokinesiology and Physical Therapy, Los Angeles, CA 90089. Offers biokinesiology (MS, PhD); physical therapy (DPT). *Accreditation:* APTA (one or more programs are accredited). *Degree requirements:* For master's, comprehensive exam; for doctorate, thesis/dissertation. *Entrance requirements:* For master's and doctorate, GRE (minimum combined score 1200, verbal 600, quantitative 600). Additional exam requirements/recommendations for international students: Required—TOEFL. Electronic applications accepted. *Expenses:* Contact institution. *Faculty research:* Exercise and aging biomechanics, musculoskeletal biomechanics, exercise and hormones related to muscle wasting, computational neurorehabilitation, motor behavior and neurorehabilitation, motor development, infant motor performance.

University of South Florida, Graduate School, College of Medicine, School of Physical Therapy, Tampa, FL 33620-9951. Offers MS, DPT. *Accreditation:* APTA. *Faculty:* 10 full-time (4 women). *Students:* 94 full-time (75 women); includes 16 minority (9 Black or African American, non-Hispanic/Latino; 2 Asian, non-Hispanic/Latino; 5 Hispanic/Latino). Average age 25. 31 applicants, 100% accepted, 31 enrolled. In 2011, 35 doctorates awarded. *Entrance requirements:* For master's, GRE General Test, minimum GPA of 3.0 in last 60 hours of coursework. Additional exam requirements/recommendations for international students: Required—TOEFL (minimum score 600 paper-based; 250 computer-based). *Application deadline:* For fall admission, 9/1 for domestic students, 2/1 for international students. Application fee: $30. *Total annual research expenditures:* $989,107. *Unit head:* David Newman, Coordinator, 813-974-1326, Fax: 813-974-8614, E-mail: dnewman1@health.usf.edu. *Application contact:* Francisco Vera, Assistant Director for Admissions, 813-974-8800, E-mail: fvera@usf.edu. Web site: http://web.health.usf.edu/ptcenter/index.html.

The University of Tennessee at Chattanooga, Graduate School, College of Health, Education and Professional Studies, Department of Physical Therapy, Chattanooga, TN 37403. Offers physical therapy (DPT); post professional (DPT). *Accreditation:* APTA. *Faculty:* 8 full-time (3 women), 7 part-time/adjunct (4 women). *Students:* 88 full-time (66 women), 17 part-time (12 women); includes 7 minority (3 Black or African American, non-Hispanic/Latino; 1 Asian, non-Hispanic/Latino; 1 Hispanic/Latino; 2 Two or more races, non-Hispanic/Latino). Average age 27. 119 applicants, 38% accepted, 43 enrolled. In 2011, 48 doctorates awarded. *Degree requirements:* For doctorate, qualifying exams, internship. *Entrance requirements:* For doctorate, interview, minimum GPA of 3.0 in science and overall. Additional exam requirements/recommendations for international students: Required—TOEFL (minimum score 550 paper-based; 213 computer-based; 79 iBT); Recommended—IELTS (minimum score 6). *Application deadline:* For fall admission, 8/1 priority date for domestic students, 6/1 for international

students; for spring admission, 12/1 priority date for domestic students, 10/1 for international students. Applications are processed on a rolling basis. Application fee: $35. Electronic applications accepted. *Expenses:* Tuition, state resident: full-time $6472; part-time $359 per credit hour. Tuition, nonresident: full-time $20,006; part-time $1111 per credit hour. *Required fees:* $1320; $160 per credit hour. *Financial support:* Career-related internships or fieldwork, scholarships/grants, and unspecified assistantships available. Support available to part-time students. *Faculty research:* Diabetes and round management, disabilities, animal physical therapy and rehabilitation, orthopedics. *Total annual research expenditures:* $4,887. *Unit head:* Dr. Randy Walker, Acting Head, 423-425-4747, Fax: 423-425-2215, E-mail: randy-walker@utc.edu. *Application contact:* Dr. Jerald Ainsworth, Dean of Graduate Studies, 423-425-4478, Fax: 423-425-5223, E-mail: jerald-ainsworth@utc.edu. Web site: http://www.utc.edu/Academic/PhysicalTherapy/.

The University of Tennessee Health Science Center, College of Allied Health Sciences, Memphis, TN 38163-0002. Offers MCP, MDH, MHIIM, MOT, MSCLS, MSPT, DPT, ScDPT, TDPT. *Accreditation:* AOTA; APTA. Part-time and evening/weekend programs available. Postbaccalaureate distance learning degree programs offered (minimal on-campus study). Terminal master's awarded for partial completion of doctoral program. *Degree requirements:* For master's, comprehensive exam, thesis; for doctorate, comprehensive exam, residency. *Entrance requirements:* For master's, GRE (MOT, MSCLS), minimum GPA of 3.0, 3 letters of reference, state license (MDH), national accreditation (MSCLS), GRE if GPA is less than 3.0 (MCP); for doctorate, GRE. Additional exam requirements/recommendations for international students: Required—TOEFL (minimum score 550 paper-based; 213 computer-based; 80 iBT). Electronic applications accepted. *Expenses:* Contact institution. *Faculty research:* Gait deviation, muscular dystrophy and strength, hemophilia and exercise, pediatric neurology, self-efficacy.

The University of Texas at El Paso, Graduate School, College of Health Sciences, Program in Physical Therapy, El Paso, TX 79968-0001. Offers MPT. *Accreditation:* APTA. *Students:* 47 (27 women); includes 30 minority (2 Black or African American, non-Hispanic/Latino; 1 Asian, non-Hispanic/Latino; 27 Hispanic/Latino), 1 international. 28 applicants, 82% accepted. In 2011, 15 master's awarded. *Entrance requirements:* For master's, GRE General Test. Additional exam requirements/recommendations for international students: Required—TOEFL. *Application deadline:* For fall admission, 8/1 for domestic students, 3/1 for international students; for spring admission, 11/1 for domestic students, 9/3 for international students. Application fee: $15 ($65 for international students). Electronic applications accepted. *Financial support:* In 2011–12, research assistantships (averaging $18,825 per year), teaching assistantships (averaging $18,000 per year) were awarded; institutionally sponsored loans and scholarships/grants also available. Financial award application deadline: 3/15. *Unit head:* Dr. Mary Carlson, Director, 915-747-7248, E-mail: mcarlson@utep.edu. *Application contact:* Dr. Benjamin Flores, Interim Dean of the Graduate School, 915-747-5491, Fax: 915-747-5788, E-mail: bflores@utep.edu.

The University of Texas Health Science Center at San Antonio, School of Health Professions, San Antonio, TX 78229-3900. Offers clinical laboratory sciences (MS); deaf education and hearing science (MED); dental hygiene (MS); occupational therapy (MOT); physical therapy (MPT); physician assistant studies (MS). *Accreditation:* AOTA; APTA; ARC-PA. *Degree requirements:* For master's, thesis. *Entrance requirements:* Additional exam requirements/recommendations for international students: Required—TOEFL (minimum score 560 paper-based; 280 computer-based; 68 iBT). Electronic applications accepted.

The University of Texas Medical Branch, School of Health Professions, Department of Physical Therapy, Galveston, TX 77555. Offers MPT, DPT. *Accreditation:* APTA. *Degree requirements:* For master's, thesis or alternative. *Entrance requirements:* For master's and doctorate, GRE, documentation of 40 hours' experience. Electronic applications accepted.

The University of Texas Southwestern Medical Center, Southwestern School of Health Professions, Physical Therapy Program, Dallas, TX 75390. Offers DPT. *Accreditation:* APTA. *Entrance requirements:* For doctorate, GRE, minimum GPA of 3.0. Additional exam requirements/recommendations for international students: Required—TOEFL (minimum score 600 paper-based; 220 computer-based). Electronic applications accepted.

University of the Pacific, Thomas J. Long School of Pharmacy and Health Sciences, Department of Physical Therapy, Stockton, CA 95211-0197. Offers MS, DPT. *Accreditation:* APTA. *Faculty:* 8 full-time (6 women), 10 part-time/adjunct (8 women). *Students:* 78 full-time (53 women), 1 (woman) part-time; includes 17 minority (2 American Indian or Alaska Native, non-Hispanic/Latino; 13 Asian, non-Hispanic/Latino; 2 Hispanic/Latino), 1 international. Average age 25. 336 applicants, 17% accepted, 38 enrolled. In 2011, 35 doctorates awarded. *Entrance requirements:* For master's, GRE General Test, minimum GPA of 3.0. Additional exam requirements/recommendations for international students: Required—TOEFL (minimum score 475 paper-based; 150 computer-based). *Application deadline:* For fall admission, 1/4 for domestic students. Application fee: $75. *Expenses:* *Tuition:* Full-time $18,900; part-time $1181 per unit. *Required fees:* $949. *Financial support:* Federal Work-Study available. Financial award application deadline: 3/1; financial award applicants required to submit FAFSA. *Unit head:* Dr. Cathy Peterson, Chair, 209-946-2947, Fax: 209-946-2410. *Application contact:* Cyndi Porter, Outreach Officer, 209-946-3957, Fax: 209-946-2410, E-mail: cporter@pacific.edu.

The University of Toledo, College of Graduate Studies, College of Medicine and Life Sciences, Department of Orthopedic Surgery, Toledo, OH 43606-3390. Offers MSBS. *Faculty:* 6. *Students:* 1 full-time (0 women), 2 part-time (both women); includes 1 minority (Asian, non-Hispanic/Latino), 2 international. Average age 36. 4 applicants, 50% accepted, 2 enrolled. In 2011, 1 master's awarded. *Degree requirements:* For master's, thesis or alternative. *Entrance requirements:* For master's, GRE, minimum undergraduate GPA of 3.0, three letters of recommendation, statement of purpose, transcripts from all prior institutions attended, resume. Additional exam requirements/recommendations for international students: Required—TOEFL (minimum score 550 paper-based; 213 computer-based; 80 iBT), IELTS (minimum score 6.5). *Application deadline:* For fall admission, 1/15 priority date for domestic students, 1/15 for international students. Application fee: $45 ($75 for international students). Electronic applications accepted. *Financial support:* Institutionally sponsored loans, tuition waivers (full and partial), and tuition scholarships available. *Unit head:* Dr. Nabil Ebraheim, Chair, 419-383-3761, E-mail: nabil.ebraheim@utoledo.edu. *Application contact:* David Kubacki, Assistant to the Chair, 419-383-4020, E-mail: david.kubacki@utoledo.edu. Web site: http://www.utoledo.edu/med/grad/.

The University of Toledo, College of Graduate Studies, Judith Herb College of Education, Health Science and Human Service, Department of Rehabilitation Sciences, Toledo, OH 43606-3390. Offers occupational therapy (OTD); physical therapy (DPT); speech-language pathology (MA). *Faculty:* 18. *Students:* 163 full-time (128 women), 24 part-time (20 women); includes 13 minority (4 Black or African American, non-Hispanic/Latino; 1 American Indian or Alaska Native, non-Hispanic/Latino; 5 Asian, non-Hispanic/Latino; 2 Hispanic/Latino; 1 Two or more races, non-Hispanic/Latino). Average age 25. 488 applicants, 23% accepted, 73 enrolled. In 2011, 29 master's, 46 doctorates awarded. *Degree requirements:* For master's, comprehensive exam, thesis; for doctorate, thesis/dissertation or alternative. *Entrance requirements:* For master's, GRE, minimum cumulative GPA of 2.7 for all previous academic work, letters of recommendation; for doctorate, GRE, minimum cumulative GPA of 3.0 for all previous academic work, letters of recommendation; OTCAS or PTCAS application and UT supplemental application (for OTD and DPT). Additional exam requirements/recommendations for international students: Required—TOEFL (minimum score 550 paper-based; 213 computer-based; 80 iBT), IELTS (minimum score 6.5). *Application deadline:* For fall admission, 11/1 for domestic and international students. Application fee: $45 ($75 for international students). Electronic applications accepted. *Financial support:* In 2011–12, 5 research assistantships with full and partial tuition reimbursements (averaging $10,705 per year), 11 teaching assistantships with full and partial tuition reimbursements (averaging $6,182 per year) were awarded; Federal Work-Study, scholarships/grants, tuition waivers (full and partial), and unspecified assistantships also available. *Unit head:* Dr. Michelle Masterson, Chair, 419-530-6671, Fax: 419-530-4780, E-mail: michelle.masterson@utoledo.edu. *Application contact:* College of Graduate Studies - HSC, 419-383-4112, Fax: 419-383-6140, E-mail: grdsch@utnet.utoledo.edu. Web site: http://www.utoledo.edu/eduhshs/.

University of Toronto, Faculty of Medicine, Department of Physical Therapy, Toronto, ON M5S 1A1, Canada. Offers M Sc PT. *Accreditation:* APTA. *Entrance requirements:* For master's, minimum B average in final year, 2 references. Additional exam requirements/recommendations for international students: Required—TOEFL (minimum score 600 paper-based; 100 iBT), TWE (minimum score 5). Electronic applications accepted.

University of Utah, Graduate School, College of Health, Department of Physical Therapy, Salt Lake City, UT 84112-1290. Offers physical therapy (DPT); rehabilitation science (PhD). *Accreditation:* APTA. *Faculty:* 12 full-time (6 women), 5 part-time/adjunct (2 women). *Students:* 136 full-time (74 women); includes 11 minority (1 Black or African American, non-Hispanic/Latino; 2 American Indian or Alaska Native, non-Hispanic/Latino; 2 Asian, non-Hispanic/Latino; 4 Hispanic/Latino; 2 Two or more races, non-Hispanic/Latino), 1 international. Average age 31. 340 applicants, 14% accepted, 46 enrolled. In 2011, 46 doctorates awarded. *Degree requirements:* For doctorate, thesis/dissertation, clinical project. *Entrance requirements:* For doctorate, minimum GPA of 3.0, volunteer work, bachelor's degree. Additional exam requirements/recommendations for international students: Recommended—TOEFL (minimum score 90 iBT). *Application deadline:* For fall admission, 10/1 priority date for domestic students, 10/1 for international students. Application fee: $55 ($65 for international students). Electronic applications accepted. *Expenses:* Contact institution. *Financial support:* In 2011–12, 20 students received support, including 1 research assistantship, 7 teaching assistantships; Federal Work-Study, institutionally sponsored loans, scholarships/grants, and tuition waivers also available. Financial award application deadline: 9/30; financial award applicants required to submit FAFSA. *Faculty research:* Rehabilitation and Parkinson's Disease, motor control and musculoskeletal dysfunction, burns/wound care, rehabilitation and multiple sclerosis, cancer. *Total annual research expenditures:* $840,500. *Unit head:* Dr. R. Scott Ward, Chair, 801-581-8681, Fax: 801-585-5629, E-mail: scott.ward@hsc.utah.edu. *Application contact:* Julia Konopasek, Academic Advisor, 801-585-8681, Fax: 801-585-5629, E-mail: julia.konopasek@hsc.utah.edu. Web site: http://www.health.utah.edu/pt.

University of Vermont, Graduate College, College of Nursing and Health Sciences, Program in Physical Therapy, Burlington, VT 05405. Offers DPT. *Accreditation:* APTA. *Students:* 92 (72 women); includes 4 minority (2 Asian, non-Hispanic/Latino; 2 Hispanic/Latino). 221 applicants, 35% accepted, 0 enrolled. In 2011, 39 doctorates awarded. *Entrance requirements:* For doctorate, GRE General Test. Additional exam requirements/recommendations for international students: Required—TOEFL (minimum score 550 paper-based; 213 computer-based; 80 iBT). *Application deadline:* For fall admission, 12/15 priority date for domestic students, 12/15 for international students. Applications are processed on a rolling basis. Application fee: $40. Electronic applications accepted. *Financial support:* Fellowships, research assistantships, teaching assistantships, and Federal Work-Study available. Financial award application deadline: 3/1. *Unit head:* Dr. Diane Jette, Chair, 802-656-3858. *Application contact:* Dr. Diane Jette, Coordinator, 802-656-3858.

University of Washington, Graduate School, School of Medicine, Graduate Programs in Medicine, Department of Rehabilitation Medicine, Seattle, WA 98195-6490. Offers occupational therapy (MOT); physical therapy (DPT); prosthetics and orthotics (MPO); rehabilitation science (PhD). *Faculty:* 65. *Students:* 200. Average age 25. In 2011, 25 master's, 30 doctorates awarded. *Degree requirements:* For doctorate, comprehensive exam (for some programs), thesis/dissertation (for some programs). *Entrance requirements:* For master's and doctorate, GRE. Additional exam requirements/recommendations for international students: Required—TOEFL. Application fee: $75. *Financial support:* In 2011–12, 1 fellowship (averaging $5,000 per year) was awarded. Financial award applicants required to submit FAFSA. *Faculty research:* Biomechanics, balance, brain injury, spinal cord injury, pain, degenerative diseases. *Unit head:* Dr. Peter C. Esselman, Professor and Chair, 206-744-3167, E-mail: esselman@u.washington.edu. *Application contact:* Dr. Deborah Kartin, Graduate Program Coordinator, 206-598-5338, Fax: 206-685-3244, E-mail: kartin@u.washington.edu. Web site: http://rehab.washington.edu/education/degree/.

The University of Western Ontario, Faculty of Graduate Studies, Biosciences Division, School of Physical Therapy, London, ON N6A 5B8, Canada. Offers manipulative therapy (CAS); physical therapy (MPT); wound healing (CAS). *Accreditation:* APTA. Part-time programs available. *Degree requirements:* For master's, thesis. *Entrance requirements:* For master's, B Sc in physical therapy. Additional exam requirements/recommendations for international students: Required—TOEFL. *Faculty research:* Muscle strength, wound healing, motor control, respiratory physiology, exercise physiology.

University of Wisconsin–La Crosse, Office of University Graduate Studies, College of Science and Health, Department of Health Professions, Program in Physical Therapy, La Crosse, WI 54601-3742. Offers MSPT, DPT. *Accreditation:* APTA. *Faculty:* 1 (woman) full-time, 2 part-time/adjunct (both women). *Students:* 90 full-time (55 women), 43 part-time (34 women); includes 5 minority (1 Black or African American, non-Hispanic/Latino; 1 American Indian or Alaska Native, non-Hispanic/Latino; 1 Hispanic/Latino; 1 Native Hawaiian or other Pacific Islander, non-Hispanic/Latino; 1 Two or more races, non-Hispanic/Latino). Average age 25. 284 applicants, 19% accepted, 45 enrolled. In 2011, 39 doctorates awarded. *Entrance requirements:* Additional exam requirements/recommendations for international students: Required—TOEFL (minimum score 550 paper-based; 213 computer-based; 79 iBT). Application fee: $56. Electronic applications accepted. *Expenses:* Contact institution. *Financial support:* Federal Work-Study, scholarships/grants, and health care benefits available. Support available to part-time students. Financial award application deadline: 11/1; financial award applicants required to submit FAFSA. *Unit head:* Dr. Michele Thorman, Director, 608-785-8466, E-mail: thorman.mich@uwlax.edu. *Application contact:* Kathryn Kiefer, Director of Admissions, 608-785-8939, E-mail: admissions@uwlax.edu. Web site: http://www.uwlax.edu/pt/.

University of Wisconsin–Milwaukee, Graduate School, College of Health Sciences, Doctor of Physical Therapy Program, Milwaukee, WI 53201-0413. Offers DPT. *Accreditation:* APTA. *Students:* 67 full-time (47 women); includes 2 minority (both Asian, non-Hispanic/Latino). Average age 31. 9 applicants, 0% accepted, 0 enrolled. *Degree requirements:* For doctorate, thesis/dissertation optional. *Entrance requirements:* For doctorate, GRE General Test, minimum GPA of 3.0. Additional exam requirements/recommendations for international students: Required—TOEFL (minimum score 550 paper-based; 79 iBT), IELTS (minimum score 6.5). One-time fee: $506.10 full-time. Tuition and fees vary according to course load and reciprocity agreements. *Financial support:* In 2011–12, 1 teaching assistantship was awarded; fellowships, research assistantships, and project assistantships also available. *Unit head:* Dr. Kristian O'Connor, Department Chair, E-mail: krisocon@uwm.edu. *Application contact:* General Information Contact, 414-229-4982, Fax: 414-229-6967, E-mail: gradschool@uwm.edu. Web site: http://www4.uwm.edu/chs/academics/doctoral/dpt/.

Utica College, Department of Physical Therapy, Utica, NY 13502-4892. Offers DPT, TDPT. *Accreditation:* APTA. Part-time and evening/weekend programs available. Postbaccalaureate distance learning degree programs offered (minimal on-campus study). *Degree requirements:* For doctorate, comprehensive exam, thesis/dissertation (for some programs). *Entrance requirements:* For doctorate, GRE, MCAT, DAT or OPT, BS, minimum GPA of 3.0. Additional exam requirements/recommendations for international students: Required—TOEFL (minimum score 525 paper-based; 195 computer-based). Electronic applications accepted. *Expenses:* Contact institution.

Virginia Commonwealth University, Graduate School, School of Allied Health Professions, Department of Physical Therapy, Richmond, VA 23284-9005. Offers advanced physical therapy (DPT); entry-level physical therapy (DPT); health related sciences (PhD); physiology/physical therapy (PhD). *Accreditation:* APTA (one or more programs are accredited). *Students:* 168 full-time (105 women), 17 part-time (12 women); includes 21 minority (6 Black or African American, non-Hispanic/Latino; 10 Asian, non-Hispanic/Latino; 4 Hispanic/Latino; 1 Two or more races, non-Hispanic/Latino; 2 international. In 2011, 85 degrees awarded. *Degree requirements:* For doctorate, thesis/dissertation. *Entrance requirements:* For doctorate, GRE General Test, Physical Therapist Centralized Application Service (PTCAS). Additional exam requirements/recommendations for international students: Required—TOEFL (minimum score 600 paper-based; 250 computer-based; 100 iBT). *Application deadline:* For fall admission, 11/2 for domestic students. Electronic applications accepted. *Expenses:* Tuition, state resident: full-time $9133; part-time $507 per credit. Tuition, nonresident: full-time $18,777; part-time $1043 per credit. *Required fees:* $77 per credit. Tuition and fees vary according to degree level, campus/location, program and student level. *Financial support:* Fellowships available. *Faculty research:* Eye movement, bilabyrinthectomy on ferret muscle fiber typing, neck disability index, cost-effective care, training effect on muscle. *Unit head:* Dr. Thomas P. Mayhew, Chair, 804-828-0234, Fax: 804-828-8111, E-mail: tpmayhew@vcu.edu. *Application contact:* Judy Kendrick, Student Coordinator, 804-828-0234, Fax: 804-828-8111, E-mail: jkendric@vcu.edu. Web site: http://www.sahp.vcu.edu/pt/.

Virginia Commonwealth University, Medical College of Virginia-Professional Programs, School of Medicine, School of Medicine Graduate Programs, Department of Physiology and Biophysics, Richmond, VA 23284-9005. Offers physical therapy (PhD); physiology (MS, PhD); MD/PhD. Terminal master's awarded for partial completion of doctoral program. *Degree requirements:* For master's, thesis; for doctorate, thesis/dissertation, comprehensive oral and written exams. *Entrance requirements:* For master's, GRE General Test, MCAT, or DAT; for doctorate, GRE, MCAT or DAT. Additional exam requirements/recommendations for international students: Required—TOEFL (minimum score 600 paper-based; 250 computer-based; 100 iBT). Electronic applications accepted. *Expenses:* Tuition, state resident: full-time $9133; part-time $507 per credit. Tuition, nonresident: full-time $18,777; part-time $1043 per credit. *Required fees:* $77 per credit. Tuition and fees vary according to degree level, campus/location, program and student level.

Walsh University, Graduate Studies, Program in Physical Therapy, North Canton, OH 44720-3396. Offers DPT. *Accreditation:* APTA. *Faculty:* 8 full-time (6 women), 25 part-time/adjunct (12 women). *Students:* 78 full-time (64 women); includes 1 minority (Asian, non-Hispanic/Latino). Average age 24. 144 applicants, 39% accepted, 32 enrolled. In 2011, 19 doctorates awarded. *Degree requirements:* For doctorate, comprehensive exam, research project, 3 clinical placements. *Entrance requirements:* For doctorate, GRE General Test, previous coursework in anatomy, physiology, chemistry, statistics, psychology, biology, and physics; minimum GPA of 3.0. Additional exam requirements/recommendations for international students: Required—TOEFL (minimum score 500 paper-based; 173 computer-based; 61 iBT). *Application deadline:* For fall admission, 7/15 priority date for domestic students. Applications are processed on a rolling basis. Application fee: $25. Electronic applications accepted. *Expenses:* Contact institution. *Financial support:* In 2011–12, 11 students received support, including 6 fellowships (averaging $1,000 per year), 3 research assistantships with partial tuition reimbursements available (averaging $11,536 per year), 4 teaching assistantships (averaging $2,163 per year); unspecified assistantships also available. Support available to part-time students. Financial award application deadline: 12/31; financial award applicants required to submit FAFSA. *Faculty research:* Interventions, diagnosis, adherence, advancing and improving learning with information technology, consumer-driven healthcare, service provider training and customer satisfaction. *Total annual research expenditures:* $750. *Unit head:* Dr. Chad Cook, Chair, 330-490-7370, Fax: 330-490-7371, E-mail: cpetrosino@walsh.edu. *Application contact:* Vanessa Freiman, Graduate and Transfer Admissions Counselor, 330-490-7177, Fax: 330-244-4925, E-mail: vfreiman@walsh.edu.

Washington University in St. Louis, School of Medicine, Graduate Programs in Medicine, Program in Physical Therapy, St. Louis, MO 63130-4899. Offers DPT, PPDPT. *Accreditation:* APTA (one or more programs are accredited). Part-time and evening/weekend programs available. Postbaccalaureate distance learning degree programs offered (minimal on-campus study). *Degree requirements:* For doctorate, thesis/dissertation (for some programs). *Entrance requirements:* For doctorate, GRE. Additional exam requirements/recommendations for international students: Required—TOEFL (minimum score 600 paper-based; 250 computer-based; 100 iBT), TWE (minimum score 5). Electronic applications accepted. *Expenses:* Contact institution. *Faculty research:* Movement and movement dysfunction.

Wayne State University, Eugene Applebaum College of Pharmacy and Health Sciences, Department of Health Care Sciences, Program in Physical Therapy, Detroit, MI 48202. Offers DPT. *Accreditation:* APTA. *Students:* 137 full-time (87 women), 19 part-time (11 women); includes 42 minority (4 Black or African American, non-Hispanic/Latino; 27 Asian, non-Hispanic/Latino; 8 Hispanic/Latino; 3 Two or more races, non-Hispanic/Latino), 7 international. Average age 26. 67 applicants, 61% accepted, 35 enrolled. In 2011, 33 doctorates awarded. *Entrance requirements:* For doctorate, personal resume, recommendations; interview; minimum of 90 undergraduate credit hours with minimum GPA of 3.0 and no less than a C in prerequisite courses, PTCAS application, essay. Additional exam requirements/recommendations for international students: Required—TOEFL (minimum score 550 paper-based; 213 computer-based); Recommended—TWE (minimum score 6). *Application deadline:* For fall admission, 11/1 for domestic and international students. Application fee: $50. Electronic applications accepted. *Expenses:* Tuition, state resident: part-time $512.85 per credit. Tuition, nonresident: part-time $1132.65 per credit. *Required fees:* $26.60 per credit. $199.65 per semester. Tuition and fees vary according to course load and program. *Financial support:* In 2011–12, 41 students received support. Scholarships/grants available. *Unit head:* Dr. Susan Talley, Academic Director, 313-577-4643, E-mail: ac1563@wayne.edu. *Application contact:* 313-577-1716, E-mail: cphsinfo@wayne.edu. Web site: http://pt.cphs.wayne.edu/.

Western Carolina University, Graduate School, College of Health and Human Sciences, Department of Physical Therapy, Cullowhee, NC 28723. Offers MPT, DPT. *Accreditation:* APTA. *Students:* 58 full-time (36 women); includes 6 minority (3 Asian, non-Hispanic/Latino; 2 Hispanic/Latino; 1 Two or more races, non-Hispanic/Latino). Average age 27. 350 applicants, 30% accepted, 32 enrolled. In 2011, 25 master's awarded. *Degree requirements:* For master's, comprehensive exam. *Entrance requirements:* For master's, GRE General Test, appropriate undergraduate degree with minimum GPA of 3.0, 3 letters of recommendation. Additional exam requirements/recommendations for international students: Required—TOEFL (minimum score 550 paper-based; 270 computer-based; 79 iBT). *Application deadline:* For fall admission, 2/1 for domestic students. Applications are processed on a rolling basis. Application fee: $50. *Expenses:* Tuition, state resident: full-time $3348. Tuition, nonresident: full-time $12,933. *Required fees:* $3155. *Financial support:* Fellowships, research assistantships with full tuition reimbursements, teaching assistantships with full tuition reimbursements, Federal Work-Study, institutionally sponsored loans, scholarships/grants, and unspecified assistantships available. Financial award application deadline: 3/31; financial award applicants required to submit FAFSA. *Faculty research:* Bone density, disability in older adults, neuroanatomy, intervention of musculoskeletal conditions. *Unit head:* Dr. Karen Lunnen, Head, 828-227-7070, Fax: 828-227-7071, E-mail: klunnen@email.wcu.edu. *Application contact:* Admissions Specialist for Physical Therapy, 828-227-7398, Fax: 828-227-7480, E-mail: gradsch@email.wcu.edu. Web site: http://www.wcu.edu/aps/pt/.

Western University of Health Sciences, College of Allied Health Professions, Program in Physical Therapy, Pomona, CA 91766-1854. Offers DPT. *Accreditation:* APTA. *Faculty:* 10 full-time (6 women), 1 (woman) part-time/adjunct. *Students:* 136 full-time (91 women), 25 part-time (18 women); includes 67 minority (2 Black or African American, non-Hispanic/Latino; 50 Asian, non-Hispanic/Latino; 11 Hispanic/Latino; 2 Native Hawaiian or other Pacific Islander, non-Hispanic/Latino; 2 Two or more races, non-Hispanic/Latino), 1 international. Average age 29. 650 applicants, 21% accepted, 52 enrolled. In 2011, 38 doctorates awarded. *Degree requirements:* For doctorate, comprehensive exam (for some programs). *Entrance requirements:* For doctorate, GRE, bachelor's degree, letters of recommendation, minimum GPA of 2.8. *Application deadline:* For fall admission, 12/1 priority date for domestic students. Applications are processed on a rolling basis. Application fee: $60. *Expenses:* Contact institution. *Financial support:* Institutionally sponsored loans, scholarships/grants, and veterans educational benefits available. Financial award application deadline: 3/2; financial award applicants required to submit FAFSA. *Unit head:* Dee Schilling, Chair, 909-469-3526, E-mail: dschilling@westernu.edu. *Application contact:* Karen Hutton-Lopez, Director of Admissions, 909-469-5650, Fax: 909-469-5570, E-mail: admissions@westernu.edu. Web site: http://www.westernu.edu/xp/edu/cahp/dpt_welcome.xml.

West Virginia University, School of Medicine, Graduate Programs in Human Performance, Division of Physical Therapy, Morgantown, WV 26506. Offers DPT. *Accreditation:* APTA. Evening/weekend programs available. Postbaccalaureate distance learning degree programs offered (minimal on-campus study). *Entrance requirements:* For doctorate, GRE, minimum cumulative GPA and prerequisite science GPA of 3.0; volunteer/work experience in physical therapy; letters of recommendation. *Expenses:* Contact institution.

Wheeling Jesuit University, Department of Physical Therapy, Wheeling, WV 26003-6295. Offers DPT. *Accreditation:* APTA. *Faculty:* 8 full-time (5 women), 10 part-time/adjunct (3 women). *Students:* 93 full-time (55 women); includes 5 minority (2 Black or African American, non-Hispanic/Latino; 3 Asian, non-Hispanic/Latino). Average age 24. 313 applicants, 16% accepted, 50 enrolled. In 2011, 36 doctorates awarded. *Degree requirements:* For doctorate, comprehensive exam, thesis/dissertation. *Entrance requirements:* For doctorate, GRE, minimum GPA of 3.0. Additional exam requirements/recommendations for international students: Required—TOEFL (minimum score 650 paper-based; 250 computer-based). *Application deadline:* For fall admission, 12/1 priority date for domestic students, 12/1 for international students. Applications are processed on a rolling basis. Application fee: $25. Electronic applications accepted. Application fee is waived when completed online. *Expenses:* Contact institution. *Financial support:* Unspecified assistantships available. Financial award application deadline: 8/1; financial award applicants required to submit FAFSA. *Faculty research:* Service-learning, clinical prediction rules, ergonomics, public health, pediatrics. *Unit head:* Dr. Craig Ruby, Director of Physical Therapy, 304-243-2068, Fax: 304-243-2042, E-mail: dpt@wju.edu. *Application contact:* Mary Ann Zandron, Office Manager, 304-243-2068, Fax: 304-243-2042, E-mail: mzandron@wju.edu. Web site: http://www.wju.edu/academics/dpt/default.asp.

Wichita State University, Graduate School, College of Health Professions, Department of Physical Therapy, Wichita, KS 67260. Offers DPT. *Accreditation:* APTA. *Expenses:* Tuition, state resident: full-time $4746; part-time $263.65 per credit. Tuition, nonresident: full-time $11,669; part-time $648.30 per credit. *Unit head:* Dr. Camilla Wilson, Chair, 316-978-5780, Fax: 316-978-3025, E-mail: camilla.wilson@wichita.edu. *Application contact:* Carrie C. Henderson, Admissions Coordinator, 316-978-3095, Fax: 316-978-3253, E-mail: carrie.henderson@wichita.edu. Web site: http://www.wichita.edu/.

Widener University, School of Human Service Professions, Institute for Physical Therapy Education, Chester, PA 19013-5792. Offers MS, DPT. *Accreditation:* APTA. *Degree requirements:* For master's, thesis. *Entrance requirements:* For master's, GRE. *Expenses:* Contact institution. *Faculty research:* Social support, aquatics, children and adults with movement dysfunction, physical therapy modalities.

Winston-Salem State University, Department of Physical Therapy, Winston-Salem, NC 27110-0003. Offers MPT. *Accreditation:* APTA. *Entrance requirements:* For master's, GRE, 3 letters of recommendation. Electronic applications accepted. *Faculty research:* Tissue healing; neuroimaging with functional recovery; visual, proprioceptive and vestibular sensor inputs roles.

Youngstown State University, Graduate School, Bitonte College of Health and Human Services, Department of Physical Therapy, Youngstown, OH 44555-0001. Offers DPT. *Accreditation:* APTA. *Entrance requirements:* Additional exam requirements/recommendations for international students: Required—TOEFL.

Physician Assistant Studies

Albany Medical College, Center for Physician Assistant Studies, Albany, NY 12208-3479. Offers MS. *Accreditation:* ARC-PA. *Faculty:* 10 full-time (6 women), 19 part-time/adjunct (9 women). *Students:* 65 full-time (46 women); includes 9 minority (2 Black or African American, non-Hispanic/Latino; 4 Asian, non-Hispanic/Latino; 3 Hispanic/Latino). Average age 24. 840 applicants, 10% accepted, 42 enrolled. In 2011, 30 degrees awarded. *Degree requirements:* For master's, comprehensive exam, clinical portfolio. *Entrance requirements:* For master's, GRE. Additional exam requirements/recommendations for international students: Required—TOEFL. *Application deadline:* For winter admission, 11/1 for domestic and international students. Applications are processed on a rolling basis. Application fee: $60. Electronic applications accepted. *Expenses:* Contact institution. *Financial support:* In 2011–12, 65 students received support. Scholarships/grants available. Financial award application deadline: 10/1; financial award applicants required to submit FAFSA. *Faculty research:* Genetics, education, informatics. *Unit head:* Dr. David F. Irvine, Director, 518-262-5251, Fax: 518-262-0484, E-mail: irvined@mail.amc.edu. *Application contact:* Rosalyn Green, Admissions Coordinator, 518-262-5251, Fax: 518-262-0484, E-mail: greenr@mail.amc.edu. Web site: http://www.amc.edu/pa/.

Alderson-Broaddus College, Program in Physician Assistant Studies, Philippi, WV 26416. Offers MPAS. *Degree requirements:* For master's, comprehensive exam, thesis. *Entrance requirements:* For master's, minimum 60 semester hours plus specific science. Electronic applications accepted.

A.T. Still University of Health Sciences, Arizona School of Health Sciences, Mesa, AZ 85206. Offers advanced occupational therapy (MS); advanced physician assistant (MS); athletic training (MS); audiology (Au D); health sciences (DHSc); human movement (MS); occupational therapy (MS); physical therapy (DPT); physician assistant (MS); transitional audiology (Au D); transitional physical therapy (DPT). *Accreditation:* AOTA (one or more programs are accredited); ASHA. Part-time and evening/weekend programs available. Postbaccalaureate distance learning degree programs offered (minimal on-campus study). *Faculty:* 44 full-time (27 women), 235 part-time/adjunct (141 women). *Students:* 410 full-time (275 women), 1,010 part-time (675 women); includes 320 minority (73 Black or African American, non-Hispanic/Latino; 18 American Indian or Alaska Native, non-Hispanic/Latino; 158 Asian, non-Hispanic/Latino; 62 Hispanic/Latino; 9 Two or more races, non-Hispanic/Latino; 6 international. Average age 35. 4,395 applicants, 18% accepted, 694 enrolled. In 2011, 221 master's, 406 doctorates awarded. *Median time to degree:* Of those who began their doctoral program in fall 2003, 98% received their degree in 8 years or less. *Degree requirements:* For master's, thesis (for some programs); for doctorate, thesis/dissertation (for some programs). *Entrance requirements:* For master's, GRE General Test; for doctorate, GRE, Evaluation of Practicing Audiologists Capabilities (Au D), Physical Therapist Evaluation Tool (DPT), current state licensure, master's degree or equivalent (Au D). Additional exam requirements/recommendations for international students: Required—TOEFL (minimum score 550 paper-based; 213 computer-based; 80 iBT). *Application deadline:* For fall admission, 8/1 priority date for domestic students, 8/1 for international students. Applications are processed on a rolling basis. Application fee: $60. *Expenses:* Contact institution. *Financial support:* In 2011–12, 272 students received support, including 14 fellowships (averaging $16,000 per year); Federal Work-Study and scholarships/grants also available. Financial award application deadline: 5/1; financial award applicants required to submit FAFSA. *Faculty research:* Physical therapy: metabolism during exercise and activity; neuromuscular function after injury, prevention of lifestyle diseases, prevention and treatment of overuse injuries; athletic training: pediatric sport-related concussion, adolescent athlete health-related quality of life; occupational therapy: spirituality and health disparities, geriatric and pediatric well-being, pain management for participation. *Total annual research expenditures:* $75,682. *Unit head:* Dr. Randy Danielsen, Dean, 480-219-6000, Fax: 480-219-6110, E-mail: rdanielsen@atsu.edu. *Application contact:* Donna Sparks, Associate Director, Admissions Processing, 660-626-2117, Fax: 660-626-2969, E-mail: admissions@atsu.edu. Web site: http://www.atsu.edu/ashs.

Augsburg College, Program in Physicians Assistant Studies, Minneapolis, MN 55454-1351. Offers MS. *Accreditation:* ARC-PA.

Barry University, Physician Assistant Program, Miami Shores, FL 33161-6695. Offers MCMS. *Accreditation:* ARC-PA. *Entrance requirements:* For master's, GRE General Test. Electronic applications accepted.

Baylor College of Medicine, School of Allied Health Sciences, Physician Assistant Program, Houston, TX 77030-3498. Offers MS. *Accreditation:* ARC-PA. *Faculty:* 5 full-time (4 women), 5 part-time/adjunct (3 women). *Students:* 117 full-time (97 women); includes 32 minority (5 Black or African American, non-Hispanic/Latino; 1 American Indian or Alaska Native, non-Hispanic/Latino; 13 Asian, non-Hispanic/Latino; 13 Hispanic/Latino). Average age 26. 835 applicants, 7% accepted, 40 enrolled. In 2011, 34 master's awarded. *Degree requirements:* For master's, comprehensive exam, thesis. *Entrance requirements:* For master's, GRE General Test, bachelor's degree. Additional exam requirements/recommendations for international students: Required—TOEFL. *Application deadline:* For fall admission, 10/1 for domestic students. Application fee: $35. Electronic applications accepted. *Expenses:* Contact institution. *Financial support:* In 2011–12, 87 students received support. Career-related internships or fieldwork, Federal Work-Study, institutionally sponsored loans, and scholarships/grants available. Financial award application deadline: 5/11; financial award applicants required to submit FAFSA. *Faculty research:* Cancer education, physician assistant studies, multiculturalism, alcoholism prevention, women's health. *Unit head:* Carl E. Fasser, Director, 713-798-5405, Fax: 713-798-6128, E-mail: cfasser@bcm.tmc.edu. *Application contact:* Dr. Florence Eddins-Folensbee, Associate Dean of Admissions, 713-798-4842, Fax: 713-798-5563, E-mail: wthomas@bcm.edu. Web site: http://www.bcm.edu/pap/.

Bethel University, Graduate Programs, McKenzie, TN 38201. Offers administration and supervision (MA Ed); business administration (MBA); conflict resolution (MA); physician assistant studies (MS). Part-time and evening/weekend programs available. *Degree requirements:* For master's, thesis (for some programs). *Entrance requirements:* For master's, GRE General Test or MAT, minimum undergraduate GPA of 2.5.

Butler University, College of Pharmacy and Health Sciences, Indianapolis, IN 46208-3485. Offers pharmaceutical science (MS, Pharm D); physician assistance studies (MS). *Accreditation:* ACPE (one or more programs are accredited). Part-time and evening/weekend programs available. *Faculty:* 18 full-time (10 women), 1 (woman) part-time/adjunct. *Students:* 273 full-time (178 women), 18 part-time (14 women); includes 20 minority (4 Black or African American, non-Hispanic/Latino; 11 Asian, non-Hispanic/Latino; 4 Hispanic/Latino; 1 Two or more races, non-Hispanic/Latino), 14 international. Average age 24. 58 applicants, 7% accepted, 4 enrolled. In 2011, 47 master's, 115 doctorates awarded. *Degree requirements:* For master's, research paper or thesis. *Application deadline:* For fall admission, 8/1 priority date for domestic students; for

spring admission, 12/15 for domestic students. Applications are processed on a rolling basis. Application fee: $35. Electronic applications accepted. *Expenses:* Contact institution. *Financial support:* Applicants required to submit FAFSA. *Faculty research:* Anti-seizure drugs, casein kinase inhibitors, speech recognition interface for prescribing drugs, pharmacoeconomics. *Total annual research expenditures:* $92,000. *Unit head:* Dr. Mary Andritz, Dean, 317-940-9451, Fax: 317-940-6172, E-mail: mandritz@butler.edu. *Application contact:* Dr. Bruce Clayton, Professor, 317-940-9830, E-mail: bclayton@butler.edu. Web site: http://www.butler.edu/pharmacy-pa/.

Carroll University, Program in Physician Assistant Studies, Waukesha, WI 53186-5593. Offers MS. *Entrance requirements:* For master's, GRE, three letters of reference, personal essay, documentation of college or community service activities, transcripts. Additional exam requirements/recommendations for international students: Required—TOEFL.

Central Michigan University, College of Graduate Studies, The Herbert H. and Grace A. Dow College of Health Professions, School of Rehabilitation and Medical Sciences, Mount Pleasant, MI 48859. Offers physical therapy (DPT); physician assistant (MS). *Accreditation:* APTA; ARC-PA. *Degree requirements:* For master's, thesis or alternative; for doctorate, thesis/dissertation or alternative. *Entrance requirements:* For master's and doctorate, GRE. Electronic applications accepted.

Chatham University, Program in Physician Assistant Studies, Pittsburgh, PA 15232-2826. Offers MPAS. *Accreditation:* ARC-PA. *Students:* 146 full-time (107 women), 2 part-time (both women); includes 37 minority (12 Black or African American, non-Hispanic/Latino; 4 American Indian or Alaska Native, non-Hispanic/Latino; 12 Asian, non-Hispanic/Latino; 8 Hispanic/Latino; 1 Two or more races, non-Hispanic/Latino), 1 international. Average age 28. 1,657 applicants, 12% accepted, 80 enrolled. In 2011, 43 master's awarded. *Degree requirements:* For master's, thesis, clinical experience, research project. *Entrance requirements:* For master's, community service, minimum GPA of 3.0, health science work or shadowing, volunteer work experience, PA shadowing form, 3 references. Additional exam requirements/recommendations for international students: Required—TOEFL (minimum score 600 paper-based; 250 computer-based; 100 iBT), IELTS (minimum score 7), TWE. *Application deadline:* For fall admission, 10/1 priority date for domestic students, 10/1 for international students. Application fee: $0. Electronic applications accepted. *Expenses:* Contact institution. *Financial support:* Career-related internships or fieldwork available. Financial award applicants required to submit FAFSA. *Faculty research:* Complementary and alternative medicine, education methods, physician assistant practice. *Unit head:* Luis Ramos, Director, 412-365-1314, Fax: 412-365-1213, E-mail: lramos@chatham.edu. *Application contact:* Maureen Stokan, Assistant Director of Graduate Admission, 412-365-2988, Fax: 412-365-1609, E-mail: gradadmissions@chatham.edu. Web site: http://www.chatham.edu/departments/healthmgmt/graduate/pa.

Christian Brothers University, School of Sciences, Memphis, TN 38104-5581. Offers physician assistant studies (MS).

Clarkson University, Graduate School, School of Arts and Sciences, Department of Physician Assistant Studies, Potsdam, NY 13699. Offers MS. *Faculty:* 4 full-time (1 woman). *Entrance requirements:* Additional exam requirements/recommendations for international students: Required—TOEFL. *Application deadline:* Applications are processed on a rolling basis. Application fee: $185. Electronic applications accepted. *Expenses: Tuition:* Full-time $14,376; part-time $1198 per credit hour. *Required fees:* $295 per semester. *Financial support:* Scholarships/grants and tuition waivers (partial) available. *Unit head:* Dr. Michael Whitehead, Chair, 315-268-7942, Fax: 315-268-7944, E-mail: mwhitehe@clarkson.edu. *Application contact:* Jennifer Reed, Graduate School Coordinator, School of Arts and Sciences, 315-268-3802, Fax: 315-268-3989, E-mail: sciencegrad@clarkson.edu. Web site: http://www.clarkson.edu/pa/.

Cleveland State University, College of Graduate Studies, College of Sciences and Health Professions, School of Health Sciences, Cleveland, OH 44115. Offers health sciences (MS), including health sciences, online health sciences; occupational therapy (MOT); physical therapy (DPT); physician's assistant (MS); speech pathology and audiology (MA). Part-time programs available. Postbaccalaureate distance learning degree programs offered (no on-campus study). *Faculty:* 22 full-time (15 women), 7 part-time/adjunct (6 women). *Students:* 231 full-time (171 women), 68 part-time (58 women); includes 36 minority (17 Black or African American, non-Hispanic/Latino; 10 Asian, non-Hispanic/Latino; 6 Hispanic/Latino; 3 Two or more races, non-Hispanic/Latino), 6 international. Average age 28. 76 applicants, 76% accepted, 52 enrolled. In 2011, 94 master's, 31 doctorates awarded. *Degree requirements:* For master's, comprehensive exam (for some programs), thesis optional, clinical/fieldwork education. *Entrance requirements:* For master's, GRE, minimum cumulative GPA of 3.0; for doctorate, GRE, BA, minimum cumulative GPA of 3.0. Additional exam requirements/recommendations for international students: Required—TOEFL (minimum score 523 paper-based; 197 computer-based), IELTS (minimum score 6). *Application deadline:* For fall admission, 7/1 for domestic and international students; for spring admission, 3/15 for domestic and international students. Application fee: $55. *Expenses:* Tuition, state resident: full-time $6416; part-time $494 per credit hour. Tuition, nonresident: full-time $12,074; part-time $929 per credit hour. *Financial support:* In 2011–12, 22 students received support, including 2 research assistantships, 20 teaching assistantships. Financial award applicants required to submit FAFSA. *Faculty research:* Psychosocial needs of children, use of technology with disabilities, effects of stroke on gait, communication variables with accentedness, grasp patterns of possums. *Unit head:* Dr. John J. Bazyk, Chair, 216-687-2379, Fax: 216-687-9316, E-mail: j.bazyk@csuohio.edu. *Application contact:* Karen Armstrong, Secretary, 216-687-3567, Fax: 216-687-9316, E-mail: k.bradley@csuohio.edu. Web site: http://www.csuohio.edu/sciences/dept/healthsciences/.

Daemen College, Physician Assistant Department, Amherst, NY 14226-3592. Offers MS. *Accreditation:* ARC-PA. *Degree requirements:* For master's, 30 credits (40 weeks) in clinical clerk-ships; 2 research courses; 3 final year seminars. *Entrance requirements:* For master's, minimum GPA of 3.0 overall and in math and science prerequisites; 120 hours of direct patient contact; admission to professional phase. Additional exam requirements/recommendations for international students: Required—TOEFL (minimum score 500 paper-based; 173 computer-based; 63 iBT), IELTS (minimum score 5.5). Electronic applications accepted.

DeSales University, Graduate Division, Program in Physician Assistant Studies, Center Valley, PA 18034-9568. Offers MSPAS. *Accreditation:* ARC-PA. Part-time and evening/weekend programs available. Postbaccalaureate distance learning degree programs offered (minimal on-campus study). *Students:* 948 applicants, 5% accepted, 21 enrolled. In 2011, 239 master's awarded. *Degree requirements:* For master's, comprehensive exam. *Entrance requirements:* For master's, GRE General Test. Additional exam requirements/recommendations for international students: Required—TOEFL (minimum

score 610 paper-based; 256 computer-based; 102 iBT). *Application deadline:* For fall admission, 1/15 for domestic and international students. Electronic applications accepted. Tuition and fees vary according to degree level. *Financial support:* Applicants required to submit FAFSA. *Unit head:* Dr. Wayne Stuart, Director, 610-282-1100 Ext. 1344, Fax: 610-282-1893, E-mail: wayne.stuart@desales.edu. *Application contact:* Caryn Stopper, Director of Graduate Admissions, 610-282-1100 Ext. 1768, Fax: 610-282-0525, E-mail: caryn.stopper@desales.edu.

Des Moines University, College of Health Sciences, Physician Assistant Program, Des Moines, IA 50312-4104. Offers MS. *Accreditation:* ARC-PA. *Degree requirements:* For master's, research project. *Entrance requirements:* For master's, GRE, interview, minimum GPA of 2.8, related work experience. Additional exam requirements/recommendations for international students: Recommended—TOEFL. Electronic applications accepted. *Expenses:* Contact institution.

Drexel University, College of Nursing and Health Professions, Physician Assistant Department, Philadelphia, PA 19104-2875. Offers MHS. *Accreditation:* ARC-PA. Electronic applications accepted.

Duke University, School of Medicine, Physician Assistant Program, Durham, NC 27701. Offers MHS. *Accreditation:* ARC-PA. *Faculty:* 16 full-time (14 women), 3 part-time/adjunct (2 women). *Students:* 159 full-time (122 women); includes 42 minority (13 Black or African American, non-Hispanic/Latino; 2 American Indian or Alaska Native, non-Hispanic/Latino; 16 Asian, non-Hispanic/Latino; 11 Hispanic/Latino), 1 international. Average age 28. 717 applicants, 13% accepted, 80 enrolled. In 2011, 72 master's awarded. *Entrance requirements:* For master's, GRE, minimum of 5 courses in biological sciences with courses in anatomy, physiology and microbiology, 8 undergraduate hours in chemistry and statistics, patient care experience. *Application deadline:* For fall admission, 10/1 for domestic students. Application fee: $0. Electronic applications accepted. *Expenses:* Contact institution. *Financial support:* Fellowships, research assistantships, teaching assistantships, institutionally sponsored loans, and scholarships/grants available. Financial award application deadline: 5/1; financial award applicants required to submit FAFSA. *Unit head:* Patricia M. Dieter, Professor/Program Director, 919-681-3161, Fax: 919-681-9666, E-mail: patricia.dieter@duke.edu. *Application contact:* Wendy Z. Elwell, Program Coordinator, 919-668-4710, Fax: 919-681-9666, E-mail: wendy.elwell@duke.edu. Web site: http://paprogram.mc.duke.edu/.

Duquesne University, John G. Rangos, Sr. School of Health Sciences, Pittsburgh, PA 15282-0001. Offers health management systems (MHMS); occupational therapy (MS); physical therapy (DPT); physician assistant studies (MPAS); rehabilitation science (MS, PhD); speech-language pathology (MS); MBA/MHMS. *Accreditation:* AOTA (one or more programs are accredited); APTA (one or more programs are accredited); ASHA. *Faculty:* 34 full-time (23 women), 20 part-time/adjunct (11 women). *Students:* 227 full-time (180 women), 12 part-time (7 women); includes 8 minority (4 Black or African American, non-Hispanic/Latino; 1 Asian, non-Hispanic/Latino; 1 Hispanic/Latino; 1 Native Hawaiian or other Pacific Islander, non-Hispanic/Latino; 1 Two or more races, non-Hispanic/Latino), 3 international. Average age 24. 537 applicants, 12% accepted, 17 enrolled. In 2011, 43 master's, 31 doctorates awarded. *Degree requirements:* For doctorate, comprehensive exam (for some programs), thesis/dissertation (for some programs). *Entrance requirements:* For master's, GRE General Test (speech-language pathology), 3 letters of recommendation; minimum GPA of 2.75 (health management systems), 3.0 (speech-language pathology and health sciences); for doctorate, GRE General Test (for physical therapy and rehabilitation science), 3 letters of recommendation, minimum GPA of 3.0, personal interview. Additional exam requirements/recommendations for international students: Required—TOEFL (minimum score 550 paper-based; 233 computer-based; 90 iBT). *Application deadline:* Applications are processed on a rolling basis. Electronic applications accepted. *Expenses:* Contact institution. *Financial support:* Federal Work-Study available. Financial award applicants required to submit FAFSA. *Faculty research:* Neuronal processing, electrical stimulation on peripheral neuropathy, CNS stimulatory and inhibitory signals, behavioral genetic methodologies to development disorders of speech, neurogenic communication disorders. *Total annual research expenditures:* $83,650. *Unit head:* Dr. Gregory H. Frazer, Dean, 412-396-5303, Fax: 412-396-5554, E-mail: frazer@duq.edu. *Application contact:* Christopher R. Hilf, Recruiter/Academic Advisor, 412-396-5653, Fax: 412-396-5554, E-mail: hilfc@duq.edu. Web site: http://www.duq.edu/healthsciences/health.html.

D'Youville College, Physician Assistant Department, Buffalo, NY 14201-1084. Offers MS. *Accreditation:* ARC-PA. *Faculty:* 5 full-time (4 women), 1 part-time/adjunct (0 women). *Students:* 162 full-time (116 women), 3 part-time (2 women); includes 21 minority (3 Black or African American, non-Hispanic/Latino; 2 American Indian or Alaska Native, non-Hispanic/Latino; 9 Asian, non-Hispanic/Latino; 5 Hispanic/Latino; 2 Two or more races, non-Hispanic/Latino), 5 international. Average age 27. 185 applicants, 24% accepted, 23 enrolled. In 2011, 38 master's awarded. *Entrance requirements:* For master's, BS, patient contact, 3 letters of recommendation. Additional exam requirements/recommendations for international students: Required—TOEFL (minimum score 500 paper-based; 173 computer-based). *Application deadline:* For fall admission, 5/1 for international students; for spring admission, 9/1 for international students. Applications are processed on a rolling basis. Application fee: $25. Electronic applications accepted. *Expenses: Tuition:* Full-time $18,960; part-time $790 per credit hour. *Required fees:* $310. Tuition and fees vary according to degree level and program. *Unit head:* Dr. Maureen F. Finney, Chair, 716-829-7730, E-mail: finneym@dyc.edu. *Application contact:* Linda Fisher, Graduate Admissions Director, 716-829-8400, Fax: 716-829-7900, E-mail: graduateadmissions@dyc.edu.

East Carolina University, Graduate School, School of Allied Health Sciences, Department of Physician Assistant Studies, Greenville, NC 27858-4353. Offers MS. *Accreditation:* ARC-PA. Application fee: $50. *Expenses:* Tuition, state resident: full-time $3557; part-time $444.63 per semester hour. Tuition, nonresident: full-time $14,351; part-time $1793.88 per semester hour. *Required fees:* $2016; $252 per semester hour. Part-time tuition and fees vary according to course load, campus/location and program. *Unit head:* Dr. Alan Gindoff, Chair, 252-744-1700, E-mail: gindoffa@ecu.edu. *Application contact:* Dean of Graduate School, 252-328-6012, Fax: 252-328-6071, E-mail: gradschool@ecu.edu.

Eastern Virginia Medical School, Master of Physician Assistant Program, Norfolk, VA 23501-1980. Offers MPA. *Accreditation:* ARC-PA. *Faculty:* 11 full-time (6 women). *Students:* 176 full-time (131 women); includes 25 minority (11 Black or African American, non-Hispanic/Latino; 13 Asian, non-Hispanic/Latino; 1 Hispanic/Latino). 1,478 applicants, 4% accepted, 55 enrolled. In 2011, 49 master's awarded. *Entrance requirements:* Additional exam requirements/recommendations for international students: Required—TOEFL. *Application deadline:* For spring admission, 3/1 for domestic students. Applications are processed on a rolling basis. Application fee: $60. Electronic applications accepted. *Expenses:* Contact institution. *Financial support:* Applicants required to submit FAFSA. *Unit head:* Dr. Thomas Parish, Director, 757-446-7126, Fax: 757-446-7403, E-mail: parishtg@evms.edu. *Application contact:* Rose Mwayungu, Admissions and Enrollment Manager, 757-446-7153, Fax: 757-446-8915, E-mail: mwayunra@evms.edu. Web site: http://www.evms.edu/evms-school-of-health-professions/physician-assistant.html.

Emory University, School of Medicine, Programs in Allied Health Professions, Physician Assistant Program, Atlanta, GA 30322-1100. Offers MM Sc. *Accreditation:* ARC-PA. *Faculty:* 8 full-time (6 women), 6 part-time/adjunct (4 women). *Students:* 160 full-time (111 women); includes 39 minority (15 Black or African American, non-Hispanic/Latino; 12 Asian, non-Hispanic/Latino; 9 Hispanic/Latino; 3 Two or more races, non-Hispanic/Latino). Average age 29. 1,060 applicants, 7% accepted, 56 enrolled. In 2011, 49 master's awarded. *Entrance requirements:* For master's, GRE General Test. Additional exam requirements/recommendations for international students: Required—TOEFL (minimum score 93 iBT). *Application deadline:* For fall admission, 10/1 for domestic and international students. Applications are processed on a rolling basis. Application fee: $55. Electronic applications accepted. *Expenses:* Contact institution. *Financial support:* In 2011–12, 92 students received support. Institutionally sponsored loans and scholarships/grants available. Financial award application deadline: 3/1; financial award applicants required to submit FAFSA. *Faculty research:* Cultural competency in medical education, farm worker health, technology in medicine, physician assistants in primary care, interprofessional education. *Unit head:* Dr. Dana Sayre-Stanhope, Director, 404-727-7825, Fax: 404-727-7836, E-mail: dsayres@emory.edu. *Application contact:* Kaye Johnson, Assistant Director of Admissions, 404-727-7857, Fax: 404-727-7836, E-mail: ljohn07@emory.edu. Web site: http://www.emory.pa.org.

Franklin Pierce University, Graduate Studies, Rindge, NH 03461-0060. Offers curriculum and instruction (M Ed); emerging network technologies (Graduate Certificate); energy and sustainability studies (MBA); health administration (MBA, Graduate Certificate); human resource management (MBA, Graduate Certificate); information technology (MBA); information technology management (MS); leadership (MBA, DA); nursing (MS); physical therapy (DPT); physician assistant studies (MPAS); special education (M Ed); sports management (MBA). *Accreditation:* APTA. Part-time programs available. Postbaccalaureate distance learning degree programs offered (no on-campus study). *Degree requirements:* For master's, concentrated original research projects; student teaching; fieldwork and/or internship; leadership project; PRAXIS I and II (for M Ed); for doctorate, concentrated original research projects, clinical fieldwork and/or internship, leadership project. *Entrance requirements:* For master's, minimum GPA of 2.5, 3 letters of recommendation; competencies in accounting, economics, statistics, and computer skills through life experience or undergraduate coursework (for MBA); certification/e-portfolio, minimum C grade in all education courses (for M Ed); license to practice as RN (for MS in nursing); for doctorate, GRE, BA/BS, 3 letters of recommendation, personal mission statement, interview, writing sample, minimum cumulative GPA of 2.8, master's degree (for DA); 80 hours of observation/work in PT settings, completion of anatomy, chemistry, physics, and statistics, minimum GPA of 3.0 (for DPT). Additional exam requirements/recommendations for international students: Required—TOEFL (minimum score 550 paper-based; 195 computer-based; 61 iBT). Electronic applications accepted. *Faculty research:* Evidence-based practice in sports physical therapy, human resource management in economic crisis, leadership in nursing, innovation in sports facility management, differentiated learning and understanding by design.

Gannon University, School of Graduate Studies, Morosky College of Health Professions and Sciences, School of Health Professions, Program in Physician Assistant, Erie, PA 16541-0001. Offers MPAS. Program requires five years to complete. *Accreditation:* ARC-PA. *Students:* 56 full-time (42 women); includes 2 minority (1 Black or African American, non-Hispanic/Latino; 1 Hispanic/Latino). Average age 24. 151 applicants, 14% accepted, 11 enrolled. In 2011, 45 master's awarded. *Degree requirements:* For master's, thesis or alternative, research project. *Entrance requirements:* For master's, interview, bachelor's degree, minimum QPA of 3.0. Additional exam requirements/recommendations for international students: Required—TOEFL (minimum score 79 iBT). *Application deadline:* For fall admission, 1/15 for domestic students. Application fee: $25. Electronic applications accepted. *Expenses:* Contact institution. *Financial support:* Scholarships/grants available. Financial award application deadline: 7/1; financial award applicants required to submit FAFSA. *Faculty research:* Diabetes/endocrinology, cardiology, amyotrophic lateral sclerosis, drug sensitivity. *Unit head:* Michele Roth-Kauffman, Chair, 814-871-5643, E-mail: rothkauf001@gannon.edu. *Application contact:* Kara Morgan, Director of Graduate Admissions, 814-871-5831, Fax: 814-871-5827, E-mail: graduate@gannon.edu.

The George Washington University, School of Medicine and Health Sciences, Health Sciences Programs, Physician Assistant Program, Washington, DC 20052. Offers MSHS, MSHS/MPH. *Accreditation:* ARC-PA. *Students:* 146 full-time (114 women), 2 part-time (1 woman); includes 23 minority (4 Black or African American, non-Hispanic/Latino; 1 American Indian or Alaska Native, non-Hispanic/Latino; 8 Asian, non-Hispanic/Latino; 7 Hispanic/Latino; 3 Native Hawaiian or other Pacific Islander, non-Hispanic/Latino), 5 international. Average age 29. 570 applicants, 18% accepted, 58 enrolled. In 2011, 60 master's awarded. *Entrance requirements:* For master's, GRE General Test, BA/BS with clinical experience. *Application deadline:* For fall admission, 10/15 for domestic students. Applications are processed on a rolling basis. Application fee: $75. Electronic applications accepted. *Unit head:* Venetia L. Orcutt, Director, 202-994-6670, E-mail: vorcutt@gwu.edu. *Application contact:* Jamie Lewis, Executive Assistant, 202-994-6661, E-mail: npajsl@gwumc.edu.

Grand Valley State University, College of Health Professions, Physician Assistant Studies Program, Allendale, MI 49401-9403. Offers MPAS. *Accreditation:* ARC-PA. *Degree requirements:* For master's, thesis, clinical rotations, project. *Entrance requirements:* For master's, interview, 250 hours of health care experience. Additional exam requirements/recommendations for international students: Required—TOEFL (minimum score 610 paper-based; 253 computer-based). Electronic applications accepted. *Faculty research:* Women's health, pain management, PA practice issues, hematology/hemostasis, patient education.

Harding University, College of Sciences, Searcy, AR 72149-0001. Offers physician assistant studies (MS). *Faculty:* 6 full-time (1 woman), 2 part-time/adjunct (1 woman). *Students:* 128 full-time (100 women), 2 part-time (both women); includes 10 minority (3 Black or African American, non-Hispanic/Latino; 2 American Indian or Alaska Native, non-Hispanic/Latino; 5 Asian, non-Hispanic/Latino). Average age 27. 390 applicants, 10% accepted, 36 enrolled. In 2011, 29 master's awarded. *Degree requirements:* For master's, project. *Entrance requirements:* For master's, GRE. *Application deadline:* For fall admission, 11/1 for domestic students. Applications are processed on a rolling basis. Application fee: $25. Electronic applications accepted. *Expenses:* Contact institution. *Financial support:* Applicants required to submit FAFSA. *Unit head:* Dr. Michael Murphy, Director, 501-279-5642, E-mail: paprogram@harding.edu. *Application contact:* Marcia Murphy, Admissions Director, Physician Assistant Program, 501-279-5642, Fax: 501-279-4188, E-mail: paprogram@harding.edu. Web site: http://www.harding.edu/paprogram.

Hofstra University, College of Liberal Arts and Sciences, Department of Biology, Hempstead, NY 11549. Offers biology (MA, MS); physician assistant studies (MS); urban ecology (MA, MS). Part-time and evening/weekend programs available. *Faculty:* 14 full-time (7 women), 3 part-time/adjunct (2 women). *Students:* 116 full-time (81 women), 10 part-time (6 women); includes 17 minority (4 Black or African American, non-Hispanic/Latino; 10 Asian, non-Hispanic/Latino; 3 Hispanic/Latino). Average age 25. 98 applicants, 89% accepted, 60 enrolled. In 2011, 5 master's awarded. *Degree*

requirements: For master's, thesis, minimum GPA of 3.0. *Entrance requirements:* For master's, GRE, bachelor's degree in biology or equivalent; 2 letters of recommendation; essay. Additional exam requirements/recommendations for international students: Required—TOEFL (minimum score 550 paper-based; 213 computer-based; 80 iBT). *Application deadline:* Applications are processed on a rolling basis. Application fee: $70 ($75 for international students). Electronic applications accepted. *Expenses: Tuition:* Full-time $18,990; part-time $1055 per credit hour. *Required fees:* $970. Tuition and fees vary according to program. *Financial support:* In 2011–12, 20 students received support, including 12 fellowships with full and partial tuition reimbursements available (averaging $4,490 per year); research assistantships with full and partial tuition reimbursements available, Federal Work-Study, institutionally sponsored loans, scholarships/grants, and tuition waivers (full and partial) also available. Support available to part-time students. Financial award applicants required to submit FAFSA. *Faculty research:* Molecular basis of sex determination in turtles; regulation of fat metabolism in Drosophimelanogaster; molecular regulation of morphological differentiation in Streptomyces; population, ecology, evolution, and behavior of mammals, reptiles, and amphibians; systematics and biology of marine polychaete worms and crustaceans. *Total annual research expenditures:* $340,650. *Unit head:* Dr. Maureen K. Krause, Program Director, 516-463-6178, Fax: 516-463-5112, E-mail: biomkk@hofstra.edu. *Application contact:* Carol Drummer, Dean of Graduate Admissions, 516-463-4876, Fax: 516-463-4664, E-mail: gradstudent@hofstra.edu. Web site: http://www.hofstra.edu/hclas.

Idaho State University, Office of Graduate Studies, Kasiska College of Health Professions, Program in Physician Assistant Studies, Pocatello, ID 83209-8253. Offers MPAS. *Accreditation:* ARC-PA. *Degree requirements:* For master's, comprehensive exam, thesis (for some programs), portfolio, clinical year, oral case presentation. *Entrance requirements:* For master's, GRE General Test, minimum GPA of 3.0, letters of reference. Additional exam requirements/recommendations for international students: Required—TOEFL (minimum score 500 paper-based; 213 computer-based). Electronic applications accepted. *Expenses:* Contact institution.

James Madison University, The Graduate School, College of Integrated Science and Technology, Department of Health Sciences, Program in Physician Assistant Studies, Harrisonburg, VA 22807. Offers MPAS. *Accreditation:* ARC-PA. Part-time programs available. *Students:* 78 full-time (53 women); includes 12 minority (2 Black or African American, non-Hispanic/Latino; 8 Asian, non-Hispanic/Latino; 1 Hispanic/Latino; 1 Two or more races, non-Hispanic/Latino), 1 international. Average age 27. In 2011, 25 master's awarded. *Entrance requirements:* For master's, GRE General Test. *Application deadline:* For fall admission, 1/15 priority date for domestic students. Application fee: $55. *Expenses:* Tuition, state resident: full-time $8016; part-time $334 per credit hour. Tuition, nonresident: full-time $22,656; part-time $944 per credit hour. *Financial support:* Application deadline: 3/1; applicants required to submit FAFSA. *Unit head:* James Hammond, Director, 540-568-2395, E-mail: hammonjb@jmu.edu. *Application contact:* Lynette M. Bible, Director of Graduate Admissions, 540-568-6395, Fax: 540-568-7860, E-mail: biblelm@jmu.edu.

Jefferson College of Health Sciences, Program in Physician Assistant, Roanoke, VA 24031-3186. Offers MS. *Accreditation:* ARC-PA. *Degree requirements:* For master's, rotations. *Entrance requirements:* For master's, GRE. Additional exam requirements/recommendations for international students: Required—TOEFL (minimum score 550 paper-based; 213 computer-based; 80 iBT). Electronic applications accepted. *Faculty research:* Community health, chronic disease management, geriatrics, rheumatology, medically underserved populations.

Keiser University, MS in Physician Assistant Program, Fort Lauderdale, FL 33309. Offers MS.

King's College, Program in Physician Assistant Studies, Wilkes-Barre, PA 18711-0801. Offers MSPAS. *Accreditation:* ARC-PA. *Degree requirements:* For master's, thesis. *Entrance requirements:* Additional exam requirements/recommendations for international students: Required—TOEFL (minimum score 600 paper-based; 250 computer-based). Electronic applications accepted.

Le Moyne College, Department of Physician Assistant Studies, Syracuse, NY 13214. Offers MS. *Accreditation:* ARC-PA. *Faculty:* 7 full-time (3 women), 14 part-time/adjunct (7 women). *Students:* 82 full-time (55 women), 1 part-time (0 women); includes 9 minority (1 Black or African American, non-Hispanic/Latino; 5 Asian, non-Hispanic/Latino; 3 Hispanic/Latino). Average age 26. 418 applicants, 15% accepted, 45 enrolled. In 2011, 40 master's awarded. *Degree requirements:* For master's, project. *Entrance requirements:* For master's, minimum GPA of 3.0, patient contact, interview, writing sample, 3 letters of recommendation. Additional exam requirements/recommendations for international students: Required—TOEFL (minimum score 550 paper-based; 213 computer-based; 79 iBT). *Application deadline:* For fall admission, 10/1 priority date for domestic students, 10/1 for international students. Electronic applications accepted. *Expenses:* Contact institution. *Financial support:* In 2011–12, 20 students received support. Career-related internships or fieldwork, scholarships/grants, and health care benefits available. Financial award applicants required to submit FAFSA. *Faculty research:* Cultural competence, educational outcomes, occupational choice, preventive medicine, health literacy. *Unit head:* Mary E. Springston, Clinical Assistant Professor and Director of Department of Physician Assistant Studies, 315-445-4163, Fax: 315-445-4602, E-mail: springme@lemoyne.edu. *Application contact:* Kristen P. Trapasso, Director of Graduate Admission, 315-445-4265, Fax: 315-445-6027, E-mail: trapaskp@lemoyne.edu. Web site: http://www.lemoyne.edu/pa.

Lock Haven University of Pennsylvania, Department of Health Science, Lock Haven, PA 17745-2390. Offers physician assistant in rural primary care (MHS). *Accreditation:* ARC-PA. *Entrance requirements:* For master's, minimum undergraduate GPA of 3.0. Additional exam requirements/recommendations for international students: Required—TOEFL. Electronic applications accepted.

Loma Linda University, School of Allied Health Professions, Department of Physician Assistant, Loma Linda, CA 92350. Offers MS. *Accreditation:* ARC-PA. *Entrance requirements:* For master's, minimum GPA of 3.0. Additional exam requirements/recommendations for international students: Required—TOEFL (minimum score 550 paper-based; 213 computer-based).

Marietta College, Program in Physician Assistant Studies, Marietta, OH 45750-4000. Offers MS. *Accreditation:* ARC-PA.

Marquette University, Graduate School, College of Health Sciences, Department of Physician Assistant Studies, Milwaukee, WI 53201-1881. Offers MPAS. Students enter the program as undergraduates. *Accreditation:* ARC-PA. *Faculty:* 9 full-time (5 women), 1 (woman) part-time/adjunct. *Students:* 109 full-time (87 women); includes 12 minority (1 Black or African American, non-Hispanic/Latino; 5 Asian, non-Hispanic/Latino; 5 Hispanic/Latino; 1 Two or more races, non-Hispanic/Latino), 1 international. Average age 25. 110 applicants, 51% accepted, 56 enrolled. In 2011, 47 master's awarded. *Degree requirements:* For master's, clinical clerkship experience, capstone project. *Entrance requirements:* For master's, GRE General Test, three letters of recommendation, minimum GPA of 3.0, official transcripts from all current and previous institutions except Marquette. Additional exam requirements/recommendations for international students: Required—TOEFL (minimum score 530 paper-based; 78 computer-based). *Application deadline:* For fall admission, 10/1 for domestic students. Application fee: $50. Electronic applications accepted. *Expenses:* Contact institution. *Financial support:* Application deadline: 2/15. *Unit head:* MaryJo Wiemiller, Chair, 414-288-7180, Fax: 414-288-7951, E-mail: maryjo.wiemiller@marquette.edu. *Application contact:* Craig Pierce, Assistant Dean of the Graduate School, 414-288-5740, Fax: 414-288-1902, E-mail: craig.pierce@marquette.edu. Web site: http://www.marquette.edu/chs/pa/index.shtml.

Marywood University, Academic Affairs, College of Health and Human Services, Department of Physician Assistant Studies, Clinical Physician Assistant Track, Scranton, PA 18509-1598. Offers MS. *Entrance requirements:* Additional exam requirements/recommendations for international students: Required—TOEFL (minimum score 550 paper-based; 213 computer-based; 79 iBT). Application fee: $35. Electronic applications accepted. *Financial support:* Career-related internships or fieldwork, scholarships/grants, and unspecified assistantships available. Support available to part-time students. Financial award application deadline: 6/30; financial award applicants required to submit FAFSA. *Unit head:* Dr. Karen E. Arscott, Director, 570-348-6211 Ext. 2175, E-mail: arscott@.marywood.edu. *Application contact:* Tammy Manka, Assistant Director of Graduate Admissions, 866-279-9663, E-mail: tmanka@marywood.edu. Web site: http://www.marywood.edu/academics/gradcatalog/.

Marywood University, Academic Affairs, College of Health and Human Services, Department of Physician Assistant Studies, Physician Assistant Studies Program, Scranton, PA 18509-1598. Offers MS. *Accreditation:* ARC-PA. Part-time and evening/weekend programs available. *Entrance requirements:* Additional exam requirements/recommendations for international students: Required—TOEFL (minimum score 550 paper-based; 213 computer-based; 79 iBT). Application fee: $35. Electronic applications accepted. *Expenses:* Contact institution. *Financial support:* Career-related internships or fieldwork, scholarships/grants, and unspecified assistantships available. Support available to part-time students. Financial award application deadline: 6/30; financial award applicants required to submit FAFSA. *Unit head:* Dr. Karen E. Arscott, Director, 570-348-6211 Ext. 2175, E-mail: arscott@es.marywood.edu. *Application contact:* Tammy Manka, Assistant Director of Graduate Admissions, 570-348-6211 Ext. 2322, E-mail: tmanka@marywood.edu. Web site: http://www.marywood.edu/academics/gradcatalog/.

Massachusetts College of Pharmacy and Health Sciences, Graduate Studies, Programs in Physician Assistant Studies, Accelerated Program in Physician Assistant Studies (Manchester/Worcester), Boston, MA 02115-5896. Offers MPAS. *Accreditation:* ARC-PA. *Students:* 212 full-time (157 women); includes 13 minority (1 Black or African American, non-Hispanic/Latino; 7 Asian, non-Hispanic/Latino; 3 Hispanic/Latino; 2 Native Hawaiian or other Pacific Islander, non-Hispanic/Latino), 2 international. Average age 28. In 2011, 71 degrees awarded. *Entrance requirements:* Additional exam requirements/recommendations for international students: Required—TOEFL (minimum score 550 paper-based; 213 computer-based; 79 iBT). *Application deadline:* For spring admission, 10/1 priority date for domestic students, 10/1 for international students. Application fee: $70. Electronic applications accepted. *Expenses: Tuition:* Full-time $30,200; part-time $945 per credit hour. *Financial support:* Application deadline: 3/15. *Unit head:* Dr. Susan WHite, Program Director, Physician Assistant Studies, 603-314-1738, E-mail: susan.white@mcphs.edu. *Application contact:* Barbara Jellie, Admission Counselor, 603-314-1701, E-mail: barbara.jellie@mcphs.edu.

Medical University of South Carolina, College of Health Professions, Department of Health Professions, Physician Assistant Studies Program, Charleston, SC 29425. Offers MS. *Accreditation:* ARC-PA. *Faculty:* 4 full-time (2 women), 4 part-time/adjunct (2 women). *Students:* 127 full-time (102 women), 1 (woman) part-time; includes 16 minority (11 Black or African American, non-Hispanic/Latino; 3 Asian, non-Hispanic/Latino; 2 Hispanic/Latino). Average age 26. 494 applicants, 17% accepted, 69 enrolled. In 2011, 69 master's awarded. *Degree requirements:* For master's, clinical clerkship, research project. *Entrance requirements:* For master's, GRE General Test, interview, minimum GPA of 3.0, 3 references. Additional exam requirements/recommendations for international students: Required—TOEFL (minimum score 600 paper-based; 250 computer-based). *Application deadline:* For fall admission, 12/1 for domestic and international students. Application fee: $85. Electronic applications accepted. *Financial support:* Federal Work-Study available. Support available to part-time students. Financial award application deadline: 3/10; financial award applicants required to submit FAFSA. *Faculty research:* Oral health, pediatric emergency medicine, simulation technology in education, health manpower needs, cultural competency. *Total annual research expenditures:* $280,111. *Unit head:* Dr. Paul F. Jacques, Interim Program Director, 843-792-2649, Fax: 843-792-0506, E-mail: jacquesp@musc.edu. *Application contact:* Kelly K. Long, Student Services Program Coordinator, 843-792-3775, Fax: 843-792-0506, E-mail: longkk@musc.edu. Web site: http://www.musc.edu/chp/pa/index.htm.

Mercy College, School of Health and Natural Sciences, Program in Physician Assistant, Dobbs Ferry, NY 10522-1189. Offers physician assistant studies (MS). *Accreditation:* ARC-PA. Evening/weekend programs available. *Degree requirements:* For master's, project. *Entrance requirements:* For master's, interview, two letters of reference, personal statement stating reason for pursuing degree in physician assistant studies, official transcripts, minimum GPA of 3.0, completed Medical and Community Experience Verification forms. Additional exam requirements/recommendations for international students: Required—TOEFL (minimum score 600 paper-based; 250 computer-based; 100 iBT), IELTS (minimum score 8). Electronic applications accepted.

Methodist University, School of Graduate Studies, Program in Physician Assistant Studies, Fayetteville, NC 28311-1498. Offers MMS. *Accreditation:* ARC-PA. *Degree requirements:* For master's, comprehensive exam. *Entrance requirements:* For master's, GRE, bachelor's degree from four-year, regionally-accredited college or university; minimum of 500 hours' clinical experience with direct patient contact; minimum GPA of 3.0 on all college level work attempted, 3.2 on medical core prerequisites (recommended). Additional exam requirements/recommendations for international students: Required—TOEFL (minimum score 500 paper-based; 173 computer-based; 60 iBT).

Midwestern University, Downers Grove Campus, College of Health Sciences, Illinois Campus, Program in Physician Assistant Studies, Downers Grove, IL 60515-1235. Offers MMS. *Accreditation:* ARC-PA. *Faculty:* 8 full-time (5 women). *Students:* 166 full-time (143 women); includes 20 minority (9 Asian, non-Hispanic/Latino; 7 Hispanic/Latino; 4 Two or more races, non-Hispanic/Latino). Average age 25. 1,267 applicants, 11% accepted, 86 enrolled. In 2011, 53.master's awarded. *Entrance requirements:* For master's, GRE General Test. *Application deadline:* Applications are processed on a rolling basis. Application fee: $50. *Expenses:* Contact institution. *Financial support:* In 2011–12, 65 students received support. Federal Work-Study available. *Unit head:* Dr. Alyson Smith, Director, 630-515-7609. *Application contact:* Michael Laken, Director of Admissions, 630-515-6171, Fax: 630-971-6086, E-mail: admissil@midwestern.edu. Web site: http://www.midwestern.edu/.

Midwestern University, Glendale Campus, College of Health Sciences, Arizona Campus, Program in Physician Assistant Studies, Glendale, AZ 85308. Offers MMS. *Accreditation:* ARC-PA. *Faculty:* 7 full-time (3 women), 3 part-time/adjunct (all women).

Students: 178 full-time (139 women), 1 part-time (0 women); includes 21 minority (8 Asian, non-Hispanic/Latino; 5 Hispanic/Latino; 1 Native Hawaiian or other Pacific Islander, non-Hispanic/Latino; 7 Two or more races, non-Hispanic/Latino), 1 international. Average age 26. 1,269 applicants, 12% accepted, 91 enrolled. In 2011, 53 master's awarded. *Entrance requirements:* For master's, GRE. *Application deadline:* Applications are processed on a rolling basis. Application fee: $50. *Expenses:* Contact institution. *Financial support:* Applicants required to submit FAFSA. *Unit head:* Kevin Lohenry, Director, 623-572-3611. *Application contact:* James Walter, Director of Admissions, 888-247-9277, Fax: 623-572-3229, E-mail: admissaz@midwestern.edu.

Missouri State University, Graduate College, College of Health and Human Services, Department of Physician Assistant Studies, Springfield, MO 65897. Offers MS. *Accreditation:* ARC-PA. *Faculty:* 4 full-time (2 women), 48 part-time/adjunct (11 women). *Students:* 53 full-time (35 women), 2 part-time (both women); includes 4 minority (1 Black or African American, non-Hispanic/Latino; 1 American Indian or Alaska Native, non-Hispanic/Latino; 1 Asian, non-Hispanic/Latino; 1 Two or more races, non-Hispanic/Latino). Average age 28. In 2011, 28 master's awarded. *Degree requirements:* For master's, comprehensive exam, thesis or alternative. *Entrance requirements:* For master's, GRE General Test, minimum GPA of 3.0. Additional exam requirements/recommendations for international students: Required—TOEFL (minimum score 550 paper-based; 213 computer-based; 79 iBT). *Application deadline:* For spring admission, 8/1 for domestic and international students. Application fee: $35 ($50 for international students). *Expenses:* Tuition, state resident: full-time $4086; part-time $227 per credit hour. Tuition, nonresident: full-time $8172; part-time $454 per credit hour. *Required fees:* $275 per semester. Tuition and fees vary according to course load, campus/location and program. *Financial support:* Application deadline: 3/31; applicants required to submit FAFSA. *Unit head:* Dr. Steven Dodge, Head, 417-836-6151, Fax: 417-836-6406, E-mail: physicianasststudies@missouristate.edu. *Application contact:* Misty Stewart, Coordinator of Graduate Recruitment, 417-836-6079, Fax: 417-836-6200, E-mail: mistystewart@missouristate.edu. Web site: http://www.missouristate.edu/pas/.

Mountain State University, School of Graduate Studies, Physician Assistant Program, Beckley, WV 25802-9003. Offers MSPA. Admittance in junior year only. *Accreditation:* ARC-PA. *Faculty:* 5 full-time (3 women), 2 part-time/adjunct (0 women). *Students:* 148 full-time (89 women), 1 part-time (0 women); includes 20 minority (5 Black or African American, non-Hispanic/Latino; 1 American Indian or Alaska Native, non-Hispanic/Latino; 6 Asian, non-Hispanic/Latino; 7 Hispanic/Latino; 1 Native Hawaiian or other Pacific Islander, non-Hispanic/Latino), 4 international. Average age 27. 233 applicants, 41% accepted, 46 enrolled. In 2011, 46 master's awarded. *Degree requirements:* For master's, comprehensive exam, thesis or alternative. *Entrance requirements:* Additional exam requirements/recommendations for international students: Required—TOEFL (minimum score 550 paper-based; 213 computer-based); Recommended—IELTS (minimum score 6.5). *Application deadline:* For fall admission, 5/31 priority date for domestic students, 5/31 for international students. Applications are processed on a rolling basis. Application fee: $25 ($50 for international students). Electronic applications accepted. *Expenses:* Contact institution. *Financial support:* Career-related internships or fieldwork, Federal Work-Study, and scholarships/grants available. Support available to part-time students. Financial award application deadline: 3/1; financial award applicants required to submit FAFSA. *Unit head:* Karen Bowling, Dean, School of Health Science, 304-929-1327, Fax: 304-256-5571, E-mail: kbowling@mountainstate.edu. *Application contact:* Debra Campbell, Graduate Program Director, 304-929-1451, Fax: 304-256-5571, E-mail: dcampbell@mountainstate.edu.

New York Institute of Technology, Graduate Division, School of Health Professions, Program in Physician Assistant, Old Westbury, NY 11568-8000. Offers MS. *Accreditation:* ARC-PA. *Students:* 152 full-time (103 women), 1 (woman) part-time; includes 33 minority (7 Black or African American, non-Hispanic/Latino; 16 Asian, non-Hispanic/Latino; 7 Hispanic/Latino; 3 Two or more races, non-Hispanic/Latino), 1 international. Average age 26. In 2011, 48 master's awarded. *Degree requirements:* For master's, thesis. *Entrance requirements:* For master's, minimum GPA of 3.0, interview, 100 hours of volunteer work, 2 letters of recommendation. Additional exam requirements/recommendations for international students: Required—TOEFL (minimum score 550 paper-based; 213 computer-based). *Application deadline:* For fall admission, 7/1 priority date for domestic students; for spring admission, 12/1 priority date for domestic students. Application fee: $50. *Expenses: Tuition:* Part-time $930 per credit hour. *Financial support:* Research assistantships with partial tuition reimbursements available. Financial award applicants required to submit FAFSA. *Unit head:* Dr. Salvatore Barese, Department Chair, 516-686-3804, Fax: 516-686-3795, E-mail: sbarese@nyit.edu. *Application contact:* Dr. Jacquelyn Nealon, Vice President for Enrollment Services, 516-686-7925, Fax: 516-686-7597, E-mail: jnealon@nyit.edu.

Northeastern University, Bouvé College of Health Sciences, Physician Assistant Program, Boston, MA 02115-5096. Offers MS. *Accreditation:* ARC-PA. *Faculty:* 8. *Students:* 67. 489 applicants, 7% accepted, 34 enrolled. In 2011, 32 master's awarded. *Entrance requirements:* For master's, minimum undergraduate GPA of 3.0; 2 semesters each of general biology plus lab and general chemistry plus lab; coursework in human anatomy, physiology, and statistics with minimum B average in each; 2,000 hours of hands-on patient care experience; interview; curriculum vitae. Additional exam requirements/recommendations for international students: Required—TOEFL (minimum score 600 paper-based; 250 computer-based; 100 iBT). *Application deadline:* For fall admission, 9/1 for domestic students. Application fee: $25. Electronic applications accepted. *Expenses:* Contact institution. *Financial support:* Federal Work-Study and institutionally sponsored loans available. Financial award application deadline: 3/1; financial award applicants required to submit FAFSA. *Faculty research:* Education and training, reimbursement. *Unit head:* Dr. Rosann M. Ippolito, Program Director, 617-373-3195, E-mail: r.ippolito@neu.edu. *Application contact:* Carol G. Goldberg, Assistant Director, 617-373-3195, E-mail: c.goldberg@neu.edu.

Northern Arizona University, Graduate College, College of Health and Human Services, Physician Assistant Program, Flagstaff, AZ 86011. Offers MPAS. *Expenses:* Tuition, state resident: full-time $7190; part-time $355 per credit hour. Tuition, nonresident: full-time $18,092; part-time $1005 per credit hour. *Required fees:* $818; $328 per semester. *Unit head:* Leslie Schulz, Executive Dean, 928-523-4331, E-mail: leslie.schulz@nau.edu. *Application contact:* April Sandoval, Coordinator, 928-523-4348, Fax: 928-523-8950, E-mail: april.sandoval@nau.edu.

Oregon Health & Science University, School of Medicine, Graduate Programs in Medicine, Division of Physician Assistant Education, Portland, OR 97239-3098. Offers MPAS. *Accreditation:* ARC-PA. *Students:* 76 full-time (51 women); includes 12 minority (2 Black or African American, non-Hispanic/Latino; 6 Asian, non-Hispanic/Latino; 4 Hispanic/Latino). Average age 28. 902 applicants, 6% accepted, 38 enrolled. In 2011, 35 master's awarded. *Application deadline:* For fall admission, 10/1 for domestic students. *Unit head:* Ted Ruback, Program Director/Division Head, 503-494-1408, E-mail: ruback@ohsu.edu. *Application contact:* Colleen Schierholtz, Director of Admissions, 503-494-1408, E-mail: schierhc@ohsu.edu. Web site: http://www.ohsu.edu/xd/education/schools/school-of-medicine/academic-programs/physician-assistant/index.cfm.

Our Lady of the Lake College, School of Arts, Sciences and Health Professions, Baton Rouge, LA 70808. Offers physician associate studies (MMS).

Pace University, Dyson College of Arts and Sciences, Program in Physician Assistant, New York, NY 10038. Offers MS. *Accreditation:* ARC-PA. *Students:* 57 full-time (42 women), 74 part-time (63 women); includes 40 minority (6 Black or African American, non-Hispanic/Latino; 23 Asian, non-Hispanic/Latino; 5 Hispanic/Latino; 6 Two or more races, non-Hispanic/Latino). Average age 25. 1,230 applicants, 8% accepted, 57 enrolled. In 2011, 62 master's awarded. *Entrance requirements:* Additional exam requirements/recommendations for international students: Required—TOEFL. *Application deadline:* For spring admission, 10/1 priority date for domestic students. Application fee: $70. *Expenses: Tuition:* Part-time $990 per credit. *Required fees:* $168 per semester. Tuition and fees vary according to course load and degree level. *Unit head:* Kathleen Roche, Program Director, 212-346-1357, E-mail: paprogram@pace.edu. *Application contact:* Susan Ford-Goldschein, Director of Admissions, 212-346-1660, Fax: 212-346-1585, E-mail: gradnyc@pace.edu.

Pacific University, School of Physician Assistant Studies, Forest Grove, OR 97116-1797. Offers MHS, MS. *Accreditation:* ARC-PA. *Degree requirements:* For master's, comprehensive exam, thesis, clinical project. *Entrance requirements:* For master's, minimum of 1000 hours of direct clinical patient care, prerequisite coursework in science with minimum C average. Additional exam requirements/recommendations for international students: Required—TOEFL (minimum score 600 paper-based; 250 computer-based). *Expenses:* Contact institution. *Faculty research:* Public health, evidenced based medicine.

Philadelphia College of Osteopathic Medicine, Graduate and Professional Programs, Physician Assistant Program, Philadelphia, PA 19131-1694. Offers health sciences (MS). *Accreditation:* ARC-PA. *Degree requirements:* For master's, thesis. *Entrance requirements:* For master's, minimum GPA of 3.0; course work in biology, chemistry, health science, math, social science; 200 hours patient contact.

See Display on next page and Close-Up on page 553.

Philadelphia University, College of Science, Health and the Liberal Arts, Program in Physician Assistant Studies, Philadelphia, PA 19144. Offers MS. *Accreditation:* ARC-PA. *Entrance requirements:* For master's, MCAT, GRE, or MAT. Additional exam requirements/recommendations for international students: Required—TOEFL (minimum score 550 paper-based; 213 computer-based; 79 iBT).

Quinnipiac University, School of Health Sciences, Program for Pathologists' Assistant, Hamden, CT 06518-1940. Offers MHS. *Accreditation:* NAACLS. *Faculty:* 2 full-time (1 woman), 6 part-time/adjunct (3 women). *Students:* 36 full-time (26 women); includes 4 minority (1 Black or African American, non-Hispanic/Latino; 3 Asian, non-Hispanic/Latino). Average age 27. 130 applicants, 14% accepted, 18 enrolled. In 2011, 18 master's awarded. *Degree requirements:* For master's, residency. *Entrance requirements:* For master's, interview, coursework in biological and health sciences, minimum GPA of 2.8. Additional exam requirements/recommendations for international students: Required—TOEFL (minimum score 575 paper-based; 233 computer-based; 90 iBT), IELTS (minimum score 6.5). *Application deadline:* For fall admission, 12/15 for domestic students. Applications are processed on a rolling basis. Application fee: $45. Electronic applications accepted. *Expenses: Tuition:* Part-time $855 per credit. *Required fees:* $35 per credit. *Financial support:* In 2011–12, 8 students received support. Career-related internships or fieldwork, tuition waivers (partial), and unspecified assistantships available. Financial award application deadline: 4/15; financial award applicants required to submit FAFSA. *Unit head:* Dr. Kenneth Kaloustian, Director, 203-582-8676, Fax: 203-582-3443, E-mail: ken.kaloustian@quinnipiac.edu. *Application contact:* Kristin Parent, Assistant Director of Graduate Health Sciences Admissions, 800-462-1944, Fax: 203-582-3443, E-mail: kristin.parent@quinnipiac.edu. Web site: http://www.quinnipiac.edu/gradpathologists.

Quinnipiac University, School of Health Sciences, Program for Physician Assistant, Hamden, CT 06518-1940. Offers MHS. *Accreditation:* ARC-PA. *Faculty:* 7 full-time (6 women), 20 part-time/adjunct (7 women). *Students:* 97 full-time (72 women), 12 part-time (7 women); includes 22 minority (9 Black or African American, non-Hispanic/Latino; 1 American Indian or Alaska Native, non-Hispanic/Latino; 6 Asian, non-Hispanic/Latino; 6 Hispanic/Latino). 823 applicants, 11% accepted, 50 enrolled. In 2011, 48 master's awarded. *Degree requirements:* For master's, comprehensive exam. *Entrance requirements:* For master's, minimum GPA of 3.0; course work in biological, physical, and behavioral sciences; interviews; 2000 hours direct patient care experience. Additional exam requirements/recommendations for international students: Required—TOEFL (minimum score 575 paper-based; 233 computer-based; 90 iBT), IELTS (minimum score 6.5). *Application deadline:* For fall admission, 9/1 for domestic students. *Expenses: Tuition:* Part-time $855 per credit. *Required fees:* $35 per credit. *Financial support:* In 2011–12, 54 students received support. Career-related internships or fieldwork, Federal Work-Study, tuition waivers (partial), and unspecified assistantships available. Financial award application deadline: 4/15; financial award applicants required to submit FAFSA. *Unit head:* Cynthia Booth-Lord, Director, 203-582-5297, Fax: 203-582-8706, E-mail: cynthia.lord@quinnipiac.edu. *Application contact:* Kristin Parent, Office of Graduate Admissions, 800-462-1944, Fax: 203-582-3443, E-mail: kristin.parent@quinnipiac.edu. Web site: http://www.quinnipiac.edu/academics/colleges-schools-and-departments/school-of-health-sciences/graduate-programs/master-of-health-science-physician-as.

Rocky Mountain College, Program in Physician Assistant Studies, Billings, MT 59102-1796. Offers MPAS. *Accreditation:* ARC-PA. *Faculty:* 4 full-time (2 women), 4 part-time/adjunct (1 woman). *Students:* 59 full-time (36 women); includes 1 minority (Asian, non-Hispanic/Latino), 1 international. Average age 26. In 2011, 26 master's awarded. *Entrance requirements:* For master's, GRE. Additional exam requirements/recommendations for international students: Required—TOEFL (minimum score 570 paper-based; 230 computer-based; 88 iBT), IELTS (minimum score 6.5). *Application deadline:* Applications are processed on a rolling basis. Application fee: $35 ($40 for international students). Electronic applications accepted. *Expenses:* Contact institution. *Financial support:* Applicants required to submit FAFSA. *Unit head:* Bob Wilmouth, Program Director, 406-657-1190, Fax: 406-657-1194, E-mail: bob.wilmouth@rocky.edu. *Application contact:* Kelly Edwards, Director of Admissions, 406-657-1026, Fax: 406-657-1189, E-mail: admissions@rocky.edu. Web site: http://www.rocky.edu/academics/academic-programs/graduate-programs/mpas/index.php.

Rosalind Franklin University of Medicine and Science, College of Health Professions, Physician Assistant Department, North Chicago, IL 60064-3095. Offers MS. *Accreditation:* ARC-PA. *Degree requirements:* For master's, thesis. *Entrance requirements:* For master's, GRE, writing sample. Additional exam requirements/recommendations for international students: Required—TOEFL. Electronic applications accepted. *Faculty research:* Ortho-spine, diabetes education, cultural competency, interprofessional medical education.

Rush University, College of Health Sciences, Physician Assistant Studies Program, Chicago, IL 60612-3832. Offers MS. *Entrance requirements:* Additional exam requirements/recommendations for international students: Required—TOEFL (minimum score 570 paper-based; 230 computer-based; 88 iBT).

Saint Francis University, Department of Physician Assistant Sciences, Loretto, PA 15940-0600. Offers health science (MHS); medical science (MMS); physician assistant

sciences (MPAS). *Accreditation:* ARC-PA. *Faculty:* 9 full-time (8 women), 3 part-time/ adjunct (0 women). *Students:* 110 full-time (87 women); includes 3 minority (2 Asian, non-Hispanic/Latino; 1 Hispanic/Latino). Average age 25. 838 applicants, 1% accepted, 7 enrolled. In 2011, 53 master's awarded. *Degree requirements:* For master's, capstone, summative evaluation. *Entrance requirements:* For master's, interview. Additional exam requirements/recommendations for international students: Required—TOEFL (minimum score 550 paper-based; 213 computer-based; 70 iBT). *Application deadline:* For fall admission, 10/1 for domestic and international students. Applications are processed on a rolling basis. Application fee: $175. Electronic applications accepted. *Expenses: Tuition:* Part-time $815 per credit. *Required fees:* $504 per semester. One-time fee: $40 part-time. Tuition and fees vary according to degree level, program and reciprocity agreements. *Financial support:* Applicants required to submit FAFSA. *Unit head:* Donna L. Yeisley, Director, 814-472-3131, Fax: 814-472-3137, E-mail: dyeisley@francis.edu. *Application contact:* Marie S. Link, Director of Research and MPAS Graduate Admission, 814-472-3138, Fax: 814-472-3137, E-mail: mlink@francis.edu. Web site: http://www.francis.edu/MPAShome.htm.

Saint Louis University, Graduate Education, Doisy College of Health Sciences, Department of Physician Assistant Education, St. Louis, MO 63103-2097. Offers MMS. *Accreditation:* ARC-PA. *Entrance requirements:* Additional exam requirements/recommendations for international students: Required—TOEFL (minimum score 86 iBT). Electronic applications accepted.

Salus University, College of Health Sciences, Elkins Park, PA 19027-1598. Offers physician assistant (MMS); public health (MPH). *Accreditation:* ARC-PA. *Entrance requirements:* For master's, GRE (recommended). Additional exam requirements/recommendations for international students: Required—TOEFL. Electronic applications accepted.

Samuel Merritt University, Department of Physician Assistant Studies, Oakland, CA 94609-3108. Offers MPA. *Accreditation:* ARC-PA. *Entrance requirements:* For master's, health care experience, minimum GPA of 3.0, previous course work in statistics.

Seton Hall University, School of Health and Medical Sciences, Physician Assistant Program, South Orange, NJ 07079-2697. Offers MS. *Accreditation:* ARC-PA. *Entrance requirements:* For master's, GRE, health care experience, interview, minimum GPA of 3.0. Additional exam requirements/recommendations for international students: Required—TOEFL. Electronic applications accepted. *Expenses: Tuition:* Part-time $1033 per credit hour. *Required fees:* $85 per semester.

Seton Hill University, Program in Physician Assistant, Greensburg, PA 15601. Offers MS. *Accreditation:* ARC-PA. *Faculty:* 6 full-time (3 women), 17 part-time/adjunct (8 women). *Students:* 66 full-time (54 women); includes 7 minority (3 Black or African American, non-Hispanic/Latino; 1 Asian, non-Hispanic/Latino; 3 Hispanic/Latino). In 2011, 24 degrees awarded. *Entrance requirements:* For master's, minimum GPA of 3.2 overall undergraduate and prerequisite courses, transcripts, 3 letters of recommendation, personal statement. Additional exam requirements/recommendations for international students: Required—TOEFL (minimum score 650 paper-based; 280 computer-based; 114 iBT), IELTS (minimum score 7). *Application deadline:* For spring admission, 1/15 priority date for domestic students. Electronic applications accepted. *Expenses: Tuition:* Full-time $13,446; part-time $747 per credit. *Required fees:* $700; $25 per credit. $50 per term. *Faculty research:* Agent Orange, use of technology in didactic and clinical education of physician assistant students, innovative methods for teaching how to perform history and physical exams, ways to improve the preparedness of medical preceptors. *Unit head:* Dr. James France, Director, 724-838-2455, E-mail: france@setonhill.edu. *Application contact:* Laurel Komarny, Program Counselor, 724-838-4209, E-mail: komarny@setonhill.edu.

Shenandoah University, School of Health Professions, Division of Physician Assistant Studies, Winchester, VA 22601-5195. Offers MS. *Accreditation:* ARC-PA. *Faculty:* 5 full-time (4 women), 1 (woman) part-time/adjunct. *Students:* 113 full-time (94 women), 1 (woman) part-time; includes 16 minority (4 Black or African American, non-Hispanic/Latino; 7 Asian, non-Hispanic/Latino; 4 Hispanic/Latino; 1 Two or more races, non-Hispanic/Latino), 2 international. Average age 27. 587 applicants, 12% accepted, 36 enrolled. In 2011, 34 master's awarded. *Degree requirements:* For master's, project. *Entrance requirements:* For master's, GRE General Test, minimum GPA of 3.0, 3 letters of reference, writing sample, interview. Additional exam requirements/recommendations for international students: Required—TOEFL (minimum score 550 paper-based; 213 computer-based; 79 iBT), IELTS (minimum score 6.5), Sakae Institute of Study Abroad (minimum score 550). *Application deadline:* For fall admission, 1/15 for domestic students. Applications are processed on a rolling basis. Application fee: $30. Electronic applications accepted. *Expenses:* Contact institution. *Financial support:* In 2011–12, 8 students received support. Career-related internships or fieldwork, institutionally sponsored loans, scholarships/grants, and federal loans, alternative loans available. Support available to part-time students. Financial award application deadline: 3/15; financial award applicants required to submit FAFSA. *Unit head:* Anthony A. Miller, Director, 540-542-6208, Fax: 540-542-6210, E-mail: amiller@su.edu. *Application contact:* David Anthony, Dean of Admissions, 540-665-4581, Fax: 540-665-4627, E-mail: admit@su.edu. Web site: http://www.su.edu.

South College, Program in Physician Assistant Studies, Knoxville, TN 37917. Offers MHS. *Accreditation:* ARC-PA.

Southern Illinois University Carbondale, Graduate School, College of Applied Science, Program in Physician Assistant Studies, Carbondale, IL 62901-4701. Offers MSPA. *Accreditation:* ARC-PA. *Students:* 56 full-time (44 women), 2 part-time (1 woman); includes 3 minority (1 Asian, non-Hispanic/Latino; 2 Hispanic/Latino). 5 applicants, 40% accepted, 1 enrolled. In 2011, 19 master's awarded. *Unit head:* Laurie Dunn-Ryznyk, Head, 618-453-8850, E-mail: jdunn@siumed.edu. *Application contact:* Lu Lyons, Supervisor, Admissions, 618-453-4512, E-mail: llyons@siu.edu.

South University, Graduate Programs, College of Health Professions, Program in Physician Assistant Studies, Savannah, GA 31406. Offers MS. *Accreditation:* ARC-PA.

See Close-Up on page 557.

Springfield College, Graduate Programs, Program in Physician Assistant, Springfield, MA 01109-3797. Offers MS. *Accreditation:* ARC-PA. Part-time programs available. *Degree requirements:* For master's, comprehensive exam. *Entrance requirements:* For master's, prerequisite courses. Additional exam requirements/recommendations for international students: Required—TOEFL (minimum score 550 paper-based; 213 computer-based). Electronic applications accepted.

Stony Brook University, State University of New York, Stony Brook University Medical Center, Health Sciences Center, School of Health Technology and Management, Stony Brook, NY 11794. Offers health care management (Advanced Certificate); health care policy and management (MS); occupational therapy (MS); physical therapy (DPT); physician assistant (MS). *Accreditation:* APTA. Part-time programs available. *Degree requirements:* For master's, thesis. *Entrance requirements:* For master's, GRE General Test, minimum GPA of 3.0, work experience in field. *Faculty research:* Health promotion and disease prevention.

Texas Tech University Health Sciences Center, School of Allied Health Sciences, Program in Physician Assistant Studies, Lubbock, TX 79430. Offers MPAS. *Accreditation:* ARC-PA. *Faculty:* 8 full-time (3 women). *Students:* 116 full-time (89 women), 1 part-time; includes 8 minority (2 Black or African American, non-Hispanic/Latino; 2 Asian, non-Hispanic/Latino; 4 Hispanic/Latino). Average age 29. 1,040

PHILADELPHIA COLLEGE OF OSTEOPATHIC MEDICINE

School Psychologist

Physician Assistant

Clinical Psychologist

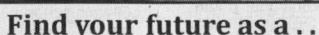
Find your future as a . . .

Organizational Leader

Mental Health Counselor

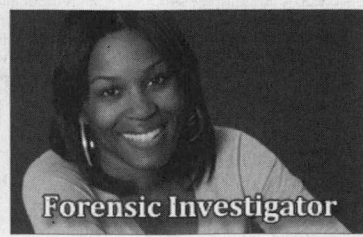
Forensic Investigator

PCOM

PCOM's **GRADUATE STUDENTS** benefit from small classes while working with faculty in a collaborative learning environment. Classes for most programs are offered evenings and on weekends. PCOM is located just minutes from center city Philadelphia and the suburbs.

215-871-6700 • pcom.edu • 4170 City Avenue, Philadelphia, PA 19131

applicants, 6% accepted, 60 enrolled. In 2011, 51 master's awarded. *Entrance requirements:* Additional exam requirements/recommendations for international students: Required—TOEFL, IELTS. *Application deadline:* For fall admission, 12/1 for domestic students. Application fee: $35. Electronic applications accepted. *Financial support:* Career-related internships or fieldwork, institutionally sponsored loans, and scholarships/grants available. Financial award applicants required to submit FAFSA. *Unit head:* Dr. Hal Larsen, Chair, 806-743-3223, E-mail: hal.larsen@ttuhsc.edu. *Application contact:* Jeri Moravcik, Assistant Director of Admissions and Student Affairs, 806-743-3220, Fax: 806-743-2994, E-mail: jeri.moravcik@ttuhsc.edu. Web site: http://www.ttuhsc.edu/sah/mpa/.

Towson University, Program in Physician Assistant Studies, Towson, MD 21252-0001. Offers MS. *Accreditation:* ARC-PA. *Students:* 62 full-time (52 women), 2 part-time (1 woman); includes 7 minority (1 Black or African American, non-Hispanic/Latino; 4 Asian, non-Hispanic/Latino; 1 Hispanic/Latino; 1 Two or more races, non-Hispanic/Latino), 2 international. *Entrance requirements:* Additional exam requirements/recommendations for international students: Required—TOEFL. Application fee: $50. *Expenses:* Contact institution. *Financial support:* Application deadline: 4/1; applicants required to submit FAFSA. *Unit head:* Marcie Weinstein, Graduate Program Director, 410-704-4049, E-mail: mweinstein@towson.edu.

Trevecca Nazarene University, College of Lifelong Learning, Graduate Physician Assistant Program, Nashville, TN 37210-2877. Offers MS. *Accreditation:* ARC-PA. *Faculty:* 5 full-time (3 women), 7 part-time/adjunct (5 women). *Students:* 89 full-time (65 women); includes 3 minority (1 Black or African American, non-Hispanic/Latino; 1 American Indian or Alaska Native, non-Hispanic/Latino; 1 Two or more races, non-Hispanic/Latino). Average age 27. In 2011, 30 master's awarded. *Degree requirements:* For master's, comprehensive exam, professional assessment, qualifying exam. *Entrance requirements:* For master's, GRE General Test, health care experience, minimum GPA of 3.25, 3 letters of recommendation. Additional exam requirements/recommendations for international students: Required—TOEFL (minimum score 550 paper-based; 213 computer-based). *Application deadline:* For fall admission, 11/1 for domestic students. Application fee: $45. *Expenses:* Contact institution. *Financial support:* Applicants required to submit FAFSA. *Unit head:* Dr. Mike Moredock, Director, 615-248-1261, Fax: 615-248-1622, E-mail: mmoredock@trevecca.edu. *Application contact:* Admissions Coordinator, 615-248-1621, Fax: 615-248-1622, E-mail: admissions_pa@trevecca.edu.

Union College, Physician Assistant Program, Lincoln, NE 68506-4300. Offers MPAS. *Accreditation:* ARC-PA. *Entrance requirements:* Additional exam requirements/recommendations for international students: Required—TOEFL (minimum score 600 paper-based; 100 iBT). Electronic applications accepted. *Faculty research:* Servant leadership, cultural competency.

The University of Alabama at Birmingham, School of Health Professions, Program in Physician Assistant Studies, Birmingham, AL 35294. Offers MSPAS. *Accreditation:* ARC-PA. *Expenses:* Tuition, state resident: full-time $5922; part-time $309 per hour. Tuition, nonresident: full-time $13,428; part-time $726 per hour. Tuition and fees vary according to program. *Unit head:* Dr. Patricia Jennings, Program Director, 205-934-4432, E-mail: prjenn@uab.edu.

University of Bridgeport, Physician Assistant Institute, Bridgeport, CT 06604. Offers MS. *Faculty:* 4 full-time (2 women), 6 part-time/adjunct (3 women). *Students:* 19 full-time (13 women); includes 9 minority (2 Black or African American, non-Hispanic/Latino; 4 Asian, non-Hispanic/Latino; 2 Hispanic/Latino; 1 Two or more races, non-Hispanic/Latino). Average age 31. 136 applicants, 20% accepted, 19 enrolled. *Degree requirements:* For master's, thesis. *Entrance requirements:* Additional exam requirements/recommendations for international students: Recommended—TOEFL (minimum score 550 paper-based; 213 computer-based; 80 iBT), IELTS (minimum score 6.5). *Application deadline:* For fall admission, 8/1 priority date for domestic students, 8/1 for international students; for spring admission, 12/1 priority date for domestic students, 12/1 for international students. Application fee: $50. *Expenses: Tuition:* Full-time $22,880; part-time $700 per credit. *Required fees:* $1870; $95 per semester. Tuition and fees vary according to course load and program. *Unit head:* Dr. Daniel Cervonka, Director, 203-576-2399, Fax: 203-576-2402, E-mail: cervonka@bridgeport.edu. *Application contact:* Karissa Peckham, Dean of Admissions, 203-576-4552, Fax: 203-576-4941, E-mail: admit@bridgeport.edu.

University of Charleston, Physician Assistant Program, Charleston, WV 25304-1099. Offers MPAS. *Unit head:* David Payne, Program Director, 304-357-4818, E-mail: davidpayne@ucwv.edu. *Application contact:* Pam Carden, Admissions Coordinator, 304-357-4968, Fax: 304-357-4832, E-mail: pamcarden@ucwv.edu. Web site: http://www.ucwv.edu/PA/.

University of Colorado Denver, School of Medicine, Physician Assistant Program, Aurora, CO 80045. Offers child health associate (MPAS), including global health, leadership, education, advocacy, development, and scholarship, rural health, urban/underserved populations. *Accreditation:* ARC-PA. *Students:* 124 full-time (107 women), 2 part-time (both women); includes 12 minority (1 American Indian or Alaska Native, non-Hispanic/Latino; 6 Asian, non-Hispanic/Latino; 5 Hispanic/Latino). Average age 26. 274 applicants, 17% accepted, 44 enrolled. In 2011, 37 master's awarded. *Degree requirements:* For master's, comprehensive exam, successful completion of all coursework and rotations. *Entrance requirements:* For master's, GRE General Test, minimum GPA of 2.8, 3 letters of recommendation, prerequisite courses in chemistry, biology, general genetics, psychology and statistics, interviews for the finalists. Additional exam requirements/recommendations for international students: Required—TOEFL (minimum score 550 paper-based; 213 computer-based). *Application deadline:* For fall admission, 10/1 for domestic students. Application fee: $170. Electronic applications accepted. *Expenses:* Contact institution. *Financial support:* Career-related internships or fieldwork and scholarships/grants available. Financial award application deadline: 3/15; financial award applicants required to submit FAFSA. *Faculty research:* Clinical genetics and genetic counseling, evidence-based medicine, pediatric allergy and asthma, childhood diabetes, standardized patient assessment. *Unit head:* Jonathan Bowser, Interim Program Director, 303-724-1349, E-mail: jonathan.bowser@ucdenver.edu. *Application contact:* Kay Denler, Director of Admissions, 303-724-1340, E-mail: kay.denler@ucdenver.edu. Web site: http://www.ucdenver.edu/academics/colleges/medicalschool/education/degree_programs/PAProgram/Pages/Home.aspx.

University of Detroit Mercy, College of Health Professions, Physician Assistant Program, Detroit, MI 48221. Offers MS. *Accreditation:* ARC-PA. *Degree requirements:* For master's, thesis or alternative. *Entrance requirements:* For master's, GRE General Test, minimum GPA of 3.0. *Expenses:* Contact institution. *Faculty research:* Substance abuse prevention, international health care, public health.

The University of Findlay, Graduate and Professional Studies, College of Health Professions, Master of Physician Assistant Program, Findlay, OH 45840-3653. Offers MPA. *Faculty:* 6 full-time (4 women), 1 part-time/adjunct (0 women). *Students:* 35 full-time (18 women), 1 (woman) part-time; includes 3 minority (1 Black or African American, non-Hispanic/Latino; 2 Asian, non-Hispanic/Latino), 2 international. Average age 25. 219 applicants, 36% accepted, 18 enrolled. *Entrance requirements:* For master's, bachelor's degree from accredited institution, minimum overall GPA of 3.0, 500 hours of health care experience, C or better in program prerequisites. Additional exam requirements/recommendations for international students: Required—TOEFL (minimum score 550 paper-based; 213 computer-based; 80 iBT). *Application deadline:* For fall admission, 1/15 for domestic and international students. Applications are processed on a rolling basis. Application fee: $25. Electronic applications accepted. *Expenses: Tuition:* Full-time $6300; part-time $700 per semester hour. *Required fees:* $35 per semester hour. One-time fee: $25. Tuition and fees vary according to course load, degree level and program. *Financial support:* In 2011–12, 1 teaching assistantship with full and partial tuition reimbursement (averaging $3,600 per year) was awarded; Federal Work-Study, health care benefits, and unspecified assistantships also available. Financial award application deadline: 4/1; financial award applicants required to submit FAFSA. *Unit head:* Dr. Paul Davis, Chair, Physician Assistant Program, 419-434-6983, Fax: 419-434-4822. *Application contact:* Heather Riffle, Assistant Director, Graduate and Professional Studies, 419-434-4640, Fax: 419-434-5517, E-mail: riffle@findlay.edu.

University of Florida, College of Medicine, Program in Physician Assistant, Gainesville, FL 32611. Offers MPAS. *Accreditation:* ARC-PA. *Entrance requirements:* For master's, GRE General Test, interview. Electronic applications accepted.

The University of Iowa, Roy J. and Lucille A. Carver College of Medicine and Graduate College, Graduate Programs in Medicine, Program in Physician Assistant, Iowa City, IA 52242-1316. Offers MPAS. *Accreditation:* ARC-PA. *Faculty:* 3 full-time (2 women), 2 part-time/adjunct (1 woman). *Students:* 51 full-time (32 women); includes 4 minority (1 Black or African American, non-Hispanic/Latino; 2 American Indian or Alaska Native, non-Hispanic/Latino; 1 Hispanic/Latino). Average age 25. 602 applicants, 4% accepted, 25 enrolled. In 2011, 24 master's awarded. *Degree requirements:* For master's, comprehensive exam, comprehensive clinical exam, clinical presentation. *Entrance requirements:* For master's, GRE General Test or MCAT, health care/research experience. Additional exam requirements/recommendations for international students: Required—TOEFL (minimum score 93 iBT). *Application deadline:* For spring admission, 11/1 for domestic students. Applications are processed on a rolling basis. Application fee: $60. Electronic applications accepted. *Financial support:* In 2011–12, 49 students received support. Institutionally sponsored loans and scholarships/grants available. Financial award application deadline: 3/1; financial award applicants required to submit FAFSA. *Unit head:* Dr. David P. Asprey, Director, 319-335-8922, Fax: 319-335-8923, E-mail: david-asprey@uiowa.edu. *Application contact:* Janet L. Steenlage, Program Administrator, 319-353-5956, Fax: 319-335-8923, E-mail: janet-steenlage@uiowa.edu. Web site: http://paprogram.medicine.uiowa.edu.

University of Kentucky, Graduate School, College of Health Sciences, Program in Physician Assistant Studies, Lexington, KY 40506-0032. Offers MSPAS. *Accreditation:* ARC-PA. *Degree requirements:* For master's, comprehensive exam. *Entrance requirements:* For master's, GRE General Test, minimum undergraduate GPA of 2.75. Additional exam requirements/recommendations for international students: Required—TOEFL (minimum score 550 paper-based; 213 computer-based). Electronic applications accepted.

University of Medicine and Dentistry of New Jersey, School of Health Related Professions, Department of Primary Care, Physician Assistant Program–Piscataway, Newark, NJ 07107-1709. Offers MS. *Accreditation:* ARC-PA. *Faculty:* 9 full-time (5 women), 9 part-time/adjunct (all women). *Students:* 127 full-time, 4 part-time; includes 45 minority (10 Black or African American, non-Hispanic/Latino; 22 Asian, non-Hispanic/Latino; 13 Hispanic/Latino). Average age 27. 1,403 applicants, 6% accepted, 45 enrolled. In 2011, 42 degrees awarded. *Degree requirements:* For master's, internship. *Entrance requirements:* For master's, GRE, interview, minimum GPA of 3.0, BS, 3 reference letters. Additional exam requirements/recommendations for international students: Required—TOEFL. *Application deadline:* For fall admission, 10/1 for domestic students, 3/1 for international students. Applications are processed on a rolling basis. Application fee: $50. Electronic applications accepted. *Unit head:* Ruth Fixelle, Director, 732-235-4444, E-mail: fixellru@umdnj.edu. *Application contact:* Diane Hanrahan, Manager of Admissions, 973-972-5336, Fax: 973-972-7463, E-mail: shrpadm@umdnj.edu.

University of Nebraska Medical Center, School of Allied Health Professions, Division of Physician Assistant Education, Omaha, NE 68198-4300. Offers MPAS. *Accreditation:* ARC-PA. *Degree requirements:* For master's, comprehensive exam, research paper. *Entrance requirements:* For master's, GRE General Test, 16 undergraduate hours of course work in both biology and chemistry, 3 in math, 6 in English, 9 in psychology; minimum GPA of 3.0. Additional exam requirements/recommendations for international students: Required—TOEFL (minimum score 600 paper-based; 250 computer-based; 100 iBT). Electronic applications accepted. *Faculty research:* Substance abuse, mental health, women's health, geriatrics.

University of New England, Westbrook College of Health Professions, Program in Physician Assistant, Biddeford, ME 04005-9526. Offers MS. *Accreditation:* ARC-PA. *Faculty:* 6 full-time, 3 part-time/adjunct. *Students:* 90 full-time (65 women). In 2011, 48 master's awarded. *Degree requirements:* For master's, 12-month rotations. *Entrance requirements:* For master's, minimum GPA of 2.5. Additional exam requirements/recommendations for international students: Required—TOEFL. *Application deadline:* For fall admission, 11/1 for domestic students. Applications are processed on a rolling basis. Application fee: $40. *Expenses:* Contact institution. *Financial support:* Scholarships/grants available. Financial award application deadline: 5/1; financial award applicants required to submit FAFSA. *Unit head:* George S. Bottomley, Program Director, 207-221-4527, Fax: 207-221-4711, E-mail: gbottomley@une.edu. *Application contact:* Stacy Gato, Assistant Director of Graduate Admissions, 207-221-4225, Fax: 207-221-4898, E-mail: gradadmissions@une.edu. Web site: http://www.une.edu/.

University of New Mexico, Health Sciences Center Graduate Programs, Program in Physician Assistant Studies, Albuquerque, NM 87131. Offers MS. *Accreditation:* ARC-PA. *Faculty:* 4 full-time (2 women), 1 (woman) part-time/adjunct. *Students:* 32 full-time (18 women); includes 14 minority (1 Black or African American, non-Hispanic/Latino; 1 American Indian or Alaska Native, non-Hispanic/Latino; 4 Asian, non-Hispanic/Latino; 8 Hispanic/Latino). Average age 33. *Degree requirements:* For master's, comprehensive exam. *Entrance requirements:* For master's, GRE. Additional exam requirements/recommendations for international students: Recommended—TOEFL. *Application deadline:* For spring admission, 5/1 for domestic students. Application fee: $50. Electronic applications accepted. *Financial support:* In 2011–12, 10 students received support. Application deadline: 6/30; applicants required to submit FAFSA. *Unit head:* Dr. Nikki Katalanos, Program Director, 505-272-9864, E-mail: paprogram@salud.unm.edu. *Application contact:* Marlys Harrison, Program Manager, 505-272-9864, E-mail: mharrison@salud.unm.edu. Web site: http://hsc.unm.edu/som/fcm/pap.

University of North Dakota, Graduate School and Graduate School, Graduate Programs in Medicine, Physician Assistant Program, Grand Forks, ND 58202. Offers MPAS. *Accreditation:* ARC-PA. *Entrance requirements:* For master's, current RN licensure, minimum of 4 years of clinical experience, current ACLS certification, interview, letters of recommendation. Additional exam requirements/recommendations for international students: Required—TOEFL (minimum score 550 paper-based; 213 computer-based; 79 iBT), IELTS (minimum score 6.5).

SECTION 20: ALLIED HEALTH

Physician Assistant Studies

University of North Texas Health Science Center at Fort Worth, Texas College of Osteopathic Medicine, School of Health Professions, Fort Worth, TX 76107-2699. Offers MPAS. *Accreditation:* ARC-PA. *Degree requirements:* For master's, thesis or alternative, research paper. *Entrance requirements:* For master's, minimum GPA of 2.85. *Faculty research:* Impact of mid-level providers on medical treatment, curriculum development, pain in geriatric patients, biopsychosocial risk factors.

University of Pittsburgh, School of Health and Rehabilitation Sciences, Physician Assistant Studies Program, Pittsburgh, PA 15260. Offers MS. *Faculty:* 5 full-time (4 women), 1 part-time/adjunct (0 women). *Students:* 52 full-time (42 women), 1 part-time (0 women); includes 3 minority (1 Black or African American, non-Hispanic/Latino; 1 Asian, non-Hispanic/Latino; 1 Two or more races, non-Hispanic/Latino). Average age 28. 721 applicants, 9% accepted, 35 enrolled. In 2011, 18 master's awarded. *Entrance requirements:* Additional exam requirements/recommendations for international students: Required—TOEFL (minimum score 550 paper-based; 213 computer-based; 80 iBT), IELTS (minimum score 6.5). *Application deadline:* For spring admission, 9/1 for domestic students. Application fee: $135. *Expenses:* Contact institution. *Unit head:* Dr. Deborah A. Opacic, Program Director, 412-647-4646, E-mail: dopacic@pitt.edu. *Application contact:* Marsha LaCovey, Program Administrator, 412-624-6719, Fax: 412-624-7934, E-mail: mlacovey@pitt.edu. Web site: http://www.shrs.pitt.edu/pa/.

University of St. Francis, College of Arts and Sciences, Joliet, IL 60435-6169. Offers advanced generalist forensic social work (Post-Master's Certificate); physician assistant practice (MS); social work (MSW). *Faculty:* 8 full-time (6 women). *Students:* 94 full-time (67 women), 23 part-time (22 women); includes 43 minority (15 Black or African American, non-Hispanic/Latino; 6 Asian, non-Hispanic/Latino; 17 Hispanic/Latino; 2 Native Hawaiian or other Pacific Islander, non-Hispanic/Latino; 3 Two or more races, non-Hispanic/Latino), 2 international. Average age 31. 62 applicants, 61% accepted, 26 enrolled. In 2011, 41 degrees awarded. *Entrance requirements:* For degree, minimum undergraduate GPA of 3.0, 2 letters recommendation, personal statement. Additional exam requirements/recommendations for international students: Required—TOEFL (minimum score 550 paper-based; 213 computer-based). *Application deadline:* Applications are processed on a rolling basis. Application fee: $30. Electronic applications accepted. *Expenses: Tuition:* Part-time $656 per credit hour. Part-time tuition and fees vary according to degree level, campus/location and program. *Financial support:* In 2011–12, 12 students received support. Scholarships/grants, tuition waivers (partial), and unspecified assistantships available. Support available to part-time students. Financial award applicants required to submit FAFSA. *Unit head:* Dr. Robert Kase, Dean, 815-740-3367, Fax: 815-740-6366. *Application contact:* Sandra Sloka, Director of Admissions for Graduate and Degree Completion Programs, 800-735-7500, Fax: 815-740-5032, E-mail: ssloka@stfrancis.edu.

University of Saint Francis, Graduate School, Department of Allied Health, Fort Wayne, IN 46808-3994. Offers nursing (MSN); physician assistant studies (MS). *Accreditation:* ARC-PA. Part-time programs available. Postbaccalaureate distance learning degree programs offered (minimal on-campus study). *Students:* 99 full-time (86 women), 97 part-time (88 women); includes 15 minority (11 Black or African American, non-Hispanic/Latino; 2 Asian, non-Hispanic/Latino; 2 Hispanic/Latino). In 2011, 57 master's awarded. *Entrance requirements:* For master's, GRE or MCAT, previous courses in biology, chemistry, and psychology, previous direct patient care. Additional exam requirements/recommendations for international students: Required—TOEFL. *Application deadline:* Applications are processed on a rolling basis. Application fee: $20. Application fee is waived when completed online. *Financial support:* Career-related internships or fieldwork, scholarships/grants, tuition waivers (full and partial), and unspecified assistantships available. Support available to part-time students. Financial award applicants required to submit FAFSA. *Unit head:* Dr. Nancy Gillespie, Dean, 260-399-7700 Ext. 8504, Fax: 260-399-8167, E-mail: ngillespie@sf.edu. *Application contact:* James Cashdollar, Admissions Counselor, 260-399-7700 Ext. 6302, E-mail: jcashdollar@sf.edu.

University of South Alabama, Graduate School, College of Allied Health Professions, Department of Physician Assistant Studies, Mobile, AL 36688-0002. Offers MHS. *Accreditation:* ARC-PA. *Faculty:* 5 full-time (2 women). *Students:* 77 full-time (57 women); includes 6 minority (2 Black or African American, non-Hispanic/Latino; 3 Asian, non-Hispanic/Latino; 1 Native Hawaiian or other Pacific Islander, non-Hispanic/Latino), 1 international. In 2011, 35 master's awarded. *Degree requirements:* For master's, thesis optional, externship; 121 hours consisting of 73 credit hours of didactic course work and 48 hours of clinical work. *Entrance requirements:* For master's, GRE General Test, minimum GPA of 3.0. *Application deadline:* For fall admission, 11/1 priority date for domestic students. Applications are processed on a rolling basis. Application fee: $110. *Expenses:* Tuition, state resident: full-time $7968; part-time $332 per credit hour. Tuition, nonresident: full-time $15,936; part-time $664 per credit hour. *Financial support:* Application deadline: 4/1. *Unit head:* Dr. Zarrintaj Alibadi, Chair, 251-445-9334. *Application contact:* Dr. Julio Turrens, Director of Graduate Studies, 251-445-9250. Web site: http://www.southalabama.edu/alliedhealth/pa/.

The University of South Dakota, Graduate School, School of Health Sciences, Department of Physician Assistant Studies, Vermillion, SD 57069-2390. Offers MS. *Accreditation:* ARC-PA. *Entrance requirements:* Additional exam requirements/recommendations for international students: Required—TOEFL (minimum score 550 paper-based; 213 computer-based). Electronic applications accepted. *Expenses:* Contact institution. *Faculty research:* Neuroscience, teaching techniques in physician assistant education.

University of Southern California, Keck School of Medicine and Graduate School, Graduate Programs in Medicine, Primary Care Physician Assistant Program, Alhambra, CA 91803. Offers MPAP. *Accreditation:* ARC-PA. *Faculty:* 9 full-time (5 women), 5 part-time/adjunct (4 women). *Students:* 148 full-time (117 women); includes 82 minority (4 Black or African American, non-Hispanic/Latino; 4 American Indian or Alaska Native, non-Hispanic/Latino; 39 Asian, non-Hispanic/Latino; 28 Hispanic/Latino; 2 Native Hawaiian or other Pacific Islander, non-Hispanic/Latino; 5 Two or more races, non-Hispanic/Latino). Average age 24. 745 applicants, 10% accepted, 53 enrolled. In 2011, 38 master's awarded. *Degree requirements:* For master's, comprehensive exam, clinical training. *Entrance requirements:* For master's, GRE or MCAT, minimum cumulative GPA of 3.0, science 2.75. Additional exam requirements/recommendations for international students: Required—TOEFL (minimum score 600 paper-based; 200 computer-based; 100 iBT). *Application deadline:* For fall admission, 12/1 for domestic and international students. Applications are processed on a rolling basis. Application fee: $85. Electronic applications accepted. *Financial support:* Institutionally sponsored loans and scholarships/grants available. Financial award application deadline: 5/4; financial award applicants required to submit FAFSA. *Unit head:* Dr. Kevin Lohenry, Program Director, 626-457-4262, Fax: 626-457-4245, E-mail: lohenry@med.usc.edu. *Application contact:* Janice Tramel, Chair, Physician Assistant Admissions Committee, 626-457-4250, Fax: 626-457-4245, E-mail: jtramel@med.usc.edu. Web site: http://www.usc.edu/schools/medicine/pa/.

The University of Texas Health Science Center at San Antonio, School of Health Professions, San Antonio, TX 78229-3900. Offers clinical laboratory sciences (MS); deaf education and hearing science (MED); dental hygiene (MS); occupational therapy (MOT); physical therapy (MPT); physician assistant studies (MS). *Accreditation:* AOTA; APTA; ARC-PA. *Degree requirements:* For master's, thesis. *Entrance requirements:* Additional exam requirements/recommendations for international students: Required—TOEFL (minimum score 560 paper-based; 280 computer-based; 68 iBT). Electronic applications accepted.

The University of Texas Medical Branch, School of Health Professions, Department of Physician Assistant Studies, Galveston, TX 77555. Offers MPAS. *Accreditation:* ARC-PA. *Entrance requirements:* For master's, GRE, interview. Electronic applications accepted.

The University of Texas Southwestern Medical Center, Southwestern School of Health Professions, Physician Assistant Studies Program, Dallas, TX 75390. Offers MPAS. *Accreditation:* ARC-PA. *Entrance requirements:* For master's, GRE, minimum GPA of 3.0. Electronic applications accepted.

University of the Cumberlands, Program in Physician Assistant Studies, Williamsburg, KY 40769-1372. Offers MPAS. *Accreditation:* ARC-PA. *Entrance requirements:* Additional exam requirements/recommendations for international students: Required—TOEFL. Electronic applications accepted.

The University of Toledo, College of Graduate Studies, College of Medicine and Life Sciences, Department of Physician Assistant Studies, Toledo, OH 43606-3390. Offers MSBS. *Accreditation:* ARC-PA. *Faculty:* 8. *Students:* 67 full-time (50 women), 37 part-time (27 women); includes 13 minority (8 Black or African American, non-Hispanic/Latino; 4 Asian, non-Hispanic/Latino; 1 Hispanic/Latino). Average age 27. 34 applicants, 100% accepted, 33 enrolled. In 2011, 32 master's awarded. *Degree requirements:* For master's, thesis or alternative, scholarly project. *Entrance requirements:* For master's, GRE, interview, minimum undergraduate GPA of 3.0, writing sample; UT supplemental application; transcripts. Additional exam requirements/recommendations for international students: Required—TOEFL (minimum score 550 paper-based; 213 computer-based; 80 iBT), IELTS (minimum score 6.5). *Application deadline:* For fall admission, 10/1 for domestic and international students. Application fee: $45 ($75 for international students). Electronic applications accepted. *Expenses:* Contact institution. *Financial support:* Federal Work-Study, institutionally sponsored loans, scholarships/grants, tuition waivers (partial), and tuition scholarships available. *Unit head:* Dr. Patricia Hogue, Director, 419-383-4807, E-mail: patricia.hogue@utoledo.edu. *Application contact:* Kristi Hayes, Secretary, 419-383-5408, E-mail: kristi.hayes@utoledo.edu. Web site: http://www.utoledo.edu/med/grad/pa/index.html.

University of Utah, School of Medicine and Graduate School, Graduate Programs in Medicine, Department of Family and Preventive Medicine, Utah Physician Assistant Program, Salt Lake City, UT 84112-1107. Offers MPAS. *Accreditation:* ARC-PA. *Degree requirements:* For master's, comprehensive exam, thesis or alternative. *Entrance requirements:* Additional exam requirements/recommendations for international students: Required—TOEFL (minimum score 550 paper-based). Electronic applications accepted. *Expenses:* Contact institution. *Faculty research:* Physical assistant education, evidence-based medicine, technology and education, international medicine education.

University of Wisconsin–La Crosse, Office of University Graduate Studies, College of Science and Health, Department of Health Professions, Program in Physician Assistant Studies, La Crosse, WI 54601-3742. Offers MS. *Accreditation:* ARC-PA. *Faculty:* 1 (woman) full-time, 3 part-time/adjunct (2 women). *Students:* 38 full-time (29 women); includes 4 minority (2 Asian, non-Hispanic/Latino; 1 Hispanic/Latino; 1 Two or more races, non-Hispanic/Latino). Average age 26. 285 applicants, 9% accepted, 18 enrolled. In 2011, 13 master's awarded. *Degree requirements:* For master's, comprehensive exam. *Entrance requirements:* For master's, GRE. Additional exam requirements/recommendations for international students: Required—TOEFL (minimum score 550 paper-based; 213 computer-based; 79 iBT). Application fee: $56. Electronic applications accepted. *Expenses:* Contact institution. *Financial support:* Federal Work-Study and scholarships/grants available. Support available to part-time students. *Unit head:* Dr. Edward Malone, Director, 608-785-8470, E-mail: malone.edwa@uwlax.edu. *Application contact:* Kathryn Kiefer, Director of Admissions, 608-785-8939, E-mail: admissions@uwlax.edu. Web site: http://www.uwlax.edu/pastudies/.

Wagner College, Division of Graduate Studies, Department of Biological Sciences, Program in Advanced Physician Assistant Studies, Staten Island, NY 10301-4495. Offers MS. *Accreditation:* ARC-PA. Part-time programs available. *Faculty:* 2 full-time (both women), 9 part-time/adjunct (5 women). *Students:* 27 full-time (25 women); includes 7 minority (2 Black or African American, non-Hispanic/Latino; 2 Asian, non-Hispanic/Latino; 3 Hispanic/Latino). Average age 24. 26 applicants, 100% accepted, 26 enrolled. In 2011, 18 master's awarded. *Degree requirements:* For master's, thesis. *Entrance requirements:* For master's, minimum GPA of 3.0; bachelor's degree in one of the biological sciences, chemistry or physician assistant studies; physician assistant certification. Additional exam requirements/recommendations for international students: Required—TOEFL (minimum score 550 paper-based; 217 computer-based; 79 iBT). *Application deadline:* For fall admission, 5/1 priority date for domestic students, 5/1 for international students; for spring admission, 11/1 for domestic and international students. Applications are processed on a rolling basis. Application fee: $50 ($85 for international students). *Expenses: Tuition:* Full-time $16,200; part-time $890 per credit. *Financial support:* Career-related internships or fieldwork, Federal Work-Study, unspecified assistantships, and alumni fellowship grant available. Financial award applicants required to submit FAFSA. *Unit head:* Nora Lowy, Director, 718-390-4610, Fax: 718-420-4004, E-mail: nora.lowy@wagner.edu. *Application contact:* Patricia Clancy, Administrative Assistant, 718-420-4464, Fax: 718-390-3105, E-mail: patricia.clancy@wagner.edu.

Wayne State University, Eugene Applebaum College of Pharmacy and Health Sciences, Department of Health Care Sciences, Program in Physician Assistant Studies, Detroit, MI 48202. Offers MS. *Accreditation:* ARC-PA. *Students:* 85 full-time (67 women); includes 3 minority (2 Asian, non-Hispanic/Latino; 1 Two or more races, non-Hispanic/Latino), 1 international. Average age 28. In 2011, 45 master's awarded. *Entrance requirements:* For master's, GRE General Test, minimum GPA of 3.0, course work in science, 500 hours of work experience in health services, recommendations, interview, bachelor's degree from accredited institution before start of PA program with minimum GPA of 3.0 overall and in prerequisites, CASPA application. Additional exam requirements/recommendations for international students: Required—TOEFL (minimum score 550 paper-based; 213 computer-based); Recommended—TWE (minimum score 6). *Application deadline:* For fall admission, 9/1 for domestic and international students. Application fee: $50. Electronic applications accepted. *Expenses:* Tuition, state resident: part-time $512.85 per credit. Tuition, nonresident: part-time $1132.65 per credit. *Required fees:* $26.60 per credit. $199.65 per semester. Tuition and fees vary according to course load and program. *Financial support:* In 2011–12, 9 students received support. Career-related internships or fieldwork and scholarships/grants available. Financial award applicants required to submit FAFSA. *Faculty research:* Medical treatment outcomes, learning and performance evaluation, service-learning research. *Unit head:* Stephanie Gilkey, Academic Director, 313-577-9666, E-mail: sgilkey@wayne.edu. *Application contact:* 313-577-1368, E-mail: paadmit@wayne.edu. Web site: http://www.pa.wayne.edu/.

Weill Cornell Medical College, Weill Cornell Graduate School of Medical Sciences, Physician Assistant Program, New York, NY 10022. Offers health sciences (MS),

including surgery. *Accreditation:* ARC-PA. *Faculty:* 7 full-time (3 women), 55 part-time/adjunct (31 women). *Students:* 88 full-time (66 women); includes 12 minority (1 Black or African American, non-Hispanic/Latino; 8 Asian, non-Hispanic/Latino; 3 Hispanic/Latino), 1 international. Average age 26. 725 applicants, 7% accepted, 33 enrolled. In 2011, 32 master's awarded. *Degree requirements:* For master's, thesis. *Entrance requirements:* For master's, GRE. Additional exam requirements/recommendations for international students: Required—TOEFL. *Application deadline:* For fall admission, 9/1 priority date for domestic students. Applications are processed on a rolling basis. Application fee: $60. Electronic applications accepted. *Expenses:* Tuition: Full-time $46,001. *Financial support:* Fellowships, research assistantships, teaching assistantships, and scholarships/grants available. Financial award application deadline: 3/31; financial award applicants required to submit FAFSA. *Unit head:* Gerard Jude Marciano, 646-962-7277, Fax: 646-962-7290, E-mail: gjm2001@med.cornell.edu. *Application contact:* William Joseph Ameres, 646-962-7277, Fax: 646-962-7290, E-mail: wja2001@med.cornell.edu. Web site: http://weill.cornell.edu/education/programs/phy_ass.html.

Western Michigan University, Graduate College, College of Health and Human Services, Department of Physician Assistant, Kalamazoo, MI 49008. Offers MS. *Accreditation:* ARC-PA. Part-time programs available.

Western University of Health Sciences, College of Allied Health Professions, Program in Physician Assistant Studies, Pomona, CA 91766-1854. Offers MS. *Accreditation:* ARC-PA. *Faculty:* 10 full-time (6 women), 1 (woman) part-time/adjunct. *Students:* 192 full-time (144 women); includes 83 minority (7 Black or African American, non-Hispanic/Latino; 50 Asian, non-Hispanic/Latino; 10 Hispanic/Latino; 16 Two or more races, non-Hispanic/Latino), 1 international. Average age 27. 1,587 applicants, 8% accepted, 97 enrolled. In 2011, 91 master's awarded. *Degree requirements:* For master's,

comprehensive exam, thesis (for some programs). *Entrance requirements:* For master's, minimum GPA of 2.7, letters of recommendation, interview. *Application deadline:* For fall admission, 11/1 for domestic students; for spring admission, 3/1 for domestic students. Application fee: $50. *Expenses:* Contact institution. *Financial support:* Institutionally sponsored loans, scholarships/grants, and veterans educational benefits available. Financial award applicants required to submit FAFSA. *Unit head:* Roy Guizado, Chair, 909-469-5445, Fax: 909-469-5407. *Application contact:* Karen Hutton-Lopez, Director of Admissions, 909-469-5650, Fax: 909-469-5570, E-mail: admissions@westernu.edu. Web site: http://www.westernu.edu/xp/edu/cahp/mspas_welcome.xml.

Wichita State University, Graduate School, College of Health Professions, Department of Physician Assistant, Wichita, KS 67260. Offers MPA. *Accreditation:* ARC-PA. *Expenses:* Tuition, state resident: full-time $4746; part-time $263.65 per credit. Tuition, nonresident: full-time $11,669; part-time $648.30 per credit. *Unit head:* Dr. Sue Nyberg, Chair, 316-978-3011, Fax: 316-978-3669. *Application contact:* Carrie C. Henderson, Admissions Coordinator, 316-978-3095, Fax: 316-978-3253, E-mail: carrie.henderson@wichita.edu. Web site: http://www.wichita.edu/pa.

Yale University, School of Medicine, Physician Associate Program, New Haven, CT 06510. Offers MM Sc, MM Sc/MPH. *Accreditation:* ARC-PA. *Degree requirements:* For master's, thesis. *Entrance requirements:* For master's, GRE General Test, course work in science. Additional exam requirements/recommendations for international students: Required—TOEFL. Electronic applications accepted. *Expenses:* Contact institution. *Faculty research:* Correlation of GRE scores and program performance, relationship of PA programs and pharmaceutical companies, career patterns in physician assistants, PA utilization and satisfaction with care, factors influencing PAs in their decision to pursue postgraduate residencies.

Rehabilitation Sciences

Appalachian State University, Cratis D. Williams Graduate School, Department of Health, Leisure, and Exercise Science, Boone, NC 28608. Offers exercise science (MS), including clinical exercise physiology, research, strength and conditioning. *Faculty:* 22 full-time (5 women), 3 part-time/adjunct (1 woman). *Students:* 28 full-time (14 women), 2 part-time (0 women); includes 2 minority (1 Asian, non-Hispanic/Latino; 1 Hispanic/Latino). 54 applicants, 50% accepted, 14 enrolled. In 2011, 14 master's awarded. *Degree requirements:* For master's, comprehensive exam, thesis optional. *Entrance requirements:* For master's, GRE General Test, 3 letters of recommendation. Additional exam requirements/recommendations for international students: Required—TOEFL (minimum score 570 paper-based; 230 computer-based; 79 iBT), IELTS (minimum score 6.5). *Application deadline:* For fall admission, 3/1 priority date for domestic students, 2/1 for international students; for spring admission, 11/1 for domestic students, 7/1 for international students. Applications are processed on a rolling basis. Application fee: $55. Electronic applications accepted. *Expenses:* Tuition, state resident: full-time $4040; part-time $180 per semester hour. Tuition, nonresident: full-time $15,900; part-time $760 per semester hour. *Required fees:* $2500; $20 per semester hour. Tuition and fees vary according to campus/location. *Financial support:* In 2011–12, 20 research assistantships (averaging $9,500 per year) were awarded; career-related internships or fieldwork, Federal Work-Study, scholarships/grants, and unspecified assistantships also available. Financial award application deadline: 4/1; financial award applicants required to submit FAFSA. *Faculty research:* Exercise immunology, biomechanics, exercise and chronic disease, muscle damage, strength and conditioning. *Total annual research expenditures:* $1 million. *Unit head:* Dr. Paul Gaskill, Head, 828-262-6336, E-mail: gaskillpl@appstate.edu. *Application contact:* Dr. Jeff McBride, Director, 828-262-7148, E-mail: mcbridejm@appstate.edu. Web site: http://www.hles.appstate.edu.

Boston University, College of Health and Rehabilitation Sciences: Sargent College, Department of Physical Therapy and Athletic Training, Boston, MA 02215. Offers physical therapy (DPT); rehabilitation sciences (D Sc). *Accreditation:* APTA (one or more programs are accredited). Postbaccalaureate distance learning degree programs offered (minimal on-campus study). *Faculty:* 13 full-time (10 women), 26 part-time/adjunct (12 women). *Students:* 142 full-time (107 women), 53 part-time (33 women); includes 28 minority (2 Black or African American, non-Hispanic/Latino; 2 American Indian or Alaska Native, non-Hispanic/Latino; 16 Asian, non-Hispanic/Latino; 5 Hispanic/Latino; 1 Native Hawaiian or other Pacific Islander, non-Hispanic/Latino; 2 Two or more races, non-Hispanic/Latino), 6 international. Average age 28. 542 applicants, 26% accepted, 38 enrolled. In 2011, 97 doctorates awarded. *Degree requirements:* For doctorate, comprehensive exam, thesis/dissertation. *Entrance requirements:* For doctorate, GRE General Test, master's degree (for Sc D), bachelor's degree (for DPT). Additional exam requirements/recommendations for international students: Required—TOEFL (minimum score 550 paper-based; 84 computer-based). *Application deadline:* For fall admission, 1/7 priority date for domestic students, 1/7 for international students. Applications are processed on a rolling basis. Application fee: $120. Electronic applications accepted. *Expenses:* Tuition: Full-time $40,848; part-time $1276 per credit hour. *Required fees:* $572; $286 per semester. *Financial support:* In 2011–12, 125 students received support, including 14 fellowships (averaging $16,000 per year), 10 teaching assistantships with partial tuition reimbursements available (averaging $3,000 per year); career-related internships or fieldwork, Federal Work-Study, institutionally sponsored loans, scholarships/grants, and tuition waivers (partial) also available. Financial award application deadline: 4/15; financial award applicants required to submit FAFSA. *Faculty research:* Gait, balance, motor control, dynamic systems analysis, spinal cord injury. *Total annual research expenditures:* $1.3 million. *Unit head:* Dr. Melanie Matthies, Chairman, 617-353-2724, E-mail: pt@bu.edu. *Application contact:* Sharon Sankey, Director, Student Services, 617-353-2713, Fax: 617-353-7500, E-mail: ssankey@bu.edu. Web site: http://www.bu.edu/sargent/.

California University of Pennsylvania, School of Graduate Studies and Research, College of Education and Human Services, Program in Exercise Science and Health Promotion, California, PA 15419-1394. Offers performance enhancement and injury prevention (MS); rehabilitation science (MS); sport psychology (MS); wellness and fitness (MS). Part-time and evening/weekend programs available. Postbaccalaureate distance learning degree programs offered (no on-campus study). *Degree requirements:* For master's, comprehensive exam, thesis optional. *Entrance requirements:* For master's, minimum QPA of 3.0. Additional exam requirements/recommendations for international students: Required—TOEFL (minimum score 550 paper-based; 213 computer-based; 80 iBT). Electronic applications accepted. *Expenses:* Contact institution. *Faculty research:* Reducing obesity in children, sport performance, creating unique biomechanical assessment techniques, Web-based training for fitness professionals, Webcams.

Central Michigan University, College of Graduate Studies, The Herbert H. and Grace A. Dow College of Health Professions, School of Rehabilitation and Medical Sciences, Mount Pleasant, MI 48859. Offers physical therapy (DPT); physician assistant (MS). *Accreditation:* APTA; ARC-PA. *Degree requirements:* For master's, thesis or alternative; for doctorate, thesis/dissertation or alternative. *Entrance requirements:* For master's and doctorate, GRE. Electronic applications accepted.

Clarion University of Pennsylvania, Office of Graduate Programs, Master of Science in Rehabilitative Sciences Program, Clarion, PA 16214. Offers MS. *Students:* 24 full-time (14 women), 25 part-time (19 women); includes 7 minority (3 Black or African American, non-Hispanic/Latino; 4 Two or more races, non-Hispanic/Latino). In 2011, 16 master's awarded. *Degree requirements:* For master's, thesis or alternative. *Entrance requirements:* For master's, GRE General Test or MAT, minimum QPA of 3.0. Additional exam requirements/recommendations for international students: Required—TOEFL (minimum score 550 paper-based; 213 computer-based; 80 iBT). *Application deadline:* For fall admission, 8/1 priority date for domestic students, 4/15 for international students; for spring admission, 12/1 priority date for domestic students, 9/15 for international students. Applications are processed on a rolling basis. Application fee: $30. Electronic applications accepted. *Expenses:* Tuition, state resident: part-time $429 per credit. Tuition, nonresident: part-time $644 per credit. *Financial support:* Research assistantships available. *Unit head:* Dr. Richard Sabousky, Chair, 814-393-2325, Fax: 814-393-1951. Web site: http://www.clarion.edu/85993/.

Concordia University Wisconsin, Graduate Programs, School of Human Services, Program in Rehabilitation Science, Mequon, WI 53097-2402. Offers MSRS. *Students:* 3 full-time (2 women), 7 part-time (4 women), 3 international. Average age 33. *Unit head:* Dr. Marsha K. Konz, Dean of Graduate Studies, 262-243-4253, Fax: 262-243-4428, E-mail: marsha.konz@cuw.edu. *Application contact:* Mary Eberhardt, Graduate Admissions, 262-243-4551, Fax: 262-243-4428, E-mail: mary.eberhardt@cuw.edu.

Duquesne University, John G. Rangos, Sr. School of Health Sciences, Pittsburgh, PA 15282-0001. Offers health management systems (MHMS); occupational therapy (MS); physical therapy (DPT); physician assistant studies (MPAS); rehabilitation science (MS, PhD); speech-language pathology (MS); MBA/MHMS. *Accreditation:* AOTA (one or more programs are accredited); APTA (one or more programs are accredited); ASHA. *Faculty:* 34 full-time (23 women), 20 part-time/adjunct (11 women). *Students:* 227 full-time (180 women), 12 part-time (7 women); includes 8 minority (4 Black or African American, non-Hispanic/Latino; 1 Asian, non-Hispanic/Latino; 1 Hispanic/Latino; 1 Native Hawaiian or other Pacific Islander, non-Hispanic/Latino; 1 Two or more races, non-Hispanic/Latino), 3 international. Average age 24. 537 applicants, 12% accepted, 17 enrolled. In 2011, 43 master's, 31 doctorates awarded. *Degree requirements:* For doctorate, comprehensive exam (for some programs), thesis/dissertation (for some programs). *Entrance requirements:* For master's, GRE General Test (speech-language pathology), 3 letters of recommendation; minimum GPA of 2.75 (health management systems), 3.0 (speech-language pathology and health sciences); for doctorate, GRE General Test (for physical therapy and rehabilitation science), 3 letters of recommendation, minimum GPA of 3.0, personal interview. Additional exam requirements/recommendations for international students: Required—TOEFL (minimum score 550 paper-based; 233 computer-based; 90 iBT). *Application deadline:* Applications are processed on a rolling basis. Electronic applications accepted. *Expenses:* Contact institution. *Financial support:* Federal Work-Study available. Financial award applicants required to submit FAFSA. *Faculty research:* Neuronal processing, electrical stimulation on peripheral neuropathy, CNS stimulatory and inhibitory signals, behavioral genetic methodologies to development disorders of speech, neurogenic communication disorders. *Total annual research expenditures:* $83,650. *Unit head:* Dr. Gregory H. Frazer, Dean, 412-396-5303, Fax: 412-396-5554, E-mail: frazer@duq.edu. *Application contact:* Christopher R. Hilf, Recruiter/Academic Advisor, 412-396-5653, Fax: 412-396-5554, E-mail: hilfc@duq.edu. Web site: http://www.duq.edu/healthsciences/health.html.

East Carolina University, Graduate School, School of Allied Health Sciences, Department of Addictions and Rehabilitation Studies, Greenville, NC 27858-4353. Offers rehabilitation counseling (MS); rehabilitation counseling and administration (PhD); substance abuse and clinical counseling (MS); vocational evaluation (Certificate). *Accreditation:* CORE. Part-time and evening/weekend programs available. *Degree requirements:* For master's, comprehensive exam, thesis or alternative, internship. *Entrance requirements:* For master's, GRE General Test or MAT. Additional exam requirements/recommendations for international students: Required—TOEFL. *Application deadline:* For fall admission, 3/1 priority date for domestic students; for spring admission, 10/1 priority date for domestic students. Applications are processed on a rolling basis. Application fee: $50. *Expenses:* Tuition, state resident: full-time

$3557; part-time $444.63 per semester hour. Tuition, nonresident: full-time $14,351; part-time $1793.88 per semester hour. *Required fees:* $2016; $252 per semester hour. Part-time tuition and fees vary according to course load, campus/location and program. *Financial support:* Research assistantships with partial tuition reimbursements, teaching assistantships with partial tuition reimbursements, Federal Work-Study, and scholarships/grants available. Support available to part-time students. Financial award application deadline: 3/1. *Unit head:* Dr. Lloyd Goodwin, Interim Chair, 252-744-6292, E-mail: goodwinl@ecu.edu. *Application contact:* Dean of Graduate School, 252-328-6012, Fax: 252-328-6071, E-mail: gradschool@ecu.edu. Web site: http://www.ecu.edu/rehb/.

East Stroudsburg University of Pennsylvania, Graduate School, College of Health Sciences, Department of Exercise Science, East Stroudsburg, PA 18301-2999. Offers cardiac rehabilitation and exercise science (MS). Part-time and evening/weekend programs available. *Degree requirements:* For master's, comprehensive exam, thesis or alternative, computer literacy. *Entrance requirements:* Additional exam requirements/recommendations for international students: Required—TOEFL (minimum score 560 paper-based; 220 computer-based; 83 iBT).

George Mason University, College of Health and Human Services, Department of Rehabilitation Science, Fairfax, VA 22030. Offers PhD. *Expenses:* Tuition, state resident: full-time $8750; part-time $364.58 per credit. Tuition, nonresident: full-time $24,092; part-time $1003.83 per credit. *Required fees:* $2514; $104.75 per credit. *Application contact:* Dr. Janet Boyd, Assistant Dean, Academic Outreach, 703-993-1910, Fax: 703-993-1622, E-mail: jboyd1@gmu.edu.

Indiana University–Purdue University Indianapolis, School of Health and Rehabilitation Sciences, Indianapolis, IN 46202-2896. Offers health sciences education (MS); nutrition and dietetics (MS); occupational therapy (MS); physical therapy (DPT). Part-time and evening/weekend programs available. *Faculty:* 8 full-time (5 women). *Students:* 197 full-time (162 women), 1 part-time (0 women); includes 13 minority (1 Black or African American, non-Hispanic/Latino; 4 Asian, non-Hispanic/Latino; 2 Hispanic/Latino; 1 Native Hawaiian or other Pacific Islander, non-Hispanic/Latino; 5 Two or more races, non-Hispanic/Latino). Average age 26. 213 applicants, 31% accepted, 62 enrolled. In 2011, 35 master's, 34 doctorates awarded. *Degree requirements:* For master's, thesis (for some programs). *Entrance requirements:* For master's, GRE General Test, minimum GPA of 3.0. Additional exam requirements/recommendations for international students: Required—TOEFL. *Application deadline:* For fall admission, 1/15 priority date for domestic students; for spring admission, 10/15 for domestic students. Application fee: $55 ($65 for international students). *Financial support:* Fellowships, research assistantships, teaching assistantships, Federal Work-Study, institutionally sponsored loans, and scholarships/grants available. Support available to part-time students. Financial award applicants required to submit FAFSA. *Unit head:* Dr. Augustine Agho, Dean, 317-274-4704, E-mail: aagho@iupui.edu. *Application contact:* Dr. Sherry Queener, Director, Graduate Studies and Associate Dean, 317-274-1577, Fax: 317-278-2380. Web site: http://www.shrs.iupui.edu/.

Logan University–College of Chiropractic, University Programs, Chesterfield, MO 63006-1065. Offers nutrition and human performance (MS); sports science and rehabilitation (MS). *Faculty:* 10 full-time (6 women), 16 part-time/adjunct (6 women). *Students:* 27 full-time (12 women), 39 part-time (10 women); includes 12 minority (7 Black or African American, non-Hispanic/Latino; 4 Asian, non-Hispanic/Latino; 1 Hispanic/Latino). Average age 26. 45 applicants, 98% accepted, 34 enrolled. In 2011, 51 master's awarded. *Degree requirements:* For master's, comprehensive exam. *Entrance requirements:* For master's, GRE or National Board of Chiropractic Examiners test, minimum GPA of 2.5. Additional exam requirements/recommendations for international students: Required—TOEFL (minimum score 79 iBT). *Application deadline:* For fall admission, 7/15 priority date for domestic students, 7/15 for international students; for winter admission, 11/15 priority date for domestic students, 11/15 for international students; for spring admission, 3/15 priority date for domestic students, 3/15 for international students. Application fee: $50. *Expenses:* Contact institution. *Financial support:* In 2011–12, 35 students received support. Federal Work-Study and scholarships/grants available. Support available to part-time students. Financial award applicants required to submit FAFSA. *Faculty research:* Ankle injury prevention in high school athletes, low back pain in college football players, short arc banding and low back pain, the effects of enzymes on inflammatory blood markers, gait analysis in high school and college athletes. *Unit head:* Dr. Elizabeth A. Goodman, Dean, 636-227-2100, Fax: 636-207-2431, E-mail: elizabeth.goodman@logan.edu. *Application contact:* Steve Held, Director of Admissions, 636-227-2100 Ext. 1754, Fax: 636-207-2425, E-mail: loganadm@logan.edu.

Marquette University, Graduate School, College of Health Sciences, Cllinical and Translational Rehabilitation Science Program, Milwaukee, WI 53201-1881. Offers MA, PhD. *Expenses: Tuition:* Full-time $17,010; part-time $945 per credit hour. Tuition and fees vary according to program.

Marquette University, Graduate School, College of Health Sciences, Department of Physical Therapy, Milwaukee, WI 53201-1881. Offers clinical and translational rehabilitation science (MS, PhD); physical therapy (DPT). *Accreditation:* APTA. *Faculty:* 12 full-time (6 women), 31 part-time/adjunct (23 women). *Students:* 98 full-time (80 women), 2 part-time (1 woman); includes 14 minority (1 Black or African American, non-Hispanic/Latino; 5 Asian, non-Hispanic/Latino; 7 Hispanic/Latino; 1 Two or more races, non-Hispanic/Latino). Average age 24. 99 applicants, 34% accepted, 18 enrolled. In 2011, 56 doctorates awarded. *Degree requirements:* For doctorate, clinical rotations. *Entrance requirements:* For doctorate, GRE General Test. Additional exam requirements/recommendations for international students: Required—TOEFL. Application fee: $50. Electronic applications accepted. *Expenses:* Contact institution. *Financial support:* In 2011–12, 2 students received support, including 2 research assistantships with full tuition reimbursements available (averaging $21,750 per year); health care benefits and unspecified assistantships also available. Financial award application deadline: 2/15. *Faculty research:* Urban health issues, mechanisms and management of pain, kinesiologic principles, brain and spinal cord control of human locomotion, mechanisms of motor impairment. *Total annual research expenditures:* $377,810. *Unit head:* Dr. Lawrence Pan, Dean, 414-288-7161, Fax: 414-288-5987, E-mail: lawrence.pan@marquette.edu. *Application contact:* Craig Pierce, Assistant Dean of the Graduate School, 414-288-5740, Fax: 414-288-1902, E-mail: craig.pierce@marquette.edu. Web site: http://www.marquette.edu/chs/pt/.

McGill University, Faculty of Graduate and Postdoctoral Studies, Faculty of Medicine, School of Physical and Occupational Therapy, Montréal, QC H3A 2T5, Canada. Offers assessing driving capability (PGC); rehabilitation science (M Sc, PhD).

McMaster University, Faculty of Health Sciences and School of Graduate Studies, Program in Rehabilitation Science (course-based), Hamilton, ON L8S 4M2, Canada. Offers M Sc. Part-time programs available. *Degree requirements:* For master's, online courses and scholarly paper. *Entrance requirements:* For master's, minimum B+ average in final year of a 4-year undergraduate health professional program or other relevant program. Additional exam requirements/recommendations for international students: Required—TOEFL (minimum score 600 paper-based; 250 computer-based).

McMaster University, Faculty of Health Sciences and School of Graduate Studies, Program in Rehabilitation Science (Thesis Option), Hamilton, ON L8S 4M2, Canada. Offers M Sc, PhD. Part-time programs available. *Degree requirements:* For master's, thesis. *Entrance requirements:* For master's, minimum B+ average in final year of a 4-year undergraduate health professional program or other relevant program. Additional exam requirements/recommendations for international students: Required—TOEFL (minimum score 600 paper-based; 250 computer-based).

Medical University of South Carolina, College of Health Professions, Department of Health Sciences and Research, PhD Program in Health and Rehabilitation Science, Charleston, SC 29425. Offers PhD. *Faculty:* 2 full-time (1 woman). *Students:* 14 full-time (11 women), 2 part-time (1 woman); includes 3 minority (2 Black or African American, non-Hispanic/Latino; 1 Hispanic/Latino), 1 international. Average age 34. 8 applicants, 75% accepted, 6 enrolled. *Degree requirements:* For doctorate, comprehensive exam, thesis/dissertation. *Entrance requirements:* Additional exam requirements/recommendations for international students: Required—TOEFL (minimum score 600 paper-based; 250 computer-based). Application fee: $85. Electronic applications accepted. *Financial support:* Career-related internships or fieldwork, Federal Work-Study, scholarships/grants, and tuition waivers (partial) available. Support available to part-time students. Financial award application deadline: 3/10; financial award applicants required to submit FAFSA. *Faculty research:* Spinal cord injury, geriatrics, health economics, health psychology, behavioral medicine. *Unit head:* Dr. Bonnie Martin-Harris, Director, 843-792-7162, E-mail: harrisbm@musc.edu. *Application contact:* Melissa Freeland, Director of Student Services, 843-792-8510, Fax: 843-792-03327, E-mail: freelan@musc.edu. Web site: http://academicdepartments.musc.edu/chp/hrs/index.htm.

Northwestern University, Northwestern University Feinberg School of Medicine, Department of Physical Therapy and Human Movement Sciences, Chicago, IL 60611-2814. Offers movement and rehabilitation science (PhD); physical therapy (DPT). *Accreditation:* APTA. *Faculty:* 24 full-time (14 women), 4 part-time/adjunct (3 women). *Students:* 211 full-time (170 women); includes 27 minority (4 Black or African American, non-Hispanic/Latino; 8 Asian, non-Hispanic/Latino; 11 Hispanic/Latino; 1 Native Hawaiian or other Pacific Islander, non-Hispanic/Latino; 3 Two or more races, non-Hispanic/Latino). Average age 24. 486 applicants, 44% accepted, 81 enrolled. *Degree requirements:* For doctorate, synthesis research project. *Entrance requirements:* For doctorate, GRE General Test (DPT), baccalaureate degree with minimum GPA of 3.0 in required course work (DPT). Additional exam requirements/recommendations for international students: Required—TOEFL (minimum score 265 computer-based). *Application deadline:* For fall admission, 10/1 for domestic and international students. Applications are processed on a rolling basis. Application fee: $40. Electronic applications accepted. *Expenses:* Contact institution. *Financial support:* In 2011–12, 184 students received support. Federal Work-Study, institutionally sponsored loans, and scholarships/grants available. Financial award application deadline: 2/15; financial award applicants required to submit FAFSA. *Faculty research:* Motor control, robotics, neuromuscular imaging, student performance (academic/professional), clinical outcomes. *Total annual research expenditures:* $3.8 million. *Unit head:* Dr. Julius P. A. Dewald, Professor and Chair, 312-908-6788, Fax: 312-908-0741, E-mail: j-dewald@northwestern.edu. *Application contact:* Dr. Jane Sullivan, Associate Professor and Assistant Chair for Recruitment and Admissions, 312-908-6789, Fax: 312-908-0741, E-mail: j-sullivan@northwestern.edu.

The Ohio State University, College of Medicine, School of Allied Medical Professions, Columbus, OH 43210. Offers allied health (MS); health and rehabilitation sciences (PhD); occupational therapy (MOT); physical therapy (DPT). *Accreditation:* AOTA; APTA. Part-time programs available. *Degree requirements:* For master's, thesis or alternative. *Entrance requirements:* Additional exam requirements/recommendations for international students: Required—TOEFL (paper-based 550; computer-based 213) or Michigan English Language Assessment Battery (82). Electronic applications accepted. *Expenses:* Tuition, state resident: full-time $11,400. Tuition, nonresident: full-time $28,125. Tuition and fees vary according to course load, degree level, campus/location and program. *Faculty research:* Geriatrics, quality assurance, nutrition, interdisciplinary health care.

Queen's University at Kingston, School of Graduate Studies and Research, Faculty of Health Sciences, School of Rehabilitation Therapy, Kingston, ON K7L 3N6, Canada. Offers occupational therapy (M Sc OT); physical therapy (M Sc PT); rehabilitation science (M Sc, PhD). Part-time programs available. *Degree requirements:* For master's, thesis; for doctorate, comprehensive exam, thesis/dissertation. *Entrance requirements:* Additional exam requirements/recommendations for international students: Required—TOEFL. *Faculty research:* Disability, community, motor performance, rehabilitation, treatment efficiency.

Salus University, College of Education and Rehabilitation, Elkins Park, PA 19027-1598. Offers education of children and youth with visual and multiple impairments (M Ed, Certificate); low vision rehabilitation (MS, Certificate); orientation and mobility therapy (MS, Certificate); vision rehabilitation therapy (MS, Certificate); OD/MS. Part-time programs available. Postbaccalaureate distance learning degree programs offered. *Entrance requirements:* For master's, GRE or MAT, letters of reference (3), interviews (2). Additional exam requirements/recommendations for international students: Required—TOEFL, TWE. *Expenses:* Contact institution. *Faculty research:* Knowledge utilization, technology transfer.

Texas Tech University Health Sciences Center, School of Allied Health Sciences, Program in Rehabilitation Sciences, Lubbock, TX 79430. Offers PhD. Part-time programs available. *Faculty:* 5 full-time (4 women). *Students:* 5 full-time (1 woman), 4 part-time (3 women); includes 2 minority (1 Black or African American, non-Hispanic/Latino; 1 Asian, non-Hispanic/Latino), 1 international. Average age 30. 15 applicants, 27% accepted, 4 enrolled. *Entrance requirements:* Additional exam requirements/recommendations for international students: Required—TOEFL, IELTS. *Application deadline:* For spring admission, 3/1 for domestic students. Application fee: $35. *Financial support:* Application deadline: 9/1; applicants required to submit FAFSA. *Unit head:* Dr. Steve Sawyer, Chair, 806-743-3220. *Application contact:* Jeri Moravcik, Assistant Director of Admissions and Student Affairs, 806-743-3220, Fax: 806-743-2994, E-mail: jeri.moravcik@ttuhsc.edu.

Université de Montréal, Faculty of Medicine, Program in Mobility and Posture, Montréal, QC H3C 3J7, Canada. Offers DESS.

University at Buffalo, the State University of New York, Graduate School, School of Public Health and Health Professions, Department of Rehabilitation Science, Buffalo, NY 14214. Offers assistive and rehabilitation technology (Certificate); occupational therapy (MS), including physical disabilities/developmental disabilities, school-based therapy/early intervention; physical therapy (DPT). *Faculty:* 19 full-time (12 women), 4 part-time/adjunct (2 women). *Students:* 180 full-time (109 women), 1 part-time (0 women); includes 25 minority (3 Black or African American, non-Hispanic/Latino; 18 Asian, non-Hispanic/Latino; 4 Hispanic/Latino). Average age 26. 112 applicants, 47% accepted, 46 enrolled. In 2011, 53 master's, 41 doctorates, 1 other advanced degree awarded. *Degree requirements:* For doctorate, comprehensive exam, thesis/dissertation. *Entrance requirements:* For master's, BS in occupational therapy; for

doctorate, GRE General Test. Additional exam requirements/recommendations for international students: Required—TOEFL (minimum score 550 paper-based; 213 computer-based; 79 iBT). Application fee: $50. Electronic applications accepted. *Financial support:* In 2011–12, 4 students received support, including 2 research assistantships with full and partial tuition reimbursements available (averaging $15,000 per year), 2 teaching assistantships with full and partial tuition reimbursements available (averaging $10,000 per year); scholarships/grants and unspecified assistantships also available. *Faculty research:* Occupational therapy, physical therapy, exercise physiology. *Total annual research expenditures:* $239,825. *Unit head:* Dr. Robert Burkard, Chair, 716-829-6720, Fax: 716-829-2317, E-mail: phhpadv@buffalo.edu. *Application contact:* Cassandra Walker-Whiteside, Director, Student Advisement and Recruitment Services, 716-829-6769, Fax: 716-829-2034, E-mail: phhpadv@buffalo.edu. Web site: http://www.sphhp.buffalo.edu/rs/.

The University of Alabama at Birmingham, School of Health Professions, Program in Rehabilitation Science, Birmingham, AL 35294. Offers PhD. Program offered jointly by Departments of Occupational Therapy and Physical Therapy. *Entrance requirements:* For doctorate, GRE, minimum GPA of 3.0, interview. *Expenses:* Tuition, state resident: full-time $5922; part-time $309 per hour. Tuition, nonresident: full-time $13,428; part-time $726 per hour. Tuition and fees vary according to program. *Unit head:* Dr. Sharon E. Shaw, Dean, 205-934-3566, Fax: 205-934-2412, E-mail: sshaw@uab.edu. Web site: http://www.uab.edu/pt/rsphd.

University of Alberta, Faculty of Graduate Studies and Research, Faculty of Rehabilitation Medicine, Edmonton, AB T6G 2E1, Canada. Offers PhD. *Degree requirements:* For doctorate, thesis/dissertation. *Entrance requirements:* For doctorate, GRE, minimum GPA of 7.0 on a 9.0 scale. Additional exam requirements/recommendations for international students: Required—TOEFL. Electronic applications accepted. *Faculty research:* Musculoskeletal disorders, neuromotor control, exercise physiology, motor speech disorders, assistive technologies, cardiac rehabilitation/therapeutic exercise.

The University of British Columbia, Faculty of Medicine, School of Rehabilitation Sciences, Vancouver, BC V6T 1Z1, Canada. Offers M Sc, MOT, MPT, MRSc, PhD. *Degree requirements:* For master's, thesis; for doctorate, comprehensive exam, thesis/dissertation. *Entrance requirements:* For master's, minimum B+ average; for doctorate, minimum B+ average, master's degree. Additional exam requirements/recommendations for international students: Required—TOEFL (minimum score 600 paper-based; 250 computer-based). Electronic applications accepted. *Faculty research:* Disability, rehabilitation and society, exercise science and rehabilitation, neurorehabilitation and motor control.

University of Cincinnati, Graduate School, College of Allied Health Sciences, Department of Rehabilitation Sciences, Cincinnati, OH 45221. Offers DPT. *Accreditation:* APTA. *Entrance requirements:* For doctorate, GRE General Test, bachelor's degree with minimum GPA of 3.0, 50 hours volunteer/work in physical therapy setting. Additional exam requirements/recommendations for international students: Required—TOEFL. Electronic applications accepted. *Faculty research:* Biomechanics, sports-related injuries, motor learning, stroke rehabilitation.

University of Colorado Denver, School of Medicine, Program in Rehabilitation Science, Aurora, CO 80045. Offers PhD. *Students:* 3 full-time (1 woman). Average age 28. 3 applicants, 100% accepted, 3 enrolled. *Degree requirements:* For doctorate, comprehensive exam, thesis/dissertation, 60 credit hours (30 of core coursework and 30 of thesis). *Entrance requirements:* For doctorate, GRE, bachelor's degree with minimum GPA of 3.0, research experience (preferred), three letters of recommendation, list of faculty with which student is interested in working, interviews for applicant finalists. Additional exam requirements/recommendations for international students: Required—TOEFL (minimum score 570 paper-based; 230 computer-based; 89 iBT). *Application deadline:* For fall admission, 1/1 for domestic students, 12/1 for international students. Application fee: $50 ($75 for international students). Electronic applications accepted. *Financial support:* Application deadline: 4/1; applicants required to submit FAFSA. *Unit head:* Dr. Katrina Maluf, Director of Physical Therapy Program, 303-724-9139, E-mail: katrina.maluf@ucdenver.edu. *Application contact:* M. J. Stewart, Program Administrator, 303-724-3102, E-mail: mj.stewart@ucdenver.edu. Web site: http://www.ucdenver.edu/academics/colleges/medicalschool/education/degree_programs/pt/PhD/Pages/Overview.aspx.

University of Florida, Graduate School, College of Public Health and Health Professions, Program in Rehabilitation Science, Gainesville, FL 32611. Offers PhD. *Students:* 33 full-time (18 women), 4 part-time (2 women); includes 9 minority (1 Black or African American, non-Hispanic/Latino; 3 Asian, non-Hispanic/Latino; 5 Hispanic/Latino), 16 international. Average age 34. 25 applicants, 20% accepted, 5 enrolled. In 2011, 5 doctorates awarded. *Degree requirements:* For doctorate, comprehensive exam, thesis/dissertation. *Entrance requirements:* For doctorate, GRE General Test, minimum GPA of 3.0. Additional exam requirements/recommendations for international students: Required—TOEFL (minimum score 550 paper-based; 213 computer-based; 80 iBT), IELTS (minimum score 6). *Application deadline:* For fall admission, 3/15 for domestic and international students; for spring admission, 7/15 for domestic and international students. Applications are processed on a rolling basis. Application fee: $30. Electronic applications accepted. *Financial support:* In 2011–12, 6 students received support, including 2 fellowships, 4 research assistantships. Financial award application deadline: 4/1; financial award applicants required to submit FAFSA. *Faculty research:* Movement science, applied neuroscience, community mobility, rehabilitation outcomes, assistive technology/environmental interventions. *Total annual research expenditures:* $4 million. *Unit head:* Dr. William C. Mann, Chair, Department of Occupational Therapy, 352-273-6883, E-mail: wmann@phhp.ufl.edu. *Application contact:* Office of Admissions, 352-392-1365, E-mail: gradinfo@ufl.edu. Web site: http://rehabsci.phhp.ufl.edu/.

University of Illinois at Urbana–Champaign, Graduate College, College of Applied Health Sciences, Department of Kinesiology and Community Health, Champaign, IL 61820. Offers community health (MS, MSPH, PhD); kinesiology (MS, PhD); public health (MPH); rehabilitation (MS). *Faculty:* 25 full-time (12 women). *Students:* 137 full-time (83 women), 10 part-time (8 women); includes 35 minority (16 Black or African American, non-Hispanic/Latino; 14 Asian, non-Hispanic/Latino; 3 Hispanic/Latino; 2 Two or more races, non-Hispanic/Latino), 38 international. 167 applicants, 40% accepted, 45 enrolled. In 2011, 22 master's, 11 doctorates awarded. *Entrance requirements:* For master's, GRE, minimum GPA of 3.0; for doctorate, GRE, minimum graduate GPA of 3.5. Additional exam requirements/recommendations for international students: Required—TOEFL. *Application deadline:* Applications are processed on a rolling basis. Application fee: $75 ($90 for international students). Electronic applications accepted. *Financial support:* In 2011–12, 15 fellowships, 37 research assistantships, 71 teaching assistantships were awarded; tuition waivers (full and partial) also available. *Unit head:* Wojciech Chodzko-Zajko, Head, 217-244-0823, Fax: 217-244-7322, E-mail: wojtek@illinois.edu. *Application contact:* Tina M. Candler, Office Manager, 217-333-1083, Fax: 217-244-7322, E-mail: tcandler@illinois.edu. Web site: http://www.kch.illinois.edu/.

The University of Iowa, Roy J. and Lucille A. Carver College of Medicine and Graduate College, Graduate Programs in Medicine, Graduate Program in Physical Therapy and Rehabilitation Science, Iowa City, IA 52242-1316. Offers physical therapy (DPT);

rehabilitation science (PhD). *Accreditation:* APTA (one or more programs are accredited). *Faculty:* 7 full-time (3 women), 47 part-time/adjunct (28 women). *Students:* 116 full-time (85 women), 4 part-time (1 woman); includes 4 minority (1 Black or African American, non-Hispanic/Latino; 2 Asian, non-Hispanic/Latino; 1 Hispanic/Latino), 3 international. Average age 24. 352 applicants, 14% accepted, 36 enrolled. In 2011, 3 doctorates awarded. Terminal master's awarded for partial completion of doctoral program. *Degree requirements:* For doctorate, thesis/dissertation (for some programs). *Entrance requirements:* For doctorate, GRE. Additional exam requirements/recommendations for international students: Required—TOEFL. *Application deadline:* For fall admission, 12/1 priority date for domestic students, 5/15 for international students; for winter admission, 10/15 for international students; for spring admission, 3/15 for international students. Application fee: $60 ($85 for international students). Electronic applications accepted. *Expenses:* Contact institution. *Financial support:* In 2011–12, 94 students received support, including 1 fellowship with partial tuition reimbursement available (averaging $9,000 per year), 6 research assistantships with partial tuition reimbursements available (averaging $10,129 per year), teaching assistantships with partial tuition reimbursements available (averaging $10,129 per year); Federal Work-Study, institutionally sponsored loans, scholarships/grants, health care benefits, and unspecified assistantships also available. Support available to part-time students. Financial award application deadline: 6/30; financial award applicants required to submit FAFSA. *Faculty research:* Muscle fatigue, motor control, pain mechanisms, body composition, sports medicine, occupational safety, neuromuscular physiology, neural control of movement. *Total annual research expenditures:* $1.4 million. *Unit head:* Dr. Richard K. Shields, Director, 319-335-9791, Fax: 319-335-9707, E-mail: physical-therapy@uiowa.edu. *Application contact:* Carol Leigh, Project Assistant, 319-335-9792, Fax: 319-335-9707, E-mail: carol-leigh@uiowa.edu. Web site: http://www.healthcare.uiowa.edu/physicaltherapy/index.html.

The University of Kansas, University of Kansas Medical Center, School of Health Professions, Department of Occupational Therapy Education, Kansas City, KS 66160. Offers occupational therapy (MOT, MS, OTD); therapeutic science (PhD). *Accreditation:* AOTA. Part-time programs available. *Faculty:* 11. *Students:* 66 full-time (55 women), 17 part-time (16 women); includes 8 minority (2 Black or African American, non-Hispanic/Latino; 1 American Indian or Alaska Native, non-Hispanic/Latino; 4 Asian, non-Hispanic/Latino; 1 Hispanic/Latino), 2 international. Average age 28. 105 applicants, 34% accepted, 34 enrolled. In 2011, 27 master's, 2 doctorates awarded. *Degree requirements:* For doctorate, comprehensive exam, thesis/dissertation, oral defense. *Entrance requirements:* For master's, 40 hours of paid work or volunteer experience working directly with people with special needs, 3 letters of recommendation, personal statement and program statement of interest, 90 hours of elective course work with 40 hours of prerequisite work, minimum GPA of 3.0; for doctorate, 24 hours of master's-level research. Additional exam requirements/recommendations for international students: Required—TOEFL. *Application deadline:* For fall admission, 12/31 for domestic students, 4/1 for international students. Applications are processed on a rolling basis. Application fee: $60. Electronic applications accepted. Tuition and fees vary according to course load, campus/location, program and reciprocity agreements. *Financial support:* Research assistantships with partial tuition reimbursements, teaching assistantships with full and partial tuition reimbursements, traineeships, and unspecified assistantships available. Financial award application deadline: 2/14; financial award applicants required to submit FAFSA. *Faculty research:* Impact of sensory processing in everyday life; improving balance, motor skills, and independence with community nonprofit organizations serving people with special needs; improving self-confidence and self-sufficiency with poverty-based services in community; working with autism population in a community-wide aquatics program. *Total annual research expenditures:* $42,046. *Unit head:* Dr. Winifred W. Dunn, Professor/Chair, 913-588-7195, Fax: 913-588-4568, E-mail: wdunn@kumc.edu. *Application contact:* Wendy Hildenbrand, Admissions Representative, 913-588-7174, Fax: 913-588-4568, E-mail: whildenb@kumc.edu. Web site: http://ot.kumc.edu.

The University of Kansas, University of Kansas Medical Center, School of Health Professions, Department of Physical Therapy and Rehabilitation Science, Kansas City, KS 66160. Offers physical therapy (DPT); rehabilitation science (PhD). *Accreditation:* APTA. *Faculty:* 30. *Students:* 123 full-time (86 women), 29 part-time (22 women); includes 9 minority (2 Black or African American, non-Hispanic/Latino; 1 American Indian or Alaska Native, non-Hispanic/Latino; 5 Asian, non-Hispanic/Latino; 1 Hispanic/Latino), 10 international. Average age 29. 150 applicants, 31% accepted, 46 enrolled. In 2011, 55 doctorates awarded. *Degree requirements:* For doctorate, comprehensive exam, research project with paper. *Entrance requirements:* For doctorate, GRE General Test, minimum GPA of 3.0. Additional exam requirements/recommendations for international students: Required—TOEFL. *Application deadline:* For fall admission, 11/1 for domestic students. Applications are processed on a rolling basis. Application fee: $60. Electronic applications accepted. *Expenses:* Contact institution. *Financial support:* Research assistantships with tuition reimbursements, teaching assistantships with full and partial tuition reimbursements, career-related internships or fieldwork, Federal Work-Study, institutionally sponsored loans, scholarships/grants, traineeships, and unspecified assistantships available. Financial award application deadline: 2/14; financial award applicants required to submit FAFSA. *Faculty research:* Stroke rehabilitation and the effects on balance and coordination; deep brain stimulation and Parkinson's Disease; peripheral neuropathies, pain and the effects of exercise; islet transplants for Type 1 diabetes; cardiac disease associated with diabetes. *Total annual research expenditures:* $615,660. *Unit head:* Dr. Lisa Stehno-Bittel, Chair, 913-588-6733, Fax: 913-588-4568, E-mail: lbittel@kumc.edu. *Application contact:* Robert Bagley, Admission Coordinator, 913-588-6799, Fax: 913-588-4568, E-mail: rbagley@kumc.edu. Web site: http://ptrs.kumc.edu.

University of Kentucky, Graduate School, College of Health Sciences, Program in Rehabilitation Sciences, Lexington, KY 40506-0032. Offers PhD. *Degree requirements:* For doctorate, comprehensive exam, thesis/dissertation. *Entrance requirements:* For doctorate, GRE General Test, minimum undergraduate GPA of 2.75. Additional exam requirements/recommendations for international students: Required—TOEFL (minimum score 550 paper-based; 213 computer-based). Electronic applications accepted.

University of Manitoba, Faculty of Graduate Studies, School of Medical Rehabilitation, Winnipeg, MB R3T 2N2, Canada. Offers applied health sciences (PhD); occupational therapy (MOT); physical therapy (MPT); rehabilitation (M Sc).

University of Manitoba, Faculty of Medicine and Faculty of Graduate Studies, Graduate Programs in Medicine, Department of Medical Rehabilitation, Winnipeg, MB R3T 2N2, Canada. Offers rehabilitation (M Sc). Part-time programs available. *Faculty research:* Understanding of human dynamics, motor control and neurological dysfunction, exercise physiology, functional motion of the upper extremity and effects of musculoskeletal disorders.

University of Maryland, Baltimore, Graduate School, Graduate Program in Life Sciences, Program in Physical Rehabilitation Science, Baltimore, MD 21201. Offers PhD. *Students:* 5 full-time (3 women), 1 (woman) part-time; includes 1 minority (Black or African American, non-Hispanic/Latino), 4 international. Average age 27. 28 applicants, 25% accepted, 4 enrolled. In 2011, 3 doctorates awarded. *Degree requirements:* For doctorate, comprehensive exam, thesis/dissertation. *Entrance requirements:* For

doctorate, GRE. Additional exam requirements/recommendations for international students: Required—TOEFL (minimum score 550 paper-based; 80 iBT); Recommended—IELTS (minimum score 7). *Application deadline:* For fall admission, 1/15 for domestic and international students. Application fee: $50. Electronic applications accepted. *Financial support:* In 2011–12, research assistantships with partial tuition reimbursements (averaging $25,000 per year) were awarded; health care benefits and unspecified assistantships also available. Financial award application deadline: 3/1. *Faculty research:* Applied physiology, biomechanics, epidemiology of disability, neuromotor control. *Unit head:* Dr. Mark Rogers, Program Director, 410-706-0841, Fax: 410-706-4903, E-mail: mrogers@som.umaryland.edu. *Application contact:* Terry Heron, Academic Coordinator, 410-706-7721, E-mail: theron@som.umaryland.edu. Web site: http://rehabscience.umaryland.edu.

University of Maryland, Baltimore, School of Medicine, Department of Physical Therapy and Rehabilitation Science, Baltimore, MD 21201. Offers physical rehabilitation science (PhD); physical therapy and rehabilitation science (DPT). *Accreditation:* APTA. *Students:* 120 full-time (76 women), 48 part-time (33 women); includes 34 minority (12 Black or African American, non-Hispanic/Latino; 12 Asian, non-Hispanic/Latino; 6 Hispanic/Latino; 4 Two or more races, non-Hispanic/Latino), 5 international. Average age 25. In 2011, 80 doctorates awarded. *Entrance requirements:* For doctorate, GRE General Test, BS, science coursework. Additional exam requirements/recommendations for international students: Required—TOEFL (minimum score 213 computer-based; 80 iBT). Electronic applications accepted. *Expenses:* Contact institution. *Financial support:* Career-related internships or fieldwork, Federal Work-Study, scholarships/grants, traineeships, health care benefits, and unspecified assistantships available. Financial award application deadline: 3/1; financial award applicants required to submit FAFSA. *Unit head:* Dr. Mary Rodgers, Chair, 410-706-5216, Fax: 410-706-4903, E-mail: mrodgers@som.umaryland.edu. *Application contact:* Terry Heron, Program Coordinator, 410-706-5215, Fax: 410-706-6387, E-mail: theron@som.umaryland.edu. Web site: http://pt.umaryland.edu/pros.asp.

University of Maryland Eastern Shore, Graduate Programs, Department of Rehabilitation Services, Princess Anne, MD 21853-1299. Offers rehabilitation counseling (MS). *Accreditation:* CORE. Part-time and evening/weekend programs available. *Degree requirements:* For master's, internship. *Entrance requirements:* For master's, interview. Additional exam requirements/recommendations for international students: Required—TOEFL (minimum score 213 computer-based; 80 iBT). Electronic applications accepted. *Faculty research:* Long-term rehabilitation training.

University of Northern Iowa, Graduate College, College of Education, School of Health, Physical Education, and Leisure Services, Program in Athletic Training, Cedar Falls, IA 50614. Offers athletic training (MS); rehabilitation studies (Ed D). Part-time and evening/weekend programs available. *Students:* 13 full-time (9 women), 5 part-time (3 women). 26 applicants, 62% accepted, 6 enrolled. In 2011, 5 degrees awarded. *Degree requirements:* For master's, comprehensive exam. *Entrance requirements:* Additional exam requirements/recommendations for international students: Required—TOEFL (minimum score 550 paper-based; 213 computer-based; 79 iBT). *Application deadline:* For fall admission, 4/1 for international students; for winter admission, 10/1 for international students. Applications are processed on a rolling basis. Application fee: $50 ($70 for international students). Electronic applications accepted. *Expenses:* Tuition, state resident: full-time $7476. Tuition, nonresident: full-time $16,410. *Required fees:* $942. *Financial support:* Unspecified assistantships available. Financial award application deadline: 2/1; financial award applicants required to submit FAFSA. *Unit head:* Jody Brucker, Coordinator, 319-273-6477, Fax: 319-273-5958, E-mail: jody.brucker@uni.edu. *Application contact:* Laurie S. Russell, Record Analyst, 319-273-2623, Fax: 319-273-6792, E-mail: laurie.russell@uni.edu. Web site: http://www.uni.edu/coe/departments/school-health-physical-education-leisure-services/athletic-training.

University of North Texas, Toulouse Graduate School, College of Public Affairs and Community Service, Department of Rehabilitation, Social Work, and Addictions, Denton, TX 76203. Offers rehabilitation counseling (MS). *Accreditation:* CORE. Part-time and evening/weekend programs available. Postbaccalaureate distance learning degree programs offered (no on-campus study). *Degree requirements:* For master's, comprehensive exam, thesis optional, 100 hour practicum, 600 hour internship. *Entrance requirements:* For master's, GRE General Test or 2 years experience, minimum overall GPA of 2.8, 3.0 in last 60 hours. Additional exam requirements/recommendations for international students: Recommended—TOEFL (minimum score 550 paper-based; 213 computer-based; 79 iBT). Electronic applications accepted. *Expenses:* Tuition, state resident: part-time $100 per credit hour. Tuition, nonresident: part-time $413 per credit hour. *Faculty research:* Resiliency, multiculturalism, substance abuse and co-existing disabilities, social work pedagogy, spiritual aspects of disability and aging.

University of Oklahoma Health Sciences Center, Graduate College, College of Allied Health, Department of Rehabilitation Sciences, Oklahoma City, OK 73190. Offers MS. *Degree requirements:* For master's, comprehensive exam, thesis optional. *Entrance requirements:* For master's, GRE General Test, 2 years clinical experience, 3 letters of reference. Additional exam requirements/recommendations for international students: Required—TOEFL (minimum score 550 paper-based).

University of Ottawa, Faculty of Graduate and Postdoctoral Studies, Faculty of Health Sciences, School of Rehabilitation Sciences, Ottawa, ON K1N 6N5, Canada. Offers audiology (M Sc); orthophony (M Sc). Part-time and evening/weekend programs available. *Entrance requirements:* For master's, honors degree or equivalent, minimum B average. Electronic applications accepted.

University of Pittsburgh, School of Health and Rehabilitation Sciences, Master's Programs in Health and Rehabilitation Sciences, Pittsburgh, PA 15260. Offers health and rehabilitation sciences (MS), including clinical dietetics and nutrition, health care supervision and management, health information systems, occupational therapy, physical therapy, rehabilitation counseling, rehabilitation science and technology, sports medicine, wellness and human performance. *Accreditation:* APTA. Part-time and evening/weekend programs available. *Faculty:* 22 full-time (16 women), 4 part-time/adjunct (2 women). *Students:* 144 full-time (91 women), 35 part-time (23 women); includes 23 minority (8 Black or African American, non-Hispanic/Latino; 8 Asian, non-Hispanic/Latino; 3 Hispanic/Latino; 4 Two or more races, non-Hispanic/Latino), 74 international. Average age 28. 399 applicants, 61% accepted, 121 enrolled. In 2011, 86 master's awarded. *Degree requirements:* For master's, comprehensive exam (for some programs), thesis optional. *Entrance requirements:* For master's, minimum GPA of 3.0. Additional exam requirements/recommendations for international students: Required—TOEFL (minimum score 550 paper-based; 213 computer-based; 80 iBT), IELTS (minimum score 6.5). *Application deadline:* For fall admission, 3/1 for international students; for spring admission, 7/31 for international students. Applications are processed on a rolling basis. Application fee: $50. Electronic applications accepted. *Expenses:* Contact institution. *Financial support:* Research assistantships, teaching assistantships, Federal Work-Study, institutionally sponsored loans, traineeships, and unspecified assistantships available. Financial award applicants required to submit FAFSA. *Faculty research:* Assistive technology, seating and wheeled mobility, cellular neurophysiology, low back syndrome, augmentative communication. *Total annual research expenditures:* $7.8 million. *Unit head:* Dr. Clifford E. Brubaker, Dean, 412-383-

6560, Fax: 412-383-6535, E-mail: cliffb@pitt.edu. *Application contact:* Shameem Gangjee, Director of Admissions, 412-383-6558, Fax: 412-383-6535, E-mail: admissions@shrs.pitt.edu. Web site: http://www.shrs.pitt.edu/.

University of Pittsburgh, School of Health and Rehabilitation Sciences, PhD Program in Rehabilitation Science, Pittsburgh, PA 15260. Offers PhD. Part-time programs available. *Faculty:* 46 full-time (20 women), 11 part-time/adjunct (3 women). *Students:* 64 full-time (21 women), 22 part-time (14 women); includes 6 minority (3 Black or African American, non-Hispanic/Latino; 2 Asian, non-Hispanic/Latino; 1 Hispanic/Latino), 45 international. Average age 33. 42 applicants, 60% accepted, 18 enrolled. In 2011, 7 doctorates awarded. *Degree requirements:* For doctorate, comprehensive exam, thesis/dissertation. *Entrance requirements:* For doctorate, GRE General Test. Additional exam requirements/recommendations for international students: Required—TOEFL (minimum score 550 paper-based; 213 computer-based; 80 iBT), IELTS (minimum score 6.5). *Application deadline:* For fall admission, 3/1 for international students; for spring admission, 9/1 for international students. Applications are processed on a rolling basis. Application fee: $50. Electronic applications accepted. *Expenses:* Tuition, state resident: full-time $18,774; part-time $760 per credit. Tuition, nonresident: full-time $30,736; part-time $1258 per credit. *Required fees:* $740; $200 per term. Tuition and fees vary according to program. *Financial support:* In 2011–12, 40 research assistantships with full and partial tuition reimbursements (averaging $18,955 per year), 4 teaching assistantships with full tuition reimbursements (averaging $21,585 per year) were awarded. *Faculty research:* Measurement and study of motion, balance disorders, human performance, neuropsychological parameters, telerehabilitation, wheelchair performance and design, injury prevention and treatment, nutrition, data mining. *Total annual research expenditures:* $2.8 million. *Unit head:* Dr. Joan Rogers, Associate Dean of Graduate Studies, 412-383-6620, Fax: 412-383-6613, E-mail: jcr@pitt.edu. *Application contact:* Shameem Gangjee, Director of Admissions, 412-383-6558, Fax: 412-383-6535, E-mail: admissions@shrs.pitt.edu. Web site: http://shrs.pitt.edu.

University of Pittsburgh, School of Health and Rehabilitation Sciences, Prosthetics and Orthotics Program, Pittsburgh, PA 15260. Offers MS. Part-time programs available. *Faculty:* 3 full-time (2 women), 5 part-time/adjunct (2 women). *Students:* 30 full-time (16 women), 1 part-time (0 women); includes 4 minority (1 Black or African American, non-Hispanic/Latino; 3 Hispanic/Latino). Average age 25. 40 applicants, 68% accepted, 19 enrolled. In 2011, 14 master's awarded. *Entrance requirements:* Additional exam requirements/recommendations for international students: Required—TOEFL (minimum score 550 paper-based; 213 computer-based; 80 iBT), IELTS (minimum score 6.5). *Application deadline:* For fall admission, 3/1 for international students. Application fee: $50. *Expenses:* Contact institution. *Unit head:* Dr. Ray Burdett, Director, 412-383-6704, E-mail: rgb@pitt.edu. *Application contact:* Shameem Gangjee, Director of Admissions, 412-383-6558, Fax: 412-383-6535, E-mail: admissions@shrs.pitt.edu. Web site: http://www.shrs.pitt.edu/po/.

University of South Carolina, School of Medicine and The Graduate School, Graduate Programs in Medicine, Program in Rehabilitation Counseling, Columbia, SC 29208. Offers psychiatric rehabilitation (Certificate); rehabilitation counseling (MRC). *Accreditation:* CORE. Part-time and evening/weekend programs available. *Degree requirements:* For master's, comprehensive exam, internship, practicum. *Entrance requirements:* For master's and Certificate, GRE General Test or GMAT. Electronic applications accepted. *Expenses:* Contact institution. *Faculty research:* Quality of life, alcohol dependency, technology for disabled, psychiatric rehabilitation, women with disabilities.

University of Toronto, Faculty of Medicine, Department of Rehabilitation Science, Toronto, ON M5S 1A1, Canada. Offers M Sc, PhD. *Degree requirements:* For master's, thesis. *Entrance requirements:* For master's, B Sc or equivalent; specialization in occupational therapy, physical therapy, or a related field; minimum B+ average in final 2 years. Additional exam requirements/recommendations for international students: Required—TOEFL (minimum score 580 paper-based; 93 iBT), TWE (minimum score 5). Electronic applications accepted.

University of Utah, Graduate School, College of Health, Department of Physical Therapy, Salt Lake City, UT 84112-1290. Offers physical therapy (DPT); rehabilitation science (PhD). *Accreditation:* APTA. *Faculty:* 12 full-time (6 women), 5 part-time/adjunct (2 women). *Students:* 136 full-time (74 women); includes 11 minority (1 Black or African American, non-Hispanic/Latino; 2 American Indian or Alaska Native, non-Hispanic/Latino; 2 Asian, non-Hispanic/Latino; 4 Hispanic/Latino; 2 Two or more races, non-Hispanic/Latino), 1 international. Average age 31. 340 applicants, 14% accepted, 46 enrolled. In 2011, 46 doctorates awarded. *Degree requirements:* For doctorate, thesis/dissertation, clinical project. *Entrance requirements:* For doctorate, minimum GPA of 3.0, volunteer work, bachelor's degree. Additional exam requirements/recommendations for international students: Recommended—TOEFL (minimum score 90 iBT). *Application deadline:* For fall admission, 10/1 priority date for domestic students, 10/1 for international students. Application fee: $55 ($65 for international students). Electronic applications accepted. *Expenses:* Contact institution. *Financial support:* In 2011–12, 20 students received support, including 1 research assistantship, 7 teaching assistantships; Federal Work-Study, institutionally sponsored loans, scholarships/grants, and tuition waivers also available. Financial award application deadline: 9/30; financial award applicants required to submit FAFSA. *Faculty research:* Rehabilitation and Parkinson's Disease, motor control and musculoskeletal dysfunction, burns/wound care, rehabilitation and multiple sclerosis, cancer. *Total annual research expenditures:* $840,500. *Unit head:* Dr. R. Scott Ward, Chair, 801-581-8681, Fax: 801-585-5629, E-mail: scott.ward@hsc.utah.edu. *Application contact:* Julia Konopasek, Academic Advisor, 801-585-8681, Fax: 801-585-5629, E-mail: julia.konopasek@hsc.utah.edu. Web site: http://www.health.utah.edu/pt.

University of Washington, Graduate School, School of Medicine, Graduate Programs in Medicine, Department of Rehabilitation Medicine, Seattle, WA 98195-6490. Offers occupational therapy (MOT); physical therapy (DPT); prosthetics and orthotics (MPO); rehabilitation science (PhD). *Faculty:* 65. *Students:* 200. Average age 25. In 2011, 25 master's, 30 doctorates awarded. *Degree requirements:* For doctorate, comprehensive exam (for some programs), thesis/dissertation (for some programs). *Entrance requirements:* For master's and doctorate, GRE. Additional exam requirements/recommendations for international students: Required—TOEFL. Application fee: $75. *Financial support:* In 2011–12, 1 fellowship (averaging $5,000 per year) was awarded. Financial award applicants required to submit FAFSA. *Faculty research:* Biomechanics, balance, brain injury, spinal cord injury, pain, degenerative diseases. *Unit head:* Dr. Peter C. Esselman, Professor and Chair, 206-744-3167, E-mail: esselman@u.washington.edu. *Application contact:* Dr. Deborah Kartin, Graduate Program Coordinator, 206-598-5338, Fax: 206-685-3244, E-mail: kartin@u.washington.edu. Web site: http://rehab.washington.edu/education/degree/.

University of Wisconsin–La Crosse, Office of University Graduate Studies, College of Science and Health, Department of Exercise and Sport Science, Program in Clinical Exercise Physiology, La Crosse, WI 54601-3742. Offers MS. *Students:* 16 full-time (10 women); includes 2 minority (1 Asian, non-Hispanic/Latino; 1 Hispanic/Latino), 1 international. Average age 24. 1 applicant, 0% accepted, 0 enrolled. In 2011, 14 master's awarded. *Degree requirements:* For master's, thesis optional. *Entrance requirements:* Additional exam requirements/recommendations for international

students: Required—TOEFL (minimum score 550 paper-based; 213 computer-based; 79 iBT). *Application deadline:* For fall admission, 2/1 priority date for domestic students, 2/1 for international students. Application fee: $56. Electronic applications accepted. *Expenses:* Tuition, state resident: full-time $8391; part-time $481.17 per credit. Tuition, nonresident: full-time $17,850; part-time $1006.68 per credit. *Required fees:* $2 per credit. $18.25 per semester. Tuition and fees vary according to course load, program, reciprocity agreements and student level. *Financial support:* Federal Work-Study, scholarships/grants, health care benefits, and tuition waivers (partial) available. Support available to part-time students. Financial award application deadline: 3/15; financial award applicants required to submit FAFSA. *Unit head:* Dr. John Porcari, Director, 608-785-8684, Fax: 608-785-8686, E-mail: porcari.john@uwlax.edu. *Application contact:* Kathryn Kiefer, Director of Admissions, 608-785-8939, E-mail: admissions@uwlax.edu. Web site: http://www.uwlax.edu/sah/ess/cep/.

University of Wisconsin–Madison, Graduate School, School of Education, Department of Kinesiology, Therapeutic Science Program, Madison, WI 53706-1380. Offers MS. *Accreditation:* AOTA. *Entrance requirements:* For master's, GRE General Test. Application fee: $56. *Expenses:* Tuition, state resident: full-time $10,296; part-time $643.51 per credit. Tuition, nonresident: full-time $24,054; part-time $1503.40 per credit. *Required fees:* $70.06 per credit. Tuition and fees vary according to course load, campus/location, program and reciprocity agreements. *Financial support:* Fellowships with full tuition reimbursements, research assistantships with full tuition reimbursements, teaching assistantships with full tuition reimbursements, traineeships, and project assistantships available. *Unit head:* Dr. Dorothy Edwards, Chair, 608-262-1654, E-mail: dfedwards@education.wisc.edu. *Application contact:* 608-262-2433, Fax: 608-262-5134, E-mail: gradadmiss@mail.bascom.wisc.edu. Web site: http://www.education.wisc.edu/kinesiology.

Virginia Commonwealth University, Graduate School, School of Education, Department of Health and Human Performance, Program in Rehabilitation and Movement Science, Richmond, VA 23284-9005. Offers PhD. *Entrance requirements:* Additional exam requirements/recommendations for international students: Required—TOEFL (minimum score 250 paper-based; 250 computer-based; 100 iBT). Electronic applications accepted. *Expenses:* Tuition, state resident: full-time $9133; part-time $507 per credit. Tuition, nonresident: full-time $18,777; part-time $1043 per credit. *Required fees:* $77 per credit. Tuition and fees vary according to degree level, campus/location, program and student level.

Washington University in St. Louis, School of Medicine, Graduate Programs in Medicine, Program in Rehabilitation and Participation Science, St. Louis, MO 63130-4899. Offers PhD.

Western Michigan University, Graduate College, College of Health and Human Services, Department of Blindness and Low Vision Studies, Kalamazoo, MI 49008. Offers orientation and mobility (MA); orientation and mobility of children (MA); vision rehabilitation teaching (MA). *Accreditation:* CORE.

PHILADELPHIA COLLEGE OF OSTEOPATHIC MEDICINE
Physician Assistant Program

Program of Study

The Physician Assistant (PA) program is a twenty-six-month program that leads to a Master of Science degree in health sciences. Students are prepared for clinical practice, using a variety of learning strategies: formal lectures, practical laboratory classes, clinical education, and clinical research. Students develop patient communication skills and advanced clinical problem-solving skills in addition to acquiring technical proficiency in areas related to professional practice. The program is highly intensive. Most of the program is provided by experienced physician assistants with clinical backgrounds in multiple specialites.

In addition to admission through the standard application process, there are also two 5-year cooperative programs with Philadelphia College of Osteopathic Medicine (PCOM) and either University of the Sciences in Philadelphia (USP) or Brenau University in Gainesville, Georgia. The programs consist of two distinct phases: the preprofessional phase and the professional phase. After successful completion of the fourth year, students earn a B.S. in health science from USP or Brenau and an M.S. from PCOM after completion of the fifth year. The B.S. degree does not qualify the student as a PA. Students must complete the entire professional phase of the program (years four and five) and obtain an M.S. from PCOM to become eligible to be certified as a PA. PCOM has the ultimate responsibility for granting the M.S. degree.

The Physician Assistant program at PCOM provides students with the ability to positively affect the lives of their patients, their families, their employers, and their communities. Students become lifelong learners, developing a baseline of analytic and critical thinking skills that prepare them for the challenges of caring for the entire patient, young or old, from the emergency room to the operating room.

Research Facilities

PCOM's library features both a well-developed collection of medical journals and texts and new capabilities for access to online medical references and Internet searching in a facility that provides individual student stations, Internet terminals, advanced audiovisual resources, and a large student computer lab.

Financial Aid

The Financial Aid Office at PCOM offers financial assistance to students through the Federal Direct Loan program, institutional grants, and various alternative private loan programs.

Cost of Study

In 2012–13, the tuition for PCOM's Physician Assistant program is $31,833 annually.

Living and Housing Costs

Students live off campus within the Philadelphia metropolitan and suburban areas, as there is no on-campus housing. Room and board costs vary by each student's individual preferences.

Student Group

Admission to the PA program is competitive and selective. The College looks for academically and socially well-rounded individuals who are committed to caring for patients. The class of 2013 totals 56 students, 47 women and 9 men, ranging in age from 21 to 43. Sixteen percent of the class self-identified as minority. Thirty were residents of Pennsylvania. The average GPA of the entering class was 3.46.

Location

Philadelphia College of Osteopathic Medicine is one of the largest of twenty-six osteopathic colleges in the United States, with campuses in both Philadelphia and suburban Atlanta. The PA studies program is offered only on the Philadelphia campus, which is located in a suburban setting on City Avenue, minutes away from Fairmount Park, Philadelphia's historic district, art museums, theaters, restaurants, and professional sports complexes. PCOM's facilities include two large lecture halls, small classrooms, labs for teaching and research, a state-of-the-art library, and scenic landscaping, all in a suburban setting.

The College

PCOM, chartered in 1899, enrolls approximately 2,400 students in its various programs across both campuses, and is committed to educating community-responsive, primary-care–oriented physicians and physician assistants to practice medicine in the twenty-first century. Supported by the latest in medical and educational technology, PCOM emphasizes treating the whole person, not merely the symptoms. Students have a committed, professional, humanistic faculty who are leaders in the osteopathic and physician assistant national health-care community. The PA Program provides a thorough foundation in health-care delivery that focuses on comprehensive, humanistic health care.

Applying

Selection for the Physician Assistant program is very competitive. Applicants must complete a baccalaureate degree at a regionally accredited college or university in the United States, Canada, or the United Kingdom with a minimum GPA of 3.0 (on a 4.0 scale), document in their CASPA application 200 hours of experience in volunteer or employment in or related to the health-care industry, and fulfill the following course requirements: five semesters of biology, three semesters of chemistry, one semester of physics or another health related science, two semesters of mathematics, and three semesters of social science courses. All requirements must have been completed within the last ten years, unless the applicant has completed an advanced degree or has extensive experience in the field of patient care. Applications are not accepted from graduates of medical schools. Selected applicants are invited to interview on campus. Application and deadline information is available online at http://www.caspaonline.org and http://www.pcom.edu/Admissions/admissions.html.

Correspondence and Information

Philadelphia College of Osteopathic Medicine
4170 City Avenue
Philadelphia, Pennsylvania 19131
Phone: 215-871-6700
        800-999-6998 (toll-free)
Fax: 215-871-6719
E-mail: PAAdmissions@pcom.edu
Web site: http://www.pcom.edu

THE FACULTY AND THEIR RESEARCH

Full-Time Faculty

Gregory McDonald, D.O., Philadelphia College of Osteopathic Medicine. Medical Director, Department of Physician Assistant Studies. Pathology.

John Cavenagh, Ph.D., Union (Ohio); PA-C. Professor, Chairman, Department of Physician Assistant Studies. Emergency medicine.

Jill Cunningham, M.H.S., Drexel; PA-C. Assistant Professor, Department of Physician Assistant Studies. Internal medicine.

Marilyn DeFeliciantonio, M.S.L.S., Villanova; PA-C. Assistant Professor, Department of Physician Assistant Studies. Hematology and oncology.

Sean Guinane, M.S., Philadelphia College of Osteopathic Medicine; PA-C. Assistant Professor, Department of Physician Assistant Studies. Family medicine.

Paul Krajewski, M.S., Philadelphia College of Osteopathic Medicine; PA-C. Associate Professor, Department of Physician Assistant Studies. Orthopedic surgery, emergency medicine.

Laura Molloy, M.M.S., Saint Francis (Pennsylvania); PA-C. Associate Professor, Assistant Program Director, Department of Physician Assistant Studies. Family medicine, women's health.

Christine Mount, M.S., University of Medicine and Dentistry of New Jersey; PA-C. Assistant Professor, Department of Physician Assistant Studies. Neurology, emergency medicine, trauma.

Jennifer Windstein, M.S., Wagner; PA-C. Assistant Professor, Department of Physician Assistant Studies. Family practice.

Adjunct Faculty

Patrick Auth, Ph.D., Drexel; PA-C. Emergency medicine, orthopedics.

Matt Baker, D.H.Sc., Nova Southeastern; PA-C. Geriatrics and gerontology.

Robert Cuzzolino, Ed.D., Temple. Academic policy.

Daniel DuPont, D.O., Philadelphia College of Osteopathic Medicine. Pulmonology.

Jeff Gutting, M.S., Philadelphia College of Osteopathic Medicine; PA-C. Cardiology.

Robert D. Howard, M.D., Hahnemann. Emergency medicine.

Michael Kirifides, Ph.D., Maryland. Human physiology.

Brian Levine, M.D., Vermont. Emergency medicine.

Burton Mark, D.O., Kirksville College of Osteopathic Medicine. Psychiatry.

Amanda Murphy, M.S., Philadelphia College of Osteopathic Medicine; PA-C. Dermatology.

Joseph Norris, M.S., D.C., Philadelphia College of Osteopathic Medicine; PA-C. Family medicine.

Richard Pascucci, D.O., Philadelphia College of Osteopathic Medicine; FACOI. Rheumatology.

Margaret Reinhart, M.M.A.; M.T., Penn State; ASCP. Laboratory diagnostics.

Gretchen Reynolds, M.S., Philadelphia College of Osteopathic Medicine; PA-C. Occupational health.

Gary Sloskey, Pharm.D., University of the Sciences in Philadelphia. Pharmacology.

Lauren Tavani, M.S., Philadelphia College of Osteopathic Medicine; PA-C. Critical care.

Rosemary Vickers, D.O., Philadelphia College of Osteopathic Medicine. Pediatrics.

SOUTH UNIVERSITY

Savannah Campus
Anesthesiologist Assistant Program

Program of Study

South University, Savannah and the Mercer University School of Medicine based in Macon, and Savannah, Georgia, have developed a relationship to bring together the unique resources of each institution to establish an Anesthesiologist Assistant program of the highest quality. The Master of Medical Science (M.M.Sc.) in Anesthesia Science program is designed to provide classroom, laboratory, and clinical experiences that prepare competent, entry-level Anesthesiologist Assistants to provide safe and efficacious anesthesia care, under the direction of a qualified physician of anesthesiology, to patients of all ages and degrees of illness for a complete range of surgical procedures. The degree program consists of 160 quarter hours of classroom, laboratory, and clinical work taking place over the course of nine quarters or 28 months. The first year of the program is in the classroom and laboratory with escalating clinical responsibilities, while the second year of the program involves multiple, full-time, month-long clinical rotations in practice settings incorporating a full range of surgical procedures from infants through geriatrics.

The Anesthesiologist Assistant program at South University strives to enhance the overall knowledge and practice of the anesthesia care team by providing students with proficiencies in physiology, pharmacology, patient monitoring, anesthesia equipment, and the principles of safe anesthesia care.

Research Facilities

Facilities for the anesthesiologist assistant program include a sophisticated mock operating room with SimMan, a lifelike simulator that provides students with the opportunity to practice real-world scenarios before stepping into a hospital. A unique, fully equipped, anesthesia-learning laboratory was built specifically for the program and features industry-standard technology and equipment.

The University recently opened a new on-campus library, more than doubling its previous library space. The new facility features comfortable study space for students, wireless Internet capabilities for laptop network connectivity, separate computer labs, and reference and interlibrary loan services.

The open-stack book collection includes access to reference, reserve, and circulating materials, along with tutorial aides and program-specific resources for class assignments. An extensive periodical collection also supports the curricula by way of authoritative journals in both print and electronic formats. Similarly, the adjoining research center, which is furnished with multiple computer workstations, offers students access to the Internet, online database services such as the MEDLINE office suite, tutorials, and class-support software.

Financial Aid

A range of financial aid options is available to students who qualify. The Savannah campus of South University offers access to federal and state programs, including grants, loans, and work-study programs. Eligible students may apply for veterans' educational benefits and are encouraged to investigate the availability of grants and scholarships through community resources. As a first step, students should complete the Free Application for Federal Student Aid (FAFSA). Students may apply electronically at http://www.fafsa.ed.gov or through the program.

Cost of Study

Tuition information for the Anesthesiologist Assistant program may be obtained by contacting the Anesthesiologist Assistant program via the South University website at http://www.southuniversity.edu/anesthesiologistassistant.

Living and Housing Costs

South University offers school-sponsored student housing at its Savannah, Georgia, campus in conjunction with a local apartment complex. Due to the full-time nature of the program, Anesthesiologist Assistant program students typically live in rental homes, town homes, or apartments in the Savannah area. More information may be obtained by contacting the Director of Student Housing at 912-201-8000.

Student Group

The Savannah campus of South University has a diverse student body enrolled in both day and evening classes.

Location

Located on the south side of the historic city of Savannah, the campus is situated on 9 acres of land. It is convenient to the city's bustling midtown section and a full range of educational and cultural activities. The Atlantic Ocean and recreational amenities of Tybee Island, including beaches and numerous outdoor activities, are just minutes away. In addition, the campus is located just a short drive from Hilton Head Island and Charleston, South Carolina.

The University

The Anesthesiologist Assistant program is accredited by the Commission for Accreditation of Allied Health Education Programs upon the recommendation of the Accreditation Review Committee for the Anesthesiologist Assistant (ARC-AA) (CAAHEP; 1361 Park Street, Clearwater, Florida 33756; phone: 727-210-2350). South University is accredited by the Southern Association of Colleges and Schools Commission on Colleges to award associate, baccalaureate, masters, and doctorate degrees. Contact the Commission on Colleges at 1866 Southern Lane, Decatur, Georgia 30033-4097 or call 404-679-4500 for questions about the accreditation of South University.

Applying

Students are accepted into South University's Anesthesiologist Assistant program once each year in June. Entrance into the

South University

Anesthesiologist Assistant program is gained through a formal application review and assessment of the applicant's potential for professional and academic achievement. Applicants to the program must be familiar with the practice of anesthesia, including related activities in the operating room. Those with no current familiarity must spend at least 8 hours with an anesthetist or an anesthesiologist in an operating room observing the conduct of anesthetics. Applicants must also have a bachelor's degree from a regionally accredited university, including above-average performance in courses required in a premed curriculum. The admissions process requires official transcripts from all colleges and universities attended, scores from the Graduate Record Examinations (GRE) or the Medical College Admission Test (MCAT) that are not more than five years old, three letters of recommendation, and a summary of an article published in a current anesthesia journal. For the GRE, the program must receive official score reports directly from the Educational Testing Service. The code for South University is 5157. Additional admission and application information may be found by visiting the University website: (http://www.southuniversity.edu).

Correspondence and Information

Applications for admission to the South University Anesthesiologist Assistant program are available by contacting:

Anesthesiologist Assistant Program
South University
709 Mall Boulevard
Savannah, Georgia 31406-4805
United States
Phone: 912-201-8080
Fax: 912-201-8070
E-mail: aaprograminfo@southuniversity.edu
Website: http://www.southuniversity.edu

See suprograms.info for program duration; tuition, fees, and other costs; median debt; federal salary data; alumni success; and other important information. http://www.southuniversity.edu/programs-info/form/

THE FACULTY

One of the most outstanding aspects of South University's Anesthesiologist Assistant program is the dedication of the faculty members and their ability to cultivate a supportive learning environment. Faculty members are committed to their roles as mentors, teachers, and co-learners. They are also dedicated to the training of students who can assume positions of leadership within the field of anesthesiology. A current list of program faculty members is available at the South University website (http://www.southuniversity.edu).

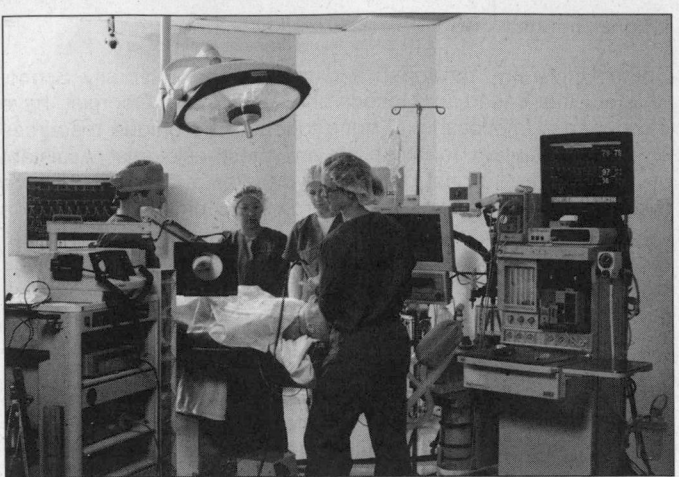

One of the main features of South University's Anesthesiologist Assistant program is its mock operating room. Modeled after actual operating rooms, the room is complete with current anesthesia equipment and SimMan, a model patient that is used to simulate real-life scenarios.

SOUTH UNIVERSITY

Savannah Campus
College of Health Professions
Physician Assistant Studies Program

Program of Study

The Master of Science in Physician Assistant Studies (M.S.P.A.S.) degree program at South University is an intensive curriculum structured around full-time course work. The Physician Assistant courses at South University, Savannah offer fundamental medical concepts and theories while also providing students with the knowledge, skills, and attitudes necessary to function, with physician supervision, as medical professionals who will serve as valued members of the healthcare team. Physician Assistants perform medical functions that include, but are not limited to, evaluation, monitoring, diagnostics, therapeutics, counseling, and referral. The scope of the practice varies according to state laws, the medical setting, and the training of the physician assistant. Students in the Physician Assistant program at South University will have the opportunity to benefit from classes designed to prepare them to perform to their expected competencies in an ethical, legal, safe, and effective manner upon graduation. South University Physician Assistant graduates are eligible to pursue licensure in all 50 states across the United States once they have passed the national Physician Assistant National Certifying Exam (PANCE). Once certified, graduates have the opportunity to pursue a medical career in family practice or a specialized area.

Research Facilities

The Physician Assistant (PA) Studies Program is housed in the School of Health Professions building at South University's campus in historic Savannah, Georgia. The campus features dedicated PA classrooms and lab facilities. The University recently opened a new on-campus library, more than doubling its previous library space. The new facility features comfortable study space for students, wireless Internet capabilities for laptop network connectivity, separate computer labs, and reference and interlibrary loan services.

Financial Aid

A range of financial aid options is available to students who qualify. The Savannah campus of South University offers access to federal and state programs, including grants, loans, and work-study programs. Eligible students may apply for veterans' educational benefits and are encouraged to investigate the availability of grants and scholarships through community resources. As a first step, students should complete the Free Application for Federal Student Aid (FAFSA). Students may apply electronically at http://www.fafsa.ed.gov or through the program.

Cost of Study

Tuition information for the Physician Assistant Studies Program may be obtained by contacting Physician Assistant Studies Program Admissions at South University's Savannah campus.

Living and Housing Costs

South University offers school-sponsored student housing at its Savannah, Georgia, campus in conjunction with a local apartment complex. Due to the full-time nature of the program, PA students typically live in rental homes or apartments in the Savannah area. More information may be obtained by contacting the Director of Student Housing at 912-201-8000.

Student Group

The Savannah campus of South University has a diverse student body enrolled in both day and evening classes. Students are primarily commuters who live within 50 miles of the city.

Location

Located on the south side of the historic city of Savannah, the campus is situated on 9 acres of land. It is convenient to the city's bustling midtown section and a full range of educational and cultural activities. The Atlantic Ocean and recreational amenities of Tybee Island, including beaches and numerous outdoor activities, are just minutes away. In addition, the campus is located just a short drive from Hilton Head Island and Charleston, South Carolina.

The University

Accreditation for South University's Physician Assistant Studies Program has been granted by the Accreditation Review Commission on Education for the Physician Assistant, Inc. (ARC-PA), 1000 North Oak Avenue, Marshfield, Wisconsin 54449-5788; 715-389-3785. The program is also a member of the Association of Physician Assistants Programs, the national organization representing physician assistant education programs. South University is accredited by the Southern Association of Colleges and Schools Commission on Colleges to award associate, baccalaureate, masters, and doctorate degrees. Contact the Commission on Colleges at 1866 Southern Lane, Decatur, Georgia 30033-4097 or call 404-679-4500 for questions about the accreditation of South University.

Applying

Students are accepted into the Physician Assistant Studies (PA) program once each year in January. Entrance to the program is gained through a formal application review and on-campus interview and is highly competitive. Only those applications meeting the admission requirements will be considered for admission. Application to the program is made through the Central Application Service for Physician Assistants (CASPA). Submission of scores from the Graduate Record Examination (GRE) are required, and all applicants must have earned a bachelor's degree from an American, accredited university with an overall minimum cumulative GPA of 2.8 (on a 4.0 scale) and a recommended science prerequisite GPA of 3.0 (on a 4.0 scale). Additional information on the application process can

be obtained through the South University PA program website (http://www.southuniversity.edu) or by calling 912-201-8025.

Correspondence and Information

Applications for admission to the South University Master of Science in Physician Assistant Studies degree program are available by contacting:

Physician Assistant Studies Program
South University
709 Mall Boulevard
Savannah, Georgia 31406-4805
United States
Phone: 912-201-8025
      866-629-2901 (toll-free)
Fax: 912-790-4199
E-mail: paprogram@southuniversity.edu
Website: http://www.southuniversity.edu

See suprograms.info for program duration; tuition, fees, and other costs; median debt; federal salary data; alumni success; and other important information. http://www.southuniversity.edu/programs-info/form/

THE FACULTY

One of the most outstanding aspects of South University's Physician Assistant Studies Program is the dedication of the faculty members and their ability to cultivate a supportive learning environment. Faculty members are committed to their roles as mentors, teachers, and co-learners. They are also dedicated to the training of students who can assume positions of leadership within the medical field. A current list of program faculty members is available in the South University catalog, which is located on the South University website (http://www.southuniversity.edu).

South University PA students celebrate the completion of their first year of study and the beginning of clinical rotations.

Section 21
Health Sciences

This section contains a directory of institutions offering graduate work in health sciences. Additional information about programs listed in the directory but not augmented by an in-depth entry may be obtained by writing directly to the dean of a graduate school or chair of a department at the address given in the directory.

For programs offering related work, see also in this book *Biological and Biomedical Sciences, Biophysics (Radiation Biology), Dentistry and Dental Sciences, Health Services, Medicine, Nursing,* and *Public Health.* In the other guides in this series:

Graduate Programs in the Physical Sciences, Mathematics, Agricultural Sciences, the Environment & Natural Resources
See *Physics*

Graduate Programs in Engineering & Applied Sciences
See *Agricultural Engineering and Bioengineering (Bioengineering), Biomedical Engineering and Biotechnology,* and *Energy and Power Engineering (Nuclear Engineering)*

CONTENTS

Program Directories

Health Physics/Radiological Health

Bloomsburg University of Pennsylvania, School of Graduate Studies, College of Science and Technology, Department of Biological and Allied Health Sciences, Radiologist Assistant Program, Bloomsburg, PA 17815-1301. Offers MS. *Entrance requirements:* For master's, ARRT certificate and Regis in radiography receptor agreement, curriculum vitae, 3 letters of recommendation. Additional exam requirements/recommendations for international students: Required—TOEFL (minimum score 550 paper-based; 213 computer-based; 79 iBT).

East Carolina University, Graduate School, Thomas Harriot College of Arts and Sciences, Department of Physics, Greenville, NC 27858-4353. Offers applied physics (MS); biomedical physics (PhD); health physics (MS); medical physics (MS). Part-time programs available. *Degree requirements:* For master's, one foreign language, comprehensive exam. *Entrance requirements:* For master's, GRE General Test. Additional exam requirements/recommendations for international students: Required—TOEFL. *Application deadline:* Applications are processed on a rolling basis. Application fee: $50. *Expenses:* Tuition, state resident: full-time $3557; part-time $444.63 per semester hour. Tuition, nonresident: full-time $14,351; part-time $1793.88 per semester hour. *Required fees:* $2016; $252 per semester hour. Part-time tuition and fees vary according to course load, campus/location and program. *Financial support:* Research assistantships with partial tuition reimbursements, teaching assistantships with partial tuition reimbursements, and Federal Work-Study available. Support available to part-time students. Financial award application deadline: 6/1. *Unit head:* Dr. John Sutherland, Chair, 252-328-2023, E-mail: sutherlandj@ecu.edu. *Application contact:* Dean of Graduate School, 252-328-6012, Fax: 252-328-6071, E-mail: gradschool@ecu.edu. Web site: http://www.ecu.edu/cs-cas/physics/Graduate-Program.cfm#.

Georgetown University, Graduate School of Arts and Sciences, Programs in Biomedical Sciences, Department of Health Physics, Washington, DC 20057. Offers health physics (MS); radiobiology (MS). *Degree requirements:* For master's, thesis. *Entrance requirements:* Additional exam requirements/recommendations for international students: Required—TOEFL.

Georgia Institute of Technology, Graduate Studies and Research, College of Engineering, George W. Woodruff School of Mechanical Engineering, Nuclear and Radiological Engineering and Medical Physics Programs, Atlanta, GA 30332-0001. Offers medical physics (MS); nuclear and radiological engineering (MSNE, PhD). Part-time programs available. Postbaccalaureate distance learning degree programs offered (no on-campus study). Terminal master's awarded for partial completion of doctoral program. *Degree requirements:* For master's, thesis optional; for doctorate, comprehensive exam, thesis/dissertation. *Entrance requirements:* For master's and doctorate, GRE General Test, minimum GPA of 3.0. Additional exam requirements/recommendations for international students: Required—TOEFL (minimum score 580 paper-based; 240 computer-based). *Faculty research:* Reactor physics, nuclear materials, plasma physics, radiation detection, radiological assessment.

Idaho State University, Office of Graduate Studies, College of Science and Engineering, Department of Physics, Pocatello, ID 83209-8106. Offers applied physics (PhD); health physics (MS); physics (MNS). Part-time programs available. *Degree requirements:* For master's, comprehensive exam, thesis (for some programs), oral exam (for some programs); for doctorate, comprehensive exam, thesis/dissertation (for some programs), oral exam, written qualifying exam in physics or health physics after 1st year. *Entrance requirements:* For master's, GRE General Test, 3 letters of recommendation, BS or BA in physics, teaching certificate (MNS); for doctorate, GRE General Test (minimum 50th percentile), 3 letters of recommendation, statement of career goals. Additional exam requirements/recommendations for international students: Required—TOEFL (minimum score 550 paper-based; 213 computer-based; 80 iBT). Electronic applications accepted. *Faculty research:* Ion beam applications, low-energy nuclear physics, relativity and cosmology, observational astronomy.

Illinois Institute of Technology, Graduate College, College of Science and Letters, Department of Biological, Chemical and Physical Sciences, Physics Division, Chicago, IL 60616. Offers health physics (MHP); physics (MS, PhD). Part-time and evening/weekend programs available. Postbaccalaureate distance learning degree programs offered (minimal on-campus study). Terminal master's awarded for partial completion of doctoral program. *Degree requirements:* For master's, comprehensive exam (for some programs), thesis (for some programs); for doctorate, comprehensive exam, thesis/dissertation. *Entrance requirements:* For master's, GRE General Test (minimum score 1000 Quantitative and Verbal, 2.5 Analytical Writing), minimum undergraduate GPA of 3.0; for doctorate, GRE General Test (minimum score 1100 Quantitative and Verbal, 3.0 Analytical Writing), minimum undergraduate GPA of 3.0. Additional exam requirements/recommendations for international students: Required—TOEFL (minimum score 523 paper-based; 213 computer-based; 70 iBT); Recommended—IELTS (minimum score 5.5). Electronic applications accepted. *Faculty research:* Experimental, condensed-matter physics; experimental elementary particle physics; membrane biophysics; synchroton radiation techniques; experimental high energy physics, especially symmetry violation and rare decays of hyperons and charm and beauty hadrons.

McMaster University, School of Graduate Studies, Faculty of Science, Department of Medical Physics and Applied Radiation Sciences, Hamilton, ON L8S 4M2, Canada. Offers health and radiation physics (M Sc); medical physics (M Sc, PhD). Part-time programs available. *Degree requirements:* For master's, thesis or alternative. *Entrance requirements:* For master's, minimum B+ average. Additional exam requirements/recommendations for international students: Required—TOEFL (minimum score 550 paper-based; 213 computer-based). *Faculty research:* Imaging, toxicology, dosimetry, body composition, medical lasers.

Midwestern State University, Graduate Studies, College of Health Sciences and Human Services, Program in Radiology, Wichita Falls, TX 76308. Offers radiologic administration (MSR); radiologic education (MSR); radiologic sciences (MSR); radiologist assistant (MSR). Part-time and evening/weekend programs available. Postbaccalaureate distance learning degree programs offered (minimal on-campus study). *Degree requirements:* For master's, comprehensive exam, thesis optional. *Entrance requirements:* For master's, GRE General Test, MAT or GMAT, credentials in one of the medical imaging modalities or radiation therapy; 1 year of experience; 3 letters of recommendation from past and/or present educators and employers. Additional exam requirements/recommendations for international students: Required—TOEFL (minimum score 550 paper-based; 213 computer-based). Electronic applications accepted. *Faculty research:* Bone densitometry, radiologic dose trends, teaching of radiologic science, radiographic positioning landmarks.

New York Chiropractic College, Program in Diagnostic Imaging, Seneca Falls, NY 13148-0800. Offers MS. *Degree requirements:* For master's, thesis. *Entrance requirements:* For master's, DC, minimum GPA of 3.0. *Faculty research:* Ultrasound, MRI and back pain, educational theory.

Northwestern State University of Louisiana, Graduate Studies and Research, College of Nursing and Allied Health, Department of Radiologic Sciences, Natchitoches, LA 71497. Offers MS. *Faculty:* 1 (woman) full-time. *Students:* 27 part-time (23 women); includes 3 minority (all Black or African American, non-Hispanic/Latino). Average age 30. 11 applicants, 100% accepted, 10 enrolled. In 2011, 2 master's awarded. *Degree requirements:* For master's, comprehensive exam, thesis (for some programs). *Entrance requirements:* Additional exam requirements/recommendations for international students: Required—TOEFL. *Application deadline:* For fall admission, 3/15 priority date for domestic students; for spring admission, 10/15 priority date for domestic students. Applications are processed on a rolling basis. Application fee: $20 ($30 for international students). Electronic applications accepted. *Expenses:* Tuition, state resident: full-time $3440. Tuition, nonresident: full-time $12,010. *Financial support:* Application deadline: 5/1; applicants required to submit FAFSA. *Unit head:* Laura Aaron, Department Head, 318-677-3072, E-mail: carwilel@nsula.edu. *Application contact:* Dr. Steven G. Horton, Associate Provost/Dean, Graduate Studies, Research, and Information Systems, 318-357-5851, Fax: 318-357-5019, E-mail: grad_school@nsula.edu. Web site: http://radiologicsciences.nsula.edu/.

Oregon State University, Graduate School, College of Engineering, Department of Nuclear Engineering and Radiation Health Physics, Corvallis, OR 97331. Offers nuclear engineering (M Eng, MS, PhD); radiation health physics (MA, MHP, MS, PhD). Part-time programs available. Terminal master's awarded for partial completion of doctoral program. *Degree requirements:* For master's, thesis; for doctorate, thesis/dissertation. *Entrance requirements:* For master's and doctorate, GRE General Test, minimum GPA of 3.0 in last 90 hours. Additional exam requirements/recommendations for international students: Required—TOEFL (minimum score 550 paper-based; 213 computer-based). *Faculty research:* Reactor thermal hydraulics and safety, applications of radiation and nuclear techniques, computational methods development, environmental transport of radioactive materials.

Purdue University, Graduate School, College of Health and Human Sciences, School of Health Sciences, West Lafayette, IN 47907. Offers health physics (MS, PhD); medical physics (MS, PhD); occupational and environmental health science (MS, PhD), including aerosol deposition and lung disease , ergonomics, exposure and risk assessment, indoor air quality and bioaerosols (PhD), liver/lung toxicology; occupational and environmental health science` (PhD), including indoor air quality and bioaerosols; radiation biology (PhD); toxicology (PhD); MS/PhD. Part-time programs available. *Faculty:* 10 full-time (3 women), 24 part-time/adjunct (3 women). *Students:* 24 full-time (9 women), 7 part-time (2 women); includes 2 minority (both Asian, non-Hispanic/Latino), 13 international. Average age 30. 49 applicants, 37% accepted, 7 enrolled. In 2011, 18 master's, 5 doctorates awarded. *Degree requirements:* For master's, thesis optional; for doctorate, one foreign language, thesis/dissertation. *Entrance requirements:* For master's and doctorate, GRE General Test, minimum undergraduate GPA of 3.0 or equivalent. Additional exam requirements/recommendations for international students: Required—TOEFL (minimum score 550 computer-based; 77 iBT); Recommended—TWE. *Application deadline:* For fall admission, 5/15 for domestic and international students; for spring admission, 10/15 for domestic and international students. Applications are processed on a rolling basis. Application fee: $60 ($75 for international students). Electronic applications accepted. *Financial support:* In 2011–12, fellowships with tuition reimbursements (averaging $14,400 per year), research assistantships with tuition reimbursements (averaging $12,000 per year), teaching assistantships with tuition reimbursements (averaging $12,000 per year) were awarded; career-related internships or fieldwork and traineeships also available. Support available to part-time students. Financial award applicants required to submit FAFSA. *Faculty research:* Environmental toxicology, industrial hygiene, radiation dosimetry. *Unit head:* Dr. Wei Zheng, Head, 765-494-1419, E-mail: wz18@purdue.edu. *Application contact:* Jennifer S. Franklin, Graduate Contact, 765-494-0248, E-mail: jfranklin@purdue.edu. Web site: http://www.healthsciences.purdue.edu/.

Quinnipiac University, School of Health Sciences, Program for Radiologist Assistant, Hamden, CT 06518-1940. Offers MHS. *Faculty:* 3 full-time (1 woman), 1 part-time/adjunct (0 women). *Students:* 5 full-time (2 women), 6 part-time (4 women); includes 5 minority (1 Black or African American, non-Hispanic/Latino; 2 Asian, non-Hispanic/Latino; 2 Hispanic/Latino). 10 applicants, 80% accepted, 6 enrolled. In 2011, 9 master's awarded. *Entrance requirements:* For master's, proof of certification from American Registry of Radiologic Technologists; 2000 hours of direct patient care; CPR certification. Additional exam requirements/recommendations for international students: Required—TOEFL (minimum score 575 paper-based; 233 computer-based; 90 iBT), IELTS (minimum score 6.5). *Application deadline:* For fall admission, 4/30 priority date for domestic students, 4/30 for international students. Applications are processed on a rolling basis. Application fee: $45. Electronic applications accepted. *Expenses: Tuition:* Part-time $855 per credit. *Required fees:* $35 per credit. *Financial support:* In 2011–12, 4 students received support. Career-related internships or fieldwork, tuition waivers (partial), and unspecified assistantships available. Financial award application deadline: 4/15; financial award applicants required to submit FAFSA. *Unit head:* Dr. Ramon Gonzalez, Director, 203-582-3765, Fax: 203-582-8706, E-mail: ramon.gonzalez@quinnipiac.edu. *Application contact:* Kristin Parent, Assistant Director of Graduate Health Sciences Admissions, 800-462-1944, Fax: 203-582-3443, E-mail: kristin.parent@quinnipiac.edu. Web site: http://www.quinnipiac.edu/gradradiologistasst.

San Diego State University, Graduate and Research Affairs, College of Sciences, Department of Physics, Program in Radiological Physics, San Diego, CA 92182. Offers MS. Part-time programs available. *Degree requirements:* For master's, thesis optional, oral or written exam. *Entrance requirements:* For master's, GRE General Test, GRE Subject Test (physics), 2 letters of recommendation. Additional exam requirements/recommendations for international students: Required—TOEFL. Electronic applications accepted. *Faculty research:* Computational radiological physics; medical physics.

Texas A&M University, Dwight Look College of Engineering, Department of Nuclear Engineering, College Station, TX 77843. Offers health physics (MS, PhD); nuclear engineering (M Eng, MS, PhD). *Faculty:* 17. *Students:* 110 full-time (20 women), 24 part-time (3 women); includes 18 minority (2 Black or African American, non-Hispanic/Latino; 5 Asian, non-Hispanic/Latino; 9 Hispanic/Latino; 2 Two or more races, non-Hispanic/Latino), 38 international. Average age 28. In 2011, 20 master's, 5 doctorates awarded. *Degree requirements:* For master's, thesis or alternative; for doctorate, thesis/dissertation, departmental qualifying exams. *Entrance requirements:* For master's and doctorate, GRE General Test, 3 letters of recommendation. Additional exam requirements/recommendations for international students: Required—TOEFL. *Application deadline:* For fall admission, 3/1 for domestic and international students; for spring admission, 8/1 for domestic and international students. Applications are processed on a rolling basis. Application fee: $50 ($75 for international students). Electronic applications accepted. *Expenses:* Tuition, state resident: full-time $5437; part-time $226.55 per credit hour. Tuition, nonresident: full-time $12,949; part-time

$539.55 per credit hour. *Required fees:* $2741. *Financial support:* Fellowships, research assistantships, career-related internships or fieldwork, scholarships/grants, and unspecified assistantships available. Financial award application deadline: 4/1; financial award applicants required to submit FAFSA. *Faculty research:* Accelerators, aerosols, computational transport, fission, fusion. *Total annual research expenditures:* $4.2 million. *Unit head:* Dr. Yassin A. Hassan, Head, 979-845-7090, E-mail: y-hassan@tamu.edu. *Application contact:* Graduate Coordinator, 979-845-7090, E-mail: nuclear@tamu.edu. Web site: http://nuclear.tamu.edu/.

Thomas Jefferson University, Jefferson School of Health Professions, Department of Radiologic Sciences, Philadelphia, PA 19107. Offers radiologic and imaging sciences (MS).

Université Laval, Faculty of Medicine, Post-Professional Programs in Medical Studies, Québec, QC G1K 7P4, Canada. Offers anatomy–pathology (DESS); anesthesiology (DESS); cardiology (DESS); care of older people (Diploma); clinical research (DESS); community health (DESS); dermatology (DESS); diagnostic radiology (DESS); emergency medicine (Diploma); family medicine (DESS); general surgery (DESS); geriatrics (DESS); hematology (DESS); internal medicine (DESS); maternal and fetal medicine (Diploma); medical biochemistry (DESS); medical microbiology and infectious diseases (DESS); medical oncology (DESS); nephrology (DESS); neurology (DESS); neurosurgery (DESS); obstetrics and gynecology (DESS); ophthalmology (DESS); orthopedic surgery (DESS); oto-rhino-laryngology (DESS); palliative medicine (Diploma); pediatrics (DESS); plastic surgery (DESS); psychiatry (DESS); pulmonary medicine (DESS); radiology–oncology (DESS); thoracic surgery (DESS); urology (DESS). *Degree requirements:* For other advanced degree, comprehensive exam. *Entrance requirements:* For degree, knowledge of French. Electronic applications accepted.

University of Alberta, Faculty of Medicine and Dentistry and Faculty of Graduate Studies and Research, Graduate Programs in Medicine, Department of Radiology and Diagnostic Imaging, Edmonton, AB T6G 2E1, Canada. Offers medical sciences (PhD); radiology and diagnostic imaging (M Sc). Terminal master's awarded for partial completion of doctoral program. *Degree requirements:* For master's, thesis; for doctorate, thesis/dissertation. *Entrance requirements:* For master's, minimum GPA of 6.5 on a 9.0 scale; for doctorate, M Sc. *Faculty research:* Spectroscopic attenuation correction, nuclear medicine technology, monoclonal antibody labeling, bone mineral analysis using ultrasound.

University of Cincinnati, Graduate School, College of Engineering and Applied Science, Department of Mechanical, Industrial and Nuclear Engineering, Program in Health Physics, Cincinnati, OH 45221. Offers MS. *Degree requirements:* For master's, thesis or alternative. *Entrance requirements:* For master's, GRE General Test. Additional exam requirements/recommendations for international students: Required—TOEFL (minimum score 575 paper-based; 233 computer-based). Electronic applications accepted.

University of Cincinnati, Graduate School, College of Medicine, Graduate Programs in Biomedical Sciences, Department of Radiological Sciences, Cincinnati, OH 45267. Offers medical physics (MS). Part-time programs available. *Degree requirements:* For master's, comprehensive exam, project. *Entrance requirements:* For master's, GRE General Test. Additional exam requirements/recommendations for international students: Required—TOEFL (minimum score 575 paper-based). Electronic applications accepted. *Faculty research:* Radiation oncology, radiologic imaging, dosimetry, radiation biology, radiation therapy.

University of Kentucky, Graduate School, College of Health Sciences, Program in Radiation Sciences, Lexington, KY 40506-0032. Offers health physics (MSHP); radiological medical physics (MSRMP). Offered in cooperation with Graduate Programs in Medicine. Part-time programs available. *Degree requirements:* For master's, comprehensive exam, thesis. *Entrance requirements:* For master's, GRE General Test, minimum undergraduate GPA of 2.75. Additional exam requirements/recommendations for international students: Required—TOEFL (minimum score 550 paper-based; 213 computer-based). Electronic applications accepted. *Faculty research:* Dosimetry, manpower studies, diagnostic imaging physics, shielding.

University of Massachusetts Lowell, College of Sciences, Department of Physics and Applied Physics, Program in Radiological Science and Protection, Lowell, MA 01854-2881. Offers MS. *Degree requirements:* For master's, one foreign language, thesis. *Entrance requirements:* For master's, GRE General Test, 3 letters of reference. Additional exam requirements/recommendations for international students: Required—TOEFL. Electronic applications accepted.

University of Medicine and Dentistry of New Jersey, School of Health Related Professions, Department of Medical Imaging Sciences, Newark, NJ 07107-1709. Offers radiologist assistant (MS). Part-time and evening/weekend programs available. *Faculty:* 1 (woman) full-time, 1 (woman) part-time/adjunct. *Students:* 9 part-time (3 women); includes 8 minority (3 Black or African American, non-Hispanic/Latino; 1 American Indian or Alaska Native, non-Hispanic/Latino; 3 Asian, non-Hispanic/Latino; 1 Hispanic/Latino). Average age 40. 11 applicants, 82% accepted, 7 enrolled. In 2011, 2 degrees awarded. *Entrance requirements:* For master's, BS with minimum GPA of 3.0, RT license, coursework in intro to pathopsychology, interview, all transcripts, personal statement, BCLS certification. Additional exam requirements/recommendations for international students: Required—TOEFL (minimum score 500 paper-based; 79 iBT). *Application deadline:* For fall admission, 5/1 for domestic students, 3/1 for international students. Applications are processed on a rolling basis. Application fee: $75. Electronic applications accepted. *Unit head:* Cynthia Silkowski, Chairperson, 973-972-8528. *Application contact:* Diane Hanrahan, Assistant Dean, 973-972-5336, Fax: 973-972-7463, E-mail: shrpadm@umdnj.edu.

University of Michigan, College of Engineering, Department of Nuclear Engineering and Radiological Sciences, Ann Arbor, MI 48109. Offers nuclear engineering (Nuc E); nuclear engineering and radiological sciences (MSE, PhD); nuclear science (MS, PhD). *Students:* 135 full-time (21 women). 145 applicants, 50% accepted, 39 enrolled. In 2011, 28 master's, 11 doctorates awarded. Terminal master's awarded for partial completion of doctoral program. *Degree requirements:* For master's, thesis optional; for doctorate, thesis/dissertation, oral defense of dissertation, preliminary exams. *Entrance requirements:* For master's and doctorate, GRE General Test. Additional exam requirements/recommendations for international students: Required—TOEFL (minimum score 560 paper-based; 220 computer-based). *Application deadline:* Applications are processed on a rolling basis. Application fee: $65 ($75 for international students). Electronic applications accepted. *Financial support:* Fellowships, research assistantships, teaching assistantships, career-related internships or fieldwork, institutionally sponsored loans, scholarships/grants, traineeships, health care benefits, and unspecified assistantships available. *Faculty research:* Radiation safety, environmental sciences, medical physics, fission systems and radiation transport, materials, plasmas and fusion, radiation measurements and imaging. *Unit head:* Dr. Ronald Gilgenbach, Chair, 734-936-0122, Fax: 734-763-4540, E-mail: rongilg@umich.edu. *Application contact:* Peggy Jo Gramer, Graduate Program Coordinator, 734-615-8810, Fax: 734-763-4540, E-mail: pjgramer@umich.edu. Web site: http://www.ners.engin.umich.edu/.

University of Missouri, Graduate School, Nuclear Science and Engineering Institute, Columbia, MO 65211. Offers nuclear power engineering (MS, PhD), including health physics (MS), medical physics (MS), nuclear power engineering (MS). *Faculty:* 5 full-time (0 women). *Students:* 58 full-time (11 women), 7 part-time (2 women); includes 8 minority (5 Asian, non-Hispanic/Latino; 3 Hispanic/Latino), 15 international. Average age 29. 44 applicants, 48% accepted, 8 enrolled. In 2011, 6 master's, 8 doctorates awarded. *Degree requirements:* For master's, research project; for doctorate, thesis/dissertation. *Entrance requirements:* For master's and doctorate, GRE General Test. Additional exam requirements/recommendations for international students: Required—TOEFL (minimum score 500 paper-based; 173 computer-based; 61 iBT). *Application deadline:* For fall admission, 3/15 priority date for domestic students. Application fee: $55 ($75 for international students). *Expenses:* Tuition, state resident: full-time $5881. Tuition, nonresident: full-time $15,183. *Required fees:* $952. Tuition and fees vary according to campus/location and program. *Financial support:* Fellowships, research assistantships, teaching assistantships, and institutionally sponsored loans available. *Unit head:* Dr. Wynn Volkert, Department Chair, E-mail: volkertw@missouri.edu. *Application contact:* Latricia Vaughn, 573-882-8201, E-mail: vaughnlj@missouri.edu. Web site: http://nsei.missouri.edu/.

University of Missouri, School of Health Professions, Program in Cardiopulmonary and Diagnostic Sciences, Columbia, MO 65211. Offers diagnostic medical ultrasound (MHS). *Faculty:* 12 full-time (9 women), 2 part-time/adjunct (1 woman). *Students:* 17 full-time (14 women); includes 3 minority (1 Hispanic/Latino; 2 Two or more races, non-Hispanic/Latino). Average age 28. 88 applicants, 18% accepted, 13 enrolled. In 2011, 7 degrees awarded. *Entrance requirements:* Additional exam requirements/recommendations for international students: Required—TOEFL (minimum score 500 paper-based; 173 computer-based; 61 iBT). *Application deadline:* For fall admission, 1/15 for domestic students; for winter admission, 10/15 for domestic students. Application fee: $55 ($75 for international students). *Expenses:* Tuition, state resident: full-time $5881. Tuition, nonresident: full-time $15,183. *Required fees:* $952. Tuition and fees vary according to campus/location and program. *Faculty research:* Auditory memory, infant vocalization and language development, children's semantic knowledge, swallowing disorders (dysphagia), laryngeal physiology, and clinical and professional voice issues, speech science, language-learning disabilities in school-age children, vocabulary development and measurement, childhood fluency disorders. *Unit head:* Dr. Glen Heggie, Department Chair, 573-884-7843, E-mail: heggieg@missouri.edu. *Application contact:* Kathy Hagen, 573-884-6262, E-mail: hagenk@missouri.edu. Web site: http://shp.missouri.edu/cpd/index.php.

University of Nevada, Las Vegas, Graduate College, School of Allied Health Sciences, Department of Health Physics, Las Vegas, NV 89154-3037. Offers MS. *Accreditation:* ABET. Part-time programs available. *Faculty:* 4 full-time (0 women), 4 part-time/adjunct (0 women). *Students:* 4 full-time (1 woman), 3 part-time (2 women); includes 3 minority (2 Asian, non-Hispanic/Latino; 1 Hispanic/Latino). Average age 24. 3 applicants, 100% accepted, 3 enrolled. In 2011, 2 master's awarded. *Degree requirements:* For master's, thesis optional, professional paper, oral exam. *Entrance requirements:* Additional exam requirements/recommendations for international students: Required—TOEFL (minimum score 550 paper-based; 213 computer-based; 80 iBT), IELTS (minimum score 7). *Application deadline:* For fall admission, 6/15 priority date for domestic students, 5/1 for international students; for spring admission, 11/15 priority date for domestic students, 10/1 for international students. Applications are processed on a rolling basis. Application fee: $60 ($95 for international students). Electronic applications accepted. *Financial support:* In 2011–12, 7 students received support, including 6 research assistantships with partial tuition reimbursements available (averaging $10,213 per year), 1 teaching assistantship with partial tuition reimbursement available (averaging $5,000 per year); institutionally sponsored loans, scholarships/grants, health care benefits, and unspecified assistantships also available. Financial award application deadline: 3/1. *Faculty research:* Nuclear forensics, medical physics, radioanalytical method development and application, radioactive waste management, biomedical optics. *Total annual research expenditures:* $469,358. *Unit head:* Dr. Steen Madsen, Chair/Associate Professor, 702-895-1805, Fax: 702-895-4819, E-mail: steen.madsen@unlv.edu. *Application contact:* Graduate College Admissions Evaluator, 702-895-3320, Fax: 702-895-4180, E-mail: gradcollege@unlv.edu. Web site: http://healthphysics.unlv.edu/.

University of Oklahoma Health Sciences Center, College of Medicine and Graduate College, Graduate Programs in Medicine, Department of Radiological Sciences, Oklahoma City, OK 73190. Offers medical radiation physics (MS, PhD), including diagnostic radiology, nuclear medicine, radiation therapy, ultrasound. Part-time programs available. Terminal master's awarded for partial completion of doctoral program. *Degree requirements:* For master's, thesis; for doctorate, thesis/dissertation. *Entrance requirements:* For master's, GRE General Test; for doctorate, GRE General Test, 3 letters of recommendation. Additional exam requirements/recommendations for international students: Required—TOEFL. *Faculty research:* Monte Carlo applications in radiation therapy, observer-performed studies in diagnostic radiology, error analysis in gated cardiac nuclear medicine studies, nuclear medicine absorbed fraction determinations.

University of Toronto, Faculty of Medicine, Institute of Medical Science, Toronto, ON M5S 1A1, Canada. Offers bioethics (MH Sc); biomedical communications (M Sc BMC); medical radiation science (MH Sc); medical science (M Sc, PhD). *Degree requirements:* For master's, thesis; for doctorate, thesis/dissertation, thesis defense. *Entrance requirements:* For master's, minimum GPA of 3.7 in 3 of 4 years (M Sc), interview; for doctorate, M Sc or equivalent, defended thesis, minimum A- average, interview. Additional exam requirements/recommendations for international students: Required—TOEFL (minimum score 600 paper-based; 93 iBT), TWE (minimum score 5). Electronic applications accepted.

Virginia Commonwealth University, Graduate School, School of Allied Health Professions, Doctoral Program in Health Related Sciences, Richmond, VA 23284-9005. Offers clinical laboratory sciences (PhD); gerontology (PhD); health administration (PhD); nurse anesthesia (PhD); occupational therapy (PhD); physical therapy (PhD); radiation sciences (PhD); rehabilitation leadership (PhD). *Faculty:* 2 full-time (1 woman). *Students:* 23 full-time (15 women), 34 part-time (23 women); includes 7 minority (4 Black or African American, non-Hispanic/Latino; 1 Asian, non-Hispanic/Latino; 1 Hispanic/Latino; 1 Two or more races, non-Hispanic/Latino), 2 international. 37 applicants, 38% accepted, 11 enrolled. In 2011, 11 doctorates awarded. *Entrance requirements:* For doctorate, GRE General Test or MAT, minimum GPA of 3.3 in master's degree. Additional exam requirements/recommendations for international students: Required—TOEFL (minimum score 600 paper-based; 250 computer-based; 100 iBT); Recommended—IELTS (minimum score 6.5). *Application deadline:* For fall admission, 3/15 for domestic students. Application fee: $50. Electronic applications accepted. *Expenses:* Tuition, state resident: full-time $9133; part-time $507 per credit. Tuition, nonresident: full-time $18,777; part-time $1043 per credit. *Required fees:* $77 per credit. Tuition and fees vary according to degree level, campus/location, program and student level. *Unit head:* Dr. Paula K. Kupstas, Director, Health Related Sciences Program, 804-828-7247, E-mail: pkupstas@vcu.edu. *Application contact:* Monica L. White, Director of Student Services, 804-828-3273, Fax: 804-828-8656, E-mail: mlwhite1@vcu.edu. Web site: http://www.pubapps.vcu.edu/BULLETINS/prog_search/?did=20005.

Wayne State University, Eugene Applebaum College of Pharmacy and Health Sciences, Department of Health Care Sciences, Program in Radiologist Assistant Studies, Detroit, MI 48202. Offers MS. *Students:* 1 (woman) part-time. 2 applicants, 0% accepted, 0 enrolled. *Entrance requirements:* For master's, bachelor's degree from accredited institution with minimum GPA of 3.0, graduation from radiologic technology program accredited by JRCERT, employment as radiologic technologist for at least 3 years, proof of American Registry of Radiologic Technologist registration, proof of Basic Life support certification, three letters of recommendation. Additional exam requirements/recommendations for international students: Required—TOEFL (minimum score 550 paper-based; 213 computer-based); Recommended—TWE (minimum score 5.5). *Application deadline:* For fall admission, 1/30 priority date for domestic students, 1/1 for international students. Application fee: $50. Electronic applications accepted. *Expenses:* Tuition, state resident: part-time $512.85 per credit. Tuition, nonresident: part-time $1132.65 per credit. *Required fees:* $26.60 per credit. $199.65 per semester. Tuition and fees vary according to course load and program. *Unit head:* Kathy Kath, Director, 313-916-1348, E-mail: kathykath@wayne.edu. *Application contact:* 313-577-1716, E-mail: cphsinfo@wayne.edu. Web site: http://www.cphs.wayne.edu/program/ra-ms.php.

Wayne State University, School of Medicine, Department of Radiology, Detroit, MI 48202. Offers medical physics (PhD); radiological physics (MS). Part-time and evening/weekend programs available. *Students:* 22 full-time (6 women), 10 part-time (0 women); includes 3 minority (all Asian, non-Hispanic/Latino), 7 international. Average age 28. 75 applicants, 40% accepted, 13 enrolled. In 2011, 8 master's, 2 doctorates awarded. *Degree requirements:* For master's, essay, exam; for doctorate, thesis/dissertation. *Entrance requirements:* For master's, GRE General Test, BS in physics or related area; for doctorate, GRE, BS in physics or related area. Additional exam requirements/recommendations for international students: Required—TOEFL (minimum score 600 paper-based; 250 computer-based; 100 iBT); Recommended—TWE (minimum score 6). *Application deadline:* For fall admission, 6/1 priority date for domestic students, 5/1 for international students; for winter admission, 10/1 priority date for domestic students, 9/1 for international students; for spring admission, 2/1 priority date for domestic students, 1/1 for international students. Applications are processed on a rolling basis. Application fee: $50. Electronic applications accepted. *Expenses:* Tuition, state resident: part-time $512.85 per credit. Tuition, nonresident: part-time $1132.65 per

credit. *Required fees:* $26.60 per credit. $199.65 per semester. Tuition and fees vary according to course load and program. *Financial support:* In 2011–12, 4 students received support. Fellowships with tuition reimbursements available, research assistantships with tuition reimbursements available, teaching assistantships with tuition reimbursements available, and career-related internships or fieldwork available. Support available to part-time students. Financial award application deadline: 2/1. *Faculty research:* Interventional radiology, magnetic resonance imaging, neuroimaging, pediatric imaging, emergency radiology. *Unit head:* Dr. Wilbur Smith, Chair, 313-745-3430, E-mail: wlsmith@med.wayne.edu. Web site: http://www.med.wayne.edu/diagRadiology/wsuhomepage.html.

Wayne State University, School of Medicine, Graduate Programs in Medicine, Department of Radiation Oncology, Detroit, MI 48202. Offers medical physics (PhD); radiological physics (MS). Part-time and evening/weekend programs available. In 2011, 1 doctorate awarded. Terminal master's awarded for partial completion of doctoral program. *Degree requirements:* For master's, thesis, essay, exit exam; for doctorate, thesis/dissertation, qualifying exam. *Entrance requirements:* For master's, GRE General Test, BS in physics or related area; for doctorate, GRE General Test, GRE Subject Test, BS in physics or related area. Additional exam requirements/recommendations for international students: Required—TOEFL (minimum score 550 paper-based; 213 computer-based); Recommended—TWE (minimum score 6). *Application deadline:* For fall admission, 1/15 for domestic students, 6/1 for international students; for winter admission, 10/1 for international students; for spring admission, 2/1 for international students. Applications are processed on a rolling basis. Application fee: $50. Electronic applications accepted. *Expenses:* Tuition, state resident: part-time $512.85 per credit. Tuition, nonresident: part-time $1132.65 per credit. *Required fees:* $26.60 per credit. $199.65 per semester. Tuition and fees vary according to course load and program. *Financial support:* In 2011–12, 1 research assistantship (averaging $20,787 per year) was awarded; fellowships, teaching assistantships, and career-related internships or fieldwork also available. Support available to part-time students. Financial award application deadline: 1/15. *Unit head:* Maria Vlachaki, Chair, 313-966-2774, Fax: 313-745-2314, E-mail: 661250@wayne.edu. *Application contact:* Michael Joiner, Professor, 313-745-2489, E-mail: joinerm@kci.wayne.edu. Web site: http://gradprograms.med.wayne.edu/program-spotlight.php?id=30.

Medical Imaging

Boston University, School of Medicine, Division of Graduate Medical Sciences, Program in Bioimaging, Boston, MA 02215. Offers MA. *Faculty:* 4 full-time (0 women). *Students:* 17 full-time (8 women), 5 part-time (4 women); includes 4 minority (3 Black or African American, non-Hispanic/Latino; 1 Asian, non-Hispanic/Latino), 5 international. Average age 28. 21 applicants, 76% accepted, 10 enrolled. In 2011, 7 master's awarded. *Degree requirements:* For master's, thesis. *Entrance requirements:* For master's, GRE. Additional exam requirements/recommendations for international students: Required—TOEFL. *Application deadline:* Applications are processed on a rolling basis. Application fee: $75. Electronic applications accepted. *Expenses: Tuition:* Full-time $40,848; part-time $1276 per credit hour. *Required fees:* $572; $286 per semester. *Financial support:* Applicants required to submit FAFSA. *Unit head:* Dr. Mark Moss, Chair, 617-638-4200, E-mail: markmoss@bu.edu. *Application contact:* Patricia Jones, Program Manager and Admissions Director, 617-414-2315, E-mail: psterlin@bu.edu. Web site: http://www.bumc.bu.edu/mbi/.

Cleveland State University, College of Graduate Studies, College of Sciences and Health Professions, Department of Physics, Cleveland, OH 44115. Offers applied optics (MS); condensed matter physics (MS); medical physics (MS); optics and materials (MS); optics and medical imaging (MS). Part-time and evening/weekend programs available. *Faculty:* 4 full-time (0 women), 1 part-time/adjunct (0 women). *Students:* 2 full-time (0 women), 12 part-time (3 women), 1 international. Average age 36. 29 applicants, 55% accepted, 7 enrolled. In 2011, 7 master's awarded. *Entrance requirements:* For master's, undergraduate degree in engineering, physics, chemistry or mathematics. Additional exam requirements/recommendations for international students: Required—TOEFL (minimum score 525 paper-based; 197 computer-based). *Application deadline:* For fall admission, 7/15 priority date for domestic students, 7/15 for international students. Applications are processed on a rolling basis. Application fee: $30. Electronic applications accepted. *Expenses:* Tuition, state resident: full-time $6416; part-time $494 per credit hour. Tuition, nonresident: full-time $12,074; part-time $929 per credit hour. *Financial support:* In 2011–12, 1 research assistantship with full and partial tuition reimbursement (averaging $5,666 per year) was awarded; fellowships with tuition reimbursements, teaching assistantships, and tuition waivers (full) also available. *Faculty research:* Statistical physics, experimental solid-state physics, theoretical optics, experimental biological physics (macromolecular crystallography), experimental optics. *Total annual research expenditures:* $350,000. *Unit head:* Dr. Miron Kaufman, Chairperson, 216-687-2436, Fax: 216-523-7268, E-mail: m.kaufman@csuohio.edu. *Application contact:* Dr. James A. Lock, Director, 216-687-2420, Fax: 216-523-7268, E-mail: j.lock@csuohio.edu. Web site: http://www.csuohio.edu/sciences/dept/physics/index.html.

Illinois Institute of Technology, Graduate College, Armour College of Engineering, Department of Electrical and Computer Engineering, Chicago, IL 60616-3793. Offers biomedical imaging and signals (MBMI); computer engineering (MS, PhD); electrical and computer engineering (MECE); electrical engineering (MS, PhD); electricity markets (MEM); network engineering (MNE); power engineering (MPE); telecommunications and software engineering (MTSE); VLSI and microelectronics (MVM). Part-time and evening/weekend programs available. Postbaccalaureate distance learning degree programs offered (minimal on-campus study). Terminal master's awarded for partial completion of doctoral program. *Degree requirements:* For master's, comprehensive exam (for some programs), thesis (for some programs); for doctorate, comprehensive exam, thesis/dissertation. *Entrance requirements:* For master's and doctorate, GRE General Test (minimum score 1100 Quantitative and Verbal, 3.5 Analytical Writing), minimum undergraduate GPA of 3.0. Additional exam requirements/recommendations for international students: Required—TOEFL (minimum score 523 paper-based; 70 iBT); Recommended—IELTS (minimum score 5.5). Electronic applications accepted. *Faculty research:* Communication systems, computer systems and micro-electronics, electromagnetics and electronics, power and control systems, signal and image processing.

Medical College of Wisconsin, Graduate School of Biomedical Sciences, Program in Functional Imaging, Milwaukee, WI 53226-0509. Offers PhD. *Entrance requirements:*

For doctorate, GRE, official transcripts, three letters of recommendation. Additional exam requirements/recommendations for international students: Required—TOEFL.

Medical University of South Carolina, College of Graduate Studies, Program in Molecular and Cellular Biology and Pathobiology, Charleston, SC 29425. Offers cancer biology (PhD); cardiovascular biology (PhD); cardiovascular imaging (PhD); cell regulation (PhD); craniofacial biology (PhD); genetics and development (PhD); marine biomedicine (PhD); DMD/PhD; MD/PhD. *Faculty:* 137 full-time (33 women). *Students:* 28 full-time (23 women); includes 5 minority (4 Black or African American, non-Hispanic/Latino; 1 Hispanic/Latino), 5 international. Average age 30. In 2011, 16 doctorates awarded. *Degree requirements:* For doctorate, thesis/dissertation, oral and written exams. *Entrance requirements:* For doctorate, GRE General Test, interview, minimum GPA of 3.0. Additional exam requirements/recommendations for international students: Required—TOEFL (minimum score 600 paper-based; 250 computer-based; 100 iBT). *Application deadline:* For fall admission, 1/15 priority date for domestic students, 1/15 for international students. Applications are processed on a rolling basis. Application fee: $0 ($85 for international students). Electronic applications accepted. *Financial support:* In 2011–12, 39 research assistantships with partial tuition reimbursements (averaging $23,000 per year) were awarded; Federal Work-Study and scholarships/grants also available. Support available to part-time students. Financial award application deadline: 3/10; financial award applicants required to submit FAFSA. *Unit head:* Dr. Donald R. Menick, Director, 843-876-5045, Fax: 843-792-6590, E-mail: menickd@musc.edu. *Application contact:* Dr. Cynthia F. Wright, Associate Dean for Admissions and Career Development, 843-792-2564, Fax: 843-792-6590, E-mail: wrightcf@musc.edu. Web site: http://www.musc.edu/mcbp/.

National University of Health Sciences, Lincoln College of Postprofessional, Graduate and Continuing Education, Lombard, IL 60148-4583. Offers advanced clinical practice (MS); diagnostic imaging (MS). Evening/weekend programs available. *Degree requirements:* For master's, comprehensive exam, thesis, capstone. *Entrance requirements:* Additional exam requirements/recommendations for international students: Required—TOEFL. Electronic applications accepted.

New York University, School of Medicine, New York, NY 10012-1019. Offers biomedical sciences (PhD), including biomedical imaging, cellular and molecular biology, computational biology, developmental genetics, medical and molecular parasitology, microbiology, molecular oncobiology and immunology, neuroscience and physiology, pathobiology, pharmacology, structural biology; clinical investigation (MS); medicine (MD); MD/MA; MD/MPA; MD/MS; MD/PhD. *Accreditation:* LCME/AMA (one or more programs are accredited). *Degree requirements:* For master's, comprehensive exam, thesis; for doctorate, comprehensive exam (for some programs), thesis/dissertation (for some programs). *Entrance requirements:* For doctorate, MCAT (for MD). Additional exam requirements/recommendations for international students: Required—TOEFL. *Expenses:* Contact institution. *Faculty research:* AIDS, cancer, neuroscience, molecular biology, neuroscience, cell biology and molecular genetics, structural biology, microbial pathogenesis and host defense, pharmacology, molecular oncology and immunology.

New York University, School of Medicine and Graduate School of Arts and Science, Sackler Institute of Graduate Biomedical Sciences, Program in Biomedical Imaging, New York, NY 10012-1019. Offers PhD. *Students:* 14 full-time (7 women); includes 5 minority (all Asian, non-Hispanic/Latino), 6 international. *Unit head:* Dr. Joel D. Oppenheim, Senior Associate Dean for Graduate Studies, 212-263-8001, Fax: 212-263-7600. *Application contact:* Lisabeth Greene, Program Coordinator, 212-263-5648, Fax: 212-263-7600, E-mail: sackler-info@med.nyu.edu.

Northwestern Health Sciences University, College of Graduate Health Sciences, Bloomington, MN 55431-1599. Offers clinical chiropractic orthopedics (MHS); clinical nutrition (MHS); diagnostic imaging (MHS).

University of Cincinnati, Graduate School, College of Engineering and Applied Science, Department of Biomedical Engineering, Cincinnati, OH 45221. Offers bioinformatics (PhD); biomechanics (PhD); medical imaging (PhD); tissue engineering (PhD). Part-time programs available. *Degree requirements:* For doctorate, one foreign

language, thesis/dissertation. *Entrance requirements:* For doctorate, GRE General Test. Additional exam requirements/recommendations for international students: Required—TOEFL (minimum score 600 paper-based; 250 computer-based).

University of Colorado Denver, College of Engineering and Applied Science, Department of Bioengineering, Aurora, CO 80045-2560. Offers bioengineering (PhD); clinical application (PhD); clinical imaging (MS); commercialization of medical technologies (MS, PhD); device design and entrepreneurship (MS); research (MS). Part-time programs available. *Faculty:* 3 full-time (1 woman). *Students:* 38 full-time (13 women), 1 part-time; includes 7 minority (3 Black or African American, non-Hispanic/Latino; 2 Asian, non-Hispanic/Latino; 1 Hispanic/Latino; 1 Two or more races, non-Hispanic/Latino), 2 international. Average age 27. 56 applicants, 48% accepted, 24 enrolled. Terminal master's awarded for partial completion of doctoral program. *Degree requirements:* For master's, thesis or alternative, 30 credit hours; for doctorate, comprehensive exam, thesis/dissertation, 36 credit hours of classwork (18 core, 18 elective), additional 30 hours of thesis work, three formal examinations, approval of dissertations. *Entrance requirements:* For master's and doctorate, GRE, transcripts, three letters of recommendation, resume, statement of purpose. Additional exam requirements/recommendations for international students: Required—TOEFL (minimum score 550 paper-based; 213 computer-based; 79 iBT), TOEFL (minimum score 600 paper-based; 250 computer-based; 100 iBT) for Ph D. *Application deadline:* For fall admission, 2/15 for domestic students. Application fee: $50. Electronic applications accepted. *Expenses:* Contact institution. *Financial support:* Fellowships, research assistantships, teaching assistantships, and Federal Work-Study available. Financial award application deadline: 4/1; financial award applicants required to submit FAFSA. *Faculty research:* Imaging and biophotonics, cardiovascular biomechanics and hemodynamics, orthopedic biomechanics, ophthalmology, neuroscience engineering, diabetes, surgery and urological sciences. *Unit head:* Dr. Robin Shandas, Chair, 303-724-4196, E-mail: robin.shandas@ucdenver.edu. *Application contact:* Graduate School Admissions, 303-556-2704, E-mail: admissions@ucdenver.edu. Web site: http://bioengineering.ucdenver.edu/.

University of Guelph, Ontario Veterinary College and Graduate Studies, Graduate Programs in Veterinary Sciences, Department of Clinical Studies, Guelph, ON N1G 2W1, Canada. Offers anesthesiology (M Sc, DV Sc); cardiology (DV Sc, Diploma); clinical studies (Diploma); dermatology (M Sc); diagnostic imaging (M Sc, DV Sc); emergency/critical care (M Sc, DV Sc, Diploma); medicine (M Sc, DV Sc); neurology (M Sc, DV Sc); ophthalmology (M Sc, DV Sc); surgery (M Sc, DV Sc). *Degree requirements:* For master's, thesis; for doctorate, comprehensive exam, thesis/dissertation. *Entrance requirements:* Additional exam requirements/recommendations for international students: Required—TOEFL (minimum score 550 paper-based; 213 computer-based), IELTS (minimum score 6.5). Electronic applications accepted. *Faculty research:* Orthopedics, respirology, oncology, exercise physiology, cardiology.

University of Medicine and Dentistry of New Jersey, School of Health Related Professions, Department of Medical Imaging Sciences, Newark, NJ 07107-1709. Offers radiologist assistant (MS). Part-time and evening/weekend programs available. *Faculty:* 1 (woman) full-time, 1 (woman) part-time/adjunct. *Students:* 9 part-time (3 women); includes 8 minority (3 Black or African American, non-Hispanic/Latino; 1 American Indian or Alaska Native, non-Hispanic/Latino; 3 Asian, non-Hispanic/Latino; 1 Hispanic/Latino). Average age 40. 11 applicants, 82% accepted, 7 enrolled. In 2011, 2 degrees awarded. *Entrance requirements:* For master's, BS with minimum GPA of 3.0, RT license, coursework in intro to pathopsychology, interview, all transcripts, personal statement, BCLS certification. Additional exam requirements/recommendations for international students: Required—TOEFL (minimum score 500 paper-based; 79 iBT). *Application deadline:* For fall admission, 5/1 for domestic students, 3/1 for international students. Applications are processed on a rolling basis. Application fee: $75. Electronic applications accepted. *Unit head:* Cynthia Silkowski, Chairperson, 973-972-8528. *Application contact:* Diane Hanrahan, Assistant Dean, 973-972-5336, Fax: 973-972-7463, E-mail: shrpadm@umdnj.edu.

University of Southern California, Graduate School, Viterbi School of Engineering, Department of Biomedical Engineering, Los Angeles, CA 90089. Offers biomedical engineering (PhD); medical device and diagnostic engineering (MS); medical imaging and imaging informatics (MS). Postbaccalaureate distance learning degree programs offered (minimal on-campus study). Terminal master's awarded for partial completion of doctoral program. *Degree requirements:* For master's, thesis optional; for doctorate, thesis/dissertation. *Entrance requirements:* For master's and doctorate, GRE General Test. Additional exam requirements/recommendations for international students: Recommended—TOEFL. Electronic applications accepted. *Faculty research:* Medical ultrasound, BioMEMS, neural prosthetics, computational bioengineering, bioengineering of vision, medical devices.

Medical Physics

Cleveland State University, College of Graduate Studies, College of Sciences and Health Professions, Department of Physics, Cleveland, OH 44115. Offers applied optics (MS); condensed matter physics (MS); medical physics (MS); optics and materials (MS); optics and medical imaging (MS). Part-time and evening/weekend programs available. *Faculty:* 4 full-time (0 women), 1 part-time/adjunct (0 women). *Students:* 2 full-time (0 women), 12 part-time (3 women), 1 international. Average age 36. 29 applicants, 55% accepted, 7 enrolled. In 2011, 7 master's awarded. *Entrance requirements:* For master's, undergraduate degree in engineering, physics, chemistry or mathematics. Additional exam requirements/recommendations for international students: Required—TOEFL (minimum score 525 paper-based; 197 computer-based). *Application deadline:* For fall admission, 7/15 priority date for domestic students, 7/15 for international students. Applications are processed on a rolling basis. Application fee: $30. Electronic applications accepted. *Expenses:* Tuition, state resident: full-time $6416; part-time $494 per credit hour. Tuition, nonresident: full-time $12,074; part-time $929 per credit hour. *Financial support:* In 2011–12, 1 research assistantship with full and partial tuition reimbursement (averaging $5,666 per year) was awarded; fellowships with tuition reimbursements, teaching assistantships, and tuition waivers (full) also available. *Faculty research:* Statistical physics, experimental solid-state physics, theoretical optics, experimental biological physics (macromolecular crystallography), experimental optics. *Total annual research expenditures:* $350,000. *Unit head:* Dr. Miron Kaufman, Chairperson, 216-687-2436, Fax: 216-523-7268, E-mail: m.kaufman@csuohio.edu. *Application contact:* Dr. James A. Lock, Director, 216-687-2420, Fax: 216-523-7268, E-mail: j.lock@csuohio.edu. Web site: http://www.csuohio.edu/sciences/dept/physics/index.html.

Columbia University, The Fu Foundation School of Engineering and Applied Science, Department of Applied Physics and Applied Mathematics, New York, NY 10027. Offers applied physics (Eng Sc D); applied physics and applied mathematics (MS, PhD, Engr); materials science and engineering (MS, Eng Sc D, PhD); medical physics (MS). Part-time programs available. Postbaccalaureate distance learning degree programs offered (no on-campus study). *Faculty:* 32 full-time (2 women), 23 part-time/adjunct (2 women). *Students:* 98 full-time (22 women), 38 part-time (10 women); includes 19 minority (14 Asian, non-Hispanic/Latino; 1 Hispanic/Latino; 4 Two or more races, non-Hispanic/Latino), 50 international. Average age 28. 371 applicants, 18% accepted, 41 enrolled. In 2011, 57 master's, 18 doctorates awarded. Terminal master's awarded for partial completion of doctoral program. *Degree requirements:* For master's, comprehensive exam; for doctorate, thesis/dissertation, qualifying exam. *Entrance requirements:* For master's, GRE General Test, GRE Subject Test (strongly recommended); for doctorate, GRE General Test, GRE Subject Test (applied physics); for Engr, GRE General Test. Additional exam requirements/recommendations for international students: Required—TOEFL, IELTS. *Application deadline:* For fall admission, 12/1 priority date for domestic students, 12/1 for international students; for spring admission, 10/1 priority date for domestic students, 10/1 for international students. Application fee: $95. Electronic applications accepted. *Financial support:* In 2011–12, 71 students received support, including 2 fellowships with full tuition reimbursements available (averaging $31,140 per year), 55 research assistantships with full tuition reimbursements available (averaging $31,133 per year), 16 teaching assistantships with full tuition reimbursements available (averaging $31,133 per year); health care benefits also available. Financial award application deadline: 12/1; financial award applicants required to submit FAFSA. *Faculty research:* Plasma physics and fusion energy; optical and laser physics; atmospheric, oceanic and earth physics; applied mathematics; solid state science and processing of materials, their properties, and their structure; medical physics. *Unit head:* Dr. Ismail C. Noyan, Professor and Department Chairman, 212-854-8919, E-mail: icn2@columbia.edu. *Application contact:* Montserrat Fernandez-Pinkley, Student Services Coordinator, 212-854-4457, Fax: 212-854-8257, E-mail: mf2157@columbia.edu. Web site: http://www.apam.columbia.edu/.

East Carolina University, Graduate School, Thomas Harriot College of Arts and Sciences, Department of Physics, Greenville, NC 27858-4353. Offers applied physics (MS); biomedical physics (PhD); health physics (MS); medical physics (MS). Part-time programs available. *Degree requirements:* For master's, one foreign language, comprehensive exam. *Entrance requirements:* For master's, GRE General Test. Additional exam requirements/recommendations for international students: Required—TOEFL. *Application deadline:* Applications are processed on a rolling basis. Application fee: $50. *Expenses:* Tuition, state resident: full-time $3557; part-time $444.63 per semester hour. Tuition, nonresident: full-time $14,351; part-time $1793.88 per semester hour. *Required fees:* $2016; $252 per semester hour. Part-time tuition and fees vary according to course load, campus/location and program. *Financial support:* Research assistantships with partial tuition reimbursements, teaching assistantships with partial tuition reimbursements, and Federal Work-Study available. Support available to part-time students. Financial award application deadline: 6/1. *Unit head:* Dr. John Sutherland, Chair, 252-328-2023, E-mail: sutherlandj@ecu.edu. *Application contact:* Dean of Graduate School, 252-328-6012, Fax: 252-328-6071, E-mail: gradschool@ecu.edu. Web site: http://www.ecu.edu/cs-cas/physics/Graduate-Program.cfm#.

Georgia Institute of Technology, Graduate Studies and Research, College of Engineering, George W. Woodruff School of Mechanical Engineering, Nuclear and Radiological Engineering and Medical Physics Programs, Atlanta, GA 30332-0001. Offers medical physics (MS); nuclear and radiological engineering (MSNE, PhD). Part-time programs available. Postbaccalaureate distance learning degree programs offered (no on-campus study). Terminal master's awarded for partial completion of doctoral program. *Degree requirements:* For master's, thesis optional; for doctorate, comprehensive exam, thesis/dissertation. *Entrance requirements:* For master's and doctorate, GRE General Test, minimum GPA of 3.0. Additional exam requirements/recommendations for international students: Required—TOEFL (minimum score 580 paper-based; 240 computer-based). *Faculty research:* Reactor physics, nuclear materials, plasma physics, radiation detection, radiological assessment.

Hampton University, Graduate College, Department of Physics, Hampton, VA 23668. Offers atmospheric physics (MS, PhD); medical physics (MS, PhD); nuclear physics (MS, PhD); optical physics (MS, PhD). Part-time and evening/weekend programs available. Terminal master's awarded for partial completion of doctoral program. *Degree requirements:* For master's, thesis optional; for doctorate, thesis/dissertation, oral defense, qualifying exam. *Entrance requirements:* For master's, GRE General Test; for doctorate, GRE General Test, minimum GPA of 3.0 or master's degree in physics or related field. *Faculty research:* Laser optics, remote sensing.

Harvard University, Graduate School of Arts and Sciences, Department of Physics, Cambridge, MA 02138. Offers experimental physics (PhD); medical engineering/medical physics (PhD), including applied physics, engineering sciences, physics; theoretical physics (PhD). *Degree requirements:* For doctorate, thesis/dissertation, final exams, laboratory experience. *Entrance requirements:* For doctorate, GRE General Test, GRE Subject Test. Additional exam requirements/recommendations for international students: Required—TOEFL. *Expenses:* Tuition: Full-time $36,304. *Required fees:* $1186. Full-time tuition and fees vary according to program. *Faculty research:* Particle physics, condensed matter physics, atomic physics.

Harvard University, Harvard Medical School and Graduate School of Arts and Sciences, Division of Health Sciences and Technology and Department of Physics and School of Engineering and Applied Sciences, Program in Medical Engineering/Medical Physics, Cambridge, MA 02138. Offers medical engineering (PhD); medical engineering/medical physics (Sc D); medical physics (PhD). Programs offered jointly with Massachusetts Institute of Technology. *Students:* 112 full-time (38 women); includes 33 minority (2 Black or African American, non-Hispanic/Latino; 22 Asian, non-Hispanic/Latino; 6 Hispanic/Latino; 3 Two or more races, non-Hispanic/Latino), 38 international. Average age 26. 222 applicants, 13% accepted, 18 enrolled. In 2011, 14 doctorates awarded. *Degree requirements:* For doctorate, comprehensive exam, thesis/dissertation, oral and written qualifying exams. *Entrance requirements:* For doctorate, GRE, bachelor's degree in engineering or science. Additional exam requirements/recommendations for international students: Required—TOEFL; Recommended—IELTS. *Application deadline:* For fall admission, 12/15 for domestic and international students. Application fee: $75. Electronic applications accepted. *Expenses:* Contact institution. *Financial support:* In 2011–12, 94 students received support, including 70 fellowships with full and partial tuition reimbursements available (averaging $55,371 per

year), 45 research assistantships with full and partial tuition reimbursements available (averaging $43,229 per year), 9 teaching assistantships with full and partial tuition reimbursements available (averaging $5,603 per year); career-related internships or fieldwork, institutionally sponsored loans, traineeships, health care benefits, and unspecified assistantships also available. Financial award application deadline: 12/15; financial award applicants required to submit FAFSA. *Faculty research:* Regenerative biomedical technologies, biomedical imaging and optics, biophysics, systems physiology, bioinstrumentation, biomedical informatics/integrative genomics. *Unit head:* Director, 617-253 Ext. 4418. *Application contact:* Laurie Ward, Administrator, 617-253-3609, Fax: 617-253-6692, E-mail: laurie@mit.edu.

Indiana University Bloomington, University Graduate School, College of Arts and Sciences, Department of Physics, Bloomington, IN 47405-4201. Offers medical physics (MS); physics (MAT, MS, PhD). Part-time programs available. Postbaccalaureate distance learning degree programs offered (no on-campus study). *Faculty:* 36 full-time (5 women), 11 part-time/adjunct (0 women). *Students:* 88 full-time (19 women), 1 part-time (0 women); includes 7 minority (2 Asian, non-Hispanic/Latino; 5 Hispanic/Latino), 42 international. Average age 27. 197 applicants, 18% accepted, 8 enrolled. In 2011, 11 master's, 6 doctorates awarded. Terminal master's awarded for partial completion of doctoral program. *Degree requirements:* For master's, comprehensive exam (for some programs), thesis (for some programs), qualifying exam; for doctorate, comprehensive exam, thesis/dissertation, qualifying exam. *Entrance requirements:* For master's and doctorate, GRE General Test, GRE Subject Test (physics), minimum GPA of 3.0. Additional exam requirements/recommendations for international students: Required—TOEFL (minimum score 550 paper-based; 213 computer-based; 80 iBT). *Application deadline:* For fall admission, 1/15 priority date for domestic students, 12/1 for international students; for spring admission, 10/1 priority date for domestic students, 9/1 for international students. Applications are processed on a rolling basis. Application fee: $55 ($65 for international students). Electronic applications accepted. *Financial support:* In 2011–12, 1 fellowship with full and partial tuition reimbursement (averaging $18,000 per year), 48 research assistantships with partial tuition reimbursements (averaging $18,800 per year), 30 teaching assistantships with partial tuition reimbursements (averaging $15,530 per year) were awarded; health care benefits also available. *Faculty research:* Accelerator physics, astrophysics and cosmology, biophysics (biocomplexity, neural networks, visual systems, chemical signaling), condensed matter physics (neutron scattering, low-dim. highly correlated systems, complex fluids, quantum computing), particle physics (collider physics, hybrid mesons, lattice gauge, symmetries, collider phenomenology), neutrino physics, nuclear physics (proton and neutron physics, neutrinos, symmetries, nuclear astrophysics, QCD, hadron structure). *Total annual research expenditures:* $13.2 million. *Unit head:* Prof. Rick Van Kooten, Department Chair, 812-855-1247, Fax: 812-855-5533, E-mail: iubphys@indiana.edu. *Application contact:* June Dizer, Director of Academic Support, 812-856-7059, Fax: 812-855-5533, E-mail: gradphys@indiana.edu. Web site: http://physics.indiana.edu/.

Louisiana State University and Agricultural and Mechanical College, Graduate School, College of Science, Department of Physics and Astronomy, Baton Rouge, LA 70803. Offers astronomy (PhD); astrophysics (PhD); medical physics (MS); physics (MS, PhD). *Faculty:* 47 full-time (5 women), 2 part-time/adjunct (0 women). *Students:* 106 full-time (23 women), 1 part-time (0 women); includes 5 minority (3 Black or African American, non-Hispanic/Latino; 2 Hispanic/Latino), 48 international. Average age 27. 166 applicants, 14% accepted, 21 enrolled. In 2011, 5 master's, 11 doctorates awarded. Terminal master's awarded for partial completion of doctoral program. *Degree requirements:* For master's, thesis or alternative; for doctorate, thesis/dissertation. *Entrance requirements:* For master's and doctorate, GRE General Test, minimum GPA of 3.0. Additional exam requirements/recommendations for international students: Required—TOEFL (minimum score 550 paper-based; 213 computer-based; 79 iBT) or IELTS (minimum score 6.5). *Application deadline:* For fall admission, 1/25 priority date for domestic students, 5/15 for international students; for spring admission, 10/15 for international students. Applications are processed on a rolling basis. Application fee: $50 ($70 for international students). Electronic applications accepted. *Financial support:* In 2011–12, 107 students received support, including 8 fellowships with full tuition reimbursements available (averaging $19,566 per year), 57 research assistantships with full and partial tuition reimbursements available (averaging $22,634 per year), 39 teaching assistantships with full and partial tuition reimbursements available (averaging $19,774 per year); Federal Work-Study, institutionally sponsored loans, health care benefits, tuition waivers (full and partial), and unspecified assistantships also available. Financial award application deadline: 3/15; financial award applicants required to submit FAFSA. *Faculty research:* Experimentation and numerical relativity, condensed matter astrophysics, quantum computing, medical physics. *Total annual research expenditures:* $8.1 million. *Unit head:* Dr. Michael Cherry, Chair, 225-578-2262, Fax: 225-578-5855, E-mail: cherry@phys.lsu.edu. *Application contact:* Arnell Dangerfield, Administrative Coordinator, 225-578-1193, Fax: 225-578-5855, E-mail: adanger@lsu.edu. Web site: http://www.phys.lsu.edu/.

Massachusetts Institute of Technology, Harvard-MIT Division of Health Sciences and Technology, Medical Engineering/Medical Physics Program, Cambridge, MA 02139-4307. Offers medical engineering (PhD); medical engineering and medical physics (Sc D); medical physics (PhD). PhD and Sc D offered jointly with Harvard University. *Students:* 112 full-time (38 women); includes 33 minority (2 Black or African American, non-Hispanic/Latino; 22 Asian, non-Hispanic/Latino; 6 Hispanic/Latino; 3 Two or more races, non-Hispanic/Latino), 38 international. Average age 26. 222 applicants, 13% accepted, 18 enrolled. In 2011, 14 doctorates awarded. *Degree requirements:* For doctorate, comprehensive exam, thesis/dissertation, oral and written departmental qualifying exams. *Entrance requirements:* For doctorate, GRE, bachelor's degree in engineering or science. Additional exam requirements/recommendations for international students: Required—TOEFL; Recommended—IELTS. *Application deadline:* For fall admission, 12/15 for domestic and international students. Application fee: $75. Electronic applications accepted. *Expenses: Tuition:* Full-time $40,460; part-time $630 per credit hour. *Required fees:* $272. *Financial support:* In 2011–12, 94 students received support, including 70 fellowships with full and partial tuition reimbursements available (averaging $55,371 per year), 45 research assistantships with full and partial tuition reimbursements available (averaging $43,229 per year), 9 teaching assistantships with full and partial tuition reimbursements available (averaging $5,603 per year); career-related internships or fieldwork, institutionally sponsored loans, traineeships, health care benefits, and unspecified assistantships also available. Financial award application deadline: 12/15; financial award applicants required to submit FAFSA. *Faculty research:* Regenerative biomedical technologies, biomedical imaging and optics, biophysics, systems physiology, bioinstrumentation, biomedical informatics/integrative genomics. *Unit head:* Director. *Application contact:* Laurie Ward, Graduate Administrator, 617-253-3609, Fax: 617-253-6692, E-mail: laurie@mit.edu. Web site: http://hst.mit.edu/.

McGill University, Faculty of Graduate and Postdoctoral Studies, Faculty of Medicine, Medical Physics Unit, Montréal, QC H3A 2T5, Canada. Offers M Sc, PhD. *Entrance requirements:* Additional exam requirements/recommendations for international students: Required—TOEFL.

McMaster University, School of Graduate Studies, Faculty of Science, Department of Medical Physics and Applied Radiation Sciences, Hamilton, ON L8S 4M2, Canada. Offers health and radiation physics (M Sc); medical physics (M Sc, PhD). Part-time programs available. *Degree requirements:* For master's, thesis or alternative. *Entrance requirements:* For master's, minimum B+ average. Additional exam requirements/recommendations for international students: Required—TOEFL (minimum score 550 paper-based; 213 computer-based). *Faculty research:* Imaging, toxicology, dosimetry, body composition, medical lasers.

Oakland University, Graduate Study and Lifelong Learning, College of Arts and Sciences, Department of Physics, Rochester, MI 48309-4401. Offers medical physics (PhD); physics (MS). *Degree requirements:* For doctorate, thesis/dissertation. *Entrance requirements:* For master's, minimum GPA of 3.0 for unconditional admission; for doctorate, GRE Subject Test, GRE General Test, minimum GPA of 3.0 for unconditional admission. Additional exam requirements/recommendations for international students: Required—TOEFL (minimum score 550 paper-based; 213 computer-based). Electronic applications accepted. *Expenses:* Contact institution. *Faculty research:* Quantitative molecular imagings of articular cartilage, multifunctional ferrite-ferroelectric layered structures for microwave and millimeter wave devices, magnoelectric materials for antenna structures.

Purdue University, Graduate School, College of Health and Human Sciences, School of Health Sciences, West Lafayette, IN 47907. Offers health physics (MS, PhD); medical physics (MS, PhD); occupational and environmental health science (MS, PhD), including aerosol deposition and lung disease , ergonomics, exposure and risk assessment, indoor air quality and bioaerosols (PhD), liver/lung toxicology; occupational and environmental health science` (PhD), including indoor air quality and bioaerosols; radiation biology (PhD); toxicology (PhD); MS/PhD. Part-time programs available. *Faculty:* 10 full-time (3 women), 24 part-time/adjunct (3 women). *Students:* 24 full-time (9 women), 7 part-time (2 women); includes 2 minority (both Asian, non-Hispanic/Latino), 13 international. Average age 30. 49 applicants, 37% accepted, 7 enrolled. In 2011, 18 master's, 5 doctorates awarded. *Degree requirements:* For master's, thesis optional; for doctorate, one foreign language, thesis/dissertation. *Entrance requirements:* For master's and doctorate, GRE General Test, minimum undergraduate GPA of 3.0 or equivalent. Additional exam requirements/recommendations for international students: Required—TOEFL (minimum score 550 computer-based; 77 iBT); Recommended—TWE. *Application deadline:* For fall admission, 5/15 for domestic and international students; for spring admission, 10/15 for domestic and international students. Applications are processed on a rolling basis. Application fee: $60 ($75 for international students). Electronic applications accepted. *Financial support:* In 2011–12, fellowships with tuition reimbursements (averaging $14,400 per year), research assistantships with tuition reimbursements (averaging $12,000 per year), teaching assistantships with tuition reimbursements (averaging $12,000 per year) were awarded; career-related internships or fieldwork and traineeships also available. Support available to part-time students. Financial award applicants required to submit FAFSA. *Faculty research:* Environmental toxicology, industrial hygiene, radiation dosimetry. *Unit head:* Dr. Wei Zheng, Head, 765-494-1419, E-mail: wz18@purdue.edu. *Application contact:* Jennifer S. Franklin, Graduate Contact, 765-494-0248, E-mail: jfranklin@purdue.edu. Web site: http://www.healthsciences.purdue.edu/.

Rosalind Franklin University of Medicine and Science, College of Health Professions, Department of Medical Radiation Physics, North Chicago, IL 60064-3095. Offers MS. Terminal master's awarded for partial completion of doctoral program. *Entrance requirements:* For master's, GRE General Test. Additional exam requirements/recommendations for international students: Required—TOEFL. *Expenses:* Contact institution.

Rush University, Graduate College, Department of Medical Physics, Chicago, IL 60612-3832. Offers MS, PhD. Terminal master's awarded for partial completion of doctoral program. *Degree requirements:* For master's, thesis, qualifying exam; for doctorate, thesis/dissertation, preliminary and qualifying exams. *Entrance requirements:* For master's, GRE General Test, BS in physics or physical science; for doctorate, GRE General Test, GRE Subject Test. Additional exam requirements/recommendations for international students: Required—TOEFL. Electronic applications accepted. *Faculty research:* Radiation therapy treatment planning, dosimetry, diagnostic radiology and nuclear imaging.

Stony Brook University, State University of New York, Graduate School, College of Engineering and Applied Sciences, Department of Biomedical Engineering, Program in Medical Physics, Stony Brook, NY 11794. Offers MS, PhD.

University of Alberta, Faculty of Graduate Studies and Research, Department of Physics, Edmonton, AB T6G 2E1, Canada. Offers astrophysics (M Sc, PhD); condensed matter (M Sc, PhD); geophysics (M Sc, PhD); medical physics (M Sc, PhD); subatomic physics (M Sc, PhD). *Degree requirements:* For master's, thesis; for doctorate, thesis/dissertation. *Entrance requirements:* For master's and doctorate, minimum GPA of 7.0 on a 9.0 scale. Additional exam requirements/recommendations for international students: Required—TOEFL. *Faculty research:* Cosmology, astroparticle physics, high-intermediate energy, magnetism, superconductivity.

University of California, Los Angeles, David Geffen School of Medicine and Graduate Division, Graduate Programs in Medicine, Program in Biomedical Physics, Los Angeles, CA 90095. Offers MS, PhD. *Students:* 35 full-time (10 women); includes 11 minority (1 American Indian or Alaska Native, non-Hispanic/Latino; 5 Asian, non-Hispanic/Latino; 4 Hispanic/Latino; 1 Two or more races, non-Hispanic/Latino), 5 international. Average age 28. 91 applicants, 14% accepted, 6 enrolled. In 2011, 3 master's, 2 doctorates awarded. *Degree requirements:* For master's, comprehensive exam or thesis; for doctorate, thesis/dissertation, oral and written qualifying exams. *Entrance requirements:* For master's and doctorate, GRE General Test. Additional exam requirements/recommendations for international students: Required—TOEFL. Application fee: $70 ($90 for international students). Electronic applications accepted. *Financial support:* In 2011–12, 31 fellowships, 21 research assistantships, 22 teaching assistantships were awarded; Federal Work-Study, institutionally sponsored loans, scholarships/grants, and tuition waivers (full and partial) also available. Financial award application deadline: 3/1. *Unit head:* Dr. Michael McNitt-Gray, Chair, 310-794-8979, E-mail: mmcnittgray@mednet.ucla.edu. *Application contact:* Departmental Office, 310-825-7811, E-mail: biomedphysics@mednet.ucla.edu. Web site: http://www.bmp.ucla.edu/.

University of Central Arkansas, Graduate School, College of Health and Behavioral Sciences, Department of Health Sciences, Conway, AR 72035-0001. Offers health education (MS); health systems (MS). *Faculty:* 9 full-time (5 women), 1 part-time/adjunct (0 women). *Students:* 17 full-time (14 women), 17 part-time (12 women); includes 18 minority (17 Black or African American, non-Hispanic/Latino; 1 Asian, non-Hispanic/Latino), 1 international. Average age 29. 13 applicants, 92% accepted, 10 enrolled. In 2011, 9 master's awarded. *Degree requirements:* For master's, comprehensive exam, thesis optional. *Entrance requirements:* For master's, GRE General Test, minimum GPA of 2.7. Additional exam requirements/recommendations for international students: Required—TOEFL (minimum score 550 paper-based; 213 computer-based). *Application deadline:* For fall admission, 3/1 priority date for domestic students; for spring admission, 10/1 for domestic students. Applications are processed on a rolling basis.

Application fee: $25 ($50 for international students). *Expenses:* Tuition, state resident: full-time $4834; part-time $398.35 per credit hour. Tuition, nonresident: full-time $8686. *Financial support:* In 2011–12, 4 research assistantships (averaging $5,700 per year) were awarded; Federal Work-Study, scholarships/grants, tuition waivers (partial), and unspecified assistantships also available. Financial award application deadline: 2/15; financial award applicants required to submit FAFSA. *Unit head:* Dr. Emogene Fox, Chairperson, 501-450-5508, Fax: 501-450-5515, E-mail: emogenef@uca.edu. *Application contact:* Susan Wood, Administrative Specialist, 501-450-5063, Fax: 501-450-5678, E-mail: swood@uca.edu. Web site: http://www.uca.edu/divisions/academic/healthsci/.

University of Chicago, Division of Biological Sciences, Committee on Medical Physics, Chicago, IL 60637-1513. Offers PhD. *Degree requirements:* For doctorate, thesis/dissertation, ethics class, 2 teaching assistantships. *Entrance requirements:* For doctorate, GRE General Test, GRE Subject Test. Additional exam requirements/recommendations for international students: Required—TOEFL (minimum score 600 paper-based; 250 computer-based; 104 iBT), IELTS (minimum score 7). Electronic applications accepted.

University of Cincinnati, Graduate School, College of Medicine, Graduate Programs in Biomedical Sciences, Department of Radiological Sciences, Cincinnati, OH 45267. Offers medical physics (MS). Part-time programs available. *Degree requirements:* For master's, comprehensive exam, project. *Entrance requirements:* For master's, GRE General Test. Additional exam requirements/recommendations for international students: Required—TOEFL (minimum score 575 paper-based). Electronic applications accepted. *Faculty research:* Radiation oncology, radiologic imaging, dosimetry, radiation biology, radiation therapy.

University of Colorado Boulder, Graduate School, College of Arts and Sciences, Department of Physics, Boulder, CO 80309. Offers chemical physics (PhD); geophysics (PhD); liquid crystal science and technology (PhD); mathematical physics (PhD); medical physics (PhD); optical sciences and engineering (PhD); physics (MS, PhD). *Faculty:* 51 full-time (7 women). *Students:* 157 full-time (28 women), 66 part-time (11 women); includes 11 minority (6 Asian, non-Hispanic/Latino; 5 Hispanic/Latino), 75 international. Average age 26. 551 applicants, 25% accepted, 47 enrolled. In 2011, 29 master's, 28 doctorates awarded. Terminal master's awarded for partial completion of doctoral program. *Degree requirements:* For master's, comprehensive exam, thesis or alternative; for doctorate, comprehensive exam, thesis/dissertation. *Entrance requirements:* For master's and doctorate, GRE General Test, GRE Subject Test, minimum undergraduate GPA of 3.0. Additional exam requirements/recommendations for international students: Required—TOEFL. *Application deadline:* For fall admission, 1/15 priority date for domestic students, 1/15 for international students. Applications are processed on a rolling basis. Application fee: $50 ($60 for international students). Electronic applications accepted. *Financial support:* In 2011–12, 216 students received support, including 85 fellowships (averaging $9,233 per year), 131 research assistantships with full and partial tuition reimbursements available (averaging $24,425 per year), 31 teaching assistantships with full and partial tuition reimbursements available (averaging $20,162 per year); institutionally sponsored loans, scholarships/grants, health care benefits, and unspecified assistantships also available. Financial award application deadline: 1/15; financial award applicants required to submit FAFSA. *Faculty research:* Atomic and molecular physics, nuclear physics, condensed matter, elementary particle physics, laser or optical physics, plasma physics, geophysics, OSEP, astrophysics and chemical physics. *Total annual research expenditures:* $26.1 million. *Application contact:* E-mail: physics@colorado.edu. Web site: http://physics.colorado.edu/.

University of Kentucky, Graduate School, College of Health Sciences, Program in Radiation Sciences, Lexington, KY 40506-0032. Offers health physics (MSHP); radiological medical physics (MSRMP). Offered in cooperation with Graduate Programs in Medicine. Part-time programs available. *Degree requirements:* For master's, comprehensive exam, thesis. *Entrance requirements:* For master's, GRE General Test, minimum undergraduate GPA of 2.75. Additional exam requirements/recommendations for international students: Required—TOEFL (minimum score 550 paper-based; 213 computer-based). Electronic applications accepted. *Faculty research:* Dosimetry, manpower studies, diagnostic imaging physics, shielding.

University of Minnesota, Twin Cities Campus, Graduate School, Program in Biophysical Sciences and Medical Physics, Minneapolis, MN 55455-0213. Offers MS, PhD. Part-time programs available. *Degree requirements:* For master's, thesis optional, research paper, oral exam; for doctorate, thesis/dissertation, oral/written preliminary exam, oral final exam. *Faculty research:* Theoretical biophysics, radiological physics, cellular and molecular biophysics.

University of Missouri, Graduate School, Nuclear Science and Engineering Institute, Columbia, MO 65211. Offers nuclear power engineering (MS, PhD), including health physics (MS), medical physics (MS), nuclear power engineering (MS). *Faculty:* 5 full-time (0 women). *Students:* 58 full-time (11 women), 7 part-time (2 women); includes 8 minority (5 Asian, non-Hispanic/Latino; 3 Hispanic/Latino), 15 international. Average age 29. 44 applicants, 48% accepted, 8 enrolled. In 2011, 6 master's, 8 doctorates awarded. *Degree requirements:* For master's, research project; for doctorate, thesis/dissertation. *Entrance requirements:* For master's and doctorate, GRE General Test. Additional exam requirements/recommendations for international students: Required—TOEFL (minimum score 500 paper-based; 173 computer-based; 61 iBT). *Application deadline:* For fall admission, 3/15 priority date for domestic students. Application fee: $55 ($75 for international students). *Expenses:* Tuition, state resident: full-time $5881. Tuition, nonresident: full-time $15,183. *Required fees:* $952. Tuition and fees vary according to campus/location and program. *Financial support:* Fellowships, research assistantships, teaching assistantships, and institutionally sponsored loans available. *Unit head:* Dr. Wynn Volkert, Department Chair, E-mail: volkertw@missouri.edu. *Application contact:* Latricia Vaughn, 573-882-8201, E-mail: vaughnlj@missouri.edu. Web site: http://nsei.missouri.edu/.

University of Oklahoma Health Sciences Center, College of Medicine and Graduate College, Graduate Programs in Medicine, Department of Radiological Sciences, Oklahoma City, OK 73190. Offers medical radiation physics (MS, PhD), including diagnostic radiology, nuclear medicine, radiation therapy, ultrasound. Part-time programs available. Terminal master's awarded for partial completion of doctoral program. *Degree requirements:* For master's, thesis; for doctorate, thesis/dissertation. *Entrance requirements:* For master's, GRE General Test; for doctorate, GRE General Test, 3 letters of recommendation. Additional exam requirements/recommendations for international students: Required—TOEFL. *Faculty research:* Monte Carlo applications in radiation therapy, observer-performed studies in diagnostic radiology, error analysis in gated cardiac nuclear medicine studies, nuclear medicine absorbed fraction determinations.

University of Pennsylvania, School of Arts and Sciences, Graduate Group in Physics and Astronomy, Philadelphia, PA 19104. Offers medical physics (MS); physics (PhD). Part-time programs available. *Faculty:* 43 full-time (5 women), 17 part-time/adjunct (1 woman). *Students:* 101 full-time (23 women), 1 part-time (0 women); includes 12 minority (11 Asian, non-Hispanic/Latino; 1 Hispanic/Latino), 17 international. 401

applicants, 9% accepted, 11 enrolled. In 2011, 18 master's, 13 doctorates awarded. *Degree requirements:* For doctorate, thesis/dissertation, oral, preliminary, and final exams. *Entrance requirements:* For doctorate, GRE General Test, GRE Subject Test (recommended). Additional exam requirements/recommendations for international students: Required—TOEFL. *Application deadline:* For fall admission, 12/1 priority date for domestic students. Application fee: $70. Electronic applications accepted. *Expenses:* Tuition: Full-time $26,660; part-time $4944 per course. *Required fees:* $2318; $291 per course. Tuition and fees vary according to course load, degree level and program. *Financial support:* Fellowships, research assistantships, teaching assistantships, institutionally sponsored loans, scholarships/grants, traineeships, health care benefits, and unspecified assistantships available. Financial award application deadline: 12/15. *Faculty research:* Astrophysics, condensed matter experiment, condensed matter theory, particle experiment, particle theory. *Total annual research expenditures:* $7.3 million. *Unit head:* Larry Gladney, Department Chair, 215-898-8152, E-mail: gladney@sas.upenn.edu. *Application contact:* Millicent Minnick, Academic Coordinator, 215-898-3125, E-mail: admiss@physics.upenn.edu.

The University of Texas Health Science Center at Houston, Graduate School of Biomedical Sciences, Program in Medical Physics, Houston, TX 77225-0036. Offers MS, PhD, MD/PhD. *Degree requirements:* For master's, thesis; for doctorate, thesis/dissertation. *Entrance requirements:* For master's and doctorate, GRE General Test. Additional exam requirements/recommendations for international students: Required—TOEFL. Electronic applications accepted. *Faculty research:* Medical physics, radiation oncology physics, diagnostic imaging physics, medical nuclear physics, image-guided therapy.

The University of Texas Health Science Center at San Antonio, Graduate School of Biomedical Sciences, Radiological Sciences Graduate Program, San Antonio, TX 78229-3900. Offers MS, PhD. *Degree requirements:* For master's, thesis; for doctorate, comprehensive exam, thesis/dissertation. *Entrance requirements:* For master's and doctorate, GRE General Test. Additional exam requirements/recommendations for international students: Required—TOEFL (minimum score 550 paper-based; 220 computer-based; 68 iBT). Electronic applications accepted. *Faculty research:* Positron emission tomography, functional magnetic resonance imaging, transcranial magnetic stimulation, neuroinformatics through network analysis, statistical parametric imaging, stroke, retinal imaging, primate aging studies, cerebral blood flow and metabolism, attention deficit hyperactivity disorder, depression and schizophrenia, motor speech disorders, motor skills disorders, Parkinson's disease, post-traumatic stress disorders.

The University of Toledo, College of Graduate Studies, College of Medicine and Life Sciences, Program in Medical Physics, Toledo, OH 43606-3390. Offers MSBS. *Faculty:* 5. *Students:* 12 full-time (2 women), 4 part-time (1 woman), 2 international. Average age 26. 23 applicants, 43% accepted, 5 enrolled. In 2011, 2 master's awarded. *Degree requirements:* For master's, thesis. *Entrance requirements:* For master's, GRE, minimum undergraduate GPA of 3.0, three letters of recommendation, statement of purpose, transcripts from all prior institutions attended, resume. Additional exam requirements/recommendations for international students: Required—TOEFL (minimum score 550 paper-based; 213 computer-based; 80 iBT), IELTS (minimum score 6.5). *Application deadline:* For fall admission, 3/31 priority date for domestic students, 3/31 for international students. Applications are processed on a rolling basis. Application fee: $45 ($75 for international students). Electronic applications accepted. *Financial support:* In 2011–12, 2 research assistantships with full tuition reimbursements (averaging $10,000 per year) were awarded; Federal Work-Study, institutionally sponsored loans, scholarships/grants, tuition waivers (full), unspecified assistantships, and tuition scholarships also available. *Unit head:* Dr. E. Ishmael Parsai, Director, 419-383-4541, E-mail: e.parsai@utoledo.edu. *Application contact:* Dianne Adams, Department Secretary, 419-383-5109, E-mail: dianne.adams@utoledo.edu. Web site: http://www.utoledo.edu/med/grad/.

The University of Toledo, College of Graduate Studies, College of Natural Sciences and Mathematics, Department of Physics and Astronomy, Toledo, OH 43606-3390. Offers physics (MS, PhD), including astrophysics (PhD), materials science (PhD), medical physics (PhD). *Faculty:* 26. *Students:* 65 full-time (13 women), 3 part-time (0 women); includes 1 minority (Asian, non-Hispanic/Latino), 24 international. Average age 29. 94 applicants, 15% accepted, 13 enrolled. In 2011, 2 master's, 8 doctorates awarded. *Degree requirements:* For master's, thesis; for doctorate, thesis/dissertation, departmental qualifying exam. *Entrance requirements:* For master's and doctorate, GRE General Test, GRE Subject Test, minimum cumulative point-hour ratio of 2.7 for all previous academic work, three letters of recommendation, statement of purpose, transcripts from all prior institutions attended. Additional exam requirements/recommendations for international students: Required—TOEFL (minimum score 550 paper-based; 213 computer-based; 80 iBT), IELTS (minimum score 6.5). *Application deadline:* For fall admission, 1/15 priority date for domestic students, 1/15 for international students. Applications are processed on a rolling basis. Application fee: $45 ($75 for international students). Electronic applications accepted. *Financial support:* In 2011–12, 47 research assistantships with full and partial tuition reimbursements (averaging $17,484 per year), 22 teaching assistantships with full and partial tuition reimbursements (averaging $19,131 per year) were awarded; Federal Work-Study, institutionally sponsored loans, scholarships/grants, tuition waivers (full), and unspecified assistantships also available. Support available to part-time students. *Faculty research:* Atomic physics, solid-state physics, materials science, astrophysics. *Unit head:* Dr. Lawrence Anderson-Huang, Chair, 419-530-7257, E-mail: lawrence.anderson@utoledo.edu. *Application contact:* Graduate School Office, 419-530-4723, Fax: 419-537-4724, E-mail: grdsch@utnet.utoledo.edu. Web site: http://www.utoledo.edu/nsm/.

University of Utah, Graduate School, College of Science, Department of Physics and Astronomy, Program in Medical Physics, Salt Lake City, UT 84112-1107. Offers MS, PhD. Part-time programs available. *Students:* 10 applicants, 20% accepted, 0 enrolled. *Degree requirements:* For master's, comprehensive exam, project or thesis; for doctorate, comprehensive exam, thesis/dissertation. *Entrance requirements:* For master's, GRE General and Subject Tests, minimum undergraduate GPA of 3.0; for doctorate, GRE General and Subject Tests, minimum GPA of 3.0. Additional exam requirements/recommendations for international students: Required—TOEFL (minimum score 500 paper-based; 173 computer-based; 69 iBT). *Application deadline:* For fall admission, 2/1 for domestic and international students. Application fee: $55 ($65 for international students). *Financial support:* In 2011–12, 4 research assistantships with full tuition reimbursements (averaging $18,500 per year), 1 teaching assistantship with full tuition reimbursement (averaging $16,200 per year) were awarded; career-related internships or fieldwork, scholarships/grants, and health care benefits also available. *Faculty research:* Improving acquisition, reconstruction, and post-processing of dynamic MRI, with particular emphasis on cardiac applications; developing new technologies for positron emission tomography (PET) imaging; image reconstruction and processing algorithms; evaluation of image quality and testing of new PET tracers for image-guided personalized medicine. *Unit head:* Dr. Brian Saam, Program Director, 801-581-6958, Fax: 801-585-3169, E-mail: saam@physics.utah.edu. *Application contact:* Jackie Hadley, Information Contact, 801-581-6861, Fax: 801-581-4801, E-mail: jackie@physics.utah.edu.

Medical Physics

University of Victoria, Faculty of Graduate Studies, Faculty of Science, Department of Physics and Astronomy, Victoria, BC V8W 2Y2, Canada. Offers astronomy and astrophysics (M Sc, PhD); condensed matter physics (M Sc, PhD); experimental particle physics (M Sc, PhD); medical physics (M Sc, PhD); ocean physics (M Sc, PhD); theoretical physics (M Sc, PhD). *Degree requirements:* For master's, thesis; for doctorate, comprehensive exam, thesis/dissertation, candidacy exam. *Entrance requirements:* For master's and doctorate, GRE. Additional exam requirements/recommendations for international students: Required—TOEFL (minimum score 575 paper-based; 233 computer-based), IELTS (minimum score 7). Electronic applications accepted. *Faculty research:* Old stellar populations; observational cosmology and large scale structure; cp violation; atlas.

University of Wisconsin–Madison, School of Medicine and Public Health and Graduate School, Graduate Programs in Medicine, Department of Medical Physics, Madison, WI 53705-2275. Offers health physics (MS); medical physics (MS, PhD). Part-time programs available. *Faculty:* 31 full-time (2 women), 13 part-time/adjunct (1 woman). *Students:* 104 full-time (31 women); includes 19 minority (4 Black or African American, non-Hispanic/Latino; 3 American Indian or Alaska Native, non-Hispanic/Latino; 4 Asian, non-Hispanic/Latino; 7 Hispanic/Latino; 1 Two or more races, non-Hispanic/Latino), 25 international. Average age 26. 111 applicants, 34% accepted, 19 enrolled. In 2011, 17 master's, 13 doctorates awarded. Terminal master's awarded for partial completion of doctoral program. *Degree requirements:* For master's, comprehensive exam; for doctorate, comprehensive exam, thesis/dissertation. *Entrance requirements:* For master's and doctorate, GRE General Test, GRE Subject Test (physics), minimum GPA of 3.0. Additional exam requirements/recommendations for international students: Required—TOEFL. *Application deadline:* For fall admission, 12/1 priority date for domestic students, 11/15 for international students. Application fee: $54. Electronic applications accepted. *Expenses:* Tuition, state resident: full-time $10,296; part-time $643.51 per credit. Tuition, nonresident: full-time $24,054; part-time $1503.40 per credit. *Required fees:* $70.06 per credit. Tuition and fees vary according to course load, campus/location, program and reciprocity agreements. *Financial support:* In 2011–12, 104 students received support, including 11 fellowships with full tuition reimbursements available (averaging $24,480 per year), 86 research assistantships with full tuition reimbursements available (averaging $22,032 per year), 7 teaching assistantships with full tuition reimbursements available (averaging $22,748 per year); traineeships, health care benefits, and unspecified assistantships also available. Financial award application deadline: 11/15. *Faculty research:* Biomagnetism: imaging and physiology, medical imaging processing, radiation therapy and radiation physics. *Total annual research expenditures:* $5.5 million. *Unit head:* Dr. James A. Zagzebski, Chair, 608-262-2171, Fax: 608-262-2413, E-mail: jazagzeb@wisc.edu. *Application contact:* Debra A. Torgerson, Graduate Coordinator, 608-265-6504, Fax: 608-262-2413, E-mail: datorger@wisc.edu. Web site: http://www.medphysics.wisc.edu/.

Vanderbilt University, School of Medicine, Program in Medical Physics, Nashville, TN 37240-1001. Offers MS. Part-time programs available. *Degree requirements:* For master's, comprehensive exam, thesis optional. *Entrance requirements:* For master's, GRE General Test, physics major, physics minor or physics minor equivalent; minimum undergraduate GPA of 3.0. Additional exam requirements/recommendations for international students: Required—TOEFL (minimum score 600 paper-based). Electronic applications accepted. *Faculty research:* MRI imaging, PET imaging, nuclear medicine dosimetry, Monte Carlo dosimetry.

Virginia Commonwealth University, Graduate School, College of Humanities and Sciences, Department of Physics, Programs in Medical Physics, Richmond, VA 23284-9005. Offers MS, PhD. *Students:* 25 full-time (6 women), 4 part-time (2 women); includes 4 minority (2 Black or African American, non-Hispanic/Latino; 1 Asian, non-Hispanic/Latino; 1 Hispanic/Latino), 10 international. 76 applicants, 22% accepted, 5 enrolled. In 2011, 5 master's, 4 doctorates awarded. *Entrance requirements:* For master's and doctorate, GRE General Test. Additional exam requirements/recommendations for international students: Required—TOEFL (minimum score 600 paper-based; 250 computer-based; 100 iBT); Recommended—IELTS (minimum score 6.5). *Application deadline:* For fall admission, 3/1 for domestic students. Applications are processed on a rolling basis. Application fee: $50. Electronic applications accepted. *Expenses:* Tuition, state resident: full-time $9133; part-time $507 per credit. Tuition, nonresident: full-time $18,777; part-time $1043 per credit. *Required fees:* $77 per credit. Tuition and fees vary according to degree level, campus/location, program and student level. *Financial support:* Federal Work-Study and institutionally sponsored loans available. Support available to part-time students. *Faculty research:* Functional imaging using PET and NMR, CT image artifact removal and deformation, intensity-modulated radiation therapy, radiation therapy dose calculations, 4D radiation therapy, brachytherapy dose calculations. *Unit head:* Dr. Jeffrey V. Siebers, Director, Medical Physics Graduate Program, 804-628-0981, Fax: 804-628-4709, E-mail: jsiebers@vcu.edu. *Application contact:* Deanna Pace, Administrator, Medical Physics Graduate Program, 804-628-7780, Fax: 804-628-4709, E-mail: medphys@vcu.edu.

Wayne State University, School of Medicine, Department of Radiology, Detroit, MI 48202. Offers medical physics (MS); radiological physics (MS). Part-time and evening/weekend programs available. *Students:* 22 full-time (6 women), 10 part-time (0 women); includes 3 minority (all Asian, non-Hispanic/Latino), 7 international. Average age 28. 75 applicants, 40% accepted, 13 enrolled. In 2011, 8 master's, 2 doctorates awarded. *Degree requirements:* For master's, essay, exam; for doctorate, thesis/dissertation. *Entrance requirements:* For master's, GRE General Test, BS in physics or related area; for doctorate, GRE, BS in physics or related area. Additional exam requirements/recommendations for international students: Required—TOEFL (minimum score 600 paper-based; 250 computer-based; 100 iBT); Recommended—TWE (minimum score 6). *Application deadline:* For fall admission, 6/1 priority date for domestic students, 5/1 for international students; for winter admission, 10/1 priority date for domestic students, 9/1 for international students; for spring admission, 2/1 priority date for domestic students, 1/1 for international students. Applications are processed on a rolling basis. Application fee: $50. Electronic applications accepted. *Expenses:* Tuition, state resident: part-time $512.85 per credit. Tuition, nonresident: part-time $1132.65 per credit. *Required fees:* $26.60 per credit. $199.65 per semester. Tuition and fees vary according to course load and program. *Financial support:* In 2011–12, 4 students received support. Fellowships with tuition reimbursements available, research assistantships with tuition reimbursements available, teaching assistantships with tuition reimbursements available, and career-related internships or fieldwork available. Support available to part-time students. Financial award application deadline: 2/1. *Faculty research:* Interventional radiology, magnetic resonance imaging, neuroimaging, pediatric imaging, emergency radiology. *Unit head:* Dr. Wilbur Smith, Chair, 313-745-3430, E-mail: wlsmith@med.wayne.edu. Web site: http://www.med.wayne.edu/diagRadiology/wsuhomepage.html.

Wayne State University, School of Medicine, Graduate Programs in Medicine, Department of Radiation Oncology, Detroit, MI 48202. Offers medical physics (PhD); radiological physics (MS). Part-time and evening/weekend programs available. In 2011, 1 doctorate awarded. Terminal master's awarded for partial completion of doctoral program. *Degree requirements:* For master's, thesis, essay, exit exam; for doctorate, thesis/dissertation, qualifying exam. *Entrance requirements:* For master's, GRE General Test, BS in physics or related area; for doctorate, GRE General Test, GRE Subject Test, BS in physics or related area. Additional exam requirements/recommendations for international students: Required—TOEFL (minimum score 550 paper-based; 213 computer-based); Recommended—TWE (minimum score 6). *Application deadline:* For fall admission, 1/15 for domestic students, 6/1 for international students; for winter admission, 10/1 for international students; for spring admission, 2/1 for international students. Applications are processed on a rolling basis. Application fee: $50. Electronic applications accepted. *Expenses:* Tuition, state resident: part-time $512.85 per credit. Tuition, nonresident: part-time $1132.65 per credit. *Required fees:* $26.60 per credit. $199.65 per semester. Tuition and fees vary according to course load and program. *Financial support:* In 2011–12, 1 research assistantship (averaging $20,787 per year) was awarded; fellowships, teaching assistantships, and career-related internships or fieldwork also available. Support available to part-time students. Financial award application deadline: 1/15. *Unit head:* Maria Vlachaki, Chair, 313-966-2774, Fax: 313-745-2314, E-mail: 661250@wayne.edu. *Application contact:* Michael Joiner, Professor, 313-745-2489, E-mail: joinerm@kci.wayne.edu. Web site: http://gradprograms.med.wayne.edu/program-spotlight.php?id=30.

Wright State University, School of Graduate Studies, College of Science and Mathematics, Department of Physics, Program in Physics, Dayton, OH 45435. Offers geophysics (MS); medical physics (MS). Part-time and evening/weekend programs available. *Degree requirements:* For master's, thesis. *Entrance requirements:* Additional exam requirements/recommendations for international students: Required—TOEFL. *Faculty research:* Solid-state physics, optics, geophysics.

Section 22
Health Services

This section contains a directory of institutions offering graduate work in health services, followed by in-depth entries submitted by institutions that chose to prepare detailed program descriptions. Additional information about programs listed in the directory but not augmented by an in-depth entry may be obtained by writing directly to the dean of a graduate school or chair of a department at the address given in the directory.

For programs offering related work, see also in this book *Allied Health, Nursing,* and *Public Health.* In another book in this series:

Graduate Programs in Business, Education, Information Studies, Law & Social Work

See *Business Administration and Management*

CONTENTS

Program Directories

Close-Ups

Health Services Management and Hospital Administration

Alaska Pacific University, Graduate Programs, Business Administration Department, Program in Business Administration, Anchorage, AK 99508-4672. Offers business administration (MBA); health services administration (MBA). Part-time and evening/weekend programs available. *Degree requirements:* For master's, capstone course. *Entrance requirements:* For master's, GMAT or GRE General Test, minimum GPA of 3.0.

Albany State University, College of Arts and Humanities, Albany, GA 31705-2717. Offers English education (M Ed); public administration (MPA), including community and economic development administration, criminal justice administration, general administration, health administration and policy, human resources management, public policy, water resources management; social work (MSW). Part-time programs available. *Faculty:* 13 full-time (6 women). *Students:* 47 full-time (38 women), 38 part-time (22 women); includes 77 minority (all Black or African American, non-Hispanic/Latino), 1 international. Average age 35. 43 applicants, 70% accepted, 23 enrolled. In 2011, 20 master's awarded. *Degree requirements:* For master's, comprehensive exam, professional portfolio (for MPA), internship, capstone report. *Entrance requirements:* For master's, GRE, MAT, minimum GPA of 3.0, official transcript, pre-medical record/certificate of immunization, letters of reference. *Application deadline:* For fall admission, 6/1 for domestic students, 5/1 for international students; for spring admission, 11/1 for domestic students, 10/1 for international students. Applications are processed on a rolling basis. Application fee: $20. Electronic applications accepted. *Expenses:* Tuition, state resident: full-time $3204; part-time $178 per credit hour. Tuition, nonresident: full-time $12,816; part-time $712 per credit hour. *Required fees:* $379 per semester. *Financial support:* Application deadline: 4/15; applicants required to submit FAFSA. *Faculty research:* HIV prevention for minority students . *Total annual research expenditures:* $2,000. *Unit head:* Dr. Leroy Bynum, Dean, 229-430-1877, Fax: 229-430-4296, E-mail: leroy.bynum@asurams.edu. *Application contact:* Jeffrey Pierce, II, Graduate Admissions Counselor, 229-430-4646, Fax: 229-430-4105, E-mail: jeffrey.pierce@asurams.edu. Web site: http://asu-sacs.asurams.edu/ASUCatalog/Graduate/index.html.

Albany State University, College of Business, Albany, GA 31705-2717. Offers accounting (MBA); general (MBA); healthcare (MBA). *Accreditation:* ACBSP. Part-time and evening/weekend programs available. *Faculty:* 3 full-time (0 women), 1 part-time/adjunct (0 women). *Students:* 4 full-time (2 women), 22 part-time (16 women); includes 24 minority (all Black or African American, non-Hispanic/Latino), 1 international. Average age 33. 22 applicants, 77% accepted, 9 enrolled. In 2011, 5 master's awarded. *Degree requirements:* For master's, comprehensive exam, internship, 3 hours of physical education. *Entrance requirements:* For master's, GMAT (minimum score of 450)/GRE (minimum score of 800) for those without earned master's degree or higher, minimum undergraduate GPA of 2.5, 2 letters of reference, official transcript, pre-entrance medical record and certificate of immunization. *Application deadline:* For fall admission, 6/1 for domestic students, 5/1 for international students; for spring admission, 11/1 for domestic students, 10/1 for international students. Applications are processed on a rolling basis. Application fee: $20. Electronic applications accepted. *Expenses:* Tuition, state resident: full-time $3204; part-time $178 per credit hour. Tuition, nonresident: full-time $12,816; part-time $712 per credit hour. *Required fees:* $379 per semester. *Financial support:* Application deadline: 4/15; applicants required to submit FAFSA. *Faculty research:* Diversity issues, ancestry, understanding finance through use of technology. *Unit head:* Dr. Fidelis Ikem, Interim Dean, 229-430-7009, Fax: 229-430-5119, E-mail: fidelis.ikem@asurams.edu. *Application contact:* Jeffrey Pierce, II, Graduate Counselor, 229-430-4646, Fax: 229-430-4105, E-mail: jeffrey.pierce@asurams.edu. Web site: http://asu-sacs.asurams.edu/ASUCatalog/Graduate/index.html.

American InterContinental University Online, Program in Business Administration, Hoffman Estates, IL 60192. Offers accounting and finance (MBA); finance (MBA); healthcare management (MBA); human resource management (MBA); international business (MBA); management (MBA); marketing (MBA); operations management (MBA); organizational psychology and development (MBA); project management (MBA). Evening/weekend programs available. Postbaccalaureate distance learning degree programs offered (no on-campus study). *Entrance requirements:* Additional exam requirements/recommendations for international students: Required—TOEFL (minimum score 550 paper-based; 213 computer-based). Electronic applications accepted.

American Public University System, AMU/APU Graduate Programs, Charles Town, WV 25414. Offers accounting (MBA, MS); administration and supervision (M Ed); criminal justice (MA); emergency and disaster management (MA); entrepreneurship (MBA); environmental policy and management (MS), including environmental planning, environmental sustainability, fish and wildlife management, general (MA, MS), global environmental management; finance (MBA); general (MBA); global business management (MBA); guidance and counseling (M Ed); history (MA), including American history, ancient and classical history, European history, global history, military and diplomatic history, public history; homeland security (MA); homeland security resource allocation (MBA); humanities (MA); information technology (MS), including digital forensics, enterprise software development, information assurance and security, IT project management; information technology management (MBA); intelligence studies (MA), including criminal intelligence, general (MA, MS), homeland security, intelligence analysis, intelligence collection, intelligence operations, terrorism studies; international relations and conflict resolution (MA), including comparative and security issues, conflict resolution, international and transnational security issues, peacekeeping; legal studies (MA); management (MA), including defense management, general (MA, MS), human resource management, organizational leadership, public administration, reverse logistics, strategic consulting; marketing (MBA); military history (MA), including American military history, American revolution, civil war, war since 1946, World War II; military studies (MA), including air warfare, asymmetrical warfare, joint warfare, land warfare, naval warfare, strategic leadership; national security studies (MA), including general (MA, MS), homeland security, regional security studies, security and intelligence analysis, terrorism studies; nonprofit management (MBA); political science (MA), including American politics and government, comparative government and development, public policy; psychology (MA); public administration (MA, MPA), including disaster management (MPA), environmental policy (MA), health policy (MPA), human resources (MPA), national security (MPA), organizational management (MPA), security management (MPA); public health (MA, MPH), including emergency management (MPH), environmental health (MPH), public administration (MA); reverse logistics management (MA); security management (MA); space studies (MS), including aerospace science, planetary science; sports and health sciences (MS); sports management (MS), including coaching theory and strategy, sports administration; teaching (M Ed), including curriculum and instruction for elementary teachers, elementary, elementary reading, English language learners, instructional leadership, online learning, secondary social sciences, special education; transportation and logistics management (MA), including maritime engineering management. Programs offered via distance learning only. Part-time and evening/weekend programs available. Postbaccalaureate distance learning degree programs offered (no on-campus study). *Faculty:* 445 full-time (241 women), 1,360 part-time/adjunct (617 women). *Students:* 688 full-time (338 women), 10,168 part-time (3,706 women); includes 3,130 minority (1,007 Black or African American, non-Hispanic/Latino; 103 American Indian or Alaska Native, non-Hispanic/Latino; 825 Asian, non-Hispanic/Latino; 810 Hispanic/Latino; 51 Native Hawaiian or other Pacific Islander, non-Hispanic/Latino; 334 Two or more races, non-Hispanic/Latino), 134 international. Average age 35. In 2011, 2,386 master's awarded. *Degree requirements:* For master's, comprehensive exam or practicum. *Entrance requirements:* For master's, official transcript showing earned bachelor's degree from institution accredited by recognized accrediting body. Additional exam requirements/recommendations for international students: Required—TOEFL (minimum score 550 paper-based; 213 computer-based), IELTS (minimum score 6.5). *Application deadline:* Applications are processed on a rolling basis. Application fee: $0. Electronic applications accepted. *Expenses: Tuition:* Part-time $325 per credit hour. *Financial support:* Applicants required to submit FAFSA. *Faculty research:* Military history, criminal justice, management performance, national security. *Unit head:* Dr. Karan Powell, Executive Vice President and Provost, 877-468-6268, Fax: 304-724-3780. *Application contact:* Terry Grant, Vice President of Enrollment Management, 877-468-6268, Fax: 304-724-3780, E-mail: info@apus.edu. Web site: http://www.apus.edu.

American Sentinel University, Graduate Programs, Aurora, CO 80014. Offers business administration (MBA); business intelligence (MS); computer science (MSCS); health information management (MS); healthcare (MBA); information systems (MSIS); nursing (MSN). Part-time and evening/weekend programs available. Postbaccalaureate distance learning degree programs offered (no on-campus study). *Entrance requirements:* Additional exam requirements/recommendations for international students: Required—TOEFL (minimum score 600 paper-based; 215 computer-based). Electronic applications accepted.

The American University in Dubai, Master in Business Administration Program, Dubai, United Arab Emirates. Offers general (MBA); healthcare management (MBA); international finance (MBA); international marketing (MBA); management of construction enterprises (MBA). Part-time and evening/weekend programs available. *Degree requirements:* For master's, thesis optional. *Entrance requirements:* For master's, GMAT, Interview. Additional exam requirements/recommendations for international students: Required—TOEFL (minimum score 550 paper-based; 213 computer-based; 79 iBT). Electronic applications accepted.

American University of Beirut, Graduate Programs, Faculty of Health Sciences, Beirut, Lebanon. Offers environmental sciences (MSES), including environmental health; epidemiology (MS); epidemiology and biostatistics (MPH); health management and policy (MPH); health promotion and community health (MPH); population health (MS). Part-time programs available. *Faculty:* 29 full-time (19 women), 5 part-time/adjunct (2 women). *Students:* 63 full-time (52 women), 103 part-time (87 women). Average age 27. 156 applicants, 71% accepted, 56 enrolled. In 2011, 69 master's awarded. *Degree requirements:* For master's, one foreign language, comprehensive exam, thesis (for some programs). *Entrance requirements:* For master's, 2 letters of recommendation, personal statement, transcripts. Additional exam requirements/recommendations for international students: Required—TOEFL (minimum score 600 paper-based; 250 computer-based; 97 iBT), IELTS (minimum score 7). *Application deadline:* For fall admission, 2/20 for domestic and international students; for spring admission, 11/1 for domestic and international students. Application fee: $50. Electronic applications accepted. *Expenses: Tuition:* Full-time $12,780; part-time $710 per credit. Tuition and fees vary according to course load and program. *Financial support:* In 2011–12, 62 students received support. Scholarships/grants, health care benefits, and unspecified assistantships available. Financial award application deadline: 2/20. *Faculty research:* Tobacco control; health of the elderly; youth health; mental health; women's health; reproductive and sexual health, including HIV/AIDS; water quality; health systems; quality in health care delivery; health human resources; health policy; occupational and environmental health; social inequality; social determinants of health; chronic diseases. *Total annual research expenditures:* $722,649. *Unit head:* Iman Adel Nuwayhid, Dean, 961-1340119, Fax: 961-1744470, E-mail: nuwayhid@aub.edu.lb. *Application contact:* Mitra Tauk, Administrative Coordinator, 961-1350000 Ext. 4687, Fax: 961-1744470, E-mail: mt12@aub.edu.lb. Web site: http://fhs.aub.edu.lb.

Aquinas College, School of Management, Grand Rapids, MI 49506-1799. Offers health care administration (M Mgt); marketing management (M Mgt); organizational leadership (M Min); sustainable business (M Mgt, MSB). Part-time and evening/weekend programs available. *Faculty:* 11 full-time (3 women), 7 part-time/adjunct (0 women). *Students:* 12 full-time (6 women), 56 part-time (32 women); includes 7 minority (3 Black or African American, non-Hispanic/Latino; 1 Asian, non-Hispanic/Latino; 3 Hispanic/Latino). *Entrance requirements:* For master's, GMAT, minimum undergraduate GPA of 2.75, 2 years of work experience. Additional exam requirements/recommendations for international students: Required—TOEFL (minimum score 550 paper-based; 213 computer-based). *Application deadline:* Applications are processed on a rolling basis. *Expenses:* Contact institution. *Financial support:* Scholarships/grants available. Support available to part-time students. Financial award application deadline: 3/15; financial award applicants required to submit FAFSA. *Unit head:* Brian DiVita, Director, 616-632-2922, Fax: 616-732-4489. *Application contact:* Lynn Atkins-Rykert, Administrative Assistant, 616-632-2924, Fax: 616-732-4489, E-mail: atkinlyn@aquinas.edu.

Aquinas Institute of Theology, Graduate and Professional Programs, St. Louis, MO 63108. Offers biblical studies (Certificate); church music (MM); health care mission (MAHCM); ministry (M Div); pastoral care (Certificate); pastoral ministry (MAPM); pastoral studies (MAPS); preaching (D Min); spiritual direction (Certificate); theology (M Div, MA); Thomistic studies (Certificate); M Div/MA; MA/PhD; MAPS/MSW. *Accreditation:* ATS (one or more programs are accredited). Part-time and evening/weekend programs available. Postbaccalaureate distance learning degree programs offered (minimal on-campus study). *Faculty:* 10 full-time (6 women), 20 part-time/adjunct (6 women). *Students:* 59 full-time (16 women), 133 part-time (81 women); includes 29 minority (13 Black or African American, non-Hispanic/Latino; 6 Asian, non-Hispanic/Latino; 10 Hispanic/Latino), 6 international. *Degree requirements:* For master's, variable

foreign language requirement, comprehensive exam (for some programs); for doctorate, thesis/dissertation. *Entrance requirements:* For master's and Certificate, MAT; for doctorate, 3 years of ministerial experience, 6 hours of graduate course work in homiletics, M Div or the equivalent, minimum GPA of 3.0. Additional exam requirements/recommendations for international students: Required—TOEFL. *Application deadline:* For fall admission, 3/15 priority date for domestic students, 3/15 for international students; for spring admission, 11/15 priority date for domestic students, 11/15 for international students. Applications are processed on a rolling basis. Application fee: $50. *Expenses: Tuition:* Full-time $15,360; part-time $640 per credit. *Required fees:* $195 per semester. Tuition and fees vary according to degree level. *Financial support:* Career-related internships or fieldwork, scholarships/grants, health care benefits, and tuition waivers (partial) available. Support available to part-time students. Financial award application deadline: 3/15; financial award applicants required to submit CSS PROFILE or FAFSA. *Faculty research:* Theology of preaching, hermeneutics, lay ecclesial ministry, pastoral and practical theology. *Unit head:* Fr. Gregory Heille, Vice-President/Academic Dean, 314-256-8800, Fax: 314-256-8888, E-mail: heille@ai.edu. *Application contact:* David Werthmann, Director of Admissions, 314-256-8806, Fax: 314-256-8888, E-mail: admissions@ai.edu. Web site: http://www.ai.edu/.

Argosy University, Atlanta, College of Business, Atlanta, GA 30328. Offers accounting (DBA); corporate compliance (MBA); customized professional concentration (MBA, DBA); finance (MBA); healthcare administration (MBA); information systems (DBA); information systems management (MBA); international business (MBA, DBA); management (MBA, MSM, DBA); marketing (MBA, DBA).

Argosy University, Chicago, College of Business, Chicago, IL 60601. Offers accounting (DBA); customized professional concentration (MBA, DBA); finance (MBA); fraud examination (MBA); global business sustainability (DBA); healthcare administration (MBA); information systems (DBA); information systems management (MBA); international business (MBA, DBA); management (MBA, MSM, DBA); marketing (MBA, DBA); organizational leadership (Ed D); public administration (MBA); sustainable management (MBA). Postbaccalaureate distance learning degree programs offered (minimal on-campus study).

Argosy University, Dallas, College of Business, Farmers Branch, TX 75244. Offers accounting (DBA, AGC); corporate compliance (MBA, Graduate Certificate); customized professional concentration (MBA); finance (MBA, Graduate Certificate); fraud examination (MBA, Graduate Certificate); global business sustainability (DBA, AGC); healthcare administration (Graduate Certificate); healthcare management (MBA); information systems (MBA, DBA, AGC); information systems management (Graduate Certificate); international business (MBA, DBA, AGC, Graduate Certificate); management (MBA, DBA, AGC, Graduate Certificate); marketing (MBA, DBA, AGC, Graduate Certificate); public administration (MBA, Graduate Certificate); sustainable management (MBA, Graduate Certificate).

Argosy University, Denver, College of Business, Denver, CO 80231. Offers accounting (DBA); corporate compliance (MBA); customized professional concentration (MBA, DBA); finance (MBA); fraud examination (MBA); global business sustainability (DBA); healthcare administration (MBA); information systems (DBA); information systems management (MBA); international business (MBA, DBA); management (MBA, MSM, DBA); marketing (MBA, DBA); organizational leadership (Ed D); public administration (MBA); sustainable management (MBA).

Argosy University, Hawai`i, College of Business, Honolulu, HI 96813. Offers accounting (DBA); corporate compliance (MBA); customized professional concentration (MBA, DBA); finance (MBA, Certificate); fraud examination (MBA); global business sustainability (DBA); healthcare administration (MBA, Certificate); information systems (DBA); information systems management (MBA, Certificate); international business (MBA, DBA, Certificate); management (MBA, MSM, DBA); marketing (MBA, DBA, Certificate); organizational leadership (Ed D); public administration (MBA); sustainable management (MBA).

Argosy University, Inland Empire, College of Business, San Bernardino, CA 92408. Offers accounting (DBA); corporate compliance (MBA); customized professional concentration (MBA, DBA); finance (MBA); fraud examination (MBA); global business sustainability (DBA); healthcare administration (MBA); information systems (DBA); information systems management (MBA); international business (MBA, DBA); management (MBA, MSM, DBA); marketing (MBA, DBA); organizational leadership (Ed D); public administration (MBA); sustainable management (MBA).

Argosy University, Los Angeles, College of Business, Santa Monica, CA 90045. Offers accounting (DBA); corporate compliance (MBA); customized professional concentration (MBA, DBA); finance (MBA); fraud examination (MBA); global business sustainability (DBA); healthcare administration (MBA); information systems (DBA); information systems management (MBA); international business (MBA, DBA); management (MBA, MSM, DBA); marketing (MBA, DBA); organizational leadership (Ed D); public administration (MBA); sustainable management (MBA).

Argosy University, Nashville, College of Business, Nashville, TN 37214. Offers accounting (DBA); customized professional concentration (MBA, DBA); finance (MBA); healthcare administration (MBA); information systems (MBA, DBA); international business (MBA, DBA); management (MBA, MSM, DBA); marketing (MBA, DBA).

Argosy University, Orange County, College of Business, Orange, CA 92868. Offers accounting (DBA, Adv C); corporate compliance (MBA); customized professional concentration (MBA, DBA); finance (MBA, Certificate); fraud examination (MBA); global business sustainability (DBA); healthcare administration (MBA, Certificate); information systems (DBA, Adv C, Certificate); information systems management (MBA); international business (MBA, DBA, Adv C, Certificate); management (MBA, MSM, DBA, Adv C); marketing (MBA, DBA, Adv C, Certificate); organizational leadership (Ed D); public administration (MBA, Certificate); sustainable management (MBA).

Argosy University, Phoenix, College of Business, Phoenix, AZ 85021. Offers accounting (DBA); corporate compliance (MBA); customized professional concentration (MBA, DBA); finance (MBA); fraud examination (MBA); global business sustainability (DBA); healthcare administration (MBA); information systems (DBA); information systems management (MBA); international business (MBA, DBA); management (MBA, DBA); marketing (MBA, DBA); public administration (MBA); sustainable management (MBA).

Argosy University, Salt Lake City, College of Business, Draper, UT 84020. Offers accounting (DBA); corporate compliance (MBA); customized professional concentration (MBA, DBA); finance (MBA); fraud examination (MBA); global business sustainability (DBA); healthcare administration (MBA); information systems (DBA); information systems management (MBA); international business (MBA, DBA); management (MBA, DBA); marketing (MBA, DBA); public administration (MBA); sustainable management (MBA).

Argosy University, San Francisco Bay Area, College of Business, Alameda, CA 94501. Offers accounting (DBA); corporate compliance (MBA); customized professional concentration (MBA, DBA); finance (MBA); fraud examination (MBA); global business sustainability (DBA); healthcare administration (MBA); information systems (DBA); information systems management (MBA); international business (MBA, DBA);

management (MBA, MSM, DBA); marketing (MBA, DBA); organizational leadership (Ed D); public administration (MBA); sustainable management (MBA).

Argosy University, Sarasota, College of Business, Sarasota, FL 34235. Offers accounting (DBA, Adv C); corporate compliance (MBA, DBA, Certificate); customized professional concentration (MBA, DBA); finance (MBA, Certificate); fraud examination (MBA, Certificate); global business sustainability (DBA, Adv C); healthcare administration (MBA, Certificate); information systems (DBA, Adv C, Certificate); information systems management (MBA); international business (MBA, DBA, Adv C, Certificate); management (MBA, MSM, DBA, Adv C, Certificate); marketing (MBA, DBA, Adv C, Certificate); organizational leadership (Ed D); public administration (MBA, Certificate); sustainable management (MBA, Certificate).

Argosy University, Schaumburg, College of Business, Schaumburg, IL 60173-5403. Offers accounting (DBA, Adv C); customized professional concentration (MBA, DBA); finance (MBA, Certificate); fraud examination (MBA); global business sustainability (DBA); healthcare administration (MBA, Certificate); information systems (DBA, Adv C, Certificate); information systems management (MBA); international business (MBA, DBA, Adv C, Certificate); management (MBA, MSM, DBA, Adv C, Certificate); marketing (MBA, DBA, Adv C, Certificate); organizational leadership (Ed D); public administration (MBA); sustainable management (MBA).

Argosy University, Seattle, College of Business, Seattle, WA 98121. Offers accounting (DBA); corporate compliance (MBA); customized professional concentration (MBA, DBA); finance (MBA); fraud examination (MBA); global business sustainability (DBA); healthcare administration (MBA); information systems (DBA); information systems management (MBA); international business (MBA, DBA); management (MBA, MSM, DBA); marketing (MBA, DBA); organizational leadership (Ed D); public administration (MBA); sustainable management (MBA).

Argosy University, Tampa, College of Business, Tampa, FL 33607. Offers accounting (DBA); corporate compliance (MBA); customized professional concentration (MBA, DBA); finance (MBA); fraud examination (MBA); global business sustainability (DBA); healthcare administration (MBA); information systems (DBA); information systems management (MBA); international business (MBA, DBA); management (MBA, MSM, DBA); marketing (MBA, DBA); organizational leadership (Ed D); public administration (MBA); sustainable management (MBA).

Argosy University, Twin Cities, College of Business, Eagan, MN 55121. Offers accounting (DBA); customized professional concentration (MBA, DBA); finance (MBA); fraud examination (MBA); global business sustainability (DBA); healthcare administration (MBA); information systems (DBA); information systems management (MBA); international business (MBA, DBA); management (MBA, MSM, DBA); marketing (MBA, DBA); organizational leadership (Ed D); public administration (MBA); sustainable management (MBA).

Argosy University, Twin Cities, College of Health Sciences, Eagan, MN 55121. Offers health services management (MS); public health (MPH).

Argosy University, Washington DC, College of Business, Arlington, VA 22209. Offers accounting (DBA); customized professional concentration (MBA, DBA); finance (MBA); fraud examination (MBA); global business sustainability (DBA); healthcare administration (MBA); information systems (DBA); information systems management (MBA); international business (MBA, DBA, Certificate); management (MBA, MSM, DBA); marketing (MBA, DBA, Certificate); organizational leadership (Ed D); public administration (MBA); sustainable management (MBA).

Arkansas State University, Graduate School, College of Nursing and Health Professions, School of Nursing, Jonesboro, State University, AR 72467. Offers aging studies (Certificate); disaster preparedness and emergency management (MS, Certificate); health care management (Certificate); health communications (Certificate); health sciences (MS); health sciences education (Certificate); nurse anesthesia (MSN); nursing (MSN). *Accreditation:* AANA/CANAEP (one or more programs are accredited); NLN. Part-time programs available. *Faculty:* 14 full-time (all women). *Students:* 107 full-time (49 women), 118 part-time (110 women); includes 32 minority (27 Black or African American, non-Hispanic/Latino; 3 Asian, non-Hispanic/Latino; 2 Hispanic/Latino). Average age 33. 96 applicants, 25% accepted, 21 enrolled. In 2011, 83 master's awarded. *Degree requirements:* For master's, comprehensive exam, thesis or alternative. *Entrance requirements:* For master's, GRE General Test or MAT, appropriate bachelor's degree, current Arkansas nursing license, CPR certification, physical examination, professional liability insurance, critical care experience, ACLS Certification, PALS Certification, interview, immunization records, personal goal statement, health assessment. Additional exam requirements/recommendations for international students: Required—TOEFL (minimum score 550 paper-based; 213 computer-based; 79 iBT), IELTS (minimum score 6), Pearson Test of English Academic (minimum score 56). *Application deadline:* Applications are processed on a rolling basis. Application fee: $30 ($40 for international students). Electronic applications accepted. *Expenses:* Contact institution. *Financial support:* In 2011–12, 5 students received support. Career-related internships or fieldwork, scholarships/grants, and unspecified assistantships available. Financial award application deadline: 7/1; financial award applicants required to submit FAFSA. *Unit head:* Dr. Sue McLarry, Chair, 870-972-3074, Fax: 870-972-2954, E-mail: smclarry@astate.edu. *Application contact:* Dr. Andrew Sustich, Dean of the Graduate School, 870-972-3029, Fax: 870-972-3857, E-mail: sustich@astate.edu. Web site: http://www.astate.edu/a/conhp/nursing/index.dot.

Armstrong Atlantic State University, School of Graduate Studies, Program in Health Science, Savannah, GA 31419-1997. Offers health services administration (MHSA); public health (MPH). *Accreditation:* CAHME; CEPH. Part-time and evening/weekend programs available. Postbaccalaureate distance learning degree programs offered (no on-campus study). *Faculty:* 9 full-time (4 women), 2 part-time/adjunct (1 woman). *Students:* 56 full-time (37 women), 25 part-time (21 women); includes 31 minority (22 Black or African American, non-Hispanic/Latino; 2 American Indian or Alaska Native, non-Hispanic/Latino; 6 Asian, non-Hispanic/Latino; 1 Hispanic/Latino), 5 international. Average age 30. 78 applicants, 49% accepted, 29 enrolled. In 2011, 30 master's awarded. *Degree requirements:* For master's, comprehensive exam, thesis optional, internship. *Entrance requirements:* For master's, GMAT or GRE General Test, MAT, minimum GPA of 2.8, letter of intent, letters of recommendation. Additional exam requirements/recommendations for international students: Required—TOEFL (minimum score 523 paper-based; 193 computer-based). *Application deadline:* For fall admission, 7/1 priority date for domestic students, 5/1 for international students; for spring admission, 11/15 priority date for domestic students, 9/15 for international students. Applications are processed on a rolling basis. Application fee: $30. Electronic applications accepted. *Expenses: Tuition,* state resident: full-time $3402. Tuition, nonresident: full-time $12,636. *Financial support:* In 2011–12, research assistantships with full tuition reimbursements (averaging $5,000 per year) were awarded; career-related internships or fieldwork, Federal Work-Study, scholarships/grants, tuition waivers (full), and unspecified assistantships also available. Support available to part-time students. Financial award applicants required to submit FAFSA. *Faculty research:* Health administration, community health, health education. *Unit head:* Dr. James Streater, Department Head, 912-344-2548, E-mail: sandy.streater@armstrong.edu. *Application contact:* Jill Bell, Director, Graduate Enrollment Services, 912-344-2798,

Fax: 912-344-3488, E-mail: graduate@armstrong.edu. Web site: http://www.armstrong.edu/Health_Professions/Health_Sciences/healthsciences_welcome.

Ashworth College, Graduate Programs, Norcross, GA 30092. Offers business administration (MBA); criminal justice (MS); health care administration (MBA, MS); human resource management (MBA, MS); international business (MBA); management (MS); marketing (MBA, MS).

A.T. Still University of Health Sciences, School of Health Management, Kirksville, MO 63501. Offers dental emphasis (MPH); health administration (MHA); health education (MH Ed, DH Ed); public health (MPH). Part-time and evening/weekend programs available. Postbaccalaureate distance learning degree programs offered (no on-campus study). *Faculty:* 15 full-time (8 women), 52 part-time/adjunct (27 women). *Students:* 50 full-time (36 women), 391 part-time (245 women); includes 125 minority (48 Black or African American, non-Hispanic/Latino; 4 American Indian or Alaska Native, non-Hispanic/Latino; 42 Asian, non-Hispanic/Latino; 26 Hispanic/Latino; 5 Two or more races, non-Hispanic/Latino). Average age 32. 121 applicants, 90% accepted, 89 enrolled. In 2011, 156 master's, 38 doctorates awarded. *Degree requirements:* For master's, thesis, integrated terminal project; for doctorate, thesis/dissertation. *Entrance requirements:* For master's, minimum GPA of 3.0, bachelor's degree or equivalent from U.S. institution; for doctorate, minimum GPA of 3.0, master's or terminal degree. Additional exam requirements/recommendations for international students: Required—TOEFL (minimum score 550 paper-based; 213 computer-based; 80 iBT). *Application deadline:* For fall admission, 7/9 for domestic students, 7/6 for international students; for winter admission, 9/28 for domestic and international students; for spring admission, 1/11 for domestic and international students. Application fee: $60. Electronic applications accepted. *Expenses:* Contact institution. *Financial support:* In 2011–12, 72 students received support. Scholarships/grants available. Financial award application deadline: 5/1; financial award applicants required to submit FAFSA. *Faculty research:* Public health: cultural health disparities, emergency preparedness, infectious disease, maternal and child health, environmental health; health education: overweight and obesity; health administration: leadership, strategic thinking, governance, healthcare reform economics, patient-centered care. *Unit head:* Dr. Kimberly O'Reilly, Interim Dean, 660-626-2820, Fax: 660-626-2826, E-mail: koreilley@atsu.edu. *Application contact:* Sarah Spencer, Associate Director, Admissions, 660-626-2820 Ext. 2669, Fax: 660-626-2826, E-mail: sspencer@atsu.edu. Web site: http://www.atsu.edu/shm.

Avila University, School of Business, Kansas City, MO 64145-1698. Offers accounting (MBA); finance (MBA); general management (MBA); health care administration (MBA); international business (MBA); management information systems (MBA); marketing (MBA). Part-time and evening/weekend programs available. *Faculty:* 9 full-time (3 women), 14 part-time/adjunct (5 women). *Students:* 102 full-time (49 women), 53 part-time (31 women); includes 36 minority (29 Black or African American, non-Hispanic/Latino; 1 American Indian or Alaska Native, non-Hispanic/Latino; 3 Asian, non-Hispanic/Latino; 2 Hispanic/Latino; 1 Native Hawaiian or other Pacific Islander, non-Hispanic/Latino), 33 international. Average age 32. 25 applicants, 76% accepted, 19 enrolled. In 2011, 59 master's awarded. *Degree requirements:* For master's, comprehensive exam, capstone course. *Entrance requirements:* For master's, GMAT (minimum score 420), minimum GPA of 3.0, interview. Additional exam requirements/recommendations for international students: Required—TOEFL (minimum score 550 paper-based). *Application deadline:* For fall admission, 7/30 priority date for domestic students, 7/30 for international students; for winter admission, 11/30 priority date for domestic students, 11/30 for international students; for spring admission, 2/28 priority date for domestic students, 2/28 for international students. Applications are processed on a rolling basis. Application fee: $0. Electronic applications accepted. *Expenses:* Contact institution. *Financial support:* In 2011–12, 102 students received support. Career-related internships or fieldwork and competitive merit scholarships available. Support available to part-time students. Financial award applicants required to submit FAFSA. *Faculty research:* Leadership characteristics, financial hedging, group dynamics. *Unit head:* Dr. Richard Woodall, Dean, 816-501-3720, Fax: 816-501-2463, E-mail: richard.woodall@avila.edu. *Application contact:* JoAnna Giffin, MBA Admissions Director, 816-501-3601, Fax: 816-501-2463, E-mail: joanna.giffin@avila.edu. Web site: http://www.avila.edu/mba.

Baker College Center for Graduate Studies - Online, Graduate Programs, Flint, MI 48507-9843. Offers accounting (MBA); business administration (DBA); finance (MBA); general business (MBA); health care management (MBA); human resources management (MBA); information management (MBA); leadership studies (MBA); management information systems (MSIS); marketing (MBA). Part-time and evening/weekend programs available. Postbaccalaureate distance learning degree programs offered. *Degree requirements:* For master's, portfolio. *Entrance requirements:* For master's, 3 years of work experience, minimum undergraduate GPA of 2.5, writing sample, 3 letters of recommendation; for doctorate, MBA or acceptable related master's degree from accredited association, 5 years work experience, minimum graduate GPA of 3.25, writing sample, 3 professional references. Additional exam requirements/recommendations for international students: Required—TOEFL (minimum score 550 paper-based; 213 computer-based). Electronic applications accepted.

Baldwin Wallace University, Graduate Programs, Division of Business, Program in Health Care Management, Berea, OH 44017-2088. Offers MBA. Part-time and evening/weekend programs available. *Students:* 46 full-time (22 women), 15 part-time (12 women); includes 4 minority (1 Black or African American, non-Hispanic/Latino; 2 Asian, non-Hispanic/Latino; 1 Two or more races, non-Hispanic/Latino), 2 international. Average age 39. 24 applicants, 75% accepted, 13 enrolled. In 2011, 10 master's awarded. *Degree requirements:* For master's, minimum overall GPA of 3.0, completion of all required courses. *Entrance requirements:* For master's, GMAT, interview, work experience, bachelor's degree in any field. Additional exam requirements/recommendations for international students: Required—TOEFL (minimum score 523 paper-based; 193 computer-based; 70 iBT). *Application deadline:* For fall admission, 7/25 priority date for domestic students, 4/30 for international students; for spring admission, 12/10 priority date for domestic students, 9/30 for international students. Applications are processed on a rolling basis. Application fee: $25. Electronic applications accepted. Application fee is waived when completed online. *Expenses: Tuition:* Full-time $17,016; part-time $727 per credit hour. Tuition and fees vary according to program. *Financial support:* Career-related internships or fieldwork available. Support available to part-time students. Financial award application deadline: 5/1; financial award applicants required to submit FAFSA. *Unit head:* Tom Campanella, Director, 440-826-3818, Fax: 440-826-3868, E-mail: tcampane@bw.edu. *Application contact:* Laura Spencer, Graduate Application Specialist, 440-826-2191, Fax: 440-826-3868, E-mail: lspencer@bw.edu. Web site: http://www.bw.edu/academics/bus/programs/hcmba/.

Barry University, Andreas School of Business, Graduate Certificate Programs, Miami Shores, FL 33161-6695. Offers finance (Certificate); health services administration (Certificate); international business (Certificate); management (Certificate); management information systems (Certificate); marketing (Certificate).

Barry University, College of Health Sciences, Graduate Certificate Programs, Miami Shores, FL 33161-6695. Offers health care leadership (Certificate); health care planning and informatics (Certificate); histotechnology (Certificate); long term care management (Certificate); medical group practice management (Certificate); quality improvement and outcomes management (Certificate).

Barry University, College of Health Sciences, Program in Health Services Administration, Miami Shores, FL 33161-6695. Offers MS. Part-time and evening/weekend programs available. *Degree requirements:* For master's, comprehensive exam. *Entrance requirements:* For master's, GMAT or GRE General Test, 2 years of experience in the health field, minimum GPA of 3.0, 1 semester of course work in computer applications or the equivalent (business). Electronic applications accepted.

Baylor University, Graduate School, Military Programs, Program in Health Care Administration, Waco, TX 76798. Offers MHA. Program offered jointly with the U.S. Army. *Accreditation:* CAHME. *Students:* 97 full-time (43 women); includes 14 minority (4 Black or African American, non-Hispanic/Latino; 1 American Indian or Alaska Native, non-Hispanic/Latino; 1 Asian, non-Hispanic/Latino; 5 Hispanic/Latino; 1 Native Hawaiian or other Pacific Islander, non-Hispanic/Latino; 2 Two or more races, non-Hispanic/Latino). In 2011, 34 master's awarded. *Entrance requirements:* For master's, GRE General Test. *Application deadline:* For fall admission, 6/15 for domestic students. Applications are processed on a rolling basis. Application fee: $25. *Faculty research:* Data quality, public health policy, organizational behavior, AIDS. *Unit head:* Lt. Cdr. Lee Bewley, Graduate Program Director, 210-221-8857 Ext. 6443, E-mail: lee.bewley@us.army.mil. *Application contact:* Rene Pryor, Program Administrator, 210-221-6443, Fax: 210-221-6010, E-mail: rene.pryor@cen.amedd.army.mil. Web site: http://www.cs.amedd.army.mil/baylorhca/.

Bellevue University, Graduate School, College of Arts and Sciences, Bellevue, NE 68005-3098. Offers clinical counseling (MS); healthcare administration (MHA); human services (MA); international security and intelligence studies (MS); managerial communication (MA). Postbaccalaureate distance learning degree programs offered.

Benedictine University, Graduate Programs, Program in Business Administration, Lisle, IL 60532-0900. Offers accounting (MBA); entrepreneurship and managing innovation (MBA); financial management (MBA); health administration (MBA); human resource management (MBA); information systems security (MBA); international business (MBA); management consulting (MBA); management information systems (MBA); marketing management (MBA); operations management and logistics (MBA); organizational leadership (MBA); MBA/MPH; MBA/MS. Part-time and evening/weekend programs available. Postbaccalaureate distance learning degree programs offered (minimal on-campus study). *Faculty:* 4 full-time (2 women), 24 part-time/adjunct (3 women). *Students:* 165 full-time (101 women), 766 part-time (381 women); includes 201 minority (118 Black or African American, non-Hispanic/Latino; 4 American Indian or Alaska Native, non-Hispanic/Latino; 37 Asian, non-Hispanic/Latino; 40 Hispanic/Latino; 2 Native Hawaiian or other Pacific Islander, non-Hispanic/Latino), 14 international. Average age 34. 313 applicants, 73% accepted, 166 enrolled. In 2011, 379 master's awarded. *Entrance requirements:* For master's, GMAT. Additional exam requirements/recommendations for international students: Required—TOEFL (minimum score 550 paper-based; 213 computer-based). *Application deadline:* For fall admission, 9/1 for domestic students; for winter admission, 12/1 for domestic students; for spring admission, 2/15 for domestic students. Applications are processed on a rolling basis. Application fee: $40. Electronic applications accepted. *Financial support:* Career-related internships or fieldwork and health care benefits available. Support available to part-time students. *Faculty research:* Strategic leadership in professional organizations, sociology of professions, organizational change, social identity theory, applications to change management. *Unit head:* Dr. Sharon Borowicz, Director, 630-829-6219, E-mail: sborowicz@ben.edu. *Application contact:* Kari Gibbons, Director, Admissions, 630-829-6200, Fax: 630-829-6584, E-mail: kgibbons@ben.edu.

Benedictine University, Graduate Programs, Program in Public Health, Lisle, IL 60532-0900. Offers administration of health care institutions (MPH); dietetics (MPH); disaster management (MPH); health education (MPH); health information systems (MPH); MBA/MPH; MPH/MS. Part-time and evening/weekend programs available. Postbaccalaureate distance learning degree programs offered. *Faculty:* 2 full-time (0 women), 8 part-time/adjunct (3 women). *Students:* 85 full-time (61 women), 437 part-time (333 women); includes 217 minority (133 Black or African American, non-Hispanic/Latino; 1 American Indian or Alaska Native, non-Hispanic/Latino; 65 Asian, non-Hispanic/Latino; 18 Hispanic/Latino), 28 international. Average age 33. 172 applicants, 80% accepted, 113 enrolled. In 2011, 116 master's awarded. *Entrance requirements:* For master's, MAT, GRE, or GMAT. Additional exam requirements/recommendations for international students: Required—TOEFL (minimum score 550 paper-based; 213 computer-based). *Application deadline:* For fall admission, 9/1 for domestic students; for winter admission, 12/1 for domestic students; for spring admission, 2/15 for domestic students. Application fee: $40. *Financial support:* Career-related internships or fieldwork and health care benefits available. Support available to part-time students. *Unit head:* Dr. Georgeen Polyak, Director, 630-829-6217, E-mail: gpolyak@ben.edu. *Application contact:* Kari Gibbons, Associate Vice President, Enrollment Center, 630-829-6200, Fax: 630-829-6584, E-mail: kgibbons@ben.edu.

Benedictine University at Springfield, Program in Business Administration, Springfield, IL 62702. Offers health administration (MBA); organizational leadership (MBA). Part-time and evening/weekend programs available. *Entrance requirements:* For master's, GMAT.

Bernard M. Baruch College of the City University of New York, School of Public Affairs, Program in Public Administration, New York, NY 10010-5585. Offers general public administration (MPA); health care policy (MPA); nonprofit administration (MPA); policy analysis and evaluation (MPA); public management (MPA); MS/MPA. *Accreditation:* NASPAA. Part-time and evening/weekend programs available. *Faculty:* 45 full-time (17 women), 34 part-time/adjunct (12 women). *Students:* 177 full-time (121 women), 493 part-time (327 women); includes 347 minority (152 Black or African American, non-Hispanic/Latino; 2 American Indian or Alaska Native, non-Hispanic/Latino; 68 Asian, non-Hispanic/Latino; 107 Hispanic/Latino; 18 Two or more races, non-Hispanic/Latino). *Degree requirements:* For master's, thesis, capstone. *Entrance requirements:* For master's, GRE General Test. Additional exam requirements/recommendations for international students: Required—TOEFL. *Application deadline:* For fall admission, 4/1 priority date for domestic students, 4/1 for international students; for spring admission, 11/15 priority date for domestic students, 11/15 for international students. Applications are processed on a rolling basis. Application fee: $125. Electronic applications accepted. *Expenses:* Contact institution. *Financial support:* In 2011–12, fellowships (averaging $1,500 per year), research assistantships (averaging $12,000 per year) were awarded; career-related internships or fieldwork, Federal Work-Study, scholarships/grants, tuition waivers (partial), and unspecified assistantships also available. Support available to part-time students. Financial award application deadline: 5/15; financial award applicants required to submit FAFSA. *Faculty research:* Urbanization, population and poverty in the developing world, housing and community development, labor unions and housing, government-nongovernment relations, immigration policy, social network analysis, cross-sectoral governance, comparative healthcare systems, program evaluation, social welfare policy, health outcomes, educational policy and leadership, transnationalism, infant health, welfare reform, racial/ethnic disparities in health, urban politics, homelessness, race and ethnic relations. *Total annual research expenditures:* $2.6 million. *Unit head:* David S. Birdsell, Dean, 646-660-

6700, Fax: 646-660-6721, E-mail: david.birdsell@baruch.cuny.edu. *Application contact:* Michael J. Lovaglio, Director of Student Affairs and Graduate Admissions, 646-660-6760, Fax: 646-660-6751, E-mail: michael.lovaglio@baruch.cuny.edu. Web site: http://www.baruch.cuny.edu/spa/.

Bernard M. Baruch College of the City University of New York, Zicklin School of Business, Zicklin Executive Programs, Baruch/Mt. Sinai Program in Health Care Administration, New York, NY 10010-5585. Offers MBA. *Accreditation:* CAHME. Part-time and evening/weekend programs available. *Entrance requirements:* For master's, GMAT, personal interview, work experience in health care. Additional exam requirements/recommendations for international students: Required—TOEFL. Electronic applications accepted. *Expenses:* Contact institution. *Faculty research:* Economics of reproductive health, multivariate point estimation.

Boston University, School of Medicine, Division of Graduate Medical Sciences, Program in Medical Sciences, Boston, MA 02215. Offers MA, MA/MA, MBA/MA, MPH/MA. Part-time programs available. *Students:* 332 full-time (147 women), 19 part-time (13 women); includes 159 minority (13 Black or African American, non-Hispanic/Latino; 109 Asian, non-Hispanic/Latino; 25 Hispanic/Latino; 1 Native Hawaiian or other Pacific Islander, non-Hispanic/Latino; 11 Two or more races, non-Hispanic/Latino), 14 international. Average age 24. 769 applicants, 54% accepted, 190 enrolled. In 2011, 176 master's awarded. *Degree requirements:* For master's, thesis. *Entrance requirements:* For master's, MCAT or GRE. Additional exam requirements/recommendations for international students: Required—TOEFL. *Application deadline:* Applications are processed on a rolling basis. Application fee: $75. Electronic applications accepted. *Expenses: Tuition:* Full-time $40,848; part-time $1276 per credit hour. *Required fees:* $572; $286 per semester. *Financial support:* In 2011–12, 3 students received support. Federal Work-Study available. Financial award applicants required to submit FAFSA. *Unit head:* Dr. Gwynneth D. Offner, Director, 617-638-8221, E-mail: goffner@bu.edu. *Application contact:* Natasha Hall, 617-638-5217, E-mail: tashah@bu.edu. Web site: http://www.bumc.bu.edu/gms/academics/masters-in-medical-sciences/.

Boston University, School of Public Health, Health Policy and Management Department, Boston, MA 02118. Offers health policy and management (MPH); health services research (MS, PhD). *Accreditation:* CAHME. Part-time and evening/weekend programs available. *Faculty:* 37 full-time, 31 part-time/adjunct. *Students:* 93 full-time (59 women), 72 part-time (55 women); includes 39 minority (5 Black or African American, non-Hispanic/Latino; 1 American Indian or Alaska Native, non-Hispanic/Latino; 19 Asian, non-Hispanic/Latino; 9 Hispanic/Latino; 1 Native Hawaiian or other Pacific Islander, non-Hispanic/Latino; 4 Two or more races, non-Hispanic/Latino), 17 international. Average age 28. 507 applicants, 44% accepted, 77 enrolled. In 2011, 187 master's, 2 doctorates awarded. *Degree requirements:* For master's, comprehensive exam (for some programs), thesis (for some programs); for doctorate, comprehensive exam, thesis/dissertation. *Entrance requirements:* For master's, GRE, MCAT, LSAT, GMAT, or DAT; for doctorate, GRE, MCAT, GMAT, LSAT. Additional exam requirements/recommendations for international students: Required—TOEFL (minimum score 600 paper-based; 250 computer-based; 100 iBT) or IELTS (minimum score 6). *Application deadline:* For fall admission, 2/1 priority date for domestic students, 2/1 for international students; for spring admission, 10/15 priority date for domestic students, 10/15 for international students. Applications are processed on a rolling basis. Application fee: $115. Electronic applications accepted. *Expenses: Tuition:* Full-time $40,848; part-time $1276 per credit hour. *Required fees:* $572; $286 per semester. *Financial support:* Career-related internships or fieldwork, Federal Work-Study, institutionally sponsored loans, scholarships/grants, and tuition waivers (partial) available. Support available to part-time students. Financial award application deadline: 3/1; financial award applicants required to submit FAFSA. *Unit head:* Dr. Alan Jette, Acting Chair, 617-638-5042. *Application contact:* LePhan Quan, Associate Director of Admissions, 617-638-4640, Fax: 617-638-5299, E-mail: asksph@bu.edu. Web site: http://sph.bu.edu/hpm.

Brandeis University, The Heller School for Social Policy and Management, Program in Nonprofit Management, Waltham, MA 02454-9110. Offers child, youth, and family management (MBA); health care management (MBA); social impact management (MBA); social policy and management (MBA); sustainable development (MBA); MBA/MA; MBA/MD. MBA/MD program offered in conjunction with Tufts University School of Medicine. *Accreditation:* AACSB. Part-time programs available. *Students:* 82 full-time (50 women), 7 part-time (5 women); includes 8 minority (2 Black or African American, non-Hispanic/Latino; 4 Asian, non-Hispanic/Latino; 2 Hispanic/Latino), 5 international. Average age 27. 130 applicants, 73% accepted, 56 enrolled. In 2011, 47 master's awarded. *Degree requirements:* For master's, team consulting project. *Entrance requirements:* For master's, GMAT (preferred) or GRE, 2 letters of recommendation, problem statement analysis, 3-5 years of professional experience. Additional exam requirements/recommendations for international students: Required—TOEFL (minimum score 600 paper-based; 250 computer-based; 100 iBT). *Application deadline:* For fall admission, 3/15 for domestic and international students. Applications are processed on a rolling basis. Application fee: $55. Electronic applications accepted. *Expenses:* Contact institution. *Financial support:* In 2011–12, 89 students received support. Career-related internships or fieldwork, scholarships/grants, and tuition waivers (partial) available. Support available to part-time students. Financial award application deadline: 3/15; financial award applicants required to submit FAFSA. *Faculty research:* Health care; children and families; elder and disabled services; social impact management; organizations in the non-profit, for-profit, or public sector. *Unit head:* Dr. Brenda Anderson, Program Director, 781-736-8423, E-mail: banderson@brandeis.edu. *Application contact:* Shana Sconyers, Assistant Director for Admissions and Financial Aid, 781-736-4229, E-mail: sconyers@brandeis.edu. Web site: http://heller.brandeis.edu/academic/mba.html.

Brandman University, School of Nursing and Health Professions, Irvine, CA 92618. Offers health administration (MHA); health risk and crisis communication (MS).

Brenau University, Sydney O. Smith Graduate School, School of Business and Mass Communication, Gainesville, GA 30501. Offers accounting (MBA); business administration (MBA); healthcare management (MBA); organizational leadership (MS); project management (MBA). Part-time and evening/weekend programs available. Postbaccalaureate distance learning degree programs offered (no on-campus study). *Degree requirements:* For master's, comprehensive exam (for some programs). *Entrance requirements:* For master's, resume, minimum undergraduate GPA of 2.5. Additional exam requirements/recommendations for international students: Required—TOEFL (minimum score 500 paper-based; 173 computer-based; 61 iBT); Recommended—IELTS (minimum score 5). Electronic applications accepted. *Expenses:* Contact institution.

Broadview University–West Jordan, Graduate Programs, West Jordan, UT 84088. Offers business administration (MBA); health care management (MSM); information technology (MSM); managerial leadership (MSM).

Brooklyn College of the City University of New York, Division of Graduate Studies, Department of Health and Nutrition Science, Program in Community Health, Brooklyn, NY 11210-2889. Offers community health education (MA); computer science and health science (MS); health care management (MPH); health care policy and administration (MPH); thanatology (MA). *Accreditation:* CEPH. *Degree requirements:* For master's, thesis or alternative. *Entrance requirements:* For master's, 2 letters of recommendation, essay. Additional exam requirements/recommendations for international students: Required—TOEFL. Electronic applications accepted. *Faculty research:* Diet restriction, religious practices in bereavement, diabetes, stress management, palliative care.

California Coast University, School of Administration and Management, Santa Ana, CA 92701. Offers business marketing (MBA); health care management (MBA); human resource management (MBA); management (MBA, MS). Postbaccalaureate distance learning degree programs offered (no on-campus study). Electronic applications accepted.

California Intercontinental University, School of Healthcare, Diamond Bar, CA 91765. Offers healthcare management and leadership (MBA, DBA).

California State University, Bakersfield, Division of Graduate Studies, School of Business and Public Administration, Administration–Health Care Management Program, Bakersfield, CA 93311. Offers MSA. *Entrance requirements:* For master's, GRE. *Application deadline:* Applications are processed on a rolling basis. Application fee: $55. *Expenses: Required fees:* $1302 per unit. Part-time tuition and fees vary according to course load and program. *Unit head:* Dr. B.J. Moore, 661-654-3026, E-mail: bjmoore@csub.edu.

California State University, Chico, Office of Graduate Studies, College of Behavioral and Social Sciences, Department of Political Science, Program in Public Administration, Chico, CA 95929-0722. Offers health administration (MPA); local government management (MPA). *Accreditation:* NASPAA. Part-time programs available. *Students:* 31 full-time (18 women), 26 part-time (17 women); includes 24 minority (3 Black or African American, non-Hispanic/Latino; 1 American Indian or Alaska Native, non-Hispanic/Latino; 7 Asian, non-Hispanic/Latino; 13 Hispanic/Latino), 3 international. Average age 31. 45 applicants, 71% accepted, 18 enrolled. In 2011, 21 master's awarded. *Entrance requirements:* For master's, 2 letters of recommendation. Additional exam requirements/recommendations for international students: Required—TOEFL (minimum score 550 paper-based; 213 computer-based; 80 iBT), IELTS (minimum score 6.5). *Application deadline:* For fall admission, 3/1 priority date for domestic students, 3/1 for international students; for spring admission, 9/15 priority date for domestic students, 9/15 for international students. Applications are processed on a rolling basis. Application fee: $55. Electronic applications accepted. Tuition and fees vary according to class time, course load and degree level. *Financial support:* Fellowships and career-related internships or fieldwork available. *Unit head:* Dr. Donna Kemp, Graduate Coordinator, 530-898-5734. *Application contact:* School of Graduate, International, and Interdisciplinary Studies, 530-898-6880, Fax: 530-898-6889, E-mail: grin@csuchico.edu.

California State University, East Bay, Office of Academic Programs and Graduate Studies, College of Letters, Arts, and Social Sciences, Department of Public Affairs and Administration, Program in Health Care Administration, Hayward, CA 94542-3000. Offers management and change in health care (MS). Part-time and evening/weekend programs available. Postbaccalaureate distance learning degree programs offered (no on-campus study). *Faculty:* 1 (woman) full-time, 2 part-time/adjunct (1 woman). *Students:* 43 full-time (36 women), 77 part-time (51 women); includes 60 minority (12 Black or African American, non-Hispanic/Latino; 40 Asian, non-Hispanic/Latino; 6 Hispanic/Latino; 1 Native Hawaiian or other Pacific Islander, non-Hispanic/Latino; 1 Two or more races, non-Hispanic/Latino), 21 international. Average age 31. 108 applicants, 72% accepted, 51 enrolled. In 2011, 47 master's awarded. *Degree requirements:* For master's, thesis or alternative, final project. *Entrance requirements:* For master's, minimum undergraduate cumulative GPA of 2.5, statement of purpose, two letters of academic and/or professional recommendation, professional resume/curriculum vitae, all undergraduate/graduate transcripts. Additional exam requirements/recommendations for international students: Required—TOEFL (minimum score 550 paper-based; 213 computer-based). *Application deadline:* For fall admission, 6/18 for domestic and international students. Application fee: $55. Electronic applications accepted. *Expenses:* Tuition, state resident: full-time $6738; part-time $1302 per quarter. Tuition, nonresident: full-time $12,690; part-time $2294 per quarter. *Required fees:* $449 per quarter. Tuition and fees vary according to degree level, program and reciprocity agreements. *Financial support:* Career-related internships or fieldwork, Federal Work-Study, institutionally sponsored loans, and scholarships/grants available. Support available to part-time students. Financial award application deadline: 3/2; financial award applicants required to submit FAFSA. *Unit head:* Dr. Toni Fogarty, Chair/HCA Graduate Advisor, 510-885-3282, Fax: 510-885-3726, E-mail: toni.fogarty@csueastbay.edu. Web site: http://class.csueastbay.edu/publicadmin/Healthcare_Admin.php.

California State University, East Bay, Office of Academic Programs and Graduate Studies, College of Letters, Arts, and Social Sciences, Department of Public Affairs and Administration, Program in Public Administration, Hayward, CA 94542-3000. Offers health care administration (MPA); management of human resources and change (MPA); public management and policy analysis (MPA). Part-time and evening/weekend programs available. *Faculty:* 5 full-time (1 woman). *Students:* 10 full-time (5 women), 135 part-time (92 women); includes 81 minority (25 Black or African American, non-Hispanic/Latino; 25 Asian, non-Hispanic/Latino; 23 Hispanic/Latino; 4 Native Hawaiian or other Pacific Islander, non-Hispanic/Latino; 4 Two or more races, non-Hispanic/Latino), 4 international. Average age 33. 132 applicants, 51% accepted, 45 enrolled. In 2011, 77 master's awarded. *Degree requirements:* For master's, comprehensive exam (for some programs), comprehensive exam or thesis. *Entrance requirements:* For master's, minimum GPA of 2.5; statement of purpose; 2 letters of recommendation; professional resume/curriculum vitae. Additional exam requirements/recommendations for international students: Required—TOEFL (minimum score 550 paper-based; 213 computer-based; 79 iBT). *Application deadline:* For fall admission, 6/18 for domestic and international students. Application fee: $55. Electronic applications accepted. *Expenses:* Tuition, state resident: full-time $6738; part-time $1302 per quarter. Tuition, nonresident: full-time $12,690; part-time $2294 per quarter. *Required fees:* $449 per quarter. Tuition and fees vary according to degree level, program and reciprocity agreements. *Financial support:* Fellowships, teaching assistantships, career-related internships or fieldwork, Federal Work-Study, institutionally sponsored loans, and scholarships/grants available. Support available to part-time students. Financial award application deadline: 3/2; financial award applicants required to submit FAFSA. *Unit head:* Dr. Toni Fogarty, Coordinator, 510-885-3282, Fax: 510-885-3726, E-mail: toni.fogarty@csueastbay.edu. *Application contact:* Prof. Michael Moon, Public Administration Graduate Advisor, 510-885-2545, Fax: 510-885-3726, E-mail: michael.moon@csueastbay.edu. Web site: http://class.csueastbay.edu/publicadmin/Public_Admin.php.

California State University, Fresno, Division of Graduate Studies, College of Health and Human Services, Department of Public Health, Fresno, CA 93740-8027. Offers health policy and management (MPH); health promotion (MPH). *Accreditation:* CEPH. Part-time and evening/weekend programs available. *Degree requirements:* For master's, thesis or alternative. *Entrance requirements:* For master's, GRE General Test, minimum GPA of 2.5. Additional exam requirements/recommendations for international

students: Required—TOEFL. Electronic applications accepted. *Faculty research:* Foster parent training, geriatrics, tobacco control.

California State University, Long Beach, Graduate Studies, College of Health and Human Services, Program in Health Care Administration, Long Beach, CA 90840. Offers MS. *Accreditation:* CAHME. Part-time programs available. *Faculty:* 3 full-time (2 women), 6 part-time/adjunct (1 woman). *Students:* 20 full-time (15 women), 13 part-time (6 women); includes 18 minority (4 Black or African American, non-Hispanic/Latino; 9 Asian, non-Hispanic/Latino; 4 Hispanic/Latino; 1 Two or more races, non-Hispanic/ Latino), 7 international. Average age 29. 117 applicants, 46% accepted, 10 enrolled. In 2011, 33 master's awarded. *Degree requirements:* For master's, comprehensive exam or thesis. *Entrance requirements:* For master's, minimum GPA of 3.0. *Application deadline:* For fall admission, 6/15 for domestic students; for spring admission, 11/15 for domestic students. Applications are processed on a rolling basis. Application fee: $55. Electronic applications accepted. *Financial support:* Federal Work-Study, institutionally sponsored loans, and scholarships/grants available. Financial award application deadline: 3/2. *Faculty research:* Long-term care, Immigration Reform Act and health care, physician reimbursement. *Unit head:* Dr. C. Kevin Malotte, Chair, 562-985-2177, Fax: 562-985-2180, E-mail: kmalotte@csulb.edu. *Application contact:* Dr. Tony Sinay, Program Director, 562-985-5304.

California State University, Los Angeles, Graduate Studies, College of Business and Economics, Department of Management, Los Angeles, CA 90032-8530. Offers health care management (MS); management (MBA, MS). *Accreditation:* AACSB. Part-time and evening/weekend programs available. *Faculty:* 4 part-time/adjunct (1 woman). *Students:* 10 full-time (7 women), 42 part-time (27 women); includes 31 minority (2 Black or African American, non-Hispanic/Latino; 16 Asian, non-Hispanic/Latino; 11 Hispanic/Latino; 2 Two or more races, non-Hispanic/Latino), 9 international. Average age 31. 96 applicants, 33% accepted, 14 enrolled. In 2011, 39 degrees awarded. *Entrance requirements:* For master's, GMAT, minimum GPA of 2.5 during previous 2 years of course work. Additional exam requirements/recommendations for international students: Required—TOEFL (minimum score 550 paper-based; 213 computer-based). *Application deadline:* For fall admission, 5/1 for domestic and international students. Applications are processed on a rolling basis. Application fee: $55. Electronic applications accepted. *Expenses:* Tuition, state resident: full-time $8225. *Financial support:* Application deadline: 3/1. *Unit head:* Dr. Angela Young, Chair, 323-343-2890, Fax: 323-343-6461, E-mail: ayoung3@calstatela.edu. *Application contact:* Dr. Karin Brown, Acting Associate Dean of Graduate Studies, 323-343-3820 Ext. 3827, Fax: 323-343-5653, E-mail: kbrown5@calstatela.edu. Web site: http://cbe.calstatela.edu/mgmt/.

California State University, Northridge, Graduate Studies, College of Health and Human Development, Department of Health Sciences, Northridge, CA 91330. Offers health administration (MS); public health (MPH). *Accreditation:* CEPH. *Entrance requirements:* For master's, GRE General Test or minimum GPA of 3.0. Additional exam requirements/recommendations for international students: Required—TOEFL. *Faculty research:* Labor market needs assessment, health education products, dental hygiene, independent practice prototype.

California State University, San Bernardino, Graduate Studies, College of Natural Sciences, Program in Health Services Administration, San Bernardino, CA 92407-2397. Offers MS. *Students:* 8 full-time (6 women), 12 part-time (10 women); includes 10 minority (4 Black or African American, non-Hispanic/Latino; 4 Asian, non-Hispanic/ Latino; 2 Hispanic/Latino), 4 international. Average age 27. 31 applicants, 55% accepted, 12 enrolled. In 2011, 9 master's awarded. *Degree requirements:* For master's, thesis or alternative. *Entrance requirements:* For master's, GRE, writing exam, minimum GPA of 3.0. *Application deadline:* For fall admission, 8/31 priority date for domestic students. Application fee: $55. *Expenses:* Tuition, state resident: full-time $7356. Tuition, nonresident: full-time $7356. *Required fees:* $1077. Tuition and fees vary according to program. *Financial support:* Fellowships, research assistantships, and teaching assistantships available. *Faculty research:* Smoking and health, oral hygiene, menopause, health services research. *Unit head:* Dr. Cynthia Paxton, Assistant Dean, 909-537-5343, Fax: 909-537-7037, E-mail: cpaxton@csusb.edu. *Application contact:* Sandra Kamusikiri, Associate Vice-President/Dean of Graduate Studies, 909-537-5058, E-mail: skamusik@csusb.edu.

Cambridge College, School of Management, Cambridge, MA 02138-5304. Offers business negotiation and conflict resolution (M Mgt); general business (M Mgt); health care informatics (M Mgt); health care management (M Mgt); leadership in human and organizational dynamics (M Mgt); non-profit and public organization management (M Mgt); small business development (M Mgt); technology management (M Mgt). Part-time and evening/weekend programs available. *Degree requirements:* For master's, thesis, seminars. *Entrance requirements:* For master's, resume, 2 professional references. Additional exam requirements/recommendations for international students: Required—TOEFL (minimum score 550 paper-based; 213 computer-based; 79 iBT); Recommended—IELTS (minimum score 6). Electronic applications accepted. *Expenses:* Contact institution. *Faculty research:* Negotiation, mediation and conflict resolution; leadership; management of diverse organizations; case studies and simulation methodologies for management education, digital as a second language: social networking for digital immigrants, non-profit and public management.

Capella University, School of Business and Technology, Minneapolis, MN 55402. Offers accounting (MBA), including system design and programming; business (Certificate), including human resource management (MS, PhD, Certificate), information technology management (MS, PhD, Certificate), leadership (MBA, MS, PhD, Certificate); finance (MBA); general business (MBA); health care management (MBA); information technology (MS, Certificate), including general information technology (MS), information security, network architecture and design (MS), professional projects management (Certificate), project management and leadership (MS), system design and development (MS),); information technology management (MBA); marketing (MBA); organization and management (MBA, MS, PhD), including general business (PhD), general organization and management (MBA, MS), human resource management (MS, PhD, Certificate), information technology management (MS, PhD, Certificate), leadership (MBA, MS, PhD, Certificate); project management (MBA). Part-time and evening/weekend programs available. Postbaccalaureate distance learning degree programs offered (minimal on-campus study). Terminal master's awarded for partial completion of doctoral program. *Degree requirements:* For master's, thesis optional, integrative project; for doctorate, comprehensive exam, thesis/dissertation. *Entrance requirements:* Additional exam requirements/recommendations for international students: Required—TOEFL (minimum score 550 paper-based; 213 computer-based), TWE (minimum score 4). Electronic applications accepted. *Faculty research:* Business policies: strategic, corporate, and financial management; interplay of technological, organizational and social change.

Capella University, School of Human Services, Minneapolis, MN 55402. Offers addictions counseling (Certificate); counseling studies (MS, PhD); criminal justice (MS, PhD, Certificate); diversity studies (Certificate); general human services (MS, PhD); health care administration (MS, PhD, Certificate); management of nonprofit agencies (MS, PhD, Certificate); marital, couple and family counseling/therapy (MS); marriage and family services (Certificate); mental health counseling (MS); professional counseling (Certificate); social and community services (MS, PhD, Certificate). Part-time and evening/weekend programs available. Postbaccalaureate distance learning degree programs offered (minimal on-campus study). Terminal master's awarded for partial completion of doctoral program. *Degree requirements:* For master's, thesis optional, integrative project; for doctorate, comprehensive exam, thesis/dissertation. *Entrance requirements:* Additional exam requirements/recommendations for international students: Required—TOEFL (minimum score 550 paper-based; 213 computer-based), TWE (minimum score 4). Electronic applications accepted. *Faculty research:* Compulsive and addictive behaviors, substance abuse, assessment of psychopathology and neuropsychology.

Capella University, School of Public Service Leadership, Minneapolis, MN 55402. Offers criminal justice (MS, PhD); emergency management (MS, PhD); general human services (MS, PhD); general public administration (MPA, DPA); gerontology (MS); health care administration (MS, PhD); health management and policy (MSPH); management of nonprofit agencies (MS, PhD); nurse educator (MS); public safety leadership (MS, PhD); social and community services (MS, PhD); social behavioral sciences (MSPH).

Carnegie Mellon University, Heinz College, School of Public Policy and Management, Master of Science Program in Health Care Policy and Management, Pittsburgh, PA 15213-3891. Offers MSHCPM. Part-time and evening/weekend programs available. *Degree requirements:* For master's, internship. *Entrance requirements:* For master's, GRE or GMAT, college-level course in advanced algebra/pre-calculus; college-level courses in economics and statistics (recommended). Additional exam requirements/ recommendations for international students: Required—TOEFL or IELTS. Electronic applications accepted.

Carnegie Mellon University, Heinz College, School of Public Policy and Management, Programs in Medical Management, Pittsburgh, PA 15213-3891. Offers MMM.

Central Michigan University, Central Michigan University Global Campus, Program in Administration, Mount Pleasant, MI 48859. Offers acquisitions administration (MSA, Certificate); general administration (MSA, Certificate); health services administration (MSA, Certificate); human resources administration (MSA, Certificate); information resource management (MSA, Certificate); international administration (MSA, Certificate); leadership (MSA, Certificate); public administration (MSA, Certificate); research administration (MSA, Certificate). Part-time and evening/weekend programs available. Postbaccalaureate distance learning degree programs offered (no on-campus study). *Students:* Average age 38. *Entrance requirements:* For master's, minimum GPA of 2.7 in major. *Application deadline:* Applications are processed on a rolling basis. Application fee: $50. Electronic applications accepted. *Financial support:* Scholarships/ grants available. Support available to part-time students. Financial award applicants required to submit FAFSA. *Unit head:* Dr. Nana Korsah, Director, 989-774-6525, E-mail: korsa1na@cmich.edu. *Application contact:* 877-268-4636, E-mail: cmuglobal@ cmich.edu.

Central Michigan University, Central Michigan University Global Campus, Program in Health Administration, Mount Pleasant, MI 48859. Offers health administration (DHA); international health (Certificate); nutrition and dietetics (MS). Part-time and evening/ weekend programs available. Postbaccalaureate distance learning degree programs offered (minimal on-campus study). Electronic applications accepted. *Financial support:* Scholarships/grants available. Support available to part-time students. Financial award applicants required to submit FAFSA. *Unit head:* Steven D. Berkshire, Director, 989-774-1640, E-mail: berks1sd@cmich.edu. *Application contact:* Off-Campus Programs Call Center, 877-268-4636, E-mail: cmuoffcampus@cmich.edu.

Central Michigan University, College of Graduate Studies, The Herbert H. and Grace A. Dow College of Health Professions, School of Health Sciences, Mount Pleasant, MI 48859. Offers exercise science (MA); health administration (DHA). Part-time and evening/weekend programs available. Postbaccalaureate distance learning degree programs offered (no on-campus study). *Degree requirements:* For doctorate, comprehensive exam, thesis/dissertation. *Entrance requirements:* For doctorate, accredited master's or doctoral degree, 5 years related work experience. Electronic applications accepted.

Central Michigan University, College of Graduate Studies, Interdisciplinary Administration Programs, Mount Pleasant, MI 48859. Offers acquisitions administration (MSA, Graduate Certificate); general administration (MSA, Graduate Certificate); health services administration (MSA, Graduate Certificate); human resource administration (Graduate Certificate); human resources administration (MSA); information resource management (MSA, Graduate Certificate); international administration (MSA, Graduate Certificate); leadership (MSA, Graduate Certificate); organizational communication (MSA, Graduate Certificate); public administration (MSA, Graduate Certificate); recreation and park administration (MSA); sport administration (MSA). *Accreditation:* AACSB. Part-time and evening/weekend programs available. Postbaccalaureate distance learning degree programs offered (no on-campus study). *Degree requirements:* For master's, thesis or alternative. *Entrance requirements:* For master's, bachelor's degree with minimum GPA of 2.7. Electronic applications accepted. *Faculty research:* Interdisciplinary studies in acquisitions administration, health services administration, sport administration, recreation and park administration, and international administration.

Champlain College, Graduate Studies, Burlington, VT 05402-0670. Offers business (MBA); digital forensic management (MS); education (M Ed); emergent media (MFA); health care management (MS); law (MS); managing innovation and information technology (MS); mediation and applied conflict studies (MS). Part-time programs available. Postbaccalaureate distance learning degree programs offered (no on-campus study). *Faculty:* 11 full-time (1 woman), 26 part-time/adjunct (11 women). *Students:* 328 full-time (213 women), 66 part-time (36 women); includes 17 minority (11 Black or African American, non-Hispanic/Latino; 1 Asian, non-Hispanic/Latino; 4 Hispanic/Latino; 1 Two or more races, non-Hispanic/Latino). Average age 37. 132 applicants, 90% accepted, 102 enrolled. In 2011, 8 master's awarded. *Degree requirements:* For master's, capstone project. *Entrance requirements:* Additional exam requirements/ recommendations for international students: Required—TOEFL. *Application deadline:* For fall admission, 8/1 priority date for domestic students, 8/1 for international students; for spring admission, 1/1 priority date for domestic students, 1/1 for international students. Applications are processed on a rolling basis. Application fee: $50. Electronic applications accepted. *Expenses: Tuition:* Part-time $746 per credit. Tuition and fees vary according to program. *Financial support:* Applicants required to submit FAFSA. *Unit head:* Dr. Donald Haggerty, Associate Provost, 802-865-6403, Fax: 802-865-6447. *Application contact:* Jon Walsh, Assistant Vice President, Graduate Admission, 800-570-5858, E-mail: walsh@champlain.edu. Web site: http://www.champlain.edu/master/.

Charleston Southern University, Program in Business, Charleston, SC 29423-8087. Offers accounting (MBA); finance (MBA); health care administration (MBA); information systems (MBA); organizational development (MBA). Part-time and evening/weekend programs available. *Degree requirements:* For master's, thesis optional. *Entrance requirements:* For master's, GMAT. Additional exam requirements/recommendations for international students: Required—TOEFL (minimum score 550 paper-based; 213 computer-based; 79 iBT).

Clark University, Graduate School, Graduate School of Management, Business Administration Program, Worcester, MA 01610-1477. Offers accounting (MBA); finance (MBA); global business (MBA); health care management (MBA); management (MBA); management of information technology (MBA); marketing (MBA). *Accreditation:* AACSB. Part-time and evening/weekend programs available. *Students:* 103 full-time (47 women), 108 part-time (41 women); includes 16 minority (7 Black or African American, non-Hispanic/Latino; 5 Asian, non-Hispanic/Latino; 4 Hispanic/Latino), 69 international. Average age 30. 371 applicants, 48% accepted, 77 enrolled. In 2011, 112 master's awarded. *Degree requirements:* For master's, thesis optional. *Application deadline:* For fall admission, 6/1 priority date for domestic students; for spring admission, 12/1 priority date for domestic students. Applications are processed on a rolling basis. Application fee: $50. Electronic applications accepted. *Expenses: Tuition:* Full-time $37,000; part-time $1156 per credit hour. *Financial support:* In 2011–12, research assistantships with partial tuition reimbursements (averaging $4,800 per year), teaching assistantships with partial tuition reimbursements (averaging $4,800 per year) were awarded; fellowships, career-related internships or fieldwork, Federal Work-Study, institutionally sponsored loans, and tuition waivers (partial) also available. Support available to part-time students. Financial award application deadline: 5/31. *Faculty research:* Marketing, accounting, human resource management, management information systems, business finance. *Unit head:* Dr. Catherine Usoff, Dean, 508-793-8822, Fax: 508-793-8822, E-mail: clarkmba@clarku.edu. *Application contact:* Patrick Oroszko, Enrollment and Marketing Director, 508-793-8822, Fax: 508-793-8822, E-mail: clarkmba@clarku.edu. Web site: http://www.clarku.edu/gsom/prospective/mba/.

Clayton State University, School of Graduate Studies, Program in Health Administration, Morrow, GA 30260-0285. Offers MHA. Part-time and evening/weekend programs available. *Faculty:* 5 full-time (1 woman). *Students:* 29 full-time (15 women), 29 part-time (18 women); includes 41 minority (35 Black or African American, non-Hispanic/Latino; 2 Asian, non-Hispanic/Latino; 2 Hispanic/Latino; 2 Two or more races, non-Hispanic/Latino), 4 international. Average age 32. 23 applicants, 91% accepted, 15 enrolled. In 2011, 5 master's awarded. *Degree requirements:* For master's, comprehensive exam, thesis. *Entrance requirements:* For master's, GRE/GMAT, 2 official copies of transcripts, 3 letters of recommendation, statement of purpose. Additional exam requirements/recommendations for international students: Required—TOEFL (minimum score 550 paper-based; 213 computer-based; 80 iBT). *Application deadline:* For fall admission, 6/15 priority date for domestic students, 5/1 for international students; for spring admission, 11/15 priority date for domestic students, 9/1 for international students. Applications are processed on a rolling basis. Application fee: $75. Electronic applications accepted. *Expenses:* Contact institution. *Financial support:* Application deadline: 7/1; applicants required to submit FAFSA. *Unit head:* Dr. Thomas McIlwain, Dean, School of Graduate Studies/Director, 678-466-4500, Fax: 678-466-4669, E-mail: thomasmcilwain@clayton.edu. *Application contact:* Michelle Terrell, Program Manager, 678-466-4500, Fax: 678-466-4669, E-mail: michelleterrell@clayton.edu. Web site: http://business.clayton.edu/MHA/.

Cleveland State University, College of Graduate Studies, Maxine Goodman Levin College of Urban Affairs, Program in Public Administration, Cleveland, OH 44115. Offers city management (MPA); economic development (MPA); healthcare administration (MPA); local and urban management (Certificate); non-profit management (Certificate); public financial management (MPA); public management (MPA); urban economic development (Certificate); JD/MPA. *Accreditation:* NASPAA. Part-time and evening/weekend programs available. *Faculty:* 26 full-time (10 women), 14 part-time/adjunct (8 women). *Students:* 36 full-time (22 women), 70 part-time (41 women); includes 31 minority (26 Black or African American, non-Hispanic/Latino; 1 American Indian or Alaska Native, non-Hispanic/Latino; 1 Asian, non-Hispanic/Latino; 2 Hispanic/Latino; 1 Two or more races, non-Hispanic/Latino), 4 international. Average age 36. 122 applicants, 52% accepted, 41 enrolled. In 2011, 45 master's awarded. *Degree requirements:* For master's, thesis or alternative, capstone course. *Entrance requirements:* For master's, GRE General Test (minimum scores in 40th percentile verbal and quantitative, 4.0 writing), minimum GPA of 3.0. Additional exam requirements/recommendations for international students: Required—TOEFL (minimum score 525 paper-based; 197 computer-based; 65 iBT). *Application deadline:* For fall admission, 7/15 priority date for domestic students, 5/15 for international students; for spring admission, 11/1 for international students. Applications are processed on a rolling basis. Application fee: $30. Electronic applications accepted. *Expenses:* Tuition, state resident: full-time $6416; part-time $494 per credit hour. Tuition, nonresident: full-time $12,074; part-time $929 per credit hour. *Financial support:* In 2011–12, 9 students received support, including 6 research assistantships with full and partial tuition reimbursements available (averaging $7,200 per year), 3 teaching assistantships with full and partial tuition reimbursements available (averaging $4,800 per year); career-related internships or fieldwork, scholarships/grants, traineeships, and unspecified assistantships also available. Support available to part-time students. Financial award application deadline: 3/1; financial award applicants required to submit FAFSA. *Faculty research:* Health care administration, public management, economic development, city management, nonprofit management. *Unit head:* Dr. Nancy Meyer-Emerick, Director, 216-687-2261, Fax: 216-687-9342, E-mail: n.meyeremerick@csuohio.edu. *Application contact:* Joan Demko, Graduate Academic Programs Specialist, 216-523-7522, Fax: 216-687-5398, E-mail: urbanprograms@csuohio.edu. Web site: http://urban.csuohio.edu/academics/graduate/mpa/.

Cleveland State University, College of Graduate Studies, Monte Ahuja College of Business, MBA Programs, Cleveland, OH 44115. Offers business administration (AMBA, MBA); executive business administration (EMBA); health care administration (MBA); off-campus programs (MBA); JD/MBA; MSN/MBA. *Accreditation:* AACSB. Part-time and evening/weekend programs available. *Faculty:* 33 full-time (9 women), 16 part-time/adjunct (2 women). *Students:* 169 full-time (72 women), 490 part-time (205 women); includes 99 minority (47 Black or African American, non-Hispanic/Latino; 33 Asian, non-Hispanic/Latino; 17 Hispanic/Latino; 2 Two or more races, non-Hispanic/Latino), 83 international. Average age 30. 716 applicants, 55% accepted, 231 enrolled. In 2011, 391 master's awarded. *Entrance requirements:* For master's, GMAT or GRE. Additional exam requirements/recommendations for international students: Required—TOEFL (minimum score 550 paper-based; 213 computer-based; 79 iBT). *Application deadline:* For fall admission, 7/15 priority date for domestic students, 5/15 for international students; for spring admission, 12/15 priority date for domestic students, 11/1 for international students. Applications are processed on a rolling basis. Application fee: $30. *Expenses:* Tuition, state resident: full-time $6416; part-time $494 per credit hour. Tuition, nonresident: full-time $12,074; part-time $929 per credit hour. *Financial support:* In 2011–12, 45 research assistantships with full and partial tuition reimbursements (averaging $6,960 per year), 1 teaching assistantship with full and partial tuition reimbursement (averaging $7,800 per year) were awarded; tuition waivers (full) and unspecified assistantships also available. Financial award application deadline: 5/15; financial award applicants required to submit FAFSA. *Total annual research expenditures:* $70,000. *Unit head:* Bruce Gottschalk, MBA Programs Administrator, 216-687-3730, Fax: 216-687-5311, E-mail: cbacsu@csuohio.edu. *Application contact:* Patricia Hite, Director, Academic Program Support, 216-687-6925, Fax: 216-687-6888, E-mail: p.hite@csuohio.edu. Web site: http://www.csuohio.edu/cba/.

The College at Brockport, State University of New York, School of Education and Human Services, Department of Public Administration, Brockport, NY 14420-2997. Offers arts administration (AGC); nonprofit management (AGC); public administration (MPA), including general public administration, health care management, nonprofit management. *Accreditation:* NASPAA. Part-time and evening/weekend programs available. *Students:* 24 full-time (20 women), 68 part-time (56 women); includes 19 minority (13 Black or African American, non-Hispanic/Latino; 4 Asian, non-Hispanic/Latino; 2 Hispanic/Latino). 49 applicants, 65% accepted, 21 enrolled. In 2011, 31 degrees awarded. *Degree requirements:* For master's, thesis or alternative. *Entrance requirements:* For master's, GRE or minimum GPA of 3.0, letters of recommendation, statement of objectives; current resume. Additional exam requirements/recommendations for international students: Required—TOEFL (minimum score 550 paper-based; 213 computer-based; 79 iBT). *Application deadline:* For fall admission, 3/1 priority date for domestic students, 3/1 for international students; for spring admission, 10/1 priority date for domestic students, 10/1 for international students. Application fee: $50. Electronic applications accepted. *Financial support:* In 2011–12, teaching assistantships with full tuition reimbursements (averaging $6,000 per year) were awarded; Federal Work-Study, scholarships/grants, and unspecified assistantships also available. Support available to part-time students. Financial award application deadline: 3/15; financial award applicants required to submit FAFSA. *Faculty research:* E-government, performance management, nonprofits and policy implementation, Medicaid and disabilities. *Unit head:* Dr. Ed Downey, Chairperson, 585-395-5568, Fax: 585-395-2172, E-mail: edowney@brockport.edu. *Application contact:* Dr. Ed Downey, Chairperson, 585-395-5568, Fax: 585-395-2172, E-mail: edowney@brockport.edu. Web site: http://www.brockport.edu/graduate/.

College of Saint Elizabeth, Department of Health Professions and Related Sciences, Morristown, NJ 07960-6989. Offers health care management (MS). Part-time and evening/weekend programs available. *Faculty:* 3 full-time (all women), 6 part-time/adjunct (3 women). *Students:* 4 full-time (3 women), 179 part-time (137 women); includes 47 minority (19 Black or African American, non-Hispanic/Latino; 1 American Indian or Alaska Native, non-Hispanic/Latino; 14 Asian, non-Hispanic/Latino; 12 Hispanic/Latino; 1 Native Hawaiian or other Pacific Islander, non-Hispanic/Latino), 2 international. Average age 45. 22 applicants, 50% accepted, 9 enrolled. In 2011, 7 master's awarded. *Degree requirements:* For master's, thesis optional, culminating experience. *Entrance requirements:* For master's, minimum GPA of 3.0. Additional exam requirements/recommendations for international students: Required—TOEFL (minimum score 550 paper-based). *Application deadline:* Applications are processed on a rolling basis. Application fee: $35. Electronic applications accepted. *Expenses: Tuition:* Part-time $899 per credit. *Required fees:* $73 per credit. *Financial support:* Career-related internships or fieldwork, tuition waivers (partial), and unspecified assistantships available. Support available to part-time students. Financial award application deadline: 3/15; financial award applicants required to submit FAFSA. *Faculty research:* Consumer protection in health care. *Unit head:* Linda Hunter, Director of the Graduate Program in Health Care Management, 973-290-4040, Fax: 973-290-4167, E-mail: lhunter@cse.edu. *Application contact:* Donna Tatarka, Dean of Admission, 973-290-4705, Fax: 973-290-4710, E-mail: dtatarka@cse.edu. Web site: http://www.cse.edu/academics/academic-areas/health-wellness/health-care-management/?tabID-tabGraduate&divID-progGraduate.

Colorado Technical University Sioux Falls, Programs in Business Administration and Management, Sioux Falls, SD 57108. Offers business administration (MBA); business management (MSM); health science management (MSM); human resources management (MSM); information technology (MSM); organizational leadership (MSM); project management (MBA); technology management (MBA). Evening/weekend programs available. *Degree requirements:* For master's, thesis optional. *Entrance requirements:* For master's, minimum 2 years work experience, resume.

Columbia Southern University, MBA Program, Orange Beach, AL 36561. Offers electronic business and technology (MBA); finance (MBA); general (MBA); healthcare management (MBA); hospitality and tourism (MBA); human resources management (MBA); international management (MBA); marketing (MBA); project management (MBA); public administration (MBA); sport management (MBA). Part-time and evening/weekend programs available. Postbaccalaureate distance learning degree programs offered (no on-campus study). *Entrance requirements:* For master's, bachelor's degree from accredited/approved institution. Additional exam requirements/recommendations for international students: Required—TOEFL. Electronic applications accepted.

Columbia University, Columbia University Mailman School of Public Health, Department of Health Policy and Management, New York, NY 10032. Offers Exec MPH, MPH. *Accreditation:* CAHME. Evening/weekend programs available. *Students:* 163 full-time (133 women), 156 part-time (98 women); includes 115 minority (21 Black or African American, non-Hispanic/Latino; 1 American Indian or Alaska Native, non-Hispanic/Latino; 70 Asian, non-Hispanic/Latino; 21 Hispanic/Latino; 2 Two or more races, non-Hispanic/Latino), 31 international. Average age 31. 477 applicants, 67% accepted, 160 enrolled. In 2011, 145 master's awarded. *Degree requirements:* For master's, thesis optional. *Entrance requirements:* For master's, GRE General Test. Additional exam requirements/recommendations for international students: Required—TOEFL (minimum score 600 paper-based; 250 computer-based; 100 iBT). *Application deadline:* For fall admission, 1/5 for domestic students. Application fee: $60. Electronic applications accepted. *Financial support:* Research assistantships, teaching assistantships, career-related internships or fieldwork, and Federal Work-Study available. Support available to part-time students. Financial award application deadline: 2/1; financial award applicants required to submit FAFSA. *Faculty research:* Health care reform, health care disparities, state and national and cross-national health policy, health care quality, organization structure and performance. *Unit head:* Dr. Michael Sparer, Chairperson, 212-305-3924. *Application contact:* Dr. Joseph Korevec, Director of Admissions and Financial Aid, 212-305-8698, Fax: 212-342-1861, E-mail: ph-admit@columbia.edu. Web site: http://mallman.hs.columbia.edu/hpm/index.html.

Concordia University, School of Graduate Studies, John Molson School of Business, Montréal, QC H3G 1M8, Canada. Offers administration (M Sc, Diploma); aviation management (Certificate, Diploma); business administration (MBA, UA Undergraduate Associate, PhD), including international aviation (UA Undergraduate Associate); chartered accountancy (Diploma); community organizational development (Certificate); event management and fundraising (Certificate); executive business administration (EMBA); investment management (Diploma); investment management option (MBA); management accounting (Certificate); management of healthcare organizations (Certificate); sport administration (Diploma). PhD program offered jointly with HEC Montreal, McGill University, and Université du Québec à Montréal. *Accreditation:* AACSB. Part-time and evening/weekend programs available. *Degree requirements:* For master's, one foreign language, thesis (for some programs), research project; for doctorate, one foreign language, thesis/dissertation; for other advanced degree, one foreign language. *Entrance requirements:* For master's and doctorate, GMAT. Additional exam requirements/recommendations for international students: Required—TOEFL. *Expenses:* Contact institution. *Faculty research:* General business, capital markets, international business.

Health Services Management and Hospital Administration

Concordia University, St. Paul, College of Business and Organizational Leadership, St. Paul, MN 55104-5494. Offers business and organizational leadership (MBA); criminal justice leadership (MA); health care management (MBA); human resources management (MA); leadership and management (MA). *Accreditation:* ACBSP. Evening/weekend programs available. Postbaccalaureate distance learning degree programs offered (minimal on-campus study). *Faculty:* 16 full-time (6 women), 31 part-time/adjunct (12 women). *Students:* 417 full-time (230 women), 11 part-time (5 women); includes 83 minority (40 Black or African American, non-Hispanic/Latino; 2 American Indian or Alaska Native, non-Hispanic/Latino; 25 Asian, non-Hispanic/Latino; 5 Hispanic/Latino; 1 Native Hawaiian or other Pacific Islander, non-Hispanic/Latino; 10 Two or more races, non-Hispanic/Latino), 5 international. Average age 35. 316 applicants, 74% accepted, 198 enrolled. In 2011, 204 master's awarded. *Application deadline:* Applications are processed on a rolling basis. Application fee: $50. Electronic applications accepted. *Expenses: Tuition:* Full-time $8100; part-time $435 per credit. Tuition and fees vary according to program. *Financial support:* Applicants required to submit FAFSA. *Unit head:* Dr. Bruce Corrie, Dean, 651-641-8226, Fax: 651-641-8807, E-mail: corrie@csp.edu. *Application contact:* Kimberly Craig, Director of Graduate and Cohort Admission, 651-603-6223, Fax: 651-603-6320, E-mail: craig@csp.edu.

Concordia University Wisconsin, Graduate Programs, School of Business and Legal Studies, MBA Program, Mequon, WI 53097-2402. Offers finance (MBA); health care administration (MBA); human resource management (MBA); international business (MBA); international business-bilingual English/Chinese (MBA); management (MBA); management information systems (MBA); managerial communications (MBA); marketing (MBA); public administration (MBA); risk management (MBA). Postbaccalaureate distance learning degree programs offered (minimal on-campus study). *Students:* 308 full-time (146 women), 536 part-time (288 women); includes 126 minority (76 Black or African American, non-Hispanic/Latino; 9 American Indian or Alaska Native, non-Hispanic/Latino; 15 Asian, non-Hispanic/Latino; 12 Hispanic/Latino; 14 Two or more races, non-Hispanic/Latino), 276 international. Average age 35. In 2011, 110 master's awarded. *Degree requirements:* For master's, comprehensive exam, thesis or alternative. *Entrance requirements:* Additional exam requirements/recommendations for international students: Required—TOEFL. *Application deadline:* For fall admission, 8/1 priority date for domestic students; for spring admission, 1/15 for domestic students. Applications are processed on a rolling basis. Application fee: $50. *Expenses:* Contact institution. *Financial support:* Application deadline: 8/1. *Unit head:* Dr. David Borst, Director, 262-243-4298, Fax: 262-243-4428, E-mail: david.borst@cuw.edu. *Application contact:* Mary Eberhardt, Graduate Admissions, 262-243-4551, Fax: 262-243-4428, E-mail: mary.eberhardt@cuw.edu.

Copenhagen Business School, Graduate Programs, Copenhagen, Denmark. Offers business administration (Exec MBA, MBA, PhD); business administration and information systems (M Sc); business, language and culture (M Sc); economics and business administration (M Sc); health management (MHM); international business and politics (M Sc); public administration (MPA); shipping and logistics (Exec MBA); technology, market and organization (MBA).

Cornell University, Graduate School, Graduate Fields of Human Ecology, Field of Policy Analysis and Management, Ithaca, NY 14853-0001. Offers consumer policy (PhD); evaluation (PhD); family and social welfare policy (PhD); health administration (MHA); health management and policy (PhD). *Faculty:* 33 full-time (13 women). *Students:* 63 full-time (36 women); includes 15 minority (6 Black or African American, non-Hispanic/Latino; 1 American Indian or Alaska Native, non-Hispanic/Latino; 8 Asian, non-Hispanic/Latino), 7 international. Average age 25. 137 applicants, 35% accepted, 29 enrolled. In 2011, 33 master's, 1 doctorate awarded. *Degree requirements:* For master's, thesis; for doctorate, thesis/dissertation. *Entrance requirements:* For master's, GRE General Test or GMAT, 2 letters of recommendation; for doctorate, GRE General Test, 2 letters of recommendation. Additional exam requirements/recommendations for international students: Required—TOEFL (minimum score 550 paper-based; 213 computer-based; 77 iBT). *Application deadline:* For fall admission, 1/15 for domestic students. Application fee: $95. Electronic applications accepted. *Financial support:* In 2011–12, 17 students received support, including 2 fellowships with full and partial tuition reimbursements available, 6 research assistantships with full and partial tuition reimbursements available, 7 teaching assistantships with full and partial tuition reimbursements available; institutionally sponsored loans, scholarships/grants, health care benefits, tuition waivers (full and partial), and unspecified assistantships also available. Financial award applicants required to submit FAFSA. *Faculty research:* Health policy, family policy, social welfare policy, program evaluation, consumer policy. *Unit head:* Director of Graduate Studies, 607-255-7772. *Application contact:* Graduate Field Assistant, 607-255-7772, Fax: 607-255-4071, E-mail: pam_phd@cornell.edu. Web site: http://www.gradschool.cornell.edu/fields.php?id-69&a-2.

Daemen College, Program in Executive Leadership and Change, Amherst, NY 14226-3592. Offers business (MS); health professions (MS); not-for-profit organizations (MS). Part-time and evening/weekend programs available. *Degree requirements:* For master's, thesis, cohort learning sequence (2 years for weekend cohort; 3 years for weeknight cohort). *Entrance requirements:* For master's, 2 letters of recommendation, interview, goal statement, official transcripts, resume. Additional exam requirements/recommendations for international students: Required—TOEFL (minimum score 500 paper-based; 173 computer-based; 63 iBT), IELTS (minimum score 5.5). Electronic applications accepted.

Dalhousie University, Faculty of Health Professions, School of Health Administration, Halifax, NS B3H 1R2, Canada. Offers MAHSR, MHA, MPH, PhD, LL B/MHA, MBA/MHA, MHA/MN. *Accreditation:* CAHME. Part-time programs available. Postbaccalaureate distance learning degree programs offered (minimal on-campus study). *Entrance requirements:* For master's, GMAT. Additional exam requirements/recommendations for international students: Required—TOEFL, IELTS, CANTEST, CAEL, or Michigan English Language Assessment Battery. Electronic applications accepted. *Expenses:* Contact institution. *Faculty research:* Hospital, nursing, long-term, public, and community health administration; government administration in health areas.

Dallas Baptist University, College of Business, Business Administration Program, Dallas, TX 75211-9299. Offers accounting (MBA); business communication (MBA); conflict resolution management (MBA); entrepreneurship (MBA); finance (MBA); health care management (MBA); international business (MBA); leading the non-profit organization (MBA); management (MBA); management information systems (MBA); marketing (MBA); project management (MBA); technology and engineering management (MBA). *Accreditation:* ACBSP. Part-time and evening/weekend programs available. *Entrance requirements:* For master's, GMAT, minimum GPA of 3.0. Additional exam requirements/recommendations for international students: Required—TOEFL, IELTS. *Application deadline:* Applications are processed on a rolling basis. Application fee: $25. Electronic applications accepted. *Expenses: Tuition:* Full-time $12,060; part-time $670 per credit hour. *Required fees:* $100; $50 per semester. *Financial support:* Federal Work-Study, institutionally sponsored loans, scholarships/grants, and tuition waivers (full and partial) available. Support available to part-time students. Financial award applicants required to submit FAFSA. *Faculty research:* Sports management, services marketing, retailing, strategic management, financial planning/investments. *Unit head:* Dr. Sandra S. Reid, Director, 214-333-5280, Fax: 214-333-5293, E-mail:

graduate@dbu.edu. *Application contact:* Kit P. Montgomery, Director of Graduate Programs, 214-333-5242, Fax: 214-333-5579, E-mail: graduate@dbu.edu. Web site: http://www3.dbu.edu/graduate/mba.asp.

Dallas Baptist University, College of Business, Management Program, Dallas, TX 75211-9299. Offers conflict resolution management (MA); general management (MA); health care management (MA); human resource management (MA). Part-time and evening/weekend programs available. *Entrance requirements:* For master's, GRE General Test, minimum GPA of 3.0. Additional exam requirements/recommendations for international students: Required—TOEFL, IELTS. *Application deadline:* Applications are processed on a rolling basis. Application fee: $25. Electronic applications accepted. *Expenses: Tuition:* Full-time $12,060; part-time $670 per credit hour. *Required fees:* $100; $50 per semester. *Financial support:* Federal Work-Study, institutionally sponsored loans, scholarships/grants, and tuition waivers (full and partial) available. Support available to part-time students. Financial award applicants required to submit FAFSA. *Faculty research:* Organizational behavior, conflict personalities. *Unit head:* Joanne Hix, Director, 214-333-5280, Fax: 214-333-5293, E-mail: graduate@dbu.edu. *Application contact:* Kit P. Montgomery, Director of Graduate Programs, 214-333-5242, Fax: 214-333-5579, E-mail: graduate@dbu.edu. Web site: http://www3.dbu.edu/graduate/maom.asp.

Dartmouth College, The Dartmouth Institute, Program in Health Policy and Clinical Practice, Hanover, NH 03755. Offers evaluative clinical sciences (MS, PhD). Part-time programs available. *Degree requirements:* For master's, research project or practicum; for doctorate, thesis/dissertation. *Entrance requirements:* For master's and doctorate, GRE or MCAT, 3 letters of recommendation. Additional exam requirements/recommendations for international students: Required—TOEFL. *Faculty research:* Prevention and treatment of cardiovascular diseases, health care cost containment, variation of delivery of care, health care improvement, decision evaluation.

Davenport University, Sneden Graduate School, Grand Rapids, MI 49512. Offers accounting (MBA); business administration (EMBA); finance (MBA); health care management (MBA); human resources (MBA); information assurance (MS); public health (MPH); strategic management (MBA). Evening/weekend programs available. *Entrance requirements:* For master's, GMAT, minimum undergraduate GPA of 2.75. Additional exam requirements/recommendations for international students: Required—TOEFL. Electronic applications accepted. *Faculty research:* Leadership, management, marketing, organizational culture.

Davenport University, Sneden Graduate School, Warren, MI 48092-5209. Offers accounting (MBA); business administration (EMBA); finance (MBA); health care management (MBA); human resources management (MBA); information assurance (MS); public health (MPH); strategic management (MBA). *Entrance requirements:* For master's, minimum undergraduate GPA of 2.7.

Davenport University, Sneden Graduate School, Dearborn, MI 48126-3799. Offers accounting (MBA); business administration (EMBA); finance (MBA); health care management (MBA); human resources management (MBA); information assurance (MS); marketing (MBA); public health (MPH); strategic management (MBA). Part-time and evening/weekend programs available. Postbaccalaureate distance learning degree programs offered (no on-campus study). *Entrance requirements:* For master's, minimum GPA of 2.7, previous course work in accounting and statistics. *Faculty research:* Accounting, international accounting, social and environmental accounting, finance.

Defiance College, Program in Business Administration, Defiance, OH 43512-1610. Offers criminal justice (MBA); health care (MBA); leadership (MBA); sport management (MBA). Part-time and evening/weekend programs available. *Faculty:* 3 full-time (0 women), 2 part-time/adjunct (1 woman). *Students:* 49 part-time (21 women); includes 2 minority (both Hispanic/Latino). *Degree requirements:* For master's, thesis. *Entrance requirements:* For master's, minimum GPA of 2.5. Additional exam requirements/recommendations for international students: Recommended—TOEFL. *Application deadline:* For fall admission, 8/1 for domestic and international students. Applications are processed on a rolling basis. Application fee: $25. *Expenses: Tuition:* Full-time $10,800; part-time $450 per credit hour. *Required fees:* $95; $35 per semester. *Unit head:* Dr. Susan Wajert, Coordinator, 419-783-2372, Fax: 419-784-0426, E-mail: swajert@defiance.edu. *Application contact:* Sally Bissell, Director of Continuing Education, 419-783-2350, Fax: 419-784-0426, E-mail: sbissell@defiance.edu. Web site: http://www.defiance.edu.

Delta State University, Graduate Programs, School of Nursing, Cleveland, MS 38733-0001. Offers family nurse practitioner (MSN); nurse administrator (MSN); nurse educator (MSN). *Accreditation:* AACN. Part-time programs available. *Degree requirements:* For master's, thesis optional. *Entrance requirements:* For master's, GRE General Test. Electronic applications accepted. *Expenses:* Tuition, state resident: full-time $4702; part-time $294 per credit hour. Tuition, nonresident: full-time $12,516; part-time $760 per credit hour. *Required fees:* $586.

DePaul University, Charles H. Kellstadt Graduate School of Business, Department of Management, Chicago, IL 60604-2287. Offers entrepreneurship (MBA); health sector management (MBA); human resource management (MBA, MSHR); leadership/change management (MBA); management planning and strategy (MBA); operations management (MBA). Part-time and evening/weekend programs available. *Faculty:* 36 full-time (7 women), 35 part-time/adjunct (16 women). *Students:* 280 full-time (116 women), 121 part-time (47 women); includes 78 minority (20 Black or African American, non-Hispanic/Latino; 37 Asian, non-Hispanic/Latino; 16 Hispanic/Latino; 1 Native Hawaiian or other Pacific Islander, non-Hispanic/Latino; 4 Two or more races, non-Hispanic/Latino), 33 international. Average age 30. In 2011, 112 master's awarded. *Entrance requirements:* For master's, GMAT, GRE (MSHR), 2 letters of recommendation, resume. Additional exam requirements/recommendations for international students: Required—TOEFL (minimum score 550 paper-based; 213 computer-based). *Application deadline:* For fall admission, 7/1 for domestic students; for winter admission, 10/1 for domestic students; for spring admission, 2/1 for domestic students. Applications are processed on a rolling basis. Application fee: $60. Electronic applications accepted. *Financial support:* Research assistantships available. Financial award application deadline: 4/1. *Faculty research:* Growth management, creativity and innovation, quality management and business process design, entrepreneurship. *Unit head:* Robert T. Ryan, Assistant Dean and Director, 312-362-8810, Fax: 312-362-6677, E-mail: rryan1@depaul.edu. *Application contact:* Christopher E. Kinsella, Director of Cohort MBA Programs, 312-362-8810, Fax: 312-362-6677, E-mail: kgsb@depaul.edu.

DePaul University, School of Public Service, Chicago, IL 60604. Offers administrative foundations (Certificate); community development (Certificate); financial administration management (Certificate); health administration (Certificate); health law and policy (MS); international public services (MS); leadership and policy studies (MS); metropolitan planning (Certificate); nonprofit leadership (Certificate); nonprofit management (MNM); public administration (MPA); public service management (MS), including association management, fundraising and philanthropy, healthcare administration, higher education administration, metropolitan planning; public services (Certificate); JD/MS. Part-time and evening/weekend programs available. Postbaccalaureate distance learning degree programs offered (minimal on-campus study). *Faculty:* 14 full-time (3 women), 43 part-time/adjunct (24 women). *Students:* 366 full-time (266 women), 316 part-time (216

women); includes 283 minority (143 Black or African American, non-Hispanic/Latino; 1 American Indian or Alaska Native, non-Hispanic/Latino; 35 Asian, non-Hispanic/Latino; 88 Hispanic/Latino; 16 Two or more races, non-Hispanic/Latino), 13 international. Average age 29. 162 applicants, 100% accepted, 94 enrolled. In 2011, 108 master's awarded. *Degree requirements:* For master's, thesis or integrative seminar. *Entrance requirements:* For master's, minimum GPA of 2.7. Additional exam requirements/recommendations for international students: Required—TOEFL (minimum score 550 paper-based; 213 computer-based; 80 iBT), IELTS (minimum score 6.5). *Application deadline:* Applications are processed on a rolling basis. Application fee: $40. Electronic applications accepted. *Financial support:* In 2011–12, 60 students received support, including 3 research assistantships with full tuition reimbursements available (averaging $7,000 per year); career-related internships or fieldwork, Federal Work-Study, institutionally sponsored loans, scholarships/grants, tuition waivers (partial), and unspecified assistantships also available. Support available to part-time students. Financial award application deadline: 7/1; financial award applicants required to submit FAFSA. *Faculty research:* Government financing, transportation, leadership, health care, volunteerism and organizational behavior, non-profit organizations. *Total annual research expenditures:* $20,000. *Unit head:* Dr. J. Patrick Murphy, Director, 312-362-5608, Fax: 312-362-5506, E-mail: jpmurphy@depaul.edu. *Application contact:* Megan B. Balderston, Director of Admissions and Marketing, 312-362-5565, Fax: 312-362-5506, E-mail: pubserv@depaul.edu. Web site: http://las.depaul.edu/sps/.

DeSales University, Graduate Division, MBA Program, Center Valley, PA 18034-9568. Offers accounting (MBA); computer information systems (MBA); finance (MBA); health care systems management (MBA); human resources management (MBA); management (MBA); marketing (MBA); project management (MBA); self-design (MBA). *Accreditation:* ACBSP. Part-time programs available. Postbaccalaureate distance learning degree programs offered (no on-campus study). *Entrance requirements:* For master's, GMAT, minimum GPA of 3.0, 2 years of work experience. Additional exam requirements/recommendations for international students: Required—TOEFL. *Application deadline:* Applications are processed on a rolling basis. Electronic applications accepted. Tuition and fees vary according to degree level. *Faculty research:* Quality improvement, executive development, productivity, cross-cultural managerial differences, leadership. *Unit head:* Dr. David Gilfoil, Director, 610-282-1100 Ext. 1828, Fax: 610-282-2869, E-mail: david.gilfoil@desales.edu. *Application contact:* Caryn Stopper, Director of Graduate Admissions, 610-282-1100 Ext. 1768, Fax: 610-282-0525, E-mail: caryn.stopper@desales.edu.

Des Moines University, College of Health Sciences, Program in Healthcare Administration, Des Moines, IA 50312-4104. Offers MHA. Part-time and evening/weekend programs available. *Entrance requirements:* For master's, minimum GPA of 3.0. Additional exam requirements/recommendations for international students: Required—TOEFL (minimum score 600 paper-based). Electronic applications accepted. *Expenses:* Contact institution. *Faculty research:* Quality improvement, rural sociology, women's health, health promotion, patient education.

Dowling College, School of Business, Oakdale, NY 11769-1999. Offers aviation management (MBA, Certificate); banking and finance (MBA, Certificate); corporate finance (MBA); financial planning (Certificate); health care management (MBA, Certificate); human resource management (Certificate); information systems management (MBA); management and leadership (MBA); marketing (Certificate); project management (Certificate); public management (MBA, Certificate); sport, event and entertainment management (Certificate); JD/MBA. Part-time and evening/weekend programs available. Postbaccalaureate distance learning degree programs offered (minimal on-campus study). *Faculty:* 10 full-time (4 women), 54 part-time/adjunct (6 women). *Students:* 237 full-time (99 women), 403 part-time (199 women); includes 186 minority (95 Black or African American, non-Hispanic/Latino; 62 Asian, non-Hispanic/Latino; 28 Hispanic/Latino; 1 Native Hawaiian or other Pacific Islander, non-Hispanic/Latino), 1 international. Average age 35. 345 applicants, 83% accepted, 193 enrolled. In 2011, 350 master's, 7 other advanced degrees awarded. *Degree requirements:* For master's, comprehensive exam, thesis optional. *Entrance requirements:* For master's, minimum GPA of 2.8, 2 letters of recommendation, courses or seminar in accounting and finance, resume. Additional exam requirements/recommendations for international students: Required—TOEFL (minimum score 550 paper-based). *Application deadline:* For fall admission, 9/1 priority date for domestic students; for winter admission, 1/1 priority date for domestic students; for spring admission, 2/1 priority date for domestic students. Applications are processed on a rolling basis. Application fee: $50. Electronic applications accepted. *Expenses: Tuition:* Full-time $19,162; part-time $933 per credit. *Required fees:* $1330; $700 per year. Tuition and fees vary according to course load. *Financial support:* Career-related internships or fieldwork and Federal Work-Study available. Support available to part-time students. Financial award application deadline: 6/30; financial award applicants required to submit FAFSA. *Faculty research:* International finance, computer applications, labor relations, executive development. *Unit head:* Antonia Loschiavo, Assistant Dean, 631-244-3266, Fax: 631-244-1018, E-mail: loschiat@dowling.edu. *Application contact:* Ronnie S. Macdonald, Assistant Vice President for Enrollment Services/Dean of Admissions, 631-244-3357, Fax: 631-244-1059, E-mail: macdonar@dowling.edu.

Duquesne University, John G. Rangos, Sr. School of Health Sciences, Pittsburgh, PA 15282-0001. Offers health management systems (MHMS); occupational therapy (MS); physical therapy (DPT); physician assistant studies (MPAS); rehabilitation science (MS, PhD); speech-language pathology (MS); MBA/MHMS. *Accreditation:* AOTA (one or more programs are accredited); APTA (one or more programs are accredited); ASHA. *Faculty:* 34 full-time (23 women), 20 part-time/adjunct (11 women). *Students:* 227 full-time (180 women), 12 part-time (7 women); includes 8 minority (4 Black or African American, non-Hispanic/Latino; 1 Asian, non-Hispanic/Latino; 1 Hispanic/Latino; 1 Native Hawaiian or other Pacific Islander, non-Hispanic/Latino; 1 Two or more races, non-Hispanic/Latino), 3 international. Average age 24. 537 applicants, 12% accepted, 17 enrolled. In 2011, 43 master's, 31 doctorates awarded. *Degree requirements:* For doctorate, comprehensive exam (for some programs), thesis/dissertation (for some programs). *Entrance requirements:* For master's, GRE General Test (speech-language pathology), 3 letters of recommendation; minimum GPA of 2.75 (health management systems), 3.0 (speech-language pathology and health sciences); for doctorate, GRE General Test (for physical therapy and rehabilitation science), 3 letters of recommendation, minimum GPA of 3.0, personal interview. Additional exam requirements/recommendations for international students: Required—TOEFL (minimum score 550 paper-based; 233 computer-based; 90 iBT). *Application deadline:* Applications are processed on a rolling basis. Electronic applications accepted. *Expenses:* Contact institution. *Financial support:* Federal Work-Study available. Financial award applicants required to submit FAFSA. *Faculty research:* Neuronal processing, electrical stimulation on peripheral neuropathy, CNS stimulatory and inhibitory signals, behavioral genetic methodologies to development disorders of speech, neurogenic communication disorders. *Total annual research expenditures:* $83,650. *Unit head:* Dr. Gregory H. Frazer, Dean, 412-396-5303, Fax: 412-396-5554, E-mail: frazer@duq.edu. *Application contact:* Christopher R. Hilf, Recruiter/Academic Advisor, 412-396-5653, Fax: 412-396-5554, E-mail: hilfc@duq.edu. Web site: http://www.duq.edu/healthsciences/health.html.

D'Youville College, Department of Health Services Administration, Buffalo, NY 14201-1084. Offers clinical research associate (Certificate); health services administration (MS, Certificate); long term care administration (Certificate). Part-time and evening/weekend programs available. *Faculty:* 4 full-time (2 women), 4 part-time/adjunct (0 women). *Students:* 17 full-time (12 women), 60 part-time (48 women); includes 21 minority (19 Black or African American, non-Hispanic/Latino; 2 Hispanic/Latino), 16 international. Average age 34. 41 applicants, 66% accepted, 19 enrolled. In 2011, 5 master's awarded. *Degree requirements:* For master's, project or thesis. *Entrance requirements:* For master's, minimum GPA of 3.0 in major. Additional exam requirements/recommendations for international students: Required—TOEFL (minimum score 500 paper-based; 173 computer-based). *Application deadline:* For fall admission, 5/1 for international students; for spring admission, 9/1 for international students. Applications are processed on a rolling basis. Application fee: $25. Electronic applications accepted. *Expenses: Tuition:* Full-time $18,960; part-time $790 per credit hour. *Required fees:* $310. Tuition and fees vary according to degree level and program. *Financial support:* In 2011–12, 1 research assistantship with partial tuition reimbursement (averaging $3,000 per year) was awarded; career-related internships or fieldwork, Federal Work-Study, and scholarships/grants also available. Support available to part-time students. Financial award application deadline: 3/1; financial award applicants required to submit FAFSA. *Faculty research:* Outcomes research in rehabilitation medicine, cost/benefit analysis of prospective payment systems. *Unit head:* Dr. Lisa Rafalson, Chair, 716-829-8489, Fax: 716-829-8184. *Application contact:* Linda Fisher, Graduate Admissions Director, 716-829-8400, Fax: 716-829-7900, E-mail: graduateadmissions@dyc.edu.

D'Youville College, Doctoral Programs, Buffalo, NY 14201-1084. Offers educational leadership (Ed D); health education (Ed D); health policy (Ed D). Part-time and evening/weekend programs available. *Faculty:* 6 full-time (2 women), 23 part-time/adjunct (13 women). *Students:* 28 full-time (14 women), 32 part-time (25 women); includes 3 minority (2 Black or African American, non-Hispanic/Latino; 1 Hispanic/Latino), 14 international. Average age 44. 38 applicants, 58% accepted, 18 enrolled. In 2011, 13 doctorates awarded. *Degree requirements:* For doctorate, comprehensive exam, thesis/dissertation, fieldwork. *Entrance requirements:* For doctorate, MS/MA; professional experience. *Expenses: Tuition:* Full-time $18,960; part-time $790 per credit hour. *Required fees:* $310. Tuition and fees vary according to degree level and program. *Financial support:* In 2011–12, research assistantships with tuition reimbursements (averaging $3,000 per year) were awarded; scholarships/grants also available. *Faculty research:* Educational assessment, assessment reform, culture and education, market-based reform, men's health, electronic records. *Unit head:* Dr. Mark Garrison, Director, 716-829-8125, E-mail: garrisonm@dyc.edu. *Application contact:* Linda Fisher, Graduate Admissions Director, 716-829-8400, Fax: 716-829-7900, E-mail: graduateadmissions@dyc.edu.

Eastern Kentucky University, The Graduate School, College of Arts and Sciences, Department of Government, Program in General Public Administration, Richmond, KY 40475-3102. Offers community development (MPA); community health administration (MPA); general public administration (MPA). *Accreditation:* NASPAA. Part-time and evening/weekend programs available. *Entrance requirements:* For master's, GRE General Test, minimum GPA of 2.5.

Eastern Michigan University, Graduate School, College of Arts and Sciences, Department of Political Science, Programs in Public Administration, Ypsilanti, MI 48197. Offers local government management (Graduate Certificate); management of public healthcare services (Graduate Certificate); public administration (MPA, Graduate Certificate); public budget management (Graduate Certificate); public land planning (Graduate Certificate); public management (Graduate Certificate); public personnel management (Graduate Certificate); public policy analysis (Graduate Certificate). *Accreditation:* NASPAA. *Students:* 21 full-time (12 women), 124 part-time (62 women); includes 48 minority (36 Black or African American, non-Hispanic/Latino; 1 American Indian or Alaska Native, non-Hispanic/Latino; 4 Asian, non-Hispanic/Latino; 5 Hispanic/Latino; 2 Two or more races, non-Hispanic/Latino), 2 international. Average age 33. 68 applicants, 68% accepted, 26 enrolled. In 2011, 20 master's, 15 other advanced degrees awarded. Application fee: $35. *Expenses:* Tuition, state resident: full-time $10,367; part-time $432 per credit hour. Tuition, nonresident: full-time $20,435; part-time $851 per credit hour. *Required fees:* $39 per credit hour. $46 per semester. One-time fee: $100. Tuition and fees vary according to course level, degree level and reciprocity agreements. *Unit head:* Dr. Joseph Ohren, Program Director, 734-487-2522, Fax: 734-487-3340, E-mail: joseph.ohren@emich.edu. *Application contact:* Graduate Admissions, 734-487-2400, Fax: 734-487-6559, E-mail: graduate.admissions@emich.edu.

Eastern Michigan University, Graduate School, College of Health and Human Services, Interdisciplinary Program in Health and Human Services, Ypsilanti, MI 48197. Offers community building (Graduate Certificate). Part-time and evening/weekend programs available. *Students:* 4 part-time (3 women); includes 1 minority (Hispanic/Latino). Average age 42. 2 applicants, 50% accepted, 1 enrolled. In 2011, 3 Graduate Certificates awarded. *Entrance requirements:* Additional exam requirements/recommendations for international students: Required—TOEFL. Application fee: $35. *Expenses:* Tuition, state resident: full-time $10,367; part-time $432 per credit hour. Tuition, nonresident: full-time $20,435; part-time $851 per credit hour. *Required fees:* $39 per credit hour. $46 per semester. One-time fee: $100. Tuition and fees vary according to course level, degree level and reciprocity agreements. *Unit head:* Dr. Marcia Bombyk, Program Coordinator, 734-487-4173, Fax: 734-487-8536, E-mail: marcia.bombyk@emich.edu. *Application contact:* Graduate Admissions, 734-487-2400, Fax: 734-487-6559, E-mail: graduate.admissions@emich.edu.

Eastern Michigan University, Graduate School, College of Health and Human Services, School of Health Sciences, Program in Health Administration, Ypsilanti, MI 48197. Offers MHA, MS, Graduate Certificate. *Students:* 12 full-time (8 women), 57 part-time (47 women); includes 28 minority (22 Black or African American, non-Hispanic/Latino; 6 Asian, non-Hispanic/Latino), 4 international. Average age 34. 62 applicants, 68% accepted, 22 enrolled. In 2011, 16 master's, 4 other advanced degrees awarded. Application fee: $35. *Expenses:* Tuition, state resident: full-time $10,367; part-time $432 per credit hour. Tuition, nonresident: full-time $20,435; part-time $851 per credit hour. *Required fees:* $39 per credit hour. $46 per semester. One-time fee: $100. Tuition and fees vary according to course level, degree level and reciprocity agreements. *Unit head:* Dr. Colleen Croxall, Program Director, 734-487-2072, Fax: 734-487-4095, E-mail: ccroxall@emich.edu. *Application contact:* Graduate Admissions, 734-487-2400, Fax: 734-487-6559, E-mail: graduate.admissions@emich.edu.

Eastern Michigan University, Graduate School, College of Health and Human Services, School of Nursing, Ypsilanti, MI 48197. Offers nursing (MSN); quality improvement in health care systems (Graduate Certificate); teaching in health care systems (MSN, Graduate Certificate). *Accreditation:* AACN. Part-time and evening/weekend programs available. Postbaccalaureate distance learning degree programs offered (minimal on-campus study). *Faculty:* 20 full-time (18 women). *Students:* 2 full-time (both women), 33 part-time (27 women); includes 20 minority (14 Black or African American, non-Hispanic/Latino; 5 Asian, non-Hispanic/Latino; 1 Hispanic/Latino). Average age 46. 32 applicants, 56% accepted, 8 enrolled. In 2011, 11 master's, 15 other advanced degrees awarded. *Degree requirements:* For master's, thesis optional.

Health Services Management and Hospital Administration

Entrance requirements: For master's, GRE General Test, Michigan RN license. Additional exam requirements/recommendations for international students: Required—TOEFL. *Application deadline:* Applications are processed on a rolling basis. Application fee: $35. *Expenses:* Tuition, state resident: full-time $10,367; part-time $432 per credit hour. Tuition, nonresident: full-time $20,435; part-time $851 per credit hour. *Required fees:* $39 per credit hour. $46 per semester. One-time fee: $100. Tuition and fees vary according to course level, degree level and reciprocity agreements. *Financial support:* Fellowships, research assistantships with full tuition reimbursements, teaching assistantships with full tuition reimbursements, career-related internships or fieldwork, Federal Work-Study, institutionally sponsored loans, scholarships/grants, tuition waivers (partial), and unspecified assistantships available. Support available to part-time students. Financial award applicants required to submit FAFSA. *Unit head:* Dr. Peggy Trewn, Interim Director, 734-487-2310, Fax: 734-487-6946, E-mail: ptrewn@emich.edu. *Application contact:* Dr. Virginia Lan, MSN Coordinator, 734-487-2310, Fax: 734-487-6946, E-mail: vlan@emich.edu. Web site: http://www.emich.edu/nursing.

Eastern University, School of Management Studies, St. Davids, PA 19087-3696. Offers health administration (MBA); management (MBA).

East Tennessee State University, School of Graduate Studies, College of Business and Technology, Department of Management and Marketing, Johnson City, TN 37614. Offers business administration (MBA, Postbaccalaureate Certificate); health care management (Postbaccalaureate Certificate). Part-time and evening/weekend programs available. *Faculty:* 17 full-time (4 women), 1 (woman) part-time/adjunct. *Students:* 71 full-time (24 women), 27 part-time (11 women); includes 7 minority (1 Asian, non-Hispanic/Latino; 4 Hispanic/Latino; 2 Two or more races, non-Hispanic/Latino), 5 international. Average age 30. 148 applicants, 51% accepted, 52 enrolled. In 2011, 62 master's, 7 other advanced degrees awarded. *Degree requirements:* For master's, comprehensive exam, capstone, strategic experience. *Entrance requirements:* For master's, GMAT, minimum GPA of 2.5. Additional exam requirements/recommendations for international students: Required—TOEFL (minimum score 550 paper-based; 213 computer-based; 79 iBT). *Application deadline:* For fall admission, 6/1 for domestic students, 4/30 for international students; for spring admission, 11/1 for domestic students, 9/30 for international students. Application fee: $35 ($45 for international students). Electronic applications accepted. *Expenses:* Tuition, state resident: full-time $7312; part-time $350 per credit hour. Tuition, nonresident: full-time $18,490; part-time $621 per credit hour. *Required fees:* $63 per credit hour. Tuition and fees vary according to course load and program. *Financial support:* In 2011–12, 34 students received support, including 17 research assistantships with full tuition reimbursements available (averaging $6,000 per year), 1 teaching assistantship with full tuition reimbursement available (averaging $6,000 per year); career-related internships or fieldwork, institutionally sponsored loans, scholarships/grants, and unspecified assistantships also available. Financial award application deadline: 7/1; financial award applicants required to submit FAFSA. *Faculty research:* Sustainability, healthcare effectiveness, consumer behavior, merchandizing trends, organizational management issues. *Total annual research expenditures:* $100,000. *Unit head:* Dr. Phillip E. Miller, Chair, 423-439-4422, Fax: 423-439-5661, E-mail: millerpe@etsu.edu. *Application contact:* Cindy Hill, Graduate Specialist, 423-439-6590, Fax: 423-439-5624, E-mail: hillcc@etsu.edu.

East Tennessee State University, School of Graduate Studies, College of Public Health, Master of Public Health Programs, Johnson City, TN 37614. Offers biostatistics (MPH); community health (MPH); environmental health (MPH); epidemiology (MPH); public health administration (MPH). Part-time programs available. Postbaccalaureate distance learning degree programs offered (no on-campus study). *Students:* 45 full-time (27 women), 31 part-time (21 women); includes 14 minority (8 Black or African American, non-Hispanic/Latino; 3 Asian, non-Hispanic/Latino; 2 Hispanic/Latino; 1 Two or more races, non-Hispanic/Latino), 11 international. 92 applicants, 45% accepted, 40 enrolled. In 2011, 24 master's awarded. *Degree requirements:* For master's, comprehensive exam, field experience. *Entrance requirements:* For master's, GRE General Test, SOPHAS application, minimum GPA of 2.75, letters of recommendation. Additional exam requirements/recommendations for international students: Required—TOEFL (minimum score 550 paper-based; 213 computer-based; 79 iBT). *Application deadline:* For fall admission, 3/1 for domestic and international students. Application fee: $35 ($45 for international students). Electronic applications accepted. *Expenses:* Tuition, state resident: full-time $7312; part-time $350 per credit hour. Tuition, nonresident: full-time $18,490; part-time $621 per credit hour. *Required fees:* $63 per credit hour. Tuition and fees vary according to course load and program. *Financial support:* In 2011–12, 31 students received support, including 14 research assistantships with full tuition reimbursements available (averaging $6,000 per year), 2 teaching assistantships with full tuition reimbursements available (averaging $6,000 per year); career-related internships or fieldwork, institutionally sponsored loans, scholarships/grants, and unspecified assistantships also available. Financial award application deadline: 7/1; financial award applicants required to submit FAFSA. *Faculty research:* Rural health issues, youth and adolescent health, health of the elderly, environmental epidemiology, spatial analysis of data. *Unit head:* Dr. Brian Martin, Graduate Program Coordinator, 423-439-4429, Fax: 423-439-6491, E-mail: martinb@etsu.edu. *Application contact:* Mary Duncan, Graduate Specialist, 423-439-4302, Fax: 423-439-5624, E-mail: duncanm@etsu.edu. Web site: http://www.etsu.edu/cph/academics/graduate/MPHHome.aspx.

East Tennessee State University, School of Graduate Studies, College of Public Health, Public Health Certificate Programs, Johnson City, TN 37614. Offers biostatistics (Postbaccalaureate Certificate); epidemiology (Postbaccalaureate Certificate); gerontology (Postbaccalaureate Certificate); health care management (Postbaccalaureate Certificate); rural health (Postbaccalaureate Certificate). Part-time programs available. *Students:* 2 full-time (both women), 5 part-time (all women); includes 4 minority (all Black or African American, non-Hispanic/Latino). 18 applicants, 28% accepted, 5 enrolled. In 2011, 7 Postbaccalaureate Certificates awarded. *Degree requirements:* For Postbaccalaureate Certificate, culminating experience or community-based project. *Entrance requirements:* For degree, minimum GPA of 2.5, 3 letters of recommendation, resume (gerontology). Additional exam requirements/recommendations for international students: Required—TOEFL (minimum score 550 paper-based; 213 computer-based; 79 iBT). *Application deadline:* For fall admission, 6/1 for domestic students, 4/29 for international students; for spring admission, 11/1 for domestic students, 9/30 for international students. Application fee: $35 ($45 for international students). Electronic applications accepted. *Expenses:* Tuition, state resident: full-time $7312; part-time $350 per credit hour. Tuition, nonresident: full-time $18,490; part-time $621 per credit hour. *Required fees:* $63 per credit hour. Tuition and fees vary according to course load and program. *Financial support:* Institutionally sponsored loans and scholarships/grants available. Financial award application deadline: 7/1; financial award applicants required to submit FAFSA. *Faculty research:* Rural health issues, youth and adolescent health, health of the elderly, environmental epidemiology, spatial analysis of data. *Unit head:* Dr. Randy Wykoff, Dean, 423-439-4243, Fax: 423-439-5238, E-mail: wykoff@etsu.edu. *Application contact:* Mary Duncan, Graduate Specialist, 423-439-4302, Fax: 423-439-5624, E-mail: duncanm@etsu.edu.

Ellis University, MBA Program, Chicago, IL 60606-7204. Offers e-commerce (MBA); finance (MBA); general business (MBA); global management (MBA); health care administration (MBA); leadership (MBA); management of information systems (MBA); marketing (MBA); professional accounting (MBA); project management (MBA); public accounting (MBA); risk management (MBA).

Emory University, Rollins School of Public Health, Department of Health Policy and Management, Atlanta, GA 30322-1100. Offers health policy (MPH); health policy research (MSPH); health services management (MPH); health services research and health policy (PhD). Part-time programs available. *Students:* 77 full-time. Average age 27. 37 applicants, 14% accepted, 2 enrolled. *Degree requirements:* For master's, thesis (for some programs), practicum, capstone course. *Entrance requirements:* For master's, GRE General Test. Additional exam requirements/recommendations for international students: Required—TOEFL (minimum score 550 paper-based; 215 computer-based; 80 iBT). *Application deadline:* For fall admission, 1/3 priority date for domestic students, 1/3 for international students. Application fee: $95. Electronic applications accepted. *Expenses: Tuition:* Full-time $34,800. *Required fees:* $1300. *Financial support:* Fellowships with full and partial tuition reimbursements, career-related internships or fieldwork, Federal Work-Study, institutionally sponsored loans, scholarships/grants, traineeships, health care benefits, and unspecified assistantships available. Support available to part-time students. Financial award application deadline: 1/5; financial award applicants required to submit FAFSA. *Faculty research:* U. S. health policy and financing, healthcare organization and financing. *Unit head:* Dr. Kenneth E. Thorpe, Chair, 404-727-3487, Fax: 404-727-9198. *Application contact:* Prof. Walter M. Burnett, Director of Graduate Studies, 404-712-9546, Fax: 404-727-9198, E-mail: wmburne@emory.edu.

Fairleigh Dickinson University, College at Florham, Silberman College of Business, Executive MBA Programs, Executive MBA Program for Health Care and Life Sciences Professionals, Madison, NJ 07940-1099. Offers EMBA.

Fairleigh Dickinson University, Metropolitan Campus, Silberman College of Business, Program in Healthcare and Life Sciences, Teaneck, NJ 07666-1914. Offers EMBA.

Felician College, Program in Health Care Administration, Lodi, NJ 07644-2117. Offers MSHA. *Expenses: Tuition:* Part-time $925 per credit. *Required fees:* $262.50 per semester. Part-time tuition and fees vary according to class time and student level. *Application contact:* Nicole Vitale, Assistant Director of Graduate Admissions, 201-559-6077, Fax: 201-559-6138, E-mail: graduate@felician.edu.

Florida Institute of Technology, Graduate Programs, Nathan M. Bisk College of Business, Online Programs, Melbourne, FL 32901-6975. Offers accounting (MBA); accounting and finance (MBA); business administration (MBA); finance (MBA); healthcare management (MBA); information technology (MS); information technology cybersecurity (MS); information technology management (MBA); international business (MBA); Internet marketing (MBA); management (MBA); marketing (MBA); project management (MBA). Part-time and evening/weekend programs available. Postbaccalaureate distance learning degree programs offered (no on-campus study). *Faculty:* 47 part-time/adjunct (15 women). *Students:* 8 full-time (4 women), 1,122 part-time (547 women); includes 418 minority (271 Black or African American, non-Hispanic/Latino; 5 American Indian or Alaska Native, non-Hispanic/Latino; 55 Asian, non-Hispanic/Latino; 81 Hispanic/Latino; 6 Native Hawaiian or other Pacific Islander, non-Hispanic/Latino), 23 international. Average age 36. In 2011, 329 degrees awarded. *Entrance requirements:* For master's, GMAT or resume showing 8 years of supervised experience, 2 letters of recommendation, resume, competency in math past college algebra. Additional exam requirements/recommendations for international students: Required—TOEFL (minimum score 550 paper-based; 213 computer-based; 79 iBT). *Application deadline:* For fall admission, 4/1 for international students; for spring admission, 9/30 for international students. Applications are processed on a rolling basis. Electronic applications accepted. *Expenses:* Contact institution. *Financial support:* Available to part-time students. Application deadline: 3/1; applicants required to submit FAFSA. *Unit head:* Dr. Mary S. Bonhomme, Dean, Florida Tech Online/Associate Provost for Online Learning, 321-674-8202, Fax: 321-674-8216, E-mail: bonhomme@fit.edu. *Application contact:* Carolyn Farrior, Director of Graduate Admissions, Online Learning and Off-Campus Programs, 321-674-7118, Fax: 321-674-8216, E-mail: cfarrior@fit.edu. Web site: http://online.fit.edu.

Florida International University, Robert Stempel College of Public Health and Social Work, Department of Health Policy and Management, Miami, FL 33199. Offers MHSA. Part-time and evening/weekend programs available. *Entrance requirements:* For master's, GRE General Test, minimum GPA of 3.0. Additional exam requirements/recommendations for international students: Required—TOEFL (minimum score 550 paper-based; 80 iBT). Electronic applications accepted.

Florida International University, Robert Stempel College of Public Health and Social Work, Programs in Public Health, Miami, FL 33199. Offers biostatistics (MPH); environmental and occupational health (MPH, PhD); epidemiology (MPH, PhD); health policy and management (MPH); health promotion and disease prevention (PhD); health promotion and diseases prevention (MPH). Ph D is fall admission only; MPH offered jointly with University of Miami. *Accreditation:* CEPH. Part-time and evening/weekend programs available. Postbaccalaureate distance learning degree programs offered (no on-campus study). *Degree requirements:* For master's, thesis optional; for doctorate, comprehensive exam, thesis/dissertation. *Entrance requirements:* For master's, minimum GPA of 3.0, letters of recommendation; for doctorate, GRE, resume, minimum GPA of 3.0, letters of recommendation, letter of intent. Additional exam requirements/recommendations for international students: Required—TOEFL (minimum score 550 paper-based; 80 iBT). Electronic applications accepted. *Expenses:* Contact institution. *Faculty research:* Drugs/AIDS intervention among migrant workers, provision of services for active/recovering drug users with HIV.

Florida State University, The Graduate School, College of Nursing, Tallahassee, FL 32312. Offers family nurse practitioner (DNP); health systems leadership (DNP); nurse educator (MSN, Certificate); nurse leader (MSN); nursing leadership (Certificate, Post-Graduate Certificate). *Accreditation:* AACN. Part-time programs available. Postbaccalaureate distance learning degree programs offered (no on-campus study). *Faculty:* 13 full-time (12 women). *Students:* 24 full-time (21 women), 63 part-time (58 women); includes 15 minority (4 Black or African American, non-Hispanic/Latino; 1 Asian, non-Hispanic/Latino; 8 Hispanic/Latino; 2 Two or more races, non-Hispanic/Latino). Average age 38. 33 applicants, 100% accepted, 33 enrolled. In 2011, 9 master's, 4 doctorates awarded. *Degree requirements:* For master's, thesis optional. *Entrance requirements:* For master's, GRE General Test, MAT, minimum GPA of 3.0, BSN, Florida RN license; for doctorate, GRE General Test, MAT, minimum GPA of 3.0, BSN or MSN, Florida RN license. Additional exam requirements/recommendations for international students: Required—TOEFL (minimum score 550 paper-based). *Application deadline:* For fall admission, 7/1 for domestic and international students. Application fee: $30. Electronic applications accepted. *Expenses:* Tuition, state resident: full-time $9474; part-time $350.88 per credit hour. Tuition, nonresident: full-time $16,236; part-time $601.34 per credit hour. *Required fees:* $630 per semester. One-time fee: $20. Tuition and fees vary according to course load and campus/location. *Financial support:* In 2011–12, 75 students received support, including fellowships with partial tuition reimbursements available (averaging $6,300 per year), research

assistantships with partial tuition reimbursements available (averaging $3,000 per year), 3 teaching assistantships with partial tuition reimbursements available (averaging $3,000 per year); career-related internships or fieldwork, Federal Work-Study, institutionally sponsored loans, scholarships/grants, traineeships, and tuition waivers (partial) also available. Financial award application deadline: 4/15; financial award applicants required to submit FAFSA. *Faculty research:* Distance learning, gerontology, health promotion, educational strategies, rehabilitation of brain injured patients. *Unit head:* Dr. Diane Speake, Interim Dean, 850-644-6846, Fax: 850-644-7660, E-mail: dspeake@nursing.fsu.edu. *Application contact:* Carlos G. Urrutia, Director of Student Services, 850-644-5638, Fax: 850-645-7249, E-mail: currutia@fsu.edu. Web site: http://nursing.fsu.edu/.

Framingham State University, Division of Graduate and Continuing Education, Program in Health Care Administration, Framingham, MA 01701-9101. Offers MA. Part-time and evening/weekend programs available.

Francis Marion University, Graduate Programs, School of Business, Florence, SC 29502-0547. Offers business (MBA); health management (MBA). *Accreditation:* AACSB. Part-time and evening/weekend programs available. *Faculty:* 21 full-time (6 women). *Students:* 5 full-time (4 women), 32 part-time (25 women); includes 9 minority (7 Black or African American, non-Hispanic/Latino; 2 Asian, non-Hispanic/Latino), 1 international. Average age 30. 23 applicants, 43% accepted, 10 enrolled. In 2011, 15 master's awarded. *Degree requirements:* For master's, comprehensive exam. *Entrance requirements:* For master's, GMAT. *Application deadline:* For fall admission, 3/15 priority date for domestic students; for spring admission, 10/15 priority date for domestic students. Applications are processed on a rolling basis. Application fee: $31. *Expenses:* Tuition, state resident: full-time $8467; part-time $443.35 per credit hour. Tuition, nonresident: full-time $16,934; part-time $866.70 per credit hour. *Required fees:* $335; $12.25 per credit hour. $30 per semester. *Financial support:* Research assistantships available. Support available to part-time students. Financial award application deadline: 3/1; financial award applicants required to submit FAFSA. *Faculty research:* Ethics, directions of MBA, international business, regional economics, environmental issues. *Unit head:* Dr. M. Barry O'Brien, Dean, 843-661-1419, Fax: 843-661-1432, E-mail: mbobrien@fmarion.edu. *Application contact:* Rannie Gamble, Administrative Manager, 843-661-1286, Fax: 843-661-4688, E-mail: rgamble@fmarion.edu. Web site: http://alpha1.fmarion.edu/~mba/.

Franklin Pierce University, Graduate Studies, Rindge, NH 03461-0060. Offers curriculum and instruction (M Ed); emerging network technologies (Graduate Certificate); energy and sustainability studies (MBA); health administration (MBA, Graduate Certificate); human resource management (MBA, Graduate Certificate); information technology (MBA); information technology management (MS); leadership (MBA, DA); nursing (MS); physical therapy (DPT); physician assistant studies (MPAS); special education (M Ed); sports management (MBA). *Accreditation:* APTA. Part-time programs available. Postbaccalaureate distance learning degree programs offered (no on-campus study). *Degree requirements:* For master's, concentrated original research projects; student teaching; fieldwork and/or internship; leadership project; PRAXIS I and II (for M Ed); for doctorate, concentrated original research projects, clinical fieldwork and/or internship, leadership project. *Entrance requirements:* For master's, minimum GPA of 2.5, 3 letters of recommendation; competencies in accounting, economics, statistics, and computer skills through life experience or undergraduate coursework (for MBA); certification/e-portfolio, minimum C grade in all education courses (for M Ed); license to practice as RN (for MS in nursing); for doctorate, GRE, BA/BS, 3 letters of recommendation, personal mission statement, interview, writing sample, minimum cumulative GPA of 2.8, master's degree (for DA); 80 hours of observation/work in PT settings, completion of anatomy, chemistry, physics, and statistics, minimum GPA of 3.0 (for DPT). Additional exam requirements/recommendations for international students: Required—TOEFL (minimum score 550 paper-based; 195 computer-based; 61 iBT). Electronic applications accepted. *Faculty research:* Evidence-based practice in sports physical therapy, human resource management in economic crisis, leadership in nursing, innovation in sports facility management, differentiated learning and understanding by design.

Friends University, Graduate School, Wichita, KS 67213. Offers accounting (MBA); business administration (MBA); business law (MBL); Christian ministry (MACM); environment science (MSES); family therapy (MSFT); global leadership and management (MA); health care leadership (MHCL); management information systems (MMIS); operations management (MSOM); organization development (MSOD); teaching (MAT). Part-time and evening/weekend programs available. Postbaccalaureate distance learning degree programs offered (no on-campus study). *Faculty:* 14 full-time (5 women), 2 part-time/adjunct (1 woman). *Students:* 158 full-time (114 women), 616 part-time (367 women); includes 159 minority (83 Black or African American, non-Hispanic/Latino; 12 American Indian or Alaska Native, non-Hispanic/Latino; 26 Asian, non-Hispanic/Latino; 22 Hispanic/Latino; 2 Native Hawaiian or other Pacific Islander, non-Hispanic/Latino; 14 Two or more races, non-Hispanic/Latino). Average age 36. 497 applicants, 68% accepted, 256 enrolled. In 2011, 341 degrees awarded. *Degree requirements:* For master's, research project. *Entrance requirements:* For master's, bachelor's degree from accredited institution, official transcripts from institution granting bachelor's degree, interview with program director, letter(s) of recommendation. Additional exam requirements/recommendations for international students: Required—TOEFL (minimum score 560 paper-based; 220 computer-based). *Application deadline:* Applications are processed on a rolling basis. Application fee: $45 ($65 for international students). Electronic applications accepted. *Expenses: Tuition:* Part-time $601 per credit hour. One-time fee: $45 full-time. Tuition and fees vary according to campus/location and program. *Financial support:* Applicants required to submit FAFSA. *Unit head:* Dr. Evelyn Hume, Dean, 800-794-6945 Ext. 5859, Fax: 316-295-5040, E-mail: evelyn_hume@friends.edu. *Application contact:* Jeanette Hanson, Executive Director of Adult Recruitment, 800-794-6945, Fax: 316-295-5050, E-mail: jeanette@friends.edu. Web site: http://www.friends.edu/.

George Mason University, College of Health and Human Services, Department of Health Administration and Policy, Fairfax, VA 22030. Offers health and medical policy (MS); health information systems (Certificate); health systems management (MS); quality improvement and outcomes management in health care systems (Certificate); senior housing administration (MS, Certificate). *Accreditation:* CAHME. *Faculty:* 18 full-time (5 women), 11 part-time/adjunct (7 women). *Students:* 45 full-time (31 women), 110 part-time (77 women); includes 75 minority (27 Black or African American, non-Hispanic/Latino; 32 Asian, non-Hispanic/Latino; 12 Hispanic/Latino; 4 Two or more races, non-Hispanic/Latino), 8 international. Average age 32. 113 applicants, 60% accepted, 49 enrolled. In 2011, 31 master's, 6 other advanced degrees awarded. *Degree requirements:* For master's, comprehensive exam, internship. *Entrance requirements:* For master's, GRE recommended if undergraduate GPA is below 3.0 (for senior housing administration MS only), 2 official transcripts; expanded goals statement; 3 letters of recommendation; resume; 1 year of work experience (for MHA in health systems management); for Certificate, 2 official transcripts; expanded goals statement; 3 letters of recommendation; resume. Additional exam requirements/recommendations for international students: Required—TOEFL (minimum score 575 paper-based; 230 computer-based; 88 iBT), IELTS, Pearson Test of English. *Application deadline:* For fall admission, 4/1 priority date for domestic students; for spring admission, 11/1 priority date for domestic students. Applications are processed on a rolling basis. Application fee: $65 ($80 for international students). Electronic applications accepted. *Expenses:* Tuition, state resident: full-time $8750; part-time $364.58 per credit. Tuition, nonresident: full-time $24,092; part-time $1003.83 per credit. *Required fees:* $2514; $104.75 per credit. *Financial support:* In 2011–12, 3 students received support, including 2 research assistantships with full and partial tuition reimbursements available (averaging $15,000 per year), 1 teaching assistantship (averaging $12,760 per year); career-related internships or fieldwork, Federal Work-Study, scholarships/grants, unspecified assistantships, and health care benefits (full-time research or teaching assistantship recipients) also available. Support available to part-time students. Financial award application deadline: 3/1; financial award applicants required to submit FAFSA. *Faculty research:* Universal health care, publications, relationships between malpractice pressure and rates of Cesarean section and VBAC, seniors and Wii gaming, relationships between changes in physician's incomes and practice settings and their care to Medicaid and charity patients. *Total annual research expenditures:* $517,468. *Unit head:* Dr. P. J. Maddox, Chair, 703-993-1982, Fax: 703-993-1982, E-mail: pmaddox@gmu.edu. *Application contact:* Valerie Bartush, Office Manager, 703-993-1929, Fax: 703-993-1953, E-mail: vbartush@gmu.edu. Web site: http://chhs.gmu.edu/hap/index.

George Mason University, School of Public Policy, Program in Health and Medical Policy, Fairfax, VA 22030. Offers global medical policy (Certificate); health and medical policy (MS). *Expenses:* Tuition, state resident: full-time $8750; part-time $364.58 per credit. Tuition, nonresident: full-time $24,092; part-time $1003.83 per credit. *Required fees:* $2514; $104.75 per credit. *Application contact:* Tennille Haegele, Director of Graduate Admissions, School of Public Policy, 703-993-3183, Fax: 703-993-4876, E-mail: thaegele@gmu.edu.

The George Washington University, College of Professional Studies, Program in Healthcare Corporate Compliance, Washington, DC 20052. Offers Graduate Certificate. Postbaccalaureate distance learning degree programs offered. *Students:* 32 part-time (22 women); includes 10 minority (6 Black or African American, non-Hispanic/Latino; 4 Hispanic/Latino). Average age 45. 38 applicants, 97% accepted, 21 enrolled. In 2011, 30 Graduate Certificates awarded. *Application deadline:* For fall admission, 8/31 for domestic students. *Unit head:* Phyllis C. Borzi, Director, 202-530-2312, E-mail: borziph@gwu.edu. *Application contact:* Kristin Williams, Assistant Vice President for Graduate and Special Enrollment Management, 202-994-0467, Fax: 202-994-0371, E-mail: ksw@gwu.edu. Web site: http://cps.gwu.edu/hcc.html.

The George Washington University, School of Medicine and Health Sciences, Health Sciences Programs, Washington, DC 20052. Offers clinical practice management (MSHS); clinical research administration (MSHS); emergency services management (MSHS); end-of-life care (MSHS); immunohematology (MSHS); physical therapy (DPT); physician assistant (MSHS); MSHS/MPH. Postbaccalaureate distance learning degree programs offered (no on-campus study). *Students:* 268 full-time (197 women), 255 part-time (194 women); includes 131 minority (52 Black or African American, non-Hispanic/Latino; 3 American Indian or Alaska Native, non-Hispanic/Latino; 43 Asian, non-Hispanic/Latino; 26 Hispanic/Latino; 7 Native Hawaiian or other Pacific Islander, non-Hispanic/Latino), 24 international. Average age 32. 922 applicants, 32% accepted. In 2011, 140 master's, 29 doctorates awarded. *Entrance requirements:* Additional exam requirements/recommendations for international students: Required—TOEFL (minimum score 550 paper-based; 213 computer-based). *Application deadline:* Applications are processed on a rolling basis. Application fee: $75. *Expenses:* Contact institution. *Unit head:* Jean E. Johnson, Senior Associate Dean, 202-994-3725, E-mail: jejohns@gwu.edu. *Application contact:* Joke Ogundiran, Director of Admission, 202-994-1668, Fax: 202-994-0870, E-mail: jokeogun@gwu.edu.

The George Washington University, School of Public Health and Health Services, Department of Health Policy, Washington, DC 20052. Offers MPH, MS. *Faculty:* 35 full-time (24 women), 95 part-time/adjunct (47 women). *Students:* 136 full-time (91 women), 201 part-time (140 women); includes 135 minority (60 Black or African American, non-Hispanic/Latino; 3 American Indian or Alaska Native, non-Hispanic/Latino; 50 Asian, non-Hispanic/Latino; 13 Hispanic/Latino; 1 Native Hawaiian or other Pacific Islander, non-Hispanic/Latino; 8 Two or more races, non-Hispanic/Latino), 14 international. Average age 32. 424 applicants, 83% accepted, 51 enrolled. In 2011, 93 master's awarded. *Degree requirements:* For master's, case study or special project. *Entrance requirements:* For master's, GMAT, GRE General Test, or MCAT. Additional exam requirements/recommendations for international students: Required—TOEFL. *Application deadline:* For fall admission, 4/15 priority date for domestic students, 4/15 for international students; for spring admission, 11/1 for domestic and international students. Applications are processed on a rolling basis. Application fee: $75. *Financial support:* In 2011–12, 10 students received support. Tuition waivers available. Financial award application deadline: 2/15. *Unit head:* Sara Rosenbaum, Chair, 202-994-4230, Fax: 202-296-0025, E-mail: sarar@gwu.edu. *Application contact:* Jane Smith, Director of Admissions, 202-994-0248, Fax: 202-994-1860, E-mail: sphhsinfo@gwumc.edu.

The George Washington University, School of Public Health and Health Services, Department of Health Services Management and Leadership, Washington, DC 20052. Offers health management and leadership (MHSA); health policy (MHSA); health services administration (Specialist); public health management (MPH). *Accreditation:* CAHME (one or more programs are accredited). *Faculty:* 8 full-time (2 women), 25 part-time/adjunct (3 women). *Degree requirements:* For master's, internship or residency. *Entrance requirements:* For master's, GMAT or GRE; for Specialist, GMAT or GRE, master's degree in related field. Additional exam requirements/recommendations for international students: Required—TOEFL. *Application deadline:* For fall admission, 5/15 priority date for domestic students; for winter admission, 11/15 for domestic students; for spring admission, 4/1 for domestic students. Applications are processed on a rolling basis. Application fee: $75. *Financial support:* Career-related internships or fieldwork, Federal Work-Study, and institutionally sponsored loans available. Financial award application deadline: 6/1. *Faculty research:* Hospital administration, ambulatory health care, social gerontology, health care financing, health care ethics. *Unit head:* Dr. Robert Burke, Chair, 202-994-5560, Fax: 202-416-0075, E-mail: bobburke@gwu.edu. *Application contact:* Jane Smith, Director of Admissions, 202-994-0248, Fax: 202-994-1860, E-mail: sphhsinfo@gwumc.edu. Web site: http://sphhs.gwumc.edu/departments/healthservicesmanagementleadership.

Georgia College & State University, Graduate School, The J. Whitney Bunting School of Business, Milledgeville, GA 31061. Offers accountancy (MACCT); accounting (MBA); business (MBA); health services administration (MBA); information systems (MIS); management information services (MBA). *Accreditation:* AACSB. Part-time and evening/weekend programs available. Postbaccalaureate distance learning degree programs offered (no on-campus study). *Students:* 61 full-time (26 women), 134 part-time (55 women); includes 34 minority (18 Black or African American, non-Hispanic/Latino; 9 Asian, non-Hispanic/Latino; 5 Hispanic/Latino; 2 Two or more races, non-Hispanic/Latino), 17 international. Average age 30. 162 applicants, 41% accepted, 45 enrolled. In 2011, 99 master's awarded. *Entrance requirements:* For master's, GMAT or GRE. Additional exam requirements/recommendations for international students: Recommended—TOEFL (minimum score 550 paper-based; 213 computer-based; 79

iBT). *Application deadline:* For fall admission, 7/1 priority date for domestic students, 4/1 for international students; for spring admission, 11/15 priority date for domestic students, 8/1 for international students. Applications are processed on a rolling basis. Application fee: $40. Electronic applications accepted. *Expenses:* Tuition, state resident: full-time $4806; part-time $267 per credit hour. Tuition, nonresident: full-time $17,802; part-time $989 per credit hour. *Required fees:* $936 per semester. Tuition and fees vary according to course load and campus/location. *Financial support:* In 2011–12, 34 research assistantships with full tuition reimbursements were awarded; career-related internships or fieldwork and unspecified assistantships also available. Support available to part-time students. Financial award application deadline: 3/1; financial award applicants required to submit FAFSA. *Unit head:* Dr. Matthew Liao-Troth, Dean, School of Business, 478-445-5497, E-mail: matthew.liao-troth@gcsu.edu. *Application contact:* Lynn Hanson, Director of Graduate Programs, 478-445-5115, E-mail: lynn.hanson@gcsu.edu. Web site: http://www.gcsu.edu/business/graduateprograms/index.htm.

Georgia Institute of Technology, Graduate Studies and Research, College of Engineering, School of Industrial and Systems Engineering, Program in Health Systems, Atlanta, GA 30332-0001. Offers MSHS. *Entrance requirements:* For master's, GRE General Test, minimum GPA of 3.0. Additional exam requirements/recommendations for international students: Required—TOEFL. Electronic applications accepted. *Faculty research:* Emergency medical services, health development planning, health services evaluations.

Georgia Southern University, Jack N. Averitt College of Graduate Studies, Jiann-Ping Hsu College of Public Health, Program in Healthcare Administration, Statesboro, GA 30460. Offers MHA. Part-time and evening/weekend programs available. *Students:* 7 full-time (6 women), 6 part-time (4 women); includes 4 minority (1 Asian, non-Hispanic/Latino; 1 Hispanic/Latino; 2 Two or more races, non-Hispanic/Latino). Average age 30. 10 applicants, 90% accepted, 6 enrolled. In 2011, 6 master's awarded. *Degree requirements:* For master's, practicum. *Entrance requirements:* For master's, GRE, GMAT, personal statement, minimum cumulative undergraduate GPA of 2.75, resume, 3 letters of recommendation. Additional exam requirements/recommendations for international students: Required—TOEFL (minimum score 550 paper-based; 213 computer-based; 80 iBT). *Application deadline:* For fall admission, 3/1 priority date for domestic students, 3/1 for international students; for spring admission, 10/1 priority date for domestic students, 10/1 for international students. Applications are processed on a rolling basis. Electronic applications accepted. *Expenses:* Contact institution. *Financial support:* In 2011–12, 6 students received support, including research assistantships with partial tuition reimbursements available (averaging $7,200 per year); unspecified assistantships also available. Financial award application deadline: 4/15; financial award applicants required to submit FAFSA. *Faculty research:* Health disparity elimination, cost effectiveness analysis, epidemiology of rural public health, health care system assessment, rural health care, health policy and healthcare financing. *Unit head:* Dr. James Stephens, Program Director, 912-478-5958, Fax: 912-478-0171, E-mail: jstephens@georgiasouthern.edu. *Application contact:* Amanda Gilliland, Coordinator for Graduate Student Recruitment, 912-478-5384, Fax: 912-478-0740, E-mail: gradadmissions@georgiasouthern.edu.

Georgia Southern University, Jack N. Averitt College of Graduate Studies, Jiann-Ping Hsu College of Public Health, Program in Public Health, Statesboro, GA 30460. Offers biostatistics (MPH, Dr PH); community health behavior and education (Dr PH); community health education (MPH); environmental health sciences (MPH); epidemiology (MPH); health services policy management (MPH); public health leadership (Dr PH). *Accreditation:* CEPH. Part-time programs available. *Students:* 87 full-time (60 women), 39 part-time (25 women); includes 68 minority (58 Black or African American, non-Hispanic/Latino; 6 Asian, non-Hispanic/Latino; 4 Hispanic/Latino), 20 international. Average age 30. 73 applicants, 84% accepted, 42 enrolled. In 2011, 22 master's, 4 doctorates awarded. *Degree requirements:* For master's, thesis optional, practicum; for doctorate, comprehensive exam, thesis/dissertation, practicum. *Entrance requirements:* For master's, GRE General Test, minimum GPA of 2.75, resume, 3 letters of reference; for doctorate, GRE, GMAT, MCAT, LSAT, 3 letters of reference, statement of purpose, resume or curriculum vitae. Additional exam requirements/recommendations for international students: Required—TOEFL (minimum score 550 paper-based; 213 computer-based; 80 iBT). *Application deadline:* For fall admission, 3/1 priority date for domestic students, 3/1 for international students; for spring admission, 10/1 priority date for domestic students, 10/1 for international students. Applications are processed on a rolling basis. Application fee: $50. Electronic applications accepted. *Expenses:* Contact institution. *Financial support:* In 2011–12, 59 students received support, including research assistantships with partial tuition reimbursements available (averaging $7,200 per year), teaching assistantships with partial tuition reimbursements available (averaging $7,200 per year); career-related internships or fieldwork, Federal Work-Study, scholarships/grants, tuition waivers (partial), and unspecified assistantships also available. Support available to part-time students. Financial award application deadline: 4/15; financial award applicants required to submit FAFSA. *Faculty research:* Rural public health best practices, health disparity elimination, community initiatives to enhance public health, cost effectiveness analysis, epidemiology of rural public health, environmental health issues, health care system assessment, rural health care, health policy and healthcare financing. *Unit head:* Dr. Charles Hardy, Dean, 912-478-2674, Fax: 912-478-5811, E-mail: chardy@georgiasouthern.edu. *Application contact:* Amanda Gilliland, Coordinator for Graduate Student Recruitment, 912-478-5384, Fax: 912-478-0740, E-mail: gradadmissions@georgiasouthern.edu. Web site: http://chhs.georgiasouthern.edu/health/.

Georgia State University, J. Mack Robinson College of Business, Institute of Health Administration, Atlanta, GA 30302-3083. Offers MBA, MHA, MSHA. *Accreditation:* CAHME. *Entrance requirements:* For master's, GMAT. Additional exam requirements/recommendations for international students: Required—TOEFL (minimum score 610 paper-based; 255 computer-based; 101 iBT). Electronic applications accepted.

Globe University–Woodbury, Minnesota School of Business, Woodbury, MN 55125. Offers business administration (MBA); health care management (MSM); information technology (MSM); managerial leadership (MSM).

Goldey-Beacom College, Graduate Program, Wilmington, DE 19808-1999. Offers business administration (MBA); finance (MS); financial management (MBA); health care management (MBA); human resource management (MBA); information technology (MBA); international business management (MBA); major finance (MBA); major taxation (MBA); management (MM); marketing management (MBA); taxation (MBA, MS). *Accreditation:* ACBSP. Part-time and evening/weekend programs available. *Faculty:* 19 full-time (7 women), 35 part-time/adjunct (12 women). *Students:* 58 full-time (32 women), 388 part-time (164 women); includes 89 minority (34 Black or African American, non-Hispanic/Latino; 2 American Indian or Alaska Native, non-Hispanic/Latino; 44 Asian, non-Hispanic/Latino; 9 Hispanic/Latino), 229 international. Average age 30. In 2011, 243 master's awarded. *Entrance requirements:* For master's, GMAT, MAT, GRE, minimum GPA of 3.0. Additional exam requirements/recommendations for international students: Required—TOEFL (minimum score 65 computer-based); Recommended—IELTS (minimum score 5). *Application deadline:* Applications are processed on a rolling basis. Application fee: $0. Electronic applications accepted. *Expenses: Tuition:* Full-time $15,750; part-time $875 per credit. *Required fees:* $10 per credit. *Financial support:* Scholarships/grants available. Support available to part-time students. Financial award application deadline: 4/1; financial award applicants required to submit FAFSA. *Unit head:* Larry W. Eby, Director of Admissions, 302-225-6289, Fax: 302-996-5408, E-mail: ebylw@gbc.edu. *Application contact:* Ashley E. Mashington, Graduate Admissions Representative, 302-225-6259, Fax: 302-996-5408, E-mail: mashina@gbc.edu. Web site: http://www.gbc.edu/programs/graduate/.

Goldfarb School of Nursing at Barnes-Jewish College, Graduate Programs, St. Louis, MO 63110. Offers adult acute care nurse practitioner (MSN); adult nurse practitioner (MSN); nurse anesthesia (MSN); nurse educator (MSN); nurse executive (MSN); DNP/PhD. *Accreditation:* AACN; AANA/CANAEP. Part-time and evening/weekend programs available. Postbaccalaureate distance learning degree programs offered (minimal on-campus study). *Faculty:* 38 full-time (35 women), 14 part-time/adjunct (11 women). *Students:* 79 full-time (68 women), 92 part-time (86 women); includes 45 minority (29 Black or African American, non-Hispanic/Latino; 1 American Indian or Alaska Native, non-Hispanic/Latino; 3 Asian, non-Hispanic/Latino; 3 Hispanic/Latino; 6 Native Hawaiian or other Pacific Islander, non-Hispanic/Latino; 3 Two or more races, non-Hispanic/Latino), 1 international. Average age 40. 134 applicants, 66% accepted, 51 enrolled. In 2011, 31 degrees awarded. *Degree requirements:* For master's, thesis or alternative. *Entrance requirements:* For master's, 2 references, personal statement, curriculum vitae or resume. Additional exam requirements/recommendations for international students: Required—TOEFL (minimum score 575 paper-based; 240 computer-based; 85 iBT). *Application deadline:* For fall admission, 2/1 for international students; for spring admission, 10/1 for international students. Applications are processed on a rolling basis. Application fee: $50. *Expenses: Tuition:* Full-time $14,685; part-time $630 per credit hour. *Required fees:* $280. *Financial support:* Fellowships, research assistantships, Federal Work-Study, institutionally sponsored loans, and scholarships/grants available. Support available to part-time students. Financial award applicants required to submit FAFSA. *Faculty research:* HIV Stigma, HIV symptom management, palliative care with children and their families, heart disease prevention in Hispanic women, depression in the well elderly, alternative therapies in pre-term infants. *Unit head:* Dr. Connie K. Koch, Interim Dean, 314-36-26590, Fax: 314-362-0984, E-mail: ckoch@bjc.org. *Application contact:* Dr. Michael Ward, Associate Dean for Student Programs, 314-362-9155, Fax: 314-362-0984, E-mail: mward@bjc.org.

Governors State University, College of Health Professions, Program in Health Administration, University Park, IL 60484. Offers MHA. *Accreditation:* CAHME. *Students:* 22 full-time (11 women), 36 part-time (27 women); includes 35 minority (27 Black or African American, non-Hispanic/Latino; 3 Asian, non-Hispanic/Latino; 3 Hispanic/Latino; 2 Two or more races, non-Hispanic/Latino), 9 international. Average age 35. *Degree requirements:* For master's, comprehensive exam, field experience or internship. *Entrance requirements:* For master's, minimum GPA of 3.0 in last 60 hours of undergraduate course work or 9 hours of graduate course work. *Application deadline:* For fall admission, 7/15 priority date for domestic students; for spring admission, 11/10 for domestic students. Applications are processed on a rolling basis. Application fee: $25. *Financial support:* Research assistantships, career-related internships or fieldwork, Federal Work-Study, institutionally sponsored loans, scholarships/grants, and tuition waivers (full and partial) available. Financial award application deadline: 5/1. *Unit head:* Dr. Elizabeth Cada, Dean, 708-534-7295. *Application contact:* Interim Director of Admission.

Grambling State University, School of Graduate Studies and Research, College of Arts and Sciences, Program in Public Administration, Grambling, LA 71270. Offers health service administration (MPA); human resource management (MPA); public management (MPA); state and local government (MPA). *Accreditation:* NASPAA. Part-time programs available. *Degree requirements:* For master's, comprehensive exam (for some programs), thesis optional. *Entrance requirements:* For master's, GRE, minimum GPA of 2.75 on last degree. Additional exam requirements/recommendations for international students: Required—TOEFL (minimum score 500 paper-based; 173 computer-based; 61 iBT). Electronic applications accepted. *Expenses:* Tuition, state resident: full-time $3546; part-time $192 per credit hour. Tuition, nonresident: full-time $3456; part-time $192 per credit hour. *Required fees:* $1829; $1829 per semester hour.

Grand Canyon University, College of Business, Phoenix, AZ 85017-1097. Offers accounting (MBA); corporate business administration (MBA); disaster preparedness and crisis management (MBA); executive fire service leadership (MS); finance (MBA); general management (MBA); government and policy (MPA); health care management (MPA); health systems management (MBA); human resource management (MBA); innovation (MBA); leadership (MBA, MS); management of information system (MBA); marketing (MBA); project-based (MBA); six sigma (MBA); strategic human resource management (MBA). *Accreditation:* ACBSP. Part-time and evening/weekend programs available. Postbaccalaureate distance learning degree programs offered (no on-campus study). *Entrance requirements:* For master's, equivalent of two years full-time professional work experience. Additional exam requirements/recommendations for international students: Required—TOEFL (minimum score 575 paper-based; 233 computer-based; 90 iBT), IELTS (minimum score 7). Electronic applications accepted.

Grand Canyon University, College of Nursing, Phoenix, AZ 85017-1097. Offers acute care nurse practitioner (MS, PMC); clinical nurse specialist (PMC), including clinical nurse specialist, education; family nurse practitioner (MS); leadership in health care systems (MS); nurse education (MS). *Accreditation:* AACN. Part-time and evening/weekend programs available. Postbaccalaureate distance learning degree programs offered (no on-campus study). *Degree requirements:* For master's and PMC, comprehensive exam (for some programs). *Entrance requirements:* For master's, minimum cumulative and science course undergraduate GPA of 3.0. Additional exam requirements/recommendations for international students: Required—TOEFL (minimum score 575 paper-based; 233 computer-based; 90 iBT), IELTS (minimum score 7).

Grand Canyon University, College of Nursing and Health Sciences, Phoenix, AZ 85017-1097. Offers addiction counseling (MS); health care administration (MS); health care informatics (MS); marriage and family therapy (MS); professional counseling (MS); public health (MS). Part-time and evening/weekend programs available. Postbaccalaureate distance learning degree programs offered (no on-campus study). *Entrance requirements:* For master's, undergraduate degree with minimum GPA of 2.8. Additional exam requirements/recommendations for international students: Required—TOEFL (minimum score 575 paper-based; 233 computer-based; 90 iBT), IELTS (minimum score 7).

Grand Valley State University, College of Community and Public Service, School of Public and Nonprofit Administration, Program in Health Administration, Allendale, MI 49401-9403. Offers MHA. Part-time and evening/weekend programs available. *Entrance requirements:* Additional exam requirements/recommendations for international students: Required—TOEFL. Electronic applications accepted. *Faculty research:* Long-term care and aging, Medicare and Medicaid finance and administration, health economics.

Grand Valley State University, Kirkhof College of Nursing, Allendale, MI 49401-9403. Offers advanced practice (MSN); case management (MSN); nursing administration (MSN); nursing education (MSN); nursing practice (DNP); MSN/MBA. *Accreditation:*

AACN. Part-time programs available. *Degree requirements:* For master's, thesis optional. *Entrance requirements:* For master's, GRE, minimum GPA of 3.0 in upper-division course work, course work in statistics, Michigan RN license. Additional exam requirements/recommendations for international students: Required—TOEFL. Electronic applications accepted. *Faculty research:* Multigenerational health promotion, chronic disease prevention, end-of-life issues, nursing workload, family caregiver health.

Grantham University, College of Arts and Sciences, Kansas City, MO 64153. Offers case management (MSN); health systems management (MS); healthcare administration (MHA); nursing (MSN); nursing education (MSN); nursing informatics (MSN); nursing management and organizational leadership (MSN). Part-time and evening/weekend programs available. Postbaccalaureate distance learning degree programs offered (no on-campus study). *Degree requirements:* For master's, thesis (for some programs), capstone project. *Entrance requirements:* For master's, bachelor's degree from accredited degree-granting institution. Additional exam requirements/recommendations for international students: Required—TOEFL (minimum score 500 paper-based; 213 computer-based; 61 iBT). Electronic applications accepted.

Hampton University, Hampton U Online, Hampton, VA 23668. Offers business administration (PhD); educational management (PhD); health administration (MHA); nursing (MSN, PhD).

Harding University, Paul R. Carter College of Business Administration, Searcy, AR 72149-0001. Offers health care management (MBA); information technology management (MBA); international business (MBA); leadership and organizational management (MBA). *Accreditation:* ACBSP. Part-time and evening/weekend programs available. Postbaccalaureate distance learning degree programs offered (no on-campus study). *Faculty:* 30 part-time/adjunct (6 women). *Students:* 60 full-time (25 women), 140 part-time (63 women); includes 33 minority (26 Black or African American, non-Hispanic/Latino; 1 American Indian or Alaska Native, non-Hispanic/Latino; 3 Asian, non-Hispanic/Latino; 1 Hispanic/Latino; 2 Two or more races, non-Hispanic/Latino), 24 international. Average age 30. 65 applicants, 98% accepted, 64 enrolled. In 2011, 120 master's awarded. *Degree requirements:* For master's, portfolio. *Entrance requirements:* For master's, GMAT (minimum score of 500) or GRE (minimum score of 300), minimum GPA of 3.0, 2 letters of recommendation, resume, 3 essays, all official transcripts. Additional exam requirements/recommendations for international students: Required—TOEFL (minimum score 550 paper-based; 213 computer-based; 79 iBT). *Application deadline:* For fall admission, 8/1 priority date for domestic students, 8/1 for international students; for spring admission, 12/1 priority date for domestic students, 12/1 for international students. Applications are processed on a rolling basis. Application fee: $40. *Expenses: Tuition:* Full-time $10,512; part-time $584 per credit hour. *Required fees:* $500; $25 per credit hour. Tuition and fees vary according to course load, degree level and program. *Financial support:* In 2011–12, 19 students received support. Unspecified assistantships available. Financial award application deadline: 7/30; financial award applicants required to submit FAFSA. *Unit head:* Glen Metheny, Director of Graduate Studies, 501-279-5851, Fax: 501-279-4805, E-mail: gmetheny@harding.edu. *Application contact:* Melanie Kiihnl, Recruiting Manager/Director of Marketing, 501-279-4523, Fax: 501-279-4805, E-mail: mba@harding.edu. Web site: http://www.harding.edu/mba.

Harrisburg University of Science and Technology, Program in Information Systems Engineering and Management, Harrisburg, PA 17101. Offers digital government specialization (MS); digital health specialization (MS); entrepreneurship specialization (MS). Part-time programs available. *Degree requirements:* For master's, comprehensive exam, thesis optional. *Entrance requirements:* For master's, baccalaureate degree. Additional exam requirements/recommendations for international students: Required—TOEFL (minimum score 520 paper-based; 200 computer-based; 80 iBT). Electronic applications accepted.

Harvard University, Graduate School of Arts and Sciences, Committee on Higher Degrees in Health Policy, Cambridge, MA 02138. Offers PhD. *Degree requirements:* For doctorate, thesis/dissertation. *Entrance requirements:* For doctorate, GMAT, GRE General Test, or MCAT. Additional exam requirements/recommendations for international students: Required—TOEFL. *Expenses: Tuition:* Full-time $36,304. *Required fees:* $1186. Full-time tuition and fees vary according to program.

Harvard University, Harvard Business School, Doctoral Programs in Management, Boston, MA 02163. Offers accounting and management (DBA); business economics (PhD); health policy management (PhD); management (DBA); marketing (DBA); organizational behavior (PhD); science, technology and management (PhD); strategy (DBA); technology and operations management (DBA). *Degree requirements:* For doctorate, comprehensive exam (for some programs), thesis/dissertation. *Entrance requirements:* For doctorate, GRE General Test or GMAT. Additional exam requirements/recommendations for international students: Required—TOEFL. *Expenses: Tuition:* Full-time $36,304. *Required fees:* $1186. Full-time tuition and fees vary according to program.

Harvard University, Harvard School of Public Health, Department of Health Policy and Management, Boston, MA 02115-6096. Offers health policy (PhD); health policy and management (SM, SD). Part-time programs available. *Faculty:* 43 full-time (12 women), 30 part-time/adjunct (12 women). *Students:* 116 full-time, 54 part-time; includes 42 minority (4 Black or African American, non-Hispanic/Latino; 24 Asian, non-Hispanic/Latino; 10 Hispanic/Latino; 4 Two or more races, non-Hispanic/Latino), 23 international. Average age 35. 304 applicants, 24% accepted, 67 enrolled. In 2011, 39 master's, 1 doctorate awarded. *Degree requirements:* For doctorate, thesis/dissertation, qualifying exam. *Entrance requirements:* For master's, GRE, GMAT; for doctorate, GRE. Additional exam requirements/recommendations for international students: Required—TOEFL (minimum score 595 paper-based; 240 computer-based; 95 iBT); Recommended—IELTS (minimum score 7). *Application deadline:* For fall admission, 12/15 for domestic and international students. Application fee: $115. *Expenses: Tuition:* Full-time $36,304. *Required fees:* $1186. Full-time tuition and fees vary according to program. *Financial support:* Fellowships, research assistantships, teaching assistantships, Federal Work-Study, scholarships/grants, traineeships, and unspecified assistantships available. Support available to part-time students. Financial award application deadline: 2/17; financial award applicants required to submit FAFSA. *Faculty research:* Environmental science and risk management. *Unit head:* Dr. Arnold Epstein, Chair, 617-432-3895, Fax: 617-432-4494, E-mail: aepstein@hsph.harvard.edu. *Application contact:* Vincent W. James, Director of Admissions, 617-432-1031, Fax: 617-432-7080, E-mail: admissions@hsph.harvard.edu. Web site: http://www.hsph.harvard.edu/departments/health-policy-and-management/.

Herzing University Online, Program in Business Administration, Milwaukee, WI 53203. Offers accounting (MBA); business administration (MBA); business management (MBA); healthcare management (MBA); human resources (MBA); marketing (MBA); project management (MBA); technology management (MBA). Postbaccalaureate distance learning degree programs offered (no on-campus study).

Hofstra University, Frank G. Zarb School of Business, Department of Management, Entrepreneurship and General Management, Hempstead, NY 11549. Offers business administration (MBA), including health services management, management, sports and entertainment management; general management (Advanced Certificate); human resource management (MS, Advanced Certificate). Part-time and evening/weekend programs available. Postbaccalaureate distance learning degree programs offered (minimal on-campus study). *Faculty:* 7 full-time (2 women), 8 part-time/adjunct (1 woman). *Students:* 92 full-time (36 women), 151 part-time (62 women); includes 58 minority (25 Black or African American, non-Hispanic/Latino; 23 Asian, non-Hispanic/Latino; 10 Hispanic/Latino), 24 international. Average age 32. 227 applicants, 72% accepted, 93 enrolled. In 2011, 74 master's awarded. *Degree requirements:* For master's, thesis optional, capstone course (for MBA); thesis (for MS); minimum GPA of 3.0. *Entrance requirements:* For master's, GMAT/GRE, 2 letters of recommendation; resume; essay. Additional exam requirements/recommendations for international students: Required—TOEFL (minimum score 550 paper-based; 213 computer-based; 80 iBT); Recommended—IELTS (minimum score 6). *Application deadline:* Applications are processed on a rolling basis. Application fee: $70 ($75 for international students). Electronic applications accepted. *Expenses:* Contact institution. *Financial support:* In 2011–12, 23 students received support, including 18 fellowships with full and partial tuition reimbursements available (averaging $5,605 per year), 1 research assistantship with full and partial tuition reimbursement available (averaging $11,370 per year); career-related internships or fieldwork, Federal Work-Study, institutionally sponsored loans, scholarships/grants, tuition waivers (full and partial), and unspecified assistantships also available. Support available to part-time students. Financial award applicants required to submit FAFSA. *Faculty research:* Business/personal ethics, sustainability, innovation, decision-making, supply chain management, learning and pedagogical issues, family business, small business, entrepreneurship. *Unit head:* Dr. Li-Lian Gao, Chairperson, 516-463-5729, Fax: 516-463-4834, E-mail: mgblzg@hofstra.edu. *Application contact:* Carol Drummer, Dean of Graduate Admissions, 516-463-4876, Fax: 516-463-4664, E-mail: gradstudent@hofstra.edu. Web site: http://www.hofstra.edu/Academics/Colleges/Zarb/MGMT/.

Hofstra University, School of Education, Health, and Human Services, Programs in Health, Hempstead, NY 11549. Offers community health (MS); health administration (MHA); public health (MPH). Part-time and evening/weekend programs available. *Students:* 66 full-time (43 women), 70 part-time (52 women); includes 60 minority (39 Black or African American, non-Hispanic/Latino; 11 Asian, non-Hispanic/Latino; 8 Hispanic/Latino; 2 Two or more races, non-Hispanic/Latino), 4 international. Average age 30. 90 applicants, 83% accepted, 48 enrolled. In 2011, 50 master's awarded. *Degree requirements:* For master's, internship, minimum GPA of 3.0. *Entrance requirements:* For master's, interview, 2 letters of recommendation, essay, resume. Additional exam requirements/recommendations for international students: Required—TOEFL (minimum score 550 paper-based; 213 computer-based; 80 iBT). *Application deadline:* Applications are processed on a rolling basis. Application fee: $70 ($75 for international students). Electronic applications accepted. *Expenses: Tuition:* Full-time $18,990; part-time $1055 per credit hour. *Required fees:* $970. Tuition and fees vary according to program. *Financial support:* In 2011–12, 25 students received support, including 17 fellowships with full and partial tuition reimbursements available (averaging $2,588 per year), 2 research assistantships with full and partial tuition reimbursements available (averaging $14,226 per year); career-related internships or fieldwork, Federal Work-Study, institutionally sponsored loans, scholarships/grants, tuition waivers (full and partial), and unspecified assistantships also available. Support available to part-time students. Financial award applicants required to submit FAFSA. *Faculty research:* Integrated long-term care, health care policy, cost-benefit analysis, chronic illness management, long-term care policy form. *Unit head:* Dr. Liora P. Schmelkin, Chairperson, 516-463-4680, Fax: 516-463-6505, E-mail: prolps@hofstra.edu. *Application contact:* Carol Drummer, Dean of Graduate Admissions, 516-463-4876, Fax: 516-463-4664, E-mail: gradstudent@hofstra.edu. Web site: http://www.hofstra.edu/education/.

Holy Family University, Division of Extended Learning, Philadelphia, PA 19114. Offers business administration (MBA); finance (MBA); health care administration (MBA). *Accreditation:* ACBSP. Part-time and evening/weekend programs available. *Entrance requirements:* For master's, interview, essay. Additional exam requirements/recommendations for international students: Required—TOEFL. Electronic applications accepted.

Houston Baptist University, College of Business and Economics, Program in Health Administration, Houston, TX 77074-3298. Offers MSHA. Part-time and evening/weekend programs available. *Entrance requirements:* For master's, GMAT, minimum GPA of 2.5. Additional exam requirements/recommendations for international students: Required—TOEFL (minimum score 550 paper-based; 213 computer-based).

Hunter College of the City University of New York, Graduate School, Schools of the Health Professions, School of Health Sciences, Programs in Urban Public Health, Program in Health Policy Management, New York, NY 10021-5085. Offers MPH. Part-time and evening/weekend programs available. *Faculty:* 1 (woman) full-time, 3 part-time/adjunct (2 women). *Students:* 4 full-time (1 woman), 68 part-time (48 women); includes 27 minority (15 Black or African American, non-Hispanic/Latino; 7 Asian, non-Hispanic/Latino; 5 Hispanic/Latino), 4 international. Average age 32. 64 applicants, 61% accepted, 28 enrolled. In 2011, 17 master's awarded. *Degree requirements:* For master's, comprehensive exam, thesis optional, internship. *Entrance requirements:* For master's, GRE General Test, previous course work in calculus and statistics. Additional exam requirements/recommendations for international students: Required—TOEFL. *Application deadline:* For fall admission, 4/1 for domestic students; for spring admission, 11/1 for domestic students. Application fee: $125. *Expenses:* Tuition, state resident: full-time $8210; part-time $345 per credit. Tuition, nonresident: full-time $15,360; part-time $640 per credit. *Required fees:* $280 per semester. One-time fee: $125. Tuition and fees vary according to class time, campus/location and program. *Financial support:* In 2011–12, 6 fellowships were awarded; career-related internships or fieldwork, Federal Work-Study, institutionally sponsored loans, and tuition waivers (partial) also available. Support available to part-time students. *Unit head:* Stacey Plichta, Coordinator, 212-481-7674, Fax: 212-481-5260, E-mail: splichta@hunter.cuny.edu. *Application contact:* Milena Solo, Director for Graduate Admissions, 212-772-4288, Fax: 212-650-3336, E-mail: milena.solo@hunter.cuny.edu. Web site: http://www.hunter.cuny.edu/uph/grad-test/health-policy-management-2.

Husson University, School of Graduate and Professional Studies, Master of Business Administration Program, Bangor, ME 04401-2999. Offers general (corporate) (MSB); health care management (MSB); hospitality management (MSB); nonprofit management (MSB). Part-time and evening/weekend programs available. *Faculty:* 9 full-time (3 women), 12 part-time/adjunct (2 women). *Students:* 111 full-time (66 women), 60 part-time (37 women); includes 8 minority (3 Black or African American, non-Hispanic/Latino; 1 American Indian or Alaska Native, non-Hispanic/Latino; 2 Asian, non-Hispanic/Latino; 2 Hispanic/Latino). 67 applicants, 35 enrolled. In 2011, 90 master's awarded. *Degree requirements:* For master's, comprehensive exam (for some programs), thesis optional. *Entrance requirements:* For master's, GMAT or GRE, minimum GPA of 3.0. Additional exam requirements/recommendations for international students: Required—TOEFL (minimum score 550 paper-based). *Application deadline:* Applications are processed on a rolling basis. Application fee: $40. Electronic applications accepted. *Expenses:* Contact institution. *Financial support:* In 2011–12, 1 student received support. Career-related internships or fieldwork, Federal Work-Study, scholarships/grants, and

unspecified assistantships available. Financial award application deadline: 4/15; financial award applicants required to submit FAFSA. *Unit head:* Dr. Ronald Nykiel, Dean, College of Business, 207-941-7111, E-mail: nykielr@husson.edu. *Application contact:* Kristen M. Card, Director of Graduate Admissions, 207-404-5660, Fax: 207-941-7935, E-mail: cardk@husson.edu. Web site: http://www.husson.edu/mba.

Independence University, Program in Business Administration in Health Care, Salt Lake City, UT 84107. Offers health care administration (MBA). Part-time and evening/weekend programs available. Postbaccalaureate distance learning degree programs offered (no on-campus study). *Degree requirements:* For master's, fieldwork/internship.

Independence University, Program in Health Care Administration, Salt Lake City, UT 84107. Offers MSHCA. Part-time and evening/weekend programs available. Postbaccalaureate distance learning degree programs offered (no on-campus study). *Degree requirements:* For master's, fieldwork, internship. *Entrance requirements:* For master's, previous course work in psychology.

Independence University, Program in Health Services, Salt Lake City, UT 84107. Offers community health (MSHS); wellness promotion (MSHS). Part-time and evening/weekend programs available. Postbaccalaureate distance learning degree programs offered (no on-campus study). *Degree requirements:* For master's, fieldwork, internship, final project (wellness promotion). *Entrance requirements:* For master's, previous course work in psychology.

Indiana Tech, Program in Business Administration, Fort Wayne, IN 46803-1297. Offers accounting (MBA); health care administration (MBA); human resources (MBA); management (MBA); marketing (MBA). Part-time and evening/weekend programs available. Postbaccalaureate distance learning degree programs offered (no on-campus study). *Entrance requirements:* For master's, GMAT, minimum undergraduate GPA of 2.5, 3 letters of recommendation. Electronic applications accepted.

Indiana University Bloomington, School of Health, Physical Education and Recreation, Department of Applied Health Science, Bloomington, IN 47405-7000. Offers biostatistics (MPH); environmental health (MPH, PhD); epidemiology (MPH, PhD); health behavior (PhD); health promotion (MS); human development/family studies (MS); nutrition science (MS); public health administration (MPH); safety management (MS); school and college health programs (MS); social, behavioral and community health (MPH). *Accreditation:* CEPH (one or more programs are accredited). *Faculty:* 24 full-time (12 women). *Students:* 169 full-time (126 women), 25 part-time (17 women); includes 56 minority (39 Black or African American, non-Hispanic/Latino; 2 American Indian or Alaska Native, non-Hispanic/Latino; 4 Asian, non-Hispanic/Latino; 9 Hispanic/Latino; 2 Two or more races, non-Hispanic/Latino), 29 international. Average age 30. 170 applicants, 74% accepted, 79 enrolled. In 2011, 52 master's, 9 doctorates awarded. *Degree requirements:* For master's, thesis optional; for doctorate, thesis/dissertation. *Entrance requirements:* For master's, GRE (MS in nutrition science), 3 recommendations; for doctorate, GRE, 3 recommendations. Additional exam requirements/recommendations for international students: Required—TOEFL (minimum score 550 paper-based; 213 computer-based; 79 iBT). *Application deadline:* For fall admission, 4/30 priority date for domestic students, 12/1 for international students; for spring admission, 11/15 priority date for domestic students, 9/1 for international students. Application fee: $55 ($65 for international students). *Financial support:* Fellowships, research assistantships with full and partial tuition reimbursements, teaching assistantships with full and partial tuition reimbursements, career-related internships or fieldwork, Federal Work-Study, institutionally sponsored loans, scholarships/grants, tuition waivers (partial), and fee remissions available. Financial award application deadline: 3/1. *Faculty research:* Cancer education, HIV/AIDS and drug education, public health, parent-child interactions, safety education. *Total annual research expenditures:* $2.8 million. *Unit head:* Dr. David K. Lohrmann, Chair, 812-856-5101, Fax: 812-855-3936, E-mail: dlohrman@indiana.edu. *Application contact:* Dr. Susan Middlestadt, Associate Professor and Graduate Coordinator, 812-856-5768, Fax: 812-855-3936, E-mail: semiddle@indiana.edu. Web site: http://www.indiana.edu/~aphealth/.

Indiana University of Pennsylvania, School of Graduate Studies and Research, College of Health and Human Services, Department of Nursing and Allied Health, Indiana, PA 15705-1087. Offers health service administration (MS); nursing (MS, PhD); nursing administration (MS); nursing education (MS). Part-time programs available. *Faculty:* 6 full-time (5 women). *Students:* 4 full-time (all women), 63 part-time (61 women); includes 4 minority (3 Black or African American, non-Hispanic/Latino; 1 Hispanic/Latino). Average age 42. 34 applicants, 47% accepted, 14 enrolled. In 2011, 12 master's awarded. *Degree requirements:* For master's, thesis optional. *Entrance requirements:* For master's, 2 letters of recommendation. Additional exam requirements/recommendations for international students: Required—TOEFL (minimum score 540 paper-based; 207 computer-based). *Application deadline:* Applications are processed on a rolling basis. Application fee: $50. Electronic applications accepted. *Expenses:* Tuition, state resident: full-time $7488; part-time $416 per credit. Tuition, nonresident: full-time $11,232; part-time $624 per credit. *Required fees:* $2070; $192.20 per credit. $90 per semester. *Financial support:* In 2011–12, 5 fellowships (averaging $5,179 per year), 4 research assistantships with full and partial tuition reimbursements (averaging $3,599 per year) were awarded; teaching assistantships and Federal Work-Study also available. Support available to part-time students. Financial award application deadline: 4/15; financial award applicants required to submit FAFSA. *Unit head:* Dr. Elizabeth Palmer, Chairperson, 724-357-2558, E-mail: lpalmer@iup.edu. *Application contact:* Dr. Kristy S. Chunta, Assistant Chairperson and Graduate Coordinator, 724-357-2408, E-mail: kchunta@iup.edu. Web site: http://www.iup.edu/upper.aspx?id=216.

Indiana University–Purdue University Indianapolis, Indiana University School of Medicine, Department of Public Health, Indianapolis, IN 46202-2896. Offers behavioral health science (MPH); epidemiology (MPH); health policy and management (MPH). *Accreditation:* CEPH. *Students:* 134 full-time (86 women), 134 part-time (93 women); includes 53 minority (25 Black or African American, non-Hispanic/Latino; 1 American Indian or Alaska Native, non-Hispanic/Latino; 14 Asian, non-Hispanic/Latino; 10 Hispanic/Latino; 3 Two or more races, non-Hispanic/Latino), 13 international. Average age 30. 236 applicants, 58% accepted, 106 enrolled. In 2011, 81 master's awarded. Application fee: $55 ($65 for international students). *Expenses:* Contact institution. *Financial support:* In 2011–12, teaching assistantships (averaging $14,058 per year) were awarded. *Unit head:* Dr. Carole Kacius, Director, 317-274-3126. *Application contact:* Robert M. Stump, Jr., Director of Admissions, 317-274-3772, E-mail: inmedadm@iupui.edu.

Indiana University South Bend, School of Public and Environmental Affairs, South Bend, IN 46634-7111. Offers health systems administration and policy (MPA); health systems management (Certificate); nonprofit management (Certificate); public and community services administration and policy (MPA); public management (Certificate); urban affairs (Certificate). *Accreditation:* NASPAA. Part-time and evening/weekend programs available. *Faculty:* 4 full-time (1 woman). *Students:* 7 part-time (5 women); includes 3 minority (2 Black or African American, non-Hispanic/Latino; 1 Hispanic/Latino). Average age 43. In 2011, 6 master's awarded. *Entrance requirements:* For master's, GRE General Test, minimum undergraduate GPA of 2.5. *Application deadline:* For fall admission, 7/1 priority date for domestic students; for spring admission, 11/1 for domestic students. Applications are processed on a rolling basis. Application fee: $50 ($60 for international students). *Financial support:* Fellowships, research assistantships, career-related internships or fieldwork, Federal Work-Study, and institutionally sponsored loans available. Support available to part-time students. Financial award application deadline: 3/1; financial award applicants required to submit FAFSA. *Unit head:* Leda M. Hall, Dean, 574-520-4803. *Application contact:* Admissions Counselor, 574-520-4839, Fax: 574-520-4834, E-mail: graduate@iusb.edu.

Institute of Public Administration, Programs in Public Administration, Dublin, Ireland. Offers healthcare management (MA); local government management (MA); public management (MA, Diploma).

Iona College, Hagan School of Business, Department of Management, New Rochelle, NY 10801-1890. Offers business administration (MBA); health care management (MBA, AC); human resource management (MBA, PMC); long term care services management (AC); management (MBA, PMC). Part-time and evening/weekend programs available. *Faculty:* 7 full-time (1 woman), 4 part-time/adjunct (1 woman). *Students:* 29 full-time (13 women), 112 part-time (55 women); includes 27 minority (10 Black or African American, non-Hispanic/Latino; 8 Asian, non-Hispanic/Latino; 9 Hispanic/Latino). Average age 32. 60 applicants, 65% accepted, 30 enrolled. In 2011, 64 master's, 13 other advanced degrees awarded. *Entrance requirements:* For master's, GMAT, 2 letters of recommendation; for other advanced degree, GMAT. Additional exam requirements/recommendations for international students: Required—TOEFL (minimum score 550 paper-based; 213 computer-based; 80 iBT). *Application deadline:* For fall admission, 8/15 priority date for domestic students, 8/1 for international students; for winter admission, 11/15 priority date for domestic students, 11/1 for international students; for spring admission, 2/15 priority date for domestic students, 2/1 for international students. Applications are processed on a rolling basis. Application fee: $50. Electronic applications accepted. *Expenses:* Contact institution. *Financial support:* Scholarships/grants, tuition waivers (partial), and unspecified assistantships available. Support available to part-time students. Financial award application deadline: 4/15; financial award applicants required to submit FAFSA. *Faculty research:* Information systems, strategic management, corporate values and ethics. *Unit head:* Dr. Fredrica Rudell, Acting Chair, 914-637-2748, E-mail: frudell@iona.edu. *Application contact:* Ben Fan, Director of MBA Admissions, 914-633-2289, Fax: 914-637-2708, E-mail: sfan@iona.edu.

The Johns Hopkins University, Bloomberg School of Public Health, Department of Health Policy and Management, Baltimore, MD 21205-1996. Offers bioethics and policy (PhD); health and public policy (PhD); health care management and leadership (Dr PH); health economics (MHS); health economics and policy (PhD); health finance and management (MHA); health policy (MHS); health services research and policy (PhD). *Accreditation:* CAHME (one or more programs are accredited). Part-time programs available. *Degree requirements:* For master's, thesis (for some programs), internship (for some programs); for doctorate, comprehensive exam, thesis/dissertation, 1 year full-time residency (for some programs), oral and written exams. *Entrance requirements:* For master's, GRE General Test or GMAT, 3 letters of recommendation, curriculum vitae/resume; for doctorate, GRE General Test or GMAT, 3 letters of recommendation, curriculum vitae, transcripts. Additional exam requirements/recommendations for international students: Recommended—TOEFL (minimum score 600 paper-based; 250 computer-based; 100 iBT), IELTS. Electronic applications accepted. *Faculty research:* Quality of care and health outcomes, health care finance and technology, health disparities and vulnerable populations, injury prevention, health policy and health care policy.

The Johns Hopkins University, Bloomberg School of Public Health, Department of International Health, Baltimore, MD 21205. Offers global disease epidemiology and control (MHS, PhD); health systems (MHS, PhD); human nutrition (MHS, PhD); international health (Dr PH); social and behavioral interventions (MHS, PhD). *Degree requirements:* For master's, comprehensive exam, thesis (for some programs), 1 year full-time residency, 4-9 month internship; for doctorate, comprehensive exam, thesis/dissertation or alternative, 1.5 years full-time residency, oral and written exams. *Entrance requirements:* For master's, GRE General Test or MCAT, 3 letters of recommendation, resume; for doctorate, GRE General Test or MCAT, 3 letters of recommendation, resume, transcripts. Additional exam requirements/recommendations for international students: Required—TOEFL (minimum score 600 paper-based; 250 computer-based; 100 iBT); Recommended—IELTS (minimum score 7). Electronic applications accepted. *Faculty research:* Nutrition, infectious diseases, health systems, health economics, humanitarian emergencies.

The Johns Hopkins University, Carey Business School, Business of Health Program, Baltimore, MD 21218-2699. Offers business of medicine (Certificate); business of nursing (Certificate); leadership and management in the life sciences (MBA); medical services management (MBA); MBA/MPH; MBA/MS; MBA/MSN. Part-time and evening/weekend programs available. *Degree requirements:* For master's, 54 credits including capstone project. *Entrance requirements:* For master's, GMAT or GRE, minimum GPA of 3.0, resume, work experience, two letters of recommendation; for Certificate, minimum GPA of 3.0, resume, work experience, two letters of recommendation. Additional exam requirements/recommendations for international students: Required—TOEFL (minimum score 600 paper-based; 250 computer-based; 100 iBT). Electronic applications accepted. *Faculty research:* Clinical practice optimization, operations management, supply chain risk management.

Jones International University, School of Business, Centennial, CO 80112. Offers accounting (MBA); business communication (MABC); entrepreneurship (MABC, MBA); finance (MBA); global enterprise management (MBA); health care management (MBA); information security management (MBA); information technology management (MBA); leadership and influence (MABC); leading the customer-driven organization (MABC); negotiation and conflict management (MBA); project management (MABC, MBA). Program only offered online. Part-time and evening/weekend programs available. Postbaccalaureate distance learning degree programs offered (no on-campus study). *Degree requirements:* For master's, capstone project. *Entrance requirements:* For master's, minimum cumulative GPA of 2.5. Additional exam requirements/recommendations for international students: Recommended—TOEFL (minimum score 550 paper-based; 213 computer-based). Electronic applications accepted.

Kaplan University, Davenport Campus, School of Business, Davenport, IA 52807-2095. Offers business administration (MBA); change leadership (MS); entrepreneurship (MBA); finance (MBA); health care management (MBA, MS); human resource (MBA); international business (MBA); management (MS); marketing (MBA); project management (MBA, MS); supply chain management and logistics (MBA, MS). Part-time and evening/weekend programs available. Postbaccalaureate distance learning degree programs offered (no on-campus study). *Entrance requirements:* Additional exam requirements/recommendations for international students: Required—TOEFL (minimum score 550 paper-based; 218 computer-based; 80 iBT). Electronic applications accepted.

Kaplan University, Davenport Campus, School of Legal Studies, Davenport, IA 52807-2095. Offers health care delivery (MS); pathway to paralegal (Postbaccalaureate Certificate); state and local government (MS). Part-time and evening/weekend programs available. Postbaccalaureate distance learning degree programs offered (no on-campus

study). *Entrance requirements:* Additional exam requirements/recommendations for international students: Required—TOEFL (minimum score 550 paper-based; 218 computer-based; 80 iBT).

Kean University, College of Business and Public Management, Program in Public Administration, Union, NJ 07083. Offers environmental management (MPA); health services administration (MPA); non-profit management (MPA); public administration (MPA). *Accreditation:* NASPAA. *Faculty:* 14 full-time (7 women). *Students:* 65 full-time (34 women), 77 part-time (41 women); includes 92 minority (68 Black or African American, non-Hispanic/Latino; 7 Asian, non-Hispanic/Latino; 17 Hispanic/Latino), 4 international. Average age 32. 69 applicants, 70% accepted, 32 enrolled. In 2011, 48 master's awarded. *Degree requirements:* For master's, thesis, internship, research seminar. *Entrance requirements:* For master's, minimum GPA of 3.0, 2 letters of recommendation, interview, writing sample, transcripts, resume. Additional exam requirements/recommendations for international students: Required—TOEFL (minimum score 79 iBT). *Application deadline:* For fall admission, 6/1 for domestic and international students; for spring admission, 12/1 for domestic and international students. Applications are processed on a rolling basis. Application fee: $75 ($150 for international students). Electronic applications accepted. *Expenses:* Tuition, state resident: full-time $11,302; part-time $550 per credit. Tuition, nonresident: full-time $15,318; part-time $674 per credit. *Required fees:* $2849; $130 per credit. Tuition and fees vary according to degree level. *Financial support:* In 2011–12, 14 research assistantships with full tuition reimbursements (averaging $3,263 per year) were awarded; unspecified assistantships also available. Financial award applicants required to submit FAFSA. *Unit head:* Dr. Patricia Moore, Program Coordinator, 908-737-4314, E-mail: pmoore@kean.edu. *Application contact:* Heenat Hasan, Admissions Counselor, 908-737-5923, Fax: 908-737-5925, E-mail: hasanr@kean.edu. Web site: http://www.kean.edu/KU/Public-Administration.

Keiser University, Master of Business Administration Program, Fort Lauderdale, FL 33309. Offers accounting (MBA); health services management (MBA); international business (MBA); leadership for managers (MBA); marketing (MBA). Leadership for Managers and International Business concentrations also offered in Spanish. Part-time programs available. Postbaccalaureate distance learning degree programs offered (minimal on-campus study). *Entrance requirements:* For master's, minimum GPA of 2.7 from an accredited institution. Additional exam requirements/recommendations for international students: Required—TOEFL. Electronic applications accepted.

Kennesaw State University, College of Health and Human Services, Program in Advanced Care Management and Leadership, Kennesaw, GA 30144-5591. Offers MSN. Part-time and evening/weekend programs available. Postbaccalaureate distance learning degree programs offered (minimal on-campus study). *Students:* 9 full-time (8 women); includes 5 minority (4 Black or African American, non-Hispanic/Latino; 1 Native Hawaiian or other Pacific Islander, non-Hispanic/Latino). Average age 40. 12 applicants, 67% accepted, 4 enrolled. In 2011, 4 degrees awarded. *Entrance requirements:* For master's, GRE General Test, minimum GPA of 3.0, 3 years experience, RN license. Additional exam requirements/recommendations for international students: Required—TOEFL (minimum score 550 paper-based; 213 computer-based; 80 iBT), IELTS (minimum score 6). *Application deadline:* For fall admission, 6/1 for domestic and international students. Application fee: $60. Electronic applications accepted. *Expenses:* Tuition, state resident: full-time $3000; part-time $250 per semester hour. Tuition, nonresident: full-time $10,836; part-time $903 per semester hour. *Required fees:* $774 per semester. *Financial support:* In 2011–12, 2 research assistantships with tuition reimbursements (averaging $4,000 per year) were awarded; unspecified assistantships also available. *Unit head:* Dr. Marilyn King, Director, 770-423-6172, Fax: 770-423-6870, E-mail: mking71@kennesaw.edu. *Application contact:* Tamara Hutto, Admissions Counselor, 770-420-4377, Fax: 770-423-6885, E-mail: ksugrad@kennesaw.edu.

King's College, William G. McGowan School of Business, Wilkes-Barre, PA 18711-0801. Offers health care administration (MS). *Accreditation:* AACSB. Part-time programs available. *Entrance requirements:* Additional exam requirements/recommendations for international students: Required—TOEFL (minimum score 600 paper-based; 250 computer-based).

Lake Erie College, School of Business, Painesville, OH 44077-3389. Offers general management (MBA); management healthcare administration (MBA). Part-time and evening/weekend programs available. *Faculty:* 5 full-time (3 women), 6 part-time/adjunct (1 woman). *Students:* 28 full-time (14 women), 117 part-time (57 women); includes 27 minority (15 Black or African American, non-Hispanic/Latino; 6 Asian, non-Hispanic/Latino; 2 Hispanic/Latino; 4 Two or more races, non-Hispanic/Latino), 2 international. Average age 36. 66 applicants, 71% accepted, 37 enrolled. In 2011, 86 master's awarded. *Entrance requirements:* For master's, GMAT or minimum GPA of 3.0, resume, references. Additional exam requirements/recommendations for international students: Required—TOEFL (minimum score 550 paper-based; 79 computer-based). *Application deadline:* For fall admission, 8/1 priority date for domestic students, 6/1 for international students; for spring admission, 12/15 for domestic students, 10/1 for international students. Applications are processed on a rolling basis. Application fee: $30. Electronic applications accepted. Application fee is waived when completed online. *Expenses: Tuition:* Full-time $9594; part-time $533 per credit hour. *Required fees:* $51 per credit hour. Tuition and fees vary according to program. *Financial support:* Career-related internships or fieldwork and unspecified assistantships available. Financial award applicants required to submit FAFSA. *Faculty research:* Organizational effectiveness. *Unit head:* Prof. Robert Trebar, Dean of the School of Business, 440-375-7115, Fax: 440-375-7005, E-mail: rtrebar@lec.edu. *Application contact:* Christopher Harris, Dean of Admissions and Financial Aid, 800-533-4996, Fax: 440-375-7000, E-mail: admissions@lec.edu. Web site: http://www.lec.edu/parkermba.

Lake Forest Graduate School of Management, The Leadership MBA Program (LMBA), Lake Forest, IL 60045. Offers finance (MBA); global business (MBA); healthcare management (MBA); management (MBA); marketing (MBA); organizational behavior (MBA). Part-time and evening/weekend programs available. *Faculty:* 136 part-time/adjunct (41 women). *Students:* 734 part-time (306 women); includes 161 minority (34 Black or African American, non-Hispanic/Latino; 4 American Indian or Alaska Native, non-Hispanic/Latino; 87 Asian, non-Hispanic/Latino; 14 Hispanic/Latino; 4 Native Hawaiian or other Pacific Islander, non-Hispanic/Latino; 18 Two or more races, non-Hispanic/Latino). Average age 38. In 2011, 213 master's awarded. *Entrance requirements:* For master's, 4 years of work experience in field, interview, 2 letters of recommendation. *Application deadline:* For fall admission, 7/1 for domestic students; for winter admission, 1/5 for domestic students; for spring admission, 3/1 for domestic students. Applications are processed on a rolling basis. Application fee: $75. Electronic applications accepted. *Expenses: Tuition:* Part-time $2932 per unit. *Required fees:* $50 per unit. *Financial support:* Scholarships/grants available. Support available to part-time students. Financial award applicants required to submit FAFSA. *Unit head:* Chris Multhauf, Executive Vice President of Educational Programs and Solutions, 847-574-5270, Fax: 847-295-3656, E-mail: cmulthauf@lfgsm.edu. *Application contact:* Carolyn Brune, Director of Admissions, 800-737-4MBA, Fax: 847-295-3656, E-mail: admiss@lfgsm.edu. Web site: http://www.lakeforestmba.edu/lake_forest_mba_program/LFGSM-Leadership-MBA.aspx.

Lakeland College, Graduate Studies Division, Program in Business Administration, Sheboygan, WI 53082-0359. Offers accounting (MBA); finance (MBA); healthcare management (MBA); project management (MBA). *Entrance requirements:* For master's, GMAT. *Expenses:* Contact institution.

Lamar University, College of Graduate Studies, College of Business, Beaumont, TX 77710. Offers accounting (MBA); experiential business and entrepreneurship (MBA); financial management (MBA); healthcare administration (MBA); information systems (MBA); management (MBA). *Accreditation:* AACSB. Part-time and evening/weekend programs available. *Faculty:* 18 full-time (5 women), 5 part-time/adjunct (0 women). *Students:* 74 full-time (33 women), 72 part-time (27 women); includes 24 minority (7 Black or African American, non-Hispanic/Latino; 9 Asian, non-Hispanic/Latino; 8 Hispanic/Latino), 34 international. Average age 29. 69 applicants, 84% accepted, 16 enrolled. In 2011, 62 master's awarded. *Degree requirements:* For master's, comprehensive exam (for some programs), thesis optional. *Entrance requirements:* For master's, GMAT. Additional exam requirements/recommendations for international students: Required—TOEFL (minimum score 525 paper-based; 197 computer-based). *Application deadline:* For fall admission, 3/15 priority date for domestic students; for spring admission, 10/1 priority date for domestic students. Applications are processed on a rolling basis. Application fee: $25 ($50 for international students). *Expenses:* Tuition, state resident: full-time $5430; part-time $272 per credit hour. Tuition, nonresident: full-time $11,540; part-time $577 per credit hour. *Required fees:* $1916. *Financial support:* In 2011–12, 12 students received support, including 4 research assistantships with partial tuition reimbursements available; fellowships with tuition reimbursements available, career-related internships or fieldwork, Federal Work-Study, institutionally sponsored loans, scholarships/grants, and tuition waivers (partial) also available. Support available to part-time students. Financial award application deadline: 4/1; financial award applicants required to submit FAFSA. *Faculty research:* Marketing, finance, quantitative methods, management information systems, legal, environmental. *Unit head:* Dr. Enrique R. Venta, Dean, 409-880-8604, Fax: 409-880-8088, E-mail: henry.venta@lamar.edu. *Application contact:* Dr. Brad Mayer, Professor and Associate Dean, 409-880-2383, Fax: 409-880-8605, E-mail: bradley.mayer@lamar.edu. Web site: http://mba.lamar.edu.

Lehigh University, P.C. Rossin College of Engineering and Applied Science, Department of Industrial and Systems Engineering, Program in Healthcare Systems Engineering, Bethlehem, PA 18015. Offers M Eng. Part-time programs available. Postbaccalaureate distance learning degree programs offered (no on-campus study). *Faculty:* 1 full-time (0 women). *Students:* 11 full-time (4 women), 7 part-time (2 women); includes 4 minority (1 Black or African American, non-Hispanic/Latino; 2 Asian, non-Hispanic/Latino; 1 Two or more races, non-Hispanic/Latino), 4 international. Average age 27. 84 applicants, 24% accepted, 17 enrolled. *Entrance requirements:* For master's, GRE (minimum scores in the 75th percentile). Additional exam requirements/recommendations for international students: Required—TOEFL. *Application deadline:* For fall admission, 7/15 for domestic and international students; for spring admission, 12/1 for domestic and international students. Applications are processed on a rolling basis. Application fee: $75. Electronic applications accepted. *Expenses:* Contact institution. *Financial support:* Application deadline: 1/15. *Faculty research:* Project management, engineering economics, statistics and stochastic processes, operations research, simulation and optimization and IT. *Unit head:* Prof. Hisham Nabaa, Professor of Practice, 610-758-3865, Fax: 610-758-6766, E-mail: hia206@lehigh.edu. *Application contact:* Linda Wismer, Coordinator, 610-758-5867, Fax: 610-758-6766, E-mail: liw511@lehigh.edu. Web site: http://www.lehigh.edu/ise/hse.html.

LeTourneau University, School of Graduate and Professional Studies, Longview, TX 75607-7001. Offers business administration (MBA); counseling (MA); education (M Ed); engineering (M Sc); health care administration (MS); psychology (MA); strategic leadership (MSL). Part-time and evening/weekend programs available. Postbaccalaureate distance learning degree programs offered (no on-campus study). *Faculty:* 19 full-time (5 women), 62 part-time/adjunct (25 women). *Students:* 12 full-time (6 women), 347 part-time (273 women); includes 191 minority (162 Black or African American, non-Hispanic/Latino; 2 American Indian or Alaska Native, non-Hispanic/Latino; 3 Asian, non-Hispanic/Latino; 20 Hispanic/Latino; 1 Native Hawaiian or other Pacific Islander, non-Hispanic/Latino; 3 Two or more races, non-Hispanic/Latino), 1 international. Average age 37. 138 applicants, 90% accepted, 120 enrolled. In 2011, 129 master's awarded. *Degree requirements:* For master's, thesis (for some programs). *Entrance requirements:* For master's, GRE (for counseling and engineering programs), minimum GPA of 2.8 (3.0 for counseling and engineering programs). Additional exam requirements/recommendations for international students: Required—TOEFL. *Application deadline:* Applications are processed on a rolling basis. Electronic applications accepted. *Expenses: Tuition:* Full-time $13,020; part-time $620 per credit hour. *Financial support:* In 2011–12, 15 students received support, including 5 research assistantships (averaging $9,600 per year); institutionally sponsored loans and unspecified assistantships also available. *Unit head:* Dr. Carol Green, Vice President, 903-233-4010, Fax: 903-233-3227, E-mail: carolgreen@letu.edu. *Application contact:* Chris Fontaine, Assistant Vice President for Enrollment Management and Marketing, 903-233-4071, Fax: 903-233-3227, E-mail: chrisfontaine@letu.edu. Web site: http://www.adults.letu.edu/.

Lewis University, College of Business, Graduate School of Management, Program in Business Administration, Romeoville, IL 60446. Offers accounting (MBA); custom elective option (MBA); e-business (MBA); finance (MBA); healthcare management (MBA); human resources management (MBA); information security (MBA); international business (MBA); management information systems (MBA); marketing (MBA); project management (MBA); technology and operations management (MBA). Part-time and evening/weekend programs available. *Students:* 112 full-time (60 women), 232 part-time (118 women); includes 104 minority (62 Black or African American, non-Hispanic/Latino; 1 American Indian or Alaska Native, non-Hispanic/Latino; 7 Asian, non-Hispanic/Latino; 33 Hispanic/Latino; 1 Native Hawaiian or other Pacific Islander, non-Hispanic/Latino), 9 international. Average age 28. In 2011, 99 master's awarded. *Entrance requirements:* For master's, interview, bachelor's degree, resume, 2 recommendations. Additional exam requirements/recommendations for international students: Required—TOEFL (minimum score 550 paper-based; 213 computer-based). *Application deadline:* For fall admission, 8/15 priority date for domestic students, 5/1 for international students; for spring admission, 11/15 for international students. Applications are processed on a rolling basis. Application fee: $40. Electronic applications accepted. *Financial support:* Career-related internships or fieldwork, Federal Work-Study, scholarships/grants, and unspecified assistantships available. Financial award application deadline: 5/1; financial award applicants required to submit FAFSA. *Unit head:* Dr. Maureen Culleeney, Academic Program Director, 815-838-0500 Ext. 5631, E-mail: culleema@lewisu.edu. *Application contact:* Michele Ryan, Director of Admission, 815-838-0500 Ext. 5384, E-mail: gsm@lewisu.edu.

Lindenwood University, Graduate Programs, College of Individualized Education, St. Charles, MO 63301-1695. Offers administration (MSA); business administration (MBA); communications (MA); criminal justice and administration (MS); gerontology (MA); health management (MS); human resource management (MS); information technology (MBA, Certificate); managing information technology (MS); writing (MFA). Part-time and

evening/weekend programs available. *Faculty:* 18 full-time (9 women), 128 part-time/adjunct (53 women). *Students:* 858 full-time (586 women), 69 part-time (43 women); includes 330 minority (296 Black or African American, non-Hispanic/Latino; 9 American Indian or Alaska Native, non-Hispanic/Latino; 4 Asian, non-Hispanic/Latino; 1 Hispanic/Latino; 20 Two or more races, non-Hispanic/Latino), 16 international. Average age 35. 229 applicants, 80% accepted, 172 enrolled. In 2011, 428 degrees awarded. *Degree requirements:* For master's, thesis (for some programs), 1 colloquium per term. *Entrance requirements:* For master's, interview, minimum GPA of 3.0. Additional exam requirements/recommendations for international students: Required—TOEFL (minimum score 550 paper-based; 213 computer-based; 80 iBT). *Application deadline:* For fall admission, 10/1 priority date for domestic students, 10/1 for international students; for winter admission, 1/7 priority date for domestic students, 1/7 for international students; for spring admission, 4/7 priority date for domestic students, 4/7 for international students. Applications are processed on a rolling basis. Application fee: $30 ($100 for international students). Electronic applications accepted. *Expenses: Tuition:* Full-time $13,650; part-time $395 per credit hour. *Required fees:* $150 per semester. Tuition and fees vary according to course level and course load. *Financial support:* In 2011–12, 386 students received support. Career-related internships or fieldwork, institutionally sponsored loans, tuition waivers (partial), and unspecified assistantships available. Financial award application deadline: 6/30; financial award applicants required to submit FAFSA. *Unit head:* Dan Kemper, Dean, 636-949-4501, Fax: 636-949-4505, E-mail: dkemper@lindenwood.edu. *Application contact:* Brett Barger, Dean of Evening Admissions and Extension Campuses, 636-949-4934, Fax: 636-949-4109, E-mail: adultadmissions@lindenwood.edu.

Lipscomb University, College of Business, Nashville, TN 37204-3951. Offers accounting (MBA); business administration (general) (MBA); conflict management (MBA); financial services (MBA); healthcare management (MBA); human resources (MHR); leadership (MBA); nonprofit management (MBA); sports management (MBA); sustainability (MBA). *Accreditation:* ACBSP. Part-time and evening/weekend programs available. *Faculty:* 13 full-time (3 women), 7 part-time/adjunct (1 woman). *Students:* 51 full-time (21 women), 83 part-time (48 women); includes 20 minority (16 Black or African American, non-Hispanic/Latino; 3 Asian, non-Hispanic/Latino; 1 Hispanic/Latino), 1 international. Average age 33. 190 applicants, 43% accepted, 54 enrolled. In 2011, 85 master's awarded. *Entrance requirements:* For master's, GMAT, interview, 2 references, resume. Additional exam requirements/recommendations for international students: Required—TOEFL (minimum score 570 paper-based; 230 computer-based). *Application deadline:* For fall admission, 6/15 for domestic students, 2/1 for international students; for winter admission, 6/1 for international students; for spring admission, 11/15 for domestic students. Applications are processed on a rolling basis. Application fee: $50 ($75 for international students). Electronic applications accepted. *Expenses:* Contact institution. *Financial support:* Career-related internships or fieldwork, scholarships/grants, tuition waivers (partial), and unspecified assistantships available. Support available to part-time students. Financial award application deadline: 7/1; financial award applicants required to submit FAFSA. *Faculty research:* Impact of spirituality on organization commitment, leadership, psychological empowerment, training. *Unit head:* Dr. Mike Kendrick, Associate Dean of Graduate Business Programs, 615-966-1833, Fax: 615-966-1818, E-mail: mikekendrick@lipscomb.edu. *Application contact:* Lisa Shacklett, Executive Director of Enrollment and Marketing, 615-966-5968, E-mail: lisa.shacklett@lipscomb.edu. Web site: http://mba.lipscomb.edu.

Loma Linda University, School of Public Health, Programs in Health Administration, Loma Linda, CA 92350. Offers MBA, MHA, MPH. *Entrance requirements:* For master's, GMAT (MHA). Additional exam requirements/recommendations for international students: Required—Michigan Test of English Language Proficiency or TOEFL.

Long Island University–Brooklyn Campus, School of Health Professions, Department of Community Health, Brooklyn, NY 11201-8423. Offers community mental health (MS); family health (MS); health management (MS). Part-time and evening/weekend programs available. *Entrance requirements:* For master's, 2 letters of recommendation. Additional exam requirements/recommendations for international students: Required—TOEFL (minimum score 500 paper-based; 173 computer-based). Electronic applications accepted.

Long Island University–C. W. Post Campus, College of Management, Department of Health Care and Public Administration, Brookville, NY 11548-1300. Offers gerontology (Certificate); health care administration (MPA); health care administration/gerontology (MPA); nonprofit management (MPA, Certificate); public administration (MPA). *Accreditation:* NASPAA (one or more programs are accredited). Part-time and evening/weekend programs available. *Degree requirements:* For master's, thesis. *Entrance requirements:* For master's, GMAT, minimum GPA of 2.5; for Certificate, minimum GPA of 2.5. Electronic applications accepted. *Faculty research:* Critical issues in sexuality, social work in religious communities, gerontological social work.

Long Island University–Hudson at Rockland, Graduate School, Master of Business Administration Program, Orangeburg, NY 10962. Offers business administration (Post Master's Certificate); entrepreneurship (MBA); finance (MBA); healthcare sector management (MBA); management (MBA). Part-time and evening/weekend programs available. *Entrance requirements:* For master's, GMAT, college transcripts, two letters of recommendation, personal statement, resume.

Long Island University–Hudson at Rockland, Graduate School, Programs in Health and Public Administration, Orangeburg, NY 10962. Offers gerontology (Advanced Certificate); health administration (MPA); public administration (MPA). Part-time and evening/weekend programs available. *Degree requirements:* For master's, thesis. *Entrance requirements:* For master's, college transcripts, letters of recommendation, personal statement, resume.

Louisiana State University Health Sciences Center, School of Public Health, New Orleans, LA 70112. Offers behavioral and community health sciences (MPH); biostatistics (MPH, MS, PhD); community health sciences (PhD); environmental and occupational health sciences (MPH); epidemiology (MPH, PhD); health policy and systems management (MPH). Part-time programs available. *Entrance requirements:* For master's, GRE General Test.

Louisiana State University in Shreveport, College of Business, Education, and Human Development, Program in Health Administration, Shreveport, LA 71115-2399. Offers MHA. Part-time and evening/weekend programs available. Postbaccalaureate distance learning degree programs offered (no on-campus study). *Students:* 8 full-time (7 women), 13 part-time (7 women); includes 2 minority (both Black or African American, non-Hispanic/Latino). Average age 32. 29 applicants, 69% accepted, 7 enrolled. In 2011, 16 master's awarded. *Entrance requirements:* For master's, GRE or GMAT, minimum GPA of 3.0, recommendations. Additional exam requirements/recommendations for international students: Required—TOEFL (minimum score 550 paper-based; 213 computer-based; 80 iBT). *Application deadline:* For fall admission, 6/30 for domestic and international students; for spring admission, 11/30 for domestic and international students. Applications are processed on a rolling basis. Application fee: $10 ($20 for international students). *Financial support:* In 2011–12, 3 students received support. *Faculty research:* Healthcare marketing, law and ethics, leadership. *Unit head:* Dr. John Fortenberry, Program Director, 318-212-0240, E-mail: john.fortenberry@lsus.edu. *Application contact:* Christianne Wojcik, Secretary, Graduate Studies, 318-797-5247, Fax: 318-798-4120, E-mail: christianne.wojcik@lsus.edu.

Loyola University Chicago, Graduate School, Marcella Niehoff School of Nursing, Doctor of Nursing Practice Program, Maywood, IL 60153. Offers healthcare quality using education in safety and technology (DNP); informatics and outcomes (DNP); nursing practice (DNP). Evening/weekend programs available. Postbaccalaureate distance learning degree programs offered (minimal on-campus study). *Faculty:* 45 full-time (44 women). *Students:* 27 part-time (22 women); includes 4 minority (3 Black or African American, non-Hispanic/Latino; 1 Asian, non-Hispanic/Latino). Average age 46. 31 applicants, 45% accepted, 12 enrolled. *Degree requirements:* For doctorate, capstone project. *Entrance requirements:* For doctorate, BSN or MSN, minimum GPA of 3.25, Illinois nursing license, 3 letters of recommendation, 1000 hours experience and certification in area of specialty, curriculum vitae. Additional exam requirements/recommendations for international students: Required—TOEFL. *Expenses: Tuition:* Full-time $15,660; part-time $870 per credit hour. *Required fees:* $125 per semester. Tuition and fees vary according to course load and program. *Unit head:* Dr. Mary K. Walker, Dean, Marcella Niehoff School of Nursing, 708-216-5448, Fax: 708-216-9555, E-mail: mwalker@luc.edu. *Application contact:* Amy Weatherford, Enrollment Advisor, School of Nursing, 773-508-3249, Fax: 773-508-3241, E-mail: aweatherford@luc.edu. Web site: http://www.luc.edu/nursing/dnp/.

Loyola University Chicago, Graduate School, Marcella Niehoff School of Nursing, Nursing Administration Program, Chicago, IL 60660. Offers MSN. Part-time and evening/weekend programs available. Postbaccalaureate distance learning degree programs offered (minimal on-campus study). *Students:* 3 full-time (all women), 34 part-time (32 women); includes 6 minority (2 Black or African American, non-Hispanic/Latino; 2 Asian, non-Hispanic/Latino; 1 Hispanic/Latino; 1 Native Hawaiian or other Pacific Islander, non-Hispanic/Latino). Average age 37. 8 applicants, 88% accepted, 7 enrolled. In 2011, 21 master's awarded. *Degree requirements:* For master's, comprehensive exam or oral thesis defense. *Entrance requirements:* For master's, BSN, minimum nursing GPA of 3.0, IL nursing license, 1000 hours experience before starting clinical. *Application deadline:* Applications are processed on a rolling basis. Application fee: $50. Electronic applications accepted. *Expenses: Tuition:* Full-time $15,660; part-time $870 per credit hour. *Required fees:* $125 per semester. Tuition and fees vary according to course load and program. *Financial support:* Traineeships available. Financial award application deadline: 3/1. *Faculty research:* Patient classification systems, career/job mobility. *Unit head:* Dr. Ida Androwich, Professor, 708-216-9276, Fax: 708-216-9555, E-mail: iandrow@luc.edu. *Application contact:* Amy Weatherford, Enrollment Advisor, School of Nursing, 773-508-3249, Fax: 773-508-3241, E-mail: aweatherford@luc.edu. Web site: http://www.luc.edu/quinlan/mba/mba-degrees/mbamsn-nursing/.

Loyola University Chicago, Graduate School, Program in Bioethics and Health Policy, Chicago, IL 60660. Offers Certificate, MD/MA. Postbaccalaureate distance learning degree programs offered (no on-campus study). *Students:* 2 full-time (1 woman), 92 part-time (49 women); includes 11 minority (6 Black or African American, non-Hispanic/Latino; 1 Asian, non-Hispanic/Latino; 2 Hispanic/Latino; 2 Two or more races, non-Hispanic/Latino), 2 international. 43 applicants, 86% accepted, 30 enrolled. *Expenses: Tuition:* Full-time $15,660; part-time $870 per credit hour. *Required fees:* $125 per semester. Tuition and fees vary according to course load and program. *Financial support:* Scholarships/grants available. *Unit head:* Dr. Samuel Attoh, Dean, 773-508-3459, Fax: 773-508-2460, E-mail: sattoh@luc.edu. *Application contact:* Ron Martin, Assistant Director of Enrollment Management, 312-915-8950, Fax: 312-915-8905, E-mail: gradapp@luc.edu.

Loyola University New Orleans, College of Social Sciences, School of Nursing, New Orleans, LA 70118-6195. Offers adult nurse practitioner (MSN); family nurse practitioner (MSN); health care systems management (MSN); nursing (MSN, DNP). *Accreditation:* NLN. Part-time and evening/weekend programs available. Postbaccalaureate distance learning degree programs offered. *Students:* 108 full-time (99 women), 428 part-time (385 women); includes 151 minority (110 Black or African American, non-Hispanic/Latino; 5 American Indian or Alaska Native, non-Hispanic/Latino; 14 Asian, non-Hispanic/Latino; 20 Hispanic/Latino; 2 Native Hawaiian or other Pacific Islander, non-Hispanic/Latino). Average age 46. 213 applicants, 91% accepted, 153 enrolled. In 2011, 241 master's awarded. *Degree requirements:* For doctorate, capstone project. *Entrance requirements:* For master's, BSN, Louisiana nursing license, 1 year of work experience in clinical nursing, minimum undergraduate GPA of 2.8, interview, resume. Additional exam requirements/recommendations for international students: Required—TOEFL (minimum score 550 paper-based; 213 computer-based). *Application deadline:* For fall admission, 8/1 priority date for domestic students, 8/1 for international students; for winter admission, 12/15 priority date for domestic students, 12/15 for international students; for spring admission, 5/15 priority date for domestic students, 5/15 for international students. Applications are processed on a rolling basis. Application fee: $20. Electronic applications accepted. *Financial support:* Traineeships and Incumbent Workers Training Program grants available. Financial award application deadline: 5/1; financial award applicants required to submit FAFSA. *Faculty research:* Increasing compliance with treatment, patient satisfaction with care provided by nurse practitioners. *Unit head:* Dr. Ann H. Cary, Director, 800-488-6257, Fax: 504-865-3254, E-mail: nursing@loyno.edu. *Application contact:* Deborah Smith, Assistant to the Director, 504-865-2823, Fax: 504-865-3254, E-mail: dhsmith@loyno.edu. Web site: http://css.loyno.edu/nursing.

Madonna University, Program in Health Services, Livonia, MI 48150-1173. Offers MSHS. Part-time programs available. *Degree requirements:* For master's, thesis or alternative. *Entrance requirements:* For master's, GRE General Test or minimum GPA of 3.25. Additional exam requirements/recommendations for international students: Required—TOEFL, TWE. Electronic applications accepted.

Marlboro College, Graduate School, Program in (Management) Healthcare Administration, Brattleboro, VT 05301. Offers MSM. Part-time and evening/weekend programs available. Postbaccalaureate distance learning degree programs offered (minimal on-campus study). *Degree requirements:* For master's, 36 credits including capstone project. *Entrance requirements:* For master's, letter of intent, 2 letters of recommendation, transcripts. Electronic applications accepted.

Marquette University, Graduate School, College of Professional Studies, Milwaukee, WI 53201-1881. Offers criminal justice administration (MLS); dispute resolution (MDR, MLS); engineering (MLS); health care administration (MLS); law enforcement leadership and management (Certificate); leadership studies (Certificate); non-profit sector (MLS); public service (MAPS, MLS); sports leadership (MLS). Part-time and evening/weekend programs available. Postbaccalaureate distance learning degree programs offered (no on-campus study). *Faculty:* 9 full-time (8 women), 10 part-time/adjunct (5 women). *Students:* 26 full-time (13 women), 142 part-time (90 women); includes 29 minority (19 Black or African American, non-Hispanic/Latino; 1 American Indian or Alaska Native, non-Hispanic/Latino; 3 Asian, non-Hispanic/Latino; 5 Hispanic/Latino; 1 Two or more races, non-Hispanic/Latino), 3 international. Average age 37. 88 applicants, 78% accepted, 36 enrolled. In 2011, 36 master's, 29 Certificates awarded. *Degree requirements:* For master's, comprehensive exam (for some programs). *Entrance requirements:* For master's, GRE General Test (preferred), GMAT, or LSAT, official transcripts from all current and previous colleges/universities except Marquette, three

letters of recommendation, statement of purpose. Additional exam requirements/recommendations for international students: Required—TOEFL. *Application deadline:* Applications are processed on a rolling basis. Application fee: $50. Electronic applications accepted. *Expenses: Tuition:* Full-time $17,010; part-time $945 per credit hour. Tuition and fees vary according to program. *Financial support:* In 2011–12, 9 students received support, including 8 fellowships with full tuition reimbursements available (averaging $16,247 per year). Financial award application deadline: 2/15. *Unit head:* Dr. Johnette Caulfield, Adjunct Assistant Professor/Director, 414-288-5556, E-mail: jay.caulfield@marquette.edu. *Application contact:* Craig Pierce, Assistant Director for Recruitment, 414-288-5740, Fax: 414-288-1902, E-mail: craig.pierce@marquette.edu.

Marshall University, Academic Affairs Division, College of Business, Program in Health Care Administration, Huntington, WV 25755. Offers MS, DMPNA. Part-time and evening/weekend programs available. *Students:* 112 full-time (64 women), 26 part-time (19 women); includes 12 minority (5 Black or African American, non-Hispanic/Latino; 5 Asian, non-Hispanic/Latino; 2 Hispanic/Latino), 5 international. Average age 31. In 2011, 18 master's awarded. *Degree requirements:* For master's, comprehensive assessment. *Entrance requirements:* For master's, GMAT or GRE General Test. *Application deadline:* Applications are processed on a rolling basis. Application fee: $40. *Financial support:* Career-related internships or fieldwork and tuition waivers (full) available. Support available to part-time students. Financial award applicants required to submit FAFSA. *Unit head:* Dr. Andrew Sikula, Associate Dean, 304-746-1956, E-mail: sikula@marshall.edu. *Application contact:* Wesley Spradlin, Academic Advisor, 304-746-8964, Fax: 304-746-1902, E-mail: spradlin2@marshall.edu.

Marylhurst University, Department of Business Administration, Marylhurst, OR 97036-0261. Offers finance (MBA); general management (MBA); government policy and administration (MBA); green development (MBA); health care management (MBA); marketing (MBA); natural and organic resources (MBA); nonprofit management (MBA); organizational behavior (MBA); real estate (MBA); renewable energy (MBA); sustainable business (MBA). Part-time and evening/weekend programs available. Postbaccalaureate distance learning degree programs offered (no on-campus study). *Faculty:* 3 full-time (0 women), 36 part-time/adjunct (6 women). *Students:* 29 full-time (15 women), 675 part-time (373 women); includes 178 minority (59 Black or African American, non-Hispanic/Latino; 6 American Indian or Alaska Native, non-Hispanic/Latino; 34 Asian, non-Hispanic/Latino; 46 Hispanic/Latino; 4 Native Hawaiian or other Pacific Islander, non-Hispanic/Latino; 29 Two or more races, non-Hispanic/Latino), 14 international. Average age 37. 262 applicants, 91% accepted, 194 enrolled. In 2011, 352 master's awarded. *Degree requirements:* For master's, comprehensive exam, capstone course. *Entrance requirements:* For master's, GMAT (if GPA less than 3.0 and fewer than 5 years of work experience), interview, resume, 2 letters of recommendation. Additional exam requirements/recommendations for international students: Recommended—TOEFL (minimum score 550 paper-based; 213 computer-based; 80 iBT). *Application deadline:* For fall admission, 9/11 priority date for domestic students, 9/11 for international students; for winter admission, 12/15 priority date for domestic students, 12/15 for international students; for spring admission, 3/15 priority date for domestic students, 3/17 for international students. Applications are processed on a rolling basis. Application fee: $50. Electronic applications accepted. *Expenses: Tuition:* Full-time $14,796; part-time $548 per quarter hour. Tuition and fees vary according to program. *Financial support:* Scholarships/grants available. Support available to part-time students. Financial award applicants required to submit FAFSA. *Unit head:* David McNamee, Interim Chair, 503-636-8141, Fax: 503-697-5597, E-mail: mba@marylhurst.edu. *Application contact:* Maruska Lynch, Graduate Admissions Specialist, 800-634-9982 Ext. 6322, Fax: 503-699-6320, E-mail: admissions@marylhurst.edu. Web site: http://www.marylhurst.edu/.

Marymount University, Educational Partnerships Program, Arlington, VA 22207-4299. Offers business administration (MBA); health care management (MS); management studies (Certificate); organization development (Certificate). Part-time and evening/weekend programs available. *Faculty:* 1 full-time (0 women), 4 part-time/adjunct (2 women). *Students:* 1 (woman) full-time, 26 part-time (16 women); includes 11 minority (9 Black or African American, non-Hispanic/Latino; 2 Asian, non-Hispanic/Latino), 1 international. Average age 42. *Entrance requirements:* For master's, GRE General Test or GMAT, resume; for Certificate, resume. Additional exam requirements/recommendations for international students: Required—TOEFL (minimum score 600 paper-based; 250 computer-based; 96 iBT), IELTS (minimum score 6.5). *Application deadline:* For fall admission, 7/1 for international students; for spring admission, 11/15 for international students. Applications are processed on a rolling basis. Application fee: $40. Electronic applications accepted. *Expenses: Tuition:* Part-time $770 per credit hour. *Required fees:* $8 per credit hour. One-time fee: $180 full-time. *Financial support:* Career-related internships or fieldwork, Federal Work-Study, scholarships/grants, and unspecified assistantships available. Support available to part-time students. Financial award applicants required to submit FAFSA. *Unit head:* Dr. Sherri Hughes, Vice President for Academic Affairs and Provost, 703-284-1550, E-mail: sherri.hughes@marymount.edu. *Application contact:* Francesca Reed, Director, Graduate Admissions, 703-284-5901, Fax: 703-527-3815, E-mail: grad.admissions@marymount.edu.

Marymount University, School of Business Administration, Program in Health Care Management, Arlington, VA 22207-4299. Offers MS. *Accreditation:* CAHME. Part-time and evening/weekend programs available. *Faculty:* 1 (woman) full-time, 3 part-time/adjunct (1 woman). *Students:* 20 full-time (11 women), 23 part-time (15 women); includes 23 minority (9 Black or African American, non-Hispanic/Latino; 1 American Indian or Alaska Native, non-Hispanic/Latino; 8 Asian, non-Hispanic/Latino; 4 Hispanic/Latino; 1 Two or more races, non-Hispanic/Latino), 7 international. Average age 31. 46 applicants, 93% accepted, 27 enrolled. In 2011, 21 master's awarded. *Degree requirements:* For master's, thesis or alternative. *Entrance requirements:* For master's, GMAT or GRE General Test, resume. Additional exam requirements/recommendations for international students: Required—TOEFL (minimum score 600 paper-based; 250 computer-based; 96 iBT), IELTS (minimum score 6.5). *Application deadline:* For fall admission, 7/1 priority date for domestic students, 7/1 for international students; for spring admission, 11/15 for domestic and international students. Applications are processed on a rolling basis. Application fee: $40. Electronic applications accepted. *Expenses: Tuition:* Part-time $770 per credit hour. *Required fees:* $8 per credit hour. One-time fee: $180 full-time. *Financial support:* In 2011–12, 4 students received support. Research assistantships with full tuition reimbursements available, career-related internships or fieldwork, Federal Work-Study, scholarships/grants, and unspecified assistantships available. Support available to part-time students. Financial award applicants required to submit FAFSA. *Unit head:* Dr. Alyson Eisenhardt, Interim Director, 703-284-4984, Fax: 703-527-3830, E-mail: alyson.eisenhardt@marymount.edu. *Application contact:* Francesca Reed, Director, Graduate Admissions, 703-284-5901, Fax: 703-527-3815, E-mail: grad.admissions@marymount.edu. Web site: http://www.marymount.edu/academics/programs/healthcareMgt.

Marywood University, Academic Affairs, College of Health and Human Services, School of Social Work and Administrative Services, Program in Health Services Administration, Scranton, PA 18509-1598. Offers MHSA. *Students:* 6 full-time (0 women), 18 part-time (16 women); includes 1 minority (Hispanic/Latino), 5 international. Average age 35. In 2011, 6 degrees awarded. *Entrance requirements:* Additional exam requirements/recommendations for international students: Required—TOEFL (minimum score 550 paper-based; 213 computer-based; 79 iBT). *Application deadline:* For fall admission, 4/1 priority date for domestic students, 3/31 for international students; for spring admission, 11/1 priority date for domestic students, 8/31 for international students. Applications are processed on a rolling basis. Application fee: $35. Electronic applications accepted. *Financial support:* Career-related internships or fieldwork, scholarships/grants, and unspecified assistantships available. Support available to part-time students. Financial award application deadline: 6/30; financial award applicants required to submit FAFSA. *Unit head:* Dr. Diane Haleem, Chair, 570-348-6211 Ext. 2540, E-mail: dhaleem@marywood.edu. *Application contact:* Tammy Manka, Assistant Director of Graduate Admissions, 866-279-9663, E-mail: tmanka@marywood.edu. Web site: http://www.marywood.edu/academics/gradcatalog/.

Massachusetts College of Pharmacy and Health Sciences, Graduate Studies, Program in Drug Regulatory Affairs and Health Policy, Boston, MA 02115-5896. Offers MS. Part-time and evening/weekend programs available. *Students:* 3 full-time (1 woman). Average age 30. In 2011, 2 master's awarded. *Degree requirements:* For master's, thesis, oral defense of thesis. *Entrance requirements:* For master's, GRE General Test, minimum GPA of 3.0. Additional exam requirements/recommendations for international students: Required—TOEFL (minimum score 550 paper-based; 213 computer-based; 79 iBT). *Application deadline:* For fall admission, 7/1 priority date for domestic students, 2/1 for international students. Application fee: $70. Electronic applications accepted. *Expenses: Tuition:* Full-time $30,200; part-time $945 per credit hour. *Financial support:* Application deadline: 3/15. *Faculty research:* Epidemiology, drug policy, drug regulation, ethics. *Unit head:* Bernard Tyrell, 617-732-2220. *Application contact:* Brian Barilone, Coordinator of Graduate Admission, 617-879-5032, E-mail: admissions@mcphs.edu.

McGill University, Faculty of Graduate and Postdoctoral Studies, Faculty of Medicine, Department of Epidemiology and Biostatistics, Montréal, QC H3A 2T5, Canada. Offers community health (M Sc); environmental health (M Sc); epidemiology and biostatistics (M Sc, PhD, Diploma); health care evaluation (M Sc); medical statistics (M Sc). *Accreditation:* CEPH (one or more programs are accredited).

Medical University of South Carolina, College of Health Professions, Department of Health Professions, Program in Health Administration-Executive, Charleston, SC 29425. Offers MHA. Part-time programs available. Postbaccalaureate distance learning degree programs offered (no on-campus study). *Faculty:* 6 full-time (3 women), 7 part-time/adjunct (3 women). *Students:* 32 full-time (22 women), 25 part-time (16 women); includes 7 minority (5 Black or African American, non-Hispanic/Latino; 1 Asian, non-Hispanic/Latino; 1 Hispanic/Latino), 2 international. Average age 36. 24 applicants, 83% accepted, 20 enrolled. In 2011, 19 master's awarded. *Degree requirements:* For master's, 20 hours of community service. *Entrance requirements:* For master's, GRE General Test or GMAT, minimum GPA of 3.0. Additional exam requirements/recommendations for international students: Required—TOEFL (minimum score 600 paper-based; 250 computer-based). *Application deadline:* For fall admission, 2/1 priority date for domestic students, 2/1 for international students; for spring admission, 11/15 priority date for domestic students, 11/15 for international students. Application fee: $85. Electronic applications accepted. *Financial support:* Federal Work-Study and scholarships/grants available. Support available to part-time students. Financial award application deadline: 3/10; financial award applicants required to submit FAFSA. *Faculty research:* Electronic health records; telemedicine; fraud prediction and prevention; decision modeling; continuous quality improvement; empathy, caring, patient-centered health care and health outcomes; health policy. *Total annual research expenditures:* $38,131. *Unit head:* Dr. Andrea W. White, Program Director, 843-792-4493, Fax: 843-792-3327, E-mail: whiteand@musc.edu. *Application contact:* Ann Brown, Student Services Program Coordinator, 843-792-2115, Fax: 843-792-3327, E-mail: brownah@musc.edu. Web site: http://academicdepartments.musc.edu/chp/dha/executive/index.htm.

Medical University of South Carolina, College of Health Professions, Department of Health Professions, Program in Health Administration-Global, Charleston, SC 29425. Offers MHA. *Entrance requirements:* Additional exam requirements/recommendations for international students: Required—TOEFL. *Unit head:* Dr. Emily L. Moore, Program Director, 843-792-4840, E-mail: mooreemi@musc.edu. *Application contact:* Melissa Freeland, Director of Student Services, 843-792-8510, Fax: 843-792-3327, E-mail: freelan@musc.edu.

Medical University of South Carolina, College of Health Professions, Department of Health Professions, Program in Health Administration-Residential, Charleston, SC 29425. Offers MHA. *Accreditation:* CAHME. Part-time programs available. Postbaccalaureate distance learning degree programs offered (minimal on-campus study). *Faculty:* 6 full-time (3 women), 6 part-time/adjunct (3 women). *Students:* 71 full-time (30 women); includes 11 minority (5 Black or African American, non-Hispanic/Latino; 3 Asian, non-Hispanic/Latino; 3 Hispanic/Latino), 1 international. Average age 25. 61 applicants, 75% accepted, 41 enrolled. In 2011, 32 master's awarded. *Degree requirements:* For master's, 20 hours of community service, internship or field project. *Entrance requirements:* For master's, GRE General Test, GMAT, minimum GPA of 3.0, 3 references, interview. Additional exam requirements/recommendations for international students: Required—TOEFL (minimum score 550 paper-based; 213 computer-based). *Application deadline:* For fall admission, 3/1 priority date for domestic students, 3/1 for international students. Application fee: $85. *Financial support:* Federal Work-Study and scholarships/grants available. Support available to part-time students. Financial award application deadline: 3/10; financial award applicants required to submit FAFSA. *Faculty research:* Electronic health records; telemedicine; fraud prediction and prevention; decision modeling; continuous quality improvement; empathy, caring, patient-centered health care; health policy; health outcomes. *Total annual research expenditures:* $38,131. *Unit head:* Dr. Andrea W. White, Program Director, 843-792-4493, Fax: 843-792-3327, E-mail: whiteand@musc.edu. *Application contact:* Ann Brown, Student Services Program Coordinator, 843-792-2115, Fax: 843-792-3327, E-mail: brownah@musc.edu. Web site: http://academicdepartments.musc.edu/chp/mha/details.htm.

Medical University of South Carolina, College of Health Professions, Department of Health Sciences and Research, Doctoral Program in Health Administration, Charleston, SC 29425. Offers DHA. *Faculty:* 2 full-time (1 woman), 2 part-time/adjunct (1 woman). *Students:* 67 full-time (41 women); includes 24 minority (22 Black or African American, non-Hispanic/Latino; 1 Asian, non-Hispanic/Latino; 1 Hispanic/Latino). Average age 43. 21 applicants, 95% accepted, 18 enrolled. In 2011, 15 doctorates awarded. *Degree requirements:* For doctorate, comprehensive exam, thesis/dissertation. *Entrance requirements:* For doctorate, experience in health care, interview, master's degree in relevant field, resume, 3 references. Additional exam requirements/recommendations for international students: Required—TOEFL (minimum score 600 paper-based; 250 computer-based). *Application deadline:* For fall admission, 8/15 for domestic and international students. Applications are processed on a rolling basis. Application fee: $85. *Financial support:* Federal Work-Study and scholarships/grants available. Support available to part-time students. Financial award application deadline: 3/10; financial award applicants required to submit FAFSA. *Faculty research:* HIV outcomes, health

outcomes and statistics, inter-professional education. *Unit head:* Dr. James S. Zoller, Program Director, 843-792-3849, E-mail: zollerjs@musc.edu. *Application contact:* Melissa Freeland, Director of Student Services, 843-792-8510, Fax: 843-792-3327, E-mail: freelan@musc.edu. Web site: http://www.musc.edu/chp/dha/index.htm.

Meharry Medical College, School of Graduate Studies, Division of Community Health Sciences, Nashville, TN 37208-9989. Offers occupational medicine (MSPH); public health administration (MSPH). *Accreditation:* CEPH. Part-time and evening/weekend programs available. *Degree requirements:* For master's, thesis, externship. *Entrance requirements:* For master's, GRE General Test, GMAT. *Expenses:* Contact institution. *Faculty research:* Policy and management, health care financing, health education and promotion.

Mercy College, School of Social and Behavioral Sciences, Program in Health Services Management, Dobbs Ferry, NY 10522-1189. Offers MPA, MS. Part-time and evening/weekend programs available. Postbaccalaureate distance learning degree programs offered (no on-campus study). *Entrance requirements:* For master's, interview, letters of recommendation from two instructors in the major area of study or professional letters from employers, minimum GPA of 3.0, 3- to 5-page essay on reason for pursuing master's degree in health services management, 8 years of work experience in health care (MS). Additional exam requirements/recommendations for international students: Required—TOEFL (minimum score 600 paper-based; 250 computer-based; 100 iBT), IELTS (minimum score 8). Electronic applications accepted.

Middle Tennessee State University, College of Graduate Studies, College of Basic and Applied Sciences, Program in Health Care Management, Murfreesboro, TN 37132. Offers Graduate Certificate. *Students:* 5 part-time (4 women); includes 2 minority (both Black or African American, non-Hispanic/Latino). 9 applicants, 44% accepted. *Entrance requirements:* Additional exam requirements/recommendations for international students: Required—TOEFL (minimum score 525 paper-based; 195 computer-based; 71 iBT) or IELTS (minimum score 6). *Expenses:* Tuition, state resident: full-time $10,008. Tuition, nonresident: full-time $25,056. *Financial support:* Application deadline: 5/1. *Unit head:* Dr. Robert W. Fischer, Jr., Dean, 615-898-2613, Fax: 615-898-2615. *Application contact:* Dr. Michael D. Allen, Dean and Vice Provost for Research, 615-898-2840, Fax: 615-904-8020, E-mail: michael.allen@mtsu.edu.

Midwestern State University, Graduate Studies, College of Health Sciences and Human Services, Nursing Program, Wichita Falls, TX 76308. Offers family nurse practitioner (MSN); family psychiatric mental health nurse practitioner (MSN); health services administration (MSN); nurse educator (MSN). *Accreditation:* AACN. Part-time and evening/weekend programs available. *Degree requirements:* For master's, comprehensive exam, thesis optional. *Entrance requirements:* For master's, GRE General Test or MAT. Additional exam requirements/recommendations for international students: Required—TOEFL (minimum score 550 paper-based; 213 computer-based). Electronic applications accepted. *Faculty research:* Infant feeding, musculoskeletal disorders, diabetes, community health education, water quality reporting.

Midwestern State University, Graduate Studies, College of Health Sciences and Human Services, Program in Health Services and Public Administration, Wichita Falls, TX 76308. Offers health services administration (MHA); public administration (MPA); public administration (administrative justice) (MPA); public administration (health services administration) with certificate (MPA); public administration (health services) (MPA). Part-time and evening/weekend programs available. *Degree requirements:* For master's, comprehensive exam, thesis. *Entrance requirements:* For master's, GRE. Additional exam requirements/recommendations for international students: Required—TOEFL (minimum score 550 paper-based; 213 computer-based). Electronic applications accepted. *Faculty research:* Universal service policy, telehealth, bullying, healthcare financial management, public health ethics.

Mississippi College, Graduate School, Program in Health Services Administration, Clinton, MS 39058. Offers MHSA. Part-time programs available. *Degree requirements:* For master's, comprehensive exam. *Entrance requirements:* For master's, GRE General Test, minimum GPA of 2.5. Additional exam requirements/recommendations for international students: Recommended—TOEFL, IELTS. Electronic applications accepted.

Missouri State University, Graduate College, College of Business Administration, Department of Management, Springfield, MO 65897. Offers health administration (MHA). Part-time and evening/weekend programs available. *Faculty:* 11 full-time (3 women). *Students:* 20 full-time (9 women), 19 part-time (12 women); includes 4 minority (2 Hispanic/Latino; 1 Native Hawaiian or other Pacific Islander, non-Hispanic/Latino; 1 Two or more races, non-Hispanic/Latino), 5 international. Average age 31. 22 applicants, 73% accepted, 9 enrolled. In 2011, 12 master's awarded. *Degree requirements:* For master's, thesis optional. *Entrance requirements:* For master's, GMAT or GRE, minimum GPA of 2.75. Additional exam requirements/recommendations for international students: Required—TOEFL (minimum score 550 paper-based; 213 computer-based; 79 iBT), IELTS (minimum score 6). *Application deadline:* For fall admission, 7/20 priority date for domestic students, 5/1 for international students; for spring admission, 12/20 priority date for domestic students, 9/1 for international students. Applications are processed on a rolling basis. Application fee: $35 ($50 for international students). Electronic applications accepted. *Expenses:* Tuition, state resident: full-time $4086; part-time $227 per credit hour. Tuition, nonresident: full-time $8172; part-time $454 per credit hour. *Required fees:* $275 per semester. Tuition and fees vary according to course load, campus/location and program. *Financial support:* Career-related internships or fieldwork, institutionally sponsored loans, scholarships/grants, tuition waivers, and unspecified assistantships available. Support available to part-time students. Financial award application deadline: 3/31; financial award applicants required to submit FAFSA. *Faculty research:* Health care management, human resource management, strategic management. *Unit head:* Dr. Barry Wisdom, Head, 417-836-5415, E-mail: barrywisdom@missouristate.edu. *Application contact:* Misty Stewart, Program Director, 417-836-6079, E-mail: mistystewart@missouristate.edu. Web site: http://mgt.missouristate.edu/.

Monmouth University, The Graduate School, Leon Hess Business School, West Long Branch, NJ 07764-1898. Offers accounting (MBA, Post-Master's Certificate); business (MBA); finance (MBA); healthcare management (MBA, Post-Master's Certificate); real estate (MBA). *Accreditation:* AACSB. Part-time and evening/weekend programs available. *Faculty:* 29 full-time (10 women), 8 part-time/adjunct (2 women). *Students:* 107 full-time (44 women), 161 part-time (61 women); includes 42 minority (8 Black or African American, non-Hispanic/Latino; 19 Asian, non-Hispanic/Latino; 12 Hispanic/Latino; 3 Two or more races, non-Hispanic/Latino), 23 international. Average age 28. 193 applicants, 84% accepted, 111 enrolled. In 2011, 87 master's awarded. *Degree requirements:* For master's, capstone course. *Entrance requirements:* For master's, GMAT, minimum GPA of 3.0 in major; 2.75 overall. Additional exam requirements/recommendations for international students: Required—TOEFL (minimum score 550 paper-based; 213 computer-based; 79 iBT), IELTS (minimum score 5), Michigan English Language Assessment Battery (minimum score 77), Cambridge A, B, C. *Application deadline:* For fall admission, 7/15 priority date for domestic students, 6/1 for international students; for spring admission, 11/15 priority date for domestic students, 11/1 for international students. Applications are processed on a rolling basis. Application fee: $50. Electronic applications accepted. *Financial support:* In 2011–12, 190 students received support, including 183 fellowships (averaging $1,638 per year), 21 research assistantships (averaging $9,311 per year); career-related internships or fieldwork, scholarships/grants, and unspecified assistantships also available. Support available to part-time students. Financial award applicants required to submit FAFSA. *Faculty research:* Information technology and marketing, behavioral research in accounting, human resources, management of technology. *Unit head:* Douglas Stives, MBA Program Director, 732-263-5894, Fax: 732-263-5517, E-mail: dstives@monmouth.edu. *Application contact:* Kevin Roane, Director, Office of Graduate Admission, 732-571-3452, Fax: 732-263-5123, E-mail: gradadm@monmouth.edu. Web site: http://www.monmouth.edu/mba.

Montana State University Billings, College of Allied Health Professions, Department of Health Administration, Billings, MT 59101-0298. Offers MHA. Postbaccalaureate distance learning degree programs offered (minimal on-campus study). *Degree requirements:* For master's, thesis or professional paper and/or field experience. *Entrance requirements:* For master's, GRE General Test or GMAT, minimum undergraduate GPA of 3.0, graduate 3.25; 3 years' clinical or administrative experience in health care delivery or 5 years' experience in business or industry management.

Morehouse School of Medicine, Master of Public Health Program, Atlanta, GA 30310-1495. Offers epidemiology (MPH); health administration, management and policy (MPH); health education/health promotion (MPH); international health (MPH). *Accreditation:* CEPH. Part-time programs available. *Degree requirements:* For master's, thesis, practicum, public health leadership seminar. *Entrance requirements:* For master's, GRE General Test, writing test, public health or human service experience. Additional exam requirements/recommendations for international students: Required—TOEFL (minimum score 550 paper-based; 200 computer-based). Electronic applications accepted. *Expenses:* Contact institution. *Faculty research:* Women's and adolescent health, violence prevention, cancer epidemiology/disparities, substance abuse prevention.

Mount St. Mary's College, Graduate Division, Program in Counseling Psychology, Los Angeles, CA 90049-1599. Offers counseling psychology (MS); general psychology (MS); marriage and family therapy (MS); mental health administration (MS). Part-time and evening/weekend programs available. *Degree requirements:* For master's, research project. *Entrance requirements:* For master's, minimum GPA of 3.0. *Application deadline:* For fall admission, 7/15 for domestic students; for spring admission, 11/15 for domestic students. Electronic applications accepted. *Expenses: Tuition:* Part-time $752 per unit. Part-time tuition and fees vary according to degree level and program. *Financial support:* Institutionally sponsored loans, scholarships/grants, and tuition waivers (partial) available. Support available to part-time students. Financial award application deadline: 3/15; financial award applicants required to submit FAFSA. *Unit head:* Dr. Gregory Travis, Director, Graduate Psychology, 213-477-2654, E-mail: gtravis@msmc.la.edu. Web site: http://www.msmc.la.edu/graduate-programs/counseling-psychology.asp.

Mount St. Mary's University, Program in Health Administration, Emmitsburg, MD 21727-7799. Offers MHA. Part-time and evening/weekend programs available. *Faculty:* 2 part-time/adjunct (1 woman). *Students:* 1 full-time (0 women), 18 part-time (16 women); includes 2 minority (1 American Indian or Alaska Native, non-Hispanic/Latino; 1 Hispanic/Latino). Average age 39. *Entrance requirements:* For master's, undergraduate degree, minimum cumulative undergraduate GPA of 2.75. Additional exam requirements/recommendations for international students: Required—TOEFL (minimum score 550 paper-based; 83 computer-based). *Expenses: Tuition:* Full-time $9000; part-time $500 per credit hour. Part-time tuition and fees vary according to program. *Unit head:* Dr. Edward A. Dolan, Director, 301-447-6122. *Application contact:* Deb Powell, Director of Graduate and Adult Business Programs, 301-447-5326, Fax: 301-447-5335, E-mail: dpowell@msmary.edu. Web site: http://www.msmary.edu/School_of_business/Graduate_Programs/mha/.

National University, Academic Affairs, School of Health and Human Services, Department of Community Health, La Jolla, CA 92037-1011. Offers health informatics (MS); healthcare administration (MHA); public health (MPH). Part-time and evening/weekend programs available. Postbaccalaureate distance learning degree programs offered. *Degree requirements:* For master's, thesis. *Entrance requirements:* Additional exam requirements/recommendations for international students: Required—TOEFL (minimum score 550 paper-based; 213 computer-based; 79 iBT). Application fee: $60 ($65 for international students). *Financial support:* Career-related internships or fieldwork, institutionally sponsored loans, and scholarships/grants available. Support available to part-time students. Financial award application deadline: 6/30; financial award applicants required to submit FAFSA. *Unit head:* Dr. Gina Piane, 858-309-3474, E-mail: gpiane@nu.edu. *Application contact:* Dominick Giovanniello, Associate Regional Dean, 800-NAT-UNIV, Fax: 858-541-7792, E-mail: dgiovann@nu.edu. Web site: http://www.nu.edu/OurPrograms/SchoolOfHealthAndHumanServices/CommunityHealth.html.

National University, Academic Affairs, School of Health and Human Services, Department of Health Sciences, La Jolla, CA 92037-1011. Offers clinical affairs (MS); clinical regulatory affairs (MS); health coaching (Certificate). Part-time and evening/weekend programs available. Postbaccalaureate distance learning degree programs offered. *Degree requirements:* For master's, thesis. *Entrance requirements:* For master's, interview, minimum GPA of 2.5. Additional exam requirements/recommendations for international students: Required—TOEFL (minimum score 550 paper-based; 213 computer-based; 79 iBT). Application fee: $60 ($65 for international students). *Financial support:* Career-related internships or fieldwork, institutionally sponsored loans, and scholarships/grants available. Support available to part-time students. Financial award application deadline: 6/30; financial award applicants required to submit FAFSA. *Unit head:* Dr. Patric Schiltz, Chair, 858-309-3476, Fax: 858-309-3480, E-mail: pschiltz@nu.edu. *Application contact:* Dominick Giovanniello, Associate Regional Dean, 800-NAT-UNIV, Fax: 858-541-7792, E-mail: dgiovann@nu.edu. Web site: http://www.nu.edu/OurPrograms/SchoolOfHealthAndHumanServices.html.

National University of Health Sciences, Lincoln College of Postprofessional, Graduate and Continuing Education, Lombard, IL 60148-4583. Offers advanced clinical practice (MS); diagnostic imaging (MS). Evening/weekend programs available. *Degree requirements:* For master's, comprehensive exam, thesis, capstone. *Entrance requirements:* Additional exam requirements/recommendations for international students: Required—TOEFL. Electronic applications accepted.

Nebraska Methodist College, Program in Medical Group Administration, Omaha, NE 68114. Offers MS. Evening/weekend programs available. Postbaccalaureate distance learning degree programs offered (no on-campus study). *Degree requirements:* For master's, thesis or alternative, capstone. *Entrance requirements:* Additional exam requirements/recommendations for international students: Required—TOEFL (minimum score 550 paper-based; 213 computer-based; 80 iBT).

New Charter University, College of Business, Birmingham, AL 35244. Offers finance (MBA); health care management (MBA); management (MBA). Part-time and evening/weekend programs available. Postbaccalaureate distance learning degree programs offered (no on-campus study). *Entrance requirements:* For master's, course work in calculus, statistics, macroeconomics. Additional exam requirements/recommendations

for international students: Required—TOEFL (minimum score 550 paper-based; 213 computer-based). Electronic applications accepted.

New England College, Program in Management, Henniker, NH 03242-3293. Offers accounting (MSA); healthcare administration (MS); international relations (MA); marketing management (MS); nonprofit leadership (MS); project management (MS); strategic leadership (MS). Part-time and evening/weekend programs available. *Degree requirements:* For master's, independent research project. Electronic applications accepted.

New Jersey City University, Graduate Studies and Continuing Education, College of Professional Studies, Department of Health Sciences, Jersey City, NJ 07305-1597. Offers community health education (MS); health administration (MS); school health education (MS). Part-time and evening/weekend programs available. *Students:* 6 full-time (5 women), 45 part-time (37 women); includes 19 minority (13 Black or African American, non-Hispanic/Latino; 4 Asian, non-Hispanic/Latino; 2 Hispanic/Latino), 2 international. Average age 41. In 2011, 16 master's awarded. *Degree requirements:* For master's, thesis or alternative, internship. *Entrance requirements:* Additional exam requirements/recommendations for international students: Required—TOEFL. *Application deadline:* For fall admission, 8/1 priority date for domestic students; for spring admission, 12/1 for domestic students. Applications are processed on a rolling basis. Application fee: $0. *Expenses:* Tuition, state resident: part-time $494 per credit. Tuition, nonresident: part-time $911.30 per credit. *Required fees:* $95.90 per year. *Financial support:* Career-related internships or fieldwork and unspecified assistantships available. *Unit head:* Dr. Lilliam Rosado, Chairperson, 201-200-3431, E-mail: lrosado@njcu.edu. *Application contact:* Dr. William Bajor, Dean of Graduate Studies, 201-200-3409, Fax: 201-200-3411, E-mail: wbajor@njcu.edu.

New Jersey Institute of Technology, Office of Graduate Studies, Newark College of Engineering, Department of Mechanical Engineering, Program in Healthcare Systems Management, Newark, NJ 07102. Offers MS. *Students:* 3 full-time (2 women), 9 part-time (6 women); includes 7 minority (3 Black or African American, non-Hispanic/Latino; 2 Asian, non-Hispanic/Latino; 2 Hispanic/Latino), 3 international. Average age 35. 16 applicants, 69% accepted, 6 enrolled. In 2011, 2 master's awarded. *Entrance requirements:* Additional exam requirements/recommendations for international students: Required—TOEFL (minimum score 550 paper-based; 213 computer-based; 79 iBT). *Application deadline:* For fall admission, 6/1 priority date for domestic students, 5/1 for international students; for spring admission, 11/15 priority date for domestic students, 11/15 for international students. Applications are processed on a rolling basis. Application fee: $65. Electronic applications accepted. *Expenses:* Tuition, state resident: full-time $7980; part-time $867 per credit. Tuition, nonresident: full-time $11,336; part-time $1196 per credit. *Required fees:* $230 per credit. *Financial support:* Application deadline: 1/15. *Unit head:* Dr. Rajpal S. Sodhi, Interim Chair, 973-596-3333, E-mail: rajpal.s.sodhi@njit.edu. *Application contact:* Kathryn Kelly, Director of Admissions, 973-596-3300, Fax: 973-596-3461, E-mail: admissions@njit.edu. Web site: http://mechanical.njit.edu/academics/graduate/ms-healthcare-systems.php.

New York Medical College, School of Health Sciences and Practice, Department of Health Policy and Management, Valhalla, NY 10595-1691. Offers emergency preparedness (Graduate Certificate); global health (Graduate Certificate); health policy and management (MPH, Dr PH). Part-time and evening/weekend programs available. *Faculty:* 6 full-time, 23 part-time/adjunct. *Students:* 55 full-time, 98 part-time. Average age 32. 125 applicants, 62% accepted, 59 enrolled. *Degree requirements:* For master's, thesis; for doctorate, comprehensive exam, thesis/dissertation. *Entrance requirements:* For master's, minimum GPA of 3.0, some work experience; for doctorate, GRE, minimum graduate GPA of 3.4. Additional exam requirements/recommendations for international students: Required—TOEFL (minimum score 600 paper-based; 250 computer-based; 100 iBT), IELTS (minimum score 7). *Application deadline:* For fall admission, 8/1 priority date for domestic students, 5/15 for international students; for spring admission, 12/1 priority date for domestic students, 10/15 for international students. Applications are processed on a rolling basis. Application fee: $50 ($100 for international students). Electronic applications accepted. *Financial support:* Research assistantships, teaching assistantships, career-related internships or fieldwork, Federal Work-Study, institutionally sponsored loans, health care benefits, and tuition reimbursements available. Support available to part-time students. Financial award applicants required to submit FAFSA. *Unit head:* Annette Choolfaian, Chair, 914-594-4250, Fax: 914-594-4292, E-mail: annette_choolfaian@nymc.edu. *Application contact:* Pamela Suett, Director of Recruitment, 914-594-4510, Fax: 914-594-4292, E-mail: shsp_admissions@nymc.edu. Web site: http://www.nymc.edu/shsp.

New York University, Robert F. Wagner Graduate School of Public Service, Program in Health Policy and Management, New York, NY 10012. Offers health finance (MPA); health policy analysis (MPA); health policy and management (Advanced Certificate); health services management (MPA); international health (MPA); MBA/MPA; MD/MPA. *Accreditation:* CAHME (one or more programs are accredited). Part-time programs available. *Faculty:* 8 full-time (2 women), 9 part-time/adjunct (6 women). *Students:* 96 full-time (68 women), 63 part-time (46 women); includes 54 minority (14 Black or African American, non-Hispanic/Latino; 24 Asian, non-Hispanic/Latino; 11 Hispanic/Latino; 5 Two or more races, non-Hispanic/Latino), 8 international. Average age 28. 194 applicants, 55% accepted, 45 enrolled. In 2011, 53 master's awarded. *Degree requirements:* For master's, thesis or alternative, residency (internship) or capstone end event. *Entrance requirements:* Additional exam requirements/recommendations for international students: Required—TOEFL, IELTS, TWE. *Application deadline:* For fall admission, 5/15 for domestic students, 1/5 for international students; for spring admission, 10/15 for domestic students, 9/1 for international students. Application fee: $85. Electronic applications accepted. *Expenses:* Contact institution. *Financial support:* In 2011–12, 27 students received support, including 27 fellowships (averaging $13,500 per year); career-related internships or fieldwork, Federal Work-Study, scholarships/grants, health care benefits, and unspecified assistantships also available. Support available to part-time students. Financial award application deadline: 1/5; financial award applicants required to submit FAFSA. *Unit head:* Prof. John Billings, Director, 212-998-7455, Fax: 212-995-4162. *Application contact:* Christopher Alexander, Communications Coordinator, 212-998-7400, Fax: 212-995-4611, E-mail: wagner.admissions@nyu.edu. Web site: http://www.nyu.edu/wagner/.

Northeastern University, College of Social Sciences and Humanities, Department of Political Science, Boston, MA 02115-5096. Offers political science (MA); public administration (MPA, Certificate), including development administration (MPA), health administration and policy (MPA), state and local government (MPA), urban studies (Certificate); public and international affairs (PhD). Part-time and evening/weekend programs available. *Faculty:* 22 full-time, 10 part-time/adjunct. *Students:* 64 full-time, 12 part-time. Average age 30. 132 applicants, 47% accepted, 23 enrolled. In 2011, 21 master's, 3 doctorates awarded. *Degree requirements:* For master's, thesis optional; for doctorate, thesis/dissertation. *Entrance requirements:* For master's, GRE General Test. Additional exam requirements/recommendations for international students: Required—TOEFL. *Application deadline:* Applications are processed on a rolling basis. Application fee: $50. *Financial support:* In 2011–12, 12 fellowships, 1 research assistantship with tuition reimbursement, 17 teaching assistantships with tuition reimbursements (averaging $14,035 per year) were awarded; career-related internships or fieldwork, Federal Work-Study, tuition waivers (full and partial), and unspecified assistantships also available. Support available to part-time students. Financial award application deadline: 2/1; financial award applicants required to submit FAFSA. *Faculty research:* Presidency, public opinion, Congress, democratization, national identity. *Unit head:* Dr. John Portz, Chair, 617-373-2796, Fax: 617-373-5311, E-mail: gradpolisci@neu.edu. *Application contact:* Brynn Thompson, Graduate Programs Assistant, 617-373-4404, Fax: 617-373-5311, E-mail: gradpolisci@neu.edu. Web site: http://www.polisci.neu.edu/

Northeastern University, College of Social Sciences and Humanities, School of Public Policy and Urban Affairs, Program in Public Administration, Boston, MA 02115-5096. Offers development administration (MPA); health administration and policy (MPA); state and local government (MPA); urban studies (Certificate). *Accreditation:* NASPAA (one or more programs are accredited). Part-time and evening/weekend programs available. *Faculty:* 22 full-time, 10 part-time/adjunct. *Students:* 74 full-time (48 women), 44 part-time (30 women). 149 applicants, 77% accepted, 56 enrolled. In 2011, 18 master's awarded. *Degree requirements:* For master's, thesis optional. *Entrance requirements:* For master's, GRE General Test. Additional exam requirements/recommendations for international students: Required—TOEFL. *Application deadline:* For fall admission, 2/1 priority date for domestic students, 5/1 for international students. Applications are processed on a rolling basis. Application fee: $50. *Financial support:* In 2011–12, 2 research assistantships with tuition reimbursements (averaging $14,035 per year) were awarded; teaching assistantships with tuition reimbursements, career-related internships or fieldwork, Federal Work-Study, tuition waivers (full and partial), and unspecified assistantships also available. Support available to part-time students. Financial award application deadline: 2/1; financial award applicants required to submit FAFSA. *Faculty research:* National health care, Third World development, leadership and ethics, science and technology, budgeting. *Unit head:* Dr. Ronald D. Hedlund, Graduate Coordinator, 617-373-2796, Fax: 617-373-5311, E-mail: gradpolisci@neu.edu. *Application contact:* Brynn Thompson, Graduate Programs Assistant, 617-373-4404, Fax: 617-373-5311, E-mail: gradpolisci@neu.edu. Web site: http://www.polisci.neu.edu/.

Northern Arizona University, Graduate College, College of Health and Human Services, Program in Interdisciplinary Health Policy, Flagstaff, AZ 86011. Offers Certificate. Part-time programs available. *Entrance requirements:* For degree, bachelor's degree from regionally-accredited university. Additional exam requirements/recommendations for international students: Required—TOEFL (minimum score 550 paper-based; 213 computer-based; 80 iBT), IELTS (minimum score 7). *Application deadline:* For fall admission, 3/1 for international students; for spring admission, 9/15 for international students. Applications are processed on a rolling basis. Application fee: $65. Electronic applications accepted. *Expenses:* Tuition, state resident: full-time $7190; part-time $355 per credit hour. Tuition, nonresident: full-time $18,092; part-time $1005 per credit hour. *Required fees:* $818; $328 per semester. *Financial support:* Applicants required to submit FAFSA. *Unit head:* Bill Wiist, Director, 928-523-5852, Fax: 928-523-7290, E-mail: bill.wiist@nau.edu. *Application contact:* April Sandoval, Coordinator, 928-523-4348, Fax: 928-523-8950, E-mail: april.sandoval@nau.edu. Web site: http://nau.edu/CHHS/IHPI/.

Northwest Nazarene University, Graduate Studies, Program in Business Administration, Nampa, ID 83686-5897. Offers business administration (MBA); business administration-health care (MBA). *Accreditation:* ACBSP. Part-time and evening/weekend programs available. Postbaccalaureate distance learning degree programs offered (no on-campus study). *Faculty:* 15 full-time (5 women), 23 part-time/adjunct (8 women). *Students:* 79 full-time (36 women), 26 part-time (11 women); includes 10 minority (3 Asian, non-Hispanic/Latino; 6 Hispanic/Latino; 1 Two or more races, non-Hispanic/Latino), 5 international. Average age 34. 13 applicants, 54% accepted, 7 enrolled. In 2011, 39 master's awarded. *Entrance requirements:* For master's, GMAT, minimum GPA of 3.0. *Application deadline:* Applications are processed on a rolling basis. Application fee: $40. Electronic applications accepted. *Expenses:* Contact institution. *Unit head:* Dr. Brenda Johnson, Director, 208-467-8415, Fax: 208-467-8440, E-mail: mba@nnu.edu. *Application contact:* Maureen Matlock, MBA Program Coordinator, 208-467-8123, Fax: 208-467-8440, E-mail: nnu-mba@nnu.edu. Web site: http://nnu.edu/mba.

The Ohio State University, College of Public Health, Columbus, OH 43210. Offers MHA, MPH, MS, PhD, JD/MHA, MHA/MBA, MHA/MD, MHA/MPA, MHA/MS, MPH/JD, MPH/MD, OD/MPH. *Accreditation:* CAHME; CEPH. *Faculty:* 40. *Students:* 208 full-time (143 women), 100 part-time (71 women); includes 56 minority (25 Black or African American, non-Hispanic/Latino; 22 Asian, non-Hispanic/Latino; 7 Hispanic/Latino; 2 Two or more races, non-Hispanic/Latino), 18 international. Average age 29. In 2011, 73 master's, 7 doctorates awarded. *Degree requirements:* For master's, thesis optional, practicum. *Entrance requirements:* For master's, GRE. Additional exam requirements/recommendations for international students: Required—TOEFL (minimum score 550 paper-based; 79 iBT), Michigan English Language Assessment Battery (minimum score 82). *Application deadline:* Applications are processed on a rolling basis. Application fee: $40 ($50 for international students). Electronic applications accepted. *Expenses:* Tuition, state resident: full-time $11,400. Tuition, nonresident: full-time $28,125. Tuition and fees vary according to course load, degree level, campus/location and program. *Financial support:* Fellowships and research assistantships available. *Unit head:* Stanley Lemeshow, Dean, 614-247-8196, E-mail: lemeshow.1@osu.edu. *Application contact:* Judy Dawson, Coordinator of Admissions and Recruitment, 614-292-8350, Fax: 614-247-0013, E-mail: jdawson@cph.osu.edu. Web site: http://cph.osu.edu/.

Ohio University, Graduate College, College of Health Sciences and Professions, Department of Social and Public Health, Athens, OH 45701-2979. Offers early child development and family life (MS); family studies (MS); health administration (MHA); public health (MPH); social work (MSW). *Accreditation:* CEPH. Part-time and evening/weekend programs available. Postbaccalaureate distance learning degree programs offered (no on-campus study). *Students:* 17 full-time (15 women), 380 part-time (259 women); includes 64 minority (38 Black or African American, non-Hispanic/Latino; 1 American Indian or Alaska Native, non-Hispanic/Latino; 14 Asian, non-Hispanic/Latino; 8 Hispanic/Latino; 3 Two or more races, non-Hispanic/Latino), 10 international. 114 applicants, 83% accepted, 72 enrolled. In 2011, 63 master's awarded. *Degree requirements:* For master's, capstone (MPH). *Entrance requirements:* For master's, GMAT, GRE General Test, previous course work in accounting, management, and statistics, previous public health background (MHA, MPH). Additional exam requirements/recommendations for international students: Required—TOEFL (minimum score 550 paper-based; 80 iBT) or IELTS (minimum score 6.5). *Application deadline:* Applications are processed on a rolling basis. Application fee: $50 ($55 for international students). Electronic applications accepted. *Expenses:* Contact institution. *Financial support:* Research assistantships with full tuition reimbursements, career-related internships or fieldwork, Federal Work-Study, institutionally sponsored loans, and unspecified assistantships available. Financial award applicants required to submit FAFSA. *Faculty research:* Health care management, health policy, managed care, health behavior, disease prevention. *Unit head:* Dr. Matthew Adeyanju, School Director, 740-593-1849, Fax: 740-593-0555, E-mail: adeyanju@ohio.edu. *Application contact:* Dr.

Health Services Management and Hospital Administration

Ruth Ann Althaus, Graduate Coordinator, Master of Health Administration Program, 740-597-2981, E-mail: althaus@ohio.edu. Web site: http://www.ohio.edu/chsp/sph/.

Oklahoma City University, Meinders School of Business, Program in Business Administration, Oklahoma City, OK 73106-1402. Offers finance (MBA); health administration (MBA); information technology (MBA); integrated marketing communications (MBA); international business (MBA); marketing (MBA); JD/MBA. *Accreditation:* ACBSP. Part-time and evening/weekend programs available. *Faculty:* 15 full-time (6 women), 14 part-time/adjunct (6 women). *Students:* 136 full-time (59 women), 112 part-time (34 women); includes 38 minority (14 Black or African American, non-Hispanic/Latino; 4 American Indian or Alaska Native, non-Hispanic/Latino; 11 Asian, non-Hispanic/Latino; 3 Hispanic/Latino; 6 Two or more races, non-Hispanic/Latino), 100 international. Average age 30. 252 applicants, 83% accepted, 30 enrolled. In 2011, 148 master's awarded. *Degree requirements:* For master's, comprehensive exam. *Entrance requirements:* For master's, GRE or GMAT. Additional exam requirements/recommendations for international students: Required—TOEFL (minimum score 560 paper-based; 220 computer-based; 83 iBT). *Application deadline:* Applications are processed on a rolling basis. Application fee: $50 ($70 for international students). Electronic applications accepted. *Expenses: Tuition:* Full-time $16,848; part-time $936 per credit hour. *Required fees:* $2070; $115 per credit hour. One-time fee: $300. *Financial support:* Career-related internships or fieldwork, Federal Work-Study, institutionally sponsored loans, and tuition waivers (partial) available. Support available to part-time students. Financial award application deadline: 6/1; financial award applicants required to submit FAFSA. *Faculty research:* Management information systems, international business strategies. *Unit head:* Dr. Steven Agee, Dean, 405-208-5130, Fax: 405-208-5098, E-mail: sagee@okcu.edu. *Application contact:* Michelle Cook, Director, Graduate Admissions, 800-633-7242, Fax: 405-208-5916, E-mail: gadmissions@okcu.edu. Web site: http://msb.okcu.edu/graduate/.

Oklahoma State University Center for Health Sciences, Program in Health Care Administration, Tulsa, OK 74107-1898. Offers MS. *Application deadline:* For fall admission, 7/1 for domestic students; for spring admission, 12/1 for domestic students. *Unit head:* Dr. Leigh Goodson, Director, 918-561-1406, Fax: 918-561-1416, E-mail: leigh.goodson@okstate.edu. *Application contact:* Leah Haines, Associate Director of Admissions and Registrar, 800-677-1972, Fax: 918-561-8243, E-mail: leah.haines@okstate.edu. Web site: http://www.healthsciences.okstate.edu/hca/index.cfm.

Oregon Health & Science University, School of Medicine, Graduate Programs in Medicine, Division of Management, Portland, OR 97239-3098. Offers healthcare management (MBA, MS). Part-time programs available. *Faculty:* 4 full-time (2 women), 29 part-time/adjunct (8 women). *Students:* 158 part-time (84 women); includes 36 minority (4 Black or African American, non-Hispanic/Latino; 2 American Indian or Alaska Native, non-Hispanic/Latino; 14 Asian, non-Hispanic/Latino; 10 Hispanic/Latino; 1 Native Hawaiian or other Pacific Islander, non-Hispanic/Latino; 5 Two or more races, non-Hispanic/Latino), 6 international. Average age 39. 70 applicants, 89% accepted, 54 enrolled. In 2011, 12 master's awarded. *Degree requirements:* For master's, thesis optional. *Entrance requirements:* For master's, GRE General Test (minimum scores: 153 Verbal/148 Quantitative/4.5 Analytical) or GMAT. Additional exam requirements/recommendations for international students: Required—TOEFL (minimum score 625 paper-based). *Application deadline:* For fall admission, 7/15 for domestic and international students; for winter admission, 10/15 for domestic and international students; for spring admission, 1/15 for domestic and international students. Applications are processed on a rolling basis. Application fee: $70. Electronic applications accepted. *Financial support:* Health care benefits available. *Faculty research:* Enhancing quality and reducing cost for healthcare by improving patient activation, identifying factors in hospital readmissions using system dynamics modeling, human and organizational dimensions of creating healthy communities. *Unit head:* Jim Huntzicker, Division Head, 503-346-0368, E-mail: hcmanagement@ohsu.edu. *Application contact:* Jessica Walter, Program Coordinator, 503-346-0369, E-mail: hcmanagement@ohsu.edu.

Oregon State University, Graduate School, College of Public Health and Human Sciences, Programs in Public Health, Corvallis, OR 97331. Offers biostatistics (MPH); environmental and occupational health and safety (MPH, PhD); epidemiology (MPH); health management and policy (MPH, PhD); health promotion and health behavior (MPH, PhD); international health (MPH). *Accreditation:* CEPH. Terminal master's awarded for partial completion of doctoral program. *Degree requirements:* For doctorate, one foreign language, thesis/dissertation. *Entrance requirements:* For master's and doctorate, minimum GPA of 3.0 in last 90 hours. Additional exam requirements/recommendations for international students: Required—TOEFL. *Faculty research:* Traffic safety, health safety, injury control, health promotion.

Our Lady of the Lake University of San Antonio, School of Business and Leadership, Program in Healthcare Management, San Antonio, TX 78207-4689. Offers MBA. Part-time and evening/weekend programs available.

Pace University, Dyson College of Arts and Sciences, Department of Public Administration, New York, NY 10038. Offers environmental management (MPA); government management (MPA); health care administration (MPA); management for public safety and homeland security (MA); nonprofit management (MPA); JD/MPA. Offered at White Plains, NY location only. Part-time and evening/weekend programs available. *Faculty:* 4 full-time (2 women), 6 part-time/adjunct (1 woman). *Students:* 66 full-time (41 women), 76 part-time (47 women); includes 73 minority (40 Black or African American, non-Hispanic/Latino; 1 American Indian or Alaska Native, non-Hispanic/Latino; 7 Asian, non-Hispanic/Latino; 21 Hispanic/Latino; 4 Two or more races, non-Hispanic/Latino), 10 international. Average age 31. 73 applicants, 89% accepted, 33 enrolled. In 2011, 49 master's awarded. *Degree requirements:* For master's, capstone project. *Entrance requirements:* For master's, GRE General Test. Additional exam requirements/recommendations for international students: Required—TOEFL. *Application deadline:* For fall admission, 8/1 priority date for domestic students; for spring admission, 12/1 priority date for domestic students. Applications are processed on a rolling basis. Application fee: $70. Electronic applications accepted. *Expenses: Tuition:* Part-time $990 per credit. *Required fees:* $168 per semester. Tuition and fees vary according to course load and degree level. *Financial support:* Research assistantships, career-related internships or fieldwork, Federal Work-Study, and tuition waivers (partial) available. Support available to part-time students. Financial award applicants required to submit FAFSA. *Unit head:* Dr. Farrokh Hormozi, Chairperson, 914-422-4285, E-mail: fhormozi@pace.edu. *Application contact:* Susan Ford-Goldschein, Director of Admissions, 914-422-4283, Fax: 914-422-4287, E-mail: gradwp@pace.edu.

Pacific University, Healthcare Administration Program, Forest Grove, OR 97116-1797. Offers MHA.

Park University, College of Graduate and Professional Studies, Kansas City, MO 54105. Offers adult education (M Ed); at-risk students (M Ed); disaster and emergency management (MPA); educational administration (M Ed); entrepreneurship (MBA); general business (MBA); general education (M Ed); government/business relations (MPA); healthcare/services management (MBA, MPA); international business (MBA); K-12 certification (MAT); management information systems (MBA); management of

information systems (MPA); middle school certification (MAT); multi-cultural education (M Ed); nonprofit management (MPA); public management (MPA); school law (M Ed); secondary school certification (MAT); special education (M Ed). Part-time and evening/weekend programs available. Postbaccalaureate distance learning degree programs offered (no on-campus study). *Degree requirements:* For master's, comprehensive exam, thesis (for some programs). *Entrance requirements:* For master's, GRE, GMAT, teacher certification (M Ed). Additional exam requirements/recommendations for international students: Required—TOEFL (minimum score 550 paper-based). Electronic applications accepted. *Faculty research:* Literacy, leadership, brain based research, multicultural education, diversity.

Penn State Harrisburg, Graduate School, School of Public Affairs, Middletown, PA 17057-4898. Offers criminal justice (MA); health administration (MHA); homeland security (MPS); public administration (MPA). *Accreditation:* NASPAA. *Unit head:* Dr. Steven A. Peterson, Director, 717-948-6154, E-mail: sap12@psu.edu. *Application contact:* Robert Coffman, Director of Admissions, 717-948-6250, Fax: 717-948-6325, E-mail: ric1@psu.edu. Web site: http://harrisburg.psu.edu/public-affairs.

Penn State University Park, Graduate School, College of Health and Human Development, Department of Health Policy and Administration, State College, University Park, PA 16802-1503. Offers MHA, MS, PhD. *Accreditation:* CAHME. *Unit head:* Dr. Ann C. Crouter, Dean, 814-865-1428, Fax: 814-865-3282, E-mail: ac1@psu.edu. *Application contact:* Cynthia E. Nicosia, Director, Graduate Enrollment Services, 814-865-1795, Fax: 814-865-4627, E-mail: cey1@psu.edu. Web site: http://www.hhdev.psu.edu/hpa/.

Pfeiffer University, Program in Health Administration, Misenheimer, NC 28109-0960. Offers MHA, MBA/MHA.

Philadelphia University, School of Business Administration, Program in Business Administration, Philadelphia, PA 19144. Offers business administration (MBA); finance (MBA); health care management (MBA); international business (MBA); marketing (MBA); MBA/MS. Part-time and evening/weekend programs available. Postbaccalaureate distance learning degree programs offered (no on-campus study). *Entrance requirements:* For master's, GMAT. Additional exam requirements/recommendations for international students: Required—TOEFL (minimum score 550 paper-based; 213 computer-based; 79 iBT).

Portland State University, Graduate Studies, College of Urban and Public Affairs, School of Community Health, Program in Health Studies, Portland, OR 97207-0751. Offers health administration (MPA, MPH). Part-time and evening/weekend programs available. *Degree requirements:* For master's, internship (MPA), practicum (MPH). *Entrance requirements:* For master's, minimum GPA of 3.0 in upper-division course work or 2.75 overall, resume, 3 recommendation forms. Additional exam requirements/recommendations for international students: Required—TOEFL (minimum score 550 paper-based; 213 computer-based).

Queen's University at Kingston, School of Graduate Studies and Research, Faculty of Health Sciences, Department of Community Health and Epidemiology, Kingston, ON K7L 3N6, Canada. Offers epidemiology (PhD); epidemiology and population health (M Sc); health services (M Sc); policy research and clinical epidemiology (M Sc); public health (MPH). Part-time programs available. *Degree requirements:* For master's, thesis. *Entrance requirements:* For master's, GRE General Test (strongly recommended). Additional exam requirements/recommendations for international students: Required—TOEFL (minimum score 600 paper-based; 250 computer-based). *Faculty research:* Cancer epidemiology, clinical trials, biostatistics health services research, health policy.

Quinnipiac University, School of Business, Program in Health Care Management, Hamden, CT 06518-1940. Offers MBA, JD/MBA. Part-time and evening/weekend programs available. Postbaccalaureate distance learning degree programs offered (no on-campus study). *Faculty:* 19 full-time (4 women), 2 part-time/adjunct (1 woman). *Students:* 17 full-time (12 women), 40 part-time (16 women); includes 10 minority (2 Black or African American, non-Hispanic/Latino; 3 Asian, non-Hispanic/Latino; 5 Hispanic/Latino), 1 international. Average age 31. 45 applicants, 67% accepted, 24 enrolled. In 2011, 8 master's awarded. *Degree requirements:* For master's, thesis or alternative, internship. *Entrance requirements:* For master's, GMAT or GRE, minimum GPA of 3.0. Additional exam requirements/recommendations for international students: Required—TOEFL (minimum score 575 paper-based; 233 computer-based; 90 iBT), IELTS (minimum score 6.5). *Application deadline:* For fall admission, 7/30 priority date for domestic students, 4/30 for international students; for spring admission, 12/15 priority date for domestic students, 9/15 for international students. Applications are processed on a rolling basis. Application fee: $45. Electronic applications accepted. *Expenses: Tuition:* Part-time $855 per credit. *Required fees:* $35 per credit. *Financial support:* Career-related internships or fieldwork, Federal Work-Study, scholarships/grants, tuition waivers (partial), and unspecified assistantships available. Support available to part-time students. Financial award application deadline: 4/15; financial award applicants required to submit FAFSA. *Faculty research:* Health care financing, health policy, health care marketing, health economics, health care management information systems. *Unit head:* Lisa Braiewa, MBA Director, 203-582-3710, Fax: 203-582-8664, E-mail: lisa.braiewa@quinnipiac.edu. *Application contact:* Katie Ludovico, Associate Director of Graduate Admissions, 800-462-1944, Fax: 203-582-3443, E-mail: katie.ludovico@quinnipiac.edu. Web site: http://www.quinnipiac.edu/mbahcm.

Regis College, School of Nursing, Science and Health Professions, Weston, MA 02493. Offers biomedical sciences (MS); health administration (MS); nurse practitioner (Certificate); nursing (MS, DNP); nursing education (Certificate). *Accreditation:* NLN. Part-time and evening/weekend programs available. *Degree requirements:* For master's, thesis. *Entrance requirements:* For master's, GRE General Test or MAT, minimum GPA of 3.0; for doctorate, MAT or GRE if GPA from master's lower than 3.5. Additional exam requirements/recommendations for international students: Required—TOEFL (minimum score 550 paper-based; 213 computer-based). Electronic applications accepted. *Faculty research:* Health policy, education, aging, job satisfaction, psychiatric nursing, critical thinking.

Regis University, College for Professional Studies, School of Management, Denver, CO 80221-1099. Offers accounting (MS, Certificate); executive international management (Certificate); executive leadership (Certificate); executive project management (Certificate); finance and accounting (MBA); general business administration (MBA); health care management (MBA); human resource management and leadership (MSOL); information technology leadership and management (MSOL); international business (MBA); marketing (MBA); operations management (MBA); organizational leadership and management (MSOL); project leadership and management (MSOL); project management (Certificate); strategic business management (Certificate); strategic human resource management (Certificate); strategic management (MBA). Offered at Colorado Springs Campus, Northwest Denver Campus, Southeast Denver Campus, Fort Collins Campus, Broomfield Campus, Henderson (Nevada) Campus, and Summerlin (Nevada) Campus and online. Part-time and evening/weekend programs available. Postbaccalaureate distance learning degree programs offered (no on-campus study). *Degree requirements:* For master's, thesis optional, capstone project. *Entrance requirements:* For master's, GMAT or essays, interview, 2 years of full-time business work experience, resume; for Certificate, GMAT.

Additional exam requirements/recommendations for international students: Required—TOEFL, TWE (minimum score 5) or university-based test. Electronic applications accepted. *Faculty research:* Impact of information technology on small business regulation of accounting, international project financing, mineral development, delivery of healthcare to rural indigenous communities.

Regis University, Rueckert-Hartman College for Health Professions, Denver, CO 80221-1099. Offers family nurse practitioner (MSN); health informatics (Postbaccalaureate Certificate); health services administration (MS); leadership in healthcare systems (MSN); neonatal nurse practitioner (MSN); nursing (MSN); pharmacy (Pharm D); physical therapy (DPT, TDPT). *Entrance requirements:* Additional exam requirements/recommendations for international students: Required—TOEFL (minimum score 550 paper-based; 213 computer-based; 82 iBT). Electronic applications accepted. *Expenses:* Contact institution. *Faculty research:* Normal and pathological balance and gait research, normal/pathological upper limb motor control/biomechanics, exercise energy/metabolism research, optical treatment protocols for therapeutic modalities.

Rice University, Graduate Programs, Wiess School–Professional Science Master's Programs, Professional Master's Program in Bioscience Research and Health Policy, Houston, TX 77251-1892. Offers MS.

Robert Morris University Illinois, Morris Graduate School of Management, Chicago, IL 60605. Offers accounting (MBA); accounting/finance (MBA); design and media (MM); health care administration (MM); higher education administration (MM); human resource management (MBA); information systems (MIS); law enforcement administration (MM); management (MBA); management/finance (MIS); management/human resource management (MBA); sports administration (MM). Part-time and evening/weekend programs available. *Faculty:* 7 full-time (1 woman), 21 part-time/adjunct (5 women). *Students:* 296 full-time (172 women), 216 part-time (136 women); includes 273 minority (160 Black or African American, non-Hispanic/Latino; 1 American Indian or Alaska Native, non-Hispanic/Latino; 32 Asian, non-Hispanic/Latino; 78 Hispanic/Latino; 2 Two or more races, non-Hispanic/Latino), 28 international. Average age 32. 247 applicants, 69% accepted, 152 enrolled. In 2011, 244 master's awarded. *Entrance requirements:* Additional exam requirements/recommendations for international students: Required—TOEFL (minimum score 550 paper-based; 173 computer-based). *Application deadline:* Applications are processed on a rolling basis. Application fee: $20 ($100 for international students). Electronic applications accepted. *Expenses: Tuition:* Full-time $13,800; part-time $2300 per course. *Financial support:* In 2011–12, 643 students received support. Federal Work-Study, scholarships/grants, tuition waivers, and leadership and athletic scholarships available. Support available to part-time students. Financial award applicants required to submit FAFSA. *Unit head:* Kayed Akkawi, Dean, 312-935-6025, Fax: 312-935-6020, E-mail: kakkawi@robertmorris.edu. *Application contact:* Fernando Villeda, Dean of Morris Graduate School of Management, 312-935-6050, Fax: 312-935-6020, E-mail: fvilleda@robertmorris.edu.

Roberts Wesleyan College, Division of Adult Professional Studies, Rochester, NY 14624-1997. Offers health administration (MS). Evening/weekend programs available. *Degree requirements:* For master's, thesis or alternative. *Entrance requirements:* For master's, minimum GPA of 3.0, verifiable work experience or recommendation. *Faculty research:* Small business entrepreneurship, church management.

Rochester Institute of Technology, Graduate Enrollment Services, College of Health Sciences and Technology, Program in Health Systems Administration, Rochester, NY 14623-5603. Offers elements of health care leadership (AC); health information resources (AC); health systems administration (MS); health systems administration executive leader (MS); health systems-finance (AC). Part-time and evening/weekend programs available. Postbaccalaureate distance learning degree programs offered (no on-campus study). *Students:* 13 full-time (3 women), 25 part-time (16 women); includes 6 minority (2 Black or African American, non-Hispanic/Latino; 3 Asian, non-Hispanic/Latino; 1 Hispanic/Latino), 13 international. Average age 35. 27 applicants, 67% accepted, 9 enrolled. In 2011, 13 master's, 1 other advanced degree awarded. *Degree requirements:* For master's, thesis. *Entrance requirements:* For master's, minimum GPA of 3.0; related professional work experience; for AC, minimum GPA of 3.0. Additional exam requirements/recommendations for international students: Required—TOEFL (minimum score 550 paper-based; 213 computer-based; 79 iBT) or IELTS (minimum score 6.5). *Application deadline:* For fall admission, 2/15 priority date for domestic students, 2/15 for international students; for winter admission, 11/1 priority date for domestic students; for spring admission, 2/1 priority date for domestic students. Applications are processed on a rolling basis. Electronic applications accepted. *Expenses: Tuition:* Full-time $34,659; part-time $963 per credit hour. *Required fees:* $228; $76 per quarter. *Financial support:* Research assistantships with partial tuition reimbursements, teaching assistantships with partial tuition reimbursements, career-related internships or fieldwork, scholarships/grants, and unspecified assistantships available. Support available to part-time students. Financial award applicants required to submit FAFSA. *Unit head:* Dr. Linda Underhill, Program Director, 585-475-7359, E-mail: lmuism@rit.edu. *Application contact:* Diane Ellison, Assistant Vice President, Graduate Enrollment Services, 585-475-2229, Fax: 585-475-7164, E-mail: gradinfo@rit.edu.

Rosalind Franklin University of Medicine and Science, College of Health Professions, Department of Interprofessional Healthcare Studies, Healthcare Administration and Management Program, North Chicago, IL 60064-3095. Offers MS, Certificate. Part-time and evening/weekend programs available. Postbaccalaureate distance learning degree programs offered (no on-campus study). *Degree requirements:* For master's, capstone portfolio. *Entrance requirements:* For master's, minimum GPA of 2.75, BS/BA from accredited college or university. Additional exam requirements/recommendations for international students: Required—TOEFL.

Royal Roads University, Graduate Studies, Applied Leadership and Management Program, Victoria, BC V9B 5Y2, Canada. Offers executive coaching (Graduate Certificate); health systems leadership (Graduate Certificate); project management (Graduate Certificate); public relations management (Graduate Certificate); strategic human resources management (Graduate Certificate).

Rush University, College of Health Sciences, Department of Health Systems Management, Chicago, IL 60612-3832. Offers MS, DHSc. *Accreditation:* CAHME. Part-time and evening/weekend programs available. *Degree requirements:* For master's, thesis; for doctorate, thesis/dissertation. *Entrance requirements:* For master's, GMAT or GRE General Test, previous undergraduate course work in accounting and statistics; for doctorate, GRE General Test, master's degree preferably in a health discipline. Additional exam requirements/recommendations for international students: Required—TOEFL. Electronic applications accepted. *Faculty research:* Organizational performance, occupational health, quality of care indicators, leadership development, entrepreneurship, health insurance and disability, managed care.

Rutgers, The State University of New Jersey, Newark, Graduate School, Program in Public Administration, Newark, NJ 07102. Offers health care administration (MPA); human resources administration (MPA); public administration (PhD); public management (MPA); public policy analysis (MPA); urban systems and issues (MPA). *Accreditation:* NASPAA (one or more programs are accredited). Part-time and evening/weekend programs available. *Degree requirements:* For master's, comprehensive exam, thesis or alternative; for doctorate, thesis/dissertation. *Entrance requirements:* For master's, GRE, minimum undergraduate B average; for doctorate, GRE, MPA, minimum B average. Electronic applications accepted. *Faculty research:* Government finance, municipal and state government, public productivity.

Sacred Heart University, Graduate Programs, College of Health Professions, Department of Nursing, Fairfield, CT 06825-1000. Offers clinical nurse leader (MSN); clinical practice in health care (DNP); family nurse practitioner (MSN); leadership in health care (DNP); nursing (DN Sc); patient care services administration (MSN). *Accreditation:* AACN. Part-time and evening/weekend programs available. Postbaccalaureate distance learning degree programs offered (minimal on-campus study). *Entrance requirements:* For master's, BSN, minimum GPA of 3.0. Additional exam requirements/recommendations for international students: Required—TOEFL (minimum score 550 paper-based; 213 computer-based). Electronic applications accepted. *Expenses:* Contact institution.

Sage Graduate School, School of Health Sciences, Department of Nursing, Troy, NY 12180-4115. Offers adult health (MS); adult nurse practitioner (MS, Post Master's Certificate); clinical nurse leader/specialist (Post Master's Certificate); community health (MS); education and leadership (DNS); family nurse practitioner (MS, Post Master's Certificate); gerontological nurse practitioner (Post Master's Certificate); nurse administrator/executive (Post Master's Certificate); nursing (Post Master's Certificate); psychiatric mental health nurse practitioner (MS, Post Master's Certificate), including psychiatric mental health. *Accreditation:* AACN. Part-time and evening/weekend programs available. *Faculty:* 5 full-time (all women), 10 part-time/adjunct (all women). *Students:* 35 full-time (31 women), 158 part-time (152 women); includes 20 minority (8 Black or African American, non-Hispanic/Latino; 1 American Indian or Alaska Native, non-Hispanic/Latino; 8 Asian, non-Hispanic/Latino; 3 Hispanic/Latino), 7 international. Average age 42. 143 applicants, 32% accepted, 34 enrolled. In 2011, 30 master's, 1 doctorate, 5 other advanced degrees awarded. *Degree requirements:* For master's, thesis or alternative. *Entrance requirements:* For master's, BS in nursing, minimum GPA of 2.75, resume, 2 letters of recommendation. Additional exam requirements/recommendations for international students: Required—TOEFL (minimum score 550 paper-based; 213 computer-based). *Application deadline:* Applications are processed on a rolling basis. Application fee: $40. *Expenses: Tuition:* Full-time $11,880; part-time $660 per credit hour. Tuition and fees vary according to program. *Financial support:* Fellowships, research assistantships, Federal Work-Study, scholarships/grants, and unspecified assistantships available. Support available to part-time students. Financial award application deadline: 3/1; financial award applicants required to submit FAFSA. *Unit head:* Dr. Esther Haskevitz, Dean, School of Health Sciences, 518-244-2296, Fax: 518-244-4571, E-mail: haskve@sage.edu. *Application contact:* Dr. Glenda Kelman, Director, 518-244-2001, Fax: 518-244-2009, E-mail: kelmag@sage.edu.

Sage Graduate School, School of Management, Program in Health Services Administration, Troy, NY 12180-4115. Offers dietetic internship (Certificate); gerontology (MS). Part-time and evening/weekend programs available. *Faculty:* 2 full-time (both women), 8 part-time/adjunct (1 woman). *Students:* 5 full-time (4 women), 24 part-time (17 women); includes 5 minority (4 Black or African American, non-Hispanic/Latino; 1 Hispanic/Latino). Average age 30. 33 applicants, 48% accepted, 11 enrolled. In 2011, 12 master's awarded. *Entrance requirements:* For master's, minimum GPA of 2.75, resume, 2 letters of recommendation. Additional exam requirements/recommendations for international students: Required—TOEFL (minimum score 550 paper-based; 213 computer-based). Application fee: $40. *Expenses: Tuition:* Full-time $11,880; part-time $660 per credit hour. Tuition and fees vary according to program. *Financial support:* Fellowships, research assistantships, Federal Work-Study, scholarships/grants, and unspecified assistantships available. Support available to part-time students. Financial award application deadline: 3/1; financial award applicants required to submit FAFSA. *Unit head:* Dr. Kimberly Fredricks, Program Director, 518-292-1782, Fax: 518-292-1964, E-mail: fredek1@sage.edu. *Application contact:* Wendy D. Diefendorf, Director of Graduate and Adult Admission, 518-244-2443, Fax: 518-244-6880, E-mail: diefew@sage.edu.

Saginaw Valley State University, Crystal M. Lange College of Nursing and Health Sciences, Program in Health Leadership, University Center, MI 48710. Offers MS. *Students:* 9 full-time (3 women), 15 part-time (8 women); includes 1 minority (Black or African American, non-Hispanic/Latino), 5 international. Average age 38. 9 applicants, 67% accepted, 3 enrolled. *Expenses:* Tuition, state resident: full-time $8300; part-time $5333 per year. Tuition, nonresident: full-time $15,613; part-time $10,209 per year. *International tuition:* $15,631 full-time. *Financial support:* Federal Work-Study and scholarships/grants available. Support available to part-time students. *Unit head:* Dr. Janalou Blecke, Dean, 989-964-4145, Fax: 989-964-4024, E-mail: blecke@svsu.edu. *Application contact:* P. Laine Blasch, Graduate Recruitment Coordinator, 989-964-2182, Fax: 989-790-0180, E-mail: blasch@svsu.edu.

St. Ambrose University, College of Business, Program in Business Administration, Davenport, IA 52803-2898. Offers business administration (DBA); health care (MBA); human resources (MBA). *Accreditation:* ACBSP. Part-time and evening/weekend programs available. *Faculty:* 17 full-time (4 women), 4 part-time/adjunct (1 woman). *Students:* 44 full-time (21 women), 208 part-time (92 women); includes 23 minority (7 Black or African American, non-Hispanic/Latino; 2 American Indian or Alaska Native, non-Hispanic/Latino; 3 Asian, non-Hispanic/Latino; 11 Hispanic/Latino), 5 international. Average age 34. 133 applicants, 80% accepted, 74 enrolled. In 2011, 110 master's, 2 doctorates awarded. *Degree requirements:* For master's, comprehensive exam (for some programs), thesis or alternative, capstone seminar; for doctorate, comprehensive exam, thesis/dissertation, oral and written exams. *Entrance requirements:* For master's, GMAT; for doctorate, GMAT, master's degree. Additional exam requirements/recommendations for international students: Required—TOEFL. *Application deadline:* For fall admission, 8/15 priority date for domestic students; for winter admission, 12/15 for domestic students; for spring admission, 1/1 for domestic students. Applications are processed on a rolling basis. Application fee: $25. Electronic applications accepted. *Expenses:* Contact institution. *Financial support:* In 2011–12, 54 students received support, including 5 research assistantships with partial tuition reimbursements available (averaging $3,600 per year); career-related internships or fieldwork, scholarships/grants, tuition waivers (partial), and unspecified assistantships also available. Financial award application deadline: 3/15; financial award applicants required to submit FAFSA. *Unit head:* Dr. Linda K. Brown, MBA Director, 563-333-6343, Fax: 563-333-6243, E-mail: brownlindak@sau.edu. *Application contact:* Elizabeth Loveless, Director of Graduate Student Recruitment, 563-333-6271, Fax: 563-333-6268, E-mail: lovelesselizabethb@sau.edu. Web site: http://www.sau.edu/mba.

St. Joseph's College, Long Island Campus, Program in Management, Patchogue, NY 11772-2399. Offers health care (AC); health care management (MS); human resource management (AC); human resources management (MS); organizational management (MS).

St. Joseph's College, New York, Graduate Programs, Program in Health Care Management, Brooklyn, NY 11205-3688. Offers MBA.

Saint Joseph's College of Maine, Master of Health Administration Program, Standish, ME 04084. Offers MHA. Degree program is external; available only by correspondence

and online. Part-time programs available. Postbaccalaureate distance learning degree programs offered (minimal on-campus study). *Faculty:* 3 full-time (2 women), 28 part-time/adjunct (19 women). *Students:* 257 part-time (167 women); includes 46 minority (23 Black or African American, non-Hispanic/Latino; 1 American Indian or Alaska Native, non-Hispanic/Latino; 11 Asian, non-Hispanic/Latino; 11 Hispanic/Latino). Average age 43. In 2011, 35 master's awarded. *Entrance requirements:* For master's, two years of experience in health care. *Application deadline:* Applications are processed on a rolling basis. Application fee: $50. Electronic applications accepted. One-time fee: $50. *Financial support:* Institutionally sponsored loans available. Support available to part-time students. Financial award applicants required to submit FAFSA. *Faculty research:* Health care organization, policy, and management; long-term care. *Unit head:* Twila Weiszbrod, Interim Director, 207-893-7841, Fax: 207-893-7987, E-mail: tweiszbrod@sjcme.edu. *Application contact:* Lynne Robinson, Director of Admissions, 800-752-4723, Fax: 207-892-7480, E-mail: info@sjcme.edu. Web site: http://online.sjcme.edu/master-health-administration.php.

Saint Joseph's University, College of Arts and Sciences, Department of Health Services, Philadelphia, PA 19131-1395. Offers health administration (MS, Post-Master's Certificate); health care ethics (Post-Master's Certificate); health education (MS, Post-Master's Certificate); health informatics (Post-Master's Certificate); healthcare ethics (MS); long-term care administration (MS); nurse anesthesia (MS); school nurse certification (MS). Part-time and evening/weekend programs available. *Faculty:* 9 full-time (1 woman), 21 part-time/adjunct (11 women). *Students:* 76 full-time (53 women), 261 part-time (204 women); includes 106 minority (79 Black or African American, non-Hispanic/Latino; 2 American Indian or Alaska Native, non-Hispanic/Latino; 12 Asian, non-Hispanic/Latino; 10 Hispanic/Latino; 1 Native Hawaiian or other Pacific Islander, non-Hispanic/Latino; 2 Two or more races, non-Hispanic/Latino), 17 international. Average age 35. 143 applicants, 69% accepted, 91 enrolled. In 2011, 67 master's awarded. *Entrance requirements:* For master's, GRE (if GPA less than 2.75), 2 letters of recommendation, minimum GPA of 2.75, resume. Additional exam requirements/recommendations for international students: Required—TOEFL (minimum score 550 paper-based; 213 computer-based; 79 iBT). *Application deadline:* For fall admission, 7/15 priority date for domestic students, 4/15 for international students; for winter admission, 1/15 for international students; for spring admission, 11/15 priority date for domestic students, 10/15 for international students. Applications are processed on a rolling basis. Application fee: $35. Electronic applications accepted. *Expenses: Tuition:* Part-time $735 per credit hour. Tuition and fees vary according to degree level and program. *Financial support:* Career-related internships or fieldwork and unspecified assistantships available. Financial award applicants required to submit FAFSA. *Unit head:* Nakia Henderson, Director, 610-660-2952, E-mail: nakia.henderson@sju.edu. *Application contact:* Kate McConnell, Director, Graduate College of Arts and Sciences Admissions and Retention, 610-660-3184, Fax: 610-660-3230, E-mail: kate.mcconnell@sju.edu.

Saint Joseph's University, Erivan K. Haub School of Business, Professional MBA Program, Philadelphia, PA 19131-1395. Offers accounting (MBA); finance (MBA), including finance; general business (MBA); health and medical services administration (MBA); human resource management (MBA); international business (MBA); international marketing (MBA); management (MBA); marketing (MBA); DO/MBA. DO/MBA offered jointly with Philadelphia College of Osteopathic Medicine. Part-time and evening/weekend programs available. Postbaccalaureate distance learning degree programs offered (no on-campus study). *Students:* 98 full-time (42 women), 528 part-time (208 women); includes 102 minority (47 Black or African American, non-Hispanic/Latino; 1 American Indian or Alaska Native, non-Hispanic/Latino; 28 Asian, non-Hispanic/Latino; 20 Hispanic/Latino; 1 Native Hawaiian or other Pacific Islander, non-Hispanic/Latino; 5 Two or more races, non-Hispanic/Latino), 45 international. Average age 31. In 2011, 290 master's awarded. *Entrance requirements:* For master's, GMAT or GRE, 2 letters of recommendation, resume, personal statement. Additional exam requirements/recommendations for international students: Required—TOEFL (minimum score 550 paper-based; 213 computer-based; 80 iBT), IELTS (minimum score 6.5), or Pearson Test of English (minimum score 60). *Application deadline:* For fall admission, 7/15 priority date for domestic students, 4/15 for international students; for spring admission, 11/15 priority date for domestic students, 10/15 for international students. Applications are processed on a rolling basis. Application fee: $35. Electronic applications accepted. *Expenses: Tuition:* Part-time $735 per credit hour. Tuition and fees vary according to degree level and program. *Financial support:* Scholarships/grants and unspecified assistantships available. Financial award application deadline: 5/1; financial award applicants required to submit FAFSA. *Unit head:* Adele C. Foley, Associate Dean/Director, Graduate Business Programs, 610-660-1691, Fax: 610-660-1599, E-mail: afoley@sju.edu. *Application contact:* Dr. Janine N. Guerra, Associate Director, Professional MBA Program, 610-660-1695, Fax: 610-660-1599, E-mail: jguerra@sju.edu. Web site: http://www.sju.edu/mba.

Saint Leo University, Graduate Business Studies, Saint Leo, FL 33574-6665. Offers accounting (MBA); business (MBA); health services management (MBA); human resource management (MBA); information security management (MBA); marketing (MBA); sport business (MBA). Part-time and evening/weekend programs available. Postbaccalaureate distance learning degree programs offered (no on-campus study). *Faculty:* 39 full-time (7 women), 56 part-time/adjunct (17 women). *Students:* 1,506 full-time (901 women); includes 620 minority (480 Black or African American, non-Hispanic/Latino; 5 American Indian or Alaska Native, non-Hispanic/Latino; 21 Asian, non-Hispanic/Latino; 100 Hispanic/Latino; 1 Native Hawaiian or other Pacific Islander, non-Hispanic/Latino; 13 Two or more races, non-Hispanic/Latino), 20 international. Average age 38. In 2011, 574 master's awarded. *Entrance requirements:* For master's, GMAT (minimum score 500 if applicant does not have 5 years of professional work experience), bachelor's degree with minimum GPA of 3.0 in the last 60 hours of coursework from regionally-accredited college or university; 5 years of professional work experience; resume; 2 letters of recommendation. Additional exam requirements/recommendations for international students: Required—TOEFL (minimum score 550 paper-based; 213 computer-based; 80 iBT). *Application deadline:* For fall admission, 7/1 priority date for domestic students, 7/1 for international students; for spring admission, 11/12 priority date for domestic students, 11/1 for international students. Applications are processed on a rolling basis. Application fee: $80. Electronic applications accepted. *Expenses: Tuition:* Full-time $11,340; part-time $630 per semester hour. Tuition and fees vary according to campus/location and program. *Financial support:* In 2011–12, 72 students received support. Career-related internships or fieldwork, Federal Work-Study, scholarships/grants, and health care benefits available. Financial award application deadline: 3/1; financial award applicants required to submit FAFSA. *Unit head:* Dr. Lorrie McGovern, Director, 352-588-7390, Fax: 352-588-8585, E-mail: mbaslu@saintleo.edu. *Application contact:* Jared Welling, Director of Graduate Admission, 800-707-8846, Fax: 352-588-7873, E-mail: grad.admissions@saintleo.edu. Web site: http://www.saintleo.edu/Academics/School-of-Business/Graduate-Degree-Programs.

Saint Louis University, Graduate Education, School of Public Health and Graduate Education, Department of Health Management and Policy, St. Louis, MO 63103-2097. Offers health administration (MHA); health policy (MPH); public health studies (PhD). *Accreditation:* CAHME. Part-time programs available. *Degree requirements:* For master's, comprehensive exam, internship. *Entrance requirements:* For master's, GMAT or GRE General Test, LSAT, MCAT, letters of recommendation, resume. Additional exam requirements/recommendations for international students: Required—TOEFL (minimum score 525 paper-based; 194 computer-based). *Faculty research:* Management of HIV/AIDS, rural health services, prevention of asthma, genetics and health services use, health insurance and access to care.

Saint Mary's University of Minnesota, Schools of Graduate and Professional Programs, Graduate School of Health and Human Services, Health and Human Services Administration Program, Winona, MN 55987-1399. Offers MA. *Unit head:* Laurel Anderson, Director, 612-728-5549, E-mail: lqander@smumn.edu. *Application contact:* Yasin Alsaidi, Director of Admissions for Graduate and Professional Programs, 612-728-5207, Fax: 612-728-5121, E-mail: yalsaidi@smumn.edu. Web site: http://www.smumn.edu/graduate-home/areas-of-study/graduate-school-of-health-human-services/ma-in-health-human-services-administration.

Saint Peter's University, Graduate Business Programs, MBA Program, Jersey City, NJ 07306-5997. Offers finance (MBA); health care administration (MBA); human resource management (MBA); international business (MBA); management (MBA); management information systems (MBA); marketing (MBA); risk management (MBA); MBA/MS. Part-time and evening/weekend programs available. *Entrance requirements:* Additional exam requirements/recommendations for international students: Required—TOEFL (minimum score 79 computer-based). Electronic applications accepted. *Faculty research:* Finance, health care management, human resource management, international business, management, management information systems, marketing, risk management.

St. Thomas University, School of Business, Department of Management, Miami Gardens, FL 33054-6459. Offers accounting (MBA); general management (MSM, Certificate); health management (MBA, MSM, Certificate); human resource management (MBA, MSM, Certificate); international business (MBA, MIB, MSM, Certificate); justice administration (MSM, Certificate); management accounting (MSM, Certificate); public management (MSM, Certificate); sports administration (MS). Part-time and evening/weekend programs available. *Degree requirements:* For master's, comprehensive exam. *Entrance requirements:* For master's, interview, minimum GPA of 3.0 or GMAT. Additional exam requirements/recommendations for international students: Required—TOEFL (minimum score 550 paper-based; 213 computer-based; 79 iBT). Electronic applications accepted.

Saint Xavier University, Graduate Studies, Graham School of Management, Chicago, IL 60655-3105. Offers employee health benefits (Certificate); finance (MBA); financial fraud examination and management (MBA, Certificate); financial planning (MBA, Certificate); generalist/individualized (MBA); health administration (MBA); managed care (Certificate); management (MBA); marketing (MBA); project management (MBA, Certificate); MBA/MS. *Accreditation:* ACBSP. Part-time and evening/weekend programs available. *Entrance requirements:* For master's, GMAT, minimum GPA of 3.0, 2 years of work experience. *Application deadline:* For fall admission, 8/15 for domestic students. Applications are processed on a rolling basis. Application fee: $35. Electronic applications accepted. *Expenses:* Contact institution. *Financial support:* Career-related internships or fieldwork available. Support available to part-time students. Financial award applicants required to submit FAFSA. *Unit head:* Dr. John E. Eber, Dean, 773-298-3601, Fax: 773-298-3601, E-mail: eber@sxu.edu. *Application contact:* Beth Gierach, Managing Director of Admission, 773-298-3053, Fax: 773-298-3076, E-mail: gierach@sxu.edu. Web site: http://www.sxu.edu/academics/colleges_schools/gsm/.

Salve Regina University, Program in Healthcare Administration and Management, Newport, RI 02840-4192. Offers MS, Certificate. Part-time and evening/weekend programs available. *Faculty:* 4 part-time/adjunct (0 women). *Students:* 5 full-time (all women), 53 part-time (41 women); includes 3 minority (2 Black or African American, non-Hispanic/Latino; 1 Hispanic/Latino), 1 international. Average age 45. *Degree requirements:* For master's, internship. *Entrance requirements:* For master's, GMAT, GRE General Test, or MAT, health care work experience or 250 internship hours. Additional exam requirements/recommendations for international students: Required—TOEFL (minimum score 600 paper-based; 250 computer-based; 100 iBT) or IELTS. *Application deadline:* For fall admission, 3/15 priority date for domestic students, 3/15 for international students; for spring admission, 9/15 priority date for domestic students, 9/15 for international students. Applications are processed on a rolling basis. Application fee: $60. Electronic applications accepted. *Expenses: Tuition:* Full-time $7740; part-time $430 per credit. *Required fees:* $40 per semester. Tuition and fees vary according to program. *Financial support:* Career-related internships or fieldwork and Federal Work-Study available. Support available to part-time students. Financial award application deadline: 3/1; financial award applicants required to submit FAFSA. *Unit head:* Mark Hough, Director, 401-341-3123, E-mail: mark.hough@salve.edu. *Application contact:* Kelly Alverson, Associate Director of Graduate Admissions, 401-341-2153, Fax: 401-341-2973, E-mail: kelly.alverson@salve.edu. Web site: http://www.salve.edu/graduatestudies/programs/ghs/.

San Diego State University, Graduate and Research Affairs, College of Health and Human Services, Graduate School of Public Health, San Diego, CA 92182. Offers environmental health (MPH); epidemiology (MPH, PhD), including biostatistics (MPH); global emergency preparedness and response (MS); global health (PhD); health behavior (PhD); health promotion (MPH); health services administration (MPH); toxicology (MS); MPH/MA; MSW/MPH. *Accreditation:* ABET (one or more programs are accredited); CAHME (one or more programs are accredited); CEPH (one or more programs are accredited). Part-time programs available. *Degree requirements:* For master's, comprehensive exam (for some programs), thesis (for some programs); for doctorate, thesis/dissertation. *Entrance requirements:* For master's, GMAT (MPH in health services administration), GRE General Test; for doctorate, GRE General Test. Additional exam requirements/recommendations for international students: Required—TOEFL. *Faculty research:* Evaluation of tobacco, AIDS prevalence and prevention, mammography, infant death project, Alzheimer's in elderly Chinese.

Seton Hall University, College of Arts and Sciences, Department of Political Science and Public Affairs, South Orange, NJ 07079-2697. Offers healthcare administration (MHA, Graduate Certificate); nonprofit organization management (Graduate Certificate); public administration (MPA), including health policy and management, nonprofit organization management, public service: leadership, governance, and policy. *Accreditation:* NASPAA. Part-time and evening/weekend programs available. Postbaccalaureate distance learning degree programs offered (minimal on-campus study). *Degree requirements:* For master's, thesis or alternative, internship or practicum. *Entrance requirements:* Additional exam requirements/recommendations for international students: Required—TOEFL. Electronic applications accepted. *Expenses: Tuition:* Part-time $1033 per credit hour. *Required fees:* $85 per semester.

Seton Hall University, College of Nursing, South Orange, NJ 07079-2697. Offers advanced practice in primary health care (MSN, DNP), including adult/gerontological nurse practitioner, pediatric nurse practitioner; entry into practice (MSN); health systems administration (MSN, DNP); nursing (PhD); nursing case management (MSN); nursing education (MA); school nurse (MSN); MSN/MA. *Accreditation:* AACN. Part-time programs available. Postbaccalaureate distance learning degree programs offered (minimal on-campus study). *Faculty:* 10 full-time (all women), 3 part-time/adjunct (1

woman). *Students:* 12 full-time (11 women), 217 part-time (197 women); includes 38 minority (15 Black or African American, non-Hispanic/Latino; 1 American Indian or Alaska Native, non-Hispanic/Latino; 12 Asian, non-Hispanic/Latino; 10 Hispanic/Latino). 180 applicants, 51% accepted, 82 enrolled. *Degree requirements:* For master's, research project; for doctorate, dissertation or scholarly project. *Entrance requirements:* For doctorate, GRE (waived for students with GPA of 3.5 or higher). Additional exam requirements/recommendations for international students: Required—TOEFL. *Application deadline:* For fall admission, 4/15 priority date for domestic students. Applications are processed on a rolling basis. Electronic applications accepted. *Expenses: Tuition:* Part-time $1033 per credit hour. *Required fees:* $85 per semester. *Financial support:* Institutionally sponsored loans, scholarships/grants, traineeships, tuition waivers (partial), and unspecified assistantships available. Support available to part-time students. Financial award applicants required to submit FAFSA. *Faculty research:* Parent/child, adult, and gerontological nursing; breast cancer; families of children with HIV; parish nursing. *Unit head:* Dr. Phyllis Shanley Hansell, Dean, 973-761-9014, E-mail: phyllis.hansell@shu.edu. *Application contact:* Kristyn Kent Wuillermin, Director of Strategic Alliances, Marketing and Enrollment, 973-761-9291, Fax: 973-761-9607, E-mail: kristyn.kent@shu.edu.

Simmons College, School of Management, Boston, MA 02115. Offers communications management (MS); entrepreneurship (Certificate); health administration (MHA); health care administration (CAGS); management (MBA); MS/MA. *Accreditation:* AACSB. *Unit head:* Cathy Minehan, Dean. *Application contact:* 617-521-3840, Fax: 617-521-3880, E-mail: somadm@simmons.edu. Web site: http://www.simmons.edu/som.

Southeast Missouri State University, School of Graduate Studies, Harrison College of Business, Cape Girardeau, MO 63701-4799. Offers accounting (MBA); entrepreneurship (MBA); financial management (MBA); general management (MBA); health administration (MBA); industrial management (MBA); international business (MBA); sport management (MBA). *Accreditation:* AACSB. Part-time and evening/weekend programs available. Postbaccalaureate distance learning degree programs offered (no on-campus study). *Faculty:* 31 full-time (10 women). *Students:* 49 full-time (23 women), 77 part-time (30 women); includes 5 minority (1 Black or African American, non-Hispanic/Latino; 1 American Indian or Alaska Native, non-Hispanic/Latino; 2 Hispanic/Latino; 1 Two or more races, non-Hispanic/Latino), 35 international. Average age 27. 78 applicants, 69% accepted, 43 enrolled. In 2011, 47 degrees awarded. *Degree requirements:* For master's, variable foreign language requirement, comprehensive exam, applied research project related to field. *Entrance requirements:* For master's, GMAT (minimum score of 450), minimum undergraduate GPA of 2.5, C or better in prerequisite courses. Additional exam requirements/recommendations for international students: Required—TOEFL (minimum score 550 paper-based; 213 computer-based; 79 iBT); Recommended—IELTS (minimum score 6). *Application deadline:* For fall admission, 8/1 for domestic students, 7/1 for international students; for spring admission, 11/21 for domestic students, 11/1 for international students. Applications are processed on a rolling basis. Application fee: $30 ($40 for international students). Electronic applications accepted. *Expenses:* Tuition, state resident: full-time $4896; part-time $272 per credit hour. Tuition, nonresident: full-time $8649; part-time $480.50 per credit hour. *Financial support:* In 2011–12, 46 students received support, including 12 teaching assistantships with full tuition reimbursements available (averaging $7,600 per year); career-related internships or fieldwork, Federal Work-Study, scholarships/grants, tuition waivers (full), and unspecified assistantships also available. Financial award application deadline: 6/30; financial award applicants required to submit FAFSA. *Faculty research:* Human resources, laws impacting accounting, advertising. *Unit head:* Dr. Kenneth A. Heischmidt, Director, Graduate Programs in Business, 573-651-5116, Fax: 573-651-5032, E-mail: kheischmidt@semo.edu. *Application contact:* Gail Amick, Administrative Secretary, 573-651-2049, Fax: 573-651-2001, E-mail: gamick@semo.edu. Web site: http://www.semo.edu/mba.

Southern Adventist University, School of Business and Management, Collegedale, TN 37315-0370. Offers accounting (MBA); church administration (MSA); church and nonprofit leadership (MBA); financial management (MFM); healthcare administration (MBA); management (MBA); marketing management (MBA); outdoor education (MSA). Part-time and evening/weekend programs available. Postbaccalaureate distance learning degree programs offered (no on-campus study). *Entrance requirements:* For master's, GMAT. Additional exam requirements/recommendations for international students: Required—TOEFL (minimum score 600 paper-based; 250 computer-based; 100 iBT). Electronic applications accepted.

Southern Illinois University Carbondale, School of Law, Program in Legal Studies, Carbondale, IL 62901-4701. Offers general law (MLS); health law and policy (MLS). *Students:* 5 full-time (2 women), 4 part-time (all women); includes 3 minority (all Black or African American, non-Hispanic/Latino), 1 international. 9 applicants, 78% accepted, 3 enrolled. In 2011, 3 master's awarded. *Unit head:* Thomas Britton, Director, 618-453-8980, E-mail: llmadmit@siu.edu. *Application contact:* Barb Smith, Office Specialist, 618-453-8858, E-mail: mlsadmit@siu.edu.

Southern Nazarene University, Graduate College, School of Business, Bethany, OK 73008. Offers business administration (MBA); health care management (MBA); management (MS Mgt). *Accreditation:* ACBSP. Part-time and evening/weekend programs available. Postbaccalaureate distance learning degree programs offered (minimal on-campus study). *Degree requirements:* For master's, thesis optional. *Entrance requirements:* For master's, GMAT, English proficiency exam, minimum GPA of 3.0 in last 60 hours/major, 2.7 overall. *Application deadline:* For fall admission, 8/1 priority date for domestic students. Applications are processed on a rolling basis. Application fee: $25 ($35 for international students). Electronic applications accepted. *Expenses: Tuition:* Full-time $17,009; part-time $639 per credit hour. *Required fees:* $2668. *Unit head:* Dr. Thomas Herskowitz, Chair, 405-491-6358. *Application contact:* Jeff Seyfert, MBA Director, 405-491-6358, E-mail: jseyfert@snu.edu. Web site: http://snu.edu/business.

South University, Graduate Programs, College of Business, Savannah, GA 31406. Offers corrections (MBA); entrepreneurship and small business (MBA); healthcare administration (MBA); hospitality management (MBA); leadership (MS); sustainability (MBA).

South University, Program in Business Administration, Royal Palm Beach, FL 33411. Offers business administration (MBA); healthcare administration (MBA).

South University, Program in Healthcare Administration, Columbia, SC 29203. Offers MBA.

See Close-Up on page 613.

South University, Program in Healthcare Administration, Montgomery, AL 36116-1120. Offers MBA.

See Close-Up on page 615.

South University, Program in Healthcare Administration, Tampa, FL 33614. Offers MBA.

See Close-Up on page 617.

Southwest Baptist University, Program in Business, Bolivar, MO 65613-2597. Offers business administration (MBA); health administration (MBA). *Accreditation:* ACBSP. Part-time programs available. Postbaccalaureate distance learning degree programs offered (no on-campus study). *Degree requirements:* For master's, comprehensive exam. *Entrance requirements:* For master's, interviews, minimum GPA of 2.75. Additional exam requirements/recommendations for international students: Required—TOEFL (minimum score 550 paper-based; 213 computer-based).

Springfield College, Graduate Programs, Program in Health Care Management, Springfield, MA 01109-3797. Offers M Ed, MS. Part-time programs available. *Degree requirements:* For master's, comprehensive exam. *Entrance requirements:* Additional exam requirements/recommendations for international students: Required—TOEFL (minimum score 550 paper-based; 213 computer-based). Electronic applications accepted.

State University of New York at Binghamton, Graduate School, School of Management, Program in Business Administration, Binghamton, NY 13902-6000. Offers business administration (MBA, PhD); health care professional executive (MBA). *Accreditation:* AACSB. *Students:* 120 full-time (47 women), 11 part-time (2 women); includes 25 minority (5 Black or African American, non-Hispanic/Latino; 9 Hispanic/Latino; 11 Native Hawaiian or other Pacific Islander, non-Hispanic/Latino), 33 international. Average age 28. 317 applicants, 48% accepted, 96 enrolled. In 2011, 89 master's, 5 doctorates awarded. *Degree requirements:* For doctorate, thesis/dissertation. *Entrance requirements:* For master's and doctorate, GMAT. Additional exam requirements/recommendations for international students: Required—TOEFL (minimum score 550 paper-based; 213 computer-based; 80 iBT). *Application deadline:* For fall admission, 3/1 priority date for domestic students, 3/1 for international students; for spring admission, 10/15 priority date for domestic students, 10/15 for international students. Applications are processed on a rolling basis. Application fee: $60. Electronic applications accepted. *Financial support:* In 2011–12, 39 students received support, including 14 fellowships with full tuition reimbursements available (averaging $17,000 per year), 13 teaching assistantships with full tuition reimbursements available (averaging $17,000 per year); research assistantships, career-related internships or fieldwork, Federal Work-Study, institutionally sponsored loans, scholarships/grants, health care benefits, tuition waivers (full and partial), and unspecified assistantships also available. Financial award application deadline: 2/15; financial award applicants required to submit FAFSA. *Unit head:* Dr. George Bobinski, Associate Dean, 607-777-2315, E-mail: gbobins@binghamton.edu. *Application contact:* Catherine Smith, Recruiting and Admissions Coordinator, 607-777-2151, Fax: 607-777-2501, E-mail: cmsmith@binghamton.edu.

Stony Brook University, State University of New York, Graduate School, College of Business, Program in Business Administration, Stony Brook, NY 11794. Offers finance (MBA, Certificate); health care management (MBA, Certificate); human resource management (Certificate); human resources (MBA); information systems management (MBA, Certificate); management (MBA); marketing (MBA).

Stony Brook University, State University of New York, Stony Brook University Medical Center, Health Sciences Center, School of Health Technology and Management, Stony Brook, NY 11794. Offers health care management (Advanced Certificate); health care policy and management (MS); occupational therapy (MS); physical therapy (DPT); physician assistant (MS). *Accreditation:* APTA. Part-time programs available. *Degree requirements:* For master's, thesis. *Entrance requirements:* For master's, GRE General Test, minimum GPA of 3.0, work experience in field. *Faculty research:* Health promotion and disease prevention.

Stony Brook University, State University of New York, Stony Brook University Medical Center, Health Sciences Center, School of Nursing, Program in Nursing Practice, Stony Brook, NY 11794. Offers DNP. Postbaccalaureate distance learning degree programs offered. *Degree requirements:* For doctorate, project. *Entrance requirements:* For doctorate, minimum GPA of 3.0. Additional exam requirements/recommendations for international students: Required—TOEFL.

Strayer University, Graduate Studies, Washington, DC 20005-2603. Offers accounting (MS); acquisition (MBA); business administration (MBA); communications technology (MS); educational management (M Ed); finance (MBA); health services administration (MHSA); hospitality and tourism management (MBA); human resource management (MBA); information systems (MS), including computer security management, decision support system management, enterprise resource management, network management, software engineering management, systems development management; management (MBA); management information systems (MS); marketing (MBA); professional accounting (MS), including accounting information systems, controllership, taxation; public administration (MPA); supply chain management (MBA); technology in education (M Ed). Programs also offered at campus locations in Birmingham, AL; Chamblee, GA; Cobb County, GA; Morrow, GA; White Marsh, MD; Charleston, SC; Columbia, SC; Greensboro, NC; Greenville, SC; Lexington, KY; Louisville, KY; Nashville, TN; North Raleigh, NC; Washington, DC. Part-time and evening/weekend programs available. Postbaccalaureate distance learning degree programs offered (minimal on-campus study). *Degree requirements:* For master's, thesis. *Entrance requirements:* For master's, GMAT, GRE General Test, bachelor's degree from an accredited college or university, minimum undergraduate GPA of 2.75. Electronic applications accepted.

Suffolk University, Sawyer Business School, Master of Business Administration Program, Boston, MA 02108-2770. Offers accounting (MBA); business administration (APC); corporate financial executive track (MBA); entrepreneurship (MBA); executive business administration (EMBA); finance (MBA); global business administration (GMBA); health administration (MBA); international business (MBA); marketing (MBA); organizational behavior (MBA); strategic management (MBA); taxation (MBA); JD/MBA; MBA/GDPA; MBA/MHA; MBA/MSA; MBA/MSF; MBA/MST. *Accreditation:* AACSB. Part-time and evening/weekend programs available. Postbaccalaureate distance learning degree programs offered (no on-campus study). *Faculty:* 98 full-time (30 women), 14 part-time/adjunct (3 women). *Students:* 139 full-time (49 women), 321 part-time (138 women); includes 53 minority (17 Black or African American, non-Hispanic/Latino; 1 American Indian or Alaska Native, non-Hispanic/Latino; 21 Asian, non-Hispanic/Latino; 11 Hispanic/Latino; 1 Native Hawaiian or other Pacific Islander, non-Hispanic/Latino; 2 Two or more races, non-Hispanic/Latino), 64 international. Average age 30. 437 applicants, 61% accepted, 121 enrolled. In 2011, 283 master's awarded. *Entrance requirements:* For master's, GMAT, minimum undergraduate GPA of 2.75 (MBA), 5 years of managerial experience (EMBA). Additional exam requirements/recommendations for international students: Required—TOEFL (minimum score 550 paper-based; 213 computer-based). *Application deadline:* For fall admission, 6/15 priority date for domestic students, 6/15 for international students; for spring admission, 11/1 priority date for domestic students, 11/1 for international students. Applications are processed on a rolling basis. Application fee: $50. Electronic applications accepted. Tuition and fees vary according to program. *Financial support:* In 2011–12, 273 students received support, including 73 fellowships with full and partial tuition reimbursements available (averaging $12,415 per year); career-related internships or fieldwork, Federal Work-Study, and institutionally sponsored loans also available. Support available to part-time students. Financial award application deadline: 4/1; financial award applicants required to submit FAFSA. *Faculty research:* Foreign

investments; career strategies and boundaryless careers; corporate ethics codes; interest rates, inflation, and growth options; innovation and product development performance. *Unit head:* Lillian Hallberg, Assistant Dean of Graduate Programs/Director of MBA Programs, 617-573-8306, E-mail: lhallber@suffolk.edu. *Application contact:* Ellen Driscoll, Director of Graduate Admissions, 617-573-8302, Fax: 617-305-1733, E-mail: grad.admission@suffolk.edu. Web site: http://www.suffolk.edu/mba.

Suffolk University, Sawyer Business School, Program in Health Administration, Boston, MA 02108-2770. Offers MBAH, MHA. Part-time and evening/weekend programs available. *Faculty:* 4 full-time (2 women), 3 part-time/adjunct (2 women). *Students:* 20 full-time (15 women), 56 part-time (37 women); includes 14 minority (7 Black or African American, non-Hispanic/Latino; 3 Asian, non-Hispanic/Latino; 4 Hispanic/Latino), 11 international. Average age 30. 54 applicants, 78% accepted, 24 enrolled. In 2011, 24 master's awarded. *Entrance requirements:* Additional exam requirements/recommendations for international students: Required—TOEFL (minimum score 550 paper-based; 213 computer-based; 80 iBT). *Application deadline:* For fall admission, 6/15 priority date for domestic students, 6/15 for international students; for spring admission, 11/1 priority date for domestic students, 11/1 for international students. Applications are processed on a rolling basis. Application fee: $50. Electronic applications accepted. *Expenses:* Contact institution. *Financial support:* In 2011–12, 50 students received support, including 24 fellowships with full and partial tuition reimbursements available (averaging $11,726 per year); career-related internships or fieldwork, Federal Work-Study, and institutionally sponsored loans also available. Support available to part-time students. Financial award application deadline: 4/1; financial award applicants required to submit FAFSA. *Faculty research:* Mental health, federal policy, health care. *Unit head:* Richard Gregg, Director, 617-994-4246, E-mail: rgregg@suffolk.edu. *Application contact:* Ellen Driscoll, Director of Graduate Admissions, 617-573-8302, Fax: 617-305-1733, E-mail: grad.admission@suffolk.edu. Web site: http://www.suffolk.edu/business/8494.html.

Syracuse University, Maxwell School of Citizenship and Public Affairs, Program in Health Services Management and Policy, Syracuse, NY 13244. Offers CAS. Part-time programs available. *Students:* 1 (woman) part-time; minority (Black or African American, non-Hispanic/Latino). Average age 32. 13 applicants, 92% accepted, 1 enrolled. In 2011, 4 degrees awarded. *Entrance requirements:* For degree, 7 years of mid-career experience. Additional exam requirements/recommendations for international students: Required—TOEFL (minimum score 100 iBT). Application fee: $75. *Expenses: Tuition:* Part-time $1206 per credit. *Financial support:* Application deadline: 1/1. *Unit head:* Dr. Thomas Dennison, Head, 315-443-9215, Fax: 315-443-9721, E-mail: thdennis@syr.edu. *Application contact:* Tammy Salisbury, Graduate Coordinator, 315-443-3192, Fax: 315-443-3423, E-mail: mtsalisb@maxwell.syr.edu.

Temple University, Fox School of Business, MBA Programs, Philadelphia, PA 19122-6096. Offers accounting (MBA); business management (MBA); financial management (MBA); healthcare and life sciences innovation (MBA); human resource management (MBA); international business (IMBA); IT management (MBA); marketing management (MBA); pharmaceutical management (MBA); strategic management (EMBA, MBA). EMBA offered in Philadelphia, PA and Tokyo, Japan. *Accreditation:* AACSB. Part-time and evening/weekend programs available. Postbaccalaureate distance learning degree programs offered (minimal on-campus study). *Entrance requirements:* For master's, GMAT, minimum undergraduate GPA of 3.0. Additional exam requirements/recommendations for international students: Required—TOEFL (minimum score 600 paper-based; 250 computer-based; 100 iBT), IELTS (minimum score 7.5). *Expenses:* Tuition, state resident: full-time $12,366; part-time $687 per credit hour. Tuition, nonresident: full-time $17,298; part-time $961 per credit hour. *Required fees:* $590; $213 per year.

Texas A&M Health Science Center, School of Rural Public Health, College Station, TX 77840. Offers environmental/occupational health (MPH); epidemiology/biostatistics (MPH); health policy/management (MPH); social and behavioral health (MPH). *Accreditation:* CEPH. Part-time programs available. Postbaccalaureate distance learning degree programs offered (no on-campus study). *Degree requirements:* For master's, thesis optional. *Entrance requirements:* For master's, GRE General Test, minimum undergraduate GPA of 3.0. Electronic applications accepted. *Faculty research:* Tobacco cessation, youth health risk.

Texas A&M University–Corpus Christi, Graduate Studies and Research, College of Business, Corpus Christi, TX 78412-5503. Offers accounting (M Acc); health care administration (MBA); international business (MBA). *Accreditation:* AACSB. Part-time and evening/weekend programs available. *Degree requirements:* For master's, comprehensive exam, thesis (for some programs). *Entrance requirements:* For master's, GMAT. Additional exam requirements/recommendations for international students: Required—TOEFL. Electronic applications accepted.

Texas A&M University–Corpus Christi, Graduate Studies and Research, College of Nursing and Health Sciences, Corpus Christi, TX 78412-5503. Offers clinical nurse specialist (MSN); family nurse practitioner (MSN); health care administration (MSN); leadership in nursing systems (MSN). *Accreditation:* AACN. Part-time and evening/weekend programs available. *Degree requirements:* For master's, comprehensive exam, thesis (for some programs). *Entrance requirements:* For master's, GRE General Test. Additional exam requirements/recommendations for international students: Required—TOEFL. Electronic applications accepted.

Texas A&M University–San Antonio, School of Business, San Antonio, TX 78224. Offers business administration (MBA); enterprise resource planning systems (MBA); finance (MBA); healthcare management (MBA); human resources management (MBA); information assurance and security (MBA); international business (MBA); professional accounting (MPA); project management (MBA); supply chain management (MBA). Part-time and evening/weekend programs available. *Faculty:* 18 full-time (6 women), 1 part-time/adjunct (0 women). *Students:* 91 full-time (45 women), 278 part-time (150 women). Average age 33. In 2011, 20 master's awarded. *Entrance requirements:* For master's, GMAT. Additional exam requirements/recommendations for international students: Required—TOEFL (minimum score 550 paper-based; 213 computer-based; 80 iBT), IELTS (minimum score 6). *Application deadline:* For fall admission, 7/1 priority date for domestic students, 6/1 for international students; for spring admission, 11/15 priority date for domestic students, 10/1 for international students. Applications are processed on a rolling basis. Application fee: $35 ($50 for international students). Electronic applications accepted. *Expenses:* Tuition, state resident: part-time $691.11 per course. Tuition, nonresident: part-time $1621.11 per course. *Financial support:* Application deadline: 3/31; applicants required to submit FAFSA. *Unit head:* Dr. Tracy Hurley, MBA Coordinator, 210-932-6200, E-mail: tracy.hurley@tamusa.tamus.edu. *Application contact:* Melissa A. Villanueva, Graduate Admissions Specialist, 210-932-6200, Fax: 210-932-6209, E-mail: melissa.villanueva@tamusa.tamus.edu. Web site: http://www.tamusa.tamus.edu.

Texas State University–San Marcos, Graduate School, College of Health Professions, School of Health Administration, Program in Healthcare Administration, San Marcos, TX 78666. Offers MHA. Part-time and evening/weekend programs available. *Faculty:* 11 full-time (4 women), 1 part-time/adjunct (0 women). *Students:* 41 full-time (19 women), 27 part-time (21 women); includes 20 minority (7 Black or African American, non-Hispanic/Latino; 4 Asian, non-Hispanic/Latino; 9 Hispanic/Latino), 1 international. Average age 27. 92 applicants, 30% accepted, 18 enrolled. In 2011, 27 master's awarded. *Degree requirements:* For master's, comprehensive exam, thesis optional, committee review. *Entrance requirements:* For master's, GRE General Test, 3 letters of reference; resume; interview. Additional exam requirements/recommendations for international students: Required—TOEFL (minimum score 550 paper-based; 213 computer-based; 78 iBT). *Application deadline:* For fall admission, 6/1 priority date for domestic students, 6/1 for international students; for spring admission, 10/1 priority date for domestic students, 10/1 for international students. Applications are processed on a rolling basis. Application fee: $40 ($90 for international students). Electronic applications accepted. *Expenses:* Tuition, state resident: full-time $6408; part-time $3204 per semester. Tuition, nonresident: full-time $14,832; part-time $7416 per semester. *Required fees:* $1824; $912 per semester. Tuition and fees vary according to course load. *Financial support:* In 2011–12, 40 students received support, including 1 research assistantship (averaging $9,855 per year), 9 teaching assistantships (averaging $9,576 per year); career-related internships or fieldwork, Federal Work-Study, institutionally sponsored loans, scholarships/grants, and unspecified assistantships also available. Support available to part-time students. Financial award application deadline: 4/1; financial award applicants required to submit FAFSA. *Unit head:* Dr. Michael Nowicki, Advisor, 512-245-3556, E-mail: mn03@txstate.edu. *Application contact:* Dr. J. Michael Willoughby, Dean of Graduate School, 512-245-2581, Fax: 512-245-8365, E-mail: gradcollege@txstate.edu. Web site: http://www.health.txstate.edu/ha/degrees-programs/master-health-administration.html.

Texas State University–San Marcos, Graduate School, College of Health Professions, School of Health Administration, Program in Healthcare Human Resources, San Marcos, TX 78666. Offers MS. *Accreditation:* CAHME. Part-time and evening/weekend programs available. *Faculty:* 1 full-time (0 women). *Students:* 2 full-time (both women), 7 part-time (5 women); includes 3 minority (2 Black or African American, non-Hispanic/Latino; 1 Hispanic/Latino). Average age 37. 2 applicants, 100% accepted, 1 enrolled. In 2011, 2 master's awarded. *Degree requirements:* For master's, comprehensive exam, thesis optional, committee review. *Entrance requirements:* For master's, GRE General Test, department interview; 3 letters of reference; resume. Additional exam requirements/recommendations for international students: Required—TOEFL (minimum score 550 paper-based; 213 computer-based; 78 iBT). *Application deadline:* For fall admission, 6/15 priority date for domestic students, 6/1 for international students; for spring admission, 10/15 priority date for domestic students, 10/1 for international students. Applications are processed on a rolling basis. Application fee: $40 ($90 for international students). Electronic applications accepted. *Expenses:* Tuition, state resident: full-time $6408; part-time $3204 per semester. Tuition, nonresident: full-time $14,832; part-time $7416 per semester. *Required fees:* $1824; $912 per semester. Tuition and fees vary according to course load. *Financial support:* In 2011–12, 4 students received support. Research assistantships, teaching assistantships, career-related internships or fieldwork, Federal Work-Study, institutionally sponsored loans, scholarships/grants, and unspecified assistantships available. Support available to part-time students. Financial award application deadline: 4/1; financial award applicants required to submit FAFSA. *Unit head:* Dr. Michael Nowicki, Program Advisor, 512-245-3556, Fax: 512-245-8712, E-mail: mn03@txstate.edu. *Application contact:* Dr. J. Michael Willoughby, Dean of Graduate School, 512-245-2581, Fax: 512-245-8365, E-mail: gradcollege@txstate.edu. Web site: http://www.health.txstate.edu/hsr.

Texas Tech University, Graduate School, Rawls College of Business Administration, Area of Information Systems and Quantitative Sciences, Lubbock, TX 79409. Offers business statistics (MS, PhD); healthcare management (MS); management information systems (MS, PhD); production and operations management (MS, PhD); risk management (MS). Part-time programs available. *Faculty:* 15 full-time (0 women). *Students:* 46 full-time (13 women), 8 part-time (0 women); includes 4 minority (1 American Indian or Alaska Native, non-Hispanic/Latino; 1 Asian, non-Hispanic/Latino; 2 Hispanic/Latino), 38 international. Average age 27. 101 applicants, 65% accepted, 18 enrolled. In 2011, 35 master's, 2 doctorates awarded. Terminal master's awarded for partial completion of doctoral program. *Degree requirements:* For master's, comprehensive exam or capstone course; for doctorate, thesis/dissertation, qualifying exams. *Entrance requirements:* For master's and doctorate, GMAT, holistic profile of academic credentials. Additional exam requirements/recommendations for international students: Required—TOEFL (minimum score 550 paper-based; 213 computer-based; 79 iBT). *Application deadline:* For fall admission, 4/1 priority date for domestic students, 1/15 for international students; for spring admission, 9/1 priority date for domestic students, 6/15 for international students. Applications are processed on a rolling basis. Application fee: $50 ($75 for international students). Electronic applications accepted. *Expenses:* Tuition, state resident: full-time $5899; part-time $245.80 per credit hour. Tuition, nonresident: full-time $13,411; part-time $558.80 per credit hour. *Required fees:* $2680.60; $86.50 per credit hour. $920.30 per semester. *Financial support:* In 2011–12; 5 research assistantships (averaging $16,160 per year), 5 teaching assistantships (averaging $18,000 per year) were awarded; Federal Work-Study, scholarships/grants, and unspecified assistantships also available. *Faculty research:* Database management systems, systems management and engineering, expert systems and adaptive knowledge-based sciences, statistical analysis and design. *Unit head:* Dr. Glenn Browne, Area Coordinator, 806-834-0969, Fax: 806-742-3193, E-mail: glenn.browne@ttu.edu. *Application contact:* Elizabeth Stuart, Director, Graduate Services Center, 806-742-3184, Fax: 806-742-3958, E-mail: ba_grad@ttu.edu. Web site: http://is.ba.ttu.edu.

Texas Tech University, Graduate School, Rawls College of Business Administration, Programs in Business Administration, Lubbock, TX 79409. Offers agricultural business (MBA); business administration (IMBA); business statistics (MBA); entrepreneurship and innovation (MBA); general business (MBA); health organization management (MBA); international business (MBA); management and leadership skills (MBA); management information systems (MBA); marketing (MBA); real estate (MBA); JD/MBA; MBA/M Arch; MBA/MA; MBA/MD; MBA/MS; MBA/Pharm D. Part-time and evening/weekend programs available. *Faculty:* 49 full-time (8 women), 2 part-time/adjunct (0 women). *Students:* 195 full-time (55 women), 397 part-time (101 women); includes 123 minority (27 Black or African American, non-Hispanic/Latino; 4 American Indian or Alaska Native, non-Hispanic/Latino; 31 Asian, non-Hispanic/Latino; 61 Hispanic/Latino), 38 international. Average age 31. 374 applicants, 83% accepted, 255 enrolled. In 2011, 256 degrees awarded. *Degree requirements:* For master's, capstone course. *Entrance requirements:* For master's, GMAT, holistic review of academic credentials. Additional exam requirements/recommendations for international students: Required—TOEFL (minimum score 550 paper-based; 213 computer-based; 79 iBT). *Application deadline:* For fall admission, 4/1 priority date for domestic students, 1/15 for international students; for spring admission, 9/1 priority date for domestic students, 6/15 for international students. Applications are processed on a rolling basis. Application fee: $50 ($75 for international students). Electronic applications accepted. *Expenses:* Tuition, state resident: full-time $5899; part-time $245.80 per credit hour. Tuition, nonresident: full-time $13,411; part-time $558.80 per credit hour. *Required fees:* $2680.60; $86.50 per credit hour. $920.30 per semester. *Financial support:* In 2011–12, 22 research assistantships (averaging $8,800 per year) were awarded; teaching assistantships, career-related internships or fieldwork, Federal Work-Study, scholarships/grants, health care benefits, and unspecified assistantships also available. Support available to part-

time students. Financial award applicants required to submit FAFSA. *Unit head:* Dr. W. Jay Conover, Director, 806-742-1546, Fax: 806-742-3958, E-mail: jay.conover@ttu.edu. *Application contact:* Elizabeth Stuart, Director, Graduate Services Center, 806-742-3184, Fax: 806-742-3958, E-mail: ba_grad@ttu.edu. Web site: http://mba.ba.ttu.edu/.

Texas Tech University Health Sciences Center, School of Allied Health Sciences, Program in Clinical Practice Management, Lubbock, TX 79430. Offers MS. *Accreditation:* CORE. Part-time programs available. *Faculty:* 5 full-time (1 woman). *Students:* 32 full-time (19 women), 113 part-time (75 women); includes 51 minority (19 Black or African American, non-Hispanic/Latino; 8 Asian, non-Hispanic/Latino; 22 Hispanic/Latino; 2 Two or more races, non-Hispanic/Latino). Average age 29. 116 applicants, 81% accepted, 94 enrolled. In 2011, 30 master's awarded. *Entrance requirements:* Additional exam requirements/recommendations for international students: Required—TOEFL, IELTS. *Application deadline:* For fall admission, 8/1 for domestic students; for spring admission, 12/1 for domestic students. Applications are processed on a rolling basis. Application fee: $35. Electronic applications accepted. *Financial support:* Institutionally sponsored loans available. *Unit head:* Dr. Robin Satterwhite, Chair, 806-743-2263, Fax: 806-743-3249, E-mail: robin.satterwhite@ttuhsc.edu. *Application contact:* Jeri Moravcik, Assistant Director of Admissions and Student Affairs, 806-743-3220, Fax: 806-743-2994, E-mail: jeri.moravcik@ttuhsc.edu. Web site: http://www.ttuhsc.edu/sah/mscpm.

Texas Wesleyan University, Graduate Programs, Graduate Business Programs, Fort Worth, TX 76105-1536. Offers business administration (MBA); health services administration (MS); management (MiM). *Accreditation:* ACBSP. Part-time and evening/weekend programs available. *Faculty:* 16 full-time (6 women), 6 part-time/adjunct (4 women). *Students:* 7 full-time (5 women), 32 part-time (20 women); includes 8 minority (3 Black or African American, non-Hispanic/Latino; 1 Asian, non-Hispanic/Latino; 4 Hispanic/Latino), 3 international. Average age 32. 42 applicants, 24% accepted, 9 enrolled. In 2011, 25 master's awarded. *Degree requirements:* For master's, capstone course. *Entrance requirements:* For master's, GMAT, 3 letters of recommendation. *Application deadline:* For fall admission, 7/7 priority date for domestic students; for spring admission, 11/1 priority date for domestic students. Applications are processed on a rolling basis. Application fee: $50. *Expenses:* Contact institution. *Financial support:* Federal Work-Study, scholarships/grants, and tuition waivers (full and partial) available. Support available to part-time students. Financial award application deadline: 3/15; financial award applicants required to submit FAFSA. *Unit head:* Dr. Hector Quintanilla, Dean, 817-531-4840, Fax: 817-531-6585. *Application contact:* Admissions Office, 817-531-4444. Web site: http://www.txwes.edu/academics/business.

Texas Woman's University, Graduate School, College of Arts and Sciences, School of Management, Denton, TX 76201. Offers business administration (MBA); health systems management (MHSM). Part-time programs available. *Faculty:* 17 full-time (10 women), 1 part-time/adjunct (0 women). *Students:* 660 full-time (555 women), 436 part-time (364 women); includes 714 minority (465 Black or African American, non-Hispanic/Latino; 8 American Indian or Alaska Native, non-Hispanic/Latino; 116 Asian, non-Hispanic/Latino; 121 Hispanic/Latino; 4 Native Hawaiian or other Pacific Islander, non-Hispanic/Latino), 46 international. Average age 35. 428 applicants, 93% accepted, 318 enrolled. In 2011, 550 master's awarded. *Degree requirements:* For master's, thesis optional. *Entrance requirements:* For master's, 2 letters of reference, resume, 5 years relevant experience (EMBA only). Additional exam requirements/recommendations for international students: Required—TOEFL (minimum score 550 paper-based; 213 computer-based; 79 iBT). *Application deadline:* For fall admission, 8/1 priority date for domestic students, 3/1 for international students; for spring admission, 12/1 priority date for domestic students, 7/1 for international students. Applications are processed on a rolling basis. Application fee: $50 ($75 for international students). Electronic applications accepted. *Expenses:* Tuition, state resident: full-time $3834; part-time $213 per credit hour. Tuition, nonresident: full-time $9468; part-time $526 per credit hour. *Required fees:* $213 per credit hour. Tuition and fees vary according to course load. *Financial support:* In 2011–12, 254 students received support, including 15 research assistantships (averaging $11,520 per year); career-related internships or fieldwork, Federal Work-Study, institutionally sponsored loans, scholarships/grants, traineeships, health care benefits, and unspecified assistantships also available. Support available to part-time students. Financial award application deadline: 3/1; financial award applicants required to submit FAFSA. *Faculty research:* Tax research, privacy issues in Web-based marketing, multitasking, leadership, women in management, global comparative studies, corporate sustainability and responsibility. *Unit head:* Dr. P. Ann Hughes, Director, 940-898-2121, Fax: 940-898-2120, E-mail: pahughes@twu.edu. *Application contact:* Dr. Samuel Wheeler, Assistant Director of Admissions, 940-898-3188, Fax: 940-898-3081, E-mail: wheelersr@twu.edu. Web site: http://www.twu.edu/som/.

Texas Woman's University, Graduate School, College of Health Sciences, Program in Health Care Administration-Houston Center, Denton, TX 76201. Offers MHA. *Accreditation:* CAHME. Part-time and evening/weekend programs available. *Faculty:* 7 full-time (2 women). *Students:* 25 full-time (21 women), 82 part-time (67 women); includes 70 minority (40 Black or African American, non-Hispanic/Latino; 1 American Indian or Alaska Native, non-Hispanic/Latino; 19 Asian, non-Hispanic/Latino; 10 Hispanic/Latino), 4 international. Average age 32. 39 applicants, 85% accepted, 22 enrolled. In 2011, 39 master's awarded. *Degree requirements:* For master's, comprehensive exam, thesis or alternative. *Entrance requirements:* For master's, GMAT (preferred minimum score 450) or GRE General Test (preferred minimum scores 150 [450 old version] Verbal, 141 [450 old version] Quantitative), interview, resume, 3 letters of reference, essay. Additional exam requirements/recommendations for international students: Required—TOEFL (minimum score 550 paper-based; 213 computer-based; 79 iBT). *Application deadline:* For fall admission, 5/30 priority date for domestic students, 3/1 for international students; for spring admission, 9/30 priority date for domestic students, 7/1 for international students. Applications are processed on a rolling basis. Application fee: $50 ($75 for international students). Electronic applications accepted. *Expenses:* Tuition, state resident: full-time $3834; part-time $213 per credit hour. Tuition, nonresident: full-time $9468; part-time $526 per credit hour. *Required fees:* $213 per credit hour. Tuition and fees vary according to course load. *Financial support:* In 2011–12, 30 students received support, including 1 research assistantship (averaging $11,520 per year); career-related internships or fieldwork, Federal Work-Study, institutionally sponsored loans, scholarships/grants, traineeships, health care benefits, and unspecified assistantships also available. Support available to part-time students. Financial award application deadline: 3/1; financial award applicants required to submit FAFSA. *Faculty research:* Organizational culture, medical errors, ethical analysis in health care, leadership and professional development, strategic management, recruitment and retention issues, elderly health care. *Unit head:* Dr. Kelley Moseley, Program Director, 713-794-2061, Fax: 713-794-2350, E-mail: healthcareadministration@twu.edu. *Application contact:* Dr. Samuel Wheeler, Assistant Director of Admissions, 940-898-3188, Fax: 940-898-3081, E-mail: wheelersr@twu.edu. Web site: http://www.twu.edu/health-care-administration/.

Texas Woman's University, Graduate School, College of Nursing, Denton, TX 76201. Offers acute care nurse practitioner (MS); adult health clinical nurse specialist (MS); adult health nurse practitioner (MS); child health clinical nurse specialist (MS); clinical nurse leader (MS); family nurse practitioner (MS); health systems management (MS); nursing education (MS); nursing practice (DNP); nursing science (PhD); pediatric nurse practitioner (MS); women's health clinical nurse specialist (MS); women's health nurse practitioner (MS). *Accreditation:* AACN. Part-time programs available. Postbaccalaureate distance learning degree programs offered. *Faculty:* 70 full-time (69 women), 7 part-time/adjunct (all women). *Students:* 87 full-time (78 women), 870 part-time (815 women); includes 489 minority (235 Black or African American, non-Hispanic/Latino; 5 American Indian or Alaska Native, non-Hispanic/Latino; 169 Asian, non-Hispanic/Latino; 78 Hispanic/Latino; 2 Native Hawaiian or other Pacific Islander, non-Hispanic/Latino), 19 international. Average age 38. 368 applicants, 71% accepted, 205 enrolled. In 2011, 147 master's, 21 doctorates awarded. *Degree requirements:* For master's, comprehensive exam, thesis or alternative; for doctorate, comprehensive exam, thesis/dissertation. *Entrance requirements:* For master's, GRE or MAT, minimum GPA of 3.0 on last 60 hours in undergraduate nursing degree and overall, RN license, BS in nursing, basic statistics course; for doctorate, GRE (preferred minimum score 153 [500 old version] Verbal, 144 [500 old version] Quantitative, 4 Analytical), MS in nursing, minimum preferred GPA of 3.5, RN license, statistics, 2 letters of reference, curriculum vitae, graduate nursing-theory course, graduate research course, statement of professional goals and research interests. Additional exam requirements/recommendations for international students: Required—TOEFL (minimum score 550 paper-based; 213 computer-based; 79 iBT). *Application deadline:* For fall admission, 5/1 priority date for domestic students, 3/1 for international students; for spring admission, 9/15 priority date for domestic students, 7/1 for international students. Applications are processed on a rolling basis. Application fee: $50 ($75 for international students). Electronic applications accepted. *Expenses:* Tuition, state resident: full-time $3834; part-time $213 per credit hour. Tuition, nonresident: full-time $9468; part-time $526 per credit hour. *Required fees:* $213 per credit hour. Tuition and fees vary according to course load. *Financial support:* In 2011–12, 149 students received support, including 10 research assistantships (averaging $12,942 per year), 1 teaching assistantship (averaging $12,942 per year); career-related internships or fieldwork, Federal Work-Study, institutionally sponsored loans, scholarships/grants, traineeships, health care benefits, and unspecified assistantships also available. Support available to part-time students. Financial award application deadline: 3/1; financial award applicants required to submit FAFSA. *Faculty research:* Screening, prevention, and treatment for intimate partner violence; needs of adolescents during childbirth intervention; a network analysis decision tool for nurse managers (Social Network Analysis); support for adolescents with implantable cardioverter defibrillators; informatics: nurse staffing, safety, quality, and financial data as they relate to patient care outcomes; prevention and treatment of obesity; improving infant outcomes related to premature birth. *Total annual research expenditures:* $462,088. *Unit head:* Dr. Patricia Holden-Huchton, Interim Dean, 940-898-2401, Fax: 940-898-2437, E-mail: nursing@twu.edu. *Application contact:* Dr. Samuel Wheeler, Assistant Director of Admissions, 940-898-3188, Fax: 940-898-3081, E-mail: wheelersr@twu.edu. Web site: http://www.twu.edu/nursing/.

Thomas Jefferson University, Jefferson School of Population Health, Program in Healthcare Quality and Safety, Philadelphia, PA 19107. Offers MS, PhD, Certificate. Part-time and evening/weekend programs available. Postbaccalaureate distance learning degree programs offered (no on-campus study). *Entrance requirements:* For master's, GRE or other graduate examination, 2 letters of recommendation, interview, curriculum vitae; for doctorate, GRE within the last 5 years, 3 letters of recommendation, interview, curriculum vitae. Additional exam requirements/recommendations for international students: Required—TOEFL.

Thomas Jefferson University, Jefferson School of Population Health, Program in Health Policy, Philadelphia, PA 19107. Offers MS, PhD, Certificate. Part-time and evening/weekend programs available. Postbaccalaureate distance learning degree programs offered. *Entrance requirements:* For master's, GRE or other graduate exam, two letters of recommendation, curriculum vitae/resume, interview; for doctorate, GRE within the last 5 years, three letters of recommendation, curriculum vitae/resume, interview. Additional exam requirements/recommendations for international students: Required—TOEFL. Electronic applications accepted.

Tiffin University, Program in Business Administration, Tiffin, OH 44883-2161. Offers finance (MBA); general management (MBA); healthcare administration (MBA); human resources (MBA); international business (MBA); leadership (MBA); marketing (MBA); sports management (MBA). *Accreditation:* ACBSP. Part-time and evening/weekend programs available. Postbaccalaureate distance learning degree programs offered (no on-campus study). *Faculty:* 30 full-time (15 women), 22 part-time/adjunct (6 women). *Students:* 209 full-time (107 women), 340 part-time (172 women); includes 112 minority (91 Black or African American, non-Hispanic/Latino; 4 Asian, non-Hispanic/Latino; 17 Hispanic/Latino), 71 international. Average age 31. 237 applicants, 76% accepted. In 2011, 170 master's awarded. *Entrance requirements:* For master's, minimum undergraduate GPA of 2.5, work experience. Additional exam requirements/recommendations for international students: Required—TOEFL (minimum score 550 paper-based; 213 computer-based; 79 iBT). *Application deadline:* For fall admission, 8/15 for domestic students, 8/1 for international students; for spring admission, 1/9 for domestic students, 12/1 for international students. Applications are processed on a rolling basis. Electronic applications accepted. *Expenses: Tuition:* Full-time $11,200; part-time $700 per credit. Tuition and fees vary according to program. *Financial support:* Available to part-time students. Application deadline: 7/31; applicants required to submit FAFSA. *Faculty research:* Small business, executive development operations, research and statistical analysis, market research, management information systems. *Unit head:* Dr. Lillian Schumacher, Dean of the School of Business, 419-448-3053, Fax: 419-443-5002, E-mail: schumacherlb@tiffin.edu. *Application contact:* Nikki Hintze, Director of Graduate Admissions and Student Services, 800-968-6446 Ext. 3445, Fax: 419-443-5002, E-mail: hintzenm@tiffin.edu. Web site: http://www.tiffin.edu/graduateprograms/.

Towson University, Program in Clinician-Administrator Transition, Towson, MD 21252-0001. Offers Postbaccalaureate Certificate. *Students:* 11 full-time (all women), 6 part-time (all women); includes 2 minority (both Black or African American, non-Hispanic/Latino), 3 international. *Entrance requirements:* For degree, minimum GPA of 3.0; bachelor's or master's degree in a clinical field; licensure, licensure eligibility, or certificate in a clinical field. *Application deadline:* Applications are processed on a rolling basis. Application fee: $50. Electronic applications accepted. *Expenses:* Tuition, state resident: part-time $337 per credit. Tuition, nonresident: part-time $709 per credit. *Required fees:* $99 per credit. *Financial support:* Application deadline: 4/1; applicants required to submit FAFSA. *Unit head:* Marcie Weinstein, Graduate Program Director, 410-704-4049, E-mail: mweinstein@towson.edu.

Trident University International, College of Health Sciences, Cypress, CA 90630. Offers MS, PhD, Certificate. Part-time and evening/weekend programs available. Postbaccalaureate distance learning degree programs offered (no on-campus study). *Degree requirements:* For doctorate, comprehensive exam, thesis/dissertation. *Entrance requirements:* For master's, minimum GPA of 2.5 (students with GPA 3.0 or greater may transfer up to 30% of graduate level credits); for doctorate, minimum GPA of 3.4. Additional exam requirements/recommendations for international students: Required—TOEFL. Electronic applications accepted.

Trinity University, Department of Health Care Administration, San Antonio, TX 78212-7200. Offers MS. *Accreditation:* CAHME. Part-time programs available.

Health Services Management and Hospital Administration

Postbaccalaureate distance learning degree programs offered (minimal on-campus study). *Degree requirements:* For master's, research projects. *Entrance requirements:* For master's, GMAT, GRE General Test, previous course work in accounting, economics, and statistics.

Trinity Western University, School of Graduate Studies, Program in Leadership, Langley, BC V2Y 1Y1, Canada. Offers business (MA, Certificate); Christian ministry (MA); education (MA, Certificate); healthcare (MA, Certificate); non-profit (MA, Certificate). Postbaccalaureate distance learning degree programs offered (minimal on-campus study). *Degree requirements:* For master's, major project. *Entrance requirements:* For master's, minimum GPA of 2.7. Additional exam requirements/recommendations for international students: Required—TOEFL (minimum score 620 paper-based; 260 computer-based; 105 iBT). Electronic applications accepted. *Expenses:* Contact institution. *Faculty research:* Servant leadership.

Troy University, Graduate School, College of Arts and Sciences, Program in Public Administration, Troy, AL 36082. Offers education (MPA); environmental management (MPA); government contracting (MPA); health care administration (MPA); justice administration (MPA); national security affairs (MPA); nonprofit management (MPA); public human resources management (MPA); public management (MPA). *Accreditation:* NASPAA. Part-time and evening/weekend programs available. Postbaccalaureate distance learning degree programs offered (no on-campus study). *Faculty:* 17 full-time (10 women), 10 part-time/adjunct (3 women). *Students:* 97 full-time (71 women), 400 part-time (259 women); includes 298 minority (264 Black or African American, non-Hispanic/Latino; 5 American Indian or Alaska Native, non-Hispanic/Latino; 15 Asian, non-Hispanic/Latino; 11 Hispanic/Latino; 3 Two or more races, non-Hispanic/Latino). Average age 33. 323 applicants, 63% accepted, 97 enrolled. In 2011, 249 master's awarded. *Degree requirements:* For master's, capstone course, minimum GPA of 3.0, admission to candidacy. *Entrance requirements:* For master's, GRE (minimum score of 920), MAT (minimum score of 400) or GMAT (minimum score of 490), minimum undergraduate GPA of 2.5, letter of recommendation, essay. Additional exam requirements/recommendations for international students: Required—TOEFL (minimum score 523 paper-based; 193 computer-based; 70 iBT), IELTS (minimum score 6). *Application deadline:* Applications are processed on a rolling basis. Application fee: $50. Electronic applications accepted. *Expenses:* Tuition, state resident: full-time $6960; part-time $290 per credit hour. Tuition, nonresident: full-time $13,920; part-time $580 per credit hour. *Required fees:* $386 per term. *Financial support:* Available to part-time students. Applicants required to submit FAFSA. *Unit head:* Dr. Charles Kruprick, Chairman, 334-670-5968, Fax: 334-670-5647, E-mail: ckrupnickl@troy.edu. *Application contact:* Brenda K. Campbell, Director of Graduate Admissions, 334-670-3178, Fax: 334-670-3733, E-mail: bcamp@troy.edu.

Troy University, Graduate School, College of Business, Program in Business Administration, Troy, AL 36082. Offers accounting (EMBA, MBA); criminal justice (EMBA); finance (MBA); general management (EMBA, MBA); healthcare management (EMBA); information systems (EMBA, MBA); international economic development (MBA). *Accreditation:* ACBSP. Part-time and evening/weekend programs available. *Faculty:* 50 full-time (14 women), 12 part-time/adjunct (0 women). *Students:* 326 full-time (168 women), 596 part-time (358 women); includes 524 minority (402 Black or African American, non-Hispanic/Latino; 12 American Indian or Alaska Native, non-Hispanic/Latino; 85 Asian, non-Hispanic/Latino; 21 Hispanic/Latino; 4 Two or more races, non-Hispanic/Latino). Average age 29. 644 applicants, 67% accepted, 204 enrolled. In 2011, 388 master's awarded. *Degree requirements:* For master's, minimum GPA of 3.0, capstone course, research course. *Entrance requirements:* For master's, GMAT (minimum score 500) or GRE General Test (minimum score 900), minimum GPA of 2.5; letter of recommendation, bachelor's degree. Additional exam requirements/recommendations for international students: Required—TOEFL (minimum score 523 paper-based; 193 computer-based; 70 iBT), IELTS (minimum score 6), or ACT COMPASS ESL (minimum listening, reading, and grammar score 270). *Application deadline:* Applications are processed on a rolling basis. Application fee: $50. *Expenses:* Tuition, state resident: full-time $6960; part-time $290 per credit hour. Tuition, nonresident: full-time $13,920; part-time $580 per credit hour. *Required fees:* $386 per term. *Unit head:* Dr. Edward Merkel, Director, Graduate Business Programs, 334-670-3194, Fax: 334-670-3599, E-mail: emerkel@troy.edu. *Application contact:* Brenda K. Campbell, Director of Graduate Admissions, 334-670-3178, Fax: 334-670-3733, E-mail: bcamp@troy.edu.

Troy University, Graduate School, College of Business, Program in Management, Troy, AL 36082. Offers applied management (MSM); healthcare management (MSM); human resources management (MSM); information systems (MSM); international hospitality management (MSM); international management (MSM); leadership and organizational effectiveness (MSM); public management (MS, MSM). *Accreditation:* ACBSP. Evening/weekend programs available. *Faculty:* 21 full-time (6 women), 7 part-time/adjunct (2 women). *Students:* 52 full-time (33 women), 284 part-time (183 women); includes 222 minority (186 Black or African American, non-Hispanic/Latino; 5 American Indian or Alaska Native, non-Hispanic/Latino; 11 Asian, non-Hispanic/Latino; 13 Hispanic/Latino; 1 Native Hawaiian or other Pacific Islander, non-Hispanic/Latino; 6 Two or more races, non-Hispanic/Latino). Average age 35. 157 applicants, 76% accepted, 55 enrolled. In 2011, 234 master's awarded. *Degree requirements:* For master's, Graduate Educational Testing Service Major Field Test, capstone exam, minimum GPA of 3.0. *Entrance requirements:* For master's, GMAT (minimum score 500) or GRE General Test (minimum score 900), minimum GPA of 2.5, bachelor's degree, letter of recommendation. Additional exam requirements/recommendations for international students: Required—TOEFL (minimum score 523 paper-based; 193 computer-based; 70 iBT), IELTS (minimum score 6), or ACT COMPASS ESL (minimum listening, reading, and grammar score 270). *Application deadline:* Applications are processed on a rolling basis. Application fee: $50. Electronic applications accepted. *Expenses:* Contact institution. *Unit head:* Dr. Edward Merkel, Director, Graduate Business Programs, 334-670-3194, Fax: 334-670-3599, E-mail: emerkel@troy.edu. *Application contact:* Brenda K. Campbell, Director of Graduate Admissions, 334-670-3178, Fax: 334-670-3733, E-mail: bcamp@troy.edu.

Tulane University, School of Public Health and Tropical Medicine, Department of Health Systems Management, New Orleans, LA 70118-5669. Offers MHA, MMM, MPH, PhD, Sc D, JD/MHA, MD/MPH. *Accreditation:* CAHME (one or more programs are accredited). *Degree requirements:* For doctorate, comprehensive exam, thesis/dissertation. *Entrance requirements:* For master's, GMAT, GRE General Test; for doctorate, GRE General Test. Additional exam requirements/recommendations for international students: Required—TOEFL. Electronic applications accepted. *Faculty research:* Health policy, organizational governance, international health administration.

Uniformed Services University of the Health Sciences, School of Medicine, Graduate Programs in the Biomedical Sciences and Public Health, Bethesda, MD 20814. Offers emerging infectious diseases (PhD); medical and clinical psychology (PhD), including clinical psychology, medical and clinical psychology, medical psychology; molecular and cell biology (MS, PhD); neuroscience (PhD); preventive medicine and biometrics (MPH, MS, MSPH, MTMH, Dr PH, PhD), including environmental health sciences (PhD), healthcare administration and policy (MS), medical zoology (PhD), public health (MPH, MSPH, Dr PH), tropical medicine and hygiene (MTMH). *Faculty:* 372 full-time (119 women), 4,044 part-time/adjunct (908 women). *Students:* 176 full-time (96 women); includes 31 minority (6 Black or African American, non-Hispanic/Latino; 4 American Indian or Alaska Native, non-Hispanic/Latino; 14 Asian, non-Hispanic/Latino; 7 Hispanic/Latino), 11 international. Average age 28. 278 applicants, 20% accepted, 47 enrolled. In 2011, 36 master's, 17 doctorates awarded. Terminal master's awarded for partial completion of doctoral program. *Degree requirements:* For master's, comprehensive exam, thesis or alternative; for doctorate, comprehensive exam, thesis/dissertation, qualifying exam. *Entrance requirements:* For master's, GRE General Test; for doctorate, GRE General Test, minimum GPA of 3.0. Additional exam requirements/recommendations for international students: Required—TOEFL. *Application deadline:* For fall admission, 1/1 priority date for domestic students, 1/1 for international students. Applications are processed on a rolling basis. Application fee: $0. Electronic applications accepted. *Financial support:* In 2011–12, fellowships with full tuition reimbursements (averaging $26,000 per year), research assistantships with full tuition reimbursements (averaging $26,000 per year) were awarded; career-related internships or fieldwork, scholarships/grants, health care benefits, and tuition waivers (full) also available. *Unit head:* Dr. Eleanor S. Metcalf, Associate Dean, 301-295-1104, E-mail: emetcalf@usuhs.edu. *Application contact:* Elena Marina Sherman, Program Administrative Specialist, 301-295-3913, Fax: 301-295-6772, E-mail: elena.sherman@usuhs.mil. Web site: http://www.usuhs.mil/graded.

Uniformed Services University of the Health Sciences, School of Medicine, Graduate Programs in the Biomedical Sciences and Public Health, Department of Preventive Medicine and Biometrics, Program in Healthcare Administration and Policy, Bethesda, MD 20814-4799. Offers MS. *Unit head:* Dr. Glen Diehl, Director, 301-295-9769, E-mail: glen.diehl@usuhs.edu. *Application contact:* Elena Marina Sherman, Program Administrative Specialist, 301-295-3913, Fax: 301-295-6772, E-mail: elena.sherman@usuhs.mil.

Union Graduate College, Center for Bioethics and Clinical Leadership, Schenectady, NY 12308-3107. Offers bioethics (MS); clinical ethics (AC); clinical leadership in health management (MS); health, policy and law (AC). Part-time and evening/weekend programs available. Postbaccalaureate distance learning degree programs offered (minimal on-campus study). *Faculty:* 2 full-time (0 women), 10 part-time/adjunct (7 women). *Students:* 7 full-time (4 women), 92 part-time (52 women); includes 38 minority (6 Black or African American, non-Hispanic/Latino; 26 Asian, non-Hispanic/Latino; 4 Hispanic/Latino; 2 Two or more races, non-Hispanic/Latino), 3 international. Average age 32. 32 applicants, 78% accepted, 21 enrolled. In 2011, 21 master's, 3 other advanced degrees awarded. *Entrance requirements:* For master's, letters of recommendation. Additional exam requirements/recommendations for international students: Required—TOEFL (minimum score 550 paper-based; 213 computer-based). *Application deadline:* Applications are processed on a rolling basis. Application fee: $60. Electronic applications accepted. *Expenses:* Contact institution. *Financial support:* In 2011–12, 10 students received support. Federal Work-Study, scholarships/grants, health care benefits, and tuition waivers (partial) available. Support available to part-time students. Financial award applicants required to submit FAFSA. *Faculty research:* Bioethics education, clinical ethics consultation, research ethics, history of biomedical ethics, international bioethics/research ethics. *Unit head:* Dr. Robert B. Baker, Director, 518-631-9860, Fax: 518-631-9903, E-mail: bakerr@union.edu. *Application contact:* Ann Nolte, Assistant Director, 518-631-9860, Fax: 518-631-9903, E-mail: noltea@uniongraduatecollege.edu.

Union Graduate College, School of Management, Schenectady, NY 12308-3107. Offers business administration (MBA); financial management (Certificate); general management (Certificate); health systems administration (MBA, Certificate); human resources (Certificate). *Accreditation:* AACSB. Part-time and evening/weekend programs available. *Faculty:* 18 full-time (4 women), 25 part-time/adjunct (4 women). *Students:* 122 full-time (53 women), 102 part-time (59 women); includes 47 minority (6 Black or African American, non-Hispanic/Latino; 35 Asian, non-Hispanic/Latino; 4 Hispanic/Latino; 2 Two or more races, non-Hispanic/Latino), 5 international. Average age 27. 101 applicants, 75% accepted, 68 enrolled. In 2011, 73 master's, 9 other advanced degrees awarded. *Degree requirements:* For master's, internship, capstone course. *Entrance requirements:* For master's, GMAT, GRE, minimum GPA of 3.0, 3 letters of recommendation. Additional exam requirements/recommendations for international students: Required—TOEFL (minimum score 550 paper-based; 213 computer-based). *Application deadline:* Applications are processed on a rolling basis. Application fee: $60. *Expenses: Tuition:* Full-time $22,000; part-time $775 per credit. One-time fee: $410 full-time. Tuition and fees vary according to course load and program. *Financial support:* In 2011–12, 79 students received support. Research assistantships, career-related internships or fieldwork, Federal Work-Study, scholarships/grants, health care benefits, and tuition waivers (partial) available. Support available to part-time students. Financial award applicants required to submit FAFSA. *Unit head:* Bela Musits, Dean, 518-631-9890, Fax: 518-631-9902, E-mail: musitsb@uniongraduatecollege.edu. *Application contact:* Diane Trzaskos, Admissions Coordinator, 518-631-9837, Fax: 518-631-9901, E-mail: trzaskod@uniongraduatecollege.edu. Web site: http://www.uniongraduatecollege.edu.

Universidad de Ciencias Medicas, Graduate Programs, San Jose, Costa Rica. Offers dermatology (SP); family health (MS); health service center administration (MHA); human anatomy (MS); medical and surgery (MD); occupational medicine (MS); pharmacy (Pharm D). Part-time programs available. *Degree requirements:* For master's, thesis; for doctorate and SP, comprehensive exam. *Entrance requirements:* For master's, MD or bachelor's degree; for doctorate, admissions test; for SP, admissions test, MD.

Universidad de Iberoamerica, Graduate School, San Jose, Costa Rica. Offers clinical neuropsychology (PhD); clinical psychology (M Psych); educational psychology (M Psych); forensic psychology (M Psych); hospital management (MHA); intensive care nursing (MN); medicine (MD).

Université de Montréal, Faculty of Medicine, Department of Health Administration, Montréal, QC H3C 3J7, Canada. Offers M Sc, DESS. *Accreditation:* CAHME. *Degree requirements:* For master's, thesis. *Entrance requirements:* For master's, proficiency in French. Electronic applications accepted.

University at Albany, State University of New York, School of Public Health, Department of Health Policy, Management, and Behavior, Albany, NY 12222-0001. Offers MS. *Degree requirements:* For master's, thesis. *Entrance requirements:* For master's, GRE General Test. Additional exam requirements/recommendations for international students: Required—TOEFL (minimum score 550 paper-based; 213 computer-based). Electronic applications accepted.

University at Buffalo, the State University of New York, Graduate School, School of Nursing, Buffalo, NY 14214. Offers adult clinical nurse specialist (DNP); adult nurse practitioner (DNP); family nurse practitioner (DNP); health care systems and leadership (MS); nurse anesthetist (DNP); nursing (PhD); nursing education (Certificate); post-master's track (DNP); psychiatric mental health nurse practitioner (DNP). *Accreditation:* AACN; AANA/CANAEP (one or more programs are accredited). Part-time programs available. Postbaccalaureate distance learning degree programs offered (minimal on-campus study). *Faculty:* 29 full-time (25 women), 18 part-time/adjunct (17 women).

Students: 101 full-time (76 women), 100 part-time (90 women); includes 19 minority (10 Black or African American, non-Hispanic/Latino; 2 American Indian or Alaska Native, non-Hispanic/Latino; 2 Asian, non-Hispanic/Latino; 2 Hispanic/Latino; 3 Native Hawaiian or other Pacific Islander, non-Hispanic/Latino), 34 international. Average age 34. 342 applicants, 26% accepted, 67 enrolled. In 2011, 51 master's, 3 doctorates awarded. *Median time to degree:* Of those who began their doctoral program in fall 2003, 75% received their degree in 8 years or less. *Degree requirements:* For master's, thesis optional, comprehensive exams or project; for doctorate, comprehensive exam (for some programs), capstone (for DNP), dissertation (for PhD). *Entrance requirements:* For doctorate, GRE or MAT, minimum GPA of 3.0 (3.25 for PhD), RN license, BS or MS in nursing, 3 references, writing sample; for Certificate, interview, minimum GPA of 3.0 or GRE General Test, RN license, MS in nursing. Additional exam requirements/recommendations for international students: Required—TOEFL (minimum score 550 paper-based; 213 computer-based; 79 iBT), IELTS (minimum score 6.5). *Application deadline:* For fall admission, 8/15 for domestic students, 4/1 for international students; for spring admission, 12/15 for domestic students, 10/1 for international students. Application fee: $75. Electronic applications accepted. *Financial support:* In 2011–12, 80 students received support, including 6 fellowships with full tuition reimbursements available (averaging $17,000 per year), 3 research assistantships with full tuition reimbursements available (averaging $10,600 per year), 5 teaching assistantships with full tuition reimbursements available (averaging $10,600 per year); scholarships/grants, traineeships, health care benefits, and unspecified assistantships also available. Financial award application deadline: 3/15; financial award applicants required to submit FAFSA. *Faculty research:* Oncology, palliative care, gerontology, addictions, mental health, community wellness. *Total annual research expenditures:* $1.3 million. *Unit head:* Dr. Marsha L. Lewis, Dean and Professor, 716-829-2533, Fax: 716-829-2566, E-mail: ubnursingdean@buffalo.edu. *Application contact:* Dr. David J. Lang, Director of Student Affairs, 716-829-2537, Fax: 716-829-2067, E-mail: nursing@buffalo.edu. Web site: http://nursing.buffalo.edu/.

The University of Akron, Graduate School, College of Business Administration, Department of Management, Program in Health Services Administration, Akron, OH 44325. Offers MSM. *Students:* 2 full-time (0 women), 10 part-time (4 women), 3 international. Average age 30. 12 applicants, 50% accepted, 3 enrolled. In 2011, 12 master's awarded. *Entrance requirements:* For master's, GMAT, minimum GPA of 2.75, two letters of recommendation, statement of purpose, resume. Additional exam requirements/recommendations for international students: Required—TOEFL (minimum score 550 paper-based; 213 computer-based; 79 iBT). *Application deadline:* For fall admission, 7/15 for domestic and international students; for spring admission, 11/15 for domestic and international students. Electronic applications accepted. *Expenses:* Tuition, state resident: full-time $7038; part-time $391 per credit hour. Tuition, nonresident: full-time $12,051; part-time $670 per credit hour. *Required fees:* $1274; $34 per credit hour. *Unit head:* Dr. Steve Ash, Interim Chair, 330-972-6429, E-mail: ash@uakron.edu. *Application contact:* Dr. Susan Hanlon, Director of Graduate Business Programs, 330-972-7043, Fax: 330-972-6588, E-mail: shanlon@uakron.edu.

The University of Alabama at Birmingham, School of Health Professions, Program in Administration/Health Services, Birmingham, AL 35294. Offers D Sc, PhD. *Degree requirements:* For doctorate, thesis/dissertation. *Entrance requirements:* For doctorate, GMAT or GRE General Test. *Expenses:* Tuition, state resident: full-time $5922; part-time $309 per hour. Tuition, nonresident: full-time $13,428; part-time $726 per hour. Tuition and fees vary according to program. *Financial support:* In 2011–12, 4 fellowships, 6 research assistantships, 1 teaching assistantship were awarded; career-related internships or fieldwork, institutionally sponsored loans, and unspecified assistantships also available. Financial award application deadline: 4/15. *Faculty research:* Healthcare strategic management, marketing, and organization studies. *Unit head:* Dr. Gerald Glandon, Co-Director, 205-934-5665, Fax: 205-975-6608. *Application contact:* Julie Bryant.

The University of Alabama at Birmingham, School of Health Professions, Program in Health Administration, Birmingham, AL 35294. Offers MSHA. *Accreditation:* CAHME. *Degree requirements:* For master's, administrative residency. *Entrance requirements:* For master's, GMAT, GRE General Test, minimum GPA of 3.0 in final 60 hours of undergraduate course work. *Application deadline:* Applications are processed on a rolling basis. Electronic applications accepted. *Expenses:* Tuition, state resident: full-time $5922; part-time $309 per hour. Tuition, nonresident: full-time $13,428; part-time $726 per hour. Tuition and fees vary according to program. *Financial support:* Career-related internships or fieldwork, Federal Work-Study, scholarships/grants, and traineeships available. Financial award application deadline: 5/1. *Unit head:* Dr. Gerald Glandon, Director, 205-934-5665. *Application contact:* Julie Bryant, Director of Graduate Admissions, 205-934-8227, Fax: 205-934-8413, E-mail: jbryant@uab.edu. Web site: http://www.uab.edu/hsa/msha.

The University of Alabama in Huntsville, School of Graduate Studies, College of Nursing, Huntsville, AL 35899. Offers family nurse practitioner (Certificate); nursing (MSN, DNP), including acute care nurse practitioner (MSN), adult clinical nursing specialist (MSN), clinical nurse leader (MSN), family nurse practitioner (MSN), leadership in health care systems (MSN); nursing education (Certificate). DNP offered jointly with The University of Alabama at Birmingham. *Accreditation:* AACN. Part-time and evening/weekend programs available. Postbaccalaureate distance learning degree programs offered (minimal on-campus study). *Faculty:* 19 full-time (18 women), 8 part-time/adjunct (7 women). *Students:* 57 full-time (43 women), 162 part-time (139 women); includes 22 minority (15 Black or African American, non-Hispanic/Latino; 3 American Indian or Alaska Native, non-Hispanic/Latino; 1 Asian, non-Hispanic/Latino; 3 Hispanic/Latino), 2 international. Average age 37. 193 applicants, 79% accepted, 112 enrolled. In 2011, 42 master's, 11 doctorates, 11 other advanced degrees awarded. *Degree requirements:* For master's, comprehensive exam, thesis or alternative, oral and written exams. *Entrance requirements:* For master's, MAT or GRE, Alabama RN license, BSN, minimum GPA of 3.0; for doctorate, master's degree in nursing in an advanced practice area; for Certificate, MAT or GRE, minimum GPA of 3.0. Additional exam requirements/recommendations for international students: Required—TOEFL (minimum score 500 paper-based; 173 computer-based; 62 iBT). *Application deadline:* For fall admission, 7/15 for domestic students, 4/1 for international students; for spring admission, 11/30 for domestic students, 9/1 for international students. Applications are processed on a rolling basis. Application fee: $40 ($50 for international students). Electronic applications accepted. *Expenses:* Tuition, state resident: full-time $7830; part-time $473.50 per credit. Tuition, nonresident: full-time $18,748; part-time $1128.33 per credit. Tuition and fees vary according to course load and program. *Financial support:* In 2011–12, 9 students received support, including 9 teaching assistantships with full tuition reimbursements available (averaging $9,596 per year); career-related internships or fieldwork, Federal Work-Study, institutionally sponsored loans, scholarships/grants, traineeships, health care benefits, and unspecified assistantships also available. Support available to part-time students. Financial award application deadline: 4/1; financial award applicants required to submit FAFSA. *Faculty research:* Home health care, gerontology, pediatric nursing, family nurse practitioner, adult acute care administration. *Total annual research expenditures:* $235,384. *Unit head:* Dr. Fay Raines, Dean, 256-824-6345, Fax: 256-824-6026, E-mail: rainesc@uah.edu. *Application contact:* Charles Davis, Director of Graduate Nursing Admissions and Advising, 256-824-2433, Fax: 256-824-6026, E-mail: charles.davis@uah.edu. Web site: http://www.uah.edu/nursing/welcome.

University of Alberta, School of Public Health, Department of Public Health Sciences, Edmonton, AB T6G 2E1, Canada. Offers clinical epidemiology (M Sc, MPH); environmental and occupational health (MPH); environmental health sciences (M Sc); epidemiology (M Sc); global health (M Sc, MPH); health policy and management (MPH); health policy research (M Sc); health technology assessment (MPH); occupational health (M Sc); population health (M Sc); public health leadership (MPH); public health sciences (PhD); quantitative methods (MPH). *Accreditation:* CEPH (one or more programs are accredited). Terminal master's awarded for partial completion of doctoral program. *Degree requirements:* For master's, thesis (for some programs); for doctorate, thesis/dissertation. *Entrance requirements:* For master's, GMAT or GRE General Test. Additional exam requirements/recommendations for international students: Required—TOEFL (minimum score 550 paper-based; 213 computer-based) or IELTS (minimum score 6). Electronic applications accepted. *Faculty research:* Biostatistics, health promotion and socio-behavioral health science.

University of Atlanta, Graduate Programs, Atlanta, GA 30360. Offers business (MS); business administration (Exec MBA, MBA); computer science (MS); educational leadership (MS, Ed D); healthcare administration (MS, D Sc, Graduate Certificate); information technology for management (Graduate Certificate); international project management (Graduate Certificate); law (JD); managerial science (DBA); project management (Graduate Certificate); social science (MS). Postbaccalaureate distance learning degree programs offered. *Entrance requirements:* For master's, minimum cumulative GPA of 2.5.

University of Baltimore, Graduate School, The Yale Gordon College of Liberal Arts, Program in Health Systems Management, Baltimore, MD 21201-5779. Offers MS. Part-time and evening/weekend programs available. *Entrance requirements:* For master's, minimum undergraduate GPA of 3.0. Additional exam requirements/recommendations for international students: Required—TOEFL (minimum score 550 paper-based; 213 computer-based).

The University of British Columbia, Faculty of Medicine, School of Population and Public Health, Vancouver, BC V6T 1Z3, Canada. Offers health administration (MHA); health care and epidemiology (MH Sc, PhD); public health (MPH). *Accreditation:* CEPH (one or more programs are accredited). Postbaccalaureate distance learning degree programs offered (minimal on-campus study). *Degree requirements:* For master's, thesis (for some programs), major paper (MH Sc), research project (MHA); for doctorate, thesis/dissertation. *Entrance requirements:* For master's, GRE General Test or GMAT, PCAT, MCAT (MHA), MD or equivalent (for MH Sc); 4-year undergraduate degree from accredited university with minimum B+ overall academic average and in math or statistics course at undergraduate level (for MPH); 4-year undergraduate degree from accredited university with minimum B+ overall academic average plus work experience (for MHA); for doctorate, master's degree from accredited university with minimum B+ overall academic average and in math or statistics course at undergraduate level. Additional exam requirements/recommendations for international students: Required—TOEFL. Electronic applications accepted. *Faculty research:* Population and public health, clinical epidemiology, epidemiology and biostatistics, global health and vulnerable populations, health care services and systems, occupational and environmental health, public health emerging threats and rapid response, social and life course determinants of health, health administration.

University of California, Berkeley, Graduate Division, School of Public Health, Group in Health Services and Policy Analysis, Berkeley, CA 94720-1500. Offers PhD. *Degree requirements:* For doctorate, thesis/dissertation, qualifying exam. *Entrance requirements:* For doctorate, GRE General Test, minimum GPA of 3.0, 3 letters of recommendation.

University of California, Irvine, The Paul Merage School of Business, Health Care Executive MBA Program, Irvine, CA 92697. Offers MBA. *Students:* 33 full-time (10 women), 29 part-time (16 women); includes 19 minority (1 Black or African American, non-Hispanic/Latino; 10 Asian, non-Hispanic/Latino; 8 Hispanic/Latino), 1 international. Average age 41. 48 applicants, 81% accepted, 27 enrolled. In 2011, 35 master's awarded. Application fee: $80 ($100 for international students). *Unit head:* Anthony Hansford, Assistant Dean, 949-824-3801, E-mail: hansfora@uci.edu. *Application contact:* Sofia Trinidad Dang, Associate Director, Student Affairs, 949-824-5374, Fax: 949-824-0522, E-mail: sofia.dang@uci.edu. Web site: http://merage.uci.edu/HealthCareExecutiveMBA/Default.aspx.

University of California, Los Angeles, Graduate Division, School of Public Health, Department of Health Services, Los Angeles, CA 90095. Offers MPH, MS, Dr PH, PhD, JD/MPH, MBA/MPH, MD/MPH. *Degree requirements:* For master's, comprehensive exam or thesis; for doctorate, thesis/dissertation, oral and written qualifying exams. *Entrance requirements:* For master's, GRE General Test, minimum GPA of 3.0; for doctorate, GRE General Test, minimum undergraduate GPA of 3.0. Electronic applications accepted.

University of California, San Diego, Office of Graduate Studies, Program in Health Law, La Jolla, CA 92093. Offers MAS. Program offered jointly with School of Medicine and California Western School of Law. Part-time programs available. *Degree requirements:* For master's, capstone project. *Entrance requirements:* For master's, undergraduate degree in healthcare, law, or related field; 3 years work experience; 3 letters of recommendation; resume.

University of California, San Diego, School of Medicine, Program in Leadership in Healthcare Organizations, La Jolla, CA 92093. Offers MAS.

University of Central Florida, College of Health and Public Affairs, Department of Health Management and Informatics, Orlando, FL 32816. Offers health care informatics (MS, Certificate); health sciences (MS). *Accreditation:* CAHME. Part-time and evening/weekend programs available. *Faculty:* 17 full-time (8 women), 25 part-time/adjunct (18 women). *Students:* 146 full-time (100 women), 248 part-time (178 women); includes 175 minority (90 Black or African American, non-Hispanic/Latino; 1 American Indian or Alaska Native, non-Hispanic/Latino; 32 Asian, non-Hispanic/Latino; 47 Hispanic/Latino; 5 Two or more races, non-Hispanic/Latino), 9 international. Average age 29. 288 applicants, 81% accepted, 138 enrolled. In 2011, 44 master's, 2 other advanced degrees awarded. *Degree requirements:* For master's, comprehensive exam, thesis or alternative, research report. *Entrance requirements:* For master's, GRE General Test. Additional exam requirements/recommendations for international students: Required—TOEFL. *Application deadline:* For fall admission, 7/15 for domestic students; for spring admission, 10/1 for domestic students. Application fee: $30. Electronic applications accepted. *Expenses:* Tuition, state resident: part-time $277.08 per credit hour. Tuition, nonresident: part-time $277.08 per credit hour. Part-time tuition and fees vary according to degree level and program. *Financial support:* In 2011–12, 4 students received support, including 1 fellowship with partial tuition reimbursement available (averaging $10,000 per year), 3 research assistantships (averaging $4,600 per year), 1 teaching assistantship (averaging $6,700 per year); career-related internships or fieldwork, Federal Work-Study, institutionally sponsored loans, and unspecified assistantships also available. Financial award application deadline: 3/1; financial award applicants required to submit FAFSA. *Unit head:* Dr. Dawn Oetjen, Interim Chair, 407-823-3729, E-mail:

dawn.oetjen@ucf.edu. *Application contact:* Barbara Rodriguez, Director, Admissions and Registration, 407-823-2766, Fax: 407-823-6442, E-mail: gradadmissions@ucf.edu. Web site: http://www.cohpa.ucf.edu/hmi/.

University of Chicago, Booth School of Business, Full-Time MBA Program, Chicago, IL 60637. Offers accounting (MBA); analytic finance (MBA); analytic management (MBA); business administration (PhD); econometrics and statistics (MBA); economics (MBA); entrepreneurship (MBA); finance (MBA); general management (MBA); health administration and policy (Certificate); human resource management (MBA); international business (IMBA, MBA); managerial and organizational behavior (MBA); marketing management (MBA); operations management (MBA); strategic management (MBA); MBA/AM; MBA/JD; MBA/MA; MBA/MD; MBA/MPP. *Accreditation:* AACSB. Part-time and evening/weekend programs available. *Faculty:* 166 full-time, 32 part-time/adjunct. *Students:* 1,160 full-time (412 women); includes 316 minority (61 Black or African American, non-Hispanic/Latino; 173 Asian, non-Hispanic/Latino; 63 Hispanic/Latino; 19 Two or more races, non-Hispanic/Latino), 372 international. Average age 28. 4,169 applicants, 575 enrolled. In 2011, 1,423 master's, 19 doctorates awarded. Terminal master's awarded for partial completion of doctoral program. *Entrance requirements:* For master's, GMAT, 2 letters of recommendation, 3 essays, resume, interview. Additional exam requirements/recommendations for international students: Required—TOEFL (minimum score 600 paper-based; 250 computer-based; 104 iBT), IELTS. *Application deadline:* For fall admission, 10/12 priority date for domestic students, 10/12 for international students; for winter admission, 1/4 for domestic and international students; for spring admission, 4/4 for domestic and international students. Application fee: $200. Electronic applications accepted. *Expenses:* Contact institution. *Financial support:* Fellowships available. Financial award applicants required to submit FAFSA. *Faculty research:* Finance, marketing, economics, entrepreneurship, strategy, management. *Unit head:* Stacey Kole, Deputy Dean, 773-702-7121. *Application contact:* Kurt Ahlm, Associate Dean of Student Recruitment and Admissions, 773-702-7369, Fax: 773-702-9085, E-mail: admissions@chicagobooth.edu. Web site: http://chicagobooth.edu/.

University of Colorado Denver, Business School, Master of Business Administration Program, Denver, CO 80217. Offers business intelligence (MBA); business strategy (MBA); business to business marketing (MBA); business to consumer marketing (MBA); change management (MBA); corporate financial management (MBA); enterprise technology management (MBA); entrepreneurship (MBA); health administration (MBA), including financial management, health administration, health information technologies, international health management and policy; human resources management (MBA); investment management (MBA); managing for sustainability (MBA); services management (MBA); sports and entertainment management (MBA). *Accreditation:* AACSB. Part-time and evening/weekend programs available. Postbaccalaureate distance learning degree programs offered (no on-campus study). *Students:* 784 full-time (306 women), 203 part-time (81 women); includes 135 minority (18 Black or African American, non-Hispanic/Latino; 5 American Indian or Alaska Native, non-Hispanic/Latino; 50 Asian, non-Hispanic/Latino; 58 Hispanic/Latino; 4 Two or more races, non-Hispanic/Latino), 38 international. Average age 31. 433 applicants, 76% accepted, 212 enrolled. In 2011, 326 master's awarded. *Degree requirements:* For master's, 48 semester hours, including 30 of core courses, 3 in international business, and 15 in electives from over 50 other graduate business courses. *Entrance requirements:* For master's, GMAT, resume, official transcripts, essay, two letters of recommendation, financial statements (for international applicants). Additional exam requirements/recommendations for international students: Required—TOEFL (minimum score 560 paper-based; 197 computer-based; 83 iBT). *Application deadline:* For fall admission, 4/15 priority date for domestic students, 3/15 for international students; for spring admission, 10/15 priority date for domestic students, 10/1 for international students. Applications are processed on a rolling basis. Application fee: $50 ($75 for international students). Electronic applications accepted. *Expenses:* Contact institution. *Financial support:* Scholarships/grants available. Support available to part-time students. Financial award application deadline: 4/1; financial award applicants required to submit FAFSA. *Faculty research:* Marketing, management, entrepreneurship, finance, health administration. *Unit head:* Elizabeth Cooperman, Professor of Finance and Managing for Sustainability/MBA Program Director, 303-315-8422, E-mail: elizabeth.cooperman@ucdenver.edu. *Application contact:* Shelly Townley, Admissions Director, Graduate Programs, 303-315-8202, E-mail: shelly.townley@ucdenver.edu. Web site: http://www.ucdenver.edu/academics/colleges/business/degrees/ms/accounting/Pages/Accounting.aspx.

University of Colorado Denver, Business School, Program in Health Administration, Denver, CO 80217. Offers MS. *Accreditation:* CAHME. Part-time and evening/weekend programs available. *Students:* 4 full-time (1 woman). Average age 35. 9 applicants, 22% accepted, 1 enrolled. In 2011, 5 master's awarded. *Degree requirements:* For master's, 30 credit hours. *Entrance requirements:* For master's, GMAT, resume, essay, two letters of reference, financial statements (for international applicants). Additional exam requirements/recommendations for international students: Required—TOEFL (minimum score 525 paper-based; 197 computer-based; 71 iBT). *Application deadline:* For fall admission, 4/15 priority date for domestic students, 3/15 for international students; for spring admission, 10/15 priority date for domestic students, 10/1 for international students. Applications are processed on a rolling basis. Application fee: $50 ($75 for international students). Electronic applications accepted. *Expenses:* Contact institution. *Financial support:* Federal Work-Study and scholarships/grants available. Support available to part-time students. Financial award application deadline: 4/1; financial award applicants required to submit FAFSA. *Faculty research:* Cost containment, financial management, governance, rural health-care delivery systems. *Unit head:* Dr. Blair Gifford, Associate Professor/Director of MS in Health Administration, 303-315-8400, E-mail: blair.gifford@ucdenver.edu. *Application contact:* Shelly Townley, Admissions Director, Graduate Programs, 303-315-8202, E-mail: shelly.townley@ucdenver.edu. Web site: http://www.ucdenver.edu/academics/colleges/business/degrees/ms/health-admin/Pages/Health-Administration.aspx.

University of Colorado Denver, Business School, Program in Information Systems, Denver, CO 80217. Offers accounting and information systems audit and control (PhD); business intelligence (MS); enterprise technology management (MS); geographic information systems (MS); health information technology management (MS); web and mobile computing (MS). Part-time and evening/weekend programs available. Postbaccalaureate distance learning degree programs offered (no on-campus study). *Students:* 53 full-time (17 women), 34 part-time (5 women); includes 13 minority (1 Black or African American, non-Hispanic/Latino; 9 Asian, non-Hispanic/Latino; 3 Hispanic/Latino), 11 international. Average age 34. 36 applicants, 61% accepted, 12 enrolled. In 2011, 16 master's awarded. *Degree requirements:* For master's, 30 credit hours. *Entrance requirements:* For master's, GMAT, resume, essay, two letters of recommendation, financial statements (for international applicants). Additional exam requirements/recommendations for international students: Required—TOEFL (minimum score 525 paper-based; 197 computer-based; 71 iBT). *Application deadline:* For fall admission, 4/15 priority date for domestic students, 3/15 for international students; for spring admission, 10/15 priority date for domestic students, 10/1 for international students. Applications are processed on a rolling basis. Application fee: $50 ($75 for international students). Electronic applications accepted. *Expenses:* Contact institution. *Financial support:* Federal Work-Study and scholarships/grants available. Support available to part-time students. Financial award application deadline: 4/1; financial award applicants required to submit FAFSA. *Faculty research:* Human-computer interaction, expert systems, database management, electronic commerce, object-oriented software development. *Unit head:* Dr. Jahangir Karimi, Director of Information Systems Programs, 303-315-8430, E-mail: jahangir.karimi@ucdenver.edu. *Application contact:* Shelly Townley, Admissions Director, Graduate Programs, 303-315-8202, E-mail: shelly.townley@ucdenver.edu. Web site: http://ucdenver.edu/academics/colleges/business/degrees/ms/IS/Pages/Information-Systems.aspx.

University of Colorado Denver, Colorado School of Public Health, Program in Public Health, Aurora, CO 80045. Offers community and behavioral health (MPH, Dr PH); environmental and occupational health (MPH); epidemiology (MPH); health systems, management and policy (MPH). *Accreditation:* CEPH. Part-time and evening/weekend programs available. *Students:* 216 full-time (177 women), 47 part-time (38 women); includes 48 minority (10 Black or African American, non-Hispanic/Latino; 5 American Indian or Alaska Native, non-Hispanic/Latino; 14 Asian, non-Hispanic/Latino; 17 Hispanic/Latino; 1 Native Hawaiian or other Pacific Islander, non-Hispanic/Latino; 1 Two or more races, non-Hispanic/Latino), 7 international. Average age 33. 670 applicants, 51% accepted, 160 enrolled. In 2011, 83 degrees awarded. *Degree requirements:* For master's, thesis or alternative, 42 credit hours; for doctorate, comprehensive exam, thesis/dissertation, 67 credit hours. *Entrance requirements:* For master's, GRE, baccalaureate degree or equivalent; minimum GPA of 3.0; transcripts; references; resume; essay; for doctorate, GRE, MPH or master's or higher degree in related field or equivalent; 2 years previous work experience in public health, essay, resume. Additional exam requirements/recommendations for international students: Required—TOEFL (minimum score 550 paper-based; 213 computer-based). *Application deadline:* For fall admission, 2/1 for domestic students. Application fee: $65. Electronic applications accepted. *Expenses:* Contact institution. *Financial support:* Fellowships, research assistantships, Federal Work-Study, scholarships/grants, and unspecified assistantships available. Support available to part-time students. Financial award application deadline: 3/15; financial award applicants required to submit FAFSA. *Faculty research:* Cancer prevention by nutrition, cancer survivorship outcomes, social and cultural factors related to health. *Unit head:* Dr. Jack Barnette, Program Director, 303-724-4472, E-mail: jack.barnette@ucdenver.edu. *Application contact:* Jennifer Pacheco, Admissions Specialist, 303-724-5585, E-mail: jennifer.pacheco@ucdenver.edu. Web site: http://www.ucdenver.edu/academics/colleges/PublicHealth/departments/CommunityBehavioralHealth/Pages/CommunityBehavioralHealth.aspx.

University of Connecticut, Graduate School, School of Business, Storrs, CT 06269. Offers accounting (MS, PhD); business administration (Exec MBA, MBA, PhD); finance (PhD); health care management and insurance studies (MBA); management (PhD); management consulting (MBA); marketing (PhD); marketing intelligence (MBA); MA/MBA; MBA/MSW. *Accreditation:* AACSB. *Degree requirements:* For master's, comprehensive exam; for doctorate, thesis/dissertation. *Entrance requirements:* For master's and doctorate, GMAT. Additional exam requirements/recommendations for international students: Required—TOEFL (minimum score 550 paper-based; 213 computer-based). Electronic applications accepted.

University of Dallas, Graduate School of Management, Irving, TX 75062-4736. Offers accounting (MBA, MM, MS); business management (MBA, MM); corporate finance (MBA, MM); financial services (MBA); global business (MBA, MM); health services management (MBA, MM); human resource management (MBA, MM); information assurance (MBA, MM, MS); information technology (MBA, MM, MS); information technology service management (MBA, MM, MS); marketing management (MBA, MM); organization development (MBA, MM); project management (MBA, MM); sports and entertainment management (MBA, MM); strategic leadership (MBA, MM); supply chain management (MBA); supply chain management and market logistics (MM). *Accreditation:* ACBSP. Part-time and evening/weekend programs available. Postbaccalaureate distance learning degree programs offered (no on-campus study). *Entrance requirements:* Additional exam requirements/recommendations for international students: Required—TOEFL. Electronic applications accepted. *Expenses:* Contact institution.

University of Denver, University College, Denver, CO 80208. Offers arts and culture (MLS, Certificate), including art, literature, and culture, arts development and program management (Certificate), creative writing; environmental policy and management (MAS, Certificate), including energy and sustainability (Certificate), environmental assessment of nuclear power (Certificate), environmental health and safety (Certificate), environmental management, natural resource management (Certificate); geographic information systems (MAS, Certificate); global affairs (MLS, Certificate), including translation studies, world history and culture; healthcare leadership (MPH, Certificate), including healthcare policy, law, and ethics, medical and healthcare information technologies, strategic management of healthcare; information and communications technology (MCIS, Certificate), including database design and administration (Certificate), geographic information systems (MCIS), information security systems security (Certificate), information systems security (MCIS), project management (MCIS, MPS, Certificate), software design and administration (Certificate), software design and programming (MCIS), technology management, telecommunications technology (MCIS), Web design and development; leadership and organizations (MPS, Certificate), including human capital in organizations, philanthropic leadership, project management (MCIS, MPS, Certificate), strategic innovation and change; organizational and professional communication (MPS, Certificate), including alternative dispute resolution, organizational communication, organizational development and training, public relations and marketing; security management (MAS, Certificate), including emergency planning and response, information security (MAS), organizational security; strategic human resource management (MPS, Certificate), including global human resources (MPS), human resource management and development (MPS). Part-time and evening/weekend programs available. Postbaccalaureate distance learning degree programs offered (no on-campus study). *Faculty:* 204 part-time/adjunct (80 women). *Students:* 56 full-time (26 women), 1,096 part-time (647 women); includes 196 minority (81 Black or African American, non-Hispanic/Latino; 7 American Indian or Alaska Native, non-Hispanic/Latino; 30 Asian, non-Hispanic/Latino; 66 Hispanic/Latino; 3 Native Hawaiian or other Pacific Islander, non-Hispanic/Latino; 9 Two or more races, non-Hispanic/Latino), 76 international. Average age 36. 572 applicants, 95% accepted, 410 enrolled. In 2011, 404 master's, 123 other advanced degrees awarded. *Degree requirements:* For master's, capstone project. *Entrance requirements:* For master's, two letters of recommendation, personal statement, resume. Additional exam requirements/recommendations for international students: Required—TOEFL (minimum score 550 paper-based; 80 iBT). *Application deadline:* For fall admission, 7/20 priority date for domestic students, 6/8 for international students; for winter admission, 10/26 priority date for domestic students, 9/14 for international students; for spring admission, 2/1 priority date for domestic students, 12/14 for international students. Applications are processed on a rolling basis. Application fee: $75. Electronic applications accepted. *Expenses:* Contact institution. *Financial support:* Applicants required to submit FAFSA. *Unit head:* Dr. James Davis, Dean, 303-871-2291, Fax: 303-871-4047, E-mail: jdavis@du.edu. *Application contact:* Information Contact, 303-871-3155, Fax: 303-871-4047, E-mail: ucolinfo@du.edu. Web site: http://www.universitycollege.du.edu/.

University of Detroit Mercy, College of Health Professions, Program in Health Services Administration, Detroit, MI 48221. Offers MHSA. *Degree requirements:* For master's, thesis. *Entrance requirements:* For master's, GRE General Test, minimum GPA of 3.0. *Faculty research:* Health systems issues, organizational theory.

University of Detroit Mercy, College of Health Professions, Program in Health Systems Management, Detroit, MI 48221. Offers MSN.

University of Evansville, College of Education and Health Sciences, Department of Nursing and Health Sciences, Evansville, IN 47722. Offers health services administration (MS). Part-time and evening/weekend programs available. *Entrance requirements:* For master's, GRE or GMAT, 2 letters of reference, interview. Additional exam requirements/recommendations for international students: Required—TOEFL (minimum score 530 paper-based; 71 iBT), IELTS (minimum score 6.5). *Expenses:* Contact institution. *Faculty research:* International health systems, health care ethics, health care marketing.

The University of Findlay, Graduate and Professional Studies, College of Business, Findlay, OH 45840-3653. Offers health care management (MBA); hospitality management (MBA); organizational leadership (MBA); public management (MBA). Part-time and evening/weekend programs available. Postbaccalaureate distance learning degree programs offered (no on-campus study). *Faculty:* 18 full-time (5 women), 1 part-time/adjunct (0 women). *Students:* 25 full-time (15 women), 184 part-time (100 women); includes 13 minority (3 Black or African American, non-Hispanic/Latino; 7 Asian, non-Hispanic/Latino; 3 Hispanic/Latino), 78 international. Average age 25. 72 applicants, 82% accepted, 24 enrolled. In 2011, 168 master's awarded. *Degree requirements:* For master's, thesis, cumulative project. *Entrance requirements:* For master's, GMAT or GRE, bachelor's degree from accredited institution, minimum undergraduate GPA of 3.0. Additional exam requirements/recommendations for international students: Required—TOEFL (minimum score 550 paper-based; 213 computer-based; 80 iBT). *Application deadline:* Applications are processed on a rolling basis. Application fee: $25. Electronic applications accepted. *Expenses:* Contact institution. *Financial support:* In 2011–12, 5 research assistantships with full and partial tuition reimbursements (averaging $4,200 per year) were awarded; career-related internships or fieldwork, Federal Work-Study, health care benefits, and unspecified assistantships also available. Financial award application deadline: 4/1; financial award applicants required to submit FAFSA. *Faculty research:* Health care management, operations and logistics management. *Unit head:* Dr. Paul Sears, Dean, 419-434-4704, Fax: 419-434-4822. *Application contact:* Heather Riffle, Assistant Director, Graduate and Professional Studies, 419-434-4640, Fax: 419-434-5517, E-mail: riffle@findlay.edu. Web site: http://www.findlay.edu/.

University of Florida, Graduate School, College of Pharmacy and Graduate School, Graduate Programs in Pharmacy, Department of Pharmaceutical Outcomes and Policy, Gainesville, FL 32611. Offers MSP, PhD. Part-time programs available. Postbaccalaureate distance learning degree programs offered (minimal on-campus study). *Faculty:* 11 full-time (6 women). *Students:* 29 full-time (20 women), 142 part-time (84 women); includes 59 minority (26 Black or African American, non-Hispanic/Latino; 3 American Indian or Alaska Native, non-Hispanic/Latino; 22 Asian, non-Hispanic/Latino; 8 Hispanic/Latino), 14 international. Average age 37. 171 applicants, 42% accepted, 57 enrolled. In 2011, 72 master's, 3 doctorates awarded. *Degree requirements:* For doctorate, thesis/dissertation. *Entrance requirements:* For master's and doctorate, GRE General Test (minimum score of 1000), minimum GPA of 3.0. Additional exam requirements/recommendations for international students: Required—TOEFL (minimum score 550 paper-based; 213 computer-based; 80 iBT), IELTS (minimum score 6). *Application deadline:* For fall admission, 1/15 priority date for domestic students. Applications are processed on a rolling basis. Application fee: $30. Electronic applications accepted. *Financial support:* In 2011–12, 12 students received support, including 2 fellowships, 4 research assistantships, 6 teaching assistantships; tuition waivers (full) also available. Financial award applicants required to submit FAFSA. *Faculty research:* Pharmaceutical care, drug use systems, drug-related morbidity. *Unit head:* Dr. Richard Segal, Chair, 352-273-6268, Fax: 352-273-6270, E-mail: segal@cop.health.ufl.edu. *Application contact:* Dr. Carole Kimberlin, Graduate Coordinator, 352-273-6263, Fax: 352-273-6270, E-mail: kimber@cop.ufl.edu. Web site: http://www.cop.ufl.edu/education/graduate-programs/pharmaceutical-outcomes-and-policy/.

University of Florida, Graduate School, College of Public Health and Health Professions, Department of Health Services Research, Management and Policy, Gainesville, FL 32611. Offers health services research (PhD). *Accreditation:* CAHME. Part-time programs available. *Students:* 59 full-time (29 women), 2 part-time (0 women); includes 18 minority (9 Black or African American, non-Hispanic/Latino; 3 Asian, non-Hispanic/Latino; 6 Hispanic/Latino), 5 international. Average age 29. 17 applicants, 18% accepted, 1 enrolled. In 2011, 2 doctorates awarded. *Entrance requirements:* For doctorate, GRE General Test, minimum GPA of 3.0. Additional exam requirements/recommendations for international students: Required—TOEFL (minimum score 550 paper-based; 213 computer-based; 80 iBT), IELTS (minimum score 6). *Application deadline:* Applications are processed on a rolling basis. Application fee: $30. Electronic applications accepted. *Financial support:* Fellowships, research assistantships, teaching assistantships, career-related internships or fieldwork, and unspecified assistantships available. Financial award applicants required to submit FAFSA. *Faculty research:* Hospital profitability, indigent care, rural health care systems, AIDS education, managed care, outcomes. *Unit head:* Dr. R. Paul Duncan, Department Chair, 352-273-6065, Fax: 352-273-6075, E-mail: pduncan@phhp.ufl.edu. *Application contact:* Barbara Ross, Student Services Coordinator, 352-273-6074, Fax: 352-273-6075, E-mail: bross@phhp.ufl.edu. Web site: http://www.phhp.ufl.edu/hsrmp/.

University of Florida, Graduate School, Warrington College of Business Administration, Hough Graduate School of Business, Department of Management, Gainesville, FL 32611. Offers geriatric care management (MSM); health care risk management (MSM); international business (MAIB); management (MSM, PhD). *Accreditation:* AACSB. Postbaccalaureate distance learning degree programs offered. *Faculty:* 11 full-time (2 women). *Students:* 235 full-time (122 women), 75 part-time (44 women); includes 79 minority (18 Black or African American, non-Hispanic/Latino; 13 Asian, non-Hispanic/Latino; 48 Hispanic/Latino), 60 international. Average age 25. 58 applicants, 78% accepted, 40 enrolled. In 2011, 239 master's, 2 doctorates awarded. *Degree requirements:* For master's, comprehensive exam, thesis; for doctorate, comprehensive exam, thesis/dissertation. *Entrance requirements:* For master's and doctorate, GMAT or GRE General Test, minimum GPA of 3.0. Additional exam requirements/recommendations for international students: Required—TOEFL (minimum score 550 paper-based; 213 computer-based; 80 iBT), IELTS (minimum score 6). *Application deadline:* For fall admission, 1/1 for domestic and international students. Applications are processed on a rolling basis. Application fee: $30. Electronic applications accepted. *Financial support:* Fellowships, research assistantships, teaching assistantships, and unspecified assistantships available. Financial award applicants required to submit FAFSA. *Faculty research:* Job attitudes, personality and individual differences, organizational entry and exit, knowledge management, competitive dynamics. *Unit head:* Dr. Robert E. Thomas, Chair, 352-392-0136, Fax: 352-392-6020, E-mail: rethomas@ufl.edu. *Application contact:* Dr. Jason A. Colquitt, Graduate Coordinator, 352-846-0507, Fax: 352-392-6020, E-mail: colquitt@ufl.edu. Web site: http://www.cba.ufl.edu/mang/.

University of Florida, Graduate School, Warrington College of Business Administration, Hough Graduate School of Business, Programs in Business Administration, Gainesville, FL 32611. Offers accounting (MBA); arts administration (MBA); business strategy and public policy (MBA); competitive strategy (MBA); decision and information sciences (MBA); electronic commerce (MBA); finance (MBA); general business (MBA); global management (MBA); Graham-Buffett security analysis (MBA); health administration (MBA); human resources management (MBA); international studies (MBA); Latin American business (MBA); management (MBA); marketing (MBA); sports administration (MBA); JD/MBA; MBA/MS; MBA/PhD; MBA/Pharm D; MD/MBA. *Accreditation:* AACSB. Part-time and evening/weekend programs available. *Faculty:* 71 full-time (10 women). *Students:* 412 full-time (111 women), 467 part-time (135 women); includes 235 minority (39 Black or African American, non-Hispanic/Latino; 7 American Indian or Alaska Native, non-Hispanic/Latino; 79 Asian, non-Hispanic/Latino; 109 Hispanic/Latino; 1 Native Hawaiian or other Pacific Islander, non-Hispanic/Latino), 44 international. Average age 32. 589 applicants, 52% accepted, 247 enrolled. In 2011, 505 master's awarded. *Degree requirements:* For master's, capstone course. *Entrance requirements:* For master's, GMAT, minimum GPA of 3.0, interview. Additional exam requirements/recommendations for international students: Required—TOEFL (minimum score 550 paper-based; 213 computer-based; 80 iBT), IELTS (minimum score 6). *Application deadline:* For fall admission, 7/1 for domestic students, 1/1 for international students; for spring admission, 12/1 for domestic and international students. Applications are processed on a rolling basis. Application fee: $30. Electronic applications accepted. *Financial support:* Teaching assistantships, career-related internships or fieldwork, scholarships/grants, and unspecified assistantships available. Support available to part-time students. Financial award applicants required to submit FAFSA. *Faculty research:* Accounting, finance, insurance, management, real estate, urban analysis marketing. *Unit head:* Prof. Alexander D. Sevilla, Assistant Dean/Director, 352-273-3252 Ext. 1206, E-mail: alex.sevilla@warrington.ufl.edu. *Application contact:* Prof. Kelli Gust, Associate Director, 352-273-3255, Fax: 352-392-8791, E-mail: kelly.gust@warrington.ufl.edu. Web site: http://www.floridamba.ufl.edu/.

University of Georgia, College of Public Health, Department of Health Policy and Management, Athens, GA 30602. Offers MPH. *Unit head:* Dr. Joel M. Lee, Dean, 706-542-3709, E-mail: joellee@uga.edu. *Application contact:* Mitchela Salum, Graduate Coordinator, 706-583-0885, E-mail: msalum@uga.edu. Web site: http://www.publichealth.uga.edu/hpam/.

University of Houston–Clear Lake, School of Business, Program in Healthcare Administration, Houston, TX 77058-1098. Offers MHA, MHA/MBA. *Degree requirements:* For master's, thesis optional. *Entrance requirements:* For master's, GMAT. Additional exam requirements/recommendations for international students: Required—TOEFL (minimum score 550 paper-based; 213 computer-based).

University of Illinois at Chicago, Graduate College, School of Public Health, Division of Health Policy and Administration, Chicago, IL 60607-7128. Offers clinical translational science (MS); health policy (PhD); health policy and administration (Dr PH); health services research (PhD); healthcare (MHA); public health policy management (MPH). Part-time programs available. Terminal master's awarded for partial completion of doctoral program. *Degree requirements:* For master's, thesis, field practicum; for doctorate, thesis/dissertation, independent research, internship. *Entrance requirements:* For master's and doctorate, GRE General Test, minimum GPA of 2.75. Additional exam requirements/recommendations for international students: Required—TOEFL. Electronic applications accepted.

The University of Iowa, Graduate College, College of Public Health, Department of Health Management and Policy, Iowa City, IA 52242-1316. Offers MHA, PhD, JD/MHA, MBA/MHA, MHA/MA, MHA/MS. *Accreditation:* CAHME (one or more programs are accredited). *Degree requirements:* For doctorate, comprehensive exam, thesis/dissertation. *Entrance requirements:* For master's, GRE General Test or equivalent, minimum GPA of 3.0; for doctorate, GRE General Test, minimum GPA of 3.0. Additional exam requirements/recommendations for international students: Required—TOEFL (minimum score 550 paper-based; 213 computer-based; 81 iBT). Electronic applications accepted. *Expenses:* Contact institution.

The University of Kansas, University of Kansas Medical Center, School of Medicine, Department of Health Policy and Management, Kansas City, KS 66160. Offers health policy and management (PhD); health services administration (MHSA); JD/MHSA; MBA/MHSA; MD/MHSA; MHSA/MS. *Accreditation:* CAHME. Part-time programs available. *Faculty:* 15. *Students:* 46 full-time (26 women), 23 part-time (17 women); includes 15 minority (3 Black or African American, non-Hispanic/Latino; 1 American Indian or Alaska Native, non-Hispanic/Latino; 6 Asian, non-Hispanic/Latino; 4 Hispanic/Latino; 1 Two or more races, non-Hispanic/Latino). Average age 31. 47 applicants, 62% accepted, 22 enrolled. In 2011, 22 master's awarded. *Degree requirements:* For master's, internship or research practicum; for doctorate, comprehensive exam, thesis/dissertation. *Entrance requirements:* For master's, college-level statistics; for doctorate, GRE, course work in health delivery system, healthcare finance, health behavior/organizations, healthcare economics, healthcare management, health policy, graduate statistics. Additional exam requirements/recommendations for international students: Required—TOEFL (minimum score 570 paper-based; 90 iBT). *Application deadline:* For fall admission, 4/15 for domestic and international students. Applications are processed on a rolling basis. Application fee: $60. Electronic applications accepted. Tuition and fees vary according to course load, campus/location, program and reciprocity agreements. *Financial support:* Career-related internships or fieldwork and departmental scholarships available. Support available to part-time students. Financial award application deadline: 2/14; financial award applicants required to submit FAFSA. *Faculty research:* Economic analysis of long-term care facilities, healthcare workforce supply and demand, the impact of disaster preparedness on individuals with developmental disabilities, policy analysis and readiness for biological outbreaks, gender issues in health roles and functions. *Total annual research expenditures:* $40,006. *Unit head:* Dr. Glendon G. Cox, Chair, 913-588-0357, Fax: 913-588-8236, E-mail: gcox@kumc.edu. *Application contact:* Deborah S. Lewis, Student Support Manager, 913-588-3763, Fax: 913-588-8236, E-mail: dlewis4@kumc.edu. Web site: http://www.kumc.edu/hpm/.

University of Kentucky, Graduate School, Program in Health Administration, Lexington, KY 40506-0032. Offers MHA. *Accreditation:* CAHME. *Degree requirements:* For master's, comprehensive exam. *Entrance requirements:* For master's, GRE General Test, minimum undergraduate GPA of 2.75. Additional exam requirements/recommendations for international students: Required—TOEFL (minimum score 550 paper-based; 213 computer-based). Electronic applications accepted. *Faculty research:* Health economy, health finance, health policy.

University of La Verne, College of Business and Public Management, Graduate Programs in Business Administration, La Verne, CA 91750-4443. Offers accounting (MBA); executive management (MBA-EP); finance (MBA, MBA-EP); health services management (MBA); information technology (MBA, MBA-EP); international business (MBA, MBA-EP); leadership (MBA-EP); managed care (MBA); management (MBA, MBA-EP); marketing (MBA, MBA-EP). Part-time and evening/weekend programs

available. *Faculty:* 34 full-time (15 women), 38 part-time/adjunct (13 women). *Students:* 525 full-time (243 women), 231 part-time (114 women); includes 199 minority (27 Black or African American, non-Hispanic/Latino; 1 American Indian or Alaska Native, non-Hispanic/Latino; 55 Asian, non-Hispanic/Latino; 113 Hispanic/Latino; 3 Two or more races, non-Hispanic/Latino), 436 international. Average age 28. In 2011, 403 master's awarded. *Entrance requirements:* For master's, minimum undergraduate GPA of 3.0, 2 letters of recommendation, resume. Additional exam requirements/recommendations for international students: Required—TOEFL (minimum score 550 paper-based; 213 computer-based). *Application deadline:* Applications are processed on a rolling basis. Application fee: $50. *Expenses:* Contact institution. *Financial support:* Career-related internships or fieldwork, institutionally sponsored loans, and scholarships/grants available. Financial award application deadline: 3/2; financial award applicants required to submit FAFSA. *Unit head:* Dr. Abe Helou, Chairperson, 909-593-3511 Ext. 4211, Fax: 909-392-2704, E-mail: ihelou@laverne.edu. *Application contact:* Rina Lazarian, Program and Admission Specialist, 909-593-3511 Ext. 4819, Fax: 909-392-2704, E-mail: cbpm@ulv.edu.

University of La Verne, College of Business and Public Management, Program in Gerontology, La Verne, CA 91750-4443. Offers gerontology (Certificate); gerontology administration (MS). Part-time programs available. *Faculty:* 34 full-time (15 women), 38 part-time/adjunct (13 women). *Students:* 15 full-time (11 women), 14 part-time (12 women); includes 22 minority (7 Black or African American, non-Hispanic/Latino; 1 Asian, non-Hispanic/Latino; 13 Hispanic/Latino; 1 Two or more races, non-Hispanic/Latino), 3 international. Average age 39. In 2011, 13 master's awarded. *Entrance requirements:* For master's, minimum GPA of 2.5. Additional exam requirements/recommendations for international students: Required—TOEFL (minimum score 550 paper-based; 213 computer-based). *Application deadline:* Applications are processed on a rolling basis. Application fee: $50. *Expenses:* Contact institution. *Financial support:* Institutionally sponsored loans available. Financial award application deadline: 3/2; financial award applicants required to submit FAFSA. *Unit head:* Terrell Ford, Program Director, 909-593-3511 Ext. 4796, E-mail: tford@laverne.edu. *Application contact:* Barbara Cox, Program and Admissions Specialist, 909-593-3511 Ext. 4004, Fax: 909-392-2761, E-mail: bcox@laverne.edu. Web site: http://laverne.edu/business-and-public-administration/healthadmin-gerontology/.

University of La Verne, College of Business and Public Management, Program in Health Administration, La Verne, CA 91750-4443. Offers financial management (MHA); health administration (MHA); human resources (MHA); information management (MHA); leadership and management (MHA); managed care (MHA); marketing and business development (MHA). Part-time programs available. *Faculty:* 34 full-time (15 women), 28 part-time/adjunct (13 women). *Students:* 55 full-time (37 women), 35 part-time (27 women); includes 52 minority (15 Black or African American, non-Hispanic/Latino; 9 Asian, non-Hispanic/Latino; 27 Hispanic/Latino; 1 Native Hawaiian or other Pacific Islander, non-Hispanic/Latino), 13 international. Average age 32. In 2011, 16 master's awarded. *Entrance requirements:* For master's, minimum undergraduate GPA of 2.5, 3 letters of reference, curriculum vitae or resume, writing sample. Additional exam requirements/recommendations for international students: Required—TOEFL (minimum score 550 paper-based; 213 computer-based). *Application deadline:* Applications are processed on a rolling basis. Application fee: $50. *Expenses:* Contact institution. *Financial support:* Application deadline: 3/2; applicants required to submit FAFSA. *Unit head:* Terrell Ford, Program Director, 909-593-3511 Ext. 4796, E-mail: tford@laverne.edu. *Application contact:* Barbara Cox, Program and Admissions Specialist, 909-593-3511 Ext. 4004, Fax: 909-392-2761, E-mail: bcox@laverne.edu. Web site: http://laverne.edu/catalog/program/mha-master-of-health-administration/.

University of La Verne, Regional Campus Administration, Graduate Programs, Central Coast/Vandenberg Air Force Base Campuses, La Verne, CA 91750-4443. Offers business (MBA-EP), including health services management, information technology; health administration (MHA); leadership and management (MS). *Entrance requirements:* For master's, 2 letters of recommendation, resume. *Expenses:* Contact institution.

University of La Verne, Regional Campus Administration, Graduate Programs, Inland Empire Campus, Rancho Cucamonga, CA 91730. Offers business (MBA-EP), including health services management, information technology, management, marketing; leadership and management (MS). *Entrance requirements:* For master's, 2 letters of recommendation, resume. *Expenses:* Contact institution.

University of La Verne, Regional Campus Administration, Graduate Programs, Kern County Campus, Bakersfield, CA 93301. Offers business (MBA-EP); health administration (MHA); leadership and management (MS). *Entrance requirements:* For master's, 2 letters of recommendation, resume. *Expenses:* Contact institution.

University of La Verne, Regional Campus Administration, Graduate Programs, Orange County Campus, Garden Grove, CA 92840. Offers business (MBA); health administration (MHA); leadership and management (MS). *Entrance requirements:* For master's, 2 letters of recommendation, resume. *Expenses:* Contact institution.

University of Louisville, Graduate School, College of Business, MBA Programs, Louisville, KY 40292-0001. Offers entrepreneurship (MBA); global business (MBA); health sector management (weekend format) (MBA). *Accreditation:* AACSB. Part-time and evening/weekend programs available. *Faculty:* 28 full-time (8 women), 3 part-time/adjunct (1 woman). *Students:* 111 full-time (35 women), 112 part-time (33 women); includes 19 minority (4 Black or African American, non-Hispanic/Latino; 1 American Indian or Alaska Native, non-Hispanic/Latino; 7 Asian, non-Hispanic/Latino; 3 Hispanic/Latino; 4 Two or more races, non-Hispanic/Latino), 12 international. Average age 29. 223 applicants, 53% accepted, 94 enrolled. In 2011, 119 degrees awarded. *Degree requirements:* For master's, international learning experience. *Entrance requirements:* For master's, GMAT, 2 letters of reference, personal interview, resume, personal statement, college transcript(s). Additional exam requirements/recommendations for international students: Required—TOEFL (minimum score 83 iBT). *Application deadline:* For fall admission, 7/1 for domestic students; for spring admission, 12/1 for domestic students. Applications are processed on a rolling basis. Application fee: $50. *Expenses:* Tuition, state resident: full-time $9692; part-time $539 per credit hour. Tuition, nonresident: full-time $20,168; part-time $1121 per credit hour. Tuition and fees vary according to program and reciprocity agreements. *Financial support:* In 2011–12, 16 students received support, including 3 fellowships with full tuition reimbursements available (averaging $15,500 per year), 10 research assistantships with full tuition reimbursements available (averaging $12,000 per year); health care benefits and unspecified assistantships also available. Financial award application deadline: 3/31; financial award applicants required to submit FAFSA. *Faculty research:* Entrepreneurship, venture capital, retailing/franchising, corporate governance and leadership, supply chain management. *Unit head:* Dr. R. Charles Moyer, Dean, 502-852-6443, Fax: 502-852-7557, E-mail: charlie.moyer@louisville.edu. *Application contact:* L. Eddie Smith, Director of IT and Master's Programs Admissions/Recruiting Manager, 502-852-7257, Fax: 502-852-4901, E-mail: eddie.smith@louisville.edu. Web site: http://business.louisville.edu/mba.

University of Louisville, Graduate School, School of Public Health and Information Sciences, Department of Health Management and Systems Sciences, Louisville, KY 40202. Offers public health sciences - health management (PhD). Part-time programs available. *Degree requirements:* For doctorate, comprehensive exam, thesis/dissertation. *Entrance requirements:* For doctorate, GRE, official transcripts, statement of purpose, resume/curriculum vitae, letters of recommendation. Additional exam requirements/recommendations for international students: Required—TOEFL (minimum score 600 paper-based; 250 computer-based; 100 iBT). Electronic applications accepted. *Expenses:* Tuition, state resident: full-time $9692; part-time $539 per credit hour. Tuition, nonresident: full-time $20,168; part-time $1121 per credit hour. Tuition and fees vary according to program and reciprocity agreements. *Faculty research:* Health information, health care administration, health policy, quality of life.

University of Mary, Gary Tharaldson School of Business, Bismarck, ND 58504-9652. Offers accountancy (MBA); business administration (MBA); health care (MBA); human resource management (MBA); management (MBA); project management (MPM); strategic leadership (MSSL). Part-time and evening/weekend programs available. *Faculty:* 8 full-time (5 women), 66 part-time/adjunct (22 women). *Students:* 340 full-time (190 women), 189 part-time (91 women); includes 69 minority (28 Black or African American, non-Hispanic/Latino; 25 American Indian or Alaska Native, non-Hispanic/Latino; 7 Asian, non-Hispanic/Latino; 7 Hispanic/Latino; 1 Native Hawaiian or other Pacific Islander, non-Hispanic/Latino; 1 Two or more races, non-Hispanic/Latino), 14 international. Average age 35. 207 applicants, 95% accepted, 148 enrolled. In 2011, 265 master's awarded. *Degree requirements:* For master's, strategic planning seminar. *Entrance requirements:* For master's, minimum GPA of 2.5. Additional exam requirements/recommendations for international students: Required—TOEFL (minimum score 500 paper-based; 197 computer-based; 71 iBT). *Application deadline:* Applications are processed on a rolling basis. Application fee: $40. *Financial support:* Application deadline: 8/1; applicants required to submit FAFSA. *Unit head:* Dr. Shanda Traiser, Director of the School of Accelerated and Distance Education, 701-355-8160, Fax: 701-255-7687, E-mail: straiser@umary.edu. *Application contact:* Wayne G. Maruska, Graduate Program Advisor, 701-355-8134, Fax: 701-255-7687, E-mail: wmaruska@umary.edu.

University of Maryland, Baltimore County, Graduate School, College of Arts, Humanities and Social Sciences, Department of Emergency Health Services, Baltimore, MD 21250. Offers administration, planning, and policy (MS); education (MS); emergency health services (MS); emergency management (Postbaccalaureate Certificate); preventive medicine and epidemiology (MS). Part-time and evening/weekend programs available. Postbaccalaureate distance learning degree programs offered (no on-campus study). *Faculty:* 2 full-time (0 women), 7 part-time/adjunct (1 woman). *Students:* 20 full-time (8 women), 21 part-time (10 women); includes 2 minority (both Black or African American, non-Hispanic/Latino), 6 international. Average age 32. 13 applicants, 85% accepted, 10 enrolled. In 2011, 13 master's awarded. *Degree requirements:* For master's, comprehensive exam, thesis (for some programs). *Entrance requirements:* For master's, GRE General Test, minimum GPA of 3.0. Additional exam requirements/recommendations for international students: Required—TOEFL (minimum score 85 iBT). *Application deadline:* For fall admission, 7/1 for domestic students, 4/1 for international students. Applications are processed on a rolling basis. Application fee: $45. Electronic applications accepted. *Financial support:* In 2011–12, 2 students received support, including 1 fellowship with tuition reimbursement available (averaging $70,000 per year), 1 research assistantship with tuition reimbursement available (averaging $21,000 per year); career-related internships or fieldwork, Federal Work-Study, health care benefits, and unspecified assistantships also available. Financial award application deadline: 5/30; financial award applicants required to submit FAFSA. *Faculty research:* EMS management, disaster health services, emergency management. *Total annual research expenditures:* $50,000. *Unit head:* Dr. Bruce Walz, Chairman, 410-455-3223. *Application contact:* Dr. Rick Bissell, Program Director, 410-455-3776, Fax: 410-455-3045, E-mail: bissell@umbc.edu. Web site: http://ehs.umbc.edu/.

University of Maryland, Baltimore County, Graduate School, College of Arts, Humanities and Social Sciences, Department of Public Policy, Program in Public Policy, Baltimore, MD 21250. Offers economics (PhD); educational policy (MPP, PhD); evaluation and analytical methods (MPP, PhD); health policy (MPP, PhD); policy history (PhD); public management (MPP, PhD); urban policy (MPP, PhD). Part-time and evening/weekend programs available. *Faculty:* 10 full-time (2 women), 2 part-time/adjunct (0 women). *Students:* 61 full-time (30 women), 88 part-time (45 women); includes 26 minority (14 Black or African American, non-Hispanic/Latino; 5 Asian, non-Hispanic/Latino; 3 Hispanic/Latino; 1 Native Hawaiian or other Pacific Islander, non-Hispanic/Latino; 3 Two or more races, non-Hispanic/Latino), 14 international. Average age 36. 101 applicants, 60% accepted, 22 enrolled. In 2011, 10 master's, 8 doctorates awarded. Terminal master's awarded for partial completion of doctoral program. *Degree requirements:* For master's, thesis optional, public analysis paper, internship for pre-service; for doctorate, thesis/dissertation, comprehensive and field qualifying exams. *Entrance requirements:* For master's, GRE General Test, 3 academic letters of reference, transcripts, resume; for doctorate, GRE General Test, 3 academic letters of reference, transcripts, resume, research paper. Additional exam requirements/recommendations for international students: Required—TOEFL (minimum score 550 paper-based; 213 computer-based; 80 iBT). *Application deadline:* For fall admission, 1/15 priority date for domestic students, 1/1 for international students; for spring admission, 11/1 priority date for domestic students, 5/1 for international students. Applications are processed on a rolling basis. Application fee: $50. Electronic applications accepted. *Financial support:* In 2011–12, 26 students received support, including 6 fellowships with full tuition reimbursements available (averaging $17,400 per year), 23 research assistantships with full tuition reimbursements available (averaging $17,400 per year), 1 teaching assistantship with full tuition reimbursement available (averaging $17,400 per year); career-related internships or fieldwork, Federal Work-Study, scholarships/grants, health care benefits, and unspecified assistantships also available. Support available to part-time students. Financial award application deadline: 1/15; financial award applicants required to submit FAFSA. *Faculty research:* Health policy, education policy, urban policy, public management, evaluation and analytical methods. *Unit head:* Dr. Donald Norris, Chair, 410-455-1455, E-mail: norris@umbc.edu. *Application contact:* Sally F. Helms, Administrator of Academic Affairs, 410-455-3202, Fax: 410-455-1172, E-mail: gradposi@umbc.edu. Web site: http://www.umbc.edu/pubpol.

University of Maryland, Baltimore County, Graduate School, Erickson School of Aging Studies, Baltimore, MD 21228. Offers management of aging services (MA). *Faculty:* 3 full-time (0 women), 5 part-time/adjunct (1 woman). *Students:* 19 full-time (12 women); includes 4 minority (2 Black or African American, non-Hispanic/Latino; 1 Asian, non-Hispanic/Latino; 1 Two or more races, non-Hispanic/Latino). Average age 39. In 2011, 30 master's awarded. *Degree requirements:* For master's, thesis or alternative. *Entrance requirements:* For master's, essays. *Application deadline:* Applications are processed on a rolling basis. Application fee: $50. Electronic applications accepted. *Expenses:* Contact institution. *Financial support:* In 2011–12, 8 students received support, including 1 teaching assistantship with tuition reimbursement available (averaging $21,600 per year). Financial award applicants required to submit FAFSA. *Faculty research:* Policy implications of entitlement programs, demographic impact of aging population, person-centered care for dementia, changing culture in long-term care. *Unit head:* Dr. Joseph Gribbin, Graduate Program Director, 443-543-5603, E-mail:

gribbin@umbc.edu. *Application contact:* Megan Risavi, Administrative Assistant, 443-543-5633, E-mail: meganr2@umbc.edu. Web site: http://www.umbc.edu/erickson/.

University of Maryland, College Park, Academic Affairs, School of Public Health, Department of Health Services Administration, College Park, MD 20742. Offers MHA, PhD. *Faculty:* 18 full-time (10 women), 6 part-time/adjunct (3 women). *Students:* 15 full-time (11 women), 8 part-time (7 women); includes 10 minority (7 Black or African American, non-Hispanic/Latino; 2 Asian, non-Hispanic/Latino; 1 Hispanic/Latino), 5 international. 70 applicants, 34% accepted, 7 enrolled. In 2011, 3 master's awarded. *Application deadline:* For fall admission, 1/15 for domestic and international students; for spring admission, 6/1 for international students. Application fee: $75. *Expenses:* Tuition, state resident: part-time $525 per credit hour. Tuition, nonresident: part-time $1131 per credit hour. *Required fees:* $386.31 per term. Tuition and fees vary according to program. *Financial support:* In 2011–12, 2 fellowships with partial tuition reimbursements (averaging $10,000 per year), 7 teaching assistantships with tuition reimbursements (averaging $15,902 per year) were awarded; research assistantships also available. *Total annual research expenditures:* $1.5 million. *Unit head:* Dr. Laura Wilson, Chair, 301-405-2469, E-mail: lwilson@umd.edu. *Application contact:* Dr. Charles A. Caramello, Dean of Graduate School, 301-405-0358, Fax: 301-314-9305.

University of Maryland University College, Graduate School of Management and Technology, Program in Health Care Administration, Adelphi, MD 20783. Offers MS, Certificate. Part-time and evening/weekend programs available. Postbaccalaureate distance learning degree programs offered (no on-campus study). *Students:* 11 full-time (9 women), 486 part-time (379 women); includes 318 minority (245 Black or African American, non-Hispanic/Latino; 3 American Indian or Alaska Native, non-Hispanic/Latino; 26 Asian, non-Hispanic/Latino; 35 Hispanic/Latino; 1 Native Hawaiian or other Pacific Islander, non-Hispanic/Latino; 8 Two or more races, non-Hispanic/Latino), 6 international. Average age 36. 155 applicants, 100% accepted, 83 enrolled. In 2011, 126 degrees awarded. *Degree requirements:* For master's, thesis or alternative. *Application deadline:* Applications are processed on a rolling basis. Application fee: $50. Electronic applications accepted. *Financial support:* Federal Work-Study and scholarships/grants available. Support available to part-time students. Financial award application deadline: 6/1; financial award applicants required to submit FAFSA. *Unit head:* Dr. Diane Bartoo, Head, 240-684-2400, Fax: 240-684-2401, E-mail: dbartoo@umuc.edu. *Application contact:* Coordinator, Graduate Admissions, 800-888-8682, Fax: 240-684-2151, E-mail: newgrad@umuc.edu. Web site: http://www.umuc.edu/grad/hcad/hcad_home.shtml.

University of Massachusetts Amherst, Graduate School, School of Public Health and Health Sciences, Department of Public Health, Amherst, MA 01003. Offers biostatistics (MPH, MS, PhD); community health education (MPH, MS, PhD); environmental health sciences (MPH, MS, PhD); epidemiology (MPH, MS, PhD); health policy and management (MPH, MS, PhD); nutrition (MPH, PhD); public health practice (MPH); MPH/MPPA. *Accreditation:* CEPH (one or more programs are accredited). Part-time and evening/weekend programs available. Postbaccalaureate distance learning degree programs offered (no on-campus study). *Faculty:* 46 full-time (26 women). *Students:* 118 full-time (88 women), 249 part-time (183 women); includes 75 minority (28 Black or African American, non-Hispanic/Latino; 21 Asian, non-Hispanic/Latino; 20 Hispanic/Latino; 6 Two or more races, non-Hispanic/Latino), 55 international. Average age 36. 377 applicants, 67% accepted, 91 enrolled. In 2011, 83 master's, 4 doctorates awarded. Terminal master's awarded for partial completion of doctoral program. *Degree requirements:* For master's, thesis (for some programs); for doctorate, comprehensive exam, thesis/dissertation. *Entrance requirements:* For master's and doctorate, GRE General Test. Additional exam requirements/recommendations for international students: Required—TOEFL (minimum score 550 paper-based; 213 computer-based; 80 iBT), IELTS (minimum score 6.5). *Application deadline:* For fall admission, 2/1 for domestic and international students. Applications are processed on a rolling basis. Application fee: $40 ($65 for international students). Electronic applications accepted. Tuition and fees vary according to course load, campus/location and program. *Financial support:* Fellowships with full and partial tuition reimbursements, research assistantships with full and partial tuition reimbursements, teaching assistantships with full and partial tuition reimbursements, career-related internships or fieldwork, Federal Work-Study, scholarships/grants, traineeships, health care benefits, tuition waivers (full and partial), and unspecified assistantships available. Support available to part-time students. Financial award application deadline: 2/1. *Unit head:* Dr. Paula Stamps, Graduate Program Director, 413-545-2861, Fax: 413-545-1645. *Application contact:* Lindsay DeSantis, Interim Supervisor of Admissions, 413-545-0722, Fax: 413-577-0010, E-mail: gradadm@grad.umass.edu. Web site: http://www.umass.edu/sphhs/public_health/.

University of Massachusetts Boston, Office of Graduate Studies, John W. McCormack Graduate School of Policy Studies, Program in Gerontology, Boston, MA 02125-3393. Offers gerontology (MS, PhD, Certificate); gerontology research (MA); management in aging services (MA). Part-time programs available. *Degree requirements:* For doctorate, comprehensive exam, thesis/dissertation. *Entrance requirements:* For doctorate, GRE General Test, minimum GPA of 3.0. *Faculty research:* Aging with a chronic disability, pension policy and social security system, elderly minorities, health services research, living arrangements.

University of Massachusetts Lowell, School of Health and Environment, Department of Community Health and Sustainability, Lowell, MA 01854-2881. Offers health management and policy (MS, Graduate Certificate). Part-time programs available. *Degree requirements:* For master's, thesis optional. *Entrance requirements:* For master's, GRE General Test. *Faculty research:* Alzheimer's disease, total quality management systems, information systems, market analysis.

University of Medicine and Dentistry of New Jersey, School of Health Related Professions, Department of Interdisciplinary Studies, Program in Health Care Management, Newark, NJ 07107-1709. Offers MS. Part-time and evening/weekend programs available. Postbaccalaureate distance learning degree programs offered (no on-campus study). *Faculty:* 1 (woman) part-time/adjunct. *Students:* 18 part-time (11 women); includes 10 minority (5 Black or African American, non-Hispanic/Latino; 4 Asian, non-Hispanic/Latino; 1 Hispanic/Latino). Average age 40. 11 applicants, 91% accepted, 5 enrolled. In 2011, 6 degrees awarded. *Entrance requirements:* For master's, minimum GPA of 3.0, bachelor's degree, statement of career goals, curriculum vitae, transcript of highest degree. Additional exam requirements/recommendations for international students: Required—TOEFL (minimum score 500 paper-based; 79 iBT). *Application deadline:* For fall admission, 6/15 for domestic students, 3/1 for international students; for winter admission, 4/15 for domestic students; for spring admission, 10/15 for domestic students, 7/1 for international students. Applications are processed on a rolling basis. Application fee: $75. Electronic applications accepted. *Unit head:* Dr. Ann W. Tucker, Chairperson, 856-566-6434, Fax: 856-566-6458, E-mail: tuckeraw@umdnj.edu. *Application contact:* Diane Hanrahan, Assistant Dean, 973-972-7336, Fax: 973-972-7463, E-mail: shrpadm@umdnj.edu.

University of Medicine and Dentistry of New Jersey, UMDNJ–School of Public Health (UMDNJ, Rutgers, NJIT) Newark Campus, Newark, NJ 07107-1709. Offers clinical epidemiology (Certificate); dental public health (MPH); general public health (Certificate); public policy and oral health services administration (Certificate); quantitative methods (MPH); urban health (MPH); DMD/MPH; MD/MPH; MS/MPH. *Accreditation:* CEPH. Part-time and evening/weekend programs available. *Degree requirements:* For master's, thesis, internship. *Entrance requirements:* For master's, GRE General Test. Additional exam requirements/recommendations for international students: Required—TOEFL. Electronic applications accepted.

University of Medicine and Dentistry of New Jersey, UMDNJ–School of Public Health (UMDNJ, Rutgers, NJIT) Piscataway/New Brunswick Campus, Piscataway, NJ 08854. Offers biostatistics (MPH, MS, Dr PH, PhD); clinical epidemiology (Certificate); environmental and occupational health (MPH, Dr PH, PhD, Certificate); epidemiology (MPH, Dr PH, PhD); general public health (Certificate); health education and behavioral science (MPH, Dr PH, PhD); health systems and policy (MPH, PhD); public health preparedness (Certificate); DO/MPH; JD/MPH; MD/MPH; MPH/MBA; MPH/MSPA; MS/MPH; Psy D/MPH. *Accreditation:* CEPH. Part-time and evening/weekend programs available. *Degree requirements:* For master's, thesis, internship; for doctorate, comprehensive exam, thesis/dissertation. *Entrance requirements:* For master's, GRE General Test; for doctorate, GRE General Test, MPH (Dr PH); MA, MPH, or MS (PhD). Additional exam requirements/recommendations for international students: Required—TOEFL. Electronic applications accepted.

University of Medicine and Dentistry of New Jersey, UMDNJ–School of Public Health (UMDNJ, Rutgers, NJIT) Stratford/Camden Campus, Stratford, NJ 08084. Offers general public health (Certificate); health systems and policy (MPH); DO/MPH. *Accreditation:* CEPH. Part-time and evening/weekend programs available. *Degree requirements:* For master's, thesis, internship. *Entrance requirements:* For master's, GRE General Test. Additional exam requirements/recommendations for international students: Required—TOEFL. Electronic applications accepted.

University of Memphis, Graduate School, School of Public Health, Memphis, TN 38152. Offers biostatistics (MPH); environmental health (MPH); epidemiology (MPH); health systems management (MPH); public health (MHA); social and behavioral sciences (MPH). Part-time and evening/weekend programs available. Postbaccalaureate distance learning degree programs offered. *Degree requirements:* For master's, comprehensive exam, thesis. *Entrance requirements:* For master's, GRE, letters of recommendation. Additional exam requirements/recommendations for international students: Required—TOEFL. Electronic applications accepted. *Faculty research:* Health and medical savings accounts, adoption rates, health informatics, Telehealth technologies, biostatistics, environmental health, epidemiology, health systems management, social and behavioral sciences.

University of Michigan, School of Public Health, Department of Health Management and Policy, Ann Arbor, MI 48109. Offers health management and policy (MHSA, MPH, MS); health services organization and policy (PhD); JD/MHSA; MD/MPH; MHSA/MBA; MHSA/MNA; MHSA/MPP; MHSA/MSIOE; MPH/JD; MPH/MBA; MPH/MPP. PhD and MS offered through the Horace H. Rackham School of Graduate Studies. *Accreditation:* CAHME (one or more programs are accredited). *Degree requirements:* For doctorate, thesis/dissertation, oral defense of dissertation, preliminary exam. *Entrance requirements:* For master's, GMAT, GRE General Test; for doctorate, GRE General Test. Additional exam requirements/recommendations for international students: Required—TOEFL (minimum score 600 paper-based; 250 computer-based; 100 iBT). Electronic applications accepted. *Faculty research:* Health insurance, long-term care and aging, tobacco policy, health information technology, understanding organization.

University of Minnesota, Twin Cities Campus, Carlson School of Management, Carlson Full-Time MBA Program, Minneapolis, MN 55455. Offers finance (MBA); information technology (MBA); management (MBA); marketing (MBA); medical industry orientation (MBA); supply chain and operations (MBA); JD/MBA; MBA/MPP; MD/MBA; MHA/MBA; Pharm D/MBA. *Accreditation:* AACSB. *Faculty:* 58 full-time (17 women), 23 part-time/adjunct (5 women). *Students:* 172 full-time (54 women); includes 16 minority (4 Black or African American, non-Hispanic/Latino; 10 Asian, non-Hispanic/Latino; 2 Two or more races, non-Hispanic/Latino), 41 international. Average age 28. 538 applicants, 41% accepted, 99 enrolled. In 2011, 97 master's awarded. *Entrance requirements:* For master's, GMAT or GRE. Additional exam requirements/recommendations for international students: Required—TOEFL (minimum score 580 paper-based; 240 computer-based; 84 iBT), IELTS (minimum score 7), or Pearson Test of English. *Application deadline:* For fall admission, 4/1 for domestic students, 2/1 for international students. Application fee: $60 ($90 for international students). Electronic applications accepted. *Expenses:* Contact institution. *Financial support:* In 2011–12, 116 students received support, including 116 fellowships with full and partial tuition reimbursements available (averaging $18,702 per year); research assistantships with partial tuition reimbursements available, teaching assistantships with partial tuition reimbursements available, career-related internships or fieldwork, Federal Work-Study, institutionally sponsored loans, scholarships/grants, health care benefits, and unspecified assistantships also available. Financial award application deadline: 4/1; financial award applicants required to submit FAFSA. *Faculty research:* Finance and accounting: financial reporting, asset pricing models and corporate finance; information and decision sciences: on-line auctions, information transparency and recommender systems; marketing: psychological influences on consumer behavior, brand equity, pricing and marketing channels; operations: lean manufacturing, quality management and global supply chains; strategic management and organization: global strategy, networks, entrepreneurship and innovation, sustainability. *Unit head:* Philip J. Miller, Assistant Dean, MBA Programs and Graduate Business Career Center, 612-625-5555, Fax: 612-625-1012, E-mail: mba@umn.edu. *Application contact:* Linh Gilles, Director of Admissions and Recruiting, 612-625-5555, Fax: 612-625-1012, E-mail: ftmba@umn.edu. Web site: http://www.csom.umn.edu/MBA/full-time/.

University of Minnesota, Twin Cities Campus, Graduate School, Program in Health Informatics, Minneapolis, MN 55455-0213. Offers MHI, MS, PhD, MD/MHI. Part-time programs available. *Degree requirements:* For master's, thesis or alternative; for doctorate, thesis/dissertation. *Entrance requirements:* For master's and doctorate, GRE General Test, previous course work in life sciences, programming, calculus. Additional exam requirements/recommendations for international students: Required—TOEFL (minimum score 550 paper-based; 237 computer-based). Electronic applications accepted. *Faculty research:* Medical decision making, physiological control systems, population studies, clinical information systems, telemedicine.

University of Minnesota, Twin Cities Campus, School of Public Health, Major in Health Services Research, Policy, and Administration, Minneapolis, MN 55455-0213. Offers MS, PhD, JD/MS, JD/PhD, MD/PhD, MPP/MS. Part-time programs available. Terminal master's awarded for partial completion of doctoral program. *Degree requirements:* For master's, thesis, internship, final oral exam; for doctorate, thesis/dissertation, teaching experience, written preliminary exam, final oral exam, dissertation. *Entrance requirements:* For master's, GRE General Test, course work in mathematics; for doctorate, GRE General Test, prerequisite courses in calculus and statistics. Additional exam requirements/recommendations for international students: Required—TOEFL (minimum score 600 paper-based; 250 computer-based; 100 iBT). *Faculty research:* Outcomes, economics and statistics, sociology, health care management.

University of Minnesota, Twin Cities Campus, School of Public Health, Major in Public Health Administration and Policy, Minneapolis, MN 55455-0213. Offers MPH, MPH/JD, MPH/MSN. Part-time programs available. *Degree requirements:* For master's,

thesis, field experience. *Entrance requirements:* For master's, GRE General Test. Additional exam requirements/recommendations for international students: Required—TOEFL. Electronic applications accepted. *Faculty research:* Community health service organizations, nursing services, dental services, the elderly, insurance coverage.

University of Minnesota, Twin Cities Campus, School of Public Health, Program in Healthcare Administration, Minneapolis, MN 55455-0213. Offers MHA. *Accreditation:* AACSB; CAHME. Part-time and evening/weekend programs available. Postbaccalaureate distance learning degree programs offered (minimal on-campus study). *Degree requirements:* For master's, thesis, project. *Entrance requirements:* For master's, GMAT or GRE General Test, minimum GPA of 3.0. Additional exam requirements/recommendations for international students: Required—TOEFL (minimum score 600 paper-based; 250 computer-based; 100 iBT). Electronic applications accepted. *Expenses:* Contact institution. *Faculty research:* Managed care, physician payment, structure and performance of healthcare systems, long-term care.

University of Missouri, Graduate School, Department of Health Management and Informatics, Columbia, MO 65211. Offers health administration (MHA); health ethics (Graduate Certificate); health informatics (MS, Graduate Certificate). *Accreditation:* CAHME. Part-time programs available. *Faculty:* 18 full-time (5 women), 2 part-time/adjunct (0 women). *Students:* 89 full-time (38 women), 42 part-time (23 women); includes 25 minority (14 Black or African American, non-Hispanic/Latino; 6 Asian, non-Hispanic/Latino; 3 Hispanic/Latino; 2 Two or more races, non-Hispanic/Latino), 19 international. Average age 31. 72 applicants, 60% accepted, 37 enrolled. In 2011, 54 master's, 3 other advanced degrees awarded. *Entrance requirements:* For master's, GRE General Test or GMAT, minimum GPA of 3.0. Additional exam requirements/recommendations for international students: Required—TOEFL (minimum score 500 paper-based; 173 computer-based; 61 iBT). Application fee: $55 ($75 for international students). *Expenses:* Tuition, state resident: full-time $5881. Tuition, nonresident: full-time $15,183. *Required fees:* $952. Tuition and fees vary according to campus/location and program. *Financial support:* Fellowships, research assistantships, teaching assistantships, and institutionally sponsored loans available. *Faculty research:* GUI aesthetics for physician use, application of informatics tools to day-to-day clinical operations, consumer health informatics, decision support, health literacy and numeracy, information interventions for persons with chronic illnesses, use of simulation in the education of health care professionals, statistical bioinformatics, classification, dimension reduction, ethics and end of life care, telehealth and tele-ethics, research ethics, health literacy, clinical informatics, human factors. *Unit head:* Dr. Robert DeGraaff, Director of Graduate Studies, 573-882-1783, E-mail: degraaffr@missouri.edu. *Application contact:* Adrienne Vogt, 573-884-0698, E-mail: vogtb@health.missouri.edu. Web site: http://www.hmi.missouri.edu/.

University of Missouri, Graduate School, Master of Public Health Program, Columbia, MO 65211. Offers health promotion and policy (MPH); public health (Graduate Certificate); veterinary public health (MPH); DVM/MPH; MPH/MA; MPH/MPA. *Accreditation:* CEPH. *Students:* 86 full-time (61 women), 68 part-time (49 women); includes 36 minority (20 Black or African American, non-Hispanic/Latino; 7 Asian, non-Hispanic/Latino; 4 Hispanic/Latino; 5 Two or more races, non-Hispanic/Latino), 16 international. Average age 29. 99 applicants, 85% accepted, 64 enrolled. In 2011, 44 master's, 34 other advanced degrees awarded. *Entrance requirements:* Additional exam requirements/recommendations for international students: Required—TOEFL (minimum score 550 paper-based; 215 computer-based; 80 iBT). Application fee: $55 ($75 for international students). *Expenses:* Tuition, state resident: full-time $5881. Tuition, nonresident: full-time $15,183. *Required fees:* $952. Tuition and fees vary according to campus/location and program. *Faculty research:* Health professions, health care equality, global health, communicable diseases, public health; zoonosis and infectious diseases, medical education, inquiry-based learning, social determinants of health, violence against women, health disparities, breast cancer screening, epigenetic, nursing, environmental health, cancer and chronic diseases, environmental exposures with metals, geographical information systems, substance use disorders/addictions, mental health. *Unit head:* Dr. Kristofer Hagglund, Associate Dean, 573-884-7050, E-mail: hagglundk@missouri.edu. *Application contact:* Lise Saffran, 573-884-6844, E-mail: saffranl@missouri.edu. Web site: http://publichealth.missouri.edu/.

University of Missouri–St. Louis, College of Arts and Sciences, School of Social Work, St. Louis, MO 63121. Offers gerontology (MS); long term care administration (Certificate); social work (MSW). *Accreditation:* CSWE. *Faculty:* 11 full-time (9 women), 9 part-time/adjunct (7 women). *Students:* 67 full-time (58 women), 65 part-time (60 women); includes 26 minority (22 Black or African American, non-Hispanic/Latino; 2 Asian, non-Hispanic/Latino; 1 Hispanic/Latino; 1 Two or more races, non-Hispanic/Latino), 1 international. Average age 31. 143 applicants, 45% accepted, 45 enrolled. In 2011, 49 degrees awarded. *Entrance requirements:* For master's, 3 letters of recommendation. Additional exam requirements/recommendations for international students: Required—TOEFL (minimum score 550 paper-based; 213 computer-based). *Application deadline:* For fall admission, 2/15 for domestic and international students. Application fee: $35 ($40 for international students). Electronic applications accepted. *Expenses:* Tuition, state resident: full-time $6273; part-time $3866 per year. Tuition, nonresident: full-time $14,969; part-time $9980 per year. *Required fees:* $315 per year. *Financial support:* In 2011–12, 10 teaching assistantships with full and partial tuition reimbursements (averaging $8,000 per year) were awarded. Financial award applicants required to submit FAFSA. *Faculty research:* Family violence, child abuse/neglect, immigration, community economic development. *Unit head:* Dr. Lois Pierce, Graduate Program Director, 314-516-6364, Fax: 314-516-5816, E-mail: socialwork@umsl.edu. *Application contact:* 314-516-5458, Fax: 314-516-6996, E-mail: gradadm@umsl.edu. Web site: http://www.umsl.edu/~socialwk/.

University of Missouri–St. Louis, Graduate School, Program in Public Policy Administration, St. Louis, MO 63121. Offers health policy (MPPA); local government management (MPPA, Certificate); managing human resources and organization (MPPA); nonprofit organization management (MPPA); nonprofit organization management and leadership (Certificate); policy research and analysis (MPPA). *Accreditation:* NASPAA. Part-time and evening/weekend programs available. *Faculty:* 10 full-time (5 women), 9 part-time/adjunct (4 women). *Students:* 33 full-time (17 women), 76 part-time (48 women); includes 30 minority (25 Black or African American, non-Hispanic/Latino; 2 American Indian or Alaska Native, non-Hispanic/Latino; 1 Asian, non-Hispanic/Latino; 2 Hispanic/Latino), 9 international. Average age 32. 68 applicants, 50% accepted, 27 enrolled. In 2011, 23 master's, 22 Certificates awarded. *Entrance requirements:* For master's, 3 letters of recommendation. Additional exam requirements/recommendations for international students: Required—TOEFL (minimum score 550 paper-based; 213 computer-based). *Application deadline:* For fall admission, 7/1 priority date for domestic students, 7/1 for international students; for spring admission, 12/1 priority date for domestic students, 12/1 for international students. Applications are processed on a rolling basis. Application fee: $35 ($40 for international students). Electronic applications accepted. *Expenses:* Tuition, state resident: full-time $6273; part-time $3866 per year. Tuition, nonresident: full-time $14,969; part-time $9980 per year. *Required fees:* $315 per year. *Financial support:* In 2011–12, 2 research assistantships with full and partial tuition reimbursements (averaging $12,000 per year) were awarded; career-related internships or fieldwork also available. Financial award application deadline: 4/1; financial award applicants required to submit FAFSA. *Faculty research:* Urban policy, public finance, evaluation. *Unit head:* Dr. Deborah Balser, Director, 314-516-5145, Fax: 314-516-5210, E-mail: balserd@msx.umsl.edu. *Application contact:* 314-516-5458, Fax: 314-516-6996, E-mail: gradadm@umsl.edu. Web site: http://www.umsl.edu/divisions/graduate/mppa/.

University of Nevada, Las Vegas, Graduate College, School of Community Health Sciences, Department of Health Care Administration, Las Vegas, NV 89154-3023. Offers MHA. *Faculty:* 5 full-time (0 women), 7 part-time/adjunct (2 women). *Students:* 26 full-time (16 women), 32 part-time (24 women); includes 20 minority (8 Black or African American, non-Hispanic/Latino; 4 Asian, non-Hispanic/Latino; 3 Hispanic/Latino; 1 Native Hawaiian or other Pacific Islander, non-Hispanic/Latino; 4 Two or more races, non-Hispanic/Latino), 7 international. Average age 31. 34 applicants, 68% accepted, 14 enrolled. In 2011, 15 master's awarded. *Entrance requirements:* Additional exam requirements/recommendations for international students: Required—TOEFL (minimum score 550 paper-based; 213 computer-based; 80 iBT), IELTS (minimum score 7). *Application deadline:* For fall admission, 4/1 priority date for domestic students, 5/1 for international students; for spring admission, 11/1 priority date for domestic students, 10/1 for international students. Applications are processed on a rolling basis. Application fee: $60 ($95 for international students). Electronic applications accepted. *Financial support:* In 2011–12, 2 students received support, including 2 research assistantships with partial tuition reimbursements available (averaging $7,500 per year); institutionally sponsored loans, scholarships/grants, health care benefits, and unspecified assistantships also available. Financial award application deadline: 3/1. *Faculty research:* Health management and policy; health and health disparities; management of health information technology and systems; patient safety, quality of care, and outcome research; comparative effectiveness research in health care. *Total annual research expenditures:* $1,827. *Unit head:* Dr. Charles Moseley, Chair/Associate Professor, 702-895-4413, Fax: 702-895-5573, E-mail: charles.moseley@unlv.edu. *Application contact:* Graduate College Admissions Evaluator, 702-895-3320, Fax: 702-895-4180, E-mail: gradcollege@unlv.edu. Web site: http://hca.unlv.edu.

University of New Haven, Graduate School, School of Business, Program in Health Care Administration, West Haven, CT 06516-1916. Offers health care management (Certificate); health care marketing (MS); health policy and finance (MS); human resource management in health care (MS); long-term care (MS); long-term health care (Certificate); managed care (MS); medical group management (MS). Part-time and evening/weekend programs available. *Students:* 55 full-time (33 women), 51 part-time (30 women); includes 13 minority (9 Black or African American, non-Hispanic/Latino; 2 Asian, non-Hispanic/Latino; 2 Hispanic/Latino), 51 international. Average age 30. 80 applicants, 99% accepted, 30 enrolled. In 2011, 44 master's, 4 other advanced degrees awarded. *Degree requirements:* For master's, thesis or alternative. *Entrance requirements:* Additional exam requirements/recommendations for international students: Required—TOEFL (minimum score 520 paper-based; 190 computer-based; 70 iBT), IELTS (minimum score 5.5). *Application deadline:* For fall admission, 5/31 for international students; for winter admission, 10/15 for international students; for spring admission, 1/15 for international students. Applications are processed on a rolling basis. Application fee: $50. Electronic applications accepted. *Expenses: Tuition:* Part-time $750 per credit. *Financial support:* Research assistantships with partial tuition reimbursements, teaching assistantships with partial tuition reimbursements, career-related internships or fieldwork, Federal Work-Study, scholarships/grants, tuition waivers, and unspecified assistantships available. Support available to part-time students. Financial award applicants required to submit FAFSA. *Unit head:* Cynthia Conrad, Chairman, 203-932-7486. *Application contact:* Eloise Gormley, Director of Graduate Admissions, 203-932-7449, Fax: 203-932-7137, E-mail: gradinfo@newhaven.edu. Web site: http://www.newhaven.edu/6848/.

University of New Haven, Graduate School, School of Business, Program in Public Administration, West Haven, CT 06516-1916. Offers personnel and labor relations (MPA); public administration (MPA, Certificate), including city management (MPA), community-clinical services (MPA), health care management (MPA), long-term health care (MPA), personnel and labor relations (MPA), public administration (Certificate), public management (Certificate), public personnel management (Certificate); MBA/MPA. Part-time and evening/weekend programs available. *Students:* 50 full-time (21 women), 19 part-time (9 women); includes 17 minority (14 Black or African American, non-Hispanic/Latino; 2 Asian, non-Hispanic/Latino; 1 Hispanic/Latino), 13 international. 23 applicants, 100% accepted, 13 enrolled. In 2011, 23 master's, 14 other advanced degrees awarded. *Degree requirements:* For master's, thesis or alternative. *Entrance requirements:* Additional exam requirements/recommendations for international students: Required—TOEFL (minimum score 520 paper-based; 190 computer-based; 70 iBT); Recommended—IELTS (minimum score 5.5). *Application deadline:* For fall admission, 5/31 for international students; for winter admission, 10/15 for international students; for spring admission, 1/15 for international students. Applications are processed on a rolling basis. Application fee: $50. Electronic applications accepted. *Expenses:* Contact institution. *Financial support:* Research assistantships with partial tuition reimbursements, teaching assistantships with partial tuition reimbursements, career-related internships or fieldwork, Federal Work-Study, scholarships/grants, tuition waivers, and unspecified assistantships available. Support available to part-time students. Financial award application deadline: 5/1; financial award applicants required to submit FAFSA. *Unit head:* Cynthia Conrad, Chair, 203-932-7486. *Application contact:* Eloise Gormley, Director of Graduate Admissions, 203-932-7449, Fax: 203-932-7137, E-mail: gradinfo@newhaven.edu. Web site: http://www.newhaven.edu/6854/.

University of New Orleans, Graduate School, College of Business Administration, Program in Health Care Management, New Orleans, LA 70148. Offers MS. *Degree requirements:* For master's, thesis optional. *Entrance requirements:* For master's, GRE or GMAT. Additional exam requirements/recommendations for international students: Required—TOEFL (minimum score 550 paper-based; 213 computer-based; 79 iBT). Electronic applications accepted.

The University of North Carolina at Chapel Hill, Graduate School, School of Public Health, Department of Health Policy and Management, Chapel Hill, NC 27599-7411. Offers MHA, MPH, MSPH, Dr PH, PhD, DDS/MPH, JD/MPH, MBA/MHA, MBA/MSPH, MD/MPH, MHA/MBA, MHA/MCRP, MHA/MSIS, MHA/MSLS, MSPH/MCRP, MSPH/MSIS, MSPH/MSLS. *Accreditation:* CAHME (one or more programs are accredited). Part-time programs available. Postbaccalaureate distance learning degree programs offered (minimal on-campus study). *Faculty:* 36 full-time, 107 part-time/adjunct. *Students:* 163 full-time (109 women), 163 part-time (101 women); includes 102 minority (36 Black or African American, non-Hispanic/Latino; 3 American Indian or Alaska Native, non-Hispanic/Latino; 35 Asian, non-Hispanic/Latino; 19 Hispanic/Latino; 1 Native Hawaiian or other Pacific Islander, non-Hispanic/Latino; 8 Two or more races, non-Hispanic/Latino), 24 international. In 2011, 116 master's, 15 doctorates awarded. *Median time to degree:* Of those who began their doctoral program in fall 2003, 100% received their degree in 8 years or less. *Degree requirements:* For master's, comprehensive exam, capstone course or paper; for doctorate, comprehensive exam, thesis/dissertation. *Entrance requirements:* For master's and doctorate, GRE General Test, minimum GPA of 3.0. Additional exam requirements/recommendations for international students: Required—TOEFL, IELTS. *Application deadline:* For fall

admission, 1/10 priority date for domestic students, 1/10 for international students. Applications are processed on a rolling basis. Application fee: $78. Electronic applications accepted. *Financial support:* Career-related internships or fieldwork, Federal Work-Study, institutionally sponsored loans, scholarships/grants, traineeships, health care benefits, and unspecified assistantships available. Financial award application deadline: 3/1; financial award applicants required to submit FAFSA. *Faculty research:* Organizational behavior; human resource management in healthcare; health services finance; mental health economics, service, and research; strategic planning and marketing. *Unit head:* Dr. Peggy Leatt, Chair, 919-966-9122, Fax: 919-966-6961, E-mail: leatt@email.unc.edu. *Application contact:* Lynnette Jones, Student Services Manager, 919-966-7391, Fax: 919-843-4980, E-mail: ljones3@email.unc.edu. Web site: http://www.sph.unc.edu/hpaa/.

The University of North Carolina at Charlotte, Graduate School, College of Health and Human Services, Department of Public Health Sciences, Charlotte, NC 28223-0001. Offers community health (Certificate); health administration (MHA); health services research (PhD); public health (MSPH). *Accreditation:* CAHME. Part-time programs available. *Faculty:* 16 full-time (10 women), 2 part-time/adjunct (1 woman). *Students:* 80 full-time (67 women), 40 part-time (30 women); includes 30 minority (22 Black or African American, non-Hispanic/Latino; 3 Asian, non-Hispanic/Latino; 5 Hispanic/Latino), 10 international. Average age 28. 171 applicants, 57% accepted, 46 enrolled. In 2011, 53 master's, 3 doctorates, 5 other advanced degrees awarded. Terminal master's awarded for partial completion of doctoral program. *Degree requirements:* For master's, thesis or comprehensive exam; for doctorate, thesis/dissertation. *Entrance requirements:* For master's, GRE or MAT (public health), GRE or GMAT (health administration), minimum GPA of 3.0 during previous 2 years, 2.75 overall. Additional exam requirements/recommendations for international students: Required—TOEFL (minimum score 557 paper-based; 220 computer-based; 83 iBT). *Application deadline:* For fall admission, 7/1 for domestic students, 5/1 for international students; for spring admission, 11/1 for domestic students, 10/1 for international students. Applications are processed on a rolling basis. Application fee: $65 ($75 for international students). Electronic applications accepted. *Expenses:* Tuition, state resident: full-time $3689. Tuition, nonresident: full-time $15,226. *Required fees:* $2198. Tuition and fees vary according to course load and program. *Financial support:* In 2011–12, 21 students received support, including 5 research assistantships (averaging $9,974 per year), 15 teaching assistantships (averaging $8,502 per year); career-related internships or fieldwork, Federal Work-Study, institutionally sponsored loans, scholarships/grants, unspecified assistantships, and administrative assistantship also available. Support available to part-time students. Financial award application deadline: 4/1; financial award applicants required to submit FAFSA. *Faculty research:* Pediatric asthma self-management, reproductive epidemiology, social aspects of injury prevention, chronic illness self-care, competency-based professional education. *Total annual research expenditures:* $405,550. *Unit head:* Dr. Andrew R. Harver, Chair, 704-687-8680, Fax: 704-687-6122, E-mail: arharver@uncc.edu. *Application contact:* Kathy B. Giddings, Director of Graduate Admissions, 704-687-5503, Fax: 704-687-3279, E-mail: gradadm@uncc.edu. Web site: http://publichealth.uncc.edu/.

The University of North Carolina at Charlotte, Graduate School, College of Health and Human Services, School of Nursing, Charlotte, NC 28223-0001. Offers administration (Post-Master's Certificate); advanced clinical (MSN, Post-Master's Certificate); anesthesia (MSN, Post-Master's Certificate); community health (MSN); family nurse practitioner (MSN, Post-Master's Certificate); health administration (MSN); mental health (MSN); nurse educator (MSN, Post-Master's Certificate); systems population (MSN). *Accreditation:* AACN. *Faculty:* 20 full-time (19 women), 5 part-time/adjunct (all women). *Students:* 76 full-time (65 women), 160 part-time (149 women); includes 49 minority (32 Black or African American, non-Hispanic/Latino; 1 American Indian or Alaska Native, non-Hispanic/Latino; 8 Asian, non-Hispanic/Latino; 8 Hispanic/Latino), 1 international. Average age 35. 191 applicants, 42% accepted, 71 enrolled. In 2011, 76 master's, 10 other advanced degrees awarded. *Degree requirements:* For master's, thesis or alternative, practicum. *Entrance requirements:* For master's, GRE General Test, minimum GPA of 3.0 in undergraduate major. Additional exam requirements/recommendations for international students: Required—TOEFL (minimum score 570 paper-based; 220 computer-based; 83 iBT). *Application deadline:* For fall admission, 7/15 for domestic students, 5/1 for international students; for spring admission, 11/15 for domestic students, 10/1 for international students. Application fee: $65 ($75 for international students). *Expenses:* Tuition, state resident: full-time $3689. Tuition, nonresident: full-time $15,226. *Required fees:* $2198. Tuition and fees vary according to course load and program. *Financial support:* In 2011–12, 10 students received support, including 4 research assistantships (averaging $5,284 per year), 6 teaching assistantships (averaging $2,918 per year); career-related internships or fieldwork, institutionally sponsored loans, scholarships/grants, traineeships, unspecified assistantships, and administrative assistantship also available. Support available to part-time students. Financial award application deadline: 4/1; financial award applicants required to submit FAFSA. *Total annual research expenditures:* $955,795. *Unit head:* Dr. Lucille L. Travis, Director, 704-687-7959, Fax: 704-687-6017, E-mail: ltravis1@uncc.edu. *Application contact:* Kathy B. Giddings, Director of Graduate Admissions, 704-687-5503, Fax: 704-687-3279, E-mail: gradadm@uncc.edu. Web site: http://nursing.uncc.edu/.

University of North Florida, Brooks College of Health, Department of Public Health, Jacksonville, FL 32224. Offers aging services (Certificate); community health (MPH); geriatric management (MSH); health administration (MHA); rehabilitation counseling (MS). *Accreditation:* CEPH. Part-time and evening/weekend programs available. *Faculty:* 15 full-time (10 women), 3 part-time/adjunct (2 women). *Students:* 106 full-time (77 women), 55 part-time (36 women); includes 28 minority (10 Black or African American, non-Hispanic/Latino; 2 American Indian or Alaska Native, non-Hispanic/Latino; 9 Asian, non-Hispanic/Latino; 5 Hispanic/Latino; 2 Two or more races, non-Hispanic/Latino), 7 international. Average age 30. 209 applicants, 38% accepted, 51 enrolled. In 2011, 65 master's awarded. *Degree requirements:* For master's, thesis optional. *Entrance requirements:* For master's, GRE General Test (MSH, MS, MPH); GMAT or GRE General Test (MHA), minimum GPA of 3.0 in last 60 hours. Additional exam requirements/recommendations for international students: Required—TOEFL (minimum score 500 paper-based; 173 computer-based). *Application deadline:* For fall admission, 7/1 priority date for domestic students, 5/1 for international students; for spring admission, 11/1 priority date for domestic students, 10/1 for international students. Applications are processed on a rolling basis. Application fee: $30. Electronic applications accepted. *Expenses:* Tuition, state resident: full-time $8793; part-time $366.38 per credit hour. Tuition, nonresident: full-time $23,502; part-time $979.24 per credit hour. *Required fees:* $1384; $57.66 per credit hour. Tuition and fees vary according to course load and program. *Financial support:* In 2011–12, 60 students received support. Research assistantships, teaching assistantships, career-related internships or fieldwork, Federal Work-Study, scholarships/grants, and tuition waivers (partial) available. Support available to part-time students. Financial award application deadline: 4/1; financial award applicants required to submit FAFSA. *Faculty research:* Dietary supplements; alcohol, tobacco, and other drug use prevention; turnover among health professionals; aging; psychosocial aspects of disabilities. *Total annual research expenditures:* $197,732. *Unit head:* Dr. JoAnn Nolin, Chair, 904-620-2840, Fax: 904-620-2848, E-mail: jnolin@unf.edu. *Application contact:* Heather Kenney, Director of Advising, 904-620-2810, Fax: 904-620-1030, E-mail: heather.kenney@unf.edu. Web site: http://www.unf.edu/brooks/public_health/.

University of North Texas Health Science Center at Fort Worth, School of Public Health, Fort Worth, TX 76107-2699. Offers biostatistics (MPH); community health (MPH); disease control and prevention (Dr PH); environmental and occupational health sciences (MPH); epidemiology (MPH); health administration (MHA); health policy and management (MPH, Dr PH); DO/MPH; MS/MPH; MSN/MPH. MPH offered jointly with University of North Texas; DO/MPH with Texas College of Osteopathic Medicine. *Accreditation:* CEPH. Part-time and evening/weekend programs available. *Degree requirements:* For master's, thesis or alternative, supervised internship; for doctorate, thesis/dissertation, supervised internship. *Entrance requirements:* For master's, GRE General Test. Additional exam requirements/recommendations for international students: Required—TOEFL. Electronic applications accepted.

University of Oklahoma Health Sciences Center, Graduate College, College of Public Health, Department of Health Administration and Policy, Oklahoma City, OK 73190. Offers MHA, MPH, MS, Dr PH, PhD, JD/MPH, MBA/MPH. MBA/MPH offered jointly with Oklahoma State University; JD/MPH with University of Oklahoma. *Accreditation:* CAHME. Part-time programs available. *Degree requirements:* For master's, comprehensive exam, thesis (for some programs); for doctorate, 2 foreign languages, comprehensive exam, thesis/dissertation. *Entrance requirements:* For master's, 3 letters of recommendation, resume; for doctorate, GRE General Test, letters of recommendation. Additional exam requirements/recommendations for international students: Required—TOEFL (minimum score 570 paper-based; 230 computer-based). *Faculty research:* Public health administration, health institutions management, public policy and the aged, injury control.

University of Ottawa, Faculty of Graduate and Postdoctoral Studies, Telfer School of Management, Health Administration Program, Ottawa, ON K1N 6N5, Canada. Offers MHA. Part-time programs available. *Degree requirements:* For master's, thesis optional, residency. *Entrance requirements:* For master's, GMAT, bachelor's degree or equivalent, minimum B average. Additional exam requirements/recommendations for international students: Recommended—TOEFL (minimum score 237 computer-based). Electronic applications accepted.

University of Pennsylvania, Wharton School, Health Care Management Department, Philadelphia, PA 19104. Offers MBA, PhD. *Accreditation:* CAHME (one or more programs are accredited). *Degree requirements:* For doctorate, comprehensive exam, thesis/dissertation. *Entrance requirements:* For master's, GMAT; for doctorate, GMAT or GRE. Electronic applications accepted. *Expenses: Tuition:* Full-time $26,660; part-time $4944 per course. *Required fees:* $2318; $291 per course. Tuition and fees vary according to course load, degree level and program. *Faculty research:* Health economics, health policy, health care management, health insurance and financing.

University of Phoenix–Atlanta Campus, College of Nursing, Sandy Springs, GA 30350-4153. Offers health administration (MHA); nursing (MSN); nursing/health care education (MSN); MSN/MBA; MSN/MHA. Evening/weekend programs available. Postbaccalaureate distance learning degree programs offered. *Degree requirements:* For master's, thesis (for some programs). *Entrance requirements:* For master's, minimum undergraduate GPA of 2.5, 3 years of work experience. Additional exam requirements/recommendations for international students: Required—TOEFL (minimum score 550 paper-based; 213 computer-based; 79 iBT). Electronic applications accepted.

University of Phoenix–Augusta Campus, College of Nursing, Augusta, GA 30909-4583. Offers health administration (MHA); nursing (MSN); nursing/health care education (MSN); MSN/MBA; MSN/MHA. Postbaccalaureate distance learning degree programs offered.

University of Phoenix–Austin Campus, College of Nursing, Austin, TX 78759. Offers health administration (MHA). Postbaccalaureate distance learning degree programs offered.

University of Phoenix–Bay Area Campus, School of Business, San Jose, CA 95134-1805. Offers accountancy (MS); accounting (MBA); business administration (MBA, DBA); energy management (MBA); global management (MBA); health care management (MBA); human resource management (MBA); human resources management (MM); management (MM); marketing (MBA); organizational leadership (DM); project management (MBA); public administration (MPA); technology management (MBA). Evening/weekend programs available. Postbaccalaureate distance learning degree programs offered (no on-campus study). *Degree requirements:* For master's, thesis (for some programs). *Entrance requirements:* For master's, minimum undergraduate GPA of 3.0, 3 years of work experience. Additional exam requirements/recommendations for international students: Required—TOEFL (minimum score 550 paper-based; 213 computer-based; 79 iBT). Electronic applications accepted.

University of Phoenix–Birmingham Campus, College of Health and Human Services, Birmingham, AL 35244. Offers education (MHA); gerontology (MHA); health administration (MHA); health care management (MBA); informatics (MHA); nursing (MSN); nursing/health care education (MSN); MSN/MBA; MSN/MHA.

University of Phoenix–Central Florida Campus, College of Nursing, Maitland, FL 32751-7057. Offers health administration (MHA); health and human services (MSN); nursing (MSN); nursing/health care education (MSN); MSN/MBA; MSN/MHA. Evening/weekend programs available. *Degree requirements:* For master's, thesis (for some programs). *Entrance requirements:* For master's, minimum undergraduate GPA of 2.5, 3 years work experience, RN license. Additional exam requirements/recommendations for international students: Required—TOEFL (minimum score 550 paper-based; 213 computer-based; 79 iBT). Electronic applications accepted.

University of Phoenix–Central Valley Campus, College of Nursing, Fresno, CA 93720-1562. Offers education (MHA); gerontology (MHA); health administration (MHA); nursing (MSN); MSN/MBA.

University of Phoenix–Charlotte Campus, College of Nursing, Charlotte, NC 28273-3409. Offers education (MHA); gerontology (MHA); health administration (MHA); informatics (MHA, MSN); nursing (MSN); nursing/health care education (MSN). Evening/weekend programs available. *Degree requirements:* For master's, thesis (for some programs). *Entrance requirements:* For master's, minimum undergraduate GPA of 2.5, 3 years work experience. Additional exam requirements/recommendations for international students: Required—TOEFL (minimum score 550 paper-based; 213 computer-based; 79 iBT). Electronic applications accepted.

University of Phoenix–Chattanooga Campus, College of Nursing, Chattanooga, TN 37421-3707. Offers education (MHA); gerontology (MHA); health administration (MHA).

University of Phoenix–Cheyenne Campus, College of Nursing, Cheyenne, WY 82009. Offers health administration (MHA); nursing (MSN); nursing/health care education (MSN); MSN/MBA; MSN/MHA. Postbaccalaureate distance learning degree programs offered.

University of Phoenix–Denver Campus, College of Nursing, Lone Tree, CO 80124-5453. Offers health administration (MHA); nursing (MSN); MSN/MBA; MSN/MHA. Evening/weekend programs available. Postbaccalaureate distance learning degree

programs offered. *Degree requirements:* For master's, thesis (for some programs). *Entrance requirements:* For master's, minimum undergraduate GPA of 2.5, 3 years work experience, RN license. Additional exam requirements/recommendations for international students: Required—TOEFL (minimum score 550 paper-based; 213 computer-based; 79 iBT). Electronic applications accepted.

University of Phoenix–Des Moines Campus, College of Nursing, Des Moines, IA 50266. Offers education (MHA); gerontology (MHA); health administration (MHA, DHA); informatics (MHA, MSN); nursing (MSN, PhD); nursing/health care education (MSN).

University of Phoenix–Harrisburg Campus, College of Nursing, Harrisburg, PA 17112. Offers health administration (MHA); nursing (MSN); nursing/health care education (MSN); MSN/MBA; MSN/MHA. Postbaccalaureate distance learning degree programs offered.

University of Phoenix–Hawaii Campus, College of Nursing, Honolulu, HI 96813-4317. Offers education (MHA); family nurse practitioner (MSN); gerontology (MHA); health administration (MHA); nursing (MSN); nursing/health care education (MSN); MSN/MBA. Evening/weekend programs available. *Degree requirements:* For master's, thesis (for some programs). *Entrance requirements:* For master's, minimum undergraduate GPA of 2.5, 3 years of work experience, RN license. Additional exam requirements/ recommendations for international students: Required—TOEFL (minimum score 550 paper-based; 213 computer-based; 79 iBT). Electronic applications accepted.

University of Phoenix–Houston Campus, College of Nursing, Houston, TX 77079-2004. Offers health administration (MHA). Postbaccalaureate distance learning degree programs offered. *Degree requirements:* For master's, thesis (for some programs). *Entrance requirements:* For master's, minimum undergraduate GPA of 2.5, 3 years of work experience. Additional exam requirements/recommendations for international students: Required—TOEFL (minimum score 550 paper-based; 213 computer-based; 79 iBT). Electronic applications accepted.

University of Phoenix–Indianapolis Campus, College of Nursing, Indianapolis, IN 46250-932. Offers health administration (MHA); nursing (MSN); nursing/health care education (MSN); MSN/MBA; MSN/MHA. Evening/weekend programs available. Postbaccalaureate distance learning degree programs offered. *Degree requirements:* For master's, thesis. *Entrance requirements:* For master's, 3 years work experience, minimum undergraduate GPA of 2.5. Additional exam requirements/recommendations for international students: Required—TOEFL (minimum score 500 paper-based; 213 computer-based). Electronic applications accepted.

University of Phoenix–Memphis Campus, College of Nursing, Cordova, TN 38018. Offers health administration (MHA, DHA).

University of Phoenix–Milwaukee Campus, College of Nursing, Milwaukee, WI 53045. Offers education (MHA); gerontology (MHA); health administration (MHA, DHA); informatics (MHA, MSN); nursing (MSN, PhD); nursing/health care education (MSN); MSN/MBA; MSN/MHA.

University of Phoenix–Nashville Campus, College of Nursing, Nashville, TN 37214-5048. Offers health administration (MHA). Evening/weekend programs available. *Degree requirements:* For master's, thesis (for some programs). *Entrance requirements:* For master's, minimum undergraduate GPA of 2.5, 3 years of work experience. Additional exam requirements/recommendations for international students: Required—TOEFL (minimum score 550 paper-based; 213 computer-based). Electronic applications accepted.

University of Phoenix–New Mexico Campus, College of Nursing, Albuquerque, NM 87113-1570. Offers health administration (MHA); health care education (MSN); nursing (MSN); MSN/MBA. Evening/weekend programs available. *Degree requirements:* For master's, thesis (for some programs). *Entrance requirements:* For master's, minimum undergraduate GPA of 2.5, 3 years of work experience, RN license. Additional exam requirements/recommendations for international students: Required—TOEFL (minimum score 550 paper-based; 213 computer-based; 79 iBT). Electronic applications accepted.

University of Phoenix–Northern Nevada Campus, College of Nursing, Reno, NV 89521-5862. Offers health administration (MHA); health care education (MSN); nursing (MSN); MSN/MBA; MSN/MHA.

University of Phoenix–Northern Virginia Campus, College of Nursing, Reston, VA 20190. Offers health administration (MHA); nursing (MSN).

University of Phoenix–North Florida Campus, College of Nursing, Jacksonville, FL 32216-0959. Offers health administration (MHA); health care education (MSN); nursing (MSN); MSN/MBA; MSN/MHA. Evening/weekend programs available. *Degree requirements:* For master's, thesis (for some programs). *Entrance requirements:* For master's, minimum undergraduate GPA of 2.5, 3 years work experience, RN license. Additional exam requirements/recommendations for international students: Required—TOEFL (minimum score 550 paper-based; 213 computer-based; 79 iBT). Electronic applications accepted.

University of Phoenix–Northwest Arkansas Campus, College of Nursing, Rogers, AR 72756-9615. Offers health administration (MHA); health care education (MSN); nursing (MSN); MSN/MBA.

University of Phoenix–Omaha Campus, College of Nursing, Omaha, NE 68154-5240. Offers health administration (MHA).

University of Phoenix–Online Campus, College of Natural Sciences, Phoenix, AZ 85034-7209. Offers education (MHA); gerontology (MHA, Graduate Certificate); health administration (MHA); health care informatics (Graduate Certificate); health care management (Graduate Certificate), including lifelong learning; informatics (MHA). Evening/weekend programs available. Postbaccalaureate distance learning degree programs offered. *Students:* 2,854 full-time (2,408 women); includes 1,137 minority (855 Black or African American, non-Hispanic/Latino; 24 American Indian or Alaska Native, non-Hispanic/Latino; 73 Asian, non-Hispanic/Latino; 140 Hispanic/Latino; 18 Native Hawaiian or other Pacific Islander, non-Hispanic/Latino; 27 Two or more races, non-Hispanic/Latino), 91 international. Average age 39. *Entrance requirements:* Additional exam requirements/recommendations for international students: Required—TOEFL, TOEIC (Test of English as an International Communication), Berlitz Online English Proficiency Exam, Pearson Test of English, or IELTS. *Application deadline:* Applications are processed on a rolling basis. Application fee: $45. Electronic applications accepted. *Expenses: Tuition:* Full-time $17,160. *Required fees:* $920. One-time fee: $45 full-time. Full-time tuition and fees vary according to course load, degree level, campus/location and program. *Financial support:* Scholarships/grants available. Financial award applicants required to submit FAFSA. *Unit head:* Dr. Hinrich Eylers, Dean/Associate Provost, 866-766-0766. *Application contact:* 866-766-0766. Web site: http://www.phoenix.edu/colleges_divisions/natural-sciences.html.

University of Phoenix–Online Campus, School of Advanced Studies, Phoenix, AZ 85034-7209. Offers business administration (DBA); education (Ed S); educational leadership (Ed D), including curriculum and instruction, education technology, educational leadership; health administration (DHA); higher education administration (PhD); industrial/organizational psychology (PhD); nursing (PhD); organizational leadership (DM), including information systems and technology, organizational leadership. Evening/weekend programs available. Postbaccalaureate distance learning degree programs offered. *Students:* 7,581 full-time (5,042 women); includes 3,199 minority (2,505 Black or African American, non-Hispanic/Latino; 68 American Indian or Alaska Native, non-Hispanic/Latino; 158 Asian, non-Hispanic/Latino; 395 Hispanic/ Latino; 46 Native Hawaiian or other Pacific Islander, non-Hispanic/Latino; 27 Two or more races, non-Hispanic/Latino), 397 international. Average age 44. *Degree requirements:* For doctorate, thesis/dissertation. *Entrance requirements:* Additional exam requirements/recommendations for international students: Required—TOEFL, TOEIC (Test of English as an International Communication), Berlitz Online English Proficiency Exam, Pearson Test of English, or IELTS. *Application deadline:* Applications are processed on a rolling basis. Application fee: $45. Electronic applications accepted. *Expenses:* Contact institution. *Financial support:* Scholarships/grants available. Financial award applicants required to submit FAFSA. *Unit head:* Dr. Jeremy Moreland, Executive Dean. *Application contact:* 866-766-0766. Web site: http://www.phoenix.edu/colleges_divisions/doctoral.html.

University of Phoenix–Online Campus, School of Business, Phoenix, AZ 85034-7209. Offers accountancy (MS); accounting (MBA); business administration (MBA); energy management (MBA); global management (MBA); health care management (MBA); human resource management (MBA); human resources management (MM); international (MM); management (MM); marketing (MBA, Graduate Certificate); organizational management (MA); project management (MBA, Graduate Certificate); public administration (MBA, MM, MPA); technology management (MBA). Evening/ weekend programs available. Postbaccalaureate distance learning degree programs offered. *Students:* 18,883 full-time (11,868 women); includes 6,302 minority (4,182 Black or African American, non-Hispanic/Latino; 121 American Indian or Alaska Native, non-Hispanic/Latino; 478 Asian, non-Hispanic/Latino; 1,252 Hispanic/Latino; 121 Native Hawaiian or other Pacific Islander, non-Hispanic/Latino; 148 Two or more races, non-Hispanic/Latino), 1,000 international. Average age 37. *Entrance requirements:* Additional exam requirements/recommendations for international students: Required—TOEFL, TOEIC (Test of English as an International Communication), Berlitz Online English Proficiency Exam, Pearson Test of English, or IELTS. *Application deadline:* Applications are processed on a rolling basis. Application fee: $45. Electronic applications accepted. *Expenses: Tuition:* Full-time $17,160. *Required fees:* $920. One-time fee: $45 full-time. Full-time tuition and fees vary according to course load, degree level, campus/location and program. *Financial support:* Scholarships/grants available. Financial award applicants required to submit FAFSA. *Application contact:* 866-766-0766. Web site: http://www.phoenix.edu/colleges_divisions/business.html.

University of Phoenix–Oregon Campus, College of Nursing, Tigard, OR 97223. Offers health administration (MHA); nursing (MSN); MSN/MBA. Evening/weekend programs available. *Degree requirements:* For master's, thesis (for some programs). *Entrance requirements:* For master's, minimum undergraduate GPA of 2.5, 3 years of work experience, current RN license (nursing). Additional exam requirements/ recommendations for international students: Required—TOEFL (minimum score 550 paper-based; 213 computer-based; 79 iBT). Electronic applications accepted.

University of Phoenix–Phoenix Main Campus, College of Natural Science, Tempe, AZ 85282-2371. Offers education (MHA); gerontology (MHA); gerontology health care (Certificate); health administration (MHA); informatics (MHA). Evening/weekend programs available. Postbaccalaureate distance learning degree programs offered. *Students:* 27 full-time (17 women); includes 10 minority (4 Black or African American, non-Hispanic/Latino; 1 American Indian or Alaska Native, non-Hispanic/Latino; 1 Asian, non-Hispanic/Latino; 4 Hispanic/Latino). Average age 42. *Entrance requirements:* Additional exam requirements/recommendations for international students: Required—TOEFL, TOEIC (Test of English as an International Communication), Berlitz Online English Proficiency Exam, Pearson Test of English, or IELTS. *Application deadline:* Applications are processed on a rolling basis. Application fee: $45. Electronic applications accepted. *Expenses:* Contact institution. *Financial support:* Scholarships/ grants available. Financial award applicants required to submit FAFSA. *Unit head:* Dr. Hinrich Eylers, Dean/Associate Provost, 866-766-0766. *Application contact:* 866-766-0766. Web site: http://www.phoenix.edu/colleges_divisions/natural-sciences.html.

University of Phoenix–Phoenix Main Campus, School of Business, Tempe, AZ 85282-2371. Offers accounting (MBA, MS); business administration (MBA); energy management (MBA); global management (MBA); health care management (MBA); human resource management (MBA); management (MM); marketing (MBA); project management (MBA); public administration (MPA); technology management (MBA). Evening/weekend programs available. Postbaccalaureate distance learning degree programs offered. *Students:* 1,151 full-time (531 women); includes 310 minority (99 Black or African American, non-Hispanic/Latino; 10 American Indian or Alaska Native, non-Hispanic/Latino; 39 Asian, non-Hispanic/Latino; 130 Hispanic/Latino; 15 Native Hawaiian or other Pacific Islander, non-Hispanic/Latino; 17 Two or more races, non-Hispanic/Latino), 63 international. Average age 34. *Entrance requirements:* Additional exam requirements/recommendations for international students: Required—TOEFL, TOEIC (Test of English as an International Communication), Berlitz Online English Proficiency Exam, Pearson Test of English, or IELTS. *Application deadline:* Applications are processed on a rolling basis. Application fee: $45. Electronic applications accepted. *Expenses:* Contact institution. *Financial support:* Scholarships/grants available. Financial award applicants required to submit FAFSA. *Application contact:* 866-766-0766. Web site: http://www.phoenix.edu/colleges_divisions/business.html.

University of Phoenix–Pittsburgh Campus, College of Nursing, Pittsburgh, PA 15276. Offers health administration (MHA); health care education (MSN); nursing (MSN); MSN/ MBA; MSN/MHA. Evening/weekend programs available. *Degree requirements:* For master's, thesis (for some programs). *Entrance requirements:* For master's, minimum undergraduate GPA of 2.5, 3 years work experience, current RN license (nursing). Additional exam requirements/recommendations for international students: Required—TOEFL (minimum score 550 paper-based; 213 computer-based; 79 iBT). Electronic applications accepted.

University of Phoenix–Raleigh Campus, College of Nursing, Raleigh, NC 27606. Offers education (MHA); gerontology (MHA); health administration (MHA, DHA); informatics (MHA, MSN); nursing (MSN, PhD); nursing/health care education (MSN).

University of Phoenix–Richmond Campus, College of Nursing, Richmond, VA 23230. Offers health administration (MHA); health care education (MSN); nursing (MSN); MSN/ MBA; MSN/MHA. Evening/weekend programs available. *Degree requirements:* For master's, thesis (for some programs). *Entrance requirements:* For master's, minimum undergraduate GPA of 2.5, 3 years work experience, current RN license for nursing programs. Additional exam requirements/recommendations for international students: Required—TOEFL (minimum score 500 paper-based; 213 computer-based; 79 iBT). Electronic applications accepted.

University of Phoenix–Sacramento Valley Campus, College of Nursing, Sacramento, CA 95833-3632. Offers family nurse practitioner (MSN); health administration (MHA); health care education (MSN); nursing (MSN); MSN/MBA. Evening/weekend programs available. *Degree requirements:* For master's, thesis (for some programs). *Entrance requirements:* For master's, RN license, minimum undergraduate GPA of 2.5, 3 years work experience. Additional exam requirements/recommendations for international

students: Required—TOEFL (minimum score 550 paper-based; 213 computer-based; 79 iBT). Electronic applications accepted.

University of Phoenix–San Antonio Campus, College of Nursing, San Antonio, TX 78230. Offers health administration (MHA).

University of Phoenix–Savannah Campus, College of Nursing, Savannah, GA 31405-7400. Offers health administration (MHA); nursing (MSN); nursing/health care education (MSN); MSN/MBA; MSN/MHA.

University of Phoenix–Southern California Campus, School of Business, Costa Mesa, CA 92626. Offers accounting (MIS); business administration (MBA); energy management (MBA); global management (MBA); health care management (MBA); human resource management (MBA); management (MM); marketing (MBA); project management (MBA); public administration (MPA); technology management (MBA). Evening/weekend programs available. Postbaccalaureate distance learning degree programs offered. *Students:* 699 full-time (341 women); includes 318 minority (124 Black or African American, non-Hispanic/Latino; 4 American Indian or Alaska Native, non-Hispanic/Latino; 44 Asian, non-Hispanic/Latino; 124 Hispanic/Latino; 15 Native Hawaiian or other Pacific Islander, non-Hispanic/Latino; 7 Two or more races, non-Hispanic/Latino), 29 international. Average age 38. *Entrance requirements:* Additional exam requirements/recommendations for international students: Required—TOEFL, TOEIC (Test of English as an International Communication), Berlitz Online English Proficiency Exam, Pearson Test of English, or IELTS. *Application deadline:* Applications are processed on a rolling basis. Application fee: $45. Electronic applications accepted. *Expenses:* Contact institution. *Financial support:* Scholarships/grants available. Financial award applicants required to submit FAFSA. *Application contact:* 866-766-0766. Web site: http://www.phoenix.edu/colleges_divisions/business.html.

University of Phoenix–Southern Colorado Campus, College of Nursing, Colorado Springs, CO 80919-2335. Offers education (MHA); gerontology (MHA); health administration (MHA); nursing (MSN); MSN/MBA. Evening/weekend programs available. *Degree requirements:* For master's, thesis (for some programs). *Entrance requirements:* For master's, minimum undergraduate GPA of 2.5, 3 years of work experience, RN license. Additional exam requirements/recommendations for international students: Required—TOEFL (minimum score 550 paper-based; 213 computer-based; 79 iBT). Electronic applications accepted.

University of Phoenix–South Florida Campus, College of Nursing, Fort Lauderdale, FL 33309. Offers health administration (MHA); health care education (MSN); nursing (MSN); MSN/MBA; MSN/MHA. Evening/weekend programs available. *Degree requirements:* For master's, thesis (for some programs). *Entrance requirements:* For master's, minimum undergraduate GPA of 2.5, 3 years work experience, RN license. Additional exam requirements/recommendations for international students: Required—TOEFL (minimum score 550 paper-based; 213 computer-based; 79 iBT). Electronic applications accepted.

University of Phoenix–Springfield Campus, College of Nursing, Springfield, MO 65804-7211. Offers health administration (MHA); nursing (MSN); MSN/MBA; MSN/MHA.

University of Phoenix–Vancouver Campus, The Artemis School, College of Health and Human Services, Burnaby, BC V5C 6G9, Canada. Offers health care management (MBA). Evening/weekend programs available. *Degree requirements:* For master's, thesis (for some programs). *Entrance requirements:* For master's, minimum undergraduate GPA of 2.5, 3 years work experience. Additional exam requirements/recommendations for international students: Required—TOEFL (minimum score 550 paper-based; 213 computer-based; 79 iBT). Electronic applications accepted.

University of Phoenix–Washington D.C. Campus, College of Nursing, Washington, DC 20001. Offers education (MHA); gerontology (MHA); health administration (MHA, DHA); informatics (MHA, MSN); nursing (MSN, PhD); nursing/health care education (MSN); MSN/MBA; MSN/MHA.

University of Phoenix–West Florida Campus, College of Nursing, Temple Terrace, FL 33637. Offers health administration (MHA); health care education (MSN); nursing (MSN); MSN/MBA; MSN/MHA. Evening/weekend programs available. Postbaccalaureate distance learning degree programs offered. *Degree requirements:* For master's, thesis (for some programs). *Entrance requirements:* For master's, minimum undergraduate GPA of 2.5, RN license, 3 years work experience. Additional exam requirements/recommendations for international students: Required—TOEFL (minimum score 550 paper-based; 213 computer-based; 79 iBT). Electronic applications accepted.

University of Pittsburgh, Graduate School of Public Health, Department of Behavioral and Community Health Science, Pittsburgh, PA 15260. Offers behavioral and community health sciences (MPH, Dr PH); community-based participatory research and practice (Certificate); lesbian, gay, bisexual and transgender health and wellness (Certificate); minority health and health disparities (Certificate); program evaluation (Certificate); public health preparedness (Certificate); MID/MPH; MPH/MPA; MPH/MSW; MPH/PhD. *Accreditation:* CAHME (one or more programs are accredited). Part-time programs available. *Faculty:* 15 full-time (7 women), 38 part-time/adjunct (15 women). *Students:* 80 full-time (64 women), 33 part-time (28 women); includes 28 minority (16 Black or African American, non-Hispanic/Latino; 5 Asian, non-Hispanic/Latino; 5 Hispanic/Latino; 2 Two or more races, non-Hispanic/Latino), 7 international. Average age 31. 286 applicants, 63% accepted, 25 enrolled. In 2011, 38 master's, 2 doctorates awarded. *Degree requirements:* For master's, thesis; for doctorate, comprehensive exam, thesis/dissertation, preliminary exams. *Entrance requirements:* For master's and Certificate, GRE; for doctorate, GRE, master's degree in public health or related field. Additional exam requirements/recommendations for international students: Required—TOEFL (minimum score 550 paper-based; 80 iBT) or IELTS (minimum score 6.5). *Application deadline:* For fall admission, 5/1 priority date for domestic students, 4/1 for international students; for winter admission, 9/1 for international students; for spring admission, 10/1 priority date for domestic students, 2/1 for international students. Applications are processed on a rolling basis. Application fee: $115. Electronic applications accepted. *Expenses:* Tuition, state resident: full-time $18,774; part-time $760 per credit. Tuition, nonresident: full-time $30,736; part-time $1258 per credit. *Required fees:* $740; $200 per term. Tuition and fees vary according to program. *Financial support:* In 2011–12, 21 students received support, including 10 fellowships with full and partial tuition reimbursements available (averaging $4,081 per year), 11 research assistantships with full and partial tuition reimbursements available (averaging $7,841 per year), 3 teaching assistantships with full and partial tuition reimbursements available (averaging $9,460 per year); unspecified assistantships also available. *Faculty research:* Maternal and child health, community-based participatory research, minority health and health disparities, aging. *Total annual research expenditures:* $2.6 million. *Unit head:* Dr. Ronald D. Stall, Chairman, 412-624-7933, Fax: 412-648-5975, E-mail: rstall@pitt.edu. *Application contact:* Natalie C. Arnold, Recruitment and Academic Affairs Administrator, 412-624-3107, Fax: 412-624-5510, E-mail: narnold@pitt.edu. Web site: http://www.bchs.pitt.edu/.

University of Pittsburgh, Graduate School of Public Health, Department of Health Policy and Management, Pittsburgh, PA 15260. Offers health administration (MHA); public health (MPH); JD/MPH. *Accreditation:* CAHME. Part-time programs available. *Faculty:* 18 full-time (7 women), 30 part-time/adjunct (9 women). *Students:* 62 full-time (42 women), 21 part-time (15 women); includes 23 minority (12 Black or African American, non-Hispanic/Latino; 8 Asian, non-Hispanic/Latino; 3 Two or more races, non-Hispanic/Latino), 10 international. Average age 29. 240 applicants, 52% accepted, 36 enrolled. In 2011, 33 master's awarded. *Degree requirements:* For master's, comprehensive exam (for some programs), thesis, essay. *Entrance requirements:* For master's, GRE, 3 credits each of course work in mathematics and biology, 6 in social science; bachelor's degree; recommendations; professional statement; transcripts. Additional exam requirements/recommendations for international students: Required—TOEFL (minimum score 550 paper-based; 80 iBT) or IELTS (minimum score 6.5). *Application deadline:* For fall admission, 4/30 priority date for domestic students, 1/4 for international students; for winter admission, 11/1 priority date for domestic students, 8/1 for international students; for spring admission, 3/1 priority date for domestic students, 2/1 for international students. Applications are processed on a rolling basis. Application fee: $115. Electronic applications accepted. *Expenses:* Tuition, state resident: full-time $18,774; part-time $760 per credit. Tuition, nonresident: full-time $30,736; part-time $1258 per credit. *Required fees:* $740; $200 per term. Tuition and fees vary according to program. *Financial support:* In 2011–12, 19 students received support, including 3 fellowships with full and partial tuition reimbursements available (averaging $4,167 per year), 11 research assistantships with full and partial tuition reimbursements available (averaging $12,112 per year), 5 teaching assistantships with full tuition reimbursements available (averaging $10,743 per year); career-related internships or fieldwork, scholarships/grants, health care benefits, and unspecified assistantships also available. Support available to part-time students. Financial award applicants required to submit FAFSA. *Faculty research:* Cost effectiveness analysis, mathematical modeling and decision science, long-term care and nursing home quality health policy and pharmaceutical policy, organization theory, health economics. *Total annual research expenditures:* $2.2 million. *Unit head:* Dr. Mark S. Roberts, Professor/Chair, 412-383-7049, Fax: 412-624-3146, E-mail: mroberts@pitt.edu. *Application contact:* Donna Schultz, Program Coordinator, 412-624-3123, Fax: 412-624-3146, E-mail: dschultz@pitt.edu. Web site: http://www.hpm.pitt.edu/.

University of Pittsburgh, School of Health and Rehabilitation Sciences, Master's Programs in Health and Rehabilitation Sciences, Pittsburgh, PA 15260. Offers health and rehabilitation sciences (MS), including clinical dietetics and nutrition, health care supervision and management, health information systems, occupational therapy, physical therapy, rehabilitation counseling, rehabilitation science and technology, sports medicine, wellness and human performance. *Accreditation:* APTA. Part-time and evening/weekend programs available. *Faculty:* 22 full-time (16 women), 4 part-time/adjunct (2 women). *Students:* 144 full-time (91 women), 35 part-time (23 women); includes 23 minority (8 Black or African American, non-Hispanic/Latino; 8 Asian, non-Hispanic/Latino; 3 Hispanic/Latino; 4 Two or more races, non-Hispanic/Latino), 74 international. Average age 28. 399 applicants, 61% accepted, 121 enrolled. In 2011, 86 master's awarded. *Degree requirements:* For master's, comprehensive exam (for some programs), thesis optional. *Entrance requirements:* For master's, minimum GPA of 3.0. Additional exam requirements/recommendations for international students: Required—TOEFL (minimum score 550 paper-based; 213 computer-based; 80 iBT), IELTS (minimum score 6.5). *Application deadline:* For fall admission, 3/1 for international students; for spring admission, 7/31 for international students. Applications are processed on a rolling basis. Application fee: $50. Electronic applications accepted. *Expenses:* Contact institution. *Financial support:* Research assistantships, teaching assistantships, Federal Work-Study, institutionally sponsored loans, traineeships, and unspecified assistantships available. Financial award applicants required to submit FAFSA. *Faculty research:* Assistive technology, seating and wheeled mobility, cellular neurophysiology, low back syndrome, augmentative communication. *Total annual research expenditures:* $7.8 million. *Unit head:* Dr. Clifford E. Brubaker, Dean, 412-383-6560, Fax: 412-383-6535, E-mail: cliffb@pitt.edu. *Application contact:* Shameem Gangjee, Director of Admissions, 412-383-6558, Fax: 412-383-6535, E-mail: admissions@shrs.pitt.edu. Web site: http://www.shrs.pitt.edu/.

University of Portland, Dr. Robert B. Pamplin, Jr. School of Business, Portland, OR 97203-5798. Offers business administration (MBA); entrepreneurship (MBA); finance (MBA, MS); health care management (MBA); marketing (MBA); nonprofit management (EMBA); operations and technology management (MBA); sustainability (MBA). *Accreditation:* AACSB. Part-time and evening/weekend programs available. *Faculty:* 13 full-time (1 woman), 8 part-time/adjunct (1 woman). *Students:* 50 full-time (13 women), 90 part-time (41 women); includes 19 minority (1 Black or African American, non-Hispanic/Latino; 1 American Indian or Alaska Native, non-Hispanic/Latino; 8 Asian, non-Hispanic/Latino; 5 Hispanic/Latino; 2 Native Hawaiian or other Pacific Islander, non-Hispanic/Latino; 2 Two or more races, non-Hispanic/Latino), 18 international. Average age 31. In 2011, 54 master's awarded. *Entrance requirements:* For master's, GMAT, minimum GPA of 3.0, resume, 2 letters of recommendation. Additional exam requirements/recommendations for international students: Required—TOEFL (minimum score 570 paper-based; 89 iBT), IELTS (minimum score 7). *Application deadline:* For fall admission, 7/15 priority date for domestic students, 7/15 for international students; for spring admission, 12/15 priority date for domestic students, 12/15 for international students. Applications are processed on a rolling basis. Application fee: $50. *Expenses:* Contact institution. *Financial support:* Federal Work-Study, scholarships/grants, and tuition waivers (partial) available. Support available to part-time students. Financial award application deadline: 3/1; financial award applicants required to submit FAFSA. *Unit head:* Dr. Howard Feldman, Associate Dean, 503-943-7224, E-mail: feldman@up.edu. *Application contact:* Melissa McCarthy, Academic Specialist, 503-943-7225, E-mail: mccarthy@up.edu. Web site: http://business.up.edu/.

University of Puerto Rico, Medical Sciences Campus, Graduate School of Public Health, Department of Health Services Administration, Program in Health Services Administration, San Juan, PR 00936-5067. Offers MHSA. *Accreditation:* CAHME. Part-time programs available. *Degree requirements:* For master's, thesis. *Entrance requirements:* For master's, GRE, previous course work in accounting, statistics, economics, algebra, and managerial finance.

University of Regina, Faculty of Graduate Studies and Research, Johnson-Shoyama Graduate School of Public Policy, Regina, SK S4S 0A2, Canada. Offers economic analysis for public policy (Master's Certificate); health systems management (Master's Certificate); health systems research (MPP); non-profit management (Master's Certificate); public management (MPA, Master's Certificate); public policy (MPA, MPP, PhD); public policy analysis (Master's Certificate). Part-time programs available. *Faculty:* 7 full-time (3 women). *Students:* 61 full-time (34 women), 58 part-time (33 women). 75 applicants, 73% accepted. In 2011, 73 master's awarded. *Degree requirements:* For master's, thesis; for doctorate, thesis/dissertation. *Entrance requirements:* For doctorate, master's degree, intended research program in an area of public policy. Additional exam requirements/recommendations for international students: Required—TOEFL (minimum score 580 paper-based; 80 iBT), IELTS (minimum score 6.5). *Application deadline:* For fall admission, 2/1 for domestic and international students. Application fee: $100. Electronic applications accepted. *Expenses:* Contact institution. *Financial support:* In 2011–12, 8 fellowships (averaging $6,500 per year), 10 teaching assistantships (averaging $2,298 per year) were awarded; research assistantships and

scholarships/grants also available. Financial award application deadline: 6/15. *Faculty research:* Governance and administration, public finance, public policy analysis, non-governmental organizations and alternative service delivery, micro-economics for policy analysis. *Unit head:* Dr. Michael Atkinson, Director, 306-996-1984, Fax: 306-585-5461, E-mail: michael.atkinson@usask.ca. *Application contact:* Elaine Groenendyk, Program Advisor, 306-585-5462, Fax: 306-585-5461, E-mail: elaine.groenendyk@uregina.ca.

University of Rochester, School of Nursing, Rochester, NY 14642. Offers acute care nurse practitioner (MS); adult nurse practitioner (MS); adult/geriatric nurse practitioner (MS); care of children and families/pediatric nurse practitioner (MS); care of children and families/pediatric nurse practitioner/neonatal nurse practitioner (MS); clinical nurse leader (MS); clinical research coordinator (MS); family nurse practitioner (MS); family psychiatric mental health nurse practitioner (MS); health care organization management and leadership (MS); health practice research (PhD); nursing (DNP). *Accreditation:* AACN; NLN (one or more programs are accredited). Part-time programs available. Postbaccalaureate distance learning degree programs offered (minimal on-campus study). *Faculty:* 49 full-time (42 women), 72 part-time/adjunct (60 women). *Students:* 38 full-time (32 women), 196 part-time (181 women); includes 37 minority (20 Black or African American, non-Hispanic/Latino; 9 Asian, non-Hispanic/Latino; 8 Hispanic/Latino), 5 international. Average age 36. 68 applicants, 56% accepted, 26 enrolled. In 2011, 49 master's, 7 doctorates awarded. Terminal master's awarded for partial completion of doctoral program. *Median time to degree:* Of those who began their doctoral program in fall 2003, 40% received their degree in 8 years or less. *Degree requirements:* For doctorate, thesis/dissertation. *Entrance requirements:* For master's, BS in nursing, minimum GPA of 3.0, course work in statistics; for doctorate, GRE General Test, MS in nursing, minimum GPA of 3.5. Additional exam requirements/recommendations for international students: Required—or IELTS (minimum score 6.5); Recommended—TOEFL (minimum score 560 paper-based; 230 computer-based; 88 iBT). *Application deadline:* For fall admission, 4/1 priority date for domestic students, 4/1 for international students; for spring admission, 9/1 for domestic and international students. Application fee: $50. Electronic applications accepted. *Expenses: Tuition:* Full-time $41,040. *Financial support:* In 2011–12, 49 students received support, including 1 fellowship with full and partial tuition reimbursement available (averaging $18,700 per year); scholarships/grants, traineeships, health care benefits, tuition waivers (partial), and unspecified assistantships also available. Support available to part-time students. Financial award application deadline: 6/30. *Faculty research:* Clinical research in aging, managing asthma in children, interventions to improve outcomes in critically ill children and their mothers, nurse home visitation studies, medical device evaluation, critical care clinical studies, high risk behavior and prevention, palliative care, pregnancy-related weight gain. *Total annual research expenditures:* $4.3 million. *Unit head:* Dr. Kathy H. Rideout, Interim Dean, 585-273-8902, Fax: 585-273-1268, E-mail: kathy_rideout@urmc.rochester.edu. *Application contact:* Elaine Andolina, Director of Admissions, 585-275-2375, Fax: 585-756-8299, E-mail: elaine_andolina@urmc.rochester.edu. Web site: http://www.son.rochester.edu.

University of St. Francis, College of Business and Health Administration, School of Health Administration, Joliet, IL 60435-6169. Offers MS. Part-time and evening/weekend programs available. Postbaccalaureate distance learning degree programs offered (no on-campus study). *Faculty:* 5 full-time (2 women), 22 part-time/adjunct (7 women). *Students:* 93 full-time (69 women), 310 part-time (260 women); includes 90 minority (46 Black or African American, non-Hispanic/Latino; 10 Asian, non-Hispanic/Latino; 27 Hispanic/Latino; 1 Native Hawaiian or other Pacific Islander, non-Hispanic/Latino; 6 Two or more races, non-Hispanic/Latino), 4 international. Average age 44. 160 applicants, 70% accepted, 80 enrolled. In 2011, 163 degrees awarded. *Degree requirements:* For master's, comprehensive exam. *Entrance requirements:* For master's, minimum GPA of 2.75, 2 letters recommendation, personal essay, computer proficiency. Additional exam requirements/recommendations for international students: Required—TOEFL (minimum score 550 paper-based; 213 computer-based). *Application deadline:* Applications are processed on a rolling basis. Application fee: $30. Electronic applications accepted. *Expenses: Tuition:* Part-time $656 per credit hour. Part-time tuition and fees vary according to degree level, campus/location and program. *Financial support:* In 2011–12, 76 students received support. Tuition waivers (partial) available. Support available to part-time students. Financial award applicants required to submit FAFSA. *Unit head:* Dr. Christopher Clott, Dean, 815-740-3395, Fax: 815-774-2920, E-mail: cclott@stfrancis.edu. *Application contact:* Sandra Sloka, Director of Admissions for Graduate and Degree Completion Programs, 800-735-7500, Fax: 815-740-5032, E-mail: ssloka@stfrancis.edu. Web site: http://www.stfrancis.edu/academics/college-of-business-health-administration/school-of-health/.

University of Saint Francis, Graduate School, Department of Business Administration, Fort Wayne, IN 46808-3994. Offers business administration (MBA); healthcare administration (MHA). Part-time and evening/weekend programs available. Postbaccalaureate distance learning degree programs offered (no on-campus study). *Faculty:* 8 full-time (5 women), 2 part-time/adjunct (0 women). *Students:* 5 full-time (1 woman), 16 part-time (11 women); includes 1 minority (Hispanic/Latino). In 2011, 11 master's awarded. *Entrance requirements:* For master's, GMAT, minimum AACSB index of 900, minimum GPA of 2.5. *Application deadline:* For fall admission, 7/1 priority date for domestic students; for spring admission, 11/1 priority date for domestic students. Applications are processed on a rolling basis. Application fee: $20. Application fee is waived when completed online. *Financial support:* Federal Work-Study, scholarships/grants, tuition waivers (full and partial), and unspecified assistantships available. Financial award applicants required to submit FAFSA. *Unit head:* Karen Palumbo, Director of Graduate Programs, 260-399-7700 Ext. 8312, Fax: 260-399-8174, E-mail: kpalumbo@st.edu. *Application contact:* James Cashdollar, Admissions Counselor, 260-399-7700 Ext. 6302, Fax: 260-399-8152, E-mail: jcashdollar@sf.edu. Web site: http://www.sf.edu.

University of St. Thomas, Graduate Studies, Opus College of Business, Health Care UST MBA Program, Minneapolis, MN 55403. Offers MBA. *Accreditation:* CAHME. Postbaccalaureate distance learning degree programs offered (minimal on-campus study). *Students:* 106 part-time (48 women); includes 18 minority (3 Black or African American, non-Hispanic/Latino; 11 Asian, non-Hispanic/Latino; 4 Hispanic/Latino), 1 international. Average age 40. 63 applicants, 100% accepted, 57 enrolled. In 2011, 20 master's awarded. *Entrance requirements:* For master's, minimum 5 years of work experience in related field, letters of recommendation, essays, interview. Additional exam requirements/recommendations for international students: Required—TOEFL (minimum score 80 iBT), IELTS, or Michigan English Language Assessment Battery. *Application deadline:* For fall admission, 6/1 for domestic students. Applications are processed on a rolling basis. Application fee: $75. Electronic applications accepted. *Expenses:* Contact institution. *Financial support:* In 2011–12, 15 students received support. Scholarships/grants available. *Unit head:* Dr. Jack Militello, Director, 651-962-4146, Fax: 651-962-8810. *Application contact:* Cindy Lorah, Manager of Marketing and Recruitment, 651-962-4135, Fax: 651-962-8810, E-mail: medmba@stthomas.edu. Web site: http://www.stthomas.edu/healthcaremba.

University of San Francisco, School of Management, Program in Public Administration, Concentration in Health Services Administration, San Francisco, CA 94117-1080. Offers MPA. Part-time and evening/weekend programs available. *Faculty:* 4 full-time (1 woman), 3 part-time/adjunct (1 woman). *Students:* 40 full-time (33 women), 1 (woman) part-time; includes 31 minority (6 Black or African American, non-Hispanic/Latino; 15 Asian, non-Hispanic/Latino; 9 Hispanic/Latino; 1 Two or more races, non-Hispanic/Latino). Average age 34. 12 applicants, 83% accepted, 9 enrolled. In 2011, 12 master's awarded. *Degree requirements:* For master's, thesis optional. *Entrance requirements:* For master's, minimum GPA of 3.0. Application fee: $55 ($65 for international students). *Expenses: Tuition:* Full-time $20,070; part-time $1115 per unit. Tuition and fees vary according to course load, campus/location and program. *Financial support:* In 2011–12, 1 student received support. Application deadline: 3/2; applicants required to submit FAFSA. *Unit head:* Dr. Maurice Penner. *Application contact:* 415-422-6000, E-mail: graduate@usfca.edu.

University of Saskatchewan, College of Graduate Studies and Research, Edwards School of Business, Program in Business Administration, Saskatoon, SK S7N 5A2, Canada. Offers agribusiness management (MBA); biotechnology management (MBA); health services management (MBA); indigenous management (MBA); international business management (MBA).

The University of Scranton, College of Graduate and Continuing Education, Department of Health Administration and Human Resources, Program in Health Administration, Scranton, PA 18510. Offers MHA. *Accreditation:* CAHME. Part-time and evening/weekend programs available. *Students:* 53 full-time (30 women), 9 part-time (6 women); includes 9 minority (1 Black or African American, non-Hispanic/Latino; 2 American Indian or Alaska Native, non-Hispanic/Latino; 3 Asian, non-Hispanic/Latino; 3 Hispanic/Latino), 9 international. Average age 28. 70 applicants, 80% accepted. In 2011, 17 master's awarded. *Degree requirements:* For master's, capstone experience. *Entrance requirements:* For master's, minimum GPA of 2.75. Additional exam requirements/recommendations for international students: Required—TOEFL (minimum score 550 paper-based; 173 computer-based), IELTS (minimum score 5.5). *Application deadline:* For fall admission, 4/15 priority date for domestic students. Applications are processed on a rolling basis. Application fee: $0. *Financial support:* Fellowships, teaching assistantships, career-related internships or fieldwork, and unspecified assistantships available. Financial award application deadline: 3/1. *Unit head:* Steven J. Szydlowski, Director, 570-941-4367, Fax: 570-941-4201, E-mail: sjs14@scranton.edu. *Application contact:* Joseph M. Roback, Director of Admissions, 570-941-4385, Fax: 570-941-5928, E-mail: robackj2@scranton.edu.

The University of Scranton, College of Graduate and Continuing Education, Program in Business Administration, Scranton, PA 18510. Offers accounting (MBA); finance (MBA); general business administration (MBA); health care management (MBA); international business (MBA); management information systems (MBA); marketing (MBA); operations management (MBA). *Accreditation:* AACSB. Part-time and evening/weekend programs available. Postbaccalaureate distance learning degree programs offered (no on-campus study). *Faculty:* 34 full-time (8 women). *Students:* 276 full-time (94 women), 243 part-time (88 women); includes 14 minority (10 Black or African American, non-Hispanic/Latino; 3 Asian, non-Hispanic/Latino; 1 Hispanic/Latino), 49 international. Average age 33. 358 applicants, 80% accepted. In 2011, 101 master's awarded. *Degree requirements:* For master's, capstone experience. *Entrance requirements:* For master's, GMAT, minimum GPA of 2.75. Additional exam requirements/recommendations for international students: Required—TOEFL (minimum score 500 paper-based; 173 computer-based), IELTS (minimum score 5.5). *Application deadline:* Applications are processed on a rolling basis. Application fee: $0. *Financial support:* In 2011–12, 12 students received support, including 12 teaching assistantships with full and partial tuition reimbursements available (averaging $8,433 per year); fellowships, career-related internships or fieldwork, Federal Work-Study, and unspecified assistantships also available. Support available to part-time students. Financial award application deadline: 3/1. *Faculty research:* Financial markets, strategic impact of total quality management, internal accounting controls, consumer preference, information systems and the Internet. *Unit head:* Dr. Murli Rajan, Director, 570-941-4043, Fax: 570-941-4342. *Application contact:* Joseph M. Roback, Director of Admissions, 570-941-4385, Fax: 570-941-5928, E-mail: robackj2@scranton.edu. Web site: http://www.academic.scranton.edu/department/mba/.

University of Sioux Falls, Vucurevich School of Business, Sioux Falls, SD 57105-1699. Offers entrepreneurial leadership (MBA); general management (MBA); health care management (MBA); marketing (MBA). Part-time and evening/weekend programs available. *Faculty:* 8 full-time (3 women), 7 part-time/adjunct (2 women). *Students:* 119 part-time (60 women); includes 2 minority (1 Black or African American, non-Hispanic/Latino; 1 Asian, non-Hispanic/Latino). 50 applicants, 90% accepted, 45 enrolled. *Degree requirements:* For master's, project. *Entrance requirements:* For master's, minimum GPA of 3.0. Additional exam requirements/recommendations for international students: Required—TOEFL. Application fee: $25. *Expenses:* Contact institution. *Financial support:* Institutionally sponsored loans, scholarships/grants, and tuition waivers (full) available. Financial award applicants required to submit FAFSA. *Unit head:* Rebecca T. Murdock, MBA Director, 605-575-2068, E-mail: mba@usiouxfalls.edu. *Application contact:* Student Contact, 605-331-6680. Web site: http://www.usiouxfalls.edu/mba.

University of South Africa, College of Human Sciences, Pretoria, South Africa. Offers adult education (M Ed); African languages (MA, PhD); African politics (MA, PhD); Afrikaans (MA, PhD); ancient history (MA, PhD); ancient Near Eastern studies (MA, PhD); anthropology (MA, PhD); applied linguistics (MA); Arabic (MA, PhD); archaeology (MA); art history (MA); Biblical archaeology (MA); Biblical studies (M Th, D Th, PhD); Christian spirituality (M Th, D Th); church history (M Th, D Th); classical studies (MA, PhD); clinical psychology (MA); communication (MA, PhD); comparative education (M Ed, Ed D); consulting psychology (D Admin, D Com, PhD); curriculum studies (M Ed, Ed D); development studies (M Admin, MA, D Admin, PhD); didactics (M Ed, Ed D); education (M Tech); education management (M Ed, Ed D); educational psychology (M Ed); English (MA); environmental education (M Ed); French (MA, PhD); German (MA, PhD); Greek (MA); guidance and counseling (M Ed); health studies (MA, PhD), including health sciences education (MA), health services management (MA), medical and surgical nursing science (critical care general) (MA), midwifery and neonatal nursing science (MA), trauma and emergency care (MA); history (MA, PhD); history of education (Ed D); inclusive education (M Ed, Ed D); information and communications technology policy and regulation (MA); information science (MA, MIS, PhD); international politics (MA, PhD); Islamic studies (MA, PhD); Italian (MA, PhD); Judaica (MA, PhD); linguistics (MA, PhD); mathematical education (M Ed); mathematics education (MA); missiology (M Th, D Th); modern Hebrew (MA, PhD); musicology (MA, MMus, D Mus, PhD); natural science education (M Ed); New Testament (M Th, D Th); Old Testament (D Th); pastoral therapy (M Th, D Th); philosophy (MA); philosophy of education (M Ed, Ed D); politics (MA, PhD); Portuguese (MA, PhD); practical theology (M Th, D Th); psychology (MA, MS, PhD); psychology of education (M Ed, Ed D); public health (MA); religious studies (MA, D Th, PhD); Romance languages (MA); Russian (MA, PhD); Semitic languages (MA, PhD); social behavior studies in HIV/AIDS (MA); social science (mental health) (MA); social science in development studies (MA); social science in psychology (MA); social science in social work (MA); social science in sociology (MA); social work (MSW, DSW, PhD); socio-education (M Ed, Ed D); sociolinguistics (MA); sociology (MA, PhD); Spanish (MA, PhD); systematic theology (M Th, D Th); TESOL (teaching English

to speakers of other languages) (MA); theological ethics (M Th, D Th); theory of literature (MA, PhD); urban ministries (D Th); urban ministry (M Th).

University of South Carolina, The Graduate School, Arnold School of Public Health, Department of Health Services Policy and Management, Columbia, SC 29208. Offers MHA, MPH, Dr PH, PhD, JD/MHA, MPH/MSN, MSW/MPH. *Accreditation:* CAHME (one or more programs are accredited). Part-time and evening/weekend programs available. *Degree requirements:* For master's, comprehensive exam, thesis or alternative, internship (MHA); for doctorate, comprehensive exam, thesis/dissertation. *Entrance requirements:* For master's, GMAT (MHA), GRE General Test (MPH); for doctorate, GRE General Test. Additional exam requirements/recommendations for international students: Required—TOEFL (minimum score 570 paper-based; 230 computer-based). Electronic applications accepted. *Faculty research:* Health systems management, evaluation, and planning; forecast applications in health care; Medicaid process to health care services.

University of Southern California, Graduate School, School of Policy, Planning, and Development, Executive Master of Health Administration Program, Los Angeles, CA 90089. Offers EMHA. Part-time and evening/weekend programs available. Postbaccalaureate distance learning degree programs offered (minimal on-campus study). *Entrance requirements:* Additional exam requirements/recommendations for international students: Required—TOEFL (minimum score 600 paper-based; 250 computer-based; 100 iBT). Electronic applications accepted. *Expenses:* Contact institution. *Faculty research:* Health management and policy, health care systems, health care economics and financing, health care access, community health, healthy communities.

University of Southern California, Graduate School, School of Policy, Planning, and Development, Master of Health Administration Program, Los Angeles, CA 90089. Offers ambulatory care (Graduate Certificate); health administration (MHA); long-term care (Graduate Certificate); MHA/MS. *Accreditation:* CAHME. Part-time programs available. *Degree requirements:* For master's, residency placement. *Entrance requirements:* For master's, GRE, GMAT. Additional exam requirements/recommendations for international students: Required—TOEFL (minimum score 600 paper-based; 250 computer-based; 100 iBT). Electronic applications accepted. *Faculty research:* Health administration, health management and policy, health care economics and financing, health care access, community health, healthy communities.

University of Southern Indiana, Graduate Studies, College of Nursing and Health Professions, Program in Health Administration, Evansville, IN 47712-3590. Offers MHA. Part-time programs available. Postbaccalaureate distance learning degree programs offered (minimal on-campus study). *Faculty:* 1 full-time (0 women), 1 part-time/adjunct (0 women). *Students:* 29 part-time (21 women); includes 2 minority (both Black or African American, non-Hispanic/Latino). Average age 32. 14 applicants, 100% accepted, 13 enrolled. In 2011, 13 master's awarded. *Entrance requirements:* For master's, GRE or GMAT, minimum GPA of 3.0. Additional exam requirements/recommendations for international students: Required—TOEFL (minimum score 550 paper-based; 213 computer-based; 79 iBT), IELTS (minimum score 6). *Application deadline:* For fall admission, 6/1 for domestic students, 1/1 for international students. Applications are processed on a rolling basis. Application fee: $35. Electronic applications accepted. *Expenses:* Tuition, state resident: full-time $5044; part-time $280.21 per credit hour. Tuition, nonresident: full-time $9949; part-time $552.71 per credit hour. *Required fees:* $240; $22.75 per term. Tuition and fees vary according to course load and reciprocity agreements. *Financial support:* In 2011–12, 7 students received support. Federal Work-Study, scholarships/grants, tuition waivers (full and partial), and unspecified assistantships available. Financial award application deadline: 3/1; financial award applicants required to submit FAFSA. *Unit head:* Dr. Kevin Valadares, Director, 812-461-5277, E-mail: kvaladar@usi.edu. *Application contact:* Dr. Wes Durham, Interim Director, Graduate Studies, 812-465-7015, Fax: 812-464-1956, E-mail: wdurham@usi.edu. Web site: http://health.usi.edu/acadprog/hlthserv/default.asp.

University of Southern Maine, Edmund S. Muskie School of Public Service, Program in Health Policy and Management, Portland, ME 04104-9300. Offers MS, Certificate, JD/MS. *Accreditation:* CAHME. Part-time and evening/weekend programs available. Postbaccalaureate distance learning degree programs offered (minimal on-campus study). *Degree requirements:* For master's, thesis, capstone project, field experience. *Entrance requirements:* For master's, GRE General Test. Additional exam requirements/recommendations for international students: Required—TOEFL. Electronic applications accepted. *Faculty research:* Health care, child welfare, social services, aging, substance abuse, health policy.

University of Southern Maine, School of Business, Portland, ME 04104-9300. Offers accounting (MBA); business administration (MBA); finance (MBA); health management and policy (MBA); sustainability (MBA); JD/MBA; MBA/MSA; MBA/MSN; MS/MBA. *Accreditation:* AACSB. Part-time and evening/weekend programs available. *Faculty:* 20 full-time (5 women), 2 part-time/adjunct (1 woman). *Students:* 28 full-time (9 women), 91 part-time (39 women), 1 international. Average age 33. 64 applicants, 72% accepted, 33 enrolled. *Entrance requirements:* For master's, GMAT, minimum AACSB index of 1100. Additional exam requirements/recommendations for international students: Required—TOEFL (minimum score 550 paper-based; 213 computer-based; 79 iBT). *Application deadline:* For fall admission, 8/1 priority date for domestic students, 5/1 for international students; for spring admission, 12/1 priority date for domestic students, 9/1 for international students. Applications are processed on a rolling basis. Application fee: $65. Electronic applications accepted. *Financial support:* In 2011–12, 3 research assistantships with partial tuition reimbursements (averaging $9,000 per year), 3 teaching assistantships with partial tuition reimbursements (averaging $9,000 per year) were awarded; career-related internships or fieldwork, Federal Work-Study, scholarships/grants, tuition waivers (full and partial), and unspecified assistantships also available. Support available to part-time students. Financial award application deadline: 2/15; financial award applicants required to submit FAFSA. *Faculty research:* Economic development, management information systems, real options, system dynamics, simulation. *Unit head:* John Voyer, Director, 207-780-4020, Fax: 207-780-4665, E-mail: voyer@usm.maine.edu. *Application contact:* Alice B. Cash, Assistant Director for Student Affairs, 207-780-4184, Fax: 207-780-4662, E-mail: acash@usm.maine.edu. Web site: http://www.usm.maine.edu/sb.

University of Southern Mississippi, Graduate School, College of Health, Department of Community Health Sciences, Hattiesburg, MS 39406-0001. Offers epidemiology and biostatistics (MPH); health education (MPH); health policy/administration (MPH); occupational/environmental health (MPH); public health nutrition (MPH). *Accreditation:* CEPH. Part-time and evening/weekend programs available. *Faculty:* 8 full-time (4 women), 1 part-time/adjunct (0 women). *Students:* 81 full-time (66 women), 17 part-time (13 women); includes 49 minority (43 Black or African American, non-Hispanic/Latino; 1 Asian, non-Hispanic/Latino; 2 Hispanic/Latino; 3 Two or more races, non-Hispanic/Latino), 7 international. Average age 32. 70 applicants, 94% accepted, 43 enrolled. In 2011, 45 degrees awarded. *Degree requirements:* For master's, comprehensive exam, thesis (for some programs). *Entrance requirements:* For master's, GRE General Test, minimum GPA of 2.75 in last 60 hours. Additional exam requirements/recommendations for international students: Required—TOEFL, IELTS. *Application deadline:* For fall admission, 3/1 priority date for domestic students, 3/1 for international students; for spring admission, 1/10 priority date for domestic students, 1/10 for international students. Applications are processed on a rolling basis. Application fee: $50. Electronic applications accepted. *Financial support:* In 2011–12, 5 research assistantships with full tuition reimbursements (averaging $7,000 per year), 1 teaching assistantship with full tuition reimbursement (averaging $8,263 per year) were awarded; career-related internships or fieldwork, Federal Work-Study, institutionally sponsored loans, scholarships/grants, health care benefits, and unspecified assistantships also available. Financial award application deadline: 3/15; financial award applicants required to submit FAFSA. *Faculty research:* Rural health care delivery, school health, nutrition of pregnant teens, risk factor reduction, sexually transmitted diseases. *Unit head:* Dr. Emanual Ahua, Interim Chair, 601-266-5437, Fax: 601-266-5043. *Application contact:* Shonna Breland, Manager of Graduate Admissions, 601-266 6563, Fax: 601-266-5138. Web site: http://www.usm.edu/chs.

University of South Florida, Graduate School, College of Public Health, Department of Health Policy and Management, Tampa, FL 33620-9951. Offers MHA, MPH, MSPH, PhD. Part-time and evening/weekend programs available. *Degree requirements:* For master's, comprehensive exam, thesis (for some programs); for doctorate, comprehensive exam, thesis/dissertation. *Entrance requirements:* For master's, GRE General Test or GMAT, minimum GPA of 3.0 in upper-level course work, 3 professional letters of recommendation, resume/curriculum vitae; for doctorate, GRE General Test, minimum GPA of 3.0 in upper-level course work, goal statement letter, three professional letters of recommendation, resume/curriculum vitae, writing sample. Additional exam requirements/recommendations for international students: Required—TOEFL (minimum score 550 paper-based; 213 computer-based; 79 iBT). Electronic applications accepted. *Faculty research:* Tracking community health, inpatient care, discharge policies, stroke education, leadership practices.

The University of Tennessee, Graduate School, College of Education, Health and Human Sciences, Program in Public Health, Knoxville, TN 37996. Offers community health education (MPH); gerontology (MPH); health planning/administration (MPH); MS/MPH. *Accreditation:* CEPH. *Degree requirements:* For master's, thesis optional. *Entrance requirements:* For master's, minimum GPA of 2.7. Additional exam requirements/recommendations for international students: Required—TOEFL. Electronic applications accepted. *Expenses:* Tuition, state resident: full-time $8332; part-time $464 per credit hour. Tuition, nonresident: full-time $25,174; part-time $1400 per credit hour. *Required fees:* $1162; $56 per credit hour. Tuition and fees vary according to program.

The University of Texas at Arlington, Graduate School, College of Business, Program in Health Care Administration, Arlington, TX 76019. Offers MS. Part-time and evening/weekend programs available. *Students:* 11 full-time (6 women), 118 part-time (70 women); includes 68 minority (35 Black or African American, non-Hispanic/Latino; 18 Asian, non-Hispanic/Latino; 12 Hispanic/Latino; 3 Two or more races, non-Hispanic/Latino), 12 international. 69 applicants, 74% accepted, 32 enrolled. In 2011, 77 degrees awarded. *Degree requirements:* For master's, one foreign language, thesis optional. *Entrance requirements:* For master's, GRE General Test or GMAT, minimum GPA of 3.0, official undergraduate and graduate transcripts, current professional resume, personal statement, three letters of recommendation. Additional exam requirements/recommendations for international students: Required—TOEFL (minimum score 550 paper-based; 213 computer-based; 79 iBT). *Application deadline:* For fall admission, 6/1 for domestic students, 4/1 for international students; for spring admission, 10/15 for domestic students, 9/15 for international students. Application fee: $40 ($70 for international students). *Financial support:* In 2011–12, 1 student received support. Fellowships, career-related internships or fieldwork, and scholarships/grants available. Support available to part-time students. Financial award application deadline: 6/1; financial award applicants required to submit FAFSA. *Unit head:* Dr. David Gray, Associate Dean, 817-272-2881, Fax: 817-272-2073, E-mail: gray@uta.edu. *Application contact:* Demetria Wilhite, Program Director, 817-272-0698, Fax: 817-272-5799, E-mail: demetria@uta.edu. Web site: http://www2.uta.edu/gradbiz/HealthAdmin/index.htm.

The University of Texas at Dallas, Naveen Jindal School of Management, Program in Business Administration, Richardson, TX 75080. Offers cohort (MBA); executive business administration (EMBA); global leadership (EMBA); global online (MBA); healthcare management (EMBA); product lifecycle and supply chain management (EMBA); professional business administration (MBA); project management (EMBA). *Accreditation:* AACSB. Part-time and evening/weekend programs available. Postbaccalaureate distance learning degree programs offered (no on-campus study). *Faculty:* 88 full-time (16 women), 52 part-time/adjunct (13 women). *Students:* 390 full-time (129 women), 658 part-time (207 women); includes 291 minority (42 Black or African American, non-Hispanic/Latino; 4 American Indian or Alaska Native, non-Hispanic/Latino; 168 Asian, non-Hispanic/Latino; 66 Hispanic/Latino; 11 Two or more races, non-Hispanic/Latino), 161 international. Average age 32. 872 applicants, 51% accepted, 323 enrolled. In 2011, 471 master's awarded. *Degree requirements:* For master's, thesis optional. *Entrance requirements:* For master's, GMAT, 10 years of business experience (EMBA), minimum GPA of 3.0. Additional exam requirements/recommendations for international students: Required—TOEFL (minimum score 550 paper-based; 215 computer-based). *Application deadline:* For fall admission, 7/15 for domestic students, 5/1 for international students; for spring admission, 11/15 for domestic students, 9/1 for international students. Applications are processed on a rolling basis. Application fee: $50 ($100 for international students). Electronic applications accepted. *Expenses:* Contact institution. *Financial support:* In 2011–12, 223 students received support, including 1 research assistantship with partial tuition reimbursement available (averaging $13,400 per year), 24 teaching assistantships with partial tuition reimbursements available (averaging $10,050 per year); career-related internships or fieldwork, Federal Work-Study, institutionally sponsored loans, scholarships/grants, and unspecified assistantships also available. Support available to part-time students. Financial award application deadline: 4/30; financial award applicants required to submit FAFSA. *Faculty research:* Production scheduling, trade and finance, organizational decision-making, life/work planning. *Unit head:* Lisa Shatz, Director, Full-time MBA Program, 972-883-6191, E-mail: lisa.shatz@utdallas.edu. *Application contact:* James Parker, Assistant Director, 972-883-5842, E-mail: jparker@utdallas.edu. Web site: http://jindal.utdallas.edu/academic-programs/mba-programs/.

The University of Texas at Dallas, Naveen Jindal School of Management, Program in Information Systems and Operations Management, Richardson, TX 75080. Offers health care systems (MS); information technology consulting (MS). Part-time and evening/weekend programs available. *Faculty:* 14 full-time (0 women), 5 part-time/adjunct (1 woman). *Students:* 172 full-time (66 women), 117 part-time (38 women); includes 33 minority (6 Black or African American, non-Hispanic/Latino; 18 Asian, non-Hispanic/Latino; 7 Hispanic/Latino; 2 Two or more races, non-Hispanic/Latino), 220 international. Average age 27. 510 applicants, 63% accepted, 99 enrolled. In 2011, 128 master's awarded. *Degree requirements:* For master's, thesis optional. *Entrance requirements:* For master's, GMAT. Additional exam requirements/recommendations for international students: Required—TOEFL (minimum score 550 paper-based; 215 computer-based). *Application deadline:* For fall admission, 7/15 for domestic students, 5/1 for international students; for spring admission, 11/15 for domestic students, 9/1 for international students. Applications are processed on a rolling basis. Application fee:

$50 ($100 for international students). Electronic applications accepted. *Expenses:* Tuition, state resident: full-time $11,170; part-time $620.56 per credit hour. Tuition, nonresident: full-time $20,212; part-time $1122.89 per credit hour. *Financial support:* In 2011–12, 97 students received support, including 1 research assistantship with partial tuition reimbursement available (averaging $14,832 per year); 7 teaching assistantships with partial tuition reimbursements available (averaging $10,050 per year); career-related internships or fieldwork, Federal Work-Study, institutionally sponsored loans, scholarships/grants, and unspecified assistantships also available. Support available to part-time students. Financial award application deadline: 4/30; financial award applicants required to submit FAFSA. *Faculty research:* Technology marketing, measuring information work productivity, electronic commerce, decision support systems, data quality. *Unit head:* Dr. Mark Thouin, Director, 972-883-4011, E-mail: mark.thouin@utdallas.edu. *Application contact:* James Parker, Assistant Director, 972-883-5842, E-mail: jparker@utdallas.edu. Web site: http://jindal.utdallas.edu/academic-areas/information-systems-and-operations-management/.

The University of Texas at Dallas, Naveen Jindal School of Management, Program in Management and Administrative Sciences, Richardson, TX 75080. Offers electronic commerce (MS); finance (MS); healthcare administration (MS); information systems (MS); innovation and entrepreneurship (MS); international management (MS); leadership in organizations (MS); marketing (MS); operations (MS); organizations (MS); real estate (MS); strategy (MS). *Accreditation:* AACSB. Part-time and evening/weekend programs available. *Faculty:* 26 full-time (6 women), 9 part-time/adjunct (2 women). *Students:* 128 full-time (69 women), 169 part-time (95 women); includes 76 minority (18 Black or African American, non-Hispanic/Latino; 1 American Indian or Alaska Native, non-Hispanic/Latino; 37 Asian, non-Hispanic/Latino; 15 Hispanic/Latino; 1 Native Hawaiian or other Pacific Islander, non-Hispanic/Latino; 4 Two or more races, non-Hispanic/Latino), 77 international. Average age 34. 220 applicants, 63% accepted, 68 enrolled. In 2011, 58 master's awarded. *Degree requirements:* For master's, thesis optional. *Entrance requirements:* For master's, GMAT. Additional exam requirements/recommendations for international students: Required—TOEFL (minimum score 550 paper-based; 215 computer-based). *Application deadline:* For fall admission, 7/15 for domestic students, 5/1 for international students; for spring admission, 11/15 for domestic students, 9/1 for international students. Applications are processed on a rolling basis. Application fee: $50 ($100 for international students). Electronic applications accepted. *Expenses:* Tuition, state resident: full-time $11,170; part-time $620.56 per credit hour. Tuition, nonresident: full-time $20,212; part-time $1122.89 per credit hour. *Financial support:* In 2011–12, 68 students received support, including 7 teaching assistantships with partial tuition reimbursements available (averaging $16,200 per year); research assistantships with partial tuition reimbursements available, career-related internships or fieldwork, Federal Work-Study, institutionally sponsored loans, scholarships/grants, and unspecified assistantships also available. Support available to part-time students. Financial award application deadline: 4/30; financial award applicants required to submit FAFSA. *Faculty research:* Integrated and detailed knowledge of functional areas of management, analytical tools for effective appraisal and decision-making. *Unit head:* Dr. Gregory Dess, Area Coordinator, 972-883-4439, E-mail: gdess@utdallas.edu. *Application contact:* James Parker, Assistant Director, 972-883-5842, E-mail: jparker@utdallas.edu. Web site: http://jindal.utdallas.edu/academic-areas/organizations-strategy-and-international-management/.

The University of Texas at El Paso, Graduate School, School of Nursing, El Paso, TX 79968-0001. Offers evidence-based practice (Certificate); family nurse practitioner (MSN); health care leadership and management (Certificate); interdisciplinary health sciences (PhD); nurse clinical specialist (MSN); nursing (Post-Master's Certificate); nursing systems management (MSN). *Accreditation:* AACN. *Students:* 162 (131 women); includes 94 minority (22 Black or African American, non-Hispanic/Latino; 11 Asian, non-Hispanic/Latino; 61 Hispanic/Latino), 3 international. Average age 34. 55 applicants, 58% accepted, 24 enrolled. In 2011, 12 master's awarded. *Degree requirements:* For master's, thesis optional; for doctorate, thesis/dissertation. *Entrance requirements:* For master's, GRE, minimum GPA of 3.0, course work in statistics, resume; for doctorate, GRE, letters of reference, relevant personal/professional experience, master's degree in health. Additional exam requirements/recommendations for international students: Required—TOEFL; Recommended—IELTS. *Application deadline:* For fall admission, 8/1 for domestic students, 3/1 for international students; for spring admission, 11/1 for domestic students, 9/1 for international students. Applications are processed on a rolling basis. Application fee: $45 ($80 for international students). Electronic applications accepted. *Financial support:* In 2011–12, research assistantships with partial tuition reimbursements (averaging $18,825 per year), teaching assistantships with partial tuition reimbursements (averaging $18,000 per year) were awarded; fellowships with partial tuition reimbursements, institutionally sponsored loans, scholarships/grants, health care benefits, tuition waivers (partial), and unspecified assistantships also available. Support available to part-time students. Financial award application deadline: 3/15; financial award applicants required to submit FAFSA. *Unit head:* Dr. Elias Provencio-Vasquez, Dean, 915-747-7273, Fax: 915-747-8266, E-mail: eprovenciovasquez@utep.edu. *Application contact:* Dr. Benjamin Flores, Interim Dean of the Graduate School, 915-747-5491, Fax: 915-747-5788, E-mail: bflores@utep.edu. Web site: http://nursing.utep.edu/.

The University of Texas at Tyler, College of Business and Technology, School of Business Administration, Tyler, TX 75799-0001. Offers business administration (MBA); general management (MBA); health care (MBA). Part-time programs available. Postbaccalaureate distance learning degree programs offered (no on-campus study). *Entrance requirements:* Additional exam requirements/recommendations for international students: Required—TOEFL (minimum score 550 paper-based; 79 computer-based). *Faculty research:* General business, inventory control, institutional markets, service marketing, product distribution, accounting fraud, financial reporting and recognition.

University of the Incarnate Word, School of Graduate Studies and Research, H-E-B School of Business and Administration, Program in Health Administration, San Antonio, TX 78209-6397. Offers MHA. *Faculty:* 23 full-time (10 women), 26 part-time/adjunct (12 women). *Students:* 30 full-time (18 women), 2 part-time (both women); includes 15 minority (3 Black or African American, non-Hispanic/Latino; 2 Asian, non-Hispanic/Latino; 10 Hispanic/Latino), 2 international. Average age 32. 27 applicants, 85% accepted, 18 enrolled. In 2011, 3 master's awarded. *Expenses: Tuition:* Part-time $725 per credit hour. Tuition and fees vary according to degree level. *Unit head:* Dr. Dan Dominguez, Director, 210-829-3180, E-mail: domingue@uiwtx.edu. *Application contact:* Andrea Cyterski-Acosta, Dean of Enrollment, 210-829-6005, Fax: 210-829-3921, E-mail: admis@uiwtx.edu. Web site: http://www.uiw.edu/mha/.

University of the Incarnate Word, School of Graduate Studies and Research, H-E-B School of Business and Administration, Programs in Administration, San Antonio, TX 78209-6397. Offers adult education (MAA); applied administration (MAA); communication arts (MAA); healthcare administration (MAA); instructional technology (MAA); international business (Certificate); nutrition (MAA); organizational development (MAA, Certificate); project management (Certificate); sports management (MAA). Part-time and evening/weekend programs available. Postbaccalaureate distance learning degree programs offered (no on-campus study). *Faculty:* 23 full-time (10 women), 26 part-time/adjunct (12 women). *Students:* 25 full-time (18 women), 54 part-time (33 women); includes 50 minority (10 Black or African American, non-Hispanic/Latino; 40 Hispanic/Latino), 5 international. Average age 34. 35 applicants, 94% accepted, 19 enrolled. In 2011, 38 master's awarded. *Degree requirements:* For master's, capstone. *Entrance requirements:* For master's, GRE, GMAT, undergraduate degree, minimum GPA of 2.5. Additional exam requirements/recommendations for international students: Required—TOEFL (minimum score 560 paper-based; 220 computer-based; 83 iBT). *Application deadline:* Applications are processed on a rolling basis. Application fee: $20. Electronic applications accepted. *Expenses: Tuition:* Part-time $725 per credit hour. Tuition and fees vary according to degree level. *Financial support:* Federal Work-Study and scholarships/grants available. Financial award applicants required to submit FAFSA. *Unit head:* Dr. Mark Teachout, MAA Programs Director, 210-829-3177, Fax: 210-805-3564, E-mail: teachout@uiwtx.edu. *Application contact:* Andrea Cyterski-Acosta, Dean of Enrollment, 210-829-6005, Fax: 210-829-3921, E-mail: admis@uiwtx.edu. Web site: http://www.uiw.edu/maa/index.htm and http://www.uiw.edu/maa/admissions.html.

University of the Sciences in Philadelphia, College of Graduate Studies, Mayes College of Healthcare Business and Policy, Program in Public Health, Philadelphia, PA 19104-4495. Offers MPH.

University of the Sciences in Philadelphia, College of Graduate Studies, Program in Health Policy and Public Health, Philadelphia, PA 19104-4495. Offers health policy (MPH, MS); public health (MPH). Part-time and evening/weekend programs available. *Degree requirements:* For doctorate, comprehensive exam, thesis/dissertation. *Entrance requirements:* For master's and doctorate, GRE General Test. Additional exam requirements/recommendations for international students: Required—TOEFL, TWE. *Expenses:* Contact institution. *Faculty research:* Managed care, pharmacoeconomics, health law and regulation, rehabilitation, genetic technologies.

The University of Toledo, College of Graduate Studies, College of Language, Literature and Social Sciences, Department of Political Science and Public Administration, Toledo, OH 43606-3390. Offers health care policy and administration (Certificate); management of non-profit organizations (Certificate); municipal administration (Certificate); political science (MA); JD/MPA. Part-time programs available. *Faculty:* 8. *Students:* 16 full-time (8 women), 23 part-time (11 women); includes 9 minority (5 Black or African American, non-Hispanic/Latino; 4 Hispanic/Latino), 1 international. Average age 31. 34 applicants, 59% accepted, 16 enrolled. In 2011, 13 master's, 7 other advanced degrees awarded. *Degree requirements:* For master's, comprehensive exam (for some programs), thesis. *Entrance requirements:* For master's, GRE General Test, minimum cumulative point-hour ratio of 2.7 (3.0 for MPA) for all previous academic work, three letters of recommendation, statement of purpose, transcripts from all prior institutions attended; for Certificate, minimum cumulative point-hour ratio of 2.7 for all previous academic work, three letters of recommendation, statement of purpose, transcripts from all prior institutions attended. Additional exam requirements/recommendations for international students: Required—TOEFL (minimum score 550 paper-based; 213 computer-based; 80 iBT), IELTS (minimum score 6.5). *Application deadline:* For fall admission, 1/15 priority date for domestic students, 1/15 for international students. Applications are processed on a rolling basis. Application fee: $45 ($75 for international students). Electronic applications accepted. *Financial support:* In 2011–12, 1 research assistantship with full and partial tuition reimbursement (averaging $9,000 per year), 10 teaching assistantships with full and partial tuition reimbursements (averaging $6,300 per year) were awarded; career-related internships or fieldwork, Federal Work-Study, institutionally sponsored loans, scholarships/grants, tuition waivers (full), and unspecified assistantships also available. Support available to part-time students. *Faculty research:* Economic development, health care, Third World, criminal justice, Eastern Europe. *Unit head:* Dr. Mark E. Denham, Chair, 419-530-4062, E-mail: mark.denham@utoledo.edu. *Application contact:* Graduate School Office, 419-530-4723, Fax: 419-530-4724, E-mail: grdsch@utnet.utoledo.edu. Web site: http://www.utoledo.edu/llss/.

The University of Toledo, College of Graduate Studies, College of Medicine and Life Sciences, Department of Public Health and Preventative Medicine, Toledo, OH 43606-3390. Offers biostatistics and epidemiology (Certificate); contemporary gerontological practice (Certificate); environmental and occupational health and safety (MPH); epidemiology (MPH, Certificate); global public health (Certificate); health administration (MPH); health promotion (MPH); medical health and science education (Certificate); nutrition (MPH); occupational health (MSOH, Certificate); public health and emergency response (Certificate); MD/MPH. Part-time and evening/weekend programs available. *Faculty:* 6. *Students:* 95 full-time (74 women), 66 part-time (45 women); includes 37 minority (21 Black or African American, non-Hispanic/Latino; 11 Asian, non-Hispanic/Latino; 3 Hispanic/Latino; 2 Two or more races, non-Hispanic/Latino), 6 international. Average age 29. 132 applicants, 75% accepted, 70 enrolled. In 2011, 60 master's, 26 other advanced degrees awarded. *Degree requirements:* For master's, thesis or alternative. *Entrance requirements:* For master's, GRE, minimum undergraduate GPA of 3.0, three letters of recommendation, statement of purpose, transcripts from all prior institutions attended, resume; for Certificate, minimum undergraduate GPA of 3.0, three letters of recommendation, statement of purpose, transcripts from all prior institutions attended, resume. Additional exam requirements/recommendations for international students: Required—TOEFL (minimum score 550 paper-based; 213 computer-based; 80 iBT), IELTS (minimum score 6.5). *Application deadline:* For fall admission, 3/15 for domestic and international students. Applications are processed on a rolling basis. Application fee: $45 ($75 for international students). Electronic applications accepted. *Financial support:* In 2011–12, 15 research assistantships with full tuition reimbursements (averaging $10,000 per year) were awarded; Federal Work-Study, institutionally sponsored loans, scholarships/grants, tuition waivers (full and partial), and unspecified assistantships also available. *Unit head:* Dr. Sheryl A. Milz, Chair, 419-383-3976, Fax: 419-383-6140, E-mail: sheryl.milz@utoledo.edu. *Application contact:* Joan Mulligan, Admissions Analyst, 419-383-4186, Fax: 419-383-6140, E-mail: joan.mulligan@utoledo.edu. Web site: http://nocphmph.org/.

University of Toronto, Faculty of Medicine, Program in Health Administration, Toronto, ON M5S 1A1, Canada. Offers MHS. *Entrance requirements:* For master's, minimum B+ average on each of the last two years of a four-year undergraduate program, minimum of three years relevant clinical or management experience. Additional exam requirements/recommendations for international students: Required—TOEFL (minimum score 580 paper-based; 93 iBT), TWE (minimum score 5). Electronic applications accepted.

University of Toronto, Faculty of Medicine, Program in Health Policy, Management and Evaluation, Toronto, ON M5S 1A1, Canada. Offers M Sc, PhD. *Entrance requirements:* For master's, 4-year undergraduate degree with minimum B+ standing in last two years of study, 2 reference letters, statement of intent; for doctorate, master's degree with minimum B+ average, 2 reference letters, statement of intent. Additional exam requirements/recommendations for international students: Required—TOEFL (minimum score 580 paper-based; 93 iBT), TWE (minimum score 5). Electronic applications accepted.

University of Utah, Graduate School, David Eccles School of Business, Program in Healthcare Administration, Salt Lake City, UT 84112-1107. Offers MHA, MS. Part-time

and evening/weekend programs available. *Students:* 6 full-time (1 woman), 1 (woman) part-time. Average age 31. 33 applicants, 45% accepted, 7 enrolled. In 2011, 8 degrees awarded. *Entrance requirements:* For master's, GMAT, statistics course with minimum B grade; minimum undergraduate GPA of 3.0. Additional exam requirements/recommendations for international students: Required—TOEFL (minimum score 600 paper-based; 250 computer-based; 100 iBT), IELTS (minimum score 7). *Application deadline:* For fall admission, 2/15 priority date for domestic students, 2/15 for international students. Applications are processed on a rolling basis. Application fee: $55. Electronic applications accepted. *Financial support:* Scholarships/grants and unspecified assistantships available. Financial award application deadline: 2/15; financial award applicants required to submit FAFSA. *Unit head:* Dr. Don Wardell, 801-581-8774, Fax: 801-581-3666, E-mail: don.wardell@utah.edu. *Application contact:* Carly Brisbay, MHA Senior Admissions Coordinator, 801-585-7785, Fax: 801-587-3666, E-mail: mhaadmissions@business.utah.edu.

University of Virginia, School of Medicine, Department of Public Health Sciences, Charlottesville, VA 22903. Offers clinical research (MS), including clinical investigation and patient-oriented research, informatics in medicine; public health (MPH). Part-time programs available. *Faculty:* 31 full-time (15 women), 4 part-time/adjunct (1 woman). *Students:* 54 full-time (34 women), 18 part-time (10 women); includes 22 minority (11 Black or African American, non-Hispanic/Latino; 8 Asian, non-Hispanic/Latino; 2 Hispanic/Latino; 1 Two or more races, non-Hispanic/Latino), 4 international. Average age 29. 96 applicants, 46% accepted, 31 enrolled. In 2011, 30 master's awarded. *Entrance requirements:* For master's, GRE General Test or MCAT. Additional exam requirements/recommendations for international students: Required—TOEFL. *Application deadline:* Applications are processed on a rolling basis. Application fee: $60. Electronic applications accepted. *Financial support:* Career-related internships or fieldwork available. Financial award applicants required to submit FAFSA. *Unit head:* Dr. Ruth Gaare Bernheim, Chair, 434-924-8430, Fax: 434-924-8437. *Application contact:* Tracey L. Brookman, Academic Programs Administrator, 434-924-8430, Fax: 434-924-8437, E-mail: ms-hes@virginia.edu. Web site: http://www.healthsystem.virginia.edu/internet/phs/education.cfm.

University of Washington, Graduate School, School of Public Health, Department of Health Services, Programs in Health Services Administration, Seattle, WA 98195. Offers EMHA, MHA, JD/MHA, MHA/MBA, MHA/MD, MHA/MPA. *Accreditation:* CAHME. Evening/weekend programs available. *Faculty:* 13 full-time (4 women), 4 part-time/adjunct (2 women). *Students:* 32 full-time (19 women), 108 part-time (61 women); includes 34 minority (3 Black or African American, non-Hispanic/Latino; 2 American Indian or Alaska Native, non-Hispanic/Latino; 21 Asian, non-Hispanic/Latino; 7 Hispanic/Latino; 1 Native Hawaiian or other Pacific Islander, non-Hispanic/Latino), 4 international. Average age 35. 243 applicants, 47% accepted, 74 enrolled. In 2011, 60 master's awarded. *Degree requirements:* For master's, capstone project. *Entrance requirements:* For master's, GRE General Test and GMAT (for MHA), minimum GPA of 3.0. Additional exam requirements/recommendations for international students: Required—TOEFL (minimum score 580 paper-based; 237 computer-based; 70 iBT), IELTS (minimum score 7). *Application deadline:* For fall admission, 1/15 for domestic students, 11/1 for international students. Application fee: $75. Electronic applications accepted. *Financial support:* In 2011–12, 8 students received support, including 2 research assistantships with full tuition reimbursements available (averaging $16,317 per year), 1 teaching assistantship with partial tuition reimbursement available (averaging $4,299 per year); Federal Work-Study, tuition waivers (partial), and unspecified assistantships also available. *Faculty research:* Health economics, health information management, research design in health services, health policy, clinical effectiveness. *Unit head:* William E. Welton, Director, 206-543-8778, Fax: 206-543-3964, E-mail: wwelton@u.washington.edu. *Application contact:* Karen L. Wetterhahn, Program Coordinator, 206-543-8878, Fax: 206-543-3964, E-mail: karenlw@u.washington.edu. Web site: http://depts.washington.edu/mhap.

The University of Western Ontario, Richard Ivey School of Business, London, ON N6A 3K7, Canada. Offers business (EMBA, PhD); corporate strategy and leadership elective (MBA); entrepreneurship elective (MBA); finance elective (MBA); health sector stream (MBA); international management elective (MBA); marketing elective (MBA); JD/MBA. *Degree requirements:* For master's, thesis (for some programs); for doctorate, thesis/dissertation. *Entrance requirements:* For master's, GMAT, 2 years of full-time work experience, interview. Additional exam requirements/recommendations for international students: Required—TOEFL (minimum score 100 computer; 100 iBT) or IELTS (minimium score 6). Electronic applications accepted. *Faculty research:* Strategy, organizational behavior, international business, finance, operations management.

University of West Georgia, School of Nursing, Carrollton, GA 30118. Offers health systems leadership (Post-Master's Certificate); nursing (MSN); nursing education (Post-Master's Certificate). *Accreditation:* AACN. Part-time programs available. *Faculty:* 8 full-time (all women). *Students:* 36 full-time (35 women), 16 part-time (all women); includes 14 minority (all Black or African American, non-Hispanic/Latino). Average age 45. 71 applicants, 77% accepted, 25 enrolled. In 2011, 10 master's awarded. *Degree requirements:* For master's, comprehensive exam, thesis or alternative. *Entrance requirements:* For master's, GRE or MAT, BSN, Georgia RN license, minimum GPA of 3.0 for upper-division nursing courses, completion of basic undergraduate statistics course. Additional exam requirements/recommendations for international students: Required—TOEFL (minimum score 523 paper-based; 193 computer-based; 69 iBT); Recommended—IELTS (minimum score 6). *Application deadline:* For fall admission, 7/15 for domestic and international students. Applications are processed on a rolling basis. Application fee: $30. Electronic applications accepted. *Expenses:* Tuition, state resident: full-time $4336; part-time $181 per credit hour. Tuition, nonresident: full-time $17,362; part-time $724 per credit hour. Tuition and fees vary according to course load, degree level, campus/location and program. *Financial support:* In 2011–12, 1 research assistantship with full tuition reimbursement (averaging $6,000 per year) was awarded. Financial award application deadline: 7/1; financial award applicants required to submit FAFSA. *Faculty research:* Caring in nursing education, pain assessment in older adults, pain outcomes. *Unit head:* Dr. Kathryn Mary Grams, Dean, 678-839-6552, Fax: 678-839-6553, E-mail: kgrams@westga.edu. *Application contact:* Alyicia Richards, Graduate Studies Associate, 678-839-5115, Fax: 678-839-6553, E-mail: alyrich@westga.edu. Web site: http://www.westga.edu/~nurs/.

University of Wisconsin–Oshkosh, Graduate Studies, College of Letters and Science, Department of Public Administration, Oshkosh, WI 54901. Offers general agency (MPA); health care (MPA). Part-time and evening/weekend programs available. *Degree requirements:* For master's, thesis or alternative. *Entrance requirements:* For master's, public service-related experience, resume, sample of written work. Additional exam requirements/recommendations for international students: Required—TOEFL (minimum score 550 paper-based; 213 computer-based; 79 iBT). Electronic applications accepted. *Faculty research:* Drug policy, local government state revenues and expenditures, health care regulation.

Utica College, Program in Health Care Administration, Utica, NY 13502-4892. Offers MS. Part-time and evening/weekend programs available. Electronic applications accepted.

Villanova University, College of Nursing, Villanova, PA 19085-1699. Offers adult nurse practitioner (MSN, Post Master's Certificate); family nurse practitioner (MSN, Post Master's Certificate); health care administration (MSN, Post Master's Certificate); nurse anesthetist (MSN, Post Master's Certificate); nursing (PhD); nursing education (MSN, Post Master's Certificate); nursing practice (DNP); pediatric nurse practitioner (MSN, Post Master's Certificate). *Accreditation:* AACN; AANA/CANAEP. Part-time programs available. Postbaccalaureate distance learning degree programs offered (minimal on-campus study). *Faculty:* 17 full-time (all women), 4 part-time/adjunct (all women). *Students:* 36 full-time (35 women), 256 part-time (234 women); includes 27 minority (14 Black or African American, non-Hispanic/Latino; 9 Asian, non-Hispanic/Latino; 4 Hispanic/Latino), 16 international. Average age 30. 161 applicants, 55% accepted, 75 enrolled. In 2011, 55 master's, 11 doctorates, 5 other advanced degrees awarded. *Degree requirements:* For master's, independent study project; for doctorate, comprehensive exam, thesis/dissertation. *Entrance requirements:* For master's, GRE or MAT, BSN, 1 year of recent nursing experience, physical assessment, course work in statistics; for doctorate, GRE, MSN. Additional exam requirements/recommendations for international students: Required—TOEFL, IELTS. *Application deadline:* For fall admission, 7/1 priority date for domestic students, 7/1 for international students; for spring admission, 11/1 priority date for domestic students, 11/1 for international students. Applications are processed on a rolling basis. Application fee: $50. *Expenses:* Contact institution. *Financial support:* In 2011–12, 43 students received support, including 5 teaching assistantships with full tuition reimbursements available (averaging $13,100 per year); institutionally sponsored loans, scholarships/grants, traineeships, tuition waivers (full), and unspecified assistantships also available. Financial award application deadline: 7/1; financial award applicants required to submit FAFSA. *Faculty research:* Genetics, ethics, cognitive development of students, women with disabilities, nursing leadership. *Unit head:* Dr. Marguerite K. Schlag, Assistant Dean/Director, Graduate Programs, 610-519-4907, Fax: 610-519-7650, E-mail: marguerite.schlag@villanova.edu. Web site: http://www.nursing.villanova.edu/.

Villanova University, Villanova School of Business, MBA - The Fast Track Program, Villanova, PA 19085. Offers finance (MBA); health care management (MBA); international business (MBA); management information systems (MBA); marketing (MBA); real estate (MBA); strategic management (MBA). *Accreditation:* AACSB. Part-time and evening/weekend programs available. *Faculty:* 101 full-time (32 women), 38 part-time/adjunct (8 women). *Students:* 123 part-time (46 women); includes 14 minority (1 Black or African American, non-Hispanic/Latino; 3 American Indian or Alaska Native, non-Hispanic/Latino; 5 Asian, non-Hispanic/Latino; 1 Hispanic/Latino; 4 Two or more races, non-Hispanic/Latino). Average age 29. In 2011, 53 master's awarded. *Degree requirements:* For master's, minimum GPA of 3.0. *Entrance requirements:* For master's, GMAT, work experience. Additional exam requirements/recommendations for international students: Required—TOEFL (minimum score 550 paper-based; 213 computer-based; 80 iBT). *Application deadline:* For fall admission, 6/30 for domestic and international students. Application fee: $50. Electronic applications accepted. *Expenses: Tuition:* Part-time $675 per credit. Part-time tuition and fees vary according to degree level and program. *Financial support:* Scholarships/grants available. Financial award application deadline: 6/30; financial award applicants required to submit FAFSA. *Faculty research:* Business analytics; creativity, innovation and entrepreneurship; global leadership; marketing and public policy; real estate; church management. *Unit head:* Kristy Irwin, Director of Recruitment and Marketing, 610-519-6288, Fax: 610-519-6273, E-mail: kristy.irwin@villanova.edu. *Application contact:* Meredith L. Lockyer, Assistant Director, 610-519-7016, Fax: 610-519-6273, E-mail: meredith.lockyer@villanova.edu. Web site: http://www.mba.villanova.edu.

Villanova University, Villanova School of Business, MBA - The Flex Track Program, Villanova, PA 19085. Offers finance (MBA); health care management (MBA); international business (MBA); management information systems (MBA); marketing (MBA); real estate (MBA); strategic management (MBA); JD/MBA. *Accreditation:* AACSB. Part-time and evening/weekend programs available. Postbaccalaureate distance learning degree programs offered (minimal on-campus study). *Faculty:* 101 full-time (32 women), 38 part-time/adjunct (8 women). *Students:* 18 full-time (9 women), 412 part-time (127 women); includes 45 minority (7 Black or African American, non-Hispanic/Latino; 1 American Indian or Alaska Native, non-Hispanic/Latino; 25 Asian, non-Hispanic/Latino; 4 Hispanic/Latino; 1 Native Hawaiian or other Pacific Islander, non-Hispanic/Latino; 7 Two or more races, non-Hispanic/Latino). Average age 30. In 2011, 150 master's awarded. *Degree requirements:* For master's, minimum GPA of 3.0. *Entrance requirements:* For master's, GMAT, work experience. Additional exam requirements/recommendations for international students: Required—TOEFL (minimum score 550 paper-based; 213 computer-based; 80 iBT). *Application deadline:* For fall admission, 6/30 for domestic and international students; for winter admission, 11/15 for domestic and international students; for spring admission, 3/30 for domestic students, 3/31 for international students. Applications are processed on a rolling basis. Application fee: $50. Electronic applications accepted. *Expenses: Tuition:* Part-time $675 per credit. Part-time tuition and fees vary according to degree level and program. *Financial support:* In 2011–12, 18 research assistantships with full tuition reimbursements (averaging $13,100 per year) were awarded; scholarships/grants and unspecified assistantships also available. Financial award application deadline: 6/30; financial award applicants required to submit FAFSA. *Faculty research:* Business analytics; creativity, innovation and entrepreneurship; global leadership; marketing and public policy; real estate; church management. *Unit head:* Kristy Irwin, Director of Recruitment and Marketing, 610-610-6288, Fax: 610-519-6273, E-mail: kristy.irwin@villanova.edu. *Application contact:* Meredity L. Lockyer, Assistant Director, 610-519-7016, Fax: 610-519-6273, E-mail: meredith.lockyer@villanova.edu. Web site: http://www.mba.villanova.edu.

Virginia College at Birmingham, Program in Business Administration, Birmingham, AL 35209. Offers healthcare (MBA); management (MBA). Part-time and evening/weekend programs available. Postbaccalaureate distance learning degree programs offered (no on-campus study). In 2011, 3 master's awarded. *Entrance requirements:* For master's, bachelor's degree in related academic area. *Financial support:* Career-related internships or fieldwork, Federal Work-Study, institutionally sponsored loans, scholarships/grants, and military educational benefits available. Support available to part-time students. Financial award applicants required to submit FAFSA. *Unit head:* Lisa Bacon, Unit Head, 877-812-8428, E-mail: admissions@vc.edu. *Application contact:* Angela Beck, Director of Admissions, 205-802-1200, E-mail: admissions@vc.edu. Web site: http://www.vc.edu/site/program.cfm?programID-7.

Virginia Commonwealth University, Graduate School, School of Allied Health Professions, Department of Health Administration, Doctoral Program in Health Services Organization and Research, Richmond, VA 23284-9005. Offers PhD. *Students:* 6 full-time (5 women), 6 part-time (3 women), 6 international. 9 applicants, 56% accepted, 5 enrolled. In 2011, 3 doctorates awarded. *Degree requirements:* For doctorate, thesis/dissertation, residency. *Entrance requirements:* For doctorate, GMAT or GRE General Test, minimum graduate GPA of 3.0. Additional exam requirements/recommendations for international students: Required—TOEFL (minimum score 600 paper-based; 250 computer-based; 100 iBT). *Application deadline:* For fall admission, 4/15 priority date for domestic students. Application fee: $50. Electronic applications accepted. *Expenses:* Tuition, state resident: full-time $9133; part-time $507 per credit. Tuition, nonresident: full-time $18,777; part-time $1043 per credit. *Required fees:* $77 per credit. Tuition and

fees vary according to degree level, campus/location, program and student level. *Financial support:* Applicants required to submit FAFSA. *Faculty research:* Organizational studies, theory, associated analytical techniques. *Unit head:* Dr. Jan Clement, Director, 804-828-7799, Fax: 804-828-1894, E-mail: jclement@vcu.edu. *Application contact:* Carolyn Wells, Administrative Coordinator, 804-828-7799, Fax: 804-828-1894, E-mail: cwwells@vcu.edu. Web site: http://www.had.vcu.edu/.

Virginia Commonwealth University, Graduate School, School of Allied Health Professions, Department of Health Administration, Master's Program in Health Administration, Richmond, VA 23284-9005. Offers MHA, JD/MHA, MD/MHA. *Accreditation:* CAHME. *Students:* 74 full-time (36 women), 39 part-time (22 women); includes 26 minority (8 Black or African American, non-Hispanic/Latino; 13 Asian, non-Hispanic/Latino; 5 Hispanic/Latino). 158 applicants, 48% accepted, 52 enrolled. In 2011, 44 master's awarded. *Degree requirements:* For master's, residency. *Entrance requirements:* For master's, GMAT or GRE General Test (preferred minimum score of 5.0 on analytical writing), course work in accounting, economics, and statistics; minimum GPA of 3.0. Additional exam requirements/recommendations for international students: Required—TOEFL (minimum score 600 paper-based; 250 computer-based; 100 iBT). *Application deadline:* For fall admission, 2/1 priority date for domestic students. Application fee: $50. Electronic applications accepted. *Expenses:* Tuition, state resident: full-time $9133; part-time $507 per credit. Tuition, nonresident: full-time $18,777; part-time $1043 per credit. *Required fees:* $77 per credit. Tuition and fees vary according to degree level, campus/location, program and student level. *Unit head:* Dr. Dolores G. Clement, Director, 804-828-7799, E-mail: dclement@vcu.edu. *Application contact:* Suzanne Havasy, Coordinator, 804-828-0719, Fax: 804-828-1894, E-mail: shavasy@hsc.vcu.edu. Web site: http://www.had.vcu.edu/.

Virginia Commonwealth University, Graduate School, School of Allied Health Professions, Department of Health Administration, Professional Online Master's Program in Health Administration, Richmond, VA 23284-9005. Offers MSHA. *Accreditation:* CAHME. Postbaccalaureate distance learning degree programs offered (minimal on-campus study). *Students:* 43 applicants, 74% accepted, 24 enrolled. *Degree requirements:* For master's, residency. *Entrance requirements:* For master's, GMAT or GRE General Test. Additional exam requirements/recommendations for international students: Required—TOEFL (minimum score 600 paper-based; 250 computer-based; 100 iBT). *Application deadline:* For fall admission, 3/1 for domestic students. Application fee: $50. Electronic applications accepted. *Expenses:* Tuition, state resident: full-time $9133; part-time $507 per credit. Tuition, nonresident: full-time $18,777; part-time $1043 per credit. *Required fees:* $77 per credit. Tuition and fees vary according to degree level, campus/location, program and student level. *Financial support:* Applicants required to submit FAFSA. *Unit head:* Dr. Dolores G. Clement, Director, 804-828-7799, Fax: 804-828-1894, E-mail: dclement@vcu.edu. *Application contact:* Carolyn W. Wells, Coordinator, 804-828-7799, Fax: 804-828-1894, E-mail: cwwells@vcu.edu. Web site: http://www.had.vcu.edu/prospective/msha/index.html.

Virginia Commonwealth University, Graduate School, School of Allied Health Professions, Doctoral Program in Health Related Sciences, Richmond, VA 23284-9005. Offers clinical laboratory sciences (PhD); gerontology (PhD); health administration (PhD); nurse anesthesia (PhD); occupational therapy (PhD); physical therapy (PhD); radiation sciences (PhD); rehabilitation leadership (PhD). *Faculty:* 2 full-time (1 woman). *Students:* 23 full-time (15 women), 34 part-time (23 women); includes 7 minority (4 Black or African American, non-Hispanic/Latino; 1 Asian, non-Hispanic/Latino; 1 Hispanic/Latino; 1 Two or more races, non-Hispanic/Latino), 2 international. 37 applicants, 38% accepted, 11 enrolled. In 2011, 11 doctorates awarded. *Entrance requirements:* For doctorate, GRE General Test or MAT, minimum GPA of 3.3 in master's degree. Additional exam requirements/recommendations for international students: Required—TOEFL (minimum score 600 paper-based; 250 computer-based; 100 iBT); Recommended—IELTS (minimum score 6.5). *Application deadline:* For fall admission, 3/15 for domestic students. Application fee: $50. Electronic applications accepted. *Expenses:* Tuition, state resident: full-time $9133; part-time $507 per credit. Tuition, nonresident: full-time $18,777; part-time $1043 per credit. *Required fees:* $77 per credit. Tuition and fees vary according to degree level, campus/location, program and student level. *Unit head:* Dr. Paula K. Kupstas, Director, Health Related Sciences Program, 804-828-7247, E-mail: pkupstas@vcu.edu. *Application contact:* Monica L. White, Director of Student Services, 804-828-3273, Fax: 804-828-8656, E-mail: mlwhite1@vcu.edu. Web site: http://www.pubapps.vcu.edu/BULLETINS/prog_search/?did=20005.

Virginia Commonwealth University, Medical College of Virginia-Professional Programs, School of Medicine, School of Medicine Graduate Programs, Department of Healthcare Policy and Research, Richmond, VA 23284-9005. Offers PhD. *Faculty:* 9 full-time (5 women). *Entrance requirements:* For doctorate, GRE General Test. Additional exam requirements/recommendations for international students: Required—TOEFL (minimum score 600 paper-based; 100 iBT). *Application deadline:* For fall admission, 1/5 priority date for domestic students, 12/15 for international students. Application fee: $50. Electronic applications accepted. *Expenses:* Tuition, state resident: full-time $9133; part-time $507 per credit. Tuition, nonresident: full-time $18,777; part-time $1043 per credit. *Required fees:* $77 per credit. Tuition and fees vary according to degree level, campus/location, program and student level. *Financial support:* Research assistantships, health care benefits, and unspecified assistantships available. Financial award application deadline: 3/15; financial award applicants required to submit FAFSA. *Faculty research:* Evaluation of healthcare services and systems to enhance quality of care and patient safety outcomes; examination of chronic disease (e.g. cancer, HIV/AIDS) policies and practices to improve health outcomes and economic efficiency; impact of uninsurance, public insurance (such as Medicaid) and the safety net on access to care and the health of low-income, underserved, and foreign-born populations; the study of labor supply and healthcare coverage in response to health behaviors and shocks. *Unit head:* Dr. Cathy Bradley, Chair, 804-828-5217, E-mail: cjbradley@vcu.edu. *Application contact:* Dr. Gail E. Christie, Graduate Program Director and Recruitment Contact, 804-828-9093, E-mail: christie@vcu.edu. Web site: http://www.healthpolicy.vcu.edu/.

Virginia International University, School of Business, Fairfax, VA 22030. Offers accounting (MBA); executive management (Graduate Certificate); global logistics (MBA); health care management (MBA); human resources management (MBA); international business management (MBA); international finance (MBA); marketing management (MBA). Part-time programs available. *Entrance requirements:* For master's and Graduate Certificate, bachelor's degree. Additional exam requirements/recommendations for international students: Required—TOEFL (minimum score 550 paper-based; 213 computer-based; 80 iBT), IELTS (minimum score 6). Electronic applications accepted.

Wagner College, Division of Graduate Studies, Department of Business Administration, Program in Health Care Administration, Staten Island, NY 10301-4495. Offers MBA. *Faculty:* 1 (woman) full-time. *Students:* 2 full-time (1 woman), 2 part-time (0 women); includes 1 minority (Asian, non-Hispanic/Latino). Average age 30. 3 applicants, 67% accepted, 0 enrolled. In 2011, 1 master's awarded. *Degree requirements:* For master's, thesis optional. *Entrance requirements:* For master's, GMAT, minimum GPA of 2.6. Additional exam requirements/recommendations for international students: Required—TOEFL (minimum score 550 paper-based; 217 computer-based; 79 iBT). *Application deadline:* For fall admission, 5/1 priority date for domestic students, 3/1 for international students; for spring admission, 10/1 priority date for domestic students, 10/1 for international students. Applications are processed on a rolling basis. Application fee: $50 ($85 for international students). *Expenses:* *Tuition:* Full-time $16,200; part-time $890 per credit. *Financial support:* Unspecified assistantships and alumni fellowship grant available. Financial award applicants required to submit FAFSA. *Unit head:* Dr. Cathyann Tully, Director, 718-390-3439, Fax: 718-420-4274, E-mail: cathyann.tully@wagner.edu. *Application contact:* Patricia Clancy, Assistant Coordinator of Graduate Studies, 718-420-4464, Fax: 718-390-3105, E-mail: patricia.clancy@wagner.edu.

Wake Forest University, Schools of Business, Full-time MBA Program, Winston-Salem, NC 27106. Offers consulting/general management (MBA); entrepreneurship (MBA); finance (MBA); health (MBA); marketing (MBA); operations management (MBA); JD/MBA; MD/MBA; MSA/MBA. *Accreditation:* AACSB. *Faculty:* 62 full-time (16 women), 41 part-time/adjunct (14 women). *Students:* 120 full-time (28 women); includes 14 minority (8 Black or African American, non-Hispanic/Latino; 4 Asian, non-Hispanic/Latino; 1 Hispanic/Latino; 1 Two or more races, non-Hispanic/Latino), 28 international. Average age 28. In 2011, 62 master's awarded. *Degree requirements:* For master's, 65.5 credit hours. *Entrance requirements:* For master's, GMAT or GRE, letters of recommendation, official transcripts, current resume or curriculum vitae, 2 years of work experience. Additional exam requirements/recommendations for international students: Required—TOEFL (minimum score 600 paper-based; 250 computer-based; 100 iBT), Pearson Test of English. *Application deadline:* For fall admission, 4/15 for domestic and international students. Applications are processed on a rolling basis. Application fee: $100. Electronic applications accepted. *Expenses:* Contact institution. *Financial support:* In 2011–12, 84 students received support. Career-related internships or fieldwork, scholarships/grants, and unspecified assistantships available. Financial award application deadline: 2/15; financial award applicants required to submit FAFSA. *Faculty research:* The influence of personal relationships on business decision-making and management of change; drivers of perceived value and consumer behavior; impact of accounting on auditing, financial, managerial, systems and taxation stakeholders; corporate governance and executive compensation; impact of operations strategies on competitiveness. *Unit head:* Jon Duchac, Director, Full-time MBA Program, 336-758-5422, Fax: 336-758-5830, E-mail: busadmissions@wfu.edu. *Application contact:* Tamara Paquee, Administrative Assistant, 336-758-5422, Fax: 336-758-5830, E-mail: busadmissions@wfu.edu. Web site: http://www.business.wfu.edu/.

Walden University, Graduate Programs, School of Health Sciences, Minneapolis, MN 55401. Offers clinical research administration (MS, Postbaccalaureate Certificate); health informatics (MS); health services (PhD), including community health education and advocacy, general program, healthcare administration, leadership, public health policy, self-designed; healthcare administration (MHA); public health (MPH, PhD), including community health and education (PhD), epidemiology (PhD). Part-time and evening/weekend programs available. Postbaccalaureate distance learning degree programs offered (minimal on-campus study). *Faculty:* 20 full-time (13 women), 175 part-time/adjunct (81 women). *Students:* 2,777 full-time (2,158 women), 1,350 part-time (1,038 women); includes 2,379 minority (1,935 Black or African American, non-Hispanic/Latino; 33 American Indian or Alaska Native, non-Hispanic/Latino; 173 Asian, non-Hispanic/Latino; 180 Hispanic/Latino; 9 Native Hawaiian or other Pacific Islander, non-Hispanic/Latino; 49 Two or more races, non-Hispanic/Latino), 247 international. Average age 40. In 2011, 528 master's, 79 doctorates, 1 other advanced degree awarded. *Degree requirements:* For doctorate, thesis/dissertation, residency. *Entrance requirements:* For master's, bachelor's degree or equivalent in related field, minimum GPA of 2.5; for doctorate, master's degree or equivalent in related field; minimum GPA of 3.0; official transcripts; three years of related professional/academic experience (preferred); access to computer and Internet. Additional exam requirements/recommendations for international students: Required—TOEFL (minimum score 550 paper-based; 213 computer-based), IELTS (minimum score 6.5), or Michigan English Language Assessment Battery (minimum score 82). *Application deadline:* Applications are processed on a rolling basis. Application fee: $50. Electronic applications accepted. *Financial support:* Federal Work-Study, scholarships/grants, unspecified assistantships, and family tuition reduction, active duty/veteran tuition reduction, group tuition reduction, interest-free payment plans, employee tuition reduction available. Support available to part-time students. Financial award applicants required to submit FAFSA. *Unit head:* Dr. Jorg Westermann, Associate Dean, 800-925-3368. *Application contact:* Jennifer Hall, Vice President of Enrollment Management, 866-4-WALDEN, E-mail: info@waldenu.edu. Web site: http://www.waldenu.edu/Colleges-and-Schools/College-of-Health-Sciences/School-of-Health-Sciences.htm.

Walden University, Graduate Programs, School of Management, Minneapolis, MN 55401. Offers accounting (MS, DBA), including accounting for the professional (MS), CPA (MS), self-designed (MS); accounting and management (MS), including accounting for strategic managers, self-designed; accounting for managers (MBA); advanced project management (Post-Graduate Certificate); applied project management (Post-Graduate Certificate); corporate finance (MBA); entrepreneurship (MBA, DBA); finance (DBA); global management (MS); global supply chain management (DBA); healthcare management (MBA, DBA); healthcare system improvement (MBA); human resource management (MBA, MS, PhD), including functional human resource management (MS), integrating functional and strategic human resource management (MS), organizational strategy (MS); information systems management (DBA); international business (MBA, DBA); leadership (MBA, MS, DBA), including entrepreneurship (MS), general management (MS), human resources leadership (MS), innovation and technology (MS), leader development (MS), leading sustainability (MS), project management (MS), self-designed (MS); management (MS), including healthcare management; managers as leaders (MS); marketing (MBA, DBA); project management (MBA, MS, DBA); research strategies (MS); risk management (MBA); self-designed (MBA, DBA, PhD); social impact management (DBA); strategies for sustainability (MBA); strategy and operations (MS); sustainable management (MS); technology (MBA); technology entrepreneurship (DBA); technology management (MS). Part-time and evening/weekend programs available. Postbaccalaureate distance learning degree programs offered (minimal on-campus study). *Faculty:* 32 full-time (14 women), 275 part-time/adjunct (98 women). *Students:* 3,962 full-time (2,095 women), 1,557 part-time (959 women); includes 3,003 minority (2,510 Black or African American, non-Hispanic/Latino; 25 American Indian or Alaska Native, non-Hispanic/Latino; 140 Asian, non-Hispanic/Latino; 240 Hispanic/Latino; 9 Native Hawaiian or other Pacific Islander, non-Hispanic/Latino; 79 Two or more races, non-Hispanic/Latino), 395 international. Average age 41. In 2011, 586 master's, 87 doctorates, 4 other advanced degrees awarded. *Degree requirements:* For doctorate, thesis/dissertation (for some programs), residency. *Entrance requirements:* For master's, bachelor's degree or equivalent in related field; minimum GPA of 2.5; official transcripts; goal statement; access to computer and Internet; for doctorate, master's degree or equivalent in related field; minimum GPA of 3.0; 3 years of related professional/academic experience (preferred). Additional exam requirements/recommendations for international students: Required—TOEFL (minimum score 550 paper-based; 213 computer-based), IELTS (minimum score 6.5), Michigan English Language Assessment Battery (minimum score 82). *Application deadline:* Applications are processed on a rolling basis. Application fee: $50. Electronic applications accepted. *Financial support:* Federal Work-Study, scholarships/grants, unspecified assistantships,

and family tuition reduction, active duty/veteran tuition reduction, group tuition reduction, interest-free payment plans, employee tuition reduction available. Support available to part-time students. Financial award applicants required to submit FAFSA. *Unit head:* Dr. William Schulz, III, Associate Dean, 800-925-3368. *Application contact:* Jennifer Hall, Vice President of Enrollment Management, 866-4-WALDEN, E-mail: info@waldenu.edu. Web site: http://www.waldenu.edu/Colleges-and-Schools/College-of-Management-and-Technology.htm.

Walden University, Graduate Programs, School of Public Policy and Administration, Minneapolis, MN 55401. Offers criminal justice (MPA, MPP, MS), including emergency management (MS, PhD), homeland security policy (MS, PhD), homeland security policy and coordination (MS, PhD), law and public policy (MS, PhD), policy analysis (MS, PhD), public management and leadership (MS, PhD), self-designed (MS), terrorism, mediation, and peace (MS, PhD); criminal justice leadership and executive management (MS), including emergency management (MS, PhD), homeland security policy (MS, PhD), homeland security policy and coordination (MS, PhD), law and public policy (MS, PhD), policy analysis (MS, PhD), public management and leadership (MS, PhD), self-designed, terrorism, mediation, and peace (MS, PhD); emergency management (MPA, MPP, MS), including criminal justice (MS, PhD), homeland security (MS), public management and leadership (MS, PhD), terrorism and emergency management (MS); government management (Postbaccalaureate Certificate); health policy (MPA); homeland security policy (MPA, MPP); homeland security policy and coordination (MPA, MPP); interdisciplinary policy studies (MPA, MPP); international nongovernmental organizations (MPA, MPP); law and public policy (MPA, MPP); local government management for sustainable communities (MPA, MPP); nonprofit management (Postbaccalaureate Certificate); nonprofit management and leadership (MPA, MPP, MS); policy analysis (MPA); public management and leadership (MPA, MPP); public policy and administration (PhD), including criminal justice (MS, PhD), emergency management (MS, PhD), health policy, homeland security policy (MS, PhD), homeland security policy and coordination (MS, PhD), interdisciplinary policy studies, international nongovernmental organizations, law and public policy (MS, PhD), local government management for sustainable communities, nonprofit management and leadership, policy analysis (MS, PhD), public management and leadership (MS, PhD), terrorism, mediation, and peace (MS, PhD); terrorism, mediation, and peace (MPA, MPP). Part-time and evening/weekend programs available. Postbaccalaureate distance learning degree programs offered (minimal on-campus study). *Faculty:* 9 full-time (3 women), 90 part-time/adjunct (41 women). *Students:* 1,396 full-time (886 women), 902 part-time (581 women); includes 1,392 minority (1,205 Black or African American, non-Hispanic/Latino; 11 American Indian or Alaska Native, non-Hispanic/Latino; 35 Asian, non-Hispanic/Latino; 95 Hispanic/Latino; 2 Native Hawaiian or other Pacific Islander, non-Hispanic/Latino; 44 Two or more races, non-Hispanic/Latino), 82 international. Average age 41. In 2011, 265 master's, 34 doctorates, 13 other advanced degrees awarded. *Degree requirements:* For doctorate, thesis/dissertation, residency. *Entrance requirements:* For master's, bachelor's degree or equivalent in related field, minimum GPA of 2.5; for doctorate, master's degree or equivalent in related field; minimum GPA of 3.0; official transcripts; three years of related professional/academic experience (preferred); access to computer and Internet. Additional exam requirements/recommendations for international students: Required—TOEFL (minimum score 550 paper-based; 213 computer-based), IELTS (minimum score 6.5), or Michigan English Language Assessment Battery (minimum score 82). *Application deadline:* Applications are processed on a rolling basis. Application fee: $50. Electronic applications accepted. *Financial support:* Federal Work-Study, scholarships/grants, unspecified assistantships, and family tuition reduction, active duty/veteran tuition reduction, group tuition reduction, interest-free payment plans, employee tuition reduction available. Support available to part-time students. Financial award applicants required to submit FAFSA. *Unit head:* Dr. Mark Gordon, Associate Dean, 800-925-3368. *Application contact:* Jennifer Hall, Vice President of Enrollment Management, 866-4-WALDEN, E-mail: info@waldenu.edu. Web site: http://www.waldenu.edu/Colleges-and-Schools/College-of-Social-and-Behavioral-Sciences/School-of-Public-Policy-and-Administration.htm.

Walsh University, Graduate Studies, MBA Program, North Canton, OH 44720-3396. Offers health care management (MBA); integrated marketing communications (MBA); management (MBA). Part-time and evening/weekend programs available. *Faculty:* 7 full-time (2 women), 24 part-time/adjunct (7 women). *Students:* 21 full-time (11 women), 151 part-time (74 women); includes 13 minority (8 Black or African American, non-Hispanic/Latino; 2 American Indian or Alaska Native, non-Hispanic/Latino; 3 Hispanic/Latino). Average age 34. 62 applicants, 81% accepted, 45 enrolled. In 2011, 57 master's awarded. *Entrance requirements:* For master's, GMAT, minimum GPA of 3.0. Additional exam requirements/recommendations for international students: Required—TOEFL (minimum score 500 paper-based; 173 computer-based; 61 iBT). *Application deadline:* For fall admission, 7/15 priority date for domestic students. Applications are processed on a rolling basis. Application fee: $25. Electronic applications accepted. *Expenses: Tuition:* Full-time $10,170; part-time $565 per credit hour. *Financial support:* In 2011–12, 106 students received support, including 10 research assistantships with partial tuition reimbursements available (averaging $5,674 per year), 4 teaching assistantships (averaging $5,763 per year); tuition waivers (partial), unspecified assistantships, and tuition discounts also available. Support available to part-time students. Financial award application deadline: 12/31; financial award applicants required to submit FAFSA. *Faculty research:* Patient and physician satisfaction, advancing and improving learning with information technology, consumer-driven healthcare, branding and the service industry, service provider training and customer satisfaction. *Unit head:* Dr. Michael A. Petrochuk, Director of the MBA Program and Assistant Professor, 330-244-4764, Fax: 330-490-7359, E-mail: mpetrochuk@walsh.edu. *Application contact:* Audra Dice, Graduate and Transfer Admissions Counselor, 330-490-7181, Fax: 330-244-4925, E-mail: adice@walsh.edu. Web site: http://www.walsh.edu/mba-program.

Walsh University, Graduate Studies, Program in Healthcare Management, North Canton, OH 44720-3396. Offers Graduate Certificate. *Entrance requirements:* For degree, minimum GPA of 3.0, official transcripts, current resume. Application fee: $25. *Expenses: Tuition:* Full-time $10,170; part-time $565 per credit hour. *Unit head:* Dr. Chris Petrosino, Director of Graduate Studies, 330-490-7370, Fax: 330-490-7371, E-mail: cpetrosino@walsh.edu. *Application contact:* Christine Haver, Assistant Director for Graduate and Transfer Admissions, 330-490-7177, Fax: 330-244-4925, E-mail: chaver@walsh.edu. Web site: http://www.walsh.edu/certificate-in-healthcare-management.

Washington Adventist University, Program in Health Care Administration, Takoma Park, MD 20912. Offers MA. Part-time programs available. *Students:* 2 full-time (1 woman), 10 part-time (9 women); includes 11 minority (10 Black or African American, non-Hispanic/Latino; 1 Asian, non-Hispanic/Latino). Average age 35. *Application deadline:* Applications are processed on a rolling basis. *Expenses: Tuition:* Part-time $560 per credit hour. *Financial support:* Applicants required to submit FAFSA. *Unit head:* Dr. Jude Edwards, Dean, School of Graduate and Professional Studies, 301-891-4092, E-mail: jeedward@wau.edu. *Application contact:* Dean, School of Graduate and Professional Studies, 301-891-4092, E-mail: sgps@wau.edu. Web site: http://www.wau.edu/index.php?option=com_content&view=article&id=1007&Itemid=964.

Washington State University, Graduate School, College of Pharmacy, Department of Health Policy and Administration, Pullman, WA 99164. Offers MHPA. Part-time programs available. *Faculty:* 5. *Entrance requirements:* For master's, GMAT, GRE, official copies of all college transcripts, letter of intent and introduction, three letters of recommendation. Additional exam requirements/recommendations for international students: Required—TOEFL or IELTS. *Application deadline:* For fall admission, 1/10 for domestic and international students; for spring admission, 9/1 for domestic and international students. Application fee: $75. *Financial support:* Application deadline: 2/15; applicants required to submit FAFSA. *Unit head:* Dr. Joseph Coyne, Interim Chair, 509-358-7983, Fax: 509-358-7984, E-mail: jsc@wsu.edu. *Application contact:* Graduate School Admissions, 800-GRADWSU, Fax: 509-335-1949, E-mail: gradsch@wsu.edu.

Washington State University Spokane, Graduate Programs, Program in Health Policy and Administration, Spokane, WA 99210. Offers MHPA. *Accreditation:* CAHME. Part-time and evening/weekend programs available. *Faculty:* 8. *Students:* 24 full-time (14 women), 1 (woman) part-time; includes 2 minority (both Asian, non-Hispanic/Latino), 6 international. Average age 29. 24 applicants, 67% accepted, 11 enrolled. In 2011, 10 master's awarded. *Degree requirements:* For master's, comprehensive exam (for some programs), thesis (for some programs), oral exam. *Entrance requirements:* For master's, GRE General Test or GMAT, minimum GPA of 3.0, 3 letters of recommendation. Additional exam requirements/recommendations for international students: Required—TOEFL (minimum score 550 paper-based; 213 computer-based) or IELTS (minimum score 7). *Application deadline:* For fall admission, 1/10 priority date for domestic students, 1/10 for international students; for spring admission, 7/1 priority date for domestic students, 7/1 for international students. Application fee: $75. *Financial support:* In 2011–12, research assistantships with full and partial tuition reimbursements (averaging $14,634 per year), teaching assistantships (averaging $13,383 per year) were awarded; career-related internships or fieldwork also available. Support available to part-time students. Financial award application deadline: 2/15. *Total annual research expenditures:* $1.1 million. *Unit head:* Dr. Joseph Coyne, Interim Chair and Professor, 509-358-7981, E-mail: jsc@wsu.edu. *Application contact:* Graduate School Admissions, 800-GRADWSU, Fax: 509-335-1949, E-mail: gradsch@wsu.edu. Web site: http://spokane.wsu.edu/academics/Health_Sciences/HPA/.

Wayland Baptist University, Graduate Programs, Programs in Business Administration/Management, Plainview, TX 79072-6998. Offers general business (MBA); health care administration (MBA); human resource management (MBA); international management (MBA); management (MA, MBA), including health care administration (MA), human resource management (MA), organization management (MA); management information systems (MBA). Part-time and evening/weekend programs available. Postbaccalaureate distance learning degree programs offered (no on-campus study). *Degree requirements:* For master's, capstone course. *Entrance requirements:* For master's, GMAT, GRE or MAT. Additional exam requirements/recommendations for international students: Required—TOEFL (minimum score 500 paper-based; 173 computer-based; 61 iBT). Electronic applications accepted.

Waynesburg University, Graduate and Professional Studies, Waynesburg, PA 15370-1222. Offers business (MBA), including finance, health systems, human resources, leadership, market development; counseling (MA), including addictions counseling, clinical mental health; education (MAT); nursing (MSN), including administration, education, informatics, palliative care; nursing practice (DNP); special education (M Ed); technology (M Ed); MSN/MBA. *Accreditation:* AACN. Part-time and evening/weekend programs available. *Degree requirements:* For doctorate, thesis/dissertation. *Entrance requirements:* Additional exam requirements/recommendations for international students: Required—TOEFL. Electronic applications accepted.

Wayne State University, College of Liberal Arts and Sciences, Department of Political Science, Program in Public Administration, Detroit, MI 48202. Offers aging policy and management (MPA); criminal justice policy and management (MPA); economic development policy and management (MPA); health services policy and management (MPA); human resources management (MPA); information technology management (MPA); non-profit management (MPA); organizational behavior and management (MPA); public budgeting and financial management (MPA); public policy analysis and program evaluation (MPA); social welfare policy and management (MPA); urban policy and management (MPA). *Accreditation:* NASPAA. Evening/weekend programs available. *Students:* 22 full-time (17 women), 45 part-time (33 women); includes 19 minority (16 Black or African American, non-Hispanic/Latino; 1 American Indian or Alaska Native, non-Hispanic/Latino; 2 Hispanic/Latino), 1 international. Average age 31. 75 applicants, 28% accepted, 11 enrolled. In 2011, 20 master's awarded. *Degree requirements:* For master's, comprehensive exam. *Entrance requirements:* For master's, GRE General Test. Additional exam requirements/recommendations for international students: Required—TOEFL (minimum score 550 paper-based; 213 computer-based); Recommended—TWE (minimum score 5.5). *Application deadline:* For fall admission, 6/1 priority date for domestic students, 5/1 for international students; for winter admission, 10/1 priority date for domestic students, 9/1 for international students; for spring admission, 2/1 priority date for domestic students, 1/1 for international students. Applications are processed on a rolling basis. Application fee: $50. Electronic applications accepted. *Expenses:* Tuition, state resident: part-time $512.85 per credit. Tuition, nonresident: part-time $1132.65 per credit. *Required fees:* $26.60 per credit. $199.65 per semester. Tuition and fees vary according to course load and program. *Financial support:* In 2011–12, 7 students received support. Scholarships/grants available. *Faculty research:* Urban politics, urban education, state administration. *Unit head:* Dr. Brady Baybeck, Director, 313-577-2630, E-mail: mpa@wayne.edu. Web site: http://clasweb.clas.wayne.edu/mapa.

Weber State University, College of Health Professions, Program of Health Administration, Ogden, UT 84408-1001. Offers MHA. Part-time and evening/weekend programs available. *Entrance requirements:* For master's, GMAT or GRE. Additional exam requirements/recommendations for international students: Required—TOEFL.

Webster University, College of Arts and Sciences, Department of Nursing, St. Louis, MO 63119-3194. Offers healthcare leadership (Certificate); nursing (MSN). *Accreditation:* NLN. *Degree requirements:* For master's, comprehensive exam. *Entrance requirements:* For master's, 1 year of clinical experience, BSN, interview, minimum C+ average in statistics and physical assessment, minimum GPA of 3.0, RN license. Additional exam requirements/recommendations for international students: Required—TOEFL. *Expenses: Tuition:* Full-time $10,890; part-time $605 per credit hour. Tuition and fees vary according to campus/location and program. *Faculty research:* Health teaching.

Webster University, George Herbert Walker School of Business and Technology, Department of Business, St. Louis, MO 63119-3194. Offers business (MA); business and organizational security management (MBA); computer resources and information management (MBA); environmental management (MBA); finance (MA, MBA); health services management (MBA); human resources development (MBA); human resources management (MBA); international business (MA, MBA); management and leadership (MBA); marketing (MBA); procurement and acquisitions management (MBA); telecommunications management (MBA). *Accreditation:* ACBSP. Part-time and evening/weekend programs available. Postbaccalaureate distance learning degree programs offered (no on-campus study). *Degree requirements:* For master's, comprehensive

exam (for some programs), thesis (for some programs). *Entrance requirements:* Additional exam requirements/recommendations for international students: Required—TOEFL. *Expenses: Tuition:* Full-time $10,890; part-time $605 per credit hour. Tuition and fees vary according to campus/location and program.

Webster University, George Herbert Walker School of Business and Technology, Department of Management, St. Louis, MO 63119-3194. Offers business and organizational security management (MA); computer resources and information management (MA); environmental management (MS); government contracting (Certificate); health care management (MA); health services management (MA); human resources development (MA); human resources management (MA); management (DM); management and leadership (MA); marketing (MA); nonprofit management (Certificate); procurement and acquisitions management (MA); public administration (MA); quality management (MA); space systems operations management (MS); telecommunications management (MA). *Accreditation:* ACBSP. Part-time and evening/weekend programs available. Postbaccalaureate distance learning degree programs offered (no on-campus study). *Degree requirements:* For master's, thesis (for some programs); for doctorate, thesis/dissertation, written exam. *Entrance requirements:* For doctorate, GMAT, 3 years of work experience, MBA. Additional exam requirements/recommendations for international students: Required—TOEFL. *Expenses: Tuition:* Full-time $10,890; part-time $605 per credit hour. Tuition and fees vary according to campus/location and program.

West Chester University of Pennsylvania, College of Health Sciences, Department of Health, West Chester, PA 19383. Offers emergency preparedness (Certificate); health care management (MPH, Certificate), including health care management (Certificate), integrative (MPH); school health (M Ed). *Accreditation:* CEPH. Part-time and evening/weekend programs available. *Faculty:* 2 full-time (both women), 15 part-time/adjunct (11 women). *Students:* 112 full-time (85 women), 94 part-time (76 women); includes 82 minority (64 Black or African American, non-Hispanic/Latino; 2 American Indian or Alaska Native, non-Hispanic/Latino; 12 Asian, non-Hispanic/Latino; 3 Hispanic/Latino; 1 Two or more races, non-Hispanic/Latino), 16 international. Average age 29. 149 applicants, 65% accepted, 73 enrolled. In 2011, 34 master's, 3 other advanced degrees awarded. *Degree requirements:* For master's, thesis (for some programs), minimum GPA of 3.0. *Entrance requirements:* For master's, one-page statement of career objectives, two letters of reference. Additional exam requirements/recommendations for international students: Required—TOEFL (minimum score 550 paper-based; 213 computer-based; 80 iBT). *Application deadline:* For fall admission, 4/15 priority date for domestic students, 3/15 for international students; for spring admission, 10/15 priority date for domestic students, 9/1 for international students. Applications are processed on a rolling basis. Application fee: $45. Electronic applications accepted. *Expenses:* Tuition, state resident: full-time $7488; part-time $416 per credit. Tuition, nonresident: full-time $11,232; part-time $624 per credit. *Required fees:* $1784.64; $67.59 per credit. Tuition and fees vary according to program. *Financial support:* Unspecified assistantships available. Support available to part-time students. Financial award application deadline: 2/15; financial award applicants required to submit FAFSA. *Faculty research:* Health school communities, community health issues and evidence-based programs, environment and health, nutrition and health, integrative health. *Unit head:* Dr. Bethann Cinelli, Chair, 610-436-2267, E-mail: bcinelli@wcupa.edu. *Application contact:* Dr. Lynn Carson, Graduate Coordinator, 610-436-2138, E-mail: lcarson@wcupa.edu. Web site: http://www.wcupa.edu/_ACADEMICS/HealthSciences/health/.

Western Carolina University, Graduate School, College of Health and Human Sciences, School of Health Sciences, Cullowhee, NC 28723. Offers MHS. Part-time and evening/weekend programs available. *Students:* 19 full-time (14 women), 54 part-time (36 women); includes 8 minority (3 Black or African American, non-Hispanic/Latino; 2 American Indian or Alaska Native, non-Hispanic/Latino; 3 Hispanic/Latino), 2 international. Average age 33. 39 applicants, 85% accepted, 26 enrolled. In 2011, 36 master's awarded. *Degree requirements:* For master's, thesis or alternative. *Entrance requirements:* For master's, GRE General Test, appropriate undergraduate degree with minimum GPA of 3.0, 3 letters of recommendation. Additional exam requirements/recommendations for international students: Required—TOEFL (minimum score 550 paper-based; 270 computer-based; 79 iBT). *Application deadline:* For fall admission, 5/1 priority date for domestic students; for spring admission, 9/1 priority date for domestic students. Applications are processed on a rolling basis. Application fee: $50. *Expenses:* Tuition, state resident: full-time $3348. Tuition, nonresident: full-time $12,933. *Required fees:* $3155. *Financial support:* Fellowships, research assistantships with full and partial tuition reimbursements, teaching assistantships with full and partial tuition reimbursements, institutionally sponsored loans, scholarships/grants, and unspecified assistantships available. Financial award application deadline: 3/31; financial award applicants required to submit FAFSA. *Faculty research:* Epidemiology, dietetics, public health, environmental technology, water quality, occupational health. *Unit head:* Dr. Marianne Hollis, Director, 828-227-2660, Fax: 828-227-7446, E-mail: mhollis@email.wcu.edu. *Application contact:* Admissions Specialist for Health Sciences, 828-227-7398, Fax: 828-227-7480, E-mail: gradsch@email.wcu.edu. Web site: http://www.wcu.edu/4626.asp.

Western Connecticut State University, Division of Graduate Studies, Ancell School of Business, Program in Health Administration, Danbury, CT 06810-6885. Offers MHA. Part-time programs available. *Students:* 2 full-time (both women), 25 part-time (14 women); includes 6 minority (1 Black or African American, non-Hispanic/Latino; 1 American Indian or Alaska Native, non-Hispanic/Latino; 3 Asian, non-Hispanic/Latino; 1 Hispanic/Latino). Average age 37. In 2011, 3 degrees awarded. *Degree requirements:* For master's, comprehensive exam, completion of program within 6 years. *Entrance requirements:* For master's, GMAT, GRE, or MAT, minimum GPA of 2.5. Additional exam requirements/recommendations for international students: Recommended—TOEFL (minimum score 550 paper-based; 213 computer-based; 79 iBT), IELTS (minimum score 6). *Application deadline:* For fall admission, 8/5 priority date for domestic students; for spring admission, 1/5 priority date for domestic students. Applications are processed on a rolling basis. Application fee: $50. Tuition and fees vary according to course level, course load, degree level and program. *Financial support:* Application deadline: 5/1; applicants required to submit FAFSA. *Faculty research:* Organizational behavior, human resource management, health delivery systems, health services financial management, managing health services organizations, health services quality management, health policy and strategic management for health services, long-term care administration, health services marketing, health care law. *Unit head:* Dr. Neil Dworkin, Coordinator, 203-837-8475, Fax: 203-837-8527. *Application contact:* Chris Shankle, Associate Director of Graduate Studies, 203-837-9005, Fax: 203-837-8326, E-mail: shanklec@wcsu.edu. Web site: http://www.wcsu.edu/asb/grad/mha/.

Western Illinois University, School of Graduate Studies, College of Education and Human Services, Department of Health Sciences, Macomb, IL 61455-1390. Offers health education (MS); health services administration (Certificate). *Accreditation:* NCATE. Part-time programs available. *Students:* 35 full-time (25 women), 17 part-time (13 women); includes 10 minority (7 Black or African American, non-Hispanic/Latino; 2 Asian, non-Hispanic/Latino; 1 Two or more races, non-Hispanic/Latino), 9 international. Average age 31. 46 applicants, 72% accepted. In 2011, 14 degrees awarded. *Degree requirements:* For master's, comprehensive exam, thesis or alternative. *Entrance requirements:* Additional exam requirements/recommendations for international students: Required—TOEFL (minimum score 550 paper-based; 213 computer-based; 80 iBT). *Application deadline:* Applications are processed on a rolling basis. Application fee: $30. Electronic applications accepted. *Expenses:* Tuition, state resident: part-time $281.16 per credit hour. Tuition, nonresident: part-time $562.32 per credit hour. Part-time tuition and fees vary according to campus/location and reciprocity agreements. *Financial support:* In 2011–12, 11 students received support, including 11 research assistantships with full tuition reimbursements available (averaging $7,360 per year). Financial award applicants required to submit FAFSA. *Unit head:* Dr. R. Mark Kelley, Chairperson, 309-298-1076. *Application contact:* Dr. Nancy Parsons, Interim Associate Provost and Director of Graduate Studies, 309-298-1806, Fax: 309-298-2345, E-mail: grad-office@wiu.edu. Web site: http://wiu.edu/health.

Western Kentucky University, Graduate Studies, College of Health and Human Services, Department of Public Health, Bowling Green, KY 42101. Offers healthcare administration (MHA); public health (MPH). *Accreditation:* CEPH. Part-time and evening/weekend programs available. *Degree requirements:* For master's, comprehensive exam, thesis or alternative. *Entrance requirements:* For master's, GRE General Test, minimum GPA of 2.75. Additional exam requirements/recommendations for international students: Required—TOEFL (minimum score 555 paper-based; 213 computer-based; 79 iBT). *Faculty research:* Health education training, driver traffic safety, community readiness, occupational injuries, local health departments.

Western Michigan University, Graduate College, College of Arts and Sciences, School of Public Affairs and Administration, Kalamazoo, MI 49008. Offers health care administration (Graduate Certificate); nonprofit leadership and administration (Graduate Certificate); public administration (MPA, PhD). *Accreditation:* NASPAA (one or more programs are accredited). *Degree requirements:* For doctorate, thesis/dissertation, oral exams. *Entrance requirements:* For doctorate, GRE General Test.

Widener University, School of Business Administration, Program in Health and Medical Services Administration, Chester, PA 19013-5792. Offers MBA, MHA, MD/MBA, MD/MHA, Psy D/MBA, Psy D/MHA. *Accreditation:* CAHME (one or more programs are accredited). Part-time and evening/weekend programs available. *Degree requirements:* For master's, clerkship, residency. *Entrance requirements:* For master's, GMAT, interview, minimum GPA of 2.5. Electronic applications accepted. *Faculty research:* Cost containment in health care, reimbursement of hospitals, strategic behavior.

Widener University, School of Human Service Professions, Institute for Graduate Clinical Psychology, Program in Clinical Psychology and Health and Medical Services Administration, Chester, PA 19013-5792. Offers Psy D/MBA, Psy D/MHA. *Accreditation:* APA (one or more programs are accredited); CAHME. Electronic applications accepted. *Faculty research:* Psychosocial competence, family systems, medical care systems and financing.

Wilkes University, College of Graduate and Professional Studies, Jay S. Sidhu School of Business and Leadership, Wilkes-Barre, PA 18766-0002. Offers accounting (MBA); entrepreneurship (MBA); finance (MBA); health care administration (MBA); human resource management (MBA); international business (MBA); marketing (MBA); operations management (MBA); organizational leadership and development (MBA). *Accreditation:* ACBSP. Part-time and evening/weekend programs available. *Students:* 48 full-time (20 women), 134 part-time (62 women); includes 12 minority (2 Black or African American, non-Hispanic/Latino; 5 Asian, non-Hispanic/Latino; 2 Hispanic/Latino; 3 Two or more races, non-Hispanic/Latino), 9 international. Average age 30. In 2011, 69 master's awarded. *Entrance requirements:* For master's, GMAT. Additional exam requirements/recommendations for international students: Required—TOEFL (minimum score 550 paper-based; 213 computer-based; 79 iBT). *Application deadline:* Applications are processed on a rolling basis. Application fee: $45 ($65 for international students). Electronic applications accepted. *Expenses:* Contact institution. *Financial support:* Federal Work-Study and unspecified assistantships available. Financial award application deadline: 3/1; financial award applicants required to submit FAFSA. *Unit head:* Dr. Jeffrey Alves, Dean, 570-408-4702, Fax: 570-408-7846, E-mail: jeffrey.alves@wilkes.edu. *Application contact:* Erin Sutzko, Director of Extended Learning, 570-408-4253, Fax: 570-408-7846, E-mail: erin.sutzko@wilkes.edu. Web site: http://www.wilkes.edu/pages/457.asp.

William Woods University, Graduate and Adult Studies, Fulton, MO 65251-1098. Offers administration (Ed S); agriculture (MBA); athletic/activities administration (M Ed); curriculum and instruction (M Ed); curriculum leadership (Ed S); elementary administration (M Ed); health management (MBA); human resources (MBA); principalship (Ed S); secondary administration (M Ed); special education director (M Ed). Evening/weekend programs available. *Degree requirements:* For master's, capstone course (MBA), action research (M Ed); for Ed S, field experience. *Entrance requirements:* For master's, 2 recommendations, resumé, BA/BS; teaching certification (M Ed); course work in economics and accounting (MBA); for Ed S, M Ed, 2 letters of recommendation, resume, teaching certification. Additional exam requirements/recommendations for international students: Required—TOEFL (minimum score 550 paper-based). Electronic applications accepted.

Wilmington University, College of Business, New Castle, DE 19720-6491. Offers accounting (MBA, MS); business administration (MBA, DBA); environmental stewardship (MBA); finance (MBA); health care administration (MBA, MSM); homeland security (MBA, MSM); human resource management (MSM); management information systems (MBA, MSN); marketing (MSM); marketing management (MBA); military leadership (MSM); organizational leadership (MBA, MSM); public administration (MSM). Part-time and evening/weekend programs available. *Faculty:* 4 full-time (0 women). *Students:* 266 full-time (121 women), 700 part-time (505 women). Average age 34. *Entrance requirements:* Additional exam requirements/recommendations for international students: Required—TOEFL (minimum score 500 paper-based; 173 computer-based). *Application deadline:* Applications are processed on a rolling basis. Application fee: $35. Electronic applications accepted. *Expenses: Tuition:* Part-time $534 per credit hour. *Required fees:* $25 per term. *Financial support:* Applicants required to submit FAFSA. *Unit head:* Dr. Donald W. Durandetta, Dean, 302-356-6780, E-mail: donald.w.durandetta@wilmu.edu. *Application contact:* Chris Ferguson, Director of Admissions, 302-356-4636 Ext. 256, Fax: 302-328-5164, E-mail: inquire@wilmcoll.edu. Web site: http://www.wilmu.edu/business/.

Worcester State University, Graduate Studies, Program in Health Care Administration, Worcester, MA 01602-2597. Offers MS. *Faculty:* 1 (woman) full-time, 3 part-time/adjunct (2 women). *Students:* 2 full-time (1 woman), 8 part-time (5 women); includes 1 minority (Black or African American, non-Hispanic/Latino), 1 international. Average age 38. 13 applicants, 69% accepted, 4 enrolled. In 2011, 14 master's awarded. *Degree requirements:* For master's, comprehensive exam (for some programs), thesis optional. *Entrance requirements:* For master's, MAT, GRE. Additional exam requirements/recommendations for international students: Required—TOEFL (minimum score 500 paper-based; 61 iBT). *Application deadline:* For fall admission, 6/15 for domestic and international students; for spring admission, 4/1 for domestic and international students. Applications are processed on a rolling basis. Application fee: $40. Electronic applications accepted. *Expenses:* Tuition, state resident: full-time $2700; part-time $150

per credit. Tuition, nonresident: full-time $2700; part-time $150 per credit. *Required fees:* $2016; $112 per credit. *Financial support:* Career-related internships or fieldwork, scholarships/grants, and unspecified assistantships available. Financial award application deadline: 3/1; financial award applicants required to submit FAFSA. *Unit head:* Dr. Elizabeth Wark, Coordinator, 508-929-8739, Fax: 508-929-8175, E-mail: ewark@worcester.edu. *Application contact:* Sara Grady, Assistant Dean of Graduate and Continuing Education, 508-929-8787, Fax: 508-929-8100, E-mail: sara.grady@worcester.edu.

Wright State University, School of Graduate Studies, Raj Soin College of Business, Department of Management, Dayton, OH 45435. Offers flexible business (MBA); health care management (MBA); international business (MBA); management, innovation and change (MBA); project management (MBA); supply chain management (MBA); MBA/MS. *Entrance requirements:* For master's, GMAT, minimum AACSB index of 1000. Additional exam requirements/recommendations for international students: Required—TOEFL.

Xavier University, College of Social Sciences, Health and Education, Program in Health Services Administration, Cincinnati, OH 45207. Offers MHSA, MHSA/MBA. *Accreditation:* CAHME. Part-time and evening/weekend programs available. *Faculty:* 5 full-time (1 woman), 6 part-time/adjunct (2 women). *Students:* 82 full-time (29 women), 24 part-time (12 women); includes 8 minority (5 Black or African American, non-Hispanic/Latino; 1 Hispanic/Latino; 2 Two or more races, non-Hispanic/Latino). Average age 27. 58 applicants, 86% accepted, 29 enrolled. In 2011, 39 master's awarded. *Degree requirements:* For master's, thesis. *Entrance requirements:* For master's, GMAT or GRE, resume, two letters of recommendation, statement of intent, official transcripts. Additional exam requirements/recommendations for international students: Required—TOEFL (minimum score 550 paper-based; 213 computer-based; 80 iBT). *Application deadline:* For fall admission, 6/1 priority date for domestic students, 1/1 for international students. Applications are processed on a rolling basis. Application fee: $35. Electronic applications accepted. *Expenses: Tuition:* Part-time $576 per credit hour. *Financial support:* In 2011–12, 20 students received support. Unspecified assistantships available. Financial award application deadline: 4/30; financial award applicants required to submit FAFSA. *Faculty research:* Success factors of ethics committees in health care, early hospital readmission and quality, health and labor economics, clinical emergency medicine and uncompensated care. *Unit head:* Dr. Nancy Linenkugel, Director/Chair, 513-745-3716, Fax: 513-745-4301, E-mail: linenkugeln@xavier.edu. *Application contact:* Amy Hellkamp, Recruitment/Promotions Coordinator, 513-745-3687, Fax: 513-745-4301, E-mail: hellkampal@xavier.edu. Web site: http://www.xavier.edu/mhsa/.

Xavier University, Williams College of Business, Master of Business Administration Program, Cincinnati, OH 45207. Offers business administration (Exec MBA, MBA); business intelligence (MBA); finance (MBA); health industry (MBA); international business (MBA); management information systems (MBA); marketing (MBA); MBA/MHSA; MSN/MBA. *Accreditation:* AACSB. Part-time and evening/weekend programs available. *Faculty:* 45 full-time (17 women), 13 part-time/adjunct (4 women). *Students:* 188 full-time (63 women), 630 part-time (206 women); includes 112 minority (36 Black or African American, non-Hispanic/Latino; 3 American Indian or Alaska Native, non-Hispanic/Latino; 52 Asian, non-Hispanic/Latino; 17 Hispanic/Latino; 1 Native Hawaiian or other Pacific Islander, non-Hispanic/Latino; 3 Two or more races, non-Hispanic/Latino), 45 international. Average age 30. 319 applicants, 63% accepted, 149 enrolled. In 2011, 403 master's awarded. *Degree requirements:* For master's, capstone course. *Entrance requirements:* For master's, GMAT or GRE. Additional exam requirements/recommendations for international students: Required—TOEFL (minimum score 550 paper-based; 213 computer-based; 80 iBT). *Application deadline:* For fall admission, 8/1 priority date for domestic students, 5/1 for international students; for spring admission, 12/1 priority date for domestic students, 9/1 for international students. Applications are processed on a rolling basis. Application fee: $0. Electronic applications accepted. *Expenses:* Contact institution. *Financial support:* In 2011–12, 176 students received support. Scholarships/grants, tuition waivers (partial), and unspecified assistantships available. Financial award application deadline: 3/1; financial award applicants required to submit FAFSA. *Unit head:* Dr. Hema Krishnan, Associate Dean, 513-745-3420, Fax: 513-745-3455, E-mail: krishnan@xavier.edu. *Application contact:* Anna Marie Whelan, Assistant Director, MBA Programs, 513-745-3525, Fax: 513-745-2929, E-mail: whelana@xavier.edu. Web site: http://www.xavier.edu/williams/mba/.

Yale University, School of Medicine, Yale School of Public Health, New Haven, CT 06520. Offers applied biostatistics and epidemiology (APMPH); biostatistics (MPH, MS, PhD), including global health (MPH); chronic disease epidemiology (MPH, PhD), including global health (MPH); environmental health sciences (MPH, PhD), including global health (MPH); epidemiology of microbial diseases (MPH, PhD), including global health (MPH); global health (APMPH); health management (MPH), including global health; health policy (MPH), including global health; health policy and administration (APMPH, PhD); occupational and environmental medicine (APMPH); preventive medicine (APMPH); social and behavioral sciences (APMPH, MPH), including global health (MPH); JD/MPH; M Div/MPH; MBA/MPH; MD/MPH; MEM/MPH; MFS/MPH; MM Sc/MPH; MPH/MA; MSN/MPH. MS and PhD offered through the Graduate School. *Accreditation:* CEPH. Part-time programs available. Terminal master's awarded for partial completion of doctoral program. *Degree requirements:* For master's, thesis, summer internship; for doctorate, comprehensive exam, thesis/dissertation, residency. *Entrance requirements:* For master's, GMAT, GRE, or MCAT, two years of undergraduate coursework in math and science; for doctorate, GRE General Test. Additional exam requirements/recommendations for international students: Required—TOEFL (minimum score 100 iBT). Electronic applications accepted. *Expenses:* Contact institution. *Faculty research:* Genetic and emerging infections epidemiology, virology, cost/quality, vector biology, quantitative methods, aging, asthma, cancer.

Youngstown State University, Graduate School, Bitonte College of Health and Human Services, Department of Health Professions, Youngstown, OH 44555-0001. Offers health and human services (MHHS); public health (MPH). *Accreditation:* NAACLS. Part-time and evening/weekend programs available. *Degree requirements:* For master's, thesis optional. *Entrance requirements:* For master's, GRE General Test, minimum GPA of 3.0. Additional exam requirements/recommendations for international students: Required—TOEFL. *Faculty research:* Drug prevention, multiskilling in health care, organizational behavior, health care management, health behaviors, research management.

Health Services Research

Albany College of Pharmacy and Health Sciences, School of Health Sciences, Albany, NY 12208. Offers biotechnology (MS); cytotechnology and molecular cytology (MS); health outcomes research (MS). *Faculty:* 8 full-time (3 women), 6 part-time/adjunct (5 women). *Students:* 47 full-time (22 women), 2 part-time (both women); includes 1 minority (Asian, non-Hispanic/Latino), 29 international. 49 applicants, 94% accepted, 32 enrolled. *Degree requirements:* For master's, thesis. *Entrance requirements:* For master's, GRE, minimum GPA of 3.0. Additional exam requirements/recommendations for international students: Required—TOEFL (minimum score 474 paper-based; 84 iBT). *Application deadline:* For fall admission, 3/1 for domestic and international students. Applications are processed on a rolling basis. Application fee: $75. Electronic applications accepted. *Expenses: Tuition:* Full-time $29,100; part-time $855 per credit hour. *Required fees:* $1230; $680. Tuition and fees vary according to degree level. *Financial support:* Federal Work-Study and scholarships/grants available. Support available to part-time students. Financial award application deadline: 3/1; financial award applicants required to submit FAFSA. *Unit head:* Dr. Hassan El-Fawal, Dean, 888-203-8010. *Application contact:* Donna Myers, Director of Pharmacy and Graduate Admissions, 518-694-7186, Fax: 518-694-7929, E-mail: graduate@acphs.edu.

Brown University, Graduate School, Division of Biology and Medicine, Department of Community Health, Program in Health Services Research, Providence, RI 02912. Offers MS, PhD.

Case Western Reserve University, School of Medicine and School of Graduate Studies, Graduate Programs in Medicine, Department of Epidemiology and Biostatistics, Program in Health Services Research, Cleveland, OH 44106. Offers MS, PhD. *Degree requirements:* For master's, comprehensive exam, thesis; for doctorate, comprehensive exam, thesis/dissertation. *Entrance requirements:* For master's and doctorate, GRE. Additional exam requirements/recommendations for international students: Required—TOEFL (minimum score 550 paper-based; 213 computer-based).

Clarkson University, Graduate School, School of Arts and Sciences, Progam in Basic Science, Potsdam, NY 13699. Offers MS. *Students:* 6 full-time (3 women); includes 1 minority (Hispanic/Latino). Average age 26. 3 applicants, 67% accepted, 1 enrolled. In 2011, 3 master's awarded. *Entrance requirements:* For master's, GRE, transcripts of all college coursework, three letters of recommendation; resume and personal statement (recommended). Additional exam requirements/recommendations for international students: Required—TOEFL, TSE recommended. *Application deadline:* For fall admission, 1/30 priority date for domestic students, 1/30 for international students; for spring admission, 9/1 priority date for domestic students, 9/1 for international students. Applications are processed on a rolling basis. Application fee: $25 ($35 for international students). Electronic applications accepted. *Expenses: Tuition:* Full-time $14,376; part-time $1198 per credit hour. *Required fees:* $295 per semester. *Financial support:* In 2011–12, 5 students received support, including 2 research assistantships with full tuition reimbursements available (averaging $21,999 per year), 3 teaching assistantships with full tuition reimbursements available (averaging $21,999 per year); scholarships/grants, tuition waivers (partial), and unspecified assistantships also available. *Faculty research:* Health science, environmental health. *Unit head:* Dr. Peter Turner, Dean, 315-268-6544, Fax: 315-268-3989, E-mail: pturner@clarkson.edu. *Application contact:* Jennifer Reed, Graduate School Coordinator, School of Arts and Sciences, 315-268-3802, Fax: 315-268-3989, E-mail: sciencegrad@clarkson.edu. Web site: http://www.clarkson.edu/artsandsci/grad/basic_sci.html.

Dartmouth College, The Dartmouth Institute, Hanover, NH 03755. Offers MPH, MS, PhD. Part-time programs available. *Degree requirements:* For master's, research project or practicum; for doctorate, thesis/dissertation. *Entrance requirements:* For master's and doctorate, GRE or MCAT, 3 letters of recommendation.

Emory University, Rollins School of Public Health, Department of Health Policy and Management, Atlanta, GA 30322-1100. Offers health policy (MPH); health policy research (MSPH); health services management (MPH); health services research and health policy (PhD). Part-time programs available. *Students:* 77 full-time. Average age 27. 37 applicants, 14% accepted, 2 enrolled. *Degree requirements:* For master's, thesis (for some programs), practicum, capstone course. *Entrance requirements:* For master's, GRE General Test. Additional exam requirements/recommendations for international students: Required—TOEFL (minimum score 550 paper-based; 215 computer-based; 80 iBT). *Application deadline:* For fall admission, 1/3 priority date for domestic students, 1/3 for international students. Application fee: $95. Electronic applications accepted. *Expenses: Tuition:* Full-time $34,800. *Required fees:* $1300. *Financial support:* Fellowships with full and partial tuition reimbursements, career-related internships or fieldwork, Federal Work-Study, institutionally sponsored loans, scholarships/grants, traineeships, health care benefits, and unspecified assistantships available. Support available to part-time students. Financial award application deadline: 1/5; financial award applicants required to submit FAFSA. *Faculty research:* U. S. health policy and financing, healthcare organization and financing. *Unit head:* Dr. Kenneth E. Thorpe, Chair, 404-727-3487, Fax: 404-727-9198. *Application contact:* Prof. Walter M. Burnett, Director of Graduate Studies, 404-712-9546, Fax: 404-727-9198, E-mail: wmburne@emory.edu.

The George Washington University, School of Medicine and Health Sciences, Health Sciences Programs, Washington, DC 20052. Offers clinical practice management (MSHS); clinical research administration (MSHS); emergency services management (MSHS); end-of-life care (MSHS); immunohematology (MSHS); physical therapy (DPT); physician assistant (MSHS); MSHS/MPH. Postbaccalaureate distance learning degree programs offered (no on-campus study). *Students:* 268 full-time (197 women), 255 part-time (194 women); includes 131 minority (52 Black or African American, non-Hispanic/Latino; 3 American Indian or Alaska Native, non-Hispanic/Latino; 43 Asian, non-Hispanic/Latino; 26 Hispanic/Latino; 7 Native Hawaiian or other Pacific Islander, non-Hispanic/Latino), 24 international. Average age 32. 922 applicants, 32% accepted. In 2011, 140 master's, 29 doctorates awarded. *Entrance requirements:* Additional exam requirements/recommendations for international students: Required—TOEFL (minimum score 550 paper-based; 213 computer-based). *Application deadline:* Applications are processed on a rolling basis. Application fee: $75. *Expenses:* Contact institution. *Unit head:* Jean E. Johnson, Senior Associate Dean, 202-994-3725, E-mail: jejohns@gwu.edu. *Application contact:* Joke Ogundiran, Director of Admission, 202-994-1668, Fax: 202-994-0870, E-mail: jokeogun@gwu.edu.

The Johns Hopkins University, Bloomberg School of Public Health, Department of Health Policy and Management, Baltimore, MD 21205-1996. Offers bioethics and policy (PhD); health and public policy (PhD); health care management and leadership (Dr PH);

health economics (MHS); health economics and policy (PhD); health finance and management (MHA); health policy (MHS); health services research and policy (PhD). *Accreditation:* CAHME (one or more programs are accredited). Part-time programs available. *Degree requirements:* For master's, thesis (for some programs), internship (for some programs); for doctorate, comprehensive exam, thesis/dissertation, 1 year full-time residency (for some programs), oral and written exams. *Entrance requirements:* For master's, GRE General Test or GMAT, 3 letters of recommendation, curriculum vitae/ resume; for doctorate, GRE General Test or GMAT, 3 letters of recommendation, curriculum vitae, transcripts. Additional exam requirements/recommendations for international students: Recommended—TOEFL (minimum score 600 paper-based; 250 computer-based; 100 iBT), IELTS. Electronic applications accepted. *Faculty research:* Quality of care and health outcomes, health care finance and technology, health disparities and vulnerable populations, injury prevention, health policy and health care policy.

Lakehead University, Graduate Studies, Faculty of Social Sciences and Humanities, Department of Sociology, Thunder Bay, ON P7B 5E1, Canada. Offers gerontology (MA); health services and policy research (MA); sociology (MA); women's studies (MA). Part-time and evening/weekend programs available. *Degree requirements:* For master's, research project or thesis. *Entrance requirements:* For master's, minimum B average. Additional exam requirements/recommendations for international students: Required—TOEFL. *Faculty research:* Sociology of medicine, cultural and social change, health human resources, gerontology, women's studies.

McMaster University, Faculty of Health Sciences and School of Graduate Studies, Program in Health Research Methodology (course-based), Hamilton, ON L8S 4M2, Canada. Offers M Sc. Part-time programs available. *Degree requirements:* For master's, research internship, scholarly paper courses. *Entrance requirements:* For master's, 4 year honors degree, minimum B+ average in last year of course work. Additional exam requirements/recommendations for international students: Required—TOEFL (minimum score 580 paper-based; 237 computer-based).

McMaster University, Faculty of Health Sciences and School of Graduate Studies, Program in Health Research Methodology (thesis), Hamilton, ON L8S 4M2, Canada. Offers M Sc, PhD. Part-time programs available. *Degree requirements:* For master's, thesis; for doctorate, comprehensive exam, thesis/dissertation. *Entrance requirements:* For master's, honors degree, minimum B+ average in last year of undergraduate course work; for doctorate, M Sc, minimum B+ average. Additional exam requirements/ recommendations for international students: Required—TOEFL (minimum score 580 paper-based; 237 computer-based; 92 iBT).

Medical University of South Carolina, College of Health Professions, Department of Health Sciences and Research, Program in Research Administration, Charleston, SC 29425. Offers MRA. Part-time programs available. *Faculty:* 2 part-time/adjunct (1 woman). *Students:* 1 (woman) full-time, 5 part-time (4 women); includes 1 minority (Hispanic/Latino). Average age 36. 8 applicants, 100% accepted. *Entrance requirements:* For master's, GRE. Additional exam requirements/recommendations for international students: Required—TOEFL (minimum score 600 paper-based; 250 computer-based). Application fee: $85. Electronic applications accepted. *Financial support:* Career-related internships or fieldwork, Federal Work-Study, scholarships/ grants, and tuition waivers (partial) available. Support available to part-time students. Financial award application deadline: 3/10; financial award applicants required to submit FAFSA. *Unit head:* Dr. James S. Zoller, Program Director, 843-792-3849, E-mail: zollerjs@musc.edu. *Application contact:* Ann Brown, Student Services Program Coordinator, 843-792-2115, Fax: 843-792-3327, E-mail: brownah@musc.edu.

Old Dominion University, College of Health Sciences, Program in Health Services Research, Norfolk, VA 23529. Offers PhD. Evening/weekend programs available. *Faculty:* 10 full-time (7 women), 10 part-time/adjunct (7 women). *Students:* 11 full-time (10 women), 14 part-time (10 women); includes 7 minority (5 Black or African American, non-Hispanic/Latino; 2 Asian, non-Hispanic/Latino), 7 international. Average age 41. 13 applicants, 54% accepted, 7 enrolled. In 2011, 4 doctorates awarded. *Degree requirements:* For doctorate, comprehensive exam, thesis/dissertation. *Entrance requirements:* For doctorate, GRE, minimum GPA of 3.25, master's degree, degree in health profession or health services. Additional exam requirements/recommendations for international students: Required—TOEFL (minimum score 550 paper-based). *Application deadline:* For fall admission, 7/1 for domestic students, 6/1 for international students. Applications are processed on a rolling basis. Application fee: $50. Electronic applications accepted. *Expenses:* Tuition, state resident: full-time $9096; part-time $379 per credit. Tuition, nonresident: full-time $23,064; part-time $961 per credit. *Required fees:* $127 per semester. One-time fee: $50. *Financial support:* In 2011–12, 6 students received support, including 4 fellowships with full tuition reimbursements available (averaging $15,000 per year), 2 research assistantships with full tuition reimbursements available (averaging $15,000 per year); career-related internships or fieldwork, scholarships/grants, and tuition waivers (partial) also available. Financial award application deadline: 7/1; financial award applicants required to submit FAFSA. *Faculty research:* Access to health services, women's health, domestic violence, health policy and planning, economics of obesity, substance abuse, health disparities. *Total annual research expenditures:* $150,133. *Unit head:* Dr. Deanne Shuman, Graduate Program Director, 757-683-6953, Fax: 757-683-5674, E-mail: dshuman@odu.edu. *Application contact:* William Heffelfinger, Director of Graduate Admissions, 757-683-5554, Fax: 757-683-3255, E-mail: gradadmit@odu.edu. Web site: http://hs.odu.edu/commhealth/ academics/phd/.

Penn State Hershey Medical Center, College of Medicine, Graduate School Programs in the Biomedical Sciences, Graduate Program in Public Health Sciences, Hershey, PA 17033. Offers MS. Part-time programs available. *Students:* 17 full-time (11 women); includes 5 minority (1 Black or African American, non-Hispanic/Latino; 2 Asian, non-Hispanic/Latino; 1 Hispanic/Latino; 1 Two or more races, non-Hispanic/Latino), 1 international. 47 applicants, 30% accepted, 13 enrolled. In 2011, 9 master's awarded. *Degree requirements:* For master's, thesis or alternative. *Entrance requirements:* Additional exam requirements/recommendations for international students: Required—TOEFL (minimum score 550 paper-based). *Application deadline:* For fall admission, 1/ 31 priority date for domestic students, 2/1 for international students. Applications are processed on a rolling basis. Application fee: $65. Electronic applications accepted. *Financial support:* Fellowships available. Financial award applicants required to submit FAFSA. *Faculty research:* Clinical trials, statistical methods in genetic epidemiology, genetic factors in nicotine dependence and dementia syndromes, health economics, cancer. *Unit head:* Dr. Douglas Leslie, Chair, 717-531-7178, Fax: 717-531-5779, E-mail: hes-grad-hmc@psu.edu. *Application contact:* Mardi Sawyer, Program Administrator, 717-531-7178, Fax: 717-531-5779, E-mail: hes-grad-hmc@psu.edu. Web site: http:// www.pennstatehershey.org/web/phs/programs.

Stanford University, School of Medicine, Graduate Programs in Medicine, Division of Health Services Research, Stanford, CA 94305-9991. Offers MS. Division accepts internal applicants only. *Degree requirements:* For master's, thesis. Electronic applications accepted. *Expenses: Tuition:* Full-time $40,050; part-time $890 per credit. *Faculty research:* Cost and quality of life in cardiovascular disease, technology assessment, physician decision making.

Texas State University–San Marcos, Graduate School, College of Health Professions, School of Health Administration, Program in Health Services Research, San Marcos, TX 78666. Offers MS. Part-time and evening/weekend programs available. *Faculty:* 2 full-time (1 woman). *Students:* 3 full-time (all women), 4 part-time (3 women); includes 3 minority (2 Hispanic/Latino; 1 Two or more races, non-Hispanic/Latino). Average age 30. 8 applicants, 75% accepted, 3 enrolled. In 2011, 8 master's awarded. *Degree requirements:* For master's, comprehensive exam, thesis optional, committee review. *Entrance requirements:* For master's, GRE General Test, 3 letters of reference, resume, department interview. Additional exam requirements/recommendations for international students: Required—TOEFL (minimum score 550 paper-based; 213 computer-based; 78 iBT). *Application deadline:* For fall admission, 6/15 priority date for domestic students, 6/1 for international students; for spring admission, 10/15 priority date for domestic students, 10/1 for international students. Applications are processed on a rolling basis. Application fee: $40 ($90 for international students). Electronic applications accepted. *Expenses:* Tuition, state resident: full-time $6408; part-time $3204 per semester. Tuition, nonresident: full-time $14,832; part-time $7416 per semester. *Required fees:* $1824; $912 per semester. Tuition and fees vary according to course load. *Financial support:* In 2011–12, 3 students received support, including 2 teaching assistantships (averaging $10,278 per year); research assistantships, career-related internships or fieldwork, Federal Work-Study, and institutionally sponsored loans also available. Support available to part-time students. Financial award application deadline: 4/1; financial award applicants required to submit FAFSA. *Unit head:* Dr. Michael Nowicki, Advisor, 512-245-3556, E-mail: mn03@txstate.edu. *Application contact:* Dr. J. Michael Willoughby, Dean of Graduate School, 512-245-2581, Fax: 512-245-8365, E-mail: gradcollege@txstate.edu. Web site: http://www.health.txstate.edu/hsr.

Thomas Jefferson University, Jefferson College of Graduate Studies, Certificate Programs in Clinical Research, Human Clinical Investigation, and Infectious Diseases, Philadelphia, PA 19107. Offers Certificate. *Faculty:* 22 full-time (7 women), 23 part-time/ adjunct (6 women). *Students:* 14 part-time (10 women); includes 7 minority (2 Black or African American, non-Hispanic/Latino; 4 Asian, non-Hispanic/Latino; 1 Hispanic/ Latino), 3 international. 20 applicants, 75% accepted, 11 enrolled. In 2011, 6 Certificates awarded. *Entrance requirements:* For degree, GRE General Test (recommended). Additional exam requirements/recommendations for international students: Required—TOEFL (minimum score 100 iBT) or IELTS (minimum score 7). *Application deadline:* For fall admission, 8/1 priority date for domestic students, 3/1 for international students; for winter admission, 12/1 priority date for domestic students, 6/1 for international students; for spring admission, 4/1 priority date for domestic students. Applications are processed on a rolling basis. Application fee: $50. Electronic applications accepted. *Financial support:* In 2011–12, 5 students received support. Federal Work-Study and institutionally sponsored loans available. Support available to part-time students. Financial award application deadline: 5/1; financial award applicants required to submit FAFSA. *Faculty research:* Epidemiology, clinical research, statistics, planning and management, disease control. *Unit head:* Dr. Dennis M. Gross, Associate Dean, 215-503-0156, Fax: 215-503-3433, E-mail: dennis.gross@jefferson.edu. *Application contact:* Eleanor M. Gorman, Assistant Coordinator, Graduate Center Programs, 215-503-5799, Fax: 215-503-3433, E-mail: eleanor.gorman@jefferson.edu. Web site: http:// www.jefferson.edu/jcgs/cert/.

Thomas Jefferson University, Jefferson School of Population Health, Philadelphia, PA 19107. Offers applied health economics and outcomes research (MS, PhD); behavioral health science (PhD); chronic care management (MS, Certificate); health policy (MS, Certificate); healthcare quality and safety (MS, PhD); public health (MPH, Certificate). Part-time and evening/weekend programs available. Postbaccalaureate distance learning degree programs offered (no on-campus study). Terminal master's awarded for partial completion of doctoral program. *Degree requirements:* For master's, thesis; for doctorate, comprehensive exam, thesis/dissertation. *Entrance requirements:* For master's, GRE or other graduate entrance exam (MCAT, LSAT, DAT, etc.), two letters of recommendation, curriculum vitae, transcripts from all undergraduate and graduate institutions; for doctorate, GRE taken within the last 5 years, three letters of recommendation, curriculum vitae, transcripts from all undergraduate and graduate institutions. Additional exam requirements/recommendations for international students: Required—TOEFL. Electronic applications accepted. *Faculty research:* Applied health economics and outcomes research, behavioral and health sciences, chronic disease management, health policy, healthcare quality and patient safety, wellness and prevention.

University of Alberta, School of Public Health, Department of Public Health Sciences, Edmonton, AB T6G 2E1, Canada. Offers clinical epidemiology (M Sc, MPH); environmental and occupational health (MPH); environmental health sciences (M Sc); epidemiology (M Sc); global health (M Sc, MPH); health policy and management (MPH); health policy research (M Sc); health technology assessment (MPH); occupational health (M Sc); population health (M Sc); public health leadership (MPH); public health sciences (PhD); quantitative methods (MPH). *Accreditation:* CEPH (one or more programs are accredited). Terminal master's awarded for partial completion of doctoral program. *Degree requirements:* For master's, thesis (for some programs); for doctorate, thesis/dissertation. *Entrance requirements:* For master's, GMAT or GRE General Test. Additional exam requirements/recommendations for international students: Required—TOEFL (minimum score 550 paper-based; 213 computer-based) or IELTS (minimum score 6). Electronic applications accepted. *Faculty research:* Biostatistics, health promotion and socio-behavioral health science.

University of Arkansas for Medical Sciences, Graduate School, Program in Health Systems Research, Little Rock, AR 72205-7199. Offers PhD. *Degree requirements:* For doctorate, thesis/dissertation. *Entrance requirements:* For doctorate, GRE. Additional exam requirements/recommendations for international students: Required—TOEFL. *Faculty research:* Health economics, quality and health outcomes research.

University of Colorado Denver, Colorado School of Public Health, Health Services Research Program, Aurora, CO 80045. Offers PhD. Part-time programs available. *Students:* 4 full-time (all women), 10 part-time (6 women); includes 3 minority (2 Asian, non-Hispanic/Latino; 1 Hispanic/Latino), 1 international. Average age 42. 12 applicants, 50% accepted, 5 enrolled. *Degree requirements:* For doctorate, comprehensive exam, thesis/dissertation, minimum of 65 credit hours including 30 credit hours for doctoral thesis research. *Entrance requirements:* For doctorate, GRE or MCAT, minimum undergraduate GPA of 3.0. Additional exam requirements/recommendations for international students: Required—TOEFL (minimum score 550 paper-based; 213 computer-based; 80 iBT). *Application deadline:* For fall admission, 2/1 for domestic students. Application fee: $65. Electronic applications accepted. *Expenses:* Contact institution. *Financial support:* Fellowships, research assistantships, Federal Work-Study, scholarships/grants, and unspecified assistantships available. Financial award application deadline: 3/1; financial award applicants required to submit FAFSA. *Faculty research:* Drug safety and risk management, health care financing and cost, health interaction with environmental factors, quality improvement and strategic research, cardiovascular health promotion. *Unit head:* Dr. Adam Atherly, Chair, 303-724-4471, E-mail: adam.atherly@ucdenver.edu. *Application contact:* Mary Baitinger, Departmental Assistant, 303-724-6698, E-mail: mary.baitinger@ucdenver.edu. Web site: http://

www.ucdenver.edu/academics/colleges/PublicHealth/departments/HealthSystems/Pages/welcome.aspx.

University of Colorado Denver, School of Medicine, Clinical Science Graduate Program, Aurora, CO 80045. Offers clinical investigation (PhD); clinical sciences (MS); health information technology (PhD); health services research (PhD). *Students:* 24 full-time (15 women), 18 part-time (10 women); includes 6 minority (2 Black or African American, non-Hispanic/Latino; 2 American Indian or Alaska Native, non-Hispanic/Latino; 2 Asian, non-Hispanic/Latino), 1 international. Average age 38. 15 applicants, 53% accepted, 8 enrolled. In 2011, 3 master's, 6 doctorates awarded. *Degree requirements:* For master's, thesis, minimum of 30 credit hours, defense/final exam of thesis or publishable paper; for doctorate, comprehensive exam, thesis/dissertation, at least 30 credit hours of thesis work. *Entrance requirements:* For master's, GRE General Test or MCAT (waived if candidate has earned MS/MA or PhD from accredited U.S. school), minimum undergraduate GPA of 3.0; for doctorate, GRE General Test or MCAT (waived if candidate has earned MS/MA or PhD from accredited U.S. school), health care graduate, professional degree, or graduate degree related to health sciences; minimum GPA of 3.0. Additional exam requirements/recommendations for international students: Required—TOEFL (minimum score 550 paper-based; 213 computer-based). *Application deadline:* For fall admission, 2/1 for domestic students; for spring admission, 10/1 for domestic students. Application fee: $50 ($75 for international students). Electronic applications accepted. *Expenses:* Contact institution. *Financial support:* Fellowships, research assistantships, and teaching assistantships available. Financial award application deadline: 3/15; financial award applicants required to submit FAFSA. *Unit head:* Dr. Lisa Cicutto, Program Director, 303-398-1538, E-mail: cicuttol@njc.org. *Application contact:* Galit Mankin, Program Administrator, 720-848-6249, Fax: 303-848-7381, E-mail: galit.mankin@ucdenver.edu. Web site: http://cctsi.ucdenver.edu/training-and-education/CLSC/Pages/default.aspx.

University of Florida, Graduate School, College of Public Health and Health Professions, Department of Health Services Research, Management and Policy, Gainesville, FL 32611. Offers health services research (PhD). *Accreditation:* CAHME. Part-time programs available. *Students:* 59 full-time (29 women), 2 part-time (0 women); includes 18 minority (9 Black or African American, non-Hispanic/Latino; 3 Asian, non-Hispanic/Latino; 6 Hispanic/Latino), 5 international. Average age 29. 17 applicants, 18% accepted, 1 enrolled. In 2011, 2 doctorates awarded. *Entrance requirements:* For doctorate, GRE General Test, minimum GPA of 3.0. Additional exam requirements/recommendations for international students: Required—TOEFL (minimum score 550 paper-based; 213 computer-based; 80 iBT), IELTS (minimum score 6). *Application deadline:* Applications are processed on a rolling basis. Application fee: $30. Electronic applications accepted. *Financial support:* Fellowships, research assistantships, teaching assistantships, career-related internships or fieldwork, and unspecified assistantships available. Financial award applicants required to submit FAFSA. *Faculty research:* Hospital profitability, indigent care, rural health care systems, AIDS education, managed care, outcomes. *Unit head:* Dr. R. Paul Duncan, Department Chair, 352-273-6065, Fax: 352-273-6075, E-mail: pduncan@phhp.ufl.edu. *Application contact:* Barbara Ross, Student Services Coordinator, 352-273-6074, Fax: 352-273-6075, E-mail: bross@phhp.ufl.edu. Web site: http://www.phhp.ufl.edu/hsrmp/.

University of Illinois at Chicago, Graduate College, School of Public Health, Division of Health Policy and Administration, Chicago, IL 60607-7128. Offers clinical translational science (MS); health policy (PhD); health policy and administration (Dr PH); health services research (PhD); healthcare (MHA); public health policy management (MPH). Part-time programs available. Terminal master's awarded for partial completion of doctoral program. *Degree requirements:* For master's, thesis, field practicum; for doctorate, thesis/dissertation, independent research, internship. *Entrance requirements:* For master's and doctorate, GRE General Test, minimum GPA of 2.75. Additional exam requirements/recommendations for international students: Required—TOEFL. Electronic applications accepted.

University of La Verne, College of Business and Public Management, Program in Health Administration, La Verne, CA 91750-4443. Offers financial management (MHA); health administration (MHA); human resources (MHA); information management (MHA); leadership and management (MHA); managed care (MHA); marketing and business development (MHA). Part-time programs available. *Faculty:* 34 full-time (15 women), 28 part-time/adjunct (13 women). *Students:* 55 full-time (37 women), 35 part-time (27 women); includes 52 minority (15 Black or African American, non-Hispanic/Latino; 9 Asian, non-Hispanic/Latino; 27 Hispanic/Latino; 1 Native Hawaiian or other Pacific Islander, non-Hispanic/Latino), 13 international. Average age 32. In 2011, 16 master's awarded. *Entrance requirements:* For master's, minimum undergraduate GPA of 2.5, 3 letters of reference, curriculum vitae or resume, writing sample. Additional exam requirements/recommendations for international students: Required—TOEFL (minimum score 550 paper-based; 213 computer-based). *Application deadline:* Applications are processed on a rolling basis. Application fee: $50. *Expenses:* Contact institution. *Financial support:* Application deadline: 3/2; applicants required to submit FAFSA. *Unit head:* Terrell Ford, Program Director, 909-593-3511 Ext. 4796, E-mail: tford@laverne.edu. *Application contact:* Barbara Cox, Program and Admissions Specialist, 909-593-3511 Ext. 4004, Fax: 909-392-2761, E-mail: bcox@laverne.edu. Web site: http://laverne.edu/catalog/program/mha-master-of-health-administration/.

University of Maryland, Baltimore, Graduate School, Graduate Programs in Pharmacy, Department of Pharmaceutical Health Service Research, Baltimore, MD 21201. Offers epidemiology (MS); pharmacy administration (PhD); Pharm D/PhD. *Degree requirements:* For doctorate, comprehensive exam, thesis/dissertation. *Entrance requirements:* For doctorate, GRE General Test. Additional exam requirements/recommendations for international students: Required—TOEFL, IELTS. Electronic applications accepted. *Faculty research:* Pharmacoeconomics, outcomes research, public health policy, drug therapy and aging.

University of Massachusetts Worcester, Graduate School of Biomedical Sciences, Worcester, MA 01655-0115. Offers biochemistry and molecular pharmacology (PhD); bioinformatics and computational biology (PhD); cancer biology (PhD); cell biology (PhD); clinical and population health research (PhD); clinical investigation (MS); immunology and virology (PhD); interdisciplinary graduate program (PhD); molecular genetics and microbiology (PhD); neuroscience (PhD); DVM/PhD; MD/PhD. *Faculty:* 1,427 full-time (526 women), 309 part-time/adjunct (196 women). *Students:* 416 full-time (225 women); includes 47 minority (12 Black or African American, non-Hispanic/Latino; 32 Asian, non-Hispanic/Latino; 3 Hispanic/Latino), 144 international. Average age 29. 623 applicants, 17% accepted, 54 enrolled. In 2011, 5 master's, 63 doctorates awarded. Terminal master's awarded for partial completion of doctoral program. *Degree requirements:* For master's, comprehensive exam, thesis; for doctorate, comprehensive exam, thesis/dissertation. *Entrance requirements:* For master's, bachelor's degree; for doctorate, GRE General Test. Additional exam requirements/recommendations for international students: Required—TOEFL (minimum score 600 paper-based; 250 computer-based; 100 iBT) or IELTS (minimum score 7.5). *Application deadline:* For fall admission, 12/15 for domestic and international students; for spring admission, 5/15 for domestic students. Application fee: $50. Electronic applications accepted. *Expenses:* Contact institution. *Financial support:* In 2011–12, 416 students received support, including 416 research assistantships with full tuition reimbursements available (averaging $29,200 per year); scholarships/grants, health care benefits, tuition waivers (full), and unspecified assistantships also available. Financial award application deadline: 4/16. *Faculty research:* RNA interference, cell biology, bioinformatics, clinical research, infectious disease. *Total annual research expenditures:* $262.7 million. *Unit head:* Dr. Anthony Carruthers, Dean, 508-856-4135, E-mail: anthony.carruthers@umassmed.edu. *Application contact:* Dr. Kendall Knight, Associate Dean and Interim Director of Admissions and Recruitment, 508-856-5628, Fax: 508-856-3659, E-mail: kendall.knight@umassmed.edu. Web site: http://www.umassmed.edu/gsbs/.

University of Minnesota, Twin Cities Campus, School of Public Health, Major in Health Services Research, Policy, and Administration, Minneapolis, MN 55455-0213. Offers MS, PhD, JD/MS, JD/PhD, MD/PhD, MPP/MS. Part-time programs available. Terminal master's awarded for partial completion of doctoral program. *Degree requirements:* For master's, thesis, internship, final oral exam; for doctorate, thesis/dissertation, teaching experience, written preliminary exam, final oral exam, dissertation. *Entrance requirements:* For master's, GRE General Test, course work in mathematics; for doctorate, GRE General Test, prerequisite courses in calculus and statistics. Additional exam requirements/recommendations for international students: Required—TOEFL (minimum score 600 paper-based; 250 computer-based; 100 iBT). *Faculty research:* Outcomes, economics and statistics, sociology, health care management.

University of New Brunswick Fredericton, School of Graduate Studies, Applied Health Services Research Program, Fredericton, NB E3B 5A3, Canada. Offers MAHSR. Part-time programs available. Postbaccalaureate distance learning degree programs offered. *Students:* 5 full-time (all women), 3 part-time (all women). In 2011, 2 master's awarded. *Degree requirements:* For master's, thesis. *Entrance requirements:* For master's, hohours BA, minimum GPA of 3.0. Additional exam requirements/recommendations for international students: Required—TWE (minimum score 4), TOEFL (minimum score 600 paper-based; 250 computer-based; 100 iBT) or IELTS (minimum score 7). *Application deadline:* For winter admission, 3/31 for domestic and international students. Application fee: $50 Canadian dollars. *Faculty research:* Health services issues. *Unit head:* Dr. Linda Eyre, Associate Dean of Graduate Studies, 506-447-3044, Fax: 506-453-4817, E-mail: gradidst@unb.ca. *Application contact:* Janet Amurault, Graduate Secretary, 506-458-7558, Fax: 506-453-4817, E-mail: jamiraul@unb.ca. Web site: http://www.artc-hsr.ca/Home.aspx.

University of Ottawa, Faculty of Graduate and Postdoctoral Studies, Interdisciplinary Programs, Ottawa, ON K1N 6N5, Canada. Offers e-business (Certificate); e-commerce (Certificate); finance (Certificate); health services and policies research (Diploma); population health (PhD); population health risk assessment and management (Certificate); public management and governance (Certificate); systems science (Certificate).

University of Pennsylvania, Perelman School of Medicine, Program in Health Policy Research, Philadelphia, PA 19104. Offers MS, MD/MS. Part-time programs available. *Faculty:* 21 full-time (9 women). *Students:* 38 full-time (25 women); includes 22 minority (6 Black or African American, non-Hispanic/Latino; 13 Asian, non-Hispanic/Latino; 3 Hispanic/Latino). Average age 33. 19 applicants, 89% accepted, 16 enrolled. In 2011, 12 master's awarded. *Degree requirements:* For master's, thesis. *Entrance requirements:* Additional exam requirements/recommendations for international students: Recommended—TOEFL. *Application deadline:* For fall admission, 11/30 for domestic students. Applications are processed on a rolling basis. Electronic applications accepted. *Expenses: Tuition:* Full-time $26,660; part-time $4944 per course. *Required fees:* $2318; $291 per course. Tuition and fees vary according to course load, degree level and program. *Financial support:* In 2011–12, 16 fellowships with partial tuition reimbursements were awarded. *Faculty research:* Disparities in health care; cost effectiveness analysis; outcomes research; biological, clinical, behavioral and environmental factors in health care; diffusion of health care innovation; medical ethics. *Unit head:* Dr. Judith A. Long, Director, 215-898-4311. *Application contact:* Elliot M. Adler, Admissions Coordinator, 215-573-2740, Fax: 215-573-2742, E-mail: elliota@mail.med.upenn.edu. Web site: http://www.med.upenn.edu/mshp/.

University of Puerto Rico, Medical Sciences Campus, Graduate School of Public Health, Department of Health Services Administration, Program in Evaluative Research of Health Systems, San Juan, PR 00936-5067. Offers MS. Part-time programs available. *Degree requirements:* For master's, thesis. *Entrance requirements:* For master's, GRE, previous course work in algebra and statistics. *Expenses:* Contact institution.

University of Regina, Faculty of Graduate Studies and Research, Johnson-Shoyama Graduate School of Public Policy, Regina, SK S4S 0A2, Canada. Offers economic analysis for public policy (Master's Certificate); health systems management (Master's Certificate); health systems research (MPP); non-profit management (Master's Certificate); public management (MPA, Master's Certificate); public policy (MPA, MPP, PhD); public policy analysis (Master's Certificate). Part-time programs available. *Faculty:* 7 full-time (3 women). *Students:* 61 full-time (34 women), 58 part-time (33 women). 75 applicants, 73% accepted. In 2011, 73 master's awarded. *Degree requirements:* For master's, thesis; for doctorate, thesis/dissertation. *Entrance requirements:* For doctorate, master's degree, intended research program in an area of public policy. Additional exam requirements/recommendations for international students: Required—TOEFL (minimum score 580 paper-based; 80 iBT), IELTS (minimum score 6.5). *Application deadline:* For fall admission, 2/1 for domestic and international students. Application fee: $100. Electronic applications accepted. *Expenses:* Contact institution. *Financial support:* In 2011–12, 8 fellowships (averaging $6,500 per year), 10 teaching assistantships (averaging $2,298 per year) were awarded; research assistantships and scholarships/grants also available. Financial award application deadline: 6/15. *Faculty research:* Governance and administration, public finance, public policy analysis, non-governmental organizations and alternative service delivery, micro-economics for policy analysis. *Unit head:* Dr. Michael Atkinson, Director, 306-996-1984, Fax: 306-585-5461, E-mail: michael.atkinson@usask.ca. *Application contact:* Elaine Groenendyk, Program Advisor, 306-585-5462, Fax: 306-585-5461, E-mail: elaine.groenendyk@uregina.ca.

University of Rochester, School of Medicine and Dentistry, Graduate Programs in Medicine and Dentistry, Department of Community and Preventive Medicine, Program in Health Services Research and Policy, Rochester, NY 14627. Offers PhD, MPH/PhD. *Degree requirements:* For doctorate, thesis/dissertation, qualifying exam. *Entrance requirements:* For doctorate, GRE General Test. *Expenses: Tuition:* Full-time $41,040.

University of Rochester, School of Nursing, Rochester, NY 14642. Offers acute care nurse practitioner (MS); adult nurse practitioner (MS); adult/geriatric nurse practitioner (MS); care of children and families/pediatric nurse practitioner (MS); care of children and families/pediatric nurse practitioner/neonatal nurse practitioner (MS); clinical nurse leader (MS); clinical research coordinator (MS); family nurse practitioner (MS); family psychiatric mental health nurse practitioner (MS); health care organization management and leadership (MS); health practice research (PhD); nursing (DNP). *Accreditation:* AACN; NLN (one or more programs are accredited). Part-time programs available. Postbaccalaureate distance learning degree programs offered (minimal on-campus study). *Faculty:* 49 full-time (42 women), 72 part-time/adjunct (60 women). *Students:* 38 full-time (32 women), 196 part-time (181 women); includes 37 minority (20 Black or African American, non-Hispanic/Latino; 9 Asian, non-Hispanic/Latino; 8 Hispanic/Latino), 5 international. Average age 36. 68 applicants, 56% accepted, 26 enrolled. In

2011, 49 master's, 7 doctorates awarded. Terminal master's awarded for partial completion of doctoral program. *Median time to degree:* Of those who began their doctoral program in fall 2003, 40% received their degree in 8 years or less. *Degree requirements:* For doctorate, thesis/dissertation. *Entrance requirements:* For master's, BS in nursing, minimum GPA of 3.0, course work in statistics; for doctorate, GRE General Test, MS in nursing, minimum GPA of 3.5. Additional exam requirements/recommendations for international students: Required—or IELTS (minimum score 6.5); Recommended—TOEFL (minimum score 560 paper-based; 230 computer-based; 88 iBT). *Application deadline:* For fall admission, 4/1 priority date for domestic students, 4/1 for international students; for spring admission, 9/1 for domestic and international students. Application fee: $50. Electronic applications accepted. *Expenses:* Tuition: Full-time $41,040. *Financial support:* In 2011–12, 49 students received support, including 1 fellowship with full and partial tuition reimbursement available (averaging $18,700 per year); scholarships/grants, traineeships, health care benefits, tuition waivers (partial), and unspecified assistantships also available. Support available to part-time students. Financial award application deadline: 6/30. *Faculty research:* Clinical research in aging, managing asthma in children, interventions to improve outcomes in critically ill children and their mothers, nurse home visitation studies, medical device evaluation, critical care clinical studies, high risk behavior and prevention, palliative care, pregnancy-related weight gain. *Total annual research expenditures:* $4.3 million. *Unit head:* Dr. Kathy H. Rideout, Interim Dean, 585-273-8902, Fax: 585-273-1268, E-mail: kathy_rideout@urmc.rochester.edu. *Application contact:* Elaine Andolina, Director of Admissions, 585-275-2375, Fax: 585-756-8299, E-mail: elaine_andolina@urmc.rochester.edu. Web site: http://www.son.rochester.edu.

University of Southern California, Keck School of Medicine and Graduate School, Graduate Programs in Medicine, Department of Preventive Medicine, Program in Health Behavior Research, Los Angeles, CA 90032. Offers PhD. *Faculty:* 21 full-time (13 women). *Students:* 24 full-time (18 women); includes 6 minority (1 American Indian or Alaska Native, non-Hispanic/Latino; 5 Asian, non-Hispanic/Latino), 2 international. Average age 32. 33 applicants, 30% accepted, 6 enrolled. In 2011, 5 doctorates awarded. *Degree requirements:* For doctorate, comprehensive exam, thesis/dissertation. *Entrance requirements:* For doctorate, GRE General Test, minimum GPA of 3.0. Additional exam requirements/recommendations for international students: Required—TOEFL (minimum score 600 paper-based; 250 computer-based; 100 iBT). *Application deadline:* For fall admission, 12/1 priority date for domestic students, 12/1 for international students. Application fee: $85. Electronic applications accepted. *Financial support:* In 2011–12, 23 students received support, including 7 fellowships with full tuition reimbursements available (averaging $31,037 per year), 10 research assistantships with full and partial tuition reimbursements available (averaging $31,037 per year), 8 teaching assistantships with full and partial tuition reimbursements available (averaging $31,037 per year); institutionally sponsored loans, scholarships/grants, traineeships, health care benefits, and unspecified assistantships also available. Financial award application deadline: 5/4; financial award applicants required to submit CSS PROFILE or FAFSA. *Faculty research:* Obesity prevention; etiology and prevention of substance abuse, other addictive behaviors, and chronic diseases; health disparities; translational research. *Total annual research expenditures:* $3.4 million. *Unit head:* Dr. Jennifer Unger, Director, 323-442-8234, E-mail: unger@usc.edu. *Application contact:* Marny Barovich, Program Manager, 323-442-8299, E-mail: barovich@hsc.usc.edu. Web site: http://phdhbr.usc.edu.

University of Virginia, School of Medicine, Department of Public Health Sciences, Charlottesville, VA 22903. Offers clinical research (MS), including clinical investigation and patient-oriented research, informatics in medicine; public health (MPH). Part-time programs available. *Faculty:* 31 full-time (15 women), 4 part-time/adjunct (1 woman). *Students:* 54 full-time (34 women), 18 part-time (10 women); includes 22 minority (11 Black or African American, non-Hispanic/Latino; 8 Asian, non-Hispanic/Latino; 2 Hispanic/Latino; 1 Two or more races, non-Hispanic/Latino), 4 international. Average age 29. 96 applicants, 46% accepted, 31 enrolled. In 2011, 30 master's awarded. *Entrance requirements:* For master's, GRE General Test or MCAT. Additional exam requirements/recommendations for international students: Required—TOEFL. *Application deadline:* Applications are processed on a rolling basis. Application fee: $60. Electronic applications accepted. *Financial support:* Career-related internships or fieldwork available. Financial award applicants required to submit FAFSA. *Unit head:* Dr. Ruth Gaare Bernheim, Chair, 434-924-8430, Fax: 434-924-8437. *Application contact:* Tracey L. Brookman, Academic Programs Administrator, 434-924-8430, Fax: 434-924-8437, E-mail: ms-hes@virginia.edu. Web site: http://www.healthsystem.virginia.edu/internet/phs/education.cfm.

University of Washington, Graduate School, School of Public Health, Department of Health Services, Seattle, WA 98195. Offers bioinformatics (PhD); cancer prevention and control (PhD); clinical research (MS); community-oriented public health practice (MPH); economics or finance (PhD); evaluation sciences (PhD); health behavior and health promotion (PhD); health policy research (PhD); health services (MS, PhD); health services administration (EMHA, MHA); health systems policy (MPH); maternal and child health (MPH, PhD); occupational health (PhD); population health and social determinants (PhD); social and behavioral sciences (MPH); sociology and demography (PhD); JD/MHA; MHA/MBA; MHA/MD; MHA/MPA; MPH/JD; MPH/MD; MPH/MN; MPH/MPA; MPH/MS; MPH/MSD; MPH/MSW; MPH/PhD. Part-time and evening/weekend programs available. Postbaccalaureate distance learning degree programs offered (minimal on-campus study). *Faculty:* 40 full-time (23 women), 62 part-time/adjunct (25 women). *Students:* 98 full-time (78 women), 86 part-time (64 women); includes 49 minority (7 Black or African American, non-Hispanic/Latino; 3 American Indian or Alaska Native, non-Hispanic/Latino; 28 Asian, non-Hispanic/Latino; 11 Hispanic/Latino), 3 international. Average age 32. 374 applicants, 49% accepted, 104 enrolled. In 2011, 43 master's, 5 doctorates awarded. Terminal master's awarded for partial completion of doctoral program. *Degree requirements:* For master's, thesis (for some programs), practicum (MPH); for doctorate, comprehensive exam, thesis/dissertation. *Entrance requirements:* For master's and doctorate, GRE General Test, minimum GPA of 3.0. Additional exam requirements/recommendations for international students: Required—TOEFL (minimum score 580 paper-based; 237 computer-based; 92 iBT), IELTS (minimum score 7). *Application deadline:* For fall admission, 1/1 for domestic students, 11/1 for international students. Application fee: 75 Albanian leks. Electronic applications accepted. *Financial support:* In 2011–12, 47 students received support, including 10 fellowships with full and partial tuition reimbursements available (averaging $22,000 per year), 10 research assistantships with full and partial tuition reimbursements available (averaging $18,700 per year), 3 teaching assistantships with full and partial tuition reimbursements available (averaging $4,575 per year); institutionally sponsored loans, traineeships, and health care benefits also available. Financial award application deadline: 2/28; financial award applicants required to submit FAFSA. *Faculty research:* Public health practice, health promotion and disease prevention, maternal and child health, organizational behavior and culture, health policy. *Unit head:* Dr. Larry Kessler, Chair, 206-543-2930. *Application contact:* Kitty A. Andert, MPH/MS/PhD Programs

Manager, 206-616-2926, Fax: 206-543-3964, E-mail: kitander@u.washington.edu. Web site: http://depts.washington.edu/hserv/.

University of Wisconsin–Madison, School of Medicine and Public Health and Graduate School, Graduate Programs in Medicine, Department of Population Health Sciences, Madison, WI 53726. Offers epidemiology (MS, PhD); population health (MS, PhD), including clinical research, epidemiology, health services research, social and behavioral health sciences; public health (MPH); DPT/MPH; DVM/MPH; JD/MPH; MD/MPH; MPA/MPH; MS/MPH; Pharm D/MPH. Accreditation: CEPH. Part-time programs available. *Faculty:* 104 full-time (54 women), 2 part-time/adjunct (0 women). *Students:* 69 full-time (50 women), 13 part-time (9 women); includes 19 minority (8 Black or African American, non-Hispanic/Latino; 8 Asian, non-Hispanic/Latino; 3 Hispanic/Latino), 15 international. Average age 31. 96 applicants, 41% accepted, 26 enrolled. In 2011, 5 master's, 6 doctorates awarded. Terminal master's awarded for partial completion of doctoral program. *Degree requirements:* For master's, thesis, defense; for doctorate, comprehensive exam, thesis/dissertation, qualifying exam, preliminary exam, dissertation defense. *Entrance requirements:* For master's and doctorate, GRE (MCAT or LSAT acceptable for those with doctoral degrees) taken within the last 5 years, minimum GPA of 3.0, quantitative preparation (calculus, statistics, or other) with minimum B average. Additional exam requirements/recommendations for international students: Required—TOEFL (minimum score 580 paper-based; 237 computer-based; 92 iBT). *Application deadline:* For fall admission, 1/15 for domestic and international students. Application fee: $56. Electronic applications accepted. *Expenses:* Tuition, state resident: full-time $10,296; part-time $643.51 per credit. Tuition, nonresident: full-time $24,054; part-time $1503.40 per credit. *Required fees:* $70.06 per credit. Tuition and fees vary according to course load, campus/location, program and reciprocity agreements. *Financial support:* Fellowships with full tuition reimbursements, research assistantships with full tuition reimbursements, teaching assistantships with full tuition reimbursements, scholarships/grants, traineeships, health care benefits, and unspecified assistantships available. Support available to part-time students. *Faculty research:* Epidemiology (cancer, environmental, aging, infectious and genetic disease), determinants of population health, health services research, social and behavioral health sciences, biostatistics. *Total annual research expenditures:* $11.4 million. *Unit head:* Kathy Rutlin, MS/PhD Programs Coordinator, 608-265-8108, Fax: 608-263-2820, E-mail: karutlin@wisc.edu. *Application contact:* Quinn H. Fullenkamp, MS/PhD Assistant Programs Coordinator, 608-263-6583, Fax: 608-263-2820, E-mail: qhfullen@wisc.edu. Web site: http://www.pophealth.wisc.edu.

Virginia Commonwealth University, Graduate School, School of Allied Health Professions, Department of Health Administration, Doctoral Program in Health Services Organization and Research, Richmond, VA 23284-9005. Offers PhD. *Students:* 6 full-time (5 women), 6 part-time (3 women), 6 international. 9 applicants, 56% accepted, 5 enrolled. In 2011, 3 doctorates awarded. *Degree requirements:* For doctorate, thesis/dissertation, residency. *Entrance requirements:* For doctorate, GMAT or GRE General Test, minimum graduate GPA of 3.0. Additional exam requirements/recommendations for international students: Required—TOEFL (minimum score 600 paper-based; 250 computer-based; 100 iBT). *Application deadline:* For fall admission, 4/15 priority date for domestic students. Application fee: $50. Electronic applications accepted. *Expenses:* Tuition, state resident: full-time $9133; part-time $507 per credit. Tuition, nonresident: full-time $18,777; part-time $1043 per credit. *Required fees:* $77 per credit. Tuition and fees vary according to degree level, campus/location, program and student level. *Financial support:* Applicants required to submit FAFSA. *Faculty research:* Organizational studies, theory, associated analytical techniques. *Unit head:* Dr. Jan Clement, Director, 804-828-7799, Fax: 804-828-1894, E-mail: jclement@vcu.edu. *Application contact:* Carolyn Wells, Administrative Coordinator, 804-828-7799, Fax: 804-828-1894, E-mail: cwwells@vcu.edu. Web site: http://www.had.vcu.edu/.

Virginia Commonwealth University, Medical College of Virginia-Professional Programs, School of Medicine, School of Medicine Graduate Programs, Department of Healthcare Policy and Research, Richmond, VA 23284-9005. Offers PhD. *Faculty:* 9 full-time (5 women). *Entrance requirements:* For doctorate, GRE General Test. Additional exam requirements/recommendations for international students: Required—TOEFL (minimum score 600 paper-based; 100 iBT). *Application deadline:* For fall admission, 1/5 priority date for domestic students, 12/15 for international students. Application fee: $50. Electronic applications accepted. *Expenses:* Tuition, state resident: full-time $9133; part-time $507 per credit. Tuition, nonresident: full-time $18,777; part-time $1043 per credit. *Required fees:* $77 per credit. Tuition and fees vary according to degree level, campus/location, program and student level. *Financial support:* Research assistantships, health care benefits, and unspecified assistantships available. Financial award application deadline: 3/15; financial award applicants required to submit FAFSA. *Faculty research:* Evaluation of healthcare services and systems to enhance quality of care and patient safety outcomes; examination of chronic disease (e.g. cancer, HIV/AIDS) policies and practices to improve health outcomes and economic efficiency; impact of uninsurance, public insurance (such as Medicaid) and the safety net on access to care and the health of low-income, underserved, and foreign-born populations; the study of labor supply and healthcare coverage in response to health behaviors and shocks. *Unit head:* Dr. Cathy Bradley, Chair, 804-828-5217, E-mail: cjbradley@vcu.edu. *Application contact:* Dr. Gail E. Christie, Graduate Program Director and Recruitment Contact, 804-828-9093, E-mail: christie@vcu.edu. Web site: http://www.healthpolicy.vcu.edu/.

Wake Forest University, School of Medicine and Graduate School of Arts and Sciences, Graduate Programs in Medicine, Program in Health Sciences Research, Winston-Salem, NC 27109. Offers MS. *Degree requirements:* For master's, thesis. *Entrance requirements:* For master's, GRE General Test. Additional exam requirements/recommendations for international students: Required—TOEFL. Electronic applications accepted. *Faculty research:* Research methodologies, statistical methods, measurement of health outcomes, health economics.

Weill Cornell Medical College, Weill Cornell Graduate School of Medical Sciences, Program in Clinical Epidemiology and Health Services Research, New York, NY 10021. Offers MS. *Faculty:* 22 full-time (7 women). *Students:* 21 full-time (14 women); includes 8 minority (3 Black or African American, non-Hispanic/Latino; 2 Asian, non-Hispanic/Latino; 1 Hispanic/Latino; 2 Native Hawaiian or other Pacific Islander, non-Hispanic/Latino), 3 international. Average age 35. 31 applicants, 42% accepted, 11 enrolled. In 2011, 10 master's awarded. *Degree requirements:* For master's, thesis. *Entrance requirements:* For master's, 3 years of work experience, MD or RN certificate. *Application deadline:* For fall admission, 12/15 for domestic students. Application fee: $60. *Expenses:* Tuition: Full-time $46,001. *Financial support:* Scholarships/grants available. *Faculty research:* Research methodology, biostatistical techniques, data management, decision analysis, health economics. *Unit head:* Dr. Carol Mancuso, Director, 212-746-5454. *Application contact:* Alison Kenny, Administrator of Clinical and Educational Programs, 212-746-1608, Fax: 212-746-7443, E-mail: alh2006@med.cornell.edu. Web site: http://weill.cornell.edu/gradschool/program/ce_courses.html.

SOUTH UNIVERSITY

Columbia Campus
Healthcare Administration M.B.A. Program

Program of Study

The Master of Business Administration in Healthcare Administration degree program at South University is designed to prepare students for a leadership role in the healthcare delivery industry. The program is founded with the philosophy that healthcare leaders require strong business competencies and management skills to be successful. The delivery structure of the program gives students the ability to balance the rigors of work and home while pursuing their master's degree. Students can complete one or two courses each term, with each quarter lasting ten weeks.

The curriculum for the program is designed to prepare students with a sound foundation in business analysis and decision making, in addition to a specialization in healthcare administration. This is achieved by combining courses in economics, decision making, behavioral sciences, and strategic environment with specialized management courses specific to the healthcare field.

Research Facilities

Along with classrooms and offices, the campus includes a bookstore, student lounge, and career services center. The South University Library provides in-library and remote access to electronic databases so that students may retrieve periodicals in paper or electronic form. Internet access is available on all computers throughout the campus.

Financial Aid

A range of financial aid options is available to students who qualify. The Columbia campus of South University offers access to federal and state programs, including grants, loans, and work-study programs. Eligible students may apply for veterans' educational benefits and are encouraged to investigate the availability of grants and scholarships through community resources. As a first step, students should complete the Free Application for Federal Student Aid (FAFSA). Students may apply electronically at http://www.fafsa.ed.gov or through the program.

Cost of Study

Tuition information for the Healthcare Administration program may be obtained by contacting the Admissions Department at South University's Columbia campus.

Living and Housing Costs

South University does not offer or operate student housing. Healthcare Administration program students typically live in apartments in the Columbia area. Students who commute from long distances can arrange to stay at nearby hotels that offer long-term rates. More information is available by contacting the Admissions Department.

Student Group

The Columbia campus of South University has a diverse student body enrolled in both day and evening classes. Students are primarily commuters who live within 50 miles of the city.

Student Outcomes

The South University Career Services Department has been established to assist currently enrolled students in developing their career plans and reaching their employment goals. Career services include, but are not limited to, one-on-one career counseling, special career-related workshops and programs, coaching for resume and cover letter development, and resume referral to employers.

Location

South University's Columbia campus is located in the Carolina Research Park in northeast Columbia. The campus features spacious classrooms, multiple computer labs, a fully equipped medical lab, and a student lounge. The campus is located just minutes from downtown off I-77 at Farrow Road and Park Lane.

The campus surroundings are highlighted by a natural wooded landscape and vast green space featuring a tranquil campus courtyard. Convenient to malls, shopping, and the growing east side of Columbia, the new campus location provides easier access to students throughout the greater Columbia area

The University

South University is accredited by the Southern Association of Colleges and Schools Commission on Colleges to award associate, baccalaureate, masters, and doctorate degrees. Contact the Commission on Colleges at 1866 Southern Lane, Decatur, Georgia 30033-4097 or call 404-679-4500 for questions about the accreditation of South University.

Applying

Students are accepted into the Master of Business Administration in Healthcare Administration degree program every academic quarter. Entrance into the program is gained through a formal application review and interview process. Acceptance is competitive and based on the admission committee's evaluation of the applicant's academic background and personal motivation. Application packets are available by contacting the South University Admissions Department (866-629-3031, toll-free) or visiting the University's website (http://www.southuniversity.edu).

South University

Correspondence and Information

Applications for admission to the South University Healthcare Administration M.B.A. program are available by contacting:

Healthcare Administration M.B.A. Program
South University
9 Science Court
Columbia, South Carolina 29203
United States
Phone: 803-799-9082
      866-629-3031 (toll-free)
Fax: 803-935-4382
E-mail: coladmis@southuniversity.edu
Website: http://www.southuniversity.edu/Columbia

See suprograms.info for program duration; tuition, fees, and other costs; median debt; federal salary data; alumni success; and other important information. http://www.southuniversity.edu/programs-info/form/

THE FACULTY

One of the most outstanding aspects of South University's Healthcare Administration program is the dedication of the faculty members and their ability to cultivate a supportive learning environment. Faculty members are committed to their roles as mentors, teachers, and co-learners. They are also dedicated to the training of students who can assume positions of leadership within the healthcare administration field. A current list of program faculty members appears in the South University catalog, which is available on the South University website (http://www.southuniversity.edu).

Campus surroundings are highlighted by a natural wooded landscape and vast green space featuring a tranquil campus courtyard.

SOUTH UNIVERSITY

Montgomery Campus
Healthcare Administration M.B.A. Program

Program of Study

The Master of Business Administration in Healthcare Administration degree program at South University is designed to prepare students for a leadership role in the healthcare delivery industry. The program is founded with the philosophy that healthcare leaders require strong business competencies and management skills to be successful. The delivery structure of the program gives students the ability to balance the rigors of work and home while pursuing their master's degree. Students can complete one or two courses each term, with each quarter lasting ten weeks.

The curriculum for the program is designed to prepare students with a sound foundation in business analysis and decision making, in addition to a specialization in healthcare administration. This is achieved by combining courses in economics, decision making, behavioral sciences, and strategic environment with specialized management courses specific to the healthcare field.

Research Facilities

Along with classrooms and offices, the campus includes a bookstore, student lounge, and career services center. The South University Library provides in-library and remote access to electronic databases so that students may retrieve periodicals in paper or electronic form. Internet access is available on all computers throughout the campus.

Financial Aid

A range of financial aid options is available to students who qualify. The Montgomery campus of South University offers access to federal and state programs, including grants, loans, and work-study programs. Eligible students may apply for veterans' educational benefits and are encouraged to investigate the availability of grants and scholarships through community resources. As a first step, students should complete the Free Application for Federal Student Aid (FAFSA). Students may apply electronically at http://www.fafsa.ed.gov or through the program.

Cost of Study

Tuition information for the Healthcare Administration program may be obtained by contacting the Admissions Department at South University's Montgomery campus.

Living and Housing Costs

South University offers school-sponsored student housing at its Montgomery, Alabama, campus in conjunction with a local apartment complex. Students who commute from long distances can arrange to stay at nearby hotels that offer long-term rates. More information may be obtained by contacting the University toll free at 866-629-2962.

Student Group

The Montgomery campus of South University has a diverse student body enrolled in both day and evening classes. Students are primarily commuters who live within 50 miles of the city.

Student Outcomes

The South University Career Services Department has been established to assist currently enrolled students in developing their career plans and reaching their employment goals. Career services include, but are not limited to, one-on-one career counseling, special career-related workshops and programs, coaching for resume and cover letter development, and resume referral to employers.

Location

South University, Montgomery is located on the rapidly growing east side of Alabama's capital city. As the state capital, Montgomery is a hub of government, banking, and law as well as a state center for culture and entertainment. Montgomery is situated in the middle of the southeastern U.S. and is less than a 3-hour drive from Atlanta and the Gulf of Mexico.

The University

South University is accredited by the Southern Association of Colleges and Schools Commission on Colleges to award associate, baccalaureate, masters, and doctorate degrees. Contact the Commission on Colleges at 1866 Southern Lane, Decatur, Georgia 30033-4097 or call 404-679-4500 for questions about the accreditation of South University.

Applying

Students are accepted into the Master of Business Administration in Healthcare Administration degree program every academic quarter. Entrance into the program is gained through a formal application review and interview process. Acceptance is competitive and based on the admission committee's evaluation of the applicant's academic background

and personal motivation. Application packets are available by contacting the South University Admissions Department (866-629-2962, toll-free) or visiting the University's website (http://www.southuniversity.edu).

Correspondence and Information

Applications for admission to the South University Healthcare Administration M.B.A. program are available by contacting:

Healthcare Administration M.B.A. Program
South University
5355 Vaughn Road
Montgomery, Alabama 36116
United States
Phone: 334-395-8800
        866-629-2962(toll-free)
Fax: 334-395-8859
E-mail: mtgadmis@southuniversity.edu
Website: http://www.southuniversity.edu/Montgomery

See suprograms.info for program duration; tuition, fees, and other costs; median debt; federal salary data; alumni success; and other important information. http://www.southuniversity.edu/programs-info/form/

THE FACULTY

One of the most outstanding aspects of South University's Healthcare Administration program is the dedication of the faculty members and their ability to cultivate a supportive learning environment. Faculty members are committed to their roles as mentors, teachers, and co-learners. They are also dedicated to the training of students who can assume positions of leadership within the healthcare administration field. A current list of program faculty members appears in the South University catalog, which is available on the South University website (http://www.southuniversity.edu).

South University's Montgomery Campus is located on the rapidly growing east side of Alabama's capital city, a hub of government, banking, and law.

SOUTH UNIVERSITY

Tampa Campus
Healthcare Administration M.B.A. Program

Program of Study

The Master of Business Administration in Healthcare Administration degree program at South University is designed to prepare students for a leadership role in the healthcare delivery industry. The program is founded with the philosophy that healthcare leaders require strong business competencies and management skills to be successful. The delivery structure of the program gives students the ability to balance the rigors of work and home while pursuing their master's degree. Students can complete one or two courses each term, with each quarter lasting ten weeks.

The curriculum for the program is designed to prepare students with a sound foundation in business analysis and decision making, in addition to a specialization in healthcare administration. This is achieved by combining courses in economics, decision making, behavioral sciences, and strategic environment with specialized management courses specific to the healthcare field.

Research Facilities

Along with classrooms and offices, the campus includes a bookstore, student lounge, and career services center. The South University Library provides in-library and remote access to electronic databases so that students may retrieve periodicals in paper or electronic form. Internet access is available on all computers throughout the campus.

Financial Aid

A range of financial aid options is available to students who qualify. The Tampa campus of South University offers access to federal and state programs, including grants, loans, and work-study programs. Eligible students may apply for veterans' educational benefits and are encouraged to investigate the availability of grants and scholarships through community resources. As a first step, students should complete the Free Application for Federal Student Aid (FAFSA). Students may apply electronically at http://www.fafsa.ed.gov or through the program.

Cost of Study

Tuition information for the Healthcare Administration program may be obtained by contacting the Admissions Department at South University's Tampa campus.

Living and Housing Costs

South University does not offer or operate student housing. Healthcare Administration program students typically live in apartments in the Tampa area. Students who commute from long distances can arrange to stay at nearby hotels that offer long-term rates. More information is available by contacting the Admissions Department.

Student Group

The Tampa campus of South University has a diverse student body enrolled in both day and evening classes. Students are primarily commuters who live within 50 miles of the city.

Student Outcomes

The South University Career Services Department has been established to assist currently enrolled students in developing their career plans and reaching their employment goals. Career services include, but are not limited to, one-on-one career counseling, special career-related workshops and programs, coaching for resume and cover letter development, and resume referral to employers.

Location

Located on North Himes Avenue, South University's Tampa campus affords students the opportunity to enjoy all the culture and excitement a large city has to offer. Major-league sporting events, major concerts, theater, world-renowned restaurants, and a cosmopolitan social scene are all within easy reach.

The University

South University is accredited by the Southern Association of Colleges and Schools Commission on Colleges to award associate, baccalaureate, masters, and doctorate degrees. Contact the Commission on Colleges at 1866 Southern Lane, Decatur, Georgia 30033-4097 or call 404-679-4500 for questions about the accreditation of South University.

South University, Tampa is licensed by the Florida Commission for Independent Education, License No. 2987.

Applying

Students are accepted into the Master of Business Administration in Healthcare Administration degree program every academic quarter. Entrance into the program is gained through a formal application review and interview process.

South University

Acceptance is competitive and based on the admission committee's evaluation of the applicant's academic background and personal motivation. Application packets are available by contacting the South University Admissions Department (800-846-1472, toll-free) or visiting the University's website (http://www.southuniversity.edu).

Correspondence and Information

Applications for admission to the South University Healthcare Administration M.B.A. program are available by contacting:

Healthcare Administration M.B.A. Program
Michele D'Alessio, Director of Admissions
South University
4401 North Himes Avenue, Suite 175
Tampa, Florida 33614-7095
United States
Phone: 813-393-3800
         800-846-1472 (toll-free)
Fax: 813-393-3814
E-mail: sutaadm@southuniversity.edu
Website: http://www.southuniversity.edu/tampa

See suprograms.info for program duration; tuition, fees, and other costs; median debt; federal salary data; alumni success; and other important information. http://www.southuniversity.edu/programs-info/form/

THE FACULTY

One of the most outstanding aspects of South University's Healthcare Administration program is the dedication of the faculty members and their ability to cultivate a supportive learning environment. Faculty members are committed to their roles as mentors, teachers, and co-learners. They are also dedicated to the training of students who can assume positions of leadership within the healthcare administration field. A current list of program faculty members appears in the South University catalog, which is available on the South University website (http://www.southuniversity.edu).

South University's Tampa campus provides ample classroom and student service areas and features several smart classrooms with audiovisual technology.

Section 23
Nursing

This section contains a directory of institutions offering graduate work in nursing, followed by in-depth entries submitted by institutions that chose to prepare detailed program descriptions. Additional information about programs listed in the directory but not augmented by an in-depth entry may be obtained by writing directly to the dean of a graduate school or chair of a department at the address given in the directory.

For programs offering related work, see also in this book *Health Services* and *Public Health.* In another guide in this series:

Graduate Programs in the Humanities, Arts & Social Sciences
See *Family and Consumer Sciences (Gerontology)*

CONTENTS

Program Directories

Displays and Close-Ups

Nursing—General

Abilene Christian University, Graduate School, School of Nursing, Abilene, TX 79699-9100. Offers education and administration (MSN); family nurse practitioner (MSN). *Accreditation:* AACN. Part-time programs available. *Faculty:* 6 part-time/adjunct (all women). *Students:* 1 (woman) full-time, 2 part-time (1 woman). 6 applicants, 17% accepted, 1 enrolled. In 2011, 3 degrees awarded. *Degree requirements:* For master's, practicum. *Entrance requirements:* For master's, GRE General Test. Additional exam requirements/recommendations for international students: Required—TOEFL (minimum score 550 paper-based; 213 computer-based; 80 iBT), IELTS (minimum score 6). *Application deadline:* For fall admission, 4/1 priority date for domestic students; for spring admission, 11/1 for domestic students. Applications are processed on a rolling basis. Application fee: $50. Electronic applications accepted. *Expenses: Tuition:* Full-time $14,168; part-time $787 per hour. *Required fees:* $82 per hour. $10 per term. *Financial support:* Application deadline: 4/1; applicants required to submit FAFSA. *Unit head:* Dr. Becky Hammack, Graduate Director, 325-671-2361, Fax: 325-671-2386, E-mail: atoone@phssn.edu. *Application contact:* David Pittman, Graduate Admissions Counselor, 325-674-2656, Fax: 325-674-6717, E-mail: gradinfo@acu.edu.

Adelphi University, School of Nursing, Garden City, NY 11530-0701. Offers MS, PhD, Certificate. *Accreditation:* AACN. Part-time and evening/weekend programs available. *Faculty:* 36 full-time (32 women), 105 part-time/adjunct (102 women). *Students:* 4 full-time (all women), 141 part-time (130 women); includes 80 minority (48 Black or African American, non-Hispanic/Latino; 1 American Indian or Alaska Native, non-Hispanic/Latino; 15 Asian, non-Hispanic/Latino; 10 Hispanic/Latino; 2 Native Hawaiian or other Pacific Islander, non-Hispanic/Latino; 4 Two or more races, non-Hispanic/Latino). Average age 42. 102 applicants, 56% accepted, 46 enrolled. In 2011, 23 master's, 1 doctorate, 3 other advanced degrees awarded. *Degree requirements:* For master's, thesis or alternative. *Entrance requirements:* For master's, BSN, clinical experience, 1 course in basic statistics, minimum GPA of 3.0, 2 letters of recommendation, resume or curriculum vitae; for doctorate, GRE, licensure as RN in New York, professional writing sample (scholarly writing), 3 letters of recommendation, resume or curriculum vitae; for Certificate, MSN. Additional exam requirements/recommendations for international students: Required—TOEFL (minimum score 550 paper-based; 213 computer-based; 80 iBT). *Application deadline:* For fall admission, 3/15 for domestic students, 4/1 for international students; for spring admission, 11/1 for international students. Application fee: $50. Electronic applications accepted. *Expenses: Tuition:* Full-time $29,600; part-time $930 per credit. *Required fees:* $1100. *Financial support:* In 2011–12, 13 research assistantships (averaging $4,011 per year) were awarded; career-related internships or fieldwork, unspecified assistantships, and graduate achievement awards also available. Support available to part-time students. Financial award application deadline: 2/15; financial award applicants required to submit FAFSA. *Faculty research:* Social practices in healthcare, bereavement, family grief, historiography, gerontology. *Unit head:* Dr. Patrick Coonan, Dean, 516-877-4511, E-mail: coonan@adelphi.edu. *Application contact:* Christine Murphy, Director of Admissions, 516-877-3050, Fax: 516-877-3039, E-mail: graduateadmissions@adelphi.edu. Web site: http://nursing.adelphi.edu/.

See Display below and Close-Up on page 791.

Albany State University, College of Sciences and Health Professions, Albany, GA 31705-2717. Offers criminal justice (MS), including corrections, forensic science, law enforcement, public administration; mathematics education (M Ed); nursing (MSN), including RN to MSN family nurse practitioner, RN to MSN nurse educator; science education (M Ed). *Accreditation:* NLN. Part-time and evening/weekend programs available. Postbaccalaureate distance learning degree programs offered. *Faculty:* 16 full-time (7 women), 7 part-time/adjunct (3 women). *Students:* 34 full-time (26 women), 103 part-time (84 women); includes 94 minority (92 Black or African American, non-Hispanic/Latino; 2 Asian, non-Hispanic/Latino), 2 international. Average age 36. 101 applicants, 48% accepted, 33 enrolled. In 2011, 16 master's awarded. *Degree requirements:* For master's, comprehensive exam, thesis. *Entrance requirements:* For master's, GRE or MAT, official transcript, letters of recommendations, pre-medical/certificate of immunizations. *Application deadline:* For fall admission, 6/15 for domestic students, 5/1 for international students; for spring admission, 11/1 for domestic students, 10/1 for international students. Applications are processed on a rolling basis. Application fee: $20. Electronic applications accepted. *Expenses:* Tuition, state resident: full-time $3204; part-time $178 per credit hour. Tuition, nonresident: full-time $12,816; part-time $712 per credit hour. *Required fees:* $379 per semester. *Financial support:* Scholarships/grants and traineeships available. Financial award application deadline: 4/15; financial award applicants required to submit CSS PROFILE or FAFSA. *Unit head:* Dr. Joyce Johnson, Dean, 229-430-4792, Fax: 229-430-3937, E-mail: joyce.johnson@asurams.edu. *Application contact:* Jeffrey Pierce, II, Graduate Admissions Counselor, 229-430-4646, Fax: 229-430-4105, E-mail: jeffrey.pierce@asurams.edu. Web site: http://asu-sacs.asurams.edu/ASUCatalog/Graduate/index.html.

Alcorn State University, School of Graduate Studies, School of Nursing, Natchez, MS 39122-8399. Offers rural nursing (MSN). *Accreditation:* NLN.

Allen College, Program in Nursing, Waterloo, IA 50703. Offers acute care nurse practitioner (MSN, Post-Master's Certificate); adult nurse practitioner (MSN, Post-Master's Certificate); adult psychiatric-mental health nurse practitioner (MSN, Post-Master's Certificate); family nurse practitioner (MSN, Post-Master's Certificate); gerontological nurse practitioner (MSN, Post-Master's Certificate); health education (MSN); leadership in health care delivery (MSN, Post-Master's Certificate); nursing (DNP). *Accreditation:* AACN; NLN. Part-time programs available. *Faculty:* 3 full-time (all women), 16 part-time/adjunct (all women). *Students:* 34 full-time (31 women), 110 part-time (106 women); includes 5 minority (2 Asian, non-Hispanic/Latino; 3 Hispanic/Latino). Average age 36. 156 applicants, 64% accepted, 76 enrolled. In 2011, 61 master's, 1 other advanced degree awarded. *Degree requirements:* For master's, thesis optional. *Entrance requirements:* For master's, minimum GPA of 3.0; for doctorate, minimum GPA of 3.25 in graduate coursework. Additional exam requirements/recommendations for international students: Recommended—TOEFL (minimum score 550 paper-based), IELTS. *Application deadline:* For fall admission, 2/1 priority date for domestic students; for spring admission, 9/1 priority date for domestic students. Applications are processed on a rolling basis. Application fee: $50. Electronic applications accepted. *Expenses: Tuition:* Full-time $13,993; part-time $691 per credit hour. *Required fees:* $832; $69 per credit hour. One-time fee: $100 part-time. Part-time tuition and fees vary according to course load. *Financial support:* In 2011–12, 41 students received support. Institutionally sponsored loans, scholarships/grants, and traineeships available. Support available to part-time students. Financial award application deadline: 8/15; financial award applicants required to submit FAFSA. *Faculty research:* Pain and the aged, congestive heart failure. *Unit head:* Kendra Williams-Perez, Dean, School of Nursing, 319-226-2044, Fax: 319-226-2070, E-mail: williakb@ihs.org. *Application contact:* Michelle Koehn, Admissions Counselor, 319-226-2002, Fax: 319-226-2051, E-mail: koehnml@ihs.org. Web site: http://www.allencollege.edu/.

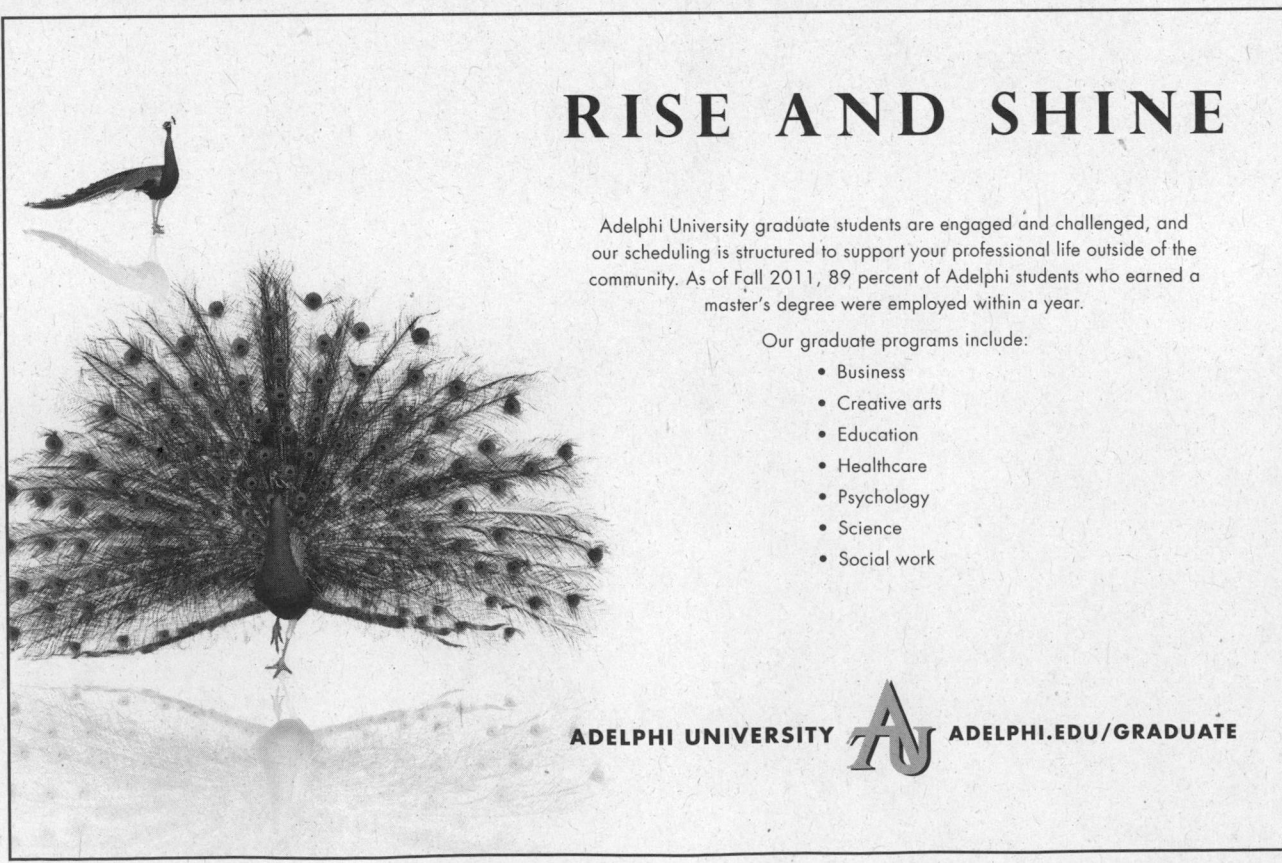

RISE AND SHINE

Adelphi University graduate students are engaged and challenged, and our scheduling is structured to support your professional life outside of the community. As of Fall 2011, 89 percent of Adelphi students who earned a master's degree were employed within a year.

Our graduate programs include:

- Business
- Creative arts
- Education
- Healthcare
- Psychology
- Science
- Social work

ADELPHI UNIVERSITY | **ADELPHI.EDU/GRADUATE**

Alverno College, School of Nursing, Milwaukee, WI 53234-3922. Offers family nurse practitioner (MSN); nursing education (MSN). *Accreditation:* AACN. Part-time and evening/weekend programs available. *Faculty:* 8 full-time (all women), 3 part-time/adjunct (all women). *Students:* 35 full-time (all women), 41 part-time (all women); includes 10 minority (8 Black or African American, non-Hispanic/Latino; 2 Hispanic/Latino), 1 international. Average age 38. 61 applicants, 54% accepted, 29 enrolled. In 2011, 8 master's awarded. *Degree requirements:* For master's, 500 clinical hours, capstone. *Entrance requirements:* For master's, BSN, current license. Additional exam requirements/recommendations for international students: Required—TOEFL. *Application deadline:* For fall admission, 7/15 priority date for domestic students, 7/15 for International students; for spring admission, 12/15 priority date for domestic students, 12/15 for international students. Applications are processed on a rolling basis. Application fee: $0. Electronic applications accepted. Application fee is waived when completed online. *Expenses:* Contact institution. *Financial support:* In 2011–12, 7 students received support. Federal Work-Study available. Support available to part-time students. Financial award application deadline: 4/15. *Faculty research:* Impact of stroke on sexuality, children's asthma management, factors affecting baccalaureate student success. *Unit head:* Dr. Catherine Knuteson, Program Director, 414-382-6287, Fax: 414-382-6354, E-mail: catherine.knuteson@alverno.edu. *Application contact:* Christy Stone, Director of Graduate and Adult Recruitment, 414-382-6108, Fax: 414-382-6354, E-mail: christy.stone@alverno.edu.

American International College, School of Health Sciences, Department of Nursing, Springfield, MA 01109-3189. Offers nursing administration (MSN); nursing education (MSN). *Accreditation:* AACN. *Entrance requirements:* For master's, BSN. Additional exam requirements/recommendations for international students: Required—TOEFL. Electronic applications accepted.

American Sentinel University, Graduate Programs, Aurora, CO 80014. Offers business administration (MBA); business intelligence (MS); computer science (MSCS); health information management (MS); healthcare (MBA); information systems (MSIS); nursing (MSN). Part-time and evening/weekend programs available. Postbaccalaureate distance learning degree programs offered (no on-campus study). *Entrance requirements:* Additional exam requirements/recommendations for international students: Required—TOEFL (minimum score 600 paper-based; 215 computer-based). Electronic applications accepted.

American University of Beirut, Graduate Programs, Rafic Hariri School of Nursing, Beirut, Lebanon. Offers adult care nursing (MSN); community health nursing (MSN); nursing administration (MSN); psychiatry mental health nursing (MSN). *Accreditation:* AACN. Part-time programs available. *Faculty:* 8 full-time (7 women), 16 part-time/adjunct (13 women). *Students:* 5 full-time (3 women), 50 part-time (39 women). Average age 29. 46 applicants, 87% accepted, 19 enrolled. In 2011, 19 master's awarded. *Degree requirements:* For master's, one foreign language, comprehensive exam, thesis optional. *Entrance requirements:* For master's, letter of recommendation. Additional exam requirements/recommendations for international students: Required—TOEFL (minimum score 600 paper-based); Recommended—IELTS. *Application deadline:* For fall admission, 2/20 for domestic and international students; for spring admission, 11/1 for domestic and international students. Applications are processed on a rolling basis. Application fee: $50. *Expenses:* Tuition: Full-time $12,780; part-time $710 per credit. Tuition and fees vary according to course load and program. *Financial support:* In 2011–12, 19 research assistantships with partial tuition reimbursements, 1 teaching assistantship with partial tuition reimbursement were awarded; career-related internships or fieldwork, institutionally sponsored loans, scholarships/grants, health care benefits, and unspecified assistantships also available. Support available to part-time students. Financial award application deadline: 2/2. *Faculty research:* Pain management and palliative care, stress and post-traumatic stress disorder, health benefits and chronic illness, health promotion and community interventions. *Total annual research expenditures:* $52,000. *Unit head:* Dr. Huda Huijer Abu-Saad, Director, 961-1374374 Ext. 5952, Fax: 961-1744476, E-mail: hh35@aub.edu.lb. *Application contact:* Dr. Salim Kanaan, Director, Admissions Office, 961-1350000 Ext. 2594, Fax: 961-1750775, E-mail: sk00@aub.edu.lb. Web site: http://staff.aub.edu.lb/~webson.

Andrews University, School of Graduate Studies, College of Arts and Sciences, Department of Nursing, Berrien Springs, MI 49104. Offers MS. *Accreditation:* NLN. Part-time and evening/weekend programs available. *Faculty:* 4 full-time (all women). *Students:* 8 full-time (7 women), 2 part-time (both women); includes 5 minority (3 Black or African American, non-Hispanic/Latino; 2 Hispanic/Latino), 2 international. Average age 42. 8 applicants, 63% accepted, 3 enrolled. In 2011, 2 master's awarded. *Degree requirements:* For master's, thesis. *Entrance requirements:* For master's, GRE, minimum GPA of 2.5, 1 year of nursing experience, RN license. Additional exam requirements/recommendations for international students: Required—TOEFL (minimum score 550 paper-based). *Application deadline:* Applications are processed on a rolling basis. Application fee: $40. *Financial support:* Institutionally sponsored loans available. *Faculty research:* Theory for nursing, salary equitability. *Unit head:* Dr. Karen A. Allen, Chairperson, 269-471-3364. *Application contact:* Carolyn Hurst, Supervisor of Graduate Admission, 800-253-2874, Fax: 269-471-6321, E-mail: graduate@andrews.edu.

Arizona State University, College of Nursing and Health Innovation, Phoenix, AZ 85004. Offers advanced nursing practice (DNP); child/family mental health nurse practitioner (Graduate Certificate); clinical research management (MS); community and public health practice (Graduate Certificate); community health (MS); exercise and wellness (MS), including exercise and wellness; family nurse practitioner (Graduate Certificate); healthcare innovation (MHI); international health for healthcare (Graduate Certificate); kinesiology (MS, PhD); nursing (MS, Graduate Certificate); nursing and healthcare innovation (PhD); nutrition (MS); physical activity nutrition and wellness (PhD), including physical activity, nutrition and wellness; public health (MPH); regulatory science and health safety (MS). *Accreditation:* AACN. Postbaccalaureate distance learning degree programs offered (minimal on-campus study). *Degree requirements:* For master's, comprehensive exam (for some programs), thesis (for some programs), interactive Program of Study (iPOS) submitted before completing 50 percent of required credit hours; for doctorate, comprehensive exam, thesis/dissertation, interactive Program of Study (iPOS) submitted before completing 50 percent of required credit hours. *Entrance requirements:* For master's and doctorate, GRE, minimum GPA of 3.0 or equivalent in last 2 years of work leading to bachelor's degree. Additional exam requirements/recommendations for international students: Required—TOEFL (minimum score 80 iBT), TOEFL, IELTS, or Pearson Test of English. Electronic applications accepted. *Expenses:* Contact institution.

Arkansas State University, Graduate School, College of Nursing and Health Professions, School of Nursing, Jonesboro, State University, AR 72467. Offers aging studies (Certificate); disaster preparedness and emergency management (MS, Certificate); health care management (Certificate); health communications (Certificate); health sciences (MS); health sciences education (Certificate); nurse anesthesia (MSN); nursing (MSN). *Accreditation:* AANA/CANAEP (one or more programs are accredited); NLN. Part-time programs available. *Faculty:* 14 full-time (all women). *Students:* 107 full-time (49 women), 118 part-time (110 women); includes 32 minority (27 Black or African American, non-Hispanic/Latino; 3 Asian, non-Hispanic/Latino; 2 Hispanic/Latino). Average age 33. 96 applicants, 25% accepted, 21 enrolled. In 2011, 83 master's

awarded. *Degree requirements:* For master's, comprehensive exam, thesis or alternative. *Entrance requirements:* For master's, GRE General Test or MAT, appropriate bachelor's degree, current Arkansas nursing license, CPR certification, physical examination, professional liability insurance, critical care experience, ACLS Certification, PALS Certification, interview, immunization records, personal goal statement, health assessment. Additional exam requirements/recommendations for international students: Required—TOEFL (minimum score 550 paper-based; 213 computer-based; 79 iBT), IELTS (minimum score 6), Pearson Test of English Academic (minimum score 56). *Application deadline:* Applications are processed on a rolling basis. Application fee: $30 ($40 for international students). Electronic applications accepted. *Expenses:* Contact institution. *Financial support:* In 2011–12, 5 students received support. Career-related internships or fieldwork, scholarships/grants, and unspecified assistantships available. Financial award application deadline: 7/1; financial award applicants required to submit FAFSA. *Unit head:* Dr. Sue McLarry, Chair, 870-972-3074, Fax: 870-972-2954, E-mail: smclarry@astate.edu. *Application contact:* Dr. Andrew Sustich, Dean of the Graduate School, 870-972-3029, Fax: 870-972-3857, E-mail: sustich@astate.edu. Web site: http://www.astate.edu/a/conhp/nursing/index.dot.

Arkansas Tech University, Center for Leadership and Learning, College of Natural and Health Sciences, Russellville, AR 72801. Offers fisheries and wildlife biology (MS); health informatics (MS); nursing (MSN). Part-time programs available. *Students:* 6 full-time (4 women), 45 part-time (34 women); includes 2 minority (1 Black or African American, non-Hispanic/Latino; 1 American Indian or Alaska Native, non-Hispanic/Latino), 1 international. Average age 40. In 2011, 9 master's awarded. *Degree requirements:* For master's, thesis (for some programs), project. *Entrance requirements:* For master's, GRE General Test. Additional exam requirements/recommendations for international students: Required—TOEFL (minimum score 550 paper-based; 213 computer-based; 79 iBT), IELTS (minimum score 6). *Application deadline:* For fall admission, 3/1 priority date for domestic students, 5/1 for international students; for spring admission, 10/1 priority date for domestic students, 10/1 for international students. Applications are processed on a rolling basis. Application fee: $25 ($75 for international students). Electronic applications accepted. *Expenses:* Tuition, state resident: full-time $4968; part-time $207 per credit hour. Tuition, nonresident: full-time $9936; part-time $414 per credit hour. *Required fees:* $375 per semester. Tuition and fees vary according to course load. *Financial support:* In 2011–12, teaching assistantships with full tuition reimbursements (averaging $4,800 per year) were awarded; research assistantships with full tuition reimbursements, career-related internships or fieldwork, Federal Work-Study, scholarships/grants, health care benefits, and unspecified assistantships also available. Support available to part-time students. Financial award application deadline: 4/15; financial award applicants required to submit FAFSA. *Unit head:* Dr. Jeff Robertson, Dean, 479-968-0498, E-mail: jrobertson@atu.edu. *Application contact:* Dr. Mary B. Gunter, Dean of Graduate College, 479-968-0398, Fax: 479-964-0542, E-mail: gradcollege@atu.edu. Web site: http://www.atu.edu/nhs/.

Armstrong Atlantic State University, School of Graduate Studies, Program in Nursing, Savannah, GA 31419-1997. Offers MSN. *Accreditation:* AACN. Part-time and evening/weekend programs available. *Faculty:* 9 full-time (all women), 1 (woman) part-time/adjunct. *Students:* 23 full-time (20 women), 20 part-time (16 women); includes 8 minority (5 Black or African American, non-Hispanic/Latino; 1 Asian, non-Hispanic/Latino; 2 Hispanic/Latino). Average age 37. 28 applicants, 57% accepted, 16 enrolled. In 2011, 12 master's awarded. *Degree requirements:* For master's, comprehensive exam, thesis optional, project. *Entrance requirements:* For master's, GRE General Test or MAT, minimum GPA of 2.5, letter of recommendation, letter of intent. Additional exam requirements/recommendations for international students: Required—TOEFL (minimum score 523 paper-based; 193 computer-based). *Application deadline:* For fall admission, 7/1 priority date for domestic students, 5/1 for international students; for spring admission, 11/15 priority date for domestic students, 9/15 for international students. Applications are processed on a rolling basis. Application fee: $30. Electronic applications accepted. *Expenses:* Tuition, state resident: full-time $3402. Tuition, nonresident: full-time $12,636. *Financial support:* In 2011–12, research assistantships with full tuition reimbursements (averaging $5,000 per year) were awarded; Federal Work-Study, scholarships/grants, and unspecified assistantships also available. Support available to part-time students. Financial award applicants required to submit FAFSA. *Faculty research:* Osteoporosis, cancer, tai chi, heart disease. *Unit head:* Dr. Helen Taggart, Department Head, 912-344-2667, E-mail: helen.taggart@armstrong.edu. *Application contact:* Jill Bell, Director/Graduate Enrollment Coordinator, 912-344-2798, Fax: 912-344-3488, E-mail: graduate@armstrong.edu. Web site: http://www.don.armstrong.edu/.

Athabasca University, Centre for Nursing and Health Studies, Athabasca, AB T9S 3A3, Canada. Offers advanced nursing practice (MN, Advanced Diploma); generalist (MN); health studies-leadership (MHS). Part-time programs available. Postbaccalaureate distance learning degree programs offered. *Degree requirements:* For master's, comprehensive exam (for some programs). *Entrance requirements:* For master's, bachelor's degree in health-related field, 2 years professional health service experience (MHS), bachelor's degree in nursing, 2 years nursing experience (MN), minimum GPA of 3.0 in final 30 credits; for Advanced Diploma, RN license, 2 years health care experience. Electronic applications accepted. *Expenses:* Contact institution.

Auburn University, Graduate School, School of Nursing, Auburn University, AL 36849. Offers nursing education (MSN); primary care practitioner option (MSN). *Accreditation:* AACN. *Faculty:* 10 full-time (8 women). *Students:* 1 (woman) full-time, 40 part-time (35 women); includes 7 minority (6 Black or African American, non-Hispanic/Latino; 1 Asian, non-Hispanic/Latino). Average age 36. 39 applicants, 62% accepted, 19 enrolled. In 2011, 10 master's awarded. *Expenses:* Tuition, state resident: full-time $7290; part-time $405 per credit hour. Tuition, nonresident: full-time $21,870; part-time $1215 per credit hour. *International tuition:* $22,000 full-time. *Required fees:* $1402. *Unit head:* Dr. Gregg Newschwander, Dean, 334-844-3658, E-mail: gen0002@auburn.edu. *Application contact:* Dr. George Flowers, Dean of the Graduate School, 334-844-4700, E-mail: gradadm@auburn.edu. Web site: http://www.nursing.auburn.edu/.

Augsburg College, Program in Transcultural Community Health Nursing, Minneapolis, MN 55454-1351. Offers MA. *Accreditation:* AACN. *Degree requirements:* For master's, thesis or alternative.

Aurora University, College of Professional Studies, Aurora, IL 60506-4892. Offers business (MBA); criminal justice (MS); nursing (MSN); social work (MSW, DSW). Part-time and evening/weekend programs available. *Entrance requirements:* Additional exam requirements/recommendations for international students: Required—TOEFL (minimum score 550 paper-based; 213 computer-based). Electronic applications accepted.

Austin Peay State University, College of Graduate Studies, College of Behavioral and Health Sciences, School of Nursing, Clarksville, TN 37044. Offers advanced practice (MSN); nursing administration (MSN); nursing education (MSN); nursing informatics (MSN). Part-time programs available. Postbaccalaureate distance learning degree programs offered. *Faculty:* 6 full-time (all women). *Students:* 21 full-time (16 women), 79 part-time (74 women); includes 12 minority (9 Black or African American, non-Hispanic/Latino; 2 Hispanic/Latino; 1 Two or more races, non-Hispanic/Latino). Average age 38.

42 applicants, 100% accepted, 29 enrolled. In 2011, 24 master's awarded. *Degree requirements:* For master's, comprehensive exam. *Entrance requirements:* For master's, GRE General Test, minimum GPA of 3.0, RN license eligibility, 3 letters of recommendation. Additional exam requirements/recommendations for international students: Required—TOEFL (minimum score 600 paper-based). *Application deadline:* For fall admission, 8/1 priority date for domestic students. Applications are processed on a rolling basis. Application fee: $25. Electronic applications accepted. *Expenses:* Tuition, state resident: part-time $350 per credit hour. Tuition, nonresident: full-time $20,644; part-time $971 per credit hour. *Required fees:* $1224; $61.20 per credit hour. *Financial support:* In 2011–12, research assistantships with full tuition reimbursements (averaging $5,184 per year) were awarded; career-related internships or fieldwork, Federal Work-Study, institutionally sponsored loans, scholarships/grants, and unspecified assistantships also available. Support available to part-time students. *Unit head:* Dr. Patty Orr, Director, 931-221-7710, Fax: 931-221-7595, E-mail: orrp@apsu.edu. *Application contact:* Kendra Bryant, Graduate Admissions, 800-844-2778, Fax: 931-221-6188, E-mail: admissionsweb@apsu.edu. Web site: http://www.apsu.edu/nursing.

Azusa Pacific University, School of Nursing, Azusa, CA 91702-7000. Offers nursing (MSN); nursing education (PhD). *Accreditation:* AACN. Part-time and evening/weekend programs available. *Degree requirements:* For master's, thesis optional. *Entrance requirements:* For master's, BSN.

Ball State University, Graduate School, College of Applied Science and Technology, School of Nursing, Muncie, IN 47306-1099. Offers MS, DNP. *Accreditation:* AACN. Part-time programs available. *Faculty:* 17 full-time (all women), 8 part-time/adjunct (7 women). *Students:* 8 full-time (7 women), 445 part-time (410 women); includes 42 minority (23 Black or African American, non-Hispanic/Latino; 2 American Indian or Alaska Native, non-Hispanic/Latino; 2 Asian, non-Hispanic/Latino; 9 Hispanic/Latino; 1 Native Hawaiian or other Pacific Islander, non-Hispanic/Latino; 5 Two or more races, non-Hispanic/Latino). Average age 42. 189 applicants, 18% accepted, 28 enrolled. In 2011, 94 master's awarded. *Entrance requirements:* For master's, bachelor's degree in nursing, minimum GPA of 2.8 in upper-level course work, interview, resume. Application fee: $50. Tuition and fees vary according to program and reciprocity agreements. *Financial support:* In 2011–12, 109 students received support. Research assistantships and career-related internships or fieldwork available. Financial award application deadline: 3/1. *Unit head:* Dr. Linda Siktberg, Director, 765-285-5570, Fax: 765-285-2169. Web site: http://www.bsu.edu/nursing/.

Barry University, School of Adult and Continuing Education, Division of Nursing, Miami Shores, FL 33161-6695. Offers MSN, PhD, Certificate, MSN/MBA. Part-time and evening/weekend programs available. *Degree requirements:* For master's, research project or thesis; for doctorate, thesis/dissertation. *Entrance requirements:* For master's, GRE General Test or MAT, BSN, minimum GPA of 3.0, course work in statistics and research, Florida RN license; for doctorate, GRE General Test or MAT, minimum GPA of 3.3, MSN. Electronic applications accepted. *Faculty research:* Adult education, nurse practitioner, stress reduction in pregnancy, prevention of cardiac problems, in children, level of school age children.

Baylor University, Graduate School, Louise Herrington School of Nursing, Waco, TX 76798. Offers family nurse practitioner (MSN); neonatal nurse practitioner (MSN); nurse-midwifery (DNP). *Accreditation:* AACN. Part-time programs available. *Faculty:* 9 full-time (all women), 3 part-time/adjunct (2 women). *Students:* 33 full-time (32 women), 45 part-time (39 women); includes 17 minority (4 Black or African American, non-Hispanic/Latino; 4 Asian, non-Hispanic/Latino; 3 Hispanic/Latino; 6 Two or more races, non-Hispanic/Latino), 1 international. 62 applicants, 63% accepted, 37 enrolled. In 2011, 24 master's, 3 doctorates awarded. *Entrance requirements:* For master's, GRE General Test or MAT; for doctorate, GRE General Test. *Application deadline:* For fall admission, 4/1 for domestic students. Application fee: $40. Electronic applications accepted. *Financial support:* Applicants required to submit FAFSA. *Unit head:* Dr. Linda Plank, Graduate Program Director, 214-818-7847, Fax: 214-818-8692, E-mail: linda_plank@baylor.edu. *Application contact:* Beverly Kurfees, Academic Support Specialist, 214-367-3752, Fax: 254-710-3870, E-mail: beverly_kurfees@baylor.edu. Web site: http://www.baylor.edu/nursing/.

Bellarmine University, Donna and Allan Lansing School of Nursing and Health Sciences, Louisville, KY 40205-0671. Offers family nurse practitioner (MSN); nursing administration (MSN); nursing education (MSN); nursing practice (DNP); physical therapy (DPT). *Accreditation:* AACN; APTA. Part-time and evening/weekend programs available. *Faculty:* 21 full-time (16 women), 7 part-time/adjunct (2 women). *Students:* 128 full-time (82 women), 116 part-time (111 women); includes 13 minority (5 Black or African American, non-Hispanic/Latino; 1 American Indian or Alaska Native, non-Hispanic/Latino; 2 Asian, non-Hispanic/Latino; 3 Hispanic/Latino; 2 Two or more races, non-Hispanic/Latino). Average age 31. In 2011, 19 master's, 50 doctorates awarded. *Degree requirements:* For doctorate, comprehensive exam, thesis/dissertation. *Entrance requirements:* For master's, GRE General Test, RN license; for doctorate, GRE General Test, Physical Therapist Centralized Application Service (for DPT). Additional exam requirements/recommendations for international students: Required—TOEFL (minimum score 550 paper-based; 213 computer-based; 80 iBT). Application fee: $25. Electronic applications accepted. *Expenses:* Contact institution. *Financial support:* Career-related internships or fieldwork and scholarships/grants available. *Faculty research:* Nursing: pain, empathy, leadership styles, control; physical therapy: service-learning; exercise in chronic and pre-operative conditions, athletes; women's health; aging. *Unit head:* Dr. Susan H. Davis, Dean, 800-274-4723 Ext. 8217, E-mail: sdavis@bellarmine.edu. *Application contact:* Julie Armstrong-Binnix, Health Science Recruiter, 800-274-4723 Ext. 8364, E-mail: julieab@bellarmine.edu. Web site: http://www.bellarmine.edu/lansing.

Bellin College, Program in Nursing, Green Bay, WI 54305. Offers administrator (MSN); educator (MSN). *Accreditation:* AACN.

Belmont University, College of Health Sciences, School of Nursing, Nashville, TN 37212-3757. Offers family nurse practitioner (MSN). *Accreditation:* AACN. Part-time programs available. *Faculty:* 1 (woman) full-time, 3 part-time/adjunct (all women). *Students:* 22 full-time (all women), 46 part-time (43 women); includes 7 minority (5 Black or African American, non-Hispanic/Latino; 2 Hispanic/Latino), 1 international. Average age 30. 65 applicants, 58% accepted, 33 enrolled. In 2011, 25 master's awarded. *Degree requirements:* For master's, comprehensive exam. *Entrance requirements:* For master's, GRE, BSN, minimum GPA of 3.0. Additional exam requirements/recommendations for international students: Required—TOEFL (minimum score 550 paper-based; 213 computer-based; 80 iBT). *Application deadline:* For fall admission, 8/1 for domestic students, 3/1 for international students; for spring admission, 10/15 priority date for domestic students, 10/1 for international students. Applications are processed on a rolling basis. Application fee: $50. Electronic applications accepted. *Expenses:* Contact institution. *Financial support:* In 2011–12, 21 students received support. Scholarships/grants and traineeships available. Financial award application deadline: 3/1; financial award applicants required to submit FAFSA. *Faculty research:* Postpartum post-operative care, adherence/compliance behavior in chronic illness, women's health in primary care, geriatrics. *Unit head:* Dr. Leslie J. Higgins, Director, Graduate Program, 615-460-6027, Fax: 615-460-6125, E-mail: leslie.higgins@belmont.edu. *Application contact:* Heather Germain, Program Assistant, 615-460-6142, Fax: 615-460-6125, E-mail: hether.germain@belmont.edu. Web site: http://www.belmont.edu/nursing/.

Benedictine University, Graduate Programs, Program in Nursing, Lisle, IL 60532-0900. Offers MSN. *Accreditation:* AACN. *Students:* 47 full-time (42 women), 341 part-time (321 women); includes 84 minority (51 Black or African American, non-Hispanic/Latino; 2 American Indian or Alaska Native, non-Hispanic/Latino; 22 Asian, non-Hispanic/Latino; 8 Hispanic/Latino; 1 Native Hawaiian or other Pacific Islander, non-Hispanic/Latino), 2 international. 110 applicants, 95% accepted, 86 enrolled. In 2011, 69 master's awarded. *Unit head:* Elizabeth Ritt, Department Chair, 630-829-1933, E-mail: eritt@ben.edu. *Application contact:* Kari Gibbons, Associate Vice President, Enrollment Center, 630-829-6200, Fax: 630-829-6584, E-mail: kgibbons@ben.edu.

Bethel College, Division of Graduate Studies, Program in Nursing, Mishawaka, IN 46545-5591. Offers MSN. *Accreditation:* NLN. Part-time and evening/weekend programs available. *Faculty:* 4 part-time/adjunct (all women). *Students:* 26 part-time (all women); includes 2 minority (1 American Indian or Alaska Native, non-Hispanic/Latino; 1 Hispanic/Latino). 20 applicants, 100% accepted, 19 enrolled. In 2011, 4 master's awarded. *Degree requirements:* For master's, thesis. *Entrance requirements:* Additional exam requirements/recommendations for international students: Required—TOEFL (minimum score 540 paper-based; 207 computer-based). *Application deadline:* For fall admission, 8/15 for domestic students, 5/1 for international students; for spring admission, 10/1 for international students. Application fee: $25. Electronic applications accepted. *Financial support:* Career-related internships or fieldwork available. Financial award applicants required to submit FAFSA. *Unit head:* Dr. Karon Schwartz, Director, 574-257-3382, E-mail: schwark@bethelcollege.edu.

Bethel University, Graduate School, St. Paul, MN 55112-6999. Offers autism spectrum disorders (Certificate); business administration (MBA); communication (MA); counseling psychology (MA); education (M Ed); educational leadership (Ed D); gerontology (MA, Certificate); international baccalaureate education (Certificate); K-12 education (MA); literacy education (MA); nursing (MA); nursing education (Certificate); nursing leadership (Certificate); organizational leadership (MA); postsecondary teaching (Certificate); special education (MA); teaching (MA). Part-time and evening/weekend programs available. Postbaccalaureate distance learning degree programs offered (minimal on-campus study). *Faculty:* 8 full-time (3 women), 98 part-time/adjunct (46 women). *Students:* 651 full-time (419 women), 312 part-time (212 women); includes 79 minority (35 Black or African American, non-Hispanic/Latino; 2 American Indian or Alaska Native, non-Hispanic/Latino; 19 Asian, non-Hispanic/Latino; 17 Hispanic/Latino; 6 Two or more races, non-Hispanic/Latino), 6 international. Average age 36. In 2011, 245 master's, 4 doctorates, 32 other advanced degrees awarded. *Degree requirements:* For master's, comprehensive exam (for some programs), thesis (for some programs); for doctorate, comprehensive exam, thesis/dissertation. *Entrance requirements:* Additional exam requirements/recommendations for international students: Required—TOEFL (minimum score 550 paper-based; 213 computer-based; 80 iBT). *Application deadline:* Applications are processed on a rolling basis. Electronic applications accepted. Tuition and fees vary according to course load, degree level and program. *Financial support:* Applicants required to submit FAFSA. *Unit head:* Dick Crombie, Vice-President/Dean, 651-635-8000, Fax: 651-635-8004, E-mail: gs@bethel.edu. *Application contact:* Paul Ives, Director of Admissions, 651-635-8000, Fax: 651-635-8004, E-mail: gs@bethel.edu. Web site: http://gs.bethel.edu/.

Blessing-Rieman College of Nursing, Program in Nursing, Quincy, IL 62305-7005. Offers MSN. *Accreditation:* AACN. Part-time programs available. *Faculty:* 7 full-time (all women). *Students:* 17 part-time (16 women). *Degree requirements:* For master's, thesis. *Entrance requirements:* For master's, proof of RN license; BSN from CCNE- or NLNAC-accredited program; minimum GPA of 3.0 for last 60 semester hours of undergraduate course work; completion of statistics, nursing research, physical assessment or equivalent with minimum grade of C. *Application deadline:* For fall admission, 4/1 for domestic students. *Unit head:* Dr. Karen Mayville, Administrative Coordinator, 217-228-5520 Ext. 6968, Fax: 217-223-4661, E-mail: kmayville@brcn.edu. *Application contact:* Heather Mutter, Admissions Counselor, 217-228-5520 Ext. 6964, Fax: 217-223-4661, E-mail: hmutter@brcn.edu.

Bloomsburg University of Pennsylvania, School of Graduate Studies, College of Science and Technology, Department of Nursing, Bloomsburg, PA 17815-1301. Offers adult and family nurse practitioner (MSN); adult health and illness (MSN); community health (MSN); nursing (MSN); nursing administration (MSN). *Accreditation:* AACN; AANA/CANAEP. *Degree requirements:* For master's, thesis. *Entrance requirements:* For master's, minimum QPA of 3.0. Additional exam requirements/recommendations for international students: Required—TOEFL. Electronic applications accepted. *Faculty research:* Cardiopulmonary nursing, cancer topics, women's health.

Boston College, William F. Connell School of Nursing, Chestnut Hill, MA 02467-3800. Offers adult-gerontology nursing (MS); community health nursing (MS); family health (MS); forensic nursing (MS); maternal/child health nursing (MS), including pediatric and women's health; nurse anesthesia (MS); nursing (PhD); palliative care (MS), including adult and pediatric; psychiatric-mental health nursing (MS); MBA/MS; MS/MA; MS/PhD. *Accreditation:* AACN; AANA/CANAEP (one or more programs are accredited). Part-time programs available. *Faculty:* 48 full-time (46 women), 31 part-time/adjunct (29 women). *Students:* 225 full-time (207 women), 90 part-time (88 women); includes 47 minority (15 Black or African American, non-Hispanic/Latino; 3 American Indian or Alaska Native, non-Hispanic/Latino; 17 Asian, non-Hispanic/Latino; 8 Hispanic/Latino; 4 Two or more races, non-Hispanic/Latino), 6 international. Average age 31. 369 applicants, 43% accepted, 80 enrolled. In 2011, 113 master's, 8 doctorates awarded. *Degree requirements:* For master's, comprehensive exam, research project; for doctorate, comprehensive exam, thesis/dissertation, computer literacy exam or foreign language. *Entrance requirements:* For master's, bachelor's degree in nursing; for doctorate, GRE General Test, MS in nursing. Additional exam requirements/recommendations for international students: Required—TOEFL (minimum score 600 paper-based; 250 computer-based; 100 iBT). *Application deadline:* For fall admission, 11/1 for domestic and international students; for winter admission, 12/31 for domestic and international students; for spring admission, 4/30 for domestic and international students. Applications are processed on a rolling basis. Application fee: $40. Electronic applications accepted. *Financial support:* In 2011–12, 167 students received support, including 9 fellowships with full tuition reimbursements available (averaging $15,300 per year), 7 teaching assistantships (averaging $13,612 per year); research assistantships, Federal Work-Study, institutionally sponsored loans, scholarships/grants, traineeships, health care benefits, tuition waivers (partial), and unspecified assistantships also available. Support available to part-time students. Financial award application deadline: 3/1; financial award applicants required to submit FAFSA. *Faculty research:* Pre-term labor, palliative care, support during chronic illness, violence, eating disorders. *Total annual research expenditures:* $2.1 million. *Unit head:* Dr. Susan Gennaro, Dean, 617-552-4251, Fax: 617-552-0931, E-mail: susan.gennaro@bc.edu. *Application contact:* MaryBeth Crowley, Graduate Programs Assistant, 617-552-4928, Fax: 617-552-2121, E-mail: csongrad@bc.edu. Web site: http://www.bc.edu/nursing/.

Bowie State University, Graduate Programs, Department of Nursing, Bowie, MD 20715-9465. Offers administration of nursing services (MS); family nurse practitioner (MS); nursing education (MS). *Accreditation:* NLN. Part-time programs available.

Faculty: 7 full-time (4 women), 14 part-time/adjunct (9 women). *Students:* 41 full-time (35 women), 55 part-time (50 women); includes 80 minority (77 Black or African American, non-Hispanic/Latino; 2 Asian, non-Hispanic/Latino; 1 Hispanic/Latino), 11 international. Average age 42. 7 applicants, 100% accepted, 5 enrolled. In 2011, 7 master's awarded. *Degree requirements:* For master's, comprehensive exam, thesis, research paper. *Entrance requirements:* For master's, minimum GPA of 2.5. *Application deadline:* For fall admission, 5/15 for domestic students. Applications are processed on a rolling basis. Application fee: $40. Electronic applications accepted. *Expenses:* Tuition, state resident: full-time $4140; part-time $3105 per semester. Tuition, nonresident: full-time $7836; part-time $5877 per semester. *Required fees:* $1715; $648 per semester. *Financial support:* Institutionally sponsored loans and traineeships available. Financial award application deadline: 4/1. *Faculty research:* Minority health, women's health, gerontology, leadership management. *Unit head:* Dr. Bonita Jenkins, Acting Chairperson, 301-860-3210, E-mail: mccaskill@bowiestate.edu. *Application contact:* Angela Issac, Information Contact, 301-860-4000.

Bradley University, Graduate School, College of Education and Health Sciences, Department of Nursing, Peoria, IL 61625-0002. Offers nurse administered anesthesia (MSN); nursing administration (MSN). *Accreditation:* AANA/CANAEP; NLN. Part-time and evening/weekend programs available. *Degree requirements:* For master's, comprehensive exam, thesis optional. *Entrance requirements:* For master's, GRE General Test or MAT, interview, Illinois RN license, advanced cardiac life support certification, pediatric advanced life support certification, 3 letters of recommendation. Additional exam requirements/recommendations for international students: Required—TOEFL (minimum score 550 paper-based; 213 computer-based; 79 iBT).

Briar Cliff University, Program in Nursing, Sioux City, IA 51104-0100. Offers MSN. *Accreditation:* NLN. Part-time and evening/weekend programs available. *Degree requirements:* For master's, thesis optional. *Entrance requirements:* For master's, minimum undergraduate GPA of 3.0 for last 60 undergraduate credits; current RN license. *Expenses:* Contact institution. *Faculty research:* The process/experience of trying something new (or change), the experience of taking a risk.

Brigham Young University, Graduate Studies, College of Nursing, Provo, UT 84602. Offers family nurse practitioner (MS). *Accreditation:* AACN. *Faculty:* 14 full-time (13 women), 4 part-time/adjunct (3 women). *Students:* 28 full-time (21 women); includes 3 minority (2 Asian, non-Hispanic/Latino; 1 Hispanic/Latino). Average age 34. 36 applicants, 42% accepted, 13 enrolled. In 2011, 13 master's awarded. *Degree requirements:* For master's, thesis. *Entrance requirements:* For master's, GRE, minimum GPA of 3.0 in last 60 hours, interview, BS in nursing, pathophysiology class within undergraduate program, course work in basic statistics. Additional exam requirements/recommendations for international students: Required—TOEFL; Recommended—IELTS. *Application deadline:* For spring admission, 12/1 for domestic students. Applications are processed on a rolling basis. Application fee: $50. Electronic applications accepted. *Expenses: Tuition:* Full-time $5760; part-time $320 per credit. Tuition and fees vary according to student's religious affiliation. *Financial support:* In 2011–12, 28 students received support, including 2 research assistantships with full and partial tuition reimbursements available (averaging $10,000 per year), 3 teaching assistantships with full and partial tuition reimbursements available (averaging $10,000 per year); institutionally sponsored loans, scholarships/grants, tuition waivers (full), and unspecified assistantships also available. Support available to part-time students. Financial award application deadline: 2/1; financial award applicants required to submit FAFSA. *Faculty research:* Cardiovascular risk factors, stroke patients, nutrition, stress among children, family response to life-threatening illness. *Total annual research expenditures:* $1,200. *Unit head:* Dr. Beth Vaughan Cole, Dean, 801-422-8296, Fax: 801-422-0536, E-mail: beth-cole@byu.edu. *Application contact:* Stephanie Von Forell,

Graduate Secretary, 801-422-4142, Fax: 801-422-0538, E-mail: stephanie-wilson@byu.edu. Web site: http://nursing.byu.edu/.

See Display below and Close-Up on page 793.

California Baptist University, Program in Nursing, Riverside, CA 92504-3206. Offers administering nursing services (MSN); teaching nursing (MSN). Part-time programs available. *Faculty:* 21 full-time (all women). *Students:* 58 full-time (44 women); includes 28 minority (5 Black or African American, non-Hispanic/Latino; 2 American Indian or Alaska Native, non-Hispanic/Latino; 7 Asian, non-Hispanic/Latino; 12 Hispanic/Latino; 1 Native Hawaiian or other Pacific Islander, non-Hispanic/Latino; 1 Two or more races, non-Hispanic/Latino). Average age 32. 35 applicants, 60% accepted, 19 enrolled. *Degree requirements:* For master's, comprehensive exam or thesis. *Entrance requirements:* For master's, GRE or California Critical Thinking Skills Test; Test of Essential Academic Skills (TEAS), minimum GPA of 3.25; health clearance; health insurance; CPR certification; vehicle insurance; criminal background clearance; passport photo; three recommendations; comprehensive essay; interview. Additional exam requirements/recommendations for international students: Required—TOEFL (minimum score 575 paper-based; 230 computer-based; 89 iBT). *Application deadline:* For fall admission, 8/1 priority date for domestic students, 7/1 for international students; for spring admission, 12/1 priority date for domestic students, 11/1 for international students. Applications are processed on a rolling basis. Application fee: $45. Electronic applications accepted. *Expenses: Tuition:* Full-time $9540; part-time $530 per unit. *Required fees:* $355 per semester. One-time fee: $45. Tuition and fees vary according to course load and program. *Financial support:* Federal Work-Study and institutionally sponsored loans available. Financial award applicants required to submit FAFSA. *Faculty research:* Qualitative research using Parse Methodology, gerontology, disaster preparedness, medical-surgical nursing, maternal-child nursing. *Unit head:* Dr. Geneva Oaks, Dean, School of Nursing, 951-343-4738, E-mail: goaks@calbaptist.edu. *Application contact:* Gail Ronveaux, Dean of Graduate Enrollment, 951-343-4246, Fax: 951-343-5095, E-mail: graduateadmissions@calbaptist.edu. Web site: http://www.calbaptist.edu/msn/.

California State University, Chico, Office of Graduate Studies, College of Natural Sciences, School of Nursing, Chico, CA 95929-0722. Offers MS. *Accreditation:* Part-time programs available. Postbaccalaureate distance learning degree programs offered. *Faculty:* 2 full-time (both women). *Students:* 1 full-time (0 women), 11 part-time (10 women); includes 4 minority (1 American Indian or Alaska Native, non-Hispanic/Latino; 2 Asian, non-Hispanic/Latino; 1 Hispanic/Latino). Average age 38. In 2011, 4 master's awarded. *Degree requirements:* For master's, thesis, oral exam. *Entrance requirements:* For master's, GRE, statement of purpose, course work in statistics in the last seven years, BSN, California nursing license. Additional exam requirements/recommendations for international students: Required—TOEFL (minimum score 550 paper-based; 213 computer-based; 80 iBT), IELTS (minimum score 6.5), Pearson Test of English (minimum score 59). *Application deadline:* For fall admission, 3/1 for domestic and international students. Application fee: $55. Electronic applications accepted. Tuition and fees vary according to class time, course load and degree level. *Financial support:* Career-related internships or fieldwork and scholarships/grants available. Financial award application deadline: 3/1; financial award applicants required to submit FAFSA. *Unit head:* Dr. Carol L. Houston, Director, 530-898-5891. *Application contact:* Judy L. Rice, Graduate Admissions Coordinator, 530-898-5416, Fax: 530-898-3342, E-mail: jlrice@csuchico.edu. Web site: http://www.csuchico.edu/nurs.

California State University, Dominguez Hills, College of Professional Studies, School of Health and Human Services, Program in Nursing, Carson, CA 90747-0001. Offers MSN. *Accreditation:* AACN. Part-time programs available. Postbaccalaureate distance learning degree programs offered. *Faculty:* 8 full-time (all women), 33 part-time/adjunct

BRIGHAM YOUNG UNIVERSITY
College of Nursing

- Master of Science (M.S.) degree prepares students as family nurse practitioners (FNP).
- Post-Master's Family Nurse Practitioner degree available for those who have already received a master's degree in nursing.
- Graduates are eligible to apply for certification examinations.
- Program can be completed in six semesters of full-time study.

For more information, please contact:
Stephanie Wilson
Nursing Masters Program
Brigham Young University
400 SWKT
Provo, UT 84602
801-422-4142
Stephanie-Wilson@byu.edu
http://nursing.byu.edu/

(29 women). *Students:* 72 full-time (58 women), 432 part-time (394 women); includes 261 minority (67 Black or African American, non-Hispanic/Latino; 2 American Indian or Alaska Native, non-Hispanic/Latino; 108 Asian, non-Hispanic/Latino; 70 Hispanic/Latino; 14 Two or more races, non-Hispanic/Latino), 4 international. Average age 41. 223 applicants, 81% accepted, 99 enrolled. In 2011, 174 master's awarded. *Degree requirements:* For master's, comprehensive exam. *Entrance requirements:* For master's, minimum GPA of 2.5, 3.0 in prior coursework in statistics, research, pathophysiology and assessment. Additional exam requirements/recommendations for international students: Required—TOEFL. *Application deadline:* For fall admission, 6/1 for domestic students; for spring admission, 11/1 for domestic students. Applications are processed on a rolling basis. Application fee: $55. Electronic applications accepted. *Faculty research:* AIDS/HIV, health promotion, elderly. *Unit head:* Dr. Cynthia Johnson, Acting Chair, 310-243-2522, E-mail: cjohnson@csudh.edu. *Application contact:* 310-243-3426. Web site: http://www.csudh.edu/cps/son/.

California State University, Fresno, Division of Graduate Studies, College of Health and Human Services, Department of Nursing, Fresno, CA 93740-8027. Offers nursing (MS), including clinical nurse, primary care nurse practitioner, specialist/nurse educator. *Accreditation:* AACN. Part-time and evening/weekend programs available. *Degree requirements:* For master's, thesis or alternative. *Entrance requirements:* For master's, GRE General Test, 1 year of clinical practice, previous course work in statistics, BSN, minimum GPA of 3.0 in nursing. Additional exam requirements/recommendations for international students: Required—TOEFL. Electronic applications accepted. *Faculty research:* Training grant, HIV assessment.

California State University, Fullerton, Graduate Studies, College of Health and Human Development, Department of Nursing, Fullerton, CA 92834-9480. Offers MS. *Accreditation:* AACN; AANA/CANAEP. Part-time programs available. *Students:* 145 full-time (112 women), 183 part-time (175 women); includes 146 minority (10 Black or African American, non-Hispanic/Latino; 85 Asian, non-Hispanic/Latino; 42 Hispanic/Latino; 9 Two or more races, non-Hispanic/Latino), 3 international. Average age 36. 358 applicants, 40% accepted, 121 enrolled. In 2011, 114 master's awarded. Application fee: $55. *Financial support:* Career-related internships or fieldwork, Federal Work-Study, institutionally sponsored loans, scholarships/grants, and traineeships available. Support available to part-time students. Financial award application deadline: 3/1; financial award applicants required to submit FAFSA. *Unit head:* Dr. Cindy Greenberg,, Chair, 657-278-3336. *Application contact:* Admissions/Applications, 657-278-2371.

California State University, Long Beach, Graduate Studies, College of Health and Human Services, Department of Nursing, Long Beach, CA 90840. Offers MSN, MSN/MPH. *Accreditation:* AACN. Part-time programs available. *Faculty:* 14 full-time (11 women), 8 part-time/adjunct (all women). *Students:* 243 full-time (213 women), 199 part-time (169 women); includes 283 minority (45 Black or African American, non-Hispanic/Latino; 1 American Indian or Alaska Native, non-Hispanic/Latino; 167 Asian, non-Hispanic/Latino; 56 Hispanic/Latino; 4 Native Hawaiian or other Pacific Islander, non-Hispanic/Latino; 10 Two or more races, non-Hispanic/Latino), 11 international. Average age 35. 225 applicants, 53% accepted, 78 enrolled. In 2011, 113 master's awarded. *Degree requirements:* For master's, thesis optional. *Entrance requirements:* For master's, minimum GPA of 3.0. *Application deadline:* For fall admission, 7/1 for domestic students. Applications are processed on a rolling basis. Application fee: $55. Electronic applications accepted. *Financial support:* Federal Work-Study, institutionally sponsored loans, and scholarships/grants available. Financial award application deadline: 3/2. *Faculty research:* Newborns of drug-dependent mothers, abuse of residents in nursing homes, interventions in care of Alzheimer's patients. *Unit head:* Dr. Lucy Huckabay, Director, 562-985-4582, Fax: 562-985-2382, E-mail: huckabay@csulb.edu. *Application contact:* Dr. David Kumrow, Graduate Advisor, 562-985-8082, Fax: 562-985-2382, E-mail: dkumrow@csulb.edu.

California State University, Los Angeles, Graduate Studies, College of Health and Human Services, School of Nursing, Los Angeles, CA 90032-8530. Offers health science (MA); nursing (MS). *Accreditation:* AACN. Part-time and evening/weekend programs available. *Faculty:* 6 full-time (5 women), 17 part-time/adjunct (16 women). *Students:* 115 full-time (100 women), 101 part-time (82 women); includes 154 minority (18 Black or African American, non-Hispanic/Latino; 90 Asian, non-Hispanic/Latino; 39 Hispanic/Latino; 2 Native Hawaiian or other Pacific Islander, non-Hispanic/Latino; 5 Two or more races, non-Hispanic/Latino), 4 international. Average age 34. 259 applicants, 30% accepted, 41 enrolled. In 2011, 57 master's awarded. *Degree requirements:* For master's, comprehensive exam, project or thesis. *Entrance requirements:* For master's, minimum GPA of 3.0 in nursing, course work in nursing and statistics. Additional exam requirements/recommendations for international students: Required—TOEFL (minimum score 500 paper-based; 173 computer-based). *Application deadline:* For fall admission, 5/1 for domestic and international students. Applications are processed on a rolling basis. Application fee: $55. *Expenses:* Tuition, state resident: full-time $8225. *Financial support:* Federal Work-Study available. Support available to part-time students. Financial award application deadline: 3/1. *Faculty research:* Family stress, geripsychiatric nursing, self-care counseling, holistic nursing, adult health. *Unit head:* Dr. Cynthia Hughes, Director, 323-343-4700, Fax: 323-343-6454, E-mail: chughes2@calstatela.edu. *Application contact:* Dr. Karin Brown, Acting Associate Dean of Graduate Studies, 323-343-3820, Fax: 323-343-5653, E-mail: kbrown5@calstatela.edu. Web site: http://www.calstatela.edu/dept/nursing/index.htm.

California State University, Sacramento, Office of Graduate Studies, College of Health and Human Services, School of Nursing, Sacramento, CA 95819. Offers MS. *Accreditation:* AACN. Part-time programs available. *Faculty:* 19 full-time (all women), 52 part-time/adjunct (43 women). *Students:* 48 full-time, 53 part-time; includes 35 minority (3 Black or African American, non-Hispanic/Latino; 2 American Indian or Alaska Native, non-Hispanic/Latino; 13 Asian, non-Hispanic/Latino; 7 Hispanic/Latino; 6 Native Hawaiian or other Pacific Islander, non-Hispanic/Latino; 4 Two or more races, non-Hispanic/Latino), 2 international. Average age 38. 77 applicants, 31% accepted, 15 enrolled. In 2011, 20 master's awarded. *Degree requirements:* For master's, thesis or project; writing proficiency exam. *Entrance requirements:* For master's, GRE, bachelor's degree in nursing, minimum GPA of 3.0. Additional exam requirements/recommendations for international students: Required—TOEFL. *Application deadline:* For fall admission, 3/1 for domestic and international students; for spring admission, 9/30 for international students. Applications are processed on a rolling basis. Application fee: $55. Electronic applications accepted. *Financial support:* Research assistantships, teaching assistantships, career-related internships or fieldwork, and Federal Work-Study available. Support available to part-time students. Financial award application deadline: 3/1; financial award applicants required to submit FAFSA. *Unit head:* Carolyn Goetze, Chair, 916-278-7543, Fax: 916-278-6311, E-mail: cgoetze@csus.edu. *Application contact:* Jose Martinez, Outreach and Graduate Diversity Coordinator, 916-278-6470, Fax: 916-278-5669, E-mail: martinj@skymail.csus.edu. Web site: http://www.csus.edu/hhs/nrs/programs/graduate.html.

California State University, San Bernardino, Graduate Studies, College of Natural Sciences, Department of Nursing, San Bernardino, CA 92407-2397. Offers MS. *Accreditation:* AACN. *Students:* 12 full-time (11 women), 10 part-time (9 women); includes 7 minority (2 Black or African American, non-Hispanic/Latino; 3 Asian, non-Hispanic/Latino; 2 Hispanic/Latino), 1 international. Average age 44. 23 applicants, 26% accepted, 5 enrolled. In 2011, 4 master's awarded. *Degree requirements:* For master's, thesis optional. *Entrance requirements:* For master's, writing exam, BSN or BS, minimum GPA of 3.0, California RN license. Application fee: $55. *Expenses:* Tuition, state resident: full-time $7356. Tuition, nonresident: full-time $7356. *Required fees:* $1077. Tuition and fees vary according to program. *Unit head:* Dwight P. Sweeney, Interim Chair, 909-537-5385, Fax: 909-537-7089, E-mail: dsweeney@csusb.edu. *Application contact:* Sandra Kamusikiri, Associate Vice-President/Dean of Graduate Studies, 909-537-5058`, E-mail: skamusik@csusb.edu.

California State University, Stanislaus, College of Human and Health Sciences, Program in Nursing (MS), Turlock, CA 95382. Offers gerontological nursing (MS); nursing education (MS). Part-time programs available. *Degree requirements:* For master's, comprehensive exam, thesis or alternative. *Entrance requirements:* For master's, GRE or MAT, minimum GPA of 3.0, 3 letters of reference, RN. Additional exam requirements/recommendations for international students: Required—TOEFL (minimum score 550 paper-based; 213 computer-based). *Application deadline:* For fall admission, 5/1 for domestic students. Application fee: $55. Electronic applications accepted. *Expenses: Required fees:* $4616 per year. *Unit head:* Dr. Margaret Hodge, Chair, 209-667-3141, Fax: 209-667-3690, E-mail: phodge@csustan.edu. *Application contact:* Graduate School, 209-667-3129, Fax: 209-664-7025, E-mail: graduate_school@csustan.edu. Web site: http://www.csustan.edu/nursing/.

Capital University, School of Nursing, Columbus, OH 43209-2394. Offers administration (MSN); legal studies (MSN); theological studies (MSN); JD/MSN; MBA/MSN; MSN/MTS. *Accreditation:* AACN. Part-time and evening/weekend programs available. *Degree requirements:* For master's, thesis or alternative. *Entrance requirements:* For master's, BSN, current RN license, minimum GPA of 3.0, undergraduate courses in statistics and research. Additional exam requirements/recommendations for international students: Required—TOEFL (minimum score 550 paper-based). *Expenses:* Contact institution. *Faculty research:* Bereavement, wellness/health promotion, emergency cardiac care, critical thinking, complementary and alternative healthcare.

Cardinal Stritch University, College of Nursing, Milwaukee, WI 53217-3985. Offers MSN. *Accreditation:* NLN. Part-time and evening/weekend programs available. *Degree requirements:* For master's, thesis. *Entrance requirements:* For master's, interview; minimum GPA of 3.0; RN license; 3 letters of recommendation; undergraduate coursework in statistics and nursing research; computer literacy; curriculum vitae. Electronic applications accepted. *Expenses:* Contact institution.

Carlow University, School of Nursing, Doctor of Nursing Practice Program, Pittsburgh, PA 15213-3165. Offers DNP. Part-time and evening/weekend programs available. Postbaccalaureate distance learning degree programs offered (minimal on-campus study). *Students:* 39 full-time (36 women), 10 part-time (all women); includes 6 minority (5 Black or African American, non-Hispanic/Latino; 1 Hispanic/Latino), 1 international. Average age 46. 66 applicants, 56% accepted, 21 enrolled. In 2011, 18 doctorates awarded. *Entrance requirements:* For doctorate, master's degree with minimum GPA of 3.0; BSN; current RN license; official transcripts from all undergraduate and graduate institutions; current curriculum vitae; two letters of recommendation; reflective essay. Additional exam requirements/recommendations for international students: Required—TOEFL (minimum score 550 paper-based; 213 computer-based). *Application deadline:* For fall admission, 4/1 priority date for domestic students. Application fee: $20. Electronic applications accepted. Application fee is waived when completed online. *Expenses: Tuition:* Full-time $10,290; part-time $686 per credit. Tuition and fees vary according to course load, degree level and program. *Unit head:* Dr. Peggy M. Slota, Director, DNP Program, 412-578-6102, Fax: 412-578-6114, E-mail: mmslota@carlow.edu. *Application contact:* Jo Danhires, Administrative Assistant, Admissions, 412-578-6059, Fax: 412-578-6321, E-mail: gradstudies@carlow.edu. Web site: http://gradstudies.carlow.edu/dnp/index.html.

Carson-Newman College, Department of Nursing, Jefferson City, TN 37760. Offers family nurse practitioner (MSN); nurse educator (MSN). *Accreditation:* AACN. *Faculty:* 2 full-time (both women), 10 part-time/adjunct (9 women). *Students:* 16 full-time (15 women), 46 part-time (36 women); includes 3 minority (2 American Indian or Alaska Native, non-Hispanic/Latino; 1 Two or more races, non-Hispanic/Latino). Average age 32. In 2011, 17 master's awarded. *Application deadline:* For fall admission, 7/15 priority date for domestic students. Applications are processed on a rolling basis. Application fee: $50. *Expenses: Tuition:* Full-time $6750; part-time $375 per credit hour. *Required fees:* $200. *Unit head:* Dr. Gregory A. Casalenuovo, Dean, 865-471-3426. *Application contact:* Graduate Admissions and Services Adviser, 865-473-3468, Fax: 865-472-3475.

Case Western Reserve University, Frances Payne Bolton School of Nursing, Doctor of Nursing Practice Program, Cleveland, OH 44106. Offers acute care nurse practitioner (DNP); adult gerontology nurse practitioner (DNP); educational leadership (DNP); family nurse practitioner (DNP); family systems psychiatric mental health nursing (DNP); midwifery/family nursing (DNP); neonatal nurse practitioner (DNP); pediatric nurse practitioner (DNP); practice leadership (DNP); women's health nurse practitioner (DNP). *Students:* 73 full-time, 194 part-time; includes 11 minority (6 Black or African American, non-Hispanic/Latino; 3 Asian, non-Hispanic/Latino; 2 Hispanic/Latino). 122 applicants, 74% accepted, 49 enrolled. In 2011, 47 doctorates awarded. Terminal master's awarded for partial completion of doctoral program. *Degree requirements:* For doctorate, thesis/dissertation. *Entrance requirements:* For doctorate, GRE General Test or MAT. Additional exam requirements/recommendations for international students: Required—TOEFL (minimum score 577 paper-based; 90 iBT), IELTS (minimum score 7). *Application deadline:* For fall admission, 6/1 priority date for domestic students, 6/1 for international students; for spring admission, 10/1 for domestic and international students. Applications are processed on a rolling basis. Application fee: $75. *Financial support:* In 2011–12, 6 students received support, including 1 teaching assistantship; research assistantships, Federal Work-Study, institutionally sponsored loans, and tuition waivers (partial) also available. Support available to part-time students. Financial award application deadline: 6/30; financial award applicants required to submit FAFSA. *Faculty research:* Clinical nursing, acute care, gerontology, mental health, critical care. *Unit head:* Dr. Donna Dowling, Director, 216-368-1869, Fax: 216-368-3542, E-mail: dad10@case.edu. *Application contact:* Donna Hassik, Admissions Coordinator, 216-368-5253, Fax: 216-368-0124, E-mail: dmh7@case.edu. Web site: http://fpb.case.edu/DNP/.

Case Western Reserve University, Frances Payne Bolton School of Nursing, Master's Programs in Nursing, Cleveland, OH 44106. Offers nurse anesthesia (MSN); nurse midwifery (MSN); nurse practitioner (MSN), including acute care cardiovascular nursing, acute care nurse practitioner, acute care/flight nurse, family nurse practitioner, neonatal nurse practitioner, pediatric nurse practitioner, women's health nurse practitioner; pre-licensure generalist nursing (MN). *Accreditation:* NLN. Part-time programs available. Postbaccalaureate distance learning degree programs offered (minimal on-campus study). *Faculty:* 54 full-time (50 women), 5 part-time/adjunct (3 women). *Students:* 112 full-time, 177 part-time; includes 17 minority (11 Black or African American, non-Hispanic/Latino; 4 Asian, non-Hispanic/Latino; 2 Hispanic/Latino), 18 international. Average age 35. 230 applicants, 45% accepted, 72 enrolled. In 2011, 75 master's awarded. *Degree requirements:* For master's, thesis optional. *Entrance requirements:* For master's, GRE General Test or MAT. Additional exam requirements/

recommendations for international students: Required—TOEFL (minimum score 577 paper-based; 90 iBT), IELTS (minimum score 7). *Application deadline:* For fall admission, 6/1 for domestic and international students; for spring admission, 10/1 for domestic and international students. Applications are processed on a rolling basis. Application fee: $75. *Financial support:* In 2011–12, 7 teaching assistantships with tuition reimbursements were awarded; fellowships, research assistantships, institutionally sponsored loans, traineeships, and tuition waivers (partial) also available. Support available to part-time students. Financial award application deadline: 6/30; financial award applicants required to submit FAFSA. *Faculty research:* Preterm skin contact effects on electrophysiological sleep, intergenerational care giving to at-risk youth, maintaining exercise in cardiac rehabilitation, left ventricular function and duration of mechanical ventilation. *Unit head:* Dr. Carol L. Savrin, Director, 216-368-5304, Fax: 215-368-3542, E-mail: cls18@case.edu. *Application contact:* Donna Hassik, Admissions Coordinator, 216-368-5253, Fax: 216-368-0124, E-mail: dmh7@case.edu. Web site: http://fpb.case.edu/MSN/.

Case Western Reserve University, Frances Payne Bolton School of Nursing and Department of Anthropology, Nursing/Anthropology Program, Cleveland, OH 44106. Offers MSN/MA. *Application deadline:* For fall admission, 6/1 for domestic and international students; for spring admission, 10/1 for domestic and international students. Applications are processed on a rolling basis. Application fee: $75. *Financial support:* Fellowships, research assistantships, and teaching assistantships available. Financial award application deadline: 6/30; financial award applicants required to submit FAFSA. *Unit head:* Dr. Carol Savrin, Head, 216-368-6304, E-mail: cls18@case.edu. *Application contact:* Donna Hassik, Admissions Coordinator, 216-368-5253, Fax: 216-368-0124, E-mail: dmh7@case.edu. Web site: http://fpb.case.edu/MSN/.

Case Western Reserve University, Frances Payne Bolton School of Nursing, Nursing/Bioethics Program, Cleveland, OH 44106. Offers MSN/MA. *Application deadline:* For fall admission, 6/1 for domestic and international students; for spring admission, 10/1 for domestic and international students. Applications are processed on a rolling basis. Application fee: $75. *Financial support:* Fellowships, research assistantships, and teaching assistantships available. Financial award application deadline: 6/30; financial award applicants required to submit FAFSA. *Unit head:* Dr. Barbara Daly, Head, 216-368-5994, E-mail: barbara.daly@case.edu. *Application contact:* Donna Hassik, Admissions Coordinator, 216-368-5253, Fax: 216-368-0124, E-mail: dmh7@case.edu. Web site: http://fpb.case.edu/MSN/.

Case Western Reserve University, Frances Payne Bolton School of Nursing, PhD in Nursing Program, Cleveland, OH 44106. Offers PhD. *Faculty:* 34 full-time (32 women), 6 part-time/adjunct (5 women). *Students:* 32 full-time (28 women), 4 part-time (3 women). Average age 40. 23 applicants, 74% accepted, 5 enrolled. In 2011, 7 doctorates awarded. *Degree requirements:* For doctorate, comprehensive exam, thesis/dissertation, 240-hour research practicum. *Entrance requirements:* For doctorate, GRE General Test. Additional exam requirements/recommendations for international students: Required—TOEFL (minimum score 577 paper-based; 90 iBT), IELTS (minimum score 7). *Application deadline:* For fall admission, 6/1 priority date for domestic students, 6/1 for international students; for spring admission, 10/1 for domestic students, 9/1 for international students. Applications are processed on a rolling basis. Application fee: $50. Electronic applications accepted. *Financial support:* In 2011–12, 7 research assistantships, 3 teaching assistantships (averaging $1,800 per year) were awarded; institutionally sponsored loans and traineeships also available. Financial award application deadline: 5/15; financial award applicants required to submit FAFSA. *Faculty research:* Cardiopulmonary, gerontology, health services, maternal-child, mental health. *Total annual research expenditures:* $5.1 million. *Unit head:* Dr. Jaclene A. Zauszniewski, Associate Dean, 216-368-3612, E-mail: jaz@case.edu. *Application contact:* Donna Hassik, Admissions Coordinator, Graduate Programs, 216-368-5253, Fax: 216-368-0124, E-mail: donna.hassik@case.edu. Web site: http://fpb.cwru.edu/PhD/.

The Catholic University of America, School of Nursing, Washington, DC 20064. Offers MSN, DNP, PhD, Certificate. *Accreditation:* AACN. Part-time programs available. *Faculty:* 18 full-time (16 women), 37 part-time/adjunct (33 women). *Students:* 20 full-time (all women), 78 part-time (76 women); includes 27 minority (19 Black or African American, non-Hispanic/Latino; 1 American Indian or Alaska Native, non-Hispanic/Latino; 6 Asian, non-Hispanic/Latino; 1 Two or more races, non-Hispanic/Latino), 4 international. Average age 41. 75 applicants, 63% accepted, 31 enrolled. In 2011, 17 master's, 8 doctorates, 3 other advanced degrees awarded. *Degree requirements:* For master's, comprehensive exam, thesis optional; for doctorate, comprehensive exam, thesis/dissertation, minimum GPA of 3.0, oral proposal defense. *Entrance requirements:* For master's, GRE General Test, 3 letters of recommendation, BA in nursing, RN registration, official copies of academic transcripts, some post-baccalaureate nursing experience; for doctorate, GRE General Test, BA in nursing, professional portfolio (including statements, resume, copy of RN license, 3 letters of recommendation, narrative description of clinical practice, proposal), copy of research/scholarly paper related to clinical nursing; for Certificate, GRE General Test. Additional exam requirements/recommendations for international students: Required—TOEFL (minimum score 580 paper-based; 237 computer-based). *Application deadline:* For fall admission, 8/1 priority date for domestic students, 7/15 for international students; for spring admission, 12/1 priority date for domestic students, 10/15 for international students. Applications are processed on a rolling basis. Application fee: $55. Electronic applications accepted. *Expenses: Tuition:* Full-time $35,260; part-time $1380 per credit. *Required fees:* $80; $40 per semester hour. One-time fee: $425. *Financial support:* Fellowships, research assistantships, teaching assistantships, Federal Work-Study, scholarships/grants, tuition waivers (full and partial), and unspecified assistantships available. Financial award application deadline: 2/1; financial award applicants required to submit FAFSA. *Faculty research:* Community involvement in health care services, primary health care services, pediatrics, chronic illness, cardiovascular disease. *Total annual research expenditures:* $128,590. *Unit head:* Dr. Patricia McMullen, Dean, 202-319-5403, Fax: 202-319-6485, E-mail: mcmullep@cua.edu. *Application contact:* Andrew Woodall, Director of Graduate Admissions, 202-319-5057, Fax: 202-319-6533, E-mail: cua-admissions@cua.edu. Web site: http://nursing.cua.edu/.

Cedar Crest College, Program in Nursing, Allentown, PA 18104-6196. Offers nursing administration (MS); nursing education (MS). Part-time programs available. *Faculty:* 5 full-time (all women). *Students:* 3 full-time, 16 part-time (all women). In 2011, 19 master's awarded. *Expenses: Tuition:* Part-time $590 per credit. Tuition and fees vary according to program. *Unit head:* Dr. Wendy Robb, Director, 610-606-4666, E-mail: wjrobb@cedarcrest.edu. *Application contact:* Bonnie Sofarelli, Director of School of Adult and Graduate Education, 610-606-4666, E-mail: sage@cedarcrest.edu. Web site: http://sage.cedarcrest.edu/degrees/graduate/nursing-science/.

Cedarville University, Graduate Programs, Cedarville, OH 45314-0601. Offers family nurse practitioner (MSN); global health nursing (MSN); nurse educator (MSN); teacher leader (M Ed). Part-time programs available. *Faculty:* 27 part-time/adjunct (14 women). *Students:* 13 full-time (11 women), 66 part-time (51 women), 2 international. Average age 33. 65 applicants, 83% accepted, 38 enrolled. In 2011, 2 master's awarded. *Degree requirements:* For master's, thesis. *Entrance requirements:* For master's, GRE, 2 professional recommendations. Additional exam requirements/recommendations for international students: Required—TOEFL (minimum score 550 paper-based; 80 iBT). *Application deadline:* For fall admission, 5/1 priority date for domestic students, 5/1 for international students; for spring admission, 11/1 priority date for domestic students, 11/1 for international students. Applications are processed on a rolling basis. Application fee: $30. Electronic applications accepted. *Financial support:* Scholarships/grants and unspecified assistantships available. Support available to part-time students. Financial award applicants required to submit FAFSA. *Unit head:* Dr. Andrew A. Runyan, Senior Associate Academic Vice-President/Dean of Graduate Studies, 937-766-3840, E-mail: arunyan@cedarville.edu. *Application contact:* Roscoe F. Smith, Associate Vice-President of Enrollment, 937-766-7700, Fax: 937-766-7575, E-mail: smithr@cedarville.edu. Web site: http://www.cedarville.edu/academics/graduate/.

Central Methodist University, College of Graduate and Extended Studies, Fayette, MO 65248-1198. Offers clinical counseling (MS); clinical nurse leader (MSN); education (M Ed). Part-time and evening/weekend programs available. Postbaccalaureate distance learning degree programs offered (no on-campus study). *Degree requirements:* For master's, thesis. *Entrance requirements:* For master's, GRE General Test, minimum GPA of 2.75. Electronic applications accepted.

Chatham University, Nursing Programs, Pittsburgh, PA 15232-2826. Offers education/leadership (MSN); nursing (DNP). *Accreditation:* AACN. Postbaccalaureate distance learning degree programs offered (minimal on-campus study). *Faculty:* 10 full-time (8 women), 11 part-time/adjunct (9 women). *Students:* 37 full-time (31 women), 62 part-time (58 women); includes 19 minority (16 Black or African American, non-Hispanic/Latino; 1 Asian, non-Hispanic/Latino; 1 Hispanic/Latino; 1 Native Hawaiian or other Pacific Islander, non-Hispanic/Latino). Average age 45. 163 applicants, 72% accepted, 84 enrolled. In 2011, 20 master's, 73 doctorates awarded. *Entrance requirements:* For master's, RN license, BSN, minimum GPA of 3.0; for doctorate, RN license, MSN. Additional exam requirements/recommendations for international students: Required—TOEFL (minimum score 600 paper-based; 250 computer-based; 100 iBT), IELTS (minimum score 6.5), TWE. *Application deadline:* For fall admission, 5/1 priority date for domestic students, 5/1 for international students. Applications are processed on a rolling basis. Application fee: $0. Electronic applications accepted. Application fee is waived when completed online. *Expenses: Tuition:* Full-time $13,896. Tuition and fees vary according to program. *Financial support:* Applicants required to submit FAFSA. *Unit head:* Dr. Elizabeth Gazza, Director, 412-365-2746, E-mail: egazza@chatham.edu. *Application contact:* David Vey, Admissions Support Specialist, 412-365-1498, Fax: 412-365-1720, E-mail: dvey@chatham.edu. Web site: http://www.chatham.edu/nursing.

Clarion University of Pennsylvania, Office of Graduate Programs, Master of Science in Nursing Program, Clarion, PA 16214. Offers family nurse practitioner (MSN, Post-Master's Certificate); nurse educator (MSN). Program offered jointly with Slippery Rock University of Pennsylvania. *Accreditation:* NLN. *Students:* 3 full-time (2 women), 60 part-time (59 women); includes 2 minority (both Black or African American, non-Hispanic/Latino). Average age 39. In 2011, 25 master's awarded. *Degree requirements:* For master's, comprehensive exam, thesis. *Entrance requirements:* For master's, minimum QPA of 2.75. Additional exam requirements/recommendations for international students: Required—TOEFL (minimum score 550 paper-based; 213 computer-based; 80 iBT). *Application deadline:* For fall admission, 6/1 for domestic students, 4/15 for international students; for spring admission, 11/1 for domestic students, 9/15 for international students. Application fee: $30. *Expenses:* Tuition, state resident: part-time $429 per credit. Tuition, nonresident: part-time $644 per credit. *Financial support:* Research assistantships with full tuition reimbursements available. Financial award application deadline: 3/1. *Unit head:* Dr. Debbie Ciesielka, Graduate Coordinator, 412-578-7277, E-mail: dciesielka@clarion.edu. *Application contact:* Dr. Brenda Sanders Dede, Assistant Vice President for Academic Affairs, 814-393-2337, Fax: 814-393-2030, E-mail: bdede@clarion.edu.

Clarke University, Department of Nursing and Health, Dubuque, IA 52001-3198. Offers administration of nursing systems (MSN); advanced practice nursing (MSN); education (MSN); family nurse practitioner (MSN, PMC). *Accreditation:* AACN. Part-time programs available. *Faculty:* 5 full-time (all women), 2 part-time/adjunct (1 woman). *Students:* 42 full-time (41 women), 25 part-time (all women); includes 1 minority (Black or African American, non-Hispanic/Latino). Average age 35. In 2011, 13 master's awarded. *Entrance requirements:* For master's, GRE General Test or MAT, BSN, minimum GPA of 3.0. *Application deadline:* For fall admission, 2/15 priority date for domestic students; for spring admission, 12/15 priority date for domestic students. Applications are processed on a rolling basis. Application fee: $25. Electronic applications accepted. *Expenses: Tuition:* Part-time $690 per credit hour. *Required fees:* $35 per credit hour. Tuition and fees vary according to program and student level. *Financial support:* In 2011–12, 6 students received support. Career-related internships or fieldwork available. Support available to part-time students. Financial award applicants required to submit FAFSA. *Faculty research:* Narrative pedagogy, ethics, end-of-life care, pedagogy, family systems. *Unit head:* Dr. Susan DeCrane, Chair, 800-224-2736, Fax: 319-584-8684. *Application contact:* Carrie Kirk, Information Contact, 563-588-6635, Fax: 563-588-6789, E-mail: graduate@clarke.edu. Web site: http://www.clarke.edu/.

Clarkson College, Master of Science in Nursing Program, Omaha, NE 68131. Offers adult nurse practitioner (MSN, Post-Master's Certificate); family nurse practitioner (MSN, Post-Master's Certificate); nursing education (MSN, Post-Master's Certificate); nursing health care leadership (MSN, Post-Master's Certificate). *Accreditation:* AANA/CANAEP; NLN. Part-time and evening/weekend programs available. Postbaccalaureate distance learning degree programs offered (minimal on-campus study). *Degree requirements:* For master's, on-campus skills assessment (family nurse practitioner, adult nurse practitioner), comprehensive exam or thesis. *Entrance requirements:* For master's, minimum GPA of 3.0, 2 references, resume. Additional exam requirements/recommendations for international students: Required—TOEFL (minimum score 600 paper-based; 250 computer-based; 100 iBT). Electronic applications accepted.

Clayton State University, School of Graduate Studies, Program in Nursing, Morrow, GA 30260-0285. Offers MSN. *Accreditation:* AACN. *Faculty:* 7 full-time (all women). *Students:* 6 full-time (4 women), 15 part-time (12 women); includes 12 minority (11 Black or African American, non-Hispanic/Latino; 1 Asian, non-Hispanic/Latino). Average age 41. 7 applicants, 100% accepted, 6 enrolled. In 2011, 2 master's awarded. *Degree requirements:* For master's, thesis. *Entrance requirements:* For master's, GRE, 2 official transcripts, 3 letters of recommendation, statement of purpose, on-campus interview. Additional exam requirements/recommendations for international students: Required—TOEFL (minimum score 550 paper-based; 213 computer-based; 80 iBT). *Application deadline:* For fall admission, 6/15 priority date for domestic students, 5/1 for international students; for spring admission, 11/15 priority date for domestic students, 9/1 for international students. Applications are processed on a rolling basis. Application fee: $75. Electronic applications accepted. *Expenses:* Contact institution. *Financial support:* Application deadline: 7/1; applicants required to submit FAFSA. *Unit head:* Dr. Betty Glenn Lane, Program Director, Master of Science in Nursing, 678-466-4953, Fax: 678-466-4999, E-mail: katherinewillock@clayton.edu. *Application contact:* Christy Hicks, Coordinator, 678-466-4959, Fax: 678-466-4999, E-mail: christyhicks@clayton.edu. Web site: http://nursing.clayton.edu/MSN/.

Clemson University, Graduate School, College of Health, Education, and Human Development, School of Nursing, Clemson, SC 29634. Offers healthcare genetics

(PhD); nursing (MS). *Accreditation:* AACN. Part-time programs available. Postbaccalaureate distance learning degree programs offered. *Faculty:* 16 full-time (15 women). *Students:* 53 full-time (48 women), 47 part-time (40 women); includes 11 minority (7 Black or African American, non-Hispanic/Latino; 1 Hispanic/Latino; 3 Two or more races, non-Hispanic/Latino), 3 international. Average age 35. 50 applicants, 62% accepted, 24 enrolled. In 2011, 27 master's awarded. *Degree requirements:* For master's, thesis or alternative; for doctorate, comprehensive exam, thesis/dissertation. *Entrance requirements:* For master's, GRE General Test, RN license; for doctorate, GRE General Test. Additional exam requirements/recommendations for international students: Required—TOEFL. *Application deadline:* For fall admission, 4/1 for domestic students; for spring admission, 10/1 for domestic students. Applications are processed on a rolling basis. Application fee: $70 ($80 for international students). Electronic applications accepted. *Expenses:* Contact institution. *Financial support:* In 2011–12, 25 students received support, including 2 research assistantships with partial tuition reimbursements available (averaging $2,000 per year), teaching assistantships with partial tuition reimbursements available (averaging $5,122 per year); fellowships with full and partial tuition reimbursements available, career-related internships or fieldwork, institutionally sponsored loans, scholarships/grants, health care benefits, and unspecified assistantships also available. Support available to part-time students. Financial award applicants required to submit FAFSA. *Faculty research:* Risk behaviors and chronic risk-taking in early adolescents, stress in older caregivers, home care of elderly, cancer awareness, pain. *Total annual research expenditures:* $175,758. *Unit head:* Dr. Rosanne Pruitt, Director, 864-656-7622, Fax: 864-656-5488, E-mail: prosan@clemson.edu. *Application contact:* Dr. Margaret Ann Wetsel, Graduate Studies Coordinator, 864-656-5527, Fax: 864-656-5488, E-mail: mwetsel@clemson.edu. Web site: http://www.clemson.edu/hehd/departments/nursing/.

Cleveland State University, College of Graduate Studies, School of Nursing, Cleveland, OH 44115. Offers clinical nurse leader (MSN); forensic nursing (MSN); nursing education (MSN); specialized population (MSN); urban education (PhD), including nursing education; MSN/MBA. *Accreditation:* AACN. Part-time programs available. Postbaccalaureate distance learning degree programs offered (no on-campus study). *Faculty:* 4 full-time (all women), 1 (woman) part-time/adjunct. *Students:* 5 full-time (3 women), 50 part-time (47 women); includes 8 minority (7 Black or African American, non-Hispanic/Latino; 1 Hispanic/Latino), 1 international. Average age 43. 41 applicants, 73% accepted, 13 enrolled. In 2011, 7 master's awarded. *Degree requirements:* For master's, thesis or alternative, portfolio, population health project; for doctorate, comprehensive exam, thesis/dissertation. *Entrance requirements:* For master's, RN license, BSN, course work in statistics; for doctorate, GRE (for PhD in urban education). Additional exam requirements/recommendations for international students: Required—TOEFL (minimum score 525 paper-based; 197 computer-based), IELTS (minimum score 6). *Application deadline:* For fall admission, 3/1 priority date for domestic students, 3/1 for international students. Application fee: $55. Electronic applications accepted. *Expenses:* Tuition, state resident: full-time $6416; part-time $494 per credit hour. Tuition, nonresident: full-time $12,074; part-time $929 per credit hour. *Financial support:* In 2011–12, 4 students received support. Tuition waivers (full), unspecified assistantships, and Nurse Faculty Loan Program (NFLP) available. Support available to part-time students. Financial award application deadline: 3/1; financial award applicants required to submit FAFSA. *Faculty research:* Diabetes management, African-American elders medication compliance, risk in home visiting, suffering, COPD and stress, nursing education, disaster health preparedness. *Total annual research expenditures:* $59,000. *Unit head:* Dr. Vida Lock, Dean, 216-523-7237, Fax: 216-687-3556, E-mail: v.lock@csuohio.edu. *Application contact:* Carol Ivan, Recruiter/Advisor, 216-687-5517, Fax: 216-687-3556, E-mail: c.ivan@csuohio.edu. Web site: http://www.csuohio.edu/nursing/.

College of Mount St. Joseph, Doctor of Nursing Practice Program, Cincinnati, OH 45233-1670. Offers administration (DNP); advanced practice (DNP). Part-time programs available. *Entrance requirements:* For doctorate, essay; MSN from regionally-accredited university; minimum graduate GPA of 3.5; professional resume; three professional references; interview; 2 years of clinical nursing experience; active RN license; criminal background check. Additional exam requirements/recommendations for international students: Required—TOEFL (minimum score 560 paper-based; 220 computer-based; 83 iBT). Application fee: $50. Electronic applications accepted. *Expenses: Tuition:* Full-time $24,200; part-time $540 per credit hour. *Required fees:* $112.50 per semester. One-time fee: $200. *Financial support:* Applicants required to submit FAFSA. *Unit head:* Dr. Lynn Bertsch, Director, 513-244-4200, E-mail: lynn_bertsch@mail.msj.edu. *Application contact:* Marilyn Hoskins, Assistant Director for Graduate Recruitment, 513-244-4723, Fax: 513-244-4629, E-mail: marilyn_hoskins@mail.msj.edu. Web site: http://www.msj.edu/view/academics/graduate-programs/doctor-of-nursing-practice.aspx.

College of Mount St. Joseph, Master of Science in Nursing Program, Cincinnati, OH 45233-1670. Offers administration (MSN); education (MSN). Part-time programs available. *Entrance requirements:* For master's, essay; BSN from regionally-accredited university; minimum undergraduate GPA of 3.25 or GRE; professional resume; three professional references; interview; 2 years of clinical nursing experience; active RN license; criminal background check. Additional exam requirements/recommendations for international students: Required—TOEFL (minimum score 560 paper-based; 220 computer-based; 83 iBT). Application fee: $50. Electronic applications accepted. *Expenses: Tuition:* Full-time $24,200; part-time $540 per credit hour. *Required fees:* $112.50 per semester. One-time fee: $200. *Financial support:* Applicants required to submit FAFSA. *Unit head:* Dr. Lynn Bertsch, Director, 513-244-4200, E-mail: lynn_bertsch@mail.msj.edu. *Application contact:* Marilyn Hoskins, Assistant Director for Graduate Recruitment, 513-244-4723, Fax: 513-244-4629, E-mail: marilyn_hoskins@mail.msj.edu. Web site: http://www.msj.edu/view/academics/graduate-programs/master-of-science-in-nursing-.aspx.

College of Mount St. Joseph, Master's Graduate Entry-Level into Nursing (MAGELIN) Program, Cincinnati, OH 45233-1670. Offers MN. *Accreditation:* AACN. *Faculty:* 17 full-time (15 women), 16 part-time/adjunct (all women). *Students:* 65 full-time (54 women); includes 12 minority (6 Black or African American, non-Hispanic/Latino; 1 Asian, non-Hispanic/Latino; 4 Hispanic/Latino; 1 Two or more races, non-Hispanic/Latino). Average age 29. 87 applicants, 34% accepted, 24 enrolled. In 2011, 40 master's awarded. *Degree requirements:* For master's, evidence-based project, preceptorship. *Entrance requirements:* For master's, GRE (or minimum GPA of 3.0), interview; course work in chemistry, anatomy, physiology, microbiology, psychology, sociology, statistics, life span development, and nutrition; non-nursing bachelor's degree; statement of goals; transcripts; criminal background check. Additional exam requirements/recommendations for international students: Required—TOEFL (minimum score 560 paper-based; 220 computer-based; 83 iBT). *Application deadline:* Applications are processed on a rolling basis. Application fee: $50. Electronic applications accepted. *Expenses:* Contact institution. *Financial support:* In 2011–12, 2 students received support. Scholarships/grants available. Financial award application deadline: 3/1; financial award applicants required to submit FAFSA. *Faculty research:* Utilizing technology in learning, assessment of student learning, critical thinking, women's health and nursing education. *Unit head:* Dr. Gail Burns, BSN and MN Program Director, 513-244-4726, Fax: 513-451-2547, E-mail: gail_burns@mail.msj.edu. *Application contact:* Marilyn Hoskins, Assistant Director of Graduate Recruitment, 513-244-4723, Fax: 513-244-4629, E-mail: marilyn_hoskins@mail.msj.edu. Web site: http://www.msj.edu/view/academics/graduate-programs/nursing_2.aspx.

College of Mount Saint Vincent, School of Professional and Continuing Studies, Department of Nursing, Riverdale, NY 10471-1093. Offers adult nurse practitioner (MSN, PMC); family nurse practitioner (MSN, PMC); nurse educator (PMC); nursing administration (MSN); nursing for the adult and aged (MSN). *Accreditation:* AACN. Part-time programs available. *Entrance requirements:* For master's, BSN, interview, RN license, minimum GPA of 3.0, letters of reference. Additional exam requirements/recommendations for international students: Required—TOEFL. *Expenses:* Contact institution.

The College of New Jersey, Graduate Studies, School of Nursing, Health and Exercise Science, Program in Nursing, Ewing, NJ 08628. Offers MSN, Certificate. *Accreditation:* AACN. Part-time programs available. *Degree requirements:* For master's, comprehensive exam. *Entrance requirements:* For master's, GRE, minimum GPA of 3.0 in field or 2.75 overall. Additional exam requirements/recommendations for international students: Required—TOEFL. Electronic applications accepted.

The College of New Rochelle, Graduate School, Program in Nursing, New Rochelle, NY 10805-2308. Offers acute care nurse practitioner (MS, Certificate); clinical specialist in holistic nursing (MS, Certificate); family nurse practitioner (MS, Certificate); nursing and health care management (MS); nursing education (Certificate). *Accreditation:* AACN. Part-time programs available. *Entrance requirements:* For master's, GRE General Test or MAT, BSN, malpractice insurance, minimum GPA of 3.0, RN license. *Expenses:* Contact institution. *Faculty research:* Holistic modalities, academic success variables.

College of Saint Elizabeth, Department of Nursing, Morristown, NJ 07960-6989. Offers MSN. *Accreditation:* NLN. Part-time and evening/weekend programs available. *Faculty:* 3 full-time (all women), 2 part-time/adjunct (both women). *Students:* 1 (woman) full-time, 39 part-time (36 women); includes 11 minority (4 Black or African American, non-Hispanic/Latino; 3 Asian, non-Hispanic/Latino; 4 Hispanic/Latino). Average age 49. 16 applicants, 100% accepted, 10 enrolled. *Entrance requirements:* Additional exam requirements/recommendations for international students: Required—TOEFL (minimum score 550 paper-based). Application fee: $35. *Expenses: Tuition:* Part-time $899 per credit. *Required fees:* $73 per credit. *Unit head:* Director of Graduate Program, 973-290-1074. *Application contact:* Donna Tatarka, Dean of Admission, 973-290-4705, Fax: 973-290-4710, E-mail: dtatarka@cse.edu. Web site: http://www.cse.edu/academics/academic-areas/health-wellness/nursing/?tabID-tabGraduate&divID-progGraduate.

College of Saint Mary, Program in Nursing, Omaha, NE 68106. Offers MSN. *Accreditation:* NLN. Part-time programs available. *Entrance requirements:* For master's, bachelor's degree in nursing, Nebraska RN license, essay or scholarly writing, minimum cumulative GPA of 3.0, 2 references. Additional exam requirements/recommendations for international students: Required—TOEFL.

The College of St. Scholastica, Graduate Studies, Department of Nursing, Duluth, MN 55811-4199. Offers MA, PMC. *Accreditation:* AACN. Part-time programs available. *Faculty:* 8 full-time (all women), 6 part-time/adjunct (all women). *Students:* 139 full-time (126 women), 43 part-time (41 women); includes 13 minority (7 Black or African American, non-Hispanic/Latino; 1 American Indian or Alaska Native, non-Hispanic/Latino; 3 Asian, non-Hispanic/Latino; 1 Hispanic/Latino; 1 Two or more races, non-Hispanic/Latino), 2 international. Average age 36. 111 applicants, 61% accepted, 68 enrolled. In 2011, 38 master's awarded. *Degree requirements:* For master's, thesis. *Entrance requirements:* For master's, GRE General Test, bachelor's degree in nursing, interview, RN license, minimum GPA of 3.0. Additional exam requirements/recommendations for international students: Required—TOEFL (minimum score 550 paper-based; 213 computer-based; 79 iBT). *Application deadline:* For fall admission, 2/1 priority date for domestic students, 2/1 for international students. Applications are processed on a rolling basis. Application fee: $50. Electronic applications accepted. *Financial support:* In 2011–12, 99 students received support. Scholarships/grants and traineeships available. Support available to part-time students. Financial award applicants required to submit FAFSA. *Faculty research:* Critical thinking and professional development, social organization of responsibility, rural health HIV/AIDS prevention, Web-based instruction in nursing. *Unit head:* Director. *Application contact:* Lindsay Lahti, Director of Graduate and Extended Studies Recruitment, 218-733-2240, Fax: 218-733-2275, E-mail: gradstudies@css.edu. Web site: http://www.css.edu/Academics/School-of-Nursing.html.

College of Staten Island of the City University of New York, Graduate Programs, Department of Nursing, Staten Island, NY 10314-6600. Offers adult health nursing (MS, 6th Year Certificate); cultural competence (6th Year Certificate); gerontological nursing (MS, 6th Year Certificate); nursing education (6th Year Certificate). *Accreditation:* NLN. *Students:* 47. Average age 40. 27 applicants, 63% accepted, 10 enrolled. In 2011, 8 master's, 2 other advanced degrees awarded. *Entrance requirements:* Additional exam requirements/recommendations for international students: Required—TOEFL (minimum score 550 paper-based; 213 computer-based; 79 iBT). *Application deadline:* Applications are processed on a rolling basis. Application fee: $125. Electronic applications accepted. *Expenses:* Tuition, state resident: full-time $8210; part-time $345 per credit. Tuition, nonresident: part-time $640 per credit. *Required fees:* $128 per semester. *Financial support:* In 2011–12, 1 student received support. Applicants required to submit FAFSA. *Unit head:* Dr. Mary O'Donnell, Chairperson, 718-982-3812, Fax: 718-982-3813, E-mail: mary.odonnell@csi.cuny.edu. *Application contact:* Sasha Spence, Assistant Director for Graduate Recruitment and Admissions, 718-982-2699, Fax: 718-982-2500, E-mail: sasha.spence@csi.cuny.edu. Web site: http://www.csi.cuny.edu/nursing/graduate.html.

Colorado State University–Pueblo, College of Education, Engineering and Professional Studies, Nursing Department, Pueblo, CO 81001-4901. Offers MS. *Accreditation:* NLN. *Degree requirements:* For master's, comprehensive exam or thesis. *Entrance requirements:* Additional exam requirements/recommendations for international students: Required—TOEFL.

Columbia University, School of Nursing, New York, NY 10032. Offers MS, DN Sc, DNP, Adv C, MBA/MS, MPH/MS. *Accreditation:* AACN. Part-time programs available. *Degree requirements:* For doctorate, thesis/dissertation. *Entrance requirements:* For master's, GRE General Test, BSN, 1 year of clinical experience (preferred); for doctorate, GRE General Test, MSN; course work in statistics, research, and theory. Additional exam requirements/recommendations for international students: Required—TOEFL. Electronic applications accepted. *Expenses:* Contact institution. *Faculty research:* HIV/AIDS, health promotion/disease prevention, health policies, advanced practice, urban health.

Concordia University Wisconsin, Graduate Programs, School of Human Services, Program in Nursing, Mequon, WI 53097-2402. Offers family nurse practitioner (MSN); geriatric nurse practitioner (MSN); nurse educator (MSN). *Accreditation:* AACN. Postbaccalaureate distance learning degree programs offered (minimal on-campus study). *Faculty:* 2 full-time (1 woman), 5 part-time/adjunct (all women). *Students:* 84 full-time (77 women), 359 part-time (347 women); includes 52 minority (20 Black or African American, non-Hispanic/Latino; 2 American Indian or Alaska Native, non-Hispanic/Latino; 11 Asian, non-Hispanic/Latino; 9 Hispanic/Latino; 10 Two or more races, non-

Hispanic/Latino), 1 international. Average age 36. In 2011, 37 master's awarded. *Degree requirements:* For master's, comprehensive exam, thesis or alternative. *Entrance requirements:* Additional exam requirements/recommendations for international students: Required—TOEFL. *Application deadline:* For fall admission, 8/1 priority date for domestic students. Applications are processed on a rolling basis. Application fee: $35. *Expenses:* Contact institution. *Financial support:* Application deadline: 8/1. *Unit head:* Dr. Ruth Gresley, Director, 262-243-4452, E-mail: ruth.gresley@cuw.edu. *Application contact:* Mary Eberhardt, Graduate Admissions, 262-243-4551, Fax: 262-243-4428, E-mail: mary.eberhardt@cuw.edu.

Coppin State University, Division of Graduate Studies, Helene Fuld School of Nursing, Baltimore, MD 21216-3698. Offers family nurse practitioner (PMC); nursing (MSN). *Accreditation:* AACN; NLN. Part-time and evening/weekend programs available. *Degree requirements:* For master's, comprehensive exam, thesis, clinical internship. *Entrance requirements:* For master's, GRE, bachelor's degree in nursing, interview, minimum GPA of 3.0,. RN license. Additional exam requirements/recommendations for international students: Required—TOEFL (minimum score 550 paper-based).

Cox College, Programs in Nursing, Springfield, MO 65802. Offers clinical nurse leader (MSN); family nurse practitioner (MSN); nurse educator (MSN). *Accreditation:* AACN. *Entrance requirements:* For master's, RN license, essay, 2 letters of recommendation, official transcripts. Electronic applications accepted.

Creighton University, School of Nursing, Omaha, NE 68178-0001. Offers MS, DNP. *Accreditation:* AACN. Part-time programs available. Postbaccalaureate distance learning degree programs offered (minimal on-campus study). Terminal master's awarded for partial completion of doctoral program. *Degree requirements:* For master's, thesis optional, capstone project; for doctorate, thesis/dissertation, scholarly research project. *Entrance requirements:* For master's, BSN, minimum GPA of 3.0, RN license; for doctorate, BSN or MSN, minimum GPA of 3.0, RN license. Additional exam requirements/recommendations for international students: Required—TOEFL (minimum score 600 paper-based; 250 computer-based; 100 iBT). Electronic applications accepted. *Expenses: Tuition:* Full-time $12,672; part-time $704 per credit hour. *Required fees:* $1410; $136 per semester. Tuition and fees vary according to campus/location and reciprocity agreements. *Faculty research:* Obesity prevention in children, evaluation of simulated clinical experiences, vitamin D3 and calcium for cancer risk education in post menopausal women, online support and education to reduce stress for prenatal patients on bed rest, behavioral counseling to increase physical activity in women.

Curry College, Graduate Studies, Program in Nursing, Milton, MA 02186-9984. Offers MSN.

Daemen College, Department of Nursing, Amherst, NY 14226-3592. Offers adult nurse practitioner (MS, Post Master's Certificate); nurse executive leadership (Post Master's Certificate); nursing education (MS, Post Master's Certificate); nursing executive leadership (MS); nursing practice (DNP); palliative care nursing (Post Master's Certificate). *Accreditation:* NLN. Part-time programs available. *Degree requirements:* For master's, thesis or alternative, degree completed in 4 years; minimum GPA of 3.0; for doctorate, degree completed in 5 years; 500 post-master's clinical hours. *Entrance requirements:* For master's, BN, 1 year medical/surgical experience, RN license and state registration, statistics course with minimum C grade, 3 letters of recommendation, minimum GPA of 3.25, interview; for doctorate, MS in advance nursing practice; New York state RN license; goal statement; resume; interview; statistics course with minimum grade of 'C'; for Post Master's Certificate, master's degree in clinical area; RN license and current registration; one year of clinical experience; statistics course with minimum grade of 'C'; 3 letters of recommendation; interview; letter of intent. Additional exam requirements/recommendations for international students: Required—TOEFL (minimum score 500 paper-based; 173 computer-based; 63 iBT), IELTS (minimum score 5.5). Electronic applications accepted. *Faculty research:* Professional stress, client behavior, drug therapy, treatment modalities and pulmonary cancers, chemical dependency.

Dalhousie University, Faculty of Health Professions, School of Nursing, Halifax, NS B3H 3J5, Canada. Offers MN, PhD, MN/MHSA. Part-time programs available. Postbaccalaureate distance learning degree programs offered (minimal on-campus study). *Degree requirements:* For master's, thesis optional. *Entrance requirements:* For master's, minimum GPA of 3.0; for doctorate, written support of faculty member who has agreed to be thesis supervisor. Additional exam requirements/recommendations for international students: Required—TOEFL, IELTS, CANTEST, CAEL, or Michigan English Language Assessment Battery. Electronic applications accepted. *Faculty research:* Coping, social support, health promotion, aging, feminist studies.

Delaware State University, Graduate Programs, College of Education, Health and Public Policy, Department of Nursing, Dover, DE 19901-2277. Offers MS. *Accreditation:* AACN. *Entrance requirements:* Additional exam requirements/recommendations for international students: Required—TOEFL (minimum score 550 paper-based). Electronic applications accepted.

Delta State University, Graduate Programs, School of Nursing, Cleveland, MS 38733-0001. Offers family nurse practitioner (MSN); nurse administrator (MSN); nurse educator (MSN). *Accreditation:* AACN. Part-time programs available. *Degree requirements:* For master's, thesis optional. *Entrance requirements:* For master's, GRE General Test. Electronic applications accepted. *Expenses:* Tuition, state resident: full-time $4702; part-time $294 per credit hour. Tuition, nonresident: full-time $12,516; part-time $760 per credit hour. *Required fees:* $586.

DePaul University, College of Science and Health, Department of Nursing, Chicago, IL 60614. Offers adult nurse practitioner (Certificate); adult nursing (MS); family nurse practitioner (Certificate); family nursing (MS); generalist nursing (MS); nurse anesthesia (MS); MS/DNP. MS in nurse anesthesia offered jointly with Ravenswood Hospital Medical Center. *Accreditation:* AACN; AANA/CANAEP (one or more programs are accredited). *Faculty:* 13 full-time (11 women), 12 part-time/adjunct (11 women). *Students:* 256 full-time (220 women), 53 part-time (48 women); includes 81 minority (15 Black or African American, non-Hispanic/Latino; 1 American Indian or Alaska Native, non-Hispanic/Latino; 39 Asian, non-Hispanic/Latino; 16 Hispanic/Latino; 5 Native Hawaiian or other Pacific Islander, non-Hispanic/Latino; 5 Two or more races, non-Hispanic/Latino), 5 international. Average age 29. 238 applicants, 46% accepted, 74 enrolled. In 2011, 70 master's awarded. Terminal master's awarded for partial completion of doctoral program. *Degree requirements:* For master's, comprehensive exam (for some programs), thesis optional. *Entrance requirements:* For master's, GRE (if bachelor's GPA less than 3.2), bachelor's degree from regionally-accredited college or university; personal statement; prerequisite worksheet; resume; 2 letters of recommendation. Additional exam requirements/recommendations for international students: Required—TOEFL (minimum score 590 paper-based; 243 computer-based; 96 iBT), IELTS (minimum score 7.5), Pearson Test of English. *Application deadline:* For fall admission, 3/1 priority date for domestic students, 3/1 for international students; for winter admission, 8/15 priority date for domestic students, 8/15 for international students. Application fee: $40. Electronic applications accepted. *Financial support:* In 2011–12, 5 students received support, including 6 fellowships (averaging $1,500 per year); traineeships also available. Financial award applicants required to submit FAFSA.

Faculty research: Children's health, women's health, health promotion. *Unit head:* Dr. Kim Amer, Interim Chair, 773-325-1160, E-mail: kamer@depaul.edu. *Application contact:* Ann Spittle, Director of Graduate Admissions, 773-325-7315, Fax: 312-476-3244, E-mail: graddepaul@depaul.edu.

DeSales University, Graduate Division, Division of Healthcare and Natural Sciences, Center Valley, PA 18034-9568. Offers adult advanced practice nurse specialist (MSN); certified nurse midwives (MSN); certified nurse practitioners (MSN); clinical leadership (DNP); family nurse practitioner (MSN); nurse educator (MSN); nurse practitioner (Post-Master's Certificate); MSN/MBA. *Accreditation:* NLN. Part-time programs available. *Degree requirements:* For master's, thesis optional. *Entrance requirements:* For master's, GRE General Test, MAT, minimum B average in undergraduate course work, health assessment course or equivalent, course work in statistics. Additional exam requirements/recommendations for international students: Required—TOEFL. *Application deadline:* Applications are processed on a rolling basis. Application fee: $35. Electronic applications accepted. Tuition and fees vary according to degree level. *Financial support:* Applicants required to submit FAFSA. *Unit head:* Dr. Carol Gullo Mest, Director, 610-282-1100 Ext. 1394, Fax: 610-282-2091, E-mail: carol.mest@desales.edu. *Application contact:* Caryn Stopper, Director of Graduate Admissions, 610-282-1100 Ext. 1768, Fax: 610-282-2254, E-mail: caryn.stopper@desales.edu.

Dominican College, Division of Nursing, Department of Nursing, Orangeburg, NY 10962-1210. Offers family nurse practitioner (MSN). *Accreditation:* AACN. Part-time and evening/weekend programs available. *Degree requirements:* For master's, guided research project, 750 hours clinical practice with a final written project. *Entrance requirements:* For master's, bachelor's degree in nursing, minimum GPA of 3.0, RN license, 1 year of nursing experience, 3 letters of recommendation. Additional exam requirements/recommendations for international students: Required—TOEFL (minimum score 550 paper-based; 213 computer-based).

Dominican University of California, Graduate Programs, School of Health and Natural Sciences, Program in Nursing, San Rafael, CA 94901-2298. Offers clinical nurse leader (MS). *Accreditation:* AACN. Part-time and evening/weekend programs available. *Students:* 15 full-time (13 women), 15 part-time (13 women); includes 7 minority (2 Black or African American, non-Hispanic/Latino; 3 Asian, non-Hispanic/Latino; 2 Hispanic/Latino). Average age 45. 27 applicants, 44% accepted, 8 enrolled. In 2011, 6 master's awarded. *Degree requirements:* For master's, thesis. *Entrance requirements:* For master's, minimum GPA of 3.0; current California RN License; clinical experience; course work in nursing research and statistics; CPR certification; professional liability and malpractice insurance; interview. Additional exam requirements/recommendations for international students: Required—TOEFL (minimum score 550 paper-based; 213 computer-based; 80 iBT), IELTS (minimum score 7). *Application deadline:* For fall admission, 6/15 priority date for domestic students; for spring admission, 11/15 priority date for domestic students. Applications are processed on a rolling basis. Application fee: $40. Electronic applications accepted. *Expenses: Tuition:* Full-time $15,660. *Required fees:* $300. Tuition and fees vary according to program. *Financial support:* In 2011–12, 12 students received support. Scholarships/grants available. Support available to part-time students. Financial award application deadline: 3/2; financial award applicants required to submit FAFSA. *Unit head:* Dr. Eira Klich-Heartt, Director, 415-257-1314, Fax: 415-485-0120, E-mail: eira.klich-heartt@dominican.edu. *Application contact:* Shannon Lovelace-White, Assistant Vice President, 415-485-3287, Fax: 415-485-3214, E-mail: shannon.lovelace-white@dominican.edu. Web site: http://www.dominican.edu/admissions/graduate/programs/ms-in-nursing-clinical-nurse-leader.

Drexel University, College of Nursing and Health Professions, Division of Graduate Nursing, Philadelphia, PA 19104-2875. Offers adult acute care (MSN); adult psychiatric/mental health (MSN); advanced practice nursing (MSN); clinical trials research (MSN); family nurse practitioner (MSN); leadership in health systems management (MSN); nursing education (MSN); pediatric primary care (MSN); women's health (MSN). *Accreditation:* AACN; NLN. Electronic applications accepted.

Drexel University, College of Nursing and Health Professions, Doctor of Nursing Practice Program, Philadelphia, PA 19104-2875. Offers Dr NP.

Duke University, School of Nursing, Program in Nursing, Durham, NC 27708-0586. Offers PhD. *Faculty:* 31 full-time (27 women). *Students:* 19 full-time (15 women); includes 5 minority (1 Black or African American, non-Hispanic/Latino; 2 Asian, non-Hispanic/Latino; 2 Two or more races, non-Hispanic/Latino). Average age 36. 23 applicants, 35% accepted, 6 enrolled. In 2011, 3 doctorates awarded. *Degree requirements:* For doctorate, comprehensive exam, thesis/dissertation. *Entrance requirements:* For doctorate, GRE General Test. Additional exam requirements/recommendations for international students: Required—TOEFL (minimum score 550 paper-based; 213 computer-based; 83 iBT), IELTS (minimum score 7). *Application deadline:* For fall admission, 12/8 for domestic and international students. Application fee: $75. Electronic applications accepted. *Expenses: Tuition:* Full-time $40,720. *Required fees:* $3107. *Financial support:* Institutionally sponsored loans, scholarships/grants, and health care benefits available. *Faculty research:* Nursing management practices, adolescents and families undergoing intense treatments, psychosocial and chronic disease. Total annual research expenditures: $3.5 million. *Unit head:* Dr. Debra H. Brandon, Director of Graduate Studies, 919-684-3813, Fax: 919-681-8899, E-mail: debra.brandon@duke.edu. *Application contact:* Revonda P. Huppert, Program Coordinator, 919-668-4797, Fax: 919-681-8899, E-mail: huppert@duke.edu. Web site: http://www.nursing.duke.edu.

Duquesne University, School of Nursing, Doctor of Nursing Practice Program, Pittsburgh, PA 15282-0001. Offers DNP. Part-time and evening/weekend programs available. Postbaccalaureate distance learning degree programs offered (minimal on-campus study). *Faculty:* 19 full-time (17 women). *Students:* 35 full-time (all women), 4 part-time (all women); includes 6 minority (5 Black or African American, non-Hispanic/Latino; 1 Asian, non-Hispanic/Latino), 1 international. Average age 47. 22 applicants, 95% accepted, 20 enrolled. In 2011, 19 degrees awarded. *Degree requirements:* For doctorate, thesis/dissertation, capstone project. *Entrance requirements:* For doctorate, current RN license; BSN; MSN with minimum GPA of 3.0; current certifications; phone interview. Additional exam requirements/recommendations for international students: Required—TOEFL (minimum score 600 paper-based; 80 iBT). *Application deadline:* For fall admission, 2/1 for domestic and international students. Application fee: $0. *Expenses: Tuition:* Full-time $16,596; part-time $922 per credit. *Required fees:* $1584; $88 per credit. Tuition and fees vary according to program. *Financial support:* In 2011–12, 36 students received support, including 4 research assistantships with partial tuition reimbursements available (averaging $1,170 per year); teaching assistantships with partial tuition reimbursements available, institutionally sponsored loans, traineeships, and unspecified assistantships also available. Support available to part-time students. Financial award application deadline: 7/1; financial award applicants required to submit FAFSA. *Faculty research:* Vulnerable populations, social justice, cultural competence, health disparities, wellness within chronic illness. *Unit head:* Dr. Joan Such Lockhart, Professor and Associate Dean of Academic Affairs, 412-396-6540, Fax: 412-396-1821, E-mail: lockhart@duq.edu. *Application contact:* Susan Hardner, Nurse Recruiter, 412-396-4945, Fax: 412-396-6346, E-mail: nursing@duq.edu. Web site: http://www.nursing.duq.edu/.

Nursing—General

Duquesne University, School of Nursing, Doctor of Philosophy in Nursing Program, Pittsburgh, PA 15282-0001. Offers PhD. Part-time and evening/weekend programs available. Postbaccalaureate distance learning degree programs offered (minimal on-campus study). *Faculty:* 16 full-time (14 women), 2 part-time/adjunct (1 woman). *Students:* 39 full-time (38 women), 15 part-time (13 women); includes 10 minority (3 Black or African American, non-Hispanic/Latino; 2 Asian, non-Hispanic/Latino; 5 Hispanic/Latino), 2 international. Average age 47. 15 applicants, 80% accepted, 8 enrolled. In 2011, 8 degrees awarded. *Median time to degree:* Of those who began their doctoral program in fall 2003, 78% received their degree in 8 years or less. *Degree requirements:* For doctorate, thesis/dissertation, preliminary exam. *Entrance requirements:* For doctorate, current RN license; BSN; master's degree with minimum GPA of 3.5; phone interview. Additional exam requirements/recommendations for international students: Required—TOEFL (minimum score 600 paper-based; 80 iBT). *Application deadline:* For fall admission, 1/15 for domestic and international students. Application fee: $0. Electronic applications accepted. *Expenses: Tuition:* Full-time $16,596; part-time $922 per credit. *Required fees:* $1584; $88 per credit. Tuition and fees vary according to program. *Financial support:* In 2011–12, 32 students received support, including 7 research assistantships with partial tuition reimbursements available (averaging $1,170 per year), 5 teaching assistantships with partial tuition reimbursements available (averaging $1,170 per year); institutionally sponsored loans, scholarships/grants, traineeships, and unspecified assistantships also available. Support available to part-time students. Financial award application deadline: 7/1; financial award applicants required to submit FAFSA. *Faculty research:* Vulnerable populations, social justice, cultural competence, health disparities, wellness within chronic illness. *Total annual research expenditures:* $171,844. *Unit head:* Dr. Joan Such Lockhart, Professor and Associate Dean of Academic Affairs, 412-396-6540, Fax: 412-396-1821, E-mail: lockhart@duq.edu. *Application contact:* Susan Hardner, Nurse Recruiter, 412-396-4945, Fax: 412-396-6346, E-mail: nursing@duq.edu. Web site: http://www.nursing.duq.edu.

Duquesne University, School of Nursing, Master of Science in Nursing Program, Pittsburgh, PA 15282-0001. Offers family nurse practitioner (MSN); forensic nursing (MSN); nursing education (MSN). *Accreditation:* AACN. Part-time and evening/weekend programs available. Postbaccalaureate distance learning degree programs offered (minimal on-campus study). *Faculty:* 18 full-time (16 women), 4 part-time/adjunct (all women). *Students:* 57 full-time (55 women), 48 part-time (47 women); includes 13 minority (7 Black or African American, non-Hispanic/Latino; 3 Asian, non-Hispanic/Latino; 1 Hispanic/Latino; 2 Two or more races, non-Hispanic/Latino), 1 international. Average age 34. 72 applicants, 74% accepted, 39 enrolled. In 2011, 38 degrees awarded. *Degree requirements:* For master's, culminating paper. *Entrance requirements:* For master's, current RN license; BSN with minimum GPA of 3.0; minimum of 1 year full-time work experience as RN prior to registration in clinical or specialty course. Additional exam requirements/recommendations for international students: Required—TOEFL (minimum score 600 paper-based; 80 iBT). *Application deadline:* For fall admission, 3/1 for domestic and international students. Application fee: $0. Electronic applications accepted. *Expenses: Tuition:* Full-time $16,596; part-time $922 per credit. *Required fees:* $1584; $88 per credit. Tuition and fees vary according to program. *Financial support:* In 2011–12, 36 students received support, including 7 research assistantships with partial tuition reimbursements available (averaging $1,170 per year); 2 teaching assistantships with partial tuition reimbursements available (averaging $1,170 per year); institutionally sponsored loans, scholarships/grants, traineeships, and tuition waivers (partial) also available. Support available to part-time students. Financial award application deadline: 7/1; financial award applicants required to submit FAFSA. *Faculty research:* Vulnerable populations, social justice, cultural competence, health disparities, wellness within chronic illness. *Unit head:* Dr. Joan Such Lockhart, Professor and Associate Dean of Academic Affairs, 412-396-6540, Fax: 412-396-1821, E-mail: lockhart@duq.edu. *Application contact:* Susan Hardner, Nurse Recruiter, 412-396-4945, Fax: 412-396-6346, E-mail: nursing@duq.edu. Web site: http://www.nursing.duq.edu.

Duquesne University, School of Nursing, Post Master's Certificate Program, Pittsburgh, PA 15282-0001. Offers family nurse practitioner (Post-Master's Certificate); forensic nursing (Post-Master's Certificate); nursing education (Post-Master's Certificate); transcultural/international nursing (Post-Master's Certificate). Part-time and evening/weekend programs available. Postbaccalaureate distance learning degree programs offered (minimal on-campus study). *Faculty:* 11 full-time (10 women), 3 part-time/adjunct (all women). *Students:* 5 full-time (all women), 7 part-time (all women); includes 1 minority (Black or African American, non-Hispanic/Latino). Average age 39. 17 applicants, 71% accepted, 9 enrolled. In 2011, 2 degrees awarded. *Entrance requirements:* For degree, current RN license, BSN, MSN. Additional exam requirements/recommendations for international students: Required—TOEFL (minimum score 600 paper-based; 80 iBT). *Application deadline:* For fall admission, 3/1 for domestic and international students. Application fee: $0. *Expenses: Tuition:* Full-time $16,596; part-time $922 per credit. *Required fees:* $1584; $88 per credit. Tuition and fees vary according to program. *Financial support:* In 2011–12, 5 students received support, including 2 teaching assistantships with partial tuition reimbursements available (averaging $1,170 per year); institutionally sponsored loans, scholarships/grants, traineeships, and tuition waivers (partial) also available. Support available to part-time students. Financial award application deadline: 7/1; financial award applicants required to submit FAFSA. *Faculty research:* Vulnerable populations, social justice, cultural competence, health disparities, wellness within chronic illness. *Unit head:* Dr. Joan Such Lockhart, Professor and Associate Dean of Academic Affairs, 412-396-6540, Fax: 412-396-1821, E-mail: lockhart@duq.edu. *Application contact:* Susan Hardner, Nurse Recruiter, 412-396-4945, Fax: 412-396-6346, E-mail: nursing@duq.edu. Web site: http://www.duq.edu/nursing/post-masters-certificates/index.cfm.

D'Youville College, School of Nursing, Buffalo, NY 14201-1084. Offers community health nursing/education (MSN); community health nursing/management (MSN); family nurse practitioner (MS, Post-Master's Certificate); nursing and health-related professions (Certificate); nursing with clinical focus choice (MSN). *Accreditation:* AACN. Part-time programs available. *Faculty:* 7 full-time (all women), 7 part-time/adjunct (6 women). *Students:* 78 full-time (72 women), 133 part-time (117 women); includes 33 minority (23 Black or African American, non-Hispanic/Latino; 2 American Indian or Alaska Native, non-Hispanic/Latino; 1 Asian, non-Hispanic/Latino; 6 Hispanic/Latino; 1 Two or more races, non-Hispanic/Latino), 86 international. Average age 35. 226 applicants, 39% accepted, 57 enrolled. In 2011, 54 master's, 1 other advanced degree awarded. *Degree requirements:* For master's, thesis or alternative, membership on board of community agency, publishable paper. *Entrance requirements:* For master's, BS in nursing, minimum GPA of 3.0, course work in statistics and computers. Additional exam requirements/recommendations for international students: Required—TOEFL (minimum score 500 paper-based; 173 computer-based). *Application deadline:* For fall admission, 5/1 for international students; for spring admission, 9/1 for international students. Applications are processed on a rolling basis. Application fee: $25. Electronic applications accepted. *Expenses: Tuition:* Full-time $18,960; part-time $790 per credit hour. *Required fees:* $310. Tuition and fees vary according to degree level and program. *Financial support:* Federal Work-Study, scholarships/grants, traineeships, and unspecified assistantships available. Support available to part-time students. Financial award application deadline: 3/1; financial award applicants required to submit FAFSA. *Faculty research:* Nursing curriculum, nursing theory-testing, wellness research, communication and socialization patterns. *Unit head:* Dr. Eileen Nahigian, Chair, 716-829-7856, Fax: 716-829-8159. *Application contact:* Linda Fisher, Graduate Admissions Director, 716-829-8400, Fax: 716-829-7900, E-mail: graduateadmissions@dyc.edu.

See Display on next page and Close-Up on page 795.

East Carolina University, Graduate School, College of Nursing, Greenville, NC 27858-4353. Offers MSN, PhD. *Accreditation:* AACN; AANA/CANAEP (one or more programs are accredited); ACNM/ACME (one or more programs are accredited). Part-time programs available. *Degree requirements:* For master's, comprehensive exam, thesis optional. *Entrance requirements:* For master's, GRE General Test or MAT, bachelor's degree in nursing, professional license, minimum B average in nursing. *Application deadline:* For fall admission, 6/1 priority date for domestic students. Applications are processed on a rolling basis. Application fee: $50. *Expenses:* Tuition, state resident: full-time $3557; part-time $444.63 per semester hour. Tuition, nonresident: full-time $14,351; part-time $1793.88 per semester hour. *Required fees:* $2016; $252 per semester hour. Part-time tuition and fees vary according to course load, campus/location and program. *Financial support:* Research assistantships with partial tuition reimbursements, teaching assistantships with partial tuition reimbursements, and Federal Work-Study available. Support available to part-time students. Financial award application deadline: 6/1. *Unit head:* Dr. Sylvia Brown, Interim Dean, 252-744-6372, E-mail: brownsy@ecu.edu. *Application contact:* Dean of Graduate School, 252-328-6012, Fax: 252-328-6071, E-mail: gradschool@ecu.edu. Web site: http://www.nursing.ecu.edu/home.htm.

Eastern Kentucky University, The Graduate School, College of Health Sciences, Department of Nursing, Richmond, KY 40475-3102. Offers rural community health care (MSN); rural health family nurse practitioner (MSN). *Accreditation:* AACN. *Entrance requirements:* For master's, GRE General Test, minimum GPA of 2.75.

Eastern Mennonite University, Program in Nursing, Harrisonburg, VA 22802-2462. Offers leadership and management (MSN); leadership/school nursing (MSN). Part-time programs available. Postbaccalaureate distance learning degree programs offered (minimal on-campus study). *Degree requirements:* For master's, clinical hours.

East Tennessee State University, School of Graduate Studies, College of Nursing, Doctoral Nursing Programs, Johnson City, TN 37614. Offers adult/gerontological nurse practitioner (DNP); executive leadership in nursing (DNP); family nurse practitioner (DNP); nursing (PhD); psychiatric/mental health nurse practitioner (DNP). Part-time and evening/weekend programs available. *Students:* 22 full-time (21 women), 27 part-time (26 women); includes 3 minority (2 Black or African American, non-Hispanic/Latino; 1 Asian, non-Hispanic/Latino). 74 applicants, 41% accepted, 30 enrolled. In 2011, 3 doctorates awarded. *Degree requirements:* For doctorate, comprehensive exam, dissertation (PhD); residency internship and capstone project (DNP). *Entrance requirements:* For doctorate, GRE General Test, minimum GPA of 3.0, RN license, minimum two years RN experience, 3 letters of recommendation, interview, writing sample, resume. Additional exam requirements/recommendations for international students: Required—TOEFL (minimum score 600 paper-based; 250 computer-based; 100 iBT). *Application deadline:* For fall admission, 2/1 for domestic and international students; for spring admission, 7/1 for domestic and international students. Application fee: $35 ($45 for international students). Electronic applications accepted. *Expenses:* Tuition, state resident: full-time $7312; part-time $350 per credit hour. Tuition, nonresident: full-time $18,490; part-time $621 per credit hour. *Required fees:* $63 per credit hour. Tuition and fees vary according to course load and program. *Financial support:* In 2011–12, 2 students received support, including 1 research assistantship with partial tuition reimbursement available (averaging $3,000 per year); career-related internships or fieldwork, institutionally sponsored loans, scholarships/grants, and unspecified assistantships also available. Financial award application deadline: 7/1; financial award applicants required to submit FAFSA. *Faculty research:* Rural primary care, healthcare for the homeless and underserved, community health problems across the lifespan, nursing education research, school health services. *Unit head:* Dr. Kathleen Rayman, Director of Graduate Programs, 423-439-5626, Fax: 423-439-4100, E-mail: raymank@etsu.edu. *Application contact:* Linda Raines, Graduate Specialist, 423-439-6158, Fax: 423-439-5624, E-mail: rainesl t@etsu.edu.

East Tennessee State University, School of Graduate Studies, College of Nursing, Master's Nursing Programs, Johnson City, TN 37614. Offers advanced practice nursing (MSN); nursing (MSN); nursing administration (MSN); nursing education (MSN); nursing informatics (MSN). Part-time programs available. Postbaccalaureate distance learning degree programs offered. *Students:* 50 full-time (47 women), 137 part-time (126 women); includes 4 minority (1 American Indian or Alaska Native, non-Hispanic/Latino; 2 Hispanic/Latino; 1 Two or more races, non-Hispanic/Latino), 1 international. 151 applicants, 29% accepted, 44 enrolled. In 2011, 74 master's awarded. *Degree requirements:* For master's, comprehensive exam (for some programs), culminating project (for some programs). *Entrance requirements:* For master's, minimum GPA of 3.0, RN license, resume, 3 letters of recommendation. Additional exam requirements/recommendations for international students: Required—TOEFL (minimum score 600 paper-based; 250 computer-based; 100 iBT). *Application deadline:* For fall admission, 2/1 for domestic and international students; for spring admission, 7/1 for domestic and international students. Application fee: $35 ($45 for international students). Electronic applications accepted. *Expenses:* Tuition, state resident: full-time $7312; part-time $350 per credit hour. Tuition, nonresident: full-time $18,490; part-time $621 per credit hour. *Required fees:* $63 per credit hour. Tuition and fees vary according to course load and program. *Financial support:* In 2011–12, 2 students received support. Institutionally sponsored loans, scholarships/grants, tuition waivers (full), and unspecified assistantships available. Support available to part-time students. Financial award application deadline: 7/1; financial award applicants required to submit FAFSA. *Faculty research:* Rural primary care, healthcare for the homeless and underserved, community health problems across the lifespan, nursing education research, school health services. *Unit head:* Dr. Nancy Cameron, Coordinator, 423-439-4874, Fax: 423-439-4100, E-mail: cameronng@etsu.edu. *Application contact:* Linda Raines, Graduate Specialist, 423-439-6158, Fax: 423-439-5624, E-mail: rainesl t@etsu.edu.

Edgewood College, Program in Nursing, Madison, WI 53711-1997. Offers MS. *Accreditation:* AACN. *Students:* 2 full-time (both women), 51 part-time (48 women); includes 3 minority (1 Black or African American, non-Hispanic/Latino; 1 Asian, non-Hispanic/Latino; 1 Hispanic/Latino), 1 international. Average age 39. In 2011, 5 master's awarded. *Degree requirements:* For master's, practicum, research project. *Entrance requirements:* For master's, minimum GPA of 3.0, 2 letters of reference, current RN license. Additional exam requirements/recommendations for international students: Required—TOEFL. *Application deadline:* For fall admission, 8/15 priority date for domestic students, 5/1 for international students; for spring admission, 1/8 priority date for domestic students, 11/1 for international students. Applications are processed on a rolling basis. Application fee: $25. Electronic applications accepted. *Expenses: Tuition:* Part-time $747 per credit. Part-time tuition and fees vary according to program. *Unit head:* Dr. Margaret Noreuil, Dean, 608-663-2820, Fax: 608-663-3291, E-mail: mnoreuil@edgewood.edu. *Application contact:* Tracy Kantor, Enrollment and

Applications Manager, 608-663-3297, Fax: 608-663-3496, E-mail: gps@edgewood.edu. Web site: http://www.edgewood.edu/Academics/Graduate.aspx.

Edinboro University of Pennsylvania, College of Arts and Sciences, Department of Nursing, Edinboro, PA 16444. Offers nurse educator (Certificate); nursing (MSN); palliative and end-of-life care (Certificate). *Accreditation:* NLN. Part-time and evening/weekend programs available. *Faculty:* 3 full-time (all women). *Students:* 40 part-time (37 women). Average age 39. In 2011, 20 master's awarded. *Degree requirements:* For master's, thesis, competency exam. *Entrance requirements:* For master's, GRE or MAT, minimum QPA of 2.5. *Application deadline:* Applications are processed on a rolling basis. *Application fee:* $30. Electronic applications accepted. *Financial support:* In 2011–12, 2 research assistantships with full and partial tuition reimbursements (averaging $4,050 per year) were awarded; career-related internships or fieldwork, Federal Work-Study, scholarships/grants, and unspecified assistantships also available. Support available to part-time students. Financial award application deadline: 2/15; financial award applicants required to submit FAFSA. *Unit head:* Dr. Alice Conway, Program Head, 814-732-2285, E-mail: aconwayt@edinboro.edu. *Application contact:* Dr. Alan Biel, Dean, 814-732-2752, Fax: 814-732-2268, E-mail: biel@edinboro.edu.

Elmhurst College, Graduate Programs, Program in Nursing, Elmhurst, IL 60126-3296. Offers MSN. *Accreditation:* AACN. Part-time and evening/weekend programs available. *Faculty:* 3 full-time (all women). *Students:* 21 part-time (20 women); includes 8 minority (1 Black or African American, non-Hispanic/Latino; 6 Asian, non-Hispanic/Latino; 1 Hispanic/Latino). Average age 39. 21 applicants, 67% accepted, 12 enrolled. In 2011, 12 master's awarded. *Entrance requirements:* For master's, 3 recommendations, resume, statement of purpose, current RN licensure in Illinois, interview. Additional exam requirements/recommendations for international students: Required—TOEFL (minimum score 550 paper-based; 213 computer-based). *Application deadline:* Applications are processed on a rolling basis. Application fee: $0. Electronic applications accepted. *Expenses:* Contact institution. *Financial support:* In 2011–12, 4 students received support. Federal Work-Study and scholarships/grants available. Support available to part-time students. Financial award application deadline: 6/1; financial award applicants required to submit FAFSA. *Unit head:* Elizabeth D. Kuebler, Director of Adult and Graduate Admission, 630-617-3300, Fax: 630-617-5501, E-mail: oaga@elmhurst.edu. *Application contact:* Elizabeth D. Kuebler, Director of Adult and Graduate Admission, 630-617-3300, Fax: 630-617-5501, E-mail: oaga@elmhurst.edu.

Elms College, Division of Nursing, Chicopee, MA 01013-2839. Offers nursing and health services management (MSN); nursing education (MSN). *Accreditation:* AACN. Part-time and evening/weekend programs available. *Entrance requirements:* Additional exam requirements/recommendations for international students: Required—TOEFL.

Emmanuel College, Graduate and Professional Programs, Graduate Program in Nursing, Boston, MA 02115. Offers nursing education (MSN); nursing management/administration (MSN). Part-time and evening/weekend programs available. *Faculty:* 5 full-time (all women). *Students:* 21 part-time (20 women); includes 4 minority (3 Black or African American, non-Hispanic/Latino; 1 Asian, non-Hispanic/Latino). Average age 49. 44 applicants, 68% accepted, 21 enrolled. *Degree requirements:* For master's, 36 credits, including 6-credit practicum. *Entrance requirements:* For master's, essay, resume, proof of RN license (nursing applicants only), interview. Additional exam requirements/recommendations for international students: Required—TOEFL (minimum score 600 paper-based; 250 computer-based; 106 iBT) or IELTS (minimum score 6.5). *Application deadline:* For fall admission, 4/30 for domestic students. Applications are processed on a rolling basis. Application fee: $0. Electronic applications accepted. *Expenses: Tuition:* Part-time $2139 per course. Tuition and fees vary according to program and reciprocity agreements. *Financial support:* Applicants required to submit FAFSA. *Unit head:* Dr. Joyce DeLeo, Vice President of Academic Affairs, 617-735-9700,

Fax: 617-507-0434, E-mail: gpp@emmanuel.edu. *Application contact:* Enrollment Counselor, 617-735-9700, Fax: 617-507-0434, E-mail: gpp@emmanuel.edu. Web site: http://gpp.emmanuel.edu.

Emory University, Nell Hodgson Woodruff School of Nursing, Atlanta, GA 30322-1100. Offers adult nurse practitioner (MSN); emergency nurse practitioner (MSN); family nurse practitioner (MSN); family nurse-midwife (MSN); health systems leadership (MSN); nurse-midwifery (MSN); pediatric nurse practitioner acute and primary care (MSN); women's health care (Title X) (MSN); women's health nurse practitioner (MSN); women's health/adult health nurse practitioner (MSN); MSN/MPH. *Accreditation:* AACN; ACNM/ACME (one or more programs are accredited). Part-time programs available. *Faculty:* 30 full-time (29 women), 11 part-time/adjunct (10 women). *Students:* 110 full-time (106 women), 53 part-time (51 women); includes 49 minority (35 Black or African American, non-Hispanic/Latino; 2 American Indian or Alaska Native, non-Hispanic/Latino; 10 Asian, non-Hispanic/Latino; 2 Hispanic/Latino), 4 international. Average age 32. 182 applicants, 63% accepted, 86 enrolled. In 2011, 81 master's awarded. *Entrance requirements:* For master's, GRE General Test or MAT, minimum GPA of 3.0, BS in nursing from an accredited institution, RN license and additional course work, 3 letters of recommendation. Additional exam requirements/recommendations for international students: Required—TOEFL (minimum score 600 paper-based; 100 iBT). *Application deadline:* For fall admission, 1/15 priority date for domestic students, 1/15 for international students; for spring admission, 10/1 priority date for domestic students, 10/1 for international students. Applications are processed on a rolling basis. Application fee: $50. Electronic applications accepted. *Expenses:* Contact institution. *Financial support:* In 2011–12, 14 fellowships (averaging $28,000 per year) were awarded; career-related internships or fieldwork, Federal Work-Study, institutionally sponsored loans, and scholarships/grants also available. Support available to part-time students. Financial award application deadline: 3/1; financial award applicants required to submit CSS PROFILE or FAFSA. *Faculty research:* Older adult falls and injuries, minority health issues, cardiac symptoms and quality of life, bio-ethics and decision-making, menopausal issues. *Unit head:* Dr. Linda McCauley, Dean, 404-727-7976, Fax: 404-727-9800, E-mail: linda.mccauley@emory.edu. Web site: http://www.nursing.emory.edu/.

Endicott College, Van Loan School of Graduate and Professional Studies, Program in Nursing, Beverly, MA 01915-2096. Offers MSN. *Faculty:* 1 (woman) full-time, 1 (woman) part-time/adjunct. *Students:* 16 full-time (all women), 1 (woman) part-time; includes 2 minority (both Black or African American, non-Hispanic/Latino). Average age 38. 7 applicants, 57% accepted, 4 enrolled. *Entrance requirements:* For master's, MAT or GRE, statement of professional goals, official transcripts of all undergraduate and graduate course work, two letters of recommendation, photocopy of current and unrestricted RN license, basic statistics course, interview. Additional exam requirements/recommendations for international students: Required—TOEFL. *Application deadline:* Applications are processed on a rolling basis. Application fee: $50. Electronic applications accepted. Tuition and fees vary according to degree level and program. *Financial support:* Applicants required to submit FAFSA. *Unit head:* Mary Findeisen, Program Director, 978-232-2332, E-mail: mfindeis@endicott.edu. Web site: http://www.endicott.edu/GradProf/GPSGradMSNursing.aspx.

Excelsior College, School of Nursing, Albany, NY 12203-5159. Offers clinical systems management (MS); nursing (MS); nursing education (MS); nursing informatics (MS). *Accreditation:* NLN. Part-time and evening/weekend programs available. Postbaccalaureate distance learning degree programs offered (no on-campus study). *Entrance requirements:* For master's, RN license. Electronic applications accepted. *Faculty research:* Leadership development, test anxiety, use of technology in online learning.

D'Youville honors its Catholic heritage and the spirit of St. Marguerite d'Youville by providing, academic, social, spiritual and professional development in programs that emphasize leadership and service, while teaching students to contribute to the world community by leading compassionate, productive and responsible lives.

D'Youville
COLLEGE
Educating for life

www.dyc.edu
1.800.777.3921

when you're here, you're almost there

D'Youville College, located in Buffalo, New York, offers 5 doctoral and 13 master's programs in the fields of:

- Business
- Chiropractic
- Teacher Education
- Educational Leadership
- Family Nurse Practitioner
- Health Services Administration
- Health Policy/Health Education
- Nursing
- Occupational Therapy
- Pharmacy
- Physical Therapy

D'Youville also features accelerated 5-year dual degree programs in:

- International Business
- Nursing
- Physician Assistant
- Occupational Therapy
- Dietetics

Nursing—General

Fairfield University, School of Nursing, Fairfield, CT 06824-5195. Offers clinical nurse leader (MSN); family nurse practitioner (MSN, DNP); nurse anesthesia (DNP); psychiatric nurse practitioner (MSN, DNP). *Accreditation:* AACN; AANA/CANAEP. Part-time programs available. *Faculty:* 15 full-time (all women). *Students:* 17 full-time (15 women), 145 part-time (127 women); includes 14 minority (6 Black or African American, non-Hispanic/Latino; 1 American Indian or Alaska Native, non-Hispanic/Latino; 4 Asian, non-Hispanic/Latino; 3 Hispanic/Latino), 1 international. Average age 38. 97 applicants, 29% accepted, 24 enrolled. In 2011, 24 master's awarded. *Degree requirements:* For master's, capstone project. *Entrance requirements:* For master's, minimum QPA of 3.0, RN license, resume, 2 recommendations; for doctorate, GRE (nurse anesthesia applicants only), MSN (minimum QPA of 3.2) or BSN (minimum QPA of 3.0); critical care nursing experience (for nurse anesthesia DNP candidates). Additional exam requirements/recommendations for international students: Required—TOEFL (minimum score 550 paper-based; 213 computer-based; 80 iBT) or IELTS (minimum score 6.5). *Application deadline:* For fall admission, 5/15 for international students; for spring admission, 10/15 for international students. Applications are processed on a rolling basis. Application fee: $60. Electronic applications accepted. *Expenses:* Contact institution. *Financial support:* In 2011–12, 2 students received support. Unspecified assistantships available. Financial award applicants required to submit FAFSA. *Faculty research:* Care of older adults, palliative care, spirituality and innovative partnerships, diabetes. *Unit head:* Dr. Suzanne Campbell, Dean, 203-254-4000 Ext. 2701, Fax: 203-254-4126, E-mail: scampbell@fairfield.edu. *Application contact:* Marianne Gumpper, Director of Graduate and Continuing Studies Admission, 203-254-4184, Fax: 203-254-4073, E-mail: gradadmis@fairfield.edu. Web site: http://www.fairfield.edu/son/son_grad_1.html.

Fairleigh Dickinson University, Metropolitan Campus, University College: Arts, Sciences, and Professional Studies, Henry P. Becton School of Nursing and Allied Health, Program in Nursing, Teaneck, NJ 07666-1914. Offers MSN, Certificate. *Accreditation:* AACN.

Fairleigh Dickinson University, Metropolitan Campus, University College: Arts, Sciences, and Professional Studies, Henry P. Becton School of Nursing and Allied Health, Program in Nursing Practice, Teaneck, NJ 07666-1914. Offers DNP.

Felician College, Doctor of Nursing Practice Program, Lodi, NJ 07644-2117. Offers DNP. Postbaccalaureate distance learning degree programs offered (no on-campus study). *Degree requirements:* For doctorate, project, residency. *Expenses: Tuition:* Full-time $925 per credit. *Required fees:* $262.50 per semester. Part-time tuition and fees vary according to class time and student level. *Application contact:* Nicole Vitale, Assistant Director of Graduate Admissions, 201-559-6077, Fax: 201-559-6138, E-mail: graduate@felician.edu.

Felician College, Program in Nursing, Lodi, NJ 07644-2117. Offers adult nurse practitioner (MSN, PMC); family nurse practitioner (MSN, PMC); nursing (MSN); nursing education (MSN). *Accreditation:* AACN. Part-time and evening/weekend programs available. Postbaccalaureate distance learning degree programs offered (no on-campus study). *Students:* 4 full-time (all women), 74 part-time (64 women); includes 18 minority (10 Black or African American, non-Hispanic/Latino; 5 Asian, non-Hispanic/Latino; 3 Hispanic/Latino). Average age 42. 29 applicants, 90% accepted, 24 enrolled. *Degree requirements:* For master's, scholarly project. *Entrance requirements:* For master's, BS in nursing or equivalent, minimum GPA of 3.0, 2 letters of recommendation, RN license; for PMC, RN license, minimum GPA of 2.75. Additional exam requirements/recommendations for international students: Recommended—TOEFL (minimum score 550 paper-based; 213 computer-based). *Application deadline:* Applications are processed on a rolling basis. Application fee: $40. *Expenses: Tuition:* Part-time $925 per credit. *Required fees:* $262.50 per semester. Part-time tuition and fees vary according to

class time and student level. *Financial support:* In 2011–12, 10 students received support. Traineeships available. Financial award applicants required to submit FAFSA. *Faculty research:* Anxiety and fear, curriculum innovation, health promotion. *Unit head:* Dr. Muriel Shore, Dean, Division of Health Sciences, 201-559-6030, E-mail: shorem@felician.edu. *Application contact:* Elizabeth Barca, Senior Assistant Director, Graduate Admissions, 201-559-6077, Fax: 201-559-6138, E-mail: graduate@felician.edu.

See Display below and Close-Up on page 797.

Ferris State University, College of Allied Health Sciences, School of Nursing, Big Rapids, MI 49307. Offers nursing (MSN); nursing administration (MSN); nursing education (MSN); nursing informatics (MSN). *Accreditation:* NLN. Part-time and evening/weekend programs available. Postbaccalaureate distance learning degree programs offered (minimal on-campus study). *Faculty:* 5 full-time (all women), 1 (woman) part-time/adjunct. *Students:* 7 full-time (all women), 80 part-time (70 women); includes 3 minority (1 Black or African American, non-Hispanic/Latino; 2 Two or more races, non-Hispanic/Latino). Average age 42. 34 applicants, 85% accepted, 24 enrolled. In 2011, 16 master's awarded. *Degree requirements:* For master's, comprehensive exam, practicum, scholarly project. *Entrance requirements:* For master's, BS in nursing or related with registered nurse license, writing sample, letters of reference, 2 years' clinical experience. Additional exam requirements/recommendations for international students: Required—TOEFL (minimum score 550 paper-based; 173 computer-based; 61 iBT). *Application deadline:* For fall admission, 4/15 priority date for domestic students; for spring admission, 10/15 for domestic students. Applications are processed on a rolling basis. Application fee: $30. Electronic applications accepted. Application fee is waived when completed online. *Financial support:* In 2011–12, 4 students received support. Fellowships, research assistantships, teaching assistantships, career-related internships or fieldwork, and scholarships/grants available. Financial award application deadline: 4/15. *Faculty research:* Nursing education-minority student focus, student attitudes toward aging. *Unit head:* Dr. Marietta Bell-Scriber, Program Coordinator, 231-591-2288, Fax: 231-591-2325, E-mail: bellscm@ferris.edu. *Application contact:* Debby Buck, Off-Campus Program Secretary, 231-591-2270, Fax: 231-591-3788, E-mail: buckd@ferris.edu.

Florida Agricultural and Mechanical University, Division of Graduate Studies, Research, and Continuing Education, School of Nursing, Tallahassee, FL 32307-3200. Offers MS. *Accreditation:* NLN. *Entrance requirements:* Additional exam requirements/recommendations for international students: Required—TOEFL.

Florida Atlantic University, Christine E. Lynn College of Nursing, Boca Raton, FL 33431-0991. Offers MS, DNP, PhD, Post Master's Certificate. *Accreditation:* AACN. Part-time programs available. *Faculty:* 36 full-time (32 women), 20 part-time/adjunct (all women). *Students:* 33 full-time (31 women), 362 part-time (334 women); includes 181 minority (104 Black or African American, non-Hispanic/Latino; 1 American Indian or Alaska Native, non-Hispanic/Latino; 21 Asian, non-Hispanic/Latino; 45 Hispanic/Latino; 1 Native Hawaiian or other Pacific Islander, non-Hispanic/Latino; 9 Two or more races, non-Hispanic/Latino), 6 international. Average age 40. 273 applicants, 33% accepted, 50 enrolled. In 2011, 131 master's, 25 doctorates awarded. *Degree requirements:* For master's, thesis or alternative; for doctorate, comprehensive exam, thesis/dissertation. *Entrance requirements:* For master's, GRE General Test, bachelor's degree in nursing, Florida RN license, minimum GPA of 3.0; for doctorate, GRE General Test, curriculum vitae, Florida RN license, minimum GPA of 3.5, MS in nursing. *Application deadline:* For fall admission, 6/1 for domestic students, 2/15 for international students; for spring admission, 10/1 for domestic students, 7/15 for international students. Applications are processed on a rolling basis. Application fee: $30. *Expenses: Tuition, area resident:* Part-time $343.02 per credit hour. Tuition, state resident: full-time $8232. Tuition, nonresident: full-time $23,931; part-time $997.14 per credit hour. *Financial support:*

FELICIAN COLLEGE HAS DESIGNED RIGOROUS AND REWARDING GRADUATE PROGRAMS **WITH YOU IN MIND.**

- Master of Business Administration (MBA) in Innovation and Entrepreneurship
- Master of Science in Healthcare Administration
- Master of Science in Nursing (MSN) – with tracks in:
  – Family Nurse Practicner (online)
  – Adult & Gerontology Nurse Practicner (online)
  – Education
  – Executive Leadership
- Doctor of Nursing Practice
- Master of Arts in Education
- Master of Arts in Education: Leadership
- Master of Arts in Education: School Nursing & Health Education
- Master of Arts in Education: School Nursing
- Master of Arts in Education: Health Education
- Certificate in School Nursing and Health Education
- Master of Arts in Counseling Psychology
- Master of Arts in Religious Education (online)

FELICIAN COLLEGE
The Franciscan College of New Jersey

STUDENTS FIRST • 201.559.6077 • graduate@felician.edu • felician.edu • Lodi and Rutherford, NJ

Research assistantships with partial tuition reimbursements, teaching assistantships with partial tuition reimbursements, career-related internships or fieldwork, Federal Work-Study, institutionally sponsored loans, scholarships/grants, and traineeships available. Support available to part-time students. *Faculty research:* Econometrics of nurse-patient relationship, Alzheimer's disease, community-based programs, falls, self-healing. *Unit head:* Dr. Marlaine Smith, Dean, 561-297-3206, Fax: 561-297-3687, E-mail: msmit230@fau.edu. *Application contact:* Carol Kruse, Graduate Coordinator, 561-297-3261, Fax: 561-297-0088, E-mail: ckruse@fau.edu. Web site: http://nursing.fau.edu/.

Florida International University, College of Nursing and Health Sciences, Nursing Program, Miami, FL 33199. Offers MSN, PhD. *Accreditation:* AACN; AANA/CANAEP. Part-time and evening/weekend programs available. *Degree requirements:* For master's, thesis or alternative; for doctorate, comprehensive exam, thesis/dissertation. *Entrance requirements:* For master's, bachelor's degree in nursing, minimum undergraduate GPA of 3.0 in upper-level coursework, letters of recommendation; for doctorate, GRE, letters of recommendation, minimum undergraduate GPA of 3.0 in upper-level coursework, interview. Additional exam requirements/recommendations for international students: Required—TOEFL (minimum score 550 paper-based; 213 computer-based; 80 iBT). Electronic applications accepted. *Faculty research:* Adult health nursing.

Florida Southern College, Program in Nursing, Lakeland, FL 33801-5698. Offers clinical nurse specialist (MSN); nurse educator (MSN); nurse practitioner (MSN). *Accreditation:* AACN. Part-time and evening/weekend programs available. *Entrance requirements:* For master's, Florida RN license, 3 letters of recommendation, personal statement, minimum GPA of 3.0, resume. Additional exam requirements/recommendations for international students: Required—TOEFL (minimum score 550 paper-based). *Expenses:* Contact institution. *Faculty research:* End of life care, dementia, health promotion.

Florida State University, The Graduate School, College of Nursing, Tallahassee, FL 32312. Offers family nurse practitioner (DNP); health systems leadership (DNP); nurse educator (MSN, Certificate); nurse leader (MSN); nursing leadership (Certificate, Post-Graduate Certificate). *Accreditation:* AACN. Part-time programs available. Postbaccalaureate distance learning degree programs offered (no on-campus study). *Faculty:* 13 full-time (12 women). *Students:* 24 full-time (21 women), 63 part-time (58 women); includes 15 minority (4 Black or African American, non-Hispanic/Latino; 1 Asian, non-Hispanic/Latino; 8 Hispanic/Latino; 2 Two or more races, non-Hispanic/Latino). Average age 38. 33 applicants, 100% accepted, 33 enrolled. In 2011, 9 master's, 4 doctorates awarded. *Degree requirements:* For master's, thesis optional. *Entrance requirements:* For master's, GRE General Test, MAT, minimum GPA of 3.0, BSN, Florida RN license; for doctorate, GRE General Test, MAT, minimum GPA of 3.0, BSN or MSN, Florida RN license. Additional exam requirements/recommendations for international students: Required—TOEFL (minimum score 550 paper-based). *Application deadline:* For fall admission, 7/1 for domestic and international students. Application fee: $30. Electronic applications accepted. *Expenses:* Tuition, state resident: full-time $9474; part-time $350.88 per credit hour. Tuition, nonresident: full-time $16,236; part-time $601.34 per credit hour. *Required fees:* $630 per semester. One-time fee: $20. Tuition and fees vary according to course load and campus/location. *Financial support:* In 2011–12, 75 students received support, including fellowships with partial tuition reimbursements available (averaging $6,300 per year), research assistantships with partial tuition reimbursements available (averaging $3,000 per year), 3 teaching assistantships with partial tuition reimbursements available (averaging $3,000 per year); career-related internships or fieldwork, Federal Work-Study, institutionally sponsored loans, scholarships/grants, traineeships, and tuition waivers (partial) also available. Financial award application deadline: 4/15; financial award applicants required to submit FAFSA. *Faculty research:* Distance learning, gerontology, health promotion, educational strategies, rehabilitation of brain injured patients. *Unit head:* Dr. Diane Speake, Interim Dean, 850-644-6846, Fax: 850-644-7660, E-mail: dspeake@nursing.fsu.edu. *Application contact:* Carlos G. Urrutia, Director of Student Services, 850-644-5638, Fax: 850-645-7249, E-mail: currutia@fsu.edu. Web site: http://nursing.fsu.edu/.

Fort Hays State University, Graduate School, College of Health and Life Sciences, Department of Nursing, Hays, KS 67601-4099. Offers MSN. *Accreditation:* AACN. *Degree requirements:* For master's, comprehensive exam, thesis optional. *Entrance requirements:* For master's, GRE General Test or MAT. Additional exam requirements/recommendations for international students: Required—TOEFL (minimum score 550 paper-based; 213 computer-based). Electronic applications accepted.

Framingham State University, Division of Graduate and Continuing Education, Program in Nursing, Framingham, MA 01701-9101. Offers nursing education (MSN); nursing leadership (MSN). *Accreditation:* AACN. *Entrance requirements:* For master's, BSN; minimum cumulative undergraduate GPA of 3.0, 3.25 in nursing courses; coursework in statistics; 2 letters of recommendation; interview. Electronic applications accepted.

Franciscan University of Steubenville, Graduate Programs, Department of Nursing, Steubenville, OH 43952-1763. Offers MSN. *Accreditation:* NLN. Part-time and evening/weekend programs available. *Degree requirements:* For master's, thesis. *Entrance requirements:* For master's, GRE General Test, MAT.

Franklin Pierce University, Graduate Studies, Rindge, NH 03461-0060. Offers curriculum and instruction (M Ed); emerging network technologies (Graduate Certificate); energy and sustainability studies (MBA); health administration (MBA, Graduate Certificate); human resource management (MBA, Graduate Certificate); information technology (MBA); information technology management (MS); leadership (MBA, DA); nursing (MS); physical therapy (DPT); physician assistant studies (MPAS); special education (M Ed); sports management (MBA). *Accreditation:* APTA. Part-time programs available. Postbaccalaureate distance learning degree programs offered (no on-campus study). *Degree requirements:* For master's, concentrated original research projects; student teaching; fieldwork and/or internship; leadership project; PRAXIS I and II (for M Ed); for doctorate, concentrated original research projects, clinical fieldwork and/or internship, leadership project. *Entrance requirements:* For master's, minimum GPA of 2.5, 3 letters of recommendation; competencies in accounting, economics, statistics, and computer skills through life experience or undergraduate coursework (for MBA); certification/e-portfolio, minimum C grade in all education courses (for M Ed); license to practice as RN (for MS in nursing); for doctorate, GRE, BA/BS, 3 letters of recommendation, personal mission statement, interview, writing sample, minimum cumulative GPA of 2.8, master's degree (for DA); 80 hours of observation/work in PT settings, completion of anatomy, chemistry, physics, and statistics, minimum GPA of 3.0 (for DPT). Additional exam requirements/recommendations for international students: Required—TOEFL (minimum score 550 paper-based; 195 computer-based; 61 iBT). Electronic applications accepted. *Faculty research:* Evidence-based practice in sports physical therapy, human resource management in economic crisis, leadership in nursing, innovation in sports facility management, differentiated learning and understanding by design.

Frontier Nursing University, Graduate Programs, Hyden, KY 41749. Offers community-based family nurse practitioner (MSN, Post Master's Certificate); community-based nurse-midwifery education (MSN, Post Master's Certificate); community-based women?s health care nurse practitioner (MSN, Post Master's Certificate). *Accreditation:* ACNM; NLN.

Gannon University, School of Graduate Studies, Morosky College of Health Professions and Sciences, School of Health Professions, Villa Maria School of Nursing, Erie, PA 16541-0001. Offers anesthesia (MSN); business administration (MSN); family nurse practitioner (Certificate); medical-surgical nursing (MSN); nurse anesthesia (Certificate); nursing rural practitioner (MSN). *Accreditation:* AACN; AANA/CANAEP (one or more programs are accredited). Part-time and evening/weekend programs available. *Students:* 2 full-time (both women), 68 part-time (49 women); includes 3 minority (1 Black or African American, non-Hispanic/Latino; 1 American Indian or Alaska Native, non-Hispanic/Latino; 1 Hispanic/Latino). Average age 44. 15 applicants, 67% accepted, 0 enrolled. In 2011, 20 master's, 3 other advanced degrees awarded. *Degree requirements:* For master's, thesis. *Entrance requirements:* For master's, GRE General Test, degree in nursing. Additional exam requirements/recommendations for international students: Required—TOEFL (minimum score 79 iBT). *Application deadline:* For spring admission, 8/1 for domestic students. Application fee: $25. Electronic applications accepted. *Financial support:* Scholarships/grants available. Financial award application deadline: 7/1; financial award applicants required to submit FAFSA. *Faculty research:* Accurate assessment of delirium in the ICU using CAM, factors affecting caregiver fatigue in dialysis nurses, hours worked by nurses and treatment error reporting. *Unit head:* Dr. Kathleen Patterson, Director, 814-871-5547, E-mail: patterso018@gannon.edu. *Application contact:* Kara Morgan, Director of Graduate Admissions, 814-871-5831, Fax: 814-871-5827, E-mail: graduate@gannon.edu.

Gardner-Webb University, Graduate School, School of Nursing, Boiling Springs, NC 28017. Offers MSN, DNP, PMC. *Accreditation:* NLN. Part-time programs available. Postbaccalaureate distance learning degree programs offered (no on-campus study). *Faculty:* 4 full-time (all women), 3 part-time/adjunct (all women). *Students:* 5 full-time (all women), 157 part-time (140 women); includes 18 minority (13 Black or African American, non-Hispanic/Latino; 1 American Indian or Alaska Native, non-Hispanic/Latino; 3 Asian, non-Hispanic/Latino; 1 Hispanic/Latino). Average age 41. In 2011, 38 master's awarded. *Entrance requirements:* For master's, GRE or MAT, minimum undergraduate GPA of 2.7; unrestricted licensure to practice as an RN. *Expenses:* Tuition: Full-time $6300; part-time $350 per credit hour. *Unit head:* Dr. Suzie B. Little, Dean, 704-406-4358, Fax: 704-406-4329, E-mail: gradschool@gardner-webb.edu. *Application contact:* Office of Graduate Admissions, 877-498-4723, Fax: 704-406-3895, E-mail: gradinfo@gardner-webb.edu.

George Mason University, College of Health and Human Services, School of Nursing, Fairfax, VA 22030. Offers forensic nursing (Certificate); nursing (MSN, PhD); nursing administration (Certificate); nursing education (Certificate); nursing practice (DNP). *Faculty:* 32 full-time (all women), 45 part-time/adjunct (43 women). *Students:* 70 full-time (69 women), 284 part-time (275 women); includes 109 minority (51 Black or African American, non-Hispanic/Latino; 1 American Indian or Alaska Native, non-Hispanic/Latino; 41 Asian, non-Hispanic/Latino; 12 Hispanic/Latino; 4 Two or more races, non-Hispanic/Latino), 11 international. Average age 41. 220 applicants, 56% accepted, 86 enrolled. In 2011, 79 master's, 4 doctorates, 1 other advanced degree awarded. *Degree requirements:* For master's, comprehensive exam (for some programs), thesis in clinical classes; for doctorate, comprehensive exam (for some programs), thesis/dissertation (for some programs). *Entrance requirements:* For master's, 2 official transcripts; expanded goals statement; resume; BSN from accredited institution; minimum GPA of 3.0 in last 60 credits of undergraduate work; 2 letters of recommendation; completion of undergraduate statistics and graduate-level bivariate statistics; certification in professional CPR; for doctorate, 2 official transcripts; expanded goals statement; resume; 3 recommendation letters, nursing license, at least 1 year of work experience as an RN; interview, writing sample, evidence of graduate-level course in applied statistics; master's in nursing with minimum GPA of 3.5; for Certificate, 2 official transcripts; expanded goals statement; resume; master's degree from accredited institution or currently enrolled with minimum GPA of 3.0. Additional exam requirements/recommendations for international students: Required—TOEFL (minimum score 575 paper-based; 230 computer-based; 88 iBT), IELTS, Pearson Test of English. *Application deadline:* For fall admission, 3/1 priority date for domestic students; for spring admission, 11/1 for domestic students. Application fee: $65 ($80 for international students). Electronic applications accepted. *Expenses:* Tuition, state resident: full-time $8750; part-time $364.58 per credit. Tuition, nonresident: full-time $24,092; part-time $1003.83 per credit. *Required fees:* $2514; $104.75 per credit. *Financial support:* In 2011–12, 5 students received support, including 4 research assistantships with full and partial tuition reimbursements available (averaging $26,672 per year), 1 teaching assistantship with full and partial tuition reimbursement available (averaging $15,000 per year); career-related internships or fieldwork, Federal Work-Study, scholarships/grants, unspecified assistantships, and nurse faculty loan, health care benefits (full-time research or teaching assistantship recipients) also available. Financial award application deadline: 3/1; financial award applicants required to submit FAFSA. *Total annual research expenditures:* $607,543. *Unit head:* Robin Remsburg, Associate Dean/Director, 703-993-1904, Fax: 703-993-1949, E-mail: rremsbur@gmu.edu. *Application contact:* Janice Lee-Beverly, Program Support, 703-993-1947, Fax: 703-993-1943, E-mail: jleebev1@gmu.edu. Web site: http://chhs.gmu.edu/nursing.

Georgetown University, Graduate School of Arts and Sciences, School of Nursing and Health Studies, Washington, DC 20057. Offers acute care nurse practitioner (MS); clinical nurse specialist (MS); family nurse practitioner (MS); nurse anesthesia (MS); nurse-midwifery (MS); nursing education (MS). *Accreditation:* AACN; AANA/CANAEP; ACNM/ACME. *Degree requirements:* For master's, thesis optional. *Entrance requirements:* For master's, GRE General Test or MAT, bachelor's degree in nursing from NLN-accredited school, minimum undergraduate GPA of 3.0. Additional exam requirements/recommendations for international students: Required—TOEFL.

The George Washington University, School of Nursing, Washington, DC 20052. Offers adult nurse practitioner (MSN, Post-Master's Certificate); clinical research administration (MSN); family nurse practitioner (MSN, Post-Master's Certificate); health care quality (MSN, Post-Master's Certificate); nursing (DNP); nursing leadership and management (MSN); palliative care nurse practitioner (Post-Master's Certificate). *Accreditation:* AACN. *Faculty:* 19 full-time (all women), 32 part-time/adjunct (29 women). *Students:* 27 full-time (25 women), 360 part-time (330 women); includes 89 minority (44 Black or African American, non-Hispanic/Latino; 9 American Indian or Alaska Native, non-Hispanic/Latino; 25 Asian, non-Hispanic/Latino; 11 Hispanic/Latino), 15 international. Average age 39. 287 applicants, 87% accepted, 176 enrolled. In 2011, 45 master's, 19 doctorates awarded. *Unit head:* Jean E. Johnson, Dean, 202-994-3725, E-mail: sonjej@gwumc.edu. *Application contact:* Kristin Williams, Assistant Vice President for Graduate and Special Enrollment Management, 202-994-0467, Fax: 202-994-0371, E-mail: ksw@gwu.edu. Web site: http://nursing.gwumc.edu/.

Georgia College & State University, Graduate School, College of Health Sciences, Graduate Nursing Program, Milledgeville, GA 31061. Offers adult health (MSN); family nurse practitioner (MSN); nursing administration (MSN); MSN/MBA. *Accreditation:* NLN.

Part-time and evening/weekend programs available. *Students:* 10 full-time (9 women), 63 part-time (60 women); includes 16 minority (all Black or African American, non-Hispanic/Latino). Average age 36. 64 applicants, 44% accepted, 20 enrolled. In 2011, 7 master's awarded. *Degree requirements:* For master's, comprehensive exam, thesis optional. *Entrance requirements:* For master's, GMAT, GRE General Test, or MAT, bachelor's degree in nursing, RN license, 1 year clinical experience. Additional exam requirements/recommendations for international students: Recommended—TOEFL (minimum score 550 paper-based; 213 computer-based; 79 iBT). *Application deadline:* For fall admission, 7/1 priority date for domestic students; for spring admission, 4/1 priority date for domestic students. Applications are processed on a rolling basis. Application fee: $40. Electronic applications accepted. *Expenses:* Tuition, state resident: full-time $4806; part-time $267 per credit hour. Tuition, nonresident: full-time $17,802; part-time $989 per credit hour. *Required fees:* $936 per semester. Tuition and fees vary according to course load and campus/location. *Financial support:* In 2011–12, 1 research assistantship with full tuition reimbursement was awarded; unspecified assistantships also available. Financial award applicants required to submit FAFSA. *Unit head:* Dr. Judith Malachowski, Director, School of Nursing, 478-445-5122, E-mail: judith.malachowski@gcsu.edu. *Application contact:* Lora Crowe, MSN Coordinator, 478-445-5122, E-mail: lora.crowe@gcsu.edu.

Georgia Health Sciences University, College of Graduate Studies, Doctor of Nursing Practice Program, Augusta, GA 30912. Offers DNP. *Students:* 46 part-time (40 women); includes 18 minority (14 Black or African American, non-Hispanic/Latino; 3 Hispanic/Latino; 1 Two or more races, non-Hispanic/Latino). Average age 47. 43 applicants, 33% accepted, 14 enrolled. *Degree requirements:* For doctorate, thesis/dissertation or alternative. *Entrance requirements:* For doctorate, GRE General Test or MAT, master's degree in nursing or related field, current professional nurse licensure. Additional exam requirements/recommendations for international students: Required—TOEFL (minimum score 600 paper-based; 250 computer-based; 100 iBT). *Application deadline:* For fall admission, 3/1 for domestic and international students; for spring admission, 7/1 for domestic and international students. Applications are processed on a rolling basis. Application fee: $50. Electronic applications accepted. *Unit head:* Dr. Lucy Marion, Dean, 706-721-3771, Fax: 706-721-8169, E-mail: lumarion@georgiahealth.edu. *Application contact:* Karen Sturgill, Program Coordinator, 706-721-3676, Fax: 706-721-8169, E-mail: ksturgill@georgiahealth.edu. Web site: http://www.mcg.edu/son/futurestudents.htm.

Georgia Health Sciences University, College of Graduate Studies, Nursing PhD Program, Augusta, GA 30912. Offers PhD. *Faculty:* 21 full-time (17 women), 6 part-time/adjunct (all women). *Students:* 8 full-time (all women), 7 part-time (6 women); includes 3 minority (2 Black or African American, non-Hispanic/Latino; 1 Asian, non-Hispanic/Latino). Average age 44. 3 applicants, 33% accepted, 0 enrolled. In 2011, 1 doctorate awarded. *Degree requirements:* For doctorate, thesis/dissertation. *Entrance requirements:* For doctorate, GRE General Test, current GA nurse licensure. Additional exam requirements/recommendations for international students: Required—TOEFL (minimum score 550 paper-based; 213 computer-based; 79 iBT). *Application deadline:* For fall admission, 5/1 for domestic and international students; for spring admission, 10/1 for domestic and international students. Application fee: $50. Electronic applications accepted. *Financial support:* In 2011–12, 7 research assistantships with partial tuition reimbursements (averaging $23,000 per year) were awarded. Financial award applicants required to submit FAFSA. *Unit head:* Dr. Lucy Marion, Dean, 706-721-3771, Fax: 706-721-8169, E-mail: lumarion@mail.mcg.edu. *Application contact:* Sarah Thomas, Program Manager, 706-721-4862, Fax: 706-721-7390. Web site: http://www.georgiahealth.edu/nursing/PhDinNursing.html.

Georgia Southern University, Jack N. Averitt College of Graduate Studies, College of Health and Human Sciences, School of Nursing, Program in Nursing Science, Statesboro, GA 30460. Offers DNP. Part-time programs available. Postbaccalaureate distance learning degree programs offered. *Students:* 25 part-time (23 women); includes 3 minority (all Black or African American, non-Hispanic/Latino), 1 international. Average age 45. 17 applicants, 82% accepted, 8 enrolled. In 2011, 11 doctorates awarded. *Entrance requirements:* Additional exam requirements/recommendations for international students: Required—TOEFL (minimum score 550 paper-based; 213 computer-based; 80 iBT). *Application deadline:* For fall admission, 3/1 priority date for domestic students, 3/1 for international students; for spring admission, 10/1 priority date for domestic students, 10/1 for international students. Applications are processed on a rolling basis. Application fee: $50. Electronic applications accepted. *Expenses:* Tuition, state resident: full-time $6300; part-time $263 per semester hour. Tuition, nonresident: full-time $25,174; part-time $1049 per semester hour. *Required fees:* $1872. *Financial support:* In 2011–12, 12 students received support, including research assistantships (averaging $6,850 per year), teaching assistantships (averaging $6,850 per year); career-related internships or fieldwork, Federal Work-Study, scholarships/grants, traineeships, tuition waivers, and unspecified assistantships also available. Support available to part-time students. Financial award application deadline: 4/15; financial award applicants required to submit FAFSA. *Faculty research:* Vulnerable populations, breast cancer, diabetes mellitus, advanced practice nursing issues. *Total annual research expenditures:* $25,000. *Unit head:* Dr. Deborah Allen, Chair, 912-478-5056, Fax: 912-478-0536, E-mail: jbartels@georgiasouthern.edu. *Application contact:* Amanda Gilliland, Coordinator for Graduate Student Recruitment, 912-478-5384, Fax: 912-478-0740, E-mail: gradadmissionss@georgiasouthern.edu.

Georgia State University, College of Health and Human Sciences, Byrdine F. Lewis School of Nursing, Atlanta, GA 30302-3083. Offers adult health (MS); adult health nursing (Certificate); child health (MS); family nurse practitioner (MS, Certificate); health promotion, protection and restoration (PhD); perinatal/women's health (MS); psychiatric mental health nursing (Certificate); psychiatric/mental health (MS); women's health nursing (Certificate). *Accreditation:* AACN. Part-time and evening/weekend programs available. Postbaccalaureate distance learning degree programs offered (minimal on-campus study). *Degree requirements:* For master's, research activity; for doctorate, comprehensive exam, thesis/dissertation. *Entrance requirements:* For master's, MAT (preferred) or GRE, interview, RN license; for doctorate, GRE General Test. Additional exam requirements/recommendations for international students: Required—TOEFL (minimum score 550 paper-based; 213 computer-based). Electronic applications accepted. *Expenses:* Contact institution. *Faculty research:* Breast cancer prevention, sexually compulsive behaviors, health risks in minority youth, asthma treatment strategies, adolescent alcohol-related issues.

Goldfarb School of Nursing at Barnes-Jewish College, Graduate Programs, St. Louis, MO 63110. Offers adult acute care nurse practitioner (MSN); adult nurse practitioner (MSN); nurse anesthesia (MSN); nurse educator (MSN); nurse executive (MSN); DNP/PhD. *Accreditation:* AACN; AANA/CANAEP. Part-time and evening/weekend programs available. Postbaccalaureate distance learning degree programs offered (minimal on-campus study). *Faculty:* 38 full-time (35 women), 14 part-time/adjunct (11 women). *Students:* 79 full-time (68 women), 92 part-time (86 women); includes 45 minority (29 Black or African American, non-Hispanic/Latino; 1 American Indian or Alaska Native, non-Hispanic/Latino; 3 Asian, non-Hispanic/Latino; 3 Hispanic/Latino; 6 Native Hawaiian or other Pacific Islander, non-Hispanic/Latino; 3 Two or more races, non-Hispanic/Latino), 1 international. Average age 40. 134 applicants, 66%

accepted, 51 enrolled. In 2011, 31 degrees awarded. *Degree requirements:* For master's, thesis or alternative. *Entrance requirements:* For master's, 2 references, personal statement, curriculum vitae or resume. Additional exam requirements/recommendations for international students: Required—TOEFL (minimum score 575 paper-based; 240 computer-based; 85 iBT). *Application deadline:* For fall admission, 2/1 for international students; for spring admission, 10/1 for international students. Applications are processed on a rolling basis. Application fee: $50. *Expenses:* Tuition: Full-time $14,685; part-time $630 per credit hour. *Required fees:* $280. *Financial support:* Fellowships, research assistantships, Federal Work-Study, institutionally sponsored loans, and scholarships/grants available. Support available to part-time students. Financial award applicants required to submit FAFSA. *Faculty research:* HIV Stigma, HIV symptom management, palliative care with children and their families, heart disease prevention in Hispanic women, depression in the well elderly, alternative therapies in pre-term infants. *Unit head:* Dr. Connie K. Koch, Interim Dean, 314-36-26590, Fax: 314-362-0984, E-mail: ckoch@bjc.org. *Application contact:* Dr. Michael Ward, Associate Dean for Student Programs, 314-362-9155, Fax: 314-362-0984, E-mail: mward@bjc.org.

Gonzaga University, School of Professional Studies, Department of Nursing, Spokane, WA 99258. Offers MSN. *Accreditation:* AACN. Postbaccalaureate distance learning degree programs offered. *Entrance requirements:* For master's, MAT, minimum B average in undergraduate course work. Additional exam requirements/recommendations for international students: Required—TOEFL.

Goshen College, Program in Nursing, Goshen, IN 46526-4794. Offers family nurse practitioner (MSN). *Accreditation:* AACN. Part-time and evening/weekend programs available. *Faculty:* 6 full-time (all women), 4 part-time/adjunct (all women). *Students:* 27 part-time (26 women), 2 international. *Degree requirements:* For master's, comprehensive exam (for some programs). *Entrance requirements:* Additional exam requirements/recommendations for international students: Required—TOEFL (minimum score 650 paper-based; 213 computer-based; 79 iBT), IELTS (minimum score 6). *Application deadline:* Applications are processed on a rolling basis. Application fee: $50. *Expenses:* Contact institution. *Financial support:* Scholarships/grants available. Financial award applicants required to submit FAFSA. *Unit head:* Dr. Brenda Srof, Chair, 574-535-7375, E-mail: brendajs@goshen.edu. Web site: http://www.goshen.edu/nursing/masters.

Governors State University, College of Health Professions, Program in Nursing, University Park, IL 60484. Offers MSN. *Accreditation:* NLN. *Students:* 19 full-time (17 women), 161 part-time (147 women); includes 124 minority (104 Black or African American, non-Hispanic/Latino; 1 American Indian or Alaska Native, non-Hispanic/Latino; 6 Asian, non-Hispanic/Latino; 11 Hispanic/Latino; 2 Two or more races, non-Hispanic/Latino). Average age 35. *Degree requirements:* For master's, comprehensive exam, thesis or alternative, practicum. *Entrance requirements:* For master's, GRE General Test, minimum GPA of 3.0 in upper-division nursing course work, 2.5 overall; BSN verification of AAS or employment as registered nurse; Illinois licensure; BSN from NLN-accredited institution. *Application deadline:* For fall admission, 7/15 priority date for domestic students; for spring admission, 11/10 for domestic students. Applications are processed on a rolling basis. Application fee: $25. *Financial support:* Research assistantships, career-related internships or fieldwork, Federal Work-Study, institutionally sponsored loans, and tuition waivers (full and partial) available. Support available to part-time students. Financial award application deadline: 5/1. *Unit head:* Dr. Elizabeth Cada, Dean, 708-534-7295.

Graceland University, School of Nursing, Independence, MO 64050-3434. Offers family nurse practitioner (MSN, PMC); nurse educator (MSN, PMC). Part-time programs available. Postbaccalaureate distance learning degree programs offered (minimal on-campus study). *Faculty:* 9 full-time (all women), 9 part-time/adjunct (7 women). *Students:* 197 full-time (181 women), 204 part-time (186 women); includes 14 minority (8 Black or African American, non-Hispanic/Latino; 1 American Indian or Alaska Native, non-Hispanic/Latino; 4 Asian, non-Hispanic/Latino; 1 Hispanic/Latino). Average age 40. 263 applicants, 71% accepted, 138 enrolled. In 2011, 88 master's, 2 other advanced degrees awarded. *Degree requirements:* For master's, comprehensive exam (for some programs), thesis optional. *Entrance requirements:* For master's, BSN from nationally-accredited program, portfolio, RN license, minimum GPA of 3.0. Additional exam requirements/recommendations for international students: Recommended—TOEFL. *Application deadline:* For fall admission, 6/1 priority date for domestic students; for winter admission, 10/1 priority date for domestic students; for spring admission, 3/1 priority date for domestic students. Application fee: $50. Electronic applications accepted. *Expenses:* Contact institution. *Financial support:* Institutionally sponsored loans and traineeships available. Support available to part-time students. Financial award applicants required to submit FAFSA. *Faculty research:* International nursing, family care-giving, health promotion. *Unit head:* Dr. Claudia D. Horton, Dean, 816-833-0524 Ext. 4214, Fax: 816-833-2990, E-mail: horton@graceland.edu. *Application contact:* Cara Hakes, Program Consultant, 816-833-0524 Ext. 4803, Fax: 816-833-2990, E-mail: chakes@graceland.edu. Web site: http://www.graceland.edu/nursing.

Graduate School and University Center of the City University of New York, Graduate Studies, Program in Nursing Science, New York, NY 10016-4039. Offers DNS. *Degree requirements:* For doctorate, thesis/dissertation, exams. *Entrance requirements:* For doctorate, GRE, 2 letters of recommendation. Additional exam requirements/recommendations for international students: Required—TOEFL. Electronic applications accepted.

Grambling State University, School of Graduate Studies and Research, College of Professional Studies, School of Nursing, Grambling, LA 71245. Offers family nurse practitioner (MSN, PMC); nurse educator (MSN). *Accreditation:* NLN. Part-time programs available. *Degree requirements:* For master's, comprehensive exam (for some programs), thesis (for some programs). *Entrance requirements:* For master's, GRE, minimum GPA of 3.0 on last degree, interview, 2 years experience as RN. Additional exam requirements/recommendations for international students: Required—TOEFL (minimum score 500 paper-based; 173 computer-based; 61 iBT). Electronic applications accepted. *Expenses:* Tuition, state resident: full-time $3546; part-time $192 per credit hour. Tuition, nonresident: full-time $3456; part-time $192 per credit hour. *Required fees:* $1829; $1829 per semester hour.

Grand Canyon University, College of Nursing, Phoenix, AZ 85017-1097. Offers acute care nurse practitioner (MS, PMC); clinical nurse specialist (PMC), including clinical nurse specialist, education; family nurse practitioner (MS); leadership in health care systems (MS); nurse education (MS). *Accreditation:* AACN. Part-time and evening/weekend programs available. Postbaccalaureate distance learning degree programs offered (no on-campus study). *Degree requirements:* For master's and PMC, comprehensive exam (for some programs). *Entrance requirements:* For master's, minimum cumulative and science course undergraduate GPA of 3.0. Additional exam requirements/recommendations for international students: Required—TOEFL (minimum score 575 paper-based; 233 computer-based; 90 iBT), IELTS (minimum score 7).

Grand Valley State University, Kirkhof College of Nursing, Allendale, MI 49401-9403. Offers advanced practice (MSN); case management (MSN); nursing administration (MSN); nursing education (MSN); nursing practice (DNP); MSN/MBA. *Accreditation:*

AACN. Part-time programs available. *Degree requirements:* For master's, thesis optional. *Entrance requirements:* For master's, GRE, minimum GPA of 3.0 in upper-division course work, course work in statistics, Michigan RN license. Additional exam requirements/recommendations for international students: Required—TOEFL. Electronic applications accepted. *Faculty research:* Multigenerational health promotion, chronic disease prevention, end-of-life issues, nursing workload, family caregiver health.

Grand View University, Master of Science in Innovative Leadership Program, Des Moines, IA 50316-1599. Offers business (MS); education (MS); nursing (MS). Part-time and evening/weekend programs available. *Faculty:* 7 full-time (3 women). *Students:* 31 part-time (23 women). Average age 32. In 2011, 16 master's awarded. *Degree requirements:* For master's, completion of all required coursework in common core and selected track with minimum cumulative GPA of 3.0 and no more than two grades of C. *Entrance requirements:* For master's, GRE, GMAT, or essay, minimum undergraduate GPA of 3.0, professional resume, 3 letters of recommendation, interview. Additional exam requirements/recommendations for international students: Required—TOEFL (minimum score 550 paper-based; 210 computer-based). *Application deadline:* Applications are processed on a rolling basis. Application fee: $40. Electronic applications accepted. *Expenses: Tuition:* Part-time $501 per credit. *Required fees:* $115 per semester. *Unit head:* Dr. Patricia Rinke, Dean of Graduate and Adult Programs, 515-263-2912, E-mail: prinke@grandview.edu. *Application contact:* Michael Norris, Director of Graduate Admissions, 515-263-2830, E-mail: gradadmissions@grandview.edu. Web site: http://www.grandview.edu.

Gwynedd-Mercy College, School of Nursing, Gwynedd Valley, PA 19437-0901. Offers clinical nurse specialist (MSN), including gerontology, oncology, pediatrics; nurse practitioner (MSN), including adult health, pediatric health. *Accreditation:* NLN. *Faculty:* 3 full-time (all women), 2 part-time/adjunct (both women). *Students:* 14 full-time (13 women), 28 part-time (25 women); includes 11 minority (4 Black or African American, non-Hispanic/Latino; 6 Asian, non-Hispanic/Latino; 1 Hispanic/Latino). Average age 40. 23 applicants, 83% accepted, 11 enrolled. In 2011, 7 master's awarded. *Degree requirements:* For master's, thesis optional. *Entrance requirements:* For master's, GRE General Test or MAT, current nursing experience, physical assessment, course work in statistics, BSN from NLNAC-accredited program, 2 letters of recommendation, personal interview. Additional exam requirements/recommendations for international students: Required—TOEFL (minimum score 575 paper-based). *Application deadline:* For fall admission, 8/1 priority date for domestic students; for winter admission, 12/1 priority date for domestic students. Applications are processed on a rolling basis. Application fee: $25. Electronic applications accepted. *Expenses:* Contact institution. *Financial support:* In 2011–12, 21 students received support. Scholarships/grants, traineeships, and unspecified assistantships available. Financial award application deadline: 8/30. *Faculty research:* Critical thinking, primary care, domestic violence, multiculturalism, nursing centers. *Unit head:* Dr. Andrea D. Hollingsworth, Dean, 215-646-7300 Ext. 539, Fax: 215-641-5517, E-mail: hollingsworth.a@gmc.edu. *Application contact:* Dr. Barbara A. Jones, Director, 215-646-7300 Ext. 407, Fax: 215-641-5564, E-mail: jones.b@gmc.edu. Web site: http://www.gmc.edu/academics/nursing/.

Hampton University, Graduate College, School of Nursing, Hampton, VA 23668. Offers advanced adult nursing (MS); community health nursing (MS); community mental health/psychiatric nursing (MS); family nursing (MS); gerontological nursing for the nurse practitioner (MS); pediatric nursing (MS); women's health nursing (MS). *Accreditation:* AACN; NLN. Part-time and evening/weekend programs available. *Degree requirements:* For master's, thesis optional. *Entrance requirements:* For master's, GRE General Test. *Faculty research:* Curriculum development, physical and mental assessment.

Hampton University, Hampton U Online, Hampton, VA 23668. Offers business administration (PhD); educational management (PhD); health administration (MHA); nursing (MSN, PhD).

Hardin-Simmons University, Graduate School, Patty Hanks Shelton School of Nursing, Abilene, TX 79698-0001. Offers advanced healthcare delivery (MSN); family nurse practitioner (MSN). Programs offered jointly with Abilene Christian University and McMurry University. *Accreditation:* AACN. Part-time programs available. *Faculty:* 6 full-time (all women), 3 part-time/adjunct (all women). *Students:* 10 full-time (9 women), 7 part-time (2 women); includes 5 minority (3 Black or African American, non-Hispanic/Latino; 2 Hispanic/Latino). Average age 35. 12 applicants, 100% accepted, 11 enrolled. In 2011, 4 master's awarded. *Degree requirements:* For master's, comprehensive exam, thesis or alternative. *Entrance requirements:* For master's, GRE, minimum undergraduate GPA of 3.0 in major, 2.8 overall; interview; upper-level course work in statistics; CPR certification; letters of recommendation. Additional exam requirements/recommendations for international students: Required—TOEFL (minimum score 550 paper-based; 213 computer-based; 75 iBT). *Application deadline:* For fall admission, 8/15 priority date for domestic students, 4/1 for international students; for spring admission, 1/5 priority date for domestic students, 9/1 for international students. Applications are processed on a rolling basis. Application fee: $50. *Expenses:* Contact institution. *Financial support:* In 2011–12, 14 students received support. Career-related internships or fieldwork and scholarships/grants available. Support available to part-time students. Financial award application deadline: 6/30; financial award applicants required to submit FAFSA. *Faculty research:* Child abuse, alternative medicine, pediatric chronic disease, health promotion. *Unit head:* Dr. Amy Toone, Director, 325-671-2361, Fax: 325-671-2386, E-mail: atoone@phssn.edu. *Application contact:* Dr. Nancy Kucinski, Dean of Graduate Studies, 325-670-1298, Fax: 325-670-1564, E-mail: gradoff@hsutx.edu. Web site: http://www.phssn.edu/.

Hawai`i Pacific University, College of Nursing and Health Sciences, Honolulu, HI 96813. Offers community clinical nurse specialist (MSN); community clinical nurse specialist educator option (MSN); family nurse practitioner (MSN). *Accreditation:* NLN. Part-time and evening/weekend programs available. *Faculty:* 5 full-time (4 women), 2 part-time/adjunct (1 woman). *Students:* 45 full-time (34 women), 13 part-time (10 women); includes 38 minority (3 Black or African American, non-Hispanic/Latino; 2 American Indian or Alaska Native, non-Hispanic/Latino; 16 Asian, non-Hispanic/Latino; 6 Hispanic/Latino; 4 Native Hawaiian or other Pacific Islander, non-Hispanic/Latino; 7 Two or more races, non-Hispanic/Latino). Average age 38. 32 applicants, 78% accepted, 19 enrolled. In 2011, 11 master's awarded. *Degree requirements:* For master's, practicum, professional paper. *Entrance requirements:* For master's, bachelor's degree in nursing, minimum GPA of 3.0. Additional exam requirements/recommendations for international students: Recommended—TOEFL (minimum score 550 paper-based; 213 computer-based; 80 iBT), TWE (minimum score 5). *Application deadline:* Applications are processed on a rolling basis. Application fee: $50. Electronic applications accepted. *Expenses: Tuition:* Full-time $13,230; part-time $735 per credit. Tuition and fees vary according to course load and program. *Financial support:* In 2011–12, 11 students received support. Career-related internships or fieldwork, Federal Work-Study, scholarships/grants, traineeships, and tuition waivers available. Financial award application deadline: 3/1; financial award applicants required to submit FAFSA. *Faculty research:* Hawaiian elders, traditional healing and nursing center. *Unit head:* Dr. Patricia Burrell, Chair, Graduate and Post Baccalaureate Programs, 808-236-5813, Fax: 808-236-5818, E-mail: pburrell@hpu.edu. *Application contact:* Chad Schempp, Director of Graduate Admissions, 808-543-8035, Fax: 808-544-0280, E-mail: graduate@hpu.edu. Web site: http://www.hpu.edu/CNHS/index.html.

See Display below and Close-Up on page 799.

Hawai`i Pacific University

» Recognized as a "Best in the West" college by *Princeton Review*

» Rated a "Best Buy" by *Barron's* and "Best Return on Investment" by *Bloomberg Businessweek*

» Choose from more than 50 programs from International Business to Nursing to Marine Biology

» Receive individual attention in classes under 25 students

1-866-CALL-HPU • admissions@hpu.edu
www.hpu.edu/petersons

Nursing—General

Herzing University Online, Program in Nursing, Milwaukee, WI 53203. Offers nursing (MSN); nursing education (MSN); nursing management (MSN). Postbaccalaureate distance learning degree programs offered (no on-campus study).

Holy Family University, Graduate School, School of Nursing and Allied Health Professions, Philadelphia, PA 19114. Offers community health nursing (MSN); nursing administration (MSN); nursing education (MSN). *Accreditation:* AACN. Part-time and evening/weekend programs available. *Degree requirements:* For master's, thesis or alternative. *Entrance requirements:* For master's, bachelor's degree in nursing, RN license, minimum GPA of 3.0, 2 letters of reference.

See Display below and Close-Up on page 801.

Holy Names University, Graduate Division, Department of Nursing, Oakland, CA 94619-1699. Offers administration/management (MS, Certificate); clinical faculty (MS, Certificate); community health nursing/case manager (MS); family nurse practitioner (MS, Certificate); MSN/Certificate; MSN/MBA. *Accreditation:* AACN. Part-time and evening/weekend programs available. *Entrance requirements:* For master's, bachelor's degree in nursing or related field, California RN license or eligibility, minimum GPA of 3.0, previous course work in research or statistics. Additional exam requirements/recommendations for international students: Required—TOEFL (minimum score 500 paper-based). *Faculty research:* Women's reproductive health, gerontology, attitudes about aging, schizophrenic families, international health issues.

Howard University, College of Nursing and Allied Health Sciences, Division of Nursing, Washington, DC 20059-0002. Offers nurse practitioner (Certificate); primary family health nursing (MSN). *Accreditation:* AACN. Part-time programs available. *Degree requirements:* For master's, comprehensive exam, thesis optional. *Entrance requirements:* For master's, RN license, minimum GPA of 3.0, BS in nursing. *Faculty research:* Urinary incontinence, breast cancer prevention, depression in the elderly, adolescent pregnancy.

Hunter College of the City University of New York, Graduate School, Schools of the Health Professions, Hunter-Bellevue School of Nursing, New York, NY 10021-5085. Offers MS, AC, MS/MPH. *Accreditation:* AACN. Part-time programs available. *Faculty:* 20 full-time (16 women), 20 part-time/adjunct (18 women). *Students:* 4 full-time (2 women), 236 part-time (195 women); includes 122 minority (56 Black or African American, non-Hispanic/Latino; 1 American Indian or Alaska Native, non-Hispanic/Latino; 49 Asian, non-Hispanic/Latino; 16 Hispanic/Latino), 23 international. Average age 39. 116 applicants, 60% accepted, 57 enrolled. In 2011, 69 master's, 9 other advanced degrees awarded. *Degree requirements:* For master's, practicum, portfolio. *Entrance requirements:* For master's, BSN, minimum GPA of 3.0, New York RN license, course work in basic statistics, resume; for AC, MSN, minimum GPA of 3.0. Additional exam requirements/recommendations for international students: Required—TOEFL. *Application deadline:* For fall admission, 4/1 for domestic students; for spring admission, 11/1 for domestic students. Applications are processed on a rolling basis. Application fee: $125. *Expenses:* Tuition, state resident: full-time $8210; part-time $345 per credit. Tuition, nonresident: full-time $15,360; part-time $640 per credit. *Required fees:* $280 per semester. One-time fee: $125. Tuition and fees vary according to class time, campus/location and program. *Financial support:* In 2011–12, 9 students received support. Federal Work-Study, scholarships/grants, traineeships, and tuition waivers (partial) available. Support available to part-time students. Financial award application deadline: 5/1; financial award applicants required to submit FAFSA. *Faculty research:* Aging, high-risk mothers and babies, adolescent health, care of HIV/AIDS clients, critical care nursing. *Unit head:* Dr. Diane Rendon, Director, 212-481-7596, Fax: 212-481-5078, E-mail: drendon@hunter.cuny.edu. *Application contact:* Milena Solo, Director for Graduate Admissions, 212-772-4482, Fax: 212-650-3336, E-mail: milena.solo@hunter.cuny.edu. Web site: http://www.hunter.cuny.edu/nursing/.

Husson University, School of Graduate and Professional Studies, Graduate Nursing Program, Bangor, ME 04401-2999. Offers advanced practice psychiatric nursing (MSN, PMC); family and community nurse practitioner (MSN, PMC); nursing education (MSN, PMC). *Accreditation:* AACN. Part-time programs available. *Faculty:* 6 full-time (all women), 6 part-time/adjunct (all women). *Students:* 49 full-time (42 women), 33 part-time (29 women); includes 2 minority (1 American Indian or Alaska Native, non-Hispanic/Latino; 1 Two or more races, non-Hispanic/Latino). 18 applicants, 13 enrolled. In 2011, 25 master's awarded. *Degree requirements:* For master's, comprehensive exam (for some programs). *Entrance requirements:* For master's, bachelor's degree in nursing, RN license. Additional exam requirements/recommendations for international students: Required—TOEFL (minimum score 550 paper-based). *Application deadline:* For fall admission, 6/30 for domestic students; for spring admission, 10/30 for domestic students. Application fee: $40. *Expenses:* Contact institution. *Financial support:* In 2011–12, 31 students received support. Federal Work-Study, institutionally sponsored loans, traineeships, and unspecified assistantships available. Financial award application deadline: 4/15; financial award applicants required to submit FAFSA. *Unit head:* Dr. Barbara Higgins, Director, Nurse Practitioner Program, 207-947-7057. *Application contact:* Kristen Card, Director of Graduate Admissions, 207-404-5660, Fax: 207-941-7935, E-mail: cardk@husson.edu.

Idaho State University, Office of Graduate Studies, Kasiska College of Health Professions, Department of Nursing, Pocatello, ID 83209-8101. Offers nursing (MS, Post-Master's Certificate). *Accreditation:* AACN. Part-time programs available. *Degree requirements:* For master's, comprehensive exam, thesis optional and/or clinical hours; for Post-Master's Certificate, comprehensive exam, thesis optional, practicum. *Entrance requirements:* For master's, GRE General Test, interview, 3 letters of reference, active RN license; for Post-Master's Certificate, GRE General Test, 3 letters of reference, practicum or nursing license, graduate degree. Additional exam requirements/recommendations for international students: Required—TOEFL (minimum score 600 paper-based; 213 computer-based). Electronic applications accepted. *Faculty research:* Health promotions, health of homeless, exercise and elderly, student stress, midwifery.

Illinois State University, Graduate School, Mennonite College of Nursing, Normal, IL 61790. Offers family nurse practitioner (PMC); nursing (MSN, PhD). *Accreditation:* AACN. *Faculty research:* Expanding the teaching-nursing home culture in the state of Illinois, advanced education nursing traineeship program, collaborative doctoral program-caring for older adults.

Immaculata University, College of Graduate Studies, Department of Nursing, Immaculata, PA 19345. Offers MSN. *Accreditation:* AACN. Part-time and evening/weekend programs available. *Entrance requirements:* For master's, MAT or GRE, BSN. Additional exam requirements/recommendations for international students: Required—TOEFL.

Independence University, Program in Nursing, Salt Lake City, UT 84107. Offers community health (MSN); gerontology (MSN); nursing administration (MSN); wellness promotion (MSN).

Indiana State University, College of Graduate and Professional Studies, College of Nursing, Health and Human Services, Department of Nursing, Terre Haute, IN 47809. Offers MS. *Accreditation:* NLN. Part-time programs available. *Degree requirements:* For master's, thesis or alternative. *Entrance requirements:* For master's, BSN, RN license, minimum undergraduate GPA of 3.0. Electronic applications accepted. *Faculty research:* Nursing faculty-student interactions, clinical evaluation, program evaluation, sexual dysfunction, faculty attitudes.

Indiana University East, School of Nursing, Richmond, IN 47374-1289. Offers MSN.

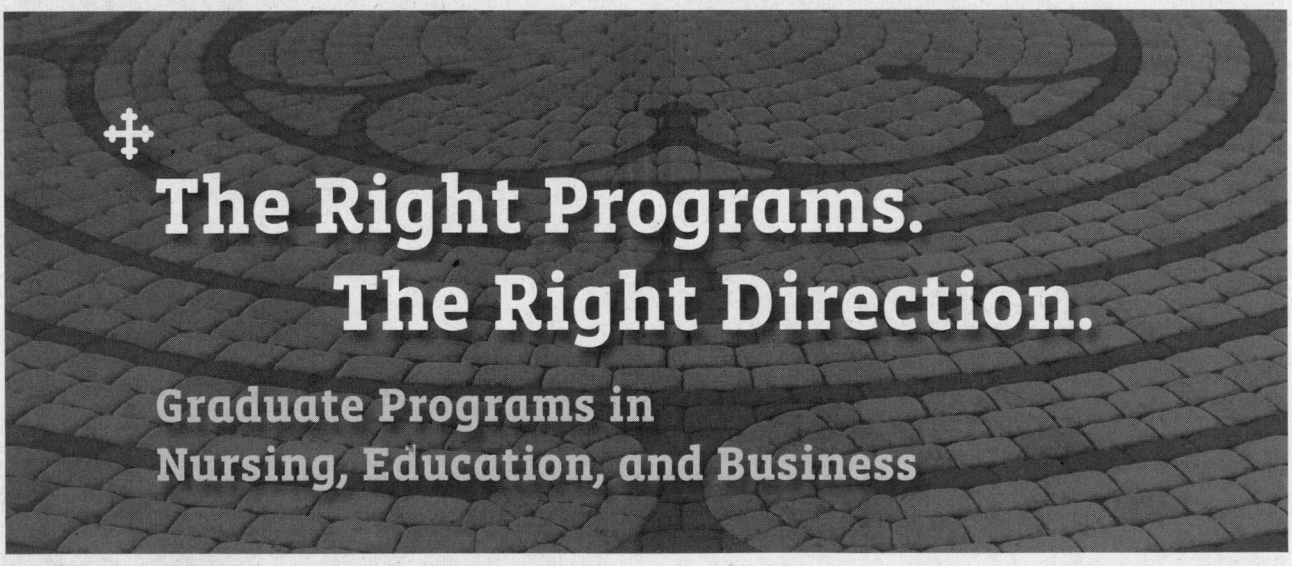

The Right Programs.
The Right Direction.

Graduate Programs in
Nursing, Education, and Business

Holy Family
U N I V E R S I T Y

holyfamily.edu

Indiana University of Pennsylvania, School of Graduate Studies and Research, College of Health and Human Services, Department of Nursing and Allied Health, PhD in Nursing Program, Indiana, PA 15705-1087. Offers PhD. *Faculty:* 6 full-time (5 women). *Students:* 1 (woman) full-time, 20 part-time (19 women); includes 1 minority (Hispanic/Latino). Average age 46. 4 applicants, 0% accepted, 0 enrolled. *Degree requirements:* For doctorate, thesis/dissertation. *Entrance requirements:* For doctorate, GRE, master's degree in nursing or related field, two letters of recommendation, statement of career and academic goals, official transcripts from all colleges and universities attended, nursing license, current curriculum vitae. Additional exam requirements/recommendations for international students: Required—TOEFL (minimum score 540 paper-based; 207 computer-based). *Application deadline:* Applications are processed on a rolling basis. Application fee: $50. Electronic applications accepted. *Expenses:* Tuition, state resident: full-time $7488; part-time $416 per credit. Tuition, nonresident: full-time $11,232; part-time $624 per credit. *Required fees:* $2070; $192.20 per credit. $90 per semester. *Financial support:* In 2011–12, 5 fellowships (averaging $5,179 per year), 1 research assistantship (averaging $3,515 per year) were awarded. Financial award application deadline: 4/15; financial award applicants required to submit FAFSA. *Unit head:* Dr. Michele Gerwick, Chairperson, 724-357-2557, E-mail: mgerwick@iup.edu. *Application contact:* Dr. Nashat Zuraikat, Graduate Coordinator, 724-357-3262, E-mail: zuraikat@iup.edu. Web site: http://www.iup.edu/rn-alliedhealth/programs/nursingphd/default.aspx.

Indiana University–Purdue University Fort Wayne, College of Health and Human Services, Department of Nursing, Fort Wayne, IN 46805-1499. Offers adult nursing practitioner (MS); nurse executive (MS); nursing administration (Certificate); nursing education (MS); women's health nurse practitioner (MS). Part-time programs available. *Faculty:* 10 full-time (all women). *Students:* 3 full-time (all women), 33 part-time (31 women); includes 3 minority (1 American Indian or Alaska Native, non-Hispanic/Latino; 1 Asian, non-Hispanic/Latino; 1 Hispanic/Latino). Average age 36. 13 applicants, 92% accepted, 10 enrolled. In 2011, 14 master's awarded. *Entrance requirements:* For master's, GRE Writing Test (if GPA below 3.0), BS in nursing, eligibility for Indiana RN license, minimum GPA of 3.0, essay, copy of resume, three references, undergraduate course work in research and statistics within last 5 years. Additional exam requirements/recommendations for international students: Required—TOEFL (minimum score 550 paper-based; 213 computer-based; 77 iBT); Recommended—TWE. *Application deadline:* For fall admission, 5/1 priority date for domestic students, 5/1 for international students; for spring admission, 11/15 priority date for domestic students. Applications are processed on a rolling basis. Application fee: $55 ($60 for international students). Electronic applications accepted. *Financial support:* In 2011–12, 11 teaching assistantships with partial tuition reimbursements (averaging $12,930 per year) were awarded; scholarships/grants also available. Support available to part-time students. Financial award application deadline: 3/1; financial award applicants required to submit FAFSA. *Faculty research:* Child psychiatric nursing. *Total annual research expenditures:* $296,680. *Unit head:* Dr. Carol Sternberger, Chair, 260-481-5798, Fax: 260-481-5767, E-mail: sternber@ipfw.edu. *Application contact:* Dr. Deborah Poling, Director of Graduate Program, 260-481-6276, Fax: 260-481-5767, E-mail: polingd@ipfw.edu. Web site: http://www.ipfw.edu/nursing/.

Indiana University–Purdue University Indianapolis, School of Nursing, Doctor of Nursing Practice Program, Indianapolis, IN 46202-2896. Offers DNP. Part-time programs available. Postbaccalaureate distance learning degree programs offered (minimal on-campus study). *Students:* 8 full-time (all women), 14 part-time (all women); includes 2 minority (both Black or African American, non-Hispanic/Latino), 1 international. Average age 48. 16 applicants, 100% accepted, 12 enrolled. *Degree requirements:* For doctorate, comprehensive exam, inquiry project: evidence-based practice implementation or intervention. *Entrance requirements:* For doctorate, background check. Additional exam requirements/recommendations for international students: Required—TOEFL, IELTS. *Application deadline:* For spring admission, 3/1 for domestic and international students. Application fee: $60. Electronic applications accepted. *Financial support:* In 2011–12, 13 teaching assistantships with partial tuition reimbursements (averaging $2,100 per year) were awarded; tuition waivers (partial) also available. Financial award application deadline: 5/1; financial award applicants required to submit FAFSA. *Unit head:* Dr. Mary Beth Riner, Coordinator, 317-274-4325, E-mail: mriner@iupui.edu. *Application contact:* Deborah Jean Grew, Graduate Advisor for Doctoral Programs, 317-274-2806, Fax: 317-274-2996, E-mail: dgrew@iupui.edu. Web site: http://nursing.iupui.edu/degrees/dnp/index.shtml.

Indiana University–Purdue University Indianapolis, School of Nursing, MSN Program in Nursing, Indianapolis, IN 46202-2896. Offers nursing administration (MSN); nursing education (MSN). *Students:* 2 full-time (both women), 39 part-time (37 women); includes 5 minority (2 Black or African American, non-Hispanic/Latino; 1 Asian, non-Hispanic/Latino; 2 Hispanic/Latino), 2 international. 50 applicants, 50% accepted, 9 enrolled. In 2011, 17 master's awarded. *Entrance requirements:* For master's, background check, statistics. *Unit head:* Associate Dean for Graduate Programs, 317-274-2806, E-mail: nursing@iupui.edu. *Application contact:* Janet Moon, Information Contact, 317-278-2205. Web site: http://nursing.iupui.edu/degrees/msn/index.shtml.

Indiana University–Purdue University Indianapolis, School of Nursing, PhD Program in Nursing Science, Indianapolis, IN 46202-2896. Offers PhD. Part-time programs available. Postbaccalaureate distance learning degree programs offered (minimal on-campus study). *Faculty:* 31 full-time (29 women). *Students:* 7 full-time (6 women), 32 part-time (31 women); includes 4 minority (all Black or African American, non-Hispanic/Latino), 4 international. Average age 45. 15 applicants, 53% accepted, 5 enrolled. In 2011, 10 doctorates awarded. *Degree requirements:* For doctorate, comprehensive exam, thesis/dissertation. *Entrance requirements:* For doctorate, GRE. Additional exam requirements/recommendations for international students: Required—TOEFL, IELTS. *Application deadline:* For fall admission, 8/15 for domestic and international students; for winter admission, 1/15 for domestic and international students. Application fee: $60. Electronic applications accepted. *Financial support:* In 2011–12, 4 fellowships with full tuition reimbursements (averaging $6,000 per year), 3 teaching assistantships with partial tuition reimbursements (averaging $2,100 per year) were awarded; Federal Work-Study, institutionally sponsored loans, scholarships/grants, traineeships, tuition waivers (partial), and unspecified assistantships also available. Support available to part-time students. Financial award application deadline: 5/1; financial award applicants required to submit FAFSA. *Unit head:* Dr. Patricia Ebright, Associate Dean for Graduate Programs, 317-274-2806, E-mail: prebrigh@iupui.edu. *Application contact:* Deborah Jean Grew, Graduate Advisor for Doctoral Programs, 317-274-2806, Fax: 317-274-2996, E-mail: dgrew@iupui.edu. Web site: http://nursing.iupui.edu/degrees/phd/index.shtml.

Indiana Wesleyan University, Graduate School, School of Nursing, Marion, IN 46953-4974. Offers community health nursing (MS); nursing (Post Master's Certificate); nursing administration (MS); nursing education (MS); primary care nursing (MS). *Accreditation:* AACN. Part-time programs available. Postbaccalaureate distance learning degree programs offered (minimal on-campus study). *Degree requirements:* For master's, capstone project or thesis. *Entrance requirements:* For master's, writing sample, RN license, 1 year of related experience, graduate statistics course. Additional exam requirements/recommendations for international students: Required—TOEFL. *Expenses:* Contact institution. *Faculty research:* Primary health care with international emphasis, international nursing.

Inter American University of Puerto Rico, Arecibo Campus, Program in Nursing, Arecibo, PR 00614-4050. Offers critical care nursing (MSN); surgical nursing (MSN). *Entrance requirements:* For master's, EXADEP or GRE General Test or MAT, 2 letters of recommendation, bachelor's degree in nursing, minimum GPA of 2.5 in last 60 credits, minimum 1 year nursing experience, nursing license.

Jacksonville State University, College of Graduate Studies and Continuing Education, College of Nursing, Jacksonville, AL 36265-1602. Offers MSN. *Accreditation:* AACN. Part-time and evening/weekend programs available. *Degree requirements:* For master's, comprehensive exam, thesis (for some programs). *Entrance requirements:* For master's, GRE General Test or MAT. Additional exam requirements/recommendations for international students: Required—TOEFL (minimum score 500 paper-based; 173 computer-based; 61 iBT). Electronic applications accepted. *Expenses:* Tuition, state resident: part-time $336 per hour. Tuition, nonresident: part-time $672 per hour. Part-time tuition and fees vary according to degree level.

Jacksonville University, School of Nursing, Jacksonville, FL 32211. Offers MSN, DNP. *Accreditation:* AACN. Part-time programs available. *Degree requirements:* For master's, thesis. *Entrance requirements:* For master's, GRE General Test, BS in nursing from an accredited program, course work in statistics within last 5 years, Florida nursing license. Additional exam requirements/recommendations for international students: Required—TOEFL (minimum score 550 paper-based). *Expenses:* Contact institution.

James Madison University, The Graduate School, College of Integrated Science and Technology, Department of Nursing, Harrisonburg, VA 22807. Offers MSN. *Accreditation:* AACN. *Faculty:* 6 full-time (all women). *Students:* 11 full-time (10 women), 50 part-time (41 women); includes 4 minority (1 Black or African American, non-Hispanic/Latino; 1 American Indian or Alaska Native, non-Hispanic/Latino; 2 Two or more races, non-Hispanic/Latino). Average age 27. In 2011, 15 master's awarded. *Entrance requirements:* For master's, GRE General Test. *Application deadline:* For fall admission, 4/1 priority date for domestic students; for spring admission, 4/1 priority date for domestic students. Application fee: $55. *Expenses:* Tuition, state resident: full-time $8016; part-time $334 per credit hour. Tuition, nonresident: full-time $22,656; part-time $944 per credit hour. *Financial support:* In 2011–12, 2 students received support. 2 graduate assistantships ($7382) available. Financial award application deadline: 3/1; financial award applicants required to submit FAFSA. *Unit head:* Julie Sanford, Academic Unit Head, 540-568-6314, E-mail: sanforjt@jmu.edu. *Application contact:* Dr. Patty Hale, Graduate Program Coordinator, 540-568-1700.

Jefferson College of Health Sciences, Program in Nursing, Roanoke, VA 24031-3186. Offers nursing education (MSN); nursing management (MSN). *Accreditation:* AACN. Part-time programs available. *Degree requirements:* For master's, project. *Entrance requirements:* For master's, MAT. Additional exam requirements/recommendations for international students: Required—TOEFL (minimum score 550 paper-based; 213 computer-based; 80 iBT). Electronic applications accepted. *Faculty research:* Nursing, teaching and learning techniques, cultural competence, spirituality and nursing.

The Johns Hopkins University, School of Nursing, Baltimore, MD 21218-2699. Offers MSN, DNP, PhD, Certificate, MSN/MBA, MSN/MPH. *Accreditation:* AACN; NLN (one or more programs are accredited). Part-time programs available. *Faculty:* 65 full-time (62 women), 2 part-time/adjunct (both women). *Students:* 92 full-time (87 women), 243 part-time (224 women); includes 103 minority (41 Black or African American, non-Hispanic/Latino; 1 American Indian or Alaska Native, non-Hispanic/Latino; 37 Asian, non-Hispanic/Latino; 16 Hispanic/Latino; 1 Native Hawaiian or other Pacific Islander, non-Hispanic/Latino; 7 Two or more races, non-Hispanic/Latino), 10 international. Average age 33. In 2011, 80 master's, 3 doctorates awarded. *Degree requirements:* For master's, thesis optional, portfolio or scholarly project; for doctorate, comprehensive exam, thesis/dissertation. *Entrance requirements:* For master's, minimum GPA of 3.0, BSN, RN license, goal statement, letters of recommendation; for doctorate, GRE (for PhD), minimum GPA of 3.0, BSN, RN license, goal statement, letters of recommendation; graded writing sample (for PhD), capstone project proposal (for DNP); for Certificate, letters of recommendation, goal statement, minimum GPA of 3.0, MSN, resume, RN license (for some certificates). Additional exam requirements/recommendations for international students: Required—TOEFL (minimum score 550 paper-based; 213 computer-based). *Application deadline:* For fall admission, 2/1 priority date for domestic students, 2/1 for international students; for winter admission, 7/1 priority date for domestic students, 7/1 for international students; for spring admission, 7/1 priority date for domestic students, 7/1 for international students. Applications are processed on a rolling basis. Application fee: $75. Electronic applications accepted. *Expenses:* Contact institution. *Financial support:* In 2011–12, 79 students received support, including 6 fellowships with partial tuition reimbursements available (averaging $23,272 per year); research assistantships with full tuition reimbursements available, teaching assistantships with full tuition reimbursements available, career-related internships or fieldwork, Federal Work-Study, scholarships/grants, traineeships, and tuition waivers (partial) also available. Support available to part-time students. Financial award application deadline: 3/1; financial award applicants required to submit FAFSA. *Faculty research:* Hypertension, violence, cardiovascular risk symptom management, symptom management, health disparities. *Unit head:* Dr. Martha N. Hill, Dean, 410-955-7544, Fax: 410-955-4890, E-mail: mnhill@son.jhmi.edu. *Application contact:* Mary O'Rourke, Director of Admissions and Student Services, 410-955-7548, Fax: 410-614-7086, E-mail: orourke@son.jhmi.edu. Web site: http://www.son.jhmi.edu/.

Kaplan University, Davenport Campus, School of Nursing, Davenport, IA 52807-2095. Offers nurse administrator (MS); nurse educator (MS). Part-time and evening/weekend programs available. Postbaccalaureate distance learning degree programs offered (no on-campus study). *Entrance requirements:* For master's, RN. Additional exam requirements/recommendations for international students: Required—TOEFL (minimum score 550 paper-based; 80 computer-based).

Kean University, College of Natural, Applied and Health Sciences, Program in Nursing, Union, NJ 07083. Offers clinical management (MSN), including transcultural focus; community health nursing (MSN); school nursing (MSN). *Accreditation:* NLN. *Faculty:* 9 full-time (all women). *Students:* 7 full-time (6 women), 95 part-time (86 women); includes 49 minority (40 Black or African American, non-Hispanic/Latino; 5 Asian, non-Hispanic/Latino; 3 Hispanic/Latino; 1 Native Hawaiian or other Pacific Islander, non-Hispanic/Latino). Average age 45. 38 applicants, 97% accepted, 27 enrolled. In 2011, 34 master's awarded. *Degree requirements:* For master's, thesis or alternative, clinical field experience. *Entrance requirements:* For master's, minimum GPA of 3.0; BS in nursing; RN license; 2 letters of recommendation; interview; 1 completed course of the following: basic health assessment and human growth and development across the life span; minimum B grade in prerequisite courses; transcripts. Additional exam requirements/recommendations for international students: Required—TOEFL (minimum score 79 computer-based). *Application deadline:* For fall admission, 6/1 for domestic and international students; for spring admission, 12/1 for domestic and international students. Applications are processed on a rolling basis. Application fee: $75 ($150 for international students). Electronic applications accepted. *Expenses:* Tuition, state resident: full-time $11,302; part-time $550 per credit. Tuition, nonresident: full-time

$15,318; part-time $674 per credit. *Required fees:* $2849; $130 per credit. Tuition and fees vary according to degree level. *Financial support:* In 2011–12, 1 research assistantship with full tuition reimbursement (averaging $3,263 per year) was awarded; unspecified assistantships also available. Financial award applicants required to submit FAFSA. *Unit head:* Dr. Minnie Campbell, Program Coordinator, 908-527-3396, E-mail: mcampbel@kean.edu. *Application contact:* Ann-Marie Kay, Assistant Director of Graduate Admissions, 908-737-5922, Fax: 908-737-5925, E-mail: akay@kean.edu. Web site: http://www.kean.edu/KU/School-of-Nursing.

Keiser University, Master of Science in Nursing Program, Fort Lauderdale, FL 33309. Offers MSN.

Kennesaw State University, College of Health and Human Services, Doctor of Nursing Science Program, Kennesaw, GA 30144-5591. Offers DNS. Part-time programs available. *Students:* 3 full-time (2 women), 7 part-time (all women). Average age 49. 7 applicants, 57% accepted, 4 enrolled. *Degree requirements:* For doctorate, thesis/dissertation. *Entrance requirements:* For doctorate, GRE, master's degree in nursing, RN licensure. Additional exam requirements/recommendations for international students: Required—TOEFL (minimum score 550 paper-based; 213 computer-based; 80 iBT), IELTS (minimum score 6). *Application deadline:* For fall admission, 3/1 for domestic and international students. Applications are processed on a rolling basis. Application fee: $60. Electronic applications accepted. *Expenses:* Tuition, state resident: full-time $3000; part-time $250 per semester hour. Tuition, nonresident: full-time $10,836; part-time $903 per semester hour. *Required fees:* $774 per semester. *Financial support:* In 2011–12, 2 research assistantships with full tuition reimbursements (averaging $4,000 per year) were awarded. Financial award application deadline: 4/1; financial award applicants required to submit FAFSA. *Unit head:* Dr. Tommie Nelms, Director, 678-797-2088, E-mail: tnelms1@kennesaw.edu. *Application contact:* Tamara Hutto, Admissions Counselor, 770-420-4377, Fax: 770-423-6885, E-mail: ksugrad@kennesaw.edu.

Kennesaw State University, College of Health and Human Services, Program in Primary Care Nurse Practitioner, Kennesaw, GA 30144-5591. Offers MSN. *Accreditation:* AACN. Part-time and evening/weekend programs available. *Students:* 75 full-time (64 women), 13 part-time (8 women); includes 36 minority (17 Black or African American, non-Hispanic/Latino; 7 Asian, non-Hispanic/Latino; 10 Hispanic/Latino; 2 Two or more races, non-Hispanic/Latino), 2 international. Average age 37. 91 applicants, 33% accepted, 25 enrolled. In 2011, 39 master's awarded. *Entrance requirements:* For master's, GRE General Test, minimum GPA of 2.5, RN license, 3 years of professional experience. Additional exam requirements/recommendations for international students: Required—TOEFL (minimum score 550 paper-based; 213 computer-based), IELTS (minimum score 6). *Application deadline:* For fall admission, 6/1 for domestic and international students. Application fee: $60. Electronic applications accepted. *Expenses:* Tuition, state resident: full-time $3000; part-time $250 per semester hour. Tuition, nonresident: full-time $10,836; part-time $903 per semester hour. *Required fees:* $774 per semester. *Financial support:* In 2011–12, 2 research assistantships with full tuition reimbursements (averaging $4,000 per year) were awarded; Federal Work-Study and unspecified assistantships also available. Support available to part-time students. Financial award application deadline: 6/15; financial award applicants required to submit FAFSA. *Unit head:* Dr. Marilyn King, Director, 770-423-6172, Fax: 770-423-6627, E-mail: mking71@kennesaw.edu. *Application contact:* Tamara Hutto, Admissions Counselor, 770-420-4377, Fax: 770-423-6885, E-mail: ksugrad@kennesaw.edu.

Kent State University, College of Nursing, Kent, OH 44242-0001. Offers acute care nurse practitioner (MSN); adult nurse practitioner (MSN); clinical nurse specialist (MSN); family nurse practitioner (MSN); geriatric nurse practitioner (MSN); health care management (MSN); nurse educator (MSN); nursing (PhD); nursing practice (DNP); pediatric nurse practitioner (MSN); psychiatric/mental health nurse practitioner (MSN); women's health nurse practitioner (MSN). PhD program offered jointly with The University of Akron. *Accreditation:* AACN. Part-time programs available. *Degree requirements:* For master's, thesis optional; for doctorate, comprehensive exam, thesis/dissertation. *Entrance requirements:* For master's, GRE (if undergraduate GPA less than 3.0), minimum GPA of 2.75; for doctorate, GRE, MSN. Additional exam requirements/recommendations for international students: Required—TOEFL. Electronic applications accepted. *Expenses:* Contact institution. *Faculty research:* Women and violence, methodological specialties, osteoporosis in women, new caregivers and the elderly.

Keuka College, Program in Nursing, Keuka Park, NY 14478-0098. Offers MS. *Accreditation:* AACN.

Lamar University, College of Graduate Studies, College of Arts and Sciences, Department of Nursing, Beaumont, TX 77710. Offers nursing administration (MSN); nursing education (MSN); MSN/MBA. *Accreditation:* NLN. Part-time and evening/weekend programs available. Postbaccalaureate distance learning degree programs offered. *Faculty:* 6 full-time (all women). *Students:* 5 full-time (all women), 29 part-time (27 women); includes 12 minority (11 Black or African American, non-Hispanic/Latino; 1 Hispanic/Latino). Average age 40. 18 applicants, 100% accepted, 10 enrolled. In 2011, 5 master's awarded. *Degree requirements:* For master's, comprehensive exam, practicum project presentation, evidence-based project. *Entrance requirements:* For master's, GRE General Test, MAT, criminal background check, RN license, NLN-accredited BSN, college course work in graduate statistics in past 5 years, letters of recommendation, minimum undergraduate GPA of 3.0. Additional exam requirements/recommendations for international students: Required—TOEFL. *Application deadline:* For fall admission, 8/1 priority date for domestic students; for spring admission, 12/1 priority date for domestic students. Applications are processed on a rolling basis. Application fee: $25 ($50 for international students). *Expenses:* Tuition, state resident: full-time $5430; part-time $272 per credit hour. Tuition, nonresident: full-time $11,540; part-time $577 per credit hour. *Required fees:* $1916. *Financial support:* In 2011–12, 3 students received support, including 2 teaching assistantships (averaging $24,000 per year); scholarships/grants and traineeships also available. Financial award application deadline: 4/1. *Faculty research:* Student retention, theory, caregiving, online course and research. *Unit head:* Dr. Nancy Blume, Director of Graduate Nursing Studies, 409-880-8820, Fax: 409-880-8698, E-mail: nancy.blume@lamar.edu. *Application contact:* Shelly R. Belk, Administrative Associate, 409-880-7720.

La Roche College, School of Graduate Studies and Adult Education, Program in Nursing, Pittsburgh, PA 15237-5898. Offers nursing education (MSN); nursing management (MSN). *Accreditation:* AANA/CANAEP; NLN. Part-time and evening/weekend programs available. Postbaccalaureate distance learning degree programs offered (minimal on-campus study). *Faculty:* 5 full-time (all women), 1 (woman) part-time/adjunct. *Students:* 8 full-time (6 women), 12 part-time (11 women), 2 international. Average age 41. 8 applicants, 63% accepted, 3 enrolled. In 2011, 4 master's awarded. *Degree requirements:* For master's, thesis optional, internship, practicum. *Entrance requirements:* For master's, GRE General Test, BSN, nursing license, work experience. Additional exam requirements/recommendations for international students: Recommended—TOEFL (minimum score 550 paper-based; 220 computer-based). *Application deadline:* For fall admission, 8/15 priority date for domestic students, 8/15 for international students; for spring admission, 12/15 priority date for domestic students, 12/15 for international students. Applications are processed on a rolling basis. Application fee: $50. Electronic applications accepted. *Expenses:* Contact institution. *Financial support:* Application deadline: 3/31; applicants required to submit FAFSA. *Faculty research:* Patient education, perception. *Unit head:* Dr. Kathleen Sullivan, Division Chair, 412-536-1173, Fax: 412-536-1175, E-mail: sullivk1@laroche.edu. *Application contact:* Hope Schiffgens, Director of Graduate Studies and Adult Education, 412-536-1266, Fax: 412-536-1283, E-mail: schombh1@laroche.edu.

La Salle University, School of Nursing and Health Sciences, Program in Nursing, Philadelphia, PA 19141-1199. Offers MSN, Certificate. *Accreditation:* AANA/CANAEP. Part-time programs available. Postbaccalaureate distance learning degree programs offered (minimal on-campus study). *Entrance requirements:* For master's, GRE or MAT, 1 year of professional work experience, BSN, Pennsylvania RN license. *Expenses:* Contact institution. *Faculty research:* Medication errors, wound care, metacognition, education of RN students.

Laurentian University, School of Graduate Studies and Research, Programme in Nursing, Sudbury, ON P3E 2C6, Canada. Offers M Sc N.

Lehman College of the City University of New York, Division of Natural and Social Sciences, Department of Nursing, Bronx, NY 10468-1589. Offers adult health nursing (MS); nursing of older adults (MS); parent-child nursing (MS); pediatric nurse practitioner (MS). *Accreditation:* AACN. Part-time and evening/weekend programs available. *Entrance requirements:* For master's, bachelor's degree in nursing, New York RN license.

Le Moyne College, Department of Nursing, Syracuse, NY 13214. Offers nursing administration (MS, CAS); nursing education (MS, CAS). *Accreditation:* AACN. Part-time and evening/weekend programs available. *Faculty:* 4 full-time (all women), 3 part-time/adjunct (all women). *Students:* 19 part-time (all women); includes 1 minority (Black or African American, non-Hispanic/Latino). Average age 45. 9 applicants, 89% accepted, 5 enrolled. In 2011, 8 master's awarded. *Degree requirements:* For master's, scholarly project. *Entrance requirements:* For master's, bachelor's degree, interview, minimum GPA of 3.0, New York RN license, 2 letters of recommendation, writing sample, transcripts. Additional exam requirements/recommendations for international students: Required—TOEFL (minimum score 550 paper-based; 213 computer-based; 79 iBT). *Application deadline:* For fall admission, 6/1 priority date for domestic students, 6/1 for international students; for spring admission, 11/1 priority date for domestic students, 11/1 for international students. Applications are processed on a rolling basis. Application fee: $50. *Expenses:* Contact institution. *Financial support:* In 2011–12, 5 students received support. Career-related internships or fieldwork, scholarships/grants, health care benefits, unspecified assistantships, and NFLP Federal Loan Program (Nurse Faculty Loan Program) available. Support available to part-time students. Financial award applicants required to submit FAFSA. *Faculty research:* Inter-profession education, eldercare, utilization of free healthcare services by the insured, health promotion education, innovative undergraduate nursing education models. *Unit head:* Dr. Susan B. Bastable, Chair and Professor, Department of Nursing, 315-445-5436, Fax: 315-445-6024, E-mail: bastabsb@lemoyne.edu. *Application contact:* Kristen P. Trapasso, Director of Graduate Admission, 315-445-4265, Fax: 315-445-6027, E-mail: trapaskp@lemoyne.edu. Web site: http://www.lemoyne.edu/nursing.

Lewis University, College of Nursing and Health Professions, Program in Nursing, Romeoville, IL 60446. Offers adult nurse practitioner (MSN); nursing administration (MSN); nursing education (MSN). *Accreditation:* AACN. Part-time and evening/weekend programs available. Postbaccalaureate distance learning degree programs offered (no on-campus study). *Students:* 11 full-time (all women), 237 part-time (232 women); includes 65 minority (42 Black or African American, non-Hispanic/Latino; 14 Asian, non-Hispanic/Latino; 9 Hispanic/Latino), 1 international. Average age 42. In 2011, 29 master's awarded. *Degree requirements:* For master's, clinical practicum. *Entrance requirements:* For master's, minimum undergraduate GPA of 3.0, degree in nursing, RN license, letter of recommendation, interview, resume or curriculum vitae. Additional exam requirements/recommendations for international students: Required—TOEFL (minimum score 550 paper-based; 213 computer-based; 80 iBT). *Application deadline:* For fall admission, 5/1 for international students; for spring admission, 11/15 for international students. Applications are processed on a rolling basis. Application fee: $40. Electronic applications accepted. *Financial support:* Federal Work-Study, scholarships/grants, tuition waivers (full and partial), and unspecified assistantships available. Financial award application deadline: 5/1; financial award applicants required to submit FAFSA. *Faculty research:* Cancer prevention, phenomenological methods, public policy analysis. *Total annual research expenditures:* $1,000. *Unit head:* 815-836-5610. *Application contact:* Nancy Wiksten, Adult Admission Counselor, 815-836-5628, Fax: 815-836-5578, E-mail: wikstena@lewisu.edu. Web site: http://www.lewisu.edu/.

Lewis University, College of Nursing and Health Professions and College of Business, Program in Nursing/Business, Romeoville, IL 60446. Offers MSN/MBA. Part-time and evening/weekend programs available. *Students:* 5 full-time (3 women), 30 part-time (28 women); includes 19 minority (10 Black or African American, non-Hispanic/Latino; 2 Asian, non-Hispanic/Latino; 7 Hispanic/Latino). Average age 38. *Entrance requirements:* Additional exam requirements/recommendations for international students: Required—TOEFL (minimum score 550 paper-based; 213 computer-based; 80 iBT). *Application deadline:* For fall admission, 4/2 priority date for domestic students, 5/1 for international students; for spring admission, 11/15 for international students. Applications are processed on a rolling basis. Electronic applications accepted. *Financial support:* Scholarships/grants, tuition waivers (full and partial), and unspecified assistantships available. Financial award application deadline: 5/1; financial award applicants required to submit FAFSA. *Faculty research:* Cancer prevention, phenomenological methods, public policy analysis. *Total annual research expenditures:* $1,000. *Unit head:* Dr. Linda Niedringhaus, Interim Director, 815-838-0500 Ext. 5878, E-mail: niedrili@lewisu.edu. *Application contact:* Nancy Wiksten, Adult Admission Counselor, 815-838-0500 Ext. 5628, Fax: 815-836-5578, E-mail: wikstena@lewisu.edu.

Liberty University, College of Arts and Sciences, Lynchburg, VA 24502. Offers counseling (MA); human services (MA); nursing (MSN); pastoral care and counseling (PhD); professional counseling (PhD). *Accreditation:* AACN. Part-time programs available. Postbaccalaureate distance learning degree programs offered (minimal on-campus study). *Students:* 2,550 full-time (2,026 women), 5,408 part-time (4,324 women); includes 2,079 minority (1,619 Black or African American, non-Hispanic/Latino; 24 American Indian or Alaska Native, non-Hispanic/Latino; 46 Asian, non-Hispanic/Latino; 231 Hispanic/Latino; 11 Native Hawaiian or other Pacific Islander, non-Hispanic/Latino; 148 Two or more races, non-Hispanic/Latino), 155 international. Average age 36. In 2011, 1,179 master's, 5 doctorates awarded. *Degree requirements:* For master's, comprehensive exam (for some programs); for doctorate, comprehensive exam, thesis/dissertation. *Entrance requirements:* For master's, GRE General Test (MSN), minimum undergraduate GPA of 3.0; for doctorate, GRE General Test, minimum master's GPA of 3.25. Additional exam requirements/recommendations for international students: Required—TOEFL (minimum score 600 paper-based; 250 computer-based; 100 iBT). *Application deadline:* For fall admission, 6/1 priority date for domestic students; for spring admission, 11/1 priority date for domestic students. Applications are processed on a rolling basis. Application fee: $50. Electronic applications accepted. *Financial support:* Teaching assistantships with tuition reimbursements and Federal Work-Study available. *Faculty research:* God concept and adult attachment, building marital

strength, image of God and gender, breastfeeding behavior among adolescent mothers, osteoporosis. *Unit head:* Dr. Ronald E. Hawkins, Dean, 434-592-4030, Fax: 434-522-0416, E-mail: rehawkin@liberty.edu. *Application contact:* Jay Bridge, Director of Graduate Admissions, 800-424-9595, Fax: 800-628-7977, E-mail: gradadmissions@liberty.edu.

Lincoln Memorial University, Caylor School of Nursing, Harrogate, TN 37752-1901. Offers family nurse practitioner (MSN); nurse anesthesia (MSN); psychiatric mental health nurse practitioner (MSN). *Accreditation:* AANA/CANAEP; NLN. Part-time programs available. *Entrance requirements:* For master's, GRE.

Loma Linda University, Department of Graduate Nursing, Loma Linda, CA 92350. Offers adult and aging family nursing (MS); growing family nursing (MS); nursing administration (MS). *Accreditation:* AACN; AANA/CANAEP. Part-time programs available. *Degree requirements:* For master's, thesis or alternative. *Entrance requirements:* For master's, GRE General Test, BSN, minimum GPA of 3.0, RN license. Additional exam requirements/recommendations for international students: Required—TOEFL (minimum score 550 paper-based; 213 computer-based). Electronic applications accepted.

Long Island University–Brooklyn Campus, School of Nursing, Brooklyn, NY 11201-8423. Offers MS, Certificate. *Accreditation:* AACN. *Entrance requirements:* For master's, New York RN license, 2 letters of recommendation. Additional exam requirements/recommendations for international students: Required—TOEFL (minimum score 500 paper-based; 173 computer-based). Electronic applications accepted.

Long Island University–C. W. Post Campus, School of Health Professions and Nursing, Department of Nursing, Brookville, NY 11548-1300. Offers clinical nurse specialist (MS); family nurse practitioner (MS, Certificate). *Accreditation:* AACN. Part-time and evening/weekend programs available. *Degree requirements:* For master's, thesis. *Entrance requirements:* For master's, minimum GPA of 3.0 in major, bachelor's degree in nursing, NYS registered nurse, interview. Electronic applications accepted. *Faculty research:* Lactation/breast cancer, early discharge in maternity.

Louisiana State University Health Sciences Center, School of Nursing, New Orleans, LA 70112-2223. Offers advanced public/community health nursing (MN); clinical nurse specialist (MN); nurse anesthesia (MN); nurse practitioner (MN); nursing (DNS). *Accreditation:* AACN; AANA/CANAEP (one or more programs are accredited). Part-time programs available. *Degree requirements:* For master's, thesis optional; for doctorate, thesis/dissertation. *Entrance requirements:* For master's, GRE General Test, MAT, minimum GPA of 3.0; for doctorate, GRE General Test, minimum GPA of 3.5. Additional exam requirements/recommendations for international students: Required—TOEFL. Electronic applications accepted. *Faculty research:* Advanced clinical practice, nursing education, health, social support, nursing administration.

Loyola University Chicago, Graduate School, Marcella Niehoff School of Nursing, Doctor of Nursing Practice Program, Maywood, IL 60153. Offers healthcare quality using education in safety and technology (DNP); informatics and outcomes (DNP); nursing practice (DNP). Evening/weekend programs available. Postbaccalaureate distance learning degree programs offered (minimal on-campus study). *Faculty:* 45 full-time (44 women). *Students:* 27 part-time (22 women); includes 4 minority (3 Black or African American, non-Hispanic/Latino; 1 Asian, non-Hispanic/Latino). Average age 46. 31 applicants, 45% accepted, 12 enrolled. *Degree requirements:* For doctorate, capstone project. *Entrance requirements:* For doctorate, BSN or MSN, minimum GPA of 3.25, Illinois nursing license, 3 letters of recommendation, 1000 hours experience and certification in area of specialty, curriculum vitae. Additional exam requirements/recommendations for international students: Required—TOEFL. *Expenses: Tuition:* Full-time $15,660; part-time $870 per credit hour. *Required fees:* $125 per semester. Tuition and fees vary according to course load and program. *Unit head:* Dr. Mary K. Walker, Dean, Marcella Niehoff School of Nursing, 708-216-5448, Fax: 708-216-9555, E-mail: mwalker@luc.edu. *Application contact:* Amy Weatherford, Enrollment Advisor, School of Nursing, 773-508-3249, Fax: 773-508-3241, E-mail: aweatherford@luc.edu. Web site: http://www.luc.edu/nursing/dnp/.

Loyola University Chicago, Graduate School, Marcella Niehoff School of Nursing, MSN General Nursing Program, Chicago, IL 60660. Offers MSN. *Students:* 5 full-time (all women), 11 part-time (10 women); includes 1 minority (Asian, non-Hispanic/Latino), 4 international. Average age 37. 9 applicants, 56% accepted, 5 enrolled. *Expenses: Tuition:* Full-time $15,660; part-time $870 per credit hour. *Required fees:* $125 per semester. Tuition and fees vary according to course load and program. *Unit head:* Enrollment Advisor, School of Nursing. *Application contact:* Amy Weatherford, Enrollment Advisor, 708-216-3751, E-mail: aweatherford@luc.edu. Web site: http://www.luc.edu/nursing/msn/.

Loyola University Chicago, Graduate School, Marcella Niehoff School of Nursing, PhD Program in Nursing, Maywood, IL 60153. Offers PhD. *Faculty:* 21 full-time (20 women). *Students:* 26 full-time (24 women), 9 part-time (8 women), 2 international. Average age 48. 10 applicants, 40% accepted, 2 enrolled. In 2011, 3 degrees awarded. *Median time to degree:* Of those who began their doctoral program in fall 2003, 100% received their degree in 8 years or less. *Degree requirements:* For doctorate, comprehensive exam, thesis/dissertation, research internship. *Entrance requirements:* For doctorate, GRE General Test, master's degree in nursing or related field, minimum GPA of 3.0, active nursing license, 3 letters of recommendation. Additional exam requirements/recommendations for international students: Required—TOEFL (minimum score 650 paper-based; 280 computer-based; 114 iBT) or IELTS. *Application deadline:* For fall admission, 7/1 for domestic and international students. Applications are processed on a rolling basis. Application fee: $0. *Expenses: Tuition:* Full-time $15,660; part-time $870 per credit hour. *Required fees:* $125 per semester. Tuition and fees vary according to course load and program. *Financial support:* In 2011–12, 3 students received support, including 3 research assistantships with full tuition reimbursements available (averaging $18,000 per year). Financial award application deadline: 5/1; financial award applicants required to submit FAFSA. *Faculty research:* Women's health, adolescent health and chronic illness, psychoneuroimmunology, grief and bereavement, nurse staffing and outcomes. *Unit head:* Dr. Lee Schmidt, Director, 708-216-3573, Fax: 708-216-9555, E-mail: lschm3@luc.edu. *Application contact:* Amy Weatherford, Enrollment Advisor, School of Nursing, 773-508-3249, Fax: 773-508-3241, E-mail: aweatherford@luc.edu.

Loyola University Chicago, Graduate School, Marcella Niehoff School of Nursing, Program in Emergency Nurse Practitioner, Chicago, IL 60660. Offers MSN. *Entrance requirements:* For master's, Illinois nursing license, 3 letters of recommendation, minimum nursing GPA of 3.0, 1000 hours experience before starting clinical. Application fee: $50. *Expenses: Tuition:* Full-time $15,660; part-time $870 per credit hour. *Required fees:* $125 per semester. Tuition and fees vary according to course load and program. *Financial support:* Traineeships available. *Unit head:* Dr. Vicki A. Keough, Associate Professor/Director, 708-216-3582, Fax: 708-216-9555, E-mail: vkeough@luc.edu. *Application contact:* Amy Weatherford, Enrollment Advisor, School of Nursing, 773-508-3249, Fax: 773-508-3241, E-mail: aweatherford@luc.edu. Web site: http://www.luc.edu/media/lucedu/nursing/graduate/FNP-ENP.pdf.

Loyola University New Orleans, College of Social Sciences, School of Nursing, New Orleans, LA 70118-6195. Offers adult nurse practitioner (MSN); family nurse practitioner (MSN); health care systems management (MSN); nursing (MSN, DNP). *Accreditation:*

NLN. Part-time and evening/weekend programs available. Postbaccalaureate distance learning degree programs offered. *Students:* 108 full-time (99 women), 428 part-time (385 women); includes 151 minority (110 Black or African American, non-Hispanic/Latino; 5 American Indian or Alaska Native, non-Hispanic/Latino; 14 Asian, non-Hispanic/Latino; 20 Hispanic/Latino; 2 Native Hawaiian or other Pacific Islander, non-Hispanic/Latino). Average age 46. 213 applicants, 91% accepted, 153 enrolled. In 2011, 241 master's awarded. *Degree requirements:* For doctorate, capstone project. *Entrance requirements:* For master's, BSN, Louisiana nursing license, 1 year of work experience in clinical nursing, minimum undergraduate GPA of 2.8, interview, resume. Additional exam requirements/recommendations for international students: Required—TOEFL (minimum score 550 paper-based; 213 computer-based). *Application deadline:* For fall admission, 8/1 priority date for domestic students, 8/1 for international students; for winter admission, 12/15 priority date for domestic students, 12/15 for international students; for spring admission, 5/15 priority date for domestic students, 5/15 for international students. Applications are processed on a rolling basis. Application fee: $20. Electronic applications accepted. *Financial support:* Traineeships and Incumbent Workers Training Program grants available. Financial award application deadline: 5/1; financial award applicants required to submit FAFSA. *Faculty research:* Increasing compliance with treatment, patient satisfaction with care provided by nurse practitioners. *Unit head:* Dr. Ann H. Cary, Director, 800-488-6257, Fax: 504-865-3254, E-mail: nursing@loyno.edu. *Application contact:* Deborah Smith, Assistant to the Director, 504-865-2823, Fax: 504-865-3254, E-mail: dhsmith@loyno.edu. Web site: http://css.loyno.edu/nursing.

Lynchburg College, Graduate Studies, School of Health Sciences and Human Performance, MS Program in Nursing, Lynchburg, VA 24501-3199. Offers clinical nurse leader (MS); nursing education (MS). *Accreditation:* AACN. Part-time and evening/weekend programs available. Postbaccalaureate distance learning degree programs offered (minimal on-campus study). *Faculty:* 3 full-time (all women), 1 (woman) part-time/adjunct. *Students:* 1 (woman) full-time, 6 part-time (all women), 1 international. Average age 39. In 2011, 4 master's awarded. *Degree requirements:* For master's, practicum. *Entrance requirements:* For master's, GRE or 2 years professional nursing experience, official transcripts, personal essay, 3 letters of recommendation, current unrestricted registered nurse license in Virginia. Additional exam requirements/recommendations for international students: Required—TOEFL (minimum score 550 paper-based; 213 computer-based; 79 iBT), IELTS (minimum score 6.5). *Application deadline:* For fall admission, 7/31 for domestic students, 6/1 for international students; for spring admission, 11/30 for domestic students, 10/15 for international students. Applications are processed on a rolling basis. Application fee: $30. Electronic applications accepted. Application fee is waived when completed online. *Expenses: Tuition:* Full-time $7740; part-time $430 per credit hour. *Financial support:* Fellowships, Federal Work-Study, scholarships/grants, health care benefits, and unspecified assistantships available. Support available to part-time students. Financial award application deadline: 7/31; financial award applicants required to submit FAFSA. *Unit head:* Dr. Jean St. Clair, Associate Professor/Director of MSN Program, 434-544-8740, E-mail: stclair.j@lynchburg.edu. *Application contact:* Anne Pingstock, Executive Assistant, Graduate Studies, 434-544-8383, E-mail: gradstudies@lynchburg.edu. Web site: http://www.lynchburg.edu/msn.xml.

Madonna University, Program in Nursing, Livonia, MI 48150-1173. Offers adult health: chronic health conditions (MSN); adult nurse practitioner (MSN); nursing administration (MSN); MSN/MSBA. *Accreditation:* AACN. Part-time programs available. *Degree requirements:* For master's, thesis or alternative. *Entrance requirements:* For master's, GRE General Test, Michigan nursing license. Electronic applications accepted. *Faculty research:* Coping, caring.

Malone University, Graduate Program in Nursing, Canton, OH 44709. Offers clinical nurse specialist (MSN); family nurse practitioner (MSN). *Accreditation:* AACN. Part-time and evening/weekend programs available. *Faculty:* 8 full-time (all women), 19 part-time/adjunct (17 women). *Students:* 62 part-time (52 women); includes 3 minority (1 Black or African American, non-Hispanic/Latino; 1 American Indian or Alaska Native, non-Hispanic/Latino; 1 Hispanic/Latino). Average age 36. 77 applicants, 57% accepted, 27 enrolled. In 2011, 22 master's awarded. *Degree requirements:* For master's, thesis. *Entrance requirements:* For master's, minimum GPA of 3.0 from BSN program, interview, Ohio RN license. Additional exam requirements/recommendations for international students: Required—TOEFL (minimum score 550 paper-based; 213 computer-based; 79 iBT). *Application deadline:* Applications are processed on a rolling basis. *Expenses:* Contact institution. *Financial support:* Tuition waivers (partial) available. Support available to part-time students. Financial award application deadline: 6/30. *Faculty research:* Home heath care and geriatrics, community settings, culture, Hispanics, TB, geriatrics, Neuman Systems Model, nursing education. *Unit head:* Dr. Kathleen M. Flaherty, Director, 330-471-8330, Fax: 330-471-8607, E-mail: kflaherty@malone.edu. *Application contact:* Mona McAuliffe, Recruiter/Adviser, 330-471-8623, Fax: 330-471-8343, E-mail: mmcauliffe@malone.edu. Web site: http://www.malone.edu/admissions/graduate/nursing/.

Mansfield University of Pennsylvania, Graduate Studies, Program in Nursing, Mansfield, PA 16933. Offers MSN. *Accreditation:* NLN. Part-time and evening/weekend programs available. Postbaccalaureate distance learning degree programs offered. *Degree requirements:* For master's, comprehensive exam, thesis optional. *Entrance requirements:* For master's, minimum GPA of 3.0. Additional exam requirements/recommendations for international students: Required—TOEFL (minimum score 550 paper-based; 220 computer-based). Electronic applications accepted. *Expenses:* Tuition, state resident: full-time $7488; part-time $416 per credit. Tuition, nonresident: full-time $11,232; part-time $624 per credit. *Faculty research:* Women's health, gyniatrics, art therapy, nursing empowerment.

Marian University, School of Nursing, Fond du Lac, WI 54935-4699. Offers adult nurse practitioner (MSN); nurse educator (MSN). *Accreditation:* AACN. Part-time and evening/weekend programs available. *Faculty:* 6 full-time (all women), 10 part-time/adjunct (9 women). *Students:* 58 full-time (52 women), 33 part-time (32 women); includes 5 minority (2 Black or African American, non-Hispanic/Latino; 2 Asian, non-Hispanic/Latino; 1 Hispanic/Latino). Average age 36. 20 applicants, 90% accepted, 18 enrolled. In 2011, 25 master's awarded. *Degree requirements:* For master's, thesis, 675 clinical practicum hours. *Entrance requirements:* For master's, 3 letters of professional recommendation; undergraduate work in nursing research, statistics, health assessment. Additional exam requirements/recommendations for international students: Required—TOEFL (minimum score 525 paper-based; 193 computer-based; 70 iBT). *Application deadline:* Applications are processed on a rolling basis. Application fee: $50. Electronic applications accepted. *Expenses:* Contact institution. *Financial support:* In 2011–12, 3 students received support. Institutionally sponsored loans and scholarships/grants available. Support available to part-time students. Financial award application deadline: 3/1; financial award applicants required to submit FAFSA. *Unit head:* Dr. Julie Luetschwager, Dean, 920-923-8094, Fax: 920-923-8770, E-mail: jaluetschwager25@marianuniversity.edu. *Application contact:* Dr. Nancy L. Stuever, Director, 920-923-8597, Fax: 920-923-8770, E-mail: nstuever44@marianuniversity.edu.

Marquette University, Graduate School, College of Nursing, Milwaukee, WI 53201-1881. Offers acute care nurse practitioner (Certificate); adult clinical nurse specialist

(Certificate); adult nurse practitioner (Certificate); advanced practice nursing (MSN, DNP), including acute care, adults, neonatal nurse practitioner (MSN), nurse midwifery (DNP), nurse-midwifery (MSN), older adults, pediatrics acute care (DNP, PhD), pediatrics primary care; clinical nurse leader (MSN); gerontologic clinical nurse specialist (Certificate); gerontologic nurse practitioner (Certificate); health care systems leadership (MSN, DNP); nurse-midwifery (Certificate); nursing (PhD), including pediatrics acute care (DNP, PhD); pediatrics acute care (Certificate); pediatrics primary care (Certificate). *Accreditation:* AACN. *Faculty:* 32 full-time (30 women), 47 part-time/adjunct (all women). *Students:* 93 full-time (88 women), 244 part-time (220 women); includes 31 minority (9 Black or African American, non-Hispanic/Latino; 7 Asian, non-Hispanic/Latino; 8 Hispanic/Latino; 7 Two or more races, non-Hispanic/Latino), 1 international. Average age 30. 282 applicants, 57% accepted, 98 enrolled. In 2011, 76 master's, 8 doctorates, 7 other advanced degrees awarded. Terminal master's awarded for partial completion of doctoral program. *Degree requirements:* For master's, comprehensive exam, thesis or alternative. *Entrance requirements:* For master's, GRE General Test, BSN, Wisconsin RN license, official transcripts from all current and previous colleges/universities except Marquette, three completed recommendation forms, resume, written statement of professional goals; for doctorate, GRE General Test, official transcripts from all current and previous colleges/universities except Marquette, three letters of recommendation, resume, written statement of professional goals, sample of scholarly writing. Additional exam requirements/recommendations for international students: Required—TOEFL (minimum score 530 paper-based; 78 computer-based). *Application deadline:* For fall admission, 2/15 for domestic and international students. Application fee: $50. Electronic applications accepted. *Expenses: Tuition:* Full-time $17,010; part-time $945 per credit hour. Tuition and fees vary according to program. *Financial support:* In 2011–12, 41 students received support, including 1 fellowship with partial tuition reimbursement available (averaging $17,500 per year), 2 research assistantships with full tuition reimbursements available (averaging $13,285 per year), 8 teaching assistantships with full tuition reimbursements available (averaging $13,912 per year); career-related internships or fieldwork, Federal Work-Study, scholarships/grants, health care benefits, tuition waivers (partial), and unspecified assistantships also available. Support available to part-time students. Financial award application deadline: 2/15. *Faculty research:* Psychosocial adjustment to chronic illness, gerontology, reminiscence, health policy: uninsured and access, hospital care delivery systems. *Total annual research expenditures:* $312,575. *Unit head:* Dr. Margaret Callahan, Dean, 414-288-3800, Fax: 414-288-1578. *Application contact:* Karen Nest, Graduate Program Coordinator, 414-288-3810, Fax: 414-288-1578. Web site: http://www.marquette.edu/nursing/academicprograms-graduate.shtml.

Marshall University, Academic Affairs Division, College of Health Professions, Department of Nursing, Huntington, WV 25755. Offers MSN. *Faculty:* 8 full-time (7 women). *Students:* 15 full-time (13 women), 165 part-time (143 women); includes 7 minority (4 Black or African American, non-Hispanic/Latino; 2 Asian, non-Hispanic/Latino; 1 Hispanic/Latino), 1 international. Average age 35. In 2011, 42 master's awarded. *Entrance requirements:* For master's, GRE General Test. Application fee: $40. *Unit head:* Dr. Diana Stotts, Associate Dean, 304-696-2623, E-mail: stotts@marshall.edu. *Application contact:* Information Contact, 304-746-1900, Fax: 304-746-1902, E-mail: services@marshall.edu.

Marymount University, School of Health Professions, Program in Nursing, Arlington, VA 22207-4299. Offers family nurse practitioner (MSN, Certificate); nursing (DNP); nursing education (MSN, Certificate); RN to MSN (MSN). *Accreditation:* AACN. Part-time and evening/weekend programs available. *Faculty:* 8 full-time (all women), 3 part-time/adjunct (2 women). *Students:* 13 full-time (12 women), 65 part-time (62 women); includes 32 minority (19 Black or African American, non-Hispanic/Latino; 2 American Indian or Alaska Native, non-Hispanic/Latino; 8 Asian, non-Hispanic/Latino; 3 Hispanic/Latino), 4 international. Average age 40. 51 applicants, 57% accepted, 21 enrolled. In 2011, 26 master's, 2 other advanced degrees awarded. *Degree requirements:* For master's, comprehensive exam; for doctorate, thesis/dissertation or alternative. *Entrance requirements:* For master's, 2 letters of recommendation, interview, resume, RN license, personal statement; for doctorate, 2 letters of recommendation, interview, resume, RN license, minimum MSN GPA of 3.5 or BSN 3.3; for Certificate, interview, master's degree in nursing. Additional exam requirements/recommendations for international students: Required—TOEFL (minimum score 600 paper-based; 250 computer-based; 96 iBT), IELTS (minimum score 6.5). *Application deadline:* For fall admission, 4/1 for domestic students, 7/1 for international students; for spring admission, 9/15 for international students. Application fee: $40. Electronic applications accepted. *Expenses: Tuition:* Part-time $770 per credit hour. *Required fees:* $8 per credit hour. One-time fee: $180 full-time. *Financial support:* In 2011–12, 1 student received support. Research assistantships with partial tuition reimbursements available, career-related internships or fieldwork, Federal Work-Study, scholarships/grants, and unspecified assistantships available. Support available to part-time students. Financial award applicants required to submit FAFSA. *Unit head:* Dr. Susan Bidwell, Chair, 703-284-1593, Fax: 703-284-3819, E-mail: susan.bidwell@marymount.edu. *Application contact:* Francesca Reed, Director, Graduate Admissions, 703-284-5901, Fax: 703-527-3815, E-mail: grad.admissions@marymount.edu. Web site: http://www.marymount.edu/academics/programs/nursingDNP.

Maryville University of Saint Louis, School of Health Professions, Nursing Program, St. Louis, MO 63141-7299. Offers accelerated RN to MSN (MSN); adult nurse practitioner (MSN); advanced practice nursing (DNP); family nurse practitioner (MSN); geriatric nurse practitioner (MSN); nursing education (MSN). *Accreditation:* AACN. Postbaccalaureate distance learning degree programs offered. *Students:* 16 full-time (14 women), 136 part-time (127 women); includes 9 minority (5 Black or African American, non-Hispanic/Latino; 3 Asian, non-Hispanic/Latino; 1 Two or more races, non-Hispanic/Latino). Average age 35. In 2011, 21 master's awarded. *Degree requirements:* For master's, practicum. *Entrance requirements:* For master's, BSN, current licensure, minimum GPA of 3.0, 3 letters of recommendation, curriculum vitae. Additional exam requirements/recommendations for international students: Required—TOEFL (minimum score 550 paper-based). *Application deadline:* Applications are processed on a rolling basis. Application fee: $40 ($60 for international students). Electronic applications accepted. *Expenses: Tuition:* Full-time $21,922; part-time $675 per credit hour. *Required fees:* $233.75 per semester. *Financial support:* Federal Work-Study and campus employment available. Support available to part-time students. Financial award application deadline: 3/1; financial award applicants required to submit FAFSA. *Unit head:* Dr. Elizabeth Buck, Director, 314-529-9453, Fax: 314-529-9139, E-mail: ebuck@maryville.edu. *Application contact:* Dr. Donna Payne, Vice President, Adult and Continuing Education, 314-529-9676, Fax: 314-529-9927, E-mail: dpayne@maryville.edu. Web site: http://www.maryville.edu/academics-hp-nursing.

Massachusetts College of Pharmacy and Health Sciences, Graduate Studies, Program in Nursing, Boston, MA 02115-5896. Offers MS. Part-time programs available. Postbaccalaureate distance learning degree programs offered (minimal on-campus study). *Students:* 3 full-time (1 woman), 48 part-time (44 women); includes 7 minority (3 Black or African American, non-Hispanic/Latino; 4 Asian, non-Hispanic/Latino). Average age 33. 13 applicants, 92% accepted, 9 enrolled. *Entrance requirements:* For master's, BSN. Additional exam requirements/recommendations for international students: Required—TOEFL (minimum score 550 paper-based; 213 computer-based; 79 iBT). *Application deadline:* Applications are processed on a rolling basis. Electronic applications accepted. *Expenses: Tuition:* Full-time $30,200; part-time $945 per credit hour. *Unit head:* Dr. Carol Eliadi, Assistant Dean/Chief Nurse Administrator, School of Nursing, 508-373-5680, E-mail: carol.eliadi@mcphs.edu. *Application contact:* Bryan Witham, Director of Admission, Worcester/Manchester, 508-373-5623, E-mail: bryan.witham@mcphs.edu.

McGill University, Faculty of Graduate and Postdoctoral Studies, Faculty of Medicine, School of Nursing, Montréal, QC H3A 2T5, Canada. Offers nurse practitioner (Graduate Diploma); nursing (M Sc A, PhD). PhD offered jointly with Université du Québec à Montréal.

McKendree University, Graduate Programs, Master of Science in Nursing Program, Lebanon, IL 62254-1299. Offers nursing education (MSN); nursing management/administration (MSN). *Accreditation:* AACN. Part-time and evening/weekend programs available. Postbaccalaureate distance learning degree programs offered (no on-campus study). *Degree requirements:* For master's, research project or thesis. *Entrance requirements:* For master's, resume, references, valid Professional Registered Nurse license. Additional exam requirements/recommendations for international students: Required—TOEFL. Electronic applications accepted.

McMaster University, Faculty of Health Sciences and School of Graduate Studies, Program in Nursing (course-based), Hamilton, ON L8S 4M2, Canada. Offers M Sc. *Degree requirements:* For master's, scholarly paper. *Entrance requirements:* For master's, 4 year honors BSCN, minimum B+ average in last 60 units. Additional exam requirements/recommendations for international students: Required—TOEFL (minimum score 580 paper-based; 237 computer-based; 92 iBT).

McMaster University, Faculty of Health Sciences and School of Graduate Studies, Program in Nursing (thesis), Hamilton, ON L8S 4M2, Canada. Offers M Sc, PhD. *Degree requirements:* For master's, thesis; for doctorate, comprehensive exam, thesis/dissertation. *Entrance requirements:* For master's, honors B Sc N, B+ average in last 60 units; for doctorate, M Sc, minimum B+ average. Additional exam requirements/recommendations for international students: Required—TOEFL (minimum score 580 paper-based; 237 computer-based; 92 iBT).

McNeese State University, Doré School of Graduate Studies, College of Nursing, Lake Charles, LA 70609. Offers clinical nurse specialist (MSN); nurse educator (MSN); nurse practitioner (MSN); nursing leadership and administration (MSN). Program offered jointly with Southeastern Louisiana University and Southern University and Agricultural and Mechanical College. *Accreditation:* AACN. *Faculty:* 4 full-time (all women), 3 part-time/adjunct (2 women). *Students:* 10 full-time (9 women), 94 part-time (79 women); includes 21 minority (15 Black or African American, non-Hispanic/Latino; 1 Asian, non-Hispanic/Latino; 4 Hispanic/Latino; 1 Two or more races, non-Hispanic/Latino). In 2011, 25 master's awarded. *Degree requirements:* For master's, comprehensive exam. *Entrance requirements:* For master's, GRE, eligibility for unencumbered licensure as RN in Louisiana. *Application deadline:* For fall admission, 5/15 priority date for domestic students, 5/15 for international students; for spring admission, 10/15 priority date for domestic students, 10/15 for international students. Applications are processed on a rolling basis. Application fee: $20 ($30 for international students). *Expenses:* Tuition, state resident: part-time $519 per credit hour. Tuition and fees vary according to course load. *Financial support:* Application deadline: 5/1. *Unit head:* Dr. Peggy L. Wolfe, Dean, 337-475-5820, Fax: 337-475-5924, E-mail: pwolfe@mcneese.edu. *Application contact:* Valarie Waldmeier, Coordinator, 337-475-5285, Fax: 337-475-5702, E-mail: vwaldmeier@mcneese.edu.

Medical University of South Carolina, College of Nursing, Doctor of Nursing Practice Program, Charleston, SC 29425. Offers advanced practice nursing (DNP). Part-time programs available. Postbaccalaureate distance learning degree programs offered (minimal on-campus study). *Faculty:* 10 full-time (all women), 3 part-time/adjunct (2 women). *Students:* 114 full-time (107 women), 37 part-time (33 women); includes 26 minority (16 Black or African American, non-Hispanic/Latino; 2 American Indian or Alaska Native, non-Hispanic/Latino; 4 Asian, non-Hispanic/Latino; 4 Hispanic/Latino). Average age 33. 34 applicants, 74% accepted, 17 enrolled. *Entrance requirements:* For doctorate, BSN or MSN, minimum GPA of 3.0, course work in statistics, RN license, 3 references, interview (if requested). Additional exam requirements/recommendations for international students: Required—TOEFL (minimum score 600 paper-based; 250 computer-based). *Application deadline:* For fall admission, 2/1 priority date for domestic students, 2/1 for international students. Application fee: $85. Electronic applications accepted. *Financial support:* Federal Work-Study, scholarships/grants, and traineeships available. Support available to part-time students. Financial award applicants required to submit FAFSA. *Faculty research:* Primary and palliative care, use of PDAs. *Unit head:* Dr. Robin L. Bissinger, Director of Graduate Programs, 843-792-0531, Fax: 843-792-9258, E-mail: bissinrl@musc.edu. *Application contact:* Carolyn F. Page, Director, Student Services, 843-792-3844, Fax: 843-792-5395, E-mail: pagecf@musc.edu. Web site: http://www.musc.edu/nursing/academics/DNP.

Medical University of South Carolina, College of Nursing, PhD in Nursing Program, Charleston, SC 29425. Offers PhD. *Accreditation:* AACN. Part-time programs available. Postbaccalaureate distance learning degree programs offered (minimal on-campus study). *Faculty:* 11 full-time (all women), 2 part-time/adjunct (1 woman). *Students:* 18 full-time (all women), 34 part-time (32 women); includes 5 minority (1 Black or African American, non-Hispanic/Latino; 1 American Indian or Alaska Native, non-Hispanic/Latino; 1 Asian, non-Hispanic/Latino; 2 Hispanic/Latino). Average age 45. 19 applicants, 84% accepted, 15 enrolled. In 2011, 3 doctorates awarded. *Degree requirements:* For doctorate, comprehensive exam, thesis/dissertation, mentored teaching and research seminar. *Entrance requirements:* For doctorate, interview, minimum GPA of 3.5, BSN or MSN, RN license, curriculum vitae, essay, three references. Additional exam requirements/recommendations for international students: Required—TOEFL (minimum score 600 paper-based; 250 computer-based). *Application deadline:* For fall admission, 2/1 priority date for domestic students, 2/1 for international students. Application fee: $85. Electronic applications accepted. *Financial support:* Federal Work-Study and scholarships/grants available. Support available to part-time students. Financial award application deadline: 3/10; financial award applicants required to submit FAFSA. *Faculty research:* Health disparities, community partnerships, ethics, skin temperature in venous disease, spinal cord injury, smoking cessation. *Unit head:* Dr. Gail A. Gilden, Director, 843-792-3815, Fax: 843-792-9258, E-mail: barbosag@musc.edu. *Application contact:* Yolanda M. Long, Administrative Coordinator, 843-792-3815, Fax: 843-792-9258, E-mail: morrisym@musc.edu. Web site: http://www.musc.edu/nursing/academics/phd/index.htm.

Memorial University of Newfoundland, School of Graduate Studies, School of Nursing, St. John's, NL A1C 5S7, Canada. Offers MN, PMD. Part-time programs available. *Degree requirements:* For master's, thesis optional; for PMD, clinical placement. *Entrance requirements:* For master's, bachelor's degree in nursing, 1 year experience in nursing practice, practicing license; for PMD, 2 years clinical nursing experience, practicing license (Canada) or proof of registration as a practicing nurse (international), letter from a health care agency guaranteeing clinical placement. Electronic applications accepted. *Faculty research:* Women's health, infant feeding practices, nursing management, care of the elderly, children's health.

Mercer University, Graduate Studies, Cecil B. Day Campus, Georgia Baptist College of Nursing, Macon, GA 31207-0003. Offers adult critical care (MSN); family nurse practitioner (MSN); nurse education (MSN, Certificate); nursing (MSN, PhD); nursing practice (DNP). *Accreditation:* AACN. Part-time programs available. *Faculty:* 13 full-time (all women), 1 (woman) part-time/adjunct. *Students:* 50 full-time (47 women), 24 part-time (23 women); includes 31 minority (27 Black or African American, non-Hispanic/Latino; 2 Asian, non-Hispanic/Latino; 2 Hispanic/Latino). Average age 40. In 2011, 7 master's awarded. *Degree requirements:* For master's, thesis or alternative; for doctorate, comprehensive exam, thesis/dissertation. *Entrance requirements:* For master's, MAT or GRE, bachelor's degree from an accredited nursing program, registered GA nursing license (unencumbered); for doctorate, GRE, master's degree from accredited nursing program, RN licensure. Additional exam requirements/recommendations for international students: Required—TOEFL (minimum score 80 iBT). *Application deadline:* For fall admission, 6/1 for domestic students, 4/1 for international students; for winter admission, 11/1 for domestic students, 9/1 for international students; for spring admission, 4/1 for domestic students, 2/1 for international students. Applications are processed on a rolling basis. Application fee: $50. *Expenses:* Contact institution. *Financial support:* Institutionally sponsored loans, scholarships/grants, and traineeships available. Support available to part-time students. Financial award application deadline: 5/1; financial award applicants required to submit FAFSA. *Faculty research:* Osteoporosis, honor system, women and alcoholism, nursing assessment measures. *Unit head:* Dr. Linda Streit, Dean/Professor, 678-547-6793, Fax: 678-547-6796, E-mail: gunby_ss@mercer.edu. *Application contact:* Lynn Vines, Director of Admissions, 678-547-6700, Fax: 678-547-6794, E-mail: vines_ml@mercer.edu. Web site: http://www.mercer.edu/nursing.

Mercy College, School of Health and Natural Sciences, Programs in Nursing, Dobbs Ferry, NY 10522-1189. Offers nursing administration (MS, Certificate); nursing education (MS, Certificate). *Accreditation:* AACN. Part-time and evening/weekend programs available. Postbaccalaureate distance learning degree programs offered (no on-campus study). *Degree requirements:* For master's, written comprehensive exam or the production of a comprehensive project. *Entrance requirements:* For master's, bachelor's degree, two letters of reference, interview/assessment, RN registration in the U.S. Additional exam requirements/recommendations for international students: Required—TOEFL (minimum score 600 paper-based; 250 computer-based; 100 iBT), IELTS (minimum score 8). Electronic applications accepted.

Metropolitan State University, College of Health, Community and Professional Studies, St. Paul, MN 55106-5000. Offers advanced dental therapy (MS); leadership and management (MSN); nursing (DNP); psychology (MA). *Accreditation:* AACN. Part-time programs available. *Students:* 26 full-time (24 women), 160 part-time (158 women); includes 20 minority (7 Black or African American, non-Hispanic/Latino; 2 American Indian or Alaska Native, non-Hispanic/Latino; 2 Asian, non-Hispanic/Latino; 2 Hispanic/Latino; 7 Two or more races, non-Hispanic/Latino), 7 international. Average age 36. *Degree requirements:* For master's, thesis or alternative; for doctorate, thesis/dissertation or alternative. *Entrance requirements:* For master's, GRE General Test, minimum GPA of 3.0, RN license, BS/BAN; for doctorate, minimum GPA of 3.0; RN license, MSN. Additional exam requirements/recommendations for international students: Required—TOEFL (minimum score 550 paper-based; 213 computer-based). *Application deadline:* For fall admission, 1/15 for domestic students; for winter admission, 1/15 for international students. Application fee: $20. *Expenses:* Tuition, state resident: full-time $5799.06; part-time $322.17 per credit. Tuition, nonresident: full-time $11,411; part-time $633.92 per credit. Tuition and fees vary according to degree level, program and reciprocity agreements. *Financial support:* Fellowships, career-related internships or fieldwork, Federal Work-Study, institutionally sponsored loans, and traineeships available. Financial award applicants required to submit FAFSA. *Faculty research:* Women's health, gerontology. *Unit head:* Ann Leja, Interim Dean, 651-793-1402, Fax: 651-793-1382, E-mail: ann.leja@metrostate.edu. *Application contact:* Lynda Zimmerman, Academic Advisor, 651-793-1378, Fax: 651-793-1382, E-mail: lynda.zimmerman@metrostate.edu. Web site: http://www.metrostate.edu/cnhs/.

MGH Institute of Health Professions, School of Nursing, Boston, MA 02129. Offers advanced practice nursing (MSN); gerontological nursing (MSN); nursing (DNP); pediatric nursing (MSN); psychiatric nursing (MSN); teaching and learning for health care education (Certificate); women's health nursing (MSN). *Accreditation:* AACN; NLN (one or more programs are accredited). *Faculty:* 41 full-time (36 women), 14 part-time/adjunct (13 women). *Students:* 418 full-time (365 women), 72 part-time (63 women); includes 51 minority (20 Black or African American, non-Hispanic/Latino; 1 American Indian or Alaska Native, non-Hispanic/Latino; 24 Asian, non-Hispanic/Latino; 5 Hispanic/Latino; 1 Native Hawaiian or other Pacific Islander, non-Hispanic/Latino). Average age 32. 1,041 applicants, 36% accepted, 148 enrolled. In 2011, 85 master's, 12 doctorates, 98 other advanced degrees awarded. *Degree requirements:* For master's, thesis or alternative. *Entrance requirements:* For master's, GRE General Test, bachelor's degree from regionally-accredited college or university. Additional exam requirements/recommendations for international students: Required—TOEFL (minimum score 550 paper-based; 213 computer-based; 80 iBT). *Application deadline:* For fall admission, 1/10 for domestic and international students; for spring admission, 11/1 for domestic and international students. Application fee: $65. Electronic applications accepted. *Expenses:* Tuition: Full-time $12,720; part-time $1060 per credit. Required fees: $1725; $430 per semester. One-time fee: $350. *Financial support:* In 2011–12, 75 students received support, including 4 research assistantships (averaging $1,200 per year), 17 teaching assistantships (averaging $1,200 per year); career-related internships or fieldwork, scholarships/grants, traineeships, and unspecified assistantships also available. Support available to part-time students. Financial award application deadline: 4/1; financial award applicants required to submit FAFSA. *Faculty research:* Biobehavioral nursing, HIV/AIDS, gerontological nursing, women's health, vulnerable populations, health systems. *Unit head:* Dr. Laurie Lauzon-Clabo, Dean, 617-643-0605, Fax: 617-726-8022, E-mail: llauzonclabo@mghihp.edu. *Application contact:* Maureen Rika Judd, Director of Admissions, 617-726-6069, Fax: 617-726-8010, E-mail: admissions@mghihp.edu. Web site: http://www.mghihp.edu/academics/nursing/.

Michigan State University, The Graduate School, College of Nursing, East Lansing, MI 48824. Offers MSN, PhD. *Accreditation:* AACN; AANA/CANAEP. Part-time programs available. Postbaccalaureate distance learning degree programs offered (no on-campus study). *Entrance requirements:* Additional exam requirements/recommendations for international students: Required—TOEFL (minimum score 580 paper-based; 213 computer-based), Michigan State University ELT (minimum score 85), Michigan English Language Assessment Battery (minimum score 83). Electronic applications accepted. *Faculty research:* Hormone replacement therapy, end of life research, human-animal bond, chronic disease, family home care for cancer.

Middle Tennessee State University, College of Graduate Studies, University College, School of Nursing, Murfreesboro, TN 37132. Offers MSN, Graduate Certificate. Part-time and evening/weekend programs available. Postbaccalaureate distance learning degree programs offered. *Faculty:* 12 full-time (all women), 13 part-time/adjunct (10 women). *Students:* 3 full-time (all women), 111 part-time (106 women); includes 22 minority (11 Black or African American, non-Hispanic/Latino; 1 American Indian or Alaska Native, non-Hispanic/Latino; 5 Asian, non-Hispanic/Latino; 3 Hispanic/Latino; 2 Two or more races, non-Hispanic/Latino). Average age 35. 1 applicant, 0% accepted. In 2011, 24 master's awarded. *Entrance requirements:* Additional exam requirements/recommendations for international students: Required—TOEFL (minimum score 525 paper-based; 195 computer-based; 71 iBT) or IELTS (minimum score 6). *Application deadline:* For fall admission, 6/1 for domestic and international students. Applications are processed on a rolling basis. Application fee: $25 ($30 for international students). Electronic applications accepted. *Expenses:* Tuition, state resident: full-time $10,008. Tuition, nonresident: full-time $25,056. *Financial support:* In 2011–12, 2 students received support. Tuition waivers available. Support available to part-time students. Financial award application deadline: 5/1. *Unit head:* Dr. Mike Boyle, Dean, 615-494-7714, Fax: 615-896-7925, E-mail: mike.boyle@mtsu.edu. *Application contact:* Dr. Michael D. Allen, Dean and Vice Provost for Research, 615-898-2840, Fax: 615-904-8020, E-mail: michael.allen@mtsu.edu.

Midwestern State University, Graduate Studies, College of Health Sciences and Human Services, Nursing Program, Wichita Falls, TX 76308. Offers family nurse practitioner (MSN); family psychiatric mental health nurse practitioner (MSN); health services administration (MSN); nurse educator (MSN). *Accreditation:* AACN. Part-time and evening/weekend programs available. *Degree requirements:* For master's, comprehensive exam, thesis optional. *Entrance requirements:* For master's, GRE General Test or MAT. Additional exam requirements/recommendations for international students: Required—TOEFL (minimum score 550 paper-based; 213 computer-based). Electronic applications accepted. *Faculty research:* Infant feeding, musculoskeletal disorders, diabetes, community health education, water quality reporting.

Millersville University of Pennsylvania, College of Graduate and Professional Studies, School of Science and Mathematics, Department of Nursing, Millersville, PA 17551-0302. Offers MSN. *Accreditation:* NLN. Part-time and evening/weekend programs available. *Faculty:* 4 full-time (all women), 2 part-time/adjunct (both women). *Students:* 1 full-time (0 women), 82 part-time (75 women); includes 16 minority (9 Black or African American, non-Hispanic/Latino; 2 Asian, non-Hispanic/Latino; 5 Hispanic/Latino). Average age 39. 26 applicants, 92% accepted, 21 enrolled. In 2011, 15 master's awarded. *Degree requirements:* For master's, internship, scholarly project. *Entrance requirements:* For master's, 3 letters of recommendation; interview; resume; copy of RN license. Additional exam requirements/recommendations for international students: Required—TOEFL (minimum score 500 paper-based; 183 computer-based; 65 iBT). *Application deadline:* For fall admission, 1/15 priority date for domestic students, 1/15 for international students; for winter admission, 10/1 priority date for domestic students, 10/1 for international students; for spring admission, 10/1 priority date for domestic students, 10/1 for international students. Applications are processed on a rolling basis. Application fee: $40 ($50 for international students). Electronic applications accepted. *Expenses:* Tuition, state resident: full-time $3744; part-time $416 per credit. Tuition, nonresident: full-time $5616; part-time $624 per credit. Required fees: $1130; $125.50 per credit. Tuition and fees vary according to course load. *Financial support:* In 2011–12, 2 students received support, including 2 research assistantships with partial tuition reimbursements available (averaging $1,871 per year); institutionally sponsored loans and unspecified assistantships also available. Support available to part-time students. Financial award application deadline: 3/15; financial award applicants required to submit FAFSA. *Unit head:* Dr. Barbara J. Zimmerman, Chair, 717-872-3376, Fax: 717-871-4877, E-mail: barbara.zimmerman@millersville.edu. *Application contact:* Dr. Victor S. DeSantis, Dean, College of Graduate and Professional Studies, 717-872-3099, Fax: 717-872-3453, E-mail: victor.desantis@millersville.edu. Web site: http://www.millersville.edu/nursing/msn/.

Millikin University, School of Nursing, Decatur, IL 62522-2084. Offers clinical nurse leader (MSN); entry into nursing practice: pre-licensure (MSN); nurse anesthesia (MSN); nurse educator (MSN). *Accreditation:* AACN; AANA/CANAEP. Part-time programs available. *Faculty:* 17 full-time (15 women), 4 part-time/adjunct (3 women). *Students:* 30 full-time (21 women), 10 part-time (9 women); includes 2 minority (both Black or African American, non-Hispanic/Latino). Average age 32. 110 applicants, 39% accepted, 40 enrolled. In 2011, 6 master's awarded. *Degree requirements:* For master's, thesis or alternative, research project. *Entrance requirements:* For master's, GRE, official academic transcript(s), written essay, immunizations, statistics course, 2 letters of recommendation, CPR certification, professional liability/malpractice insurance. Additional exam requirements/recommendations for international students: Required—TOEFL (minimum score 550 paper-based; 79 iBT). *Application deadline:* For spring admission, 11/1 priority date for domestic students. Applications are processed on a rolling basis. Application fee: $0. Electronic applications accepted. *Expenses: Tuition:* Full-time $24,890; part-time $681 per credit hour. Tuition and fees vary according to program. *Financial support:* Institutionally sponsored loans available. Financial award applicants required to submit FAFSA. *Faculty research:* Congestive heart failure, quality of life, transcultural nursing issues, teaching/learning strategies, maternal - newborn. *Unit head:* Dr. Deborah Slayton, Director, 217-424-6348, Fax: 217-420-6731, E-mail: dslayton@millikin.edu. *Application contact:* Marianne Taylor, Administrative Assistant, 800-373-7733 Ext. 5034, Fax: 217-420-6677, E-mail: mgtaylor@millikin.edu. Web site: http://www.millikin.edu/academics/cps/nursing/msn/.

Minnesota State University Mankato, College of Graduate Studies, College of Allied Health and Nursing, School of Nursing, Mankato, MN 56001. Offers family nursing (MSN), including family nurse practitioner; nursing (DNP). MSN offered jointly with Metropolitan State University; DNP with Metropolitan State University, Minnesota State University Moorhead, Winona State University. *Accreditation:* AACN. *Students:* 9 full-time (all women), 49 part-time (46 women). *Degree requirements:* For master's, comprehensive exam, internships, research project or thesis; for doctorate, capstone project. *Entrance requirements:* For master's, GRE General Test or on-campus essay, minimum GPA of 3.0 during previous 2 years, BSN or equivalent references; for doctorate, master's degree in nursing. Additional exam requirements/recommendations for international students: Required—TOEFL. *Application deadline:* For fall admission, 2/15 priority date for domestic students, 2/15 for international students. Applications are processed on a rolling basis. Application fee: $40. Electronic applications accepted. *Financial support:* Research assistantships with full tuition reimbursements and teaching assistantships with full tuition reimbursements available. Financial award application deadline: 3/15; financial award applicants required to submit FAFSA. *Faculty research:* Psychosocial nursing, computers in nursing, family adaptation. *Unit head:* Dr. Sue Ellen Bell, Graduate Coordinator, 507-389-6814. *Application contact:* Collaborative MSN Program Admissions, 507-389-6022. Web site: http://www.mnsu.edu/nursing/.

Minnesota State University Moorhead, Graduate Studies, College of Education and Human Services, Moorhead, MN 56563-0002. Offers counseling and student affairs (MS); curriculum and instruction (MS); educational leadership (MS, Ed S); nursing (MS); reading (MS); special education (MS); speech-language pathology (MS). *Accreditation:* NCATE. Part-time and evening/weekend programs available. *Degree requirements:* For master's, comprehensive exam, final oral exam, project or thesis. *Entrance requirements:* Additional exam requirements/recommendations for international students: Required—TOEFL. Electronic applications accepted.

Misericordia University, College of Health Sciences, Department of Nursing, Dallas, PA 18612-1098. Offers MSN. *Accreditation:* AACN. Part-time and evening/weekend programs available. Postbaccalaureate distance learning degree programs offered.

Nursing—General

Faculty: 5 full-time (all women), 5 part-time/adjunct (all women). *Students:* 52 part-time (51 women); includes 1 minority (Hispanic/Latino). Average age 36. 29 applicants, 83% accepted, 20 enrolled. In 2011, 5 master's awarded. *Degree requirements:* For master's, thesis optional, practicum. *Entrance requirements:* For master's, interview, minimum GPA of 3.0. *Application deadline:* For fall admission, 8/7 priority date for domestic students; for spring admission, 1/3 for domestic students. Applications are processed on a rolling basis. Application fee: $25. Electronic applications accepted. *Expenses:* Contact institution. *Financial support:* In 2011–12, 29 students received support. Teaching assistantships, career-related internships or fieldwork, scholarships/grants, traineeships, tuition waivers (partial), and unspecified assistantships available. Support available to part-time students. Financial award application deadline: 6/30; financial award applicants required to submit FAFSA. *Faculty research:* Quality of life, maternal-child, spirituality, critical thinking, adult health. *Unit head:* Dr. Brenda Hage, Coordinator of Graduate Nursing, 570-674-6760, E-mail: bhage@misericordia.edu. *Application contact:* Larree Brown, Assistant Director of Admissions, Part-Time Undergraduate and Graduate Programs, 570-674-6451, Fax: 570-674-6232, E-mail: lbrown@misericordia.edu. Web site: http://www.misericordia.edu/nursing.

Mississippi University for Women, Graduate School, College of Nursing and Speech Language Pathology, Columbus, MS 39701-9998. Offers nursing (MSN, PMC); speech-language pathology (MS). *Accreditation:* AACN. Part-time programs available. *Degree requirements:* For master's, comprehensive exam, thesis. *Entrance requirements:* For master's, GRE General Test, bachelor's degree in nursing, previous course work in statistics, proficiency in English.

Missouri Southern State University, Program in Nursing, Joplin, MO 64801-1595. Offers MSN. Program offered jointly with University of Missouri–Kansas City. *Accreditation:* AACN. Part-time programs available. *Entrance requirements:* For master's, minimum cumulative GPA of 3.2 for the last 60 hours of the BSN program, resume, RN licensure, CPR certification, course work in statistics and health assessment. Electronic applications accepted.

Missouri State University, Graduate College, College of Health and Human Services, Department of Nursing, Springfield, MO 65897. Offers nursing (MSN), including family nurse practitioner, nurse educator. *Accreditation:* AACN. *Faculty:* 9 full-time (all women), 12 part-time/adjunct (10 women). *Students:* 24 full-time (20 women), 25 part-time (23 women); includes 2 minority (1 Asian, non-Hispanic/Latino; 1 Two or more races, non-Hispanic/Latino). Average age 37. 14 applicants, 93% accepted, 5 enrolled. In 2011, 10 master's awarded. *Degree requirements:* For master's, comprehensive exam, thesis or alternative. *Entrance requirements:* For master's, GRE General Test, minimum GPA of 3.0, RN license (MSN), 1 year work experience (MPH). Additional exam requirements/recommendations for international students: Required—TOEFL (minimum score 550 paper-based; 213 computer-based; 79 iBT). *Application deadline:* For fall admission, 7/20 priority date for domestic students, 5/1 for international students; for spring admission, 12/20 priority date for domestic students, 9/1 for international students. Applications are processed on a rolling basis. Application fee: $35 ($50 for international students). Electronic applications accepted. *Expenses:* Tuition, state resident: full-time $4086; part-time $227 per credit hour. Tuition, nonresident: full-time $8172; part-time $454 per credit hour. *Required fees:* $275 per semester. Tuition and fees vary according to course load, campus/location and program. *Financial support:* Federal Work-Study, institutionally sponsored loans, scholarships/grants, and unspecified assistantships available. Financial award application deadline: 3/31; financial award applicants required to submit FAFSA. *Faculty research:* Preconceptual health, women's health, nursing satisfaction, nursing education. *Unit head:* Dr. Kathryn Hope, Head, 417-836-5310, Fax: 417-836-5484, E-mail: nursing@missouristate.edu. *Application contact:* Eric Eckert, Coordinator of Admissions and Recruitment, 417-836-5331, Fax: 417-836-6200, E-mail: tobinbushman@missouristate.edu. Web site: http://www.missouristate.edu/nursing/.

Missouri Western State University, Program in Health Care Leadership, St. Joseph, MO 64507-2294. Offers MSN. Part-time programs available. *Application deadline:* For fall admission, 7/15 for domestic and international students; for spring admission, 10/1 for domestic and international students. Applications are processed on a rolling basis. Application fee: $45 ($50 for international students). Electronic applications accepted. *Expenses:* Tuition, state resident: full-time $4697; part-time $261 per credit hour. Tuition, nonresident: full-time $9355; part-time $520 per credit hour. *Required fees:* $343; $19.10 per credit hour. $30 per semester. Tuition and fees vary according to course load. *Unit head:* Dr. Kathleen O'Connor, Coordinator, 816-271-5910, E-mail: koconnor5@missouriwestern.edu. *Application contact:* Dr. Brian C. Cronk, Dean of the Graduate School, 816-271-4394, E-mail: graduate@missouriwestern.edu. Web site: http://www.missouriwestern.edu/nursing/msn/.

Molloy College, Division of Nursing, Rockville Centre, NY 11571-5002. Offers adult nurse practitioner (Advanced Certificate); clinical nurse specialist: adult health (Advanced Certificate); family nurse practitioner (Advanced Certificate); nurse practitioner psychiatry (Advanced Certificate); nursing (MS); nursing administration (Advanced Certificate); nursing administration with informatics (Advanced Certificate); nursing education (Advanced Certificate); nursing informatics (Advanced Certificate); pediatric nurse practitioner (Advanced Certificate). *Accreditation:* AACN. Part-time and evening/weekend programs available. *Faculty:* 20 full-time (19 women), 12 part-time/adjunct (11 women). *Students:* 19 full-time (15 women), 483 part-time (452 women); includes 238 minority (132 Black or African American, non-Hispanic/Latino; 61 Asian, non-Hispanic/Latino; 35 Hispanic/Latino; 2 Native Hawaiian or other Pacific Islander, non-Hispanic/Latino; 8 Two or more races, non-Hispanic/Latino), 5 international. Average age 40. 186 applicants, 82% accepted, 110 enrolled. In 2011, 94 master's awarded. *Degree requirements:* For master's, thesis optional. *Entrance requirements:* For master's, 3 letters of reference, BS in nursing, minimum undergraduate GPA of 3.0; for Advanced Certificate, 3 letters of reference, master's degree in nursing. *Application deadline:* For fall admission, 9/2 priority date for domestic students; for spring admission, 1/20 priority date for domestic students. Applications are processed on a rolling basis. Application fee: $60. *Financial support:* Research assistantships with partial tuition reimbursements, teaching assistantships with partial tuition reimbursements, institutionally sponsored loans, scholarships/grants, and unspecified assistantships available. Support available to part-time students. Financial award application deadline: 4/1; financial award applicants required to submit FAFSA. *Unit head:* Dr. Denise Walsh, Associate Dean, Graduate Nursing, 516-678-5000, Fax: 516-678-9718, E-mail: dwalsh@molloy.edu. *Application contact:* Alina Haitz, Assistant Director of Graduate Admissions, 516-678-5000, Fax: 516-256-2247, E-mail: ahaitz@molloy.edu. Web site: http://www.molloy.edu/academics/nursing-division.

Monmouth University, The Graduate School, The Marjorie K. Unterberg School of Nursing and Health Studies, West Long Branch, NJ 07764-1898. Offers adult nurse practitioner (MSN); adult psychiatric and mental health advanced practice nursing (MSN, Post-Master's Certificate); advanced practice nursing (Post-Master's Certificate); family nurse practitioner (MSN, Post-Master's Certificate); forensic nursing (MSN, Certificate); nursing (MSN); nursing administration (MSN, Post-Master's Certificate); nursing education (MSN, Post-Master's Certificate); nursing practice (DNP); school nursing (MSN, Certificate). *Accreditation:* AACN. Part-time and evening/weekend programs available. *Faculty:* 12 full-time (all women), 2 part-time/adjunct (both women). *Students:* 16 full-time (11 women), 244 part-time (238 women); includes 73 minority (23 Black or African American, non-Hispanic/Latino; 2 American Indian or Alaska Native, non-Hispanic/Latino; 34 Asian, non-Hispanic/Latino; 12 Hispanic/Latino; 1 Native Hawaiian or other Pacific Islander, non-Hispanic/Latino; 1 Two or more races, non-Hispanic/Latino), 1 international. Average age 41. 107 applicants, 92% accepted, 67 enrolled. In 2011, 55 master's awarded. *Degree requirements:* For master's, practicum (for some tracks). *Entrance requirements:* For master's, GRE General Test, RN license, 1 year of work experience, minimum undergraduate GPA of 2.75. Additional exam requirements/recommendations for international students: Required—TOEFL (minimum score 550 paper-based; 213 computer-based; 79 iBT), IELTS (minimum score 5) or Michigan English Language Assessment Battery (minimum score 77), Cambridge A, B, C. *Application deadline:* For fall admission, 7/15 priority date for domestic students, 6/1 for international students; for spring admission, 11/15 priority date for domestic students, 11/1 for international students. Applications are processed on a rolling basis. Application fee: $50. Electronic applications accepted. *Financial support:* In 2011–12, 138 students received support, including 138 fellowships (averaging $1,423 per year), 4 research assistantships (averaging $5,240 per year); career-related internships or fieldwork, scholarships/grants, and unspecified assistantships also available. Support available to part-time students. Financial award applicants required to submit FAFSA. *Faculty research:* Relationship of undergraduate GPA and GRE to succeed in a graduate nursing program. *Unit head:* Dr. Janet Mahoney, Dean, 732-571-3443, Fax: 732-263-5131, E-mail: jmahoney@monmouth.edu. *Application contact:* Kevin Roane, Director, Office of Graduate Admission, 732-571-3452, Fax: 732-263-5123, E-mail: gradadm@monmouth.edu. Web site: http://www.monmouth.edu/nursingschool.

Moravian College, Moravian College Comenius Center, St. Luke's School of Nursing, Bethlehem, PA 18018-6650. Offers nurse administrator (MS); nurse educator (MS); nurse leadership (MS). Part-time and evening/weekend programs available. *Degree requirements:* For master's, comprehensive exam (for some programs), evidence-based practice project. *Entrance requirements:* For master's, GRE or MAT. Additional exam requirements/recommendations for international students: Required—TOEFL (minimum score 550 paper-based; 260 computer-based; 90 iBT).

Morgan State University, School of Graduate Studies, School of Community Health and Policy, Department of Nursing, Baltimore, MD 21251. Offers MS, PhD.

Mountain State University, Program in Nursing, Beckley, WV 25802-9003. Offers administration/education (MSN); family nurse practitioner (MSN). *Accreditation:* NLN. Part-time programs available. Postbaccalaureate distance learning degree programs offered (minimal on-campus study). *Faculty:* 3 full-time (all women), 2 part-time/adjunct (both women). *Students:* 65 full-time (61 women), 9 part-time (8 women); includes 11 minority (8 Black or African American, non-Hispanic/Latino; 1 American Indian or Alaska Native, non-Hispanic/Latino; 2 Asian, non-Hispanic/Latino), 1 international. Average age 37. 85 applicants, 27% accepted, 20 enrolled. In 2011, 46 master's awarded. *Degree requirements:* For master's, comprehensive exam, thesis or alternative. *Entrance requirements:* For master's, GRE. Additional exam requirements/recommendations for international students: Required—TOEFL (minimum score 550 paper-based; 213 computer-based); Recommended—IELTS (minimum score 6.5). *Application deadline:* For spring admission, 6/30 for domestic and international students. Applications are processed on a rolling basis. Application fee: $25 ($50 for international students). Electronic applications accepted. *Expenses:* Contact institution. *Financial support:* Federal Work-Study, scholarships/grants, and unspecified assistantships available. Support available to part-time students. Financial award applicants required to submit FAFSA. *Unit head:* Dr. Sheila Garland, Dean, School of Health Sciences, 304-929-1516, Fax: 304-929-1601, E-mail: sgarland@mountainstate.edu.

Mount Carmel College of Nursing, Nursing Program, Columbus, OH 43222. Offers adult health clinical nurse specialist (MS); family nurse practitioner (MS); nursing administration (MS); nursing education (MS). *Accreditation:* AACN. Part-time programs available. *Faculty:* 11 full-time (10 women), 4 part-time/adjunct (2 women). *Students:* 69 full-time (66 women), 33 part-time (30 women); includes 19 minority (11 Black or African American, non-Hispanic/Latino; 1 American Indian or Alaska Native, non-Hispanic/Latino; 5 Asian, non-Hispanic/Latino; 1 Native Hawaiian or other Pacific Islander, non-Hispanic/Latino; 1 Two or more races, non-Hispanic/Latino). Average age 38. 23 applicants, 100% accepted, 20 enrolled. In 2011, 16 master's awarded. *Degree requirements:* For master's, professional manuscript. *Entrance requirements:* For master's, letters of recommendation, current resume, baccalaureate degree in nursing, current Ohio RN license, minimum cumulative GPA of 3.0. Additional exam requirements/recommendations for international students: Required—TOEFL (minimum score 550 paper-based; 213 computer-based; 80 iBT). *Application deadline:* For fall admission, 6/15 priority date for domestic students; for winter admission, 11/1 priority date for domestic students. Applications are processed on a rolling basis. Application fee: $30. *Expenses: Tuition:* Full-time $7839; part-time $402 per credit. *Required fees:* $75. *Financial support:* In 2011–12, 6 students received support. Institutionally sponsored loans and scholarships/grants available. Financial award application deadline: 7/1; financial award applicants required to submit FAFSA. *Unit head:* Dr. Angela Phillips-Lowe, Associate Dean, 614-234-5717, Fax: 614-234-2875, E-mail: aphillips-lowe@mccn.edu. *Application contact:* Elsie Sexton, Program Coordinator, 614-234-5169, Fax: 614-234-2875, E-mail: ksexton@mccn.edu. Web site: http://www.mccn.edu/.

Mount Marty College, Graduate Studies Division, Yankton, SD 57078-3724. Offers business administration (MBA); nurse anesthesia (MS); nursing (MSN); pastoral ministries (MPM). *Accreditation:* AANA/CANAEP (one or more programs are accredited). *Degree requirements:* For master's, thesis or alternative. *Entrance requirements:* For master's, GRE General Test, minimum GPA of 3.0. Electronic applications accepted. *Faculty research:* Clinical anesthesia, professional characteristics, motivations of applicants.

Mount Saint Mary College, Division of Nursing, Newburgh, NY 12550-3494. Offers adult nurse practitioner (MS, Advanced Certificate), including nursing education (MS), nursing management (MS); clinical nurse specialist-adult health (MS), including nursing education, nursing management; family nurse practitioner (Advanced Certificate). *Accreditation:* AACN. Part-time and evening/weekend programs available. *Faculty:* 3 full-time (all women), 1 (woman) part-time/adjunct. *Students:* 3 full-time (2 women), 58 part-time (54 women); includes 16 minority (11 Black or African American, non-Hispanic/Latino; 1 Asian, non-Hispanic/Latino; 1 Hispanic/Latino; 3 Native Hawaiian or other Pacific Islander, non-Hispanic/Latino), 2 international. Average age 38. 47 applicants, 53% accepted, 18 enrolled. In 2011, 17 master's, 5 other advanced degrees awarded. *Degree requirements:* For master's, research utilization project. *Entrance requirements:* For master's, BSN, minimum GPA of 3.0, RN license. *Application deadline:* For fall admission, 6/3 priority date for domestic students; for spring admission, 10/31 priority date for domestic students. Applications are processed on a rolling basis. Application fee: $45. Application fee is waived when completed online. *Expenses: Tuition:* Full-time $13,356; part-time $742 per credit. *Required fees:* $70 per semester. *Financial support:* In 2011–12, 8 students received support. Unspecified assistantships available. Financial award application deadline: 4/15; financial award applicants required to submit FAFSA. *Unit head:* Dr. Karen Baldwin, Coordinator, 845-569-3512, Fax: 845-562-6762, E-mail: baldwin@msmc.edu. *Application contact:* Courtney McDermott, Graduate Recruiter,

845-569-3402, Fax: 845-569-3450, E-mail: courtney.mcdermott@msmc.edu. Web site: http://www.msmc.edu/Academics/Graduate_Programs/Master_of_Science_in_Nursing.

Mount St. Mary's College, Graduate Division, Program in Nursing, Los Angeles, CA 90049-1599. Offers educator (MSN); leadership and administration (MSN). *Accreditation:* AACN. *Entrance requirements:* For master's, baccalaureate degree; current CA nursing license; minimum cumulative GPA of 3.0 in last 60 semester units or last 90 quarter units of undergraduate and/or graduate course work; essay; two letters of recommendation; official transcript. Additional exam requirements/recommendations for international students: Required—TOEFL (minimum score 550 paper-based). *Application deadline:* For fall admission, 7/15 priority date for domestic students; for spring admission, 11/15 priority date for domestic students. Application fee: $50. Electronic applications accepted. *Expenses: Tuition:* Part-time $752 per unit. Part-time tuition and fees vary according to degree level and program. *Financial support:* Scholarships/grants available. *Unit head:* Dr. Marsha Sato, Director, 213-477-2980, E-mail: msato@msmc.la.edu. Web site: http://www.msmc.la.edu/graduate-programs/nursing.asp.

Murray State University, College of Health Sciences and Human Services, Program in Nursing, Murray, KY 42071. Offers clinical nurse specialist (MSN); family nurse practitioner (MSN); nurse anesthesia (MSN). *Accreditation:* AACN; AANA/CANAEP. *Degree requirements:* For master's, research project. *Entrance requirements:* For master's, GRE General Test, BSN, interview, RN licensure. Additional exam requirements/recommendations for international students: Required—TOEFL (minimum score 550 paper-based). *Faculty research:* Fibromyalgis, primary care, rural health.

Nazareth College of Rochester, Graduate Studies, Department of Nursing, Rochester, NY 14618-3790. Offers gerontological nurse practitioner (MS). *Accreditation:* AACN. Part-time programs available. *Entrance requirements:* For master's, minimum GPA of 3.0, RN license.

Nebraska Methodist College, Program in Nursing, Omaha, NE 68114. Offers nurse educator (MSN); nurse executive (MSN). *Accreditation:* AACN. Evening/weekend programs available. Postbaccalaureate distance learning degree programs offered (no on-campus study). *Degree requirements:* For master's, thesis or alternative, Evidence Based Practice (EBP) project. *Entrance requirements:* For master's, interview. Additional exam requirements/recommendations for international students: Required—TOEFL (minimum score 550 paper-based; 213 computer-based; 80 iBT). *Faculty research:* Spirituality, student outcomes, service-learning, leadership and administration, women's issues.

Nebraska Wesleyan University, University College, Program in Nursing, Lincoln, NE 68504-2796. Offers MSN. *Accreditation:* NLN. Part-time programs available.

Neumann University, Program in Nursing and Health Sciences, Aston, PA 19014-1298. Offers MS. *Accreditation:* NLN. Part-time programs available. *Entrance requirements:* For master's, GRE or MAT. Additional exam requirements/recommendations for international students: Required—TOEFL. *Expenses:* Contact institution.

New Mexico State University, Graduate School, College of Health and Social Services, School of Nursing, Las Cruces, NM 88003-8001. Offers adult/gerontology nurse practitioner (DNP); family nurse practitioner (DNP); nursing (MSN, PhD); public/community health (DNP). *Accreditation:* AACN. Postbaccalaureate distance learning degree programs offered (minimal on-campus study). *Faculty:* 9 full-time (all women). *Students:* 44 full-time (38 women), 72 part-time (59 women); includes 48 minority (9 Black or African American, non-Hispanic/Latino; 5 American Indian or Alaska Native, non-Hispanic/Latino; 2 Asian, non-Hispanic/Latino; 31 Hispanic/Latino; 1 Two or more races, non-Hispanic/Latino), 2 international. Average age 43. 37 applicants, 86% accepted, 25 enrolled. In 2011, 35 master's, 3 doctorates awarded. *Degree requirements:* For master's, comprehensive exam, thesis optional, clinical practice; for doctorate, comprehensive exam, thesis/dissertation. *Entrance requirements:* For master's, NCLEX exam, BSN, minimum GPA of 3.0, course work in statistics, 3 letters of reference, writing sample, RN license, CPR certification, proof of liability, immunizations, criminal background check; for doctorate, NCLEX exam, MSN, minimum GPA of 3.0, 3 letters of reference, writing sample, RN license, CPR certification, proof of liability, immunizations, criminal background check, statistics course. Additional exam requirements/recommendations for international students: Required—TOEFL (minimum score 550 paper-based; 79 iBT), IELTS (minimum score 6.5). *Application deadline:* For spring admission, 10/1 priority date for domestic students. Application fee: $40 ($50 for international students). Electronic applications accepted. *Expenses:* Tuition, state resident: full-time $5004; part-time $208.50 per credit. Tuition, nonresident: full-time $17,446; part-time $726.90 per credit. *Financial support:* In 2011–12, 1 teaching assistantship (averaging $28,242 per year) was awarded; fellowships, research assistantships, career-related internships or fieldwork, Federal Work-Study, scholarships/grants, traineeships, and health care benefits also available. Financial award application deadline: 3/1. *Faculty research:* Public policy, community health, health disparities, self efficacy and self management, psychiatric mental health. *Unit head:* Dr. Pamela Schultz, Director, 575-646-3812, Fax: 575-646-2167, E-mail: pschultz@nmsu.edu. *Application contact:* Dr. Kathleen Huttlinger, Associate Director for Graduate Studies, 575-646-4387, Fax: 575-646-2167. Web site: http://www.nmsu.edu/~nursing/.

New York University, College of Nursing, Doctor of Nursing Practice Program, New York, NY 10012-1019. Offers advanced practice nursing (DNP), including adult acute care, adult nurse practitioner/holistic nursing, adult nurse practitioner/palliative care nursing, adult primary care, adult primary care/geriatrics, family, geriatrics, mental health nursing, nurse-midwifery, pediatrics. Part-time and evening/weekend programs available. *Faculty:* 7 full-time (all women). *Students:* 23 part-time (19 women); includes 6 minority (4 Black or African American, non-Hispanic/Latino; 1 Asian, non-Hispanic/Latino; 1 Hispanic/Latino), 1 international. Average age 46. 20 applicants, 80% accepted, 11 enrolled. In 2011, 8 doctorates awarded. *Degree requirements:* For doctorate, thesis/dissertation. *Entrance requirements:* For doctorate, MS, RN license, interview, NP Certification. Additional exam requirements/recommendations for international students: Required—TOEFL, IELTS. *Application deadline:* For fall admission, 4/1 priority date for domestic students, 4/1 for international students. Applications are processed on a rolling basis. Application fee: $75. Electronic applications accepted. *Financial support:* In 2011–12, 15 students received support. Fellowships with full and partial tuition reimbursements available, institutionally sponsored loans, scholarships/grants, and tuition waivers (partial) available. Support available to part-time students. Financial award application deadline: 2/1; financial award applicants required to submit FAFSA. *Faculty research:* Elderly black diabetics, families and illness, oral systemic connection. *Unit head:* Dr. Jamesetta A. Newland, Director, 212-998-5319, Fax: 212-995-3143, E-mail: jan7@nyu.edu. *Application contact:* Gail Wolfmeyer, Assistant Director, Graduate Student Affairs and Admissions, 212-992-7653, Fax: 212-995-4302, E-mail: gail.wolfmeyer@nyu.edu.

New York University, College of Nursing, Doctor of Philosophy in Nursing Program, New York, NY 10012-1019. Offers research and theory development in nursing science (PhD). Part-time and evening/weekend programs available. *Faculty:* 8 full-time (all women), 6 part-time/adjunct (5 women). *Students:* 7 full-time (5 women), 32 part-time

(28 women); includes 8 minority (5 Black or African American, non-Hispanic/Latino; 2 Asian, non-Hispanic/Latino; 1 Two or more races, non-Hispanic/Latino), 3 international. Average age 43. 20 applicants, 80% accepted, 11 enrolled. In 2011, 5 doctorates awarded. *Degree requirements:* For doctorate, thesis/dissertation. *Entrance requirements:* For doctorate, GRE General Test, interview. Additional exam requirements/recommendations for international students: Required—TOEFL. *Application deadline:* For fall admission, 3/1 priority date for domestic students, 3/1 for international students. Applications are processed on a rolling basis. Application fee: $75. Electronic applications accepted. *Financial support:* In 2011–12, 18 students received support, including 2 research assistantships with full and partial tuition reimbursements available (averaging $23,000 per year); fellowships with full and partial tuition reimbursements available, institutionally sponsored loans, scholarships/grants, and tuition waivers (partial) also available. Support available to part-time students. Financial award application deadline: 2/1; financial award applicants required to submit FAFSA. *Faculty research:* Geriatrics, infectious diseases/global public health, chronic disease prevention and management, health systems/education. *Unit head:* Dr. Deborah Chyun, Director, 212-998-5264, Fax: 212-995-4561, E-mail: dc116@nyu.edu. *Application contact:* Gail Wolfmeyer, Assistant Director, Graduate Student Affairs and Admissions, 212-992-7653, Fax: 212-995-4302, E-mail: gail.wolfmeyer@nyu.edu.

New York University, College of Nursing, Programs in Advanced Practice Nursing, New York, NY 10012-1019. Offers advanced practice nursing: adult acute care (MS, Advanced Certificate); advanced practice nursing: adult nurse practitioner/holistic nurse practitioner (Advanced Certificate); advanced practice nursing: adult nurse practitioner/palliative care nurse practitioner (Advanced Certificate); advanced practice nursing: adult primary care (MS, Advanced Certificate); advanced practice nursing: family (MS, Advanced Certificate); advanced practice nursing: geriatrics (Advanced Certificate); advanced practice nursing: mental health (MS); advanced practice nursing: mental health nursing (Advanced Certificate); advanced practice nursing: pediatrics (MS, Advanced Certificate); nurse midwifery (MS, Advanced Certificate); nursing administration (MS, Advanced Certificate); nursing education (MS, Advanced Certificate); nursing informatics (MS, Advanced Certificate); MS/MPA; MS/MPH. *Accreditation:* AACN; ACNM/ACME. Part-time programs available. *Faculty:* 23 full-time (all women), 60 part-time/adjunct (47 women). *Students:* 27 full-time (23 women), 552 part-time (514 women); includes 251 minority (91 Black or African American, non-Hispanic/Latino; 115 Asian, non-Hispanic/Latino; 34 Hispanic/Latino; 11 Native Hawaiian or other Pacific Islander, non-Hispanic/Latino), 8 international. Average age 33. 325 applicants, 81% accepted, 179 enrolled. In 2011, 89 master's awarded. *Degree requirements:* For master's, thesis (for some programs). *Entrance requirements:* For master's, BS in nursing, AS in nursing with another BS/BA, interview, RN license, 1 year of clinical experience (3 for nursing education program); for Advanced Certificate, master's degree. Additional exam requirements/recommendations for international students: Required—TOEFL, IELTS. *Application deadline:* For fall admission, 7/1 priority date for domestic students, 7/1 for international students; for spring admission, 12/1 for domestic and international students. Applications are processed on a rolling basis. Application fee: $75. Electronic applications accepted. *Financial support:* In 2011–12, 36 students received support. Career-related internships or fieldwork, institutionally sponsored loans, scholarships/grants, traineeships, and tuition waivers (partial) available. Support available to part-time students. Financial award application deadline: 2/1; financial award applicants required to submit FAFSA. *Faculty research:* Elderly black diabetics, families and illness, oral systemic connection. *Unit head:* Dr. Judith Haber, Associate Dean, 212-998-9020, Fax: 212-995-3143, E-mail: jh33@nyu.edu. *Application contact:* Gail Wolfmeyer, Assistant Director, Graduate Student Affairs and Admissions, 212-992-7653, Fax: 212-995-4302, E-mail: gail.wolfmeyer@nyu.edu.

North Dakota State University, College of Graduate and Interdisciplinary Studies, College of Pharmacy, Nursing and Allied Sciences, Graduate Nursing Program, Fargo, ND 58108. Offers MS, DNP. *Accreditation:* AACN. Part-time programs available. Postbaccalaureate distance learning degree programs offered (minimal on-campus study). *Faculty:* 7 full-time (all women), 1 part-time/adjunct (0 women). *Students:* 34 full-time (32 women), 10 part-time (all women); includes 2 minority (1 American Indian or Alaska Native, non-Hispanic/Latino; 1 Two or more races, non-Hispanic/Latino), 4 international. Average age 35. 31 applicants, 45% accepted, 10 enrolled. In 2011, 3 master's, 14 doctorates awarded. *Degree requirements:* For master's, thesis or alternative, oral defense; for doctorate, thesis/dissertation or alternative, oral defense. *Entrance requirements:* For master's, bachelor's degree with nursing major, minimum GPA of 3.0 in nursing courses, RN license; for doctorate, bachelor's or master's degree with a nursing major, minimum GPA of 3.0 in nursing courses, RN license. Additional exam requirements/recommendations for international students: Required—TOEFL, IELTS. *Application deadline:* For fall admission, 5/1 priority date for domestic students; for spring admission, 11/1 priority date for domestic students. Applications are processed on a rolling basis. Application fee: $35. Electronic applications accepted. *Expenses:* Contact institution. *Financial support:* In 2011–12, 1 research assistantship with full tuition reimbursement (averaging $1,600 per year), 6 teaching assistantships with full tuition reimbursements (averaging $4,668 per year) were awarded; traineeships and unspecified assistantships also available. Financial award application deadline: 8/15; financial award applicants required to submit CSS PROFILE or FAFSA. *Faculty research:* Prevention of farmers' hearing loss, breast cancer in Native American women, colon cancer, quality improvement in a wellness center. *Unit head:* Dr. Carla Gross, Department Chair, 701-231-5692, Fax: 701-231-7606, E-mail: carla.gross@ndsu.edu. Web site: http://www.ndsu.edu/ndsu/nursing.

Northeastern University, Bouvé College of Health Sciences, School of Nursing, Program in Primary Care Nursing, Boston, MA 02115-5096. Offers MS, CAGS, CAS. *Accreditation:* AACN. *Faculty:* 25 full-time, 4 part-time/adjunct. *Students:* 28 full-time, 13 part-time. 27 applicants, 74% accepted, 15 enrolled. In 2011, 10 master's awarded. *Entrance requirements:* For master's, GRE General Test; for other advanced degree, MS in nursing. Additional exam requirements/recommendations for international students: Required—TOEFL (minimum score 100 iBT). *Application deadline:* For fall admission, 7/1 for domestic students. Applications are processed on a rolling basis. Application fee: $50. Electronic applications accepted. *Financial support:* Research assistantships with tuition reimbursements, teaching assistantships with tuition reimbursements, scholarships/grants, traineeships, and tuition waivers (partial) available. Financial award application deadline: 7/1; financial award applicants required to submit FAFSA. *Unit head:* Dr. Susan Jo Roberts, Director, 617-373-3130, Fax: 617-373-3050, E-mail: s.roberts@neu.edu. *Application contact:* Margaret Schnabel, Director of Graduate Admissions, 617-373-2708, E-mail: bouvegrad@neu.edu. Web site: http://www.northeastern.edu/bouve/programs/cprimarycarenurse.html.

Northern Arizona University, Graduate College, College of Health and Human Services, School of Nursing, Flagstaff, AZ 86011. Offers family nurse practitioner (MSN, Certificate); nurse generalist (MSN); nursing (MSN); nursing practice (DNP). *Accreditation:* AACN. Part-time programs available. *Faculty:* 36 full-time (31 women). *Students:* 25 full-time (22 women), 68 part-time (57 women); includes 17 minority (1 Black or African American, non-Hispanic/Latino; 1 American Indian or Alaska Native, non-Hispanic/Latino; 3 Asian, non-Hispanic/Latino; 10 Hispanic/Latino; 1 Native Hawaiian or other Pacific Islander, non-Hispanic/Latino; 1 Two or more races, non-Hispanic/Latino). Average age 30. 71 applicants, 17% accepted, 8 enrolled. In 2011, 19

degrees awarded. *Degree requirements:* For master's, thesis (for some programs), project or thesis. *Entrance requirements:* For master's, GRE General Test or minimum GPA of 3.0, undergraduate statistics or health assessment with minimum grade of B in last 5 years or 3 years of RN experience (nursing education). Additional exam requirements/recommendations for international students: Required—TOEFL (minimum score 550 paper-based; 213 computer-based; 80 iBT), IELTS (minimum score 7). *Application deadline:* For fall admission, 1/15 priority date for domestic students, 1/15 for international students. Applications are processed on a rolling basis. Application fee: $65. Electronic applications accepted. *Expenses:* Tuition, state resident: full-time $7190; part-time $355 per credit hour. Tuition, nonresident: full-time $18,092; part-time $1005 per credit hour. *Required fees:* $818; $328 per semester. *Financial support:* Career-related internships or fieldwork, Federal Work-Study, scholarships/grants, traineeships, health care benefits, tuition waivers, and unspecified assistantships available. Financial award applicants required to submit FAFSA. *Unit head:* Dr. Debera Thomas, Chair, 928-523-2656, Fax: 928-523-7171, E-mail: debera.thomas@nau.edu. *Application contact:* Penny Susan Walior, Student Academic Specialist, 928-523-6717, Fax: 928-523-9155, E-mail: nursing@nau.edu. Web site: http://nau.edu/CHHS/Nursing/Welcome/.

Northern Illinois University, Graduate School, College of Health and Human Sciences, School of Nursing and Health Studies, De Kalb, IL 60115-2854. Offers nursing (MS); public health (MPH). *Accreditation:* AACN. Part-time programs available. *Faculty:* 12 full-time (11 women), 1 (woman) part-time/adjunct. *Students:* 28 full-time (21 women), 232 part-time (214 women); includes 61 minority (20 Black or African American, non-Hispanic/Latino; 24 Asian, non-Hispanic/Latino; 14 Hispanic/Latino; 3 Two or more races, non-Hispanic/Latino), 9 international. Average age 35. 118 applicants, 40% accepted, 20 enrolled. In 2011, 77 master's awarded. *Degree requirements:* For master's, thesis optional, internship. *Entrance requirements:* For master's, minimum GPA of 3.0 in last 60 hours, BA in nursing, nursing license. Additional exam requirements/recommendations for international students: Required—TOEFL (minimum score 550 paper-based; 213 computer-based). *Application deadline:* For fall admission, 6/1 for domestic students, 5/1 for international students; for spring admission, 11/1 for domestic students, 10/1 for international students. Applications are processed on a rolling basis. Application fee: $40. Electronic applications accepted. *Financial support:* In 2011–12, 7 research assistantships with full tuition reimbursements, 16 teaching assistantships with full tuition reimbursements were awarded; fellowships with full tuition reimbursements, career-related internships or fieldwork, Federal Work-Study, scholarships/grants, tuition waivers (full), and unspecified assistantships also available. Support available to part-time students. Financial award applicants required to submit FAFSA. *Faculty research:* Neonatal intensive care, stress and coping, refugee and immigrant issues, older adults, autoimmune disorders. *Unit head:* Dr. Brigid Lusk, Chair, 815-753-6550, Fax: 815-753-0814, E-mail: blusk@niu.edu. *Application contact:* Graduate School Office, 815-753-0395, E-mail: gradsch@niu.edu. Web site: http://www.chhs.niu.edu/nursing/.

Northern Kentucky University, Office of Graduate Programs, School of Nursing and Health Professions, Online Doctor of Nursing Practice Program, Highland Heights, KY 41099. Offers DNP. Part-time programs available. Postbaccalaureate distance learning degree programs offered. *Students:* 13 part-time (all women); includes 2 minority (both Hispanic/Latino). Average age 50. 28 applicants, 61% accepted, 13 enrolled. *Degree requirements:* For doctorate, thesis/dissertation. *Entrance requirements:* For doctorate, RN License, master's degree in nursing, minimum GPA of 3.25, course in statistics. Additional exam requirements/recommendations for international students: Required—TOEFL (minimum score 550 paper-based; 213 computer-based; 79 iBT); Recommended—IELTS (minimum score 6.5). *Application deadline:* For fall admission, 4/2 for domestic students, 6/1 for international students. Application fee: $50. *Expenses:* Contact institution. *Faculty research:* Pathways to nursing degree, lead poisoning in children, predictors for NCLEX success in BSN and ABSN programs, work life balanced and deans of baccalaureate nursing programs, heart failure self management. *Unit head:* Dr. Marilyn C. Schleyer, Program Director, 859-572-5240, Fax: 859-572-1934, E-mail: schleyerm1@nku.edu. *Application contact:* Dr. Peg Griffin, Director of Graduate Programs, 859-572-6934, Fax: 859-572-6670, E-mail: griffinp@nku.edu. Web site: http://advancednursing.nku.edu/programs/dnp/index.php.

Northern Kentucky University, Office of Graduate Programs, School of Nursing and Health Professions, Program in Nursing, Highland Heights, KY 41099. Offers MSN, Certificate, Post-Master's Certificate. *Accreditation:* NLN. Part-time and evening/weekend programs available. Postbaccalaureate distance learning degree programs offered (no on-campus study). *Students:* 15 full-time (12 women), 289 part-time (267 women); includes 18 minority (9 Black or African American, non-Hispanic/Latino; 5 Asian, non-Hispanic/Latino; 2 Hispanic/Latino; 2 Two or more races, non-Hispanic/Latino). Average age 38. 215 applicants, 49% accepted, 93 enrolled. In 2011, 64 master's, 17 other advanced degrees awarded. *Degree requirements:* For master's, comprehensive exam. *Entrance requirements:* For master's, minimum cumulative GPA of 2.75; one year of experience as RN; college courses in statistics, nursing research, physical assessment and nursing theory, proof of current nursing licensure, updated resume. Additional exam requirements/recommendations for international students: Required—TOEFL (minimum score 550 paper-based; 213 computer-based; 79 iBT); Recommended—IELTS (minimum score 6.5). *Application deadline:* For fall admission, 2/1 for domestic and international students; for spring admission, 10/15 for domestic and international students. Application fee: $40. Electronic applications accepted. *Expenses:* Tuition, state resident: full-time $7614; part-time $423 per credit hour. Tuition, nonresident: full-time $13,104; part-time $728 per credit hour. Tuition and fees vary according to degree level and reciprocity agreements. *Financial support:* Unspecified assistantships available. Financial award applicants required to submit FAFSA. *Faculty research:* Career planning for middle school students, technology skills for workforce, diabetes, factors affecting NCLEX scores. *Unit head:* Dr. Marilyn Schleyer, Program Director, 859-572-5240, Fax: 859-572-1934, E-mail: schleyerm1@nku.edu. *Application contact:* Dr. Peg Griffin, Director of Graduate Programs, 859-572-6934, Fax: 859-572-6670, E-mail: griffinp@nku.edu. Web site: http://advancednursing.nku.edu/index.php.

Northern Michigan University, College of Graduate Studies, College of Professional Studies, School of Nursing, Marquette, MI 49855-5301. Offers MSN. *Accreditation:* AACN. Part-time and evening/weekend programs available. *Degree requirements:* For master's, thesis or alternative. *Entrance requirements:* For master's, GRE General Test, minimum GPA of 3.0.

North Park University, School of Nursing, Chicago, IL 60625-4895. Offers advanced practice nursing (MS); leadership and management (MS); MBA/MS; MM/MSN; MS/MHR; MS/MNA. *Accreditation:* AACN. Part-time and evening/weekend programs available. *Degree requirements:* For master's, thesis. *Entrance requirements:* For master's, GMAT, MAT. *Faculty research:* Aging, consultation roles, critical thinking skills, family breakdown, science of caring.

Northwestern State University of Louisiana, Graduate Studies and Research, College of Nursing and Allied Health, Shreveport, LA 71101-4653. Offers MS, MSN. *Accreditation:* AACN. Part-time programs available. *Faculty:* 8 full-time (all women), 5 part-time/adjunct (all women). *Students:* 14 full-time (all women), 160 part-time (145 women); includes 25 minority (22 Black or African American, non-Hispanic/Latino; 2

American Indian or Alaska Native, non-Hispanic/Latino; 1 Hispanic/Latino), 2 international. Average age 34. 73 applicants, 96% accepted, 33 enrolled. In 2011, 59 master's awarded. *Degree requirements:* For master's, comprehensive exam, thesis or alternative. *Entrance requirements:* For master's, GRE General Test, 6 months of clinical nursing experience, BS in nursing, minimum GPA of 3.0. Additional exam requirements/recommendations for international students: Required—TOEFL. *Application deadline:* For fall admission, 3/15 priority date for domestic students; for spring admission, 10/15 priority date for domestic students. Applications are processed on a rolling basis. Application fee: $20 ($30 for international students). Electronic applications accepted. *Expenses:* Tuition, state resident: full-time $3440. Tuition, nonresident: full-time $12,010. *Financial support:* Career-related internships or fieldwork and Federal Work-Study available. Support available to part-time students. Financial award application deadline: 5/1; financial award applicants required to submit FAFSA. *Unit head:* Dr. Norann Planchock, Director, 318-677-3100, Fax: 318-676-7887, E-mail: planchockn@alpha.nsula.edu. *Application contact:* Dr. Steven G. Horton, Associate Provost/Dean, Graduate Studies, Research, and Information Systems, 318-357-5851, Fax: 318-357-5019, E-mail: grad_school@nsula.edu. Web site: http://nursing.nsula.edu/.

Norwich University, College of Graduate and Continuing Studies, Master of Science in Nursing Program, Northfield, VT 05663. Offers nursing administration (MSN); nursing education (MSN). *Accreditation:* AACN. Evening/weekend programs available. *Faculty:* 8 part-time/adjunct (5 women). *Students:* 31 full-time (29 women); includes 3 minority (1 Black or African American, non-Hispanic/Latino; 1 Asian, non-Hispanic/Latino; 1 Hispanic/Latino). Average age 44. 17 applicants, 59% accepted, 10 enrolled. In 2011, 28 master's awarded. *Entrance requirements:* For master's, minimum undergraduate GPA of 2.75. Additional exam requirements/recommendations for international students: Required—TOEFL (minimum score 550 paper-based; 212 computer-based; 83 iBT). *Application deadline:* For fall admission, 8/10 for domestic and international students; for winter admission, 11/7 for domestic and international students; for spring admission, 2/6 for domestic and international students. Applications are processed on a rolling basis. Application fee: $50. Electronic applications accepted. *Expenses:* Tuition: Full-time $16,174. *Required fees:* $2130. Full-time tuition and fees vary according to program. *Financial support:* In 2011–12, 7 students received support. Scholarships/grants available. Financial award applicants required to submit FAFSA. *Application contact:* Rija Ramahatra, Associate Program Director, 802-485-2892, Fax: 802-485-2533, E-mail: rramahatr@norwich.edu. Web site: http://nursing.norwich.edu/.

Nova Southeastern University, Health Professions Division, College of Nursing, Fort Lauderdale, FL 33314-7796. Offers advanced practice registered nurse (APRN) (MSN); nursing (MSN); nursing education (PhD); nursing practice (DNP). *Accreditation:* AACN. Part-time and evening/weekend programs available. Postbaccalaureate distance learning degree programs offered (no on-campus study). *Faculty:* 16 full-time (all women), 32 part-time/adjunct (all women). *Students:* 170 full-time (159 women), 5 part-time (4 women); includes 90 minority (55 Black or African American, non-Hispanic/Latino; 5 American Indian or Alaska Native, non-Hispanic/Latino; 9 Asian, non-Hispanic/Latino; 19 Hispanic/Latino; 2 Native Hawaiian or other Pacific Islander, non-Hispanic/Latino). Average age 44. 70 applicants, 89% accepted, 57 enrolled. In 2011, 59 degrees awarded. *Degree requirements:* For doctorate, comprehensive exam, thesis/dissertation. *Entrance requirements:* For master's, minimum GPA of 3.0, RN, BSN; for doctorate, minimum GPA of 3.5, BSN, RN. Additional exam requirements/recommendations for international students: Recommended—TOEFL. *Application deadline:* For fall admission, 3/1 for domestic and international students; for winter admission, 11/1 for domestic and international students. Applications are processed on a rolling basis. Application fee: $50. Electronic applications accepted. *Faculty research:* Nursing education, curriculum, clinical research, interdisciplinary research. *Unit head:* Dr. Marcella Rutherford, Dean, 954-262-1963, E-mail: rmarcell@nova.edu. *Application contact:* Keatta Jerry, Application Contact, 954-262-1114, E-mail: keatta@nova.edu. Web site: http://www.nova.edu/nursing/.

Oakland University, Graduate Study and Lifelong Learning, School of Nursing, Rochester, MI 48309-4401. Offers MSN, DNP, Certificate. *Accreditation:* AACN. Part-time and evening/weekend programs available. *Entrance requirements:* For master's, GRE General Test, minimum GPA of 3.0 for unconditional admission. Electronic applications accepted. *Faculty research:* Accelerated Health Care Career Training Initiative.

The Ohio State University, Graduate School, College of Nursing, Columbus, OH 43210. Offers MS, DNP, PhD. *Accreditation:* AACN; ACNM/ACME. Part-time programs available. *Faculty:* 30. *Students:* 215 full-time (180 women), 213 part-time (195 women); includes 51 minority (20 Black or African American, non-Hispanic/Latino; 1 American Indian or Alaska Native, non-Hispanic/Latino; 14 Asian, non-Hispanic/Latino; 9 Hispanic/Latino; 7 Two or more races, non-Hispanic/Latino), 5 international. Average age 35. In 2011, 93 master's, 11 doctorates awarded. *Degree requirements:* For master's, thesis optional; for doctorate, thesis/dissertation. *Entrance requirements:* Additional exam requirements/recommendations for international students: Required—TOEFL (minimum score 600 paper-based; 250 computer-based; 79 iBT), Michigan English Language Assessment Battery (minimum score 82). *Application deadline:* For fall admission, 8/15 priority date for domestic students, 7/1 for international students; for winter admission, 12/1 priority date for domestic students, 11/1 for international students; for spring admission, 3/1 priority date for domestic students, 2/1 for international students. Applications are processed on a rolling basis. Application fee: $40 ($50 for international students). Electronic applications accepted. *Expenses:* Tuition, state resident: full-time $11,400. Tuition, nonresident: full-time $28,125. Tuition and fees vary according to course load, degree level, campus/location and program. *Financial support:* Fellowships, research assistantships, teaching assistantships, Federal Work-Study, institutionally sponsored loans, and unspecified assistantships available. Support available to part-time students. *Unit head:* Bernadette M. Melnyk, Dean, 614-292-4844, Fax: 614-292-4535, E-mail: melnyk.15@osu.edu. *Application contact:* Graduate Admissions, 614-292-6031, Fax: 614-292-3656, E-mail: domestic.grad@osu.edu. Web site: http://nursing.osu.edu/.

Ohio University, Graduate College, College of Health Sciences and Professions, School of Nursing, Athens, OH 45701-2979. Offers acute care nurse practitioner (MSN); acute care nurse practitioner and family nurse practitioner (MSN); acute care nurse practitioner and nurse administrator (MSN); acute care nurse practitioner and nurse educator (MSN); family nurse practitioner (MSN); nurse administrator (MSN); nurse administrator and family nurse practitioner (MSN); nurse educator (MSN); nurse educator and family nurse practitioner (MSN); nurse educator and nurse administrator (MSN). *Accreditation:* AACN. *Students:* 33 full-time (29 women), 91 part-time (84 women); includes 16 minority (8 Black or African American, non-Hispanic/Latino; 2 Asian, non-Hispanic/Latino; 1 Hispanic/Latino; 5 Two or more races, non-Hispanic/Latino), 3 international. 86 applicants, 86% accepted, 61 enrolled. In 2011, 24 master's awarded. *Degree requirements:* For master's, capstone project. *Entrance requirements:* For master's, GRE, bachelor's degree in nursing from an accredited college or university, minimum overall undergraduate GPA of 3.0, official transcripts, statement of goals and objectives, resume, 3 letters of recommendation. Additional exam requirements/recommendations for international students: Required—TOEFL (minimum

score 550 paper-based; 80 iBT) or IELTS (minimum score 6.5). *Application deadline:* For fall admission, 3/1 priority date for domestic students, 2/1 for international students. Applications are processed on a rolling basis. Application fee: $50 ($55 for international students). Electronic applications accepted. *Financial support:* Research assistantships, Federal Work-Study, institutionally sponsored loans, and unspecified assistantships available. Financial award application deadline: 3/1. *Unit head:* Dr. Deborah Henderson, Professor and Interim Director, 740-593-4497, Fax: 740-593-0286, E-mail: hendersd@ohio.edu. *Application contact:* Cheryl Brimner, Administrative Associate, 740-593-4494, Fax: 740-593-0286, E-mail: brimner@ohio.edu. Web site: http://www.ohio.edu/chsp/nrse/index.cfm.

Oklahoma City University, Kramer School of Nursing, Oklahoma City, OK 73106-1402. Offers MSN, DNP, PhD. *Accreditation:* NLN. *Faculty:* 7 full-time (6 women), 7 part-time/adjunct (5 women). *Students:* 13 full-time (11 women), 67 part-time (7 women); includes 20 minority (6 Black or African American, non-Hispanic/Latino; 6 American Indian or Alaska Native, non-Hispanic/Latino; 3 Asian, non-Hispanic/Latino; 2 Hispanic/Latino; 3 Two or more races, non-Hispanic/Latino), 7 international. Average age 40. 15 applicants, 87% accepted, 7 enrolled. In 2011, 10 degrees awarded. *Degree requirements:* For master's, thesis; for doctorate, comprehensive exam, thesis/dissertation. *Entrance requirements:* For master's, registered nurse licensure, minimum undergraduate GPA of 3.0, BSN from nationally accredited nursing program, completion of courses in health assessment and statistics. Additional exam requirements/recommendations for international students: Required—TOEFL (minimum score 550 paper-based). *Application deadline:* Applications are processed on a rolling basis. Application fee: $50 ($70 for international students). Electronic applications accepted. *Expenses: Tuition:* Full-time $16,848; part-time $936 per credit hour. *Required fees:* $2070; $115 per credit hour. One-time fee: $300. *Financial support:* Applicants required to submit FAFSA. *Unit head:* Dr. Marvel L. Williamson, Dean, 405-208-5900, Fax: 405-208-5914, E-mail: mwilliamson@okcu.edu. *Application contact:* Michelle Cook, Director, Admissions, 405-208-5340, Fax: 405-208-5916, E-mail: gadmissions@okcu.edu. Web site: http://www.okcu.edu/nursing/.

Old Dominion University, College of Health Sciences, Doctor of Nursing Practice Program, Norfolk, VA 23529. Offers DNP. Part-time programs available. Postbaccalaureate distance learning degree programs offered (minimal on-campus study). *Faculty:* 4 full-time (all women), 2 part-time/adjunct (both women). *Students:* 12 full-time (11 women), 20 part-time (all women); includes 11 minority (6 Black or African American, non-Hispanic/Latino; 1 American Indian or Alaska Native, non-Hispanic/Latino; 2 Asian, non-Hispanic/Latino; 2 Hispanic/Latino). Average age 49. 26 applicants, 100% accepted, 24 enrolled. In 2011, 23 doctorates awarded. *Degree requirements:* For doctorate, thesis/dissertation, capstone project. *Entrance requirements:* Additional exam requirements/recommendations for international students: Required—TOEFL. *Application deadline:* For spring admission, 9/15 priority date for domestic students. Applications are processed on a rolling basis. Application fee: $50. Electronic applications accepted. *Expenses:* Tuition, state resident: full-time $9096; part-time $379 per credit. Tuition, nonresident: full-time $23,064; part-time $961 per credit. *Required fees:* $127 per semester. One-time fee: $50. *Financial support:* In 2011–12, 2 students received support, including 1 fellowship with full tuition reimbursement available (averaging $15,000 per year), 2 teaching assistantships with full tuition reimbursements available (averaging $15,000 per year); scholarships/grants, traineeships, and unspecified assistantships also available. *Faculty research:* Cultural competency, sleep disorders, self-care in HIV positive African-American women, ethical decision-making in pediatric cases. *Unit head:* Dr. Carolyn M. Rutledge, Director, 757-683-5009, Fax: 757-683-5253, E-mail: crutledg@odu.edu. *Application contact:* Sue Parker, Coordinator, Graduate Student Services, 757-683-4298, Fax: 757-683-5124, E-mail: sparker@odu.edu. Web site: http://www.odu.edu/dnp.

Old Dominion University, College of Health Sciences, School of Nursing, Norfolk, VA 23529. Offers family nurse practitioner (MSN); nurse administrator (MSN); nurse anesthesia (MSN); nurse educator (MSN); nurse midwifery (MSN); women's health nurse practitioner (MSN). *Accreditation:* AACN; AANA/CANAEP (one or more programs are accredited). Part-time programs available. Postbaccalaureate distance learning degree programs offered (no on-campus study). *Faculty:* 11 full-time (10 women), 15 part-time/adjunct (14 women). *Students:* 101 full-time (90 women), 98 part-time (94 women); includes 43 minority (27 Black or African American, non-Hispanic/Latino; 4 Asian, non-Hispanic/Latino; 8 Hispanic/Latino; 2 Native Hawaiian or other Pacific Islander, non-Hispanic/Latino; 2 Two or more races, non-Hispanic/Latino). Average age 35. 211 applicants, 57% accepted, 93 enrolled. In 2011, 81 master's awarded. *Degree requirements:* For master's, comprehensive exam; for doctorate, capstone project. *Entrance requirements:* For master's, GRE or MAT, BSN, minimum GPA of 3.0 in nursing and overall. Additional exam requirements/recommendations for international students: Required—TOEFL. *Application deadline:* For fall admission, 5/1 for domestic students, 4/15 for international students. Applications are processed on a rolling basis. Application fee: $50. Electronic applications accepted. *Expenses:* Tuition, state resident: full-time $9096; part-time $379 per credit. Tuition, nonresident: full-time $23,064; part-time $961 per credit. *Required fees:* $127 per semester. One-time fee: $50. *Financial support:* In 2011–12, 18 students received support, including 2 research assistantships with partial tuition reimbursements available (averaging $10,000 per year); teaching assistantships, career-related internships or fieldwork, scholarships/grants, traineeships, and tuition waivers (partial) also available. Support available to part-time students. Financial award application deadline: 2/15; financial award applicants required to submit FAFSA. *Faculty research:* Health and culture, cardiovascular health, transition of military families, genetics, cultural diversity. *Total annual research expenditures:* $231,117. *Unit head:* Dr. Karen Karlowicz, Chair, 757-683-5262, Fax: 757-683-5253, E-mail: nursgpd@odu.edu. *Application contact:* Sue Parker, Coordinator, Graduate Student Services, 757-683-4298, Fax: 757-683-5253, E-mail: sparker@odu.edu. Web site: http://hs.odu.edu/nursing/.

Oregon Health & Science University, School of Nursing, Portland, OR 97239-3098. Offers MN, MPH, MS, DNP, PhD, Post Master's Certificate. *Accreditation:* AACN; ACNM/ACME (one or more programs are accredited). Part-time programs available. *Degree requirements:* For master's, thesis optional; for doctorate, thesis/dissertation. *Entrance requirements:* For master's, GRE General Test, bachelor's degree in nursing, minimum undergraduate GPA of 3.0, previous course work in statistics; for doctorate, GRE General Test, master's degree in nursing; minimum undergraduate GPA of 3.0, 3.5 graduate; for Post Master's Certificate, master's degree in nursing. Electronic applications accepted. *Expenses:* Contact institution. *Faculty research:* Nursing care of older persons; families in health, illness, and transition; family caregiving; end of life care/decision making; mother-infant interactions; pregnancy outcomes; enteral feeding; psychoactive drugs in long-term care.

Otterbein University, Department of Nursing, Westerville, OH 43081. Offers advanced practice nurse educator (Certificate); clinical nurse leader (MSN); family nurse practitioner (MSN, Certificate); nurse anesthesia (MSN, Certificate); nursing (DNP); nursing service administration (MSN). *Accreditation:* AACN; AANA/CANAEP; NLN. Part-time and evening/weekend programs available. Postbaccalaureate distance learning degree programs offered (minimal on-campus study). *Degree requirements:* For master's, comprehensive exam (for some programs), thesis (for some programs).

Entrance requirements: For master's, 2 reference forms, resume; for Certificate, official transcripts, 2 reference forms, essay, resumé. Additional exam requirements/recommendations for international students: Required—TOEFL (minimum score 550 paper-based; 213 computer-based; 79 iBT). *Faculty research:* Patient education, women's health, trauma curriculum development, administration.

Our Lady of the Lake College, School of Nursing, Baton Rouge, LA 70808. Offers nurse anesthesia (MS); nursing (MS), including administration, education. *Accreditation:* NLN.

Pace University, Lienhard School of Nursing, New York, NY 10038. Offers family nurse practitioner (MS); nursing education (MA); nursing leadership (Advanced Certificate); nursing practice (DNP). *Accreditation:* AACN. Part-time and evening/weekend programs available. Postbaccalaureate distance learning degree programs offered. *Faculty:* 10 full-time (8 women), 37 part-time/adjunct (30 women). *Students:* 32 full-time (26 women), 417 part-time (381 women); includes 187 minority (88 Black or African American, non-Hispanic/Latino; 1 American Indian or Alaska Native, non-Hispanic/Latino; 49 Asian, non-Hispanic/Latino; 43 Hispanic/Latino; 1 Native Hawaiian or other Pacific Islander, non-Hispanic/Latino; 5 Two or more races, non-Hispanic/Latino), 5 international. Average age 36. 437 applicants, 41% accepted, 84 enrolled. In 2011, 96 master's, 20 doctorates, 3 other advanced degrees awarded. *Degree requirements:* For master's, thesis. *Entrance requirements:* For master's, GRE General Test or MAT, RN license, resume, personal statement, 2 letters of recommendation, official transcripts; for doctorate, RN license, resume, personal statement, 2 letters of recommendation, official transcripts, accredited master's degree in nursing, minimum GPA of 3.3, state certification; for Advanced Certificate, RN license, completion of 2nd degree in nursing. Additional exam requirements/recommendations for international students: Required—TOEFL. *Application deadline:* For fall admission, 7/31 priority date for domestic students, 4/30 for international students; for spring admission, 10/14 for domestic students, 9/14 for international students. Applications are processed on a rolling basis. Application fee: $70. Electronic applications accepted. *Expenses:* Contact institution. *Financial support:* Research assistantships, career-related internships or fieldwork, Federal Work-Study, and tuition waivers (partial) available. Support available to part-time students. Financial award applicants required to submit FAFSA. *Unit head:* Dr. Geraldine Colombraro, Interim Dean, 914-773-3341, E-mail: gcolombraro@pace.edu. *Application contact:* Susan Ford-Goldschein, Director of Graduate Admissions, 914-422-4283, Fax: 914-422-4287, E-mail: gradwp@pace.edu. Web site: http://www.pace.edu/.

Pacific Lutheran University, Division of Graduate Studies, School of Nursing, Tacoma, WA 98447. Offers MSN. *Accreditation:* AACN. Part-time programs available. *Faculty:* 4 full-time (3 women), 3 part-time/adjunct (2 women). *Students:* 55 full-time (44 women), 1 (woman) part-time; includes 3 minority (2 Asian, non-Hispanic/Latino; 1 Hispanic/Latino). Average age 32. In 2011, 22 master's awarded. *Degree requirements:* For master's, thesis or alternative. *Entrance requirements:* For master's, GRE General Test, minimum undergraduate GPA of 3.0. Additional exam requirements/recommendations for international students: Required—TOEFL (minimum score 550 paper-based; 213 computer-based). *Application deadline:* For fall admission, 4/1 priority date for domestic students. Applications are processed on a rolling basis. Application fee: $40. *Expenses: Tuition:* Part-time $915 per semester hour. *Financial support:* Fellowships, Federal Work-Study, scholarships/grants, and unspecified assistantships available. Financial award application deadline: 3/1; financial award applicants required to submit FAFSA. *Unit head:* Dr. Terry Miller, Dean and Graduate Program Director, 253-535-7672, Fax: 253-535-7590, E-mail: millertw@plu.edu. *Application contact:* Rachel Christopherson, Director, Graduate Admission, 253-535-8570, Fax: 253-536-5136, E-mail: admission@plu.edu.

Penn State University Park, Graduate School, College of Health and Human Development, School of Nursing, State College, University Park, PA 16802-1503. Offers MS, PhD. *Accreditation:* AACN; NLN. *Unit head:* Dr. Ann C. Crouter, Dean, 814-865-1428, Fax: 814-865-3282, E-mail: ac1@psu.edu. *Application contact:* Cynthia E. Nicosia, Director, Graduate Enrollment Services, 814-865-1795, Fax: 814-865-4627, E-mail: cey1@psu.edu. Web site: http://www.nursing.psu.edu/.

Pittsburg State University, Graduate School, College of Arts and Sciences, Department of Nursing, Pittsburg, KS 66762. Offers MSN. *Accreditation:* AACN. *Entrance requirements:* For master's, GRE General Test. *Expenses:* Tuition, state resident: full-time $5056; part-time $211 per credit hour. Tuition, nonresident: full-time $13,410; part-time $559 per credit hour. *Required fees:* $50 per credit hour.

Point Loma Nazarene University, Program in Nursing, San Diego, CA 92106-2899. Offers MSN, Post-MSN Certificate. *Accreditation:* AACN. Part-time programs available. *Entrance requirements:* For master's, MAT, BS in nursing, interview, minimum GPA of 3.0, RN license.

Pontifical Catholic University of Puerto Rico, College of Sciences, Department of Nursing, Ponce, PR 00717-0777. Offers medical-surgical nursing (MSN); mental health and psychiatric nursing (MSN). *Accreditation:* NLN. Part-time and evening/weekend programs available. *Degree requirements:* For master's, comprehensive exam (for some programs), thesis, clinical research paper. *Entrance requirements:* For master's, GRE General Test, 2 letters of recommendation, interview, minimum GPA of 2.5. Electronic applications accepted.

Prairie View A&M University, College of Nursing, Houston, TX 77030. Offers family nurse practitioner (MSN); nursing administration (MSN); nursing education (MSN). *Accreditation:* AACN; NLN. Part-time programs available. *Degree requirements:* For master's, comprehensive exam, thesis. *Entrance requirements:* For master's, MAT or GRE, BS in nursing; 2 years of experience as a registered nurse; 1 course each in statistics, basic health and assessment. *Faculty research:* Software development and violence prevention, health promotion and disease prevention.

Purdue University Calumet, Graduate Studies Office, School of Nursing, Hammond, IN 46323-2094. Offers adult health clinical nurse specialist (MS); critical care clinical nurse specialist (MS); family nurse practitioner (MS); nurse executive (MS). *Accreditation:* AACN; NLN. Part-time programs available. Postbaccalaureate distance learning degree programs offered (minimal on-campus study). *Entrance requirements:* For master's, BSN. Additional exam requirements/recommendations for international students: Required—TOEFL. Electronic applications accepted. *Faculty research:* Adult health, cardiovascular and pulmonary nursing.

Queen's University at Kingston, School of Graduate Studies and Research, Faculty of Health Sciences, School of Nursing, Kingston, ON K7L 3N6, Canada. Offers health and chronic illness (M Sc); nurse scientist (PhD); primary health care nurse practitioner (Certificate); women's and children's health (M Sc). *Degree requirements:* For master's, thesis. *Entrance requirements:* For master's, RN license. Additional exam requirements/recommendations for international students: Required—TOEFL. *Faculty research:* Women and children's health, health and chronic illness.

Queens University of Charlotte, Presbyterian School of Nursing, Charlotte, NC 28274-0002. Offers nursing management (MSN). *Accreditation:* AACN. *Degree requirements:* For master's, research project. *Entrance requirements:* For master's, minimum GPA of 3.0. Additional exam requirements/recommendations for international students: Required—TOEFL. Electronic applications accepted. *Expenses:* Contact institution.

Nursing—General

Quinnipiac University, School of Nursing, Hamden, CT 06518-1940. Offers MSN, DNP. Part-time programs available. *Faculty:* 6 full-time (5 women), 7 part-time/adjunct (4 women). *Students:* 33 full-time (30 women), 97 part-time (91 women); includes 30 minority (15 Black or African American, non-Hispanic/Latino; 9 Asian, non-Hispanic/Latino; 6 Hispanic/Latino), 2 international. 78 applicants, 71% accepted, 46 enrolled. In 2011, 38 master's awarded. *Degree requirements:* For master's, thesis optional, clinical practicum. *Entrance requirements:* For master's, RN license, minimum GPA of 3.0. Additional exam requirements/recommendations for international students: Required—TOEFL (minimum score 575 paper-based; 233 computer-based; 90 iBT), IELTS (minimum score 6.5). *Application deadline:* For fall admission, 6/1 priority date for domestic students, 4/30 for international students. Applications are processed on a rolling basis. Application fee: $45. Electronic applications accepted. *Expenses: Tuition:* Part-time $855 per credit. *Required fees:* $35 per credit. *Financial support:* In 2011–12, 54 students received support. Traineeships, tuition waivers (partial), and unspecified assistantships available. Support available to part-time students. Financial award application deadline: 4/15; financial award applicants required to submit FAFSA. *Unit head:* Dr. Jeanne LeVasseur, Director of Graduate Admissions, 203-582-3484, Fax: 203-582-3230, E-mail: jeanne.levasseur@quinnipiac.edu. *Application contact:* Kristin Parent, Assistant Director of Graduate Health Sciences Admissions, 800-462-1944, Fax: 203-582-3443, E-mail: kristin.parent@quinnipiac.edu. Web site: http://www.quinnipiac.edu/gradnursing.

Radford University, College of Graduate and Professional Studies, Waldron College of Health and Human Services, School of Nursing, Radford, VA 24142. Offers MSN, DNP. *Accreditation:* AACN. Part-time programs available. *Faculty:* 13 full-time (11 women), 3 part-time/adjunct (1 woman). *Students:* 9 full-time (all women), 34 part-time (all women); includes 2 minority (1 Black or African American, non-Hispanic/Latino; 1 Asian, non-Hispanic/Latino), 1 international. Average age 41. 35 applicants, 74% accepted, 22 enrolled. In 2011, 12 master's awarded. *Degree requirements:* For master's, comprehensive exam, thesis optional. *Entrance requirements:* For master's, GRE, minimum undergraduate GPA of 3.0, 3 letters of reference from professional contacts, letter of intent, resume, professional writing sample, official transcripts. Additional exam requirements/recommendations for international students: Required—TOEFL (minimum score 550 paper-based; 213 computer-based; 79 iBT). *Application deadline:* For fall admission, 2/15 priority date for domestic students, 12/1 for international students; for spring admission, 7/1 for international students. Applications are processed on a rolling basis. Application fee: $50. Electronic applications accepted. *Expenses:* Tuition, state resident: full-time $6262; part-time $261 per credit hour. Tuition, nonresident: full-time $14,540; part-time $606 per credit hour. *Required fees:* $2812; $117 per credit hour. Tuition and fees vary according to program. *Financial support:* In 2011–12, 3 students received support, including 3 teaching assistantships with partial tuition reimbursements available (averaging $8,420 per year); career-related internships or fieldwork, Federal Work-Study, institutionally sponsored loans, scholarships/grants, and unspecified assistantships also available. Financial award application deadline: 3/1; financial award applicants required to submit FAFSA. *Unit head:* Dr. Kimberly F. Carter, Director, 540-831-7700, Fax: 540-831-7716, E-mail: kcarter@radford.edu. *Application contact:* Rebecca Conner, Graduate Admissions, 540-831-5431, Fax: 540-831-6061, E-mail: gradcollege@radford.edu. Web site: http://www.radford.edu/content/wchs/home/nursing.html/.

Ramapo College of New Jersey, Master of Science in Nursing Program, Mahwah, NJ 07430. Offers nursing education (MSN). *Accreditation:* NLN. Part-time programs available. Postbaccalaureate distance learning degree programs offered (minimal on-campus study). *Faculty:* 2 full-time (both women), 2 part-time/adjunct (1 woman). *Students:* 2 full-time (both women), 42 part-time (40 women); includes 6 minority (3 Black or African American, non-Hispanic/Latino; 2 Asian, non-Hispanic/Latino; 1 Two or more races, non-Hispanic/Latino). Average age 41. 21 applicants, 90% accepted, 15 enrolled. In 2011, 13 master's awarded. *Degree requirements:* For master's, capstone project. *Entrance requirements:* For master's, interview; 2 letters of reference; immunizations; official transcript from accredited higher education institution with minimum cumulative GPA of 3.0; 1 year recent experience as RN; evidence of undergraduate statistics course; background check; current licensure as RN in NJ or eligibility for licensure. Additional exam requirements/recommendations for international students: Required—TOEFL (minimum score 550 paper-based; 213 computer-based; 95 iBT). *Application deadline:* Applications are processed on a rolling basis. Application fee: $60. *Expenses: Tuition, area resident:* Part-time $551.05 per credit. Tuition, nonresident: part-time $708.30 per credit. *Required fees:* $122.50 per credit. *Financial support:* In 2011–12, 10 students received support, including 10 fellowships with partial tuition reimbursements available (averaging $1,992 per year); traineeships also available. Financial award applicants required to submit FAFSA. *Faculty research:* Learning styles and critical thinking, evidence-based education, outcomes measurement. *Unit head:* Dr. Kathleen M. Burke, Assistant Dean, 201-684-7737, E-mail: kmburke@ramapo.edu. *Application contact:* Ulysses Simpkins, Program Assistant, 201-684-7749, E-mail: usimpkin@ramapo.edu. Web site: http://www.ramapo.edu/msn/.

Regis College, School of Nursing, Science and Health Professions, Weston, MA 02493. Offers biomedical sciences (MS); health administration (MS); nurse practitioner (Certificate); nursing (MS, DNP); nursing education (Certificate). *Accreditation:* NLN. Part-time and evening/weekend programs available. *Degree requirements:* For master's, thesis. *Entrance requirements:* For master's, GRE General Test or MAT, minimum GPA of 3.0; for doctorate, MAT or GRE if GPA from master's lower than 3.5. Additional exam requirements/recommendations for international students: Required—TOEFL (minimum score 550 paper-based; 213 computer-based). Electronic applications accepted. *Faculty research:* Health policy, education, aging, job satisfaction, psychiatric nursing, critical thinking.

Regis University, Rueckert-Hartman College for Health Professions, Denver, CO 80221-1099. Offers family nurse practitioner (MSN); health informatics (Postbaccalaureate Certificate); health services administration (MS); leadership in healthcare systems (MSN); neonatal nurse practitioner (MSN); nursing (MSN); pharmacy (Pharm D); physical therapy (DPT, TDPT). *Entrance requirements:* Additional exam requirements/recommendations for international students: Required—TOEFL (minimum score 550 paper-based; 213 computer-based; 82 iBT). Electronic applications accepted. *Expenses:* Contact institution. *Faculty research:* Normal and pathological balance and gait research, normal/pathological upper limb motor control/biomechanics, exercise energy/metabolism research, optical treatment protocols for therapeutic modalities.

Research College of Nursing, Nursing Program, Kansas City, MO 64132. Offers clinical nurse leader (MSN); executive nurse practitioner (MSN); family nurse practitioner (MSN); nurse educator (MSN). *Accreditation:* AACN. Part-time programs available. Postbaccalaureate distance learning degree programs offered (no on-campus study). *Faculty:* 8 full-time (all women), 1 (woman) part-time/adjunct. *Students:* 9 full-time (7 women), 132 part-time (121 women). Average age 30. In 2011, 23 master's awarded. *Degree requirements:* For master's, research project. *Entrance requirements:* For master's, 3 letters of recommendation, official transcripts, resume. Additional exam requirements/recommendations for international students: Required—TOEFL (minimum score 550 paper-based; 213 computer-based), TWE. *Application deadline:* Applications are processed on a rolling basis. Application fee: $50. *Expenses: Tuition:* Part-time $425 per credit hour. *Required fees:* $25 per credit hour. *Financial support:* Applicants required to submit FAFSA. *Unit head:* Dr. Nancy O. DeBasio, President and Dean, 816-995-2815, Fax: 816-995-2817, E-mail: nancy.debasio@researchcollege.edu. *Application contact:* Leslie Mendenhall, Director of Transfer and Graduate Recruitment, 816-995-2820, Fax: 816-995-2813, E-mail: leslie.mendenhall@researchcollege.edu.

Resurrection University, Nursing Program, Oak Park, IL 60302. Offers MSN. *Entrance requirements:* For master's, letter of recommendation.

Rhode Island College, School of Graduate Studies, School of Nursing, Providence, RI 02908-1991. Offers MSN. *Accreditation:* AACN. Part-time programs available. *Faculty:* 6 full-time (all women), 2 part-time/adjunct (both women). *Students:* 4 full-time (3 women), 42 part-time (37 women); includes 3 minority (2 Black or African American, non-Hispanic/Latino; 1 Hispanic/Latino), 1 international. Average age 44. In 2011, 10 master's awarded. *Entrance requirements:* For master's, GRE, undergraduate transcripts; minimum undergraduate GPA of 3.0; 3 letters of recommendation; evidence of current unrestricted Rhode Island RN licensure; professional resume; letter of intent. Additional exam requirements/recommendations for international students: Recommended—TOEFL (minimum score 550 paper-based; 213 computer-based; 79 iBT). *Application deadline:* For fall admission, 2/15 for domestic students. Applications are processed on a rolling basis. Application fee: $50. *Expenses:* Tuition, state resident: full-time $8592; part-time $358 per credit hour. Tuition, nonresident: full-time $16,800; part-time $700 per credit hour. *Required fees:* $602; $22 per credit. $72 per term. *Financial support:* Teaching assistantships with full tuition reimbursements, Federal Work-Study, scholarships/grants, health care benefits, and unspecified assistantships available. Support available to part-time students. Financial award application deadline: 5/15; financial award applicants required to submit FAFSA. *Unit head:* Dr. Jane Williams, Dean, 401-456-8013, Fax: 401-456-9608, E-mail: jwilliams@ric.edu. *Application contact:* Graduate Studies, 401-456-8700. Web site: http://www.ric.edu/nursing/.

The Richard Stockton College of New Jersey, School of Graduate and Continuing Studies, Program in Nursing, Pomona, NJ 08240-0195. Offers MSN. *Accreditation:* AACN. Part-time programs available. *Faculty:* 5 full-time (4 women). *Students:* 10 full-time (8 women), 29 part-time (25 women); includes 10 minority (1 Black or African American, non-Hispanic/Latino; 3 Asian, non-Hispanic/Latino; 4 Hispanic/Latino; 2 Two or more races, non-Hispanic/Latino). Average age 42. 17 applicants, 76% accepted, 11 enrolled. In 2011, 11 master's awarded. *Degree requirements:* For master's, 300 clinical hours. *Entrance requirements:* For master's, CPR certification, minimum GPA of 3.0, RN license. Additional exam requirements/recommendations for international students: Required—TOEFL. *Application deadline:* For fall admission, 7/1 for domestic and international students; for spring admission, 12/1 for domestic and international students. Applications are processed on a rolling basis. Application fee: $50. Electronic applications accepted. *Expenses:* Tuition, state resident: full-time $13,035; part-time $543 per credit. Tuition, nonresident: full-time $20,065; part-time $836 per credit. *Required fees:* $3920; $163 per credit. Tuition and fees vary according to degree level. *Financial support:* In 2011–12, 4 students received support, including 9 research assistantships with partial tuition reimbursements available; fellowships, career-related internships or fieldwork, Federal Work-Study, scholarships/grants, and unspecified assistantships also available. Support available to part-time students. Financial award application deadline: 3/1; financial award applicants required to submit FAFSA. *Faculty research:* Psychoneuroimmunology, relationship of nutrition and disease, mental health as affected by chronic disease states, home care for elderly relatives. *Unit head:* Dr. Michelle Sabatini, Program Director, 609-626-3640, E-mail: michelle.sabatini@stockton.edu. *Application contact:* Tara Williams, Associate Director of Admissions, 609-626-3640, Fax: 609-626-6050, E-mail: gradschool@stockton.edu.

Rivier University, School of Graduate Studies, Division of Nursing, Nashua, NH 03060. Offers adult psychiatric/mental health practitioner (MS); family nurse practitioner (MS); nursing education (MS). *Accreditation:* NLN. Part-time and evening/weekend programs available. *Entrance requirements:* For master's, GRE, MAT. Electronic applications accepted.

Robert Morris University, Graduate Studies, School of Nursing and Health Sciences, Moon Township, PA 15108-1189. Offers MSN, DNP. *Accreditation:* AACN. Part-time and evening/weekend programs available. *Faculty:* 7 full-time (3 women), 4 part-time/adjunct (3 women). *Students:* 146 part-time (131 women); includes 10 minority (5 Black or African American, non-Hispanic/Latino; 3 Asian, non-Hispanic/Latino; 2 Hispanic/Latino), 2 international. *Entrance requirements:* For master's, letters of recommendation. Additional exam requirements/recommendations for international students: Required—TOEFL (minimum score 550 paper-based; 213 computer-based; 79 iBT). *Application deadline:* For fall admission, 7/1 priority date for domestic students, 7/1 for international students; for spring admission, 11/1 priority date for domestic students, 11/1 for international students. Applications are processed on a rolling basis. Application fee: $35. Electronic applications accepted. *Expenses:* Contact institution. *Financial support:* Federal Work-Study, institutionally sponsored loans, and unspecified assistantships available. Financial award application deadline: 5/1; financial award applicants required to submit FAFSA. *Unit head:* Dr. Lynda J. Davidson, Dean, 412-397-6801, Fax: 412-397-3277, E-mail: davidson@rmu.edu. *Application contact:* Deborah Roach, Assistant Dean, Graduate Admissions, 412-397-5200, Fax: 412-397-2425, E-mail: graduateadmissions@rmu.edu. Web site: http://www.rmu.edu/web/cms/schools/snhs/.

Roberts Wesleyan College, Division of Nursing, Rochester, NY 14624-1997. Offers nursing administration (MSN); nursing education (MSN). *Accreditation:* AACN. *Entrance requirements:* For master's, minimum GPA of 3.0; BS in nursing; interview; RN license; resume; course work in statistics and health assessment. Additional exam requirements/recommendations for international students: Required—TOEFL.

Rocky Mountain University of Health Professions, MSN Program in Nursing, Provo, UT 84606. Offers MSN.

Rocky Mountain University of Health Professions, PhD Program in Nursing, Provo, UT 84606. Offers PhD. *Degree requirements:* For doctorate, thesis/dissertation.

Rush University, College of Nursing, Chicago, IL 60612-3832. Offers MSN, DNP, PhD, Post-Master's Certificate. *Accreditation:* AACN; AANA/CANAEP (one or more programs are accredited). Part-time programs available. Postbaccalaureate distance learning degree programs offered (minimal on-campus study). Terminal master's awarded for partial completion of doctoral program. *Degree requirements:* For master's, capstone project; for doctorate, thesis/dissertation, DNP leadership project. *Entrance requirements:* For master's, GRE General Test (waived if nursing GPA is greater than 3.0 or cumulative GPA is greater than 3.25), interview; for doctorate, GRE General Test. Additional exam requirements/recommendations for international students: Required—TOEFL, TWE. Electronic applications accepted. *Faculty research:* Parenting intervention, immigrant mental health, caregiver interventions, immune function, cardiac risk reduction.

Rutgers, The State University of New Jersey, Newark, Graduate School, Program in Nursing, Newark, NJ 07102. Offers nursing (MS), including acute care of adults and aged, advanced practice in pediatric nursing, advanced practice with childbearing families, community health nursing, family nurse practitioner, primary care of adults and

aged, psychiatric/mental health nursing. *Accreditation:* AACN. Part-time programs available. *Degree requirements:* For master's, comprehensive exam. *Entrance requirements:* For master's, GRE General Test, RN license, minimum B average, BS in nursing. Additional exam requirements/recommendations for international students: Required—TOEFL. Electronic applications accepted. *Faculty research:* HIV/AIDS, quality of life: MS and breast cancer, sleep patterns of cardiac patients.

Sacred Heart University, Graduate Programs, College of Health Professions, Department of Nursing, Fairfield, CT 06825-1000. Offers clinical nurse leader (MSN); clinical practice in health care (DNP); family nurse practitioner (MSN); leadership in health care (DNP); nursing (DN Sc); patient care services administration (MSN). *Accreditation:* AACN. Part-time and evening/weekend programs available. Postbaccalaureate distance learning degree programs offered (minimal on-campus study). *Entrance requirements:* For master's, BSN, minimum GPA of 3.0. Additional exam requirements/recommendations for international students: Required—TOEFL (minimum score 550 paper-based; 213 computer-based). Electronic applications accepted. *Expenses:* Contact institution.

Sage Graduate School, School of Health Sciences, Department of Nursing, Troy, NY 12180-4115. Offers adult health (MS); adult nurse practitioner (MS, Post Master's Certificate); clinical nurse leader/specialist (Post Master's Certificate); community health (MS); education and leadership (DNS); family nurse practitioner (MS, Post Master's Certificate); gerontological nurse practitioner (Post Master's Certificate); nurse administrator/executive (Post Master's Certificate); nursing (Post Master's Certificate); psychiatric mental health nurse practitioner (MS, Post Master's Certificate), including psychiatric mental health. *Accreditation:* AACN. Part-time and evening/weekend programs available. *Faculty:* 5 full-time (all women), 10 part-time/adjunct (all women). *Students:* 35 full-time (31 women), 158 part-time (152 women); includes 20 minority (8 Black or African American, non-Hispanic/Latino; 1 American Indian or Alaska Native, non-Hispanic/Latino; 8 Asian, non-Hispanic/Latino; 3 Hispanic/Latino), 7 international. Average age 42. 143 applicants, 32% accepted, 34 enrolled. In 2011, 30 master's, 1 doctorate, 5 other advanced degrees awarded. *Degree requirements:* For master's, thesis or alternative. *Entrance requirements:* For master's, BS in nursing, minimum GPA of 2.75, resume, 2 letters of recommendation. Additional exam requirements/recommendations for international students: Required—TOEFL (minimum score 550 paper-based; 213 computer-based). *Application deadline:* Applications are processed on a rolling basis. Application fee: $40. *Expenses: Tuition:* Full-time $11,880; part-time $660 per credit hour. Tuition and fees vary according to program. *Financial support:* Fellowships, research assistantships, Federal Work-Study, scholarships/grants, and unspecified assistantships available. Support available to part-time students. Financial award application deadline: 3/1; financial award applicants required to submit FAFSA. *Unit head:* Dr. Esther Haskevitz, Dean, School of Health Sciences, 518-244-2296, Fax: 518-244-4571, E-mail: haskve@sage.edu. *Application contact:* Dr. Glenda Kelman, Director, 518-244-2001, Fax: 518-244-2009, E-mail: kelmag@sage.edu.

Saginaw Valley State University, Crystal M. Lange College of Nursing and Health Sciences, Program in Clinical Nurse Specialist, University Center, MI 48710. Offers MSN. *Accreditation:* AACN. Part-time and evening/weekend programs available. *Students:* 1 (woman) part-time. Average age 36. *Degree requirements:* For master's, thesis optional. *Entrance requirements:* For master's, GRE. Additional exam requirements/recommendations for international students: Required—TOEFL (minimum score 525 paper-based; 237 computer-based; 92 iBT). *Application deadline:* Applications are processed on a rolling basis. Application fee: $25. Electronic applications accepted. *Expenses:* Tuition, state resident: full-time $8300; part-time $5333 per year. Tuition, nonresident: full-time $15,613; part-time $10,209 per year. *International tuition:* $15,631 full-time. *Financial support:* Federal Work-Study and scholarships/grants available. Support available to part-time students. Financial award application deadline: 4/1; financial award applicants required to submit FAFSA. *Unit head:* Dr. Sally Decker, Professor of Nursing, 989-964-4098, E-mail: decker@svsu.edu. *Application contact:* P. Laine Blasch, Graduate Recruitment Coordinator, 989-964-2182, Fax: 989-790-0180, E-mail: blasch@svsu.edu.

Saginaw Valley State University, Crystal M. Lange College of Nursing and Health Sciences, Program in Nursing, University Center, MI 48710. Offers MSN. *Accreditation:* AACN. *Students:* 2 full-time (both women), 1 (woman) part-time. Average age 41. 2 applicants, 100% accepted, 2 enrolled. *Expenses:* Tuition, state resident: full-time $8300; part-time $5333 per year. Tuition, nonresident: full-time $15,613; part-time $10,209 per year. *International tuition:* $15,631 full-time. *Financial support:* Federal Work-Study and scholarships/grants available. Support available to part-time students. *Unit head:* Dr. Sally Decker, Professor, 989-964-4098, E-mail: decker@svsu.edu. *Application contact:* P. Laine Blasch, Graduate Recruitment Coordinator, 989-964-2182, Fax: 989-790-0180, E-mail: blasch@svsu.edu.

St. Ambrose University, College of Education and Health Sciences, Program in Nursing, Davenport, IA 52803-2898. Offers MSN. *Accreditation:* AACN. Part-time and evening/weekend programs available. *Faculty:* 3 full-time (all women), 1 (woman) part-time/adjunct. *Students:* 20 part-time (all women); includes 2 minority (1 Asian, non-Hispanic/Latino; 1 Hispanic/Latino). Average age 46. 9 applicants, 78% accepted, 7 enrolled. *Entrance requirements:* Additional exam requirements/recommendations for international students: Required—TOEFL. *Application deadline:* Applications are processed on a rolling basis. Application fee: $25. Electronic applications accepted. *Expenses: Tuition:* Full-time $13,770; part-time $765 per credit hour. *Required fees:* $60 per semester. Tuition and fees vary according to degree level, program and reciprocity agreements. *Financial support:* In 2011–12, 2 students received support. Career-related internships or fieldwork, scholarships/grants, tuition waivers (partial), and unspecified assistantships available. *Unit head:* Kathryn M. McKnight, Director, 563-333-6069, Fax: 563-333-6063, E-mail: mcknightkathrynm@sau.edu. *Application contact:* Laura R. Hudson, Academic Advisor and Recruiter, 563-333-6082, Fax: 563-333-6063, E-mail: hudsonlaurar@sau.edu. Web site: http://web.sau.edu/nursing/msn/index.htm.

Saint Anthony College of Nursing, Graduate Program, Rockford, IL 61108-2468. Offers MSN. *Accreditation:* AACN. Part-time programs available.

St. Catherine University, Graduate Programs, Program in Nursing, St. Paul, MN 55105. Offers adult-gerontological nurse practitioner (MA); neonatal nurse practitioner (MA); nurse educator (MA); nursing (DNP); pediatric nurse practitioner (MA). *Accreditation:* NLN. Part-time and evening/weekend programs available. *Degree requirements:* For master's, thesis; for doctorate, portfolio, systems change project. *Entrance requirements:* For master's, GRE General Test, bachelor's degree in nursing, current nursing license, 2 years of recent clinical practice; for doctorate, master's degree in nursing, RN license, advanced nursing position. Additional exam requirements/recommendations for international students: Required—TOEFL (minimum score 600 paper-based; 250 computer-based; 100 iBT). *Expenses: Required fees:* $30 per semester. Tuition and fees vary according to program.

Saint Francis Medical Center College of Nursing, Graduate Programs, Peoria, IL 61603-3783. Offers child and family nurse practitioner (MSN); clinical nurse leader (MSN); family nurse practitioner (MSN); family psychiatric mental health nurse practitioner (MSN); medical-surgical nursing (MSN); neonatal nurse practitioner (MSN); nurse clinician (Post-Graduate Certificate); nurse educator (MSN, Post-Graduate Certificate); nursing (DNP); nursing management leadership (MSN). *Accreditation:* NLN. Part-time programs available. Postbaccalaureate distance learning degree programs offered (minimal on-campus study). *Faculty:* 6 full-time (all women), 5 part-time/adjunct (all women). *Students:* 26 full-time (25 women), 174 part-time (166 women); includes 19 minority (8 Black or African American, non-Hispanic/Latino; 1 American Indian or Alaska Native, non-Hispanic/Latino; 3 Asian, non-Hispanic/Latino; 6 Hispanic/Latino; 1 Native Hawaiian or other Pacific Islander, non-Hispanic/Latino). Average age 37. 123 applicants, 93% accepted, 93 enrolled. In 2011, 29 degrees awarded. *Degree requirements:* For master's, research experience, portfolio, practicum; for doctorate, practicum hours. *Entrance requirements:* For master's, nursing research, health assessment, graduate course work in statistics, RN license; for doctorate, master's degree in nursing, professional portfolio, graduate statistics, transcripts, RN license. Additional exam requirements/recommendations for international students: Required—TOEFL. *Application deadline:* For fall admission, 6/1 priority date for domestic students, 6/1 for international students; for spring admission, 11/15 priority date for domestic students, 11/15 for international students. Applications are processed on a rolling basis. Application fee: $50. Electronic applications accepted. *Expenses: Tuition:* Full-time $6120; part-time $510 per semester hour. *Required fees:* $300. *Financial support:* In 2011–12, 3 students received support. Scholarships/grants and tuition waivers (partial) available. Support available to part-time students. Financial award application deadline: 6/15; financial award applicants required to submit FAFSA. *Faculty research:* Outcome and curriculum planning, health promotion, NCLEX-RN results, decision-making program evaluation. *Unit head:* Dr. Patti A. Stockert, President of the College, 309-655-4124, Fax: 309-624-8973, E-mail: patricia.a.stockert@osfhealthcare.org. *Application contact:* Dr. Janice F. Boundy, Dean, 309-655-2230, Fax: 309-624-8973, E-mail: jan.f.boundy@osfhealthcare.org. Web site: http://www.sfmccon.edu/graduate-programs/.

St. John Fisher College, Wegmans School of Nursing, Advanced Practice Nursing Program, Rochester, NY 14618-3597. Offers advanced practice nursing (MS); clinical nurse specialist (Certificate); family nurse practitioner (Certificate); nurse educator (Certificate). *Accreditation:* AACN. Part-time and evening/weekend programs available. *Faculty:* 11 full-time (10 women), 4 part-time/adjunct (3 women). *Students:* 4 full-time (3 women), 98 part-time (96 women); includes 10 minority (7 Black or African American, non-Hispanic/Latino; 1 Asian, non-Hispanic/Latino; 2 Hispanic/Latino), 2 international. Average age 33. 35 applicants, 74% accepted, 21 enrolled. In 2011, 20 master's, 1 other advanced degree awarded. *Degree requirements:* For master's, clinical practice, project; for Certificate, clinical practice. *Entrance requirements:* For master's, BSN; undergraduate course work in statistics, health assessment, and nursing research; current New York State RN License; 2 letters of recommendation; current resume. Additional exam requirements/recommendations for international students: Required—TOEFL (minimum score 575 paper-based; 233 computer-based; 80 iBT). *Application deadline:* Applications are processed on a rolling basis. Application fee: $30. Electronic applications accepted. *Expenses: Tuition:* Part-time $735 per credit. One-time fee: $50 part-time. Tuition and fees vary according to course load, degree level and program. *Financial support:* In 2011–12, 39 students received support. Scholarships/grants and traineeships available. Financial award applicants required to submit FAFSA. *Faculty research:* Chronic illness, pediatric injury, women's health, public health policy, health care teams. *Unit head:* Dr. Cynthia McCloskey, Graduate Director, 585-385-8471, Fax: 585-385-8466, E-mail: cmccloskey@sjfc.edu. *Application contact:* Jose Perales, Director of Graduate Admissions, 585-385-8067, E-mail: jperales@sjfc.edu.

St. John Fisher College, Wegmans School of Nursing, Doctor of Nursing Practice Program, Rochester, NY 14618-3597. Offers DNP. Part-time and evening/weekend programs available. *Faculty:* 11 full-time (10 women), 4 part-time/adjunct (3 women). *Students:* 14 full-time (all women), 10 part-time (9 women); includes 4 minority (3 Black or African American, non-Hispanic/Latino; 1 Hispanic/Latino). Average age 43. 12 applicants, 100% accepted, 11 enrolled. In 2011, 5 doctorates awarded. *Degree requirements:* For doctorate, 1,000 hours of clinical practice, clinical scholarship project. *Entrance requirements:* For doctorate, New York State RN License; New York State Certificate as advanced practice nurse or eligibility and National Professional Certification in advanced practice nurse (APN) specialty; currently practicing as APN; 2 letters of recommendation; writing sample. *Application deadline:* For fall admission, 8/1 for domestic students; for spring admission, 12/1 for domestic students. Applications are processed on a rolling basis. Application fee: $0. Electronic applications accepted. *Expenses:* Contact institution. *Financial support:* In 2011–12, 20 students received support. Scholarships/grants available. Financial award applicants required to submit FAFSA. *Unit head:* Dr. Mary S. Collins, Program Director, 585-385-8397, E-mail: mscollins@sjfc.edu. *Application contact:* Jose Perales, Director of Graduate Admissions, 585-385-8067, E-mail: jperales@sjfc.edu. Web site: http://www.sjfc.edu/academics/nursing/departments/dnp/.

St. Joseph's College, Long Island Campus, Program in Nursing, Patchogue, NY 11772-2399. Offers MS.

St. Joseph's College, New York, Graduate Programs, Program in Nursing, Brooklyn, NY 11205-3688. Offers MS. *Accreditation:* NLN.

See Display on next page and Close-Up on page 803.

Saint Joseph's College of Maine, Master of Science in Nursing Program, Standish, ME 04084. Offers administration (MSN); education (MSN); family nurse practitioner (MSN); nursing administration and leadership (Certificate); nursing and health care education (Certificate). *Accreditation:* AACN. Part-time programs available. Postbaccalaureate distance learning degree programs offered (no on-campus study). *Faculty:* 2 full-time (both women), 22 part-time/adjunct (20 women). *Students:* 768 part-time (665 women); includes 85 minority (48 Black or African American, non-Hispanic/Latino; 21 Asian, non-Hispanic/Latino; 16 Hispanic/Latino). Average age 43. In 2011, 26 master's awarded. *Entrance requirements:* For master's, MAT. *Application deadline:* Applications are processed on a rolling basis. Application fee: $50. Electronic applications accepted. One-time fee: $50. *Financial support:* Institutionally sponsored loans available. Support available to part-time students. Financial award applicants required to submit FAFSA. *Unit head:* Joyce Murphy, Program Director, 207-893-7841, Fax: 207-892-7423, E-mail: jmurphy@sjcme.edu. *Application contact:* Lynne Robinson, Director of Admissions, 800-752-4723, Fax: 207-892-7480, E-mail: info@sjcme.edu. Web site: http://online.sjcme.edu/master-science-nursing.php.

Saint Louis University, Graduate Education, Doisy College of Health Sciences, School of Nursing, St. Louis, MO 63104-1099. Offers MSN, DNP, PhD, Certificate. *Accreditation:* AACN. Part-time programs available. Postbaccalaureate distance learning degree programs offered (minimal on-campus study). *Degree requirements:* For master's, comprehensive exam, thesis optional; for doctorate, comprehensive exam, thesis/dissertation, preliminary exams. *Entrance requirements:* For master's, 3 letters of recommendation, resumé, transcripts; for doctorate, GRE General Test, 3 letters of recommendation, curriculum vitae; for Certificate, 3 letters of recommendation, resumé, transcripts, copy of RN license, personal statement. Additional exam requirements/recommendations for international students: Required—TOEFL (minimum score 525 paper-based; 194 computer-based). Electronic applications accepted. *Faculty research:*

Nursing—General

Sensory enhancement to the elderly, fall prevention in elderly, tube feeding placement and gastroenterology, patient outcomes, exercise behavior in the older adult.

Saint Peter's University, School of Nursing, Nursing Program, Jersey City, NJ 07306-5997. Offers adult nurse practitioner (MSN, Certificate); advanced practice (DNP); case management (MSN, DNP). *Accreditation:* AACN. Part-time and evening/weekend programs available. *Entrance requirements:* Additional exam requirements/recommendations for international students: Required—TOEFL (minimum score 79 computer-based). Electronic applications accepted.

Saint Xavier University, Graduate Studies, School of Nursing, Chicago, IL 60655-3105. Offers MSN, Certificate, MBA/MS. *Accreditation:* AACN. Part-time and evening/weekend programs available. *Entrance requirements:* For master's, GRE General Test or MAT, minimum GPA of 3.0, RN license. *Application deadline:* For fall admission, 2/15 for domestic students; for spring admission, 9/15 for domestic students. Applications are processed on a rolling basis. Application fee: $35. *Expenses: Tuition:* Part-time $750 per credit hour. *Required fees:* $135 per semester. Tuition and fees vary according to program. *Financial support:* Available to part-time students. Applicants required to submit FAFSA. *Unit head:* Gloria Jacobson, Dean, 773-298-3706, Fax: 773-298-3076, E-mail: jacobson@sxu.edu. *Application contact:* Beth Gierach, Managing Director of Admission, 773-298-3053, Fax: 773-298-3076, E-mail: gierach@sxu.edu. Web site: http://www.sxu.edu/academics/colleges_schools/son/.

Salem State University, School of Graduate Studies, Program in Nursing, Salem, MA 01970-5353. Offers direct entry nursing (MSN); MBA/MSN. *Accreditation:* AACN. Part-time and evening/weekend programs available. *Entrance requirements:* For master's, GRE or MAT. Additional exam requirements/recommendations for international students: Required—TOEFL (minimum score 550 paper-based; 80 iBT) or IELTS (minimum score 5.5).

Salisbury University, Graduate Division, Program in Nursing, Salisbury, MD 21801-6837. Offers MS. *Accreditation:* AACN. Part-time programs available. *Faculty:* 7 full-time (6 women), 1 part-time/adjunct (0 women). *Students:* 7 full-time (all women), 35 part-time (30 women); includes 10 minority (6 Black or African American, non-Hispanic/Latino; 3 Hispanic/Latino; 1 Two or more races, non-Hispanic/Latino), 1 international. Average age 35. 18 applicants, 72% accepted, 13 enrolled. In 2011, 14 master's awarded. *Degree requirements:* For master's, thesis optional, thesis, capstone project, or internship. *Entrance requirements:* For master's, NLN- or CCNE-accredited baccalaureate degree in nursing, minimum undergraduate GPA of 3.0, personal statement, resume or curriculum vitae, 2 recommendations, evidence of current RN license in state where practicing, interview, CPR certification, passport photo, proof of immunizations. Additional exam requirements/recommendations for international students: Required—TOEFL (minimum score 550 paper-based; 79 iBT). *Application deadline:* For fall admission, 2/15 for domestic students; for spring admission, 10/15 for domestic students. Applications are processed on a rolling basis. Application fee: $45. Electronic applications accepted. *Expenses: Tuition, area resident:* Part-time $306 per credit hour. Tuition, state resident: Part-time $306 per credit hour. Tuition, nonresident: part-time $595 per credit hour. *Required fees:* $68 per credit hour. *Financial support:* In 2011–12, 18 students received support. Career-related internships or fieldwork, institutionally sponsored loans, scholarships/grants, and unspecified assistantships available. Support available to part-time students. Financial award application deadline: 3/1; financial award applicants required to submit FAFSA. *Faculty research:* UMB Susan Komen Breast Cancer. *Total annual research expenditures:* $366,293. *Unit head:* Dr. Mary Parsons, Director, 410-543-6416, Fax: 410-548-3313, E-mail: mtparsons@salisbury.edu. *Application contact:* Carmel Boger, Administrative Assistant, 410-543-6420, Fax: 410-548-3313, E-mail: ciboger@salisbury.edu. Web site: http://www.salisbury.edu/nursing/ms.html.

Samford University, Ida V. Moffett School of Nursing, Birmingham, AL 35229. Offers advance practice (DNP); anesthesia (MSN); family nurse practitioner (MSN); nurse educator (MSN); nurse executive (DNP); nurse manager (MSN). *Accreditation:* AACN; AANA/CANAEP (one or more programs are accredited). Part-time programs available. Postbaccalaureate distance learning degree programs offered (minimal on-campus study). *Faculty:* 14 full-time (all women), 2 part-time/adjunct (0 women). *Students:* 226 full-time (152 women), 42 part-time (20 women); includes 43 minority (14 Black or African American, non-Hispanic/Latino; 4 American Indian or Alaska Native, non-Hispanic/Latino; 15 Asian, non-Hispanic/Latino; 9 Hispanic/Latino; 1 Native Hawaiian or other Pacific Islander, non-Hispanic/Latino), 2 international. Average age 39. 50 applicants, 88% accepted, 44 enrolled. In 2011, 95 master's, 14 doctorates awarded. *Median time to degree:* Of those who began their doctoral program in fall 2003, 100% received their degree in 8 years or less. *Degree requirements:* For master's and doctorate, capstone project with oral presentation. *Entrance requirements:* For master's, MAT; GRE (for nurse anesthesia). Additional exam requirements/recommendations for international students: Required—TOEFL (minimum score 550 paper-based; 213 computer-based; 80 iBT). *Application deadline:* For fall admission, 7/1 priority date for domestic students, 7/1 for international students; for spring admission, 10/1 priority date for domestic students, 10/1 for international students. Application fee: $65. Electronic applications accepted. *Expenses:* Contact institution. *Financial support:* In 2011–12, 166 students received support. Institutionally sponsored loans, scholarships/grants, and traineeships available. Financial award application deadline: 3/1; financial award applicants required to submit FAFSA. *Faculty research:* Issues in rural health care, vulnerable populations, genetics and disabilities in pediatrics, geriatrics, Parrish nursing research. *Unit head:* Dr. Nena F. Sanders, Dean, 205-726-2629, E-mail: nfsander@samford.edu. *Application contact:* Dr. Marian Carter, Director of Graduate Student Services, 205-726-2047, Fax: 205-726-4269, E-mail: mwcarter@samford.edu. Web site: http://samford.edu/nursing.

Samuel Merritt University, School of Nursing, Oakland, CA 94609-3108. Offers case management (MSN); family nurse practitioner (MSN, Certificate); nurse anesthetist (MSN, Certificate); nursing (MSN, DNP). *Accreditation:* AACN; AANA/CANAEP (one or more programs are accredited). Part-time and evening/weekend programs available. *Degree requirements:* For master's, thesis or alternative. *Entrance requirements:* For master's, minimum GPA of 2.5 in science, 3.0 overall; previous course work in statistics; current RN license. Additional exam requirements/recommendations for international students: Required—TOEFL. *Faculty research:* Gerontology, community health, maternal-child health, sexually transmitted diseases, substance abuse, oncology.

San Diego State University, Graduate and Research Affairs, College of Health and Human Services, School of Nursing, San Diego, CA 92182. Offers MS. *Accreditation:* AACN; ACNM/ACME. Part-time and evening/weekend programs available. *Entrance requirements:* For master's, GRE General Test, previous course work in statistics and physical assessment, 3 letters of recommendation, California RN license. Additional exam requirements/recommendations for international students: Required—TOEFL. Electronic applications accepted. *Faculty research:* Health promotion, nursing systems and leadership, maternal-child nursing, advanced practice nursing, child oral health.

San Francisco State University, Division of Graduate Studies, College of Health and Human Services, School of Nursing, San Francisco, CA 94132-1722. Offers clinical nurse specialist (MS); community/public health nursing (MS); family nurse practitioner (MS, Certificate); nursing administration (MS); nursing education (MS). *Accreditation:* AACN. Part-time programs available. *Application deadline:* Applications are processed on a rolling basis. *Financial support:* Career-related internships or fieldwork available. *Unit head:* Dr. Lynette Landry, Director, 415-338-1802, E-mail: llandry@sfsu.edu. *Application contact:* Dr. Mary-Ann van Dam, Associate Director, 415-338-1802, E-mail: vandam@sfsu.edu. Web site: http://nursing.sfsu.edu.

sjcny.edu

An Ambition Fulfilled

Graduate Degree Programs

MANAGEMENT · NURSING · EDUCATION · HUMAN SERVICES · CREATIVE WRITING

Looking for a more exciting, challenging career? A St. Joseph's education can provide the critical knowledge and skills you need to get ahead.

- Undergraduate, graduate and certificate programs
- Emphasis on career preparation and enhancement
- Strong academic, and value-oriented education
- Affordable

A St. Joseph's College graduate degree. Take a look, and give us a call.

St. Joseph's College
NEW YORK
SCHOOL OF PROFESSIONAL AND GRADUATE STUDIES

Transforming lives—one student at a time.

LONG ISLAND **631.687.4501** BROOKLYN **718.940.5800**

"My professors inspired me with their intense passion for teaching."

Michelle-Lee '02, Director of Compliance, Maxim Group

San Jose State University, Graduate Studies and Research, College of Applied Sciences and Arts, School of Nursing, San Jose, CA 95192-0001. Offers gerontology nurse practitioner (MS); nursing (Certificate); nursing administration (MS); nursing education (MS). *Accreditation:* AACN. Part-time and evening/weekend programs available. *Degree requirements:* For master's, thesis. *Entrance requirements:* For master's, BS in nursing, RN license. Electronic applications accepted. *Faculty research:* Nurse-managed clinics, computers in nursing.

Seattle Pacific University, MS in Nursing Program, Seattle, WA 98119-1997. Offers administration (MSN); adult/gerontology nurse practitioner (MSN); clinical nurse specialist (MSN); family nurse practitioner (MSN, Certificate); informatics (MSN); nurse educator (MSN). *Accreditation:* AACN. Part-time programs available. *Degree requirements:* For master's, thesis. Electronic applications accepted. *Expenses:* Contact institution.

Seattle University, College of Nursing, Program in Advanced Practice Nursing Immersion, Seattle, WA 98122-1090. Offers adult/gerontological nurse practitioner (MSN); advanced community public health (MSN); certified nurse midwifery (MSN); family nurse practitioner (MSN); psychiatric mental health nurse practitioner (MSN). *Faculty:* 43 full-time, 63 part-time/adjunct. *Students:* 104 full-time (91 women); includes 24 minority (2 Black or African American, non-Hispanic/Latino; 12 Asian, non-Hispanic/Latino; 7 Hispanic/Latino; 3 Two or more races, non-Hispanic/Latino). Average age 30. *Degree requirements:* For master's, thesis or scholarly project. *Entrance requirements:* For master's, GRE, bachelor's degree, minimum GPA of 3.0, professional resume, two recommendations, letter of intent, English proficiency (for non-English speakers). Additional exam requirements/recommendations for international students: Required—TOEFL (minimum score 92 iBT), IELTS. *Application deadline:* For fall admission, 12/1 for domestic and international students. Application fee: $55. Electronic applications accepted. *Financial support:* Scholarships/grants and traineeships available. Financial award applicants required to submit FAFSA. *Unit head:* Dr. Azita Emami, Dean, 206-296-5660. *Application contact:* Janet Shandley, Associate Dean of Graduate Admissions, 206-296-5900, Fax: 206-298-5656, E-mail: grad_admissions@seattleu.edu.

Seattle University, College of Nursing, Program in Nursing, Seattle, WA 98122-1090. Offers adult/gerontological nurse practitioner (MSN); advanced community public health (MSN); psychiatric mental health nurse practitioner (MSN). *Faculty:* 43 full-time, 63 part-time/adjunct. *Students:* 22 full-time (20 women); includes 4 minority (1 Black or African American, non-Hispanic/Latino; 1 Asian, non-Hispanic/Latino; 1 Hispanic/Latino; 1 Two or more races, non-Hispanic/Latino). *Degree requirements:* For master's, thesis or scholarly project. *Entrance requirements:* For master's, GRE, bachelor's degree in nursing or associate degree in nursing with baccalaureate in different major, 5-quarter statistics course, minimum cumulative GPA of 3.0, professional resume, two recommendations, letter of intent, English proficiency (for non-English speakers), copy of current RN license or ability to obtain RN license in WA state. Additional exam requirements/recommendations for international students: Required—TOEFL (minimum score 92 iBT), IELTS. *Application deadline:* For fall admission, 12/1 for domestic and international students. Application fee: $55. Electronic applications accepted. *Financial support:* In 2011–12, 2 teaching assistantships were awarded; scholarships/grants and traineeships also available. Financial award applicants required to submit FAFSA. *Unit head:* Dr. Azita Emami, Dean, 206-296-5660. *Application contact:* Janet Shandley, Associate Dean of Graduate Admissions, 206-296-5900, Fax: 206-298-5656, E-mail: grad_admissions@seattleu.edu.

Seton Hall University, College of Nursing, South Orange, NJ 07079-2697. Offers advanced practice in primary health care (MSN, DNP), including adult/gerontological nurse practitioner, pediatric nurse practitioner; entry into practice (MSN); health systems administration (MSN, DNP); nursing (PhD); nursing case management (MSN); nursing education (MA); school nurse (MSN); MSN/MA. *Accreditation:* AACN. Part-time programs available. Postbaccalaureate distance learning degree programs offered (minimal on-campus study). *Faculty:* 10 full-time (all women), 3 part-time/adjunct (1 woman). *Students:* 12 full-time (11 women), 217 part-time (197 women); includes 38 minority (15 Black or African American, non-Hispanic/Latino; 1 American Indian or Alaska Native, non-Hispanic/Latino; 12 Asian, non-Hispanic/Latino; 10 Hispanic/Latino). 180 applicants, 51% accepted, 82 enrolled. *Degree requirements:* For master's, research project; for doctorate, dissertation or scholarly project. *Entrance requirements:* For doctorate, GRE (waived for students with GPA of 3.5 or higher). Additional exam requirements/recommendations for international students: Required—TOEFL. *Application deadline:* For fall admission, 4/15 priority date for domestic students. Applications are processed on a rolling basis. Electronic applications accepted. *Expenses: Tuition:* Part-time 1033 per credit hour. *Required fees:* $85 per semester. *Financial support:* Institutionally sponsored loans, scholarships/grants, traineeships, tuition waivers (partial), and unspecified assistantships available. Support available to part-time students. Financial award applicants required to submit FAFSA. *Faculty research:* Parent/child, adult, and gerontological nursing; breast cancer; families of children with HIV; parish nursing. *Unit head:* Dr. Phyllis Shanley Hansell, Dean, 973-761-9014, E-mail: phyllis.hansell@shu.edu. *Application contact:* Kristyn Kent Wuillermin, Director of Strategic Alliances, Marketing and Enrollment, 973-761-9291, Fax: 973-761-9607, E-mail: kristyn.kent@shu.edu.

Shenandoah University, School of Health Professions, Division of Nursing, Winchester, VA 22601-5195. Offers family nurse practitioner (Certificate); nurse-midwifery (Certificate); nurse-midwifery endorsement (Certificate); nursing (MSN, DNP); post-master's in nursing education (Certificate); psychiatric mental health nurse practitioner (Certificate). *Accreditation:* AACN; ACNM/ACME. Part-time programs available. *Faculty:* 11 full-time (all women), 2 part-time/adjunct (both women). *Students:* 40 full-time (34 women), 102 part-time (96 women); includes 32 minority (22 Black or African American, non-Hispanic/Latino; 1 American Indian or Alaska Native, non-Hispanic/Latino; 5 Asian, non-Hispanic/Latino; 3 Hispanic/Latino; 1 Two or more races, non-Hispanic/Latino), 2 international. Average age 39. 69 applicants, 90% accepted, 45 enrolled. In 2011, 15 master's, 2 doctorates, 17 other advanced degrees awarded. *Degree requirements:* For master's, research project, clinical hours; for doctorate and Certificate, clinical hours. *Entrance requirements:* For master's, GRE General Test, previous course work in statistics, community nursing, and physical assessment; RN license; BSN; minimum undergraduate GPA of 3.0; appropriate clinical experience; curriculum vitae; 3 letters of recommendation; for doctorate, MSN, minimum GPA of 3.0, 3 letters of recommendation, essay, interview; for Certificate, MSN, minimum GPA of 3.0, 3 letters of recommendation, minimum of one year (2,080 hours) clinical nursing experience, interview. Additional exam requirements/recommendations for international students: Required—TOEFL (minimum score 550 paper-based; 213 computer-based; 79 iBT), IELTS (minimum score 6.5), Sakae Institute of Study Abroad (minimum score 550). *Application deadline:* For fall admission, 6/15 priority date for domestic students, 6/15 for international students. Applications are processed on a rolling basis. Application fee: $30. Electronic applications accepted. *Expenses: Tuition:* Full-time $17,952; part-time $748 per credit. *Required fees:* $500 per term. Tuition and fees vary according to course level, course load and program. *Financial support:* In 2011–12, 13 students received support, including 3 teaching assistantships with partial tuition reimbursements available (averaging $4,224 per year); career-related internships or fieldwork, institutionally

sponsored loans, scholarships/grants, unspecified assistantships, and federal loans, alternative loans also available. Support available to part-time students. Financial award application deadline: 3/15; financial award applicants required to submit FAFSA. *Faculty research:* Moral reasoning in nurses, improving health care access to under-served rural women, screening for depression and anxiety in the obese in a rural free clinic, health care outcomes among patients in a free clinic setting cared for by nurse practitioners, effects of depression on diabetes as evidenced by the relationship between the patient healthcare questionnaire (PHQ-9) scores and the patient's glycohemoglobin (HbA1c). *Unit head:* Dr. Kathryn Ganske, Director, 540-678-4374, Fax: 540-665-5519, E-mail: kganske@su.edu. *Application contact:* David Anthony, Dean of Admissions, 540-665-4581, Fax: 540-665-4627, E-mail: admit@su.edu. Web site: http://www.su.edu/nurse.

Simmons College, School of Nursing and Health Sciences, Boston, MA 02115. Offers didactic dietetics (Certificate); health professions education (CAGS); nursing (MS); nursing administration (MS); nursing practice (DNP); nutrition (MS, Certificate); physical therapy (DPT); sports nutrition (Certificate); sports nutrition/didactic dietetics (Certificate); MS/Certificate. *Unit head:* Dr. Judy Beal, Dean, 617-521-2139, Fax: 617-521-3137, E-mail: judy.beal@simmons.edu. *Application contact:* Carmen Fortin, Assistant Dean/Director of Admission, 617-521-2651, Fax: 617-521-3137, E-mail: gshsadm@simmons.edu. Web site: http://www.simmons.edu/snhs/.

South Dakota State University, Graduate School, College of Nursing, Brookings, SD 57007. Offers MS, PhD. *Accreditation:* AACN. Part-time and evening/weekend programs available. Postbaccalaureate distance learning degree programs offered. *Degree requirements:* For master's, comprehensive exam, thesis (for some programs), oral exam. *Entrance requirements:* For master's, nurse registration; for doctorate, nurse registration, MS. Additional exam requirements/recommendations for international students: Required—TOEFL (minimum score 525 paper-based; 197 computer-based; 71 iBT). *Expenses:* Contact institution. *Faculty research:* Rural health, aging, health promotion, Native American health, woman's health, underserved populations, quality of life.

Southeastern Louisiana University, College of Nursing and Health Sciences, School of Nursing, Hammond, LA 70402. Offers adult psychiatric/mental health nurse practitioner/clinical nurse specialist (MSN); education (MSN); nurse executive (MSN); nurse practitioner (MSN). *Accreditation:* AACN. Part-time and evening/weekend programs available. *Faculty:* 12 full-time (11 women), 7 part-time/adjunct (4 women). *Students:* 17 full-time (16 women), 108 part-time (94 women); includes 12 minority (8 Black or African American, non-Hispanic/Latino; 2 Asian, non-Hispanic/Latino; 1 Hispanic/Latino; 1 Two or more races, non-Hispanic/Latino), 1 international. Average age 35. 50 applicants, 100% accepted, 29 enrolled. In 2011, 27 degrees awarded. *Degree requirements:* For master's, thesis. *Entrance requirements:* For master's, GRE (verbal and quantitative), baccalaureate degree in nursing from accredited undergraduate nursing program; minimum GPA of 2.7; all transcripts from undergraduate school and any work attempted at the graduate level; curriculum vitae; valid Louisiana Registered Nurse license; letters of recommendation; letter of intent/statement of purpose. Additional exam requirements/recommendations for international students: Required—TOEFL (minimum score 500 paper-based; 173 computer-based; 61 iBT). *Application deadline:* For fall admission, 7/15 priority date for domestic students, 6/1 for international students; for spring admission, 12/1 priority date for domestic students, 10/1 for international students. Applications are processed on a rolling basis. Application fee: $20 ($30 for international students). Electronic applications accepted. *Expenses:* Tuition, state resident: full-time $3977; part-time $283 per semester hour. Tuition, nonresident: full-time $13,482; part-time $811 per semester hour. *Financial support:* Federal Work-Study, institutionally sponsored loans, scholarships/grants, traineeships, and unspecified assistantships available. Support available to part-time students. Financial award application deadline: 5/1; financial award applicants required to submit FAFSA. *Faculty research:* Gender issues, LGBT issues, occupational health/safety, accelerated students, caring development. Total annual research expenditures: $245,268. *Unit head:* Dr. Lorinda Sealy, Graduate Coordinator, 985-549-5045, Fax: 985-549-5087, E-mail: lorinda.sealy@selu.edu. *Application contact:* Sandra Meyers, Graduate Admissions Analyst, 985-549-5620, Fax: 985-549-5632, E-mail: admissions@selu.edu. Web site: http://www.selu.edu/acad_research/depts/nurs.

Southeast Missouri State University, School of Graduate Studies, Department of Nursing, Cape Girardeau, MO 63701-4799. Offers MSN. Fall semester admission only. *Accreditation:* AACN. *Faculty:* 15 full-time (all women). *Students:* 38 part-time (33 women); includes 2 minority (both American Indian or Alaska Native, non-Hispanic/Latino). Average age 34. 39 applicants, 31% accepted, 11 enrolled. In 2011, 15 master's awarded. *Degree requirements:* For master's, research paper and comprehensive exam or thesis and oral defense. *Entrance requirements:* For master's, minimum GPA of 3.25; current Missouri license as a Registered Professional Nurse; CPR certification; BSN; professional liability insurance; minimum B grade in statistics; statement of academic goals and objectives. Additional exam requirements/recommendations for international students: Required—TOEFL (minimum score 550 paper-based; 213 computer-based; 79 iBT); Recommended—IELTS (minimum score 6). *Application deadline:* For fall admission, 8/1 priority date for domestic students, 7/1 for international students. Applications are processed on a rolling basis. Application fee: $30 ($40 for international students). Electronic applications accepted. *Expenses:* Tuition, state resident: full-time $4896; part-time $272 per credit hour. Tuition, nonresident: full-time $8649; part-time $480.50 per credit hour. *Financial support:* In 2011–12, 10 students received support, including 6 teaching assistantships with full tuition reimbursements available (averaging $7,600 per year); career-related internships or fieldwork, Federal Work-Study, scholarships/grants, tuition waivers (full), and unspecified assistantships also available. Financial award application deadline: 6/30; financial award applicants required to submit FAFSA. *Faculty research:* Gerontology, teaching methodology, addictions, student transition into leadership, health outcomes. *Unit head:* Dr. Gloria J. Green, Chairperson, 573-651-5154, E-mail: gjgreen@semo.edu. *Application contact:* Alisa Aleen McFerron, Assistant Director of Admissions for Operations, 573-651-5937, Fax: 573-651-5936, E-mail: amcferron@semo.edu. Web site: http://www2.semo.edu/nursing/.

Southern Adventist University, School of Nursing, Collegedale, TN 37315-0370. Offers acute care nurse practitioner (MSN); adult nurse practitioner (MSN); family nurse practitioner (MSN); nurse educator (MSN); MSN/MSBA. *Accreditation:* NLN. Part-time programs available. *Degree requirements:* For master's, thesis or project. *Entrance requirements:* For master's, RN license. Additional exam requirements/recommendations for international students: Required—TOEFL (minimum score 600 paper-based; 250 computer-based). Electronic applications accepted. *Faculty research:* Pain management, ethics, corporate wellness, caring spirituality, stress.

Southern Connecticut State University, School of Graduate Studies, School of Health and Human Services, Department of Nursing, New Haven, CT 06515-1355. Offers nursing administration (MSN); nursing education (MSN). *Accreditation:* AACN; AANA/CANAEP. Part-time and evening/weekend programs available. *Faculty:* 3 full-time (all women), 1 (woman) part-time/adjunct. *Students:* 9 full-time (8 women), 23 part-time (19 women); includes 3 minority (1 Black or African American, non-Hispanic/Latino; 1 Asian, non-Hispanic/Latino; 1 Hispanic/Latino). 120 applicants, 12% accepted, 11 enrolled. In 2011, 1 master's awarded. *Degree requirements:* For master's, thesis. *Entrance*

requirements: For master's, GRE, MAT, interview, minimum QPA of 2.8, RN license, minimum 1 year of professional nursing experience. *Application deadline:* For fall admission, 7/15 priority date for domestic students. Applications are processed on a rolling basis. Application fee: $50. Electronic applications accepted. *Expenses:* Tuition, state resident: full-time $5137; part-time $413 per credit. *Required fees:* $4008; $55 per term. *Financial support:* Application deadline: 4/15; applicants required to submit FAFSA. *Unit head:* Dr. Lisa Rebeschi, Chairperson, 203-392-6485, E-mail: rebeschil1@southernct.edu. *Application contact:* Dr. Antonia Nelson, Graduate Coordinator, 203-392-6480, Fax: 203-392-6493, E-mail: nelsona13@southernct.edu.

Southern Illinois University Edwardsville, Graduate School, School of Nursing, Edwardsville, IL 62026. Offers MS, DNP, Post-Master's Certificate. *Accreditation:* AACN. Part-time programs available. *Faculty:* 28 full-time (26 women). *Students:* 69 full-time (43 women), 169 part-time (155 women); includes 31 minority (12 Black or African American, non-Hispanic/Latino; 1 American Indian or Alaska Native, non-Hispanic/Latino; 11 Asian, non-Hispanic/Latino; 3 Hispanic/Latino; 4 Two or more races, non-Hispanic/Latino), 3 international. 218 applicants, 33% accepted. In 2011, 51 master's awarded. *Degree requirements:* For master's, comprehensive exam. *Entrance requirements:* For master's, appropriate bachelor's degree, RN license; for Post-Master's Certificate, minimum graduate nursing GPA of 3.0, completion of graduate-level statistics and epidemiology courses with minimum B grade, current unencumbered RN licensure. Additional exam requirements/recommendations for international students: Required—TOEFL (minimum score 550 paper-based; 213 computer-based; 79 iBT), IELTS (minimum score 6.5). *Application deadline:* For fall admission, 3/1 for domestic and international students. Application fee: $30. Electronic applications accepted. Tuition and fees vary according to course load and program. *Financial support:* In 2011–12, 3 fellowships with full tuition reimbursements (averaging $8,370 per year), 2 research assistantships with full tuition reimbursements (averaging $9,927 per year), 2 teaching assistantships with full tuition reimbursements (averaging $9,927 per year) were awarded; institutionally sponsored loans, scholarships/grants, and unspecified assistantships also available. Financial award application deadline: 3/1; financial award applicants required to submit FAFSA. *Unit head:* Dr. Marcia Maurer, Dean, 618-650-3959, E-mail: mamaure@siue.edu. *Application contact:* Dr. Kathy Ketchum, Director, 618-650-3936, E-mail: kketchu@siue.edu. Web site: http://www.siue.edu/nursing/graduate.

Southern Nazarene University, Graduate College, School of Nursing, Bethany, OK 73008. Offers nursing education (MS); nursing leadership (MS). *Accreditation:* AACN. Part-time and evening/weekend programs available. *Degree requirements:* For master's, thesis. *Entrance requirements:* For master's, minimum undergraduate cumulative GPA of 3.0; baccalaureate degree in nursing from nationally-accredited program; current unencumbered registered nurse licensure in Oklahoma or eligibility for same; documentation of basic computer skills; basic statistics course; statement of professional goals; three letters of recommendation. Additional exam requirements/recommendations for international students: Required—TOEFL (minimum score 550 paper-based; 213 computer-based). *Expenses: Tuition:* Full-time $17,009; part-time $639 per credit hour. *Required fees:* $2668. *Unit head:* Dr. Katie Sigler, Interim Chair, 405-717-6217, E-mail: ksigler@snu.edu. *Application contact:* Dr. Mary Hibbert, Program Director, 405-491-6612, Fax: 405-491-6302, E-mail: mhibbert@snu.edu. Web site: http://snu.edu/school-of-nursing.

Southern University and Agricultural and Mechanical College, School of Nursing, Baton Rouge, LA 70813. Offers educator/administrator (PhD); family health nursing (MSN); family nurse practitioner (Post Master's Certificate); geriatric nurse practitioner/gerontology (PhD). *Accreditation:* AACN. Part-time programs available. *Degree requirements:* For master's, comprehensive exam, thesis; for doctorate, comprehensive exam, thesis/dissertation. *Entrance requirements:* For master's, GRE General Test, BSN, minimum GPA of 2.7; for doctorate, GRE General Test; for Post Master's Certificate, MSN. Additional exam requirements/recommendations for international students: Required—TOEFL (minimum score 525 paper-based; 193 computer-based). *Faculty research:* Health promotions, vulnerable populations, (community-based) cardiovascular participating research, health disparities chronic diseases, care of the elderly.

South University, Graduate Programs, College of Nursing, Savannah, GA 31406. Offers nurse educator (MS).

South University, Program in Nursing, Tampa, FL 33614. Offers adult health nurse practitioner (MS); family nurse practitioner (MS); nurse educator (MS).

South University, Program in Nursing, Royal Palm Beach, FL 33411. Offers family nurse practitioner (MS).

Spalding University, Graduate Studies, College of Health and Natural Sciences, School of Nursing, Louisville, KY 40203-2188. Offers adult nurse practitioner (MSN); family nurse practitioner (MSN); leadership in nursing and healthcare (MSN); pediatric nurse practitioner (MSN). *Accreditation:* AACN. Part-time and evening/weekend programs available. *Faculty:* 6 full-time (all women), 5 part-time/adjunct (all women). *Students:* 90 full-time (82 women), 24 part-time (all women); includes 21 minority (16 Black or African American, non-Hispanic/Latino; 3 Asian, non-Hispanic/Latino; 1 Hispanic/Latino; 1 Native Hawaiian or other Pacific Islander, non-Hispanic/Latino). Average age 36. 85 applicants, 24% accepted, 15 enrolled. In 2011, 23 master's awarded. *Degree requirements:* For master's, comprehensive exam (for some programs), thesis. *Entrance requirements:* For master's, GRE General Test, BSN or bachelor's degree and RN licensure. Additional exam requirements/recommendations for international students: Required—TOEFL (minimum score 535 paper-based; 203 computer-based). *Application deadline:* For fall admission, 3/1 priority date for domestic students. Applications are processed on a rolling basis. Application fee: $30. *Expenses: Tuition:* Full-time $12,438. Tuition and fees vary according to course load, degree level and program. *Financial support:* In 2011–12, 21 students received support, including 1 research assistantship with partial tuition reimbursement available (averaging $4,260 per year); career-related internships or fieldwork, scholarships/grants, and traineeships also available. Support available to part-time students. Financial award application deadline: 3/15; financial award applicants required to submit FAFSA. *Faculty research:* Nurse educational administration, gerontology, bioterrorism, healthcare ethics, leadership. *Unit head:* Dr. Paula Travis, Chair, 502-873-4298, E-mail: clewis@spalding.edu. *Application contact:* Dr. Pam King, 502-873-4292, E-mail: pking@spalding.edu. Web site: http://www.spalding.edu/nursing/.

Spring Arbor University, School of Graduate and Professional Studies, Spring Arbor, MI 49283-9799. Offers counseling (MAC); family studies (MAFS); nursing (MSN); organizational management (MSM). Part-time and evening/weekend programs available. Postbaccalaureate distance learning degree programs offered (no on-campus study). *Faculty:* 12 full-time (5 women), 113 part-time/adjunct (67 women). *Students:* 363 full-time (300 women), 344 part-time (265 women); includes 166 minority (142 Black or African American, non-Hispanic/Latino; 4 American Indian or Alaska Native, non-Hispanic/Latino; 5 Asian, non-Hispanic/Latino; 13 Hispanic/Latino; 2 Two or more races, non-Hispanic/Latino), 1 international. Average age 40. In 2011, 276 master's awarded. *Entrance requirements:* For master's, bachelor's degree from regionally-accredited college or university, minimum GPA of 3.0 for at least the last two years of the bachelor's degree, at least two recommendations from professional/academic individuals. Additional exam requirements/recommendations for international students: Required—TOEFL (minimum score 600 paper-based; 220 computer-based). *Application deadline:* Applications are processed on a rolling basis. Application fee: $40. Electronic applications accepted. *Expenses: Tuition:* Full-time $5500; part-time $490 per credit hour. *Required fees:* $240; $120 per term. Tuition and fees vary according to program. *Financial support:* Scholarships/grants available. Support available to part-time students. Financial award applicants required to submit FAFSA. *Unit head:* Natalie Gianetti, Dean, 517-750-1200 Ext. 1343, Fax: 517-750-6602, E-mail: gianetti@arbor.edu. *Application contact:* Greg Bentle, Coordinator of Graduate Recruitment, 517-750-6763, Fax: 517-750-6624, E-mail: gbentle@arbor.edu. Web site: http://www.arbor.edu/.

Spring Hill College, Graduate Programs, Program in Nursing, Mobile, AL 36608-1791. Offers clinical nurse leader (MSN). *Accreditation:* AACN. Part-time and evening/weekend programs available. Postbaccalaureate distance learning degree programs offered (no on-campus study). *Faculty:* 4 full-time (all women). *Students:* 27 part-time (all women); includes 13 minority (all Black or African American, non-Hispanic/Latino). Average age 44. In 2011, 18 master's, 2 other advanced degrees awarded. *Degree requirements:* For master's, comprehensive exam, capstone courses, completion of program within 6 calendar years; for Post-Master's Certificate, 460 clinical integration hours. *Entrance requirements:* For master's, RN license in state where practicing nursing; 1 year of clinical nursing experience; work in clinical setting or have access to health care facility for clinical integration/research; 3 written references; employer verification; resume; 500-word essay explaining how becoming a CNL will help applicant achieve personal and professional goals; for Post-Master's Certificate, RN license; master's degree in nursing. Additional exam requirements/recommendations for international students: Required—TOEFL (minimum score 550 paper-based; 213 computer-based; 80 iBT), IELTS (minimum score 6.5), CPE or CAE (minimum score C), Michigan English Language Assessment Battery (minimum score 90). *Application deadline:* For fall admission, 8/1 priority date for domestic students, 8/1 for international students; for spring admission, 12/1 priority date for domestic students, 12/1 for international students. Applications are processed on a rolling basis. Application fee: $25 ($35 for international students). Electronic applications accepted. *Expenses:* Contact institution. *Financial support:* Applicants required to submit FAFSA. *Unit head:* Dr. Ola H. Fox, Director, 251-380-4486, Fax: 251-460-4495, E-mail: ofox@shc.edu. *Application contact:* Donna B. Tarasavage, Director of Admissions, Graduate and Continuing Studies, 251-380-3067, Fax: 251-460-2190, E-mail: dtarasavage@shc.edu. Web site: http://www.shc.edu/grad/academics/nursing.

State University of New York at Binghamton, Graduate School, Decker School of Nursing, Binghamton, NY 13902-6000. Offers MS, PhD, Certificate. *Accreditation:* AACN. Part-time and evening/weekend programs available. *Faculty:* 42 full-time (39 women), 46 part-time/adjunct (42 women). *Students:* 93 full-time (86 women), 109 part-time (101 women); includes 30 minority (10 Black or African American, non-Hispanic/Latino; 8 Asian, non-Hispanic/Latino; 7 Hispanic/Latino; 5 Native Hawaiian or other Pacific Islander, non-Hispanic/Latino), 7 international. Average age 37. 110 applicants, 80% accepted, 77 enrolled. In 2011, 41 master's, 3 doctorates, 71 other advanced degrees awarded. *Degree requirements:* For master's, comprehensive exam, thesis; for doctorate, thesis/dissertation. *Entrance requirements:* For master's, GRE General Test. Additional exam requirements/recommendations for international students: Required—TOEFL. *Application deadline:* For fall admission, 4/15 priority date for domestic students, 1/15 for international students; for spring admission, 11/1 for domestic students, 10/1 for international students. Applications are processed on a rolling basis. Application fee: $60. Electronic applications accepted. *Financial support:* In 2011–12, 22 students received support, including 4 fellowships with partial tuition reimbursements available (averaging $8,250 per year), 1 research assistantship with full tuition reimbursement available (averaging $10,000 per year), 8 teaching assistantships with full tuition reimbursements available (averaging $10,000 per year); career-related internships or fieldwork, Federal Work-Study, institutionally sponsored loans, traineeships, health care benefits, tuition waivers (full and partial), and unspecified assistantships also available. Financial award application deadline: 2/15; financial award applicants required to submit FAFSA. *Unit head:* Dr. Joyce Ferrario, Dean, 607-777-2311, Fax: 607-777-4440, E-mail: jferrari@binghamton.edu. *Application contact:* Catherine Smith, Director of Graduate Studies, 607-777-2151, Fax: 607-777-2501, E-mail: cmsmith@binghamton.edu. Web site: http://dson.binghamton.edu/.

State University of New York Downstate Medical Center, College of Nursing, Graduate Program in Nursing, Brooklyn, NY 11203-2098. Offers clinical nurse specialist (MS, Post Master's Certificate); nurse anesthesia (MS); nurse midwifery (MS, Post Master's Certificate); nurse practitioner (MS, Post Master's Certificate); nursing (MS). *Accreditation:* AACN. Part-time programs available. *Degree requirements:* For master's, thesis optional, clinical research project. *Entrance requirements:* For master's, GRE, BSN; minimum GPA of 3.0; previous undergraduate course work in statistics, health assessment, and nursing research; RN license; for Post Master's Certificate, BSN; minimum GPA of 3.0; RN license; previous undergraduate course work in statistics, health assessment, and nursing research. *Faculty research:* AIDS, continuity of care, case management, self-care.

State University of New York Upstate Medical University, College of Nursing, Syracuse, NY 13210-2334. Offers nurse practitioner (Post Master's Certificate); nursing (MS). *Accreditation:* AACN. Part-time programs available. Postbaccalaureate distance learning degree programs offered (no on-campus study). *Degree requirements:* For master's, thesis or alternative. *Entrance requirements:* For master's, 3 years of work experience. Electronic applications accepted.

Stevenson University, Program in Nursing, Stevenson, MD 21153. Offers MS.

Stony Brook University, State University of New York, Stony Brook University Medical Center, Health Sciences Center, School of Nursing, Stony Brook, NY 11794. Offers MS, DNP, Certificate. *Accreditation:* AACN; ACNM/ACME. Postbaccalaureate distance learning degree programs offered. *Degree requirements:* For master's, thesis. *Entrance requirements:* For master's, BSN, minimum GPA of 3.0, course work in statistics.

Temple University, Health Sciences Center, College of Health Professions and Social Work, Department of Nursing, Philadelphia, PA 19122-6096. Offers MSN. *Accreditation:* AACN. Part-time programs available. *Faculty:* 3 full-time (all women). *Students:* 8 full-time (6 women), 76 part-time (69 women); includes 31 minority (19 Black or African American, non-Hispanic/Latino; 9 Asian, non-Hispanic/Latino; 3 Hispanic/Latino), 7 international. Average age 42. 35 applicants, 97% accepted, 27 enrolled. In 2011, 18 master's awarded. *Degree requirements:* For master's, thesis or research project. *Entrance requirements:* For master's, GRE General Test, current RN license, interview. Additional exam requirements/recommendations for international students: Required—TOEFL (minimum score 550 paper-based; 213 computer-based; 79 iBT). *Application deadline:* For fall admission, 8/15 priority date for domestic students, 12/15 for international students; for spring admission, 12/15 for domestic students, 8/1 for international students. Applications are processed on a rolling basis. Application fee: $50. Electronic applications accepted. *Expenses:* Tuition, state resident: full-time $12,366; part-time $687 per credit hour. Tuition, nonresident: full-time $17,298; part-

time $961 per credit hour. *Required fees:* $590; $213 per year. *Financial support:* Teaching assistantships with full tuition reimbursements, career-related internships or fieldwork, institutionally sponsored loans, and traineeships available. Support available to part-time students. Financial award application deadline: 1/15; financial award applicants required to submit FAFSA. *Faculty research:* Osteoporosis, sensory deprivation in elderly, child abuse, attitudes towards AIDS, management styles. *Unit head:* Dr. Frances Ward, Chair, 215-707-4688, Fax: 215-707-1599, E-mail: nursing@temple.edu. *Application contact:* Tara Schumacher, Coordinator of Outreach, 215-204-6575, Fax: 215-204-8781, E-mail: tara.schumacher@temple.edu. Web site: http://www.temple.edu/chp/departments/nursing/.

Tennessee State University, The School of Graduate Studies and Research, School of Nursing, Nashville, TN 37209-1561. Offers family nurse practitioner (MSN); holistic nursing (MSN); nursing administration (MSN); nursing education (MSN); nursing informatics (MSN). *Accreditation:* NLN. *Entrance requirements:* For master's, GRE General Test or MAT, BSN, current RN license, minimum GPA of 3.0.

Tennessee Technological University, Whitson-Hester School of Nursing, Cookeville, TN 38505. Offers family nurse practitioner (MSN); informatics (MSN); nursing administration (MSN); nursing education (MSN). Part-time and evening/weekend programs available. Postbaccalaureate distance learning degree programs offered (no on-campus study). *Students:* 3 full-time (2 women), 43 part-time (39 women); includes 3 minority (1 Black or African American, non-Hispanic/Latino; 2 Hispanic/Latino). 48 applicants, 46% accepted, 15 enrolled. In 2011, 13 master's awarded. *Degree requirements:* For master's, comprehensive exam, thesis or alternative. *Entrance requirements:* Additional exam requirements/recommendations for international students: Required—TOEFL (minimum score 550 paper-based; 79 iBT), IELTS (minimum score 5.5), Pearson Test of English Academic. *Application deadline:* For fall admission, 8/1 for domestic students, 5/1 for international students; for spring admission, 12/1 for domestic students, 10/1 for international students. Application fee: $25 ($30 for international students). Electronic applications accepted. *Expenses:* Tuition, state resident: full-time $8094; part-time $422 per credit hour. Tuition, nonresident: full-time $20,574; part-time $1046 per credit hour. *Financial support:* Application deadline: 4/1. *Unit head:* Dr. Sherry Gaines, Director, 931-372-3203, Fax: 931-372-6244, E-mail: sgaines@tntech.edu. *Application contact:* Shelia K. Kendrick, Coordinator of Graduate Admissions, 931-372-3808, Fax: 931-372-3497, E-mail: skendrick@tntech.edu.

Texas A&M International University, Office of Graduate Studies and Research, College of Nursing and Health Sciences, Laredo, TX 78041-1900. Offers family nurse practitioner (MSN). *Accreditation:* NLN. *Faculty:* 4 full-time (all women). *Students:* 29 part-time (24 women); includes 27 minority (1 Asian, non-Hispanic/Latino; 26 Hispanic/Latino). Average age 34. 26 applicants, 81% accepted, 16 enrolled. *Entrance requirements:* Additional exam requirements/recommendations for international students: Required—TOEFL (minimum score 550 paper-based; 213 computer-based; 79 iBT). *Application deadline:* For fall admission, 4/30 for domestic and international students; for spring admission, 11/30 for domestic students, 10/1 for international students. Application fee: $35 ($50 for international students). *Expenses:* Tuition, state resident: full-time $5063. *Unit head:* Regina Aune, Dean, 956-326-2574, E-mail: regina.aune@tamiu.edu. *Application contact:* Suzanne Hansen-Alford, Director of Graduate Recruiting, 956-326-3023, Fax: 956-326-3021, E-mail: enroll@tamiu.edu. Web site: http://www.tamiu.edu/cson/.

Texas A&M University–Corpus Christi, Graduate Studies and Research, College of Nursing and Health Sciences, Corpus Christi, TX 78412-5503. Offers clinical nurse specialist (MSN); family nurse practitioner (MSN); health care administration (MSN); leadership in nursing systems (MSN). *Accreditation:* AACN. Part-time and evening/weekend programs available. *Degree requirements:* For master's, comprehensive exam, thesis (for some programs). *Entrance requirements:* For master's, GRE General Test. Additional exam requirements/recommendations for international students: Required—TOEFL. Electronic applications accepted.

Texas Christian University, Harris College of Nursing and Health Sciences, Program in Nursing, Fort Worth, TX 76129-0002. Offers advanced practice registered nurse (DNP); clinical nurse leader (MSN); clinical nurse specialist: adult/gerontology nursing (MSN); clinical nurse specialist: pediatric nursing (MSN); nursing administration (DNP); nursing education (MSN). *Accreditation:* AACN; AANA/CANAEP (one or more programs are accredited). Part-time programs available. Postbaccalaureate distance learning degree programs offered (no on-campus study). *Faculty:* 18 full-time (16 women), 2 part-time/adjunct (both women). *Students:* 2 full-time (both women), 105 part-time (96 women); includes 16 minority (8 Black or African American, non-Hispanic/Latino; 4 Asian, non-Hispanic/Latino; 2 Hispanic/Latino; 1 Native Hawaiian or other Pacific Islander, non-Hispanic/Latino; 1 Two or more races, non-Hispanic/Latino), 1 international. Average age 44. 58 applicants, 93% accepted, 46 enrolled. In 2011, 11 master's, 21 doctorates awarded. *Degree requirements:* For master's and doctorate, professional project. *Entrance requirements:* For master's, GRE General Test or MAT, 3 letters of reference, 2 years preferred full-time experience as registered nurse, current nursing license, minimum GPA of 3.0; for doctorate, APRN recognition (national certification), minimum GPA of 3.0, 3 professional references, essay, 2 years post-master's experience (preferrred). Additional exam requirements/recommendations for international students: Required—TOEFL, Spoken English Test for DNP. *Expenses:* Tuition: Full-time $20,250; part-time $1125 per credit hour. Part-time tuition and fees vary according to course load and program. *Financial support:* In 2011–12, teaching assistantships (averaging $5,000 per year) were awarded; tuition waivers also available. *Unit head:* Dr. Pamela Frable, Associate Dean and Director of Nursing, 817-257-5840, E-mail: p.frable@tcu.edu. *Application contact:* Dr. Kathy Baker, Director of Graduate Studies and Director of DNP Program, 817-257-6726, E-mail: kathy.baker@tcu.edu. Web site: http://www.nursing.tcu.edu/graduate.asp.

Texas Tech University Health Sciences Center, School of Nursing, Lubbock, TX 79430. Offers acute care nurse practitioner (MSN, Certificate); administration (MSN); advanced practice (DNP); education (MSN); executive leadership (DNP); family nurse practitioner (MSN, Certificate); geriatric nurse practitioner (MSN, Certificate); pediatric nurse practitioner (MSN, Certificate). *Accreditation:* AACN. Part-time programs available. Postbaccalaureate distance learning degree programs offered (minimal on-campus study). *Degree requirements:* For master's, thesis optional. *Entrance requirements:* For master's, minimum GPA of 3.0, 3 letters of reference, BSN, RN license; for Certificate, minimum GPA of 3.0, 3 letters of reference, RN license. Additional exam requirements/recommendations for international students: Required—TOEFL (minimum score 550 paper-based; 213 computer-based). *Faculty research:* Diabetes/obesity, nurse competency, disease management, intervention and measurements, health disparities.

Texas Woman's University, Graduate School, College of Nursing, Denton, TX 76201. Offers acute care nurse practitioner (MS); adult health clinical nurse specialist (MS); adult health nurse practitioner (MS); child health clinical nurse specialist (MS); clinical nurse leader (MS); family nurse practitioner (MS); health systems management (MS); nursing education (MS); nursing practice (DNP); nursing science (PhD); pediatric nurse practitioner (MS); women's health clinical nurse specialist (MS); women's health nurse practitioner (MS). *Accreditation:* AACN. Part-time programs available. Postbaccalaureate distance learning degree programs offered. *Faculty:* 70 full-time (69 women), 7 part-time/adjunct (all women). *Students:* 87 full-time (78 women), 870 part-time (815 women); includes 489 minority (235 Black or African American, non-Hispanic/Latino; 5 American Indian or Alaska Native, non-Hispanic/Latino; 169 Asian, non-Hispanic/Latino; 78 Hispanic/Latino; 2 Native Hawaiian or other Pacific Islander, non-Hispanic/Latino), 19 international. Average age 38. 368 applicants, 71% accepted, 205 enrolled. In 2011, 147 master's, 21 doctorates awarded. *Degree requirements:* For master's, comprehensive exam, thesis or alternative; for doctorate, comprehensive exam, thesis/dissertation. *Entrance requirements:* For master's, GRE or MAT, minimum GPA of 3.0 on last 60 hours in undergraduate nursing degree and overall, RN license, BS in nursing, basic statistics course, for doctorate, GRE (preferred minimum score 153 [500 old version] Verbal, 144 [500 old version] Quantitative, 4 Analytical), MS in nursing, minimum preferred GPA of 3.5, RN license, statistics, 2 letters of reference, curriculum vitae, graduate nursing-theory course, graduate research course, statement of professional goals and research interests. Additional exam requirements/recommendations for international students: Required—TOEFL (minimum score 550 paper-based; 213 computer-based; 79 iBT). *Application deadline:* For fall admission, 5/1 priority date for domestic students, 3/1 for international students; for spring admission, 9/15 priority date for domestic students, 7/1 for international students. Applications are processed on a rolling basis. Application fee: $50 ($75 for international students). Electronic applications accepted. *Expenses:* Tuition, state resident: full-time $3834; part-time $213 per credit hour. Tuition, nonresident: full-time $9468; part-time $526 per credit hour. *Required fees:* $213 per credit hour. Tuition and fees vary according to course load. *Financial support:* In 2011–12, 149 students received support, including 10 research assistantships (averaging $12,942 per year), 1 teaching assistantship (averaging $12,942 per year); career-related internships or fieldwork, Federal Work-Study, institutionally sponsored loans, scholarships/grants, traineeships, health care benefits, and unspecified assistantships also available. Support available to part-time students. Financial award application deadline: 3/1; financial award applicants required to submit FAFSA. *Faculty research:* Screening, prevention, and treatment for intimate partner violence; needs of adolescents during childbirth intervention; a network analysis decision tool for nurse managers (Social Network Analysis); support for adolescents with implantable cardioverter defibrillators; informatics: nurse staffing, safety, quality, and financial data as they relate to patient care outcomes; prevention and treatment of obesity; improving infant outcomes related to premature birth. *Total annual research expenditures:* $462,088. *Unit head:* Dr. Patricia Holden-Huchton, Interim Dean, 940-898-2401, Fax: 940-898-2437, E-mail: nursing@twu.edu. *Application contact:* Dr. Samuel Wheeler, Assistant Director of Admissions, 940-898-3188, Fax: 940-898-3081, E-mail: wheelersr@twu.edu. Web site: http://www.twu.edu/nursing/.

Thomas Edison State College, School of Nursing, Program in Nursing, Trenton, NJ 08608-1176. Offers MSN. *Accreditation:* AACN. Part-time programs available. Postbaccalaureate distance learning degree programs offered (no on-campus study). *Students:* 405 part-time (378 women); includes 112 minority (56 Black or African American, non-Hispanic/Latino; 1 American Indian or Alaska Native, non-Hispanic/Latino; 22 Asian, non-Hispanic/Latino; 30 Hispanic/Latino; 1 Native Hawaiian or other Pacific Islander, non-Hispanic/Latino; 2 Two or more races, non-Hispanic/Latino), 1 international. Average age 46. In 2011, 30 master's awarded. *Degree requirements:* For master's, nursing education seminar, onground practicum, online practicum. *Entrance requirements:* For master's, BSN. Additional exam requirements/recommendations for international students: Required—TOEFL (minimum score 550 paper-based; 213 computer-based; 79 iBT). *Application deadline:* For fall admission, 8/15 for domestic and international students; for winter admission, 11/15 for domestic and international students; for spring admission, 2/15 for domestic and international students. Application fee: $75. Electronic applications accepted. *Financial support:* Applicants required to submit FAFSA. *Unit head:* Dr. Susan O'Brien, Dean, School of Nursing, 609-633-6460, Fax: 609-292-8279, E-mail: nursing@tesc.edu. *Application contact:* David Hoftiezer, Director of Admissions, 888-442-8372, Fax: 609-984-8447, E-mail: admissions@tesc.edu. Web site: http://www.tesc.edu/nursing/msn.cfm.

Thomas Jefferson University, Jefferson School of Nursing, Philadelphia, PA 19107. Offers MS. *Accreditation:* AACN; AANA/CANAEP. Part-time programs available. Postbaccalaureate distance learning degree programs offered (no on-campus study). *Entrance requirements:* For master's, GRE or MAT, BSN or equivalent, CPR certification, professional RN license, previous undergraduate course work in statistics and nursing research, minimum GPA of 3.0. Additional exam requirements/recommendations for international students: Required—TOEFL (minimum score 213 computer-based). Electronic applications accepted. *Expenses:* Contact institution. *Faculty research:* Interdisciplinary primary care, women and HIV, health promotion and disease prevention, psychosocial impact of disability, ethical decision making.

Thomas University, Department of Nursing, Thomasville, GA 31792-7499. Offers MSN. *Accreditation:* NLN. Part-time programs available. *Entrance requirements:* For master's, resume, 3 academic/professional references. Additional exam requirements/recommendations for international students: Required—TOEFL (minimum score 600 paper-based; 250 computer-based). Electronic applications accepted.

Towson University, Program in Nursing, Towson, MD 21252-0001. Offers nursing (MS); nursing education (Postbaccalaureate Certificate). *Accreditation:* AACN. Part-time programs available. *Students:* 43 full-time (42 women), 65 part-time (63 women); includes 34 minority (29 Black or African American, non-Hispanic/Latino; 3 Asian, non-Hispanic/Latino; 2 Two or more races, non-Hispanic/Latino), 2 international. *Degree requirements:* For master's, thesis optional. *Entrance requirements:* For master's, minimum GPA of 3.0, copy of current nursing license, bachelor's degree in nursing, curriculum vitae; for Postbaccalaureate Certificate, minimum GPA of 3.0, copy of current nursing license, curriculum vitae, bachelor's degree in nursing. *Application deadline:* Applications are processed on a rolling basis. Application fee: $50. Electronic applications accepted. *Expenses:* Tuition, state resident: part-time $337 per credit. Tuition, nonresident: part-time $709 per credit. *Required fees:* $99 per credit. *Financial support:* Application deadline: 4/1; applicants required to submit FAFSA. *Unit head:* Kathleen Ogle, Graduate Program Director, 410-704-4389, E-mail: kogle@towson.edu.

Trinity Western University, School of Graduate Studies, School of Nursing, Langley, BC V2Y 1Y1, Canada. Offers MSN.

Troy University, Graduate School, College of Health and Human Services, Program in Nursing, Troy, AL 36082. Offers adult health (MSN); clinical nurse specialist adult health (DNP); clinical nurse specialist maternal infant (DNP); family nurse practitioner (MSN, DNP, PMC); informatics specialist (MSN); maternal infant (MSN). *Accreditation:* NLN. Part-time and evening/weekend programs available. *Faculty:* 11 full-time (10 women), 7 part-time/adjunct (4 women). *Students:* 58 full-time (43 women), 181 part-time (165 women); includes 91 minority (76 Black or African American, non-Hispanic/Latino; 8 American Indian or Alaska Native, non-Hispanic/Latino; 1 Asian, non-Hispanic/Latino; 3 Hispanic/Latino; 1 Native Hawaiian or other Pacific Islander, non-Hispanic/Latino; 2 Two or more races, non-Hispanic/Latino). Average age 38. 144 applicants, 63% accepted, 73 enrolled. In 2011, 35 master's, 8 doctorates awarded. *Degree requirements:* For master's, comprehensive exam, minimum GPA of 3.0, candidacy; for doctorate, minimum GPA of 3.0, submission of approved comprehensive e-portfolio, completion of residency synthesis project, minimum of 1000 hours of clinical practice, score of 80% or

better on qualifying exam. *Entrance requirements:* For master's, MAT (minimum score 396) or GRE (minimum score 850), minimum GPA of 3.0, BSN, current RN licensure; 2 letters of reference; for doctorate, GRE (minimum score of 850), BSN or MSN, minimum GPA of 3.0, 2 letters of reference, current RN licensure, essay. Additional exam requirements/recommendations for international students: Required—TOEFL (minimum score 523 paper-based; 193 computer-based; 70 iBT), IELTS (minimum score 6), or ACT COMPASS ESL (minimum listening, reading, and grammar score 270). *Application deadline:* Applications are processed on a rolling basis. Application fee: $50. Electronic applications accepted. *Expenses:* Tuition, state resident: full-time $6960; part-time $290 per credit hour. Tuition, nonresident: full-time $13,920; part-time $580 per credit hour. *Required fees:* $386 per term. *Financial support:* Available to part-time students. Applicants required to submit FAFSA. *Unit head:* Dr. Bernita K. Hamilton, Director, School of Nursing, 334-670-3428, Fax: 334-670-3743, E-mail: bernitah@troy.edu. *Application contact:* Brenda K. Campbell, Director of Graduate Admissions, 334-670-3178, Fax: 334-670-3733, E-mail: bcamp@troy.edu.

Uniformed Services University of the Health Sciences, Graduate School of Nursing, Bethesda, MD 20814-4799. Offers family nurse practitioner (MSN); nurse anesthesia (MSN); nursing science (PhD); perioperative clinical nurse specialty (MSN); psychiatric mental health nurse practitioner (MSN). Program available to military officers only. *Accreditation:* AACN; AANA/CANAEP. *Faculty:* 36 full-time (21 women), 2 part-time/adjunct (0 women). *Students:* 71 full-time (35 women); includes 17 minority (11 Black or African American, non-Hispanic/Latino; 3 Asian, non-Hispanic/Latino; 3 Hispanic/Latino). Average age 36. 120 applicants, 59% accepted, 71 enrolled. In 2011, 57 master's, 2 doctorates awarded. *Degree requirements:* For master's, thesis or alternative. *Entrance requirements:* For master's, GRE, BSN, clinical experience, minimum GPA of 3.0, previous course work in science, writing paper; for doctorate, GRE, written papers, articles. *Application deadline:* For fall admission, 7/1 for domestic students; for winter admission, 2/15 for domestic students. Application fee: $0. Electronic applications accepted. *Faculty research:* Prenatal care, military health care, military readiness, distance learning. *Unit head:* Dr. Carol A. Romano, Associate Dean for Academic Affairs, 301-295-1180, Fax: 301-295-1707, E-mail: carol.romano@usuhs.edu. *Application contact:* Terry Lynn Malavakis, Recording Secretary for Admissions Committee, 301-295-1055, Fax: 301-295-1707, E-mail: terry.malavakis@usuhs.edu. Web site: http://www.usuhs.mil/gsn/.

Union University, School of Nursing, Jackson, TN 38305-3697. Offers executive leadership (DNP); nurse anesthesia (DNP); nurse anesthetist (PMC); nurse practitioner (DNP); nursing education (MSN, PMC). *Accreditation:* AACN; AANA/CANAEP. *Degree requirements:* For master's, thesis or alternative. *Entrance requirements:* For master's, GRE, 3 letters of reference, bachelor's degree in nursing, minimum GPA of 3.0. Additional exam requirements/recommendations for international students: Required—TOEFL (minimum score 560 paper-based; 220 computer-based). Electronic applications accepted. *Faculty research:* Children's health, occupational rehabilitation, informatics, health promotion.

United States University, School of Nursing, Cypress, CA 90630. Offers administrator (MSN); educator (MSN).

Universidad del Turabo, Graduate Programs, School of Health Sciences, Programs in Nursing, Program in Clinical Nurse Leader, Gurabo, PR 00778-3030. Offers MSN. *Accreditation:* AACN. *Students:* 1 applicant, 0% accepted, 0 enrolled. *Unit head:* Dr. Maria Rosa, Dean, 787-743-7979. *Application contact:* Virginia Gonzalez, Admissions Officer, 787-746-3009.

Universidad Metropolitana, School of Health Sciences, Department of Nursing, San Juan, PR 00928-1150. Offers case management (Certificate); nursing (MSN); oncology nursing (Certificate). *Accreditation:* NLN.

Université de Montréal, Faculty of Nursing, Montréal, QC H3C 3J7, Canada. Offers M Sc, PhD, Certificate, DESS. PhD offered jointly with McGill University. Part-time programs available. *Degree requirements:* For master's, one foreign language, thesis optional; for doctorate, thesis/dissertation, general exam; for other advanced degree, one foreign language. *Entrance requirements:* For master's, doctorate, and other advanced degree, proficiency in French. Electronic applications accepted. *Faculty research:* Mental and physical care of chronic patients, care of the hospitalized aged, cancer nursing, home care of caregivers, AIDS patients.

Université du Québec à Rimouski, Graduate Programs, Program in Nursing Studies, Rimouski, QC G5L 3A1, Canada. Offers M Sc, Diploma. Programs offered jointly with Université du Québec à Chicoutimi, Université du Québec à Trois-Rivières, and Université du Québec en Outaouais.

Université du Québec à Trois-Rivières, Graduate Programs, Program in Nursing Sciences, Trois-Rivières, QC G9A 5H7, Canada. Offers M Sc, DESS. Part-time programs available.

Université du Québec en Outaouais, Graduate Programs, Program in Nursing, Gatineau, QC J8X 3X7, Canada. Offers M Sc, DESS, Diploma. Part-time and evening/weekend programs available. *Students:* 12 full-time, 28 part-time. *Degree requirements:* For master's, thesis (for some programs). *Application deadline:* For fall admission, 6/1 priority date for domestic students, 3/1 for international students; for winter admission, 8/1 priority date for domestic students, 10/1 for international students. Application fee: $30. *Unit head:* Chantal Saint-Pierre, Director, 819-595-3900 Ext. 2347, Fax: 819-595-3804, E-mail: chantal.saint-pierre@uqo.ca. *Application contact:* Registrar's Office, 819-773-1850, Fax: 819-773-1835, E-mail: registraire@ugo.ca.

Université Laval, Faculty of Nursing, Programs in Nursing, Québec, QC G1K 7P4, Canada. Offers M Sc, PhD, DESS, Diploma. *Degree requirements:* For master's, thesis (for some programs). *Entrance requirements:* For master's, French exam, knowledge of English; for other advanced degree, knowledge of French. Electronic applications accepted.

University at Buffalo, the State University of New York, Graduate School, School of Nursing, Buffalo, NY 14214. Offers adult clinical nurse specialist (DNP); adult nurse practitioner (DNP); family nurse practitioner (DNP); health care systems and leadership (MS); nurse anesthetist (DNP); nursing (PhD); nursing education (Certificate); post-master's track (DNP); psychiatric mental health nurse practitioner (DNP). *Accreditation:* AACN; AANA/CANAEP (one or more programs are accredited). Part-time programs available. Postbaccalaureate distance learning degree programs offered (minimal on-campus study). *Faculty:* 29 full-time (25 women), 18 part-time/adjunct (17 women). *Students:* 101 full-time (76 women), 100 part-time (90 women); includes 19 minority (10 Black or African American, non-Hispanic/Latino; 2 American Indian or Alaska Native, non-Hispanic/Latino; 2 Asian, non-Hispanic/Latino; 2 Hispanic/Latino; 3 Native Hawaiian or other Pacific Islander, non-Hispanic/Latino), 34 international. Average age 34. 342 applicants, 26% accepted, 67 enrolled. In 2011, 51 master's, 3 doctorates awarded. *Median time to degree:* Of those who began their doctoral program in fall 2003, 75% received their degree in 8 years or less. *Degree requirements:* For master's, thesis optional, comprehensive exams or project; for doctorate, comprehensive exam (for some programs), capstone (for DNP), dissertation (for PhD). *Entrance requirements:* For doctorate, GRE or MAT, minimum GPA of 3.0 (3.25 for PhD), RN license, BS or MS in nursing, 3 references, writing sample; for Certificate, interview, minimum GPA of 3.0 or GRE General Test, RN license, MS in nursing. Additional exam requirements/recommendations for international students: Required—TOEFL (minimum score 550 paper-based; 213 computer-based; 79 iBT), IELTS (minimum score 6.5). *Application deadline:* For fall admission, 8/15 for domestic students, 4/1 for international students; for spring admission, 12/15 for domestic students, 10/1 for international students. Application fee: $75. Electronic applications accepted. *Financial support:* In 2011–12, 80 students received support, including 6 fellowships with full tuition reimbursements available (averaging $17,000 per year), 3 research assistantships with full tuition reimbursements available (averaging $10,600 per year), 5 teaching assistantships with full tuition reimbursements available (averaging $10,600 per year); scholarships/grants, traineeships, health care benefits, and unspecified assistantships also available. Financial award application deadline: 3/15; financial award applicants required to submit FAFSA. *Faculty research:* Oncology, palliative care, gerontology, addictions, mental health, community wellness. *Total annual research expenditures:* $1.3 million. *Unit head:* Dr. Marsha L. Lewis, Dean and Professor, 716-829-2533, Fax: 716-829-2566, E-mail: ubnursingdean@buffalo.edu. *Application contact:* Dr. David J. Lang, Director of Student Affairs, 716-829-2537, Fax: 716-829-2067, E-mail: nursing@buffalo.edu. Web site: http://nursing.buffalo.edu/.

The University of Akron, Graduate School, College of Nursing, Akron, OH 44325. Offers nursing (MSN, PhD); public health (MPH). PhD offered jointly with Kent State University. *Accreditation:* AACN; AANA/CANAEP (one or more programs are accredited). Part-time programs available. *Faculty:* 41 full-time (40 women), 60 part-time/adjunct (58 women). *Students:* 68 full-time (59 women), 287 part-time (252 women); includes 32 minority (20 Black or African American, non-Hispanic/Latino; 5 Asian, non-Hispanic/Latino; 3 Hispanic/Latino; 4 Two or more races, non-Hispanic/Latino), 5 international. Average age 34. 202 applicants, 72% accepted, 85 enrolled. In 2011, 87 master's, 1 doctorate awarded. *Degree requirements:* For doctorate, one foreign language, thesis/dissertation, qualifying exam. *Entrance requirements:* For master's, current Ohio state license as registered nurse, three letters of reference, 300-word essay, interview with program coordinator; for doctorate, GRE, minimum GPA of 3.0, MSN, nursing license or eligibility for licensure, writing sample, letters of recommendation, interview, resume, personal statement of research interests and career goals. Additional exam requirements/recommendations for international students: Required—TOEFL (minimum score 550 paper-based; 213 computer-based; 79 iBT). *Application deadline:* For fall admission, 7/15 for domestic and international students. Applications are processed on a rolling basis. Application fee: $30 ($40 for international students). Electronic applications accepted. *Expenses:* Tuition, state resident: full-time $7038; part-time $391 per credit hour. Tuition, nonresident: full-time $12,051; part-time $670 per credit hour. *Required fees:* $1274; $34 per credit hour. *Financial support:* In 2011–12, 10 teaching assistantships with full tuition reimbursements were awarded; career-related internships or fieldwork and Federal Work-Study also available. *Faculty research:* Health promotion and chronic disease prevention; mental health and psychosocial resilience; gerontological health, trauma and violence; gut oxygenation during shock and trauma, simulation and the pedagogy of teaching and learning. *Total annual research expenditures:* $618,835. *Unit head:* Dr. Roberta DePompei, Interim Dean, 330-972-6114, E-mail: rdepom1@uakron.edu. *Application contact:* Dr. Marlene Huff, Graduate Director, 330-972-7555, E-mail: mhuff@uakron.edu. Web site: http://www.uakron.edu/nursing/.

The University of Alabama, Graduate School, Capstone College of Nursing, Tuscaloosa, AL 35487. Offers MSN, DNP, Ed D, MSN/Ed D. *Accreditation:* AACN. Part-time programs available. Postbaccalaureate distance learning degree programs offered (no on-campus study). *Faculty:* 16 full-time (14 women), 1 (woman) part-time/adjunct. *Students:* 73 full-time (67 women), 254 part-time (225 women); includes 113 minority (79 Black or African American, non-Hispanic/Latino; 5 American Indian or Alaska Native, non-Hispanic/Latino; 6 Asian, non-Hispanic/Latino; 16 Hispanic/Latino; 1 Native Hawaiian or other Pacific Islander, non-Hispanic/Latino; 6 Two or more races, non-Hispanic/Latino). Average age 44. 218 applicants, 86% accepted, 132 enrolled. In 2011, 36 master's, 68 doctorates awarded. *Degree requirements:* For doctorate, comprehensive exam, thesis/dissertation. *Entrance requirements:* For master's, GRE or MAT (if GPA is below 3.0), BSN, RN licensure, minimum GPA of 3.0; for doctorate, GRE or MAT, MSN, RN licensure, minimum GPA of 3.0, references, writing sample, curriculum vitae (Ed D). *Application deadline:* For fall admission, 6/1 priority date for domestic students; for winter admission, 1/1 priority date for domestic students; for spring admission, 4/15 priority date for domestic students. Applications are processed on a rolling basis. Application fee: $50 ($60 for international students). Electronic applications accepted. *Expenses:* Tuition, state resident: full-time $8600. Tuition, nonresident: full-time $21,900. *Financial support:* In 2011–12, 2 fellowships with full tuition reimbursements (averaging $14,000 per year) were awarded; scholarships/grants and traineeships also available. Financial award application deadline: 8/1; financial award applicants required to submit FAFSA. *Faculty research:* Diabetes education, childhood asthma, HIV/AIDS prevention and care, breast cancer in rural minority women, nursing labor cost, nursing case management, sleep. *Total annual research expenditures:* $492,552. *Unit head:* Dr. Sara E. Barger, Dean, 205-348-1040, Fax: 205-348-5559, E-mail: sbarger@bama.ua.edu. *Application contact:* Dr. Marietta Stanton, Assistant Dean, Graduate Programs, 205-348-1020, Fax: 205-348-5559, E-mail: mstanton@bama.ua.edu. Web site: http://nursing.ua.edu/.

The University of Alabama at Birmingham, School of Nursing, Birmingham, AL 35294. Offers nurse anesthesia (MNA); nursing (MSN, DNP, PhD). *Accreditation:* AACN. Terminal master's awarded for partial completion of doctoral program. *Degree requirements:* For doctorate, thesis/dissertation, research mentorship experience. *Entrance requirements:* For master's, GRE General Test, BS in nursing, interview; for doctorate, GRE General Test, computer literacy, course work in statistics, interview, minimum GPA of 3.0, MS in nursing. Additional exam requirements/recommendations for international students: Required—TOEFL. *Application deadline:* Applications are processed on a rolling basis. Electronic applications accepted. *Expenses:* Contact institution. *Financial support:* Fellowships, research assistantships, teaching assistantships, and Federal Work-Study available. Support available to part-time students. *Unit head:* Dr. Doreen C. Harper, Dean, 205-934-5360, E-mail: dcharper@uab.edu. Web site: http://www.uab.edu/son/.

The University of Alabama in Huntsville, School of Graduate Studies, College of Nursing, Huntsville, AL 35899. Offers family nurse practitioner (Certificate); nursing (MSN, DNP), including acute care nurse practitioner (MSN), adult clinical nursing specialist (MSN), clinical nurse leader (MSN), family nurse practitioner (MSN), leadership in health care systems (MSN); nursing education (Certificate). DNP offered jointly with The University of Alabama at Birmingham. *Accreditation:* AACN. Part-time and evening/weekend programs available. Postbaccalaureate distance learning degree programs offered (minimal on-campus study). *Faculty:* 19 full-time (18 women), 8 part-time/adjunct (7 women). *Students:* 57 full-time (43 women), 162 part-time (139 women); includes 22 minority (15 Black or African American, non-Hispanic/Latino; 3 American Indian or Alaska Native, non-Hispanic/Latino; 1 Asian, non-Hispanic/Latino; 3 Hispanic/Latino), 2 international. Average age 37. 193 applicants, 79% accepted, 112 enrolled. In 2011, 42 master's, 11 doctorates, 11 other advanced degrees awarded. *Degree requirements:* For master's, comprehensive exam, thesis or alternative, oral and written exams. *Entrance requirements:* For master's, MAT or GRE, Alabama RN license, BSN,

minimum GPA of 3.0; for doctorate, master's degree in nursing in an advanced practice area; for Certificate, MAT or GRE, minimum GPA of 3.0. Additional exam requirements/recommendations for international students: Required—TOEFL (minimum score 500 paper-based; 173 computer-based; 62 iBT). *Application deadline:* For fall admission, 7/15 for domestic students, 4/1 for international students; for spring admission, 11/30 for domestic students, 9/1 for international students. Applications are processed on a rolling basis. Application fee: $40 ($50 for international students). Electronic applications accepted. *Expenses:* Tuition, state resident: full-time $7830; part-time $473.50 per credit. Tuition, nonresident: full-time $18,748; part-time $1128.33 per credit. Tuition and fees vary according to course load and program. *Financial support:* In 2011–12, 9 students received support, including 9 teaching assistantships with full tuition reimbursements available (averaging $9,596 per year); career-related internships or fieldwork, Federal Work-Study, institutionally sponsored loans, scholarships/grants, traineeships, health care benefits, and unspecified assistantships also available. Support available to part-time students. Financial award application deadline: 4/1; financial award applicants required to submit FAFSA. *Faculty research:* Home health care, gerontology, pediatric nursing, family nurse practitioner, adult acute care administration. *Total annual research expenditures:* $235,384. *Unit head:* Dr. Fay Raines, Dean, 256-824-6345, Fax: 256-824-6026, E-mail: rainesc@uah.edu. *Application contact:* Charles Davis, Director of Graduate Nursing Admissions and Advising, 256-824-2433, Fax: 256-824-6026, E-mail: charles.davis@uah.edu. Web site: http://www.uah.edu/nursing/welcome.

University of Alaska Anchorage, College of Health, School of Nursing, Anchorage, AK 99508. Offers family nurse practitioner (Certificate); nursing (MS); nursing education (Certificate); psychiatric nurse practitioner (Certificate). *Accreditation:* NLN. Part-time and evening/weekend programs available. *Degree requirements:* For master's, comprehensive exam, individual project. *Entrance requirements:* For master's, GRE or MAT, BS in nursing, interview, minimum GPA of 3.0, RN license, 1 year of part-time or 6 months of full-time clinical experience. Additional exam requirements/recommendations for international students: Required—TOEFL (minimum score 550 paper-based; 213 computer-based).

University of Alberta, Faculty of Graduate Studies and Research, Faculty of Nursing, Edmonton, AB T6G 2E1, Canada. Offers MN, PhD. Part-time programs available. *Degree requirements:* For master's, thesis optional, clinical practice; for doctorate, thesis/dissertation. *Entrance requirements:* For master's, B Sc N, 1 year of clinical nursing experience in specialty area; for doctorate, MN. Additional exam requirements/recommendations for international students: Required—TOEFL (minimum score 550 paper-based; 213 computer-based). *Faculty research:* Symptom management, healthy human development, health policy, teaching excellence and information.

The University of Arizona, College of Nursing, Tucson, AZ 85721. Offers health care informatics (Certificate); nurse practitioner (MS, Certificate); nursing (DNP, PhD); rural health (Certificate). *Accreditation:* AACN. Part-time programs available. Postbaccalaureate distance learning degree programs offered (minimal on-campus study). *Faculty:* 19 full-time (18 women). *Students:* 279 full-time (241 women), 36 part-time (32 women); includes 84 minority (13 Black or African American, non-Hispanic/Latino; 4 American Indian or Alaska Native, non-Hispanic/Latino; 19 Asian, non-Hispanic/Latino; 31 Hispanic/Latino; 1 Native Hawaiian or other Pacific Islander, non-Hispanic/Latino; 16 Two or more races, non-Hispanic/Latino), 3 international. Average age 38. In 2011, 1 master's, 19 doctorates awarded. Terminal master's awarded for partial completion of doctoral program. *Degree requirements:* For master's, thesis optional; for doctorate, comprehensive exam, thesis/dissertation. *Entrance requirements:* For master's, BSN, eligibility for RN license; for doctorate, BSN; for Certificate, GRE General Test, Arizona RN license, BSN, minimum GPA of 3.0. Additional exam requirements/recommendations for international students: Required—TOEFL (minimum score 550 paper-based; 213 computer-based; 79 iBT). *Application deadline:* For fall admission, 1/15 for domestic and international students. Applications are processed on a rolling basis. Application fee: $75. Electronic applications accepted. *Expenses:* Contact institution. *Financial support:* In 2011–12, 4 research assistantships with full tuition reimbursements (averaging $18,220 per year), 3 teaching assistantships (averaging $18,327 per year) were awarded; career-related internships or fieldwork, institutionally sponsored loans, scholarships/grants, traineeships, health care benefits, tuition waivers (full), and unspecified assistantships also available. Financial award application deadline: 6/1. *Faculty research:* Vulnerable populations, injury mechanisms and biobehavioral responses, health care systems, informatics, rural health. *Total annual research expenditures:* $5.5 million. *Unit head:* Dr. Joan Shaver, Dean, 520-626-7124, Fax: 520-626-6424, E-mail: cmurdaugh@nursing.arizona.edu. *Application contact:* Sally J. Reel, Assistant Dean, Student Affairs, 520-626-6154, Fax: 520-626-2211, E-mail: info@nursing.arizona.edu. Web site: http://www.nursing.arizona.edu/.

University of Arkansas, Graduate School, College of Education and Health Professions, Eleanor Mann School of Nursing, Fayetteville, AR 72701-1201. Offers MSN. *Accreditation:* AACN. Postbaccalaureate distance learning degree programs offered. *Students:* 10 full-time (all women), 17 part-time (all women); includes 1 minority (American Indian or Alaska Native, non-Hispanic/Latino). In 2011, 6 master's awarded. *Application deadline:* For fall admission, 4/1 for international students; for spring admission, 10/1 for international students. Applications are processed on a rolling basis. Application fee: $40 ($50 for international students). Electronic applications accepted. *Financial support:* Fellowships, research assistantships, and teaching assistantships available. *Unit head:* Dr. Nan A. Smith-Blair, Director, 479-575-3904, Fax: 479-575-3218, E-mail: nsblair@uark.edu. *Application contact:* Dr. Kathleen Barta, Graduate Admissions, 479-575-5871, E-mail: kbarta@uark.edu. Web site: http://nurs.uark.edu/.

University of Arkansas for Medical Sciences, Graduate School, College of Nursing, Little Rock, AR 72205-7199. Offers PhD. *Accreditation:* AACN. Part-time programs available. *Entrance requirements:* For doctorate, GRE. Additional exam requirements/recommendations for international students: Required—TOEFL.

The University of British Columbia, Faculty of Applied Science, Program in Nursing, Vancouver, BC V6T 1Z1, Canada. Offers MSN, PhD. Part-time programs available. *Degree requirements:* For master's, essay or thesis; for doctorate, comprehensive exam, thesis/dissertation. *Entrance requirements:* For master's, GRE, bachelor's degree in nursing; for doctorate, GRE, master's degree in nursing. Additional exam requirements/recommendations for international students: Required—TOEFL. Electronic applications accepted. *Faculty research:* Women and children, aging, critical care, cross-cultural.

University of Calgary, Faculty of Graduate Studies, Faculty of Nursing, Calgary, AB T2N 1N4, Canada. Offers MN, PhD, PMD. Part-time programs available. *Degree requirements:* For master's, comprehensive exam (for some programs), thesis (for some programs); for doctorate, thesis/dissertation; for PMD, comprehensive exam. *Entrance requirements:* For master's and PMD, nursing experience, nursing registration; for doctorate, nursing registration. Additional exam requirements/recommendations for international students: Required—TOEFL (minimum score 600 paper-based; 250 computer-based), IELTS (minimum score 7), Michigan English Language Battery (MELAB). Electronic applications accepted. *Expenses:* Contact institution. *Faculty research:* Health outcomes across multiple populations and multiple settings including patients and families with chronic health problems, culturally diverse, and vulnerable populations; family health; core processes; professional, educational and health services delivery.

University of California, Irvine, College of Health Sciences, Program in Nursing Science, Irvine, CA 92697. Offers MSN. *Accreditation:* AACN. *Students:* 10 full-time (8 women), 22 part-time (20 women); includes 20 minority (1 Black or African American, non-Hispanic/Latino; 13 Asian, non-Hispanic/Latino; 5 Hispanic/Latino; 1 Two or more races, non-Hispanic/Latino). Average age 31. 52 applicants, 52% accepted, 15 enrolled. In 2011, 6 degrees awarded. Application fee: $80 ($100 for international students). *Unit head:* Linda Hill, Management Service Officer, 949-824-0468, E-mail: lshill@uci.edu. *Application contact:* Sheree McPeak, Graduate Division, 949-824-4611, Fax: 949-824-9096, E-mail: ogsfront@uci.edu. Web site: http://www.nursing.uci.edu/.

University of California, Los Angeles, Graduate Division, School of Nursing, Los Angeles, CA 90095. Offers MSN, PhD, MBA/MSN. *Accreditation:* AACN. *Faculty:* 32 full-time (31 women). *Students:* 352 full-time (308 women); includes 182 minority (27 Black or African American, non-Hispanic/Latino; 2 American Indian or Alaska Native, non-Hispanic/Latino; 81 Asian, non-Hispanic/Latino; 45 Hispanic/Latino; 3 Native Hawaiian or other Pacific Islander, non-Hispanic/Latino; 24 Two or more races, non-Hispanic/Latino), 8 international. Average age 32. 751 applicants, 28% accepted, 149 enrolled. In 2011, 148 master's, 6 doctorates awarded. *Degree requirements:* For master's, comprehensive exam; for doctorate, thesis/dissertation, oral and written qualifying exams. *Entrance requirements:* For master's, minimum GPA of 3.0, bachelor's degree in nursing; for doctorate, GRE General Test, minimum undergraduate GPA of 3.5, bachelor's or master's degree in nursing, licensed as registered nurse. Additional exam requirements/recommendations for international students: Required—TOEFL. *Application deadline:* For fall admission, 12/1 priority date for domestic students, 12/1 for international students. Application fee: $70 ($90 for international students). Electronic applications accepted. *Financial support:* In 2011–12, 254 fellowships with full and partial tuition reimbursements, 10 research assistantships with full and partial tuition reimbursements, 43 teaching assistantships with full and partial tuition reimbursements were awarded; Federal Work-Study, institutionally sponsored loans, scholarships/grants, health care benefits, tuition waivers (full and partial), and unspecified assistantships also available. Financial award application deadline: 3/1; financial award applicants required to submit FAFSA. *Faculty research:* AIDS, adolescents, gerontology, homeless, activity/mobility. *Unit head:* Dr. Barbara H. Bates-Jensen, Dean, 310-206-5739, E-mail: bbatesjensen@sonnet.ucla.edu. *Application contact:* Departmental Office, 310-794-7461, E-mail: sonsaff@sonnet.ucla.edu. Web site: http://www.nursing.ucla.edu/.

University of California, San Francisco, Graduate Division, School of Nursing, Program in Nursing, San Francisco, CA 94143. Offers MS, PhD. *Accreditation:* AACN; ACNM/ACME (one or more programs are accredited). *Degree requirements:* For master's, comprehensive exam, thesis or alternative; for doctorate, thesis/dissertation. *Entrance requirements:* For master's and doctorate, GRE General Test. *Expenses:* Contact institution.

University of Central Arkansas, Graduate School, College of Health and Behavioral Sciences, Department of Nursing, Conway, AR 72035-0001. Offers clinical nurse specialist (MSN); nurse practitioner (MSN). *Accreditation:* AACN. *Faculty:* 7 full-time (all women). *Students:* 6 full-time (5 women), 147 part-time (138 women); includes 14 minority (7 Black or African American, non-Hispanic/Latino; 5 American Indian or Alaska Native, non-Hispanic/Latino; 2 Hispanic/Latino). Average age 35. 45 applicants, 64% accepted, 26 enrolled. In 2011, 27 master's awarded. *Degree requirements:* For master's, comprehensive exam, thesis optional, clinicals. *Entrance requirements:* For master's, GRE General Test, minimum GPA of 2.7. Additional exam requirements/recommendations for international students: Required—TOEFL (minimum score 550 paper-based; 213 computer-based). *Application deadline:* For fall admission, 3/1 priority date for domestic students; for spring admission, 10/1 for domestic students. Applications are processed on a rolling basis. Application fee: $25 ($50 for international students). *Expenses:* Contact institution. *Financial support:* Federal Work-Study, traineeships, and unspecified assistantships available. Financial award application deadline: 2/15; financial award applicants required to submit FAFSA. *Total annual research expenditures:* $216,643. *Unit head:* Dr. Barbara Williams, Chairperson, 501-450-3119, Fax: 501-450-5503, E-mail: barbaraw@uca.edu. *Application contact:* Susan Wood, Administrative Assistant, 501-450-3124, Fax: 501-450-5678, E-mail: swood@uca.edu. Web site: http://www.uca.edu/divisions/academic/chas/nurse2ab.asp.

University of Central Florida, College of Nursing, Orlando, FL 32816. Offers adult-gerontology clinical nurse specialist (Post-Master's Certificate); adult-gerontology nurse practitioner (Post-Master's Certificate); clinical nurse leader (Post-Master's Certificate); family nurse practitioner (Post-Master's Certificate); nursing (MSN, PhD); nursing education (Post-Master's Certificate); nursing practice (DNP). *Accreditation:* AACN. Part-time and evening/weekend programs available. *Faculty:* 44 full-time (39 women), 72 part-time/adjunct (71 women). *Students:* 75 full-time (68 women), 350 part-time (332 women); includes 109 minority (54 Black or African American, non-Hispanic/Latino; 1 American Indian or Alaska Native, non-Hispanic/Latino; 19 Asian, non-Hispanic/Latino; 33 Hispanic/Latino; 1 Native Hawaiian or other Pacific Islander, non-Hispanic/Latino; 1 Two or more races, non-Hispanic/Latino), 5 international. Average age 40. 203 applicants, 60% accepted, 98 enrolled. In 2011, 110 master's, 17 doctorates, 11 other advanced degrees awarded. *Degree requirements:* For master's, thesis or alternative. *Entrance requirements:* For master's, GRE General Test, minimum GPA of 3.0 in last 60 hours. Additional exam requirements/recommendations for international students: Required—TOEFL. *Application deadline:* For fall admission, 2/15 for domestic students; for spring admission, 9/15 for domestic students. Application fee: $30. Electronic applications accepted. *Expenses:* Tuition, state resident: part-time $277.08 per credit hour. Tuition, nonresident: part-time $277.08 per credit hour. Part-time tuition and fees vary according to degree level and program. *Financial support:* In 2011–12, 92 students received support, including 92 fellowships with partial tuition reimbursements available (averaging $1,100 per year), 2 teaching assistantships with partial tuition reimbursements available (averaging $8,100 per year); research assistantships with partial tuition reimbursements available, career-related internships or fieldwork, Federal Work-Study, institutionally sponsored loans, traineeships, and unspecified assistantships also available. Financial award application deadline: 3/1; financial award applicants required to submit FAFSA. *Unit head:* Dr. Jean D. Leuner, Dean, 407-823-5496, Fax: 407-823-5675, E-mail: jean.leuner@ucf.edu. *Application contact:* Barbara Rodriguez, Director, Admissions and Registration, 407-823-2766, Fax: 407-823-6442, E-mail: gradadmissions@ucf.edu. Web site: http://nursing.ucf.edu/.

University of Central Missouri, The Graduate School, College of Health and Human Services, Warrensburg, MO 64093. Offers criminal justice (MS); industrial hygiene (MS); occupational safety management (MS); physical education/exercise and sport science (MS); rural family nursing (MS); social gerontology (MS); sociology (MA); speech language pathology and audiology (MS). *Accreditation:* NCATE. Part-time programs available. Postbaccalaureate distance learning degree programs offered. *Entrance requirements:* Additional exam requirements/recommendations for international students: Required—TOEFL (minimum score 550 paper-based; 79 computer-based). Electronic applications accepted.

Nursing—General

University of Cincinnati, Graduate School, College of Nursing, Cincinnati, OH 45221-0038. Offers clinical nurse specialist (MSN), including adult health, community health, neonatal, nursing administration, occupational health, pediatric health, psychiatric nursing, women's health; nurse anesthesia (MSN); nurse midwifery (MSN); nurse practitioner (MSN), including acute care, ambulatory care, family, family/psychiatric, women's health; nursing (PhD); MBA/MSN. *Accreditation:* AACN; AANA/CANAEP (one or more programs are accredited); ACNM/ACME. Part-time programs available. Postbaccalaureate distance learning degree programs offered (no on-campus study). Terminal master's awarded for partial completion of doctoral program. *Degree requirements:* For master's, thesis or alternative; for doctorate, comprehensive exam, thesis/dissertation. *Entrance requirements:* For master's and doctorate, GRE General Test. Additional exam requirements/recommendations for international students: Required—TOEFL (minimum score 520 paper-based; 190 computer-based). Electronic applications accepted. *Faculty research:* Substance abuse, injury and violence, symptom management.

University of Colorado at Colorado Springs, Beth-El College of Nursing and Health Sciences, Colorado Springs, CO 80933-7150. Offers adult health nurse practitioner and clinical specialist (MSN); family practitioner (MSN), including community clinical specialist, forensic clinical specialist, holistic clinical specialist; neonatal nurse practitioner and clinical specialist (MSN); nursing administration (MSN); nursing practice (DNP); women nurse practitioner (MSN). *Accreditation:* AACN. Part-time programs available. Postbaccalaureate distance learning degree programs offered (minimal on-campus study). *Faculty:* 31 full-time (28 women), 6 part-time/adjunct (all women). *Students:* 122 full-time (103 women), 68 part-time (64 women); includes 36 minority (4 Black or African American, non-Hispanic/Latino; 2 American Indian or Alaska Native, non-Hispanic/Latino; 9 Asian, non-Hispanic/Latino; 18 Hispanic/Latino; 3 Two or more races, non-Hispanic/Latino), 5 international. Average age 35. 153 applicants, 71% accepted, 60 enrolled. In 2011, 41 master's, 15 doctorates awarded. *Degree requirements:* For master's, comprehensive exam, thesis optional; for doctorate, capstone project. *Entrance requirements:* For master's, GRE General Test or MAT, BSN, minimum GPA of 3.0, unrestricted RN license; for doctorate, interview; active RN license; MA; minimum GPA of 3.3; National Certification as NP or CNS; portfolio. Additional exam requirements/recommendations for international students: Required—TOEFL. *Application deadline:* For fall admission, 6/15 priority date for domestic students; for spring admission, 11/15 for domestic students. Application fee: $60 ($75 for international students). Electronic applications accepted. *Expenses:* Contact institution. *Financial support:* In 2011–12, 33 students received support, including 1 fellowship (averaging $2,500 per year); career-related internships or fieldwork, Federal Work-Study, and scholarships/grants also available. Support available to part-time students. Financial award application deadline: 3/1; financial award applicants required to submit FAFSA. *Faculty research:* Women's health, uncertainty, empowerment, family experience in chronic illness. *Total annual research expenditures:* $322,604. *Unit head:* Dr. Nancy Smith, Dean, 719-255-4411, Fax: 719-255-4416, E-mail: nsmith2@uccs.edu. *Application contact:* Diane Busch, Director, 719-255-4424, Fax: 719-255-4416, E-mail: dbusch@uccs.edu. Web site: http://www.uccs.edu/~bethel/.

University of Colorado Denver, College of Nursing, Aurora, CO 80045. Offers adult clinical nurse specialist (MS); adult nurse practitioner (MS); family nurse practitioner (MS); family psychiatric mental health nurse practitioner (MS); health care informatics (MS); nurse-midwifery (MS); nursing (DNP, PhD); nursing leadership and health care systems (MS); pediatric nurse practitioner (MS); pediatric nursing leadership (MS); special studies (MS); women's health care (MS); MS/PhD. *Accreditation:* ACNM/ACME (one or more programs are accredited); NLN (one or more programs are accredited). Part-time and evening/weekend programs available. Postbaccalaureate distance learning degree programs offered (minimal on-campus study). *Faculty:* 69 full-time (65 women), 68 part-time/adjunct (64 women). *Students:* 308 full-time (288 women), 134 part-time (118 women); includes 59 minority (11 Black or African American, non-Hispanic/Latino; 8 American Indian or Alaska Native, non-Hispanic/Latino; 10 Asian, non-Hispanic/Latino; 27 Hispanic/Latino; 3 Two or more races, non-Hispanic/Latino), 8 international. Average age 39. 298 applicants, 46% accepted, 110 enrolled. In 2011, 72 master's, 19 doctorates awarded. Terminal master's awarded for partial completion of doctoral program. *Degree requirements:* For master's, thesis optional; for doctorate, comprehensive exam, thesis/dissertation, 42 credits of coursework, 30 credits of dissertation. *Entrance requirements:* For master's, GRE if cumulative undergraduate GPA is less than 3.0, undergraduate nursing degree from NLNAC- or CCNE-accredited school or university; completion of research and statistics courses with minimum grade of C; copy of current and unencumbered nursing license; for doctorate, GRE, bachelor's and/or master's degrees in nursing from NLN- or CCNE-accredited institution; portfolio; minimum undergraduate GPA of 3.0, graduate 3.5; graduate-level intermediate statistics and master's-level nursing theory courses with minimum B grade; interview. Additional exam requirements/recommendations for international students: Required—TOEFL (minimum score 560 paper-based; 220 computer-based; 83 iBT). *Application deadline:* For fall admission, 4/1 for domestic students; for spring admission, 9/1 for domestic students. Application fee: $65. Electronic applications accepted. *Expenses:* Contact institution. *Financial support:* In 2011–12, 40 students received support. Fellowships, research assistantships, teaching assistantships, Federal Work-Study, scholarships/grants, and unspecified assistantships available. Support available to part-time students. Financial award application deadline: 4/1; financial award applicants required to submit FAFSA. *Faculty research:* Biological and behavioral phenomena in pregnancy and postpartum; patterns of glycemia during the insulin resistance of pregnancy; obesity, gestational diabetes, and relationship to neonatal adiposity; men's awareness and knowledge of male breast cancer; cognitive-behavioral therapy for chronic insomnia after breast cancer treatment; massage therapy for the treatment of tension-type headaches. *Total annual research expenditures:* $5.2 million. *Unit head:* Dr. Patricia Moritz, Dean, 303-724-1679, E-mail: pat.moritz@ucdenver.edu. *Application contact:* Judy Campbell, Graduate Programs Coordinator, 303-724-8503, E-mail: judy.campbell@ucdenver.edu. Web site: http://www.ucdenver.edu/academics/colleges/nursing/Pages/default.aspx.

University of Connecticut, Graduate School, School of Nursing, Storrs, CT 06269. Offers MS, PhD, Post-Master's Certificate. *Accreditation:* AACN. *Degree requirements:* For master's, comprehensive exam; for doctorate, thesis/dissertation. *Entrance requirements:* Additional exam requirements/recommendations for international students: Required—TOEFL (minimum score 550 paper-based; 213 computer-based). Electronic applications accepted.

University of Delaware, College of Health Sciences, School of Nursing, Newark, DE 19716. Offers adult nurse practitioner (MSN, PMC); cardiopulmonary clinical nurse specialist (MSN, PMC); cardiopulmonary clinical nurse specialist/adult nurse practitioner (MSN, PMC); family nurse practitioner (MSN, PMC); gerontology clinical nurse specialist (MSN, PMC); gerontology clinical nurse specialist geriatric nurse practitioner (PMC); gerontology clinical nurse specialist/geriatric nurse practitioner (MSN); health services administration (MSN, PMC); nursing of children clinical nurse specialist (MSN, PMC); nursing of children clinical nurse specialist/pediatric nurse practitioner (MSN, PMC); oncology/immune deficiency clinical nurse specialist (MSN, PMC); oncology/immune deficiency clinical nurse specialist/adult nurse practitioner (MSN, PMC); perinatal/women's health clinical nurse specialist (MSN, PMC); perinatal/women's health clinical nurse specialist/women's health nurse practitioner (MSN, PMC); psychiatric nursing clinical nurse specialist (MSN, PMC). *Accreditation:* AACN; NLN (one or more programs are accredited). Part-time and evening/weekend programs available. Postbaccalaureate distance learning degree programs offered (minimal on-campus study). *Degree requirements:* For master's, thesis optional. *Entrance requirements:* For master's, BSN, interview, RN license. Electronic applications accepted. *Faculty research:* Marriage and chronic illness, health promotion, congestive heart failure patient outcomes, school nursing, diabetes in children, culture, health disparities, cardiovascular, prison nursing, oncology, public policy, child obesity, smoking and teen pregnancy, blood pressure measurements, men's health.

University of Florida, Graduate School, College of Nursing, Gainesville, FL 32611. Offers MSN, DNP, PhD. *Accreditation:* AACN; ACNM/ACME (one or more programs are accredited). Part-time programs available. *Faculty:* 20 full-time (19 women), 1 (woman) part-time/adjunct. *Students:* 75 full-time (70 women), 67 part-time (64 women); includes 17 minority (6 Black or African American, non-Hispanic/Latino; 3 Asian, non-Hispanic/Latino; 8 Hispanic/Latino), 2 international. Average age 35. 97 applicants, 64% accepted, 56 enrolled. In 2011, 45 master's awarded. *Degree requirements:* For master's, thesis optional; for doctorate, thesis/dissertation. *Entrance requirements:* For master's and doctorate, GRE General Test, minimum GPA of 3.0. Additional exam requirements/recommendations for international students: Required—TOEFL (minimum score 550 paper-based; 213 computer-based; 80 iBT), IELTS (minimum score 6). *Application deadline:* For fall admission, 3/15 priority date for domestic students, 3/15 for international students. Applications are processed on a rolling basis. Application fee: $30. Electronic applications accepted. *Financial support:* In 2011–12, 12 students received support, including 12 fellowships with partial tuition reimbursements available; career-related internships or fieldwork and Federal Work-Study also available. Support available to part-time students. Financial award applicants required to submit FAFSA. *Faculty research:* Aging and health: cancer survivorship, interventions to promote healthy aging, and symptom management; women's health, fetal and infant development; biobehavioral interventions: interrelationships among the biological, behavioral, psychological, social and spiritual factors that influence wellness and disease; health policy: influence of local and national policy on physical and psychological health. *Unit head:* Dr. Kathleen A. Long, PhD, Dean and Professor, 352-273-6324, Fax: 352-273-6505, E-mail: longka@ufl.edu. *Application contact:* Cecile Kiley, Academic Graduate Advisor, 352-273-36613. Web site: http://www.con.ufl.edu/.

University of Hartford, College of Education, Nursing, and Health Professions, Program in Nursing, West Hartford, CT 06117-1599. Offers community/public health nursing (MSN); nursing education (MSN); nursing management (MSN). *Accreditation:* AACN. Part-time and evening/weekend programs available. *Degree requirements:* For master's, research project. *Entrance requirements:* For master's, BSN, Connecticut RN license. Additional exam requirements/recommendations for international students: Required—TOEFL (minimum score 550 paper-based; 213 computer-based). Electronic applications accepted. *Expenses:* Contact institution. *Faculty research:* Child development, women in doctoral study, applying feminist theory in teaching methods, near death experience, grandmothers as primary care providers.

University of Hawaii at Manoa, Graduate Division, School of Nursing and Dental Hygiene, Honolulu, HI 96822. Offers clinical nurse specialist (MS), including adult health, community mental health; nurse practitioner (MS), including adult health, community mental health, family nurse practitioner; nursing (PhD, Graduate Certificate); nursing administration (MS). *Accreditation:* AACN; NLN (one or more programs are accredited). Part-time programs available. Postbaccalaureate distance learning degree programs offered (minimal on-campus study). *Degree requirements:* For master's, thesis optional; for doctorate, comprehensive exam, thesis/dissertation. *Entrance requirements:* For master's, Hawaii RN license. Additional exam requirements/recommendations for international students: Required—TOEFL (minimum score 580 paper-based; 237 computer-based; 92 iBT), IELTS (minimum score 5). *Expenses:* Contact institution.

University of Houston–Victoria, School of Nursing, Victoria, TX 77901-4450. Offers MSN. *Accreditation:* AACN. *Entrance requirements:* For master's, GRE or MAT, minimum GPA of 3.0 in last 60 hours of academic course work, valid Texas RN licensure, 2 letters of recommendation. Electronic applications accepted.

University of Illinois at Chicago, Graduate College, College of Nursing, Chicago, IL 60607-7128. Offers MS, DNP, PhD, MBA/MS, MPH/MS. *Accreditation:* AACN. Part-time programs available. *Degree requirements:* For master's, thesis or alternative; for doctorate, thesis/dissertation. *Entrance requirements:* For master's and doctorate, GRE General Test, minimum GPA of 2.75. Additional exam requirements/recommendations for international students: Required—TOEFL. Electronic applications accepted. *Expenses:* Contact institution.

University of Indianapolis, Graduate Programs, School of Nursing, Indianapolis, IN 46227-3697. Offers family practice (post-RN) (MSN); gerontological nurse practitioner (MSN); nurse-midwifery (MSN); nursing (MSN); nursing administration (MSN); nursing education (MSN); MBA/MSN. *Accreditation:* AACN; ACNM. *Faculty:* 1 full-time (0 women), 4 part-time/adjunct (1 woman). *Students:* 14 full-time (13 women), 168 part-time (159 women); includes 23 minority (13 Black or African American, non-Hispanic/Latino; 1 American Indian or Alaska Native, non-Hispanic/Latino; 4 Asian, non-Hispanic/Latino; 2 Hispanic/Latino; 3 Two or more races, non-Hispanic/Latino), 5 international. Average age 36. In 2011, 51 master's awarded. *Entrance requirements:* For master's, minimum GPA of 3.0, interview, letters of recommendation, resume, IN nursing license, 1 year professional practice. Additional exam requirements/recommendations for international students: Required—TOEFL (minimum score 550 paper-based; 213 computer-based). *Application deadline:* For fall admission, 8/1 for domestic students; for winter admission, 12/15 for domestic students; for spring admission, 4/15 for domestic students. Applications are processed on a rolling basis. Application fee: $50. Tuition and fees vary according to degree level and program. *Financial support:* Federal Work-Study available. *Unit head:* Dr. Anne Thomas, Dean, 317-788-3206, E-mail: athomas@uindy.edu. *Application contact:* Sueann Meagher, Graduate Administrative Assistant, 317-788-8005, Fax: 317-788-3542, E-mail: meaghers@uindy.edu. Web site: http://nursing.uindy.edu/.

The University of Iowa, Graduate College, College of Nursing, Iowa City, IA 52242-1316. Offers MSN, DNP, PhD, MBA/MSN, MSN/MPH. *Accreditation:* AACN; AANA/CANAEP (one or more programs are accredited). *Degree requirements:* For master's, thesis optional, portfolio, project; for doctorate, comprehensive exam, thesis/dissertation. *Entrance requirements:* For master's, minimum GPA of 3.0; for doctorate, GRE General Test, minimum GPA of 3.0. Additional exam requirements/recommendations for international students: Required—TOEFL (minimum score 550 paper-based; 213 computer-based; 81 iBT). Electronic applications accepted. *Expenses:* Contact institution.

The University of Kansas, University of Kansas Medical Center, School of Nursing, Kansas City, KS 66160. Offers adult/gerontological clinical nurse specialist (PMC); adult/gerontological nurse practitioner (PMC); clinical research management (PMC); family nurse practitioner (PMC); health care informatics (PMC); health professions educator (PMC); nurse midwife (PMC); nursing (MS, DNP, PhD); organizational

leadership (PMC); psychiatric/mental health nurse practitioner (PMC); public health nursing (PMC). *Accreditation:* AACN; ACNM/ACME. Part-time programs available. Postbaccalaureate distance learning degree programs offered (minimal on-campus study). *Faculty:* 80. *Students:* 79 full-time (71 women), 336 part-time (317 women); includes 63 minority (24 Black or African American, non-Hispanic/Latino; 2 American Indian or Alaska Native, non-Hispanic/Latino; 18 Asian, non-Hispanic/Latino; 15 Hispanic/Latino; 4 Two or more races, non-Hispanic/Latino), 6 international. Average age 37. 155 applicants, 82% accepted, 127 enrolled. In 2011, 79 master's, 15 doctorates, 12 other advanced degrees awarded. Terminal master's awarded for partial completion of doctoral program. *Degree requirements:* For master's, comprehensive exam, thesis optional, general oral exam; for doctorate, variable foreign language requirement, thesis/dissertation, comprehensive oral exam (for DNP); comprehensive written and oral exam (for PhD). *Entrance requirements:* For master's, bachelor's degree in nursing, minimum GPA of 3.0, RN license, 1 year of clinical experience, RN license in KS and MO; for doctorate, GRE General Test, master's degree in nursing, minimum GPA of 3.5, RN license in KS and MO; national certification (for some specialties). Additional exam requirements/recommendations for international students: Required—TOEFL. *Application deadline:* For fall admission, 4/1 for domestic and international students; for spring admission, 9/1 for domestic and international students. Application fee: $60. Electronic applications accepted. Tuition and fees vary according to course load, campus/location, program and reciprocity agreements. *Financial support:* Research assistantships with full and partial tuition reimbursements, teaching assistantships with full and partial tuition reimbursements, and traineeships available. Financial award application deadline: 2/14; financial award applicants required to submit FAFSA. *Faculty research:* Breastfeeding practices of teen mothers, national database of nursing quality indicators, caregiving of families of patients using technology in the home, simulation in nursing education, diaphragm fatigue. *Total annual research expenditures:* $6.1 million. *Unit head:* Dr. Karen L. Miller, Dean, 913-588-1601, Fax: 913-588-1660, E-mail: kmiller@kumc.edu. *Application contact:* Dr. Debra J. Ford, Associate Dean, Student Affairs, 913-588-1619, Fax: 913-588-1615, E-mail: dford@kumc.edu. Web site: http://nursing.kumc.edu.

University of Kentucky, Graduate School, Graduate School Programs in the College of Nursing, Program in Nursing, Lexington, KY 40506-0032. Offers MSN, PhD. *Accreditation:* AACN. *Degree requirements:* For master's, comprehensive exam, thesis optional, research project; for doctorate, comprehensive exam, thesis/dissertation. *Entrance requirements:* For master's, GRE General Test, minimum undergraduate GPA of 2.75; for doctorate, GRE General Test, minimum undergraduate GPA of 2.75, graduate 3.0. Additional exam requirements/recommendations for international students: Required—TOEFL (minimum score 550 paper-based; 213 computer-based). Electronic applications accepted.

University of Lethbridge, School of Graduate Studies, Lethbridge, AB T1K 3M4, Canada. Offers accounting (MScM); addictions counseling (M Sc); agricultural biotechnology (M Sc); agricultural studies (M Sc, MA); anthropology (MA); archaeology (MA); art (MA, MFA); biochemistry (M Sc); biological sciences (M Sc); biomolecular science (PhD); biosystems and biodiversity (PhD); Canadian studies (MA); chemistry (M Sc); computer science (M Sc); computer science and geographical information science (M Sc); counseling psychology (M Ed); dramatic arts (MA); earth, space, and physical science (PhD); economics (MA); educational leadership (M Ed); English (MA); environmental science (M Sc); evolution and behavior (PhD); exercise science (M Sc); finance (MScM); French (MA); French/German (MA); French/Spanish (MA); general education (M Ed); general management (MScM); geography (M Sc, MA); German (MA); health science (M Sc); history (MA); human resource management and labour relations (MScM); individualized multidisciplinary (M Sc, MA); information systems (MScM); international management (MScM); kinesiology (M Sc, MA); management (M Sc, MA); marketing (MScM); mathematics (M Sc); music (M Mus, MA); Native American studies (MA); neuroscience (M Sc, PhD); new media (MA); nursing (M Sc); philosophy (MA); physics (M Sc); policy and strategy (MScM); political science (MA); psychology (M Sc, MA); religious studies (MA); social sciences (MA); sociology (MA); theatre and dramatic arts (MFA); theoretical and computational science (PhD); urban and regional studies (MA); women's studies (MA). Part-time and evening/weekend programs available. *Degree requirements:* For doctorate, comprehensive exam, thesis/dissertation. *Entrance requirements:* For master's, GMAT (M Sc in management), bachelor's degree in related field, minimum GPA of 3.0 during previous 20 graded semester courses, 2 years teaching or related experience (M Ed); for doctorate, master's degree, minimum graduate GPA of 3.5. Additional exam requirements/recommendations for international students: Required—TOEFL. *Faculty research:* Movement and brain plasticity, gibberellin physiology, photosynthesis, carbon cycling, molecular properties of main-group ring components.

University of Louisiana at Lafayette, College of Nursing, Lafayette, LA 70504. Offers MSN. Program offered jointly with Southern Louisiana University, McNeese State University, Southern University and Agricultural and Mechanical College. *Accreditation:* AACN. *Degree requirements:* For master's, thesis or alternative. *Entrance requirements:* For master's, GRE General Test, minimum GPA of 2.75. Additional exam requirements/recommendations for international students: Required—TOEFL (minimum score 550 paper-based; 213 computer-based). Electronic applications accepted.

University of Louisville, Graduate School, School of Nursing, Louisville, KY 40202. Offers adult nurse practitioner (MSN); family nurse practitioner (MSN); health professions education (MSN); neonatal nurse practitioner (MSN); nursing research (PhD); psychiatric mental health nurse practitioner (MSN). *Accreditation:* AACN. Part-time programs available. *Faculty:* 24 full-time (22 women), 4 part-time/adjunct (3 women). *Students:* 82 full-time (74 women), 65 part-time (58 women); includes 20 minority (13 Black or African American, non-Hispanic/Latino; 1 American Indian or Alaska Native, non-Hispanic/Latino; 1 Asian, non-Hispanic/Latino; 1 Hispanic/Latino; 4 Two or more races, non-Hispanic/Latino), 2 international. Average age 34. 41 applicants, 56% accepted, 19 enrolled. In 2011, 42 master's, 2 doctorates awarded. Terminal master's awarded for partial completion of doctoral program. *Degree requirements:* For master's, thesis optional; for doctorate, comprehensive exam, thesis/dissertation. *Entrance requirements:* For master's, GRE General Test, bachelor's degree in nursing, minimum GPA of 3.0, RN license; for doctorate, GRE General Test, BSN or MSN with recommended minimum GPA of 3.0. Additional exam requirements/recommendations for international students: Required—TOEFL. *Application deadline:* For fall admission, 4/1 priority date for domestic students, 4/1 for international students. Applications are processed on a rolling basis. Application fee: $50. Electronic applications accepted. *Expenses:* Tuition, state resident: full-time $9692; part-time $539 per credit hour. Tuition, nonresident: full-time $20,168; part-time $1121 per credit hour. Tuition and fees vary according to program and reciprocity agreements. *Financial support:* In 2011–12, 45 students received support, including 6 research assistantships with full tuition reimbursements available (averaging $20,000 per year), 6 teaching assistantships with full tuition reimbursements available (averaging $19,167 per year); fellowships with full tuition reimbursements available, institutionally sponsored loans, scholarships/grants, traineeships, health care benefits, and unspecified assistantships also available. Support available to part-time students. Financial award application deadline: 4/15; financial award applicants required to submit FAFSA. *Faculty research:* Maternal-child/family stress after pregnancy loss, postpartum depression, access to healthcare (underserved populations), quality of life issues, physical activity (impact on chronic/acute conditions). *Total annual research expenditures:* $795,250. *Unit head:* Dr. Marcia J. Hern, Dean, 502-852-8300, Fax: 502-852-5044, E-mail: m.hern@gwise.louisville.edu. *Application contact:* Dr. Lee Ridner, Interim Associate Dean for Academic Affairs and Director of MSN Programs, 502-852-8518, Fax: 502-852-0704, E-mail: romain01@louisville.edu. Web site: http://www.louisville.edu/nursing/.

University of Maine, Graduate School, College of Natural Sciences, Forestry, and Agriculture, School of Nursing, Orono, ME 04469. Offers individualized (MS); individualized track (CAS); rural health family nurse practitioner (MS, CAS). *Accreditation:* AACN. *Faculty:* 16 full-time (13 women), 29 part-time/adjunct (25 women). *Students:* 15 full-time (all women), 11 part-time (9 women); includes 1 minority (Asian, non-Hispanic/Latino). Average age 38. 6 applicants, 33% accepted, 2 enrolled. In 2011, 5 master's, 1 other advanced degree awarded. *Entrance requirements:* For master's, GRE General Test. Additional exam requirements/recommendations for international students: Required—TOEFL. *Application deadline:* Applications are processed on a rolling basis. Application fee: $65. Electronic applications accepted. *Expenses:* Tuition, state resident: full-time $5016. Tuition, nonresident: full-time $14,424. *Financial support:* Career-related internships or fieldwork, Federal Work-Study, institutionally sponsored loans, and tuition waivers (full and partial) available. Support available to part-time students. Financial award application deadline: 3/1. *Unit head:* Dr. Nancy Fishwick, Director, 207-581-2505, Fax: 207-581-2585. *Application contact:* Scott G. Delcourt, Associate Dean of the Graduate School, 207-581-3291, Fax: 207-581-3232, E-mail: graduate@maine.edu. Web site: http://www2.umaine.edu/graduate/.

The University of Manchester, School of Nursing, Midwifery and Social Work, Manchester, United Kingdom. Offers nursing (M Phil, PhD); social work (M Phil, PhD).

University of Manitoba, Faculty of Graduate Studies, Faculty of Nursing, Winnipeg, MB R3T 2N2, Canada. Offers cancer nursing (MN); nursing (MN). *Degree requirements:* For master's, thesis.

University of Mary, School of Health Sciences, Division of Nursing, Bismarck, ND 58504-9652. Offers family nurse practitioner (MSN); nurse administrator (MSN); nursing educator (MSN). *Accreditation:* AACN. Part-time and evening/weekend programs available. Postbaccalaureate distance learning degree programs offered (minimal on-campus study). *Faculty:* 6 full-time (all women), 16 part-time/adjunct (all women). *Students:* 157 full-time (148 women), 91 part-time (85 women); includes 14 minority (5 Black or African American, non-Hispanic/Latino; 4 American Indian or Alaska Native, non-Hispanic/Latino; 1 Asian, non-Hispanic/Latino; 4 Hispanic/Latino), 2 international. Average age 37. 92 applicants. In 2011, 80 master's awarded. *Degree requirements:* For master's, comprehensive exam (for some programs), thesis (for some programs), internship (family nurse practitioner), teaching practice. *Entrance requirements:* For master's, minimum GPA of 2.75 in nursing, interview, letters of recommendation, criminal background check, immunizations, statement of professional goals. Additional exam requirements/recommendations for international students: Required—TOEFL (minimum score 500 paper-based; 197 computer-based; 71 iBT). *Application deadline:* Applications are processed on a rolling basis. Application fee: $40. Electronic applications accepted. *Financial support:* In 2011–12, 14 fellowships with partial tuition reimbursements, 3 teaching assistantships with partial tuition reimbursements were awarded. Financial award application deadline: 8/1; financial award applicants required to submit FAFSA. *Faculty research:* Gerontology issues, rural nursing, health policy, primary care, women's health. *Unit head:* Glenda Reemts, Director, 701-255-7500 Ext. 8041, Fax: 701-255-7687, E-mail: greemts@umary.edu. *Application contact:* Joanne Lassiter, Nurse Recruiter, 701-355-8379, Fax: 701-255-7687, E-mail: jllassiter@umary.edu.

University of Mary Hardin-Baylor, Graduate Studies in Nursing, Belton, TX 76513. Offers clinical nurse leader (MSN); family nurse practitioner (MSN); nursing education (MSN). *Accreditation:* AACN. Part-time and evening/weekend programs available. *Faculty:* 8 full-time (all women), 1 (woman) part-time/adjunct. *Students:* 30 full-time (28 women), 2 part-time (both women); includes 9 minority (5 Black or African American, non-Hispanic/Latino; 1 Asian, non-Hispanic/Latino; 3 Hispanic/Latino), 6 international. Average age 34. 48 applicants, 83% accepted, 25 enrolled. In 2011, 3 master's awarded. *Degree requirements:* For master's, practicum. *Entrance requirements:* For master's, GRE General Test, RN, BSN, minimum GPA of 3.0 in last 60 hours of undergraduate program. *Application deadline:* For fall admission, 6/1 priority date for domestic students; for spring admission, 11/1 priority date for domestic students. Applications are processed on a rolling basis. Application fee: $35 ($135 for international students). Electronic applications accepted. *Expenses: Tuition:* Full-time $12,780. *Required fees:* $2350. *Financial support:* Applicants required to submit FAFSA. *Unit head:* Dr. Margaret Prydun, Director of Master's Program in Nursing, 254-295-4674, E-mail: margaret.prydun@umhb.edu. *Application contact:* Melissa Ford, Director of Graduate Admissions, 254-295-4020, Fax: 254-295-5301, E-mail: mford@umhb.edu. Web site: http://graduate.umhb.edu/nursing/.

University of Maryland, Baltimore, Graduate School, School of Nursing, Doctoral Program in Nursing, Baltimore, MD 21201. Offers direct nursing (PhD); indirect nursing (PhD). *Students:* 20 full-time (18 women), 29 part-time (26 women); includes 13 minority (4 Black or African American, non-Hispanic/Latino; 6 Asian, non-Hispanic/Latino; 1 Hispanic/Latino; 2 Two or more races, non-Hispanic/Latino), 8 international. Average age 43. 49 applicants, 24% accepted, 2 enrolled. In 2011, 10 doctorates awarded. *Degree requirements:* For doctorate, thesis/dissertation. *Entrance requirements:* For doctorate, GRE General Test, minimum GPA of 3.0, MS in nursing. Additional exam requirements/recommendations for international students: Required—TOEFL (minimum score 550 paper-based; 80 iBT); Recommended—IELTS (minimum score 7). *Application deadline:* For fall admission, 1/15 for domestic and international students. Application fee: $50. Electronic applications accepted. *Financial support:* Fellowships, research assistantships, and teaching assistantships available. Financial award application deadline: 2/15, financial award applicants required to submit FAFSA. *Unit head:* Dr. Susan Thomas, Director, 410-706-3716, Fax: 410-706-3769. *Application contact:* Janice Anarino, Program Coordinator. Web site: http://nursing.umaryland.edu/.

University of Maryland, Baltimore, Graduate School, School of Nursing, Doctor of Nursing Practice Program, Baltimore, MD 21201. Offers DNP. *Students:* 8 full-time (all women), 70 part-time (64 women); includes 15 minority (13 Black or African American, non-Hispanic/Latino; 1 American Indian or Alaska Native, non-Hispanic/Latino; 1 Asian, non-Hispanic/Latino), 1 international. Average age 46. In 2011, 15 doctorates awarded. *Unit head:* Dr. Jane Kapustin, Professor/Director of Master's Program, 410-706-3890. *Application contact:* Keith T. Brooks, Assistant Dean, 410-706-7131, Fax: 410-706-3473, E-mail: kbrooks@umaryland.edu. Web site: http://nursing.umaryland.edu/academic-programs/grad/doctoral-degree/dnp.

University of Maryland, Baltimore, Graduate School, School of Nursing, Master's Program in Nursing, Baltimore, MD 21201. Offers community health nursing (MS); gerontological nursing (MS); maternal-child nursing (MS); medical-surgical nursing (MS); nurse-midwifery education (MS); nursing administration (MS); nursing education (MS); nursing health policy (MS); primary care nursing (MS); psychiatric nursing (MS); MS/MBA. MS/MBA offered jointly with University of Baltimore. *Accreditation:* AACN;

AANA/CANAEP; NLN (one or more programs are accredited). Part-time programs available. *Students:* 370 full-time (314 women), 480 part-time (441 women); includes 308 minority (176 Black or African American, non-Hispanic/Latino; 2 American Indian or Alaska Native, non-Hispanic/Latino; 70 Asian, non-Hispanic/Latino; 33 Hispanic/Latino; 27 Two or more races, non-Hispanic/Latino), 9 international. Average age 35. 990 applicants, 30% accepted, 204 enrolled. In 2011, 301 master's awarded. *Degree requirements:* For master's, comprehensive exam (for some programs), thesis or alternative. *Entrance requirements:* For master's, minimum GPA of 2.75, course work in statistics, BS in nursing. Additional exam requirements/recommendations for international students: Required—TOEFL (minimum score 550 paper-based; 80 iBT) or IELTS (minimum score 7). *Application deadline:* For fall admission, 2/1 for domestic students, 1/15 for international students. Application fee: $50. Electronic applications accepted. *Financial support:* Fellowships, research assistantships, teaching assistantships, career-related internships or fieldwork, and traineeships available. Support available to part-time students. Financial award application deadline: 2/15; financial award applicants required to submit FAFSA. *Unit head:* Dr. Jane Kapustin, Assistant Dean, 410-706-6741, Fax: 410-706-4231. *Application contact:* Marjorie Fass, Admissions Director, 410-706-0501, Fax: 410-706-7238.

University of Maryland, Baltimore, Graduate School, School of Nursing, Post Baccalaureate Certificate Program in Nursing, Baltimore, MD 21201. Offers Postbaccalaureate Certificate. *Students:* 17 part-time (all women); includes 3 minority (1 Black or African American, non-Hispanic/Latino; 1 Asian, non-Hispanic/Latino; 1 Two or more races, non-Hispanic/Latino). Average age 50. *Unit head:* Dr. Jane Kapustin, Professor/Director of Master's Program, 410-706-3890. *Application contact:* Keith T. Brooks, Assistant Dean, 410-706-7131, Fax: 410-706-3473, E-mail: kbrooks@umaryland.edu.

University of Massachusetts Amherst, Graduate School, School of Nursing, Amherst, MA 01003. Offers clinical nurse leader (MS); family nurse practitioner (DNP); nursing (PhD); public health nurse leader (DNP). *Accreditation:* AACN. Part-time programs available. Postbaccalaureate distance learning degree programs offered (minimal on-campus study). *Faculty:* 12 full-time (11 women). *Students:* 56 full-time (51 women), 155 part-time (142 women); includes 57 minority (24 Black or African American, non-Hispanic/Latino; 5 Asian, non-Hispanic/Latino; 25 Hispanic/Latino; 3 Two or more races, non-Hispanic/Latino), 11 international. Average age 42. 125 applicants, 66% accepted, 53 enrolled. In 2011, 11 master's, 26 doctorates awarded. Terminal master's awarded for partial completion of doctoral program. *Degree requirements:* For master's, thesis optional; for doctorate, comprehensive exam, thesis/dissertation. *Entrance requirements:* For master's and doctorate, GRE General Test. Additional exam requirements/recommendations for international students: Required—TOEFL (minimum score 550 paper-based; 213 computer-based; 80 iBT), IELTS (minimum score 6.5). *Application deadline:* For fall admission, 2/1 for domestic and international students. Applications are processed on a rolling basis. Application fee: $50 ($65 for international students). Electronic applications accepted. Tuition and fees vary according to course load, campus/location and program. *Financial support:* Fellowships with full and partial tuition reimbursements, research assistantships with full and partial tuition reimbursements, teaching assistantships with full and partial tuition reimbursements, career-related internships or fieldwork, Federal Work-Study, scholarships/grants, traineeships, health care benefits, tuition waivers (full and partial), and unspecified assistantships available. Support available to part-time students. Financial award application deadline: 2/1. *Faculty research:* Health of older adults and their caretakers, mental health of individuals and families, health of children and adolescents, power and decision-making, transcultural health. *Unit head:* Dr. Donna Zucker, Graduate Program Director, 413-577-2322, Fax: 413-577-2550. *Application contact:* Lindsay DeSantis, Interim Supervisor of Admissions, 413-545-0722, Fax: 413-577-0010, E-mail: gradadm@grad.umass.edu. Web site: http://www.umass.edu/nursing/.

University of Massachusetts Boston, Office of Graduate Studies, College of Nursing and Health Sciences, Boston, MA 02125-3393. Offers MS, PhD, MS/MBA. *Accreditation:* AACN. Part-time and evening/weekend programs available. *Degree requirements:* For master's, comprehensive exam; for doctorate, comprehensive exam, thesis/dissertation. *Entrance requirements:* For master's, minimum GPA of 2.75; for doctorate, GRE General Test, master's degree, minimum GPA of 3.3. *Faculty research:* Domestic abuse and pregnancy, health policy and home health care, caregiving burdens of families, the chronically ill, health care delivery models and their impact on outcomes, health promotion and disease prevention among the elderly.

University of Massachusetts Dartmouth, Graduate School, College of Nursing, Graduate Nursing Programs, North Dartmouth, MA 02747-2300. Offers adult health/adult nurse practitioner (MS); adult health/advanced practice (MS); adult health/nurse educator (MS); adult health/nurse manager (MS); adult nurse practitioner (PMC); community nursing/advanced practice (MS); community nursing/nurse educator (MS); community nursing/nurse manager (MS); individualized nursing (PMC); nursing (DNP, PhD). Part-time programs available. *Faculty:* 27 full-time (all women), 42 part-time/adjunct (41 women). *Students:* 8 full-time (all women), 99 part-time (93 women); includes 11 minority (4 Black or African American, non-Hispanic/Latino; 2 Asian, non-Hispanic/Latino; 4 Hispanic/Latino; 1 Two or more races, non-Hispanic/Latino), 1 international. Average age 38. 65 applicants, 75% accepted, 26 enrolled. In 2011, 12 master's, 1 other advanced degree awarded. *Degree requirements:* For master's, thesis; for doctorate, thesis/dissertation. *Entrance requirements:* For master's, GRE General Test, BSN, minimum undergraduate GPA of 3.0, RN license, 3 letters of recommendation, 1 year experience as registered nurse; for doctorate, GRE General Test, minimum undergraduate GPA of 3.0, graduate 3.3; 3 letters of recommendation; personal statement; current Massachusetts RN license or eligibility for licensure in Massachusetts; 1 year professional nursing experience; example of scholarly writing. Additional exam requirements/recommendations for international students: Required—TOEFL (minimum score 533 paper-based; 200 computer-based; 72 iBT). *Application deadline:* For fall admission, 3/15 for domestic students, 2/15 for international students. Application fee: $40 ($60 for international students). Electronic applications accepted. *Expenses:* Tuition, state resident: full-time $2071; part-time $86.29 per credit. Tuition, nonresident: full-time $8099; part-time $337.46 per credit. *Required fees:* $438.58 per credit. Part-time tuition and fees vary according to class time, course load, degree level and reciprocity agreements. *Financial support:* In 2011–12, 14 teaching assistantships with partial tuition reimbursements (averaging $2,571 per year) were awarded; Federal Work-Study also available. Support available to part-time students. Financial award application deadline: 3/1; financial award applicants required to submit FAFSA. *Faculty research:* Chronic illness management, risk reduction activities in Type 2 diabetes, diabetes care and education, clinical decision-making, quantitative methodologies. *Total annual research expenditures:* $31,049. *Unit head:* Dr. Gail Russell, Graduate Program Director, 508-999-8251, Fax: 508-999-9127, E-mail: grussell@umassd.edu. *Application contact:* Elan Turcotte-Shamski, Graduate Admissions Officer, 508-999-8604, Fax: 508-999-8183, E-mail: graduate@umassd.edu. Web site: http://www.umassd.edu/nursing/graduateprograms.

University of Massachusetts Lowell, School of Health and Environment, Department of Nursing, Lowell, MA 01854-2881. Offers adult psychiatric and mental health nursing (MS, Graduate Certificate); family health nursing (MS); gerontological nursing (MS, Graduate Certificate); geropsychiatric nursing (Graduate Certificate); nursing (PhD); nursing education (Graduate Certificate); palliative and end-of-life nursing care (Graduate Certificate). *Accreditation:* AACN. *Degree requirements:* For master's, thesis optional; for doctorate, thesis/dissertation. *Entrance requirements:* For master's and doctorate, GRE General Test. *Faculty research:* Gerontology, women's health issues, long-term care, alcoholism, health promotion.

University of Massachusetts Worcester, Graduate School of Nursing, Worcester, MA 01655-0115. Offers adult acute/critical care nurse practitioner (MS, Post Master's Certificate); adult acute/critical care nurse practitioner and gerontological nurse practitioner (MS, Post Master's Certificate); adult primary care nurse practitioner (MS, Post Master's Certificate); adult primary care nurse practitioner and gerontological nurse practitioner (MS, Post Master's Certificate); advanced practice nursing (DNP); family nurse practitioner (MS); gerontological nurse practitioner (Post Master's Certificate); leadership (DNP); nurse education (Post Master's Certificate); nurse educator (MS); nursing (PhD). *Accreditation:* AACN. *Faculty:* 20 full-time (17 women), 60 part-time/adjunct (50 women). *Students:* 162 full-time (141 women), 36 part-time (30 women); includes 29 minority (13 Black or African American, non-Hispanic/Latino; 10 Asian, non-Hispanic/Latino; 6 Hispanic/Latino), 1 international. Average age 36. 252 applicants, 38% accepted, 82 enrolled. In 2011, 38 master's, 6 doctorates awarded. *Degree requirements:* For doctorate, comprehensive exam, thesis/dissertation. *Entrance requirements:* For master's, GRE General Test, bachelor's degree, course work in statistics; for doctorate, GRE General Test, bachelor's or master's degree, RN licensure; for Post Master's Certificate, GRE General Test, MS in nursing. Additional exam requirements/recommendations for international students: Required—TOEFL. *Application deadline:* For fall admission, 1/15 priority date for domestic students. Applications are processed on a rolling basis. Application fee: $40 ($60 for international students). *Expenses:* Contact institution. *Financial support:* In 2011–12, 38 students received support. Institutionally sponsored loans, scholarships/grants, traineeships, and tuition waivers (for some) available. Support available to part-time students. Financial award application deadline: 5/16; financial award applicants required to submit FAFSA. *Faculty research:* Decision-making of partners and men with prostate cancer, coinfection (HIV and Hepatitus C) and treatment decisions, parent management of children with T1DM, health literacy and discharge planning, Ghanian women and self-care. *Total annual research expenditures:* $939,567. *Unit head:* Dr. Paulette Seymour-Route, Dean, 508-856-5801, Fax: 508-856-6552, E-mail: paulette.seymour-route@umassmed.edu. *Application contact:* Diane Brescia, Admissions Coordinator, 508-856-3488, Fax: 508-856-5851, E-mail: diane.brescia@umassmed.edu. Web site: http://www.umassmed.edu/gsn/.

University of Medicine and Dentistry of New Jersey, School of Nursing, Program in Advanced Practice Nursing, Newark, NJ 07107-1709. Offers MSN, Post Master's Certificate. *Entrance requirements:* Additional exam requirements/recommendations for international students: Required—TOEFL. Electronic applications accepted.

University of Memphis, Loewenberg School of Nursing, Memphis, TN 38152. Offers advance practice-family nurse practitioner (MSN); executive nursing leadership (MSN); nursing (Graduate Certificate); nursing administration (MSN); nursing education (MSN); nursing informatics (MSN). *Accreditation:* AACN. Part-time and evening/weekend programs available. Postbaccalaureate distance learning degree programs offered. *Degree requirements:* For master's, comprehensive exam, thesis optional, scholarly project; completion of clinical practicum hours. *Entrance requirements:* For master's, NCLEX Exam, interview. Additional exam requirements/recommendations for international students: Required—TOEFL (minimum score 550 paper-based; 213 computer-based; 79 iBT). *Faculty research:* Technology in nursing, nurse retention, cultural competence, health policy, health access.

University of Miami, Graduate School, School of Nursing and Health Studies, Coral Gables, FL 33124. Offers acute care (MSN), including acute care nurse practitioner, nurse anesthesia; nursing (PhD); primary care (MSN), including adult nurse practitioner, family nurse practitioner, nurse midwifery, women's health practitioner. *Accreditation:* AACN; AANA/CANAEP; ACNM/ACME (one or more programs are accredited). Part-time programs available. *Degree requirements:* For master's, thesis optional; for doctorate, thesis/dissertation. *Entrance requirements:* For master's, GRE General Test, BSN, minimum GPA of 3.0, Florida RN license; for doctorate, GRE General Test, BSN or MSN, minimum GPA of 3.0. Additional exam requirements/recommendations for international students: Required—TOEFL (minimum score 550 paper-based; 213 computer-based). Electronic applications accepted. *Faculty research:* Transcultural nursing, exercise and depression in Alzheimer's disease, infectious diseases/HIV–AIDS, postpartum depression, outcomes assessment.

University of Michigan, Horace H. Rackham School of Graduate Studies, School of Nursing, Ann Arbor, MI 48109. Offers MS, PhD, Post Master's Certificate, MBA/MS, MHSA/MS, MS/MSI. *Accreditation:* AACN; ACNM/ACME (one or more programs are accredited). Part-time programs available. Postbaccalaureate distance learning degree programs offered (minimal on-campus study). Terminal master's awarded for partial completion of doctoral program. *Degree requirements:* For doctorate, thesis/dissertation, oral defense of dissertation, preliminary exam. *Entrance requirements:* For master's, GRE General Test (if undergraduate GPA less than 3.25), minimum B average, nursing license; for doctorate, GRE General Test, nursing license, minimum B average, 2 original papers. Electronic applications accepted. *Faculty research:* Preparation of clinical nurse researchers, biobehavior, women's health, health promotion, substance abuse, psychobiology of menopause, fertility, obesity, health care systems.

University of Michigan–Flint, School of Health Professions and Studies, Program in Nursing, Flint, MI 48502-1950. Offers DNP. *Accreditation:* AACN. Part-time programs available. *Entrance requirements:* Additional exam requirements/recommendations for international students: Required—TOEFL (minimum score 560 paper-based; 220 computer-based), IELTS (minimum score 6.5). Electronic applications accepted. *Expenses:* Contact institution. *Faculty research:* Family system stress, self breast exam, family roads evaluation, causal model testing for psychosocial development, basic needs.

University of Minnesota, Twin Cities Campus, Graduate School, School of Nursing, Minneapolis, MN 55455-0213. Offers MN, MS, DNP, PhD. *Accreditation:* AACN; AANA/CANAEP; ACNM/ACME (one or more programs are accredited). Part-time programs available. Postbaccalaureate distance learning degree programs offered (minimal on-campus study). Terminal master's awarded for partial completion of doctoral program. *Degree requirements:* For master's, final oral exam, project or thesis; for doctorate, thesis/dissertation. *Entrance requirements:* For master's and doctorate, GRE General Test. Additional exam requirements/recommendations for international students: Required—TOEFL (minimum score 586 paper-based; 240 computer-based). *Expenses:* Contact institution. *Faculty research:* Child and family health promotion, nursing research on elders.

University of Mississippi Medical Center, School of Graduate Studies in the Health Sciences, Program in Nursing, Jackson, MS 39216-4505. Offers MSN, PhD. *Accreditation:* AACN. Part-time and evening/weekend programs available. *Degree requirements:* For master's, thesis optional; for doctorate, comprehensive exam, thesis/

dissertation, publishable paper. *Entrance requirements:* For master's, GRE, 1 year of clinical experience, RN license; for doctorate, GRE, RN license, professional nursing experience. Electronic applications accepted. *Expenses:* Contact institution. *Faculty research:* Quality of life, neuroscience nursing, adult learning, gerontology, child birthing/parenting education.

University of Missouri, Graduate School, Sinclair School of Nursing, Columbia, MO 65211. Offers MS, PhD. *Accreditation:* AACN. Part-time programs available. *Faculty:* 20 full-time (18 women), 6 part-time/adjunct (all women). *Students:* 43 full-time (40 women), 280 part-time (262 women); includes 18 minority (10 Black or African American, non-Hispanic/Latino; 2 American Indian or Alaska Native, non-Hispanic/Latino; 2 Asian, non-Hispanic/Latino; 2 Hispanic/Latino; 2 Two or more races, non-Hispanic/Latino), 2 international. Average age 38. 276 applicants, 44% accepted, 92 enrolled. In 2011, 43 master's, 4 doctorates awarded. *Degree requirements:* For master's, thesis optional, oral exam; for doctorate, thesis/dissertation. *Entrance requirements:* For master's, GRE General Test, BSN, minimum GPA of 3.0 during last 60 hours, nursing license. Additional exam requirements/recommendations for international students: Required—TOEFL (minimum score 550 paper-based; 213 computer-based; 79 iBT). *Application deadline:* For fall admission, 2/1 priority date for domestic students. Applications are processed on a rolling basis. Application fee: $55 ($75 for international students). *Expenses:* Tuition, state resident: full-time $5881. Tuition, nonresident: full-time $15,183. *Required fees:* $952. Tuition and fees vary according to campus/location and program. *Financial support:* Fellowships, research assistantships, teaching assistantships, career-related internships or fieldwork, institutionally sponsored loans, traineeships, and tuition waivers (full) available. *Faculty research:* Pain, stepfamilies, chemotherapy-related nausea and vomiting, stress management, self-care deficit theory. *Unit head:* Dr. Roxanne W. McDaniel, Department Chair, E-mail: mcdanielr@missouri.edu. *Application contact:* Amie Orth, 573-882-0200, E-mail: ortha@missouri.edu. Web site: http://nursing.missouri.edu/.

University of Missouri–Kansas City, School of Nursing, Kansas City, MO 64110-2499. Offers adult clinical nurse specialist (MSN), including adult nurse practitioner, women's health nurse practitioner; family nurse practitioner (MSN); neonatal nurse practitioner (MSN); nurse educator (MSN); nurse executive (MSN); nursing (PhD); nursing practice (DNP); pediatric nurse practitioner (MSN). *Accreditation:* AACN. Part-time programs available. Postbaccalaureate distance learning degree programs offered (minimal on-campus study). *Faculty:* 40 full-time (35 women), 57 part-time/adjunct (52 women). *Students:* 51 full-time (48 women), 381 part-time (352 women); includes 41 minority (22 Black or African American, non-Hispanic/Latino; 7 Asian, non-Hispanic/Latino; 12 Hispanic/Latino). Average age 37. 195 applicants, 49% accepted, 90 enrolled. In 2011, 78 master's, 19 doctorates awarded. *Degree requirements:* For master's, thesis or alternative. *Entrance requirements:* For master's, minimum undergraduate GPA of 3.2; for doctorate, GRE, 3 letters of reference, interview by invitation. Additional exam requirements/recommendations for international students: Required—TOEFL (minimum score 550 paper-based; 213 computer-based; 80 iBT). *Application deadline:* For fall admission, 2/1 priority date for domestic students, 2/1 for international students; for spring admission, 9/1 priority date for domestic students, 9/1 for international students. Application fee: $45 ($50 for international students). *Expenses:* Tuition, state resident: full-time $5798; part-time $322.10 per credit hour. Tuition, nonresident: full-time $14,969; part-time $831.60 per credit hour. *Required fees:* $93.51 per credit hour. *Financial support:* In 2011–12, 25 teaching assistantships with partial tuition reimbursements (averaging $6,927 per year) were awarded; fellowships, research assistantships, career-related internships or fieldwork, Federal Work-Study, institutionally sponsored loans, and tuition waivers (full and partial) also available. Support available to part-time students. Financial award application deadline: 3/1; financial award applicants required to submit FAFSA. *Faculty research:* Geriatrics/gerontology, children's pain, neonatology, Alzheimer's care, cancer caregivers. *Unit head:* Dr. Lora Lacey-Haun, Dean, 816-235-1700, Fax: 816-235-1701, E-mail: lacey-haunc@umkc.edu. *Application contact:* Leah Wilder, Coordinator for Admissions and Recruitment, 816-235-5768, Fax: 816-235-1701, E-mail: wilderl@umkc.edu. Web site: http://nursing.umkc.edu/.

University of Missouri–St. Louis, College of Nursing, St. Louis, MO 63121. Offers adult nurse practitioner (DNP, Post Master's Certificate); clinical nurse specialist (DNP); family mental health nurse practitioner (DNP); family nurse practitioner (MSN, DNP, Post Master's Certificate); neonatal nurse practitioner (MSN); nurse educator (MSN); nurse leader (MSN); nurse practitioner (Post Master's Certificate); nursing (PhD); pediatric clinical nurse specialist (DNP); pediatric nurse practitioner (MSN, DNP, Post Master's Certificate); women's health nurse practitioner (MSN, Post Master's Certificate). *Accreditation:* AACN. Part-time programs available. *Faculty:* 12 full-time (11 women), 14 part-time/adjunct (all women). *Students:* 240 part-time (226 women); includes 30 minority (26 Black or African American, non-Hispanic/Latino; 1 Asian, non-Hispanic/Latino; 2 Hispanic/Latino; 1 Two or more races, non-Hispanic/Latino). Average age 37. 228 applicants, 28% accepted, 53 enrolled. In 2011, 66 master's, 2 doctorates, 2 other advanced degrees awarded. *Degree requirements:* For doctorate, comprehensive exam, thesis/dissertation; for Post Master's Certificate, thesis. *Entrance requirements:* For master's, 2 recommendation letters; minimum GPA of 3.0; BSN; nursing licensure; statement of purpose; course in differential/inferential statistics; for doctorate, GRE, 2 letters of recommendation, MSN, minimum GPA of 3.2, course in differential/inferential statistics; for Post Master's Certificate, 2 recommendation letters; MSN; advanced practice certificate; minimum GPA of 3.0; essay. Additional exam requirements/recommendations for international students: Required—TOEFL (minimum score 550 paper-based; 213 computer-based). *Application deadline:* For fall admission, 2/15 for domestic and international students. Application fee: $35 ($40 for international students). Electronic applications accepted. *Expenses:* Tuition, state resident: full-time $6273; part-time $3866 per year. Tuition, nonresident: full-time $14,969; part-time $9980 per year. *Required fees:* $315 per year. *Financial support:* In 2011–12, 3 research assistantships with full and partial tuition reimbursements (averaging $12,339 per year) were awarded. Financial award application deadline: 4/1; financial award applicants required to submit FAFSA. *Faculty research:* Health promotion and restoration, family disruption, violence, abuse, battered women, health survey methods. *Unit head:* Dr. Nancy Magnuson, Director, 314-516-6066. *Application contact:* 314-516-5458, Fax: 314-516-6996, E-mail: gradadm@umsl.edu. Web site: http://www.umsl.edu/divisions/nursing/.

University of Mobile, Graduate Programs, Program in Nursing, Mobile, AL 36613. Offers MSN. *Accreditation:* AACN. Part-time and evening/weekend programs available. *Faculty:* 2 full-time (1 woman), 1 (woman) part-time/adjunct. *Students:* 14 full-time (13 women), 11 part-time (9 women); includes 16 minority (all Black or African American, non-Hispanic/Latino), 1 international. Average age 38. 6 applicants, 100% accepted, 2 enrolled. In 2011, 10 master's awarded. *Degree requirements:* For master's, comprehensive exam, thesis or alternative. *Entrance requirements:* For master's, GRE or MAT. Additional exam requirements/recommendations for international students: Required—TOEFL (minimum score 550 paper-based; 213 computer-based; 80 iBT). *Application deadline:* For fall admission, 8/3 priority date for domestic students; for spring admission, 12/23 for domestic students. Applications are processed on a rolling basis. Application fee: $40 ($50 for international students). *Expenses: Tuition:* Full-time $8262; part-time $459 per credit hour. *Required fees:* $110 per term. *Financial support:* Application deadline: 8/1. *Faculty research:* Nursing management, transcultural nursing, spiritual aspects, educational expectations. *Unit head:* Dr. Richard McElhaney, Dean, School of Nursing, 251-442-2256, Fax: 251-442-2520, E-mail: rmcelhaney@umobile.edu. *Application contact:* Tammy C. Eubanks, Administrative Assistant to Dean of Graduate Programs, 251-442-2270, Fax: 251-442-2523, E-mail: teubanks@umobile.edu. Web site: http://www.umobile.edu/.

University of Nebraska Medical Center, Graduate Studies, Program in Nursing, Omaha, NE 68198. Offers MSN, PhD. *Accreditation:* AACN. Part-time programs available. Postbaccalaureate distance learning degree programs offered. *Degree requirements:* For master's, comprehensive exam, research project or thesis; for doctorate, comprehensive exam, thesis/dissertation. *Entrance requirements:* For master's, minimum GPA of 3.0; for doctorate, GRE General Test, minimum GPA of 3.2. Additional exam requirements/recommendations for international students: Required—TOEFL (minimum score 550 paper-based; 213 computer-based). Electronic applications accepted. *Expenses:* Contact institution. *Faculty research:* Health promotion, sleep and fatigue in cancer patients, symptoms management in cardiovascular disease, prevention of osteoporosis in breast cancer survivors, impact of quality end of life care in nursing homes.

University of Nevada, Las Vegas, Graduate College, School of Nursing, Las Vegas, NV 89154-3018. Offers family nurse practitioner (Advanced Certificate); nursing (MS, DNP, PhD); nursing education (Advanced Certificate); pediatric nurse practitioner (Post-Master's Certificate). *Accreditation:* AACN. Part-time programs available. Postbaccalaureate distance learning degree programs offered (minimal on-campus study). *Faculty:* 17 full-time (all women), 22 part-time/adjunct (6 women). *Students:* 49 full-time (46 women), 82 part-time (73 women); includes 28 minority (7 Black or African American, non-Hispanic/Latino; 1 American Indian or Alaska Native, non-Hispanic/Latino; 8 Asian, non-Hispanic/Latino; 5 Hispanic/Latino; 1 Native Hawaiian or other Pacific Islander, non-Hispanic/Latino; 6 Two or more races, non-Hispanic/Latino), 3 international. Average age 41. 125 applicants, 43% accepted, 40 enrolled. In 2011, 29 master's, 8 doctorates, 2 other advanced degrees awarded. *Entrance requirements:* For doctorate, GRE General Test. Additional exam requirements/recommendations for international students: Recommended—TOEFL (minimum score 550 paper-based; 213 computer-based; 80 iBT), IELTS (minimum score 7). *Application deadline:* For fall admission, 2/15 priority date for domestic students, 5/1 for international students; for spring admission, 10/1 for international students. Applications are processed on a rolling basis. Application fee: $60 ($95 for international students). Electronic applications accepted. *Financial support:* In 2011–12, 3 students received support, including 3 teaching assistantships with partial tuition reimbursements available (averaging $9,334 per year); institutionally sponsored loans, scholarships/grants, health care benefits, and unspecified assistantships also available. Financial award application deadline: 3/1. *Faculty research:* Physiological stress reactions, leukocyte response and skeletal muscle injury, depression in lay caregivers, incivility in nursing practice, work-related injuries in healthcare and construction workers. *Total annual research expenditures:* $1.7 million. *Unit head:* Dr. Carolyn Yucha, Interim Dean, 702-895-3906, Fax: 702-895-5050, E-mail: carolyn.yucha@unlv.edu. *Application contact:* Graduate College Admissions Evaluator, 702-895-3320, Fax: 702-895-4180, E-mail: gradcollege@unlv.edu. Web site: http://nursing.unlv.edu/.

University of Nevada, Reno, Graduate School, Division of Health Sciences, Orvis School of Nursing, Reno, NV 89557. Offers MSN, DNP, MPH/MSN. *Accreditation:* AACN. *Degree requirements:* For master's, thesis optional. *Entrance requirements:* For master's, minimum GPA of 3.0 in bachelor's degree from accredited school. Additional exam requirements/recommendations for international students: Required—TOEFL (minimum score 500 paper-based; 173 computer-based; 61 iBT), IELTS (minimum score 6). Electronic applications accepted. *Faculty research:* Analysis and evaluation of nursing theory, strategies for nursing applications.

University of New Brunswick Fredericton, School of Graduate Studies, Faculty of Nursing, Fredericton, NB E3B 5A3, Canada. Offers nurse educator (MN); nurse practitioner (MN); nursing (MN). Part-time programs available. Postbaccalaureate distance learning degree programs offered. *Faculty:* 24 full-time (all women), 1 part-time/adjunct (0 women). *Students:* 10 full-time (8 women), 35 part-time (34 women). In 2011, 14 master's awarded. *Degree requirements:* For master's, comprehensive exam (for some programs), thesis (for some programs). *Entrance requirements:* For master's, undergraduate coursework in statistics and nursing research, minimum GPA of 3.3, registration as a nurse (or eligibility) in New Brunswick. Additional exam requirements/recommendations for international students: Required—TOEFL (minimum score 600 paper-based; 250 computer-based). *Application deadline:* For winter admission, 2/5 for domestic students. Application fee: $50 Canadian dollars. Electronic applications accepted. *Financial support:* In 2011–12, 9 fellowships, 1 research assistantship, 1 teaching assistantship were awarded. *Faculty research:* Violence and abuse; healthy child development, chronic illness and addiction; rural populations access to health care and primary healthcare; teaching and learning in classroom, clinical lab, and by distance; Aboriginal nursing. *Unit head:* Kathy Wilson, Assistant Dean of Graduate and Advanced RN Studies, 506-458-7640, Fax: 506-447-3057, E-mail: kewilson@unb.ca. *Application contact:* Francis Perry, Graduate Secretary, 506-451-6844, Fax: 506-447-3057, E-mail: fperry@unb.ca. Web site: http://www.unbf.ca/nursing/.

University of New Hampshire, Graduate School, School of Health and Human Services, Department of Nursing, Durham, NH 03824. Offers family practitioner (Postbaccalaureate Certificate); nursing (MS). *Accreditation:* AACN. Part-time programs available. *Faculty:* 12 full-time (11 women). *Students:* 51 full-time (46 women), 66 part-time (53 women); includes 5 minority (1 Black or African American, non-Hispanic/Latino; 1 American Indian or Alaska Native, non-Hispanic/Latino; 1 Asian, non-Hispanic/Latino; 2 Hispanic/Latino), 1 international. Average age 34. 59 applicants, 49% accepted, 16 enrolled. In 2011, 43 master's, 4 other advanced degrees awarded. *Degree requirements:* For master's, thesis or alternative. *Entrance requirements:* For master's, GRE General Test or MAT. Additional exam requirements/recommendations for international students: Required—TOEFL (minimum score 550 paper-based; 213 computer-based; 80 iBT). *Application deadline:* For fall admission, 4/1 priority date for domestic students, 4/1 for international students; for spring admission, 11/1 for domestic students. Applications are processed on a rolling basis. Application fee: $65. Electronic applications accepted. *Expenses:* Tuition, state resident: full-time $12,360; part-time $687 per credit hour. Tuition, nonresident: full-time $25,680; part-time $1058 per credit hour. *International tuition:* $29,550 full-time. *Required fees:* $1666; $833 per course. $416.50 per semester. Tuition and fees vary according to course load and degree level. *Financial support:* In 2011–12, 21 students received support, including 2 teaching assistantships; fellowships, research assistantships, Federal Work-Study, scholarships/grants, and tuition waivers (full and partial) also available. Financial award application deadline: 2/15. *Faculty research:* Adult health, nursing administration, family nurse practitioner. *Unit head:* Dr. Gene Harkless, Chairperson, 603-862-2285. *Application contact:* Jane Dufresne, Administrative Assistant, 603-862-2299, E-mail: nursing.department@unh.edu. Web site: http://www.unh.edu/nursing/.

University of New Mexico, Graduate School, College of Nursing, Albuquerque, NM 87131-0001. Offers MSN, PhD, MSN/MA. *Accreditation:* AACN; ACNM/ACME (one or more programs are accredited). Part-time programs available. Postbaccalaureate

distance learning degree programs offered (minimal on-campus study). *Faculty:* 50 full-time (44 women), 1 (woman) part-time/adjunct. *Students:* 55 full-time (51 women), 124 part-time (109 women); includes 59 minority (3 Black or African American, non-Hispanic/Latino; 7 American Indian or Alaska Native, non-Hispanic/Latino; 7 Asian, non-Hispanic/Latino; 41 Hispanic/Latino; 1 Two or more races, non-Hispanic/Latino). Average age 42. 33 applicants, 61% accepted, 19 enrolled. In 2011, 68 master's, 3 doctorates awarded. *Degree requirements:* For master's, comprehensive exam, thesis optional; for doctorate, comprehensive exam, thesis/dissertation. *Entrance requirements:* For master's, minimum GPA of 3.0, course work in statistics (recommended), interview (for some concentrations), BSN or RN with BA; for doctorate, interview, minimum GPA of 3.0, writing sample, MSN or BSN with MA. Additional exam requirements/recommendations for international students: Required—TOEFL. Application fee: $50. Electronic applications accepted. *Financial support:* In 2011–12, 55 students received support, including 10 fellowships (averaging $10,863 per year), 2 research assistantships with partial tuition reimbursements available (averaging $6,183 per year), 14 teaching assistantships with partial tuition reimbursements available (averaging $7,276 per year); institutionally sponsored loans, scholarships/grants, traineeships, and unspecified assistantships also available. Support available to part-time students. Financial award application deadline: 3/1; financial award applicants required to submit FAFSA. *Faculty research:* Women's and children's health, pregnancy prevention in teens, vulnerable populations, nursing education, chronic illness, symptom appraisal and management. *Unit head:* Dr. Nancy Ridenour, Dean, 505-272-6284, Fax: 505-272-4343, E-mail: nridenour@salud.unm.edu. *Application contact:* Karen Wells, Student Academic Advisor, 505-272-4223, Fax: 505-272-3970, E-mail: kwells@salud.unm.edu. Web site: http://nursing.unm.edu/.

University of North Alabama, College of Nursing and Allied Health, Florence, AL 35632-0001. Offers MSN. *Accreditation:* AACN. *Faculty:* 4 part-time/adjunct (all women). *Students:* 8 full-time (all women), 50 part-time (45 women); includes 11 minority (9 Black or African American, non-Hispanic/Latino; 1 American Indian or Alaska Native, non-Hispanic/Latino; 1 Two or more races, non-Hispanic/Latino). Average age 40. In 2011, 12 master's awarded. *Unit head:* Dr. Birdie Bailey, Dean, 256-765-4984, E-mail: bibailey@una.edu. *Application contact:* Kim Mauldin, Director of Admissions, 256-465-4608, Fax: 256-765-4960, E-mail: komauldin@una.edu. Web site: http://www.una.edu/nursing/.

The University of North Carolina at Chapel Hill, School of Nursing, Chapel Hill, NC 27599-7460. Offers nursing (MSN, PhD, PMC), including adult nurse practitioner (MSN, PMC), children's health advanced practice (MSN, PMC), family nurse practitioner (MSN, PMC), health care systems (MSN, PMC), psychiatric/mental health nursing (MSN, PMC), women's health nursing (MSN, PMC). *Accreditation:* AACN; NLN (one or more programs are accredited). Part-time programs available. *Degree requirements:* For master's, comprehensive exam, thesis; for doctorate, thesis/dissertation, 3 exams. *Entrance requirements:* For master's and doctorate, GRE General Test. *Faculty research:* Chronic illness, parenting, cardiovascular health in children, elderly, HIV-AIDS.

The University of North Carolina at Charlotte, Graduate School, College of Health and Human Services, School of Nursing, Charlotte, NC 28223-0001. Offers administration (Post-Master's Certificate); advanced clinical (MSN, Post-Master's Certificate); anesthesia (MSN, Post-Master's Certificate); community health (MSN); family nurse practitioner (MSN, Post-Master's Certificate); health administration (MSN); mental health (MSN); nurse educator (MSN, Post-Master's Certificate); systems population (MSN). *Accreditation:* AACN. *Faculty:* 20 full-time (19 women), 5 part-time/adjunct (all women). *Students:* 76 full-time (65 women), 160 part-time (149 women); includes 49 minority (32 Black or African American, non-Hispanic/Latino; 1 American Indian or Alaska Native, non-Hispanic/Latino; 8 Asian, non-Hispanic/Latino; 8 Hispanic/Latino), 1 international. Average age 35. 191 applicants, 42% accepted, 71 enrolled. In 2011, 76 master's, 10 other advanced degrees awarded. *Degree requirements:* For master's, thesis or alternative, practicum. *Entrance requirements:* For master's, GRE General Test, minimum GPA of 3.0 in undergraduate major. Additional exam requirements/recommendations for international students: Required—TOEFL (minimum score 570 paper-based; 220 computer-based; 83 iBT). *Application deadline:* For fall admission, 7/15 for domestic students, 5/1 for international students; for spring admission, 11/15 for domestic students, 10/1 for international students. Application fee: $65 ($75 for international students). *Expenses:* Tuition, state resident: full-time $3689. Tuition, nonresident: full-time $15,226. *Required fees:* $2198. Tuition and fees vary according to course load and program. *Financial support:* In 2011–12, 10 students received support, including 4 research assistantships (averaging $5,284 per year), 6 teaching assistantships (averaging $2,918 per year); career-related internships or fieldwork, institutionally sponsored loans, scholarships/grants, traineeships, unspecified assistantships, and administrative assistanship also available. Support available to part-time students. Financial award application deadline: 4/1; financial award applicants required to submit FAFSA. *Total annual research expenditures:* $955,795. *Unit head:* Dr. Lucille L. Travis, Director, 704-687-7959, Fax: 704-687-6017, E-mail: ltravis1@uncc.edu. *Application contact:* Kathy B. Giddings, Director of Graduate Admissions, 704-687-5503, Fax: 704-687-3279, E-mail: gradadm@uncc.edu. Web site: http://nursing.uncc.edu/.

The University of North Carolina at Greensboro, Graduate School, School of Nursing, Greensboro, NC 27412-5001. Offers adult clinical nurse specialist (MSN, PMC); adult/gerontological nurse practitioner (MSN, PMC); nurse anesthesia (MSN, PMC); nursing (PhD); nursing administration (MSN); nursing education (MSN); MSN/MBA. *Accreditation:* AACN; AANA/CANAEP; NLN. *Degree requirements:* For master's, thesis or alternative. *Entrance requirements:* For master's, GRE General Test or MAT, BSN, clinical experience, liability insurance, RN license; for PMC, liability insurance, MSN, RN license. Additional exam requirements/recommendations for international students: Required—TOEFL. Electronic applications accepted.

The University of North Carolina Wilmington, School of Nursing, Wilmington, NC 28403-3297. Offers family nurse practitioner (MSN); nurse educator (MSN). *Accreditation:* AACN; NLN. *Degree requirements:* For master's, comprehensive exam, thesis or project. *Entrance requirements:* For master's, GRE General Test, bachelor's degree in nursing. Additional exam requirements/recommendations for international students: Required—TOEFL (minimum score 550 paper-based; 217 computer-based; 79 iBT), IELTS (minimum score 6.5). Electronic applications accepted.

University of North Dakota, Graduate School, College of Nursing, Grand Forks, ND 58202. Offers advanced public health nursing (MS); family nurse practitioner (MS); gerontological nursing (MS); nurse anesthesia (MS); nursing (MS, PhD); nursing education (MS); psychiatric and mental health (MS). *Accreditation:* AACN; AANA/CANAEP (one or more programs are accredited). Part-time and evening/weekend programs available. Postbaccalaureate distance learning degree programs offered (minimal on-campus study). *Degree requirements:* For master's, thesis or alternative. *Entrance requirements:* For master's, minimum GPA of 3.0; for doctorate, GRE or MAT, minimum GPA of 3.0. Additional exam requirements/recommendations for international students: Required—TOEFL (minimum score 550 paper-based; 213 computer-based; 79 iBT), IELTS (minimum score 6.5). Electronic applications accepted. *Faculty research:* Adult health, anesthesia, rural health, health administration, family nurse practitioner.

University of Northern Colorado, Graduate School, College of Natural and Health Sciences, School of Nursing, Greeley, CO 80639. Offers clinical nurse specialist in chronic illness (MS); family nurse practitioner (MS); nursing education (MS, PhD). *Accreditation:* AACN. Postbaccalaureate distance learning degree programs offered. *Degree requirements:* For master's, comprehensive exam, thesis or alternative; for doctorate, comprehensive exam, thesis/dissertation. *Entrance requirements:* For master's and doctorate, GRE General Test, minimum GPA of 3.0 in last 60 hours, BS in nursing, 2 letters of recommendation. Electronic applications accepted.

University of North Florida, Brooks College of Health, School of Nursing, Jacksonville, FL 32224. Offers clinical nurse leader (MSN); clinical nurse specialist (MSN); family nurse practitioner (Certificate); nurse anesthetist (CRNA) (MSN); nursing practice (DNP); primary care nurse practitioner (MSN). *Accreditation:* AACN; AANA/CANAEP. Part-time programs available. *Faculty:* 28 full-time (21 women), 1 (woman) part-time/adjunct. *Students:* 97 full-time (69 women), 69 part-time (60 women); includes 41 minority (17 Black or African American, non-Hispanic/Latino; 1 American Indian or Alaska Native, non-Hispanic/Latino; 10 Asian, non-Hispanic/Latino; 11 Hispanic/Latino; 2 Two or more races, non-Hispanic/Latino). Average age 34. 215 applicants, 23% accepted, 31 enrolled. In 2011, 55 master's, 4 doctorates awarded. *Degree requirements:* For master's, thesis optional. *Entrance requirements:* For master's, GRE General Test, minimum GPA of 3.0 in last 60 hours of course work, BSN, clinical experience, resume; for doctorate, GRE (minimum score of 1000) or MAT (minimum score of 410), master's degree in nursing specialty from nationally-accredited program; national certification in one of the following APRN roles: CNE, CNM, CNS, CRNA, CNP; minimum graduate GPA of 3.3; three letters of reference which address academic ability and clinical skills; active license as registered nurse or advanced practice registered nurse. Additional exam requirements/recommendations for international students: Required—TOEFL (minimum score 500 paper-based; 173 computer-based; 61 iBT). *Application deadline:* For fall admission, 3/15 for domestic students, 4/1 for international students. Applications are processed on a rolling basis. Application fee: $30. Electronic applications accepted. *Expenses:* Tuition, state resident: full-time $8793; part-time $366.38 per credit hour. Tuition, nonresident: full-time $23,502; part-time $979.24 per credit hour. *Required fees:* $1384; $57.66 per credit hour. Tuition and fees vary according to course load and program. *Financial support:* In 2011–12, 59 students received support. Research assistantships available. Financial award application deadline: 4/1; financial award applicants required to submit FAFSA. *Faculty research:* Teen pregnancy, diabetes, ethical decision-making, family caregivers. *Total annual research expenditures:* $545,563. *Unit head:* Dr. John McDonough, Director, 904-620-2684, E-mail: jmcdonou@unf.edu. *Application contact:* Beth Dibble, 904-620-2684, Fax: 904-620-1832, E-mail: nursingadmissions@unf.edu. Web site: http://www.unf.edu/brooks/nursing.

University of Oklahoma Health Sciences Center, Graduate College, College of Nursing, Oklahoma City, OK 73190. Offers MS, MS/MBA. MS/MBA offered jointly with Oklahoma State University, University of Oklahoma. *Accreditation:* NLN. Part-time programs available. *Degree requirements:* For master's, comprehensive exam, thesis optional. *Entrance requirements:* For master's, 3 letters of recommendation, Oklahoma RN license, statistics course, research methods, computer course or completion of a computer literacy test. *Faculty research:* Parenting and Native Americans, elderly reminiscence, diabetes in Native Americans.

University of Ottawa, Faculty of Graduate and Postdoctoral Studies, Faculty of Health Sciences, School of Nursing, Ottawa, ON K1N 6N5, Canada. Offers nurse practitioner (Certificate); nursing (M Sc, PhD); nursing/primary health care (M Sc). Part-time and evening/weekend programs available. *Degree requirements:* For master's, thesis or alternative. *Entrance requirements:* For master's, honors degree or equivalent, minimum B average. Electronic applications accepted. *Faculty research:* Decision making in nursing, evaluating complete nursing interventions.

University of Pennsylvania, School of Nursing, Philadelphia, PA 19104. Offers MSN, PhD, Certificate, MBA/MSN, MBA/PhD, MSN/PhD. *Accreditation:* AACN; AANA/CANAEP. Part-time programs available. Postbaccalaureate distance learning degree programs offered. *Faculty:* 58 full-time (53 women), 41 part-time/adjunct (36 women). *Students:* 261 full-time (228 women), 242 part-time (228 women); includes 93 minority (31 Black or African American, non-Hispanic/Latino; 4 American Indian or Alaska Native, non-Hispanic/Latino; 32 Asian, non-Hispanic/Latino; 18 Hispanic/Latino; 8 Two or more races, non-Hispanic/Latino), 18 international. 676 applicants, 37% accepted, 227 enrolled. In 2011, 220 master's, 12 doctorates awarded. Terminal master's awarded for partial completion of doctoral program. *Degree requirements:* For doctorate, thesis/dissertation. *Entrance requirements:* For master's, GRE General Test, BSN, minimum GPA of 3.0; for doctorate, GRE General Test, BSN or MSN, minimum GPA of 3.0. Additional exam requirements/recommendations for international students: Required—TOEFL. *Application deadline:* For fall admission, 2/15 priority date for domestic students. Applications are processed on a rolling basis. Application fee: $70. *Expenses:* Contact institution. *Financial support:* In 2011–12, 71 students received support. Fellowships, research assistantships, teaching assistantships, institutionally sponsored loans, scholarships/grants, traineeships, health care benefits, and unspecified assistantships available. Financial award application deadline: 12/15. *Faculty research:* Nursing and patient outcomes research. *Unit head:* Assistant Dean of Admissions and Financial Aid, 866-867-6877, Fax: 215-573-8439, E-mail: admissions@nursing.upenn.edu. *Application contact:* Sylvia V. J. English, Enrollment Management Coordinator, 866-867-6877, Fax: 215-573-8439, E-mail: admissions@nursing.upenn.edu. Web site: http://www.nursing.upenn.edu/.

University of Phoenix–Atlanta Campus, College of Nursing, Sandy Springs, GA 30350-4153. Offers health administration (MHA); nursing (MSN); nursing/health care education (MSN); MSN/MBA; MSN/MHA. Evening/weekend programs available. Postbaccalaureate distance learning degree programs offered. *Degree requirements:* For master's, thesis (for some programs). *Entrance requirements:* For master's, minimum undergraduate GPA of 2.5, 3 years of work experience. Additional exam requirements/recommendations for international students: Required—TOEFL (minimum score 550 paper-based; 213 computer-based; 79 iBT). Electronic applications accepted.

University of Phoenix–Augusta Campus, College of Nursing, Augusta, GA 30909-4583. Offers health administration (MHA); nursing (MSN); nursing/health care education (MSN); MSN/MBA; MSN/MHA. Postbaccalaureate distance learning degree programs offered.

University of Phoenix–Austin Campus, College of Nursing, Austin, TX 78759. Offers health administration (MHA). Postbaccalaureate distance learning degree programs offered.

University of Phoenix–Bay Area Campus, College of Nursing, San Jose, CA 95134-1805. Offers education (MHA); gerontology (MHA); health administration (MHA, DHA); informatics (MHA, MSN); nursing (MSN, PhD); nursing/health care education (MSN); MSN/MBA. Evening/weekend programs available. Postbaccalaureate distance learning degree programs offered (no on-campus study). *Degree requirements:* For master's, thesis (for some programs). *Entrance requirements:* For master's, minimum undergraduate GPA of 2.5, 3 years of work experience, RN license. Additional exam

requirements/recommendations for international students: Required—TOEFL (minimum score 550 paper-based; 213 computer-based; 79 iBT). Electronic applications accepted.

University of Phoenix–Birmingham Campus, College of Health and Human Services, Birmingham, AL 35244. Offers education (MHA); gerontology (MHA); health administration (MHA); health care management (MBA); informatics (MHA); nursing (MSN); nursing/health care education (MSN); MSN/MBA; MSN/MHA.

University of Phoenix–Central Florida Campus, College of Nursing, Maitland, FL 32751-7057. Offers health administration (MHA); health and human services (MSN); nursing (MSN); nursing/health care education (MSN); MSN/MBA; MSN/MHA. Evening/weekend programs available. *Degree requirements:* For master's, thesis (for some programs). *Entrance requirements:* For master's, minimum undergraduate GPA of 2.5, 3 years work experience, RN license. Additional exam requirements/recommendations for international students: Required—TOEFL (minimum score 550 paper-based; 213 computer-based; 79 iBT). Electronic applications accepted.

University of Phoenix–Central Valley Campus, College of Nursing, Fresno, CA 93720-1562. Offers education (MHA); gerontology (MHA); health administration (MHA); nursing (MSN); MSN/MBA.

University of Phoenix–Charlotte Campus, College of Nursing, Charlotte, NC 28273-3409. Offers education (MHA); gerontology (MHA); health administration (MHA); informatics (MHA, MSN); nursing (MSN); nursing/health care education (MSN). Evening/weekend programs available. *Degree requirements:* For master's, thesis (for some programs). *Entrance requirements:* For master's, minimum undergraduate GPA of 2.5, 3 years work experience. Additional exam requirements/recommendations for international students: Required—TOEFL (minimum score 550 paper-based; 213 computer-based; 79 iBT). Electronic applications accepted.

University of Phoenix–Chattanooga Campus, College of Nursing, Chattanooga, TN 37421-3707. Offers education (MHA); gerontology (MHA); health administration (MHA).

University of Phoenix–Cheyenne Campus, College of Nursing, Cheyenne, WY 82009. Offers health administration (MHA); nursing (MSN); nursing/health care education (MSN); MSN/MBA; MSN/MHA. Postbaccalaureate distance learning degree programs offered.

University of Phoenix–Cleveland Campus, College of Nursing, Independence, OH 44131-2194. Offers MSN, PhD. Evening/weekend programs available. Postbaccalaureate distance learning degree programs offered. *Degree requirements:* For master's, thesis (for some programs). *Entrance requirements:* For master's, minimum undergraduate GPA of 2.5, 3 years of work experience. Additional exam requirements/recommendations for international students: Required—TOEFL (minimum score 550 paper-based; 213 computer-based; 79 iBT). Electronic applications accepted.

University of Phoenix–Columbus Georgia Campus, College of Nursing, Columbus, GA 31904-6321. Offers health administration (MHA); nursing (MSN). Postbaccalaureate distance learning degree programs offered. *Degree requirements:* For master's, thesis (for some programs). *Entrance requirements:* For master's, minimum undergraduate GPA of 2.5, 3 years of work experience. Additional exam requirements/ recommendations for international students: Required—TOEFL (minimum score 550 paper-based; 213 computer-based; 79 iBT). Electronic applications accepted.

University of Phoenix–Columbus Ohio Campus, College of Nursing, Columbus, OH 43240-4032. Offers MSN, PhD. Evening/weekend programs available. Postbaccalaureate distance learning degree programs offered. *Degree requirements:* For master's, thesis (for some programs). *Entrance requirements:* For master's, minimum undergraduate GPA of 2.5, 3 years work experience. Additional exam requirements/recommendations for international students: Required—TOEFL (minimum score 550 paper-based; 213 computer-based; 79 iBT). Electronic applications accepted.

University of Phoenix–Denver Campus, College of Nursing, Lone Tree, CO 80124-5453. Offers health administration (MHA); nursing (MSN); MSN/MBA; MSN/MHA. Evening/weekend programs available. Postbaccalaureate distance learning degree programs offered. *Degree requirements:* For master's, thesis (for some programs). *Entrance requirements:* For master's, minimum undergraduate GPA of 2.5, 3 years work experience, RN license. Additional exam requirements/recommendations for international students: Required—TOEFL (minimum score 550 paper-based; 213 computer-based; 79 iBT). Electronic applications accepted.

University of Phoenix–Des Moines Campus, College of Nursing, Des Moines, IA 50266. Offers education (MHA); gerontology (MHA); health administration (MHA, DHA); informatics (MHA, MSN); nursing (MSN, PhD); nursing/health care education (MSN).

University of Phoenix–Harrisburg Campus, College of Nursing, Harrisburg, PA 17112. Offers health administration (MHA); nursing (MSN); nursing/health care education (MSN); MSN/MBA; MSN/MHA. Postbaccalaureate distance learning degree programs offered.

University of Phoenix–Hawaii Campus, College of Nursing, Honolulu, HI 96813-4317. Offers education (MHA); family nurse practitioner (MSN); gerontology (MHA); health administration (MHA); nursing (MSN); nursing/health care education (MSN); MSN/MBA. Evening/weekend programs available. *Degree requirements:* For master's, thesis (for some programs). *Entrance requirements:* For master's, minimum undergraduate GPA of 2.5, 3 years of work experience, RN license. Additional exam requirements/recommendations for international students: Required—TOEFL (minimum score 550 paper-based; 213 computer-based; 79 iBT). Electronic applications accepted.

University of Phoenix–Houston Campus, College of Nursing, Houston, TX 77079-2004. Offers health administration (MHA). Postbaccalaureate distance learning degree programs offered. *Degree requirements:* For master's, thesis (for some programs). *Entrance requirements:* For master's, minimum undergraduate GPA of 2.5, 3 years of work experience. Additional exam requirements/recommendations for international students: Required—TOEFL (minimum score 550 paper-based; 213 computer-based; 79 iBT). Electronic applications accepted.

University of Phoenix–Idaho Campus, College of Nursing, Meridian, ID 83642-5114. Offers health administration (MHA); nursing (MSN); nursing/health care education (MSN); MSN/MBA. Evening/weekend programs available. Postbaccalaureate distance learning degree programs offered. *Degree requirements:* For master's, thesis (for some programs). *Entrance requirements:* For master's, minimum undergraduate GPA of 2.5, 3 years of work experience. Additional exam requirements/recommendations for international students: Required—TOEFL (minimum score 550 paper-based; 213 computer-based). Electronic applications accepted.

University of Phoenix–Indianapolis Campus, College of Nursing, Indianapolis, IN 46250-932. Offers health administration (MHA); nursing (MSN); nursing/health care education (MSN); MSN/MBA; MSN/MHA. Evening/weekend programs available. Postbaccalaureate distance learning degree programs offered. *Degree requirements:* For master's, thesis. *Entrance requirements:* For master's, 3 years work experience, minimum undergraduate GPA of 2.5. Additional exam requirements/recommendations for international students: Required—TOEFL (minimum score 500 paper-based; 213 computer-based). Electronic applications accepted.

University of Phoenix–Louisiana Campus, College of Nursing, Metairie, LA 70001-2082. Offers health administration (MHA); nursing (MSN); MSN/MBA. Evening/weekend

programs available. Postbaccalaureate distance learning degree programs offered (no on-campus study). *Degree requirements:* For master's, thesis (for some programs). *Entrance requirements:* For master's, minimum undergraduate GPA of 2.5, 3 years work experience, RN license. Additional exam requirements/recommendations for international students: Required—TOEFL (minimum score 550 paper-based; 213 computer-based; 79 iBT). Electronic applications accepted.

University of Phoenix–Memphis Campus, College of Nursing, Cordova, TN 38018. Offers health administration (MHA, DHA).

University of Phoenix–Metro Detroit Campus, College of Nursing, Southfield, MI 48076. Offers health care education (MSN); nursing (MSN). Evening/weekend programs available. *Degree requirements:* For master's, thesis (for some programs). *Entrance requirements:* For master's, minimum undergraduate GPA of 2.5, 3 years of work experience, RN license. Additional exam requirements/recommendations for international students: Required—TOEFL (minimum score 550 paper-based; 213 computer-based; 79 iBT). Electronic applications accepted.

University of Phoenix–Milwaukee Campus, College of Nursing, Milwaukee, WI 53045. Offers education (MHA); gerontology (MHA); health administration (MHA, DHA); informatics (MHA, MSN); nursing (MSN, PhD); nursing/health care education (MSN); MSN/MBA; MSN/MHA.

University of Phoenix–Nashville Campus, College of Nursing, Nashville, TN 37214-5048. Offers health administration (MHA). Evening/weekend programs available. *Degree requirements:* For master's, thesis (for some programs). *Entrance requirements:* For master's, minimum undergraduate GPA of 2.5, 3 years of work experience. Additional exam requirements/recommendations for international students: Required—TOEFL (minimum score 550 paper-based; 213 computer-based). Electronic applications accepted.

University of Phoenix–New Mexico Campus, College of Nursing, Albuquerque, NM 87113-1570. Offers health administration (MHA); health care education (MSN); nursing (MSN); MSN/MBA. Evening/weekend programs available. *Degree requirements:* For master's, thesis (for some programs). *Entrance requirements:* For master's, minimum undergraduate GPA of 2.5, 3 years of work experience, RN license. Additional exam requirements/recommendations for international students: Required—TOEFL (minimum score 550 paper-based; 213 computer-based; 79 iBT). Electronic applications accepted.

University of Phoenix–Northern Nevada Campus, College of Nursing, Reno, NV 89521-5862. Offers health administration (MHA); health care education (MSN); nursing (MSN); MSN/MBA; MSN/MHA.

University of Phoenix–Northern Virginia Campus, College of Nursing, Reston, VA 20190. Offers health administration (MHA); nursing (MSN).

University of Phoenix–North Florida Campus, College of Nursing, Jacksonville, FL 32216-0959. Offers health administration (MHA); health care education (MSN); nursing (MSN); MSN/MBA; MSN/MHA. Evening/weekend programs available. *Degree requirements:* For master's, thesis (for some programs). *Entrance requirements:* For master's, minimum undergraduate GPA of 2.5, 3 years work experience, RN license. Additional exam requirements/recommendations for international students: Required—TOEFL (minimum score 550 paper-based; 213 computer-based; 79 iBT). Electronic applications accepted.

University of Phoenix–Northwest Arkansas Campus, College of Nursing, Rogers, AR 72756-9615. Offers health administration (MHA); health care education (MSN); nursing (MSN); MSN/MBA.

University of Phoenix–Oklahoma City Campus, College of Nursing, Oklahoma City, OK 73116-8244. Offers MSN.

University of Phoenix–Omaha Campus, College of Nursing, Omaha, NE 68154-5240. Offers health administration (MHA).

University of Phoenix–Online Campus, College of Nursing, Phoenix, AZ 85034-7209. Offers informatics (MSN); international (MSN); nurse practitioner (MSN); nursing (MSN); nursing/health care education (MSN); MSN/Certificate; MSN/MBA; MSN/MHA. *Accreditation:* AACN. Evening/weekend programs available. Postbaccalaureate distance learning degree programs offered. *Students:* 5,257 full-time (4,805 women); includes 1,381 minority (803 Black or African American, non-Hispanic/Latino; 36 American Indian or Alaska Native, non-Hispanic/Latino; 271 Asian, non-Hispanic/Latino; 188 Hispanic/Latino; 51 Native Hawaiian or other Pacific Islander, non-Hispanic/Latino; 32 Two or more races, non-Hispanic/Latino), 244 international. Average age 43. *Entrance requirements:* Additional exam requirements/recommendations for international students: Required—TOEFL, TOEIC (Test of English as an International Communication), Berlitz Online English Proficiency Exam, Pearson Test of English, or IELTS. *Application deadline:* Applications are processed on a rolling basis. Application fee: $45. Electronic applications accepted. *Expenses:* Contact institution. *Financial support:* Scholarships/grants available. Financial award applicants required to submit FAFSA. *Application contact:* 866-766-0766. Web site: http://www.phoenix.edu/colleges_divisions/nursing.html.

University of Phoenix–Online Campus, School of Advanced Studies, Phoenix, AZ 85034-7209. Offers business administration (DBA); education (Ed S); educational leadership (Ed D), including curriculum and instruction, education technology, educational leadership; health administration (DHA); higher education administration (PhD); industrial/organizational psychology (PhD); nursing (PhD); organizational leadership (DM), including information systems and technology, organizational leadership. Evening/weekend programs available. Postbaccalaureate distance learning degree programs offered. *Students:* 7,581 full-time (5,042 women); includes 3,199 minority (2,505 Black or African American, non-Hispanic/Latino; 68 American Indian or Alaska Native, non-Hispanic/Latino; 158 Asian, non-Hispanic/Latino; 395 Hispanic/Latino; 46 Native Hawaiian or other Pacific Islander, non-Hispanic/Latino; 27 Two or more races, non-Hispanic/Latino), 397 international. Average age 44. *Degree requirements:* For doctorate, thesis/dissertation. *Entrance requirements:* Additional exam requirements/recommendations for international students: Required—TOEFL, TOEIC (Test of English as an International Communication), Berlitz Online English Proficiency Exam, Pearson Test of English, or IELTS. *Application deadline:* Applications are processed on a rolling basis. Application fee: $45. Electronic applications accepted. *Expenses:* Contact institution. *Financial support:* Scholarships/grants available. Financial award applicants required to submit FAFSA. *Unit head:* Dr. Jeremy Moreland, Executive Dean. *Application contact:* 866-766-0766. Web site: http://www.phoenix.edu/colleges_divisions/doctoral.html.

University of Phoenix–Oregon Campus, College of Nursing, Tigard, OR 97223. Offers health administration (MHA); nursing (MSN); MSN/MBA. Evening/weekend programs available. *Degree requirements:* For master's, thesis (for some programs). *Entrance requirements:* For master's, minimum undergraduate GPA of 2.5, 3 years of work experience, current RN license (nursing). Additional exam requirements/recommendations for international students: Required—TOEFL (minimum score 550 paper-based; 213 computer-based; 79 iBT). Electronic applications accepted.

University of Phoenix–Phoenix Main Campus, College of Nursing, Tempe, AZ 85282-2371. Offers family nurse practitioner (MSN, Certificate); informatics (MSN);

nursing (MSN); nursing/health care education (MSN); MSN/Certificate; MSN/MBA; MSN/MHA. Evening/weekend programs available. Postbaccalaureate distance learning degree programs offered. *Students:* 172 full-time (148 women); includes 25 minority (4 Black or African American, non-Hispanic/Latino; 8 Asian, non-Hispanic/Latino; 13 Hispanic/Latino), 10 international. Average age 40. *Entrance requirements:* Additional exam requirements/recommendations for international students: Required—TOEFL, TOEIC (Test of English as an International Communication), Berlitz Online English Proficiency Exam, Pearson Test of English, or IELTS. *Application deadline:* Applications are processed on a rolling basis. Application fee: $45. Electronic applications accepted. *Expenses:* Contact institution. *Financial support:* Scholarships/grants available. Financial award applicants required to submit FAFSA. *Application contact:* 866-766-0766. Web site: http://www.phoenix.edu/colleges_divisions/nursing.html.

University of Phoenix–Pittsburgh Campus, College of Nursing, Pittsburgh, PA 15276. Offers health administration (MHA); health care education (MSN); nursing (MSN); MSN/MBA; MSN/MHA. Evening/weekend programs available. *Degree requirements:* For master's, thesis (for some programs). *Entrance requirements:* For master's, minimum undergraduate GPA of 2.5, 3 years work experience, current RN license (nursing). Additional exam requirements/recommendations for international students: Required—TOEFL (minimum score 550 paper-based; 213 computer-based; 79 iBT). Electronic applications accepted.

University of Phoenix–Raleigh Campus, College of Nursing, Raleigh, NC 27606. Offers education (MHA); gerontology (MHA); health administration (MHA, DHA); informatics (MHA, MSN); nursing (MSN, PhD); nursing/health care education (MSN).

University of Phoenix–Richmond Campus, College of Nursing, Richmond, VA 23230. Offers health administration (MHA); health care education (MSN); nursing (MSN); MSN/MBA; MSN/MHA. Evening/weekend programs available. *Degree requirements:* For master's, thesis (for some programs). *Entrance requirements:* For master's, minimum undergraduate GPA of 2.5, 3 years work experience, current RN license for nursing programs. Additional exam requirements/recommendations for international students: Required—TOEFL (minimum score 500 paper-based; 213 computer-based; 79 iBT). Electronic applications accepted.

University of Phoenix–Sacramento Valley Campus, College of Nursing, Sacramento, CA 95833-3632. Offers family nurse practitioner (MSN); health administration (MHA); health care education (MSN); nursing (MSN); MSN/MBA. Evening/weekend programs available. *Degree requirements:* For master's, thesis (for some programs). *Entrance requirements:* For master's, RN license, minimum undergraduate GPA of 2.5, 3 years work experience. Additional exam requirements/recommendations for international students: Required—TOEFL (minimum score 550 paper-based; 213 computer-based; 79 iBT). Electronic applications accepted.

University of Phoenix–San Antonio Campus, College of Nursing, San Antonio, TX 78230. Offers health administration (MHA).

University of Phoenix–San Diego Campus, College of Nursing, San Diego, CA 92123. Offers health care education (MSN); nursing (MSN); MSN/MBA. Evening/weekend programs available. *Degree requirements:* For master's, thesis (for some programs). *Entrance requirements:* For master's, minimum undergraduate GPA of 2.5, 3 years work experience, RN license. Additional exam requirements/recommendations for international students: Required—TOEFL (minimum score 550 paper-based; 213 computer-based; 79 iBT). Electronic applications accepted.

University of Phoenix–Savannah Campus, College of Nursing, Savannah, GA 31405-7400. Offers health administration (MHA); nursing (MSN); nursing/health care education (MSN); MSN/MBA; MSN/MHA.

University of Phoenix–Southern California Campus, College of Nursing, Costa Mesa, CA 92626. Offers family nurse practitioner (MSN, Certificate); informatics (MSN); nursing (MSN); nursing/health care education (MSN); MSN/Certificate; MSN/MBA; MSN/MHA. Evening/weekend programs available. Postbaccalaureate distance learning degree programs offered. *Students:* 281 full-time (244 women); includes 129 minority (47 Black or African American, non-Hispanic/Latino; 1 American Indian or Alaska Native, non-Hispanic/Latino; 44 Asian, non-Hispanic/Latino; 26 Hispanic/Latino; 9 Native Hawaiian or other Pacific Islander, non-Hispanic/Latino; 2 Two or more races, non-Hispanic/Latino), 13 international. Average age 43. *Entrance requirements:* Additional exam requirements/recommendations for international students: Required—TOEFL, TOEIC (Test of English as an International Communication), Berlitz Online English Proficiency Exam, Pearson Test of English, or IELTS. *Application deadline:* Applications are processed on a rolling basis. Application fee: $45. Electronic applications accepted. *Expenses:* Contact institution. *Financial support:* Scholarships/grants available. Financial award applicants required to submit FAFSA. *Application contact:* 866-766-0766. Web site: http://www.phoenix.edu/colleges_divisions/nursing.html.

University of Phoenix–Southern Colorado Campus, College of Nursing, Colorado Springs, CO 80919-2335. Offers education (MHA); gerontology (MHA); health administration (MHA); nursing (MSN); MSN/MBA. Evening/weekend programs available. *Degree requirements:* For master's, thesis (for some programs). *Entrance requirements:* For master's, minimum undergraduate GPA of 2.5, 3 years of work experience, RN license. Additional exam requirements/recommendations for international students: Required—TOEFL (minimum score 550 paper-based; 213 computer-based; 79 iBT). Electronic applications accepted.

University of Phoenix–South Florida Campus, College of Nursing, Fort Lauderdale, FL 33309. Offers health administration (MHA); health care education (MSN); nursing (MSN); MSN/MBA; MSN/MHA. Evening/weekend programs available. *Degree requirements:* For master's, thesis (for some programs). *Entrance requirements:* For master's, minimum undergraduate GPA of 2.5, 3 years work experience, RN license. Additional exam requirements/recommendations for international students: Required—TOEFL (minimum score 550 paper-based; 213 computer-based; 79 iBT). Electronic applications accepted.

University of Phoenix–Springfield Campus, College of Nursing, Springfield, MO 65804-7211. Offers health administration (MHA); nursing (MSN); MSN/MBA; MSN/MHA.

University of Phoenix–Tulsa Campus, College of Nursing, Tulsa, OK 74134-1412. Offers MSN.

University of Phoenix–Utah Campus, College of Nursing, Salt Lake City, UT 84123-4617. Offers health care education (MSN); nursing (MSN); MSN/MBA. Evening/weekend programs available. *Degree requirements:* For master's, thesis (for some programs). *Entrance requirements:* For master's, minimum undergraduate GPA of 2.5, 3 years work experience, RN license. Additional exam requirements/recommendations for international students: Required—TOEFL (minimum score 550 paper-based; 213 computer-based; 79 iBT). Electronic applications accepted.

University of Phoenix–Vancouver Campus, The Artemis School, College of Health and Human Services, Burnaby, BC V5C 6G9, Canada. Offers health care management (MBA). Evening/weekend programs available. *Degree requirements:* For master's, thesis (for some programs). *Entrance requirements:* For master's, minimum undergraduate GPA of 2.5, 3 years work experience. Additional exam requirements/recommendations for international students: Required—TOEFL (minimum score 550 paper-based; 213 computer-based; 79 iBT). Electronic applications accepted.

University of Phoenix–Washington D.C. Campus, College of Nursing, Washington, DC 20001. Offers education (MHA); gerontology (MHA); health administration (MHA, DHA); informatics (MHA, MSN); nursing (MSN, PhD); nursing/health care education (MSN); MSN/MBA; MSN/MHA.

University of Phoenix–West Florida Campus, College of Nursing, Temple Terrace, FL 33637. Offers health administration (MHA); health care education (MSN); nursing (MSN); MSN/MBA; MSN/MHA. Evening/weekend programs available. Postbaccalaureate distance learning degree programs offered. *Degree requirements:* For master's, thesis (for some programs). *Entrance requirements:* For master's, minimum undergraduate GPA of 2.5, RN license, 3 years work experience. Additional exam requirements/recommendations for international students: Required—TOEFL (minimum score 550 paper-based; 213 computer-based; 79 iBT). Electronic applications accepted.

University of Pittsburgh, School of Nursing, Clinical Nurse Specialist Program, Pittsburgh, PA 15260. Offers medical/surgical clinical nurse specialist (MSN, DNP); psychiatric and mental health clinical nurse specialist (MSN, DNP). *Accreditation:* AACN. Part-time programs available. *Students:* 4 full-time (all women), 20 part-time (18 women); includes 2 minority (both Asian, non-Hispanic/Latino). Average age 43. 18 applicants, 67% accepted, 10 enrolled. In 2011, 5 master's, 2 doctorates awarded. *Degree requirements:* For master's, comprehensive exam, thesis optional. *Entrance requirements:* For master's, GRE or MAT, BSN, RN license, letters of recommendation, resume, course work in statistics, 1-3 years of nursing experience. Additional exam requirements/recommendations for international students: Required—TOEFL (minimum score 550 paper-based; 213 computer-based; 80 iBT). *Application deadline:* For fall admission, 6/1 priority date for domestic students, 6/1 for international students. Applications are processed on a rolling basis. Application fee: $50. Electronic applications accepted. *Expenses:* Tuition, state resident: full-time $18,774; part-time $760 per credit. Tuition, nonresident: full-time $30,736; part-time $1258 per credit. *Required fees:* $740; $200 per term. Tuition and fees vary according to program. *Financial support:* In 2011–12, 2 students received support, including 1 fellowship with full tuition reimbursement available (averaging $22,724 per year), 1 teaching assistantship with partial tuition reimbursement available (averaging $5,596 per year); scholarships/grants, traineeships, health care benefits, and unspecified assistantships also available. Support available to part-time students. *Unit head:* Dr. Sandra Engberg, Associate Dean for Clinical Education, 412-624-3835, Fax: 412-624-8521, E-mail: sje1@pitt.edu. *Application contact:* Laurie Lapsley, Administrator of Graduate Student Services, 412-624-9670, Fax: 412-624-2409, E-mail: lapsleyl@pitt.edu.

University of Pittsburgh, School of Nursing, Nurse Specialty Role Program, Pittsburgh, PA 15260. Offers clinical nurse leader (MSN); nursing administration (MSN, DNP); nursing informatics (MSN). *Accreditation:* AACN. Part-time programs available. *Students:* 5 full-time (3 women), 63 part-time (60 women); includes 5 minority (2 Black or African American, non-Hispanic/Latino; 3 Asian, non-Hispanic/Latino). Average age 43. 42 applicants, 71% accepted, 25 enrolled. In 2011, 9 master's, 5 doctorates awarded. *Degree requirements:* For master's, comprehensive exam, thesis optional. *Entrance requirements:* For master's, GRE or MAT, BSN, RN license, letters of recommendation, resume, course work in statistics, 1-3 years of nursing experience. Additional exam requirements/recommendations for international students: Required—TOEFL (minimum score 550 paper-based; 213 computer-based; 80 iBT). *Application deadline:* For fall admission, 6/1 priority date for domestic students, 6/1 for international students; for spring admission, 2/15 priority date for domestic students, 2/15 for international students. Applications are processed on a rolling basis. Application fee: $50. Electronic applications accepted. *Expenses:* Tuition, state resident: full-time $18,774; part-time $760 per credit. Tuition, nonresident: full-time $30,736; part-time $1258 per credit. *Required fees:* $740; $200 per term. Tuition and fees vary according to program. *Unit head:* Dr. Sandra Engberg, Associate Dean for Clinical Education, 412-624-3835, Fax: 412-624-8521, E-mail: sje1@pitt.edu. *Application contact:* Laurie Lapsley, Administrator of Graduate Student Services, 412-624-9670, Fax: 412-624-2409, E-mail: lapsleyl@pitt.edu. Web site: http://www.nursing.pitt.edu/.

University of Pittsburgh, School of Nursing, PhD Program in Nursing, Pittsburgh, PA 15261. Offers PhD. Part-time programs available. *Students:* 30 full-time (27 women), 8 part-time (all women); includes 8 minority (3 Black or African American, non-Hispanic/Latino; 5 Asian, non-Hispanic/Latino). Average age 35. 14 applicants, 64% accepted, 7 enrolled. In 2011, 4 doctorates awarded. *Degree requirements:* For doctorate, comprehensive exam, thesis/dissertation. *Entrance requirements:* For doctorate, GRE General Test. Additional exam requirements/recommendations for international students: Required—TOEFL (minimum score 550 paper-based; 213 computer-based; 79 iBT) or IELTS (minimum score 6.5). *Application deadline:* For fall admission, 6/1 priority date for domestic students, 5/1 for international students. Applications are processed on a rolling basis. Application fee: $50. Electronic applications accepted. *Expenses:* Tuition, state resident: full-time $18,774; part-time $760 per credit. Tuition, nonresident: full-time $30,736; part-time $1258 per credit. *Required fees:* $740; $200 per term. Tuition and fees vary according to program. *Financial support:* In 2011–12, 29 students received support, including 11 fellowships with full and partial tuition reimbursements available (averaging $21,718 per year), 15 research assistantships with full and partial tuition reimbursements available (averaging $12,331 per year), 3 teaching assistantships with full and partial tuition reimbursements available (averaging $11,936 per year); scholarships/grants, traineeships, health care benefits, and unspecified assistantships also available. Support available to part-time students. *Faculty research:* Behavioral management of chronic disorders, patient management in critical care, consumer informatics, genetic applications, technology. *Unit head:* Dr. Judith Erlen, Coordinator, 412-624-1905, Fax: 412-624-2401, E-mail: jae001@pitt.edu. *Application contact:* Laurie Lapsley, Administrator of Graduate Student Services, 412-624-9670, Fax: 412-624-2409, E-mail: lapsleyl@pitt.edu. Web site: http://www.nursing.pitt.edu/.

University of Portland, School of Nursing, Portland, OR 97203-5798. Offers clinical nurse leader (MS); nursing (DNP). *Accreditation:* AACN. Part-time and evening/weekend programs available. Postbaccalaureate distance learning degree programs offered (minimal on-campus study). *Faculty:* 16 full-time (15 women), 10 part-time/adjunct (8 women). *Students:* 54 full-time (45 women), 62 part-time (54 women); includes 13 minority (2 Black or African American, non-Hispanic/Latino; 1 American Indian or Alaska Native, non-Hispanic/Latino; 5 Asian, non-Hispanic/Latino; 2 Hispanic/Latino; 3 Two or more races, non-Hispanic/Latino), 2 international. Average age 33. In 2011, 11 master's, 4 doctorates awarded. *Entrance requirements:* For master's, GRE General Test or MAT, Oregon RN license, BSN, course work in statistics, resume, letters of recommendation, writing sample; for doctorate, GRE General Test or MAT, Oregon RN license, BSN or MSN, 2 letters of recommendation, resume, writing sample, official transcripts. Additional exam requirements/recommendations for international students: Required—TOEFL (minimum score 550 paper-based; 80 iBT), IELTS (minimum score 7). *Application deadline:* For fall admission, 11/2 priority date for domestic students, 11/2 for international students; for spring admission, 1/7 priority date for domestic students, 1/7 for international students. Applications are processed on a

rolling basis. Application fee: $50. *Expenses:* Contact institution. *Financial support:* Fellowships, research assistantships, Federal Work-Study, and scholarships/grants available. Support available to part-time students. Financial award application deadline: 3/1; financial award applicants required to submit FAFSA. *Unit head:* Dr. Joanne Warner, 503-943-7509, Fax: 503-943-7729, E-mail: warner@up.edu. *Application contact:* Dr. Katherine Crabtree, Associate Dean, 503-943-8142, E-mail: crabtrek@up.edu.

University of Puerto Rico, Medical Sciences Campus, School of Nursing, San Juan, PR 00936-5067. Offers adult and elderly nursing (MSN); child and adolescent nursing (MSN); critical care nursing (MSN); family and community nursing (MSN); family nurse practitioner (MSN); maternity nursing (MSN); mental health and psychiatric nursing (MSN). *Accreditation:* AACN; AANA/CANAEP. *Entrance requirements:* For master's, GRE or EXADEP, interview, Puerto Rico RN license or professional license for international students, general and specific point average, article analysis. Electronic applications accepted. *Faculty research:* HIV, health disparities, teen violence, women and violence, neurological disorders.

University of Rhode Island, Graduate School, College of Nursing, Kingston, RI 02881. Offers administration (MS); clinical nurse leader (MS); clinical specialist in gerontology (MS); clinical specialist in psychiatric/mental health (MS); family nurse practitioner (MS); gerontological nurse practitioner (MS); nursing (DNP, PhD); nursing education (MS). *Accreditation:* AACN; ACNM/ACME (one or more programs are accredited). Part-time programs available. *Faculty:* 29 full-time (28 women), 2 part-time/adjunct (1 woman). *Students:* 33 full-time (30 women), 81 part-time (77 women); includes 6 minority (1 Asian, non-Hispanic/Latino; 5 Hispanic/Latino). In 2011, 17 master's, 6 doctorates awarded. *Degree requirements:* For master's, comprehensive exam; for doctorate, comprehensive exam, thesis/dissertation. *Entrance requirements:* For master's, GRE or MAT, 2 letters of recommendation, scholarly papers; for doctorate, GRE, 3 letters of recommendation, scholarly papers. Additional exam requirements/recommendations for international students: Required—TOEFL (minimum score 550 paper-based; 213 computer-based). *Application deadline:* For fall admission, 4/15 for domestic students, 2/1 for international students; for spring admission, 11/15 for domestic students, 7/15 for international students. Application fee: $65. Electronic applications accepted. *Expenses:* Tuition, state resident: full-time $10,432; part-time $580 per credit hour. Tuition, nonresident: full-time $23,130; part-time $1285 per credit hour. *Required fees:* $1362; $36 per credit hour. $35 per semester. One-time fee: $130. *Financial support:* In 2011–12, 5 teaching assistantships with full and partial tuition reimbursements (averaging $12,596 per year) were awarded. Financial award application deadline: 4/15; financial award applicants required to submit FAFSA. *Faculty research:* Group intervention for grieving women in prison, translating Best Practice in non-drug interventions for postoperative pain management, further development and testing of the pain assessment inventory, preschool motor and functional performance of two cohorts, neuroactivation of brain motor areas in preterm children. *Unit head:* Dr. Dayle Joseph, Dean, 401-874-2766, Fax: 401-874-2061, E-mail: dayle@uri.edu. *Application contact:* Dr. Mary C. Sullivan, Director of Graduate Studies, 401-874-5339, Fax: 401-874-2061, E-mail: mcsullivan@uri.edu. Web site: http://www.uri.edu/nursing/.

University of Rochester, School of Nursing, Rochester, NY 14642. Offers acute care nurse practitioner (MS); adult nurse practitioner (MS); adult/geriatric nurse practitioner (MS); care of children and families/pediatric nurse practitioner (MS); care of children and families/pediatric nurse practitioner/neonatal nurse practitioner (MS); clinical nurse leader (MS); clinical research coordinator (MS); family nurse practitioner (MS); family psychiatric mental health nurse practitioner (MS); health care organization management and leadership (MS); health practice research (PhD); nursing (DNP). *Accreditation:* AACN; NLN (one or more programs are accredited). Part-time programs available. Postbaccalaureate distance learning degree programs offered (minimal on-campus study). *Faculty:* 49 full-time (42 women), 72 part-time/adjunct (60 women). *Students:* 38 full-time (32 women), 196 part-time (181 women); includes 37 minority (20 Black or African American, non-Hispanic/Latino; 9 Asian, non-Hispanic/Latino; 8 Hispanic/Latino), 5 international. Average age 36. 68 applicants, 56% accepted, 26 enrolled. In 2011, 49 master's, 7 doctorates awarded. Terminal master's awarded for partial completion of doctoral program. *Median time to degree:* Of those who began their doctoral program in fall 2003, 40% received their degree in 8 years or less. *Degree requirements:* For doctorate, thesis/dissertation. *Entrance requirements:* For master's, BS in nursing, minimum GPA of 3.0, course work in statistics; for doctorate, GRE General Test, MS in nursing, minimum GPA of 3.5. Additional exam requirements/recommendations for international students: Required—or IELTS (minimum score 6.5); Recommended—TOEFL (minimum score 560 paper-based; 230 computer-based; 88 iBT). *Application deadline:* For fall admission, 4/1 priority date for domestic students, 4/1 for international students; for spring admission, 9/1 for domestic and international students. Application fee: $50. Electronic applications accepted. *Expenses: Tuition:* Full-time $41,040. *Financial support:* In 2011–12, 49 students received support, including 1 fellowship with full and partial tuition reimbursement available (averaging $18,700 per year); scholarships/grants, traineeships, health care benefits, tuition waivers (partial), and unspecified assistantships also available. Support available to part-time students. Financial award application deadline: 6/30. *Faculty research:* Clinical research in aging, managing asthma in children, interventions to improve outcomes in critically ill children and their mothers, nurse home visitation studies, medical device evaluation, critical care clinical studies, high risk behavior and prevention, palliative care, pregnancy-related weight gain. *Total annual research expenditures:* $4.3 million. *Unit head:* Dr. Kathy H. Rideout, Interim Dean, 585-273-8902, Fax: 585-273-1268, E-mail: kathy_rideout@urmc.rochester.edu. *Application contact:* Elaine Andolina, Director of Admissions, 585-275-2375, Fax: 585-756-8299, E-mail: elaine_andolina@urmc.rochester.edu. Web site: http://www.son.rochester.edu.

University of St. Francis, College of Nursing, Joliet, IL 60435-6169. Offers adult health clinical nurse specialist (Post-Master's Certificate); adult nurse practitioner (MSN, Post-Master's Certificate); family nurse practitioner (Post-Master's Certificate); nursing administration (MSN); nursing practice (DNP). *Accreditation:* AACN. Part-time and evening/weekend programs available. Postbaccalaureate distance learning degree programs offered (no on-campus study). *Faculty:* 11 full-time (10 women), 16 part-time/adjunct (all women). *Students:* 59 full-time (52 women), 254 part-time (232 women); includes 80 minority (31 Black or African American, non-Hispanic/Latino; 11 Asian, non-Hispanic/Latino; 33 Hispanic/Latino; 5 Two or more races, non-Hispanic/Latino), 15 international. Average age 41. 340 applicants, 46% accepted, 117 enrolled. In 2011, 20 master's, 4 doctorates, 4 other advanced degrees awarded. *Entrance requirements:* Additional exam requirements/recommendations for international students: Required—TOEFL (minimum score 550 paper-based; 213 computer-based). *Application deadline:* Applications are processed on a rolling basis. Application fee: $30. Electronic applications accepted. *Expenses:* Contact institution. *Financial support:* In 2011–12, 87 students received support. Scholarships/grants, traineeships, and tuition waivers (partial) available. Support available to part-time students. Financial award applicants required to submit FAFSA. *Unit head:* Dr. Carol Wilson, Dean, 815-740-3840, Fax: 815-740-4243, E-mail: cwilson@stfrancis.edu. *Application contact:* Sandra Sloka, Director of Admissions for Graduate and Degree Completion Programs, 800-735-7500, Fax: 815-740-5032, E-mail: ssloka@stfrancis.edu. Web site: http://www.stfrancis.edu/academics/college-of-nursing-allied-health/graduate-programs/.

University of Saint Francis, Graduate School, Department of Allied Health, Fort Wayne, IN 46808-3994. Offers nursing (MSN); physician assistant studies (MS). *Accreditation:* ARC-PA. Part-time programs available. Postbaccalaureate distance learning degree programs offered (minimal on-campus study). *Students:* 99 full-time (86 women), 97 part-time (88 women); includes 15 minority (11 Black or African American, non-Hispanic/Latino; 2 Asian, non-Hispanic/Latino; 2 Hispanic/Latino). In 2011, 57 master's awarded. *Entrance requirements:* For master's, GRE or MCAT, previous courses in biology, chemistry, and psychology, previous direct patient care. Additional exam requirements/recommendations for international students: Required—TOEFL. *Application deadline:* Applications are processed on a rolling basis. Application fee: $20. Application fee is waived when completed online. *Financial support:* Career-related internships or fieldwork, scholarships/grants, tuition waivers (full and partial), and unspecified assistantships available. Support available to part-time students. Financial award applicants required to submit FAFSA. *Unit head:* Dr. Nancy Gillespie, Dean, 260-399-7700 Ext. 8504, Fax: 260-399-8167, E-mail: ngillespie@sf.edu. *Application contact:* James Cashdollar, Admissions Counselor, 260-399-7700 Ext. 6302, E-mail: jcashdollar@sf.edu.

University of Saint Francis, Graduate School, Department of Nursing, Fort Wayne, IN 46808-3994. Offers MSN. *Accreditation:* AACN. Part-time and evening/weekend programs available. Postbaccalaureate distance learning degree programs offered (no on-campus study). *Students:* 8 full-time (all women), 56 part-time (52 women); includes 1 minority (Asian, non-Hispanic/Latino). In 2011, 6 master's awarded. *Degree requirements:* For master's, research project. *Entrance requirements:* For master's, GRE, minimum GPA of 3.2, Indiana RN license. *Application deadline:* For fall admission, 7/1 priority date for domestic students; for spring admission, 11/1 priority date for domestic students. Applications are processed on a rolling basis. Application fee: $20. Application fee is waived when completed online. *Financial support:* Federal Work-Study, scholarships/grants, tuition waivers (full and partial), and unspecified assistantships available. Financial award applicants required to submit FAFSA. *Unit head:* Dr. Nancy Gillespie, Dean, 260-399-7700 Ext. 8504, Fax: 260-399-8167, E-mail: ngillespie@sf.edu. *Application contact:* James Cashdollar, Admissions Counselor, 260-399-7700 Ext. 6302, Fax: 260-399-8152, E-mail: jcashdollar@sf.edu.

University of Saint Joseph, Department of Nursing, West Hartford, CT 06117-2700. Offers MS. *Accreditation:* AACN. Part-time and evening/weekend programs available. *Students:* 8 full-time (6 women), 96 part-time (93 women); includes 20 minority (12 Black or African American, non-Hispanic/Latino; 4 Asian, non-Hispanic/Latino; 4 Hispanic/Latino), 3 international. Average age 39. *Degree requirements:* For master's, thesis. *Entrance requirements:* For master's, 2 letters of recommendation. *Application deadline:* Applications are processed on a rolling basis. Application fee: $50. Electronic applications accepted. Application fee is waived when completed online. *Expenses: Tuition:* Part-time $670 per credit. *Required fees:* $40 per credit. Tuition and fees vary according to course load, degree level, campus/location and program. *Financial support:* Career-related internships or fieldwork and unspecified assistantships available. Support available to part-time students. Financial award applicants required to submit FAFSA. *Application contact:* Graduate Admissions Office, 860-231-5261, E-mail: graduate@usj.edu.

University of San Diego, Hahn School of Nursing and Health Science, San Diego, CA 92110-2492. Offers adult-gerontology clinical nurse specialist (MSN); adult-gerontology nurse practitioner/family nurse practitioner (MSN); clinical nursing (MSN); entry-level nursing (for non-RNs) (MSN); executive nurse leader (MSN); family nurse practitioner (MSN); family/lifespan psychiatric-mental health nurse practitioner (MSN); healthcare informatics (MS, MSN); nursing (PhD); nursing practice (DNP); pediatric nurse practitioner/family nurse practitioner (MSN). *Accreditation:* AACN. Part-time and evening/weekend programs available. *Faculty:* 23 full-time (21 women), 37 part-time/adjunct (34 women). *Students:* 157 full-time (131 women), 182 part-time (162 women); includes 121 minority (21 Black or African American, non-Hispanic/Latino; 6 American Indian or Alaska Native, non-Hispanic/Latino; 51 Asian, non-Hispanic/Latino; 36 Hispanic/Latino; 2 Native Hawaiian or other Pacific Islander, non-Hispanic/Latino; 5 Two or more races, non-Hispanic/Latino), 7 international. Average age 36. 506 applicants, 47% accepted, 150 enrolled. In 2011, 87 master's, 26 doctorates awarded. *Degree requirements:* For doctorate, thesis/dissertation (for some programs), residency (DNP). *Entrance requirements:* For master's, GRE General Test (entry-level nursing), BSN, current California RN licensure (except for entry-level nursing); minimum GPA of 3.0; for doctorate, minimum GPA of 3.5, MSN, current California RN licensure. Additional exam requirements/recommendations for international students: Required—TOEFL (minimum score 580 paper-based; 237 computer-based; 83 iBT), TWE. *Application deadline:* For fall admission, 3/1 priority date for domestic students, 3/1 for international students; for spring admission, 11/1 priority date for domestic students, 11/1 for international students. Applications are processed on a rolling basis. Application fee: $45. Electronic applications accepted. *Expenses: Tuition:* Full-time $22,482; part-time $1249 per unit. *Required fees:* $224. Full-time tuition and fees vary according to course load and degree level. *Financial support:* In 2011–12, 232 students received support. Scholarships/grants and traineeships available. Support available to part-time students. Financial award application deadline: 4/1; financial award applicants required to submit FAFSA. *Faculty research:* Palliative and end of life care, maternal/child health, childhood obesity, health care disparities, cognitive functioning. *Unit head:* Dr. Sally Hardin, Dean, 619-260-4550, Fax: 619-260-6814. *Application contact:* Monica Mahon, Associate Director of Graduate Admissions, 619-260-4524, Fax: 619-260-4158, E-mail: grads@sandiego.edu. Web site: http://www.sandiego.edu/academics/nursing/.

University of San Francisco, School of Nursing and Health Professions, San Francisco, CA 94117-1080. Offers clinical nurse leader (MSN); healthcare systems leadership (MSN); nursing practice (DNP), including family nurse practitioner, healthcare systems leadership; public health (MPH); MSN/MBA; MSN/MPA; MSN/MSIS. *Accreditation:* AACN. Part-time programs available. *Faculty:* 5 full-time (all women), 38 part-time/adjunct (36 women). *Students:* 321 full-time (272 women), 55 part-time (52 women); includes 163 minority (18 Black or African American, non-Hispanic/Latino; 2 American Indian or Alaska Native, non-Hispanic/Latino; 76 Asian, non-Hispanic/Latino; 46 Hispanic/Latino; 1 Native Hawaiian or other Pacific Islander, non-Hispanic/Latino; 20 Two or more races, non-Hispanic/Latino), 3 international. Average age 38. 538 applicants, 30% accepted, 110 enrolled. In 2011, 121 master's, 7 doctorates awarded. *Entrance requirements:* For master's, minimum GPA of 3.0. *Application deadline:* Applications are processed on a rolling basis. *Expenses: Tuition:* Full-time $20,070; part-time $1115 per unit. Tuition and fees vary according to course load, campus/location and program. *Financial support:* In 2011–12, 63 students received support. Institutionally sponsored loans available. Financial award application deadline: 3/2. *Faculty research:* Direct patient/client care, providers of health care. *Unit head:* Dr. Judith Karshmer, Dean, 415-422-6681, Fax: 415-422-6877, E-mail: nursing@usfca.edu. *Application contact:* Information Contact, 415-422-4723, Fax: 415-422-2217. Web site: http://www.usfca.edu/nursing/.

University of Saskatchewan, College of Graduate Studies and Research, College of Nursing, Saskatoon, SK S7N 5E5, Canada. Offers MN. Part-time programs available. *Entrance requirements:* Additional exam requirements/recommendations for international students: Required—TOEFL.

Nursing—General

The University of Scranton, College of Graduate and Continuing Education, Department of Nursing, Scranton, PA 18510. Offers adult health nursing (MSN); family nurse practitioner (MSN, PMC); nurse anesthesia (MSN, PMC). Applicants accepted in odd-numbered years only. *Accreditation:* AACN; AANA/CANAEP. Part-time and evening/weekend programs available. *Faculty:* 13 full-time (all women), 2 part-time/adjunct (both women). *Students:* 50 full-time (45 women), 27 part-time (20 women); includes 7 minority (4 Black or African American, non-Hispanic/Latino; 1 Asian, non-Hispanic/Latino; 2 Hispanic/Latino). Average age 35. 100 applicants, 32% accepted. In 2011, 26 master's awarded. *Degree requirements:* For master's, thesis (for some programs), capstone experience. *Entrance requirements:* For master's, BSN, minimum GPA of 3.0, Pennsylvania RN license. Additional exam requirements/recommendations for international students: Required—TOEFL (minimum score 500 paper-based; 173 computer-based), IELTS (minimum score 5.5). *Application deadline:* For fall admission, 9/1 for domestic students. Applications are processed on a rolling basis. Application fee: $0. *Financial support:* In 2011–12, 7 students received support, including 7 teaching assistantships with full and partial tuition reimbursements available (averaging $6,914 per year); career-related internships or fieldwork, Federal Work-Study, and unspecified assistantships also available. Support available to part-time students. Financial award application deadline: 3/1. *Faculty research:* Home care, doctoral education, health care of women and children, pain, health promotion and adolescence. *Unit head:* Dr. Patricia Harrington, Chair, 570-941-7673, Fax: 570-941-4201, E-mail: harringtonp1@uofs.edu. *Application contact:* Dr. Mary Jane Hanson, Director, 570-941-4060, Fax: 570-941-4201, E-mail: hansonm2@scranton.edu. Web site: http://academic.uofs.edu/department/nursing/.

University of South Alabama, Graduate School, College of Nursing, Mobile, AL 36688. Offers adult health nursing (MSN); community/mental health nursing (MSN); maternal/child nursing (MSN); nursing (DNP). *Accreditation:* AACN. *Faculty:* 21 full-time (20 women). *Students:* 1,335 full-time (1,200 women), 172 part-time (147 women); includes 280 minority (164 Black or African American, non-Hispanic/Latino; 15 American Indian or Alaska Native, non-Hispanic/Latino; 41 Asian, non-Hispanic/Latino; 45 Hispanic/Latino; 2 Native Hawaiian or other Pacific Islander, non-Hispanic/Latino; 13 Two or more races, non-Hispanic/Latino), 10 international. 1,327 applicants, 38% accepted, 388 enrolled. In 2011, 266 master's, 21 doctorates awarded. *Degree requirements:* For master's, thesis optional. *Entrance requirements:* For master's, BSN, RN licensure, minimum GPA of 3.0, resume documenting clinical experience, background check, drug screening; for doctorate, GRE. *Application deadline:* For fall admission, 7/15 for domestic students; for spring admission, 12/1 for domestic students. Application fee: $35. *Expenses:* Tuition, state resident: full-time $7968; part-time $332 per credit hour. Tuition, nonresident: full-time $15,936; part-time $664 per credit hour. *Unit head:* Dr. Rosemary Rhodes, Director of Graduate Education, 251-445-9409, Fax: 251-445-9416. *Application contact:* Dr. B. Keith Harrison, Dean of the Graduate School, 251-460-6310, Fax: 251-461-1513, E-mail: kharriso@usouthal.edu. Web site: http://www.southalabama.edu/nursing.

University of South Carolina, The Graduate School, College of Nursing, Program in Advanced Practice Clinical Nursing, Columbia, SC 29208. Offers acute care nurse practitioner (Certificate); advanced practice clinical nursing (MSN). *Accreditation:* AACN. Part-time programs available. Postbaccalaureate distance learning degree programs offered (minimal on-campus study). *Entrance requirements:* For master's, master's degree in nursing, RN license; for Certificate, MSN. Additional exam requirements/recommendations for international students: Required—TOEFL (minimum score 570 paper-based; 213 computer-based). Electronic applications accepted. *Faculty research:* Systems research, evidence based practice, breast cancer, violence.

University of South Carolina, The Graduate School, College of Nursing, Program in Advanced Practice Nursing in Primary Care, Columbia, SC 29208. Offers MSN, Certificate. *Accreditation:* AACN. *Entrance requirements:* For master's, master's degree in nursing, RN license; for Certificate, MSN. Additional exam requirements/recommendations for international students: Required—TOEFL (minimum score 570 paper-based; 230 computer-based). Electronic applications accepted. *Faculty research:* Systems research, evidence based practice, breast cancer, violence.

University of Southern Indiana, Graduate Studies, College of Nursing and Health Professions, Program in Nursing, Evansville, IN 47712-3590. Offers MSN, DNP. Part-time programs available. Postbaccalaureate distance learning degree programs offered (minimal on-campus study). *Faculty:* 9 full-time (7 women), 2 part-time/adjunct (both women). *Students:* 24 full-time (22 women), 406 part-time (380 women); includes 27 minority (16 Black or African American, non-Hispanic/Latino; 6 Asian, non-Hispanic/Latino; 4 Hispanic/Latino; 1 Native Hawaiian or other Pacific Islander, non-Hispanic/Latino), 6 international. Average age 38. 261 applicants, 59% accepted, 103 enrolled. In 2011, 86 master's, 15 doctorates awarded. *Entrance requirements:* For master's, minimum GPA of 3.0, licensure or eligibility for licensure in Indiana, 1 year or 2000 hours of clinical practice, bachelor's degree in nursing from accredited school. Additional exam requirements/recommendations for international students: Required—TOEFL (minimum score 550 paper-based; 213 computer-based; 79 iBT), IELTS (minimum score 6). *Application deadline:* For fall admission, 2/1 for domestic students, 1/1 for international students. Applications are processed on a rolling basis. Application fee: $35. Electronic applications accepted. *Expenses:* Tuition, state resident: full-time $5044; part-time $280.21 per credit hour. Tuition, nonresident: full-time $9949; part-time $552.71 per credit hour. *Required fees:* $240; $22.75 per term. Tuition and fees vary according to course load and reciprocity agreements. *Financial support:* In 2011–12, 7 students received support. Federal Work-Study, scholarships/grants, tuition waivers (full and partial), and unspecified assistantships available. Financial award application deadline: 3/1; financial award applicants required to submit FAFSA. *Unit head:* Dr. Mayola Rowser, Director, 812-465-1154, E-mail: mrowser@usi.edu. *Application contact:* Dr. Wes Durham, Interim Director, Graduate Studies, 812-465-7015, Fax: 812-464-1956, E-mail: wdurham@usi.edu. Web site: http://health.usi.edu/acadprog/nursing/default.asp.

University of Southern Maine, School of Nursing, Portland, ME 04104-9300. Offers adult health nursing (PMC); adult psychiatric/mental health nurse practitioner (MS); clinical nurse leader (MS); clinical nurse specialist psychiatric-mental health nursing (MS); education (MS); family nursing (PMC); family psychiatric/mental health nurse practitioner (MS); management (MS); medical/surgical nursing (MS); nurse practitioner adult health nursing (MS); nurse practitioner family nursing (MS); nursing (DNP); psychiatric-mental health nursing (PMC); MBA/MSN. *Accreditation:* AACN. Part-time programs available. *Degree requirements:* For master's, thesis optional. *Entrance requirements:* For master's, GRE General Test or MAT, minimum GPA of 3.0; for doctorate, GRE. Additional exam requirements/recommendations for international students: Required—TOEFL (minimum score 550 paper-based; 213 computer-based). Electronic applications accepted. *Faculty research:* Women's health, nursing history, weight control, community services, substance abuse.

University of Southern Mississippi, Graduate School, College of Health, School of Nursing, Hattiesburg, MS 39406-0001. Offers family nurse practitioner (MSN); nursing (DNP, PhD); nursing executive (MSN); psychiatric nurse practitioner (MSN). *Accreditation:* AACN. Part-time and evening/weekend programs available. *Faculty:* 17 full-time (16 women), 1 part-time/adjunct (0 women). *Students:* 115 full-time (98 women), 43 part-time (38 women); includes 42 minority (35 Black or African American, non-Hispanic/Latino; 1 American Indian or Alaska Native, non-Hispanic/Latino; 3 Asian, non-Hispanic/Latino; 3 Two or more races, non-Hispanic/Latino). Average age 40. 128 applicants, 52% accepted, 58 enrolled. In 2011, 42 master's, 2 doctorates awarded. *Degree requirements:* For master's, comprehensive exam, thesis optional; for doctorate, comprehensive exam, thesis/dissertation. *Entrance requirements:* For master's, GRE General Test, minimum GPA of 2.75 during last 60 hours, nursing license, BS in nursing; for doctorate, GRE General Test, master's degree in nursing, minimum GPA of 3.5. Additional exam requirements/recommendations for international students: Required—TOEFL, IELTS. *Application deadline:* For fall admission, 3/15 priority date for domestic students, 5/1 for international students; for spring admission, 1/10 priority date for domestic students, 1/10 for international students. Applications are processed on a rolling basis. Application fee: $50. Electronic applications accepted. *Financial support:* In 2011–12, 14 research assistantships with full tuition reimbursements (averaging $12,577 per year), teaching assistantships (averaging $12,000 per year) were awarded; Federal Work-Study, institutionally sponsored loans, scholarships/grants, traineeships, health care benefits, and unspecified assistantships also available. Financial award application deadline: 3/15; financial award applicants required to submit FAFSA. *Faculty research:* Gerontology, caregivers, HIV, bereavement, pain, nursing leadership. *Unit head:* Dr. Katherine Nugent, Director and Associate Dean, 601-266-5500, Fax: 601-266-5927. *Application contact:* Dr. Sandra Bishop, Graduate Coordinator, 601-266-5500, Fax: 601-266-5927. Web site: http://www.usm.edu/graduateschool/table.php.

University of South Florida, Graduate School, College of Nursing, Tampa, FL 33620-9951. Offers MS, DNP, PhD. *Accreditation:* AACN; AANA/CANAEP; NLN (one or more programs are accredited). Part-time programs available. *Faculty:* 46 full-time (39 women), 6 part-time/adjunct (4 women). *Students:* 97 full-time (83 women), 526 part-time (468 women); includes 163 minority (63 Black or African American, non-Hispanic/Latino; 3 American Indian or Alaska Native, non-Hispanic/Latino; 25 Asian, non-Hispanic/Latino; 69 Hispanic/Latino; 1 Native Hawaiian or other Pacific Islander, non-Hispanic/Latino; 2 Two or more races, non-Hispanic/Latino), 10 international. Average age 37. 377 applicants, 28% accepted, 93 enrolled. In 2011, 224 master's, 16 doctorates awarded. *Degree requirements:* For master's, comprehensive exam, thesis optional; for doctorate, comprehensive exam, thesis/dissertation. *Entrance requirements:* For master's and doctorate, GRE General Test. Additional exam requirements/recommendations for international students: Required—TOEFL (minimum score 550 paper-based; 213 computer-based). *Application deadline:* For fall admission, 2/15 for domestic students, 1/2 for international students; for spring admission, 10/15 for domestic students, 6/1 for international students. Application fee: $30. Electronic applications accepted. *Financial support:* In 2011–12, 36 students received support, including 7 research assistantships with tuition reimbursements available (averaging $18,935 per year), 29 teaching assistantships with tuition reimbursements available (averaging $30,814 per year); tuition waivers (partial) and unspecified assistantships also available. Financial award application deadline: 2/1; financial award applicants required to submit FAFSA. *Faculty research:* Women's health, palliative and end-of-life care, cardiac rehabilitation, complementary therapies for chronic illness and cancer. *Total annual research expenditures:* $4 million. *Unit head:* Dr. Rita D'Aoust, Associate Dean, 813-974-3195, Fax: 813-974-5762, E-mail: rdaoust@health.usf.edu. *Application contact:* Dr. Connie Visovsky, Associate Dean of Student Affairs, 813-396-9641, Fax: 813-974-3118, E-mail: cvisovsk@health.usf.edu. Web site: http://www.hsc.usf.edu/nocms/nursing/index.html.

The University of Tampa, Nursing Programs, Tampa, FL 33606-1490. Offers adult nurse practitioner (MSN); family nurse practitioner (MSN). *Accreditation:* NLN. Part-time programs available. *Faculty:* 12 full-time (all women), 7 part-time/adjunct (all women). *Students:* 3 full-time (all women), 134 part-time (125 women); includes 28 minority (13 Black or African American, non-Hispanic/Latino; 1 Asian, non-Hispanic/Latino; 13 Hispanic/Latino; 1 Two or more races, non-Hispanic/Latino), 1 international. Average age 34. 148 applicants, 59% accepted, 52 enrolled. In 2011, 14 master's awarded. *Degree requirements:* For master's, comprehensive exam, oral exam, practicum. *Entrance requirements:* For master's, GRE (minimum score of 1000, 4.0 on Analytical Writing portion), bachelor's degree in nursing, current Florida RN license, minimum GPA of 3.0. Additional exam requirements/recommendations for international students: Required—TOEFL or IELTS. *Application deadline:* Applications are processed on a rolling basis. Application fee: $40. Electronic applications accepted. *Expenses:* Tuition: Full-time $8320; part-time $520 per credit hour. *Required fees:* $40 per semester. Tuition and fees vary according to program. *Financial support:* In 2011–12, 18 students received support. Unspecified assistantships available. Financial award applicants required to submit FAFSA. *Faculty research:* Vaccinations and public health, osteoporosis, cultural diversity, ethics, nursing practice. *Unit head:* Dr. Maria Warda, Director/Chair, 813-257-3302, Fax: 813-258-7214, E-mail: mwarda@ut.edu. *Application contact:* Brent Benner, Director of Admissions, 813-257-3642, E-mail: ctobie@ut.edu.

The University of Tennessee, Graduate School, College of Nursing, Knoxville, TN 37996. Offers MSN, PhD. *Accreditation:* AACN; AANA/CANAEP. Part-time programs available. *Degree requirements:* For master's, thesis or alternative; for doctorate, thesis/dissertation. *Entrance requirements:* For master's and doctorate, GRE General Test, minimum GPA of 2.7. Additional exam requirements/recommendations for international students: Required—TOEFL. Electronic applications accepted. *Expenses:* Tuition, state resident: full-time $8332; part-time $464 per credit hour. Tuition, nonresident: full-time $25,174; part-time $1400 per credit hour. *Required fees:* $1162; $56 per credit hour. Tuition and fees vary according to program.

The University of Tennessee at Chattanooga, Graduate School, College of Health, Education and Professional Studies, School of Nursing, Chattanooga, TN 37403. Offers administration (MSN); certified nurse anesthetist (Post-Master's Certificate); education (MSN); family nurse practitioner (MSN, Post-Master's Certificate); health care informatics (Post-Master's Certificate); nurse anesthesia (MSN); nurse education (Post-Master's Certificate); nursing (DNP). *Accreditation:* AACN; AANA/CANAEP (one or more programs are accredited). *Faculty:* 15 full-time (13 women), 4 part-time/adjunct (all women). *Students:* 68 full-time (45 women), 37 part-time (33 women); includes 8 minority (6 Black or African American, non-Hispanic/Latino; 2 Hispanic/Latino). Average age 33. 5 applicants, 100% accepted, 3 enrolled. In 2011, 52 degrees awarded. *Degree requirements:* For master's, thesis optional, qualifying exams, professional project; for Post-Master's Certificate, thesis or alternative, practicum, seminar. *Entrance requirements:* For master's, GRE General Test, MAT, BSN, minimum GPA of 3.0, eligibility for Tennessee RN license, 1 year direct patient care experience; for Post-Master's Certificate, GRE General Test, MAT, MSN, minimum GPA of 3.0, eligibility for Tennessee RN license, one year of direct patient care experience. Additional exam requirements/recommendations for international students: Required—TOEFL (minimum score 550 paper-based; 213 computer-based; 79 iBT), IELTS (minimum score 6). *Application deadline:* For fall admission, 8/1 priority date for domestic students, 6/1 for international students; for spring admission, 12/1 priority date for domestic students, 10/1 for international students. Applications are processed on a rolling basis. Application fee: $35. Electronic applications accepted. *Expenses:* Tuition, state resident: full-time $6472; part-time $359 per credit hour. Tuition, nonresident: full-time $20,006; part-time $1111 per credit hour. *Required fees:* $1320; $160 per credit hour. *Financial support:* Career-related internships or fieldwork and scholarships/grants available. Support

available to part-time students. *Faculty research:* Diabetes in women, health care for elderly, alternative medicine, hypertension, nurse anesthesia. *Total annual research expenditures:* $1.9 million. *Unit head:* Dr. Kay R. Lindgren, Head, 423-425-4646, Fax: 423-425-4668, E-mail: kay-lindgren@utc.edu. *Application contact:* Dr. Jerald Ainsworth, Dean of Graduate Studies, 423-425-4478, Fax: 423-425-5223, E-mail: jerald-ainsworth@utc.edu. Web site: http://www.utc.edu/Academic/Nursing/.

The University of Tennessee Health Science Center, College of Nursing, Memphis, TN 38163-0002. Offers MSN, DNP, PhD. *Accreditation:* AACN; AANA/CANAEP. Postbaccalaureate distance learning degree programs offered (minimal on-campus study). *Degree requirements:* For master's, thesis; for doctorate, thesis/dissertation. *Entrance requirements:* For master's, GRE General Test, BSN, minimum GPA of 3.0; for doctorate, minimum GPA of 3.0. Additional exam requirements/recommendations for international students: Required—TOEFL. Electronic applications accepted. *Expenses:* Contact institution.

The University of Texas at Arlington, Graduate School, College of Nursing, Arlington, TX 76019. Offers nurse practitioner (MSN); nursing administration (MSN); nursing education (MSN); nursing practice (DNP); nursing science (PhD). *Accreditation:* AACN. Part-time and evening/weekend programs available. Postbaccalaureate distance learning degree programs offered (no on-campus study). *Faculty:* 15 full-time (all women), 2 part-time/adjunct (both women). *Students:* 58 full-time (48 women), 720 part-time (654 women); includes 281 minority (133 Black or African American, non-Hispanic/Latino; 3 American Indian or Alaska Native, non-Hispanic/Latino; 73 Asian, non-Hispanic/Latino; 53 Hispanic/Latino; 4 Native Hawaiian or other Pacific Islander, non-Hispanic/Latino; 15 Two or more races, non-Hispanic/Latino), 22 international. Average age 37. 686 applicants, 48% accepted, 265 enrolled. In 2011, 117 master's, 4 doctorates awarded. *Degree requirements:* For master's, practicum course; for doctorate, comprehensive exam (for some programs), thesis/dissertation (for some programs), proposal defense dissertation (for PhD); scholarship project (for DNP). *Entrance requirements:* For master's, GRE General Test if GPA less than 3.0, minimum GPA of 3.0, Texas nursing license, minimum C grade in undergraduate statistics course; for doctorate, GRE General Test (waived for MSN-to-PhD applicants), minimum undergraduate, graduate and statistics GPA of 3.0; Texas RN license; interview; written statement of goals. Additional exam requirements/recommendations for international students: Required—TOEFL (minimum score 550 paper-based; 213 computer-based), IELTS (minimum score 7). *Application deadline:* For fall admission, 2/1 for domestic students, 4/1 for international students; for spring admission, 10/15 for domestic students, 9/5 for international students. Applications are processed on a rolling basis. Application fee: $40 ($70 for international students). *Financial support:* In 2011–12, 46 students received support, including 22 fellowships with partial tuition reimbursements available (averaging $4,473 per year), 6 research assistantships (averaging $8,873 per year), 24 teaching assistantships (averaging $6,202 per year); career-related internships or fieldwork, scholarships/grants, and traineeships also available. Financial award application deadline: 6/1; financial award applicants required to submit FAFSA. *Faculty research:* Simulation in clinical education and practice, cultural diversity, vulnerable populations, substance abuse. *Unit head:* Dr. Elizabeth C. Poster, Dean, 817-272-2776, Fax: 817-272-5006, E-mail: poster@uta.edu. *Application contact:* Dr. Jennifer Gray, Graduate Advisor/Associate Dean, 817-272-5295, Fax: 817-272-2065, E-mail: jgray@uta.edu. Web site: http://www.uta.edu/nursing.

The University of Texas at Austin, Graduate School, School of Nursing, Austin, TX 78712-1111. Offers adult -gerontology clinical nurse specialist (MSN); child health (MSN), including administration, public health nursing; child health (MSN), including teaching; family nurse practitioner (MSN); family psychiatric/mental health nurse practitioner (MSN); holistic adult health (MSN), including administration, education; maternity (MSN), including administration, public health nursing; maternity (MSN), including teaching; nursing (PhD); nursing administration and healthcare systems management (MSN); pediatric nurse practitioner (MSN); public health nursing (MSN). *Accreditation:* AACN. Part-time programs available. *Degree requirements:* For master's, thesis optional; for doctorate, thesis/dissertation. *Entrance requirements:* For master's and doctorate, GRE General Test. Additional exam requirements/recommendations for international students: Required—TOEFL (minimum score 550 paper-based; 213 computer-based). *Application deadline:* For fall admission, 12/1 for domestic students. Application fee: $50 ($75 for international students). Electronic applications accepted. *Financial support:* Fellowships, research assistantships, teaching assistantships, scholarships/grants, and traineeships available. Financial award application deadline: 2/1. *Faculty research:* Chronic illness management, memory and aging, health promotion, women's health, adolescent health. *Unit head:* Dr. Alexa Stuifbergen, Dean, 512-471-4100, Fax: 512-471-4910, E-mail: astuifbergen@mail.utexas.edu. Web site: http://www.utexas.edu/nursing/.

The University of Texas at El Paso, Graduate School, School of Nursing, El Paso, TX 79968-0001. Offers evidence-based practice (Certificate); family nurse practitioner (MSN); health care leadership and management (Certificate); interdisciplinary health sciences (PhD); nurse clinical specialist (MSN); nursing (Post-Master's Certificate); nursing systems management (MSN). *Accreditation:* AACN. *Students:* 162 (131 women); includes 94 minority (22 Black or African American, non-Hispanic/Latino; 11 Asian, non-Hispanic/Latino; 61 Hispanic/Latino), 3 international. Average age 34. 55 applicants, 58% accepted, 24 enrolled. In 2011, 12 master's awarded. *Degree requirements:* For master's, thesis optional; for doctorate, thesis/dissertation. *Entrance requirements:* For master's, GRE, minimum GPA of 3.0, course work in statistics, resume; for doctorate, GRE, letters of reference, relevant personal/professional experience, master's degree in health. Additional exam requirements/recommendations for international students: Required—TOEFL; Recommended—IELTS. *Application deadline:* For fall admission, 8/1 for domestic students, 3/1 for international students; for spring admission, 11/1 for domestic students, 9/1 for international students. Applications are processed on a rolling basis. Application fee: $45 ($80 for international students). Electronic applications accepted. *Financial support:* In 2011–12, research assistantships with partial tuition reimbursements (averaging $18,825 per year), teaching assistantships with partial tuition reimbursements (averaging $18,000 per year) were awarded; fellowships with partial tuition reimbursements, institutionally sponsored loans, scholarships/grants, health care benefits, tuition waivers (partial), and unspecified assistantships also available. Support available to part-time students. Financial award application deadline: 3/15; financial award applicants required to submit FAFSA. *Unit head:* Dr. Elias Provencio-Vasquez, Dean, 915-747-7273, Fax: 915-747-8266, E-mail: eprovenciovasquez@utep.edu. *Application contact:* Dr. Benjamin Flores, Interim Dean of the Graduate School, 915-747-5491, Fax: 915-747-5788, E-mail: bflores@utep.edu. Web site: http://nursing.utep.edu/.

The University of Texas at Tyler, College of Nursing and Health Sciences, Program in Nursing, Tyler, TX 75799-0001. Offers nurse practitioner (MSN); nursing (PhD); nursing administration (MSN); nursing education (MSN); MSN/MBA. *Accreditation:* AACN. Part-time and evening/weekend programs available. Postbaccalaureate distance learning degree programs offered (no on-campus study). *Degree requirements:* For master's, comprehensive exam (for some programs), thesis (for some programs); for doctorate, thesis/dissertation. *Entrance requirements:* For master's, GRE General Test or MAT, GMAT, minimum undergraduate GPA of 3.0, course work in statistics, RN license, BSN.

Additional exam requirements/recommendations for international students: Required—TOEFL (minimum score 79 computer-based). Electronic applications accepted. *Faculty research:* Psychosocial adjustment, aging, support/commitment of caregivers, psychological abuse and violence, hope/hopelessness, professional values, end of life care, suicidology, clinical supervision, workforce retention and issues, global health issues, health promotion.

The University of Texas Health Science Center at Houston, School of Nursing, Houston, TX 77030. Offers MSN, DNP, PhD, MSN/MPH. *Accreditation:* AACN; AANA/CANAEP. Part-time programs available. *Degree requirements:* For master's, thesis, research project, or clinical project; for doctorate, thesis/dissertation. *Entrance requirements:* For master's, GRE or MAT, BSN, Texas RN license, related work experience, interview, writing sample; for doctorate, GRE, interview, Texas RN license, portfolio, master's degree. Additional exam requirements/recommendations for international students: Required—TOEFL (minimum score 550 paper-based; 213 computer-based; 86 iBT). Electronic applications accepted. *Faculty research:* Malnutrition in institutionalized elderly, defining nursing, sensitive outcome measures, substance abuse in mothers during pregnancy, psychoeducational intervention among caregivers of stroke patients.

The University of Texas Health Science Center at San Antonio, School of Nursing, San Antonio, TX 78229-3900. Offers MSN, PhD. *Accreditation:* AACN. Part-time programs available. Terminal master's awarded for partial completion of doctoral program. *Degree requirements:* For master's, thesis optional; for doctorate, comprehensive exam, thesis/dissertation. *Entrance requirements:* For master's, minimum GPA of 3.0, references, goal statement; for doctorate, GRE, MAT, minimum GPA of 3.0, personal interview. Additional exam requirements/recommendations for international students: Required—TOEFL (minimum score 560 paper-based; 220 computer-based; 83 iBT). Electronic applications accepted. *Faculty research:* Pain, organizational structure, aging, quality and safety.

The University of Texas Medical Branch, Graduate School of Biomedical Sciences, Doctoral Program in Nursing, Galveston, TX 77555. Offers PhD. *Degree requirements:* For doctorate, comprehensive exam, thesis/dissertation. *Entrance requirements:* For doctorate, GRE General Test, minimum GPA of 3.0, BSN and MSN or equivalent advanced degree, 2 writing samples, 3 letters of reference, curriculum vitae or resume. Additional exam requirements/recommendations for international students: Required—TOEFL (minimum score 550 paper-based; 213 computer-based). Electronic applications accepted.

The University of Texas Medical Branch, School of Nursing, Master's Program in Nursing, Galveston, TX 77555. Offers MSN. Part-time programs available. Postbaccalaureate distance learning degree programs offered. *Entrance requirements:* For master's, GRE General Test or MAT, minimum BSN GPA of 3.0, 3 references, interview, 1 year nursing experience. Additional exam requirements/recommendations for international students: Required—TOEFL (minimum score 550 paper-based).

The University of Texas–Pan American, College of Health Sciences and Human Services, Department of Nursing, Edinburg, TX 78539. Offers adult health nursing (MSN); family nurse practitioner (MSN). *Accreditation:* AACN. Part-time and evening/weekend programs available. *Degree requirements:* For master's, thesis optional. *Entrance requirements:* For master's, Texas RN licensure, undergraduate physical statistic course. Additional exam requirements/recommendations for international students: Required—TOEFL (minimum score 550 paper-based). *Application deadline:* For fall admission, 7/1 priority date for domestic students, 7/1 for international students; for spring admission, 10/1 priority date for domestic students, 10/1 for international students. Applications are processed on a rolling basis. Application fee: $35. Electronic applications accepted. *Expenses:* Contact institution. *Financial support:* Scholarships/grants and traineeships available. *Faculty research:* Health promotion, adolescent pregnancy, herbal and nontraditional approaches, healing touch stress. *Unit head:* Dr. Carolina G. Huerta, Chair, 956-665-3496, Fax: 956-381-2384, E-mail: chuerta@utpa.edu. *Application contact:* Dr. Janice A. Maville, Professor and Assistant Dean, 956-665-2111, Fax: 956-665-2875, E-mail: jmaville@utpa.edu. Web site: http://www.panam.edu/dept/nursing/.

University of the Incarnate Word, School of Graduate Studies and Research, School of Nursing and Health Professions, Program in Nursing, San Antonio, TX 78209-6397. Offers MSN, DNP. *Accreditation:* AACN. Part-time and evening/weekend programs available. *Faculty:* 14 full-time (all women), 2 part-time/adjunct (both women). *Students:* 5 full-time (4 women), 59 part-time (51 women); includes 21 minority (5 Black or African American, non-Hispanic/Latino; 4 Asian, non-Hispanic/Latino; 12 Hispanic/Latino), 28 international. Average age 41. 25 applicants, 96% accepted, 16 enrolled. In 2011, 5 master's awarded. *Degree requirements:* For master's, capstone, clinical hours. *Entrance requirements:* For master's, baccalaureate degree in nursing from CCNE- or NLN-accredited program including courses in statistics and health assessment; minimum undergraduate cumulative GPA of 2.5, 3.0 in upper-division nursing courses; three professional references; license to practice nursing in Texas or recognized state. Additional exam requirements/recommendations for international students: Required—TOEFL (minimum score 560 paper-based; 220 computer-based; 83 iBT). *Application deadline:* Applications are processed on a rolling basis. Application fee: $20. Electronic applications accepted. *Expenses: Tuition:* Part-time $725 per credit hour. Tuition and fees vary according to degree level. *Financial support:* Federal Work-Study, scholarships/grants, and traineeships available. Support available to part-time students. Financial award applicants required to submit FAFSA. *Unit head:* Dr. Holly Cassells, Chair, Graduate Programs, 210-829-3977, Fax: 210-829-3174, E-mail: cassells@uiwtx.edu. *Application contact:* Andrea Cyterski-Acosta, Dean of Enrollment, 210-829-6005, Fax: 210-829-3921, E-mail: admis@uiwtx.edu. Web site: http://www.uiw.edu/msn/.

The University of Toledo, College of Graduate Studies, College of Nursing, Toledo, OH 43606-3390. Offers MSN, DNP, Certificate. *Accreditation:* AACN. Part-time programs available. Postbaccalaureate distance learning degree programs offered (no on-campus study). *Faculty:* 43. *Students:* 77 full-time (63 women), 208 part-time (190 women); includes 31 minority (14 Black or African American, non-Hispanic/Latino; 1 American Indian or Alaska Native, non-Hispanic/Latino; 4 Asian, non-Hispanic/Latino; 9 Hispanic/Latino; 3 Two or more races, non-Hispanic/Latino), 1 international. Average age 34. 184 applicants, 55% accepted, 90 enrolled. In 2011, 66 master's, 6 doctorates, 10 other advanced degrees awarded. *Degree requirements:* For master's, thesis or scholarly project; for doctorate, thesis/dissertation or alternative, evidence-based project. *Entrance requirements:* For master's, GRE, BS in nursing, minimum undergraduate GPA of 3.0, statement of purpose, two letters of recommendation, transcripts from all prior institutions attended, resume, Nursing CAS application, UT supplemental application; for doctorate, minimum undergraduate GPA of 3.0, statement of purpose, three letters of recommendation, transcripts from all prior institutions attended, resume, Nursing CAS application, UT supplemental application. Additional exam requirements/recommendations for international students: Required—TOEFL (minimum score 550 paper-based; 213 computer-based; 80 iBT), IELTS (minimum score 6.5). Application fee: $45 ($75 for international students). Electronic applications accepted. *Expenses:* Contact institution. *Financial support:* In 2011–12, 6 students received support. Federal Work-Study, institutionally sponsored loans, scholarships/

grants, traineeships, and tuition waivers (full and partial) available. *Faculty research:* Sexuality issues, prenatal testing, health care of homeless, nursing education, chronic/acute pain, eating disorders, low birth weight infants. *Unit head:* Dr. Timothy Gaspar, Dean, 419-383-5858, E-mail: admitnurse@utoledo.edu. *Application contact:* Kathleen Mitchell, Nursing Advisor, 419-383-5841, E-mail: kathleen.mitchell@utoledo.edu. Web site: http://www.utoledo.edu/nursing/.

University of Toronto, School of Graduate Studies, Lawrence S. Bloomberg Faculty of Nursing, Toronto, ON M5S 1A1, Canada. Offers MN, PhD, MHSc/MN. Part-time programs available. *Degree requirements:* For doctorate, thesis/dissertation, departmental and final oral exam/thesis defense. *Entrance requirements:* For master's, B Sc N or equivalent, minimum B average in next-to-final year, resume, 3 letters of reference; for doctorate, minimum B+ average, master's degree in nursing or a related area, resume, 2 letters of recommendation. Additional exam requirements/recommendations for international students: Required—TOEFL (minimum score 580 paper-based; 93 iBT), TWE (minimum score 5). Electronic applications accepted. *Expenses:* Contact institution.

University of Utah, Graduate School, College of Nursing, Program in Nursing, Salt Lake City, UT 84112. Offers MS, DNP, PhD. Part-time programs available. Postbaccalaureate distance learning degree programs offered (minimal on-campus study). *Faculty:* 48 full-time (42 women), 20 part-time/adjunct (18 women). *Students:* 218 full-time (179 women), 89 part-time (77 women); includes 37 minority (5 Black or African American, non-Hispanic/Latino; 1 American Indian or Alaska Native, non-Hispanic/Latino; 13 Asian, non-Hispanic/Latino; 17 Hispanic/Latino; 1 Two or more races, non-Hispanic/Latino), 6 international. Average age 39. 230 applicants, 55% accepted, 104 enrolled. In 2011, 38 master's, 50 doctorates awarded. *Median time to degree:* Of those who began their doctoral program in fall 2003, 80% received their degree in 8 years or less. *Degree requirements:* For master's, thesis optional, thesis or project; for doctorate, comprehensive exam, thesis/dissertation. *Entrance requirements:* For master's, GRE General Test (if cumulative GPA less than 3.2), RN licensure in one of the jurisdictions of the National Council of State Boards of Nursing, goal statement, professional references; for doctorate, GRE General Test, interview, curriculum vitae/resume, goal statement, professional and academic references, writing sample. Additional exam requirements/recommendations for international students: Required—TOEFL (minimum score 500 paper-based; 173 computer-based; 85 iBT). *Application deadline:* For fall admission, 1/15 priority date for domestic students, 1/15 for international students. Application fee: $55 ($65 for international students). Electronic applications accepted. *Expenses:* Contact institution. *Financial support:* In 2011–12, 141 students received support, including 103 fellowships with full and partial tuition reimbursements available (averaging $10,900 per year), 9 research assistantships with full and partial tuition reimbursements available (averaging $10,500 per year), 13 teaching assistantships with partial tuition reimbursements available (averaging $5,800 per year); scholarships/grants, traineeships, health care benefits, and unspecified assistantships also available. Support available to part-time students. Financial award application deadline: 1/15; financial award applicants required to submit FAFSA. *Faculty research:* Symptom management, patient-provider communication, patient safety/informatics, gerontology/geriatric nursing, end-of-life bereavement. *Total annual research expenditures:* $2.9 million. *Unit head:* Dr. Maureen Keefe, Dean, 801-581-8262, Fax: 801-581-4642, E-mail: maureen.keefe@nurs.utah.edu. *Application contact:* Melissa Pederson, Program Administrator, 801-585-1671, Fax: 801-585-9705, E-mail: melissa.pederson@nurs.utah.edu. Web site: http://www.nursing.utah.edu/.

University of Vermont, Graduate College, College of Nursing and Health Sciences, Department of Nursing, Burlington, VT 05405. Offers MS. *Accreditation:* AACN. *Students:* 88 (79 women); includes 6 minority (1 American Indian or Alaska Native, non-Hispanic/Latino; 3 Asian, non-Hispanic/Latino; 2 Hispanic/Latino), 1 international. 149 applicants, 35% accepted, 29 enrolled. In 2011, 16 master's awarded. *Entrance requirements:* For master's, GRE General Test. Additional exam requirements/recommendations for international students: Required—TOEFL (minimum score 550 paper-based; 213 computer-based; 80 iBT). *Application deadline:* For fall admission, 4/15 priority date for domestic students, 4/15 for international students. Applications are processed on a rolling basis. Application fee: $40. Electronic applications accepted. *Financial support:* Application deadline: 3/1. *Unit head:* Diane Jette, Chair, 802-656-3830. *Application contact:* Prof. Carol Buck-Rolland, Coordinator, 802-656-3858.

University of Victoria, Faculty of Graduate Studies, Faculty of Human and Social Development, School of Nursing, Victoria, BC V8W 2Y2, Canada. Offers advanced nursing practice (advanced practice leadership option) (MN); advanced nursing practice (nurse educator option) (MN); advanced nursing practice (nurse practitioner option) (MN); nursing (PhD). Part-time programs available. Postbaccalaureate distance learning degree programs offered (no on-campus study). *Entrance requirements:* Additional exam requirements/recommendations for international students: Required—TOEFL (minimum score 575 paper-based; 233 computer-based), IELTS (minimum score 7). Electronic applications accepted.

University of Virginia, School of Nursing, Charlottesville, VA 22903. Offers acute and specialty care (MSN); acute care nurse practitioner (MSN); clinical nurse leadership (MSN); community-public health leadership (MSN); nursing (DNP, PhD); psychiatric mental health counseling (MSN); MSN/MBA. *Accreditation:* AACN. Part-time programs available. *Faculty:* 44 full-time (43 women), 2 part-time/adjunct (both women). *Students:* 174 full-time (152 women), 151 part-time (139 women); includes 57 minority (28 Black or African American, non-Hispanic/Latino; 1 American Indian or Alaska Native, non-Hispanic/Latino; 14 Asian, non-Hispanic/Latino; 10 Hispanic/Latino; 4 Two or more races, non-Hispanic/Latino), 11 international. Average age 37. 236 applicants, 40% accepted, 74 enrolled. In 2011, 70 master's, 15 doctorates awarded. *Degree requirements:* For doctorate, comprehensive exam (for some programs), capstone project (DNP), dissertation (PhD). *Entrance requirements:* For master's, GRE General Test, MAT; for doctorate, GRE General Test. Additional exam requirements/recommendations for international students: Required—TOEFL, IELTS. *Application deadline:* Applications are processed on a rolling basis. Application fee: $60. Electronic applications accepted. *Expenses:* Contact institution. *Financial support:* Fellowships, research assistantships, teaching assistantships, Federal Work-Study, and scholarships/grants available. Financial award applicants required to submit FAFSA. *Unit head:* Dorrie K. Fontaine, Dean, 434-924-0141, Fax: 434-982-1809. *Application contact:* Clay Hysell, Assistant Dean for Admissions and Financial Services, 434-924-0141, Fax: 434-982-1809, E-mail: nur-osa@virginia.edu. Web site: http://www.nursing.virginia.edu/.

University of Washington, Graduate School, School of Nursing, Seattle, WA 98195. Offers MN, MS, DNP, PhD, Graduate Certificate, MN/MPH. *Accreditation:* AACN; ACNM/ACME (one or more programs are accredited). Part-time programs available. *Degree requirements:* For master's, thesis (for some programs); for doctorate, thesis/dissertation. *Entrance requirements:* For master's, GRE, minimum GPA of 3.0, resume; for doctorate, GRE, minimum GPA of 3.0. Additional exam requirements/recommendations for international students: Required—TOEFL. *Faculty research:* High risk youth, pain management, women's health, oncology, sleep.

University of Washington, Bothell, Program in Nursing, Bothell, WA 98011-8246. Offers MN. Part-time programs available. *Faculty:* 11 full-time (10 women). *Students:* 1 (woman) full-time, 82 part-time (74 women); includes 24 minority (8 Black or African American, non-Hispanic/Latino; 10 Asian, non-Hispanic/Latino; 3 Hispanic/Latino; 1 Native Hawaiian or other Pacific Islander, non-Hispanic/Latino; 2 Two or more races, non-Hispanic/Latino). Average age 42. 48 applicants, 73% accepted, 30 enrolled. In 2011, 36 master's awarded. *Degree requirements:* For master's, scholarly project. *Entrance requirements:* For master's, BSN (or other bachelor's degree with additional prerequisite work); current license as registered nurse in Washington state; minimum GPA of 3.0 in last 90 college credits, 2.0 in college statistics course. Additional exam requirements/recommendations for international students: Required—TOEFL (minimum score 580 paper-based; 237 computer-based). *Application deadline:* For fall admission, 3/1 priority date for domestic students, 3/1 for international students. Applications are processed on a rolling basis. Application fee: $75. Electronic applications accepted. *Expenses:* Contact institution. *Financial support:* In 2011–12, 21 students received support. Federal Work-Study, scholarships/grants, traineeships, and tuition waivers (partial) available. Financial award application deadline: 2/28; financial award applicants required to submit FAFSA. *Faculty research:* Health of special populations, nursing education, higher education technology, healing through patient's narratives, women's health care issues, end of life issues in nursing. *Unit head:* Prof. David Allen, Director and Professor, 425-352-5376, Fax: 425-352-3237, E-mail: dallen@uwb.edu. *Application contact:* Linda R. Bale, MN Academic Advisor, 425-352-3238, Fax: 425-352-3237, E-mail: lbale@uwb.edu. Web site: http://www.uwb.edu/nursing.

University of Washington, Tacoma, Graduate Programs, Program in Nursing, Tacoma, WA 98402-3100. Offers communities, populations and health (MN); leadership in healthcare (MN); nurse educator (MN). Part-time programs available. *Degree requirements:* For master's, thesis (for some programs), advance fieldwork. *Entrance requirements:* For master's, Washington State NCLEX exam, minimum GPA of 3.0. Additional exam requirements/recommendations for international students: Required—TOEFL (minimum score 580 paper-based; 237 computer-based; 70 iBT); Recommended—IELTS (minimum score 7). *Faculty research:* Hospice and palliative care; clinical trial decision-making; minority nurse retention; asthma and public health; injustice, suffering, difference: Linking Them to Us; adolescent health.

The University of Western Ontario, Faculty of Graduate Studies, Health Sciences Division, School of Nursing, London, ON N6A 5B8, Canada. Offers M Sc N, MN NP, PhD. Part-time programs available. *Degree requirements:* For master's, thesis; for doctorate, thesis/dissertation. *Entrance requirements:* Additional exam requirements/recommendations for international students: Required—TOEFL. *Faculty research:* Empowerment, self-efficacy, family health, community health, gerontology.

University of West Florida, College of Arts and Sciences: Sciences, School of Allied Health and Life Sciences, Department of Nursing, Pensacola, FL 32514-5750. Offers MSN. Part-time and evening/weekend programs available. *Faculty:* 2 full-time (both women). *Students:* 4 full-time (3 women), 3 part-time (all women). Average age 43. 5 applicants, 80% accepted, 3 enrolled. *Entrance requirements:* For master's, GRE or MAT, letter of intent; current curriculum vitae/resume. Additional exam requirements/recommendations for international students: Required—TOEFL (minimum score 550 paper-based; 213 computer-based). *Application deadline:* For fall admission, 5/1 for domestic students, 6/1 for international students; for spring admission, 10/1 for domestic students. Applications are processed on a rolling basis. Application fee: $30. *Expenses:* Tuition, state resident: full-time $5729; part-time $302 per credit hour. Tuition, nonresident: full-time $20,059; part-time $961 per credit hour. *Required fees:* $1509; $63 per credit hour. *Unit head:* Dr. Diane Gardner, Chairperson, 850-474-7761. *Application contact:* Terry McCray, Assistant Director of Graduate Admissions, 850-473-7718, Fax: 850-473-7714, E-mail: gradadmissions@uwf.edu. Web site: http://uwf.edu/nursing/.

University of West Georgia, School of Nursing, Carrollton, GA 30118. Offers health systems leadership (Post-Master's Certificate); nursing (MSN); nursing education (Post-Master's Certificate). *Accreditation:* AACN. Part-time programs available. *Faculty:* 8 full-time (all women). *Students:* 36 full-time (35 women), 16 part-time (all women); includes 14 minority (all Black or African American, non-Hispanic/Latino). Average age 45. 71 applicants, 77% accepted, 25 enrolled. In 2011, 10 master's awarded. *Degree requirements:* For master's, comprehensive exam, thesis or alternative. *Entrance requirements:* For master's, GRE or MAT, BSN, Georgia RN license, minimum GPA of 3.0 for upper-division nursing courses, completion of basic undergraduate statistics course. Additional exam requirements/recommendations for international students: Required—TOEFL (minimum score 523 paper-based; 193 computer-based; 69 iBT); Recommended—IELTS (minimum score 6). *Application deadline:* For fall admission, 7/15 for domestic and international students. Applications are processed on a rolling basis. Application fee: $30. Electronic applications accepted. *Expenses:* Tuition, state resident: full-time $4336; part-time $181 per credit hour. Tuition, nonresident: full-time $17,362; part-time $724 per credit hour. Tuition and fees vary according to course load, degree level, campus/location and program. *Financial support:* In 2011–12, 1 research assistantship with full tuition reimbursement (averaging $6,000 per year) was awarded. Financial award application deadline: 7/1; financial award applicants required to submit FAFSA. *Faculty research:* Caring in nursing education, pain assessment in older adults, pain outcomes. *Unit head:* Dr. Kathryn Mary Grams, Dean, 678-839-6552, Fax: 678-839-6553, E-mail: kgrams@westga.edu. *Application contact:* Alyicia Richards, Graduate Studies Associate, 678-839-5115, Fax: 678-839-6553, E-mail: alyrich@westga.edu. Web site: http://www.westga.edu/~nurs/.

University of Windsor, Faculty of Graduate Studies, Faculty of Nursing, Windsor, ON N9B 3P4, Canada. Offers M Sc, MN. *Degree requirements:* For master's, thesis or alternative. *Entrance requirements:* For master's, minimum B average, certificate of competence (nurse registration). Additional exam requirements/recommendations for international students: Required—TOEFL (minimum score 560 paper-based; 220 computer-based). Electronic applications accepted.

University of Wisconsin–Eau Claire, College of Nursing and Health Sciences, Program in Nursing, Eau Claire, WI 54702-4004. Offers adult-gerontologic administration (MSN); adult-gerontologic clinical nurse specialist (MSN); adult-gerontologic education (MSN); adult-gerontologic nurse practitioner (MSN); family health administration (MSN); family health in education (MSN); family health nurse practitioner (MSN); nursing practice (DNP). Part-time programs available. *Faculty:* 13 full-time (all women), 1 (woman) part-time/adjunct. *Students:* 42 full-time (40 women), 68 part-time (66 women); includes 3 minority (1 Black or African American, non-Hispanic/Latino; 1 Asian, non-Hispanic/Latino; 1 Hispanic/Latino). Average age 37. 74 applicants, 70% accepted, 41 enrolled. In 2011, 35 master's awarded. Terminal master's awarded for partial completion of doctoral program. *Degree requirements:* For master's, thesis optional, 500-600 hours clinical practicum, oral and written exams. *Entrance requirements:* For master's, Wisconsin RN license, minimum GPA of 3.0, undergraduate statistics, course work in health assessment. Additional exam requirements/recommendations for international students: Required—TOEFL (minimum score 550 paper-based; 213 computer-based; 79 iBT); Recommended—IELTS (minimum score 7). *Application deadline:* For fall admission, 1/15 priority date for domestic students, 1/15 for international students. Applications are processed on a rolling basis. Application fee: $86. *Expenses:* Tuition, state resident: full-time $7312; part-time $406 per credit. Tuition, nonresident: full-time $16,771; part-time $932 per credit. *Required fees:* $1101;

$61 per credit. *Financial support:* In 2011–12, 16 students received support. Federal Work-Study and unspecified assistantships available. Financial award application deadline: 3/1; financial award applicants required to submit FAFSA. *Unit head:* Dr. Linda Young, Dean, 715-836-4904, Fax: 715-836-5925, E-mail: younglk@uwec.edu. *Application contact:* Dr. Mary Zwygart-Stauffacher, Director, 715-836-5287, E-mail: zwygarmc@uwec.edu. Web site: http://www.uwec.edu/conhs/programs/grad/index.htm.

University of Wisconsin–Madison, School of Nursing, Madison, WI 53706-1380. Offers adult/gerontology (DNP); nursing (PhD); pediatrics (DNP); psychiatric mental health (DNP); MS/MPH. *Accreditation:* AACN. Part-time programs available. *Degree requirements:* For doctorate, comprehensive exam, thesis/dissertation. *Entrance requirements:* For doctorate, GRE General Test, 2 samples of scholarly written work, BS in nursing from an accredited program, minimum undergraduate GPA of 3.0 in last 60 credits (for PhD); licensure as professional nurse (for DNP). Additional exam requirements/recommendations for international students: Required—TOEFL (minimum score 600 paper-based; 250 computer-based; 100 iBT). Electronic applications accepted. *Expenses:* Tuition, state resident: full-time $10,296; part-time $643.51 per credit. Tuition, nonresident: full-time $24,054; part-time $1503.40 per credit. *Required fees:* $70.06 per credit. Tuition and fees vary according to course load, campus/location, program and reciprocity agreements. *Faculty research:* Nursing informatics to promote self-care and disease management skills among patients and caregivers; quality of care to frail, vulnerable, and chronically ill populations; study of health-related and health-seeking behaviors; eliminating health disparities; pain and symptom management for patients with cancer.

University of Wisconsin–Milwaukee, Graduate School, College of Nursing, Milwaukee, WI 53201-0413. Offers family nursing practitioner (Post Master's Certificate); health professional education (Certificate); nursing (MS, PhD); public health (Certificate). *Accreditation:* AACN. Part-time programs available. *Faculty:* 30 full-time (29 women), 2 part-time/adjunct (both women). *Students:* 125 full-time (114 women), 122 part-time (108 women); includes 34 minority (15 Black or African American, non-Hispanic/Latino; 1 American Indian or Alaska Native, non-Hispanic/Latino; 7 Asian, non-Hispanic/Latino; 1 Hispanic/Latino; 10 Two or more races, non-Hispanic/Latino), 6 international. Average age 39. 128 applicants, 49% accepted, 41 enrolled. In 2011, 52 master's, 16 doctorates awarded. *Degree requirements:* For master's, thesis; for doctorate, thesis/dissertation. *Entrance requirements:* For master's, GRE General Test or MAT, autobiographical sketch; for doctorate, GRE, minimum GPA of 3.2. Additional exam requirements/recommendations for international students: Required—TOEFL (minimum score 550 paper-based; 79 iBT), IELTS (minimum score 6.5). *Application deadline:* For fall admission, 1/1 priority date for domestic students; for spring admission, 9/1 for domestic students. Applications are processed on a rolling basis. Application fee: $56 ($96 for international students). Electronic applications accepted. One-time fee: $506.10 full-time. Tuition and fees vary according to course load and reciprocity agreements. *Financial support:* In 2011–12, 3 fellowships, 1 research assistantship, 9 teaching assistantships were awarded; career-related internships or fieldwork, Federal Work-Study, health care benefits, unspecified assistantships, and project assistantships also available. Support available to part-time students. Financial award application deadline: 4/15; financial award applicants required to submit FAFSA. *Total annual research expenditures:* $3.3 million. *Unit head:* Dr. Sally Lundeen, Dean, 414-229-4189, E-mail: slundeen@uwm.edu. *Application contact:* Kim Litwack, Representative, 414-229-5098. Web site: http://www.uwm.edu/Dept/Nursing/.

University of Wisconsin–Oshkosh, Graduate Studies, College of Nursing, Oshkosh, WI 54901. Offers adult health and illness (MSN); family nurse practitioner (MSN). *Accreditation:* AACN. Part-time programs available. *Degree requirements:* For master's, thesis or alternative, clinical paper. *Entrance requirements:* For master's, RN license, BSN, previous course work in statistics and health assessment, minimum undergraduate GPA of 3.0, letters of recommendation. Additional exam requirements/recommendations for international students: Required—TOEFL (minimum score 550 paper-based; 213 computer-based; 79 iBT). Electronic applications accepted. *Faculty research:* Adult health and illness, nurse practitioners practice, health care service, advanced practitioner roles, natural alternative complementary healthcare.

University of Wyoming, College of Health Sciences, Fay W. Whitney School of Nursing, Laramie, WY 82070. Offers MS. *Accreditation:* AACN. Part-time programs available. Postbaccalaureate distance learning degree programs offered (no on-campus study). *Degree requirements:* For master's, thesis. *Entrance requirements:* For master's, GRE General Test, BSN from CCNE or NCN-accredited school, minimum GPA of 3.0. Additional exam requirements/recommendations for international students: Required—TOEFL. *Faculty research:* Support systems for the elderly, fetal alcohol syndrome, teen pregnancy, rehabilitation with chronic mental illness, global peace building among women.

Urbana University, College of Nursing and Allied Health, Urbana, OH 43078-2091. Offers nursing (MSN). *Accreditation:* AACN. *Entrance requirements:* For master's, baccalaureate degree in nursing with minimum cumulative undergraduate GPA of 3.0, official transcripts, Ohio RN license, background check, statement of goals and objectives, resume, 3 letters of recommendation, interview.

Ursuline College, School of Graduate Studies, Programs in Nursing, Pepper Pike, OH 44124-4398. Offers care management (MSN); nurse practitioner (MSN); nursing (DNP); nursing education (MSN); palliative care (MSN). *Accreditation:* AACN. Part-time programs available. *Faculty:* 2 full-time (both women), 9 part-time/adjunct (7 women). *Students:* 1 (woman) full-time, 133 part-time (124 women); includes 27 minority (23 Black or African American, non-Hispanic/Latino; 3 Asian, non-Hispanic/Latino; 1 Two or more races, non-Hispanic/Latino), 1 international. Average age 38. 61 applicants, 87% accepted, 47 enrolled. In 2011, 21 master's awarded. *Degree requirements:* For master's, comprehensive exam. *Entrance requirements:* For master's, minimum undergraduate GPA of 3.0, bachelor's degree in nursing, eligibility for or current Ohio RN license. Additional exam requirements/recommendations for international students: Required—TOEFL (minimum score 500 paper-based, 173 computer-based). *Application deadline:* For fall admission, 8/1 priority date for domestic students. Applications are processed on a rolling basis. Application fee: $25. *Expenses:* Tuition: Part-time $875 per credit hour. *Required fees:* $170 per semester. *Financial support:* In 2011–12, 11 students received support. Federal Work-Study available. Financial award application deadline: 3/1. *Unit head:* Dr. Janet Baker, Director, 440-864-8172, Fax: 440-684-6053, E-mail: jbaker@ursuline.edu. *Application contact:* Melanie Steele, Graduate Admission Assistant, 440-646-8199, Fax: 440-684-6138, E-mail: graduateadmissions@ursuline.edu.

Utah Valley University, Program in Nursing, Orem, UT 84058-5999. Offers MSN. Part-time programs available. *Faculty:* 8 full-time (7 women). *Students:* 9 full-time (7 women), 2 part-time (both women). Average age 44. Terminal master's awarded for partial completion of doctoral program. *Degree requirements:* For master's, project or thesis. *Entrance requirements:* For master's, GRE, baccalaureate degree in nursing, nurse licensure, undergraduate course in statistics, minimum undergraduate GPA of 3.2 overall or in last 60 semester hours of coursework, 3 letters of recommendation. Additional exam requirements/recommendations for international students: Required—TOEFL (minimum score 83 iBT). *Application deadline:* For fall admission, 4/1 for domestic and international students. Application fee: $45 ($100 for international

students). Electronic applications accepted. *Financial support:* Application deadline: 5/1; applicants required to submit FAFSA. *Unit head:* Sam Rushforth, Dean of the College of Science and Health, 801-863-6441. *Application contact:* Eric Wilding, Intermediate Research Analyst, 801-863-7925, E-mail: eric.wilding@uvu.edu. Web site: http://www.uvu.edu/csh/nursing/degrees/ms.html.

Valparaiso University, Graduate School, College of Nursing, Valparaiso, IN 46383. Offers management (Certificate); nursing education (MSN, Certificate, MSN/MBA); MSN/MBA. *Accreditation:* AACN. Part-time and evening/weekend programs available. Postbaccalaureate distance learning degree programs offered (minimal on-campus study). *Faculty:* 10 part-time/adjunct (all women). *Students:* 20 full-time (19 women), 43 part-time (42 women); includes 12 minority (7 Black or African American, non-Hispanic/Latino; 1 Asian, non-Hispanic/Latino; 4 Hispanic/Latino), 1 international. Average age 39. In 2011, 12 master's, 21 other advanced degrees awarded. *Entrance requirements:* For master's, minimum GPA of 3.0, undergraduate major in nursing, Indiana registered nursing license, undergraduate courses in research and statistics. Additional exam requirements/recommendations for international students: Required—TOEFL (minimum score 550 paper-based; 213 computer-based; 80 iBT). *Application deadline:* Applications are processed on a rolling basis. Application fee: $30 ($50 for international students). Electronic applications accepted. *Expenses:* Contact institution. *Financial support:* Available to part-time students. Applicants required to submit FAFSA. *Unit head:* Dr. Janet Brown, Dean, 219-464-5289, Fax: 219-464-5425, E-mail: janet.brown@valpo.edu. *Application contact:* Dustin Jesch, Coordinator, U.S. Student Engagement, 219-464-5313, Fax: 219-464-5381, E-mail: dustin.jesch@valpo.edu. Web site: http://valpo.edu/nursing/.

Vanderbilt University, Graduate School, Program in Nursing Science, Nashville, TN 37240-1001. Offers PhD. *Faculty:* 31 full-time (23 women). *Students:* 23 full-time (18 women), 5 part-time (4 women); includes 2 minority (1 Black or African American, non-Hispanic/Latino; 1 Hispanic/Latino). Average age 42. 32 applicants, 31% accepted, 9 enrolled. In 2011, 2 doctorates awarded. *Degree requirements:* For doctorate, comprehensive exam, thesis/dissertation, final and qualifying exams. *Entrance requirements:* For doctorate, GRE General Test. Additional exam requirements/recommendations for international students: Required—TOEFL (minimum score 570 paper-based; 230 computer-based; 88 iBT). *Application deadline:* For fall admission, 1/15 for domestic and international students. Application fee: $0. Electronic applications accepted. *Financial support:* Fellowships with full tuition reimbursements, research assistantships with full tuition reimbursements, teaching assistantships with full tuition reimbursements, career-related internships or fieldwork, Federal Work-Study, institutionally sponsored loans, scholarships/grants, health care benefits, and tuition waivers (full and partial) available. Financial award application deadline: 1/15; financial award applicants required to submit CSS PROFILE or FAFSA. *Faculty research:* Adaptation to chronic illness/conditions, health problems related to stress and coping, vulnerable childbearing and child rearing families. *Unit head:* Dr. Susan M. Adams, Director, 615-343-3324, Fax: 615-936-0228, E-mail: susie.adams@vanderbilt.edu. *Application contact:* Dr. Ann Minnick, Director of Graduate Studies, 615-343-2998, Fax: 615-343-5898, E-mail: ann.minnick@vanderbilt.edu. Web site: http://www.nursing.vanderbilt.edu/.

Vanderbilt University, Vanderbilt University School of Nursing, Nashville, TN 37240. Offers acute care nurse practitioner (MSN), including intensivist; adult-gerontology primary care nurse practitioner (MSN); emergency nurse practitioner (MSN); family nurse practitioner (MSN); family psychiatric and mental health nurse practitioner (MSN); health systems management (MSN); neonatal nurse practitioner (MSN); nurse midwifery (MSN); nurse midwifery/family nurse practitioner (MSN); nursing informatics (MSN); nursing practice (DNP); nursing science (PhD); pediatric acute care nurse practitioner (MSN); pediatric primary care nurse practitioner (MSN); women's health nurse practitioner (MSN), including urogynecology, women's health; women's health nurse practitioner/adult gerontology nurse practitioner (MSN); MSN/M Div; MSN/MTS. *Accreditation:* ACNM/ACME; NLN (one or more programs are accredited). Part-time programs available. Postbaccalaureate distance learning degree programs offered (minimal on-campus study). *Faculty:* 120 full-time (105 women), 415 part-time/adjunct (302 women). *Students:* 570 full-time (503 women), 395 part-time (364 women); includes 107 minority (57 Black or African American, non-Hispanic/Latino; 1 American Indian or Alaska Native, non-Hispanic/Latino; 19 Asian, non-Hispanic/Latino; 19 Hispanic/Latino; 2 Native Hawaiian or other Pacific Islander, non-Hispanic/Latino; 9 Two or more races, non-Hispanic/Latino), 10 international. Average age 32. 1,116 applicants, 56% accepted, 455 enrolled. In 2011, 341 master's, 33 doctorates awarded. *Degree requirements:* For doctorate, comprehensive exam, thesis/dissertation. *Entrance requirements:* For master's, GRE General Test (within the past 5 years), minimum B average in undergraduate course work, 3 letters of recommendation; for doctorate, GRE General Test, interview, 3 letters of recommendation from doctorally-prepared faculty, MSN, essay. Additional exam requirements/recommendations for international students: Required—TOEFL (minimum score 570 paper-based; 88 computer-based), IELTS (minimum score 6.5). *Application deadline:* For fall admission, 12/1 priority date for domestic students, 12/1 for international students. Applications are processed on a rolling basis. Application fee: $50. Electronic applications accepted. *Expenses:* Contact institution. *Financial support:* In 2011–12, 392 students received support. Scholarships/grants and health care benefits available. Support available to part-time students. Financial award application deadline: 3/15; financial award applicants required to submit FAFSA. *Faculty research:* Lymphedema, palliative care and bereavement, health services research including workforce, safety and quality of care, gerontology, better birth outcomes including nutrition . *Total annual research expenditures:* $1.8 million. *Unit head:* Dr. Colleen Conway-Welch, Dean, 615-343-8776, Fax: 615-343-7711, E-mail: colleen.conway-welch@vanderbilt.edu. *Application contact:* Patricia Peerman, Assistant Dean for Enrollment Management, 615-322-3800, Fax: 615-343-0333, E-mail: vusn-admissions@vanderbilt.edu. Web site: http://www.nursing.vanderbilt.edu.

Villanova University, College of Nursing, Villanova, PA 19085-1699. Offers adult nurse practitioner (MSN, Post Master's Certificate); family nurse practitioner (MSN, Post Master's Certificate); health care administration (MSN, Post Master's Certificate); nurse anesthetist (MSN, Post Master's Certificate); nursing (PhD); nursing education (MSN, Post Master's Certificate); nursing practice (DNP); pediatric nurse practitioner (MSN, Post Master's Certificate). *Accreditation:* AACN; AANA/CANAEP. Part-time programs available. Postbaccalaureate distance learning degree programs offered (minimal on-campus study). *Faculty:* 17 full-time (all women), 4 part-time/adjunct (all women). *Students:* 36 full-time (35 women), 256 part-time (234 women); includes 27 minority (14 Black or African American, non-Hispanic/Latino; 9 Asian, non-Hispanic/Latino; 4 Hispanic/Latino), 16 international. Average age 30. 161 applicants, 55% accepted, 75 enrolled. In 2011, 55 master's, 11 doctorates, 5 other advanced degrees awarded. *Degree requirements:* For master's, independent study project; for doctorate, comprehensive exam, thesis/dissertation. *Entrance requirements:* For master's, GRE or MAT, BSN, 1 year of recent nursing experience, physical assessment, course work in statistics; for doctorate, GRE, MSN. Additional exam requirements/recommendations for international students: Required—TOEFL, IELTS. *Application deadline:* For fall admission, 7/1 priority date for domestic students, 7/1 for international students; for spring admission, 11/1 priority date for domestic students, 11/1 for international students. Applications are processed on a rolling basis. Application fee: $50. *Expenses:*

Nursing—General

Contact institution. *Financial support:* In 2011–12, 43 students received support, including 5 teaching assistantships with full tuition reimbursements available (averaging $13,100 per year); institutionally sponsored loans, scholarships/grants, traineeships, tuition waivers (full), and unspecified assistantships also available. Financial award application deadline: 7/1; financial award applicants required to submit FAFSA. *Faculty research:* Genetics, ethics, cognitive development of students, women with disabilities, nursing leadership. *Unit head:* Dr. Marguerite K. Schlag, Assistant Dean/Director, Graduate Programs, 610-519-4907, Fax: 610-519-7650, E-mail: marguerite.schlag@villanova.edu. Web site: http://www.nursing.villanova.edu/.

Virginia Commonwealth University, Graduate School, School of Nursing, Richmond, VA 23284-9005. Offers adult health acute nursing (MS); adult health primary nursing (MS); biobehavioral clinical research (PhD); child health nursing (MS); clinical nurse leader (MS); family health nursing (MS); nurse educator (MS); nurse practitioner (MS); nursing (Certificate); nursing administration (MS), including clinical nurse manager; psychiatric-mental health nursing (MS); women's health nursing (MS). *Accreditation:* NLN (one or more programs are accredited). Part-time and evening/weekend programs available. *Degree requirements:* For master's, thesis optional; for doctorate, thesis/dissertation. *Entrance requirements:* For master's, GRE General Test, BSN, minimum GPA of 2.8; for doctorate, GRE General Test. Additional exam requirements/recommendations for international students: Required—TOEFL (minimum score 600 paper-based; 250 computer-based; 100 iBT). Electronic applications accepted. *Expenses:* Tuition, state resident: full-time $9133; part-time $507 per credit. Tuition, nonresident: full-time $18,777; part-time $1043 per credit. *Required fees:* $77 per credit. Tuition and fees vary according to degree level, campus/location, program and student level.

Viterbo University, Graduate Program in Nursing, La Crosse, WI 54601-4797. Offers MSN. *Accreditation:* AACN. Part-time programs available. Postbaccalaureate distance learning degree programs offered (minimal on-campus study). *Entrance requirements:* For master's, GRE General Test or MAT, bachelor's degree in nursing, minimum GPA of 3.0, RN license. *Expenses:* Contact institution.

Wagner College, Division of Graduate Studies, Department of Nursing, Program in Nursing, Staten Island, NY 10301-4495. Offers MS. *Accreditation:* NLN. Part-time and evening/weekend programs available. *Faculty:* 8 full-time (all women), 25 part-time/adjunct (22 women). *Students:* 10 full-time (all women), 107 part-time (95 women); includes 29 minority (12 Black or African American, non-Hispanic/Latino; 8 Asian, non-Hispanic/Latino; 5 Hispanic/Latino; 4 Two or more races, non-Hispanic/Latino). Average age 33. 28 applicants, 96% accepted, 22 enrolled. In 2011, 21 master's awarded. *Degree requirements:* For master's, thesis optional. *Entrance requirements:* For master's, BS in nursing, current clinical experience, minimum GPA of 2.75. *Application deadline:* For fall admission, 5/1 priority date for domestic students; for spring admission, 12/1 for domestic students. Applications are processed on a rolling basis. Application fee: $50 ($80 for international students). *Expenses: Tuition:* Full-time $16,200; part-time $890 per credit. *Financial support:* Traineeships, unspecified assistantships, and alumni fellowship grant available. Financial award applicants required to submit FAFSA. *Unit head:* Dr. Paula Tropello, Associate Professor/Chairman, Department of Nursing, 718-390-3452, Fax: 718-420-4009, E-mail: ptropell@wagner.edu. *Application contact:* Patricia Clancy, Administrative Assistant, 718-420-4464, Fax: 718-390-3105, E-mail: patricia.clancy@wagner.edu.

Walden University, Graduate Programs, School of Nursing, Minneapolis, MN 55401. Offers education (MSN); informatics (MSN); leadership and management (MSN); nursing (DNP, Post-Master's Certificate), including nursing education (Post-Master's Certificate), nursing informatics (Post-Master's Certificate), nursing leadership and management (Post-Master's Certificate). *Accreditation:* AACN. Part-time and evening/weekend programs available. Postbaccalaureate distance learning degree programs offered (no on-campus study). *Faculty:* 13 full-time (10 women), 142 part-time/adjunct (123 women). *Students:* 4,064 full-time (3,749 women), 1,418 part-time (1,321 women); includes 1,448 minority (975 Black or African American, non-Hispanic/Latino; 27 American Indian or Alaska Native, non-Hispanic/Latino; 207 Asian, non-Hispanic/Latino; 178 Hispanic/Latino; 8 Native Hawaiian or other Pacific Islander, non-Hispanic/Latino; 53 Two or more races, non-Hispanic/Latino), 181 international. Average age 43. In 2011, 1,141 master's, 31 other advanced degrees awarded. *Entrance requirements:* For master's, bachelor's degree or equivalent in related field or RN; minimum GPA of 2.5; goal statement; for doctorate, master's degree or higher, three years of related professional or academic experience, RN, goal statement. Additional exam requirements/recommendations for international students: Required—TOEFL (minimum score 550 paper-based; 213 computer-based), IELTS (minimum score 6.5), or Michigan English Language Assessment Battery (minimum score 82). *Application deadline:* Applications are processed on a rolling basis. Application fee: $50. Electronic applications accepted. *Financial support:* Federal Work-Study, scholarships/grants, unspecified assistantships, and family tuition reduction, active duty/veteran tuition reduction, group tuition reduction, interest-free payment plans, employee tuition reduction available. Support available to part-time students. Financial award applicants required to submit FAFSA. *Unit head:* Dr. Sara Torres, Associate Dean, 800-925-3368. *Application contact:* Jennifer Hall, Vice President of Enrollment Management, 866-4-WALDEN, E-mail: info@walden.edu. Web site: http://www.waldenu.edu/Colleges-and-Schools/College-of-Health-Sciences/School-of-Nursing.htm.

Walsh University, Graduate Studies, School of Nursing, North Canton, OH 44720-3396. Offers clinical nurse leader (MSN); nursing practice (DNP). Part-time and evening/weekend programs available. Postbaccalaureate distance learning degree programs offered (minimal on-campus study). *Faculty:* 5 full-time (4 women). *Students:* 4 full-time (all women), 10 part-time (all women); includes 1 minority (Black or African American, non-Hispanic/Latino). Average age 48. *Degree requirements:* For doctorate, project; manuscript for publication (peer reviewed); presentation at regional or national meeting. *Entrance requirements:* For master's, current unencumbered RN license, completion of an undergraduate or graduate statistics course, essay, interview; for doctorate, BSN; master's degree; statistics and research courses; essay; interview. Additional exam requirements/recommendations for international students: Required—TOEFL. *Expenses: Tuition:* Full-time $10,170; part-time $565 per credit hour. *Financial support:* Research assistantships, tuition waivers (partial), and tuition discounts available. Financial award application deadline: 12/31; financial award applicants required to submit FAFSA. *Faculty research:* Faith community nursing, gerontology, women's health, global nursing education, nursing assessment, grief and reconstitution, health needs of psychiatric patients. *Unit head:* Dr. Linda Linc, Dean, School of Nursing, 330-490-7250, Fax: 330-490-7371, E-mail: llinc@walsh.edu. *Application contact:* Dr. Karen R. Gehrling, Director, Graduate Program in Nursing, 330-244-4659, Fax: 330-490-7206, E-mail: kgehrling@walsh.edu. Web site: http://www.walsh.edu/master-of-science-in-nursing.

Washburn University, School of Nursing, Topeka, KS 66621. Offers adult nurse practitioner (MSN); clinical nurse leader (MSN); family nurse practitioner (MSN). *Accreditation:* AACN. Part-time programs available. *Faculty:* 13 full-time (all women), 1 (woman) part-time/adjunct. *Students:* 23 full-time (all women), 78 part-time (73 women). 52 applicants, 77% accepted, 40 enrolled. In 2011, 23 master's awarded. *Entrance requirements:* Additional exam requirements/recommendations for international

students: Required—TOEFL. *Application deadline:* For fall admission, 3/15 for international students. Application fee: $35. *Expenses:* Tuition, state resident: full-time $5346; part-time $297 per credit hour. Tuition, nonresident: full-time $10,908; part-time $606 per credit hour. *Required fees:* $86; $43 per semester. *Financial support:* Application deadline: 2/15. *Unit head:* Dr. Monica S. Scheibmeir, Dean, 785-670-1526, E-mail: monica.scheibmeir@washburn.edu. *Application contact:* Mary V. Allen, Director of Student Academic Support Services, 785-670-1533, E-mail: mary.allen@washburn.edu. Web site: http://www.washburn.edu/sonu.

Washington Adventist University, Program in Nursing - Business Leadership, Takoma Park, MD 20912. Offers MSN. Part-time programs available. *Students:* 6 full-time (5 women), 14 part-time (13 women); includes 18 minority (17 Black or African American, non-Hispanic/Latino; 1 Asian, non-Hispanic/Latino). Average age 39. *Application deadline:* Applications are processed on a rolling basis. *Expenses:* Tuition: Part-time $560 per credit hour. *Financial support:* Applicants required to submit FAFSA. *Unit head:* Dr. Jude Edwards, Dean of School of Graduate and Professional Studies, 301-891-4092, E-mail: jeedward@wau.edu. *Application contact:* Rahneeka Hazelton, Director, 301-891-4092, E-mail: rhazelto@wau.edu. Web site: http://www.wau.edu/index.php?option=com_content&view=article&id=408&Itemid=965.

Washington State University Spokane, Graduate Programs, Intercollegiate College of Nursing, Spokane, WA 99210. Offers MN. *Accreditation:* AACN. *Faculty:* 30. *Students:* 44 full-time (42 women), 58 part-time (47 women); includes 10 minority (1 Black or African American, non-Hispanic/Latino; 1 American Indian or Alaska Native, non-Hispanic/Latino; 2 Asian, non-Hispanic/Latino; 5 Hispanic/Latino; 1 Two or more races, non-Hispanic/Latino), 1 international. Average age 42. 73 applicants, 37% accepted, 26 enrolled. In 2011, 8 master's awarded. *Degree requirements:* For master's, comprehensive exam (for some programs), thesis (for some programs), oral exam, research project. *Entrance requirements:* For master's, minimum GPA of 3.0, Washington state RN license, physical assessment skills, course work in statistics, recommendations, written interview (nurse practitioner). *Application deadline:* For fall admission, 1/10 priority date for domestic students, 1/10 for international students; for spring admission, 7/1 priority date for domestic students, 7/1 for international students. Application fee: $75. *Financial support:* Teaching assistantships with tuition reimbursements available. Financial award application deadline: 4/1. *Faculty research:* Cardiovascular and Type 2 diabetes in children, evaluation of strategies to increase physical activity in sedentary people. *Total annual research expenditures:* $2.1 million. *Unit head:* Dr. Patricia Butterfield, Dean, 509-324-7292, Fax: 509-858-7336. *Application contact:* Graduate School Admissions, 800-GRADWSU, Fax: 509-335-1949, E-mail: gradsch@wsu.edu. Web site: http://www.nursing.wsu.edu.

Washington State University Tri-Cities, Graduate Programs, College of Nursing, Richland, WA 99354. Offers MN, PhD. Part-time programs available. Postbaccalaureate distance learning degree programs offered (minimal on-campus study). *Faculty:* 30. *Students:* 9 full-time (all women), 20 part-time (17 women); includes 2 minority (both Hispanic/Latino). Average age 40. 28 applicants, 29% accepted, 7 enrolled. In 2011, 12 degrees awarded. *Degree requirements:* For master's, comprehensive exam (for some programs), thesis (for some programs), oral exam, research project. *Entrance requirements:* For master's, current Washington state RN license; minimum cumulative GPA of 2.5, 2.0 in each nursing course. Additional exam requirements/recommendations for international students: Required—TOEFL. *Application deadline:* For fall admission, 1/10 priority date for domestic students, 1/10 for international students; for spring admission, 7/1 priority date for domestic students, 7/1 for international students. Application fee: $75. *Financial support:* In 2011–12, 24 students received support, including fellowships (averaging $4,050 per year), teaching assistantships with tuition reimbursements available (averaging $13,056 per year). Financial award application deadline: 4/1; financial award applicants required to submit FAFSA. *Unit head:* Phyllis Morris, Interim Director, 509-372-7196, Fax: 509-372-7116, E-mail: pmorris@tricity.wsu.edu. *Application contact:* Graduate School Admissions, 800-GRADWSU, Fax: 509-335-1949, E-mail: gradsch@wsu.edu. Web site: http://www.tricity.wsu.edu/nursing/.

Washington State University Vancouver, Graduate Programs, Intercollegiate College of Nursing, Vancouver, WA 98686. Offers MN. *Faculty:* 30. *Students:* 11 full-time (7 women), 108 part-time (97 women); includes 20 minority (3 Black or African American, non-Hispanic/Latino; 2 American Indian or Alaska Native, non-Hispanic/Latino; 7 Asian, non-Hispanic/Latino; 6 Hispanic/Latino; 2 Two or more races, non-Hispanic/Latino). Average age 44. 85 applicants, 41% accepted, 33 enrolled. In 2011, 8 degrees awarded. *Degree requirements:* For master's, comprehensive exam (for some programs), thesis (for some programs), research project. *Entrance requirements:* For master's, Washington RN license, minimum GPA of 3.0. Additional exam requirements/recommendations for international students: Required—TOEFL. *Application deadline:* For fall admission, 1/10 priority date for domestic students, 1/10 for international students; for spring admission, 7/1 priority date for domestic students, 7/1 for international students. Applications are processed on a rolling basis. Application fee: $75. Electronic applications accepted. *Financial support:* In 2011–12, research assistantships (averaging $14,634 per year), teaching assistantships with tuition reimbursements (averaging $13,383 per year) were awarded. Financial award application deadline: 2/15. *Faculty research:* Cultural competence in nursing, prescribing controlled substances by Advanced Registered Nurse Practitioners, decreasing health disparities, workforce diversity. *Total annual research expenditures:* $1.5 million. *Unit head:* Dr. Ginny Guido, Regional Director, 360-546-9244, Fax: 360-546-9038, E-mail: ginny_guido@vancouver.wsu.edu. *Application contact:* Tami Kelly, Principal Assistant, 509-324-7334, E-mail: kelleyt@wsu.edu. Web site: http://nursing.wsu.edu/index.html.

Waynesburg University, Graduate and Professional Studies, Waynesburg, PA 15370-1222. Offers business (MBA), including finance, health systems, human resources, leadership, market development; counseling (MA), including addictions counseling, clinical mental health; education (MAT); nursing (MSN), including administration, education, informatics, palliative care; nursing practice (DNP); special education (M Ed); technology (M Ed); MSN/MBA. *Accreditation:* AACN. Part-time and evening/weekend programs available. *Degree requirements:* For doctorate, thesis/dissertation. *Entrance requirements:* Additional exam requirements/recommendations for international students: Required—TOEFL. Electronic applications accepted.

Wayne State University, College of Nursing, Program in Nursing, Detroit, MI 48202. Offers PhD. Part-time programs available. *Students:* 28 full-time (25 women), 3 part-time (all women); includes 11 minority (10 Black or African American, non-Hispanic/Latino; 1 Two or more races, non-Hispanic/Latino), 5 international. Average age 45. 8 applicants, 13% accepted, 1 enrolled. In 2011, 4 doctorates awarded. *Degree requirements:* For doctorate, thesis/dissertation. *Entrance requirements:* For doctorate, GRE General Test, minimum GPA of 3.3, bachelor's or master's degree in nursing, current RN license, interview, goals statement, curriculum vitae, reference letters from doctorally-prepared individuals (three for PhD applicants, two for DNP). Additional exam requirements/recommendations for international students: Required—TOEFL (minimum score 550 paper-based; 213 computer-based); Recommended—TWE (minimum score 6). *Application deadline:* For fall admission, 1/15 for domestic and international students. Application fee: $50. Electronic applications accepted. *Expenses:* Tuition, state resident: part-time $512.85 per credit. Tuition, nonresident: part-time $1132.65 per

credit. *Required fees:* $26.60 per credit. $199.65 per semester. Tuition and fees vary according to course load and program. *Financial support:* In 2011–12, 10 students received support. Fellowships with tuition reimbursements available, research assistantships with tuition reimbursements available, teaching assistantships with tuition reimbursements available, institutionally sponsored loans, scholarships/grants, and unspecified assistantships available. Support available to part-time students. *Faculty research:* Self-care, transcultural care, adaptation to acute and chronic illness, urban health and health care systems. *Unit head:* Dr. Barbara Redman, Dean, 313-577-4070, Fax: 313-577-4571, E-mail: ae9080@wayne.edu. *Application contact:* Dr. Cythia Redwine, Assistant Dean for the Office of Student Affairs, 313-577-4082, E-mail: nursinginfo@wayne.edu. Web site: http://www.nursing.wayne.edu/phd/index.php.

Webster University, College of Arts and Sciences, Department of Nursing, St. Louis, MO 63119-3194. Offers healthcare leadership (Certificate); nursing (MSN). *Accreditation:* NLN. *Degree requirements:* For master's, comprehensive exam. *Entrance requirements:* For master's, 1 year of clinical experience, BSN, interview, minimum C+ average in statistics and physical assessment, minimum GPA of 3.0, RN license. Additional exam requirements/recommendations for international students: Required—TOEFL. *Expenses: Tuition:* Full-time $10,890; part-time $605 per credit hour. Tuition and fees vary according to campus/location and program. *Faculty research:* Health teaching.

Wesley College, Nursing Program, Dover, DE 19901-3875. Offers MSN. *Accreditation:* NLN. Part-time and evening/weekend programs available. *Degree requirements:* For master's, thesis optional, portfolio. *Entrance requirements:* For master's, GRE or MAT. Electronic applications accepted. *Faculty research:* Childhood obesity, organizational behavior, health promotion and wellness.

West Chester University of Pennsylvania, College of Health Sciences, Department of Nursing, West Chester, PA 19383. Offers nursing education (Certificate); public health nursing (MSN), including administration; school nursing (Teaching Certificate). *Accreditation:* AACN. Part-time and evening/weekend programs available. *Faculty:* 1 (woman) full-time, 2 part-time/adjunct (both women). *Students:* 10 full-time (all women), 31 part-time (all women); includes 8 minority (7 Black or African American, non-Hispanic/Latino; 1 Asian, non-Hispanic/Latino), 2 international. Average age 46. 20 applicants, 75% accepted, 13 enrolled. In 2011, 1 degree awarded. *Entrance requirements:* For master's, RN license, BSN or RN with bachelor's degree in another discipline, minimum GPA of 2.8, experience as a nurse providing direct clinical care, two letters of recommendation. Additional exam requirements/recommendations for international students: Required—TOEFL (minimum score 550 paper-based; 213 computer-based; 80 iBT). *Application deadline:* For fall admission, 4/15 priority date for domestic students, 3/15 for international students; for spring admission, 10/15 priority date for domestic students, 9/1 for international students. Applications are processed on a rolling basis. Application fee: $45. Electronic applications accepted. *Expenses:* Tuition, state resident: full-time $7488; part-time $416 per credit. Tuition, nonresident: full-time $11,232; part-time $624 per credit. *Required fees:* $1784.64; $67.59 per credit. Tuition and fees vary according to program. *Financial support:* Unspecified assistantships available. Support available to part-time students. Financial award application deadline: 2/15; financial award applicants required to submit FAFSA. *Unit head:* Dr. Charlotte Mackey, Chair, 610-436-3474, Fax: 610-436-3083, E-mail: cmackey@wcupa.edu. *Application contact:* Dr. Ann Coghlan Stowe, Graduate Coordinator, 610-436-2331, Fax: 610-436-3083, E-mail: astowe@wcupa.edu. Web site: http://www.wcupa.edu/_ACADEMICS/HealthSciences/nursing/.

Western Carolina University, Graduate School, College of Health and Human Sciences, School of Nursing, Cullowhee, NC 28723. Offers nurse educator (PMC); nursing (MSN). *Accreditation:* AACN; AANA/CANAEP. Part-time and evening/weekend programs available. *Students:* 31 full-time (23 women), 79 part-time (69 women); includes 13 minority (2 Black or African American, non-Hispanic/Latino; 3 American Indian or Alaska Native, non-Hispanic/Latino; 1 Asian, non-Hispanic/Latino; 4 Hispanic/Latino; 3 Two or more races, non-Hispanic/Latino). Average age 39. 54 applicants, 63% accepted, 33 enrolled. In 2011, 32 master's awarded. *Degree requirements:* For master's, comprehensive exam, thesis or alternative. *Entrance requirements:* For master's, GRE General Test, BSN with minimum GPA of 3.0, 3 references, 1 year of clinical experience. Additional exam requirements/recommendations for international students: Required—TOEFL (minimum score 550 paper-based; 270 computer-based; 79 iBT). *Application deadline:* For fall admission, 2/15 for domestic students; for spring admission, 6/15 for domestic students. Applications are processed on a rolling basis. Application fee: $50. *Expenses:* Tuition, state resident: full-time $3348. Tuition, nonresident: full-time $12,933. *Required fees:* $3155. *Financial support:* Fellowships, research assistantships with full and partial tuition reimbursements, teaching assistantships with full and partial tuition reimbursements, career-related internships or fieldwork, institutionally sponsored loans, scholarships/grants, and unspecified assistantships available. Financial award application deadline: 3/31; financial award applicants required to submit FAFSA. *Unit head:* Dr. Judy Neubrander, Director, 828-227-3521, Fax: 828-227-7052, E-mail: jneubrander@email.wcu.edu. *Application contact:* Admissions Specialist for Nursing, 828-227-7398, Fax: 828-227-7480, E-mail: gradsch@email.wcu.edu. Web site: http://www.wcu.edu/4193.asp.

Western Connecticut State University, Division of Graduate Studies, School of Professional Studies, Nursing Department, Danbury, CT 06810-6885. Offers adult nurse practitioner (MSN); clinical nurse specialist (MSN). *Accreditation:* AACN. Part-time programs available. *Faculty:* 3 full-time (all women). *Students:* 44 part-time (43 women); includes 8 minority (6 Black or African American, non-Hispanic/Latino; 1 Asian, non-Hispanic/Latino; 1 Hispanic/Latino). Average age 38. 27 applicants, 41% accepted, 9 enrolled. In 2011, 8 degrees awarded. *Degree requirements:* For master's, clinical component, thesis or research project, completion of program in 6 years. *Entrance requirements:* For master's, MAT (if GPA less than 3.0), bachelor's degree in nursing, minimum GPA of 3.0, previous course work in statistics and nursing research, RN license. Additional exam requirements/recommendations for international students: Recommended—TOEFL (minimum score 550 paper-based; 213 computer-based; 79 iBT), IELTS (minimum score 6). *Application deadline:* For fall admission, 8/5 priority date for domestic students; for spring admission, 1/5 for domestic students. Applications are processed on a rolling basis. Application fee: $50. *Expenses:* Contact institution. *Financial support:* Scholarships/grants available. Financial award application deadline: 5/1; financial award applicants required to submit FAFSA. *Faculty research:* evaluating effectiveness of Reiki and acupressure on stress reduction. *Unit head:* Dr. Karen Daley, Graduate Coordinator, 203-837-8563, Fax: 203-837-8550, E-mail: daleyk@wcsu.edu. *Application contact:* Chris Shankle, Associate Director of Graduate Studies, 203-837-9005, Fax: 203-837-8326, E-mail: shanklec@wcsu.edu. Web site: http://www.wcsu.edu/nursing/.

Western Kentucky University, Graduate Studies, College of Health and Human Services, School of Nursing, Bowling Green, KY 42101. Offers MSN. *Accreditation:* AACN. Part-time and evening/weekend programs available. *Degree requirements:* For master's, comprehensive exam, thesis optional. *Entrance requirements:* For master's, GRE General Test, minimum GPA of 2.75. Additional exam requirements/ recommendations for international students: Required—TOEFL (minimum score 555

paper-based; 213 computer-based; 79 iBT). *Faculty research:* Folic acid, disease and injury prevention, rural mobile health, mental health issues.

Western Michigan University, Graduate College, College of Health and Human Services, Bronson School of Nursing, Kalamazoo, MI 49008. Offers MSN. *Accreditation:* AACN.

Western University of Health Sciences, College of Graduate Nursing, Doctor of Nursing Practice Program, Pomona, CA 91766-1854. Offers DNP. Postbaccalaureate distance learning degree programs offered (minimal on-campus study). *Faculty:* 5 full-time (4 women). *Students:* 76 full-time (68 women); includes 35 minority (9 Black or African American, non-Hispanic/Latino; 17 Asian, non-Hispanic/Latino; 9 Hispanic/Latino), 2 international. Average age 49. 33 applicants, 55% accepted, 16 enrolled. In 2011, 25 doctorates awarded. *Degree requirements:* For doctorate, project. *Entrance requirements:* For doctorate, MSN or master's degree in related field, or nurse practitioner, minimum GPA of 3.0, 3 letters of recommendation. Additional exam requirements/recommendations for international students: Required—TOEFL. *Application deadline:* For fall admission, 3/1 for domestic students. Applications are processed on a rolling basis. Application fee: $60. *Unit head:* Karen J. Hanford, Dean, 909-469-5243, Fax: 909-469-5521, E-mail: khanford@westernu.edu. *Application contact:* Kathryn Ford, Director of Admissions/International Student Advisor, 909-469-5541, Fax: 909-469-5570, E-mail: admissions@westernu.edu. Web site: http://www.westernu.edu/nursing-dnp.

Western University of Health Sciences, College of Graduate Nursing, Master of Science in Nursing Program, Pomona, CA 91766-1854. Offers administrative nurse leader (MSN); clinical nurse leader (MSN); degree completion (MSN); entry-level (MSN); family nurse practitioner (MSN); nursing (MSN). *Faculty:* 12 full-time (all women), 18 part-time/adjunct (16 women). *Students:* 262 full-time (228 women), 12 part-time (all women); includes 150 minority (22 Black or African American, non-Hispanic/Latino; 2 American Indian or Alaska Native, non-Hispanic/Latino; 83 Asian, non-Hispanic/Latino; 33 Hispanic/Latino; 10 Two or more races, non-Hispanic/Latino), 4 international. Average age 31. 485 applicants, 38% accepted, 104 enrolled. In 2011, 55 master's awarded. *Entrance requirements:* For master's, BSN, minimum GPA of 3.0, 3 letters of recommendation. Additional exam requirements/recommendations for international students: Required—TOEFL. *Application deadline:* For fall admission, 3/1 for domestic students. Applications are processed on a rolling basis. Application fee: $60. *Unit head:* Karen J. Hanford, Dean, 909-469-5243, Fax: 909-469-5521, E-mail: khanford@westernu.edu. *Application contact:* Kathryn Ford, Director of Admissions/International Student Advisor, 909-469-5541, Fax: 909-469-5570, E-mail: admissions@westernu.edu.

Westminster College, School of Nursing and Health Sciences, Salt Lake City, UT 84105-3697. Offers family nurse practitioner (MSN); nurse anesthesia (MSNA); nurse education (MSNED); nursing (MSN); public health (MPH). *Accreditation:* AACN; AANA/CANAEP. *Faculty:* 13 full-time (7 women), 7 part-time/adjunct (4 women). *Students:* 102 full-time (54 women), 16 part-time (12 women); includes 9 minority (2 Black or African American, non-Hispanic/Latino; 1 American Indian or Alaska Native, non-Hispanic/Latino; 5 Asian, non-Hispanic/Latino; 1 Hispanic/Latino), 1 international. Average age 34. 106 applicants, 64% accepted, 38 enrolled. In 2011, 53 master's awarded. *Degree requirements:* For master's, clinical practicum, 504 clinical practice hours. *Entrance requirements:* For master's, GRE, resume, Utah RN license in good standing, minimum GPA of 3.0, 3 letters of reference, BSN from accredited nursing program, proof of clear state and federal background check, drug test results, personal interview, current PALS certification, current ACLS certification. Additional exam requirements/recommendations for international students: Required—TOEFL (minimum score 600 paper-based; 250 computer-based; 100 iBT), IELTS (minimum score 7). *Application deadline:* Applications are processed on a rolling basis. Application fee: $50. Electronic applications accepted. *Expenses:* Contact institution. *Financial support:* In 2011–12, 11 students received support. Career-related internships or fieldwork and tuition reimbursement, tuition remission available. Support available to part-time students. Financial award applicants required to submit FAFSA. *Faculty research:* Collaborative testing in nursing: student outcomes and perspectives, Implementing New Educational Paradigms into Pre-Licensure Nursing Curricula conference presentation. *Unit head:* Dr. Sheryl Steadman, Dean, 801-832-2164, Fax: 801-832-3110, E-mail: ssteadman@westminstercollege.edu. *Application contact:* Dr. Gary Daynes, Vice President for Strategic Outreach and Enrollment, 801-832-2200, Fax: 801-832-3101, E-mail: admission@westminstercollege.edu. Web site: http://www.westminstercollege.edu/msn.

West Texas A&M University, College of Nursing and Health Sciences, Department of Nursing, Canyon, TX 79016-0001. Offers family nurse practitioner (MSN); nursing (MSN). *Accreditation:* AACN. Part-time programs available. Postbaccalaureate distance learning degree programs offered (minimal on-campus study). *Degree requirements:* For master's, comprehensive exam, thesis optional. *Entrance requirements:* For master's, GRE General Test, bachelor's degree in nursing, minimum GPA of 3.0 in last 60 hours. Additional exam requirements/recommendations for international students: Required—TOEFL (minimum score 550 paper-based). Electronic applications accepted. *Faculty research:* Family-focused nursing, nursing traineeship, professional nursing.

West Virginia University, School of Nursing, Morgantown, WV 26506. Offers nurse practitioner (Certificate); nursing (MSN, DNP, PhD). *Accreditation:* AACN. Part-time programs available. Postbaccalaureate distance learning degree programs offered (minimal on-campus study). *Degree requirements:* For master's, thesis or alternative; for doctorate, comprehensive exam, thesis/dissertation. *Entrance requirements:* For master's, minimum GPA of 3.0, current U.S. RN license, BSN, course work in statistics and physical assessment, GRE General Test; for doctorate, GRE General Test (PhD), minimum graduate GPA of 3.0, minimum grade of B in graduate statistics course work. Additional exam requirements/recommendations for international students: Required—TOEFL. Electronic applications accepted. *Expenses:* Contact institution. *Faculty research:* Rural primary health/health promotion, parent/child/women's health, cardiovascular risk reduction, complementary health modalities, breast cancer detection-care.

West Virginia Wesleyan College, Department of Nursing, Buckhannon, WV 26201. Offers MS.

Wheeling Jesuit University, Department of Nursing, Wheeling, WV 26003-6295. Offers MSN. *Accreditation:* AACN. Part-time and evening/weekend programs available. Postbaccalaureate distance learning degree programs offered (minimal on-campus study). *Faculty:* 3 full-time (all women), 7 part-time/adjunct (6 women). *Students:* 11 full-time (all women), 139 part-time (124 women); includes 3 minority (2 Black or African American, non-Hispanic/Latino; 1 Hispanic/Latino). Average age 36. 123 applicants, 57% accepted, 52 enrolled. In 2011, 34 master's awarded. *Degree requirements:* For master's, comprehensive exam (for some programs), thesis (for some programs). *Entrance requirements:* For master's, GRE General Test or MAT, BSN, minimum GPA of 3.0, course work in research and statistics, U.S. nursing license. Additional exam requirements/recommendations for international students: Required—TOEFL (minimum score 600 paper-based; 250 computer-based; 100 iBT). *Application deadline:* For fall admission, 8/1 priority date for domestic students, 7/15 for international students; for spring admission, 12/15 priority date for domestic students, 12/1 for international

students. Applications are processed on a rolling basis. Application fee: $25. Electronic applications accepted. Application fee is waived when completed online. *Expenses: Tuition:* Full-time $9720; part-time $540 per credit hour. *Required fees:* $250. *Financial support:* In 2011–12, 10 students received support. Scholarships/grants and unspecified assistantships available. Financial award application deadline: 8/1; financial award applicants required to submit FAFSA. *Faculty research:* Spirituality, obesity in women, mentorship. *Unit head:* Dr. Monica Kennison, Director of Nursing, 304-243-4411, Fax: 304-243-2243, E-mail: mkennison@wju.edu. *Application contact:* Cynthia Hunter, Adult Admissions Counselor, 304-243-2359, Fax: 304-243-2397, E-mail: chunter@wju.edu. Web site: http://www.wju.edu/academics/nur/.

Wichita State University, Graduate School, College of Health Professions, School of Nursing, Wichita, KS 67260. Offers nursing (MSN); nursing practice (DNP); MSN/MBA. *Accreditation:* AACN. Part-time programs available. *Expenses:* Tuition, state resident: full-time $4746; part-time $263.65 per credit. Tuition, nonresident: full-time $11,669; part-time $648.30 per credit. *Faculty research:* Adolescent pregnancy, alcoholism, arthritis and chronic disease, health practices of elderly, diabetes. *Unit head:* Dr. Betty Smith-Campbell, Chairperson, 316-978-3610, Fax: 316-978-3025, E-mail: betty.smith-campbell@wichita.edu. *Application contact:* Dr. Alicia Huckstadt, Graduate Coordinator, 316-978-3610, Fax: 316-978-3025, E-mail: alicia.huckstadt@wichita.edu. Web site: http://www.wichita.edu/.

Widener University, School of Nursing, Chester, PA 19013-5792. Offers MSN, DN Sc, PhD, PMC. *Accreditation:* AACN; NLN (one or more programs are accredited). Part-time and evening/weekend programs available. *Degree requirements:* For doctorate, thesis/dissertation. *Entrance requirements:* For master's, GRE General Test, BSN, undergraduate course in statistics; for doctorate, GRE General Test, MSN, undergraduate course in statistics. Electronic applications accepted. *Expenses:* Contact institution. *Faculty research:* Women's health leadership, nursing education, research utilization, program evaluation, health promotion.

Wilkes University, College of Graduate and Professional Studies, Nesbitt College of Pharmacy and Nursing, Department of Nursing, Wilkes-Barre, PA 18766-0002. Offers MSN, DNP. *Accreditation:* AACN. Part-time and evening/weekend programs available. *Students:* 5 full-time (4 women), 87 part-time (81 women); includes 15 minority (8 Black or African American, non-Hispanic/Latino; 3 Asian, non-Hispanic/Latino; 1 Hispanic/Latino; 3 Two or more races, non-Hispanic/Latino). Average age 47. In 2011, 19 master's awarded. *Entrance requirements:* Additional exam requirements/recommendations for international students: Required—TOEFL (minimum score 550 paper-based; 213 computer-based; 79 iBT). *Application deadline:* Applications are processed on a rolling basis. Application fee: $45. Electronic applications accepted. *Financial support:* Federal Work-Study and unspecified assistantships available. Financial award application deadline: 3/1; financial award applicants required to submit FAFSA. *Unit head:* Dr. Mary Ann Merrigan, Chair, 570-408-4070, Fax: 570-408-7807, E-mail: maryann.merrigan@wilkes.edu. *Application contact:* Erin Sutzko, Director of Extended Learning, 570-408-4253, Fax: 570-408-7846, E-mail: erin.sutzko@wilkes.edu. Web site: http://www.wilkes.edu/pages/391.asp.

William Carey University, School of Nursing, Hattiesburg, MS 39401-5499. Offers MSN. *Accreditation:* AACN. Part-time programs available. *Degree requirements:* For master's, thesis or alternative. *Entrance requirements:* For master's, GRE, minimum GPA of 3.0, RN license. Additional exam requirements/recommendations for international students: Required—TOEFL (minimum score 500 paper-based; 213 computer-based).

William Paterson University of New Jersey, College of Science and Health, Wayne, NJ 07470-8420. Offers biotechnology (MS); communication disorders (MS); general biology (MS); nursing (MSN). Part-time and evening/weekend programs available. *Entrance requirements:* For master's, GRE General Test, minimum GPA of 2.75. Electronic applications accepted. *Faculty research:* Plant tissue culture, DNA cloning, cellular structure, language development, speech and hearing science.

Wilmington University, College of Health Professions, New Castle, DE 19720-6491. Offers adult nurse practitioner (MSN); family nurse practitioner (MSN); gerontology nurse practitioner (MSN); nursing (MSN); nursing leadership (MSN); nursing practice (DNP). *Accreditation:* AACN. Part-time programs available. *Faculty:* 3 full-time (all women). *Students:* 30 full-time (all women), 270 part-time (241 women). Average age 38. *Degree requirements:* For master's, thesis. *Entrance requirements:* For master's, BSN, RN license, interview, 3 letters of recommendation. Additional exam requirements/recommendations for international students: Required—TOEFL (minimum score 500 paper-based; 173 computer-based). *Application deadline:* For fall admission, 4/1 for domestic students; for spring admission, 9/1 for domestic students. Applications are processed on a rolling basis. Application fee: $35. Electronic applications accepted. *Expenses: Tuition:* Part-time $534 per credit hour. *Required fees:* $25 per term. *Financial support:* Fellowships with tuition reimbursements and traineeships available. Financial award applicants required to submit FAFSA. *Faculty research:* Outcomes assessment, student writing ability. *Unit head:* Denise Z. Westbrook, Dean, 302-356-6915, E-mail: denise.z.westbrook@wilmu.edu. *Application contact:* Chris Ferguson, Director of Admissions, 302-356-4636 Ext. 256, Fax: 302-328-5164, E-mail: inquire@wilmcoll.edu. Web site: http://www.wilmu.edu/health/.

Winona State University, College of Nursing and Health Sciences, Winona, MN 55987. Offers adult nurse practitioner (MS, Post Master's Certificate); clinical nurse specialist (MS, Post Master's Certificate); family nurse practitioner (MS, Post Master's Certificate); nurse administrator (MS); nurse educator (MS, Post Master's Certificate); nursing (DNP). *Accreditation:* AACN. Part-time programs available. Postbaccalaureate distance learning degree programs offered (no on-campus study). *Students:* 75 full-time (70 women), 25 part-time (22 women); includes 11 minority (4 Black or African American, non-Hispanic/Latino; 5 Asian, non-Hispanic/Latino; 1 Hispanic/Latino; 1 Two or more races, non-Hispanic/Latino), 2 international. Average age 34. In 2011, 26 master's, 2 doctorates, 3 other advanced degrees awarded. *Degree requirements:* For master's, thesis; for doctorate, capstone. *Entrance requirements:* For master's, GRE (if GPA less than 3.0). Additional exam requirements/recommendations for international students: Required—TOEFL (minimum score 550 paper-based). *Application deadline:* For fall admission, 12/1 for domestic and international students. Application fee: $20. *Financial support:* Research assistantships with partial tuition reimbursements, Federal Work-Study, traineeships, and unspecified assistantships available. Support available to part-time students. Financial award application deadline: 8/15; financial award applicants required to submit FAFSA. *Unit head:* Dr. William J. McBreen, Dean, 507-457-5122, E-mail: wmcbreen@winona.edu. *Application contact:* Patricia Cichosz, Office Manager, Graduate Studies, 507-457-5038, E-mail: pcichosz@winona.edu.

Winston-Salem State University, Program in Nursing, Winston-Salem, NC 27110-0003. Offers MSN. *Accreditation:* AACN. Part-time and evening/weekend programs available. Postbaccalaureate distance learning degree programs offered. *Entrance requirements:* For master's, GRE, MAT, resume, NC or state compact license, 3 letters of recommendation. Electronic applications accepted. *Faculty research:* Elimination of health care disparities.

Wright State University, School of Graduate Studies, College of Nursing and Health, Program in Nursing, Dayton, OH 45435. Offers acute care nurse practitioner (MS); administration of nursing and health care systems (MS); adult health (MS); child and adolescent health (MS); community health (MS); family nurse practitioner (MS); nurse practitioner (MS); school nurse (MS); MBA/MS. *Accreditation:* AACN. Part-time and evening/weekend programs available. *Degree requirements:* For master's, thesis or alternative. *Entrance requirements:* For master's, GRE General Test, BSN from NLN-accredited college, Ohio RN license. Additional exam requirements/recommendations for international students: Required—TOEFL. *Faculty research:* Clinical nursing and health, teaching, caring, pain administration, informatics and technology.

Xavier University, College of Social Sciences, Health and Education, School of Nursing, Cincinnati, OH 45207. Offers clinical nurse leader (MSN); education (MSN); forensic nursing (MSN); healthcare law (MSN); informatics (MSN); nursing administration (MSN); school nursing (MSN); MSN/M Ed; MSN/MBA; MSN/MS. *Accreditation:* AACN. Part-time and evening/weekend programs available. *Faculty:* 13 full-time (all women), 10 part-time/adjunct (all women). *Students:* 69 full-time (66 women), 158 part-time (156 women); includes 30 minority (19 Black or African American, non-Hispanic/Latino; 2 American Indian or Alaska Native, non-Hispanic/Latino; 4 Asian, non-Hispanic/Latino; 3 Hispanic/Latino; 2 Two or more races, non-Hispanic/Latino). Average age 38. 117 applicants, 81% accepted, 71 enrolled. In 2011, 63 master's awarded. *Degree requirements:* For master's, thesis, scholarly project. *Entrance requirements:* For master's, GRE. Additional exam requirements/recommendations for international students: Required—TOEFL. *Application deadline:* Applications are processed on a rolling basis. Application fee: $35. Electronic applications accepted. *Expenses: Tuition:* Part-time $576 per credit hour. *Financial support:* In 2011–12, 88 students received support. Applicants required to submit FAFSA. *Faculty research:* Clinical nurse leader, simulation, employment satisfaction, nontraditional students, holistic nursing. *Unit head:* Dr. Susan M. Schmidt, Director, 513-745-3815, Fax: 513-745-1087, E-mail: schmidt@xavier.edu. *Application contact:* Marilyn Volk Gomez, Director of Nursing Student Services, 513-745-4392, Fax: 513-745-1087, E-mail: gomez@xavier.edu. Web site: http://www.xavier.edu/msn/.

Yale University, School of Nursing, New Haven, CT 06536. Offers MSN, PhD, Post Master's Certificate, MAR/MSN, MSN/M Div, MSN/MPH. *Accreditation:* AACN. Part-time programs available. Postbaccalaureate distance learning degree programs offered (minimal on-campus study). Terminal master's awarded for partial completion of doctoral program. *Degree requirements:* For master's, thesis; for doctorate, comprehensive exam, thesis/dissertation. *Entrance requirements:* For master's, GRE General Test, bachelor's degree; for doctorate, GRE General Test, MSN; for Post Master's Certificate, MSN. Additional exam requirements/recommendations for international students: Required—TOEFL or IELTS. Electronic applications accepted. *Expenses:* Contact institution. *Faculty research:* Family-based care, chronic illness, primary care, development, policy.

York College of Pennsylvania, Department of Nursing, York, PA 17405-7199. Offers adult nurse practitioner (MS); certified nurse anesthetist (MS); clinical nurse specialist (MS), including education: administration; nurse educator (MS); nursing (DNP). *Accreditation:* AACN; AANA/CANAEP. Part-time and evening/weekend programs available. *Faculty:* 10 full-time (all women), 9 part-time/adjunct (6 women). *Students:* 31 full-time (23 women), 50 part-time (43 women); includes 4 minority (2 Black or African American, non-Hispanic/Latino; 2 Asian, non-Hispanic/Latino), 1 international. Average age 36. 49 applicants, 53% accepted, 20 enrolled. In 2011, 17 master's awarded. *Entrance requirements:* For master's, GRE General Test, minimum GPA of 3.0 with NLNAC or CCNE major. Additional exam requirements/recommendations for international students: Required—TOEFL (minimum score 530 paper-based; 200 computer-based; 72 iBT). *Application deadline:* For fall admission, 7/15 priority date for domestic students; for spring admission, 11/15 priority date for domestic students. Applications are processed on a rolling basis. Application fee: $50. Electronic applications accepted. *Expenses: Tuition:* Full-time $12,060; part-time $670 per credit hour. *Required fees:* $340 per semester. Tuition and fees vary according to degree level. *Financial support:* Federal Work-Study available. *Faculty research:* Employer and faculty beliefs about concepts in RN-BS education, evaluating effectiveness of mental health partnerships in psychiatric settings. *Unit head:* Dr. Linda Pugh, Graduate Program Director, 717-815-1243, E-mail: lwarner@ycp.edu. *Application contact:* Nancy Spataro, Director of Admissions, 717-815-1600, Fax: 717-849-1607, E-mail: admissions@ycp.edu. Web site: http://www.ycp.edu/academics/academic-departments/nursing/.

York University, Faculty of Graduate Studies, Faculty of Health, Program in Nursing, Toronto, ON M3J 1P3, Canada. Offers M Sc N.

Youngstown State University, Graduate School, Bitonte College of Health and Human Services, Department of Nursing, Youngstown, OH 44555-0001. Offers MSN. *Accreditation:* NLN. Part-time and evening/weekend programs available. *Degree requirements:* For master's, thesis optional. *Entrance requirements:* For master's, GRE General Test, BSN, CPR certification. Additional exam requirements/recommendations for international students: Required—TOEFL.

Acute Care/Critical Care Nursing

Allen College, Program in Nursing, Waterloo, IA 50703. Offers acute care nurse practitioner (MSN, Post-Master's Certificate); adult nurse practitioner (MSN, Post-Master's Certificate); adult psychiatric-mental health nurse practitioner (MSN, Post-Master's Certificate); family nurse practitioner (MSN, Post-Master's Certificate); gerontological nurse practitioner (MSN, Post-Master's Certificate); health education (MSN); leadership in health care delivery (MSN, Post-Master's Certificate); nursing (DNP). *Accreditation:* AACN; NLN. Part-time programs available. *Faculty:* 3 full-time (all women), 16 part-time/adjunct (all women). *Students:* 34 full-time (31 women), 110 part-time (106 women); includes 5 minority (2 Asian, non-Hispanic/Latino; 3 Hispanic/Latino). Average age 36. 156 applicants, 64% accepted, 76 enrolled. In 2011, 61 master's, 1

other advanced degree awarded. *Degree requirements:* For master's, thesis optional. *Entrance requirements:* For master's, minimum GPA of 3.0; for doctorate, minimum GPA of 3.25 in graduate coursework. Additional exam requirements/recommendations for international students: Recommended—TOEFL (minimum score 550 paper-based), IELTS. *Application deadline:* For fall admission, 2/1 priority date for domestic students; for spring admission, 9/1 priority date for domestic students. Applications are processed on a rolling basis. Application fee: $50. Electronic applications accepted. *Expenses: Tuition:* Full-time $13,993; part-time $691 per credit hour. *Required fees:* $832; $69 per credit hour. One-time fee: $100 part-time. Part-time tuition and fees vary according to course load. *Financial support:* In 2011–12, 41 students received support. Institutionally sponsored loans, scholarships/grants, and traineeships available. Support available to part-time students. Financial award application deadline: 8/15; financial award applicants required to submit FAFSA. *Faculty research:* Pain and the aged, congestive heart failure. *Unit head:* Kendra Williams-Perez, Dean, School of Nursing, 319-226-2044, Fax: 319-226-2070, E-mail: williakb@ihs.org. *Application contact:* Michelle Koehn, Admissions Counselor, 319-226-2002, Fax: 319-226-2051, E-mail: koehnml@ihs.org. Web site: http://www.allencollege.edu/.

Barry University, School of Adult and Continuing Education, Division of Nursing, Program in Nurse Practitioner, Miami Shores, FL 33161-6695. Offers acute care nurse practitioner (MSN); family nurse practitioner (MSN); nurse practitioner (Certificate). *Accreditation:* AACN. Part-time and evening/weekend programs available. *Degree requirements:* For master's, research project or thesis. *Entrance requirements:* For master's, GRE General Test or MAT, BSN, minimum GPA of 3.0, course work in statistics. Electronic applications accepted. *Faculty research:* Child abuse, health beliefs, teenage pregnancy, cultural and clinical studies across the lifespan.

Case Western Reserve University, Frances Payne Bolton School of Nursing, Doctor of Nursing Practice Program, Cleveland, OH 44106. Offers acute care nurse practitioner (DNP); adult gerontology nurse practitioner (DNP); educational leadership (DNP); family nurse practitioner (DNP); family systems psychiatric mental health nursing (DNP); midwifery/family nursing (DNP); neonatal nurse practitioner (DNP); pediatric nurse practitioner (DNP); practice leadership (DNP); women's health nurse practitioner (DNP). *Students:* 73 full-time, 194 part-time; includes 11 minority (6 Black or African American, non-Hispanic/Latino; 3 Asian, non-Hispanic/Latino; 2 Hispanic/Latino). 122 applicants, 74% accepted, 49 enrolled. In 2011, 47 doctorates awarded. Terminal master's awarded for partial completion of doctoral program. *Degree requirements:* For doctorate, thesis/dissertation. *Entrance requirements:* For doctorate, GRE General Test or MAT. Additional exam requirements/recommendations for international students: Required—TOEFL (minimum score 577 paper-based; 90 iBT), IELTS (minimum score 7). *Application deadline:* For fall admission, 6/1 priority date for domestic students, 6/1 for international students; for spring admission, 10/1 for domestic and international students. Applications are processed on a rolling basis. Application fee: $75. *Financial support:* In 2011–12, 6 students received support, including 1 teaching assistantship; research assistantships, Federal Work-Study, institutionally sponsored loans, and tuition waivers (partial) also available. Support available to part-time students. Financial award application deadline: 6/30; financial award applicants required to submit FAFSA. *Faculty research:* Clinical nursing, acute care, gerontology, mental health, critical care. *Unit head:* Dr. Donna Dowling, Director, 216-368-1869, Fax: 216-368-3542, E-mail: dad10@case.edu. *Application contact:* Donna Hassik, Admissions Coordinator, 216-368-5253, Fax: 216-368-0124, E-mail: dmh7@case.edu. Web site: http://fpb.case.edu/DNP/.

Case Western Reserve University, Frances Payne Bolton School of Nursing, Master's Programs in Nursing, Nurse Practitioner Program, Cleveland, OH 44106. Offers acute care cardiovascular nursing (MSN); acute care nurse practitioner (MSN); acute care/flight nurse (MSN); adult gerontology nurse practitioner (MSN); family nurse practitioner (MSN); neonatal nurse practitioner (MSN); pediatric nurse practitioner (MSN); women's health nurse practitioner (MSN). *Accreditation:* NLN. Part-time programs available. Postbaccalaureate distance learning degree programs offered (minimal on-campus study). *Faculty:* 54 full-time (50 women), 5 part-time/adjunct (3 women). *Students:* 89 full-time (69 women), 77 part-time (67 women); includes 17 minority (11 Black or African American, non-Hispanic/Latino; 5 Asian, non-Hispanic/Latino; 1 Hispanic/Latino), 17 international. Average age 35. 75 applicants, 84% accepted, 42 enrolled. In 2011, 34 master's awarded. *Degree requirements:* For master's, thesis optional. *Entrance requirements:* For master's, GRE General Test or MAT. Additional exam requirements/recommendations for international students: Required—TOEFL (minimum score 577 paper-based; 90 iBT), IELTS (minimum score 7). *Application deadline:* For fall admission, 6/1 for domestic students; for spring admission, 10/1 for domestic students. Applications are processed on a rolling basis. Application fee: $75. *Financial support:* In 2011–12, 7 teaching assistantships were awarded; research assistantships, institutionally sponsored loans, and tuition waivers (partial) also available. Support available to part-time students. Financial award application deadline: 6/30; financial award applicants required to submit FAFSA. *Faculty research:* Positive and negative mood states in parents of twins, effect of a care path on chronic obstructive pulmonary disease home care. *Unit head:* Dr. Carol Savrin, Director, 216-368-5304, Fax: 216-368-3542, E-mail: cls18@case.edu. *Application contact:* Donna Hassik, Admissions Coordinator, 216-368-5253, Fax: 216-368-0124, E-mail: dmh7@case.edu. Web site: http://fpb.cwru.edu/MSN/majors.shtm.

The College of New Rochelle, Graduate School, Program in Nursing, New Rochelle, NY 10805-2308. Offers acute care nurse practitioner (MS, Certificate); clinical specialist in holistic nursing (MS, Certificate); family nurse practitioner (MS, Certificate); nursing and health care management (MS); nursing education (Certificate). *Accreditation:* AACN. Part-time programs available. *Entrance requirements:* For master's, GRE General Test or MAT, BSN, malpractice insurance, minimum GPA of 3.0, RN license. *Expenses:* Contact institution. *Faculty research:* Holistic modalities, academic success variables.

Columbia University, School of Nursing, Program in Acute Care Nurse Practitioner, New York, NY 10032. Offers MS, Adv C. *Accreditation:* AACN. Part-time programs available. *Entrance requirements:* For master's, GRE General Test, 1 year of clinical experience (preferred), BSN; for Adv C, MSN. Electronic applications accepted.

Drexel University, College of Nursing and Health Professions, Division of Graduate Nursing, Philadelphia, PA 19104-2875. Offers adult acute care (MSN); adult psychiatric/mental health (MSN); advanced practice nursing (MSN); clinical trials research (MSN); family nurse practitioner (MSN); leadership in health systems management (MSN); nursing education (MSN); pediatric primary care (MSN); women's health (MSN). *Accreditation:* AACN; NLN. Electronic applications accepted.

Duke University, School of Nursing, Durham, NC 27708-0586. Offers adult acute care (Certificate); adult cardiovascular (Certificate); adult oncology (Certificate); adult primary care (Certificate); clinical nurse specialist (MSN), including adult oncology, gerontology, neonatal, pediatric; clinical research management (MSN, Certificate); family (Certificate); gerontology (Certificate); health and nursing ministries (MSN, Certificate); health systems leadership and outcomes (Certificate); neonatal (Certificate); neonatal/pediatric in rural health (MSN, Certificate); nurse anesthetist (MSN, Certificate); nurse practitioner (MSN), including adult acute care, adult cardiovascular, adult oncology, adult primary care, family, gerontology, neonatal, pediatric, pediatric acute care; nursing (DNP, PhD); nursing and healthcare leadership (MSN); nursing education (MSN);

nursing informatics (MSN, Certificate); pediatric (Certificate); pediatric acute care (Certificate); MBA/MSN; MSN/MCM. *Accreditation:* AACN; AANA/CANAEP. Part-time and evening/weekend programs available. Postbaccalaureate distance learning degree programs offered (minimal on-campus study). *Faculty:* 56 full-time (47 women), 2 part-time/adjunct (1 woman). *Students:* 127 full-time (108 women), 395 part-time (358 women); includes 92 minority (42 Black or African American, non-Hispanic/Latino; 3 American Indian or Alaska Native, non-Hispanic/Latino; 21 Asian, non-Hispanic/Latino; 14 Hispanic/Latino; 12 Two or more races, non-Hispanic/Latino), 10 international. Average age 36. 432 applicants, 45% accepted, 143 enrolled. In 2011, 117 master's, 29 doctorates, 32 other advanced degrees awarded. Terminal master's awarded for partial completion of doctoral program. *Degree requirements:* For master's, thesis optional; for doctorate, capstone project. *Entrance requirements:* For master's, GRE General Test, 1 year of nursing experience, BSN, minimum GPA of 3.0, previous course work in statistics; for doctorate, BSN or MSN, minimum GPA of 3.0, portfolio; for Certificate, MSN. Additional exam requirements/recommendations for international students: Required—TOEFL (minimum score 550 paper-based; 213 computer-based). *Application deadline:* For fall admission, 12/1 for domestic and international students; for spring admission, 5/1 for domestic and international students. Application fee: $50. Electronic applications accepted. *Expenses:* Contact institution. *Financial support:* Career-related internships or fieldwork, institutionally sponsored loans, scholarships/grants, traineeships, and tuition waivers (partial) available. Support available to part-time students. Financial award application deadline: 4/1; financial award applicants required to submit FAFSA. *Faculty research:* Cardiovascular disease, caregiver skill training, data mining, prostate cancer, neonatal immune system. *Total annual research expenditures:* $4.7 million. *Unit head:* Dr. Catherine L. Gilliss, Dean/Vice Chancellor for Nursing Affairs, 919-684-9444, Fax: 919-684-9414, E-mail: gilli025@mc.duke.edu. *Application contact:* Bebe T. Mills, Director of Admissions, 919-684-9151, Fax: 919-668-4693, E-mail: mills031@mc.duke.edu. Web site: http://www.nursing.duke.edu/.

Georgetown University, Graduate School of Arts and Sciences, School of Nursing and Health Studies, Washington, DC 20057. Offers acute care nurse practitioner (MS); clinical nurse specialist (MS); family nurse practitioner (MS); nurse anesthesia (MS); nurse-midwifery (MS); nursing education (MS). *Accreditation:* AACN; AANA/CANAEP; ACNM/ACME. *Degree requirements:* For master's, thesis optional. *Entrance requirements:* For master's, GRE General Test or MAT, bachelor's degree in nursing from NLN-accredited school, minimum undergraduate GPA of 3.0. Additional exam requirements/recommendations for international students: Required—TOEFL.

Grand Canyon University, College of Nursing, Phoenix, AZ 85017-1097. Offers acute care nurse practitioner (MS, PMC); clinical nurse specialist (PMC), including clinical nurse specialist, education; family nurse practitioner (MS); leadership in health care systems (MS); nurse education (MS). *Accreditation:* AACN. Part-time and evening/weekend programs available. Postbaccalaureate distance learning degree programs offered (no on-campus study). *Degree requirements:* For master's and PMC, comprehensive exam (for some programs). *Entrance requirements:* For master's, minimum cumulative and science course undergraduate GPA of 3.0. Additional exam requirements/recommendations for international students: Required—TOEFL (minimum score 575 paper-based; 233 computer-based; 90 iBT), IELTS (minimum score 7).

Indiana University–Purdue University Indianapolis, School of Nursing, Indianapolis, IN 46202-2896. Offers acute care nurse practitioner (MSN); adult health clinical nurse specialist (MSN); adult health nursing (MSN), including adult clinical nurse specialist; adult nurse practitioner (MSN); adult psychiatric/mental health nursing (MSN); child psychiatric/mental health nursing (MSN); community health nursing (MSN); family nurse practitioner (MSN); neonatal nurse practitioner (MSN); nursing (MSN, DNP), including nursing education (MSN); nursing (MSN), including nursing administration; nursing science (PhD); pediatric clinical nurse specialist (MSN); women's health nurse practitioner (MSN); MSN/MPA; MSN/MPH. *Accreditation:* AACN; NLN (one or more programs are accredited). Part-time programs available. *Faculty:* 85 full-time (82 women), 60 part-time/adjunct (all women). *Students:* 35 full-time (32 women), 360 part-time (340 women); includes 47 minority (28 Black or African American, non-Hispanic/Latino; 9 Asian, non-Hispanic/Latino; 4 Hispanic/Latino; 1 Native Hawaiian or other Pacific Islander, non-Hispanic/Latino; 5 Two or more races, non-Hispanic/Latino), 5 international. Average age 38. 119 applicants, 76% accepted, 54 enrolled. In 2011, 89 master's, 10 doctorates awarded. Terminal master's awarded for partial completion of doctoral program. *Degree requirements:* For master's, thesis; for doctorate, thesis/dissertation. *Entrance requirements:* For master's, minimum GPA of 3.0, RN license; for doctorate, GRE General Test, minimum GPA of 3.0, MSN, RN license, graduate statistics course with minimum B grade (not older than 3 years). Additional exam requirements/recommendations for international students: Required—TOEFL. *Application deadline:* For fall admission, 2/15 for domestic students; for spring admission, 9/15 for domestic students. Application fee: $55 ($65 for international students). *Financial support:* In 2011–12, 93 students received support, including 9 fellowships with full tuition reimbursements available (averaging $7,039 per year), 7 teaching assistantships with full tuition reimbursements available (averaging $5,300 per year); research assistantships with full tuition reimbursements available, Federal Work-Study, institutionally sponsored loans, scholarships/grants, and tuition waivers (full) also available. Support available to part-time students. Financial award application deadline: 5/1. *Faculty research:* Clinical science, health systems. *Total annual research expenditures:* $3 million. *Unit head:* Associate Dean for Graduate Programs, 317-274-2806, E-mail: nursing@iupui.edu. *Application contact:* Information Contact, 317-274-2806. Web site: http://nursing.iupui.edu/.

Inter American University of Puerto Rico, Arecibo Campus, Program in Nursing, Arecibo, PR 00614-4050. Offers critical care nursing (MSN); surgical nursing (MSN). *Entrance requirements:* For master's, EXADEP or GRE General Test or MAT, 2 letters of recommendation, bachelor's degree in nursing, minimum GPA of 2.5 in last 60 credits, minimum 1 year nursing experience, nursing license.

The Johns Hopkins University, School of Nursing, Nurse Practitioner Program, Baltimore, MD 21218-2699. Offers adult acute/critical care (MSN, Certificate); adult and pediatric primary care (MSN); adult or pediatric primary care (Certificate); emergency preparedness/disaster response (Certificate); family primary care (MSN, Certificate); women's health (Certificate). *Accreditation:* AACN; NLN (one or more programs are accredited). Part-time programs available. *Degree requirements:* For master's, thesis optional, scholarly project or portfolio. *Entrance requirements:* For master's, GRE, interview, minimum GPA of 3.0, BSN, Maryland RN license. Additional exam requirements/recommendations for international students: Required—TOEFL (minimum score 550 paper-based; 213 computer-based). Electronic applications accepted. *Expenses:* Contact institution. *Faculty research:* Community outreach, primary care of underserved populations, substance-abusing individuals, childhood violence, women's health.

Kent State University, College of Nursing, Kent, OH 44242-0001. Offers acute care nurse practitioner (MSN); adult nurse practitioner (MSN); clinical nurse specialist (MSN); family nurse practitioner (MSN); geriatric nurse practitioner (MSN); health care management (MSN); nurse educator (MSN); nursing (PhD); nursing practice (DNP); pediatric nurse practitioner (MSN); psychiatric/mental health nurse practitioner (MSN); women's health nurse practitioner (MSN). PhD program offered jointly with The

Acute Care/Critical Care Nursing

University of Akron. *Accreditation:* AACN. Part-time programs available. *Degree requirements:* For master's, thesis optional; for doctorate, comprehensive exam, thesis/dissertation. *Entrance requirements:* For master's, GRE (if undergraduate GPA less than 3.0), minimum GPA of 2.75; for doctorate, GRE, MSN. Additional exam requirements/recommendations for international students: Required—TOEFL. Electronic applications accepted. *Expenses:* Contact institution. *Faculty research:* Women and violence, methodological specialties, osteoporosis in women, new caregivers and the elderly.

Loyola University Chicago, Graduate School, Marcella Niehoff School of Nursing, Acute Care Nurse Practitioner Program, Chicago, IL 60660. Offers MSN. *Accreditation:* AACN. Part-time and evening/weekend programs available. *Students:* 10 full-time (8 women), 28 part-time (24 women); includes 3 minority (2 Black or African American, non-Hispanic/Latino; 1 Asian, non-Hispanic/Latino). Average age 34. 22 applicants, 82% accepted, 8 enrolled. In 2011, 17 master's awarded. *Degree requirements:* For master's, comprehensive exam or oral thesis defense. *Entrance requirements:* For master's, Illinois nursing license, BSN, minimum nursing GPA of 3.0, 3 letters of recommendation, 2,000 hours experience in acute care prior to clinical. *Application deadline:* Applications are processed on a rolling basis. Application fee: $40. Electronic applications accepted. *Expenses: Tuition:* Full-time $15,660; part-time $870 per credit hour. *Required fees:* $125 per semester. Tuition and fees vary according to course load and program. *Financial support:* Traineeships available. Financial award application deadline: 3/1. *Unit head:* Dr. Judith Jennrich, Associate Professor, 708-216-3813, E-mail: jjrennri@luc.edu. *Application contact:* Amy Weatherford, Enrollment Advisor, 708-216-3751, Fax: 708-216-9555, E-mail: aweatherford@luc.edu.

Marquette University, Graduate School, College of Nursing, Milwaukee, WI 53201-1881. Offers acute care nurse practitioner (Certificate); adult clinical nurse specialist (Certificate); adult nurse practitioner (Certificate); advanced practice nursing (MSN, DNP), including acute care, adults, neonatal nurse practitioner (MSN), nurse midwifery (DNP), nurse-midwifery (MSN), older adults, pediatrics acute care (DNP, PhD), pediatrics primary care; clinical nurse leader (MSN); gerontologic clinical nurse specialist (Certificate); gerontologic nurse practitioner (Certificate); health care systems leadership (MSN, DNP); nurse-midwifery (Certificate); nursing (PhD), including pediatrics acute care (DNP, PhD); pediatrics acute care (Certificate); pediatrics primary care (Certificate). *Accreditation:* AACN. *Faculty:* 32 full-time (30 women), 47 part-time/adjunct (all women). *Students:* 93 full-time (88 women), 244 part-time (220 women); includes 31 minority (9 Black or African American, non-Hispanic/Latino; 7 Asian, non-Hispanic/Latino; 8 Hispanic/Latino; 7 Two or more races, non-Hispanic/Latino), 1 international. Average age 30. 282 applicants, 57% accepted, 98 enrolled. In 2011, 76 master's, 8 doctorates, 7 other advanced degrees awarded. Terminal master's awarded for partial completion of doctoral program. *Degree requirements:* For master's, comprehensive exam, thesis or alternative. *Entrance requirements:* For master's, GRE General Test, BSN, Wisconsin RN license, official transcripts from all current and previous colleges/universities except Marquette, three completed recommendation forms, resume, written statement of professional goals; for doctorate, GRE General Test, official transcripts from all current and previous colleges/universities except Marquette, three letters of recommendation, resume, written statement of professional goals, sample of scholarly writing. Additional exam requirements/recommendations for international students: Required—TOEFL (minimum score 530 paper-based; 78 computer-based). *Application deadline:* For fall admission, 2/15 for domestic and international students. Application fee: $50. Electronic applications accepted. *Expenses: Tuition:* Full-time $17,010; part-time $945 per credit hour. Tuition and fees vary according to program. *Financial support:* In 2011–12, 41 students received support, including 1 fellowship with partial tuition reimbursement available (averaging $17,500 per year), 2 research assistantships with full tuition reimbursements available (averaging $13,285 per year), 8 teaching assistantships with full tuition reimbursements available (averaging $13,912 per year); career-related internships or fieldwork, Federal Work-Study, scholarships/grants, health care benefits, tuition waivers (partial), and unspecified assistantships also available. Support available to part-time students. Financial award application deadline: 2/15. *Faculty research:* Psychosocial adjustment to chronic illness, gerontology, reminiscence, health policy: uninsured and access, hospital care delivery systems. *Total annual research expenditures:* $312,575. *Unit head:* Dr. Margaret Callahan, Dean, 414-288-3800, Fax: 414-288-1578. *Application contact:* Karen Nest, Graduate Program Coordinator, 414-288-3810, Fax: 414-288-1578. Web site: http://www.marquette.edu/nursing/academicprograms-graduate.shtml.

New York University, College of Nursing, Doctor of Nursing Practice Program, New York, NY 10012-1019. Offers advanced practice nursing (DNP), including adult acute care, adult nurse practitioner/holistic nursing, adult nurse practitioner/palliative care nursing, adult primary care, adult primary care/geriatrics, family, geriatrics, mental health nursing, nurse-midwifery, pediatrics. Part-time and evening/weekend programs available. *Faculty:* 7 full-time (all women). *Students:* 23 part-time (19 women); includes 6 minority (4 Black or African American, non-Hispanic/Latino; 1 Asian, non-Hispanic/Latino; 1 Hispanic/Latino), 1 international. Average age 46. 20 applicants, 80% accepted, 11 enrolled. In 2011, 8 doctorates awarded. *Degree requirements:* For doctorate, thesis/dissertation. *Entrance requirements:* For doctorate, MS, RN license, interview, NP Certification. Additional exam requirements/recommendations for international students: Required—TOEFL, IELTS. *Application deadline:* For fall admission, 4/1 priority date for domestic students, 4/1 for international students. Applications are processed on a rolling basis. Application fee: $75. Electronic applications accepted. *Financial support:* In 2011–12, 15 students received support. Fellowships with full and partial tuition reimbursements available, institutionally sponsored loans, scholarships/grants, and tuition waivers (partial) available. Support available to part-time students. Financial award application deadline: 2/1; financial award applicants required to submit FAFSA. *Faculty research:* Elderly black diabetics, families and illness, oral systemic connection. *Unit head:* Dr. Jamesetta A. Newland, Director, 212-998-5319, Fax: 212-995-3143, E-mail: jan7@nyu.edu. *Application contact:* Gail Wolfmeyer, Assistant Director, Graduate Student Affairs and Admissions, 212-992-7653, Fax: 212-995-4302, E-mail: gail.wolfmeyer@nyu.edu.

New York University, College of Nursing, Programs in Advanced Practice Nursing, New York, NY 10012-1019. Offers advanced practice nursing: adult acute care (MS, Advanced Certificate); advanced practice nursing: adult nurse practitioner/holistic nurse practitioner (Advanced Certificate); advanced practice nursing: adult nurse practitioner/palliative care nurse practitioner (Advanced Certificate); advanced practice nursing: adult primary care (MS, Advanced Certificate); advanced practice nursing: family (MS, Advanced Certificate); advanced practice nursing: geriatrics (Advanced Certificate); advanced practice nursing: mental health (MS); advanced practice nursing: mental health nursing (Advanced Certificate); advanced practice nursing: pediatrics (MS, Advanced Certificate); nurse midwifery (MS, Advanced Certificate); nursing administration (MS, Advanced Certificate); nursing education (MS, Advanced Certificate); nursing informatics (MS, Advanced Certificate); MS/MPA; MS/MPH. *Accreditation:* AACN; ACNM/ACME. Part-time programs available. *Faculty:* 23 full-time (all women), 60 part-time/adjunct (47 women). *Students:* 27 full-time (23 women), 552 part-time (514 women); includes 251 minority (91 Black or African American, non-Hispanic/Latino; 115 Asian, non-Hispanic/Latino; 34 Hispanic/Latino; 11 Native Hawaiian or other Pacific Islander, non-Hispanic/Latino), 8 international. Average age 33. 325 applicants, 81% accepted, 179 enrolled. In 2011, 89 master's awarded. *Degree requirements:* For master's, thesis (for some programs). *Entrance requirements:* For master's, BS in nursing, AS in nursing with another BS/BA, interview, RN license, 1 year of clinical experience (3 for nursing education program); for Advanced Certificate, master's degree. Additional exam requirements/recommendations for international students: Required—TOEFL, IELTS. *Application deadline:* For fall admission, 7/1 priority date for domestic students, 7/1 for international students; for spring admission, 12/1 for domestic and international students. Applications are processed on a rolling basis. Application fee: $75. Electronic applications accepted. *Financial support:* In 2011–12, 36 students received support. Career-related internships or fieldwork, institutionally sponsored loans, scholarships/grants, traineeships, and tuition waivers (partial) available. Support available to part-time students. Financial award application deadline: 2/1; financial award applicants required to submit FAFSA. *Faculty research:* Elderly black diabetics, families and illness, oral systemic connection. *Unit head:* Dr. Judith Haber, Associate Dean, 212-998-9020, Fax: 212-995-3143, E-mail: jh33@nyu.edu. *Application contact:* Gail Wolfmeyer, Assistant Director, Graduate Student Affairs and Admissions, 212-992-7653, Fax: 212-995-4302, E-mail: gail.wolfmeyer@nyu.edu.

Northeastern University, Bouvé College of Health Sciences, School of Nursing, Program in Critical Care-Acute Care Nurse Practitioner, Boston, MA 02115-5096. Offers MS, CAGS, CAS. *Accreditation:* AACN. *Faculty:* 25 full-time, 4 part-time/adjunct. *Students:* 13 full-time, 16 part-time. 12 applicants, 75% accepted, 8 enrolled. In 2011, 12 master's awarded. *Degree requirements:* For master's, thesis or alternative. *Entrance requirements:* For master's, GRE General Test; for other advanced degree, MS in nursing. Additional exam requirements/recommendations for international students: Required—TOEFL (minimum score 100 iBT). *Application deadline:* For fall admission, 7/1 for domestic students. Applications are processed on a rolling basis. Application fee: $50. Electronic applications accepted. *Financial support:* Research assistantships with tuition reimbursements, teaching assistantships with tuition reimbursements, scholarships/grants, traineeships, and tuition waivers (partial) available. Financial award application deadline: 7/1; financial award applicants required to submit FAFSA. *Unit head:* Prof. John Kenna, Director, 617-373-6543, Fax: 617-373-6543, E-mail: j.kenna@neu.edu. *Application contact:* Margaret Schnabel, Director of Graduate Admissions, 617-373-2708, E-mail: bouvegrad@neu.edu. Web site: http://www.northeastern.edu/bouve/programs/cacutecare.html.

Northeastern University, Bouvé College of Health Sciences, School of Nursing, Program in Critical Care-Neonatal Nurse Practitioner, Boston, MA 02115-5096. Offers MS, CAS. *Accreditation:* AACN. *Faculty:* 25 full-time, 4 part-time/adjunct. *Students:* 4 full-time, 3 part-time. 7 applicants, 100% accepted, 5 enrolled. *Degree requirements:* For master's, thesis or alternative. *Entrance requirements:* For master's, GRE General Test, minimum GPA of 3.0, previous course work in statistics, 1-2 years of nursing experience, RN license, ICU experience. Additional exam requirements/recommendations for international students: Required—TOEFL (minimum score 100 iBT). *Application deadline:* For fall admission, 7/1 for domestic students. Application fee: $50. Electronic applications accepted. *Financial support:* Research assistantships, teaching assistantships, scholarships/grants, traineeships, and tuition waivers (partial) available. Financial award application deadline: 7/1; financial award applicants required to submit FAFSA. *Unit head:* Prof. Gretchen R. Hamn, Director, 617-373-6543, E-mail: g.hamn@neu.edu. *Application contact:* Margaret Schnabel, Director of Graduate Admissions, 617-373-2708, E-mail: bouvegrad@neu.edu. Web site: http://www.northeastern.edu/bouve/programs/cneonatal.html.

Ohio University, Graduate College, College of Health Sciences and Professions, School of Nursing, Athens, OH 45701-2979. Offers acute care nurse practitioner (MSN); acute care nurse practitioner and family nurse practitioner (MSN); acute care nurse practitioner and nurse administrator (MSN); acute care nurse practitioner and nurse educator (MSN); family nurse practitioner (MSN); nurse administrator (MSN); nurse administrator and family nurse practitioner (MSN); nurse educator (MSN); nurse educator and family nurse practitioner (MSN); nurse educator and nurse administrator (MSN). *Accreditation:* AACN. *Students:* 33 full-time (29 women), 91 part-time (84 women); includes 16 minority (8 Black or African American, non-Hispanic/Latino; 2 Asian, non-Hispanic/Latino; 1 Hispanic/Latino; 5 Two or more races, non-Hispanic/Latino), 3 international. 86 applicants, 86% accepted, 61 enrolled. In 2011, 24 master's awarded. *Degree requirements:* For master's, capstone project. *Entrance requirements:* For master's, GRE, bachelor's degree in nursing from an accredited college or university, minimum overall undergraduate GPA of 3.0, official transcripts, statement of goals and objectives, resume, 3 letters of recommendation. Additional exam requirements/recommendations for international students: Required—TOEFL (minimum score 550 paper-based; 80 iBT) or IELTS (minimum score 6.5). *Application deadline:* For fall admission, 3/1 priority date for domestic students, 2/1 for international students. Applications are processed on a rolling basis. Application fee: $50 ($55 for international students). Electronic applications accepted. *Financial support:* Research assistantships, Federal Work-Study, institutionally sponsored loans, and unspecified assistantships available. Financial award application deadline: 3/1. *Unit head:* Dr. Deborah Henderson, Professor and Interim Director, 740-593-4497, Fax: 740-593-0286, E-mail: hendersd@ohio.edu. *Application contact:* Cheryl Brimner, Administrative Associate, 740-593-4494, Fax: 740-593-0286, E-mail: brimner@ohio.edu. Web site: http://www.ohio.edu/chsp/nrse/index.cfm.

Purdue University Calumet, Graduate Studies Office, School of Nursing, Hammond, IN 46323-2094. Offers adult health clinical nurse specialist (MS); critical care clinical nurse specialist (MS); family nurse practitioner (MS); nurse executive (MS). *Accreditation:* AACN; NLN. Part-time programs available. Postbaccalaureate distance learning degree programs offered (minimal on-campus study). *Entrance requirements:* For master's, BSN. Additional exam requirements/recommendations for international students: Required—TOEFL. Electronic applications accepted. *Faculty research:* Adult health, cardiovascular and pulmonary nursing.

Rush University, College of Nursing, Department of Adult Health Nursing, Chicago, IL 60612-3832. Offers acute care nurse practitioner (MSN, Post-Master's Certificate); adult health nursing (DNP, PhD); adult nurse practitioner (MSN, Post-Master's Certificate); adult/gerontological nurse practitioner (MSN); anesthesia nurse practitioner (MSN, Post-Master's Certificate); critical care clinical specialist (MSN); gerontological nurse practitioner (MSN, Post-Master's Certificate); medical surgical clinical specialist (MSN). *Accreditation:* AACN; AANA/CANAEP (one or more programs are accredited). Part-time programs available. Postbaccalaureate distance learning degree programs offered (minimal on-campus study). Terminal master's awarded for partial completion of doctoral program. *Degree requirements:* For master's, capstone project; for doctorate, thesis/dissertation, DNP leadership project. *Entrance requirements:* For master's, GRE General Test (waived if nursing GPA is above 3.0 or cumulative GPA is above 3.25), interview; for doctorate, GRE General Test, interview, course work in statistics (PhD). Additional exam requirements/recommendations for international students: Required—TOEFL, TWE. Electronic applications accepted. *Faculty research:* Complementary/alternative medicine, critical care outcomes, cardiac risk reduction, Alzheimer's Disease, telehealth monitoring.

Rush University, College of Nursing, Department of Women's and Children's Health Nursing, Chicago, IL 60612-3832. Offers neonatal nurse practitioner (MSN, Post-

Master's Certificate); pediatric acute/chronic care nurse practitioner (MSN); pediatric clinical nurse specialist (MSN); pediatric nurse practitioner (MSN, Post-Master's Certificate); women's and children's health nursing (DNP, PhD). *Accreditation:* AACN. Part-time programs available. Postbaccalaureate distance learning degree programs offered (minimal on-campus study). Terminal master's awarded for partial completion of doctoral program. *Degree requirements:* For master's, capstone project; for doctorate, thesis/dissertation, DNP leadership project. *Entrance requirements:* For master's, GRE General Test (waived if nursing GPA is above 3.0 or cumulative GPA is above 3.25), interview; for doctorate, GRE General Test, interview, course work in statistics (PhD). Additional exam requirements/recommendations for international students: Required—TOEFL, TWE. Electronic applications accepted. *Faculty research:* Family-centered care, women's health, health outcomes of human milk feeding for VhBW infants.

Southern Adventist University, School of Nursing, Collegedale, TN 37315-0370. Offers acute care nurse practitioner (MSN); adult nurse practitioner (MSN); family nurse practitioner (MSN); nurse educator (MSN); MSN/MSBA. *Accreditation:* NLN. Part-time programs available. *Degree requirements:* For master's, thesis or project. *Entrance requirements:* For master's, RN license. Additional exam requirements/recommendations for international students: Required—TOEFL (minimum score 600 paper-based; 250 computer-based). Electronic applications accepted. *Faculty research:* Pain management, ethics, corporate wellness, caring spirituality, stress.

Texas Tech University Health Sciences Center, School of Nursing, Lubbock, TX 79430. Offers acute care nurse practitioner (MSN, Certificate); administration (MSN); advanced practice (DNP); education (MSN); executive leadership (DNP); family nurse practitioner (MSN, Certificate); geriatric nurse practitioner (MSN, Certificate); pediatric nurse practitioner (MSN, Certificate). *Accreditation:* AACN. Part-time programs available. Postbaccalaureate distance learning degree programs offered (minimal on-campus study). *Degree requirements:* For master's, thesis optional. *Entrance requirements:* For master's, minimum GPA of 3.0, 3 letters of reference, BSN, RN license; for Certificate, minimum GPA of 3.0, 3 letters of reference, RN license. Additional exam requirements/recommendations for international students: Required—TOEFL (minimum score 550 paper-based; 213 computer-based). *Faculty research:* Diabetes/obesity, nurse competency, disease management, intervention and measurements, health disparities.

Texas Woman's University, Graduate School, College of Nursing, Denton, TX 76201. Offers acute care nurse practitioner (MS); adult health clinical nurse specialist (MS); adult health nurse practitioner (MS); child health clinical nurse specialist (MS); clinical nurse leader (MS); family nurse practitioner (MS); health systems management (MS); nursing education (MS); nursing practice (DNP); nursing science (PhD); pediatric nurse practitioner (MS); women's health clinical nurse specialist (MS); women's health nurse practitioner (MS). *Accreditation:* AACN. Part-time programs available. Postbaccalaureate distance learning degree programs offered. *Faculty:* 70 full-time (69 women), 7 part-time/adjunct (all women). *Students:* 87 full-time (78 women), 870 part-time (815 women); includes 489 minority (235 Black or African American, non-Hispanic/Latino; 5 American Indian or Alaska Native, non-Hispanic/Latino; 169 Asian, non-Hispanic/Latino; 78 Hispanic/Latino; 2 Native Hawaiian or other Pacific Islander, non-Hispanic/Latino), 19 international. Average age 38. 368 applicants, 71% accepted, 205 enrolled. In 2011, 147 master's, 21 doctorates awarded. *Degree requirements:* For master's, comprehensive exam, thesis or alternative; for doctorate, comprehensive exam, thesis/dissertation. *Entrance requirements:* For master's, GRE or MAT, minimum GPA of 3.0 on last 60 hours in undergraduate nursing degree and overall, RN license, BS in nursing, basic statistics course; for doctorate, GRE (preferred minimum score 153 [500 old version] Verbal, 144 [500 old version] Quantitative, 4 Analytical), MS in nursing, minimum preferred GPA of 3.5, RN license, statistics, 2 letters of reference, curriculum vitae, graduate nursing-theory course, graduate research course, statement of professional goals and research interests. Additional exam requirements/recommendations for international students: Required—TOEFL (minimum score 550 paper-based; 213 computer-based; 79 iBT). *Application deadline:* For fall admission, 5/1 priority date for domestic students, 3/1 for international students; for spring admission, 9/15 priority date for domestic students, 7/1 for international students. Applications are processed on a rolling basis. Application fee: $50 ($75 for international students). Electronic applications accepted. *Expenses:* Tuition, state resident: full-time $3834; part-time $213 per credit hour. Tuition, nonresident: full-time $9468; part-time $526 per credit hour. *Required fees:* $213 per credit hour. Tuition and fees vary according to course load. *Financial support:* In 2011–12, 149 students received support, including 10 research assistantships (averaging $12,942 per year), 1 teaching assistantship (averaging $12,942 per year); career-related internships or fieldwork, Federal Work-Study, institutionally sponsored loans, scholarships/grants, traineeships, health care benefits, and unspecified assistantships also available. Support available to part-time students. Financial award application deadline: 3/1; financial award applicants required to submit FAFSA. *Faculty research:* Screening, prevention, and treatment for intimate partner violence; needs of adolescents during childbirth intervention; a network analysis decision tool for nurse managers (Social Network Analysis); support for adolescents with implantable cardioverter defibrillators; informatics: nurse staffing, safety, quality, and financial data as they relate to patient care outcomes; prevention and treatment of obesity; improving infant outcomes related to premature birth. *Total annual research expenditures:* $462,088. *Unit head:* Dr. Patricia Holden-Huchton, Interim Dean, 940-898-2401, Fax: 940-898-2437, E-mail: nursing@twu.edu. *Application contact:* Dr. Samuel Wheeler, Assistant Director of Admissions, 940-898-3188, Fax: 940-898-3081, E-mail: wheelersr@twu.edu. Web site: http://www.twu.edu/nursing/.

Universidad de Iberoamerica, Graduate School, San Jose, Costa Rica. Offers clinical neuropsychology (PhD); clinical psychology (M Psych); educational psychology (M Psych); forensic psychology (M Psych); hospital management (MHA); intensive care nursing (MN); medicine (MD).

The University of Alabama in Huntsville, School of Graduate Studies, College of Nursing, Huntsville, AL 35899. Offers family nurse practitioner (Certificate); nursing (MSN, DNP), including acute care nurse practitioner (MSN), adult clinical nursing specialist (MSN), clinical nurse leader (MSN), family nurse practitioner (MSN), leadership in health care systems (MSN); nursing education (Certificate). DNP offered jointly with The University of Alabama at Birmingham. *Accreditation:* AACN. Part-time and evening/weekend programs available. Postbaccalaureate distance learning degree programs offered (minimal on-campus study). *Faculty:* 19 full-time (18 women), 8 part-time/adjunct (7 women). *Students:* 57 full-time (43 women), 162 part-time (139 women); includes 22 minority (15 Black or African American, non-Hispanic/Latino; 3 American Indian or Alaska Native, non-Hispanic/Latino; 1 Asian, non-Hispanic/Latino; 3 Hispanic/Latino), 2 international. Average age 37. 193 applicants, 79% accepted, 112 enrolled. In 2011, 42 master's, 11 doctorates, 11 other advanced degrees awarded. *Degree requirements:* For master's, comprehensive exam, thesis or alternative, oral and written exams. *Entrance requirements:* For master's, MAT or GRE, Alabama RN license, BSN, minimum GPA of 3.0; for doctorate, master's degree in nursing in an advanced practice area; for Certificate, MAT or GRE, minimum GPA of 3.0. Additional exam requirements/recommendations for international students: Required—TOEFL (minimum score 500 paper-based; 173 computer-based; 62 iBT). *Application deadline:* For fall admission, 7/15 for domestic students, 4/1 for international students; for spring admission, 11/30 for domestic students, 9/1 for international students. Applications are processed on a rolling basis. Application fee: $40 ($50 for international students). Electronic applications accepted. *Expenses:* Tuition, state resident: full-time $7830; part-time $473.50 per credit. Tuition, nonresident: full-time $18,748; part-time $1128.33 per credit. Tuition and fees vary according to course load and program. *Financial support:* In 2011–12, 9 students received support, including 9 teaching assistantships with full tuition reimbursements available (averaging $9,596 per year); career-related internships or fieldwork, Federal Work-Study, institutionally sponsored loans, scholarships/grants, traineeships, health care benefits, and unspecified assistantships also available. Support available to part-time students. Financial award application deadline: 4/1; financial award applicants required to submit FAFSA. *Faculty research:* Home health care, gerontology, pediatric nursing, family nurse practitioner, adult acute care administration. *Total annual research expenditures:* $235,384. *Unit head:* Dr. Fay Raines, Dean, 256-824-6345, Fax: 256-824-6026, E-mail: rainesc@uah.edu. *Application contact:* Charles Davis, Director of Graduate Nursing Admissions and Advising, 256-824-2433, Fax: 256-824-6026, E-mail: charles.davis@uah.edu. Web site: http://www.uah.edu/nursing/welcome.

University of Cincinnati, Graduate School, College of Nursing, Cincinnati, OH 45221-0038. Offers clinical nurse specialist (MSN), including adult health, community health, neonatal, nursing administration, occupational health, pediatric health, psychiatric nursing, women's health; nurse anesthesia (MSN); nurse midwifery (MSN); nurse practitioner (MSN), including acute care, ambulatory care, family, family/psychiatric, women's health; nursing (PhD); MBA/MSN. *Accreditation:* AACN; AANA/CANAEP (one or more programs are accredited); ACNM/ACME. Part-time programs available. Postbaccalaureate distance learning degree programs offered (no on-campus study). Terminal master's awarded for partial completion of doctoral program. *Degree requirements:* For master's, thesis or alternative; for doctorate, comprehensive exam, thesis/dissertation. *Entrance requirements:* For master's and doctorate, GRE General Test. Additional exam requirements/recommendations for international students: Required—TOEFL (minimum score 520 paper-based; 190 computer-based). Electronic applications accepted. *Faculty research:* Substance abuse, injury and violence, symptom management.

University of Guelph, Ontario Veterinary College and Graduate Studies, Graduate Programs in Veterinary Sciences, Department of Clinical Studies, Guelph, ON N1G 2W1, Canada. Offers anesthesiology (M Sc, DV Sc); cardiology (DV Sc, Diploma); clinical studies (Diploma); dermatology (M Sc); diagnostic imaging (M Sc, DV Sc); emergency/critical care (M Sc, DV Sc, Diploma); medicine (M Sc, DV Sc); neurology (M Sc, DV Sc); ophthalmology (M Sc, DV Sc); surgery (M Sc, DV Sc). *Degree requirements:* For master's, thesis; for doctorate, comprehensive exam, thesis/dissertation. *Entrance requirements:* Additional exam requirements/recommendations for international students: Required—TOEFL (minimum score 550 paper-based; 213 computer-based), IELTS (minimum score 6.5). Electronic applications accepted. *Faculty research:* Orthopedics, respirology, oncology, exercise physiology, cardiology.

University of Illinois at Chicago, Graduate College, College of Nursing, Program in Nursing, Chicago, IL 60607-7128. Offers acute care clinical nurse specialist (MS); acute care nurse practitioner (MS); administrative studies in nursing (MS); adult nurse practitioner (MS); adult/geriatric nurse practitioner (MS); advanced community health nurse specialist (MS); family nurse practitioner (MS); geriatric clinical nurse specialist (MS); geriatric nurse practitioner (MS); mental health clinical nurse specialist (MS); mental health nurse practitioner (MS); nurse midwifery (MS); occupational health/advanced community health nurse specialist (MS); occupational health/family nurse practitioner (MS); pediatric clinical nurse specialist (MS); pediatric nurse practitioner (MS); perinatal clinical nurse specialist (MS); school/advanced community health nurse specialist (MS); school/family nurse practitioner (MS); women's health nurse practitioner (MS). *Accreditation:* AACN. Part-time programs available. *Degree requirements:* For master's, thesis or alternative. *Entrance requirements:* For master's, GRE General Test, minimum GPA of 2.75. Additional exam requirements/recommendations for international students: Required—TOEFL. Electronic applications accepted.

University of Massachusetts Worcester, Graduate School of Nursing, Worcester, MA 01655-0115. Offers adult acute/critical care nurse practitioner (MS, Post Master's Certificate); adult acute/critical care nurse practitioner and gerontological nurse practitioner (MS, Post Master's Certificate); adult primary care nurse practitioner (MS, Post Master's Certificate); adult primary care nurse practitioner and gerontological nurse practitioner (MS, Post Master's Certificate); advanced practice nursing (DNP); family nurse practitioner (MS); gerontological nurse practitioner (Post Master's Certificate); leadership (DNP); nurse education (Post Master's Certificate); nurse educator (MS); nursing (PhD). *Accreditation:* AACN. *Faculty:* 20 full-time (17 women), 60 part-time/adjunct (50 women). *Students:* 162 full-time (141 women), 36 part-time (30 women); includes 29 minority (13 Black or African American, non-Hispanic/Latino; 10 Asian, non-Hispanic/Latino; 6 Hispanic/Latino), 1 international. Average age 36. 252 applicants, 38% accepted, 82 enrolled. In 2011, 38 master's, 6 doctorates awarded. *Degree requirements:* For doctorate, comprehensive exam, thesis/dissertation. *Entrance requirements:* For master's, GRE General Test, bachelor's degree, course work in statistics; for doctorate, GRE General Test, bachelor's or master's degree, RN licensure; for Post Master's Certificate, GRE General Test, MS in nursing. Additional exam requirements/recommendations for international students: Required—TOEFL. *Application deadline:* For fall admission, 1/15 priority date for domestic students. Applications are processed on a rolling basis. Application fee: $40 ($60 for international students). *Expenses:* Contact institution. *Financial support:* In 2011–12, 38 students received support. Institutionally sponsored loans, scholarships/grants, traineeships, and tuition waivers (for some) available. Support available to part-time students. Financial award application deadline: 5/16; financial award applicants required to submit FAFSA. *Faculty research:* Decision-making of partners and men with prostate cancer, coinfection (HIV and Hepatitus C) and treatment decisions, parent management of children with T1DM, health literacy and discharge planning, Ghanian women and self-care. *Total annual research expenditures:* $939,567. *Unit head:* Dr. Paulette Seymour-Route, Dean, 508-856-5801, Fax: 508-856-6552, E-mail: paulette.seymour-route@umassmed.edu. *Application contact:* Diane Brescia, Admissions Coordinator, 508-856-3488, Fax: 508-856-5851, E-mail: diane.brescia@umassmed.edu. Web site: http://www.umassmed.edu/gsn/.

University of Miami, Graduate School, School of Nursing and Health Studies, Coral Gables, FL 33124. Offers acute care (MSN), including acute care nurse practitioner, nurse anesthesia; nursing (PhD); primary care (MSN), including adult nurse practitioner, family nurse practitioner, nurse midwifery, women's health practitioner. *Accreditation:* AACN; AANA/CANAEP; ACNM/ACME (one or more programs are accredited). Part-time programs available. *Degree requirements:* For master's, thesis optional; for doctorate, thesis/dissertation. *Entrance requirements:* For master's, GRE General Test, BSN, minimum GPA of 3.0, Florida RN license; for doctorate, GRE General Test, BSN or MSN, minimum GPA of 3.0. Additional exam requirements/recommendations for international students: Required—TOEFL (minimum score 550 paper-based; 213 computer-based). Electronic applications accepted. *Faculty research:* Transcultural nursing, exercise and depression in Alzheimer's disease, infectious diseases/HIV–AIDS, postpartum depression, outcomes assessment.

Acute Care/Critical Care Nursing

University of Michigan, Horace H. Rackham School of Graduate Studies, School of Nursing, Division of Acute, Critical and Long-term Care, Program in Adult Acute Care Nurse Practitioner, Ann Arbor, MI 48109. Offers MS. *Accreditation:* AACN. Part-time programs available. *Degree requirements:* For master's, thesis. *Entrance requirements:* For master's, GRE General Test (if BSN GPA less than 3.25), Michigan licensure, minimum of B average in BSN program. Additional exam requirements/ recommendations for international students: Required—TOEFL (minimum score 560 paper-based; 220 computer-based). Electronic applications accepted. *Faculty research:* The functional outcomes and quality of life in women with breast cancer, hypertension.

University of Pennsylvania, School of Nursing, Adult Acute Care Nurse Practitioner Program, Philadelphia, PA 19104. Offers acute care nurse practitioner (MSN). *Accreditation:* AACN. Part-time programs available. *Students:* 32 full-time (29 women), 62 part-time (58 women); includes 17 minority (4 Black or African American, non-Hispanic/Latino; 1 American Indian or Alaska Native, non-Hispanic/Latino; 8 Asian, non-Hispanic/Latino; 3 Hispanic/Latino; 1 Two or more races, non-Hispanic/Latino), 2 international. 74 applicants, 43% accepted, 31 enrolled. In 2011, 44 degrees awarded. *Entrance requirements:* For master's, GRE General Test, BSN, minimum GPA of 3.0, previous course work in statistics. *Application deadline:* For fall admission, 2/15 priority date for domestic students. Applications are processed on a rolling basis. Application fee: $70. *Expenses:* Contact institution. *Financial support:* Fellowships, research assistantships, teaching assistantships, Federal Work-Study, and institutionally sponsored loans available. Support available to part-time students. Financial award application deadline: 4/1. *Faculty research:* Post-injury disability, bereavement and attributions in fire survivors, stress in staff nurses. *Unit head:* Assistant Dean of Admissions and Financial Aid, 866-867-6877, Fax: 215-573-8439, E-mail: admissions@nursing.upenn.edu. *Application contact:* Deborah Becker, Program Director, 215-898-0432, E-mail: debecker@nursing.upenn.edu. Web site: http://www.nursing.upenn.edu/.

University of Pennsylvania, School of Nursing, Pediatric Acute/Chronic Care Nurse Practitioner Program, Philadelphia, PA 19104. Offers MSN. *Accreditation:* AACN. Part-time programs available. Postbaccalaureate distance learning degree programs offered. *Students:* 7 full-time (all women), 20 part-time (all women); includes 5 minority (2 Asian, non-Hispanic/Latino; 2 Hispanic/Latino; 1 Two or more races, non-Hispanic/Latino), 1 international. 42 applicants, 60% accepted, 25 enrolled. In 2011, 12 degrees awarded. *Entrance requirements:* For master's, GRE General Test, 1 year of clinical course work, BSN, minimum GPA of 3.0, previous course work in statistics. Additional exam requirements/recommendations for international students: Required—TOEFL. *Application deadline:* For fall admission, 2/15 priority date for domestic students. Applications are processed on a rolling basis. Application fee: $70. *Expenses:* Contact institution. *Financial support:* Research assistantships, teaching assistantships, career-related internships or fieldwork, and institutionally sponsored loans available. Support available to part-time students. Financial award application deadline: 4/1. *Faculty research:* Hispanic health, bereavement, pediatric AIDS, chronically ill children and their families. *Unit head:* Assistant Dean of Admissions and Financial Aid, 866-867-6877, Fax: 215-573-8439, E-mail: admissions@nursing.upenn.edu. *Application contact:* Terri Lipman, Program Director, 215-898-4271, E-mail: lipman@nursing.upenn.edu. Web site: http://www.nursing.upenn.edu/academic_programs/grad/masters/program_detail.asp?prid-16.

University of Pennsylvania, School of Nursing, Pediatric Critical Care Nurse Practitioner Program, Philadelphia, PA 19104. Offers MSN. *Accreditation:* AACN. *Students:* 8 full-time (all women), 4 part-time (all women); includes 1 minority (Hispanic/Latino), 1 international. 23 applicants, 48% accepted, 11 enrolled. In 2011, 13 degrees awarded. *Entrance requirements:* For master's, GRE General Test, BSN, minimum GPA of 3.0, previous course work in statistics, 1 year of clinical course work. Additional exam requirements/recommendations for international students: Required—TOEFL. *Application deadline:* For fall admission, 2/15 priority date for domestic students. Applications are processed on a rolling basis. Application fee: $70. *Expenses:* Contact institution. *Financial support:* Application deadline: 4/1. *Unit head:* Assistant Dean of Admissions and Financial Aid, 866-867-6877, Fax: 215-573-8439, E-mail: admissions@nursing.upenn.edu. *Application contact:* Judy Verger, 215-898-4271, E-mail: jtv@nursing.upenn.edu. Web site: http://www.nursing.upenn.edu/peds/.

University of Pittsburgh, School of Nursing, Nurse Practitioner Program, Pittsburgh, PA 15261. Offers acute care nurse practitioner (MSN, DNP); adult nurse practitioner (MSN, DNP); family nurse practitioner (MSN, DNP); neonatal (MSN, DNP); nursing practice (DNP); pediatric nurse practitioner (MSN, DNP); psychiatric primary care nurse practitioner (MSN, DNP). *Accreditation:* AACN. Part-time programs available. *Students:* 46 full-time (44 women), 135 part-time (123 women); includes 13 minority (6 Black or African American, non-Hispanic/Latino; 1 American Indian or Alaska Native, non-Hispanic/Latino; 6 Asian, non-Hispanic/Latino). Average age 32. 126 applicants, 71% accepted, 70 enrolled. In 2011, 24 master's, 4 doctorates awarded. *Degree requirements:* For master's, comprehensive exam, thesis optional. *Entrance requirements:* For master's, GRE General Test or MAT, BSN, RN license, letters of recommendation, resume, course work in statistics, 1-3 years of nursing experience; for doctorate, GRE General Test, BSN, RN license, minimum GPA of 3.5, 3 letters of recommendation. Additional exam requirements/recommendations for international students: Required—TOEFL (minimum score 550 paper-based; 213 computer-based; 80 iBT). *Application deadline:* Applications are processed on a rolling basis. Application fee: $50. Electronic applications accepted. *Expenses:* Tuition, state resident: full-time $18,774; part-time $760 per credit. Tuition, nonresident: full-time $30,736; part-time $1258 per credit. *Required fees:* $740; $200 per term. Tuition and fees vary according to program. *Financial support:* In 2011–12, 5 students received support, including 1 fellowship with partial tuition reimbursement available (averaging $11,330 per year), 1 research assistantship with full tuition reimbursement available (averaging $35,942 per year), 3 teaching assistantships with full and partial tuition reimbursements available (averaging $27,470 per year); scholarships/grants, traineeships, health care benefits, and unspecified assistantships also available. Support available to part-time students. *Unit head:* Dr. Sandra Engberg, Associate Dean for Clinical Education, 412-624-3835, Fax: 412-624-8521, E-mail: sje1@pitt.edu. *Application contact:* Laurie Lapsley, Administrator of Graduate Student Services, 412-624-9670, Fax: 412-624-2409, E-mail: lapsleyl@pitt.edu. Web site: http://www.nursing.pitt.edu.

University of Puerto Rico, Medical Sciences Campus, School of Nursing, San Juan, PR 00936-5067. Offers adult and elderly nursing (MSN); child and adolescent nursing (MSN); critical care nursing (MSN); family and community nursing (MSN); family nurse practitioner (MSN); maternity nursing (MSN); mental health and psychiatric nursing (MSN). *Accreditation:* AACN; AANA/CANAEP. *Entrance requirements:* For master's, GRE or EXADEP, interview, Puerto Rico RN license or professional license for international students, general and specific point average, article analysis. Electronic applications accepted. *Faculty research:* HIV, health disparities, teen violence, women and violence, neurological disorders.

University of Rochester, School of Nursing, Rochester, NY 14642. Offers acute care nurse practitioner (MS); adult nurse practitioner (MS); adult/geriatric nurse practitioner (MS); care of children and families/pediatric nurse practitioner (MS); care of children and families/pediatric nurse practitioner/neonatal nurse practitioner (MS); clinical nurse leader (MS); clinical research coordinator (MS); family nurse practitioner (MS); family psychiatric mental health nurse practitioner (MS); health care organization management and leadership (MS); health practice research (PhD); nursing (DNP). *Accreditation:* AACN; NLN (one or more programs are accredited). Part-time programs available. Postbaccalaureate distance learning degree programs offered (minimal on-campus study). *Faculty:* 49 full-time (42 women), 72 part-time/adjunct (60 women). *Students:* 38 full-time (32 women), 196 part-time (181 women); includes 37 minority (20 Black or African American, non-Hispanic/Latino; 9 Asian, non-Hispanic/Latino; 8 Hispanic/Latino), 5 international. Average age 36. 68 applicants, 56% accepted, 26 enrolled. In 2011, 49 master's, 7 doctorates awarded. Terminal master's awarded for partial completion of doctoral program. *Median time to degree:* Of those who began their doctoral program in fall 2003, 40% received their degree in 8 years or less. *Degree requirements:* For doctorate, thesis/dissertation. *Entrance requirements:* For master's, BS in nursing, minimum GPA of 3.0, course work in statistics; for doctorate, GRE General Test, MS in nursing, minimum GPA of 3.5. Additional exam requirements/recommendations for international students: Required—or IELTS (minimum score 6.5); Recommended—TOEFL (minimum score 560 paper-based; 230 computer-based; 88 iBT). *Application deadline:* For fall admission, 4/1 priority date for domestic students, 4/1 for international students; for spring admission, 9/1 for domestic and international students. Application fee: $50. Electronic applications accepted. *Expenses: Tuition:* Full-time $41,040. *Financial support:* In 2011–12, 49 students received support, including 1 fellowship with full and partial tuition reimbursement available (averaging $18,700 per year); scholarships/grants, traineeships, health care benefits, tuition waivers (partial), and unspecified assistantships also available. Support available to part-time students. Financial award application deadline: 6/30. *Faculty research:* Clinical research in aging, managing asthma in children, interventions to improve outcomes in critically ill children and their mothers, nurse home visitation studies, medical device evaluation, critical care clinical studies, high risk behavior and prevention, palliative care, pregnancy-related weight gain. *Total annual research expenditures:* $4.3 million. *Unit head:* Dr. Kathy H. Rideout, Interim Dean, 585-273-8902, Fax: 585-273-1268, E-mail: kathy_rideout@urmc.rochester.edu. *Application contact:* Elaine Andolina, Director of Admissions, 585-275-2375, Fax: 585-756-8299, E-mail: elaine_andolina@urmc.rochester.edu. Web site: http://www.son.rochester.edu.

University of South Africa, College of Human Sciences, Pretoria, South Africa. Offers adult education (M Ed); African languages (MA, PhD); African politics (MA, PhD); Afrikaans (MA, PhD); ancient history (MA, PhD); ancient Near Eastern studies (MA, PhD); anthropology (MA, PhD); applied linguistics (MA); Arabic (MA, PhD); archaeology (MA); art history (MA); Biblical archaeology (MA); Biblical studies (M Th, D Th, PhD); Christian spirituality (M Th, D Th); church history (M Th, D Th); classical studies (MA, PhD); clinical psychology (MA); communication (MA, PhD); comparative education (M Ed, Ed D); consulting psychology (D Admin, D Com, PhD); curriculum studies (M Ed, Ed D); development studies (M Admin, MA, D Admin, PhD); didactics (M Ed, Ed D); education (M Tech); education management (M Ed, Ed D); educational psychology (M Ed); English (MA); environmental education (M Ed); French (MA, PhD); German (MA, PhD); Greek (MA); guidance and counseling (M Ed); health studies (MA, PhD), including health sciences education (MA), health services management (MA), medical and surgical nursing science (critical care general) (MA), midwifery and neonatal nursing science (MA), trauma and emergency care (MA); history (MA, PhD); history of education (Ed D); inclusive education (M Ed, Ed D); information and communications technology policy and regulation (MA); information science (MA, MIS, PhD); international politics (MA, PhD); Islamic studies (MA, PhD); Italian (MA, PhD); Judaica (MA, PhD); linguistics (MA, PhD); mathematical education (M Ed); mathematics education (MA); missiology (M Th, D Th); modern Hebrew (MA, PhD); musicology (MA, MMus, D Mus, PhD); natural science education (M Ed); New Testament (M Th, D Th); Old Testament (D Th); pastoral therapy (M Th, D Th); philosophy (MA); philosophy of education (M Ed, Ed D); politics (MA, PhD); Portuguese (MA, PhD); practical theology (M Th, D Th); psychology (MA, MS, PhD); psychology of education (M Ed, Ed D); public health (MA); religious studies (MA, D Th, PhD); Romance languages (MA); Russian (MA, PhD); Semitic languages (MA, PhD); social behavior studies in HIV/AIDS (MA); social science (mental health) (MA); social science in development studies (MA); social science in psychology (MA); social science in social work (MA); social science in sociology (MA); social work (MSW, DSW, PhD); socio-education (M Ed, Ed D); sociolinguistics (MA); sociology (MA, PhD); Spanish (MA, PhD); systematic theology (M Th, D Th); TESOL (teaching English to speakers of other languages) (MA); theological ethics (M Th, D Th); theory of literature (MA, PhD); urban ministries (D Th); urban ministry (M Th).

University of South Carolina, The Graduate School, College of Nursing, Program in Advanced Practice Clinical Nursing, Columbia, SC 29208. Offers acute care nurse practitioner (Certificate); advanced practice clinical nursing (MSN). *Accreditation:* AACN. Part-time programs available. Postbaccalaureate distance learning degree programs offered (minimal on-campus study). *Entrance requirements:* For master's, master's degree in nursing, RN license; for Certificate, MSN. Additional exam requirements/recommendations for international students: Required—TOEFL (minimum score 570 paper-based; 213 computer-based). Electronic applications accepted. *Faculty research:* Systems research, evidence based practice, breast cancer, violence.

University of South Carolina, The Graduate School, College of Nursing, Program in Clinical Nursing, Columbia, SC 29208. Offers acute care clinical specialist (MSN); acute care nurse practitioner (MSN); women's health nurse practitioner (MSN). *Accreditation:* AACN. Part-time programs available. *Degree requirements:* For master's, thesis or alternative. *Entrance requirements:* For master's, GRE General Test or MAT, BS in nursing, RN licensure. Additional exam requirements/recommendations for international students: Required—TOEFL (minimum score 570 paper-based; 230 computer-based). Electronic applications accepted. *Faculty research:* Systems research, evidence based practice, breast cancer, violence.

University of Virginia, School of Nursing, Charlottesville, VA 22903. Offers acute and specialty care (MSN); acute care nurse practitioner (MSN); clinical nurse leadership (MSN); community-public health leadership (MSN); nursing (DNP, PhD); psychiatric mental health counseling (MSN); MSN/MBA. *Accreditation:* AACN. Part-time programs available. *Faculty:* 44 full-time (43 women), 2 part-time/adjunct (both women). *Students:* 174 full-time (152 women), 151 part-time (139 women); includes 57 minority (28 Black or African American, non-Hispanic/Latino; 1 American Indian or Alaska Native, non-Hispanic/Latino; 14 Asian, non-Hispanic/Latino; 10 Hispanic/Latino; 4 Two or more races, non-Hispanic/Latino), 11 international. Average age 37. 236 applicants, 40% accepted, 74 enrolled. In 2011, 70 master's, 15 doctorates awarded. *Degree requirements:* For doctorate, comprehensive exam (for some programs), capstone project (DNP), dissertation (PhD). *Entrance requirements:* For master's, GRE General Test, MAT; for doctorate, GRE General Test. Additional exam requirements/recommendations for international students: Required—TOEFL, IELTS. *Application deadline:* Applications are processed on a rolling basis. Application fee: $60. Electronic applications accepted. *Expenses:* Contact institution. *Financial support:* Fellowships, research assistantships, teaching assistantships, Federal Work-Study, and scholarships/grants available. Financial award applicants required to submit FAFSA. *Unit head:* Dorrie K. Fontaine, Dean, 434-924-0141, Fax: 434-982-1809. *Application contact:* Clay Hysell, Assistant Dean for Admissions and Financial Services, 434-924-0141, Fax: 434-982-1809, E-mail: nur-osa@virginia.edu. Web site: http://www.nursing.virginia.edu/.

Vanderbilt University, Vanderbilt University School of Nursing, Nashville, TN 37240. Offers acute care nurse practitioner (MSN), including intensivist; adult-gerontology primary care nurse practitioner (MSN); emergency nurse practitioner (MSN); family nurse practitioner (MSN); family psychiatric and mental health nurse practitioner (MSN); health systems management (MSN); neonatal nurse practitioner (MSN); nurse midwifery (MSN); nurse midwifery/family nurse practitioner (MSN); nursing informatics (MSN); nursing practice (DNP); nursing science (PhD); pediatric acute care nurse practitioner (MSN); pediatric primary care nurse practitioner (MSN); women's health nurse practitioner (MSN), including urogynecology, women's health; women's health nurse practitioner/adult gerontology nurse practitioner (MSN); MSN/M Div; MSN/MTS. *Accreditation:* ACNM/ACME; NLN (one or more programs are accredited). Part-time programs available. Postbaccalaureate distance learning degree programs offered (minimal on-campus study). *Faculty:* 120 full-time (105 women), 415 part-time/adjunct (302 women). *Students:* 570 full-time (503 women), 395 part-time (364 women); includes 107 minority (57 Black or African American, non-Hispanic/Latino; 1 American Indian or Alaska Native, non-Hispanic/Latino; 19 Asian, non-Hispanic/Latino; 19 Hispanic/Latino; 2 Native Hawaiian or other Pacific Islander, non-Hispanic/Latino; 9 Two or more races, non-Hispanic/Latino), 10 international. Average age 32. 1,116 applicants, 56% accepted, 455 enrolled. In 2011, 341 master's, 33 doctorates awarded. *Degree requirements:* For doctorate, comprehensive exam, thesis/dissertation. *Entrance requirements:* For master's, GRE General Test (within the past 5 years), minimum B average in undergraduate course work, 3 letters of recommendation; for doctorate, GRE General Test, interview, 3 letters of recommendation from doctorally-prepared faculty, MSN, essay. Additional exam requirements/recommendations for international students: Required—TOEFL (minimum score 570 paper-based; 88 computer-based), IELTS (minimum score 6.5). *Application deadline:* For fall admission, 12/1 priority date for domestic students, 12/1 for international students. Applications are processed on a rolling basis. Application fee: $50. Electronic applications accepted. *Expenses:* Contact institution. *Financial support:* In 2011–12, 392 students received support. Scholarships/grants and health care benefits available. Support available to part-time students. Financial award application deadline: 3/15; financial award applicants required to submit FAFSA. *Faculty research:* Lymphedema, palliative care and bereavement, health services research including workforce, safety and quality of care, gerontology, better birth outcomes including nutrition . *Total annual research expenditures:* $1.8 million. *Unit head:* Dr. Colleen Conway-Welch, Dean, 615-343-8776, Fax: 615-343-7711, E-mail: colleen.conway-welch@vanderbilt.edu. *Application contact:* Patricia Peerman, Assistant Dean for Enrollment Management, 615-322-3800, Fax: 615-343-0333, E-mail: vusn-admissions@vanderbilt.edu. Web site: http://www.nursing.vanderbilt.edu.

Wayne State University, College of Nursing, Program in Adult Acute Care Nursing, Detroit, MI 48202. Offers MSN. *Accreditation:* AACN. Part-time programs available. *Students:* 1 (woman) full-time, 41 part-time (34 women); includes 4 minority (1 Black or African American, non-Hispanic/Latino; 3 Asian, non-Hispanic/Latino), 2 international. Average age 37. 6 applicants, 17% accepted, 0 enrolled. In 2011, 42 master's awarded. *Degree requirements:* For master's, thesis or alternative. *Entrance requirements:* For master's, GRE General Test, minimum honor point average of 2.8 in upper-division course work; BA from NLN- or CCNE-accredited program; references; current RN license; personal statement. Additional exam requirements/recommendations for international students: Required—TOEFL (minimum score 550 paper-based; 213 computer-based); Recommended—TWE (minimum score 6). *Application deadline:* For fall admission, 6/1 priority date for domestic students, 5/1 for international students; for winter admission, 10/1 priority date for domestic students, 9/1 for international students; for spring admission, 2/1 priority date for domestic students, 1/1 for international students. Applications are processed on a rolling basis. Application fee: $50. Electronic applications accepted. *Expenses:* Tuition, state resident: part-time $512.85 per credit. Tuition, nonresident: part-time $1132.65 per credit. *Required fees:* $26.60 per credit. $199.65 per semester. Tuition and fees vary according to course load and program. *Financial support:* In 2011–12, 2 students received support. Fellowships with tuition reimbursements available, research assistantships with tuition reimbursements available, teaching assistantships with tuition reimbursements available, institutionally sponsored loans, scholarships/grants, traineeships, and unspecified assistantships available. Financial award applicants required to submit FAFSA. *Faculty research:* Cardiovascular nursing with vulnerable populations, wound healing, symptom management. *Unit head:* Dr. Barbara Redman, Dean, 313-577-4070, Fax: 313-577-4571, E-mail: ao9080@wayne.edu. *Application contact:* Dr. Cynthia Redwine, Assistant Dean for the Office of Student Affairs, 313-577-4082, E-mail: nursinginfo@wayne.edu. Web site: http://www.nursing.wayne.edu/msn/AACCNPCurriculum.php.

Wright State University, School of Graduate Studies, College of Nursing and Health, Program in Nursing, Dayton, OH 45435. Offers acute care nurse practitioner (MS); administration of nursing and health care systems (MS); adult health (MS); child and adolescent health (MS); community health (MS); family nurse practitioner (MS); nurse practitioner (MS); school nurse (MS); MBA/MS. *Accreditation:* AACN. Part-time and evening/weekend programs available. *Degree requirements:* For master's, thesis or alternative. *Entrance requirements:* For master's, GRE General Test, BSN from NLN-accredited college, Ohio RN license. Additional exam requirements/recommendations for international students: Required—TOEFL. *Faculty research:* Clinical nursing and health, teaching, caring, pain administration, informatics and technology.

Adult Nursing

Allen College, Program in Nursing, Waterloo, IA 50703. Offers acute care nurse practitioner (MSN, Post-Master's Certificate); adult nurse practitioner (MSN, Post-Master's Certificate); adult psychiatric-mental health nurse practitioner (MSN, Post-Master's Certificate); family nurse practitioner (MSN, Post-Master's Certificate); gerontological nurse practitioner (MSN, Post-Master's Certificate); health education (MSN); leadership in health care delivery (MSN, Post-Master's Certificate); nursing (DNP). *Accreditation:* AACN; NLN. Part-time programs available. *Faculty:* 3 full-time (all women), 16 part-time/adjunct (all women). *Students:* 34 full-time (31 women), 110 part-time (106 women); includes 5 minority (2 Asian, non-Hispanic/Latino; 3 Hispanic/Latino). Average age 36. 156 applicants, 64% accepted, 76 enrolled. In 2011, 61 master's, 1 other advanced degree awarded. *Degree requirements:* For master's, thesis optional. *Entrance requirements:* For master's, minimum GPA of 3.0; for doctorate, minimum GPA of 3.25 in graduate coursework. Additional exam requirements/recommendations for international students: Recommended—TOEFL (minimum score 550 paper-based), IELTS. *Application deadline:* For fall admission, 2/1 priority date for domestic students; for spring admission, 9/1 priority date for domestic students. Applications are processed on a rolling basis. Application fee: $50. Electronic applications accepted. *Expenses: Tuition:* Full-time $13,993; part-time $691 per credit hour. *Required fees:* $832; $69 per credit hour. One-time fee: $100 part-time. Part-time tuition and fees vary according to course load. *Financial support:* In 2011–12, 41 students received support. Institutionally sponsored loans, scholarships/grants, and traineeships available. Support available to part-time students. Financial award application deadline: 8/15; financial award applicants required to submit FAFSA. *Faculty research:* Pain and the aged, congestive heart failure. *Unit head:* Kendra Williams-Perez, Dean, School of Nursing, 319-226-2044, Fax: 319-226-2070, E-mail: williakb@ihs.org. *Application contact:* Michelle Koehn, Admissions Counselor, 319-226-2002, Fax: 319-226-2051, E-mail: koehnml@ihs.org. Web site: http://www.allencollege.edu/.

American University of Beirut, Graduate Programs, Rafic Hariri School of Nursing, Beirut, Lebanon. Offers adult care nursing (MSN); community health nursing (MSN); nursing administration (MSN); psychiatry mental health nursing (MSN). *Accreditation:* AACN. Part-time programs available. *Faculty:* 8 full-time (7 women), 16 part-time/adjunct (13 women). *Students:* 5 full-time (3 women), 50 part-time (39 women). Average age 29. 46 applicants, 87% accepted, 19 enrolled. In 2011, 19 master's awarded. *Degree requirements:* For master's, one foreign language, comprehensive exam, thesis optional. *Entrance requirements:* For master's, letter of recommendation. Additional exam requirements/recommendations for international students: Required—TOEFL (minimum score 600 paper-based); Recommended—IELTS. *Application deadline:* For fall admission, 2/20 for domestic and international students; for spring admission, 11/1 for domestic and international students. Applications are processed on a rolling basis. Application fee: $50. *Expenses: Tuition:* Full-time $12,780; part-time $710 per credit. Tuition and fees vary according to course load and program. *Financial support:* In 2011–12, 19 research assistantships with partial tuition reimbursements, 1 teaching assistantship with partial tuition reimbursement were awarded; career-related internships or fieldwork, institutionally sponsored loans, scholarships/grants, health care benefits, and unspecified assistantships also available. Support available to part-time students. Financial award application deadline: 2/2. *Faculty research:* Pain management and palliative care, stress and post-traumatic stress disorder, health benefits and chronic illness, health promotion and community interventions. *Total annual research expenditures:* $52,000. *Unit head:* Dr. Huda Huijer Abu-Saad, Director, 961-1374374 Ext. 5952, Fax: 961-1744476, E-mail: hh35@aub.edu.lb. *Application contact:* Dr. Salim Kanaan, Director, Admissions Office, 961-1350000 Ext. 2594, Fax: 961-1750775, E-mail: sk00@aub.edu.lb. Web site: http://staff.aub.edu.lb/~webson.

Angelo State University, College of Graduate Studies, College of Health and Human Services, Department of Nursing and Rehabilitation Sciences, San Angelo, TX 76909. Offers advanced practice registered nurse (MSN); nurse educator (MSN); nursing - RN to MSN (MSN). *Accreditation:* NLN. Part-time and evening/weekend programs available. Postbaccalaureate distance learning degree programs offered (no on-campus study). *Faculty:* 7 full-time (all women). *Students:* 23 full-time (20 women), 89 part-time (80 women); includes 12 minority (3 Black or African American, non-Hispanic/Latino; 1 American Indian or Alaska Native, non-Hispanic/Latino; 3 Asian, non-Hispanic/Latino; 5 Hispanic/Latino). Average age 41. 143 applicants, 25% accepted, 25 enrolled. In 2011, 9 master's awarded. *Degree requirements:* For master's, comprehensive exam. *Entrance requirements:* For master's, essay, three letters of recommendation. Additional exam requirements/recommendations for international students: Required—TOEFL or IELTS. *Application deadline:* For fall admission, 7/15 priority date for domestic students, 6/10 for international students; for spring admission, 12/1 priority date for domestic students, 11/1 for international students. Applications are processed on a rolling basis. Application fee: $40 ($50 for international students). Electronic applications accepted. *Financial support:* In 2011–12, 24 students received support. Career-related internships or fieldwork, Federal Work-Study, and scholarships/grants available. Support available to part-time students. Financial award application deadline: 3/1. *Unit head:* Dr. Susan S. Wilkinson, Department Head, 325-942-2060 Ext. 290, Fax: 325-942-2236, E-mail: susan.wilkinson@angelo.edu. *Application contact:* Dr. Molly J. Walker, Graduate Advisor, 325-942-2060 Ext. 246, Fax: 325-942-2236, E-mail: molly.walker@angelo.edu. Web site: http://www.angelo.edu/dept/nursing/.

Bloomsburg University of Pennsylvania, School of Graduate Studies, College of Science and Technology, Department of Nursing, Bloomsburg, PA 17815-1301. Offers adult and family nurse practitioner (MSN); adult health and illness (MSN); community health (MSN); nursing (MSN); nursing administration (MSN). *Accreditation:* AACN; AANA/CANAEP. *Degree requirements:* For master's, thesis. *Entrance requirements:* For master's, minimum QPA of 3.0. Additional exam requirements/recommendations for international students: Required—TOEFL. Electronic applications accepted. *Faculty research:* Cardiopulmonary nursing, cancer topics, women's health.

Boston College, William F. Connell School of Nursing, Chestnut Hill, MA 02467-3800. Offers adult-gerontology nursing (MS); community health nursing (MS); family health (MS); forensic nursing (MS); maternal/child health nursing (MS), including pediatric and women's health; nurse anesthesia (MS); nursing (PhD); palliative care (MS), including adult and pediatric; psychiatric-mental health nursing (MS); MBA/MS; MS/MA; MS/PhD. *Accreditation:* AACN; AANA/CANAEP (one or more programs are accredited). Part-time programs available. *Faculty:* 48 full-time (46 women), 31 part-time/adjunct (29 women). *Students:* 225 full-time (207 women), 90 part-time (88 women); includes 47 minority (15 Black or African American, non-Hispanic/Latino; 3 American Indian or Alaska Native, non-Hispanic/Latino; 17 Asian, non-Hispanic/Latino; 8 Hispanic/Latino; 4 Two or more races, non-Hispanic/Latino), 6 international. Average age 31. 369 applicants, 43% accepted, 80 enrolled. In 2011, 113 master's, 8 doctorates awarded. *Degree requirements:* For master's, comprehensive exam, research project; for doctorate, comprehensive exam, thesis/dissertation, computer literacy exam or foreign language. *Entrance requirements:* For master's, bachelor's degree in nursing; for doctorate, GRE General Test, MS in nursing. Additional exam requirements/recommendations for international students: Required—TOEFL (minimum score 600 paper-based; 250 computer-based; 100 iBT). *Application deadline:* For fall admission, 11/1 for domestic and international students; for winter admission, 12/31 for domestic and international students; for spring admission, 4/30 for domestic and international students. Applications are processed on a rolling basis. Application fee: $40. Electronic applications accepted. *Financial support:* In 2011–12, 167 students received support, including 9 fellowships with full tuition reimbursements available (averaging $15,300 per year), 7 teaching assistantships (averaging $13,612 per year); research assistantships, Federal Work-Study, institutionally sponsored loans, scholarships/grants, traineeships, health care benefits, tuition waivers (partial), and unspecified assistantships also available. Support available to part-time students. Financial award application deadline: 3/1; financial award applicants required to submit FAFSA. *Faculty research:* Pre-term labor, palliative care, support during chronic illness, violence, eating disorders. *Total*

annual research expenditures: $2.1 million. *Unit head:* Dr. Susan Gennaro, Dean, 617-552-4251, Fax: 617-552-0931, E-mail: susan.gennaro@bc.edu. *Application contact:* MaryBeth Crowley, Graduate Programs Assistant, 617-552-4928, Fax: 617-552-2121, E-mail: csongrad@bc.edu. Web site: http://www.bc.edu/nursing/.

Clarkson College, Master of Science in Nursing Program, Omaha, NE 68131. Offers adult nurse practitioner (MSN, Post-Master's Certificate); family nurse practitioner (MSN, Post-Master's Certificate); nursing education (MSN, Post-Master's Certificate); nursing health care leadership (MSN, Post-Master's Certificate). *Accreditation:* AANA/CANAEP; NLN. Part-time and evening/weekend programs available. Postbaccalaureate distance learning degree programs offered (minimal on-campus study). *Degree requirements:* For master's, on-campus skills assessment (family nurse practitioner, adult nurse practitioner), comprehensive exam or thesis. *Entrance requirements:* For master's, minimum GPA of 3.0, 2 references, resume. Additional exam requirements/recommendations for international students: Required—TOEFL (minimum score 600 paper-based; 250 computer-based; 100 iBT). Electronic applications accepted.

College of Mount Saint Vincent, School of Professional and Continuing Studies, Department of Nursing, Riverdale, NY 10471-1093. Offers adult nurse practitioner (MSN, PMC); family nurse practitioner (MSN, PMC); nurse educator (PMC); nursing administration (MSN); nursing for the adult and aged (MSN). *Accreditation:* AACN. Part-time programs available. *Entrance requirements:* For master's, BSN, interview, RN license, minimum GPA of 3.0, letters of reference. Additional exam requirements/recommendations for international students: Required—TOEFL. *Expenses:* Contact institution.

College of Staten Island of the City University of New York, Graduate Programs, Department of Nursing, Program in Adult Health Nursing, Staten Island, NY 10314-6600. Offers MS, 6th Year Certificate. Part-time and evening/weekend programs available. *Faculty:* 5 full-time (all women), 3 part-time/adjunct (2 women). *Students:* 43. Average age 39. 28 applicants, 54% accepted, 12 enrolled. In 2011, 7 master's, 2 other advanced degrees awarded. *Degree requirements:* For master's, thesis optional. *Entrance requirements:* For master's, minimum undergraduate GPA of 3.0 in nursing courses, New York RN license, 2 professional references; for 6th Year Certificate, master's degree in nursing. Additional exam requirements/recommendations for international students: Required—TOEFL (minimum score 550 paper-based; 213 computer-based; 79 iBT), IELTS (minimum score 6.5). *Application deadline:* For fall admission, 4/18 priority date for domestic students, 4/18 for international students; for spring admission, 11/21 priority date for domestic students, 11/21 for international students. Applications are processed on a rolling basis. Application fee: $125. Electronic applications accepted. *Expenses:* Tuition, state resident: full-time $8210; part-time $345 per credit. Tuition, nonresident: part-time $640 per credit. *Required fees:* $128 per semester. *Financial support:* Career-related internships or fieldwork, Federal Work-Study, and scholarships/grants available. Support available to part-time students. Financial award applicants required to submit FAFSA. *Unit head:* Prof. Mary Ellen McMorrow, Coordinator, 718-982-3823, Fax: 718-982-3813, E-mail: maryellen.mcmorrow@csi.cuny.edu. *Application contact:* Sasha Spence, Assistant Director for Graduate Admissions, 718-982-2699, Fax: 718-982-2500, E-mail: spence@mail.csi.cuny.edu. Web site: http://www.csi.cuny.edu/catalog/graduate/nursing.php3.

Columbia University, School of Nursing, Program in Adult Nurse Practitioner, New York, NY 10032. Offers MS, Adv C. *Accreditation:* AACN. Part-time programs available. *Entrance requirements:* For master's, GRE General Test, BSN, 1 year of clinical experience (preferred); for Adv C, MSN. Electronic applications accepted.

Daemen College, Department of Nursing, Amherst, NY 14226-3592. Offers adult nurse practitioner (MS, Post Master's Certificate); nurse executive leadership (Post Master's Certificate); nursing education (MS, Post Master's Certificate); nursing executive leadership (MS); nursing practice (DNP); palliative care nursing (Post Master's Certificate). *Accreditation:* NLN. Part-time programs available. *Degree requirements:* For master's, thesis or alternative, degree completed in 4 years; minimum GPA of 3.0; for doctorate, degree completed in 5 years; 500 post-master's clinical hours. *Entrance requirements:* For master's, BN, 1 year medical/surgical experience, RN license and state registration, statistics course with minimum C grade, 3 letters of recommendation, minimum GPA of 3.25, interview; for doctorate, MS in advance nursing practice; New York state RN license; goal statement; resume; interview; statistics course with minimum grade of 'C'; for Post Master's Certificate, master's degree in clinical area; RN license and current registration; one year of clinical experience; statistics course with minimum grade of 'C'; 3 letters of recommendation; interview; letter of intent. Additional exam requirements/recommendations for international students: Required—TOEFL (minimum score 500 paper-based; 173 computer-based; 63 iBT), IELTS (minimum score 5.5). Electronic applications accepted. *Faculty research:* Professional stress, client behavior, drug therapy, treatment modalities and pulmonary cancers, chemical dependency.

DePaul University, College of Science and Health, Department of Nursing, Chicago, IL 60614. Offers adult nurse practitioner (Certificate); adult nursing (MS); family nurse practitioner (Certificate); family nursing (MS); generalist nursing (MS); nurse anesthesia (MS); MS/DNP. MS in nurse anesthesia offered jointly with Ravenswood Hospital Medical Center. *Accreditation:* AACN; AANA/CANAEP (one or more programs are accredited). *Faculty:* 13 full-time (11 women), 12 part-time/adjunct (11 women). *Students:* 256 full-time (220 women), 53 part-time (48 women); includes 81 minority (15 Black or African American, non-Hispanic/Latino; 1 American Indian or Alaska Native, non-Hispanic/Latino; 39 Asian, non-Hispanic/Latino; 16 Hispanic/Latino; 5 Native Hawaiian or other Pacific Islander, non-Hispanic/Latino; 5 Two or more races, non-Hispanic/Latino), 5 international. Average age 29. 238 applicants, 46% accepted, 74 enrolled. In 2011, 70 master's awarded. Terminal master's awarded for partial completion of doctoral program. *Degree requirements:* For master's, comprehensive exam (for some programs), thesis optional. *Entrance requirements:* For master's, GRE (if bachelor's GPA less than 3.2), bachelor's degree from regionally-accredited college or university; personal statement; prerequisite worksheet; resume; 2 letters of recommendation. Additional exam requirements/recommendations for international students: Required—TOEFL (minimum score 590 paper-based; 243 computer-based; 96 iBT), IELTS (minimum score 7.5), Pearson Test of English. *Application deadline:* For fall admission, 3/1 priority date for domestic students, 3/1 for international students; for winter admission, 8/15 priority date for domestic students, 8/15 for international students. Application fee: $40. Electronic applications accepted. *Financial support:* In 2011–12, 5 students received support, including 6 fellowships (averaging $1,500 per year); traineeships also available. Financial award applicants required to submit FAFSA. *Faculty research:* Children's health, women's health, health promotion. *Unit head:* Dr. Kim Amer, Interim Chair, 773-325-1160, E-mail: kamer@depaul.edu. *Application contact:* Ann Spittle, Director of Graduate Admissions, 773-325-7315, Fax: 312-476-3244, E-mail: graddepaul@depaul.edu.

DeSales University, Graduate Division, Division of Healthcare and Natural Sciences, Center Valley, PA 18034-9568. Offers adult advanced practice nurse specialist (MSN); certified nurse midwives (MSN); certified nurse practitioners (MSN); clinical leadership (DNP); family nurse practitioner (MSN); nurse educator (MSN); nurse practitioner (Post-Master's Certificate); MSN/MBA. *Accreditation:* NLN. Part-time programs available. *Degree requirements:* For master's, thesis optional. *Entrance requirements:* For master's, GRE General Test, MAT, minimum B average in undergraduate course work, health assessment course or equivalent, course work in statistics. Additional exam requirements/recommendations for international students: Required—TOEFL. *Application deadline:* Applications are processed on a rolling basis. Application fee: $35. Electronic applications accepted. Tuition and fees vary according to degree level. *Financial support:* Applicants required to submit FAFSA. *Unit head:* Dr. Carol Gullo Mest, Director, 610-282-1100 Ext. 1394, Fax: 610-282-2091, E-mail: carol.mest@desales.edu. *Application contact:* Caryn Stopper, Director of Graduate Admissions, 610-282-1100 Ext. 1768, Fax: 610-282-2254, E-mail: caryn.stopper@desales.edu.

Duke University, School of Nursing, Durham, NC 27708-0586. Offers adult acute care (Certificate); adult cardiovascular (Certificate); adult oncology (Certificate); adult primary care (Certificate); clinical nurse specialist (MSN), including adult oncology, gerontology, neonatal, pediatric; clinical research management (MSN, Certificate); family (Certificate); gerontology (Certificate); health and nursing ministries (MSN, Certificate); health systems leadership and outcomes (Certificate); neonatal (Certificate); neonatal/pediatric in rural health (MSN, Certificate); nurse anesthetist (MSN, Certificate); nurse practitioner (MSN), including adult acute care, adult cardiovascular, adult oncology, adult primary care, family, gerontology, neonatal, pediatric, pediatric acute care; nursing (DNP, PhD); nursing and healthcare leadership (MSN); nursing education (MSN); nursing informatics (MSN, Certificate); pediatric (Certificate); pediatric acute care (Certificate); MBA/MSN; MSN/MCM. *Accreditation:* AACN; AANA/CANAEP. Part-time and evening/weekend programs available. Postbaccalaureate distance learning degree programs offered (minimal on-campus study). *Faculty:* 56 full-time (47 women), 2 part-time/adjunct (1 woman). *Students:* 127 full-time (108 women), 395 part-time (358 women); includes 92 minority (42 Black or African American, non-Hispanic/Latino; 3 American Indian or Alaska Native, non-Hispanic/Latino; 21 Asian, non-Hispanic/Latino; 14 Hispanic/Latino; 12 Two or more races, non-Hispanic/Latino), 10 international. Average age 36. 432 applicants, 45% accepted, 143 enrolled. In 2011, 117 master's, 29 doctorates, 32 other advanced degrees awarded. Terminal master's awarded for partial completion of doctoral program. *Degree requirements:* For master's, thesis optional; for doctorate, capstone project. *Entrance requirements:* For master's, GRE General Test, 1 year of nursing experience, BSN, minimum GPA of 3.0, previous course work in statistics; for doctorate, BSN or MSN, minimum GPA of 3.0, portfolio; for Certificate, MSN. Additional exam requirements/recommendations for international students: Required—TOEFL (minimum score 550 paper-based; 213 computer-based). *Application deadline:* For fall admission, 12/1 for domestic and international students; for spring admission, 5/1 for domestic and international students. Application fee: $50. Electronic applications accepted. *Expenses:* Contact institution. *Financial support:* Career-related internships or fieldwork, institutionally sponsored loans, scholarships/grants, traineeships, and tuition waivers (partial) available. Support available to part-time students. Financial award application deadline: 4/1; financial award applicants required to submit FAFSA. *Faculty research:* Cardiovascular disease, caregiver skill training, data mining, prostate cancer, neonatal immune system. *Total annual research expenditures:* $4.7 million. *Unit head:* Dr. Catherine L. Gilliss, Dean/Vice Chancellor for Nursing Affairs, 919-684-9444, Fax: 919-684-9414, E-mail: gilli025@mc.duke.edu. *Application contact:* Bebe T. Mills, Director of Admissions, 919-684-9151, Fax: 919-668-4693, E-mail: mills031@mc.duke.edu. Web site: http://www.nursing.duke.edu/.

Eastern Michigan University, Graduate School, College of Health and Human Services, School of Nursing, Ypsilanti, MI 48197. Offers nursing (MSN); quality improvement in health care systems (Graduate Certificate); teaching in health care systems (MSN, Graduate Certificate). *Accreditation:* AACN. Part-time and evening/weekend programs available. Postbaccalaureate distance learning degree programs offered (minimal on-campus study). *Faculty:* 20 full-time (18 women). *Students:* 2 full-time (both women), 33 part-time (27 women); includes 20 minority (14 Black or African American, non-Hispanic/Latino; 5 Asian, non-Hispanic/Latino; 1 Hispanic/Latino). Average age 46. 32 applicants, 56% accepted, 8 enrolled. In 2011, 11 master's, 15 other advanced degrees awarded. *Degree requirements:* For master's, thesis optional. *Entrance requirements:* For master's, GRE General Test, Michigan RN license. Additional exam requirements/recommendations for international students: Required—TOEFL. *Application deadline:* Applications are processed on a rolling basis. Application fee: $35. *Expenses:* Tuition, state resident: full-time $10,367; part-time $432 per credit hour. Tuition, nonresident: full-time $20,435; part-time $851 per credit hour. *Required fees:* $39 per credit hour. $46 per semester. One-time fee: $100. Tuition and fees vary according to course level, degree level and reciprocity agreements. *Financial support:* Fellowships, research assistantships with full tuition reimbursements, teaching assistantships with full tuition reimbursements, career-related internships or fieldwork, Federal Work-Study, institutionally sponsored loans, scholarships/grants, tuition waivers (partial), and unspecified assistantships available. Support available to part-time students. Financial award applicants required to submit FAFSA. *Unit head:* Dr. Peggy Trewn, Interim Director, 734-487-2310, Fax: 734-487-6946, E-mail: ptrewn@emich.edu. *Application contact:* Dr. Virginia Lan, MSN Coordinator, 734-487-2310, Fax: 734-487-6946, E-mail: vlan@emich.edu. Web site: http://www.emich.edu/nursing.

East Tennessee State University, School of Graduate Studies, College of Nursing, Doctoral Nursing Programs, Johnson City, TN 37614. Offers adult/gerontological nurse practitioner (DNP); executive leadership in nursing (DNP); family nurse practitioner (DNP); nursing (PhD); psychiatric/mental health nurse practitioner (DNP). Part-time and evening/weekend programs available. *Students:* 22 full-time (21 women), 27 part-time (26 women); includes 3 minority (2 Black or African American, non-Hispanic/Latino; 1 Asian, non-Hispanic/Latino). 74 applicants, 41% accepted, 30 enrolled. In 2011, 3 doctorates awarded. *Degree requirements:* For doctorate, comprehensive exam, dissertation (PhD); residency internship and capstone project (DNP). *Entrance requirements:* For doctorate, GRE General Test, minimum GPA of 3.0, RN license, minimum two years RN experience, 3 letters of recommendation, interview, writing sample, resume. Additional exam requirements/recommendations for international students: Required—TOEFL (minimum score 600 paper-based; 250 computer-based; 100 iBT). *Application deadline:* For fall admission, 2/1 for domestic and international students; for spring admission, 7/1 for domestic and international students. Application fee: $35 ($45 for international students). Electronic applications accepted. *Expenses:* Tuition, state resident: full-time $7312; part-time $350 per credit hour. Tuition, nonresident: full-time $18,490; part-time $621 per credit hour. *Required fees:* $63 per credit hour. Tuition and fees vary according to course load and program. *Financial support:* In 2011–12, 2 students received support, including 1 research assistantship with partial tuition reimbursement available (averaging $3,000 per year); career-related internships or fieldwork, institutionally sponsored loans, scholarships/grants, and unspecified assistantships also available. Financial award application deadline: 7/1; financial award applicants required to submit FAFSA. *Faculty research:* Rural primary care, healthcare for the homeless and underserved, community health problems across the lifespan, nursing education research, school health services. *Unit head:* Dr. Kathleen Rayman, Director of Graduate Programs, 423-439-5626, Fax: 423-439-4100, E-mail: raymank@etsu.edu. *Application contact:* Linda Raines, Graduate Specialist, 423-439-6158, Fax: 423-439-5624, E-mail: rainesIt@etsu.edu.

East Tennessee State University, School of Graduate Studies, College of Nursing, Master's Nursing Programs, Johnson City, TN 37614. Offers advanced practice nursing (MSN); nursing (MSN); nursing administration (MSN); nursing education (MSN); nursing

informatics (MSN). Part-time programs available. Postbaccalaureate distance learning degree programs offered. *Students:* 50 full-time (47 women), 137 part-time (126 women); includes 4 minority (1 American Indian or Alaska Native, non-Hispanic/Latino; 2 Hispanic/Latino; 1 Two or more races, non-Hispanic/Latino), 1 international. 151 applicants, 29% accepted, 44 enrolled. In 2011, 74 master's awarded. *Degree requirements:* For master's, comprehensive exam (for some programs), culminating project (for some programs). *Entrance requirements:* For master's, minimum GPA of 3.0, RN license, resume, 3 letters of recommendation. Additional exam requirements/recommendations for international students: Required—TOEFL (minimum score 600 paper-based; 250 computer-based; 100 iBT). *Application deadline:* For fall admission, 2/1 for domestic and international students; for spring admission, 7/1 for domestic and international students. Application fee: $35 ($45 for international students). Electronic applications accepted. *Expenses:* Tuition: state resident: full-time $7312; part-time $350 per credit hour. Tuition, nonresident: full-time $18,490; part-time $621 per credit hour. *Required fees:* $63 per credit hour. Tuition and fees vary according to course load and program. *Financial support:* In 2011–12, 2 students received support. Institutionally sponsored loans, scholarships/grants, tuition waivers (full), and unspecified assistantships available. Support available to part-time students. Financial award application deadline: 7/1; financial award applicants required to submit FAFSA. *Faculty research:* Rural primary care, healthcare for the homeless and underserved, community health problems across the lifespan, nursing education research, school health services. *Unit head:* Dr. Nancy Cameron, Coordinator, 423-439-4874, Fax: 423-439-4100, E-mail: cameronng@etsu.edu. *Application contact:* Linda Raines, Graduate Specialist, 423-439-6158, Fax: 423-439-5624, E-mail: raineslt@etsu.edu.

Emory University, Nell Hodgson Woodruff School of Nursing, Atlanta, GA 30322-1100. Offers adult nurse practitioner (MSN); emergency nurse practitioner (MSN); family nurse practitioner (MSN); family nurse-midwife (MSN); health systems leadership (MSN); nurse-midwifery (MSN); pediatric nurse practitioner acute and primary care (MSN); women's health care (Title X) (MSN); women's health nurse practitioner (MSN); women's health/adult health nurse practitioner (MSN); MSN/MPH. *Accreditation:* AACN; ACNM/ACME (one or more programs are accredited). Part-time programs available. *Faculty:* 30 full-time (29 women), 11 part-time/adjunct (10 women). *Students:* 110 full-time (106 women), 53 part-time (51 women); includes 49 minority (35 Black or African American, non-Hispanic/Latino; 2 American Indian or Alaska Native, non-Hispanic/Latino; 10 Asian, non-Hispanic/Latino; 2 Hispanic/Latino), 4 international. Average age 32. 182 applicants, 63% accepted, 86 enrolled. In 2011, 81 master's awarded. *Entrance requirements:* For master's, GRE General Test or MAT, minimum GPA of 3.0, BS in nursing from an accredited institution, RN license and additional course work, 3 letters of recommendation. Additional exam requirements/recommendations for international students: Required—TOEFL (minimum score 600 paper-based; 100 iBT). *Application deadline:* For fall admission, 1/15 priority date for domestic students, 1/15 for international students; for spring admission, 10/1 priority date for domestic students, 10/1 for international students. Applications are processed on a rolling basis. Application fee: $50. Electronic applications accepted. *Expenses:* Contact institution. *Financial support:* In 2011–12, 14 fellowships (averaging $28,000 per year) were awarded; career-related internships or fieldwork, Federal Work-Study, institutionally sponsored loans, and scholarships/grants also available. Support available to part-time students. Financial award application deadline: 3/1; financial award applicants required to submit CSS PROFILE or FAFSA. *Faculty research:* Older adult falls and injuries, minority health issues, cardiac symptoms and quality of life, bio-ethics and decision-making, menopausal issues. *Unit head:* Dr. Linda McCauley, Dean, 404-727-7976, Fax: 404-727-9800, E-mail: linda.mccauley@emory.edu. Web site: http://www.nursing.emory.edu/.

Felician College, Program in Nursing, Lodi, NJ 07644-2117. Offers adult nurse practitioner (MSN, PMC); family nurse practitioner (MSN, PMC); nursing (MSN); nursing education (MSN). *Accreditation:* AACN. Part-time and evening/weekend programs available. Postbaccalaureate distance learning degree programs offered (no on-campus study). *Students:* 4 full-time (all women), 74 part-time (64 women); includes 18 minority (10 Black or African American, non-Hispanic/Latino; 5 Asian, non-Hispanic/Latino; 3 Hispanic/Latino). Average age 42. 29 applicants, 90% accepted, 24 enrolled. *Degree requirements:* For master's, scholarly project. *Entrance requirements:* For master's, BS in nursing or equivalent, minimum GPA of 3.0, 2 letters of recommendation, RN license; for PMC, RN license, minimum GPA of 2.75. Additional exam requirements/recommendations for international students: Recommended—TOEFL (minimum score 550 paper-based; 213 computer-based). *Application deadline:* Applications are processed on a rolling basis. Application fee: $40. *Expenses: Tuition:* Part-time $925 per credit. *Required fees:* $262.50 per semester. Part-time tuition and fees vary according to class time and student level. *Financial support:* In 2011–12, 10 students received support. Traineeships available. Financial award applicants required to submit FAFSA. *Faculty research:* Anxiety and fear, curriculum innovation, health promotion. *Unit head:* Dr. Muriel Shore, Dean, Division of Health Sciences, 201-559-6030, E-mail: shorem@felician.edu. *Application contact:* Elizabeth Barca, Senior Assistant Director, Graduate Admissions, 201-559-6077, Fax: 201-559-6138, E-mail: graduate@felician.edu.

See Display on page 630 and Close-Up on page 797.

Florida Southern College, Program in Nursing, Lakeland, FL 33801-5698. Offers clinical nurse specialist (MSN); nurse educator (MSN); nurse practitioner (MSN). *Accreditation:* AACN. Part-time and evening/weekend programs available. *Entrance requirements:* For master's, Florida RN license, 3 letters of recommendation, personal statement, minimum GPA of 3.0, resume. Additional exam requirements/recommendations for international students: Required—TOEFL (minimum score 550 paper-based). *Expenses:* Contact institution. *Faculty research:* End of life care, dementia, health promotion.

The George Washington University, School of Nursing, Washington, DC 20052. Offers adult nurse practitioner (MSN, Post-Master's Certificate); clinical research administration (MSN); family nurse practitioner (MSN, Post-Master's Certificate); health care quality (MSN, Post-Master's Certificate); nursing (DNP); nursing leadership and management (MSN); palliative care nurse practitioner (Post-Master's Certificate). *Accreditation:* AACN. *Faculty:* 19 full-time (all women), 32 part-time/adjunct (29 women). *Students:* 27 full-time (25 women), 360 part-time (330 women); includes 89 minority (44 Black or African American, non-Hispanic/Latino; 9 American Indian or Alaska Native, non-Hispanic/Latino; 25 Asian, non-Hispanic/Latino; 11 Hispanic/Latino), 15 international. Average age 39. 287 applicants, 87% accepted, 176 enrolled. In 2011, 45 master's, 19 doctorates awarded. *Unit head:* Jean E. Johnson, Dean, 202-994-3725, E-mail: sonjej@gwumc.edu. *Application contact:* Kristin Williams, Assistant Vice President for Graduate and Special Enrollment Management, 202-994-0467, Fax: 202-994-0371, E-mail: ksw@gwu.edu. Web site: http://nursing.gwumc.edu/.

Georgia College & State University, Graduate School, College of Health Sciences, Graduate Nursing Program, Milledgeville, GA 31061. Offers adult health (MSN); family nurse practitioner (MSN); nursing administration (MSN); MSN/MBA. *Accreditation:* NLN. Part-time and evening/weekend programs available. *Students:* 10 full-time (9 women), 63 part-time (60 women); includes 16 minority (all Black or African American, non-Hispanic/Latino). Average age 36. 64 applicants, 44% accepted, 20 enrolled. In 2011, 7 master's awarded. *Degree requirements:* For master's, comprehensive exam, thesis optional. *Entrance requirements:* For master's, GMAT, GRE General Test, or MAT, bachelor's degree in nursing, RN license, 1 year clinical experience. Additional exam requirements/recommendations for international students: Recommended—TOEFL (minimum score 550 paper-based; 213 computer-based; 79 iBT). *Application deadline:* For fall admission, 7/1 priority date for domestic students; for spring admission, 4/1 priority date for domestic students. Applications are processed on a rolling basis. Application fee: $40. Electronic applications accepted. *Expenses:* Tuition, state resident: full-time $4806; part-time $267 per credit hour. Tuition, nonresident: full-time $17,802; part-time $989 per credit hour. *Required fees:* $936 per semester. Tuition and fees vary according to course load and campus/location. *Financial support:* In 2011–12, 1 research assistantship with full tuition reimbursement was awarded; unspecified assistantships also available. Financial award applicants required to submit FAFSA. *Unit head:* Dr. Judith Malachowski, Director, School of Nursing, 478-445-5122, E-mail: judith.malachowski@gcsu.edu. *Application contact:* Lora Crowe, MSN Coordinator, 478-445-5122, E-mail: lora.crowe@gcsu.edu.

Georgia State University, College of Health and Human Sciences, Byrdine F. Lewis School of Nursing, Atlanta, GA 30302-3083. Offers adult health (MS); adult health nursing (Certificate); child health (MS); family nurse practitioner (MS, Certificate); health promotion, protection and restoration (PhD); perinatal/women's health (MS); psychiatric mental health nursing (Certificate); psychiatric/mental health (MS); women's health nursing (Certificate). *Accreditation:* AACN. Part-time and evening/weekend programs available. Postbaccalaureate distance learning degree programs offered (minimal on-campus study). *Degree requirements:* For master's, research activity; for doctorate, comprehensive exam, thesis/dissertation. *Entrance requirements:* For master's, MAT (preferred) or GRE, interview, RN license; for doctorate, GRE General Test. Additional exam requirements/recommendations for international students: Required—TOEFL (minimum score 550 paper-based; 213 computer-based). Electronic applications accepted. *Expenses:* Contact institution. *Faculty research:* Breast cancer prevention, sexually compulsive behaviors, health risks in minority youth, asthma treatment strategies, adolescent alcohol-related issues.

Goldfarb School of Nursing at Barnes-Jewish College, Graduate Programs, St. Louis, MO 63110. Offers adult acute care nurse practitioner (MSN); adult nurse practitioner (MSN); nurse anesthesia (MSN); nurse educator (MSN); nurse executive (MSN); DNP/PhD. *Accreditation:* AACN; AANA/CANAEP. Part-time and evening/weekend programs available. Postbaccalaureate distance learning degree programs offered (minimal on-campus study). *Faculty:* 38 full-time (35 women), 14 part-time/adjunct (11 women). *Students:* 79 full-time (68 women), 92 part-time (86 women); includes 45 minority (29 Black or African American, non-Hispanic/Latino; 1 American Indian or Alaska Native, non-Hispanic/Latino; 3 Asian, non-Hispanic/Latino; 3 Hispanic/Latino; 6 Native Hawaiian or other Pacific Islander, non-Hispanic/Latino; 3 Two or more races, non-Hispanic/Latino), 1 international. Average age 40. 134 applicants, 66% accepted, 51 enrolled. In 2011, 31 degrees awarded. *Degree requirements:* For master's, thesis or alternative. *Entrance requirements:* For master's, 2 references, personal statement, curriculum vitae or resume. Additional exam requirements/recommendations for international students: Required—TOEFL (minimum score 575 paper-based; 240 computer-based; 85 iBT). *Application deadline:* For fall admission, 2/1 for international students; for spring admission, 10/1 for international students. Applications are processed on a rolling basis. Application fee: $50. *Expenses: Tuition:* Full-time $14,685; part-time $630 per credit hour. *Required fees:* $280. *Financial support:* Fellowships, research assistantships, Federal Work-Study, institutionally sponsored loans, and scholarships/grants available. Support available to part-time students. Financial award applicants required to submit FAFSA. *Faculty research:* HIV Stigma, HIV symptom management, palliative care with children and their families, heart disease prevention in Hispanic women, depression in the well elderly, alternative therapies in pre-term infants. *Unit head:* Dr. Connie K. Koch, Interim Dean, 314-36-26590, Fax: 314-362-0984, E-mail: ckoch@bjc.org. *Application contact:* Dr. Michael Ward, Associate Dean for Student Programs, 314-362-9155, Fax: 314-362-0984, E-mail: mward@bjc.org.

Grantham University, College of Arts and Sciences, Kansas City, MO 64153. Offers case management (MSN); health systems management (MS); healthcare administration (MHA); nursing (MSN); nursing education (MSN); nursing informatics (MSN); nursing management and organizational leadership (MSN). Part-time and evening/weekend programs available. Postbaccalaureate distance learning degree programs offered (no on-campus study). *Degree requirements:* For master's, thesis (for some programs), capstone project. *Entrance requirements:* For master's, bachelor's degree from accredited degree-granting institution. Additional exam requirements/recommendations for international students: Required—TOEFL (minimum score 500 paper-based; 213 computer-based; 61 iBT). Electronic applications accepted.

Gwynedd-Mercy College, School of Nursing, Gwynedd Valley, PA 19437-0901. Offers clinical nurse specialist (MSN), including gerontology, oncology, pediatrics; nurse practitioner (MSN), including adult health, pediatric health. *Accreditation:* NLN. *Faculty:* 3 full-time (all women), 2 part-time/adjunct (both women). *Students:* 14 full-time (13 women), 28 part-time (25 women); includes 11 minority (4 Black or African American, non-Hispanic/Latino; 6 Asian, non-Hispanic/Latino; 1 Hispanic/Latino). Average age 40. 23 applicants, 83% accepted, 11 enrolled. In 2011, 7 master's awarded. *Degree requirements:* For master's, thesis optional. *Entrance requirements:* For master's, GRE General Test or MAT, current nursing experience, physical assessment, course work in statistics, BSN from NLNAC-accredited program, 2 letters of recommendation, personal interview. Additional exam requirements/recommendations for international students: Required—TOEFL (minimum score 575 paper-based). *Application deadline:* For fall admission, 8/1 priority date for domestic students; for winter admission, 12/1 priority date for domestic students. Applications are processed on a rolling basis. Application fee: $25. Electronic applications accepted. *Expenses:* Contact institution. *Financial support:* In 2011–12, 21 students received support. Scholarships/grants, traineeships, and unspecified assistantships available. Financial award application deadline: 8/30. *Faculty research:* Critical thinking, primary care, domestic violence, multiculturalism, nursing centers. *Unit head:* Dr. Andrea D. Hollingsworth, Dean, 215-646-7300 Ext. 539, Fax: 215-641-5517, E-mail: hollingsworth.a@gmc.edu. *Application contact:* Dr. Barbara A. Jones, Director, 215-646-7300 Ext. 407, Fax: 215-641-5564, E-mail: jones.b@gmc.edu. Web site: http://www.gmc.edu/academics/nursing/.

Hampton University, Graduate College, School of Nursing, Hampton, VA 23668. Offers advanced adult nursing (MS); community health nursing (MS); community mental health/psychiatric nursing (MS); family nursing (MS); gerontological nursing for the nurse practitioner (MS); pediatric nursing (MS); women's health nursing (MS). *Accreditation:* AACN; NLN. Part-time and evening/weekend programs available. *Degree requirements:* For master's, thesis optional. *Entrance requirements:* For master's, GRE General Test. *Faculty research:* Curriculum development, physical and mental assessment.

Hunter College of the City University of New York, Graduate School, Schools of the Health Professions, Hunter-Bellevue School of Nursing, Program in Adult Nurse Practitioner, New York, NY 10021-5085. Offers MS. *Accreditation:* AACN. *Faculty:* 20 full-time (16 women), 20 part-time/adjunct (18 women). *Students:* 33 part-time (29 women); includes 9 minority (3 Black or African American, non-Hispanic/Latino; 4 Asian,

non-Hispanic/Latino; 2 Hispanic/Latino), 6 international. Average age 32. 27 applicants, 63% accepted, 13 enrolled. *Degree requirements:* For master's, practicum. *Entrance requirements:* For master's, minimum GPA of 3.0, New York RN license, 2 years of professional practice experience, BSN. Additional exam requirements/recommendations for international students: Required—TOEFL. *Application deadline:* For fall admission, 4/1 for domestic students, 2/1 for international students; for spring admission, 11/1 for domestic students, 9/1 for international students. Applications are processed on a rolling basis. Application fee: $125. *Expenses:* Tuition, state resident: full-time $8210; part-time $345 per credit. Tuition, nonresident: full-time $15,360; part-time $640 per credit. *Required fees:* $280 per semester. One-time fee: $125. Tuition and fees vary according to class time, campus/location and program. *Financial support:* Federal Work-Study, scholarships/grants, and traineeships available. Support available to part-time students. Financial award application deadline: 5/1. *Faculty research:* Adult primary care, critical care. *Unit head:* Dr. Joanna Hofmann, Graduate Advisor, 212-481-4454, Fax: 212-481-5078, E-mail: jhofmann@hunter.cuny.edu. *Application contact:* William Zlata, Director for Graduate Admissions, 212-772-4482, Fax: 212-650-3336, E-mail: admissions@hunter.cuny.edu. Web site: http://www.hunter.cuny.edu/graduateadmissions/program-requirements/schools-of-health-professions/nursing/adult-nurse-practitioner.

Indiana University–Purdue University Fort Wayne, College of Health and Human Services, Department of Nursing, Fort Wayne, IN 46805-1499. Offers adult nursing practitioner (MS); nurse executive (MS); nursing administration (Certificate); nursing education (MS); women's health nurse practitioner (MS). Part-time programs available. *Faculty:* 10 full-time (all women). *Students:* 3 full-time (all women), 33 part-time (31 women); includes 3 minority (1 American Indian or Alaska Native, non-Hispanic/Latino; 1 Asian, non-Hispanic/Latino; 1 Hispanic/Latino). Average age 36. 13 applicants, 92% accepted, 10 enrolled. In 2011, 14 master's awarded. *Entrance requirements:* For master's, GRE Writing Test (if GPA below 3.0), BS in nursing, eligibility for Indiana RN license, minimum GPA of 3.0, essay, copy of resume, three references, undergraduate course work in research and statistics within last 5 years. Additional exam requirements/recommendations for international students: Required—TOEFL (minimum score 550 paper-based; 213 computer-based; 77 iBT); Recommended—TWE. *Application deadline:* For fall admission, 5/1 priority date for domestic students, 5/1 for international students; for spring admission, 11/15 priority date for domestic students. Applications are processed on a rolling basis. Application fee: $55 ($60 for international students). Electronic applications accepted. *Financial support:* In 2011–12, 11 teaching assistantships with partial tuition reimbursements (averaging $12,930 per year) were awarded; scholarships/grants also available. Support available to part-time students. Financial award application deadline: 3/1; financial award applicants required to submit FAFSA. *Faculty research:* Child psychiatric nursing. *Total annual research expenditures:* $296,680. *Unit head:* Dr. Carol Sternberger, Chair, 260-481-5798, Fax: 260-481-5767, E-mail: sternber@ipfw.edu. *Application contact:* Dr. Deborah Poling, Director of Graduate Program, 260-481-6276, Fax: 260-481-5767, E-mail: polingd@ipfw.edu. Web site: http://www.ipfw.edu/nursing/.

Indiana University–Purdue University Indianapolis, School of Nursing, Indianapolis, IN 46202-2896. Offers acute care nurse practitioner (MSN); adult health clinical nurse specialist (MSN); adult health nursing (MSN), including adult clinical nurse specialist; adult nurse practitioner (MSN); adult psychiatric/mental health nursing (MSN); child psychiatric/mental health nursing (MSN); community health nursing (MSN); family nurse practitioner (MSN); neonatal nurse practitioner (MSN); nursing (MSN, DNP), including nursing education (MSN); nursing (MSN), including nursing administration; nursing science (PhD); pediatric clinical nurse specialist (MSN); women's health nurse practitioner (MSN); MSN/MPA; MSN/MPH. *Accreditation:* AACN; NLN (one or more programs are accredited). Part-time programs available. *Faculty:* 85 full-time (82 women), 60 part-time/adjunct (all women). *Students:* 35 full-time (32 women), 360 part-time (340 women); includes 47 minority (28 Black or African American, non-Hispanic/Latino; 9 Asian, non-Hispanic/Latino; 4 Hispanic/Latino; 1 Native Hawaiian or other Pacific Islander, non-Hispanic/Latino; 5 Two or more races, non-Hispanic/Latino), 5 international. Average age 38. 119 applicants, 76% accepted, 54 enrolled. In 2011, 89 master's, 10 doctorates awarded. Terminal master's awarded for partial completion of doctoral program. *Degree requirements:* For master's, thesis; for doctorate, thesis/dissertation. *Entrance requirements:* For master's, minimum GPA of 3.0, RN license; for doctorate, GRE General Test, minimum GPA of 3.0, MSN, RN license, graduate statistics course with minimum B grade (not older than 3 years). Additional exam requirements/recommendations for international students: Required—TOEFL. *Application deadline:* For fall admission, 2/15 for domestic students; for spring admission, 9/15 for domestic students. Application fee: $55 ($65 for international students). *Financial support:* In 2011–12, 93 students received support, including 9 fellowships with full tuition reimbursements available (averaging $7,039 per year), 7 teaching assistantships with full tuition reimbursements available (averaging $5,300 per year); research assistantships with full tuition reimbursements available, Federal Work-Study, institutionally sponsored loans, scholarships/grants, and tuition waivers (full) also available. Support available to part-time students. Financial award application deadline: 5/1. *Faculty research:* Clinical science, health systems. *Total annual research expenditures:* $3 million. *Unit head:* Associate Dean for Graduate Programs, 317-274-2806, E-mail: nursing@iupui.edu. *Application contact:* Information Contact, 317-274-2806. Web site: http://nursing.iupui.edu/.

The Johns Hopkins University, School of Nursing, Nurse Practitioner Program, Baltimore, MD 21218-2699. Offers adult acute/critical care (MSN, Certificate); adult and pediatric primary care (MSN); adult or pediatric primary care (Certificate); emergency preparedness/disaster response (Certificate); family primary care (MSN, Certificate); women's health (Certificate). *Accreditation:* AACN; NLN (one or more programs are accredited). Part-time programs available. *Degree requirements:* For master's, thesis optional, scholarly project or portfolio. *Entrance requirements:* For master's, GRE, interview, minimum GPA of 3.0, BSN, Maryland RN license. Additional exam requirements/recommendations for international students: Required—TOEFL (minimum score 550 paper-based; 213 computer-based). Electronic applications accepted. *Expenses:* Contact institution. *Faculty research:* Community outreach, primary care of underserved populations, substance-abusing individuals, childhood violence, women's health.

Kent State University, College of Nursing, Kent, OH 44242-0001. Offers acute care nurse practitioner (MSN); adult nurse practitioner (MSN); clinical nurse specialist (MSN); family nurse practitioner (MSN); geriatric nurse practitioner (MSN); health care management (MSN); nurse educator (MSN); nursing (PhD); nursing practice (DNP); pediatric nurse practitioner (MSN); psychiatric/mental health nurse practitioner (MSN); women's health nurse practitioner (MSN). PhD program offered jointly with The University of Akron. *Accreditation:* AACN. Part-time programs available. *Degree requirements:* For master's, thesis optional; for doctorate, comprehensive exam, thesis/dissertation. *Entrance requirements:* For master's, GRE (if undergraduate GPA less than 3.0), minimum GPA of 2.75; for doctorate, GRE, MSN. Additional exam requirements/recommendations for international students: Required—TOEFL. Electronic applications accepted. *Expenses:* Contact institution. *Faculty research:* Women and violence, methodological specialties, osteoporosis in women, new caregivers and the elderly.

Lehman College of the City University of New York, Division of Natural and Social Sciences, Department of Nursing, Bronx, NY 10468-1589. Offers adult health nursing (MS); nursing of older adults (MS); parent-child nursing (MS); pediatric nurse practitioner (MS). *Accreditation:* AACN. Part-time and evening/weekend programs available. *Entrance requirements:* For master's, bachelor's degree in nursing, New York RN license.

Lewis University, College of Nursing and Health Professions, Program in Nursing, Romeoville, IL 60446. Offers adult nurse practitioner (MSN); nursing administration (MSN); nursing education (MSN). *Accreditation:* AACN. Part-time and evening/weekend programs available. Postbaccalaureate distance learning degree programs offered (no on-campus study). *Students:* 11 full-time (all women), 237 part-time (232 women); includes 65 minority (42 Black or African American, non-Hispanic/Latino; 14 Asian, non-Hispanic/Latino; 9 Hispanic/Latino), 1 international. Average age 42. In 2011, 29 master's awarded. *Degree requirements:* For master's, clinical practicum. *Entrance requirements:* For master's, minimum undergraduate GPA of 3.0, degree in nursing, RN license, letter of recommendation, interview, resume or curriculum vitae. Additional exam requirements/recommendations for international students: Required—TOEFL (minimum score 550 paper-based; 213 computer-based; 80 iBT). *Application deadline:* For fall admission, 5/1 for international students; for spring admission, 11/15 for international students. Applications are processed on a rolling basis. Application fee: $40. Electronic applications accepted. *Financial support:* Federal Work-Study, scholarships/grants, tuition waivers (full and partial), and unspecified assistantships available. Financial award application deadline: 5/1; financial award applicants required to submit FAFSA. *Faculty research:* Cancer prevention, phenomenological methods, public policy analysis. *Total annual research expenditures:* $1,000. *Unit head:* 815-836-5610. *Application contact:* Nancy Wiksten, Adult Admission Counselor, 815-836-5628, Fax: 815-836-5578, E-mail: wikstena@lewisu.edu. Web site: http://www.lewisu.edu/.

Loma Linda University, Department of Graduate Nursing, Program in Adult and Aging Family Nursing, Loma Linda, CA 92350. Offers MS. *Accreditation:* AACN. Part-time programs available. *Degree requirements:* For master's, thesis or alternative. *Entrance requirements:* For master's, GRE General Test, BSN, minimum GPA of 3.0, RN license. Additional exam requirements/recommendations for international students: Required—TOEFL. Electronic applications accepted. *Faculty research:* Coping, integration of research.

Long Island University–Brooklyn Campus, School of Nursing, Department of Adult Nurse Practitioner, Brooklyn, NY 11201-8423. Offers MS, Certificate. *Accreditation:* AACN. *Entrance requirements:* For master's, New York RN license, 2 letters of recommendation. Additional exam requirements/recommendations for international students: Required—TOEFL (minimum score 500 paper-based; 173 computer-based). Electronic applications accepted.

Louisiana State University Health Sciences Center, School of Nursing, New Orleans, LA 70112-2223. Offers advanced public/community health nursing (MN); clinical nurse specialist (MN); nurse anesthesia (MN); nurse practitioner (MN); nursing (DNS). *Accreditation:* AACN; AANA/CANAEP (one or more programs are accredited). Part-time programs available. *Degree requirements:* For master's, thesis optional; for doctorate, thesis/dissertation. *Entrance requirements:* For master's, GRE General Test, MAT, minimum GPA of 3.0; for doctorate, GRE General Test, minimum GPA of 3.5. Additional exam requirements/recommendations for international students: Required—TOEFL. Electronic applications accepted. *Faculty research:* Advanced clinical practice, nursing education, health, social support, nursing administration.

Loyola University Chicago, Graduate School, Marcella Niehoff School of Nursing, Adult Clinical Nurse Specialist Program, Chicago, IL 60660. Offers adult clinical nurse specialist (MSN, Certificate). Part-time and evening/weekend programs available. Postbaccalaureate distance learning degree programs offered (minimal on-campus study). *Students:* 25 part-time (all women); includes 4 minority (2 Asian, non-Hispanic/Latino; 2 Hispanic/Latino), 1 international. Average age 33. 5 applicants, 80% accepted, 1 enrolled. In 2011, 3 master's awarded. *Entrance requirements:* For master's, Illinois nursing license, BSN, minimum nursing GPA of 3.0, 3 letters of recommendation, 1,000 hours experience in area of specialty. *Expenses: Tuition:* Full-time $15,660; part-time $870 per credit hour. *Required fees:* $125 per semester. Tuition and fees vary according to course load and program. *Unit head:* Dr. Meg Gulanick, Professor, 708-216-9687, Fax: 708-216-9555, E-mail: mgulani@luc.edu. *Application contact:* Amy Weatherford, Enrollment Advisor, School of Nursing, 773-508-3249, Fax: 773-508-3241, E-mail: aweatherford@luc.edu.

Loyola University Chicago, Graduate School, Marcella Niehoff School of Nursing, Adult Nurse Practitioner Program, Chicago, IL 60660. Offers adult clinical nurse practitioner (MSN), including cardiovascular ; adult health (Certificate); adult nurse practitioner (MSN); cardiovascular (MSN); cardiovascular nursing (Certificate). *Accreditation:* AACN. Part-time and evening/weekend programs available. *Students:* 1 (woman) full-time, 55 part-time (53 women); includes 9 minority (1 Black or African American, non-Hispanic/Latino; 6 Asian, non-Hispanic/Latino; 2 Hispanic/Latino). Average age 34. 23 applicants, 48% accepted, 8 enrolled. In 2011, 23 master's awarded. *Degree requirements:* For master's, comprehensive exam or oral thesis defense. *Entrance requirements:* For master's, BSN, minimum nursing GPA of 3.0, Illinois nursing license, 3 letters of recommendation, 1000 hours experience before starting clinical. *Application deadline:* Applications are processed on a rolling basis. Application fee: $50. Electronic applications accepted. *Expenses: Tuition:* Full-time $15,660; part-time $870 per credit hour. *Required fees:* $125 per semester. Tuition and fees vary according to course load and program. *Financial support:* Traineeships available. *Faculty research:* Menopause. *Unit head:* Dr. Marijo Letizia, Associate Professor, 708-216-9325, Fax: 708-216-9555, E-mail: mletizi@luc.edu. *Application contact:* Amy Weatherford, Enrollment Advisor, School of Nursing, 773-508-3249, Fax: 773-508-3241, E-mail: aweatherford@luc.edu. Web site: http://www.luc.edu/nursing/np/

Loyola University New Orleans, College of Social Sciences, School of Nursing, New Orleans, LA 70118-6195. Offers adult nurse practitioner (MSN); family nurse practitioner (MSN); health care systems management (MSN); nursing (MSN, DNP). *Accreditation:* NLN. Part-time and evening/weekend programs available. Postbaccalaureate distance learning degree programs offered. *Students:* 108 full-time (99 women), 428 part-time (385 women); includes 151 minority (110 Black or African American, non-Hispanic/Latino; 5 American Indian or Alaska Native, non-Hispanic/Latino; 14 Asian, non-Hispanic/Latino; 20 Hispanic/Latino; 2 Native Hawaiian or other Pacific Islander, non-Hispanic/Latino). Average age 46. 213 applicants, 91% accepted, 153 enrolled. In 2011, 241 master's awarded. *Degree requirements:* For doctorate, capstone project. *Entrance requirements:* For master's, BSN, Louisiana nursing license, 1 year of work experience in clinical nursing, minimum undergraduate GPA of 2.8, interview, resume. Additional exam requirements/recommendations for international students: Required—TOEFL (minimum score 550 paper-based; 213 computer-based). *Application deadline:* For fall admission, 8/1 priority date for domestic students, 8/1 for international students; for winter admission, 12/15 priority date for domestic students, 12/15 for international students; for spring admission, 5/15 priority date for domestic students, 5/15 for international students. Applications are processed on a rolling basis. Application fee: $20. Electronic applications accepted. *Financial support:* Traineeships and Incumbent

Workers Training Program grants available. Financial award application deadline: 5/1; financial award applicants required to submit FAFSA. *Faculty research:* Increasing compliance with treatment, patient satisfaction with care provided by nurse practitioners. *Unit head:* Dr. Ann H. Cary, Director, 800-488-6257, Fax: 504-865-3254, E-mail: nursing@loyno.edu. *Application contact:* Deborah Smith, Assistant to the Director, 504-865-2823, Fax: 504-865-3254, E-mail: dhsmith@loyno.edu. Web site: http://css.loyno.edu/nursing.

Madonna University, Program in Nursing, Livonia, MI 48150-1173. Offers adult health: chronic health conditions (MSN); adult nurse practitioner (MSN); nursing administration (MSN); MSN/MSBA. *Accreditation:* AACN. Part-time programs available. *Degree requirements:* For master's, thesis or alternative. *Entrance requirements:* For master's, GRE General Test, Michigan nursing license. Electronic applications accepted. *Faculty research:* Coping, caring.

Marian University, School of Nursing, Fond du Lac, WI 54935-4699. Offers adult nurse practitioner (MSN); nurse educator (MSN). *Accreditation:* AACN. Part-time and evening/weekend programs available. *Faculty:* 6 full-time (all women), 10 part-time/adjunct (9 women). *Students:* 58 full-time (52 women), 33 part-time (32 women); includes 5 minority (2 Black or African American, non-Hispanic/Latino; 2 Asian, non-Hispanic/Latino; 1 Hispanic/Latino). Average age 36. 20 applicants, 90% accepted, 18 enrolled. In 2011, 25 master's awarded. *Degree requirements:* For master's, thesis, 675 clinical practicum hours. *Entrance requirements:* For master's, 3 letters of professional recommendation; undergraduate work in nursing research, statistics, health assessment. Additional exam requirements/recommendations for international students: Required—TOEFL (minimum score 525 paper-based; 193 computer-based; 70 iBT). *Application deadline:* Applications are processed on a rolling basis. Application fee: $50. Electronic applications accepted. *Expenses:* Contact institution. *Financial support:* In 2011–12, 3 students received support. Institutionally sponsored loans and scholarships/grants available. Support available to part-time students. Financial award application deadline: 3/1; financial award applicants required to submit FAFSA. *Unit head:* Dr. Julie Luetschwager, Dean, 920-923-8094, Fax: 920-923-8770, E-mail: jaluetschwager25@marianuniversity.edu. *Application contact:* Dr. Nancy L. Stuever, Director, 920-923-8597, Fax: 920-923-8770, E-mail: nstuever44@marianuniversity.edu.

Marquette University, Graduate School, College of Nursing, Milwaukee, WI 53201-1881. Offers acute care nurse practitioner (Certificate); adult clinical nurse specialist (Certificate); adult nurse practitioner (Certificate); advanced practice nursing (MSN, DNP), including acute care, adults, neonatal nurse practitioner (MSN), nurse midwifery (DNP), nurse-midwifery (MSN), older adults, pediatrics acute care (DNP, PhD), pediatrics primary care; clinical nurse leader (MSN); gerontologic clinical nurse specialist (Certificate); gerontologic nurse practitioner (Certificate); health care systems leadership (MSN, DNP); nurse-midwifery (Certificate); nursing (PhD), including pediatrics acute care (DNP, PhD); pediatrics acute care (Certificate); pediatrics primary care (Certificate). *Accreditation:* AACN. *Faculty:* 32 full-time (30 women), 47 part-time/adjunct (all women). *Students:* 93 full-time (88 women), 244 part-time (220 women); includes 31 minority (9 Black or African American, non-Hispanic/Latino; 7 Asian, non-Hispanic/Latino; 8 Hispanic/Latino; 7 Two or more races, non-Hispanic/Latino), 1 international. Average age 30. 282 applicants, 57% accepted, 98 enrolled. In 2011, 76 master's, 8 doctorates, 7 other advanced degrees awarded. Terminal master's awarded for partial completion of doctoral program. *Degree requirements:* For master's, comprehensive exam, thesis or alternative. *Entrance requirements:* For master's, GRE General Test, BSN, Wisconsin RN license, official transcripts from all current and previous colleges/universities except Marquette, three completed recommendation forms, resume, written statement of professional goals; for doctorate, GRE General Test, official transcripts from all current and previous colleges/universities except Marquette, three letters of recommendation, resume, written statement of professional goals, sample of scholarly writing. Additional exam requirements/recommendations for international students: Required—TOEFL (minimum score 530 paper-based; 78 computer-based). *Application deadline:* For fall admission, 2/15 for domestic and international students. Application fee: $50. Electronic applications accepted. *Expenses: Tuition:* Full-time $17,010; part-time $945 per credit hour. Tuition and fees vary according to program. *Financial support:* In 2011–12, 41 students received support, including 1 fellowship with partial tuition reimbursement available (averaging $17,500 per year), 2 research assistantships with full tuition reimbursements available (averaging $13,285 per year), 8 teaching assistantships with full tuition reimbursements available (averaging $13,912 per year); career-related internships or fieldwork, Federal Work-Study, scholarships/grants, health care benefits, tuition waivers (partial), and unspecified assistantships also available. Support available to part-time students. Financial award application deadline: 2/15. *Faculty research:* Psychosocial adjustment to chronic illness, gerontology, reminiscence, health policy: uninsured and access, hospital care delivery systems. *Total annual research expenditures:* $312,575. *Unit head:* Dr. Margaret Callahan, Dean, 414-288-3800, Fax: 414-288-1578. *Application contact:* Karen Nest, Graduate Program Coordinator, 414-288-3810, Fax: 414-288-1578. Web site: http://www.marquette.edu/nursing/academicprograms-graduate.shtml.

Maryville University of Saint Louis, School of Health Professions, Nursing Program, St. Louis, MO 63141-7299. Offers accelerated RN to MSN (MSN); adult nurse practitioner (MSN); advanced practice nursing (DNP); family nurse practitioner (MSN); geriatric nurse practitioner (MSN); nursing education (MSN). *Accreditation:* AACN. Postbaccalaureate distance learning degree programs offered. *Students:* 16 full-time (14 women), 136 part-time (127 women); includes 9 minority (5 Black or African American, non-Hispanic/Latino; 3 Asian, non-Hispanic/Latino; 1 Two or more races, non-Hispanic/Latino). Average age 35. In 2011, 21 master's awarded. *Degree requirements:* For master's, practicum. *Entrance requirements:* For master's, BSN, current licensure, minimum GPA of 3.0, 3 letters of recommendation, curriculum vitae. Additional exam requirements/recommendations for international students: Required—TOEFL (minimum score 550 paper-based). *Application deadline:* Applications are processed on a rolling basis. Application fee: $40 ($60 for international students). Electronic applications accepted. *Expenses: Tuition:* Full-time $21,922; part-time $675 per credit hour. *Required fees:* $233.75 per semester. *Financial support:* Federal Work-Study and campus employment available. Support available to part-time students. Financial award application deadline: 3/1; financial award applicants required to submit FAFSA. *Unit head:* Dr. Elizabeth Buck, Director, 314-529-9453, Fax: 314-529-9139, E-mail: ebuck@maryville.edu. *Application contact:* Dr. Donna Payne, Vice President, Adult and Continuing Education, 314-529-9676, Fax: 314-529-9927, E-mail: dpayne@maryville.edu. Web site: http://www.maryville.edu/academics-hp-nursing.

Medical University of South Carolina, College of Nursing, Adult Nurse Practitioner Program, Charleston, SC 29425. Offers MSN. Part-time programs available. Postbaccalaureate distance learning degree programs offered (minimal on-campus study). *Faculty:* 10 full-time (all women), 3 part-time/adjunct (2 women). *Students:* 3 full-time (all women), 2 part-time (both women). Average age 34. 52 applicants, 17% accepted. In 2011, 4 master's awarded. *Degree requirements:* For master's, comprehensive exam (for some programs), thesis optional. *Entrance requirements:* For master's, BSN, course work in statistics, nursing license, minimum GPA of 3.0, current curriculum vitae, essay, three references. Additional exam requirements/recommendations for international students: Required—TOEFL (minimum score 600 paper-based; 250 computer-based). *Application deadline:* For fall admission, 2/1 priority date for domestic students, 2/1 for international students. Application fee: $85. Electronic applications accepted. *Financial support:* Federal Work-Study, scholarships/grants, and traineeships available. Support available to part-time students. Financial award application deadline: 3/10; financial award applicants required to submit FAFSA. *Faculty research:* Primary and palliative care, use of PDAs, diabetes. *Unit head:* Dr. Barbara J. Edlund, Lead Faculty, 843-792-4653, Fax: 843-792-2104, E-mail: edlundb@musc.edu. *Application contact:* Carolyn F. Page, Director, Student Services, 843-792-3844, Fax: 843-792-5395, E-mail: pagecf@musc.edu. Web site: http://www.musc.edu/nursing/academics/masters/anp.htm.

Molloy College, Division of Nursing, Rockville Centre, NY 11571-5002. Offers adult nurse practitioner (Advanced Certificate); clinical nurse specialist: adult health (Advanced Certificate); family nurse practitioner (Advanced Certificate); nurse practitioner psychiatry (Advanced Certificate); nursing (MS); nursing administration (Advanced Certificate); nursing administration with informatics (Advanced Certificate); nursing education (Advanced Certificate); nursing informatics (Advanced Certificate); pediatric nurse practitioner (Advanced Certificate). *Accreditation:* AACN. Part-time and evening/weekend programs available. *Faculty:* 20 full-time (19 women), 12 part-time/adjunct (11 women). *Students:* 19 full-time (15 women), 483 part-time (452 women); includes 238 minority (132 Black or African American, non-Hispanic/Latino; 61 Asian, non-Hispanic/Latino; 35 Hispanic/Latino; 2 Native Hawaiian or other Pacific Islander, non-Hispanic/Latino; 8 Two or more races, non-Hispanic/Latino), 5 international. Average age 40. 186 applicants, 82% accepted, 110 enrolled. In 2011, 94 master's awarded. *Degree requirements:* For master's, thesis optional. *Entrance requirements:* For master's, 3 letters of reference, BS in nursing, minimum undergraduate GPA of 3.0; for Advanced Certificate, 3 letters of reference, master's degree in nursing. *Application deadline:* For fall admission, 9/2 priority date for domestic students; for spring admission, 1/20 priority date for domestic students. Applications are processed on a rolling basis. Application fee: $60. *Financial support:* Research assistantships with partial tuition reimbursements, teaching assistantships with partial tuition reimbursements, institutionally sponsored loans, scholarships/grants, and unspecified assistantships available. Support available to part-time students. Financial award application deadline: 4/1; financial award applicants required to submit FAFSA. *Unit head:* Dr. Denise Walsh, Associate Dean, Graduate Nursing, 516-678-5000, Fax: 516-678-9718, E-mail: dwalsh@molloy.edu. *Application contact:* Alina Haitz, Assistant Director of Graduate Admissions, 516-678-5000, Fax: 516-256-2247, E-mail: ahaitz@molloy.edu. Web site: http://www.molloy.edu/academics/nursing-division.

Monmouth University, The Graduate School, The Marjorie K. Unterberg School of Nursing and Health Studies, West Long Branch, NJ 07764-1898. Offers adult nurse practitioner (MSN); adult psychiatric and mental health advanced practice nursing (MSN, Post-Master's Certificate); advanced practice nursing (Post-Master's Certificate); family nurse practitioner (MSN, Post-Master's Certificate); forensic nursing (MSN, Certificate); nursing (MSN); nursing administration (MSN, Post-Master's Certificate); nursing education (MSN, Post-Master's Certificate); nursing practice (DNP); school nursing (MSN, Certificate). *Accreditation:* AACN. Part-time and evening/weekend programs available. *Faculty:* 12 full-time (all women), 2 part-time/adjunct (both women). *Students:* 16 full-time (11 women), 244 part-time (238 women); includes 73 minority (23 Black or African American, non-Hispanic/Latino; 2 American Indian or Alaska Native, non-Hispanic/Latino; 34 Asian, non-Hispanic/Latino; 12 Hispanic/Latino; 1 Native Hawaiian or other Pacific Islander, non-Hispanic/Latino; 1 Two or more races, non-Hispanic/Latino), 1 international. Average age 41. 107 applicants, 92% accepted, 67 enrolled. In 2011, 55 master's awarded. *Degree requirements:* For master's, practicum (for some tracks). *Entrance requirements:* For master's, GRE General Test, RN license, 1 year of work experience, minimum undergraduate GPA of 2.75. Additional exam requirements/recommendations for international students: Required—TOEFL (minimum score 550 paper-based; 213 computer-based; 79 iBT), IELTS (minimum score 5) or Michigan English Language Assessment Battery (minimum score 77), Cambridge A, B, C. *Application deadline:* For fall admission, 7/15 priority date for domestic students, 6/1 for international students; for spring admission, 11/15 priority date for domestic students, 11/1 for international students. Applications are processed on a rolling basis. Application fee: $50. Electronic applications accepted. *Financial support:* In 2011–12, 138 students received support, including 138 fellowships (averaging $1,423 per year), 4 research assistantships (averaging $5,240 per year); career-related internships or fieldwork, scholarships/grants, and unspecified assistantships also available. Support available to part-time students. Financial award applicants required to submit FAFSA. *Faculty research:* Relationship of undergraduate GPA and GRE to succeed in a graduate nursing program. *Unit head:* Dr. Janet Mahoney, Dean, 732-571-3443, Fax: 732-263-5131, E-mail: jmahoney@monmouth.edu. *Application contact:* Kevin Roane, Director, Office of Graduate Admission, 732-571-3452, Fax: 732-263-5123, E-mail: gradadm@monmouth.edu. Web site: http://www.monmouth.edu/nursingschool.

Mount Carmel College of Nursing, Nursing Program, Columbus, OH 43222. Offers adult health clinical nurse specialist (MS); family nurse practitioner (MS); nursing administration (MS); nursing education (MS). *Accreditation:* AACN. Part-time programs available. *Faculty:* 11 full-time (10 women), 4 part-time/adjunct (2 women). *Students:* 69 full-time (66 women), 33 part-time (30 women); includes 19 minority (11 Black or African American, non-Hispanic/Latino; 1 American Indian or Alaska Native, non-Hispanic/Latino; 5 Asian, non-Hispanic/Latino; 1 Native Hawaiian or other Pacific Islander, non-Hispanic/Latino; 1 Two or more races, non-Hispanic/Latino). Average age 38. 23 applicants, 100% accepted, 20 enrolled. In 2011, 16 master's awarded. *Degree requirements:* For master's, professional manuscript. *Entrance requirements:* For master's, letters of recommendation, current resume, baccalaureate degree in nursing, current Ohio RN license, minimum cumulative GPA of 3.0. Additional exam requirements/recommendations for international students: Required—TOEFL (minimum score 550 paper-based; 213 computer-based; 80 iBT). *Application deadline:* For fall admission, 6/15 priority date for domestic students; for winter admission, 11/1 priority date for domestic students. Applications are processed on a rolling basis. Application fee: $30. *Expenses: Tuition:* Full-time $7839; part-time $402 per credit. *Required fees:* $75. *Financial support:* In 2011–12, 6 students received support. Institutionally sponsored loans and scholarships/grants available. Financial award application deadline: 7/1; financial award applicants required to submit FAFSA. *Unit head:* Dr. Angela Phillips-Lowe, Associate Dean, 614-234-5717, Fax: 614-234-2875, E-mail: aphillips-lowe@mccn.edu. *Application contact:* Elsie Sexton, Program Coordinator, 614-234-5169, Fax: 614-234-2875, E-mail: ksexton@mccn.edu. Web site: http://www.mccn.edu/.

Mount Saint Mary College, Division of Nursing, Newburgh, NY 12550-3494. Offers adult nurse practitioner (MS, Advanced Certificate), including nursing education (MS), nursing management (MS); clinical nurse specialist-adult health (MS), including nursing education, nursing management; family nurse practitioner (Advanced Certificate). *Accreditation:* AACN. Part-time and evening/weekend programs available. *Faculty:* 3 full-time (all women), 1 (woman) part-time/adjunct. *Students:* 3 full-time (2 women), 58 part-time (54 women); includes 16 minority (11 Black or African American, non-Hispanic/Latino; 1 Asian, non-Hispanic/Latino; 1 Hispanic/Latino; 3 Native Hawaiian or other Pacific Islander, non-Hispanic/Latino), 2 international. Average age 38. 47 applicants, 53% accepted, 18 enrolled. In 2011, 17 master's, 5 other advanced degrees awarded.

Degree requirements: For master's, research utilization project. *Entrance requirements:* For master's, BSN, minimum GPA of 3.0, RN license. *Application deadline:* For fall admission, 6/3 priority date for domestic students; for spring admission, 10/31 priority date for domestic students. Applications are processed on a rolling basis. Application fee: $45. Application fee is waived when completed online. *Expenses: Tuition:* Full-time $13,356; part-time $742 per credit. *Required fees:* $70 per semester. *Financial support:* In 2011–12, 8 students received support. Unspecified assistantships available. Financial award application deadline: 4/15; financial award applicants required to submit FAFSA. *Unit head:* Dr. Karen Baldwin, Coordinator, 845-569-3512, Fax: 845-562-6762, E-mail: baldwin@msmc.edu. *Application contact:* Courtney McDermott, Graduate Recruiter, 845-569-3402, Fax: 845-569-3450, E-mail: courtney.mcdermott@msmc.edu. Web site: http://www.msmc.edu/Academics/Graduate_Programs/Master_of_Science_in_Nursing.

New Mexico State University, Graduate School, College of Health and Social Services, School of Nursing, Las Cruces, NM 88003-8001. Offers adult/gerontology nurse practitioner (DNP); family nurse practitioner (DNP); nursing (MSN, PhD); public/community health (DNP). *Accreditation:* AACN. Postbaccalaureate distance learning degree programs offered (minimal on-campus study). *Faculty:* 9 full-time (all women). *Students:* 44 full-time (38 women), 72 part-time (59 women); includes 48 minority (9 Black or African American, non-Hispanic/Latino; 5 American Indian or Alaska Native, non-Hispanic/Latino; 2 Asian, non-Hispanic/Latino; 31 Hispanic/Latino; 1 Two or more races, non-Hispanic/Latino), 2 international. Average age 43. 37 applicants, 86% accepted, 25 enrolled. In 2011, 35 master's, 3 doctorates awarded. *Degree requirements:* For master's, comprehensive exam, thesis optional, clinical practice; for doctorate, comprehensive exam, thesis/dissertation. *Entrance requirements:* For master's, NCLEX exam, BSN, minimum GPA of 3.0, course work in statistics, 3 letters of reference, writing sample, RN license, CPR certification, proof of liability, immunizations, criminal background check; for doctorate, NCLEX exam, MSN, minimum GPA of 3.0, 3 letters of reference, writing sample, RN license, CPR certification, proof of liability, immunizations, criminal background check, statistics course. Additional exam requirements/recommendations for international students: Required—TOEFL (minimum score 550 paper-based; 79 iBT), IELTS (minimum score 6.5). *Application deadline:* For spring admission, 10/1 priority date for domestic students. Application fee: $40 ($50 for international students). Electronic applications accepted. *Expenses:* Tuition, state resident: full-time $5004; part-time $208.50 per credit. Tuition, nonresident: full-time $17,446; part-time $726.90 per credit. *Financial support:* In 2011–12, 1 teaching assistantship (averaging $28,242 per year) was awarded; fellowships, research assistantships, career-related internships or fieldwork, Federal Work-Study, scholarships/grants, traineeships, and health care benefits also available. Financial award application deadline: 3/1. *Faculty research:* Public policy, community health, health disparities, self efficacy and self management, psychiatric mental health. *Unit head:* Dr. Pamela Schultz, Director, 575-646-3812, Fax: 575-646-2167, E-mail: pschultz@nmsu.edu. *Application contact:* Dr. Kathleen Huttlinger, Associate Director for Graduate Studies, 575-646-4387, Fax: 575-646-2167. Web site: http://www.nmsu.edu/~nursing/.

New York University, College of Nursing, Doctor of Nursing Practice Program, New York, NY 10012-1019. Offers advanced practice nursing (DNP), including adult acute care, adult nurse practitioner/holistic nursing, adult nurse practitioner/palliative care nursing, adult primary care, adult primary care/geriatrics, family, geriatrics, mental health nursing, nurse-midwifery, pediatrics. Part-time and evening/weekend programs available. *Faculty:* 7 full-time (all women). *Students:* 23 part-time (19 women); includes 6 minority (4 Black or African American, non-Hispanic/Latino; 1 Asian, non-Hispanic/Latino; 1 Hispanic/Latino), 1 international. Average age 46. 20 applicants, 80% accepted, 11 enrolled. In 2011, 8 doctorates awarded. *Degree requirements:* For doctorate, thesis/dissertation. *Entrance requirements:* For doctorate, MS, RN license, interview, NP Certification. Additional exam requirements/recommendations for international students: Required—TOEFL, IELTS. *Application deadline:* For fall admission, 4/1 priority date for domestic students, 4/1 for international students. Applications are processed on a rolling basis. Application fee: $75. Electronic applications accepted. *Financial support:* In 2011–12, 15 students received support. Fellowships with full and partial tuition reimbursements available, institutionally sponsored loans, scholarships/grants, and tuition waivers (partial) available. Support available to part-time students. Financial award application deadline: 2/1; financial award applicants required to submit FAFSA. *Faculty research:* Elderly black diabetics, families and illness, oral systemic connection. *Unit head:* Dr. Jamesetta A. Newland, Director, 212-998-5319, Fax: 212-995-3143, E-mail: jan7@nyu.edu. *Application contact:* Gail Wolfmeyer, Assistant Director, Graduate Student Affairs and Admissions, 212-992-7653, Fax: 212-995-4302, E-mail: gail.wolfmeyer@nyu.edu.

New York University, College of Nursing, Programs in Advanced Practice Nursing, New York, NY 10012-1019. Offers advanced practice nursing: adult acute care (MS, Advanced Certificate); advanced practice nursing: adult nurse practitioner/holistic nurse practitioner (Advanced Certificate); advanced practice nursing: adult nurse practitioner/palliative care nurse practitioner (Advanced Certificate); advanced practice nursing: adult primary care (MS, Advanced Certificate); advanced practice nursing: family (MS, Advanced Certificate); advanced practice nursing: geriatrics (Advanced Certificate); advanced practice nursing: mental health (MS); advanced practice nursing: mental health nursing (Advanced Certificate); advanced practice nursing: pediatrics (MS, Advanced Certificate); nurse midwifery (MS, Advanced Certificate); nursing administration (MS, Advanced Certificate); nursing education (MS, Advanced Certificate); nursing informatics (MS, Advanced Certificate); MS/MPA; MS/MPH. *Accreditation:* AACN; ACNM/ACME. Part-time programs available. *Faculty:* 23 full-time (all women), 60 part-time/adjunct (47 women). *Students:* 27 full-time (23 women), 552 part-time (514 women); includes 251 minority (91 Black or African American, non-Hispanic/Latino; 115 Asian, non-Hispanic/Latino; 34 Hispanic/Latino; 11 Native Hawaiian or other Pacific Islander, non-Hispanic/Latino), 8 international. Average age 33. 325 applicants, 81% accepted, 179 enrolled. In 2011, 89 master's awarded. *Degree requirements:* For master's, thesis (for some programs). *Entrance requirements:* For master's, BS in nursing, AS in nursing with another BS/BA, interview, RN license, 1 year of clinical experience (3 for nursing education program); for Advanced Certificate, master's degree. Additional exam requirements/recommendations for international students: Required—TOEFL, IELTS. *Application deadline:* For fall admission, 7/1 priority date for domestic students, 7/1 for international students; for spring admission, 12/1 for domestic and international students. Applications are processed on a rolling basis. Application fee: $75. Electronic applications accepted. *Financial support:* In 2011–12, 36 students received support. Career-related internships or fieldwork, institutionally sponsored loans, scholarships/grants, traineeships, and tuition waivers (partial) available. Support available to part-time students. Financial award application deadline: 2/1; financial award applicants required to submit FAFSA. *Faculty research:* Elderly black diabetics, families and illness, oral systemic connection. *Unit head:* Dr. Judith Haber, Associate Dean, 212-998-9020, Fax: 212-995-3143, E-mail: jh33@nyu.edu. *Application contact:* Gail Wolfmeyer, Assistant Director, Graduate Student Affairs and Admissions, 212-992-7653, Fax: 212-995-4302, E-mail: gail.wolfmeyer@nyu.edu.

North Park University, School of Nursing, Chicago, IL 60625-4895. Offers advanced practice nursing (MS); leadership and management (MS); MBA/MS; MM/MSN; MS/MHR; MS/MNA. *Accreditation:* AACN. Part-time and evening/weekend programs available. *Degree requirements:* For master's, thesis. *Entrance requirements:* For master's, GMAT, MAT. *Faculty research:* Aging, consultation roles, critical thinking skills, family breakdown, science of caring.

Oakland University, Graduate Study and Lifelong Learning, School of Nursing, Program in Adult Health, Rochester, MI 48309-4401. Offers MSN. *Accreditation:* AACN. *Degree requirements:* For master's, thesis (for some programs). *Entrance requirements:* For master's, GRE General Test, minimum GPA of 3.0 for unconditional admission. Electronic applications accepted.

Purdue University Calumet, Graduate Studies Office, School of Nursing, Hammond, IN 46323-2094. Offers adult health clinical nurse specialist (MS); critical care clinical nurse specialist (MS); family nurse practitioner (MS); nurse executive (MS). *Accreditation:* AACN; NLN. Part-time programs available. Postbaccalaureate distance learning degree programs offered (minimal on-campus study). *Entrance requirements:* For master's, BSN. Additional exam requirements/recommendations for international students: Required—TOEFL. Electronic applications accepted. *Faculty research:* Adult health, cardiovascular and pulmonary nursing.

Quinnipiac University, School of Nursing, Adult Nurse Practitioner Track, Hamden, CT 06518-1940. Offers DNP. *Accreditation:* NLN. Part-time programs available. *Faculty:* 6 full-time (5 women), 7 part-time/adjunct (4 women). *Students:* 10 full-time (8 women), 61 part-time (55 women); includes 24 minority (13 Black or African American, non-Hispanic/Latino; 6 Asian, non-Hispanic/Latino; 5 Hispanic/Latino). Average age 30. 28 applicants, 71% accepted, 17 enrolled. *Entrance requirements:* Additional exam requirements/recommendations for international students: Required—TOEFL (minimum score 575 paper-based; 233 computer-based; 90 iBT), IELTS (minimum score 6.5). *Application deadline:* For fall admission, 6/1 priority date for domestic students, 4/30 for international students. Applications are processed on a rolling basis. Application fee: $45. Electronic applications accepted. *Expenses: Tuition:* Part-time $855 per credit. *Required fees:* $35 per credit. *Financial support:* Traineeships, tuition waivers (partial), and unspecified assistantships available. Support available to part-time students. Financial award application deadline: 4/15; financial award applicants required to submit FAFSA. *Unit head:* Dr. Jeanne LeVasseur, Professor of Nursing, 203-582-5397, Fax: 203-582-3230, E-mail: jeanne.levasseur@quinnipiac.edu. *Application contact:* Kristin Parent, Associate Director of Graduate Health Sciences Admissions, 800-462-1944, Fax: 203-582-3443, E-mail: kristin.parent@quinnipiac.edu. Web site: http://www.quinnipiac.edu/gradnursing.

Rush University, College of Nursing, Department of Adult Health Nursing, Chicago, IL 60612-3832. Offers acute care nurse practitioner (MSN, Post-Master's Certificate); adult health nursing (DNP, PhD); adult nurse practitioner (MSN, Post-Master's Certificate); adult/gerontological nurse practitioner (MSN); anesthesia nurse practitioner (MSN, Post-Master's Certificate); critical care clinical specialist (MSN); gerontological nurse practitioner (MSN, Post-Master's Certificate); medical surgical clinical specialist (MSN). *Accreditation:* AACN; AANA/CANAEP (one or more programs are accredited). Part-time programs available. Postbaccalaureate distance learning degree programs offered (minimal on-campus study). Terminal master's awarded for partial completion of doctoral program. *Degree requirements:* For master's, capstone project; for doctorate, thesis/dissertation, DNP leadership project. *Entrance requirements:* For master's, GRE General Test (waived if nursing GPA is above 3.0 or cumulative GPA is above 3.25), interview; for doctorate, GRE General Test, interview, course work in statistics (PhD). Additional exam requirements/recommendations for international students: Required—TOEFL, TWE. Electronic applications accepted. *Faculty research:* Complementary/alternative medicine, critical care outcomes, cardiac risk reduction, Alzheimer's Disease, telehealth monitoring.

Rush University, College of Nursing, Department of Community Systems and Mental Health Nursing, Chicago, IL 60612-3832. Offers community and mental health nursing (DNP, PhD); family nurse practitioner (MSN, Post-Master's Certificate); psychiatric clinical specialist (MSN); psychiatric nurse practitioner - adult (MSN); psychiatric nurse practitioner - family (MSN); psychiatric-mental health clinical specialist (Post-Master's Certificate); psychiatric-mental health nurse practitioner (Post-Master's Certificate); public health nursing (MSN). *Accreditation:* AACN. Part-time programs available. Postbaccalaureate distance learning degree programs offered (minimal on-campus study). Terminal master's awarded for partial completion of doctoral program. *Degree requirements:* For master's, capstone project; for doctorate, thesis/dissertation, DNP leadership project. *Entrance requirements:* For master's, GRE General Test (waived if nursing GPA is above 3.0 or cumulative GPA is above 3.25), interview; for doctorate, GRE General Test, interview, course work in statistics (DN Sc). Electronic applications accepted. *Faculty research:* Immigrant mental health, de-escalation strategies, caregiver interventions, parent-teacher training, restraint use.

Rutgers, The State University of New Jersey, Newark, Graduate School, Program in Nursing, Newark, NJ 07102. Offers nursing (MS), including acute care of adults and aged, advanced practice in pediatric nursing, advanced practice with childbearing families, community health nursing, family nurse practitioner, primary care of adults and aged, psychiatric/mental health nursing. *Accreditation:* AACN. Part-time programs available. *Degree requirements:* For master's, comprehensive exam. *Entrance requirements:* For master's, GRE General Test, RN license, minimum B average, BS in nursing. Additional exam requirements/recommendations for international students: Required—TOEFL. Electronic applications accepted. *Faculty research:* HIV/AIDS, quality of life: MS and breast cancer, sleep patterns of cardiac patients.

Sage Graduate School, School of Health Sciences, Department of Nursing, Program in Adult Health, Troy, NY 12180-4115. Offers MS, Post Master's Certificate. *Accreditation:* AACN. Part-time and evening/weekend programs available. *Faculty:* 5 full-time (all women), 9 part-time/adjunct (all women). *Students:* 10 full-time (8 women), 32 part-time (30 women); includes 4 minority (2 Black or African American, non-Hispanic/Latino; 2 Asian, non-Hispanic/Latino), 5 international. Average age 42. 26 applicants, 23% accepted, 3 enrolled. In 2011, 6 master's, 3 other advanced degrees awarded. *Degree requirements:* For master's, thesis or alternative. *Entrance requirements:* For master's, BS in nursing, minimum GPA of 2.75, resume, 2 letters of recommendation. Additional exam requirements/recommendations for international students: Required—TOEFL (minimum score 550 paper-based; 213 computer-based). *Application deadline:* Applications are processed on a rolling basis. Application fee: $40. *Expenses: Tuition:* Full-time $11,880; part-time $660 per credit hour. Tuition and fees vary according to program. *Financial support:* Fellowships, research assistantships, Federal Work-Study, scholarships/grants, and unspecified assistantships available. Support available to part-time students. Financial award application deadline: 3/1; financial award applicants required to submit FAFSA. *Unit head:* Dr. Esther Haskevitz, Dean, School of Health Sciences, 518-244-2296, Fax: 518-244-4571, E-mail: haskve@sage.edu. *Application contact:* Arlene Pericak, Director, 518-244-2012, Fax: 518-244-2009, E-mail: perica@sage.edu.

Sage Graduate School, School of Health Sciences, Department of Nursing, Program in Adult Nurse Practitioner, Troy, NY 12180-4115. Offers MS, Post Master's Certificate. *Accreditation:* AACN. Part-time and evening/weekend programs available. *Faculty:* 5 full-time (all women), 9 part-time/adjunct (all women). *Students:* 9 full-time (7 women), 24 part-time (22 women); includes 7 minority (2 Black or African American, non-

Hispanic/Latino; 4 Asian, non-Hispanic/Latino; 1 Hispanic/Latino), 2 international. Average age 38. 25 applicants, 24% accepted, 6 enrolled. In 2011, 8 degrees awarded. *Degree requirements:* For master's, thesis or alternative. *Entrance requirements:* For master's, BS in nursing, minimum GPA of 2.75, resume, 2 letters of recommendation. Additional exam requirements/recommendations for international students: Required—TOEFL (minimum score 550 paper-based; 213 computer-based). *Application deadline:* Applications are processed on a rolling basis. Application fee: $40. *Expenses: Tuition:* Full-time $11,880; part-time $660 per credit hour. Tuition and fees vary according to program. *Financial support:* Fellowships, research assistantships, Federal Work-Study, scholarships/grants, and unspecified assistantships available. Support available to part-time students. Financial award application deadline: 3/1; financial award applicants required to submit FAFSA. *Unit head:* Dr. Esther Haskevitz, Dean, School of Health Sciences, 518-244-2296, Fax: 518-244-4571, E-mail: haskve@sage.edu. *Application contact:* Arlene Pericak, Director, 518-244-2012, Fax: 518-244-2009, E-mail: perica@sage.edu.

St. Catherine University, Graduate Programs, Program in Nursing, St. Paul, MN 55105. Offers adult-gerontological nurse practitioner (MA); neonatal nurse practitioner (MA); nurse educator (MA); nursing (DNP); pediatric nurse practitioner (MA). *Accreditation:* NLN. Part-time and evening/weekend programs available. *Degree requirements:* For master's, thesis; for doctorate, portfolio, systems change project. *Entrance requirements:* For master's, GRE General Test, bachelor's degree in nursing, current nursing license, 2 years of recent clinical practice; for doctorate, master's degree in nursing, RN license, advanced nursing position. Additional exam requirements/recommendations for international students: Required—TOEFL (minimum score 600 paper-based; 250 computer-based; 100 iBT). *Expenses: Required fees:* $30 per semester. Tuition and fees vary according to program.

Saint Peter's University, School of Nursing, Nursing Program, Jersey City, NJ 07306-5997. Offers adult nurse practitioner (MSN, Certificate); advanced practice (DNP); case management (MSN, DNP). *Accreditation:* AACN. Part-time and evening/weekend programs available. *Entrance requirements:* Additional exam requirements/recommendations for international students: Required—TOEFL (minimum score 79 computer-based). Electronic applications accepted.

Seattle Pacific University, MS in Nursing Program, Seattle, WA 98119-1997. Offers administration (MSN); adult/gerontology nurse practitioner (MSN); clinical nurse specialist (MSN); family nurse practitioner (MSN, Certificate); informatics (MSN); nurse educator (MSN). *Accreditation:* AACN. Part-time programs available. *Degree requirements:* For master's, thesis. Electronic applications accepted. *Expenses:* Contact institution.

Seattle University, College of Nursing, Program in Advanced Practice Nursing Immersion, Seattle, WA 98122-1090. Offers adult/gerontological nurse practitioner (MSN); advanced community public health (MSN); certified nurse midwifery (MSN); family nurse practitioner (MSN); psychiatric mental health nurse practitioner (MSN). *Faculty:* 43 full-time; 63 part-time/adjunct. *Students:* 104 full-time (91 women); includes 24 minority (2 Black or African American, non-Hispanic/Latino; 12 Asian, non-Hispanic/Latino; 7 Hispanic/Latino; 3 Two or more races, non-Hispanic/Latino). Average age 30. *Degree requirements:* For master's, thesis or scholarly project. *Entrance requirements:* For master's, GRE, bachelor's degree, minimum GPA of 3.0, professional resume, two recommendations, letter of intent, English proficiency (for non-English speakers). Additional exam requirements/recommendations for international students: Required—TOEFL (minimum score 92 iBT), IELTS. *Application deadline:* For fall admission, 12/1 for domestic and international students. Application fee: $55. Electronic applications accepted. *Financial support:* Scholarships/grants and traineeships available. Financial award applicants required to submit FAFSA. *Unit head:* Dr. Azita Emami, Dean, 206-296-5660. *Application contact:* Janet Shandley, Associate Dean of Graduate Admissions, 206-296-5900, Fax: 206-298-5656, E-mail: grad_admissions@seattleu.edu.

Seattle University, College of Nursing, Program in Nursing, Seattle, WA 98122-1090. Offers adult/gerontological nurse practitioner (MSN); advanced community public health (MSN); psychiatric mental health nurse practitioner (MSN). *Faculty:* 43 full-time, 63 part-time/adjunct. *Students:* 22 full-time (20 women); includes 4 minority (1 Black or African American, non-Hispanic/Latino; 1 Asian, non-Hispanic/Latino; 1 Hispanic/Latino; 1 Two or more races, non-Hispanic/Latino). *Degree requirements:* For master's, thesis or scholarly project. *Entrance requirements:* For master's, GRE, bachelor's degree in nursing or associate degree in nursing with baccalaureate in different major, 5-quarter statistics course, minimum cumulative GPA of 3.0, professional resume, two recommendations, letter of intent, English proficiency (for non-English speakers), copy of current RN license or ability to obtain RN license in WA state. Additional exam requirements/recommendations for international students: Required—TOEFL (minimum score 92 iBT), IELTS. *Application deadline:* For fall admission, 12/1 for domestic and international students. Application fee: $55. Electronic applications accepted. *Financial support:* In 2011–12, 2 teaching assistantships were awarded; scholarships/grants and traineeships also available. Financial award applicants required to submit FAFSA. *Unit head:* Dr. Azita Emami, Dean, 206-296-5660. *Application contact:* Janet Shandley, Associate Dean of Graduate Admissions, 206-296-5900, Fax: 206-298-5656, E-mail: grad_admissions@seattleu.edu.

Seton Hall University, College of Nursing, South Orange, NJ 07079-2697. Offers advanced practice in primary health care (MSN, DNP), including adult/gerontological nurse practitioner, pediatric nurse practitioner; entry into practice (MSN); health systems administration (MSN, DNP); nursing (PhD); nursing case management (MSN); nursing education (MA); school nurse (MSN); MSN/MA. *Accreditation:* AACN. Part-time programs available. Postbaccalaureate distance learning degree programs offered (minimal on-campus study). *Faculty:* 10 full-time (all women), 3 part-time/adjunct (1 woman). *Students:* 12 full-time (11 women), 217 part-time (197 women); includes 38 minority (15 Black or African American, non-Hispanic/Latino; 1 American Indian or Alaska Native, non-Hispanic/Latino; 12 Asian, non-Hispanic/Latino; 10 Hispanic/Latino). 180 applicants, 51% accepted, 82 enrolled. *Degree requirements:* For master's, research project; for doctorate, dissertation or scholarly project. *Entrance requirements:* For doctorate, GRE (waived for students with GPA of 3.5 or higher). Additional exam requirements/recommendations for international students: Required—TOEFL. *Application deadline:* For fall admission, 4/15 priority date for domestic students. Applications are processed on a rolling basis. Electronic applications accepted. *Expenses: Tuition:* Part-time $1033 per credit hour. *Required fees:* $85 per semester. *Financial support:* Institutionally sponsored loans, scholarships/grants, traineeships, tuition waivers (partial), and unspecified assistantships available. Support available to part-time students. Financial award applicants required to submit FAFSA. *Faculty research:* Parent/child, adult, and gerontological nursing; breast cancer; families of children with HIV; parish nursing. *Unit head:* Dr. Phyllis Shanley Hansell, Dean, 973-761-9014, E-mail: phyllis.hansell@shu.edu. *Application contact:* Kristyn Kent Wuillermin, Director of Strategic Alliances, Marketing and Enrollment, 973-761-9291, Fax: 973-761-9607, E-mail: kristyn.kent@shu.edu.

Southeastern Louisiana University, College of Nursing and Health Sciences, School of Nursing, Hammond, LA 70402. Offers adult psychiatric/mental health nurse practitioner/clinical nurse specialist (MSN); education (MSN); nurse executive (MSN);

nurse practitioner (MSN). *Accreditation:* AACN. Part-time and evening/weekend programs available. *Faculty:* 12 full-time (11 women), 7 part-time/adjunct (4 women). *Students:* 17 full-time (16 women), 108 part-time (94 women); includes 12 minority (8 Black or African American, non-Hispanic/Latino; 2 Asian, non-Hispanic/Latino; 1 Hispanic/Latino; 1 Two or more races, non-Hispanic/Latino), 1 international. Average age 35. 50 applicants, 100% accepted, 29 enrolled. In 2011, 27 degrees awarded. *Degree requirements:* For master's, thesis. *Entrance requirements:* For master's, GRE (verbal and quantitative), baccalaureate degree in nursing from accredited undergraduate nursing program; minimum GPA of 2.7; all transcripts from undergraduate school and any work attempted at the graduate level; curriculum vitae; valid Louisiana Registered Nurse license; letters of recommendation; letter of intent/statement of purpose. Additional exam requirements/recommendations for international students: Required—TOEFL (minimum score 500 paper-based; 173 computer-based; 61 iBT). *Application deadline:* For fall admission, 7/15 priority date for domestic students, 6/1 for international students; for spring admission, 12/1 priority date for domestic students, 10/1 for international students. Applications are processed on a rolling basis. Application fee: $20 ($30 for international students). Electronic applications accepted. *Expenses:* Tuition, state resident: full-time $3977; part-time $283 per semester hour. Tuition, nonresident: full-time $13,482; part-time $811 per semester hour. *Financial support:* Federal Work-Study, institutionally sponsored loans, scholarships/grants, traineeships, and unspecified assistantships available. Support available to part-time students. Financial award application deadline: 5/1; financial award applicants required to submit FAFSA. *Faculty research:* Gender issues, LGBT issues, occupational health/safety, accelerated students, caring development. *Total annual research expenditures:* $245,268. *Unit head:* Dr. Lorinda Sealy, Graduate Coordinator, 985-549-5045, Fax: 985-549-5087, E-mail: lorinda.sealy@selu.edu. *Application contact:* Sandra Meyers, Graduate Admissions Analyst, 985-549-5620, Fax: 985-549-5632, E-mail: admissions@selu.edu. Web site: http://www.selu.edu/acad_research/depts/nurs.

Southern Adventist University, School of Nursing, Collegedale, TN 37315-0370. Offers acute care nurse practitioner (MSN); adult nurse practitioner (MSN); family nurse practitioner (MSN); nurse educator (MSN); MSN/MSBA. *Accreditation:* NLN. Part-time programs available. *Degree requirements:* For master's, thesis or project. *Entrance requirements:* For master's, RN license. Additional exam requirements/recommendations for international students: Required—TOEFL (minimum score 600 paper-based; 250 computer-based). Electronic applications accepted. *Faculty research:* Pain management, ethics, corporate wellness, caring spirituality, stress.

South University, Program in Nursing, Tampa, FL 33614. Offers adult health nurse practitioner (MS); family nurse practitioner (MS); nurse educator (MS).

Spalding University, Graduate Studies, College of Health and Natural Sciences, School of Nursing, Louisville, KY 40203-2188. Offers adult nurse practitioner (MSN); family nurse practitioner (MSN); leadership in nursing and healthcare (MSN); pediatric nurse practitioner (MSN). *Accreditation:* AACN. Part-time and evening/weekend programs available. *Faculty:* 6 full-time (all women), 5 part-time/adjunct (all women). *Students:* 90 full-time (82 women), 24 part-time (all women); includes 21 minority (16 Black or African American, non-Hispanic/Latino; 3 Asian, non-Hispanic/Latino; 1 Hispanic/Latino; 1 Native Hawaiian or other Pacific Islander, non-Hispanic/Latino). Average age 36. 85 applicants, 24% accepted, 15 enrolled. In 2011, 23 master's awarded. *Degree requirements:* For master's, comprehensive exam (for some programs), thesis. *Entrance requirements:* For master's, GRE General Test, BSN or bachelor's degree and RN licensure. Additional exam requirements/recommendations for international students: Required—TOEFL (minimum score 535 paper-based; 203 computer-based). *Application deadline:* For fall admission, 3/1 priority date for domestic students. Applications are processed on a rolling basis. Application fee: $30. *Expenses: Tuition:* Full-time $12,438. Tuition and fees vary according to course load, degree level and program. *Financial support:* In 2011–12, 21 students received support, including 1 research assistantship with partial tuition reimbursement available (averaging $4,260 per year); career-related internships or fieldwork, scholarships/grants, and traineeships also available. Support available to part-time students. Financial award application deadline: 3/15; financial award applicants required to submit FAFSA. *Faculty research:* Nurse educational administration, gerontology, bioterrorism, healthcare ethics, leadership. *Unit head:* Dr. Paula Travis, Chair, 502-873-4298, E-mail: clewis@spalding.edu. *Application contact:* Dr. Pam King, 502-873-4292, E-mail: pking@spalding.edu. Web site: http://www.spalding.edu/nursing/.

State University of New York Institute of Technology, Program in Adult Nurse Practitioner, Utica, NY 13504-3050. Offers MS, CAS. *Accreditation:* AACN. Part-time programs available. *Degree requirements:* For master's, thesis or project. *Entrance requirements:* For master's, GRE General Test (if undergraduate GPA less than 3.3), minimum GPA of 3.0 in last 30 hours of undergraduate coursework, BS in nursing, 1 year of RN experience, RN license, interview, 2 letters of recommendation. Additional exam requirements/recommendations for international students: Required—TOEFL (minimum score 550 paper-based; 213 computer-based). *Faculty research:* Adult health care, critical thinking, epidemiology, ethics, moral reasoning.

Stony Brook University, State University of New York, Stony Brook University Medical Center, Health Sciences Center, School of Nursing, Program in Adult Health/Primary Care Nursing, Stony Brook, NY 11794. Offers adult health nurse practitioner (Certificate); adult health/primary care nursing (MS). *Accreditation:* AACN. Postbaccalaureate distance learning degree programs offered. *Degree requirements:* For master's, thesis. *Entrance requirements:* For master's, BSN, minimum GPA of 3.0, course work in statistics.

Texas Christian University, Harris College of Nursing and Health Sciences, Program in Nursing, Fort Worth, TX 76129-0002. Offers advanced practice registered nurse (DNP); clinical nurse leader (MSN); clinical nurse specialist: adult/gerontology nursing (MSN); clinical nurse specialist: pediatric nursing (MSN); nursing administration (DNP); nursing education (MSN). *Accreditation:* AACN; AANA/CANAEP (one or more programs are accredited). Part-time programs available. Postbaccalaureate distance learning degree programs offered (no on-campus study). *Faculty:* 18 full-time (16 women), 2 part-time/adjunct (both women). *Students:* 2 full-time (both women), 105 part-time (96 women); includes 16 minority (8 Black or African American, non-Hispanic/Latino; 4 Asian, non-Hispanic/Latino; 2 Hispanic/Latino; 1 Native Hawaiian or other Pacific Islander, non-Hispanic/Latino; 1 Two or more races, non-Hispanic/Latino), 1 international. Average age 44. 58 applicants, 93% accepted, 46 enrolled. In 2011, 11 master's, 21 doctorates awarded. *Degree requirements:* For master's and doctorate, professional project. *Entrance requirements:* For master's, GRE General Test or MAT, 3 letters of reference, 2 years preferred full-time experience as registered nurse, current nursing license, minimum GPA of 3.0; for doctorate, APRN recognition (national certification), minimum GPA of 3.0, 3 professional references, essay, 2 years post-master's experience (preferrred). Additional exam requirements/recommendations for international students: Required—TOEFL, Spoken English Test for DNP. *Expenses: Tuition:* Full-time $20,250; part-time $1125 per credit hour. Part-time tuition and fees vary according to course load and program. *Financial support:* In 2011–12, teaching assistantships (averaging $5,000 per year) were awarded; tuition waivers also available. *Unit head:* Dr. Pamela Frable, Associate Dean and Director of Nursing, 817-257-5840,

E-mail: p.frable@tcu.edu. *Application contact:* Dr. Kathy Baker, Director of Graduate Studies and Director of DNP Program, 817-257-6726, E-mail: kathy.baker@tcu.edu. Web site: http://www.nursing.tcu.edu/graduate.asp.

Texas Woman's University, Graduate School, College of Nursing, Denton, TX 76201. Offers acute care nurse practitioner (MS); adult health clinical nurse specialist (MS); adult health nurse practitioner (MS); child health clinical nurse specialist (MS); clinical nurse leader (MS); family nurse practitioner (MS); health systems management (MS); nursing education (MS); nursing practice (DNP); nursing science (PhD); pediatric nurse practitioner (MS); women's health clinical nurse specialist (MS); women's health nurse practitioner (MS). *Accreditation:* AACN. Part-time programs available. Postbaccalaureate distance learning degree programs offered. *Faculty:* 70 full-time (69 women), 7 part-time/adjunct (all women). *Students:* 87 full-time (78 women), 870 part-time (815 women); includes 489 minority (235 Black or African American, non-Hispanic/Latino; 5 American Indian or Alaska Native, non-Hispanic/Latino; 169 Asian, non-Hispanic/Latino; 78 Hispanic/Latino; 2 Native Hawaiian or other Pacific Islander, non-Hispanic/Latino), 19 international. Average age 38. 368 applicants, 71% accepted, 205 enrolled. In 2011, 147 master's, 21 doctorates awarded. *Degree requirements:* For master's, comprehensive exam, thesis or alternative; for doctorate, comprehensive exam, thesis/dissertation. *Entrance requirements:* For master's, GRE or MAT, minimum GPA of 3.0 on last 60 hours in undergraduate nursing degree and overall, RN license, BS in nursing, basic statistics course; for doctorate, GRE (preferred minimum score 153 [500 old version] Verbal, 144 [500 old version] Quantitative, 4 Analytical), MS in nursing, minimum preferred GPA of 3.5, RN license, statistics, 2 letters of reference, curriculum vitae, graduate nursing-theory course, graduate research course, statement of professional goals and research interests. Additional exam requirements/recommendations for international students: Required—TOEFL (minimum score 550 paper-based; 213 computer-based; 79 iBT). *Application deadline:* For fall admission, 5/1 priority date for domestic students, 3/1 for international students; for spring admission, 9/15 priority date for domestic students, 7/1 for international students. Applications are processed on a rolling basis. Application fee: $50 ($75 for international students). Electronic applications accepted. *Expenses:* Tuition, state resident: full-time $3834; part-time $213 per credit hour. Tuition, nonresident: full-time $9468; part-time $526 per credit hour. *Required fees:* $213 per credit hour. Tuition and fees vary according to course load. *Financial support:* In 2011–12, 149 students received support, including 10 research assistantships (averaging $12,942 per year), 1 teaching assistantship (averaging $12,942 per year); career-related internships or fieldwork, Federal Work-Study, institutionally sponsored loans, scholarships/grants, traineeships, health care benefits, and unspecified assistantships also available. Support available to part-time students. Financial award application deadline: 3/1; financial award applicants required to submit FAFSA. *Faculty research:* Screening, prevention, and treatment for intimate partner violence; needs of adolescents during childbirth intervention; a network analysis decision tool for nurse managers (Social Network Analysis); support for adolescents with implantable cardioverter defibrillators; informatics: nurse staffing, safety, quality, and financial data as they relate to patient care outcomes; prevention and treatment of obesity; improving infant outcomes related to premature birth. *Total annual research expenditures:* $462,088. *Unit head:* Dr. Patricia Holden-Huchton, Interim Dean, 940-898-2401, Fax: 940-898-2437, E-mail: nursing@twu.edu. *Application contact:* Dr. Samuel Wheeler, Assistant Director of Admissions, 940-898-3188, Fax: 940-898-3081, E-mail: wheelersr@twu.edu. Web site: http://www.twu.edu/nursing/.

Troy University, Graduate School, College of Health and Human Services, Program in Nursing, Troy, AL 36082. Offers adult health (MSN); clinical nurse specialist adult health (DNP); clinical nurse specialist maternal infant (DNP); family nurse practitioner (MSN, DNP, PMC); informatics specialist (MSN); maternal infant (MSN). *Accreditation:* NLN. Part-time and evening/weekend programs available. *Faculty:* 11 full-time (10 women), 7 part-time/adjunct (4 women). *Students:* 58 full-time (43 women), 181 part-time (165 women); includes 91 minority (76 Black or African American, non-Hispanic/Latino; 8 American Indian or Alaska Native, non-Hispanic/Latino; 1 Asian, non-Hispanic/Latino; 3 Hispanic/Latino; 1 Native Hawaiian or other Pacific Islander, non-Hispanic/Latino; 2 Two or more races, non-Hispanic/Latino). Average age 38. 144 applicants, 63% accepted, 73 enrolled. In 2011, 35 master's, 8 doctorates awarded. *Degree requirements:* For master's, comprehensive exam, minimum GPA of 3.0, candidacy; for doctorate, minimum GPA of 3.0, submission of approved comprehensive e-portfolio, completion of residency synthesis project, minimum of 1000 hours of clinical practice, score of 80% or better on qualifying exam. *Entrance requirements:* For master's, MAT (minimum score 396) or GRE (minimum score 850), minimum GPA of 3.0, BSN, current RN licensure; 2 letters of reference; for doctorate, GRE (minimum score of 850), BSN or MSN, minimum GPA of 3.0, 2 letters of reference, current RN licensure, essay. Additional exam requirements/recommendations for international students: Required—TOEFL (minimum score 523 paper-based; 193 computer-based; 70 iBT), IELTS (minimum score 6), or ACT COMPASS ESL (minimum listening, reading, and grammar score 270). *Application deadline:* Applications are processed on a rolling basis. Application fee: $50. Electronic applications accepted. *Expenses:* Tuition, state resident: full-time $6960; part-time $290 per credit hour. Tuition, nonresident: full-time $13,920; part-time $580 per credit hour. *Required fees:* $386 per term. *Financial support:* Available to part-time students. Applicants required to submit FAFSA. *Unit head:* Dr. Bernita K. Hamilton, Director, School of Nursing, 334-670-3428, Fax: 334-670-3743, E-mail: bernitah@troy.edu. *Application contact:* Brenda K. Campbell, Director of Graduate Admissions, 334-670-3178, Fax: 334-670-3733, E-mail: bcamp@troy.edu.

Universidad del Turabo, Graduate Programs, School of Health Sciences, Programs in Nursing, Program in Family Nurse Practitioner - Adult Nursing, Gurabo, PR 00778-3030. Offers MSN, Certificate. *Students:* 6 applicants, 0% accepted, 0 enrolled. In 2011, 2 degrees awarded. *Unit head:* David Mendez, Head, 787-743-7979. *Application contact:* Virginia Gonzalez, Admissions Officer, 787-746-3009.

University at Buffalo, the State University of New York, Graduate School, School of Nursing, Buffalo, NY 14214. Offers adult clinical nurse specialist (DNP); adult nurse practitioner (DNP); family nurse practitioner (DNP); health care systems and leadership (MS); nurse anesthetist (DNP); nursing (PhD); nursing education (Certificate); post-master's track (DNP); psychiatric mental health nurse practitioner (DNP). *Accreditation:* AACN; AANA/CANAEP (one or more programs are accredited). Part-time programs available. Postbaccalaureate distance learning degree programs offered (minimal on-campus study). *Faculty:* 29 full-time (25 women), 18 part-time/adjunct (17 women). *Students:* 101 full-time (76 women), 100 part-time (90 women); includes 19 minority (10 Black or African American, non-Hispanic/Latino; 2 American Indian or Alaska Native, non-Hispanic/Latino; 2 Asian, non-Hispanic/Latino; 2 Hispanic/Latino; 3 Native Hawaiian or other Pacific Islander, non-Hispanic/Latino), 34 international. Average age 34. 342 applicants, 26% accepted, 67 enrolled. In 2011, 51 master's, 3 doctorates awarded. *Median time to degree:* Of those who began their doctoral program in fall 2003, 75% received their degree in 8 years or less. *Degree requirements:* For master's, thesis optional, comprehensive exams or project; for doctorate, comprehensive exam (for some programs), capstone (for DNP), dissertation (for PhD). *Entrance requirements:* For doctorate, GRE or MAT, minimum GPA of 3.0 (3.25 for PhD), RN license, BS or MS in nursing, 3 references, writing sample; for Certificate, interview, minimum GPA of 3.0 or GRE General Test, RN license, MS in nursing. Additional exam requirements/recommendations for international students: Required—TOEFL (minimum score 550 paper-based; 213 computer-based; 79 iBT), IELTS (minimum score 6.5). *Application deadline:* For fall admission, 8/15 for domestic students, 4/1 for international students; for spring admission, 12/15 for domestic students, 10/1 for international students. Application fee: $75. Electronic applications accepted. *Financial support:* In 2011–12, 80 students received support, including 6 fellowships with full tuition reimbursements available (averaging $17,000 per year), 3 research assistantships with full tuition reimbursements available (averaging $10,600 per year), 5 teaching assistantships with full tuition reimbursements available (averaging $10,600 per year); scholarships/grants, traineeships, health care benefits, and unspecified assistantships also available. Financial award application deadline: 3/15; financial award applicants required to submit FAFSA. *Faculty research:* Oncology, palliative care, gerontology, addictions, mental health, community wellness. *Total annual research expenditures:* $1.3 million. *Unit head:* Dr. Marsha L. Lewis, Dean and Professor, 716-829-2533, Fax: 716-829-2566, E-mail: ubnursingdean@buffalo.edu. *Application contact:* Dr. David J. Lang, Director of Student Affairs, 716-829-2537, Fax: 716-829-2067, E-mail: nursing@buffalo.edu. Web site: http://nursing.buffalo.edu/.

University of Central Florida, College of Nursing, Orlando, FL 32816. Offers adult-gerontology clinical nurse specialist (Post-Master's Certificate); adult-gerontology nurse practitioner (Post-Master's Certificate); clinical nurse leader (Post-Master's Certificate); family nurse practitioner (Post-Master's Certificate); nursing (MSN, PhD); nursing education (Post-Master's Certificate); nursing practice (DNP). *Accreditation:* AACN. Part-time and evening/weekend programs available. *Faculty:* 44 full-time (39 women), 72 part-time/adjunct (71 women). *Students:* 75 full-time (68 women), 350 part-time (332 women); includes 109 minority (54 Black or African American, non-Hispanic/Latino; 1 American Indian or Alaska Native, non-Hispanic/Latino; 19 Asian, non-Hispanic/Latino; 33 Hispanic/Latino; 1 Native Hawaiian or other Pacific Islander, non-Hispanic/Latino; 1 Two or more races, non-Hispanic/Latino), 5 international. Average age 40. 203 applicants, 60% accepted, 98 enrolled. In 2011, 110 master's, 17 doctorates, 11 other advanced degrees awarded. *Degree requirements:* For master's, thesis or alternative. *Entrance requirements:* For master's, GRE General Test, minimum GPA of 3.0 in last 60 hours. Additional exam requirements/recommendations for international students: Required—TOEFL. *Application deadline:* For fall admission, 2/15 for domestic students; for spring admission, 9/15 for domestic students. Application fee: $30. Electronic applications accepted. *Expenses:* Tuition, state resident: part-time $277.08 per credit hour. Tuition, nonresident: part-time $277.08 per credit hour. Part-time tuition and fees vary according to degree level and program. *Financial support:* In 2011–12, 92 students received support, including 92 fellowships with partial tuition reimbursements available (averaging $1,100 per year), 2 teaching assistantships with partial tuition reimbursements available (averaging $8,100 per year); research assistantships with partial tuition reimbursements available, career-related internships or fieldwork, Federal Work-Study, institutionally sponsored loans, traineeships, and unspecified assistantships also available. Financial award application deadline: 3/1; financial award applicants required to submit FAFSA. *Unit head:* Dr. Jean D. Leuner, Dean, 407-823-5496, Fax: 407-823-5675, E-mail: jean.leuner@ucf.edu. *Application contact:* Barbara Rodriguez, Director, Admissions and Registration, 407-823-2766, Fax: 407-823-6442, E-mail: gradadmissions@ucf.edu. Web site: http://nursing.ucf.edu/.

University of Cincinnati, Graduate School, College of Nursing, Cincinnati, OH 45221-0038. Offers clinical nurse specialist (MSN), including adult health, community health, neonatal, nursing administration, occupational health, pediatric health, psychiatric nursing, women's health; nurse anesthesia (MSN); nurse midwifery (MSN); nurse practitioner (MSN), including acute care, ambulatory care, family, family/psychiatric, women's health; nursing (PhD); MBA/MSN. *Accreditation:* AACN; AANA/CANAEP (one or more programs are accredited); ACNM/ACME. Part-time programs available. Postbaccalaureate distance learning degree programs offered (no on-campus study). Terminal master's awarded for partial completion of doctoral program. *Degree requirements:* For master's, thesis or alternative; for doctorate, comprehensive exam, thesis/dissertation. *Entrance requirements:* For master's and doctorate, GRE General Test. Additional exam requirements/recommendations for international students: Required—TOEFL (minimum score 520 paper-based; 190 computer-based). Electronic applications accepted. *Faculty research:* Substance abuse, injury and violence, symptom management.

University of Colorado at Colorado Springs, Beth-El College of Nursing and Health Sciences, Colorado Springs, CO 80933-7150. Offers adult health nurse practitioner and clinical specialist (MSN); family practitioner (MSN), including community clinical specialist, forensic clinical specialist, holistic clinical specialist; neonatal nurse practitioner and clinical specialist (MSN); nursing administration (MSN); nursing practice (DNP); women nurse practitioner (MSN). *Accreditation:* AACN. Part-time programs available. Postbaccalaureate distance learning degree programs offered (minimal on-campus study). *Faculty:* 31 full-time (28 women), 6 part-time/adjunct (all women). *Students:* 122 full-time (103 women), 68 part-time (64 women); includes 36 minority (4 Black or African American, non-Hispanic/Latino; 2 American Indian or Alaska Native, non-Hispanic/Latino; 9 Asian, non-Hispanic/Latino; 18 Hispanic/Latino; 3 Two or more races, non-Hispanic/Latino), 5 international. Average age 35. 153 applicants, 71% accepted, 60 enrolled. In 2011, 41 master's, 15 doctorates awarded. *Degree requirements:* For master's, comprehensive exam, thesis optional; for doctorate, capstone project. *Entrance requirements:* For master's, GRE General Test or MAT, BSN, minimum GPA of 3.0, unrestricted RN license; for doctorate, interview; active RN license; MA; minimum GPA of 3.3; National Certification as NP or CNS; portfolio. Additional exam requirements/recommendations for international students: Required—TOEFL. *Application deadline:* For fall admission, 6/15 priority date for domestic students; for spring admission, 11/15 for domestic students. Application fee: $60 ($75 for international students). Electronic applications accepted. *Expenses:* Contact institution. *Financial support:* In 2011–12, 33 students received support, including 1 fellowship (averaging $2,500 per year); career-related internships or fieldwork, Federal Work-Study, and scholarships/grants also available. Support available to part-time students. Financial award application deadline: 3/1; financial award applicants required to submit FAFSA. *Faculty research:* Women's health, uncertainty, empowerment, family experience in chronic illness. *Total annual research expenditures:* $322,604. *Unit head:* Dr. Nancy Smith, Dean, 719-255-4411, Fax: 719-255-4416, E-mail: nsmith2@uccs.edu. *Application contact:* Diane Busch, Director, 719-255-4424, Fax: 719-255-4416, E-mail: dbusch@uccs.edu. Web site: http://www.uccs.edu/~bethel/.

University of Colorado Denver, College of Nursing, Aurora, CO 80045. Offers adult clinical nurse specialist (MS); adult nurse practitioner (MS); family nurse practitioner (MS); family psychiatric mental health nurse practitioner (MS); health care informatics (MS); nurse-midwifery (MS); nursing (DNP, PhD); nursing leadership and health care systems (MS); pediatric nurse practitioner (MS); pediatric nursing leadership (MS); special studies (MS); women's health care (MS); MS/PhD. *Accreditation:* ACNM/ACME (one or more programs are accredited); NLN (one or more programs are accredited). Part-time and evening/weekend programs available. Postbaccalaureate distance learning degree programs offered (minimal on-campus study). *Faculty:* 69 full-time (65 women), 68 part-time/adjunct (64 women). *Students:* 308 full-time (288 women), 134 part-time (118 women); includes 59 minority (11 Black or African American, non-Hispanic/Latino; 8 American Indian or Alaska Native, non-Hispanic/Latino; 10 Asian, non-Hispanic/Latino; 27 Hispanic/Latino; 3 Two or more races, non-Hispanic/Latino), 8

international. Average age 39. 298 applicants, 46% accepted, 110 enrolled. In 2011, 72 master's, 19 doctorates awarded. Terminal master's awarded for partial completion of doctoral program. *Degree requirements:* For master's, thesis optional; for doctorate, comprehensive exam, thesis/dissertation, 42 credits of coursework, 30 credits of dissertation. *Entrance requirements:* For master's, GRE if cumulative undergraduate GPA is less than 3.0, undergraduate nursing degree from NLNAC- or CCNE-accredited school or university; completion of research and statistics courses with minimum grade of C; copy of current and unencumbered nursing license; for doctorate, GRE, bachelor's and/or master's degrees in nursing from NLN- or CCNE-accredited institution; portfolio; minimum undergraduate GPA of 3.0, graduate 3.5; graduate-level intermediate statistics and master's-level nursing theory courses with minimum B grade; interview. Additional exam requirements/recommendations for international students: Required—TOEFL (minimum score 560 paper-based; 220 computer-based; 83 iBT). *Application deadline:* For fall admission, 4/1 for domestic students; for spring admission, 9/1 for domestic students. Application fee: $65. Electronic applications accepted. *Expenses:* Contact institution. *Financial support:* In 2011–12, 40 students received support. Fellowships, research assistantships, teaching assistantships, Federal Work-Study, scholarships/grants, and unspecified assistantships available. Support available to part-time students. Financial award application deadline: 4/1; financial award applicants required to submit FAFSA. *Faculty research:* Biological and behavioral phenomena in pregnancy and postpartum; patterns of glycemia during the insulin resistance of pregnancy; obesity, gestational diabetes, and relationship to neonatal adiposity; men's awareness and knowledge of male breast cancer; cognitive-behavioral therapy for chronic insomnia after breast cancer treatment; massage therapy for the treatment of tension-type headaches. *Total annual research expenditures:* $5.2 million. *Unit head:* Dr. Patricia Moritz, Dean, 303-724-1679, E-mail: pat.moritz@ucdenver.edu. *Application contact:* Judy Campbell, Graduate Programs Coordinator, 303-724-8503, E-mail: judy.campbell@ucdenver.edu. Web site: http://www.ucdenver.edu/academics/colleges/nursing/Pages/default.aspx.

University of Delaware, College of Health Sciences, School of Nursing, Newark, DE 19716. Offers adult nurse practitioner (MSN, PMC); cardiopulmonary clinical nurse specialist (MSN, PMC); cardiopulmonary clinical nurse specialist/adult nurse practitioner (MSN, PMC); family nurse practitioner (MSN, PMC); gerontology clinical nurse specialist (MSN, PMC); gerontology clinical nurse specialist geriatric nurse practitioner (PMC); gerontology clinical nurse specialist/geriatric nurse practitioner (MSN); health services administration (MSN, PMC); nursing of children clinical nurse specialist (MSN, PMC); nursing of children clinical nurse specialist/pediatric nurse practitioner (MSN, PMC); oncology/immune deficiency clinical nurse specialist (MSN, PMC); oncology/immune deficiency clinical nurse specialist/adult nurse practitioner (MSN, PMC); perinatal/women's health clinical nurse specialist (MSN, PMC); perinatal/women's health clinical nurse specialist/women's health nurse practitioner (MSN, PMC); psychiatric nursing clinical nurse specialist (MSN, PMC). *Accreditation:* AACN; NLN (one or more programs are accredited). Part-time and evening/weekend programs available. Postbaccalaureate distance learning degree programs offered (minimal on-campus study). *Degree requirements:* For master's, thesis optional. *Entrance requirements:* For master's, BSN, interview, RN license. Electronic applications accepted. *Faculty research:* Marriage and chronic illness, health promotion, congestive heart failure patient outcomes, school nursing, diabetes in children, culture, health disparities, cardiovascular, prison nursing, oncology, public policy, child obesity, smoking and teen pregnancy, blood pressure measurements, men's health.

University of Hawaii at Manoa, Graduate Division, School of Nursing and Dental Hygiene, Honolulu, HI 96822. Offers clinical nurse specialist (MS), including adult health, community mental health; nurse practitioner (MS), including adult health, community mental health, family nurse practitioner; nursing (PhD, Graduate Certificate); nursing administration (MS). *Accreditation:* AACN; NLN (one or more programs are accredited). Part-time programs available. Postbaccalaureate distance learning degree programs offered (minimal on-campus study). *Degree requirements:* For master's, thesis optional; for doctorate, comprehensive exam, thesis/dissertation. *Entrance requirements:* For master's, Hawaii RN license. Additional exam requirements/recommendations for international students: Required—TOEFL (minimum score 580 paper-based; 237 computer-based; 92 iBT), IELTS (minimum score 5). *Expenses:* Contact institution.

University of Illinois at Chicago, Graduate College, College of Nursing, Program in Nursing, Chicago, IL 60607-7128. Offers acute care clinical nurse specialist (MS); acute care nurse practitioner (MS); administrative studies in nursing (MS); adult nurse practitioner (MS); adult/geriatric nurse practitioner (MS); advanced community health nurse specialist (MS); family nurse practitioner (MS); geriatric clinical nurse specialist (MS); geriatric nurse practitioner (MS); mental health clinical nurse specialist (MS); mental health nurse practitioner (MS); nurse midwifery (MS); occupational health/advanced community health nurse specialist (MS); occupational health/family nurse practitioner (MS); pediatric clinical nurse specialist (MS); pediatric nurse practitioner (MS); perinatal clinical nurse specialist (MS); school/advanced community health nurse specialist (MS); school/family nurse practitioner (MS); women's health nurse practitioner (MS). *Accreditation:* AACN. Part-time programs available. *Degree requirements:* For master's, thesis or alternative. *Entrance requirements:* For master's, GRE General Test, minimum GPA of 2.75. Additional exam requirements/recommendations for international students: Required—TOEFL. Electronic applications accepted.

The University of Kansas, University of Kansas Medical Center, School of Nursing, Kansas City, KS 66160. Offers adult/gerontological clinical nurse specialist (PMC); adult/gerontological nurse practitioner (PMC); clinical research management (PMC); family nurse practitioner (PMC); health care informatics (PMC); health professions educator (PMC); nurse midwife (PMC); nursing (MS, DNP, PhD); organizational leadership (PMC); psychiatric/mental health nurse practitioner (PMC); public health nursing (PMC). *Accreditation:* AACN; ACNM/ACME. Part-time programs available. Postbaccalaureate distance learning degree programs offered (minimal on-campus study). *Faculty:* 80. *Students:* 79 full-time (71 women), 336 part-time (317 women). Includes 63 minority (24 Black or African American, non-Hispanic/Latino; 2 American Indian or Alaska Native, non-Hispanic/Latino; 18 Asian, non-Hispanic/Latino; 15 Hispanic/Latino; 4 Two or more races, non-Hispanic/Latino), 6 international. Average age 37. 155 applicants, 82% accepted, 127 enrolled. In 2011, 79 master's, 15 doctorates, 12 other advanced degrees awarded. Terminal master's awarded for partial completion of doctoral program. *Degree requirements:* For master's, comprehensive exam, thesis optional, general oral exam; for doctorate, variable foreign language requirement, thesis/dissertation, comprehensive oral exam (for DNP); comprehensive written and oral exam (for PhD). *Entrance requirements:* For master's, bachelor's degree in nursing, minimum GPA of 3.0, RN license, 1 year of clinical experience, RN license in KS and MO; for doctorate, GRE General Test, master's degree in nursing, minimum GPA of 3.5, RN license in KS and MO; national certification (for some specialties). Additional exam requirements/recommendations for international students: Required—TOEFL. *Application deadline:* For fall admission, 4/1 for domestic and international students; for spring admission, 9/1 for domestic and international students. Application fee: $60. Electronic applications accepted. Tuition and fees vary according to course load, campus/location, program and reciprocity agreements. *Financial support:* Research assistantships with full and partial tuition reimbursements, teaching

assistantships with full and partial tuition reimbursements, and traineeships available. Financial award application deadline: 2/14; financial award applicants required to submit FAFSA. *Faculty research:* Breastfeeding practices of teen mothers, national database of nursing quality indicators, caregiving of families of patients using technology in the home, simulation in nursing education, diaphragm fatigue. *Total annual research expenditures:* $6.1 million. *Unit head:* Dr. Karen L. Miller, Dean, 913-588-1601, Fax: 913-588-1660, E-mail: kmiller@kumc.edu. *Application contact:* Dr. Debra J. Ford, Associate Dean, Student Affairs, 913-588-1619, Fax: 913-588-1615, E-mail: dford@kumc.edu. Web site: http://nursing.kumc.edu.

University of Louisville, Graduate School, School of Nursing, Louisville, KY 40202. Offers adult nurse practitioner (MSN); family nurse practitioner (MSN); health professions education (MSN); neonatal nurse practitioner (MSN); nursing research (PhD); psychiatric mental health nurse practitioner (MSN). *Accreditation:* AACN. Part-time programs available. *Faculty:* 24 full-time (22 women), 4 part-time/adjunct (3 women). *Students:* 82 full-time (74 women), 65 part-time (58 women); includes 20 minority (13 Black or African American, non-Hispanic/Latino; 1 American Indian or Alaska Native, non-Hispanic/Latino; 1 Asian, non-Hispanic/Latino; 1 Hispanic/Latino; 4 Two or more races, non-Hispanic/Latino), 2 international. Average age 34. 41 applicants, 56% accepted, 19 enrolled. In 2011, 42 master's, 2 doctorates awarded. Terminal master's awarded for partial completion of doctoral program. *Degree requirements:* For master's, thesis optional; for doctorate, comprehensive exam, thesis/dissertation. *Entrance requirements:* For master's, GRE General Test, bachelor's degree in nursing, minimum GPA of 3.0, RN license; for doctorate, GRE General Test, BSN or MSN with recommended minimum GPA of 3.0. Additional exam requirements/recommendations for international students: Required—TOEFL. *Application deadline:* For fall admission, 4/1 priority date for domestic students, 4/1 for international students. Applications are processed on a rolling basis. Application fee: $50. Electronic applications accepted. *Expenses:* Tuition, state resident: full-time $9692; part-time $539 per credit hour. Tuition, nonresident: full-time $20,168; part-time $1121 per credit hour. Tuition and fees vary according to program and reciprocity agreements. *Financial support:* In 2011–12, 45 students received support, including 6 research assistantships with full tuition reimbursements available (averaging $20,000 per year), 6 teaching assistantships with full tuition reimbursements available (averaging $19,167 per year); fellowships with full tuition reimbursements available, institutionally sponsored loans, scholarships/grants, traineeships, health care benefits, and unspecified assistantships also available. Support available to part-time students. Financial award application deadline: 4/15; financial award applicants required to submit FAFSA. *Faculty research:* Maternal-child/family stress after pregnancy loss, postpartum depression, access to healthcare (underserved populations), quality of life issues, physical activity (impact on chronic/acute conditions). *Total annual research expenditures:* $795,250. *Unit head:* Dr. Marcia J. Hern, Dean, 502-852-8300, Fax: 502-852-5044, E-mail: m.hern@gwise.louisville.edu. *Application contact:* Dr. Lee Ridner, Interim Associate Dean for Academic Affairs and Director of MSN Programs, 502-852-8518, Fax: 502-852-0704, E-mail: romain01@louisville.edu. Web site: http://www.louisville.edu/nursing/.

University of Massachusetts Dartmouth, Graduate School, College of Nursing, Graduate Nursing Programs, North Dartmouth, MA 02747-2300. Offers adult health/adult nurse practitioner (MS); adult health/advanced practice (MS); adult health/nurse educator (MS); adult health/nurse manager (MS); adult nurse practitioner (PMC); community nursing/advanced practice (MS); community nursing/nurse educator (MS); community nursing/nurse manager (MS); individualized nursing (PMC); nursing (DNP, PhD). Part-time programs available. *Faculty:* 27 full-time (all women), 42 part-time/adjunct (41 women). *Students:* 8 full-time (all women), 99 part-time (93 women); includes 11 minority (4 Black or African American, non-Hispanic/Latino; 2 Asian, non-Hispanic/Latino; 4 Hispanic/Latino; 1 Two or more races, non-Hispanic/Latino), 1 international. Average age 38. 65 applicants, 75% accepted, 26 enrolled. In 2011, 12 master's, 1 other advanced degree awarded. *Degree requirements:* For master's, thesis; for doctorate, thesis/dissertation. *Entrance requirements:* For master's, GRE General Test, BSN, minimum undergraduate GPA of 3.0, RN license, 3 letters of recommendation, 1 year experience as registered nurse; for doctorate, GRE General Test, minimum undergraduate GPA of 3.0, graduate 3.3; 3 letters of recommendation; personal statement; current Massachusetts RN license or eligibility for licensure in Massachusetts; 1 year professional nursing experience; example of scholarly writing. Additional exam requirements/recommendations for international students: Required—TOEFL (minimum score 533 paper-based; 200 computer-based; 72 iBT). *Application deadline:* For fall admission, 3/15 for domestic students, 2/15 for international students. Application fee: $40 ($60 for international students). Electronic applications accepted. *Expenses:* Tuition, state resident: full-time $2071; part-time $86.29 per credit. Tuition, nonresident: full-time $8099; part-time $337.46 per credit. *Required fees:* $438.58 per credit. Part-time tuition and fees vary according to class time, course load, degree level and reciprocity agreements. *Financial support:* In 2011–12, 14 teaching assistantships with partial tuition reimbursements (averaging $2,571 per year) were awarded; Federal Work-Study also available. Support available to part-time students. Financial award application deadline: 3/1; financial award applicants required to submit FAFSA. *Faculty research:* Chronic illness management, risk reduction activities in Type 2 diabetes, diabetes care and education, clinical decision-making, quantitative methodologies. *Total annual research expenditures:* $31,049. *Unit head:* Dr. Gail Russell, Graduate Program Director, 508-999-8251, Fax: 508-999-9127, E-mail: grussell@umassd.edu. *Application contact:* Elan Turcotte-Shamski, Graduate Admissions Officer, 508-999-8604, Fax: 508-999-8183, E-mail: graduate@umassd.edu. Web site: http://www.umassd.edu/nursing/graduateprograms.

University of Massachusetts Worcester, Graduate School of Nursing, Worcester, MA 01655-0115. Offers adult acute/critical care nurse practitioner (MS, Post Master's Certificate); adult acute/critical care nurse practitioner and gerontological nurse practitioner (MS, Post Master's Certificate); adult primary care nurse practitioner (MS, Post Master's Certificate); adult primary care nurse practitioner and gerontological nurse practitioner (MS, Post Master's Certificate); advanced practice nursing (DNP); family nurse practitioner (MS); gerontological nurse practitioner (Post Master's Certificate); leadership (DNP); nurse education (Post Master's Certificate); nurse educator (MS); nursing (PhD). *Accreditation:* AACN. *Faculty:* 20 full-time (17 women), 60 part-time/adjunct (50 women). *Students:* 162 full-time (141 women), 36 part-time (30 women); includes 29 minority (13 Black or African American, non-Hispanic/Latino; 10 Asian, non-Hispanic/Latino; 6 Hispanic/Latino), 1 international. Average age 36. 252 applicants, 38% accepted, 82 enrolled. In 2011, 38 master's, 6 doctorates awarded. *Degree requirements:* For doctorate, comprehensive exam, thesis/dissertation. *Entrance requirements:* For master's, GRE General Test, bachelor's degree, course work in statistics; for doctorate, GRE General Test, bachelor's or master's degree, RN licensure; for Post Master's Certificate, GRE General Test, MS in nursing. Additional exam requirements/recommendations for international students: Required—TOEFL. *Application deadline:* For fall admission, 1/15 priority date for domestic students. Applications are processed on a rolling basis. Application fee: $40 ($60 for international students). *Expenses:* Contact institution. *Financial support:* In 2011–12, 38 students received support. Institutionally sponsored loans, scholarships/grants, traineeships, and tuition waivers (for some) available. Support available to part-time students. Financial award application deadline: 5/16; financial award applicants required to submit FAFSA.

Faculty research: Decision-making of partners and men with prostate cancer, coinfection (HIV and Hepatitus C) and treatment decisions, parent management of children with T1DM, health literacy and discharge planning, Ghanian women and self-care. *Total annual research expenditures:* $939,567. *Unit head:* Dr. Paulette Seymour-Route, Dean, 508-856-5801, Fax: 508-856-6552, E-mail: paulette.seymour-route@umassmed.edu. *Application contact:* Diane Brescia, Admissions Coordinator, 508-856-3488, Fax: 508-856-5851, E-mail: diane.brescia@umassmed.edu. Web site: http://www.umassmed.edu/gsn/.

University of Medicine and Dentistry of New Jersey, School of Nursing, Newark, NJ 07107-3001. Offers adult health (MSN); adult occupational health (MSN); advanced practice nursing (MSN, Post Master's Certificate); family nurse practitioner (MSN); nurse anesthesia (MSN); nursing (MSN); nursing informatics (MSN); urban health (PhD); women's health practitioner (MSN). *Accreditation:* AANA/CANAEP; NLN (one or more programs are accredited). Part-time programs available. *Entrance requirements:* For master's, GRE, RN license; basic life support, statistics, and health assessment experience. Additional exam requirements/recommendations for international students: Required—TOEFL. Electronic applications accepted. *Expenses:* Contact institution. *Faculty research:* HIV/AIDS, diabetes education, learned helplessness, nursing science, psychoeducation.

University of Miami, Graduate School, School of Nursing and Health Studies, Coral Gables, FL 33124. Offers acute care (MSN), including acute care nurse practitioner, nurse anesthesia; nursing (PhD); primary care (MSN), including adult nurse practitioner, family nurse practitioner, nurse midwifery, women's health practitioner. *Accreditation:* AACN; AANA/CANAEP; ACNM/ACME (one or more programs are accredited). Part-time programs available. *Degree requirements:* For master's, thesis optional; for doctorate, thesis/dissertation. *Entrance requirements:* For master's, GRE General Test, BSN, minimum GPA of 3.0, Florida RN license; for doctorate, GRE General Test, BSN or MSN, minimum GPA of 3.0. Additional exam requirements/recommendations for international students: Required—TOEFL (minimum score 550 paper-based; 213 computer-based). Electronic applications accepted. *Faculty research:* Transcultural nursing, exercise and depression in Alzheimer's disease, infectious diseases/HIV–AIDS, postpartum depression, outcomes assessment.

University of Michigan, Horace H. Rackham School of Graduate Studies, School of Nursing, Division of Acute, Critical and Long-term Care, Program in Adult Acute Care Nurse Practitioner, Ann Arbor, MI 48109. Offers MS. *Accreditation:* AACN. Part-time programs available. *Degree requirements:* For master's, thesis. *Entrance requirements:* For master's, GRE General Test (if BSN GPA less than 3.25), Michigan licensure, minimum of B average in BSN program. Additional exam requirements/recommendations for international students: Required—TOEFL (minimum score 560 paper-based; 220 computer-based). Electronic applications accepted. *Faculty research:* The functional outcomes and quality of life in women with breast cancer, hypertension.

University of Michigan, Horace H. Rackham School of Graduate Studies, School of Nursing, Division of Health Promotion and Risk Reduction, Program in Community Health Nursing, Ann Arbor, MI 48109. Offers adult nurse practitioner (Post Master's Certificate); adult primary care/adult nurse practitioner (MS); community care (Post Master's Certificate); community care/home care (MS); family nurse practitioner (MS, Post Master's Certificate); occupational health nursing (MS). *Accreditation:* AACN. Part-time and evening/weekend programs available. *Degree requirements:* For master's, thesis. *Entrance requirements:* For master's, GRE General Test (if cumulative BSN GPA less than 3.25), licensure, minimum GPA of 3.0 in BSN program. Additional exam requirements/recommendations for international students: Required—TOEFL (minimum score 560 paper-based; 220 computer-based).

University of Minnesota, Twin Cities Campus, Graduate School, School of Nursing, Program in Adult Health Clinical Nurse Specialist, Minneapolis, MN 55455-0213. Offers MS. *Accreditation:* AACN. *Degree requirements:* For master's, final oral exam, project or thesis. *Entrance requirements:* Additional exam requirements/recommendations for international students: Required—TOEFL (minimum score 586 paper-based; 240 computer-based).

University of Missouri–Kansas City, School of Nursing, Kansas City, MO 64110-2499. Offers adult clinical nurse specialist (MSN), including adult nurse practitioner, women's health nurse practitioner; family nurse practitioner (MSN); neonatal nurse practitioner (MSN); nurse educator (MSN); nurse executive (MSN); nursing (PhD); nursing practice (DNP); pediatric nurse practitioner (MSN). *Accreditation:* AACN. Part-time programs available. Postbaccalaureate distance learning degree programs offered (minimal on-campus study). *Faculty:* 40 full-time (35 women), 57 part-time/adjunct (52 women). *Students:* 51 full-time (48 women), 381 part-time (352 women); includes 41 minority (22 Black or African American, non-Hispanic/Latino; 7 Asian, non-Hispanic/Latino; 12 Hispanic/Latino). Average age 37. 195 applicants, 49% accepted, 90 enrolled. In 2011, 78 master's, 19 doctorates awarded. *Degree requirements:* For master's, thesis or alternative. *Entrance requirements:* For master's, minimum undergraduate GPA of 3.2; for doctorate, GRE, 3 letters of reference, interview by invitation. Additional exam requirements/recommendations for international students: Required—TOEFL (minimum score 550 paper-based; 213 computer-based; 80 iBT). *Application deadline:* For fall admission, 2/1 priority date for domestic students, 2/1 for international students; for spring admission, 9/1 priority date for domestic students, 9/1 for international students. Application fee: $45 ($50 for international students). *Expenses:* Tuition, state resident: full-time $5798; part-time $322.10 per credit hour. Tuition, nonresident: full-time $14,969; part-time $831.60 per credit hour. *Required fees:* $93.51 per credit hour. *Financial support:* In 2011–12, 25 teaching assistantships with partial tuition reimbursements (averaging $6,927 per year) were awarded; fellowships, research assistantships, career-related internships or fieldwork, Federal Work-Study, institutionally sponsored loans, and tuition waivers (full and partial) also available. Support available to part-time students. Financial award application deadline: 3/1; financial award applicants required to submit FAFSA. *Faculty research:* Geriatrics/gerontology, children's pain, neonatology, Alzheimer's care, cancer caregivers. *Unit head:* Dr. Lora Lacey-Haun, Dean, 816-235-1700, Fax: 816-235-1701, E-mail: laceyhaunc@umkc.edu. *Application contact:* Leah Wilder, Coordinator for Admissions and Recruitment, 816-235-5768, Fax: 816-235-1701, E-mail: wilderl@umkc.edu. Web site: http://nursing.umkc.edu/.

University of Missouri–St. Louis, College of Nursing, St. Louis, MO 63121. Offers adult nurse practitioner (DNP, Post Master's Certificate); clinical nurse specialist (DNP); family mental health nurse practitioner (DNP); family nurse practitioner (MSN, DNP, Post Master's Certificate); neonatal nurse practitioner (MSN); nurse educator (MSN); nurse leader (MSN); nurse practitioner (Post Master's Certificate); nursing (PhD); pediatric clinical nurse specialist (DNP); pediatric nurse practitioner (MSN, DNP, Post Master's Certificate); women's health nurse practitioner (MSN, Post Master's Certificate). *Accreditation:* AACN. Part-time programs available. *Faculty:* 12 full-time (11 women), 14 part-time/adjunct (all women). *Students:* 240 part-time (226 women); includes 30 minority (26 Black or African American, non-Hispanic/Latino; 1 Asian, non-Hispanic/Latino; 2 Hispanic/Latino; 1 Two or more races, non-Hispanic/Latino). Average age 37. 228 applicants, 28% accepted, 53 enrolled. In 2011, 66 master's, 2 doctorates, 2 other advanced degrees awarded. *Degree requirements:* For doctorate, comprehensive exam, thesis/dissertation; for Post Master's Certificate, thesis. *Entrance requirements:* For master's, 2 recommendation letters; minimum GPA of 3.0; BSN; nursing licensure; statement of purpose; course in differential/inferential statistics; for doctorate, GRE, 2 letters of recommendation, MSN, minimum GPA of 3.2, course in differential/inferential statistics; for Post Master's Certificate, 2 recommendation letters; MSN; advanced practice certificate; minimum GPA of 3.0; essay. Additional exam requirements/recommendations for international students: Required—TOEFL (minimum score 550 paper-based; 213 computer-based). *Application deadline:* For fall admission, 2/15 for domestic and international students. Application fee: $35 ($40 for international students). Electronic applications accepted. *Expenses:* Tuition, state resident: full-time $6273; part-time $3866 per year. Tuition, nonresident: full-time $14,969; part-time $9980 per year. *Required fees:* $315 per year. *Financial support:* In 2011–12, 3 research assistantships with full and partial tuition reimbursements (averaging $12,339 per year) were awarded. Financial award application deadline: 4/1; financial award applicants required to submit FAFSA. *Faculty research:* Health promotion and restoration, family disruption, violence, abuse, battered women, health survey methods. *Unit head:* Dr. Nancy Magnuson, Director, 314-516-6066. *Application contact:* 314-516-5458, Fax: 314-516-6996, E-mail: gradadm@umsl.edu. Web site: http://www.umsl.edu/divisions/nursing/.

The University of North Carolina at Chapel Hill, School of Nursing, Chapel Hill, NC 27599-7460. Offers nursing (MSN, PhD, PMC), including adult nurse practitioner (MSN, PMC), children's health advanced practice (MSN, PMC), family nurse practitioner (MSN, PMC), health care systems (MSN, PMC), psychiatric/mental health nursing (MSN, PMC), women's health nursing (MSN, PMC). *Accreditation:* AACN; NLN (one or more programs are accredited). Part-time programs available. *Degree requirements:* For master's, comprehensive exam, thesis; for doctorate, thesis/dissertation, 3 exams. *Entrance requirements:* For master's and doctorate, GRE General Test. *Faculty research:* Chronic illness, parenting, cardiovascular health in children, elderly, HIV-AIDS.

The University of North Carolina at Charlotte, Graduate School, College of Health and Human Services, School of Nursing, Charlotte, NC 28223-0001. Offers administration (Post-Master's Certificate); advanced clinical (MSN, Post-Master's Certificate); anesthesia (MSN, Post-Master's Certificate); community health (MSN); family nurse practitioner (MSN, Post-Master's Certificate); health administration (MSN); mental health (MSN); nurse educator (MSN, Post-Master's Certificate); systems population (MSN). *Accreditation:* AACN. *Faculty:* 20 full-time (19 women), 5 part-time/adjunct (all women). *Students:* 76 full-time (65 women), 160 part-time (149 women); includes 49 minority (32 Black or African American, non-Hispanic/Latino; 1 American Indian or Alaska Native, non-Hispanic/Latino; 8 Asian, non-Hispanic/Latino; 8 Hispanic/Latino), 1 international. Average age 35. 191 applicants, 42% accepted, 71 enrolled. In 2011, 76 master's, 10 other advanced degrees awarded. *Degree requirements:* For master's, thesis or alternative, practicum. *Entrance requirements:* For master's, GRE General Test, minimum GPA of 3.0 in undergraduate major. Additional exam requirements/recommendations for international students: Required—TOEFL (minimum score 570 paper-based; 220 computer-based; 83 iBT). *Application deadline:* For fall admission, 7/15 for domestic students, 5/1 for international students; for spring admission, 11/15 for domestic students, 10/1 for international students. Application fee: $65 ($75 for international students). *Expenses:* Tuition, state resident: full-time $3689. Tuition, nonresident: full-time $15,226. *Required fees:* $2198. Tuition and fees vary according to course load and program. *Financial support:* In 2011–12, 10 students received support, including 4 research assistantships (averaging $5,284 per year), 6 teaching assistantships (averaging $2,918 per year); career-related internships or fieldwork, institutionally sponsored loans, scholarships/grants, traineeships, unspecified assistantships, and administrative assistanship also available. Support available to part-time students. Financial award application deadline: 4/1; financial award applicants required to submit FAFSA. *Total annual research expenditures:* $955,795. *Unit head:* Dr. Lucille L. Travis, Director, 704-687-7959, Fax: 704-687-6017, E-mail: ltravis1@uncc.edu. *Application contact:* Kathy B. Giddings, Director of Graduate Admissions, 704-687-5503, Fax: 704-687-3279, E-mail: gradadm@uncc.edu. Web site: http://nursing.uncc.edu/.

The University of North Carolina at Greensboro, Graduate School, School of Nursing, Greensboro, NC 27412-5001. Offers adult clinical nurse specialist (MSN, PMC); adult/gerontological nurse practitioner (MSN, PMC); nurse anesthesia (MSN, PMC); nursing (PhD); nursing administration (MSN); nursing education (MSN); MSN/MBA. *Accreditation:* AACN; AANA/CANAEP; NLN. *Degree requirements:* For master's, thesis or alternative. *Entrance requirements:* For master's, GRE General Test or MAT, BSN, clinical experience, liability insurance, RN license; for PMC, liability insurance, MSN, RN license. Additional exam requirements/recommendations for international students: Required—TOEFL. Electronic applications accepted.

University of North Florida, Brooks College of Health, School of Nursing, Jacksonville, FL 32224. Offers clinical nurse leader (MSN); clinical nurse specialist (MSN); family nurse practitioner (Certificate); nurse anesthetist (CRNA) (MSN); nursing practice (DNP); primary care nurse practitioner (MSN). *Accreditation:* AACN; AANA/CANAEP. Part-time programs available. *Faculty:* 28 full-time (21 women), 1 (woman) part-time/adjunct. *Students:* 97 full-time (69 women), 69 part-time (60 women); includes 41 minority (17 Black or African American, non-Hispanic/Latino; 1 American Indian or Alaska Native, non-Hispanic/Latino; 10 Asian, non-Hispanic/Latino; 11 Hispanic/Latino; 2 Two or more races, non-Hispanic/Latino). Average age 34. 215 applicants, 23% accepted, 31 enrolled. In 2011, 55 master's, 4 doctorates awarded. *Degree requirements:* For master's, thesis optional. *Entrance requirements:* For master's, GRE General Test, minimum GPA of 3.0 in last 60 hours of course work, BSN, clinical experience, resume; for doctorate, GRE (minimum score of 1000) or MAT (minimum score of 410), master's degree in nursing specialty from nationally-accredited program; national certification in one of the following APRN roles: CNE, CNM, CNS, CRNA, CNP; minimum graduate GPA of 3.3; three letters of reference which address academic ability and clinical skills; active license as registered nurse or advanced practice registered nurse. Additional exam requirements/recommendations for international students: Required—TOEFL (minimum score 500 paper-based; 173 computer-based; 61 iBT). *Application deadline:* For fall admission, 3/15 for domestic students, 4/1 for international students. Applications are processed on a rolling basis. Application fee: $30. Electronic applications accepted. *Expenses:* Tuition, state resident: full-time $8793; part-time $366.38 per credit hour. Tuition, nonresident: full-time $23,502; part-time $979.24 per credit hour. *Required fees:* $1384; $57.66 per credit hour. Tuition and fees vary according to course load and program. *Financial support:* In 2011–12, 59 students received support. Research assistantships available. Financial award application deadline: 4/1; financial award applicants required to submit FAFSA. *Faculty research:* Teen pregnancy, diabetes, ethical decision-making, family caregivers. *Total annual research expenditures:* $545,563. *Unit head:* Dr. John McDonough, Director, 904-620-2684, E-mail: jmcdonou@unf.edu. *Application contact:* Beth Dibble, 904-620-2684, Fax: 904-620-1832, E-mail: nursingadmissions@unf.edu. Web site: http://www.unf.edu/brooks/nursing.

University of Pennsylvania, School of Nursing, Adult Acute Care Nurse Practitioner Program, Philadelphia, PA 19104. Offers acute care nurse practitioner (MSN). *Accreditation:* AACN. Part-time programs available. *Students:* 32 full-time (29 women),

62 part-time (58 women); includes 17 minority (4 Black or African American, non-Hispanic/Latino; 1 American Indian or Alaska Native, non-Hispanic/Latino; 8 Asian, non-Hispanic/Latino; 3 Hispanic/Latino; 1 Two or more races, non-Hispanic/Latino), 2 international. 74 applicants, 43% accepted, 31 enrolled. In 2011, 44 degrees awarded. *Entrance requirements:* For master's, GRE General Test, BSN, minimum GPA of 3.0, previous course work in statistics. *Application deadline:* For fall admission, 2/15 priority date for domestic students. Applications are processed on a rolling basis. Application fee: $70. *Expenses:* Contact institution. *Financial support:* Fellowships, research assistantships, teaching assistantships, Federal Work-Study, and institutionally sponsored loans available. Support available to part-time students. Financial award application deadline: 4/1. *Faculty research:* Post-injury disability, bereavement and attributions in fire survivors, stress in staff nurses. *Unit head:* Assistant Dean of Admissions and Financial Aid, 866-867-6877, Fax: 215-573-8439, E-mail: admissions@nursing.upenn.edu. *Application contact:* Deborah Becker, Program Director, 215-898-0432, E-mail: debecker@nursing.upenn.edu. Web site: http://www.nursing.upenn.edu/.

University of Pennsylvania, School of Nursing, Adult Health Nurse Practitioner Program, Philadelphia, PA 19104. Offers MSN. *Accreditation:* AACN. Part-time programs available. *Students:* 22 full-time (18 women), 24 part-time (22 women); includes 9 minority (4 Black or African American, non-Hispanic/Latino; 2 Asian, non-Hispanic/Latino; 1 Hispanic/Latino; 2 Two or more races, non-Hispanic/Latino), 3 international. 46 applicants, 65% accepted, 28 enrolled. In 2011, 14 degrees awarded. *Entrance requirements:* For master's, GRE General Test, BSN, minimum GPA of 3.0, previous course work in basic statistics. Additional exam requirements/recommendations for international students: Required—TOEFL. *Application deadline:* For fall admission, 2/15 priority date for domestic students. Applications are processed on a rolling basis. Application fee: $70. *Expenses:* Contact institution. *Financial support:* Fellowships, research assistantships, teaching assistantships, career-related internships or fieldwork, Federal Work-Study, and institutionally sponsored loans available. Support available to part-time students. Financial award application deadline: 4/1. *Faculty research:* Restraints, incontinence, discharge planning, frail elders, quality of life across continuum of care. *Unit head:* Assistant Dean of Admissions and Financial Aid, 866-867-6877, Fax: 215-573-8439, E-mail: admissions@nursing.upenn.edu. *Application contact:* Valerie Cotter, Program Director, 215-898-1795, E-mail: cottervt@nursing.upenn.edu. Web site: http://www.nursing.upenn.edu/ahnp/.

University of Pittsburgh, School of Nursing, Nurse Practitioner Program, Pittsburgh, PA 15261. Offers acute care nurse practitioner (MSN, DNP); adult nurse practitioner (MSN, DNP); family nurse practitioner (MSN, DNP); neonatal (MSN, DNP); nursing practice (DNP); pediatric nurse practitioner (MSN, DNP); psychiatric primary care nurse practitioner (MSN, DNP). *Accreditation:* AACN. Part-time programs available. *Students:* 46 full-time (44 women), 135 part-time (123 women); includes 13 minority (6 Black or African American, non-Hispanic/Latino; 1 American Indian or Alaska Native, non-Hispanic/Latino; 6 Asian, non-Hispanic/Latino). Average age 32. 126 applicants, 71% accepted, 70 enrolled. In 2011, 24 master's, 4 doctorates awarded. *Degree requirements:* For master's, comprehensive exam, thesis optional. *Entrance requirements:* For master's, GRE General Test or MAT, BSN, RN license, letters of recommendation, resume, course work in statistics, 1-3 years of nursing experience; for doctorate, GRE General Test, BSN, RN license, minimum GPA of 3.5, 3 letters of recommendation. Additional exam requirements/recommendations for international students: Required—TOEFL (minimum score 550 paper-based; 213 computer-based; 80 iBT). *Application deadline:* Applications are processed on a rolling basis. Application fee: $50. Electronic applications accepted. *Expenses:* Tuition, state resident: full-time $18,774; part-time $760 per credit. Tuition, nonresident: full-time $30,736; part-time $1258 per credit. *Required fees:* $740; $200 per term. Tuition and fees vary according to program. *Financial support:* In 2011–12, 5 students received support, including 1 fellowship with partial tuition reimbursement available (averaging $11,330 per year), 1 research assistantship with full tuition reimbursement available (averaging $35,942 per year), 3 teaching assistantships with full and partial tuition reimbursements available (averaging $27,470 per year); scholarships/grants, traineeships, health care benefits, and unspecified assistantships also available. Support available to part-time students. *Unit head:* Dr. Sandra Engberg, Associate Dean for Clinical Education, 412-624-3835, Fax: 412-624-8521, E-mail: sje1@pitt.edu. *Application contact:* Laurie Lapsley, Administrator of Graduate Student Services, 412-624-9670, Fax: 412-624-2409, E-mail: lapsleyl@pitt.edu. Web site: http://www.nursing.pitt.edu.

University of Puerto Rico, Medical Sciences Campus, School of Nursing, San Juan, PR 00936-5067. Offers adult and elderly nursing (MSN); child and adolescent nursing (MSN); critical care nursing (MSN); family and community nursing (MSN); family nurse practitioner (MSN); maternity nursing (MSN); mental health and psychiatric nursing (MSN). *Accreditation:* AACN; AANA/CANAEP. *Entrance requirements:* For master's, GRE or EXADEP, interview, Puerto Rico RN license or professional license for international students, general and specific point average, article analysis. Electronic applications accepted. *Faculty research:* HIV, health disparities, teen violence, women and violence, neurological disorders.

University of Rochester, School of Nursing, Rochester, NY 14642. Offers acute care nurse practitioner (MS); adult nurse practitioner (MS); adult/geriatric nurse practitioner (MS); care of children and families/pediatric nurse practitioner (MS); care of children and families/pediatric nurse practitioner/neonatal nurse practitioner (MS); clinical nurse leader (MS); clinical research coordinator (MS); family nurse practitioner (MS); family psychiatric mental health nurse practitioner (MS); health care organization management and leadership (MS); health practice research (PhD); nursing (DNP). *Accreditation:* AACN; NLN (one or more programs are accredited). Part-time programs available. Postbaccalaureate distance learning degree programs offered (minimal on-campus study). *Faculty:* 49 full-time (42 women), 72 part-time/adjunct (60 women). *Students:* 38 full-time (32 women), 196 part-time (181 women); includes 37 minority (20 Black or African American, non-Hispanic/Latino; 9 Asian, non-Hispanic/Latino; 8 Hispanic/Latino), 5 international. Average age 36. 68 applicants, 56% accepted, 26 enrolled. In 2011, 49 master's, 7 doctorates awarded. Terminal master's awarded for partial completion of doctoral program. *Median time to degree:* Of those who began their doctoral program in fall 2003, 40% received their degree in 8 years or less. *Degree requirements:* For doctorate, thesis/dissertation. *Entrance requirements:* For master's, BS in nursing, minimum GPA of 3.0, course work in statistics; for doctorate, GRE General Test, MS in nursing, minimum GPA of 3.5. Additional exam requirements/recommendations for international students: Required—or IELTS (minimum score 6.5); Recommended—TOEFL (minimum score 560 paper-based; 230 computer-based; 88 iBT). *Application deadline:* For fall admission, 4/1 priority date for domestic students, 4/1 for international students; for spring admission, 9/1 for domestic and international students. Application fee: $50. Electronic applications accepted. *Expenses:* Tuition: Full-time $41,040. *Financial support:* In 2011–12, 49 students received support, including 1 fellowship with full and partial tuition reimbursement available (averaging $18,700 per year); scholarships/grants, traineeships, health care benefits, tuition waivers (partial), and unspecified assistantships also available. Support available to part-time students. Financial award application deadline: 6/30. *Faculty research:* Clinical research in aging, managing asthma in children, interventions to improve outcomes in critically ill children and their mothers, nurse home visitation studies, medical device evaluation, critical care clinical studies, high risk behavior and prevention, palliative care, pregnancy-related weight gain. *Total annual research expenditures:* $4.3 million. *Unit head:* Dr. Kathy H. Rideout, Interim Dean, 585-273-8902, Fax: 585-273-1268, E-mail: kathy_rideout@urmc.rochester.edu. *Application contact:* Elaine Andolina, Director of Admissions, 585-275-2375, Fax: 585-756-8299, E-mail: elaine_andolina@urmc.rochester.edu. Web site: http://www.son.rochester.edu.

University of St. Francis, College of Nursing, Joliet, IL 60435-6169. Offers adult health clinical nurse specialist (Post-Master's Certificate); adult nurse practitioner (MSN, Post-Master's Certificate); family nurse practitioner (Post-Master's Certificate); nursing administration (MSN); nursing practice (DNP). *Accreditation:* AACN. Part-time and evening/weekend programs available. Postbaccalaureate distance learning degree programs offered (no on-campus study). *Faculty:* 11 full-time (10 women), 16 part-time/adjunct (all women). *Students:* 59 full-time (52 women), 254 part-time (232 women); includes 80 minority (31 Black or African American, non-Hispanic/Latino; 11 Asian, non-Hispanic/Latino; 33 Hispanic/Latino; 5 Two or more races, non-Hispanic/Latino), 15 international. Average age 41. 340 applicants, 46% accepted, 117 enrolled. In 2011, 20 master's, 4 doctorates, 4 other advanced degrees awarded. *Entrance requirements:* Additional exam requirements/recommendations for international students: Required—TOEFL (minimum score 550 paper-based; 213 computer-based). *Application deadline:* Applications are processed on a rolling basis. Application fee: $30. Electronic applications accepted. *Expenses:* Contact institution. *Financial support:* In 2011–12, 87 students received support. Scholarships/grants, traineeships, and tuition waivers (partial) available. Support available to part-time students. Financial award applicants required to submit FAFSA. *Unit head:* Dr. Carol Wilson, Dean, 815-740-3840, Fax: 815-740-4243, E-mail: cwilson@stfrancis.edu. *Application contact:* Sandra Sloka, Director of Admissions for Graduate and Degree Completion Programs, 800-735-7500, Fax: 815-740-5032, E-mail: ssloka@stfrancis.edu. Web site: http://www.stfrancis.edu/academics/college-of-nursing-allied-health/graduate-programs/.

University of San Diego, Hahn School of Nursing and Health Science, San Diego, CA 92110-2492. Offers adult-gerontology clinical nurse specialist (MSN); adult-gerontology nurse practitioner/family nurse practitioner (MSN); clinical nursing (MSN); entry-level nursing (for non-RNs) (MSN); executive nurse leader (MSN); family nurse practitioner (MSN); family/lifespan psychiatric-mental health nurse practitioner (MSN); healthcare informatics (MS, MSN); nursing (PhD); nursing practice (DNP); pediatric nurse practitioner/family nurse practitioner (MSN). *Accreditation:* AACN. Part-time and evening/weekend programs available. *Faculty:* 23 full-time (21 women), 37 part-time/adjunct (34 women). *Students:* 157 full-time (131 women), 182 part-time (162 women); includes 121 minority (21 Black or African American, non-Hispanic/Latino; 6 American Indian or Alaska Native, non-Hispanic/Latino; 51 Asian, non-Hispanic/Latino; 36 Hispanic/Latino; 2 Native Hawaiian or other Pacific Islander, non-Hispanic/Latino; 5 Two or more races, non-Hispanic/Latino), 7 international. Average age 36. 506 applicants, 47% accepted, 150 enrolled. In 2011, 87 master's, 26 doctorates awarded. *Degree requirements:* For doctorate, thesis/dissertation (for some programs), residency (DNP). *Entrance requirements:* For master's, GRE General Test (entry-level nursing), BSN, current California RN licensure (except for entry-level nursing); minimum GPA of 3.0; for doctorate, minimum GPA of 3.5, MSN, current California RN licensure. Additional exam requirements/recommendations for international students: Required—TOEFL (minimum score 580 paper-based; 237 computer-based; 83 iBT), TWE. *Application deadline:* For fall admission, 3/1 priority date for domestic students, 3/1 for international students; for spring admission, 11/1 priority date for domestic students, 11/1 for international students. Applications are processed on a rolling basis. Application fee: $45. Electronic applications accepted. *Expenses:* Tuition: Full-time $22,482; part-time $1249 per unit. *Required fees:* $224. Full-time tuition and fees vary according to course load and degree level. *Financial support:* In 2011–12, 232 students received support. Scholarships/grants and traineeships available. Support available to part-time students. Financial award application deadline: 4/1; financial award applicants required to submit FAFSA. *Faculty research:* Palliative and end of life care, maternal/child health, childhood obesity, health care disparities, cognitive functioning. *Unit head:* Dr. Sally Hardin, Dean, 619-260-4550, Fax: 619-260-6814. *Application contact:* Monica Mahon, Associate Director of Graduate Admissions, 619-260-4524, Fax: 619-260-4158, E-mail: grads@sandiego.edu. Web site: http://www.sandiego.edu/academics/nursing/.

The University of Scranton, College of Graduate and Continuing Education, Department of Nursing, Scranton, PA 18510. Offers adult health nursing (MSN); family nurse practitioner (MSN, PMC); nurse anesthesia (MSN, PMC). Applicants accepted in odd-numbered years only. *Accreditation:* AACN; AANA/CANAEP. Part-time and evening/weekend programs available. *Faculty:* 13 full-time (all women), 2 part-time/adjunct (both women). *Students:* 50 full-time (45 women), 27 part-time (20 women); includes 7 minority (4 Black or African American, non-Hispanic/Latino; 1 Asian, non-Hispanic/Latino; 2 Hispanic/Latino). Average age 35. 100 applicants, 32% accepted. In 2011, 26 master's awarded. *Degree requirements:* For master's, thesis (for some programs), capstone experience. *Entrance requirements:* For master's, BSN, minimum GPA of 3.0, Pennsylvania RN license. Additional exam requirements/recommendations for international students: Required—TOEFL (minimum score 500 paper-based; 173 computer-based), IELTS (minimum score 5.5). *Application deadline:* For fall admission, 9/1 for domestic students. Applications are processed on a rolling basis. Application fee: $0. *Financial support:* In 2011–12, 7 students received support, including 7 teaching assistantships with full and partial tuition reimbursements available (averaging $6,914 per year); career-related internships or fieldwork, Federal Work-Study, and unspecified assistantships also available. Support available to part-time students. Financial award application deadline: 3/1. *Faculty research:* Home care, doctoral education, health care of women and children, pain, health promotion and adolescence. *Unit head:* Dr. Patricia Harrington, Chair, 570-941-7673, Fax: 570-941-4201, E-mail: harringtonp1@uofs.edu. *Application contact:* Dr. Mary Jane Hanson, Director, 570-941-4060, Fax: 570-941-4201, E-mail: hansonm2@scranton.edu. Web site: http://academic.uofs.edu/department/nursing/.

University of South Alabama, Graduate School, College of Nursing, Mobile, AL 36688. Offers adult health nursing (MSN); community/mental health nursing (MSN); maternal/child nursing (MSN); nursing (DNP). *Accreditation:* AACN. *Faculty:* 21 full-time (20 women). *Students:* 1,335 full-time (1,200 women), 172 part-time (147 women); includes 280 minority (164 Black or African American, non-Hispanic/Latino; 15 American Indian or Alaska Native, non-Hispanic/Latino; 41 Asian, non-Hispanic/Latino; 45 Hispanic/Latino; 2 Native Hawaiian or other Pacific Islander, non-Hispanic/Latino; 13 Two or more races, non-Hispanic/Latino), 10 international. 1,327 applicants, 38% accepted, 388 enrolled. In 2011, 266 master's, 21 doctorates awarded. *Degree requirements:* For master's, thesis optional. *Entrance requirements:* For master's, BSN, RN licensure, minimum GPA of 3.0, resume documenting clinical experience, background check, drug screening; for doctorate, GRE. *Application deadline:* For fall admission, 7/15 for domestic students; for spring admission, 12/1 for domestic students. Application fee: $35. *Expenses:* Tuition, state resident: full-time $7968; part-time $332 per credit hour. Tuition, nonresident: full-time $15,936; part-time $664 per credit hour. *Unit head:* Dr. Rosemary Rhodes, Director of Graduate Education, 251-445-9409, Fax: 251-445-9416. *Application contact:* Dr. B. Keith Harrison, Dean of the Graduate School, 251-460-6310, Fax: 251-461-1513, E-mail: kharriso@usouthal.edu. Web site: http://www.southalabama.edu/nursing.

Adult Nursing

University of South Carolina, The Graduate School, College of Nursing, Program in Health Nursing, Columbia, SC 29208. Offers adult nurse practitioner (MSN); community/public health clinical nurse specialist (MSN); family nurse practitioner (MSN); pediatric nurse practitioner (MSN). *Accreditation:* AACN. Part-time programs available. *Degree requirements:* For master's, thesis or alternative. *Entrance requirements:* For master's, GRE General Test or MAT, BS in nursing, nursing license. Additional exam requirements/recommendations for international students: Required—TOEFL (minimum score 570 paper-based; 230 computer-based). Electronic applications accepted. *Faculty research:* System research, evidence based practice, breast cancer, violence.

University of Southern Maine, School of Nursing, Portland, ME 04104-9300. Offers adult health nursing (PMC); adult psychiatric/mental health nurse practitioner (MS); clinical nurse leader (MS); clinical nurse specialist psychiatric-mental health nursing (MS); education (MS); family nursing (PMC); family psychiatric/mental health nurse practitioner (MS); management (MS); medical/surgical nursing (MS); nurse practitioner adult health nursing (MS); nurse practitioner family nursing (MS); nursing (DNP); psychiatric-mental health nursing (PMC); MBA/MSN. *Accreditation:* AACN. Part-time programs available. *Degree requirements:* For master's, thesis optional. *Entrance requirements:* For master's, GRE General Test or MAT, minimum GPA of 3.0; for doctorate, GRE. Additional exam requirements/recommendations for international students: Required—TOEFL (minimum score 550 paper-based; 213 computer-based). Electronic applications accepted. *Faculty research:* Women's health, nursing history, weight control, community services, substance abuse.

The University of Tampa, Nursing Programs, Tampa, FL 33606-1490. Offers adult nurse practitioner (MSN); family nurse practitioner (MSN). *Accreditation:* NLN. Part-time programs available. *Faculty:* 12 full-time (all women), 7 part-time/adjunct (all women). *Students:* 3 full-time (all women), 134 part-time (125 women); includes 28 minority (13 Black or African American, non-Hispanic/Latino; 1 Asian, non-Hispanic/Latino; 13 Hispanic/Latino; 1 Two or more races, non-Hispanic/Latino), 1 international. Average age 34. 148 applicants, 59% accepted, 52 enrolled. In 2011, 14 master's awarded. *Degree requirements:* For master's, comprehensive exam, oral exam, practicum. *Entrance requirements:* For master's, GRE (minimum score of 1000, 4.0 on Analytical Writing portion), bachelor's degree in nursing, current Florida RN license, minimum GPA of 3.0. Additional exam requirements/recommendations for international students: Required—TOEFL or IELTS. *Application deadline:* Applications are processed on a rolling basis. Application fee: $40. Electronic applications accepted. *Expenses: Tuition:* Full-time $8320; part-time $520 per credit hour. *Required fees:* $40 per semester. Tuition and fees vary according to program. *Financial support:* In 2011–12, 18 students received support. Unspecified assistantships available. Financial award applicants required to submit FAFSA. *Faculty research:* Vaccinations and public health, osteoporosis, cultural diversity, ethics, nursing practice. *Unit head:* Dr. Maria Warda, Director/Chair, 813-257-3302, Fax: 813-258-7214, E-mail: mwarda@ut.edu. *Application contact:* Brent Benner, Director of Admissions, 813-257-3642, E-mail: ctobie@ut.edu.

The University of Texas at Austin, Graduate School, School of Nursing, Austin, TX 78712-1111. Offers adult -gerontology clinical nurse specialist (MSN); child health (MSN), including administration, public health nursing; child health (MSN), including teaching; family nurse practitioner (MSN); family psychiatric/mental health nurse practitioner (MSN); holistic adult health (MSN), including administration, education; maternity (MSN), including administration, public health nursing; maternity (MSN), including teaching; nursing (PhD); nursing administration and healthcare systems management (MSN); pediatric nurse practitioner (MSN); public health nursing (MSN). *Accreditation:* AACN. Part-time programs available. *Degree requirements:* For master's, thesis optional; for doctorate, thesis/dissertation. *Entrance requirements:* For master's and doctorate, GRE General Test. Additional exam requirements/recommendations for international students: Required—TOEFL (minimum score 550 paper-based; 213 computer-based). *Application deadline:* For fall admission, 12/1 for domestic students. Application fee: $50 ($75 for international students). Electronic applications accepted. *Financial support:* Fellowships, research assistantships, teaching assistantships, scholarships/grants, and traineeships available. Financial award application deadline: 2/1. *Faculty research:* Chronic illness management, memory and aging, health promotion, women's health, adolescent health. *Unit head:* Dr. Alexa Stuifbergen, Dean, 512-471-4100, Fax: 512-471-4910, E-mail: astuifbergen@mail.utexas.edu. Web site: http://www.utexas.edu/nursing/.

The University of Texas–Pan American, College of Health Sciences and Human Services, Department of Nursing, Edinburg, TX 78539. Offers adult health nursing (MSN); family nurse practitioner (MSN). *Accreditation:* AACN. Part-time and evening/weekend programs available. *Degree requirements:* For master's, thesis optional. *Entrance requirements:* For master's, Texas RN licensure, undergraduate physical statistic course. Additional exam requirements/recommendations for international students: Required—TOEFL (minimum score 550 paper-based). *Application deadline:* For fall admission, 7/1 priority date for domestic students, 7/1 for international students; for spring admission, 10/1 priority date for domestic students, 10/1 for international students. Applications are processed on a rolling basis. Application fee: $35. Electronic applications accepted. *Expenses:* Contact institution. *Financial support:* Scholarships/grants and traineeships available. *Faculty research:* Health promotion, adolescent pregnancy, herbal and nontraditional approaches, healing touch stress. *Unit head:* Dr. Carolina G. Huerta, Chair, 956-665-3496, Fax: 956-381-2384, E-mail: chuerta@utpa.edu. *Application contact:* Dr. Janice A. Maville, Professor and Assistant Dean, 956-665-2111, Fax: 956-665-2875, E-mail: jmaville@utpa.edu. Web site: http://www.panam.edu/dept/nursing/.

The University of Toledo, College of Graduate Studies, College of Nursing, Department of Population and Community Care, Toledo, OH 43606-3390. Offers adult nurse practitioner (Certificate); adult nurse practitioner/clinical nurse specialist (MSN); clinical nurse leader (MSN); family nurse practitioner (MSN, Certificate); nurse educator (MSN, Certificate); pediatric nurse practitioner (MSN, Certificate); psychiatric-mental health clinical nurse specialist (MSN, Certificate). Part-time programs available. *Faculty:* 43. *Students:* 77 full-time (63 women), 198 part-time (180 women); includes 30 minority (14 Black or African American, non-Hispanic/Latino; 1 American Indian or Alaska Native, non-Hispanic/Latino; 4 Asian, non-Hispanic/Latino; 8 Hispanic/Latino; 3 Two or more races, non-Hispanic/Latino), 1 international. Average age 33. 172 applicants, 53% accepted, 82 enrolled. In 2011, 66 master's, 10 other advanced degrees awarded. *Degree requirements:* For master's, thesis or alternative. *Entrance requirements:* For master's, GRE, BS in nursing, minimum undergraduate GPA of 3.0, statement of purpose, three letters of recommendation, transcripts from all prior institutions attended, Nursing CAS application, UT supplemental application; for Certificate, BS in nursing, minimum undergraduate GPA of 3.0, statement of purpose, three letters of recommendation, transcripts from all prior institutions attended. Additional exam requirements/recommendations for international students: Required—TOEFL (minimum score 550 paper-based; 213 computer-based; 80 iBT), IELTS (minimum score 6.5). Application fee: $45 ($75 for international students). Electronic applications accepted. *Financial support:* Research assistantships, Federal Work-Study, scholarships/grants, traineeships, and tuition waivers (full and partial) available. *Application contact:* Joan Mulligan, Admissions Analyst, 419-383-4168, Fax: 419-383-6140, E-mail: joan.mulligan@utoledo.edu. Web site: http://www.utoledo.edu/nursing/.

University of Wisconsin–Eau Claire, College of Nursing and Health Sciences, Program in Nursing, Eau Claire, WI 54702-4004. Offers adult-gerontologic administration (MSN); adult-gerontologic clinical nurse specialist (MSN); adult-gerontologic education (MSN); adult-gerontologic nurse practitioner (MSN); family health administration (MSN); family health in education (MSN); family health nurse practitioner (MSN); nursing practice (DNP). Part-time programs available. *Faculty:* 13 full-time (all women), 1 (woman) part-time/adjunct. *Students:* 42 full-time (40 women), 68 part-time (66 women); includes 3 minority (1 Black or African American, non-Hispanic/Latino; 1 Asian, non-Hispanic/Latino; 1 Hispanic/Latino). Average age 37. 74 applicants, 70% accepted, 41 enrolled. In 2011, 35 master's awarded. Terminal master's awarded for partial completion of doctoral program. *Degree requirements:* For master's, thesis optional, 500-600 hours clinical practicum, oral and written exams. *Entrance requirements:* For master's, Wisconsin RN license, minimum GPA of 3.0, undergraduate statistics, course work in health assessment. Additional exam requirements/recommendations for international students: Required—TOEFL (minimum score 550 paper-based; 213 computer-based; 79 iBT). Recommended—IELTS (minimum score 7). *Application deadline:* For fall admission, 1/15 priority date for domestic students, 1/15 for international students. Applications are processed on a rolling basis. Application fee: $86. *Expenses:* Tuition, state resident: full-time $7312; part-time $406 per credit. Tuition, nonresident: full-time $16,771; part-time $932 per credit. *Required fees:* $1101; $61 per credit. *Financial support:* In 2011–12, 16 students received support. Federal Work-Study and unspecified assistantships available. Financial award application deadline: 3/1; financial award applicants required to submit FAFSA. *Unit head:* Dr. Linda Young, Dean, 715-836-4904, Fax: 715-836-5925, E-mail: younglk@uwec.edu. *Application contact:* Dr. Mary Zwygart-Stauffacher, Director, 715-836-5287, E-mail: zwygarmc@uwec.edu. Web site: http://www.uwec.edu/conhs/programs/grad/index.htm.

University of Wisconsin–Madison, School of Nursing, Madison, WI 53706-1380. Offers adult/gerontology (DNP); nursing (PhD); pediatrics (DNP); psychiatric mental health (DNP); MS/MPH. *Accreditation:* AACN. Part-time programs available. *Degree requirements:* For doctorate, comprehensive exam, thesis/dissertation. *Entrance requirements:* For doctorate, GRE General Test, 2 samples of scholarly written work, BS in nursing from an accredited program, minimum undergraduate GPA of 3.0 in last 60 credits (for PhD); licensure as professional nurse (for DNP). Additional exam requirements/recommendations for international students: Required—TOEFL (minimum score 600 paper-based; 250 computer-based; 100 iBT). Electronic applications accepted. *Expenses:* Tuition, state resident: full-time $10,296; part-time $643.51 per credit. Tuition, nonresident: full-time $24,054; part-time $1503.40 per credit. *Required fees:* $70.06 per credit. Tuition and fees vary according to course load, campus/location, program and reciprocity agreements. *Faculty research:* Nursing informatics to promote self-care and disease management skills among patients and caregivers; quality of care to frail, vulnerable, and chronically ill populations; study of health-related and health-seeking behaviors; eliminating health disparities; pain and symptom management for patients with cancer.

University of Wisconsin–Oshkosh, Graduate Studies, College of Nursing, Oshkosh, WI 54901. Offers adult health and illness (MSN); family nurse practitioner (MSN). *Accreditation:* AACN. Part-time programs available. *Degree requirements:* For master's, thesis or alternative, clinical paper. *Entrance requirements:* For master's, RN license, BSN, previous course work in statistics and health assessment, minimum undergraduate GPA of 3.0, letters of recommendation. Additional exam requirements/recommendations for international students: Required—TOEFL (minimum score 550 paper-based; 213 computer-based; 79 iBT). Electronic applications accepted. *Faculty research:* Adult health and illness, nurse practitioners practice, health care service, advanced practitioner roles, natural alternative complementary healthcare.

Vanderbilt University, Vanderbilt University School of Nursing, Nashville, TN 37240. Offers acute care nurse practitioner (MSN), including intensivist; adult-gerontology primary care nurse practitioner (MSN); emergency nurse practitioner (MSN); family nurse practitioner (MSN); family psychiatric and mental health nurse practitioner (MSN); health systems management (MSN); neonatal nurse practitioner (MSN); nurse midwifery (MSN); nurse midwifery/family nurse practitioner (MSN); nursing informatics (MSN); nursing practice (DNP); nursing science (PhD); pediatric acute care nurse practitioner (MSN); pediatric primary care nurse practitioner (MSN); women's health nurse practitioner (MSN), including urogynecology, women's health; women's health nurse practitioner/adult gerontology nurse practitioner (MSN); MSN/M Div; MSN/MTS. *Accreditation:* ACNM/ACME; NLN (one or more programs are accredited). Part-time programs available. Postbaccalaureate distance learning degree programs offered (minimal on-campus study). *Faculty:* 120 full-time (105 women), 415 part-time/adjunct (302 women). *Students:* 570 full-time (503 women), 395 part-time (364 women); includes 107 minority (57 Black or African American, non-Hispanic/Latino; 1 American Indian or Alaska Native, non-Hispanic/Latino; 19 Asian, non-Hispanic/Latino; 19 Hispanic/Latino; 2 Native Hawaiian or other Pacific Islander, non-Hispanic/Latino; 9 Two or more races, non-Hispanic/Latino), 10 international. Average age 32. 1,116 applicants, 56% accepted, 455 enrolled. In 2011, 341 master's, 33 doctorates awarded. *Degree requirements:* For doctorate, comprehensive exam, thesis/dissertation. *Entrance requirements:* For master's, GRE General Test (within the past 5 years), minimum B average in undergraduate course work, 3 letters of recommendation; for doctorate, GRE General Test, interview, 3 letters of recommendation from doctorally-prepared faculty, MSN, essay. Additional exam requirements/recommendations for international students: Required—TOEFL (minimum score 570 paper-based; 88 computer-based), IELTS (minimum score 6.5). *Application deadline:* For fall admission, 12/1 priority date for domestic students, 12/1 for international students. Applications are processed on a rolling basis. Application fee: $50. Electronic applications accepted. *Expenses:* Contact institution. *Financial support:* In 2011–12, 392 students received support. Scholarships/grants and health care benefits available. Support available to part-time students. Financial award application deadline: 3/15; financial award applicants required to submit FAFSA. *Faculty research:* Lymphedema, palliative care and bereavement, health services research including workforce, safety and quality of care, gerontology, better birth outcomes including nutrition . *Total annual research expenditures:* $1.8 million. *Unit head:* Dr. Colleen Conway-Welch, Dean, 615-343-8776, Fax: 615-343-7711, E-mail: colleen.conway-welch@vanderbilt.edu. *Application contact:* Patricia Peerman, Assistant Dean for Enrollment Management, 615-322-3800, Fax: 615-343-0333, E-mail: vusn-admissions@vanderbilt.edu. Web site: http://www.nursing.vanderbilt.edu.

Villanova University, College of Nursing, Villanova, PA 19085-1699. Offers adult nurse practitioner (MSN, Post Master's Certificate); family nurse practitioner (MSN, Post Master's Certificate); health care administration (MSN, Post Master's Certificate); nurse anesthetist (MSN, Post Master's Certificate); nursing (PhD); nursing education (MSN, Post Master's Certificate); nursing practice (DNP); pediatric nurse practitioner (MSN, Post Master's Certificate). *Accreditation:* AACN; AANA/CANAEP. Part-time programs available. Postbaccalaureate distance learning degree programs offered (minimal on-campus study). *Faculty:* 17 full-time (all women), 4 part-time/adjunct (all women). *Students:* 36 full-time (35 women), 256 part-time (234 women); includes 27 minority (14 Black or African American, non-Hispanic/Latino; 9 Asian, non-Hispanic/Latino; 4 Hispanic/Latino), 16 international. Average age 30. 161 applicants, 55% accepted, 75 enrolled. In 2011, 55 master's, 11 doctorates, 5 other advanced degrees awarded. *Degree requirements:* For master's, independent study project; for doctorate,

comprehensive exam, thesis/dissertation. *Entrance requirements:* For master's, GRE or MAT, BSN, 1 year of recent nursing experience, physical assessment, course work in statistics; for doctorate, GRE, MSN. Additional exam requirements/recommendations for international students: Required—TOEFL, IELTS. *Application deadline:* For fall admission, 7/1 priority date for domestic students, 7/1 for international students; for spring admission, 11/1 priority date for domestic students, 11/1 for international students. Applications are processed on a rolling basis. Application fee: $50. *Expenses:* Contact institution. *Financial support:* In 2011–12, 43 students received support, including 5 teaching assistantships with full tuition reimbursements available (averaging $13,100 per year); institutionally sponsored loans, scholarships/grants, traineeships, tuition waivers (full), and unspecified assistantships also available. Financial award application deadline: 7/1; financial award applicants required to submit FAFSA. *Faculty research:* Genetics, ethics, cognitive development of students, women with disabilities, nursing leadership. *Unit head:* Dr. Marguerite K. Schlag, Assistant Dean/Director, Graduate Programs, 610-519-4907, Fax: 610-519-7650, E-mail: marguerite.schlag@villanova.edu. Web site: http://www.nursing.villanova.edu/.

Virginia Commonwealth University, Graduate School, School of Nursing, Richmond, VA 23284-9005. Offers adult health acute nursing (MS); adult health primary nursing (MS); biobehavioral clinical research (PhD); child health nursing (MS); clinical nurse leader (MS); family health nursing (MS); nurse educator (MS); nurse practitioner (MS); nursing (Certificate); nursing administration (MS), including clinical nurse manager; psychiatric-mental health nursing (MS); women's health nursing (MS). *Accreditation:* NLN (one or more programs are accredited). Part-time and evening/weekend programs available. *Degree requirements:* For master's, thesis optional; for doctorate, thesis/dissertation. *Entrance requirements:* For master's, GRE General Test, BSN, minimum GPA of 2.8; for doctorate, GRE General Test. Additional exam requirements/recommendations for international students: Required—TOEFL (minimum score 600 paper-based; 250 computer-based; 100 iBT). Electronic applications accepted. *Expenses:* Tuition, state resident: full-time $9133; part-time $507 per credit. Tuition, nonresident: full-time $18,777; part-time $1043 per credit. *Required fees:* $77 per credit. Tuition and fees vary according to degree level, campus/location, program and student level.

Washburn University, School of Nursing, Topeka, KS 66621. Offers adult nurse practitioner (MSN); clinical nurse leader (MSN); family nurse practitioner (MSN). *Accreditation:* AACN. Part-time programs available. *Faculty:* 13 full-time (all women), 1 (woman) part-time/adjunct. *Students:* 23 full-time (all women), 78 part-time (73 women). 52 applicants, 77% accepted, 40 enrolled. In 2011, 23 master's awarded. *Entrance requirements:* Additional exam requirements/recommendations for international students: Required—TOEFL. *Application deadline:* For fall admission, 3/15 for international students. Application fee: $35. *Expenses:* Tuition, state resident: full-time $5346; part-time $297 per credit hour. Tuition, nonresident: full-time $10,908; part-time $606 per credit hour. *Required fees:* $86; $43 per semester. *Financial support:* Application deadline: 2/15. *Unit head:* Dr. Monica S. Scheibmeir, Dean, 785-670-1526, E-mail: monica.scheibmeir@washburn.edu. *Application contact:* Mary V. Allen, Director of Student Academic Support Services, 785-670-1533, E-mail: mary.allen@washburn.edu. Web site: http://www.washburn.edu/sonu.

Wayne State University, College of Nursing, Program in Adult Acute Care Nursing, Detroit, MI 48202. Offers MSN. *Accreditation:* AACN. Part-time programs available. *Students:* 1 (woman) full-time, 41 part-time (34 women); includes 4 minority (1 Black or African American, non-Hispanic/Latino; 3 Asian, non-Hispanic/Latino), 2 international. Average age 37. 6 applicants, 17% accepted, 0 enrolled. In 2011, 42 master's awarded. *Degree requirements:* For master's, thesis or alternative. *Entrance requirements:* For master's, GRE General Test, minimum honor point average of 2.8 in upper-division course work; BA from NLN- or CCNE-accredited program; references; current RN license; personal statement. Additional exam requirements/recommendations for international students: Required—TOEFL (minimum score 550 paper-based; 213 computer-based); Recommended—TWE (minimum score 6). *Application deadline:* For fall admission, 6/1 priority date for domestic students, 5/1 for international students; for winter admission, 10/1 priority date for domestic students, 9/1 for international students; for spring admission, 2/1 priority date for domestic students, 1/1 for international students. Applications are processed on a rolling basis. Application fee: $50. Electronic applications accepted. *Expenses:* Tuition, state resident: part-time $512.85 per credit. Tuition, nonresident: part-time $1132.65 per credit. *Required fees:* $26.60 per credit. $199.65 per semester. Tuition and fees vary according to course load and program. *Financial support:* In 2011–12, 2 students received support. Fellowships with tuition reimbursements available, research assistantships with tuition reimbursements available, teaching assistantships with tuition reimbursements available, institutionally sponsored loans, scholarships/grants, traineeships, and unspecified assistantships available. Financial award applicants required to submit FAFSA. *Faculty research:* Cardiovascular nursing with vulnerable populations, wound healing, symptom management. *Unit head:* Dr. Barbara Redman, Dean, 313-577-4070, Fax: 313-577-4571, E-mail: ae9080@wayne.edu. *Application contact:* Dr. Cynthia Redwine, Assistant Dean for the Office of Student Affairs, 313-577-4082, E-mail: nursinginfo@wayne.edu. Web site: http://www.nursing.wayne.edu/msn/AACCNPCurriculum.php.

Wayne State University, College of Nursing, Program in Adult Primary Care Nursing, Detroit, MI 48202. Offers MSN. *Accreditation:* AACN. Part-time programs available. *Students:* 9 full-time (7 women), 132 part-time (117 women); includes 51 minority (29 Black or African American, non-Hispanic/Latino; 15 Asian, non-Hispanic/Latino; 4 Hispanic/Latino; 3 Two or more races, non-Hispanic/Latino), 3 international. Average age 36. 10 applicants, 100% accepted, 10 enrolled. In 2011, 19 master's awarded. *Degree requirements:* For master's, thesis or alternative. *Entrance requirements:* For master's, minimum honor point average of 2.8 in upper-division course work; BA from NLN- or CCNE-accredited program; references; current RN license; personal statement. Additional exam requirements/recommendations for international students: Required—TOEFL (minimum score 550 paper-based; 213 computer-based); Recommended—TWE (minimum score 6). *Application deadline:* For fall admission, 6/1 priority date for domestic students, 6/1 for international students; for winter admission, 10/1 priority date for domestic students, 9/1 for international students; for spring admission, 2/1 priority date for domestic students, 1/1 for international students. Applications are processed on a rolling basis. Application fee: $50. Electronic applications accepted. *Expenses:* Tuition, state resident: part-time $512.85 per credit. Tuition, nonresident: part-time $1132.65 per credit. *Required fees:* $26.60 per credit. $199.65 per semester. Tuition and fees vary according to course load and program. *Financial support:* In 2011–12, 16 students received support. Fellowships with tuition reimbursements available, research assistantships with tuition reimbursements available, teaching assistantships with tuition reimbursements available, scholarships/grants, traineeships, and unspecified assistantships available. Support available to part-time students. Financial award applicants required to submit FAFSA. *Faculty research:* Smoking risk behaviors in adolescents, sleep disturbances in postmenopausal women, health disparities in urban

environments, nurse practitioner interventions, caregiving and pain management. *Unit head:* Dr. Barbara Redman, Dean, 313-577-4070, Fax: 313-577-4571, E-mail: ae9080@wayne.edu. *Application contact:* Dr. Cynthia Redwine, Assistant Dean for the Office of Student Affairs, 313-577-4082, E-mail: nursinginfo@wayne.edu. Web site: http://www.nursing.wayne.edu/msn/APCNPCurriculum.php.

Western Connecticut State University, Division of Graduate Studies, School of Professional Studies, Nursing Department, Danbury, CT 06810-6885. Offers adult nurse practitioner (MSN); clinical nurse specialist (MSN). *Accreditation:* AACN. Part-time programs available. *Faculty:* 3 full-time (all women). *Students:* 44 part-time (43 women); includes 8 minority (6 Black or African American, non-Hispanic/Latino; 1 Asian, non-Hispanic/Latino; 1 Hispanic/Latino). Average age 38. 27 applicants, 41% accepted, 9 enrolled. In 2011, 8 degrees awarded. *Degree requirements:* For master's, clinical component, thesis or research project, completion of program in 6 years. *Entrance requirements:* For master's, MAT (if GPA less than 3.0), bachelor's degree in nursing, minimum GPA of 3.0, previous course work in statistics and nursing research, RN license. Additional exam requirements/recommendations for international students: Recommended—TOEFL (minimum score 550 paper-based; 213 computer-based; 79 iBT), IELTS (minimum score 6). *Application deadline:* For fall admission, 8/5 priority date for domestic students; for spring admission, 1/5 for domestic students. Applications are processed on a rolling basis. Application fee: $50. *Expenses:* Contact institution. *Financial support:* Scholarships/grants available. Financial award application deadline: 5/1; financial award applicants required to submit FAFSA. *Faculty research:* evaluating effectiveness of Reiki and acupressure on stress reduction. *Unit head:* Dr. Karen Daley, Graduate Coordinator, 203-837-8563, Fax: 203-837-8550, E-mail: daleyk@wcsu.edu. *Application contact:* Chris Shankle, Associate Director of Graduate Studies, 203-837-9005, Fax: 203-837-8326, E-mail: shanklec@wcsu.edu. Web site: http://www.wcsu.edu/nursing/.

Wilmington University, College of Health Professions, New Castle, DE 19720-6491. Offers adult nurse practitioner (MSN); family nurse practitioner (MSN); gerontology nurse practitioner (MSN); nursing (MSN); nursing leadership (MSN); nursing practice (DNP). *Accreditation:* AACN. Part-time programs available. *Faculty:* 3 full-time (all women). *Students:* 30 full-time (all women), 270 part-time (241 women). Average age 38. *Degree requirements:* For master's, thesis. *Entrance requirements:* For master's, BSN, RN license, interview, 3 letters of recommendation. Additional exam requirements/recommendations for international students: Required—TOEFL (minimum score 500 paper-based; 173 computer-based). *Application deadline:* For fall admission, 4/1 for domestic students; for spring admission, 9/1 for domestic students. Applications are processed on a rolling basis. Application fee: $35. Electronic applications accepted. *Expenses:* Tuition: Part-time $534 per credit hour. *Required fees:* $25 per term. *Financial support:* Fellowships with tuition reimbursements and traineeships available. Financial award applicants required to submit FAFSA. *Faculty research:* Outcomes assessment, student writing ability. *Unit head:* Denise Z. Westbrook, Dean, 302-356-6915, E-mail: denise.z.westbrook@wilmu.edu. *Application contact:* Chris Ferguson, Director of Admissions, 302-356-4636 Ext. 256, Fax: 302-328-5164, E-mail: inquire@wilmcoll.edu. Web site: http://www.wilmu.edu/health/.

Winona State University, College of Nursing and Health Sciences, Winona, MN 55987. Offers adult nurse practitioner (MS, Post Master's Certificate); clinical nurse specialist (MS, Post Master's Certificate); family nurse practitioner (MS, Post Master's Certificate); nurse administrator (MS); nurse educator (MS, Post Master's Certificate); nursing (DNP). *Accreditation:* AACN. Part-time programs available. Postbaccalaureate distance learning degree programs offered (no on-campus study). *Students:* 75 full-time (70 women), 25 part-time (22 women); includes 11 minority (4 Black or African American, non-Hispanic/Latino; 5 Asian, non-Hispanic/Latino; 1 Hispanic/Latino; 1 Two or more races, non-Hispanic/Latino), 2 international. Average age 34. In 2011, 26 master's, 2 doctorates, 3 other advanced degrees awarded. *Degree requirements:* For master's, thesis; for doctorate, capstone. *Entrance requirements:* For master's, GRE (if GPA less than 3.0). Additional exam requirements/recommendations for international students: Required—TOEFL (minimum score 550 paper-based). *Application deadline:* For fall admission, 12/1 for domestic and international students. Application fee: $20. *Financial support:* Research assistantships with partial tuition reimbursements, Federal Work-Study, traineeships, and unspecified assistantships available. Support available to part-time students. Financial award application deadline: 8/15; financial award applicants required to submit FAFSA. *Unit head:* Dr. William J. McBreen, Dean, 507-457-5122, E-mail: wmcbreen@winona.edu. *Application contact:* Patricia Cichosz, Office Manager, Graduate Studies, 507-457-5038, E-mail: pcichosz@winona.edu.

Wright State University, School of Graduate Studies, College of Nursing and Health, Program in Nursing, Dayton, OH 45435. Offers acute care nurse practitioner (MS); administration of nursing and health care systems (MS); adult health (MS); child and adolescent health (MS); community health (MS); family nurse practitioner (MS); nurse practitioner (MS); school nurse (MS); MBA/MS. *Accreditation:* AACN. Part-time and evening/weekend programs available. *Degree requirements:* For master's, thesis or alternative. *Entrance requirements:* For master's, GRE General Test, BSN from NLN-accredited college, Ohio RN license. Additional exam requirements/recommendations for international students: Required—TOEFL. *Faculty research:* Clinical nursing and health, teaching, caring, pain administration, informatics and technology.

York College of Pennsylvania, Department of Nursing, York, PA 17405-7199. Offers adult nurse practitioner (MS); certified nurse anesthetist (MS); clinical nurse specialist (MS), including education: administration; nurse educator (MS); nursing (DNP). *Accreditation:* AACN; AANA/CANAEP. Part-time and evening/weekend programs available. *Faculty:* 10 full-time (all women), 9 part-time/adjunct (6 women). *Students:* 31 full-time (23 women), 50 part-time (43 women); includes 4 minority (2 Black or African American, non-Hispanic/Latino; 2 Asian, non-Hispanic/Latino), 1 international. Average age 36. 49 applicants, 53% accepted, 20 enrolled. In 2011, 17 master's awarded. *Entrance requirements:* For master's, GRE General Test, minimum GPA of 3.0 with NLNAC or CCNE major. Additional exam requirements/recommendations for international students: Required—TOEFL (minimum score 530 paper-based; 200 computer-based; 72 iBT). *Application deadline:* For fall admission, 7/15 priority date for domestic students; for spring admission, 11/15 priority date for domestic students. Applications are processed on a rolling basis. Application fee: $50. Electronic applications accepted. *Expenses: Tuition:* Full-time $12,060; part-time $670 per credit hour. *Required fees:* $340 per semester. Tuition and fees vary according to degree level. *Financial support:* Federal Work-Study available. *Faculty research:* Employer and faculty beliefs about concepts in RN-BS education, evaluating effectiveness of mental health partnerships in psychiatric settings. *Unit head:* Dr. Linda Pugh, Graduate Program Director, 717-815-1243, E-mail: lwarner@ycp.edu. *Application contact:* Nancy Spataro, Director of Admissions, 717-815-1600, Fax: 717-849-1607, E-mail: admissions@ycp.edu. Web site: http://www.ycp.edu/academics/academic-departments/nursing/.

Community Health Nursing

American University of Beirut, Graduate Programs, Rafic Hariri School of Nursing, Beirut, Lebanon. Offers adult care nursing (MSN); community health nursing (MSN); nursing administration (MSN); psychiatry mental health nursing (MSN). *Accreditation:* AACN. Part-time programs available. *Faculty:* 8 full-time (7 women), 16 part-time/adjunct (13 women). *Students:* 5 full-time (3 women), 50 part-time (39 women). Average age 29. 46 applicants, 87% accepted, 19 enrolled. In 2011, 19 master's awarded. *Degree requirements:* For master's, one foreign language, comprehensive exam, thesis optional. *Entrance requirements:* For master's, letter of recommendation. Additional exam requirements/recommendations for international students: Required—TOEFL (minimum score 600 paper-based); Recommended—IELTS. *Application deadline:* For fall admission, 2/20 for domestic and international students; for spring admission, 11/1 for domestic and international students. Applications are processed on a rolling basis. Application fee: $50. *Expenses: Tuition:* Full-time $12,780; part-time $710 per credit. Tuition and fees vary according to course load and program. *Financial support:* In 2011–12, 19 research assistantships with partial tuition reimbursements, 1 teaching assistantship with partial tuition reimbursement were awarded; career-related internships or fieldwork, institutionally sponsored loans, scholarships/grants, health care benefits, and unspecified assistantships also available. Support available to part-time students. Financial award application deadline: 2/2. *Faculty research:* Pain management and palliative care, stress and post-traumatic stress disorder, health benefits and chronic illness, health promotion and community interventions. *Total annual research expenditures:* $52,000. *Unit head:* Dr. Huda Huijer Abu-Saad, Director, 961-1374374 Ext. 5952, Fax: 961-1744476, E-mail: hh35@aub.edu.lb. *Application contact:* Dr. Salim Kanaan, Director, Admissions Office, 961-1350000 Ext. 2594, Fax: 961-1750775, E-mail: sk00@aub.edu.lb. Web site: http://staff.aub.edu.lb/~webson.

Arizona State University, College of Nursing and Health Innovation, Phoenix, AZ 85004. Offers advanced nursing practice (DNP); child/family mental health nurse practitioner (Graduate Certificate); clinical research management (MS); community and public health practice (Graduate Certificate); community health (MS); exercise and wellness (MS), including exercise and wellness; family nurse practitioner (Graduate Certificate); healthcare innovation (MHI); international health for healthcare (Graduate Certificate); kinesiology (MS, PhD); nursing (MS, Graduate Certificate); nursing and healthcare innovation (PhD); nutrition (MS); physical activity nutrition and wellness (PhD), including physical activity, nutrition and wellness; public health (MPH); regulatory science and health safety (MS). *Accreditation:* AACN. Postbaccalaureate distance learning degree programs offered (minimal on-campus study). *Degree requirements:* For master's, comprehensive exam (for some programs), thesis (for some programs), interactive Program of Study (iPOS) submitted before completing 50 percent of required credit hours; for doctorate, comprehensive exam, thesis/dissertation, interactive Program of Study (iPOS) submitted before completing 50 percent of required credit hours. *Entrance requirements:* For master's and doctorate, GRE, minimum GPA of 3.0 or equivalent in last 2 years of work leading to bachelor's degree. Additional exam requirements/recommendations for international students: Required—TOEFL (minimum score 80 iBT), TOEFL, IELTS, or Pearson Test of English. Electronic applications accepted. *Expenses:* Contact institution.

Augsburg College, Program in Transcultural Community Health Nursing, Minneapolis, MN 55454-1351. Offers MA. *Accreditation:* AACN. *Degree requirements:* For master's, thesis or alternative.

Boston College, William F. Connell School of Nursing, Chestnut Hill, MA 02467-3800. Offers adult-gerontology nursing (MS); community health nursing (MS); family health (MS); forensic nursing (MS); maternal/child health nursing (MS), including pediatric and women's health; nurse anesthesia (MS); nursing (PhD); palliative care (MS), including adult and pediatric; psychiatric-mental health nursing (MS); MBA/MS; MS/MA; MS/PhD. *Accreditation:* AACN; AANA/CANAEP (one or more programs are accredited). Part-time programs available. *Faculty:* 48 full-time (46 women), 31 part-time/adjunct (29 women). *Students:* 225 full-time (207 women), 90 part-time (88 women); includes 47 minority (15 Black or African American, non-Hispanic/Latino; 3 American Indian or Alaska Native, non-Hispanic/Latino; 17 Asian, non-Hispanic/Latino; 8 Hispanic/Latino; 4 Two or more races, non-Hispanic/Latino), 6 international. Average age 31. 369 applicants, 43% accepted, 80 enrolled. In 2011, 113 master's, 8 doctorates awarded. *Degree requirements:* For master's, comprehensive exam, research project; for doctorate, comprehensive exam, thesis/dissertation, computer literacy exam or foreign language. *Entrance requirements:* For master's, bachelor's degree in nursing; for doctorate, GRE General Test, MS in nursing. Additional exam requirements/recommendations for international students: Required—TOEFL (minimum score 600 paper-based; 250 computer-based; 100 iBT). *Application deadline:* For fall admission, 11/1 for domestic and international students; for winter admission, 12/31 for domestic and international students; for spring admission, 4/30 for domestic and international students. Applications are processed on a rolling basis. Application fee: $40. Electronic applications accepted. *Financial support:* In 2011–12, 167 students received support, including 9 fellowships with full tuition reimbursements available (averaging $15,300 per year), 7 teaching assistantships (averaging $13,612 per year); research assistantships, Federal Work-Study, institutionally sponsored loans, scholarships/grants, traineeships, health care benefits, tuition waivers (partial), and unspecified assistantships also available. Support available to part-time students. Financial award application deadline: 3/1; financial award applicants required to submit FAFSA. *Faculty research:* Pre-term labor, palliative care, support during chronic illness, violence, eating disorders. *Total annual research expenditures:* $2.1 million. *Unit head:* Dr. Susan Gennaro, Dean, 617-552-4251, Fax: 617-552-0931, E-mail: susan.gennaro@bc.edu. *Application contact:* MaryBeth Crowley, Graduate Programs Assistant, 617-552-4928, Fax: 617-552-2121, E-mail: csongrad@bc.edu. Web site: http://www.bc.edu/nursing/.

Cleveland State University, College of Graduate Studies, School of Nursing, Cleveland, OH 44115. Offers clinical nurse leader (MSN); forensic nursing (MSN); nursing education (MSN); specialized population (MSN); urban education (PhD), including nursing education; MSN/MBA. *Accreditation:* AACN. Part-time programs available. Postbaccalaureate distance learning degree programs offered (no on-campus study). *Faculty:* 4 full-time (all women), 1 (woman) part-time/adjunct. *Students:* 5 full-time (3 women), 50 part-time (47 women); includes 8 minority (7 Black or African American, non-Hispanic/Latino; 1 Hispanic/Latino), 1 international. Average age 43. 41 applicants, 73% accepted, 13 enrolled. In 2011, 7 master's awarded. *Degree requirements:* For master's, thesis or alternative, portfolio, population health project; for doctorate, comprehensive exam, thesis/dissertation. *Entrance requirements:* For master's, RN license, BSN, course work in statistics; for doctorate, GRE (for PhD in urban education). Additional exam requirements/recommendations for international students: Required—TOEFL (minimum score 525 paper-based; 197 computer-based), IELTS (minimum score 6). *Application deadline:* For fall admission, 3/1 priority date for domestic students, 3/1 for international students. Application fee: $55. Electronic

applications accepted. *Expenses:* Tuition, state resident: full-time $6416; part-time $494 per credit hour. Tuition, nonresident: full-time $12,074; part-time $929 per credit hour. *Financial support:* In 2011–12, 4 students received support. Tuition waivers (full), unspecified assistantships, and Nurse Faculty Loan Program (NFLP) available. Support available to part-time students. Financial award application deadline: 3/1; financial award applicants required to submit FAFSA. *Faculty research:* Diabetes management, African-American elders medication compliance, risk in home visiting, suffering, COPD and stress, nursing education, disaster health preparedness. *Total annual research expenditures:* $59,000. *Unit head:* Dr. Vida Lock, Dean, 216-523-7237, Fax: 216-687-3556, E-mail: v.lock@csuohio.edu. *Application contact:* Carol Ivan, Recruiter/Advisor, 216-687-5517, Fax: 216-687-3556, E-mail: c.ivan@csuohio.edu. Web site: http://www.csuohio.edu/nursing/.

D'Youville College, School of Nursing, Buffalo, NY 14201-1084. Offers community health nursing/education (MSN); community health nursing/management (MSN); family nurse practitioner (MS, Post-Master's Certificate); nursing and health-related professions (Certificate); nursing with clinical focus choice (MSN). *Accreditation:* AACN. Part-time programs available. *Faculty:* 7 full-time (all women), 7 part-time/adjunct (6 women). *Students:* 78 full-time (72 women), 133 part-time (117 women); includes 33 minority (23 Black or African American, non-Hispanic/Latino; 2 American Indian or Alaska Native, non-Hispanic/Latino; 1 Asian, non-Hispanic/Latino; 6 Hispanic/Latino; 1 Two or more races, non-Hispanic/Latino), 86 international. Average age 35. 226 applicants, 39% accepted, 57 enrolled. In 2011, 54 master's, 1 other advanced degree awarded. *Degree requirements:* For master's, thesis or alternative, membership on board of community agency, publishable paper. *Entrance requirements:* For master's, BS in nursing, minimum GPA of 3.0, course work in statistics and computers. Additional exam requirements/recommendations for international students: Required—TOEFL (minimum score 500 paper-based; 173 computer-based). *Application deadline:* For fall admission, 5/1 for international students; for spring admission, 9/1 for international students. Applications are processed on a rolling basis. Application fee: $25. Electronic applications accepted. *Expenses: Tuition:* Full-time $18,960; part-time $790 per credit hour. *Required fees:* $310. Tuition and fees vary according to degree level and program. *Financial support:* Federal Work-Study, scholarships/grants, traineeships, and unspecified assistantships available. Support available to part-time students. Financial award application deadline: 3/1; financial award applicants required to submit FAFSA. *Faculty research:* Nursing curriculum, nursing theory-testing, wellness research, communication and socialization patterns. *Unit head:* Dr. Eileen Nahigian, Chair, 716-829-7856, Fax: 716-829-8159. *Application contact:* Linda Fisher, Graduate Admissions Director, 716-829-8400, Fax: 716-829-7900, E-mail: graduateadmissions@dyc.edu.

See Display on page 629 and Close-Up on page 795.

Georgia Southern University, Jack N. Averitt College of Graduate Studies, College of Health and Human Sciences, School of Nursing, Statesboro, GA 30460. Offers nurse practitioner (MSN, Certificate); nursing science (DNP); rural community health nurse practitioner (MSN); rural community health nurse specialist (Certificate); rural family nurse practitioner (MSN, Certificate); women's health nurse practitioner (MSN, Certificate). *Accreditation:* AACN. Part-time programs available. Postbaccalaureate distance learning degree programs offered. *Students:* 3 full-time (all women), 79 part-time (74 women); includes 13 minority (9 Black or African American, non-Hispanic/Latino; 1 Asian, non-Hispanic/Latino; 1 Hispanic/Latino; 1 Native Hawaiian or other Pacific Islander, non-Hispanic/Latino; 1 Two or more races, non-Hispanic/Latino), 1 international. Average age 37. 75 applicants, 57% accepted, 34 enrolled. In 2011, 23 master's, 11 doctorates awarded. *Degree requirements:* For master's, comprehensive exam, thesis optional; for doctorate, clinical immersion project, capstone practicum. *Entrance requirements:* For master's, GRE General Test or MAT, minimum GPA of 3.0, Georgia nursing license, 2 years of clinical experience, CPR certification; for doctorate, GRE, MAT, portfolio, certification, RN licensure, clinical hours; for Certificate, MSN. Additional exam requirements/recommendations for international students: Required—TOEFL (minimum score 550 paper-based; 213 computer-based; 80 iBT). *Application deadline:* For fall admission, 3/1 priority date for domestic students, 3/1 for international students; for spring admission, 10/1 priority date for domestic students, 10/1 for international students. Applications are processed on a rolling basis. Application fee: $50. Electronic applications accepted. *Expenses:* Tuition, state resident: full-time $6300; part-time $263 per semester hour. Tuition, nonresident: full-time $25,174; part-time $1049 per semester hour. *Required fees:* $1872. *Financial support:* In 2011–12, 44 students received support, including research assistantships with partial tuition reimbursements available (averaging $7,200 per year), teaching assistantships with partial tuition reimbursements available (averaging $7,200 per year); career-related internships or fieldwork, Federal Work-Study, scholarships/grants, traineeships, tuition waivers (partial), and unspecified assistantships also available. Support available to part-time students. Financial award application deadline: 4/15; financial award applicants required to submit FAFSA. *Faculty research:* Obesity, diabetes mellitus, vulnerable populations, breast cancer, nursing education, literacy. *Total annual research expenditures:* $50,000. *Unit head:* Dr. Donna Hodnicki, Chair, 912-478-5056, Fax: 912-478-0536, E-mail: dhodnick@georgiasouthern.edu. *Application contact:* Amanda Gilliland, Coordinator for Graduate Student Recruitment, 912-478-5384, Fax: 912-478-0740, E-mail: gradadmissions@georgiasouthern.edu. Web site: http://www.chhs.georgiasouthern.edu/nursing/.

Hampton University, Graduate College, School of Nursing, Hampton, VA 23668. Offers advanced adult nursing (MS); community health nursing (MS); community mental health/psychiatric nursing (MS); family nursing (MS); gerontological nursing for the nurse practitioner (MS); pediatric nursing (MS); women's health nursing (MS). *Accreditation:* AACN; NLN. Part-time and evening/weekend programs available. *Degree requirements:* For master's, thesis optional. *Entrance requirements:* For master's, GRE General Test. *Faculty research:* Curriculum development, physical and mental assessment.

Hawai`i Pacific University, College of Nursing and Health Sciences, Honolulu, HI 96813. Offers community clinical nurse specialist (MSN); community clinical nurse specialist educator option (MSN); family nurse practitioner (MSN). *Accreditation:* NLN. Part-time and evening/weekend programs available. *Faculty:* 5 full-time (4 women), 2 part-time/adjunct (1 woman). *Students:* 45 full-time (34 women), 13 part-time (10 women); includes 38 minority (3 Black or African American, non-Hispanic/Latino; 2 American Indian or Alaska Native, non-Hispanic/Latino; 16 Asian, non-Hispanic/Latino; 6 Hispanic/Latino; 4 Native Hawaiian or other Pacific Islander, non-Hispanic/Latino; 7 Two or more races, non-Hispanic/Latino). Average age 38. 32 applicants, 78% accepted, 19 enrolled. In 2011, 11 master's awarded. *Degree requirements:* For master's, practicum, professional paper. *Entrance requirements:* For master's, bachelor's degree in nursing, minimum GPA of 3.0. Additional exam requirements/

recommendations for international students: Recommended—TOEFL (minimum score 550 paper-based; 213 computer-based; 80 iBT), TWE (minimum score 5). *Application deadline:* Applications are processed on a rolling basis. Application fee: $50. Electronic applications accepted. *Expenses: Tuition:* Full-time $13,230; part-time $735 per credit. Tuition and fees vary according to course load and program. *Financial support:* In 2011–12, 11 students received support. Career-related internships or fieldwork, Federal Work-Study, scholarships/grants, traineeships, and tuition waivers available. Financial award application deadline: 3/1; financial award applicants required to submit FAFSA. *Faculty research:* Hawaiian elders, traditional healing and nursing center. *Unit head:* Dr. Patricia Burrell, Chair, Graduate and Post Baccalaureate Programs, 808-236-5813, Fax: 808-236-5818, E-mail: pburrell@hpu.edu. *Application contact:* Chad Schempp, Director of Graduate Admissions, 808-543-8035, Fax: 808-544-0280, E-mail: graduate@hpu.edu. Web site: http://www.hpu.edu/CNHS/index.html.

See Display on page 633 and Close-Up on page 799.

Holy Family University, Graduate School, School of Nursing and Allied Health Professions, Philadelphia, PA 19114. Offers community health nursing (MSN); nursing administration (MSN); nursing education (MSN). *Accreditation:* AACN. Part-time and evening/weekend programs available. *Degree requirements:* For master's, thesis or alternative. *Entrance requirements:* For masters, bachelor's degree in nursing, RN license, minimum GPA of 3.0, 2 letters of reference.

See Display on page 634 and Close-Up on page 801.

Holy Names University, Graduate Division, Department of Nursing, Oakland, CA 94619-1699. Offers administration/management (MS, Certificate); clinical faculty (MS, Certificate); community health nursing/case manager (MS); family nurse practitioner (MS, Certificate); MSN/Certificate; MSN/MBA. *Accreditation:* AACN. Part-time and evening/weekend programs available. *Entrance requirements:* For master's, bachelor's degree in nursing or related field, California RN license or eligibility, minimum GPA of 3.0, previous course work in research or statistics. Additional exam requirements/recommendations for international students: Required—TOEFL (minimum score 500 paper-based). *Faculty research:* Women's reproductive health, gerontology, attitudes about aging, schizophrenic families, international health issues.

Hunter College of the City University of New York, Graduate School, Schools of the Health Professions, Hunter-Bellevue School of Nursing, Community Health Nursing Program, New York, NY 10021-5085. Offers MS. *Accreditation:* AACN. Part-time programs available. *Faculty:* 20 full-time (16 women), 20 part-time/adjunct (18 women). *Students:* 31 part-time (26 women); includes 18 minority (10 Black or African American, non-Hispanic/Latino; 4 Asian, non-Hispanic/Latino; 4 Hispanic/Latino), 5 international. Average age 34. 23 applicants, 61% accepted, 14 enrolled. In 2011, 3 master's awarded. *Degree requirements:* For master's, practicum. *Entrance requirements:* For master's, minimum GPA of 3.0, New York RN license, BSN. Additional exam requirements/recommendations for international students: Required—TOEFL. *Application deadline:* For fall admission, 4/1 for domestic students, 2/1 for international students; for spring admission, 11/1 for domestic students, 9/1 for international students. Applications are processed on a rolling basis. Application fee: $125. *Expenses:* Tuition, state resident: full-time $8210; part-time $345 per credit. Tuition, nonresident: full-time $15,360; part-time $640 per credit. *Required fees:* $280 per semester. One-time fee: $125. Tuition and fees vary according to class time, campus/location and program. *Financial support:* Federal Work-Study, scholarships/grants, traineeships, and tuition waivers (partial) available. Support available to part-time students. Financial award application deadline: 5/1; financial award applicants required to submit FAFSA. *Faculty research:* HIV/AIDS, health promotion with vulnerable populations. *Unit head:* Dr. Patricia Hill, Coordinator, 212-481-3478, E-mail: psthil@hunter.cuny.edu. *Application contact:* William Zlata, Director for Graduate Admissions, 212-772-4482, Fax: 212-650-3336, E-mail: admissions@hunter.cuny.edu.

Hunter College of the City University of New York, Graduate School, Schools of the Health Professions, Hunter-Bellevue School of Nursing, Community/Public Health Nursing/Urban Public Health Program, New York, NY 10021-5085. Offers MS/MPH. *Accreditation:* AACN. Part-time programs available. *Faculty:* 20 full-time (16 women), 20 part-time/adjunct (18 women). *Students:* 1 full-time (0 women), 36 part-time (34 women); includes 17 minority (14 Black or African American, non-Hispanic/Latino; 1 Asian, non-Hispanic/Latino; 2 Hispanic/Latino), 6 international. Average age 39. 7 applicants, 71% accepted, 5 enrolled. *Entrance requirements:* Additional exam requirements/recommendations for international students: Required—TOEFL. *Application deadline:* For fall admission, 4/1 for domestic students, 2/1 for international students; for spring admission, 11/1 for domestic students, 9/1 for international students. Applications are processed on a rolling basis. Application fee: $125. *Expenses:* Tuition, state resident: full-time $8210; part-time $345 per credit. Tuition, nonresident: full-time $15,360; part-time $640 per credit. *Required fees:* $280 per semester. One-time fee: $125. Tuition and fees vary according to class time, campus/location and program. *Financial support:* Federal Work-Study, scholarships/grants, traineeships, and tuition waivers (partial) available. Support available to part-time students. Financial award application deadline: 5/1; financial award applicants required to submit FAFSA. *Faculty research:* HIV/AIDS, health promotion with vulnerable populations, immigrant health. *Unit head:* Dr. Kathleen Nokes, Coordinator, 212-481-7594, Fax: 212-481-5078, E-mail: knokes@hejira.hunter.cuny.edu. *Application contact:* William Zlata, Director for Graduate Admissions, 212-772-4482, Fax: 212-650-3336, E-mail: admissions@hunter.cuny.edu. Web site: http://www.hunter.cuny.edu/uph/grad-test/community-health-education-1.

Husson University, School of Graduate and Professional Studies, Graduate Nursing Program, Bangor, ME 04401-2999. Offers advanced practice psychiatric nursing (MSN, PMC); family and community nurse practitioner (MSN, PMC); nursing education (MSN, PMC). *Accreditation:* AACN. Part-time programs available. *Faculty:* 6 full-time (all women), 6 part-time/adjunct (all women). *Students:* 49 full-time (42 women), 33 part-time (29 women); includes 2 minority (1 American Indian or Alaska Native, non-Hispanic/Latino; 1 Two or more races, non-Hispanic/Latino). 18 applicants, 13 enrolled. In 2011, 25 master's awarded. *Degree requirements:* For master's, comprehensive exam (for some programs). *Entrance requirements:* For master's, MAT or GRE, BSN. Additional exam requirements/recommendations for international students: Required—TOEFL (minimum score 550 paper-based). *Application deadline:* For fall admission, 6/30 for domestic students; for spring admission, 10/30 for domestic students. Application fee: $40. *Expenses:* Contact institution. *Financial support:* In 2011–12, 31 students received support. Federal Work-Study, institutionally sponsored loans, traineeships, and unspecified assistantships available. Financial award application deadline: 4/15; financial award applicants required to submit FAFSA. *Unit head:* Dr. Barbara Higgins, Director, Nurse Practitioner Program, 207-947-7057. *Application contact:* Kristen Card, Director of Graduate Admissions, 207-404-5660, Fax: 207-941-7935, E-mail: cardk@husson.edu.

Independence University, Program in Nursing, Salt Lake City, UT 84107. Offers community health (MSN); gerontology (MSN); nursing administration (MSN); wellness promotion (MSN).

Indiana University–Purdue University Indianapolis, School of Nursing, Indianapolis, IN 46202-2896. Offers acute care nurse practitioner (MSN); adult health clinical nurse specialist (MSN); adult health nursing (MSN), including adult clinical nurse specialist; adult nurse practitioner (MSN); adult psychiatric/mental health nursing (MSN); child psychiatric/mental health nursing (MSN); community health nursing (MSN); family nurse practitioner (MSN); neonatal nurse practitioner (MSN); nursing (MSN, DNP), including nursing education (MSN); nursing (MSN), including nursing administration; nursing science (PhD); pediatric clinical nurse specialist (MSN); women's health nurse practitioner (MSN); MSN/MPA; MSN/MPH. *Accreditation:* AACN; NLN (one or more programs are accredited). Part-time programs available. *Faculty:* 85 full-time (82 women), 60 part-time/adjunct (all women). *Students:* 35 full-time (32 women), 360 part-time (340 women); includes 47 minority (28 Black or African American, non-Hispanic/Latino; 9 Asian, non-Hispanic/Latino; 4 Hispanic/Latino; 1 Native Hawaiian or other Pacific Islander, non-Hispanic/Latino; 5 Two or more races, non-Hispanic/Latino), 5 international. Average age 38. 119 applicants, 76% accepted, 54 enrolled. In 2011, 89 master's, 10 doctorates awarded. Terminal master's awarded for partial completion of doctoral program. *Degree requirements:* For master's, thesis; for doctorate, thesis/dissertation. *Entrance requirements:* For master's, minimum GPA of 3.0, RN license; for doctorate, GRE General Test, minimum GPA of 3.0, MSN, RN license, graduate statistics course with minimum B grade (not older than 3 years). Additional exam requirements/recommendations for international students: Required—TOEFL. *Application deadline:* For fall admission, 2/15 for domestic students; for spring admission, 9/15 for domestic students. Application fee: $55 ($65 for international students). *Financial support:* In 2011–12, 93 students received support, including 9 fellowships with full tuition reimbursements available (averaging $7,039 per year), 7 teaching assistantships with full tuition reimbursements available (averaging $5,300 per year); research assistantships with full tuition reimbursements available, Federal Work-Study, institutionally sponsored loans, scholarships/grants, and tuition waivers (full) also available. Support available to part-time students. Financial award application deadline: 5/1. *Faculty research:* Clinical science, health systems. *Total annual research expenditures:* $3 million. *Unit head:* Associate Dean for Graduate Programs, 317-274-2806, E-mail: nursing@iupui.edu. *Application contact:* Information Contact, 317-274-2806. Web site: http://nursing.iupui.edu/.

Indiana Wesleyan University, Graduate School, School of Nursing, Marion, IN 46953-4974. Offers community health nursing (MS); nursing (Post Master's Certificate); nursing administration (MS); nursing education (MS); primary care nursing (MS). *Accreditation:* AACN. Part-time programs available. Postbaccalaureate distance learning degree programs offered (minimal on-campus study). *Degree requirements:* For master's, capstone project or thesis. *Entrance requirements:* For master's, writing sample, RN license, 1 year of related experience, graduate statistics course. Additional exam requirements/recommendations for international students: Required—TOEFL. *Expenses:* Contact institution. *Faculty research:* Primary health care with international emphasis, international nursing.

The Johns Hopkins University, School of Nursing and Bloomberg School of Public Health, Joint Degree Program in Nursing and Public Health, Baltimore, MD 21218-2699. Offers MSN/MPH. *Accreditation:* AACN; CEPH. Part-time programs available. *Entrance requirements:* Additional exam requirements/recommendations for international students: Required—TOEFL (minimum score 550 paper-based; 213 computer-based). Electronic applications accepted. *Expenses:* Contact institution. *Faculty research:* Asthma, tuberculosis control, injury, violence, international health, women's health, substance abuse.

The Johns Hopkins University, School of Nursing, Program in Public Health Nursing, Baltimore, MD 21218-2699. Offers MSN. *Accreditation:* AACN. Part-time programs available. *Degree requirements:* For master's, thesis optional, scholarly project or portfolio. *Entrance requirements:* For master's, interview, minimum GPA of 3.0, BSN, Maryland RN license. Additional exam requirements/recommendations for international students: Required—TOEFL (minimum score 550 paper-based; 213 computer-based). Electronic applications accepted. *Expenses:* Contact institution. *Faculty research:* Violence, community outreach, outcomes, asthma, HIV.

Kean University, College of Natural, Applied and Health Sciences, Program in Nursing, Union, NJ 07083. Offers clinical management (MSN), including transcultural focus; community health nursing (MSN); school nursing (MSN). *Accreditation:* NLN. *Faculty:* 9 full-time (all women). *Students:* 7 full-time (6 women), 95 part-time (86 women); includes 49 minority (40 Black or African American, non-Hispanic/Latino; 5 Asian, non-Hispanic/Latino; 3 Hispanic/Latino; 1 Native Hawaiian or other Pacific Islander, non-Hispanic/Latino). Average age 45. 38 applicants, 97% accepted, 27 enrolled. In 2011, 34 master's awarded. *Degree requirements:* For master's, thesis or alternative, clinical field experience. *Entrance requirements:* For master's, minimum GPA of 3.0; BS in nursing; RN license; 2 letters of recommendation; interview; 1 completed course of the following: basic health assessment and human growth and development across the life span; minimum B grade in prerequisite courses; transcripts. Additional exam requirements/recommendations for international students: Required—TOEFL (minimum score 79 computer-based). *Application deadline:* For fall admission, 6/1 for domestic and international students; for spring admission, 12/1 for domestic and international students. Applications are processed on a rolling basis. Application fee: $75 ($150 for international students). Electronic applications accepted. *Expenses:* Tuition, state resident: full-time $11,302; part-time $550 per credit. Tuition, nonresident: full-time $15,318; part-time $674 per credit. *Required fees:* $2849; $130 per credit. Tuition and fees vary according to degree level. *Financial support:* In 2011–12, 1 research assistantship with full tuition reimbursement (averaging $3,263 per year) was awarded; unspecified assistantships also available. Financial award applicants required to submit FAFSA. *Unit head:* Dr. Minnie Campbell, Program Coordinator, 908-527-3396, E-mail: mcampbel@kean.edu. *Application contact:* Ann-Marie Kay, Assistant Director of Graduate Admissions, 908-737-5922, Fax: 908-737-5925, E-mail: akay@kean.edu. Web site: http://www.kean.edu/KU/School-of-Nursing.

Louisiana State University Health Sciences Center, School of Nursing, New Orleans, LA 70112-2223. Offers advanced public/community health nursing (MN); clinical nurse specialist (MN); nurse anesthesia (MN); nurse practitioner (MN); nursing (DNS). *Accreditation:* AACN; AANA/CANAEP (one or more programs are accredited). Part-time programs available. *Degree requirements:* For master's, thesis optional; for doctorate, thesis/dissertation. *Entrance requirements:* For master's, GRE General Test, MAT, minimum GPA of 3.0; for doctorate, GRE General Test, minimum GPA of 3.5. Additional exam requirements/recommendations for international students: Required—TOEFL. Electronic applications accepted. *Faculty research:* Advanced clinical practice, nursing education, health, social support, nursing administration.

New Mexico State University, Graduate School, College of Health and Social Services, School of Nursing, Las Cruces, NM 88003-8001. Offers adult/gerontology nurse practitioner (DNP); family nurse practitioner (DNP); nursing (MSN, PhD); public/community health (DNP). *Accreditation:* AACN. Postbaccalaureate distance learning degree programs offered (minimal on-campus study). *Faculty:* 9 full-time (all women). *Students:* 44 full-time (38 women), 72 part-time (59 women); includes 48 minority (9 Black or African American, non-Hispanic/Latino; 5 American Indian or Alaska Native, non-Hispanic/Latino; 2 Asian, non-Hispanic/Latino; 31 Hispanic/Latino; 1 Two or more races, non-Hispanic/Latino), 2 international. Average age 43. 37 applicants, 86% accepted, 25 enrolled. In 2011, 35 master's, 3 doctorates awarded. *Degree requirements:* For master's, comprehensive exam, thesis optional, clinical practice; for

doctorate, comprehensive exam, thesis/dissertation. *Entrance requirements:* For master's, NCLEX exam, BSN, minimum GPA of 3.0, course work in statistics, 3 letters of reference, writing sample, RN license, CPR certification, proof of liability, immunizations, criminal background check; for doctorate, NCLEX exam, MSN, minimum GPA of 3.0, 3 letters of reference, writing sample, RN license, CPR certification, proof of liability, immunizations, criminal background check, statistics course. Additional exam requirements/recommendations for international students: Required—TOEFL (minimum score 550 paper-based; 79 iBT), IELTS (minimum score 6.5). *Application deadline:* For spring admission, 10/1 priority date for domestic students. Application fee: $40 ($50 for international students). Electronic applications accepted. *Expenses:* Tuition, state resident: full-time $5004; part-time $208.50 per credit. Tuition, nonresident: full-time $17,446; part-time $726.90 per credit. *Financial support:* In 2011–12, 1 teaching assistantship (averaging $28,242 per year) was awarded; fellowships, research assistantships, career-related internships or fieldwork, Federal Work-Study, scholarships/grants, traineeships, and health care benefits also available. Financial award application deadline: 3/1. *Faculty research:* Public policy, community health, health disparities, self efficacy and self management, psychiatric mental health. *Unit head:* Dr. Pamela Schultz, Director, 575-646-3812, Fax: 575-646-2167, E-mail: pschultz@nmsu.edu. *Application contact:* Dr. Kathleen Huttlinger, Associate Director for Graduate Studies, 575-646-4387, Fax: 575-646-2167. Web site: http://www.nmsu.edu/~nursing/.

Oregon Health & Science University, School of Nursing, Program in Nursing Education, Portland, OR 97239-3098. Offers MN, MS, Post Master's Certificate.

Oregon Health & Science University, School of Nursing, Program in Public Health Nursing, Portland, OR 97239-3098. Offers primary care and disparities (MPH); public health (MPH, Post Master's Certificate). *Accreditation:* AACN. *Degree requirements:* For master's, thesis optional. *Entrance requirements:* For master's, GRE General Test, bachelor's degree in nursing, minimum undergraduate GPA of 3.0, previous course work in statistics.

Rush University, College of Nursing, Department of Community Systems and Mental Health Nursing, Chicago, IL 60612-3832. Offers community and mental health nursing (DNP, PhD); family nurse practitioner (MSN, Post-Master's Certificate); psychiatric clinical specialist (MSN); psychiatric nurse practitioner - adult (MSN); psychiatric nurse practitioner - family (MSN); psychiatric-mental health clinical specialist (Post-Master's Certificate); psychiatric-mental health nurse practitioner (Post-Master's Certificate); public health nursing (MSN). *Accreditation:* AACN. Part-time programs available. Postbaccalaureate distance learning degree programs offered (minimal on-campus study). Terminal master's awarded for partial completion of doctoral program. *Degree requirements:* For master's, capstone project; for doctorate, thesis/dissertation, DNP leadership project. *Entrance requirements:* For master's, GRE General Test (waived if nursing GPA is above 3.0 or cumulative GPA is above 3.25), interview; for doctorate, GRE General Test, interview, course work in statistics (DN Sc). Electronic applications accepted. *Faculty research:* Immigrant mental health, de-escalation strategies, caregiver interventions, parent-teacher training, restraint use.

Rutgers, The State University of New Jersey, Newark, Graduate School, Program in Nursing, Newark, NJ 07102. Offers nursing (MS), including acute care of adults and aged, advanced practice in pediatric nursing, advanced practice with childbearing families, community health nursing, family nurse practitioner, primary care of adults and aged, psychiatric/mental health nursing. *Accreditation:* AACN. Part-time programs available. *Degree requirements:* For master's, comprehensive exam. *Entrance requirements:* For master's, GRE General Test, RN license, minimum B average, BS in nursing. Additional exam requirements/recommendations for international students: Required—TOEFL. Electronic applications accepted. *Faculty research:* HIV/AIDS, quality of life: MS and breast cancer, sleep patterns of cardiac patients.

Sage Graduate School, School of Health Sciences, Department of Nursing, Program in Community Health, Troy, NY 12180-4115. Offers MS, Post Master's Certificate. *Accreditation:* AACN. Part-time programs available. *Faculty:* 5 full-time (all women), 9 part-time/adjunct (all women). *Students:* 1 (woman) part-time. Average age 26. 13 applicants, 8% accepted, 0 enrolled. In 2011, 4 degrees awarded. *Degree requirements:* For master's, thesis or alternative. *Entrance requirements:* For master's, BS in nursing, minimum GPA of 2.75, resume, 2 letters of recommendation. Additional exam requirements/recommendations for international students: Required—TOEFL (minimum score 550 paper-based; 213 computer-based). *Application deadline:* Applications are processed on a rolling basis. Application fee: $40. *Expenses: Tuition:* Full-time $11,880; part-time $660 per credit hour. Tuition and fees vary according to program. *Financial support:* Fellowships, research assistantships, Federal Work-Study, scholarships/grants, and unspecified assistantships available. Support available to part-time students. Financial award application deadline: 3/1; financial award applicants required to submit FAFSA. *Unit head:* Dr. Esther Haskevitz, Dean, School of Health Sciences, 518-244-2296, Fax: 518-244-4571, E-mail: haskve@sage.edu. *Application contact:* Arlene Pericak, Director, 518-244-2012, Fax: 518-244-2009, E-mail: perica@sage.edu.

San Francisco State University, Division of Graduate Studies, College of Health and Human Services, School of Nursing, San Francisco, CA 94132-1722. Offers clinical nurse specialist (MS); community/public health nursing (MS); family nurse practitioner (MS, Certificate); nursing administration (MS); nursing education (MS). *Accreditation:* AACN. Part-time programs available. *Application deadline:* Applications are processed on a rolling basis. *Financial support:* Career-related internships or fieldwork available. *Unit head:* Dr. Lynette Landry, Director, 415-338-1802, E-mail: llandry@sfsu.edu. *Application contact:* Dr. Mary-Ann van Dam, Associate Director, 415-338-1802, E-mail: vandam@sfsu.edu. Web site: http://nursing.sfsu.edu.

Seattle University, College of Nursing, Program in Advanced Practice Nursing Immersion, Seattle, WA 98122-1090. Offers adult/gerontological nurse practitioner (MSN); advanced community public health (MSN); certified nurse midwifery (MSN); family nurse practitioner (MSN); psychiatric mental health nurse practitioner (MSN). *Faculty:* 43 full-time, 63 part-time/adjunct. *Students:* 104 full-time (91 women); includes 24 minority (2 Black or African American, non-Hispanic/Latino; 12 Asian, non-Hispanic/Latino; 7 Hispanic/Latino; 3 Two or more races, non-Hispanic/Latino). Average age 30. *Degree requirements:* For master's, thesis or scholarly project. *Entrance requirements:* For master's, GRE, bachelor's degree, minimum GPA of 3.0, professional resume, two recommendations, letter of intent, English proficiency (for non-English speakers). Additional exam requirements/recommendations for international students: Required—TOEFL (minimum score 92 iBT), IELTS. *Application deadline:* For fall admission, 12/1 for domestic and international students. Application fee: $55. Electronic applications accepted. *Financial support:* Scholarships/grants and traineeships available. Financial award applicants required to submit FAFSA. *Unit head:* Dr. Azita Emami, Dean, 206-296-5660. *Application contact:* Janet Shandley, Associate Dean of Graduate Admissions, 206-296-5900, Fax: 206-298-5656, E-mail: grad_admissions@seattleu.edu.

Seattle University, College of Nursing, Program in Nursing, Seattle, WA 98122-1090. Offers adult/gerontological nurse practitioner (MSN); advanced community public health (MSN); psychiatric mental health nurse practitioner (MSN). *Faculty:* 43 full-time, 63 part-time/adjunct. *Students:* 22 full-time (20 women); includes 4 minority (1 Black or African American, non-Hispanic/Latino; 1 Asian, non-Hispanic/Latino; 1 Hispanic/Latino; 1 Two or more races, non-Hispanic/Latino). *Degree requirements:* For master's, thesis or scholarly project. *Entrance requirements:* For master's, GRE, bachelor's degree in nursing or associate degree in nursing with baccalaureate in different major, 5-quarter statistics course, minimum cumulative GPA of 3.0, professional resume, two recommendations, letter of intent, English proficiency (for non-English speakers), copy of current RN license or ability to obtain RN license in WA state. Additional exam requirements/recommendations for international students: Required—TOEFL (minimum score 92 iBT), IELTS. *Application deadline:* For fall admission, 12/1 for domestic and international students. Application fee: $55. Electronic applications accepted. *Financial support:* In 2011–12, 2 teaching assistantships were awarded; scholarships/grants and traineeships also available. Financial award applicants required to submit FAFSA. *Unit head:* Dr. Azita Emami, Dean, 206-296-5660. *Application contact:* Janet Shandley, Associate Dean of Graduate Admissions, 206-296-5900, Fax: 206-298-5656, E-mail: grad_admissions@seattleu.edu.

University of Cincinnati, Graduate School, College of Nursing, Cincinnati, OH 45221-0038. Offers clinical nurse specialist (MSN), including adult health, community health, neonatal, nursing administration, occupational health, pediatric health, psychiatric nursing, women's health; nurse anesthesia (MSN); nurse midwifery (MSN); nurse practitioner (MSN), including acute care, ambulatory care, family, family/psychiatric, women's health; nursing (PhD); MBA/MSN. *Accreditation:* AACN; AANA/CANAEP (one or more programs are accredited); ACNM/ACME. Part-time programs available. Postbaccalaureate distance learning degree programs offered (no on-campus study). Terminal master's awarded for partial completion of doctoral program. *Degree requirements:* For master's, thesis or alternative; for doctorate, comprehensive exam, thesis/dissertation. *Entrance requirements:* For master's and doctorate, GRE General Test. Additional exam requirements/recommendations for international students: Required—TOEFL (minimum score 520 paper-based; 190 computer-based). Electronic applications accepted. *Faculty research:* Substance abuse, injury and violence, symptom management.

University of Colorado at Colorado Springs, Beth-El College of Nursing and Health Sciences, Colorado Springs, CO 80933-7150. Offers adult health nurse practitioner and clinical specialist (MSN); family practitioner (MSN), including community clinical specialist, forensic clinical specialist, holistic clinical specialist; neonatal nurse practitioner and clinical specialist (MSN); nursing administration (MSN); nursing practice (DNP); women nurse practitioner (MSN). *Accreditation:* AACN. Part-time programs available. Postbaccalaureate distance learning degree programs offered (minimal on-campus study). *Faculty:* 31 full-time (28 women), 6 part-time/adjunct (all women). *Students:* 122 full-time (103 women), 68 part-time (64 women); includes 36 minority (4 Black or African American, non-Hispanic/Latino; 2 American Indian or Alaska Native, non-Hispanic/Latino; 9 Asian, non-Hispanic/Latino; 18 Hispanic/Latino; 3 Two or more races, non-Hispanic/Latino), 5 international. Average age 35. 153 applicants, 71% accepted, 60 enrolled. In 2011, 41 master's, 15 doctorates awarded. *Degree requirements:* For master's, comprehensive exam, thesis optional; for doctorate, capstone project. *Entrance requirements:* For master's, GRE General Test or MAT, BSN, minimum GPA of 3.0, unrestricted RN license; for doctorate, interview; active RN license; MA; minimum GPA of 3.3; National Certification as NP or CNS; portfolio. Additional exam requirements/recommendations for international students: Required—TOEFL. *Application deadline:* For fall admission, 6/15 priority date for domestic students; for spring admission, 11/15 for domestic students. Application fee: $60 ($75 for international students). Electronic applications accepted. *Expenses:* Contact institution. *Financial support:* In 2011–12, 33 students received support, including 1 fellowship (averaging $2,500 per year); career-related internships or fieldwork, Federal Work-Study, and scholarships/grants also available. Support available to part-time students. Financial award application deadline: 3/1; financial award applicants required to submit FAFSA. *Faculty research:* Women's health, uncertainty, empowerment, family experience in chronic illness. *Total annual research expenditures:* $322,604. *Unit head:* Dr. Nancy Smith, Dean, 719-255-4411, Fax: 719-255-4416, E-mail: nsmith2@uccs.edu. *Application contact:* Diane Busch, Director, 719-255-4424, Fax: 719-255-4416, E-mail: dbusch@uccs.edu. Web site: http://www.uccs.edu/~bethel/.

University of Hartford, College of Education, Nursing, and Health Professions, Program in Nursing, West Hartford, CT 06117-1599. Offers community/public health nursing (MSN); nursing education (MSN); nursing management (MSN). *Accreditation:* AACN. Part-time and evening/weekend programs available. *Degree requirements:* For master's, research project. *Entrance requirements:* For master's, BSN, Connecticut RN license. Additional exam requirements/recommendations for international students: Required—TOEFL (minimum score 550 paper-based; 213 computer-based). Electronic applications accepted. *Expenses:* Contact institution. *Faculty research:* Child development, women in doctoral study, applying feminist theory in teaching methods, near death experience, grandmothers as primary care providers.

University of Hawaii at Manoa, Graduate Division, School of Nursing and Dental Hygiene, Honolulu, HI 96822. Offers clinical nurse specialist (MS), including adult health, community mental health; nurse practitioner (MS), including adult health, community mental health, family nurse practitioner; nursing (PhD, Graduate Certificate); nursing administration (MS). *Accreditation:* AACN; NLN (one or more programs are accredited). Part-time programs available. Postbaccalaureate distance learning degree programs offered (minimal on-campus study). *Degree requirements:* For master's, thesis optional; for doctorate, comprehensive exam, thesis/dissertation. *Entrance requirements:* For master's, Hawaii RN license. Additional exam requirements/recommendations for international students: Required—TOEFL (minimum score 580 paper-based; 237 computer-based; 92 iBT), IELTS (minimum score 5). *Expenses:* Contact institution.

University of Illinois at Chicago, Graduate College, College of Nursing, Program in Nursing, Chicago, IL 60607-7128. Offers acute care clinical nurse specialist (MS); acute care nurse practitioner (MS); administrative studies in nursing (MS); adult nurse practitioner (MS); adult/geriatric nurse practitioner (MS); advanced community health nurse specialist (MS); family nurse practitioner (MS); geriatric clinical nurse specialist (MS); geriatric nurse practitioner (MS); mental health clinical nurse specialist (MS); mental health nurse practitioner (MS); nurse midwifery (MS); occupational health/advanced community health nurse specialist (MS); occupational health/family nurse practitioner (MS); pediatric clinical nurse specialist (MS); pediatric nurse practitioner (MS); perinatal clinical nurse specialist (MS); school/advanced community health nurse specialist (MS); school/family nurse practitioner (MS); women's health nurse practitioner (MS). *Accreditation:* AACN. Part-time programs available. *Degree requirements:* For master's, thesis or alternative. *Entrance requirements:* For master's, GRE General Test, minimum GPA of 2.75. Additional exam requirements/recommendations for international students: Required—TOEFL. Electronic applications accepted.

The University of Kansas, University of Kansas Medical Center, School of Nursing, Kansas City, KS 66160. Offers adult/gerontological clinical nurse specialist (PMC); adult/gerontological nurse practitioner (PMC); clinical research management (PMC); family nurse practitioner (PMC); health care informatics (PMC); health professions educator (PMC); nurse midwife (PMC); nursing (MS, DNP, PhD); organizational leadership (PMC); psychiatric/mental health nurse practitioner (PMC); public health

nursing (PMC). *Accreditation:* AACN; ACNM/ACME. Part-time programs available. Postbaccalaureate distance learning degree programs offered (minimal on-campus study). *Faculty:* 80. *Students:* 79 full-time (71 women), 336 part-time (317 women); includes 63 minority (24 Black or African American, non-Hispanic/Latino; 2 American Indian or Alaska Native, non-Hispanic/Latino; 18 Asian, non-Hispanic/Latino; 15 Hispanic/Latino; 4 Two or more races, non-Hispanic/Latino), 6 international. Average age 37. 155 applicants, 82% accepted, 127 enrolled. In 2011, 79 master's, 15 doctorates, 12 other advanced degrees awarded. Terminal master's awarded for partial completion of doctoral program. *Degree requirements:* For master's, comprehensive exam, thesis optional, general oral exam; for doctorate, variable foreign language requirement, thesis/dissertation, comprehensive oral exam (for DNP); comprehensive written and oral exam (for PhD). *Entrance requirements:* For master's, bachelor's degree in nursing, minimum GPA of 3.0, RN license, 1 year of clinical experience, RN license in KS and MO; for doctorate, GRE General Test, master's degree in nursing, minimum GPA of 3.5, RN license in KS and MO; national certification (for some specialties). Additional exam requirements/recommendations for international students: Required—TOEFL. *Application deadline:* For fall admission, 4/1 for domestic and international students; for spring admission, 9/1 for domestic and international students. Application fee: $60. Electronic applications accepted. Tuition and fees vary according to course load, campus/location, program and reciprocity agreements. *Financial support:* Research assistantships with full and partial tuition reimbursements, teaching assistantships with full and partial tuition reimbursements, and traineeships available. Financial award application deadline: 2/14; financial award applicants required to submit FAFSA. *Faculty research:* Breastfeeding practices of teen mothers, national database of nursing quality indicators, caregiving of families of patients using technology in the home, simulation in nursing education, diaphragm fatigue. *Total annual research expenditures:* $6.1 million. *Unit head:* Dr. Karen L. Miller, Dean, 913-588-1601, Fax: 913-588-1660, E-mail: kmiller@kumc.edu. *Application contact:* Dr. Debra J. Ford, Associate Dean, Student Affairs, 913-588-1619, Fax: 913-588-1615, E-mail: dford@kumc.edu. Web site: http://nursing.kumc.edu.

University of Maryland, Baltimore, Graduate School, School of Nursing, Master's Program in Nursing, Baltimore, MD 21201. Offers community health nursing (MS); gerontological nursing (MS); maternal-child nursing (MS); medical-surgical nursing (MS); nurse-midwifery education (MS); nursing administration (MS); nursing education (MS); nursing health policy (MS); primary care nursing (MS); psychiatric nursing (MS); MS/MBA. MS/MBA offered jointly with University of Baltimore. *Accreditation:* AACN; AANA/CANAEP; NLN (one or more programs are accredited). Part-time programs available. *Students:* 370 full-time (314 women), 480 part-time (441 women); includes 308 minority (176 Black or African American, non-Hispanic/Latino; 2 American Indian or Alaska Native, non-Hispanic/Latino; 70 Asian, non-Hispanic/Latino; 33 Hispanic/Latino; 27 Two or more races, non-Hispanic/Latino), 9 international. Average age 35. 990 applicants, 30% accepted, 204 enrolled. In 2011, 301 master's awarded. *Degree requirements:* For master's, comprehensive exam (for some programs), thesis or alternative. *Entrance requirements:* For master's, minimum GPA of 2.75, course work in statistics, BS in nursing. Additional exam requirements/recommendations for international students: Required—TOEFL (minimum score 550 paper-based; 80 iBT) or IELTS (minimum score 7). *Application deadline:* For fall admission, 2/1 for domestic students, 1/15 for international students. Application fee: $50. Electronic applications accepted. *Financial support:* Fellowships, research assistantships, teaching assistantships, career-related internships or fieldwork, and traineeships available. Support available to part-time students. Financial award application deadline: 2/15; financial award applicants required to submit FAFSA. *Unit head:* Dr. Jane Kapustin, Assistant Dean, 410-706-6741, Fax: 410-706-4231. *Application contact:* Marjorie Fass, Admissions Director, 410-706-0501, Fax: 410-706-7238.

University of Massachusetts Amherst, Graduate School, School of Nursing, Amherst, MA 01003. Offers clinical nurse leader (MS); family nurse practitioner (DNP); nursing (PhD); public health nurse leader (DNP). *Accreditation:* AACN. Part-time programs available. Postbaccalaureate distance learning degree programs offered (minimal on-campus study). *Faculty:* 12 full-time (11 women). *Students:* 56 full-time (51 women), 155 part-time (142 women); includes 57 minority (24 Black or African American, non-Hispanic/Latino; 5 Asian, non-Hispanic/Latino; 25 Hispanic/Latino; 3 Two or more races, non-Hispanic/Latino), 11 international. Average age 42. 125 applicants, 66% accepted, 53 enrolled. In 2011, 11 master's, 26 doctorates awarded. Terminal master's awarded for partial completion of doctoral program. *Degree requirements:* For master's, thesis optional; for doctorate, comprehensive exam, thesis/dissertation. *Entrance requirements:* For master's and doctorate, GRE General Test. Additional exam requirements/recommendations for international students: Required—TOEFL (minimum score 550 paper-based; 213 computer-based; 80 iBT), IELTS (minimum score 6.5). *Application deadline:* For fall admission, 2/1 for domestic and international students. Applications are processed on a rolling basis. Application fee: $50 ($65 for international students). Electronic applications accepted. Tuition and fees vary according to course load, campus/location and program. *Financial support:* Fellowships with full and partial tuition reimbursements, research assistantships with full and partial tuition reimbursements, teaching assistantships with full and partial tuition reimbursements, career-related internships or fieldwork, Federal Work-Study, scholarships/grants, traineeships, health care benefits, tuition waivers (full and partial), and unspecified assistantships available. Support available to part-time students. Financial award application deadline: 2/1. *Faculty research:* Health of older adults and their caretakers, mental health of individuals and families, health of children and adolescents, power and decision-making, transcultural health. *Unit head:* Dr. Donna Zucker, Graduate Program Director, 413-577-2322, Fax: 413-577-2550. *Application contact:* Lindsay DeSantis, Interim Supervisor of Admissions, 413-545-0722, Fax: 413-577-0010, E-mail: gradadm@grad.umass.edu. Web site: http://www.umass.edu/nursing/.

University of Massachusetts Dartmouth, Graduate School, College of Nursing, Graduate Nursing Programs, North Dartmouth, MA 02747-2300. Offers adult health/adult nurse practitioner (MS); adult health/advanced practice (MS); adult health/nurse educator (MS); adult health/nurse manager (MS); adult nurse practitioner (PMC); community nursing/advanced practice (MS); community nursing/nurse educator (MS); community nursing/nurse manager (MS); individualized nursing (PMC); nursing (DNP, PhD). Part-time programs available. *Faculty:* 27 full-time (all women), 42 part-time/adjunct (41 women). *Students:* 8 full-time (all women), 99 part-time (93 women); includes 11 minority (4 Black or African American, non-Hispanic/Latino; 2 Asian, non-Hispanic/Latino; 4 Hispanic/Latino; 1 Two or more races, non-Hispanic/Latino), 1 international. Average age 38. 65 applicants, 75% accepted, 26 enrolled. In 2011, 12 master's, 1 other advanced degree awarded. *Degree requirements:* For master's, thesis; for doctorate, thesis/dissertation. *Entrance requirements:* For master's, GRE General Test, BSN, minimum undergraduate GPA of 3.0, RN license, 3 letters of recommendation, 1 year experience as registered nurse; for doctorate, GRE General Test, minimum undergraduate GPA of 3.0, graduate 3.3; 3 letters of recommendation; personal statement; current Massachusetts RN license or eligibility for licensure in Massachusetts; 1 year professional nursing experience; example of scholarly writing. Additional exam requirements/recommendations for international students: Required—TOEFL (minimum score 533 paper-based; 200 computer-based; 72 iBT). *Application deadline:* For fall admission, 3/15 for domestic students, 2/15 for international students.

Application fee: $40 ($60 for international students). Electronic applications accepted. *Expenses:* Tuition, state resident: full-time $2071; part-time $86.29 per credit. Tuition, nonresident: full-time $8099; part-time $337.46 per credit. *Required fees:* $438.58 per credit. Part-time tuition and fees vary according to class time, course load, degree level and reciprocity agreements. *Financial support:* In 2011–12, 14 teaching assistantships with partial tuition reimbursements (averaging $2,571 per year) were awarded; Federal Work-Study also available. Support available to part-time students. Financial award application deadline: 3/1; financial award applicants required to submit FAFSA. *Faculty research:* Chronic illness management, risk reduction activities in Type 2 diabetes, diabetes care and education, clinical decision-making, quantitative methodologies. *Total annual research expenditures:* $31,049. *Unit head:* Dr. Gail Russell, Graduate Program Director, 508-999-8251, Fax: 508-999-9127, E-mail: grussell@umassd.edu. *Application contact:* Elan Turcotte-Shamski, Graduate Admissions Officer, 508-999-8604, Fax: 508-999-8183, E-mail: graduate@umassd.edu. Web site: http://www.umassd.edu/nursing/graduateprograms.

University of Michigan, Horace H. Rackham School of Graduate Studies, School of Nursing, Division of Health Promotion and Risk Reduction, Program in Community Health Nursing, Ann Arbor, MI 48109. Offers adult nurse practitioner (Post Master's Certificate); adult primary care/adult nurse practitioner (MS); community care (Post Master's Certificate); community care/home care (MS); family nurse practitioner (MS, Post Master's Certificate); occupational health nursing (MS). *Accreditation:* AACN. Part-time and evening/weekend programs available. *Degree requirements:* For master's, thesis. *Entrance requirements:* For master's, GRE General Test (if cumulative BSN GPA less than 3.25), licensure, minimum GPA of 3.0 in BSN program. Additional exam requirements/recommendations for international students: Required—TOEFL (minimum score 560 paper-based; 220 computer-based).

University of Minnesota, Twin Cities Campus, Graduate School, School of Nursing, Program in Public Health Nursing, Minneapolis, MN 55455-0213. Offers MS. *Accreditation:* AACN. Part-time programs available. Postbaccalaureate distance learning degree programs offered (minimal on-campus study). *Degree requirements:* For master's, final oral exam, project or thesis. *Entrance requirements:* Additional exam requirements/recommendations for international students: Required—TOEFL (minimum score 586 paper-based; 240 computer-based).

The University of North Carolina at Chapel Hill, Graduate School, School of Public Health, Public Health Leadership Program, Chapel Hill, NC 27599. Offers health care and prevention (MPH); leadership (MPH); occupational health nursing (MPH); public health nursing (MS). Part-time programs available. Postbaccalaureate distance learning degree programs offered (minimal on-campus study). *Degree requirements:* For master's, comprehensive exam, thesis (MS), paper (MPH). *Entrance requirements:* For master's, GRE General Test, minimum GPA of 3.0, public health experience. Additional exam requirements/recommendations for international students: Required—TOEFL. Electronic applications accepted. *Faculty research:* Occupational health issues, clinical outcomes, prenatal and early childcare, adolescent health, effectiveness of home visiting, issues in occupational health nursing, community-based interventions.

University of North Dakota, Graduate School, College of Nursing, Grand Forks, ND 58202. Offers advanced public health nursing (MS); family nurse practitioner (MS); gerontological nursing (MS); nurse anesthesia (MS); nursing (MS, PhD); nursing education (MS); psychiatric and mental health (MS). *Accreditation:* AACN; AANA/CANAEP (one or more programs are accredited). Part-time and evening/weekend programs available. Postbaccalaureate distance learning degree programs offered (minimal on-campus study). *Degree requirements:* For master's, thesis or alternative. *Entrance requirements:* For master's, minimum GPA of 3.0; for doctorate, GRE or MAT, minimum GPA of 3.0. Additional exam requirements/recommendations for international students: Required—TOEFL (minimum score 550 paper-based; 213 computer-based; 79 iBT), IELTS (minimum score 6.5). Electronic applications accepted. *Faculty research:* Adult health, anesthesia, rural health, health administration, family nurse practitioner.

University of Puerto Rico, Medical Sciences Campus, School of Nursing, San Juan, PR 00936-5067. Offers adult and elderly nursing (MSN); child and adolescent nursing (MSN); critical care nursing (MSN); family and community nursing (MSN); family nurse practitioner (MSN); maternity nursing (MSN); mental health and psychiatric nursing (MSN). *Accreditation:* AACN; AANA/CANAEP. *Entrance requirements:* For master's, GRE or EXADEP, interview, Puerto Rico RN license or professional license for international students, general and specific point average, article analysis. Electronic applications accepted. *Faculty research:* HIV, health disparities, teen violence, women and violence, neurological disorders.

University of South Alabama, Graduate School, College of Nursing, Mobile, AL 36688. Offers adult health nursing (MSN); community/mental health nursing (MSN); maternal/child nursing (MSN); nursing (DNP). *Accreditation:* AACN. *Faculty:* 21 full-time (20 women). *Students:* 1,335 full-time (1,200 women), 172 part-time (147 women); includes 280 minority (164 Black or African American, non-Hispanic/Latino; 15 American Indian or Alaska Native, non-Hispanic/Latino; 41 Asian, non-Hispanic/Latino; 45 Hispanic/Latino; 2 Native Hawaiian or other Pacific Islander, non-Hispanic/Latino; 13 Two or more races, non-Hispanic/Latino), 10 international. 1,327 applicants, 38% accepted, 388 enrolled. In 2011, 266 master's, 21 doctorates awarded. *Degree requirements:* For master's, thesis optional. *Entrance requirements:* For master's, BSN, RN licensure, minimum GPA of 3.0, resume documenting clinical experience, background check, drug screening; for doctorate, GRE. *Application deadline:* For fall admission, 7/15 for domestic students; for spring admission, 12/1 for domestic students. Application fee: $35. *Expenses:* Tuition, state resident: full-time $7968; part-time $332 per credit hour. Tuition, nonresident: full-time $15,936; part-time $664 per credit hour. *Unit head:* Dr. Rosemary Rhodes, Director of Graduate Education, 251-445-9409, Fax: 251-445-9416. *Application contact:* Dr. B. Keith Harrison, Dean of the Graduate School, 251-460-6310, Fax: 251-461-1513, E-mail: kharriso@usouthal.edu. Web site: http://www.southalabama.edu/nursing.

University of South Carolina, The Graduate School, College of Nursing, Program in Health Nursing, Columbia, SC 29208. Offers adult nurse practitioner (MSN); community/public health clinical nurse specialist (MSN); family nurse practitioner (MSN); pediatric nurse practitioner (MSN). *Accreditation:* AACN. Part-time programs available. *Degree requirements:* For master's, thesis or alternative. *Entrance requirements:* For master's, GRE General Test or MAT, BS in nursing, nursing license. Additional exam requirements/recommendations for international students: Required—TOEFL (minimum score 570 paper-based; 230 computer-based). Electronic applications accepted. *Faculty research:* System research, evidence based practice, breast cancer, violence.

University of South Carolina, The Graduate School, College of Nursing, Program in Nursing and Public Health, Columbia, SC 29208. Offers MPH/MSN. *Accreditation:* AACN; CEPH. Part-time programs available. *Entrance requirements:* Additional exam requirements/recommendations for international students: Required—TOEFL (minimum score 570 paper-based; 230 computer-based). Electronic applications accepted. *Faculty research:* System research, evidence based practice, breast cancer, violence.

The University of Texas at Austin, Graduate School, School of Nursing, Austin, TX 78712-1111. Offers adult -gerontology clinical nurse specialist (MSN); child health (MSN), including administration, public health nursing; child health (MSN), including

teaching; family nurse practitioner (MSN); family psychiatric/mental health nurse practitioner (MSN); holistic adult health (MSN), including administration, education; maternity (MSN), including administration, public health nursing; maternity (MSN), including teaching; nursing (PhD); nursing administration and healthcare systems management (MSN); pediatric nurse practitioner (MSN); public health nursing (MSN). *Accreditation:* AACN. Part-time programs available. *Degree requirements:* For master's, thesis optional; for doctorate, thesis/dissertation. *Entrance requirements:* For master's and doctorate, GRE General Test. Additional exam requirements/recommendations for international students: Required—TOEFL (minimum score 550 paper-based; 213 computer-based). *Application deadline:* For fall admission, 12/1 for domestic students. Application fee: $50 ($75 for international students). Electronic applications accepted. *Financial support:* Fellowships, research assistantships, teaching assistantships, scholarships/grants, and traineeships available. Financial award application deadline: 2/1. *Faculty research:* Chronic illness management, memory and aging, health promotion, women's health, adolescent health. *Unit head:* Dr. Alexa Stuifbergen, Dean, 512-471-4100, Fax: 512-471-4910, E-mail: astuifbergen@mail.utexas.edu. Web site: http://www.utexas.edu/nursing/.

The University of Texas at Brownsville, Graduate Studies, School of Health Sciences, Brownsville, TX 78520-4991. Offers MSN. *Accreditation:* NLN. *Degree requirements:* For master's, comprehensive exam, thesis optional.

The University of Toledo, College of Graduate Studies, College of Nursing, Department of Population and Community Care, Toledo, OH 43606-3390. Offers adult nurse practitioner (Certificate); adult nurse practitioner/clinical nurse specialist (MSN); clinical nurse leader (MSN); family nurse practitioner (MSN, Certificate); nurse educator (MSN, Certificate); pediatric nurse practitioner (MSN, Certificate); psychiatric-mental health clinical nurse specialist (MSN, Certificate). Part-time programs available. *Faculty:* 43. *Students:* 77 full-time (63 women), 198 part-time (180 women); includes 30 minority (14 Black or African American, non-Hispanic/Latino; 1 American Indian or Alaska Native, non-Hispanic/Latino; 4 Asian, non-Hispanic/Latino; 8 Hispanic/Latino; 3 Two or more races, non-Hispanic/Latino), 1 international. Average age 33. 172 applicants, 53% accepted, 82 enrolled. In 2011, 66 master's, 10 other advanced degrees awarded. *Degree requirements:* For master's, thesis or alternative. *Entrance requirements:* For master's, GRE, BS in nursing, minimum undergraduate GPA of 3.0, statement of purpose, three letters of recommendation, transcripts from all prior institutions attended, Nursing CAS application, UT supplemental application; for Certificate, BS in nursing, minimum undergraduate GPA of 3.0, statement of purpose, three letters of recommendation, transcripts from all prior institutions attended. Additional exam requirements/recommendations for international students: Required—TOEFL (minimum score 550 paper-based; 213 computer-based; 80 iBT), IELTS (minimum score 6.5). Application fee: $45 ($75 for international students). Electronic applications accepted. *Financial support:* Research assistantships, Federal Work-Study, scholarships/grants, traineeships, and tuition waivers (full and partial) available. *Application contact:* Joan Mulligan, Admissions Analyst, 419-383-4168, Fax: 419-383-6140, E-mail: joan.mulligan@utoledo.edu. Web site: http://www.utoledo.edu/nursing/.

University of Washington, Tacoma, Graduate Programs, Program in Nursing, Tacoma, WA 98402-3100. Offers communities, populations and health (MN); leadership in healthcare (MN); nurse educator (MN). Part-time programs available. *Degree requirements:* For master's, thesis (for some programs), advance fieldwork. *Entrance requirements:* For master's, Washington State NCLEX exam, minimum GPA of 3.0. Additional exam requirements/recommendations for international students: Required—TOEFL (minimum score 580 paper-based; 237 computer-based; 70 iBT); Recommended—IELTS (minimum score 7). *Faculty research:* Hospice and palliative care; clinical trial decision-making; minority nurse retention; asthma and public health; injustice, suffering, difference: Linking Them to Us; adolescent health.

Wayne State University, College of Nursing, Program in Community Health Nursing, Detroit, MI 48202. Offers MSN. *Accreditation:* AACN. Part-time programs available. *Students:* 3 full-time (all women), 9 part-time (all women); includes 4 minority (all Black or African American, non-Hispanic/Latino), 2 international. Average age 42. 6 applicants, 33% accepted, 2 enrolled. In 2011, 2 master's awarded. *Degree requirements:* For master's, thesis or alternative. *Entrance requirements:* For master's, minimum honor point average of 2.8 in upper-division course work; BA from NLN- or CCNE-accredited program; references; current RN license; personal statement. Additional exam requirements/recommendations for international students: Required—TOEFL (minimum score 550 paper-based; 213 computer-based); Recommended—TWE (minimum score 6). *Application deadline:* For fall admission, 6/1 priority date for domestic students, 5/1 for international students; for winter admission, 10/1 priority date for domestic students, 9/1 for international students; for spring admission, 2/1 priority date for domestic students, 1/1 for international students. Applications are processed on a rolling basis. Application fee: $50. Electronic applications accepted. *Expenses:* Tuition, state resident: part-time $512.85 per credit. Tuition, nonresident: part-time $1132.65 per credit. *Required fees:* $26.60 per credit. $199.65 per semester. Tuition and fees vary according to course load and program. *Financial support:* In 2011–12, 4 students received support, including 2 fellowships with tuition reimbursements available (averaging $13,708 per year); research assistantships with tuition reimbursements available, teaching assistantships with tuition reimbursements available, institutionally sponsored loans, scholarships/grants, traineeships, and unspecified assistantships also available. Support available to part-time students. Financial award applicants required to submit FAFSA. *Faculty research:* Alternative therapies, end-of-life issues, health literacy communication, physical activity and exercise, quality of nursing care. *Total annual research expenditures:* $572,858. *Unit head:* Dr. Barbara Redman, Dean, 313-577-4070, Fax: 313-577-4571, E-mail: ae9080@wayne.edu. *Application contact:* Dr. Cynthia Redwine, Assistant Dean for the Office of Student Affairs, 313-577-4082, E-mail: nursinginfo@wayne.edu. Web site: http://www.nursing.wayne.edu/msn/CNSCHNCurriculum.php.

West Chester University of Pennsylvania, College of Health Sciences, Department of Nursing, West Chester, PA 19383. Offers nursing education (Certificate); public health nursing (MSN), including administration; school nursing (Teaching Certificate). *Accreditation:* AACN. Part-time and evening/weekend programs available. *Faculty:* 1 (woman) full-time, 2 part-time/adjunct (both women). *Students:* 10 full-time (all women), 31 part-time (all women); includes 8 minority (7 Black or African American, non-Hispanic/Latino; 1 Asian, non-Hispanic/Latino), 2 international. Average age 46. 20 applicants, 75% accepted, 13 enrolled. In 2011, 1 degree awarded. *Entrance requirements:* For master's, RN license, BSN or RN with bachelor's degree in another discipline, minimum GPA of 2.8, experience as a nurse providing direct clinical care, two letters of recommendation. Additional exam requirements/recommendations for international students: Required—TOEFL (minimum score 550 paper-based; 213 computer-based; 80 iBT). *Application deadline:* For fall admission, 4/15 priority date for domestic students, 3/15 for international students; for spring admission, 10/15 priority date for domestic students, 9/1 for international students. Applications are processed on a rolling basis. Application fee: $45. Electronic applications accepted. *Expenses:* Tuition, state resident: full-time $7488; part-time $416 per credit. Tuition, nonresident: full-time $11,232; part-time $624 per credit. *Required fees:* $1784.64; $67.59 per credit. Tuition and fees vary according to program. *Financial support:* Unspecified assistantships available. Support available to part-time students. Financial award application deadline: 2/15; financial award applicants required to submit FAFSA. *Unit head:* Dr. Charlotte Mackey, Chair, 610-436-3474, Fax: 610-436-3083, E-mail: cmackey@wcupa.edu. *Application contact:* Dr. Ann Coghlan Stowe, Graduate Coordinator, 610-436-2331, Fax: 610-436-3083, E-mail: astowe@wcupa.edu. Web site: http://www.wcupa.edu/_ACADEMICS/HealthSciences/nursing/.

Worcester State University, Graduate Studies, Department of Nursing, Program in Community and Public Health Nursing, Worcester, MA 01602-2597. Offers MSN. Part-time programs available. *Faculty:* 2 full-time (both women), 4 part-time/adjunct (3 women). *Students:* 10 full-time (9 women), 19 part-time (18 women); includes 7 minority (4 Black or African American, non-Hispanic/Latino; 2 Asian, non-Hispanic/Latino; 1 Hispanic/Latino). Average age 44. 35 applicants, 86% accepted, 10 enrolled. In 2011, 3 master's awarded. *Degree requirements:* For master's, final project and practicum. *Entrance requirements:* For master's, GRE, MAT, unencumbered license to practice as a Registered Nurse in Massachusetts. Additional exam requirements/recommendations for international students: Required—TOEFL (minimum score 500 paper-based; 61 iBT). *Application deadline:* For fall admission, 6/15 for domestic and international students; for spring admission, 4/1 for domestic and international students. Applications are processed on a rolling basis. Application fee: $40. Electronic applications accepted. *Expenses:* Tuition, state resident: full-time $2700; part-time $150 per credit. Tuition, nonresident: full-time $2700; part-time $150 per credit. *Required fees:* $2016; $112 per credit. *Financial support:* In 2011–12, 2 students received support, including 2 research assistantships (averaging $4,800 per year). Financial award application deadline: 3/1; financial award applicants required to submit FAFSA. *Unit head:* Dr. Stephanie Chalupka, Coordinator, 508-929-8680, E-mail: schalupka@worcester.edu. *Application contact:* Sara Grady, Assistant Dean of Continuing Education, 508-929-8787, Fax: 508-929-8100, E-mail: sara.grady@worcester.edu.

Wright State University, School of Graduate Studies, College of Nursing and Health, Program in Nursing, Dayton, OH 45435. Offers acute care nurse practitioner (MS); administration of nursing and health care systems (MS); adult health (MS); child and adolescent health (MS); community health (MS); family nurse practitioner (MS); nurse practitioner (MS); school nurse (MS); MBA/MS. *Accreditation:* AACN. Part-time and evening/weekend programs available. *Degree requirements:* For master's, thesis or alternative. *Entrance requirements:* For master's, GRE General Test, BSN from NLN-accredited college, Ohio RN license. Additional exam requirements/recommendations for international students: Required—TOEFL. *Faculty research:* Clinical nursing and health, teaching, caring, pain administration, informatics and technology.

Family Nurse Practitioner Studies

Abilene Christian University, Graduate School, School of Nursing, Abilene, TX 79699-9100. Offers education and administration (MSN); family nurse practitioner (MSN). *Accreditation:* AACN. Part-time programs available. *Faculty:* 6 part-time/adjunct (all women). *Students:* 1 (woman) full-time, 2 part-time (1 woman). 6 applicants, 17% accepted, 1 enrolled. In 2011, 3 degrees awarded. *Degree requirements:* For master's, practicum. *Entrance requirements:* For master's, GRE General Test. Additional exam requirements/recommendations for international students: Required—TOEFL (minimum score 550 paper-based; 213 computer-based; 80 iBT), IELTS (minimum score 6). *Application deadline:* For fall admission, 4/1 priority date for domestic students; for spring admission, 11/1 for domestic students. Applications are processed on a rolling basis. Application fee: $50. Electronic applications accepted. *Expenses: Tuition:* Full-time $14,168; part-time $787 per hour. *Required fees:* $82 per hour. $10 per term. *Financial support:* Application deadline: 4/1; applicants required to submit FAFSA. *Unit head:* Dr. Becky Hammack, Graduate Director, 325-671-2361, Fax: 325-671-2386, E-mail: atoone@phssn.edu. *Application contact:* David Pittman, Graduate Admissions Counselor, 325-674-2656, Fax: 325-674-6717, E-mail: gradinfo@acu.edu.

Albany State University, College of Sciences and Health Professions, Albany, GA 31705-2717. Offers criminal justice (MS), including corrections, forensic science, law enforcement, public administration; mathematics education (M Ed); nursing (MSN), including RN to MSN family nurse practitioner, RN to MSN nurse educator; science education (M Ed). *Accreditation:* NLN. Part-time and evening/weekend programs available. Postbaccalaureate distance learning degree programs offered. *Faculty:* 16 full-time (7 women), 7 part-time/adjunct (3 women). *Students:* 34 full-time (26 women), 103 part-time (84 women); includes 94 minority (92 Black or African American, non-Hispanic/Latino; 2 Asian, non-Hispanic/Latino), 2 international. Average age 36. 101 applicants, 48% accepted, 33 enrolled. In 2011, 16 master's awarded. *Degree requirements:* For master's, comprehensive exam, thesis. *Entrance requirements:* For master's, GRE or MAT, official transcript, letters of recommendations, pre-medical/certificate of immunizations. *Application deadline:* For fall admission, 6/15 for domestic students, 5/1 for international students; for spring admission, 11/1 for domestic students, 10/1 for international students. Applications are processed on a rolling basis. Application fee: $20. Electronic applications accepted. *Expenses:* Tuition, state resident: full-time $3204; part-time $178 per credit hour. Tuition, nonresident: full-time $12,816; part-time $712 per credit hour. *Required fees:* $379 per semester. *Financial support:* Scholarships/grants and traineeships available. Financial award application deadline: 4/15; financial award applicants required to submit CSS PROFILE or FAFSA. *Unit head:* Dr. Joyce Johnson, Dean, 229-430-4792, Fax: 229-430-3937, E-mail: joyce.johnson@asurams.edu. *Application contact:* Jeffrey Pierce, II, Graduate Admissions Counselor, 229-430-4646, Fax: 229-430-4105, E-mail: jeffrey.pierce@asurams.edu. Web site: http://asu-sacs.asurams.edu/ASUCatalog/Graduate/index.html.

Allen College, Program in Nursing, Waterloo, IA 50703. Offers acute care nurse practitioner (MSN, Post-Master's Certificate); adult nurse practitioner (MSN, Post-Master's Certificate); adult psychiatric-mental health nurse practitioner (MSN, Post-Master's Certificate); family nurse practitioner (MSN, Post-Master's Certificate); gerontological nurse practitioner (MSN, Post-Master's Certificate); health education (MSN); leadership in health care delivery (MSN, Post-Master's Certificate); nursing

(DNP). *Accreditation:* AACN; NLN. Part-time programs available. *Faculty:* 3 full-time (all women), 16 part-time/adjunct (all women). *Students:* 34 full-time (31 women), 110 part-time (106 women); includes 5 minority (2 Asian, non-Hispanic/Latino; 3 Hispanic/Latino). Average age 36. 156 applicants, 64% accepted, 76 enrolled. In 2011, 61 master's, 1 other advanced degree awarded. *Degree requirements:* For master's, thesis optional. *Entrance requirements:* For master's, minimum GPA of 3.0; for doctorate, minimum GPA of 3.25 in graduate coursework. Additional exam requirements/recommendations for international students: Recommended—TOEFL (minimum score 550 paper-based), IELTS. *Application deadline:* For fall admission, 2/1 priority date for domestic students; for spring admission, 9/1 priority date for domestic students. Applications are processed on a rolling basis. Application fee: $50. Electronic applications accepted. *Expenses: Tuition:* Full-time $13,993; part-time $691 per credit hour. *Required fees:* $832; $69 per credit hour. One-time fee: $100 part-time. Part-time tuition and fees vary according to course load. *Financial support:* In 2011–12, 41 students received support. Institutionally sponsored loans; scholarships/grants, and traineeships available. Support available to part-time students. Financial award application deadline: 8/15; financial award applicants required to submit FAFSA. *Faculty research:* Pain and the aged, congestive heart failure. *Unit head:* Kendra Williams-Perez, Dean, School of Nursing, 319-226-2044, Fax: 319-226-2070, E-mail: williakb@ihs.org. *Application contact:* Michelle Koehn, Admissions Counselor, 319-226-2002, Fax: 319-226-2051, E-mail: koehnml@ihs.org. Web site: http://www.allencollege.edu/.

Alverno College, School of Nursing, Milwaukee, WI 53234-3922. Offers family nurse practitioner (MSN); nursing education (MSN). *Accreditation:* AACN. Part-time and evening/weekend programs available. *Faculty:* 8 full-time (all women), 3 part-time/adjunct (all women). *Students:* 35 full-time (all women), 41 part-time (all women); includes 10 minority (8 Black or African American, non-Hispanic/Latino; 2 Hispanic/Latino), 1 international. Average age 38. 61 applicants, 54% accepted, 29 enrolled. In 2011, 8 master's awarded. *Degree requirements:* For master's, 500 clinical hours, capstone. *Entrance requirements:* For master's, BSN, current license. Additional exam requirements/recommendations for international students: Required—TOEFL. *Application deadline:* For fall admission, 7/15 priority date for domestic students, 7/15 for international students; for spring admission, 12/15 priority date for domestic students, 12/15 for international students. Applications are processed on a rolling basis. Application fee: $0. Electronic applications accepted. Application fee is waived when completed online. *Expenses:* Contact institution. *Financial support:* In 2011–12, 7 students received support. Federal Work-Study available. Support available to part-time students. Financial award application deadline: 4/15. *Faculty research:* Impact of stroke on sexuality, children's asthma management, factors affecting baccalaureate student success. *Unit head:* Dr. Catherine Knuteson, Program Director, 414-382-6287, Fax: 414-382-6354, E-mail: catherine.knuteson@alverno.edu. *Application contact:* Christy Stone, Director of Graduate and Adult Recruitment, 414-382-6108, Fax: 414-382-6354, E-mail: christy.stone@alverno.edu.

Arizona State University, College of Nursing and Health Innovation, Phoenix, AZ 85004. Offers advanced nursing practice (DNP); child/family mental health nurse practitioner (Graduate Certificate); clinical research management (MS); community and public health practice (Graduate Certificate); community health (MS); exercise and wellness (MS), including exercise and wellness; family nurse practitioner (Graduate Certificate); healthcare innovation (MHI); international health for healthcare (Graduate Certificate); kinesiology (MS, PhD); nursing (MS, Graduate Certificate); nursing and healthcare innovation (PhD); nutrition (MS); physical activity nutrition and wellness (PhD), including physical activity, nutrition and wellness; public health (MPH); regulatory science and health safety (MS). *Accreditation:* AACN. Postbaccalaureate distance learning degree programs offered (minimal on-campus study). *Degree requirements:* For master's, comprehensive exam (for some programs), thesis (for some programs), interactive Program of Study (iPOS) submitted before completing 50 percent of required credit hours; for doctorate, comprehensive exam, thesis/dissertation, interactive Program of Study (iPOS) submitted before completing 50 percent of required credit hours. *Entrance requirements:* For master's and doctorate, GRE, minimum GPA of 3.0 or equivalent in last 2 years of work leading to bachelor's degree. Additional exam requirements/recommendations for international students: Required—TOEFL (minimum score 80 iBT), TOEFL, IELTS, or Pearson Test of English. Electronic applications accepted. *Expenses:* Contact institution.

Barry University, School of Adult and Continuing Education, Division of Nursing, Program in Nurse Practitioner, Miami Shores, FL 33161-6695. Offers acute care nurse practitioner (MSN); family nurse practitioner (MSN); nurse practitioner (Certificate). *Accreditation:* AACN. Part-time and evening/weekend programs available. *Degree requirements:* For master's, research project or thesis. *Entrance requirements:* For master's, GRE General Test or MAT, BSN, minimum GPA of 3.0, course work in statistics. Electronic applications accepted. *Faculty research:* Child abuse, health beliefs, teenage pregnancy, cultural and clinical studies across the lifespan.

Baylor University, Graduate School, Louise Herrington School of Nursing, Waco, TX 76798. Offers family nurse practitioner (MSN); neonatal nurse practitioner (MSN); nurse-midwifery (DNP). *Accreditation:* AACN. Part-time programs available. *Faculty:* 9 full-time (all women), 3 part-time/adjunct (2 women). *Students:* 33 full-time (32 women), 45 part-time (39 women); includes 17 minority (4 Black or African American, non-Hispanic/Latino; 4 Asian, non-Hispanic/Latino; 3 Hispanic/Latino; 6 Two or more races, non-Hispanic/Latino), 1 international. 62 applicants, 63% accepted, 37 enrolled. In 2011, 24 master's, 3 doctorates awarded. *Entrance requirements:* For master's, GRE General Test or MAT; for doctorate, GRE General Test. *Application deadline:* For fall admission, 4/1 for domestic students. Application fee: $40. Electronic applications accepted. *Financial support:* Applicants required to submit FAFSA. *Unit head:* Dr. Linda Plank, Graduate Program Director, 214-818-7847, Fax: 214-818-8692, E-mail: linda_plank@baylor.edu. *Application contact:* Beverly Kurfees, Academic Support Specialist, 214-367-3752, Fax: 254-710-3870, E-mail: beverly_kurfees@baylor.edu. Web site: http://www.baylor.edu/nursing/.

Bellarmine University, Donna and Allan Lansing School of Nursing and Health Sciences, Louisville, KY 40205-0671. Offers family nurse practitioner (MSN); nursing administration (MSN); nursing education (MSN); nursing practice (DNP); physical therapy (DPT). *Accreditation:* AACN; APTA. Part-time and evening/weekend programs available. *Faculty:* 21 full-time (16 women), 7 part-time/adjunct (2 women). *Students:* 128 full-time (82 women), 116 part-time (111 women); includes 13 minority (5 Black or African American, non-Hispanic/Latino; 1 American Indian or Alaska Native, non-Hispanic/Latino; 2 Asian, non-Hispanic/Latino; 3 Hispanic/Latino; 2 Two or more races, non-Hispanic/Latino). Average age 31. In 2011, 19 master's, 50 doctorates awarded. *Degree requirements:* For doctorate, comprehensive exam, thesis/dissertation. *Entrance requirements:* For master's, GRE General Test, RN license; for doctorate, GRE General Test, Physical Therapist Centralized Application Service (for DPT). Additional exam requirements/recommendations for international students: Required—TOEFL (minimum score 550 paper-based; 213 computer-based; 80 iBT). Application fee: $25. Electronic applications accepted. *Expenses:* Contact institution. *Financial support:* Career-related internships or fieldwork and scholarships/grants available. *Faculty research:* Nursing: pain, empathy, leadership styles, control; physical therapy: service-learning; exercise in chronic and pre-operative conditions, athletes; women's

health; aging. *Unit head:* Dr. Susan H. Davis, Dean, 800-274-4723 Ext. 8217, E-mail: sdavis@bellarmine.edu. *Application contact:* Julie Armstrong-Binnix, Health Science Recruiter, 800-274-4723 Ext. 8364, E-mail: julieab@bellarmine.edu. Web site: http://www.bellarmine.edu/lansing.

Belmont University, College of Health Sciences, School of Nursing, Nashville, TN 37212-3757. Offers family nurse practitioner (MSN). *Accreditation:* AACN. Part-time programs available. *Faculty:* 1 (woman) full-time, 3 part-time/adjunct (all women). *Students:* 22 full-time (all women), 46 part-time (43 women); includes 7 minority (5 Black or African American, non-Hispanic/Latino; 2 Hispanic/Latino), 1 international. Average age 30. 65 applicants, 58% accepted, 33 enrolled. In 2011, 25 master's awarded. *Degree requirements:* For master's, comprehensive exam. *Entrance requirements:* For master's, GRE, BSN, minimum GPA of 3.0. Additional exam requirements/recommendations for international students: Required—TOEFL (minimum score 550 paper-based; 213 computer-based; 80 iBT). *Application deadline:* For fall admission, 8/1 for domestic students, 3/1 for international students; for spring admission, 10/15 priority date for domestic students, 10/1 for international students. Applications are processed on a rolling basis. Application fee: $50. Electronic applications accepted. *Expenses:* Contact institution. *Financial support:* In 2011–12, 21 students received support. Scholarships/grants and traineeships available. Financial award application deadline: 3/1; financial award applicants required to submit FAFSA. *Faculty research:* Postpartum post-operative care, adherence/compliance behavior in chronic illness, women's health in primary care, geriatrics. *Unit head:* Dr. Leslie J. Higgins, Director, Graduate Program, 615-460-6027, Fax: 615-460-6125, E-mail: leslie.higgins@belmont.edu. *Application contact:* Heather Germain, Program Assistant, 615-460-6142, Fax: 615-460-6125, E-mail: hether.germain@belmont.edu. Web site: http://www.belmont.edu/nursing/.

Bloomsburg University of Pennsylvania, School of Graduate Studies, College of Science and Technology, Department of Nursing, Bloomsburg, PA 17815-1301. Offers adult and family nurse practitioner (MSN); adult health and illness (MSN); community health (MSN); nursing (MSN); nursing administration (MSN). *Accreditation:* AACN; AANA/CANAEP. *Degree requirements:* For master's, thesis. *Entrance requirements:* For master's, minimum QPA of 3.0. Additional exam requirements/recommendations for international students: Required—TOEFL. Electronic applications accepted. *Faculty research:* Cardiopulmonary nursing, cancer topics, women's health.

Bowie State University, Graduate Programs, Department of Nursing, Bowie, MD 20715-9465. Offers administration of nursing services (MS); family nurse practitioner (MS); nursing education (MS). *Accreditation:* NLN. Part-time programs available. *Faculty:* 7 full-time (4 women), 14 part-time/adjunct (9 women). *Students:* 41 full-time (35 women), 55 part-time (50 women); includes 80 minority (77 Black or African American, non-Hispanic/Latino; 2 Asian, non-Hispanic/Latino; 1 Hispanic/Latino), 11 international. Average age 42. 7 applicants, 100% accepted, 5 enrolled. In 2011, 7 master's awarded. *Degree requirements:* For master's, comprehensive exam, thesis, research paper. *Entrance requirements:* For master's, minimum GPA of 2.5. *Application deadline:* For fall admission, 5/15 for domestic students. Applications are processed on a rolling basis. Application fee: $40. Electronic applications accepted. *Expenses: Tuition,* state resident: full-time $4140; part-time $3105 per semester. Tuition, nonresident: full-time $7836; part-time $5877 per semester. *Required fees:* $1715; $648 per semester. *Financial support:* Institutionally sponsored loans and traineeships available. Financial award application deadline: 4/1. *Faculty research:* Minority health, women's health, gerontology, leadership management. *Unit head:* Dr. Bonita Jenkins, Acting Chairperson, 301-860-3210, E-mail: mccaskill@bowiestate.edu. *Application contact:* Angela Issac, Information Contact, 301-860-4000.

Brenau University, Sydney O. Smith Graduate School, College of Health and Science, Gainesville, GA 30501. Offers family nurse practitioner (MSN); nurse educator (MSN); nursing management (MSN); occupational therapy (MS); psychology (MS). *Accreditation:* AOTA; NLN. Part-time and evening/weekend programs available. *Degree requirements:* For master's, comprehensive exam (for some programs), thesis (for some programs), clinical practicum hours. *Entrance requirements:* For master's, GRE General Test or MAT (for some programs), interview, writing sample, references (for some programs). Additional exam requirements/recommendations for international students: Required—TOEFL (minimum score 500 paper-based; 173 computer-based; 61 iBT); Recommended—IELTS (minimum score 5). Electronic applications accepted. *Expenses:* Contact institution.

Brigham Young University, Graduate Studies, College of Nursing, Provo, UT 84602. Offers family nurse practitioner (MS). *Accreditation:* AACN. *Faculty:* 14 full-time (13 women), 4 part-time/adjunct (3 women). *Students:* 28 full-time (21 women); includes 3 minority (2 Asian, non-Hispanic/Latino; 1 Hispanic/Latino). Average age 34. 36 applicants, 42% accepted, 13 enrolled. In 2011, 13 master's awarded. *Degree requirements:* For master's, thesis. *Entrance requirements:* For master's, GRE, minimum GPA of 3.0 in last 60 hours, interview, BS in nursing, pathophysiology class within undergraduate program, course work in basic statistics. Additional exam requirements/recommendations for international students: Required—TOEFL; Recommended—IELTS. *Application deadline:* For spring admission, 12/1 for domestic students. Applications are processed on a rolling basis. Application fee: $50. Electronic applications accepted. *Expenses: Tuition:* Full-time $5760; part-time $320 per credit. Tuition and fees vary according to student's religious affiliation. *Financial support:* In 2011–12, 28 students received support, including 2 research assistantships with full and partial tuition reimbursements available (averaging $10,000 per year), 3 teaching assistantships with full and partial tuition reimbursements available (averaging $10,000 per year); institutionally sponsored loans, scholarships/grants, tuition waivers (full), and unspecified assistantships also available. Support available to part-time students. Financial award application deadline: 2/1; financial award applicants required to submit FAFSA. *Faculty research:* Cardiovascular risk factors, stroke patients, nutrition, stress among children, family response to life-threatening illness. *Total annual research expenditures:* $1,200. *Unit head:* Dr. Beth Vaughan Cole, Dean, 801-422-8296, Fax: 801-422-0536, E-mail: beth-cole@byu.edu. *Application contact:* Stephanie Von Forell, Graduate Secretary, 801-422-4142, Fax: 801-422-0538, E-mail: stephanie-wilson@byu.edu. Web site: http://nursing.byu.edu/.

See Display on page 623 and Close-Up on page 793.

California State University, Fresno, Division of Graduate Studies, College of Health and Human Services, Department of Nursing, Fresno, CA 93740-8027. Offers nursing (MS), including clinical nurse, primary care nurse practitioner, specialist/nurse educator. *Accreditation:* AACN. Part-time and evening/weekend programs available. *Degree requirements:* For master's, thesis or alternative. *Entrance requirements:* For master's, GRE General Test, 1 year of clinical practice, previous course work in statistics, BSN, minimum GPA of 3.0 in nursing. Additional exam requirements/recommendations for international students: Required—TOEFL. Electronic applications accepted. *Faculty research:* Training grant, HIV assessment.

Carlow University, School of Nursing, Program in Family Nurse Practitioner, Pittsburgh, PA 15213-3165. Offers MSN, Certificate. Part-time programs available. *Students:* 143 full-time (128 women), 36 part-time (31 women); includes 10 minority (4 Black or African American, non-Hispanic/Latino; 3 Asian, non-Hispanic/Latino; 3 Hispanic/Latino). Average age 34. 128 applicants, 54% accepted, 50 enrolled. *Entrance*

requirements: For master's, minimum undergraduate GPA of 3.0 from accredited BSN program; current license as RN in Pennsylvania; at least one year of recent clinical (bedside) nursing experience; course in statistics in past 6 years; two recommendations; personal statement; personal interview. Additional exam requirements/recommendations for international students: Required—TOEFL (minimum score 550 paper-based; 213 computer-based). *Application deadline:* Applications are processed on a rolling basis. Application fee: $20. Application fee is waived when completed online. *Expenses: Tuition:* Full-time $10,290; part-time $686 per credit. Tuition and fees vary according to course load, degree level and program. *Unit head:* Dr. Karen A. Cummins, Director, Family Nurse Practitioner Program, 412-578-6112, Fax: 412-578-6114, E-mail: kacummins@carlow.edu. *Application contact:* Jo Danhires, Administrative Assistant, Admissions, 412-578-6059, Fax: 412-578-6321, E-mail: gradstudies@carlow.edu.

Carson-Newman College, Department of Nursing, Jefferson City, TN 37760. Offers family nurse practitioner (MSN); nurse educator (MSN). *Accreditation:* AACN. *Faculty:* 2 full-time (both women), 10 part-time/adjunct (9 women). *Students:* 16 full-time (15 women), 46 part-time (36 women); includes 3 minority (2 American Indian or Alaska Native, non-Hispanic/Latino; 1 Two or more races, non-Hispanic/Latino). Average age 32. In 2011, 17 master's awarded. *Application deadline:* For fall admission, 7/15 priority date for domestic students. Applications are processed on a rolling basis. Application fee: $50. *Expenses: Tuition:* Full-time $6750; part-time $375 per credit hour. *Required fees:* $200. *Unit head:* Dr. Gregory A. Casalenuovo, Dean, 865-471-3426. *Application contact:* Graduate Admissions and Services Adviser, 865-473-3468, Fax: 865-472-3475.

Case Western Reserve University, Frances Payne Bolton School of Nursing, Doctor of Nursing Practice Program, Cleveland, OH 44106. Offers acute care nurse practitioner (DNP); adult gerontology nurse practitioner (DNP); educational leadership (DNP); family nurse practitioner (DNP); family systems psychiatric mental health nursing (DNP); midwifery/family nursing (DNP); neonatal nurse practitioner (DNP); pediatric nurse practitioner (DNP); practice leadership (DNP); women's health nurse practitioner (DNP). *Students:* 73 full-time, 194 part-time; includes 11 minority (6 Black or African American, non-Hispanic/Latino; 3 Asian, non-Hispanic/Latino; 2 Hispanic/Latino). 122 applicants, 74% accepted, 49 enrolled. In 2011, 47 doctorates awarded. Terminal master's awarded for partial completion of doctoral program. *Degree requirements:* For doctorate, thesis/dissertation. *Entrance requirements:* For doctorate, GRE General Test or MAT. Additional exam requirements/recommendations for international students: Required—TOEFL (minimum score 577 paper-based; 90 iBT), IELTS (minimum score 7). *Application deadline:* For fall admission, 6/1 priority date for domestic students, 6/1 for international students; for spring admission, 10/1 for domestic and international students. Applications are processed on a rolling basis. Application fee: $75. *Financial support:* In 2011–12, 6 students received support, including 1 teaching assistantship; research assistantships, Federal Work-Study, institutionally sponsored loans, and tuition waivers (partial) also available. Support available to part-time students. Financial award application deadline: 6/30; financial award applicants required to submit FAFSA. *Faculty research:* Clinical nursing, acute care, gerontology, mental health, critical care. *Unit head:* Dr. Donna Dowling, Director, 216-368-1869, Fax: 216-368-3542, E-mail: dad10@case.edu. *Application contact:* Donna Hassik, Admissions Coordinator, 216-368-5253, Fax: 216-368-0124, E-mail: dmh7@case.edu. Web site: http://fpb.case.edu/DNP/.

Case Western Reserve University, Frances Payne Bolton School of Nursing, Master's Programs in Nursing, Nurse Practitioner Program, Cleveland, OH 44106. Offers acute care cardiovascular nursing (MSN); acute care nurse practitioner (MSN); acute care/flight nurse (MSN); adult gerontology nurse practitioner (MSN); family nurse practitioner (MSN); neonatal nurse practitioner (MSN); pediatric nurse practitioner (MSN); women's health nurse practitioner (MSN). *Accreditation:* NLN. Part-time programs available. Postbaccalaureate distance learning degree programs offered (minimal on-campus study). *Faculty:* 54 full-time (50 women), 5 part-time/adjunct (3 women). *Students:* 89 full-time (69 women), 77 part-time (67 women); includes 17 minority (11 Black or African American, non-Hispanic/Latino; 5 Asian, non-Hispanic/Latino; 1 Hispanic/Latino), 17 international. Average age 35. 75 applicants, 84% accepted, 42 enrolled. In 2011, 34 master's awarded. *Degree requirements:* For master's, thesis optional. *Entrance requirements:* For master's, GRE General Test or MAT. Additional exam requirements/recommendations for international students: Required—TOEFL (minimum score 577 paper-based; 90 iBT), IELTS (minimum score 7). *Application deadline:* For fall admission, 6/1 for domestic students; for spring admission, 10/1 for domestic students. Applications are processed on a rolling basis. Application fee: $75. *Financial support:* In 2011–12, 7 teaching assistantships were awarded; research assistantships, institutionally sponsored loans, and tuition waivers (partial) also available. Support available to part-time students. Financial award application deadline: 6/30; financial award applicants required to submit FAFSA. *Faculty research:* Positive and negative mood states in parents of twins, effect of a care path on chronic obstructive pulmonary disease home care. *Unit head:* Dr. Carol Savrin, Director, 216-368-5304, Fax: 216-368-3542, E-mail: cls18@case.edu. *Application contact:* Donna Hassik, Admissions Coordinator, 216-368-5253, Fax: 216-368-0124, E-mail: dmh7@case.edu. Web site: http://fpb.cwru.edu/MSN/majors.shtm.

Cedarville University, Graduate Programs, Cedarville, OH 45314-0601. Offers family nurse practitioner (MSN); global health nursing (MSN); nurse educator (MSN); teacher leader (M Ed). Part-time programs available. *Faculty:* 27 part-time/adjunct (14 women). *Students:* 13 full-time (11 women), 66 part-time (51 women), 2 international. Average age 33. 65 applicants, 83% accepted, 38 enrolled. In 2011, 2 master's awarded. *Degree requirements:* For master's, thesis. *Entrance requirements:* For master's, GRE, 2 professional recommendations. Additional exam requirements/recommendations for international students: Required—TOEFL (minimum score 550 paper-based; 80 iBT). *Application deadline:* For fall admission, 5/1 priority date for domestic students, 5/1 for international students; for spring admission, 11/1 priority date for domestic students, 11/1 for international students. Applications are processed on a rolling basis. Application fee: $30. Electronic applications accepted. *Financial support:* Scholarships/grants and unspecified assistantships available. Support available to part-time students. Financial award applicants required to submit FAFSA. *Unit head:* Dr. Andrew A. Runyan, Senior Associate Academic Vice-President/Dean of Graduate Studies, 937-766-3840, E-mail: arunyan@cedarville.edu. *Application contact:* Roscoe F. Smith, Associate Vice-President of Enrollment, 937-766-7700, Fax: 937-766-7575, E-mail: smithr@cedarville.edu. Web site: http://www.cedarville.edu/academics/graduate/.

Clarion University of Pennsylvania, Office of Graduate Programs, Master of Science in Nursing Program, Clarion, PA 16214. Offers family nurse practitioner (MSN, Post-Master's Certificate); nurse educator (MSN). Program offered jointly with Slippery Rock University of Pennsylvania. *Accreditation:* NLN. *Students:* 3 full-time (2 women), 60 part-time (59 women); includes 2 minority (both Black or African American, non-Hispanic/Latino). Average age 39. In 2011, 25 master's awarded. *Degree requirements:* For master's, comprehensive exam, thesis. *Entrance requirements:* For master's, minimum QPA of 2.75. Additional exam requirements/recommendations for international students: Required—TOEFL (minimum score 550 paper-based; 213 computer-based; 80 iBT). *Application deadline:* For fall admission, 6/1 for domestic students, 4/15 for international students; for spring admission, 11/1 for domestic students, 9/15 for international students. Application fee: $30. *Expenses:* Tuition, state resident: part-time $429 per credit. Tuition, nonresident: part-time $644 per credit. *Financial support:* Research assistantships with full tuition reimbursements available. Financial award application deadline: 3/1. *Unit head:* Dr. Debbie Ciesielka, Graduate Coordinator, 412-578-7277, E-mail: dciesielka@clarion.edu. *Application contact:* Dr. Brenda Sanders Dede, Assistant Vice President for Academic Affairs, 814-393-2337, Fax: 814-393-2030, E-mail: bdede@clarion.edu.

Clarke University, Department of Nursing and Health, Dubuque, IA 52001-3198. Offers administration of nursing systems (MSN); advanced practice nursing (MSN); education (MSN); family nurse practitioner (MSN, PMC). *Accreditation:* AACN. Part-time programs available. *Faculty:* 5 full-time (all women), 2 part-time/adjunct (1 woman). *Students:* 42 full-time (41 women), 25 part-time (all women); includes 1 minority (Black or African American, non-Hispanic/Latino). Average age 35. In 2011, 13 master's awarded. *Entrance requirements:* For master's, GRE General Test or MAT, BSN, minimum GPA of 3.0. *Application deadline:* For fall admission, 2/15 priority date for domestic students; for spring admission, 12/15 priority date for domestic students. Applications are processed on a rolling basis. Application fee: $25. Electronic applications accepted. *Expenses: Tuition:* Part-time $690 per credit hour. *Required fees:* $35 per credit hour. Tuition and fees vary according to program and student level. *Financial support:* In 2011–12, 6 students received support. Career-related internships or fieldwork available. Support available to part-time students. Financial award applicants required to submit FAFSA. *Faculty research:* Narrative pedagogy, ethics, end-of-life care, pedagogy, family systems. *Unit head:* Dr. Susan DeCrane, Chair, 800-224-2736, Fax: 319-584-8684. *Application contact:* Carrie Kirk, Information Contact, 563-588-6635, Fax: 563-588-6789, E-mail: graduate@clarke.edu. Web site: http://www.clarke.edu/.

Clarkson College, Master of Science in Nursing Program, Omaha, NE 68131. Offers adult nurse practitioner (MSN, Post-Master's Certificate); family nurse practitioner (MSN, Post-Master's Certificate); nursing education (MSN, Post-Master's Certificate); nursing health care leadership (MSN, Post-Master's Certificate). *Accreditation:* AANA/CANAEP; NLN. Part-time and evening/weekend programs available. Postbaccalaureate distance learning degree programs offered (minimal on-campus study). *Degree requirements:* For master's, on-campus skills assessment (family nurse practitioner, adult nurse practitioner), comprehensive exam or thesis. *Entrance requirements:* For master's, minimum GPA of 3.0, 2 references, resume. Additional exam requirements/recommendations for international students: Required—TOEFL (minimum score 600 paper-based; 250 computer-based; 100 iBT). Electronic applications accepted.

College of Mount Saint Vincent, School of Professional and Continuing Studies, Department of Nursing, Riverdale, NY 10471-1093. Offers adult nurse practitioner (MSN, PMC); family nurse practitioner (MSN, PMC); nurse educator (PMC); nursing administration (MSN); nursing for the adult and aged (MSN). *Accreditation:* AACN. Part-time programs available. *Entrance requirements:* For master's, BSN, interview, RN license, minimum GPA of 3.0, letters of reference. Additional exam requirements/recommendations for international students: Required—TOEFL. *Expenses:* Contact institution.

The College of New Rochelle, Graduate School, Program in Nursing, New Rochelle, NY 10805-2308. Offers acute care nurse practitioner (MS, Certificate); clinical specialist in holistic nursing (MS, Certificate); family nurse practitioner (MS, Certificate); nursing and health care management (MS); nursing education (Certificate). *Accreditation:* AACN. Part-time programs available. *Entrance requirements:* For master's, GRE General Test or MAT, BSN, malpractice insurance, minimum GPA of 3.0, RN license. *Expenses:* Contact institution. *Faculty research:* Holistic modalities, academic success variables.

Columbia University, School of Nursing, Program in Family Nurse Practitioner, New York, NY 10032. Offers MS, Adv C. *Accreditation:* AACN. Part-time programs available. *Entrance requirements:* For master's, GRE General Test, BSN, 1 year of clinical experience (preferred); for Adv C, MSN. Electronic applications accepted.

Concordia University Wisconsin, Graduate Programs, School of Human Services, Program in Nursing, Mequon, WI 53097-2402. Offers family nurse practitioner (MSN); geriatric nurse practitioner (MSN); nurse educator (MSN). *Accreditation:* AACN. Postbaccalaureate distance learning degree programs offered (minimal on-campus study). *Faculty:* 2 full-time (1 woman), 5 part-time/adjunct (all women). *Students:* 84 full-time (77 women), 359 part-time (347 women); includes 52 minority (20 Black or African American, non-Hispanic/Latino; 2 American Indian or Alaska Native, non-Hispanic/Latino; 11 Asian, non-Hispanic/Latino; 9 Hispanic/Latino; 10 Two or more races, non-Hispanic/Latino), 1 international. Average age 36. In 2011, 37 master's awarded. *Degree requirements:* For master's, comprehensive exam, thesis or alternative. *Entrance requirements:* Additional exam requirements/recommendations for international students: Required—TOEFL. *Application deadline:* For fall admission, 8/1 priority date for domestic students. Applications are processed on a rolling basis. Application fee: $35. *Expenses:* Contact institution. *Financial support:* Application deadline: 8/1. *Unit head:* Dr. Ruth Gresley, Director, 262-243-4452, E-mail: ruth.gresley@cuw.edu. *Application contact:* Mary Eberhardt, Graduate Admissions, 262-243-4551, Fax: 262-243-4428, E-mail: mary.eberhardt@cuw.edu.

Coppin State University, Division of Graduate Studies, Helene Fuld School of Nursing, Baltimore, MD 21216-3698. Offers family nurse practitioner (PMC); nursing (MSN). *Accreditation:* AACN; NLN. Part-time and evening/weekend programs available. *Degree requirements:* For master's, comprehensive exam, thesis, clinical internship. *Entrance requirements:* For master's, GRE, bachelor's degree in nursing, interview, minimum GPA of 3.0, RN license. Additional exam requirements/recommendations for international students: Required—TOEFL (minimum score 550 paper-based).

Cox College, Programs in Nursing, Springfield, MO 65802. Offers clinical nurse leader (MSN); family nurse practitioner (MSN); nurse educator (MSN). *Accreditation:* AACN. *Entrance requirements:* For master's, RN license, essay, 2 letters of recommendation, official transcripts. Electronic applications accepted.

Delta State University, Graduate Programs, School of Nursing, Cleveland, MS 38733-0001. Offers family nurse practitioner (MSN); nurse administrator (MSN); nurse educator (MSN). *Accreditation:* AACN. Part-time programs available. *Degree requirements:* For master's, thesis optional. *Entrance requirements:* For master's, GRE General Test. Electronic applications accepted. *Expenses:* Tuition, state resident: full-time $4702; part-time $294 per credit hour. Tuition, nonresident: full-time $12,516; part-time $760 per credit hour. *Required fees:* $586.

DePaul University, College of Science and Health, Department of Nursing, Chicago, IL 60614. Offers adult nurse practitioner (Certificate); adult nursing (MS); family nurse practitioner (Certificate); family nursing (MS); generalist nursing (MS); nurse anesthesia (MS); MS/DNP. MS in nurse anesthesia offered jointly with Ravenswood Hospital Medical Center. *Accreditation:* AACN; AANA/CANAEP (one or more programs are accredited). *Faculty:* 13 full-time (11 women), 12 part-time/adjunct (11 women). *Students:* 256 full-time (220 women), 53 part-time (48 women); includes 81 minority (15 Black or African American, non-Hispanic/Latino; 1 American Indian or Alaska Native, non-Hispanic/Latino; 39 Asian, non-Hispanic/Latino; 16 Hispanic/Latino; 5 Native Hawaiian or other Pacific Islander, non-Hispanic/Latino; 5 Two or more races, non-Hispanic/Latino), 5 international. Average age 29. 238 applicants, 46% accepted, 74 enrolled. In 2011, 70 master's awarded. Terminal master's awarded for partial

completion of doctoral program. *Degree requirements:* For master's, comprehensive exam (for some programs), thesis optional. *Entrance requirements:* For master's, GRE (if bachelor's GPA less than 3.2), bachelor's degree from regionally-accredited college or university; personal statement; prerequisite worksheet; resume; 2 letters of recommendation. Additional exam requirements/recommendations for international students: Required—TOEFL (minimum score 590 paper-based; 243 computer-based; 96 iBT), IELTS (minimum score 7.5), Pearson Test of English. *Application deadline:* For fall admission, 3/1 priority date for domestic students, 3/1 for international students; for winter admission, 8/15 priority date for domestic students, 8/15 for international students. Application fee: $40. Electronic applications accepted. *Financial support:* In 2011–12, 5 students received support, including 6 fellowships (averaging $1,500 per year); traineeships also available. Financial award applicants required to submit FAFSA. *Faculty research:* Children's health, women's health, health promotion. *Unit head:* Dr. Kim Amer, Interim Chair, 773-325-1160, E-mail: kamer@depaul.edu. *Application contact:* Ann Spittle, Director of Graduate Admissions, 773-325-7315, Fax: 312-476-3244, E-mail: graddepaul@depaul.edu.

DeSales University, Graduate Division, Division of Healthcare and Natural Sciences, Center Valley, PA 18034-9568. Offers adult advanced practice nurse specialist (MSN); certified nurse midwives (MSN); certified nurse practitioners (MSN); clinical leadership (DNP); family nurse practitioner (MSN); nurse educator (MSN); nurse practitioner (Post-Master's Certificate); MSN/MBA. *Accreditation:* NLN. Part-time programs available. *Degree requirements:* For master's, thesis optional. *Entrance requirements:* For master's, GRE General Test, MAT, minimum B average in undergraduate course work, health assessment course or equivalent, course work in statistics. Additional exam requirements/recommendations for international students: Required—TOEFL. *Application deadline:* Applications are processed on a rolling basis. Application fee: $35. Electronic applications accepted. Tuition and fees vary according to degree level. *Financial support:* Applicants required to submit FAFSA. *Unit head:* Dr. Carol Gullo Mest, Director, 610-282-1100 Ext. 1394, Fax: 610-282-2091, E-mail: carol.mest@desales.edu. *Application contact:* Caryn Stopper, Director of Graduate Admissions, 610-282-1100 Ext. 1768, Fax: 610-282-2254, E-mail: caryn.stopper@desales.edu.

Dominican College, Division of Nursing, Department of Nursing, Orangeburg, NY 10962-1210. Offers family nurse practitioner (MSN). *Accreditation:* AACN. Part-time and evening/weekend programs available. *Degree requirements:* For master's, guided research project, 750 hours clinical practice with a final written project. *Entrance requirements:* For master's, bachelor's degree in nursing, minimum GPA of 3.0, RN license, 1 year of nursing experience, 3 letters of recommendation. Additional exam requirements/recommendations for international students: Required—TOEFL (minimum score 550 paper-based; 213 computer-based).

Drexel University, College of Nursing and Health Professions, Division of Graduate Nursing, Philadelphia, PA 19104-2875. Offers adult acute care (MSN); adult psychiatric/mental health (MSN); advanced practice nursing (MSN); clinical trials research (MSN); family nurse practitioner (MSN); leadership in health systems management (MSN); nursing education (MSN); pediatric primary care (MSN); women's health (MSN). *Accreditation:* AACN; NLN. Electronic applications accepted.

Duke University, School of Nursing, Durham, NC 27708-0586. Offers adult acute care (Certificate); adult cardiovascular (Certificate); adult oncology (Certificate); adult primary care (Certificate); clinical nurse specialist (MSN), including adult oncology, gerontology, neonatal, pediatric; clinical research management (MSN, Certificate); family (Certificate); gerontology (Certificate); health and nursing ministries (MSN, Certificate); health systems leadership and outcomes (Certificate); neonatal (Certificate); neonatal/pediatric in rural health (MSN, Certificate); nurse anesthetist (MSN, Certificate); nurse practitioner (MSN), including adult acute care, adult cardiovascular, adult oncology, adult primary care, family, gerontology, neonatal, pediatric, pediatric acute care; nursing (DNP, PhD); nursing and healthcare leadership (MSN); nursing education (MSN); nursing informatics (MSN, Certificate); pediatric (Certificate); pediatric acute care (Certificate); MBA/MSN; MSN/MCM. *Accreditation:* AACN; AANA/CANAEP. Part-time and evening/weekend programs available. Postbaccalaureate distance learning degree programs offered (minimal on-campus study). *Faculty:* 56 full-time (47 women), 2 part-time/adjunct (1 woman). *Students:* 127 full-time (108 women), 395 part-time (358 women); includes 92 minority (42 Black or African American, non-Hispanic/Latino; 3 American Indian or Alaska Native, non-Hispanic/Latino; 21 Asian, non-Hispanic/Latino; 14 Hispanic/Latino; 12 Two or more races, non-Hispanic/Latino), 10 international. Average age 36. 432 applicants, 45% accepted, 143 enrolled. In 2011, 117 master's, 29 doctorates, 32 other advanced degrees awarded. Terminal master's awarded for partial completion of doctoral program. *Degree requirements:* For master's, thesis optional; for doctorate, capstone project. *Entrance requirements:* For master's, GRE General Test, 1 year of nursing experience, BSN, minimum GPA of 3.0, previous course work in statistics; for doctorate, BSN or MSN, minimum GPA of 3.0, portfolio; for Certificate, MSN. Additional exam requirements/recommendations for international students: Required—TOEFL (minimum score 550 paper-based; 213 computer-based). *Application deadline:* For fall admission, 12/1 for domestic and international students; for spring admission, 5/1 for domestic and international students. Application fee: $50. Electronic applications accepted. *Expenses:* Contact institution. *Financial support:* Career-related internships or fieldwork, institutionally sponsored loans, scholarships/grants, traineeships, and tuition waivers (partial) available. Support available to part-time students. Financial award application deadline: 4/1; financial award applicants required to submit FAFSA. *Faculty research:* Cardiovascular disease, caregiver skill training, data mining, prostate cancer, neonatal immune system. *Total annual research expenditures:* $4.7 million. *Unit head:* Dr. Catherine L. Gilliss, Dean/Vice Chancellor for Nursing Affairs, 919-684-9444, Fax: 919-684-9414, E-mail: gilli025@mc.duke.edu. *Application contact:* Bebe T. Mills, Director of Admissions, 919-684-9151, Fax: 919-668-4693, E-mail: mills031@mc.duke.edu. Web site: http://www.nursing.duke.edu/.

Duquesne University, School of Nursing, Master of Science in Nursing Program, Pittsburgh, PA 15282-0001. Offers family nurse practitioner (MSN); forensic nursing (MSN); nursing education (MSN). *Accreditation:* AACN. Part-time and evening/weekend programs available. Postbaccalaureate distance learning degree programs offered (minimal on-campus study). *Faculty:* 18 full-time (16 women), 4 part-time/adjunct (all women). *Students:* 57 full-time (55 women), 48 part-time (47 women); includes 13 minority (7 Black or African American, non-Hispanic/Latino; 3 Asian, non-Hispanic/Latino; 1 Hispanic/Latino; 2 Two or more races, non-Hispanic/Latino), 1 international. Average age 34. 72 applicants, 74% accepted, 39 enrolled. In 2011, 38 degrees awarded. *Degree requirements:* For master's, culminating paper. *Entrance requirements:* For master's, current RN license; BSN with minimum GPA of 3.0; minimum of 1 year full-time work experience as RN prior to registration in clinical or specialty course. Additional exam requirements/recommendations for international students: Required—TOEFL (minimum score 600 paper-based; 80 iBT). *Application deadline:* For fall admission, 3/1 for domestic and international students. Application fee: $0. Electronic applications accepted. *Expenses: Tuition:* Full-time $16,596; part-time $922 per credit. *Required fees:* $1584; $88 per credit. Tuition and fees vary according to program. *Financial support:* In 2011–12, 36 students received support, including 7 research assistantships with partial tuition reimbursements available (averaging $1,170 per year), 2 teaching assistantships with partial tuition reimbursements available (averaging $1,170 per year); institutionally sponsored loans, scholarships/grants, traineeships, and tuition waivers (partial) also available. Support available to part-time students. Financial award application deadline: 7/1; financial award applicants required to submit FAFSA. *Faculty research:* Vulnerable populations, social justice, cultural competence, health disparities, wellness within chronic illness. *Unit head:* Dr. Joan Such Lockhart, Professor and Associate Dean of Academic Affairs, 412-396-6540, Fax: 412-396-1821, E-mail: lockhart@duq.edu. *Application contact:* Susan Hardner, Nurse Recruiter, 412-396-4945, Fax: 412-396-6346, E-mail: nursing@duq.edu. Web site: http://www.nursing.duq.edu.

Duquesne University, School of Nursing, Post Master's Certificate Program, Pittsburgh, PA 15282-0001. Offers family nurse practitioner (Post-Master's Certificate); forensic nursing (Post-Master's Certificate); nursing education (Post-Master's Certificate); transcultural/international nursing (Post-Master's Certificate). Part-time and evening/weekend programs available. Postbaccalaureate distance learning degree programs offered (minimal on-campus study). *Faculty:* 11 full-time (10 women), 3 part-time/adjunct (all women). *Students:* 5 full-time (all women), 7 part-time (all women); includes 1 minority (Black or African American, non-Hispanic/Latino). Average age 39. 17 applicants, 71% accepted, 9 enrolled. In 2011, 2 degrees awarded. *Entrance requirements:* For degree, current RN license, BSN, MSN. Additional exam requirements/recommendations for international students: Required—TOEFL (minimum score 600 paper-based; 80 iBT). *Application deadline:* For fall admission, 3/1 for domestic and international students. Application fee: $0. *Expenses: Tuition:* Full-time $16,596; part-time $922 per credit. *Required fees:* $1584; $88 per credit. Tuition and fees vary according to program. *Financial support:* In 2011–12, 5 students received support, including 2 teaching assistantships with partial tuition reimbursements available (averaging $1,170 per year); institutionally sponsored loans, scholarships/grants, traineeships, and tuition waivers (partial) also available. Support available to part-time students. Financial award application deadline: 7/1; financial award applicants required to submit FAFSA. *Faculty research:* Vulnerable populations, social justice, cultural competence, health disparities, wellness within chronic illness. *Unit head:* Dr. Joan Such Lockhart, Professor and Associate Dean of Academic Affairs, 412-396-6540, Fax: 412-396-1821, E-mail: lockhart@duq.edu. *Application contact:* Susan Hardner, Nurse Recruiter, 412-396-4945, Fax: 412-396-6346, E-mail: nursing@duq.edu. Web site: http://www.duq.edu/nursing/post-masters-certificates/index.cfm.

D'Youville College, School of Nursing, Buffalo, NY 14201-1084. Offers community health nursing/education (MSN); community health nursing/management (MSN); family nurse practitioner (MS, Post-Master's Certificate); nursing and health-related professions (Certificate); nursing with clinical focus choice (MSN). *Accreditation:* AACN. Part-time programs available. *Faculty:* 7 full-time (all women), 7 part-time/adjunct (6 women). *Students:* 78 full-time (72 women), 133 part-time (117 women); includes 33 minority (23 Black or African American, non-Hispanic/Latino; 2 American Indian or Alaska Native, non-Hispanic/Latino; 1 Asian, non-Hispanic/Latino; 6 Hispanic/Latino; 1 Two or more races, non-Hispanic/Latino), 86 international. Average age 35. 226 applicants, 39% accepted, 57 enrolled. In 2011, 54 master's, 1 other advanced degree awarded. *Degree requirements:* For master's, thesis or alternative, membership on board of community agency, publishable paper. *Entrance requirements:* For master's, BS in nursing, minimum GPA of 3.0, course work in statistics and computers. Additional exam requirements/recommendations for international students: Required—TOEFL (minimum score 500 paper-based; 173 computer-based). *Application deadline:* For fall admission, 5/1 for international students; for spring admission, 9/1 for international students. Applications are processed on a rolling basis. Application fee: $25. Electronic applications accepted. *Expenses: Tuition:* Full-time $18,960; part-time $790 per credit hour. *Required fees:* $310. Tuition and fees vary according to degree level and program. *Financial support:* Federal Work-Study, scholarships/grants, traineeships, and unspecified assistantships available. Support available to part-time students. Financial award application deadline: 3/1; financial award applicants required to submit FAFSA. *Faculty research:* Nursing curriculum, nursing theory-testing, wellness research, communication and socialization patterns. *Unit head:* Dr. Eileen Nahigian, Chair, 716-829-7856, Fax: 716-829-8159. *Application contact:* Linda Fisher, Graduate Admissions Director, 716-829-8400, Fax: 716-829-7900, E-mail: graduateadmissions@dyc.edu.

See Display on page 629 and Close-Up on page 795.

Eastern Kentucky University, The Graduate School, College of Health Sciences, Department of Nursing, Richmond, KY 40475-3102. Offers rural community health care (MSN); rural health family nurse practitioner (MSN). *Accreditation:* AACN. *Entrance requirements:* For master's, GRE General Test, minimum GPA of 2.75.

East Tennessee State University, School of Graduate Studies, College of Nursing, Certificate Nursing Programs, Johnson City, TN 37614. Offers family nurse practitioner (Post-Master's Certificate); health care management (Postbaccalaureate Certificate). Part-time programs available. Postbaccalaureate distance learning degree programs offered (no on-campus study). *Students:* 2 full-time (1 woman), 20 part-time (15 women); includes 4 minority (3 Black or African American, non-Hispanic/Latino; 1 Hispanic/Latino), 1 international. 21 applicants, 62% accepted, 13 enrolled. In 2011, 10 Post-Master's Certificates awarded. *Degree requirements:* For other advanced degree, practical experience. *Entrance requirements:* For degree, minimum of GPA of 2.5, 3 letters of recommendation; RN license (nursing post-master's certificate). Additional exam requirements/recommendations for international students: Required—TOEFL. *Application deadline:* For fall admission, 2/1 for domestic and international students; for spring admission, 7/1 for domestic and international students. Application fee: $35 ($45 for international students). Electronic applications accepted. *Expenses:* Tuition, state resident: full-time $7312; part-time $350 per credit hour. Tuition, nonresident: full-time $18,490; part-time $621 per credit hour. *Required fees:* $63 per credit hour. Tuition and fees vary according to course load and program. *Faculty research:* Rural primary care, healthcare for the homeless and underserved, community health problems across the lifespan, nursing education research, school health services. *Unit head:* Dr. Nancy Cameron, Graduate Program Coordinator, 423-439-4874, Fax: 423-439-4100, E-mail: camerong@etsu.edu. *Application contact:* Linda Raines, Graduate Specialist, 423-439-6158, Fax: 423-439-5624, E-mail: raineslt@etsu.edu.

East Tennessee State University, School of Graduate Studies, College of Nursing, Doctoral Nursing Programs, Johnson City, TN 37614. Offers adult/gerontological nurse practitioner (DNP); executive leadership in nursing (DNP); family nurse practitioner (DNP); nursing (PhD); psychiatric/mental health nurse practitioner (DNP). Part-time and evening/weekend programs available. *Students:* 22 full-time (21 women), 27 part-time (26 women); includes 3 minority (2 Black or African American, non-Hispanic/Latino; 1 Asian, non-Hispanic/Latino). 74 applicants, 41% accepted, 30 enrolled. In 2011, 3 doctorates awarded. *Degree requirements:* For doctorate, comprehensive exam, dissertation (PhD); residency internship and capstone project (DNP). *Entrance requirements:* For doctorate, GRE General Test, minimum GPA of 3.0, RN license, minimum two years RN experience, 3 letters of recommendation, interview, writing sample, resume. Additional exam requirements/recommendations for international students: Required—TOEFL (minimum score 600 paper-based; 250 computer-based; 100 iBT). *Application deadline:* For fall admission, 2/1 for domestic and international students; for spring admission, 7/1 for domestic and international students. Application fee: $35 ($45 for international students). Electronic applications accepted. *Expenses:*

Family Nurse Practitioner Studies

Tuition, state resident: full-time $7312; part-time $350 per credit hour. Tuition, nonresident: full-time $18,490; part-time $621 per credit hour. *Required fees:* $63 per credit hour. Tuition and fees vary according to course load and program. *Financial support:* In 2011–12, 2 students received support, including 1 research assistantship with partial tuition reimbursement available (averaging $3,000 per year); career-related internships or fieldwork, institutionally sponsored loans, scholarships/grants, and unspecified assistantships also available. Financial award application deadline: 7/1; financial award applicants required to submit FAFSA. *Faculty research:* Rural primary care, healthcare for the homeless and underserved, community health problems across the lifespan, nursing education research, school health services. *Unit head:* Dr. Kathleen Rayman, Director of Graduate Programs, 423-439-5626, Fax: 423-439-4100, E-mail: raymank@etsu.edu. *Application contact:* Linda Raines, Graduate Specialist, 423-439-6158, Fax: 423-439-5624, E-mail: raineslt@etsu.edu.

Emory University, Nell Hodgson Woodruff School of Nursing, Atlanta, GA 30322-1100. Offers adult nurse practitioner (MSN); emergency nurse practitioner (MSN); family nurse practitioner (MSN); family nurse-midwife (MSN); health systems leadership (MSN); nurse-midwifery (MSN); pediatric nurse practitioner acute and primary care (MSN); women's health care (Title X) (MSN); women's health nurse practitioner (MSN); women's health/adult health nurse practitioner (MSN); MSN/MPH. *Accreditation:* AACN; ACNM/ACME (one or more programs are accredited). Part-time programs available. *Faculty:* 30 full-time (29 women), 11 part-time/adjunct (10 women). *Students:* 110 full-time (106 women), 53 part-time (51 women); includes 49 minority (35 Black or African American, non-Hispanic/Latino; 2 American Indian or Alaska Native, non-Hispanic/Latino; 10 Asian, non-Hispanic/Latino; 2 Hispanic/Latino), 4 international. Average age 32. 182 applicants, 63% accepted, 86 enrolled. In 2011, 81 master's awarded. *Entrance requirements:* For master's, GRE General Test or MAT, minimum GPA of 3.0, BS in nursing from an accredited institution, RN license and additional course work, 3 letters of recommendation. Additional exam requirements/recommendations for international students: Required—TOEFL (minimum score 600 paper-based; 100 iBT). *Application deadline:* For fall admission, 1/15 priority date for domestic students, 1/15 for international students; for spring admission, 10/1 priority date for domestic students, 10/1 for international students. Applications are processed on a rolling basis. Application fee: $50. Electronic applications accepted. *Expenses:* Contact institution. *Financial support:* In 2011–12, 14 fellowships (averaging $28,000 per year) were awarded; career-related internships or fieldwork, Federal Work-Study, institutionally sponsored loans, and scholarships/grants also available. Support available to part-time students. Financial award application deadline: 3/1; financial award applicants required to submit CSS PROFILE or FAFSA. *Faculty research:* Older adult falls and injuries, minority health issues, cardiac symptoms and quality of life, bio-ethics and decision-making, menopausal issues. *Unit head:* Dr. Linda McCauley, Dean, 404-727-7976, Fax: 404-727-9800, E-mail: linda.mccauley@emory.edu. Web site: http://www.nursing.emory.edu/.

Fairfield University, School of Nursing, Fairfield, CT 06824-5195. Offers clinical nurse leader (MSN); family nurse practitioner (MSN, DNP); nurse anesthesia (DNP); psychiatric nurse practitioner (MSN, DNP). *Accreditation:* AACN; AANA/CANAEP. Part-time programs available. *Faculty:* 15 full-time (all women). *Students:* 17 full-time (15 women), 145 part-time (127 women); includes 14 minority (6 Black or African American, non-Hispanic/Latino; 1 American Indian or Alaska Native, non-Hispanic/Latino; 4 Asian, non-Hispanic/Latino; 3 Hispanic/Latino), 1 international. Average age 38. 97 applicants, 29% accepted, 24 enrolled. In 2011, 24 master's awarded. *Degree requirements:* For master's, capstone project. *Entrance requirements:* For master's, minimum QPA of 3.0, RN license, resume, 2 recommendations; for doctorate, GRE (nurse anesthesia applicants only), MSN (minimum QPA of 3.2) or BSN (minimum QPA of 3.0); critical care nursing experience (for nurse anesthesia DNP candidates). Additional exam requirements/recommendations for international students: Required—TOEFL (minimum score 550 paper-based; 213 computer-based; 80 iBT) or IELTS (minimum score 6.5). *Application deadline:* For fall admission, 5/15 for international students; for spring admission, 10/15 for international students. Applications are processed on a rolling basis. Application fee: $60. Electronic applications accepted. *Expenses:* Contact institution. *Financial support:* In 2011–12, 2 students received support. Unspecified assistantships available. Financial award applicants required to submit FAFSA. *Faculty research:* Care of older adults, palliative care, spirituality and innovative partnerships, diabetes. *Unit head:* Dr. Suzanne Campbell, Dean, 203-254-4000 Ext. 2701, Fax: 203-254-4126, E-mail: scampbell@fairfield.edu. *Application contact:* Marianne Gumpper, Director of Graduate and Continuing Studies Admission, 203-254-4184, Fax: 203-254-4073, E-mail: gradadmis@fairfield.edu. Web site: http://www.fairfield.edu/son/son_grad_1.html.

Felician College, Program in Nursing, Lodi, NJ 07644-2117. Offers adult nurse practitioner (MSN, PMC); family nurse practitioner (MSN, PMC); nursing (MSN); nursing education (MSN). *Accreditation:* AACN. Part-time and evening/weekend programs available. Postbaccalaureate distance learning degree programs offered (no on-campus study). *Students:* 4 full-time (all women), 74 part-time (64 women); includes 18 minority (10 Black or African American, non-Hispanic/Latino; 5 Asian, non-Hispanic/Latino; 3 Hispanic/Latino). Average age 42. 29 applicants, 90% accepted, 24 enrolled. *Degree requirements:* For master's, scholarly project. *Entrance requirements:* For master's, BS in nursing or equivalent, minimum GPA of 3.0, 2 letters of recommendation, RN license; for PMC, RN license, minimum GPA of 2.75. Additional exam requirements/recommendations for international students: Recommended—TOEFL (minimum score 550 paper-based; 213 computer-based). *Application deadline:* Applications are processed on a rolling basis. Application fee: $40. *Expenses: Tuition:* Part-time $925 per credit. *Required fees:* $262.50 per semester. Part-time tuition and fees vary according to class time and student level. *Financial support:* In 2011–12, 10 students received support. Traineeships available. Financial award applicants required to submit FAFSA. *Faculty research:* Anxiety and fear, curriculum innovation, health promotion. *Unit head:* Dr. Muriel Shore, Dean, Division of Health Sciences, 201-559-6030, E-mail: shorem@felician.edu. *Application contact:* Elizabeth Barca, Senior Assistant Director, Graduate Admissions, 201-559-6077, Fax: 201-559-6138, E-mail: graduate@felician.edu.

See Display on page 630 and Close-Up on page 797.

Florida Southern College, Program in Nursing, Lakeland, FL 33801-5698. Offers clinical nurse specialist (MSN); nurse educator (MSN); nurse practitioner (MSN). *Accreditation:* AACN. Part-time and evening/weekend programs available. *Entrance requirements:* For master's, Florida RN license, 3 letters of recommendation, personal statement, minimum GPA of 3.0, resume. Additional exam requirements/recommendations for international students: Required—TOEFL (minimum score 550 paper-based). *Expenses:* Contact institution. *Faculty research:* End of life care, dementia, health promotion.

Florida State University, The Graduate School, College of Nursing, Tallahassee, FL 32312. Offers family nurse practitioner (DNP); health systems leadership (DNP); nurse educator (MSN, Certificate); nurse leader (MSN); nursing leadership (Certificate, Post-Graduate Certificate). *Accreditation:* AACN. Part-time programs available. Postbaccalaureate distance learning degree programs offered (no on-campus study). *Faculty:* 13 full-time (12 women). *Students:* 24 full-time (21 women), 63 part-time (58 women); includes 15 minority (4 Black or African American, non-Hispanic/Latino; 1

Asian, non-Hispanic/Latino; 8 Hispanic/Latino; 2 Two or more races, non-Hispanic/Latino). Average age 38. 33 applicants, 100% accepted, 33 enrolled. In 2011, 9 master's, 4 doctorates awarded. *Degree requirements:* For master's, thesis optional. *Entrance requirements:* For master's, GRE General Test, MAT, minimum GPA of 3.0, BSN, Florida RN license; for doctorate, GRE General Test, MAT, minimum GPA of 3.0, BSN or MSN, Florida RN license. Additional exam requirements/recommendations for international students: Required—TOEFL (minimum score 550 paper-based). *Application deadline:* For fall admission, 7/1 for domestic and international students. Application fee: $30. Electronic applications accepted. *Expenses:* Tuition, state resident: full-time $9474; part-time $350.88 per credit hour. Tuition, nonresident: full-time $16,236; part-time $601.34 per credit hour. *Required fees:* $630 per semester. One-time fee: $20. Tuition and fees vary according to course load and campus/location. *Financial support:* In 2011–12, 75 students received support, including fellowships with partial tuition reimbursements available (averaging $6,300 per year), research assistantships with partial tuition reimbursements available (averaging $3,000 per year), 3 teaching assistantships with partial tuition reimbursements available (averaging $3,000 per year); career-related internships or fieldwork, Federal Work-Study, institutionally sponsored loans, scholarships/grants, traineeships, and tuition waivers (partial) also available. Financial award application deadline: 4/15; financial award applicants required to submit FAFSA. *Faculty research:* Distance learning, gerontology, health promotion, educational strategies, rehabilitation of brain injured patients. *Unit head:* Dr. Diane Speake, Interim Dean, 850-644-6846, Fax: 850-644-7660, E-mail: dspeake@nursing.fsu.edu. *Application contact:* Carlos G. Urrutia, Director of Student Services, 850-644-5638, Fax: 850-645-7249, E-mail: currutia@fsu.edu. Web site: http://nursing.fsu.edu/.

Frontier Nursing University, Graduate Programs, Hyden, KY 41749. Offers community-based family nurse practitioner (MSN, Post Master's Certificate); community-based nurse-midwifery education (MSN, Post Master's Certificate); community-based women?s health care nurse practitioner (MSN, Post Master's Certificate). *Accreditation:* ACNM; NLN.

Gannon University, School of Graduate Studies, Morosky College of Health Professions and Sciences, School of Health Professions, Villa Maria School of Nursing, Erie, PA 16541-0001. Offers anesthesia (MSN); business administration (MSN); family nurse practitioner (Certificate); medical-surgical nursing (MSN); nurse anesthesia (Certificate); nursing rural practitioner (MSN). *Accreditation:* AACN; AANA/CANAEP (one or more programs are accredited). Part-time and evening/weekend programs available. *Students:* 2 full-time (both women), 68 part-time (49 women); includes 3 minority (1 Black or African American, non-Hispanic/Latino; 1 American Indian or Alaska Native, non-Hispanic/Latino; 1 Hispanic/Latino). Average age 44. 15 applicants, 67% accepted, 0 enrolled. In 2011, 20 master's, 3 other advanced degrees awarded. *Degree requirements:* For master's, thesis. *Entrance requirements:* For master's, GRE General Test, degree in nursing. Additional exam requirements/recommendations for international students: Required—TOEFL (minimum score 79 iBT). *Application deadline:* For spring admission, 8/1 for domestic students. Application fee: $25. Electronic applications accepted. *Financial support:* Scholarships/grants available. Financial award application deadline: 7/1; financial award applicants required to submit FAFSA. *Faculty research:* Accurate assessment of delirium in the ICU using CAM, factors affecting caregiver fatigue in dialysis nurses, hours worked by nurses and treatment error reporting. *Unit head:* Dr. Kathleen Patterson, Director, 814-871-5547, E-mail: patterso018@gannon.edu. *Application contact:* Kara Morgan, Director of Graduate Admissions, 814-871-5831, Fax: 814-871-5827, E-mail: graduate@gannon.edu.

Georgetown University, Graduate School of Arts and Sciences, School of Nursing and Health Studies, Washington, DC 20057. Offers acute care nurse practitioner (MS); clinical nurse specialist (MS); family nurse practitioner (MS); nurse anesthesia (MS); nurse-midwifery (MS); nursing education (MS). *Accreditation:* AACN; AANA/CANAEP; ACNM/ACME. *Degree requirements:* For master's, thesis optional. *Entrance requirements:* For master's, GRE General Test or MAT, bachelor's degree in nursing from NLN-accredited school, minimum undergraduate GPA of 3.0. Additional exam requirements/recommendations for international students: Required—TOEFL.

The George Washington University, School of Nursing, Washington, DC 20052. Offers adult nurse practitioner (MSN, Post-Master's Certificate); clinical research administration (MSN); family nurse practitioner (MSN, Post-Master's Certificate); health care quality (MSN, Post-Master's Certificate); nursing (DNP); nursing leadership and management (MSN); palliative care nurse practitioner (Post-Master's Certificate). *Accreditation:* AACN. *Faculty:* 19 full-time (all women), 32 part-time/adjunct (29 women). *Students:* 27 full-time (25 women), 360 part-time (330 women); includes 89 minority (44 Black or African American, non-Hispanic/Latino; 9 American Indian or Alaska Native, non-Hispanic/Latino; 25 Asian, non-Hispanic/Latino; 11 Hispanic/Latino), 15 international. Average age 39. 287 applicants, 87% accepted, 176 enrolled. In 2011, 45 master's, 19 doctorates awarded. *Unit head:* Jean E. Johnson, Dean, 202-994-3725, E-mail: sonjej@gwumc.edu. *Application contact:* Kristin Williams, Assistant Vice President for Graduate and Special Enrollment Management, 202-994-0467, Fax: 202-994-0371, E-mail: ksw@gwu.edu. Web site: http://nursing.gwumc.edu/.

Georgia College & State University, Graduate School, College of Health Sciences, Graduate Nursing Program, Milledgeville, GA 31061. Offers adult health (MSN); family nurse practitioner (MSN); nursing administration (MSN); MSN/MBA. *Accreditation:* NLN. Part-time and evening/weekend programs available. *Students:* 10 full-time (9 women), 63 part-time (60 women); includes 16 minority (all Black or African American, non-Hispanic/Latino). Average age 36. 64 applicants, 44% accepted, 20 enrolled. In 2011, 7 master's awarded. *Degree requirements:* For master's, comprehensive exam, thesis optional. *Entrance requirements:* For master's, GMAT, GRE General Test, or MAT, bachelor's degree in nursing, RN license, 1 year clinical experience. Additional exam requirements/recommendations for international students: Recommended—TOEFL (minimum score 550 paper-based; 213 computer-based; 79 iBT). *Application deadline:* For fall admission, 7/1 priority date for domestic students; for spring admission, 4/1 priority date for domestic students. Applications are processed on a rolling basis. Application fee: $40. Electronic applications accepted. *Expenses:* Tuition, state resident: full-time $4806; part-time $267 per credit hour. Tuition, nonresident: full-time $17,802; part-time $989 per credit hour. *Required fees:* $936 per semester. Tuition and fees vary according to course load and campus/location. *Financial support:* In 2011–12, 1 research assistantship with full tuition reimbursement was awarded; unspecified assistantships also available. Financial award applicants required to submit FAFSA. *Unit head:* Dr. Judith Malachowski, Director, School of Nursing, 478-445-5122, E-mail: judith.malachowski@gcsu.edu. *Application contact:* Lora Crowe, MSN Coordinator, 478-445-5122, E-mail: lora.crowe@gcsu.edu.

Georgia Health Sciences University, College of Graduate Studies, Family Nurse Practitioner Program, Augusta, GA 30912. Offers MSN, Post-Master's Certificate. *Students:* 26 full-time (24 women), 42 part-time (39 women); includes 11 minority (8 Black or African American, non-Hispanic/Latino; 2 Asian, non-Hispanic/Latino; 1 Hispanic/Latino). Average age 34. 29 applicants, 52% accepted, 13 enrolled. In 2011, 16 master's awarded. *Entrance requirements:* For master's, GRE General Test or MAT, Georgia registered professional nurse license. Additional exam requirements/recommendations for international students: Required—TOEFL (minimum score 550

paper-based; 213 computer-based; 79 iBT). *Application deadline:* For fall admission, 2/1 for domestic and international students; for spring admission, 10/1 for domestic and international students. Application fee: $50. Electronic applications accepted. *Unit head:* Dr. Lucy Marion, Dean, 706-721-3771, Fax: 706-721-8169, E-mail: lumarion@georgiahealth.edu. *Application contact:* Karen Sturgill, Program Coordinator, 706-721-3676, Fax: 706-721-8169, E-mail: ksturgillt@georgiahealth.edu. Web site: http://www.mcg.edu/son.futurestudents.htm.

Georgia Southern University, Jack N. Averitt College of Graduate Studies, College of Health and Human Sciences, School of Nursing, Program in Nurse Practitioner, Statesboro, GA 30460. Offers MSN, Certificate. Part-time programs available. Postbaccalaureate distance learning degree programs offered. *Students:* 3 full-time (all women), 54 part-time (51 women); includes 10 minority (6 Black or African American, non-Hispanic/Latino; 1 Asian, non-Hispanic/Latino; 1 Hispanic/Latino; 1 Native Hawaiian or other Pacific Islander, non-Hispanic/Latino; 1 Two or more races, non-Hispanic/Latino). Average age 33. 58 applicants, 50% accepted, 26 enrolled. In 2011, 19 master's awarded. *Entrance requirements:* For master's, GRE General Test or MAT, minimum GPA of 3.0, Georgia nursing license, 2 years of clinical experience, CPR certification. Additional exam requirements/recommendations for international students: Required—TOEFL (minimum score 550 paper-based; 213 computer-based; 80 iBT). *Application deadline:* For fall admission, 3/1 priority date for domestic students, 3/1 for international students; for spring admission, 10/1 priority date for domestic students, 10/1 for international students. Applications are processed on a rolling basis. Application fee: $50. Electronic applications accepted. *Expenses:* Tuition, state resident: full-time $6300; part-time $263 per semester hour. Tuition, nonresident: full-time $25,174; part-time $1049 per semester hour. *Required fees:* $1872. *Financial support:* In 2011–12, 32 students received support, including research assistantships with partial tuition reimbursements available (averaging $6,850 per year), teaching assistantships with partial tuition reimbursements available (averaging $6,850 per year); career-related internships or fieldwork, Federal Work-Study, scholarships/grants, traineeships, tuition waivers (partial), and unspecified assistantships also available. Support available to part-time students. Financial award application deadline: 4/15. *Faculty research:* Vulnerable populations, breast cancer, diabetes, mellitus, advanced practice nursing issues. *Total annual research expenditures:* $25,000. *Unit head:* Dr. Deborah Allen, Graduate Program Director, 912-478-5056, Fax: 912-478-5036, E-mail: debbieallen@georgiasouthern.edu. *Application contact:* Amanda Gilliland, Coordinator for Graduate Student Recruitment, 912-478-5384, Fax: 912-478-0740, E-mail: gradadmissions@georgiasouthern.edu.

Georgia State University, College of Health and Human Sciences, Byrdine F. Lewis School of Nursing, Atlanta, GA 30302-3083. Offers adult health (MS); adult health nursing (Certificate); child health (MS); family nurse practitioner (MS, Certificate); health promotion, protection and restoration (PhD); perinatal/women's health (MS); psychiatric mental health nursing (Certificate); psychiatric/mental health (MS); women's health nursing (Certificate). *Accreditation:* AACN. Part-time and evening/weekend programs available. Postbaccalaureate distance learning degree programs offered (minimal on-campus study). *Degree requirements:* For master's, research activity; for doctorate, comprehensive exam, thesis/dissertation. *Entrance requirements:* For master's, MAT (preferred) or GRE, interview, RN license; for doctorate, GRE General Test. Additional exam requirements/recommendations for international students: Required—TOEFL (minimum score 550 paper-based; 213 computer-based). Electronic applications accepted. *Expenses:* Contact institution. *Faculty research:* Breast cancer prevention, sexually compulsive behaviors, health risks in minority youth, asthma treatment strategies, adolescent alcohol-related issues.

Goshen College, Program in Nursing, Goshen, IN 46526-4794. Offers family nurse practitioner (MSN). *Accreditation:* AACN. Part-time and evening/weekend programs available. *Faculty:* 6 full-time (all women), 4 part-time/adjunct (all women). *Students:* 27 part-time (26 women), 2 international. *Degree requirements:* For master's, comprehensive exam (for some programs). *Entrance requirements:* Additional exam requirements/recommendations for international students: Required—TOEFL (minimum score 650 paper-based; 213 computer-based; 79 iBT), IELTS (minimum score 6). *Application deadline:* Applications are processed on a rolling basis. Application fee: $50. *Expenses:* Contact institution. *Financial support:* Scholarships/grants available. Financial award applicants required to submit FAFSA. *Unit head:* Dr. Brenda Srof, Chair, 574-535-7375, E-mail: brendajs@goshen.edu. Web site: http://www.goshen.edu/nursing/masters.

Graceland University, School of Nursing, Independence, MO 64050-3434. Offers family nurse practitioner (MSN, PMC); nurse educator (MSN, PMC). Part-time programs available. Postbaccalaureate distance learning degree programs offered (minimal on-campus study). *Faculty:* 9 full-time (all women), 9 part-time/adjunct (7 women). *Students:* 197 full-time (181 women), 204 part-time (186 women); includes 14 minority (8 Black or African American, non-Hispanic/Latino; 1 American Indian or Alaska Native, non-Hispanic/Latino; 4 Asian, non-Hispanic/Latino; 1 Hispanic/Latino). Average age 40. 263 applicants, 71% accepted, 138 enrolled. In 2011, 88 master's, 2 other advanced degrees awarded. *Degree requirements:* For master's, comprehensive exam (for some programs), thesis optional. *Entrance requirements:* For master's, BSN from nationally-accredited program, portfolio, RN license, minimum GPA of 3.0. Additional exam requirements/recommendations for international students: Recommended—TOEFL. *Application deadline:* For fall admission, 6/1 priority date for domestic students; for winter admission, 10/1 priority date for domestic students; for spring admission, 3/1 priority date for domestic students. Application fee: $50. Electronic applications accepted. *Expenses:* Contact institution. *Financial support:* Institutionally sponsored loans and traineeships available. Support available to part-time students. Financial award applicants required to submit FAFSA. *Faculty research:* International nursing, family care-giving, health promotion. *Unit head:* Dr. Claudia D. Horton, Dean, 816-833-0524 Ext. 4214, Fax: 816-833-2990, E-mail: horton@graceland.edu. *Application contact:* Cara Hakes, Program Consultant, 816-833-0524 Ext. 4803, Fax: 816-833-2990, E-mail: chakes@graceland.edu. Web site: http://www.graceland.edu/nursing.

Grambling State University, School of Graduate Studies and Research, College of Professional Studies, School of Nursing, Grambling, LA 71245. Offers family nurse practitioner (MSN, PMC); nurse educator (MSN). *Accreditation:* NLN. Part-time programs available. *Degree requirements:* For master's, comprehensive exam (for some programs), thesis (for some programs). *Entrance requirements:* For master's, GRE, minimum GPA of 3.0 on last degree, interview, 2 years experience as RN. Additional exam requirements/recommendations for international students: Required—TOEFL (minimum score 500 paper-based; 173 computer-based; 61 iBT). Electronic applications accepted. *Expenses:* Tuition, state resident: full-time $3546; part-time $192 per credit hour. Tuition, nonresident: full-time $3456; part-time $192 per credit hour. *Required fees:* $1829; $1829 per semester hour.

Grand Canyon University, College of Nursing, Phoenix, AZ 85017-1097. Offers acute care nurse practitioner (MS, PMC); clinical nurse specialist (PMC), including clinical nurse specialist, education; family nurse practitioner (MS); leadership in health care systems (MS); nurse education (MS). *Accreditation:* AACN. Part-time and evening/weekend programs available. Postbaccalaureate distance learning degree programs offered (no on-campus study). *Degree requirements:* For master's and PMC, comprehensive exam (for some programs). *Entrance requirements:* For master's, minimum cumulative and science course undergraduate GPA of 3.0. Additional exam requirements/recommendations for international students: Required—TOEFL (minimum score 575 paper-based; 233 computer-based; 90 iBT), IELTS (minimum score 7).

Gwynedd-Mercy College, School of Nursing, Gwynedd Valley, PA 19437-0901. Offers clinical nurse specialist (MSN), including gerontology, oncology, pediatrics; nurse practitioner (MSN), including adult health, pediatric health. *Accreditation:* NLN. *Faculty:* 3 full-time (all women), 2 part-time/adjunct (both women). *Students:* 14 full-time (13 women), 28 part-time (25 women); includes 11 minority (4 Black or African American, non-Hispanic/Latino; 6 Asian, non-Hispanic/Latino; 1 Hispanic/Latino). Average age 40. 23 applicants, 83% accepted, 11 enrolled. In 2011, 7 master's awarded. *Degree requirements:* For master's, thesis optional. *Entrance requirements:* For master's, GRE General Test or MAT, current nursing experience, physical assessment, course work in statistics, BSN from NLNAC-accredited program, 2 letters of recommendation, personal interview. Additional exam requirements/recommendations for international students: Required—TOEFL (minimum score 575 paper-based). *Application deadline:* For fall admission, 8/1 priority date for domestic students; for winter admission, 12/1 priority date for domestic students. Applications are processed on a rolling basis. Application fee: $25. Electronic applications accepted. *Expenses:* Contact institution. *Financial support:* In 2011–12, 21 students received support. Scholarships/grants, traineeships, and unspecified assistantships available. Financial award application deadline: 8/30. *Faculty research:* Critical thinking, primary care, domestic violence, multiculturalism, nursing centers. *Unit head:* Dr. Andrea D. Hollingsworth, Dean, 215-646-7300 Ext. 539, Fax: 215-641-5517, E-mail: hollingsworth.a@gmc.edu. *Application contact:* Dr. Barbara A. Jones, Director, 215-646-7300 Ext. 407, Fax: 215-641-5564, E-mail: jones.b@gmc.edu. Web site: http://www.gmc.edu/academics/nursing/.

Hardin-Simmons University, Graduate School, Patty Hanks Shelton School of Nursing, Abilene, TX 79698-0001. Offers advanced healthcare delivery (MSN); family nurse practitioner (MSN). Programs offered jointly with Abilene Christian University and McMurry University. *Accreditation:* AACN. Part-time programs available. *Faculty:* 6 full-time (all women), 3 part-time/adjunct (all women). *Students:* 10 full-time (9 women), 7 part-time (2 women); includes 5 minority (3 Black or African American, non-Hispanic/Latino; 2 Hispanic/Latino). Average age 35. 12 applicants, 100% accepted, 11 enrolled. In 2011, 4 master's awarded. *Degree requirements:* For master's, comprehensive exam, thesis or alternative. *Entrance requirements:* For master's, GRE, minimum undergraduate GPA of 3.0 in major, 2.8 overall; interview; upper-level course work in statistics; CPR certification; letters of recommendation. Additional exam requirements/recommendations for international students: Required—TOEFL (minimum score 550 paper-based; 213 computer-based; 75 iBT). *Application deadline:* For fall admission, 8/15 priority date for domestic students, 4/1 for international students; for spring admission, 1/5 priority date for domestic students, 9/1 for international students. Applications are processed on a rolling basis. Application fee: $50. *Expenses:* Contact institution. *Financial support:* In 2011–12, 14 students received support. Career-related internships or fieldwork and scholarships/grants available. Support available to part-time students. Financial award application deadline: 6/30; financial award applicants required to submit FAFSA. *Faculty research:* Child abuse, alternative medicine, pediatric chronic disease, health promotion. *Unit head:* Dr. Amy Toone, Director, 325-671-2361, Fax: 325-671-2386, E-mail: atoone@phssn.edu. *Application contact:* Dr. Nancy Kucinski, Dean of Graduate Studies, 325-670-1298, Fax: 325-670-1564, E-mail: gradoff@hsutx.edu. Web site: http://www.phssn.edu/.

Hawai`i Pacific University, College of Nursing and Health Sciences, Honolulu, HI 96813. Offers community clinical nurse specialist (MSN); community clinical nurse specialist educator option (MSN); family nurse practitioner (MSN). *Accreditation:* NLN. Part-time and evening/weekend programs available. *Faculty:* 5 full-time (4 women), 2 part-time/adjunct (1 woman). *Students:* 45 full-time (34 women), 13 part-time (10 women); includes 38 minority (3 Black or African American, non-Hispanic/Latino; 2 American Indian or Alaska Native, non-Hispanic/Latino; 16 Asian, non-Hispanic/Latino; 6 Hispanic/Latino; 4 Native Hawaiian or other Pacific Islander, non-Hispanic/Latino; 7 Two or more races, non-Hispanic/Latino). Average age 38. 32 applicants, 78% accepted, 19 enrolled. In 2011, 11 master's awarded. *Degree requirements:* For master's, practicum, professional paper. *Entrance requirements:* For master's, bachelor's degree in nursing, minimum GPA of 3.0. Additional exam requirements/recommendations for international students: Recommended—TOEFL (minimum score 550 paper-based; 213 computer-based; 80 iBT), TWE (minimum score 5). *Application deadline:* Applications are processed on a rolling basis. Application fee: $50. Electronic applications accepted. *Expenses: Tuition:* Full-time $13,230; part-time $735 per credit. Tuition and fees vary according to course load and program. *Financial support:* In 2011–12, 11 students received support. Career-related internships or fieldwork, Federal Work-Study, scholarships/grants, traineeships, and tuition waivers available. Financial award application deadline: 3/1; financial award applicants required to submit FAFSA. *Faculty research:* Hawaiian elders, traditional healing and nursing center. *Unit head:* Dr. Patricia Burrell, Chair, Graduate and Post Baccalaureate Programs, 808-236-5813, Fax: 808-236-5818, E-mail: pburrell@hpu.edu. *Application contact:* Chad Schempp, Director of Graduate Admissions, 808-543-8035, Fax: 808-544-0280, E-mail: graduate@hpu.edu. Web site: http://www.hpu.edu/CNHS/index.html.

See Display on page 633 and Close-Up on page 799.

Holy Names University, Graduate Division, Department of Nursing, Oakland, CA 94619-1699. Offers administration/management (MS, Certificate); clinical faculty (MS, Certificate); community health nursing/case manager (MS); family nurse practitioner (MS, Certificate); MSN/Certificate; MSN/MBA. *Accreditation:* AACN. Part-time and evening/weekend programs available. *Entrance requirements:* For master's, bachelor's degree in nursing or related field, California RN license or eligibility, minimum GPA of 3.0, previous course work in research or statistics. Additional exam requirements/recommendations for international students: Required—TOEFL (minimum score 500 paper-based). *Faculty research:* Women's reproductive health, gerontology, attitudes about aging, schizophrenic families, international health issues.

Howard University, College of Nursing and Allied Health Sciences, Division of Nursing, Washington, DC 20059-0002. Offers nurse practitioner (Certificate); primary family health nursing (MSN). *Accreditation:* AACN. Part-time programs available. *Degree requirements:* For master's, comprehensive exam, thesis optional. *Entrance requirements:* For master's, RN license, minimum GPA of 3.0, BS in nursing. *Faculty research:* Urinary incontinence, breast cancer prevention, depression in the elderly, adolescent pregnancy.

Husson University, School of Graduate and Professional Studies, Graduate Nursing Program, Bangor, ME 04401-2999. Offers advanced practice psychiatric nursing (MSN, PMC); family and community nurse practitioner (MSN, PMC); nursing education (MSN, PMC). *Accreditation:* AACN. Part-time programs available. *Faculty:* 6 full-time (all women), 6 part-time/adjunct (all women). *Students:* 49 full-time (42 women), 33 part-time (29 women); includes 2 minority (1 American Indian or Alaska Native, non-Hispanic/Latino; 1 Two or more races, non-Hispanic/Latino). 18 applicants, 13 enrolled. In 2011, 25 master's awarded. *Degree requirements:* For master's, comprehensive exam (for some programs). *Entrance requirements:* For master's, MAT or GRE, BSN.

Additional exam requirements/recommendations for international students: Required—TOEFL (minimum score 550 paper-based). *Application deadline:* For fall admission, 6/30 for domestic students; for spring admission, 10/30 for domestic students. Application fee: $40. *Expenses:* Contact institution. *Financial support:* In 2011–12, 31 students received support. Federal Work-Study, institutionally sponsored loans, traineeships, and unspecified assistantships available. Financial award application deadline: 4/15; financial award applicants required to submit FAFSA. *Unit head:* Dr. Barbara Higgins, Director, Nurse Practitioner Program, 207-947-7057. *Application contact:* Kristen Card, Director of Graduate Admissions, 207-404-5660, Fax: 207-941-7935, E-mail: cardk@husson.edu.

Illinois State University, Graduate School, Mennonite College of Nursing, Normal, IL 61790. Offers family nurse practitioner (PMC); nursing (MSN, PhD). *Accreditation:* AACN. *Faculty research:* Expanding the teaching-nursing home culture in the state of Illinois, advanced education nursing traineeship program, collaborative doctoral program-caring for older adults.

Indiana University–Purdue University Indianapolis, School of Nursing, Indianapolis, IN 46202-2896. Offers acute care nurse practitioner (MSN); adult health clinical nurse specialist (MSN); adult health nursing (MSN), including adult clinical nurse specialist; adult nurse practitioner (MSN); adult psychiatric/mental health nursing (MSN); child psychiatric/mental health nursing (MSN); community health nursing (MSN); family nurse practitioner (MSN); neonatal nurse practitioner (MSN); nursing (MSN, DNP), including nursing education (MSN); nursing (MSN), including nursing administration; nursing science (PhD); pediatric clinical nurse specialist (MSN); women's health nurse practitioner (MSN); MSN/MPA; MSN/MPH. *Accreditation:* AACN; NLN (one or more programs are accredited). Part-time programs available. *Faculty:* 85 full-time (82 women), 60 part-time/adjunct (all women). *Students:* 35 full-time (32 women), 360 part-time (340 women); includes 47 minority (28 Black or African American, non-Hispanic/Latino; 9 Asian, non-Hispanic/Latino; 4 Hispanic/Latino; 1 Native Hawaiian or other Pacific Islander, non-Hispanic/Latino; 5 Two or more races, non-Hispanic/Latino), 5 international. Average age 38. 119 applicants, 76% accepted, 54 enrolled. In 2011, 89 master's, 10 doctorates awarded. Terminal master's awarded for partial completion of doctoral program. *Degree requirements:* For master's, thesis; for doctorate, thesis/dissertation. *Entrance requirements:* For master's, minimum GPA of 3.0, RN license; for doctorate, GRE General Test, minimum GPA of 3.0, MSN, RN license, graduate statistics course with minimum B grade (not older than 3 years). Additional exam requirements/recommendations for international students: Required—TOEFL. *Application deadline:* For fall admission, 2/15 for domestic students; for spring admission, 9/15 for domestic students. Application fee: $55 ($65 for international students). *Financial support:* In 2011–12, 93 students received support, including 9 fellowships with full tuition reimbursements available (averaging $7,039 per year), 7 teaching assistantships with full tuition reimbursements available (averaging $5,300 per year); research assistantships with full tuition reimbursements available, Federal Work-Study, institutionally sponsored loans, scholarships/grants, and tuition waivers (full) also available. Support available to part-time students. Financial award application deadline: 5/1. *Faculty research:* Clinical science, health systems. *Total annual research expenditures:* $3 million. *Unit head:* Associate Dean for Graduate Programs, 317-274-2806, E-mail: nursing@iupui.edu. *Application contact:* Information Contact, 317-274-2806. Web site: http://nursing.iupui.edu/.

The Johns Hopkins University, School of Nursing, Nurse Practitioner Program, Baltimore, MD 21218-2699. Offers adult acute/critical care (MSN, Certificate); adult and pediatric primary care (MSN); adult or pediatric primary care (Certificate); emergency preparedness/disaster response (Certificate); family primary care (MSN, Certificate); women's health (Certificate). *Accreditation:* AACN; NLN (one or more programs are accredited). Part-time programs available. *Degree requirements:* For master's, thesis optional, scholarly project or portfolio. *Entrance requirements:* For master's, GRE, interview, minimum GPA of 3.0, BSN, Maryland RN license. Additional exam requirements/recommendations for international students: Required—TOEFL (minimum score 550 paper-based; 213 computer-based). Electronic applications accepted. *Expenses:* Contact institution. *Faculty research:* Community outreach, primary care of underserved populations, substance-abusing individuals, childhood violence, women's health.

Kent State University, College of Nursing, Kent, OH 44242-0001. Offers acute care nurse practitioner (MSN); adult nurse practitioner (MSN); clinical nurse specialist (MSN); family nurse practitioner (MSN); geriatric nurse practitioner (MSN); health care management (MSN); nurse educator (MSN); nursing (PhD); nursing practice (DNP); pediatric nurse practitioner (MSN); psychiatric/mental health nurse practitioner (MSN); women's health nurse practitioner (MSN). PhD program offered jointly with The University of Akron. *Accreditation:* AACN. Part-time programs available. *Degree requirements:* For master's, thesis optional; for doctorate, comprehensive exam, thesis/dissertation. *Entrance requirements:* For master's, GRE (if undergraduate GPA less than 3.0), minimum GPA of 2.75; for doctorate, GRE, MSN. Additional exam requirements/recommendations for international students: Required—TOEFL. Electronic applications accepted. *Expenses:* Contact institution. *Faculty research:* Women and violence, methodological specialties, osteoporosis in women, new caregivers and the elderly.

Lincoln Memorial University, Caylor School of Nursing, Harrogate, TN 37752-1901. Offers family nurse practitioner (MSN); nurse anesthesia (MSN); psychiatric mental health nurse practitioner (MSN). *Accreditation:* AANA/CANAEP; NLN. Part-time programs available. *Entrance requirements:* For master's, GRE.

Long Island University–C. W. Post Campus, School of Health Professions and Nursing, Department of Nursing, Brookville, NY 11548-1300. Offers clinical nurse specialist (MS); family nurse practitioner (MS, Certificate). *Accreditation:* AACN. Part-time and evening/weekend programs available. *Degree requirements:* For master's, thesis. *Entrance requirements:* For master's, minimum GPA of 3.0 in major, bachelor's degree in nursing, NYS registered nurse, interview. Electronic applications accepted. *Faculty research:* Lactation/breast cancer, early discharge in maternity.

Loyola University Chicago, Graduate School, Marcella Niehoff School of Nursing, Family Nurse Practitioner Program, Chicago, IL 60660. Offers emergency (Certificate); family nurse practitioner (MSN); family practice nurse practitioner (Certificate). Part-time and evening/weekend programs available. *Students:* 10 full-time (9 women), 115 part-time (109 women); includes 31 minority (7 Black or African American, non-Hispanic/Latino; 14 Asian, non-Hispanic/Latino; 9 Hispanic/Latino; 1 Two or more races, non-Hispanic/Latino). Average age 31. 63 applicants, 49% accepted, 23 enrolled. In 2011, 9 master's awarded. *Entrance requirements:* For master's, BSN, Illinois nursing license, minimum nursing GPA of 3.0, 1000 hours experience before starting clinical. *Application deadline:* Applications are processed on a rolling basis. Application fee: $50. Electronic applications accepted. *Expenses: Tuition:* Full-time $15,660; part-time $870 per credit hour. *Required fees:* $125 per semester. Tuition and fees vary according to course load and program. *Financial support:* Traineeships available. Financial award applicants required to submit FAFSA. *Unit head:* Dr. Marijo Letizia, Associate Professor, 708-216-9325, Fax: 708-216-9555, E-mail: mletizi@luc.edu. *Application contact:* Amy Weatherford, Enrollment Advisor, School of Nursing, 773-508-3249, Fax: 773-508-3241, E-mail: aweatherford@luc.edu.

Loyola University New Orleans, College of Social Sciences, School of Nursing, New Orleans, LA 70118-6195. Offers adult nurse practitioner (MSN); family nurse practitioner (MSN); health care systems management (MSN); nursing (MSN, DNP). *Accreditation:* NLN. Part-time and evening/weekend programs available. Postbaccalaureate distance learning degree programs offered. *Students:* 108 full-time (99 women), 428 part-time (385 women); includes 151 minority (110 Black or African American, non-Hispanic/Latino; 5 American Indian or Alaska Native, non-Hispanic/Latino; 14 Asian, non-Hispanic/Latino; 20 Hispanic/Latino; 2 Native Hawaiian or other Pacific Islander, non-Hispanic/Latino). Average age 46. 213 applicants, 91% accepted, 153 enrolled. In 2011, 241 master's awarded. *Degree requirements:* For doctorate, capstone project. *Entrance requirements:* For master's, BSN, Louisiana nursing license, 1 year of work experience in clinical nursing, minimum undergraduate GPA of 2.8, interview, resume. Additional exam requirements/recommendations for international students: Required—TOEFL (minimum score 550 paper-based; 213 computer-based). *Application deadline:* For fall admission, 8/1 priority date for domestic students, 8/1 for international students; for winter admission, 12/15 priority date for domestic students, 12/15 for international students; for spring admission, 5/15 priority date for domestic students, 5/15 for international students. Applications are processed on a rolling basis. Application fee: $20. Electronic applications accepted. *Financial support:* Traineeships and Incumbent Workers Training Program grants available. Financial award application deadline: 5/1; financial award applicants required to submit FAFSA. *Faculty research:* Increasing compliance with treatment, patient satisfaction with care provided by nurse practitioners. *Unit head:* Dr. Ann H. Cary, Director, 800-488-6257, Fax: 504-865-3254, E-mail: nursing@loyno.edu. *Application contact:* Deborah Smith, Assistant to the Director, 504-865-2823, Fax: 504-865-3254, E-mail: dhsmith@loyno.edu. Web site: http://css.loyno.edu/nursing.

Malone University, Graduate Program in Nursing, Canton, OH 44709. Offers clinical nurse specialist (MSN); family nurse practitioner (MSN). *Accreditation:* AACN. Part-time and evening/weekend programs available. *Faculty:* 8 full-time (all women), 19 part-time/adjunct (17 women). *Students:* 62 part-time (52 women); includes 3 minority (1 Black or African American, non-Hispanic/Latino; 1 American Indian or Alaska Native, non-Hispanic/Latino; 1 Hispanic/Latino). Average age 36. 77 applicants, 57% accepted, 27 enrolled. In 2011, 22 master's awarded. *Degree requirements:* For master's, thesis. *Entrance requirements:* For master's, minimum GPA of 3.0 from BSN program, interview, Ohio RN license. Additional exam requirements/recommendations for international students: Required—TOEFL (minimum score 550 paper-based; 213 computer-based; 79 iBT). *Application deadline:* Applications are processed on a rolling basis. *Expenses:* Contact institution. *Financial support:* Tuition waivers (partial) available. Support available to part-time students. Financial award application deadline: 6/30. *Faculty research:* Home heath care and geriatrics, community settings, culture, Hispanics, TB, geriatrics, Neuman Systems Model, nursing education. *Unit head:* Dr. Kathleen M. Flaherty, Director, 330-471-8330, Fax: 330-471-8607, E-mail: kflaherty@malone.edu. *Application contact:* Mona McAuliffe, Recruiter/Adviser, 330-471-8623, Fax: 330-471-8343, E-mail: mmcauliffe@malone.edu. Web site: http://www.malone.edu/admissions/graduate/nursing/.

Marymount University, School of Health Professions, Program in Nursing, Arlington, VA 22207-4299. Offers family nurse practitioner (MSN, Certificate); nursing (DNP); nursing education (MSN, Certificate); RN to MSN (MSN). *Accreditation:* AACN. Part-time and evening/weekend programs available. *Faculty:* 8 full-time (all women), 3 part-time/adjunct (2 women). *Students:* 13 full-time (12 women), 65 part-time (62 women); includes 32 minority (19 Black or African American, non-Hispanic/Latino; 2 American Indian or Alaska Native, non-Hispanic/Latino; 8 Asian, non-Hispanic/Latino; 3 Hispanic/Latino), 4 international. Average age 40. 51 applicants, 57% accepted, 21 enrolled. In 2011, 26 master's, 2 other advanced degrees awarded. *Degree requirements:* For master's, comprehensive exam; for doctorate, thesis/dissertation or alternative. *Entrance requirements:* For master's, 2 letters of recommendation, interview, resume, RN license, personal statement; for doctorate, 2 letters of recommendation, interview, resume, RN license, minimum MSN GPA of 3.5 or BSN 3.3; for Certificate, interview, master's degree in nursing. Additional exam requirements/recommendations for international students: Required—TOEFL (minimum score 600 paper-based; 250 computer-based; 96 iBT), IELTS (minimum score 6.5). *Application deadline:* For fall admission, 4/1 for domestic students, 7/1 for international students; for spring admission, 9/15 for international students. Application fee: $40. Electronic applications accepted. *Expenses: Tuition:* Part-time $770 per credit hour. *Required fees:* $8 per credit hour. One-time fee: $180 full-time. *Financial support:* In 2011–12, 1 student received support. Research assistantships with partial tuition reimbursements available, career-related internships or fieldwork, Federal Work-Study, scholarships/grants, and unspecified assistantships available. Support available to part-time students. Financial award applicants required to submit FAFSA. *Unit head:* Dr. Susan Bidwell, Chair, 703-284-1593, Fax: 703-284-3819, E-mail: susan.bidwell@marymount.edu. *Application contact:* Francesca Reed, Director, Graduate Admissions, 703-284-5901, Fax: 703-527-3815, E-mail: grad.admissions@marymount.edu. Web site: http://www.marymount.edu/academics/programs/nursingDNP.

Maryville University of Saint Louis, School of Health Professions, Nursing Program, St. Louis, MO 63141-7299. Offers accelerated RN to MSN (MSN); adult nurse practitioner (MSN); advanced practice nursing (DNP); family nurse practitioner (MSN); geriatric nurse practitioner (MSN); nursing education (MSN). *Accreditation:* AACN. Postbaccalaureate distance learning degree programs offered. *Students:* 16 full-time (14 women), 136 part-time (127 women); includes 9 minority (5 Black or African American, non-Hispanic/Latino; 3 Asian, non-Hispanic/Latino; 1 Two or more races, non-Hispanic/Latino). Average age 35. In 2011, 21 master's awarded. *Degree requirements:* For master's, practicum. *Entrance requirements:* For master's, BSN, current licensure, minimum GPA of 3.0, 3 letters of recommendation, curriculum vitae. Additional exam requirements/recommendations for international students: Required—TOEFL (minimum score 550 paper-based). *Application deadline:* Applications are processed on a rolling basis. Application fee: $40 ($60 for international students). Electronic applications accepted. *Expenses: Tuition:* Full-time $21,922; part-time $675 per credit hour. *Required fees:* $233.75 per semester. *Financial support:* Federal Work-Study and campus employment available. Support available to part-time students. Financial award application deadline: 3/1; financial award applicants required to submit FAFSA. *Unit head:* Dr. Elizabeth Buck, Director, 314-529-9453, Fax: 314-529-9139, E-mail: ebuck@maryville.edu. *Application contact:* Dr. Donna Payne, Vice President, Adult and Continuing Education, 314-529-9676, Fax: 314-529-9927, E-mail: dpayne@maryville.edu. Web site: http://www.maryville.edu/academics-hp-nursing.

McGill University, Faculty of Graduate and Postdoctoral Studies, Faculty of Medicine, School of Nursing, Montréal, QC H3A 2T5, Canada. Offers nurse practitioner (Graduate Diploma); nursing (M Sc A, PhD). PhD offered jointly with Université du Québec à Montréal.

McNeese State University, Doré School of Graduate Studies, College of Nursing, Lake Charles, LA 70609. Offers clinical nurse specialist (MSN); nurse educator (MSN); nurse practitioner (MSN); nursing leadership and administration (MSN). Program offered jointly with Southeastern Louisiana University and Southern University and Agricultural and Mechanical College. *Accreditation:* AACN. *Faculty:* 4 full-time (all women), 3 part-time/

adjunct (2 women). *Students:* 10 full-time (9 women), 94 part-time (79 women); includes 21 minority (15 Black or African American, non-Hispanic/Latino; 1 Asian, non-Hispanic/Latino; 4 Hispanic/Latino; 1 Two or more races, non-Hispanic/Latino). In 2011, 25 master's awarded. *Degree requirements:* For master's, comprehensive exam. *Entrance requirements:* For master's, GRE, eligibility for unencumbered licensure as RN in Louisiana. *Application deadline:* For fall admission, 5/15 priority date for domestic students, 5/15 for international students; for spring admission, 10/15 priority date for domestic students, 10/15 for international students. Applications are processed on a rolling basis. Application fee: $20 ($30 for international students). *Expenses:* Tuition, state resident: part-time $519 per credit hour. Tuition and fees vary according to course load. *Financial support:* Application deadline: 5/1. *Unit head:* Dr. Peggy L. Wolfe, Dean, 337-475-5820, Fax: 337-475-5924, E-mail: pwolfe@mcneese.edu. *Application contact:* Valarie Waldmeier, Coordinator, 337-475-5285, Fax: 337-475-5702, E-mail: vwaldmeier@mcneese.edu.

Medical University of South Carolina, College of Nursing, Family Nurse Practitioner Program, Charleston, SC 29425. Offers MSN. Part-time programs available. *Faculty:* 10 full-time (all women), 3 part-time/adjunct (2 women). *Students:* 6 full-time (all women), 4 part-time (all women). Average age 29. 153 applicants, 53% accepted. In 2011, 10 master's awarded. *Degree requirements:* For master's, thesis optional. *Entrance requirements:* For master's, BSN, course work in statistics, nursing license, minimum GPA of 3.0, current curriculum vitae, essay, three references. Additional exam requirements/recommendations for international students: Required—TOEFL (minimum score 600 paper-based; 250 computer-based). *Application deadline:* For fall admission, 2/1 priority date for domestic students, 2/1 for international students. Application fee: $85. Electronic applications accepted. *Financial support:* Federal Work-Study, scholarships/grants, and traineeships available. Support available to part-time students. Financial award application deadline: 3/10; financial award applicants required to submit FAFSA. *Faculty research:* Use of PDAs in clinical practice, palliative care, diabetes, smoking cessation, feeding with late stage dementia. *Unit head:* Margaret P. Spain, Lead Faculty, 843-792-2315, Fax: 843-792-2104, E-mail: spainm@musc.edu. *Application contact:* Carolyn F. Page, Director, Student Services, 843-792-3844, Fax: 843-792-5395, E-mail: pagecf@musc.edu. Web site: http://www.musc.edu/nursing/academics/masters/fnp.htm.

Middle Tennessee State University, College of Graduate Studies, University College, School of Nursing, Program in Family Nurse Practitioner, Murfreesboro, TN 37132. Offers MSN, Graduate Certificate. Part-time and evening/weekend programs available. Postbaccalaureate distance learning degree programs offered. *Students:* 4 part-time (3 women). In 2011, 1 other advanced degree awarded. *Entrance requirements:* Additional exam requirements/recommendations for international students: Required—TOEFL (minimum score 525 paper-based; 195 computer-based; 71 iBT) or IELTS (minimum score 6). *Expenses:* Tuition, state resident: full-time $10,008. Tuition, nonresident: full-time $25,056. *Financial support:* Institutionally sponsored loans available. Support available to part-time students. Financial award application deadline: 5/1. *Unit head:* Dr. Mike Boyle, Dean, 615-494-7714, Fax: 615-896-7925, E-mail: mike.boyle@mtsu.edu. *Application contact:* Dr. Michael D. Allen, Dean and Vice Provost for Research, 615-898-2840, Fax: 615-904-8020, E-mail: michael.allen@mtsu.edu.

Midwestern State University, Graduate Studies, College of Health Sciences and Human Services, Nursing Program, Wichita Falls, TX 76308. Offers family nurse practitioner (MSN); family psychiatric mental health nurse practitioner (MSN); health services administration (MSN); nurse educator (MSN). *Accreditation:* AACN. Part-time and evening/weekend programs available. *Degree requirements:* For master's, comprehensive exam, thesis optional. *Entrance requirements:* For master's, GRE General Test or MAT. Additional exam requirements/recommendations for international students: Required—TOEFL (minimum score 550 paper-based; 213 computer-based). Electronic applications accepted. *Faculty research:* Infant feeding, musculoskeletal disorders, diabetes, community health education, water quality reporting.

Minnesota State University Mankato, College of Graduate Studies, College of Allied Health and Nursing, School of Nursing, Mankato, MN 56001. Offers family nursing (MSN), including family nurse practitioner; nursing (DNP). MSN offered jointly with Metropolitan State University; DNP with Metropolitan State University, Minnesota State University Moorhead, Winona State University. *Accreditation:* AACN. *Students:* 9 full-time (all women), 49 part-time (46 women). *Degree requirements:* For master's, comprehensive exam, internships, research project or thesis; for doctorate, capstone project. *Entrance requirements:* For master's, GRE General Test or on-campus essay, minimum GPA of 3.0 during previous 2 years, BSN or equivalent references; for doctorate, master's degree in nursing. Additional exam requirements/recommendations for international students: Required—TOEFL. *Application deadline:* For fall admission, 2/15 priority date for domestic students, 2/15 for international students. Applications are processed on a rolling basis. Application fee: $40. Electronic applications accepted. *Financial support:* Research assistantships with full tuition reimbursements and teaching assistantships with full tuition reimbursements available. Financial award application deadline: 3/15; financial award applicants required to submit FAFSA. *Faculty research:* Psychosocial nursing, computers in nursing, family adaptation. *Unit head:* Dr. Sue Ellen Bell, Graduate Coordinator, 507-389-6814. *Application contact:* Collaborative MSN Program Admissions, 507-389-6022. Web site: http://www.mnsu.edu/nursing/.

Missouri State University, Graduate College, College of Health and Human Services, Department of Nursing, Springfield, MO 65897. Offers nursing (MSN), including family nurse practitioner, nurse educator. *Accreditation:* AACN. *Faculty:* 9 full-time (all women), 12 part-time/adjunct (10 women). *Students:* 24 full-time (20 women), 25 part-time (23 women); includes 2 minority (1 Asian, non-Hispanic/Latino; 1 Two or more races, non-Hispanic/Latino). Average age 37. 14 applicants, 93% accepted, 5 enrolled. In 2011, 10 master's awarded. *Degree requirements:* For master's, comprehensive exam, thesis or alternative. *Entrance requirements:* For master's, GRE General Test, minimum GPA of 3.0, RN license (MSN), 1 year work experience (MPH). Additional exam requirements/recommendations for international students: Required—TOEFL (minimum score 550 paper-based; 213 computer-based; 79 iBT). *Application deadline:* For fall admission, 7/20 priority date for domestic students, 5/1 for international students; for spring admission, 12/20 priority date for domestic students, 9/1 for international students. Applications are processed on a rolling basis. Application fee: $35 ($50 for international students). Electronic applications accepted. *Expenses:* Tuition, state resident: full-time $4086; part-time $227 per credit hour. Tuition, nonresident: full-time $8172; part-time $454 per credit hour. *Required fees:* $275 per semester. Tuition and fees vary according to course load, campus/location and program. *Financial support:* Federal Work-Study, institutionally sponsored loans, scholarships/grants, and unspecified assistantships available. Financial award application deadline: 3/31; financial award applicants required to submit FAFSA. *Faculty research:* Preconceptual health, women's health, nursing satisfaction, nursing education. *Unit head:* Dr. Kathryn Hope, Head, 417-836-5310, Fax: 417-836-5484, E-mail: nursing@missouristate.edu. *Application contact:* Eric Eckert, Coordinator of Admissions and Recruitment, 417-836-5331, Fax: 417-836-6200, E-mail: tobinbushman@missouristate.edu. Web site: http://www.missouristate.edu/nursing/.

Molloy College, Division of Nursing, Rockville Centre, NY 11571-5002. Offers adult nurse practitioner (Advanced Certificate); clinical nurse specialist: adult health (Advanced Certificate); family nurse practitioner (Advanced Certificate); nurse practitioner psychiatry (Advanced Certificate); nursing (MS); nursing administration (Advanced Certificate); nursing administration with informatics (Advanced Certificate); nursing education (Advanced Certificate); nursing informatics (Advanced Certificate); pediatric nurse practitioner (Advanced Certificate). *Accreditation:* AACN. Part-time and evening/weekend programs available. *Faculty:* 20 full-time (19 women), 12 part-time/adjunct (11 women). *Students:* 19 full-time (15 women), 483 part-time (452 women); includes 238 minority (132 Black or African American, non-Hispanic/Latino; 61 Asian, non-Hispanic/Latino; 35 Hispanic/Latino; 2 Native Hawaiian or other Pacific Islander, non-Hispanic/Latino; 8 Two or more races, non-Hispanic/Latino), 5 international. Average age 40. 186 applicants, 82% accepted, 110 enrolled. In 2011, 94 master's awarded. *Degree requirements:* For master's, thesis optional. *Entrance requirements:* For master's, 3 letters of reference, BS in nursing, minimum undergraduate GPA of 3.0; for Advanced Certificate, 3 letters of reference, master's degree in nursing. *Application deadline:* For fall admission, 9/2 priority date for domestic students; for spring admission, 1/20 priority date for domestic students. Applications are processed on a rolling basis. Application fee: $60. *Financial support:* Research assistantships with partial tuition reimbursements, teaching assistantships with partial tuition reimbursements, institutionally sponsored loans, scholarships/grants, and unspecified assistantships available. Support available to part-time students. Financial award application deadline: 4/1; financial award applicants required to submit FAFSA. *Unit head:* Dr. Denise Walsh, Associate Dean, Graduate Nursing, 516-678-5000, Fax: 516-678-9718, E-mail: dwalsh@molloy.edu. *Application contact:* Alina Haitz, Assistant Director of Graduate Admissions, 516-678-5000, Fax: 516-256-2247, E-mail: ahaitz@molloy.edu. Web site: http://www.molloy.edu/academics/nursing-division.

Monmouth University, The Graduate School, The Marjorie K. Unterberg School of Nursing and Health Studies, West Long Branch, NJ 07764-1898. Offers adult nurse practitioner (MSN); adult psychiatric and mental health advanced practice nursing (MSN, Post-Master's Certificate); advanced practice nursing (Post-Master's Certificate); family nurse practitioner (MSN, Post-Master's Certificate); forensic nursing (MSN, Certificate); nursing (MSN); nursing administration (MSN, Post-Master's Certificate); nursing education (MSN, Post-Master's Certificate); nursing practice (DNP); school nursing (MSN, Certificate). *Accreditation:* AACN. Part-time and evening/weekend programs available. *Faculty:* 12 full-time (all women), 2 part-time/adjunct (both women). *Students:* 16 full-time (11 women), 244 part-time (238 women); includes 73 minority (23 Black or African American, non-Hispanic/Latino; 2 American Indian or Alaska Native, non-Hispanic/Latino; 34 Asian, non-Hispanic/Latino; 12 Hispanic/Latino; 1 Native Hawaiian or other Pacific Islander, non-Hispanic/Latino; 1 Two or more races, non-Hispanic/Latino), 1 international. Average age 41. 107 applicants, 92% accepted, 67 enrolled. In 2011, 55 master's awarded. *Degree requirements:* For master's, practicum (for some tracks). *Entrance requirements:* For master's, GRE General Test, RN license, 1 year of work experience, minimum undergraduate GPA of 2.75. Additional exam requirements/recommendations for international students: Required—TOEFL (minimum score 550 paper-based; 213 computer-based; 79 iBT), IELTS (minimum score 5) or Michigan English Language Assessment Battery (minimum score 77), Cambridge A, B, C. *Application deadline:* For fall admission, 7/15 priority date for domestic students, 6/1 for international students; for spring admission, 11/15 priority date for domestic students, 11/1 for international students. Applications are processed on a rolling basis. Application fee: $50. Electronic applications accepted. *Financial support:* In 2011–12, 138 students received support, including 138 fellowships (averaging $1,423 per year), 4 research assistantships (averaging $5,240 per year); career-related internships or fieldwork, scholarships/grants, and unspecified assistantships also available. Support available to part-time students. Financial award applicants required to submit FAFSA. *Faculty research:* Relationship of undergraduate GPA and GRE to succeed in a graduate nursing program. *Unit head:* Dr. Janet Mahoney, Dean, 732-571-3443, Fax: 732-263-5131, E-mail: jmahoney@monmouth.edu. *Application contact:* Kevin Roane, Director, Office of Graduate Admission, 732-571-3452, Fax: 732-263-5123, E-mail: gradadm@monmouth.edu. Web site: http://www.monmouth.edu/nursingschool.

Montana State University, College of Graduate Studies, College of Nursing, Bozeman, MT 59717. Offers clinical nurse leader (MN); family nurse practitioner (MN, Post-Master's Certificate); nursing education (Certificate, Post-Master's Certificate); psychiatric mental health nurse practitioner (MN). *Accreditation:* AACN. Part-time programs available. Postbaccalaureate distance learning degree programs offered (minimal on-campus study). *Degree requirements:* For master's, comprehensive exam, thesis (for some programs). *Entrance requirements:* For master's, GRE General Test, minimum GPA of 3.0 for undergraduate and post-baccalaureate work. Additional exam requirements/recommendations for international students: Required—TOEFL (minimum score 580 paper-based; 213 computer-based). Electronic applications accepted. *Faculty research:* Rural nursing, health disparities, environmental/public health, oral health, resilience.

Mountain State University, Program in Nursing, Beckley, WV 25802-9003. Offers administration/education (MSN); family nurse practitioner (MSN). *Accreditation:* NLN. Part-time programs available. Postbaccalaureate distance learning degree programs offered (minimal on-campus study). *Faculty:* 3 full-time (all women), 2 part-time/adjunct (both women). *Students:* 65 full-time (61 women), 9 part-time (8 women); includes 11 minority (8 Black or African American, non-Hispanic/Latino; 1 American Indian or Alaska Native, non-Hispanic/Latino; 2 Asian, non-Hispanic/Latino), 1 international. Average age 37. 85 applicants, 27% accepted, 20 enrolled. In 2011, 46 master's awarded. *Degree requirements:* For master's, comprehensive exam, thesis or alternative. *Entrance requirements:* For master's, GRE. Additional exam requirements/recommendations for international students: Required—TOEFL (minimum score 550 paper-based; 213 computer-based); Recommended—IELTS (minimum score 6.5). *Application deadline:* For spring admission, 6/30 for domestic and international students. Applications are processed on a rolling basis. Application fee: $25 ($50 for international students). Electronic applications accepted. *Expenses:* Contact institution. *Financial support:* Federal Work-Study, scholarships/grants, and unspecified assistantships available. Support available to part-time students. Financial award applicants required to submit FAFSA. *Unit head:* Dr. Sheila Garland, Dean, School of Health Sciences, 304-929-1516, Fax: 304-929-1601, E-mail: sgarland@mountainstate.edu.

Mount Carmel College of Nursing, Nursing Program, Columbus, OH 43222. Offers adult health clinical nurse specialist (MS); family nurse practitioner (MS); nursing administration (MS); nursing education (MS). *Accreditation:* AACN. Part-time programs available. *Faculty:* 11 full-time (10 women), 4 part-time/adjunct (2 women). *Students:* 69 full-time (66 women), 33 part-time (30 women); includes 19 minority (11 Black or African American, non-Hispanic/Latino; 1 American Indian or Alaska Native, non-Hispanic/Latino; 5 Asian, non-Hispanic/Latino; 1 Native Hawaiian or other Pacific Islander, non-Hispanic/Latino; 1 Two or more races, non-Hispanic/Latino). Average age 38. 23 applicants, 100% accepted, 20 enrolled. In 2011, 16 master's awarded. *Degree requirements:* For master's, professional manuscript. *Entrance requirements:* For master's, letters of recommendation, current resume, baccalaureate degree in nursing, current Ohio RN license, minimum cumulative GPA of 3.0. Additional exam requirements/recommendations for international students: Required—TOEFL (minimum score 550 paper-based; 213 computer-based; 80 iBT). *Application deadline:* For fall admission, 6/15 priority date for domestic students; for winter admission, 11/1 priority date for domestic students. Applications are processed on a rolling basis. Application

fee: $30. *Expenses: Tuition:* Full-time $7839; part-time $402 per credit. *Required fees:* $75. *Financial support:* In 2011–12, 6 students received support. Institutionally sponsored loans and scholarships/grants available. Financial award application deadline: 7/1; financial award applicants required to submit FAFSA. *Unit head:* Dr. Angela Phillips-Lowe, Associate Dean, 614-234-5717, Fax: 614-234-2875, E-mail: aphillips-lowe@mccn.edu. *Application contact:* Elsie Sexton, Program Coordinator, 614-234-5169, Fax: 614-234-2875, E-mail: ksexton@mccn.edu. Web site: http://www.mccn.edu/.

Mount Saint Mary College, Division of Nursing, Newburgh, NY 12550-3494. Offers adult nurse practitioner (MS, Advanced Certificate), including nursing education (MS), nursing management (MS); clinical nurse specialist-adult health (MS), including nursing education, nursing management; family nurse practitioner (Advanced Certificate). *Accreditation:* AACN. Part-time and evening/weekend programs available. *Faculty:* 3 full-time (all women), 1 (woman) part-time/adjunct. *Students:* 3 full-time (2 women), 58 part-time (54 women); includes 16 minority (11 Black or African American, non-Hispanic/Latino; 1 Asian, non-Hispanic/Latino; 1 Hispanic/Latino; 3 Native Hawaiian or other Pacific Islander, non-Hispanic/Latino), 2 international. Average age 38. 47 applicants, 53% accepted, 18 enrolled. In 2011, 17 master's, 5 other advanced degrees awarded. *Degree requirements:* For master's, research utilization project. *Entrance requirements:* For master's, BSN, minimum GPA of 3.0, RN license. *Application deadline:* For fall admission, 6/3 priority date for domestic students; for spring admission, 10/31 priority date for domestic students. Applications are processed on a rolling basis. Application fee: $45. Application fee is waived when completed online. *Expenses: Tuition:* Full-time $13,356; part-time $742 per credit. *Required fees:* $70 per semester. *Financial support:* In 2011–12, 8 students received support. Unspecified assistantships available. Financial award application deadline: 4/15; financial award applicants required to submit FAFSA. *Unit head:* Dr. Karen Baldwin, Coordinator, 845-569-3512, Fax: 845-562-6762, E-mail: baldwin@msmc.edu. *Application contact:* Courtney McDermott, Graduate Recruiter, 845-569-3402, Fax: 845-569-3450, E-mail: courtney.mcdermott@msmc.edu. Web site: http://www.msmc.edu/Academics/Graduate_Programs/Master_of_Science_in_Nursing.

Murray State University, College of Health Sciences and Human Services, Program in Nursing, Murray, KY 42071. Offers clinical nurse specialist (MSN); family nurse practitioner (MSN); nurse anesthesia (MSN). *Accreditation:* AACN; AANA/CANAEP. *Degree requirements:* For master's, research project. *Entrance requirements:* For master's, GRE General Test, BSN, interview, RN licensure. Additional exam requirements/recommendations for international students: Required—TOEFL (minimum score 550 paper-based). *Faculty research:* Fibromyalgis, primary care, rural health.

New Mexico State University, Graduate School, College of Health and Social Services, School of Nursing, Las Cruces, NM 88003-8001. Offers adult/gerontology nurse practitioner (DNP); family nurse practitioner (DNP); nursing (MSN, PhD); public/community health (DNP). *Accreditation:* AACN. Postbaccalaureate distance learning degree programs offered (minimal on-campus study). *Faculty:* 9 full-time (all women). *Students:* 44 full-time (38 women), 72 part-time (59 women); includes 48 minority (9 Black or African American, non-Hispanic/Latino; 5 American Indian or Alaska Native, non-Hispanic/Latino; 2 Asian, non-Hispanic/Latino; 31 Hispanic/Latino; 1 Two or more races, non-Hispanic/Latino), 2 international. Average age 43. 37 applicants, 86% accepted, 25 enrolled. In 2011, 35 master's, 3 doctorates awarded. *Degree requirements:* For master's, comprehensive exam, thesis optional, clinical practice; for doctorate, comprehensive exam, thesis/dissertation. *Entrance requirements:* For master's, NCLEX exam, BSN, minimum GPA of 3.0, course work in statistics, 3 letters of reference, writing sample, RN license, CPR certification, proof of liability, immunizations, criminal background check; for doctorate, NCLEX exam, MSN, minimum GPA of 3.0, 3 letters of reference, writing sample, RN license, CPR certification, proof of liability, immunizations, criminal background check, statistics course. Additional exam requirements/recommendations for international students: Required—TOEFL (minimum score 550 paper-based; 79 iBT), IELTS (minimum score 6.5). *Application deadline:* For spring admission, 10/1 priority date for domestic students. Application fee: $40 ($50 for international students). Electronic applications accepted. *Expenses: Tuition,* state resident: full-time $5004; part-time $208.50 per credit. Tuition, nonresident: full-time $17,446; part-time $726.90 per credit. *Financial support:* In 2011–12, 1 teaching assistantship (averaging $28,242 per year) was awarded; fellowships, research assistantships, career-related internships or fieldwork, Federal Work-Study, scholarships/grants, traineeships, and health care benefits also available. Financial award application deadline: 3/1. *Faculty research:* Public policy, community health, health disparities, self efficacy and self management, psychiatric mental health. *Unit head:* Dr. Pamela Schultz, Director, 575-646-3812, Fax: 575-646-2167, E-mail: pschultz@nmsu.edu. *Application contact:* Dr. Kathleen Huttlinger, Associate Director for Graduate Studies, 575-646-4387, Fax: 575-646-2167. Web site: http://www.nmsu.edu/~nursing/.

New York University, College of Nursing, Doctor of Nursing Practice Program, New York, NY 10012-1019. Offers advanced practice nursing (DNP), including adult acute care, adult nurse practitioner/holistic nursing, adult nurse practitioner/palliative care nursing, adult primary care, adult primary care/geriatrics, family, geriatrics, mental health nursing, nurse-midwifery, pediatrics. Part-time and evening/weekend programs available. *Faculty:* 7 full-time (all women). *Students:* 23 part-time (19 women); includes 6 minority (4 Black or African American, non-Hispanic/Latino; 1 Asian, non-Hispanic/Latino; 1 Hispanic/Latino), 1 international. Average age 46. 20 applicants, 80% accepted, 11 enrolled. In 2011, 8 doctorates awarded. *Degree requirements:* For doctorate, thesis/dissertation. *Entrance requirements:* For doctorate, MS, RN license, interview, NP Certification. Additional exam requirements/recommendations for international students: Required—TOEFL, IELTS. *Application deadline:* For fall admission, 4/1 priority date for domestic students, 4/1 for international students. Applications are processed on a rolling basis. Application fee: $75. Electronic applications accepted. *Financial support:* In 2011–12, 15 students received support. Fellowships with full and partial tuition reimbursements available, institutionally sponsored loans, scholarships/grants, and tuition waivers (partial) available. Support available to part-time students. Financial award application deadline: 2/1; financial award applicants required to submit FAFSA. *Faculty research:* Elderly black diabetics, families and illness, oral systemic connection. *Unit head:* Dr. Jamesetta A. Newland, Director, 212-998-5319, Fax: 212-995-3143, E-mail: jan7@nyu.edu. *Application contact:* Gail Wolfmeyer, Assistant Director, Graduate Student Affairs and Admissions, 212-992-7653, Fax: 212-995-4302, E-mail: gail.wolfmeyer@nyu.edu.

New York University, College of Nursing, Programs in Advanced Practice Nursing, New York, NY 10012-1019. Offers advanced practice nursing: adult acute care (MS, Advanced Certificate); advanced practice nursing: adult nurse practitioner/holistic nurse practitioner (Advanced Certificate); advanced practice nursing: adult nurse practitioner/palliative care nurse practitioner (Advanced Certificate); advanced practice nursing: adult primary care (MS, Advanced Certificate); advanced practice nursing: family (MS, Advanced Certificate); advanced practice nursing: geriatrics (Advanced Certificate); advanced practice nursing: mental health (MS); advanced practice nursing: mental health nursing (Advanced Certificate); advanced practice nursing: pediatrics (MS, Advanced Certificate); nurse midwifery (MS, Advanced Certificate); nursing administration (MS, Advanced Certificate); nursing education (MS, Advanced

Certificate); nursing informatics (MS, Advanced Certificate); MS/MPA; MS/MPH. *Accreditation:* AACN; ACNM/ACME. Part-time programs available. *Faculty:* 23 full-time (all women), 60 part-time/adjunct (47 women). *Students:* 27 full-time (23 women), 552 part-time (514 women); includes 251 minority (91 Black or African American, non-Hispanic/Latino; 115 Asian, non-Hispanic/Latino; 34 Hispanic/Latino; 11 Native Hawaiian or other Pacific Islander, non-Hispanic/Latino), 8 international. Average age 33. 325 applicants, 81% accepted, 179 enrolled. In 2011, 89 master's awarded. *Degree requirements:* For master's, thesis (for some programs). *Entrance requirements:* For master's, BS in nursing, AS in nursing with another BS/BA, interview, RN license, 1 year of clinical experience (3 for nursing education program); for Advanced Certificate, master's degree. Additional exam requirements/recommendations for international students: Required—TOEFL, IELTS. *Application deadline:* For fall admission, 7/1 priority date for domestic students, 7/1 for international students; for spring admission, 12/1 for domestic and international students. Applications are processed on a rolling basis. Application fee: $75. Electronic applications accepted. *Financial support:* In 2011–12, 36 students received support. Career-related internships or fieldwork, institutionally sponsored loans, scholarships/grants, traineeships, and tuition waivers (partial) available. Support available to part-time students. Financial award application deadline: 2/1; financial award applicants required to submit FAFSA. *Faculty research:* Elderly black diabetics, families and illness, oral systemic connection. *Unit head:* Dr. Judith Haber, Associate Dean, 212-998-9020, Fax: 212-995-3143, E-mail: jh33@nyu.edu. *Application contact:* Gail Wolfmeyer, Assistant Director, Graduate Student Affairs and Admissions, 212-992-7653, Fax: 212-995-4302, E-mail: gail.wolfmeyer@nyu.edu.

Northern Arizona University, Graduate College, College of Health and Human Services, School of Nursing, Flagstaff, AZ 86011. Offers family nurse practitioner (MSN, Certificate); nurse generalist (MSN); nursing (MSN); nursing practice (DNP). *Accreditation:* AACN. Part-time programs available. *Faculty:* 36 full-time (31 women). *Students:* 25 full-time (22 women), 68 part-time (57 women); includes 17 minority (1 Black or African American, non-Hispanic/Latino; 1 American Indian or Alaska Native, non-Hispanic/Latino; 3 Asian, non-Hispanic/Latino; 10 Hispanic/Latino; 1 Native Hawaiian or other Pacific Islander, non-Hispanic/Latino; 1 Two or more races, non-Hispanic/Latino). Average age 30. 71 applicants, 17% accepted, 8 enrolled. In 2011, 19 degrees awarded. *Degree requirements:* For master's, thesis (for some programs), project or thesis. *Entrance requirements:* For master's, GRE General Test or minimum GPA of 3.0, undergraduate statistics or health assessment with minimum grade of B in last 5 years or 3 years of RN experience (nursing education). Additional exam requirements/recommendations for international students: Required—TOEFL (minimum score 550 paper-based; 213 computer-based; 80 iBT), IELTS (minimum score 7). *Application deadline:* For fall admission, 1/15 priority date for domestic students, 1/15 for international students. Applications are processed on a rolling basis. Application fee: $65. Electronic applications accepted. *Expenses: Tuition,* state resident: full-time $7190; part-time $355 per credit hour. Tuition, nonresident: full-time $18,092; part-time $1005 per credit hour. *Required fees:* $818; $328 per semester. *Financial support:* Career-related internships or fieldwork, Federal Work-Study, scholarships/grants, traineeships, health care benefits, tuition waivers, and unspecified assistantships available. Financial award applicants required to submit FAFSA. *Unit head:* Dr. Debera Thomas, Chair, 928-523-2656, Fax: 928-523-7171, E-mail: debera.thomas@nau.edu. *Application contact:* Penny Susan Walior, Student Academic Specialist, 928-523-6717, Fax: 928-523-9155, E-mail: nursing@nau.edu. Web site: http://nau.edu/CHHS/Nursing/Welcome/.

North Georgia College & State University, Department of Nursing, Dahlonega, GA 30597. Offers family nurse practitioner (MSN); nursing education (MSN). *Accreditation:* NLN. Part-time programs available. *Faculty:* 9 full-time (8 women), 3 part-time/adjunct (2 women). *Students:* 23 full-time (21 women), 53 part-time (49 women); includes 9 minority (5 Black or African American, non-Hispanic/Latino; 1 Asian, non-Hispanic/Latino; 1 Hispanic/Latino; 2 Two or more races, non-Hispanic/Latino), 1 international. Average age 39. 105 applicants, 44% accepted, 33 enrolled. In 2011, 21 master's awarded. *Degree requirements:* For master's, one foreign language, comprehensive exam, thesis. *Entrance requirements:* For master's, GRE General Test or MAT, minimum GPA of 2.75, 3 letters of recommendation, current Georgia RN license, 1 year of post-licensure work, BSN, ASN. Additional exam requirements/recommendations for international students: Required—TOEFL (minimum score 550 paper-based; 213 computer-based; 79 iBT), IELTS (minimum score 6.5). *Application deadline:* For fall admission, 7/1 priority date for domestic students, 6/1 for international students. Application fee: $40. Electronic applications accepted. *Expenses: Tuition,* state resident: full-time $3528; part-time $196 per credit hour. Tuition, nonresident: full-time $14,094; part-time $783 per credit hour. *Required fees:* $1718; $859 per semester. Tuition and fees vary according to course load, campus/location and program. *Financial support:* Career-related internships or fieldwork and unspecified assistantships available. Financial award application deadline: 5/1; financial award applicants required to submit CSS PROFILE or FAFSA. *Faculty research:* Diabetes, hypertension, access to woman's health screening, simulation in nursing education, health care of undeserved populations. *Unit head:* Dr. Diane Nelson, Department Head, 706-864-1930, Fax: 706-864-1845, E-mail: denelson@northgeorgia.edu. *Application contact:* Susan L. Perry, Graduate Admissions Coordinator, 706-864-1543, Fax: 706-867-2795, E-mail: slperry@northgeorgia.edu.

Oakland University, Graduate Study and Lifelong Learning, School of Nursing, Program in Family Nurse Practitioner, Rochester, MI 48309-4401. Offers MSN, Certificate. *Accreditation:* AACN. *Degree requirements:* For master's, thesis. *Entrance requirements:* For master's, GRE General Test, minimum GPA of 3.0 for unconditional admission. Additional exam requirements/recommendations for international students: Required—TOEFL (minimum score 550 paper-based; 213 computer-based). Electronic applications accepted. *Expenses:* Contact institution.

Ohio University, Graduate College, College of Health Sciences and Professions, School of Nursing, Athens, OH 45701-2979. Offers acute care nurse practitioner (MSN); acute care nurse practitioner and family nurse practitioner (MSN); acute care nurse practitioner and nurse administrator (MSN); acute care nurse practitioner and nurse educator (MSN); family nurse practitioner (MSN); nurse administrator (MSN); nurse administrator and family nurse practitioner (MSN); nurse educator (MSN); nurse educator and family nurse practitioner (MSN); nurse educator and nurse administrator (MSN). *Accreditation:* AACN. *Students:* 33 full-time (29 women), 91 part-time (84 women); includes 16 minority (8 Black or African American, non-Hispanic/Latino; 2 Asian, non-Hispanic/Latino; 1 Hispanic/Latino; 5 Two or more races, non-Hispanic/Latino), 3 international. 86 applicants, 86% accepted, 61 enrolled. In 2011, 24 master's awarded. *Degree requirements:* For master's, capstone project. *Entrance requirements:* For master's, GRE, bachelor's degree in nursing from an accredited college or university, minimum overall undergraduate GPA of 3.0, official transcripts, statement of goals and objectives, resume, 3 letters of recommendation. Additional exam requirements/recommendations for international students: Required—TOEFL (minimum score 550 paper-based; 80 iBT) or IELTS (minimum score 6.5). *Application deadline:* For fall admission, 3/1 priority date for domestic students, 2/1 for international students. Applications are processed on a rolling basis. Application fee: $50 ($55 for international students). Electronic applications accepted. *Financial support:* Research assistantships, Federal Work-Study, institutionally sponsored loans, and unspecified

assistantships available. Financial award application deadline: 3/1. *Unit head:* Dr. Deborah Henderson, Professor and Interim Director, 740-593-4497, Fax: 740-593-0286, E-mail: hendersd@ohio.edu. *Application contact:* Cheryl Brimner, Administrative Associate, 740-593-4494, Fax: 740-593-0286, E-mail: brimner@ohio.edu. Web site: http://www.ohio.edu/chsp/nrse/index.cfm.

Old Dominion University, College of Health Sciences, School of Nursing, Family Nurse Practitioner Emphasis, Norfolk, VA 23529. Offers MSN. Part-time programs available. Postbaccalaureate distance learning degree programs offered (minimal on-campus study). *Faculty:* 3 full-time (all women), 9 part-time/adjunct (all women). *Students:* 60 full-time (56 women), 69 part-time (66 women); includes 17 minority (12 Black or African American, non-Hispanic/Latino; 2 Asian, non-Hispanic/Latino; 2 Hispanic/Latino; 1 Native Hawaiian or other Pacific Islander, non-Hispanic/Latino). Average age 35. 137 applicants, 52% accepted, 54 enrolled. In 2011, 41 master's awarded. *Degree requirements:* For master's, comprehensive exam. *Entrance requirements:* For master's, GRE or MAT. Additional exam requirements/recommendations for international students: Required—TOEFL. *Application deadline:* For fall admission, 3/1 for domestic students, 4/15 for international students. Application fee: $50. *Expenses:* Tuition, state resident: full-time $9096; part-time $379 per credit. Tuition, nonresident: full-time $23,064; part-time $961 per credit. *Required fees:* $127 per semester. One-time fee: $50. *Financial support:* In 2011–12, 2 research assistantships with partial tuition reimbursements (averaging $10,000 per year) were awarded; career-related internships or fieldwork, scholarships/grants, and traineeships also available. Support available to part-time students. *Faculty research:* Military families, nurse practitioner student reaching modalities, gerontology, pediatrics, ethics. *Unit head:* Dr. Micah Scott, Graduate Program Director, 757-683-5255, E-mail: mscott@odu.edu. *Application contact:* Sue Parker, Coordinator, Graduate Student Services, 757-683-4298, Fax: 757-683-5253, E-mail: sparker@odu.edu. Web site: http://hs.odu.edu/nursing/academics/family_nurse/family_nurse.shtml.

Oregon Health & Science University, School of Nursing, Family Nurse Practitioner Program, Portland, OR 97239-3098. Offers MN, MS, Post Master's Certificate.

Otterbein University, Department of Nursing, Westerville, OH 43081. Offers advanced practice nurse educator (Certificate); clinical nurse leader (MSN); family nurse practitioner (MSN, Certificate); nurse anesthesia (MSN, Certificate); nursing (DNP); nursing service administration (MSN). *Accreditation:* AACN; AANA/CANAEP; NLN. Part-time and evening/weekend programs available. Postbaccalaureate distance learning degree programs offered (minimal on-campus study). *Degree requirements:* For master's, comprehensive exam (for some programs), thesis (for some programs). *Entrance requirements:* For master's, 2 reference forms, resume; for Certificate, official transcripts, 2 reference forms, essay, resumé. Additional exam requirements/recommendations for international students: Required—TOEFL (minimum score 550 paper-based; 213 computer-based; 79 iBT). *Faculty research:* Patient education, women's health, trauma curriculum development, administration.

Pace University, Lienhard School of Nursing, New York, NY 10038. Offers family nurse practitioner (MS); nursing education (MA); nursing leadership (Advanced Certificate); nursing practice (DNP). *Accreditation:* AACN. Part-time and evening/weekend programs available. Postbaccalaureate distance learning degree programs offered. *Faculty:* 10 full-time (8 women), 37 part-time/adjunct (30 women). *Students:* 32 full-time (26 women), 417 part-time (381 women); includes 187 minority (88 Black or African American, non-Hispanic/Latino; 1 American Indian or Alaska Native, non-Hispanic/Latino; 49 Asian, non-Hispanic/Latino; 43 Hispanic/Latino; 1 Native Hawaiian or other Pacific Islander, non-Hispanic/Latino; 5 Two or more races, non-Hispanic/Latino), 5 international. Average age 36. 437 applicants, 41% accepted, 84 enrolled. In 2011, 96 master's, 20 doctorates, 3 other advanced degrees awarded. *Degree requirements:* For master's, thesis. *Entrance requirements:* For master's, GRE General Test or MAT, RN license, resume, personal statement, 2 letters of recommendation, official transcripts; for doctorate, RN license, resume, personal statement, 2 letters of recommendation, official transcripts, accredited master's degree in nursing, minimum GPA of 3.3, state certification; for Advanced Certificate, RN license, completion of 2nd degree in nursing. Additional exam requirements/recommendations for international students: Required—TOEFL. *Application deadline:* For fall admission, 7/31 priority date for domestic students, 4/30 for international students; for spring admission, 10/14 for domestic students, 9/14 for international students. Applications are processed on a rolling basis. Application fee: $70. Electronic applications accepted. *Expenses:* Contact institution. *Financial support:* Research assistantships, career-related internships or fieldwork, Federal Work-Study, and tuition waivers (partial) available. Support available to part-time students. Financial award applicants required to submit FAFSA. *Unit head:* Dr. Geraldine Colombraro, Interim Dean, 914-773-3341, E-mail: gcolombraro@pace.edu. *Application contact:* Susan Ford-Goldschein, Director of Graduate Admissions, 914-422-4283, Fax: 914-422-4287, E-mail: gradwp@pace.edu. Web site: http://www.pace.edu/.

Pacific Lutheran University, Division of Graduate Studies, School of Nursing, Program in Family Nurse Practitioner, Tacoma, WA 98447. Offers MSN. *Accreditation:* AACN. Part-time and evening/weekend programs available. *Faculty:* 5 full-time (2 women), 1 (woman) part-time/adjunct. *Students:* 5 full-time (all women), 2 part-time (both women). Average age 39. 10 applicants, 50% accepted, 4 enrolled. In 2011, 12 master's awarded. *Degree requirements:* For master's, thesis or alternative. *Entrance requirements:* For master's, GRE General Test, minimum undergraduate GPA of 3.0. Additional exam requirements/recommendations for international students: Required—TOEFL (minimum score 550 paper-based; 213 computer-based). *Application deadline:* For fall admission, 4/1 priority date for domestic students. Applications are processed on a rolling basis. Application fee: $40. *Expenses:* Contact institution. *Financial support:* In 2011–12, 6 students received support. Federal Work-Study, scholarships/grants, and unspecified assistantships available. Financial award application deadline: 3/1. *Unit head:* Dr. Ruth Schaffler, Unit Head, 253-535-7680. *Application contact:* Linda DuBay, Senior Office Assistant, 253-535-7151, Fax: 253-536-5136, E-mail: admissions@plu.edu.

Prairie View A&M University, College of Nursing, Houston, TX 77030. Offers family nurse practitioner (MSN); nursing administration (MSN); nursing education (MSN). *Accreditation:* AACN; NLN. Part-time programs available. *Degree requirements:* For master's, comprehensive exam, thesis. *Entrance requirements:* For master's, MAT or GRE, BS in nursing; 2 years of experience as a registered nurse; 1 course each in statistics, basic health and assessment. *Faculty research:* Software development and violence prevention, health promotion and disease prevention.

Purdue University Calumet, Graduate Studies Office, School of Nursing, Hammond, IN 46323-2094. Offers adult health clinical nurse specialist (MS); critical care clinical nurse specialist (MS); family nurse practitioner (MS); nurse executive (MS). *Accreditation:* AACN; NLN. Part-time programs available. Postbaccalaureate distance learning degree programs offered (minimal on-campus study). *Entrance requirements:* For master's, BSN. Additional exam requirements/recommendations for international students: Required—TOEFL. Electronic applications accepted. *Faculty research:* Adult health, cardiovascular and pulmonary nursing.

Queen's University at Kingston, School of Graduate Studies and Research, Faculty of Health Sciences, School of Nursing, Kingston, ON K7L 3N6, Canada. Offers health and chronic illness (M Sc); nurse scientist (PhD); primary health care nurse practitioner (Certificate); women's and children's health (M Sc). *Degree requirements:* For master's, thesis. *Entrance requirements:* For master's, RN license. Additional exam requirements/recommendations for international students: Required—TOEFL. *Faculty research:* Women and children's health, health and chronic illness.

Quinnipiac University, School of Nursing, Family Nurse Practitioner Track, Hamden, CT 06518-1940. Offers DNP. *Accreditation:* NLN. *Faculty:* 6 full-time (5 women), 7 part-time/adjunct (4 women). *Students:* 23 full-time (22 women), 46 part-time (all women); includes 10 minority (6 Black or African American, non-Hispanic/Latino; 3 Asian, non-Hispanic/Latino; 1 Hispanic/Latino). 37 applicants, 62% accepted, 18 enrolled. *Entrance requirements:* Additional exam requirements/recommendations for international students: Required—TOEFL (minimum score 575 paper-based; 233 computer-based; 90 iBT), IELTS (minimum score 6.5). *Application deadline:* For fall admission, 6/1 priority date for domestic students, 4/30 for international students; for spring admission, 9/15 for international students. Applications are processed on a rolling basis. Application fee: $45. Electronic applications accepted. *Expenses: Tuition:* Part-time $855 per credit. *Required fees:* $35 per credit. *Financial support:* Traineeships and unspecified assistantships available. Support available to part-time students. Financial award application deadline: 4/15. *Unit head:* Dr. Jeanne LeVasseur, Professor of Nursing, 203-582-3483, Fax: 203-582-3230, E-mail: jeanne.levasseur@quinnipiac.edu. *Application contact:* Kristin Parent, Associate Director of Graduate Health Sciences Admissions, 800-462-1944, Fax: 203-582-3443, E-mail: kristin.parent@quinnipiac.edu. Web site: http://www.quinnipiac.edu/gradnursing.

Regis College, School of Nursing, Science and Health Professions, Weston, MA 02493. Offers biomedical sciences (MS); health administration (MS); nurse practitioner (Certificate); nursing (MS, DNP), nursing education (Certificate). *Accreditation:* NLN. Part-time and evening/weekend programs available. *Degree requirements:* For master's, thesis. *Entrance requirements:* For master's, GRE General Test or MAT, minimum GPA of 3.0; for doctorate, MAT or GRE if GPA from master's lower than 3.5. Additional exam requirements/recommendations for international students: Required—TOEFL (minimum score 550 paper-based; 213 computer-based). Electronic applications accepted. *Faculty research:* Health policy, education, aging, job satisfaction, psychiatric nursing, critical thinking.

Regis University, Rueckert-Hartman College for Health Professions, Denver, CO 80221-1099. Offers family nurse practitioner (MSN); health informatics (Postbaccalaureate Certificate); health services administration (MS); leadership in healthcare systems (MSN); neonatal nurse practitioner (MSN); nursing (MSN); pharmacy (Pharm D); physical therapy (DPT, TDPT). *Entrance requirements:* Additional exam requirements/recommendations for international students: Required—TOEFL (minimum score 550 paper-based; 213 computer-based; 82 iBT). Electronic applications accepted. *Expenses:* Contact institution. *Faculty research:* Normal and pathological balance and gait research, normal/pathological upper limb motor control/biomechanics, exercise energy/metabolism research, optical treatment protocols for therapeutic modalities.

Research College of Nursing, Nursing Program, Kansas City, MO 64132. Offers clinical nurse leader (MSN); executive nurse practitioner (MSN); family nurse practitioner (MSN); nurse educator (MSN). *Accreditation:* AACN. Part-time programs available. Postbaccalaureate distance learning degree programs offered (no on-campus study). *Faculty:* 8 full-time (all women), 1 (woman) part-time/adjunct. *Students:* 9 full-time (7 women), 132 part-time (121 women). Average age 30. In 2011, 23 master's awarded. *Degree requirements:* For master's, research project. *Entrance requirements:* For master's, 3 letters of recommendation, official transcripts, resume. Additional exam requirements/recommendations for international students: Required—TOEFL (minimum score 550 paper-based; 213 computer-based), TWE. *Application deadline:* Applications are processed on a rolling basis. Application fee: $50. *Expenses: Tuition:* Part-time $425 per credit hour. *Required fees:* $25 per credit hour. *Financial support:* Applicants required to submit FAFSA. *Unit head:* Dr. Nancy O. DeBasio, President and Dean, 816-995-2815, Fax: 816-995-2817, E-mail: nancy.debasio@researchcollege.edu. *Application contact:* Leslie Mendenhall, Director of Transfer and Graduate Recruitment, 816-995-2820, Fax: 816-995-2813, E-mail: leslie.mendenhall@researchcollege.edu.

Rivier University, School of Graduate Studies, Division of Nursing, Nashua, NH 03060. Offers adult psychiatric/mental health practitioner (MS); family nurse practitioner (MS); nursing education (MS). *Accreditation:* NLN. Part-time and evening/weekend programs available. *Entrance requirements:* For master's, GRE, MAT. Electronic applications accepted.

Rocky Mountain University of Health Professions, Doctor of Nursing Practice Program, Provo, UT 84606. Offers DNP. *Faculty:* 2 full-time (both women), 10 part-time/adjunct (8 women). *Students:* 44 full-time (39 women); includes 16 minority (8 Black or African American, non-Hispanic/Latino; 4 Asian, non-Hispanic/Latino; 3 Hispanic/Latino; 1 Two or more races, non-Hispanic/Latino). Average age 42. Application fee: $150. *Unit head:* Dr. Marie-Eileen Onieal, Program Director, 801-375-5125, E-mail: monieal@rmuohp.edu. *Application contact:* Bryce Greenberg, Director of Admissions, 801-734-6832, Fax: 801-734-6833, E-mail: bgreenberg@rmuohp.edu.

Rush University, College of Nursing, Department of Community Systems and Mental Health Nursing, Chicago, IL 60612-3832. Offers community and mental health nursing (DNP, PhD); family nurse practitioner (MSN, Post-Master's Certificate); psychiatric clinical specialist (MSN); psychiatric nurse practitioner - adult (MSN); psychiatric nurse practitioner - family (MSN); psychiatric-mental health clinical specialist (Post-Master's Certificate); psychiatric-mental health nurse practitioner (Post-Master's Certificate); public health nursing (MSN). *Accreditation:* AACN. Part-time programs available. Postbaccalaureate distance learning degree programs offered (minimal on-campus study). Terminal master's awarded for partial completion of doctoral program. *Degree requirements:* For master's, capstone project; for doctorate, thesis/dissertation, DNP leadership project. *Entrance requirements:* For master's, GRE General Test (waived if nursing GPA is above 3.0 or cumulative GPA is above 3.25), interview; for doctorate, GRE General Test, interview, course work in statistics (DN Sc). Electronic applications accepted. *Faculty research:* Immigrant mental health, de-escalation strategies, caregiver interventions, parent-teacher training, restraint use.

Rutgers, The State University of New Jersey, Newark, Graduate School, Program in Nursing, Newark, NJ 07102. Offers nursing (MS), including acute care of adults and aged, advanced practice in pediatric nursing, advanced practice with childbearing families, community health nursing, family nurse practitioner, primary care of adults and aged, psychiatric/mental health nursing. *Accreditation:* AACN. Part-time programs available. *Degree requirements:* For master's, comprehensive exam. *Entrance requirements:* For master's, GRE General Test, RN license, minimum B average, BS in nursing. Additional exam requirements/recommendations for international students: Required—TOEFL. Electronic applications accepted. *Faculty research:* HIV/AIDS, quality of life: MS and breast cancer, sleep patterns of cardiac patients.

Sacred Heart University, Graduate Programs, College of Health Professions, Department of Nursing, Fairfield, CT 06825-1000. Offers clinical nurse leader (MSN); clinical practice in health care (DNP); family nurse practitioner (MSN); leadership in health care (DNP); nursing (DN Sc); patient care services administration (MSN).

Family Nurse Practitioner Studies

Accreditation: AACN. Part-time and evening/weekend programs available. Postbaccalaureate distance learning degree programs offered (minimal on-campus study). *Entrance requirements:* For master's, BSN, minimum GPA of 3.0. Additional exam requirements/recommendations for international students: Required—TOEFL (minimum score 550 paper-based; 213 computer-based). Electronic applications accepted. *Expenses:* Contact institution.

Sage Graduate School, School of Health Sciences, Department of Nursing, Program in Family Nurse Practitioner, Troy, NY 12180-4115. Offers MS, Post Master's Certificate. *Accreditation:* AACN. Part-time and evening/weekend programs available. *Faculty:* 5 full-time (all women), 9 part-time/adjunct (all women). *Students:* 11 full-time (10 women), 38 part-time (37 women); includes 5 minority (3 Black or African American, non-Hispanic/Latino; 1 Asian, non-Hispanic/Latino; 1 Hispanic/Latino). Average age 37. 53 applicants, 26% accepted, 11 enrolled. In 2011, 7 master's awarded. *Degree requirements:* For master's, thesis or alternative. *Entrance requirements:* For master's, BS in nursing, minimum GPA of 2.75, resume, 2 letters of recommendation. Additional exam requirements/recommendations for international students: Required—TOEFL (minimum score 550 paper-based; 213 computer-based). *Application deadline:* Applications are processed on a rolling basis. Application fee: $40. *Expenses:* Tuition: Full-time $11,880; part-time $660 per credit hour. Tuition and fees vary according to program. *Financial support:* Fellowships, research assistantships, teaching assistantships, Federal Work-Study, scholarships/grants, and unspecified assistantships available. Support available to part-time students. Financial award application deadline: 3/1; financial award applicants required to submit FAFSA. *Unit head:* Dr. Esther Haskevitz, Dean, School of Health Sciences, 518-244-2296, Fax: 518-244-4571, E-mail: haskve@sage.edu. *Application contact:* Arlene Pericak, Director, 518-244-2012, Fax: 518-244-2009, E-mail: perica@sage.edu.

Saginaw Valley State University, Crystal M. Lange College of Nursing and Health Sciences, Program in Nurse Practitioner, University Center, MI 48710. Offers MSN. *Accreditation:* AACN. Part-time and evening/weekend programs available. *Students:* 12 full-time (11 women), 79 part-time (74 women); includes 6 minority (2 Black or African American, non-Hispanic/Latino; 2 Asian, non-Hispanic/Latino; 2 Hispanic/Latino), 4 international. Average age 37. 28 applicants, 82% accepted, 21 enrolled. In 2011, 13 master's awarded. *Degree requirements:* For master's, thesis optional. *Entrance requirements:* For master's, GRE. Additional exam requirements/recommendations for international students: Required—TOEFL (minimum score 525 paper-based; 237 computer-based; 92 iBT). *Application deadline:* Applications are processed on a rolling basis. Application fee: $25. Electronic applications accepted. *Expenses:* Tuition, state resident: full-time $8300; part-time $5333 per year. Tuition, nonresident: full-time $15,613; part-time $10,209 per year. International tuition: $15,631 full-time. *Financial support:* Federal Work-Study and scholarships/grants available. Support available to part-time students. Financial award application deadline: 4/1; financial award applicants required to submit FAFSA. *Unit head:* Dr. Sally Decker, Professor of Nursing, 989-964-4098, E-mail: decker@svsu.edu. *Application contact:* P. Laine Blasch, Graduate Recruitment Coordinator, 989-964-2182, Fax: 989-790-0180, E-mail: blasch@svsu.edu.

Saint Francis Medical Center College of Nursing, Graduate Programs, Peoria, IL 61603-3783. Offers child and family nurse practitioner (MSN); clinical nurse leader (MSN); family nurse practitioner (MSN); family psychiatric mental health nurse practitioner (MSN); medical-surgical nursing (MSN); neonatal nurse practitioner (MSN); nurse clinician (Post-Graduate Certificate); nurse educator (MSN, Post-Graduate Certificate); nursing (DNP); nursing management leadership (MSN). *Accreditation:* NLN. Part-time programs available. Postbaccalaureate distance learning degree programs offered (minimal on-campus study). *Faculty:* 6 full-time (all women), 5 part-time/adjunct (all women). *Students:* 26 full-time (25 women), 174 part-time (166 women); includes 19 minority (8 Black or African American, non-Hispanic/Latino; 1 American Indian or Alaska Native, non-Hispanic/Latino; 3 Asian, non-Hispanic/Latino; 6 Hispanic/Latino; 1 Native Hawaiian or other Pacific Islander, non-Hispanic/Latino). Average age 37. 123 applicants, 93% accepted, 93 enrolled. In 2011, 29 degrees awarded. *Degree requirements:* For master's, research experience, portfolio, practicum; for doctorate, practicum hours. *Entrance requirements:* For master's, nursing research, health assessment, graduate course work in statistics, RN license; for doctorate, master's degree in nursing, professional portfolio, graduate statistics, transcripts, RN license. Additional exam requirements/recommendations for international students: Required—TOEFL. *Application deadline:* For fall admission, 6/1 priority date for domestic students, 6/1 for international students; for spring admission, 11/15 priority date for domestic students, 11/15 for international students. Applications are processed on a rolling basis. Application fee: $50. Electronic applications accepted. *Expenses:* Tuition: Full-time $6120; part-time $510 per semester hour. Required fees: $300. *Financial support:* In 2011–12, 3 students received support. Scholarships/grants and tuition waivers (partial) available. Support available to part-time students. Financial award application deadline: 6/15; financial award applicants required to submit FAFSA. *Faculty research:* Outcome and curriculum planning, health promotion, NCLEX-RN results, decision-making program evaluation. *Unit head:* Dr. Patti A. Stockert, President of the College, 309-655-4124, Fax: 309-624-8973, E-mail: patricia.a.stockert@osfhealthcare.org. *Application contact:* Dr. Janice F. Boundy, Dean, 309-655-2230, Fax: 309-624-8973, E-mail: jan.f.boundy@osfhealthcare.org. Web site: http://www.sfmccon.edu/graduate-programs/.

St. John Fisher College, Wegmans School of Nursing, Advanced Practice Nursing Program, Rochester, NY 14618-3597. Offers advanced practice nursing (MS); clinical nurse specialist (Certificate); family nurse practitioner (Certificate); nurse educator (Certificate). *Accreditation:* AACN. Part-time and evening/weekend programs available. *Faculty:* 11 full-time (10 women), 4 part-time/adjunct (3 women). *Students:* 4 full-time (3 women), 98 part-time (96 women); includes 10 minority (7 Black or African American, non-Hispanic/Latino; 1 Asian, non-Hispanic/Latino; 2 Hispanic/Latino), 2 international. Average age 33. 35 applicants, 74% accepted, 21 enrolled. In 2011, 20 master's, 1 other advanced degree awarded. *Degree requirements:* For master's, clinical practice, project; for Certificate, clinical practice. *Entrance requirements:* For master's, BSN; undergraduate course work in statistics, health assessment, and nursing research; current New York State RN License; 2 letters of recommendation; current resume. Additional exam requirements/recommendations for international students: Required—TOEFL (minimum score 575 paper-based; 233 computer-based; 80 iBT). *Application deadline:* Applications are processed on a rolling basis. Application fee: $30. Electronic applications accepted. *Expenses:* Tuition: Part-time $735 per credit. One-time fee: $50 part-time. Tuition and fees vary according to course load, degree level and program. *Financial support:* In 2011–12, 39 students received support. Scholarships/grants and traineeships available. Financial award applicants required to submit FAFSA. *Faculty research:* Chronic illness, pediatric injury, women's health, public health policy, health care teams. *Unit head:* Dr. Cynthia McCloskey, Graduate Director, 585-385-8471, Fax: 585-385-8466, E-mail: cmccloskey@sjfc.edu. *Application contact:* Jose Perales, Director of Graduate Admissions, 585-385-8067, E-mail: jperales@sjfc.edu.

Saint Joseph's College of Maine, Master of Science in Nursing Program, Standish, ME 04084. Offers administration (MSN); education (MSN); family nurse practitioner (MSN); nursing administration and leadership (Certificate); nursing and health care education (Certificate). *Accreditation:* AACN. Part-time programs available. Postbaccalaureate distance learning degree programs offered (no on-campus study). *Faculty:* 2 full-time (both women), 22 part-time/adjunct (20 women). *Students:* 768 part-time (665 women); includes 85 minority (48 Black or African American, non-Hispanic/Latino; 21 Asian, non-Hispanic/Latino; 16 Hispanic/Latino). Average age 43. In 2011, 26 master's awarded. *Entrance requirements:* For master's, MAT. *Application deadline:* Applications are processed on a rolling basis. Application fee: $50. Electronic applications accepted. One-time fee: $50. *Financial support:* Institutionally sponsored loans available. Support available to part-time students. Financial award applicants required to submit FAFSA. *Unit head:* Joyce Murphy, Program Director, 207-893-7841, Fax: 207-892-7423, E-mail: jmurphy@sjcme.edu. *Application contact:* Lynne Robinson, Director of Admissions, 800-752-4723, Fax: 207-892-7480, E-mail: info@sjcme.edu. Web site: http://online.sjcme.edu/master-science-nursing.php.

Samford University, Ida V. Moffett School of Nursing, Birmingham, AL 35229. Offers advance practice (DNP); anesthesia (MSN); family nurse practitioner (MSN); nurse educator (MSN); nurse executive (DNP); nurse manager (MSN). *Accreditation:* AACN; AANA/CANAEP (one or more programs are accredited). Part-time programs available. Postbaccalaureate distance learning degree programs offered (minimal on-campus study). *Faculty:* 14 full-time (all women), 2 part-time/adjunct (0 women). *Students:* 226 full-time (152 women), 42 part-time (20 women); includes 43 minority (14 Black or African American, non-Hispanic/Latino; 4 American Indian or Alaska Native, non-Hispanic/Latino; 15 Asian, non-Hispanic/Latino; 9 Hispanic/Latino; 1 Native Hawaiian or other Pacific Islander, non-Hispanic/Latino), 2 international. Average age 39. 50 applicants, 88% accepted, 44 enrolled. In 2011, 95 master's, 14 doctorates awarded. *Median time to degree:* Of those who began their doctoral program in fall 2003, 100% received their degree in 8 years or less. *Degree requirements:* For master's and doctorate, capstone project with oral presentation. *Entrance requirements:* For master's, MAT; GRE (for nurse anesthesia). Additional exam requirements/recommendations for international students: Required—TOEFL (minimum score 550 paper-based; 213 computer-based; 80 iBT). *Application deadline:* For fall admission, 7/1 priority date for domestic students, 7/1 for international students; for spring admission, 10/1 priority date for domestic students, 10/1 for international students. Application fee: $65. Electronic applications accepted. *Expenses:* Contact institution. *Financial support:* In 2011–12, 166 students received support. Institutionally sponsored loans, scholarships/grants, and traineeships available. Financial award application deadline: 3/1; financial award applicants required to submit FAFSA. *Faculty research:* Issues in rural health care, vulnerable populations, genetics and disabilities in pediatrics, geriatrics, Parrish nursing research. *Unit head:* Dr. Nena F. Sanders, Dean, 205-726-2629, E-mail: nfsander@samford.edu. *Application contact:* Dr. Marian Carter, Director of Graduate Student Services, 205-726-2047, Fax: 205-726-4269, E-mail: mwcarter@samford.edu. Web site: http://samford.edu/nursing.

Samuel Merritt University, School of Nursing, Oakland, CA 94609-3108. Offers case management (MSN); family nurse practitioner (MSN, Certificate); nurse anesthetist (MSN, Certificate); nursing (MSN, DNP). *Accreditation:* AACN; AANA/CANAEP (one or more programs are accredited). Part-time and evening/weekend programs available. *Degree requirements:* For master's, thesis or alternative. *Entrance requirements:* For master's, minimum GPA of 2.5 in science, 3.0 overall; previous course work in statistics; current RN license. Additional exam requirements/recommendations for international students: Required—TOEFL. *Faculty research:* Gerontology, community health, maternal-child health, sexually transmitted diseases, substance abuse, oncology.

San Francisco State University, Division of Graduate Studies, College of Health and Human Services, School of Nursing, San Francisco, CA 94132-1722. Offers clinical nurse specialist (MS); community/public health nursing (MS); family nurse practitioner (MS, Certificate); nursing administration (MS); nursing education (MS). *Accreditation:* AACN. Part-time programs available. *Application deadline:* Applications are processed on a rolling basis. *Financial support:* Career-related internships or fieldwork available. *Unit head:* Dr. Lynette Landry, Director, 415-338-1802, E-mail: llandry@sfsu.edu. *Application contact:* Dr. Mary-Ann van Dam, Associate Director, 415-338-1802, E-mail: vandam@sfsu.edu. Web site: http://nursing.sfsu.edu.

Seattle Pacific University, MS in Nursing Program, Seattle, WA 98119-1997. Offers administration (MSN); adult/gerontology nurse practitioner (MSN); clinical nurse specialist (MSN); family nurse practitioner (MSN, Certificate); informatics (MSN); nurse educator (MSN). *Accreditation:* AACN. Part-time programs available. *Degree requirements:* For master's, thesis. Electronic applications accepted. *Expenses:* Contact institution.

Seattle University, College of Nursing, Program in Advanced Practice Nursing Immersion, Seattle, WA 98122-1090. Offers adult/gerontological nurse practitioner (MSN); advanced community public health (MSN); certified nurse midwifery (MSN); family nurse practitioner (MSN); psychiatric mental health nurse practitioner (MSN). *Faculty:* 43 full-time, 63 part-time/adjunct. *Students:* 104 full-time (91 women); includes 24 minority (2 Black or African American, non-Hispanic/Latino; 12 Asian, non-Hispanic/Latino; 7 Hispanic/Latino; 3 Two or more races, non-Hispanic/Latino). Average age 30. *Degree requirements:* For master's, thesis or scholarly project. *Entrance requirements:* For master's, GRE, bachelor's degree, minimum GPA of 3.0, professional resume, two recommendations, letter of intent, English proficiency (for non-English speakers). Additional exam requirements/recommendations for international students: Required—TOEFL (minimum score 92 iBT), IELTS. *Application deadline:* For fall admission, 12/1 for domestic and international students. Application fee: $55. Electronic applications accepted. *Financial support:* Scholarships/grants and traineeships available. Financial award applicants required to submit FAFSA. *Unit head:* Dr. Azita Emami, Dean, 206-296-5660. *Application contact:* Janet Shandley, Associate Dean of Graduate Admissions, 206-296-5900, Fax: 206-298-5656, E-mail: grad_admissions@seattleu.edu.

Shenandoah University, School of Health Professions, Division of Nursing, Winchester, VA 22601-5195. Offers family nurse practitioner (Certificate); nurse-midwifery (Certificate); nurse-midwifery endorsement (Certificate); nursing (MSN, DNP); post-master's in nursing education (Certificate); psychiatric mental health nurse practitioner (Certificate). *Accreditation:* AACN; ACNM/ACME. Part-time programs available. *Faculty:* 11 full-time (all women), 2 part-time/adjunct (both women). *Students:* 40 full-time (34 women), 102 part-time (96 women); includes 32 minority (22 Black or African American, non-Hispanic/Latino; 1 American Indian or Alaska Native, non-Hispanic/Latino; 5 Asian, non-Hispanic/Latino; 3 Hispanic/Latino; 1 Two or more races, non-Hispanic/Latino), 2 international. Average age 39. 69 applicants, 90% accepted, 45 enrolled. In 2011, 15 master's, 2 doctorates, 17 other advanced degrees awarded. *Degree requirements:* For master's, research project, clinical hours; for doctorate and Certificate, clinical hours. *Entrance requirements:* For master's, GRE General Test, previous course work in statistics, community nursing, and physical assessment; RN license; BSN; minimum undergraduate GPA of 3.0; appropriate clinical experience; curriculum vitae; 3 letters of recommendation; for doctorate, MSN, minimum GPA of 3.0, 3 letters of recommendation, essay, interview; for Certificate, MSN, minimum GPA of 3.0, 3 letters of recommendation, minimum of one year (2,080 hours) clinical nursing experience, interview. Additional exam requirements/recommendations for international students: Required—TOEFL (minimum score 550 paper-based; 213 computer-based; 79 iBT), IELTS (minimum score 6.5), Sakae Institute of Study Abroad (minimum score 550). *Application deadline:* For fall

admission, 6/15 priority date for domestic students, 6/15 for international students. Applications are processed on a rolling basis. Application fee: $30. Electronic applications accepted. *Expenses: Tuition:* Full-time $17,952; part-time $748 per credit. *Required fees:* $500 per term. Tuition and fees vary according to course level, course load and program. *Financial support:* In 2011–12, 13 students received support, including 3 teaching assistantships with partial tuition reimbursements available (averaging $4,224 per year); career-related internships or fieldwork, institutionally sponsored loans, scholarships/grants, unspecified assistantships, and federal loans, alternative loans also available. Support available to part-time students. Financial award application deadline: 3/15; financial award applicants required to submit FAFSA. *Faculty research:* Moral reasoning in nurses, improving health care access to under-served rural women, screening for depression and anxiety in the obese in a rural free clinic, health care outcomes among patients in a free clinic setting cared for by nurse practitioners, effects of depression on diabetes as evidenced by the relationship between the patient healthcare questionnaire (PHQ-9) scores and the patient's glycohemoglobin (HbA1c). *Unit head:* Dr. Kathryn Ganske, Director, 540-678-4374, Fax: 540-665-5519, E-mail: kganske@su.edu. *Application contact:* David Anthony, Dean of Admissions, 540-665-4581, Fax: 540-665-4627, E-mail: admit@su.edu. Web site: http://www.su.edu/nurse.

Sonoma State University, School of Science and Technology, Family Nurse Practitioner Program, Rohnert Park, CA 94928-3609. Offers MS. *Accreditation:* NLN. Part-time programs available. *Faculty:* 12 full-time (all women), 6 part-time/adjunct (all women). *Students:* 26 full-time (18 women), 122 part-time (104 women); includes 47 minority (10 Black or African American, non-Hispanic/Latino; 1 American Indian or Alaska Native, non-Hispanic/Latino; 19 Asian, non-Hispanic/Latino; 11 Hispanic/Latino; 6 Two or more races, non-Hispanic/Latino). Average age 38. 109 applicants, 61% accepted, 38 enrolled. In 2011, 74 master's awarded. *Degree requirements:* For master's, comprehensive exam, thesis or alternative, oral exams. *Entrance requirements:* For master's, GRE General Test, BSN, minimum GPA of 3.0, course work in statistics, physical assessment, RN license. Additional exam requirements/recommendations for international students: Required—TOEFL (minimum score 500 paper-based; 173 computer-based). *Application deadline:* For fall admission, 11/30 for domestic students. Application fee: $55. *Financial support:* Fellowships and traineeships available. Financial award applicants required to submit FAFSA. *Faculty research:* Neonatal ethics. *Unit head:* Dr. Elizabeth Close, Chair, 707-664-2465, E-mail: elizabeth.close@sonoma.edu. *Application contact:* Dr. Wendy Smith, Director, 707-664-2276, E-mail: wendy.smith@sonoma.edu. Web site: http://www.sonoma.edu/nursing/fnpp/default.

Southeastern Louisiana University, College of Nursing and Health Sciences, School of Nursing, Hammond, LA 70402. Offers adult psychiatric/mental health nurse practitioner/clinical nurse specialist (MSN); education (MSN); nurse executive (MSN); nurse practitioner (MSN). *Accreditation:* AACN. Part-time and evening/weekend programs available. *Faculty:* 12 full-time (11 women), 7 part-time/adjunct (4 women). *Students:* 17 full-time (16 women), 108 part-time (94 women); includes 12 minority (8 Black or African American, non-Hispanic/Latino; 2 Asian, non-Hispanic/Latino; 1 Hispanic/Latino; 1 Two or more races, non-Hispanic/Latino), 1 international. Average age 35. 50 applicants, 100% accepted, 29 enrolled. In 2011, 27 degrees awarded. *Degree requirements:* For master's, thesis. *Entrance requirements:* For master's, GRE (verbal and quantitative), baccalaureate degree in nursing from accredited undergraduate nursing program; minimum GPA of 2.7; all transcripts from undergraduate school and any work attempted at the graduate level; curriculum vitae; valid Louisiana Registered Nurse license; letters of recommendation; letter of intent/statement of purpose. Additional exam requirements/recommendations for international students: Required—TOEFL (minimum score 500 paper-based; 173 computer-based; 61 iBT). *Application deadline:* For fall admission, 7/15 priority date for domestic students, 6/1 for international students; for spring admission, 12/1 priority date for domestic students, 10/1 for international students. Applications are processed on a rolling basis. Application fee: $20 ($30 for international students). Electronic applications accepted. *Expenses:* Tuition, state resident: full-time $3977; part-time $283 per semester hour. Tuition, nonresident: full-time $13,482; part-time $811 per semester hour. *Financial support:* Federal Work-Study, institutionally sponsored loans, scholarships/grants, traineeships, and unspecified assistantships available. Support available to part-time students. Financial award application deadline: 5/1; financial award applicants required to submit FAFSA. *Faculty research:* Gender issues, LGBT issues, occupational health/safety, accelerated students, caring development. *Total annual research expenditures:* $245,268. *Unit head:* Dr. Lorinda Sealy, Graduate Coordinator, 985-549-5045, Fax: 985-549-5087, E-mail: lorinda.sealy@selu.edu. *Application contact:* Sandra Meyers, Graduate Admissions Analyst, 985-549-5620, Fax: 985-549-5632, E-mail: admissions@selu.edu. Web site: http://www.selu.edu/acad_research/depts/nurs.

Southern Adventist University, School of Nursing, Collegedale, TN 37315-0370. Offers acute care nurse practitioner (MSN); adult nurse practitioner (MSN); family nurse practitioner (MSN); nurse educator (MSN); MSN/MSBA. *Accreditation:* NLN. Part-time programs available. *Degree requirements:* For master's, thesis or project. *Entrance requirements:* For master's, RN license. Additional exam requirements/recommendations for international students: Required—TOEFL (minimum score 600 paper-based; 250 computer-based). Electronic applications accepted. *Faculty research:* Pain management, ethics, corporate wellness, caring spirituality, stress.

Southern Illinois University Edwardsville, Graduate School, School of Nursing, Program in Family Nurse Practitioner, Edwardsville, IL 62026-0001. Offers MS, Post-Master's Certificate. *Accreditation:* AACN. Part-time programs available. *Students:* 97 part-time (88 women); includes 8 minority (3 Black or African American, non-Hispanic/Latino; 2 Asian, non-Hispanic/Latino; 1 Hispanic/Latino; 2 Two or more races, non-Hispanic/Latino), 1 international. 129 applicants, 27% accepted. In 2011, 19 degrees awarded. *Degree requirements:* For master's, comprehensive exam. *Entrance requirements:* For master's, appropriate bachelor's degree, RN license. Additional exam requirements/recommendations for international students: Required—TOEFL (minimum score 550 paper-based; 213 computer-based; 79 iBT), IELTS (minimum score 6.5). *Application deadline:* For fall admission, 3/1 for domestic and international students. Application fee: $30. Electronic applications accepted. Tuition and fees vary according to course load and program. *Financial support:* Fellowships with full tuition reimbursements, research assistantships, teaching assistantships, institutionally sponsored loans, scholarships/grants, and unspecified assistantships available. Financial award application deadline: 3/1; financial award applicants required to submit FAFSA. *Unit head:* Dr. Kathy Ketchum, Director, 618-650-3936, E-mail: kketchu@siue.edu. *Application contact:* Dr. Kathy Ketchum, Director, 618-650-3936, E-mail: kketchu@siue.edu. Web site: http://www.siue.edu/nursing/graduate.

Southern Illinois University Edwardsville, Graduate School, School of Nursing, Program in Nursing Practice, Edwardsville, IL 62026. Offers DNP. Part-time programs available. *Faculty:* 28 full-time (26 women). *Students:* 21 part-time (19 women); includes 3 minority (2 Black or African American, non-Hispanic/Latino; 1 American Indian or Alaska Native, non-Hispanic/Latino). 22 applicants, 77% accepted. *Degree requirements:* For doctorate, thesis/dissertation or alternative, project. *Entrance requirements:* Additional exam requirements/recommendations for international students: Required—TOEFL (minimum score 550 paper-based; 213 computer-based; 79 iBT), IELTS (minimum score 6.5). *Application deadline:* For spring admission, 3/1 priority date for domestic students, 3/1 for international students. Application fee: $30. Electronic applications accepted. Tuition and fees vary according to course load and program. *Financial support:* Institutionally sponsored loans, scholarships/grants, and unspecified assistantships available. Financial award application deadline: 3/1; financial award applicants required to submit FAFSA. *Unit head:* Dr. Marcia Maurer, Dean, 618-650-3959, E-mail: mamaure@siue.edu. *Application contact:* Dr. Kathy Ketchum, Assistant Dean for Graduate Programs, 618-650-3975, E-mail: kketchu@siue.edu. Web site: http://www.siue.edu/nursing/graduate/dnp/overview.shtml.

Southern University and Agricultural and Mechanical College, School of Nursing, Baton Rouge, LA 70813. Offers educator/administrator (PhD); family health nursing (MSN); family nurse practitioner (Post Master's Certificate); geriatric nurse practitioner/gerontology (PhD). *Accreditation:* AACN. Part-time programs available. *Degree requirements:* For master's, comprehensive exam, thesis; for doctorate, comprehensive exam, thesis/dissertation. *Entrance requirements:* For master's, GRE General Test, BSN, minimum GPA of 2.7; for doctorate, GRE General Test; for Post Master's Certificate, MSN. Additional exam requirements/recommendations for international students: Required—TOEFL (minimum score 525 paper-based; 193 computer-based). *Faculty research:* Health promotions, vulnerable populations, (community-based) cardiovascular participating research, health disparities chronic diseases, care of the elderly.

South University, Program in Nursing, Tampa, FL 33614. Offers adult health nurse practitioner (MS); family nurse practitioner (MS); nurse educator (MS).

South University, Program in Nursing, Royal Palm Beach, FL 33411. Offers family nurse practitioner (MS).

Spalding University, Graduate Studies, College of Health and Natural Sciences, School of Nursing, Louisville, KY 40203-2188. Offers adult nurse practitioner (MSN); family nurse practitioner (MSN); leadership in nursing and healthcare (MSN); pediatric nurse practitioner (MSN). *Accreditation:* AACN. Part-time and evening/weekend programs available. *Faculty:* 6 full-time (all women), 5 part-time/adjunct (all women). *Students:* 90 full-time (82 women), 24 part-time (all women); includes 21 minority (16 Black or African American, non-Hispanic/Latino; 3 Asian, non-Hispanic/Latino; 1 Hispanic/Latino; 1 Native Hawaiian or other Pacific Islander, non-Hispanic/Latino). Average age 36. 85 applicants, 24% accepted, 15 enrolled. In 2011, 23 master's awarded. *Degree requirements:* For master's, comprehensive exam (for some programs), thesis. *Entrance requirements:* For master's, GRE General Test, BSN or bachelor's degree and RN licensure. Additional exam requirements/recommendations for international students: Required—TOEFL (minimum score 535 paper-based; 203 computer-based). *Application deadline:* For fall admission, 3/1 priority date for domestic students. Applications are processed on a rolling basis. Application fee: $30. *Expenses: Tuition:* Full-time $12,438. Tuition and fees vary according to course load, degree level and program. *Financial support:* In 2011–12, 21 students received support, including 1 research assistantship with partial tuition reimbursement available (averaging $4,260 per year); career-related internships or fieldwork, scholarships/grants, and traineeships also available. Support available to part-time students. Financial award application deadline: 3/15; financial award applicants required to submit FAFSA. *Faculty research:* Nurse educational administration, gerontology, bioterrorism, healthcare ethics, leadership. *Unit head:* Dr. Paula Travis, Chair, 502-873-4298, E-mail: clewis@spalding.edu. *Application contact:* Dr. Pam King, 502-873-4292, E-mail: pking@spalding.edu. Web site: http://www.spalding.edu/nursing/.

State University of New York Downstate Medical Center, College of Nursing, Graduate Program in Nursing, Nurse Practitioner Program, Brooklyn, NY 11203-2098. Offers MS, Post Master's Certificate. *Accreditation:* AACN. Part-time programs available. *Degree requirements:* For master's, thesis optional. *Entrance requirements:* For master's, GRE, BSN; minimum GPA of 3.0; previous undergraduate course work in statistics, health assessment, and nursing research; RN license; for Post Master's Certificate, BSN; minimum GPA of 3.0; RN license; previous undergraduate course work in statistics, health assessment, and nursing research. *Faculty research:* Women's health.

State University of New York Institute of Technology, Program in Family Nurse Practitioner, Utica, NY 13504-3050. Offers MS, CAS. *Accreditation:* AACN. Part-time programs available. *Degree requirements:* For master's, thesis or project. *Entrance requirements:* For master's, GRE (if undergraduate GPA less than 3.3), minimum GPA of 3.0 in last 30 undergraduate hours, bachelor's degree in nursing, 1 year professional experience, RN license, interview, 2 letters of recommendation. Additional exam requirements/recommendations for international students: Required—TOEFL (minimum score 550 paper-based; 213 computer-based). *Faculty research:* Adult and family healthcare, critical thinking, epidemiology, refugee and women's health, child obesity.

State University of New York Upstate Medical University, College of Nursing, Syracuse, NY 13210-2334. Offers nurse practitioner (Post Master's Certificate); nursing (MS). *Accreditation:* AACN. Part-time programs available. Postbaccalaureate distance learning degree programs offered (no on-campus study). *Degree requirements:* For master's, thesis or alternative. *Entrance requirements:* For master's, 3 years of work experience. Electronic applications accepted.

Stony Brook University, State University of New York, Stony Brook University Medical Center, Health Sciences Center, School of Nursing, Program in Family Nurse Practitioner, Stony Brook, NY 11794. Offers MS, Certificate. *Accreditation:* AACN. Postbaccalaureate distance learning degree programs offered. *Degree requirements:* For master's, thesis. *Entrance requirements:* For master's, BSN, minimum GPA of 3.0, course work in statistics.

Stony Brook University, State University of New York, Stony Brook University Medical Center, Health Sciences Center, School of Nursing, Program in Perinatal Women's Health Nursing, Stony Brook, NY 11794. Offers MS, Certificate. *Accreditation:* AACN. Postbaccalaureate distance learning degree programs offered. *Degree requirements:* For master's, thesis. *Entrance requirements:* For master's, BSN, minimum GPA of 3.0, course work in statistics.

Tennessee State University, The School of Graduate Studies and Research, School of Nursing, Nashville, TN 37209-1561. Offers family nurse practitioner (MSN); holistic nursing (MSN); nursing administration (MSN); nursing education (MSN); nursing informatics (MSN). *Accreditation:* NLN. *Entrance requirements:* For master's, GRE General Test or MAT, BSN, current RN license, minimum GPA of 3.0.

Tennessee Technological University, Whitson-Hester School of Nursing, Cookeville, TN 38505. Offers family nurse practitioner (MSN); informatics (MSN); nursing administration (MSN); nursing education (MSN). Part-time and evening/weekend programs available. Postbaccalaureate distance learning degree programs offered (no on-campus study). *Students:* 3 full-time (2 women), 43 part-time (39 women); includes 3 minority (1 Black or African American, non-Hispanic/Latino; 2 Hispanic/Latino). 48 applicants, 46% accepted, 15 enrolled. In 2011, 13 master's awarded. *Degree requirements:* For master's, comprehensive exam, thesis or alternative. *Entrance requirements:* Additional exam requirements/recommendations for international

students: Required—TOEFL (minimum score 550 paper-based; 79 iBT), IELTS (minimum score 5.5), Pearson Test of English Academic. *Application deadline:* For fall admission, 8/1 for domestic students, 5/1 for international students; for spring admission, 12/1 for domestic students, 10/1 for international students. Application fee: $25 ($30 for international students). Electronic applications accepted. *Expenses:* Tuition, state resident: full-time $8094; part-time $422 per credit hour. Tuition, nonresident: full-time $20,574; part-time $1046 per credit hour. *Financial support:* Application deadline: 4/1. *Unit head:* Dr. Sherry Gaines, Director, 931-372-3203, Fax: 931-372-6244, E-mail: sgaines@tntech.edu. *Application contact:* Shelia K. Kendrick, Coordinator of Graduate Admissions, 931-372-3808, Fax: 931-372-3497, E-mail: skendrick@tntech.edu.

Texas A&M International University, Office of Graduate Studies and Research, College of Nursing and Health Sciences, Laredo, TX 78041-1900. Offers family nurse practitioner (MSN). *Accreditation:* NLN. *Faculty:* 4 full-time (all women). *Students:* 29 part-time (24 women); includes 27 minority (1 Asian, non-Hispanic/Latino; 26 Hispanic/Latino). Average age 34. 26 applicants, 81% accepted, 16 enrolled. *Entrance requirements:* Additional exam requirements/recommendations for international students: Required—TOEFL (minimum score 550 paper-based; 213 computer-based; 79 iBT). *Application deadline:* For fall admission, 4/30 for domestic and international students; for spring admission, 11/30 for domestic students, 10/1 for international students. Application fee: $35 ($50 for international students). *Expenses:* Tuition, state resident: full-time $5063. *Unit head:* Regina Aune, Dean, 956-326-2574, E-mail: regina.aune@tamiu.edu. *Application contact:* Suzanne Hansen-Alford, Director of Graduate Recruiting, 956-326-3023, Fax: 956-326-3021, E-mail: enroll@tamiu.edu. Web site: http://www.tamiu.edu/cson/.

Texas A&M University–Corpus Christi, Graduate Studies and Research, College of Nursing and Health Sciences, Corpus Christi, TX 78412-5503. Offers clinical nurse specialist (MSN); family nurse practitioner (MSN); health care administration (MSN); leadership in nursing systems (MSN). *Accreditation:* AACN. Part-time and evening/weekend programs available. *Degree requirements:* For master's, comprehensive exam, thesis (for some programs). *Entrance requirements:* For master's, GRE General Test. Additional exam requirements/recommendations for international students: Required—TOEFL. Electronic applications accepted.

Texas Tech University Health Sciences Center, School of Nursing, Lubbock, TX 79430. Offers acute care nurse practitioner (MSN, Certificate); administration (MSN); advanced practice (DNP); education (MSN); executive leadership (DNP); family nurse practitioner (MSN, Certificate); geriatric nurse practitioner (MSN, Certificate); pediatric nurse practitioner (MSN, Certificate). *Accreditation:* AACN. Part-time programs available. Postbaccalaureate distance learning degree programs offered (minimal on-campus study). *Degree requirements:* For master's, thesis optional. *Entrance requirements:* For master's, minimum GPA of 3.0, 3 letters of reference, BSN, RN license; for Certificate, minimum GPA of 3.0, 3 letters of reference, RN license. Additional exam requirements/recommendations for international students: Required—TOEFL (minimum score 550 paper-based; 213 computer-based). *Faculty research:* Diabetes/obesity, nurse competency, disease management, intervention and measurements, health disparities.

Texas Woman's University, Graduate School, College of Nursing, Denton, TX 76201. Offers acute care nurse practitioner (MS); adult health clinical nurse specialist (MS); adult health nurse practitioner (MS); child health clinical nurse specialist (MS); clinical nurse leader (MS); family nurse practitioner (MS); health systems management (MS); nursing education (MS); nursing practice (DNP); nursing science (PhD); pediatric nurse practitioner (MS); women's health clinical nurse specialist (MS); women's health nurse practitioner (MS). *Accreditation:* AACN. Part-time programs available. Postbaccalaureate distance learning degree programs offered. *Faculty:* 70 full-time (69 women), 7 part-time/adjunct (all women). *Students:* 87 full-time (78 women), 870 part-time (815 women); includes 489 minority (235 Black or African American, non-Hispanic/Latino; 5 American Indian or Alaska Native, non-Hispanic/Latino; 169 Asian, non-Hispanic/Latino; 78 Hispanic/Latino; 2 Native Hawaiian or other Pacific Islander, non-Hispanic/Latino), 19 international. Average age 38. 368 applicants, 71% accepted, 205 enrolled. In 2011, 147 master's, 21 doctorates awarded. *Degree requirements:* For master's, comprehensive exam, thesis or alternative; for doctorate, comprehensive exam, thesis/dissertation. *Entrance requirements:* For master's, GRE or MAT, minimum GPA of 3.0 on last 60 hours in undergraduate nursing degree and overall, RN license, BS in nursing, basic statistics course; for doctorate, GRE (preferred minimum score 153 [500 old version] Verbal, 144 [500 old version] Quantitative, 4 Analytical), MS in nursing, minimum preferred GPA of 3.5, RN license, statistics, 2 letters of reference, curriculum vitae, graduate nursing-theory course, graduate research course, statement of professional goals and research interests. Additional exam requirements/recommendations for international students: Required—TOEFL (minimum score 550 paper-based; 213 computer-based; 79 iBT). *Application deadline:* For fall admission, 5/1 priority date for domestic students, 3/1 for international students; for spring admission, 9/15 priority date for domestic students, 7/1 for international students. Applications are processed on a rolling basis. Application fee: $50 ($75 for international students). Electronic applications accepted. *Expenses:* Tuition, state resident: full-time $3834; part-time $213 per credit hour. Tuition, nonresident: full-time $9468; part-time $526 per credit hour. *Required fees:* $213 per credit hour. Tuition and fees vary according to course load. *Financial support:* In 2011–12, 149 students received support, including 10 research assistantships (averaging $12,942 per year), 1 teaching assistantship (averaging $12,942 per year); career-related internships or fieldwork, Federal Work-Study, institutionally sponsored loans, scholarships/grants, traineeships, health care benefits, and unspecified assistantships also available. Support available to part-time students. Financial award application deadline: 3/1; financial award applicants required to submit FAFSA. *Faculty research:* Screening, prevention, and treatment for intimate partner violence; needs of adolescents during childbirth intervention; a network analysis decision tool for nurse managers (Social Network Analysis); support for adolescents with implantable cardioverter defibrillators; informatics: nurse staffing, safety, quality, and financial data as they relate to patient care outcomes; prevention and treatment of obesity; improving infant outcomes related to premature birth. *Total annual research expenditures:* $462,088. *Unit head:* Dr. Patricia Holden-Huchton, Interim Dean, 940-898-2401, Fax: 940-898-2437, E-mail: nursing@twu.edu. *Application contact:* Dr. Samuel Wheeler, Assistant Director of Admissions, 940-898-3188, Fax: 940-898-3081, E-mail: wheelersr@twu.edu. Web site: http://www.twu.edu/nursing/.

Troy University, Graduate School, College of Health and Human Services, Program in Nursing, Troy, AL 36082. Offers adult health (MSN); clinical nurse specialist adult health (DNP); clinical nurse specialist maternal infant (DNP); family nurse practitioner (MSN, DNP, PMC); informatics specialist (MSN); maternal infant (MSN). *Accreditation:* NLN. Part-time and evening/weekend programs available. *Faculty:* 11 full-time (10 women), 7 part-time/adjunct (4 women). *Students:* 58 full-time (43 women), 181 part-time (165 women); includes 91 minority (76 Black or African American, non-Hispanic/Latino; 8 American Indian or Alaska Native, non-Hispanic/Latino; 1 Asian, non-Hispanic/Latino; 3 Hispanic/Latino; 1 Native Hawaiian or other Pacific Islander, non-Hispanic/Latino; 2 Two or more races, non-Hispanic/Latino). Average age 38. 144 applicants, 63% accepted, 73 enrolled. In 2011, 35 master's, 8 doctorates awarded. *Degree requirements:* For

master's, comprehensive exam, minimum GPA of 3.0, candidacy; for doctorate, minimum GPA of 3.0, submission of approved comprehensive e-portfolio, completion of residency synthesis project, minimum of 1000 hours of clinical practice, score of 80% or better on qualifying exam. *Entrance requirements:* For master's, MAT (minimum score 396) or GRE (minimum score 850), minimum GPA of 3.0, BSN, current RN licensure; 2 letters of reference; for doctorate, GRE (minimum score of 850), BSN or MSN, minimum GPA of 3.0, 2 letters of reference, current RN licensure, essay. Additional exam requirements/recommendations for international students: Required—TOEFL (minimum score 523 paper-based; 193 computer-based; 70 iBT), IELTS (minimum score 6), or ACT COMPASS ESL (minimum listening, reading, and grammar score 270). *Application deadline:* Applications are processed on a rolling basis. Application fee: $50. Electronic applications accepted. *Expenses:* Tuition, state resident: full-time $6960; part-time $290 per credit hour. Tuition, nonresident: full-time $13,920; part-time $580 per credit hour. *Required fees:* $386 per term. *Financial support:* Available to part-time students. Applicants required to submit FAFSA. *Unit head:* Dr. Bernita K. Hamilton, Director, School of Nursing, 334-670-3428, Fax: 334-670-3743, E-mail: bernitah@troy.edu. *Application contact:* Brenda K. Campbell, Director of Graduate Admissions, 334-670-3178, Fax: 334-670-3733, E-mail: bcamp@troy.edu.

Uniformed Services University of the Health Sciences, Graduate School of Nursing, Bethesda, MD 20814-4799. Offers family nurse practitioner (MSN); nurse anesthesia (MSN); nursing science (PhD); perioperative clinical nurse specialty (MSN); psychiatric mental health nurse practitioner (MSN). Program available to military officers only. *Accreditation:* AACN; AANA/CANAEP. *Faculty:* 36 full-time (21 women), 2 part-time/adjunct (0 women). *Students:* 71 full-time (35 women); includes 17 minority (11 Black or African American, non-Hispanic/Latino; 3 Asian, non-Hispanic/Latino; 3 Hispanic/Latino). Average age 36. 120 applicants, 59% accepted, 71 enrolled. In 2011, 57 master's, 2 doctorates awarded. *Degree requirements:* For master's, thesis or alternative. *Entrance requirements:* For master's, GRE, BSN, clinical experience, minimum GPA of 3.0, previous course work in science, writing paper; for doctorate, GRE, written papers, articles. *Application deadline:* For fall admission, 7/1 for domestic students; for winter admission, 2/15 for domestic students. Application fee: $0. Electronic applications accepted. *Faculty research:* Prenatal care, military health care, military readiness, distance learning. *Unit head:* Dr. Carol A. Romano, Associate Dean for Academic Affairs, 301-295-1180, Fax: 301-295-1707, E-mail: carol.romano@usuhs.edu. *Application contact:* Terry Lynn Malavakis, Recording Secretary for Admissions Committee, 301-295-1055, Fax: 301-295-1707, E-mail: terry.malavakis@usuhs.edu. Web site: http://www.usuhs.mil/gsn/.

Union University, School of Nursing, Jackson, TN 38305-3697. Offers executive leadership (DNP); nurse anesthesia (DNP); nurse anesthetist (PMC); nurse practitioner (DNP); nursing education (MSN, PMC). *Accreditation:* AACN; AANA/CANAEP. *Degree requirements:* For master's, thesis or alternative. *Entrance requirements:* For master's, GRE, 3 letters of reference, bachelor's degree in nursing, minimum GPA of 3.0. Additional exam requirements/recommendations for international students: Required—TOEFL (minimum score 560 paper-based; 220 computer-based). Electronic applications accepted. *Faculty research:* Children's health, occupational rehabilitation, informatics, health promotion.

United States University, Family Nurse Practitioner Program, Chula Vista, CA 91911. Offers MSN. *Degree requirements:* For master's, project. *Entrance requirements:* For master's, RN license, minimum cumulative undergraduate GPA of 2.5, background check, official transcripts, personal goal statement. Additional exam requirements/recommendations for international students: Required—TOEFL (minimum score 550 paper-based; 213 computer-based; 80 iBT).

Universidad del Turabo, Graduate Programs, School of Health Sciences, Programs in Nursing, Program in Family Nurse Practitioner, Gurabo, PR 00778-3030. Offers MSN. *Students:* 24 full-time (15 women), 9 part-time (3 women); includes 23 minority (all Hispanic/Latino). Average age 37. 44 applicants, 61% accepted, 21 enrolled. *Unit head:* Dr. Maria Rosa, Dean, 787-743-7979. *Application contact:* Virginia Gonzalez, Admissions Officer, 787-746-3009.

University at Buffalo, the State University of New York, Graduate School, School of Nursing, Buffalo, NY 14214. Offers adult clinical nurse specialist (DNP); adult nurse practitioner (DNP); family nurse practitioner (DNP); health care systems and leadership (MS); nurse anesthetist (DNP); nursing (PhD); nursing education (Certificate); post-master's track (DNP); psychiatric mental health nurse practitioner (DNP). *Accreditation:* AACN; AANA/CANAEP (one or more programs are accredited). Part-time programs available. Postbaccalaureate distance learning degree programs offered (minimal on-campus study). *Faculty:* 29 full-time (25 women), 18 part-time/adjunct (17 women). *Students:* 101 full-time (76 women), 100 part-time (90 women); includes 19 minority (10 Black or African American, non-Hispanic/Latino; 2 American Indian or Alaska Native, non-Hispanic/Latino; 2 Asian, non-Hispanic/Latino; 2 Hispanic/Latino; 3 Native Hawaiian or other Pacific Islander, non-Hispanic/Latino), 34 international. Average age 34. 342 applicants, 26% accepted, 67 enrolled. In 2011, 51 master's, 3 doctorates awarded. *Median time to degree:* Of those who began their doctoral program in fall 2003, 75% received their degree in 8 years or less. *Degree requirements:* For master's, thesis optional, comprehensive exams or project; for doctorate, comprehensive exam (for some programs), capstone (for DNP), dissertation (for PhD). *Entrance requirements:* For doctorate, GRE or MAT, minimum GPA of 3.0 (3.25 for PhD), RN license, BS or MS in nursing, 3 references, writing sample; for Certificate, interview, minimum GPA of 3.0 or GRE General Test, RN license, MS in nursing. Additional exam requirements/recommendations for international students: Required—TOEFL (minimum score 550 paper-based; 213 computer-based; 79 iBT), IELTS (minimum score 6.5). *Application deadline:* For fall admission, 8/15 for domestic students, 4/1 for international students; for spring admission, 12/15 for domestic students, 10/1 for international students. Application fee: $75. Electronic applications accepted. *Financial support:* In 2011–12, 80 students received support, including 6 fellowships with full tuition reimbursements available (averaging $17,000 per year), 3 research assistantships with full tuition reimbursements available (averaging $10,600 per year), 5 teaching assistantships with full tuition reimbursements available (averaging $10,600 per year); scholarships/grants, traineeships, health care benefits, and unspecified assistantships also available. Financial award application deadline: 3/15; financial award applicants required to submit FAFSA. *Faculty research:* Oncology, palliative care, gerontology, addictions, mental health, community wellness. *Total annual research expenditures:* $1.3 million. *Unit head:* Dr. Marsha L. Lewis, Dean and Professor, 716-829-2533, Fax: 716-829-2566, E-mail: ubnursingdean@buffalo.edu. *Application contact:* Dr. David J. Lang, Director of Student Affairs, 716-829-2537, Fax: 716-829-2067, E-mail: nursing@buffalo.edu. Web site: http://nursing.buffalo.edu/.

The University of Alabama in Huntsville, School of Graduate Studies, College of Nursing, Huntsville, AL 35899. Offers family nurse practitioner (Certificate); nursing (MSN, DNP), including acute care nurse practitioner (MSN), adult clinical nursing specialist (MSN), clinical nurse leader (MSN), family nurse practitioner (MSN), leadership in health care systems (MSN); nursing education (Certificate). DNP offered jointly with The University of Alabama at Birmingham. *Accreditation:* AACN. Part-time and evening/weekend programs available. Postbaccalaureate distance learning degree programs offered (minimal on-campus study). *Faculty:* 19 full-time (18 women), 8 part-

time/adjunct (7 women). *Students:* 57 full-time (43 women), 162 part-time (139 women); includes 22 minority (15 Black or African American, non-Hispanic/Latino; 3 American Indian or Alaska Native, non-Hispanic/Latino; 1 Asian, non-Hispanic/Latino; 3 Hispanic/Latino), 2 international. Average age 37. 193 applicants, 79% accepted, 112 enrolled. In 2011, 42 master's, 11 doctorates, 11 other advanced degrees awarded. *Degree requirements:* For master's, comprehensive exam, thesis or alternative, oral and written exams. *Entrance requirements:* For master's, MAT or GRE, Alabama RN license, BSN, minimum GPA of 3.0; for doctorate, master's degree in nursing in an advanced practice area; for Certificate, MAT or GRE, minimum GPA of 3.0. Additional exam requirements/recommendations for international students: Required TOEFL (minimum score 500 paper-based; 173 computer-based; 62 iBT). *Application deadline:* For fall admission, 7/15 for domestic students, 4/1 for international students; for spring admission, 11/30 for domestic students, 9/1 for international students. Applications are processed on a rolling basis. Application fee: $40 ($50 for international students). Electronic applications accepted. *Expenses:* Tuition, state resident: full-time $7830; part-time $473.50 per credit. Tuition, nonresident: full-time $18,748; part-time $1128.33 per credit. Tuition and fees vary according to course load and program. *Financial support:* In 2011–12, 9 students received support, including 9 teaching assistantships with full tuition reimbursements available (averaging $9,596 per year); career-related internships or fieldwork, Federal Work-Study, institutionally sponsored loans, scholarships/grants, traineeships, health care benefits, and unspecified assistantships also available. Support available to part-time students. Financial award application deadline: 4/1; financial award applicants required to submit FAFSA. *Faculty research:* Home health care, gerontology, pediatric nursing, family nurse practitioner, adult acute care administration. *Total annual research expenditures:* $235,384. *Unit head:* Dr. Fay Raines, Dean, 256-824-6345, Fax: 256-824-6026, E-mail: rainesc@uah.edu. *Application contact:* Charles Davis, Director of Graduate Nursing Admissions and Advising, 256-824-2433, Fax: 256-824-6026, E-mail: charles.davis@uah.edu. Web site: http://www.uah.edu/nursing/welcome.

University of Alaska Anchorage, College of Health, School of Nursing, Anchorage, AK 99508. Offers family nurse practitioner (Certificate); nursing (MS); nursing education (Certificate); psychiatric nurse practitioner (Certificate). *Accreditation:* NLN. Part-time and evening/weekend programs available. *Degree requirements:* For master's, comprehensive exam, individual project. *Entrance requirements:* For master's, GRE or MAT, BS in nursing, interview, minimum GPA of 3.0, RN license, 1 year of part-time or 6 months of full-time clinical experience. Additional exam requirements/recommendations for international students: Required—TOEFL (minimum score 550 paper-based; 213 computer-based).

The University of Arizona, College of Nursing, Tucson, AZ 85721. Offers health care informatics (Certificate); nurse practitioner (MS, Certificate); nursing (DNP, PhD); rural health (Certificate). *Accreditation:* AACN. Part-time programs available. Postbaccalaureate distance learning degree programs offered (minimal on-campus study). *Faculty:* 19 full-time (18 women). *Students:* 279 full-time (241 women), 36 part-time (32 women); includes 84 minority (13 Black or African American, non-Hispanic/Latino; 4 American Indian or Alaska Native, non-Hispanic/Latino; 19 Asian, non-Hispanic/Latino; 31 Hispanic/Latino; 1 Native Hawaiian or other Pacific Islander, non-Hispanic/Latino; 16 Two or more races, non-Hispanic/Latino), 3 international. Average age 38. In 2011, 1 master's, 19 doctorates awarded. Terminal master's awarded for partial completion of doctoral program. *Degree requirements:* For master's, thesis optional; for doctorate, comprehensive exam, thesis/dissertation. *Entrance requirements:* For master's, BSN, eligibility for RN license; for doctorate, BSN; for Certificate, GRE General Test, Arizona RN license, BSN, minimum GPA of 3.0. Additional exam requirements/recommendations for international students: Required—TOEFL (minimum score 550 paper-based; 213 computer-based; 79 iBT). *Application deadline:* For fall admission, 1/15 for domestic and international students. Applications are processed on a rolling basis. Application fee: $75. Electronic applications accepted. *Expenses:* Contact institution. *Financial support:* In 2011–12, 4 research assistantships with full tuition reimbursements (averaging $18,220 per year), 3 teaching assistantships (averaging $18,327 per year) were awarded; career-related internships or fieldwork, institutionally sponsored loans, scholarships/grants, traineeships, health care benefits, tuition waivers (full), and unspecified assistantships also available. Financial award application deadline: 6/1. *Faculty research:* Vulnerable populations, injury mechanisms and biobehavioral responses, health care systems, informatics, rural health. *Total annual research expenditures:* $5.5 million. *Unit head:* Dr. Joan Shaver, Dean, 520-626-7124, Fax: 520-626-6424, E-mail: cmurdaugh@nursing.arizona.edu. *Application contact:* Sally J. Reel, Assistant Dean, Student Affairs, 520-626-6154, Fax: 520-626-2211, E-mail: info@nursing.arizona.edu. Web site: http://www.nursing.arizona.edu/.

University of Central Arkansas, Graduate School, College of Health and Behavioral Sciences, Department of Nursing, Conway, AR 72035-0001. Offers clinical nurse specialist (MSN); nurse practitioner (MSN). *Accreditation:* AACN. *Faculty:* 7 full-time (all women). *Students:* 6 full-time (5 women), 147 part-time (138 women); includes 14 minority (7 Black or African American, non-Hispanic/Latino; 5 American Indian or Alaska Native, non-Hispanic/Latino; 2 Hispanic/Latino). Average age 35. 45 applicants, 64% accepted, 26 enrolled. In 2011, 27 master's awarded. *Degree requirements:* For master's, comprehensive exam, thesis optional, clinicals. *Entrance requirements:* For master's, GRE General Test, minimum GPA of 2.7. Additional exam requirements/recommendations for international students: Required—TOEFL (minimum score 550 paper-based; 213 computer-based). *Application deadline:* For fall admission, 3/1 priority date for domestic students; for spring admission, 10/1 for domestic students. Applications are processed on a rolling basis. Application fee: $25 ($50 for international students). *Expenses:* Contact institution. *Financial support:* Federal Work-Study, traineeships, and unspecified assistantships available. Financial award application deadline: 2/15; financial award applicants required to submit FAFSA. *Total annual research expenditures:* $216,643. *Unit head:* Dr. Barbara Williams, Chairperson, 501-450-3119, Fax: 501-450-5503, E-mail: barbaraw@uca.edu. *Application contact:* Susan Wood, Administrative Assistant, 501-450-3124, Fax: 501-450-5678, E-mail: swood@uca.edu. Web site: http://www.uca.edu/divisions/academic/chas/nurse2ab.asp.

University of Central Florida, College of Nursing, Orlando, FL 32816. Offers adult-gerontology clinical nurse specialist (Post-Master's Certificate); adult-gerontology nurse practitioner (Post-Master's Certificate); clinical nurse leader (Post-Master's Certificate); family nurse practitioner (Post-Master's Certificate); nursing (MSN, PhD); nursing education (Post-Master's Certificate); nursing practice (DNP). *Accreditation:* AACN. Part-time and evening/weekend programs available. *Faculty:* 44 full-time (39 women), 72 part-time/adjunct (71 women). *Students:* 75 full-time (68 women), 350 part-time (332 women); includes 109 minority (54 Black or African American, non-Hispanic/Latino; 1 American Indian or Alaska Native, non-Hispanic/Latino; 19 Asian, non-Hispanic/Latino; 33 Hispanic/Latino; 1 Native Hawaiian or other Pacific Islander, non-Hispanic/Latino; 1 Two or more races, non-Hispanic/Latino), 5 international. Average age 40. 203 applicants, 60% accepted, 98 enrolled. In 2011, 110 master's, 17 doctorates, 11 other advanced degrees awarded. *Degree requirements:* For master's, thesis or alternative. *Entrance requirements:* For master's, GRE General Test, minimum GPA of 3.0 in last 60 hours. Additional exam requirements/recommendations for international students: Required—TOEFL. *Application deadline:* For fall admission, 2/15 for domestic students; for spring admission, 9/15 for domestic students. Application fee: $30. Electronic applications accepted. *Expenses:* Tuition, state resident: part-time $277.08 per credit hour. Tuition, nonresident: part-time $277.08 per credit hour. Part-time tuition and fees vary according to degree level and program. *Financial support:* In 2011–12, 92 students received support, including 92 fellowships with partial tuition reimbursements available (averaging $1,100 per year), 2 teaching assistantships with partial tuition reimbursements available (averaging $8,100 per year); research assistantships with partial tuition reimbursements available, career-related internships or fieldwork, Federal Work-Study, institutionally sponsored loans, traineeships, and unspecified assistantships also available. Financial award application deadline: 3/1; financial award applicants required to submit FAFSA. *Unit head:* Dr. Jean D. Leuner, Dean, 407-823-5496, Fax: 407-823-5675, E-mail: jean.leuner@ucf.edu. *Application contact:* Barbara Rodriguez, Director, Admissions and Registration, 407-823-2766, Fax: 407-823-6442, E-mail: gradadmissions@ucf.edu. Web site: http://nursing.ucf.edu/.

University of Colorado at Colorado Springs, Beth-El College of Nursing and Health Sciences, Colorado Springs, CO 80933-7150. Offers adult health nurse practitioner and clinical specialist (MSN); family practitioner (MSN), including community clinical specialist, forensic clinical specialist, holistic clinical specialist; neonatal nurse practitioner and clinical specialist (MSN); nursing administration (MSN); nursing practice (DNP); women nurse practitioner (MSN). *Accreditation:* AACN. Part-time programs available. Postbaccalaureate distance learning degree programs offered (minimal on-campus study). *Faculty:* 31 full-time (28 women), 6 part-time/adjunct (all women). *Students:* 122 full-time (103 women), 68 part-time (64 women); includes 36 minority (4 Black or African American, non-Hispanic/Latino; 2 American Indian or Alaska Native, non-Hispanic/Latino; 9 Asian, non-Hispanic/Latino; 18 Hispanic/Latino; 3 Two or more races, non-Hispanic/Latino), 5 international. Average age 35. 153 applicants, 71% accepted, 60 enrolled. In 2011, 41 master's, 15 doctorates awarded. *Degree requirements:* For master's, comprehensive exam, thesis optional; for doctorate, capstone project. *Entrance requirements:* For master's, GRE General Test or MAT, BSN, minimum GPA of 3.0, unrestricted RN license; for doctorate, interview; active RN license; MA; minimum GPA of 3.3; National Certification as NP or CNS; portfolio. Additional exam requirements/recommendations for international students: Required—TOEFL. *Application deadline:* For fall admission, 6/15 priority date for domestic students; for spring admission, 11/15 for domestic students. Application fee: $60 ($75 for international students). Electronic applications accepted. *Expenses:* Contact institution. *Financial support:* In 2011–12, 33 students received support, including 1 fellowship (averaging $2,500 per year); career-related internships or fieldwork, Federal Work-Study, and scholarships/grants also available. Support available to part-time students. Financial award application deadline: 3/1; financial award applicants required to submit FAFSA. *Faculty research:* Women's health, uncertainty, empowerment, family experience in chronic illness. *Total annual research expenditures:* $322,604. *Unit head:* Dr. Nancy Smith, Dean, 719-255-4411, Fax: 719-255-4416, E-mail: nsmith2@uccs.edu. *Application contact:* Diane Busch, Director, 719-255-4424, Fax: 719-255-4416, E-mail: dbusch@uccs.edu. Web site: http://www.uccs.edu/~bethel/.

University of Colorado Denver, College of Nursing, Aurora, CO 80045. Offers adult clinical nurse specialist (MS); adult nurse practitioner (MS); family nurse practitioner (MS); family psychiatric mental health nurse practitioner (MS); health care informatics (MS); nurse-midwifery (MS); nursing (DNP, PhD); nursing leadership and health care systems (MS); pediatric nurse practitioner (MS); pediatric nursing leadership (MS); special studies (MS); women's health care (MS); MS/PhD. *Accreditation:* ACNM/ACME (one or more programs are accredited); NLN (one or more programs are accredited). Part-time and evening/weekend programs available. Postbaccalaureate distance learning degree programs offered (minimal on-campus study). *Faculty:* 69 full-time (65 women), 68 part-time/adjunct (64 women). *Students:* 308 full-time (288 women), 134 part-time (118 women); includes 59 minority (11 Black or African American, non-Hispanic/Latino; 8 American Indian or Alaska Native, non-Hispanic/Latino; 10 Asian, non-Hispanic/Latino; 27 Hispanic/Latino; 3 Two or more races, non-Hispanic/Latino), 8 international. Average age 39. 298 applicants, 46% accepted, 110 enrolled. In 2011, 72 master's, 19 doctorates awarded. Terminal master's awarded for partial completion of doctoral program. *Degree requirements:* For master's, thesis optional; for doctorate, comprehensive exam, thesis/dissertation, 42 credits of coursework, 30 credits of dissertation. *Entrance requirements:* For master's, GRE if cumulative undergraduate GPA is less than 3.0, undergraduate nursing degree from NLNAC- or CCNE-accredited school or university; completion of research and statistics courses with minimum grade of C; copy of current and unencumbered nursing license; for doctorate, GRE, bachelor's and/or master's degrees in nursing from NLN- or CCNE-accredited institution; portfolio; minimum undergraduate GPA of 3.0, graduate 3.5; graduate-level intermediate statistics and master's-level nursing theory courses with minimum B grade; interview. Additional exam requirements/recommendations for international students: Required—TOEFL (minimum score 560 paper-based; 220 computer-based; 83 iBT). *Application deadline:* For fall admission, 4/1 for domestic students; for spring admission, 9/1 for domestic students. Application fee: $65. Electronic applications accepted. *Expenses:* Contact institution. *Financial support:* In 2011–12, 40 students received support. Fellowships, research assistantships, teaching assistantships, Federal Work-Study, scholarships/grants, and unspecified assistantships available. Support available to part-time students. Financial award application deadline: 4/1; financial award applicants required to submit FAFSA. *Faculty research:* Biological and behavioral phenomena in pregnancy and postpartum; patterns of glycemia during the insulin resistance of pregnancy; obesity, gestational diabetes, and relationship to neonatal adiposity; men's awareness and knowledge of male breast cancer; cognitive-behavioral therapy for chronic insomnia after breast cancer treatment; massage therapy for the treatment of tension-type headaches. *Total annual research expenditures:* $5.2 million. *Unit head:* Dr. Patricia Moritz, Dean, 303-724-1679, E-mail: pat.moritz@ucdenver.edu. *Application contact:* Judy Campbell, Graduate Programs Coordinator, 303-724-8503, E-mail: judy.campbell@ucdenver.edu. Web site: http://www.ucdenver.edu/academics/colleges/nursing/Pages/default.aspx.

University of Delaware, College of Health Sciences, School of Nursing, Newark, DE 19716. Offers adult nurse practitioner (MSN, PMC); cardiopulmonary clinical nurse specialist (MSN, PMC); cardiopulmonary clinical nurse specialist/adult nurse practitioner (MSN, PMC); family nurse practitioner (MSN, PMC); gerontology clinical nurse specialist (MSN, PMC); gerontology clinical nurse specialist geriatric nurse practitioner (PMC); gerontology clinical nurse specialist/geriatric nurse practitioner (MSN); health services administration (MSN, PMC); nursing of children clinical nurse specialist (MSN, PMC); nursing of children clinical nurse specialist/pediatric nurse practitioner (MSN, PMC); oncology/immune deficiency clinical nurse specialist (MSN, PMC); oncology/immune deficiency clinical nurse specialist/adult nurse practitioner (MSN, PMC); perinatal/women's health clinical nurse specialist (MSN, PMC); perinatal/women's health clinical nurse specialist/women's health nurse practitioner (MSN, PMC); psychiatric nursing clinical nurse specialist (MSN, PMC). *Accreditation:* AACN; NLN (one or more programs are accredited). Part-time and evening/weekend programs available. Postbaccalaureate distance learning degree programs offered (minimal on-campus study). *Degree requirements:* For master's, thesis optional. *Entrance requirements:* For master's, BSN, interview, RN license. Electronic applications accepted. *Faculty research:* Marriage and chronic illness, health promotion, congestive heart failure patient outcomes, school nursing, diabetes in children, culture, health disparities, cardiovascular, prison nursing,

oncology, public policy, child obesity, smoking and teen pregnancy, blood pressure measurements, men's health.

University of Detroit Mercy, College of Health Professions, Program in Family Nurse Practitioner, Detroit, MI 48221. Offers MSN, Certificate. *Accreditation:* AACN.

University of Hawaii at Manoa, Graduate Division, School of Nursing and Dental Hygiene, Honolulu, HI 96822. Offers clinical nurse specialist (MS), including adult health, community mental health; nurse practitioner (MS), including adult health, community mental health, family nurse practitioner; nursing (PhD, Graduate Certificate); nursing administration (MS). *Accreditation:* AACN; NLN (one or more programs are accredited). Part-time programs available. Postbaccalaureate distance learning degree programs offered (minimal on-campus study). *Degree requirements:* For master's, thesis optional; for doctorate, comprehensive exam, thesis/dissertation. *Entrance requirements:* For master's, Hawaii RN license. Additional exam requirements/recommendations for international students: Required—TOEFL (minimum score 580 paper-based; 237 computer-based; 92 iBT), IELTS (minimum score 5). *Expenses:* Contact institution.

University of Illinois at Chicago, Graduate College, College of Nursing, Program in Nursing, Chicago, IL 60607-7128. Offers acute care clinical nurse specialist (MS); acute care nurse practitioner (MS); administrative studies in nursing (MS); adult nurse practitioner (MS); adult/geriatric nurse practitioner (MS); advanced community health nurse specialist (MS); family nurse practitioner (MS); geriatric clinical nurse specialist (MS); geriatric nurse practitioner (MS); mental health clinical nurse specialist (MS); mental health nurse practitioner (MS); nurse midwifery (MS); occupational health/advanced community health nurse specialist (MS); occupational health/family nurse practitioner (MS); pediatric clinical nurse specialist (MS); pediatric nurse practitioner (MS); perinatal clinical nurse specialist (MS); school/advanced community health nurse specialist (MS); school/family nurse practitioner (MS); women's health nurse practitioner (MS). *Accreditation:* AACN. Part-time programs available. *Degree requirements:* For master's, thesis or alternative. *Entrance requirements:* For master's, GRE General Test, minimum GPA of 2.75. Additional exam requirements/recommendations for international students: Required—TOEFL. Electronic applications accepted.

The University of Kansas, University of Kansas Medical Center, School of Nursing, Kansas City, KS 66160. Offers adult/gerontological clinical nurse specialist (PMC); adult/gerontological nurse practitioner (PMC); clinical research management (PMC); family nurse practitioner (PMC); health care informatics (PMC); health professions educator (PMC); nurse midwife (PMC); nursing (MS, DNP, PhD); organizational leadership (PMC); psychiatric/mental health nurse practitioner (PMC); public health nursing (PMC). *Accreditation:* AACN; ACNM/ACME. Part-time programs available. Postbaccalaureate distance learning degree programs offered (minimal on-campus study). *Faculty:* 80. *Students:* 79 full-time (71 women), 336 part-time (317 women); includes 63 minority (24 Black or African American, non-Hispanic/Latino; 2 American Indian or Alaska Native, non-Hispanic/Latino; 18 Asian, non-Hispanic/Latino; 15 Hispanic/Latino; 4 Two or more races, non-Hispanic/Latino), 6 international. Average age 37. 155 applicants, 82% accepted, 127 enrolled. In 2011, 79 master's, 15 doctorates, 12 other advanced degrees awarded. Terminal master's awarded for partial completion of doctoral program. *Degree requirements:* For master's, comprehensive exam, thesis optional, general oral exam; for doctorate, variable foreign language requirement, thesis/dissertation, comprehensive oral exam (for DNP); comprehensive written and oral exam (for PhD). *Entrance requirements:* For master's, bachelor's degree in nursing, minimum GPA of 3.0, RN license, 1 year of clinical experience, RN license in KS and MO; for doctorate, GRE General Test, master's degree in nursing, minimum GPA of 3.5, RN license in KS and MO; national certification (for some specialties). Additional exam requirements/recommendations for international students: Required—TOEFL. *Application deadline:* For fall admission, 4/1 for domestic and international students; for spring admission, 9/1 for domestic and international students. Application fee: $60. Electronic applications accepted. Tuition and fees vary according to course load, campus/location, program and reciprocity agreements. *Financial support:* Research assistantships with full and partial tuition reimbursements, teaching assistantships with full and partial tuition reimbursements, and traineeships available. Financial award application deadline: 2/14; financial award applicants required to submit FAFSA. *Faculty research:* Breastfeeding practices of teen mothers, national database of nursing quality indicators, caregiving of families of patients using technology in the home, simulation in nursing education, diaphragm fatigue. *Total annual research expenditures:* $6.1 million. *Unit head:* Dr. Karen L. Miller, Dean, 913-588-1601, Fax: 913-588-1660, E-mail: kmiller@kumc.edu. *Application contact:* Dr. Debra J. Ford, Associate Dean, Student Affairs, 913-588-1619, Fax: 913-588-1615, E-mail: dford@kumc.edu. Web site: http://nursing.kumc.edu.

University of Louisville, Graduate School, School of Nursing, Louisville, KY 40202. Offers adult nurse practitioner (MSN); family nurse practitioner (MSN); health professions education (MSN); neonatal nurse practitioner (MSN); nursing research (PhD); psychiatric mental health nurse practitioner (MSN). *Accreditation:* AACN. Part-time programs available. *Faculty:* 24 full-time (22 women), 4 part-time/adjunct (3 women). *Students:* 82 full-time (74 women), 65 part-time (58 women); includes 20 minority (13 Black or African American, non-Hispanic/Latino; 1 American Indian or Alaska Native, non-Hispanic/Latino; 1 Asian, non-Hispanic/Latino; 1 Hispanic/Latino; 4 Two or more races, non-Hispanic/Latino), 2 international. Average age 34. 41 applicants, 56% accepted, 19 enrolled. In 2011, 42 master's, 2 doctorates awarded. Terminal master's awarded for partial completion of doctoral program. *Degree requirements:* For master's, thesis optional; for doctorate, comprehensive exam, thesis/dissertation. *Entrance requirements:* For master's, GRE General Test, bachelor's degree in nursing, minimum GPA of 3.0, RN license; for doctorate, GRE General Test, BSN or MSN with recommended minimum GPA of 3.0. Additional exam requirements/recommendations for international students: Required—TOEFL. *Application deadline:* For fall admission, 4/1 priority date for domestic students, 4/1 for international students. Applications are processed on a rolling basis. Application fee: $50. Electronic applications accepted. *Expenses:* Tuition, state resident: full-time $9692; part-time $539 per credit hour. Tuition, nonresident: full-time $20,168; part-time $1121 per credit hour. Tuition and fees vary according to program and reciprocity agreements. *Financial support:* In 2011–12, 45 students received support, including 6 research assistantships with full tuition reimbursements available (averaging $20,000 per year), 6 teaching assistantships with full tuition reimbursements available (averaging $19,167 per year); fellowships with full tuition reimbursements available, institutionally sponsored loans, scholarships/grants, traineeships, health care benefits, and unspecified assistantships also available. Support available to part-time students. Financial award application deadline: 4/15; financial award applicants required to submit FAFSA. *Faculty research:* Maternal-child/family stress after pregnancy loss, postpartum depression, access to healthcare (underserved populations), quality of life issues, physical activity (impact on chronic/acute conditions). *Total annual research expenditures:* $795,250. *Unit head:* Dr. Marcia J. Hern, Dean, 502-852-8300, Fax: 502-852-5044, E-mail: m.hern@gwise.louisville.edu. *Application contact:* Dr. Lee Ridner, Interim Associate Dean for Academic Affairs and Director of MSN Programs, 502-852-8518, Fax: 502-852-0704, E-mail: romain01@louisville.edu. Web site: http://www.louisville.edu/nursing/.

University of Maine, Graduate School, College of Natural Sciences, Forestry, and Agriculture, School of Nursing, Orono, ME 04469. Offers individualized (MS); individualized track (CAS); rural health family nurse practitioner (MS, CAS). *Accreditation:* AACN. *Faculty:* 16 full-time (13 women), 29 part-time/adjunct (25 women). *Students:* 15 full-time (all women), 11 part-time (9 women); includes 1 minority (Asian, non-Hispanic/Latino). Average age 38. 6 applicants, 33% accepted, 2 enrolled. In 2011, 5 master's, 1 other advanced degree awarded. *Entrance requirements:* For master's, GRE General Test. Additional exam requirements/recommendations for international students: Required—TOEFL. *Application deadline:* Applications are processed on a rolling basis. Application fee: $65. Electronic applications accepted. *Expenses:* Tuition, state resident: full-time $5016. Tuition, nonresident: full-time $14,424. *Financial support:* Career-related internships or fieldwork, Federal Work-Study, institutionally sponsored loans, and tuition waivers (full and partial) available. Support available to part-time students. Financial award application deadline: 3/1. *Unit head:* Dr. Nancy Fishwick, Director, 207-581-2505, Fax: 207-581-2585. *Application contact:* Scott G. Delcourt, Associate Dean of the Graduate School, 207-581-3291, Fax: 207-581-3232, E-mail: graduate@maine.edu. Web site: http://www2.umaine.edu/graduate/.

University of Mary, School of Health Sciences, Division of Nursing, Bismarck, ND 58504-9652. Offers family nurse practitioner (MSN); nurse administrator (MSN); nursing educator (MSN). *Accreditation:* AACN. Part-time and evening/weekend programs available. Postbaccalaureate distance learning degree programs offered (minimal on-campus study). *Faculty:* 6 full-time (all women), 16 part-time/adjunct (all women). *Students:* 157 full-time (148 women), 91 part-time (85 women); includes 14 minority (5 Black or African American, non-Hispanic/Latino; 4 American Indian or Alaska Native, non-Hispanic/Latino; 1 Asian, non-Hispanic/Latino; 4 Hispanic/Latino), 2 international. Average age 37. 92 applicants. In 2011, 80 master's awarded. *Degree requirements:* For master's, comprehensive exam (for some programs), thesis (for some programs), internship (family nurse practitioner), teaching practice. *Entrance requirements:* For master's, minimum GPA of 2.75 in nursing, interview, letters of recommendation, criminal background check, immunizations, statement of professional goals. Additional exam requirements/recommendations for international students: Required—TOEFL (minimum score 500 paper-based; 197 computer-based; 71 iBT). *Application deadline:* Applications are processed on a rolling basis. Application fee: $40. Electronic applications accepted. *Financial support:* In 2011–12, 14 fellowships with partial tuition reimbursements, 3 teaching assistantships with partial tuition reimbursements were awarded. Financial award application deadline: 8/1; financial award applicants required to submit FAFSA. *Faculty research:* Gerontology issues, rural nursing, health policy, primary care, women's health. *Unit head:* Glenda Reemts, Director, 701-255-7500 Ext. 8041, Fax: 701-255-7687, E-mail: greemts@umary.edu. *Application contact:* Joanne Lassiter, Nurse Recruiter, 701-355-8379, Fax: 701-255-7687, E-mail: jllassiter@umary.edu.

University of Mary Hardin-Baylor, Graduate Studies in Nursing, Belton, TX 76513. Offers clinical nurse leader (MSN); family nurse practitioner (MSN); nursing education (MSN). *Accreditation:* AACN. Part-time and evening/weekend programs available. *Faculty:* 8 full-time (all women), 1 (woman) part-time/adjunct. *Students:* 30 full-time (28 women), 2 part-time (both women); includes 9 minority (5 Black or African American, non-Hispanic/Latino; 1 Asian, non-Hispanic/Latino; 3 Hispanic/Latino), 6 international. Average age 34. 48 applicants, 83% accepted, 25 enrolled. In 2011, 3 master's awarded. *Degree requirements:* For master's, practicum. *Entrance requirements:* For master's, GRE General Test, RN, BSN, minimum GPA of 3.0 in last 60 hours of undergraduate program. *Application deadline:* For fall admission, 6/1 priority date for domestic students; for spring admission, 11/1 priority date for domestic students. Applications are processed on a rolling basis. Application fee: $35 ($135 for international students). Electronic applications accepted. *Expenses: Tuition:* Full-time $12,780. *Required fees:* $2350. *Financial support:* Applicants required to submit FAFSA. *Unit head:* Dr. Margaret Prydun, Director of Master's Program in Nursing, 254-295-4674, E-mail: margaret.prydun@umhb.edu. *Application contact:* Melissa Ford, Director of Graduate Admissions, 254-295-4020, Fax: 254-295-5301, E-mail: mford@umhb.edu. Web site: http://graduate.umhb.edu/nursing/.

University of Massachusetts Amherst, Graduate School, School of Nursing, Amherst, MA 01003. Offers clinical nurse leader (MS); family nurse practitioner (DNP); nursing (PhD); public health nurse leader (DNP). *Accreditation:* AACN. Part-time programs available. Postbaccalaureate distance learning degree programs offered (minimal on-campus study). *Faculty:* 12 full-time (11 women). *Students:* 56 full-time (51 women), 155 part-time (142 women); includes 57 minority (24 Black or African American, non-Hispanic/Latino; 5 Asian, non-Hispanic/Latino; 25 Hispanic/Latino; 3 Two or more races, non-Hispanic/Latino), 11 international. Average age 42. 125 applicants, 66% accepted, 53 enrolled. In 2011, 11 master's, 26 doctorates awarded. Terminal master's awarded for partial completion of doctoral program. *Degree requirements:* For master's, thesis optional; for doctorate, comprehensive exam, thesis/dissertation. *Entrance requirements:* For master's and doctorate, GRE General Test. Additional exam requirements/recommendations for international students: Required—TOEFL (minimum score 550 paper-based; 213 computer-based; 80 iBT), IELTS (minimum score 6.5). *Application deadline:* For fall admission, 2/1 for domestic and international students. Applications are processed on a rolling basis. Application fee: $50 ($65 for international students). Electronic applications accepted. Tuition and fees vary according to course load, campus/location and program. *Financial support:* Fellowships with full and partial tuition reimbursements, research assistantships with full and partial tuition reimbursements, teaching assistantships with full and partial tuition reimbursements, career-related internships or fieldwork, Federal Work-Study, scholarships/grants, traineeships, health care benefits, tuition waivers (full and partial), and unspecified assistantships available. Support available to part-time students. Financial award application deadline: 2/1. *Faculty research:* Health of older adults and their caretakers, mental health of individuals and families, health of children and adolescents, power and decision-making, transcultural health. *Unit head:* Dr. Donna Zucker, Graduate Program Director, 413-577-2322, Fax: 413-577-2550. *Application contact:* Lindsay DeSantis, Interim Supervisor of Admissions, 413-545-0722, Fax: 413-577-0010, E-mail: gradadm@grad.umass.edu. Web site: http://www.umass.edu/nursing/.

University of Massachusetts Lowell, School of Health and Environment, Department of Nursing, Program in Family Health Nursing, Lowell, MA 01854-2881. Offers MS. *Accreditation:* AACN. *Degree requirements:* For master's, thesis optional. *Entrance requirements:* For master's, GRE General Test, minimum GPA of 3.0, MA nursing license, interview, 3 letters of recommendation.

University of Massachusetts Worcester, Graduate School of Nursing, Worcester, MA 01655-0115. Offers adult acute/critical care nurse practitioner (MS, Post Master's Certificate); adult acute/critical care nurse practitioner and gerontological nurse practitioner (MS, Post Master's Certificate); adult primary care nurse practitioner (MS, Post Master's Certificate); adult primary care nurse practitioner and gerontological nurse practitioner (MS, Post Master's Certificate); advanced practice nursing (DNP); family nurse practitioner (MS); gerontological nurse practitioner (Post Master's Certificate); leadership (DNP); nurse education (Post Master's Certificate); nurse educator (MS); nursing (PhD). *Accreditation:* AACN. *Faculty:* 20 full-time (17 women), 60 part-time/

adjunct (50 women). *Students:* 162 full-time (141 women), 36 part-time (30 women); includes 29 minority (13 Black or African American, non-Hispanic/Latino; 10 Asian, non-Hispanic/Latino; 6 Hispanic/Latino), 1 international. Average age 36. 252 applicants, 38% accepted, 82 enrolled. In 2011, 38 master's, 6 doctorates awarded. *Degree requirements:* For doctorate, comprehensive exam, thesis/dissertation. *Entrance requirements:* For master's, GRE General Test, bachelor's degree, course work in statistics; for doctorate, GRE General Test, bachelor's or master's degree, RN licensure; for Post Master's Certificate, GRE General Test, MS in nursing. Additional exam requirements/recommendations for international students: Required—TOEFL. *Application deadline:* For fall admission, 1/15 priority date for domestic students. Applications are processed on a rolling basis. Application fee: $40 ($60 for international students). *Expenses:* Contact institution. *Financial support:* In 2011–12, 38 students received support. Institutionally sponsored loans, scholarships/grants, traineeships, and tuition waivers (for some) available. Support available to part-time students. Financial award application deadline: 5/16; financial award applicants required to submit FAFSA. *Faculty research:* Decision-making of partners and men with prostate cancer, coinfection (HIV and Hepatitus C) and treatment decisions, parent management of children with T1DM, health literacy and discharge planning, Ghanian women and self-care. *Total annual research expenditures:* $939,567. *Unit head:* Dr. Paulette Seymour-Route, Dean, 508-856-5801, Fax: 508-856-6552, E-mail: paulette.seymour-route@umassmed.edu. *Application contact:* Diane Brescia, Admissions Coordinator, 508-856-3488, Fax: 508-856-5851, E-mail: diane.brescia@umassmed.edu. Web site: http://www.umassmed.edu/gsn/.

University of Medicine and Dentistry of New Jersey, School of Nursing, Newark, NJ 07107-3001. Offers adult health (MSN); adult occupational health (MSN); advanced practice nursing (MSN, Post Master's Certificate); family nurse practitioner (MSN); nurse anesthesia (MSN); nursing (MSN); nursing informatics (MSN); urban health (PhD); women's health practitioner (MSN). *Accreditation:* AANA/CANAEP; NLN (one or more programs are accredited). Part-time programs available. *Entrance requirements:* For master's, GRE, RN license; basic life support, statistics, and health assessment experience. Additional exam requirements/recommendations for international students: Required—TOEFL. Electronic applications accepted. *Expenses:* Contact institution. *Faculty research:* HIV/AIDS, diabetes education, learned helplessness, nursing science, psychoeducation.

University of Memphis, Loewenberg School of Nursing, Memphis, TN 38152. Offers advance practice-family nurse practitioner (MSN); executive nursing leadership (MSN); nursing (Graduate Certificate); nursing administration (MSN); nursing education (MSN); nursing informatics (MSN). *Accreditation:* AACN. Part-time and evening/weekend programs available. Postbaccalaureate distance learning degree programs offered. *Degree requirements:* For master's, comprehensive exam, thesis optional, scholarly project; completion of clinical practicum hours. *Entrance requirements:* For master's, NCLEX Exam, interview. Additional exam requirements/recommendations for international students: Required—TOEFL (minimum score 550 paper-based; 213 computer-based; 79 iBT). *Faculty research:* Technology in nursing, nurse retention, cultural competence, health policy, health access.

University of Miami, Graduate School, School of Nursing and Health Studies, Coral Gables, FL 33124. Offers acute care (MSN), including acute care nurse practitioner, nurse anesthesia; nursing (PhD); primary care (MSN), including adult nurse practitioner, family nurse practitioner, nurse midwifery, women's health practitioner. *Accreditation:* AACN; AANA/CANAEP; ACNM/ACME (one or more programs are accredited). Part-time programs available. *Degree requirements:* For master's, thesis optional; for doctorate, thesis/dissertation. *Entrance requirements:* For master's, GRE General Test, BSN, minimum GPA of 3.0, Florida RN license; for doctorate, GRE General Test, BSN or MSN, minimum GPA of 3.0. Additional exam requirements/recommendations for international students: Required—TOEFL (minimum score 550 paper-based; 213 computer-based). Electronic applications accepted. *Faculty research:* Transcultural nursing, exercise and depression in Alzheimer's disease, infectious diseases/HIV–AIDS, postpartum depression, outcomes assessment.

University of Michigan, Horace H. Rackham School of Graduate Studies, School of Nursing, Division of Health Promotion and Risk Reduction, Program in Community Health Nursing, Ann Arbor, MI 48109. Offers adult nurse practitioner (Post Master's Certificate); adult primary care/adult nurse practitioner (MS); community care (Post Master's Certificate); community care/home care (MS); family nurse practitioner (MS, Post Master's Certificate); occupational health nursing (MS). *Accreditation:* AACN. Part-time and evening/weekend programs available. *Degree requirements:* For master's, thesis. *Entrance requirements:* For master's, GRE General Test (if cumulative BSN GPA less than 3.25), licensure, minimum GPA of 3.0 in BSN program. Additional exam requirements/recommendations for international students: Required—TOEFL (minimum score 560 paper-based; 220 computer-based).

University of Minnesota, Twin Cities Campus, Graduate School, School of Nursing, Family Nurse Practitioner Program, Minneapolis, MN 55455-0213. Offers MS. *Accreditation:* AACN. *Degree requirements:* For master's, final oral exam, project or thesis. *Entrance requirements:* Additional exam requirements/recommendations for international students: Required—TOEFL (minimum score 586 paper-based; 240 computer-based).

University of Missouri–Kansas City, School of Nursing, Kansas City, MO 64110-2499. Offers adult clinical nurse specialist (MSN), including adult nurse practitioner, women's health nurse practitioner; family nurse practitioner (MSN); neonatal nurse practitioner (MSN); nurse educator (MSN); nurse executive (MSN); nursing (PhD); nursing practice (DNP); pediatric nurse practitioner (MSN). *Accreditation:* AACN. Part-time programs available. Postbaccalaureate distance learning degree programs offered (minimal on-campus study). *Faculty:* 40 full-time (35 women), 57 part-time/adjunct (52 women). *Students:* 51 full-time (48 women), 381 part-time (352 women); includes 41 minority (22 Black or African American, non-Hispanic/Latino; 7 Asian, non-Hispanic/Latino; 12 Hispanic/Latino). Average age 37. 195 applicants, 49% accepted, 90 enrolled. In 2011, 78 master's, 19 doctorates awarded. *Degree requirements:* For master's, thesis or alternative. *Entrance requirements:* For master's, minimum undergraduate GPA of 3.2; for doctorate, GRE, 3 letters of reference, interview by invitation. Additional exam requirements/recommendations for international students: Required—TOEFL (minimum score 550 paper-based; 213 computer-based; 80 iBT). *Application deadline:* For fall admission, 2/1 priority date for domestic students, 2/1 for international students; for spring admission, 9/1 priority date for domestic students, 9/1 for international students. Application fee: $45 ($50 for international students). *Expenses:* Tuition, state resident: full-time $5798; part-time $322.10 per credit hour. Tuition, nonresident: full-time $14,969; part-time $831.60 per credit hour. *Required fees:* $93.51 per credit hour. *Financial support:* In 2011–12, 25 teaching assistantships with partial tuition reimbursements (averaging $6,927 per year) were awarded; fellowships, research assistantships, career-related internships or fieldwork, Federal Work-Study, institutionally sponsored loans, and tuition waivers (full and partial) also available. Support available to part-time students. Financial award application deadline: 3/1; financial award applicants required to submit FAFSA. *Faculty research:* Geriatrics/gerontology, children's pain, neonatology, Alzheimer's care, cancer caregivers. *Unit head:* Dr. Lora Lacey-Haun, Dean, 816-235-1700, Fax: 816-235-1701, E-mail: laceyhaunc@umkc.edu. *Application contact:* Leah Wilder, Coordinator for Admissions and Recruitment, 816-235-5768, Fax: 816-235-1701, E-mail: wilderl@umkc.edu. Web site: http://nursing.umkc.edu/.

University of Missouri–St. Louis, College of Nursing, St. Louis, MO 63121. Offers adult nurse practitioner (DNP, Post Master's Certificate); clinical nurse specialist (DNP); family mental health nurse practitioner (DNP); family nurse practitioner (MSN, DNP, Post Master's Certificate); neonatal nurse practitioner (MSN); nurse educator (MSN); nurse leader (MSN); nurse practitioner (Post Master's Certificate); nursing (PhD); pediatric clinical nurse specialist (DNP); pediatric nurse practitioner (MSN, DNP, Post Master's Certificate); women's health nurse practitioner (MSN, Post Master's Certificate). *Accreditation:* AACN. Part-time programs available. *Faculty:* 12 full-time (11 women), 14 part-time/adjunct (all women). *Students:* 240 part-time (226 women); includes 30 minority (26 Black or African American, non-Hispanic/Latino; 1 Asian, non-Hispanic/Latino; 2 Hispanic/Latino; 1 Two or more races, non-Hispanic/Latino). Average age 37. 228 applicants, 28% accepted, 53 enrolled. In 2011, 66 master's, 2 doctorates, 2 other advanced degrees awarded. *Degree requirements:* For doctorate, comprehensive exam, thesis/dissertation; for Post Master's Certificate, thesis. *Entrance requirements:* For master's, 2 recommendation letters; minimum GPA of 3.0; BSN; nursing licensure; statement of purpose; course in differential/inferential statistics; for doctorate, GRE, 2 letters of recommendation, MSN, minimum GPA of 3.2, course in differential/inferential statistics; for Post Master's Certificate, 2 recommendation letters; MSN; advanced practice certificate; minimum GPA of 3.0; essay. Additional exam requirements/recommendations for international students: Required—TOEFL (minimum score 550 paper-based; 213 computer-based). *Application deadline:* For fall admission, 2/15 for domestic and international students. Application fee: $35 ($40 for international students). Electronic applications accepted. *Expenses:* Tuition, state resident: full-time $6273; part-time $3866 per year. Tuition, nonresident: full-time $14,969; part-time $9980 per year. *Required fees:* $315 per year. *Financial support:* In 2011–12, 3 research assistantships with full and partial tuition reimbursements (averaging $12,339 per year) were awarded. Financial award application deadline: 4/1; financial award applicants required to submit FAFSA. *Faculty research:* Health promotion and restoration, family disruption, violence, abuse, battered women, health survey methods. *Unit head:* Dr. Nancy Magnuson, Director, 314-516-6066. *Application contact:* 314-516-5458, Fax: 314-516-6996, E-mail: gradadm@umsl.edu. Web site: http://www.umsl.edu/divisions/nursing/.

University of Nevada, Las Vegas, Graduate College, School of Nursing, Las Vegas, NV 89154-3018. Offers family nurse practitioner (Advanced Certificate); nursing (MS, DNP, PhD); nursing education (Advanced Certificate); pediatric nurse practitioner (Post-Master's Certificate). *Accreditation:* AACN. Part-time programs available. Postbaccalaureate distance learning degree programs offered (minimal on-campus study). *Faculty:* 17 full-time (all women), 22 part-time/adjunct (6 women). *Students:* 49 full-time (46 women), 82 part-time (73 women); includes 28 minority (7 Black or African American, non-Hispanic/Latino; 1 American Indian or Alaska Native, non-Hispanic/Latino; 8 Asian, non-Hispanic/Latino; 5 Hispanic/Latino; 1 Native Hawaiian or other Pacific Islander, non-Hispanic/Latino; 6 Two or more races, non-Hispanic/Latino), 3 international. Average age 41. 125 applicants, 43% accepted, 40 enrolled. In 2011, 29 master's, 8 doctorates, 2 other advanced degrees awarded. *Entrance requirements:* For doctorate, GRE General Test. Additional exam requirements/recommendations for international students: Recommended—TOEFL (minimum score 550 paper-based; 213 computer-based; 80 iBT), IELTS (minimum score 7). *Application deadline:* For fall admission, 2/15 priority date for domestic students, 5/1 for international students; for spring admission, 10/1 for international students. Applications are processed on a rolling basis. Application fee: $60 ($95 for international students). Electronic applications accepted. *Financial support:* In 2011–12, 3 students received support, including 3 teaching assistantships with partial tuition reimbursements available (averaging $9,334 per year); institutionally sponsored loans, scholarships/grants, health care benefits, and unspecified assistantships also available. Financial award application deadline: 3/1. *Faculty research:* Physiological stress reactions, leukocyte response and skeletal muscle injury, depression in lay caregivers, incivility in nursing practice, work-related injuries in healthcare and construction workers. *Total annual research expenditures:* $1.7 million. *Unit head:* Dr. Carolyn Yucha, Interim Dean, 702-895-3906, Fax: 702-895-5050, E-mail: carolyn.yucha@unlv.edu. *Application contact:* Graduate College Admissions Evaluator, 702-895-3320, Fax: 702-895-4180, E-mail: gradcollege@unlv.edu. Web site: http://nursing.unlv.edu/.

University of New Hampshire, Graduate School, School of Health and Human Services, Department of Nursing, Durham, NH 03824. Offers family practitioner (Postbaccalaureate Certificate); nursing (MS). *Accreditation:* AACN. Part-time programs available. *Faculty:* 12 full-time (11 women). *Students:* 51 full-time (46 women), 66 part-time (53 women); includes 5 minority (1 Black or African American, non-Hispanic/Latino; 1 American Indian or Alaska Native, non-Hispanic/Latino; 1 Asian, non-Hispanic/Latino; 2 Hispanic/Latino), 1 international. Average age 34. 59 applicants, 49% accepted, 16 enrolled. In 2011, 43 master's, 4 other advanced degrees awarded. *Degree requirements:* For master's, thesis or alternative. *Entrance requirements:* For master's, GRE General Test or MAT. Additional exam requirements/recommendations for international students: Required—TOEFL (minimum score 550 paper-based; 213 computer-based; 80 iBT). *Application deadline:* For fall admission, 4/1 priority date for domestic students, 4/1 for international students; for spring admission, 11/1 for domestic students. Applications are processed on a rolling basis. Application fee: $65. Electronic applications accepted. *Expenses:* Tuition, state resident: full-time $12,360; part-time $687 per credit hour. Tuition, nonresident: full-time $25,680; part-time $1058 per credit hour. *International tuition:* $29,550 full-time. *Required fees:* $1666; $833 per course. $416.50 per semester. Tuition and fees vary according to course load and degree level. *Financial support:* In 2011–12, 21 students received support, including 2 teaching assistantships; fellowships, research assistantships, Federal Work-Study, scholarships/grants, and tuition waivers (full and partial) also available. Financial award application deadline: 2/15. *Faculty research:* Adult health, nursing administration, family nurse practitioner. *Unit head:* Dr. Gene Harkless, Chairperson, 603-862-2285. *Application contact:* Jane Dufresne, Administrative Assistant, 603-862-2299, E-mail: nursing.department@unh.edu. Web site: http://www.unh.edu/nursing/.

The University of North Carolina at Chapel Hill, School of Nursing, Chapel Hill, NC 27599-7460. Offers nursing (MSN, PhD, PMC), including adult nurse practitioner (MSN, PMC), children's health advanced practice (MSN, PMC), family nurse practitioner (MSN, PMC), health care systems (MSN, PMC), psychiatric/mental health nursing (MSN, PMC), women's health nursing (MSN, PMC). *Accreditation:* AACN; NLN (one or more programs are accredited). Part-time programs available. *Degree requirements:* For master's, comprehensive exam, thesis; for doctorate, thesis/dissertation, 3 exams. *Entrance requirements:* For master's and doctorate, GRE General Test. *Faculty research:* Chronic illness, parenting, cardiovascular health in children, elderly, HIV-AIDS.

The University of North Carolina at Charlotte, Graduate School, College of Health and Human Services, School of Nursing, Charlotte, NC 28223-0001. Offers administration (Post-Master's Certificate); advanced clinical (MSN, Post-Master's Certificate); anesthesia (MSN, Post-Master's Certificate); community health (MSN);

family nurse practitioner (MSN, Post-Master's Certificate); health administration (MSN); mental health (MSN); nurse educator (MSN, Post-Master's Certificate); systems population (MSN). *Accreditation:* AACN. *Faculty:* 20 full-time (19 women), 5 part-time/adjunct (all women). *Students:* 76 full-time (65 women), 160 part-time (149 women); includes 49 minority (32 Black or African American, non-Hispanic/Latino; 1 American Indian or Alaska Native, non-Hispanic/Latino; 8 Asian, non-Hispanic/Latino; 8 Hispanic/Latino), 1 international. Average age 35. 191 applicants, 42% accepted, 71 enrolled. In 2011, 76 master's, 10 other advanced degrees awarded. *Degree requirements:* For master's, thesis or alternative, practicum. *Entrance requirements:* For master's, GRE General Test, minimum GPA of 3.0 in undergraduate major. Additional exam requirements/recommendations for international students: Required—TOEFL (minimum score 570 paper-based; 220 computer-based; 83 iBT). *Application deadline:* For fall admission, 7/15 for domestic students, 5/1 for international students; for spring admission, 11/15 for domestic students, 10/1 for international students. Application fee: $65 ($75 for international students). *Expenses:* Tuition, state resident: full-time $3689. Tuition, nonresident: full-time $15,226. *Required fees:* $2198. Tuition and fees vary according to course load and program. *Financial support:* In 2011–12, 10 students received support, including 4 research assistantships (averaging $5,284 per year), 6 teaching assistantships (averaging $2,918 per year); career-related internships or fieldwork, institutionally sponsored loans, scholarships/grants, traineeships, unspecified assistantships, and administrative assistanship also available. Support available to part-time students. Financial award application deadline: 4/1; financial award applicants required to submit FAFSA. *Total annual research expenditures:* $955,795. *Unit head:* Dr. Lucille L. Travis, Director, 704-687-7959, Fax: 704-687-6017, E-mail: ltravis1@uncc.edu. *Application contact:* Kathy B. Giddings, Director of Graduate Admissions, 704-687-5503, Fax: 704-687-3279, E-mail: gradadm@uncc.edu. Web site: http://nursing.uncc.edu/.

The University of North Carolina Wilmington, School of Nursing, Wilmington, NC 28403-3297. Offers family nurse practitioner (MSN); nurse educator (MSN). *Accreditation:* AACN; NLN. *Degree requirements:* For master's, comprehensive exam, thesis or project. *Entrance requirements:* For master's, GRE General Test, bachelor's degree in nursing. Additional exam requirements/recommendations for international students: Required—TOEFL (minimum score 550 paper-based; 217 computer-based; 79 iBT), IELTS (minimum score 6.5). Electronic applications accepted.

University of North Dakota, Graduate School, College of Nursing, Grand Forks, ND 58202. Offers advanced public health nursing (MS); family nurse practitioner (MS); gerontological nursing (MS); nurse anesthesia (MS); nursing (MS, PhD); nursing education (MS); psychiatric and mental health (MS). *Accreditation:* AACN; AANA/CANAEP (one or more programs are accredited). Part-time and evening/weekend programs available. Postbaccalaureate distance learning degree programs offered (minimal on-campus study). *Degree requirements:* For master's, thesis or alternative. *Entrance requirements:* For master's, minimum GPA of 3.0; for doctorate, GRE or MAT, minimum GPA of 3.0. Additional exam requirements/recommendations for international students: Required—TOEFL (minimum score 550 paper-based; 213 computer-based; 79 iBT), IELTS (minimum score 6.5). Electronic applications accepted. *Faculty research:* Adult health, anesthesia, rural health, health administration, family nurse practitioner.

University of Northern Colorado, Graduate School, College of Natural and Health Sciences, School of Nursing, Greeley, CO 80639. Offers clinical nurse specialist in chronic illness (MS); family nurse practitioner (MS); nursing education (MS, PhD). *Accreditation:* AACN. Postbaccalaureate distance learning degree programs offered. *Degree requirements:* For master's, comprehensive exam, thesis or alternative; for doctorate, comprehensive exam, thesis/dissertation. *Entrance requirements:* For master's and doctorate, GRE General Test, minimum GPA of 3.0 in last 60 hours, BS in nursing, 2 letters of recommendation. Electronic applications accepted.

University of North Florida, Brooks College of Health, School of Nursing, Jacksonville, FL 32224. Offers clinical nurse leader (MSN); clinical nurse specialist (MSN); family nurse practitioner (Certificate); nurse anesthetist (CRNA) (MSN); nursing practice (DNP); primary care nurse practitioner (MSN). *Accreditation:* AACN; AANA/CANAEP. Part-time programs available. *Faculty:* 28 full-time (21 women), 1 (woman) part-time/adjunct. *Students:* 97 full-time (69 women), 69 part-time (60 women); includes 41 minority (17 Black or African American, non-Hispanic/Latino; 1 American Indian or Alaska Native, non-Hispanic/Latino; 10 Asian, non-Hispanic/Latino; 11 Hispanic/Latino; 2 Two or more races, non-Hispanic/Latino). Average age 34. 215 applicants, 23% accepted, 31 enrolled. In 2011, 55 master's, 4 doctorates awarded. *Degree requirements:* For master's, thesis optional. *Entrance requirements:* For master's, GRE General Test, minimum GPA of 3.0 in last 60 hours of course work, BSN, clinical experience, resume; for doctorate, GRE (minimum score of 1000) or MAT (minimum score of 410), master's degree in nursing specialty from nationally-accredited program; national certification in one of the following APRN roles: CNE, CNM, CNS, CRNA, CNP; minimum graduate GPA of 3.3; three letters of reference which address academic ability and clinical skills; active license as registered nurse or advanced practice registered nurse. Additional exam requirements/recommendations for international students: Required—TOEFL (minimum score 500 paper-based; 173 computer-based; 61 iBT). *Application deadline:* For fall admission, 3/15 for domestic students, 4/1 for international students. Applications are processed on a rolling basis. Application fee: $30. Electronic applications accepted. *Expenses:* Tuition, state resident: full-time $8793; part-time $366.38 per credit hour. Tuition, nonresident: full-time $23,502; part-time $979.24 per credit hour. *Required fees:* $1384; $57.66 per credit hour. Tuition and fees vary according to course load and program. *Financial support:* In 2011–12, 59 students received support. Research assistantships available. Financial award application deadline: 4/1; financial award applicants required to submit FAFSA. *Faculty research:* Teen pregnancy, diabetes, ethical decision-making, family caregivers. *Total annual research expenditures:* $545,563. *Unit head:* Dr. John McDonough, Director, 904-620-2684, E-mail: jmcdonou@unf.edu. *Application contact:* Beth Dibble, 904-620-2684, Fax: 904-620-1832, E-mail: nursingadmissions@unf.edu. Web site: http://www.unf.edu/brooks/nursing.

University of Pennsylvania, School of Nursing, Family Health Nurse Practitioner Program, Philadelphia, PA 19104. Offers MSN, Certificate. *Accreditation:* AACN. Part-time programs available. *Students:* 19 full-time (18 women), 33 part-time (all women); includes 10 minority (2 Black or African American, non-Hispanic/Latino; 4 Asian, non-Hispanic/Latino; 3 Hispanic/Latino; 1 Two or more races, non-Hispanic/Latino), 1 international. 47 applicants, 26% accepted, 12 enrolled. In 2011, 31 degrees awarded. *Entrance requirements:* For master's, GRE General Test, 1 year of clinical experience in area of interest, BSN, minimum GPA of 3.0, previous course work in statistics. Additional exam requirements/recommendations for international students: Required—TOEFL. *Application deadline:* For fall admission, 2/15 priority date for domestic students. Applications are processed on a rolling basis. Application fee: $70. *Expenses:* Contact institution. *Financial support:* Research assistantships, teaching assistantships, career-related internships or fieldwork, Federal Work-Study, and institutionally sponsored loans available. Support available to part-time students. Financial award application deadline: 4/1. *Faculty research:* Evaluation of primary care practitioner practice, access to primary care. *Unit head:* Assistant Dean of Admissions and Financial Aid, 866-867-6877, Fax: 215-573-8439, E-mail: admissions@nursing.upenn.edu. *Application contact:* Ann O'Sullivan, Program Director, 215-898-4272, E-mail: osull@nursing.upenn.edu. Web site: http://www.nursing.upenn.edu/fnp/.

University of Phoenix–Hawaii Campus, College of Nursing, Honolulu, HI 96813-4317. Offers education (MHA); family nurse practitioner (MSN); gerontology (MHA); health administration (MHA); nursing (MSN); nursing/health care education (MSN); MSN/MBA. Evening/weekend programs available. *Degree requirements:* For master's, thesis (for some programs). *Entrance requirements:* For master's, minimum undergraduate GPA of 2.5, 3 years of work experience, RN license. Additional exam requirements/recommendations for international students: Required—TOEFL (minimum score 550 paper-based; 213 computer-based; 79 iBT). Electronic applications accepted.

University of Phoenix–Online Campus, College of Nursing, Phoenix, AZ 85034-7209. Offers informatics (MSN); international (MSN); nurse practitioner (MSN); nursing (MSN); nursing/health care education (MSN); MSN/Certificate; MSN/MBA; MSN/MHA. *Accreditation:* AACN. Evening/weekend programs available. Postbaccalaureate distance learning degree programs offered. *Students:* 5,257 full-time (4,805 women); includes 1,381 minority (803 Black or African American, non-Hispanic/Latino; 36 American Indian or Alaska Native, non-Hispanic/Latino; 271 Asian, non-Hispanic/Latino; 188 Hispanic/Latino; 51 Native Hawaiian or other Pacific Islander, non-Hispanic/Latino; 32 Two or more races, non-Hispanic/Latino), 244 international. Average age 43. *Entrance requirements:* Additional exam requirements/recommendations for international students: Required—TOEFL, TOEIC (Test of English as an International Communication), Berlitz Online English Proficiency Exam, Pearson Test of English, or IELTS. *Application deadline:* Applications are processed on a rolling basis. Application fee: $45. Electronic applications accepted. *Expenses:* Contact institution. *Financial support:* Scholarships/grants available. Financial award applicants required to submit FAFSA. *Application contact:* 866-766-0766. Web site: http://www.phoenix.edu/colleges_divisions/nursing.html.

University of Phoenix–Phoenix Main Campus, College of Nursing, Tempe, AZ 85282-2371. Offers family nurse practitioner (MSN, Certificate); informatics (MSN); nursing (MSN); nursing/health care education (MSN); MSN/Certificate; MSN/MBA; MSN/MHA. Evening/weekend programs available. Postbaccalaureate distance learning degree programs offered. *Students:* 172 full-time (148 women); includes 25 minority (4 Black or African American, non-Hispanic/Latino; 8 Asian, non-Hispanic/Latino; 13 Hispanic/Latino), 10 international. Average age 40. *Entrance requirements:* Additional exam requirements/recommendations for international students: Required—TOEFL, TOEIC (Test of English as an International Communication), Berlitz Online English Proficiency Exam, Pearson Test of English, or IELTS. *Application deadline:* Applications are processed on a rolling basis. Application fee: $45. Electronic applications accepted. *Expenses:* Contact institution. *Financial support:* Scholarships/grants available. Financial award applicants required to submit FAFSA. *Application contact:* 866-766-0766. Web site: http://www.phoenix.edu/colleges_divisions/nursing.html.

University of Phoenix–Sacramento Valley Campus, College of Nursing, Sacramento, CA 95833-3632. Offers family nurse practitioner (MSN); health administration (MHA); health care education (MSN); nursing (MSN); MSN/MBA. Evening/weekend programs available. *Degree requirements:* For master's, thesis (for some programs). *Entrance requirements:* For master's, RN license, minimum undergraduate GPA of 2.5, 3 years work experience. Additional exam requirements/recommendations for international students: Required—TOEFL (minimum score 550 paper-based; 213 computer-based; 79 iBT). Electronic applications accepted.

University of Phoenix–Southern California Campus, College of Nursing, Costa Mesa, CA 92626. Offers family nurse practitioner (MSN, Certificate); informatics (MSN); nursing (MSN); nursing/health care education (MSN); MSN/Certificate; MSN/MBA; MSN/MHA. Evening/weekend programs available. Postbaccalaureate distance learning degree programs offered. *Students:* 281 full-time (244 women); includes 129 minority (47 Black or African American, non-Hispanic/Latino; 1 American Indian or Alaska Native, non-Hispanic/Latino; 44 Asian, non-Hispanic/Latino; 26 Hispanic/Latino; 9 Native Hawaiian or other Pacific Islander, non-Hispanic/Latino; 2 Two or more races, non-Hispanic/Latino), 13 international. Average age 43. *Entrance requirements:* Additional exam requirements/recommendations for international students: Required—TOEFL, TOEIC (Test of English as an International Communication), Berlitz Online English Proficiency Exam, Pearson Test of English, or IELTS. *Application deadline:* Applications are processed on a rolling basis. Application fee: $45. Electronic applications accepted. *Expenses:* Contact institution. *Financial support:* Scholarships/grants available. Financial award applicants required to submit FAFSA. *Application contact:* 866-766-0766. Web site: http://www.phoenix.edu/colleges_divisions/nursing.html.

University of Pittsburgh, School of Nursing, Nurse Practitioner Program, Pittsburgh, PA 15261. Offers acute care nurse practitioner (MSN, DNP); adult nurse practitioner (MSN, DNP); family nurse practitioner (MSN, DNP); neonatal (MSN, DNP); nursing practice (DNP); pediatric nurse practitioner (MSN, DNP); psychiatric primary care nurse practitioner (MSN, DNP). *Accreditation:* AACN. Part-time programs available. *Students:* 46 full-time (44 women), 135 part-time (123 women); includes 13 minority (6 Black or African American, non-Hispanic/Latino; 1 American Indian or Alaska Native, non-Hispanic/Latino; 6 Asian, non-Hispanic/Latino). Average age 32. 126 applicants, 71% accepted, 70 enrolled. In 2011, 24 master's, 4 doctorates awarded. *Degree requirements:* For master's, comprehensive exam, thesis optional. *Entrance requirements:* For master's, GRE General Test or MAT, BSN, RN license, letters of recommendation, resume, course work in statistics, 1-3 years of nursing experience; for doctorate, GRE General Test, BSN, RN license, minimum GPA of 3.5, 3 letters of recommendation. Additional exam requirements/recommendations for international students: Required—TOEFL (minimum score 550 paper-based; 213 computer-based; 80 iBT). *Application deadline:* Applications are processed on a rolling basis. Application fee: $50. Electronic applications accepted. *Expenses:* Tuition, state resident: full-time $18,774; part-time $760 per credit. Tuition, nonresident: full-time $30,736; part-time $1258 per credit. *Required fees:* $740; $200 per term. Tuition and fees vary according to program. *Financial support:* In 2011–12, 5 students received support, including 1 fellowship with partial tuition reimbursement available (averaging $11,330 per year), 1 research assistantship with full tuition reimbursement available (averaging $35,942 per year), 3 teaching assistantships with full and partial tuition reimbursements available (averaging $27,470 per year); scholarships/grants, traineeships, health care benefits, and unspecified assistantships also available. Support available to part-time students. *Unit head:* Dr. Sandra Engberg, Associate Dean for Clinical Education, 412-624-3835, Fax: 412-624-8521, E-mail: sje1@pitt.edu. *Application contact:* Laurie Lapsley, Administrator of Graduate Student Services, 412-624-9670, Fax: 412-624-2409, E-mail: lapsleyl@pitt.edu. Web site: http://www.nursing.pitt.edu.

University of Puerto Rico, Medical Sciences Campus, School of Nursing, San Juan, PR 00936-5067. Offers adult and elderly nursing (MSN); child and adolescent nursing (MSN); critical care nursing (MSN); family and community nursing (MSN); family nurse practitioner (MSN); maternity nursing (MSN); mental health and psychiatric nursing (MSN). *Accreditation:* AACN; AANA/CANAEP. *Entrance requirements:* For master's, GRE or EXADEP, interview, Puerto Rico RN license or professional license for international students, general and specific point average, article analysis. Electronic applications accepted. *Faculty research:* HIV, health disparities, teen violence, women and violence, neurological disorders.

University of Rhode Island, Graduate School, College of Nursing, Kingston, RI 02881. Offers administration (MS); clinical nurse leader (MS); clinical specialist in gerontology (MS); clinical specialist in psychiatric/mental health (MS); family nurse practitioner (MS); gerontological nurse practitioner (MS); nursing (DNP, PhD); nursing education (MS). *Accreditation:* AACN; ACNM/ACME (one or more programs are accredited). Part-time programs available. *Faculty:* 29 full-time (28 women), 2 part-time/adjunct (1 woman). *Students:* 33 full-time (30 women), 81 part-time (77 women); includes 6 minority (1 Asian, non-Hispanic/Latino; 5 Hispanic/Latino). In 2011, 17 master's, 6 doctorates awarded. *Degree requirements:* For master's, comprehensive exam; for doctorate, comprehensive exam, thesis/dissertation. *Entrance requirements:* For master's, GRE or MAT, 2 letters of recommendation, scholarly papers; for doctorate, GRE, 3 letters of recommendation, scholarly papers. Additional exam requirements/recommendations for international students: Required—TOEFL (minimum score 550 paper-based; 213 computer-based). *Application deadline:* For fall admission, 4/15 for domestic students, 2/1 for international students; for spring admission, 11/15 for domestic students, 7/15 for international students. Application fee: $65. Electronic applications accepted. *Expenses:* Tuition, state resident: full-time $10,432; part-time $580 per credit hour. Tuition, nonresident: full-time $23,130; part-time $1285 per credit hour. *Required fees:* $1362; $36 per credit hour. $35 per semester. One-time fee: $130. *Financial support:* In 2011–12, 5 teaching assistantships with full and partial tuition reimbursements (averaging $12,596 per year) were awarded. Financial award application deadline: 4/15; financial award applicants required to submit FAFSA. *Faculty research:* Group intervention for grieving women in prison, translating Best Practice in non-drug interventions for postoperative pain management, further development and testing of the pain assessment inventory, preschool motor and functional performance of two cohorts, neuroactivation of brain motor areas in preterm children. *Unit head:* Dr. Dayle Joseph, Dean, 401-874-2766, Fax: 401-874-2061, E-mail: dayle@uri.edu. *Application contact:* Dr. Mary C. Sullivan, Director of Graduate Studies, 401-874-5339, Fax: 401-874-2061, E-mail: mcsullivan@uri.edu. Web site: http://www.uri.edu/nursing/.

University of Rochester, School of Nursing, Rochester, NY 14642. Offers acute care nurse practitioner (MS); adult nurse practitioner (MS); adult/geriatric nurse practitioner (MS); care of children and families/pediatric nurse practitioner (MS); care of children and families/pediatric nurse practitioner/neonatal nurse practitioner (MS); clinical nurse leader (MS); clinical research coordinator (MS); family nurse practitioner (MS); family psychiatric mental health nurse practitioner (MS); health care organization management and leadership (MS); health practice research (PhD); nursing (DNP). *Accreditation:* AACN; NLN (one or more programs are accredited). Part-time programs available. Postbaccalaureate distance learning degree programs offered (minimal on-campus study). *Faculty:* 49 full-time (42 women), 72 part-time/adjunct (60 women). *Students:* 38 full-time (32 women), 196 part-time (181 women); includes 37 minority (20 Black or African American, non-Hispanic/Latino; 9 Asian, non-Hispanic/Latino; 8 Hispanic/Latino), 5 international. Average age 36. 68 applicants, 56% accepted, 26 enrolled. In 2011, 49 master's, 7 doctorates awarded. Terminal master's awarded for partial completion of doctoral program. *Median time to degree:* Of those who began their doctoral program in fall 2003, 40% received their degree in 8 years or less. *Degree requirements:* For doctorate, thesis/dissertation. *Entrance requirements:* For master's, BS in nursing, minimum GPA of 3.0, course work in statistics; for doctorate, GRE General Test, MS in nursing, minimum GPA of 3.5. Additional exam requirements/recommendations for international students: Required—or IELTS (minimum score 6.5); Recommended—TOEFL (minimum score 560 paper-based; 230 computer-based; 88 iBT). *Application deadline:* For fall admission, 4/1 priority date for domestic students, 4/1 for international students; for spring admission, 9/1 for domestic and international students. Application fee: $50. Electronic applications accepted. *Expenses: Tuition:* Full-time $41,040. *Financial support:* In 2011–12, 49 students received support, including 1 fellowship with full and partial tuition reimbursement available (averaging $18,700 per year); scholarships/grants, traineeships, health care benefits, tuition waivers (partial), and unspecified assistantships also available. Support available to part-time students. Financial award application deadline: 6/30. *Faculty research:* Clinical research in aging, managing asthma in children, interventions to improve outcomes in critically ill children and their mothers, nurse home visitation studies, medical device evaluation, critical care clinical studies, high risk behavior and prevention, palliative care, pregnancy-related weight gain. *Total annual research expenditures:* $4.3 million. *Unit head:* Dr. Kathy H. Rideout, Interim Dean, 585-273-8902, Fax: 585-273-1268, E-mail: kathy_rideout@urmc.rochester.edu. *Application contact:* Elaine Andolina, Director of Admissions, 585-275-2375, Fax: 585-756-8299, E-mail: elaine_andolina@urmc.rochester.edu. Web site: http://www.son.rochester.edu.

University of St. Francis, College of Nursing, Joliet, IL 60435-6169. Offers adult health clinical nurse specialist (Post-Master's Certificate); adult nurse practitioner (MSN, Post-Master's Certificate); family nurse practitioner (Post-Master's Certificate); nursing administration (MSN); nursing practice (DNP). *Accreditation:* AACN. Part-time and evening/weekend programs available. Postbaccalaureate distance learning degree programs offered (no on-campus study). *Faculty:* 11 full-time (10 women), 16 part-time/adjunct (all women). *Students:* 59 full-time (52 women), 254 part-time (232 women); includes 80 minority (31 Black or African American, non-Hispanic/Latino; 11 Asian, non-Hispanic/Latino; 33 Hispanic/Latino; 5 Two or more races, non-Hispanic/Latino), 15 international. Average age 41. 340 applicants, 46% accepted, 117 enrolled. In 2011, 20 master's, 4 doctorates, 4 other advanced degrees awarded. *Entrance requirements:* Additional exam requirements/recommendations for international students: Required—TOEFL (minimum score 550 paper-based; 213 computer-based). *Application deadline:* Applications are processed on a rolling basis. Application fee: $30. Electronic applications accepted. *Expenses:* Contact institution. *Financial support:* In 2011–12, 87 students received support. Scholarships/grants, traineeships, and tuition waivers (partial) available. Support available to part-time students. Financial award applicants required to submit FAFSA. *Unit head:* Dr. Carol Wilson, Dean, 815-740-3840, Fax: 815-740-4243, E-mail: cwilson@stfrancis.edu. *Application contact:* Sandra Sloka, Director of Admissions for Graduate and Degree Completion Programs, 800-735-7500, Fax: 815-740-5032, E-mail: ssloka@stfrancis.edu. Web site: http://www.stfrancis.edu/academics/college-of-nursing-allied-health/graduate-programs/.

University of San Diego, Hahn School of Nursing and Health Science, San Diego, CA 92110-2492. Offers adult-gerontology clinical nurse specialist (MSN); adult-gerontology nurse practitioner/family nurse practitioner (MSN); clinical nursing (MSN); entry-level nursing (for non-RNs) (MSN); executive nurse leader (MSN); family nurse practitioner (MSN); family/lifespan psychiatric-mental health nurse practitioner (MSN); healthcare informatics (MS, MSN); nursing (PhD); nursing practice (DNP); pediatric nurse practitioner/family nurse practitioner (MSN). *Accreditation:* AACN. Part-time and evening/weekend programs available. *Faculty:* 23 full-time (21 women), 37 part-time/adjunct (34 women). *Students:* 157 full-time (131 women), 182 part-time (162 women); includes 121 minority (21 Black or African American, non-Hispanic/Latino; 6 American Indian or Alaska Native, non-Hispanic/Latino; 51 Asian, non-Hispanic/Latino; 36 Hispanic/Latino; 2 Native Hawaiian or other Pacific Islander, non-Hispanic/Latino; 5 Two or more races, non-Hispanic/Latino), 7 international. Average age 36. 506 applicants, 47% accepted, 150 enrolled. In 2011, 87 master's, 26 doctorates awarded. *Degree requirements:* For doctorate, thesis/dissertation (for some programs), residency (DNP). *Entrance requirements:* For master's, GRE General Test (entry-level nursing), BSN,

current California RN licensure (except for entry-level nursing); minimum GPA of 3.0; for doctorate, minimum GPA of 3.5, MSN, current California RN licensure. Additional exam requirements/recommendations for international students: Required—TOEFL (minimum score 580 paper-based; 237 computer-based; 83 iBT), TWE. *Application deadline:* For fall admission, 3/1 priority date for domestic students, 3/1 for international students; for spring admission, 11/1 priority date for domestic students, 11/1 for international students. Applications are processed on a rolling basis. Application fee: $45. Electronic applications accepted. *Expenses: Tuition:* Full-time $22,482; part-time $1249 per unit. *Required fees:* $224. Full-time tuition and fees vary according to course load and degree level. *Financial support:* In 2011–12, 232 students received support. Scholarships/grants and traineeships available. Support available to part-time students. Financial award application deadline: 4/1; financial award applicants required to submit FAFSA. *Faculty research:* Palliative and end of life care, maternal/child health, childhood obesity, health care disparities, cognitive functioning. *Unit head:* Dr. Sally Hardin, Dean, 619-260-4550, Fax: 619-260-6814. *Application contact:* Monica Mahon, Associate Director of Graduate Admissions, 619-260-4524, Fax: 619-260-4158, E-mail: grads@sandiego.edu. Web site: http://www.sandiego.edu/academics/nursing/.

University of San Francisco, School of Nursing and Health Professions, Program in Nursing Practice, San Francisco, CA 94117-1080. Offers family nurse practitioner (DNP); healthcare systems leadership (DNP). *Faculty:* 3 full-time (all women), 7 part-time/adjunct (6 women). *Students:* 73 full-time (67 women), 25 part-time (24 women); includes 35 minority (5 Black or African American, non-Hispanic/Latino; 1 American Indian or Alaska Native, non-Hispanic/Latino; 15 Asian, non-Hispanic/Latino; 10 Hispanic/Latino; 4 Two or more races, non-Hispanic/Latino), 1 international. Average age 48. 59 applicants, 58% accepted, 25 enrolled. In 2011, 7 doctorates awarded. *Entrance requirements:* For doctorate, nursing bachelor's degree, valid RN license in California. *Expenses: Tuition:* Full-time $20,070; part-time $1115 per unit. Tuition and fees vary according to course load, campus/location and program. *Financial support:* In 2011–12, 2 students received support. *Unit head:* Dr. Judith Karshmer, Dean, 415-422-6681, Fax: 415-422-6877, E-mail: nursing@usfca.edu. *Application contact:* Information Contact, 415-422-4723, Fax: 415-422-2217.

The University of Scranton, College of Graduate and Continuing Education, Department of Nursing, Scranton, PA 18510. Offers adult health nursing (MSN); family nurse practitioner (MSN, PMC); nurse anesthesia (MSN, PMC). Applicants accepted in odd-numbered years only. *Accreditation:* AACN; AANA/CANAEP. Part-time and evening/weekend programs available. *Faculty:* 13 full-time (all women), 2 part-time/adjunct (both women). *Students:* 50 full-time (45 women), 27 part-time (20 women); includes 7 minority (4 Black or African American, non-Hispanic/Latino; 1 Asian, non-Hispanic/Latino; 2 Hispanic/Latino). Average age 35. 100 applicants, 32% accepted. In 2011, 26 master's awarded. *Degree requirements:* For master's, thesis (for some programs), capstone experience. *Entrance requirements:* For master's, BSN, minimum GPA of 3.0, Pennsylvania RN license. Additional exam requirements/recommendations for international students: Required—TOEFL (minimum score 500 paper-based; 173 computer-based), IELTS (minimum score 5.5). *Application deadline:* For fall admission, 9/1 for domestic students. Applications are processed on a rolling basis. Application fee: $0. *Financial support:* In 2011–12, 7 students received support, including 7 teaching assistantships with full and partial tuition reimbursements available (averaging $6,914 per year); career-related internships or fieldwork, Federal Work-Study, and unspecified assistantships also available. Support available to part-time students. Financial award application deadline: 3/1. *Faculty research:* Home care, doctoral education, health care of women and children, pain, health promotion and adolescence. *Unit head:* Dr. Patricia Harrington, Chair, 570-941-7673, Fax: 570-941-4201, E-mail: harringtonp1@uofs.edu. *Application contact:* Dr. Mary Jane Hanson, Director, 570-941-4060, Fax: 570-941-4201, E-mail: hansonm2@scranton.edu. Web site: http://academic.uofs.edu/department/nursing/.

University of South Carolina, The Graduate School, College of Nursing, Program in Health Nursing, Columbia, SC 29208. Offers adult nurse practitioner (MSN); community/public health clinical nurse specialist (MSN); family nurse practitioner (MSN); pediatric nurse practitioner (MSN). *Accreditation:* AACN. Part-time programs available. *Degree requirements:* For master's, thesis or alternative. *Entrance requirements:* For master's, GRE General Test or MAT, BS in nursing, nursing license. Additional exam requirements/recommendations for international students: Required—TOEFL (minimum score 570 paper-based; 230 computer-based). Electronic applications accepted. *Faculty research:* System research, evidence based practice, breast cancer, violence.

University of Southern Maine, School of Nursing, Portland, ME 04104-9300. Offers adult health nursing (PMC); adult psychiatric/mental health nurse practitioner (MS); clinical nurse leader (MS); clinical nurse specialist psychiatric-mental health nursing (MS); education (MS); family nursing (PMC); family psychiatric/mental health nurse practitioner (MS); management (MS); medical/surgical nursing (MS); nurse practitioner adult health nursing (MS); nurse practitioner family nursing (MS); nursing (DNP); psychiatric-mental health nursing (PMC); MBA/MSN. *Accreditation:* AACN. Part-time programs available. *Degree requirements:* For master's, thesis optional. *Entrance requirements:* For master's, GRE General Test or MAT, minimum GPA of 3.0; for doctorate, GRE. Additional exam requirements/recommendations for international students: Required—TOEFL (minimum score 550 paper-based; 213 computer-based). Electronic applications accepted. *Faculty research:* Women's health, nursing history, weight control, community services, substance abuse.

University of Southern Mississippi, Graduate School, College of Health, School of Nursing, Hattiesburg, MS 39406-0001. Offers family nurse practitioner (MSN); nursing (DNP, PhD); nursing executive (MSN); psychiatric nurse practitioner (MSN). *Accreditation:* AACN. Part-time and evening/weekend programs available. *Faculty:* 17 full-time (16 women), 1 part-time/adjunct (0 women). *Students:* 115 full-time (98 women), 43 part-time (38 women); includes 42 minority (35 Black or African American, non-Hispanic/Latino; 1 American Indian or Alaska Native, non-Hispanic/Latino; 3 Asian, non-Hispanic/Latino; 3 Two or more races, non-Hispanic/Latino). Average age 40. 128 applicants, 52% accepted, 58 enrolled. In 2011, 42 master's, 2 doctorates awarded. *Degree requirements:* For master's, comprehensive exam, thesis optional; for doctorate, comprehensive exam, thesis/dissertation. *Entrance requirements:* For master's, GRE General Test, minimum GPA of 2.75 during last 60 hours, nursing license, BS in nursing; for doctorate, GRE General Test, master's degree in nursing, minimum GPA of 3.5. Additional exam requirements/recommendations for international students: Required—TOEFL, IELTS. *Application deadline:* For fall admission, 3/15 priority date for domestic students, 5/1 for international students; for spring admission, 1/10 priority date for domestic students, 1/10 for international students. Applications are processed on a rolling basis. Application fee: $50. Electronic applications accepted. *Financial support:* In 2011–12, 14 research assistantships with full tuition reimbursements (averaging $12,577 per year), teaching assistantships (averaging $12,000 per year) were awarded; Federal Work-Study, institutionally sponsored loans, scholarships/grants, traineeships, health care benefits, and unspecified assistantships also available. Financial award application deadline: 3/15; financial award applicants required to submit FAFSA. *Faculty research:* Gerontology, caregivers, HIV, bereavement, pain, nursing leadership. *Unit head:* Dr. Katherine Nugent, Director and Associate Dean, 601-266-5500, Fax: 601-266-

5927. *Application contact:* Dr. Sandra Bishop, Graduate Coordinator, 601-266-5500, Fax: 601-266-5927. Web site: http://www.usm.edu/graduateschool/table.php.

The University of Tampa, Nursing Programs, Tampa, FL 33606-1490. Offers adult nurse practitioner (MSN); family nurse practitioner (MSN). *Accreditation:* NLN. Part-time programs available. *Faculty:* 12 full-time (all women), 7 part-time/adjunct (all women). *Students:* 3 full-time (all women), 134 part-time (125 women); includes 28 minority (13 Black or African American, non-Hispanic/Latino; 1 Asian, non-Hispanic/Latino; 13 Hispanic/Latino; 1 Two or more races, non-Hispanic/Latino), 1 international. Average age 34. 148 applicants, 59% accepted, 52 enrolled. In 2011, 14 master's awarded. *Degree requirements:* For master's, comprehensive exam, oral exam, practicum. *Entrance requirements:* For master's, GRE (minimum score of 1000, 4.0 on Analytical Writing portion), bachelor's degree in nursing, current Florida RN license, minimum GPA of 3.0. Additional exam requirements/recommendations for international students: Required—TOEFL or IELTS. *Application deadline:* Applications are processed on a rolling basis. Application fee: $40. Electronic applications accepted. *Expenses: Tuition:* Full-time $8320; part-time $520 per credit hour. *Required fees:* $40 per semester. Tuition and fees vary according to program. *Financial support:* In 2011–12, 18 students received support. Unspecified assistantships available. Financial award applicants required to submit FAFSA. *Faculty research:* Vaccinations and public health, osteoporosis, cultural diversity, ethics, nursing practice. *Unit head:* Dr. Maria Warda, Director/Chair, 813-257-3302, Fax: 813-258-7214, E-mail: mwarda@ut.edu. *Application contact:* Brent Benner, Director of Admissions, 813-257-3642, E-mail: ctobie@ut.edu.

The University of Tennessee at Chattanooga, Graduate School, College of Health, Education and Professional Studies, School of Nursing, Chattanooga, TN 37403. Offers administration (MSN); certified nurse anesthetist (Post-Master's Certificate); education (MSN); family nurse practitioner (MSN, Post-Master's Certificate); health care informatics (Post-Master's Certificate); nurse anesthesia (MSN); nurse education (Post-Master's Certificate); nursing (DNP). *Accreditation:* AACN; AANA/CANAEP (one or more programs are accredited). *Faculty:* 15 full-time (13 women), 4 part-time/adjunct (all women). *Students:* 68 full-time (45 women), 37 part-time (33 women); includes 8 minority (6 Black or African American, non-Hispanic/Latino; 2 Hispanic/Latino). Average age 33. 5 applicants, 100% accepted, 3 enrolled. In 2011, 52 degrees awarded. *Degree requirements:* For master's, thesis optional, qualifying exams, professional project; for Post-Master's Certificate, thesis or alternative, practicum, seminar. *Entrance requirements:* For master's, GRE General Test, MAT, BSN, minimum GPA of 3.0, eligibility for Tennessee RN license, 1 year direct patient care experience; for Post-Master's Certificate, GRE General Test, MAT, MSN, minimum GPA of 3.0, eligibility for Tennessee RN license, one year of direct patient care experience. Additional exam requirements/recommendations for international students: Required—TOEFL (minimum score 550 paper-based; 213 computer-based; 79 iBT), IELTS (minimum score 6). *Application deadline:* For fall admission, 8/1 priority date for domestic students, 6/1 for international students; for spring admission, 12/1 priority date for domestic students, 10/1 for international students. Applications are processed on a rolling basis. Application fee: $35. Electronic applications accepted. *Expenses:* Tuition, state resident: full-time $6472; part-time $359 per credit hour. Tuition, nonresident: full-time $20,006; part-time $1111 per credit hour. *Required fees:* $1320; $160 per credit hour. *Financial support:* Career-related internships or fieldwork and scholarships/grants available. Support available to part-time students. *Faculty research:* Diabetes in women, health care for elderly, alternative medicine, hypertension, nurse anesthesia. *Total annual research expenditures:* $1.9 million. *Unit head:* Dr. Kay R. Lindgren, Head, 423-425-4646, Fax: 423-425-4668, E-mail: kay-lindgren@utc.edu. *Application contact:* Dr. Jerald Ainsworth, Dean of Graduate Studies, 423-425-4478, Fax: 423-425-5223, E-mail: jerald-ainsworth@utc.edu. Web site: http://www.utc.edu/Academic/Nursing/.

The University of Texas at Arlington, Graduate School, College of Nursing, Arlington, TX 76019. Offers nurse practitioner (MSN); nursing administration (MSN); nursing education (MSN); nursing practice (DNP); nursing science (PhD). *Accreditation:* AACN. Part-time and evening/weekend programs available. Postbaccalaureate distance learning degree programs offered (no on-campus study). *Faculty:* 15 full-time (all women), 2 part-time/adjunct (both women). *Students:* 58 full-time (48 women), 720 part-time (654 women); includes 281 minority (133 Black or African American, non-Hispanic/Latino; 3 American Indian or Alaska Native, non-Hispanic/Latino; 73 Asian, non-Hispanic/Latino; 53 Hispanic/Latino; 4 Native Hawaiian or other Pacific Islander, non-Hispanic/Latino; 15 Two or more races, non-Hispanic/Latino), 22 international. Average age 37. 686 applicants, 48% accepted, 265 enrolled. In 2011, 117 master's, 4 doctorates awarded. *Degree requirements:* For master's, practicum course; for doctorate, comprehensive exam (for some programs), thesis/dissertation (for some programs), proposal defense dissertation (for PhD); scholarship project (for DNP). *Entrance requirements:* For master's, GRE General Test if GPA less than 3.0, minimum GPA of 3.0, Texas nursing license, minimum C grade in undergraduate statistics course; for doctorate, GRE General Test (waived for MSN-to-PhD applicants), minimum undergraduate, graduate and statistics GPA of 3.0; Texas RN license; interview; written statement of goals. Additional exam requirements/recommendations for international students: Required—TOEFL (minimum score 550 paper-based; 213 computer-based), IELTS (minimum score 7). *Application deadline:* For fall admission, 2/1 for domestic students, 4/1 for international students; for spring admission, 10/15 for domestic students, 9/5 for international students. Applications are processed on a rolling basis. Application fee: $40 ($70 for international students). *Financial support:* In 2011–12, 46 students received support, including 22 fellowships with partial tuition reimbursements available (averaging $4,473 per year), 6 research assistantships (averaging $8,873 per year), 24 teaching assistantships (averaging $6,202 per year); career-related internships or fieldwork, scholarships/grants, and traineeships also available. Financial award application deadline: 6/1; financial award applicants required to submit FAFSA. *Faculty research:* Simulation in clinical education and practice, cultural diversity, vulnerable populations, substance abuse. *Unit head:* Dr. Elizabeth C. Poster, Dean, 817-272-2776, Fax: 817-272-5006, E-mail: poster@uta.edu. *Application contact:* Dr. Jennifer Gray, Graduate Advisor/Associate Dean, 817-272-5295, Fax: 817-272-2065, E-mail: jgray@uta.edu. Web site: http://www.uta.edu/nursing.

The University of Texas at Austin, Graduate School, School of Nursing, Austin, TX 78712-1111. Offers adult -gerontology clinical nurse specialist (MSN); child health (MSN), including administration, public health nursing; child health (MSN), including teaching; family nurse practitioner (MSN); family psychiatric/mental health nurse practitioner (MSN); holistic adult health (MSN), including administration, education; maternity (MSN), including administration, public health nursing; maternity (MSN), including teaching; nursing (PhD); nursing administration and healthcare systems management (MSN); pediatric nurse practitioner (MSN); public health nursing (MSN). *Accreditation:* AACN. Part-time programs available. *Degree requirements:* For master's, thesis optional; for doctorate, thesis/dissertation. *Entrance requirements:* For master's and doctorate, GRE General Test. Additional exam requirements/recommendations for international students: Required—TOEFL (minimum score 550 paper-based; 213 computer-based). *Application deadline:* For fall admission, 12/1 for domestic students. Application fee: $50 ($75 for international students). Electronic applications accepted. *Financial support:* Fellowships, research assistantships, teaching assistantships, scholarships/grants, and traineeships available. Financial award application deadline: 2/1. *Faculty research:* Chronic illness management, memory and aging, health promotion, women's health, adolescent health. *Unit head:* Dr. Alexa Stuifbergen, Dean, 512-471-4100, Fax: 512-471-4910, E-mail: astuifbergen@mail.utexas.edu. Web site: http://www.utexas.edu/nursing/.

The University of Texas at El Paso, Graduate School, School of Nursing, El Paso, TX 79968-0001. Offers evidence-based practice (Certificate); family nurse practitioner (MSN); health care leadership and management (Certificate); interdisciplinary health sciences (PhD); nurse clinical specialist (MSN); nursing (Post-Master's Certificate); nursing systems management (MSN). *Accreditation:* AACN. *Students:* 162 (131 women); includes 94 minority (22 Black or African American, non-Hispanic/Latino; 11 Asian, non-Hispanic/Latino; 61 Hispanic/Latino), 3 international. Average age 34. 55 applicants, 58% accepted, 24 enrolled. In 2011, 12 master's awarded. *Degree requirements:* For master's, thesis optional; for doctorate, thesis/dissertation. *Entrance requirements:* For master's, GRE, minimum GPA of 3.0, course work in statistics, resume; for doctorate, GRE, letters of reference, relevant personal/professional experience, master's degree in health. Additional exam requirements/recommendations for international students: Required—TOEFL; Recommended—IELTS. *Application deadline:* For fall admission, 8/1 for domestic students, 3/1 for international students; for spring admission, 11/1 for domestic students, 9/1 for international students. Applications are processed on a rolling basis. Application fee: $45 ($80 for international students). Electronic applications accepted. *Financial support:* In 2011–12, research assistantships with partial tuition reimbursements (averaging $18,825 per year), teaching assistantships with partial tuition reimbursements (averaging $18,000 per year) were awarded; fellowships with partial tuition reimbursements, institutionally sponsored loans, scholarships/grants, health care benefits, tuition waivers (partial), and unspecified assistantships also available. Support available to part-time students. Financial award application deadline: 3/15; financial award applicants required to submit FAFSA. *Unit head:* Dr. Elias Provencio-Vasquez, Dean, 915-747-7273, Fax: 915-747-8266, E-mail: eprovenciovasquez@utep.edu. *Application contact:* Dr. Benjamin Flores, Interim Dean of the Graduate School, 915-747-5491, Fax: 915-747-5788, E-mail: bflores@utep.edu. Web site: http://nursing.utep.edu/.

The University of Texas at Tyler, College of Nursing and Health Sciences, Program in Nursing, Tyler, TX 75799-0001. Offers nurse practitioner (MSN); nursing (PhD); nursing administration (MSN); nursing education (MSN); MSN/MBA. *Accreditation:* AACN. Part-time and evening/weekend programs available. Postbaccalaureate distance learning degree programs offered (no on-campus study). *Degree requirements:* For master's, comprehensive exam (for some programs), thesis (for some programs); for doctorate, thesis/dissertation. *Entrance requirements:* For master's, GRE General Test or MAT, GMAT, minimum undergraduate GPA of 3.0, course work in statistics, RN license, BSN. Additional exam requirements/recommendations for international students: Required—TOEFL (minimum score 79 computer-based). Electronic applications accepted. *Faculty research:* Psychosocial adjustment, aging, support/commitment of caregivers, psychological abuse and violence, hope/hopelessness, professional values, end of life care, suicidology, clinical supervision, workforce retention and issues, global health issues, health promotion.

The University of Texas–Pan American, College of Health Sciences and Human Services, Department of Nursing, Edinburg, TX 78539. Offers adult health nursing (MSN); family nurse practitioner (MSN). *Accreditation:* AACN. Part-time and evening/weekend programs available. *Degree requirements:* For master's, thesis optional. *Entrance requirements:* For master's, Texas RN licensure, undergraduate physical statistic course. Additional exam requirements/recommendations for international students: Required—TOEFL (minimum score 550 paper-based). *Application deadline:* For fall admission, 7/1 priority date for domestic students, 7/1 for international students; for spring admission, 10/1 priority date for domestic students, 10/1 for international students. Applications are processed on a rolling basis. Application fee: $35. Electronic applications accepted. *Expenses:* Contact institution. *Financial support:* Scholarships/grants and traineeships available. *Faculty research:* Health promotion, adolescent pregnancy, herbal and nontraditional approaches, healing touch stress. *Unit head:* Dr. Carolina G. Huerta, Chair, 956-665-3496, Fax: 956-381-2384, E-mail: chuerta@utpa.edu. *Application contact:* Dr. Janice A. Maville, Professor and Assistant Dean, 956-665-2111, Fax: 956-665-2875, E-mail: jmaville@utpa.edu. Web site: http://www.panam.edu/dept/nursing/.

The University of Toledo, College of Graduate Studies, College of Nursing, Department of Population and Community Care, Toledo, OH 43606-3390. Offers adult nurse practitioner (Certificate); adult nurse practitioner/clinical nurse specialist (MSN); clinical nurse leader (MSN); family nurse practitioner (MSN, Certificate); nurse educator (MSN, Certificate); pediatric nurse practitioner (MSN, Certificate); psychiatric-mental health clinical nurse specialist (MSN, Certificate). Part-time programs available. *Faculty:* 43. *Students:* 77 full-time (63 women), 198 part-time (180 women); includes 30 minority (14 Black or African American, non-Hispanic/Latino; 1 American Indian or Alaska Native, non-Hispanic/Latino; 4 Asian, non-Hispanic/Latino; 8 Hispanic/Latino; 3 Two or more races, non-Hispanic/Latino), 1 international. Average age 33. 172 applicants, 53% accepted, 82 enrolled. In 2011, 66 master's, 10 other advanced degrees awarded. *Degree requirements:* For master's, thesis or alternative. *Entrance requirements:* For master's, GRE, BS in nursing, minimum undergraduate GPA of 3.0, statement of purpose, three letters of recommendation, transcripts from all prior institutions attended, Nursing CAS application, UT supplemental application; for Certificate, BS in nursing, minimum undergraduate GPA of 3.0, statement of purpose, three letters of recommendation, transcripts from all prior institutions attended. Additional exam requirements/recommendations for international students: Required—TOEFL (minimum score 550 paper-based; 213 computer-based; 80 iBT), IELTS (minimum score 6.5). Application fee: $45 ($75 for international students). Electronic applications accepted. *Financial support:* Research assistantships, Federal Work-Study, scholarships/grants, traineeships, and tuition waivers (full and partial) available. *Application contact:* Joan Mulligan, Admissions Analyst, 419-383-4168, Fax: 419-383-6140, E-mail: joan.mulligan@utoledo.edu. Web site: http://www.utoledo.edu/nursing/.

University of Victoria, Faculty of Graduate Studies, Faculty of Human and Social Development, School of Nursing, Victoria, BC V8W 2Y2, Canada. Offers advanced nursing practice (advanced practice leadership option) (MN); advanced nursing practice (nurse educator option) (MN); advanced nursing practice (nurse practitioner option) (MN); nursing (PhD). Part-time programs available. Postbaccalaureate distance learning degree programs offered (no on-campus study). *Entrance requirements:* Additional exam requirements/recommendations for international students: Required—TOEFL (minimum score 575 paper-based; 233 computer-based), IELTS (minimum score 7). Electronic applications accepted.

University of Wisconsin–Eau Claire, College of Nursing and Health Sciences, Program in Nursing, Eau Claire, WI 54702-4004. Offers adult-gerontologic administration (MSN); adult-gerontologic clinical nurse specialist (MSN); adult-gerontologic education (MSN); adult-gerontologic nurse practitioner (MSN); family health administration (MSN); family health in education (MSN); family health nurse practitioner (MSN); nursing practice (DNP). Part-time programs available. *Faculty:* 13 full-time (all women), 1 (woman) part-time/adjunct. *Students:* 42 full-time (40 women), 68 part-time (66 women); includes 3 minority (1 Black or African American, non-Hispanic/Latino; 1 Asian, non-Hispanic/Latino; 1 Hispanic/Latino). Average age 37. 74 applicants,

70% accepted, 41 enrolled. In 2011, 35 master's awarded. Terminal master's awarded for partial completion of doctoral program. *Degree requirements:* For master's, thesis optional, 500-600 hours clinical practicum, oral and written exams. *Entrance requirements:* For master's, Wisconsin RN license, minimum GPA of 3.0, undergraduate statistics, course work in health assessment. Additional exam requirements/recommendations for international students: Required—TOEFL (minimum score 550 paper-based; 213 computer-based; 79 iBT); Recommended—IELTS (minimum score 7). *Application deadline:* For fall admission, 1/15 priority date for domestic students, 1/15 for international students. Applications are processed on a rolling basis. Application fee: $86. *Expenses:* Tuition, state resident: full-time $7312; part-time $406 per credit. Tuition, nonresident: full-time $16,771; part-time $932 per credit. *Required fees:* $1101; $61 per credit. *Financial support:* In 2011–12, 16 students received support. Federal Work-Study and unspecified assistantships available. Financial award application deadline: 3/1; financial award applicants required to submit FAFSA. *Unit head:* Dr. Linda Young, Dean, 715-836-4904, Fax: 715-836-5925, E-mail: younglk@uwec.edu. *Application contact:* Dr. Mary Zwygart-Stauffacher, Director, 715-836-5287, E-mail: zwygarmc@uwec.edu. Web site: http://www.uwec.edu/conhs/programs/grad/index.htm.

University of Wisconsin–Milwaukee, Graduate School, College of Nursing, Milwaukee, WI 53201-0413. Offers family nursing practitioner (Post Master's Certificate); health professional education (Certificate); nursing (MS, PhD); public health (Certificate). *Accreditation:* AACN. Part-time programs available. *Faculty:* 30 full-time (29 women), 2 part-time/adjunct (both women). *Students:* 125 full-time (114 women), 122 part-time (108 women); includes 34 minority (15 Black or African American, non-Hispanic/Latino; 1 American Indian or Alaska Native, non-Hispanic/Latino; 7 Asian, non-Hispanic/Latino; 1 Hispanic/Latino; 10 Two or more races, non-Hispanic/Latino), 6 international. Average age 39. 128 applicants, 49% accepted, 41 enrolled. In 2011, 52 master's, 16 doctorates awarded. *Degree requirements:* For master's, thesis; for doctorate, thesis/dissertation. *Entrance requirements:* For master's, GRE General Test or MAT, autobiographical sketch; for doctorate, GRE, minimum GPA of 3.2. Additional exam requirements/recommendations for international students: Required—TOEFL (minimum score 550 paper-based; 79 iBT), IELTS (minimum score 6.5). *Application deadline:* For fall admission, 1/1 priority date for domestic students; for spring admission, 9/1 for domestic students. Applications are processed on a rolling basis. Application fee: $56 ($96 for international students). Electronic applications accepted. One-time fee: $506.10 full-time. Tuition and fees vary according to course load and reciprocity agreements. *Financial support:* In 2011–12, 3 fellowships, 1 research assistantship, 9 teaching assistantships were awarded; career-related internships or fieldwork, Federal Work-Study, health care benefits, unspecified assistantships, and project assistantships also available. Support available to part-time students. Financial award application deadline: 4/15; financial award applicants required to submit FAFSA. *Total annual research expenditures:* $3.3 million. *Unit head:* Dr. Sally Lundeen, Dean, 414-229-4189, E-mail: slundeen@uwm.edu. *Application contact:* Kim Litwack, Representative, 414-229-5098. Web site: http://www.uwm.edu/Dept/Nursing/.

University of Wisconsin–Oshkosh, Graduate Studies, College of Nursing, Oshkosh, WI 54901. Offers adult health and illness (MSN); family nurse practitioner (MSN). *Accreditation:* AACN. Part-time programs available. *Degree requirements:* For master's, thesis or alternative, clinical paper. *Entrance requirements:* For master's, RN license, BSN, previous course work in statistics and health assessment, minimum undergraduate GPA of 3.0, letters of recommendation. Additional exam requirements/recommendations for international students: Required—TOEFL (minimum score 550 paper-based; 213 computer-based; 79 iBT). Electronic applications accepted. *Faculty research:* Adult health and illness, nurse practitioners practice, health care service, advanced practitioner roles, natural alternative complementary healthcare.

Vanderbilt University, Vanderbilt University School of Nursing, Nashville, TN 37240. Offers acute care nurse practitioner (MSN), including intensivist; adult-gerontology primary care nurse practitioner (MSN); emergency nurse practitioner (MSN); family nurse practitioner (MSN); family psychiatric and mental health nurse practitioner (MSN); health systems management (MSN); neonatal nurse practitioner (MSN); nurse midwifery (MSN); nurse midwifery/family nurse practitioner (MSN); nursing informatics (MSN); nursing practice (DNP); nursing science (PhD); pediatric acute care nurse practitioner (MSN); pediatric primary care nurse practitioner (MSN); women's health nurse practitioner (MSN), including urogynecology, women's health; women's health nurse practitioner/adult gerontology nurse practitioner (MSN); MSN/M Div; MSN/MTS. *Accreditation:* ACNM/ACME; NLN (one or more programs are accredited). Part-time programs available. Postbaccalaureate distance learning degree programs offered (minimal on-campus study). *Faculty:* 120 full-time (105 women), 415 part-time/adjunct (302 women). *Students:* 570 full-time (503 women), 395 part-time (364 women); includes 107 minority (57 Black or African American, non-Hispanic/Latino; 1 American Indian or Alaska Native, non-Hispanic/Latino; 19 Asian, non-Hispanic/Latino; 19 Hispanic/Latino; 2 Native Hawaiian or other Pacific Islander, non-Hispanic/Latino; 9 Two or more races, non-Hispanic/Latino), 10 international. Average age 32. 1,116 applicants, 56% accepted, 455 enrolled. In 2011, 341 master's, 33 doctorates awarded. *Degree requirements:* For doctorate, comprehensive exam, thesis/dissertation. *Entrance requirements:* For master's, GRE General Test (within the past 5 years), minimum B average in undergraduate course work, 3 letters of recommendation; for doctorate, GRE General Test, interview, 3 letters of recommendation from doctorally-prepared faculty, MSN, essay. Additional exam requirements/recommendations for international students: Required—TOEFL (minimum score 570 paper-based; 88 computer-based), IELTS (minimum score 6.5). *Application deadline:* For fall admission, 12/1 priority date for domestic students, 12/1 for international students. Applications are processed on a rolling basis. Application fee: $50. Electronic applications accepted. *Expenses:* Contact institution. *Financial support:* In 2011–12, 392 students received support. Scholarships/grants and health care benefits available. Support available to part-time students. Financial award application deadline: 3/15; financial award applicants required to submit FAFSA. *Faculty research:* Lymphedema, palliative care and bereavement, health services research including workforce, safety and quality of care, gerontology, better birth outcomes including nutrition . *Total annual research expenditures:* $1.8 million. *Unit head:* Dr. Colleen Conway-Welch, Dean, 615-343-8776, Fax: 615-343-7711, E-mail: colleen.conway-welch@vanderbilt.edu. *Application contact:* Patricia Peerman, Assistant Dean for Enrollment Management, 615-322-3800, Fax: 615-343-0333, E-mail: vusn-admissions@vanderbilt.edu. Web site: http://www.nursing.vanderbilt.edu.

Villanova University, College of Nursing, Villanova, PA 19085-1699. Offers adult nurse practitioner (MSN, Post Master's Certificate); family nurse practitioner (MSN, Post Master's Certificate); health care administration (MSN, Post Master's Certificate); nurse anesthetist (MSN, Post Master's Certificate); nursing (PhD); nursing education (MSN, Post Master's Certificate); nursing practice (DNP); pediatric nurse practitioner (MSN, Post Master's Certificate). *Accreditation:* AACN; AANA/CANAEP. Part-time programs available. Postbaccalaureate distance learning degree programs offered (minimal on-campus study). *Faculty:* 17 full-time (all women), 4 part-time/adjunct (all women). *Students:* 36 full-time (35 women), 256 part-time (234 women); includes 27 minority (14 Black or African American, non-Hispanic/Latino; 9 Asian, non-Hispanic/Latino; 4 Hispanic/Latino), 16 international. Average age 30. 161 applicants, 55% accepted, 75 enrolled. In 2011, 55 master's, 11 doctorates, 5 other advanced degrees awarded. *Degree requirements:* For master's, independent study project; for doctorate, comprehensive exam, thesis/dissertation. *Entrance requirements:* For master's, GRE or MAT, BSN, 1 year of recent nursing experience, physical assessment, course work in statistics; for doctorate, GRE, MSN. Additional exam requirements/recommendations for international students: Required—TOEFL, IELTS. *Application deadline:* For fall admission, 7/1 priority date for domestic students, 7/1 for international students; for spring admission, 11/1 priority date for domestic students, 11/1 for international students. Applications are processed on a rolling basis. Application fee: $50. *Expenses:* Contact institution. *Financial support:* In 2011–12, 43 students received support, including 5 teaching assistantships with full tuition reimbursements available (averaging $13,100 per year); institutionally sponsored loans, scholarships/grants, traineeships, tuition waivers (full), and unspecified assistantships also available. Financial award application deadline: 7/1; financial award applicants required to submit FAFSA. *Faculty research:* Genetics, ethics, cognitive development of students, women with disabilities, nursing leadership. *Unit head:* Dr. Marguerite K. Schlag, Assistant Dean/Director, Graduate Programs, 610-519-4907, Fax: 610-519-7650, E-mail: marguerite.schlag@villanova.edu. Web site: http://www.nursing.villanova.edu/.

Virginia Commonwealth University, Graduate School, School of Nursing, Nurse Practitioner Program, Richmond, VA 23284-9005. Offers MS, Certificate. Part-time programs available. *Entrance requirements:* For master's, GRE General Test, minimum GPA of 2.8. Additional exam requirements/recommendations for international students: Required—TOEFL (minimum score 600 paper-based; 250 computer-based; 100 iBT). Electronic applications accepted. *Expenses:* Tuition, state resident: full-time $9133; part-time $507 per credit. Tuition, nonresident: full-time $18,777; part-time $1043 per credit. *Required fees:* $77 per credit. Tuition and fees vary according to degree level, campus/location, program and student level.

Wagner College, Division of Graduate Studies, Department of Nursing, Program in Family Nurse Practitioner, Staten Island, NY 10301-4495. Offers Certificate. Part-time and evening/weekend programs available. *Faculty:* 3 part-time/adjunct (all women). *Students:* 2 part-time (both women); includes 1 minority (Two or more races, non-Hispanic/Latino). Average age 51. 1 applicant, 100% accepted, 1 enrolled. In 2011, 1 Certificate awarded. *Entrance requirements:* For degree, master's degree in nursing from an NLN-accredited program, minimum GPA of 3.0, current NY State licensure as Professional Registered Nurse, malpractice insurance coverage, current immunization and physical exam. *Application deadline:* For fall admission, 5/1 priority date for domestic students; for spring admission, 12/1 for domestic students. Applications are processed on a rolling basis. Application fee: $50 ($80 for international students). *Expenses: Tuition:* Full-time $16,200; part-time $890 per credit. *Financial support:* Unspecified assistantships and alumni fellowship grant available. Financial award applicants required to submit FAFSA. *Unit head:* Dr. Paula Tropello, Associate Professor/Chairman, Department of Nursing, 718-390-3452, Fax: 718-420-4009, E-mail: ptropell@wagner.edu. *Application contact:* Patricia Clancy, Administrative Assistant, 718-420-4464, Fax: 718-390-3105, E-mail: patricia.clancy@wagner.edu.

Washburn University, School of Nursing, Topeka, KS 66621. Offers adult nurse practitioner (MSN); clinical nurse leader (MSN); family nurse practitioner (MSN). *Accreditation:* AACN. Part-time programs available. *Faculty:* 13 full-time (all women), 1 (woman) part-time/adjunct. *Students:* 23 full-time (all women), 78 part-time (73 women). 52 applicants, 77% accepted, 40 enrolled. In 2011, 23 master's awarded. *Entrance requirements:* Additional exam requirements/recommendations for international students: Required—TOEFL. *Application deadline:* For fall admission, 3/15 for international students. Application fee: $35. *Expenses:* Tuition, state resident: full-time $5346; part-time $297 per credit hour. Tuition, nonresident: full-time $10,908; part-time $606 per credit hour. *Required fees:* $86; $43 per semester. *Financial support:* Application deadline: 2/15. *Unit head:* Dr. Monica S. Scheibmeir, Dean, 785-670-1526, E-mail: monica.scheibmeir@washburn.edu. *Application contact:* Mary V. Allen, Director of Student Academic Support Services, 785-670-1533, E-mail: mary.allen@washburn.edu. Web site: http://www.washburn.edu/sonu.

Western University of Health Sciences, College of Graduate Nursing, Master of Science in Nursing Program, Pomona, CA 91766-1854. Offers administrative nurse leader (MSN); clinical nurse leader (MSN); degree completion (MSN); entry-level (MSN); family nurse practitioner (MSN); nursing (MSN). *Faculty:* 12 full-time (all women), 18 part-time/adjunct (16 women). *Students:* 262 full-time (228 women), 12 part-time (all women); includes 150 minority (22 Black or African American, non-Hispanic/Latino; 2 American Indian or Alaska Native, non-Hispanic/Latino; 83 Asian, non-Hispanic/Latino; 33 Hispanic/Latino; 10 Two or more races, non-Hispanic/Latino), 4 international. Average age 31. 485 applicants, 38% accepted, 104 enrolled. In 2011, 55 master's awarded. *Entrance requirements:* For master's, BSN, minimum GPA of 3.0, 3 letters of recommendation. Additional exam requirements/recommendations for international students: Required—TOEFL. *Application deadline:* For fall admission, 3/1 for domestic students. Applications are processed on a rolling basis. Application fee: $60. *Unit head:* Karen J. Hanford, Dean, 909-469-5243, Fax: 909-469-5521, E-mail: khanford@westernu.edu. *Application contact:* Kathryn Ford, Director of Admissions/International Student Advisor, 909-469-5541, Fax: 909-469-5570, E-mail: admissions@westernu.edu.

Westminster College, School of Nursing and Health Sciences, Salt Lake City, UT 84105-3697. Offers family nurse practitioner (MSN); nurse anesthesia (MSNA); nurse education (MSNED); nursing (MSN); public health (MPH). *Accreditation:* AACN; AANA/CANAEP. *Faculty:* 13 full-time (7 women), 7 part-time/adjunct (4 women). *Students:* 102 full-time (54 women), 16 part-time (12 women); includes 9 minority (2 Black or African American, non-Hispanic/Latino; 1 American Indian or Alaska Native, non-Hispanic/Latino; 5 Asian, non-Hispanic/Latino; 1 Hispanic/Latino), 1 international. Average age 34. 106 applicants, 64% accepted, 38 enrolled. In 2011, 53 master's awarded. *Degree requirements:* For master's, clinical practicum, 504 clinical practice hours. *Entrance requirements:* For master's, GRE, resume, Utah RN license in good standing, minimum GPA of 3.0, 3 letters of reference, BSN from accredited nursing program, proof of clear state and federal background check, drug test results, personal interview, current PALS certification, current ACLS certification. Additional exam requirements/recommendations for international students: Required—TOEFL (minimum score 600 paper-based; 250 computer-based; 100 iBT), IELTS (minimum score 7). *Application deadline:* Applications are processed on a rolling basis. Application fee: $50. Electronic applications accepted. *Expenses:* Contact institution. *Financial support:* In 2011–12, 11 students received support. Career-related internships or fieldwork and tuition reimbursement, tuition remission available. Support available to part-time students. Financial award applicants required to submit FAFSA. *Faculty research:* Collaborative testing in nursing: student outcomes and perspectives, Implementing New Educational Paradigms into Pre-Licensure Nursing Curricula conference presentation. *Unit head:* Dr. Sheryl Steadman, Dean, 801-832-2164, Fax: 801-832-3110, E-mail: ssteadman@westminstercollege.edu. *Application contact:* Dr. Gary Daynes, Vice President for Strategic Outreach and Enrollment, 801-832-2200, Fax: 801-832-3101, E-mail: admission@westminstercollege.edu. Web site: http://www.westminstercollege.edu/msn.

West Texas A&M University, College of Nursing and Health Sciences, Department of Nursing, Canyon, TX 79016-0001. Offers family nurse practitioner (MSN); nursing (MSN). *Accreditation:* AACN. Part-time programs available. Postbaccalaureate distance learning degree programs offered (minimal on-campus study). *Degree requirements:*

For master's, comprehensive exam, thesis optional. *Entrance requirements:* For master's, GRE General Test, bachelor's degree in nursing, minimum GPA of 3.0 in last 60 hours. Additional exam requirements/recommendations for international students: Required—TOEFL (minimum score 550 paper-based). Electronic applications accepted. *Faculty research:* Family-focused nursing, nursing traineeship, professional nursing.

Wilmington University, College of Health Professions, New Castle, DE 19720-6491. Offers adult nurse practitioner (MSN); family nurse practitioner (MSN); gerontology nurse practitioner (MSN); nursing (MSN); nursing leadership (MSN); nursing practice (DNP). *Accreditation:* AACN. Part-time programs available. *Faculty:* 3 full-time (all women). *Students:* 30 full-time (all women), 270 part-time (241 women). Average age 38. *Degree requirements:* For master's, thesis. *Entrance requirements:* For master's, BSN, RN license, interview, 3 letters of recommendation. Additional exam requirements/recommendations for international students: Required—TOEFL (minimum score 500 paper-based; 173 computer-based). *Application deadline:* For fall admission, 4/1 for domestic students; for spring admission, 9/1 for domestic students. Applications are processed on a rolling basis. Application fee: $35. Electronic applications accepted. *Expenses: Tuition:* Part-time $534 per credit hour. *Required fees:* $25 per term. *Financial support:* Fellowships with tuition reimbursements and traineeships available. Financial award applicants required to submit FAFSA. *Faculty research:* Outcomes assessment, student writing ability. *Unit head:* Denise Z. Westbrook, Dean, 302-356-6915, E-mail: denise.z.westbrook@wilmu.edu. *Application contact:* Chris Ferguson, Director of Admissions, 302-356-4636 Ext. 256, Fax: 302-328-5164, E-mail: inquire@wilmcoll.edu. Web site: http://www.wilmu.edu/health/.

Winona State University, College of Nursing and Health Sciences, Winona, MN 55987. Offers adult nurse practitioner (MS, Post Master's Certificate); clinical nurse specialist (MS, Post Master's Certificate); family nurse practitioner (MS, Post Master's Certificate); nurse administrator (MS); nurse educator (MS, Post Master's Certificate); nursing (DNP). *Accreditation:* AACN. Part-time programs available. Postbaccalaureate distance learning degree programs offered (no on-campus study). *Students:* 75 full-time (70 women), 25 part-time (22 women); includes 11 minority (4 Black or African American, non-Hispanic/Latino; 5 Asian, non-Hispanic/Latino; 1 Hispanic/Latino; 1 Two or more races, non-Hispanic/Latino), 2 international. Average age 34. In 2011, 26 master's, 2 doctorates, 3 other advanced degrees awarded. *Degree requirements:* For master's, thesis; for doctorate, capstone. *Entrance requirements:* For master's, GRE (if GPA less than 3.0). Additional exam requirements/recommendations for international students: Required—TOEFL (minimum score 550 paper-based). *Application deadline:* For fall admission, 12/1 for domestic and international students. Application fee: $20. *Financial support:* Research assistantships with partial tuition reimbursements, Federal Work-Study, traineeships, and unspecified assistantships available. Support available to part-time students. Financial award application deadline: 8/15; financial award applicants required to submit FAFSA. *Unit head:* Dr. William J. McBreen, Dean, 507-457-5122, E-mail: wmcbreen@winona.edu. *Application contact:* Patricia Cichosz, Office Manager, Graduate Studies, 507-457-5038, E-mail: pcichosz@winona.edu.

Wright State University, School of Graduate Studies, College of Nursing and Health, Program in Nursing, Dayton, OH 45435. Offers acute care nurse practitioner (MS); administration of nursing and health care systems (MS); adult health (MS); child and adolescent health (MS); community health (MS); family nurse practitioner (MS); nurse practitioner (MS); school nurse (MS); MBA/MS. *Accreditation:* AACN. Part-time and evening/weekend programs available. *Degree requirements:* For master's, thesis or alternative. *Entrance requirements:* For master's, GRE General Test, BSN from NLN-accredited college, Ohio RN license. Additional exam requirements/recommendations for international students: Required—TOEFL. *Faculty research:* Clinical nursing and health, teaching, caring, pain administration, informatics and technology.

Forensic Nursing

Boston College, William F. Connell School of Nursing, Chestnut Hill, MA 02467-3800. Offers adult-gerontology nursing (MS); community health nursing (MS); family health (MS); forensic nursing (MS); maternal/child health nursing (MS), including pediatric and women's health; nurse anesthesia (MS); nursing (PhD); palliative care (MS), including adult and pediatric; psychiatric-mental health nursing (MS); MBA/MS; MS/MA; MS/PhD. *Accreditation:* AACN; AANA/CANAEP (one or more programs are accredited). Part-time programs available. *Faculty:* 48 full-time (46 women), 31 part-time/adjunct (29 women). *Students:* 225 full-time (207 women), 90 part-time (88 women); includes 47 minority (15 Black or African American, non-Hispanic/Latino; 3 American Indian or Alaska Native, non-Hispanic/Latino; 17 Asian, non-Hispanic/Latino; 8 Hispanic/Latino; 4 Two or more races, non-Hispanic/Latino), 6 international. Average age 31. 369 applicants, 43% accepted, 80 enrolled. In 2011, 113 master's, 8 doctorates awarded. *Degree requirements:* For master's, comprehensive exam, research project; for doctorate, comprehensive exam, thesis/dissertation, computer literacy exam or foreign language. *Entrance requirements:* For master's, bachelor's degree in nursing; for doctorate, GRE General Test, MS in nursing. Additional exam requirements/recommendations for international students: Required—TOEFL (minimum score 600 paper-based; 250 computer-based; 100 iBT). *Application deadline:* For fall admission, 11/1 for domestic and international students; for winter admission, 12/31 for domestic and international students; for spring admission, 4/30 for domestic and international students. Applications are processed on a rolling basis. Application fee: $40. Electronic applications accepted. *Financial support:* In 2011–12, 167 students received support, including 9 fellowships with full tuition reimbursements available (averaging $15,300 per year), 7 teaching assistantships (averaging $13,612 per year); research assistantships, Federal Work-Study, institutionally sponsored loans, scholarships/grants, traineeships, health care benefits, tuition waivers (partial), and unspecified assistantships also available. Support available to part-time students. Financial award application deadline: 3/1; financial award applicants required to submit FAFSA. *Faculty research:* Pre-term labor, palliative care, support during chronic illness, violence, eating disorders. *Total annual research expenditures:* $2.1 million. *Unit head:* Dr. Susan Gennaro, Dean, 617-552-4251, Fax: 617-552-0931, E-mail: susan.gennaro@bc.edu. *Application contact:* MaryBeth Crowley, Graduate Programs Assistant, 617-552-4928, Fax: 617-552-2121, E-mail: csongrad@bc.edu. Web site: http://www.bc.edu/nursing/.

Cleveland State University, College of Graduate Studies, School of Nursing, Cleveland, OH 44115. Offers clinical nurse leader (MSN); forensic nursing (MSN); nursing education (MSN); specialized population (MSN); urban education (PhD), including nursing education; MSN/MBA. *Accreditation:* AACN. Part-time programs available. Postbaccalaureate distance learning degree programs offered (no on-campus study). *Faculty:* 4 full-time (all women), 1 (woman) part-time/adjunct. *Students:* 5 full-time (3 women), 50 part-time (47 women); includes 8 minority (7 Black or African American, non-Hispanic/Latino; 1 Hispanic/Latino), 1 international. Average age 43. 41 applicants, 73% accepted, 13 enrolled. In 2011, 7 master's awarded. *Degree requirements:* For master's, thesis or alternative, portfolio, population health project; for doctorate, comprehensive exam, thesis/dissertation. *Entrance requirements:* For master's, RN license, BSN, course work in statistics; for doctorate, GRE (for PhD in urban education). Additional exam requirements/recommendations for international students: Required—TOEFL (minimum score 525 paper-based; 197 computer-based), IELTS (minimum score 6). *Application deadline:* For fall admission, 3/1 priority date for domestic students, 3/1 for international students. Application fee: $55. Electronic applications accepted. *Expenses:* Tuition, state resident: full-time $6416; part-time $494 per credit hour. Tuition, nonresident: full-time $12,074; part-time $929 per credit hour. *Financial support:* In 2011–12, 4 students received support. Tuition waivers (full), unspecified assistantships, and Nurse Faculty Loan Program (NFLP) available. Support available to part-time students. Financial award application deadline: 3/1; financial award applicants required to submit FAFSA. *Faculty research:* Diabetes management, African-American elders medication compliance, risk in home visiting, suffering, COPD and stress, nursing education, disaster health preparedness. *Total annual research expenditures:* $59,000. *Unit head:* Dr. Vida Lock, Dean, 216-523-7237, Fax: 216-687-3556, E-mail: v.lock@csuohio.edu. *Application contact:* Carol Ivan, Recruiter/Advisor, 216-687-5517, Fax: 216-687-3556, E-mail: c.ivan@csuohio.edu. Web site: http://www.csuohio.edu/nursing/.

Duquesne University, School of Nursing, Master of Science in Nursing Program, Pittsburgh, PA 15282-0001. Offers family nurse practitioner (MSN); forensic nursing (MSN); nursing education (MSN). *Accreditation:* AACN. Part-time and evening/weekend programs available. Postbaccalaureate distance learning degree programs offered (minimal on-campus study). *Faculty:* 18 full-time (16 women), 4 part-time/adjunct (all women). *Students:* 57 full-time (55 women), 48 part-time (47 women); includes 13 minority (7 Black or African American, non-Hispanic/Latino; 3 Asian, non-Hispanic/Latino; 1 Hispanic/Latino; 2 Two or more races, non-Hispanic/Latino), 1 international. Average age 34. 72 applicants, 74% accepted, 39 enrolled. In 2011, 38 degrees awarded. *Degree requirements:* For master's, culminating paper. *Entrance requirements:* For master's, current RN license; BSN with minimum GPA of 3.0; minimum of 1 year full-time work experience as RN prior to registration in clinical or specialty course. Additional exam requirements/recommendations for international students: Required—TOEFL (minimum score 600 paper-based; 80 iBT). *Application deadline:* For fall admission, 3/1 for domestic and international students. Application fee: $0. Electronic applications accepted. *Expenses: Tuition:* Full-time $16,596; part-time $922 per credit. *Required fees:* $1584; $88 per credit. Tuition and fees vary according to program. *Financial support:* In 2011–12, 36 students received support, including 7 research assistantships with partial tuition reimbursements available (averaging $1,170 per year), 2 teaching assistantships with partial tuition reimbursements available (averaging $1,170 per year); institutionally sponsored loans, scholarships/grants, traineeships, and tuition waivers (partial) also available. Support available to part-time students. Financial award application deadline: 7/1; financial award applicants required to submit FAFSA. *Faculty research:* Vulnerable populations, social justice, cultural competence, health disparities, wellness within chronic illness. *Unit head:* Dr. Joan Such Lockhart, Professor and Associate Dean of Academic Affairs, 412-396-6540, Fax: 412-396-1821, E-mail: lockhart@duq.edu. *Application contact:* Susan Hardner, Nurse Recruiter, 412-396-4945, Fax: 412-396-6346, E-mail: nursing@duq.edu. Web site: http://www.nursing.duq.edu.

Duquesne University, School of Nursing, Post Master's Certificate Program, Pittsburgh, PA 15282-0001. Offers family nurse practitioner (Post-Master's Certificate); forensic nursing (Post-Master's Certificate); nursing education (Post-Master's Certificate); transcultural/international nursing (Post-Master's Certificate). Part-time and evening/weekend programs available. Postbaccalaureate distance learning degree programs offered (minimal on-campus study). *Faculty:* 11 full-time (10 women), 3 part-time/adjunct (all women). *Students:* 5 full-time (all women), 7 part-time (all women); includes 1 minority (Black or African American, non-Hispanic/Latino). Average age 39. 17 applicants, 71% accepted, 9 enrolled. In 2011, 2 degrees awarded. *Entrance requirements:* For degree, current RN license, BSN, MSN. Additional exam requirements/recommendations for international students: Required—TOEFL (minimum score 600 paper-based; 80 iBT). *Application deadline:* For fall admission, 3/1 for domestic and international students. Application fee: $0. *Expenses: Tuition:* Full-time $16,596; part-time $922 per credit. *Required fees:* $1584; $88 per credit. Tuition and fees vary according to program. *Financial support:* In 2011–12, 5 students received support, including 2 teaching assistantships with partial tuition reimbursements available (averaging $1,170 per year); institutionally sponsored loans, scholarships/grants, traineeships, and tuition waivers (partial) also available. Support available to part-time students. Financial award application deadline: 7/1; financial award applicants required to submit FAFSA. *Faculty research:* Vulnerable populations, social justice, cultural competence, health disparities, wellness within chronic illness. *Unit head:* Dr. Joan Such Lockhart, Professor and Associate Dean of Academic Affairs, 412-396-6540, Fax: 412-396-1821, E-mail: lockhart@duq.edu. *Application contact:* Susan Hardner, Nurse Recruiter, 412-396-4945, Fax: 412-396-6346, E-mail: nursing@duq.edu. Web site: http://www.duq.edu/nursing/post-masters-certificates/index.cfm.

Fitchburg State University, Division of Graduate and Continuing Education, Program in Forensic Nursing, Fitchburg, MA 01420-2697. Offers MS, Certificate. *Accreditation:* AACN. Part-time and evening/weekend programs available. Postbaccalaureate distance learning degree programs offered (no on-campus study). *Students:* 17 part-time (all women). Average age 38. 4 applicants, 100% accepted, 2 enrolled. In 2011, 6 master's awarded. *Entrance requirements:* Additional exam requirements/recommendations for international students: Required—TOEFL (minimum score 550 paper-based; 213 computer-based; 79 iBT). *Application deadline:* For fall admission, 7/15 for international students; for spring admission, 12/1 for international students. Applications are processed on a rolling basis. Application fee: $25 ($50 for international students). Electronic applications accepted. *Expenses:* Tuition, state resident: full-time $2700; part-time $150 per credit. Tuition, nonresident: full-time $2700; part-time $150 per credit. *Required fees:* $2286; $127 per credit. *Financial support:* In 2011–12, research assistantships with partial tuition reimbursements (averaging $5,500 per year) were awarded; Federal Work-Study, scholarships/grants, and unspecified assistantships also available. Support available to part-time students. Financial award application deadline: 3/1; financial award applicants required to submit FAFSA. *Unit head:* Dr. Robert Dumas,

Chair, 978-665-3026, Fax: 978-665-3658, E-mail: gce@fitchburgstate.edu. *Application contact:* Kay Reynolds, Director of Admissions, 978-665-3144, Fax: 978-665-4540, E-mail: admissions@fitchburgstate.edu. Web site: http://www.fitchburgstate.edu/.

George Mason University, College of Health and Human Services, School of Nursing, Fairfax, VA 22030. Offers forensic nursing (Certificate); nursing (MSN, PhD); nursing administration (Certificate); nursing education (Certificate); nursing practice (DNP). *Faculty:* 32 full-time (all women), 45 part-time/adjunct (43 women). *Students:* 70 full-time (69 women), 284 part-time (275 women); includes 109 minority (51 Black or African American, non-Hispanic/Latino; 1 American Indian or Alaska Native, non-Hispanic/Latino; 41 Asian, non-Hispanic/Latino; 12 Hispanic/Latino; 4 Two or more races, non-Hispanic/Latino), 11 international. Average age 41. 220 applicants, 56% accepted, 86 enrolled. In 2011, 79 master's, 4 doctorates, 1 other advanced degree awarded. *Degree requirements:* For master's, comprehensive exam (for some programs), thesis in clinical classes; for doctorate, comprehensive exam (for some programs), thesis/dissertation (for some programs). *Entrance requirements:* For master's, 2 official transcripts; expanded goals statement; resume; BSN from accredited institution; minimum GPA of 3.0 in last 60 credits of undergraduate work; 2 letters of recommendation; completion of undergraduate statistics and graduate-level bivariate statistics; certification in professional CPR; for doctorate, 2 official transcripts; expanded goals statement; resume; 3 recommendation letters, nursing license, at least 1 year of work experience as an RN; interview, writing sample, evidence of graduate-level course in applied statistics; master's in nursing with minimum GPA of 3.5; for Certificate, 2 official transcripts; expanded goals statement; resume; master's degree from accredited institution or currently enrolled with minimum GPA of 3.0. Additional exam requirements/recommendations for international students: Required—TOEFL (minimum score 575 paper-based; 230 computer-based; 88 iBT), IELTS, Pearson Test of English. *Application deadline:* For fall admission, 3/1 priority date for domestic students; for spring admission, 11/1 for domestic students. Application fee: $65 ($80 for international students). Electronic applications accepted. *Expenses:* Tuition, state resident: full-time $8750; part-time $364.58 per credit. Tuition, nonresident: full-time $24,092; part-time $1003.83 per credit. *Required fees:* $2514; $104.75 per credit. *Financial support:* In 2011–12, 5 students received support, including 4 research assistantships with full and partial tuition reimbursements available (averaging $26,672 per year), 1 teaching assistantship with full and partial tuition reimbursement available (averaging $15,000 per year); career-related internships or fieldwork, Federal Work-Study, scholarships/grants, unspecified assistantships, and nurse faculty loan, health care benefits (full-time research or teaching assistantship recipients) also available. Financial award application deadline: 3/1; financial award applicants required to submit FAFSA. *Total annual research expenditures:* $607,543. *Unit head:* Robin Remsburg, Associate Dean/Director, 703-993-1904, Fax: 703-993-1949, E-mail: rremsbur@gmu.edu. *Application contact:* Janice Lee-Beverly, Program Support, 703-993-1947, Fax: 703-993-1943, E-mail: jleebev1@gmu.edu. Web site: http://chhs.gmu.edu/nursing.

Monmouth University, The Graduate School, The Marjorie K. Unterberg School of Nursing and Health Studies, West Long Branch, NJ 07764-1898. Offers adult nurse practitioner (MSN); adult psychiatric and mental health advanced practice nursing (MSN, Post-Master's Certificate); advanced practice nursing (Post-Master's Certificate); family nurse practitioner (MSN, Post-Master's Certificate); forensic nursing (MSN, Certificate); nursing (MSN); nursing administration (MSN, Post-Master's Certificate); nursing education (MSN, Post-Master's Certificate); nursing practice (DNP); school nursing (MSN, Certificate). *Accreditation:* AACN. Part-time and evening/weekend programs available. *Faculty:* 12 full-time (all women), 2 part-time/adjunct (both women). *Students:* 16 full-time (11 women), 244 part-time (238 women); includes 73 minority (23 Black or African American, non-Hispanic/Latino; 2 American Indian or Alaska Native,

non-Hispanic/Latino; 34 Asian, non-Hispanic/Latino; 12 Hispanic/Latino; 1 Native Hawaiian or other Pacific Islander, non-Hispanic/Latino; 1 Two or more races, non-Hispanic/Latino), 1 international. Average age 41. 107 applicants, 92% accepted, 67 enrolled. In 2011, 55 master's awarded. *Degree requirements:* For master's, practicum (for some tracks). *Entrance requirements:* For master's, GRE General Test, RN license, 1 year of work experience, minimum undergraduate GPA of 2.75. Additional exam requirements/recommendations for international students: Required—TOEFL (minimum score 550 paper-based; 213 computer-based; 79 iBT), IELTS (minimum score 5) or Michigan English Language Assessment Battery (minimum score 77), Cambridge A, B, C. *Application deadline:* For fall admission, 7/15 priority date for domestic students, 6/1 for international students; for spring admission, 11/15 priority date for domestic students, 11/1 for international students. Applications are processed on a rolling basis. Application fee: $50. Electronic applications accepted. *Financial support:* In 2011–12, 138 students received support, including 138 fellowships (averaging $1,423 per year), 4 research assistantships (averaging $5,240 per year); career-related internships or fieldwork, scholarships/grants, and unspecified assistantships also available. Support available to part-time students. Financial award applicants required to submit FAFSA. *Faculty research:* Relationship of undergraduate GPA and GRE to succeed in a graduate nursing program. *Unit head:* Dr. Janet Mahoney, Dean, 732-571-3443, Fax: 732-263-5131, E-mail: jmahoney@monmouth.edu. *Application contact:* Kevin Roane, Director, Office of Graduate Admission, 732-571-3452, Fax: 732-263-5123, E-mail: gradadm@monmouth.edu. Web site: http://www.monmouth.edu/nursingschool.

University of Colorado at Colorado Springs, Beth-El College of Nursing and Health Sciences, Colorado Springs, CO 80933-7150. Offers adult health nurse practitioner and clinical specialist (MSN); family practitioner (MSN), including community clinical specialist, forensic clinical specialist, holistic clinical specialist; neonatal nurse practitioner and clinical specialist (MSN); nursing administration (MSN); nursing practice (DNP); women nurse practitioner (MSN). *Accreditation:* AACN. Part-time programs available. Postbaccalaureate distance learning degree programs offered (minimal on-campus study). *Faculty:* 31 full-time (28 women), 6 part-time/adjunct (all women). *Students:* 122 full-time (103 women), 68 part-time (64 women); includes 36 minority (4 Black or African American, non-Hispanic/Latino; 2 American Indian or Alaska Native, non-Hispanic/Latino; 9 Asian, non-Hispanic/Latino; 18 Hispanic/Latino; 3 Two or more races, non-Hispanic/Latino), 5 international. Average age 35. 153 applicants, 71% accepted, 60 enrolled. In 2011, 41 master's, 15 doctorates awarded. *Degree requirements:* For master's, comprehensive exam, thesis optional; for doctorate, capstone project. *Entrance requirements:* For master's, GRE General Test or MAT, BSN, minimum GPA of 3.0, unrestricted RN license; for doctorate, interview; active RN license; MA, minimum GPA of 3.3; National Certification as NP or CNS; portfolio. Additional exam requirements/recommendations for international students: Required—TOEFL. *Application deadline:* For fall admission, 6/15 priority date for domestic students; for spring admission, 11/15 for domestic students. Application fee: $60 ($75 for international students). Electronic applications accepted. *Expenses:* Contact institution. *Financial support:* In 2011–12, 33 students received support, including 1 fellowship (averaging $2,500 per year); career-related internships or fieldwork, Federal Work-Study, and scholarships/grants also available. Support available to part-time students. Financial award application deadline: 3/1; financial award applicants required to submit FAFSA. *Faculty research:* Women's health, uncertainty, empowerment, family experience in chronic illness. *Total annual research expenditures:* $322,604. *Unit head:* Dr. Nancy Smith, Dean, 719-255-4411, Fax: 719-255-4416, E-mail: nsmith2@uccs.edu. *Application contact:* Diane Busch, Director, 719-255-4424, Fax: 719-255-4416, E-mail: dbusch@uccs.edu. Web site: http://www.uccs.edu/~bethel/.

Gerontological Nursing

Allen College, Program in Nursing, Waterloo, IA 50703. Offers acute care nurse practitioner (MSN, Post-Master's Certificate); adult nurse practitioner (MSN, Post-Master's Certificate); adult psychiatric-mental health nurse practitioner (MSN, Post-Master's Certificate); family nurse practitioner (MSN, Post-Master's Certificate); gerontological nurse practitioner (MSN, Post-Master's Certificate); health education (MSN); leadership in health care delivery (MSN, Post-Master's Certificate); nursing (DNP). *Accreditation:* AACN; NLN. Part-time programs available. *Faculty:* 3 full-time (all women), 16 part-time/adjunct (all women). *Students:* 34 full-time (31 women), 110 part-time (106 women); includes 5 minority (2 Asian, non-Hispanic/Latino; 3 Hispanic/Latino). Average age 36. 156 applicants, 64% accepted, 76 enrolled. In 2011, 61 master's, 1 other advanced degree awarded. *Degree requirements:* For master's, thesis optional. *Entrance requirements:* For master's, minimum GPA of 3.0; for doctorate, minimum GPA of 3.25 in graduate coursework. Additional exam requirements/recommendations for international students: Recommended—TOEFL (minimum score 550 paper-based), IELTS. *Application deadline:* For fall admission, 2/1 priority date for domestic students; for spring admission, 9/1 priority date for domestic students. Applications are processed on a rolling basis. Application fee: $50. Electronic applications accepted. *Expenses:* Tuition: Full-time $13,993; part-time $691 per credit hour. *Required fees:* $832; $69 per credit hour. One-time fee: $100 part-time. Part-time tuition and fees vary according to course load. *Financial support:* In 2011–12, 41 students received support. Institutionally sponsored loans, scholarships/grants, and traineeships available. Support available to part-time students. Financial award application deadline: 8/15; financial award applicants required to submit FAFSA. *Faculty research:* Pain and the aged, congestive heart failure. *Unit head:* Kendra Williams-Perez, Dean, School of Nursing, 319-226-2044, Fax: 319-226-2070, E-mail: williakb@ihs.org. *Application contact:* Michelle Koehn, Admissions Counselor, 319-226-2002, Fax: 319-226-2051, E-mail: koehnml@ihs.org. Web site: http://www.allencollege.edu/.

Boston College, William F. Connell School of Nursing, Chestnut Hill, MA 02467-3800. Offers adult-gerontology nursing (MS); community health nursing (MS); family health (MS); forensic nursing (MS); maternal/child health nursing (MS), including pediatric and women's health; nurse anesthesia (MS); nursing (PhD); palliative care (MS), including adult and pediatric; psychiatric-mental health nursing (MS); MBA/MS; MS/MA; MS/PhD. *Accreditation:* AACN; AANA/CANAEP (one or more programs are accredited). Part-time programs available. *Faculty:* 48 full-time (46 women), 31 part-time/adjunct (29 women). *Students:* 225 full-time (207 women), 90 part-time (88 women); includes 47 minority (15 Black or African American, non-Hispanic/Latino; 3 American Indian or Alaska Native, non-Hispanic/Latino; 17 Asian, non-Hispanic/Latino; 8 Hispanic/Latino; 4 Two or more races, non-Hispanic/Latino), 6 international. Average age 31. 369 applicants, 43% accepted, 80 enrolled. In 2011, 113 master's, 8 doctorates awarded. *Degree requirements:* For master's, comprehensive exam, research project; for doctorate, comprehensive exam, thesis/dissertation, computer literacy exam or foreign language.

Entrance requirements: For master's, bachelor's degree in nursing; for doctorate, GRE General Test, MS in nursing. Additional exam requirements/recommendations for international students: Required—TOEFL (minimum score 600 paper-based; 250 computer-based; 100 iBT). *Application deadline:* For fall admission, 11/1 for domestic and international students; for winter admission, 12/31 for domestic and international students; for spring admission, 4/30 for domestic and international students. Applications are processed on a rolling basis. Application fee: $40. Electronic applications accepted. *Financial support:* In 2011–12, 167 students received support, including 9 fellowships with full tuition reimbursements available (averaging $15,300 per year), 7 teaching assistantships (averaging $13,612 per year); research assistantships, Federal Work-Study, institutionally sponsored loans, scholarships/grants, traineeships, health care benefits, tuition waivers (partial), and unspecified assistantships also available. Support available to part-time students. Financial award application deadline: 3/1; financial award applicants required to submit FAFSA. *Faculty research:* Pre-term labor, palliative care, support during chronic illness, violence, eating disorders. *Total annual research expenditures:* $2.1 million. *Unit head:* Dr. Susan Gennaro, Dean, 617-552-4251, Fax: 617-552-0931, E-mail: susan.gennaro@bc.edu. *Application contact:* MaryBeth Crowley, Graduate Programs Assistant, 617-552-4928, Fax: 617-552-2121, E-mail: csongrad@bc.edu. Web site: http://www.bc.edu/nursing/.

California State University, Stanislaus, College of Human and Health Sciences, Program in Nursing (MS), Turlock, CA 95382. Offers gerontological nursing (MS); nursing education (MS). Part-time programs available. *Degree requirements:* For master's, comprehensive exam, thesis or alternative. *Entrance requirements:* For master's, GRE or MAT, minimum GPA of 3.0, 3 letters of reference, RN. Additional exam requirements/recommendations for international students: Required—TOEFL (minimum score 550 paper-based; 213 computer-based). *Application deadline:* For fall admission, 5/1 for domestic students. Application fee: $55. Electronic applications accepted. *Expenses: Required fees:* $4616 per year. *Unit head:* Dr. Margaret Hodge, Chair, 209-667-3141, Fax: 209-667-3690, E-mail: phodge@csustan.edu. *Application contact:* Graduate School, 209-667-3129, Fax: 209-664-7025, E-mail: graduate_school@csustan.edu. Web site: http://www.csustan.edu/nursing/.

Caribbean University, Graduate School, Bayamón, PR 00960-0493. Offers administration and supervision (MA Ed); criminal justice (MA); curriculum and instruction (MA Ed, PhD), including elementary education (MA Ed), English education (MA Ed), history education (MA Ed), mathematics education (MA Ed), primary education (MA Ed), science education (MA Ed), Spanish education (MA Ed); educational technology in instructional systems (MA Ed); gerontology (MSN); human resources (MBA); museology, archiving and art history (MA Ed); neonatal pediatrics (MSN); physical education (MA Ed); special education (MA Ed). *Entrance requirements:* For master's, interview, minimum GPA of 2.5.

Gerontological Nursing

Case Western Reserve University, Frances Payne Bolton School of Nursing, Doctor of Nursing Practice Program, Cleveland, OH 44106. Offers acute care nurse practitioner (DNP); adult gerontology nurse practitioner (DNP); educational leadership (DNP); family nurse practitioner (DNP); family systems psychiatric mental health nursing (DNP); midwifery/family nursing (DNP); neonatal nurse practitioner (DNP); pediatric nurse practitioner (DNP); practice leadership (DNP); women's health nurse practitioner (DNP). *Students:* 73 full-time, 194 part-time; includes 11 minority (6 Black or African American, non-Hispanic/Latino; 3 Asian, non-Hispanic/Latino; 2 Hispanic/Latino). 122 applicants, 74% accepted, 49 enrolled. In 2011, 47 doctorates awarded. Terminal master's awarded for partial completion of doctoral program. *Degree requirements:* For doctorate, thesis/dissertation. *Entrance requirements:* For doctorate, GRE General Test or MAT. Additional exam requirements/recommendations for international students: Required—TOEFL (minimum score 577 paper-based; 90 iBT), IELTS (minimum score 7). *Application deadline:* For fall admission, 6/1 priority date for domestic students, 6/1 for international students; for spring admission, 10/1 for domestic and international students. Applications are processed on a rolling basis. Application fee: $75. *Financial support:* In 2011–12, 6 students received support, including 1 teaching assistantship; research assistantships, Federal Work-Study, institutionally sponsored loans, and tuition waivers (partial) also available. Support available to part-time students. Financial award application deadline: 6/30; financial award applicants required to submit FAFSA. *Faculty research:* Clinical nursing, acute care, gerontology, mental health, critical care. *Unit head:* Dr. Donna Dowling, Director, 216-368-1869, Fax: 216-368-3542, E-mail: dad10@case.edu. *Application contact:* Donna Hassik, Admissions Coordinator, 216-368-5253, Fax: 216-368-0124, E-mail: dmh7@case.edu. Web site: http://fpb.case.edu/DNP/.

Case Western Reserve University, Frances Payne Bolton School of Nursing, Master's Programs in Nursing, Nurse Practitioner Program, Cleveland, OH 44106. Offers acute care cardiovascular nursing (MSN); acute care nurse practitioner (MSN); acute care/flight nurse (MSN); adult gerontology nurse practitioner (MSN); family nurse practitioner (MSN); neonatal nurse practitioner (MSN); pediatric nurse practitioner (MSN); women's health nurse practitioner (MSN). *Accreditation:* NLN. Part-time programs available. Postbaccalaureate distance learning degree programs offered (minimal on-campus study). *Faculty:* 54 full-time (50 women), 5 part-time/adjunct (3 women). *Students:* 89 full-time (69 women), 77 part-time (67 women); includes 17 minority (11 Black or African American, non-Hispanic/Latino; 5 Asian, non-Hispanic/Latino; 1 Hispanic/Latino), 17 international. Average age 35. 75 applicants, 84% accepted, 42 enrolled. In 2011, 34 master's awarded. *Degree requirements:* For master's, thesis optional. *Entrance requirements:* For master's, GRE General Test or MAT. Additional exam requirements/recommendations for international students: Required—TOEFL (minimum score 577 paper-based; 90 iBT), IELTS (minimum score 7). *Application deadline:* For fall admission, 6/1 for domestic students; for spring admission, 10/1 for domestic students. Applications are processed on a rolling basis. Application fee: $75. *Financial support:* In 2011–12, 7 teaching assistantships were awarded; research assistantships, institutionally sponsored loans, and tuition waivers (partial) also available. Support available to part-time students. Financial award application deadline: 6/30; financial award applicants required to submit FAFSA. *Faculty research:* Positive and negative mood states in parents of twins, effect of a care path on chronic obstructive pulmonary disease home care. *Unit head:* Dr. Carol Savrin, Director, 216-368-5304, Fax: 216-368-3542, E-mail: cls18@case.edu. *Application contact:* Donna Hassik, Admissions Coordinator, 216-368-5253, Fax: 216-368-0124, E-mail: dmh7@case.edu. Web site: http://fpb.cwru.edu/MSN/majors.shtm.

College of Mount Saint Vincent, School of Professional and Continuing Studies, Department of Nursing, Riverdale, NY 10471-1093. Offers adult nurse practitioner (MSN, PMC); family nurse practitioner (MSN, PMC); nurse educator (PMC); nursing administration (MSN); nursing for the adult and aged (MSN). *Accreditation:* AACN. Part-time programs available. *Entrance requirements:* For master's, BSN, interview, RN license, minimum GPA of 3.0, letters of reference. Additional exam requirements/recommendations for international students: Required—TOEFL. *Expenses:* Contact institution.

College of Staten Island of the City University of New York, Graduate Programs, Department of Nursing, Program in Gerontological Nursing, Staten Island, NY 10314-6600. Offers MS, 6th Year Certificate. Part-time programs available. *Faculty:* 5 full-time (all women), 3 part-time/adjunct (2 women). *Students:* 4. 8 applicants, 13% accepted, 1 enrolled. In 2011, 1 master's awarded. *Degree requirements:* For master's, thesis or alternative. *Entrance requirements:* For master's, BS in nursing, minimum undergraduate GPA of 3.0 in nursing courses, RN license, 2 letters of references, 1 year of full-time experience as a nurse or its equivalent, goal statement; for 6th Year Certificate, master's degree in nursing. Additional exam requirements/recommendations for international students: Required—TOEFL (minimum score 550 paper-based; 213 computer-based; 79 iBT), IELTS (minimum score 6.5). *Application deadline:* For fall admission, 4/18 priority date for domestic students, 4/18 for international students; for spring admission, 11/21 priority date for domestic students, 11/21 for international students. Applications are processed on a rolling basis. Application fee: $125. Electronic applications accepted. *Expenses:* Tuition, state resident: full-time $8210; part-time $345 per credit. Tuition, nonresident: part-time $640 per credit. *Required fees:* $128 per semester. *Financial support:* Career-related internships or fieldwork, Federal Work-Study, scholarships/grants, and traineeships available. Support available to part-time students. Financial award applicants required to submit FAFSA. *Unit head:* Prof. Mary Ellen McMorrow, Interim Director of Graduate Nursing Programs, 718-982-3823, Fax: 718-982-3813, E-mail: maryellen.mcmorrow@csi.cuny.edu. *Application contact:* Sasha Spence, Assistant Director for Graduate Admissions, 718-982-2699, Fax: 718-982-2500, E-mail: spence@mail.csi.cuny.edu. Web site: http://www.csi.cuny.edu/nursing/graduate.html.

Columbia University, School of Nursing, Program in Geriatric Nurse Practitioner, New York, NY 10032. Offers MS, Adv C. *Accreditation:* AACN. Part-time programs available. *Entrance requirements:* For master's, GRE General Test, BSN, 1 year of clinical experience (preferred); for Adv C, MSN. Electronic applications accepted.

Concordia University Wisconsin, Graduate Programs, School of Human Services, Program in Nursing, Mequon, WI 53097-2402. Offers family nurse practitioner (MSN); geriatric nurse practitioner (MSN); nurse educator (MSN). *Accreditation:* AACN. Postbaccalaureate distance learning degree programs offered (minimal on-campus study). *Faculty:* 2 full-time (1 woman), 5 part-time/adjunct (all women). *Students:* 84 full-time (77 women), 359 part-time (347 women); includes 52 minority (20 Black or African American, non-Hispanic/Latino; 2 American Indian or Alaska Native, non-Hispanic/Latino; 11 Asian, non-Hispanic/Latino; 9 Hispanic/Latino; 10 Two or more races, non-Hispanic/Latino), 1 international. Average age 36. In 2011, 37 master's awarded. *Degree requirements:* For master's, comprehensive exam, thesis or alternative. *Entrance requirements:* Additional exam requirements/recommendations for international students: Required—TOEFL. *Application deadline:* For fall admission, 8/1 priority date for domestic students. Applications are processed on a rolling basis. Application fee: $35. *Expenses:* Contact institution. *Financial support:* Application deadline: 8/1. *Unit head:* Dr. Ruth Gresley, Director, 262-243-4452, E-mail: ruth.gresley@cuw.edu. *Application contact:* Mary Eberhardt, Graduate Admissions, 262-243-4551, Fax: 262-243-4428, E-mail: mary.eberhardt@cuw.edu.

Duke University, School of Nursing, Durham, NC 27708-0586. Offers adult acute care (Certificate); adult cardiovascular (Certificate); adult oncology (Certificate); adult primary care (Certificate); clinical nurse specialist (MSN), including adult oncology, gerontology, neonatal, pediatric; clinical research management (MSN, Certificate); family (Certificate); gerontology (Certificate); health and nursing ministries (MSN, Certificate); health systems leadership and outcomes (Certificate); neonatal (Certificate); neonatal/pediatric in rural health (MSN, Certificate); nurse anesthetist (MSN, Certificate); nurse practitioner (MSN), including adult acute care, adult cardiovascular, adult oncology, adult primary care, family, gerontology, neonatal, pediatric, pediatric acute care; nursing (DNP, PhD); nursing and healthcare leadership (MSN); nursing education (MSN); nursing informatics (MSN, Certificate); pediatric (Certificate); pediatric acute care (Certificate); MBA/MSN; MSN/MCM. *Accreditation:* AACN; AANA/CANAEP. Part-time and evening/weekend programs available. Postbaccalaureate distance learning degree programs offered (minimal on-campus study). *Faculty:* 56 full-time (47 women); 2 part-time/adjunct (1 woman). *Students:* 127 full-time (108 women), 395 part-time (358 women); includes 92 minority (42 Black or African American, non-Hispanic/Latino; 3 American Indian or Alaska Native, non-Hispanic/Latino; 21 Asian, non-Hispanic/Latino; 14 Hispanic/Latino; 12 Two or more races, non-Hispanic/Latino), 10 international. Average age 36. 432 applicants, 45% accepted, 143 enrolled. In 2011, 117 master's, 29 doctorates, 32 other advanced degrees awarded. Terminal master's awarded for partial completion of doctoral program. *Degree requirements:* For master's, thesis optional; for doctorate, capstone project. *Entrance requirements:* For master's, GRE General Test, 1 year of nursing experience, BSN, minimum GPA of 3.0, previous course work in statistics; for doctorate, BSN or MSN, minimum GPA of 3.0, portfolio; for Certificate, MSN. Additional exam requirements/recommendations for international students: Required—TOEFL (minimum score 550 paper-based; 213 computer-based). *Application deadline:* For fall admission, 12/1 for domestic and international students; for spring admission, 5/1 for domestic and international students. Application fee: $50. Electronic applications accepted. *Expenses:* Contact institution. *Financial support:* Career-related internships or fieldwork, institutionally sponsored loans, scholarships/grants, traineeships, and tuition waivers (partial) available. Support available to part-time students. Financial award application deadline: 4/1; financial award applicants required to submit FAFSA. *Faculty research:* Cardiovascular disease, caregiver skill training, data mining, prostate cancer, neonatal immune system. *Total annual research expenditures:* $4.7 million. *Unit head:* Dr. Catherine L. Gilliss, Dean/Vice Chancellor for Nursing Affairs, 919-684-9444, Fax: 919-684-9414, E-mail: gilli025@mc.duke.edu. *Application contact:* Bebe T. Mills, Director of Admissions, 919-684-9151, Fax: 919-668-4693, E-mail: mills031@mc.duke.edu. Web site: http://www.nursing.duke.edu/.

East Tennessee State University, School of Graduate Studies, College of Nursing, Doctoral Nursing Programs, Johnson City, TN 37614. Offers adult/gerontological nurse practitioner (DNP); executive leadership in nursing (DNP); family nurse practitioner (DNP); nursing (PhD); psychiatric/mental health nurse practitioner (DNP). Part-time and evening/weekend programs available. *Students:* 22 full-time (21 women), 27 part-time (26 women); includes 3 minority (2 Black or African American, non-Hispanic/Latino; 1 Asian, non-Hispanic/Latino). 74 applicants, 41% accepted, 30 enrolled. In 2011, 3 doctorates awarded. *Degree requirements:* For doctorate, comprehensive exam, dissertation (PhD); residency internship and capstone project (DNP). *Entrance requirements:* For doctorate, GRE General Test, minimum GPA of 3.0, RN license, minimum two years RN experience, 3 letters of recommendation, interview, writing sample, resume. Additional exam requirements/recommendations for international students: Required—TOEFL (minimum score 600 paper-based; 250 computer-based; 100 iBT). *Application deadline:* For fall admission, 2/1 for domestic and international students; for spring admission, 7/1 for domestic and international students. Application fee: $35 ($45 for international students). Electronic applications accepted. *Expenses:* Tuition, state resident: full-time $7312; part-time $350 per credit hour. Tuition, nonresident: full-time $18,490; part-time $621 per credit hour. *Required fees:* $63 per credit hour. Tuition and fees vary according to course load and program. *Financial support:* In 2011–12, 2 students received support, including 1 research assistantship with partial tuition reimbursement available (averaging $3,000 per year); career-related internships or fieldwork, institutionally sponsored loans, scholarships/grants, and unspecified assistantships also available. Financial award application deadline: 7/1; financial award applicants required to submit FAFSA. *Faculty research:* Rural primary care, healthcare for the homeless and underserved, community health problems across the lifespan, nursing education research, school health services. *Unit head:* Dr. Kathleen Rayman, Director of Graduate Programs, 423-439-5626, Fax: 423-439-4100, E-mail: raymank@etsu.edu. *Application contact:* Linda Raines, Graduate Specialist, 423-439-6158, Fax: 423-439-5624, E-mail: raineslt@etsu.edu.

Gwynedd-Mercy College, School of Nursing, Gwynedd Valley, PA 19437-0901. Offers clinical nurse specialist (MSN), including gerontology, oncology, pediatrics; nurse practitioner (MSN), including adult health, pediatric health. *Accreditation:* NLN. *Faculty:* 3 full-time (all women), 2 part-time/adjunct (both women). *Students:* 14 full-time (13 women), 28 part-time (25 women); includes 11 minority (4 Black or African American, non-Hispanic/Latino; 6 Asian, non-Hispanic/Latino; 1 Hispanic/Latino). Average age 40. 23 applicants, 83% accepted, 11 enrolled. In 2011, 7 master's awarded. *Degree requirements:* For master's, thesis optional. *Entrance requirements:* For master's, GRE General Test or MAT, current nursing experience, physical assessment, course work in statistics, BSN from NLNAC-accredited program, 2 letters of recommendation, personal interview. Additional exam requirements/recommendations for international students: Required—TOEFL (minimum score 575 paper-based). *Application deadline:* For fall admission, 8/1 priority date for domestic students; for winter admission, 12/1 priority date for domestic students. Applications are processed on a rolling basis. Application fee: $25. Electronic applications accepted. *Expenses:* Contact institution. *Financial support:* In 2011–12, 21 students received support. Scholarships/grants, traineeships, and unspecified assistantships available. Financial award application deadline: 8/30. *Faculty research:* Critical thinking, primary care, domestic violence, multiculturalism, nursing centers. *Unit head:* Dr. Andrea D. Hollingsworth, Dean, 215-646-7300 Ext. 539, Fax: 215-641-5517, E-mail: hollingsworth.a@gmc.edu. *Application contact:* Dr. Barbara A. Jones, Director, 215-646-7300 Ext. 407, Fax: 215-641-5564, E-mail: jones.b@gmc.edu. Web site: http://www.gmc.edu/academics/nursing/.

Hampton University, Graduate College, School of Nursing, Hampton, VA 23668. Offers advanced adult nursing (MS); community health nursing (MS); community mental health/psychiatric nursing (MS); family nursing (MS); gerontological nursing for the nurse practitioner (MS); pediatric nursing (MS); women's health nursing (MS). *Accreditation:* AACN; NLN. Part-time and evening/weekend programs available. *Degree requirements:* For master's, thesis optional. *Entrance requirements:* For master's, GRE General Test. *Faculty research:* Curriculum development, physical and mental assessment.

Hunter College of the City University of New York, Graduate School, Schools of the Health Professions, Hunter-Bellevue School of Nursing, Gerontological Nurse Practitioner Program, New York, NY 10021-5085. Offers MS. *Accreditation:* AACN. Part-time programs available. *Faculty:* 20 full-time (16 women), 20 part-time/adjunct (18 women). *Students:* 2 full-time (1 woman), 101 part-time (85 women); includes 57 minority (21 Black or African American, non-Hispanic/Latino; 1 American Indian or Alaska Native, non-Hispanic/Latino; 31 Asian, non-Hispanic/Latino; 4 Hispanic/Latino), 5

international. Average age 34. 18 applicants, 67% accepted, 10 enrolled. In 2011, 14 master's awarded. *Degree requirements:* For master's, practicum. *Entrance requirements:* For master's, minimum GPA of 3.0, New York RN license, 2 years of professional practice experience, BSN. Additional exam requirements/recommendations for international students: Required—TOEFL. *Application deadline:* For fall admission, 4/1 for domestic students, 2/1 for international students; for spring admission, 11/1 for domestic students, 9/1 for international students. Applications are processed on a rolling basis. Application fee: $125. *Expenses:* Tuition, state resident: full-time $8210; part-time $345 per credit. Tuition, nonresident: full-time $15,360; part-time $640 per credit. *Required fees:* $280 per semester. One-time fee: $125. Tuition and fees vary according to class time, campus/location and program. *Financial support:* Federal Work-Study, scholarships/grants, traineeships, and tuition waivers (partial) available. Support available to part-time students. Financial award application deadline: 5/1; financial award applicants required to submit FAFSA. *Faculty research:* Primary care of older adults, lived experiences of elders. *Unit head:* Dr. Steven Baumann, Coordinator, 212-481-4457, Fax: 212-481-5078, E-mail: sbaumann@shiva.hunter.cuny.edu. *Application contact:* William Zlata, Director for Graduate Admissions, 212-772-4482, Fax: 212-650-3336, E-mail: admissions@hunter.cuny.edu.

Independence University, Program in Nursing, Salt Lake City, UT 84107. Offers community health (MSN); gerontology (MSN); nursing administration (MSN); wellness promotion (MSN).

Kent State University, College of Nursing, Kent, OH 44242-0001. Offers acute care nurse practitioner (MSN); adult nurse practitioner (MSN); clinical nurse specialist (MSN); family nurse practitioner (MSN); geriatric nurse practitioner (MSN); health care management (MSN); nurse educator (MSN); nursing (PhD); nursing practice (DNP); pediatric nurse practitioner (MSN); psychiatric/mental health nurse practitioner (MSN); women's health nurse practitioner (MSN). PhD program offered jointly with The University of Akron. *Accreditation:* AACN. Part-time programs available. *Degree requirements:* For master's, thesis optional; for doctorate, comprehensive exam, thesis/dissertation. *Entrance requirements:* For master's, GRE (if undergraduate GPA less than 3.0), minimum GPA of 2.75; for doctorate, GRE, MSN. Additional exam requirements/recommendations for international students: Required—TOEFL. Electronic applications accepted. *Expenses:* Contact institution. *Faculty research:* Women and violence, methodological specialties, osteoporosis in women, new caregivers and the elderly.

Lehman College of the City University of New York, Division of Natural and Social Sciences, Department of Nursing, Bronx, NY 10468-1589. Offers adult health nursing (MS); nursing of older adults (MS); parent-child nursing (MS); pediatric nurse practitioner (MS). *Accreditation:* AACN. Part-time and evening/weekend programs available. *Entrance requirements:* For master's, bachelor's degree in nursing, New York RN license.

Loma Linda University, Department of Graduate Nursing, Program in Adult and Aging Family Nursing, Loma Linda, CA 92350. Offers MS. *Accreditation:* AACN. Part-time programs available. *Degree requirements:* For master's, thesis or alternative. *Entrance requirements:* For master's, GRE General Test, BSN, minimum GPA of 3.0, RN license. Additional exam requirements/recommendations for international students: Required—TOEFL. Electronic applications accepted. *Faculty research:* Coping, integration of research.

Marquette University, Graduate School, College of Nursing, Milwaukee, WI 53201-1881. Offers acute care nurse practitioner (Certificate); adult clinical nurse specialist (Certificate); adult nurse practitioner (Certificate); advanced practice nursing (MSN, DNP), including acute care, adults, neonatal nurse practitioner (MSN), nurse midwifery (DNP), nurse-midwifery (MSN), older adults, pediatrics acute care (DNP, PhD), pediatrics primary care; clinical nurse leader (MSN); gerontologic clinical nurse specialist (Certificate); gerontologic nurse practitioner (Certificate); health care systems leadership (MSN, DNP); nurse-midwifery (Certificate); nursing (PhD), including pediatrics acute care (DNP, PhD); pediatrics acute care (Certificate); pediatrics primary care (Certificate). *Accreditation:* AACN. *Faculty:* 32 full-time (30 women), 47 part-time/adjunct (all women). *Students:* 93 full-time (88 women), 244 part-time (220 women); includes 31 minority (9 Black or African American, non-Hispanic/Latino; 7 Asian, non-Hispanic/Latino; 8 Hispanic/Latino; 7 Two or more races, non-Hispanic/Latino), 1 international. Average age 30. 282 applicants, 57% accepted, 98 enrolled. In 2011, 76 master's, 8 doctorates, 7 other advanced degrees awarded. Terminal master's awarded for partial completion of doctoral program. *Degree requirements:* For master's, comprehensive exam, thesis or alternative. *Entrance requirements:* For master's, GRE General Test, BSN, Wisconsin RN license, official transcripts from all current and previous colleges/universities except Marquette, three completed recommendation forms, resume, written statement of professional goals; for doctorate, GRE General Test, official transcripts from all current and previous colleges/universities except Marquette, three letters of recommendation, resume, written statement of professional goals, sample of scholarly writing. Additional exam requirements/recommendations for international students: Required—TOEFL (minimum score 530 paper-based; 78 computer-based). *Application deadline:* For fall admission, 2/15 for domestic and international students. Application fee: $50. Electronic applications accepted. *Expenses: Tuition:* Full-time $17,010; part-time $945 per credit hour. Tuition and fees vary according to program. *Financial support:* In 2011–12, 41 students received support, including 1 fellowship with partial tuition reimbursement available (averaging $17,500 per year), 2 research assistantships with full tuition reimbursements available (averaging $13,285 per year), 8 teaching assistantships with full tuition reimbursements available (averaging $13,912 per year); career-related internships or fieldwork, Federal Work-Study, scholarships/grants, health care benefits, tuition waivers (partial), and unspecified assistantships also available. Support available to part-time students. Financial award application deadline: 2/15. *Faculty research:* Psychosocial adjustment to chronic illness, gerontology, reminiscence, health policy: uninsured and access, hospital care delivery systems. *Total annual research expenditures:* $312,575. *Unit head:* Dr. Margaret Callahan, Dean, 414-288-3800, Fax: 414-288-1578. *Application contact:* Karen Nest, Graduate Program Coordinator, 414-288-3810, Fax: 414-288-1578. Web site: http://www.marquette.edu/nursing/academicprograms-graduate.shtml.

Maryville University of Saint Louis, School of Health Professions, Nursing Program, St. Louis, MO 63141-7299. Offers accelerated RN to MSN (MSN); adult nurse practitioner (MSN); advanced practice nursing (DNP); family nurse practitioner (MSN); geriatric nurse practitioner (MSN); nursing education (MSN). *Accreditation:* AACN. Postbaccalaureate distance learning degree programs offered. *Students:* 16 full-time (14 women), 136 part-time (127 women); includes 9 minority (5 Black or African American, non-Hispanic/Latino; 3 Asian, non-Hispanic/Latino; 1 Two or more races, non-Hispanic/Latino). Average age 35. In 2011, 21 master's awarded. *Degree requirements:* For master's, practicum. *Entrance requirements:* For master's, BSN, current licensure, minimum GPA of 3.0, 3 letters of recommendation, curriculum vitae. Additional exam requirements/recommendations for international students: Required—TOEFL (minimum score 550 paper-based). *Application deadline:* Applications are processed on a rolling basis. Application fee: $40 ($60 for international students). Electronic applications accepted. *Expenses: Tuition:* Full-time $21,922; part-time $675 per credit hour. *Required fees:* $233.75 per semester. *Financial support:* Federal Work-Study and campus employment available. Support available to part-time students. Financial award application deadline: 3/1; financial award applicants required to submit FAFSA. *Unit head:* Dr. Elizabeth Buck, Director, 314-529-9453, Fax: 314-529-9139, E-mail: ebuck@maryville.edu. *Application contact:* Dr. Donna Payne, Vice President, Adult and Continuing Education, 314-529-9676, Fax: 314-529-9927, E-mail: dpayne@maryville.edu. Web site: http://www.maryville.edu/academics-hp-nursing.

MGH Institute of Health Professions, School of Nursing, Boston, MA 02129. Offers advanced practice nursing (MSN); gerontological nursing (MSN); nursing (DNP); pediatric nursing (MSN); psychiatric nursing (MSN); teaching and learning for health care education (Certificate); women's health nursing (MSN). *Accreditation:* AACN; NLN (one or more programs are accredited). *Faculty:* 41 full-time (36 women), 14 part-time/adjunct (13 women). *Students:* 418 full-time (365 women), 72 part-time (63 women); includes 51 minority (20 Black or African American, non-Hispanic/Latino; 1 American Indian or Alaska Native, non-Hispanic/Latino; 24 Asian, non-Hispanic/Latino; 5 Hispanic/Latino; 1 Native Hawaiian or other Pacific Islander, non-Hispanic/Latino). Average age 32. 1,041 applicants, 36% accepted, 148 enrolled. In 2011, 85 master's, 12 doctorates, 98 other advanced degrees awarded. *Degree requirements:* For master's, thesis or alternative. *Entrance requirements:* For master's, GRE General Test, bachelor's degree from regionally-accredited college or university. Additional exam requirements/recommendations for international students: Required—TOEFL (minimum score 550 paper-based; 213 computer-based; 80 iBT). *Application deadline:* For fall admission, 1/10 for domestic and international students; for spring admission, 11/1 for domestic and international students. Application fee: $65. Electronic applications accepted. *Expenses: Tuition:* Full-time $12,720; part-time $1060 per credit. *Required fees:* $1725; $430 per semester. One-time fee: $350. *Financial support:* In 2011–12, 75 students received support, including 4 research assistantships (averaging $1,200 per year), 17 teaching assistantships (averaging $1,200 per year); career-related internships or fieldwork, scholarships/grants, traineeships, and unspecified assistantships also available. Support available to part-time students. Financial award application deadline: 4/1; financial award applicants required to submit FAFSA. *Faculty research:* Biobehavioral nursing, HIV/AIDS, gerontological nursing, women's health, vulnerable populations, health systems. *Unit head:* Dr. Laurie Lauzon-Clabo, Dean, 617-643-0605, Fax: 617-726-8022, E-mail: llauzonclabo@mghihp.edu. *Application contact:* Maureen Rika Judd, Director of Admissions, 617-726-6069, Fax: 617-726-8010, E-mail: admissions@mghihp.edu. Web site: http://www.mghihp.edu/academics/nursing/.

Nazareth College of Rochester, Graduate Studies, Department of Nursing, Gerontological Nurse Practitioner Program, Rochester, NY 14618-3790. Offers MS. *Accreditation:* AACN. Part-time programs available. *Entrance requirements:* For master's, minimum GPA of 3.0, RN license.

New Mexico State University, Graduate School, College of Health and Social Services, School of Nursing, Las Cruces, NM 88003-8001. Offers adult/gerontology nurse practitioner (DNP); family nurse practitioner (DNP); nursing (MSN, PhD); public/community health (DNP). *Accreditation:* AACN. Postbaccalaureate distance learning degree programs offered (minimal on-campus study). *Faculty:* 9 full-time (all women). *Students:* 44 full-time (38 women), 72 part-time (59 women); includes 48 minority (9 Black or African American, non-Hispanic/Latino; 5 American Indian or Alaska Native, non-Hispanic/Latino; 2 Asian, non-Hispanic/Latino; 31 Hispanic/Latino; 1 Two or more races, non-Hispanic/Latino), 2 international. Average age 43. 37 applicants, 86% accepted, 25 enrolled. In 2011, 35 master's, 3 doctorates awarded. *Degree requirements:* For master's, comprehensive exam, thesis optional, clinical practice; for doctorate, comprehensive exam, thesis/dissertation. *Entrance requirements:* For master's, NCLEX exam, BSN, minimum GPA of 3.0, course work in statistics, 3 letters of reference, writing sample, RN license, CPR certification, proof of liability, immunizations, criminal background check; for doctorate, NCLEX exam, MSN, minimum GPA of 3.0, 3 letters of reference, writing sample, RN license, CPR certification, proof of liability, immunizations, criminal background check, statistics course. Additional exam requirements/recommendations for international students: Required—TOEFL (minimum score 550 paper-based; 79 iBT), IELTS (minimum score 6.5). *Application deadline:* For spring admission, 10/1 priority date for domestic students. Application fee: $40 ($50 for international students). Electronic applications accepted. *Expenses:* Tuition, state resident: full-time $5004; part-time $208.50 per credit. Tuition, nonresident: full-time $17,446; part-time $726.90 per credit. *Financial support:* In 2011–12, 1 teaching assistantship (averaging $28,242 per year) was awarded; fellowships, research assistantships, career-related internships or fieldwork, Federal Work-Study, scholarships/grants, traineeships, and health care benefits also available. Financial award application deadline: 3/1. *Faculty research:* Public policy, community health, health disparities, self efficacy and self management, psychiatric mental health. *Unit head:* Dr. Pamela Schultz, Director, 575-646-3812, Fax: 575-646-2167, E-mail: pschultz@nmsu.edu. *Application contact:* Dr. Kathleen Huttlinger, Associate Director for Graduate Studies, 575-646-4387, Fax: 575-646-2167. Web site: http://www.nmsu.edu/~nursing/.

New York University, College of Nursing, Doctor of Nursing Practice Program, New York, NY 10012-1019. Offers advanced practice nursing (DNP), including adult acute care, adult nurse practitioner/holistic nursing, adult nurse practitioner/palliative care nursing, adult primary care, adult primary care/geriatrics, family, geriatrics, mental health nursing, nurse-midwifery, pediatrics. Part-time and evening/weekend programs available. *Faculty:* 7 full-time (all women). *Students:* 23 part-time (19 women); includes 6 minority (4 Black or African American, non-Hispanic/Latino; 1 Asian, non-Hispanic/Latino; 1 Hispanic/Latino), 1 international. Average age 46. 20 applicants, 80% accepted, 11 enrolled. In 2011, 8 doctorates awarded. *Degree requirements:* For doctorate, thesis/dissertation. *Entrance requirements:* For doctorate, MS, RN license, interview, NP Certification. Additional exam requirements/recommendations for international students: Required—TOEFL, IELTS. *Application deadline:* For fall admission, 4/1 priority date for domestic students, 4/1 for international students. Applications are processed on a rolling basis. Application fee: $75. Electronic applications accepted. *Financial support:* In 2011–12, 15 students received support. Fellowships with full and partial tuition reimbursements available, institutionally sponsored loans, scholarships/grants, and tuition waivers (partial) available. Support available to part-time students. Financial award application deadline: 2/1; financial award applicants required to submit FAFSA. *Faculty research:* Elderly black diabetics, families and illness, oral systemic connection. *Unit head:* Dr. Jamesetta A. Newland, Director, 212-998-5319, Fax: 212-995-3143, E-mail: jan7@nyu.edu. *Application contact:* Gail Wolfmeyer, Assistant Director, Graduate Student Affairs and Admissions, 212-992-7653, Fax: 212-995-4302, E-mail: gail.wolfmeyer@nyu.edu.

New York University, College of Nursing, Programs in Advanced Practice Nursing, New York, NY 10012-1019. Offers advanced practice nursing: adult acute care (MS, Advanced Certificate); advanced practice nursing: adult nurse practitioner/holistic nurse practitioner (Advanced Certificate); advanced practice nursing: adult nurse practitioner/palliative care nurse practitioner (Advanced Certificate); advanced practice nursing: adult primary care (MS, Advanced Certificate); advanced practice nursing: family (MS, Advanced Certificate); advanced practice nursing: geriatrics (Advanced Certificate); advanced practice nursing: mental health (MS); advanced practice nursing: mental health nursing (Advanced Certificate); advanced practice nursing: pediatrics (MS,

Advanced Certificate); nurse midwifery (MS, Advanced Certificate); nursing administration (MS, Advanced Certificate); nursing education (MS, Advanced Certificate); nursing informatics (MS, Advanced Certificate); MS/MPA; MS/MPH. *Accreditation:* AACN; ACNM/ACME. Part-time programs available. *Faculty:* 23 full-time (all women), 60 part-time/adjunct (47 women). *Students:* 27 full-time (23 women), 552 part-time (514 women); includes 251 minority (91 Black or African American, non-Hispanic/Latino; 115 Asian, non-Hispanic/Latino; 34 Hispanic/Latino; 11 Native Hawaiian or other Pacific Islander, non-Hispanic/Latino), 8 international. Average age 33. 325 applicants, 81% accepted, 179 enrolled. In 2011, 89 master's awarded. *Degree requirements:* For master's, thesis (for some programs). *Entrance requirements:* For master's, BS in nursing, AS in nursing with another BS/BA, interview, RN license, 1 year of clinical experience (3 for nursing education program); for Advanced Certificate, master's degree. Additional exam requirements/recommendations for international students: Required—TOEFL, IELTS. *Application deadline:* For fall admission, 7/1 priority date for domestic students, 7/1 for international students; for spring admission, 12/1 for domestic and international students. Applications are processed on a rolling basis. Application fee: $75. Electronic applications accepted. *Financial support:* In 2011–12, 36 students received support. Career-related internships or fieldwork, institutionally sponsored loans, scholarships/grants, traineeships, and tuition waivers (partial) available. Support available to part-time students. Financial award application deadline: 2/1; financial award applicants required to submit FAFSA. *Faculty research:* Elderly black diabetics, families and illness, oral systemic connection. *Unit head:* Dr. Judith Haber, Associate Dean, 212-998-9020, Fax: 212-995-3143, E-mail: jh33@nyu.edu. *Application contact:* Gail Wolfmeyer, Assistant Director, Graduate Student Affairs and Admissions, 212-992-7653, Fax: 212-995-4302, E-mail: gail.wolfmeyer@nyu.edu.

Oakland University, Graduate Study and Lifelong Learning, School of Nursing, Adult Gerontological Nurse Practitioner Program, Rochester, MI 48309-4401. Offers MSN, Certificate.

Oregon Health & Science University, School of Nursing, Program in Gerontological Nursing, Portland, OR 97239-3098. Offers Post Master's Certificate. *Accreditation:* AACN. *Entrance requirements:* For degree, master's or associate's degree in nursing.

Rush University, College of Nursing, Department of Adult Health Nursing, Chicago, IL 60612-3832. Offers acute care nurse practitioner (MSN, Post-Master's Certificate); adult health nursing (DNP, PhD); adult nurse practitioner (MSN, Post-Master's Certificate); adult/gerontological nurse practitioner (MSN); anesthesia nurse practitioner (MSN, Post-Master's Certificate); critical care clinical specialist (MSN); gerontological nurse practitioner (MSN, Post-Master's Certificate); medical surgical clinical specialist (MSN). *Accreditation:* AACN; AANA/CANAEP (one or more programs are accredited). Part-time programs available. Postbaccalaureate distance learning degree programs offered (minimal on-campus study). Terminal master's awarded for partial completion of doctoral program. *Degree requirements:* For master's, capstone project; for doctorate, thesis/dissertation, DNP leadership project. *Entrance requirements:* For master's, GRE General Test (waived if nursing GPA is above 3.0 or cumulative GPA is above 3.25), interview; for doctorate, GRE General Test, interview, course work in statistics (PhD). Additional exam requirements/recommendations for international students: Required—TOEFL, TWE. Electronic applications accepted. *Faculty research:* Complementary/alternative medicine, critical care outcomes, cardiac risk reduction, Alzheimer's Disease, telehealth monitoring.

Rutgers, The State University of New Jersey, Newark, Graduate School, Program in Nursing, Newark, NJ 07102. Offers nursing (MS), including acute care of adults and aged, advanced practice in pediatric nursing, advanced practice with childbearing families, community health nursing, family nurse practitioner, primary care of adults and aged, psychiatric/mental health nursing. *Accreditation:* AACN. Part-time programs available. *Degree requirements:* For master's, comprehensive exam. *Entrance requirements:* For master's, GRE General Test, RN license, minimum B average, BS in nursing. Additional exam requirements/recommendations for international students: Required—TOEFL. Electronic applications accepted. *Faculty research:* HIV/AIDS, quality of life: MS and breast cancer, sleep patterns of cardiac patients.

Sage Graduate School, School of Health Sciences, Department of Nursing, Troy, NY 12180-4115. Offers adult health (MS); adult nurse practitioner (MS, Post Master's Certificate); clinical nurse leader/specialist (Post Master's Certificate); community health (MS); education and leadership (DNS); family nurse practitioner (MS, Post Master's Certificate); gerontological nurse practitioner (Post Master's Certificate); nurse administrator/executive (Post Master's Certificate); nursing (Post Master's Certificate); psychiatric mental health nurse practitioner (MS, Post Master's Certificate), including psychiatric mental health. *Accreditation:* AACN. Part-time and evening/weekend programs available. *Faculty:* 5 full-time (all women), 10 part-time/adjunct (all women). *Students:* 35 full-time (31 women), 158 part-time (152 women); includes 20 minority (8 Black or African American, non-Hispanic/Latino; 1 American Indian or Alaska Native, non-Hispanic/Latino; 8 Asian, non-Hispanic/Latino; 3 Hispanic/Latino), 7 international. Average age 42. 143 applicants, 32% accepted, 34 enrolled. In 2011, 30 master's, 1 doctorate, 5 other advanced degrees awarded. *Degree requirements:* For master's, thesis or alternative. *Entrance requirements:* For master's, BS in nursing, minimum GPA of 2.75, resume, 2 letters of recommendation. Additional exam requirements/recommendations for international students: Required—TOEFL (minimum score 550 paper-based; 213 computer-based). *Application deadline:* Applications are processed on a rolling basis. Application fee: $40. *Expenses: Tuition:* Full-time $11,880; part-time $660 per credit hour. Tuition and fees vary according to program. *Financial support:* Fellowships, research assistantships, Federal Work-Study, scholarships/grants, and unspecified assistantships available. Support available to part-time students. Financial award application deadline: 3/1; financial award applicants required to submit FAFSA. *Unit head:* Dr. Esther Haskevitz, Dean, School of Health Sciences, 518-244-2296, Fax: 518-244-4571, E-mail: haskve@sage.edu. *Application contact:* Dr. Glenda Kelman, Director, 518-244-2001, Fax: 518-244-2009, E-mail: kelmag@sage.edu.

St. Catherine University, Graduate Programs, Program in Nursing, St. Paul, MN 55105. Offers adult-gerontological nurse practitioner (MA); neonatal nurse practitioner (MA); nurse educator (MA); nursing (DNP); pediatric nurse practitioner (MA). *Accreditation:* NLN. Part-time and evening/weekend programs available. *Degree requirements:* For master's, thesis; for doctorate, portfolio, systems change project. *Entrance requirements:* For master's, GRE General Test, bachelor's degree in nursing, current nursing license, 2 years of recent clinical practice; for doctorate, master's degree in nursing, RN license, advanced nursing position. Additional exam requirements/recommendations for international students: Required—TOEFL (minimum score 600 paper-based; 250 computer-based; 100 iBT). *Expenses: Required fees:* $30 per semester. Tuition and fees vary according to program.

San Jose State University, Graduate Studies and Research, College of Applied Sciences and Arts, School of Nursing, San Jose, CA 95192-0001. Offers gerontology nurse practitioner (MS); nursing (Certificate); nursing administration (MS); nursing education (MS). *Accreditation:* AACN. Part-time and evening/weekend programs available. *Degree requirements:* For master's, thesis. *Entrance requirements:* For master's, BS in nursing, RN license. Electronic applications accepted. *Faculty research:* Nurse-managed clinics, computers in nursing.

Seattle Pacific University, MS in Nursing Program, Seattle, WA 98119-1997. Offers administration (MSN); adult/gerontology nurse practitioner (MSN); clinical nurse specialist (MSN); family nurse practitioner (MSN, Certificate); informatics (MSN); nurse educator (MSN). *Accreditation:* AACN. Part-time programs available. *Degree requirements:* For master's, thesis. Electronic applications accepted. *Expenses:* Contact institution.

Seattle University, College of Nursing, Program in Advanced Practice Nursing Immersion, Seattle, WA 98122-1090. Offers adult/gerontological nurse practitioner (MSN); advanced community public health (MSN); certified nurse midwifery (MSN); family nurse practitioner (MSN); psychiatric mental health nurse practitioner (MSN). *Faculty:* 43 full-time, 63 part-time/adjunct. *Students:* 104 full-time (91 women); includes 24 minority (2 Black or African American, non-Hispanic/Latino; 12 Asian, non-Hispanic/Latino; 7 Hispanic/Latino; 3 Two or more races, non-Hispanic/Latino). Average age 30. *Degree requirements:* For master's, thesis or scholarly project. *Entrance requirements:* For master's, GRE, bachelor's degree, minimum GPA of 3.0, professional resume, two recommendations, letter of intent, English proficiency (for non-English speakers). Additional exam requirements/recommendations for international students: Required—TOEFL (minimum score 92 iBT), IELTS. *Application deadline:* For fall admission, 12/1 for domestic and international students. Application fee: $55. Electronic applications accepted. *Financial support:* Scholarships/grants and traineeships available. Financial award applicants required to submit FAFSA. *Unit head:* Dr. Azita Emami, Dean, 206-296-5660. *Application contact:* Janet Shandley, Associate Dean of Graduate Admissions, 206-296-5900, Fax: 206-298-5656, E-mail: grad_admissions@seattleu.edu.

Seattle University, College of Nursing, Program in Nursing, Seattle, WA 98122-1090. Offers adult/gerontological nurse practitioner (MSN); advanced community public health (MSN); psychiatric mental health nurse practitioner (MSN). *Faculty:* 43 full-time, 63 part-time/adjunct. *Students:* 22 full-time (20 women); includes 4 minority (1 Black or African American, non-Hispanic/Latino; 1 Asian, non-Hispanic/Latino; 1 Hispanic/Latino; 1 Two or more races, non-Hispanic/Latino). *Degree requirements:* For master's, thesis or scholarly project. *Entrance requirements:* For master's, GRE, bachelor's degree in nursing or associate degree in nursing with baccalaureate in different major, 5-quarter statistics course, minimum cumulative GPA of 3.0, professional resume, two recommendations, letter of intent, English proficiency (for non-English speakers), copy of current RN license or ability to obtain RN license in WA state. Additional exam requirements/recommendations for international students: Required—TOEFL (minimum score 92 iBT), IELTS. *Application deadline:* For fall admission, 12/1 for domestic and international students. Application fee: $55. Electronic applications accepted. *Financial support:* In 2011–12, 2 teaching assistantships were awarded; scholarships/grants and traineeships also available. Financial award applicants required to submit FAFSA. *Unit head:* Dr. Azita Emami, Dean, 206-296-5660. *Application contact:* Janet Shandley, Associate Dean of Graduate Admissions, 206-296-5900, Fax: 206-298-5656, E-mail: grad_admissions@seattleu.edu.

Seton Hall University, College of Nursing, South Orange, NJ 07079-2697. Offers advanced practice in primary health care (MSN, DNP), including adult/gerontological nurse practitioner, pediatric nurse practitioner; entry into practice (MSN); health systems administration (MSN, DNP); nursing (PhD); nursing case management (MSN); nursing education (MA); school nurse (MSN); MSN/MA. *Accreditation:* AACN. Part-time programs available. Postbaccalaureate distance learning degree programs offered (minimal on-campus study). *Faculty:* 10 full-time (all women), 3 part-time/adjunct (1 woman). *Students:* 12 full-time (11 women), 217 part-time (197 women); includes 38 minority (15 Black or African American, non-Hispanic/Latino; 1 American Indian or Alaska Native, non-Hispanic/Latino; 12 Asian, non-Hispanic/Latino; 10 Hispanic/Latino). 180 applicants, 51% accepted, 82 enrolled. *Degree requirements:* For master's, research project; for doctorate, dissertation or scholarly project. *Entrance requirements:* For doctorate, GRE (waived for students with GPA of 3.5 or higher). Additional exam requirements/recommendations for international students: Required—TOEFL. *Application deadline:* For fall admission, 4/15 priority date for domestic students. Applications are processed on a rolling basis. Electronic applications accepted. *Expenses: Tuition:* Part-time $1033 per credit hour. *Required fees:* $85 per semester. *Financial support:* Institutionally sponsored loans, scholarships/grants, traineeships, tuition waivers (partial), and unspecified assistantships available. Support available to part-time students. Financial award applicants required to submit FAFSA. *Faculty research:* Parent/child, adult, and gerontological nursing; breast cancer; families of children with HIV; parish nursing. *Unit head:* Dr. Phyllis Shanley Hansell, Dean, 973-761-9014, E-mail: phyllis.hansell@shu.edu. *Application contact:* Kristyn Kent Wuillermin, Director of Strategic Alliances, Marketing and Enrollment, 973-761-9291, Fax: 973-761-9607, E-mail: kristyn.kent@shu.edu.

Southern University and Agricultural and Mechanical College, School of Nursing, Baton Rouge, LA 70813. Offers educator/administrator (PhD); family health nursing (MSN); family nurse practitioner (Post Master's Certificate); geriatric nurse practitioner/gerontology (PhD). *Accreditation:* AACN. Part-time programs available. *Degree requirements:* For master's, comprehensive exam, thesis; for doctorate, comprehensive exam, thesis/dissertation. *Entrance requirements:* For master's, GRE General Test, BSN, minimum GPA of 2.7; for doctorate, GRE General Test; for Post Master's Certificate, MSN. Additional exam requirements/recommendations for international students: Required—TOEFL (minimum score 525 paper-based; 193 computer-based). *Faculty research:* Health promotions, vulnerable populations, (community-based) cardiovascular participating research, health disparities chronic diseases, care of the elderly.

State University of New York Institute of Technology, Program in Gerontological Nurse Practitioner, Utica, NY 13504-3050. Offers MS, CAS. *Entrance requirements:* For master's, GRE General Test (if undergraduate GPA less than, minimum GPA of 3.0 in last 30 hours of undergraduate work, bachelor's degree in nursing, 1 year professional experience, RN license, interview, 2 letters of recommendation. Additional exam requirements/recommendations for international students: Required—TOEFL (minimum score 550 paper-based; 213 computer-based). *Faculty research:* Gerontological health issues, assessment of eldercare, nursing shortages, nursing faculty shortages.

Texas Christian University, Harris College of Nursing and Health Sciences, Program in Nursing, Fort Worth, TX 76129-0002. Offers advanced practice registered nurse (DNP); clinical nurse leader (MSN); clinical nurse specialist: adult/gerontology nursing (MSN); clinical nurse specialist: pediatric nursing (MSN); nursing administration (DNP); nursing education (MSN). *Accreditation:* AACN; AANA/CANAEP (one or more programs are accredited). Part-time programs available. Postbaccalaureate distance learning degree programs offered (no on-campus study). *Faculty:* 18 full-time (16 women), 2 part-time/adjunct (both women). *Students:* 2 full-time (both women), 105 part-time (96 women); includes 16 minority (8 Black or African American, non-Hispanic/Latino; 4 Asian, non-Hispanic/Latino; 2 Hispanic/Latino; 1 Native Hawaiian or other Pacific Islander, non-Hispanic/Latino; 1 Two or more races, non-Hispanic/Latino), 1 international. Average age 44. 58 applicants, 93% accepted, 46 enrolled. In 2011, 11 master's, 21 doctorates awarded. *Degree requirements:* For master's and doctorate, professional project. *Entrance requirements:* For master's, GRE General Test or MAT, 3 letters of reference, 2 years preferred full-time experience as registered nurse, current

nursing license, minimum GPA of 3.0; for doctorate, APRN recognition (national certification), minimum GPA of 3.0, 3 professional references, essay, 2 years post-master's experience (preferrred). Additional exam requirements/recommendations for international students: Required—TOEFL, Spoken English Test for DNP. *Expenses: Tuition:* Full-time $20,250; part-time $1125 per credit hour. Part-time tuition and fees vary according to course load and program. *Financial support:* In 2011–12, teaching assistantships (averaging $5,000 per year) were awarded; tuition waivers also available. *Unit head:* Dr. Pamela Frable, Associate Dean and Director of Nursing, 817-257-5840, E-mail: p.frable@tcu.edu. *Application contact:* Dr. Kathy Baker, Director of Graduate Studies and Director of DNP Program, 817-257-6726, E-mail: kathy.baker@tcu.edu. Web site: http://www.nursing.tcu.edu/graduate.asp.

Texas Tech University Health Sciences Center, School of Nursing, Lubbock, TX 79430. Offers acute care nurse practitioner (MSN, Certificate); administration (MSN); advanced practice (DNP); education (MSN); executive leadership (DNP); family nurse practitioner (MSN, Certificate); geriatric nurse practitioner (MSN, Certificate); pediatric nurse practitioner (MSN, Certificate). *Accreditation:* AACN. Part-time programs available. Postbaccalaureate distance learning degree programs offered (minimal on-campus study). *Degree requirements:* For master's, thesis optional. *Entrance requirements:* For master's, minimum GPA of 3.0, 3 letters of reference, BSN, RN license; for Certificate, minimum GPA of 3.0, 3 letters of reference, RN license. Additional exam requirements/recommendations for international students: Required—TOEFL (minimum score 550 paper-based; 213 computer-based). *Faculty research:* Diabetes/obesity, nurse competency, disease management, intervention and measurements, health disparities.

University of Central Florida, College of Nursing, Orlando, FL 32816. Offers adult-gerontology clinical nurse specialist (Post-Master's Certificate); adult-gerontology nurse practitioner (Post-Master's Certificate); clinical nurse leader (Post-Master's Certificate); family nurse practitioner (Post-Master's Certificate); nursing (MSN, PhD); nursing education (Post-Master's Certificate); nursing practice (DNP). *Accreditation:* AACN. Part-time and evening/weekend programs available. *Faculty:* 44 full-time (39 women), 72 part-time/adjunct (71 women). *Students:* 75 full-time (68 women), 350 part-time (332 women); includes 109 minority (54 Black or African American, non-Hispanic/Latino; 1 American Indian or Alaska Native, non-Hispanic/Latino; 19 Asian, non-Hispanic/Latino; 33 Hispanic/Latino; 1 Native Hawaiian or other Pacific Islander, non-Hispanic/Latino; 1 Two or more races, non-Hispanic/Latino), 5 international. Average age 40. 203 applicants, 60% accepted, 98 enrolled. In 2011, 110 master's, 17 doctorates, 11 other advanced degrees awarded. *Degree requirements:* For master's, thesis or alternative. *Entrance requirements:* For master's, GRE General Test, minimum GPA of 3.0 in last 60 hours. Additional exam requirements/recommendations for international students: Required—TOEFL. *Application deadline:* For fall admission, 2/15 for domestic students; for spring admission, 9/15 for domestic students. Application fee: $30. Electronic applications accepted. *Expenses:* Tuition, state resident: part-time $277.08 per credit hour. Tuition, nonresident: part-time $277.08 per credit hour. Part-time tuition and fees vary according to degree level and program. *Financial support:* In 2011–12, 92 students received support, including 92 fellowships with partial tuition reimbursements available (averaging $1,100 per year), 2 teaching assistantships with partial tuition reimbursements available (averaging $8,100 per year); research assistantships with partial tuition reimbursements available, career-related internships or fieldwork, Federal Work-Study, institutionally sponsored loans, traineeships, and unspecified assistantships also available. Financial award application deadline: 3/1; financial award applicants required to submit FAFSA. *Unit head:* Dr. Jean D. Leuner, Dean, 407-823-5496, Fax: 407-823-5675, E-mail: jean.leuner@ucf.edu. *Application contact:* Barbara Rodriguez, Director, Admissions and Registration, 407-823-2766, Fax: 407-823-6442, E-mail: gradadmissions@ucf.edu. Web site: http://nursing.ucf.edu/.

University of Delaware, College of Health Sciences, School of Nursing, Newark, DE 19716. Offers adult nurse practitioner (MSN, PMC); cardiopulmonary clinical nurse specialist (MSN, PMC); cardiopulmonary clinical nurse specialist/adult nurse practitioner (MSN, PMC); family nurse practitioner (MSN, PMC); gerontology clinical nurse specialist (MSN, PMC); gerontology clinical nurse specialist geriatric nurse practitioner (PMC); gerontology clinical nurse specialist/geriatric nurse practitioner (MSN); health services administration (MSN, PMC); nursing of children clinical nurse specialist (MSN, PMC); nursing of children clinical nurse specialist/pediatric nurse practitioner (MSN, PMC); oncology/immune deficiency clinical nurse specialist (MSN, PMC); oncology/immune deficiency clinical nurse specialist/adult nurse practitioner (MSN, PMC); perinatal/women's health clinical nurse specialist (MSN, PMC); perinatal/women's health clinical nurse specialist/women's health nurse practitioner (MSN, PMC); psychiatric nursing clinical nurse specialist (MSN, PMC). *Accreditation:* AACN; NLN (one or more programs are accredited). Part-time and evening/weekend programs available. Postbaccalaureate distance learning degree programs offered (minimal on-campus study). *Degree requirements:* For master's, thesis optional. *Entrance requirements:* For master's, BSN, interview, RN license. Electronic applications accepted. *Faculty research:* Marriage and chronic illness, health promotion, congestive heart failure patient outcomes, school nursing, diabetes in children, culture, health disparities, cardiovascular, prison nursing, oncology, public policy, child obesity, smoking and teen pregnancy, blood pressure measurements, men's health.

University of Illinois at Chicago, Graduate College, College of Nursing, Program in Nursing, Chicago, IL 60607-7128. Offers acute care clinical nurse specialist (MS); acute care nurse practitioner (MS); administrative studies in nursing (MS); adult nurse practitioner (MS); adult/geriatric nurse practitioner (MS); advanced community health nurse specialist (MS); family nurse practitioner (MS); geriatric clinical nurse specialist (MS); geriatric nurse practitioner (MS); mental health clinical nurse specialist (MS); mental health nurse practitioner (MS); nurse midwifery (MS); occupational health/advanced community health nurse specialist (MS); occupational health/family nurse practitioner (MS); pediatric clinical nurse specialist (MS); pediatric nurse practitioner (MS); perinatal clinical nurse specialist (MS); school/advanced community health nurse specialist (MS); school/family nurse practitioner (MS); women's health nurse practitioner (MS). *Accreditation:* AACN. Part-time programs available. *Degree requirements:* For master's, thesis or alternative. *Entrance requirements:* For master's, GRE General Test, minimum GPA of 2.75. Additional exam requirements/recommendations for international students: Required—TOEFL. Electronic applications accepted.

The University of Kansas, University of Kansas Medical Center, School of Nursing, Kansas City, KS 66160. Offers adult/gerontological clinical nurse specialist (PMC); adult/gerontological nurse practitioner (PMC); clinical research management (PMC); family nurse practitioner (PMC); health care informatics (PMC); health professions educator (PMC); nurse midwife (PMC); nursing (MS, DNP, PhD); organizational leadership (PMC); psychiatric/mental health nurse practitioner (PMC); public health nursing (PMC). *Accreditation:* AACN; ACNM/ACME. Part-time programs available. Postbaccalaureate distance learning degree programs offered (minimal on-campus study). *Faculty:* 80. *Students:* 79 full-time (71 women), 336 part-time (317 women); includes 63 minority (24 Black or African American, non-Hispanic/Latino; 2 American Indian or Alaska Native, non-Hispanic/Latino; 18 Asian, non-Hispanic/Latino; 15 Hispanic/Latino; 4 Two or more races, non-Hispanic/Latino), 6 international. Average age 37. 155 applicants, 82% accepted, 127 enrolled. In 2011, 79 master's, 15 doctorates, 12 other advanced degrees awarded. Terminal master's awarded for partial completion of doctoral program. *Degree requirements:* For master's, comprehensive exam, thesis optional, general oral exam; for doctorate, variable foreign language requirement, thesis/dissertation, comprehensive oral exam (for DNP); comprehensive written and oral exam (for PhD). *Entrance requirements:* For master's, bachelor's degree in nursing, minimum GPA of 3.0, RN license, 1 year of clinical experience, RN license in KS and MO; for doctorate, GRE General Test, master's degree in nursing, minimum GPA of 3.5, RN license in KS and MO; national certification (for some specialties). Additional exam requirements/recommendations for international students: Required—TOEFL. *Application deadline:* For fall admission, 4/1 for domestic and international students; for spring admission, 9/1 for domestic and international students. Application fee: $60. Electronic applications accepted. Tuition and fees vary according to course load, campus/location, program and reciprocity agreements. *Financial support:* Research assistantships with full and partial tuition reimbursements, teaching assistantships with full and partial tuition reimbursements, and traineeships available. Financial award application deadline: 2/14; financial award applicants required to submit FAFSA. *Faculty research:* Breastfeeding practices of teen mothers, national database of nursing quality indicators, caregiving of families of patients using technology in the home, simulation in nursing education, diaphragm fatigue. *Total annual research expenditures:* $6.1 million. *Unit head:* Dr. Karen L. Miller, Dean, 913-588-1601, Fax: 913-588-1660, E-mail: kmiller@kumc.edu. *Application contact:* Dr. Debra J. Ford, Associate Dean, Student Affairs, 913-588-1619, Fax: 913-588-1615, E-mail: dford@kumc.edu. Web site: http://nursing.kumc.edu.

University of Maryland, Baltimore, Graduate School, School of Nursing, Master's Program in Nursing, Baltimore, MD 21201. Offers community health nursing (MS); gerontological nursing (MS); maternal-child nursing (MS); medical-surgical nursing (MS); nurse-midwifery education (MS); nursing administration (MS); nursing education (MS); nursing health policy (MS); primary care nursing (MS); psychiatric nursing (MS); MS/MBA. MS/MBA offered jointly with University of Baltimore. *Accreditation:* AACN; AANA/CANAEP; NLN (one or more programs are accredited). Part-time programs available. *Students:* 370 full-time (314 women), 480 part-time (441 women); includes 308 minority (176 Black or African American, non-Hispanic/Latino; 2 American Indian or Alaska Native, non-Hispanic/Latino; 70 Asian, non-Hispanic/Latino; 33 Hispanic/Latino; 27 Two or more races, non-Hispanic/Latino), 9 international. Average age 35. 990 applicants, 30% accepted, 204 enrolled. In 2011, 301 master's awarded. *Degree requirements:* For master's, comprehensive exam (for some programs), thesis or alternative. *Entrance requirements:* For master's, minimum GPA of 2.75, course work in statistics, BS in nursing. Additional exam requirements/recommendations for international students: Required—TOEFL (minimum score 550 paper-based; 80 iBT) or IELTS (minimum score 7). *Application deadline:* For fall admission, 2/1 for domestic students, 1/15 for international students. Application fee: $50. Electronic applications accepted. *Financial support:* Fellowships, research assistantships, teaching assistantships, career-related internships or fieldwork, and traineeships available. Support available to part-time students. Financial award application deadline: 2/15; financial award applicants required to submit FAFSA. *Unit head:* Dr. Jane Kapustin, Assistant Dean, 410-706-6741, Fax: 410-706-4231. *Application contact:* Marjorie Fass, Admissions Director, 410-706-0501, Fax: 410-706-7238.

University of Massachusetts Lowell, School of Health and Environment, Department of Nursing, Program in Gerontological Nursing, Lowell, MA 01854-2881. Offers MS, Graduate Certificate. *Accreditation:* AACN. *Degree requirements:* For master's, thesis optional. *Entrance requirements:* For master's, GRE General Test, minimum GPA of 3.0, MA nursing license, interview, 3 letters of recommendation.

University of Massachusetts Worcester, Graduate School of Nursing, Worcester, MA 01655-0115. Offers adult acute/critical care nurse practitioner (MS, Post Master's Certificate); adult acute/critical care nurse practitioner and gerontological nurse practitioner (MS, Post Master's Certificate); adult primary care nurse practitioner (MS, Post Master's Certificate); adult primary care nurse practitioner and gerontological nurse practitioner (MS, Post Master's Certificate); advanced practice nursing (DNP); family nurse practitioner (MS); gerontological nurse practitioner (Post Master's Certificate); leadership (DNP); nurse education (Post Master's Certificate); nurse educator (MS); nursing (PhD). *Accreditation:* AACN. *Faculty:* 20 full-time (17 women), 60 part-time/adjunct (50 women). *Students:* 162 full-time (141 women), 36 part-time (30 women); includes 29 minority (13 Black or African American, non-Hispanic/Latino; 10 Asian, non-Hispanic/Latino; 6 Hispanic/Latino), 1 international. Average age 36. 252 applicants, 38% accepted, 82 enrolled. In 2011, 38 master's, 6 doctorates awarded. *Degree requirements:* For doctorate, comprehensive exam, thesis/dissertation. *Entrance requirements:* For master's, GRE General Test, bachelor's degree, course work in statistics; for doctorate, GRE General Test, bachelor's or master's degree, RN licensure; for Post Master's Certificate, GRE General Test, MS in nursing. Additional exam requirements/recommendations for international students: Required—TOEFL. *Application deadline:* For fall admission, 1/15 priority date for domestic students. Applications are processed on a rolling basis. Application fee: $40 ($60 for international students). *Expenses:* Contact institution. *Financial support:* In 2011–12, 38 students received support. Institutionally sponsored loans, scholarships/grants, traineeships, and tuition waivers (for some) available. Support available to part-time students. Financial award application deadline: 5/16; financial award applicants required to submit FAFSA. *Faculty research:* Decision-making of partners and men with prostate cancer, coinfection (HIV and Hepatitus C) and treatment decisions, parent management of children with T1DM, health literacy and discharge planning, Ghanian women and self-care. *Total annual research expenditures:* $939,567. *Unit head:* Dr. Paulette Seymour-Route, Dean, 508-856-5801, Fax: 508-856-6552, E-mail: paulette.seymour-route@umassmed.edu. *Application contact:* Diane Brescia, Admissions Coordinator, 508-856-3488, Fax: 508-856-5851, E-mail: diane.brescia@umassmed.edu. Web site: http://www.umassmed.edu/gsn/.

University of Michigan, Horace H. Rackham School of Graduate Studies, School of Nursing, Division of Acute, Critical and Long-term Care, Program in Gerontology Nursing, Ann Arbor, MI 48109. Offers gerontology nurse practitioner (MS); gerontology-clinical nurse specialist (MS). *Accreditation:* AACN. Part-time programs available. *Degree requirements:* For master's, thesis. *Entrance requirements:* For master's, GRE General Test (if BSN GPA less than 3.25), Michigan licensure, minimum of B average in BSN program. Additional exam requirements/recommendations for international students: Required—TOEFL (minimum score 560 paper-based; 220 computer-based). Electronic applications accepted. *Faculty research:* Wandering in the elderly, Alzheimer's, clinical specialist and nurse practitioner roles, enhancement of cognitive function.

University of Minnesota, Twin Cities Campus, Graduate School, School of Nursing, Gerontological Nurse Practitioner Program, Minneapolis, MN 55455-0213. Offers MS. *Accreditation:* AACN. *Degree requirements:* For master's, final oral exam, project or thesis. *Entrance requirements:* Additional exam requirements/recommendations for international students: Required—TOEFL (minimum score 586 paper-based; 240 computer-based).

University of Minnesota, Twin Cities Campus, Graduate School, School of Nursing, Program in Gerontological Clinical Nurse Specialist, Minneapolis, MN 55455-0213.

Gerontological Nursing

Offers advanced clinical specialist in gerontology (MS). *Accreditation:* AACN. Part-time programs available. *Degree requirements:* For master's, final oral exam, project or thesis. *Entrance requirements:* Additional exam requirements/recommendations for international students: Required—TOEFL (minimum score 586 paper-based; 240 computer-based).

The University of North Carolina at Greensboro, Graduate School, School of Nursing, Greensboro, NC 27412-5001. Offers adult clinical nurse specialist (MSN, PMC); adult/gerontological nurse practitioner (MSN, PMC); nurse anesthesia (MSN, PMC); nursing (PhD); nursing administration (MSN); nursing education (MSN); MSN/MBA. *Accreditation:* AACN; AANA/CANAEP; NLN. *Degree requirements:* For master's, thesis or alternative. *Entrance requirements:* For master's, GRE General Test or MAT, BSN, clinical experience, liability insurance, RN license; for PMC, liability insurance, MSN, RN license. Additional exam requirements/recommendations for international students: Required—TOEFL. Electronic applications accepted.

University of North Dakota, Graduate School, College of Nursing, Grand Forks, ND 58202. Offers advanced public health nursing (MS); family nurse practitioner (MS); gerontological nursing (MS); nurse anesthesia (MS); nursing (MS, PhD); nursing education (MS); psychiatric and mental health (MS). *Accreditation:* AACN; AANA/CANAEP (one or more programs are accredited). Part-time and evening/weekend programs available. Postbaccalaureate distance learning degree programs offered (minimal on-campus study). *Degree requirements:* For master's, thesis or alternative. *Entrance requirements:* For master's, minimum GPA of 3.0; for doctorate, GRE or MAT, minimum GPA of 3.0. Additional exam requirements/recommendations for international students: Required—TOEFL (minimum score 550 paper-based; 213 computer-based; 79 iBT), IELTS (minimum score 6.5). Electronic applications accepted. *Faculty research:* Adult health, anesthesia, rural health, health administration, family nurse practitioner.

University of Phoenix–Bay Area Campus, College of Nursing, San Jose, CA 95134-1805. Offers education (MHA); gerontology (MHA); health administration (MHA, DHA); informatics (MHA, MSN); nursing (MSN, PhD); nursing/health care education (MSN); MSN/MBA. Evening/weekend programs available. Postbaccalaureate distance learning degree programs offered (no on-campus study). *Degree requirements:* For master's, thesis (for some programs). *Entrance requirements:* For master's, minimum undergraduate GPA of 2.5, 3 years of work experience, RN license. Additional exam requirements/recommendations for international students: Required—TOEFL (minimum score 550 paper-based; 213 computer-based; 79 iBT). Electronic applications accepted.

University of Phoenix–Phoenix Main Campus, College of Natural Science, Tempe, AZ 85282-2371. Offers education (MHA); gerontology (MHA); gerontology health care (Certificate); health administration (MHA); informatics (MHA). Evening/weekend programs available. Postbaccalaureate distance learning degree programs offered. *Students:* 27 full-time (17 women); includes 10 minority (4 Black or African American, non-Hispanic/Latino; 1 American Indian or Alaska Native, non-Hispanic/Latino; 1 Asian, non-Hispanic/Latino; 4 Hispanic/Latino). Average age 42. *Entrance requirements:* Additional exam requirements/recommendations for international students: Required—TOEFL, TOEIC (Test of English as an International Communication), Berlitz Online English Proficiency Exam, Pearson Test of English, or IELTS. *Application deadline:* Applications are processed on a rolling basis. Application fee: $45. Electronic applications accepted. *Expenses:* Contact institution. *Financial support:* Scholarships/grants available. Financial award applicants required to submit FAFSA. *Unit head:* Dr. Hinrich Eylers, Dean/Associate Provost, 866-766-0766. *Application contact:* 866-766-0766. Web site: http://www.phoenix.edu/colleges_divisions/natural-sciences.html.

University of Puerto Rico, Medical Sciences Campus, School of Nursing, San Juan, PR 00936-5067. Offers adult and elderly nursing (MSN); child and adolescent nursing (MSN); critical care nursing (MSN); family and community nursing (MSN); family nurse practitioner (MSN); maternity nursing (MSN); mental health and psychiatric nursing (MSN). *Accreditation:* AACN; AANA/CANAEP. *Entrance requirements:* For master's, GRE or EXADEP, interview, Puerto Rico RN license or professional license for international students, general and specific point average, article analysis. Electronic applications accepted. *Faculty research:* HIV, health disparities, teen violence, women and violence, neurological disorders.

University of Rhode Island, Graduate School, College of Nursing, Kingston, RI 02881. Offers administration (MS); clinical nurse leader (MS); clinical specialist in gerontology (MS); clinical specialist in psychiatric/mental health (MS); family nurse practitioner (MS); gerontological nurse practitioner (MS); nursing (DNP, PhD); nursing education (MS). *Accreditation:* AACN; ACNM/ACME (one or more programs are accredited). Part-time programs available. *Faculty:* 29 full-time (28 women), 2 part-time/adjunct (1 woman). *Students:* 33 full-time (30 women), 81 part-time (77 women); includes 6 minority (1 Asian, non-Hispanic/Latino; 5 Hispanic/Latino). In 2011, 17 master's, 6 doctorates awarded. *Degree requirements:* For master's, comprehensive exam; for doctorate, comprehensive exam, thesis/dissertation. *Entrance requirements:* For master's, GRE or MAT, 2 letters of recommendation, scholarly papers; for doctorate, GRE, 3 letters of recommendation, scholarly papers. Additional exam requirements/recommendations for international students: Required—TOEFL (minimum score 550 paper-based; 213 computer-based). *Application deadline:* For fall admission, 4/15 for domestic students, 2/1 for international students; for spring admission, 11/15 for domestic students, 7/15 for international students. Application fee: $65. Electronic applications accepted. *Expenses:* Tuition, state resident: full-time $10,432; part-time $580 per credit hour. Tuition, nonresident: full-time $23,130; part-time $1285 per credit hour. *Required fees:* $1362; $36 per credit hour. $35 per semester. One-time fee: $130. *Financial support:* In 2011–12, 5 teaching assistantships with full and partial tuition reimbursements (averaging $12,596 per year) were awarded. Financial award application deadline: 4/15; financial award applicants required to submit FAFSA. *Faculty research:* Group intervention for grieving women in prison, translating Best Practice in non-drug interventions for postoperative pain management, further development and testing of the pain assessment inventory, preschool motor and functional performance of two cohorts, neuroactivation of brain motor areas in preterm children. *Unit head:* Dr. Dayle Joseph, Dean, 401-874-2766, Fax: 401-874-2061, E-mail: dayle@uri.edu. *Application contact:* Dr. Mary C. Sullivan, Director of Graduate Studies, 401-874-5339, Fax: 401-874-2061, E-mail: mcsullivan@uri.edu. Web site: http://www.uri.edu/nursing/.

University of Rochester, School of Nursing, Rochester, NY 14642. Offers acute care nurse practitioner (MS); adult nurse practitioner (MS); adult/geriatric nurse practitioner (MS); care of children and families/pediatric nurse practitioner (MS); care of children and families/pediatric nurse practitioner/neonatal nurse practitioner (MS); clinical nurse leader (MS); clinical research coordinator (MS); family nurse practitioner (MS); family psychiatric mental health nurse practitioner (MS); health care organization management and leadership (MS); health practice research (PhD); nursing (DNP). *Accreditation:* AACN; NLN (one or more programs are accredited). Part-time programs available. Postbaccalaureate distance learning degree programs offered (minimal on-campus study). *Faculty:* 49 full-time (42 women), 72 part-time/adjunct (60 women). *Students:* 38 full-time (32 women), 196 part-time (181 women); includes 37 minority (20 Black or African American, non-Hispanic/Latino; 9 Asian, non-Hispanic/Latino; 8 Hispanic/Latino), 5 international. Average age 36. 68 applicants, 56% accepted, 26 enrolled. In 2011, 49 master's, 7 doctorates awarded. Terminal master's awarded for partial completion of doctoral program. *Median time to degree:* Of those who began their doctoral program in fall 2003, 40% received their degree in 8 years or less. *Degree requirements:* For doctorate, thesis/dissertation. *Entrance requirements:* For master's, BS in nursing, minimum GPA of 3.0, course work in statistics; for doctorate, GRE General Test, MS in nursing, minimum GPA of 3.5. Additional exam requirements/recommendations for international students: Required—or IELTS (minimum score 6.5); Recommended—TOEFL (minimum score 560 paper-based; 230 computer-based; 88 iBT). *Application deadline:* For fall admission, 4/1 priority date for domestic students, 4/1 for international students; for spring admission, 9/1 for domestic and international students. Application fee: $50. Electronic applications accepted. *Expenses: Tuition:* Full-time $41,040. *Financial support:* In 2011–12, 49 students received support, including 1 fellowship with full and partial tuition reimbursement available (averaging $18,700 per year); scholarships/grants, traineeships, health care benefits, tuition waivers (partial), and unspecified assistantships also available. Support available to part-time students. Financial award application deadline: 6/30. *Faculty research:* Clinical research in aging, managing asthma in children, interventions to improve outcomes in critically ill children and their mothers, nurse home visitation studies, medical device evaluation, critical care clinical studies, high risk behavior and prevention, palliative care, pregnancy-related weight gain. *Total annual research expenditures:* $4.3 million. *Unit head:* Dr. Kathy H. Rideout, Interim Dean, 585-273-8902, Fax: 585-273-1268, E-mail: kathy_rideout@urmc.rochester.edu. *Application contact:* Elaine Andolina, Director of Admissions, 585-275-2375, Fax: 585-756-8299, E-mail: elaine_andolina@urmc.rochester.edu. Web site: http://www.son.rochester.edu.

University of San Diego, Hahn School of Nursing and Health Science, San Diego, CA 92110-2492. Offers adult-gerontology clinical nurse specialist (MSN); adult-gerontology nurse practitioner/family nurse practitioner (MSN); clinical nursing (MSN); entry-level nursing (for non-RNs) (MSN); executive nurse leader (MSN); family nurse practitioner (MSN); family/lifespan psychiatric-mental health nurse practitioner (MSN); healthcare informatics (MS, MSN); nursing (PhD); nursing practice (DNP); pediatric nurse practitioner/family nurse practitioner (MSN). *Accreditation:* AACN. Part-time and evening/weekend programs available. *Faculty:* 23 full-time (21 women), 37 part-time/adjunct (34 women). *Students:* 157 full-time (131 women), 182 part-time (162 women); includes 121 minority (21 Black or African American, non-Hispanic/Latino; 6 American Indian or Alaska Native, non-Hispanic/Latino; 51 Asian, non-Hispanic/Latino; 36 Hispanic/Latino; 2 Native Hawaiian or other Pacific Islander, non-Hispanic/Latino; 5 Two or more races, non-Hispanic/Latino), 7 international. Average age 36. 506 applicants, 47% accepted, 150 enrolled. In 2011, 87 master's, 26 doctorates awarded. *Degree requirements:* For doctorate, thesis/dissertation (for some programs), residency (DNP). *Entrance requirements:* For master's, GRE General Test (entry-level nursing), BSN, current California RN licensure (except for entry-level nursing); minimum GPA of 3.0; for doctorate, minimum GPA of 3.5, MSN, current California RN licensure. Additional exam requirements/recommendations for international students: Required—TOEFL (minimum score 580 paper-based; 237 computer-based; 83 iBT), TWE. *Application deadline:* For fall admission, 3/1 priority date for domestic students, 3/1 for international students; for spring admission, 11/1 priority date for domestic students, 11/1 for international students. Applications are processed on a rolling basis. Application fee: $45. Electronic applications accepted. *Expenses: Tuition:* Full-time $22,482; part-time $1249 per unit. *Required fees:* $224. Full-time tuition and fees vary according to course load and degree level. *Financial support:* In 2011–12, 232 students received support. Scholarships/grants and traineeships available. Support available to part-time students. Financial award application deadline: 4/1; financial award applicants required to submit FAFSA. *Faculty research:* Palliative and end of life care, maternal/child health, childhood obesity, health care disparities, cognitive functioning. *Unit head:* Dr. Sally Hardin, Dean, 619-260-4550, Fax: 619-260-6814. *Application contact:* Monica Mahon, Associate Director of Graduate Admissions, 619-260-4524, Fax: 619-260-4158, E-mail: grads@sandiego.edu. Web site: http://www.sandiego.edu/academics/nursing/.

The University of Texas at Austin, Graduate School, School of Nursing, Austin, TX 78712-1111. Offers adult -gerontology clinical nurse specialist (MSN); child health (MSN), including administration, public health nursing; child health (MSN), including teaching; family nurse practitioner (MSN); family psychiatric/mental health nurse practitioner (MSN); holistic adult health (MSN), including administration, education; maternity (MSN), including administration, public health nursing; maternity (MSN), including teaching; nursing (PhD); nursing administration and healthcare systems management (MSN); pediatric nurse practitioner (MSN); public health nursing (MSN). *Accreditation:* AACN. Part-time programs available. *Degree requirements:* For master's, thesis optional; for doctorate, thesis/dissertation. *Entrance requirements:* For master's and doctorate, GRE General Test. Additional exam requirements/recommendations for international students: Required—TOEFL (minimum score 550 paper-based; 213 computer-based). *Application deadline:* For fall admission, 12/1 for domestic students. Application fee: $50 ($75 for international students). Electronic applications accepted. *Financial support:* Fellowships, research assistantships, teaching assistantships, scholarships/grants, and traineeships available. Financial award application deadline: 2/1. *Faculty research:* Chronic illness management, memory and aging, health promotion, women's health, adolescent health. *Unit head:* Dr. Alexa Stuifbergen, Dean, 512-471-4100, Fax: 512-471-4910, E-mail: astuifbergen@mail.utexas.edu. Web site: http://www.utexas.edu/nursing/.

University of Utah, Graduate School, College of Nursing, Gerontology Interdisciplinary Program, Salt Lake City, UT 84112. Offers MS, Certificate. *Accreditation:* AACN. Part-time programs available. *Students:* 14 full-time (11 women), 4 part-time (all women); includes 2 minority (1 Asian, non-Hispanic/Latino; 1 Two or more races, non-Hispanic/Latino), 3 international. Average age 38. 15 applicants, 67% accepted, 6 enrolled. In 2011, 6 master's awarded. *Degree requirements:* For master's, thesis optional, thesis or project. *Entrance requirements:* For master's, GRE General Test (if cumulative GPA is less than 3.2), minimum undergraduate GPA of 3.0. Additional exam requirements/recommendations for international students: Required—TOEFL (minimum score 500 paper-based; 173 computer-based; 85 iBT). *Application deadline:* For fall admission, 1/15 priority date for domestic students, 1/15 for international students. Application fee: $55 ($65 for international students). Electronic applications accepted. *Expenses:* Contact institution. *Financial support:* In 2011–12, 8 students received support, including 7 fellowships with partial tuition reimbursements available (averaging $1,800 per year), 1 teaching assistantship with partial tuition reimbursement available (averaging $6,000 per year); scholarships/grants also available. Support available to part-time students. Financial award application deadline: 1/15; financial award applicants required to submit FAFSA. *Faculty research:* Spousal bereavement, family caregiving, healthy promotion and self-care, environmental issues, geriatric care management, technology and aging. *Unit head:* Dr. Maureen R. Keefe, Dean/Interim Director, 801-581-8262, E-mail: maureen.keefe@nurs.utah.edu. *Application contact:* Brent E. Vawdrey, Program Manager, 801-581-8198, Fax: 801-585-9705, E-mail: brent.vawdrey@nurs.utah.edu. Web site: http://www.nursing.utah.edu/gerontology/.

University of Wisconsin–Eau Claire, College of Nursing and Health Sciences, Program in Nursing, Eau Claire, WI 54702-4004. Offers adult-gerontologic administration (MSN); adult-gerontologic clinical nurse specialist (MSN); adult-gerontologic education (MSN); adult-gerontologic nurse practitioner (MSN); family health administration (MSN); family health in education (MSN); family health nurse practitioner (MSN); nursing practice (DNP). Part-time programs available. *Faculty:* 13

full-time (all women), 1 (woman) part-time/adjunct. *Students:* 42 full-time (40 women), 68 part-time (66 women); includes 3 minority (1 Black or African American, non-Hispanic/Latino; 1 Asian, non-Hispanic/Latino; 1 Hispanic/Latino). Average age 37. 74 applicants, 70% accepted, 41 enrolled. In 2011, 35 master's awarded. Terminal master's awarded for partial completion of doctoral program. *Degree requirements:* For master's, thesis optional, 500-600 hours clinical practicum, oral and written exams. *Entrance requirements:* For master's, Wisconsin RN license, minimum GPA of 3.0, undergraduate statistics, course work in health assessment. Additional exam requirements/recommendations for international students: Required—TOEFL (minimum score 550 paper-based; 213 computer-based; 79 iBT); Recommended—IELTS (minimum score 7). *Application deadline:* For fall admission, 1/15 priority date for domestic students, 1/15 for international students. Applications are processed on a rolling basis. Application fee: $86. *Expenses:* Tuition, state resident: full-time $7312; part-time $406 per credit. Tuition, nonresident: full-time $16,771; part-time $932 per credit. *Required fees:* $1101; $61 per credit. *Financial support:* In 2011–12, 16 students received support. Federal Work-Study and unspecified assistantships available. Financial award application deadline: 3/1; financial award applicants required to submit FAFSA. *Unit head:* Dr. Linda Young, Dean, 715-836-4904, Fax: 715-836-5925, E-mail: younglk@uwec.edu. *Application contact:* Dr. Mary Zwygart-Stauffacher, Director, 715-836-5287, E-mail: zwygarmc@uwec.edu. Web site: http://www.uwec.edu/conhs/programs/grad/index.htm.

University of Wisconsin–Madison, School of Nursing, Madison, WI 53706-1380. Offers adult/gerontology (DNP); nursing (PhD); pediatrics (DNP); psychiatric mental health (DNP); MS/MPH. *Accreditation:* AACN. Part-time programs available. *Degree requirements:* For doctorate, comprehensive exam, thesis/dissertation. *Entrance requirements:* For doctorate, GRE General Test, 2 samples of scholarly written work, BS in nursing from an accredited program, minimum undergraduate GPA of 3.0 in last 60 credits (for PhD); licensure as professional nurse (for DNP). Additional exam requirements/recommendations for international students: Required—TOEFL (minimum score 600 paper-based; 250 computer-based; 100 iBT). Electronic applications accepted. *Expenses:* Tuition, state resident: full-time $10,296; part-time $643.51 per credit. Tuition, nonresident: full-time $24,054; part-time $1503.40 per credit. *Required fees:* $70.06 per credit. Tuition and fees vary according to course load, campus/location, program and reciprocity agreements. *Faculty research:* Nursing informatics to promote self-care and disease management skills among patients and caregivers; quality of care to frail, vulnerable, and chronically ill populations; study of health-related and health-seeking behaviors; eliminating health disparities; pain and symptom management for patients with cancer.

Vanderbilt University, Vanderbilt University School of Nursing, Nashville, TN 37240. Offers acute care nurse practitioner (MSN), including intensivist; adult-gerontology primary care nurse practitioner (MSN); emergency nurse practitioner (MSN); family nurse practitioner (MSN); family psychiatric and mental health nurse practitioner (MSN); health systems management (MSN); neonatal nurse practitioner (MSN); nurse midwifery (MSN); nurse midwifery/family nurse practitioner (MSN); nursing informatics (MSN); nursing practice (DNP); nursing science (PhD); pediatric acute care nurse practitioner (MSN); pediatric primary care nurse practitioner (MSN); women's health nurse practitioner (MSN), including urogynecology, women's health; women's health nurse practitioner/adult gerontology nurse practitioner (MSN); MSN/M Div; MSN/MTS. *Accreditation:* ACNM/ACME; NLN (one or more programs are accredited). Part-time programs available. Postbaccalaureate distance learning degree programs offered (minimal on-campus study). *Faculty:* 120 full-time (105 women), 415 part-time/adjunct (302 women). *Students:* 570 full-time (503 women), 395 part-time (364 women); includes 107 minority (57 Black or African American, non-Hispanic/Latino; 1 American Indian or Alaska Native, non-Hispanic/Latino; 19 Asian, non-Hispanic/Latino; 19 Hispanic/Latino; 2 Native Hawaiian or other Pacific Islander, non-Hispanic/Latino; 9 Two or more races, non-Hispanic/Latino), 10 international. Average age 32. 1,116 applicants, 56% accepted, 455 enrolled. In 2011, 341 master's, 33 doctorates awarded. *Degree requirements:* For doctorate, comprehensive exam, thesis/dissertation. *Entrance requirements:* For master's, GRE General Test (within the past 5 years), minimum B average in undergraduate course work, 3 letters of recommendation; for doctorate, GRE General Test, interview, 3 letters of recommendation from doctorally-prepared faculty, MSN, essay. Additional exam requirements/recommendations for international students: Required—TOEFL (minimum score 570 paper-based; 88 computer-based), IELTS (minimum score 6.5). *Application deadline:* For fall admission, 12/1 priority date for domestic students, 12/1 for international students. Applications are processed on a rolling basis. Application fee: $50. Electronic applications accepted. *Expenses:* Contact institution. *Financial support:* In 2011–12, 392 students received support. Scholarships/grants and health care benefits available. Support available to part-time students. Financial award application deadline: 3/15; financial award applicants required to submit FAFSA. *Faculty research:* Lymphedema, palliative care and bereavement, health services research including workforce, safety and quality of care, gerontology, better birth outcomes including nutrition . *Total annual research expenditures:* $1.8 million. *Unit head:* Dr. Colleen Conway-Welch, Dean, 615-343-8776, Fax: 615-343-7711, E-mail: colleen.conway-welch@vanderbilt.edu. *Application contact:* Patricia Peerman, Assistant

Dean for Enrollment Management, 615-322-3800, Fax: 615-343-0333, E-mail: vusn-admissions@vanderbilt.edu. Web site: http://www.nursing.vanderbilt.edu.

Virginia Polytechnic Institute and State University, Graduate School, College of Liberal Arts and Human Sciences, Department of Human Development, Blacksburg, VA 24061. Offers gerontology (Certificate); human development (MS, PhD); marriage and family therapy (Certificate). *Accreditation:* AAMFT/COAMFTE (one or more programs are accredited). *Degree requirements:* For master's, comprehensive exam (for some programs), thesis (for some programs); for doctorate, comprehensive exam (for some programs), thesis/dissertation (for some programs). *Entrance requirements:* For master's and doctorate, GRE. Additional exam requirements/recommendations for international students: Required—TOEFL (minimum score 550 paper-based; 213 computer-based). *Application deadline:* For fall admission, 7/1 for domestic and international students; for spring admission, 12/1 for domestic and international students. Applications are processed on a rolling basis. Application fee: $65. Electronic applications accepted. *Expenses:* Tuition, state resident: full-time $10,048; part-time $558.25 per credit hour. Tuition, nonresident: full-time $19,497; part-time $1083.25 per credit hour. *Required fees:* $405 per semester. Tuition and fees vary according to course load, campus/location and program. *Financial support:* Research assistantships with full tuition reimbursements, teaching assistantships with full tuition reimbursements, career-related internships or fieldwork, Federal Work-Study, scholarships/grants, health care benefits, and unspecified assistantships available. Financial award application deadline: 1/15. *Faculty research:* Stress management, children's play, dual-career families, social cognition, relationships of elderly. *Unit head:* Dr. Sharron E. Jarrott, Unit Head, 540-231-5434, Fax: 540-231-7012, E-mail: sjarrott@vt.edu. *Application contact:* Mark Benson, Information Contact, 540-231-5720, Fax: 540-231-7012, E-mail: mbenson@vt.edu. Web site: http://www.humandevelopment.vt.edu/grad.html.

Wayne State University, College of Liberal Arts and Sciences, Department of Political Science, Program in Public Administration, Detroit, MI 48202. Offers aging policy and management (MPA); criminal justice policy and management (MPA); economic development policy and management (MPA); health services policy and management (MPA); human resources management (MPA); information technology management (MPA); non-profit management (MPA); organizational behavior and management (MPA); public budgeting and financial management (MPA); public policy analysis and program evaluation (MPA); social welfare policy and management (MPA); urban policy and management (MPA). *Accreditation:* NASPAA. Evening/weekend programs available. *Students:* 22 full-time (17 women), 45 part-time (33 women); includes 19 minority (16 Black or African American, non-Hispanic/Latino; 1 American Indian or Alaska Native, non-Hispanic/Latino; 2 Hispanic/Latino), 1 international. Average age 31. 75 applicants, 28% accepted, 11 enrolled. In 2011, 20 master's awarded. *Degree requirements:* For master's, comprehensive exam. *Entrance requirements:* For master's, GRE General Test. Additional exam requirements/recommendations for international students: Required—TOEFL (minimum score 550 paper-based; 213 computer-based); Recommended—TWE (minimum score 5.5). *Application deadline:* For fall admission, 6/1 priority date for domestic students, 5/1 for international students; for winter admission, 10/1 priority date for domestic students, 9/1 for international students; for spring admission, 2/1 priority date for domestic students, 1/1 for international students. Applications are processed on a rolling basis. Application fee: $50. Electronic applications accepted. *Expenses:* Tuition, state resident: part-time $512.85 per credit. Tuition, nonresident: part-time $1132.65 per credit. *Required fees:* $26.60 per credit. $199.65 per semester. Tuition and fees vary according to course load and program. *Financial support:* In 2011–12, 7 students received support. Scholarships/grants available. *Faculty research:* Urban politics, urban education, state administration. *Unit head:* Dr. Brady Baybeck, Director, 313-577-2630, E-mail: mpa@wayne.edu. Web site: http://clasweb.clas.wayne.edu/mapa.

Wilmington University, College of Health Professions, New Castle, DE 19720-6491. Offers adult nurse practitioner (MSN); family nurse practitioner (MSN); gerontology nurse practitioner (MSN); nursing (MSN); nursing leadership (MSN); nursing practice (DNP). *Accreditation:* AACN. Part-time programs available. *Faculty:* 3 full-time (all women). *Students:* 30 full-time (all women), 270 part-time (241 women). Average age 38. *Degree requirements:* For master's, thesis. *Entrance requirements:* For master's, BSN, RN license, interview, 3 letters of recommendation. Additional exam requirements/recommendations for international students: Required—TOEFL (minimum score 500 paper-based; 173 computer-based). *Application deadline:* For fall admission, 4/1 for domestic students; for spring admission, 9/1 for domestic students. Applications are processed on a rolling basis. Application fee: $35. Electronic applications accepted. *Expenses: Tuition:* Part-time $534 per credit hour. *Required fees:* $25 per term. *Financial support:* Fellowships with tuition reimbursements and traineeships available. Financial award applicants required to submit FAFSA. *Faculty research:* Outcomes assessment, student writing ability. *Unit head:* Denise Z. Westbrook, Dean, 302-356-6915, E-mail: denise.z.westbrook@wilmu.edu. *Application contact:* Chris Ferguson, Director of Admissions, 302-356-4636 Ext. 256, Fax: 302-328-5164, E-mail: inquire@wilmcoll.edu. Web site: http://www.wilmu.edu/health/.

HIV/AIDS Nursing

University of Delaware, College of Health Sciences, School of Nursing, Newark, DE 19716. Offers adult nurse practitioner (MSN, PMC); cardiopulmonary clinical nurse specialist (MSN, PMC); cardiopulmonary clinical nurse specialist/adult nurse practitioner (MSN, PMC); family nurse practitioner (MSN, PMC); gerontology clinical nurse specialist (MSN, PMC); gerontology clinical nurse specialist geriatric nurse practitioner (PMC); gerontology clinical nurse specialist/geriatric nurse practitioner (MSN); health services administration (MSN, PMC); nursing of children clinical nurse specialist (MSN, PMC); nursing of children clinical nurse specialist/pediatric nurse practitioner (MSN, PMC); oncology/immune deficiency clinical nurse specialist (MSN, PMC); oncology/immune deficiency clinical nurse specialist/adult nurse practitioner (MSN, PMC); perinatal/women's health clinical nurse specialist (MSN, PMC); perinatal/women's health clinical

nurse specialist/women's health nurse practitioner (MSN, PMC); psychiatric nursing clinical nurse specialist (MSN, PMC). *Accreditation:* AACN; NLN (one or more programs are accredited). Part-time and evening/weekend programs available. Postbaccalaureate distance learning degree programs offered (minimal on-campus study). *Degree requirements:* For master's, thesis optional. *Entrance requirements:* For master's, BSN, interview, RN license. Electronic applications accepted. *Faculty research:* Marriage and chronic illness, health promotion, congestive heart failure patient outcomes, school nursing, diabetes in children, culture, health disparities, cardiovascular, prison nursing, oncology, public policy, child obesity, smoking and teen pregnancy, blood pressure measurements, men's health.

Hospice Nursing

Madonna University, Program in Hospice, Livonia, MI 48150-1173. Offers MSH. Part-time and evening/weekend programs available. *Degree requirements:* For master's, thesis or alternative. *Entrance requirements:* For master's, GRE General Test, minimum undergraduate GPA of 3.0, 2 letters of recommendation, interview. Electronic applications accepted.

Maternal and Child/Neonatal Nursing

Baylor University, Graduate School, Louise Herrington School of Nursing, Waco, TX 76798. Offers family nurse practitioner (MSN); neonatal nurse practitioner (MSN); nurse-midwifery (DNP). *Accreditation:* AACN. Part-time programs available. *Faculty:* 9 full-time (all women), 3 part-time/adjunct (2 women). *Students:* 33 full-time (32 women), 45 part-time (39 women); includes 17 minority (4 Black or African American, non-Hispanic/Latino; 4 Asian, non-Hispanic/Latino; 3 Hispanic/Latino; 6 Two or more races, non-Hispanic/Latino), 1 international. 62 applicants, 63% accepted, 37 enrolled. In 2011, 24 master's, 3 doctorates awarded. *Entrance requirements:* For master's, GRE General Test or MAT; for doctorate, GRE General Test. *Application deadline:* For fall admission, 4/1 for domestic students. Application fee: $40. Electronic applications accepted. *Financial support:* Applicants required to submit FAFSA. *Unit head:* Dr. Linda Plank, Graduate Program Director, 214-818-7847, Fax: 214-818-8692, E-mail: linda_plank@baylor.edu. *Application contact:* Beverly Kurfees, Academic Support Specialist, 214-367-3752, Fax: 254-710-3870, E-mail: beverly_kurfees@baylor.edu. Web site: http://www.baylor.edu/nursing/.

Boston College, William F. Connell School of Nursing, Chestnut Hill, MA 02467-3800. Offers adult-gerontology nursing (MS); community health nursing (MS); family health (MS); forensic nursing (MS); maternal/child health nursing (MS), including pediatric and women's health; nurse anesthesia (MS); nursing (PhD); palliative care (MS), including adult and pediatric; psychiatric-mental health nursing (MS); MBA/MS; MS/MA; MS/PhD. *Accreditation:* AACN; AANA/CANAEP (one or more programs are accredited). Part-time programs available. *Faculty:* 48 full-time (46 women), 31 part-time/adjunct (29 women). *Students:* 225 full-time (207 women), 90 part-time (88 women); includes 47 minority (15 Black or African American, non-Hispanic/Latino; 3 American Indian or Alaska Native, non-Hispanic/Latino; 17 Asian, non-Hispanic/Latino; 8 Hispanic/Latino; 4 Two or more races, non-Hispanic/Latino), 6 international. Average age 31. 369 applicants, 43% accepted, 80 enrolled. In 2011, 113 master's, 8 doctorates awarded. *Degree requirements:* For master's, comprehensive exam, research project; for doctorate, comprehensive exam, thesis/dissertation, computer literacy exam or foreign language. *Entrance requirements:* For master's, bachelor's degree in nursing; for doctorate, GRE General Test, MS in nursing. Additional exam requirements/recommendations for international students: Required—TOEFL (minimum score 600 paper-based; 250 computer-based; 100 iBT). *Application deadline:* For fall admission, 11/1 for domestic and international students; for winter admission, 12/31 for domestic and international students; for spring admission, 4/30 for domestic and international students. Applications are processed on a rolling basis. Application fee: $40. Electronic applications accepted. *Financial support:* In 2011–12, 167 students received support, including 9 fellowships with full tuition reimbursements available (averaging $15,300 per year), 7 teaching assistantships (averaging $13,612 per year); research assistantships, Federal Work-Study, institutionally sponsored loans, scholarships/grants, traineeships, health care benefits, tuition waivers (partial), and unspecified assistantships also available. Support available to part-time students. Financial award application deadline: 3/1; financial award applicants required to submit FAFSA. *Faculty research:* Pre-term labor, palliative care, support during chronic illness, violence, eating disorders. *Total annual research expenditures:* $2.1 million. *Unit head:* Dr. Susan Gennaro, Dean, 617-552-4251, Fax: 617-552-0931, E-mail: susan.gennaro@bc.edu. *Application contact:* MaryBeth Crowley, Graduate Programs Assistant, 617-552-4928, Fax: 617-552-2121, E-mail: csongrad@bc.edu. Web site: http://www.bc.edu/nursing/.

Case Western Reserve University, Frances Payne Bolton School of Nursing, Doctor of Nursing Practice Program, Cleveland, OH 44106. Offers acute care nurse practitioner (DNP); adult gerontology nurse practitioner (DNP); educational leadership (DNP); family nurse practitioner (DNP); family systems psychiatric mental health nursing (DNP); midwifery/family nursing (DNP); neonatal nurse practitioner (DNP); pediatric nurse practitioner (DNP); practice leadership (DNP); women's health nurse practitioner (DNP). *Students:* 73 full-time, 194 part-time; includes 11 minority (6 Black or African American, non-Hispanic/Latino; 3 Asian, non-Hispanic/Latino; 2 Hispanic/Latino). 122 applicants, 74% accepted, 49 enrolled. In 2011, 47 doctorates awarded. Terminal master's awarded for partial completion of doctoral program. *Degree requirements:* For doctorate, thesis/dissertation. *Entrance requirements:* For doctorate, GRE General Test or MAT. Additional exam requirements/recommendations for international students: Required—TOEFL (minimum score 577 paper-based; 90 iBT), IELTS (minimum score 7). *Application deadline:* For fall admission, 6/1 priority date for domestic students, 6/1 for international students; for spring admission, 10/1 for domestic and international students. Applications are processed on a rolling basis. Application fee: $75. *Financial support:* In 2011–12, 6 students received support, including 1 teaching assistantship; research assistantships, Federal Work-Study, institutionally sponsored loans, and tuition waivers (partial) also available. Support available to part-time students. Financial award application deadline: 6/30; financial award applicants required to submit FAFSA. *Faculty research:* Clinical nursing, acute care, gerontology, mental health, critical care. *Unit head:* Dr. Donna Dowling, Director, 216-368-1869, Fax: 216-368-3542, E-mail: dad10@case.edu. *Application contact:* Donna Hassik, Admissions Coordinator, 216-368-5253, Fax: 216-368-0124, E-mail: dmh7@case.edu. Web site: http://fpb.case.edu/DNP/.

Case Western Reserve University, Frances Payne Bolton School of Nursing, Master's Programs in Nursing, Nurse Practitioner Program, Cleveland, OH 44106. Offers acute care cardiovascular nursing (MSN); acute care nurse practitioner (MSN); acute care/flight nurse (MSN); adult gerontology nurse practitioner (MSN); family nurse practitioner (MSN); neonatal nurse practitioner (MSN); pediatric nurse practitioner (MSN); women's health nurse practitioner (MSN). *Accreditation:* NLN. Part-time programs available. Postbaccalaureate distance learning degree programs offered (minimal on-campus study). *Faculty:* 54 full-time (50 women), 5 part-time/adjunct (3 women). *Students:* 89 full-time (69 women), 77 part-time (67 women); includes 17 minority (11 Black or African American, non-Hispanic/Latino; 5 Asian, non-Hispanic/Latino; 1 Hispanic/Latino), 17 international. Average age 35. 75 applicants, 84% accepted, 42 enrolled. In 2011, 34 master's awarded. *Degree requirements:* For master's, thesis optional. *Entrance requirements:* For master's, GRE General Test or MAT. Additional exam requirements/recommendations for international students: Required—TOEFL (minimum score 577 paper-based; 90 iBT), IELTS (minimum score 7). *Application deadline:* For fall admission, 6/1 for domestic students; for spring admission, 10/1 for domestic students. Applications are processed on a rolling basis. Application fee: $75. *Financial support:* In 2011–12, 7 teaching assistantships were awarded; research assistantships, institutionally sponsored loans, and tuition waivers (partial) also available. Support available to part-time students. Financial award application deadline: 6/30; financial award applicants required to submit FAFSA. *Faculty research:* Positive and negative mood states in parents of twins, effect of a care path on chronic obstructive pulmonary disease home care. *Unit head:* Dr. Carol Savrin, Director, 216-368-5304, Fax: 216-368-3542, E-mail: cls18@case.edu. *Application contact:* Donna Hassik, Admissions Coordinator, 216-368-5253, Fax: 216-368-0124, E-mail: dmh7@case.edu. Web site: http://fpb.cwru.edu/MSN/majors.shtm.

Columbia University, School of Nursing, Program in Neonatal Nurse Practitioner, New York, NY 10032. Offers MS, Adv C. *Accreditation:* AACN. Part-time programs available. *Entrance requirements:* For master's, GRE General Test, BSN, 1 year of neonatal intensive care unit experience; for Adv C, MSN. Electronic applications accepted.

Duke University, School of Nursing, Durham, NC 27708-0586. Offers adult acute care (Certificate); adult cardiovascular (Certificate); adult oncology (Certificate); adult primary care (Certificate); clinical nurse specialist (MSN), including adult oncology, gerontology, neonatal, pediatric; clinical research management (MSN, Certificate); family (Certificate); gerontology (Certificate); health and nursing ministries (MSN, Certificate); health systems leadership and outcomes (Certificate); neonatal (Certificate); neonatal/pediatric in rural health (MSN, Certificate); nurse anesthetist (MSN, Certificate); nurse practitioner (MSN), including adult acute care, adult cardiovascular, adult oncology, adult primary care, family, gerontology, neonatal, pediatric, pediatric acute care; nursing (DNP, PhD); nursing and healthcare leadership (MSN); nursing education (MSN); nursing informatics (MSN, Certificate); pediatric (Certificate); pediatric acute care (Certificate); MBA/MSN; MSN/MCM. *Accreditation:* AACN; AANA/CANAEP. Part-time and evening/weekend programs available. Postbaccalaureate distance learning degree programs offered (minimal on-campus study). *Faculty:* 56 full-time (47 women), 2 part-time/adjunct (1 woman). *Students:* 127 full-time (108 women), 395 part-time (358 women); includes 92 minority (42 Black or African American, non-Hispanic/Latino; 3 American Indian or Alaska Native, non-Hispanic/Latino; 21 Asian, non-Hispanic/Latino; 14 Hispanic/Latino; 12 Two or more races, non-Hispanic/Latino), 10 international. Average age 36. 432 applicants, 45% accepted, 143 enrolled. In 2011, 117 master's, 29 doctorates, 32 other advanced degrees awarded. Terminal master's awarded for partial completion of doctoral program. *Degree requirements:* For master's, thesis optional; for doctorate, capstone project. *Entrance requirements:* For master's, GRE General Test, 1 year of nursing experience, BSN, minimum GPA of 3.0, previous course work in statistics; for doctorate, BSN or MSN, minimum GPA of 3.0, portfolio; for Certificate, MSN. Additional exam requirements/recommendations for international students: Required—TOEFL (minimum score 550 paper-based; 213 computer-based). *Application deadline:* For fall admission, 12/1 for domestic and international students; for spring admission, 5/1 for domestic and international students. Application fee: $50. Electronic applications accepted. *Expenses:* Contact institution. *Financial support:* Career-related internships or fieldwork, institutionally sponsored loans, scholarships/grants, traineeships, and tuition waivers (partial) available. Support available to part-time students. Financial award application deadline: 4/1; financial award applicants required to submit FAFSA. *Faculty research:* Cardiovascular disease, caregiver skill training, data mining, prostate cancer, neonatal immune system. *Total annual research expenditures:* $4.7 million. *Unit head:* Dr. Catherine L. Gilliss, Dean/Vice Chancellor for Nursing Affairs, 919-684-9444, Fax: 919-684-9414, E-mail: gilli025@mc.duke.edu. *Application contact:* Bebe T. Mills, Director of Admissions, 919-684-9151, Fax: 919-668-4693, E-mail: mills031@mc.duke.edu. Web site: http://www.nursing.duke.edu/.

Hardin-Simmons University, Graduate School, Patty Hanks Shelton School of Nursing, Abilene, TX 79698-0001. Offers advanced healthcare delivery (MSN); family nurse practitioner (MSN). Programs offered jointly with Abilene Christian University and McMurry University. *Accreditation:* AACN. Part-time programs available. *Faculty:* 6 full-time (all women), 3 part-time/adjunct (all women). *Students:* 10 full-time (9 women), 7 part-time (2 women); includes 5 minority (3 Black or African American, non-Hispanic/Latino; 2 Hispanic/Latino). Average age 35. 12 applicants, 100% accepted, 11 enrolled. In 2011, 4 master's awarded. *Degree requirements:* For master's, comprehensive exam, thesis or alternative. *Entrance requirements:* For master's, GRE, minimum undergraduate GPA of 3.0 in major, 2.8 overall; interview; upper-level course work in statistics; CPR certification; letters of recommendation. Additional exam requirements/recommendations for international students: Required—TOEFL (minimum score 550 paper-based; 213 computer-based; 75 iBT). *Application deadline:* For fall admission, 8/15 priority date for domestic students, 4/1 for international students; for spring admission, 1/5 priority date for domestic students, 9/1 for international students. Applications are processed on a rolling basis. Application fee: $50. *Expenses:* Contact institution. *Financial support:* In 2011–12, 14 students received support. Career-related internships or fieldwork and scholarships/grants available. Support available to part-time students. Financial award application deadline: 6/30; financial award applicants required to submit FAFSA. *Faculty research:* Child abuse, alternative medicine, pediatric chronic disease, health promotion. *Unit head:* Dr. Amy Toone, Director, 325-671-2361, Fax: 325-671-2386, E-mail: atoone@phssn.edu. *Application contact:* Dr. Nancy Kucinski, Dean of Graduate Studies, 325-670-1298, Fax: 325-670-1564, E-mail: gradoff@hsutx.edu. Web site: http://www.phssn.edu/.

Indiana University–Purdue University Indianapolis, School of Nursing, Indianapolis, IN 46202-2896. Offers acute care nurse practitioner (MSN); adult health clinical nurse specialist (MSN); adult health nursing (MSN), including adult clinical nurse specialist; adult nurse practitioner (MSN); adult psychiatric/mental health nursing (MSN); child

psychiatric/mental health nursing (MSN); community health nursing (MSN); family nurse practitioner (MSN); neonatal nurse practitioner (MSN); nursing (MSN, DNP), including nursing education (MSN); nursing (MSN), including nursing administration; nursing science (PhD); pediatric clinical nurse specialist (MSN); women's health nurse practitioner (MSN); MSN/MPA; MSN/MPH. *Accreditation:* AACN; NLN (one or more programs are accredited). Part-time programs available. *Faculty:* 85 full-time (82 women), 60 part-time/adjunct (all women). *Students:* 35 full-time (32 women), 360 part-time (340 women); includes 47 minority (28 Black or African American, non-Hispanic/Latino; 9 Asian, non-Hispanic/Latino; 4 Hispanic/Latino; 1 Native Hawaiian or other Pacific Islander, non-Hispanic/Latino; 5 Two or more races, non-Hispanic/Latino), 5 international. Average age 38. 119 applicants, 76% accepted, 54 enrolled. In 2011, 89 master's, 10 doctorates awarded. Terminal master's awarded for partial completion of doctoral program. *Degree requirements:* For master's, thesis; for doctorate, thesis/dissertation. *Entrance requirements:* For master's, minimum GPA of 3.0, RN license; for doctorate, GRE General Test, minimum GPA of 3.0, MSN, RN license, graduate statistics course with minimum B grade (not older than 3 years). Additional exam requirements/recommendations for international students: Required—TOEFL. *Application deadline:* For fall admission, 2/15 for domestic students; for spring admission, 9/15 for domestic students. Application fee: $55 ($65 for international students). *Financial support:* In 2011–12, 93 students received support, including 9 fellowships with full tuition reimbursements available (averaging $7,039 per year), 7 teaching assistantships with full tuition reimbursements available (averaging $5,300 per year); research assistantships with full tuition reimbursements available, Federal Work-Study, institutionally sponsored loans, scholarships/grants, and tuition waivers (full) also available. Support available to part-time students. Financial award application deadline: 5/1. *Faculty research:* Clinical science, health systems. *Total annual research expenditures:* $3 million. *Unit head:* Associate Dean for Graduate Programs, 317-274-2806, E-mail: nursing@iupui.edu. *Application contact:* Information Contact, 317-274-2806. Web site: http://nursing.iupui.edu/.

Lehman College of the City University of New York, Division of Natural and Social Sciences, Department of Nursing, Bronx, NY 10468-1589. Offers adult health nursing (MS); nursing of older adults (MS); parent-child nursing (MS); pediatric nurse practitioner (MS). *Accreditation:* AACN. Part-time and evening/weekend programs available. *Entrance requirements:* For master's, bachelor's degree in nursing, New York RN license.

Marquette University, Graduate School, College of Nursing, Milwaukee, WI 53201-1881. Offers acute care nurse practitioner (Certificate); adult clinical nurse specialist (Certificate); adult nurse practitioner (Certificate); advanced practice nursing (MSN, DNP), including acute care, adults, neonatal nurse practitioner (MSN), nurse midwifery (DNP), nurse-midwifery (MSN), older adults, pediatrics acute care (DNP, PhD); pediatrics primary care; clinical nurse leader (MSN); gerontologic clinical nurse specialist (Certificate); gerontologic nurse practitioner (Certificate); health care systems leadership (MSN, DNP); nurse-midwifery (Certificate); nursing (PhD), including pediatrics acute care (DNP, PhD); pediatrics acute care (Certificate); pediatrics primary care (Certificate). *Accreditation:* AACN. *Faculty:* 32 full-time (30 women), 47 part-time/adjunct (all women). *Students:* 93 full-time (88 women), 244 part-time (220 women); includes 31 minority (9 Black or African American, non-Hispanic/Latino; 7 Asian, non-Hispanic/Latino; 8 Hispanic/Latino; 7 Two or more races, non-Hispanic/Latino), 1 international. Average age 30. 282 applicants, 57% accepted, 98 enrolled. In 2011, 76 master's, 8 doctorates, 7 other advanced degrees awarded. Terminal master's awarded for partial completion of doctoral program. *Degree requirements:* For master's, comprehensive exam, thesis or alternative. *Entrance requirements:* For master's, GRE General Test, BSN, Wisconsin RN license, official transcripts from all current and previous colleges/universities except Marquette, three completed recommendation forms, resume, written statement of professional goals; for doctorate, GRE General Test, official transcripts from all current and previous colleges/universities except Marquette, three letters of recommendation, resume, written statement of professional goals, sample of scholarly writing. Additional exam requirements/recommendations for international students: Required—TOEFL (minimum score 530 paper-based; 78 computer-based). *Application deadline:* For fall admission, 2/15 for domestic and international students. Application fee: $50. Electronic applications accepted. *Expenses: Tuition:* Full-time $17,010; part-time $945 per credit hour. Tuition and fees vary according to program. *Financial support:* In 2011–12, 41 students received support, including 1 fellowship with partial tuition reimbursement available (averaging $17,500 per year), 2 research assistantships with full tuition reimbursements available (averaging $13,285 per year), 8 teaching assistantships with full tuition reimbursements available (averaging $13,912 per year); career-related internships or fieldwork, Federal Work-Study, scholarships/grants, health care benefits, tuition waivers (partial), and unspecified assistantships also available. Support available to part-time students. Financial award application deadline: 2/15. *Faculty research:* Psychosocial adjustment to chronic illness, gerontology, reminiscence, health policy: uninsured and access, hospital care delivery systems. *Total annual research expenditures:* $312,575. *Unit head:* Dr. Margaret Callahan, Dean, 414-288-3800, Fax: 414-288-1578. *Application contact:* Karen Nest, Graduate Program Coordinator, 414-288-3810, Fax: 414-288-1578. Web site: http://www.marquette.edu/nursing/academicprograms-graduate.shtml.

Medical University of South Carolina, College of Nursing, Pediatric Nurse Practitioner Program, Charleston, SC 29425. Offers MSN. *Accreditation:* AACN. Part-time programs available. *Faculty:* 7 full-time (all women), 3 part-time/adjunct (2 women). *Students:* 1 (woman) full-time, 3 part-time (all women); includes 1 minority (Hispanic/Latino). Average age 28. 44 applicants, 52% accepted. In 2011, 8 master's awarded. *Degree requirements:* For master's, comprehensive exam (for some programs), thesis optional. *Entrance requirements:* For master's, BSN, course work in statistics, nursing license, minimum GPA of 3.0, current curriculum vitae, essay, three references. Additional exam requirements/recommendations for international students: Required—TOEFL (minimum score 600 paper-based; 250 computer-based). *Application deadline:* For fall admission, 2/1 priority date for domestic students, 2/1 for international students. Application fee: $85. Electronic applications accepted. *Financial support:* Federal Work-Study, scholarships/grants, and traineeships available. Support available to part-time students. Financial award application deadline: 3/10; financial award applicants required to submit FAFSA. *Faculty research:* Epilepsy management, ADHD/ADD management, school-based clinics. *Unit head:* Georgette M. Smith, Lead Faculty, 843-792-4611, Fax: 843-792-5395, E-mail: smithgi@musc.edu. *Application contact:* Carolyn F. Page, Director, Student Services, 843-792-3844, Fax: 843-792-5395, E-mail: pagecf@musc.edu. Web site: http://www.musc.edu/nursing/academics/masters/pediatricnursing.htm.

Northeastern University, Bouvé College of Health Sciences, School of Nursing, Program in Critical Care-Neonatal Nurse Practitioner, Boston, MA 02115-5096. Offers MS, CAS. *Accreditation:* AACN. *Faculty:* 25 full-time, 4 part-time/adjunct. *Students:* 4 full-time, 3 part-time. 7 applicants, 100% accepted, 5 enrolled. *Degree requirements:* For master's, thesis or alternative. *Entrance requirements:* For master's, GRE General Test, minimum GPA of 3.0, previous course work in statistics, 1-2 years of nursing experience, RN license, ICU experience. Additional exam requirements/recommendations for international students: Required—TOEFL (minimum score 100 iBT). *Application deadline:* For fall admission, 7/1 for domestic students. Application fee: $50. Electronic applications accepted. *Financial support:* Research assistantships, teaching assistantships, scholarships/grants, traineeships, and tuition waivers (partial) available. Financial award application deadline: 7/1; financial award applicants required to submit FAFSA. *Unit head:* Prof. Gretchen R. Hamn, Director, 617-373-6543, E-mail: g.hamn@neu.edu. *Application contact:* Margaret Schnabel, Director of Graduate Admissions, 617-373-2708, E-mail: bouvegrad@neu.edu. Web site: http://www.northeastern.edu/bouve/programs/cneonatal.html.

Regis University, Rueckert-Hartman College for Health Professions, Denver, CO 80221-1099. Offers family nurse practitioner (MSN); health informatics (Postbaccalaureate Certificate); health services administration (MS); leadership in healthcare systems (MSN); neonatal nurse practitioner (MSN); nursing (MSN); pharmacy (Pharm D); physical therapy (DPT, TDPT). *Entrance requirements:* Additional exam requirements/recommendations for international students: Required—TOEFL (minimum score 550 paper-based; 213 computer-based; 82 iBT). Electronic applications accepted. *Expenses:* Contact institution. *Faculty research:* Normal and pathological balance and gait research, normal/pathological upper limb motor control/biomechanics, exercise energy/metabolism research, optical treatment protocols for therapeutic modalities.

Rush University, College of Nursing, Department of Women's and Children's Health Nursing, Chicago, IL 60612-3832. Offers neonatal nurse practitioner (MSN, Post-Master's Certificate); pediatric acute/chronic care nurse practitioner (MSN); pediatric clinical nurse specialist (MSN); pediatric nurse practitioner (MSN, Post-Master's Certificate); women's and children's health nursing (DNP, PhD). *Accreditation:* AACN. Part-time programs available. Postbaccalaureate distance learning degree programs offered (minimal on-campus study). Terminal master's awarded for partial completion of doctoral program. *Degree requirements:* For master's, capstone project; for doctorate, thesis/dissertation, DNP leadership project. *Entrance requirements:* For master's, GRE General Test (waived if nursing GPA is above 3.0 or cumulative GPA is above 3.25), interview; for doctorate, GRE General Test, interview, course work in statistics (PhD). Additional exam requirements/recommendations for international students: Required—TOEFL, TWE. Electronic applications accepted. *Faculty research:* Family-centered care, women's health, health outcomes of human milk feeding for VhBW infants.

Rutgers, The State University of New Jersey, Newark, Graduate School, Program in Nursing, Newark, NJ 07102. Offers nursing (MS), including acute care of adults and aged, advanced practice in pediatric nursing, advanced practice with childbearing families, community health nursing, family nurse practitioner, primary care of adults and aged, psychiatric/mental health nursing. *Accreditation:* AACN. Part-time programs available. *Degree requirements:* For master's, comprehensive exam. *Entrance requirements:* For master's, GRE General Test, RN license, minimum B average, BS in nursing. Additional exam requirements/recommendations for international students: Required—TOEFL. Electronic applications accepted. *Faculty research:* HIV/AIDS, quality of life: MS and breast cancer, sleep patterns of cardiac patients.

St. Catherine University, Graduate Programs, Program in Nursing, St. Paul, MN 55105. Offers adult-gerontological nurse practitioner (MA); neonatal nurse practitioner (MA); nurse educator (MA); nursing (DNP); pediatric nurse practitioner (MA). *Accreditation:* NLN. Part-time and evening/weekend programs available. *Degree requirements:* For master's, thesis; for doctorate, portfolio, systems change project. *Entrance requirements:* For master's, GRE General Test, bachelor's degree in nursing, current nursing license, 2 years of recent clinical practice; for doctorate, master's degree in nursing, RN license, advanced nursing position. Additional exam requirements/recommendations for international students: Required—TOEFL (minimum score 600 paper-based; 250 computer-based; 100 iBT). *Expenses: Required fees:* $30 per semester. Tuition and fees vary according to program.

Saint Francis Medical Center College of Nursing, Graduate Programs, Peoria, IL 61603-3783. Offers child and family nurse practitioner (MSN); clinical nurse leader (MSN); family nurse practitioner (MSN); family psychiatric mental health nurse practitioner (MSN); medical-surgical nursing (MSN); neonatal nurse practitioner (MSN); nurse clinician (Post-Graduate Certificate); nurse educator (MSN, Post-Graduate Certificate); nursing (DNP); nursing management leadership (MSN). *Accreditation:* NLN. Part-time programs available. Postbaccalaureate distance learning degree programs offered (minimal on-campus study). *Faculty:* 6 full-time (all women), 5 part-time/adjunct (all women). *Students:* 26 full-time (25 women), 174 part-time (166 women); includes 19 minority (8 Black or African American, non-Hispanic/Latino; 1 American Indian or Alaska Native, non-Hispanic/Latino; 3 Asian, non-Hispanic/Latino; 6 Hispanic/Latino; 1 Native Hawaiian or other Pacific Islander, non-Hispanic/Latino). Average age 37. 123 applicants, 93% accepted, 93 enrolled. In 2011, 29 degrees awarded. *Degree requirements:* For master's, research experience, portfolio, practicum; for doctorate, practicum hours. *Entrance requirements:* For master's, nursing research, health assessment, graduate course work in statistics, RN license; for doctorate, master's degree in nursing, professional portfolio, graduate statistics, transcripts, RN license. Additional exam requirements/recommendations for international students: Required—TOEFL. *Application deadline:* For fall admission, 6/1 priority date for domestic students, 6/1 for international students; for spring admission, 11/15 priority date for domestic students, 11/15 for international students. Applications are processed on a rolling basis. Application fee: $50. Electronic applications accepted. *Expenses: Tuition:* Full-time $6120; part-time $510 per semester hour. *Required fees:* $300. *Financial support:* In 2011–12, 3 students received support. Scholarships/grants and tuition waivers (partial) available. Support available to part-time students. Financial award application deadline: 6/15; financial award applicants required to submit FAFSA. *Faculty research:* Outcome and curriculum planning, health promotion, NCLEX-RN results, decision-making program evaluation. *Unit head:* Dr. Patti A. Stockert, President of the College, 309-655-4124, Fax: 309-624-8973, E-mail: patricia.a.stockert@osfhealthcare.org. *Application contact:* Dr. Janice F. Boundy, Dean, 309-655-2230, Fax: 309-624-8973, E-mail: jan.f.boundy@osfhealthcare.org. Web site: http://www.sfmccon.edu/graduate-programs/.

Stony Brook University, State University of New York, Stony Brook University Medical Center, Health Sciences Center, School of Nursing, Program in Neonatal Nursing, Stony Brook, NY 11794. Offers neonatal nurse practitioner (Certificate); neonatal nursing (MS). *Accreditation:* AACN. Postbaccalaureate distance learning degree programs offered. *Degree requirements:* For master's, thesis. *Entrance requirements:* For master's, BSN, minimum GPA of 3.0, course work in statistics.

Stony Brook University, State University of New York, Stony Brook University Medical Center, Health Sciences Center, School of Nursing, Program in Perinatal Women's Health Nursing, Stony Brook, NY 11794. Offers MS, Certificate. *Accreditation:* AACN. Postbaccalaureate distance learning degree programs offered. *Degree requirements:* For master's, thesis. *Entrance requirements:* For master's, BSN, minimum GPA of 3.0, course work in statistics.

University of Alberta, Faculty of Medicine and Dentistry and Faculty of Graduate Studies and Research, Graduate Programs in Medicine, Department of Obstetrics and Gynecology, Edmonton, AB T6G 2E1, Canada. Offers MD. *Entrance requirements:* Additional exam requirements/recommendations for international students: Required—TOEFL. *Faculty research:* Parturition, fetal/neonatal lung development, nitric oxide, vascular reactivity, pre-eclampsia gestational diabetes.

Maternal and Child/Neonatal Nursing

University of Cincinnati, Graduate School, College of Nursing, Cincinnati, OH 45221-0038. Offers clinical nurse specialist (MSN), including adult health, community health, neonatal, nursing administration, occupational health, pediatric health, psychiatric nursing, women's health; nurse anesthesia (MSN); nurse midwifery (MSN); nurse practitioner (MSN), including acute care, ambulatory care, family, family/psychiatric, women's health; nursing (PhD); MBA/MSN. *Accreditation:* AACN; AANA/CANAEP (one or more programs are accredited); ACNM/ACME. Part-time programs available. Postbaccalaureate distance learning degree programs offered (no on-campus study). Terminal master's awarded for partial completion of doctoral program. *Degree requirements:* For master's, thesis or alternative; for doctorate, comprehensive exam, thesis/dissertation. *Entrance requirements:* For master's and doctorate, GRE General Test. Additional exam requirements/recommendations for international students: Required—TOEFL (minimum score 520 paper-based; 190 computer-based). Electronic applications accepted. *Faculty research:* Substance abuse, injury and violence, symptom management.

University of Colorado at Colorado Springs, Beth-El College of Nursing and Health Sciences, Colorado Springs, CO 80933-7150. Offers adult health nurse practitioner and clinical specialist (MSN); family practitioner (MSN), including community clinical specialist, forensic clinical specialist, holistic clinical specialist; neonatal nurse practitioner and clinical specialist (MSN); nursing administration (MSN); nursing practice (DNP); women nurse practitioner (MSN). *Accreditation:* AACN. Part-time programs available. Postbaccalaureate distance learning degree programs offered (minimal on-campus study). *Faculty:* 31 full-time (28 women), 6 part-time/adjunct (all women). *Students:* 122 full-time (103 women), 68 part-time (64 women); includes 36 minority (4 Black or African American, non-Hispanic/Latino; 2 American Indian or Alaska Native, non-Hispanic/Latino; 9 Asian, non-Hispanic/Latino; 18 Hispanic/Latino; 3 Two or more races, non-Hispanic/Latino), 5 international. Average age 35. 153 applicants, 71% accepted, 60 enrolled. In 2011, 41 master's, 15 doctorates awarded. *Degree requirements:* For master's, comprehensive exam, thesis optional; for doctorate, capstone project. *Entrance requirements:* For master's, GRE General Test or MAT, BSN, minimum GPA of 3.0, unrestricted RN license; for doctorate, interview; active RN license; MA; minimum GPA of 3.3; National Certification as NP or CNS; portfolio. Additional exam requirements/recommendations for international students: Required—TOEFL. *Application deadline:* For fall admission, 6/15 priority date for domestic students; for spring admission, 11/15 for domestic students. Application fee: $60 ($75 for international students). Electronic applications accepted. *Expenses:* Contact institution. *Financial support:* In 2011–12, 33 students received support, including 1 fellowship (averaging $2,500 per year); career-related internships or fieldwork, Federal Work-Study, and scholarships/grants also available. Support available to part-time students. Financial award application deadline: 3/1; financial award applicants required to submit FAFSA. *Faculty research:* Women's health, uncertainty, empowerment, family experience in chronic illness. *Total annual research expenditures:* $322,604. *Unit head:* Dr. Nancy Smith, Dean, 719-255-4411, Fax: 719-255-4416, E-mail: nsmith2@uccs.edu. *Application contact:* Diane Busch, Director, 719-255-4424, Fax: 719-255-4416, E-mail: dbusch@uccs.edu. Web site: http://www.uccs.edu/~bethel.

University of Delaware, College of Health Sciences, School of Nursing, Newark, DE 19716. Offers adult nurse practitioner (MSN, PMC); cardiopulmonary clinical nurse specialist (MSN, PMC); cardiopulmonary clinical nurse specialist/adult nurse practitioner (MSN, PMC); family nurse practitioner (MSN, PMC); gerontology clinical nurse specialist (MSN, PMC); gerontology clinical nurse specialist geriatric nurse practitioner (PMC); gerontology clinical nurse specialist/geriatric nurse practitioner (MSN); health services administration (MSN, PMC); nursing of children clinical nurse specialist (MSN, PMC); nursing of children clinical nurse specialist/pediatric nurse practitioner (MSN, PMC); oncology/immune deficiency clinical nurse specialist (MSN, PMC); oncology/immune deficiency clinical nurse specialist/adult nurse practitioner (MSN, PMC); perinatal/women's health clinical nurse specialist (MSN, PMC); perinatal/women's health clinical nurse specialist/women's health nurse practitioner (MSN, PMC); psychiatric nursing clinical nurse specialist (MSN, PMC). *Accreditation:* AACN; NLN (one or more programs are accredited). Part-time and evening/weekend programs available. Postbaccalaureate distance learning degree programs offered (minimal on-campus study). *Degree requirements:* For master's, thesis optional. *Entrance requirements:* For master's, BSN, interview, RN license. Electronic applications accepted. *Faculty research:* Marriage and chronic illness, health promotion, congestive heart failure patient outcomes, school nursing, diabetes in children, culture, health disparities, cardiovascular, prison nursing, oncology, public policy, child obesity, smoking and teen pregnancy, blood pressure measurements, men's health.

University of Illinois at Chicago, Graduate College, College of Nursing, Program in Nursing, Chicago, IL 60607-7128. Offers acute care clinical nurse specialist (MS); acute care nurse practitioner (MS); administrative studies in nursing (MS); adult nurse practitioner (MS); adult/geriatric nurse practitioner (MS); advanced community health nurse specialist (MS); family nurse practitioner (MS); geriatric clinical nurse specialist (MS); geriatric nurse practitioner (MS); mental health clinical nurse specialist (MS); mental health nurse practitioner (MS); nurse midwifery (MS); occupational health/advanced community health nurse specialist (MS); occupational health/family nurse practitioner (MS); pediatric clinical nurse specialist (MS); pediatric nurse practitioner (MS); perinatal clinical nurse specialist (MS); school/advanced community health nurse specialist (MS); school/family nurse practitioner (MS); women's health nurse practitioner (MS). *Accreditation:* AACN. Part-time programs available. *Degree requirements:* For master's, thesis or alternative. *Entrance requirements:* For master's, GRE General Test, minimum GPA of 2.75. Additional exam requirements/recommendations for international students: Required—TOEFL. Electronic applications accepted.

University of Louisville, Graduate School, School of Nursing, Louisville, KY 40202. Offers adult nurse practitioner (MSN); family nurse practitioner (MSN); health professions education (MSN); neonatal nurse practitioner (MSN); nursing research (PhD); psychiatric mental health nurse practitioner (MSN). *Accreditation:* AACN. Part-time programs available. *Faculty:* 24 full-time (22 women), 4 part-time/adjunct (3 women). *Students:* 82 full-time (74 women), 65 part-time (58 women); includes 20 minority (13 Black or African American, non-Hispanic/Latino; 1 American Indian or Alaska Native, non-Hispanic/Latino; 1 Asian, non-Hispanic/Latino; 1 Hispanic/Latino; 4 Two or more races, non-Hispanic/Latino), 2 international. Average age 34. 41 applicants, 56% accepted, 19 enrolled. In 2011, 42 master's, 2 doctorates awarded. Terminal master's awarded for partial completion of doctoral program. *Degree requirements:* For master's, thesis optional; for doctorate, comprehensive exam, thesis/dissertation. *Entrance requirements:* For master's, GRE General Test, bachelor's degree in nursing, minimum GPA of 3.0, RN license; for doctorate, GRE General Test, BSN or MSN with recommended minimum GPA of 3.0. Additional exam requirements/recommendations for international students: Required—TOEFL. *Application deadline:* For fall admission, 4/1 priority date for domestic students, 4/1 for international students. Applications are processed on a rolling basis. Application fee: $50. Electronic applications accepted. *Expenses:* Tuition, state resident: full-time $9692; part-time $539 per credit hour. Tuition, nonresident: full-time $20,168; part-time $1121 per credit hour. Tuition and fees vary according to program and reciprocity agreements. *Financial support:* In 2011–12, 45 students received support, including 6 research assistantships with full tuition reimbursements available (averaging $20,000 per year), 6 teaching assistantships with full tuition reimbursements available (averaging $19,167 per year); fellowships with full tuition reimbursements available, institutionally sponsored loans, scholarships/grants, traineeships, health care benefits, and unspecified assistantships also available. Support available to part-time students. Financial award application deadline: 4/15; financial award applicants required to submit FAFSA. *Faculty research:* Maternal-child/family stress after pregnancy loss, postpartum depression, access to healthcare (underserved populations), quality of life issues, physical activity (impact on chronic/acute conditions). *Total annual research expenditures:* $795,250. *Unit head:* Dr. Marcia J. Hern, Dean, 502-852-8300, Fax: 502-852-5044, E-mail: m.hern@gwise.louisville.edu. *Application contact:* Dr. Lee Ridner, Interim Associate Dean for Academic Affairs and Director of MSN Programs, 502-852-8518, Fax: 502-852-0704, E-mail: romain01@louisville.edu. Web site: http://www.louisville.edu/nursing/.

University of Maryland, Baltimore, Graduate School, School of Nursing, Master's Program in Nursing, Baltimore, MD 21201. Offers community health nursing (MS); gerontological nursing (MS); maternal-child nursing (MS); medical-surgical nursing (MS); nurse-midwifery education (MS); nursing administration (MS); nursing education (MS); nursing health policy (MS); primary care nursing (MS); psychiatric nursing (MS); MS/MBA. MS/MBA offered jointly with University of Baltimore. *Accreditation:* AACN; AANA/CANAEP; NLN (one or more programs are accredited). Part-time programs available. *Students:* 370 full-time (314 women), 480 part-time (441 women); includes 308 minority (176 Black or African American, non-Hispanic/Latino; 2 American Indian or Alaska Native, non-Hispanic/Latino; 70 Asian, non-Hispanic/Latino; 33 Hispanic/Latino; 27 Two or more races, non-Hispanic/Latino), 9 international. Average age 35. 990 applicants, 30% accepted, 204 enrolled. In 2011, 301 master's awarded. *Degree requirements:* For master's, comprehensive exam (for some programs), thesis or alternative. *Entrance requirements:* For master's, minimum GPA of 2.75, course work in statistics, BS in nursing. Additional exam requirements/recommendations for international students: Required—TOEFL (minimum score 550 paper-based; 80 iBT) or IELTS (minimum score 7). *Application deadline:* For fall admission, 2/1 for domestic students, 1/15 for international students. Application fee: $50. Electronic applications accepted. *Financial support:* Fellowships, research assistantships, teaching assistantships, career-related internships or fieldwork, and traineeships available. Support available to part-time students. Financial award application deadline: 2/15; financial award applicants required to submit FAFSA. *Unit head:* Dr. Jane Kapustin, Assistant Dean, 410-706-6741, Fax: 410-706-4231. *Application contact:* Marjorie Fass, Admissions Director, 410-706-0501, Fax: 410-706-7238.

University of Missouri–Kansas City, School of Nursing, Kansas City, MO 64110-2499. Offers adult clinical nurse specialist (MSN), including adult nurse practitioner, women's health nurse practitioner; family nurse practitioner (MSN); neonatal nurse practitioner (MSN); nurse educator (MSN); nurse executive (MSN); nursing (PhD); nursing practice (DNP); pediatric nurse practitioner (MSN). *Accreditation:* AACN. Part-time programs available. Postbaccalaureate distance learning degree programs offered (minimal on-campus study). *Faculty:* 40 full-time (35 women), 57 part-time/adjunct (52 women). *Students:* 51 full-time (48 women), 381 part-time (352 women); includes 41 minority (22 Black or African American, non-Hispanic/Latino; 7 Asian, non-Hispanic/Latino; 12 Hispanic/Latino). Average age 37. 195 applicants, 49% accepted, 90 enrolled. In 2011, 78 master's, 19 doctorates awarded. *Degree requirements:* For master's, thesis or alternative. *Entrance requirements:* For master's, minimum undergraduate GPA of 3.2; for doctorate, GRE, 3 letters of reference, interview by invitation. Additional exam requirements/recommendations for international students: Required—TOEFL (minimum score 550 paper-based; 213 computer-based; 80 iBT). *Application deadline:* For fall admission, 2/1 priority date for domestic students, 2/1 for international students; for spring admission, 9/1 priority date for domestic students, 9/1 for international students. Application fee: $45 ($50 for international students). *Expenses:* Tuition, state resident: full-time $5798; part-time $322.10 per credit hour. Tuition, nonresident: full-time $14,969; part-time $831.60 per credit hour. Required fees: $93.51 per credit hour. *Financial support:* In 2011–12, 25 teaching assistantships with partial tuition reimbursements (averaging $6,927 per year) were awarded; fellowships, research assistantships, career-related internships or fieldwork, Federal Work-Study, institutionally sponsored loans, and tuition waivers (full and partial) also available. Support available to part-time students. Financial award application deadline: 3/1; financial award applicants required to submit FAFSA. *Faculty research:* Geriatrics/gerontology, children's pain, neonatology, Alzheimer's care, cancer caregivers. *Unit head:* Dr. Lora Lacey-Haun, Dean, 816-235-1700, Fax: 816-235-1701, E-mail: lacey-haunc@umkc.edu. *Application contact:* Leah Wilder, Coordinator for Admissions and Recruitment, 816-235-5768, Fax: 816-235-1701, E-mail: wilderl@umkc.edu. Web site: http://nursing.umkc.edu/.

University of Missouri–St. Louis, College of Nursing, St. Louis, MO 63121. Offers adult nurse practitioner (DNP, Post Master's Certificate); clinical nurse specialist (DNP); family mental health nurse practitioner (DNP); family nurse practitioner (MSN, DNP, Post Master's Certificate); neonatal nurse practitioner (MSN); nurse educator (MSN); nurse leader (MSN); nurse practitioner (Post Master's Certificate); nursing (PhD); pediatric clinical nurse specialist (DNP); pediatric nurse practitioner (MSN, DNP, Post Master's Certificate); women's health nurse practitioner (MSN, Post Master's Certificate). *Accreditation:* AACN. Part-time programs available. *Faculty:* 12 full-time (11 women), 14 part-time/adjunct (all women). *Students:* 240 part-time (226 women); includes 30 minority (26 Black or African American, non-Hispanic/Latino; 1 Asian, non-Hispanic/Latino; 2 Hispanic/Latino; 1 Two or more races, non-Hispanic/Latino). Average age 37. 228 applicants, 28% accepted, 53 enrolled. In 2011, 66 master's, 2 doctorates, 2 other advanced degrees awarded. *Degree requirements:* For doctorate, comprehensive exam, thesis/dissertation; for Post Master's Certificate, thesis. *Entrance requirements:* For master's, 2 recommendation letters; minimum GPA of 3.0; BSN; nursing licensure; statement of purpose; course in differential/inferential statistics; for doctorate, GRE, 2 letters of recommendation, MSN, minimum GPA of 3.2, course in differential/inferential statistics; for Post Master's Certificate, 2 recommendation letters; MSN; advanced practice certificate; minimum GPA of 3.0; essay. Additional exam requirements/recommendations for international students: Required—TOEFL (minimum score 550 paper-based; 213 computer-based). *Application deadline:* For fall admission, 2/15 for domestic and international students. Application fee: $35 ($40 for international students). Electronic applications accepted. *Expenses:* Tuition, state resident: full-time $6273; part-time $3866 per year. Tuition, nonresident: full-time $14,969; part-time $9980 per year. Required fees: $315 per year. *Financial support:* In 2011–12, 3 research assistantships with full and partial tuition reimbursements (averaging $12,339 per year) were awarded. Financial award application deadline: 4/1; financial award applicants required to submit FAFSA. *Faculty research:* Health promotion and restoration, family disruption, violence, abuse, battered women, health survey methods. *Unit head:* Dr. Nancy Magnuson, Director, 314-516-6066. *Application contact:* 314-516-5458, Fax: 314-516-6996, E-mail: gradadm@umsl.edu. Web site: http://www.umsl.edu/divisions/nursing/.

University of Pennsylvania, School of Nursing, Family Health Nurse Practitioner Program, Philadelphia, PA 19104. Offers MSN, Certificate. *Accreditation:* AACN. Part-time programs available. *Students:* 19 full-time (18 women), 33 part-time (all women); includes 10 minority (2 Black or African American, non-Hispanic/Latino; 4 Asian, non-Hispanic/Latino; 3 Hispanic/Latino; 1 Two or more races, non-Hispanic/Latino), 1

international. 47 applicants, 26% accepted, 12 enrolled. In 2011, 31 degrees awarded. *Entrance requirements:* For master's, GRE General Test, 1 year of clinical experience in area of interest, BSN, minimum GPA of 3.0, previous course work in statistics. Additional exam requirements/recommendations for international students: Required—TOEFL. *Application deadline:* For fall admission, 2/15 priority date for domestic students. Applications are processed on a rolling basis. Application fee: $70. *Expenses:* Contact institution. *Financial support:* Research assistantships, teaching assistantships, career-related internships or fieldwork, Federal Work-Study, and institutionally sponsored loans available. Support available to part-time students. Financial award application deadline: 4/1. *Faculty research:* Evaluation of primary care practitioner practice, access to primary care. *Unit head:* Assistant Dean of Admissions and Financial Aid, 866-867-6877, Fax: 215-573-8439, E-mail: admissions@nursing.upenn.edu. *Application contact:* Ann O'Sullivan, Program Director, 215-898-4272, E-mail: osull@nursing.upenn.edu. Web site: http://www.nursing.upenn.edu/fnp/.

University of Pennsylvania, School of Nursing, Neonatal Nurse Practitioner Program, Philadelphia, PA 19104. Offers MSN. *Accreditation:* AACN. Part-time programs available. *Students:* 3 full-time (all women), 6 part-time (5 women); includes 1 minority (Asian, non-Hispanic/Latino), 1 international. 11 applicants, 55% accepted, 6 enrolled. In 2011, 8 degrees awarded. *Entrance requirements:* For master's, GRE General Test, BSN, minimum GPA of 3.0, previous course work in statistics, 1 year of experience in a neonatal intensive care unit. Additional exam requirements/recommendations for international students: Required—TOEFL. *Application deadline:* For fall admission, 2/15 priority date for domestic students. Applications are processed on a rolling basis. Application fee: $70. *Expenses:* Contact institution. *Financial support:* Fellowships, research assistantships, teaching assistantships, career-related internships or fieldwork, Federal Work-Study, and institutionally sponsored loans available. Support available to part-time students. Financial award application deadline: 4/1. *Faculty research:* Neurobehavioral development, temperament, newborn sucking behaviors, parenting pre-term infants. *Unit head:* Assistant Dean of Admissions and Financial Aid, 866-867-6877, Fax: 215-573-8439, E-mail: admissions@nursing.upenn.edu. *Application contact:* Judy Verger, Program Director, 215-898-4271, E-mail: jtv@nursing.upenn.edu. Web site: http://www.nursing.upenn.edu/.

University of Pennsylvania, School of Nursing, Perinatal Advanced Practice Nurse Specialist Program, Philadelphia, PA 19104. Offers MSN. *Accreditation:* AACN. Part-time programs available. *Students:* 5 full-time (all women), 12 part-time (all women); includes 1 minority (Asian, non-Hispanic/Latino). 15 applicants, 40% accepted, 4 enrolled. In 2011, 18 degrees awarded. *Entrance requirements:* For master's, GRE General Test, BSN, minimum GPA of 3.0, previous course work in statistics. Additional exam requirements/recommendations for international students: Required—TOEFL. *Application deadline:* For fall admission, 2/15 priority date for domestic students. Applications are processed on a rolling basis. Application fee: $70. *Expenses:* Contact institution. *Financial support:* Fellowships, research assistantships, teaching assistantships, career-related internships or fieldwork, Federal Work-Study, and institutionally sponsored loans available. Support available to part-time students. Financial award application deadline: 4/1. *Unit head:* Assistant Dean of Admissions and Financial Aid, 866-867-6877, Fax: 215-573-8439, E-mail: admissions@nursing.upenn.edu. *Application contact:* Sylvia V. J. English, Enrollment Management Coordinator, 866-867-6877, Fax: 215-573-8439, E-mail: admissions@nursing.upenn.edu.

University of Pittsburgh, School of Nursing, Nurse Practitioner Program, Pittsburgh, PA 15261. Offers acute care nurse practitioner (MSN, DNP); adult nurse practitioner (MSN, DNP); family nurse practitioner (MSN, DNP); neonatal (MSN, DNP); nursing practice (DNP); pediatric nurse practitioner (MSN, DNP); psychiatric primary care nurse practitioner (MSN, DNP). *Accreditation:* AACN. Part-time programs available. *Students:* 46 full-time (44 women), 135 part-time (123 women); includes 13 minority (6 Black or African American, non-Hispanic/Latino; 1 American Indian or Alaska Native, non-Hispanic/Latino; 6 Asian, non-Hispanic/Latino). Average age 32. 126 applicants, 71% accepted, 70 enrolled. In 2011, 24 master's, 4 doctorates awarded. *Degree requirements:* For master's, comprehensive exam, thesis optional. *Entrance requirements:* For master's, GRE General Test or MAT, BSN, RN license, letters of recommendation, resume, course work in statistics, 1-3 years of nursing experience; for doctorate, GRE General Test, BSN, RN license, minimum GPA of 3.5, 3 letters of recommendation. Additional exam requirements/recommendations for international students: Required—TOEFL (minimum score 550 paper-based; 213 computer-based; 80 iBT). *Application deadline:* Applications are processed on a rolling basis. Application fee: $50. Electronic applications accepted. *Expenses:* Tuition, state resident: full-time $18,774; part-time $760 per credit. Tuition, nonresident: full-time $30,736; part-time $1258 per credit. *Required fees:* $740; $200 per term. Tuition and fees vary according to program. *Financial support:* In 2011–12, 5 students received support, including 1 fellowship with partial tuition reimbursement available (averaging $11,330 per year), 1 research assistantship with full tuition reimbursement available (averaging $35,942 per year), 3 teaching assistantships with full and partial tuition reimbursements available (averaging $27,470 per year); scholarships/grants, traineeships, health care benefits, and unspecified assistantships also available. Support available to part-time students. *Unit head:* Dr. Sandra Engberg, Associate Dean for Clinical Education, 412-624-3835, Fax: 412-624-8521, E-mail: sje1@pitt.edu. *Application contact:* Laurie Lapsley, Administrator of Graduate Student Services, 412-624-9670, Fax: 412-624-2409, E-mail: lapsleyl@pitt.edu. Web site: http://www.nursing.pitt.edu.

University of Puerto Rico, Medical Sciences Campus, School of Nursing, San Juan, PR 00936-5067. Offers adult and elderly nursing (MSN); child and adolescent nursing (MSN); critical care nursing (MSN); family and community nursing (MSN); family nurse practitioner (MSN); maternity nursing (MSN); mental health and psychiatric nursing (MSN). *Accreditation:* AACN; AANA/CANAEP. *Entrance requirements:* For master's, GRE or EXADEP, interview, Puerto Rico RN license or professional license for international students, general and specific point average, article analysis. Electronic applications accepted. *Faculty research:* HIV, health disparities, teen violence, women and violence, neurological disorders.

University of Rochester, School of Nursing, Rochester, NY 14642. Offers acute care nurse practitioner (MS); adult nurse practitioner (MS); adult/geriatric nurse practitioner (MS); care of children and families/pediatric nurse practitioner (MS); care of children and families/pediatric nurse practitioner/neonatal nurse practitioner (MS); clinical nurse leader (MS); clinical research coordinator (MS); family nurse practitioner (MS); family psychiatric mental health nurse practitioner (MS); health care organization management and leadership (MS); health practice research (PhD); nursing (DNP). *Accreditation:* AACN; NLN (one or more programs are accredited). Part-time programs available. Postbaccalaureate distance learning degree programs offered (minimal on-campus study). *Faculty:* 49 full-time (42 women), 72 part-time/adjunct (60 women). *Students:* 38 full-time (32 women), 196 part-time (181 women); includes 37 minority (20 Black or African American, non-Hispanic/Latino; 9 Asian, non-Hispanic/Latino; 8 Hispanic/Latino), 5 international. Average age 36. 68 applicants, 56% accepted, 26 enrolled. In 2011, 49 master's, 7 doctorates awarded. Terminal master's awarded for partial completion of doctoral program. *Median time to degree:* Of those who began their doctoral program in fall 2003, 40% received their degree in 8 years or less. *Degree*

requirements: For doctorate, thesis/dissertation. *Entrance requirements:* For master's, BS in nursing, minimum GPA of 3.0, course work in statistics; for doctorate, GRE General Test, MS in nursing, minimum GPA of 3.5. Additional exam requirements/recommendations for international students: Required—or IELTS (minimum score 6.5); Recommended—TOEFL (minimum score 560 paper-based; 230 computer-based; 88 iBT). *Application deadline:* For fall admission, 4/1 priority date for domestic students, 4/1 for international students; for spring admission, 9/1 for domestic and international students. Application fee: $50. Electronic applications accepted. *Expenses: Tuition:* Full-time $41,040. *Financial support:* In 2011–12, 49 students received support, including 1 fellowship with full and partial tuition reimbursement available (averaging $18,700 per year); scholarships/grants, traineeships, health care benefits, tuition waivers (partial), and unspecified assistantships also available. Support available to part-time students. Financial award application deadline: 6/30. *Faculty research:* Clinical research in aging, managing asthma in children, interventions to improve outcomes in critically ill children and their mothers, nurse home visitation studies, medical device evaluation, critical care clinical studies, high risk behavior and prevention, palliative care, pregnancy-related weight gain. *Total annual research expenditures:* $4.3 million. *Unit head:* Dr. Kathy H. Rideout, Interim Dean, 585-273-8902, Fax: 585-273-1268, E-mail: kathy_rideout@urmc.rochester.edu. *Application contact:* Elaine Andolina, Director of Admissions, 585-275-2375, Fax: 585-756-8299, E-mail: elaine_andolina@urmc.rochester.edu. Web site: http://www.son.rochester.edu.

University of South Africa, College of Human Sciences, Pretoria, South Africa. Offers adult education (M Ed); African languages (MA, PhD); African politics (MA, PhD); Afrikaans (MA, PhD); ancient history (MA, PhD); ancient Near Eastern studies (MA, PhD); anthropology (MA, PhD); applied linguistics (MA); Arabic (MA, PhD); archaeology (MA); art history (MA); Biblical archaeology (MA); Biblical studies (M Th, D Th, PhD); Christian spirituality (M Th, D Th); church history (M Th, D Th); classical studies (MA, PhD); clinical psychology (MA); communication (MA, PhD); comparative education (M Ed, Ed D); consulting psychology (D Admin, D Com, PhD); curriculum studies (M Ed, Ed D); development studies (M Admin, MA, D Admin, PhD); didactics (M Ed, Ed D); education (M Tech); education management (M Ed, Ed D); educational psychology (M Ed); English (MA); environmental education (M Ed); French (MA, PhD); German (MA, PhD); Greek (MA); guidance and counseling (M Ed); health studies (MA, PhD), including health sciences education (MA), health services management (MA), medical and surgical nursing science (critical care general) (MA), midwifery and neonatal nursing science (MA), trauma and emergency care (MA); history (MA, PhD); history of education (Ed D); inclusive education (M Ed, Ed D); information and communications technology policy and regulation (MA); information science (MA, MIS, PhD); international politics (MA, PhD); Islamic studies (MA, PhD); Italian (MA, PhD); Judaica (MA, PhD); linguistics (MA, PhD); mathematical education (M Ed); mathematics education (MA); missiology (M Th, D Th); modern Hebrew (MA, PhD); musicology (MA, MMus, D Mus, PhD); natural science education (M Ed); New Testament (M Th, D Th); Old Testament (D Th); pastoral therapy (M Th, D Th); philosophy (MA); philosophy of education (M Ed, Ed D); politics (MA, PhD); Portuguese (MA, PhD); practical theology (M Th, D Th); psychology (MA, MS, PhD); psychology of education (M Ed, Ed D); public health (MA); religious studies (MA, D Th, PhD); Romance languages (MA); Russian (MA, PhD); Semitic languages (MA, PhD); social behavior studies in HIV/AIDS (MA); social science (mental health) (MA); social science in development studies (MA); social science in psychology (MA); social science in social work (MA); social science in sociology (MA); social work (MSW, DSW, PhD); socio-education (M Ed, Ed D); sociolinguistics (MA); sociology (MA, PhD); Spanish (MA, PhD); systematic theology (M Th, D Th); TESOL (teaching English to speakers of other languages) (MA); theological ethics (M Th, D Th); theory of literature (MA, PhD); urban ministries (D Th); urban ministry (M Th).

University of South Alabama, Graduate School, College of Nursing, Mobile, AL 36688. Offers adult health nursing (MSN); community/mental health nursing (MSN); maternal/child nursing (MSN); nursing (DNP). *Accreditation:* AACN. *Faculty:* 21 full-time (20 women). *Students:* 1,335 full-time (1,200 women), 172 part-time (147 women); includes 280 minority (164 Black or African American, non-Hispanic/Latino; 15 American Indian or Alaska Native, non-Hispanic/Latino; 41 Asian, non-Hispanic/Latino; 45 Hispanic/Latino; 2 Native Hawaiian or other Pacific Islander, non-Hispanic/Latino; 13 Two or more races, non-Hispanic/Latino), 10 international. 1,327 applicants, 38% accepted, 388 enrolled. In 2011, 266 master's, 21 doctorates awarded. *Degree requirements:* For master's, thesis optional. *Entrance requirements:* For master's, BSN, RN licensure, minimum GPA of 3.0, resume documenting clinical experience, background check, drug screening; for doctorate, GRE. *Application deadline:* For fall admission, 7/15 for domestic students; for spring admission, 12/1 for domestic students. Application fee: $35. *Expenses:* Tuition, state resident: full-time $7968; part-time $332 per credit hour. Tuition, nonresident: full-time $15,936; part-time $664 per credit hour. *Unit head:* Dr. Rosemary Rhodes, Director of Graduate Education, 251-445-9409, Fax: 251-445-9416. *Application contact:* Dr. B. Keith Harrison, Dean of the Graduate School, 251-460-6310, Fax: 251-461-1513, E-mail: kharriso@usouthal.edu. Web site: http://www.southalabama.edu/nursing.

University of Southern Mississippi, Graduate School, College of Health, School of Nursing, Hattiesburg, MS 39406-0001. Offers family nurse practitioner (MSN); nursing (DNP, PhD); nursing executive (MSN); psychiatric nurse practitioner (MSN). *Accreditation:* AACN. Part-time and evening/weekend programs available. *Faculty:* 17 full-time (16 women), 1 part-time/adjunct (0 women). *Students:* 115 full-time (98 women), 43 part-time (38 women); includes 42 minority (35 Black or African American, non-Hispanic/Latino; 1 American Indian or Alaska Native, non-Hispanic/Latino; 3 Asian, non-Hispanic/Latino; 3 Two or more races, non-Hispanic/Latino). Average age 40. 128 applicants, 52% accepted, 58 enrolled. In 2011, 42 master's, 2 doctorates awarded. *Degree requirements:* For master's, comprehensive exam, thesis optional; for doctorate, comprehensive exam, thesis/dissertation. *Entrance requirements:* For master's, GRE General Test, minimum GPA of 2.75 during last 60 hours, nursing license, BS in nursing; for doctorate, GRE General Test, master's degree in nursing, minimum GPA of 3.5. Additional exam requirements/recommendations for international students: Required—TOEFL, IELTS. *Application deadline:* For fall admission, 3/15 priority date for domestic students, 5/1 for international students; for spring admission, 1/10 priority date for domestic students, 1/10 for international students. Applications are processed on a rolling basis. Application fee: $50. Electronic applications accepted. *Financial support:* In 2011–12, 14 research assistantships with full tuition reimbursements (averaging $12,577 per year), teaching assistantships (averaging $12,000 per year) were awarded; Federal Work-Study, institutionally sponsored loans, scholarships/grants, traineeships, health care benefits, and unspecified assistantships also available. Financial award application deadline: 3/15; financial award applicants required to submit FAFSA. *Faculty research:* Gerontology, caregivers, HIV, bereavement, pain, nursing leadership. *Unit head:* Dr. Katherine Nugent, Director and Associate Dean, 601-266-5500, Fax: 601-266-5927. *Application contact:* Dr. Sandra Bishop, Graduate Coordinator, 601-266-5500, Fax: 601-266-5927. Web site: http://www.usm.edu/graduateschool/table.php.

The University of Texas at Austin, Graduate School, School of Nursing, Austin, TX 78712-1111. Offers adult -gerontology clinical nurse specialist (MSN); child health (MSN), including administration, public health nursing; child health (MSN), including teaching; family nurse practitioner (MSN); family psychiatric/mental health nurse practitioner (MSN); holistic adult health (MSN), including administration, education;

maternity (MSN), including administration, public health nursing; maternity (MSN), including teaching; nursing (PhD); nursing administration and healthcare systems management (MSN); pediatric nurse practitioner (MSN); public health nursing (MSN). *Accreditation:* AACN. Part-time programs available. *Degree requirements:* For master's, thesis optional; for doctorate, thesis/dissertation. *Entrance requirements:* For master's and doctorate, GRE General Test. Additional exam requirements/recommendations for international students: Required—TOEFL (minimum score 550 paper-based; 213 computer-based). *Application deadline:* For fall admission, 12/1 for domestic students. Application fee: $50 ($75 for international students). Electronic applications accepted. *Financial support:* Fellowships, research assistantships, teaching assistantships, scholarships/grants, and traineeships available. Financial award application deadline: 2/1. *Faculty research:* Chronic illness management, memory and aging, health promotion, women's health, adolescent health. *Unit head:* Dr. Alexa Stuifbergen, Dean, 512-471-4100, Fax: 512-471-4910, E-mail: astuifbergen@mail.utexas.edu. Web site: http://www.utexas.edu/nursing/.

Vanderbilt University, Vanderbilt University School of Nursing, Nashville, TN 37240. Offers acute care nurse practitioner (MSN), including intensivist; adult-gerontology primary care nurse practitioner (MSN); emergency nurse practitioner (MSN); family nurse practitioner (MSN); family psychiatric and mental health nurse practitioner (MSN); health systems management (MSN); neonatal nurse practitioner (MSN); nurse midwifery (MSN); nurse midwifery/family nurse practitioner (MSN); nursing informatics (MSN); nursing practice (DNP); nursing science (PhD); pediatric acute care nurse practitioner (MSN); pediatric primary care nurse practitioner (MSN); women's health nurse practitioner (MSN), including urogynecology, women's health; women's health nurse practitioner/adult gerontology nurse practitioner (MSN); MSN/M Div; MSN/MTS. *Accreditation:* ACNM/ACME; NLN (one or more programs are accredited). Part-time programs available. Postbaccalaureate distance learning degree programs offered (minimal on-campus study). *Faculty:* 120 full-time (105 women), 415 part-time/adjunct (302 women). *Students:* 570 full-time (503 women), 395 part-time (364 women); includes 107 minority (57 Black or African American, non-Hispanic/Latino; 1 American Indian or Alaska Native, non-Hispanic/Latino; 19 Asian, non-Hispanic/Latino; 19 Hispanic/Latino; 2 Native Hawaiian or other Pacific Islander, non-Hispanic/Latino; 9 Two or more races, non-Hispanic/Latino), 10 international. Average age 32. 1,116 applicants, 56% accepted, 455 enrolled. In 2011, 341 master's, 33 doctorates awarded. *Degree requirements:* For doctorate, comprehensive exam, thesis/dissertation. *Entrance requirements:* For master's, GRE General Test (within the past 5 years), minimum B average in undergraduate course work, 3 letters of recommendation; for doctorate, GRE General Test, interview, 3 letters of recommendation from doctorally-prepared faculty, MSN, essay. Additional exam requirements/recommendations for international students: Required—TOEFL (minimum score 570 paper-based; 88 computer-based), IELTS (minimum score 6.5). *Application deadline:* For fall admission, 12/1 priority date for domestic students, 12/1 for international students. Applications are processed on a rolling basis. Application fee: $50. Electronic applications accepted. *Expenses:* Contact institution. *Financial support:* In 2011–12, 392 students received support. Scholarships/grants and health care benefits available. Support available to part-time students. Financial award application deadline: 3/15; financial award applicants required to submit FAFSA. *Faculty research:* Lymphedema, palliative care and bereavement, health services research including workforce, safety and quality of care, gerontology, better birth outcomes including nutrition . *Total annual research expenditures:* $1.8 million. *Unit head:* Dr. Colleen Conway-Welch, Dean, 615-343-8776, Fax: 615-343-7711, E-mail: colleen.conway-welch@vanderbilt.edu. *Application contact:* Patricia Peerman, Assistant Dean for Enrollment Management, 615-322-3800, Fax: 615-343-0333, E-mail: vusn-admissions@vanderbilt.edu. Web site: http://www.nursing.vanderbilt.edu.

Wayne State University, College of Nursing, Program in Advanced Practice Nursing with Women, Neonates and Children, Detroit, MI 48202. Offers MSN. *Accreditation:* AACN. Part-time programs available. *Students:* 48 full-time (47 women), 69 part-time (65 women); includes 16 minority (11 Black or African American, non-Hispanic/Latino; 5 Hispanic/Latino), 2 international. Average age 33. 44 applicants, 68% accepted, 27 enrolled. In 2011, 30 master's awarded. *Degree requirements:* For master's, thesis or alternative. *Entrance requirements:* For master's, minimum honor point average of 2.8 in upper-division course work; BA from NLN- or CCNE-accredited program; references; current RN license; personal statement. Additional exam requirements/recommendations for international students: Required—TOEFL (minimum score 550 paper-based; 213 computer-based); Recommended—TWE (minimum score 6). *Application deadline:* For fall admission, 6/1 priority date for domestic students, 5/1 for international students; for winter admission, 10/1 priority date for domestic students, 9/1 for international students; for spring admission, 2/1 priority date for domestic students, 1/1 for international students. Applications are processed on a rolling basis. Application fee: $50. Electronic applications accepted. *Expenses:* Tuition, state resident: part-time $512.85 per credit. Tuition, nonresident: part-time $1132.65 per credit. *Required fees:* $26.60 per credit. $199.65 per semester. Tuition and fees vary according to course load and program. *Financial support:* In 2011–12, 17 students received support. Fellowships with tuition reimbursements available, research assistantships with tuition reimbursements available, teaching assistantships with tuition reimbursements available, institutionally sponsored loans, scholarships/grants, traineeships, and unspecified assistantships available. Financial award applicants required to submit FAFSA. *Faculty research:* Acculturation and parenting, domestic violence, evidence-based midwifery practice, pain in children, trauma and community violence. *Unit head:* Dr. Barbara Redman, Dean, 313-577-4070, Fax: 313-577-4571, E-mail: ae9080@wayne.edu. *Application contact:* Dr. Cynthia Redwine, Assistant Dean for the Office of Student Affairs, 313-577-4082, E-mail: nursinginfo@wayne.edu. Web site: http://www.nursing.wayne.edu/msn/nnpcurriculum.php.

Medical/Surgical Nursing

Angelo State University, College of Graduate Studies, College of Health and Human Services, Department of Nursing and Rehabilitation Sciences, San Angelo, TX 76909. Offers advanced practice registered nurse (MSN); nurse educator (MSN); nursing - RN to MSN (MSN). *Accreditation:* NLN. Part-time and evening/weekend programs available. Postbaccalaureate distance learning degree programs offered (no on-campus study). *Faculty:* 7 full-time (all women). *Students:* 23 full-time (20 women), 89 part-time (80 women); includes 12 minority (3 Black or African American, non-Hispanic/Latino; 1 American Indian or Alaska Native, non-Hispanic/Latino; 3 Asian, non-Hispanic/Latino; 5 Hispanic/Latino). Average age 41. 143 applicants, 25% accepted, 25 enrolled. In 2011, 9 master's awarded. *Degree requirements:* For master's, comprehensive exam. *Entrance requirements:* For master's, essay, three letters of recommendation. Additional exam requirements/recommendations for international students: Required—TOEFL or IELTS. *Application deadline:* For fall admission, 7/15 priority date for domestic students, 6/10 for international students; for spring admission, 12/1 priority date for domestic students, 11/1 for international students. Applications are processed on a rolling basis. Application fee: $40 ($50 for international students). Electronic applications accepted. *Financial support:* In 2011–12, 24 students received support. Career-related internships or fieldwork, Federal Work-Study, and scholarships/grants available. Support available to part-time students. Financial award application deadline: 3/1. *Unit head:* Dr. Susan S. Wilkinson, Department Head, 325-942-2060 Ext. 290, Fax: 325-942-2236, E-mail: susan.wilkinson@angelo.edu. *Application contact:* Dr. Molly J. Walker, Graduate Advisor, 325-942-2060 Ext. 246, Fax: 325-942-2236, E-mail: molly.walker@angelo.edu. Web site: http://www.angelo.edu/dept/nursing/.

Boston College, William F. Connell School of Nursing, Chestnut Hill, MA 02467-3800. Offers adult-gerontology nursing (MS); community health nursing (MS); family health (MS); forensic nursing (MS); maternal/child health nursing (MS), including pediatric and women's health; nurse anesthesia (MS); nursing (PhD); palliative care (MS), including adult and pediatric; psychiatric-mental health nursing (MS); MBA/MS; MS/MA; MS/PhD. *Accreditation:* AACN; AANA/CANAEP (one or more programs are accredited). Part-time programs available. *Faculty:* 48 full-time (46 women), 31 part-time/adjunct (29 women). *Students:* 225 full-time (207 women), 90 part-time (88 women); includes 47 minority (15 Black or African American, non-Hispanic/Latino; 3 American Indian or Alaska Native, non-Hispanic/Latino; 17 Asian, non-Hispanic/Latino; 8 Hispanic/Latino; 4 Two or more races, non-Hispanic/Latino), 6 international. Average age 31. 369 applicants, 43% accepted, 80 enrolled. In 2011, 113 master's, 8 doctorates awarded. *Degree requirements:* For master's, comprehensive exam, research project; for doctorate, comprehensive exam, thesis/dissertation, computer literacy exam or foreign language. *Entrance requirements:* For master's, bachelor's degree in nursing; for doctorate, GRE General Test, MS in nursing. Additional exam requirements/recommendations for international students: Required—TOEFL (minimum score 600 paper-based; 250 computer-based; 100 iBT). *Application deadline:* For fall admission, 11/1 for domestic and international students; for winter admission, 12/31 for domestic and international students; for spring admission, 4/30 for domestic and international students. Applications are processed on a rolling basis. Application fee: $40. Electronic applications accepted. *Financial support:* In 2011–12, 167 students received support, including 9 fellowships with full tuition reimbursements available (averaging $15,300 per year), 7 teaching assistantships (averaging $13,612 per year); research assistantships, Federal Work-Study, institutionally sponsored loans, scholarships/grants, traineeships, health care benefits, tuition waivers (partial), and unspecified assistantships also available. Support available to part-time students. Financial award application deadline: 3/1; financial award applicants required to submit FAFSA. *Faculty research:* Pre-term labor, palliative care, support during chronic illness, violence, eating disorders. *Total annual research expenditures:* $2.1 million. *Unit head:* Dr. Susan Gennaro, Dean, 617-552-4251, Fax: 617-552-0931, E-mail: susan.gennaro@bc.edu. *Application contact:* MaryBeth Crowley, Graduate Programs Assistant, 617-552-4928, Fax: 617-552-2121, E-mail: csongrad@bc.edu. Web site: http://www.bc.edu/nursing/.

Columbia University, School of Nursing, Program in Acute Care Nurse Practitioner, New York, NY 10032. Offers MS, Adv C. *Accreditation:* AACN. Part-time programs available. *Entrance requirements:* For master's, GRE General Test, 1 year of clinical experience (preferred), BSN; for Adv C, MSN. Electronic applications accepted.

Daemen College, Department of Nursing, Amherst, NY 14226-3592. Offers adult nurse practitioner (MS, Post Master's Certificate); nurse executive leadership (Post Master's Certificate); nursing education (MS, Post Master's Certificate); nursing executive leadership (MS); nursing practice (DNP); palliative care nursing (Post Master's Certificate). *Accreditation:* NLN. Part-time programs available. *Degree requirements:* For master's, thesis or alternative, degree completed in 4 years; minimum GPA of 3.0; for doctorate, degree completed in 5 years; 500 post-master's clinical hours. *Entrance requirements:* For master's, BN, 1 year medical/surgical experience, RN license and state registration, statistics course with minimum C grade, 3 letters of recommendation, minimum GPA of 3.25, interview; for doctorate, MS in advance nursing practice; New York state RN license; goal statement; resume; interview; statistics course with minimum grade of 'C'; for Post Master's Certificate, master's degree in clinical area; RN license and current registration; one year of clinical experience; statistics course with minimum grade of 'C'; 3 letters of recommendation; interview; letter of intent. Additional exam requirements/recommendations for international students: Required—TOEFL (minimum score 500 paper-based; 173 computer-based; 63 iBT), IELTS (minimum score 5.5). Electronic applications accepted. *Faculty research:* Professional stress, client behavior, drug therapy, treatment modalities and pulmonary cancers, chemical dependency.

Eastern Virginia Medical School, Surgical Assistant Program, Norfolk, VA 23501-1980. Offers Graduate Certificate. *Faculty:* 8. *Students:* 24 full-time (16 women); includes 7 minority (4 Black or African American, non-Hispanic/Latino; 3 Asian, non-Hispanic/Latino). 22 applicants, 68% accepted, 14 enrolled. *Application deadline:* For fall admission, 2/1 for domestic students. Applications are processed on a rolling basis. Application fee: $60. Electronic applications accepted. *Expenses:* Contact institution. *Unit head:* R. Clinton Crews, Program Director, 757-446-8961, Fax: 757-446-6179, E-mail: crewsrc@evms.edu. *Application contact:* Michelle Hammer, Administrative Support Coordinator, 757-446-5076, Fax: 757-446-6179, E-mail: hammermr@evms.edu. Web site: http://www.evms.edu/evms-school-of-health-professions/surgical-assistant.html.

Gannon University, School of Graduate Studies, Morosky College of Health Professions and Sciences, School of Health Professions, Villa Maria School of Nursing, Erie, PA 16541-0001. Offers anesthesia (MSN); business administration (MSN); family nurse practitioner (Certificate); medical-surgical nursing (MSN); nurse anesthesia (Certificate); nursing rural practitioner (MSN). *Accreditation:* AACN; AANA/CANAEP (one or more programs are accredited). Part-time and evening/weekend programs available. *Students:* 2 full-time (both women), 68 part-time (49 women); includes 3 minority (1 Black or African American, non-Hispanic/Latino; 1 American Indian or Alaska Native, non-Hispanic/Latino; 1 Hispanic/Latino). Average age 44. 15 applicants, 67% accepted, 0 enrolled. In 2011, 20 master's, 3 other advanced degrees awarded. *Degree requirements:* For master's, thesis. *Entrance requirements:* For master's, GRE General Test, degree in nursing. Additional exam requirements/recommendations for international students: Required—TOEFL (minimum score 79 iBT). *Application deadline:* For spring admission, 8/1 for domestic students. Application fee: $25. Electronic applications accepted. *Financial support:* Scholarships/grants available. Financial

award application deadline: 7/1; financial award applicants required to submit FAFSA. *Faculty research:* Accurate assessment of delirium in the ICU using CAM, factors affecting caregiver fatigue in dialysis nurses, hours worked by nurses and treatment error reporting. *Unit head:* Dr. Kathleen Patterson, Director, 814-871-5547, E-mail: patterso018@gannon.edu. *Application contact:* Kara Morgan, Director of Graduate Admissions, 814-871-5831, Fax: 814-871-5827, E-mail: graduate@gannon.edu.

Inter American University of Puerto Rico, Arecibo Campus, Program in Nursing, Arecibo, PR 00614-4050. Offers critical care nursing (MSN); surgical nursing (MSN). *Entrance requirements:* For master's, EXADEP or GRE General Test or MAT, 2 letters of recommendation, bachelor's degree in nursing, minimum GPA of 2.5 in last 60 credits, minimum 1 year nursing experience, nursing license.

Pontifical Catholic University of Puerto Rico, College of Sciences, Department of Nursing, Program in Medical-Surgical Nursing, Ponce, PR 00717-0777. Offers MSN. Part-time and evening/weekend programs available. *Degree requirements:* For master's, comprehensive exam (for some programs), thesis, clinical research paper. *Entrance requirements:* For master's, GRE General Test, 2 letters of recommendation, interview, minimum GPA of 2.75. Electronic applications accepted.

Rush University, College of Nursing, Department of Adult Health Nursing, Chicago, IL 60612-3832. Offers acute care nurse practitioner (MSN, Post-Master's Certificate); adult health nursing (DNP, PhD); adult nurse practitioner (MSN, Post-Master's Certificate); adult/gerontological nurse practitioner (MSN); anesthesia nurse practitioner (MSN, Post-Master's Certificate); critical care clinical specialist (MSN); gerontological nurse practitioner (MSN, Post-Master's Certificate); medical surgical clinical specialist (MSN). *Accreditation:* AACN; AANA/CANAEP (one or more programs are accredited). Part-time programs available. Postbaccalaureate distance learning degree programs offered (minimal on-campus study). Terminal master's awarded for partial completion of doctoral program. *Degree requirements:* For master's, capstone project; for doctorate, thesis/dissertation, DNP leadership project. *Entrance requirements:* For master's, GRE General Test (waived if nursing GPA is above 3.0 or cumulative GPA is above 3.25), interview; for doctorate, GRE General Test, interview, course work in statistics (PhD). Additional exam requirements/recommendations for international students: Required—TOEFL, TWE. Electronic applications accepted. *Faculty research:* Complementary/alternative medicine, critical care outcomes, cardiac risk reduction, Alzheimer's Disease, telehealth monitoring.

Saint Francis Medical Center College of Nursing, Graduate Programs, Peoria, IL 61603-3783. Offers child and family nurse practitioner (MSN); clinical nurse leader (MSN); family nurse practitioner (MSN); family psychiatric mental health nurse practitioner (MSN); medical-surgical nursing (MSN); neonatal nurse practitioner (MSN); nurse clinician (Post-Graduate Certificate); nurse educator (MSN, Post-Graduate Certificate); nursing (DNP); nursing management leadership (MSN). *Accreditation:* NLN. Part-time programs available. Postbaccalaureate distance learning degree programs offered (minimal on-campus study). *Faculty:* 6 full-time (all women), 5 part-time/adjunct (all women). *Students:* 26 full-time (25 women), 174 part-time (166 women); includes 19 minority (8 Black or African American, non-Hispanic/Latino; 1 American Indian or Alaska Native, non-Hispanic/Latino; 3 Asian, non-Hispanic/Latino; 6 Hispanic/Latino; 1 Native Hawaiian or other Pacific Islander, non-Hispanic/Latino). Average age 37. 123 applicants, 93% accepted, 93 enrolled. In 2011, 29 degrees awarded. *Degree requirements:* For master's, research experience, portfolio, practicum; for doctorate, practicum hours. *Entrance requirements:* For master's, nursing research, health assessment, graduate course work in statistics, RN license; for doctorate, master's degree in nursing, professional portfolio, graduate statistics, transcripts, RN license. Additional exam requirements/recommendations for international students: Required—TOEFL. *Application deadline:* For fall admission, 6/1 priority date for domestic students, 6/1 for international students; for spring admission, 11/15 priority date for domestic students, 11/15 for international students. Applications are processed on a rolling basis. Application fee: $50. Electronic applications accepted. *Expenses: Tuition:* Full-time $6120; part-time $510 per semester hour. *Required fees:* $300. *Financial support:* In 2011–12, 3 students received support. Scholarships/grants and tuition waivers (partial) available. Support available to part-time students. Financial award application deadline: 6/15; financial award applicants required to submit FAFSA. *Faculty research:* Outcome and curriculum planning, health promotion, NCLEX-RN results, decision-making program evaluation. *Unit head:* Dr. Patti A. Stockert, President of the College, 309-655-4124, Fax: 309-624-8973, E-mail: patricia.a.stockert@osfhealthcare.org. *Application contact:* Dr. Janice F. Boundy, Dean, 309-655-2230, Fax: 309-624-8973, E-mail: jan.f.boundy@osfhealthcare.org. Web site: http://www.sfmccon.edu/graduate-programs/.

State University of New York Downstate Medical Center, College of Nursing, Graduate Program in Nursing, Program in Clinical Nurse Specialist, Brooklyn, NY 11203-2098. Offers MS, Post Master's Certificate.

Uniformed Services University of the Health Sciences, Graduate School of Nursing, Bethesda, MD 20814-4799. Offers family nurse practitioner (MSN); nurse anesthesia (MSN); nursing science (PhD); perioperative clinical nurse specialty (MSN); psychiatric mental health nurse practitioner (MSN). Program available to military officers only. *Accreditation:* AACN; AANA/CANAEP. *Faculty:* 36 full-time (21 women), 2 part-time/adjunct (0 women). *Students:* 71 full-time (35 women); includes 17 minority (11 Black or African American, non-Hispanic/Latino; 3 Asian, non-Hispanic/Latino; 3 Hispanic/Latino). Average age 36. 120 applicants, 59% accepted, 71 enrolled. In 2011, 57 master's, 2 doctorates awarded. *Degree requirements:* For master's, thesis or alternative. *Entrance requirements:* For master's, GRE, BSN, clinical experience, minimum GPA of 3.0, previous course work in science, writing paper; for doctorate, GRE, written papers, articles. *Application deadline:* For fall admission, 7/1 for domestic students; for winter admission, 2/15 for domestic students. Application fee: $0. Electronic applications accepted. *Faculty research:* Prenatal care, military health care, military readiness, distance learning. *Unit head:* Dr. Carol A. Romano, Associate Dean for Academic Affairs, 301-295-1180, Fax: 301-295-1707, E-mail: carol.romano@usuhs.edu. *Application contact:* Terry Lynn Malavakis, Recording Secretary for Admissions Committee, 301-295-1055, Fax: 301-295-1707, E-mail: terry.malavakis@usuhs.edu. Web site: http://www.usuhs.mil/gsn/.

Universidad Adventista de las Antillas, EGECED Department, Mayagüez, PR 00681-0118. Offers curriculum and instruction (M Ed); health education (M Ed); medical surgical nursing (MN); pastoral theology (M Div); school administration and supervision (M Ed). *Degree requirements:* For master's, comprehensive exam (for some programs), thesis (for some programs). *Entrance requirements:* For master's, EXADEP or GRE General Test, recommendations. Electronic applications accepted.

University of Maryland, Baltimore, Graduate School, School of Nursing, Master's Program in Nursing, Baltimore, MD 21201. Offers community health nursing (MS); gerontological nursing (MS); maternal-child nursing (MS); medical-surgical nursing (MS); nurse-midwifery education (MS); nursing administration (MS); nursing education (MS); nursing health policy (MS); primary care nursing (MS); psychiatric nursing (MS); MS/MBA. MS/MBA offered jointly with University of Baltimore. *Accreditation:* AACN; AANA/CANAEP; NLN (one or more programs are accredited). Part-time programs available. *Students:* 370 full-time (314 women), 480 part-time (441 women); includes 308 minority (176 Black or African American, non-Hispanic/Latino; 2 American Indian or Alaska Native, non-Hispanic/Latino; 70 Asian, non-Hispanic/Latino; 33 Hispanic/Latino; 27 Two or more races, non-Hispanic/Latino), 9 international. Average age 35. 990 applicants, 30% accepted, 204 enrolled. In 2011, 301 master's awarded. *Degree requirements:* For master's, comprehensive exam (for some programs), thesis or alternative. *Entrance requirements:* For master's, minimum GPA of 2.75, course work in statistics, BS in nursing. Additional exam requirements/recommendations for international students: Required—TOEFL (minimum score 550 paper-based; 80 iBT) or IELTS (minimum score 7). *Application deadline:* For fall admission, 2/1 for domestic students, 1/15 for international students. Application fee: $50. Electronic applications accepted. *Financial support:* Fellowships, research assistantships, teaching assistantships, career-related internships or fieldwork, and traineeships available. Support available to part-time students. Financial award application deadline: 2/15; financial award applicants required to submit FAFSA. *Unit head:* Dr. Jane Kapustin, Assistant Dean, 410-706-6741, Fax: 410-706-4231. *Application contact:* Marjorie Fass, Admissions Director, 410-706-0501, Fax: 410-706-7238.

University of Massachusetts Lowell, School of Health and Environment, Department of Nursing, Lowell, MA 01854-2881. Offers adult psychiatric and mental health nursing (MS, Graduate Certificate); family health nursing (MS); gerontological nursing (MS, Graduate Certificate); geropsychiatric nursing (Graduate Certificate); nursing (PhD); nursing education (Graduate Certificate); palliative and end-of-life nursing care (Graduate Certificate). *Accreditation:* AACN. *Degree requirements:* For master's, thesis optional; for doctorate, thesis/dissertation. *Entrance requirements:* For master's and doctorate, GRE General Test. *Faculty research:* Gerontology, women's health issues, long-term care, alcoholism, health promotion.

University of Michigan, Horace H. Rackham School of Graduate Studies, School of Nursing, Division of Acute, Critical and Long-term Care, Program in Medical-Surgical Clinical Nurse Specialist, Ann Arbor, MI 48109. Offers MS. *Accreditation:* AACN. Part-time programs available. *Degree requirements:* For master's, thesis. *Entrance requirements:* For master's, GRE General Test (if BSN GPA less than 3.25), Michigan licensure, B average in BSN. Additional exam requirements/recommendations for international students: Required—TOEFL (minimum score 560 paper-based; 220 computer-based). Electronic applications accepted. *Faculty research:* Clinical specialist and nurse practitioner roles, obesity, breast cancer, Alzheimer's, neurological disorders.

University of South Africa, College of Human Sciences, Pretoria, South Africa. Offers adult education (M Ed); African languages (MA, PhD); African politics (MA, PhD); Afrikaans (MA, PhD); ancient history (MA, PhD); ancient Near Eastern studies (MA, PhD); anthropology (MA, PhD); applied linguistics (MA); Arabic (MA, PhD); archaeology (MA); art history (MA); Biblical archaeology (MA); Biblical studies (M Th, D Th, PhD); Christian spirituality (M Th, D Th); church history (M Th, D Th); classical studies (MA, PhD); clinical psychology (MA); communication (MA, PhD); comparative education (M Ed, Ed D); consulting psychology (D Admin, D Com, PhD); curriculum studies (M Ed, Ed D); development studies (M Admin, MA, D Admin, PhD); didactics (M Ed, Ed D); education (M Tech); education management (M Ed, Ed D); educational psychology (M Ed); English (MA); environmental education (M Ed); French (MA, PhD); German (MA, PhD); Greek (MA); guidance and counseling (M Ed); health studies (MA, PhD), including health sciences education (MA), health services management (MA), medical and surgical nursing science (critical care general) (MA), midwifery and neonatal nursing science (MA), trauma and emergency care (MA); history (MA, PhD); history of education (Ed D); inclusive education (M Ed, Ed D); information and communications technology policy and regulation (MA); information science (MA, MIS, PhD); international politics (MA, PhD); Islamic studies (MA, PhD); Italian (MA, PhD); Judaica (MA, PhD); linguistics (MA, PhD); mathematical education (M Ed); mathematics education (MA); missiology (M Th, D Th); modern Hebrew (MA, PhD); musicology (MA, MMus, D Mus, PhD); natural science education (M Ed); New Testament (M Th, D Th); Old Testament (D Th); pastoral therapy (M Th, D Th); philosophy (MA); philosophy of education (M Ed, Ed D); politics (MA, PhD); Portuguese (MA, PhD); practical theology (M Th, D Th); psychology (MA, MS, PhD); psychology of education (M Ed, Ed D); public health (MA); religious studies (MA, D Th, PhD); Romance languages (MA); Russian (MA, PhD); Semitic languages (MA, PhD); social behavior studies in HIV/AIDS (MA); social science (mental health) (MA); social science in development studies (MA); social science in psychology (MA); social science in social work (MA); social science in sociology (MA); social work (MSW, DSW, PhD); socio-education (M Ed, Ed D); sociolinguistics (MA); sociology (MA, PhD); Spanish (MA, PhD); systematic theology (M Th, D Th); TESOL (teaching English to speakers of other languages) (MA); theological ethics (M Th, D Th); theory of literature (MA, PhD); urban ministries (D Th); urban ministry (M Th).

University of South Carolina, The Graduate School, College of Nursing, Program in Clinical Nursing, Columbia, SC 29208. Offers acute care clinical specialist (MSN); acute care nurse practitioner (MSN); women's health nurse practitioner (MSN). *Accreditation:* AACN. Part-time programs available. *Degree requirements:* For master's, thesis or alternative. *Entrance requirements:* For master's, GRE General Test or MAT, BS in nursing, RN licensure. Additional exam requirements/recommendations for international students: Required—TOEFL (minimum score 570 paper-based; 230 computer-based). Electronic applications accepted. *Faculty research:* Systems research, evidence based practice, breast cancer, violence.

University of Southern Maine, School of Nursing, Portland, ME 04104-9300. Offers adult health nursing (PMC); adult psychiatric/mental health nurse practitioner (MS); clinical nurse leader (MS); clinical nurse specialist psychiatric-mental health nursing (MS); education (MS); family nursing (PMC); family psychiatric/mental health nurse practitioner (MS); management (MS); medical/surgical nursing (MS); nurse practitioner adult health nursing (MS); nurse practitioner family nursing (MS); nursing (DNP); psychiatric-mental health nursing (PMC); MBA/MSN. *Accreditation:* AACN. Part-time programs available. *Degree requirements:* For master's, thesis optional. *Entrance requirements:* For master's, GRE General Test or MAT, minimum GPA of 3.0; for doctorate, GRE. Additional exam requirements/recommendations for international students: Required—TOEFL (minimum score 550 paper-based; 213 computer-based). Electronic applications accepted. *Faculty research:* Women's health, nursing history, weight control, community services, substance abuse.

Ursuline College, School of Graduate Studies, Programs in Nursing, Pepper Pike, OH 44124-4398. Offers care management (MSN); nurse practitioner (MSN); nursing (DNP); nursing education (MSN); palliative care (MSN). *Accreditation:* AACN. Part-time programs available. *Faculty:* 2 full-time (both women), 9 part-time/adjunct (7 women). *Students:* 1 (woman) full-time, 133 part-time (124 women); includes 27 minority (23 Black or African American, non-Hispanic/Latino; 3 Asian, non-Hispanic/Latino; 1 Two or more races, non-Hispanic/Latino), 1 international. Average age 38. 61 applicants, 87% accepted, 47 enrolled. In 2011, 21 master's awarded. *Degree requirements:* For master's, comprehensive exam. *Entrance requirements:* For master's, minimum undergraduate GPA of 3.0, bachelor's degree in nursing, eligibility for or current Ohio RN license. Additional exam requirements/recommendations for international students: Required—TOEFL (minimum score 500 paper-based; 173 computer-based). *Application deadline:* For fall admission, 8/1 priority date for domestic students. Applications are processed on a rolling basis. Application fee: $25. *Expenses: Tuition:* Part-time $875 per credit hour. *Required fees:* $170 per semester. *Financial support:* In 2011–12, 11

students received support. Federal Work-Study available. Financial award application deadline: 3/1. *Unit head:* Dr. Janet Baker, Director, 440-864-8172, Fax: 440-684-6053, E-mail: jbaker@ursuline.edu. *Application contact:* Melanie Steele, Graduate Admission Assistant, 440-646-8199, Fax: 440-684-6138, E-mail: graduateadmissions@ursuline.edu.

Waynesburg University, Graduate and Professional Studies, Waynesburg, PA 15370-1222. Offers business (MBA), including finance, health systems, human resources, leadership, market development; counseling (MA), including addictions counseling, clinical mental health; education (MAT); nursing (MSN), including administration, education, informatics, palliative care; nursing practice (DNP); special education (M Ed); technology (M Ed); MSN/MBA. *Accreditation:* AACN. Part-time and evening/weekend programs available. *Degree requirements:* For doctorate, thesis/dissertation. *Entrance requirements:* Additional exam requirements/recommendations for international students: Required—TOEFL. Electronic applications accepted.

Nurse Anesthesia

Albany Medical College, Center for Nurse Anesthesiology, Albany, NY 12208. Offers anesthesia (MS). *Accreditation:* AANA/CANAEP. *Faculty:* 4 full-time (all women), 1 (woman) part-time/adjunct. *Students:* 43 full-time (35 women); includes 11 minority (3 Black or African American, non-Hispanic/Latino; 4 Asian, non-Hispanic/Latino; 2 Hispanic/Latino; 1 Native Hawaiian or other Pacific Islander, non-Hispanic/Latino; 1 Two or more races, non-Hispanic/Latino), 2 international. Average age 31. 80 applicants, 29% accepted, 23 enrolled. In 2011, 18 degrees awarded. *Degree requirements:* For master's, thesis, thesis proposal/clinical research. *Entrance requirements:* For master's, GRE General Test, BSN or appropriate bachelor's degree, current RN license, critical care experience, organic chemistry, research methods. *Application deadline:* For fall admission, 5/1 for domestic students. Applications are processed on a rolling basis. Application fee: $100. Electronic applications accepted. *Expenses:* Contact institution. *Financial support:* Scholarships/grants and traineeships available. Financial award applicants required to submit FAFSA. *Unit head:* Eileen Falcone, Director, 518-262-4303, Fax: 518-262-5170, E-mail: amcnap@mail.amc.edu. *Application contact:* Helene M. Gregory, Coordinator, 518-262-4303, Fax: 518-262-5170, E-mail: amcnap@mail.amc.edu.

Arkansas State University, Graduate School, College of Nursing and Health Professions, School of Nursing, Jonesboro, State University, AR 72467. Offers aging studies (Certificate); disaster preparedness and emergency management (MS, Certificate); health care management (Certificate); health communications (Certificate); health sciences (MS); health sciences education (Certificate); nurse anesthesia (MSN); nursing (MSN). *Accreditation:* AANA/CANAEP (one or more programs are accredited); NLN. Part-time programs available. *Faculty:* 14 full-time (all women). *Students:* 107 full-time (49 women), 118 part-time (110 women); includes 32 minority (27 Black or African American, non-Hispanic/Latino; 3 Asian, non-Hispanic/Latino; 2 Hispanic/Latino). Average age 33. 96 applicants, 25% accepted, 21 enrolled. In 2011, 83 master's awarded. *Degree requirements:* For master's, comprehensive exam, thesis or alternative. *Entrance requirements:* For master's, GRE General Test or MAT, appropriate bachelor's degree, current Arkansas nursing license, CPR certification, physical examination, professional liability insurance, critical care experience, ACLS Certification, PALS Certification, interview, immunization records, personal goal statement, health assessment. Additional exam requirements/recommendations for international students: Required—TOEFL (minimum score 550 paper-based; 213 computer-based; 79 iBT), IELTS (minimum score 6), Pearson Test of English Academic (minimum score 56). *Application deadline:* Applications are processed on a rolling basis. Application fee: $30 ($40 for international students). Electronic applications accepted. *Expenses:* Contact institution. *Financial support:* In 2011–12, 5 students received support. Career-related internships or fieldwork, scholarships/grants, and unspecified assistantships available. Financial award application deadline: 7/1; financial award applicants required to submit FAFSA. *Unit head:* Dr. Sue McLarry, Chair, 870-972-3074, Fax: 870-972-2954, E-mail: smclarry@astate.edu. *Application contact:* Dr. Andrew Sustich, Dean of the Graduate School, 870-972-3029, Fax: 870-972-3857, E-mail: sustich@astate.edu. Web site: http://www.astate.edu/a/conhp/nursing/index.dot.

Barry University, College of Health Sciences, Program in Anesthesiology, Miami Shores, FL 33161-6695. Offers MS. *Accreditation:* AANA/CANAEP. *Degree requirements:* For master's, comprehensive exam. *Entrance requirements:* For master's, GRE General Test, minimum GPA of 3.0; 2 courses in chemistry (1 with lab); minimum 1 year critical care experience; BSN or RN; 4-year bachelor's degree in health sciences, nursing, biology, or chemistry. Electronic applications accepted. *Faculty research:* Use of computers in education, psychological well-bring of health care providers.

Baylor College of Medicine, School of Allied Health Sciences, Graduate Program in Nurse Anesthesia, Houston, TX 77030-3498. Offers MS, DNP. *Accreditation:* AANA/CANAEP. *Faculty:* 12 full-time (5 women). *Students:* 55 full-time (35 women); includes 20 minority (4 Black or African American, non-Hispanic/Latino; 7 Asian, non-Hispanic/Latino; 6 Hispanic/Latino; 3 Two or more races, non-Hispanic/Latino). Average age 32. 55 applicants, 40% accepted, 20 enrolled. In 2011, 12 master's awarded. *Degree requirements:* For master's, comprehensive exam, thesis; for doctorate, comprehensive exam, thesis/dissertation. *Entrance requirements:* For doctorate, GRE General Test, Texas nursing license, 1 year of work experience in critical care nursing, minimum GPA of 3.0, BSN, statistics, organic chemistry. *Application deadline:* For spring admission, 7/1 for domestic and international students. Application fee: $90. Electronic applications accepted. *Expenses:* Contact institution. *Financial support:* Career-related internships or fieldwork, Federal Work-Study, institutionally sponsored loans, scholarships/grants, and traineeships available. Financial award application deadline: 10/1; financial award applicants required to submit FAFSA. *Faculty research:* Education, simulation. *Total annual research expenditures:* $300,000. *Unit head:* Dr. James R. Walker, Director, 713-798-8650, Fax: 713-798-2743, E-mail: jrwalker@bcm.edu. Web site: http://www.bcm.edu/crna.

Boston College, William F. Connell School of Nursing, Chestnut Hill, MA 02467-3800. Offers adult-gerontology nursing (MS); community health nursing (MS); family health (MS); forensic nursing (MS); maternal/child health nursing (MS), including pediatric and women's health; nurse anesthesia (MS); nursing (PhD); palliative care (MS), including adult and pediatric; psychiatric-mental health nursing (MS); MBA/MS; MS/MA; MS/PhD. *Accreditation:* AACN; AANA/CANAEP (one or more programs are accredited). Part-time programs available. *Faculty:* 48 full-time (46 women), 31 part-time/adjunct (29 women). *Students:* 225 full-time (207 women), 90 part-time (88 women); includes 47 minority (15 Black or African American, non-Hispanic/Latino; 3 American Indian or Alaska Native, non-Hispanic/Latino; 17 Asian, non-Hispanic/Latino; 8 Hispanic/Latino; 4 Two or more races, non-Hispanic/Latino), 6 international. Average age 31. 369 applicants, 43% accepted, 80 enrolled. In 2011, 113 master's, 8 doctorates awarded. *Degree requirements:* For master's, comprehensive exam, research project; for doctorate, comprehensive exam, thesis/dissertation, computer literacy exam or foreign language. *Entrance requirements:* For master's, bachelor's degree in nursing; for doctorate, GRE General Test, MS in nursing. Additional exam requirements/recommendations for international students: Required—TOEFL (minimum score 600 paper-based; 250 computer-based; 100 iBT). *Application deadline:* For fall admission, 11/1 for domestic and international students; for winter admission, 12/31 for domestic and international students; for spring admission, 4/30 for domestic and international students. Applications are processed on a rolling basis. Application fee: $40. Electronic applications accepted. *Financial support:* In 2011–12, 167 students received support, including 9 fellowships with full tuition reimbursements available (averaging $15,300 per year), 7 teaching assistantships (averaging $13,612 per year); research assistantships, Federal Work-Study, institutionally sponsored loans, scholarships/grants, traineeships, health care benefits, tuition waivers (partial), and unspecified assistantships also available. Support available to part-time students. Financial award application deadline: 3/1; financial award applicants required to submit FAFSA. *Faculty research:* Pre-term labor, palliative care, support during chronic illness, violence, eating disorders. *Total annual research expenditures:* $2.1 million. *Unit head:* Dr. Susan Gennaro, Dean, 617-552-4251, Fax: 617-552-0931, E-mail: susan.gennaro@bc.edu. *Application contact:* MaryBeth Crowley, Graduate Programs Assistant, 617-552-4928, Fax: 617-552-2121, E-mail: csongrad@bc.edu. Web site: http://www.bc.edu/nursing/.

Bradley University, Graduate School, College of Education and Health Sciences, Department of Nursing, Peoria, IL 61625-0002. Offers nurse administered anesthesia (MSN); nursing administration (MSN). *Accreditation:* AANA/CANAEP; NLN. Part-time and evening/weekend programs available. *Degree requirements:* For master's, comprehensive exam, thesis optional. *Entrance requirements:* For master's, GRE General Test or MAT, interview, Illinois RN license, advanced cardiac life support certification, pediatric advanced life support certification, 3 letters of recommendation. Additional exam requirements/recommendations for international students: Required—TOEFL (minimum score 550 paper-based; 213 computer-based; 79 iBT).

BryanLGH College of Health Sciences, School of Nurse Anesthesia, Lincoln, NE 68506-1398. Offers MS. *Accreditation:* AANA/CANAEP.

Case Western Reserve University, Frances Payne Bolton School of Nursing, Master's Programs in Nursing, Program in Nurse Anesthesia, Cleveland, OH 44106. Offers MSN. *Accreditation:* AANA/CANAEP. *Students:* 52 full-time (32 women); includes 3 minority (1 Black or African American, non-Hispanic/Latino; 1 Asian, non-Hispanic/Latino; 1 Hispanic/Latino). 112 applicants, 29% accepted, 28 enrolled. In 2011, 32 master's awarded. *Degree requirements:* For master's, thesis optional. *Entrance requirements:* For master's, GRE General Test or MAT. *Application deadline:* For fall admission, 1/15 for domestic students. Application fee: $75. *Financial support:* Research assistantships, teaching assistantships, institutionally sponsored loans, and tuition waivers (partial) available. Support available to part-time students. Financial award application deadline: 6/30. *Faculty research:* Mechanical ventilation antioxidant trial, intravenous function and mechanical ventilation, impact of taxane on peripheral nerve function. *Unit head:* Dr. Jack Kless, Head, 216-368-0221, E-mail: jrk@case.edu. *Application contact:* Donna Hassik, Admissions Coordinator, 216-368-5253, Fax: 216-368-0124, E-mail: dmh7@case.edu. Web site: http://fpb.cwru.edu/MSN/anesthesia.shtm.

Central Connecticut State University, School of Graduate Studies, School of Arts and Sciences, Department of Biology, New Britain, CT 06050-4010. Offers biological sciences (MA, MS), including anesthesia (MS), ecology and environmental sciences (MA), general biology (MA), health sciences specialization (MS), professional education program (MS); biology (Certificate). Part-time and evening/weekend programs available. *Faculty:* 13 full-time (5 women), 6 part-time/adjunct (5 women). *Students:* 133 full-time (74 women), 40 part-time (27 women); includes 35 minority (9 Black or African American, non-Hispanic/Latino; 1 American Indian or Alaska Native, non-Hispanic/Latino; 11 Asian, non-Hispanic/Latino; 11 Hispanic/Latino; 3 Two or more races, non-Hispanic/Latino). Average age 31. 25 applicants, 60% accepted, 8 enrolled. In 2011, 40 master's, 4 other advanced degrees awarded. *Degree requirements:* For master's, comprehensive exam, thesis or alternative; for Certificate, qualifying exam. *Entrance requirements:* For master's, minimum undergraduate GPA of 2.7, essay. Additional exam requirements/recommendations for international students: Required—TOEFL (minimum score 550 paper-based; 213 computer-based). *Application deadline:* For fall admission, 6/1 for domestic students, 5/1 for international students; for spring admission, 11/1 for domestic and international students. Applications are processed on a rolling basis. Application fee: $50. Electronic applications accepted. *Expenses: Tuition, area resident:* Full-time $5137; part-time $482 per credit. Tuition, state resident: full-time $7707; part-time $494 per credit. Tuition, nonresident: full-time $14,311; part-time $494 per credit. *Required fees:* $3865. One-time fee: $62 part-time. *Financial support:* In 2011–12, 6 students received support, including 3 research assistantships; career-related internships or fieldwork, Federal Work-Study, scholarships/grants, and unspecified assistantships also available. Support available to part-time students. Financial award application deadline: 4/15; financial award applicants required to submit FAFSA. *Faculty research:* Environmental science, anesthesia, health sciences, zoology, animal behavior. *Unit head:* Dr. Jeremiah Jarrett, Chair, 860-832-2645, E-mail: jarrettj@ccsu.edu. *Application contact:* Patricia Gardner, Associate Director of Graduate Studies, 860-832-2350, Fax: 860-832-2352, E-mail: graduateadmissions@ccsu.edu. Web site: http://www.biology.ccsu.edu/.

Columbia University, School of Nursing, Program in Nurse Anesthesia, New York, NY 10032. Offers MS, Adv C. *Accreditation:* AACN; AANA/CANAEP. *Entrance requirements:* For master's, GRE General Test, BSN, 1 year of intensive care unit experience; for Adv C, MSN, 1 year of intensive care unit experience. Electronic applications accepted.

DePaul University, College of Science and Health, Department of Nursing, Chicago, IL 60614. Offers adult nurse practitioner (Certificate); adult nursing (MS); family nurse practitioner (Certificate); family nursing (MS); generalist nursing (MS); nurse anesthesia (MS); MS/DNP. MS in nurse anesthesia offered jointly with Ravenswood Hospital Medical Center. *Accreditation:* AACN; AANA/CANAEP (one or more programs are accredited). *Faculty:* 13 full-time (11 women), 12 part-time/adjunct (11 women). *Students:* 256 full-time (220 women), 53 part-time (48 women); includes 81 minority (15

Black or African American, non-Hispanic/Latino; 1 American Indian or Alaska Native, non-Hispanic/Latino; 39 Asian, non-Hispanic/Latino; 16 Hispanic/Latino; 5 Native Hawaiian or other Pacific Islander, non-Hispanic/Latino; 5 Two or more races, non-Hispanic/Latino; 5 international. Average age 29. 238 applicants, 46% accepted, 74 enrolled. In 2011, 70 master's awarded. Terminal master's awarded for partial completion of doctoral program. *Degree requirements:* For master's, comprehensive exam (for some programs), thesis optional. *Entrance requirements:* For master's, GRE (if bachelor's GPA less than 3.2), bachelor's degree from regionally-accredited college or university; personal statement; prerequisite worksheet; resume; 2 letters of recommendation. Additional exam requirements/recommendations for international students: Required—TOEFL (minimum score 590 paper-based; 243 computer-based; 96 iBT), IELTS (minimum score 7.5), Pearson Test of English. *Application deadline:* For fall admission, 3/1 priority date for domestic students, 3/1 for international students; for winter admission, 8/15 priority date for domestic students, 8/15 for international students. Application fee: $40. Electronic applications accepted. *Financial support:* In 2011–12, 5 students received support, including 6 fellowships (averaging $1,500 per year); traineeships also available. Financial award applicants required to submit FAFSA. *Faculty research:* Children's health, women's health, health promotion. *Unit head:* Dr. Kim Amer, Interim Chair, 773-325-1160, E-mail: kamer@depaul.edu. *Application contact:* Ann Spittle, Director of Graduate Admissions, 773-325-7315, Fax: 312-476-3244, E-mail: graddepaul@depaul.edu.

Drexel University, College of Nursing and Health Professions, Department of Nurse Anesthesia, Philadelphia, PA 19104-2875. Offers MSN. *Accreditation:* AACN; AANA/CANAEP. Electronic applications accepted.

Duke University, School of Nursing, Durham, NC 27708-0586. Offers adult acute care (Certificate); adult cardiovascular (Certificate); adult oncology (Certificate); adult primary care (Certificate); clinical nurse specialist (MSN), including adult oncology, gerontology, neonatal, pediatric; clinical research management (MSN, Certificate); family (Certificate); gerontology (Certificate); health and nursing ministries (MSN, Certificate); health systems leadership and outcomes (Certificate); neonatal (Certificate); neonatal/pediatric in rural health (MSN, Certificate); nurse anesthetist (MSN, Certificate); nurse practitioner (MSN), including adult acute care, adult cardiovascular, adult oncology, adult primary care, family, gerontology, neonatal, pediatric, pediatric acute care; nursing (DNP, PhD); nursing and healthcare leadership (MSN); nursing education (MSN); nursing informatics (MSN, Certificate); pediatric (Certificate); pediatric acute care (Certificate); MBA/MSN; MSN/MCM. *Accreditation:* AACN; AANA/CANAEP. Part-time and evening/weekend programs available. Postbaccalaureate distance learning degree programs offered (minimal on-campus study). *Faculty:* 56 full-time (47 women), 2 part-time/adjunct (1 woman). *Students:* 127 full-time (108 women), 395 part-time (358 women); includes 92 minority (42 Black or African American, non-Hispanic/Latino; 3 American Indian or Alaska Native, non-Hispanic/Latino; 21 Asian, non-Hispanic/Latino; 14 Hispanic/Latino; 12 Two or more races, non-Hispanic/Latino), 10 international. Average age 36. 432 applicants, 45% accepted, 143 enrolled. In 2011, 117 master's, 29 doctorates, 32 other advanced degrees awarded. Terminal master's awarded for partial completion of doctoral program. *Degree requirements:* For master's, thesis optional; for doctorate, capstone project. *Entrance requirements:* For master's, GRE General Test, 1 year of nursing experience, BSN, minimum GPA of 3.0, previous course work in statistics; for doctorate, BSN or MSN, minimum GPA of 3.0, portfolio; for Certificate, MSN. Additional exam requirements/recommendations for international students: Required—TOEFL (minimum score 550 paper-based; 213 computer-based). *Application deadline:* For fall admission, 12/1 for domestic and international students; for spring admission, 5/1 for domestic and international students. Application fee: $50. Electronic applications accepted. *Expenses:* Contact institution. *Financial support:* Career-related internships or fieldwork, institutionally sponsored loans, scholarships/grants, traineeships, and tuition waivers (partial) available. Support available to part-time students. Financial award application deadline: 4/1; financial award applicants required to submit FAFSA. *Faculty research:* Cardiovascular disease, caregiver skill training, data mining, prostate cancer, neonatal immune system. *Total annual research expenditures:* $4.7 million. *Unit head:* Dr. Catherine L. Gilliss, Dean/Vice Chancellor for Nursing Affairs, 919-684-9444, Fax: 919-684-9414, E-mail: gilli025@mc.duke.edu. *Application contact:* Bebe T. Mills, Director of Admissions, 919-684-9151, Fax: 919-668-4693, E-mail: mills031@mc.duke.edu. Web site: http://www.nursing.duke.edu/.

Fairfield University, School of Nursing, Fairfield, CT 06824-5195. Offers clinical nurse leader (MSN); family nurse practitioner (MSN, DNP); nurse anesthesia (DNP); psychiatric nurse practitioner (MSN, DNP). *Accreditation:* AACN; AANA/CANAEP. Part-time programs available. *Faculty:* 15 full-time (all women). *Students:* 17 full-time (15 women), 145 part-time (127 women); includes 14 minority (6 Black or African American, non-Hispanic/Latino; 1 American Indian or Alaska Native, non-Hispanic/Latino; 4 Asian, non-Hispanic/Latino; 3 Hispanic/Latino), 1 international. Average age 38. 97 applicants, 29% accepted, 24 enrolled. In 2011, 24 master's awarded. *Degree requirements:* For master's, capstone project. *Entrance requirements:* For master's, minimum QPA of 3.0, RN license, resume, 2 recommendations; for doctorate, GRE (nurse anesthesia applicants only), MSN (minimum QPA of 3.2) or BSN (minimum QPA of 3.0); critical care nursing experience (for nurse anesthesia DNP candidates). Additional exam requirements/recommendations for international students: Required—TOEFL (minimum score 550 paper-based; 213 computer-based; 80 iBT) or IELTS (minimum score 6.5). *Application deadline:* For fall admission, 5/15 for international students; for spring admission, 10/15 for international students. Applications are processed on a rolling basis. Application fee: $60. Electronic applications accepted. *Expenses:* Contact institution. *Financial support:* In 2011–12, 2 students received support. Unspecified assistantships available. Financial award applicants required to submit FAFSA. *Faculty research:* Care of older adults, palliative care, spirituality and innovative partnerships, diabetes. *Unit head:* Dr. Suzanne Campbell, Dean, 203-254-4000 Ext. 2701, Fax: 203-254-4126, E-mail: scampbell@fairfield.edu. *Application contact:* Marianne Gumpper, Director of Graduate and Continuing Studies Admission, 203-254-4184, Fax: 203-254-4073, E-mail: gradadmis@fairfield.edu. Web site: http://www.fairfield.edu/son/son_grad_1.html.

Florida Gulf Coast University, College of Health Professions, Program in Nurse Anesthesia, Fort Myers, FL 33965-6565. Offers MSN. *Accreditation:* AACN; AANA/CANAEP. Part-time programs available. *Faculty:* 45 full-time (32 women), 22 part-time/adjunct (14 women). *Students:* 26 full-time (22 women); includes 3 minority (1 Black or African American, non-Hispanic/Latino; 1 Asian, non-Hispanic/Latino; 1 Hispanic/Latino). Average age 33. 7 applicants, 0% accepted. In 2011, 11 master's awarded. *Degree requirements:* For master's, thesis or alternative. *Entrance requirements:* For master's, GRE General Test, MAT, minimum GPA of 3.0. Additional exam requirements/recommendations for international students: Required—TOEFL (minimum score 550 paper-based; 213 computer-based). *Application deadline:* For fall admission, 4/15 priority date for domestic students; for spring admission, 6/1 for domestic students. Applications are processed on a rolling basis. Application fee: $30. Electronic applications accepted. *Expenses:* Tuition, state resident: full-time $8289. Tuition, nonresident: full-time $28,895. *Required fees:* $1831. One-time fee: $30 full-time. *Faculty research:* Gerontology, community health, ethical and legal aspects of health care, critical care. *Total annual research expenditures:* $181,623. *Unit head:* Dr. Anne Nolen, Interim Director, 239-590-7513, Fax: 239-590-7474, E-mail: anolan@fgcu.edu.

Application contact: Lynn O'Hare, Administrative Assistant, 239-590-7451, Fax: 239-590-7474, E-mail: lohare@fgcu.edu.

Florida Hospital College of Health Sciences, Program in Nurse Anesthesia, Orlando, FL 32803. Offers MS. *Entrance requirements:* For master's, GRE or MAT, minimum undergraduate cumulative GPA of 3.0, 1 year of intensive critical care nursing experience, 3 recommendations, interview.

Gannon University, School of Graduate Studies, Morosky College of Health Professions and Sciences, School of Health Professions, Villa Maria School of Nursing, Erie, PA 16541-0001. Offers anesthesia (MSN); business administration (MSN); family nurse practitioner (Certificate); medical-surgical nursing (MSN); nurse anesthesia (Certificate); nursing rural practitioner (MSN). *Accreditation:* AACN; AANA/CANAEP (one or more programs are accredited). Part-time and evening/weekend programs available. *Students:* 2 full-time (both women), 68 part-time (49 women); includes 3 minority (1 Black or African American, non-Hispanic/Latino; 1 American Indian or Alaska Native, non-Hispanic/Latino; 1 Hispanic/Latino). Average age 44. 15 applicants, 67% accepted, 0 enrolled. In 2011, 20 master's, 3 other advanced degrees awarded. *Degree requirements:* For master's, thesis. *Entrance requirements:* For master's, GRE General Test, degree in nursing. Additional exam requirements/recommendations for international students: Required—TOEFL (minimum score 79 iBT). *Application deadline:* For spring admission, 8/1 for domestic students. Application fee: $25. Electronic applications accepted. *Financial support:* Scholarships/grants available. Financial award application deadline: 7/1; financial award applicants required to submit FAFSA. *Faculty research:* Accurate assessment of delirium in the ICU using CAM, factors affecting caregiver fatigue in dialysis nurses, hours worked by nurses and treatment error reporting. *Unit head:* Dr. Kathleen Patterson, Director, 814-871-5547, E-mail: patterso018@gannon.edu. *Application contact:* Kara Morgan, Director of Graduate Admissions, 814-871-5831, Fax: 814-871-5827, E-mail: graduate@gannon.edu.

Georgetown University, Graduate School of Arts and Sciences, School of Nursing and Health Studies, Washington, DC 20057. Offers acute care nurse practitioner (MS); clinical nurse specialist (MS); family nurse practitioner (MS); nurse anesthesia (MS); nurse-midwifery (MS); nursing education (MS). *Accreditation:* AACN; AANA/CANAEP; ACNM/ACME. *Degree requirements:* For master's, thesis optional. *Entrance requirements:* For master's, GRE General Test or MAT, bachelor's degree in nursing from NLN-accredited school, minimum undergraduate GPA of 3.0. Additional exam requirements/recommendations for international students: Required—TOEFL.

Georgia Health Sciences University, College of Graduate Studies, Nursing Anesthesia Program, Augusta, GA 30912. Offers MSN. *Accreditation:* AACN; AANA/CANAEP. *Students:* 59 full-time (43 women); includes 12 minority (7 Black or African American, non-Hispanic/Latino; 4 Hispanic/Latino; 1 Two or more races, non-Hispanic/Latino). Average age 31. 108 applicants, 24% accepted, 18 enrolled. In 2011, 15 master's awarded. *Entrance requirements:* For master's, GRE General Test, Georgia RN license, at least 1 year of critical care RN experience. Additional exam requirements/recommendations for international students: Required—TOEFL (minimum score 550 paper-based; 213 computer-based; 79 iBT). *Application deadline:* For fall admission, 11/1 for domestic and international students. Application fee: $50. Electronic applications accepted. *Unit head:* Dr. Lucy Marion, Dean, 706-721-3771, Fax: 706-721-8169, E-mail: lumarion@georgiahealth.edu. *Application contact:* Melvenia Blanchard, Office Specialist, 706-721-9558, Fax: 706-721-8169, E-mail: mblanchard@georgiahealth.edu. Web site: http://www.georgiahealth.edu/nursing/nap.html.

Goldfarb School of Nursing at Barnes-Jewish College, Graduate Programs, St. Louis, MO 63110. Offers adult acute care nurse practitioner (MSN); adult nurse practitioner (MSN); nurse anesthesia (MSN); nurse educator (MSN); nurse executive (MSN); DNP/PhD. *Accreditation:* AACN; AANA/CANAEP. Part-time and evening/weekend programs available. Postbaccalaureate distance learning degree programs offered (minimal on-campus study). *Faculty:* 38 full-time (35 women), 14 part-time/adjunct (11 women). *Students:* 79 full-time (68 women), 92 part-time (86 women); includes 45 minority (29 Black or African American, non-Hispanic/Latino; 1 American Indian or Alaska Native, non-Hispanic/Latino; 3 Asian, non-Hispanic/Latino; 3 Hispanic/Latino; 6 Native Hawaiian or other Pacific Islander, non-Hispanic/Latino; 3 Two or more races, non-Hispanic/Latino), 1 international. Average age 40. 134 applicants, 66% accepted, 51 enrolled. In 2011, 31 degrees awarded. *Degree requirements:* For master's, thesis or alternative. *Entrance requirements:* For master's, 2 references, personal statement, curriculum vitae or resume. Additional exam requirements/recommendations for international students: Required—TOEFL (minimum score 575 paper-based; 240 computer-based; 85 iBT). *Application deadline:* For fall admission, 2/1 for international students; for spring admission, 10/1 for international students. Applications are processed on a rolling basis. Application fee: $50. *Expenses:* Tuition: Full-time $14,685; part-time $630 per credit hour. *Required fees:* $280. *Financial support:* Fellowships, research assistantships, Federal Work-Study, institutionally sponsored loans, and scholarships/grants available. Support available to part-time students. Financial award applicants required to submit FAFSA. *Faculty research:* HIV Stigma, HIV symptom management, palliative care with children and their families, heart disease prevention in Hispanic women, depression in the well elderly, alternative therapies in pre-term infants. *Unit head:* Dr. Connie K. Koch, Interim Dean, 314-36-26590, Fax: 314-362-0984, E-mail: ckoch@bjc.org. *Application contact:* Dr. Michael Ward, Associate Dean for Student Programs, 314-362-9155, Fax: 314-362-0984, E-mail: mward@bjc.org.

Gonzaga University, School of Education, Program in Anesthesiology Education, Spokane, WA 99258. Offers M Anesth Ed. *Accreditation:* AANA/CANAEP. *Degree requirements:* For master's, comprehensive exam. *Entrance requirements:* For master's, GRE General Test or MAT. Additional exam requirements/recommendations for international students: Required—TOEFL.

Gooding Institute of Nurse Anesthesia, Program in Nurse Anesthesia, Panama City, FL 32401. Offers MS. *Accreditation:* AANA/CANAEP. *Degree requirements:* For master's, comprehensive exam, thesis. *Entrance requirements:* For master's, GRE General Test, BSN or BA, RN license.

Inter American University of Puerto Rico, Arecibo Campus, Program in Anesthesia, Arecibo, PR 00614-4050. Offers MS. *Accreditation:* AANA/CANAEP. *Degree requirements:* For master's, comprehensive exam, thesis optional. *Entrance requirements:* For master's, GRE, EXADEP, 2 letters of recommendation, bachelor's degree in nursing, interview, minimum GPA of 3.0 in last 60 credits, minimum 1 year experience.

La Roche College, School of Graduate Studies and Adult Education, Program in Health Sciences, Pittsburgh, PA 15237-5898. Offers nurse anesthesia (MS). *Accreditation:* AANA/CANAEP. *Faculty:* 2 full-time (0 women), 1 part-time/adjunct (0 women). *Students:* 31 full-time (10 women); includes 1 minority (Asian, non-Hispanic/Latino), 1 international. Average age 31. 17 applicants, 100% accepted, 17 enrolled. In 2011, 15 master's awarded. *Degree requirements:* For master's, thesis optional. *Entrance requirements:* For master's, GRE General Test, prior acceptance to the Allegheny Valley School of Anesthesia. *Application deadline:* For fall admission, 12/31 for domestic students. Application fee: $50. Electronic applications accepted. *Expenses:* Tuition: Full-time $11,250; part-time $625 per credit hour. *Financial support:*

Application deadline: 3/31; applicants required to submit FAFSA. *Unit head:* Dr. Don Fujito, Coordinator, 412-536-1157, Fax: 412-536-1175, E-mail: fujitod1@laroche.edu. *Application contact:* Hope Schiffgens, Director of Graduate Studies and Adult Education, 412-536-1266, Fax: 412-536-1283, E-mail: schombh1@laroche.edu.

Lincoln Memorial University, Caylor School of Nursing, Harrogate, TN 37752-1901. Offers family nurse practitioner (MSN); nurse anesthesia (MSN); psychiatric mental health nurse practitioner (MSN). *Accreditation:* AANA/CANAEP; NLN. Part-time programs available. *Entrance requirements:* For master's, GRE.

Louisiana State University Health Sciences Center, School of Nursing, New Orleans, LA 70112-2223. Offers advanced public/community health nursing (MN); clinical nurse specialist (MN); nurse anesthesia (MN); nurse practitioner (MN); nursing (DNS). *Accreditation:* AACN; AANA/CANAEP (one or more programs are accredited). Part-time programs available. *Degree requirements:* For master's, thesis optional; for doctorate, thesis/dissertation. *Entrance requirements:* For master's, GRE General Test, MAT, minimum GPA of 3.0; for doctorate, GRE General Test, minimum GPA of 3.5. Additional exam requirements/recommendations for international students: Required—TOEFL. Electronic applications accepted. *Faculty research:* Advanced clinical practice, nursing education, health, social support, nursing administration.

Marshall University, Academic Affairs Division, Program in Nurse Anesthesia, Huntington, WV 25755. Offers DMPNA.

Mayo School of Health Sciences, Program in Nurse Anesthesia, Rochester, MN 55905. Offers MNA. *Accreditation:* AANA/CANAEP. *Faculty:* 1 (woman) full-time, 3 part-time/adjunct (2 women). *Students:* 76 full-time (52 women); includes 9 minority (5 Black or African American, non-Hispanic/Latino; 1 American Indian or Alaska Native, non-Hispanic/Latino; 3 Asian, non-Hispanic/Latino). Average age 30. 112 applicants, 23% accepted, 24 enrolled. In 2011, 26 master's awarded. *Degree requirements:* For master's, comprehensive exam, research project. *Entrance requirements:* For master's, GRE General Test, minimum GPA of 3.0, minimum 1 year of critical care experience. Additional exam requirements/recommendations for international students: Required—TOEFL. *Application deadline:* For fall admission, 10/1 for domestic students. Application fee: $50. Electronic applications accepted. *Expenses:* Contact institution. *Financial support:* Scholarships/grants, health care benefits, and stipends available. Financial award applicants required to submit FAFSA. *Unit head:* Mary Shirk Marienau, Director, 507-284-3293, Fax: 507-284-2818, E-mail: marienau.mary@mayo.edu. *Application contact:* Tammy Neis, Administrative Assistant, 507-284-8331, Fax: 507-284-2818, E-mail: neis.tamra@mayo.edu. Web site: http://www.mayo.edu/mshs.

Medical University of South Carolina, College of Health Professions, Department of Health Professions, Anesthesia for Nurses Program, Charleston, SC 29425. Offers MSNA. *Accreditation:* AANA/CANAEP. *Faculty:* 2 full-time (1 woman), 4 part-time/adjunct (1 woman). *Students:* 81 full-time (59 women); includes 5 minority (2 Black or African American, non-Hispanic/Latino; 1 Asian, non-Hispanic/Latino; 2 Hispanic/Latino). Average age 30. 134 applicants, 22% accepted, 27 enrolled. In 2011, 24 master's awarded. *Degree requirements:* For master's, comprehensive exam, research project, clinical practica. *Entrance requirements:* For master's, GRE General Test, interview, minimum GPA of 3.0, 2 years of RN (ICU) experience, RN license. Additional exam requirements/recommendations for international students: Required—TOEFL (minimum score 600 paper-based; 250 computer-based). *Application deadline:* For fall admission, 11/30 priority date for domestic students, 11/30 for international students. Application fee: $85. Electronic applications accepted. *Financial support:* In 2011–12, 2 students received support. Federal Work-Study, scholarships/grants, and tuition waivers (partial) available. Support available to part-time students. Financial award application deadline: 3/10; financial award applicants required to submit FAFSA. *Faculty research:* Stress in nurse anesthesia, economic changes and continuing education. *Unit head:* Dr. Anthony Chipas, Director, 843-792-3785, Fax: 843-792-1984, E-mail: chipas@musc.edu. *Application contact:* Ann H. Brown, Student Services Program Coordinator, 843-792-2115, Fax: 843-792-3327, E-mail: brownah@musc.edu. Web site: http://www.musc.edu/chp/afn/index.htm.

Middle Tennessee School of Anesthesia, Program in Nurse Anesthesia, Madison, TN 37116. Offers MS. *Accreditation:* AANA/CANAEP. *Degree requirements:* For master's, project. *Entrance requirements:* For master's, GRE General Test, RN license, 1 year of critical-care nursing experience, BSN, general chemistry (minimum of 3 semester hours).

Midwestern University, Glendale Campus, College of Health Sciences, Arizona Campus, Program in Nurse Anesthesia, Glendale, AZ 85308. Offers MS. *Accreditation:* AANA/CANAEP. *Faculty:* 55 full-time (25 women), 1 part-time/adjunct (0 women). *Students:* 56 full-time (34 women); includes 13 minority (3 Black or African American, non-Hispanic/Latino; 2 Asian, non-Hispanic/Latino; 7 Hispanic/Latino; 1 Two or more races, non-Hispanic/Latino). Average age 32. 237 applicants, 16% accepted, 28 enrolled. In 2011, 13 master's awarded. Application fee: $50. *Expenses:* Contact institution. *Unit head:* Mary Wojnakowski, Head, 623-572-3763. *Application contact:* James Walter, Director of Admissions, 888-247-9277, Fax: 623-572-3229, E-mail: admissaz@midwestern.edu. Web site: http://www.midwestern.edu/crna/.

Millikin University, School of Nursing, Decatur, IL 62522-2084. Offers clinical nurse leader (MSN); entry into nursing practice: pre-licensure (MSN); nurse anesthesia (MSN); nurse educator (MSN). *Accreditation:* AACN; AANA/CANAEP. Part-time programs available. *Faculty:* 17 full-time (15 women), 4 part-time/adjunct (3 women). *Students:* 30 full-time (21 women), 10 part-time (9 women); includes 2 minority (both Black or African American, non-Hispanic/Latino). Average age 32. 110 applicants, 39% accepted, 40 enrolled. In 2011, 6 master's awarded. *Degree requirements:* For master's, thesis or alternative, research project. *Entrance requirements:* For master's, GRE, official academic transcript(s), written essay, immunizations, statistics course, 2 letters of recommendation, CPR certification, professional liability/malpractice insurance. Additional exam requirements/recommendations for international students: Required—TOEFL (minimum score 550 paper-based; 79 iBT). *Application deadline:* For spring admission, 11/1 priority date for domestic students. Applications are processed on a rolling basis. Application fee: $0. Electronic applications accepted. *Expenses:* Tuition: Full-time $24,890; part-time $681 per credit hour. Tuition and fees vary according to program. *Financial support:* Institutionally sponsored loans available. Financial award applicants required to submit FAFSA. *Faculty research:* Congestive heart failure, quality of life, transcultural nursing issues, teaching/learning strategies, maternal - newborn. *Unit head:* Dr. Deborah Slayton, Director, 217-424-6348, Fax: 217-420-6731, E-mail: dslayton@millikin.edu. *Application contact:* Marianne Taylor, Administrative Assistant, 800-373-7733 Ext. 5034, Fax: 217-420-6677, E-mail: mgtaylor@millikin.edu. Web site: http://www.millikin.edu/academics/cps/nursing/msn/.

Missouri State University, Graduate College, College of Health and Human Services, Department of Biomedical Sciences, Program in Nurse Anesthesia, Springfield, MO 65897. Offers MS. *Accreditation:* AANA/CANAEP. *Students:* 28 full-time (14 women), 2 part-time (1 woman); includes 3 minority (1 Asian, non-Hispanic/Latino; 1 Hispanic/Latino; 1 Two or more races, non-Hispanic/Latino), 1 international. Average age 33. 12 applicants, 92% accepted, 7 enrolled. In 2011, 12 master's awarded. *Degree requirements:* For master's, comprehensive exam, thesis or alternative, oral exams. *Entrance requirements:* For master's, GRE General Test, 1 year of experience in acute care nursing, current RN license, interview, minimum GPA of 3.0 during final 60 hours of course work. Additional exam requirements/recommendations for international students: Required—TOEFL (minimum score 550 paper-based; 213 computer-based; 79 iBT). *Application deadline:* For fall admission, 11/1 priority date for domestic students, 11/1 for international students; for spring admission, 7/1 priority date for domestic students, 7/1 for international students. Application fee: $35. *Expenses:* Tuition, state resident: full-time $4086; part-time $227 per credit hour. Tuition, nonresident: full-time $8172; part-time $454 per credit hour. *Required fees:* $275 per semester. Tuition and fees vary according to course load, campus/location and program. *Financial support:* Career-related internships or fieldwork and institutionally sponsored loans available. Support available to part-time students. Financial award application deadline: 3/31; financial award applicants required to submit FAFSA. *Unit head:* Benjamin Timson, Didactic Director, 417-838-4145, E-mail: bentimson@missouristate.edu. *Application contact:* Eric Eckert, Coordinator of Graduate Admissions and Recruitment, 417-836-5331, Fax: 417-836-6200, E-mail: ericeckert@missouristate.edu.

Mount Marty College, Graduate Studies Division, Yankton, SD 57078-3724. Offers business administration (MBA); nurse anesthesia (MS); nursing (MSN); pastoral ministries (MPM). *Accreditation:* AANA/CANAEP (one or more programs are accredited). *Degree requirements:* For master's, thesis or alternative. *Entrance requirements:* For master's, GRE General Test, minimum GPA of 3.0. Electronic applications accepted. *Faculty research:* Clinical anesthesia, professional characteristics, motivations of applicants.

Murray State University, College of Health Sciences and Human Services, Program in Nursing, Murray, KY 42071. Offers clinical nurse specialist (MSN); family nurse practitioner (MSN); nurse anesthesia (MSN). *Accreditation:* AACN; AANA/CANAEP. *Degree requirements:* For master's, research project. *Entrance requirements:* For master's, GRE General Test, BSN, interview, RN licensure. Additional exam requirements/recommendations for international students: Required—TOEFL (minimum score 550 paper-based). *Faculty research:* Fibromyalgis, primary care, rural health.

Newman University, School of Nursing and Allied Health, Wichita, KS 67213-2097. Offers nurse anesthesia (MS). *Accreditation:* AANA/CANAEP. *Faculty:* 1 (woman) full-time, 6 part-time/adjunct (3 women). *Students:* 41 full-time (23 women), 17 part-time (12 women); includes 3 minority (1 Black or African American, non-Hispanic/Latino; 1 Hispanic/Latino; 1 Two or more races, non-Hispanic/Latino). Average age 32. 165 applicants, 13% accepted, 22 enrolled. In 2011, 19 master's awarded. *Degree requirements:* For master's, thesis optional. *Entrance requirements:* For master's, GRE General Test, registered professional nursing license in Kansas, 3 professional recommendations, BSN, statistics course, 1 year of employment, interview, minimum GPA of 3.0. Additional exam requirements/recommendations for international students: Required—TOEFL (minimum score 600 paper-based; 250 computer-based; 100 iBT). *Application deadline:* For fall admission, 11/15 for domestic and international students. Applications are processed on a rolling basis. Application fee: $25 ($40 for international students). Electronic applications accepted. *Expenses:* Contact institution. *Financial support:* Federal Work-Study available. Financial award application deadline: 8/15; financial award applicants required to submit FAFSA. *Unit head:* Prof. Sharon Niemann, Director of the Master of Science in Nurse Anesthesia Program, 316-942-4291 Ext. 2272, Fax: 316-942-4483, E-mail: niemanns@newmanu.edu. *Application contact:* Linda Kay Sabala, Director of Graduate Admissions, 316-942-4291 Ext. 2230, Fax: 316-942-4483.

Northeastern University, Bouvé College of Health Sciences, School of Nursing, Program in Nurse Anesthesia, Boston, MA 02115-5096. Offers MS, CAGS. *Accreditation:* AACN; AANA/CANAEP. *Faculty:* 25 full-time, 4 part-time/adjunct. *Students:* 163 full-time, 6 part-time. 91 applicants, 57% accepted, 49 enrolled. In 2011, 24 master's awarded. *Degree requirements:* For master's, thesis or alternative. *Entrance requirements:* For master's, GRE General Test. Additional exam requirements/recommendations for international students: Required—TOEFL (minimum score 100 iBT). *Application deadline:* For fall admission, 12/1 for domestic students. Application fee: $50. Electronic applications accepted. *Financial support:* Research assistantships, teaching assistantships, scholarships/grants, traineeships, and tuition waivers (partial) available. Financial award application deadline: 7/1; financial award applicants required to submit FAFSA. *Unit head:* Dr. Steve Alves, Director, 617-373-2985, Fax: 617-373-8672, E-mail: s.alves@neu.edu. *Application contact:* Margaret Schnabel, Director of Graduate Admissions, 617-373-2708, E-mail: bouvegrad@neu.edu. Web site: http://www.northeastern.edu/bouve/programs/cmnurseanes.html.

Oakland University, Graduate Study and Lifelong Learning, School of Nursing, Program in Nurse Anesthetist, Rochester, MI 48309-4401. Offers MSN, Certificate. Programs offered jointly with Beaumont Hospital Corporation. *Accreditation:* AACN; AANA/CANAEP. *Degree requirements:* For master's, thesis (for some programs). *Entrance requirements:* For master's, GRE General Test. Additional exam requirements/recommendations for international students: Required—TOEFL (minimum score 550 paper-based; 213 computer-based). Electronic applications accepted. *Expenses:* Contact institution.

Old Dominion University, College of Health Sciences, School of Nursing, Nurse Anesthesia Program, Norfolk, VA 23529. Offers MSN. *Faculty:* 1 full-time (0 women), 3 part-time/adjunct (2 women). *Students:* 9 full-time (8 women); includes 2 minority (1 Hispanic/Latino; 1 Two or more races, non-Hispanic/Latino). Average age 34. 70 applicants, 21% accepted, 9 enrolled. In 2011, 5 master's awarded. *Degree requirements:* For master's, comprehensive exam, statistics, organic chemistry. *Entrance requirements:* For master's, GRE, MAT. *Application deadline:* For fall admission, 11/15 priority date for domestic students; for spring admission, 3/15 for domestic and international students. Applications are processed on a rolling basis. Application fee: $50. Electronic applications accepted. *Expenses:* Tuition, state resident: full-time $9096; part-time $379 per credit. Tuition, nonresident: full-time $23,064; part-time $961 per credit. *Required fees:* $127 per semester. One-time fee: $50. *Unit head:* Dr. Nathaniel Michael Apatov, Graduate Program Director, 757-683-5263, Fax: 757-683-5253, E-mail: napatov@odu.edu. *Application contact:* Sue Parker, Coordinator, Graduate Student Services, 757-683-4298, Fax: 757-683-5253, E-mail: sparker@odu.edu. Web site: http://hs.odu.edu/nursing/academics/nurse_anesthesia/nurse_anesthesia.shtml.

Oregon Health & Science University, School of Nursing, Program in Nurse Anesthesia, Portland, OR 97239-3098. Offers MN, MS. *Accreditation:* AANA/CANAEP.

Otterbein University, Department of Nursing, Westerville, OH 43081. Offers advanced practice nurse educator (Certificate); clinical nurse leader (MSN); family nurse practitioner (MSN, Certificate); nurse anesthesia (MSN, Certificate); nursing (DNP); nursing service administration (MSN). *Accreditation:* AACN; AANA/CANAEP; NLN. Part-time and evening/weekend programs available. Postbaccalaureate distance learning degree programs offered (minimal on-campus study). *Degree requirements:* For master's, comprehensive exam (for some programs), thesis (for some programs). *Entrance requirements:* For master's, 2 reference forms, resume; for Certificate, official transcripts, 2 reference forms, essay, resumé. Additional exam requirements/recommendations for international students: Required—TOEFL (minimum score 550

paper-based; 213 computer-based; 79 iBT). *Faculty research:* Patient education, women's health, trauma curriculum development, administration.

Our Lady of the Lake College, School of Nursing, Program in Nurse Anesthesia, Baton Rouge, LA 70808. Offers MS. *Accreditation:* AANA/CANAEP. *Degree requirements:* For master's, clinical practicum. *Entrance requirements:* For master's, GRE, current RN license; baccalaureate degree in nursing; 1 year full-time experience (2 years preferred) as RN in adult critical care setting (adult intensive care unit preferred); minimum cumulative GPA of 3.0; one undergraduate or graduate chemistry course. Additional exam requirements/recommendations for international students: Required—TOEFL.

Rosalind Franklin University of Medicine and Science, College of Health Professions, Nurse Anesthesia Department, North Chicago, IL 60064-3095. Offers MS. *Accreditation:* AANA/CANAEP. *Entrance requirements:* For master's, GRE, RN license, ICU experience. Additional exam requirements/recommendations for international students: Required—TOEFL. Electronic applications accepted. *Faculty research:* Patient safety, pediatric anesthesia, instructional technology.

Rush University, College of Nursing, Department of Adult Health Nursing, Chicago, IL 60612-3832. Offers acute care nurse practitioner (MSN, Post-Master's Certificate); adult health nursing (DNP, PhD); adult nurse practitioner (MSN, Post-Master's Certificate); adult/gerontological nurse practitioner (MSN); anesthesia nurse practitioner (MSN, Post-Master's Certificate); critical care clinical specialist (MSN); gerontological nurse practitioner (MSN, Post-Master's Certificate); medical surgical clinical specialist (MSN). *Accreditation:* AACN; AANA/CANAEP (one or more programs are accredited). Part-time programs available. Postbaccalaureate distance learning degree programs offered (minimal on-campus study). Terminal master's awarded for partial completion of doctoral program. *Degree requirements:* For master's, capstone project; for doctorate, thesis/dissertation, DNP leadership project. *Entrance requirements:* For master's, GRE General Test (waived if nursing GPA is above 3.0 or cumulative GPA is above 3.25), interview; for doctorate, GRE General Test, interview, course work in statistics (PhD). Additional exam requirements/recommendations for international students: Required—TOEFL, TWE. Electronic applications accepted. *Faculty research:* Complementary/alternative medicine, critical care outcomes, cardiac risk reduction, Alzheimer's Disease, telehealth monitoring.

Saint Joseph's University, College of Arts and Sciences, Department of Health Services, Philadelphia, PA 19131-1395. Offers health administration (MS, Post-Master's Certificate); health care ethics (Post-Master's Certificate); health education (MS, Post-Master's Certificate); health informatics (Post-Master's Certificate); healthcare ethics (MS); long-term care administration (MS); nurse anesthesia (MS); school nurse certification (MS). Part-time and evening/weekend programs available. *Faculty:* 9 full-time (1 woman), 21 part-time/adjunct (11 women). *Students:* 76 full-time (53 women), 261 part-time (204 women); includes 106 minority (79 Black or African American, non-Hispanic/Latino; 2 American Indian or Alaska Native, non-Hispanic/Latino; 12 Asian, non-Hispanic/Latino; 10 Hispanic/Latino; 1 Native Hawaiian or other Pacific Islander, non-Hispanic/Latino; 2 Two or more races, non-Hispanic/Latino), 17 international. Average age 35. 143 applicants, 69% accepted, 91 enrolled. In 2011, 67 master's awarded. *Entrance requirements:* For master's, GRE (if GPA less than 2.75), 2 letters of recommendation, minimum GPA of 2.75, resume. Additional exam requirements/recommendations for international students: Required—TOEFL (minimum score 550 paper-based; 213 computer-based; 79 iBT). *Application deadline:* For fall admission, 7/15 priority date for domestic students, 4/15 for international students; for winter admission, 1/15 for international students; for spring admission, 11/15 priority date for domestic students, 10/15 for international students. Applications are processed on a rolling basis. Application fee: $35. Electronic applications accepted. *Expenses: Tuition:* Part-time $735 per credit hour. Tuition and fees vary according to degree level and program. *Financial support:* Career-related internships or fieldwork and unspecified assistantships available. Financial award applicants required to submit FAFSA. *Unit head:* Nakia Henderson, Director, 610-660-2952, E-mail: nakia.henderson@sju.edu. *Application contact:* Kate McConnell, Director, Graduate College of Arts and Sciences Admissions and Retention, 610-660-3184, Fax: 610-660-3230, E-mail: kate.mcconnell@sju.edu.

Saint Mary's University of Minnesota, Schools of Graduate and Professional Programs, Graduate School of Health and Human Services, Nurse Anesthesia Program, Winona, MN 55987-1399. Offers MS. Offered jointly with the Minneapolis School of Anesthesia. *Accreditation:* AANA/CANAEP. *Unit head:* Merri Moody, 612-728-5133. *Application contact:* Yasin Alsaidi, Director of Admissions for Graduate and Professional Programs, 612-728-5207, Fax: 612-728-5121, E-mail: yalsaidi@smumn.edu. Web site: http://www.smumn.edu/graduate-home/areas-of-study/graduate-school-of-health-human-services/ms-in-nurse-anesthesia.

Saint Vincent College, Program in Health Services, Latrobe, PA 15650-2690. Offers nurse anesthesia (MS).

Samford University, Ida V. Moffett School of Nursing, Birmingham, AL 35229. Offers advance practice (DNP); anesthesia (MSN); family nurse practitioner (MSN); nurse educator (MSN); nurse executive (DNP); nurse manager (MSN). *Accreditation:* AACN; AANA/CANAEP (one or more programs are accredited). Part-time programs available. Postbaccalaureate distance learning degree programs offered (minimal on-campus study). *Faculty:* 14 full-time (all women), 2 part-time/adjunct (0 women). *Students:* 226 full-time (152 women), 42 part-time (20 women); includes 43 minority (14 Black or African American, non-Hispanic/Latino; 4 American Indian or Alaska Native, non-Hispanic/Latino; 15 Asian, non-Hispanic/Latino; 9 Hispanic/Latino; 1 Native Hawaiian or other Pacific Islander, non-Hispanic/Latino), 2 international. Average age 39. 50 applicants, 88% accepted, 44 enrolled. In 2011, 95 master's, 14 doctorates awarded. *Median time to degree:* Of those who began their doctoral program in fall 2003, 100% received their degree in 8 years or less. *Degree requirements:* For master's and doctorate, capstone project with oral presentation. *Entrance requirements:* For master's, MAT; GRE (for nurse anesthesia). Additional exam requirements/recommendations for international students: Required—TOEFL (minimum score 550 paper-based; 213 computer-based; 80 iBT). *Application deadline:* For fall admission, 7/1 priority date for domestic students, 7/1 for international students; for spring admission, 10/1 priority date for domestic students, 10/1 for international students. Application fee: $65. Electronic applications accepted. *Expenses:* Contact institution. *Financial support:* In 2011–12, 166 students received support. Institutionally sponsored loans, scholarships/grants, and traineeships available. Financial award application deadline: 3/1; financial award applicants required to submit FAFSA. *Faculty research:* Issues in rural health care, vulnerable populations, genetics and disabilities in pediatrics, geriatrics, Parrish nursing research. *Unit head:* Dr. Nena F. Sanders, Dean, 205-726-2629, E-mail: nfsander@samford.edu. *Application contact:* Dr. Marian Carter, Director of Graduate Student Services, 205-726-2047, Fax: 205-726-4269, E-mail: mwcarter@samford.edu. Web site: http://samford.edu/nursing.

Samuel Merritt University, School of Nursing, Oakland, CA 94609-3108. Offers case management (MSN); family nurse practitioner (MSN, Certificate); nurse anesthetist (MSN, Certificate); nursing (MSN, DNP). *Accreditation:* AACN; AANA/CANAEP (one or more programs are accredited). Part-time and evening/weekend programs available. *Degree requirements:* For master's, thesis or alternative. *Entrance requirements:* For master's, minimum GPA of 2.5 in science, 3.0 overall; previous course work in statistics; current RN license. Additional exam requirements/recommendations for international students: Required—TOEFL. *Faculty research:* Gerontology, community health, maternal-child health, sexually transmitted diseases, substance abuse, oncology.

Southern Illinois University Edwardsville, Graduate School, School of Nursing, Program in Nurse Anesthesia, Edwardsville, IL 62026-0001. Offers MS, Post-Master's Certificate. *Accreditation:* AANA/CANAEP. Part-time programs available. *Students:* 69 full-time (43 women), 4 part-time (3 women); includes 14 minority (3 Black or African American, non-Hispanic/Latino; 9 Asian, non-Hispanic/Latino; 1 Hispanic/Latino; 1 Two or more races, non-Hispanic/Latino), 1 international. 8 applicants, 0% accepted. In 2011, 21 master's awarded. *Degree requirements:* For master's, comprehensive exam. *Entrance requirements:* For master's, appropriate bachelor's degree, RN license, minimum undergraduate nursing GPA of 3.0. Additional exam requirements/recommendations for international students: Required—TOEFL (minimum score 550 paper-based; 213 computer-based; 79 iBT), IELTS (minimum score 6.5). *Application deadline:* For spring admission, 6/1 for domestic and international students. Application fee: $30. Electronic applications accepted. Tuition and fees vary according to course load and program. *Financial support:* Fellowships, research assistantships, teaching assistantships, institutionally sponsored loans, scholarships/grants, and unspecified assistantships available. Financial award application deadline: 3/1; financial award applicants required to submit FAFSA. *Unit head:* Dr. Kathy Ketchum, Director, 618-650-3936, E-mail: kketchu@siue.edu. *Application contact:* Dr. Kathy Ketchum, Director, 618-650-3936, E-mail: kketchu@siue.edu. Web site: http://www.siue.edu/nursing/graduate.

State University of New York Downstate Medical Center, College of Nursing, Graduate Program in Nursing, Program in Nurse Anesthesia, Brooklyn, NY 11203-2098. Offers MS. *Accreditation:* AACN; AANA/CANAEP. *Degree requirements:* For master's, thesis optional. *Entrance requirements:* For master's, GRE, BSN; minimum GPA of 3.0; previous undergraduate course work in statistics, health assessment, and nursing research; RN license.

Texas Christian University, Harris College of Nursing and Health Sciences, School of Nurse Anesthesia, Fort Worth, TX 76129-0002. Offers DNP-A. Postbaccalaureate distance learning degree programs offered (minimal on-campus study). *Faculty:* 7 full-time (4 women), 2 part-time/adjunct (1 woman). *Students:* 55 full-time (32 women), 123 part-time (64 women); includes 28 minority (4 Black or African American, non-Hispanic/Latino; 1 American Indian or Alaska Native, non-Hispanic/Latino; 9 Asian, non-Hispanic/Latino; 11 Hispanic/Latino; 3 Two or more races, non-Hispanic/Latino). Average age 29. 29 applicants, 100% accepted, 23 enrolled. *Entrance requirements:* For doctorate, GRE, CCRN Certification. Additional exam requirements/recommendations for international students: Required—TOEFL (minimum score 600 paper-based). *Application deadline:* For fall admission, 7/1 for domestic and international students. Application fee: $50. *Expenses:* Contact institution. *Financial support:* Traineeships available. Financial award applicants required to submit FAFSA. *Unit head:* Dr. Kay K. Sanders, Director, 817-257-7887, E-mail: k.sanders@tcu.edu. *Application contact:* Admissions, TCU Graduate Studies Office, 817-257-7515, Fax: 817-257-7484, E-mail: frogmail@tcu.edu. Web site: http://www.crna.tcu.edu/.

Texas Wesleyan University, Graduate Programs, Programs in Nurse Anesthesia, Fort Worth, TX 76105-1536. Offers MHS, MSNA, DNAP. *Accreditation:* AANA/CANAEP (one or more programs are accredited). *Faculty:* 11 full-time (5 women), 1 (woman) part-time/adjunct. *Students:* 443 full-time (256 women); includes 96 minority (30 Black or African American, non-Hispanic/Latino; 3 American Indian or Alaska Native, non-Hispanic/Latino; 29 Asian, non-Hispanic/Latino; 30 Hispanic/Latino; 2 Native Hawaiian or other Pacific Islander, non-Hispanic/Latino; 2 Two or more races, non-Hispanic/Latino), 1 international. Average age 33. 483 applicants, 30% accepted, 135 enrolled. In 2011, 124 master's awarded. *Entrance requirements:* For master's, GRE General Test, master's degree; copy of current Council on Certification/Recertification card (all applicants must be Certified RN Anesthetists); minimum GPA of 3.0, science 2.75; undergraduate statistics course with minimum C grade; graduate statistics course with minimum B grade; graduate-level research course; current curriculum vitae; 3 letters of support; for doctorate, master's degree; copy of current Council on Certification/Recertification card (all applicants must be Certified RN Anesthetists); minimum GPA of 3.0, science 2.75; undergraduate statistics course with minimum C grade; graduate statistics course with minimum B grade, graduate-level research course; current curriculum vitae; 3 letters of support. *Application deadline:* For fall admission, 12/1 priority date for domestic students. Applications are processed on a rolling basis. Application fee: $50. *Expenses:* Contact institution. *Financial support:* Federal Work-Study, institutionally sponsored loans, scholarships/grants, and tuition waivers (full and partial) available. Support available to part-time students. Financial award application deadline: 3/15; financial award applicants required to submit FAFSA. *Unit head:* John Martin, Director, 817-531-4406, Fax: 817-531-6508. *Application contact:* Information Contact, 817-531-4406, Fax: 817-531-6508, E-mail: igriffin@txwes.edu. Web site: http://www.txwes.edu/academics/gpna.

Uniformed Services University of the Health Sciences, Graduate School of Nursing, Bethesda, MD 20814-4799. Offers family nurse practitioner (MSN); nurse anesthesia (MSN); nursing science (PhD); perioperative clinical nurse specialty (MSN); psychiatric mental health nurse practitioner (MSN). Program available to military officers only. *Accreditation:* AACN; AANA/CANAEP. *Faculty:* 36 full-time (21 women), 2 part-time/adjunct (0 women). *Students:* 71 full-time (35 women); includes 17 minority (11 Black or African American, non-Hispanic/Latino; 3 Asian, non-Hispanic/Latino; 3 Hispanic/Latino). Average age 36. 120 applicants, 59% accepted, 71 enrolled. In 2011, 57 master's, 2 doctorates awarded. *Degree requirements:* For master's, thesis or alternative. *Entrance requirements:* For master's, GRE, BSN, clinical experience, minimum GPA of 3.0, previous course work in science, writing paper; for doctorate, GRE, written papers, articles. *Application deadline:* For fall admission, 7/1 for domestic students; for winter admission, 2/15 for domestic students. Application fee: $0. Electronic applications accepted. *Faculty research:* Prenatal care, military health care, military readiness, distance learning. *Unit head:* Dr. Carol A. Romano, Associate Dean for Academic Affairs, 301-295-1180, Fax: 301-295-1707, E-mail: carol.romano@usuhs.edu. *Application contact:* Terry Lynn Malavakis, Recording Secretary for Admissions Committee, 301-295-1055, Fax: 301-295-1707, E-mail: terry.malavakis@usuhs.edu. Web site: http://www.usuhs.mil/gsn/.

Union University, School of Nursing, Jackson, TN 38305-3697. Offers executive leadership (DNP); nurse anesthesia (DNP); nurse anesthetist (PMC); nurse practitioner (DNP); nursing education (MSN, PMC). *Accreditation:* AACN; AANA/CANAEP. *Degree requirements:* For master's, thesis or alternative. *Entrance requirements:* For master's, GRE, 3 letters of reference, bachelor's degree in nursing, minimum GPA of 3.0. Additional exam requirements/recommendations for international students: Required—TOEFL (minimum score 560 paper-based; 220 computer-based). Electronic applications accepted. *Faculty research:* Children's health, occupational rehabilitation, informatics, health promotion.

University at Buffalo, the State University of New York, Graduate School, School of Nursing, Buffalo, NY 14214. Offers adult clinical nurse specialist (DNP); adult nurse practitioner (DNP); family nurse practitioner (DNP); health care systems and leadership (MS); nurse anesthetist (DNP); nursing (PhD); nursing education (Certificate); post-

master's track (DNP); psychiatric mental health nurse practitioner (DNP). *Accreditation:* AACN; AANA/CANAEP (one or more programs are accredited). Part-time programs available. Postbaccalaureate distance learning degree programs offered (minimal on-campus study). *Faculty:* 29 full-time (25 women), 18 part-time/adjunct (17 women). *Students:* 101 full-time (76 women), 100 part-time (90 women); includes 19 minority (10 Black or African American, non-Hispanic/Latino; 2 American Indian or Alaska Native, non-Hispanic/Latino; 2 Asian, non-Hispanic/Latino; 2 Hispanic/Latino; 3 Native Hawaiian or other Pacific Islander, non-Hispanic/Latino), 34 international. Average age 34. 342 applicants, 26% accepted, 67 enrolled. In 2011, 51 master's, 3 doctorates awarded. *Median time to degree:* Of those who began their doctoral program in fall 2003, 75% received their degree in 8 years or less. *Degree requirements:* For master's, thesis optional, comprehensive exams or project; for doctorate, comprehensive exam (for some programs), capstone (for DNP), dissertation (for PhD). *Entrance requirements:* For doctorate, GRE or MAT, minimum GPA of 3.0 (3.25 for PhD), RN license, BS or MS in nursing, 3 references, writing sample; for Certificate, interview, minimum GPA of 3.0 or GRE General Test, RN license, MS in nursing. Additional exam requirements/recommendations for international students: Required—TOEFL (minimum score 550 paper-based; 213 computer-based; 79 iBT), IELTS (minimum score 6.5). *Application deadline:* For fall admission, 8/15 for domestic students, 4/1 for international students; for spring admission, 12/15 for domestic students, 10/1 for international students. Application fee: $75. Electronic applications accepted. *Financial support:* In 2011–12, 80 students received support, including 6 fellowships with full tuition reimbursements available (averaging $17,000 per year), 3 research assistantships with full tuition reimbursements available (averaging $10,600 per year), 5 teaching assistantships with full tuition reimbursements available (averaging $10,600 per year); scholarships/grants, traineeships, health care benefits, and unspecified assistantships also available. Financial award application deadline: 3/15; financial award applicants required to submit FAFSA. *Faculty research:* Oncology, palliative care, gerontology, addictions, mental health, community wellness. *Total annual research expenditures:* $1.3 million. *Unit head:* Dr. Marsha L. Lewis, Dean and Professor, 716-829-2533, Fax: 716-829-2566, E-mail: ubnursingdean@buffalo.edu. *Application contact:* Dr. David J. Lang, Director of Student Affairs, 716-829-2537, Fax: 716-829-2067, E-mail: nursing@buffalo.edu. Web site: http://nursing.buffalo.edu/.

The University of Alabama at Birmingham, School of Nursing, Birmingham, AL 35294. Offers nurse anesthesia (MNA); nursing (MSN, DNP, PhD). *Accreditation:* AACN. Terminal master's awarded for partial completion of doctoral program. *Degree requirements:* For doctorate, thesis/dissertation, research mentorship experience. *Entrance requirements:* For master's, GRE General Test, BS in nursing, interview; for doctorate, GRE General Test, computer literacy, course work in statistics, interview, minimum GPA of 3.0, MS in nursing. Additional exam requirements/recommendations for international students: Required—TOEFL. *Application deadline:* Applications are processed on a rolling basis. Electronic applications accepted. *Expenses:* Contact institution. *Financial support:* Fellowships, research assistantships, teaching assistantships, and Federal Work-Study available. Support available to part-time students. *Unit head:* Dr. Doreen C. Harper, Dean, 205-934-5360, E-mail: dcharper@uab.edu. Web site: http://www.uab.edu/son/.

The University of British Columbia, Faculty of Medicine, Department of Anesthesiology, Pharmacology and Therapeutics, Vancouver, BC V6T 1Z3, Canada. Offers M Sc, PhD. Terminal master's awarded for partial completion of doctoral program. *Degree requirements:* For master's, thesis; for doctorate, comprehensive exam, thesis/dissertation. *Entrance requirements:* For master's, MD or appropriate bachelor's degree; for doctorate, MD or M Sc. Additional exam requirements/recommendations for international students: Required—TOEFL (minimum score 600 paper-based; 250 computer-based; 100 iBT). Electronic applications accepted. *Faculty research:* Cellular, biochemical, autonomic, cardiovascular pharmacology; neuropharmacology and pulmonary pharmacology.

University of Cincinnati, Graduate School, College of Nursing, Cincinnati, OH 45221-0038. Offers clinical nurse specialist (MSN), including adult health, community health, neonatal, nursing administration, occupational health, pediatric health, psychiatric nursing, women's health; nurse anesthesia (MSN); nurse midwifery (MSN); nurse practitioner (MSN), including acute care, ambulatory care, family, family/psychiatric, women's health; nursing (PhD); MBA/MSN. *Accreditation:* AACN; AANA/CANAEP (one or more programs are accredited); ACNM/ACME. Part-time programs available. Postbaccalaureate distance learning degree programs offered (no on-campus study). Terminal master's awarded for partial completion of doctoral program. *Degree requirements:* For master's, thesis or alternative; for doctorate, comprehensive exam, thesis/dissertation. *Entrance requirements:* For master's and doctorate, GRE General Test. Additional exam requirements/recommendations for international students: Required—TOEFL (minimum score 520 paper-based; 190 computer-based). Electronic applications accepted. *Faculty research:* Substance abuse, injury and violence, symptom management.

University of Detroit Mercy, College of Health Professions, Program in Nurse Anesthesiology, Detroit, MI 48221. Offers MS. *Accreditation:* AANA/CANAEP. *Entrance requirements:* For master's, GRE General Test, minimum GPA of 3.0. *Expenses:* Contact institution.

The University of Kansas, University of Kansas Medical Center, School of Health Professions, Department of Nurse Anesthesia Education, Kansas City, KS 66160. Offers nurse anesthesia (MS). *Accreditation:* AANA/CANAEP. *Faculty:* 8. *Students:* 66 full-time (43 women), 1 (woman) part-time; includes 10 minority (4 Black or African American, non-Hispanic/Latino; 2 Asian, non-Hispanic/Latino; 2 Hispanic/Latino; 2 Two or more races, non-Hispanic/Latino). Average age 30. 89 applicants, 44% accepted, 24 enrolled. In 2011, 19 master's awarded. *Degree requirements:* For master's, comprehensive exam, thesis or alternative. *Entrance requirements:* For master's, bachelor's degree in nursing or related field, RN license, 2 years of experience as an RN including 1 year of experience in ICU; five science classes (anatomy, physiology, microbiology and 2 chemistry) and statistics. Additional exam requirements/recommendations for international students: Required—TOEFL. *Application deadline:* For fall admission, 7/15 for domestic and international students. Application fee: $60. *Expenses:* Contact institution. *Financial support:* Traineeships available. Financial award application deadline: 2/14; financial award applicants required to submit FAFSA. *Faculty research:* Simulation training and diaphragm fatigue. *Total annual research expenditures:* $14,863. *Unit head:* Dr. Donna S. Nyght, Chair, 913-588-6612, Fax: 913-588-3334, E-mail: dnyght@kumc.edu. *Application contact:* Carrie Hewitt, Administrative Officer, 913-588-6612, Fax: 913-588-3334, E-mail: na@kumc.edu. Web site: http://na.kumc.edu.

University of Medicine and Dentistry of New Jersey, School of Nursing, Newark, NJ 07107-3001. Offers adult health (MSN); adult occupational health (MSN); advanced practice nursing (MSN, Post Master's Certificate); family nurse practitioner (MSN); nurse anesthesia (MSN); nursing (MSN); nursing informatics (MSN); urban health (PhD); women's health practitioner (MSN). *Accreditation:* AANA/CANAEP; NLN (one or more programs are accredited). Part-time programs available. *Entrance requirements:* For master's, GRE, RN license; basic life support, statistics, and health assessment experience. Additional exam requirements/recommendations for international students: Required—TOEFL. Electronic applications accepted. *Expenses:* Contact institution. *Faculty research:* HIV/AIDS, diabetes education, learned helplessness, nursing science, psychoeducation.

University of Miami, Graduate School, School of Nursing and Health Studies, Coral Gables, FL 33124. Offers acute care (MSN), including acute care nurse practitioner, nurse anesthesia; nursing (PhD); primary care (MSN), including adult nurse practitioner, family nurse practitioner, nurse midwifery, women's health practitioner. *Accreditation:* AACN; AANA/CANAEP; ACNM/ACME (one or more programs are accredited). Part-time programs available. *Degree requirements:* For master's, thesis optional; for doctorate, thesis/dissertation. *Entrance requirements:* For master's, GRE General Test, BSN, minimum GPA of 3.0, Florida RN license; for doctorate, GRE General Test, BSN or MSN, minimum GPA of 3.0. Additional exam requirements/recommendations for international students: Required—TOEFL (minimum score 550 paper-based; 213 computer-based). Electronic applications accepted. *Faculty research:* Transcultural nursing, exercise and depression in Alzheimer's disease, infectious diseases/HIV–AIDS, postpartum depression, outcomes assessment.

University of Michigan–Flint, School of Health Professions and Studies, Program in Anesthesia, Flint, MI 48502-1950. Offers MSA. *Accreditation:* AACN; AANA/CANAEP. Part-time programs available. *Degree requirements:* For master's, thesis. *Entrance requirements:* For master's, GRE, BSN or BS in science, critical care experience, RN license, minimum GPA of 3.0 in prerequisites. Additional exam requirements/recommendations for international students: Required—TOEFL (minimum score 560 paper-based; 220 computer-based; 84 iBT), IELTS (minimum score 6.5). *Expenses:* Contact institution. *Faculty research:* CRNA expected retirement patterns, factors of importance in CENA selection of first job, lidocaine 4% in ETT cuff and reducing in coughing on emergence, orientation of spinal needle benel, length of time to discharge outpatients.

University of Minnesota, Twin Cities Campus, Graduate School, School of Nursing, Program in Nurse Anesthetist, Minneapolis, MN 55455-0213. Offers MS. *Accreditation:* AANA/CANAEP. *Entrance requirements:* Additional exam requirements/recommendations for international students: Required—TOEFL (minimum score 586 paper-based; 240 computer-based).

University of New England, Westbrook College of Health Professions, Program in Nurse Anesthesia, Biddeford, ME 04005-9526. Offers MS. Offered in association with Eastern Maine Medical Center, St. Joseph Hospital, and Harlem Hospital. *Accreditation:* AANA/CANAEP. *Faculty:* 3 full-time, 2 part-time/adjunct. *Students:* 101 full-time (64 women). In 2011, 29 master's awarded. *Degree requirements:* For master's, thesis or alternative, practicum. *Entrance requirements:* For master's, GRE, RN license, 1 year of acute care experience, 3 letters of reference, recent completion of organic or biochemistry course. *Application deadline:* For fall admission, 2/1 for domestic and international students. Applications are processed on a rolling basis. Application fee: $40. Electronic applications accepted. *Expenses:* Contact institution. *Financial support:* Application deadline: 5/1; applicants required to submit FAFSA. *Faculty research:* Evaluation, faculty perceptions of student characteristics and success during clinical practicum. *Unit head:* Maribeth Massie, Interim Program Director, 207-221-4519, Fax: 207-221-4546, E-mail: mmassie@une.edu. *Application contact:* Stacy Gato, Assistant Director of Graduate Admissions, 207-221-4225, Fax: 207-221-4898, E-mail: gradadmissions@une.edu. Web site: http://www.une.edu/.

The University of North Carolina at Charlotte, Graduate School, College of Health and Human Services, School of Nursing, Charlotte, NC 28223-0001. Offers administration (Post-Master's Certificate); advanced clinical (MSN, Post-Master's Certificate); anesthesia (MSN, Post-Master's Certificate); community health (MSN); family nurse practitioner (MSN, Post-Master's Certificate); health administration (MSN); mental health (MSN); nurse educator (MSN, Post-Master's Certificate); systems population (MSN). *Accreditation:* AACN. *Faculty:* 20 full-time (19 women), 5 part-time/adjunct (all women). *Students:* 76 full-time (65 women), 160 part-time (149 women); includes 49 minority (32 Black or African American, non-Hispanic/Latino; 1 American Indian or Alaska Native, non-Hispanic/Latino; 8 Asian, non-Hispanic/Latino; 8 Hispanic/Latino), 1 international. Average age 35. 191 applicants, 42% accepted, 71 enrolled. In 2011, 76 master's, 10 other advanced degrees awarded. *Degree requirements:* For master's, thesis or alternative, practicum. *Entrance requirements:* For master's, GRE General Test, minimum GPA of 3.0 in undergraduate major. Additional exam requirements/recommendations for international students: Required—TOEFL (minimum score 570 paper-based; 220 computer-based; 83 iBT). *Application deadline:* For fall admission, 7/15 for domestic students, 5/1 for international students; for spring admission, 11/15 for domestic students, 10/1 for international students. Application fee: $65 ($75 for international students). *Expenses:* Tuition, state resident: full-time $3689. Tuition, nonresident: full-time $15,226. *Required fees:* $2198. Tuition and fees vary according to course load and program. *Financial support:* In 2011–12, 10 students received support, including 4 research assistantships (averaging $5,284 per year), 6 teaching assistantships (averaging $2,918 per year); career-related internships or fieldwork, institutionally sponsored loans, scholarships/grants, traineeships, unspecified assistantships, and administrative assistantship also available. Support available to part-time students. Financial award application deadline: 4/1; financial award applicants required to submit FAFSA. *Total annual research expenditures:* $955,795. *Unit head:* Dr. Lucille L. Travis, Director, 704-687-7959, Fax: 704-687-6017, E-mail: ltravis1@uncc.edu. *Application contact:* Kathy B. Giddings, Director of Graduate Admissions, 704-687-5503, Fax: 704-687-3279, E-mail: gradadm@uncc.edu. Web site: http://nursing.uncc.edu/.

The University of North Carolina at Greensboro, Graduate School, School of Nursing, Greensboro, NC 27412-5001. Offers adult clinical nurse specialist (MSN, PMC); adult/gerontological nurse practitioner (MSN, PMC); nurse anesthesia (MSN, PMC); nursing (PhD); nursing administration (MSN); nursing education (MSN); MSN/MBA. *Accreditation:* AACN; AANA/CANAEP; NLN. *Degree requirements:* For master's, thesis or alternative. *Entrance requirements:* For master's, GRE General Test or MAT, BSN, clinical experience, liability insurance, RN license; for PMC, liability insurance, MSN, RN license. Additional exam requirements/recommendations for international students: Required—TOEFL. Electronic applications accepted.

University of North Dakota, Graduate School, College of Nursing, Grand Forks, ND 58202. Offers advanced public health nursing (MS); family nurse practitioner (MS); gerontological nursing (MS); nurse anesthesia (MS); nursing (MS, PhD); nursing education (MS); psychiatric and mental health (MS). *Accreditation:* AACN; AANA/CANAEP (one or more programs are accredited). Part-time and evening/weekend programs available. Postbaccalaureate distance learning degree programs offered (minimal on-campus study). *Degree requirements:* For master's, thesis or alternative. *Entrance requirements:* For master's, minimum GPA of 3.0; for doctorate, GRE or MAT, minimum GPA of 3.0. Additional exam requirements/recommendations for international students: Required—TOEFL (minimum score 550 paper-based; 213 computer-based; 79 iBT), IELTS (minimum score 6.5). Electronic applications accepted. *Faculty research:* Adult health, anesthesia, rural health, health administration, family nurse practitioner.

University of North Florida, Brooks College of Health, School of Nursing, Jacksonville, FL 32224. Offers clinical nurse leader (MSN); clinical nurse specialist (MSN); family

nurse practitioner (Certificate); nurse anesthetist (CRNA) (MSN); nursing practice (DNP); primary care nurse practitioner (MSN). *Accreditation:* AACN; AANA/CANAEP. Part-time programs available. *Faculty:* 28 full-time (21 women), 1 (woman) part-time/adjunct. *Students:* 97 full-time (69 women), 69 part-time (60 women); includes 41 minority (17 Black or African American, non-Hispanic/Latino; 1 American Indian or Alaska Native, non-Hispanic/Latino; 10 Asian, non-Hispanic/Latino; 11 Hispanic/Latino; 2 Two or more races, non-Hispanic/Latino). Average age 34. 215 applicants, 23% accepted, 31 enrolled. In 2011, 55 master's, 4 doctorates awarded. *Degree requirements:* For master's, thesis optional. *Entrance requirements:* For master's, GRE General Test, minimum GPA of 3.0 in last 60 hours of course work, BSN, clinical experience, resume; for doctorate, GRE (minimum score of 1000) or MAT (minimum score of 410), master's degree in nursing specialty from nationally-accredited program; national certification in one of the following APRN roles: CNE, CNM, CNS, CRNA, CNP; minimum graduate GPA of 3.3; three letters of reference which address academic ability and clinical skills; active license as registered nurse or advanced practice registered nurse. Additional exam requirements/recommendations for international students: Required—TOEFL (minimum score 500 paper-based; 173 computer-based; 61 iBT). *Application deadline:* For fall admission, 3/15 for domestic students, 4/1 for international students. Applications are processed on a rolling basis. Application fee: $30. Electronic applications accepted. *Expenses:* Tuition, state resident: full-time $8793; part-time $366.38 per credit hour. Tuition, nonresident: full-time $23,502; part-time $979.24 per credit hour. *Required fees:* $1384; $57.66 per credit hour. Tuition and fees vary according to course load and program. *Financial support:* In 2011–12, 59 students received support. Research assistantships available. Financial award application deadline: 4/1; financial award applicants required to submit FAFSA. *Faculty research:* Teen pregnancy, diabetes, ethical decision-making, family caregivers. *Total annual research expenditures:* $545,563. *Unit head:* Dr. John McDonough, Director, 904-620-2684, E-mail: jmcdonou@unf.edu. *Application contact:* Beth Dibble, 904-620-2684, Fax: 904-620-1832, E-mail: nursingadmissions@unf.edu. Web site: http://www.unf.edu/brooks/nursing.

University of Pennsylvania, School of Nursing, Nurse Anesthetist Program, Philadelphia, PA 19104. Offers MSN. *Accreditation:* AANA/CANAEP. *Students:* 44 full-time (28 women), 3 part-time (2 women); includes 6 minority (2 Black or African American, non-Hispanic/Latino; 2 American Indian or Alaska Native, non-Hispanic/Latino; 1 Asian, non-Hispanic/Latino; 1 Hispanic/Latino). 233 applicants, 18% accepted, 36 enrolled. In 2011, 18 degrees awarded. Application fee: $70. *Expenses: Tuition:* Full-time $26,660; part-time $4944 per course. *Required fees:* $2318; $291 per course. Tuition and fees vary according to course load, degree level and program. *Unit head:* Assistant Dean of Admissions and Financial Aid, 866-867-6877, Fax: 215-573-8439, E-mail: admissions@nursing.upenn.edu. *Application contact:* Maria Magro, Program Director, 215-898-8292, E-mail: magro@nursing.upenn.edu.

University of Pittsburgh, School of Nursing, Nurse Anesthesia Program, Pittsburgh, PA 15260. Offers MSN, DNP. *Accreditation:* AACN; AANA/CANAEP. *Students:* 114 full-time (83 women), 17 part-time (14 women); includes 10 minority (5 Black or African American, non-Hispanic/Latino; 5 Asian, non-Hispanic/Latino). Average age 29. 193 applicants, 24% accepted, 41 enrolled. In 2011, 43 master's awarded. *Degree requirements:* For master's, comprehensive exam, thesis optional. *Entrance requirements:* For master's, GRE General Test, BSN, RN license, 1-3 years nursing experience, letters of recommendation, resume, course work in statistics. Additional exam requirements/recommendations for international students: Required—TOEFL (minimum score 550 paper-based; 213 computer-based; 80 iBT). *Application deadline:* For fall admission, 1/5 for domestic and international students. Application fee: $50. Electronic applications accepted. *Expenses:* Tuition, state resident: full-time $18,774; part-time $760 per credit. Tuition, nonresident: full-time $30,736; part-time $1258 per credit. *Required fees:* $740; $200 per term. Tuition and fees vary according to program. *Unit head:* John O'Donnell, Director, 412-624-4860, Fax: 412-624-2401, E-mail: jod01@pitt.edu. *Application contact:* Laurie Lapsley, Administrator of Graduate Student Services, 412-624-9670, Fax: 412-624-2409, E-mail: lapsleyl@pitt.edu. Web site: http://www.nursing.pitt.edu/.

The University of Scranton, College of Graduate and Continuing Education, Department of Nursing, Scranton, PA 18510. Offers adult health nursing (MSN); family nurse practitioner (MSN, PMC); nurse anesthesia (MSN, PMC). Applicants accepted in odd-numbered years only. *Accreditation:* AACN; AANA/CANAEP. Part-time and evening/weekend programs available. *Faculty:* 13 full-time (all women), 2 part-time/adjunct (both women). *Students:* 50 full-time (45 women), 27 part-time (20 women); includes 7 minority (4 Black or African American, non-Hispanic/Latino; 1 Asian, non-Hispanic/Latino; 2 Hispanic/Latino). Average age 35. 100 applicants, 32% accepted. In 2011, 26 master's awarded. *Degree requirements:* For master's, thesis (for some programs), capstone experience. *Entrance requirements:* For master's, BSN, minimum GPA of 3.0, Pennsylvania RN license. Additional exam requirements/recommendations for international students: Required—TOEFL (minimum score 500 paper-based; 173 computer-based), IELTS (minimum score 5.5). *Application deadline:* For fall admission, 9/1 for domestic students. Applications are processed on a rolling basis. Application fee: $0. *Financial support:* In 2011–12, 7 students received support, including 7 teaching assistantships with full and partial tuition reimbursements available (averaging $6,914 per year); career-related internships or fieldwork, Federal Work-Study, and unspecified assistantships also available. Support available to part-time students. Financial award application deadline: 3/1. *Faculty research:* Home care, doctoral education, health care of women and children, pain, health promotion and adolescence. *Unit head:* Dr. Patricia Harrington, Chair, 570-941-7673, Fax: 570-941-4201, E-mail: harringtonp1@uofs.edu. *Application contact:* Dr. Mary Jane Hanson, Director, 570-941-4060, Fax: 570-941-4201, E-mail: hansonm2@scranton.edu. Web site: http://academic.uofs.edu/department/nursing/.

University of South Carolina, School of Medicine and The Graduate School, Graduate Programs in Medicine, Program in Nurse Anesthesia, Columbia, SC 29208. Offers MNA. *Accreditation:* AACN; AANA/CANAEP. *Degree requirements:* For master's, comprehensive exam, practicum. *Entrance requirements:* For master's, GRE, 1 year of critical care experience, RN license. Electronic applications accepted. *Expenses:* Contact institution. *Faculty research:* Neuroscience, cardiovascular, hormones, stress, homeostasis.

The University of Tennessee at Chattanooga, Graduate School, College of Health, Education and Professional Studies, School of Nursing, Chattanooga, TN 37403. Offers administration (MSN); certified nurse anesthetist (Post-Master's Certificate); education (MSN); family nurse practitioner (MSN, Post-Master's Certificate); health care informatics (Post-Master's Certificate); nurse anesthesia (MSN); nurse education (Post-Master's Certificate); nursing (DNP). *Accreditation:* AACN; AANA/CANAEP (one or more programs are accredited). *Faculty:* 15 full-time (13 women), 4 part-time/adjunct (all women). *Students:* 68 full-time (45 women), 37 part-time (33 women); includes 8 minority (6 Black or African American, non-Hispanic/Latino; 2 Hispanic/Latino). Average age 33. 5 applicants, 100% accepted, 3 enrolled. In 2011, 52 degrees awarded. *Degree requirements:* For master's, thesis optional, qualifying exams, professional project; for Post-Master's Certificate, thesis or alternative, practicum, seminar. *Entrance requirements:* For master's, GRE General Test, MAT, BSN, minimum GPA of 3.0,

eligibility for Tennessee RN license, 1 year direct patient care experience; for Post-Master's Certificate, GRE General Test, MAT, MSN, minimum GPA of 3.0, eligibility for Tennessee RN license, one year of direct patient care experience. Additional exam requirements/recommendations for international students: Required—TOEFL (minimum score 550 paper-based; 213 computer-based; 79 iBT), IELTS (minimum score 6). *Application deadline:* For fall admission, 8/1 priority date for domestic students, 6/1 for international students; for spring admission, 12/1 priority date for domestic students, 10/1 for international students. Applications are processed on a rolling basis. Application fee: $35. Electronic applications accepted. *Expenses:* Tuition, state resident: full-time $6472; part-time $359 per credit hour. Tuition, nonresident: full-time $20,006; part-time $1111 per credit hour. *Required fees:* $1320; $160 per credit hour. *Financial support:* Career-related internships or fieldwork and scholarships/grants available. Support available to part-time students. *Faculty research:* Diabetes in women, health care for elderly, alternative medicine, hypertension, nurse anesthesia. *Total annual research expenditures:* $1.9 million. *Unit head:* Dr. Kay R. Lindgren, Head, 423-425-4646, Fax: 423-425-4668, E-mail: kay-lindgren@utc.edu. *Application contact:* Dr. Jerald Ainsworth, Dean of Graduate Studies, 423-425-4478, Fax: 423-425-5223, E-mail: jerald-ainsworth@utc.edu. Web site: http://www.utc.edu/Academic/Nursing/.

University of Wisconsin–La Crosse, Office of University Graduate Studies, College of Science and Health, Department of Biology, La Crosse, WI 54601-3742. Offers aquatic sciences (MS); biology (MS); cellular and molecular biology (MS); clinical microbiology (MS); microbiology (MS); nurse anesthesia (MS); physiology (MS). Part-time programs available. *Faculty:* 21 full-time (8 women), 3 part-time/adjunct (1 woman). *Students:* 45 full-time (30 women), 47 part-time (22 women); includes 10 minority (1 Black or African American, non-Hispanic/Latino; 5 Asian, non-Hispanic/Latino; 3 Hispanic/Latino; 1 Two or more races, non-Hispanic/Latino), 3 international. Average age 28. 63 applicants, 46% accepted, 24 enrolled. In 2011, 23 master's awarded. *Degree requirements:* For master's, comprehensive exam, thesis. *Entrance requirements:* For master's, GRE General Test, minimum GPA of 2.85. Additional exam requirements/recommendations for international students: Required—TOEFL (minimum score 550 paper-based; 213 computer-based; 79 iBT). *Application deadline:* For fall admission, 2/1 priority date for domestic students, 2/1 for international students; for spring admission, 1/4 priority date for domestic students, 1/4 for international students. Applications are processed on a rolling basis. Application fee: $56. Electronic applications accepted. *Expenses:* Tuition, state resident: full-time $8391; part-time $481.17 per credit. Tuition, nonresident: full-time $17,850; part-time $1006.68 per credit. *Required fees:* $2 per credit. $18.25 per semester. Tuition and fees vary according to course load, program, reciprocity agreements and student level. *Financial support:* In 2011–12, 29 research assistantships with partial tuition reimbursements (averaging $9,712 per year) were awarded; Federal Work-Study, scholarships/grants, health care benefits, and tuition waivers (partial) also available. Support available to part-time students. Financial award application deadline: 3/15; financial award applicants required to submit FAFSA. *Unit head:* Dr. Thomas Volk, Coordinator of Graduate Studies, 608-785-6972, Fax: 608-785-6959, E-mail: volk.thom@uwlax.edu. *Application contact:* Kathryn Kiefer, Director of Admissions, 608-785-8939, E-mail: admissions@uwlax.edu. Web site: http://uwlax.edu/biology/.

Villanova University, College of Nursing, Villanova, PA 19085-1699. Offers adult nurse practitioner (MSN, Post Master's Certificate); family nurse practitioner (MSN, Post Master's Certificate); health care administration (MSN, Post Master's Certificate); nurse anesthetist (MSN, Post Master's Certificate); nursing (PhD); nursing education (MSN, Post Master's Certificate); nursing practice (DNP); pediatric nurse practitioner (MSN, Post Master's Certificate). *Accreditation:* AACN; AANA/CANAEP. Part-time programs available. Postbaccalaureate distance learning degree programs offered (minimal on-campus study). *Faculty:* 17 full-time (all women), 4 part-time/adjunct (all women). *Students:* 36 full-time (35 women), 256 part-time (234 women); includes 27 minority (14 Black or African American, non-Hispanic/Latino; 9 Asian, non-Hispanic/Latino; 4 Hispanic/Latino), 16 international. Average age 30. 161 applicants, 55% accepted, 75 enrolled. In 2011, 55 master's, 11 doctorates, 5 other advanced degrees awarded. *Degree requirements:* For master's, independent study project; for doctorate, comprehensive exam, thesis/dissertation. *Entrance requirements:* For master's, GRE or MAT, BSN, 1 year of recent nursing experience, physical assessment, course work in statistics; for doctorate, GRE, MSN. Additional exam requirements/recommendations for international students: Required—TOEFL, IELTS. *Application deadline:* For fall admission, 7/1 priority date for domestic students, 7/1 for international students; for spring admission, 11/1 priority date for domestic students, 11/1 for international students. Applications are processed on a rolling basis. Application fee: $50. *Expenses:* Contact institution. *Financial support:* In 2011–12, 43 students received support, including 5 teaching assistantships with full tuition reimbursements available (averaging $13,100 per year); institutionally sponsored loans, scholarships/grants, traineeships, tuition waivers (full), and unspecified assistantships also available. Financial award application deadline: 7/1; financial award applicants required to submit FAFSA. *Faculty research:* Genetics, ethics, cognitive development of students, women with disabilities, nursing leadership. *Unit head:* Dr. Marguerite K. Schlag, Assistant Dean/Director, Graduate Programs, 610-519-4907, Fax: 610-519-7650, E-mail: marguerite.schlag@villanova.edu. Web site: http://www.nursing.villanova.edu/.

Virginia Commonwealth University, Graduate School, School of Allied Health Professions, Department of Nurse Anesthesia, Richmond, VA 23284-9005. Offers MSNA, DNAP. *Accreditation:* AANA/CANAEP. *Students:* 119 full-time (83 women), 24 part-time (18 women); includes 24 minority (6 Black or African American, non-Hispanic/Latino; 1 American Indian or Alaska Native, non-Hispanic/Latino; 10 Asian, non-Hispanic/Latino; 6 Hispanic/Latino; 1 Two or more races, non-Hispanic/Latino). 206 applicants, 33% accepted, 58 enrolled. In 2011, 37 master's, 42 doctorates awarded. *Degree requirements:* For master's, thesis. *Entrance requirements:* For master's, GRE General Test, 1 year experience in acute critical care nursing, current state RN license, minimum GPA of 3.0; for doctorate, GRE General Test, accredited MSNA, CCNA certification, minimum GPA of 3.0. Additional exam requirements/recommendations for international students: Required—TOEFL (minimum score 600 paper-based; 250 computer-based; 100 iBT). Recommended—IELTS (minimum score 6.5). *Application deadline:* For fall admission, 10/1 priority date for domestic students. Application fee: $50. Electronic applications accepted. *Expenses:* Tuition, state resident: full-time $9133; part-time $507 per credit. Tuition, nonresident: full-time $18,777; part-time $1043 per credit. *Required fees:* $77 per credit. Tuition and fees vary according to degree level, campus/location, program and student level. *Financial support:* Applicants required to submit FAFSA. *Faculty research:* Obstetrical anesthesia, ambulatory anesthesia, regional anesthesia, practice profiles, clinical practice. *Unit head:* Dr. Michael D. Fallacaro, Chair, 804-828-9808, Fax: 804-828-0581, E-mail: mdfallac@vcu.edu. *Application contact:* Marjorie T. Goodwin, Program Support Specialist, 804-828-9808, Fax: 804-828-0581, E-mail: mtgoodwin@vcu.edu. Web site: http://www.sahp.vcu.edu/nrsa/index.html.

Virginia Commonwealth University, Graduate School, School of Allied Health Professions, Doctoral Program in Health Related Sciences, Richmond, VA 23284-9005. Offers clinical laboratory sciences (PhD); gerontology (PhD); health administration (PhD); nurse anesthesia (PhD); occupational therapy (PhD); physical therapy (PhD); radiation sciences (PhD); rehabilitation leadership (PhD). *Faculty:* 2 full-time (1 woman).

Nurse Anesthesia

Students: 23 full-time (15 women), 34 part-time (23 women); includes 7 minority (4 Black or African American, non-Hispanic/Latino; 1 Asian, non-Hispanic/Latino; 1 Hispanic/Latino; 1 Two or more races, non-Hispanic/Latino), 2 international. 37 applicants, 38% accepted, 11 enrolled. In 2011, 11 doctorates awarded. *Entrance requirements:* For doctorate, GRE General Test or MAT, minimum GPA of 3.3 in master's degree. Additional exam requirements/recommendations for international students: Required—TOEFL (minimum score 600 paper-based; 250 computer-based; 100 iBT); Recommended—IELTS (minimum score 6.5). *Application deadline:* For fall admission, 3/15 for domestic students. Application fee: $50. Electronic applications accepted. *Expenses:* Tuition, state resident: full-time $9133; part-time $507 per credit. Tuition, nonresident: full-time $18,777; part-time $1043 per credit. *Required fees:* $77 per credit. Tuition and fees vary according to degree level, campus/location, program and student level. *Unit head:* Dr. Paula K. Kupstas, Director, Health Related Sciences Program, 804-828-7247, E-mail: pkupstas@vcu.edu. *Application contact:* Monica L. White, Director of Student Services, 804-828-3273, Fax: 804-828-8656, E-mail: mlwhite1@vcu.edu. Web site: http://www.pubapps.vcu.edu/BULLETINS/prog_search/?did=20005.

Wayne State University, Eugene Applebaum College of Pharmacy and Health Sciences, Department of Health Care Sciences, Program in Nursing Anesthesia, Detroit, MI 48202. Offers nurse anesthesia (MS); pediatric nurse anesthesia (Certificate). *Accreditation:* AACN; AANA/CANAEP. *Students:* 30 full-time (20 women), 4 part-time (3 women); includes 10 minority (4 Black or African American, non-Hispanic/Latino; 5 Asian, non-Hispanic/Latino; 1 Two or more races, non-Hispanic/Latino). Average age 32. 11 applicants, 27% accepted, 1 enrolled. In 2011, 20 master's awarded. *Entrance requirements:* For master's, GRE General Test. Additional exam requirements/recommendations for international students: Required—TOEFL (minimum score 550 paper-based; 213 computer-based); Recommended—TWE (minimum score 6). *Application deadline:* For fall admission, 7/1 for domestic and international students. Application fee: $50. Electronic applications accepted. *Expenses:* Tuition, state resident: part-time $512.85 per credit. Tuition, nonresident: part-time $1132.65 per credit. *Required fees:* $26.60 per credit. $199.65 per semester. Tuition and fees vary according to course load and program. *Financial support:* In 2011–12, 8 students received support. Career-related internships or fieldwork and scholarships/grants available. Support available to part-time students. *Faculty research:* Maternal oxygen administration, re-activated epidural anesthesia, temperate monitoring modalitics, sedation, anesthesia outcomes. *Unit head:* Dr. Prudentia A. Worth, Academic Director, 313-745-3610, E-mail: pworth@wayne.edu. Web site: http://www.cphs.wayne.edu/anesth/.

Webster University, College of Arts and Sciences, Department of Biological Sciences, Program in Nurse Anesthesia, St. Louis, MO 63119-3194. Offers MS. *Accreditation:* AANA/CANAEP. Postbaccalaureate distance learning degree programs offered. *Degree requirements:* For master's, thesis. *Entrance requirements:* For master's, 1 year of work-related experience, 75 hours of graduate course work, BSN, interview, minimum GPA of 3.0. Additional exam requirements/recommendations for international students: Required—TOEFL. *Expenses: Tuition:* Full-time $10,890; part-time $605 per credit hour. Tuition and fees vary according to campus/location and program. *Faculty research:* Clinical anesthesia, substance abuse education in the health professions, technology and education, clinical pharmacology.

Westminster College, School of Nursing and Health Sciences, Salt Lake City, UT 84105-3697. Offers family nurse practitioner (MSN); nurse anesthesia (MSNA); nurse education (MSNED); nursing (MSN); public health (MPH). *Accreditation:* AACN; AANA/CANAEP. *Faculty:* 13 full-time (7 women), 7 part-time/adjunct (4 women). *Students:* 102 full-time (54 women), 16 part-time (12 women); includes 9 minority (2 Black or African American, non-Hispanic/Latino; 1 American Indian or Alaska Native, non-Hispanic/Latino; 5 Asian, non-Hispanic/Latino; 1 Hispanic/Latino), 1 international. Average age 34. 106 applicants, 64% accepted, 38 enrolled. In 2011, 53 master's awarded. *Degree requirements:* For master's, clinical practicum, 504 clinical practice hours. *Entrance requirements:* For master's, GRE, resume, Utah RN license in good standing, minimum GPA of 3.0, 3 letters of reference, BSN from accredited nursing program, proof of clear state and federal background check, drug test results, personal interview, current PALS certification, current ACLS certification. Additional exam requirements/recommendations for international students: Required—TOEFL (minimum score 600 paper-based; 250 computer-based; 100 iBT), IELTS (minimum score 7). *Application deadline:* Applications are processed on a rolling basis. Application fee: $50. Electronic applications accepted. *Expenses:* Contact institution. *Financial support:* In 2011–12, 11 students received support. Career-related internships or fieldwork and tuition reimbursement, tuition remission available. Support available to part-time students. Financial award applicants required to submit FAFSA. *Faculty research:* Collaborative testing in nursing: student outcomes and perspectives, Implementing New Educational Paradigms into Pre-Licensure Nursing Curricula conference presentation. *Unit head:* Dr. Sheryl Steadman, Dean, 801-832-2164, Fax: 801-832-3110, E-mail: ssteadman@westminstercollege.edu. *Application contact:* Dr. Gary Daynes, Vice President for Strategic Outreach and Enrollment, 801-832-2200, Fax: 801-832-3101, E-mail: admission@westminstercollege.edu. Web site: http://www.westminstercollege.edu/msn.

York College of Pennsylvania, Department of Nursing, York, PA 17405-7199. Offers adult nurse practitioner (MS); certified nurse anesthetist (MS); clinical nurse specialist (MS), including education: administration; nurse educator (MS); nursing (DNP). *Accreditation:* AACN; AANA/CANAEP. Part-time and evening/weekend programs available. *Faculty:* 10 full-time (all women), 9 part-time/adjunct (6 women). *Students:* 31 full-time (23 women), 50 part-time (43 women); includes 4 minority (2 Black or African American, non-Hispanic/Latino; 2 Asian, non-Hispanic/Latino), 1 international. Average age 36. 49 applicants, 53% accepted, 20 enrolled. In 2011, 17 master's awarded. *Entrance requirements:* For master's, GRE General Test, minimum GPA of 3.0 with NLNAC or CCNE major. Additional exam requirements/recommendations for international students: Required—TOEFL (minimum score 530 paper-based; 200 computer-based; 72 iBT). *Application deadline:* For fall admission, 7/15 priority date for domestic students; for spring admission, 11/15 priority date for domestic students. Applications are processed on a rolling basis. Application fee: $50. Electronic applications accepted. *Expenses: Tuition:* Full-time $12,060; part-time $670 per credit hour. *Required fees:* $340 per semester. Tuition and fees vary according to degree level. *Financial support:* Federal Work-Study available. *Faculty research:* Employer and faculty beliefs about concepts in RN-BS education, evaluating effectiveness of mental health partnerships in psychiatric settings. *Unit head:* Dr. Linda Pugh, Graduate Program Director, 717-815-1243, E-mail: lwarner@ycp.edu. *Application contact:* Nancy Spataro, Director of Admissions, 717-815-1600, Fax: 717-849-1607, E-mail: admissions@ycp.edu. Web site: http://www.ycp.edu/academics/academic-departments/nursing/.

Nurse Midwifery

Bastyr University, School of Natural Health Arts and Sciences, Kenmore, WA 98028-4966. Offers counseling psychology (MA); holistic landscape design (Certificate); midwifery (MS); nutrition (MS); nutrition and clinical health psychology (MS). *Accreditation:* AND. Part-time programs available. *Students:* 142 full-time (136 women), 15 part-time (all women); includes 28 minority (3 Black or African American, non-Hispanic/Latino; 5 Asian, non-Hispanic/Latino; 8 Hispanic/Latino; 12 Two or more races, non-Hispanic/Latino), 5 international. Average age 30. In 2011, 36 master's awarded. *Degree requirements:* For master's, thesis optional. *Entrance requirements:* For master's, 1-2 years' basic sciences course work (depending on program). Additional exam requirements/recommendations for international students: Required—TOEFL (minimum score 550 paper-based; 213 computer-based; 79 iBT). *Application deadline:* For fall admission, 3/15 priority date for domestic students, 3/15 for international students. Applications are processed on a rolling basis. Application fee: $75. *Expenses: Tuition:* Full-time $27,653; part-time $6440 per quarter. *Required fees:* $75; $75. One-time fee: $375. Tuition and fees vary according to course load, degree level, program and student level. *Financial support:* In 2011–12, 47 students received support, including 4 teaching assistantships (averaging $2,000 per year); career-related internships or fieldwork, Federal Work-Study, and scholarships/grants also available. Support available to part-time students. Financial award application deadline: 4/15; financial award applicants required to submit FAFSA. *Faculty research:* Whole-food nutrition for type 2 diabetes; meditation in end-of-life care; stress management; Qi Gong, Tai Chi and yoga for older adults; echinacea and immunology. *Unit head:* Dr. Timothy Callahan, Vice President and Provost, 425-602-3110, Fax: 425-823-6222. *Application contact:* Admissions Office, 425-602-3330, Fax: 425-602-3090, E-mail: admissions@bastyr.edu. Web site: http://www.bastyr.edu/academics/schools-departments/school-natural-health-arts-sciences.

Baylor University, Graduate School, Louise Herrington School of Nursing, Waco, TX 76798. Offers family nurse practitioner (MSN); neonatal nurse practitioner (MSN); nurse-midwifery (DNP). *Accreditation:* AACN. Part-time programs available. *Faculty:* 9 full-time (all women), 3 part-time/adjunct (2 women). *Students:* 33 full-time (32 women), 45 part-time (39 women); includes 17 minority (4 Black or African American, non-Hispanic/Latino; 4 Asian, non-Hispanic/Latino; 3 Hispanic/Latino; 6 Two or more races, non-Hispanic/Latino), 1 international. 62 applicants, 63% accepted, 37 enrolled. In 2011, 24 master's, 3 doctorates awarded. *Entrance requirements:* For master's, GRE General Test or MAT; for doctorate, GRE General Test. *Application deadline:* For fall admission, 4/1 for domestic students. Application fee: $40. Electronic applications accepted. *Financial support:* Applicants required to submit FAFSA. *Unit head:* Dr. Linda Plank, Graduate Program Director, 214-818-7847, Fax: 214-818-8692, E-mail: linda_plank@baylor.edu. *Application contact:* Beverly Kurfees, Academic Support Specialist, 214-367-3752, Fax: 254-710-3870, E-mail: beverly_kurfees@baylor.edu. Web site: http://www.baylor.edu/nursing/.

Case Western Reserve University, Frances Payne Bolton School of Nursing, Doctor of Nursing Practice Program, Cleveland, OH 44106. Offers acute care nurse practitioner (DNP); adult gerontology nurse practitioner (DNP); educational leadership (DNP); family nurse practitioner (DNP); family systems psychiatric mental health nursing (DNP); midwifery/family nursing (DNP); neonatal nurse practitioner (DNP); pediatric nurse practitioner (DNP); practice leadership (DNP); women's health nurse practitioner (DNP). *Students:* 73 full-time, 194 part-time; includes 11 minority (6 Black or African American, non-Hispanic/Latino; 3 Asian, non-Hispanic/Latino; 2 Hispanic/Latino). 122 applicants, 74% accepted, 49 enrolled. In 2011, 47 doctorates awarded. Terminal master's awarded for partial completion of doctoral program. *Degree requirements:* For doctorate, thesis/dissertation. *Entrance requirements:* For doctorate, GRE General Test or MAT. Additional exam requirements/recommendations for international students: Required—TOEFL (minimum score 577 paper-based; 90 iBT), IELTS (minimum score 7). *Application deadline:* For fall admission, 6/1 priority date for domestic students, 6/1 for international students; for spring admission, 10/1 for domestic and international students. Applications are processed on a rolling basis. Application fee: $75. *Financial support:* In 2011–12, 6 students received support, including 1 teaching assistantship; research assistantships, Federal Work-Study, institutionally sponsored loans, and tuition waivers (partial) also available. Support available to part-time students. Financial award application deadline: 6/30; financial award applicants required to submit FAFSA. *Faculty research:* Clinical nursing, acute care, gerontology, mental health, critical care. *Unit head:* Dr. Donna Dowling, Director, 216-368-1869, Fax: 216-368-3542, E-mail: dad10@case.edu. *Application contact:* Donna Hassik, Admissions Coordinator, 216-368-5253, Fax: 216-368-0124, E-mail: dmh7@case.edu. Web site: http://fpb.case.edu/DNP/.

Case Western Reserve University, Frances Payne Bolton School of Nursing, Master's Programs in Nursing, Program in Nurse Midwifery, Cleveland, OH 44106. Offers MSN. *Accreditation:* ACNM/ACME. *Students:* 5 full-time (all women), 2 part-time (both women); includes 1 minority (Black or African American, non-Hispanic/Latino). 3 applicants, 100% accepted, 2 enrolled. In 2011, 3 master's awarded. *Degree requirements:* For master's, thesis optional. *Entrance requirements:* For master's, GRE General Test or MAT. Additional exam requirements/recommendations for international students: Required—TOEFL (minimum score 577 paper-based; 90 iBT), IELTS (minimum score 7). *Application deadline:* For fall admission, 6/1 for domestic and international students; for spring admission, 10/1 for domestic and international students. Applications are processed on a rolling basis. Application fee: $75. *Financial support:* Fellowships, research assistantships, teaching assistantships, institutionally sponsored loans, and tuition waivers (partial) available. Support available to part-time students. Financial award application deadline: 6/30; financial award applicants required to submit FAFSA. *Faculty research:* Clinical nursing, normal childbearing, descriptive studies of care, high risk pregnancy side effects of bed rest, strengthening and expanding nursing services. *Unit head:* Dr. Gretchen Mettler, Head, 216-368-0671, E-mail: ggm@case.edu. *Application contact:* Donna Hassik, Admissions Coordinator, 216-368-5253, Fax: 216-368-0124, E-mail: dmh7@case.edu. Web site: http://fpb.case.edu/MSN/midwifery.shtm.

Columbia University, School of Nursing, Program in Nurse Midwifery, New York, NY 10032. Offers MS. *Accreditation:* AACN; ACNM/ACME. Part-time programs available. *Entrance requirements:* For master's, GRE General Test, BSN, 1 year of clinical experience (preferred). Electronic applications accepted.

DeSales University, Graduate Division, Division of Healthcare and Natural Sciences, Center Valley, PA 18034-9568. Offers adult advanced practice nurse specialist (MSN); certified nurse midwives (MSN); certified nurse practitioners (MSN); clinical leadership (DNP); family nurse practitioner (MSN); nurse educator (MSN); nurse practitioner (Post-Master's Certificate); MSN/MBA. *Accreditation:* NLN. Part-time programs available. *Degree requirements:* For master's, thesis optional. *Entrance requirements:* For master's, GRE General Test, MAT, minimum B average in undergraduate course work, health assessment course or equivalent, course work in statistics. Additional exam requirements/recommendations for international students: Required—TOEFL. *Application deadline:* Applications are processed on a rolling basis. Application fee: $35. Electronic applications accepted. Tuition and fees vary according to degree level. *Financial support:* Applicants required to submit FAFSA. *Unit head:* Dr. Carol Gullo Mest, Director, 610-282-1100 Ext. 1394, Fax: 610-282-2091, E-mail: carol.mest@desales.edu. *Application contact:* Caryn Stopper, Director of Graduate Admissions, 610-282-1100 Ext. 1768, Fax: 610-282-2254, E-mail: caryn.stopper@desales.edu.

Emory University, Nell Hodgson Woodruff School of Nursing, Atlanta, GA 30322-1100. Offers adult nurse practitioner (MSN); emergency nurse practitioner (MSN); family nurse practitioner (MSN); family nurse-midwife (MSN); health systems leadership (MSN); nurse-midwifery (MSN); pediatric nurse practitioner acute and primary care (MSN); women's health care (Title X) (MSN); women's health nurse practitioner (MSN); women's health/adult health nurse practitioner (MSN); MSN/MPH. *Accreditation:* AACN; ACNM/ACME (one or more programs are accredited). Part-time programs available. *Faculty:* 30 full-time (29 women), 11 part-time/adjunct (10 women). *Students:* 110 full-time (106 women), 53 part-time (51 women); includes 49 minority (35 Black or African American, non-Hispanic/Latino; 2 American Indian or Alaska Native, non-Hispanic/Latino; 10 Asian, non-Hispanic/Latino; 2 Hispanic/Latino), 4 international. Average age 32. 182 applicants, 63% accepted, 86 enrolled. In 2011, 81 master's awarded. *Entrance requirements:* For master's, GRE General Test or MAT, minimum GPA of 3.0, BS in nursing from an accredited institution, RN license and additional course work, 3 letters of recommendation. Additional exam requirements/recommendations for international students: Required—TOEFL (minimum score 600 paper-based; 100 iBT). *Application deadline:* For fall admission, 1/15 priority date for domestic students, 1/15 for international students; for spring admission, 10/1 priority date for domestic students, 10/1 for international students. Applications are processed on a rolling basis. Application fee: $50. Electronic applications accepted. *Expenses:* Contact institution. *Financial support:* In 2011–12, 14 fellowships (averaging $28,000 per year) were awarded; career-related internships or fieldwork, Federal Work-Study, institutionally sponsored loans, and scholarships/grants also available. Support available to part-time students. Financial award application deadline: 3/1; financial award applicants required to submit CSS PROFILE or FAFSA. *Faculty research:* Older adult falls and injuries, minority health issues, cardiac symptoms and quality of life, bio-ethics and decision-making, menopausal issues. *Unit head:* Dr. Linda McCauley, Dean, 404-727-7976, Fax: 404-727-9800, E-mail: linda.mccauley@emory.edu. Web site: http://www.nursing.emory.edu/.

Frontier Nursing University, Graduate Programs, Hyden, KY 41749. Offers community-based family nurse practitioner (MSN, Post Master's Certificate); community-based nurse-midwifery education (MSN, Post Master's Certificate); community-based women?s health care nurse practitioner (MSN, Post Master's Certificate). *Accreditation:* ACNM; NLN.

Georgetown University, Graduate School of Arts and Sciences, School of Nursing and Health Studies, Washington, DC 20057. Offers acute care nurse practitioner (MS); clinical nurse specialist (MS); family nurse practitioner (MS); nurse anesthesia (MS); nurse-midwifery (MS); nursing education (MS). *Accreditation:* AACN; AANA/CANAEP; ACNM/ACME. *Degree requirements:* For master's, thesis optional. *Entrance requirements:* For master's, GRE General Test or MAT, bachelor's degree in nursing from NLN-accredited school, minimum undergraduate GPA of 3.0. Additional exam requirements/recommendations for international students: Required—TOEFL.

Marquette University, Graduate School, College of Nursing, Milwaukee, WI 53201-1881. Offers acute care nurse practitioner (Certificate); adult clinical nurse specialist (Certificate); adult nurse practitioner (Certificate); advanced practice nursing (MSN, DNP), including acute care, adults, neonatal nurse practitioner (MSN), nurse midwifery (DNP), nurse-midwifery (MSN), older adults, pediatrics acute care (DNP, PhD), pediatrics primary care; clinical nurse leader (MSN); gerontologic clinical nurse specialist (Certificate); gerontologic nurse practitioner (Certificate); health care systems leadership (MSN, DNP); nurse-midwifery (Certificate); nursing (PhD), including pediatrics acute care (DNP, PhD); pediatrics acute care (Certificate); pediatrics primary care (Certificate). *Accreditation:* AACN. *Faculty:* 32 full-time (30 women), 47 part-time/adjunct (all women). *Students:* 93 full-time (88 women), 244 part-time (220 women); includes 31 minority (9 Black or African American, non-Hispanic/Latino; 7 Asian, non-Hispanic/Latino; 8 Hispanic/Latino; 7 Two or more races, non-Hispanic/Latino), 1 international. Average age 30. 282 applicants, 57% accepted, 98 enrolled. In 2011, 76 master's, 8 doctorates, 7 other advanced degrees awarded. Terminal master's awarded for partial completion of doctoral program. *Degree requirements:* For master's, comprehensive exam, thesis or alternative. *Entrance requirements:* For master's, GRE General Test, BSN, Wisconsin RN license, official transcripts from all current and previous colleges/universities except Marquette, three completed recommendation forms, resume, written statement of professional goals; for doctorate, GRE General Test, official transcripts from all current and previous colleges/universities except Marquette, three letters of recommendation, resume, written statement of professional goals, sample of scholarly writing. Additional exam requirements/recommendations for international students: Required—TOEFL (minimum score 530 paper-based; 78 computer-based). *Application deadline:* For fall admission, 2/15 for domestic and international students. Application fee: $50. Electronic applications accepted. *Expenses:* Tuition: Full-time $17,010; part-time $945 per credit hour. Tuition and fees vary according to program. *Financial support:* In 2011–12, 41 students received support, including 1 fellowship with partial tuition reimbursement available (averaging $17,500 per year), 2 research assistantships with full tuition reimbursements available (averaging $13,285 per year), 8 teaching assistantships with full tuition reimbursements available (averaging $13,912 per year); career-related internships or fieldwork, Federal Work-Study, scholarships/grants, health care benefits, tuition waivers (partial), and unspecified assistantships also available. Support available to part-time students. Financial award application deadline: 2/15. *Faculty research:* Psychosocial adjustment to chronic illness, gerontology, reminiscence, health policy: uninsured and access, hospital care delivery systems. *Total annual research expenditures:* $312,575. *Unit head:* Dr. Margaret Callahan, Dean, 414-288-3800, Fax: 414-288-1578. *Application contact:* Karen Nest, Graduate Program Coordinator, 414-288-3810, Fax: 414-288-1578. Web site: http://www.marquette.edu/nursing/academicprograms-graduate.shtml.

Midwives College of Utah, Graduate Program, Salt Lake City, UT 84106. Offers MS. *Accreditation:* MEAC. *Degree requirements:* For master's, comprehensive exam (for some programs), thesis.

National College of Midwifery, Graduate Programs, Taos, NM 87571. Offers MS, PhD. *Accreditation:* MEAC. Part-time and evening/weekend programs available. Postbaccalaureate distance learning degree programs offered (no on-campus study).

Degree requirements: For master's, thesis, publication; for doctorate, thesis/dissertation, presentation, publication. *Entrance requirements:* For master's and doctorate, midwifery license or certification. Electronic applications accepted.

New York University, College of Nursing, Doctor of Nursing Practice Program, New York, NY 10012-1019. Offers advanced practice nursing (DNP), including adult acute care, adult nurse practitioner/holistic nursing, adult nurse practitioner/palliative care nursing, adult primary care, adult primary care/geriatrics, family, geriatrics, mental health nursing, nurse-midwifery, pediatrics. Part-time and evening/weekend programs available. *Faculty:* 7 full-time (all women). *Students:* 23 part-time (19 women); includes 6 minority (4 Black or African American, non-Hispanic/Latino; 1 Asian, non-Hispanic/Latino; 1 Hispanic/Latino), 1 international. Average age 46. 20 applicants, 80% accepted, 11 enrolled. In 2011, 8 doctorates awarded. *Degree requirements:* For doctorate, thesis/dissertation. *Entrance requirements:* For doctorate, MS, RN license, interview, NP Certification. Additional exam requirements/recommendations for international students: Required—TOEFL, IELTS. *Application deadline:* For fall admission, 4/1 priority date for domestic students, 4/1 for international students. Applications are processed on a rolling basis. Application fee: $75. Electronic applications accepted. *Financial support:* In 2011–12, 15 students received support. Fellowships with full and partial tuition reimbursements available, institutionally sponsored loans, scholarships/grants, and tuition waivers (partial) available. Support available to part-time students. Financial award application deadline: 2/1; financial award applicants required to submit FAFSA. *Faculty research:* Elderly black diabetics, families and illness, oral systemic connection. *Unit head:* Dr. Jamesetta A. Newland, Director, 212-998-5319, Fax: 212-995-3143, E-mail: jan7@nyu.edu. *Application contact:* Gail Wolfmeyer, Assistant Director, Graduate Student Affairs and Admissions, 212-992-7653, Fax: 212-995-4302, E-mail: gail.wolfmeyer@nyu.edu.

New York University, College of Nursing, Programs in Advanced Practice Nursing, New York, NY 10012-1019. Offers advanced practice nursing: adult acute care (MS, Advanced Certificate); advanced practice nursing: adult nurse practitioner/holistic nurse practitioner (Advanced Certificate); advanced practice nursing: adult nurse practitioner/palliative care nurse practitioner (Advanced Certificate); advanced practice nursing: adult primary care (MS, Advanced Certificate); advanced practice nursing: family (MS, Advanced Certificate); advanced practice nursing: geriatrics (Advanced Certificate); advanced practice nursing: mental health (MS); advanced practice nursing: mental health nursing (Advanced Certificate); advanced practice nursing: pediatrics (MS, Advanced Certificate); nurse midwifery (MS, Advanced Certificate); nursing administration (MS, Advanced Certificate); nursing education (MS, Advanced Certificate); nursing informatics (MS, Advanced Certificate); MS/MPA; MS/MPH. *Accreditation:* AACN; ACNM/ACME. Part-time programs available. *Faculty:* 23 full-time (all women), 60 part-time/adjunct (47 women). *Students:* 27 full-time (23 women), 552 part-time (514 women); includes 251 minority (91 Black or African American, non-Hispanic/Latino; 115 Asian, non-Hispanic/Latino; 34 Hispanic/Latino; 11 Native Hawaiian or other Pacific Islander, non-Hispanic/Latino), 8 international. Average age 33. 325 applicants, 81% accepted, 179 enrolled. In 2011, 89 master's awarded. *Degree requirements:* For master's, thesis (for some programs). *Entrance requirements:* For master's, BS in nursing, AS in nursing with another BS/BA, interview, RN license, 1 year of clinical experience (3 for nursing education program); for Advanced Certificate, master's degree. Additional exam requirements/recommendations for international students: Required—TOEFL, IELTS. *Application deadline:* For fall admission, 7/1 priority date for domestic students, 7/1 for international students; for spring admission, 12/1 for domestic and international students. Applications are processed on a rolling basis. Application fee: $75. Electronic applications accepted. *Financial support:* In 2011–12, 36 students received support. Career-related internships or fieldwork, institutionally sponsored loans, scholarships/grants, traineeships, and tuition waivers (partial) available. Support available to part-time students. Financial award application deadline: 2/1; financial award applicants required to submit FAFSA. *Faculty research:* Elderly black diabetics, families and illness, oral systemic connection. *Unit head:* Dr. Judith Haber, Associate Dean, 212-998-9020, Fax: 212-995-3143, E-mail: jh33@nyu.edu. *Application contact:* Gail Wolfmeyer, Assistant Director, Graduate Student Affairs and Admissions, 212-992-7653, Fax: 212-995-4302, E-mail: gail.wolfmeyer@nyu.edu.

Old Dominion University, College of Health Sciences, School of Nursing, Norfolk, VA 23529. Offers family nurse practitioner (MSN); nurse administrator (MSN); nurse anesthesia (MSN); nurse educator (MSN); nurse midwifery (MSN); women's health nurse practitioner (MSN). *Accreditation:* AACN; AANA/CANAEP (one or more programs are accredited). Part-time programs available. Postbaccalaureate distance learning degree programs offered (no on-campus study). *Faculty:* 11 full-time (10 women), 15 part-time/adjunct (14 women). *Students:* 101 full-time (90 women), 98 part-time (94 women); includes 43 minority (27 Black or African American, non-Hispanic/Latino; 4 Asian, non-Hispanic/Latino; 8 Hispanic/Latino; 2 Native Hawaiian or other Pacific Islander, non-Hispanic/Latino; 2 Two or more races, non-Hispanic/Latino). Average age 35. 211 applicants, 57% accepted, 93 enrolled. In 2011, 81 master's awarded. *Degree requirements:* For master's, comprehensive exam; for doctorate, capstone project. *Entrance requirements:* For master's, GRE or MAT, BSN, minimum GPA of 3.0 in nursing and overall. Additional exam requirements/recommendations for international students: Required—TOEFL. *Application deadline:* For fall admission, 5/1 for domestic students, 4/15 for international students. Applications are processed on a rolling basis. Application fee: $50. Electronic applications accepted. *Expenses:* Tuition, state resident: full-time $9096; part-time $379 per credit. Tuition, nonresident: full-time $23,064; part-time $961 per credit. *Required fees:* $127 per semester. One-time fee: $50. *Financial support:* In 2011–12, 18 students received support, including 2 research assistantships with partial tuition reimbursements available (averaging $10,000 per year); teaching assistantships, career-related internships or fieldwork, scholarships/grants, traineeships, and tuition waivers (partial) also available. Support available to part-time students. Financial award application deadline: 2/15; financial award applicants required to submit FAFSA. *Faculty research:* Health and culture, cardiovascular health, transition of military families, genetics, cultural diversity. *Total annual research expenditures:* $231,117. *Unit head:* Dr. Karen Karlowicz, Chair, 757-683-5262, Fax: 757-683-5253, E-mail: nursgpd@odu.edu. *Application contact:* Sue Parker, Coordinator, Graduate Student Services, 757-683-4298, Fax: 757-683-5253, E-mail: sparker@odu.edu. Web site: http://hs.odu.edu/nursing/.

Oregon Health & Science University, School of Nursing, Program in Nurse Midwifery, Portland, OR 97239-3098. Offers MN, MS, Post Master's Certificate. *Accreditation:* AACN; ACNM/ACME (one or more programs are accredited). *Degree requirements:* For master's, thesis optional. *Entrance requirements:* For master's, GRE General Test, bachelor's degree in nursing, minimum undergraduate GPA of 3.0, previous course work in statistics; for Post Master's Certificate, master's degree in nursing.

Philadelphia University, College of Science, Health and the Liberal Arts, Program in Midwifery, Philadelphia, PA 19144. Offers midwifery (MS); nurse midwifery (Postbaccalaureate Certificate). *Accreditation:* ACNM/ACME. Part-time and evening/weekend programs available. Postbaccalaureate distance learning degree programs offered (minimal on-campus study). *Entrance requirements:* For master's, GRE or MAT. Additional exam requirements/recommendations for international students: Required—

TOEFL (minimum score 550 paper-based; 213 computer-based; 79 iBT). Electronic applications accepted.

Seattle University, College of Nursing, Program in Advanced Practice Nursing Immersion, Seattle, WA 98122-1090. Offers adult/gerontological nurse practitioner (MSN); advanced community public health (MSN); certified nurse midwifery (MSN); family nurse practitioner (MSN); psychiatric mental health nurse practitioner (MSN). *Faculty:* 43 full-time, 63 part-time/adjunct. *Students:* 104 full-time (91 women); includes 24 minority (2 Black or African American, non-Hispanic/Latino; 12 Asian, non-Hispanic/Latino; 7 Hispanic/Latino; 3 Two or more races, non-Hispanic/Latino). Average age 30. *Degree requirements:* For master's, thesis or scholarly project. *Entrance requirements:* For master's, GRE, bachelor's degree, minimum GPA of 3.0, professional resume, two recommendations, letter of intent, English proficiency (for non-English speakers). Additional exam requirements/recommendations for international students: Required—TOEFL (minimum score 92 iBT), IELTS. *Application deadline:* For fall admission, 12/1 for domestic and international students. Application fee: $55. Electronic applications accepted. *Financial support:* Scholarships/grants and traineeships available. Financial award applicants required to submit FAFSA. *Unit head:* Dr. Azita Emami, Dean, 206-296-5660. *Application contact:* Janet Shandley, Associate Dean of Graduate Admissions, 206-296-5900, Fax: 206-298-5656, E-mail: grad_admissions@seattleu.edu.

Shenandoah University, School of Health Professions, Division of Nursing, Winchester, VA 22601-5195. Offers family nurse practitioner (Certificate); nurse-midwifery (Certificate); nurse-midwifery endorsement (Certificate); nursing (MSN, DNP); post-master's in nursing education (Certificate); psychiatric mental health nurse practitioner (Certificate). *Accreditation:* AACN; ACNM/ACME. Part-time programs available. *Faculty:* 11 full-time (all women), 2 part-time/adjunct (both women). *Students:* 40 full-time (34 women), 102 part-time (96 women); includes 32 minority (22 Black or African American, non-Hispanic/Latino; 1 American Indian or Alaska Native, non-Hispanic/Latino; 5 Asian, non-Hispanic/Latino; 3 Hispanic/Latino; 1 Two or more races, non-Hispanic/Latino), 2 international. Average age 39. 69 applicants, 90% accepted, 45 enrolled. In 2011, 15 master's, 2 doctorates, 17 other advanced degrees awarded. *Degree requirements:* For master's, research project, clinical hours; for doctorate and Certificate, clinical hours. *Entrance requirements:* For master's, GRE General Test, previous course work in statistics, community nursing, and physical assessment; RN license; BSN; minimum undergraduate GPA of 3.0; appropriate clinical experience; curriculum vitae; 3 letters of recommendation; for doctorate, MSN, minimum GPA of 3.0, 3 letters of recommendation, essay, interview; for Certificate, MSN, minimum GPA of 3.0, 3 letters of recommendation, minimum of one year (2,080 hours) clinical nursing experience, interview. Additional exam requirements/recommendations for international students: Required—TOEFL (minimum score 550 paper-based; 213 computer-based; 79 iBT), IELTS (minimum score 6.5), Sakae Institute of Study Abroad (minimum score 550). *Application deadline:* For fall admission, 6/15 priority date for domestic students, 6/15 for international students. Applications are processed on a rolling basis. Application fee: $30. Electronic applications accepted. *Expenses: Tuition:* Full-time $17,952; part-time $748 per credit. *Required fees:* $500 per term. Tuition and fees vary according to course level, course load and program. *Financial support:* In 2011–12, 13 students received support, including 3 teaching assistantships with partial tuition reimbursements available (averaging $4,224 per year); career-related internships or fieldwork, institutionally sponsored loans, scholarships/grants, unspecified assistantships, and federal loans, alternative loans also available. Support available to part-time students. Financial award application deadline: 3/15; financial award applicants required to submit FAFSA. *Faculty research:* Moral reasoning in nurses, improving health care access to under-served rural women, screening for depression and anxiety in the obese in a rural free clinic, health care outcomes among patients in a free clinic setting cared for by nurse practitioners, effects of depression on diabetes as evidenced by the relationship between the patient healthcare questionnaire (PHQ-9) scores and the patient's glycohemoglobin (HbA1c). *Unit head:* Dr. Kathryn Ganske, Director, 540-678-4374, Fax: 540-665-5519, E-mail: kganske@su.edu. *Application contact:* David Anthony, Dean of Admissions, 540-665-4581, Fax: 540-665-4627, E-mail: admit@su.edu. Web site: http://www.su.edu/nurse.

State University of New York Downstate Medical Center, College of Nursing, Graduate Program in Nursing, Program in Nurse Midwifery, Brooklyn, NY 11203-2098. Offers MS, Post Master's Certificate. *Accreditation:* ACNM.

Stony Brook University, State University of New York, Stony Brook University Medical Center, Health Sciences Center, School of Nursing, Program in Nurse Midwifery, Stony Brook, NY 11794. Offers MS, Certificate. *Accreditation:* AACN; ACNM/ACME. Postbaccalaureate distance learning degree programs offered. *Degree requirements:* For master's, thesis. *Entrance requirements:* For master's, BSN, minimum GPA of 3.0, course work in statistics.

University of Cincinnati, Graduate School, College of Nursing, Cincinnati, OH 45221-0038. Offers clinical nurse specialist (MSN), including adult health, community health, neonatal, nursing administration, occupational health, pediatric health, psychiatric nursing, women's health; nurse anesthesia (MSN); nurse midwifery (MSN); nurse practitioner (MSN), including acute care, ambulatory care, family, family/psychiatric, women's health; nursing (PhD); MBA/MSN. *Accreditation:* AACN; AANA/CANAEP (one or more programs are accredited); ACNM/ACME. Part-time programs available. Postbaccalaureate distance learning degree programs offered (no on-campus study). Terminal master's awarded for partial completion of doctoral program. *Degree requirements:* For master's, thesis or alternative; for doctorate, comprehensive exam, thesis/dissertation. *Entrance requirements:* For master's and doctorate, GRE General Test. Additional exam requirements/recommendations for international students: Required—TOEFL (minimum score 520 paper-based; 190 computer-based). Electronic applications accepted. *Faculty research:* Substance abuse, injury and violence, symptom management.

University of Colorado Denver, College of Nursing, Aurora, CO 80045. Offers adult clinical nurse specialist (MS); adult nurse practitioner (MS); family nurse practitioner (MS); family psychiatric mental health nurse practitioner (MS); health care informatics (MS); nurse-midwifery (MS); nursing (DNP, PhD); nursing leadership and health care systems (MS); pediatric nurse practitioner (MS); pediatric nursing leadership (MS); special studies (MS); women's health care (MS); MS/PhD. *Accreditation:* ACNM/ACME (one or more programs are accredited); NLN (one or more programs are accredited). Part-time and evening/weekend programs available. Postbaccalaureate distance learning degree programs offered (minimal on-campus study). *Faculty:* 69 full-time (65 women), 68 part-time/adjunct (64 women). *Students:* 308 full-time (288 women), 134 part-time (118 women); includes 59 minority (11 Black or African American, non-Hispanic/Latino; 8 American Indian or Alaska Native, non-Hispanic/Latino; 10 Asian, non-Hispanic/Latino; 27 Hispanic/Latino; 3 Two or more races, non-Hispanic/Latino), 8 international. Average age 39. 298 applicants, 46% accepted, 110 enrolled. In 2011, 72 master's, 19 doctorates awarded. Terminal master's awarded for partial completion of doctoral program. *Degree requirements:* For master's, thesis optional; for doctorate, comprehensive exam, thesis/dissertation, 42 credits of coursework, 30 credits of dissertation. *Entrance requirements:* For master's, GRE if cumulative undergraduate GPA is less than 3.0, undergraduate nursing degree from NLNAC- or CCNE-accredited school or university; completion of research and statistics courses with minimum grade

of C; copy of current and unencumbered nursing license; for doctorate, GRE, bachelor's and/or master's degrees in nursing from NLN- or CCNE-accredited institution; portfolio; minimum undergraduate GPA of 3.0, graduate 3.5; graduate-level intermediate statistics and master's-level nursing theory courses with minimum B grade; interview. Additional exam requirements/recommendations for international students: Required—TOEFL (minimum score 560 paper-based; 220 computer-based; 83 iBT). *Application deadline:* For fall admission, 4/1 for domestic students; for spring admission, 9/1 for domestic students. Application fee: $65. Electronic applications accepted. *Expenses:* Contact institution. *Financial support:* In 2011–12, 40 students received support. Fellowships, research assistantships, teaching assistantships, Federal Work-Study, scholarships/grants, and unspecified assistantships available. Support available to part-time students. Financial award application deadline: 4/1; financial award applicants required to submit FAFSA. *Faculty research:* Biological and behavioral phenomena in pregnancy and postpartum; patterns of glycemia during the insulin resistance of pregnancy; obesity, gestational diabetes, and relationship to neonatal adiposity; men's awareness and knowledge of male breast cancer; cognitive-behavioral therapy for chronic insomnia after breast cancer treatment; massage therapy for the treatment of tension-type headaches. *Total annual research expenditures:* $5.2 million. *Unit head:* Dr. Patricia Moritz, Dean, 303-724-1679, E-mail: pat.moritz@ucdenver.edu. *Application contact:* Judy Campbell, Graduate Programs Coordinator, 303-724-8503, E-mail: judy.campbell@ucdenver.edu. Web site: http://www.ucdenver.edu/academics/colleges/nursing/Pages/default.aspx.

University of Illinois at Chicago, Graduate College, College of Nursing, Program in Nursing, Chicago, IL 60607-7128. Offers acute care clinical nurse specialist (MS); acute care nurse practitioner (MS); administrative studies in nursing (MS); adult nurse practitioner (MS); adult/geriatric nurse practitioner (MS); advanced community health nurse specialist (MS); family nurse practitioner (MS); geriatric clinical nurse specialist (MS); geriatric nurse practitioner (MS); mental health clinical nurse specialist (MS); mental health nurse practitioner (MS); nurse midwifery (MS); occupational health/advanced community health nurse specialist (MS); occupational health/family nurse practitioner (MS); pediatric clinical nurse specialist (MS); pediatric nurse practitioner (MS); perinatal clinical nurse specialist (MS); school/advanced community health nurse specialist (MS); school/family nurse practitioner (MS); women's health nurse practitioner (MS). *Accreditation:* AACN. Part-time programs available. *Degree requirements:* For master's, thesis or alternative. *Entrance requirements:* For master's, GRE General Test, minimum GPA of 2.75. Additional exam requirements/recommendations for international students: Required—TOEFL. Electronic applications accepted.

University of Indianapolis, Graduate Programs, School of Nursing, Indianapolis, IN 46227-3697. Offers family practice (post-RN) (MSN); gerontological nurse practitioner (MSN); nurse-midwifery (MSN); nursing (MSN); nursing administration (MSN); nursing education (MSN); MBA/MSN. *Accreditation:* AACN; ACNM. *Faculty:* 1 full-time (0 women), 4 part-time/adjunct (1 woman). *Students:* 14 full-time (13 women), 168 part-time (159 women); includes 23 minority (13 Black or African American, non-Hispanic/Latino; 1 American Indian or Alaska Native, non-Hispanic/Latino; 4 Asian, non-Hispanic/Latino; 2 Hispanic/Latino; 3 Two or more races, non-Hispanic/Latino), 5 international. Average age 36. In 2011, 51 master's awarded. *Entrance requirements:* For master's, minimum GPA of 3.0, interview, letters of recommendation, resume, IN nursing license, 1 year professional practice. Additional exam requirements/recommendations for international students: Required—TOEFL (minimum score 550 paper-based; 213 computer-based). *Application deadline:* For fall admission, 8/1 for domestic students; for winter admission, 12/15 for domestic students; for spring admission, 4/15 for domestic students. Applications are processed on a rolling basis. Application fee: $50. Tuition and fees vary according to degree level and program. *Financial support:* Federal Work-Study available. *Unit head:* Dr. Anne Thomas, Dean, 317-788-3206, E-mail: athomas@uindy.edu. *Application contact:* Sueann Meagher, Graduate Administrative Assistant, 317-788-8005, Fax: 317-788-3542, E-mail: meaghers@uindy.edu. Web site: http://nursing.uindy.edu/.

The University of Kansas, University of Kansas Medical Center, School of Nursing, Kansas City, KS 66160. Offers adult/gerontological clinical nurse specialist (PMC); adult/gerontological nurse practitioner (PMC); clinical research management (PMC); family nurse practitioner (PMC); health care informatics (PMC); health professions educator (PMC); nurse midwife (PMC); nursing (MS, DNP, PhD); organizational leadership (PMC); psychiatric/mental health nurse practitioner (PMC); public health nursing (PMC). *Accreditation:* AACN; ACNM/ACME. Part-time programs available. Postbaccalaureate distance learning degree programs offered (minimal on-campus study). *Faculty:* 80. *Students:* 79 full-time (71 women), 336 part-time (317 women); includes 63 minority (24 Black or African American, non-Hispanic/Latino; 2 American Indian or Alaska Native, non-Hispanic/Latino; 18 Asian, non-Hispanic/Latino; 15 Hispanic/Latino; 4 Two or more races, non-Hispanic/Latino), 6 international. Average age 37. 155 applicants, 82% accepted, 127 enrolled. In 2011, 79 master's, 15 doctorates, 12 other advanced degrees awarded. Terminal master's awarded for partial completion of doctoral program. *Degree requirements:* For master's, comprehensive exam, thesis optional, general oral exam; for doctorate, variable foreign language requirement, thesis/dissertation, comprehensive oral exam (for DNP); comprehensive written and oral exam (for PhD). *Entrance requirements:* For master's, bachelor's degree in nursing, minimum GPA of 3.0, RN license, 1 year of clinical experience, RN license in KS and MO; for doctorate, GRE General Test, master's degree in nursing, minimum GPA of 3.5, RN license in KS and MO; national certification (for some specialties). Additional exam requirements/recommendations for international students: Required—TOEFL. *Application deadline:* For fall admission, 4/1 for domestic and international students; for spring admission, 9/1 for domestic and international students. Application fee: $60. Electronic applications accepted. Tuition and fees vary according to course load, campus/location, program and reciprocity agreements. *Financial support:* Research assistantships with full and partial tuition reimbursements, teaching assistantships with full and partial tuition reimbursements, and traineeships available. Financial award application deadline: 2/14; financial award applicants required to submit FAFSA. *Faculty research:* Breastfeeding practices of teen mothers, national database of nursing quality indicators, caregiving of families of patients using technology in the home, simulation in nursing education, diaphragm fatigue. *Total annual research expenditures:* $6.1 million. *Unit head:* Dr. Karen L. Miller, Dean, 913-588-1601, Fax: 913-588-1660, E-mail: kmiller@kumc.edu. *Application contact:* Dr. Debra J. Ford, Associate Dean, Student Affairs, 913-588-1619, Fax: 913-588-1615, E-mail: dford@kumc.edu. Web site: http://nursing.kumc.edu.

The University of Manchester, School of Nursing, Midwifery and Social Work, Manchester, United Kingdom. Offers nursing (M Phil, PhD); social work (M Phil, PhD).

University of Maryland, Baltimore, Graduate School, School of Nursing, Master's Program in Nursing, Baltimore, MD 21201. Offers community health nursing (MS); gerontological nursing (MS); maternal-child nursing (MS); medical-surgical nursing (MS); nurse-midwifery education (MS); nursing administration (MS); nursing education (MS); nursing health policy (MS); primary care nursing (MS); psychiatric nursing (MS); MS/MBA. MS/MBA offered jointly with University of Baltimore. *Accreditation:* AACN; AANA/CANAEP; NLN (one or more programs are accredited). Part-time programs available. *Students:* 370 full-time (314 women), 480 part-time (441 women); includes

308 minority (176 Black or African American, non-Hispanic/Latino; 2 American Indian or Alaska Native, non-Hispanic/Latino; 70 Asian, non-Hispanic/Latino; 33 Hispanic/Latino; 27 Two or more races, non-Hispanic/Latino), 9 international. Average age 35. 990 applicants, 30% accepted, 204 enrolled. In 2011, 301 master's awarded. *Degree requirements:* For master's, comprehensive exam (for some programs), thesis or alternative. *Entrance requirements:* For master's, minimum GPA of 2.75, course work in statistics, BS in nursing. Additional exam requirements/recommendations for international students: Required—TOEFL (minimum score 550 paper-based; 80 iBT) or IELTS (minimum score 7). *Application deadline:* For fall admission, 2/1 for domestic students, 1/15 for international students. Application fee: $50. Electronic applications accepted. *Financial support:* Fellowships, research assistantships, teaching assistantships, career-related internships or fieldwork, and traineeships available. Support available to part-time students. Financial award application deadline: 2/15; financial award applicants required to submit FAFSA. *Unit head:* Dr. Jane Kapustin, Assistant Dean, 410-706-6741, Fax: 410-706-4231. *Application contact:* Marjorie Fass, Admissions Director, 410-706-0501, Fax: 410-706-7238.

University of Medicine and Dentistry of New Jersey, School of Health Related Professions, Department of Primary Care, Newark, NJ 07107-1709. Offers nurse midwifery (Certificate); physician assistant (MS). Part-time programs available. *Entrance requirements:* For master's, bachelor's degree with prerequisite work in psychology, English, mathematics, chemistry with lab, and biological sciences with lab; personal statement; interview. Additional exam requirements/recommendations for international students: Required—TOEFL (minimum score 500 paper-based; 79 iBT). *Application deadline:* For fall admission, 10/1 for domestic students, 3/1 for international students. Applications are processed on a rolling basis. Electronic applications accepted. *Unit head:* Dr. Adam Perlman, Chairperson, 973-972-8519. *Application contact:* Douglas Lomonaco, Assistant Dean, 973-972-5454, Fax: 973-972-7463, E-mail: shrpadm@umdnj.edu.

University of Miami, Graduate School, School of Nursing and Health Studies, Coral Gables, FL 33124. Offers acute care (MSN), including acute care nurse practitioner, nurse anesthesia; nursing (PhD); primary care (MSN), including adult nurse practitioner, family nurse practitioner, nurse midwifery, women's health practitioner. *Accreditation:* AACN; AANA/CANAEP; ACNM/ACME (one or more programs are accredited). Part-time programs available. *Degree requirements:* For master's, thesis optional; for doctorate, thesis/dissertation. *Entrance requirements:* For master's, GRE General Test, BSN, minimum GPA of 3.0, Florida RN license; for doctorate, GRE General Test, BSN or MSN, minimum GPA of 3.0. Additional exam requirements/recommendations for international students: Required—TOEFL (minimum score 550 paper-based; 213 computer-based). Electronic applications accepted. *Faculty research:* Transcultural nursing, exercise and depression in Alzheimer's disease, infectious diseases/HIV–AIDS, postpartum depression, outcomes assessment.

University of Michigan, Horace H. Rackham School of Graduate Studies, School of Nursing, Division of Health Promotion and Risk Reduction, Program in Parent-Child Nursing, Ann Arbor, MI 48109. Offers infant, child, adolescent health nurse practitioner (MS); nurse midwifery (MS, Post Master's Certificate). *Accreditation:* AACN. Part-time programs available. Postbaccalaureate distance learning degree programs offered (minimal on-campus study). *Degree requirements:* For master's, thesis. *Entrance requirements:* For master's, GRE General Test (if cumulative BSN GPA less than 3.25), licensure, minimum GPA of 3.0 in BSN program. Additional exam requirements/recommendations for international students: Required—TOEFL (minimum score 560 paper-based; 220 computer-based).

University of Minnesota, Twin Cities Campus, Graduate School, School of Nursing, Nurse Midwifery Program, Minneapolis, MN 55455-0213. Offers MS. *Accreditation:* ACNM/ACME. Postbaccalaureate distance learning degree programs offered (minimal on-campus study). *Degree requirements:* For master's, final oral exam, project or thesis. *Entrance requirements:* Additional exam requirements/recommendations for international students: Required—TOEFL (minimum score 586 paper-based; 240 computer-based).

University of Pennsylvania, School of Nursing, Program in Nurse Midwifery, Philadelphia, PA 19104. Offers MSN. *Accreditation:* AACN; ACNM/ACME. Part-time programs available. *Students:* 34 full-time (all women), 5 part-time (all women); includes 8 minority (2 Black or African American, non-Hispanic/Latino; 1 American Indian or Alaska Native, non-Hispanic/Latino; 3 Asian, non-Hispanic/Latino; 2 Hispanic/Latino). 40 applicants, 20% accepted, 7 enrolled. In 2011, 18 degrees awarded. *Entrance requirements:* For master's, GRE General Test, BSN, minimum GPA of 3.0, previous course work in statistics, physical assessment. Additional exam requirements/recommendations for international students: Required—TOEFL. *Application deadline:* For fall admission, 2/15 priority date for domestic students. Applications are processed on a rolling basis. Application fee: $70. *Expenses:* Contact institution. *Financial support:* Fellowships, research assistantships, teaching assistantships, career-related internships or fieldwork, Federal Work-Study, and institutionally sponsored loans available. Support available to part-time students. Financial award application deadline: 4/1. *Faculty research:* Breast-feeding protocols, history of midwifery, hydrotherapy in labor, cocaine abuse during pregnancy, stress in pregnancy. *Unit head:* Assistant Dean of Admissions and Financial Aid, 866-867-6877, Fax: 215-573-8439, E-mail: admissions@nursing.upenn.edu. *Application contact:* William McCool, Program Director, 215-573-7679, E-mail: mccoolwf@nursing.upenn.edu. Web site: http://www.nursing.upenn.edu.

University of Puerto Rico, Medical Sciences Campus, Graduate School of Public Health, Department of Human Development, Program in Nurse Midwifery, San Juan, PR 00936-5067. Offers MPH, Certificate. *Accreditation:* ACNM/ACME. Part-time programs available. *Entrance requirements:* For master's, GRE, previous course work in algebra.

University of South Africa, College of Human Sciences, Pretoria, South Africa. Offers adult education (M Ed); African languages (MA, PhD); African politics (MA, PhD); Afrikaans (MA, PhD); ancient history (MA, PhD); ancient Near Eastern studies (MA, PhD); anthropology (MA, PhD); applied linguistics (MA); Arabic (MA, PhD); archaeology (MA); art history (MA); Biblical archaeology (MA); Biblical studies (M Th, D Th, PhD); Christian spirituality (M Th, D Th); church history (M Th, D Th); classical studies (MA, PhD); clinical psychology (MA); communication (MA, PhD); comparative education (M Ed, Ed D); consulting psychology (D Admin, D Com, PhD); curriculum studies (M Ed, Ed D); development studies (M Admin, MA, D Admin, PhD); didactics (M Ed, Ed D); education (M Tech); education management (M Ed, Ed D); educational psychology (M Ed); English (MA); environmental education (M Ed); French (MA, PhD); German (MA, PhD); Greek (MA); guidance and counseling (M Ed); health studies (MA, PhD), including health sciences education (MA), health services management (MA), medical and surgical nursing science (critical care general) (MA), midwifery and neonatal nursing science (MA), trauma and emergency care (MA); history (MA, PhD); history of education (Ed D); inclusive education (M Ed, Ed D); information and communications technology policy and regulation (MA); information science (MA, MIS, PhD); international politics (MA, PhD); Islamic studies (MA, PhD); Italian (MA, PhD); Judaica (MA, PhD); linguistics (MA, PhD); mathematical education (M Ed); mathematics education (MA); missiology (M Th, D Th); modern Hebrew (MA, PhD); musicology (MA, MMus, D Mus, PhD); natural science education (M Ed); New Testament (M Th, D Th); Old Testament (D Th); pastoral therapy (M Th, D Th); philosophy (MA); philosophy of education (M Ed, Ed D); politics (MA, PhD); Portuguese (MA, PhD); practical theology (M Th, D Th); psychology (MA, MS, PhD); psychology of education (M Ed, Ed D); public health (MA); religious studies (MA, D Th, PhD); Romance languages (MA); Russian (MA, PhD); Semitic languages (MA, PhD); social behavior studies in HIV/AIDS (MA); social science (mental health) (MA); social science in development studies (MA); social science in psychology (MA); social science in social work (MA); social science in sociology (MA); social work (MSW, DSW, PhD); socio-education (M Ed, Ed D); sociolinguistics (MA); sociology (MA, PhD); Spanish (MA, PhD); systematic theology (M Th, D Th); TESOL (teaching English to speakers of other languages) (MA); theological ethics (M Th, D Th); theory of literature (MA, PhD); urban ministries (D Th); urban ministry (M Th).

Vanderbilt University, Vanderbilt University School of Nursing, Nashville, TN 37240. Offers acute care nurse practitioner (MSN), including intensivist; adult-gerontology primary care nurse practitioner (MSN); emergency nurse practitioner (MSN); family nurse practitioner (MSN); family psychiatric and mental health nurse practitioner (MSN); health systems management (MSN); neonatal nurse practitioner (MSN); nurse midwifery (MSN); nurse midwifery/family nurse practitioner (MSN); nursing informatics (MSN); nursing practice (DNP); nursing science (PhD); pediatric acute care nurse practitioner (MSN); pediatric primary care nurse practitioner (MSN); women's health nurse practitioner (MSN), including urogynecology, women's health; women's health nurse practitioner/adult gerontology nurse practitioner (MSN); MSN/M Div; MSN/MTS. *Accreditation:* ACNM/ACME; NLN (one or more programs are accredited). Part-time programs available. Postbaccalaureate distance learning degree programs offered (minimal on-campus study). *Faculty:* 120 full-time (105 women), 415 part-time/adjunct (302 women). *Students:* 570 full-time (503 women), 395 part-time (364 women); includes 107 minority (57 Black or African American, non-Hispanic/Latino; 1 American Indian or Alaska Native, non-Hispanic/Latino; 19 Asian, non-Hispanic/Latino; 19 Hispanic/Latino; 2 Native Hawaiian or other Pacific Islander, non-Hispanic/Latino; 9 Two or more races, non-Hispanic/Latino), 10 international. Average age 32. 1,116 applicants, 56% accepted, 455 enrolled. In 2011, 341 master's, 33 doctorates awarded. *Degree requirements:* For doctorate, comprehensive exam, thesis/dissertation. *Entrance requirements:* For master's, GRE General Test (within the past 5 years), minimum B average in undergraduate course work, 3 letters of recommendation; for doctorate, GRE General Test, interview, 3 letters of recommendation from doctorally-prepared faculty, MSN, essay. Additional exam requirements/recommendations for international students: Required—TOEFL (minimum score 570 paper-based; 88 computer-based), IELTS (minimum score 6.5). *Application deadline:* For fall admission, 12/1 priority date for domestic students, 12/1 for international students. Applications are processed on a rolling basis. Application fee: $50. Electronic applications accepted. *Expenses:* Contact institution. *Financial support:* In 2011–12, 392 students received support. Scholarships/grants and health care benefits available. Support available to part-time students. Financial award application deadline: 3/15; financial award applicants required to submit FAFSA. *Faculty research:* Lymphedema, palliative care and bereavement, health services research including workforce, safety and quality of care, gerontology, better birth outcomes including nutrition . *Total annual research expenditures:* $1.8 million. *Unit head:* Dr. Colleen Conway-Welch, Dean, 615-343-8776, Fax: 615-343-7711, E-mail: colleen.conway-welch@vanderbilt.edu. *Application contact:* Patricia Peerman, Assistant Dean for Enrollment Management, 615-322-3800, Fax: 615-343-0333, E-mail: vusn-admissions@vanderbilt.edu. Web site: http://www.nursing.vanderbilt.edu.

Wayne State University, College of Nursing, Detroit, MI 48202. Offers adult acute care nursing (MSN); adult primary care nursing (MSN); advanced practice nursing with women, neonates and children (MSN); community health nursing (MSN); complementary therapies in healthcare (Certificate); infant mental health (DNP, PhD); nurse-midwifery (Certificate); nursing (PhD); nursing education (MSN, Certificate), including nursing education (Certificate), transcultural nursing; nursing practice (DNP); pediatric nurse practitioner - acute care (Certificate); pediatric nurse practitioner - primary care (Certificate); psychiatric mental health nurse practitioner (MSN, Certificate); women's health nurse practitioner (Certificate). Application deadline for DNP and PhD is January 15. *Accreditation:* AACN. Part-time programs available. *Students:* 136 full-time (124 women), 333 part-time (300 women); includes 127 minority (82 Black or African American, non-Hispanic/Latino; 1 American Indian or Alaska Native, non-Hispanic/Latino; 27 Asian, non-Hispanic/Latino; 12 Hispanic/Latino; 5 Two or more races, non-Hispanic/Latino), 17 international. Average age 37. 180 applicants, 56% accepted, 90 enrolled. In 2011, 95 master's, 6 doctorates, 21 other advanced degrees awarded. Terminal master's awarded for partial completion of doctoral program. *Degree requirements:* For master's, thesis or alternative; for doctorate, thesis/dissertation. *Entrance requirements:* For master's, minimum honor point average of 2.8 in upper-division course work; BA from NLN- or CCNE-accredited program; references; current RN license; personal statement; for doctorate, GRE General Test (for PhD applicants; DNP applicants may choose the GRE exception but must submit a writing sample), minimum GPA of 3.3, bachelor's or master's degree in nursing, current RN license, interview, goals statement, curriculum vitae, reference letters from doctorally-prepared individuals (three for PhD applicants, two for DNP); for Certificate, graduate degree in nursing, current Michigan RN license, three letters of reference, personal goal statement. Additional exam requirements/recommendations for international students: Required—TOEFL (minimum score 550 paper-based; 213 computer-based); Recommended—TWE (minimum score 6). *Application deadline:* For fall admission, 6/1 priority date for domestic students, 5/1 for international students; for winter admission, 10/1 priority date for domestic students, 9/1 for international students; for spring admission, 2/1 priority date for domestic students, 1/1 for international students. Applications are processed on a rolling basis. Application fee: $50. Electronic applications accepted. *Expenses:* Tuition, state resident: part-time $512.85 per credit. Tuition, nonresident: part-time $1132.65 per credit. *Required fees:* $26.60 per credit. $199.65 per semester. Tuition and fees vary according to course load and program. *Financial support:* In 2011–12, 81 students received support, including 2 fellowships with tuition reimbursements available (averaging $13,708 per year), 1 research assistantship with tuition reimbursement available (averaging $17,391 per year), 4 teaching assistantships with tuition reimbursements available (averaging $27,103 per year); Federal Work-Study, institutionally sponsored loans, scholarships/grants, traineeships, and unspecified assistantships also available. Support available to part-time students. Financial award applicants required to submit FAFSA. *Faculty research:* Urban self-care and care-giving, health disparities, healthy functioning across the life-span. *Total annual research expenditures:* $1.2 million. *Unit head:* Dr. Barbara Redman, Dean, 313-577-4070, Fax: 313-577-4571, E-mail: ae9080@wayne.edu. *Application contact:* Dr. Cynthia Redwine, Assistant Dean for the Office of Student Affairs, 313-577-4082, Fax: 313-577-6949, E-mail: nursinginfo@wayne.edu. Web site: http://www.nursing.wayne.edu/.

Nursing and Healthcare Administration

Abilene Christian University, Graduate School, School of Nursing, Abilene, TX 79699-9100. Offers education and administration (MSN); family nurse practitioner (MSN). *Accreditation:* AACN. Part-time programs available. *Faculty:* 6 part-time/adjunct (all women). *Students:* 1 (woman) full-time, 2 part-time (1 woman). 6 applicants, 17% accepted, 1 enrolled. In 2011, 3 degrees awarded. *Degree requirements:* For master's, practicum. *Entrance requirements:* For master's, GRE General Test. Additional exam requirements/recommendations for international students: Required—TOEFL (minimum score 550 paper-based; 213 computer-based; 80 iBT), IELTS (minimum score 6). *Application deadline:* For fall admission, 4/1 priority date for domestic students; for spring admission, 11/1 for domestic students. Applications are processed on a rolling basis. Application fee: $50. Electronic applications accepted. *Expenses: Tuition:* Full-time $14,168; part-time $787 per hour. *Required fees:* $82 per hour. $10 per term. *Financial support:* Application deadline: 4/1; applicants required to submit FAFSA. *Unit head:* Dr. Becky Hammack, Graduate Director, 325-671-2361, Fax: 325-671-2386, E-mail: atoone@phssn.edu. *Application contact:* David Pittman, Graduate Admissions Counselor, 325-674-2656, Fax: 325-674-6717; E-mail: gradinfo@acu.edu.

Allen College, Program in Nursing, Waterloo, IA 50703. Offers acute care nurse practitioner (MSN, Post-Master's Certificate); adult nurse practitioner (MSN, Post-Master's Certificate); adult psychiatric-mental health nurse practitioner (MSN, Post-Master's Certificate); family nurse practitioner (MSN, Post-Master's Certificate); gerontological nurse practitioner (MSN, Post-Master's Certificate); health education (MSN); leadership in health care delivery (MSN, Post-Master's Certificate); nursing (DNP). *Accreditation:* AACN; NLN. Part-time programs available. *Faculty:* 3 full-time (all women), 16 part-time/adjunct (all women). *Students:* 34 full-time (31 women), 110 part-time (106 women); includes 5 minority (2 Asian, non-Hispanic/Latino; 3 Hispanic/Latino). Average age 36. 156 applicants, 64% accepted, 76 enrolled. In 2011, 61 master's, 1 other advanced degree awarded. *Degree requirements:* For master's, thesis optional. *Entrance requirements:* For master's, minimum GPA of 3.0; for doctorate, minimum GPA of 3.25 in graduate coursework. Additional exam requirements/recommendations for international students: Recommended—TOEFL (minimum score 550 paper-based), IELTS. *Application deadline:* For fall admission, 2/1 priority date for domestic students; for spring admission, 9/1 priority date for domestic students. Applications are processed on a rolling basis. Application fee: $50. Electronic applications accepted. *Expenses: Tuition:* Full-time $13,993; part-time $691 per credit hour. *Required fees:* $832; $69 per credit hour. One-time fee: $100 part-time. Part-time tuition and fees vary according to course load. *Financial support:* In 2011–12, 41 students received support. Institutionally sponsored loans, scholarships/grants, and traineeships available. Support available to part-time students. Financial award application deadline: 8/15; financial award applicants required to submit FAFSA. *Faculty research:* Pain and the aged, congestive heart failure. *Unit head:* Kendra Williams-Perez, Dean, School of Nursing, 319-226-2044, Fax: 319-226-2070, E-mail: williakb@ihs.org. *Application contact:* Michelle Koehn, Admissions Counselor, 319-226-2002, Fax: 319-226-2051, E-mail: koehnml@ihs.org. Web site: http://www.allencollege.edu/.

American International College, School of Health Sciences, Department of Nursing, Springfield, MA 01109-3189. Offers nursing administration (MSN); nursing education (MSN). *Accreditation:* AACN. *Entrance requirements:* For master's, BSN. Additional exam requirements/recommendations for international students: Required—TOEFL. Electronic applications accepted.

American University of Beirut, Graduate Programs, Rafic Hariri School of Nursing, Beirut, Lebanon. Offers adult care nursing (MSN); community health nursing (MSN); nursing administration (MSN); psychiatry mental health nursing (MSN). *Accreditation:* AACN. Part-time programs available. *Faculty:* 8 full-time (7 women), 16 part-time/adjunct (13 women). *Students:* 5 full-time (3 women), 50 part-time (39 women). Average age 29. 46 applicants, 87% accepted, 19 enrolled. In 2011, 19 master's awarded. *Degree requirements:* For master's, one foreign language, comprehensive exam, thesis optional. *Entrance requirements:* For master's, letter of recommendation. Additional exam requirements/recommendations for international students: Required—TOEFL (minimum score 600 paper-based); Recommended—IELTS. *Application deadline:* For fall admission, 2/20 for domestic and international students; for spring admission, 11/1 for domestic and international students. Applications are processed on a rolling basis. Application fee: $50. *Expenses: Tuition:* Full-time $12,780; part-time $710 per credit. Tuition and fees vary according to course load and program. *Financial support:* In 2011–12, 19 research assistantships with partial tuition reimbursements, 1 teaching assistantship with partial tuition reimbursement were awarded; career-related internships or fieldwork, institutionally sponsored loans, scholarships/grants, health care benefits, and unspecified assistantships also available. Support available to part-time students. Financial award application deadline: 2/2. *Faculty research:* Pain management and palliative care, stress and post-traumatic stress disorder, health benefits and chronic illness, health promotion and community interventions. *Total annual research expenditures:* $52,000. *Unit head:* Dr. Huda Huijer Abu-Saad, Director, 961-1374374 Ext. 5952, Fax: 961-1744476, E-mail: hh35@aub.edu.lb. *Application contact:* Dr. Salim Kanaan, Director, Admissions Office, 961-1350000 Ext. 2594, Fax: 961-1750775, E-mail: sk00@aub.edu.lb. Web site: http://staff.aub.edu.lb/~webson.

Arizona State University, College of Nursing and Health Innovation, Phoenix, AZ 85004. Offers advanced nursing practice (DNP); child/family mental health nurse practitioner (Graduate Certificate); clinical research management (MS); community and public health practice (Graduate Certificate); community health (MS); exercise and wellness (MS), including exercise and wellness; family nurse practitioner (Graduate Certificate); healthcare innovation (MHI); international health for healthcare (Graduate Certificate); kinesiology (MS, PhD); nursing (MS, Graduate Certificate); nursing and healthcare innovation (PhD); nutrition (MS); physical activity nutrition and wellness (PhD), including physical activity, nutrition and wellness; public health (MPH); regulatory science and health safety (MS). *Accreditation:* AACN. Postbaccalaureate distance learning degree programs offered (minimal on-campus study). *Degree requirements:* For master's, comprehensive exam (for some programs), thesis (for some programs), interactive Program of Study (iPOS) submitted before completing 50 percent of required credit hours; for doctorate, comprehensive exam, thesis/dissertation, interactive Program of Study (iPOS) submitted before completing 50 percent of required credit hours. *Entrance requirements:* For master's and doctorate, GRE, minimum GPA of 3.0 or equivalent in last 2 years of work leading to bachelor's degree. Additional exam requirements/recommendations for international students: Required—TOEFL (minimum score 80 iBT), TOEFL, IELTS, or Pearson Test of English. Electronic applications accepted. *Expenses:* Contact institution.

Athabasca University, Centre for Nursing and Health Studies, Athabasca, AB T9S 3A3, Canada. Offers advanced nursing practice (MN, Advanced Diploma); generalist (MN); health studies-leadership (MHS). Part-time programs available. Postbaccalaureate distance learning degree programs offered. *Degree requirements:*

For master's, comprehensive exam (for some programs). *Entrance requirements:* For master's, bachelor's degree in health-related field, 2 years professional health service experience (MHS), bachelor's degree in nursing, 2 years nursing experience (MN), minimum GPA of 3.0 in final 30 credits; for Advanced Diploma, RN license, 2 years health care experience. Electronic applications accepted. *Expenses:* Contact institution.

Austin Peay State University, College of Graduate Studies, College of Behavioral and Health Sciences, School of Nursing, Clarksville, TN 37044. Offers advanced practice (MSN); nursing administration (MSN); nursing education (MSN); nursing informatics (MSN). Part-time programs available. Postbaccalaureate distance learning degree programs offered. *Faculty:* 6 full-time (all women). *Students:* 21 full-time (16 women), 79 part-time (74 women); includes 12 minority (9 Black or African American, non-Hispanic/Latino; 2 Hispanic/Latino; 1 Two or more races, non-Hispanic/Latino). Average age 38. 42 applicants, 100% accepted, 29 enrolled. In 2011, 24 master's awarded. *Degree requirements:* For master's, comprehensive exam. *Entrance requirements:* For master's, GRE General Test, minimum GPA of 3.0, RN license eligibility, 3 letters of recommendation. Additional exam requirements/recommendations for international students: Required—TOEFL (minimum score 600 paper-based). *Application deadline:* For fall admission, 8/1 priority date for domestic students. Applications are processed on a rolling basis. Application fee: $25. Electronic applications accepted. *Expenses:* Tuition, state resident: part-time $350 per credit hour. Tuition, nonresident: full-time $20,644; part-time $971 per credit hour. *Required fees:* $1224; $61.20 per credit hour. *Financial support:* In 2011–12, research assistantships with full tuition reimbursements (averaging $5,184 per year) were awarded; career-related internships or fieldwork, Federal Work-Study, institutionally sponsored loans, scholarships/grants, and unspecified assistantships also available. Support available to part-time students. *Unit head:* Dr. Patty Orr, Director, 931-221-7710, Fax: 931-221-7595, E-mail: orrp@apsu.edu. *Application contact:* Kendra Bryant, Graduate Admissions, 800-844-2778, Fax: 931-221-6188, E-mail: admissionsweb@apsu.edu. Web site: http://www.apsu.edu/nursing.

Barry University, School of Adult and Continuing Education, Division of Nursing, Program in Nursing Administration, Miami Shores, FL 33161-6695. Offers MSN, PhD, Certificate. *Accreditation:* AACN. Part-time and evening/weekend programs available. *Degree requirements:* For master's, research project or thesis. *Entrance requirements:* For master's, GRE General Test or MAT, BSN, minimum GPA of 3.0, course work in statistics. Electronic applications accepted. *Faculty research:* Power/empowerment, health delivery systems, managed care, employee health and well being.

Barry University, School of Adult and Continuing Education, Division of Nursing and Andreas School of Business, Program in Nursing Administration and Business Administration, Miami Shores, FL 33161-6695. Offers MSN/MBA. *Accreditation:* AACN. Part-time and evening/weekend programs available. Electronic applications accepted. *Faculty research:* Power/empowerment, health delivery systems, managed care, employee health well-being.

Bellarmine University, Donna and Allan Lansing School of Nursing and Health Sciences, Louisville, KY 40205-0671. Offers family nurse practitioner (MSN); nursing administration (MSN); nursing education (MSN); nursing practice (DNP); physical therapy (DPT). *Accreditation:* AACN; APTA. Part-time and evening/weekend programs available. *Faculty:* 21 full-time (16 women), 7 part-time/adjunct (2 women). *Students:* 128 full-time (82 women), 116 part-time (111 women); includes 13 minority (5 Black or African American, non-Hispanic/Latino; 1 American Indian or Alaska Native, non-Hispanic/Latino; 2 Asian, non-Hispanic/Latino; 3 Hispanic/Latino; 2 Two or more races, non-Hispanic/Latino). Average age 31. In 2011, 19 master's, 50 doctorates awarded. *Degree requirements:* For doctorate, comprehensive exam, thesis/dissertation. *Entrance requirements:* For master's, GRE General Test, RN license; for doctorate, GRE General Test, Physical Therapist Centralized Application Service (for DPT). Additional exam requirements/recommendations for international students: Required—TOEFL (minimum score 550 paper-based; 213 computer-based; 80 iBT). Application fee: $25. Electronic applications accepted. *Expenses:* Contact institution. *Financial support:* Career-related internships or fieldwork and scholarships/grants available. *Faculty research:* Nursing: pain, empathy, leadership styles, control; physical therapy: service-learning; exercise in chronic and pre-operative conditions, athletes; women's health; aging. *Unit head:* Dr. Susan H. Davis, Dean, 800-274-4723 Ext. 8217, E-mail: sdavis@bellarmine.edu. *Application contact:* Julie Armstrong-Binnix, Health Science Recruiter, 800-274-4723 Ext. 8364, E-mail: julieab@bellarmine.edu. Web site: http://www.bellarmine.edu/lansing.

Bellin College, Program in Nursing, Green Bay, WI 54305. Offers administrator (MSN); educator (MSN). *Accreditation:* AACN.

Bethel University, Graduate School, St. Paul, MN 55112-6999. Offers autism spectrum disorders (Certificate); business administration (MBA); communication (MA); counseling psychology (MA); education (M Ed); educational leadership (Ed D); gerontology (MA, Certificate); international baccalaureate education (Certificate); K-12 education (MA); literacy education (MA); nursing (MA); nursing education (Certificate); nursing leadership (Certificate); organizational leadership (MA); postsecondary teaching (Certificate); special education (MA); teaching (MA). Part-time and evening/weekend programs available. Postbaccalaureate distance learning degree programs offered (minimal on-campus study). *Faculty:* 8 full-time (3 women), 98 part-time/adjunct (46 women). *Students:* 651 full-time (419 women), 312 part-time (212 women); includes 79 minority (35 Black or African American, non-Hispanic/Latino; 2 American Indian or Alaska Native, non-Hispanic/Latino; 19 Asian, non-Hispanic/Latino; 17 Hispanic/Latino; 6 Two or more races, non-Hispanic/Latino), 6 international. Average age 36. In 2011, 245 master's, 4 doctorates, 32 other advanced degrees awarded. *Degree requirements:* For master's, comprehensive exam (for some programs), thesis (for some programs); for doctorate, comprehensive exam, thesis/dissertation. *Entrance requirements:* Additional exam requirements/recommendations for international students: Required—TOEFL (minimum score 550 paper-based; 213 computer-based; 80 iBT). *Application deadline:* Applications are processed on a rolling basis. Electronic applications accepted. Tuition and fees vary according to course load, degree level and program. *Financial support:* Applicants required to submit FAFSA. *Unit head:* Dick Crombie, Vice-President/Dean, 651-635-8000, Fax: 651-635-8004, E-mail: gs@bethel.edu. *Application contact:* Paul Ives, Director of Admissions, 651-635-8000, Fax: 651-635-8004, E-mail: gs@bethel.edu. Web site: http://gs.bethel.edu/.

Bloomsburg University of Pennsylvania, School of Graduate Studies, College of Science and Technology, Department of Nursing, Bloomsburg, PA 17815-1301. Offers adult and family nurse practitioner (MSN); adult health and illness (MSN); community health (MSN); nursing (MSN); nursing administration (MSN). *Accreditation:* AACN; AANA/CANAEP. *Degree requirements:* For master's, thesis. *Entrance requirements:* For master's, minimum QPA of 3.0. Additional exam requirements/recommendations for

international students: Required—TOEFL. Electronic applications accepted. *Faculty research:* Cardiopulmonary nursing, cancer topics, women's health.

Bowie State University, Graduate Programs, Department of Nursing, Bowie, MD 20715-9465. Offers administration of nursing services (MS); family nurse practitioner (MS); nursing education (MS). *Accreditation:* NLN. Part-time programs available. *Faculty:* 7 full-time (4 women), 14 part-time/adjunct (9 women). *Students:* 41 full-time (35 women), 55 part-time (50 women); includes 80 minority (77 Black or African American, non-Hispanic/Latino; 2 Asian, non-Hispanic/Latino; 1 Hispanic/Latino), 11 international. Average age 42. 7 applicants, 100% accepted, 5 enrolled. In 2011, 7 master's awarded. *Degree requirements:* For master's, comprehensive exam, thesis, research paper. *Entrance requirements:* For master's, minimum GPA of 2.5. *Application deadline:* For fall admission, 5/15 for domestic students. Applications are processed on a rolling basis. Application fee: $40. Electronic applications accepted. *Expenses:* Tuition, state resident: full-time $4140; part-time $3105 per semester. Tuition, nonresident: full-time $7836; part-time $5877 per semester. *Required fees:* $1715; $648 per semester. *Financial support:* Institutionally sponsored loans and traineeships available. Financial award application deadline: 4/1. *Faculty research:* Minority health, women's health, gerontology, leadership management. *Unit head:* Dr. Bonita Jenkins, Acting Chairperson, 301-860-3210, E-mail: mccaskill@bowiestate.edu. *Application contact:* Angela Issac, Information Contact, 301-860-4000.

Bradley University, Graduate School, College of Education and Health Sciences, Department of Nursing, Peoria, IL 61625-0002. Offers nurse administered anesthesia (MSN); nursing administration (MSN). *Accreditation:* AANA/CANAEP; NLN. Part-time and evening/weekend programs available. *Degree requirements:* For master's, comprehensive exam, thesis optional. *Entrance requirements:* For master's, GRE General Test or MAT, interview, Illinois RN license, advanced cardiac life support certification, pediatric advanced life support certification, 3 letters of recommendation. Additional exam requirements/recommendations for international students: Required—TOEFL (minimum score 550 paper-based; 213 computer-based; 79 iBT).

Brenau University, Sydney O. Smith Graduate School, College of Health and Science, Gainesville, GA 30501. Offers family nurse practitioner (MSN); nurse educator (MSN); nursing management (MSN); occupational therapy (MS); psychology (MS). *Accreditation:* AOTA; NLN. Part-time and evening/weekend programs available. *Degree requirements:* For master's, comprehensive exam (for some programs), thesis (for some programs), clinical practicum hours. *Entrance requirements:* For master's, GRE General Test or MAT (for some programs), interview, writing sample, references (for some programs). Additional exam requirements/recommendations for international students: Required—TOEFL (minimum score 500 paper-based; 173 computer-based; 61 iBT); Recommended—IELTS (minimum score 5). Electronic applications accepted. *Expenses:* Contact institution.

California Baptist University, Program in Nursing, Riverside, CA 92504-3206. Offers administering nursing services (MSN); teaching nursing (MSN). Part-time programs available. *Faculty:* 21 full-time (all women). *Students:* 58 full-time (44 women); includes 28 minority (5 Black or African American, non-Hispanic/Latino; 2 American Indian or Alaska Native, non-Hispanic/Latino; 7 Asian, non-Hispanic/Latino; 12 Hispanic/Latino; 1 Native Hawaiian or other Pacific Islander, non-Hispanic/Latino; 1 Two or more races, non-Hispanic/Latino). Average age 32. 35 applicants, 60% accepted, 19 enrolled. *Degree requirements:* For master's, comprehensive exam or thesis. *Entrance requirements:* For master's, GRE or California Critical Thinking Skills Test; Test of Essential Academic Skills (TEAS), minimum GPA of 3.25; health clearance; health insurance; CPR certification; vehicle insurance; criminal background clearance; passport photo; three recommendations; comprehensive essay; interview. Additional exam requirements/recommendations for international students: Required—TOEFL (minimum score 575 paper-based; 230 computer-based; 89 iBT). *Application deadline:* For fall admission, 8/1 priority date for domestic students, 7/1 for international students; for spring admission, 12/1 priority date for domestic students, 11/1 for international students. Applications are processed on a rolling basis. Application fee: $45. Electronic applications accepted. *Expenses: Tuition:* Full-time $9540; part-time $530 per unit. *Required fees:* $355 per semester. One-time fee: $45. Tuition and fees vary according to course load and program. *Financial support:* Federal Work-Study and institutionally sponsored loans available. Financial award applicants required to submit FAFSA. *Faculty research:* Qualitative research using Parse Methodology, gerontology, disaster preparedness, medical-surgical nursing, maternal-child nursing. *Unit head:* Dr. Geneva Oaks, Dean, School of Nursing, 951-343-4738, E-mail: goaks@calbaptist.edu. *Application contact:* Gail Ronveaux, Dean of Graduate Enrollment, 951-343-4246, Fax: 951-343-5095, E-mail: graduateadmissions@calbaptist.edu. Web site: http://www.calbaptist.edu/msn/.

Capital University, School of Nursing, Columbus, OH 43209-2394. Offers administration (MSN); legal studies (MSN); theological studies (MSN); JD/MSN; MBA/MSN; MSN/MTS. *Accreditation:* AACN. Part-time and evening/weekend programs available. *Degree requirements:* For master's, thesis or alternative. *Entrance requirements:* For master's, BSN, current RN license, minimum GPA of 3.0, undergraduate courses in statistics and research. Additional exam requirements/recommendations for international students: Required—TOEFL (minimum score 550 paper-based). *Expenses:* Contact institution. *Faculty research:* Bereavement, wellness/health promotion, emergency cardiac care, critical thinking, complementary and alternative healthcare.

Carlow University, School of Nursing, Program in Nursing Leadership and Education, Pittsburgh, PA 15213-3165. Offers MSN. Part-time and evening/weekend programs available. *Students:* 43 full-time (41 women), 15 part-time (all women); includes 2 minority (1 Black or African American, non-Hispanic/Latino; 1 Native Hawaiian or other Pacific Islander, non-Hispanic/Latino), 2 international. Average age 39. 31 applicants, 58% accepted, 10 enrolled. In 2011, 23 master's awarded. *Degree requirements:* For master's, internship. *Entrance requirements:* For master's, minimum undergraduate GPA of 3.0 from accredited BSN program; current license as RN in Pennsylvania; course in statistics in past 6 years; two recommendations; personal statement; personal interview. Additional exam requirements/recommendations for international students: Required—TOEFL (minimum score 550 paper-based; 213 computer-based). Application fee: $20. Application fee is waived when completed online. *Expenses: Tuition:* Full-time $10,290; part-time $686 per credit. Tuition and fees vary according to course load, degree level and program. *Unit head:* Dr. Peggy Slota, Director, Nursing Leadership and DNP Programs, 412-578-6102, Fax: 412-578-6114, E-mail: mmslota@carlow.edu. *Application contact:* Jo Danhires, Administrative Assistant, Admissions, 412-578-6059, Fax: 412-578-6321, E-mail: gradstudies@carlow.edu.

Case Western Reserve University, Frances Payne Bolton School of Nursing, Doctor of Nursing Practice Program, Cleveland, OH 44106. Offers acute care nurse practitioner (DNP); adult gerontology nurse practitioner (DNP); educational leadership (DNP); family nurse practitioner (DNP); family systems psychiatric mental health nursing (DNP); midwifery/family nursing (DNP); neonatal nurse practitioner (DNP); pediatric nurse practitioner (DNP); practice leadership (DNP); women's health nurse practitioner (DNP). *Students:* 73 full-time, 194 part-time; includes 11 minority (6 Black or African American, non-Hispanic/Latino; 3 Asian, non-Hispanic/Latino; 2 Hispanic/Latino). 122 applicants, 74% accepted, 49 enrolled. In 2011, 47 doctorates awarded. Terminal master's awarded for partial completion of doctoral program. *Degree requirements:* For doctorate, thesis/dissertation. *Entrance requirements:* For doctorate, GRE General Test or MAT. Additional exam requirements/recommendations for international students: Required—TOEFL (minimum score 577 paper-based; 90 iBT), IELTS (minimum score 7). *Application deadline:* For fall admission, 6/1 priority date for domestic students, 6/1 for international students; for spring admission, 10/1 for domestic and international students. Applications are processed on a rolling basis. Application fee: $75. *Financial support:* In 2011–12, 6 students received support, including 1 teaching assistantship; research assistantships, Federal Work-Study, institutionally sponsored loans, and tuition waivers (partial) also available. Support available to part-time students. Financial award application deadline: 6/30; financial award applicants required to submit FAFSA. *Faculty research:* Clinical nursing, acute care, gerontology, mental health, critical care. *Unit head:* Dr. Donna Dowling, Director, 216-368-1869, Fax: 216-368-3542, E-mail: dad10@case.edu. *Application contact:* Donna Hassik, Admissions Coordinator, 216-368-5253, Fax: 216-368-0124, E-mail: dmh7@case.edu. Web site: http://fpb.case.edu/DNP/.

Cedar Crest College, Program in Nursing, Allentown, PA 18104-6196. Offers nursing administration (MS); nursing education (MS). Part-time programs available. *Faculty:* 5 full-time (all women). *Students:* 3 full-time, 16 part-time (all women). In 2011, 19 master's awarded. *Expenses: Tuition:* Part-time $590 per credit. Tuition and fees vary according to program. *Unit head:* Dr. Wendy Robb, Director, 610-606-4666, E-mail: wjrobb@cedarcrest.edu. *Application contact:* Bonnie Sofarelli, Director of School of Adult and Graduate Education, 610-606-4666, E-mail: sage@cedarcrest.edu. Web site: http://sage.cedarcrest.edu/degrees/graduate/nursing-science/.

Central Methodist University, College of Graduate and Extended Studies, Fayette, MO 65248-1198. Offers clinical counseling (MS); clinical nurse leader (MSN); education (M Ed). Part-time and evening/weekend programs available. Postbaccalaureate distance learning degree programs offered (no on-campus study). *Degree requirements:* For master's, thesis. *Entrance requirements:* For master's, GRE General Test, minimum GPA of 2.75. Electronic applications accepted.

Chatham University, Nursing Programs, Pittsburgh, PA 15232-2826. Offers education/leadership (MSN); nursing (DNP). *Accreditation:* AACN. Postbaccalaureate distance learning degree programs offered (minimal on-campus study). *Faculty:* 10 full-time (8 women), 11 part-time/adjunct (9 women). *Students:* 37 full-time (31 women), 62 part-time (58 women); includes 19 minority (16 Black or African American, non-Hispanic/Latino; 1 Asian, non-Hispanic/Latino; 1 Hispanic/Latino; 1 Native Hawaiian or other Pacific Islander, non-Hispanic/Latino). Average age 45. 163 applicants, 72% accepted, 84 enrolled. In 2011, 20 master's, 73 doctorates awarded. *Entrance requirements:* For master's, RN license, BSN, minimum GPA of 3.0; for doctorate, RN license, MSN. Additional exam requirements/recommendations for international students: Required—TOEFL (minimum score 600 paper-based; 250 computer-based; 100 iBT), IELTS (minimum score 6.5), TWE. *Application deadline:* For fall admission, 5/1 priority date for domestic students, 5/1 for international students. Applications are processed on a rolling basis. Application fee: $0. Electronic applications accepted. Application fee is waived when completed online. *Expenses: Tuition:* Full-time $13,896. Tuition and fees vary according to program. *Financial support:* Applicants required to submit FAFSA. *Unit head:* Dr. Elizabeth Gazza, Director, 412-365-2746, E-mail: egazza@chatham.edu. *Application contact:* David Vey, Admissions Support Specialist, 412-365-1498, Fax: 412-365-1720, E-mail: dvey@chatham.edu. Web site: http://www.chatham.edu/nursing.

Clarke University, Department of Nursing and Health, Dubuque, IA 52001-3198. Offers administration of nursing systems (MSN); advanced practice nursing (MSN); education (MSN); family nurse practitioner (MSN, PMC). *Accreditation:* AACN. Part-time programs available. *Faculty:* 5 full-time (all women), 2 part-time/adjunct (1 woman). *Students:* 42 full-time (41 women), 25 part-time (all women); includes 1 minority (Black or African American, non-Hispanic/Latino). Average age 35. In 2011, 13 master's awarded. *Entrance requirements:* For master's, GRE General Test or MAT, BSN, minimum GPA of 3.0. *Application deadline:* For fall admission, 2/15 priority date for domestic students; for spring admission, 12/15 priority date for domestic students. Applications are processed on a rolling basis. Application fee: $25. Electronic applications accepted. *Expenses: Tuition:* Part-time $690 per credit hour. *Required fees:* $35 per credit hour. Tuition and fees vary according to program and student level. *Financial support:* In 2011–12, 6 students received support. Career-related internships or fieldwork available. Support available to part-time students. Financial award applicants required to submit FAFSA. *Faculty research:* Narrative pedagogy, ethics, end-of-life care, pedagogy, family systems. *Unit head:* Dr. Susan DeCrane, Chair, 800-224-2736, Fax: 319-584-8684. *Application contact:* Carrie Kirk, Information Contact, 563-588-6635, Fax: 563-588-6789, E-mail: graduate@clarke.edu. Web site: http://www.clarke.edu/.

Clarkson College, Master of Science in Nursing Program, Omaha, NE 68131. Offers adult nurse practitioner (MSN, Post-Master's Certificate); family nurse practitioner (MSN, Post-Master's Certificate); nursing education (MSN, Post-Master's Certificate); nursing health care leadership (MSN, Post-Master's Certificate). *Accreditation:* AANA/CANAEP; NLN. Part-time and evening/weekend programs available. Postbaccalaureate distance learning degree programs offered (minimal on-campus study). *Degree requirements:* For master's, on-campus skills assessment (family nurse practitioner, adult nurse practitioner), comprehensive exam or thesis. *Entrance requirements:* For master's, minimum GPA of 3.0, 2 references, resume. Additional exam requirements/recommendations for international students: Required—TOEFL (minimum score 600 paper-based; 250 computer-based; 100 iBT). Electronic applications accepted.

Clarkson College, Program in Health Care Administration, Omaha, NE 68131-2739. Offers MHCA. Part-time and evening/weekend programs available. Postbaccalaureate distance learning degree programs offered (no on-campus study). *Entrance requirements:* For master's, minimum GPA of 3.0, resume, references. Additional exam requirements/recommendations for international students: Required—TOEFL (minimum score 600 paper-based; 250 computer-based; 100 iBT). Electronic applications accepted.

College of Mount St. Joseph, Doctor of Nursing Practice Program, Cincinnati, OH 45233-1670. Offers administration (DNP); advanced practice (DNP). Part-time programs available. *Entrance requirements:* For doctorate, essay; MSN from regionally-accredited university; minimum graduate GPA of 3.5; professional resume; three professional references; interview; 2 years of clinical nursing experience; active RN license; criminal background check. Additional exam requirements/recommendations for international students: Required—TOEFL (minimum score 560 paper-based; 220 computer-based; 83 iBT). Application fee: $50. Electronic applications accepted. *Expenses: Tuition:* Full-time $24,200; part-time $540 per credit hour. *Required fees:* $112.50 per semester. One-time fee: $200. *Financial support:* Applicants required to submit FAFSA. *Unit head:* Dr. Lynn Bertsch, Director, 513-244-4200, E-mail: lynn_bertsch@mail.msj.edu. *Application contact:* Marilyn Hoskins, Assistant Director for Graduate Recruitment, 513-244-4723, Fax: 513-244-4629, E-mail: marilyn_hoskins@mail.msj.edu. Web site: http://www.msj.edu/view/academics/graduate-programs/doctor-of-nursing-practice.aspx.

College of Mount St. Joseph, Master of Science in Nursing Program, Cincinnati, OH 45233-1670. Offers administration (MSN); education (MSN). Part-time programs available. *Entrance requirements:* For master's, essay; BSN from regionally-accredited university; minimum undergraduate GPA of 3.25 or GRE; professional resume; three

professional references; interview; 2 years of clinical nursing experience; active RN license; criminal background check. Additional exam requirements/recommendations for international students: Required—TOEFL (minimum score 560 paper-based; 220 computer-based; 83 iBT). Application fee: $50. Electronic applications accepted. *Expenses: Tuition:* Full-time $24,200; part-time $540 per credit hour. *Required fees:* $112.50 per semester. One-time fee: $200. *Financial support:* Applicants required to submit FAFSA. *Unit head:* Dr. Lynn Bertsch, Director, 513-244-4200, E-mail: lynn_bertsch@mail.msj.edu. *Application contact:* Marilyn Hoskins, Assistant Director for Graduate Recruitment, 513-244-4723, Fax: 513-244-4629, E-mail: marilyn_hoskins@mail.msj.edu. Web site: http://www.msj.edu/view/academics/graduate-programs/master-of-science-in-nursing-.aspx.

College of Mount Saint Vincent, School of Professional and Continuing Studies, Department of Nursing, Riverdale, NY 10471-1093. Offers adult nurse practitioner (MSN, PMC); family nurse practitioner (MSN, PMC); nurse educator (PMC); nursing administration (MSN); nursing for the adult and aged (MSN). *Accreditation:* AACN. Part-time programs available. *Entrance requirements:* For master's, BSN, interview, RN license, minimum GPA of 3.0, letters of reference. Additional exam requirements/recommendations for international students: Required—TOEFL. *Expenses:* Contact institution.

The College of New Rochelle, Graduate School, Program in Nursing, New Rochelle, NY 10805-2308. Offers acute care nurse practitioner (MS, Certificate); clinical specialist in holistic nursing (MS, Certificate); family nurse practitioner (MS, Certificate); nursing and health care management (MS); nursing education (Certificate). *Accreditation:* AACN. Part-time programs available. *Entrance requirements:* For master's, GRE General Test or MAT, BSN, malpractice insurance, minimum GPA of 3.0, RN license. *Expenses:* Contact institution. *Faculty research:* Holistic modalities, academic success variables.

Cox College, Programs in Nursing, Springfield, MO 65802. Offers clinical nurse leader (MSN); family nurse practitioner (MSN); nurse educator (MSN). *Accreditation:* AACN. *Entrance requirements:* For master's, RN license, essay, 2 letters of recommendation, official transcripts. Electronic applications accepted.

Daemen College, Department of Nursing, Amherst, NY 14226-3592. Offers adult nurse practitioner (MS, Post Master's Certificate); nurse executive leadership (Post Master's Certificate); nursing education (MS, Post Master's Certificate); nursing executive leadership (MS); nursing practice (DNP); palliative care nursing (Post Master's Certificate). *Accreditation:* NLN. Part-time programs available. *Degree requirements:* For master's, thesis or alternative, degree completed in 4 years; minimum GPA of 3.0; for doctorate, degree completed in 5 years; 500 post-master's clinical hours. *Entrance requirements:* For master's, BN, 1 year medical/surgical experience, RN license and state registration, statistics course with minimum C grade, 3 letters of recommendation, minimum GPA of 3.25, interview; for doctorate, MS in advance nursing practice; New York state RN license; goal statement; resume; interview; statistics course with minimum grade of 'C'; for Post Master's Certificate, master's degree in clinical area; RN license and current registration; one year of clinical experience; statistics course with minimum grade of 'C'; 3 letters of recommendation; interview; letter of intent. Additional exam requirements/recommendations for international students: Required—TOEFL (minimum score 500 paper-based; 173 computer-based; 63 iBT), IELTS (minimum score 5.5). Electronic applications accepted. *Faculty research:* Professional stress, client behavior, drug therapy, treatment modalities and pulmonary cancers, chemical dependency.

DeSales University, Graduate Division, Division of Healthcare and Natural Sciences, Center Valley, PA 18034-9568. Offers adult advanced practice nurse specialist (MSN); certified nurse midwives (MSN); certified nurse practitioners (MSN); clinical leadership (DNP); family nurse practitioner (MSN); nurse educator (MSN); nurse practitioner (Post-Master's Certificate); MSN/MBA. *Accreditation:* NLN. Part-time programs available. *Degree requirements:* For master's, thesis optional. *Entrance requirements:* For master's, GRE General Test, MAT, minimum B average in undergraduate course work, health assessment course or equivalent, course work in statistics. Additional exam requirements/recommendations for international students: Required—TOEFL. *Application deadline:* Applications are processed on a rolling basis. Application fee: $35. Electronic applications accepted. Tuition and fees vary according to degree level. *Financial support:* Applicants required to submit FAFSA. *Unit head:* Dr. Carol Gullo Mest, Director, 610-282-1100 Ext. 1394, Fax: 610-282-2091, E-mail: carol.mest@desales.edu. *Application contact:* Caryn Stopper, Director of Graduate Admissions, 610-282-1100 Ext. 1768, Fax: 610-282-2254, E-mail: caryn.stopper@desales.edu.

Dominican University of California, Graduate Programs, School of Health and Natural Sciences, Program in Nursing, San Rafael, CA 94901-2298. Offers clinical nurse leader (MS). *Accreditation:* AACN. Part-time and evening/weekend programs available. *Students:* 15 full-time (13 women), 15 part-time (13 women); includes 7 minority (2 Black or African American, non-Hispanic/Latino; 3 Asian, non-Hispanic/Latino; 2 Hispanic/Latino). Average age 45. 27 applicants, 44% accepted, 8 enrolled. In 2011, 6 master's awarded. *Degree requirements:* For master's, thesis. *Entrance requirements:* For master's, minimum GPA of 3.0; current California RN License; clinical experience; course work in nursing research and statistics; CPR certification; professional liability and malpractice insurance; interview. Additional exam requirements/recommendations for international students: Required—TOEFL (minimum score 550 paper-based; 213 computer-based; 80 iBT), IELTS (minimum score 7). *Application deadline:* For fall admission, 6/15 priority date for domestic students; for spring admission, 11/15 priority date for domestic students. Applications are processed on a rolling basis. Application fee: $40. Electronic applications accepted. *Expenses: Tuition:* Full-time $15,660. *Required fees:* $300. Tuition and fees vary according to program. *Financial support:* In 2011–12, 12 students received support. Scholarships/grants available. Support available to part-time students. Financial award application deadline: 3/2; financial award applicants required to submit FAFSA. *Unit head:* Dr. Eira Klich-Heartt, Director, 415-257-1314, Fax: 415-485-0120, E-mail: eira.klich-heartt@dominican.edu. *Application contact:* Shannon Lovelace-White, Assistant Vice President, 415-485-3287, Fax: 415-485-3214, E-mail: shannon.lovelace-white@dominican.edu. Web site: http://www.dominican.edu/admissions/graduate/programs/ms-in-nursing-clinical-nurse-leader.

Drexel University, College of Nursing and Health Professions, Division of Graduate Nursing, Philadelphia, PA 19104-2875. Offers adult acute care (MSN); adult psychiatric/mental health (MSN); advanced practice nursing (MSN); clinical trials research (MSN); family nurse practitioner (MSN); leadership in health systems management (MSN); nursing education (MSN); pediatric primary care (MSN); women's health (MSN). *Accreditation:* AACN; NLN. Electronic applications accepted.

Duke University, School of Nursing, Durham, NC 27708-0586. Offers adult acute care (Certificate); adult cardiovascular (Certificate); adult oncology (Certificate); adult primary care (Certificate); clinical nurse specialist (MSN), including adult oncology, gerontology, neonatal, pediatric; clinical research management (MSN, Certificate); family (Certificate); gerontology (Certificate); health and nursing ministries (MSN, Certificate); health systems leadership and outcomes (Certificate); neonatal (Certificate); neonatal/pediatric in rural health (MSN, Certificate); nurse anesthetist (MSN, Certificate); nurse practitioner (MSN), including adult acute care, adult cardiovascular, adult oncology, adult primary care, family, gerontology, neonatal, pediatric, pediatric acute care; nursing (DNP, PhD); nursing and healthcare leadership (MSN); nursing education (MSN); nursing informatics (MSN, Certificate); pediatric (Certificate); pediatric acute care (Certificate); MBA/MSN; MSN/MCM. *Accreditation:* AACN; AANA/CANAEP. Part-time and evening/weekend programs available. Postbaccalaureate distance learning degree programs offered (minimal on-campus study). *Faculty:* 56 full-time (47 women), 2 part-time/adjunct (1 woman). *Students:* 127 full-time (108 women), 395 part-time (358 women); includes 92 minority (42 Black or African American, non-Hispanic/Latino; 3 American Indian or Alaska Native, non-Hispanic/Latino; 21 Asian, non-Hispanic/Latino; 14 Hispanic/Latino; 12 Two or more races, non-Hispanic/Latino), 10 international. Average age 36. 432 applicants, 45% accepted, 143 enrolled. In 2011, 117 master's, 29 doctorates, 32 other advanced degrees awarded. Terminal master's awarded for partial completion of doctoral program. *Degree requirements:* For master's, thesis optional; for doctorate, capstone project. *Entrance requirements:* For master's, GRE General Test, 1 year of nursing experience, BSN, minimum GPA of 3.0, previous course work in statistics; for doctorate, BSN or MSN, minimum GPA of 3.0, portfolio; for Certificate, MSN. Additional exam requirements/recommendations for international students: Required—TOEFL (minimum score 550 paper-based; 213 computer-based). *Application deadline:* For fall admission, 12/1 for domestic and international students; for spring admission, 5/1 for domestic and international students. Application fee: $50. Electronic applications accepted. *Expenses:* Contact institution. *Financial support:* Career-related internships or fieldwork, institutionally sponsored loans, scholarships/grants, traineeships, and tuition waivers (partial) available. Support available to part-time students. Financial award application deadline: 4/1; financial award applicants required to submit FAFSA. *Faculty research:* Cardiovascular disease, caregiver skill training, data mining, prostate cancer, neonatal immune system. *Total annual research expenditures:* $4.7 million. *Unit head:* Dr. Catherine L. Gilliss, Dean/Vice Chancellor for Nursing Affairs, 919-684-9444, Fax: 919-684-9414, E-mail: gilli025@mc.duke.edu. *Application contact:* Bebe T. Mills, Director of Admissions, 919-684-9151, Fax: 919-668-4693, E-mail: mills031@mc.duke.edu. Web site: http://www.nursing.duke.edu/.

D'Youville College, School of Nursing, Buffalo, NY 14201-1084. Offers community health nursing/education (MSN); community health nursing/management (MSN); family nurse practitioner (MS, Post-Master's Certificate); nursing and health-related professions (Certificate); nursing with clinical focus choice (MSN). *Accreditation:* AACN. Part-time programs available. *Faculty:* 7 full-time (all women), 7 part-time/adjunct (6 women). *Students:* 78 full-time (72 women), 133 part-time (117 women); includes 33 minority (23 Black or African American, non-Hispanic/Latino; 2 American Indian or Alaska Native, non-Hispanic/Latino; 1 Asian, non-Hispanic/Latino; 6 Hispanic/Latino; 1 Two or more races, non-Hispanic/Latino), 86 international. Average age 35. 226 applicants, 39% accepted, 57 enrolled. In 2011, 54 master's, 1 other advanced degree awarded. *Degree requirements:* For master's, thesis or alternative, membership on board of community agency, publishable paper. *Entrance requirements:* For master's, BS in nursing, minimum GPA of 3.0, course work in statistics and computers. Additional exam requirements/recommendations for international students: Required—TOEFL (minimum score 500 paper-based; 173 computer-based). *Application deadline:* For fall admission, 5/1 for international students; for spring admission, 9/1 for international students. Applications are processed on a rolling basis. Application fee: $25. Electronic applications accepted. *Expenses: Tuition:* Full-time $18,960; part-time $790 per credit hour. *Required fees:* $310. Tuition and fees vary according to degree level and program. *Financial support:* Federal Work-Study, scholarships/grants, traineeships, and unspecified assistantships available. Support available to part-time students. Financial award application deadline: 3/1; financial award applicants required to submit FAFSA. *Faculty research:* Nursing curriculum, nursing theory-testing, wellness research, communication and socialization patterns. *Unit head:* Dr. Eileen Nahigian, Chair, 716-829-7856, Fax: 716-829-8159. *Application contact:* Linda Fisher, Graduate Admissions Director, 716-829-8400, Fax: 716-829-7900, E-mail: graduateadmissions@dyc.edu.

See Display on page 629 and Close-Up on page 795.

Eastern Mennonite University, Program in Nursing, Harrisonburg, VA 22802-2462. Offers leadership and management (MSN); leadership/school nursing (MSN). Part-time programs available. Postbaccalaureate distance learning degree programs offered (minimal on-campus study). *Degree requirements:* For master's, clinical hours.

Eastern Michigan University, Graduate School, College of Health and Human Services, School of Health Sciences, Program in Clinical Research Administration, Ypsilanti, MI 48197. Offers MS, Graduate Certificate. Part-time and evening/weekend programs available. Postbaccalaureate distance learning degree programs offered (minimal on-campus study). *Students:* 19 full-time (9 women), 60 part-time (41 women); includes 8 minority (3 Black or African American, non-Hispanic/Latino; 2 Asian, non-Hispanic/Latino; 2 Hispanic/Latino; 1 Native Hawaiian or other Pacific Islander, non-Hispanic/Latino), 49 international. Average age 29. 174 applicants, 44% accepted, 25 enrolled. In 2011, 15 master's, 8 other advanced degrees awarded. *Entrance requirements:* Additional exam requirements/recommendations for international students: Required—TOEFL. *Application deadline:* Applications are processed on a rolling basis. Application fee: $35. *Expenses:* Tuition, state resident: full-time $10,367; part-time $432 per credit hour. Tuition, nonresident: full-time $20,435; part-time $851 per credit hour. *Required fees:* $39 per credit hour. $46 per semester. One-time fee: $100. Tuition and fees vary according to course level, degree level and reciprocity agreements. *Financial support:* Fellowships, research assistantships with full tuition reimbursements, teaching assistantships with full tuition reimbursements, career-related internships or fieldwork, Federal Work-Study, institutionally sponsored loans, scholarships/grants, tuition waivers (partial), and unspecified assistantships available. Support available to part-time students. Financial award applicants required to submit FAFSA. *Unit head:* Dr. Stephen Sonstein, Program Coordinator, 734-487-1238, Fax: 734-487-4095, E-mail: stephen.sonstein@emich.edu. *Application contact:* Graduate Admissions, 734-487-2400, Fax: 734-487-6559, E-mail: graduate.admissions@emich.edu.

East Tennessee State University, School of Graduate Studies, College of Nursing, Certificate Nursing Programs, Johnson City, TN 37614. Offers family nurse practitioner (Post-Master's Certificate); health care management (Postbaccalaureate Certificate). Part-time programs available. Postbaccalaureate distance learning degree programs offered (no on-campus study). *Students:* 2 full-time (1 woman), 20 part-time (15 women); includes 4 minority (3 Black or African American, non-Hispanic/Latino; 1 Hispanic/Latino), 1 international. 21 applicants, 62% accepted, 13 enrolled. In 2011, 10 Post-Master's Certificates awarded. *Degree requirements:* For other advanced degree, practical experience. *Entrance requirements:* For degree, minimum of GPA of 2.5, 3 letters of recommendation; RN license (nursing post-master's certificate). Additional exam requirements/recommendations for international students: Required—TOEFL. *Application deadline:* For fall admission, 2/1 for domestic and international students; for spring admission, 7/1 for domestic and international students. Application fee: $35 ($45 for international students). Electronic applications accepted. *Expenses:* Tuition, state resident: full-time $7312; part-time $350 per credit hour. Tuition, nonresident: full-time $18,490; part-time $621 per credit hour. *Required fees:* $63 per credit hour. Tuition and fees vary according to course load and program. *Faculty research:* Rural primary care,

healthcare for the homeless and underserved, community health problems across the lifespan, nursing education research, school health services. *Unit head:* Dr. Nancy Cameron, Graduate Program Coordinator, 423-439-4874, Fax: 423-439-4100, E-mail: cameronng@etsu.edu. *Application contact:* Linda Raines, Graduate Specialist, 423-439-6158, Fax: 423-439-5624, E-mail: raineslt@etsu.edu.

East Tennessee State University, School of Graduate Studies, College of Nursing, Doctoral Nursing Programs, Johnson City, TN 37614. Offers adult/gerontological nurse practitioner (DNP); executive leadership in nursing (DNP); family nurse practitioner (DNP); nursing (PhD); psychiatric/mental health nurse practitioner (DNP). Part-time and evening/weekend programs available. *Students:* 22 full-time (21 women), 27 part-time (26 women); includes 3 minority (2 Black or African American, non-Hispanic/Latino; 1 Asian, non-Hispanic/Latino). 74 applicants, 41% accepted, 30 enrolled. In 2011, 3 doctorates awarded. *Degree requirements:* For doctorate, comprehensive exam, dissertation (PhD); residency internship and capstone project (DNP). *Entrance requirements:* For doctorate, GRE General Test, minimum GPA of 3.0, RN license, minimum two years RN experience, 3 letters of recommendation, interview, writing sample, resume. Additional exam requirements/recommendations for international students: Required—TOEFL (minimum score 600 paper-based; 250 computer-based; 100 iBT). *Application deadline:* For fall admission, 2/1 for domestic and international students; for spring admission, 7/1 for domestic and international students. Application fee: $35 ($45 for international students). Electronic applications accepted. *Expenses:* Tuition, state resident: full-time $7312; part-time $350 per credit hour. Tuition, nonresident: full-time $18,490; part-time $621 per credit hour. *Required fees:* $63 per credit hour. Tuition and fees vary according to course load and program. *Financial support:* In 2011–12, 2 students received support, including 1 research assistantship with partial tuition reimbursement available (averaging $3,000 per year); career-related internships or fieldwork, institutionally sponsored loans, scholarships/grants, and unspecified assistantships also available. Financial award application deadline: 7/1; financial award applicants required to submit FAFSA. *Faculty research:* Rural primary care, healthcare for the homeless and underserved, community health problems across the lifespan, nursing education research, school health services. *Unit head:* Dr. Kathleen Rayman, Director of Graduate Programs, 423-439-5626, Fax: 423-439-4100, E-mail: raymank@etsu.edu. *Application contact:* Linda Raines, Graduate Specialist, 423-439-6158, Fax: 423-439-5624, E-mail: raineslt@etsu.edu.

East Tennessee State University, School of Graduate Studies, College of Nursing, Master's Nursing Programs, Johnson City, TN 37614. Offers advanced practice nursing (MSN); nursing (MSN); nursing administration (MSN); nursing education (MSN); nursing informatics (MSN). Part-time programs available. Postbaccalaureate distance learning degree programs offered. *Students:* 50 full-time (47 women), 137 part-time (126 women); includes 4 minority (1 American Indian or Alaska Native, non-Hispanic/Latino; 2 Hispanic/Latino; 1 Two or more races, non-Hispanic/Latino), 1 international. 151 applicants, 29% accepted, 44 enrolled. In 2011, 74 master's awarded. *Degree requirements:* For master's, comprehensive exam (for some programs), culminating project (for some programs). *Entrance requirements:* For master's, minimum GPA of 3.0, RN license, resume, 3 letters of recommendation. Additional exam requirements/recommendations for international students: Required—TOEFL (minimum score 600 paper-based; 250 computer-based; 100 iBT). *Application deadline:* For fall admission, 2/1 for domestic and international students; for spring admission, 7/1 for domestic and international students. Application fee: $35 ($45 for international students). Electronic applications accepted. *Expenses:* Tuition, state resident: full-time $7312; part-time $350 per credit hour. Tuition, nonresident: full-time $18,490; part-time $621 per credit hour. *Required fees:* $63 per credit hour. Tuition and fees vary according to course load and program. *Financial support:* In 2011–12, 2 students received support. Institutionally sponsored loans, scholarships/grants, tuition waivers (full), and unspecified assistantships available. Support available to part-time students. Financial award application deadline: 7/1; financial award applicants required to submit FAFSA. *Faculty research:* Rural primary care, healthcare for the homeless and underserved, community health problems across the lifespan, nursing education research, school health services. *Unit head:* Dr. Nancy Cameron, Coordinator, 423-439-4874, Fax: 423-439-4100, E-mail: cameronng@etsu.edu. *Application contact:* Linda Raines, Graduate Specialist, 423-439-6158, Fax: 423-439-5624, E-mail: raineslt@etsu.edu.

Elms College, Division of Nursing, Chicopee, MA 01013-2839. Offers nursing and health services management (MSN); nursing education (MSN). *Accreditation:* AACN. Part-time and evening/weekend programs available. *Entrance requirements:* Additional exam requirements/recommendations for international students: Required—TOEFL.

Emmanuel College, Graduate and Professional Programs, Graduate Program in Nursing, Boston, MA 02115. Offers nursing education (MSN); nursing management/administration (MSN). Part-time and evening/weekend programs available. *Faculty:* 5 full-time (all women). *Students:* 21 part-time (20 women); includes 4 minority (3 Black or African American, non-Hispanic/Latino; 1 Asian, non-Hispanic/Latino). Average age 49. 44 applicants, 68% accepted, 21 enrolled. *Degree requirements:* For master's, 36 credits, including 6-credit practicum. *Entrance requirements:* For master's, essay, resume, proof of RN license (nursing applicants only), interview. Additional exam requirements/recommendations for international students: Required—TOEFL (minimum score 600 paper-based; 250 computer-based; 106 iBT) or IELTS (minimum score 6.5). *Application deadline:* For fall admission, 4/30 for domestic students. Applications are processed on a rolling basis. Application fee: $0. Electronic applications accepted. *Expenses: Tuition:* Part-time $2139 per course. Tuition and fees vary according to program and reciprocity agreements. *Financial support:* Applicants required to submit FAFSA. *Unit head:* Dr. Joyce DeLeo, Vice President of Academic Affairs, 617-735-9700, Fax: 617-507-0434, E-mail: gpp@emmanuel.edu. *Application contact:* Enrollment Counselor, 617-735-9700, Fax: 617-507-0434, E-mail: gpp@emmanuel.edu. Web site: http://gpp.emmanuel.edu.

Emory University, Nell Hodgson Woodruff School of Nursing, Atlanta, GA 30322-1100. Offers adult nurse practitioner (MSN); emergency nurse practitioner (MSN); family nurse practitioner (MSN); family nurse-midwife (MSN); health systems leadership (MSN); nurse-midwifery (MSN); pediatric nurse practitioner acute and primary care (MSN); women's health care (Title X) (MSN); women's health nurse practitioner (MSN); women's health/adult health nurse practitioner (MSN); MSN/MPH. *Accreditation:* AACN; ACNM/ACME (one or more programs are accredited). Part-time programs available. *Faculty:* 30 full-time (29 women), 11 part-time/adjunct (10 women). *Students:* 110 full-time (106 women), 53 part-time (51 women); includes 49 minority (35 Black or African American, non-Hispanic/Latino; 2 American Indian or Alaska Native, non-Hispanic/Latino; 10 Asian, non-Hispanic/Latino; 2 Hispanic/Latino), 4 international. Average age 32. 182 applicants, 63% accepted, 86 enrolled. In 2011, 81 master's awarded. *Entrance requirements:* For master's, GRE General Test or MAT, minimum GPA of 3.0, BS in nursing from an accredited institution, RN license and additional course work, 3 letters of recommendation. Additional exam requirements/recommendations for international students: Required—TOEFL (minimum score 600 paper-based; 100 iBT). *Application deadline:* For fall admission, 1/15 priority date for domestic students, 1/15 for international students; for spring admission, 10/1 priority date for domestic students, 10/1 for international students. Applications are processed on a rolling basis. Application fee: $50. Electronic applications accepted. *Expenses:* Contact institution. *Financial*

support: In 2011–12, 14 fellowships (averaging $28,000 per year) were awarded; career-related internships or fieldwork, Federal Work-Study, institutionally sponsored loans, and scholarships/grants also available. Support available to part-time students. Financial award application deadline: 3/1; financial award applicants required to submit CSS PROFILE or FAFSA. *Faculty research:* Older adult falls and injuries, minority health issues, cardiac symptoms and quality of life, bio-ethics and decision-making, menopausal issues. *Unit head:* Dr. Linda McCauley, Dean, 404-727-7976, Fax: 404-727-9800, E-mail: linda.mccauley@emory.edu. Web site: http://www.nursing.emory.edu/.

Fairfield University, School of Nursing, Fairfield, CT 06824-5195. Offers clinical nurse leader (MSN); family nurse practitioner (MSN, DNP); nurse anesthesia (DNP); psychiatric nurse practitioner (MSN, DNP). *Accreditation:* AACN; AANA/CANAEP. Part-time programs available. *Faculty:* 15 full-time (all women). *Students:* 17 full-time (15 women), 145 part-time (127 women); includes 14 minority (6 Black or African American, non-Hispanic/Latino; 1 American Indian or Alaska Native, non-Hispanic/Latino; 4 Asian, non-Hispanic/Latino; 3 Hispanic/Latino), 1 international. Average age 38. 97 applicants, 29% accepted, 24 enrolled. In 2011, 24 master's awarded. *Degree requirements:* For master's, capstone project. *Entrance requirements:* For master's, minimum QPA of 3.0, RN license, resume, 2 recommendations; for doctorate, GRE (nurse anesthesia applicants only), MSN (minimum QPA of 3.2) or BSN (minimum QPA of 3.0); critical care nursing experience (for nurse anesthesia DNP candidates). Additional exam requirements/recommendations for international students: Required—TOEFL (minimum score 550 paper-based; 213 computer-based; 80 iBT) or IELTS (minimum score 6.5). *Application deadline:* For fall admission, 5/15 for international students; for spring admission, 10/15 for international students. Applications are processed on a rolling basis. Application fee: $60. Electronic applications accepted. *Expenses:* Contact institution. *Financial support:* In 2011–12, 2 students received support. Unspecified assistantships available. Financial award applicants required to submit FAFSA. *Faculty research:* Care of older adults, palliative care, spirituality and innovative partnerships, diabetes. *Unit head:* Dr. Suzanne Campbell, Dean, 203-254-4000 Ext. 2701, Fax: 203-254-4126, E-mail: scampbell@fairfield.edu. *Application contact:* Marianne Gumpper, Director of Graduate and Continuing Studies Admission, 203-254-4184, Fax: 203-254-4073, E-mail: gradadmis@fairfield.edu. Web site: http://www.fairfield.edu/son/son_grad_1.html.

Ferris State University, College of Allied Health Sciences, School of Nursing, Big Rapids, MI 49307. Offers nursing (MSN); nursing administration (MSN); nursing education (MSN); nursing informatics (MSN). *Accreditation:* NLN. Part-time and evening/weekend programs available. Postbaccalaureate distance learning degree programs offered (minimal on-campus study). *Faculty:* 5 full-time (all women), 1 (woman) part-time/adjunct. *Students:* 7 full-time (all women), 80 part-time (70 women); includes 3 minority (1 Black or African American, non-Hispanic/Latino; 2 Two or more races, non-Hispanic/Latino). Average age 42. 34 applicants, 85% accepted, 24 enrolled. In 2011, 16 master's awarded. *Degree requirements:* For master's, comprehensive exam, practicum, scholarly project. *Entrance requirements:* For master's, BS in nursing or related field with registered nurse license, writing sample, letters of reference, 2 years' clinical experience. Additional exam requirements/recommendations for international students: Required—TOEFL (minimum score 550 paper-based; 173 computer-based; 61 iBT). *Application deadline:* For fall admission, 4/15 priority date for domestic students; for spring admission, 10/15 for domestic students. Applications are processed on a rolling basis. Application fee: $30. Electronic applications accepted. Application fee is waived when completed online. *Financial support:* In 2011–12, 4 students received support. Fellowships, research assistantships, teaching assistantships, career-related internships or fieldwork, and scholarships/grants available. Financial award application deadline: 4/15. *Faculty research:* Nursing education-minority student focus, student attitudes toward aging. *Unit head:* Dr. Marietta Bell-Scriber, Program Coordinator, 231-591-2288, Fax: 231-591-2325, E-mail: bellscm@ferris.edu. *Application contact:* Debby Buck, Off-Campus Program Secretary, 231-591-2270, Fax: 231-591-3788, E-mail: buckd@ferris.edu.

Florida Agricultural and Mechanical University, Division of Graduate Studies, Research, and Continuing Education, School of Allied Health Sciences, Tallahassee, FL 32307-3200. Offers health administration (MS); occupational therapy (MOT); physical therapy (MPT). *Degree requirements:* For master's, thesis (for some programs). *Entrance requirements:* For master's, GRE General Test or GMAT, minimum GPA of 3.0. Additional exam requirements/recommendations for international students: Required—TOEFL (minimum score 550 paper-based).

Florida State University, The Graduate School, College of Nursing, Tallahassee, FL 32312. Offers family nurse practitioner (DNP); health systems leadership (DNP); nurse educator (MSN, Certificate); nurse leader (MSN); nursing leadership (Certificate, Post-Graduate Certificate). *Accreditation:* AACN. Part-time programs available. Postbaccalaureate distance learning degree programs offered (no on-campus study). *Faculty:* 13 full-time (12 women). *Students:* 24 full-time (21 women), 63 part-time (58 women); includes 15 minority (4 Black or African American, non-Hispanic/Latino; 1 Asian, non-Hispanic/Latino; 8 Hispanic/Latino; 2 Two or more races, non-Hispanic/Latino). Average age 38. 33 applicants, 100% accepted, 33 enrolled. In 2011, 9 master's, 4 doctorates awarded. *Degree requirements:* For master's, thesis optional. *Entrance requirements:* For master's, GRE General Test, MAT, minimum GPA of 3.0, BSN, Florida RN license; for doctorate, GRE General Test, MAT, minimum GPA of 3.0, BSN or MSN, Florida RN license. Additional exam requirements/recommendations for international students: Required—TOEFL (minimum score 550 paper-based). *Application deadline:* For fall admission, 7/1 for domestic and international students. Application fee: $30. Electronic applications accepted. *Expenses:* Tuition, state resident: full-time $9474; part-time $350.88 per credit hour. Tuition, nonresident: full-time $16,236; part-time $601.34 per credit hour. *Required fees:* $630 per semester. One-time fee: $20. Tuition and fees vary according to course load and campus/location. *Financial support:* In 2011–12, 75 students received support, including fellowships with partial tuition reimbursements available (averaging $6,300 per year), research assistantships with partial tuition reimbursements available (averaging $3,000 per year), 3 teaching assistantships with partial tuition reimbursements available (averaging $3,000 per year); career-related internships or fieldwork, Federal Work-Study, institutionally sponsored loans, scholarships/grants, traineeships, and tuition waivers (partial) also available. Financial award application deadline: 4/15; financial award applicants required to submit FAFSA. *Faculty research:* Distance learning, gerontology, health promotion, educational strategies, rehabilitation of brain injured patients. *Unit head:* Dr. Diane Speake, Interim Dean, 850-644-6846, Fax: 850-644-7660, E-mail: dspeake@nursing.fsu.edu. *Application contact:* Carlos G. Urrutia, Director of Student Services, 850-644-5638, Fax: 850-645-7249, E-mail: currutia@fsu.edu. Web site: http://nursing.fsu.edu/.

Framingham State University, Division of Graduate and Continuing Education, Program in Nursing, Framingham, MA 01701-9101. Offers nursing education (MSN); nursing leadership (MSN). *Accreditation:* AACN. *Entrance requirements:* For master's, BSN; minimum cumulative undergraduate GPA of 3.0, 3.25 in nursing courses; coursework in statistics; 2 letters of recommendation; interview. Electronic applications accepted.

Nursing and Healthcare Administration

Gannon University, School of Graduate Studies, Morosky College of Health Professions and Sciences, School of Health Professions, Villa Maria School of Nursing, Erie, PA 16541-0001. Offers anesthesia (MSN); business administration (MSN); family nurse practitioner (Certificate); medical-surgical nursing (MSN); nurse anesthesia (Certificate); nursing rural practitioner (MSN). *Accreditation:* AACN; AANA/CANAEP (one or more programs are accredited). Part-time and evening/weekend programs available. *Students:* 2 full-time (both women), 68 part-time (49 women); includes 3 minority (1 Black or African American, non-Hispanic/Latino; 1 American Indian or Alaska Native, non-Hispanic/Latino; 1 Hispanic/Latino). Average age 44. 15 applicants, 67% accepted, 0 enrolled. In 2011, 20 master's, 3 other advanced degrees awarded. *Degree requirements:* For master's, thesis. *Entrance requirements:* For master's, GRE General Test, degree in nursing. Additional exam requirements/recommendations for international students: Required—TOEFL (minimum score 79 iBT). *Application deadline:* For spring admission, 8/1 for domestic students. Application fee: $25. Electronic applications accepted. *Financial support:* Scholarships/grants available. Financial award application deadline: 7/1; financial award applicants required to submit FAFSA. *Faculty research:* Accurate assessment of delirium in the ICU using CAM, factors affecting caregiver fatigue in dialysis nurses, hours worked by nurses and treatment error reporting. *Unit head:* Dr. Kathleen Patterson, Director, 814-871-5547, E-mail: patterso018@gannon.edu. *Application contact:* Kara Morgan, Director of Graduate Admissions, 814-871-5831, Fax: 814-871-5827, E-mail: graduate@gannon.edu.

George Mason University, College of Health and Human Services, School of Nursing, Fairfax, VA 22030. Offers forensic nursing (Certificate); nursing (MSN, PhD); nursing administration (Certificate); nursing education (Certificate); nursing practice (DNP). *Faculty:* 32 full-time (all women), 45 part-time/adjunct (43 women). *Students:* 70 full-time (69 women), 284 part-time (275 women); includes 109 minority (51 Black or African American, non-Hispanic/Latino; 1 American Indian or Alaska Native, non-Hispanic/Latino; 41 Asian, non-Hispanic/Latino; 12 Hispanic/Latino; 4 Two or more races, non-Hispanic/Latino), 11 international. Average age 41. 220 applicants, 56% accepted, 86 enrolled. In 2011, 79 master's, 4 doctorates, 1 other advanced degree awarded. *Degree requirements:* For master's, comprehensive exam (for some programs), thesis in clinical classes; for doctorate, comprehensive exam (for some programs), thesis/dissertation (for some programs). *Entrance requirements:* For master's, 2 official transcripts; expanded goals statement; resume; BSN from accredited institution; minimum GPA of 3.0 in last 60 credits of undergraduate work; 2 letters of recommendation; completion of undergraduate statistics and graduate-level bivariate statistics; certification in professional CPR; for doctorate, 2 official transcripts; expanded goals statement; resume; 3 recommendation letters, nursing license, at least 1 year of work experience as an RN; interview, writing sample, evidence of graduate-level course in applied statistics; master's in nursing with minimum GPA of 3.5; for Certificate, 2 official transcripts; expanded goals statement; resume; master's degree from accredited institution or currently enrolled with minimum GPA of 3.0. Additional exam requirements/recommendations for international students: Required—TOEFL (minimum score 575 paper-based; 230 computer-based; 88 iBT), IELTS, Pearson Test of English. *Application deadline:* For fall admission, 3/1 priority date for domestic students; for spring admission, 11/1 for domestic students. Application fee: $65 ($80 for international students). Electronic applications accepted. *Expenses:* Tuition, state resident: full-time $8750; part-time $364.58 per credit. Tuition, nonresident: full-time $24,092; part-time $1003.83 per credit. *Required fees:* $2514; $104.75 per credit. *Financial support:* In 2011–12, 5 students received support, including 4 research assistantships with full and partial tuition reimbursements available (averaging $26,672 per year), 1 teaching assistantship with full and partial tuition reimbursement available (averaging $15,000 per year); career-related internships or fieldwork, Federal Work-Study, scholarships/grants, unspecified assistantships, and nurse faculty loan, health care benefits (full-time research or teaching assistantship recipients) also available. Financial award application deadline: 3/1; financial award applicants required to submit FAFSA. *Total annual research expenditures:* $607,543. *Unit head:* Robin Remsburg, Associate Dean/Director, 703-993-1904, Fax: 703-993-1949, E-mail: rremsbur@gmu.edu. *Application contact:* Janice Lee-Beverly, Program Support, 703-993-1947, Fax: 703-993-1943, E-mail: jleebev1@gmu.edu. Web site: http://chhs.gmu.edu/nursing.

The George Washington University, School of Nursing, Washington, DC 20052. Offers adult nurse practitioner (MSN, Post-Master's Certificate); clinical research administration (MSN); family nurse practitioner (MSN, Post-Master's Certificate); health care quality (MSN, Post-Master's Certificate); nursing (DNP); nursing leadership and management (MSN); palliative care nurse practitioner (Post-Master's Certificate). *Accreditation:* AACN. *Faculty:* 19 full-time (all women), 32 part-time/adjunct (29 women). *Students:* 27 full-time (25 women), 360 part-time (330 women); includes 89 minority (44 Black or African American, non-Hispanic/Latino; 9 American Indian or Alaska Native, non-Hispanic/Latino; 25 Asian, non-Hispanic/Latino; 11 Hispanic/Latino), 15 international. Average age 39. 287 applicants, 87% accepted, 176 enrolled. In 2011, 45 master's, 19 doctorates awarded. *Unit head:* Jean E. Johnson, Dean, 202-994-3725, E-mail: sonjej@gwumc.edu. *Application contact:* Kristin Williams, Assistant Vice President for Graduate and Special Enrollment Management, 202-994-0467, Fax: 202-994-0371, E-mail: ksw@gwu.edu. Web site: http://nursing.gwumc.edu/.

Georgia College & State University, Graduate School, College of Health Sciences, Graduate Nursing Program, Milledgeville, GA 31061. Offers adult health (MSN); family nurse practitioner (MSN); nursing administration (MSN); MSN/MBA. *Accreditation:* NLN. Part-time and evening/weekend programs available. *Students:* 10 full-time (9 women), 63 part-time (60 women); includes 16 minority (all Black or African American, non-Hispanic/Latino). Average age 36. 64 applicants, 44% accepted, 20 enrolled. In 2011, 7 master's awarded. *Degree requirements:* For master's, comprehensive exam, thesis optional. *Entrance requirements:* For master's, GMAT, GRE General Test, or MAT, bachelor's degree in nursing, RN license, 1 year clinical experience. Additional exam requirements/recommendations for international students: Recommended—TOEFL (minimum score 550 paper-based; 213 computer-based; 79 iBT). *Application deadline:* For fall admission, 7/1 priority date for domestic students; for spring admission, 4/1 priority date for domestic students. Applications are processed on a rolling basis. Application fee: $40. Electronic applications accepted. *Expenses:* Tuition, state resident: full-time $4806; part-time $267 per credit hour. Tuition, nonresident: full-time $17,802; part-time $989 per credit hour. *Required fees:* $936 per semester. Tuition and fees vary according to course load and campus/location. *Financial support:* In 2011–12, 1 research assistantship with full tuition reimbursement was awarded; unspecified assistantships also available. Financial award applicants required to submit FAFSA. *Unit head:* Dr. Judith Malachowski, Director, School of Nursing, 478-445-5122, E-mail: judith.malachowski@gcsu.edu. *Application contact:* Lora Crowe, MSN Coordinator, 478-445-5122, E-mail: lora.crowe@gcsu.edu.

Georgia Health Sciences University, College of Graduate Studies, Clinical Nurse Leader Program, Augusta, GA 30912. Offers MSN. *Students:* 179 full-time (150 women), 8 part-time (all women); includes 31 minority (18 Black or African American, non-Hispanic/Latino; 5 Asian, non-Hispanic/Latino; 2 Hispanic/Latino; 6 Two or more races, non-Hispanic/Latino). Average age 28. 96 applicants, 49% accepted, 40 enrolled. In 2011, 13 master's awarded. *Entrance requirements:* For master's, GRE General Test or MAT, bachelor's degree or higher in a non-nursing discipline. Additional exam requirements/recommendations for international students: Required—TOEFL (minimum

score 550 paper-based; 213 computer-based; 79 iBT). *Application deadline:* For fall admission, 4/1 for domestic and international students. Application fee: $50. Electronic applications accepted. *Unit head:* Dr. Lucy Marion, Dean, 706-721-3771, Fax: 706-721-8169, E-mail: lumarion@georgiahealth.edu. *Application contact:* Olivia Mitchell, Program Coordinator, 706-721-9767, Fax: 706-721-8169, E-mail: omitchel@georgiahealth.edu. Web site: http://www.mcg.edu/son/futurestudents.htm.

Grand Valley State University, Kirkhof College of Nursing, Allendale, MI 49401-9403. Offers advanced practice (MSN); case management (MSN); nursing administration (MSN); nursing education (MSN); nursing practice (DNP); MSN/MBA. *Accreditation:* AACN. Part-time programs available. *Degree requirements:* For master's, thesis optional. *Entrance requirements:* For master's, GRE, minimum GPA of 3.0 in upper-division course work, course work in statistics, Michigan RN license. Additional exam requirements/recommendations for international students: Required—TOEFL. Electronic applications accepted. *Faculty research:* Multigenerational health promotion, chronic disease prevention, end-of-life issues, nursing workload, family caregiver health.

Grantham University, College of Arts and Sciences, Kansas City, MO 64153. Offers case management (MSN); health systems management (MS); healthcare administration (MHA); nursing (MSN); nursing education (MSN); nursing informatics (MSN); nursing management and organizational leadership (MSN). Part-time and evening/weekend programs available. Postbaccalaureate distance learning degree programs offered (no on-campus study). *Degree requirements:* For master's, thesis (for some programs), capstone project. *Entrance requirements:* For master's, bachelor's degree from accredited degree-granting institution. Additional exam requirements/recommendations for international students: Required—TOEFL (minimum score 500 paper-based; 213 computer-based; 61 iBT). Electronic applications accepted.

Herzing University Online, Program in Nursing, Milwaukee, WI 53203. Offers nursing (MSN); nursing education (MSN); nursing management (MSN). Postbaccalaureate distance learning degree programs offered (no on-campus study).

Holy Family University, Graduate School, School of Nursing and Allied Health Professions, Philadelphia, PA 19114. Offers community health nursing (MSN); nursing administration (MSN); nursing education (MSN). *Accreditation:* AACN. Part-time and evening/weekend programs available. *Degree requirements:* For master's, thesis or alternative. *Entrance requirements:* For master's, bachelor's degree in nursing, RN license, minimum GPA of 3.0, 2 letters of reference.

See Display on page 634 and Close-Up on page 801.

Holy Names University, Graduate Division, Department of Nursing, Oakland, CA 94619-1699. Offers administration/management (MS, Certificate); clinical faculty (MS, Certificate); community health nursing/case manager (MS); family nurse practitioner (MS, Certificate); MSN/Certificate; MSN/MBA. *Accreditation:* AACN. Part-time and evening/weekend programs available. *Entrance requirements:* For master's, bachelor's degree in nursing or related field, California RN license or eligibility, minimum GPA of 3.0, previous course work in research or statistics. Additional exam requirements/recommendations for international students: Required—TOEFL (minimum score 500 paper-based). *Faculty research:* Women's reproductive health, gerontology, attitudes about aging, schizophrenic families, international health issues.

Independence University, Program in Nursing, Salt Lake City, UT 84107. Offers community health (MSN); gerontology (MSN); nursing administration (MSN); wellness promotion (MSN).

Indiana University of Pennsylvania, School of Graduate Studies and Research, College of Health and Human Services, Department of Nursing and Allied Health, Program in Nursing Administration, Indiana, PA 15705-1087. Offers MS. *Accreditation:* AACN. *Faculty:* 6 full-time (5 women). *Students:* 3 part-time (all women). Average age 39. 8 applicants, 38% accepted, 2 enrolled. In 2011, 4 master's awarded. *Degree requirements:* For master's, practicum. *Entrance requirements:* Additional exam requirements/recommendations for international students: Required—TOEFL (minimum score 540 paper-based; 207 computer-based). *Application deadline:* Applications are processed on a rolling basis. Application fee: $50. Electronic applications accepted. *Expenses:* Tuition, state resident: full-time $7488; part-time $416 per credit. Tuition, nonresident: full-time $11,232; part-time $624 per credit. *Required fees:* $2070; $192.20 per credit. $90 per semester. *Financial support:* Application deadline: 4/15; applicants required to submit FAFSA. *Unit head:* Dr. Michele Gerwick, Chairperson, 724-357-2557, E-mail: mgerwick@iup.edu. *Application contact:* Dr. Nashat Zuraikat, Graduate Coordinator, 724-357-3262, E-mail: zuraikat@iup.edu. Web site: http://www.iup.edu/page.aspx?id=43337.

Indiana University–Purdue University Fort Wayne, College of Health and Human Services, Department of Nursing, Fort Wayne, IN 46805-1499. Offers adult nursing practitioner (MS); nurse executive (MS); nursing administration (Certificate); nursing education (MS); women's health nurse practitioner (MS). Part-time programs available. *Faculty:* 10 full-time (all women). *Students:* 3 full-time (all women), 33 part-time (31 women); includes 3 minority (1 American Indian or Alaska Native, non-Hispanic/Latino; 1 Asian, non-Hispanic/Latino; 1 Hispanic/Latino). Average age 36. 13 applicants, 92% accepted, 10 enrolled. In 2011, 14 master's awarded. *Entrance requirements:* For master's, GRE Writing Test (if GPA below 3.0), BS in nursing, eligibility for Indiana RN license, minimum GPA of 3.0, essay, copy of resume, three references, undergraduate course work in research and statistics within last 5 years. Additional exam requirements/recommendations for international students: Required—TOEFL (minimum score 550 paper-based; 213 computer-based; 77 iBT); Recommended—TWE. *Application deadline:* For fall admission, 5/1 priority date for domestic students, 5/1 for international students; for spring admission, 11/15 priority date for domestic students. Applications are processed on a rolling basis. Application fee: $55 ($60 for international students). Electronic applications accepted. *Financial support:* In 2011–12, 11 teaching assistantships with partial tuition reimbursements (averaging $12,930 per year) were awarded; scholarships/grants also available. Support available to part-time students. Financial award application deadline: 3/1; financial award applicants required to submit FAFSA. *Faculty research:* Child psychiatric nursing. *Total annual research expenditures:* $296,680. *Unit head:* Dr. Carol Sternberger, Chair, 260-481-5798, Fax: 260-481-5767, E-mail: sternber@ipfw.edu. *Application contact:* Dr. Deborah Poling, Director of Graduate Program, 260-481-6276, Fax: 260-481-5767, E-mail: polingd@ipfw.edu. Web site: http://www.ipfw.edu/nursing/.

Indiana University–Purdue University Indianapolis, School of Nursing, MSN Program in Nursing, Indianapolis, IN 46202-2896. Offers nursing administration (MSN); nursing education (MSN). *Students:* 2 full-time (both women), 39 part-time (37 women); includes 5 minority (2 Black or African American, non-Hispanic/Latino; 1 Asian, non-Hispanic/Latino; 2 Hispanic/Latino), 2 international. 50 applicants, 50% accepted, 9 enrolled. In 2011, 17 master's awarded. *Entrance requirements:* For master's, background check, statistics. *Unit head:* Associate Dean for Graduate Programs, 317-274-2806, E-mail: nursing@iupui.edu. *Application contact:* Janet Moon, Information Contact, 317-278-2205. Web site: http://nursing.iupui.edu/degrees/msn/index.shtml.

Indiana Wesleyan University, College of Adult and Professional Studies, Graduate Studies in Business, Marion, IN 46953. Offers accounting (MBA); applied management (MBA); business administration (MBA); health care (MBA); human resources (MBA);

management (MS). Part-time and evening/weekend programs available. Postbaccalaureate distance learning degree programs offered (no on-campus study). *Degree requirements:* For master's, applied business or management project. *Entrance requirements:* For master's, minimum GPA of 2.5, 2 years of related work experience. Additional exam requirements/recommendations for international students: Required—TOEFL (minimum score 550 paper-based; 213 computer-based). Electronic applications accepted.

Indiana Wesleyan University, Graduate School, School of Nursing, Marion, IN 46953-4974. Offers community health nursing (MS); nursing (Post Master's Certificate); nursing administration (MS); nursing education (MS); primary care nursing (MS). *Accreditation:* AACN. Part-time programs available. Postbaccalaureate distance learning degree programs offered (minimal on-campus study). *Degree requirements:* For master's, capstone project or thesis. *Entrance requirements:* For master's, writing sample, RN license, 1 year of related experience, graduate statistics course. Additional exam requirements/recommendations for international students: Required—TOEFL. *Expenses:* Contact institution. *Faculty research:* Primary health care with international emphasis, international nursing.

Jefferson College of Health Sciences, Program in Nursing, Roanoke, VA 24031-3186. Offers nursing education (MSN); nursing management (MSN). *Accreditation:* AACN. Part-time programs available. *Degree requirements:* For master's, project. *Entrance requirements:* For master's, MAT. Additional exam requirements/recommendations for international students: Required—TOEFL (minimum score 550 paper-based; 213 computer-based; 80 iBT). Electronic applications accepted. *Faculty research:* Nursing, teaching and learning techniques, cultural competence, spirituality and nursing.

The Johns Hopkins University, School of Nursing, Certificate Program in Business of Nursing, Baltimore, MD 21218-2699. Offers Certificate. *Degree requirements:* For Certificate, final exam. *Entrance requirements:* For degree, BSN. Additional exam requirements/recommendations for international students: Required—TOEFL (minimum score 550 paper-based; 213 computer-based). Electronic applications accepted. *Faculty research:* Health policy, nursing administration, financial outcomes.

The Johns Hopkins University, School of Nursing, Dual Major in Clinical Nurse Specialist and Health Systems Management, Baltimore, MD 21218-2699. Offers MSN. *Accreditation:* AACN. Part-time programs available. *Degree requirements:* For master's, thesis optional, scholarly project or portfolio. *Entrance requirements:* For master's, interview, minimum GPA of 3.0, BSN, Maryland RN license. Additional exam requirements/recommendations for international students: Required—TOEFL (minimum score 550 paper-based; 213 computer-based). Electronic applications accepted. *Faculty research:* Maternal/child health, outcomes measurement, symptom management, oncology, HIV/AIDS.

The Johns Hopkins University, School of Nursing and Carey Business School, Joint Degree Program in Nursing and Business, Baltimore, MD 21218-2699. Offers MSN/MBA. Part-time programs available. *Entrance requirements:* Additional exam requirements/recommendations for international students: Required—TOEFL (minimum score 550 paper-based; 213 computer-based). Electronic applications accepted. *Expenses:* Contact institution. *Faculty research:* Program evaluation, outcomes, staff satisfaction, program development, quality and staff, outcome evaluation.

The Johns Hopkins University, School of Nursing, Program in Clinical Nurse Specialist, Baltimore, MD 21218-2699. Offers MSN. *Accreditation:* AACN. Part-time programs available. *Degree requirements:* For master's, thesis optional, scholarly project or portfolio. *Entrance requirements:* For master's, interview, minimum GPA of 3.0, BSN, Maryland RN license. Additional exam requirements/recommendations for international students: Required—TOEFL (minimum score 550 paper-based; 213 computer-based). Electronic applications accepted. *Expenses:* Contact institution. *Faculty research:* Maternal child health, symptom management, cardiovascular risk reduction, asthma, hypertension.

The Johns Hopkins University, School of Nursing, Program in Health Systems Management, Baltimore, MD 21218-2699. Offers MSN. *Accreditation:* AACN. Part-time programs available. *Degree requirements:* For master's, thesis optional, scholarly project or portfolio. *Entrance requirements:* For master's, interview, minimum GPA of 3.0, BSN, Maryland RN license. Additional exam requirements/recommendations for international students: Required—TOEFL (minimum score 550 paper-based; 213 computer-based). Electronic applications accepted. *Expenses:* Contact institution. *Faculty research:* Program evaluation, program development, staff satisfaction, quality and safety.

Kaplan University, Davenport Campus, School of Nursing, Davenport, IA 52807-2095. Offers nurse administrator (MS); nurse educator (MS). Part-time and evening/weekend programs available. Postbaccalaureate distance learning degree programs offered (no on-campus study). *Entrance requirements:* For master's, RN. Additional exam requirements/recommendations for international students: Required—TOEFL (minimum score 550 paper-based; 80 computer-based).

Kean University, College of Natural, Applied and Health Sciences, Program in Nursing, Union, NJ 07083. Offers clinical management (MSN), including transcultural focus; community health nursing (MSN); school nursing (MSN). *Accreditation:* NLN. *Faculty:* 9 full-time (all women). *Students:* 7 full-time (6 women), 95 part-time (86 women); includes 49 minority (40 Black or African American, non-Hispanic/Latino; 5 Asian, non-Hispanic/Latino; 3 Hispanic/Latino; 1 Native Hawaiian or other Pacific Islander, non-Hispanic/Latino). Average age 45. 38 applicants, 97% accepted, 27 enrolled. In 2011, 34 master's awarded. *Degree requirements:* For master's, thesis or alternative, clinical field experience. *Entrance requirements:* For master's, minimum GPA of 3.0; BS in nursing; RN license; 2 letters of recommendation; interview; 1 completed course of the following: basic health assessment and human growth and development across the life span; minimum B grade in prerequisite courses; transcripts. Additional exam requirements/recommendations for international students: Required—TOEFL (minimum score 79 computer-based). *Application deadline:* For fall admission, 6/1 for domestic and international students; for spring admission, 12/1 for domestic and international students. Applications are processed on a rolling basis. Application fee: $75 ($150 for international students). Electronic applications accepted. *Expenses:* Tuition, state resident: full-time $11,302; part-time $550 per credit. Tuition, nonresident: full-time $15,318; part-time $674 per credit. *Required fees:* $2849; $130 per credit. Tuition and fees vary according to degree level. *Financial support:* In 2011–12, 1 research assistantship with full tuition reimbursement (averaging $3,263 per year) was awarded; unspecified assistantships also available. Financial award applicants required to submit FAFSA. *Unit head:* Dr. Minnie Campbell, Program Coordinator, 908-527-3396, E-mail: mcampbel@kean.edu. *Application contact:* Ann-Marie Kay, Assistant Director of Graduate Admissions, 908-737-5922, Fax: 908-737-5925, E-mail: akay@kean.edu. Web site: http://www.kean.edu/KU/School-of-Nursing.

Kent State University, College of Nursing, Kent, OH 44242-0001. Offers acute care nurse practitioner (MSN); adult nurse practitioner (MSN); clinical nurse specialist (MSN); family nurse practitioner (MSN); geriatric nurse practitioner (MSN); health care management (MSN); nurse educator (MSN); nursing (PhD); nursing practice (DNP); pediatric nurse practitioner (MSN); psychiatric/mental health nurse practitioner (MSN); women's health nurse practitioner (MSN). PhD program offered jointly with The

University of Akron. *Accreditation:* AACN. Part-time programs available. *Degree requirements:* For master's, thesis optional; for doctorate, comprehensive exam, thesis/dissertation. *Entrance requirements:* For master's, GRE (if undergraduate GPA less than 3.0), minimum GPA of 2.75; for doctorate, GRE, MSN. Additional exam requirements/recommendations for international students: Required—TOEFL. Electronic applications accepted. *Expenses:* Contact institution. *Faculty research:* Women and violence, methodological specialties, osteoporosis in women, new caregivers and the elderly.

Lamar University, College of Graduate Studies, College of Arts and Sciences, Department of Nursing, Beaumont, TX 77710. Offers nursing administration (MSN); nursing education (MSN); MSN/MBA. *Accreditation:* NLN. Part-time and evening/weekend programs available. Postbaccalaureate distance learning degree programs offered. *Faculty:* 6 full-time (all women). *Students:* 5 full-time (all women), 29 part-time (27 women); includes 12 minority (11 Black or African American, non-Hispanic/Latino; 1 Hispanic/Latino). Average age 40. 18 applicants, 100% accepted, 10 enrolled. In 2011, 5 master's awarded. *Degree requirements:* For master's, comprehensive exam, practicum project presentation, evidence-based project. *Entrance requirements:* For master's, GRE General Test, MAT, criminal background check, RN license, NLN-accredited BSN, college course work in graduate statistics in past 5 years, letters of recommendation, minimum undergraduate GPA of 3.0. Additional exam requirements/recommendations for international students: Required—TOEFL. *Application deadline:* For fall admission, 8/1 priority date for domestic students; for spring admission, 12/1 priority date for domestic students. Applications are processed on a rolling basis. Application fee: $25 ($50 for international students). *Expenses:* Tuition, state resident: full-time $5430; part-time $272 per credit hour. Tuition, nonresident: full-time $11,540; part-time $577 per credit hour. *Required fees:* $1916. *Financial support:* In 2011–12, 3 students received support, including 2 teaching assistantships (averaging $24,000 per year); scholarships/grants and traineeships also available. Financial award application deadline: 4/1. *Faculty research:* Student retention, theory, caregiving, online course and research. *Unit head:* Dr. Nancy Blume, Director of Graduate Nursing Studies, 409-880-8820, Fax: 409-880-8698, E-mail: nancy.blume@lamar.edu. *Application contact:* Shelly R. Belk, Administrative Associate, 409-880-7720.

La Roche College, School of Graduate Studies and Adult Education, Program in Nursing, Pittsburgh, PA 15237-5898. Offers nursing education (MSN); nursing management (MSN). *Accreditation:* AANA/CANAEP; NLN. Part-time and evening/weekend programs available. Postbaccalaureate distance learning degree programs offered (minimal on-campus study). *Faculty:* 5 full-time (all women), 1 (woman) part-time/adjunct. *Students:* 8 full-time (6 women), 12 part-time (11 women), 2 international. Average age 41. 8 applicants, 63% accepted, 3 enrolled. In 2011, 4 master's awarded. *Degree requirements:* For master's, thesis optional, internship, practicum. *Entrance requirements:* For master's, GRE General Test, BSN, nursing license, work experience. Additional exam requirements/recommendations for international students: Recommended—TOEFL (minimum score 550 paper-based; 220 computer-based). *Application deadline:* For fall admission, 8/15 priority date for domestic students, 8/15 for international students; for spring admission, 12/15 priority date for domestic students, 12/15 for international students. Applications are processed on a rolling basis. Application fee: $50. Electronic applications accepted. *Expenses:* Contact institution. *Financial support:* Application deadline: 3/31; applicants required to submit FAFSA. *Faculty research:* Patient education, perception. *Unit head:* Dr. Kathleen Sullivan, Division Chair, 412-536-1173, Fax: 412-536-1175, E-mail: sullivk1@laroche.edu. *Application contact:* Hope Schiffgens, Director of Graduate Studies and Adult Education, 412-536-1266, Fax: 412-536-1283, E-mail: schombh1@laroche.edu.

Le Moyne College, Department of Nursing, Syracuse, NY 13214. Offers nursing administration (MS, CAS); nursing education (MS, CAS). *Accreditation:* AACN. Part-time and evening/weekend programs available. *Faculty:* 4 full-time (all women), 3 part-time/adjunct (all women). *Students:* 19 part-time (all women); includes 1 minority (Black or African American, non-Hispanic/Latino). Average age 45. 9 applicants, 89% accepted, 5 enrolled. In 2011, 8 master's awarded. *Degree requirements:* For master's, scholarly project. *Entrance requirements:* For master's, bachelor's degree, interview, minimum GPA of 3.0, New York RN license, 2 letters of recommendation, writing sample, transcripts. Additional exam requirements/recommendations for international students: Required—TOEFL (minimum score 550 paper-based; 213 computer-based; 79 iBT). *Application deadline:* For fall admission, 6/1 priority date for domestic students, 6/1 for international students; for spring admission, 11/1 priority date for domestic students, 11/1 for international students. Applications are processed on a rolling basis. Application fee: $50. *Expenses:* Contact institution. *Financial support:* In 2011–12, 5 students received support. Career-related internships or fieldwork, scholarships/grants, health care benefits, unspecified assistantships, and NFLP Federal Loan Program (Nurse Faculty Loan Program) available. Support available to part-time students. Financial award applicants required to submit FAFSA. *Faculty research:* Inter-profession education, eldercare, utilization of free healthcare services by the insured, health promotion education, innovative undergraduate nursing education models. *Unit head:* Dr. Susan B. Bastable, Chair and Professor, Department of Nursing, 315-445-5436, Fax: 315-445-6024, E-mail: bastabsb@lemoyne.edu. *Application contact:* Kristen P. Trapasso, Director of Graduate Admission, 315-445-4265, Fax: 315-445-6027, E-mail: trapaskp@lemoyne.edu. Web site: http://www.lemoyne.edu/nursing.

Lewis University, College of Nursing and Health Professions, Program in Nursing, Romeoville, IL 60446. Offers adult nurse practitioner (MSN); nursing administration (MSN); nursing education (MSN). *Accreditation:* AACN. Part-time and evening/weekend programs available. Postbaccalaureate distance learning degree programs offered (no on-campus study). *Students:* 11 full-time (all women), 237 part-time (232 women); includes 65 minority (42 Black or African American, non-Hispanic/Latino; 14 Asian, non-Hispanic/Latino; 9 Hispanic/Latino), 1 international. Average age 42. In 2011, 29 master's awarded. *Degree requirements:* For master's, clinical practicum. *Entrance requirements:* For master's, minimum undergraduate GPA of 3.0, degree in nursing, RN license, letter of recommendation, interview, resume or curriculum vitae. Additional exam requirements/recommendations for international students: Required—TOEFL (minimum score 550 paper-based; 213 computer-based; 80 iBT). *Application deadline:* For fall admission, 5/1 for international students; for spring admission, 11/15 for international students. Applications are processed on a rolling basis. Application fee: $40. Electronic applications accepted. *Financial support:* Federal Work-Study, scholarships/grants, tuition waivers (full and partial), and unspecified assistantships available. Financial award application deadline: 5/1; financial award applicants required to submit FAFSA. *Faculty research:* Cancer prevention, phenomenological methods, public policy analysis. *Total annual research expenditures:* $1,000. *Unit head:* 815-836-5610. *Application contact:* Nancy Wiksten, Adult Admission Counselor, 815-836-5628, Fax: 815-836-5578, E-mail: wikstena@lewisu.edu. Web site: http://www.lewisu.edu/.

Loma Linda University, Department of Graduate Nursing, Program in Nursing Administration, Loma Linda, CA 92350. Offers MS. *Accreditation:* AACN. Part-time programs available. *Degree requirements:* For master's, thesis or alternative. *Entrance requirements:* For master's, GRE General Test, BSN, minimum GPA of 3.0, RN license. Additional exam requirements/recommendations for international students: Required—TOEFL. Electronic applications accepted. *Faculty research:* Job aspects contributing to

satisfaction among leaders in health care institutions, leadership content significant to RN graduates.

Long Island University–Brooklyn Campus, School of Nursing, Department of Nurse Executive, Brooklyn, NY 11201-8423. Offers MS. *Accreditation:* AACN. *Entrance requirements:* For master's, New York RN license, 2 letters of recommendation. Additional exam requirements/recommendations for international students: Required—TOEFL (minimum score 500 paper-based; 173 computer-based).

Loyola University Chicago, Graduate School, Marcella Niehoff School of Nursing, Nursing Administration Program, Chicago, IL 60660. Offers MSN. Part-time and evening/weekend programs available. Postbaccalaureate distance learning degree programs offered (minimal on-campus study). *Students:* 3 full-time (all women), 34 part-time (32 women); includes 6 minority (2 Black or African American, non-Hispanic/Latino; 2 Asian, non-Hispanic/Latino; 1 Hispanic/Latino; 1 Native Hawaiian or other Pacific Islander, non-Hispanic/Latino). Average age 37. 8 applicants, 88% accepted, 7 enrolled. In 2011, 21 master's awarded. *Degree requirements:* For master's, comprehensive exam or oral thesis defense. *Entrance requirements:* For master's, BSN, minimum nursing GPA of 3.0, IL nursing license, 1000 hours experience before starting clinical. *Application deadline:* Applications are processed on a rolling basis. Application fee: $50. Electronic applications accepted. *Expenses: Tuition:* Full-time $15,660; part-time $870 per credit hour. *Required fees:* $125 per semester. Tuition and fees vary according to course load and program. *Financial support:* Traineeships available. Financial award application deadline: 3/1. *Faculty research:* Patient classification systems, career/job mobility. *Unit head:* Dr. Ida Androwich, Professor, 708-216-9276, Fax: 708-216-9555, E-mail: iandrow@luc.edu. *Application contact:* Amy Weatherford, Enrollment Advisor, School of Nursing, 773-508-3249, Fax: 773-508-3241, E-mail: aweatherford@luc.edu. Web site: http://www.luc.edu/quinlan/mba/mba-degrees/mbamsn-nursing/.

Lynchburg College, Graduate Studies, School of Health Sciences and Human Performance, MS Program in Nursing, Lynchburg, VA 24501-3199. Offers clinical nurse leader (MS); nursing education (MS). *Accreditation:* AACN. Part-time and evening/weekend programs available. Postbaccalaureate distance learning degree programs offered (minimal on-campus study). *Faculty:* 3 full-time (all women), 1 (woman) part-time/adjunct. *Students:* 1 (woman) full-time, 6 part-time (all women), 1 international. Average age 39. In 2011, 4 master's awarded. *Degree requirements:* For master's, practicum. *Entrance requirements:* For master's, GRE or 2 years professional nursing experience, official transcripts, personal essay, 3 letters of recommendation, current unrestricted registered nurse license in Virginia. Additional exam requirements/recommendations for international students: Required—TOEFL (minimum score 550 paper-based; 213 computer-based; 79 iBT), IELTS (minimum score 6.5). *Application deadline:* For fall admission, 7/31 for domestic students, 6/1 for international students; for spring admission, 11/30 for domestic students, 10/15 for international students. Applications are processed on a rolling basis. Application fee: $30. Electronic applications accepted. Application fee is waived when completed online. *Expenses: Tuition:* Full-time $7740; part-time $430 per credit hour. *Financial support:* Fellowships, Federal Work-Study, scholarships/grants, health care benefits, and unspecified assistantships available. Support available to part-time students. Financial award application deadline: 7/31; financial award applicants required to submit FAFSA. *Unit head:* Dr. Jean St. Clair, Associate Professor/Director of MSN Program, 434-544-8740, E-mail: stclair.j@lynchburg.edu. *Application contact:* Anne Pingstock, Executive Assistant, Graduate Studies, 434-544-8383, E-mail: gradstudies@lynchburg.edu. Web site: http://www.lynchburg.edu/msn.xml.

Madonna University, Program in Nursing, Livonia, MI 48150-1173. Offers adult health: chronic health conditions (MSN); adult nurse practitioner (MSN); nursing administration (MSN); MSN/MSBA. *Accreditation:* AACN. Part-time programs available. *Degree requirements:* For master's, thesis or alternative. *Entrance requirements:* For master's, GRE General Test, Michigan nursing license. Electronic applications accepted. *Faculty research:* Coping, caring.

Marquette University, Graduate School, College of Nursing, Milwaukee, WI 53201-1881. Offers acute care nurse practitioner (Certificate); adult clinical nurse specialist (Certificate); adult nurse practitioner (Certificate); advanced practice nursing (MSN, DNP), including acute care, adults, neonatal nurse practitioner (MSN), nurse midwifery (DNP), nurse-midwifery (MSN), older adults, pediatrics acute care (DNP, PhD), pediatrics primary care; clinical nurse leader (MSN); gerontologic clinical nurse specialist (Certificate); gerontologic nurse practitioner (Certificate); health care systems leadership (MSN, DNP); nurse-midwifery (Certificate); nursing (PhD), including pediatrics acute care (DNP, PhD); pediatrics acute care (Certificate); pediatrics primary care (Certificate). *Accreditation:* AACN. *Faculty:* 32 full-time (30 women), 47 part-time/adjunct (all women). *Students:* 93 full-time (88 women), 244 part-time (220 women); includes 31 minority (9 Black or African American, non-Hispanic/Latino; 7 Asian, non-Hispanic/Latino; 8 Hispanic/Latino; 7 Two or more races, non-Hispanic/Latino), 1 international. Average age 30. 282 applicants, 57% accepted, 98 enrolled. In 2011, 76 master's, 8 doctorates, 7 other advanced degrees awarded. Terminal master's awarded for partial completion of doctoral program. *Degree requirements:* For master's, comprehensive exam, thesis or alternative. *Entrance requirements:* For master's, GRE General Test, BSN, Wisconsin RN license, official transcripts from all current and previous colleges/universities except Marquette, three completed recommendation forms, resume, written statement of professional goals; for doctorate, GRE General Test, official transcripts from all current and previous colleges/universities except Marquette, three letters of recommendation, resume, written statement of professional goals, sample of scholarly writing. Additional exam requirements/recommendations for international students: Required—TOEFL (minimum score 530 paper-based; 78 computer-based). *Application deadline:* For fall admission, 2/15 for domestic and international students. Application fee: $50. Electronic applications accepted. *Expenses: Tuition:* Full-time $17,010; part-time $945 per credit hour. Tuition and fees vary according to program. *Financial support:* In 2011–12, 41 students received support, including 1 fellowship with partial tuition reimbursement available (averaging $17,500 per year), 2 research assistantships with full tuition reimbursements available (averaging $13,285 per year), 8 teaching assistantships with full tuition reimbursements available (averaging $13,912 per year); career-related internships or fieldwork, Federal Work-Study, scholarships/grants, health care benefits, tuition waivers (partial), and unspecified assistantships also available. Support available to part-time students. Financial award application deadline: 2/15. *Faculty research:* Psychosocial adjustment to chronic illness, gerontology, reminiscence, health policy: uninsured and access, hospital care delivery systems. *Total annual research expenditures:* $312,575. *Unit head:* Dr. Margaret Callahan, Dean, 414-288-3800, Fax: 414-288-1578. *Application contact:* Karen Nest, Graduate Program Coordinator, 414-288-3810, Fax: 414-288-1578. Web site: http://www.marquette.edu/nursing/academicprograms-graduate.shtml.

McKendree University, Graduate Programs, Master of Science in Nursing Program, Lebanon, IL 62254-1299. Offers nursing education (MSN); nursing management/administration (MSN). *Accreditation:* AACN. Part-time and evening/weekend programs available. Postbaccalaureate distance learning degree programs offered (no on-campus study). *Degree requirements:* For master's, research project or thesis. *Entrance requirements:* For master's, resume, references, valid Professional Registered Nurse license. Additional exam requirements/recommendations for international students: Required—TOEFL. Electronic applications accepted.

McNeese State University, Doré School of Graduate Studies, College of Nursing, Lake Charles, LA 70609. Offers clinical nurse specialist (MSN); nurse educator (MSN); nurse practitioner (MSN); nursing leadership and administration (MSN). Program offered jointly with Southeastern Louisiana University and Southern University and Agricultural and Mechanical College. *Accreditation:* AACN. *Faculty:* 4 full-time (all women), 3 part-time/adjunct (2 women). *Students:* 10 full-time (9 women), 94 part-time (79 women); includes 21 minority (15 Black or African American, non-Hispanic/Latino; 1 Asian, non-Hispanic/Latino; 4 Hispanic/Latino; 1 Two or more races, non-Hispanic/Latino). In 2011, 25 master's awarded. *Degree requirements:* For master's, comprehensive exam. *Entrance requirements:* For master's, GRE, eligibility for unencumbered licensure as RN in Louisiana. *Application deadline:* For fall admission, 5/15 priority date for domestic students, 5/15 for international students; for spring admission, 10/15 priority date for domestic students, 10/15 for international students. Applications are processed on a rolling basis. Application fee: $20 ($30 for international students). *Expenses:* Tuition, state resident: part-time $519 per credit hour. Tuition and fees vary according to course load. *Financial support:* Application deadline: 5/1. *Unit head:* Dr. Peggy L. Wolfe, Dean, 337-475-5820, Fax: 337-475-5924, E-mail: pwolfe@mcneese.edu. *Application contact:* Valarie Waldmeier, Coordinator, 337-475-5285, Fax: 337-475-5702, E-mail: vwaldmeier@mcneese.edu.

Medical University of South Carolina, College of Nursing, Nurse Administrator Program, Charleston, SC 29425. Offers MSN. *Accreditation:* AACN. Part-time programs available. Postbaccalaureate distance learning degree programs offered (no on-campus study). *Faculty:* 6 full-time (5 women), 2 part-time/adjunct (1 woman). *Students:* 1 (woman) full-time, 5 part-time (all women). Average age 38. 13 applicants, 0% accepted. In 2011, 4 master's awarded. *Degree requirements:* For master's, thesis optional. *Entrance requirements:* For master's, BSN, nursing license, minimum GPA of 3.0, current curriculum vitae, essay, three references. Additional exam requirements/recommendations for international students: Required—TOEFL (minimum score 600 paper-based; 250 computer-based). *Application deadline:* For fall admission, 2/1 priority date for domestic students, 2/1 for international students. Application fee: $85. Electronic applications accepted. *Financial support:* Federal Work-Study, scholarships/grants, and traineeships available. Support available to part-time students. Financial award application deadline: 3/10; financial award applicants required to submit FAFSA. *Faculty research:* Hospital billing for nursing intensity. *Unit head:* Dr. Mary M. Martin, Lead Faculty, 843-792-3084, Fax: 843-792-1741, E-mail: martinmm@musc.edu. *Application contact:* Carolyn F. Page, Director, Student Services, 843-792-3844, Fax: 843-792-5395, E-mail: pagecf@musc.edu. Web site: http://academicdepartments.musc.edu/nursing/.

Mercy College, School of Health and Natural Sciences, Programs in Nursing, Dobbs Ferry, NY 10522-1189. Offers nursing administration (MS, Certificate); nursing education (MS, Certificate). *Accreditation:* AACN. Part-time and evening/weekend programs available. Postbaccalaureate distance learning degree programs offered (no on-campus study). *Degree requirements:* For master's, written comprehensive exam or the production of a comprehensive project. *Entrance requirements:* For master's, bachelor's degree, two letters of reference, interview/assessment, RN registration in the U.S.. Additional exam requirements/recommendations for international students: Required—TOEFL (minimum score 600 paper-based; 250 computer-based; 100 iBT), IELTS (minimum score 8). Electronic applications accepted.

Metropolitan State University, College of Health, Community and Professional Studies, St. Paul, MN 55106-5000. Offers advanced dental therapy (MS); leadership and management (MSN); nursing (DNP); psychology (MA). *Accreditation:* AACN. Part-time programs available. *Students:* 26 full-time (24 women), 160 part-time (158 women); includes 20 minority (7 Black or African American, non-Hispanic/Latino; 2 American Indian or Alaska Native, non-Hispanic/Latino; 2 Asian, non-Hispanic/Latino; 2 Hispanic/Latino; 7 Two or more races, non-Hispanic/Latino), 7 international. Average age 36. *Degree requirements:* For master's, thesis or alternative; for doctorate, thesis/dissertation or alternative. *Entrance requirements:* For master's, GRE General Test, minimum GPA of 3.0, RN license, BS/BAN; for doctorate, minimum GPA of 3.0; RN license, MSN. Additional exam requirements/recommendations for international students: Required—TOEFL (minimum score 550 paper-based; 213 computer-based). *Application deadline:* For fall admission, 1/15 for domestic students; for winter admission, 1/15 for international students. Application fee: $20. *Expenses:* Tuition, state resident: full-time $5799.06; part-time $322.17 per credit. Tuition, nonresident: full-time $11,411; part-time $633.92 per credit. Tuition and fees vary according to degree level, program and reciprocity agreements. *Financial support:* Fellowships, career-related internships or fieldwork, Federal Work-Study, institutionally sponsored loans, and traineeships available. Financial award applicants required to submit FAFSA. *Faculty research:* Women's health, gerontology. *Unit head:* Ann Leja, Interim Dean, 651-793-1402, Fax: 651-793-1382, E-mail: ann.leja@metrostate.edu. *Application contact:* Lynda Zimmerman, Academic Advisor, 651-793-1378, Fax: 651-793-1382, E-mail: lynda.zimmerman@metrostate.edu. Web site: http://www.metrostate.edu/cnhs/.

Millikin University, School of Nursing, Decatur, IL 62522-2084. Offers clinical nurse leader (MSN); entry into nursing practice: pre-licensure (MSN); nurse anesthesia (MSN); nurse educator (MSN). *Accreditation:* AACN; AANA/CANAEP. Part-time programs available. *Faculty:* 17 full-time (15 women), 4 part-time/adjunct (3 women). *Students:* 30 full-time (21 women), 10 part-time (9 women); includes 2 minority (both Black or African American, non-Hispanic/Latino). Average age 32. 110 applicants, 39% accepted, 40 enrolled. In 2011, 6 master's awarded. *Degree requirements:* For master's, thesis or alternative, research project. *Entrance requirements:* For master's, GRE, official academic transcript(s), written essay, immunizations, statistics course, 2 letters of recommendation, CPR certification, professional liability/malpractice insurance. Additional exam requirements/recommendations for international students: Required—TOEFL (minimum score 550 paper-based; 79 iBT). *Application deadline:* For spring admission, 11/1 priority date for domestic students. Applications are processed on a rolling basis. Application fee: $0. Electronic applications accepted. *Expenses: Tuition:* Full-time $24,890; part-time $681 per credit hour. Tuition and fees vary according to program. *Financial support:* Institutionally sponsored loans available. Financial award applicants required to submit FAFSA. *Faculty research:* Congestive heart failure, quality of life, transcultural nursing issues, teaching/learning strategies, maternal - newborn. *Unit head:* Dr. Deborah Slayton, Director, 217-424-6348, Fax: 217-420-6731, E-mail: dslayton@millikin.edu. *Application contact:* Marianne Taylor, Administrative Assistant, 800-373-7733 Ext. 5034, Fax: 217-420-6677, E-mail: mgtaylor@millikin.edu. Web site: http://www.millikin.edu/academics/cps/nursing/msn/.

Missouri Western State University, Program in Health Care Leadership, St. Joseph, MO 64507-2294. Offers MSN. Part-time programs available. *Application deadline:* For fall admission, 7/15 for domestic and international students; for spring admission, 10/1 for domestic and international students. Applications are processed on a rolling basis. Application fee: $45 ($50 for international students). Electronic applications accepted. *Expenses:* Tuition, state resident: full-time $4697; part-time $261 per credit hour. Tuition, nonresident: full-time $9355; part-time $520 per credit hour. *Required fees:* $343; $19.10 per credit hour. $30 per semester. Tuition and fees vary according to

course load. *Unit head:* Dr. Kathleen O'Connor, Coordinator, 816-271-5910, E-mail: koconnor5@missouriwestern.edu. *Application contact:* Dr. Brian C. Cronk, Dean of the Graduate School, 816-271-4394, E-mail: graduate@missouriwestern.edu. Web site: http://www.missouriwestern.edu/nursing/msn/.

Molloy College, Division of Nursing, Rockville Centre, NY 11571-5002. Offers adult nurse practitioner (Advanced Certificate); clinical nurse specialist: adult health (Advanced Certificate); family nurse practitioner (Advanced Certificate); nurse practitioner psychiatry (Advanced Certificate); nursing (MS); nursing administration (Advanced Certificate); nursing administration with informatics (Advanced Certificate); nursing education (Advanced Certificate); nursing informatics (Advanced Certificate); pediatric nurse practitioner (Advanced Certificate). *Accreditation:* AACN. Part-time and evening/weekend programs available. *Faculty:* 20 full-time (19 women), 12 part-time/adjunct (11 women). *Students:* 19 full-time (15 women), 483 part-time (452 women); includes 238 minority (132 Black or African American, non-Hispanic/Latino; 61 Asian, non-Hispanic/Latino; 35 Hispanic/Latino; 2 Native Hawaiian or other Pacific Islander, non-Hispanic/Latino; 8 Two or more races, non-Hispanic/Latino), 5 international. Average age 40. 186 applicants, 82% accepted, 110 enrolled. In 2011, 94 master's awarded. *Degree requirements:* For master's, thesis optional. *Entrance requirements:* For master's, 3 letters of reference, BS in nursing, minimum undergraduate GPA of 3.0; for Advanced Certificate, 3 letters of reference, master's degree in nursing. *Application deadline:* For fall admission, 9/2 priority date for domestic students; for spring admission, 1/20 priority date for domestic students. Applications are processed on a rolling basis. Application fee: $60. *Financial support:* Research assistantships with partial tuition reimbursements, teaching assistantships with partial tuition reimbursements, institutionally sponsored loans, scholarships/grants, and unspecified assistantships available. Support available to part-time students. Financial award application deadline: 4/1; financial award applicants required to submit FAFSA. *Unit head:* Dr. Denise Walsh, Associate Dean, Graduate Nursing, 516-678-5000, Fax: 516-678-9718, E-mail: dwalsh@molloy.edu. *Application contact:* Alina Haitz, Assistant Director of Graduate Admissions, 516-678-5000, Fax: 516-256-2247, E-mail: ahaitz@molloy.edu. Web site: http://www.molloy.edu/academics/nursing-division.

Monmouth University, The Graduate School, The Marjorie K. Unterberg School of Nursing and Health Studies, West Long Branch, NJ 07764-1898. Offers adult nurse practitioner (MSN); adult psychiatric and mental health advanced practice nursing (MSN, Post-Master's Certificate); advanced practice nursing (Post-Master's Certificate); family nurse practitioner (MSN, Post-Master's Certificate); forensic nursing (MSN, Certificate); nursing (MSN); nursing administration (MSN, Post-Master's Certificate); nursing education (MSN, Post-Master's Certificate); nursing practice (DNP); school nursing (MSN, Certificate). *Accreditation:* AACN. Part-time and evening/weekend programs available. *Faculty:* 12 full-time (all women), 2 part-time/adjunct (both women). *Students:* 16 full-time (11 women), 244 part-time (238 women); includes 73 minority (23 Black or African American, non-Hispanic/Latino; 2 American Indian or Alaska Native, non-Hispanic/Latino; 34 Asian, non-Hispanic/Latino; 12 Hispanic/Latino; 1 Native Hawaiian or other Pacific Islander, non-Hispanic/Latino; 1 Two or more races, non-Hispanic/Latino), 1 international. Average age 41. 107 applicants, 92% accepted, 67 enrolled. In 2011, 55 master's awarded. *Degree requirements:* For master's, practicum (for some tracks). *Entrance requirements:* For master's, GRE General Test, RN license, 1 year of work experience, minimum undergraduate GPA of 2.75. Additional exam requirements/recommendations for international students: Required—TOEFL (minimum score 550 paper-based; 213 computer-based; 79 iBT), IELTS (minimum score 5) or Michigan English Language Assessment Battery (minimum score 77), Cambridge A, B, C. *Application deadline:* For fall admission, 7/15 priority date for domestic students, 6/1 for international students; for spring admission, 11/15 priority date for domestic students, 11/1 for international students. Applications are processed on a rolling basis. Application fee: $50. Electronic applications accepted. *Financial support:* In 2011–12, 138 students received support, including 138 fellowships (averaging $1,423 per year), 4 research assistantships (averaging $5,240 per year); career-related internships or fieldwork, scholarships/grants, and unspecified assistantships also available. Support available to part-time students. Financial award applicants required to submit FAFSA. *Faculty research:* Relationship of undergraduate GPA and GRE to succeed in a graduate nursing program. *Unit head:* Dr. Janet Mahoney, Dean, 732-571-3443, Fax: 732-263-5131, E-mail: jmahoney@monmouth.edu. *Application contact:* Kevin Roane, Director, Office of Graduate Admission, 732-571-3452, Fax: 732-263-5123, E-mail: gradadm@monmouth.edu. Web site: http://www.monmouth.edu/nursingschool.

Montana State University, College of Graduate Studies, College of Nursing, Bozeman, MT 59717. Offers clinical nurse leader (MN); family nurse practitioner (MN, Post-Master's Certificate); nursing education (Certificate, Post-Master's Certificate); psychiatric mental health nurse practitioner (MN). *Accreditation:* AACN. Part-time programs available. Postbaccalaureate distance learning degree programs offered (minimal on-campus study). *Degree requirements:* For master's, comprehensive exam, thesis (for some programs). *Entrance requirements:* For master's, GRE General Test, minimum GPA of 3.0 for undergraduate and post-baccalaureate work. Additional exam requirements/recommendations for international students: Required—TOEFL (minimum score 580 paper-based; 213 computer-based). Electronic applications accepted. *Faculty research:* Rural nursing, health disparities, environmental/public health, oral health, resilience.

Moravian College, Moravian College Comenius Center, St. Luke's School of Nursing, Bethlehem, PA 18018-6650. Offers nurse administrator (MS); nurse educator (MS); nurse leadership (MS). Part-time and evening/weekend programs available. *Degree requirements:* For master's, comprehensive exam (for some programs), evidence-based practice project. *Entrance requirements:* For master's, GRE or MAT. Additional exam requirements/recommendations for international students: Required—TOEFL (minimum score 550 paper-based; 260 computer-based; 90 iBT).

Mountain State University, Program in Nursing, Beckley, WV 25802-9003. Offers administration/education (MSN); family nurse practitioner (MSN). *Accreditation:* NLN. Part-time programs available. Postbaccalaureate distance learning degree programs offered (minimal on-campus study). *Faculty:* 3 full-time (all women), 2 part-time/adjunct (both women). *Students:* 65 full-time (61 women), 9 part-time (8 women); includes 11 minority (8 Black or African American, non-Hispanic/Latino; 1 American Indian or Alaska Native, non-Hispanic/Latino; 2 Asian, non-Hispanic/Latino), 1 international. Average age 37. 85 applicants, 27% accepted, 20 enrolled. In 2011, 46 master's awarded. *Degree requirements:* For master's, comprehensive exam, thesis or alternative. *Entrance requirements:* For master's, GRE. Additional exam requirements/recommendations for international students: Required—TOEFL (minimum score 550 paper-based; 213 computer-based); Recommended—IELTS (minimum score 6.5). *Application deadline:* For spring admission, 6/30 for domestic and international students. Applications are processed on a rolling basis. Application fee: $25 ($50 for international students). Electronic applications accepted. *Expenses:* Contact institution. *Financial support:* Federal Work-Study, scholarships/grants, and unspecified assistantships available. Support available to part-time students. Financial award applicants required to submit FAFSA. *Unit head:* Dr. Sheila Garland, Dean, School of Health Sciences, 304-929-1516, Fax: 304-929-1601, E-mail: sgarland@mountainstate.edu.

Mount Carmel College of Nursing, Nursing Program, Columbus, OH 43222. Offers adult health clinical nurse specialist (MS); family nurse practitioner (MS); nursing administration (MS); nursing education (MS). *Accreditation:* AACN. Part-time programs available. *Faculty:* 11 full-time (10 women), 4 part-time/adjunct (2 women). *Students:* 69 full-time (66 women), 33 part-time (30 women); includes 19 minority (11 Black or African American, non-Hispanic/Latino; 1 American Indian or Alaska Native, non-Hispanic/Latino; 5 Asian, non-Hispanic/Latino; 1 Native Hawaiian or other Pacific Islander, non-Hispanic/Latino; 1 Two or more races, non-Hispanic/Latino). Average age 38. 23 applicants, 100% accepted, 20 enrolled. In 2011, 16 master's awarded. *Degree requirements:* For master's, professional manuscript. *Entrance requirements:* For master's, letters of recommendation, current resume, baccalaureate degree in nursing, current Ohio RN license, minimum cumulative GPA of 3.0. Additional exam requirements/recommendations for international students: Required—TOEFL (minimum score 550 paper-based; 213 computer-based; 80 iBT). *Application deadline:* For fall admission, 6/15 priority date for domestic students; for winter admission, 11/1 priority date for domestic students. Applications are processed on a rolling basis. Application fee: $30. *Expenses: Tuition:* Full-time $7839; part-time $402 per credit. *Required fees:* $75. *Financial support:* In 2011–12, 6 students received support. Institutionally sponsored loans and scholarships/grants available. Financial award application deadline: 7/1; financial award applicants required to submit FAFSA. *Unit head:* Dr. Angela Phillips-Lowe, Associate Dean, 614-234-5717, Fax: 614-234-2875, E-mail: aphillips-lowe@mccn.edu. *Application contact:* Elsie Sexton, Program Coordinator, 614-234-5169, Fax: 614-234-2875, E-mail: ksexton@mccn.edu. Web site: http://www.mccn.edu/.

Mount Saint Mary College, Division of Nursing, Newburgh, NY 12550-3494. Offers adult nurse practitioner (MS, Advanced Certificate), including nursing education (MS); nursing management (MS); clinical nurse specialist-adult health (MS), including nursing education, nursing management; family nurse practitioner (Advanced Certificate). *Accreditation:* AACN. Part-time and evening/weekend programs available. *Faculty:* 3 full-time (all women), 1 (woman) part-time/adjunct. *Students:* 3 full-time (2 women), 58 part-time (54 women); includes 16 minority (11 Black or African American, non-Hispanic/Latino; 1 Asian, non-Hispanic/Latino; 1 Hispanic/Latino; 3 Native Hawaiian or other Pacific Islander, non-Hispanic/Latino), 2 international. Average age 38. 47 applicants, 53% accepted, 18 enrolled. In 2011, 17 master's, 5 other advanced degrees awarded. *Degree requirements:* For master's, research utilization project. *Entrance requirements:* For master's, BSN, minimum GPA of 3.0, RN license. *Application deadline:* For fall admission, 6/3 priority date for domestic students; for spring admission, 10/31 priority date for domestic students. Applications are processed on a rolling basis. Application fee: $45. Application fee is waived when completed online. *Expenses: Tuition:* Full-time $13,356; part-time $742 per credit. *Required fees:* $70 per semester. *Financial support:* In 2011–12, 8 students received support. Unspecified assistantships available. Financial award application deadline: 4/15; financial award applicants required to submit FAFSA. *Unit head:* Dr. Karen Baldwin, Coordinator, 845-569-3512, Fax: 845-562-6762, E-mail: baldwin@msmc.edu. *Application contact:* Courtney McDermott, Graduate Recruiter, 845-569-3402, Fax: 845-569-3450, E-mail: courtney.mcdermott@msmc.edu. Web site: http://www.msmc.edu/Academics/Graduate_Programs/Master_of_Science_in_Nursing.

Mount St. Mary's College, Graduate Division, Program in Nursing, Los Angeles, CA 90049-1599. Offers educator (MSN); leadership and administration (MSN). *Accreditation:* AACN. *Entrance requirements:* For master's, baccalaureate degree; current CA nursing license; minimum cumulative GPA of 3.0 in last 60 semester units or last 90 quarter units of undergraduate and/or graduate course work; essay; two letters of recommendation; official transcript. Additional exam requirements/recommendations for international students: Required—TOEFL (minimum score 550 paper-based). *Application deadline:* For fall admission, 7/15 priority date for domestic students; for spring admission, 11/15 priority date for domestic students. Application fee: $50. Electronic applications accepted. *Expenses: Tuition:* Part-time $752 per unit. Part-time tuition and fees vary according to degree level and program. *Financial support:* Scholarships/grants available. *Unit head:* Dr. Marsha Sato, Director, 213-477-2980, E-mail: msato@msmc.la.edu. Web site: http://www.msmc.la.edu/graduate-programs/nursing.asp.

Nebraska Methodist College, Program in Nursing, Omaha, NE 68114. Offers nurse educator (MSN); nurse executive (MSN). *Accreditation:* AACN. Evening/weekend programs available. Postbaccalaureate distance learning degree programs offered (no on-campus study). *Degree requirements:* For master's, thesis or alternative, Evidence Based Practice (EBP) project. *Entrance requirements:* For master's, interview. Additional exam requirements/recommendations for international students: Required—TOEFL (minimum score 550 paper-based; 213 computer-based; 80 iBT). *Faculty research:* Spirituality, student outcomes, service-learning, leadership and administration, women's issues.

New York University, Robert F. Wagner Graduate School of Public Service, Executive Master of Public Administration, New York, NY 10012. Offers nurse leader (EMPA); public administration (EMPA); MSW/EMPA. *Accreditation:* AACSB. Part-time programs available. *Faculty:* 10 full-time (3 women), 3 part-time/adjunct (all women). *Students:* 27 full-time (16 women), 74 part-time (52 women); includes 27 minority (11 Black or African American, non-Hispanic/Latino; 10 Asian, non-Hispanic/Latino; 6 Hispanic/Latino), 3 international. Average age 40. 82 applicants, 71% accepted, 37 enrolled. In 2011, 34 master's awarded. *Entrance requirements:* Additional exam requirements/recommendations for international students: Required—TOEFL, IELTS, TWE. *Application deadline:* For fall admission, 5/15 for domestic students; for spring admission, 10/15 for domestic students. Application fee: $85. Electronic applications accepted. *Expenses:* Contact institution. *Financial support:* In 2011–12, 7 students received support, including 9 fellowships (averaging $13,500 per year); research assistantships, scholarships/grants, health care benefits, and unspecified assistantships also available. Support available to part-time students. Financial award application deadline: 1/5; financial award applicants required to submit FAFSA. *Unit head:* David Elcott, Director, 212-992-9894, Fax: 212-995-4164, E-mail: david.elcott@nyu.edu. *Application contact:* Christopher Alexander, Communications Coordinator, 212-998-7400, Fax: 212-995-4611, E-mail: wagner.admissions@nyu.edu. Web site: http://www.nyu.edu/wagner/.

Northeastern University, Bouvé College of Health Sciences, School of Nursing, Program in Nursing Administration, Boston, MA 02115-5096. Offers MS, MS/MBA. *Accreditation:* AACN. *Faculty:* 25 full-time, 4 part-time/adjunct. *Students:* 6 full-time, 10 part-time. Average age 42. In 2011, 3 master's awarded. *Degree requirements:* For master's, thesis or alternative. *Entrance requirements:* For master's, GRE General Test. Additional exam requirements/recommendations for international students: Required—TOEFL (minimum score 100 iBT). *Application deadline:* For fall admission, 8/1 priority date for domestic students; for spring admission, 12/1 for domestic students. Applications are processed on a rolling basis. Application fee: $50. *Financial support:* Research assistantships, teaching assistantships, and tuition waivers (partial) available. Financial award application deadline: 7/1; financial award applicants required to submit FAFSA. *Faculty research:* Nursing informatics. *Unit head:* Dr. Jane Aroian, Director, 617-373-3128, E-mail: j.aroian@neu.edu. *Application contact:* Margaret Schnabel, Director of Graduate Admissions, 617-373-2708, E-mail: bouvegrad@neu.edu.

Nursing and Healthcare Administration

North Park University, School of Nursing, Chicago, IL 60625-4895. Offers advanced practice nursing (MS); leadership and management (MS); MBA/MS; MM/MSN; MS/MHR; MS/MNA. *Accreditation:* AACN. Part-time and evening/weekend programs available. *Degree requirements:* For master's, thesis. *Entrance requirements:* For master's, GMAT, MAT. *Faculty research:* Aging, consultation roles, critical thinking skills, family breakdown, science of caring.

Northwest Nazarene University, Graduate Studies, Program in Nursing, Nampa, ID 83686-5897. Offers MSN. *Accreditation:* AACN. Postbaccalaureate distance learning degree programs offered (no on-campus study). *Faculty:* 1 (woman) full-time, 4 part-time/adjunct (all women). *Students:* 15 full-time (all women). Average age 38. 18 applicants, 100% accepted, 10 enrolled. In 2011, 8 master's awarded. *Unit head:* Dr. Barbara Lester, Director, 208-467-8679, E-mail: balester@nnu.edu. *Application contact:* Stacey Little, Program Assistant, 208-467-8642, Fax: 208-467-8651, E-mail: slittle@nnu.edu. Web site: http://www.nnu.edu/msn.

Norwich University, College of Graduate and Continuing Studies, Master of Science in Nursing Program, Northfield, VT 05663. Offers nursing administration (MSN); nursing education (MSN). *Accreditation:* AACN. Evening/weekend programs available. *Faculty:* 8 part-time/adjunct (5 women). *Students:* 31 full-time (29 women); includes 3 minority (1 Black or African American, non-Hispanic/Latino; 1 Asian, non-Hispanic/Latino; 1 Hispanic/Latino). Average age 44. 17 applicants, 59% accepted, 10 enrolled. In 2011, 28 master's awarded. *Entrance requirements:* For master's, minimum undergraduate GPA of 2.75. Additional exam requirements/recommendations for international students: Required—TOEFL (minimum score 550 paper-based; 212 computer-based; 83 iBT). *Application deadline:* For fall admission, 8/10 for domestic and international students; for winter admission, 11/7 for domestic and international students; for spring admission, 2/6 for domestic and international students. Applications are processed on a rolling basis. Application fee: $50. Electronic applications accepted. *Expenses: Tuition:* Full-time $16,174. *Required fees:* $2130. Full-time tuition and fees vary according to program. *Financial support:* In 2011–12, 7 students received support. Scholarships/grants available. Financial award applicants required to submit FAFSA. *Application contact:* Rija Ramahatra, Associate Program Director, 802-485-2892, Fax: 802-485-2533, E-mail: rramahatr@norwich.edu. Web site: http://nursing.norwich.edu/.

Ohio University, Graduate College, College of Health Sciences and Professions, School of Nursing, Athens, OH 45701-2979. Offers acute care nurse practitioner (MSN); acute care nurse practitioner and family nurse practitioner (MSN); acute care nurse practitioner and nurse administrator (MSN); acute care nurse practitioner and nurse educator (MSN); family nurse practitioner (MSN); nurse administrator (MSN); nurse administrator and family nurse practitioner (MSN); nurse educator (MSN); nurse educator and family nurse practitioner (MSN); nurse educator and nurse administrator (MSN). *Accreditation:* AACN. *Students:* 33 full-time (29 women), 91 part-time (84 women); includes 16 minority (8 Black or African American, non-Hispanic/Latino; 2 Asian, non-Hispanic/Latino; 1 Hispanic/Latino; 5 Two or more races, non-Hispanic/Latino), 3 international. 86 applicants, 86% accepted, 61 enrolled. In 2011, 24 master's awarded. *Degree requirements:* For master's, capstone project. *Entrance requirements:* For master's, GRE, bachelor's degree in nursing from an accredited college or university, minimum overall undergraduate GPA of 3.0, official transcripts, statement of goals and objectives, resume, 3 letters of recommendation. Additional exam requirements/recommendations for international students: Required—TOEFL (minimum score 550 paper-based; 80 iBT) or IELTS (minimum score 6.5). *Application deadline:* For fall admission, 3/1 priority date for domestic students, 2/1 for international students. Applications are processed on a rolling basis. Application fee: $50 ($55 for international students). Electronic applications accepted. *Financial support:* Research assistantships, Federal Work-Study, institutionally sponsored loans, and unspecified assistantships available. Financial award application deadline: 3/1. *Unit head:* Dr. Deborah Henderson, Professor and Interim Director, 740-593-4497, Fax: 740-593-0286, E-mail: hendersd@ohio.edu. *Application contact:* Cheryl Brimner, Administrative Associate, 740-593-4494, Fax: 740-593-0286, E-mail: brimner@ohio.edu. Web site: http://www.ohio.edu/chsp/nrse/index.cfm.

Old Dominion University, College of Health Sciences, School of Nursing, Nurse Administrator Emphasis, Norfolk, VA 23529. Offers MSN. Part-time programs available. Postbaccalaureate distance learning degree programs offered. *Faculty:* 1 (woman) full-time, 3 part-time/adjunct (2 women). *Students:* 3 full-time (all women), 13 part-time (12 women); includes 4 minority (2 Black or African American, non-Hispanic/Latino; 1 Hispanic/Latino; 1 Native Hawaiian or other Pacific Islander, non-Hispanic/Latino). Average age 35. 14 applicants, 93% accepted, 11 enrolled. In 2011, 9 master's awarded. *Degree requirements:* For master's, comprehensive exam. *Entrance requirements:* For master's, GRE or MAT. Additional exam requirements/recommendations for international students: Required—TOEFL. *Application deadline:* For fall admission, 5/1 priority date for domestic students, 4/15 for international students. Applications are processed on a rolling basis. Application fee: $50. Electronic applications accepted. *Expenses:* Tuition, state resident: full-time $9096; part-time $379 per credit. Tuition, nonresident: full-time $23,064; part-time $961 per credit. *Required fees:* $127 per semester. One-time fee: $50. *Faculty research:* Telehealth, vulnerable populations. *Unit head:* Dr. Laurel Shepherd, Graduate Program Director, 757-683-5250, Fax: 757-683-5253, E-mail: lgarzon@odu.edu. *Application contact:* Sue Parker, Coordinator, Graduate Student Services, 757-683-4298, Fax: 757-683-5253, E-mail: sparker@odu.edu. Web site: http://hs.odu.edu/nursing/academics/nurse_admin/nurse_admin.shtml.

Otterbein University, Department of Nursing, Westerville, OH 43081. Offers advanced practice nurse educator (Certificate); clinical nurse leader (MSN); family nurse practitioner (MSN, Certificate); nurse anesthesia (MSN, Certificate); nursing (DNP); nursing service administration (MSN). *Accreditation:* AACN; AANA/CANAEP; NLN. Part-time and evening/weekend programs available. Postbaccalaureate distance learning degree programs offered (minimal on-campus study). *Degree requirements:* For master's, comprehensive exam (for some programs), thesis (for some programs). *Entrance requirements:* For master's, 2 reference forms, resume; for Certificate, official transcripts, 2 reference forms, essay, resumé. Additional exam requirements/recommendations for international students: Required—TOEFL (minimum score 550 paper-based; 213 computer-based; 79 iBT). *Faculty research:* Patient education, women's health, trauma curriculum development, administration.

Our Lady of the Lake College, School of Nursing, Program in Nursing, Baton Rouge, LA 70808. Offers administration (MS); education (MS). Part-time programs available. *Degree requirements:* For master's, capstone project. *Entrance requirements:* For master's, BSN with minimum GPA of 3.0 during the last 60 hours of undergraduate work, 1 year of clinical nursing experience as a registered nurse, current licensure or eligibility to practice as registered nurse in Louisiana, 3 professional references, 3 credit hours of undergraduate statistics with minimum C average.

Pace University, Lienhard School of Nursing, New York, NY 10038. Offers family nurse practitioner (MS); nursing education (MA); nursing leadership (Advanced Certificate); nursing practice (DNP). *Accreditation:* AACN. Part-time and evening/weekend programs available. Postbaccalaureate distance learning degree programs offered. *Faculty:* 10 full-time (8 women), 37 part-time/adjunct (30 women). *Students:* 32 full-time (26 women), 417 part-time (381 women); includes 187 minority (88 Black or African

American, non-Hispanic/Latino; 1 American Indian or Alaska Native, non-Hispanic/Latino; 49 Asian, non-Hispanic/Latino; 43 Hispanic/Latino; 1 Native Hawaiian or other Pacific Islander, non-Hispanic/Latino; 5 Two or more races, non-Hispanic/Latino), 5 international. Average age 36. 437 applicants, 41% accepted, 84 enrolled. In 2011, 96 master's, 20 doctorates, 3 other advanced degrees awarded. *Degree requirements:* For master's, thesis. *Entrance requirements:* For master's, GRE General Test or MAT, RN license, resume, personal statement, 2 letters of recommendation, official transcripts; for doctorate, RN license, resume, personal statement, 2 letters of recommendation, official transcripts, accredited master's degree in nursing, minimum GPA of 3.3, state certification; for Advanced Certificate, RN license, completion of 2nd degree in nursing. Additional exam requirements/recommendations for international students: Required—TOEFL. *Application deadline:* For fall admission, 7/31 priority date for domestic students, 4/30 for international students; for spring admission, 10/14 for domestic students, 9/14 for international students. Applications are processed on a rolling basis. Application fee: $70. Electronic applications accepted. *Expenses:* Contact institution. *Financial support:* Research assistantships, career-related internships or fieldwork, Federal Work-Study, and tuition waivers (partial) available. Support available to part-time students. Financial award applicants required to submit FAFSA. *Unit head:* Dr. Geraldine Colombraro, Interim Dean, 914-773-3341, E-mail: gcolombraro@pace.edu. *Application contact:* Susan Ford-Goldschein, Director of Graduate Admissions, 914-422-4283, Fax: 914-422-4287, E-mail: gradwp@pace.edu. Web site: http://www.pace.edu/.

Pacific Lutheran University, Division of Graduate Studies, School of Nursing, Program in Care and Outcomes Manager, Tacoma, WA 98447. Offers client systems management (MSN); health care systems management (MSN). *Accreditation:* AACN. Part-time and evening/weekend programs available. *Faculty:* 5 full-time (2 women), 1 (woman) part-time/adjunct. *Students:* 1 (woman) full-time, 3 part-time (all women); includes 1 minority (Black or African American, non-Hispanic/Latino). Average age 44. 2 applicants, 100% accepted, 1 enrolled. In 2011, 10 master's awarded. *Degree requirements:* For master's, thesis or alternative. *Entrance requirements:* For master's, GRE General Test, minimum undergraduate GPA of 3.0. Additional exam requirements/recommendations for international students: Required—TOEFL (minimum score 550 paper-based; 213 computer-based). *Application deadline:* For fall admission, 4/1 priority date for domestic students. Applications are processed on a rolling basis. Application fee: $40. *Expenses:* Contact institution. *Financial support:* In 2011–12, 2 students received support. Federal Work-Study, scholarships/grants, and unspecified assistantships available. Financial award application deadline: 3/1. *Unit head:* Dr. Patsy Maloney, Unit Head, 253-535-7685. *Application contact:* Linda DuBay, Senior Office Assistant, 253-535-7151, Fax: 253-536-5136, E-mail: admissions@plu.edu.

Prairie View A&M University, College of Nursing, Houston, TX 77030. Offers family nurse practitioner (MSN); nursing administration (MSN); nursing education (MSN). *Accreditation:* AACN; NLN. Part-time programs available. *Degree requirements:* For master's, comprehensive exam, thesis. *Entrance requirements:* For master's, MAT or GRE, BS in nursing; 2 years of experience as a registered nurse; 1 course each in statistics, basic health and assessment. *Faculty research:* Software development and violence prevention, health promotion and disease prevention.

Purdue University Calumet, Graduate Studies Office, School of Nursing, Hammond, IN 46323-2094. Offers adult health clinical nurse specialist (MS); critical care clinical nurse specialist (MS); family nurse practitioner (MS); nurse executive (MS). *Accreditation:* AACN; NLN. Part-time programs available. Postbaccalaureate distance learning degree programs offered (minimal on-campus study). *Entrance requirements:* For master's, BSN. Additional exam requirements/recommendations for international students: Required—TOEFL. Electronic applications accepted. *Faculty research:* Adult health, cardiovascular and pulmonary nursing.

Queens University of Charlotte, Presbyterian School of Nursing, Charlotte, NC 28274-0002. Offers nursing management (MSN). *Accreditation:* AACN. *Degree requirements:* For master's, research project. *Entrance requirements:* For master's, minimum GPA of 3.0. Additional exam requirements/recommendations for international students: Required—TOEFL. Electronic applications accepted. *Expenses:* Contact institution.

Regis University, Rueckert-Hartman College for Health Professions, Denver, CO 80221-1099. Offers family nurse practitioner (MSN); health informatics (Postbaccalaureate Certificate); health services administration (MS); leadership in healthcare systems (MSN); neonatal nurse practitioner (MSN); nursing (MSN); pharmacy (Pharm D); physical therapy (DPT, TDPT). *Entrance requirements:* Additional exam requirements/recommendations for international students: Required—TOEFL (minimum score 550 paper-based; 213 computer-based; 82 iBT). Electronic applications accepted. *Expenses:* Contact institution. *Faculty research:* Normal and pathological balance and gait research, normal/pathological upper limb motor control/biomechanics, exercise energy/metabolism research, optical treatment protocols for therapeutic modalities.

Research College of Nursing, Nursing Program, Kansas City, MO 64132. Offers clinical nurse leader (MSN); executive nurse practitioner (MSN); family nurse practitioner (MSN); nurse educator (MSN). *Accreditation:* AACN. Part-time programs available. Postbaccalaureate distance learning degree programs offered (no on-campus study). *Faculty:* 8 full-time (all women), 1 (woman) part-time/adjunct. *Students:* 9 full-time (7 women), 132 part-time (121 women). Average age 30. In 2011, 23 master's awarded. *Degree requirements:* For master's, research project. *Entrance requirements:* For master's, 3 letters of recommendation, official transcripts, resume. Additional exam requirements/recommendations for international students: Required—TOEFL (minimum score 550 paper-based; 213 computer-based), TWE. *Application deadline:* Applications are processed on a rolling basis. Application fee: $50. *Expenses: Tuition:* Part-time $425 per credit hour. *Required fees:* $25 per credit hour. *Financial support:* Applicants required to submit FAFSA. *Unit head:* Dr. Nancy O. DeBasio, President and Dean, 816-995-2815, Fax: 816-995-2817, E-mail: nancy.debasio@researchcollege.edu. *Application contact:* Leslie Mendenhall, Director of Transfer and Graduate Recruitment, 816-995-2820, Fax: 816-995-2813, E-mail: leslie.mendenhall@researchcollege.edu.

Roberts Wesleyan College, Division of Nursing, Rochester, NY 14624-1997. Offers nursing administration (MSN); nursing education (MSN). *Accreditation:* AACN. *Entrance requirements:* For master's, minimum GPA of 3.0; BS in nursing; interview; RN license; resume; course work in statistics and health assessment. Additional exam requirements/recommendations for international students: Required—TOEFL.

Sacred Heart University, Graduate Programs, College of Health Professions, Department of Nursing, Fairfield, CT 06825-1000. Offers clinical nurse leader (MSN); clinical practice in health care (DNP); family nurse practitioner (MSN); leadership in health care (DNP); nursing (DN Sc); patient care services administration (MSN). *Accreditation:* AACN. Part-time and evening/weekend programs available. Postbaccalaureate distance learning degree programs offered (minimal on-campus study). *Entrance requirements:* For master's, BSN, minimum GPA of 3.0. Additional exam requirements/recommendations for international students: Required—TOEFL (minimum score 550 paper-based; 213 computer-based). Electronic applications accepted. *Expenses:* Contact institution.

Sage Graduate School, School of Health Sciences, Department of Nursing, Troy, NY 12180-4115. Offers adult health (MS); adult nurse practitioner (MS, Post Master's

Certificate); clinical nurse leader/specialist (Post Master's Certificate); community health (MS); education and leadership (DNS); family nurse practitioner (MS, Post Master's Certificate); gerontological nurse practitioner (Post Master's Certificate); nurse administrator/executive (Post Master's Certificate); nursing (Post Master's Certificate); psychiatric mental health nurse practitioner (MS, Post Master's Certificate), including psychiatric mental health. *Accreditation:* AACN. Part-time and evening/weekend programs available. *Faculty:* 5 full-time (all women), 10 part-time/adjunct (all women). *Students:* 35 full-time (31 women), 158 part-time (152 women); includes 20 minority (8 Black or African American, non-Hispanic/Latino; 1 American Indian or Alaska Native, non-Hispanic/Latino; 8 Asian, non-Hispanic/Latino; 3 Hispanic/Latino), 7 international. Average age 42. 143 applicants, 32% accepted, 34 enrolled. In 2011, 30 master's, 1 doctorate, 5 other advanced degrees awarded. *Degree requirements:* For master's, thesis or alternative. *Entrance requirements:* For master's, BS in nursing, minimum GPA of 2.75, resume, 2 letters of recommendation. Additional exam requirements/recommendations for international students: Required—TOEFL (minimum score 550 paper-based; 213 computer-based). *Application deadline:* Applications are processed on a rolling basis. Application fee: $40. *Expenses: Tuition:* Full-time $11,880; part-time $660 per credit hour. Tuition and fees vary according to program. *Financial support:* Fellowships, research assistantships, Federal Work-Study, scholarships/grants, and unspecified assistantships available. Support available to part-time students. Financial award application deadline: 3/1; financial award applicants required to submit FAFSA. *Unit head:* Dr. Esther Haskevitz, Dean, School of Health Sciences, 518-244-2296, Fax: 518-244-4571, E-mail: haskve@sage.edu. *Application contact:* Dr. Glenda Kelman, Director, 518-244-2001, Fax: 518-244-2009, E-mail: kelmag@sage.edu.

Saginaw Valley State University, Crystal M. Lange College of Nursing and Health Sciences, Program in Health System Nurse Specialist, University Center, MI 48710. Offers MSN. *Accreditation:* AACN. Part-time and evening/weekend programs available. *Students:* 25 part-time (all women); includes 3 minority (2 Black or African American, non-Hispanic/Latino; 1 Hispanic/Latino). Average age 39. 9 applicants, 78% accepted, 7 enrolled. In 2011, 6 master's awarded. *Degree requirements:* For master's, thesis optional. *Entrance requirements:* For master's, GRE. Additional exam requirements/recommendations for international students: Required—TOEFL (minimum score 525 paper-based; 237 computer-based; 92 iBT). *Application deadline:* Applications are processed on a rolling basis. Application fee: $25. Electronic applications accepted. *Expenses:* Tuition, state resident: full-time $8300; part-time $5333 per year. Tuition, nonresident: full-time $15,613; part-time $10,209 per year. *International tuition:* $15,631 full-time. *Financial support:* Federal Work-Study and scholarships/grants available. Support available to part-time students. Financial award application deadline: 4/1; financial award applicants required to submit FAFSA. *Unit head:* Dr. Sally Decker, Professor of Nursing, 989-964-4098, E-mail: decker@svsu.edu. *Application contact:* P. Laine Blasch, Graduate Recruitment Coordinator, 989-964-2182, Fax: 989-790-0180, E-mail: blasch@svsu.edu.

Saint Francis Medical Center College of Nursing, Graduate Programs, Peoria, IL 61603-3783. Offers child and family nurse practitioner (MSN); clinical nurse leader (MSN); family nurse practitioner (MSN); family psychiatric mental health nurse practitioner (MSN); medical-surgical nursing (MSN); neonatal nurse practitioner (MSN); nurse clinician (Post-Graduate Certificate); nurse educator (MSN, Post-Graduate Certificate); nursing (DNP); nursing management leadership (MSN). *Accreditation:* NLN. Part-time programs available. Postbaccalaureate distance learning degree programs offered (minimal on-campus study). *Faculty:* 6 full-time (all women), 5 part-time/adjunct (all women). *Students:* 26 full-time (25 women), 174 part-time (166 women); includes 19 minority (8 Black or African American, non-Hispanic/Latino; 1 American Indian or Alaska Native, non-Hispanic/Latino; 3 Asian, non-Hispanic/Latino; 6 Hispanic/Latino; 1 Native Hawaiian or other Pacific Islander, non-Hispanic/Latino). Average age 37. 123 applicants, 93% accepted, 93 enrolled. In 2011, 29 degrees awarded. *Degree requirements:* For master's, research experience, portfolio, practicum; for doctorate, practicum hours. *Entrance requirements:* For master's, nursing research, health assessment, graduate course work in statistics, RN license; for doctorate, master's degree in nursing, professional portfolio, graduate statistics, transcripts, RN license. Additional exam requirements/recommendations for international students: Required—TOEFL. *Application deadline:* For fall admission, 6/1 priority date for domestic students, 6/1 for international students; for spring admission, 11/15 priority date for domestic students, 11/15 for international students. Applications are processed on a rolling basis. Application fee: $50. Electronic applications accepted. *Expenses: Tuition:* Full-time $6120; part-time $510 per semester hour. *Required fees:* $300. *Financial support:* In 2011–12, 3 students received support. Scholarships/grants and tuition waivers (partial) available. Support available to part-time students. Financial award application deadline: 6/15; financial award applicants required to submit FAFSA. *Faculty research:* Outcome and curriculum planning, health promotion, NCLEX-RN results, decision-making program evaluation. *Unit head:* Dr. Patti A. Stockert, President of the College, 309-655-4124, Fax: 309-624-8973, E-mail: patricia.a.stockert@osfhealthcare.org. *Application contact:* Dr. Janice F. Boundy, Dean, 309-655-2230, Fax: 309-624-8973, E-mail: jan.f.boundy@osfhealthcare.org. Web site: http://www.sfmccon.edu/graduate-programs/.

Saint Joseph's College of Maine, Master of Science in Nursing Program, Standish, ME 04084. Offers administration (MSN); education (MSN); family nurse practitioner (MSN); nursing administration and leadership (Certificate); nursing and health care education (Certificate). *Accreditation:* AACN. Part-time programs available. Postbaccalaureate distance learning degree programs offered (no on-campus study). *Faculty:* 2 full-time (both women), 22 part-time/adjunct (20 women). *Students:* 768 part-time (665 women), includes 85 minority (48 Black or African American, non-Hispanic/Latino; 21 Asian, non-Hispanic/Latino; 16 Hispanic/Latino). Average age 43. In 2011, 26 master's awarded. *Entrance requirements:* For master's, MAT. *Application deadline:* Applications are processed on a rolling basis. Application fee: $50. Electronic applications accepted. One-time fee: $50. *Financial support:* Institutionally sponsored loans available. Support available to part-time students. Financial award applicants required to submit FAFSA. *Unit head:* Joyce Murphy, Program Director, 207-893-7841, Fax: 207-892-7423, E-mail: jmurphy@sjcme.edu. *Application contact:* Lynne Robinson, Director of Admissions, 800-752-4723, Fax: 207-892-7480, E-mail: info@sjcme.edu. Web site: http://online.sjcme.edu/master-science-nursing.php.

Saint Joseph's University, College of Arts and Sciences, Department of Health Services, Philadelphia, PA 19131-1395. Offers health administration (MS, Post-Master's Certificate); health care ethics (Post-Master's Certificate); health education (MS, Post-Master's Certificate); health informatics (Post-Master's Certificate); healthcare ethics (MS); long-term care administration (MS); nurse anesthesia (MS); school nurse certification (MS). Part-time and evening/weekend programs available. *Faculty:* 9 full-time (1 woman), 21 part-time/adjunct (11 women). *Students:* 76 full-time (53 women), 261 part-time (204 women); includes 106 minority (79 Black or African American, non-Hispanic/Latino; 2 American Indian or Alaska Native, non-Hispanic/Latino; 12 Asian, non-Hispanic/Latino; 10 Hispanic/Latino; 1 Native Hawaiian or other Pacific Islander, non-Hispanic/Latino; 2 Two or more races, non-Hispanic/Latino), 17 international. Average age 35. 143 applicants, 69% accepted, 91 enrolled. In 2011, 67 master's awarded. *Entrance requirements:* For master's, GRE (if GPA less than 2.75), 2 letters of recommendation, minimum GPA of 2.75, resume. Additional exam requirements/

recommendations for international students: Required—TOEFL (minimum score 550 paper-based; 213 computer-based; 79 iBT). *Application deadline:* For fall admission, 7/15 priority date for domestic students, 4/15 for international students; for winter admission, 1/15 for international students; for spring admission, 11/15 priority date for domestic students, 10/15 for international students. Applications are processed on a rolling basis. Application fee: $35. Electronic applications accepted. *Expenses: Tuition:* Part-time $735 per credit hour. Tuition and fees vary according to degree level and program. *Financial support:* Career-related internships or fieldwork and unspecified assistantships available. Financial award applicants required to submit FAFSA. *Unit head:* Nakia Henderson, Director, 610-660-2952, E-mail: nakia.henderson@sju.edu. *Application contact:* Kate McConnell, Director, Graduate College of Arts and Sciences Admissions and Retention, 610-660-3184, Fax: 610-660-3230, E-mail: kate.mcconnell@sju.edu.

Saint Joseph's University, College of Arts and Sciences, Program in Gerontological Services, Philadelphia, PA 19131-1395. Offers gerontological counseling (MS); gerontological services (Post-Master's Certificate); long-term care administration (MS). Part-time and evening/weekend programs available. *Faculty:* 1 (woman) full-time, 3 part-time/adjunct (all women). *Students:* 1 (woman) full-time, 13 part-time (all women); includes 5 minority (all Black or African American, non-Hispanic/Latino), 1 international. Average age 37. 9 applicants, 44% accepted, 3 enrolled. In 2011, 5 master's, 1 other advanced degree awarded. *Entrance requirements:* For master's, 2 letters of recommendation. Additional exam requirements/recommendations for international students: Required—TOEFL (minimum score 550 paper-based; 213 computer-based; 79 iBT). *Application deadline:* For fall admission, 7/15 priority date for domestic students, 4/15 for international students; for winter admission, 1/15 for international students; for spring admission, 11/15 priority date for domestic students, 10/15 for international students. Applications are processed on a rolling basis. Application fee: $35. Electronic applications accepted. *Expenses: Tuition:* Part-time $735 per credit hour. Tuition and fees vary according to degree level and program. *Financial support:* Fellowships available. Financial award applicants required to submit FAFSA. *Unit head:* Dr. Catherine Murray, Director, 610-660-1805, E-mail: cmurray@sju.edu. *Application contact:* Kate McConnell, Director, Graduate College of Arts and Sciences Admissions and Retention, 610-660-3184, Fax: 610-660-3230, E-mail: kate.mcconnell@sju.edu. Web site: http://www.sju.edu/academics/cas/grad/gerontological.

Saint Peter's University, School of Nursing, Nursing Program, Jersey City, NJ 07306-5997. Offers adult nurse practitioner (MSN, Certificate); advanced practice (DNP); case management (MSN, DNP). *Accreditation:* AACN. Part-time and evening/weekend programs available. *Entrance requirements:* Additional exam requirements/recommendations for international students: Required—TOEFL (minimum score 79 computer-based). Electronic applications accepted.

Saint Vincent College, Program in Health Services Leadership, Latrobe, PA 15650-2690. Offers MS.

Samford University, Ida V. Moffett School of Nursing, Birmingham, AL 35229. Offers advance practice (DNP); anesthesia (MSN); family nurse practitioner (MSN); nurse educator (MSN); nurse executive (DNP); nurse manager (MSN). *Accreditation:* AACN, AANA/CANAEP (one or more programs are accredited). Part-time programs available. Postbaccalaureate distance learning degree programs offered (minimal on-campus study). *Faculty:* 14 full-time (all women), 2 part-time/adjunct (0 women). *Students:* 226 full-time (152 women), 42 part-time (20 women); includes 43 minority (14 Black or African American, non-Hispanic/Latino; 4 American Indian or Alaska Native, non-Hispanic/Latino; 15 Asian, non-Hispanic/Latino; 9 Hispanic/Latino; 1 Native Hawaiian or other Pacific Islander, non-Hispanic/Latino), 2 international. Average age 39. 50 applicants, 88% accepted, 44 enrolled. In 2011, 95 master's, 14 doctorates awarded. *Median time to degree:* Of those who began their doctoral program in fall 2003, 100% received their degree in 8 years or less. *Degree requirements:* For master's and doctorate, capstone project with oral presentation. *Entrance requirements:* For master's, MAT; GRE (for nurse anesthesia). Additional exam requirements/recommendations for international students: Required—TOEFL (minimum score 550 paper-based; 213 computer-based; 80 iBT). *Application deadline:* For fall admission, 7/1 priority date for domestic students, 7/1 for international students; for spring admission, 10/1 priority date for domestic students, 10/1 for international students. Application fee: $65. Electronic applications accepted. *Expenses:* Contact institution. *Financial support:* In 2011–12, 166 students received support. Institutionally sponsored loans, scholarships/grants, and traineeships available. Financial award application deadline: 3/1; financial award applicants required to submit FAFSA. *Faculty research:* Issues in rural health care, vulnerable populations, genetics and disabilities in pediatrics, geriatrics, Parrish nursing research. *Unit head:* Dr. Nena F. Sanders, Dean, 205-726-2629, E-mail: nfsander@samford.edu. *Application contact:* Dr. Marian Carter, Director of Graduate Student Services, 205-726-2047, Fax: 205-726-4269, E-mail: mwcarter@samford.edu. Web site: http://samford.edu/nursing.

Samuel Merritt University, School of Nursing, Oakland, CA 94609-3108. Offers case management (MSN); family nurse practitioner (MSN, Certificate); nurse anesthetist (MSN, Certificate); nursing (MSN, DNP). *Accreditation:* AACN; AANA/CANAEP (one or more programs are accredited). Part-time and evening/weekend programs available. *Degree requirements:* For master's, thesis or alternative. *Entrance requirements:* For master's, minimum GPA of 2.5 in science, 3.0 overall; previous course work in statistics; current RN license. Additional exam requirements/recommendations for international students: Required—TOEFL. *Faculty research:* Gerontology, community health, maternal-child health, sexually transmitted diseases, substance abuse, oncology.

San Francisco State University, Division of Graduate Studies, College of Health and Human Services, School of Nursing, San Francisco, CA 94132-1722. Offers clinical nurse specialist (MS); community/public health nursing (MS); family nurse practitioner (MS, Certificate); nursing administration (MS); nursing education (MS). *Accreditation:* AACN. Part-time programs available. *Application deadline:* Applications are processed on a rolling basis. *Financial support:* Career-related internships or fieldwork available. *Unit head:* Dr. Lynette Landry, Director, 415-338-1802, E-mail: llandry@sfsu.edu. *Application contact:* Dr. Mary-Ann van Dam, Associate Director, 415-338-1802, E-mail: vandam@sfsu.edu. Web site: http://nursing.sfsu.edu.

San Jose State University, Graduate Studies and Research, College of Applied Sciences and Arts, School of Nursing, San Jose, CA 95192-0001. Offers gerontology nurse practitioner (MS); nursing (Certificate); nursing administration (MS); nursing education (MS). *Accreditation:* AACN. Part-time and evening/weekend programs available. *Degree requirements:* For master's, thesis. *Entrance requirements:* For master's, BS in nursing, RN license. Electronic applications accepted. *Faculty research:* Nurse-managed clinics, computers in nursing.

Seattle Pacific University, MS in Nursing Program, Seattle, WA 98119-1997. Offers administration (MSN); adult/gerontology nurse practitioner (MSN); clinical nurse specialist (MSN); family nurse practitioner (MSN, Certificate); informatics (MSN); nurse educator (MSN). *Accreditation:* AACN. Part-time programs available. *Degree requirements:* For master's, thesis. Electronic applications accepted. *Expenses:* Contact institution.

Nursing and Healthcare Administration

Seton Hall University, College of Nursing, South Orange, NJ 07079-2697. Offers advanced practice in primary health care (MSN, DNP), including adult/gerontological nurse practitioner, pediatric nurse practitioner; entry into practice (MSN); health systems administration (MSN, DNP); nursing (PhD); nursing case management (MSN); nursing education (MA); school nurse (MSN); MSN/MA. *Accreditation:* AACN. Part-time programs available. Postbaccalaureate distance learning degree programs offered (minimal on-campus study). *Faculty:* 10 full-time (all women), 3 part-time/adjunct (1 woman). *Students:* 12 full-time (11 women), 217 part-time (197 women); includes 38 minority (15 Black or African American, non-Hispanic/Latino; 1 American Indian or Alaska Native, non-Hispanic/Latino; 12 Asian, non-Hispanic/Latino; 10 Hispanic/Latino). 180 applicants, 51% accepted, 82 enrolled. *Degree requirements:* For master's, research project; for doctorate, dissertation or scholarly project. *Entrance requirements:* For doctorate, GRE (waived for students with GPA of 3.5 or higher). Additional exam requirements/recommendations for international students: Required—TOEFL. *Application deadline:* For fall admission, 4/15 priority date for domestic students. Applications are processed on a rolling basis. Electronic applications accepted. *Expenses: Tuition:* Part-time $1033 per credit hour. *Required fees:* $85 per semester. *Financial support:* Institutionally sponsored loans, scholarships/grants, traineeships, tuition waivers (partial), and unspecified assistantships available. Support available to part-time students. Financial award applicants required to submit FAFSA. *Faculty research:* Parent/child, adult, and gerontological nursing; breast cancer; families of children with HIV; parish nursing. *Unit head:* Dr. Phyllis Shanley Hansell, Dean, 973-761-9014, E-mail: phyllis.hansell@shu.edu. *Application contact:* Kristyn Kent Wuillermin, Director of Strategic Alliances, Marketing and Enrollment, 973-761-9291, Fax: 973-761-9607, E-mail: kristyn.kent@shu.edu.

Simmons College, School of Nursing and Health Sciences, Boston, MA 02115. Offers didactic dietetics (Certificate); health professions education (CAGS); nursing (MS); nursing administration (MS); nursing practice (DNP); nutrition (MS, Certificate); physical therapy (DPT); sports nutrition (Certificate); sports nutrition/didactic dietetics (Certificate); MS/Certificate. *Unit head:* Dr. Judy Beal, Dean, 617-521-2139, Fax: 617-521-3137, E-mail: judy.beal@simmons.edu. *Application contact:* Carmen Fortin, Assistant Dean/Director of Admission, 617-521-2651, Fax: 617-521-3137, E-mail: gshsadm@simmons.edu. Web site: http://www.simmons.edu/snhs/.

Southeastern Louisiana University, College of Nursing and Health Sciences, School of Nursing, Hammond, LA 70402. Offers adult psychiatric/mental health nurse practitioner/clinical nurse specialist (MSN); education (MSN); nurse executive (MSN); nurse practitioner (MSN). *Accreditation:* AACN. Part-time and evening/weekend programs available. *Faculty:* 12 full-time (11 women), 7 part-time/adjunct (4 women). *Students:* 17 full-time (16 women), 108 part-time (94 women); includes 12 minority (8 Black or African American, non-Hispanic/Latino; 2 Asian, non-Hispanic/Latino; 1 Hispanic/Latino; 1 Two or more races, non-Hispanic/Latino), 1 international. Average age 35. 50 applicants, 100% accepted, 29 enrolled. In 2011, 27 degrees awarded. *Degree requirements:* For master's, thesis. *Entrance requirements:* For master's, GRE (verbal and quantitative), baccalaureate degree in nursing from accredited undergraduate nursing program; minimum GPA of 2.7; all transcripts from undergraduate school and any work attempted at the graduate level; curriculum vitae; valid Louisiana Registered Nurse license; letters of recommendation; letter of intent/statement of purpose. Additional exam requirements/recommendations for international students: Required—TOEFL (minimum score 500 paper-based; 173 computer-based; 61 iBT). *Application deadline:* For fall admission, 7/15 priority date for domestic students, 6/1 for international students; for spring admission, 12/1 priority date for domestic students, 10/1 for international students. Applications are processed on a rolling basis. Application fee: $20 ($30 for international students). Electronic applications accepted. *Expenses:* Tuition, state resident: full-time $3977; part-time $283 per semester hour. Tuition, nonresident: full-time $13,482; part-time $811 per semester hour. *Financial support:* Federal Work-Study, institutionally sponsored loans, scholarships/grants, traineeships, and unspecified assistantships available. Support available to part-time students. Financial award application deadline: 5/1; financial award applicants required to submit FAFSA. *Faculty research:* Gender issues, LGBT issues, occupational health/safety, accelerated students, caring development. *Total annual research expenditures:* $245,268. *Unit head:* Dr. Lorinda Sealy, Graduate Coordinator, 985-549-5045, Fax: 985-549-5087, E-mail: lorinda.sealy@selu.edu. *Application contact:* Sandra Meyers, Graduate Admissions Analyst, 985-549-5620, Fax: 985-549-5632, E-mail: admissions@selu.edu. Web site: http://www.selu.edu/acad_research/depts/nurs.

Southern Adventist University, School of Nursing, Collegedale, TN 37315-0370. Offers acute care nurse practitioner (MSN); adult nurse practitioner (MSN); family nurse practitioner (MSN); nurse educator (MSN); MSN/MSBA. *Accreditation:* NLN. Part-time programs available. *Degree requirements:* For master's, thesis or project. *Entrance requirements:* For master's, RN license. Additional exam requirements/recommendations for international students: Required—TOEFL (minimum score 600 paper-based; 250 computer-based). Electronic applications accepted. *Faculty research:* Pain management, ethics, corporate wellness, caring spirituality, stress.

Southern Connecticut State University, School of Graduate Studies, School of Health and Human Services, Department of Nursing, New Haven, CT 06515-1355. Offers nursing administration (MSN); nursing education (MSN). *Accreditation:* AACN; AANA/CANAEP. Part-time and evening/weekend programs available. *Faculty:* 3 full-time (all women), 1 (woman) part-time/adjunct. *Students:* 9 full-time (8 women), 23 part-time (19 women); includes 3 minority (1 Black or African American, non-Hispanic/Latino; 1 Asian, non-Hispanic/Latino; 1 Hispanic/Latino). 120 applicants, 12% accepted, 11 enrolled. In 2011, 1 master's awarded. *Degree requirements:* For master's, thesis. *Entrance requirements:* For master's, GRE, MAT, interview, minimum QPA of 2.8, RN license, minimum 1 year of professional nursing experience. *Application deadline:* For fall admission, 7/15 priority date for domestic students. Applications are processed on a rolling basis. Application fee: $50. Electronic applications accepted. *Expenses:* Tuition, state resident: full-time $5137; part-time $413 per credit. *Required fees:* $4008; $55 per term. *Financial support:* Application deadline: 4/15; applicants required to submit FAFSA. *Unit head:* Dr. Lisa Rebeschi, Chairperson, 203-392-6485, E-mail: rebeschil1@southernct.edu. *Application contact:* Dr. Antonia Nelson, Graduate Coordinator, 203-392-6480, Fax: 203-392-6493, E-mail: nelsona13@southernct.edu.

Southern Illinois University Edwardsville, Graduate School, School of Nursing, Program in Health Care and Nursing Administration, Edwardsville, IL 62026-0001. Offers MS, Post-Master's Certificate. Part-time programs available. *Students:* 13 part-time (12 women). 14 applicants, 0% accepted. In 2011, 2 master's awarded. *Degree requirements:* For master's, comprehensive exam. *Entrance requirements:* For master's, RN licensure, minimum undergraduate nursing GPA of 3.0, BS from CCNE- or NLNAC-accredited program. Additional exam requirements/recommendations for international students: Required—TOEFL (minimum score 550 paper-based; 213 computer-based; 79 iBT), IELTS (minimum score 6.5). *Application deadline:* For fall admission, 3/1 for domestic and international students. Application fee: $30. Electronic applications accepted. Tuition and fees vary according to course load and program. *Financial support:* Institutionally sponsored loans, scholarships/grants, and unspecified assistantships available. Financial award application deadline: 3/1; financial award applicants required to submit FAFSA. *Unit head:* Dr. Kathy Ketchum, Director, 618-650-3936, E-mail: kketchu@siue.edu. *Application contact:* Dr. Kathy Ketchum, Director, 618-650-3936, E-mail: kketchu@siue.edu. Web site: http://www.siue.edu/nursing/graduate.

Southern Nazarene University, Graduate College, School of Nursing, Bethany, OK 73008. Offers nursing education (MS); nursing leadership (MS). *Accreditation:* AACN. Part-time and evening/weekend programs available. *Degree requirements:* For master's, thesis. *Entrance requirements:* For master's, minimum undergraduate cumulative GPA of 3.0; baccalaureate degree in nursing from nationally-accredited program; current unencumbered registered nurse licensure in Oklahoma or eligibility for same; documentation of basic computer skills; basic statistics course; statement of professional goals; three letters of recommendation. Additional exam requirements/recommendations for international students: Required—TOEFL (minimum score 550 paper-based; 213 computer-based). *Expenses: Tuition:* Full-time $17,009; part-time $639 per credit hour. *Required fees:* $2668. *Unit head:* Dr. Katie Sigler, Interim Chair, 405-717-6217, E-mail: ksigler@snu.edu. *Application contact:* Dr. Mary Hibbert, Program Director, 405-491-6612, Fax: 405-491-6302, E-mail: mhibbert@snu.edu. Web site: http://snu.edu/school-of-nursing.

Southern University and Agricultural and Mechanical College, School of Nursing, Baton Rouge, LA 70813. Offers educator/administrator (PhD); family health nursing (MSN); family nurse practitioner (Post Master's Certificate); geriatric nurse practitioner/gerontology (PhD). *Accreditation:* AACN. Part-time programs available. *Degree requirements:* For master's, comprehensive exam, thesis; for doctorate, comprehensive exam, thesis/dissertation. *Entrance requirements:* For master's, GRE General Test, BSN, minimum GPA of 2.7; for doctorate, GRE General Test; for Post Master's Certificate, MSN. Additional exam requirements/recommendations for international students: Required—TOEFL (minimum score 525 paper-based; 193 computer-based). *Faculty research:* Health promotions, vulnerable populations, (community-based) cardiovascular participating research, health disparities chronic diseases, care of the elderly.

Spalding University, Graduate Studies, College of Health and Natural Sciences, School of Nursing, Louisville, KY 40203-2188. Offers adult nurse practitioner (MSN); family nurse practitioner (MSN); leadership in nursing and healthcare (MSN); pediatric nurse practitioner (MSN). *Accreditation:* AACN. Part-time and evening/weekend programs available. *Faculty:* 6 full-time (all women), 5 part-time/adjunct (all women). *Students:* 90 full-time (82 women), 24 part-time (all women); includes 21 minority (16 Black or African American, non-Hispanic/Latino; 3 Asian, non-Hispanic/Latino; 1 Hispanic/Latino; 1 Native Hawaiian or other Pacific Islander, non-Hispanic/Latino). Average age 36. 85 applicants, 24% accepted, 15 enrolled. In 2011, 23 master's awarded. *Degree requirements:* For master's, comprehensive exam (for some programs), thesis. *Entrance requirements:* For master's, GRE General Test, BSN or bachelor's degree and RN licensure. Additional exam requirements/recommendations for international students: Required—TOEFL (minimum score 535 paper-based; 203 computer-based). *Application deadline:* For fall admission, 3/1 priority date for domestic students. Applications are processed on a rolling basis. Application fee: $30. *Expenses: Tuition:* Full-time $12,438. Tuition and fees vary according to course load, degree level and program. *Financial support:* In 2011–12, 21 students received support, including 1 research assistantship with partial tuition reimbursement available (averaging $4,260 per year); career-related internships or fieldwork, scholarships/grants, and traineeships also available. Support available to part-time students. Financial award application deadline: 3/15; financial award applicants required to submit FAFSA. *Faculty research:* Nurse educational administration, gerontology, bioterrorism, healthcare ethics, leadership. *Unit head:* Dr. Paula Travis, Chair, 502-873-4298, E-mail: clewis@spalding.edu. *Application contact:* Dr. Pam King, 502-873-4292, E-mail: pking@spalding.edu. Web site: http://www.spalding.edu/nursing/.

Spring Hill College, Graduate Programs, Program in Nursing, Mobile, AL 36608-1791. Offers clinical nurse leader (MSN). *Accreditation:* AACN. Part-time and evening/weekend programs available. Postbaccalaureate distance learning degree programs offered (no on-campus study). *Faculty:* 4 full-time (all women). *Students:* 27 part-time (all women); includes 13 minority (all Black or African American, non-Hispanic/Latino). Average age 44. In 2011, 18 master's, 2 other advanced degrees awarded. *Degree requirements:* For master's, comprehensive exam, capstone courses, completion of program within 6 calendar years; for Post-Master's Certificate, 460 clinical integration hours. *Entrance requirements:* For master's, RN license in state where practicing nursing; 1 year of clinical nursing experience; work in clinical setting or have access to health care facility for clinical integration/research; 3 written references; employer verification; resume; 500-word essay explaining how becoming a CNL will help applicant achieve personal and professional goals; for Post-Master's Certificate, RN license; master's degree in nursing. Additional exam requirements/recommendations for international students: Required—TOEFL (minimum score 550 paper-based; 213 computer-based; 80 iBT), IELTS (minimum score 6.5), CPE or CAE (minimum score C), Michigan English Language Assessment Battery (minimum score 90). *Application deadline:* For fall admission, 8/1 priority date for domestic students, 8/1 for international students; for spring admission, 12/1 priority date for domestic students, 12/1 for international students. Applications are processed on a rolling basis. Application fee: $25 ($35 for international students). Electronic applications accepted. *Expenses:* Contact institution. *Financial support:* Applicants required to submit FAFSA. *Unit head:* Dr. Ola H. Fox, Director, 251-380-4486, Fax: 251-460-4495, E-mail: ofox@shc.edu. *Application contact:* Donna B. Tarasavage, Director of Admissions, Graduate and Continuing Studies, 251-380-3067, Fax: 251-460-2190, E-mail: dtarasavage@shc.edu. Web site: http://www.shc.edu/grad/academics/nursing.

State University of New York Institute of Technology, Program in Nursing Administration, Utica, NY 13504-3050. Offers MS, CAS. *Accreditation:* AACN. Part-time programs available. *Degree requirements:* For master's, thesis or project. *Entrance requirements:* For master's, GRE General Test (if undergraduate GPA less than 3.3), minimum GPA of 3.0, 2 letters of recommendation. Additional exam requirements/recommendations for international students: Required—TOEFL (minimum score 550 paper-based; 213 computer-based). *Faculty research:* Community health, critical thinking, leadership, nursing informatics, child obesity, evidence-based practice.

Teachers College, Columbia University, Graduate Faculty of Education, Department of Organization and Leadership, Program in Nurse Executive, New York, NY 10027. Offers administration studies (MA); nurse executive (Ed D); professional studies (MA). *Faculty:* 1 (woman) full-time, 13 part-time/adjunct (10 women). *Students:* 35 full-time (33 women), 14 part-time (13 women); includes 25 minority (17 Black or African American, non-Hispanic/Latino; 5 Asian, non-Hispanic/Latino; 2 Hispanic/Latino; 1 Two or more races, non-Hispanic/Latino), 1 international. Average age 46. 15 applicants, 87% accepted, 11 enrolled. In 2011, 3 degrees awarded. *Degree requirements:* For master's, capstone project; for doctorate, thesis/dissertation. *Entrance requirements:* For master's, BSN, minimum cumulative GPA of 3.0 from the undergraduate program, one year of continuous post-baccalaureate full-time clinical nursing practice experience in a particular area; for doctorate, GRE General Test or MAT, BSN, nursing license, graduate degree and/or minimum of 36 graduate points/credits, one year of continuous post-baccalaureate full-time nursing or healthcare management experience. Additional exam requirements/recommendations for international students: Required—TOEFL

(minimum score 600 paper-based). Application fee: $65. *Financial support:* Career-related internships or fieldwork, Federal Work-Study, institutionally sponsored loans, traineeships, and tuition waivers (full and partial) available. Support available to part-time students. Financial award application deadline: 2/1. *Faculty research:* Health care administration, health care law, nursing administration and education, consumer satisfaction with health care. *Unit head:* Prof. Elaine La Monica Rigolosi, Coordinator, 212-678-3812, E-mail: ell9@columbia.edu. *Application contact:* Debbie Lesperance, Assistant Director of Admission, 212-678-3710, Fax: 212-678-4171. Web site: http://www.tc.edu/o%26l/NurseExec/.

Tennessee Technological University, Whitson-Hester School of Nursing, Cookeville, TN 38505. Offers family nurse practitioner (MSN); informatics (MSN); nursing administration (MSN); nursing education (MSN). Part-time and evening/weekend programs available. Postbaccalaureate distance learning degree programs offered (no on-campus study). *Students:* 3 full-time (2 women), 43 part-time (39 women); includes 3 minority (1 Black or African American, non-Hispanic/Latino; 2 Hispanic/Latino). 48 applicants, 46% accepted, 15 enrolled. In 2011, 13 master's awarded. *Degree requirements:* For master's, comprehensive exam, thesis or alternative. *Entrance requirements:* Additional exam requirements/recommendations for international students: Required—TOEFL (minimum score 550 paper-based; 79 iBT), IELTS (minimum score 5.5), Pearson Test of English Academic. *Application deadline:* For fall admission, 8/1 for domestic students, 5/1 for international students; for spring admission, 12/1 for domestic students, 10/1 for international students. Application fee: $25 ($30 for international students). Electronic applications accepted. *Expenses:* Tuition, state resident: full-time $8094; part-time $422 per credit hour. Tuition, nonresident: full-time $20,574; part-time $1046 per credit hour. *Financial support:* Application deadline: 4/1. *Unit head:* Dr. Sherry Gaines, Director, 931-372-3203, Fax: 931-372-6244, E-mail: sgaines@tntech.edu. *Application contact:* Shelia K. Kendrick, Coordinator of Graduate Admissions, 931-372-3808, Fax: 931-372-3497, E-mail: skendrick@tntech.edu.

Texas A&M University–Corpus Christi, Graduate Studies and Research, College of Nursing and Health Sciences, Corpus Christi, TX 78412-5503. Offers clinical nurse specialist (MSN); family nurse practitioner (MSN); health care administration (MSN); leadership in nursing systems (MSN). *Accreditation:* AACN. Part-time and evening/weekend programs available. *Degree requirements:* For master's, comprehensive exam, thesis (for some programs). *Entrance requirements:* For master's, GRE General Test. Additional exam requirements/recommendations for international students: Required—TOEFL. Electronic applications accepted.

Texas Christian University, Harris College of Nursing and Health Sciences, Program in Nursing, Fort Worth, TX 76129-0002. Offers advanced practice registered nurse (DNP); clinical nurse leader (MSN); clinical nurse specialist: adult/gerontology nursing (MSN); clinical nurse specialist: pediatric nursing (MSN); nursing administration (DNP); nursing education (MSN). *Accreditation:* AACN; AANA/CANAEP (one or more programs are accredited). Part-time programs available. Postbaccalaureate distance learning degree programs offered (no on-campus study). *Faculty:* 18 full-time (16 women), 2 part-time/adjunct (both women). *Students:* 2 full-time (both women), 105 part-time (96 women); includes 16 minority (8 Black or African American, non-Hispanic/Latino; 4 Asian, non-Hispanic/Latino; 2 Hispanic/Latino; 1 Native Hawaiian or other Pacific Islander, non-Hispanic/Latino; 1 Two or more races, non-Hispanic/Latino), 1 international. Average age 44. 58 applicants, 93% accepted, 46 enrolled. In 2011, 11 master's, 21 doctorates awarded. *Degree requirements:* For master's and doctorate, professional project. *Entrance requirements:* For master's, GRE General Test or MAT, 3 letters of reference, 2 years preferred full-time experience as registered nurse, current nursing license, minimum GPA of 3.0; for doctorate, APRN recognition (national certification), minimum GPA of 3.0, 3 professional references, essay, 2 years post-master's experience (preferrred). Additional exam requirements/recommendations for international students: Required—TOEFL, Spoken English Test for DNP. *Expenses: Tuition:* Full-time $20,250; part-time $1125 per credit hour. Part-time tuition and fees vary according to course load and program. *Financial support:* In 2011–12, teaching assistantships (averaging $5,000 per year) were awarded; tuition waivers also available. *Unit head:* Dr. Pamela Frable, Associate Dean and Director of Nursing, 817-257-5840, E-mail: p.frable@tcu.edu. *Application contact:* Dr. Kathy Baker, Director of Graduate Studies and Director of DNP Program, 817-257-6726, E-mail: kathy.baker@tcu.edu. Web site: http://www.nursing.tcu.edu/graduate.asp.

Texas Tech University Health Sciences Center, School of Nursing, Lubbock, TX 79430. Offers acute care nurse practitioner (MSN, Certificate); administration (MSN); advanced practice (DNP); education (MSN); executive leadership (DNP); family nurse practitioner (MSN, Certificate); geriatric nurse practitioner (MSN, Certificate); pediatric nurse practitioner (MSN, Certificate). *Accreditation:* AACN. Part-time programs available. Postbaccalaureate distance learning degree programs offered (minimal on-campus study). *Degree requirements:* For master's, thesis optional. *Entrance requirements:* For master's, minimum GPA of 3.0, 3 letters of reference, BSN, RN license; for Certificate, minimum GPA of 3.0, 3 letters of reference, RN license. Additional exam requirements/recommendations for international students: Required—TOEFL (minimum score 550 paper-based; 213 computer-based). *Faculty research:* Diabetes/obesity, nurse competency, disease management, intervention and measurements, health disparities.

Texas Woman's University, Graduate School, College of Nursing, Denton, TX 76201. Offers acute care nurse practitioner (MS); adult health clinical nurse specialist (MS); adult health nurse practitioner (MS); child health clinical nurse specialist (MS); clinical nurse leader (MS); family nurse practitioner (MS); health systems management (MS); nursing education (MS); nursing practice (DNP); nursing science (PhD); pediatric nurse practitioner (MS); women's health clinical nurse specialist (MS); women's health nurse practitioner (MS). *Accreditation:* AACN. Part-time programs available. Postbaccalaureate distance learning degree programs offered. *Faculty:* 70 full-time (69 women), 7 part-time/adjunct (all women). *Students:* 87 full-time (78 women), 870 part-time (815 women); includes 489 minority (235 Black or African American, non-Hispanic/Latino; 5 American Indian or Alaska Native, non-Hispanic/Latino; 169 Asian, non-Hispanic/Latino; 78 Hispanic/Latino; 2 Native Hawaiian or other Pacific Islander, non-Hispanic/Latino), 19 international. Average age 38. 368 applicants, 71% accepted, 205 enrolled. In 2011, 147 master's, 21 doctorates awarded. *Degree requirements:* For master's, comprehensive exam, thesis or alternative; for doctorate, comprehensive exam, thesis/dissertation. *Entrance requirements:* For master's, GRE or MAT, minimum GPA of 3.0 on last 60 hours in undergraduate nursing degree and overall, RN license, BS in nursing, basic statistics course; for doctorate, GRE (preferred minimum score 153 [500 old version] Verbal, 144 [500 old version] Quantitative, 4 Analytical), MS in nursing, minimum preferred GPA of 3.5, RN license, statistics, 2 letters of reference, curriculum vitae, graduate nursing-theory course, graduate research course, statement of professional goals and research interests. Additional exam requirements/recommendations for international students: Required—TOEFL (minimum score 550 paper-based; 213 computer-based; 79 iBT). *Application deadline:* For fall admission, 5/1 priority date for domestic students, 3/1 for international students; for spring admission, 9/15 priority date for domestic students, 7/1 for international students. Applications are processed on a rolling basis. Application fee: $50 ($75 for international students). Electronic applications accepted. *Expenses:* Tuition, state resident: full-time $3834; part-time $213 per credit hour. Tuition, nonresident: full-time $9468; part-time $526 per credit hour. *Required fees:* $213 per credit hour. Tuition and fees vary according to course load. *Financial support:* In 2011–12, 149 students received support, including 10 research assistantships (averaging $12,942 per year), 1 teaching assistantship (averaging $12,942 per year); career-related internships or fieldwork, Federal Work-Study, institutionally sponsored loans, scholarships/grants, traineeships, health care benefits, and unspecified assistantships also available. Support available to part-time students. Financial award application deadline: 3/1; financial award applicants required to submit FAFSA. *Faculty research:* Screening, prevention, and treatment for intimate partner violence; needs of adolescents during childbirth intervention; a network analysis decision tool for nurse managers (Social Network Analysis); support for adolescents with implantable cardioverter defibrillators; informatics: nurse staffing, safety, quality, and financial data as they relate to patient care outcomes; prevention and treatment of obesity; improving infant outcomes related to premature birth. *Total annual research expenditures:* $462,088. *Unit head:* Dr. Patricia Holden-Huchton, Interim Dean, 940-898-2401, Fax: 940-898-2437, E-mail: nursing@twu.edu. *Application contact:* Dr. Samuel Wheeler, Assistant Director of Admissions, 940-898-3188, Fax: 940-898-3081, E-mail: wheelersr@twu.edu. Web site: http://www.twu.edu/nursing/.

Trident University International, College of Health Sciences, Program in Health Sciences, Cypress, CA 90630. Offers clinical research administration (MS, Certificate); emergency and disaster management (MS, Certificate); environmental health science (Certificate); health care administration (PhD); health care management (MS), including health informatics; health education (MS, Certificate); health informatics (Certificate); health sciences (PhD); international health (MS); international health: educator or researcher option (PhD); international health: practitioner option (PhD); law and expert witness studies (MS, Certificate); public health (MS); quality assurance (Certificate). Part-time and evening/weekend programs available. Postbaccalaureate distance learning degree programs offered (no on-campus study). *Degree requirements:* For doctorate, comprehensive exam, thesis/dissertation, defense of dissertation. *Entrance requirements:* For master's, minimum GPA of 2.5 (students with GPA 3.0 or greater may transfer up to 30% of graduate level credits); for doctorate, minimum GPA of 3.4, curriculum vitae, course work in research methods or statistics. Additional exam requirements/recommendations for international students: Required—TOEFL. Electronic applications accepted.

Union University, School of Nursing, Jackson, TN 38305-3697. Offers executive leadership (DNP); nurse anesthesia (DNP); nurse anesthetist (PMC); nurse practitioner (DNP); nursing education (MSN, PMC). *Accreditation:* AACN; AANA/CANAEP. *Degree requirements:* For master's, thesis or alternative. *Entrance requirements:* For master's, GRE, 3 letters of reference, bachelor's degree in nursing, minimum GPA of 3.0. Additional exam requirements/recommendations for international students: Required—TOEFL (minimum score 560 paper-based; 220 computer-based). Electronic applications accepted. *Faculty research:* Children's health, occupational rehabilitation, informatics, health promotion.

United States University, School of Nursing, Cypress, CA 90630. Offers administrator (MSN); educator (MSN).

Universidad Metropolitana, School of Health Sciences, Department of Nursing, San Juan, PR 00928-1150. Offers case management (Certificate); nursing (MSN); oncology nursing (Certificate). *Accreditation:* NLN.

University at Buffalo, the State University of New York, Graduate School, School of Nursing, Buffalo, NY 14214. Offers adult clinical nurse specialist (DNP); adult nurse practitioner (DNP); family nurse practitioner (DNP); health care systems and leadership (MS); nurse anesthetist (DNP); nursing (PhD); nursing education (Certificate); post-master's track (DNP); psychiatric mental health nurse practitioner (DNP). *Accreditation:* AACN; AANA/CANAEP (one or more programs are accredited). Part-time programs available. Postbaccalaureate distance learning degree programs offered (minimal on-campus study). *Faculty:* 29 full-time (25 women), 18 part-time/adjunct (17 women). *Students:* 101 full-time (76 women), 100 part-time (90 women); includes 19 minority (10 Black or African American, non-Hispanic/Latino; 2 American Indian or Alaska Native, non-Hispanic/Latino; 2 Asian, non-Hispanic/Latino; 2 Hispanic/Latino; 3 Native Hawaiian or other Pacific Islander, non-Hispanic/Latino), 34 international. Average age 34. 342 applicants, 26% accepted, 67 enrolled. In 2011, 51 master's, 3 doctorates awarded. *Median time to degree:* Of those who began their doctoral program in fall 2003, 75% received their degree in 8 years or less. *Degree requirements:* For master's, thesis optional, comprehensive exams or project; for doctorate, comprehensive exam (for some programs), capstone (for DNP), dissertation (for PhD). *Entrance requirements:* For doctorate, GRE or MAT, minimum GPA of 3.0 (3.25 for PhD), RN license, BS or MS in nursing, 3 references, writing sample; for Certificate, interview, minimum GPA of 3.0 or GRE General Test, RN license, MS in nursing. Additional exam requirements/recommendations for international students: Required—TOEFL (minimum score 550 paper-based; 213 computer-based; 79 iBT), IELTS (minimum score 6.5). *Application deadline:* For fall admission, 8/15 for domestic students, 4/1 for international students; for spring admission, 12/15 for domestic students, 10/1 for international students. Application fee: $75. Electronic applications accepted. *Financial support:* In 2011–12, 80 students received support, including 6 fellowships with full tuition reimbursements available (averaging $17,000 per year), 3 research assistantships with full tuition reimbursements available (averaging $10,600 per year), 5 teaching assistantships with full tuition reimbursements available (averaging $10,600 per year); scholarships/grants, traineeships, health care benefits, and unspecified assistantships also available. Financial award application deadline: 3/15; financial award applicants required to submit FAFSA. *Faculty research:* Oncology, palliative care, gerontology, addictions, mental health, community wellness. *Total annual research expenditures:* $1.3 million. *Unit head:* Dr. Marsha L. Lewis, Dean and Professor, 716-829-2533, Fax: 716-829-2566, E-mail: ubnursingdean@buffalo.edu. *Application contact:* Dr. David J. Lang, Director of Student Affairs, 716-829-2537, Fax: 716-829-2067, E-mail: nursing@buffalo.edu. Web site: http://nursing.buffalo.edu/.

University of Central Florida, College of Nursing, Orlando, FL 32816. Offers adult-gerontology clinical nurse specialist (Post-Master's Certificate); adult-gerontology nurse practitioner (Post-Master's Certificate); clinical nurse leader (Post-Master's Certificate); family nurse practitioner (Post-Master's Certificate); nursing (MSN, PhD); nursing education (Post-Master's Certificate); nursing practice (DNP). *Accreditation:* AACN. Part-time and evening/weekend programs available. *Faculty:* 44 full-time (39 women), 72 part-time/adjunct (71 women). *Students:* 75 full-time (68 women), 350 part-time (332 women); includes 109 minority (54 Black or African American, non-Hispanic/Latino; 1 American Indian or Alaska Native, non-Hispanic/Latino; 19 Asian, non-Hispanic/Latino; 33 Hispanic/Latino; 1 Native Hawaiian or other Pacific Islander, non-Hispanic/Latino; 1 Two or more races, non-Hispanic/Latino), 5 international. Average age 40. 203 applicants, 60% accepted, 98 enrolled. In 2011, 110 master's, 17 doctorates, 11 other advanced degrees awarded. *Degree requirements:* For master's, thesis or alternative. *Entrance requirements:* For master's, GRE General Test, minimum GPA of 3.0 in last 60 hours. Additional exam requirements/recommendations for international students: Required—TOEFL. *Application deadline:* For fall admission, 2/15 for domestic students; for spring admission, 9/15 for domestic students. Application fee: $30. Electronic

applications accepted. *Expenses:* Tuition, state resident: part-time $277.08 per credit hour. Tuition, nonresident: part-time $277.08 per credit hour. Part-time tuition and fees vary according to degree level and program. *Financial support:* In 2011–12, 92 students received support, including 92 fellowships with partial tuition reimbursements available (averaging $1,100 per year), 2 teaching assistantships with partial tuition reimbursements available (averaging $8,100 per year); research assistantships with partial tuition reimbursements available, career-related internships or fieldwork, Federal Work-Study, institutionally sponsored loans, traineeships, and unspecified assistantships also available. Financial award application deadline: 3/1; financial award applicants required to submit FAFSA. *Unit head:* Dr. Jean D. Leuner, Dean, 407-823-5496, Fax: 407-823-5675, E-mail: jean.leuner@ucf.edu. *Application contact:* Barbara Rodriguez, Director, Admissions and Registration, 407-823-2766, Fax: 407-823-6442, E-mail: gradadmissions@ucf.edu. Web site: http://nursing.ucf.edu/.

University of Cincinnati, Graduate School, College of Nursing, Cincinnati, OH 45221-0038. Offers clinical nurse specialist (MSN), including adult health, community health, neonatal, nursing administration, occupational health, pediatric health, psychiatric nursing, women's health; nurse anesthesia (MSN); nurse midwifery (MSN); nurse practitioner (MSN), including acute care, ambulatory care, family, family/psychiatric, women's health; nursing (PhD); MBA/MSN. *Accreditation:* AACN; AANA/CANAEP (one or more programs are accredited); ACNM/ACME. Part-time programs available. Postbaccalaureate distance learning degree programs offered (no on-campus study). Terminal master's awarded for partial completion of doctoral program. *Degree requirements:* For master's, thesis or alternative; for doctorate, comprehensive exam, thesis/dissertation. *Entrance requirements:* For master's and doctorate, GRE General Test. Additional exam requirements/recommendations for international students: Required—TOEFL (minimum score 520 paper-based; 190 computer-based). Electronic applications accepted. *Faculty research:* Substance abuse, injury and violence, symptom management.

University of Colorado at Colorado Springs, Beth-El College of Nursing and Health Sciences, Colorado Springs, CO 80933-7150. Offers adult health nurse practitioner and clinical specialist (MSN); family practitioner (MSN), including community clinical specialist, forensic clinical specialist, holistic clinical specialist; neonatal nurse practitioner and clinical specialist (MSN); nursing administration (MSN); nursing practice (DNP); women nurse practitioner (MSN). *Accreditation:* AACN. Part-time programs available. Postbaccalaureate distance learning degree programs offered (minimal on-campus study). *Faculty:* 31 full-time (28 women), 6 part-time/adjunct (all women). *Students:* 122 full-time (103 women), 68 part-time (64 women); includes 36 minority (4 Black or African American, non-Hispanic/Latino; 2 American Indian or Alaska Native, non-Hispanic/Latino; 9 Asian, non-Hispanic/Latino; 18 Hispanic/Latino; 3 Two or more races, non-Hispanic/Latino), 5 international. Average age 35. 153 applicants, 71% accepted, 60 enrolled. In 2011, 41 master's, 15 doctorates awarded. *Degree requirements:* For master's, comprehensive exam, thesis optional; for doctorate, capstone project. *Entrance requirements:* For master's, GRE General Test or MAT, BSN, minimum GPA of 3.0, unrestricted RN license; for doctorate, interview; active RN license; MA; minimum GPA of 3.3; National Certification as NP or CNS; portfolio. Additional exam requirements/recommendations for international students: Required—TOEFL. *Application deadline:* For fall admission, 6/15 priority date for domestic students; for spring admission, 11/15 for domestic students. Application fee: $60 ($75 for international students). Electronic applications accepted. *Expenses:* Contact institution. *Financial support:* In 2011–12, 33 students received support, including 1 fellowship (averaging $2,500 per year); career-related internships or fieldwork, Federal Work-Study, and scholarships/grants also available. Support available to part-time students. Financial award application deadline: 3/1; financial award applicants required to submit FAFSA. *Faculty research:* Women's health, uncertainty, empowerment, family experience in chronic illness. *Total annual research expenditures:* $322,604. *Unit head:* Dr. Nancy Smith, Dean, 719-255-4411, Fax: 719-255-4416, E-mail: nsmith2@uccs.edu. *Application contact:* Diane Busch, Director, 719-255-4424, Fax: 719-255-4416, E-mail: dbusch@uccs.edu. Web site: http://www.uccs.edu/~bethel/.

University of Colorado Denver, College of Nursing, Aurora, CO 80045. Offers adult clinical nurse specialist (MS); adult nurse practitioner (MS); family nurse practitioner (MS); family psychiatric mental health nurse practitioner (MS); health care informatics (MS); nurse-midwifery (MS); nursing (DNP, PhD); nursing leadership and health care systems (MS); pediatric nurse practitioner (MS); pediatric nursing leadership (MS); special studies (MS); women's health care (MS); MS/PhD. *Accreditation:* ACNM/ACME (one or more programs are accredited); NLN (one or more programs are accredited). Part-time and evening/weekend programs available. Postbaccalaureate distance learning degree programs offered (minimal on-campus study). *Faculty:* 69 full-time (65 women), 68 part-time/adjunct (64 women). *Students:* 308 full-time (288 women), 134 part-time (118 women); includes 59 minority (11 Black or African American, non-Hispanic/Latino; 8 American Indian or Alaska Native, non-Hispanic/Latino; 10 Asian, non-Hispanic/Latino; 27 Hispanic/Latino; 3 Two or more races, non-Hispanic/Latino), 8 international. Average age 39. 298 applicants, 46% accepted, 110 enrolled. In 2011, 72 master's, 19 doctorates awarded. Terminal master's awarded for partial completion of doctoral program. *Degree requirements:* For master's, thesis optional; for doctorate, comprehensive exam, thesis/dissertation, 42 credits of coursework, 30 credits of dissertation. *Entrance requirements:* For master's, GRE if cumulative undergraduate GPA is less than 3.0, undergraduate nursing degree from NLNAC- or CCNE-accredited school or university; completion of research and statistics courses with minimum grade of C; copy of current and unencumbered nursing license; for doctorate, GRE, bachelor's and/or master's degrees in nursing from NLN- or CCNE-accredited institution; portfolio; minimum undergraduate GPA of 3.0, graduate 3.5; graduate-level intermediate statistics and master's-level nursing theory courses with minimum B grade; interview. Additional exam requirements/recommendations for international students: Required—TOEFL (minimum score 560 paper-based; 220 computer-based; 83 iBT). *Application deadline:* For fall admission, 4/1 for domestic students; for spring admission, 9/1 for domestic students. Application fee: $65. Electronic applications accepted. *Expenses:* Contact institution. *Financial support:* In 2011–12, 40 students received support. Fellowships, research assistantships, teaching assistantships, Federal Work-Study, scholarships/grants, and unspecified assistantships available. Support available to part-time students. Financial award application deadline: 4/1; financial award applicants required to submit FAFSA. *Faculty research:* Biological and behavioral phenomena in pregnancy and postpartum; patterns of glycemia during the insulin resistance of pregnancy; obesity, gestational diabetes, and relationship to neonatal adiposity; men's awareness and knowledge of male breast cancer; cognitive-behavioral therapy for chronic insomnia after breast cancer treatment; massage therapy for the treatment of tension-type headaches. *Total annual research expenditures:* $5.2 million. *Unit head:* Dr. Patricia Moritz, Dean, 303-724-1679, E-mail: pat.moritz@ucdenver.edu. *Application contact:* Judy Campbell, Graduate Programs Coordinator, 303-724-8503, E-mail: judy.campbell@ucdenver.edu. Web site: http://www.ucdenver.edu/academics/colleges/nursing/Pages/default.aspx.

University of Delaware, College of Health Sciences, School of Nursing, Newark, DE 19716. Offers adult nurse practitioner (MSN, PMC); cardiopulmonary clinical nurse specialist (MSN, PMC); cardiopulmonary clinical nurse specialist/adult nurse practitioner (MSN, PMC); family nurse practitioner (MSN, PMC); gerontology clinical nurse specialist (MSN, PMC); gerontology clinical nurse specialist geriatric nurse practitioner (PMC); gerontology clinical nurse specialist/geriatric nurse practitioner (MSN); health services administration (MSN, PMC); nursing of children clinical nurse specialist (MSN, PMC); nursing of children clinical nurse specialist/pediatric nurse practitioner (MSN, PMC); oncology/immune deficiency clinical nurse specialist (MSN, PMC); oncology/immune deficiency clinical nurse specialist/adult nurse practitioner (MSN, PMC); perinatal/women's health clinical nurse specialist (MSN, PMC); perinatal/women's health clinical nurse specialist/women's health nurse practitioner (MSN, PMC); psychiatric nursing clinical nurse specialist (MSN, PMC). *Accreditation:* AACN; NLN (one or more programs are accredited). Part-time and evening/weekend programs available. Postbaccalaureate distance learning degree programs offered (minimal on-campus study). *Degree requirements:* For master's, thesis optional. *Entrance requirements:* For master's, BSN, interview, RN license. Electronic applications accepted. *Faculty research:* Marriage and chronic illness, health promotion, congestive heart failure patient outcomes, school nursing, diabetes in children, culture, health disparities, cardiovascular, prison nursing, oncology, public policy, child obesity, smoking and teen pregnancy, blood pressure measurements, men's health.

University of Hawaii at Manoa, Graduate Division, School of Nursing and Dental Hygiene, Honolulu, HI 96822. Offers clinical nurse specialist (MS), including adult health, community mental health; nurse practitioner (MS), including adult health, community mental health, family nurse practitioner; nursing (PhD, Graduate Certificate); nursing administration (MS). *Accreditation:* AACN; NLN (one or more programs are accredited). Part-time programs available. Postbaccalaureate distance learning degree programs offered (minimal on-campus study). *Degree requirements:* For master's, thesis optional; for doctorate, comprehensive exam, thesis/dissertation. *Entrance requirements:* For master's, Hawaii RN license. Additional exam requirements/recommendations for international students: Required—TOEFL (minimum score 580 paper-based; 237 computer-based; 92 iBT), IELTS (minimum score 5). *Expenses:* Contact institution.

University of Illinois at Chicago, Graduate College, College of Nursing, Program in Nursing, Chicago, IL 60607-7128. Offers acute care clinical nurse specialist (MS); acute care nurse practitioner (MS); administrative studies in nursing (MS); adult nurse practitioner (MS); adult/geriatric nurse practitioner (MS); advanced community health nurse specialist (MS); family nurse practitioner (MS); geriatric clinical nurse specialist (MS); geriatric nurse practitioner (MS); mental health clinical nurse specialist (MS); mental health nurse practitioner (MS); nurse midwifery (MS); occupational health/advanced community health nurse specialist (MS); occupational health/family nurse practitioner (MS); pediatric clinical nurse specialist (MS); pediatric nurse practitioner (MS); perinatal clinical nurse specialist (MS); school/advanced community health nurse specialist (MS); school/family nurse practitioner (MS); women's health nurse practitioner (MS). *Accreditation:* AACN. Part-time programs available. *Degree requirements:* For master's, thesis or alternative. *Entrance requirements:* For master's, GRE General Test, minimum GPA of 2.75. Additional exam requirements/recommendations for international students: Required—TOEFL. Electronic applications accepted.

University of Indianapolis, Graduate Programs, School of Nursing, Indianapolis, IN 46227-3697. Offers family practice (post-RN) (MSN); gerontological nurse practitioner (MSN); nurse-midwifery (MSN); nursing (MSN); nursing administration (MSN); nursing education (MSN); MBA/MSN. *Accreditation:* AACN; ACNM. *Faculty:* 1 full-time (0 women), 4 part-time/adjunct (1 woman). *Students:* 14 full-time (13 women), 168 part-time (159 women); includes 23 minority (13 Black or African American, non-Hispanic/Latino; 1 American Indian or Alaska Native, non-Hispanic/Latino; 4 Asian, non-Hispanic/Latino; 2 Hispanic/Latino; 3 Two or more races, non-Hispanic/Latino), 5 international. Average age 36. In 2011, 51 master's awarded. *Entrance requirements:* For master's, minimum GPA of 3.0, interview, letters of recommendation, resume, IN nursing license, 1 year professional practice. Additional exam requirements/recommendations for international students: Required—TOEFL (minimum score 550 paper-based; 213 computer-based). *Application deadline:* For fall admission, 8/1 for domestic students; for winter admission, 12/15 for domestic students; for spring admission, 4/15 for domestic students. Applications are processed on a rolling basis. Application fee: $50. Tuition and fees vary according to degree level and program. *Financial support:* Federal Work-Study available. *Unit head:* Dr. Anne Thomas, Dean, 317-788-3206, E-mail: athomas@uindy.edu. *Application contact:* Sueann Meagher, Graduate Administrative Assistant, 317-788-8005, Fax: 317-788-3542, E-mail: meaghers@uindy.edu. Web site: http://nursing.uindy.edu/.

The University of Kansas, University of Kansas Medical Center, School of Nursing, Kansas City, KS 66160. Offers adult/gerontological clinical nurse specialist (PMC); adult/gerontological nurse practitioner (PMC); clinical research management (PMC); family nurse practitioner (PMC); health care informatics (PMC); health professions educator (PMC); nurse midwife (PMC); nursing (MS, DNP, PhD); organizational leadership (PMC); psychiatric/mental health nurse practitioner (PMC); public health nursing (PMC). *Accreditation:* AACN; ACNM/ACME. Part-time programs available. Postbaccalaureate distance learning degree programs offered (minimal on-campus study). *Faculty:* 80. *Students:* 79 full-time (71 women), 336 part-time (317 women); includes 63 minority (24 Black or African American, non-Hispanic/Latino; 2 American Indian or Alaska Native, non-Hispanic/Latino; 18 Asian, non-Hispanic/Latino; 15 Hispanic/Latino; 4 Two or more races, non-Hispanic/Latino), 6 international. Average age 37. 155 applicants, 82% accepted, 127 enrolled. In 2011, 79 master's, 15 doctorates, 12 other advanced degrees awarded. Terminal master's awarded for partial completion of doctoral program. *Degree requirements:* For master's, comprehensive exam, thesis optional, general oral exam; for doctorate, variable foreign language requirement, thesis/dissertation, comprehensive oral exam (for DNP); comprehensive written and oral exam (for PhD). *Entrance requirements:* For master's, bachelor's degree in nursing, minimum GPA of 3.0, RN license, 1 year of clinical experience, RN license in KS and MO; for doctorate, GRE General Test, master's degree in nursing, minimum GPA of 3.5, RN license in KS and MO; national certification (for some specialties). Additional exam requirements/recommendations for international students: Required—TOEFL. *Application deadline:* For fall admission, 4/1 for domestic and international students; for spring admission, 9/1 for domestic and international students. Application fee: $60. Electronic applications accepted. Tuition and fees vary according to course load, campus/location, program and reciprocity agreements. *Financial support:* Research assistantships with full and partial tuition reimbursements, teaching assistantships with full and partial tuition reimbursements, and traineeships available. Financial award application deadline: 2/14; financial award applicants required to submit FAFSA. *Faculty research:* Breastfeeding practices of teen mothers, national database of nursing quality indicators, caregiving of families of patients using technology in the home, simulation in nursing education, diaphragm fatigue. *Total annual research expenditures:* $6.1 million. *Unit head:* Dr. Karen L. Miller, Dean, 913-588-1601, Fax: 913-588-1660, E-mail: kmiller@kumc.edu. *Application contact:* Dr. Debra J. Ford, Associate Dean, Student Affairs, 913-588-1619, Fax: 913-588-1615, E-mail: dford@kumc.edu. Web site: http://nursing.kumc.edu.

University of Mary, School of Health Sciences, Division of Nursing, Bismarck, ND 58504-9652. Offers family nurse practitioner (MSN); nurse administrator (MSN); nursing educator (MSN). *Accreditation:* AACN. Part-time and evening/weekend programs

available. Postbaccalaureate distance learning degree programs offered (minimal on-campus study). *Faculty:* 6 full-time (all women), 16 part-time/adjunct (all women). *Students:* 157 full-time (148 women), 91 part-time (85 women); includes 14 minority (5 Black or African American, non-Hispanic/Latino; 4 American Indian or Alaska Native, non-Hispanic/Latino; 1 Asian, non-Hispanic/Latino; 4 Hispanic/Latino), 2 international. Average age 37. 92 applicants. In 2011, 80 master's awarded. *Degree requirements:* For master's, comprehensive exam (for some programs), thesis (for some programs), internship (family nurse practitioner), teaching practice. *Entrance requirements:* For master's, minimum GPA of 2.75 in nursing, interview, letters of recommendation, criminal background check, immunizations, statement of professional goals. Additional exam requirements/recommendations for international students: Required—TOEFL (minimum score 500 paper-based; 197 computer-based; 71 iBT). *Application deadline:* Applications are processed on a rolling basis. Application fee: $40. Electronic applications accepted. *Financial support:* In 2011–12, 14 fellowships with partial tuition reimbursements, 3 teaching assistantships with partial tuition reimbursements were awarded. Financial award application deadline: 8/1; financial award applicants required to submit FAFSA. *Faculty research:* Gerontology issues, rural nursing, health policy, primary care, women's health. *Unit head:* Glenda Reemts, Director, 701-255-7500 Ext. 8041, Fax: 701-255-7687, E-mail: greemts@umary.edu. *Application contact:* Joanne Lassiter, Nurse Recruiter, 701-355-8379, Fax: 701-255-7687, E-mail: jllassiter@umary.edu.

University of Mary Hardin-Baylor, Graduate Studies in Nursing, Belton, TX 76513. Offers clinical nurse leader (MSN); family nurse practitioner (MSN); nursing education (MSN). *Accreditation:* AACN. Part-time and evening/weekend programs available. *Faculty:* 8 full-time (all women), 1 (woman) part-time/adjunct. *Students:* 30 full-time (28 women), 2 part-time (both women); includes 9 minority (5 Black or African American, non-Hispanic/Latino; 1 Asian, non-Hispanic/Latino; 3 Hispanic/Latino), 6 international. Average age 34. 48 applicants, 83% accepted, 25 enrolled. In 2011, 3 master's awarded. *Degree requirements:* For master's, practicum. *Entrance requirements:* For master's, GRE General Test, RN, BSN, minimum GPA of 3.0 in last 60 hours of undergraduate program. *Application deadline:* For fall admission, 6/1 priority date for domestic students; for spring admission, 11/1 priority date for domestic students. Applications are processed on a rolling basis. Application fee: $35 ($135 for international students). Electronic applications accepted. *Expenses: Tuition:* Full-time $12,780. *Required fees:* $2350. *Financial support:* Applicants required to submit FAFSA. *Unit head:* Dr. Margaret Prydun, Director of Master's Program in Nursing, 254-295-4674, E-mail: margaret.prydun@umhb.edu. *Application contact:* Melissa Ford, Director of Graduate Admissions, 254-295-4020, Fax: 254-295-5301, E-mail: mford@umhb.edu. Web site: http://graduate.umhb.edu/nursing/.

University of Maryland, Baltimore, Graduate School, School of Nursing, Master's Program in Nursing, Baltimore, MD 21201. Offers community health nursing (MS); gerontological nursing (MS); maternal-child nursing (MS); medical-surgical nursing (MS); nurse-midwifery education (MS); nursing administration (MS); nursing education (MS); nursing health policy (MS); primary care nursing (MS); psychiatric nursing (MS); MS/MBA. MS/MBA offered jointly with University of Baltimore. *Accreditation:* AACN; AANA/CANAEP; NLN (one or more programs are accredited). Part-time programs available. *Students:* 370 full-time (314 women), 480 part-time (441 women); includes 308 minority (176 Black or African American, non-Hispanic/Latino; 2 American Indian or Alaska Native, non-Hispanic/Latino; 70 Asian, non-Hispanic/Latino; 33 Hispanic/Latino; 27 Two or more races, non-Hispanic/Latino), 9 international. Average age 35. 990 applicants, 30% accepted, 204 enrolled. In 2011, 301 master's awarded. *Degree requirements:* For master's, comprehensive exam (for some programs), thesis or alternative. *Entrance requirements:* For master's, minimum GPA of 2.75, course work in statistics, BS in nursing. Additional exam requirements/recommendations for international students: Required—TOEFL (minimum score 550 paper-based; 80 iBT) or IELTS (minimum score 7). *Application deadline:* For fall admission, 2/1 for domestic students, 1/15 for international students. Application fee: $50. Electronic applications accepted. *Financial support:* Fellowships, research assistantships, teaching assistantships, career-related internships or fieldwork, and traineeships available. Support available to part-time students. Financial award application deadline: 2/15; financial award applicants required to submit FAFSA. *Unit head:* Dr. Jane Kapustin, Assistant Dean, 410-706-6741, Fax: 410-706-4231. *Application contact:* Marjorie Fass, Admissions Director, 410-706-0501, Fax: 410-706-7238.

University of Massachusetts Amherst, Graduate School, School of Nursing, Amherst, MA 01003. Offers clinical nurse leader (MS); family nurse practitioner (DNP); nursing (PhD); public health nurse leader (DNP). *Accreditation:* AACN. Part-time programs available. Postbaccalaureate distance learning degree programs offered (minimal on-campus study). *Faculty:* 12 full-time (11 women). *Students:* 56 full-time (51 women), 155 part-time (142 women); includes 57 minority (24 Black or African American, non-Hispanic/Latino; 5 Asian, non-Hispanic/Latino; 25 Hispanic/Latino; 3 Two or more races, non-Hispanic/Latino), 11 international. Average age 42. 125 applicants, 66% accepted, 53 enrolled. In 2011, 11 master's, 26 doctorates awarded. Terminal master's awarded for partial completion of doctoral program. *Degree requirements:* For master's, thesis optional; for doctorate, comprehensive exam, thesis/dissertation. *Entrance requirements:* For master's and doctorate, GRE General Test. Additional exam requirements/recommendations for international students: Required—TOEFL (minimum score 550 paper-based; 213 computer-based; 80 iBT), IELTS (minimum score 6.5). *Application deadline:* For fall admission, 2/1 for domestic and international students. Applications are processed on a rolling basis. Application fee: $50 ($65 for international students). Electronic applications accepted. Tuition and fees vary according to course load, campus/location and program. *Financial support:* Fellowships with full and partial tuition reimbursements, research assistantships with full and partial tuition reimbursements, teaching assistantships with full and partial tuition reimbursements, career-related internships or fieldwork, Federal Work-Study, scholarships/grants, traineeships, health care benefits, tuition waivers (full and partial), and unspecified assistantships available. Support available to part-time students. Financial award application deadline: 2/1. *Faculty research:* Health of older adults and their caretakers, mental health of individuals and families, health of children and adolescents, power and decision-making, transcultural health. *Unit head:* Dr. Donna Zucker, Graduate Program Director, 413-577-2322, Fax: 413-577-2550. *Application contact:* Lindsay DeSantis, Interim Supervisor of Admissions, 413-545-0722, Fax: 413-577-0010, E-mail: gradadm@grad.umass.edu. Web site: http://www.umass.edu/nursing/.

University of Massachusetts Dartmouth, Graduate School, College of Nursing, Graduate Nursing Programs, North Dartmouth, MA 02747-2300. Offers adult health/adult nurse practitioner (MS); adult health/advanced practice (MS); adult health/nurse educator (MS); adult health/nurse manager (MS); adult nurse practitioner (PMC); community nursing/advanced practice (MS); community nursing/nurse educator (MS); community nursing/nurse manager (MS); individualized nursing (PMC); nursing (DNP, PhD). Part-time programs available. *Faculty:* 27 full-time (all women), 42 part-time/adjunct (41 women). *Students:* 8 full-time (all women), 99 part-time (93 women); includes 11 minority (4 Black or African American, non-Hispanic/Latino; 2 Asian, non-Hispanic/Latino; 4 Hispanic/Latino; 1 Two or more races, non-Hispanic/Latino), 1 international. Average age 38. 65 applicants, 75% accepted, 26 enrolled. In 2011, 12 master's, 1 other advanced degree awarded. *Degree requirements:* For master's, thesis; for doctorate, thesis/dissertation. *Entrance requirements:* For master's, GRE General Test, BSN, minimum undergraduate GPA of 3.0, RN license, 3 letters of recommendation, 1 year experience as registered nurse; for doctorate, GRE General Test, minimum undergraduate GPA of 3.0, graduate 3.3; 3 letters of recommendation; personal statement; current Massachusetts RN license or eligibility for licensure in Massachusetts; 1 year professional nursing experience; example of scholarly writing. Additional exam requirements/recommendations for international students: Required—TOEFL (minimum score 533 paper-based; 200 computer-based; 72 iBT). *Application deadline:* For fall admission, 3/15 for domestic students, 2/15 for international students. Application fee: $40 ($60 for international students). Electronic applications accepted. *Expenses:* Tuition, state resident: full-time $2071; part-time $86.29 per credit. Tuition, nonresident: full-time $8099; part-time $337.46 per credit. *Required fees:* $438.58 per credit. Part-time tuition and fees vary according to class time, course load, degree level and reciprocity agreements. *Financial support:* In 2011–12, 14 teaching assistantships with partial tuition reimbursements (averaging $2,571 per year) were awarded; Federal Work-Study also available. Support available to part-time students. Financial award application deadline: 3/1; financial award applicants required to submit FAFSA. *Faculty research:* Chronic illness management, risk reduction activities in Type 2 diabetes, diabetes care and education, clinical decision-making, quantitative methodologies. *Total annual research expenditures:* $31,049. *Unit head:* Dr. Gail Russell, Graduate Program Director, 508-999-8251, Fax: 508-999-9127, E-mail: grussell@umassd.edu. *Application contact:* Elan Turcotte-Shamski, Graduate Admissions Officer, 508-999-8604, Fax: 508-999-8183, E-mail: graduate@umassd.edu. Web site: http://www.umassd.edu/nursing/graduateprograms.

University of Massachusetts Lowell, School of Health and Environment, Department of Nursing, Program in Nursing, Lowell, MA 01854-2881. Offers PhD. *Accreditation:* AACN. *Degree requirements:* For doctorate, thesis/dissertation, qualifying examination. *Entrance requirements:* For doctorate, GRE General Test, master's degree in nursing with minimum GPA of 3.3, current MA RN license, 2 years of professional nursing experience, 3 letters of recommendation.

University of Massachusetts Worcester, Graduate School of Nursing, Worcester, MA 01655-0115. Offers adult acute/critical care nurse practitioner (MS, Post Master's Certificate); adult acute/critical care nurse practitioner and gerontological nurse practitioner (MS, Post Master's Certificate); adult primary care nurse practitioner (MS, Post Master's Certificate); adult primary care nurse practitioner and gerontological nurse practitioner (MS, Post Master's Certificate); advanced practice nursing (DNP); family nurse practitioner (MS); gerontological nurse practitioner (Post Master's Certificate); leadership (DNP); nurse education (Post Master's Certificate); nurse educator (MS); nursing (PhD). *Accreditation:* AACN. *Faculty:* 20 full-time (17 women), 60 part-time/adjunct (50 women). *Students:* 162 full-time (141 women), 36 part-time (30 women); includes 29 minority (13 Black or African American, non-Hispanic/Latino; 10 Asian, non-Hispanic/Latino; 6 Hispanic/Latino), 1 international. Average age 36. 252 applicants, 38% accepted, 82 enrolled. In 2011, 38 master's, 6 doctorates awarded. *Degree requirements:* For doctorate, comprehensive exam, thesis/dissertation. *Entrance requirements:* For master's, GRE General Test, bachelor's degree, course work in statistics; for doctorate, GRE General Test, bachelor's or master's degree, RN licensure; for Post Master's Certificate, GRE General Test, MS in nursing. Additional exam requirements/recommendations for international students: Required—TOEFL. *Application deadline:* For fall admission, 1/15 priority date for domestic students. Applications are processed on a rolling basis. Application fee: $40 ($60 for international students). *Expenses:* Contact institution. *Financial support:* In 2011–12, 38 students received support. Institutionally sponsored loans, scholarships/grants, traineeships, and tuition waivers (for some) available. Support available to part-time students. Financial award application deadline: 5/16; financial award applicants required to submit FAFSA. *Faculty research:* Decision-making of partners and men with prostate cancer, coinfection (HIV and Hepatitus C) and treatment decisions, parent management of children with T1DM, health literacy and discharge planning, Ghanian women and self-care. *Total annual research expenditures:* $939,567. *Unit head:* Dr. Paulette Seymour-Route, Dean, 508-856-5801, Fax: 508-856-6552, E-mail: paulette.seymour-route@umassmed.edu. *Application contact:* Diane Brescia, Admissions Coordinator, 508-856-3488, Fax: 508-856-5851, E-mail: diane.brescia@umassmed.edu. Web site: http://www.umassmed.edu/gsn/.

University of Memphis, Loewenberg School of Nursing, Memphis, TN 38152. Offers advance practice-family nurse practitioner (MSN); executive nursing leadership (MSN); nursing (Graduate Certificate); nursing administration (MSN); nursing education (MSN); nursing informatics (MSN). *Accreditation:* AACN. Part-time and evening/weekend programs available. Postbaccalaureate distance learning degree programs offered. *Degree requirements:* For master's, comprehensive exam, thesis optional, scholarly project; completion of clinical practicum hours. *Entrance requirements:* For master's, NCLEX Exam, interview. Additional exam requirements/recommendations for international students: Required—TOEFL (minimum score 550 paper-based; 213 computer-based; 79 iBT). *Faculty research:* Technology in nursing, nurse retention, cultural competence, health policy, health access.

University of Michigan, Horace H. Rackham School of Graduate Studies, School of Nursing, Division of Nursing Business and Health Systems, Ann Arbor, MI 48109. Offers MS, MBA/MS, MHSA/MS, MS/MSI. MS/MSI offered with School of Information. *Accreditation:* AACN. Part-time and evening/weekend programs available. Postbaccalaureate distance learning degree programs offered (minimal on-campus study). *Degree requirements:* For master's, thesis. *Entrance requirements:* For master's, GRE General Test (if GPA less than 3.23), minimum GPA of 3.0. Electronic applications accepted. *Faculty research:* Outcomes research, nursing language, change management and innovation, nurse staffing, and informatics.

University of Minnesota, Twin Cities Campus, Graduate School, School of Nursing, Program in Nursing and Health Care Systems Administration, Minneapolis, MN 55455-0213. Offers MS. *Accreditation:* AACN. Part-time programs available. *Degree requirements:* For master's, final oral exam, project or thesis. *Entrance requirements:* Additional exam requirements/recommendations for international students: Required—TOEFL (minimum score 586 paper-based; 240 computer-based).

University of Missouri–Kansas City, School of Nursing, Kansas City, MO 64110-2499. Offers adult clinical nurse specialist (MSN), including adult nurse practitioner, women's health nurse practitioner; family nurse practitioner (MSN); neonatal nurse practitioner (MSN); nurse educator (MSN); nurse executive (MSN); nursing (PhD); nursing practice (DNP); pediatric nurse practitioner (MSN). *Accreditation:* AACN. Part-time programs available. Postbaccalaureate distance learning degree programs offered (minimal on-campus study). *Faculty:* 40 full-time (35 women), 57 part-time/adjunct (52 women). *Students:* 51 full-time (48 women), 381 part-time (352 women); includes 41 minority (22 Black or African American, non-Hispanic/Latino; 7 Asian, non-Hispanic/Latino; 12 Hispanic/Latino). Average age 37. 195 applicants, 49% accepted, 90 enrolled. In 2011, 78 master's, 19 doctorates awarded. *Degree requirements:* For master's, thesis or alternative. *Entrance requirements:* For master's, minimum undergraduate GPA of 3.2; for doctorate, GRE, 3 letters of reference, interview by invitation. Additional exam requirements/recommendations for international students: Required—TOEFL (minimum score 550 paper-based; 213 computer-based; 80 iBT). *Application deadline:* For fall

admission, 2/1 priority date for domestic students, 2/1 for international students; for spring admission, 9/1 priority date for domestic students, 9/1 for international students. Application fee: $45 ($50 for international students). *Expenses:* Tuition, state resident: full-time $5798; part-time $322.10 per credit hour. Tuition, nonresident: full-time $14,969; part-time $831.60 per credit hour. *Required fees:* $93.51 per credit hour. *Financial support:* In 2011–12, 25 teaching assistantships with partial tuition reimbursements (averaging $6,927 per year) were awarded; fellowships, research assistantships, career-related internships or fieldwork, Federal Work-Study, institutionally sponsored loans, and tuition waivers (full and partial) also available. Support available to part-time students. Financial award application deadline: 3/1; financial award applicants required to submit FAFSA. *Faculty research:* Geriatrics/ gerontology, children's pain, neonatology, Alzheimer's care, cancer caregivers. *Unit head:* Dr. Lora Lacey-Haun, Dean, 816-235-1700, Fax: 816-235-1701, E-mail: laceyhaunc@umkc.edu. *Application contact:* Leah Wilder, Coordinator for Admissions and Recruitment, 816-235-5768, Fax: 816-235-1701, E-mail: wilderl@umkc.edu. Web site: http://nursing.umkc.edu/.

University of Missouri–St. Louis, College of Nursing, St. Louis, MO 63121. Offers adult nurse practitioner (DNP, Post Master's Certificate); clinical nurse specialist (DNP); family mental health nurse practitioner (DNP); family nurse practitioner (MSN, DNP, Post Master's Certificate); neonatal nurse practitioner (MSN); nurse educator (MSN); nurse leader (MSN); nurse practitioner (Post Master's Certificate); nursing (PhD); pediatric clinical nurse specialist (DNP); pediatric nurse practitioner (MSN, DNP, Post Master's Certificate); women's health nurse practitioner (MSN, Post Master's Certificate). *Accreditation:* AACN. Part-time programs available. *Faculty:* 12 full-time (11 women), 14 part-time/adjunct (all women). *Students:* 240 part-time (226 women); includes 30 minority (26 Black or African American, non-Hispanic/Latino; 1 Asian, non-Hispanic/Latino; 2 Hispanic/Latino; 1 Two or more races, non-Hispanic/Latino). Average age 37. 228 applicants, 28% accepted, 53 enrolled. In 2011, 66 master's, 2 doctorates, 2 other advanced degrees awarded. *Degree requirements:* For doctorate, comprehensive exam, thesis/dissertation; for Post Master's Certificate, thesis. *Entrance requirements:* For master's, 2 recommendation letters; minimum GPA of 3.0; BSN; nursing licensure; statement of purpose; course in differential/inferential statistics; for doctorate, GRE, 2 letters of recommendation, MSN, minimum GPA of 3.2, course in differential/inferential statistics; for Post Master's Certificate, 2 recommendation letters; MSN; advanced practice certificate; minimum GPA of 3.0; essay. Additional exam requirements/recommendations for international students: Required—TOEFL (minimum score 550 paper-based; 213 computer-based). *Application deadline:* For fall admission, 2/15 for domestic and international students. Application fee: $35 ($40 for international students). Electronic applications accepted. *Expenses:* Tuition, state resident: full-time $6273; part-time $3866 per year. Tuition, nonresident: full-time $14,969; part-time $9980 per year. *Required fees:* $315 per year. *Financial support:* In 2011–12, 3 research assistantships with full and partial tuition reimbursements (averaging $12,339 per year) were awarded. Financial award application deadline: 4/1; financial award applicants required to submit FAFSA. *Faculty research:* Health promotion and restoration, family disruption, violence, abuse, battered women, health survey methods. *Unit head:* Dr. Nancy Magnuson, Director, 314-516-6066. *Application contact:* 314-516-5458, Fax: 314-516-6996, E-mail: gradadm@umsl.edu. Web site: http://www.umsl.edu/ divisions/nursing/.

The University of North Carolina at Chapel Hill, School of Nursing, Chapel Hill, NC 27599-7460. Offers nursing (MSN, PhD, PMC), including adult nurse practitioner (MSN, PMC), children's health advanced practice (MSN, PMC), family nurse practitioner (MSN, PMC), health care systems (MSN, PMC), psychiatric/mental health nursing (MSN, PMC), women's health nursing (MSN, PMC). *Accreditation:* AACN; NLN (one or more programs are accredited). Part-time programs available. *Degree requirements:* For master's, comprehensive exam, thesis; for doctorate, thesis/dissertation, 3 exams. *Entrance requirements:* For master's and doctorate, GRE General Test. *Faculty research:* Chronic illness, parenting, cardiovascular health in children, elderly, HIV-AIDS.

The University of North Carolina at Greensboro, Graduate School, School of Nursing, Greensboro, NC 27412-5001. Offers adult clinical nurse specialist (MSN, PMC); adult/gerontological nurse practitioner (MSN, PMC); nurse anesthesia (MSN, PMC); nursing (PhD); nursing administration (MSN); nursing education (MSN); MSN/ MBA. *Accreditation:* AACN; AANA/CANAEP; NLN. *Degree requirements:* For master's, thesis or alternative. *Entrance requirements:* For master's, GRE General Test or MAT, BSN, clinical experience, liability insurance, RN license; for PMC, liability insurance, MSN, RN license. Additional exam requirements/recommendations for international students: Required—TOEFL. Electronic applications accepted.

University of North Florida, Brooks College of Health, School of Nursing, Jacksonville, FL 32224. Offers clinical nurse leader (MSN); clinical nurse specialist (MSN); family nurse practitioner (Certificate); nurse anesthetist (CRNA) (MSN); nursing practice (DNP); primary care nurse practitioner (MSN). *Accreditation:* AACN; AANA/CANAEP. Part-time programs available. *Faculty:* 28 full-time (21 women), 1 (woman) part-time/ adjunct. *Students:* 97 full-time (69 women), 69 part-time (60 women); includes 41 minority (17 Black or African American, non-Hispanic/Latino; 1 American Indian or Alaska Native, non-Hispanic/Latino; 10 Asian, non-Hispanic/Latino; 11 Hispanic/Latino; 2 Two or more races, non-Hispanic/Latino). Average age 34. 215 applicants, 23% accepted, 31 enrolled. In 2011, 55 master's, 4 doctorates awarded. *Degree requirements:* For master's, thesis optional. *Entrance requirements:* For master's, GRE General Test, minimum GPA of 3.0 in last 60 hours of course work, BSN, clinical experience, resume; for doctorate, GRE (minimum score of 1000) or MAT (minimum score of 410), master's degree in nursing specialty from nationally-accredited program; national certification in one of the following APRN roles: CNE, CNM, CNS, CRNA, CNP; minimum graduate GPA of 3.3; three letters of reference which address academic ability and clinical skills; active license as registered nurse or advanced practice registered nurse. Additional exam requirements/recommendations for international students: Required—TOEFL (minimum score 500 paper-based; 173 computer-based; 61 iBT). *Application deadline:* For fall admission, 3/15 for domestic students, 4/1 for international students. Applications are processed on a rolling basis. Application fee: $30. Electronic applications accepted. *Expenses:* Tuition, state resident: full-time $8793; part-time $366.38 per credit hour. Tuition, nonresident: full-time $23,502; part-time $979.24 per credit hour. *Required fees:* $1384; $57.66 per credit hour. Tuition and fees vary according to course load and program. *Financial support:* In 2011–12, 59 students received support. Research assistantships available. Financial award application deadline: 4/1; financial award applicants required to submit FAFSA. *Faculty research:* Teen pregnancy, diabetes, ethical decision-making, family caregivers. *Total annual research expenditures:* $545,563. *Unit head:* Dr. John McDonough, Director, 904-620-2684, E-mail: jmcdonou@unf.edu. *Application contact:* Beth Dibble, 904-620-2684, Fax: 904-620-1832, E-mail: nursingadmissions@unf.edu. Web site: http://www.unf.edu/ brooks/nursing.

University of Pennsylvania, School of Nursing, Health Leadership Program, Philadelphia, PA 19104. Offers MSN. *Accreditation:* AACN. Part-time programs available. *Students:* 6 full-time (5 women), 12 part-time (all women); includes 4 minority (2 Black or African American, non-Hispanic/Latino; 1 Asian, non-Hispanic/Latino; 1 Hispanic/Latino), 1 international. 8 applicants, 50% accepted, 4 enrolled. In 2011, 6 degrees awarded. *Entrance requirements:* For master's, GRE General Test, BSN, minimum GPA of 3.0, previous course work in statistics, 1 year of clinical experience in area of interest. Additional exam requirements/recommendations for international students: Required—TOEFL. *Application deadline:* For fall admission, 2/15 priority date for domestic students. Applications are processed on a rolling basis. Application fee: $70. *Expenses:* Contact institution. *Financial support:* Teaching assistantships, career-related internships or fieldwork, Federal Work-Study, and institutionally sponsored loans available. Support available to part-time students. Financial award application deadline: 4/1. *Faculty research:* Payment structures for nurse practitioners, delirium in older adults. *Unit head:* Assistant Dean of Admissions and Financial Aid, 866-867-6877, Fax: 215-573-8439, E-mail: admissions@nursing.upenn.edu. *Application contact:* Susan Keim, Program Director, 215-573-9759, E-mail: skeim@nursing.upenn.edu.

University of Pennsylvania, School of Nursing, Program in Nursing and Health Care Administration, Philadelphia, PA 19104. Offers MSN, PhD, MBA/MSN. *Accreditation:* AACN. Part-time programs available. *Students:* 7 full-time (5 women), 20 part-time (19 women); includes 5 minority (3 Black or African American, non-Hispanic/Latino; 1 Asian, non-Hispanic/Latino; 1 Two or more races, non-Hispanic/Latino), 2 international. 13 applicants, 77% accepted, 10 enrolled. In 2011, 5 degrees awarded. Terminal master's awarded for partial completion of doctoral program. *Degree requirements:* For doctorate, thesis/dissertation. *Entrance requirements:* For master's, GRE General Test, BSN, minimum GPA of 3.0, previous course work in statistics; for doctorate, GRE General Test, BSN or MSN, minimum GPA of 3.0. Additional exam requirements/ recommendations for international students: Required—TOEFL. *Application deadline:* For fall admission, 2/15 priority date for domestic students. Applications are processed on a rolling basis. Application fee: $70. *Expenses:* Contact institution. *Financial support:* Research assistantships, teaching assistantships, career-related internships or fieldwork, Federal Work-Study, and institutionally sponsored loans available. Support available to part-time students. Financial award application deadline: 12/15. *Faculty research:* Nursing services and policy, home health services utilization. *Unit head:* Assistant Dean of Admissions and Financial Aid, 866-867-6877, Fax: 215-573-8439, E-mail: admissions@nursing.upenn.edu. *Application contact:* Susan Keim, Program Director, 215-573-9759, E-mail: skeim@nursing.upenn.edu. Web site: http:// www.nursing.upenn.edu/.

University of Phoenix–Bay Area Campus, College of Nursing, San Jose, CA 95134-1805. Offers education (MHA); gerontology (MHA); health administration (MHA, DHA); informatics (MHA, MSN); nursing (MSN, PhD); nursing/health care education (MSN); MSN/MBA. Evening/weekend programs available. Postbaccalaureate distance learning degree programs offered (no on-campus study). *Degree requirements:* For master's, thesis (for some programs). *Entrance requirements:* For master's, minimum undergraduate GPA of 2.5, 3 years of work experience, RN license. Additional exam requirements/recommendations for international students: Required—TOEFL (minimum score 550 paper-based; 213 computer-based; 79 iBT). Electronic applications accepted.

University of Phoenix–Washington D.C. Campus, College of Nursing, Washington, DC 20001. Offers education (MHA); gerontology (MHA); health administration (MHA, DHA); informatics (MHA, MSN); nursing (MSN, PhD); nursing/health care education (MSN); MSN/MBA; MSN/MHA.

University of Pittsburgh, School of Nursing, Nurse Specialty Role Program, Pittsburgh, PA 15260. Offers clinical nurse leader (MSN); nursing administration (MSN, DNP); nursing informatics (MSN). *Accreditation:* AACN. Part-time programs available. *Students:* 5 full-time (3 women), 63 part-time (60 women); includes 5 minority (2 Black or African American, non-Hispanic/Latino; 3 Asian, non-Hispanic/Latino). Average age 43. 42 applicants, 71% accepted, 25 enrolled. In 2011, 9 master's, 5 doctorates awarded. *Degree requirements:* For master's, comprehensive exam, thesis optional. *Entrance requirements:* For master's, GRE or MAT, BSN, RN license, letters of recommendation, resume, course work in statistics, 1-3 years of nursing experience. Additional exam requirements/recommendations for international students: Required—TOEFL (minimum score 550 paper-based; 213 computer-based; 80 iBT). *Application deadline:* For fall admission, 6/1 priority date for domestic students, 6/1 for international students; for spring admission, 2/15 priority date for domestic students, 2/15 for international students. Applications are processed on a rolling basis. Application fee: $50. Electronic applications accepted. *Expenses:* Tuition, state resident: full-time $18,774; part-time $760 per credit. Tuition, nonresident: full-time $30,736; part-time $1258 per credit. *Required fees:* $740; $200 per term. Tuition and fees vary according to program. *Unit head:* Dr. Sandra Engberg, Associate Dean for Clinical Education, 412-624-3835, Fax: 412-624-8521, E-mail: sje1@pitt.edu. *Application contact:* Laurie Lapsley, Administrator of Graduate Student Services, 412-624-9670, Fax: 412-624-2409, E-mail: lapsleyl@ pitt.edu. Web site: http://www.nursing.pitt.edu/.

University of Rhode Island, Graduate School, College of Nursing, Kingston, RI 02881. Offers administration (MS); clinical nurse leader (MS); clinical specialist in gerontology (MS); clinical specialist in psychiatric/mental health (MS); family nurse practitioner (MS); gerontological nurse practitioner (MS); nursing (DNP, PhD); nursing education (MS). *Accreditation:* AACN; ACNM/ACME (one or more programs are accredited). Part-time programs available. *Faculty:* 29 full-time (28 women), 2 part-time/adjunct (1 woman). *Students:* 33 full-time (30 women), 81 part-time (77 women); includes 6 minority (1 Asian, non-Hispanic/Latino; 5 Hispanic/Latino). In 2011, 17 master's, 6 doctorates awarded. *Degree requirements:* For master's, comprehensive exam; for doctorate, comprehensive exam, thesis/dissertation. *Entrance requirements:* For master's, GRE or MAT, 2 letters of recommendation, scholarly papers; for doctorate, GRE, 3 letters of recommendation, scholarly papers. Additional exam requirements/recommendations for international students: Required—TOEFL (minimum score 550 paper-based; 213 computer-based). *Application deadline:* For fall admission, 4/15 for domestic students, 2/1 for international students; for spring admission, 11/15 for domestic students, 7/15 for international students. Application fee: $65. Electronic applications accepted. *Expenses:* Tuition, state resident: full-time $10,432; part-time $580 per credit hour. Tuition, nonresident: full-time $23,130; part-time $1285 per credit hour. *Required fees:* $1362; $36 per credit hour. $35 per semester. One-time fee: $130. *Financial support:* In 2011–12, 5 teaching assistantships with full and partial tuition reimbursements (averaging $12,596 per year) were awarded. Financial award application deadline: 4/15; financial award applicants required to submit FAFSA. *Faculty research:* Group intervention for grieving women in prison, translating Best Practice in non-drug interventions for postoperative pain management, further development and testing of the pain assessment inventory, preschool motor and functional performance of two cohorts, neuroactivation of brain motor areas in preterm children. *Unit head:* Dr. Dayle Joseph, Dean, 401-874-2766, Fax: 401-874-2061, E-mail: dayle@uri.edu. *Application contact:* Dr. Mary C. Sullivan, Director of Graduate Studies, 401-874-5339, Fax: 401-874-2061, E-mail: mcsullivan@uri.edu. Web site: http://www.uri.edu/nursing/.

University of Rochester, School of Nursing, Rochester, NY 14642. Offers acute care nurse practitioner (MS); adult nurse practitioner (MS); adult/geriatric nurse practitioner (MS); care of children and families/pediatric nurse practitioner (MS); care of children and families/pediatric nurse practitioner/neonatal nurse practitioner (MS); clinical nurse leader (MS); clinical research coordinator (MS); family nurse practitioner (MS); family psychiatric mental health nurse practitioner (MS); health care organization management

and leadership (MS); health practice research (PhD); nursing (DNP). *Accreditation:* AACN; NLN (one or more programs are accredited). Part-time programs available. Postbaccalaureate distance learning degree programs offered (minimal on-campus study). *Faculty:* 49 full-time (42 women), 72 part-time/adjunct (60 women). *Students:* 38 full-time (32 women), 196 part-time (181 women); includes 37 minority (20 Black or African American, non-Hispanic/Latino; 9 Asian, non-Hispanic/Latino; 8 Hispanic/Latino), 5 international. Average age 36. 68 applicants, 56% accepted, 26 enrolled. In 2011, 49 master's, 7 doctorates awarded. Terminal master's awarded for partial completion of doctoral program. *Median time to degree:* Of those who began their doctoral program in fall 2003, 40% received their degree in 8 years or less. *Degree requirements:* For doctorate, thesis/dissertation. *Entrance requirements:* For master's, BS in nursing, minimum GPA of 3.0, course work in statistics; for doctorate, GRE General Test, MS in nursing, minimum GPA of 3.5. Additional exam requirements/recommendations for international students: Required—or IELTS (minimum score 6.5); Recommended—TOEFL (minimum score 560 paper-based; 230 computer-based; 88 iBT). *Application deadline:* For fall admission, 4/1 priority date for domestic students, 4/1 for international students; for spring admission, 9/1 for domestic and international students. Application fee: $50. Electronic applications accepted. *Expenses: Tuition:* Full-time $41,040. *Financial support:* In 2011–12, 49 students received support, including 1 fellowship with full and partial tuition reimbursement available (averaging $18,700 per year); scholarships/grants, traineeships, health care benefits, tuition waivers (partial), and unspecified assistantships also available. Support available to part-time students. Financial award application deadline: 6/30. *Faculty research:* Clinical research in aging, managing asthma in children, interventions to improve outcomes in critically ill children and their mothers, nurse home visitation studies, medical device evaluation, critical care clinical studies, high risk behavior and prevention, palliative care, pregnancy-related weight gain: *Total annual research expenditures:* $4.3 million. *Unit head:* Dr. Kathy H. Rideout, Interim Dean, 585-273-8902, Fax: 585-273-1268, E-mail: kathy_rideout@urmc.rochester.edu. *Application contact:* Elaine Andolina, Director of Admissions, 585-275-2375, Fax: 585-756-8299, E-mail: elaine_andolina@urmc.rochester.edu. Web site: http://www.son.rochester.edu.

University of St. Francis, College of Nursing, Joliet, IL 60435-6169. Offers adult health clinical nurse specialist (Post-Master's Certificate); adult nurse practitioner (MSN, Post-Master's Certificate); family nurse practitioner (Post-Master's Certificate); nursing administration (MSN); nursing practice (DNP). *Accreditation:* AACN. Part-time and evening/weekend programs available. Postbaccalaureate distance learning degree programs offered (no on-campus study). *Faculty:* 11 full-time (10 women), 16 part-time/adjunct (all women). *Students:* 59 full-time (52 women), 254 part-time (232 women); includes 80 minority (31 Black or African American, non-Hispanic/Latino; 11 Asian, non-Hispanic/Latino; 33 Hispanic/Latino; 5 Two or more races, non-Hispanic/Latino), 15 international. Average age 41. 340 applicants, 46% accepted, 117 enrolled. In 2011, 20 master's, 4 doctorates, 4 other advanced degrees awarded. *Entrance requirements:* Additional exam requirements/recommendations for international students: Required—TOEFL (minimum score 550 paper-based; 213 computer-based). *Application deadline:* Applications are processed on a rolling basis. Application fee: $30. Electronic applications accepted. *Expenses:* Contact institution. *Financial support:* In 2011–12, 87 students received support. Scholarships/grants, traineeships, and tuition waivers (partial) available. Support available to part-time students. Financial award applicants required to submit FAFSA. *Unit head:* Dr. Carol Wilson, Dean, 815-740-3840, Fax: 815-740-4243, E-mail: cwilson@stfrancis.edu. *Application contact:* Sandra Sloka, Director of Admissions for Graduate and Degree Completion Programs, 800-735-7500, Fax: 815-740-5032, E-mail: ssloka@stfrancis.edu. Web site: http://www.stfrancis.edu/academics/college-of-nursing-allied-health/graduate-programs/.

University of San Diego, Hahn School of Nursing and Health Science, San Diego, CA 92110-2492. Offers adult-gerontology clinical nurse specialist (MSN); adult-gerontology nurse practitioner/family nurse practitioner (MSN); clinical nursing (MSN); entry-level nursing (for non-RNs) (MSN); executive nurse leader (MSN); family nurse practitioner (MSN); family/lifespan psychiatric-mental health nurse practitioner (MSN); healthcare informatics (MS, MSN); nursing (PhD); nursing practice (DNP); pediatric nurse practitioner/family nurse practitioner (MSN). *Accreditation:* AACN. Part-time and evening/weekend programs available. *Faculty:* 23 full-time (21 women), 37 part-time/adjunct (34 women). *Students:* 157 full-time (131 women), 182 part-time (162 women); includes 121 minority (21 Black or African American, non-Hispanic/Latino; 6 American Indian or Alaska Native, non-Hispanic/Latino; 51 Asian, non-Hispanic/Latino; 36 Hispanic/Latino; 2 Native Hawaiian or other Pacific Islander, non-Hispanic/Latino; 5 Two or more races, non-Hispanic/Latino), 7 international. Average age 36. 506 applicants, 47% accepted, 150 enrolled. In 2011, 87 master's, 26 doctorates awarded. *Degree requirements:* For doctorate, thesis/dissertation (for some programs), residency (DNP). *Entrance requirements:* For master's, GRE General Test (entry-level nursing), BSN, current California RN licensure (except for entry-level nursing); minimum GPA of 3.0; for doctorate, minimum GPA of 3.5, MSN, current California RN licensure. Additional exam requirements/recommendations for international students: Required—TOEFL (minimum score 580 paper-based; 237 computer-based; 83 iBT), TWE. *Application deadline:* For fall admission, 3/1 priority date for domestic students, 3/1 for international students; for spring admission, 11/1 priority date for domestic students, 11/1 for international students. Applications are processed on a rolling basis. Application fee: $45. Electronic applications accepted. *Expenses: Tuition:* Full-time $22,482; part-time $1249 per unit. *Required fees:* $224. Full-time tuition and fees vary according to course load and degree level. *Financial support:* In 2011–12, 232 students received support. Scholarships/grants and traineeships available. Support available to part-time students. Financial award application deadline: 4/1; financial award applicants required to submit FAFSA. *Faculty research:* Palliative and end of life care, maternal/child health, childhood obesity, health care disparities, cognitive functioning. *Unit head:* Dr. Sally Hardin, Dean, 619-260-4550, Fax: 619-260-6814. *Application contact:* Monica Mahon, Associate Director of Graduate Admissions, 619-260-4524, Fax: 619-260-4158, E-mail: grads@sandiego.edu. Web site: http://www.sandiego.edu/academics/nursing/.

University of San Francisco, School of Nursing and Health Professions, Program in Nursing Practice, San Francisco, CA 94117-1080. Offers family nurse practitioner (DNP); healthcare systems leadership (DNP). *Faculty:* 3 full-time (all women), 7 part-time/adjunct (6 women). *Students:* 73 full-time (67 women), 25 part-time (24 women); includes 35 minority (5 Black or African American, non-Hispanic/Latino; 1 American Indian or Alaska Native, non-Hispanic/Latino; 15 Asian, non-Hispanic/Latino; 10 Hispanic/Latino; 4 Two or more races, non-Hispanic/Latino), 1 international. Average age 48. 59 applicants, 58% accepted, 25 enrolled. In 2011, 7 doctorates awarded. *Entrance requirements:* For doctorate, nursing bachelor's degree, valid RN license in California. *Expenses: Tuition:* Full-time $20,070; part-time $1115 per unit. Tuition and fees vary according to course load, campus/location and program. *Financial support:* In 2011–12, 2 students received support. *Unit head:* Dr. Judith Karshmer, Dean, 415-422-6681, Fax: 415-422-6877, E-mail: nursing@usfca.edu. *Application contact:* Information Contact, 415-422-4723, Fax: 415-422-2217.

University of South Carolina, The Graduate School, College of Nursing, Program in Nursing Administration, Columbia, SC 29208. Offers MSN. *Accreditation:* AACN. Part-time programs available. *Degree requirements:* For master's, thesis or alternative. *Entrance requirements:* For master's, GRE General Test or MAT, BS in nursing, nursing

license. Additional exam requirements/recommendations for international students: Required—TOEFL (minimum score 570 paper-based; 230 computer-based). Electronic applications accepted. *Faculty research:* System research, evidence based practice, breast cancer, violence.

University of Southern Maine, School of Nursing, Portland, ME 04104-9300. Offers adult health nursing (PMC); adult psychiatric/mental health nurse practitioner (MS); clinical nurse leader (MS); clinical nurse specialist psychiatric-mental health nursing (MS); education (MS); family nursing (PMC); family psychiatric/mental health nurse practitioner (MS); management (MS); medical/surgical nursing (MS); nurse practitioner adult health nursing (MS); nurse practitioner family nursing (MS); nursing (DNP); psychiatric-mental health nursing (PMC); MBA/MSN. *Accreditation:* AACN. Part-time programs available. *Degree requirements:* For master's, thesis optional. *Entrance requirements:* For master's, GRE General Test or MAT, minimum GPA of 3.0; for doctorate, GRE. Additional exam requirements/recommendations for international students: Required—TOEFL (minimum score 550 paper-based; 213 computer-based). Electronic applications accepted. *Faculty research:* Women's health, nursing history, weight control, community services, substance abuse.

University of Southern Mississippi, Graduate School, College of Health, School of Nursing, Hattiesburg, MS 39406-0001. Offers family nurse practitioner (MSN); nursing (DNP, PhD); nursing executive (MSN); psychiatric nurse practitioner (MSN). *Accreditation:* AACN. Part-time and evening/weekend programs available. *Faculty:* 17 full-time (16 women), 1 part-time/adjunct (0 women). *Students:* 115 full-time (98 women), 43 part-time (38 women); includes 42 minority (35 Black or African American, non-Hispanic/Latino; 1 American Indian or Alaska Native, non-Hispanic/Latino; 3 Asian, non-Hispanic/Latino; 3 Two or more races, non-Hispanic/Latino). Average age 40. 128 applicants, 52% accepted, 58 enrolled. In 2011, 42 master's, 2 doctorates awarded. *Degree requirements:* For master's, comprehensive exam, thesis optional; for doctorate, comprehensive exam, thesis/dissertation. *Entrance requirements:* For master's, GRE General Test, minimum GPA of 2.75 during last 60 hours, nursing license, BS in nursing; for doctorate, GRE General Test, master's degree in nursing, minimum GPA of 3.5. Additional exam requirements/recommendations for international students: Required—TOEFL, IELTS. *Application deadline:* For fall admission, 3/15 priority date for domestic students, 5/1 for international students; for spring admission, 1/10 priority date for domestic students, 1/10 for international students. Applications are processed on a rolling basis. Application fee: $50. Electronic applications accepted. *Financial support:* In 2011–12, 14 research assistantships with full tuition reimbursements (averaging $12,577 per year), teaching assistantships (averaging $12,000 per year) were awarded; Federal Work-Study, institutionally sponsored loans, scholarships/grants, traineeships, health care benefits, and unspecified assistantships also available. Financial award application deadline: 3/15; financial award applicants required to submit FAFSA. *Faculty research:* Gerontology, caregivers, HIV, bereavement, pain, nursing leadership. *Unit head:* Dr. Katherine Nugent, Director and Associate Dean, 601-266-5500, Fax: 601-266-5927. *Application contact:* Dr. Sandra Bishop, Graduate Coordinator, 601-266-5500, Fax: 601-266-5927. Web site: http://www.usm.edu/graduateschool/table.php.

The University of Tennessee at Chattanooga, Graduate School, College of Health, Education and Professional Studies, School of Nursing, Chattanooga, TN 37403. Offers administration (MSN); certified nurse anesthetist (Post-Master's Certificate); education (MSN); family nurse practitioner (MSN, Post-Master's Certificate); health care informatics (Post-Master's Certificate); nurse anesthesia (MSN); nurse education (Post-Master's Certificate); nursing (DNP). *Accreditation:* AACN; AANA/CANAEP (one or more programs are accredited). *Faculty:* 15 full-time (13 women), 4 part-time/adjunct (all women). *Students:* 68 full-time (45 women), 37 part-time (33 women); includes 8 minority (6 Black or African American, non-Hispanic/Latino; 2 Hispanic/Latino). Average age 33. 5 applicants, 100% accepted, 3 enrolled. In 2011, 52 degrees awarded. *Degree requirements:* For master's, thesis optional, qualifying exams, professional project; for Post-Master's Certificate, thesis or alternative, practicum, seminar. *Entrance requirements:* For master's, GRE General Test, MAT, BSN, minimum GPA of 3.0, eligibility for Tennessee RN license, 1 year direct patient care experience; for Post-Master's Certificate, GRE General Test, MAT, MSN, minimum GPA of 3.0, eligibility for Tennessee RN license, one year of direct patient care experience. Additional exam requirements/recommendations for international students: Required—TOEFL (minimum score 550 paper-based; 213 computer-based; 79 iBT), IELTS (minimum score 6). *Application deadline:* For fall admission, 8/1 priority date for domestic students, 6/1 for international students; for spring admission, 12/1 priority date for domestic students, 10/1 for international students. Applications are processed on a rolling basis. Application fee: $35. Electronic applications accepted. *Expenses:* Tuition, state resident: full-time $6472; part-time $359 per credit hour. Tuition, nonresident: full-time $20,006; part-time $1111 per credit hour. *Required fees:* $1320; $160 per credit hour. *Financial support:* Career-related internships or fieldwork and scholarships/grants available. Support available to part-time students. *Faculty research:* Diabetes in women, health care for elderly, alternative medicine, hypertension, nurse anesthesia. *Total annual research expenditures:* $1.9 million. *Unit head:* Dr. Kay R. Lindgren, Head, 423-425-4646, Fax: 423-425-4668, E-mail: kay-lindgren@utc.edu. *Application contact:* Dr. Jerald Ainsworth, Dean of Graduate Studies, 423-425-4478, Fax: 423-425-5223, E-mail: jerald-ainsworth@utc.edu. Web site: http://www.utc.edu/Academic/Nursing/.

The University of Texas at Arlington, Graduate School, College of Nursing, Arlington, TX 76019. Offers nurse practitioner (MSN); nursing administration (MSN); nursing education (MSN); nursing practice (DNP); nursing science (PhD). *Accreditation:* AACN. Part-time and evening/weekend programs available. Postbaccalaureate distance learning degree programs offered (no on-campus study). *Faculty:* 15 full-time (all women), 2 part-time/adjunct (both women). *Students:* 58 full-time (48 women), 720 part-time (654 women); includes 281 minority (133 Black or African American, non-Hispanic/Latino; 3 American Indian or Alaska Native, non-Hispanic/Latino; 73 Asian, non-Hispanic/Latino; 53 Hispanic/Latino; 4 Native Hawaiian or other Pacific Islander, non-Hispanic/Latino; 15 Two or more races, non-Hispanic/Latino), 22 international. Average age 37. 686 applicants, 48% accepted, 265 enrolled. In 2011, 117 master's, 4 doctorates awarded. *Degree requirements:* For master's, practicum course; for doctorate, comprehensive exam (for some programs), thesis/dissertation (for some programs), proposal defense dissertation (for PhD); scholarship project (for DNP). *Entrance requirements:* For master's, GRE General Test if GPA less than 3.0, minimum GPA of 3.0, Texas nursing license, minimum C grade in undergraduate statistics course; for doctorate, GRE General Test (waived for MSN-to-PhD applicants), minimum undergraduate, graduate and statistics GPA of 3.0; Texas RN license; interview; written statement of goals. Additional exam requirements/recommendations for international students: Required—TOEFL (minimum score 550 paper-based; 213 computer-based), IELTS (minimum score 7). *Application deadline:* For fall admission, 2/1 for domestic students, 4/1 for international students; for spring admission, 10/15 for domestic students, 9/5 for international students. Applications are processed on a rolling basis. Application fee: $40 ($70 for international students). *Financial support:* In 2011–12, 46 students received support, including 22 fellowships with partial tuition reimbursements available (averaging $4,473 per year), 6 research assistantships (averaging $8,873 per year), 24 teaching assistantships (averaging $6,202 per year); career-related internships or fieldwork, scholarships/grants, and traineeships also available. Financial award application deadline: 6/1; financial award applicants required to submit FAFSA. *Faculty*

research: Simulation in clinical education and practice, cultural diversity, vulnerable populations, substance abuse. *Unit head:* Dr. Elizabeth C. Poster, Dean, 817-272-2776, Fax: 817-272-5006, E-mail: poster@uta.edu. *Application contact:* Dr. Jennifer Gray, Graduate Advisor/Associate Dean, 817-272-5295, Fax: 817-272-2065, E-mail: jgray@uta.edu. Web site: http://www.uta.edu/nursing.

The University of Texas at Austin, Graduate School, School of Nursing, Austin, TX 78712-1111. Offers adult -gerontology clinical nurse specialist (MSN); child health (MSN), including administration, public health nursing; child health (MSN), including teaching; family nurse practitioner (MSN); family psychiatric/mental health nurse practitioner (MSN); holistic adult health (MSN), including administration, education; maternity (MSN), including administration, public health nursing; maternity (MSN), including teaching; nursing (PhD); nursing administration and healthcare systems management (MSN); pediatric nurse practitioner (MSN); public health nursing (MSN). *Accreditation:* AACN. Part-time programs available. *Degree requirements:* For master's, thesis optional; for doctorate, thesis/dissertation. *Entrance requirements:* For master's and doctorate, GRE General Test. Additional exam requirements/recommendations for international students: Required—TOEFL (minimum score 550 paper-based; 213 computer-based). *Application deadline:* For fall admission, 12/1 for domestic students. Application fee: $50 ($75 for international students). Electronic applications accepted. *Financial support:* Fellowships, research assistantships, teaching assistantships, scholarships/grants, and traineeships available. Financial award application deadline: 2/1. *Faculty research:* Chronic illness management, memory and aging, health promotion, women's health, adolescent health. *Unit head:* Dr. Alexa Stuifbergen, Dean, 512-471-4100, Fax: 512-471-4910, E-mail: astuifbergen@mail.utexas.edu. Web site: http://www.utexas.edu/nursing/.

The University of Texas at El Paso, Graduate School, School of Nursing, El Paso, TX 79968-0001. Offers evidence-based practice (Certificate); family nurse practitioner (MSN); health care leadership and management (Certificate); interdisciplinary health sciences (PhD); nurse clinical specialist (MSN); nursing (Post-Master's Certificate); nursing systems management (MSN). *Accreditation:* AACN. *Students:* 162 (131 women); includes 94 minority (22 Black or African American, non-Hispanic/Latino; 11 Asian, non-Hispanic/Latino; 61 Hispanic/Latino), 3 international. Average age 34. 55 applicants, 58% accepted, 24 enrolled. In 2011, 12 master's awarded. *Degree requirements:* For master's, thesis optional; for doctorate, thesis/dissertation. *Entrance requirements:* For master's, GRE, minimum GPA of 3.0, course work in statistics, resume; for doctorate, GRE, letters of reference, relevant personal/professional experience, master's degree in health. Additional exam requirements/recommendations for international students: Required—TOEFL; Recommended—IELTS. *Application deadline:* For fall admission, 8/1 for domestic students, 3/1 for international students; for spring admission, 11/1 for domestic students, 9/1 for international students. Applications are processed on a rolling basis. Application fee: $45 ($80 for international students). Electronic applications accepted. *Financial support:* In 2011–12, research assistantships with partial tuition reimbursements (averaging $18,825 per year), teaching assistantships with partial tuition reimbursements (averaging $18,000 per year) were awarded; fellowships with partial tuition reimbursements, institutionally sponsored loans, scholarships/grants, health care benefits, tuition waivers (partial), and unspecified assistantships also available. Support available to part-time students. Financial award application deadline: 3/15; financial award applicants required to submit FAFSA. *Unit head:* Dr. Elias Provencio-Vasquez, Dean, 915-747-7273, Fax: 915-747-8266, E-mail: eprovenciovasquez@utep.edu. *Application contact:* Dr. Benjamin Flores, Interim Dean of the Graduate School, 915-747-5491, Fax: 915-747-5788, E-mail: bflores@utep.edu. Web site: http://nursing.utep.edu/.

The University of Texas at Tyler, College of Nursing and Health Sciences, Program in Nursing, Tyler, TX 75799-0001. Offers nurse practitioner (MSN); nursing (PhD); nursing administration (MSN); nursing education (MSN); MSN/MBA. *Accreditation:* AACN. Part-time and evening/weekend programs available. Postbaccalaureate distance learning degree programs offered (no on-campus study). *Degree requirements:* For master's, comprehensive exam (for some programs), thesis (for some programs); for doctorate, thesis/dissertation. *Entrance requirements:* For master's, GRE General Test or MAT, GMAT, minimum undergraduate GPA of 3.0, course work in statistics, RN license, BSN. Additional exam requirements/recommendations for international students: Required—TOEFL (minimum score 79 computer-based). Electronic applications accepted. *Faculty research:* Psychosocial adjustment, aging, support/commitment of caregivers, psychological abuse and violence, hope/hopelessness, professional values, end of life care, suicidology, clinical supervision, workforce retention and issues, global health issues, health promotion.

The University of Toledo, College of Graduate Studies, College of Nursing, Department of Population and Community Care, Toledo, OH 43606-3390. Offers adult nurse practitioner (Certificate); adult nurse practitioner/clinical nurse specialist (MSN); clinical nurse leader (MSN); family nurse practitioner (MSN, Certificate); nurse educator (MSN, Certificate); pediatric nurse practitioner (MSN, Certificate); psychiatric-mental health clinical nurse specialist (MSN, Certificate). Part-time programs available. *Faculty:* 43. *Students:* 77 full-time (63 women), 198 part-time (180 women); includes 30 minority (14 Black or African American, non-Hispanic/Latino; 1 American Indian or Alaska Native, non-Hispanic/Latino; 4 Asian, non-Hispanic/Latino; 8 Hispanic/Latino; 3 Two or more races, non-Hispanic/Latino), 1 international. Average age 33. 172 applicants, 53% accepted, 82 enrolled. In 2011, 66 master's, 10 other advanced degrees awarded. *Degree requirements:* For master's, thesis or alternative. *Entrance requirements:* For master's, GRE, BS in nursing, minimum undergraduate GPA of 3.0, statement of purpose, three letters of recommendation, transcripts from all prior institutions attended, Nursing CAS application, UT supplemental application; for Certificate, BS in nursing, minimum undergraduate GPA of 3.0, statement of purpose, three letters of recommendation, transcripts from all prior institutions attended. Additional exam requirements/recommendations for international students: Required—TOEFL (minimum score 550 paper-based; 213 computer-based; 80 iBT), IELTS (minimum score 6.5). Application fee: $45 ($75 for international students). Electronic applications accepted. *Financial support:* Research assistantships, Federal Work-Study, scholarships/grants, traineeships, and tuition waivers (full and partial) available. *Application contact:* Joan Mulligan, Admissions Analyst, 419-383-4168, Fax: 419-383-6140, E-mail: joan.mulligan@utoledo.edu. Web site: http://www.utoledo.edu/nursing/.

University of Victoria, Faculty of Graduate Studies, Faculty of Human and Social Development, School of Nursing, Victoria, BC V8W 2Y2, Canada. Offers advanced nursing practice (advanced practice leadership option) (MN); advanced nursing practice (nurse educator option) (MN); advanced nursing practice (nurse practitioner option) (MN); nursing (PhD). Part-time programs available. Postbaccalaureate distance learning degree programs offered (no on-campus study). *Entrance requirements:* Additional exam requirements/recommendations for international students: Required—TOEFL (minimum score 575 paper-based; 233 computer-based), IELTS (minimum score 7). Electronic applications accepted.

University of Virginia, School of Nursing, Charlottesville, VA 22903. Offers acute and specialty care (MSN); acute care nurse practitioner (MSN); clinical nurse leadership (MSN); community-public health leadership (MSN); nursing (DNP, PhD); psychiatric mental health counseling (MSN); MSN/MBA. *Accreditation:* AACN. Part-time programs available. *Faculty:* 44 full-time (43 women), 2 part-time/adjunct (both women). *Students:* 174 full-time (152 women), 151 part-time (139 women); includes 57 minority (28 Black or African American, non-Hispanic/Latino; 1 American Indian or Alaska Native, non-Hispanic/Latino; 14 Asian, non-Hispanic/Latino; 10 Hispanic/Latino; 4 Two or more races, non-Hispanic/Latino), 11 international. Average age 37. 236 applicants, 40% accepted, 74 enrolled. In 2011, 70 master's, 15 doctorates awarded. *Degree requirements:* For doctorate, comprehensive exam (for some programs), capstone project (DNP), dissertation (PhD). *Entrance requirements:* For master's, GRE General Test, MAT; for doctorate, GRE General Test. Additional exam requirements/recommendations for international students: Required—TOEFL, IELTS. *Application deadline:* Applications are processed on a rolling basis. Application fee: $60. Electronic applications accepted. *Expenses:* Contact institution. *Financial support:* Fellowships, research assistantships, teaching assistantships, Federal Work-Study, and scholarships/grants available. Financial award applicants required to submit FAFSA. *Unit head:* Dorrie K. Fontaine, Dean, 434-924-0141, Fax: 434-982-1809. *Application contact:* Clay Hysell, Assistant Dean for Admissions and Financial Services, 434-924-0141, Fax: 434-982-1809, E-mail: nur-osa@virginia.edu. Web site: http://www.nursing.virginia.edu/.

University of Washington, Tacoma, Graduate Programs, Program in Nursing, Tacoma, WA 98402-3100. Offers communities, populations and health (MN); leadership in healthcare (MN); nurse educator (MN). Part-time programs available. *Degree requirements:* For master's, thesis (for some programs), advance fieldwork. *Entrance requirements:* For master's, Washington State NCLEX exam, minimum GPA of 3.0. Additional exam requirements/recommendations for international students: Required—TOEFL (minimum score 580 paper-based; 237 computer-based; 70 iBT); Recommended—IELTS (minimum score 7). *Faculty research:* Hospice and palliative care; clinical trial decision-making; minority nurse retention; asthma and public health; injustice, suffering, difference: Linking Them to Us; adolescent health.

University of West Florida, College of Professional Studies, Department of Applied Science, Technology and Administration, Program in Administration, Pensacola, FL 32514-5750. Offers acquisition and contract administration (MSA); biomedical/pharmaceutical (MSA); criminal justice administration (MSA); database administration (MSA); education leadership (MSA); healthcare administration (MSA); human performance technology (MSA); leadership (MSA); nursing administration (MSA); public administration (MSA); software engineering administration (MSA). Part-time and evening/weekend programs available. Postbaccalaureate distance learning degree programs offered (no on-campus study). *Students:* 36 full-time (28 women), 158 part-time (95 women); includes 61 minority (31 Black or African American, non-Hispanic/Latino; 4 American Indian or Alaska Native, non-Hispanic/Latino; 4 Asian, non-Hispanic/Latino; 17 Hispanic/Latino; 2 Native Hawaiian or other Pacific Islander, non-Hispanic/Latino; 3 Two or more races, non-Hispanic/Latino), 1 international. Average age 34. 102 applicants, 59% accepted, 40 enrolled. In 2011, 62 master's awarded. *Entrance requirements:* For master's, GRE General Test, letter of intent, names of references. Additional exam requirements/recommendations for international students: Required—TOEFL (minimum score 550 paper-based; 213 computer-based). *Application deadline:* For fall admission, 6/1 for domestic and international students; for spring admission, 10/1 for domestic and international students. Applications are processed on a rolling basis. Application fee: $30. *Expenses:* Tuition, state resident: full-time $5729; part-time $302 per credit hour. Tuition, nonresident: full-time $20,059; part-time $961 per credit hour. *Required fees:* $1509; $63 per credit hour. *Financial support:* Unspecified assistantships available. Financial award application deadline: 4/15; financial award applicants required to submit FAFSA. *Unit head:* Dr. Karen Rasmussen, Chairperson, 850-474-2301, Fax: 850-474-2804, E-mail: krasmuss@uwf.edu. *Application contact:* Terry McCray, Assistant Director of Graduate Admissions, 850-473-7718, Fax: 850-473-7714, E-mail: gradadmissions@uwf.edu. Web site: http://uwf.edu/msaprogram/.

University of West Florida, College of Professional Studies, Department of Research and Applied Studies, Pensacola, FL 32514-5750. Offers administration (MSA), including acquisition and contract administration, biomedical/pharmaceutical, criminal justice administration, database administration, education leadership, healthcare administration, human performance technology, leadership, nursing administration, public administration, software engineering and administration; college student personnel administration (M Ed), including college personnel administration, guidance and counseling; curriculum and instruction (M Ed, Ed S); educational leadership (M Ed); middle and secondary level education and ESOL (M Ed). Part-time and evening/weekend programs available. *Faculty:* 2 full-time (both women), 3 part-time/adjunct (2 women). *Students:* 26 full-time (15 women), 13 part-time (9 women); includes 6 minority (4 Black or African American, non-Hispanic/Latino; 1 Hispanic/Latino; 1 Two or more races, non-Hispanic/Latino), 1 international. Average age 26. 51 applicants, 51% accepted, 16 enrolled. In 2011, 17 master's, 49 Ed Ss awarded. *Entrance requirements:* For master's, GRE or MAT, official transcripts; minimum undergraduate GPA of 3.0; letter of intent; three letters of recommendation; resume. Additional exam requirements/recommendations for international students: Required—TOEFL (minimum score 550 paper-based; 213 computer-based). *Application deadline:* For fall admission, 6/1 for domestic and international students; for spring admission, 10/1 for domestic and international students. Applications are processed on a rolling basis. Application fee: $30. *Expenses:* Tuition, state resident: full-time $5729; part-time $302 per credit hour. Tuition, nonresident: full-time $20,059; part-time $961 per credit hour. *Required fees:* $1509; $63 per credit hour. *Financial support:* In 2011–12, 33 fellowships (averaging $860 per year), 10 research assistantships (averaging $3,280 per year), 2 teaching assistantships (averaging $3,760 per year) were awarded; unspecified assistantships also available. Financial award application deadline: 4/15; financial award applicants required to submit FAFSA. *Unit head:* Dr. Joyce Nichols, Chairperson, 850-857-6042, E-mail: jcoleman0@uwf.edu. *Application contact:* Terry McCray, Assistant Director of Graduate Admissions, 850-473-7718, Fax: 850-473-7714, E-mail: gradadmissions@uwf.edu. Web site: http://uwf.edu/pcl/.

University of Wisconsin–Eau Claire, College of Nursing and Health Sciences, Program in Nursing, Eau Claire, WI 54702-4004. Offers adult-gerontologic administration (MSN); adult-gerontologic clinical nurse specialist (MSN); adult-gerontologic education (MSN); adult-gerontologic nurse practitioner (MSN); family health administration (MSN); family health in education (MSN); family health nurse practitioner (MSN); nursing practice (DNP). Part-time programs available. *Faculty:* 13 full-time (all women), 1 (woman) part-time/adjunct. *Students:* 42 full-time (40 women), 68 part-time (66 women); includes 3 minority (1 Black or African American, non-Hispanic/Latino; 1 Asian, non-Hispanic/Latino; 1 Hispanic/Latino). Average age 37. 74 applicants, 70% accepted, 41 enrolled. In 2011, 35 master's awarded. Terminal master's awarded for partial completion of doctoral program. *Degree requirements:* For master's, thesis optional, 500-600 hours clinical practicum, oral and written exams. *Entrance requirements:* For master's, Wisconsin RN license, minimum GPA of 3.0, undergraduate statistics, course work in health assessment. Additional exam requirements/recommendations for international students: Required—TOEFL (minimum score 550 paper-based; 213 computer-based; 79 iBT); Recommended—IELTS (minimum score 7). *Application deadline:* For fall admission, 1/15 priority date for domestic students, 1/15 for international students. Applications are processed on a rolling basis. Application fee: $86. *Expenses:* Tuition, state resident: full-time $7312; part-time $406 per credit.

Tuition, nonresident: full-time $16,771; part-time $932 per credit. *Required fees:* $1101; $61 per credit. *Financial support:* In 2011–12, 16 students received support. Federal Work-Study and unspecified assistantships available. Financial award application deadline: 3/1; financial award applicants required to submit FAFSA. *Unit head:* Dr. Linda Young, Dean, 715-836-4904, Fax: 715-836-5925, E-mail: younglk@uwec.edu. *Application contact:* Dr. Mary Zwygart-Stauffacher, Director, 715-836-5287, E-mail: zwygarmc@uwec.edu. Web site: http://www.uwec.edu/conhs/programs/grad/index.htm.

Ursuline College, School of Graduate Studies, Programs in Nursing, Pepper Pike, OH 44124-4398. Offers care management (MSN); nurse practitioner (MSN); nursing (DNP); nursing education (MSN); palliative care (MSN). *Accreditation:* AACN. Part-time programs available. *Faculty:* 2 full-time (both women), 9 part-time/adjunct (7 women). *Students:* 1 (woman) full-time, 133 part-time (124 women); includes 27 minority (23 Black or African American, non-Hispanic/Latino; 3 Asian, non-Hispanic/Latino; 1 Two or more races, non-Hispanic/Latino), 1 international. Average age 38. 61 applicants, 87% accepted, 47 enrolled. In 2011, 21 master's awarded. *Degree requirements:* For master's, comprehensive exam. *Entrance requirements:* For master's, minimum undergraduate GPA of 3.0, bachelor's degree in nursing, eligibility for or current Ohio RN license. Additional exam requirements/recommendations for international students: Required—TOEFL (minimum score 500 paper-based; 173 computer-based). *Application deadline:* For fall admission, 8/1 priority date for domestic students. Applications are processed on a rolling basis. Application fee: $25. *Expenses: Tuition:* Part-time $875 per credit hour. *Required fees:* $170 per semester. *Financial support:* In 2011–12, 11 students received support. Federal Work-Study available. Financial award application deadline: 3/1. *Unit head:* Dr. Janet Baker, Director, 440-864-8172, Fax: 440-684-6053, E-mail: jbaker@ursuline.edu. *Application contact:* Melanie Steele, Graduate Admission Assistant, 440-646-8199, Fax: 440-684-6138, E-mail: graduateadmissions@ursuline.edu.

Vanderbilt University, Vanderbilt University School of Nursing, Nashville, TN 37240. Offers acute care nurse practitioner (MSN), including intensivist; adult-gerontology primary care nurse practitioner (MSN); emergency nurse practitioner (MSN); family nurse practitioner (MSN); family psychiatric and mental health nurse practitioner (MSN); health systems management (MSN); neonatal nurse practitioner (MSN); nurse midwifery (MSN); nurse midwifery/family nurse practitioner (MSN); nursing informatics (MSN); nursing practice (DNP); nursing science (PhD); pediatric acute care nurse practitioner (MSN); pediatric primary care nurse practitioner (MSN); women's health nurse practitioner (MSN), including urogynecology; women's health; women's health nurse practitioner/adult gerontology nurse practitioner (MSN); MSN/M Div; MSN/MTS. *Accreditation:* ACNM/ACME; NLN (one or more programs are accredited). Part-time programs available. Postbaccalaureate distance learning degree programs offered (minimal on-campus study). *Faculty:* 120 full-time (105 women), 415 part-time/adjunct (302 women). *Students:* 570 full-time (503 women), 395 part-time (364 women); includes 107 minority (57 Black or African American, non-Hispanic/Latino; 1 American Indian or Alaska Native, non-Hispanic/Latino; 19 Asian, non-Hispanic/Latino; 19 Hispanic/Latino; 2 Native Hawaiian or other Pacific Islander, non-Hispanic/Latino; 9 Two or more races, non-Hispanic/Latino), 10 international. Average age 32. 1,116 applicants, 56% accepted, 455 enrolled. In 2011, 341 master's, 33 doctorates awarded. *Degree requirements:* For doctorate, comprehensive exam, thesis/dissertation. *Entrance requirements:* For master's, GRE General Test (within the past 5 years), minimum B average in undergraduate course work, 3 letters of recommendation; for doctorate, GRE General Test, interview, 3 letters of recommendation from doctorally-prepared faculty, MSN, essay. Additional exam requirements/recommendations for international students: Required—TOEFL (minimum score 570 paper-based; 88 computer-based), IELTS (minimum score 6.5). *Application deadline:* For fall admission, 12/1 priority date for domestic students, 12/1 for international students. Applications are processed on a rolling basis. Application fee: $50. Electronic applications accepted. *Expenses:* Contact institution. *Financial support:* In 2011–12, 392 students received support. Scholarships/grants and health care benefits available. Support available to part-time students. Financial award application deadline: 3/15; financial award applicants required to submit FAFSA. *Faculty research:* Lymphedema, palliative care and bereavement, health services research including workforce, safety and quality of care, gerontology, better birth outcomes including nutrition . *Total annual research expenditures:* $1.8 million. *Unit head:* Dr. Colleen Conway-Welch, Dean, 615-343-8776, Fax: 615-343-7711, E-mail: colleen.conway-welch@vanderbilt.edu. *Application contact:* Patricia Peerman, Assistant Dean for Enrollment Management, 615-322-3800, Fax: 615-343-0333, E-mail: vusn-admissions@vanderbilt.edu. Web site: http://www.nursing.vanderbilt.edu.

Villanova University, College of Nursing, Villanova, PA 19085-1699. Offers adult nurse practitioner (MSN, Post Master's Certificate); family nurse practitioner (MSN, Post Master's Certificate); health care administration (MSN, Post Master's Certificate); nurse anesthetist (MSN, Post Master's Certificate); nursing (PhD); nursing education (MSN, Post Master's Certificate); nursing practice (DNP); pediatric nurse practitioner (MSN, Post Master's Certificate). *Accreditation:* AACN; AANA/CANAEP. Part-time programs available. Postbaccalaureate distance learning degree programs offered (minimal on-campus study). *Faculty:* 17 full-time (all women), 4 part-time/adjunct (all women). *Students:* 36 full-time (35 women), 256 part-time (234 women); includes 27 minority (14 Black or African American, non-Hispanic/Latino; 9 Asian, non-Hispanic/Latino; 4 Hispanic/Latino), 16 international. Average age 30. 161 applicants, 55% accepted, 75 enrolled. In 2011, 55 master's, 11 doctorates, 5 other advanced degrees awarded. *Degree requirements:* For master's, independent study project; for doctorate, comprehensive exam, thesis/dissertation. *Entrance requirements:* For master's, GRE or MAT, BSN, 1 year of recent nursing experience, physical assessment, course work in statistics; for doctorate, GRE, MSN. Additional exam requirements/recommendations for international students: Required—TOEFL, IELTS. *Application deadline:* For fall admission, 7/1 priority date for domestic students, 7/1 for international students; for spring admission, 11/1 priority date for domestic students, 11/1 for international students. Applications are processed on a rolling basis. Application fee: $50. *Expenses:* Contact institution. *Financial support:* In 2011–12, 43 students received support, including 5 teaching assistantships with full tuition reimbursements available (averaging $13,100 per year); institutionally sponsored loans, scholarships/grants, traineeships, tuition waivers (full), and unspecified assistantships also available. Financial award application deadline: 7/1; financial award applicants required to submit FAFSA. *Faculty research:* Genetics, ethics, cognitive development of students, women with disabilities, nursing leadership. *Unit head:* Dr. Marguerite K. Schlag, Assistant Dean/Director, Graduate Programs, 610-519-4907, Fax: 610-519-7650, E-mail: marguerite.schlag@villanova.edu. Web site: http://www.nursing.villanova.edu/.

Virginia Commonwealth University, Graduate School, School of Nursing, Richmond, VA 23284-9005. Offers adult health acute nursing (MS); adult health primary nursing (MS); biobehavioral clinical research (PhD); child health nursing (MS); clinical nurse leader (MS); family health nursing (MS); nurse educator (MS); nurse practitioner (MS); nursing (Certificate); nursing administration (MS), including clinical nurse manager; psychiatric-mental health nursing (MS); women's health nursing (MS). *Accreditation:* NLN (one or more programs are accredited). Part-time and evening/weekend programs available. *Degree requirements:* For master's, thesis optional; for doctorate, thesis/dissertation. *Entrance requirements:* For master's, GRE General Test, BSN, minimum GPA of 2.8; for doctorate, GRE General Test. Additional exam requirements/

recommendations for international students: Required—TOEFL (minimum score 600 paper-based; 250 computer-based; 100 iBT). Electronic applications accepted. *Expenses:* Tuition, state resident: full-time $9133; part-time $507 per credit. Tuition, nonresident: full-time $18,777; part-time $1043 per credit. *Required fees:* $77 per credit. Tuition and fees vary according to degree level, campus/location, program and student level.

Walden University, Graduate Programs, School of Nursing, Minneapolis, MN 55401. Offers education (MSN); informatics (MSN); leadership and management (MSN); nursing (DNP, Post-Master's Certificate), including nursing education (Post-Master's Certificate), nursing informatics (Post-Master's Certificate), nursing leadership and management (Post-Master's Certificate). *Accreditation:* AACN. Part-time and evening/weekend programs available. Postbaccalaureate distance learning degree programs offered (no on-campus study). *Faculty:* 13 full-time (10 women), 142 part-time/adjunct (123 women). *Students:* 4,064 full-time (3,749 women), 1,418 part-time (1,321 women); includes 1,448 minority (975 Black or African American, non-Hispanic/Latino; 27 American Indian or Alaska Native, non-Hispanic/Latino; 207 Asian, non-Hispanic/Latino; 178 Hispanic/Latino; 8 Native Hawaiian or other Pacific Islander, non-Hispanic/Latino; 53 Two or more races, non-Hispanic/Latino), 181 international. Average age 43. In 2011, 1,141 master's, 31 other advanced degrees awarded. *Entrance requirements:* For master's, bachelor's degree or equivalent in related field or RN; minimum GPA of 2.5; goal statement; for doctorate, master's degree or higher, three years of related professional or academic experience, RN, goal statement. Additional exam requirements/recommendations for international students: Required—TOEFL (minimum score 550 paper-based; 213 computer-based), IELTS (minimum score 6.5), or Michigan English Language Assessment Battery (minimum score 82). *Application deadline:* Applications are processed on a rolling basis. Application fee: $50. Electronic applications accepted. *Financial support:* Federal Work-Study, scholarships/grants, unspecified assistantships, and family tuition reduction, active duty/veteran tuition reduction, group tuition reduction, interest-free payment plans, employee tuition reduction available. Support available to part-time students. Financial award applicants required to submit FAFSA. *Unit head:* Dr. Sara Torres, Associate Dean, 800-925-3368. *Application contact:* Jennifer Hall, Vice President of Enrollment Management, 866-4-WALDEN, E-mail: info@walden.edu. Web site: http://www.waldenu.edu/Colleges-and-Schools/College-of-Health-Sciences/School-of-Nursing.htm.

Walsh University, Graduate Studies, School of Nursing, North Canton, OH 44720-3396. Offers clinical nurse leader (MSN); nursing practice (DNP). Part-time and evening/weekend programs available. Postbaccalaureate distance learning degree programs offered (minimal on-campus study). *Faculty:* 5 full-time (4 women). *Students:* 4 full-time (all women), 10 part-time (all women); includes 1 minority (Black or African American, non-Hispanic/Latino). Average age 48. *Degree requirements:* For doctorate, project; manuscript for publication (peer reviewed); presentation at regional or national meeting. *Entrance requirements:* For master's, current unencumbered RN license, completion of an undergraduate or graduate statistics course, essay, interview; for doctorate, BSN; master's degree; statistics and research courses; essay; interview. Additional exam requirements/recommendations for international students: Required—TOEFL. *Expenses: Tuition:* Full-time $10,170; part-time $565 per credit hour. *Financial support:* Research assistantships, tuition waivers (partial), and tuition discounts available. Financial award application deadline: 12/31; financial award applicants required to submit FAFSA. *Faculty research:* Faith community nursing, gerontology, women's health, global nursing education, nursing assessment, grief and reconstitution, health needs of psychiatric patients. *Unit head:* Dr. Linda Linc, Dean, School of Nursing, 330-490-7250, Fax: 330-490-7371, E-mail: llinc@walsh.edu. *Application contact:* Dr. Karen R. Gehrling, Director, Graduate Program in Nursing, 330-244-4659, Fax: 330-490-7206, E-mail: kgehrling@walsh.edu. Web site: http://www.walsh.edu/master-of-science-in-nursing.

Washburn University, School of Nursing, Topeka, KS 66621. Offers adult nurse practitioner (MSN); clinical nurse leader (MSN); family nurse practitioner (MSN). *Accreditation:* AACN. Part-time programs available. *Faculty:* 13 full-time (all women), 1 (woman) part-time/adjunct. *Students:* 23 full-time (all women), 78 part-time (73 women). 52 applicants, 77% accepted, 40 enrolled. In 2011, 23 master's awarded. *Entrance requirements:* Additional exam requirements/recommendations for international students: Required—TOEFL. *Application deadline:* For fall admission, 3/15 for international students. Application fee: $35. *Expenses:* Tuition, state resident: full-time $5346; part-time $297 per credit hour. Tuition, nonresident: full-time $10,908; part-time $606 per credit hour. *Required fees:* $86; $43 per semester. *Financial support:* Application deadline: 2/15. *Unit head:* Dr. Monica S. Scheibmeir, Dean, 785-670-1526, E-mail: monica.scheibmeir@washburn.edu. *Application contact:* Mary V. Allen, Director of Student Academic Support Services, 785-670-1533, E-mail: mary.allen@washburn.edu. Web site: http://www.washburn.edu/sonu.

Washington Adventist University, Program in Nursing - Business Leadership, Takoma Park, MD 20912. Offers MSN. Part-time programs available. *Students:* 6 full-time (5 women), 14 part-time (13 women); includes 18 minority (17 Black or African American, non-Hispanic/Latino; 1 Asian, non-Hispanic/Latino). Average age 39. *Application deadline:* Applications are processed on a rolling basis. *Expenses: Tuition:* Part-time $560 per credit hour. *Financial support:* Applicants required to submit FAFSA. *Unit head:* Dr. Jude Edwards, Dean of School of Graduate and Professional Studies, 301-891-4092, E-mail: jeedward@wau.edu. *Application contact:* Rahneeka Hazelton, Director, 301-891-4092, E-mail: rhazelto@wau.edu. Web site: http://www.wau.edu/index.php?option=com_content&view=article&id=408&Itemid=965.

Waynesburg University, Graduate and Professional Studies, Waynesburg, PA 15370-1222. Offers business (MBA), including finance, health systems, human resources, leadership, market development; counseling (MA), including addictions counseling, clinical mental health; education (MAT); nursing (MSN), including administration, education, informatics, palliative care; nursing practice (DNP); special education (M Ed); technology (M Ed); MSN/MBA. *Accreditation:* AACN. Part-time and evening/weekend programs available. *Degree requirements:* For doctorate, thesis/dissertation. *Entrance requirements:* Additional exam requirements/recommendations for international students: Required—TOEFL. Electronic applications accepted.

West Chester University of Pennsylvania, College of Health Sciences, Department of Nursing, West Chester, PA 19383. Offers nursing education (Certificate); public health nursing (MSN), including administration; school nursing (Teaching Certificate). *Accreditation:* AACN. Part-time and evening/weekend programs available. *Faculty:* 1 (woman) full-time, 2 part-time/adjunct (both women). *Students:* 10 full-time (all women), 31 part-time (all women); includes 8 minority (7 Black or African American, non-Hispanic/Latino; 1 Asian, non-Hispanic/Latino), 2 international. Average age 46. 20 applicants, 75% accepted, 13 enrolled. In 2011, 1 degree awarded. *Entrance requirements:* For master's, RN license, BSN or RN with bachelor's degree in another discipline, minimum GPA of 2.8, experience as a nurse providing direct clinical care, two letters of recommendation. Additional exam requirements/recommendations for international students: Required—TOEFL (minimum score 550 paper-based; 213 computer-based; 80 iBT). *Application deadline:* For fall admission, 4/15 priority date for domestic students, 3/15 for international students; for spring admission, 10/15 priority date for domestic students, 9/1 for international students. Applications are processed on

a rolling basis. Application fee: $45. Electronic applications accepted. *Expenses:* Tuition, state resident: full-time $7488; part-time $416 per credit. Tuition, nonresident: full-time $11,232; part-time $624 per credit. *Required fees:* $1784.64; $67.59 per credit. Tuition and fees vary according to program. *Financial support:* Unspecified assistantships available. Support available to part-time students. Financial award application deadline: 2/15; financial award applicants required to submit FAFSA. *Unit head:* Dr. Charlotte Mackey, Chair, 610-436-3474, Fax: 610-436-3083, E-mail: cmackey@wcupa.edu. *Application contact:* Dr. Ann Coghlan Stowe, Graduate Coordinator, 610-436-2331, Fax: 610-436-3083, E-mail: astowe@wcupa.edu. Web site: http://www.wcupa.edu/_ACADEMICS/HealthSciences/nursing/.

Western University of Health Sciences, College of Graduate Nursing, Master of Science in Nursing Program, Pomona, CA 91766-1854. Offers administrative nurse leader (MSN); clinical nurse leader (MSN); degree completion (MSN); entry-level (MSN); family nurse practitioner (MSN); nursing (MSN). *Faculty:* 12 full-time (all women), 18 part-time/adjunct (16 women). *Students:* 262 full-time (228 women), 12 part-time (all women); includes 150 minority (22 Black or African American, non-Hispanic/Latino; 2 American Indian or Alaska Native, non-Hispanic/Latino; 83 Asian, non-Hispanic/Latino; 33 Hispanic/Latino; 10 Two or more races, non-Hispanic/Latino), 4 international. Average age 31. 485 applicants, 38% accepted, 104 enrolled. In 2011, 55 master's awarded. *Entrance requirements:* For master's, BSN, minimum GPA of 3.0, 3 letters of recommendation. Additional exam requirements/recommendations for international students: Required—TOEFL. *Application deadline:* For fall admission, 3/1 for domestic students. Applications are processed on a rolling basis. Application fee: $60. *Unit head:* Karen J. Hanford, Dean, 909-469-5243, Fax: 909-469-5521, E-mail: khanford@westernu.edu. *Application contact:* Kathryn Ford, Director of Admissions/International Student Advisor, 909-469-5541, Fax: 909-469-5570, E-mail: admissions@westernu.edu.

Wilmington University, College of Health Professions, New Castle, DE 19720-6491. Offers adult nurse practitioner (MSN); family nurse practitioner (MSN); gerontology nurse practitioner (MSN); nursing (MSN); nursing leadership (MSN); nursing practice (DNP). *Accreditation:* AACN. Part-time programs available. *Faculty:* 3 full-time (all women). *Students:* 30 full-time (all women), 270 part-time (241 women). Average age 38. *Degree requirements:* For master's, thesis. *Entrance requirements:* For master's, BSN, RN license, interview, 3 letters of recommendation. Additional exam requirements/recommendations for international students: Required—TOEFL (minimum score 500 paper-based; 173 computer-based). *Application deadline:* For fall admission, 4/1 for domestic students; for spring admission, 9/1 for domestic students. Applications are processed on a rolling basis. Application fee: $35. Electronic applications accepted. *Expenses: Tuition:* Part-time $534 per credit hour. *Required fees:* $25 per term. *Financial support:* Fellowships with tuition reimbursements and traineeships available. Financial award applicants required to submit FAFSA. *Faculty research:* Outcomes assessment, student writing ability. *Unit head:* Denise Z. Westbrook, Dean, 302-356-6915, E-mail: denise.z.westbrook@wilmu.edu. *Application contact:* Chris Ferguson, Director of Admissions, 302-356-4636 Ext. 256, Fax: 302-328-5164, E-mail: inquire@wilmcoll.edu. Web site: http://www.wilmu.edu/health/.

Winona State University, College of Nursing and Health Sciences, Winona, MN 55987. Offers adult nurse practitioner (MS, Post Master's Certificate); clinical nurse specialist (MS, Post Master's Certificate); family nurse practitioner (MS, Post Master's Certificate); nurse administrator (MS); nurse educator (MS, Post Master's Certificate); nursing (DNP). *Accreditation:* AACN. Part-time programs available. Postbaccalaureate distance learning degree programs offered (no on-campus study). *Students:* 75 full-time (70 women), 25 part-time (22 women); includes 11 minority (4 Black or African American, non-Hispanic/Latino; 5 Asian, non-Hispanic/Latino; 1 Hispanic/Latino; 1 Two or more races, non-Hispanic/Latino), 2 international. Average age 34. In 2011, 26 master's, 2 doctorates, 3 other advanced degrees awarded. *Degree requirements:* For master's, thesis; for doctorate, capstone. *Entrance requirements:* For master's, GRE (if GPA less than 3.0). Additional exam requirements/recommendations for international students: Required—TOEFL (minimum score 550 paper-based). *Application deadline:* For fall admission, 12/1 for domestic and international students. Application fee: $20. *Financial support:* Research assistantships with partial tuition reimbursements, Federal Work-Study, traineeships, and unspecified assistantships available. Support available to part-time students. Financial award application deadline: 8/15; financial award applicants required to submit FAFSA. *Unit head:* Dr. William J. McBreen, Dean, 507-457-5122, E-mail: wmcbreen@winona.edu. *Application contact:* Patricia Cichosz, Office Manager, Graduate Studies, 507-457-5038, E-mail: pcichosz@winona.edu.

Wright State University, School of Graduate Studies, College of Nursing and Health, Program in Nursing, Dayton, OH 45435. Offers acute care nurse practitioner (MS); administration of nursing and health care systems (MS); adult health (MS); child and adolescent health (MS); community health (MS); family nurse practitioner (MS); nurse practitioner (MS); school nurse (MS); MBA/MS. *Accreditation:* AACN. Part-time and evening/weekend programs available. *Degree requirements:* For master's, thesis or alternative. *Entrance requirements:* For master's, GRE General Test, BSN from NLN-accredited college, Ohio RN license. Additional exam requirements/recommendations for international students: Required—TOEFL. *Faculty research:* Clinical nursing and health, teaching, caring, pain administration, informatics and technology.

Xavier University, College of Social Sciences, Health and Education, School of Nursing, Cincinnati, OH 45207. Offers clinical nurse leader (MSN); education (MSN); forensic nursing (MSN); healthcare law (MSN); informatics (MSN); nursing administration (MSN); school nursing (MSN); MSN/M Ed; MSN/MBA; MSN/MS. *Accreditation:* AACN. Part-time and evening/weekend programs available. *Faculty:* 13 full-time (all women), 10 part-time/adjunct (all women). *Students:* 69 full-time (66 women), 158 part-time (156 women); includes 30 minority (19 Black or African American, non-Hispanic/Latino; 2 American Indian or Alaska Native, non-Hispanic/Latino; 4 Asian, non-Hispanic/Latino; 3 Hispanic/Latino; 2 Two or more races, non-Hispanic/Latino). Average age 38. 117 applicants, 81% accepted, 71 enrolled. In 2011, 63 master's awarded. *Degree requirements:* For master's, thesis, scholarly project. *Entrance requirements:* For master's, GRE. Additional exam requirements/recommendations for international students: Required—TOEFL. *Application deadline:* Applications are processed on a rolling basis. Application fee: $35. Electronic applications accepted. *Expenses: Tuition:* Part-time $576 per credit hour. *Financial support:* In 2011–12, 88 students received support. Applicants required to submit FAFSA. *Faculty research:* Clinical nurse leader, simulation, employment satisfaction, nontraditional students, holistic nursing. *Unit head:* Dr. Susan M. Schmidt, Director, 513-745-3815, Fax: 513-745-1087, E-mail: schmidt@xavier.edu. *Application contact:* Marilyn Volk Gomez, Director of Nursing Student Services, 513-745-4392, Fax: 513-745-1087, E-mail: gomez@xavier.edu. Web site: http://www.xavier.edu/msn/.

York College of Pennsylvania, Department of Nursing, York, PA 17405-7199. Offers adult nurse practitioner (MS); certified nurse anesthetist (MS); clinical nurse specialist (MS), including education: administration; nurse educator (MS); nursing (DNP). *Accreditation:* AACN; AANA/CANAEP. Part-time and evening/weekend programs available. *Faculty:* 10 full-time (all women), 9 part-time/adjunct (6 women). *Students:* 31 full-time (23 women), 50 part-time (43 women); includes 4 minority (2 Black or African American, non-Hispanic/Latino; 2 Asian, non-Hispanic/Latino), 1 international. Average age 36. 49 applicants, 53% accepted, 20 enrolled. In 2011, 17 master's awarded. *Entrance requirements:* For master's, GRE General Test, minimum GPA of 3.0 with NLNAC or CCNE major. Additional exam requirements/recommendations for international students: Required—TOEFL (minimum score 530 paper-based; 200 computer-based; 72 iBT). *Application deadline:* For fall admission, 7/15 priority date for domestic students; for spring admission, 11/15 priority date for domestic students. Applications are processed on a rolling basis. Application fee: $50. Electronic applications accepted. *Expenses: Tuition:* Full-time $12,060; part-time $670 per credit hour. *Required fees:* $340 per semester. Tuition and fees vary according to degree level. *Financial support:* Federal Work-Study available. *Faculty research:* Employer and faculty beliefs about concepts in RN-BS education, evaluating effectiveness of mental health partnerships in psychiatric settings. *Unit head:* Dr. Linda Pugh, Graduate Program Director, 717-815-1243, E-mail: lwarner@ycp.edu. *Application contact:* Nancy Spataro, Director of Admissions, 717-815-1600, Fax: 717-849-1607, E-mail: admissions@ycp.edu. Web site: http://www.ycp.edu/academics/academic-departments/nursing/.

Nursing Education

Abilene Christian University, Graduate School, School of Nursing, Abilene, TX 79699-9100. Offers education and administration (MSN); family nurse practitioner (MSN). *Accreditation:* AACN. Part-time programs available. *Faculty:* 6 part-time/adjunct (all women). *Students:* 1 (woman) full-time, 2 part-time (1 woman). 6 applicants, 17% accepted, 1 enrolled. In 2011, 3 degrees awarded. *Degree requirements:* For master's, practicum. *Entrance requirements:* For master's, GRE General Test. Additional exam requirements/recommendations for international students: Required—TOEFL (minimum score 550 paper-based; 213 computer-based; 80 iBT), IELTS (minimum score 6). *Application deadline:* For fall admission, 4/1 priority date for domestic students; for spring admission, 11/1 for domestic students. Applications are processed on a rolling basis. Application fee: $50. Electronic applications accepted. *Expenses: Tuition:* Full-time $14,168; part-time $787 per hour. *Required fees:* $82 per hour. $10 per term. *Financial support:* Application deadline: 4/1; applicants required to submit FAFSA. *Unit head:* Dr. Becky Hammack, Graduate Director, 325-671-2361, Fax: 325-671-2386, E-mail: atoone@phssn.edu. *Application contact:* David Pittman, Graduate Admissions Counselor, 325-674-2656, Fax: 325-674-6717, E-mail: gradinfo@acu.edu.

Albany State University, College of Sciences and Health Professions, Albany, GA 31705-2717. Offers criminal justice (MS), including corrections, forensic science, law enforcement, public administration; mathematics education (M Ed); nursing (MSN), including RN to MSN family nurse practitioner, RN to MSN nurse educator; science education (M Ed). *Accreditation:* NLN. Part-time and evening/weekend programs available. Postbaccalaureate distance learning degree programs offered. *Faculty:* 16 full-time (7 women), 7 part-time/adjunct (3 women). *Students:* 34 full-time (26 women), 103 part-time (84 women); includes 94 minority (92 Black or African American, non-Hispanic/Latino; 2 Asian, non-Hispanic/Latino), 2 international. Average age 36. 101 applicants, 48% accepted, 33 enrolled. In 2011, 16 master's awarded. *Degree requirements:* For master's, comprehensive exam, thesis. *Entrance requirements:* For master's, GRE or MAT, official transcript, letters of recommendations, pre-medical/certificate of immunizations. *Application deadline:* For fall admission, 6/15 for domestic students, 5/1 for international students; for spring admission, 11/1 for domestic students, 10/1 for international students. Applications are processed on a rolling basis. Application fee: $20. Electronic applications accepted. *Expenses:* Tuition, state resident: full-time $3204; part-time $178 per credit hour. Tuition, nonresident: full-time $12,816; part-time $712 per credit hour. *Required fees:* $379 per semester. *Financial support:* Scholarships/grants and traineeships available. Financial award application deadline: 4/15; financial award applicants required to submit CSS PROFILE or FAFSA. *Unit head:* Dr. Joyce Johnson, Dean, 229-430-4792, Fax: 229-430-3937, E-mail: joyce.johnson@asurams.edu. *Application contact:* Jeffrey Pierce, II, Graduate Admissions Counselor, 229-430-4646, Fax: 229-430-4105, E-mail: jeffrey.pierce@asurams.edu. Web site: http://asu-sacs.asurams.edu/ASUCatalog/Graduate/index.html.

Alverno College, School of Nursing, Milwaukee, WI 53234-3922. Offers family nurse practitioner (MSN); nursing education (MSN). *Accreditation:* AACN. Part-time and evening/weekend programs available. *Faculty:* 8 full-time (all women), 3 part-time/adjunct (all women). *Students:* 35 full-time (all women), 41 part-time (all women); includes 10 minority (8 Black or African American, non-Hispanic/Latino; 2 Hispanic/Latino), 1 international. Average age 38. 61 applicants, 54% accepted; 29 enrolled. In 2011, 8 master's awarded. *Degree requirements:* For master's, 500 clinical hours, capstone. *Entrance requirements:* For master's, BSN, current license. Additional exam requirements/recommendations for international students: Required—TOEFL. *Application deadline:* For fall admission, 7/15 priority date for domestic students, 7/15 for international students; for spring admission, 12/15 priority date for domestic students, 12/15 for international students. Applications are processed on a rolling basis. Application fee: $0. Electronic applications accepted. Application fee is waived when completed online. *Expenses:* Contact institution. *Financial support:* In 2011–12, 7 students received support. Federal Work-Study available. Support available to part-time students. Financial award application deadline: 4/15. *Faculty research:* Impact of stroke on sexuality, children's asthma management, factors affecting baccalaureate student success. *Unit head:* Dr. Catherine Knuteson, Program Director, 414-382-6287, Fax: 414-382-6354, E-mail: catherine.knuteson@alverno.edu. *Application contact:* Christy Stone, Director of Graduate and Adult Recruitment, 414-382-6108, Fax: 414-382-6354, E-mail: christy.stone@alverno.edu.

American International College, School of Health Sciences, Department of Nursing, Springfield, MA 01109-3189. Offers nursing administration (MSN); nursing education (MSN). *Accreditation:* AACN. *Entrance requirements:* For master's, BSN. Additional exam requirements/recommendations for international students: Required—TOEFL. Electronic applications accepted.

Angelo State University, College of Graduate Studies, College of Health and Human Services, Department of Nursing and Rehabilitation Sciences, San Angelo, TX 76909. Offers advanced practice registered nurse (MSN); nurse educator (MSN); nursing - RN to MSN (MSN). *Accreditation:* NLN. Part-time and evening/weekend programs available. Postbaccalaureate distance learning degree programs offered (no on-campus study). *Faculty:* 7 full-time (all women). *Students:* 23 full-time (20 women), 89 part-time (80 women); includes 12 minority (3 Black or African American, non-Hispanic/Latino; 1 American Indian or Alaska Native, non-Hispanic/Latino; 3 Asian, non-Hispanic/Latino; 5 Hispanic/Latino). Average age 41. 143 applicants, 25% accepted, 25 enrolled. In 2011, 9 master's awarded. *Degree requirements:* For master's, comprehensive exam. *Entrance requirements:* For master's, essay, three letters of recommendation. Additional exam requirements/recommendations for international students: Required—TOEFL or IELTS. *Application deadline:* For fall admission, 7/15 priority date for domestic students, 6/10 for international students; for spring admission, 12/1 priority date for domestic students, 11/1 for international students. Applications are processed on a rolling basis. Application fee: $40 ($50 for international students). Electronic applications accepted. *Financial support:* In 2011–12, 24 students received support. Career-related internships or fieldwork, Federal Work-Study, and scholarships/grants available. Support available to part-time students. Financial award application deadline: 3/1. *Unit head:* Dr. Susan S. Wilkinson, Department Head, 325-942-2060 Ext. 290, Fax: 325-942-2236, E-mail: susan.wilkinson@angelo.edu. *Application contact:* Dr. Molly J. Walker, Graduate Advisor, 325-942-2060 Ext. 246, Fax: 325-942-2236, E-mail: molly.walker@angelo.edu. Web site: http://www.angelo.edu/dept/nursing/.

Auburn University, Graduate School, School of Nursing, Auburn University, AL 36849. Offers nursing education (MSN); primary care practitioner option (MSN). *Accreditation:* AACN. *Faculty:* 10 full-time (8 women). *Students:* 1 (woman) full-time, 40 part-time (35 women); includes 7 minority (6 Black or African American, non-Hispanic/Latino; 1 Asian, non-Hispanic/Latino). Average age 36. 39 applicants, 62% accepted, 19 enrolled. In 2011, 10 master's awarded. *Expenses:* Tuition, state resident: full-time $7290; part-time $405 per credit hour. Tuition, nonresident: full-time $21,870; part-time $1215 per credit hour. *International tuition:* $22,000 full-time. *Required fees:* $1402. *Unit head:* Dr. Gregg Newschwander, Dean, 334-844-3658, E-mail: gen0002@auburn.edu. *Application contact:* Dr. George Flowers, Dean of the Graduate School, 334-844-4700, E-mail: gradadm@auburn.edu. Web site: http://www.nursing.auburn.edu/.

Austin Peay State University, College of Graduate Studies, College of Behavioral and Health Sciences, School of Nursing, Clarksville, TN 37044. Offers advanced practice (MSN); nursing administration (MSN); nursing education (MSN); nursing informatics (MSN). Part-time programs available. Postbaccalaureate distance learning degree programs offered. *Faculty:* 6 full-time (all women). *Students:* 21 full-time (16 women), 79 part-time (74 women); includes 12 minority (9 Black or African American, non-Hispanic/Latino; 2 Hispanic/Latino; 1 Two or more races, non-Hispanic/Latino). Average age 38. 42 applicants, 100% accepted, 29 enrolled. In 2011, 24 master's awarded. *Degree requirements:* For master's, comprehensive exam. *Entrance requirements:* For master's, GRE General Test, minimum GPA of 3.0, RN license eligibility, 3 letters of recommendation. Additional exam requirements/recommendations for international students: Required—TOEFL (minimum score 600 paper-based). *Application deadline:* For fall admission, 8/1 priority date for domestic students. Applications are processed on a rolling basis. Application fee: $25. Electronic applications accepted. *Expenses:* Tuition, state resident: part-time $350 per credit hour. Tuition, nonresident: full-time $20,644; part-time $971 per credit hour. *Required fees:* $1224; $61.20 per credit hour. *Financial support:* In 2011–12, research assistantships with full tuition reimbursements (averaging $5,184 per year) were awarded; career-related internships or fieldwork, Federal Work-Study, institutionally sponsored loans, scholarships/grants, and unspecified assistantships also available. Support available to part-time students. *Unit head:* Dr. Patty Orr, Director, 931-221-7710, Fax: 931-221-7595, E-mail: orrp@apsu.edu. *Application contact:* Kendra Bryant, Graduate Admissions, 800-844-2778, Fax: 931-221-6188, E-mail: admissionsweb@apsu.edu. Web site: http://www.apsu.edu/nursing.

Azusa Pacific University, School of Nursing, Azusa, CA 91702-7000. Offers nursing (MSN); nursing education (PhD). *Accreditation:* AACN. Part-time and evening/weekend programs available. *Degree requirements:* For master's, thesis optional. *Entrance requirements:* For master's, BSN.

Barry University, School of Adult and Continuing Education, Division of Nursing, Program in Nursing Education, Miami Shores, FL 33161-6695. Offers MSN, Certificate. *Accreditation:* AACN. Part-time and evening/weekend programs available. *Degree requirements:* For master's, research project or thesis. *Entrance requirements:* For master's, GRE General Test or MAT, BSN, minimum GPA of 3.0, course work in statistics. Electronic applications accepted. *Faculty research:* HIV/AIDS, gerontology.

Bellarmine University, Donna and Allan Lansing School of Nursing and Health Sciences, Louisville, KY 40205-0671. Offers family nurse practitioner (MSN); nursing administration (MSN); nursing education (MSN); nursing practice (DNP); physical therapy (DPT). *Accreditation:* AACN; APTA. Part-time and evening/weekend programs available. *Faculty:* 21 full-time (16 women), 7 part-time/adjunct (2 women). *Students:* 128 full-time (82 women), 116 part-time (111 women); includes 13 minority (5 Black or African American, non-Hispanic/Latino; 1 American Indian or Alaska Native, non-Hispanic/Latino; 2 Asian, non-Hispanic/Latino; 3 Hispanic/Latino; 2 Two or more races, non-Hispanic/Latino). Average age 31. In 2011, 19 master's, 50 doctorates awarded. *Degree requirements:* For doctorate, comprehensive exam, thesis/dissertation. *Entrance requirements:* For master's, GRE General Test, RN license; for doctorate, GRE General Test, Physical Therapist Centralized Application Service (for DPT). Additional exam requirements/recommendations for international students: Required—TOEFL (minimum score 550 paper-based; 213 computer-based; 80 iBT). Application fee: $25. Electronic applications accepted. *Expenses:* Contact institution. *Financial support:* Career-related internships or fieldwork and scholarships/grants available. *Faculty research:* Nursing: pain, empathy, leadership styles, control; physical therapy: service-learning; exercise in chronic and pre-operative conditions, athletes; women's health; aging. *Unit head:* Dr. Susan H. Davis, Dean, 800-274-4723 Ext. 8217, E-mail: sdavis@bellarmine.edu. *Application contact:* Julie Armstrong-Binnix, Health Science Recruiter, 800-274-4723 Ext. 8364, E-mail: julieab@bellarmine.edu. Web site: http://www.bellarmine.edu/lansing.

Bellin College, Program in Nursing, Green Bay, WI 54305. Offers administrator (MSN); educator (MSN). *Accreditation:* AACN.

Bethel University, Graduate School, St. Paul, MN 55112-6999. Offers autism spectrum disorders (Certificate); business administration (MBA); communication (MA); counseling psychology (MA); education (M Ed); educational leadership (Ed D); gerontology (MA, Certificate); international baccalaureate education (Certificate); K-12 education (MA); literacy education (MA); nursing (MA); nursing education (Certificate); nursing leadership (Certificate); organizational leadership (MA); postsecondary teaching (Certificate); special education (MA); teaching (MA). Part-time and evening/weekend programs available. Postbaccalaureate distance learning degree programs offered (minimal on-campus study). *Faculty:* 8 full-time (3 women), 98 part-time/adjunct (46 women). *Students:* 651 full-time (419 women), 312 part-time (212 women); includes 79 minority (35 Black or African American, non-Hispanic/Latino; 2 American Indian or Alaska Native, non-Hispanic/Latino; 19 Asian, non-Hispanic/Latino; 17 Hispanic/Latino; 6 Two or more races, non-Hispanic/Latino), 6 international. Average age 36. In 2011, 245 master's, 4 doctorates, 32 other advanced degrees awarded. *Degree requirements:* For master's, comprehensive exam (for some programs), thesis (for some programs); for doctorate, comprehensive exam, thesis/dissertation. *Entrance requirements:* Additional exam requirements/recommendations for international students: Required—TOEFL (minimum score 550 paper-based; 213 computer-based; 80 iBT). *Application deadline:* Applications are processed on a rolling basis. Electronic applications accepted. Tuition and fees vary according to course load, degree level and program. *Financial support:* Applicants required to submit FAFSA. *Unit head:* Dick Crombie, Vice-President/Dean, 651-635-8000, Fax: 651-635-8004, E-mail: gs@bethel.edu. *Application contact:* Paul Ives, Director of Admissions, 651-635-8000, Fax: 651-635-8004, E-mail: gs@bethel.edu. Web site: http://gs.bethel.edu/.

Bowie State University, Graduate Programs, Department of Nursing, Bowie, MD 20715-9465. Offers administration of nursing services (MS); family nurse practitioner (MS); nursing education (MS). *Accreditation:* NLN. Part-time programs available. *Faculty:* 7 full-time (4 women), 14 part-time/adjunct (9 women). *Students:* 41 full-time (35 women), 55 part-time (50 women); includes 80 minority (77 Black or African American, non-Hispanic/Latino; 2 Asian, non-Hispanic/Latino; 1 Hispanic/Latino), 11 international. Average age 42. 7 applicants, 100% accepted, 5 enrolled. In 2011, 7 master's awarded. *Degree requirements:* For master's, comprehensive exam, thesis, research paper. *Entrance requirements:* For master's, minimum GPA of 2.5. *Application deadline:* For fall admission, 5/15 for domestic students. Applications are processed on a rolling basis. Application fee: $40. Electronic applications accepted. *Expenses:* Tuition, state resident: full-time $4140; part-time $3105 per semester. Tuition, nonresident: full-time $7836; part-time $5877 per semester. *Required fees:* $1715; $648 per semester. *Financial support:* Institutionally sponsored loans and traineeships available. Financial award application deadline: 4/1. *Faculty research:* Minority health, women's health, gerontology, leadership management. *Unit head:* Dr. Bonita Jenkins, Acting Chairperson, 301-860-3210, E-mail: mccaskill@bowiestate.edu. *Application contact:* Angela Issac, Information Contact, 301-860-4000.

Brenau University, Sydney O. Smith Graduate School, College of Health and Science, Gainesville, GA 30501. Offers family nurse practitioner (MSN); nurse educator (MSN); nursing management (MSN); occupational therapy (MS); psychology (MS). *Accreditation:* AOTA; NLN. Part-time and evening/weekend programs available. *Degree requirements:* For master's, comprehensive exam (for some programs), thesis (for some programs), clinical practicum hours. *Entrance requirements:* For master's, GRE General Test or MAT (for some programs), interview, writing sample, references (for some programs). Additional exam requirements/recommendations for international students: Required—TOEFL (minimum score 500 paper-based; 173 computer-based; 61 iBT); Recommended—IELTS (minimum score 5). Electronic applications accepted. *Expenses:* Contact institution.

California Baptist University, Program in Nursing, Riverside, CA 92504-3206. Offers administering nursing services (MSN); teaching nursing (MSN). Part-time programs available. *Faculty:* 21 full-time (all women). *Students:* 58 full-time (44 women); includes 28 minority (5 Black or African American, non-Hispanic/Latino; 2 American Indian or Alaska Native, non-Hispanic/Latino; 7 Asian, non-Hispanic/Latino; 12 Hispanic/Latino; 1 Native Hawaiian or other Pacific Islander, non-Hispanic/Latino; 1 Two or more races, non-Hispanic/Latino). Average age 32. 35 applicants, 60% accepted, 19 enrolled. *Degree requirements:* For master's, comprehensive exam or thesis. *Entrance requirements:* For master's, GRE or California Critical Thinking Skills Test; Test of Essential Academic Skills (TEAS), minimum GPA of 3.25; health clearance; health insurance; CPR certification; vehicle insurance; criminal background clearance; passport photo; three recommendations; comprehensive essay; interview. Additional exam requirements/recommendations for international students: Required—TOEFL (minimum score 575 paper-based; 230 computer-based; 89 iBT). *Application deadline:* For fall admission, 8/1 priority date for domestic students, 7/1 for international students; for spring admission, 12/1 priority date for domestic students, 11/1 for international students. Applications are processed on a rolling basis. Application fee: $45. Electronic applications accepted. *Expenses:* Tuition: Full-time $9540; part-time $530 per unit. *Required fees:* $355 per semester. One-time fee: $45. Tuition and fees vary according to course load and program. *Financial support:* Federal Work-Study and institutionally sponsored loans available. Financial award applicants required to submit FAFSA. *Faculty research:* Qualitative research using Parse Methodology, gerontology, disaster preparedness, medical-surgical nursing, maternal-child nursing. *Unit head:* Dr. Geneva Oaks, Dean, School of Nursing, 951-343-4738, E-mail: goaks@calbaptist.edu. *Application contact:* Gail Ronveaux, Dean of Graduate Enrollment, 951-343-4246, Fax: 951-343-5095, E-mail: graduateadmissions@calbaptist.edu. Web site: http://www.calbaptist.edu/msn/.

California State University, Fresno, Division of Graduate Studies, College of Health and Human Services, Department of Nursing, Fresno, CA 93740-8027. Offers nursing (MS), including clinical nurse, primary care nurse practitioner, specialist/nurse educator. *Accreditation:* AACN. Part-time and evening/weekend programs available. *Degree requirements:* For master's, thesis or alternative. *Entrance requirements:* For master's, GRE General Test, 1 year of clinical practice, previous course work in statistics, BSN, minimum GPA of 3.0 in nursing. Additional exam requirements/recommendations for international students: Required—TOEFL. Electronic applications accepted. *Faculty research:* Training grant, HIV assessment.

California State University, Stanislaus, College of Human and Health Sciences, Program in Nursing (MS), Turlock, CA 95382. Offers gerontological nursing (MS); nursing education (MS). Part-time programs available. *Degree requirements:* For master's, comprehensive exam, thesis or alternative. *Entrance requirements:* For master's, GRE or MAT, minimum GPA of 3.0, 3 letters of reference, RN. Additional exam requirements/recommendations for international students: Required—TOEFL (minimum score 550 paper-based; 213 computer-based). *Application deadline:* For fall admission, 5/1 for domestic students. Application fee: $55. Electronic applications accepted. *Expenses:* Required fees: $4616 per year. *Unit head:* Dr. Margaret Hodge, Chair, 209-667-3141, Fax: 209-667-3690, E-mail: phodge@csustan.edu. *Application contact:* Graduate School, 209-667-3129, Fax: 209-664-7025, E-mail: graduate_school@csustan.edu. Web site: http://www.csustan.edu/nursing/.

Capella University, School of Public Service Leadership, Minneapolis, MN 55402. Offers criminal justice (MS, PhD); emergency management (MS, PhD); general human services (MS, PhD); general public administration (MPA, DPA); gerontology (MS); health care administration (MS, PhD); health management and policy (MSPH); management of nonprofit agencies (MS, PhD); nurse educator (MS); public safety leadership (MS, PhD); social and community services (MS, PhD); social behavioral sciences (MSPH).

Carlow University, School of Nursing, Program in Nursing Leadership and Education, Pittsburgh, PA 15213-3165. Offers MSN. Part-time and evening/weekend programs available. *Students:* 43 full-time (41 women), 15 part-time (all women); includes 2 minority (1 Black or African American, non-Hispanic/Latino; 1 Native Hawaiian or other Pacific Islander, non-Hispanic/Latino), 2 international. Average age 39. 31 applicants, 58% accepted, 10 enrolled. In 2011, 23 master's awarded. *Degree requirements:* For

master's, internship. *Entrance requirements:* For master's, minimum undergraduate GPA of 3.0 from accredited BSN program; current license as RN in Pennsylvania; course in statistics in past 6 years; two recommendations; personal statement; personal interview. Additional exam requirements/recommendations for international students: Required—TOEFL (minimum score 550 paper-based; 213 computer-based). Application fee: $20. Application fee is waived when completed online. *Expenses: Tuition:* Full-time $10,290; part-time $686 per credit. Tuition and fees vary according to course load, degree level and program. *Unit head:* Dr. Peggy Slota, Director, Nursing Leadership and DNP Programs, 412-578-6102, Fax: 412-578-6114, E-mail: mmslota@carlow.edu. *Application contact:* Jo Danhires, Administrative Assistant, Admissions, 412-578-6059, Fax: 412-578-6321, E-mail: gradstudies@carlow.edu.

Carson-Newman College, Department of Nursing, Jefferson City, TN 37760. Offers family nurse practitioner (MSN); nurse educator (MSN). *Accreditation:* AACN. *Faculty:* 2 full-time (both women), 10 part-time/adjunct (9 women). *Students:* 16 full-time (15 women), 46 part-time (36 women); includes 3 minority (2 American Indian or Alaska Native, non-Hispanic/Latino; 1 Two or more races, non-Hispanic/Latino). Average age 32. In 2011, 17 master's awarded. *Application deadline:* For fall admission, 7/15 priority date for domestic students. Applications are processed on a rolling basis. Application fee: $50. *Expenses: Tuition:* Full-time $6750; part-time $375 per credit hour. *Required fees:* $200. *Unit head:* Dr. Gregory A. Casalenuovo, Dean, 865-471-3426. *Application contact:* Graduate Admissions and Services Adviser, 865-473-3468, Fax: 865-472-3475.

Case Western Reserve University, Frances Payne Bolton School of Nursing, Doctor of Nursing Practice Program, Cleveland, OH 44106. Offers acute care nurse practitioner (DNP); adult gerontology nurse practitioner (DNP); educational leadership (DNP); family nurse practitioner (DNP); family systems psychiatric mental health nursing (DNP); midwifery/family nursing (DNP); neonatal nurse practitioner (DNP); pediatric nurse practitioner (DNP); practice leadership (DNP); women's health nurse practitioner (DNP). *Students:* 73 full-time, 194 part-time; includes 11 minority (6 Black or African American, non-Hispanic/Latino; 3 Asian, non-Hispanic/Latino; 2 Hispanic/Latino). 122 applicants, 74% accepted, 49 enrolled. In 2011, 47 doctorates awarded. Terminal master's awarded for partial completion of doctoral program. *Degree requirements:* For doctorate, thesis/dissertation. *Entrance requirements:* For doctorate, GRE General Test or MAT. Additional exam requirements/recommendations for international students: Required—TOEFL (minimum score 577 paper-based; 90 iBT), IELTS (minimum score 7). *Application deadline:* For fall admission, 6/1 priority date for domestic students, 6/1 for international students; for spring admission, 10/1 for domestic and international students. Applications are processed on a rolling basis. Application fee: $75. *Financial support:* In 2011–12, 6 students received support, including 1 teaching assistantship; research assistantships, Federal Work-Study, institutionally sponsored loans, and tuition waivers (partial) also available. Support available to part-time students. Financial award application deadline: 6/30; financial award applicants required to submit FAFSA. *Faculty research:* Clinical nursing, acute care, gerontology, mental health, critical care. *Unit head:* Dr. Donna Dowling, Director, 216-368-1869, Fax: 216-368-3542, E-mail: dad10@case.edu. *Application contact:* Donna Hassik, Admissions Coordinator, 216-368-5253, Fax: 216-368-0124, E-mail: dmh7@case.edu. Web site: http://fpb.case.edu/DNP/.

Cedar Crest College, Program in Nursing, Allentown, PA 18104-6196. Offers nursing administration (MS); nursing education (MS). Part-time programs available. *Faculty:* 5 full-time (all women). *Students:* 3 full-time, 16 part-time (all women). In 2011, 19 master's awarded. *Expenses: Tuition:* Part-time $590 per credit. Tuition and fees vary according to program. *Unit head:* Dr. Wendy Robb, Director, 610-606-4666, E-mail: wjrobb@cedarcrest.edu. *Application contact:* Bonnie Sofarelli, Director of School of Adult and Graduate Education, 610-606-4666, E-mail: sage@cedarcrest.edu. Web site: http://sage.cedarcrest.edu/degrees/graduate/nursing-science/.

Cedarville University, Graduate Programs, Cedarville, OH 45314-0601. Offers family nurse practitioner (MSN); global health nursing (MSN); nurse educator (MSN); teacher leader (M Ed). Part-time programs available. *Faculty:* 27 part-time/adjunct (14 women). *Students:* 13 full-time (11 women), 66 part-time (51 women), 2 international. Average age 33. 65 applicants, 83% accepted, 38 enrolled. In 2011, 2 master's awarded. *Degree requirements:* For master's, thesis. *Entrance requirements:* For master's, GRE, 2 professional recommendations. Additional exam requirements/recommendations for international students: Required—TOEFL (minimum score 550 paper-based; 80 iBT). *Application deadline:* For fall admission, 5/1 priority date for domestic students, 5/1 for international students; for spring admission, 11/1 priority date for domestic students, 11/1 for international students. Applications are processed on a rolling basis. Application fee: $30. Electronic applications accepted. *Financial support:* Scholarships/grants and unspecified assistantships available. Support available to part-time students. Financial award applicants required to submit FAFSA. *Unit head:* Dr. Andrew A. Runyan, Senior Associate Academic Vice-President/Dean of Graduate Studies, 937-766-3840, E-mail: arunyan@cedarville.edu. *Application contact:* Roscoe F. Smith, Associate Vice-President of Enrollment, 937-766-7700, Fax: 937-766-7575, E-mail: smithr@cedarville.edu. Web site: http://www.cedarville.edu/academics/graduate/.

Chatham University, Nursing Programs, Pittsburgh, PA 15232-2826. Offers education/leadership (MSN); nursing (DNP). *Accreditation:* AACN. Postbaccalaureate distance learning degree programs offered (minimal on-campus study). *Faculty:* 10 full-time (8 women), 11 part-time/adjunct (9 women). *Students:* 37 full-time (31 women), 62 part-time (58 women); includes 19 minority (16 Black or African American, non-Hispanic/Latino; 1 Asian, non-Hispanic/Latino; 1 Hispanic/Latino; 1 Native Hawaiian or other Pacific Islander, non-Hispanic/Latino). Average age 45. 163 applicants, 72% accepted, 84 enrolled. In 2011, 20 master's, 73 doctorates awarded. *Entrance requirements:* For master's, RN license, BSN, minimum GPA of 3.0; for doctorate, RN license, MSN. Additional exam requirements/recommendations for international students: Required—TOEFL (minimum score 600 paper-based; 250 computer-based; 100 iBT), IELTS (minimum score 6.5), TWE. *Application deadline:* For fall admission, 5/1 priority date for domestic students, 5/1 for international students. Applications are processed on a rolling basis. Application fee: $0. Electronic applications accepted. Application fee is waived when completed online. *Expenses: Tuition:* Full-time $13,896. Tuition and fees vary according to program. *Financial support:* Applicants required to submit FAFSA. *Unit head:* Dr. Elizabeth Gazza, Director, 412-365-2746, E-mail: egazza@chatham.edu. *Application contact:* David Vey, Admissions Support Specialist, 412-365-1498, Fax: 412-365-1720, E-mail: dvey@chatham.edu. Web site: http://www.chatham.edu/nursing.

Clarion University of Pennsylvania, Office of Graduate Programs, Master of Science in Nursing Program, Clarion, PA 16214. Offers family nurse practitioner (MSN, Post-Master's Certificate); nurse educator (MSN). Program offered jointly with Slippery Rock University of Pennsylvania. *Accreditation:* NLN. *Students:* 3 full-time (2 women), 60 part-time (59 women); includes 2 minority (both Black or African American, non-Hispanic/Latino). Average age 39. In 2011, 25 master's awarded. *Degree requirements:* For master's, comprehensive exam, thesis. *Entrance requirements:* For master's, minimum QPA of 2.75. Additional exam requirements/recommendations for international students: Required—TOEFL (minimum score 550 paper-based; 213 computer-based; 80 iBT). *Application deadline:* For fall admission, 6/1 for domestic students, 4/15 for international students; for spring admission, 11/1 for domestic students, 9/15 for international students. Application fee: $30. *Expenses:* Tuition, state resident: part-time $429 per credit. Tuition, nonresident: part-time $644 per credit. *Financial support:* Research assistantships with full tuition reimbursements available. Financial award application deadline: 3/1. *Unit head:* Dr. Debbie Ciesielka, Graduate Coordinator, 412-578-7277, E-mail: dciesielka@clarion.edu. *Application contact:* Dr. Brenda Sanders Dede, Assistant Vice President for Academic Affairs, 814-393-2337, Fax: 814-393-2030, E-mail: bdede@clarion.edu.

Clarke University, Department of Nursing and Health, Dubuque, IA 52001-3198. Offers administration of nursing systems (MSN); advanced practice nursing (MSN); education (MSN); family nurse practitioner (MSN, PMC). *Accreditation:* AACN. Part-time programs available. *Faculty:* 5 full-time (all women), 2 part-time/adjunct (1 woman). *Students:* 42 full-time (41 women), 25 part-time (all women); includes 1 minority (Black or African American, non-Hispanic/Latino). Average age 35. In 2011, 13 master's awarded. *Entrance requirements:* For master's, GRE General Test or MAT, BSN, minimum GPA of 3.0. *Application deadline:* For fall admission, 2/15 priority date for domestic students; for spring admission, 12/15 priority date for domestic students. Applications are processed on a rolling basis. Application fee: $25. Electronic applications accepted. *Expenses: Tuition:* Part-time $690 per credit hour. *Required fees:* $35 per credit hour. Tuition and fees vary according to program and student level. *Financial support:* In 2011–12, 6 students received support. Career-related internships or fieldwork available. Support available to part-time students. Financial award applicants required to submit FAFSA. *Faculty research:* Narrative pedagogy, ethics, end-of-life care, pedagogy, family systems. *Unit head:* Dr. Susan DeCrane, Chair, 800-224-2736, Fax: 319-584-8684. *Application contact:* Carrie Kirk, Information Contact, 563-588-6635, Fax: 563-588-6789, E-mail: graduate@clarke.edu. Web site: http://www.clarke.edu/.

Clarkson College, Master of Science in Nursing Program, Omaha, NE 68131. Offers adult nurse practitioner (MSN, Post-Master's Certificate); family nurse practitioner (MSN, Post-Master's Certificate); nursing education (MSN, Post-Master's Certificate); nursing health care leadership (MSN, Post-Master's Certificate). *Accreditation:* AANA/CANAEP; NLN. Part-time and evening/weekend programs available. Postbaccalaureate distance learning degree programs offered (minimal on-campus study). *Degree requirements:* For master's, on-campus skills assessment (family nurse practitioner, adult nurse practitioner), comprehensive exam or thesis. *Entrance requirements:* For master's, minimum GPA of 3.0, 2 references, resume. Additional exam requirements/recommendations for international students: Required—TOEFL (minimum score 600 paper-based; 250 computer-based; 100 iBT). Electronic applications accepted.

Cleveland State University, College of Graduate Studies, School of Nursing, Cleveland, OH 44115. Offers clinical nurse leader (MSN); forensic nursing (MSN); nursing education (MSN); specialized population (MSN); urban education (PhD), including nursing education; MSN/MBA. *Accreditation:* AACN. Part-time programs available. Postbaccalaureate distance learning degree programs offered (no on-campus study). *Faculty:* 4 full-time (all women), 1 (woman) part-time/adjunct. *Students:* 5 full-time (3 women), 50 part-time (47 women); includes 8 minority (7 Black or African American, non-Hispanic/Latino; 1 Hispanic/Latino), 1 international. Average age 43. 41 applicants, 73% accepted, 13 enrolled. In 2011, 7 master's awarded. *Degree requirements:* For master's, thesis or alternative, portfolio, population health project; for doctorate, comprehensive exam, thesis/dissertation. *Entrance requirements:* For master's, RN license, BSN, course work in statistics; for doctorate, GRE (for PhD in urban education). Additional exam requirements/recommendations for international students: Required—TOEFL (minimum score 525 paper-based; 197 computer-based), IELTS (minimum score 6). *Application deadline:* For fall admission, 3/1 priority date for domestic students, 3/1 for international students. Application fee: $55. Electronic applications accepted. *Expenses:* Tuition, state resident: full-time $6416; part-time $494 per credit hour. Tuition, nonresident: full-time $12,074; part-time $929 per credit hour. *Financial support:* In 2011–12, 4 students received support. Tuition waivers (full), unspecified assistantships, and Nurse Faculty Loan Program (NFLP) available. Support available to part-time students. Financial award application deadline: 3/1; financial award applicants required to submit FAFSA. *Faculty research:* Diabetes management, African-American elders medication compliance, risk in home visiting, suffering, COPD and stress, nursing education, disaster health preparedness. *Total annual research expenditures:* $59,000. *Unit head:* Dr. Vida Lock, Dean, 216-523-7237, Fax: 216-687-3556, E-mail: v.lock@csuohio.edu. *Application contact:* Carol Ivan, Recruiter/Advisor, 216-687-5517, Fax: 216-687-3556, E-mail: c.ivan@csuohio.edu. Web site: http://www.csuohio.edu/nursing/.

College of Mount St. Joseph, Master of Science in Nursing Program, Cincinnati, OH 45233-1670. Offers administration (MSN); education (MSN). Part-time programs available. *Entrance requirements:* For master's, essay; BSN from regionally-accredited university; minimum undergraduate GPA of 3.25 or GRE; professional resume; three professional references; interview; 2 years of clinical nursing experience; active RN license; criminal background check. Additional exam requirements/recommendations for international students: Required—TOEFL (minimum score 560 paper-based; 220 computer-based; 83 iBT). Application fee: $50. Electronic applications accepted. *Expenses: Tuition:* Full-time $24,200; part-time $540 per credit hour. *Required fees:* $112.50 per semester. One-time fee: $200. *Financial support:* Applicants required to submit FAFSA. *Unit head:* Dr. Lynn Bertsch, Director, 513-244-4200, E-mail: lynn_bertsch@mail.msj.edu. *Application contact:* Marilyn Hoskins, Assistant Director for Graduate Recruitment, 513-244-4723, Fax: 513-244-4629, E-mail: marilyn_hoskins@mail.msj.edu. Web site: http://www.msj.edu/view/academics/graduate-programs/master-of-science-in-nursing-.aspx.

College of Mount Saint Vincent, School of Professional and Continuing Studies, Department of Nursing, Riverdale, NY 10471-1093. Offers adult nurse practitioner (MSN, PMC); family nurse practitioner (MSN, PMC); nurse educator (PMC); nursing administration (MSN); nursing for the adult and aged (MSN). *Accreditation:* AACN. Part-time programs available. *Entrance requirements:* For master's, BSN, interview, RN license, minimum GPA of 3.0, letters of reference. Additional exam requirements/recommendations for international students: Required—TOEFL. *Expenses:* Contact institution.

The College of New Rochelle, Graduate School, Program in Nursing, New Rochelle, NY 10805-2308. Offers acute care nurse practitioner (MS, Certificate); clinical specialist in holistic nursing (MS, Certificate); family nurse practitioner (MS, Certificate); nursing and health care management (MS); nursing education (Certificate). *Accreditation:* AACN. Part-time programs available. *Entrance requirements:* For master's, GRE General Test or MAT, BSN, malpractice insurance, minimum GPA of 3.0, RN license. *Expenses:* Contact institution. *Faculty research:* Holistic modalities, academic success variables.

College of Staten Island of the City University of New York, Graduate Programs, Department of Nursing, Program in Nursing Education, Staten Island, NY 10314-6600. Offers 6th Year Certificate. *Students:* 1. In 2011, 2 6th Year Certificates awarded. *Entrance requirements:* Additional exam requirements/recommendations for international students: Required—TOEFL (minimum score 550 paper-based; 213 computer-based; 79 iBT), IELTS (minimum score 6.5). *Application deadline:* For fall admission, 4/18 priority date for domestic students, 4/18 for international students; for spring admission, 11/21 priority date for domestic students, 11/21 for international students. Application fee: $125. *Expenses:* Tuition, state resident: full-time $8210; part-

time $345 per credit. Tuition, nonresident: part-time $640 per credit. *Required fees:* $128 per semester. *Financial support:* Career-related internships or fieldwork, Federal Work-Study, and scholarships/grants available. Support available to part-time students. Financial award applicants required to submit FAFSA. *Unit head:* Prof. Mary Ellen McMorrow, Coordinator, 718-982-3823, Fax: 718-982-3813, E-mail: maryellen.mcmorrow@csi.cuny.edu. *Application contact:* Sasha Spence, Assistant Director for Graduate Admissions, 718-982-2699, Fax: 718-982-2500, E-mail: sasha.spence@csi.cuny.edu. Web site: http://www.csi.cuny.edu/nursing/graduate.html.

Concordia University Wisconsin, Graduate Programs, School of Human Services, Program in Nursing, Mequon, WI 53097-2402. Offers family nurse practitioner (MSN); geriatric nurse practitioner (MSN); nurse educator (MSN). *Accreditation:* AACN. Postbaccalaureate distance learning degree programs offered (minimal on-campus study). *Faculty:* 2 full-time (1 woman), 5 part-time/adjunct (all women). *Students:* 84 full-time (77 women), 359 part-time (347 women); includes 52 minority (20 Black or African American, non-Hispanic/Latino; 2 American Indian or Alaska Native, non-Hispanic/Latino; 11 Asian, non-Hispanic/Latino; 9 Hispanic/Latino; 10 Two or more races, non-Hispanic/Latino; 1 international. Average age 36. In 2011, 37 master's awarded. *Degree requirements:* For master's, comprehensive exam, thesis or alternative. *Entrance requirements:* Additional exam requirements/recommendations for international students: Required—TOEFL. *Application deadline:* For fall admission, 8/1 priority date for domestic students. Applications are processed on a rolling basis. Application fee: $35. *Expenses:* Contact institution. *Financial support:* Application deadline: 8/1. *Unit head:* Dr. Ruth Gresley, Director, 262-243-4452, E-mail: ruth.gresley@cuw.edu. *Application contact:* Mary Eberhardt, Graduate Admissions, 262-243-4551, Fax: 262-243-4428, E-mail: mary.eberhardt@cuw.edu.

Cox College, Programs in Nursing, Springfield, MO 65802. Offers clinical nurse leader (MSN); family nurse practitioner (MSN); nurse educator (MSN). *Accreditation:* AACN. *Entrance requirements:* For master's, RN license, essay, 2 letters of recommendation, official transcripts. Electronic applications accepted.

Daemen College, Department of Nursing, Amherst, NY 14226-3592. Offers adult nurse practitioner (MS, Post Master's Certificate); nurse executive leadership (Post Master's Certificate); nursing education (MS, Post Master's Certificate); nursing executive leadership (MS); nursing practice (DNP); palliative care nursing (Post Master's Certificate). *Accreditation:* NLN. Part-time programs available. *Degree requirements:* For master's, thesis or alternative, degree completed in 4 years; minimum GPA of 3.0; for doctorate, degree completed in 5 years; 500 post-master's clinical hours. *Entrance requirements:* For master's, BN, 1 year medical/surgical experience, RN license and state registration, statistics course with minimum C grade, 3 letters of recommendation, minimum GPA of 3.25, interview; for doctorate, MS in advance nursing practice; New York state RN license; goal statement; resume; interview; statistics course with minimum grade of 'C'; for Post Master's Certificate, master's degree in clinical area; RN license and current registration; one year of clinical experience; statistics course with minimum grade of 'C'; 3 letters of recommendation; interview; letter of intent. Additional exam requirements/recommendations for international students: Required—TOEFL (minimum score 500 paper-based; 173 computer-based; 63 iBT), IELTS (minimum score 5.5). Electronic applications accepted. *Faculty research:* Professional stress, client behavior, drug therapy, treatment modalities and pulmonary cancers, chemical dependency.

Delta State University, Graduate Programs, School of Nursing, Cleveland, MS 38733-0001. Offers family nurse practitioner (MSN); nurse administrator (MSN); nurse educator (MSN). *Accreditation:* AACN. Part-time programs available. *Degree requirements:* For master's, thesis optional. *Entrance requirements:* For master's, GRE General Test. Electronic applications accepted. *Expenses:* Tuition, state resident: full-time $4702; part-time $294 per credit hour. Tuition, nonresident: full-time $12,516; part-time $760 per credit hour. *Required fees:* $586.

DeSales University, Graduate Division, Division of Healthcare and Natural Sciences, Center Valley, PA 18034-9568. Offers adult advanced practice nurse specialist (MSN); certified nurse midwives (MSN); certified nurse practitioners (MSN); clinical leadership (DNP); family nurse practitioner (MSN); nurse educator (MSN); nurse practitioner (Post-Master's Certificate); MSN/MBA. *Accreditation:* NLN. Part-time programs available. *Degree requirements:* For master's, thesis optional. *Entrance requirements:* For master's, GRE General Test, MAT, minimum B average in undergraduate course work, health assessment course or equivalent, course work in statistics. Additional exam requirements/recommendations for international students: Required—TOEFL. *Application deadline:* Applications are processed on a rolling basis. Application fee: $35. Electronic applications accepted. Tuition and fees vary according to degree level. *Financial support:* Applicants required to submit FAFSA. *Unit head:* Dr. Carol Gullo Mest, Director, 610-282-1100 Ext. 1394, Fax: 610-282-2091, E-mail: carol.mest@desales.edu. *Application contact:* Caryn Stopper, Director of Graduate Admissions, 610-282-1100 Ext. 1768, Fax: 610-282-2254, E-mail: caryn.stopper@desales.edu.

Drexel University, College of Nursing and Health Professions, Division of Graduate Nursing, Philadelphia, PA 19104-2875. Offers adult acute care (MSN); adult psychiatric/mental health (MSN); advanced practice nursing (MSN); clinical trials research (MSN); family nurse practitioner (MSN); leadership in health systems management (MSN); nursing education (MSN); pediatric primary care (MSN); women's health (MSN). *Accreditation:* AACN; NLN. Electronic applications accepted.

Duke University, School of Nursing, Durham, NC 27708-0586. Offers adult acute care (Certificate); adult cardiovascular (Certificate); adult oncology (Certificate); adult primary care (Certificate); clinical nurse specialist (MSN), including adult oncology, gerontology, neonatal, pediatric; clinical research management (MSN, Certificate); family (Certificate); gerontology (Certificate); health and nursing ministries (MSN, Certificate); health systems leadership and outcomes (Certificate); neonatal (Certificate); neonatal/pediatric in rural health (MSN, Certificate); nurse anesthetist (MSN, Certificate); nurse practitioner (MSN), including adult acute care, adult cardiovascular, adult oncology, adult primary care, family, gerontology, neonatal, pediatric, pediatric acute care; nursing (DNP, PhD); nursing and healthcare leadership (MSN); nursing education (MSN); nursing informatics (MSN, Certificate); pediatric (Certificate); pediatric acute care (Certificate); MBA/MSN; MSN/MCM. *Accreditation:* AACN; AANA/CANAEP. Part-time and evening/weekend programs available. Postbaccalaureate distance learning degree programs offered (minimal on-campus study). *Faculty:* 56 full-time (47 women), 2 part-time/adjunct (1 woman). *Students:* 127 full-time (108 women), 395 part-time (358 women); includes 92 minority (42 Black or African American, non-Hispanic/Latino; 3 American Indian or Alaska Native, non-Hispanic/Latino; 21 Asian, non-Hispanic/Latino; 14 Hispanic/Latino; 12 Two or more races, non-Hispanic/Latino; 10 international. Average age 36. 432 applicants, 45% accepted, 143 enrolled. In 2011, 117 master's, 29 doctorates, 32 other advanced degrees awarded. Terminal master's awarded for partial completion of doctoral program. *Degree requirements:* For master's, thesis optional; for doctorate, capstone project. *Entrance requirements:* For master's, GRE General Test, 1 year of nursing experience, BSN, minimum GPA of 3.0, previous course work in statistics; for doctorate, BSN or MSN, minimum GPA of 3.0, portfolio; for Certificate, MSN. Additional exam requirements/recommendations for international students: Required—TOEFL (minimum score 550 paper-based; 213 computer-based). *Application deadline:* For fall admission, 12/1 for domestic and international students; for spring

admission, 5/1 for domestic and international students. Application fee: $50. Electronic applications accepted. *Expenses:* Contact institution. *Financial support:* Career-related internships or fieldwork, institutionally sponsored loans, scholarships/grants, traineeships, and tuition waivers (partial) available. Support available to part-time students. Financial award application deadline: 4/1; financial award applicants required to submit FAFSA. *Faculty research:* Cardiovascular disease, caregiver skill training, data mining, prostate cancer, neonatal immune system. *Total annual research expenditures:* $4.7 million. *Unit head:* Dr. Catherine L. Gilliss, Dean/Vice Chancellor for Nursing Affairs, 919-684-9444, Fax: 919-684-9414, E-mail: gilli025@mc.duke.edu. *Application contact:* Bebe T. Mills, Director of Admissions, 919-684-9151, Fax: 919-668-4693, E-mail: mills031@mc.duke.edu. Web site: http://www.nursing.duke.edu/.

Duquesne University, School of Nursing, Master of Science in Nursing Program, Pittsburgh, PA 15282-0001. Offers family nurse practitioner (MSN); forensic nursing (MSN); nursing education (MSN). *Accreditation:* AACN. Part-time and evening/weekend programs available. Postbaccalaureate distance learning degree programs offered (minimal on-campus study). *Faculty:* 18 full-time (16 women), 4 part-time/adjunct (all women). *Students:* 57 full-time (55 women), 48 part-time (47 women); includes 13 minority (7 Black or African American, non-Hispanic/Latino; 3 Asian, non-Hispanic/Latino; 1 Hispanic/Latino; 2 Two or more races, non-Hispanic/Latino), 1 international. Average age 34. 72 applicants, 74% accepted, 39 enrolled. In 2011, 38 degrees awarded. *Degree requirements:* For master's, culminating paper. *Entrance requirements:* For master's, current RN license; BSN with minimum GPA of 3.0; minimum of 1 year full-time work experience as RN prior to registration in clinical or specialty course. Additional exam requirements/recommendations for international students: Required—TOEFL (minimum score 600 paper-based; 80 iBT). *Application deadline:* For fall admission, 3/1 for domestic and international students. Application fee: $0. Electronic applications accepted. *Expenses:* Tuition: Full-time $16,596; part-time $922 per credit. *Required fees:* $1584; $88 per credit. Tuition and fees vary according to program. *Financial support:* In 2011–12, 36 students received support, including 7 research assistantships with partial tuition reimbursements available (averaging $1,170 per year), 2 teaching assistantships with partial tuition reimbursements available (averaging $1,170 per year); institutionally sponsored loans, scholarships/grants, traineeships, and tuition waivers (partial) also available. Support available to part-time students. Financial award application deadline: 7/1; financial award applicants required to submit FAFSA. *Faculty research:* Vulnerable populations, social justice, cultural competence, health disparities, wellness within chronic illness. *Unit head:* Dr. Joan Such Lockhart, Professor and Associate Dean of Academic Affairs, 412-396-6540, Fax: 412-396-1821, E-mail: lockhart@duq.edu. *Application contact:* Susan Hardner, Nurse Recruiter, 412-396-4945, Fax: 412-396-6346, E-mail: nursing@duq.edu. Web site: http://www.nursing.duq.edu.

Duquesne University, School of Nursing, Post Master's Certificate Program, Pittsburgh, PA 15282-0001. Offers family nurse practitioner (Post-Master's Certificate); forensic nursing (Post-Master's Certificate); nursing education (Post-Master's Certificate); transcultural/international nursing (Post-Master's Certificate). Part-time and evening/weekend programs available. Postbaccalaureate distance learning degree programs offered (minimal on-campus study). *Faculty:* 11 full-time (10 women), 3 part-time/adjunct (all women). *Students:* 5 full-time (all women), 7 part-time (all women); includes 1 minority (Black or African American, non-Hispanic/Latino). Average age 39. 17 applicants, 71% accepted, 9 enrolled. In 2011, 2 degrees awarded. *Entrance requirements:* For degree, current RN license, BSN, MSN. Additional exam requirements/recommendations for international students: Required—TOEFL (minimum score 600 paper-based; 80 iBT). *Application deadline:* For fall admission, 3/1 for domestic and international students. Application fee: $0. *Expenses:* Tuition: Full-time $16,596; part-time $922 per credit. *Required fees:* $1584; $88 per credit. Tuition and fees vary according to program. *Financial support:* In 2011–12, 5 students received support, including 2 teaching assistantships with partial tuition reimbursements available (averaging $1,170 per year); institutionally sponsored loans, scholarships/grants, traineeships, and tuition waivers (partial) also available. Support available to part-time students. Financial award application deadline: 7/1; financial award applicants required to submit FAFSA. *Faculty research:* Vulnerable populations, social justice, cultural competence, health disparities, wellness within chronic illness. *Unit head:* Dr. Joan Such Lockhart, Professor and Associate Dean of Academic Affairs, 412-396-6540, Fax: 412-396-1821, E-mail: lockhart@duq.edu. *Application contact:* Susan Hardner, Nurse Recruiter, 412-396-4945, Fax: 412-396-6346, E-mail: nursing@duq.edu. Web site: http://www.duq.edu/nursing/post-masters-certificates/index.cfm.

D'Youville College, School of Nursing, Buffalo, NY 14201-1084. Offers community health nursing/education (MSN); community health nursing/management (MSN); family nurse practitioner (MS, Post-Master's Certificate); nursing and health-related professions (Certificate); nursing with clinical focus choice (MSN). *Accreditation:* AACN. Part-time programs available. *Faculty:* 7 full-time (all women), 7 part-time/adjunct (6 women). *Students:* 78 full-time (72 women), 133 part-time (117 women); includes 33 minority (23 Black or African American, non-Hispanic/Latino; 2 American Indian or Alaska Native, non-Hispanic/Latino; 1 Asian, non-Hispanic/Latino; 6 Hispanic/Latino; 1 Two or more races, non-Hispanic/Latino), 86 international. Average age 35. 226 applicants, 39% accepted, 57 enrolled. In 2011, 54 master's, 1 other advanced degree awarded. *Degree requirements:* For master's, thesis or alternative, membership on board of community agency, publishable paper. *Entrance requirements:* For master's, BS in nursing, minimum GPA of 3.0, course work in statistics and computers. Additional exam requirements/recommendations for international students: Required—TOEFL (minimum score 500 paper-based; 173 computer-based). *Application deadline:* For fall admission, 5/1 for international students; for spring admission, 9/1 for international students. Applications are processed on a rolling basis. Application fee: $25. Electronic applications accepted. *Expenses:* Tuition: Full-time $18,960; part-time $790 per credit hour. *Required fees:* $310. Tuition and fees vary according to degree level and program. *Financial support:* Federal Work-Study, scholarships/grants, traineeships, and unspecified assistantships available. Support available to part-time students. Financial award application deadline: 3/1; financial award applicants required to submit FAFSA. *Faculty research:* Nursing curriculum, nursing theory-testing, wellness research, communication and socialization patterns. *Unit head:* Dr. Eileen Nahigian, Chair, 716-829-7856, Fax: 716-829-8159. *Application contact:* Linda Fisher, Graduate Admissions Director, 716-829-8400, Fax: 716-829-7900, E-mail: graduateadmissions@dyc.edu.

See Display on page 629 and Close-Up on page 795.

Eastern Michigan University, Graduate School, College of Health and Human Services, School of Nursing, Ypsilanti, MI 48197. Offers nursing (MSN); quality improvement in health care systems (Graduate Certificate); teaching in health care systems (MSN, Graduate Certificate). *Accreditation:* AACN. Part-time and evening/weekend programs available. Postbaccalaureate distance learning degree programs offered (minimal on-campus study). *Faculty:* 20 full-time (18 women). *Students:* 2 full-time (both women), 33 part-time (27 women); includes 20 minority (14 Black or African American, non-Hispanic/Latino; 5 Asian, non-Hispanic/Latino; 1 Hispanic/Latino). Average age 46. 32 applicants, 56% accepted, 8 enrolled. In 2011, 11 master's, 15 other advanced degrees awarded. *Degree requirements:* For master's, thesis optional. *Entrance requirements:* For master's, GRE General Test, Michigan RN license.

Additional exam requirements/recommendations for international students: Required—TOEFL. *Application deadline:* Applications are processed on a rolling basis. Application fee: $35. *Expenses:* Tuition, state resident: full-time $10,367; part-time $432 per credit hour. Tuition, nonresident: full-time $20,435; part-time $851 per credit hour. *Required fees:* $39 per credit hour. $46 per semester. One-time fee: $100. Tuition and fees vary according to course level, degree level and reciprocity agreements. *Financial support:* Fellowships, research assistantships with full tuition reimbursements, teaching assistantships with full tuition reimbursements, career-related internships or fieldwork, Federal Work-Study, institutionally sponsored loans, scholarships/grants, tuition waivers (partial), and unspecified assistantships available. Support available to part-time students. Financial award applicants required to submit FAFSA. *Unit head:* Dr. Peggy Trewn, Interim Director, 734-487-2310, Fax: 734-487-6946, E-mail: ptrewn@emich.edu. *Application contact:* Dr. Virginia Lan, MSN Coordinator, 734-487-2310, Fax: 734-487-6946, E-mail: vlan@emich.edu. Web site: http://www.emich.edu/nursing.

East Tennessee State University, School of Graduate Studies, College of Nursing, Master's Nursing Programs, Johnson City, TN 37614. Offers advanced practice nursing (MSN); nursing (MSN); nursing administration (MSN); nursing education (MSN); nursing informatics (MSN). Part-time programs available. Postbaccalaureate distance learning degree programs offered. *Students:* 50 full-time (47 women), 137 part-time (126 women); includes 4 minority (1 American Indian or Alaska Native, non-Hispanic/Latino; 2 Hispanic/Latino; 1 Two or more races, non-Hispanic/Latino), 1 international. 151 applicants, 29% accepted, 44 enrolled. In 2011, 74 master's awarded. *Degree requirements:* For master's, comprehensive exam (for some programs), culminating project (for some programs). *Entrance requirements:* For master's, minimum GPA of 3.0, RN license, resume, 3 letters of recommendation. Additional exam requirements/recommendations for international students: Required—TOEFL (minimum score 600 paper-based; 250 computer-based; 100 iBT). *Application deadline:* For fall admission, 2/1 for domestic and international students; for spring admission, 7/1 for domestic and international students. Application fee: $35 ($45 for international students). Electronic applications accepted. *Expenses:* Tuition, state resident: full-time $7312; part-time $350 per credit hour. Tuition, nonresident: full-time $18,490; part-time $621 per credit hour. *Required fees:* $63 per credit hour. Tuition and fees vary according to course load and program. *Financial support:* In 2011–12, 2 students received support. Institutionally sponsored loans, scholarships/grants, tuition waivers (full), and unspecified assistantships available. Support available to part-time students. Financial award application deadline: 7/1; financial award applicants required to submit FAFSA. *Faculty research:* Rural primary care, healthcare for the homeless and underserved, community health problems across the lifespan, nursing education research, school health services. *Unit head:* Dr. Nancy Cameron, Coordinator, 423-439-4874, Fax: 423-439-4100, E-mail: cameronng@etsu.edu. *Application contact:* Linda Raines, Graduate Specialist, 423-439-6158, Fax: 423-439-5624, E-mail: raineslt@etsu.edu.

Edinboro University of Pennsylvania, College of Arts and Sciences, Department of Nursing, Edinboro, PA 16444. Offers nurse educator (Certificate); nursing (MSN); palliative and end-of-life care (Certificate). *Accreditation:* NLN. Part-time and evening/weekend programs available. *Faculty:* 3 full-time (all women). *Students:* 40 part-time (37 women). Average age 39. In 2011, 20 master's awarded. *Degree requirements:* For master's, thesis, competency exam. *Entrance requirements:* For master's, GRE or MAT, minimum QPA of 2.5. *Application deadline:* Applications are processed on a rolling basis. Application fee: $30. Electronic applications accepted. *Financial support:* In 2011–12, 2 research assistantships with full and partial tuition reimbursements (averaging $4,050 per year) were awarded; career-related internships or fieldwork, Federal Work-Study, scholarships/grants, and unspecified assistantships also available. Support available to part-time students. Financial award application deadline: 2/15; financial award applicants required to submit FAFSA. *Unit head:* Dr. Alice Conway, Program Head, 814-732-2285, E-mail: aconwayt@edinboro.edu. *Application contact:* Dr. Alan Biel, Dean, 814-732-2752, Fax: 814-732-2268, E-mail: biel@edinboro.edu.

Elms College, Division of Nursing, Chicopee, MA 01013-2839. Offers nursing and health services management (MSN); nursing education (MSN). *Accreditation:* AACN. Part-time and evening/weekend programs available. *Entrance requirements:* Additional exam requirements/recommendations for international students: Required—TOEFL.

Emmanuel College, Graduate and Professional Programs, Graduate Program in Nursing, Boston, MA 02115. Offers nursing education (MSN); nursing management/administration (MSN). Part-time and evening/weekend programs available. *Faculty:* 5 full-time (all women). *Students:* 21 part-time (20 women); includes 4 minority (3 Black or African American, non-Hispanic/Latino; 1 Asian, non-Hispanic/Latino). Average age 49. 44 applicants, 68% accepted, 21 enrolled. *Degree requirements:* For master's, 36 credits, including 6-credit practicum. *Entrance requirements:* For master's, essay, resume, proof of RN license (nursing applicants only), interview. Additional exam requirements/recommendations for international students: Required—TOEFL (minimum score 600 paper-based; 250 computer-based; 106 iBT) or IELTS (minimum score 6.5). *Application deadline:* For fall admission, 4/30 for domestic students. Applications are processed on a rolling basis. Application fee: $0. Electronic applications accepted. *Expenses: Tuition:* Part-time $2139 per course. Tuition and fees vary according to program and reciprocity agreements. *Financial support:* Applicants required to submit FAFSA. *Unit head:* Dr. Joyce DeLeo, Vice President of Academic Affairs, 617-735-9700, Fax: 617-507-0434, E-mail: gpp@emmanuel.edu. *Application contact:* Enrollment Counselor, 617-735-9700, Fax: 617-507-0434, E-mail: gpp@emmanuel.edu. Web site: http://gpp.emmanuel.edu.

Excelsior College, School of Nursing, Albany, NY 12203-5159. Offers clinical systems management (MS); nursing (MS); nursing education (MS); nursing informatics (MS). *Accreditation:* NLN. Part-time and evening/weekend programs available. Postbaccalaureate distance learning degree programs offered (no on-campus study). *Entrance requirements:* For master's, RN license. Electronic applications accepted. *Faculty research:* Leadership development, test anxiety, use of technology in online learning.

Felician College, Program in Nursing, Lodi, NJ 07644-2117. Offers adult nurse practitioner (MSN, PMC); family nurse practitioner (MSN, PMC); nursing (MSN); nursing education (MSN). *Accreditation:* AACN. Part-time and evening/weekend programs available. Postbaccalaureate distance learning degree programs offered (no on-campus study). *Students:* 4 full-time (all women), 74 part-time (64 women); includes 18 minority (10 Black or African American, non-Hispanic/Latino; 5 Asian, non-Hispanic/Latino; 3 Hispanic/Latino). Average age 42. 29 applicants, 90% accepted, 24 enrolled. *Degree requirements:* For master's, scholarly project. *Entrance requirements:* For master's, BS in nursing or equivalent, minimum GPA of 3.0, 2 letters of recommendation, RN license; for PMC, RN license, minimum GPA of 2.75. Additional exam requirements/recommendations for international students: Recommended—TOEFL (minimum score 550 paper-based; 213 computer-based). *Application deadline:* Applications are processed on a rolling basis. Application fee: $40. *Expenses: Tuition:* Part-time $925 per credit. *Required fees:* $262.50 per semester. Part-time tuition and fees vary according to class time and student level. *Financial support:* In 2011–12, 10 students received support. Traineeships available. Financial award applicants required to submit FAFSA. *Faculty research:* Anxiety and fear, curriculum innovation, health promotion. *Unit head:* Dr. Muriel Shore, Dean, Division of Health Sciences, 201-559-6030, E-mail: shorem@felician.edu. *Application contact:* Elizabeth Barca, Senior Assistant Director, Graduate Admissions, 201-559-6077, Fax: 201-559-6138, E-mail: graduate@felician.edu.

See Display on page 630 and Close-Up on page 797.

Ferris State University, College of Allied Health Sciences, School of Nursing, Big Rapids, MI 49307. Offers nursing (MSN); nursing administration (MSN); nursing education (MSN); nursing informatics (MSN). *Accreditation:* NLN. Part-time and evening/weekend programs available. Postbaccalaureate distance learning degree programs offered (minimal on-campus study). *Faculty:* 5 full-time (all women), 1 (woman) part-time/adjunct. *Students:* 7 full-time (all women), 80 part-time (70 women); includes 3 minority (1 Black or African American, non-Hispanic/Latino; 2 Two or more races, non-Hispanic/Latino). Average age 42. 34 applicants, 85% accepted, 24 enrolled. In 2011, 16 master's awarded. *Degree requirements:* For master's, comprehensive exam, practicum, scholarly project. *Entrance requirements:* For master's, BS in nursing or related field with registered nurse license, writing sample, letters of reference, 2 years' clinical experience. Additional exam requirements/recommendations for international students: Required—TOEFL (minimum score 550 paper-based; 173 computer-based; 61 iBT). *Application deadline:* For fall admission, 4/15 priority date for domestic students; for spring admission, 10/15 for domestic students. Applications are processed on a rolling basis. Application fee: $30. Electronic applications accepted. Application fee is waived when completed online. *Financial support:* In 2011–12, 4 students received support. Fellowships, research assistantships, teaching assistantships, career-related internships or fieldwork, and scholarships/grants available. Financial award application deadline: 4/15. *Faculty research:* Nursing education-minority student focus, student attitudes toward aging. *Unit head:* Dr. Marietta Bell-Scriber, Program Coordinator, 231-591-2288, Fax: 231-591-2325, E-mail: bellscm@ferris.edu. *Application contact:* Debby Buck, Off-Campus Program Secretary, 231-591-2270, Fax: 231-591-3788, E-mail: buckd@ferris.edu.

Florida Southern College, Program in Nursing, Lakeland, FL 33801-5698. Offers clinical nurse specialist (MSN); nurse educator (MSN); nurse practitioner (MSN). *Accreditation:* AACN. Part-time and evening/weekend programs available. *Entrance requirements:* For master's, Florida RN license, 3 letters of recommendation, personal statement, minimum GPA of 3.0, resume. Additional exam requirements/recommendations for international students: Required—TOEFL (minimum score 550 paper-based). *Expenses:* Contact institution. *Faculty research:* End of life care, dementia, health promotion.

Florida State University, The Graduate School, College of Nursing, Tallahassee, FL 32312. Offers family nurse practitioner (DNP); health systems leadership (DNP); nurse educator (MSN, Certificate); nurse leader (MSN); nursing leadership (Certificate, Post-Graduate Certificate). *Accreditation:* AACN. Part-time programs available. Postbaccalaureate distance learning degree programs offered (no on-campus study). *Faculty:* 13 full-time (12 women). *Students:* 24 full-time (21 women), 63 part-time (58 women); includes 15 minority (4 Black or African American, non-Hispanic/Latino; 1 Asian, non-Hispanic/Latino; 8 Hispanic/Latino; 2 Two or more races, non-Hispanic/Latino). Average age 38. 33 applicants, 100% accepted, 33 enrolled. In 2011, 9 master's, 4 doctorates awarded. *Degree requirements:* For master's, thesis optional. *Entrance requirements:* For master's, GRE General Test, MAT, minimum GPA of 3.0, BSN, Florida RN license; for doctorate, GRE General Test, MAT, minimum GPA of 3.0, BSN or MSN, Florida RN license. Additional exam requirements/recommendations for international students: Required—TOEFL (minimum score 550 paper-based). *Application deadline:* For fall admission, 7/1 for domestic and international students. Application fee: $30. Electronic applications accepted. *Expenses:* Tuition, state resident: full-time $9474; part-time $350.88 per credit hour. Tuition, nonresident: full-time $16,236; part-time $601.34 per credit hour. *Required fees:* $630 per semester. One-time fee: $20. Tuition and fees vary according to course load and campus/location. *Financial support:* In 2011–12, 75 students received support, including fellowships with partial tuition reimbursements available (averaging $6,300 per year), research assistantships with partial tuition reimbursements available (averaging $3,000 per year), 3 teaching assistantships with partial tuition reimbursements available (averaging $3,000 per year); career-related internships or fieldwork, Federal Work-Study, institutionally sponsored loans, scholarships/grants, traineeships, and tuition waivers (partial) also available. Financial award application deadline: 4/15; financial award applicants required to submit FAFSA. *Faculty research:* Distance learning, gerontology, health promotion, educational strategies, rehabilitation of brain injured patients. *Unit head:* Dr. Diane Speake, Interim Dean, 850-644-6846, Fax: 850-644-7660, E-mail: dspeake@nursing.fsu.edu. *Application contact:* Carlos G. Urrutia, Director of Student Services, 850-644-5638, Fax: 850-645-7249, E-mail: currutia@fsu.edu. Web site: http://nursing.fsu.edu/.

Framingham State University, Division of Graduate and Continuing Education, Program in Nursing, Framingham, MA 01701-9101. Offers nursing education (MSN); nursing leadership (MSN). *Accreditation:* AACN. *Entrance requirements:* For master's, BSN; minimum cumulative undergraduate GPA of 3.0, 3.25 in nursing courses; coursework in statistics; 2 letters of recommendation; interview. Electronic applications accepted.

George Mason University, College of Health and Human Services, School of Nursing, Fairfax, VA 22030. Offers forensic nursing (Certificate); nursing (MSN, PhD); nursing administration (Certificate); nursing education (Certificate); nursing practice (DNP). *Faculty:* 32 full-time (all women), 45 part-time/adjunct (43 women). *Students:* 70 full-time (69 women), 284 part-time (275 women); includes 109 minority (51 Black or African American, non-Hispanic/Latino; 1 American Indian or Alaska Native, non-Hispanic/Latino; 41 Asian, non-Hispanic/Latino; 12 Hispanic/Latino; 4 Two or more races, non-Hispanic/Latino), 11 international. Average age 41. 220 applicants, 56% accepted, 86 enrolled. In 2011, 79 master's, 4 doctorates, 1 other advanced degree awarded. *Degree requirements:* For master's, comprehensive exam (for some programs), thesis in clinical classes; for doctorate, comprehensive exam (for some programs), thesis/dissertation (for some programs). *Entrance requirements:* For master's, 2 official transcripts; expanded goals statement; resume; BSN from accredited institution; minimum GPA of 3.0 in last 60 credits of undergraduate work; 2 letters of recommendation; completion of undergraduate statistics and graduate-level bivariate statistics; certification in professional CPR; for doctorate, 2 official transcripts; expanded goals statement; resume; 3 recommendation letters, nursing license, at least 1 year of work experience as an RN; interview, writing sample, evidence of graduate-level course in applied statistics; master's in nursing with minimum GPA of 3.5; for Certificate, 2 official transcripts; expanded goals statement; resume; master's degree from accredited institution or currently enrolled with minimum GPA of 3.0. Additional exam requirements/recommendations for international students: Required—TOEFL (minimum score 575 paper-based; 230 computer-based; 88 iBT), IELTS, Pearson Test of English. *Application deadline:* For fall admission, 3/1 priority date for domestic students; for spring admission, 11/1 for domestic students. Application fee: $65 ($80 for international students). Electronic applications accepted. *Expenses:* Tuition, state resident: full-time $8750; part-time $364.58 per credit. Tuition, nonresident: full-time $24,092; part-time $1003.83 per credit. *Required fees:* $2514; $104.75 per credit. *Financial support:* In 2011–12, 5 students received support, including 4 research assistantships with full and partial tuition reimbursements available (averaging $26,672 per year), 1 teaching

assistantship with full and partial tuition reimbursement available (averaging $15,000 per year); career-related internships or fieldwork, Federal Work-Study, scholarships/grants, unspecified assistantships, and nurse faculty loan, health care benefits (full-time research or teaching assistantship recipients) also available. Financial award application deadline: 3/1; financial award applicants required to submit FAFSA. *Total annual research expenditures:* $607,543. *Unit head:* Robin Remsburg, Associate Dean/Director, 703-993-1904, Fax: 703-993-1949, E-mail: rremsbur@gmu.edu. *Application contact:* Janice Lee-Beverly, Program Support, 703-993-1947, Fax: 703-993-1943, E-mail: jleebev1@gmu.edu. Web site: http://chhs.gmu.edu/nursing.

Georgetown University, Graduate School of Arts and Sciences, School of Nursing and Health Studies, Washington, DC 20057. Offers acute care nurse practitioner (MS); clinical nurse specialist (MS); family nurse practitioner (MS); nurse anesthesia (MS); nurse-midwifery (MS); nursing education (MS). *Accreditation:* AACN; AANA/CANAEP; ACNM/ACME. *Degree requirements:* For master's, thesis optional. *Entrance requirements:* For master's, GRE General Test or MAT, bachelor's degree in nursing from NLN-accredited school, minimum undergraduate GPA of 3.0. Additional exam requirements/recommendations for international students: Required—TOEFL.

Goldfarb School of Nursing at Barnes-Jewish College, Graduate Programs, St. Louis, MO 63110. Offers adult acute care nurse practitioner (MSN); adult nurse practitioner (MSN); nurse anesthesia (MSN); nurse educator (MSN); nurse executive (MSN); DNP/PhD. *Accreditation:* AACN; AANA/CANAEP. Part-time and evening/weekend programs available. Postbaccalaureate distance learning degree programs offered (minimal on-campus study). *Faculty:* 38 full-time (35 women), 14 part-time/adjunct (11 women). *Students:* 79 full-time (68 women), 92 part-time (86 women); includes 45 minority (29 Black or African American, non-Hispanic/Latino; 1 American Indian or Alaska Native, non-Hispanic/Latino; 3 Asian, non-Hispanic/Latino; 3 Hispanic/Latino; 6 Native Hawaiian or other Pacific Islander, non-Hispanic/Latino; 3 Two or more races, non-Hispanic/Latino), 1 international. Average age 40. 134 applicants, 66% accepted, 51 enrolled. In 2011, 31 degrees awarded. *Degree requirements:* For master's, thesis or alternative. *Entrance requirements:* For master's, 2 references, personal statement, curriculum vitae or resume. Additional exam requirements/recommendations for international students: Required—TOEFL (minimum score 575 paper-based; 240 computer-based; 85 iBT). *Application deadline:* For fall admission, 2/1 for international students; for spring admission, 10/1 for international students. Applications are processed on a rolling basis. Application fee: $50. *Expenses: Tuition:* Full-time $14,685; part-time $630 per credit hour. *Required fees:* $280. *Financial support:* Fellowships, research assistantships, Federal Work-Study, institutionally sponsored loans, and scholarships/grants available. Support available to part-time students. Financial award applicants required to submit FAFSA. *Faculty research:* HIV Stigma, HIV symptom management, palliative care with children and their families, heart disease prevention in Hispanic women, depression in the well elderly, alternative therapies in pre-term infants. *Unit head:* Dr. Connie K. Koch, Interim Dean, 314-36-26590, Fax: 314-362-0984, E-mail: ckoch@bjc.org. *Application contact:* Dr. Michael Ward, Associate Dean for Student Programs, 314-362-9155, Fax: 314-362-0984, E-mail: mward@bjc.org.

Graceland University, School of Nursing, Independence, MO 64050-3434. Offers family nurse practitioner (MSN, PMC); nurse educator (MSN, PMC). Part-time programs available. Postbaccalaureate distance learning degree programs offered (minimal on-campus study). *Faculty:* 9 full-time (all women), 9 part-time/adjunct (7 women). *Students:* 197 full-time (181 women), 204 part-time (186 women); includes 14 minority (8 Black or African American, non-Hispanic/Latino; 1 American Indian or Alaska Native, non-Hispanic/Latino; 4 Asian, non-Hispanic/Latino; 1 Hispanic/Latino). Average age 40. 263 applicants, 71% accepted, 138 enrolled. In 2011, 88 master's, 2 other advanced degrees awarded. *Degree requirements:* For master's, comprehensive exam (for some programs), thesis optional. *Entrance requirements:* For master's, BSN from nationally-accredited program, portfolio, RN license, minimum GPA of 3.0. Additional exam requirements/recommendations for international students: Recommended—TOEFL. *Application deadline:* For fall admission, 6/1 priority date for domestic students; for winter admission, 10/1 priority date for domestic students; for spring admission, 3/1 priority date for domestic students. Application fee: $50. Electronic applications accepted. *Expenses:* Contact institution. *Financial support:* Institutionally sponsored loans and traineeships available. Support available to part-time students. Financial award applicants required to submit FAFSA. *Faculty research:* International nursing, family care-giving, health promotion. *Unit head:* Dr. Claudia D. Horton, Dean, 816-833-0524 Ext. 4214, Fax: 816-833-2990, E-mail: horton@graceland.edu. *Application contact:* Cara Hakes, Program Consultant, 816-833-0524 Ext. 4803, Fax: 816-833-2990, E-mail: chakes@graceland.edu. Web site: http://www.graceland.edu/nursing.

Grambling State University, School of Graduate Studies and Research, College of Professional Studies, School of Nursing, Grambling, LA 71245. Offers family nurse practitioner (MSN, PMC); nurse educator (MSN). *Accreditation:* NLN. Part-time programs available. *Degree requirements:* For master's, comprehensive exam (for some programs), thesis (for some programs). *Entrance requirements:* For master's, GRE, minimum GPA of 3.0 on last degree, interview, 2 years experience as RN. Additional exam requirements/recommendations for international students: Required—TOEFL (minimum score 500 paper-based; 173 computer-based; 61 iBT). Electronic applications accepted. *Expenses:* Tuition, state resident: full-time $3546; part-time $192 per credit hour. Tuition, nonresident: full-time $3456; part-time $192 per credit hour. *Required fees:* $1829; $1829 per semester hour.

Grand Canyon University, College of Nursing, Phoenix, AZ 85017-1097. Offers acute care nurse practitioner (MS, PMC); clinical nurse specialist (PMC), including clinical nurse specialist, education; family nurse practitioner (MS); leadership in health care systems (MS); nurse education (MS). *Accreditation:* AACN. Part-time and evening/weekend programs available. Postbaccalaureate distance learning degree programs offered (no on-campus study). *Degree requirements:* For master's and PMC, comprehensive exam (for some programs). *Entrance requirements:* For master's, minimum cumulative and science course undergraduate GPA of 3.0. Additional exam requirements/recommendations for international students: Required—TOEFL (minimum score 575 paper-based; 233 computer-based; 90 iBT), IELTS (minimum score 7).

Grand Valley State University, Kirkhof College of Nursing, Allendale, MI 49401-9403. Offers advanced practice (MSN); case management (MSN); nursing administration (MSN); nursing education (MSN); nursing practice (DNP); MSN/MBA. *Accreditation:* AACN. Part-time programs available. *Degree requirements:* For master's, thesis optional. *Entrance requirements:* For master's, GRE, minimum GPA of 3.0 in upper-division course work, course work in statistics, Michigan RN license. Additional exam requirements/recommendations for international students: Required—TOEFL. Electronic applications accepted. *Faculty research:* Multigenerational health promotion, chronic disease prevention, end-of-life issues, nursing workload, family caregiver health.

Grantham University, College of Arts and Sciences, Kansas City, MO 64153. Offers case management (MSN); health systems management (MS); healthcare administration (MHA); nursing (MSN); nursing education (MSN); nursing informatics (MSN); nursing management and organizational leadership (MSN). Part-time and evening/weekend programs available. Postbaccalaureate distance learning degree programs offered (no on-campus study). *Degree requirements:* For master's, thesis (for some programs),

capstone project. *Entrance requirements:* For master's, bachelor's degree from accredited degree-granting institution. Additional exam requirements/recommendations for international students: Required—TOEFL (minimum score 500 paper-based; 213 computer-based; 61 iBT). Electronic applications accepted.

Herzing University Online, Program in Nursing, Milwaukee, WI 53203. Offers nursing (MSN); nursing education (MSN); nursing management (MSN). Postbaccalaureate distance learning degree programs offered (no on-campus study).

Holy Family University, Graduate School, School of Nursing and Allied Health Professions, Philadelphia, PA 19114. Offers community health nursing (MSN); nursing administration (MSN); nursing education (MSN). *Accreditation:* AACN. Part-time and evening/weekend programs available. *Degree requirements:* For master's, thesis or alternative. *Entrance requirements:* For master's, bachelor's degree in nursing, RN license, minimum GPA of 3.0, 2 letters of reference.

See Display on page 634 and Close-Up on page 801.

Holy Names University, Graduate Division, Department of Nursing, Oakland, CA 94619-1699. Offers administration/management (MS, Certificate); clinical faculty (MS, Certificate); community health nursing/case manager (MS); family nurse practitioner (MS, Certificate); MSN/Certificate; MSN/MBA. *Accreditation:* AACN. Part-time and evening/weekend programs available. *Entrance requirements:* For master's, bachelor's degree in nursing or related field, California RN license or eligibility, minimum GPA of 3.0, previous course work in research or statistics. Additional exam requirements/recommendations for international students: Required—TOEFL (minimum score 500 paper-based). *Faculty research:* Women's reproductive health, gerontology, attitudes about aging, schizophrenic families, international health issues.

Husson University, School of Graduate and Professional Studies, Graduate Nursing Program, Bangor, ME 04401-2999. Offers advanced practice psychiatric nursing (MSN, PMC); family and community nurse practitioner (MSN, PMC); nursing education (MSN, PMC). *Accreditation:* AACN. Part-time programs available. *Faculty:* 6 full-time (all women), 6 part-time/adjunct (all women). *Students:* 49 full-time (42 women), 33 part-time (29 women); includes 2 minority (1 American Indian or Alaska Native, non-Hispanic/Latino; 1 Two or more races, non-Hispanic/Latino). 18 applicants, 13 enrolled. In 2011, 25 master's awarded. *Degree requirements:* For master's, comprehensive exam (for some programs). *Entrance requirements:* For master's, MAT or GRE, BSN. Additional exam requirements/recommendations for international students: Required—TOEFL (minimum score 550 paper-based). *Application deadline:* For fall admission, 6/30 for domestic students; for spring admission, 10/30 for domestic students. Application fee: $40. *Expenses:* Contact institution. *Financial support:* In 2011–12, 31 students received support. Federal Work-Study, institutionally sponsored loans, traineeships, and unspecified assistantships available. Financial award application deadline: 4/15; financial award applicants required to submit FAFSA. *Unit head:* Dr. Barbara Higgins, Director, Nurse Practitioner Program, 207-947-7057. *Application contact:* Kristen Card, Director of Graduate Admissions, 207-404-5660, Fax: 207-941-7935, E-mail: cardk@husson.edu.

Indiana University of Pennsylvania, School of Graduate Studies and Research, College of Health and Human Services, Department of Nursing and Allied Health, Program in Nursing Education, Indiana, PA 15705-1087. Offers MS. *Faculty:* 6 full-time (5 women). *Students:* 3 full-time (all women), 40 part-time (39 women); includes 3 minority (all Black or African American, non-Hispanic/Latino). Average age 40. 22 applicants, 59% accepted, 12 enrolled. In 2011, 8 master's awarded. *Degree requirements:* For master's, practicum. *Entrance requirements:* Additional exam requirements/recommendations for international students: Required—TOEFL (minimum score 540 paper-based; 207 computer-based). *Application deadline:* Applications are processed on a rolling basis. Application fee: $50. Electronic applications accepted. *Expenses:* Tuition, state resident: full-time $7488; part-time $416 per credit. Tuition, nonresident: full-time $11,232; part-time $624 per credit. *Required fees:* $2070; $192.20 per credit. $90 per semester. *Financial support:* In 2011–12, 3 research assistantships (averaging $3,626 per year) were awarded. Financial award application deadline: 4/15; financial award applicants required to submit FAFSA. *Unit head:* Dr. Michele Gerwick, Chairperson, 724-357-2557, E-mail: mgerwick@iup.edu. *Application contact:* Dr. Nashat Zuraikat, Graduate Coordinator, 724-357-3262, E-mail: zuraikat@iup.edu. Web site: http://www.iup.edu/page.aspx?id=43341.

Indiana University–Purdue University Fort Wayne, College of Health and Human Services, Department of Nursing, Fort Wayne, IN 46805-1499. Offers adult nursing practitioner (MS); nurse executive (MS); nursing administration (Certificate); nursing education (MS); women's health nurse practitioner (MS). Part-time programs available. *Faculty:* 10 full-time (all women). *Students:* 3 full-time (all women), 33 part-time (31 women); includes 3 minority (1 American Indian or Alaska Native, non-Hispanic/Latino; 1 Asian, non-Hispanic/Latino; 1 Hispanic/Latino). Average age 36. 13 applicants, 92% accepted, 10 enrolled. In 2011, 14 master's awarded. *Entrance requirements:* For master's, GRE Writing Test (if GPA below 3.0), BS in nursing, eligibility for Indiana RN license, minimum GPA of 3.0, essay, copy of resume, three references, undergraduate course work in research and statistics within last 5 years. Additional exam requirements/recommendations for international students: Required—TOEFL (minimum score 550 paper-based; 213 computer-based; 77 iBT); Recommended—TWE. *Application deadline:* For fall admission, 5/1 priority date for domestic students, 5/1 for international students; for spring admission, 11/15 priority date for domestic students. Applications are processed on a rolling basis. Application fee: $55 ($60 for international students). Electronic applications accepted. *Financial support:* In 2011–12, 11 teaching assistantships with partial tuition reimbursements (averaging $12,930 per year) were awarded; scholarships/grants also available. Support available to part-time students. Financial award application deadline: 3/1; financial award applicants required to submit FAFSA. *Faculty research:* Child psychiatric nursing. *Total annual research expenditures:* $296,680. *Unit head:* Dr. Carol Sternberger, Chair, 260-481-5798, Fax: 260-481-5767, E-mail: sternber@ipfw.edu. *Application contact:* Dr. Deborah Poling, Director of Graduate Program, 260-481-6276, Fax: 260-481-5767, E-mail: polingd@ipfw.edu. Web site: http://www.ipfw.edu/nursing/.

Indiana University–Purdue University Indianapolis, School of Nursing, MSN Program in Nursing, Indianapolis, IN 46202-2896. Offers nursing administration (MSN); nursing education (MSN). *Students:* 2 full-time (both women), 39 part-time (37 women); includes 5 minority (2 Black or African American, non-Hispanic/Latino; 1 Asian, non-Hispanic/Latino; 2 Hispanic/Latino), 2 international. 50 applicants, 50% accepted, 9 enrolled. In 2011, 17 master's awarded. *Entrance requirements:* For master's, background check, statistics. *Unit head:* Associate Dean for Graduate Programs, 317-274-2806, E-mail: nursing@iupui.edu. *Application contact:* Janet Moon, Information Contact, 317-278-2205. Web site: http://nursing.iupui.edu/degrees/msn/index.shtml.

Indiana Wesleyan University, Graduate School, School of Nursing, Marion, IN 46953-4974. Offers community health nursing (MS); nursing (Post Master's Certificate); nursing administration (MS); nursing education (MS); primary care nursing (MS). *Accreditation:* AACN. Part-time programs available. Postbaccalaureate distance learning degree programs offered (minimal on-campus study). *Degree requirements:* For master's, capstone project or thesis. *Entrance requirements:* For master's, writing sample, RN license, 1 year of related experience, graduate statistics course. Additional exam

requirements/recommendations for international students: Required—TOEFL. *Expenses:* Contact institution. *Faculty research:* Primary health care with international emphasis, international nursing.

Jefferson College of Health Sciences, Program in Nursing, Roanoke, VA 24031-3186. Offers nursing education (MSN); nursing management (MSN). *Accreditation:* AACN. Part-time programs available. *Degree requirements:* For master's, project. *Entrance requirements:* For master's, MAT. Additional exam requirements/recommendations for international students: Required—TOEFL (minimum score 550 paper-based; 213 computer-based; 80 iBT). Electronic applications accepted. *Faculty research:* Nursing, teaching and learning techniques, cultural competence, spirituality and nursing.

Kaplan University, Davenport Campus, School of Nursing, Davenport, IA 52807-2095. Offers nurse administrator (MS); nurse educator (MS). Part-time and evening/weekend programs available. Postbaccalaureate distance learning degree programs offered (no on-campus study). *Entrance requirements:* For master's, RN. Additional exam requirements/recommendations for international students: Required—TOEFL (minimum score 550 paper-based; 80 computer-based).

Kent State University, College of Nursing, Kent, OH 44242-0001. Offers acute care nurse practitioner (MSN); adult nurse practitioner (MSN); clinical nurse specialist (MSN); family nurse practitioner (MSN); geriatric nurse practitioner (MSN); health care management (MSN); nurse educator (MSN); nursing (PhD); nursing practice (DNP); pediatric nurse practitioner (MSN); psychiatric/mental health nurse practitioner (MSN); women's health nurse practitioner (MSN). PhD program offered jointly with The University of Akron. *Accreditation:* AACN. Part-time programs available. *Degree requirements:* For master's, thesis optional; for doctorate, comprehensive exam, thesis/dissertation. *Entrance requirements:* For master's, GRE (if undergraduate GPA less than 3.0), minimum GPA of 2.75; for doctorate, GRE, MSN. Additional exam requirements/recommendations for international students: Required—TOEFL. Electronic applications accepted. *Expenses:* Contact institution. *Faculty research:* Women and violence, methodological specialties, osteoporosis in women, new caregivers and the elderly.

Lamar University, College of Graduate Studies, College of Arts and Sciences, Department of Nursing, Beaumont, TX 77710. Offers nursing administration (MSN); nursing education (MSN); MSN/MBA. *Accreditation:* NLN. Part-time and evening/weekend programs available. Postbaccalaureate distance learning degree programs offered. *Faculty:* 6 full-time (all women). *Students:* 5 full-time (all women), 29 part-time (27 women); includes 12 minority (11 Black or African American, non-Hispanic/Latino; 1 Hispanic/Latino). Average age 40. 18 applicants, 100% accepted, 10 enrolled. In 2011, 5 master's awarded. *Degree requirements:* For master's, comprehensive exam, practicum project presentation, evidence-based project. *Entrance requirements:* For master's, GRE General Test, MAT, criminal background check, RN license, NLN-accredited BSN, college course work in graduate statistics in past 5 years, letters of recommendation, minimum undergraduate GPA of 3.0. Additional exam requirements/recommendations for international students: Required—TOEFL. *Application deadline:* For fall admission, 8/1 priority date for domestic students; for spring admission, 12/1 priority date for domestic students. Applications are processed on a rolling basis. Application fee: $25 ($50 for international students). *Expenses:* Tuition, state resident: full-time $5430; part-time $272 per credit hour. Tuition, nonresident: full-time $11,540; part-time $577 per credit hour. *Required fees:* $1916. *Financial support:* In 2011–12, 3 students received support, including 2 teaching assistantships (averaging $24,000 per year); scholarships/grants and traineeships also available. Financial award application deadline: 4/1. *Faculty research:* Student retention, theory, caregiving, online course and research. *Unit head:* Dr. Nancy Blume, Director of Graduate Nursing Studies, 409-880-8820, Fax: 409-880-8698, E-mail: nancy.blume@lamar.edu. *Application contact:* Shelly R. Belk, Administrative Associate, 409-880-7720.

La Roche College, School of Graduate Studies and Adult Education, Program in Nursing, Pittsburgh, PA 15237-5898. Offers nursing education (MSN); nursing management (MSN). *Accreditation:* AANA/CANAEP; NLN. Part-time and evening/weekend programs available. Postbaccalaureate distance learning degree programs offered (minimal on-campus study). *Faculty:* 5 full-time (all women), 1 (woman) part-time/adjunct. *Students:* 8 full-time (6 women), 12 part-time (11 women), 2 international. Average age 41. 8 applicants, 63% accepted, 3 enrolled. In 2011, 4 master's awarded. *Degree requirements:* For master's, thesis optional, internship, practicum. *Entrance requirements:* For master's, GRE General Test, BSN, nursing license, work experience. Additional exam requirements/recommendations for international students: Recommended—TOEFL (minimum score 550 paper-based; 220 computer-based). *Application deadline:* For fall admission, 8/15 priority date for domestic students, 8/15 for international students; for spring admission, 12/15 priority date for domestic students, 12/15 for international students. Applications are processed on a rolling basis. Application fee: $50. Electronic applications accepted. *Expenses:* Contact institution. *Financial support:* Application deadline: 3/31; applicants required to submit FAFSA. *Faculty research:* Patient education, perception. *Unit head:* Dr. Kathleen Sullivan, Division Chair, 412-536-1173, Fax: 412-536-1175, E-mail: sullivk1@laroche.edu. *Application contact:* Hope Schiffgens, Director of Graduate Studies and Adult Education, 412-536-1266, Fax: 412-536-1283, E-mail: schombh1@laroche.edu.

Le Moyne College, Department of Nursing, Syracuse, NY 13214. Offers nursing administration (MS, CAS); nursing education (MS, CAS). *Accreditation:* AACN. Part-time and evening/weekend programs available. *Faculty:* 4 full-time (all women), 3 part-time/adjunct (all women). *Students:* 19 part-time (all women); includes 1 minority (Black or African American, non-Hispanic/Latino). Average age 45. 9 applicants, 89% accepted, 5 enrolled. In 2011, 8 master's awarded. *Degree requirements:* For master's, scholarly project. *Entrance requirements:* For master's, bachelor's degree, interview, minimum GPA of 3.0, New York RN license, 2 letters of recommendation, writing sample, transcripts. Additional exam requirements/recommendations for international students: Required—TOEFL (minimum score 550 paper-based; 213 computer-based; 79 iBT). *Application deadline:* For fall admission, 6/1 priority date for domestic students, 6/1 for international students; for spring admission, 11/1 priority date for domestic students, 11/1 for international students. Applications are processed on a rolling basis. Application fee: $50. *Expenses:* Contact institution. *Financial support:* In 2011–12, 5 students received support. Career-related internships or fieldwork, scholarships/grants, health care benefits, unspecified assistantships, and NFLP Federal Loan Program (Nurse Faculty Loan Program) available. Support available to part-time students. Financial award applicants required to submit FAFSA. *Faculty research:* Inter-profession education, eldercare, utilization of free healthcare services by the insured, health promotion education, innovative undergraduate nursing education models. *Unit head:* Dr. Susan B. Bastable, Chair and Professor, Department of Nursing, 315-445-5436, Fax: 315-445-6024, E-mail: bastabsb@lemoyne.edu. *Application contact:* Kristen P. Trapasso, Director of Graduate Admission, 315-445-4265, Fax: 315-445-6027, E-mail: trapaskp@lemoyne.edu. Web site: http://www.lemoyne.edu/nursing.

Lewis University, College of Nursing and Health Professions, Program in Nursing, Romeoville, IL 60446. Offers adult nurse practitioner (MSN); nursing administration (MSN); nursing education (MSN). *Accreditation:* AACN. Part-time and evening/weekend programs available. Postbaccalaureate distance learning degree programs offered (no on-campus study). *Students:* 11 full-time (all women), 237 part-time (232 women); includes 65 minority (42 Black or African American, non-Hispanic/Latino; 14 Asian, non-Hispanic/Latino; 9 Hispanic/Latino), 1 international. Average age 42. In 2011, 29 master's awarded. *Degree requirements:* For master's, clinical practicum. *Entrance requirements:* For master's, minimum undergraduate GPA of 3.0, degree in nursing, RN license, letter of recommendation, interview, resume or curriculum vitae. Additional exam requirements/recommendations for international students: Required—TOEFL (minimum score 550 paper-based; 213 computer-based; 80 iBT). *Application deadline:* For fall admission, 5/1 for international students; for spring admission, 11/15 for international students. Applications are processed on a rolling basis. Application fee: $40. Electronic applications accepted. *Financial support:* Federal Work-Study, scholarships/grants, tuition waivers (full and partial), and unspecified assistantships available. Financial award application deadline: 5/1; financial award applicants required to submit FAFSA. *Faculty research:* Cancer prevention, phenomenological methods, public policy analysis. *Total annual research expenditures:* $1,000. *Unit head:* 815-836-5610. *Application contact:* Nancy Wiksten, Adult Admission Counselor, 815-836-5628, Fax: 815-836-5578, E-mail: wikstena@lewisu.edu. Web site: http://www.lewisu.edu/.

Lynchburg College, Graduate Studies, School of Health Sciences and Human Performance, MS Program in Nursing, Lynchburg, VA 24501-3199. Offers clinical nurse leader (MS); nursing education (MS). *Accreditation:* AACN. Part-time and evening/weekend programs available. Postbaccalaureate distance learning degree programs offered (minimal on-campus study). *Faculty:* 3 full-time (all women), 1 (woman) part-time/adjunct. *Students:* 1 (woman) full-time, 6 part-time (all women), 1 international. Average age 39. In 2011, 4 master's awarded. *Degree requirements:* For master's, practicum. *Entrance requirements:* For master's, GRE or 2 years professional nursing experience, official transcripts, personal essay, 3 letters of recommendation, current unrestricted registered nurse license in Virginia. Additional exam requirements/recommendations for international students: Required—TOEFL (minimum score 550 paper-based; 213 computer-based; 79 iBT), IELTS (minimum score 6.5). *Application deadline:* For fall admission, 7/31 for domestic students, 6/1 for international students; for spring admission, 11/30 for domestic students, 10/15 for international students. Applications are processed on a rolling basis. Application fee: $30. Electronic applications accepted. Application fee is waived when completed online. *Expenses:* *Tuition:* Full-time $7740; part-time $430 per credit hour. *Financial support:* Fellowships, Federal Work-Study, scholarships/grants, health care benefits, and unspecified assistantships available. Support available to part-time students. Financial award application deadline: 7/31; financial award applicants required to submit FAFSA. *Unit head:* Dr. Jean St. Clair, Associate Professor/Director of MSN Program, 434-544-8740, E-mail: stclair.j@lynchburg.edu. *Application contact:* Anne Pingstock, Executive Assistant, Graduate Studies, 434-544-8383, E-mail: gradstudies@lynchburg.edu. Web site: http://www.lynchburg.edu/msn.xml.

Marian University, School of Nursing, Fond du Lac, WI 54935-4699. Offers adult nurse practitioner (MSN); nurse educator (MSN). *Accreditation:* AACN. Part-time and evening/weekend programs available. *Faculty:* 6 full-time (all women), 10 part-time/adjunct (9 women). *Students:* 58 full-time (52 women), 33 part-time (32 women); includes 5 minority (2 Black or African American, non-Hispanic/Latino; 2 Asian, non-Hispanic/Latino; 1 Hispanic/Latino). Average age 36. 20 applicants, 90% accepted, 18 enrolled. In 2011, 25 master's awarded. *Degree requirements:* For master's, thesis, 675 clinical practicum hours. *Entrance requirements:* For master's, 3 letters of professional recommendation; undergraduate work in nursing research, statistics, health assessment. Additional exam requirements/recommendations for international students: Required—TOEFL (minimum score 525 paper-based; 193 computer-based; 70 iBT). *Application deadline:* Applications are processed on a rolling basis. Application fee: $50. Electronic applications accepted. *Expenses:* Contact institution. *Financial support:* In 2011–12, 3 students received support. Institutionally sponsored loans and scholarships/grants available. Support available to part-time students. Financial award application deadline: 3/1; financial award applicants required to submit FAFSA. *Unit head:* Dr. Julie Luetschwager, Dean, 920-923-8094, Fax: 920-923-8770, E-mail: jaluetschwager25@marianuniversity.edu. *Application contact:* Dr. Nancy L. Stuever, Director, 920-923-8597, Fax: 920-923-8770, E-mail: nstuever44@marianuniversity.edu.

Marymount University, School of Health Professions, Program in Nursing, Arlington, VA 22207-4299. Offers family nurse practitioner (MSN, Certificate); nursing (DNP); nursing education (MSN, Certificate); RN to MSN (MSN). *Accreditation:* AACN. Part-time and evening/weekend programs available. *Faculty:* 8 full-time (all women), 3 part-time/adjunct (2 women). *Students:* 13 full-time (12 women), 65 part-time (62 women); includes 32 minority (19 Black or African American, non-Hispanic/Latino; 2 American Indian or Alaska Native, non-Hispanic/Latino; 8 Asian, non-Hispanic/Latino; 3 Hispanic/Latino), 4 international. Average age 40. 51 applicants, 57% accepted, 21 enrolled. In 2011, 26 master's, 2 other advanced degrees awarded. *Degree requirements:* For master's, comprehensive exam; for doctorate, thesis/dissertation or alternative. *Entrance requirements:* For master's, 2 letters of recommendation, interview, resume, RN license, personal statement; for doctorate, 2 letters of recommendation, interview, resume, RN license, minimum MSN GPA of 3.5 or BSN 3.3; for Certificate, interview, master's degree in nursing. Additional exam requirements/recommendations for international students: Required—TOEFL (minimum score 600 paper-based; 250 computer-based; 96 iBT), IELTS (minimum score 6.5). *Application deadline:* For fall admission, 4/1 for domestic students, 7/1 for international students; for spring admission, 9/15 for international students. Application fee: $40. Electronic applications accepted. *Expenses:* *Tuition:* Part-time $770 per credit hour. *Required fees:* $8 per credit hour. One-time fee: $180 full-time. *Financial support:* In 2011–12, 1 student received support. Research assistantships with partial tuition reimbursements available, career-related internships or fieldwork, Federal Work-Study, scholarships/grants, and unspecified assistantships available. Support available to part-time students. Financial award applicants required to submit FAFSA. *Unit head:* Dr. Susan Bidwell, Chair, 703-284-1593, Fax: 703-284-3819, E-mail: susan.bidwell@marymount.edu. *Application contact:* Francesca Reed, Director, Graduate Admissions, 703-284-5901, Fax: 703-527-3815, E-mail: grad.admissions@marymount.edu. Web site: http://www.marymount.edu/academics/programs/nursingDNP.

Maryville University of Saint Louis, School of Health Professions, Nursing Program, St. Louis, MO 63141-7299. Offers accelerated RN to MSN (MSN); adult nurse practitioner (MSN); advanced practice nursing (DNP); family nurse practitioner (MSN); geriatric nurse practitioner (MSN); nursing education (MSN). *Accreditation:* AACN. Postbaccalaureate distance learning degree programs offered. *Students:* 16 full-time (14 women), 136 part-time (127 women); includes 9 minority (5 Black or African American, non-Hispanic/Latino; 3 Asian, non-Hispanic/Latino; 1 Two or more races, non-Hispanic/Latino). Average age 35. In 2011, 21 master's awarded. *Degree requirements:* For master's, practicum. *Entrance requirements:* For master's, BSN, current licensure, minimum GPA of 3.0, 3 letters of recommendation, curriculum vitae. Additional exam requirements/recommendations for international students: Required—TOEFL (minimum score 550 paper-based). *Application deadline:* Applications are processed on a rolling basis. Application fee: $40 ($60 for international students). Electronic applications accepted. *Expenses:* *Tuition:* Full-time $21,922; part-time $675 per credit hour. *Required fees:* $233.75 per semester. *Financial support:* Federal Work-Study and campus employment available. Support available to part-time students. Financial award application deadline: 3/1; financial award applicants required to submit FAFSA. *Unit*

head: Dr. Elizabeth Buck, Director, 314-529-9453, Fax: 314-529-9139, E-mail: ebuck@maryville.edu. *Application contact:* Dr. Donna Payne, Vice President, Adult and Continuing Education, 314-529-9676, Fax: 314-529-9927, E-mail: dpayne@maryville.edu. Web site: http://www.maryville.edu/academics-hp-nursing.

McKendree University, Graduate Programs, Master of Science in Nursing Program, Lebanon, IL 62254-1299. Offers nursing education (MSN); nursing management/administration (MSN). *Accreditation:* AACN. Part-time and evening/weekend programs available. Postbaccalaureate distance learning degree programs offered (no on-campus study). *Degree requirements:* For master's, research project or thesis. *Entrance requirements:* For master's, resume, references, valid Professional Registered Nurse license. Additional exam requirements/recommendations for international students: Required—TOEFL. Electronic applications accepted.

McNeese State University, Doré School of Graduate Studies, College of Nursing, Lake Charles, LA 70609. Offers clinical nurse specialist (MSN); nurse educator (MSN); nurse practitioner (MSN); nursing leadership and administration (MSN). Program offered jointly with Southeastern Louisiana University and Southern University and Agricultural and Mechanical College. *Accreditation:* AACN. *Faculty:* 4 full-time (all women), 3 part-time/adjunct (2 women). *Students:* 10 full-time (9 women), 94 part-time (79 women); includes 21 minority (15 Black or African American, non-Hispanic/Latino; 1 Asian, non-Hispanic/Latino; 4 Hispanic/Latino; 1 Two or more races, non-Hispanic/Latino). In 2011, 25 master's awarded. *Degree requirements:* For master's, comprehensive exam. *Entrance requirements:* For master's, GRE, eligibility for unencumbered licensure as RN in Louisiana. *Application deadline:* For fall admission, 5/15 priority date for domestic students, 5/15 for international students; for spring admission, 10/15 priority date for domestic students, 10/15 for international students. Applications are processed on a rolling basis. Application fee: $20 ($30 for international students). *Expenses:* Tuition, state resident: part-time $519 per credit hour. Tuition and fees vary according to course load. *Financial support:* Application deadline: 5/1. *Unit head:* Dr. Peggy L. Wolfe, Dean, 337-475-5820, Fax: 337-475-5924, E-mail: pwolfe@mcneese.edu. *Application contact:* Valarie Waldmeier, Coordinator, 337-475-5285, Fax: 337-475-5702, E-mail: vwaldmeier@mcneese.edu.

Medical University of South Carolina, College of Nursing, Nurse Educator Program, Charleston, SC 29425. Offers MSN. Part-time and evening/weekend programs available. Postbaccalaureate distance learning degree programs offered (no on-campus study). *Faculty:* 6 full-time (all women), 3 part-time/adjunct (2 women). *Students:* 3 part-time (all women); includes 1 minority (Black or African American, non-Hispanic/Latino). Average age 35. 33 applicants, 27% accepted, 3 enrolled. In 2011, 10 master's awarded. *Degree requirements:* For master's, thesis optional. *Entrance requirements:* For master's, BSN, course work in statistics, nursing license, minimum GPA of 3.0, current curriculum vitae, essay, three references. Additional exam requirements/recommendations for international students: Required—TOEFL (minimum score 600 paper-based; 250 computer-based). *Application deadline:* For fall admission, 2/1 priority date for domestic students, 2/1 for international students. Application fee: $85. Electronic applications accepted. *Financial support:* Federal Work-Study, scholarships/grants, and traineeships available. Support available to part-time students. Financial award application deadline: 3/10; financial award applicants required to submit FAFSA. *Faculty research:* Prenatal care outcomes, perinatal wellness in Hispanic women, use of PDAs in clinical practice. *Unit head:* Carol J. McDougall, Lead Faculty, 843-792-3682, Fax: 843-792-5395, E-mail: mcdougac@musc.edu. *Application contact:* Carolyn G. Page, Director, Student Services, 843-792-3844, Fax: 843-792-5395, E-mail: pagecf@musc.edu.

Mercy College, School of Health and Natural Sciences, Programs in Nursing, Dobbs Ferry, NY 10522-1189. Offers nursing administration (MS, Certificate); nursing education (MS, Certificate). *Accreditation:* AACN. Part-time and evening/weekend programs available. Postbaccalaureate distance learning degree programs offered (no on-campus study). *Degree requirements:* For master's, written comprehensive exam or the production of a comprehensive project. *Entrance requirements:* For master's, bachelor's degree, two letters of reference, interview/assessment, RN registration in the U.S.. Additional exam requirements/recommendations for international students: Required—TOEFL (minimum score 600 paper-based; 250 computer-based; 100 iBT), IELTS (minimum score 8). Electronic applications accepted.

MGH Institute of Health Professions, School of Nursing, Boston, MA 02129. Offers advanced practice nursing (MSN); gerontological nursing (MSN); nursing (DNP); pediatric nursing (MSN); psychiatric nursing (MSN); teaching and learning for health care education (Certificate); women's health nursing (MSN). *Accreditation:* AACN; NLN (one or more programs are accredited). *Faculty:* 41 full-time (36 women), 14 part-time/adjunct (13 women). *Students:* 418 full-time (365 women), 72 part-time (63 women); includes 51 minority (20 Black or African American, non-Hispanic/Latino; 1 American Indian or Alaska Native, non-Hispanic/Latino; 24 Asian, non-Hispanic/Latino; 5 Hispanic/Latino; 1 Native Hawaiian or other Pacific Islander, non-Hispanic/Latino). Average age 32. 1,041 applicants, 36% accepted, 148 enrolled. In 2011, 85 master's, 12 doctorates, 98 other advanced degrees awarded. *Degree requirements:* For master's, thesis or alternative. *Entrance requirements:* For master's, GRE General Test, bachelor's degree from regionally-accredited college or university. Additional exam requirements/recommendations for international students: Required—TOEFL (minimum score 550 paper-based; 213 computer-based; 80 iBT). *Application deadline:* For fall admission, 1/10 for domestic and international students; for spring admission, 11/1 for domestic and international students. Application fee: $65. Electronic applications accepted. *Expenses:* *Tuition:* Full-time $12,720; part-time $1060 per credit. *Required fees:* $1725; $430 per semester. One-time fee: $350. *Financial support:* In 2011–12, 75 students received support, including 4 research assistantships (averaging $1,200 per year), 17 teaching assistantships (averaging $1,200 per year); career-related internships or fieldwork, scholarships/grants, traineeships, and unspecified assistantships also available. Support available to part-time students. Financial award application deadline: 4/1; financial award applicants required to submit FAFSA. *Faculty research:* Biobehavioral nursing, HIV/AIDS, gerontological nursing, women's health, vulnerable populations, health systems. *Unit head:* Dr. Laurie Lauzon-Clabo, Dean, 617-643-0605, Fax: 617-726-8022, E-mail: llauzonclabo@mghihp.edu. *Application contact:* Maureen Rika Judd, Director of Admissions, 617-726-6069, Fax: 617-726-8010, E-mail: admissions@mghihp.edu. Web site: http://www.mghihp.edu/academics/nursing/.

Midwestern State University, Graduate Studies, College of Health Sciences and Human Services, Nursing Program, Wichita Falls, TX 76308. Offers family nurse practitioner (MSN); family psychiatric mental health nurse practitioner (MSN); health services administration (MSN); nurse educator (MSN). *Accreditation:* AACN. Part-time and evening/weekend programs available. *Degree requirements:* For master's, comprehensive exam, thesis optional. *Entrance requirements:* For master's, GRE General Test or MAT. Additional exam requirements/recommendations for international students: Required—TOEFL (minimum score 550 paper-based; 213 computer-based). Electronic applications accepted. *Faculty research:* Infant feeding, musculoskeletal disorders, diabetes, community health education, water quality reporting.

Millikin University, School of Nursing, Decatur, IL 62522-2084. Offers clinical nurse leader (MSN); entry into nursing practice: pre-licensure (MSN); nurse anesthesia (MSN); nurse educator (MSN). *Accreditation:* AACN; AANA/CANAEP. Part-time programs available. *Faculty:* 17 full-time (15 women), 4 part-time/adjunct (3 women). *Students:* 30 full-time (21 women), 10 part-time (9 women); includes 2 minority (both Black or African American, non-Hispanic/Latino). Average age 32. 110 applicants, 39% accepted, 40 enrolled. In 2011, 6 master's awarded. *Degree requirements:* For master's, thesis or alternative, research project. *Entrance requirements:* For master's, GRE, official academic transcript(s), written essay, immunizations, statistics course, 2 letters of recommendation, CPR certification, professional liability/malpractice insurance. Additional exam requirements/recommendations for international students: Required—TOEFL (minimum score 550 paper-based; 79 iBT). *Application deadline:* For spring admission, 11/1 priority date for domestic students. Applications are processed on a rolling basis. Application fee: $0. Electronic applications accepted. *Expenses:* *Tuition:* Full-time $24,890; part-time $681 per credit hour. Tuition and fees vary according to program. *Financial support:* Institutionally sponsored loans available. Financial award applicants required to submit FAFSA. *Faculty research:* Congestive heart failure, quality of life, transcultural nursing issues, teaching/learning strategies, maternal - newborn. *Unit head:* Dr. Deborah Slayton, Director, 217-424-6348, Fax: 217-420-6731, E-mail: dslayton@millikin.edu. *Application contact:* Marianne Taylor, Administrative Assistant, 800-373-7733 Ext. 5034, Fax: 217-420-6677, E-mail: mgtaylor@millikin.edu. Web site: http://www.millikin.edu/academics/cps/nursing/msn/.

Minnesota State University Moorhead, Graduate Studies, College of Education and Human Services, Tri-College University Nursing Consortium, Moorhead, MN 56563-0002. Offers MS. Program offered jointly with North Dakota State University and Concordia College. *Accreditation:* AACN. *Degree requirements:* For master's, thesis or alternative, final oral exam. *Entrance requirements:* For master's, 3 letters of recommendation, minimum GPA of 3.0, RN licensure, bachelor's degree with nursing major. Additional exam requirements/recommendations for international students: Required—TOEFL (minimum score 550 paper-based; 213 computer-based). Electronic applications accepted. *Expenses:* Contact institution.

Missouri State University, Graduate College, College of Health and Human Services, Department of Nursing, Springfield, MO 65897. Offers nursing (MSN), including family nurse practitioner, nurse educator. *Accreditation:* AACN. *Faculty:* 9 full-time (all women), 12 part-time/adjunct (10 women). *Students:* 24 full-time (20 women), 25 part-time (23 women); includes 2 minority (1 Asian, non-Hispanic/Latino; 1 Two or more races, non-Hispanic/Latino). Average age 37. 14 applicants, 93% accepted, 5 enrolled. In 2011, 10 master's awarded. *Degree requirements:* For master's, comprehensive exam, thesis or alternative. *Entrance requirements:* For master's, GRE General Test, minimum GPA of 3.0, RN license (MSN), 1 year work experience (MPH). Additional exam requirements/recommendations for international students: Required—TOEFL (minimum score 550 paper-based; 213 computer-based; 79 iBT). *Application deadline:* For fall admission, 7/20 priority date for domestic students, 5/1 for international students; for spring admission, 12/20 priority date for domestic students, 9/1 for international students. Applications are processed on a rolling basis. Application fee: $35 ($50 for international students). Electronic applications accepted. *Expenses:* Tuition, state resident: full-time $4086; part-time $227 per credit hour. Tuition, nonresident: full-time $8172; part-time $454 per credit hour. *Required fees:* $275 per semester. Tuition and fees vary according to course load, campus/location and program. *Financial support:* Federal Work-Study, institutionally sponsored loans, scholarships/grants, and unspecified assistantships available. Financial award application deadline: 3/31; financial award applicants required to submit FAFSA. *Faculty research:* Preconceptual health, women's health, nursing satisfaction, nursing education. *Unit head:* Dr. Kathryn Hope, Head, 417-836-5310, Fax: 417-836-5484, E-mail: nursing@missouristate.edu. *Application contact:* Eric Eckert, Coordinator of Admissions and Recruitment, 417-836-5331, Fax: 417-836-6200, E-mail: tobinbushman@missouristate.edu. Web site: http://www.missouristate.edu/nursing/.

Molloy College, Division of Nursing, Rockville Centre, NY 11571-5002. Offers adult nurse practitioner (Advanced Certificate); clinical nurse specialist: adult health (Advanced Certificate); family nurse practitioner (Advanced Certificate); nurse practitioner psychiatry (Advanced Certificate); nursing (MS); nursing administration (Advanced Certificate); nursing administration with informatics (Advanced Certificate); nursing education (Advanced Certificate); nursing informatics (Advanced Certificate); pediatric nurse practitioner (Advanced Certificate). *Accreditation:* AACN. Part-time and evening/weekend programs available. *Faculty:* 20 full-time (19 women), 12 part-time/adjunct (11 women). *Students:* 19 full-time (15 women), 483 part-time (452 women); includes 238 minority (132 Black or African American, non-Hispanic/Latino; 61 Asian, non-Hispanic/Latino; 35 Hispanic/Latino; 2 Native Hawaiian or other Pacific Islander, non-Hispanic/Latino; 8 Two or more races, non-Hispanic/Latino), 5 international. Average age 40. 186 applicants, 82% accepted, 110 enrolled. In 2011, 94 master's awarded. *Degree requirements:* For master's, thesis optional. *Entrance requirements:* For master's, 3 letters of reference, BS in nursing, minimum undergraduate GPA of 3.0; for Advanced Certificate, 3 letters of reference, master's degree in nursing. *Application deadline:* For fall admission, 9/2 priority date for domestic students; for spring admission, 1/20 priority date for domestic students. Applications are processed on a rolling basis. Application fee: $60. *Financial support:* Research assistantships with partial tuition reimbursements, teaching assistantships with partial tuition reimbursements, institutionally sponsored loans, scholarships/grants, and unspecified assistantships available. Support available to part-time students. Financial award application deadline: 4/1; financial award applicants required to submit FAFSA. *Unit head:* Dr. Denise Walsh, Associate Dean, Graduate Nursing, 516-678-5000, Fax: 516-678-9718, E-mail: dwalsh@molloy.edu. *Application contact:* Alina Haitz, Assistant Director of Graduate Admissions, 516-678-5000, Fax: 516-256-2247, E-mail: ahaitz@molloy.edu. Web site: http://www.molloy.edu/academics/nursing-division.

Monmouth University, The Graduate School, The Marjorie K. Unterberg School of Nursing and Health Studies, West Long Branch, NJ 07764-1898. Offers adult nurse practitioner (MSN); adult psychiatric and mental health advanced practice nursing (MSN, Post-Master's Certificate); advanced practice nursing (Post-Master's Certificate); family nurse practitioner (MSN, Post-Master's Certificate); forensic nursing (MSN, Certificate); nursing (MSN); nursing administration (MSN, Post-Master's Certificate); nursing education (MSN, Post-Master's Certificate); nursing practice (DNP); school nursing (MSN, Certificate). *Accreditation:* AACN. Part-time and evening/weekend programs available. *Faculty:* 12 full-time (all women), 2 part-time/adjunct (both women). *Students:* 16 full-time (11 women), 244 part-time (238 women); includes 73 minority (23 Black or African American, non-Hispanic/Latino; 2 American Indian or Alaska Native, non-Hispanic/Latino; 34 Asian, non-Hispanic/Latino; 12 Hispanic/Latino; 1 Native Hawaiian or other Pacific Islander, non-Hispanic/Latino; 1 Two or more races, non-Hispanic/Latino), 1 international. Average age 41. 107 applicants, 92% accepted, 67 enrolled. In 2011, 55 master's awarded. *Degree requirements:* For master's, practicum (for some tracks). *Entrance requirements:* For master's, GRE General Test, RN license, 1 year of work experience, minimum undergraduate GPA of 2.75. Additional exam requirements/recommendations for international students: Required—TOEFL (minimum score 550 paper-based; 213 computer-based; 79 iBT), IELTS (minimum score 5) or Michigan English Language Assessment Battery (minimum score 77), Cambridge A, B, C. *Application deadline:* For fall admission, 7/15 priority date for domestic students, 6/1 for international students; for spring admission, 11/15 priority date for domestic students, 11/1 for international students. Applications are processed on a rolling basis. Application fee: $50. Electronic applications accepted. *Financial support:* In 2011–12, 138 students

received support, including 138 fellowships (averaging $1,423 per year), 4 research assistantships (averaging $5,240 per year); career-related internships or fieldwork, scholarships/grants, and unspecified assistantships also available. Support available to part-time students. Financial award applicants required to submit FAFSA. *Faculty research:* Relationship of undergraduate GPA and GRE to succeed in a graduate nursing program. *Unit head:* Dr. Janet Mahoney, Dean, 732-571-3443, Fax: 732-263-5131, E-mail: jmahoney@monmouth.edu. *Application contact:* Kevin Roane, Director, Office of Graduate Admission, 732-571-3452, Fax: 732-263-5123, E-mail: gradadm@monmouth.edu. Web site: http://www.monmouth.edu/nursingschool.

Montana State University, College of Graduate Studies, College of Nursing, Bozeman, MT 59717. Offers clinical nurse leader (MN); family nurse practitioner (MN, Post-Master's Certificate); nursing education (Certificate, Post-Master's Certificate); psychiatric mental health nurse practitioner (MN). *Accreditation:* AACN. Part-time programs available. Postbaccalaureate distance learning degree programs offered (minimal on-campus study). *Degree requirements:* For master's, comprehensive exam, thesis (for some programs). *Entrance requirements:* For master's, GRE General Test, minimum GPA of 3.0 for undergraduate and post-baccalaureate work. Additional exam requirements/recommendations for international students: Required—TOEFL (minimum score 580 paper-based; 213 computer-based). Electronic applications accepted. *Faculty research:* Rural nursing, health disparities, environmental/public health, oral health, resilience.

Moravian College, Moravian College Comenius Center, St. Luke's School of Nursing, Bethlehem, PA 18018-6650. Offers nurse administrator (MS); nurse educator (MS); nurse leadership (MS). Part-time and evening/weekend programs available. *Degree requirements:* For master's, comprehensive exam (for some programs), evidence-based practice project. *Entrance requirements:* For master's, GRE or MAT. Additional exam requirements/recommendations for international students: Required—TOEFL (minimum score 550 paper-based; 260 computer-based; 90 iBT).

Mountain State University, Program in Nursing, Beckley, WV 25802-9003. Offers administration/education (MSN); family nurse practitioner (MSN). *Accreditation:* NLN. Part-time programs available. Postbaccalaureate distance learning degree programs offered (minimal on-campus study). *Faculty:* 3 full-time (all women), 2 part-time/adjunct (both women). *Students:* 65 full-time (61 women), 9 part-time (8 women); includes 11 minority (8 Black or African American, non-Hispanic/Latino; 1 American Indian or Alaska Native, non-Hispanic/Latino; 2 Asian, non-Hispanic/Latino; 1 international. Average age 37. 85 applicants, 27% accepted, 20 enrolled. In 2011, 46 master's awarded. *Degree requirements:* For master's, comprehensive exam, thesis or alternative. *Entrance requirements:* For master's, GRE. Additional exam requirements/recommendations for international students: Required—TOEFL (minimum score 550 paper-based; 213 computer-based); Recommended—IELTS (minimum score 6.5). *Application deadline:* For spring admission, 6/30 for domestic and international students. Applications are processed on a rolling basis. Application fee: $25 ($50 for international students). Electronic applications accepted. *Expenses:* Contact institution. *Financial support:* Federal Work-Study, scholarships/grants, and unspecified assistantships available. Support available to part-time students. Financial award applicants required to submit FAFSA. *Unit head:* Dr. Sheila Garland, Dean, School of Health Sciences, 304-929-1516, Fax: 304-929-1601, E-mail: sgarland@mountainstate.edu.

Mount Carmel College of Nursing, Nursing Program, Columbus, OH 43222. Offers adult health clinical nurse specialist (MS); family nurse practitioner (MS); nursing administration (MS); nursing education (MS). *Accreditation:* AACN. Part-time programs available. *Faculty:* 11 full-time (10 women), 4 part-time/adjunct (2 women). *Students:* 69 full-time (66 women), 33 part-time (30 women); includes 19 minority (11 Black or African American, non-Hispanic/Latino; 1 American Indian or Alaska Native, non-Hispanic/Latino; 5 Asian, non-Hispanic/Latino; 1 Native Hawaiian or other Pacific Islander, non-Hispanic/Latino; 1 Two or more races, non-Hispanic/Latino). Average age 38. 23 applicants, 100% accepted, 20 enrolled. In 2011, 16 master's awarded. *Degree requirements:* For master's, professional manuscript. *Entrance requirements:* For master's, letters of recommendation, current resume, baccalaureate degree in nursing, current Ohio RN license, minimum cumulative GPA of 3.0. Additional exam requirements/recommendations for international students: Required—TOEFL (minimum score 550 paper-based; 213 computer-based; 80 iBT). *Application deadline:* For fall admission, 6/15 priority date for domestic students; for winter admission, 11/1 priority date for domestic students. Applications are processed on a rolling basis. Application fee: $30. *Expenses: Tuition:* Full-time $7839; part-time $402 per credit. *Required fees:* $75. *Financial support:* In 2011–12, 6 students received support. Institutionally sponsored loans and scholarships/grants available. Financial award application deadline: 7/1; financial award applicants required to submit FAFSA. *Unit head:* Dr. Angela Phillips-Lowe, Associate Dean, 614-234-5717, Fax: 614-234-2875, E-mail: aphillips-lowe@mccn.edu. *Application contact:* Elsie Sexton, Program Coordinator, 614-234-5169, Fax: 614-234-2875, E-mail: ksexton@mccn.edu. Web site: http://www.mccn.edu/.

Mount Saint Mary College, Division of Nursing, Newburgh, NY 12550-3494. Offers adult nurse practitioner (MS, Advanced Certificate), including nursing education (MS), nursing management (MS); clinical nurse specialist-adult health (MS), including nursing education, nursing management; family nurse practitioner (Advanced Certificate). *Accreditation:* AACN. Part-time and evening/weekend programs available. *Faculty:* 3 full-time (all women), 1 (woman) part-time/adjunct. *Students:* 3 full-time (2 women), 58 part-time (54 women); includes 16 minority (11 Black or African American, non-Hispanic/Latino; 1 Asian, non-Hispanic/Latino; 1 Hispanic/Latino; 3 Native Hawaiian or other Pacific Islander, non-Hispanic/Latino), 2 international. Average age 38. 47 applicants, 53% accepted, 18 enrolled. In 2011, 17 master's, 5 other advanced degrees awarded. *Degree requirements:* For master's, research utilization project. *Entrance requirements:* For master's, BSN, minimum GPA of 3.0, RN license. *Application deadline:* For fall admission, 6/3 priority date for domestic students; for spring admission, 10/31 priority date for domestic students. Applications are processed on a rolling basis. Application fee: $45. Application fee is waived when completed online. *Expenses: Tuition:* Full-time $13,356; part-time $742 per credit. *Required fees:* $70 per semester. *Financial support:* In 2011–12, 8 students received support. Unspecified assistantships available. Financial award application deadline: 4/15; financial award applicants required to submit FAFSA. *Unit head:* Dr. Karen Baldwin, Coordinator, 845-569-3512, Fax: 845-562-6762, E-mail: baldwin@msmc.edu. *Application contact:* Courtney McDermott, Graduate Recruiter, 845-569-3402, Fax: 845-569-3450, E-mail: courtney.mcdermott@msmc.edu. Web site: http://www.msmc.edu/Academics/Graduate_Programs/Master_of_Science_in_Nursing.

Mount St. Mary's College, Graduate Division, Program in Nursing, Los Angeles, CA 90049-1599. Offers educator (MSN); leadership and administration (MSN). *Accreditation:* AACN. *Entrance requirements:* For master's, baccalaureate degree; current CA nursing license; minimum cumulative GPA of 3.0 in last 60 semester units or last 90 quarter units of undergraduate and/or graduate course work; essay; two letters of recommendation; official transcript. Additional exam requirements/recommendations for international students: Required—TOEFL (minimum score 550 paper-based). *Application deadline:* For fall admission, 7/15 priority date for domestic students; for spring admission, 11/15 priority date for domestic students. Application fee: $50. Electronic applications accepted. *Expenses: Tuition:* Part-time $752 per unit. Part-time

tuition and fees vary according to degree level and program. *Financial support:* Scholarships/grants available. *Unit head:* Dr. Marsha Sato, Director, 213-477-2980, E-mail: msato@msmc.la.edu. Web site: http://www.msmc.la.edu/graduate-programs/nursing.asp.

Nebraska Methodist College, Program in Nursing, Omaha, NE 68114. Offers nurse educator (MSN); nurse executive (MSN). *Accreditation:* AACN. Evening/weekend programs available. Postbaccalaureate distance learning degree programs offered (no on-campus study). *Degree requirements:* For master's, thesis or alternative, Evidence Based Practice (EBP) project. *Entrance requirements:* For master's, interview. Additional exam requirements/recommendations for international students: Required—TOEFL (minimum score 550 paper-based; 213 computer-based; 80 iBT). *Faculty research:* Spirituality, student outcomes, service-learning, leadership and administration, women's issues.

New York University, College of Nursing, Programs in Advanced Practice Nursing, New York, NY 10012-1019. Offers advanced practice nursing: adult acute care (MS, Advanced Certificate); advanced practice nursing: adult nurse practitioner/holistic nurse practitioner (Advanced Certificate); advanced practice nursing: adult nurse practitioner/palliative care nurse practitioner (Advanced Certificate); advanced practice nursing: adult primary care (MS, Advanced Certificate); advanced practice nursing: family (MS, Advanced Certificate); advanced practice nursing: geriatrics (Advanced Certificate); advanced practice nursing: mental health (MS); advanced practice nursing: mental health nursing (Advanced Certificate); advanced practice nursing: pediatrics (MS, Advanced Certificate); nurse midwifery (MS, Advanced Certificate); nursing administration (MS, Advanced Certificate); nursing education (MS, Advanced Certificate); nursing informatics (MS, Advanced Certificate); MS/MPA; MS/MPH. *Accreditation:* AACN; ACNM/ACME. Part-time programs available. *Faculty:* 23 full-time (all women), 60 part-time/adjunct (47 women). *Students:* 27 full-time (23 women), 552 part-time (514 women); includes 251 minority (91 Black or African American, non-Hispanic/Latino; 115 Asian, non-Hispanic/Latino; 34 Hispanic/Latino; 11 Native Hawaiian or other Pacific Islander, non-Hispanic/Latino), 8 international. Average age 33. 325 applicants, 81% accepted, 179 enrolled. In 2011, 89 master's awarded. *Degree requirements:* For master's, thesis (for some programs). *Entrance requirements:* For master's, BS in nursing, AS in nursing with another BS/BA, interview, RN license, 1 year of clinical experience (3 for nursing education program); for Advanced Certificate, master's degree. Additional exam requirements/recommendations for international students: Required—TOEFL, IELTS. *Application deadline:* For fall admission, 7/1 priority date for domestic students, 7/1 for international students; for spring admission, 12/1 for domestic and international students. Applications are processed on a rolling basis. Application fee: $75. Electronic applications accepted. *Financial support:* In 2011–12, 36 students received support. Career-related internships or fieldwork, institutionally sponsored loans, scholarships/grants, traineeships, and tuition waivers (partial) available. Support available to part-time students. Financial award application deadline: 2/1; financial award applicants required to submit FAFSA. *Faculty research:* Elderly black diabetics, families and illness, oral systemic connection. *Unit head:* Dr. Judith Haber, Associate Dean, 212-998-9020, Fax: 212-995-3143, E-mail: jh33@nyu.edu. *Application contact:* Gail Wolfmeyer, Assistant Director, Graduate Student Affairs and Admissions, 212-992-7653, Fax: 212-995-4302, E-mail: gail.wolfmeyer@nyu.edu.

Northeastern State University, Graduate College, College of Education, Program in Nursing Education, Muskogee, OK 74401. Offers MS. *Faculty:* 3 full-time (all women). *Students:* 1 (woman) full-time, 14 part-time (13 women); includes 6 minority (1 Black or African American, non-Hispanic/Latino; 5 American Indian or Alaska Native, non-Hispanic/Latino), 1 international. Application fee: $25. *Unit head:* Dr. Joyce Van Nostrand, Department Chair, 918-456-5511 Ext. 5410, E-mail: vannostr@nsuok.edu. *Application contact:* Margie Railey, Administrative Assistant, 918-456-5511 Ext. 2093, Fax: 918-458-2061, E-mail: railey@nsouk.edu.

North Georgia College & State University, Department of Nursing, Dahlonega, GA 30597. Offers family nurse practitioner (MSN); nursing education (MSN). *Accreditation:* NLN. Part-time programs available. *Faculty:* 9 full-time (8 women), 3 part-time/adjunct (2 women). *Students:* 23 full-time (21 women), 53 part-time (49 women); includes 9 minority (5 Black or African American, non-Hispanic/Latino; 1 Asian, non-Hispanic/Latino; 1 Hispanic/Latino; 2 Two or more races, non-Hispanic/Latino), 1 international. Average age 39. 105 applicants, 44% accepted, 33 enrolled. In 2011, 21 master's awarded. *Degree requirements:* For master's, one foreign language, comprehensive exam, thesis. *Entrance requirements:* For master's, GRE General Test or MAT, minimum GPA of 2.75, 3 letters of recommendation, current Georgia RN license, 1 year of post-licensure work, BSN, ASN. Additional exam requirements/recommendations for international students: Required—TOEFL (minimum score 550 paper-based; 213 computer-based; 79 iBT), IELTS (minimum score 6.5). *Application deadline:* For fall admission, 7/1 priority date for domestic students, 6/1 for international students. Application fee: $40. Electronic applications accepted. *Expenses:* Tuition, state resident: full-time $3528; part-time $196 per credit hour. Tuition, nonresident: full-time $14,094; part-time $783 per credit hour. *Required fees:* $1718; $859 per semester. Tuition and fees vary according to course load, campus/location and program. *Financial support:* Career-related internships or fieldwork and unspecified assistantships available. Financial award application deadline: 5/1; financial award applicants required to submit CSS PROFILE or FAFSA. *Faculty research:* Diabetes, hypertension, access to woman's health screening, simulation in nursing education, health care of undeserved populations. *Unit head:* Dr. Diane Nelson, Department Head, 706-864-1930, Fax: 706-864-1845, E-mail: denelson@northgeorgia.edu. *Application contact:* Susan L. Perry, Graduate Admissions Coordinator, 706-864-1543, Fax: 706-867-2795, E-mail: slperry@northgeorgia.edu.

Norwich University, College of Graduate and Continuing Studies, Master of Science in Nursing Program, Northfield, VT 05663. Offers nursing administration (MSN); nursing education (MSN). *Accreditation:* AACN. Evening/weekend programs available. *Faculty:* 8 part-time/adjunct (5 women). *Students:* 31 full-time (29 women); includes 3 minority (1 Black or African American, non-Hispanic/Latino; 1 Asian, non-Hispanic/Latino; 1 Hispanic/Latino). Average age 44. 17 applicants, 59% accepted, 10 enrolled. In 2011, 28 master's awarded. *Entrance requirements:* For master's, minimum undergraduate GPA of 2.75. Additional exam requirements/recommendations for international students: Required—TOEFL (minimum score 550 paper-based; 212 computer-based; 83 iBT). *Application deadline:* For fall admission, 8/10 for domestic and international students; for winter admission, 11/7 for domestic and international students; for spring admission, 2/6 for domestic and international students. Applications are processed on a rolling basis. Application fee: $50. Electronic applications accepted. *Expenses: Tuition:* Full-time $16,174. *Required fees:* $2130. Full-time tuition and fees vary according to program. *Financial support:* In 2011–12, 7 students received support. Scholarships/grants available. Financial award applicants required to submit FAFSA. *Application contact:* Rija Ramahatra, Associate Program Director, 802-485-2892, Fax: 802-485-2533, E-mail: rramahatr@norwich.edu. Web site: http://nursing.norwich.edu/.

Nova Southeastern University, Health Professions Division, College of Nursing, Fort Lauderdale, FL 33314-7796. Offers advanced practice registered nurse (APRN) (MSN); nursing (MSN); nursing education (PhD); nursing practice (DNP). *Accreditation:* AACN. Part-time and evening/weekend programs available. Postbaccalaureate distance

learning degree programs offered (no on-campus study). *Faculty:* 16 full-time (all women), 32 part-time/adjunct (all women). *Students:* 170 full-time (159 women), 5 part-time (4 women); includes 90 minority (55 Black or African American, non-Hispanic/Latino; 5 American Indian or Alaska Native, non-Hispanic/Latino; 9 Asian, non-Hispanic/Latino; 19 Hispanic/Latino; 2 Native Hawaiian or other Pacific Islander, non-Hispanic/Latino). Average age 44. 70 applicants, 89% accepted, 57 enrolled. In 2011, 59 degrees awarded. *Degree requirements:* For doctorate, comprehensive exam, thesis/dissertation. *Entrance requirements:* For master's, minimum GPA of 3.0, RN, BSN; for doctorate, minimum GPA of 3.5, BSN, RN. Additional exam requirements/recommendations for international students: Recommended—TOEFL. *Application deadline:* For fall admission, 3/1 for domestic and international students; for winter admission, 11/1 for domestic and international students. Applications are processed on a rolling basis. Application fee: $50. Electronic applications accepted. *Faculty research:* Nursing education, curriculum, clinical research, interdisciplinary research. *Unit head:* Dr. Marcella Rutherford, Dean, 954-262-1963, E-mail: rmarcell@nova.edu. *Application contact:* Keatta Jerry, Application Contact, 954-262-1114, E-mail: keatta@nova.edu. Web site: http://www.nova.edu/nursing/.

Oakland University, Graduate Study and Lifelong Learning, School of Nursing, Program in Nursing Education, Rochester, MI 48309-4401. Offers MSN, Certificate.

Ohio University, Graduate College, College of Health Sciences and Professions, School of Nursing, Athens, OH 45701-2979. Offers acute care nurse practitioner (MSN); acute care nurse practitioner and family nurse practitioner (MSN); acute care nurse practitioner and nurse administrator (MSN); acute care nurse practitioner and nurse educator (MSN); family nurse practitioner (MSN); nurse administrator (MSN); nurse administrator and family nurse practitioner (MSN); nurse educator (MSN); nurse educator and family nurse practitioner (MSN); nurse educator and nurse administrator (MSN). *Accreditation:* AACN. *Students:* 33 full-time (29 women), 91 part-time (84 women); includes 16 minority (8 Black or African American, non-Hispanic/Latino; 2 Asian, non-Hispanic/Latino; 1 Hispanic/Latino; 5 Two or more races, non-Hispanic/Latino), 3 international. 86 applicants, 86% accepted, 61 enrolled. In 2011, 24 master's awarded. *Degree requirements:* For master's, capstone project. *Entrance requirements:* For master's, GRE, bachelor's degree in nursing from an accredited college or university, minimum overall undergraduate GPA of 3.0, official transcripts, statement of goals and objectives, resume, 3 letters of recommendation. Additional exam requirements/recommendations for international students: Required—TOEFL (minimum score 550 paper-based; 80 iBT) or IELTS (minimum score 6.5). *Application deadline:* For fall admission, 3/1 priority date for domestic students, 2/1 for international students. Applications are processed on a rolling basis. Application fee: $50 ($55 for international students). Electronic applications accepted. *Financial support:* Research assistantships, Federal Work-Study, institutionally sponsored loans, and unspecified assistantships available. Financial award application deadline: 3/1. *Unit head:* Dr. Deborah Henderson, Professor and Interim Director, 740-593-4497, Fax: 740-593-0286, E-mail: hendersd@ohio.edu. *Application contact:* Cheryl Brimner, Administrative Associate, 740-593-4494, Fax: 740-593-0286, E-mail: brimner@ohio.edu. Web site: http://www.ohio.edu/chsp/nrse/index.cfm.

Old Dominion University, College of Health Sciences, School of Nursing, Nurse Educator Emphasis, Norfolk, VA 23529. Offers MSN. Part-time programs available. Postbaccalaureate distance learning degree programs offered (no on-campus study). *Faculty:* 1 (woman) full-time, 2 part-time/adjunct (both women). *Students:* 20 full-time (all women); includes 8 minority (6 Black or African American, non-Hispanic/Latino; 1 Asian, non-Hispanic/Latino; 1 Hispanic/Latino). Average age 40. 19 applicants, 100% accepted, 17 enrolled. In 2011, 15 master's awarded. *Degree requirements:* For master's, comprehensive exam, thesis optional. *Entrance requirements:* For master's, GRE/MAT. *Application deadline:* For spring admission, 5/5 for domestic students. Application fee: $50. *Expenses:* Tuition, state resident: full-time $9096; part-time $379 per credit. Tuition, nonresident: full-time $23,064; part-time $961 per credit. *Required fees:* $127 per semester. One-time fee: $50. *Financial support:* In 2011–12, 1 teaching assistantship (averaging $2,500 per year) was awarded. *Faculty research:* Technology in nursing education, evidence-based instructional strategies, clinical judgment and decision-making. *Total annual research expenditures:* $35,726. *Unit head:* Kim Curry-Lourenco, Graduate Program Director, 757-683-5261, E-mail: kcurrylo@odu.edu. *Application contact:* Sue Parker, Coordinator, Graduate Student Services, 757-683-4298, Fax: 757-683-5253, E-mail: sparker@odu.edu. Web site: http://hs.odu.edu/nursing/academics/nurse_educator/nurse_educator.shtml.

Oregon Health & Science University, School of Nursing, Program in Nursing Education, Portland, OR 97239-3098. Offers MN, MS, Post Master's Certificate.

Otterbein University, Department of Nursing, Westerville, OH 43081. Offers advanced practice nurse educator (Certificate); clinical nurse leader (MSN); family nurse practitioner (MSN, Certificate); nurse anesthesia (MSN, Certificate); nursing (DNP); nursing service administration (MSN). *Accreditation:* AACN; AANA/CANAEP; NLN. Part-time and evening/weekend programs available. Postbaccalaureate distance learning degree programs offered (minimal on-campus study). *Degree requirements:* For master's, comprehensive exam (for some programs), thesis (for some programs). *Entrance requirements:* For master's, 2 reference forms, resume; for Certificate, official transcripts, 2 reference forms, essay, resumé. Additional exam requirements/recommendations for international students: Required—TOEFL (minimum score 550 paper-based; 213 computer-based; 79 iBT). *Faculty research:* Patient education, women's health, trauma curriculum development, administration.

Our Lady of the Lake College, School of Nursing, Program in Nursing, Baton Rouge, LA 70808. Offers administration (MS); education (MS). Part-time programs available. *Degree requirements:* For master's, capstone project. *Entrance requirements:* For master's, BSN with minimum GPA of 3.0 during the last 60 hours of undergraduate work, 1 year of clinical nursing experience as a registered nurse, current licensure or eligibility to practice as registered nurse in Louisiana, 3 professional references, 3 credit hours of undergraduate statistics with minimum C average.

Pace University, Lienhard School of Nursing, New York, NY 10038. Offers family nurse practitioner (MS); nursing education (MA); nursing leadership (Advanced Certificate); nursing practice (DNP). *Accreditation:* AACN. Part-time and evening/weekend programs available. Postbaccalaureate distance learning degree programs offered. *Faculty:* 10 full-time (8 women), 37 part-time/adjunct (30 women). *Students:* 32 full-time (26 women), 417 part-time (381 women); includes 187 minority (88 Black or African American, non-Hispanic/Latino; 1 American Indian or Alaska Native, non-Hispanic/Latino; 49 Asian, non-Hispanic/Latino; 43 Hispanic/Latino; 1 Native Hawaiian or other Pacific Islander, non-Hispanic/Latino; 5 Two or more races, non-Hispanic/Latino), 5 international. Average age 36. 437 applicants, 41% accepted, 84 enrolled. In 2011, 96 master's, 20 doctorates, 3 other advanced degrees awarded. *Degree requirements:* For master's, thesis. *Entrance requirements:* For master's, GRE General Test or MAT, RN license, resume, personal statement, 2 letters of recommendation, official transcripts; for doctorate, RN license, resume, personal statement, 2 letters of recommendation, official transcripts, accredited master's degree in nursing, minimum GPA of 3.3, state certification; for Advanced Certificate, RN license, completion of 2nd degree in nursing. Additional exam requirements/recommendations for international students: Required—TOEFL. *Application deadline:* For fall admission, 7/31 priority date for domestic students, 4/30 for international students; for spring admission, 10/14 for domestic students, 9/14 for international students. Applications are processed on a rolling basis. Application fee: $70. Electronic applications accepted. *Expenses:* Contact institution. *Financial support:* Research assistantships, career-related internships or fieldwork, Federal Work-Study, and tuition waivers (partial) available. Support available to part-time students. Financial award applicants required to submit FAFSA. *Unit head:* Dr. Geraldine Colombraro, Interim Dean, 914-773-3341, E-mail: gcolombraro@pace.edu. *Application contact:* Susan Ford-Goldschein, Director of Graduate Admissions, 914-422-4283, Fax: 914-422-4287, E-mail: gradwp@pace.edu. Web site: http://www.pace.edu/.

Prairie View A&M University, College of Nursing, Houston, TX 77030. Offers family nurse practitioner (MSN); nursing administration (MSN); nursing education (MSN). *Accreditation:* AACN; NLN. Part-time programs available. *Degree requirements:* For master's, comprehensive exam, thesis. *Entrance requirements:* For master's, MAT or GRE, BS in nursing; 2 years of experience as a registered nurse; 1 course each in statistics, basic health and assessment. *Faculty research:* Software development and violence prevention, health promotion and disease prevention.

Ramapo College of New Jersey, Master of Science in Nursing Program, Mahwah, NJ 07430. Offers nursing education (MSN). *Accreditation:* NLN. Part-time programs available. Postbaccalaureate distance learning degree programs offered (minimal on-campus study). *Faculty:* 2 full-time (both women), 2 part-time/adjunct (1 woman). *Students:* 2 full-time (both women), 42 part-time (40 women); includes 6 minority (3 Black or African American, non-Hispanic/Latino; 2 Asian, non-Hispanic/Latino; 1 Two or more races, non-Hispanic/Latino). Average age 41. 21 applicants, 90% accepted, 15 enrolled. In 2011, 13 master's awarded. *Degree requirements:* For master's, capstone project. *Entrance requirements:* For master's, interview; 2 letters of reference; immunizations; official transcript from accredited higher education institution with minimum cumulative GPA of 3.0; 1 year recent experience as RN; evidence of undergraduate statistics course; background check; current licensure as RN in NJ or eligibility for licensure. Additional exam requirements/recommendations for international students: Required—TOEFL (minimum score 550 paper-based; 213 computer-based; 95 iBT). *Application deadline:* Applications are processed on a rolling basis. Application fee: $60. *Expenses: Tuition, area resident:* Part-time $551.05 per credit. Tuition, nonresident: part-time $708.30 per credit. *Required fees:* $122.50 per credit. *Financial support:* In 2011–12, 10 students received support, including 10 fellowships with partial tuition reimbursements available (averaging $1,992 per year); traineeships also available. Financial award applicants required to submit FAFSA. *Faculty research:* Learning styles and critical thinking, evidence-based education, outcomes measurement. *Unit head:* Dr. Kathleen M. Burke, Assistant Dean, 201-684-7737, E-mail: kmburke@ramapo.edu. *Application contact:* Ulysses Simpkins, Program Assistant, 201-684-7749, E-mail: usimpkin@ramapo.edu. Web site: http://www.ramapo.edu/msn/.

Regis College, School of Nursing, Science and Health Professions, Weston, MA 02493. Offers biomedical sciences (MS); health administration (MS); nurse practitioner (Certificate); nursing (MS, DNP); nursing education (Certificate). *Accreditation:* NLN. Part-time and evening/weekend programs available. *Degree requirements:* For master's, thesis. *Entrance requirements:* For master's, GRE General Test or MAT, minimum GPA of 3.0; for doctorate, MAT or GRE if GPA from master's lower than 3.5. Additional exam requirements/recommendations for international students: Required—TOEFL (minimum score 550 paper-based; 213 computer-based). Electronic applications accepted. *Faculty research:* Health policy, education, aging, job satisfaction, psychiatric nursing, critical thinking.

Research College of Nursing, Nursing Program, Kansas City, MO 64132. Offers clinical nurse leader (MSN); executive nurse practitioner (MSN); family nurse practitioner (MSN); nurse educator (MSN). *Accreditation:* AACN. Part-time programs available. Postbaccalaureate distance learning degree programs offered (no on-campus study). *Faculty:* 8 full-time (all women), 1 (woman) part-time/adjunct. *Students:* 9 full-time (7 women), 132 part-time (121 women). Average age 30. In 2011, 23 master's awarded. *Degree requirements:* For master's, research project. *Entrance requirements:* For master's, 3 letters of recommendation, official transcripts, resume. Additional exam requirements/recommendations for international students: Required—TOEFL (minimum score 550 paper-based; 213 computer-based), TWE. *Application deadline:* Applications are processed on a rolling basis. Application fee: $50. *Expenses: Tuition:* Part-time $425 per credit hour. *Required fees:* $25 per credit hour. *Financial support:* Applicants required to submit FAFSA. *Unit head:* Dr. Nancy O. DeBasio, President and Dean, 816-995-2815, Fax: 816-995-2817, E-mail: nancy.debasio@researchcollege.edu. *Application contact:* Leslie Mendenhall, Director of Transfer and Graduate Recruitment, 816-995-2820, Fax: 816-995-2813, E-mail: leslie.mendenhall@researchcollege.edu.

Rivier University, School of Graduate Studies, Division of Nursing, Nashua, NH 03060. Offers adult psychiatric/mental health practitioner (MS); family nurse practitioner (MS); nursing education (MS). *Accreditation:* NLN. Part-time and evening/weekend programs available. *Entrance requirements:* For master's, GRE, MAT. Electronic applications accepted.

Roberts Wesleyan College, Division of Nursing, Rochester, NY 14624-1997. Offers nursing administration (MSN); nursing education (MSN). *Accreditation:* AACN. *Entrance requirements:* For master's, minimum GPA of 3.0; BS in nursing; interview; RN license; resume; course work in statistics and health assessment. Additional exam requirements/recommendations for international students: Required—TOEFL.

Sage Graduate School, School of Health Sciences, Department of Nursing, Program in Education and Leadership, Troy, NY 12180-4115. Offers DNS. *Faculty:* 5 full-time (all women), 2 part-time/adjunct (both women). *Students:* 39 part-time (all women); includes 1 minority (Black or African American, non-Hispanic/Latino). Average age 50. 19 applicants, 58% accepted, 7 enrolled. In 2011, 1 doctorate awarded. *Degree requirements:* For doctorate, thesis/dissertation. *Entrance requirements:* For doctorate, master's degree in nursing from accredited institution; minimum GPA of 3.5; official transcripts; academic curriculum vitae; 3 letters of recommendation; 1-2 page personal essay; interview; current registered nurse license. Additional exam requirements/recommendations for international students: Required—TOEFL (minimum score 550 paper-based; 213 computer-based). Application fee: $40. *Expenses: Tuition:* Full-time $11,880; part-time $660 per credit hour. Tuition and fees vary according to program. *Financial support:* Fellowships, research assistantships, Federal Work-Study, scholarships/grants, and unspecified assistantships available. Support available to part-time students. *Unit head:* Dr. Esther Haskevitz, Dean, School of Health Sciences, 518-244-2296, Fax: 518-244-4571, E-mail: haskve@sage.edu. *Application contact:* Dr. Joan Dacher, Associate Professor, Nursing, 518-244-2042, Fax: 518-244-2009, E-mail: dachej@sage.edu.

St. Catherine University, Graduate Programs, Program in Nursing, St. Paul, MN 55105. Offers adult-gerontological nurse practitioner (MA); neonatal nurse practitioner (MA); nurse educator (MA); nursing (DNP); pediatric nurse practitioner (MA). *Accreditation:* NLN. Part-time and evening/weekend programs available. *Degree requirements:* For master's, thesis; for doctorate, portfolio, systems change project. *Entrance requirements:* For master's, GRE General Test, bachelor's degree in nursing, current nursing license, 2 years of recent clinical practice; for doctorate, master's degree in nursing, RN license, advanced nursing position. Additional exam requirements/

recommendations for international students: Required—TOEFL (minimum score 600 paper-based; 250 computer-based; 100 iBT). *Expenses: Required fees:* $30 per semester. Tuition and fees vary according to program.

Saint Francis Medical Center College of Nursing, Graduate Programs, Peoria, IL 61603-3783. Offers child and family nurse practitioner (MSN); clinical nurse leader (MSN); family nurse practitioner (MSN); family psychiatric mental health nurse practitioner (MSN); medical-surgical nursing (MSN); neonatal nurse practitioner (MSN); nurse clinician (Post-Graduate Certificate); nurse educator (MSN, Post-Graduate Certificate); nursing (DNP); nursing management leadership (MSN). *Accreditation:* NLN. Part-time programs available. Postbaccalaureate distance learning degree programs offered (minimal on-campus study). *Faculty:* 6 full-time (all women), 5 part-time/adjunct (all women). *Students:* 26 full-time (25 women), 174 part-time (166 women); includes 19 minority (8 Black or African American, non-Hispanic/Latino; 1 American Indian or Alaska Native, non-Hispanic/Latino; 3 Asian, non-Hispanic/Latino; 6 Hispanic/Latino; 1 Native Hawaiian or other Pacific Islander, non-Hispanic/Latino). Average age 37. 123 applicants, 93% accepted, 93 enrolled. In 2011, 29 degrees awarded. *Degree requirements:* For master's, research experience, portfolio, practicum; for doctorate, practicum hours. *Entrance requirements:* For master's, nursing research, health assessment, graduate course work in statistics, RN license; for doctorate, master's degree in nursing, professional portfolio, graduate statistics, transcripts, RN license. Additional exam requirements/recommendations for international students: Required—TOEFL. *Application deadline:* For fall admission, 6/1 priority date for domestic students, 6/1 for international students; for spring admission, 11/15 priority date for domestic students, 11/15 for international students. Applications are processed on a rolling basis. Application fee: $50. Electronic applications accepted. *Expenses: Tuition:* Full-time $6120; part-time $510 per semester hour. *Required fees:* $300. *Financial support:* In 2011–12, 3 students received support. Scholarships/grants and tuition waivers (partial) available. Support available to part-time students. Financial award application deadline: 6/15; financial award applicants required to submit FAFSA. *Faculty research:* Outcome and curriculum planning, health promotion, NCLEX-RN results, decision-making program evaluation. *Unit head:* Dr. Patti A. Stockert, President of the College, 309-655-4124, Fax: 309-624-8973, E-mail: patricia.a.stockert@osfhealthcare.org. *Application contact:* Dr. Janice F. Boundy, Dean, 309-655-2230, Fax: 309-624-8973, E-mail: jan.f.boundy@osfhealthcare.org. Web site: http://www.sfmccon.edu/graduate-programs/.

St. John Fisher College, Wegmans School of Nursing, Advanced Practice Nursing Program, Rochester, NY 14618-3597. Offers advanced practice nursing (MS); clinical nurse specialist (Certificate); family nurse practitioner (Certificate); nurse educator (Certificate). *Accreditation:* AACN. Part-time and evening/weekend programs available. *Faculty:* 11 full-time (10 women), 4 part-time/adjunct (3 women). *Students:* 4 full-time (3 women), 98 part-time (96 women); includes 10 minority (7 Black or African American, non-Hispanic/Latino; 1 Asian, non-Hispanic/Latino; 2 Hispanic/Latino), 2 international. Average age 33. 35 applicants, 74% accepted, 21 enrolled. In 2011, 20 master's, 1 other advanced degree awarded. *Degree requirements:* For master's, clinical practice, project; for Certificate, clinical practice. *Entrance requirements:* For master's, BSN; undergraduate course work in statistics, health assessment, and nursing research; current New York State RN License; 2 letters of recommendation; current resume. Additional exam requirements/recommendations for international students: Required—TOEFL (minimum score 575 paper-based; 233 computer-based; 80 iBT). *Application deadline:* Applications are processed on a rolling basis. Application fee: $30. Electronic applications accepted. *Expenses: Tuition:* Part-time $735 per credit. One-time fee: $50 part-time. Tuition and fees vary according to course load, degree level and program. *Financial support:* In 2011–12, 39 students received support. Scholarships/grants and traineeships available. Financial award applicants required to submit FAFSA. *Faculty research:* Chronic illness, pediatric injury, women's health, public health policy, health care teams. *Unit head:* Dr. Cynthia McCloskey, Graduate Director, 585-385-8471, Fax: 585-385-8466, E-mail: cmccloskey@sjfc.edu. *Application contact:* Jose Perales, Director of Graduate Admissions, 585-385-8067, E-mail: jperales@sjfc.edu.

Saint Joseph's College of Maine, Master of Science in Nursing Program, Standish, ME 04084. Offers administration (MSN); education (MSN); family nurse practitioner (MSN); nursing administration and leadership (Certificate); nursing and health care education (Certificate). *Accreditation:* AACN. Part-time programs available. Postbaccalaureate distance learning degree programs offered (no on-campus study). *Faculty:* 2 full-time (both women), 22 part-time/adjunct (20 women). *Students:* 768 part-time (665 women); includes 85 minority (48 Black or African American, non-Hispanic/Latino; 21 Asian, non-Hispanic/Latino; 16 Hispanic/Latino). Average age 43. In 2011, 26 master's awarded. *Entrance requirements:* For master's, MAT. *Application deadline:* Applications are processed on a rolling basis. Application fee: $50. Electronic applications accepted. One-time fee: $50. *Financial support:* Institutionally sponsored loans available. Support available to part-time students. Financial award applicants required to submit FAFSA. *Unit head:* Joyce Murphy, Program Director, 207-893-7841, Fax: 207-892-7423, E-mail: jmurphy@sjcme.edu. *Application contact:* Lynne Robinson, Director of Admissions, 800-752-4723, Fax: 207-892-7480, E-mail: info@sjcme.edu. Web site: http://online.sjcme.edu/master-science-nursing.php.

Samford University, Ida V. Moffett School of Nursing, Birmingham, AL 35229. Offers advance practice (DNP); anesthesia (MSN); family nurse practitioner (MSN); nurse educator (MSN); nurse executive (DNP); nurse manager (MSN). *Accreditation:* AACN; AANA/CANAEP (one or more programs are accredited). Part-time programs available. Postbaccalaureate distance learning degree programs offered (minimal on-campus study). *Faculty:* 14 full-time (all women), 2 part-time/adjunct (0 women). *Students:* 226 full-time (152 women), 42 part-time (20 women); includes 43 minority (14 Black or African American, non-Hispanic/Latino; 4 American Indian or Alaska Native, non-Hispanic/Latino; 15 Asian, non-Hispanic/Latino; 9 Hispanic/Latino; 1 Native Hawaiian or other Pacific Islander, non-Hispanic/Latino), 2 international. Average age 39. 50 applicants, 88% accepted, 44 enrolled. In 2011, 95 master's, 14 doctorates awarded. *Median time to degree:* Of those who began their doctoral program in fall 2003, 100% received their degree in 8 years or less. *Degree requirements:* For master's and doctorate, capstone project with oral presentation. *Entrance requirements:* For master's, MAT; GRE (for nurse anesthesia). Additional exam requirements/recommendations for international students: Required—TOEFL (minimum score 550 paper-based; 213 computer-based; 80 iBT). *Application deadline:* For fall admission, 7/1 priority date for domestic students, 7/1 for international students; for spring admission, 10/1 priority date for domestic students, 10/1 for international students. Application fee: $65. Electronic applications accepted. *Expenses:* Contact institution. *Financial support:* In 2011–12, 166 students received support. Institutionally sponsored loans, scholarships/grants, and traineeships available. Financial award application deadline: 3/1; financial award applicants required to submit FAFSA. *Faculty research:* Issues in rural health care, vulnerable populations, genetics and disabilities in pediatrics, geriatrics, Parrish nursing research. *Unit head:* Dr. Nena F. Sanders, Dean, 205-726-2629, E-mail: nfsander@samford.edu. *Application contact:* Dr. Marian Carter, Director of Graduate Student Services, 205-726-2047, Fax: 205-726-4269, E-mail: mwcarter@samford.edu. Web site: http://samford.edu/nursing.

San Francisco State University, Division of Graduate Studies, College of Health and Human Services, School of Nursing, San Francisco, CA 94132-1722. Offers clinical nurse specialist (MS); community/public health nursing (MS); family nurse practitioner (MS, Certificate); nursing administration (MS); nursing education (MS). *Accreditation:* AACN. Part-time programs available. *Application deadline:* Applications are processed on a rolling basis. *Financial support:* Career-related internships or fieldwork available. *Unit head:* Dr. Lynette Landry, Director, 415-338-1802, E-mail: llandry@sfsu.edu. *Application contact:* Dr. Mary-Ann van Dam, Associate Director, 415-338-1802, E-mail: vandam@sfsu.edu. Web site: http://nursing.sfsu.edu.

San Jose State University, Graduate Studies and Research, College of Applied Sciences and Arts, School of Nursing, San Jose, CA 95192-0001. Offers gerontology nurse practitioner (MS); nursing (Certificate); nursing administration (MS); nursing education (MS). *Accreditation:* AACN. Part-time and evening/weekend programs available. *Degree requirements:* For master's, thesis. *Entrance requirements:* For master's, BS in nursing, RN license. Electronic applications accepted. *Faculty research:* Nurse-managed clinics, computers in nursing.

Seattle Pacific University, MS in Nursing Program, Seattle, WA 98119-1997. Offers administration (MSN); adult/gerontology nurse practitioner (MSN); clinical nurse specialist (MSN); family nurse practitioner (MSN, Certificate); informatics (MSN); nurse educator (MSN). *Accreditation:* AACN. Part-time programs available. *Degree requirements:* For master's, thesis. Electronic applications accepted. *Expenses:* Contact institution.

Seton Hall University, College of Nursing, South Orange, NJ 07079-2697. Offers advanced practice in primary health care (MSN, DNP), including adult/gerontological nurse practitioner, pediatric nurse practitioner; entry into practice (MSN); health systems administration (MSN, DNP); nursing (PhD); nursing case management (MSN); nursing education (MA); school nurse (MSN); MSN/MA. *Accreditation:* AACN. Part-time programs available. Postbaccalaureate distance learning degree programs offered (minimal on-campus study). *Faculty:* 10 full-time (all women), 3 part-time/adjunct (1 woman). *Students:* 12 full-time (11 women), 217 part-time (197 women); includes 38 minority (15 Black or African American, non-Hispanic/Latino; 1 American Indian or Alaska Native, non-Hispanic/Latino; 12 Asian, non-Hispanic/Latino; 10 Hispanic/Latino). 180 applicants, 51% accepted, 82 enrolled. *Degree requirements:* For master's, research project; for doctorate, dissertation or scholarly project. *Entrance requirements:* For doctorate, GRE (waived for students with GPA of 3.5 or higher). Additional exam requirements/recommendations for international students: Required—TOEFL. *Application deadline:* For fall admission, 4/15 priority date for domestic students. Applications are processed on a rolling basis. Electronic applications accepted. *Expenses: Tuition:* Part-time $1033 per credit hour. *Required fees:* $85 per semester. *Financial support:* Institutionally sponsored loans, scholarships/grants, traineeships, tuition waivers (partial), and unspecified assistantships available. Support available to part-time students. Financial award applicants required to submit FAFSA. *Faculty research:* Parent/child, adult, and gerontological nursing; breast cancer; families of children with HIV; parish nursing. *Unit head:* Dr. Phyllis Shanley Hansell, Dean, 973-761-9014, E-mail: phyllis.hansell@shu.edu. *Application contact:* Kristyn Kent Wuillermin, Director of Strategic Alliances, Marketing and Enrollment, 973-761-9291, Fax: 973-761-9607, E-mail: kristyn.kent@shu.edu.

Shenandoah University, School of Health Professions, Division of Nursing, Winchester, VA 22601-5195. Offers family nurse practitioner (Certificate); nurse-midwifery (Certificate); nurse-midwifery endorsement (Certificate); nursing (MSN, DNP); post-master's in nursing education (Certificate); psychiatric mental health nurse practitioner (Certificate). *Accreditation:* AACN; ACNM/ACME. Part-time programs available. *Faculty:* 11 full-time (all women), 2 part-time/adjunct (both women). *Students:* 40 full-time (34 women), 102 part-time (96 women); includes 32 minority (22 Black or African American, non-Hispanic/Latino; 1 American Indian or Alaska Native, non-Hispanic/Latino; 5 Asian, non-Hispanic/Latino; 3 Hispanic/Latino; 1 Two or more races, non-Hispanic/Latino), 2 international. Average age 39. 69 applicants, 90% accepted, 45 enrolled. In 2011, 15 master's, 2 doctorates, 17 other advanced degrees awarded. *Degree requirements:* For master's, research project, clinical hours; for doctorate and Certificate, clinical hours. *Entrance requirements:* For master's, GRE General Test, previous course work in statistics, community nursing, and physical assessment; RN license; BSN; minimum undergraduate GPA of 3.0; appropriate clinical experience; curriculum vitae; 3 letters of recommendation; for doctorate, MSN, minimum GPA of 3.0, 3 letters of recommendation, essay, interview; for Certificate, MSN, minimum GPA of 3.0, 3 letters of recommendation, minimum of one year (2,080 hours) clinical nursing experience, interview. Additional exam requirements/recommendations for international students: Required—TOEFL (minimum score 550 paper-based; 213 computer-based; 79 iBT), IELTS (minimum score 6.5), Sakae Institute of Study Abroad (minimum score 550). *Application deadline:* For fall admission, 6/15 priority date for domestic students, 6/15 for international students. Applications are processed on a rolling basis. Application fee: $30. Electronic applications accepted. *Expenses: Tuition:* Full-time $17,952; part-time $748 per credit. *Required fees:* $500 per term. Tuition and fees vary according to course level, course load and program. *Financial support:* In 2011–12, 13 students received support, including 3 teaching assistantships with partial tuition reimbursements available (averaging $4,224 per year); career-related internships or fieldwork, institutionally sponsored loans, scholarships/grants, unspecified assistantships, and federal loans, alternative loans also available. Support available to part-time students. Financial award application deadline: 3/15; financial award applicants required to submit FAFSA. *Faculty research:* Moral reasoning in nurses, improving health care access to under-served rural women, screening for depression and anxiety in the obese in a rural free clinic, health care outcomes among patients in a free clinic setting cared for by nurse practitioners, effects of depression on diabetes as evidenced by the relationship between the patient healthcare questionnaire (PHQ-9) scores and the patient's glycohemoglobin (HbA1c). *Unit head:* Dr. Kathryn Ganske, Director, 540-678-4374, Fax: 540-665-5519, E-mail: kganske@su.edu. *Application contact:* David Anthony, Dean of Admissions, 540-665-4581, Fax: 540-665-4627, E-mail: admit@su.edu. Web site: http://www.su.edu/nurse.

Southeastern Louisiana University, College of Nursing and Health Sciences, School of Nursing, Hammond, LA 70402. Offers adult psychiatric/mental health nurse practitioner/clinical nurse specialist (MSN); education (MSN); nurse executive (MSN); nurse practitioner (MSN). *Accreditation:* AACN. Part-time and evening/weekend programs available. *Faculty:* 12 full-time (11 women), 7 part-time/adjunct (4 women). *Students:* 17 full-time (16 women), 108 part-time (94 women); includes 12 minority (8 Black or African American, non-Hispanic/Latino; 2 Asian, non-Hispanic/Latino; 1 Hispanic/Latino; 1 Two or more races, non-Hispanic/Latino), 1 international. Average age 35. 50 applicants, 100% accepted, 29 enrolled. In 2011, 27 degrees awarded. *Degree requirements:* For master's, thesis. *Entrance requirements:* For master's, GRE (verbal and quantitative), baccalaureate degree in nursing from accredited undergraduate nursing program; minimum GPA of 2.7; all transcripts from undergraduate school and any work attempted at the graduate level; curriculum vitae; valid Louisiana Registered Nurse license; letters of recommendation; letter of intent/statement of purpose. Additional exam requirements/recommendations for international students: Required—TOEFL (minimum score 500 paper-based; 173 computer-based; 61 iBT). *Application deadline:* For fall admission, 7/15 priority date for domestic

students, 6/1 for international students; for spring admission, 12/1 priority date for domestic students, 10/1 for international students. Applications are processed on a rolling basis. Application fee: $20 ($30 for international students). Electronic applications accepted. *Expenses:* Tuition, state resident: full-time $3977; part-time $283 per semester hour. Tuition, nonresident: full-time $13,482; part-time $811 per semester hour. *Financial support:* Federal Work-Study, institutionally sponsored loans, scholarships/grants, traineeships, and unspecified assistantships available. Support available to part-time students. Financial award application deadline: 5/1; financial award applicants required to submit FAFSA. *Faculty research:* Gender issues, LGBT issues, occupational health/safety, accelerated students, caring development. *Total annual research expenditures:* $245,268. *Unit head:* Dr. Lorinda Sealy, Graduate Coordinator, 985-549-5045, Fax: 985-549-5087, E-mail: lorinda.sealy@selu.edu. *Application contact:* Sandra Meyers, Graduate Admissions Analyst, 985-549-5620, Fax: 985-549-5632, E-mail: admissions@selu.edu. Web site: http://www.selu.edu/acad_research/depts/nurs.

Southern Connecticut State University, School of Graduate Studies, School of Health and Human Services, Department of Nursing, New Haven, CT 06515-1355. Offers nursing administration (MSN); nursing education (MSN). *Accreditation:* AACN; AANA/CANAEP. Part-time and evening/weekend programs available. *Faculty:* 3 full-time (all women), 1 (woman) part-time/adjunct. *Students:* 9 full-time (8 women), 23 part-time (19 women); includes 3 minority (1 Black or African American, non-Hispanic/Latino; 1 Asian, non-Hispanic/Latino; 1 Hispanic/Latino). 120 applicants, 12% accepted, 11 enrolled. In 2011, 1 master's awarded. *Degree requirements:* For master's, thesis. *Entrance requirements:* For master's, GRE, MAT, interview, minimum QPA of 2.8, RN license, minimum 1 year of professional nursing experience. *Application deadline:* For fall admission, 7/15 priority date for domestic students. Applications are processed on a rolling basis. Application fee: $50. Electronic applications accepted. *Expenses:* Tuition, state resident: full-time $5137; part-time $413 per credit. *Required fees:* $4008; $55 per term. *Financial support:* Application deadline: 4/15; applicants required to submit FAFSA. *Unit head:* Dr. Lisa Rebeschi, Chairperson, 203-392-6485, E-mail: rebeschil1@southernct.edu. *Application contact:* Dr. Antonia Nelson, Graduate Coordinator, 203-392-6480, Fax: 203-392-6493, E-mail: nelsona13@southernct.edu.

Southern Illinois University Edwardsville, Graduate School, School of Nursing, Program in Nurse Educator, Edwardsville, IL 62026-0001. Offers MS, Post-Master's Certificate. Part-time programs available. *Students:* 34 part-time (33 women); includes 6 minority (4 Black or African American, non-Hispanic/Latino; 1 Hispanic/Latino; 1 Two or more races, non-Hispanic/Latino), 1 international. 45 applicants, 47% accepted. In 2011, 9 degrees awarded. *Degree requirements:* For master's, comprehensive exam. *Entrance requirements:* For master's, RN licensure, minimum undergraduate nursing GPA of 3.0. Additional exam requirements/recommendations for international students: Required—TOEFL (minimum score 550 paper-based; 213 computer-based; 79 iBT), IELTS (minimum score 6.5). *Application deadline:* For fall admission, 3/1 for domestic and international students. Application fee: $30. Electronic applications accepted. Tuition and fees vary according to course load and program. *Financial support:* Institutionally sponsored loans, scholarships/grants, and unspecified assistantships available. Financial award application deadline: 3/1; financial award applicants required to submit FAFSA. *Unit head:* Dr. Kathy Ketchum, Director, 618-650-3936, E-mail: kketchu@siue.edu. *Application contact:* Dr. Kathy Ketchum, Director, 618-650-3936, E-mail: kketchu@siue.edu. Web site: http://www.siue.edu/nursing/graduate.

Southern Nazarene University, Graduate College, School of Nursing, Bethany, OK 73008. Offers nursing education (MS); nursing leadership (MS). *Accreditation:* AACN. Part-time and evening/weekend programs available. *Degree requirements:* For master's, thesis. *Entrance requirements:* For master's, minimum undergraduate cumulative GPA of 3.0; baccalaureate degree in nursing from nationally-accredited program; current unencumbered registered nurse licensure in Oklahoma or eligibility for same; documentation of basic computer skills; basic statistics course; statement of professional goals; three letters of recommendation. Additional exam requirements/recommendations for international students: Required—TOEFL (minimum score 550 paper-based; 213 computer-based). *Expenses: Tuition:* Full-time $17,009; part-time $639 per credit hour. *Required fees:* $2668. *Unit head:* Dr. Katie Sigler, Interim Chair, 405-717-6217, E-mail: ksigler@snu.edu. *Application contact:* Dr. Mary Hibbert, Program Director, 405-491-6612, Fax: 405-491-6302, E-mail: mhibbert@snu.edu. Web site: http://snu.edu/school-of-nursing.

Southern University and Agricultural and Mechanical College, School of Nursing, Baton Rouge, LA 70813. Offers educator/administrator (PhD); family health nursing (MSN); family nurse practitioner (Post Master's Certificate); geriatric nurse practitioner/gerontology (PhD). *Accreditation:* AACN. Part-time programs available. *Degree requirements:* For master's, comprehensive exam, thesis; for doctorate, comprehensive exam, thesis/dissertation. *Entrance requirements:* For master's, GRE General Test, BSN, minimum GPA of 2.7; for doctorate, GRE General Test; for Post Master's Certificate, MSN. Additional exam requirements/recommendations for international students: Required—TOEFL (minimum score 525 paper-based; 193 computer-based). *Faculty research:* Health promotions, vulnerable populations, (community-based) cardiovascular participating research, health disparities chronic diseases, care of the elderly.

South University, Graduate Programs, College of Nursing, Savannah, GA 31406. Offers nurse educator (MS).

South University, Program in Nursing, Tampa, FL 33614. Offers adult health nurse practitioner (MS); family nurse practitioner (MS); nurse educator (MS).

State University of New York Institute of Technology, Program in Nursing Education, Utica, NY 13504-3050. Offers MS, CAS. *Entrance requirements:* For master's, GRE General Test (if undergraduate GPA less than 3.3), minimum GPA of 3.0 in last 30 hours of undergraduate work, bachelor's in nursing, 1 year RN experience, RN license, 2 letters of recommendation, interview. Additional exam requirements/recommendations for international students: Required—TOEFL (minimum score 550 paper-based; 213 computer-based). *Faculty research:* Nursing faculty shortages, curriculum enhancements, measurement and assessment, evidence-based practice.

Tennessee Technological University, Whitson-Hester School of Nursing, Cookeville, TN 38505. Offers family nurse practitioner (MSN); informatics (MSN); nursing administration (MSN); nursing education (MSN). Part-time and evening/weekend programs available. Postbaccalaureate distance learning degree programs offered (no on-campus study). *Students:* 3 full-time (2 women), 43 part-time (39 women); includes 3 minority (1 Black or African American, non-Hispanic/Latino; 2 Hispanic/Latino). 48 applicants, 46% accepted, 15 enrolled. In 2011, 13 master's awarded. *Degree requirements:* For master's, comprehensive exam, thesis or alternative. *Entrance requirements:* Additional exam requirements/recommendations for international students: Required—TOEFL (minimum score 550 paper-based; 79 iBT), IELTS (minimum score 5.5), Pearson Test of English Academic. *Application deadline:* For fall admission, 8/1 for domestic students, 5/1 for international students; for spring admission, 12/1 for domestic students, 10/1 for international students. Application fee: $25 ($30 for international students). Electronic applications accepted. *Expenses:* Tuition, state resident: full-time $8094; part-time $422 per credit hour. Tuition,

nonresident: full-time $20,574; part-time $1046 per credit hour. *Financial support:* Application deadline: 4/1. *Unit head:* Dr. Sherry Gaines, Director, 931-372-3203, Fax: 931-372-6244, E-mail: sgaines@tntech.edu. *Application contact:* Shelia K. Kendrick, Coordinator of Graduate Admissions, 931-372-3808, Fax: 931-372-3497, E-mail: skendrick@tntech.edu.

Texas Christian University, Harris College of Nursing and Health Sciences, Program in Nursing, Fort Worth, TX 76129-0002. Offers advanced practice registered nurse (DNP); clinical nurse leader (MSN); clinical nurse specialist: adult/gerontology nursing (MSN); clinical nurse specialist: pediatric nursing (MSN); nursing administration (DNP); nursing education (MSN). *Accreditation:* AACN; AANA/CANAEP (one or more programs are accredited). Part-time programs available. Postbaccalaureate distance learning degree programs offered (no on-campus study). *Faculty:* 18 full-time (16 women), 2 part-time/adjunct (both women). *Students:* 2 full-time (both women), 105 part-time (96 women); includes 16 minority (8 Black or African American, non-Hispanic/Latino; 4 Asian, non-Hispanic/Latino; 2 Hispanic/Latino; 1 Native Hawaiian or other Pacific Islander, non-Hispanic/Latino; 1 Two or more races, non-Hispanic/Latino), 1 international. Average age 44. 58 applicants, 93% accepted, 46 enrolled. In 2011, 11 master's, 21 doctorates awarded. *Degree requirements:* For master's and doctorate, professional project. *Entrance requirements:* For master's, GRE General Test or MAT, 3 letters of reference, 2 years preferred full-time experience as registered nurse, current nursing license, minimum GPA of 3.0; for doctorate, APRN recognition (national certification), minimum GPA of 3.0, 3 professional references, essay, 2 years post-master's experience (preferrred). Additional exam requirements/recommendations for international students: Required—TOEFL, Spoken English Test for DNP. *Expenses: Tuition:* Full-time $20,250; part-time $1125 per credit hour. Part-time tuition and fees vary according to course load and program. *Financial support:* In 2011–12, teaching assistantships (averaging $5,000 per year) were awarded; tuition waivers also available. *Unit head:* Dr. Pamela Frable, Associate Dean and Director of Nursing, 817-257-5840, E-mail: p.frable@tcu.edu. *Application contact:* Dr. Kathy Baker, Director of Graduate Studies and Director of DNP Program, 817-257-6726, E-mail: kathy.baker@tcu.edu. Web site: http://www.nursing.tcu.edu/graduate.asp.

Texas Tech University Health Sciences Center, School of Nursing, Lubbock, TX 79430. Offers acute care nurse practitioner (MSN, Certificate); administration (MSN); advanced practice (DNP); education (MSN); executive leadership (DNP); family nurse practitioner (MSN, Certificate); geriatric nurse practitioner (MSN, Certificate); pediatric nurse practitioner (MSN, Certificate). *Accreditation:* AACN. Part-time programs available. Postbaccalaureate distance learning degree programs offered (minimal on-campus study). *Degree requirements:* For master's, thesis optional. *Entrance requirements:* For master's, minimum GPA of 3.0, 3 letters of reference, BSN, RN license; for Certificate, minimum GPA of 3.0, 3 letters of reference, RN license. Additional exam requirements/recommendations for international students: Required—TOEFL (minimum score 550 paper-based; 213 computer-based). *Faculty research:* Diabetes/obesity, nurse competency, disease management, intervention and measurements, health disparities.

Texas Woman's University, Graduate School, College of Nursing, Denton, TX 76201. Offers acute care nurse practitioner (MS); adult health clinical nurse specialist (MS); adult health nurse practitioner (MS); child health clinical nurse specialist (MS); clinical nurse leader (MS); family nurse practitioner (MS); health systems management (MS); nursing education (MS); nursing practice (DNP); nursing science (PhD); pediatric nurse practitioner (MS); women's health clinical nurse specialist (MS); women's health nurse practitioner (MS). *Accreditation:* AACN. Part-time programs available. Postbaccalaureate distance learning degree programs offered. *Faculty:* 70 full-time (69 women), 7 part-time/adjunct (all women). *Students:* 87 full-time (78 women), 870 part-time (815 women); includes 489 minority (235 Black or African American, non-Hispanic/Latino; 5 American Indian or Alaska Native, non-Hispanic/Latino; 169 Asian, non-Hispanic/Latino; 78 Hispanic/Latino; 2 Native Hawaiian or other Pacific Islander, non-Hispanic/Latino), 19 international. Average age 38. 368 applicants, 71% accepted, 205 enrolled. In 2011, 147 master's, 21 doctorates awarded. *Degree requirements:* For master's, comprehensive exam, thesis or alternative; for doctorate, comprehensive exam, thesis/dissertation. *Entrance requirements:* For master's, GRE or MAT, minimum GPA of 3.0 on last 60 hours in undergraduate nursing degree and overall, RN license, BS in nursing, basic statistics course; for doctorate, GRE (preferred minimum score 153 [500 old version] Verbal, 144 [500 old version] Quantitative, 4 Analytical), MS in nursing, minimum preferred GPA of 3.5, RN license, statistics, 2 letters of reference, curriculum vitae, graduate nursing-theory course, graduate research course, statement of professional goals and research interests. Additional exam requirements/recommendations for international students: Required—TOEFL (minimum score 550 paper-based; 213 computer-based; 79 iBT). *Application deadline:* For fall admission, 5/1 priority date for domestic students, 3/1 for international students; for spring admission, 9/15 priority date for domestic students, 7/1 for international students. Applications are processed on a rolling basis. Application fee: $50 ($75 for international students). Electronic applications accepted. *Expenses:* Tuition, state resident: full-time $3834; part-time $213 per credit hour. Tuition, nonresident: full-time $9468; part-time $526 per credit hour. *Required fees:* $213 per credit hour. Tuition and fees vary according to course load. *Financial support:* In 2011–12, 149 students received support, including 10 research assistantships (averaging $12,942 per year), 1 teaching assistantship (averaging $12,942 per year); career-related internships or fieldwork, Federal Work-Study, institutionally sponsored loans, scholarships/grants, traineeships, health care benefits, and unspecified assistantships also available. Support available to part-time students. Financial award application deadline: 3/1; financial award applicants required to submit FAFSA. *Faculty research:* Screening, prevention, and treatment for intimate partner violence; needs of adolescents during childbirth intervention; a network analysis decision tool for nurse managers (Social Network Analysis); support for adolescents with implantable cardioverter defibrillators; informatics: nurse staffing, safety, quality, and financial data as they relate to patient care outcomes; prevention and treatment of obesity; improving infant outcomes related to premature birth. *Total annual research expenditures:* $462,088. *Unit head:* Dr. Patricia Holden-Huchton, Interim Dean, 940-898-2401, Fax: 940-898-2437, E-mail: nursing@twu.edu. *Application contact:* Dr. Samuel Wheeler, Assistant Director of Admissions, 940-898-3188, Fax: 940-898-3081, E-mail: wheelersr@twu.edu. Web site: http://www.twu.edu/nursing/.

Thomas Edison State College, School of Nursing, Program in Nurse Educator, Trenton, NJ 08608-1176. Offers Post-Master's Certificate. *Accreditation:* AACN. Part-time programs available. Postbaccalaureate distance learning degree programs offered (no on-campus study). *Students:* 9 part-time (7 women); includes 4 minority (1 Black or African American, non-Hispanic/Latino; 3 Hispanic/Latino). Average age 58. In 2011, 2 Post-Master's Certificates awarded. *Degree requirements:* For Post-Master's Certificate, nursing education seminar and online practicum. *Entrance requirements:* For degree, master's degree in nursing, RN. Additional exam requirements/recommendations for international students: Required—TOEFL (minimum score 550 paper-based; 213 computer-based; 79 iBT). *Application deadline:* For fall admission, 8/15 for domestic and international students; for winter admission, 11/15 for domestic and international students; for spring admission, 2/15 for domestic and international students. Application fee: $75. Electronic applications accepted. *Financial support:* Applicants required to submit FAFSA. *Unit head:* Dr. Susan O'Brien, Dean, School of Nursing, 609-633-6460,

Fax: 609-292-8279, E-mail: nursing@tesc.edu. *Application contact:* David Hoftiezer, Director of Admissions, 888-442-8372, Fax: 609-984-8447, E-mail: admissions@tesc.edu. Web site: http://www.tesc.edu/nursing/msn.cfm#educator.

Towson University, Program in Nursing, Towson, MD 21252-0001. Offers nursing (MS); nursing education (Postbaccalaureate Certificate). *Accreditation:* AACN. Part-time programs available. *Students:* 43 full-time (42 women), 65 part-time (63 women); includes 34 minority (29 Black or African American, non-Hispanic/Latino; 3 Asian, non-Hispanic/Latino; 2 Two or more races, non-Hispanic/Latino), 2 international. *Degree requirements:* For master's, thesis optional. *Entrance requirements:* For master's, minimum GPA of 3.0, copy of current nursing license, bachelor's degree in nursing, curriculum vitae; for Postbaccalaureate Certificate, minimum GPA of 3.0, copy of current nursing license, curriculum vitae, bachelor's degree in nursing. *Application deadline:* Applications are processed on a rolling basis. Application fee: $50. Electronic applications accepted. *Expenses:* Tuition, state resident: part-time $337 per credit. Tuition, nonresident: part-time $709 per credit. *Required fees:* $99 per credit. *Financial support:* Application deadline: 4/1; applicants required to submit FAFSA. *Unit head:* Kathleen Ogle, Graduate Program Director, 410-704-4389, E-mail: kogle@towson.edu.

Union University, School of Nursing, Jackson, TN 38305-3697. Offers executive leadership (DNP); nurse anesthesia (DNP); nurse anesthetist (PMC); nurse practitioner (DNP); nursing education (MSN, PMC). *Accreditation:* AACN; AANA/CANAEP. *Degree requirements:* For master's, thesis or alternative. *Entrance requirements:* For master's, GRE, 3 letters of reference, bachelor's degree in nursing, minimum GPA of 3.0. Additional exam requirements/recommendations for international students: Required—TOEFL (minimum score 560 paper-based; 220 computer-based). Electronic applications accepted. *Faculty research:* Children's health, occupational rehabilitation, informatics, health promotion.

United States University, School of Nursing, Cypress, CA 90630. Offers administrator (MSN); educator (MSN).

The University of Alabama in Huntsville, School of Graduate Studies, College of Nursing, Huntsville, AL 35899. Offers family nurse practitioner (Certificate); nursing (MSN, DNP), including acute care nurse practitioner (MSN), adult clinical nursing specialist (MSN), clinical nurse leader (MSN), family nurse practitioner (MSN), leadership in health care systems (MSN); nursing education (Certificate). DNP offered jointly with The University of Alabama at Birmingham. *Accreditation:* AACN. Part-time and evening/weekend programs available. Postbaccalaureate distance learning degree programs offered (minimal on-campus study). *Faculty:* 19 full-time (18 women), 8 part-time/adjunct (7 women). *Students:* 57 full-time (43 women), 162 part-time (139 women); includes 22 minority (15 Black or African American, non-Hispanic/Latino; 3 American Indian or Alaska Native, non-Hispanic/Latino; 1 Asian, non-Hispanic/Latino; 3 Hispanic/Latino), 2 international. Average age 37. 193 applicants, 79% accepted, 112 enrolled. In 2011, 42 master's, 11 doctorates, 11 other advanced degrees awarded. *Degree requirements:* For master's, comprehensive exam, thesis or alternative, oral and written exams. *Entrance requirements:* For master's, MAT or GRE, Alabama RN license, BSN, minimum GPA of 3.0; for doctorate, master's degree in nursing in an advanced practice area; for Certificate, MAT or GRE, minimum GPA of 3.0. Additional exam requirements/recommendations for international students: Required—TOEFL (minimum score 500 paper-based; 173 computer-based; 62 iBT). *Application deadline:* For fall admission, 7/15 for domestic students, 4/1 for international students; for spring admission, 11/30 for domestic students, 9/1 for international students. Applications are processed on a rolling basis. Application fee: $40 ($50 for international students). Electronic applications accepted. *Expenses:* Tuition, state resident: full-time $7830; part-time $473.50 per credit. Tuition, nonresident: full-time $18,748; part-time $1128.33 per credit. Tuition and fees vary according to course load and program. *Financial support:* In 2011–12, 9 students received support, including 9 teaching assistantships with full tuition reimbursements available (averaging $9,596 per year); career-related internships or fieldwork, Federal Work-Study, institutionally sponsored loans, scholarships/grants, traineeships, health care benefits, and unspecified assistantships also available. Support available to part-time students. Financial award application deadline: 4/1; financial award applicants required to submit FAFSA. *Faculty research:* Home health care, gerontology, pediatric nursing, family nurse practitioner, adult acute care administration. *Total annual research expenditures:* $235,384. *Unit head:* Dr. Fay Raines, Dean, 256-824-6345, Fax: 256-824-6026, E-mail: rainesc@uah.edu. *Application contact:* Charles Davis, Director of Graduate Nursing Admissions and Advising, 256-824-2433, Fax: 256-824-6026, E-mail: charles.davis@uah.edu. Web site: http://www.uah.edu/nursing/welcome.

University of Alaska Anchorage, College of Health, School of Nursing, Anchorage, AK 99508. Offers family nurse practitioner (Certificate); nursing (MS); nursing education (Certificate); psychiatric nurse practitioner (Certificate). *Accreditation:* NLN. Part-time and evening/weekend programs available. *Degree requirements:* For master's, comprehensive exam, individual project. *Entrance requirements:* For master's, GRE or MAT, BS in nursing, interview, minimum GPA of 3.0, RN license, 1 year of part-time or 6 months of full-time clinical experience. Additional exam requirements/recommendations for international students: Required—TOEFL (minimum score 550 paper-based; 213 computer-based).

University of Central Florida, College of Nursing, Orlando, FL 32816. Offers adult-gerontology clinical nurse specialist (Post-Master's Certificate); adult-gerontology nurse practitioner (Post-Master's Certificate); clinical nurse leader (Post-Master's Certificate); family nurse practitioner (Post-Master's Certificate); nursing (MSN, PhD); nursing education (Post-Master's Certificate); nursing practice (DNP). *Accreditation:* AACN. Part-time and evening/weekend programs available. *Faculty:* 44 full-time (39 women), 72 part-time/adjunct (71 women). *Students:* 75 full-time (68 women), 350 part-time (332 women); includes 109 minority (54 Black or African American, non-Hispanic/Latino; 1 American Indian or Alaska Native, non-Hispanic/Latino; 19 Asian, non-Hispanic/Latino; 33 Hispanic/Latino; 1 Native Hawaiian or other Pacific Islander, non-Hispanic/Latino; 1 Two or more races, non-Hispanic/Latino), 5 international. Average age 40. 203 applicants, 60% accepted, 98 enrolled. In 2011, 110 master's, 17 doctorates, 11 other advanced degrees awarded. *Degree requirements:* For master's, thesis or alternative. *Entrance requirements:* For master's, GRE General Test, minimum GPA of 3.0 in last 60 hours. Additional exam requirements/recommendations for international students: Required—TOEFL. *Application deadline:* For fall admission, 2/15 for domestic students; for spring admission, 9/15 for domestic students. Application fee: $30. Electronic applications accepted. *Expenses:* Tuition, state resident: part-time $277.08 per credit hour. Tuition, nonresident: part-time $277.08 per credit hour. Part-time tuition and fees vary according to degree level and program. *Financial support:* In 2011–12, 92 students received support, including 92 fellowships with partial tuition reimbursements available (averaging $1,100 per year), 2 teaching assistantships with partial tuition reimbursements available (averaging $8,100 per year); research assistantships with partial tuition reimbursements available, career-related internships or fieldwork, Federal Work-Study, institutionally sponsored loans, traineeships, and unspecified assistantships also available. Financial award application deadline: 3/1; financial award applicants required to submit FAFSA. *Unit head:* Dr. Jean D. Leuner, Dean, 407-823-5496, Fax: 407-823-5675, E-mail: jean.leuner@ucf.edu. *Application contact:* Barbara Rodriguez, Director, Admissions and Registration, 407-823-2766, Fax: 407-823-6442, E-mail: gradadmissions@ucf.edu. Web site: http://nursing.ucf.edu/.

University of Hartford, College of Education, Nursing, and Health Professions, Program in Nursing, West Hartford, CT 06117-1599. Offers community/public health nursing (MSN); nursing education (MSN); nursing management (MSN). *Accreditation:* AACN. Part-time and evening/weekend programs available. *Degree requirements:* For master's, research project. *Entrance requirements:* For master's, BSN, Connecticut RN license. Additional exam requirements/recommendations for international students: Required—TOEFL (minimum score 550 paper-based; 213 computer-based). Electronic applications accepted. *Expenses:* Contact institution. *Faculty research:* Child development, women in doctoral study, applying feminist theory in teaching methods, near death experience, grandmothers as primary care providers.

University of Indianapolis, Graduate Programs, School of Nursing, Indianapolis, IN 46227-3697. Offers family practice (post-RN) (MSN); gerontological nurse practitioner (MSN); nurse-midwifery (MSN); nursing (MSN); nursing administration (MSN); nursing education (MSN); MBA/MSN. *Accreditation:* AACN; ACNM. *Faculty:* 1 full-time (0 women), 4 part-time/adjunct (1 woman). *Students:* 14 full-time (13 women), 168 part-time (159 women); includes 23 minority (13 Black or African American, non-Hispanic/Latino; 1 American Indian or Alaska Native, non-Hispanic/Latino; 4 Asian, non-Hispanic/Latino; 2 Hispanic/Latino; 3 Two or more races, non-Hispanic/Latino), 5 international. Average age 36. In 2011, 51 master's awarded. *Entrance requirements:* For master's, minimum GPA of 3.0, interview, letters of recommendation, resume, IN nursing license, 1 year professional practice. Additional exam requirements/recommendations for international students: Required—TOEFL (minimum score 550 paper-based; 213 computer-based). *Application deadline:* For fall admission, 8/1 for domestic students; for winter admission, 12/15 for domestic students; for spring admission, 4/15 for domestic students. Applications are processed on a rolling basis. Application fee: $50. Tuition and fees vary according to degree level and program. *Financial support:* Federal Work-Study available. *Unit head:* Dr. Anne Thomas, Dean, 317-788-3206, E-mail: athomas@uindy.edu. *Application contact:* Sueann Meagher, Graduate Administrative Assistant, 317-788-8005, Fax: 317-788-3542, E-mail: meaghers@uindy.edu. Web site: http://nursing.uindy.edu/.

University of Mary, School of Health Sciences, Division of Nursing, Bismarck, ND 58504-9652. Offers family nurse practitioner (MSN); nurse administrator (MSN); nursing educator (MSN). *Accreditation:* AACN. Part-time and evening/weekend programs available. Postbaccalaureate distance learning degree programs offered (minimal on-campus study). *Faculty:* 6 full-time (all women), 16 part-time/adjunct (all women). *Students:* 157 full-time (148 women), 91 part-time (85 women); includes 14 minority (5 Black or African American, non-Hispanic/Latino; 4 American Indian or Alaska Native, non-Hispanic/Latino; 1 Asian, non-Hispanic/Latino; 4 Hispanic/Latino), 2 international. Average age 37. 92 applicants. In 2011, 80 master's awarded. *Degree requirements:* For master's, comprehensive exam (for some programs), thesis (for some programs), internship (family nurse practitioner), teaching practice. *Entrance requirements:* For master's, minimum GPA of 2.75 in nursing, interview, letters of recommendation, criminal background check, immunizations, statement of professional goals. Additional exam requirements/recommendations for international students: Required—TOEFL (minimum score 500 paper-based; 197 computer-based; 71 iBT). *Application deadline:* Applications are processed on a rolling basis. Application fee: $40. Electronic applications accepted. *Financial support:* In 2011–12, 14 fellowships with partial tuition reimbursements, 3 teaching assistantships with partial tuition reimbursements were awarded. Financial award application deadline: 8/1; financial award applicants required to submit FAFSA. *Faculty research:* Gerontology issues, rural nursing, health policy, primary care, women's health. *Unit head:* Glenda Reemts, Director, 701-255-7500 Ext. 8041, Fax: 701-255-7687, E-mail: greemts@umary.edu. *Application contact:* Joanne Lassiter, Nurse Recruiter, 701-355-8379, Fax: 701-255-7687, E-mail: jllassiter@umary.edu.

University of Mary Hardin-Baylor, Graduate Studies in Nursing, Belton, TX 76513. Offers clinical nurse leader (MSN); family nurse practitioner (MSN); nursing education (MSN). *Accreditation:* AACN. Part-time and evening/weekend programs available. *Faculty:* 8 full-time (all women), 1 (woman) part-time/adjunct. *Students:* 30 full-time (28 women), 2 part-time (both women); includes 9 minority (5 Black or African American, non-Hispanic/Latino; 1 Asian, non-Hispanic/Latino; 3 Hispanic/Latino), 6 international. Average age 34. 48 applicants, 83% accepted, 25 enrolled. In 2011, 3 master's awarded. *Degree requirements:* For master's, practicum. *Entrance requirements:* For master's, GRE General Test, RN, BSN, minimum GPA of 3.0 in last 60 hours of undergraduate program. *Application deadline:* For fall admission, 6/1 priority date for domestic students; for spring admission, 11/1 priority date for domestic students. Applications are processed on a rolling basis. Application fee: $35 ($135 for international students). Electronic applications accepted. *Expenses: Tuition:* Full-time $12,780. *Required fees:* $2350. *Financial support:* Applicants required to submit FAFSA. *Unit head:* Dr. Margaret Prydun, Director of Master's Program in Nursing, 254-295-4674, E-mail: margaret.prydun@umhb.edu. *Application contact:* Melissa Ford, Director of Graduate Admissions, 254-295-4020, Fax: 254-295-5301, E-mail: mford@umhb.edu. Web site: http://graduate.umhb.edu/nursing/.

University of Maryland, Baltimore, Graduate School, School of Nursing, Master's Program in Nursing, Baltimore, MD 21201. Offers community health nursing (MS); gerontological nursing (MS); maternal-child nursing (MS); medical-surgical nursing (MS); nurse-midwifery education (MS); nursing administration (MS); nursing education (MS); nursing health policy (MS); primary care nursing (MS); psychiatric nursing (MS); MS/MBA. MS/MBA offered jointly with University of Baltimore. *Accreditation:* AACN; AANA/CANAEP; NLN (one or more programs are accredited). Part-time programs available. *Students:* 370 full-time (314 women), 480 part-time (441 women); includes 308 minority (176 Black or African American, non-Hispanic/Latino; 2 American Indian or Alaska Native, non-Hispanic/Latino; 70 Asian, non-Hispanic/Latino; 33 Hispanic/Latino; 27 Two or more races, non-Hispanic/Latino), 9 international. Average age 35. 990 applicants, 30% accepted, 204 enrolled. In 2011, 301 master's awarded. *Degree requirements:* For master's, comprehensive exam (for some programs), thesis or alternative. *Entrance requirements:* For master's, minimum GPA of 2.75, course work in statistics, BS in nursing. Additional exam requirements/recommendations for international students: Required—TOEFL (minimum score 550 paper-based; 80 iBT) or IELTS (minimum score 7). *Application deadline:* For fall admission, 2/1 for domestic students, 1/15 for international students. Application fee: $50. Electronic applications accepted. *Financial support:* Fellowships, research assistantships, teaching assistantships, career-related internships or fieldwork, and traineeships available. Support available to part-time students. Financial award application deadline: 2/15; financial award applicants required to submit FAFSA. *Unit head:* Dr. Jane Kapustin, Assistant Dean, 410-706-6741, Fax: 410-706-4231. *Application contact:* Marjorie Fass, Admissions Director, 410-706-0501, Fax: 410-706-7238.

University of Massachusetts Dartmouth, Graduate School, College of Nursing, Graduate Nursing Programs, North Dartmouth, MA 02747-2300. Offers adult health/adult nurse practitioner (MS); adult health/advanced practice (MS); adult health/nurse educator (MS); adult health/nurse manager (MS); adult nurse practitioner (PMC); community nursing/advanced practice (MS); community nursing/nurse educator (MS);

community nursing/nurse manager (MS); individualized nursing (PMC); nursing (DNP, PhD). Part-time programs available. *Faculty:* 27 full-time (all women), 42 part-time/adjunct (41 women). *Students:* 8 full-time (all women), 99 part-time (93 women); includes 11 minority (4 Black or African American, non-Hispanic/Latino; 2 Asian, non-Hispanic/Latino; 4 Hispanic/Latino; 1 Two or more races, non-Hispanic/Latino), 1 international. Average age 38. 65 applicants, 75% accepted, 26 enrolled. In 2011, 12 master's, 1 other advanced degree awarded. *Degree requirements:* For master's, thesis; for doctorate, thesis/dissertation. *Entrance requirements:* For master's, GRE General Test, BSN, minimum undergraduate GPA of 3.0, RN license, 3 letters of recommendation, 1 year experience as registered nurse; for doctorate, GRE General Test, minimum undergraduate GPA of 3.0, graduate 3.3; 3 letters of recommendation; personal statement; current Massachusetts RN license or eligibility for licensure in Massachusetts; 1 year professional nursing experience; example of scholarly writing. Additional exam requirements/recommendations for international students: Required—TOEFL (minimum score 533 paper-based; 200 computer-based; 72 iBT). *Application deadline:* For fall admission, 3/15 for domestic students, 2/15 for international students. Application fee: $40 ($60 for international students). Electronic applications accepted. *Expenses:* Tuition, state resident: full-time $2071; part-time $86.29 per credit. Tuition, nonresident: full-time $8099; part-time $337.46 per credit. *Required fees:* $438.58 per credit. Part-time tuition and fees vary according to class time, course load, degree level and reciprocity agreements. *Financial support:* In 2011–12, 14 teaching assistantships with partial tuition reimbursements (averaging $2,571 per year) were awarded; Federal Work-Study also available. Support available to part-time students. Financial award application deadline: 3/1; financial award applicants required to submit FAFSA. *Faculty research:* Chronic illness management, risk reduction activities in Type 2 diabetes, diabetes care and education, clinical decision making, quantitative methodologies. *Total annual research expenditures:* $31,049. *Unit head:* Dr. Gail Russell, Graduate Program Director, 508-999-8251, Fax: 508-999-9127, E-mail: grussell@umassd.edu. *Application contact:* Elan Turcotte-Shamski, Graduate Admissions Officer, 508-999-8604, Fax: 508-999-8183, E-mail: graduate@umassd.edu. Web site: http://www.umassd.edu/nursing/graduateprograms.

University of Massachusetts Lowell, School of Health and Environment, Department of Nursing, Lowell, MA 01854-2881. Offers adult psychiatric and mental health nursing (MS, Graduate Certificate); family health nursing (MS); gerontological nursing (MS, Graduate Certificate); geropsychiatric nursing (Graduate Certificate); nursing (PhD); nursing education (Graduate Certificate); palliative and end-of-life nursing care (Graduate Certificate). *Accreditation:* AACN. *Degree requirements:* For master's, thesis optional; for doctorate, thesis/dissertation. *Entrance requirements:* For master's and doctorate, GRE General Test. *Faculty research:* Gerontology, women's health issues, long-term care, alcoholism, health promotion.

University of Massachusetts Worcester, Graduate School of Nursing, Worcester, MA 01655-0115. Offers adult acute/critical care nurse practitioner (MS, Post Master's Certificate); adult acute/critical care nurse practitioner and gerontological nurse practitioner (MS, Post Master's Certificate); adult primary care nurse practitioner (MS, Post Master's Certificate); adult primary care nurse practitioner and gerontological nurse practitioner (MS, Post Master's Certificate); advanced practice nursing (DNP); family nurse practitioner (MS); gerontological nurse practitioner (Post Master's Certificate); leadership (DNP); nurse education (Post Master's Certificate); nurse educator (MS); nursing (PhD). *Accreditation:* AACN. *Faculty:* 20 full-time (17 women), 60 part-time/adjunct (50 women). *Students:* 162 full-time (141 women), 36 part-time (30 women); includes 29 minority (13 Black or African American, non-Hispanic/Latino; 10 Asian, non-Hispanic/Latino; 6 Hispanic/Latino), 1 international. Average age 36. 252 applicants, 38% accepted, 82 enrolled. In 2011, 38 master's, 6 doctorates awarded. *Degree requirements:* For doctorate, comprehensive exam, thesis/dissertation. *Entrance requirements:* For master's, GRE General Test, bachelor's degree, course work in statistics; for doctorate, GRE General Test, bachelor's or master's degree, RN licensure; for Post Master's Certificate, GRE General Test, MS in nursing. Additional exam requirements/recommendations for international students: Required—TOEFL. *Application deadline:* For fall admission, 1/15 priority date for domestic students. Applications are processed on a rolling basis. Application fee: $40 ($60 for international students). *Expenses:* Contact institution. *Financial support:* In 2011–12, 38 students received support. Institutionally sponsored loans, scholarships/grants, traineeships, and tuition waivers (for some) available. Support available to part-time students. Financial award application deadline: 5/16; financial award applicants required to submit FAFSA. *Faculty research:* Decision-making of partners and men with prostate cancer, coinfection (HIV and Hepatitus C) and treatment decisions, parent management of children with T1DM, health literacy and discharge planning, Ghanian women and self-care. *Total annual research expenditures:* $939,567. *Unit head:* Dr. Paulette Seymour-Route, Dean, 508-856-5801, Fax: 508-856-6552, E-mail: paulette.seymour-route@umassmed.edu. *Application contact:* Diane Brescia, Admissions Coordinator, 508-856-3488, Fax: 508-856-5851, E-mail: diane.brescia@umassmed.edu. Web site: http://www.umassmed.edu/gsn/.

University of Memphis, Loewenberg School of Nursing, Memphis, TN 38152. Offers advance practice-family nurse practitioner (MSN); executive nursing leadership (MSN); nursing (Graduate Certificate); nursing administration (MSN); nursing education (MSN); nursing informatics (MSN). *Accreditation:* AACN. Part-time and evening/weekend programs available. Postbaccalaureate distance learning degree programs offered. *Degree requirements:* For master's, comprehensive exam, thesis optional, scholarly project; completion of clinical practicum hours. *Entrance requirements:* For master's, NCLEX Exam, interview. Additional exam requirements/recommendations for international students: Required—TOEFL (minimum score 550 paper-based; 213 computer-based; 79 iBT). *Faculty research:* Technology in nursing, nurse retention, cultural competence, health policy, health access.

University of Missouri–Kansas City, School of Nursing, Kansas City, MO 64110-2499. Offers adult clinical nurse specialist (MSN), including adult nurse practitioner, women's health nurse practitioner; family nurse practitioner (MSN); neonatal nurse practitioner (MSN); nurse educator (MSN); nurse executive (MSN); nursing (PhD); nursing practice (DNP); pediatric nurse practitioner (MSN). *Accreditation:* AACN. Part-time programs available. Postbaccalaureate distance learning degree programs offered (minimal on-campus study). *Faculty:* 40 full-time (35 women), 57 part-time/adjunct (52 women). *Students:* 51 full-time (48 women), 381 part-time (352 women); includes 41 minority (22 Black or African American, non-Hispanic/Latino; 7 Asian, non-Hispanic/Latino; 12 Hispanic/Latino). Average age 37. 195 applicants, 49% accepted, 90 enrolled. In 2011, 78 master's, 19 doctorates awarded. *Degree requirements:* For master's, thesis or alternative. *Entrance requirements:* For master's, minimum undergraduate GPA of 3.2; for doctorate, GRE, 3 letters of reference, interview by invitation. Additional exam requirements/recommendations for international students: Required—TOEFL (minimum score 550 paper-based; 213 computer-based; 80 iBT). *Application deadline:* For fall admission, 2/1 priority date for domestic students, 2/1 for international students; for spring admission, 9/1 priority date for domestic students, 9/1 for international students. Application fee: $45 ($50 for international students). *Expenses:* Tuition, state resident: full-time $5798; part-time $322.10 per credit hour. Tuition, nonresident: full-time $14,969; part-time $831.60 per credit hour. *Required fees:* $93.51 per credit hour. *Financial support:* In 2011–12, 25 teaching assistantships with partial tuition reimbursements (averaging $6,927 per year) were awarded; fellowships, research assistantships, career-related internships or fieldwork, Federal Work-Study, institutionally sponsored loans, and tuition waivers (full and partial) also available. Support available to part-time students. Financial award application deadline: 3/1; financial award applicants required to submit FAFSA. *Faculty research:* Geriatrics/gerontology, children's pain, neonatology, Alzheimer's care, cancer caregivers. *Unit head:* Dr. Lora Lacey-Haun, Dean, 816-235-1700, Fax: 816-235-1701, E-mail: lacey-haunc@umkc.edu. *Application contact:* Leah Wilder, Coordinator for Admissions and Recruitment, 816-235-5768, Fax: 816-235-1701, E-mail: wilderl@umkc.edu. Web site: http://nursing.umkc.edu/.

University of Missouri–St. Louis, College of Nursing, St. Louis, MO 63121. Offers adult nurse practitioner (DNP, Post Master's Certificate); clinical nurse specialist (DNP); family mental health nurse practitioner (DNP); family nurse practitioner (MSN, DNP, Post Master's Certificate); neonatal nurse practitioner (MSN); nurse educator (MSN); nurse leader (MSN); nurse practitioner (Post Master's Certificate); nursing (PhD); pediatric clinical nurse specialist (DNP); pediatric nurse practitioner (MSN, DNP, Post Master's Certificate); women's health nurse practitioner (MSN, Post Master's Certificate). *Accreditation:* AACN. Part-time programs available. *Faculty:* 12 full-time (11 women), 14 part-time/adjunct (all women). *Students:* 240 part-time (226 women); includes 30 minority (26 Black or African American, non-Hispanic/Latino; 1 Asian, non-Hispanic/Latino; 2 Hispanic/Latino; 1 Two or more races, non-Hispanic/Latino). Average age 37. 228 applicants, 28% accepted, 53 enrolled. In 2011, 66 master's, 2 doctorates, 2 other advanced degrees awarded. *Degree requirements:* For doctorate, comprehensive exam, thesis/dissertation; for Post Master's Certificate, thesis. *Entrance requirements:* For master's, 2 recommendation letters; minimum GPA of 3.0; BSN; nursing licensure; statement of purpose; course in differential/inferential statistics; for doctorate, GRE, 2 letters of recommendation, MSN, minimum GPA of 3.2, course in differential/inferential statistics; for Post Master's Certificate, 2 recommendation letters; MSN; advanced practice certificate; minimum GPA of 3.0; essay. Additional exam requirements/recommendations for international students: Required—TOEFL (minimum score 550 paper-based; 213 computer-based). *Application deadline:* For fall admission, 2/15 for domestic and international students. Application fee: $35 ($40 for international students). Electronic applications accepted. *Expenses:* Tuition, state resident: full-time $6273; part-time $3866 per year. Tuition, nonresident: full-time $14,969; part-time $9980 per year. *Required fees:* $315 per year. *Financial support:* In 2011–12, 3 research assistantships with full and partial tuition reimbursements (averaging $12,339 per year) were awarded. Financial award application deadline: 4/1; financial award applicants required to submit FAFSA. *Faculty research:* Health promotion and restoration, family disruption, violence, abuse, battered women, health survey methods. *Unit head:* Dr. Nancy Magnuson, Director, 314-516-6066. *Application contact:* 314-516-5458, Fax: 314-516-6996, E-mail: gradadm@umsl.edu. Web site: http://www.umsl.edu/divisions/nursing/.

University of Nevada, Las Vegas, Graduate College, School of Nursing, Las Vegas, NV 89154-3018. Offers family nurse practitioner (Advanced Certificate); nursing (MS, DNP, PhD); nursing education (Advanced Certificate); pediatric nurse practitioner (Post-Master's Certificate). *Accreditation:* AACN. Part-time programs available. Postbaccalaureate distance learning degree programs offered (minimal on-campus study). *Faculty:* 17 full-time (all women), 22 part-time/adjunct (6 women). *Students:* 49 full-time (46 women), 82 part-time (73 women); includes 28 minority (7 Black or African American, non-Hispanic/Latino; 1 American Indian or Alaska Native, non-Hispanic/Latino; 8 Asian, non-Hispanic/Latino; 5 Hispanic/Latino; 1 Native Hawaiian or other Pacific Islander, non-Hispanic/Latino; 6 Two or more races, non-Hispanic/Latino), 3 international. Average age 41. 125 applicants, 43% accepted, 40 enrolled. In 2011, 29 master's, 8 doctorates, 2 other advanced degrees awarded. *Entrance requirements:* For doctorate, GRE General Test. Additional exam requirements/recommendations for international students: Recommended—TOEFL (minimum score 550 paper-based; 213 computer-based; 80 iBT), IELTS (minimum score 7). *Application deadline:* For fall admission, 2/15 priority date for domestic students, 5/1 for international students; for spring admission, 10/1 for international students. Applications are processed on a rolling basis. Application fee: $60 ($95 for international students). Electronic applications accepted. *Financial support:* In 2011–12, 3 students received support, including 3 teaching assistantships with partial tuition reimbursements available (averaging $9,334 per year); institutionally sponsored loans, scholarships/grants, health care benefits, and unspecified assistantships also available. Financial award application deadline: 3/1. *Faculty research:* Physiological stress reactions, leukocyte response and skeletal muscle injury, depression in lay caregivers, incivility in nursing practice, work-related injuries in healthcare and construction workers. *Total annual research expenditures:* $1.7 million. *Unit head:* Dr. Carolyn Yucha, Interim Dean, 702-895-3906, Fax: 702-895-5050, E-mail: carolyn.yucha@unlv.edu. *Application contact:* Graduate College Admissions Evaluator, 702-895-3320, Fax: 702-895-4180, E-mail: gradcollege@unlv.edu. Web site: http://nursing.unlv.edu/.

University of New Brunswick Fredericton, School of Graduate Studies, Faculty of Nursing, Fredericton, NB E3B 5A3, Canada. Offers nurse educator (MN); nurse practitioner (MN); nursing (MN). Part-time programs available. Postbaccalaureate distance learning degree programs offered. *Faculty:* 24 full-time (all women), 1 part-time/adjunct (0 women). *Students:* 10 full-time (8 women), 35 part-time (34 women). In 2011, 14 master's awarded. *Degree requirements:* For master's, comprehensive exam (for some programs), thesis (for some programs). *Entrance requirements:* For master's, undergraduate coursework in statistics and nursing research, minimum GPA of 3.3, registration as a nurse (or eligibility) in New Brunswick. Additional exam requirements/recommendations for international students: Required—TOEFL (minimum score 600 paper-based; 250 computer-based). *Application deadline:* For winter admission, 2/5 for domestic students. Application fee: $50 Canadian dollars. Electronic applications accepted. *Financial support:* In 2011–12, 9 fellowships, 1 research assistantship, 1 teaching assistantship were awarded. *Faculty research:* Violence and abuse; healthy child development, chronic illness and addiction; rural populations access to health care and primary healthcare; teaching and learning in classroom, clinical lab, and by distance; Aboriginal nursing. *Unit head:* Kathy Wilson, Assistant Dean of Graduate and Advanced RN Studies, 506-458-7640, Fax: 506-447-3057, E-mail: kewilson@unb.ca. *Application contact:* Francis Perry, Graduate Secretary, 506-451-6844, Fax: 506-447-3057, E-mail: fperry@unb.ca. Web site: http://www.unbf.ca/nursing/.

The University of North Carolina at Charlotte, Graduate School, College of Health and Human Services, School of Nursing, Charlotte, NC 28223-0001. Offers administration (Post-Master's Certificate); advanced clinical (MSN, Post-Master's Certificate); anesthesia (MSN, Post-Master's Certificate); community health (MSN); family nurse practitioner (MSN, Post-Master's Certificate); health administration (MSN); mental health (MSN); nurse educator (MSN, Post-Master's Certificate); systems population (MSN). *Accreditation:* AACN. *Faculty:* 20 full-time (19 women), 5 part-time/adjunct (all women). *Students:* 76 full-time (65 women), 160 part-time (149 women); includes 49 minority (32 Black or African American, non-Hispanic/Latino; 1 American Indian or Alaska Native, non-Hispanic/Latino; 8 Asian, non-Hispanic/Latino; 8 Hispanic/Latino), 1 international. Average age 35. 191 applicants, 42% accepted, 71 enrolled. In 2011, 76 master's, 10 other advanced degrees awarded. *Degree requirements:* For master's, thesis or alternative, practicum. *Entrance requirements:* For master's, GRE

General Test, minimum GPA of 3.0 in undergraduate major. Additional exam requirements/recommendations for international students: Required—TOEFL (minimum score 570 paper-based; 220 computer-based; 83 iBT). *Application deadline:* For fall admission, 7/15 for domestic students, 5/1 for international students; for spring admission, 11/15 for domestic students, 10/1 for international students. Application fee: $65 ($75 for international students). *Expenses:* Tuition, state resident: full-time $3689. Tuition, nonresident: full-time $15,226. *Required fees:* $2198. Tuition and fees vary according to course load and program. *Financial support:* In 2011–12, 10 students received support, including 4 research assistantships (averaging $5,284 per year), 6 teaching assistantships (averaging $2,918 per year); career-related internships or fieldwork, institutionally sponsored loans, scholarships/grants, traineeships, unspecified assistantships, and administrative assistanship also available. Support available to part-time students. Financial award application deadline: 4/1; financial award applicants required to submit FAFSA. *Total annual research expenditures:* $955,795. *Unit head:* Dr. Lucille L. Travis, Director, 704-687-7959, Fax: 704-687-6017, E-mail: ltravis1@uncc.edu. *Application contact:* Kathy B. Giddings, Director of Graduate Admissions, 704-687-5503, Fax: 704-687-3279, E-mail: gradadm@uncc.edu. Web site: http://nursing.uncc.edu/.

The University of North Carolina at Greensboro, Graduate School, School of Nursing, Greensboro, NC 27412-5001. Offers adult clinical nurse specialist (MSN, PMC); adult/gerontological nurse practitioner (MSN, PMC); nurse anesthesia (MSN, PMC); nursing (PhD); nursing administration (MSN); nursing education (MSN); MSN/MBA. *Accreditation:* AACN; AANA/CANAEP; NLN. *Degree requirements:* For master's, thesis or alternative. *Entrance requirements:* For master's, GRE General Test or MAT, BSN, clinical experience, liability insurance, RN license; for PMC, liability insurance, MSN, RN license. Additional exam requirements/recommendations for international students: Required—TOEFL. Electronic applications accepted.

The University of North Carolina Wilmington, School of Nursing, Wilmington, NC 28403-3297. Offers family nurse practitioner (MSN); nurse educator (MSN). *Accreditation:* AACN; NLN. *Degree requirements:* For master's, comprehensive exam, thesis or project. *Entrance requirements:* For master's, GRE General Test, bachelor's degree in nursing. Additional exam requirements/recommendations for international students: Required—TOEFL (minimum score 550 paper-based; 217 computer-based; 79 iBT), IELTS (minimum score 6.5). Electronic applications accepted.

University of North Dakota, Graduate School, College of Nursing, Grand Forks, ND 58202. Offers advanced public health nursing (MS); family nurse practitioner (MS); gerontological nursing (MS); nurse anesthesia (MS); nursing (MS, PhD); nursing education (MS); psychiatric and mental health (MS). *Accreditation:* AACN; AANA/CANAEP (one or more programs are accredited). Part-time and evening/weekend programs available. Postbaccalaureate distance learning degree programs offered (minimal on-campus study). *Degree requirements:* For master's, thesis or alternative. *Entrance requirements:* For master's, minimum GPA of 3.0; for doctorate, GRE or MAT, minimum GPA of 3.0. Additional exam requirements/recommendations for international students: Required—TOEFL (minimum score 550 paper-based; 213 computer-based; 79 iBT), IELTS (minimum score 6.5). Electronic applications accepted. *Faculty research:* Adult health, anesthesia, rural health, health administration, family nurse practitioner.

University of Northern Colorado, Graduate School, College of Natural and Health Sciences, School of Nursing, Greeley, CO 80639. Offers clinical nurse specialist in chronic illness (MS); family nurse practitioner (MS); nursing education (MS, PhD). *Accreditation:* AACN. Postbaccalaureate distance learning degree programs offered. *Degree requirements:* For master's, comprehensive exam, thesis or alternative; for doctorate, comprehensive exam, thesis/dissertation. *Entrance requirements:* For master's and doctorate, GRE General Test, minimum GPA of 3.0 in last 60 hours, BS in nursing, 2 letters of recommendation. Electronic applications accepted.

University of Phoenix–Atlanta Campus, College of Nursing, Sandy Springs, GA 30350-4153. Offers health administration (MHA); nursing (MSN); nursing/health care education (MSN); MSN/MBA; MSN/MHA. Evening/weekend programs available. Postbaccalaureate distance learning degree programs offered. *Degree requirements:* For master's, thesis (for some programs). *Entrance requirements:* For master's, minimum undergraduate GPA of 2.5, 3 years of work experience. Additional exam requirements/recommendations for international students: Required—TOEFL (minimum score 550 paper-based; 213 computer-based; 79 iBT). Electronic applications accepted.

University of Phoenix–Augusta Campus, College of Nursing, Augusta, GA 30909-4583. Offers health administration (MHA); nursing (MSN); nursing/health care education (MSN); MSN/MBA; MSN/MHA. Postbaccalaureate distance learning degree programs offered.

University of Phoenix–Bay Area Campus, College of Nursing, San Jose, CA 95134-1805. Offers education (MHA); gerontology (MHA); health administration (MHA, DHA); informatics (MHA, MSN); nursing (MSN, PhD); nursing/health care education (MSN); MSN/MBA. Evening/weekend programs available. Postbaccalaureate distance learning degree programs offered (no on-campus study). *Degree requirements:* For master's, thesis (for some programs). *Entrance requirements:* For master's, minimum undergraduate GPA of 2.5, 3 years of work experience, RN license. Additional exam requirements/recommendations for international students: Required—TOEFL (minimum score 550 paper-based; 213 computer-based; 79 iBT). Electronic applications accepted.

University of Phoenix–Birmingham Campus, College of Health and Human Services, Birmingham, AL 35244. Offers education (MHA); gerontology (MHA); health administration (MHA); health care management (MBA); informatics (MHA); nursing (MSN); nursing/health care education (MSN); MSN/MBA; MSN/MHA.

University of Phoenix–Central Florida Campus, College of Nursing, Maitland, FL 32751-7057. Offers health administration (MHA); health and human services (MSN); nursing (MSN); nursing/health care education (MSN); MSN/MBA; MSN/MHA. Evening/weekend programs available. *Degree requirements:* For master's, thesis (for some programs). *Entrance requirements:* For master's, minimum undergraduate GPA of 2.5, 3 years work experience, RN license. Additional exam requirements/recommendations for international students: Required—TOEFL (minimum score 550 paper-based; 213 computer-based; 79 iBT). Electronic applications accepted.

University of Phoenix–Charlotte Campus, College of Nursing, Charlotte, NC 28273-3409. Offers education (MHA); gerontology (MHA); health administration (MHA); informatics (MHA, MSN); nursing (MSN); nursing/health care education (MSN). Evening/weekend programs available. *Degree requirements:* For master's, thesis (for some programs). *Entrance requirements:* For master's, minimum undergraduate GPA of 2.5, 3 years work experience. Additional exam requirements/recommendations for international students: Required—TOEFL (minimum score 550 paper-based; 213 computer-based; 79 iBT). Electronic applications accepted.

University of Phoenix–Cheyenne Campus, College of Nursing, Cheyenne, WY 82009. Offers health administration (MHA); nursing (MSN); nursing/health care education (MSN); MSN/MBA; MSN/MHA. Postbaccalaureate distance learning degree programs offered.

University of Phoenix–Des Moines Campus, College of Nursing, Des Moines, IA 50266. Offers education (MHA); gerontology (MHA); health administration (MHA, DHA); informatics (MHA, MSN); nursing (MSN, PhD); nursing/health care education (MSN).

University of Phoenix–Harrisburg Campus, College of Nursing, Harrisburg, PA 17112. Offers health administration (MHA); nursing (MSN); nursing/health care education (MSN); MSN/MBA; MSN/MHA. Postbaccalaureate distance learning degree programs offered.

University of Phoenix–Hawaii Campus, College of Nursing, Honolulu, HI 96813-4317. Offers education (MHA); family nurse practitioner (MSN); gerontology (MHA); health administration (MHA); nursing (MSN); nursing/health care education (MSN); MSN/MBA. Evening/weekend programs available. *Degree requirements:* For master's, thesis (for some programs). *Entrance requirements:* For master's, minimum undergraduate GPA of 2.5, 3 years of work experience, RN license. Additional exam requirements/recommendations for international students: Required—TOEFL (minimum score 550 paper-based; 213 computer-based; 79 iBT). Electronic applications accepted.

University of Phoenix–Idaho Campus, College of Nursing, Meridian, ID 83642-5114. Offers health administration (MHA); nursing (MSN); nursing/health care education (MSN); MSN/MBA. Evening/weekend programs available. Postbaccalaureate distance learning degree programs offered. *Degree requirements:* For master's, thesis (for some programs). *Entrance requirements:* For master's, minimum undergraduate GPA of 2.5, 3 years of work experience. Additional exam requirements/recommendations for international students: Required—TOEFL (minimum score 550 paper-based; 213 computer-based). Electronic applications accepted.

University of Phoenix–Indianapolis Campus, College of Nursing, Indianapolis, IN 46250-932. Offers health administration (MHA); nursing (MSN); nursing/health care education (MSN); MSN/MBA; MSN/MHA. Evening/weekend programs available. Postbaccalaureate distance learning degree programs offered. *Degree requirements:* For master's, thesis. *Entrance requirements:* For master's, 3 years work experience, minimum undergraduate GPA of 2.5. Additional exam requirements/recommendations for international students: Required—TOEFL (minimum score 500 paper-based; 213 computer-based). Electronic applications accepted.

University of Phoenix–Metro Detroit Campus, College of Nursing, Southfield, MI 48076. Offers health care education (MSN); nursing (MSN). Evening/weekend programs available. *Degree requirements:* For master's, thesis (for some programs). *Entrance requirements:* For master's, minimum undergraduate GPA of 2.5, 3 years of work experience, RN license. Additional exam requirements/recommendations for international students: Required—TOEFL (minimum score 550 paper-based; 213 computer-based; 79 iBT). Electronic applications accepted.

University of Phoenix–Milwaukee Campus, College of Nursing, Milwaukee, WI 53045. Offers education (MHA); gerontology (MHA); health administration (MHA, DHA); informatics (MHA, MSN); nursing (MSN, PhD); nursing/health care education (MSN); MSN/MBA; MSN/MHA.

University of Phoenix–New Mexico Campus, College of Nursing, Albuquerque, NM 87113-1570. Offers health administration (MHA); health care education (MSN); nursing (MSN); MSN/MBA. Evening/weekend programs available. *Degree requirements:* For master's, thesis (for some programs). *Entrance requirements:* For master's, minimum undergraduate GPA of 2.5, 3 years of work experience, RN license. Additional exam requirements/recommendations for international students: Required—TOEFL (minimum score 550 paper-based; 213 computer-based; 79 iBT). Electronic applications accepted.

University of Phoenix–Northern Nevada Campus, College of Nursing, Reno, NV 89521-5862. Offers health administration (MHA); health care education (MSN); nursing (MSN); MSN/MBA; MSN/MHA.

University of Phoenix–North Florida Campus, College of Nursing, Jacksonville, FL 32216-0959. Offers health administration (MHA); health care education (MSN); nursing (MSN); MSN/MBA; MSN/MHA. Evening/weekend programs available. *Degree requirements:* For master's, thesis (for some programs). *Entrance requirements:* For master's, minimum undergraduate GPA of 2.5, 3 years work experience, RN license. Additional exam requirements/recommendations for international students: Required—TOEFL (minimum score 550 paper-based; 213 computer-based; 79 iBT). Electronic applications accepted.

University of Phoenix–Northwest Arkansas Campus, College of Nursing, Rogers, AR 72756-9615. Offers health administration (MHA); health care education (MSN); nursing (MSN); MSN/MBA.

University of Phoenix–Online Campus, College of Nursing, Phoenix, AZ 85034-7209. Offers informatics (MSN); international (MSN); nurse practitioner (MSN); nursing (MSN); nursing/health care education (MSN); MSN/Certificate; MSN/MBA; MSN/MHA. *Accreditation:* AACN. Evening/weekend programs available. Postbaccalaureate distance learning degree programs offered. *Students:* 5,257 full-time (4,805 women); includes 1,381 minority (803 Black or African American, non-Hispanic/Latino; 36 American Indian or Alaska Native, non-Hispanic/Latino; 271 Asian, non-Hispanic/Latino; 188 Hispanic/Latino; 51 Native Hawaiian or other Pacific Islander, non-Hispanic/Latino; 32 Two or more races, non-Hispanic/Latino), 244 international. Average age 43. *Entrance requirements:* Additional exam requirements/recommendations for international students: Required—TOEFL, TOEIC (Test of English as an International Communication), Berlitz Online English Proficiency Exam, Pearson Test of English, or IELTS. *Application deadline:* Applications are processed on a rolling basis. Application fee: $45. Electronic applications accepted. *Expenses:* Contact institution. *Financial support:* Scholarships/grants available. Financial award applicants required to submit FAFSA. *Application contact:* 866-766-0766. Web site: http://www.phoenix.edu/colleges_divisions/nursing.html.

University of Phoenix–Phoenix Main Campus, College of Nursing, Tempe, AZ 85282-2371. Offers family nurse practitioner (MSN, Certificate); informatics (MSN); nursing (MSN); nursing/health care education (MSN); MSN/Certificate; MSN/MBA; MSN/MHA. Evening/weekend programs available. Postbaccalaureate distance learning degree programs offered. *Students:* 172 full-time (148 women); includes 25 minority (4 Black or African American, non-Hispanic/Latino; 8 Asian, non-Hispanic/Latino; 13 Hispanic/Latino), 10 international. Average age 40. *Entrance requirements:* Additional exam requirements/recommendations for international students: Required—TOEFL, TOEIC (Test of English as an International Communication), Berlitz Online English Proficiency Exam, Pearson Test of English, or IELTS. *Application deadline:* Applications are processed on a rolling basis. Application fee: $45. Electronic applications accepted. *Expenses:* Contact institution. *Financial support:* Scholarships/grants available. Financial award applicants required to submit FAFSA. *Application contact:* 866-766-0766. Web site: http://www.phoenix.edu/colleges_divisions/nursing.html.

University of Phoenix–Pittsburgh Campus, College of Nursing, Pittsburgh, PA 15276. Offers health administration (MHA); health care education (MSN); nursing (MSN); MSN/MBA; MSN/MHA. Evening/weekend programs available. *Degree requirements:* For master's, thesis (for some programs). *Entrance requirements:* For master's, minimum undergraduate GPA of 2.5, 3 years work experience, current RN license (nursing). Additional exam requirements/recommendations for international students: Required—

TOEFL (minimum score 550 paper-based; 213 computer-based; 79 iBT). Electronic applications accepted.

University of Phoenix–Raleigh Campus, College of Nursing, Raleigh, NC 27606. Offers education (MHA); gerontology (MHA); health administration (MHA, DHA); informatics (MHA, MSN); nursing (MSN, PhD); nursing/health care education (MSN).

University of Phoenix–Richmond Campus, College of Nursing, Richmond, VA 23230. Offers health administration (MHA); health care education (MSN); nursing (MSN); MSN/MBA; MSN/MHA. Evening/weekend programs available. *Degree requirements:* For master's, thesis (for some programs). *Entrance requirements:* For master's, minimum undergraduate GPA of 2.5, 3 years work experience, current RN license for nursing programs. Additional exam requirements/recommendations for international students: Required—TOEFL (minimum score 500 paper-based; 213 computer-based; 79 iBT). Electronic applications accepted.

University of Phoenix–Sacramento Valley Campus, College of Nursing, Sacramento, CA 95833-3632. Offers family nurse practitioner (MSN); health administration (MHA); health care education (MSN); nursing (MSN); MSN/MBA. Evening/weekend programs available. *Degree requirements:* For master's, thesis (for some programs). *Entrance requirements:* For master's, RN license, minimum undergraduate GPA of 2.5, 3 years work experience. Additional exam requirements/recommendations for international students: Required—TOEFL (minimum score 550 paper-based; 213 computer-based; 79 iBT). Electronic applications accepted.

University of Phoenix–San Diego Campus, College of Nursing, San Diego, CA 92123. Offers health care education (MSN); nursing (MSN); MSN/MBA. Evening/weekend programs available. *Degree requirements:* For master's, thesis (for some programs). *Entrance requirements:* For master's, minimum undergraduate GPA of 2.5, 3 years work experience, RN license. Additional exam requirements/recommendations for international students: Required—TOEFL (minimum score 550 paper-based; 213 computer-based; 79 iBT). Electronic applications accepted.

University of Phoenix–Savannah Campus, College of Nursing, Savannah, GA 31405-7400. Offers health administration (MHA); nursing (MSN); nursing/health care education (MSN); MSN/MBA; MSN/MHA.

University of Phoenix–Southern California Campus, College of Nursing, Costa Mesa, CA 92626. Offers family nurse practitioner (MSN, Certificate); informatics (MSN); nursing (MSN); nursing/health care education (MSN); MSN/Certificate; MSN/MBA; MSN/MHA. Evening/weekend programs available. Postbaccalaureate distance learning degree programs offered. *Students:* 281 full-time (244 women); includes 129 minority (47 Black or African American, non-Hispanic/Latino; 1 American Indian or Alaska Native, non-Hispanic/Latino; 44 Asian, non-Hispanic/Latino; 26 Hispanic/Latino; 9 Native Hawaiian or other Pacific Islander, non-Hispanic/Latino; 2 Two or more races, non-Hispanic/Latino), 13 international. Average age 43. *Entrance requirements:* Additional exam requirements/recommendations for international students: Required—TOEFL, TOEIC (Test of English as an International Communication), Berlitz Online English Proficiency Exam, Pearson Test of English, or IELTS. *Application deadline:* Applications are processed on a rolling basis. Application fee: $45. Electronic applications accepted. *Expenses:* Contact institution. *Financial support:* Scholarships/grants available. Financial award applicants required to submit FAFSA. *Application contact:* 866-766-0766. Web site: http://www.phoenix.edu/colleges_divisions/nursing.html.

University of Phoenix–South Florida Campus, College of Nursing, Fort Lauderdale, FL 33309. Offers health administration (MHA); health care education (MSN); nursing (MSN); MSN/MBA; MSN/MHA. Evening/weekend programs available. *Degree requirements:* For master's, thesis (for some programs). *Entrance requirements:* For master's, minimum undergraduate GPA of 2.5, 3 years work experience, RN license. Additional exam requirements/recommendations for international students: Required—TOEFL (minimum score 550 paper-based; 213 computer-based; 79 iBT). Electronic applications accepted.

University of Phoenix–Utah Campus, College of Nursing, Salt Lake City, UT 84123-4617. Offers health care education (MSN); nursing (MSN); MSN/MBA. Evening/weekend programs available. *Degree requirements:* For master's, thesis (for some programs). *Entrance requirements:* For master's, minimum undergraduate GPA of 2.5, 3 years work experience, RN license. Additional exam requirements/recommendations for international students: Required—TOEFL (minimum score 550 paper-based; 213 computer-based; 79 iBT). Electronic applications accepted.

University of Phoenix–Washington D.C. Campus, College of Nursing, Washington, DC 20001. Offers education (MHA); gerontology (MHA); health administration (MHA, DHA); informatics (MHA, MSN); nursing (MSN, PhD); nursing/health care education (MSN); MSN/MBA; MSN/MHA.

University of Phoenix–West Florida Campus, College of Nursing, Temple Terrace, FL 33637. Offers health administration (MHA); health care education (MSN); nursing (MSN); MSN/MBA; MSN/MHA. Evening/weekend programs available. Postbaccalaureate distance learning degree programs offered. *Degree requirements:* For master's, thesis (for some programs). *Entrance requirements:* For master's, minimum undergraduate GPA of 2.5, RN license, 3 years work experience. Additional exam requirements/recommendations for international students: Required—TOEFL (minimum score 550 paper-based; 213 computer-based; 79 iBT). Electronic applications accepted.

University of Rhode Island, Graduate School, College of Nursing, Kingston, RI 02881. Offers administration (MS); clinical nurse leader (MS); clinical specialist in gerontology (MS); clinical specialist in psychiatric/mental health (MS); family nurse practitioner (MS); gerontological nurse practitioner (MS); nursing (DNP, PhD); nursing education (MS). *Accreditation:* AACN; ACNM/ACME (one or more programs are accredited). Part-time programs available. *Faculty:* 29 full-time (28 women), 2 part-time/adjunct (1 woman). *Students:* 33 full-time (30 women), 81 part-time (77 women); includes 6 minority (1 Asian, non-Hispanic/Latino; 5 Hispanic/Latino). In 2011, 17 master's, 6 doctorates awarded. *Degree requirements:* For master's, comprehensive exam; for doctorate, comprehensive exam, thesis/dissertation. *Entrance requirements:* For master's, GRE or MAT, 2 letters of recommendation, scholarly papers; for doctorate, GRE, 3 letters of recommendation, scholarly papers. Additional exam requirements/recommendations for international students: Required—TOEFL (minimum score 550 paper-based; 213 computer-based). *Application deadline:* For fall admission, 4/15 for domestic students, 2/1 for international students; for spring admission, 11/15 for domestic students, 7/15 for international students. Application fee: $65. Electronic applications accepted. *Expenses:* Tuition, state resident: full-time $10,432; part-time $580 per credit hour. Tuition, nonresident: full-time $23,130; part-time $1285 per credit hour. *Required fees:* $1362; $36 per credit hour. $35 per semester. One-time fee: $130. *Financial support:* In 2011–12, 5 teaching assistantships with full and partial tuition reimbursements (averaging $12,596 per year) were awarded. Financial award application deadline: 4/15; financial award applicants required to submit FAFSA. *Faculty research:* Group intervention for grieving women in prison, translating Best Practice in non-drug interventions for postoperative pain management, further development and testing of the pain assessment inventory, preschool motor and functional performance of two cohorts, neuroactivation of brain motor areas in preterm children. *Unit head:* Dr. Dayle Joseph, Dean, 401-874-2766, Fax: 401-874-2061, E-mail: dayle@uri.edu. *Application contact:* Dr. Mary C. Sullivan, Director of Graduate Studies, 401-874-5339, Fax: 401-874-2061, E-mail: mcsullivan@uri.edu. Web site: http://www.uri.edu/nursing/.

University of Southern Maine, School of Nursing, Portland, ME 04104-9300. Offers adult health nursing (PMC); adult psychiatric/mental health nurse practitioner (MS); clinical nurse leader (MS); clinical nurse specialist psychiatric-mental health nursing (MS); education (MS); family nursing (PMC); family psychiatric/mental health nurse practitioner (MS); management (MS); medical/surgical nursing (MS); nurse practitioner adult health nursing (MS); nurse practitioner family nursing (MS); nursing (DNP); psychiatric-mental health nursing (PMC); MBA/MSN. *Accreditation:* AACN. Part-time programs available. *Degree requirements:* For master's, thesis optional. *Entrance requirements:* For master's, GRE General Test or MAT, minimum GPA of 3.0; for doctorate, GRE. Additional exam requirements/recommendations for international students: Required—TOEFL (minimum score 550 paper-based; 213 computer-based). Electronic applications accepted. *Faculty research:* Women's health, nursing history, weight control, community services, substance abuse.

The University of Tennessee at Chattanooga, Graduate School, College of Health, Education and Professional Studies, School of Nursing, Chattanooga, TN 37403. Offers administration (MSN); certified nurse anesthetist (Post-Master's Certificate); education (MSN); family nurse practitioner (MSN, Post-Master's Certificate); health care informatics (Post-Master's Certificate); nurse anesthesia (MSN); nurse education (Post-Master's Certificate); nursing (DNP). *Accreditation:* AACN; AANA/CANAEP (one or more programs are accredited). *Faculty:* 15 full-time (13 women), 4 part-time/adjunct (all women). *Students:* 68 full-time (45 women), 37 part-time (33 women); includes 8 minority (6 Black or African American, non-Hispanic/Latino; 2 Hispanic/Latino). Average age 33. 5 applicants, 100% accepted, 3 enrolled. In 2011, 52 degrees awarded. *Degree requirements:* For master's, thesis optional, qualifying exams, professional project; for Post-Master's Certificate, thesis or alternative, practicum, seminar. *Entrance requirements:* For master's, GRE General Test, MAT, BSN, minimum GPA of 3.0, eligibility for Tennessee RN license, 1 year direct patient care experience; for Post-Master's Certificate, GRE General Test, MAT, MSN, minimum GPA of 3.0, eligibility for Tennessee RN license, one year of direct patient care experience. Additional exam requirements/recommendations for international students: Required—TOEFL (minimum score 550 paper-based; 213 computer-based; 79 iBT), IELTS (minimum score 6). *Application deadline:* For fall admission, 8/1 priority date for domestic students, 6/1 for international students; for spring admission, 12/1 priority date for domestic students, 10/1 for international students. Applications are processed on a rolling basis. Application fee: $35. Electronic applications accepted. *Expenses:* Tuition, state resident: full-time $6472; part-time $359 per credit hour. Tuition, nonresident: full-time $20,006; part-time $1111 per credit hour. *Required fees:* $1320; $160 per credit hour. *Financial support:* Career-related internships or fieldwork and scholarships/grants available. Support available to part-time students. *Faculty research:* Diabetes in women, health care for elderly, alternative medicine, hypertension, nurse anesthesia. *Total annual research expenditures:* $1.9 million. *Unit head:* Dr. Kay R. Lindgren, Head, 423-425-4646, Fax: 423-425-4668, E-mail: kay-lindgren@utc.edu. *Application contact:* Dr. Jerald Ainsworth, Dean of Graduate Studies, 423-425-4478, Fax: 423-425-5223, E-mail: jerald-ainsworth@utc.edu. Web site: http://www.utc.edu/Academic/Nursing/.

The University of Texas at Arlington, Graduate School, College of Nursing, Arlington, TX 76019. Offers nurse practitioner (MSN); nursing administration (MSN); nursing education (MSN); nursing practice (DNP); nursing science (PhD). *Accreditation:* AACN. Part-time and evening/weekend programs available. Postbaccalaureate distance learning degree programs offered (no on-campus study). *Faculty:* 15 full-time (all women), 2 part-time/adjunct (both women). *Students:* 58 full-time (48 women), 720 part-time (654 women); includes 281 minority (133 Black or African American, non-Hispanic/Latino; 3 American Indian or Alaska Native, non-Hispanic/Latino; 73 Asian, non-Hispanic/Latino; 53 Hispanic/Latino; 4 Native Hawaiian or other Pacific Islander, non-Hispanic/Latino; 15 Two or more races, non-Hispanic/Latino), 22 international. Average age 37. 686 applicants, 48% accepted, 265 enrolled. In 2011, 117 master's, 4 doctorates awarded. *Degree requirements:* For master's, practicum course; for doctorate, comprehensive exam (for some programs), thesis/dissertation (for some programs), proposal defense dissertation (for PhD); scholarship project (for DNP). *Entrance requirements:* For master's, GRE General Test if GPA less than 3.0, minimum GPA of 3.0, Texas nursing license, minimum C grade in undergraduate statistics course; for doctorate, GRE General Test (waived for MSN-to-PhD applicants), minimum undergraduate, graduate and statistics GPA of 3.0; Texas RN license; interview; written statement of goals. Additional exam requirements/recommendations for international students: Required—TOEFL (minimum score 550 paper-based; 213 computer-based), IELTS (minimum score 7). *Application deadline:* For fall admission, 2/1 for domestic students, 4/1 for international students; for spring admission, 10/15 for domestic students, 9/5 for international students. Applications are processed on a rolling basis. Application fee: $40 ($70 for international students). *Financial support:* In 2011–12, 46 students received support, including 22 fellowships with partial tuition reimbursements available (averaging $4,473 per year), 6 research assistantships (averaging $8,873 per year), 24 teaching assistantships (averaging $6,202 per year); career-related internships or fieldwork, scholarships/grants, and traineeships also available. Financial award application deadline: 6/1; financial award applicants required to submit FAFSA. *Faculty research:* Simulation in clinical education and practice, cultural diversity, vulnerable populations, substance abuse. *Unit head:* Dr. Elizabeth C. Poster, Dean, 817-272-2776, Fax: 817-272-5006, E-mail: poster@uta.edu. *Application contact:* Dr. Jennifer Gray, Graduate Advisor/Associate Dean, 817-272-5295, Fax: 817-272-2065, E-mail: jgray@uta.edu. Web site: http://www.uta.edu/nursing.

The University of Texas at Austin, Graduate School, School of Nursing, Austin, TX 78712-1111. Offers adult -gerontology clinical nurse specialist (MSN); child health (MSN), including administration, public health nursing; child health (MSN), including teaching; family nurse practitioner (MSN); family psychiatric/mental health nurse practitioner (MSN); holistic adult health (MSN), including administration, education; maternity (MSN), including administration, public health nursing; maternity (MSN), including teaching; nursing (PhD); nursing administration and healthcare systems management (MSN); pediatric nurse practitioner (MSN); public health nursing (MSN). *Accreditation:* AACN. Part-time programs available. *Degree requirements:* For master's, thesis optional; for doctorate, thesis/dissertation. *Entrance requirements:* For master's and doctorate, GRE General Test. Additional exam requirements/recommendations for international students: Required—TOEFL (minimum score 550 paper-based; 213 computer-based). *Application deadline:* For fall admission, 12/1 for domestic students. Application fee: $50 ($75 for international students). Electronic applications accepted. *Financial support:* Fellowships, research assistantships, teaching assistantships, scholarships/grants, and traineeships available. Financial award application deadline: 2/1. *Faculty research:* Chronic illness management, memory and aging, health promotion, women's health, adolescent health. *Unit head:* Dr. Alexa Stuifbergen, Dean, 512-471-4100, Fax: 512-471-4910, E-mail: astuifbergen@mail.utexas.edu. Web site: http://www.utexas.edu/nursing/.

The University of Texas at Tyler, College of Nursing and Health Sciences, Program in Nursing, Tyler, TX 75799-0001. Offers nurse practitioner (MSN); nursing (PhD); nursing

administration (MSN); nursing education (MSN); MSN/MBA. *Accreditation:* AACN. Part-time and evening/weekend programs available. Postbaccalaureate distance learning degree programs offered (no on-campus study). *Degree requirements:* For master's, comprehensive exam (for some programs), thesis (for some programs); for doctorate, thesis/dissertation. *Entrance requirements:* For master's, GRE General Test or MAT, GMAT, minimum undergraduate GPA of 3.0, course work in statistics, RN license, BSN. Additional exam requirements/recommendations for international students: Required—TOEFL (minimum score 79 computer-based). Electronic applications accepted. *Faculty research:* Psychosocial adjustment, aging, support/commitment of caregivers, psychological abuse and violence, hope/hopelessness, professional values, end of life care, suicidology, clinical supervision, workforce retention and issues, global health issues, health promotion.

The University of Toledo, College of Graduate Studies, College of Nursing, Department of Population and Community Care, Toledo, OH 43606-3390. Offers adult nurse practitioner (Certificate); adult nurse practitioner/clinical nurse specialist (MSN); clinical nurse leader (MSN); family nurse practitioner (MSN, Certificate); nurse educator (MSN, Certificate); pediatric nurse practitioner (MSN, Certificate); psychiatric-mental health clinical nurse specialist (MSN, Certificate). Part-time programs available. *Faculty:* 43. *Students:* 77 full-time (63 women), 198 part-time (180 women); includes 30 minority (14 Black or African American, non-Hispanic/Latino; 1 American Indian or Alaska Native, non-Hispanic/Latino; 4 Asian, non-Hispanic/Latino; 8 Hispanic/Latino; 3 Two or more races, non-Hispanic/Latino), 1 international. Average age 33. 172 applicants, 53% accepted, 82 enrolled. In 2011, 66 master's, 10 other advanced degrees awarded. *Degree requirements:* For master's, thesis or alternative. *Entrance requirements:* For master's, GRE, BS in nursing, minimum undergraduate GPA of 3.0, statement of purpose, three letters of recommendation, transcripts from all prior institutions attended, Nursing CAS application, UT supplemental application; for Certificate, BS in nursing, minimum undergraduate GPA of 3.0, statement of purpose, three letters of recommendation, transcripts from all prior institutions attended. Additional exam requirements/recommendations for international students: Required—TOEFL (minimum score 550 paper-based; 213 computer-based; 80 iBT), IELTS (minimum score 6.5). Application fee: $45 ($75 for international students). Electronic applications accepted. *Financial support:* Research assistantships, Federal Work-Study, scholarships/grants, traineeships, and tuition waivers (full and partial) available. *Application contact:* Joan Mulligan, Admissions Analyst, 419-383-4168, Fax: 419-383-6140, E-mail: joan.mulligan@utoledo.edu. Web site: http://www.utoledo.edu/nursing/.

University of Victoria, Faculty of Graduate Studies, Faculty of Human and Social Development, School of Nursing, Victoria, BC V8W 2Y2, Canada. Offers advanced nursing practice (advanced practice leadership option) (MN); advanced nursing practice (nurse educator option) (MN); advanced nursing practice (nurse practitioner option) (MN); nursing (PhD). Part-time programs available. Postbaccalaureate distance learning degree programs offered (no on-campus study). *Entrance requirements:* Additional exam requirements/recommendations for international students: Required—TOEFL (minimum score 575 paper-based; 233 computer-based), IELTS (minimum score 7). Electronic applications accepted.

University of Washington, Tacoma, Graduate Programs, Program in Nursing, Tacoma, WA 98402-3100. Offers communities, populations and health (MN); leadership in healthcare (MN); nurse educator (MN). Part-time programs available. *Degree requirements:* For master's, thesis (for some programs), advance fieldwork. *Entrance requirements:* For master's, Washington State NCLEX exam, minimum GPA of 3.0. Additional exam requirements/recommendations for international students: Required—TOEFL (minimum score 580 paper-based; 237 computer-based; 70 iBT); Recommended—IELTS (minimum score 7). *Faculty research:* Hospice and palliative care; clinical trial decision-making; minority nurse retention; asthma and public health; injustice, suffering, difference: Linking Them to Us; adolescent health.

University of West Georgia, School of Nursing, Carrollton, GA 30118. Offers health systems leadership (Post-Master's Certificate); nursing (MSN); nursing education (Post-Master's Certificate). *Accreditation:* AACN. Part-time programs available. *Faculty:* 8 full-time (all women). *Students:* 36 full-time (35 women), 16 part-time (all women); includes 14 minority (all Black or African American, non-Hispanic/Latino). Average age 45. 71 applicants, 77% accepted, 25 enrolled. In 2011, 10 master's awarded. *Degree requirements:* For master's, comprehensive exam, thesis or alternative. *Entrance requirements:* For master's, GRE or MAT, BSN, Georgia RN license, minimum GPA of 3.0 for upper-division nursing courses, completion of basic undergraduate statistics course. Additional exam requirements/recommendations for international students: Required—TOEFL (minimum score 523 paper-based; 193 computer-based; 69 iBT); Recommended—IELTS (minimum score 6). *Application deadline:* For fall admission, 7/15 for domestic and international students. Applications are processed on a rolling basis. Application fee: $30. Electronic applications accepted. *Expenses:* Tuition, state resident: full-time $4336; part-time $181 per credit hour. Tuition, nonresident: full-time $17,362; part-time $724 per credit hour. Tuition and fees vary according to course load, degree level, campus/location and program. *Financial support:* In 2011–12, 1 research assistantship with full tuition reimbursement (averaging $6,000 per year) was awarded. Financial award application deadline: 7/1; financial award applicants required to submit FAFSA. *Faculty research:* Caring in nursing education, pain assessment in older adults, pain outcomes. *Unit head:* Dr. Kathryn Mary Grams, Dean, 678-839-6552, Fax: 678-839-6553, E-mail: kgrams@westga.edu. *Application contact:* Alyicia Richards, Graduate Studies Associate, 678-839-5115, Fax: 678-839-6553, E-mail: alyrich@westga.edu. Web site: http://www.westga.edu/~nurs/.

University of Wisconsin–Eau Claire, College of Nursing and Health Sciences, Program in Nursing, Eau Claire, WI 54702-4004. Offers adult-gerontologic administration (MSN); adult-gerontologic clinical nurse specialist (MSN); adult-gerontologic education (MSN); adult-gerontologic nurse practitioner (MSN); family health administration (MSN); family health in education (MSN); family health nurse practitioner (MSN); nursing practice (DNP). Part-time programs available. *Faculty:* 13 full-time (all women), 1 (woman) part-time/adjunct. *Students:* 42 full-time (40 women), 68 part-time (66 women); includes 3 minority (1 Black or African American, non-Hispanic/Latino; 1 Asian, non-Hispanic/Latino; 1 Hispanic/Latino). Average age 37. 74 applicants, 70% accepted, 41 enrolled. In 2011, 35 master's awarded. Terminal master's awarded for partial completion of doctoral program. *Degree requirements:* For master's, thesis optional, 500-600 hours clinical practicum, oral and written exams. *Entrance requirements:* For master's, Wisconsin RN license, minimum GPA of 3.0, undergraduate statistics, course work in health assessment. Additional exam requirements/recommendations for international students: Required—TOEFL (minimum score 550 paper-based; 213 computer-based; 79 iBT); Recommended—IELTS (minimum score 7). *Application deadline:* For fall admission, 1/15 priority date for domestic students, 1/15 for international students. Applications are processed on a rolling basis. Application fee: $86. *Expenses:* Tuition, state resident: full-time $7312; part-time $406 per credit. Tuition, nonresident: full-time $16,771; part-time $932 per credit. *Required fees:* $1101; $61 per credit. *Financial support:* In 2011–12, 16 students received support. Federal Work-Study and unspecified assistantships available. Financial award application deadline: 3/1; financial award applicants required to submit FAFSA. *Unit head:* Dr. Linda Young, Dean, 715-836-4904, Fax: 715-836-5925, E-mail: younglk@uwec.edu.

Application contact: Dr. Mary Zwygart-Stauffacher, Director, 715-836-5287, E-mail: zwygarmc@uwec.edu. Web site: http://www.uwec.edu/conhs/programs/grad/index.htm.

Ursuline College, School of Graduate Studies, Programs in Nursing, Pepper Pike, OH 44124-4398. Offers care management (MSN); nurse practitioner (MSN); nursing (DNP); nursing education (MSN); palliative care (MSN). *Accreditation:* AACN. Part-time programs available. *Faculty:* 2 full-time (both women), 9 part-time/adjunct (7 women). *Students:* 1 (woman) full-time, 133 part-time (124 women); includes 27 minority (23 Black or African American, non-Hispanic/Latino; 3 Asian, non-Hispanic/Latino; 1 Two or more races, non-Hispanic/Latino), 1 international. Average age 38. 61 applicants, 87% accepted, 47 enrolled. In 2011, 21 master's awarded. *Degree requirements:* For master's, comprehensive exam. *Entrance requirements:* For master's, minimum undergraduate GPA of 3.0, bachelor's degree in nursing, eligibility for or current Ohio RN license. Additional exam requirements/recommendations for international students: Required—TOEFL (minimum score 500 paper-based; 173 computer-based). *Application deadline:* For fall admission, 8/1 priority date for domestic students. Applications are processed on a rolling basis. Application fee: $25. *Expenses:* Tuition: Part-time $875 per credit hour. *Required fees:* $170 per semester. *Financial support:* In 2011–12, 11 students received support. Federal Work-Study available. Financial award application deadline: 3/1. *Unit head:* Dr. Janet Baker, Director, 440-864-8172, Fax: 440-684-6053, E-mail: jbaker@ursuline.edu. *Application contact:* Melanie Steele, Graduate Admission Assistant, 440-646-8199, Fax: 440-684-6138, E-mail: graduateadmissions@ursuline.edu.

Valparaiso University, Graduate School, College of Nursing, Valparaiso, IN 46383. Offers management (Certificate); nursing education (MSN, Certificate, MSN/MBA); MSN/MBA. *Accreditation:* AACN. Part-time and evening/weekend programs available. Postbaccalaureate distance learning degree programs offered (minimal on-campus study). *Faculty:* 10 part-time/adjunct (all women). *Students:* 20 full-time (19 women), 43 part-time (42 women); includes 12 minority (7 Black or African American, non-Hispanic/Latino; 1 Asian, non-Hispanic/Latino; 4 Hispanic/Latino), 1 international. Average age 39. In 2011, 12 master's, 21 other advanced degrees awarded. *Entrance requirements:* For master's, minimum GPA of 3.0, undergraduate major in nursing, Indiana registered nursing license, undergraduate courses in research and statistics. Additional exam requirements/recommendations for international students: Required—TOEFL (minimum score 550 paper-based; 213 computer-based; 80 iBT). *Application deadline:* Applications are processed on a rolling basis. Application fee: $30 ($50 for international students). Electronic applications accepted. *Expenses:* Contact institution. *Financial support:* Available to part-time students. Applicants required to submit FAFSA. *Unit head:* Dr. Janet Brown, Dean, 219-464-5289, Fax: 219-464-5425, E-mail: janet.brown@valpo.edu. *Application contact:* Dustin Jesch, Coordinator, U.S. Student Engagement, 219-464-5313, Fax: 219-464-5381, E-mail: dustin.jesch@valpo.edu. Web site: http://valpo.edu/nursing/.

Villanova University, College of Nursing, Villanova, PA 19085-1699. Offers adult nurse practitioner (MSN, Post Master's Certificate); family nurse practitioner (MSN, Post Master's Certificate); health care administration (MSN, Post Master's Certificate); nurse anesthetist (MSN, Post Master's Certificate); nursing (PhD); nursing education (MSN, Post Master's Certificate); nursing practice (DNP); pediatric nurse practitioner (MSN, Post Master's Certificate). *Accreditation:* AACN; AANA/CANAEP. Part-time programs available. Postbaccalaureate distance learning degree programs offered (minimal on-campus study). *Faculty:* 17 full-time (all women), 4 part-time/adjunct (all women). *Students:* 36 full-time (35 women), 256 part-time (234 women); includes 27 minority (14 Black or African American, non-Hispanic/Latino; 9 Asian, non-Hispanic/Latino; 4 Hispanic/Latino), 16 international. Average age 30. 161 applicants, 55% accepted, 75 enrolled. In 2011, 55 master's, 11 doctorates, 5 other advanced degrees awarded. *Degree requirements:* For master's, independent study project; for doctorate, comprehensive exam, thesis/dissertation. *Entrance requirements:* For master's, GRE or MAT, BSN, 1 year of recent nursing experience, physical assessment, course work in statistics; for doctorate, GRE, MSN. Additional exam requirements/recommendations for international students: Required—TOEFL, IELTS. *Application deadline:* For fall admission, 7/1 priority date for domestic students, 7/1 for international students; for spring admission, 11/1 priority date for domestic students, 11/1 for international students. Applications are processed on a rolling basis. Application fee: $50. *Expenses:* Contact institution. *Financial support:* In 2011–12, 43 students received support, including 5 teaching assistantships with full tuition reimbursements available (averaging $13,100 per year); institutionally sponsored loans, scholarships/grants, traineeships, tuition waivers (full), and unspecified assistantships also available. Financial award application deadline: 7/1; financial award applicants required to submit FAFSA. *Faculty research:* Genetics, ethics, cognitive development of students, women with disabilities, nursing leadership. *Unit head:* Dr. Marguerite K. Schlag, Assistant Dean/Director, Graduate Programs, 610-519-4907, Fax: 610-519-7650, E-mail: marguerite.schlag@villanova.edu. Web site: http://www.nursing.villanova.edu/.

Virginia Commonwealth University, Graduate School, School of Nursing, Richmond, VA 23284-9005. Offers adult health acute nursing (MS); adult health primary nursing (MS); biobehavioral clinical research (PhD); child health nursing (MS); clinical nurse leader (MS); family health nursing (MS); nurse educator (MS); nurse practitioner (MS); nursing (Certificate); nursing administration (MS), including clinical nurse manager; psychiatric-mental health nursing (MS); women's health nursing (MS). *Accreditation:* NLN (one or more programs are accredited). Part-time and evening/weekend programs available. *Degree requirements:* For master's, thesis optional; for doctorate, thesis/dissertation. *Entrance requirements:* For master's, GRE General Test, BSN, minimum GPA of 2.8; for doctorate, GRE General Test. Additional exam requirements/recommendations for international students: Required—TOEFL (minimum score 600 paper-based; 250 computer-based; 100 iBT). Electronic applications accepted. *Expenses:* Tuition, state resident: full-time $9133; part-time $507 per credit. Tuition, nonresident: full-time $18,777; part-time $1043 per credit. *Required fees:* $77 per credit. Tuition and fees vary according to degree level, campus/location, program and student level.

Walden University, Graduate Programs, School of Nursing, Minneapolis, MN 55401. Offers education (MSN); informatics (MSN); leadership and management (MSN); nursing (DNP, Post-Master's Certificate), including nursing education (Post-Master's Certificate), nursing informatics (Post-Master's Certificate), nursing leadership and management (Post-Master's Certificate). *Accreditation:* AACN. Part-time and evening/weekend programs available. Postbaccalaureate distance learning degree programs offered (no on-campus study). *Faculty:* 13 full-time (10 women), 142 part-time/adjunct (123 women). *Students:* 4,064 full-time (3,749 women), 1,418 part-time (1,321 women); includes 1,448 minority (975 Black or African American, non-Hispanic/Latino; 27 American Indian or Alaska Native, non-Hispanic/Latino; 207 Asian, non-Hispanic/Latino; 178 Hispanic/Latino; 8 Native Hawaiian or other Pacific Islander, non-Hispanic/Latino; 53 Two or more races, non-Hispanic/Latino), 181 international. Average age 43. In 2011, 1,141 master's, 31 other advanced degrees awarded. *Entrance requirements:* For master's, bachelor's degree or equivalent in related field or RN; minimum GPA of 2.5; goal statement; for doctorate, master's degree or higher, three years of related professional or academic experience, RN, goal statement. Additional exam requirements/recommendations for international students: Required—TOEFL (minimum

score 550 paper-based; 213 computer-based), IELTS (minimum score 6.5), or Michigan English Language Assessment Battery (minimum score 82). *Application deadline:* Applications are processed on a rolling basis. Application fee: $50. Electronic applications accepted. *Financial support:* Federal Work-Study, scholarships/grants, unspecified assistantships, and family tuition reduction, active duty/veteran tuition reduction, group tuition reduction, interest-free payment plans, employee tuition reduction available. Support available to part-time students. Financial award applicants required to submit FAFSA. *Unit head:* Dr. Sara Torres, Associate Dean, 800-925-3368. *Application contact:* Jennifer Hall, Vice President of Enrollment Management, 866-4-WALDEN, E-mail: info@walden.edu. Web site: http://www.waldenu.edu/Colleges-and-Schools/College-of-Health-Sciences/School-of-Nursing.htm.

Washington Adventist University, Program in Nursing - Education, Takoma Park, MD 20912. Offers MS. Part-time programs available. *Students:* 2 full-time (both women), 24 part-time (23 women); includes 20 minority (16 Black or African American, non-Hispanic/Latino; 3 Asian, non-Hispanic/Latino; 1 Hispanic/Latino). *Application deadline:* Applications are processed on a rolling basis. *Expenses: Tuition:* Part-time $560 per credit hour. *Financial support:* Applicants required to submit FAFSA. *Unit head:* Dr. Jude Edwards, Dean, School of Graduate and Professional Studies, 301-891-4092, E-mail: jeedward@wau.edu. *Application contact:* Dean, School of Graduate and Professional Studies, 301-891-4092, E-mail: sgps@wau.edu. Web site: http://www.wau.edu/index.php?option=com_content&view=article&id=408&Itemid=965.

Waynesburg University, Graduate and Professional Studies, Waynesburg, PA 15370-1222. Offers business (MBA), including finance, health systems, human resources, leadership, market development; counseling (MA), including addictions counseling, clinical mental health; education (MAT); nursing (MSN), including administration, education, informatics, palliative care; nursing practice (DNP); special education (M Ed); technology (M Ed); MSN/MBA. *Accreditation:* AACN. Part-time and evening/weekend programs available. *Degree requirements:* For doctorate, thesis/dissertation. *Entrance requirements:* Additional exam requirements/recommendations for international students: Required—TOEFL. Electronic applications accepted.

Wayne State University, College of Nursing, Program in Nursing Education, Detroit, MI 48202. Offers nursing education (Certificate); transcultural nursing (MSN, Certificate). *Faculty:* 33 full-time (31 women), 2 part-time/adjunct (both women). *Students:* Average age 42. 23 applicants, 91% accepted, 18 enrolled. *Entrance requirements:* For degree, GRE General Test, minimum GPA of 2.8. Additional exam requirements/recommendations for international students: Required—TOEFL (minimum score 550 paper-based; 213 computer-based); Recommended—TWE (minimum score 6). *Application deadline:* For fall admission, 7/1 priority date for domestic students, 6/1 for international students; for winter admission, 10/1 for international students; for spring admission, 11/1 for domestic students, 2/1 for international students. Applications are processed on a rolling basis. Application fee: $30 ($50 for international students). Electronic applications accepted. *Expenses:* Tuition, state resident: part-time $512.85 per credit. Tuition, nonresident: part-time $1132.65 per credit. *Required fees:* $26.60 per credit. $199.65 per semester. Tuition and fees vary according to course load and program. *Financial support:* In 2011–12, 1 fellowship (averaging $11,712 per year), 1 teaching assistantship (averaging $26,000 per year) were awarded; institutionally sponsored loans, scholarships/grants, and traineeships also available. Financial award application deadline: 7/1. *Unit head:* Dr. Barbara Redman, Dean, 313-577-4070, Fax: 313-577-4571, E-mail: ae9080@wayne.edu. *Application contact:* Nancy Artinian, Professor, 313-577-4143, E-mail: n.artinian@wayne.edu. Web site: http://www.nursing.wayne.edu/certificate/gcnecurriculum.php.

West Chester University of Pennsylvania, College of Health Sciences, Department of Nursing, West Chester, PA 19383. Offers nursing education (Certificate); public health nursing (MSN), including administration; school nursing (Teaching Certificate). *Accreditation:* AACN. Part-time and evening/weekend programs available. *Faculty:* 1 (woman) full-time, 2 part-time/adjunct (both women). *Students:* 10 full-time (all women), 31 part-time (all women); includes 8 minority (7 Black or African American, non-Hispanic/Latino; 1 Asian, non-Hispanic/Latino), 2 international. Average age 46. 20 applicants, 75% accepted, 13 enrolled. In 2011, 1 degree awarded. *Entrance requirements:* For master's, RN license, BSN or RN with bachelor's degree in another discipline, minimum GPA of 2.8, experience as a nurse providing direct clinical care, two letters of recommendation. Additional exam requirements/recommendations for international students: Required—TOEFL (minimum score 550 paper-based; 213 computer-based; 80 iBT). *Application deadline:* For fall admission, 4/15 priority date for domestic students, 3/15 for international students; for spring admission, 10/15 priority date for domestic students, 9/1 for international students. Applications are processed on a rolling basis. Application fee: $45. Electronic applications accepted. *Expenses:* Tuition, state resident: full-time $7488; part-time $416 per credit. Tuition, nonresident: full-time $11,232; part-time $624 per credit. *Required fees:* $1784.64; $67.59 per credit. Tuition and fees vary according to program. *Financial support:* Unspecified assistantships available. Support available to part-time students. Financial award application deadline: 2/15; financial award applicants required to submit FAFSA. *Unit head:* Dr. Charlotte Mackey, Chair, 610-436-3474, Fax: 610-436-3083, E-mail: cmackey@wcupa.edu. *Application contact:* Dr. Ann Coghlan Stowe, Graduate Coordinator, 610-436-2331, Fax: 610-436-3083, E-mail: astowe@wcupa.edu. Web site: http://www.wcupa.edu/_ACADEMICS/HealthSciences/nursing/.

Western Carolina University, Graduate School, College of Health and Human Sciences, School of Nursing, Cullowhee, NC 28723. Offers nurse educator (PMC); nursing (MSN). *Accreditation:* AACN; AANA/CANAEP. Part-time and evening/weekend programs available. *Students:* 31 full-time (23 women), 79 part-time (69 women); includes 13 minority (2 Black or African American, non-Hispanic/Latino; 3 American Indian or Alaska Native, non-Hispanic/Latino; 1 Asian, non-Hispanic/Latino; 4 Hispanic/Latino; 3 Two or more races, non-Hispanic/Latino). Average age 39. 54 applicants, 63% accepted, 33 enrolled. In 2011, 32 master's awarded. *Degree requirements:* For master's, comprehensive exam, thesis or alternative. *Entrance requirements:* For master's, GRE General Test, BSN with minimum GPA of 3.0, 3 references, 1 year of clinical experience. Additional exam requirements/recommendations for international students: Required—TOEFL (minimum score 550 paper-based; 270 computer-based; 79 iBT). *Application deadline:* For fall admission, 2/15 for domestic students; for spring admission, 6/15 for domestic students. Applications are processed on a rolling basis. Application fee: $50. *Expenses:* Tuition, state resident: full-time $3348. Tuition, nonresident: full-time $12,933. *Required fees:* $3155. *Financial support:* Fellowships, research assistantships with full and partial tuition reimbursements, teaching assistantships with full and partial tuition reimbursements, career-related internships or fieldwork, institutionally sponsored loans, scholarships/grants, and unspecified assistantships available. Financial award application deadline: 3/31; financial award applicants required to submit FAFSA. *Unit head:* Dr. Judy Neubrander, Director, 828-227-3521, Fax: 828-227-7052, E-mail: jneubrander@email.wcu.edu. *Application contact:* Admissions Specialist for Nursing, 828-227-7398, Fax: 828-227-7480, E-mail: gradsch@email.wcu.edu. Web site: http://www.wcu.edu/4193.asp.

Westminster College, School of Nursing and Health Sciences, Salt Lake City, UT 84105-3697. Offers family nurse practitioner (MSN); nurse anesthesia (MSNA); nurse education (MSNED); nursing (MSN); public health (MPH). *Accreditation:* AACN; AANA/CANAEP. *Faculty:* 13 full-time (7 women), 7 part-time/adjunct (4 women). *Students:* 102 full-time (54 women), 16 part-time (12 women); includes 9 minority (2 Black or African American, non-Hispanic/Latino; 1 American Indian or Alaska Native, non-Hispanic/Latino; 5 Asian, non-Hispanic/Latino; 1 Hispanic/Latino), 1 international. Average age 34. 106 applicants, 64% accepted, 38 enrolled. In 2011, 53 master's awarded. *Degree requirements:* For master's, clinical practicum, 504 clinical practice hours. *Entrance requirements:* For master's, GRE, resume, Utah RN license in good standing, minimum GPA of 3.0, 3 letters of reference, BSN from accredited nursing program, proof of clear state and federal background check, drug test results, personal interview, current PALS certification, current ACLS certification. Additional exam requirements/recommendations for international students: Required—TOEFL (minimum score 600 paper-based; 250 computer-based; 100 iBT), IELTS (minimum score 7). *Application deadline:* Applications are processed on a rolling basis. Application fee: $50. Electronic applications accepted. *Expenses:* Contact institution. *Financial support:* In 2011–12, 11 students received support. Career-related internships or fieldwork and tuition reimbursement, tuition remission available. Support available to part-time students. Financial award applicants required to submit FAFSA. *Faculty research:* Collaborative testing in nursing: student outcomes and perspectives, Implementing New Educational Paradigms into Pre-Licensure Nursing Curricula conference presentation. *Unit head:* Dr. Sheryl Steadman, Dean, 801-832-2164, Fax: 801-832-3110, E-mail: ssteadman@westminstercollege.edu. *Application contact:* Dr. Gary Daynes, Vice President for Strategic Outreach and Enrollment, 801-832-2200, Fax: 801-832-3101, E-mail: admission@westminstercollege.edu. Web site: http://www.westminstercollege.edu/msn.

Winona State University, College of Nursing and Health Sciences, Winona, MN 55987. Offers adult nurse practitioner (MS, Post Master's Certificate); clinical nurse specialist (MS, Post Master's Certificate); family nurse practitioner (MS, Post Master's Certificate); nurse administrator (MS); nurse educator (MS, Post Master's Certificate); nursing (DNP). *Accreditation:* AACN. Part-time programs available. Postbaccalaureate distance learning degree programs offered (no on-campus study). *Students:* 75 full-time (70 women), 25 part-time (22 women); includes 11 minority (4 Black or African American, non-Hispanic/Latino; 5 Asian, non-Hispanic/Latino; 1 Hispanic/Latino; 1 Two or more races, non-Hispanic/Latino), 2 international. Average age 34. In 2011, 26 master's, 2 doctorates, 3 other advanced degrees awarded. *Degree requirements:* For master's, thesis; for doctorate, capstone. *Entrance requirements:* For master's, GRE (if GPA less than 3.0). Additional exam requirements/recommendations for international students: Required—TOEFL (minimum score 550 paper-based). *Application deadline:* For fall admission, 12/1 for domestic and international students. Application fee: $20. *Financial support:* Research assistantships with partial tuition reimbursements, Federal Work-Study, traineeships, and unspecified assistantships available. Support available to part-time students. Financial award application deadline: 8/15; financial award applicants required to submit FAFSA. *Unit head:* Dr. William J. McBreen, Dean, 507-457-5122, E-mail: wmcbreen@winona.edu. *Application contact:* Patricia Cichosz, Office Manager, Graduate Studies, 507-457-5038, E-mail: pcichosz@winona.edu.

Worcester State University, Graduate Studies, Department of Nursing, Program in Nurse Educator, Worcester, MA 01602-2597. Offers MSN. Part-time programs available. *Faculty:* 2 full-time (both women), 4 part-time/adjunct (3 women). *Students:* 10 part-time (9 women); includes 1 minority (Hispanic/Latino). Average age 45. *Degree requirements:* For master's, practicum. *Entrance requirements:* For master's, GRE, MAT, unencumbered license to practice as a Registered Nurse in Massachusetts. Additional exam requirements/recommendations for international students: Required—TOEFL (minimum score 500 paper-based; 61 iBT). *Application deadline:* For fall admission, 6/15 for domestic and international students; for spring admission, 4/1 for domestic and international students. Applications are processed on a rolling basis. Application fee: $40. Electronic applications accepted. *Expenses:* Tuition, state resident: full-time $2700; part-time $150 per credit. Tuition, nonresident: full-time $2700; part-time $150 per credit. *Required fees:* $2016; $112 per credit. *Financial support:* Application deadline: 3/1; applicants required to submit FAFSA. *Unit head:* Dr. Stephanie Chalupka, Coordinator, 508-929-8680, E-mail: schalupka@worcester.edu. *Application contact:* Sara Grady, Assistant Dean of Continuing Education, 508-929-8787, Fax: 508-929-8100, E-mail: sara.grady@worcester.edu.

Xavier University, College of Social Sciences, Health and Education, School of Nursing, Cincinnati, OH 45207. Offers clinical nurse leader (MSN); education (MSN); forensic nursing (MSN); healthcare law (MSN); informatics (MSN); nursing administration (MSN); school nursing (MSN); MSN/M Ed; MSN/MBA; MSN/MS. *Accreditation:* AACN. Part-time and evening/weekend programs available. *Faculty:* 13 full-time (all women), 10 part-time/adjunct (all women). *Students:* 69 full-time (66 women), 158 part-time (156 women); includes 30 minority (19 Black or African American, non-Hispanic/Latino; 2 American Indian or Alaska Native, non-Hispanic/Latino; 4 Asian, non-Hispanic/Latino; 3 Hispanic/Latino; 2 Two or more races, non-Hispanic/Latino). Average age 38. 117 applicants, 81% accepted, 71 enrolled. In 2011, 63 master's awarded. *Degree requirements:* For master's, thesis, scholarly project. *Entrance requirements:* For master's, GRE. Additional exam requirements/recommendations for international students: Required—TOEFL. *Application deadline:* Applications are processed on a rolling basis. Application fee: $35. Electronic applications accepted. *Expenses: Tuition:* Part-time $576 per credit hour. *Financial support:* In 2011–12, 88 students received support. Applicants required to submit FAFSA. *Faculty research:* Clinical nurse leader, simulation, employment satisfaction, nontraditional students, holistic nursing. *Unit head:* Dr. Susan M. Schmidt, Director, 513-745-3815, Fax: 513-745-1087, E-mail: schmidt@xavier.edu. *Application contact:* Marilyn Volk Gomez, Director of Nursing Student Services, 513-745-4392, Fax: 513-745-1087, E-mail: gomez@xavier.edu. Web site: http://www.xavier.edu/msn/.

York College of Pennsylvania, Department of Nursing, York, PA 17405-7199. Offers adult nurse practitioner (MS); certified nurse anesthetist (MS); clinical nurse specialist (MS), including education: administration; nurse educator (MS); nursing (DNP). *Accreditation:* AACN; AANA/CANAEP. Part-time and evening/weekend programs available. *Faculty:* 10 full-time (all women), 9 part-time/adjunct (6 women). *Students:* 31 full-time (23 women), 50 part-time (43 women); includes 4 minority (2 Black or African American, non-Hispanic/Latino; 2 Asian, non-Hispanic/Latino), 1 international. Average age 36. 49 applicants, 53% accepted, 20 enrolled. In 2011, 17 master's awarded. *Entrance requirements:* For master's, GRE General Test, minimum GPA of 3.0 with NLNAC or CCNE major. Additional exam requirements/recommendations for international students: Required—TOEFL (minimum score 530 paper-based; 200 computer-based; 72 iBT). *Application deadline:* For fall admission, 7/15 priority date for domestic students; for spring admission, 11/15 priority date for domestic students. Applications are processed on a rolling basis. Application fee: $50. Electronic applications accepted. *Expenses: Tuition:* Full-time $12,060; part-time $670 per credit hour. *Required fees:* $340 per semester. Tuition and fees vary according to degree level. *Financial support:* Federal Work-Study available. *Faculty research:* Employer and faculty beliefs about concepts in RN-BS education, evaluating effectiveness of mental health partnerships in psychiatric settings. *Unit head:* Dr. Linda Pugh, Graduate Program Director, 717-815-1243, E-mail: lwarner@ycp.edu. *Application contact:* Nancy Spataro, Director of Admissions, 717-815-1600, Fax: 717-849-1607, E-mail: admissions@ycp.edu. Web site: http://www.ycp.edu/academics/academic-departments/nursing/.

Nursing Informatics

Austin Peay State University, College of Graduate Studies, College of Behavioral and Health Sciences, School of Nursing, Clarksville, TN 37044. Offers advanced practice (MSN); nursing administration (MSN); nursing education (MSN); nursing informatics (MSN). Part-time programs available. Postbaccalaureate distance learning degree programs offered. *Faculty:* 6 full-time (all women). *Students:* 21 full-time (16 women), 79 part-time (74 women); includes 12 minority (9 Black or African American, non-Hispanic/Latino; 2 Hispanic/Latino; 1 Two or more races, non-Hispanic/Latino). Average age 38. 42 applicants, 100% accepted, 29 enrolled. In 2011, 24 master's awarded. *Degree requirements:* For master's, comprehensive exam. *Entrance requirements:* For master's, GRE General Test, minimum GPA of 3.0, RN license eligibility, 3 letters of recommendation. Additional exam requirements/recommendations for international students: Required—TOEFL (minimum score 600 paper-based). *Application deadline:* For fall admission, 8/1 priority date for domestic students. Applications are processed on a rolling basis. Application fee: $25. Electronic applications accepted. *Expenses:* Tuition, state resident: part-time $350 per credit hour. Tuition, nonresident: full-time $20,644; part-time $971 per credit hour. *Required fees:* $1224; $61.20 per credit hour. *Financial support:* In 2011–12, research assistantships with full tuition reimbursements (averaging $5,184 per year) were awarded; career-related internships or fieldwork, Federal Work-Study, institutionally sponsored loans, scholarships/grants, and unspecified assistantships also available. Support available to part-time students. *Unit head:* Dr. Patty Orr, Director, 931-221-7710, Fax: 931-221-7595, E-mail: orrp@apsu.edu. *Application contact:* Kendra Bryant, Graduate Admissions, 800-844-2778, Fax: 931-221-6188, E-mail: admissionsweb@apsu.edu. Web site: http://www.apsu.edu/nursing.

Duke University, School of Nursing, Durham, NC 27708-0586. Offers adult acute care (Certificate); adult cardiovascular (Certificate); adult oncology (Certificate); adult primary care (Certificate); clinical nurse specialist (MSN), including adult oncology, gerontology, neonatal, pediatric; clinical research management (MSN, Certificate); family (Certificate); gerontology (Certificate); health and nursing ministries (MSN, Certificate); health systems leadership and outcomes (Certificate); neonatal (Certificate); neonatal/pediatric in rural health (MSN, Certificate); nurse anesthetist (MSN, Certificate); nurse practitioner (MSN), including adult acute care, adult cardiovascular, adult oncology, adult primary care, family, gerontology, neonatal, pediatric, pediatric acute care; nursing (DNP, PhD); nursing and healthcare leadership (MSN); nursing education (MSN); nursing informatics (MSN, Certificate); pediatric (Certificate); pediatric acute care (Certificate); MBA/MSN; MSN/MCM. *Accreditation:* AACN; AANA/CANAEP. Part-time and evening/weekend programs available. Postbaccalaureate distance learning degree programs offered (minimal on-campus study). *Faculty:* 56 full-time (47 women), 2 part-time/adjunct (1 woman). *Students:* 127 full-time (108 women), 395 part-time (358 women); includes 92 minority (42 Black or African American, non-Hispanic/Latino; 3 American Indian or Alaska Native, non-Hispanic/Latino; 21 Asian, non-Hispanic/Latino; 14 Hispanic/Latino; 12 Two or more races, non-Hispanic/Latino), 10 international. Average age 36. 432 applicants, 45% accepted, 143 enrolled. In 2011, 117 master's, 29 doctorates, 32 other advanced degrees awarded. Terminal master's awarded for partial completion of doctoral program. *Degree requirements:* For master's, thesis optional; for doctorate, capstone project. *Entrance requirements:* For master's, GRE General Test, 1 year of nursing experience, BSN, minimum GPA of 3.0, previous course work in statistics; for doctorate, BSN or MSN, minimum GPA of 3.0, portfolio; for Certificate, MSN. Additional exam requirements/recommendations for international students: Required—TOEFL (minimum score 550 paper-based; 213 computer-based). *Application deadline:* For fall admission, 12/1 for domestic and international students; for spring admission, 5/1 for domestic and international students. Application fee: $50. Electronic applications accepted. *Expenses:* Contact institution. *Financial support:* Career-related internships or fieldwork, institutionally sponsored loans, scholarships/grants, traineeships, and tuition waivers (partial) available. Support available to part-time students. Financial award application deadline: 4/1; financial award applicants required to submit FAFSA. *Faculty research:* Cardiovascular disease, caregiver skill training, data mining, prostate cancer, neonatal immune system. *Total annual research expenditures:* $4.7 million. *Unit head:* Dr. Catherine L. Gilliss, Dean/Vice Chancellor for Nursing Affairs, 919-684-9444, Fax: 919-684-9414, E-mail: gilli025@mc.duke.edu. *Application contact:* Bebe T. Mills, Director of Admissions, 919-684-9151, Fax: 919-668-4693, E-mail: mills031@mc.duke.edu. Web site: http://www.nursing.duke.edu/.

East Tennessee State University, School of Graduate Studies, College of Nursing, Master's Nursing Programs, Johnson City, TN 37614. Offers advanced practice nursing (MSN); nursing (MSN); nursing administration (MSN); nursing education (MSN); nursing informatics (MSN). Part-time programs available. Postbaccalaureate distance learning degree programs offered. *Students:* 50 full-time (47 women), 137 part-time (126 women); includes 4 minority (1 American Indian or Alaska Native, non-Hispanic/Latino; 2 Hispanic/Latino; 1 Two or more races, non-Hispanic/Latino), 1 international. 151 applicants, 29% accepted, 44 enrolled. In 2011, 74 master's awarded. *Degree requirements:* For master's, comprehensive exam (for some programs), culminating project (for some programs). *Entrance requirements:* For master's, minimum GPA of 3.0, RN license, resume, 3 letters of recommendation. Additional exam requirements/recommendations for international students: Required—TOEFL (minimum score 600 paper-based; 250 computer-based; 100 iBT). *Application deadline:* For fall admission, 2/1 for domestic and international students; for spring admission, 7/1 for domestic and international students. Application fee: $35 ($45 for international students). Electronic applications accepted. *Expenses:* Tuition, state resident: full-time $7312; part-time $350 per credit hour. Tuition, nonresident: full-time $18,490; part-time $621 per credit hour. *Required fees:* $63 per credit hour. Tuition and fees vary according to course load and program. *Financial support:* In 2011–12, 2 students received support. Institutionally sponsored loans, scholarships/grants, tuition waivers (full), and unspecified assistantships available. Support available to part-time students. Financial award application deadline: 7/1; financial award applicants required to submit FAFSA. *Faculty research:* Rural primary care, healthcare for the homeless and underserved, community health problems across the lifespan, nursing education research, school health services. *Unit head:* Dr. Nancy Cameron, Coordinator, 423-439-4874, Fax: 423-439-4100, E-mail: cameronng@etsu.edu. *Application contact:* Linda Raines, Graduate Specialist, 423-439-6158, Fax: 423-439-5624, E-mail: raineslt@etsu.edu.

Excelsior College, School of Nursing, Albany, NY 12203-5159. Offers clinical systems management (MS); nursing (MS); nursing education (MS); nursing informatics (MS). *Accreditation:* NLN. Part-time and evening/weekend programs available. Postbaccalaureate distance learning degree programs offered (no on-campus study). *Entrance requirements:* For master's, RN license. Electronic applications accepted. *Faculty research:* Leadership development, test anxiety, use of technology in online learning.

Ferris State University, College of Allied Health Sciences, School of Nursing, Big Rapids, MI 49307. Offers nursing (MSN); nursing administration (MSN); nursing education (MSN); nursing informatics (MSN). *Accreditation:* NLN. Part-time and evening/weekend programs available. Postbaccalaureate distance learning degree programs offered (minimal on-campus study). *Faculty:* 5 full-time (all women), 1 (woman) part-time/adjunct. *Students:* 7 full-time (all women), 80 part-time (70 women); includes 3 minority (1 Black or African American, non-Hispanic/Latino; 2 Two or more races, non-Hispanic/Latino). Average age 42. 34 applicants, 85% accepted, 24 enrolled. In 2011, 16 master's awarded. *Degree requirements:* For master's, comprehensive exam, practicum, scholarly project. *Entrance requirements:* For master's, BS in nursing or related field with registered nurse license, writing sample, letters of reference, 2 years' clinical experience. Additional exam requirements/recommendations for international students: Required—TOEFL (minimum score 550 paper-based; 173 computer-based; 61 iBT). *Application deadline:* For fall admission, 4/15 priority date for domestic students; for spring admission, 10/15 for domestic students. Applications are processed on a rolling basis. Application fee: $30. Electronic applications accepted. Application fee is waived when completed online. *Financial support:* In 2011–12, 4 students received support. Fellowships, research assistantships, teaching assistantships, career-related internships or fieldwork, and scholarships/grants available. Financial award application deadline: 4/15. *Faculty research:* Nursing education-minority student focus, student attitudes toward aging. *Unit head:* Dr. Marietta Bell-Scriber, Program Coordinator, 231-591-2288, Fax: 231-591-2325, E-mail: bellscm@ferris.edu. *Application contact:* Debby Buck, Off-Campus Program Secretary, 231-591-2270, Fax: 231-591-3788, E-mail: buckd@ferris.edu.

Grantham University, College of Arts and Sciences, Kansas City, MO 64153. Offers case management (MSN); health systems management (MS); healthcare administration (MHA); nursing (MSN); nursing education (MSN); nursing informatics (MSN); nursing management and organizational leadership (MSN). Part-time and evening/weekend programs available. Postbaccalaureate distance learning degree programs offered (no on-campus study). *Degree requirements:* For master's, thesis (for some programs), capstone project. *Entrance requirements:* For master's, bachelor's degree from accredited degree-granting institution. Additional exam requirements/recommendations for international students: Required—TOEFL (minimum score 500 paper-based; 213 computer-based; 61 iBT). Electronic applications accepted.

Loyola University Chicago, Graduate School, Marcella Niehoff School of Nursing, Doctor of Nursing Practice Program, Maywood, IL 60153. Offers healthcare quality using education in safety and technology (DNP); informatics and outcomes (DNP); nursing practice (DNP). Evening/weekend programs available. Postbaccalaureate distance learning degree programs offered (minimal on-campus study). *Faculty:* 45 full-time (44 women). *Students:* 27 part-time (22 women); includes 4 minority (3 Black or African American, non-Hispanic/Latino; 1 Asian, non-Hispanic/Latino). Average age 46. 31 applicants, 45% accepted, 12 enrolled. *Degree requirements:* For doctorate, capstone project. *Entrance requirements:* For doctorate, BSN or MSN, minimum GPA of 3.25, Illinois nursing license, 3 letters of recommendation, 1000 hours experience and certification in area of specialty, curriculum vitae. Additional exam requirements/recommendations for international students: Required—TOEFL. *Expenses: Tuition:* Full-time $15,660; part-time $870 per credit hour. *Required fees:* $125 per semester. Tuition and fees vary according to course load and program. *Unit head:* Dr. Mary K. Walker, Dean, Marcella Niehoff School of Nursing, 708-216-5448, Fax: 708-216-9555, E-mail: mwalker@luc.edu. *Application contact:* Amy Weatherford, Enrollment Advisor, School of Nursing, 773-508-3249, Fax: 773-508-3241, E-mail: aweatherford@luc.edu. Web site: http://www.luc.edu/nursing/dnp/.

Molloy College, Division of Nursing, Rockville Centre, NY 11571-5002. Offers adult nurse practitioner (Advanced Certificate); clinical nurse specialist: adult health (Advanced Certificate); family nurse practitioner (Advanced Certificate); nurse practitioner psychiatry (Advanced Certificate); nursing (MS); nursing administration (Advanced Certificate); nursing administration with informatics (Advanced Certificate); nursing education (Advanced Certificate); nursing informatics (Advanced Certificate); pediatric nurse practitioner (Advanced Certificate). *Accreditation:* AACN. Part-time and evening/weekend programs available. *Faculty:* 20 full-time (19 women), 12 part-time/adjunct (11 women). *Students:* 19 full-time (15 women), 483 part-time (452 women); includes 238 minority (132 Black or African American, non-Hispanic/Latino; 61 Asian, non-Hispanic/Latino; 35 Hispanic/Latino; 2 Native Hawaiian or other Pacific Islander, non-Hispanic/Latino; 8 Two or more races, non-Hispanic/Latino), 5 international. Average age 40. 186 applicants, 82% accepted, 110 enrolled. In 2011, 94 master's awarded. *Degree requirements:* For master's, thesis optional. *Entrance requirements:* For master's, 3 letters of reference, BS in nursing, minimum undergraduate GPA of 3.0; for Advanced Certificate, 3 letters of reference, master's degree in nursing. *Application deadline:* For fall admission, 9/2 priority date for domestic students; for spring admission, 1/20 priority date for domestic students. Applications are processed on a rolling basis. Application fee: $60. *Financial support:* Research assistantships with partial tuition reimbursements, teaching assistantships with partial tuition reimbursements, institutionally sponsored loans, scholarships/grants, and unspecified assistantships available. Support available to part-time students. Financial award application deadline: 4/1; financial award applicants required to submit FAFSA. *Unit head:* Dr. Denise Walsh, Associate Dean, Graduate Nursing, 516-678-5000, Fax: 516-678-9718, E-mail: dwalsh@molloy.edu. *Application contact:* Alina Haitz, Assistant Director of Graduate Admissions, 516-678-5000, Fax: 516-256-2247, E-mail: ahaitz@molloy.edu. Web site: http://www.molloy.edu/academics/nursing-division.

New York University, College of Nursing, Programs in Advanced Practice Nursing, New York, NY 10012-1019. Offers advanced practice nursing: adult acute care (MS, Advanced Certificate); advanced practice nursing: adult nurse practitioner/holistic nurse practitioner (Advanced Certificate); advanced practice nursing: adult nurse practitioner/palliative care nurse practitioner (Advanced Certificate); advanced practice nursing: adult primary care (MS, Advanced Certificate); advanced practice nursing: family (MS, Advanced Certificate); advanced practice nursing: geriatrics (Advanced Certificate); advanced practice nursing: mental health (MS); advanced practice nursing: mental health nursing (Advanced Certificate); advanced practice nursing: pediatrics (MS, Advanced Certificate); nurse midwifery (MS, Advanced Certificate); nursing administration (MS, Advanced Certificate); nursing education (MS, Advanced Certificate); nursing informatics (MS, Advanced Certificate); MS/MPA; MS/MPH. *Accreditation:* AACN; ACNM/ACME. Part-time programs available. *Faculty:* 23 full-time (all women), 60 part-time/adjunct (47 women). *Students:* 27 full-time (23 women), 552 part-time (514 women); includes 251 minority (91 Black or African American, non-Hispanic/Latino; 115 Asian, non-Hispanic/Latino; 34 Hispanic/Latino; 11 Native Hawaiian or other Pacific Islander, non-Hispanic/Latino), 8 international. Average age 33. 325 applicants, 81% accepted, 179 enrolled. In 2011, 89 master's awarded. *Degree*

requirements: For master's, thesis (for some programs). *Entrance requirements:* For master's, BS in nursing, AS in nursing with another BS/BA, interview, RN license, 1 year of clinical experience (3 for nursing education program); for Advanced Certificate, master's degree. Additional exam requirements/recommendations for international students: Required—TOEFL, IELTS. *Application deadline:* For fall admission, 7/1 priority date for domestic students, 7/1 for international students; for spring admission, 12/1 for domestic and international students. Applications are processed on a rolling basis. Application fee: $75. Electronic applications accepted. *Financial support:* In 2011–12, 36 students received support. Career-related internships or fieldwork, institutionally sponsored loans, scholarships/grants, traineeships, and tuition waivers (partial) available. Support available to part-time students. Financial award application deadline: 2/1; financial award applicants required to submit FAFSA. *Faculty research:* Elderly black diabetics, families and illness, oral systemic connection. *Unit head:* Dr. Judith Haber, Associate Dean, 212-998-9020, Fax: 212-995-3143, E-mail: jh33@nyu.edu. *Application contact:* Gail Wolfmeyer, Assistant Director, Graduate Student Affairs and Admissions, 212-992-7653, Fax: 212-995-4302, E-mail: gail.wolfmeyer@nyu.edu.

Seattle Pacific University, MS in Nursing Program, Seattle, WA 98119-1997. Offers administration (MSN); adult/gerontology nurse practitioner (MSN); clinical nurse specialist (MSN); family nurse practitioner (MSN, Certificate); informatics (MSN); nurse educator (MSN). *Accreditation:* AACN. Part-time programs available. *Degree requirements:* For master's, thesis. Electronic applications accepted. *Expenses:* Contact institution.

Tennessee State University, The School of Graduate Studies and Research, School of Nursing, Nashville, TN 37209-1561. Offers family nurse practitioner (MSN); holistic nursing (MSN); nursing administration (MSN); nursing education (MSN); nursing informatics (MSN). *Accreditation:* NLN. *Entrance requirements:* For master's, GRE General Test or MAT, BSN, current RN license, minimum GPA of 3.0.

Tennessee Technological University, Whitson-Hester School of Nursing, Cookeville, TN 38505. Offers family nurse practitioner (MSN); informatics (MSN); nursing administration (MSN); nursing education (MSN). Part-time and evening/weekend programs available. Postbaccalaureate distance learning degree programs offered (no on-campus study). *Students:* 3 full-time (2 women), 43 part-time (39 women); includes 3 minority (1 Black or African* American, non-Hispanic/Latino; 2 Hispanic/Latino). 48 applicants, 46% accepted, 15 enrolled. In 2011, 13 master's awarded. *Degree requirements:* For master's, comprehensive exam, thesis or alternative. *Entrance requirements:* Additional exam requirements/recommendations for international students: Required—TOEFL (minimum score 550 paper-based; 79 iBT), IELTS (minimum score 5.5), Pearson Test of English Academic. *Application deadline:* For fall admission, 8/1 for domestic students, 5/1 for international students; for spring admission, 12/1 for domestic students, 10/1 for international students. Application fee: $25 ($30 for international students). Electronic applications accepted. *Expenses:* Tuition, state resident: full-time $8094; part-time $422 per credit hour. Tuition, nonresident: full-time $20,574; part-time $1046 per credit hour. *Financial support:* Application deadline: 4/1. *Unit head:* Dr. Sherry Gaines, Director, 931-372-3203, Fax: 931-372-6244, E-mail: sgaines@tntech.edu. *Application contact:* Shelia K. Kendrick, Coordinator of Graduate Admissions, 931-372-3808, Fax: 931-372-3497, E-mail: skendrick@tntech.edu.

Troy University, Graduate School, College of Health and Human Services, Program in Nursing, Troy, AL 36082. Offers adult health (MSN); clinical nurse specialist adult health (DNP); clinical nurse specialist maternal infant (DNP); family nurse practitioner (MSN, DNP, PMC); informatics specialist (MSN); maternal infant (MSN). *Accreditation:* NLN. Part-time and evening/weekend programs available. *Faculty:* 11 full-time (10 women), 7 part-time/adjunct (4 women). *Students:* 58 full-time (43 women), 181 part-time (165 women); includes 91 minority (76 Black or African American, non-Hispanic/Latino; 8 American Indian or Alaska Native, non-Hispanic/Latino; 1 Asian, non-Hispanic/Latino; 3 Hispanic/Latino; 1 Native Hawaiian or other Pacific Islander, non-Hispanic/Latino; 2 Two or more races, non-Hispanic/Latino). Average age 38. 144 applicants, 63% accepted, 73 enrolled. In 2011, 35 master's, 8 doctorates awarded. *Degree requirements:* For master's, comprehensive exam, minimum GPA of 3.0, candidacy; for doctorate, minimum GPA of 3.0, submission of approved comprehensive e-portfolio, completion of residency synthesis project, minimum of 1000 hours of clinical practice, score of 80% or better on qualifying exam. *Entrance requirements:* For master's, MAT (minimum score 396) or GRE (minimum score 850), minimum GPA of 3.0, BSN, current RN licensure; 2 letters of reference; for doctorate, GRE (minimum score of 850), BSN or MSN, minimum GPA of 3.0, 2 letters of reference, current RN licensure, essay. Additional exam requirements/recommendations for international students: Required—TOEFL (minimum score 523 paper-based; 193 computer-based; 70 iBT), IELTS (minimum score 6), or ACT COMPASS ESL (minimum listening, reading, and grammar score 270). *Application deadline:* Applications are processed on a rolling basis. Application fee: $50. Electronic applications accepted. *Expenses:* Tuition, state resident: full-time $6960; part-time $290 per credit hour. Tuition, nonresident: full-time $13,920; part-time $580 per credit hour. *Required fees:* $386 per term. *Financial support:* Available to part-time students. Applicants required to submit FAFSA. *Unit head:* Dr. Bernita K. Hamilton, Director, School of Nursing, 334-670-3428, Fax: 334-670-3743, E-mail: bernitah@troy.edu. *Application contact:* Brenda K. Campbell, Director of Graduate Admissions, 334-670-3178, Fax: 334-670-3733, E-mail: bcamp@troy.edu.

University of Medicine and Dentistry of New Jersey, School of Nursing, Program in Nursing Informatics - Newark, Newark, NJ 07107-1709. Offers MSN. Program offered jointly with New Jersey Institute of Technology. *Entrance requirements:* Additional exam requirements/recommendations for international students: Required—TOEFL. Electronic applications accepted.

University of Medicine and Dentistry of New Jersey, School of Nursing, Program in Nursing Informatics - Stratford, Newark, NJ 07107-1709. Offers MSN. Program offered jointly with New Jersey Institute of Technology. *Entrance requirements:* Additional exam requirements/recommendations for international students: Required—TOEFL. Electronic applications accepted.

University of Memphis, Loewenberg School of Nursing, Memphis, TN 38152. Offers advance practice-family nurse practitioner (MSN); executive nursing leadership (MSN); nursing (Graduate Certificate); nursing administration (MSN); nursing education (MSN); nursing informatics (MSN). *Accreditation:* AACN. Part-time and evening/weekend programs available. Postbaccalaureate distance learning degree programs offered. *Degree requirements:* For master's, comprehensive exam, thesis optional, scholarly project; completion of clinical practicum hours. *Entrance requirements:* For master's, NCLEX Exam, interview. Additional exam requirements/recommendations for international students: Required—TOEFL (minimum score 550 paper-based; 213 computer-based; 79 iBT). *Faculty research:* Technology in nursing, nurse retention, cultural competence, health policy, health access.

University of Phoenix–Bay Area Campus, College of Nursing, San Jose, CA 95134-1805. Offers education (MHA); gerontology (MHA); health administration (MHA, DHA); informatics (MHA, MSN); nursing (MSN, PhD); nursing/health care education (MSN); MSN/MBA. Evening/weekend programs available. Postbaccalaureate distance learning degree programs offered (no on-campus study). *Degree requirements:* For master's,

thesis (for some programs). *Entrance requirements:* For master's, minimum undergraduate GPA of 2.5, 3 years of work experience, RN license. Additional exam requirements/recommendations for international students: Required—TOEFL (minimum score 550 paper-based; 213 computer-based; 79 iBT). Electronic applications accepted.

University of Phoenix–Charlotte Campus, College of Nursing, Charlotte, NC 28273-3409. Offers education (MHA); gerontology (MHA); health administration (MHA); informatics (MHA, MSN); nursing (MSN); nursing/health care education (MSN). Evening/weekend programs available. *Degree requirements:* For master's, thesis (for some programs). *Entrance requirements:* For master's, minimum undergraduate GPA of 2.5, 3 years work experience. Additional exam requirements/recommendations for international students: Required—TOEFL (minimum score 550 paper-based; 213 computer-based; 79 iBT). Electronic applications accepted.

University of Phoenix–Des Moines Campus, College of Nursing, Des Moines, IA 50266. Offers education (MHA); gerontology (MHA); health administration (MHA, DHA); informatics (MHA, MSN); nursing (MSN, PhD); nursing/health care education (MSN).

University of Phoenix–Milwaukee Campus, College of Nursing, Milwaukee, WI 53045. Offers education (MHA); gerontology (MHA); health administration (MHA, DHA); informatics (MHA, MSN); nursing (MSN, PhD); nursing/health care education (MSN); MSN/MBA; MSN/MHA.

University of Phoenix–Online Campus, College of Nursing, Phoenix, AZ 85034-7209. Offers informatics (MSN); international (MSN); nurse practitioner (MSN); nursing (MSN); nursing/health care education (MSN); MSN/Certificate; MSN/MBA; MSN/MHA. *Accreditation:* AACN. Evening/weekend programs available. Postbaccalaureate distance learning degree programs offered. *Students:* 5,257 full-time (4,805 women); includes 1,381 minority (803 Black or African American, non-Hispanic/Latino; 36 American Indian or Alaska Native, non-Hispanic/Latino; 271 Asian, non-Hispanic/Latino; 188 Hispanic/Latino; 51 Native Hawaiian or other Pacific Islander, non-Hispanic/Latino; 32 Two or more races, non-Hispanic/Latino), 244 international. Average age 43. *Entrance requirements:* Additional exam requirements/recommendations for international students: Required—TOEFL, TOEIC (Test of English as an International Communication), Berlitz Online English Proficiency Exam, Pearson Test of English, or IELTS. *Application deadline:* Applications are processed on a rolling basis. Application fee: $45. Electronic applications accepted. *Expenses:* Contact institution. *Financial support:* Scholarships/grants available. Financial award applicants required to submit FAFSA. *Application contact:* 866-766-0766. Web site: http://www.phoenix.edu/colleges_divisions/nursing.html.

University of Phoenix–Phoenix Main Campus, College of Nursing, Tempe, AZ 85282-2371. Offers family nurse practitioner (MSN, Certificate); informatics (MSN); nursing (MSN); nursing/health care education (MSN); MSN/Certificate; MSN/MBA; MSN/MHA. Evening/weekend programs available. Postbaccalaureate distance learning degree programs offered. *Students:* 172 full-time (148 women); includes 25 minority (4 Black or African American, non-Hispanic/Latino; 8 Asian, non-Hispanic/Latino; 13 Hispanic/Latino), 10 international. Average age 40. *Entrance requirements:* Additional exam requirements/recommendations for international students: Required—TOEFL, TOEIC (Test of English as an International Communication), Berlitz Online English Proficiency Exam, Pearson Test of English, or IELTS. *Application deadline:* Applications are processed on a rolling basis. Application fee: $45. Electronic applications accepted. *Expenses:* Contact institution. *Financial support:* Scholarships/grants available. Financial award applicants required to submit FAFSA. *Application contact:* 866-766-0766. Web site: http://www.phoenix.edu/colleges_divisions/nursing.html.

University of Phoenix–Raleigh Campus, College of Nursing, Raleigh, NC 27606. Offers education (MHA); gerontology (MHA); health administration (MHA, DHA); informatics (MHA, MSN); nursing (MSN, PhD); nursing/health care education (MSN).

University of Phoenix–Southern California Campus, College of Nursing, Costa Mesa, CA 92626. Offers family nurse practitioner (MSN, Certificate); informatics (MSN); nursing (MSN); nursing/health care education (MSN); MSN/Certificate; MSN/MBA; MSN/MHA. Evening/weekend programs available. Postbaccalaureate distance learning degree programs offered. *Students:* 281 full-time (244 women); includes 129 minority (47 Black or African American, non-Hispanic/Latino; 1 American Indian or Alaska Native, non-Hispanic/Latino; 44 Asian, non-Hispanic/Latino; 26 Hispanic/Latino; 9 Native Hawaiian or other Pacific Islander, non-Hispanic/Latino; 2 Two or more races, non-Hispanic/Latino), 13 international. Average age 43. *Entrance requirements:* Additional exam requirements/recommendations for international students: Required—TOEFL, TOEIC (Test of English as an International Communication), Berlitz Online English Proficiency Exam, Pearson Test of English, or IELTS. *Application deadline:* Applications are processed on a rolling basis. Application fee: $45. Electronic applications accepted. *Expenses:* Contact institution. *Financial support:* Scholarships/grants available. Financial award applicants required to submit FAFSA. *Application contact:* 866-766-0766. Web site: http://www.phoenix.edu/colleges_divisions/nursing.html.

University of Phoenix–Washington D.C. Campus, College of Nursing, Washington, DC 20001. Offers education (MHA); gerontology (MHA); health administration (MHA, DHA); informatics (MHA, MSN); nursing (MSN, PhD); nursing/health care education (MSN); MSN/MBA; MSN/MHA.

Vanderbilt University, Vanderbilt University School of Nursing, Nashville, TN 37240. Offers acute care nurse practitioner (MSN), including intensivist; adult-gerontology primary care nurse practitioner (MSN); emergency nurse practitioner (MSN); family nurse practitioner (MSN); family psychiatric and mental health nurse practitioner (MSN); health systems management (MSN); neonatal nurse practitioner (MSN); nurse midwifery (MSN); nurse midwifery/family nurse practitioner (MSN); nursing informatics (MSN); nursing practice (DNP); nursing science (PhD); pediatric acute care nurse practitioner (MSN); pediatric primary care nurse practitioner (MSN); women's health nurse practitioner (MSN), including urogynecology; women's health; women's health nurse practitioner/adult gerontology nurse practitioner (MSN); MSN/M Div; MSN/MTS. *Accreditation:* ACNM/ACME; NLN (one or more programs are accredited). Part-time programs available. Postbaccalaureate distance learning degree programs offered (minimal on-campus study). *Faculty:* 120 full-time (105 women), 415 part-time/adjunct (302 women). *Students:* 570 full-time (503 women), 395 part-time (364 women); includes 107 minority (57 Black or African American, non-Hispanic/Latino; 1 American Indian or Alaska Native, non-Hispanic/Latino; 19 Asian, non-Hispanic/Latino; 19 Hispanic/Latino; 2 Native Hawaiian or other Pacific Islander, non-Hispanic/Latino; 9 Two or more races, non-Hispanic/Latino), 10 international. Average age 32. 1,116 applicants, 56% accepted, 455 enrolled. In 2011, 341 master's, 33 doctorates awarded. *Degree requirements:* For doctorate, comprehensive exam, thesis/dissertation. *Entrance requirements:* For master's, GRE General Test (within the past 5 years), minimum B average in undergraduate course work, 3 letters of recommendation; for doctorate, GRE General Test, interview, 3 letters of recommendation from doctorally-prepared faculty, MSN, essay. Additional exam requirements/recommendations for international students: Required—TOEFL (minimum score 570 paper-based; 88 computer-based), IELTS (minimum score 6.5). *Application deadline:* For fall admission, 12/1 priority date for domestic students, 12/1 for international students. Applications are processed on a rolling basis. Application fee: $50. Electronic applications accepted. *Expenses:* Contact institution. *Financial support:* In 2011–12, 392 students received support. Scholarships/

grants and health care benefits available. Support available to part-time students. Financial award application deadline: 3/15; financial award applicants required to submit FAFSA. *Faculty research:* Lymphedema, palliative care and bereavement, health services research including workforce, safety and quality of care, gerontology, better birth outcomes including nutrition . *Total annual research expenditures:* $1.8 million. *Unit head:* Dr. Colleen Conway-Welch, Dean, 615-343-8776; Fax: 615-343-7711, E-mail: colleen.conway-welch@vanderbilt.edu. *Application contact:* Patricia Peerman, Assistant Dean for Enrollment Management, 615-322-3800, Fax: 615-343-0333, E-mail: vusn-admissions@vanderbilt.edu. Web site: http://www.nursing.vanderbilt.edu.

Walden University, Graduate Programs, School of Nursing, Minneapolis, MN 55401. Offers education (MSN); informatics (MSN); leadership and management (MSN); nursing (DNP, Post-Master's Certificate), including nursing education (Post-Master's Certificate), nursing informatics (Post-Master's Certificate), nursing leadership and management (Post-Master's Certificate). *Accreditation:* AACN. Part-time and evening/weekend programs available. Postbaccalaureate distance learning degree programs offered (no on-campus study). *Faculty:* 13 full-time (10 women), 142 part-time/adjunct (123 women). *Students:* 4,064 full-time (3,749 women), 1,418 part-time (1,321 women); includes 1,448 minority (975 Black or African American, non-Hispanic/Latino; 27 American Indian or Alaska Native, non-Hispanic/Latino; 207 Asian, non-Hispanic/Latino; 178 Hispanic/Latino; 8 Native Hawaiian or other Pacific Islander, non-Hispanic/Latino; 53 Two or more races, non-Hispanic/Latino), 181 international. Average age 43. In 2011, 1,141 master's, 31 other advanced degrees awarded. *Entrance requirements:* For master's, bachelor's degree or equivalent in related field or RN; minimum GPA of 2.5; goal statement; for doctorate, master's degree or higher, three years of related professional or academic experience, RN, goal statement. Additional exam requirements/recommendations for international students: Required—TOEFL (minimum score 550 paper-based; 213 computer-based), IELTS (minimum score 6.5), or Michigan English Language Assessment Battery (minimum score 82). *Application deadline:* Applications are processed on a rolling basis. Application fee: $50. Electronic applications accepted. *Financial support:* Federal Work-Study, scholarships/grants, unspecified assistantships, and family tuition reduction, active duty/veteran tuition reduction, group tuition reduction, interest-free payment plans, employee tuition reduction available. Support available to part-time students. Financial award applicants required to submit FAFSA. *Unit head:* Dr. Sara Torres, Associate Dean, 800-925-3368.

Application contact: Jennifer Hall, Vice President of Enrollment Management, 866-4-WALDEN, E-mail: info@walden.edu. Web site: http://www.waldenu.edu/Colleges-and-Schools/College-of-Health-Sciences/School-of-Nursing.htm.

Waynesburg University, Graduate and Professional Studies, Waynesburg, PA 15370-1222. Offers business (MBA), including finance, health systems, human resources, leadership, market development; counseling (MA), including addictions counseling, clinical mental health; education (MAT); nursing (MSN), including administration, education, informatics, palliative care; nursing practice (DNP); special education (M Ed); technology (M Ed); MSN/MBA. *Accreditation:* AACN. Part-time and evening/weekend programs available. *Degree requirements:* For doctorate, thesis/dissertation. *Entrance requirements:* Additional exam requirements/recommendations for international students: Required—TOEFL. Electronic applications accepted.

Xavier University, College of Social Sciences, Health and Education, School of Nursing, Cincinnati, OH 45207. Offers clinical nurse leader (MSN); education (MSN); forensic nursing (MSN); healthcare law (MSN); informatics (MSN); nursing administration (MSN); school nursing (MSN); MSN/M Ed; MSN/MBA; MSN/MS. *Accreditation:* AACN. Part-time and evening/weekend programs available. *Faculty:* 13 full-time (all women), 10 part-time/adjunct (all women). *Students:* 69 full-time (66 women), 158 part-time (156 women); includes 30 minority (19 Black or African American, non-Hispanic/Latino; 2 American Indian or Alaska Native, non-Hispanic/Latino; 4 Asian, non-Hispanic/Latino; 3 Hispanic/Latino; 2 Two or more races, non-Hispanic/Latino). Average age 38. 117 applicants, 81% accepted, 71 enrolled. In 2011, 63 master's awarded. *Degree requirements:* For master's, thesis, scholarly project. *Entrance requirements:* For master's, GRE. Additional exam requirements/recommendations for international students: Required—TOEFL. *Application deadline:* Applications are processed on a rolling basis. Application fee: $35. Electronic applications accepted. *Expenses: Tuition:* Part-time $576 per credit hour. *Financial support:* In 2011–12, 88 students received support. Applicants required to submit FAFSA. *Faculty research:* Clinical nurse leader, simulation, employment satisfaction, nontraditional students, holistic nursing. *Unit head:* Dr. Susan M. Schmidt, Director, 513-745-3815, Fax: 513-745-1087, E-mail: schmidt@xavier.edu. *Application contact:* Marilyn Volk Gomez, Director of Nursing Student Services, 513-745-4392, Fax: 513-745-1087, E-mail: gomez@xavier.edu. Web site: http://www.xavier.edu/msn/.

Occupational Health Nursing

University of Cincinnati, Graduate School, College of Nursing, Cincinnati, OH 45221-0038. Offers clinical nurse specialist (MSN), including adult health, community health, neonatal, nursing administration, occupational health, pediatric health, psychiatric nursing, women's health; nurse anesthesia (MSN); nurse midwifery (MSN); nurse practitioner (MSN), including acute care, ambulatory care, family, family/psychiatric, women's health; nursing (PhD); MBA/MSN. *Accreditation:* AACN; AANA/CANAEP (one or more programs are accredited); ACNM/ACME. Part-time programs available. Postbaccalaureate distance learning degree programs offered (no on-campus study). Terminal master's awarded for partial completion of doctoral program. *Degree requirements:* For master's, thesis or alternative; for doctorate, comprehensive exam, thesis/dissertation. *Entrance requirements:* For master's and doctorate, GRE General Test. Additional exam requirements/recommendations for international students: Required—TOEFL (minimum score 520 paper-based; 190 computer-based). Electronic applications accepted. *Faculty research:* Substance abuse, injury and violence, symptom management.

University of Illinois at Chicago, Graduate College, College of Nursing, Program in Nursing, Chicago, IL 60607-7128. Offers acute care clinical nurse specialist (MS); acute care nurse practitioner (MS); administrative studies in nursing (MS); adult nurse practitioner (MS); adult/geriatric nurse practitioner (MS); advanced community health nurse specialist (MS); family nurse practitioner (MS); geriatric clinical nurse specialist (MS); geriatric nurse practitioner (MS); mental health clinical nurse specialist (MS); mental health nurse practitioner (MS); nurse midwifery (MS); occupational health/advanced community health nurse specialist (MS); occupational health/family nurse practitioner (MS); pediatric clinical nurse specialist (MS); pediatric nurse practitioner (MS); perinatal clinical nurse specialist (MS); school/advanced community health nurse specialist (MS); school/family nurse practitioner (MS); women's health nurse practitioner (MS). *Accreditation:* AACN. Part-time programs available. *Degree requirements:* For master's, thesis or alternative. *Entrance requirements:* For master's, GRE General Test, minimum GPA of 2.75. Additional exam requirements/recommendations for international students: Required—TOEFL. Electronic applications accepted.

University of Medicine and Dentistry of New Jersey, School of Nursing, Newark, NJ 07107-3001. Offers adult health (MSN); adult occupational health (MSN); advanced practice nursing (MSN, Post Master's Certificate); family nurse practitioner (MSN); nurse anesthesia (MSN); nursing (MSN); nursing informatics (MSN); urban health (PhD); women's health practitioner (MSN). *Accreditation:* AANA/CANAEP; NLN (one or more programs are accredited). Part-time programs available. *Entrance requirements:* For

master's, GRE, RN license; basic life support, statistics, and health assessment experience. Additional exam requirements/recommendations for international students: Required—TOEFL. Electronic applications accepted. *Expenses:* Contact institution. *Faculty research:* HIV/AIDS, diabetes education, learned helplessness, nursing science, psychoeducation.

University of Michigan, Horace H. Rackham School of Graduate Studies, School of Nursing, Division of Health Promotion and Risk Reduction, Program in Community Health Nursing, Ann Arbor, MI 48109. Offers adult nurse practitioner (Post Master's Certificate); adult primary care/adult nurse practitioner (MS); community care (Post Master's Certificate); community care/home care (MS); family nurse practitioner (MS, Post Master's Certificate); occupational health nursing (MS). *Accreditation:* AACN. Part-time and evening/weekend programs available. *Degree requirements:* For master's, thesis. *Entrance requirements:* For master's, GRE General Test (if cumulative BSN GPA less than 3.25), licensure, minimum GPA of 3.0 in BSN program. Additional exam requirements/recommendations for international students: Required—TOEFL (minimum score 560 paper-based; 220 computer-based).

University of Minnesota, Twin Cities Campus, School of Public Health, Division of Environmental Health Sciences, Area in Occupational Health Nursing, Minneapolis, MN 55455-0213. Offers MPH, MS, PhD, MPH/MS. *Accreditation:* AACN. *Degree requirements:* For doctorate, thesis/dissertation. *Entrance requirements:* For master's and doctorate, GRE General Test. Electronic applications accepted.

The University of North Carolina at Chapel Hill, Graduate School, School of Public Health, Public Health Leadership Program, Chapel Hill, NC 27599. Offers health care and prevention (MPH); leadership (MPH); occupational health nursing (MPH); public health nursing (MS). Part-time programs available. Postbaccalaureate distance learning degree programs offered (minimal on-campus study). *Degree requirements:* For master's, comprehensive exam, thesis (MS), paper (MPH). *Entrance requirements:* For master's, GRE General Test, minimum GPA of 3.0, public health experience. Additional exam requirements/recommendations for international students: Required—TOEFL. Electronic applications accepted. *Faculty research:* Occupational health issues, clinical outcomes, prenatal and early childcare, adolescent health, effectiveness of home visiting, issues in occupational health nursing, community-based interventions.

University of the Sacred Heart, Graduate Programs, Department of Natural Sciences, San Juan, PR 00914-0383. Offers occupational health and safety (MS); occupational nursing (MSN). Part-time and evening/weekend programs available.

Oncology Nursing

Columbia University, School of Nursing, Program in Oncology Nursing, New York, NY 10032. Offers MS, Adv C. *Accreditation:* AACN. Part-time programs available. *Entrance requirements:* For master's, GRE General Test, BSN, 1 year of clinical experience (preferred); for Adv C, MSN. Electronic applications accepted.

Duke University, School of Nursing, Durham, NC 27708-0586. Offers adult acute care (Certificate); adult cardiovascular (Certificate); adult oncology (Certificate); adult primary care (Certificate); clinical nurse specialist (MSN), including adult oncology, gerontology, neonatal, pediatric; clinical research management (MSN, Certificate); family (Certificate); gerontology (Certificate); health and nursing ministries (MSN, Certificate); health systems leadership and outcomes (Certificate); neonatal (Certificate); neonatal/pediatric in rural health (MSN, Certificate); nurse anesthetist (MSN, Certificate); nurse practitioner (MSN), including adult acute care, adult cardiovascular, adult oncology, adult primary care, family, gerontology, neonatal, pediatric, pediatric acute care; nursing

(DNP, PhD); nursing and healthcare leadership (MSN); nursing education (MSN); nursing informatics (MSN, Certificate); pediatric (Certificate); pediatric acute care (Certificate); MBA/MSN; MSN/MCM. *Accreditation:* AACN; AANA/CANAEP. Part-time and evening/weekend programs available. Postbaccalaureate distance learning degree programs offered (minimal on-campus study). *Faculty:* 56 full-time (47 women), 2 part-time/adjunct (1 woman). *Students:* 127 full-time (108 women), 395 part-time (358 women); includes 92 minority (42 Black or African American, non-Hispanic/Latino; 3 American Indian or Alaska Native, non-Hispanic/Latino; 21 Asian, non-Hispanic/Latino; 14 Hispanic/Latino; 12 Two or more races, non-Hispanic/Latino), 10 international. Average age 36. 432 applicants, 45% accepted, 143 enrolled. In 2011, 117 master's, 29 doctorates, 32 other advanced degrees awarded. Terminal master's awarded for partial completion of doctoral program. *Degree requirements:* For master's, thesis optional; for doctorate, capstone project. *Entrance requirements:* For master's, GRE General Test, 1

year of nursing experience, BSN, minimum GPA of 3.0, previous course work in statistics; for doctorate, BSN or MSN, minimum GPA of 3.0, portfolio; for Certificate, MSN. Additional exam requirements/recommendations for international students: Required—TOEFL (minimum score 550 paper-based; 213 computer-based). *Application deadline:* For fall admission, 12/1 for domestic and international students; for spring admission, 5/1 for domestic and international students. Application fee: $50. Electronic applications accepted. *Expenses:* Contact institution. *Financial support:* Career-related internships or fieldwork, institutionally sponsored loans, scholarships/grants, traineeships, and tuition waivers (partial) available. Support available to part-time students. Financial award application deadline: 4/1; financial award applicants required to submit FAFSA. *Faculty research:* Cardiovascular disease, caregiver skill training, data mining, prostate cancer, neonatal immune system. *Total annual research expenditures:* $4.7 million. *Unit head:* Dr. Catherine L. Gilliss, Dean/Vice Chancellor for Nursing Affairs, 919-684-9444, Fax: 919-684-9414, E-mail: gilli025@mc.duke.edu. *Application contact:* Bebe T. Mills, Director of Admissions, 919-684-9151, Fax: 919-668-4693, E-mail: mills031@mc.duke.edu. Web site: http://www.nursing.duke.edu/.

Goldfarb School of Nursing at Barnes-Jewish College, Graduate Programs, St. Louis, MO 63110. Offers adult acute care nurse practitioner (MSN); adult nurse practitioner (MSN); nurse anesthesia (MSN); nurse educator (MSN); nurse executive (MSN); DNP/PhD. *Accreditation:* AACN; AANA/CANAEP. Part-time and evening/weekend programs available. Postbaccalaureate distance learning degree programs offered (minimal on-campus study). *Faculty:* 38 full-time (35 women), 14 part-time/adjunct (11 women). *Students:* 79 full-time (68 women), 92 part-time (86 women); includes 45 minority (29 Black or African American, non-Hispanic/Latino; 1 American Indian or Alaska Native, non-Hispanic/Latino; 3 Asian, non-Hispanic/Latino; 3 Hispanic/Latino; 6 Native Hawaiian or other Pacific Islander, non-Hispanic/Latino; 3 Two or more races, non-Hispanic/Latino), 1 international. Average age 40. 134 applicants, 66% accepted, 51 enrolled. In 2011, 31 degrees awarded. *Degree requirements:* For master's, thesis or alternative. *Entrance requirements:* For master's, 2 references, personal statement, curriculum vitae or resume. Additional exam requirements/recommendations for international students: Required—TOEFL (minimum score 575 paper-based; 240 computer-based; 85 iBT). *Application deadline:* For fall admission, 2/1 for international students; for spring admission, 10/1 for international students. Applications are processed on a rolling basis. Application fee: $50. *Expenses: Tuition:* Full-time $14,685; part-time $630 per credit hour. *Required fees:* $280. *Financial support:* Fellowships, research assistantships, Federal Work-Study, institutionally sponsored loans, and scholarships/grants available. Support available to part-time students. Financial award applicants required to submit FAFSA. *Faculty research:* HIV Stigma, HIV symptom management, palliative care with children and their families, heart disease prevention in Hispanic women, depression in the well elderly, alternative therapies in pre-term infants. *Unit head:* Dr. Connie K. Koch, Interim Dean, 314-36-26590, Fax: 314-362-0984, E-mail: ckoch@bjc.org. *Application contact:* Dr. Michael Ward, Associate Dean for Student Programs, 314-362-9155, Fax: 314-362-0984, E-mail: mward@bjc.org.

Gwynedd-Mercy College, School of Nursing, Gwynedd Valley, PA 19437-0901. Offers clinical nurse specialist (MSN), including gerontology, oncology, pediatrics; nurse practitioner (MSN), including adult health, pediatric health. *Accreditation:* NLN. *Faculty:* 3 full-time (all women), 2 part-time/adjunct (both women). *Students:* 14 full-time (13 women), 28 part-time (25 women); includes 11 minority (4 Black or African American, non-Hispanic/Latino; 6 Asian, non-Hispanic/Latino; 1 Hispanic/Latino). Average age 40. 23 applicants, 83% accepted, 11 enrolled. In 2011, 7 master's awarded. *Degree requirements:* For master's, thesis optional. *Entrance requirements:* For master's, GRE General Test or MAT, current nursing experience, physical assessment, course work in statistics, BSN from NLNAC-accredited program, 2 letters of recommendation, personal interview. Additional exam requirements/recommendations for international students:

Required—TOEFL (minimum score 575 paper-based). *Application deadline:* For fall admission, 8/1 priority date for domestic students; for winter admission, 12/1 priority date for domestic students. Applications are processed on a rolling basis. Application fee: $25. Electronic applications accepted. *Expenses:* Contact institution. *Financial support:* In 2011–12, 21 students received support. Scholarships/grants, traineeships, and unspecified assistantships available. Financial award application deadline: 8/30. *Faculty research:* Critical thinking, primary care, domestic violence, multiculturalism, nursing centers. *Unit head:* Dr. Andrea D. Hollingsworth, Dean, 215-646-7300 Ext. 539, Fax: 215-641-5517, E-mail: hollingsworth.a@gmc.edu. *Application contact:* Dr. Barbara A. Jones, Director, 215-646-7300 Ext. 407, Fax: 215-641-5564, E-mail: jones.b@gmc.edu. Web site: http://www.gmc.edu/academics/nursing/.

Loyola University Chicago, Graduate School, Marcella Niehoff School of Nursing, Oncology Clinical Nurse Specialist Program, Chicago, IL 60660. Offers nursing oncology (Certificate); oncology clinical nurse specialist (MSN). *Accreditation:* AACN. Part-time and evening/weekend programs available. Postbaccalaureate distance learning degree programs offered (minimal on-campus study). *Students:* 15 part-time (14 women). Average age 40. 13 applicants, 85% accepted, 10 enrolled. In 2011, 2 master's awarded. *Degree requirements:* For master's, comprehensive exam or oral thesis defense. *Entrance requirements:* For master's, Illinois nursing license, BSN, minimum nursing GPA of 3.0, 3 letters of recommendation, 1000 hours experience before starting clinical. *Application deadline:* Applications are processed on a rolling basis. Application fee: $50. Electronic applications accepted. *Expenses: Tuition:* Full-time $15,660; part-time $870 per credit hour. *Required fees:* $125 per semester. Tuition and fees vary according to course load and program. *Financial support:* Teaching assistantships, traineeships, and unspecified assistantships available. Financial award application deadline: 3/1. *Faculty research:* Breast cancer, coping with cancer, pain. *Unit head:* Dr. Patricia Friend, Assistant Professor, 708-216-9553, Fax: 708-216-9555, E-mail: pfriend@luc.edu. *Application contact:* Amy Weatherford, Enrollment Advisor, School of Nursing, 773-508-3249, Fax: 773-508-3241, E-mail: aweatherford@luc.edu. Web site: http://www.luc.edu/media/lucedu/nursing/graduate/ONC%20CNS.pdf.

Universidad Metropolitana, School of Health Sciences, Department of Nursing, San Juan, PR 00928-1150. Offers case management (Certificate); nursing (MSN); oncology nursing (Certificate). *Accreditation:* NLN.

University of Delaware, College of Health Sciences, School of Nursing, Newark, DE 19716. Offers adult nurse practitioner (MSN, PMC); cardiopulmonary clinical nurse specialist (MSN, PMC); cardiopulmonary clinical nurse specialist/adult nurse practitioner (MSN, PMC); family nurse practitioner (MSN, PMC); gerontology clinical nurse specialist (MSN, PMC); gerontology clinical nurse specialist geriatric nurse practitioner (PMC); gerontology clinical nurse specialist/geriatric nurse practitioner (MSN); health services administration (MSN, PMC); nursing of children clinical nurse specialist (MSN, PMC); nursing of children clinical nurse specialist/pediatric nurse practitioner (MSN, PMC); oncology/immune deficiency clinical nurse specialist (MSN, PMC); oncology/immune deficiency clinical nurse specialist/adult nurse practitioner (MSN, PMC); perinatal/women's health clinical nurse specialist (MSN, PMC); perinatal/women's health clinical nurse specialist/women's health nurse practitioner (MSN, PMC); psychiatric nursing clinical nurse specialist (MSN, PMC). *Accreditation:* AACN; NLN (one or more programs are accredited). Part-time and evening/weekend programs available. Postbaccalaureate distance learning degree programs offered (minimal on-campus study). *Degree requirements:* For master's, thesis optional. *Entrance requirements:* For master's, BSN, interview, RN license. Electronic applications accepted. *Faculty research:* Marriage and chronic illness, health promotion, congestive heart failure patient outcomes, school nursing, diabetes in children, culture, health disparities, cardiovascular, prison nursing, oncology, public policy, child obesity, smoking and teen pregnancy, blood pressure measurements, men's health.

Pediatric Nursing

Boston College, William F. Connell School of Nursing, Chestnut Hill, MA 02467-3800. Offers adult-gerontology nursing (MS); community health nursing (MS); family health (MS); forensic nursing (MS); maternal/child health nursing (MS), including pediatric and women's health; nurse anesthesia (MS); nursing (PhD); palliative care (MS), including adult and pediatric; psychiatric-mental health nursing (MS); MBA/MS; MS/MA; MS/PhD. *Accreditation:* AACN; AANA/CANAEP (one or more programs are accredited). Part-time programs available. *Faculty:* 48 full-time (46 women), 31 part-time/adjunct (29 women). *Students:* 225 full-time (207 women), 90 part-time (88 women); includes 47 minority (15 Black or African American, non-Hispanic/Latino; 3 American Indian or Alaska Native, non-Hispanic/Latino; 17 Asian, non-Hispanic/Latino; 8 Hispanic/Latino; 4 Two or more races, non-Hispanic/Latino), 6 international. Average age 31. 369 applicants, 43% accepted, 80 enrolled. In 2011, 113 master's, 8 doctorates awarded. *Degree requirements:* For master's, comprehensive exam, research project; for doctorate, comprehensive exam, thesis/dissertation, computer literacy exam or foreign language. *Entrance requirements:* For master's, bachelor's degree in nursing; for doctorate, GRE General Test, MS in nursing. Additional exam requirements/recommendations for international students: Required—TOEFL (minimum score 600 paper-based; 250 computer-based; 100 iBT). *Application deadline:* For fall admission, 11/1 for domestic and international students; for winter admission, 12/31 for domestic and international students; for spring admission, 4/30 for domestic and international students. Applications are processed on a rolling basis. Application fee: $40. Electronic applications accepted. *Financial support:* In 2011–12, 167 students received support, including 9 fellowships with full tuition reimbursements available (averaging $15,300 per year), 7 teaching assistantships (averaging $13,612 per year); research assistantships, Federal Work-Study, institutionally sponsored loans, scholarships/grants, traineeships, health care benefits, tuition waivers (partial), and unspecified assistantships also available. Support available to part-time students. Financial award application deadline: 3/1; financial award applicants required to submit FAFSA. *Faculty research:* Pre-term labor, palliative care, support during chronic illness, violence, eating disorders. *Total annual research expenditures:* $2.1 million. *Unit head:* Dr. Susan Gennaro, Dean, 617-552-4251, Fax: 617-552-0931, E-mail: susan.gennaro@bc.edu. *Application contact:* MaryBeth Crowley, Graduate Programs Assistant, 617-552-4928, Fax: 617-552-2121, E-mail: csongrad@bc.edu. Web site: http://www.bc.edu/nursing/.

Caribbean University, Graduate School, Bayamón, PR 00960-0493. Offers administration and supervision (MA Ed); criminal justice (MA); curriculum and instruction (MA Ed, PhD), including elementary education (MA Ed), English education (MA Ed), history education (MA Ed), mathematics education (MA Ed), primary education (MA Ed), science education (MA Ed), Spanish education (MA Ed); educational technology in instructional systems (MA Ed); gerontology (MSN); human resources (MBA);

museology, archiving and art history (MA Ed); neonatal pediatrics (MSN); physical education (MA Ed); special education (MA Ed). *Entrance requirements:* For master's, interview, minimum GPA of 2.5.

Case Western Reserve University, Frances Payne Bolton School of Nursing, Doctor of Nursing Practice Program, Cleveland, OH 44106. Offers acute care nurse practitioner (DNP); adult gerontology nurse practitioner (DNP); educational leadership (DNP); family nurse practitioner (DNP); family systems psychiatric mental health nursing (DNP); midwifery/family nursing (DNP); neonatal nurse practitioner (DNP); pediatric nurse practitioner (DNP); practice leadership (DNP); women's health nurse practitioner (DNP). *Students:* 73 full-time, 194 part-time; includes 11 minority (6 Black or African American, non-Hispanic/Latino; 3 Asian, non-Hispanic/Latino; 2 Hispanic/Latino). 122 applicants, 74% accepted, 49 enrolled. In 2011, 47 doctorates awarded. Terminal master's awarded for partial completion of doctoral program. *Degree requirements:* For doctorate, thesis/dissertation. *Entrance requirements:* For doctorate, GRE General Test or MAT. Additional exam requirements/recommendations for international students: Required—TOEFL (minimum score 577 paper-based; 90 iBT), IELTS (minimum score 7). *Application deadline:* For fall admission, 6/1 priority date for domestic students, 6/1 for international students; for spring admission, 10/1 for domestic and international students. Applications are processed on a rolling basis. Application fee: $75. *Financial support:* In 2011–12, 6 students received support, including 1 teaching assistantship; research assistantships, Federal Work-Study, institutionally sponsored loans, and tuition waivers (partial) also available. Support available to part-time students. Financial award application deadline: 6/30; financial award applicants required to submit FAFSA. *Faculty research:* Clinical nursing, acute care, gerontology, mental health, critical care. *Unit head:* Dr. Donna Dowling, Director, 216-368-1869, Fax: 216-368-3542, E-mail: dad10@case.edu. *Application contact:* Donna Hassik, Admissions Coordinator, 216-368-5253, Fax: 216-368-0124, E-mail: dmh7@case.edu. Web site: http://fpb.case.edu/DNP/.

Case Western Reserve University, Frances Payne Bolton School of Nursing, Master's Programs in Nursing, Nurse Practitioner Program, Cleveland, OH 44106. Offers acute care cardiovascular nursing (MSN); acute care nurse practitioner (MSN); acute care/flight nurse (MSN); adult gerontology nurse practitioner (MSN); family nurse practitioner (MSN); neonatal nurse practitioner (MSN); pediatric nurse practitioner (MSN); women's health nurse practitioner (MSN). *Accreditation:* NLN. Part-time programs available. Postbaccalaureate distance learning degree programs offered (minimal on-campus study). *Faculty:* 54 full-time (50 women), 5 part-time/adjunct (3 women). *Students:* 89 full-time (69 women), 77 part-time (67 women); includes 17 minority (11 Black or African American, non-Hispanic/Latino; 5 Asian, non-Hispanic/Latino; 1 Hispanic/Latino), 17 international. Average age 35. 75 applicants, 84% accepted, 42 enrolled. In 2011, 34

master's awarded. *Degree requirements:* For master's, thesis optional. *Entrance requirements:* For master's, GRE General Test or MAT. Additional exam requirements/recommendations for international students: Required—TOEFL (minimum score 577 paper-based; 90 iBT), IELTS (minimum score 7). *Application deadline:* For fall admission, 6/1 for domestic students; for spring admission, 10/1 for domestic students. Applications are processed on a rolling basis. Application fee: $75. *Financial support:* In 2011–12, 7 teaching assistantships were awarded; research assistantships, institutionally sponsored loans, and tuition waivers (partial) also available. Support available to part-time students. Financial award application deadline: 6/30; financial award applicants required to submit FAFSA. *Faculty research:* Positive and negative mood states in parents of twins, effect of a care path on chronic obstructive pulmonary disease home care. *Unit head:* Dr. Carol Savrin, Director, 216-368-5304, Fax: 216-368-3542, E-mail: cls18@case.edu. *Application contact:* Donna Hassik, Admissions Coordinator, 216-368-5253, Fax: 216-368-0124, E-mail: dmh7@case.edu. Web site: http://fpb.cwru.edu/MSN/majors.shtm.

Columbia University, School of Nursing, Program in Pediatric Nurse Practitioner, New York, NY 10032. Offers MS, Adv C. *Accreditation:* AACN. Part-time programs available. *Entrance requirements:* For master's, GRE General Test, BSN, 1 year of clinical experience (preferred); for Adv C, MSN. Electronic applications accepted.

Drexel University, College of Nursing and Health Professions, Division of Graduate Nursing, Philadelphia, PA 19104-2875. Offers adult acute care (MSN); adult psychiatric/mental health (MSN); advanced practice nursing (MSN); clinical trials research (MSN); family nurse practitioner (MSN); leadership in health systems management (MSN); nursing education (MSN); pediatric primary care (MSN); women's health (MSN). *Accreditation:* AACN; NLN. Electronic applications accepted.

Duke University, School of Nursing, Durham, NC 27708-0586. Offers adult acute care (Certificate); adult cardiovascular (Certificate); adult oncology (Certificate); adult primary care (Certificate); clinical nurse specialist (MSN), including adult oncology, gerontology, neonatal, pediatric; clinical research management (MSN, Certificate); family (Certificate); gerontology (Certificate); health and nursing ministries (MSN, Certificate); health systems leadership and outcomes (Certificate); neonatal (Certificate); neonatal/pediatric in rural health (MSN, Certificate); nurse anesthetist (MSN, Certificate); nurse practitioner (MSN), including adult acute care, adult cardiovascular, adult oncology, adult primary care, family, gerontology, neonatal, pediatric, pediatric acute care; nursing (DNP, PhD); nursing and healthcare leadership (MSN); nursing education (MSN); nursing informatics (MSN, Certificate); pediatric (Certificate); pediatric acute care (Certificate); MBA/MSN; MSN/MCM. *Accreditation:* AACN; AANA/CANAEP. Part-time and evening/weekend programs available. Postbaccalaureate distance learning degree programs offered (minimal on-campus study). *Faculty:* 56 full-time (47 women), 2 part-time/adjunct (1 woman). *Students:* 127 full-time (108 women), 395 part-time (358 women); includes 92 minority (42 Black or African American, non-Hispanic/Latino; 3 American Indian or Alaska Native, non-Hispanic/Latino; 21 Asian, non-Hispanic/Latino; 14 Hispanic/Latino; 12 Two or more races, non-Hispanic/Latino), 10 international. Average age 36. 432 applicants, 45% accepted, 143 enrolled. In 2011, 117 master's, 29 doctorates, 32 other advanced degrees awarded. Terminal master's awarded for partial completion of doctoral program. *Degree requirements:* For master's, thesis optional; for doctorate, capstone project. *Entrance requirements:* For master's, GRE General Test, 1 year of nursing experience, BSN, minimum GPA of 3.0, previous course work in statistics; for doctorate, BSN or MSN, minimum GPA of 3.0, portfolio; for Certificate, MSN. Additional exam requirements/recommendations for international students: Required—TOEFL (minimum score 550 paper-based; 213 computer-based). *Application deadline:* For fall admission, 12/1 for domestic and international students; for spring admission, 5/1 for domestic and international students. Application fee: $50. Electronic applications accepted. *Expenses:* Contact institution. *Financial support:* Career-related internships or fieldwork, institutionally sponsored loans, scholarships/grants, traineeships, and tuition waivers (partial) available. Support available to part-time students. Financial award application deadline: 4/1; financial award applicants required to submit FAFSA. *Faculty research:* Cardiovascular disease, caregiver skill training, data mining, prostate cancer, neonatal immune system. *Total annual research expenditures:* $4.7 million. *Unit head:* Dr. Catherine L. Gilliss, Dean/Vice Chancellor for Nursing Affairs, 919-684-9444, Fax: 919-684-9414, E-mail: gilli025@mc.duke.edu. *Application contact:* Bebe T. Mills, Director of Admissions, 919-684-9151, Fax: 919-668-4693, E-mail: mills031@mc.duke.edu. Web site: http://www.nursing.duke.edu/.

Emory University, Nell Hodgson Woodruff School of Nursing, Atlanta, GA 30322-1100. Offers adult nurse practitioner (MSN); emergency nurse practitioner (MSN); family nurse practitioner (MSN); family nurse-midwife (MSN); health systems leadership (MSN); nurse-midwifery (MSN); pediatric nurse practitioner acute and primary care (MSN); women's health care (Title X) (MSN); women's health nurse practitioner (MSN); women's health/adult health nurse practitioner (MSN); MSN/MPH. *Accreditation:* AACN; ACNM/ACME (one or more programs are accredited). Part-time programs available. *Faculty:* 30 full-time (29 women), 11 part-time/adjunct (10 women). *Students:* 110 full-time (106 women), 53 part-time (51 women); includes 49 minority (35 Black or African American, non-Hispanic/Latino; 2 American Indian or Alaska Native, non-Hispanic/Latino; 10 Asian, non-Hispanic/Latino; 2 Hispanic/Latino), 4 international. Average age 32. 182 applicants, 63% accepted, 86 enrolled. In 2011, 81 master's awarded. *Entrance requirements:* For master's, GRE General Test or MAT, minimum GPA of 3.0, BS in nursing from an accredited institution, RN license and additional course work, 3 letters of recommendation. Additional exam requirements/recommendations for international students: Required—TOEFL (minimum score 600 paper-based; 100 iBT). *Application deadline:* For fall admission, 1/15 priority date for domestic students, 1/15 for international students; for spring admission, 10/1 priority date for domestic students, 10/1 for international students. Applications are processed on a rolling basis. Application fee: $50. Electronic applications accepted. *Expenses:* Contact institution. *Financial support:* In 2011–12, 14 fellowships (averaging $28,000 per year) were awarded; career-related internships or fieldwork, Federal Work-Study, institutionally sponsored loans, and scholarships/grants also available. Support available to part-time students. Financial award application deadline: 3/1; financial award applicants required to submit CSS PROFILE or FAFSA. *Faculty research:* Older adult falls and injuries, minority health issues, cardiac symptoms and quality of life, bio-ethics and decision-making, menopausal issues. *Unit head:* Dr. Linda McCauley, Dean, 404-727-7976, Fax: 404-727-9800, E-mail: linda.mccauley@emory.edu. Web site: http://www.nursing.emory.edu/.

Georgia Health Sciences University, College of Graduate Studies, Pediatric Nurse Practitioner Program, Augusta, GA 30912. Offers MSN, Post-Master's Certificate. *Students:* 4 full-time (all women), 7 part-time (6 women); includes 1 minority (Black or African American, non-Hispanic/Latino). Average age 27. 4 applicants, 50% accepted, 2 enrolled. In 2011, 3 master's awarded. *Entrance requirements:* For master's, GRE General Test or MAT, Georgia license as a registered professional nurse. Additional exam requirements/recommendations for international students: Required—TOEFL (minimum score 550 paper-based; 213 computer-based; 79 iBT). *Application deadline:* For fall admission, 2/1 for domestic and international students; for spring admission, 10/1 for domestic and international students. Application fee: $50. Electronic applications accepted. *Unit head:* Dr. Lucy Marion, Dean, 706-721-3771, Fax: 706-721-8169, E-mail: lumarion@georgiahealth.edu. *Application contact:* Karen Sturgill, Program Coordinator, 706-721-3676, Fax: 706-721-8169, E-mail: ksturgill@georgiahealth.edu. Web site: http://www.mcg.edu/son/futurestudents.htm.

Georgia State University, College of Health and Human Sciences, Byrdine F. Lewis School of Nursing, Atlanta, GA 30302-3083. Offers adult health (MS); adult health nursing (Certificate); child health (MS); family nurse practitioner (MS, Certificate); health promotion, protection and restoration (PhD); perinatal/women's health (MS); psychiatric mental health nursing (Certificate); psychiatric/mental health (MS); women's health nursing (Certificate). *Accreditation:* AACN. Part-time and evening/weekend programs available. Postbaccalaureate distance learning degree programs offered (minimal on-campus study). *Degree requirements:* For master's, research activity; for doctorate, comprehensive exam, thesis/dissertation. *Entrance requirements:* For master's, MAT (preferred) or GRE, interview, RN license; for doctorate, GRE General Test. Additional exam requirements/recommendations for international students: Required—TOEFL (minimum score 550 paper-based; 213 computer-based). Electronic applications accepted. *Expenses:* Contact institution. *Faculty research:* Breast cancer prevention, sexually compulsive behaviors, health risks in minority youth, asthma treatment strategies, adolescent alcohol-related issues.

Gwynedd-Mercy College, School of Nursing, Gwynedd Valley, PA 19437-0901. Offers clinical nurse specialist (MSN), including gerontology, oncology, pediatrics; nurse practitioner (MSN), including adult health, pediatric health. *Accreditation:* NLN. *Faculty:* 3 full-time (all women), 2 part-time/adjunct (both women). *Students:* 14 full-time (13 women), 28 part-time (25 women); includes 11 minority (4 Black or African American, non-Hispanic/Latino; 6 Asian, non-Hispanic/Latino; 1 Hispanic/Latino). Average age 40. 23 applicants, 83% accepted, 11 enrolled. In 2011, 7 master's awarded. *Degree requirements:* For master's, thesis optional. *Entrance requirements:* For master's, GRE General Test or MAT, current nursing experience, physical assessment, course work in statistics, BSN from NLNAC-accredited program, 2 letters of recommendation, personal interview. Additional exam requirements/recommendations for international students: Required—TOEFL (minimum score 575 paper-based). *Application deadline:* For fall admission, 8/1 priority date for domestic students; for winter admission, 12/1 priority date for domestic students. Applications are processed on a rolling basis. Application fee: $25. Electronic applications accepted. *Expenses:* Contact institution. *Financial support:* In 2011–12, 21 students received support. Scholarships/grants, traineeships, and unspecified assistantships available. Financial award application deadline: 8/30. *Faculty research:* Critical thinking, primary care, domestic violence, multiculturalism, nursing centers. *Unit head:* Dr. Andrea D. Hollingsworth, Dean, 215-646-7300 Ext. 539, Fax: 215-641-5517, E-mail: hollingsworth.a@gmc.edu. *Application contact:* Dr. Barbara A. Jones, Director, 215-646-7300 Ext. 407, Fax: 215-641-5564, E-mail: jones.b@gmc.edu. Web site: http://www.gmc.edu/academics/nursing/.

Hampton University, Graduate College, School of Nursing, Hampton, VA 23668. Offers advanced adult nursing (MS); community health nursing (MS); community mental health/psychiatric nursing (MS); family nursing (MS); gerontological nursing for the nurse practitioner (MS); pediatric nursing (MS); women's health nursing (MS). *Accreditation:* AACN; NLN. Part-time and evening/weekend programs available. *Degree requirements:* For master's, thesis optional. *Entrance requirements:* For master's, GRE General Test. *Faculty research:* Curriculum development, physical and mental assessment.

Indiana University–Purdue University Indianapolis, School of Nursing, Indianapolis, IN 46202-2896. Offers acute care nurse practitioner (MSN); adult health clinical nurse specialist (MSN); adult health nursing (MSN), including adult clinical nurse specialist; adult nurse practitioner (MSN); adult psychiatric/mental health nursing (MSN); child psychiatric/mental health nursing (MSN); community health nursing (MSN); family nurse practitioner (MSN); neonatal nurse practitioner (MSN); nursing (MSN, DNP), including nursing education (MSN); nursing (MSN), including nursing administration; nursing science (PhD); pediatric clinical nurse specialist (MSN); women's health nurse practitioner (MSN); MSN/MPA; MSN/MPH. *Accreditation:* AACN; NLN (one or more programs are accredited). Part-time programs available. *Faculty:* 85 full-time (82 women), 60 part-time/adjunct (all women). *Students:* 35 full-time (32 women), 360 part-time (340 women); includes 47 minority (28 Black or African American, non-Hispanic/Latino; 9 Asian, non-Hispanic/Latino; 4 Hispanic/Latino; 1 Native Hawaiian or other Pacific Islander, non-Hispanic/Latino; 5 Two or more races, non-Hispanic/Latino), 5 international. Average age 38. 119 applicants, 76% accepted, 54 enrolled. In 2011, 89 master's, 10 doctorates awarded. Terminal master's awarded for partial completion of doctoral program. *Degree requirements:* For master's, thesis; for doctorate, thesis/dissertation. *Entrance requirements:* For master's, minimum GPA of 3.0, RN license; for doctorate, GRE General Test, minimum GPA of 3.0, MSN, RN license, graduate statistics course with minimum B grade (not older than 3 years). Additional exam requirements/recommendations for international students: Required—TOEFL. *Application deadline:* For fall admission, 2/15 for domestic students; for spring admission, 9/15 for domestic students. Application fee: $55 ($65 for international students). *Financial support:* In 2011–12, 93 students received support, including 9 fellowships with full tuition reimbursements available (averaging $7,039 per year), 7 teaching assistantships with full tuition reimbursements available (averaging $5,300 per year); research assistantships with full tuition reimbursements available, Federal Work-Study, institutionally sponsored loans, scholarships/grants, and tuition waivers (full) also available. Support available to part-time students. Financial award application deadline: 5/1. *Faculty research:* Clinical science, health systems. *Total annual research expenditures:* $3 million. *Unit head:* Associate Dean for Graduate Programs, 317-274-2806, E-mail: nursing@iupui.edu. *Application contact:* Information Contact, 317-274-2806. Web site: http://nursing.iupui.edu/.

The Johns Hopkins University, School of Nursing, Nurse Practitioner Program, Baltimore, MD 21218-2699. Offers adult acute/critical care (MSN, Certificate); adult and pediatric primary care (MSN); adult or pediatric primary care (Certificate); emergency preparedness/disaster response (Certificate); family primary care (MSN, Certificate); women's health (Certificate). *Accreditation:* AACN; NLN (one or more programs are accredited). Part-time programs available. *Degree requirements:* For master's, thesis optional, scholarly project or portfolio. *Entrance requirements:* For master's, GRE, interview, minimum GPA of 3.0, BSN, Maryland RN license. Additional exam requirements/recommendations for international students: Required—TOEFL (minimum score 550 paper-based; 213 computer-based). Electronic applications accepted. *Expenses:* Contact institution. *Faculty research:* Community outreach, primary care of underserved populations, substance-abusing individuals, childhood violence, women's health.

Kent State University, College of Nursing, Kent, OH 44242-0001. Offers acute care nurse practitioner (MSN); adult nurse practitioner (MSN); clinical nurse specialist (MSN); family nurse practitioner (MSN); geriatric nurse practitioner (MSN); health care management (MSN); nurse educator (MSN); nursing (PhD); nursing practice (DNP); pediatric nurse practitioner (MSN); psychiatric/mental health nurse practitioner (MSN); women's health nurse practitioner (MSN). PhD program offered jointly with The University of Akron. *Accreditation:* AACN. Part-time programs available. *Degree requirements:* For master's, thesis optional; for doctorate, comprehensive exam, thesis/dissertation. *Entrance requirements:* For master's, GRE (if undergraduate GPA less

than 3.0), minimum GPA of 2.75; for doctorate, GRE, MSN. Additional exam requirements/recommendations for international students: Required—TOEFL. Electronic applications accepted. *Expenses:* Contact institution. *Faculty research:* Women and violence, methodological specialties, osteoporosis in women, new caregivers and the elderly.

Lehman College of the City University of New York, Division of Natural and Social Sciences, Department of Nursing, Bronx, NY 10468-1589. Offers adult health nursing (MS); nursing of older adults (MS); parent-child nursing (MS); pediatric nurse practitioner (MS). *Accreditation:* AACN. Part-time and evening/weekend programs available. *Entrance requirements:* For master's, bachelor's degree in nursing, New York RN license.

Loma Linda University, Department of Graduate Nursing, Program in Growing Family Nursing, Loma Linda, CA 92350. Offers MS. *Accreditation:* AACN. Part-time programs available. *Degree requirements:* For master's, thesis or alternative. *Entrance requirements:* For master's, GRE General Test, BSN, minimum GPA of 3.0, RN license. Additional exam requirements/recommendations for international students: Required—TOEFL. Electronic applications accepted. *Faculty research:* Family coping in chronic illness; women, identity, and career/family issues.

Marquette University, Graduate School, College of Nursing, Milwaukee, WI 53201-1881. Offers acute care nurse practitioner (Certificate); adult clinical nurse specialist (Certificate); adult nurse practitioner (Certificate); advanced practice nursing (MSN, DNP), including acute care, adults, neonatal nurse practitioner (MSN), nurse midwifery (DNP), nurse-midwifery (MSN), older adults, pediatrics acute care (DNP, PhD), pediatrics primary care; clinical nurse leader (MSN); gerontologic clinical nurse specialist (Certificate); gerontologic nurse practitioner (Certificate); health care systems leadership (MSN, DNP); nurse-midwifery (Certificate); nursing (PhD), including pediatrics acute care (DNP, PhD); pediatrics acute care (Certificate); pediatrics primary care (Certificate). *Accreditation:* AACN. *Faculty:* 32 full-time (30 women), 47 part-time/ adjunct (all women). *Students:* 93 full-time (88 women), 244 part-time (220 women); includes 31 minority (9 Black or African American, non-Hispanic/Latino; 7 Asian, non-Hispanic/Latino; 8 Hispanic/Latino; 7 Two or more races, non-Hispanic/Latino), 1 international. Average age 30. 282 applicants, 57% accepted, 98 enrolled. In 2011, 76 master's, 8 doctorates, 7 other advanced degrees awarded. Terminal master's awarded for partial completion of doctoral program. *Degree requirements:* For master's, comprehensive exam, thesis or alternative. *Entrance requirements:* For master's, GRE General Test, BSN, Wisconsin RN license, official transcripts from all current and previous colleges/universities except Marquette, three completed recommendation forms, resume, written statement of professional goals; for doctorate, GRE General Test, official transcripts from all current and previous colleges/universities except Marquette, three letters of recommendation, resume, written statement of professional goals, sample of scholarly writing. Additional exam requirements/recommendations for international students: Required—TOEFL (minimum score 530 paper-based; 78 computer-based). *Application deadline:* For fall admission, 2/15 for domestic and international students. Application fee: $50. Electronic applications accepted. *Expenses: Tuition:* Full-time $17,010; part-time $945 per credit hour. Tuition and fees vary according to program. *Financial support:* In 2011–12, 41 students received support, including 1 fellowship with partial tuition reimbursement available (averaging $17,500 per year), 2 research assistantships with full tuition reimbursements available (averaging $13,285 per year), 8 teaching assistantships with full tuition reimbursements available (averaging $13,912 per year); career-related internships or fieldwork, Federal Work-Study, scholarships/grants, health care benefits, tuition waivers (partial), and unspecified assistantships also available. Support available to part-time students. Financial award application deadline: 2/15. *Faculty research:* Psychosocial adjustment to chronic illness, gerontology, reminiscence, health policy: uninsured and access, hospital care delivery systems. *Total annual research expenditures:* $312,575. *Unit head:* Dr. Margaret Callahan, Dean, 414-288-3800, Fax: 414-288-1578. *Application contact:* Karen Nest, Graduate Program Coordinator, 414-288-3810, Fax: 414-288-1578. Web site: http://www.marquette.edu/nursing/academicprograms-graduate.shtml.

MGH Institute of Health Professions, School of Nursing, Boston, MA 02129. Offers advanced practice nursing (MSN); gerontological nursing (MSN); nursing (DNP); pediatric nursing (MSN); psychiatric nursing (MSN); teaching and learning for health care education (Certificate); women's health nursing (MSN). *Accreditation:* AACN; NLN (one or more programs are accredited). *Faculty:* 41 full-time (36 women), 14 part-time/ adjunct (13 women). *Students:* 418 full-time (365 women), 72 part-time (63 women); includes 51 minority (20 Black or African American, non-Hispanic/Latino; 1 American Indian or Alaska Native, non-Hispanic/Latino; 24 Asian, non-Hispanic/Latino; 5 Hispanic/ Latino; 1 Native Hawaiian or other Pacific Islander, non-Hispanic/Latino). Average age 32. 1,041 applicants, 36% accepted, 148 enrolled. In 2011, 85 master's, 12 doctorates, 98 other advanced degrees awarded. *Degree requirements:* For master's, thesis or alternative. *Entrance requirements:* For master's, GRE General Test, bachelor's degree from regionally-accredited college or university. Additional exam requirements/ recommendations for international students: Required—TOEFL (minimum score 550 paper-based; 213 computer-based; 80 iBT). *Application deadline:* For fall admission, 1/ 10 for domestic and international students; for spring admission, 11/1 for domestic and international students. Application fee: $65. Electronic applications accepted. *Expenses: Tuition:* Full-time $12,720; part-time $1060 per credit. *Required fees:* $1725; $430 per semester. One-time fee: $350. *Financial support:* In 2011–12, 75 students received support, including 4 research assistantships (averaging $1,200 per year), 17 teaching assistantships (averaging $1,200 per year); career-related internships or fieldwork, scholarships/grants, traineeships, and unspecified assistantships also available. Support available to part-time students. Financial award application deadline: 4/1; financial award applicants required to submit FAFSA. *Faculty research:* Biobehavioral nursing, HIV/AIDS, gerontological nursing, women's health, vulnerable populations, health systems. *Unit head:* Dr. Laurie Lauzon-Clabo, Dean, 617-643-0605, Fax: 617-726-8022, E-mail: llauzonclabo@mghihp.edu. *Application contact:* Maureen Rika Judd, Director of Admissions, 617-726-6069, Fax: 617-726-8010, E-mail: admissions@ mghihp.edu. Web site: http://www.mghihp.edu/academics/nursing/.

Molloy College, Division of Nursing, Rockville Centre, NY 11571-5002. Offers adult nurse practitioner (Advanced Certificate); clinical nurse specialist: adult health (Advanced Certificate); family nurse practitioner (Advanced Certificate); nurse practitioner psychiatry (Advanced Certificate); nursing (MS); nursing administration (Advanced Certificate); nursing administration with informatics (Advanced Certificate); nursing education (Advanced Certificate); nursing informatics (Advanced Certificate); pediatric nurse practitioner (Advanced Certificate). *Accreditation:* AACN. Part-time and evening/weekend programs available. *Faculty:* 20 full-time (19 women), 12 part-time/ adjunct (11 women). *Students:* 19 full-time (15 women), 483 part-time (452 women); includes 238 minority (132 Black or African American, non-Hispanic/Latino; 61 Asian, non-Hispanic/Latino; 35 Hispanic/Latino; 2 Native Hawaiian or other Pacific Islander, non-Hispanic/Latino; 8 Two or more races, non-Hispanic/Latino), 5 international. Average age 40. 186 applicants, 82% accepted, 110 enrolled. In 2011, 94 master's awarded. *Degree requirements:* For master's, thesis optional. *Entrance requirements:* For master's, 3 letters of reference, BS in nursing, minimum undergraduate GPA of 3.0; for Advanced Certificate, 3 letters of reference, master's degree in nursing. *Application*

deadline: For fall admission, 9/2 priority date for domestic students; for spring admission, 1/20 priority date for domestic students. Applications are processed on a rolling basis. Application fee: $60. *Financial support:* Research assistantships with partial tuition reimbursements, teaching assistantships with partial tuition reimbursements, institutionally sponsored loans, scholarships/grants, and unspecified assistantships available. Support available to part-time students. Financial award application deadline: 4/1; financial award applicants required to submit FAFSA. *Unit head:* Dr. Denise Walsh, Associate Dean, Graduate Nursing, 516-678-5000, Fax: 516-678-9718, E-mail: dwalsh@molloy.edu. *Application contact:* Alina Haitz, Assistant Director of Graduate Admissions, 516-678-5000, Fax: 516-256-2247, E-mail: ahaitz@ molloy.edu. Web site: http://www.molloy.edu/academics/nursing-division.

New York University, College of Nursing, Doctor of Nursing Practice Program, New York, NY 10012-1019. Offers advanced practice nursing (DNP), including adult acute care, adult nurse practitioner/holistic nursing, adult nurse practitioner/palliative care nursing, adult primary care, adult primary care/geriatrics, family, geriatrics, mental health nursing, nurse-midwifery, pediatrics. Part-time and evening/weekend programs available. *Faculty:* 7 full-time (all women). *Students:* 23 part-time (19 women); includes 6 minority (4 Black or African American, non-Hispanic/Latino; 1 Asian, non-Hispanic/ Latino; 1 Hispanic/Latino), 1 international. Average age 46. 20 applicants, 80% accepted, 11 enrolled. In 2011, 8 doctorates awarded. *Degree requirements:* For doctorate, thesis/dissertation. *Entrance requirements:* For doctorate, MS, RN license, interview, NP Certification. Additional exam requirements/recommendations for international students: Required—TOEFL, IELTS. *Application deadline:* For fall admission, 4/1 priority date for domestic students, 4/1 for international students. Applications are processed on a rolling basis. Application fee: $75. Electronic applications accepted. *Financial support:* In 2011–12, 15 students received support. Fellowships with full and partial tuition reimbursements available, institutionally sponsored loans, scholarships/grants, and tuition waivers (partial) available. Support available to part-time students. Financial award application deadline: 2/1; financial award applicants required to submit FAFSA. *Faculty research:* Elderly black diabetics, families and illness, oral systemic connection. *Unit head:* Dr. Jamesetta A. Newland, Director, 212-998-5319, Fax: 212-995-3143, E-mail: jan7@nyu.edu. *Application contact:* Gail Wolfmeyer, Assistant Director, Graduate Student Affairs and Admissions, 212-992-7653, Fax: 212-995-4302, E-mail: gail.wolfmeyer@nyu.edu.

New York University, College of Nursing, Programs in Advanced Practice Nursing, New York, NY 10012-1019. Offers advanced practice nursing: adult acute care (MS, Advanced Certificate); advanced practice nursing: adult nurse practitioner/holistic nurse practitioner (Advanced Certificate); advanced practice nursing: adult nurse practitioner/ palliative care nurse practitioner (Advanced Certificate); advanced practice nursing: adult primary care (MS, Advanced Certificate); advanced practice nursing: family (MS, Advanced Certificate); advanced practice nursing: geriatrics (Advanced Certificate); advanced practice nursing: mental health (MS); advanced practice nursing: mental health nursing (Advanced Certificate); advanced practice nursing: pediatrics (MS, Advanced Certificate); nurse midwifery (MS, Advanced Certificate); nursing administration (MS, Advanced Certificate); nursing education (MS, Advanced Certificate); nursing informatics (MS, Advanced Certificate); MS/MPA; MS/MPH. *Accreditation:* AACN; ACNM/ACME. Part-time programs available. *Faculty:* 23 full-time (all women), 60 part-time/adjunct (47 women). *Students:* 27 full-time (23 women), 552 part-time (514 women); includes 251 minority (91 Black or African American, non-Hispanic/Latino; 115 Asian, non-Hispanic/Latino; 34 Hispanic/Latino; 11 Native Hawaiian or other Pacific Islander, non-Hispanic/Latino), 8 international. Average age 33. 325 applicants, 81% accepted, 179 enrolled. In 2011, 89 master's awarded. *Degree requirements:* For master's, thesis (for some programs). *Entrance requirements:* For master's, BS in nursing, AS in nursing with another BS/BA, interview, RN license, 1 year of clinical experience (3 for nursing education program); for Advanced Certificate, master's degree. Additional exam requirements/recommendations for international students: Required—TOEFL, IELTS. *Application deadline:* For fall admission, 7/1 priority date for domestic students, 7/1 for international students; for spring admission, 12/1 for domestic and international students. Applications are processed on a rolling basis. Application fee: $75. Electronic applications accepted. *Financial support:* In 2011–12, 36 students received support. Career-related internships or fieldwork, institutionally sponsored loans, scholarships/grants, traineeships, and tuition waivers (partial) available. Support available to part-time students. Financial award application deadline: 2/1; financial award applicants required to submit FAFSA. *Faculty research:* Elderly black diabetics, families and illness, oral systemic connection. *Unit head:* Dr. Judith Haber, Associate Dean, 212-998-9020, Fax: 212-995-3143, E-mail: jh33@nyu.edu. *Application contact:* Gail Wolfmeyer, Assistant Director, Graduate Student Affairs and Admissions, 212-992-7653, Fax: 212-995-4302, E-mail: gail.wolfmeyer@nyu.edu.

Northeastern University, Bouvé College of Health Sciences, School of Nursing, Program in Pediatric Nurse Practitioner, Boston, MA 02115-5096. Offers MS, CAGS. Part-time programs available. *Faculty:* 25 full-time, 4 part-time/adjunct. *Students:* 16 full-time, 16 part-time. In 2011, 4 master's awarded. *Entrance requirements:* For master's, GRE General Test. Additional exam requirements/recommendations for international students: Required—TOEFL (minimum score 100 iBT). *Application deadline:* For fall admission, 7/1 for domestic students. Applications are processed on a rolling basis. Application fee: $50. Electronic applications accepted. *Financial support:* Research assistantships, teaching assistantships, scholarships/grants, traineeships, and unspecified assistantships available. *Unit head:* Prof. Michelle Beauchesne, Coordinator, 617-373-3621, E-mail: m.beauchesne@neu.edu. *Application contact:* Margaret Schnabel, Director of Graduate Admissions, 617-373-2708, E-mail: bouvegrad@neu.edu. Web site: http://www.northeastern.edu/bouve/programs/ cpediatricnp.html.

Queen's University at Kingston, School of Graduate Studies and Research, Faculty of Health Sciences, School of Nursing, Kingston, ON K7L 3N6, Canada. Offers health and chronic illness (M Sc); nurse scientist (PhD); primary health care nurse practitioner (Certificate); women's and children's health (M Sc). *Degree requirements:* For master's, thesis. *Entrance requirements:* For master's, RN license. Additional exam requirements/ recommendations for international students: Required—TOEFL. *Faculty research:* Women and children's health, health and chronic illness.

Rocky Mountain University of Health Professions, Program in Pediatric Science, Provo, UT 84606. Offers PhD. *Degree requirements:* For doctorate, thesis/dissertation.

Rush University, College of Nursing, Department of Women's and Children's Health Nursing, Chicago, IL 60612-3832. Offers neonatal nurse practitioner (MSN, Post-Master's Certificate); pediatric acute/chronic care nurse practitioner (MSN); pediatric clinical nurse specialist (MSN); pediatric nurse practitioner (MSN, Post-Master's Certificate); women's and children's health nursing (DNP, PhD). *Accreditation:* AACN. Part-time programs available. Postbaccalaureate distance learning degree programs offered (minimal on-campus study). Terminal master's awarded for partial completion of doctoral program. *Degree requirements:* For master's, capstone project; for doctorate, thesis/dissertation, DNP leadership project. *Entrance requirements:* For master's, GRE General Test (waived if nursing GPA is above 3.0 or cumulative GPA is above 3.25), interview; for doctorate, GRE General Test, interview, course work in statistics (PhD). Additional exam requirements/recommendations for international students: Required—

TOEFL, TWE. Electronic applications accepted. *Faculty research:* Family-centered care, women's health, health outcomes of human milk feeding for VhBW infants.

St. Catherine University, Graduate Programs, Program in Nursing, St. Paul, MN 55105. Offers adult-gerontological nurse practitioner (MA); neonatal nurse practitioner (MA); nurse educator (MA); nursing (DNP); pediatric nurse practitioner (MA). *Accreditation:* NLN. Part-time and evening/weekend programs available. *Degree requirements:* For master's, thesis; for doctorate, portfolio, systems change project. *Entrance requirements:* For master's, GRE General Test, bachelor's degree in nursing, current nursing license, 2 years of recent clinical practice; for doctorate, master's degree in nursing, RN license, advanced nursing position. Additional exam requirements/recommendations for international students: Required—TOEFL (minimum score 600 paper-based; 250 computer-based; 100 iBT). *Expenses: Required fees:* $30 per semester. Tuition and fees vary according to program.

Seton Hall University, College of Nursing, South Orange, NJ 07079-2697. Offers advanced practice in primary health care (MSN, DNP), including adult/gerontological nurse practitioner, pediatric nurse practitioner; entry into practice (MSN); health systems administration (MSN, DNP); nursing (PhD); nursing case management (MSN); nursing education (MA); school nurse (MSN); MSN/MA. *Accreditation:* AACN. Part-time programs available. Postbaccalaureate distance learning degree programs offered (minimal on-campus study). *Faculty:* 10 full-time (all women), 3 part-time/adjunct (1 woman). *Students:* 12 full-time (11 women), 217 part-time (197 women); includes 38 minority (15 Black or African American, non-Hispanic/Latino; 1 American Indian or Alaska Native, non-Hispanic/Latino; 12 Asian, non-Hispanic/Latino; 10 Hispanic/Latino). 180 applicants, 51% accepted, 82 enrolled. *Degree requirements:* For master's, research project; for doctorate, dissertation or scholarly project. *Entrance requirements:* For doctorate, GRE (waived for students with GPA of 3.5 or higher). Additional exam requirements/recommendations for international students: Required—TOEFL. *Application deadline:* For fall admission, 4/15 priority date for domestic students. Applications are processed on a rolling basis. Electronic applications accepted. *Expenses: Tuition:* Part-time $1033 per credit hour. *Required fees:* $85 per semester. *Financial support:* Institutionally sponsored loans, scholarships/grants, traineeships, tuition waivers (partial), and unspecified assistantships available. Support available to part-time students. Financial award applicants required to submit FAFSA. *Faculty research:* Parent/child, adult, and gerontological nursing; breast cancer; families of children with HIV; parish nursing. *Unit head:* Dr. Phyllis Shanley Hansell, Dean, 973-761-9014, E-mail: phyllis.hansell@shu.edu. *Application contact:* Kristyn Kent Wuillermin, Director of Strategic Alliances, Marketing and Enrollment, 973-761-9291, Fax: 973-761-9607, E-mail: kristyn.kent@shu.edu.

Spalding University, Graduate Studies, College of Health and Natural Sciences, School of Nursing, Louisville, KY 40203-2188. Offers adult nurse practitioner (MSN); family nurse practitioner (MSN); leadership in nursing and healthcare (MSN); pediatric nurse practitioner (MSN). *Accreditation:* AACN. Part-time and evening/weekend programs available. *Faculty:* 6 full-time (all women), 5 part-time/adjunct (all women). *Students:* 90 full-time (82 women), 24 part-time (all women); includes 21 minority (16 Black or African American, non-Hispanic/Latino; 3 Asian, non-Hispanic/Latino; 1 Hispanic/Latino; 1 Native Hawaiian or other Pacific Islander, non-Hispanic/Latino). Average age 36. 85 applicants, 24% accepted, 15 enrolled. In 2011, 23 master's awarded. *Degree requirements:* For master's, comprehensive exam (for some programs), thesis. *Entrance requirements:* For master's, GRE General Test, BSN or bachelor's degree and RN licensure. Additional exam requirements/recommendations for international students: Required—TOEFL (minimum score 535 paper-based; 203 computer-based). *Application deadline:* For fall admission, 3/1 priority date for domestic students. Applications are processed on a rolling basis. Application fee: $30. *Expenses: Tuition:* Full-time $12,438. Tuition and fees vary according to course load, degree level and program. *Financial support:* In 2011–12, 21 students received support, including 1 research assistantship with partial tuition reimbursement available (averaging $4,260 per year); career-related internships or fieldwork, scholarships/grants, and traineeships also available. Support available to part-time students. Financial award application deadline: 3/15; financial award applicants required to submit FAFSA. *Faculty research:* Nurse educational administration, gerontology, bioterrorism, healthcare ethics, leadership. *Unit head:* Dr. Paula Travis, Chair, 502-873-4298, E-mail: clewis@spalding.edu. *Application contact:* Dr. Pam King, 502-873-4292, E-mail: pking@spalding.edu. Web site: http://www.spalding.edu/nursing/.

Stony Brook University, State University of New York, Stony Brook University Medical Center, Health Sciences Center, School of Nursing, Program in Child Health Nursing, Stony Brook, NY 11794. Offers child health nurse practitioner (Certificate); child health nursing (MS). *Accreditation:* AACN. Postbaccalaureate distance learning degree programs offered. *Degree requirements:* For master's, thesis. *Entrance requirements:* For master's, BSN, minimum GPA of 3.0, course work in statistics.

Texas Christian University, Harris College of Nursing and Health Sciences, Program in Nursing, Fort Worth, TX 76129-0002. Offers advanced practice registered nurse (DNP); clinical nurse leader (MSN); clinical nurse specialist: adult/gerontology nursing (MSN); clinical nurse specialist: pediatric nursing (MSN); nursing administration (DNP); nursing education (MSN). *Accreditation:* AACN; AANA/CANAEP (one or more programs are accredited). Part-time programs available. Postbaccalaureate distance learning degree programs offered (no on-campus study). *Faculty:* 18 full-time (16 women), 2 part-time/adjunct (both women). *Students:* 2 full-time (both women), 105 part-time (96 women); includes 16 minority (8 Black or African American, non-Hispanic/Latino; 4 Asian, non-Hispanic/Latino; 2 Hispanic/Latino; 1 Native Hawaiian or other Pacific Islander, non-Hispanic/Latino; 1 Two or more races, non-Hispanic/Latino), 1 international. Average age 44. 58 applicants, 93% accepted, 46 enrolled. In 2011, 11 master's, 21 doctorates awarded. *Degree requirements:* For master's and doctorate, professional project. *Entrance requirements:* For master's, GRE General Test or MAT, 3 letters of reference, 2 years preferred full-time experience as registered nurse, current nursing license, minimum GPA of 3.0; for doctorate, APRN recognition (national certification), minimum GPA of 3.0, 3 professional references, essay, 2 years post-master's experience (preferrred). Additional exam requirements/recommendations for international students: Required—TOEFL, Spoken English Test for DNP. *Expenses: Tuition:* Full-time $20,250; part-time $1125 per credit hour. Part-time tuition and fees vary according to course load and program. *Financial support:* In 2011–12, teaching assistantships (averaging $5,000 per year) were awarded; tuition waivers also available. *Unit head:* Dr. Pamela Frable, Associate Dean and Director of Nursing, 817-257-5840, E-mail: p.frable@tcu.edu. *Application contact:* Dr. Kathy Baker, Director of Graduate Studies and Director of DNP Program, 817-257-6726, E-mail: kathy.baker@tcu.edu. Web site: http://www.nursing.tcu.edu/graduate.asp.

Texas Tech University Health Sciences Center, School of Nursing, Lubbock, TX 79430. Offers acute care nurse practitioner (MSN, Certificate); administration (MSN); advanced practice (DNP); education (MSN); executive leadership (DNP); family nurse practitioner (MSN, Certificate); geriatric nurse practitioner (MSN, Certificate); pediatric nurse practitioner (MSN, Certificate). *Accreditation:* AACN. Part-time programs available. Postbaccalaureate distance learning degree programs offered (minimal on-campus study). *Degree requirements:* For master's, thesis optional. *Entrance requirements:* For master's, minimum GPA of 3.0, 3 letters of reference, BSN, RN license; for Certificate, minimum GPA of 3.0, 3 letters of reference, RN license. Additional exam requirements/recommendations for international students: Required—TOEFL (minimum score 550 paper-based; 213 computer-based). *Faculty research:* Diabetes/obesity, nurse competency, disease management, intervention and measurements, health disparities.

Texas Woman's University, Graduate School, College of Nursing, Denton, TX 76201. Offers acute care nurse practitioner (MS); adult health clinical nurse specialist (MS); adult health nurse practitioner (MS); child health clinical nurse specialist (MS); clinical nurse leader (MS); family nurse practitioner (MS); health systems management (MS); nursing education (MS); nursing practice (DNP); nursing science (PhD); pediatric nurse practitioner (MS); women's health clinical nurse specialist (MS); women's health nurse practitioner (MS). *Accreditation:* AACN. Part-time programs available. Postbaccalaureate distance learning degree programs offered. *Faculty:* 70 full-time (69 women), 7 part-time/adjunct (all women). *Students:* 87 full-time (78 women), 870 part-time (815 women); includes 489 minority (235 Black or African American, non-Hispanic/Latino; 5 American Indian or Alaska Native, non-Hispanic/Latino; 169 Asian, non-Hispanic/Latino; 78 Hispanic/Latino; 2 Native Hawaiian or other Pacific Islander, non-Hispanic/Latino), 19 international. Average age 38. 368 applicants, 71% accepted, 205 enrolled. In 2011, 147 master's, 21 doctorates awarded. *Degree requirements:* For master's, comprehensive exam, thesis or alternative; for doctorate, comprehensive exam, thesis/dissertation. *Entrance requirements:* For master's, GRE or MAT, minimum GPA of 3.0 on last 60 hours in undergraduate nursing degree and overall, RN license, BS in nursing, basic statistics course; for doctorate, GRE (preferred minimum score 153 [500 old version] Verbal, 144 [500 old version] Quantitative, 4 Analytical), MS in nursing, minimum preferred GPA of 3.5, RN license, statistics, 2 letters of reference, curriculum vitae, graduate nursing-theory course, graduate research course, statement of professional goals and research interests. Additional exam requirements/recommendations for international students: Required—TOEFL (minimum score 550 paper-based; 213 computer-based; 79 iBT). *Application deadline:* For fall admission, 5/1 priority date for domestic students, 3/1 for international students; for spring admission, 9/15 priority date for domestic students, 7/1 for international students. Applications are processed on a rolling basis. Application fee: $50 ($75 for international students). Electronic applications accepted. *Expenses:* Tuition, state resident: full-time $3834; part-time $213 per credit hour. Tuition, nonresident: full-time $9468; part-time $526 per credit hour. *Required fees:* $213 per credit hour. Tuition and fees vary according to course load. *Financial support:* In 2011–12, 149 students received support, including 10 research assistantships (averaging $12,942 per year), 1 teaching assistantship (averaging $12,942 per year); career-related internships or fieldwork, Federal Work-Study, institutionally sponsored loans, scholarships/grants, traineeships, health care benefits, and unspecified assistantships also available. Support available to part-time students. Financial award application deadline: 3/1; financial award applicants required to submit FAFSA. *Faculty research:* Screening, prevention, and treatment for intimate partner violence; needs of adolescents during childbirth intervention; a network analysis decision tool for nurse managers (Social Network Analysis); support for adolescents with implantable cardioverter defibrillators; informatics: nurse staffing, safety, quality, and financial data as they relate to patient care outcomes; prevention and treatment of obesity; improving infant outcomes related to premature birth. *Total annual research expenditures:* $462,088. *Unit head:* Dr. Patricia Holden-Huchton, Interim Dean, 940-898-2401, Fax: 940-898-2437, E-mail: nursing@twu.edu. *Application contact:* Dr. Samuel Wheeler, Assistant Director of Admissions, 940-898-3188, Fax: 940-898-3081, E-mail: wheelersr@twu.edu. Web site: http://www.twu.edu/nursing/.

University of Cincinnati, Graduate School, College of Nursing, Cincinnati, OH 45221-0038. Offers clinical nurse specialist (MSN), including adult health, community health, neonatal, nursing administration, occupational health, pediatric health, psychiatric nursing, women's health; nurse anesthesia (MSN); nurse midwifery (MSN); nurse practitioner (MSN), including acute care, ambulatory care, family, family/psychiatric, women's health; nursing (PhD); MBA/MSN. *Accreditation:* AACN; AANA/CANAEP (one or more programs are accredited); ACNM/ACME. Part-time programs available. Postbaccalaureate distance learning degree programs offered (no on-campus study). Terminal master's awarded for partial completion of doctoral program. *Degree requirements:* For master's, thesis or alternative; for doctorate, comprehensive exam, thesis/dissertation. *Entrance requirements:* For master's and doctorate, GRE General Test. Additional exam requirements/recommendations for international students: Required—TOEFL (minimum score 520 paper-based; 190 computer-based). Electronic applications accepted. *Faculty research:* Substance abuse, injury and violence, symptom management.

University of Colorado Denver, College of Nursing, Aurora, CO 80045. Offers adult clinical nurse specialist (MS); adult nurse practitioner (MS); family nurse practitioner (MS); family psychiatric mental health nurse practitioner (MS); health care informatics (MS); nurse-midwifery (MS); nursing (DNP, PhD); nursing leadership and health care systems (MS); pediatric nurse practitioner (MS); pediatric nursing leadership (MS); special studies (MS); women's health care (MS); MS/PhD. *Accreditation:* ACNM/ACME (one or more programs are accredited); NLN (one or more programs are accredited). Part-time and evening/weekend programs available. Postbaccalaureate distance learning degree programs offered (minimal on-campus study). *Faculty:* 69 full-time (65 women), 68 part-time/adjunct (64 women). *Students:* 308 full-time (288 women), 134 part-time (118 women); includes 59 minority (11 Black or African American, non-Hispanic/Latino; 8 American Indian or Alaska Native, non-Hispanic/Latino; 10 Asian, non-Hispanic/Latino; 27 Hispanic/Latino; 3 Two or more races, non-Hispanic/Latino), 8 international. Average age 39. 298 applicants, 46% accepted, 110 enrolled. In 2011, 72 master's, 19 doctorates awarded. Terminal master's awarded for partial completion of doctoral program. *Degree requirements:* For master's, thesis optional; for doctorate, comprehensive exam, thesis/dissertation, 42 credits of coursework, 30 credits of dissertation. *Entrance requirements:* For master's, GRE if cumulative undergraduate GPA is less than 3.0, undergraduate nursing degree from NLNAC- or CCNE-accredited school or university; completion of research and statistics courses with minimum grade of C; copy of current and unencumbered nursing license; for doctorate, GRE, bachelor's and/or master's degrees in nursing from NLN- or CCNE-accredited institution; portfolio; minimum undergraduate GPA of 3.0, graduate 3.5; graduate-level intermediate statistics and master's-level nursing theory courses with minimum B grade; interview. Additional exam requirements/recommendations for international students: Required—TOEFL (minimum score 560 paper-based; 220 computer-based; 83 iBT). *Application deadline:* For fall admission, 4/1 for domestic students; for spring admission, 9/1 for domestic students. Application fee: $65. Electronic applications accepted. *Expenses:* Contact institution. *Financial support:* In 2011–12, 40 students received support. Fellowships, research assistantships, teaching assistantships, Federal Work-Study, scholarships/grants, and unspecified assistantships available. Support available to part-time students. Financial award application deadline: 4/1; financial award applicants required to submit FAFSA. *Faculty research:* Biological and behavioral phenomena in pregnancy and postpartum; patterns of glycemia during the insulin resistance of pregnancy; obesity, gestational diabetes, and relationship to neonatal adiposity; men's awareness and knowledge of male breast cancer; cognitive-behavioral therapy for chronic insomnia after breast cancer treatment; massage therapy for the treatment of tension-type headaches. *Total annual research expenditures:* $5.2 million. *Unit head:* Dr. Patricia

Moritz, Dean, 303-724-1679, E-mail: pat.moritz@ucdenver.edu. *Application contact:* Judy Campbell, Graduate Programs Coordinator, 303-724-8503, E-mail: judy.campbell@ucdenver.edu. Web site: http://www.ucdenver.edu/academics/colleges/nursing/Pages/default.aspx.

University of Colorado Denver, School of Medicine, Physician Assistant Program, Aurora, CO 80045. Offers child health associate (MPAS), including global health, leadership, education, advocacy, development, and scholarship, rural health, urban/underserved populations. *Accreditation:* ARC-PA. *Students:* 124 full-time (107 women), 2 part-time (both women); includes 12 minority (1 American Indian or Alaska Native, non-Hispanic/Latino; 6 Asian, non-Hispanic/Latino; 5 Hispanic/Latino). Average age 26. 274 applicants, 17% accepted, 44 enrolled. In 2011, 37 master's awarded. *Degree requirements:* For master's, comprehensive exam, successful completion of all coursework and rotations. *Entrance requirements:* For master's, GRE General Test, minimum GPA of 2.8, 3 letters of recommendation, prerequisite courses in chemistry, biology, general genetics, psychology and statistics, interviews for the finalists. Additional exam requirements/recommendations for international students: Required—TOEFL (minimum score 550 paper-based; 213 computer-based). *Application deadline:* For fall admission, 10/1 for domestic students. Application fee: $170. Electronic applications accepted. *Expenses:* Contact institution. *Financial support:* Career-related internships or fieldwork and scholarships/grants available. Financial award application deadline: 3/15; financial award applicants required to submit FAFSA. *Faculty research:* Clinical genetics and genetic counseling, evidence-based medicine, pediatric allergy and asthma, childhood diabetes, standardized patient assessment. *Unit head:* Jonathan Bowser, Interim Program Director, 303-724-1349, E-mail: jonathan.bowser@ucdenver.edu. *Application contact:* Kay Denler, Director of Admissions, 303-724-1340, E-mail: kay.denler@ucdenver.edu. Web site: http://www.ucdenver.edu/academics/colleges/medicalschool/education/degree_programs/PAProgram/Pages/Home.aspx.

University of Delaware, College of Health Sciences, School of Nursing, Newark, DE 19716. Offers adult nurse practitioner (MSN, PMC); cardiopulmonary clinical nurse specialist (MSN, PMC); cardiopulmonary clinical nurse specialist/adult nurse practitioner (MSN, PMC); family nurse practitioner (MSN, PMC); gerontology clinical nurse specialist (MSN, PMC); gerontology clinical nurse specialist geriatric nurse practitioner (PMC); gerontology clinical nurse specialist/geriatric nurse practitioner (MSN); health services administration (MSN, PMC); nursing of children clinical nurse specialist (MSN, PMC); nursing of children clinical nurse specialist/pediatric nurse practitioner (MSN, PMC); oncology/immune deficiency clinical nurse specialist (MSN, PMC); oncology/immune deficiency clinical nurse specialist/adult nurse practitioner (MSN, PMC); perinatal/women's health clinical nurse specialist (MSN, PMC); perinatal/women's health clinical nurse specialist/women's health nurse practitioner (MSN, PMC); psychiatric nursing clinical nurse specialist (MSN, PMC). *Accreditation:* AACN; NLN (one or more programs are accredited). Part-time and evening/weekend programs available. Postbaccalaureate distance learning degree programs offered (minimal on-campus study). *Degree requirements:* For master's, thesis optional. *Entrance requirements:* For master's, BSN, interview, RN license. Electronic applications accepted. *Faculty research:* Marriage and chronic illness, health promotion, congestive heart failure patient outcomes, school nursing, diabetes in children, culture, health disparities, cardiovascular, prison nursing, oncology, public policy, child obesity, smoking and teen pregnancy, blood pressure measurements, men's health.

University of Illinois at Chicago, Graduate College, College of Nursing, Program in Nursing, Chicago, IL 60607-7128. Offers acute care clinical nurse specialist (MS); acute care nurse practitioner (MS); administrative studies in nursing (MS); adult nurse practitioner (MS); adult/geriatric nurse practitioner (MS); advanced community health nurse specialist (MS); family nurse practitioner (MS); geriatric clinical nurse specialist (MS); geriatric nurse practitioner (MS); mental health clinical nurse specialist (MS); mental health nurse practitioner (MS); nurse midwifery (MS); occupational health/advanced community health nurse specialist (MS); occupational health/family nurse practitioner (MS); pediatric clinical nurse specialist (MS); pediatric nurse practitioner (MS); perinatal clinical nurse specialist (MS); school/advanced community health nurse specialist (MS); school/family nurse practitioner (MS); women's health nurse practitioner (MS). *Accreditation:* AACN. Part-time programs available. *Degree requirements:* For master's, thesis or alternative. *Entrance requirements:* For master's, GRE General Test, minimum GPA of 2.75. Additional exam requirements/recommendations for international students: Required—TOEFL. Electronic applications accepted.

University of Maryland, Baltimore, Graduate School, School of Nursing, Master's Program in Nursing, Baltimore, MD 21201. Offers community health nursing (MS); gerontological nursing (MS); maternal-child nursing (MS); medical-surgical nursing (MS); nurse-midwifery education (MS); nursing administration (MS); nursing education (MS); nursing health policy (MS); primary care nursing (MS); psychiatric nursing (MS); MS/MBA. MS/MBA offered jointly with University of Baltimore. *Accreditation:* AACN; AANA/CANAEP; NLN (one or more programs are accredited). Part-time programs available. *Students:* 370 full-time (314 women), 480 part-time (441 women); includes 308 minority (176 Black or African American, non-Hispanic/Latino; 2 American Indian or Alaska Native, non-Hispanic/Latino; 70 Asian, non-Hispanic/Latino; 33 Hispanic/Latino; 27 Two or more races, non-Hispanic/Latino), 9 international. Average age 35. 990 applicants, 30% accepted, 204 enrolled. In 2011, 301 master's awarded. *Degree requirements:* For master's, comprehensive exam (for some programs), thesis or alternative. *Entrance requirements:* For master's, minimum GPA of 2.75, course work in statistics, BS in nursing. Additional exam requirements/recommendations for international students: Required—TOEFL (minimum score 550 paper-based; 80 iBT) or IELTS (minimum score 7). *Application deadline:* For fall admission, 2/1 for domestic students, 1/15 for international students. Application fee: $50. Electronic applications accepted. *Financial support:* Fellowships, research assistantships, teaching assistantships, career-related internships or fieldwork, and traineeships available. Support available to part-time students. Financial award application deadline: 2/15; financial award applicants required to submit FAFSA. *Unit head:* Dr. Jane Kapustin, Assistant Dean, 410-706-6741, Fax: 410-706-4231. *Application contact:* Marjorie Fass, Admissions Director, 410-706-0501, Fax: 410-706-7238.

University of Michigan, Horace H. Rackham School of Graduate Studies, School of Nursing, Division of Health Promotion and Risk Reduction, Program in Parent-Child Nursing, Ann Arbor, MI 48109. Offers infant, child, adolescent health nurse practitioner (MS); nurse midwifery (MS, Post Master's Certificate). *Accreditation:* AACN. Part-time programs available. Postbaccalaureate distance learning degree programs offered (minimal on-campus study). *Degree requirements:* For master's, thesis. *Entrance requirements:* For master's, GRE General Test (if cumulative BSN GPA less than 3.25), licensure, minimum GPA of 3.0 in BSN program. Additional exam requirements/recommendations for international students: Required—TOEFL (minimum score 560 paper-based; 220 computer-based).

University of Minnesota, Twin Cities Campus, Graduate School, School of Nursing, Children with Special Health Care Needs Program, Minneapolis, MN 55455-0213. Offers MS. *Entrance requirements:* Additional exam requirements/recommendations for international students: Required—TOEFL (minimum score 586 paper-based; 240 computer-based).

University of Minnesota, Twin Cities Campus, Graduate School, School of Nursing, Pediatric Clinical Nurse Specialist Program, Minneapolis, MN 55455-0213. Offers MS. *Accreditation:* AACN. Part-time programs available. *Degree requirements:* For master's, final oral exam, project or thesis.

University of Minnesota, Twin Cities Campus, Graduate School, School of Nursing, Pediatric Nurse Practitioner Program, Minneapolis, MN 55455-0213. Offers MS. *Accreditation:* AACN. *Degree requirements:* For master's, final oral exam, project or thesis.

University of Minnesota, Twin Cities Campus, Graduate School, School of Nursing, Program in Adolescent Nursing, Minneapolis, MN 55455-0213. Offers MS. *Accreditation:* AACN. Part-time programs available. *Degree requirements:* For master's, final oral exam, project or thesis. *Entrance requirements:* Additional exam requirements/recommendations for international students: Required—TOEFL (minimum score 586 paper-based; 240 computer-based).

University of Missouri–Kansas City, School of Nursing, Kansas City, MO 64110-2499. Offers adult clinical nurse specialist (MSN), including adult nurse practitioner, women's health nurse practitioner; family nurse practitioner (MSN); neonatal nurse practitioner (MSN); nurse educator (MSN); nurse executive (MSN); nursing (PhD); nursing practice (DNP); pediatric nurse practitioner (MSN). *Accreditation:* AACN. Part-time programs available. Postbaccalaureate distance learning degree programs offered (minimal on-campus study). *Faculty:* 40 full-time (35 women), 57 part-time/adjunct (52 women). *Students:* 51 full-time (48 women), 381 part-time (352 women); includes 41 minority (22 Black or African American, non-Hispanic/Latino; 7 Asian, non-Hispanic/Latino; 12 Hispanic/Latino). Average age 37. 195 applicants, 49% accepted, 90 enrolled. In 2011, 78 master's, 19 doctorates awarded. *Degree requirements:* For master's, thesis or alternative. *Entrance requirements:* For master's, minimum undergraduate GPA of 3.2; for doctorate, GRE, 3 letters of reference, interview by invitation. Additional exam requirements/recommendations for international students: Required—TOEFL (minimum score 550 paper-based; 213 computer-based; 80 iBT). *Application deadline:* For fall admission, 2/1 priority date for domestic students, 2/1 for international students; for spring admission, 9/1 priority date for domestic students, 9/1 for international students. Application fee: $45 ($50 for international students). *Expenses:* Tuition, state resident: full-time $5798; part-time $322.10 per credit hour. Tuition, nonresident: full-time $14,969; part-time $831.60 per credit hour. *Required fees:* $93.51 per credit hour. *Financial support:* In 2011–12, 25 teaching assistantships with partial tuition reimbursements (averaging $6,927 per year) were awarded; fellowships, research assistantships, career-related internships or fieldwork, Federal Work-Study, institutionally sponsored loans, and tuition waivers (full and partial) also available. Support available to part-time students. Financial award application deadline: 3/1; financial award applicants required to submit FAFSA. *Faculty research:* Geriatrics/gerontology, children's pain, neonatology, Alzheimer's care, cancer caregivers. *Unit head:* Dr. Lora Lacey-Haun, Dean, 816-235-1700, Fax: 816-235-1701, E-mail: lacey-haunc@umkc.edu. *Application contact:* Leah Wilder, Coordinator for Admissions and Recruitment, 816-235-5768, Fax: 816-235-1701, E-mail: wilderl@umkc.edu. Web site: http://nursing.umkc.edu/.

University of Missouri–St. Louis, College of Nursing, St. Louis, MO 63121. Offers adult nurse practitioner (DNP, Post Master's Certificate); clinical nurse specialist (DNP); family mental health nurse practitioner (DNP); family nurse practitioner (MSN, DNP, Post Master's Certificate); neonatal nurse practitioner (MSN); nurse educator (MSN); nurse leader (MSN); nurse practitioner (Post Master's Certificate); nursing (PhD); pediatric clinical nurse specialist (DNP); pediatric nurse practitioner (MSN, DNP, Post Master's Certificate); women's health nurse practitioner (MSN, Post Master's Certificate). *Accreditation:* AACN. Part-time programs available. *Faculty:* 12 full-time (11 women), 14 part-time/adjunct (all women). *Students:* 240 part-time (226 women); includes 30 minority (26 Black or African American, non-Hispanic/Latino; 1 Asian, non-Hispanic/Latino; 2 Hispanic/Latino; 1 Two or more races, non-Hispanic/Latino). Average age 37. 228 applicants, 28% accepted, 53 enrolled. In 2011, 66 master's, 2 doctorates, 2 other advanced degrees awarded. *Degree requirements:* For doctorate, comprehensive exam, thesis/dissertation; for Post Master's Certificate, thesis. *Entrance requirements:* For master's, 2 recommendation letters; minimum GPA of 3.0; BSN; nursing licensure; statement of purpose; course in differential/inferential statistics; for doctorate, GRE, 2 letters of recommendation, MSN, minimum GPA of 3.2, course in differential/inferential statistics; for Post Master's Certificate, 2 recommendation letters; MSN; advanced practice certificate; minimum GPA of 3.0; essay. Additional exam requirements/recommendations for international students: Required—TOEFL (minimum score 550 paper-based; 213 computer-based). *Application deadline:* For fall admission, 2/15 for domestic and international students. Application fee: $35 ($40 for international students). Electronic applications accepted. *Expenses:* Tuition, state resident: full-time $6273; part-time $3866 per year. Tuition, nonresident: full-time $14,969; part-time $9980 per year. *Required fees:* $315 per year. *Financial support:* In 2011–12, 3 research assistantships with full and partial tuition reimbursements (averaging $12,339 per year) were awarded. Financial award application deadline: 4/1; financial award applicants required to submit FAFSA. *Faculty research:* Health promotion and restoration, family disruption, violence, abuse, battered women, health survey methods. *Unit head:* Dr. Nancy Magnuson, Director, 314-516-6066. *Application contact:* 314-516-5458, Fax: 314-516-6996, E-mail: gradadm@umsl.edu. Web site: http://www.umsl.edu/divisions/nursing/.

University of Nevada, Las Vegas, Graduate College, School of Nursing, Las Vegas, NV 89154-3018. Offers family nurse practitioner (Advanced Certificate); nursing (MS, DNP, PhD); nursing education (Advanced Certificate); pediatric nurse practitioner (Post-Master's Certificate). *Accreditation:* AACN. Part-time programs available. Postbaccalaureate distance learning degree programs offered (minimal on-campus study). *Faculty:* 17 full-time (all women), 22 part-time/adjunct (6 women). *Students:* 49 full-time (46 women), 82 part-time (73 women); includes 28 minority (7 Black or African American, non-Hispanic/Latino; 1 American Indian or Alaska Native, non-Hispanic/Latino; 8 Asian, non-Hispanic/Latino; 5 Hispanic/Latino; 1 Native Hawaiian or other Pacific Islander, non-Hispanic/Latino; 6 Two or more races, non-Hispanic/Latino), 3 international. Average age 41. 125 applicants, 43% accepted, 40 enrolled. In 2011, 29 master's, 8 doctorates, 2 other advanced degrees awarded. *Entrance requirements:* For doctorate, GRE General Test. Additional exam requirements/recommendations for international students: Recommended—TOEFL (minimum score 550 paper-based; 213 computer-based; 80 iBT), IELTS (minimum score 7). *Application deadline:* For fall admission, 2/15 priority date for domestic students, 5/1 for international students; for spring admission, 10/1 for international students. Applications are processed on a rolling basis. Application fee: $60 ($95 for international students). Electronic applications accepted. *Financial support:* In 2011–12, 3 students received support, including 3 teaching assistantships with partial tuition reimbursements available (averaging $9,334 per year); institutionally sponsored loans, scholarships/grants, health care benefits, and unspecified assistantships also available. Financial award application deadline: 3/1. *Faculty research:* Physiological stress reactions, leukocyte response and skeletal muscle injury, depression in lay caregivers, incivility in nursing practice, work-related injuries in healthcare and construction workers. *Total annual research expenditures:* $1.7 million. *Unit head:* Dr. Carolyn Yucha, Interim Dean, 702-895-3906, Fax: 702-895-

5050, E-mail: carolyn.yucha@unlv.edu. *Application contact:* Graduate College Admissions Evaluator, 702-895-3320, Fax: 702-895-4180, E-mail: gradcollege@unlv.edu. Web site: http://nursing.unlv.edu/.

The University of North Carolina at Chapel Hill, School of Nursing, Chapel Hill, NC 27599-7460. Offers nursing (MSN, PhD, PMC), including adult nurse practitioner (MSN, PMC), children's health advanced practice (MSN, PMC), family nurse practitioner (MSN, PMC), health care systems (MSN, PMC), psychiatric/mental health nursing (MSN, PMC), women's health nursing (MSN, PMC). *Accreditation:* AACN; NLN (one or more programs are accredited). Part-time programs available. *Degree requirements:* For master's, comprehensive exam, thesis; for doctorate, thesis/dissertation, 3 exams. *Entrance requirements:* For master's and doctorate, GRE General Test. *Faculty research:* Chronic illness, parenting, cardiovascular health in children, elderly, HIV-AIDS.

University of Pennsylvania, School of Nursing, Pediatric Acute/Chronic Care Nurse Practitioner Program, Philadelphia, PA 19104. Offers MSN. *Accreditation:* AACN. Part-time programs available. Postbaccalaureate distance learning degree programs offered. *Students:* 7 full-time (all women), 20 part-time (all women); includes 5 minority (2 Asian, non-Hispanic/Latino; 2 Hispanic/Latino; 1 Two or more races, non-Hispanic/Latino), 1 international. 42 applicants, 60% accepted, 25 enrolled. In 2011, 12 degrees awarded. *Entrance requirements:* For master's, GRE General Test, 1 year of clinical course work, BSN, minimum GPA of 3.0, previous course work in statistics. Additional exam requirements/recommendations for international students: Required—TOEFL. *Application deadline:* For fall admission, 2/15 priority date for domestic students. Applications are processed on a rolling basis. Application fee: $70. *Expenses:* Contact institution. *Financial support:* Research assistantships, teaching assistantships, career-related internships or fieldwork, and institutionally sponsored loans available. Support available to part-time students. Financial award application deadline: 4/1. *Faculty research:* Hispanic health, bereavement, pediatric AIDS, chronically ill children and their families. *Unit head:* Assistant Dean of Admissions and Financial Aid, 866-867-6877, Fax: 215-573-8439, E-mail: admissions@nursing.upenn.edu. *Application contact:* Terri Lipman, Program Director, 215-898-4271, E-mail: lipman@nursing.upenn.edu. Web site: http://www.nursing.upenn.edu/academic_programs/grad/masters/program_detail.asp?prid-16.

University of Pennsylvania, School of Nursing, Pediatric Critical Care Nurse Practitioner Program, Philadelphia, PA 19104. Offers MSN. *Accreditation:* AACN. *Students:* 8 full-time (all women), 4 part-time (all women); includes 1 minority (Hispanic/Latino), 1 international. 23 applicants, 48% accepted, 11 enrolled. In 2011, 13 degrees awarded. *Entrance requirements:* For master's, GRE General Test, BSN, minimum GPA of 3.0, previous course work in statistics, 1 year of clinical course work. Additional exam requirements/recommendations for international students: Required—TOEFL. *Application deadline:* For fall admission, 2/15 priority date for domestic students. Applications are processed on a rolling basis. Application fee: $70. *Expenses:* Contact institution. *Financial support:* Application deadline: 4/1. *Unit head:* Assistant Dean of Admissions and Financial Aid, 866-867-6877, Fax: 215-573-8439, E-mail: admissions@nursing.upenn.edu. *Application contact:* Judy Verger, 215-898-4271, E-mail: jtv@nursing.upenn.edu. Web site: http://www.nursing.upenn.edu/peds/.

University of Pennsylvania, School of Nursing, Pediatric Nurse Practitioner Program, Philadelphia, PA 19104. Offers MSN. *Accreditation:* AACN. Part-time programs available. *Students:* 8 full-time (all women), 21 part-time (all women); includes 5 minority (3 Black or African American, non-Hispanic/Latino; 1 Asian, non-Hispanic/Latino; 1 Two or more races, non-Hispanic/Latino). 33 applicants, 64% accepted, 20 enrolled. In 2011, 14 degrees awarded. *Entrance requirements:* For master's, GRE General Test, 1 year of clinical experience in area of interest, BSN, minimum GPA of 3.0, previous course work in statistics. Additional exam requirements/recommendations for international students: Required—TOEFL. *Application deadline:* For fall admission, 2/15 priority date for domestic students. Applications are processed on a rolling basis. Application fee: $70. *Expenses:* Contact institution. *Financial support:* Research assistantships, teaching assistantships, career-related internships or fieldwork, Federal Work-Study, and institutionally sponsored loans available. Support available to part-time students. Financial award application deadline: 4/1. *Faculty research:* Adolescent behavior change, prevention of teenage pregnancy, community schools. *Total annual research expenditures:* $500,000. *Unit head:* Assistant Dean of Admissions and Financial Aid, 866-867-6877, Fax: 215-573-8439, E-mail: admissions@nursing.upenn.edu. *Application contact:* Ann O'Sullivan, 215-898-4272, E-mail: osull@nursing.upenn.edu. Web site: http://www.nursing.upenn.edu/pnp.

University of Pittsburgh, School of Nursing, Nurse Practitioner Program, Pittsburgh, PA 15261. Offers acute care nurse practitioner (MSN, DNP); adult nurse practitioner (MSN, DNP); family nurse practitioner (MSN, DNP); neonatal (MSN, DNP); nursing practice (DNP); pediatric nurse practitioner (MSN, DNP); psychiatric primary care nurse practitioner (MSN, DNP). *Accreditation:* AACN. Part-time programs available. *Students:* 46 full-time (44 women), 135 part-time (123 women); includes 13 minority (6 Black or African American, non-Hispanic/Latino; 1 American Indian or Alaska Native, non-Hispanic/Latino; 6 Asian, non-Hispanic/Latino). Average age 32. 126 applicants, 71% accepted, 70 enrolled. In 2011, 24 master's, 4 doctorates awarded. *Degree requirements:* For master's, comprehensive exam, thesis optional. *Entrance requirements:* For master's, GRE General Test or MAT, BSN, RN license, letters of recommendation, resume, course work in statistics, 1-3 years of nursing experience; for doctorate, GRE General Test, BSN, RN license, minimum GPA of 3.5, 3 letters of recommendation. Additional exam requirements/recommendations for international students: Required—TOEFL (minimum score 550 paper-based; 213 computer-based; 80 iBT). *Application deadline:* Applications are processed on a rolling basis. Application fee: $50. Electronic applications accepted. *Expenses:* Tuition, state resident: full-time $18,774; part-time $760 per credit. Tuition, nonresident: full-time $30,736; part-time $1258 per credit. *Required fees:* $740; $200 per term. Tuition and fees vary according to program. *Financial support:* In 2011–12, 5 students received support, including 1 fellowship with partial tuition reimbursement available (averaging $11,330 per year), 1 research assistantship with full tuition reimbursement available (averaging $35,942 per year), 3 teaching assistantships with full and partial tuition reimbursements available (averaging $27,470 per year); scholarships/grants, traineeships, health care benefits, and unspecified assistantships also available. Support available to part-time students. *Unit head:* Dr. Sandra Engberg, Associate Dean for Clinical Education, 412-624-3835, Fax: 412-624-8521, E-mail: sje1@pitt.edu. *Application contact:* Laurie Lapsley, Administrator of Graduate Student Services, 412-624-9670, Fax: 412-624-2409, E-mail: lapsleyl@pitt.edu. Web site: http://www.nursing.pitt.edu.

University of Puerto Rico, Medical Sciences Campus, School of Nursing, San Juan, PR 00936-5067. Offers adult and elderly nursing (MSN); child and adolescent nursing (MSN); critical care nursing (MSN); family and community nursing (MSN); family nurse practitioner (MSN); maternity nursing (MSN); mental health and psychiatric nursing (MSN). *Accreditation:* AACN; AANA/CANAEP. *Entrance requirements:* For master's, GRE or EXADEP, interview, Puerto Rico RN license or professional license for international students, general and specific point average, article analysis. Electronic applications accepted. *Faculty research:* HIV, health disparities, teen violence, women and violence, neurological disorders.

University of Rochester, School of Nursing, Rochester, NY 14642. Offers acute care nurse practitioner (MS); adult nurse practitioner (MS); adult/geriatric nurse practitioner (MS); care of children and families/pediatric nurse practitioner (MS); care of children and families/pediatric nurse practitioner/neonatal nurse practitioner (MS); clinical nurse leader (MS); clinical research coordinator (MS); family nurse practitioner (MS); family psychiatric mental health nurse practitioner (MS); health care organization management and leadership (MS); health practice research (PhD); nursing (DNP). *Accreditation:* AACN; NLN (one or more programs are accredited). Part-time programs available. Postbaccalaureate distance learning degree programs offered (minimal on-campus study). *Faculty:* 49 full-time (42 women), 72 part-time/adjunct (60 women). *Students:* 38 full-time (32 women), 196 part-time (181 women); includes 37 minority (20 Black or African American, non-Hispanic/Latino; 9 Asian, non-Hispanic/Latino; 8 Hispanic/Latino), 5 international. Average age 36. 68 applicants, 56% accepted, 26 enrolled. In 2011, 49 master's, 7 doctorates awarded. Terminal master's awarded for partial completion of doctoral program. *Median time to degree:* Of those who began their doctoral program in fall 2003, 40% received their degree in 8 years or less. *Degree requirements:* For doctorate, thesis/dissertation. *Entrance requirements:* For master's, BS in nursing, minimum GPA of 3.0, course work in statistics; for doctorate, GRE General Test, MS in nursing, minimum GPA of 3.5. Additional exam requirements/recommendations for international students: Required—or IELTS (minimum score 6.5); Recommended—TOEFL (minimum score 560 paper-based; 230 computer-based; 88 iBT). *Application deadline:* For fall admission, 4/1 priority date for domestic students, 4/1 for international students; for spring admission, 9/1 for domestic and international students. Application fee: $50. Electronic applications accepted. *Expenses: Tuition:* Full-time $41,040. *Financial support:* In 2011–12, 49 students received support, including 1 fellowship with full and partial tuition reimbursement available (averaging $18,700 per year); scholarships/grants, traineeships, health care benefits, tuition waivers (partial), and unspecified assistantships also available. Support available to part-time students. Financial award application deadline: 6/30. *Faculty research:* Clinical research in aging, managing asthma in children, interventions to improve outcomes in critically ill children and their mothers, nurse home visitation studies, medical device evaluation, critical care clinical studies, high risk behavior and prevention, palliative care, pregnancy-related weight gain. *Total annual research expenditures:* $4.3 million. *Unit head:* Dr. Kathy H. Rideout, Interim Dean, 585-273-8902, Fax: 585-273-1268, E-mail: kathy_rideout@urmc.rochester.edu. *Application contact:* Elaine Andolina, Director of Admissions, 585-275-2375, Fax: 585-756-8299, E-mail: elaine_andolina@urmc.rochester.edu. Web site: http://www.son.rochester.edu.

University of San Diego, Hahn School of Nursing and Health Science, San Diego, CA 92110-2492. Offers adult-gerontology clinical nurse specialist (MSN); adult-gerontology nurse practitioner/family nurse practitioner (MSN); clinical nursing (MSN); entry-level nursing (for non-RNs) (MSN); executive nurse leader (MSN); family nurse practitioner (MSN); family/lifespan psychiatric-mental health nurse practitioner (MSN); healthcare informatics (MS, MSN); nursing (PhD); nursing practice (DNP); pediatric nurse practitioner/family nurse practitioner (MSN). *Accreditation:* AACN. Part-time and evening/weekend programs available. *Faculty:* 23 full-time (21 women), 37 part-time/adjunct (34 women). *Students:* 157 full-time (131 women), 182 part-time (162 women); includes 121 minority (21 Black or African American, non-Hispanic/Latino; 6 American Indian or Alaska Native, non-Hispanic/Latino; 51 Asian, non-Hispanic/Latino; 36 Hispanic/Latino; 2 Native Hawaiian or other Pacific Islander, non-Hispanic/Latino; 5 Two or more races, non-Hispanic/Latino), 7 international. Average age 36. 506 applicants, 47% accepted, 150 enrolled. In 2011, 87 master's, 26 doctorates awarded. *Degree requirements:* For doctorate, thesis/dissertation (for some programs), residency (DNP). *Entrance requirements:* For master's, GRE General Test (entry-level nursing), BSN, current California RN licensure (except for entry-level nursing); minimum GPA of 3.0; for doctorate, minimum GPA of 3.5, MSN, current California RN licensure. Additional exam requirements/recommendations for international students: Required—TOEFL (minimum score 580 paper-based; 237 computer-based; 83 iBT), TWE. *Application deadline:* For fall admission, 3/1 priority date for domestic students, 3/1 for international students; for spring admission, 11/1 priority date for domestic students, 11/1 for international students. Applications are processed on a rolling basis. Application fee: $45. Electronic applications accepted. *Expenses: Tuition:* Full-time $22,482; part-time $1249 per unit. *Required fees:* $224. Full-time tuition and fees vary according to course load and degree level. *Financial support:* In 2011–12, 232 students received support. Scholarships/grants and traineeships available. Support available to part-time students. Financial award application deadline: 4/1; financial award applicants required to submit FAFSA. *Faculty research:* Palliative and end of life care, maternal/child health, childhood obesity, health care disparities, cognitive functioning. *Unit head:* Dr. Sally Hardin, Dean, 619-260-4550, Fax: 619-260-6814. *Application contact:* Monica Mahon, Associate Director of Graduate Admissions, 619-260-4524, Fax: 619-260-4158, E-mail: grads@sandiego.edu. Web site: http://www.sandiego.edu/academics/nursing/.

University of South Carolina, The Graduate School, College of Nursing, Program in Health Nursing, Columbia, SC 29208. Offers adult nurse practitioner (MSN); community/public health clinical nurse specialist (MSN); family nurse practitioner (MSN); pediatric nurse practitioner (MSN). *Accreditation:* AACN. Part-time programs available. *Degree requirements:* For master's, thesis or alternative. *Entrance requirements:* For master's, GRE General Test or MAT, BS in nursing, nursing license. Additional exam requirements/recommendations for international students: Required—TOEFL (minimum score 570 paper-based; 230 computer-based). Electronic applications accepted. *Faculty research:* System research, evidence based practice, breast cancer, violence.

The University of Texas at Austin, Graduate School, School of Nursing, Austin, TX 78712-1111. Offers adult -gerontology clinical nurse specialist (MSN); child health (MSN), including administration, public health nursing; child health (MSN), including teaching; family nurse practitioner (MSN); family psychiatric/mental health nurse practitioner (MSN); holistic adult health (MSN), including administration, education; maternity (MSN), including administration, public health nursing; maternity (MSN), including teaching; nursing (PhD); nursing administration and healthcare systems management (MSN); pediatric nurse practitioner (MSN); public health nursing (MSN). *Accreditation:* AACN. Part-time programs available. *Degree requirements:* For master's, thesis optional; for doctorate, thesis/dissertation. *Entrance requirements:* For master's and doctorate, GRE General Test. Additional exam requirements/recommendations for international students: Required—TOEFL (minimum score 550 paper-based; 213 computer-based). *Application deadline:* For fall admission, 12/1 for domestic students. Application fee: $50 ($75 for international students). Electronic applications accepted. *Financial support:* Fellowships, research assistantships, teaching assistantships, scholarships/grants, and traineeships available. Financial award application deadline: 2/1. *Faculty research:* Chronic illness management, memory and aging, health promotion, women's health, adolescent health. *Unit head:* Dr. Alexa Stuifbergen, Dean, 512-471-4100, Fax: 512-471-4910, E-mail: astuifbergen@mail.utexas.edu. Web site: http://www.utexas.edu/nursing/.

The University of Toledo, College of Graduate Studies, College of Nursing, Department of Population and Community Care, Toledo, OH 43606-3390. Offers adult nurse practitioner (Certificate); adult nurse practitioner/clinical nurse specialist (MSN); clinical nurse leader (MSN); family nurse practitioner (MSN, Certificate); nurse educator (MSN, Certificate); pediatric nurse practitioner (MSN, Certificate); psychiatric-mental

health clinical nurse specialist (MSN, Certificate). Part-time programs available. *Faculty:* 43. *Students:* 77 full-time (63 women), 198 part-time (180 women); includes 30 minority (14 Black or African American, non-Hispanic/Latino; 1 American Indian or Alaska Native, non-Hispanic/Latino; 4 Asian, non-Hispanic/Latino; 8 Hispanic/Latino; 3 Two or more races, non-Hispanic/Latino), 1 international. Average age 33. 172 applicants, 53% accepted, 82 enrolled. In 2011, 66 master's, 10 other advanced degrees awarded. *Degree requirements:* For master's, thesis or alternative. *Entrance requirements:* For master's, GRE, BS in nursing, minimum undergraduate GPA of 3.0, statement of purpose, three letters of recommendation, transcripts from all prior institutions attended, Nursing CAS application, UT supplemental application; for Certificate, BS in nursing, minimum undergraduate GPA of 3.0, statement of purpose, three letters of recommendation, transcripts from all prior institutions attended. Additional exam requirements/recommendations for international students: Required—TOEFL (minimum score 550 paper-based; 213 computer-based; 80 iBT), IELTS (minimum score 6.5). Application fee: $45 ($75 for international students). Electronic applications accepted. *Financial support:* Research assistantships, Federal Work-Study, scholarships/grants, traineeships, and tuition waivers (full and partial) available. *Application contact:* Joan Mulligan, Admissions Analyst, 419-383-4168, Fax: 419-383-6140, E-mail: joan.mulligan@utoledo.edu. Web site: http://www.utoledo.edu/nursing/.

University of Wisconsin–Madison, School of Nursing, Madison, WI 53706-1380. Offers adult/gerontology (DNP); nursing (PhD); pediatrics (DNP); psychiatric mental health (DNP); MS/MPH. *Accreditation:* AACN. Part-time programs available. *Degree requirements:* For doctorate, comprehensive exam, thesis/dissertation. *Entrance requirements:* For doctorate, GRE General Test, 2 samples of scholarly written work, BS in nursing from an accredited program, minimum undergraduate GPA of 3.0 in last 60 credits (for PhD); licensure as professional nurse (for DNP). Additional exam requirements/recommendations for international students: Required—TOEFL (minimum score 600 paper-based; 250 computer-based; 100 iBT). Electronic applications accepted. *Expenses:* Tuition, state resident: full-time $10,296; part-time $643.51 per credit. Tuition, nonresident: full-time $24,054; part-time $1503.40 per credit. *Required fees:* $70.06 per credit. Tuition and fees vary according to course load, campus/location, program and reciprocity agreements. *Faculty research:* Nursing informatics to promote self-care and disease management skills among patients and caregivers; quality of care to frail, vulnerable, and chronically ill populations; study of health-related and health-seeking behaviors; eliminating health disparities; pain and symptom management for patients with cancer.

Vanderbilt University, Vanderbilt University School of Nursing, Nashville, TN 37240. Offers acute care nurse practitioner (MSN), including intensivist; adult-gerontology primary care nurse practitioner (MSN); emergency nurse practitioner (MSN); family nurse practitioner (MSN); family psychiatric and mental health nurse practitioner (MSN); health systems management (MSN); neonatal nurse practitioner (MSN); nurse midwifery (MSN); nurse midwifery/family nurse practitioner (MSN); nursing informatics (MSN); nursing practice (DNP); nursing science (PhD); pediatric acute care nurse practitioner (MSN); pediatric primary care nurse practitioner (MSN); women's health nurse practitioner (MSN), including urogynecology, women's health; women's health nurse practitioner/adult gerontology nurse practitioner (MSN); MSN/M Div; MSN/MTS. *Accreditation:* ACNM/ACME; NLN (one or more programs are accredited). Part-time programs available. Postbaccalaureate distance learning degree programs offered (minimal on-campus study). *Faculty:* 120 full-time (105 women), 415 part-time/adjunct (302 women). *Students:* 570 full-time (503 women), 395 part-time (364 women); includes 107 minority (57 Black or African American, non-Hispanic/Latino; 1 American Indian or Alaska Native, non-Hispanic/Latino; 19 Asian, non-Hispanic/Latino; 19 Hispanic/Latino; 2 Native Hawaiian or other Pacific Islander, non-Hispanic/Latino; 9 Two or more races, non-Hispanic/Latino), 10 international. Average age 32. 1,116 applicants, 56% accepted, 455 enrolled. In 2011, 341 master's, 33 doctorates awarded. *Degree requirements:* For doctorate, comprehensive exam, thesis/dissertation. *Entrance requirements:* For master's, GRE General Test (within the past 5 years), minimum B average in undergraduate course work, 3 letters of recommendation; for doctorate, GRE General Test, interview, 3 letters of recommendation from doctorally-prepared faculty, MSN, essay. Additional exam requirements/recommendations for international students: Required—TOEFL (minimum score 570 paper-based; 88 computer-based), IELTS (minimum score 6.5). *Application deadline:* For fall admission, 12/1 priority date for domestic students, 12/1 for international students. Applications are processed on a rolling basis. Application fee: $50. Electronic applications accepted. *Expenses:* Contact institution. *Financial support:* In 2011–12, 392 students received support. Scholarships/grants and health care benefits available. Support available to part-time students. Financial award application deadline: 3/15; financial award applicants required to submit FAFSA. *Faculty research:* Lymphedema, palliative care and bereavement, health services research including workforce, safety and quality of care, gerontology, better birth outcomes including nutrition . *Total annual research expenditures:* $1.8 million. *Unit head:* Dr. Colleen Conway-Welch, Dean, 615-343-8776, Fax: 615-343-7711, E-mail: colleen.conway-welch@vanderbilt.edu. *Application contact:* Patricia Peerman, Assistant Dean for Enrollment Management, 615-322-3800, Fax: 615-343-0333, E-mail: .vusn-admissions@vanderbilt.edu. Web site: http://www.nursing.vanderbilt.edu.

Villanova University, College of Nursing, Villanova, PA 19085-1699. Offers adult nurse practitioner (MSN, Post Master's Certificate); family nurse practitioner (MSN, Post Master's Certificate); health care administration (MSN, Post Master's Certificate); nurse anesthetist (MSN, Post-Master's Certificate); nursing (PhD); nursing education (MSN, Post Master's Certificate); nursing practice (DNP); pediatric nurse practitioner (MSN, Post Master's Certificate). *Accreditation:* AACN; AANA/CANAEP. Part-time programs available. Postbaccalaureate distance learning degree programs offered (minimal on-campus study). *Faculty:* 17 full-time (all women), 4 part-time/adjunct (all women). *Students:* 36 full-time (35 women), 256 part-time (234 women); includes 27 minority (14 Black or African American, non-Hispanic/Latino; 9 Asian, non-Hispanic/Latino; 4 Hispanic/Latino), 16 international. Average age 30. 161 applicants, 55% accepted, 75 enrolled. In 2011, 55 master's, 11 doctorates, 5 other advanced degrees awarded. *Degree requirements:* For master's, independent study project; for doctorate, comprehensive exam, thesis/dissertation. *Entrance requirements:* For master's, GRE or MAT, BSN, 1 year of recent nursing experience, physical assessment, course work in statistics; for doctorate, GRE, MSN. Additional exam requirements/recommendations for international students: Required—TOEFL, IELTS. *Application deadline:* For fall admission, 7/1 priority date for domestic students, 7/1 for international students; for spring admission, 11/1 priority date for domestic students, 11/1 for international students. Applications are processed on a rolling basis. Application fee: $50. *Expenses:* Contact institution. *Financial support:* In 2011–12, 43 students received support, including 5 teaching assistantships with full tuition reimbursements available (averaging $13,100 per year); institutionally sponsored loans, scholarships/grants, traineeships, tuition waivers (full), and unspecified assistantships also available. Financial award application deadline: 7/1; financial award applicants required to submit FAFSA. *Faculty research:* Genetics, ethics, cognitive development of students, women with disabilities, nursing leadership. *Unit head:* Dr. Marguerite K. Schlag, Assistant Dean/Director, Graduate Programs, 610-519-4907, Fax: 610-519-7650, E-mail: marguerite.schlag@villanova.edu. Web site: http://www.nursing.villanova.edu/.

Virginia Commonwealth University, Graduate School, School of Nursing, Richmond, VA 23284-9005. Offers adult health acute nursing (MS); adult health primary nursing (MS); biobehavioral clinical research (PhD); child health nursing (MS); clinical nurse leader (MS); family health nursing (MS); nurse educator (MS); nurse practitioner (MS); nursing (Certificate); nursing administration (MS), including clinical nurse manager; psychiatric-mental health nursing (MS); women's health nursing (MS). *Accreditation:* NLN (one or more programs are accredited). Part-time and evening/weekend programs available. *Degree requirements:* For master's, thesis optional; for doctorate, thesis/dissertation. *Entrance requirements:* For master's, GRE General Test, BSN, minimum GPA of 2.8; for doctorate, GRE General Test. Additional exam requirements/recommendations for international students: Required—TOEFL (minimum score 600 paper-based; 250 computer-based; 100 iBT). Electronic applications accepted. *Expenses:* Tuition, state resident: full-time $9133; part-time $507 per credit. Tuition, nonresident: full-time $18,777; part-time $1043 per credit. *Required fees:* $77 per credit. Tuition and fees vary according to degree level, campus/location, program and student level.

Wayne State University, College of Nursing, Program in Advanced Practice Nursing with Women, Neonates and Children, Detroit, MI 48202. Offers MSN. *Accreditation:* AACN. Part-time programs available. *Students:* 48 full-time (47 women), 69 part-time (65 women); includes 16 minority (11 Black or African American, non-Hispanic/Latino; 5 Hispanic/Latino), 2 international. Average age 33. 44 applicants, 68% accepted, 27 enrolled. In 2011, 30 master's awarded. *Degree requirements:* For master's, thesis or alternative. *Entrance requirements:* For master's, minimum honor point average of 2.8 in upper-division course work; BA from NLN- or CCNE-accredited program; references; current RN license; personal statement. Additional exam requirements/recommendations for international students: Required—TOEFL (minimum score 550 paper-based; 213 computer-based); Recommended—TWE (minimum score 6). *Application deadline:* For fall admission, 6/1 priority date for domestic students, 5/1 for international students; for winter admission, 10/1 priority date for domestic students, 9/1 for international students; for spring admission, 2/1 priority date for domestic students, 1/1 for international students. Applications are processed on a rolling basis. Application fee: $50. Electronic applications accepted. *Expenses:* Tuition, state resident: part-time $512.85 per credit. Tuition, nonresident: part-time $1132.65 per credit. *Required fees:* $26.60 per credit; $199.65 per semester. Tuition and fees vary according to course load and program. *Financial support:* In 2011–12, 17 students received support. Fellowships with tuition reimbursements available, research assistantships with tuition reimbursements available, teaching assistantships with tuition reimbursements available, institutionally sponsored loans, scholarships/grants, traineeships, and unspecified assistantships available. Financial award applicants required to submit FAFSA. *Faculty research:* Acculturation and parenting, domestic violence, evidence-based midwifery practice, pain in children, trauma and community violence. *Unit head:* Dr. Barbara Redman, Dean, 313-577-4070, Fax: 313-577-4571, E-mail: ae9080@wayne.edu. *Application contact:* Dr. Cynthia Redwine, Assistant Dean for the Office of Student Affairs, 313-577-4082, E-mail: nursinginfo@wayne.edu. Web site: http://www.nursing.wayne.edu/msn/nnpcurriculum.php.

Wright State University, School of Graduate Studies, College of Nursing and Health, Program in Nursing, Dayton, OH 45435. Offers acute care nurse practitioner (MS); administration of nursing and health care systems (MS); adult health (MS); child and adolescent health (MS); community health (MS); family nurse practitioner (MS); nurse practitioner (MS); school nurse (MS); MBA/MS. *Accreditation:* AACN. Part-time and evening/weekend programs available. *Degree requirements:* For master's, thesis or alternative. *Entrance requirements:* For master's, GRE General Test, BSN from NLN-accredited college, Ohio RN license. Additional exam requirements/recommendations for international students: Required—TOEFL. *Faculty research:* Clinical nursing and health, teaching, caring, pain administration, informatics and technology.

Psychiatric Nursing

Allen College, Program in Nursing, Waterloo, IA 50703. Offers acute care nurse practitioner (MSN, Post-Master's Certificate); adult nurse practitioner (MSN, Post-Master's Certificate); adult psychiatric-mental health nurse practitioner (MSN, Post-Master's Certificate); family nurse practitioner (MSN, Post-Master's Certificate); gerontological nurse practitioner (MSN, Post-Master's Certificate); health education (MSN); leadership in health care delivery (MSN, Post-Master's Certificate); nursing (DNP). *Accreditation:* AACN; NLN. Part-time programs available. *Faculty:* 3 full-time (all women), 16 part-time/adjunct (all women). *Students:* 34 full-time (31 women), 110 part-time (106 women); includes 5 minority (2 Asian, non-Hispanic/Latino; 3 Hispanic/Latino). Average age 36. 156 applicants, 64% accepted, 76 enrolled. In 2011, 61 master's, 1 other advanced degree awarded. *Degree requirements:* For master's, thesis optional. *Entrance requirements:* For master's, minimum GPA of 3.0; for doctorate, minimum GPA of 3.25 in graduate coursework. Additional exam requirements/recommendations for international students: Recommended—TOEFL (minimum score 550 paper-based), IELTS. *Application deadline:* For fall admission, 2/1 priority date for domestic students; for spring admission, 9/1 priority date for domestic students. Applications are processed on a rolling basis. Application fee: $50. Electronic applications accepted. *Expenses:* Tuition: Full-time $13,993; part-time $691 per credit hour. *Required fees:* $832; $69 per credit hour. One-time fee: $100 part-time. Part-time tuition and fees vary according to course load. *Financial support:* In 2011–12, 41 students received support. Institutionally sponsored loans, scholarships/grants, and traineeships available. Support available to part-time students. Financial award application deadline: 8/15; financial award applicants required to submit FAFSA. *Faculty research:* Pain and the aged, congestive heart failure. *Unit head:* Kendra Williams-Perez, Dean, School of Nursing, 319-226-2044, Fax: 319-226-2070, E-mail: williakb@ihs.org. *Application contact:* Michelle Koehn, Admissions Counselor, 319-226-2002, Fax: 319-226-2051, E-mail: koehnml@ihs.org. Web site: http://www.allencollege.edu/.

American University of Beirut, Graduate Programs, Rafic Hariri School of Nursing, Beirut, Lebanon. Offers adult care nursing (MSN); community health nursing (MSN);

nursing administration (MSN); psychiatry mental health nursing (MSN). *Accreditation:* AACN. Part-time programs available. *Faculty:* 8 full-time (7 women), 16 part-time/adjunct (13 women). *Students:* 5 full-time (3 women), 50 part-time (39 women). Average age 29. 46 applicants, 87% accepted, 19 enrolled. In 2011, 19 master's awarded. *Degree requirements:* For master's, one foreign language, comprehensive exam, thesis optional. *Entrance requirements:* For master's, letter of recommendation. Additional exam requirements/recommendations for international students: Required—TOEFL (minimum score 600 paper-based); Recommended—IELTS. *Application deadline:* For fall admission, 2/20 for domestic and international students; for spring admission, 11/1 for domestic and international students. Applications are processed on a rolling basis. Application fee: $50. *Expenses: Tuition:* Full-time $12,780; part-time $710 per credit. Tuition and fees vary according to course load and program. *Financial support:* In 2011–12, 19 research assistantships with partial tuition reimbursements, 1 teaching assistantship with partial tuition reimbursement were awarded; career-related internships or fieldwork, institutionally sponsored loans, scholarships/grants, health care benefits, and unspecified assistantships also available. Support available to part-time students. Financial award application deadline: 2/2. *Faculty research:* Pain management and palliative care, stress and post-traumatic stress disorder, health benefits and chronic illness, health promotion and community interventions. *Total annual research expenditures:* $52,000. *Unit head:* Dr. Huda Huijer Abu-Saad, Director, 961-1374374 Ext. 5952, Fax: 961-1744476, E-mail: hh35@aub.edu.lb. *Application contact:* Dr. Salim Kanaan, Director, Admissions Office, 961-1350000 Ext. 2594, Fax: 961-1750775, E-mail: sk00@aub.edu.lb. Web site: http://staff.aub.edu.lb/~webson.

Arizona State University, College of Nursing and Health Innovation, Phoenix, AZ 85004. Offers advanced nursing practice (DNP); child/family mental health nurse practitioner (Graduate Certificate); clinical research management (MS); community and public health practice (Graduate Certificate); community health (MS); exercise and wellness (MS), including exercise and wellness; family nurse practitioner (Graduate Certificate); healthcare innovation (MHI); international health for healthcare (Graduate Certificate); kinesiology (MS, PhD); nursing (MS, Graduate Certificate); nursing and healthcare innovation (PhD); nutrition (MS); physical activity nutrition and wellness (PhD), including physical activity, nutrition and wellness; public health (MPH); regulatory science and health safety (MS). *Accreditation:* AACN. Postbaccalaureate distance learning degree programs offered (minimal on-campus study). *Degree requirements:* For master's, comprehensive exam (for some programs), thesis (for some programs), interactive Program of Study (iPOS) submitted before completing 50 percent of required credit hours; for doctorate, comprehensive exam, thesis/dissertation, interactive Program of Study (iPOS) submitted before completing 50 percent of required credit hours. *Entrance requirements:* For master's and doctorate, GRE, minimum GPA of 3.0 or equivalent in last 2 years of work leading to bachelor's degree. Additional exam requirements/recommendations for international students: Required—TOEFL (minimum score 80 iBT), TOEFL, IELTS, or Pearson Test of English. Electronic applications accepted. *Expenses:* Contact institution.

Boston College, William F. Connell School of Nursing, Chestnut Hill, MA 02467-3800. Offers adult-gerontology nursing (MS); community health nursing (MS); family health (MS); forensic nursing (MS); maternal/child health nursing (MS), including pediatric and women's health; nurse anesthesia (MS); nursing (PhD); palliative care (MS), including adult and pediatric; psychiatric-mental health nursing (MS); MBA/MS; MS/MA; MS/PhD. *Accreditation:* AACN; AANA/CANAEP (one or more programs are accredited). Part-time programs available. *Faculty:* 48 full-time (46 women), 31 part-time/adjunct (29 women). *Students:* 225 full-time (207 women), 90 part-time (88 women); includes 47 minority (15 Black or African American, non-Hispanic/Latino; 3 American Indian or Alaska Native, non-Hispanic/Latino; 17 Asian, non-Hispanic/Latino; 8 Hispanic/Latino; 4 Two or more races, non-Hispanic/Latino), 6 international. Average age 31. 369 applicants, 43% accepted, 80 enrolled. In 2011, 113 master's, 8 doctorates awarded. *Degree requirements:* For master's, comprehensive exam, research project; for doctorate, comprehensive exam, thesis/dissertation, computer literacy exam or foreign language. *Entrance requirements:* For master's, bachelor's degree in nursing; for doctorate, GRE General Test, MS in nursing. Additional exam requirements/recommendations for international students: Required—TOEFL (minimum score 600 paper-based; 250 computer-based; 100 iBT). *Application deadline:* For fall admission, 11/1 for domestic and international students; for winter admission, 12/31 for domestic and international students; for spring admission, 4/30 for domestic and international students. Applications are processed on a rolling basis. Application fee: $40. Electronic applications accepted. *Financial support:* In 2011–12, 167 students received support, including 9 fellowships with full tuition reimbursements available (averaging $15,300 per year), 7 teaching assistantships (averaging $13,612 per year); research assistantships, Federal Work-Study, institutionally sponsored loans, scholarships/grants, traineeships, health care benefits, tuition waivers (partial), and unspecified assistantships also available. Support available to part-time students. Financial award application deadline: 3/1; financial award applicants required to submit FAFSA. *Faculty research:* Pre-term labor, palliative care, support during chronic illness, violence, eating disorders. *Total annual research expenditures:* $2.1 million. *Unit head:* Dr. Susan Gennaro, Dean, 617-552-4251, Fax: 617-552-0931, E-mail: susan.gennaro@bc.edu. *Application contact:* MaryBeth Crowley, Graduate Programs Assistant, 617-552-4928, Fax: 617-552-2121, E-mail: csongrad@bc.edu. Web site: http://www.bc.edu/nursing/.

Case Western Reserve University, Frances Payne Bolton School of Nursing, Doctor of Nursing Practice Program, Cleveland, OH 44106. Offers acute care nurse practitioner (DNP); adult gerontology nurse practitioner (DNP); educational leadership (DNP); family nurse practitioner (DNP); family systems psychiatric mental health nursing (DNP); midwifery/family nursing (DNP); neonatal nurse practitioner (DNP); pediatric nurse practitioner (DNP); practice leadership (DNP); women's health nurse practitioner (DNP). *Students:* 73 full-time, 194 part-time; includes 11 minority (6 Black or African American, non-Hispanic/Latino; 3 Asian, non-Hispanic/Latino; 2 Hispanic/Latino). 122 applicants, 74% accepted, 49 enrolled. In 2011, 47 doctorates awarded. Terminal master's awarded for partial completion of doctoral program. *Degree requirements:* For doctorate, thesis/dissertation. *Entrance requirements:* For doctorate, GRE General Test or MAT. Additional exam requirements/recommendations for international students: Required—TOEFL (minimum score 577 paper-based; 90 iBT), IELTS (minimum score 7). *Application deadline:* For fall admission, 6/1 priority date for domestic students, 6/1 for international students; for spring admission, 10/1 for domestic and international students. Applications are processed on a rolling basis. Application fee: $75. *Financial support:* In 2011–12, 6 students received support, including 1 teaching assistantship; research assistantships, Federal Work-Study, institutionally sponsored loans, and tuition waivers (partial) also available. Support available to part-time students. Financial award application deadline: 6/30; financial award applicants required to submit FAFSA. *Faculty research:* Clinical nursing, acute care, gerontology, mental health, critical care. *Unit head:* Dr. Donna Dowling, Director, 216-368-1869, Fax: 216-368-3542, E-mail: dad10@case.edu. *Application contact:* Donna Hassik, Admissions Coordinator, 216-368-5253, Fax: 216-368-0124, E-mail: dmh7@case.edu. Web site: http://fpb.case.edu/DNP/.

Columbia University, School of Nursing, Program in Psychiatric Mental Health Nursing, New York, NY 10032. Offers MS, Adv C. *Accreditation:* AACN. Part-time programs available. *Entrance requirements:* For master's, GRE General Test, BSN, 1 year of clinical experience (preferred); for Adv C, MSN. Electronic applications accepted.

Drexel University, College of Nursing and Health Professions, Division of Graduate Nursing, Philadelphia, PA 19104-2875. Offers adult acute care (MSN); adult psychiatric/mental health (MSN); advanced practice nursing (MSN); clinical trials research (MSN); family nurse practitioner (MSN); leadership in health systems management (MSN); nursing education (MSN); pediatric primary care (MSN); women's health (MSN). *Accreditation:* AACN; NLN. Electronic applications accepted.

East Tennessee State University, School of Graduate Studies, College of Nursing, Doctoral Nursing Programs, Johnson City, TN 37614. Offers adult/gerontological nurse practitioner (DNP); executive leadership in nursing (DNP); family nurse practitioner (DNP); nursing (PhD); psychiatric/mental health nurse practitioner (DNP). Part-time and evening/weekend programs available. *Students:* 22 full-time (21 women), 27 part-time (26 women); includes 3 minority (2 Black or African American, non-Hispanic/Latino; 1 Asian, non-Hispanic/Latino). 74 applicants, 41% accepted, 30 enrolled. In 2011, 3 doctorates awarded. *Degree requirements:* For doctorate, comprehensive exam, dissertation (PhD); residency internship and capstone project (DNP). *Entrance requirements:* For doctorate, GRE General Test, minimum GPA of 3.0, RN license, minimum two years RN experience, 3 letters of recommendation, interview, writing sample, resume. Additional exam requirements/recommendations for international students: Required—TOEFL (minimum score 600 paper-based; 250 computer-based; 100 iBT). *Application deadline:* For fall admission, 2/1 for domestic and international students; for spring admission, 7/1 for domestic and international students. Application fee: $35 ($45 for international students). Electronic applications accepted. *Expenses:* Tuition, state resident: full-time $7312; part-time $350 per credit hour. Tuition, nonresident: full-time $18,490; part-time $621 per credit hour. *Required fees:* $63 per credit hour. Tuition and fees vary according to course load and program. *Financial support:* In 2011–12, 2 students received support, including 1 research assistantship with partial tuition reimbursement available (averaging $3,000 per year); career-related internships or fieldwork, institutionally sponsored loans, scholarships/grants, and unspecified assistantships also available. Financial award application deadline: 7/1; financial award applicants required to submit FAFSA. *Faculty research:* Rural primary care, healthcare for the homeless and underserved, community health problems across the lifespan, nursing education research, school health services. *Unit head:* Dr. Kathleen Rayman, Director of Graduate Programs, 423-439-5626, Fax: 423-439-4100, E-mail: raymank@etsu.edu. *Application contact:* Linda Raines, Graduate Specialist, 423-439-6158, Fax: 423-439-5624, E-mail: rainesIt@etsu.edu.

Fairfield University, School of Nursing, Fairfield, CT 06824-5195. Offers clinical nurse leader (MSN); family nurse practitioner (MSN, DNP); nurse anesthesia (DNP); psychiatric nurse practitioner (MSN, DNP). *Accreditation:* AACN; AANA/CANAEP. Part-time programs available. *Faculty:* 15 full-time (all women). *Students:* 17 full-time (15 women), 145 part-time (127 women); includes 14 minority (6 Black or African American, non-Hispanic/Latino; 1 American Indian or Alaska Native, non-Hispanic/Latino; 4 Asian, non-Hispanic/Latino; 3 Hispanic/Latino), 1 international. Average age 38. 97 applicants, 29% accepted, 24 enrolled. In 2011, 24 master's awarded. *Degree requirements:* For master's, capstone project. *Entrance requirements:* For master's, minimum QPA of 3.0, RN license, resume, 2 recommendations; for doctorate, GRE (nurse anesthesia applicants only), MSN (minimum QPA of 3.2) or BSN (minimum QPA of 3.0); critical care nursing experience (for nurse anesthesia DNP candidates). Additional exam requirements/recommendations for international students: Required—TOEFL (minimum score 550 paper-based; 213 computer-based; 80 iBT) or IELTS (minimum score 6.5). *Application deadline:* For fall admission, 5/15 for international students; for spring admission, 10/15 for international students. Applications are processed on a rolling basis. Application fee: $60. Electronic applications accepted. *Expenses:* Contact institution. *Financial support:* In 2011–12, 2 students received support. Unspecified assistantships available. Financial award applicants required to submit FAFSA. *Faculty research:* Care of older adults, palliative care, spirituality and innovative partnerships, diabetes. *Unit head:* Dr. Suzanne Campbell, Dean, 203-254-4000 Ext. 2701, Fax: 203-254-4126, E-mail: scampbell@fairfield.edu. *Application contact:* Marianne Gumpper, Director of Graduate and Continuing Studies Admission, 203-254-4184, Fax: 203-254-4073, E-mail: gradadmis@fairfield.edu. Web site: http://www.fairfield.edu/son/son_grad_1.html.

Georgia State University, College of Health and Human Sciences, Byrdine F. Lewis School of Nursing, Atlanta, GA 30302-3083. Offers adult health (MS); adult health nursing (Certificate); child health (MS); family nurse practitioner (MS, Certificate); health promotion, protection and restoration (PhD); perinatal/women's health (MS); psychiatric mental health nursing (Certificate); psychiatric/mental health (MS); women's health nursing (Certificate). *Accreditation:* AACN. Part-time and evening/weekend programs available. Postbaccalaureate distance learning degree programs offered (minimal on-campus study). *Degree requirements:* For master's, research activity; for doctorate, comprehensive exam, thesis/dissertation. *Entrance requirements:* For master's, MAT (preferred) or GRE, interview, RN license; for doctorate, GRE General Test. Additional exam requirements/recommendations for international students: Required—TOEFL (minimum score 550 paper-based; 213 computer-based). Electronic applications accepted. *Expenses:* Contact institution. *Faculty research:* Breast cancer prevention, sexually compulsive behaviors, health risks in minority youth, asthma treatment strategies, adolescent alcohol-related issues.

Hampton University, Graduate College, School of Nursing, Hampton, VA 23668. Offers advanced adult nursing (MS); community health nursing (MS); community mental health/psychiatric nursing (MS); family nursing (MS); gerontological nursing for the nurse practitioner (MS); pediatric nursing (MS); women's health nursing (MS). *Accreditation:* AACN; NLN. Part-time and evening/weekend programs available. *Degree requirements:* For master's, thesis optional. *Entrance requirements:* For master's, GRE General Test. *Faculty research:* Curriculum development, physical and mental assessment.

Hunter College of the City University of New York, Graduate School, Schools of the Health Professions, Hunter-Bellevue School of Nursing, Program in Psychiatric Nursing, New York, NY 10021-5085. Offers MS, AC. *Accreditation:* AACN. Part-time programs available. *Faculty:* 20 full-time (16 women), 20 part-time/adjunct (18 women). *Students:* 1 (woman) full-time, 44 part-time (30 women); includes 21 minority (8 Black or African American, non-Hispanic/Latino; 9 Asian, non-Hispanic/Latino; 4 Hispanic/Latino), 1 international. Average age 58. 41 applicants, 54% accepted, 15 enrolled. In 2011, 10 master's awarded. *Degree requirements:* For master's, practicum. *Entrance requirements:* For master's, minimum GPA of 3.0, New York RN license, BSN. Additional exam requirements/recommendations for international students: Required—TOEFL. *Application deadline:* For fall admission, 4/1 for domestic students, 2/1 for international students; for spring admission, 11/1 for domestic students, 9/1 for international students. Applications are processed on a rolling basis. Application fee: $125. *Expenses:* Tuition, state resident: full-time $8210; part-time $345 per credit. Tuition, nonresident: full-time $15,360; part-time $640 per credit. *Required fees:* $280 per semester. One-time fee: $125. Tuition and fees vary according to class time, campus/location and program. *Financial support:* Federal Work-Study, scholarships/grants, traineeships, and tuition waivers (partial) available. Support available to part-time

students. Financial award application deadline: 5/1; financial award applicants required to submit FAFSA. *Faculty research:* Nursing approaches with the homeless, chronic mentally ill, and depressed; power and empathy. *Unit head:* Dr. Kunsook Bernstein, Coordinator, 212-481-4346, Fax: 212-481-5078, E-mail: kbernst@hunter.cuny.edu. *Application contact:* William Zlata, Director for Graduate Admissions, 212-772-4482, Fax: 212-650-3336, E-mail: admissions@hunter.cuny.edu. Web site: http://www.hunter.cuny.edu/nursing/repository/files/graduate-fact-sheets/FactPsych.NP.Jan.%2026-2012.FINAL.pdf.

Husson University, School of Graduate and Professional Studies, Graduate Nursing Program, Bangor, ME 04401-2999. Offers advanced practice psychiatric nursing (MSN, PMC); family and community nurse practitioner (MSN, PMC); nursing education (MSN, PMC). *Accreditation:* AACN. Part-time programs available. *Faculty:* 6 full-time (all women), 6 part-time/adjunct (all women). *Students:* 49 full-time (42 women), 33 part-time (29 women); includes 2 minority (1 American Indian or Alaska Native, non-Hispanic/Latino; 1 Two or more races, non-Hispanic/Latino). 18 applicants, 13 enrolled. In 2011, 25 master's awarded. *Degree requirements:* For master's, comprehensive exam (for some programs). *Entrance requirements:* For master's, MAT or GRE, BSN. Additional exam requirements/recommendations for international students: Required—TOEFL (minimum score 550 paper-based). *Application deadline:* For fall admission, 6/30 for domestic students; for spring admission, 10/30 for domestic students. Application fee: $40. *Expenses:* Contact institution. *Financial support:* In 2011–12, 31 students received support. Federal Work-Study, institutionally sponsored loans, traineeships, and unspecified assistantships available. Financial award application deadline: 4/15; financial award applicants required to submit FAFSA. *Unit head:* Dr. Barbara Higgins, Director, Nurse Practitioner Program, 207-947-7057. *Application contact:* Kristen Card, Director of Graduate Admissions, 207-404-5660, Fax: 207-941-7935, E-mail: cardk@husson.edu.

Indiana University–Purdue University Indianapolis, School of Nursing, Indianapolis, IN 46202-2896. Offers acute care nurse practitioner (MSN); adult health clinical nurse specialist (MSN); adult health nursing (MSN), including adult clinical nurse specialist; adult nurse practitioner (MSN); adult psychiatric/mental health nursing (MSN); child psychiatric/mental health nursing (MSN); community health nursing (MSN); family nurse practitioner (MSN); neonatal nurse practitioner (MSN); nursing (MSN, DNP), including nursing education (MSN); nursing (MSN), including nursing administration; nursing science (PhD); pediatric clinical nurse specialist (MSN); women's health nurse practitioner (MSN); MSN/MPA; MSN/MPH. *Accreditation:* AACN; NLN (one or more programs are accredited). Part-time programs available. *Faculty:* 85 full-time (82 women), 60 part-time/adjunct (all women). *Students:* 35 full-time (32 women), 360 part-time (340 women); includes 47 minority (28 Black or African American, non-Hispanic/Latino; 9 Asian, non-Hispanic/Latino; 4 Hispanic/Latino; 1 Native Hawaiian or other Pacific Islander, non-Hispanic/Latino; 5 Two or more races, non-Hispanic/Latino), 5 international. Average age 38. 119 applicants, 76% accepted, 54 enrolled. In 2011, 89 master's, 10 doctorates awarded. Terminal master's awarded for partial completion of doctoral program. *Degree requirements:* For master's, thesis; for doctorate, thesis/dissertation. *Entrance requirements:* For master's, minimum GPA of 3.0, RN license; for doctorate, GRE General Test, minimum GPA of 3.0, MSN, RN license, graduate statistics course with minimum B grade (not older than 3 years). Additional exam requirements/recommendations for international students: Required—TOEFL. *Application deadline:* For fall admission, 2/15 for domestic students; for spring admission, 9/15 for domestic students. Application fee: $55 ($65 for international students). *Financial support:* In 2011–12, 93 students received support, including 9 fellowships with full tuition reimbursements available (averaging $7,039 per year), 7 teaching assistantships with full tuition reimbursements available (averaging $5,300 per year); research assistantships with full tuition reimbursements available, Federal Work-Study, institutionally sponsored loans, scholarships/grants, and tuition waivers (full) also available. Support available to part-time students. Financial award application deadline: 5/1. *Faculty research:* Clinical science, health systems. *Total annual research expenditures:* $3 million. *Unit head:* Associate Dean for Graduate Programs, 317-274-2806, E-mail: nursing@iupui.edu. *Application contact:* Information Contact, 317-274-2806. Web site: http://nursing.iupui.edu/.

Kent State University, College of Nursing, Kent, OH 44242-0001. Offers acute care nurse practitioner (MSN); adult nurse practitioner (MSN); clinical nurse specialist (MSN); family nurse practitioner (MSN); geriatric nurse practitioner (MSN); health care management (MSN); nurse educator (MSN); nursing (PhD); nursing practice (DNP); pediatric nurse practitioner (MSN); psychiatric/mental health nurse practitioner (MSN); women's health nurse practitioner (MSN). PhD program offered jointly with The University of Akron. *Accreditation:* AACN. Part-time programs available. *Degree requirements:* For master's, thesis optional; for doctorate, comprehensive exam, thesis/dissertation. *Entrance requirements:* For master's, GRE (if undergraduate GPA less than 3.0), minimum GPA of 2.75; for doctorate, GRE, MSN. Additional exam requirements/recommendations for international students: Required—TOEFL. Electronic applications accepted. *Expenses:* Contact institution. *Faculty research:* Women and violence, methodological specialties, osteoporosis in women, new caregivers and the elderly.

Lincoln Memorial University, Caylor School of Nursing, Harrogate, TN 37752-1901. Offers family nurse practitioner (MSN); nurse anesthesia (MSN); psychiatric mental health nurse practitioner (MSN). *Accreditation:* AANA/CANAEP; NLN. Part-time programs available. *Entrance requirements:* For master's, GRE.

MGH Institute of Health Professions, School of Nursing, Boston, MA 02129. Offers advanced practice nursing (MSN); gerontological nursing (MSN); nursing (DNP); pediatric nursing (MSN); psychiatric nursing (MSN); teaching and learning for health care education (Certificate); women's health nursing (MSN). *Accreditation:* AACN; NLN (one or more programs are accredited). *Faculty:* 41 full-time (36 women), 14 part-time/adjunct (13 women). *Students:* 418 full-time (365 women), 72 part-time (63 women); includes 51 minority (20 Black or African American, non-Hispanic/Latino; 1 American Indian or Alaska Native, non-Hispanic/Latino; 24 Asian, non-Hispanic/Latino; 5 Hispanic/Latino; 1 Native Hawaiian or other Pacific Islander, non-Hispanic/Latino). Average age 32. 1,041 applicants, 36% accepted, 148 enrolled. In 2011, 85 master's, 12 doctorates, 98 other advanced degrees awarded. *Degree requirements:* For master's, thesis or alternative. *Entrance requirements:* For master's, GRE General Test, bachelor's degree from regionally-accredited college or university. Additional exam requirements/recommendations for international students: Required—TOEFL (minimum score 550 paper-based; 213 computer-based; 80 iBT). *Application deadline:* For fall admission, 1/10 for domestic and international students; for spring admission, 11/1 for domestic and international students. Application fee: $65. Electronic applications accepted. *Expenses: Tuition:* Full-time $12,720; part-time $1060 per credit. *Required fees:* $1725; $430 per semester. One-time fee: $350. *Financial support:* In 2011–12, 75 students received support, including 4 research assistantships (averaging $1,200 per year), 17 teaching assistantships (averaging $1,200 per year); career-related internships or fieldwork, scholarships/grants, traineeships, and unspecified assistantships also available. Support available to part-time students. Financial award application deadline: 4/1; financial award applicants required to submit FAFSA. *Faculty research:* Biobehavioral nursing, HIV/AIDS, gerontological nursing, women's health, vulnerable populations,

health systems. *Unit head:* Dr. Laurie Lauzon-Clabo, Dean, 617-643-0605, Fax: 617-726-8022, E-mail: llauzonclabo@mghihp.edu. *Application contact:* Maureen Rika Judd, Director of Admissions, 617-726-6069, Fax: 617-726-8010, E-mail: admissions@mghihp.edu. Web site: http://www.mghihp.edu/academics/nursing/.

Midwestern State University, Graduate Studies, College of Health Sciences and Human Services, Nursing Program, Wichita Falls, TX 76308. Offers family nurse practitioner (MSN); family psychiatric mental health nurse practitioner (MSN); health services administration (MSN); nurse educator (MSN). *Accreditation:* AACN. Part-time and evening/weekend programs available. *Degree requirements:* For master's, comprehensive exam, thesis optional. *Entrance requirements:* For master's, GRE General Test or MAT. Additional exam requirements/recommendations for international students: Required—TOEFL (minimum score 550 paper-based; 213 computer-based). Electronic applications accepted. *Faculty research:* Infant feeding, musculoskeletal disorders, diabetes, community health education, water quality reporting.

Molloy College, Division of Nursing, Rockville Centre, NY 11571-5002. Offers adult nurse practitioner (Advanced Certificate); clinical nurse specialist: adult health (Advanced Certificate); family nurse practitioner (Advanced Certificate); nurse practitioner psychiatry (Advanced Certificate); nursing (MS); nursing administration (Advanced Certificate); nursing administration with informatics (Advanced Certificate); nursing education (Advanced Certificate); nursing informatics (Advanced Certificate); pediatric nurse practitioner (Advanced Certificate). *Accreditation:* AACN. Part-time and evening/weekend programs available. *Faculty:* 20 full-time (19 women), 12 part-time/adjunct (11 women). *Students:* 19 full-time (15 women), 483 part-time (452 women); includes 238 minority (132 Black or African American, non-Hispanic/Latino; 61 Asian, non-Hispanic/Latino; 35 Hispanic/Latino; 2 Native Hawaiian or other Pacific Islander, non-Hispanic/Latino; 8 Two or more races, non-Hispanic/Latino), 5 international. Average age 40. 186 applicants, 82% accepted, 110 enrolled. In 2011, 94 master's awarded. *Degree requirements:* For master's, thesis optional. *Entrance requirements:* For master's, 3 letters of reference, BS in nursing, minimum undergraduate GPA of 3.0; for Advanced Certificate, 3 letters of reference, master's degree in nursing. *Application deadline:* For fall admission, 9/2 priority date for domestic students; for spring admission, 1/20 priority date for domestic students. Applications are processed on a rolling basis. Application fee: $60. *Financial support:* Research assistantships with partial tuition reimbursements, teaching assistantships with partial tuition reimbursements, institutionally sponsored loans, scholarships/grants, and unspecified assistantships available. Support available to part-time students. Financial award application deadline: 4/1; financial award applicants required to submit FAFSA. *Unit head:* Dr. Denise Walsh, Associate Dean, Graduate Nursing, 516-678-5000, Fax: 516-678-9718, E-mail: dwalsh@molloy.edu. *Application contact:* Alina Haitz, Assistant Director of Graduate Admissions, 516-678-5000, Fax: 516-256-2247, E-mail: ahaitz@molloy.edu. Web site: http://www.molloy.edu/academics/nursing-division.

Monmouth University, The Graduate School, The Marjorie K. Unterberg School of Nursing and Health Studies, West Long Branch, NJ 07764-1898. Offers adult nurse practitioner (MSN); adult psychiatric and mental health advanced practice nursing (MSN, Post-Master's Certificate); advanced practice nursing (Post-Master's Certificate); family nurse practitioner (MSN, Post-Master's Certificate); forensic nursing (MSN, Certificate); nursing (MSN); nursing administration (MSN, Post-Master's Certificate); nursing education (MSN, Post-Master's Certificate); nursing practice (DNP); school nursing (MSN, Certificate). *Accreditation:* AACN. Part-time and evening/weekend programs available. *Faculty:* 12 full-time (all women), 2 part-time/adjunct (both women). *Students:* 16 full-time (11 women), 244 part-time (238 women); includes 73 minority (23 Black or African American, non-Hispanic/Latino; 2 American Indian or Alaska Native, non-Hispanic/Latino; 34 Asian, non-Hispanic/Latino; 12 Hispanic/Latino; 1 Native Hawaiian or other Pacific Islander, non-Hispanic/Latino; 1 Two or more races, non-Hispanic/Latino), 1 international. Average age 41. 107 applicants, 92% accepted, 67 enrolled. In 2011, 55 master's awarded. *Degree requirements:* For master's, practicum (for some tracks). *Entrance requirements:* For master's, GRE General Test, RN license, 1 year of work experience, minimum undergraduate GPA of 2.75. Additional exam requirements/recommendations for international students: Required—TOEFL (minimum score 550 paper-based; 213 computer-based; 79 iBT), IELTS (minimum score 5) or Michigan English Language Assessment Battery (minimum score 77), Cambridge A, B, C. *Application deadline:* For fall admission, 7/15 priority date for domestic students, 6/1 for international students; for spring admission, 11/15 priority date for domestic students, 11/1 for international students. Applications are processed on a rolling basis. Application fee: $50. Electronic applications accepted. *Financial support:* In 2011–12, 138 students received support, including 138 fellowships (averaging $1,423 per year), 4 research assistantships (averaging $5,240 per year); career-related internships or fieldwork, scholarships/grants, and unspecified assistantships also available. Support available to part-time students. Financial award applicants required to submit FAFSA. *Faculty research:* Relationship of undergraduate GPA and GRE to succeed in a graduate nursing program. *Unit head:* Dr. Janet Mahoney, Dean, 732-571-3443, Fax: 732-263-5131, E-mail: jmahoney@monmouth.edu. *Application contact:* Kevin Roane, Director, Office of Graduate Admission, 732-571-3452, Fax: 732-263-5123, E-mail: gradadm@monmouth.edu. Web site: http://www.monmouth.edu/nursingschool.

Montana State University, College of Graduate Studies, College of Nursing, Bozeman, MT 59717. Offers clinical nurse leader (MN); family nurse practitioner (MN, Post-Master's Certificate); nursing education (Certificate, Post-Master's Certificate); psychiatric mental health nurse practitioner (MN). *Accreditation:* AACN. Part-time programs available. Postbaccalaureate distance learning degree programs offered (minimal on-campus study). *Degree requirements:* For master's, comprehensive exam, thesis (for some programs). *Entrance requirements:* For master's, GRE General Test, minimum GPA of 3.0 for undergraduate and post-baccalaureate work. Additional exam requirements/recommendations for international students: Required—TOEFL (minimum score 580 paper-based; 213 computer-based). Electronic applications accepted. *Faculty research:* Rural nursing, health disparities, environmental/public health, oral health, resilience.

New York University, College of Nursing, Doctor of Nursing Practice Program, New York, NY 10012-1019. Offers advanced practice nursing (DNP), including adult acute care, adult nurse practitioner/holistic nursing, adult nurse practitioner/palliative care nursing, adult primary care, adult primary care/geriatrics, family, geriatrics, mental health nursing, nurse-midwifery, pediatrics. Part-time and evening/weekend programs available. *Faculty:* 7 full-time (all women). *Students:* 23 part-time (19 women); includes 6 minority (4 Black or African American, non-Hispanic/Latino; 1 Asian, non-Hispanic/Latino; 1 Hispanic/Latino), 1 international. Average age 46. 20 applicants, 80% accepted, 11 enrolled. In 2011, 8 doctorates awarded. *Degree requirements:* For doctorate, thesis/dissertation. *Entrance requirements:* For doctorate, MS, RN license, interview, NP Certification. Additional exam requirements/recommendations for international students: Required—TOEFL, IELTS. *Application deadline:* For fall admission, 4/1 priority date for domestic students, 4/1 for international students. Applications are processed on a rolling basis. Application fee: $75. Electronic applications accepted. *Financial support:* In 2011–12, 15 students received support. Fellowships with full and partial tuition reimbursements available, institutionally sponsored loans, scholarships/grants, and tuition waivers (partial) available. Support

available to part-time students. Financial award application deadline: 2/1; financial award applicants required to submit FAFSA. *Faculty research:* Elderly black diabetics, families and illness, oral systemic connection. *Unit head:* Dr. Jamesetta A. Newland, Director, 212-998-5319, Fax: 212-995-3143, E-mail: jan7@nyu.edu. *Application contact:* Gail Wolfmeyer, Assistant Director, Graduate Student Affairs and Admissions, 212-992-7653, Fax: 212-995-4302, E-mail: gail.wolfmeyer@nyu.edu.

New York University, College of Nursing, Programs in Advanced Practice Nursing, New York, NY 10012-1019. Offers advanced practice nursing: adult acute care (MS, Advanced Certificate); advanced practice nursing: adult nurse practitioner/holistic nurse practitioner (Advanced Certificate); advanced practice nursing: adult nurse practitioner/ palliative care nurse practitioner (Advanced Certificate); advanced practice nursing: adult primary care (MS, Advanced Certificate); advanced practice nursing: family (MS, Advanced Certificate); advanced practice nursing: geriatrics (Advanced Certificate); advanced practice nursing: mental health (MS); advanced practice nursing: mental health nursing (Advanced Certificate); advanced practice nursing: pediatrics (MS, Advanced Certificate); nurse midwifery (MS, Advanced Certificate); nursing administration (MS, Advanced Certificate); nursing education (MS, Advanced Certificate); nursing informatics (MS, Advanced Certificate); MS/MPA; MS/MPH. *Accreditation:* AACN; ACNM/ACME. Part-time programs available. *Faculty:* 23 full-time (all women), 60 part-time/adjunct (47 women). *Students:* 27 full-time (23 women), 552 part-time (514 women); includes 251 minority (91 Black or African American, non-Hispanic/Latino; 115 Asian, non-Hispanic/Latino; 34 Hispanic/Latino; 11 Native Hawaiian or other Pacific Islander, non-Hispanic/Latino), 8 international. Average age 33. 325 applicants, 81% accepted, 179 enrolled. In 2011, 89 master's awarded. *Degree requirements:* For master's, thesis (for some programs). *Entrance requirements:* For master's, BS in nursing, AS in nursing with another BS/BA, interview, RN license, 1 year of clinical experience (3 for nursing education program); for Advanced Certificate, master's degree. Additional exam requirements/recommendations for international students: Required—TOEFL, IELTS. *Application deadline:* For fall admission, 7/1 priority date for domestic students, 7/1 for international students; for spring admission, 12/1 for domestic and international students. Applications are processed on a rolling basis. Application fee: $75. Electronic applications accepted. *Financial support:* In 2011–12, 36 students received support. Career-related internships or fieldwork, institutionally sponsored loans, scholarships/grants, traineeships, and tuition waivers (partial) available. Support available to part-time students. Financial award application deadline: 2/1; financial award applicants required to submit FAFSA. *Faculty research:* Elderly black diabetics, families and illness, oral systemic connection. *Unit head:* Dr. Judith Haber, Associate Dean, 212-998-9020, Fax: 212-995-3143, E-mail: jh33@nyu.edu. *Application contact:* Gail Wolfmeyer, Assistant Director, Graduate Student Affairs and Admissions, 212-992-7653, Fax: 212-995-4302, E-mail: gail.wolfmeyer@nyu.edu.

Northeastern University, Bouvé College of Health Sciences, School of Nursing, Program in Psychiatric-Mental Health Nursing, Boston, MA 02115-5096. Offers MS, CAGS, CAS. *Accreditation:* AACN. *Faculty:* 25 full-time, 4 part-time/adjunct. *Students:* 8 full-time, 15 part-time. Average age 45. In 2011, 2 degrees awarded. *Degree requirements:* For master's, thesis or alternative. *Entrance requirements:* For master's, GRE General Test; for other advanced degree, MS in nursing. Additional exam requirements/recommendations for international students: Required—TOEFL (minimum score 100 iBT). *Application deadline:* For fall admission, 7/1 for domestic students. Application fee: $50. Electronic applications accepted. *Financial support:* Research assistantships, teaching assistantships, scholarships/grants, traineeships, and tuition waivers (partial) available. Financial award application deadline: 7/1; financial award applicants required to submit FAFSA. *Faculty research:* Clinical psychopharmacology, access to mental health care, child abuse, seasonal affective disorder (SAD), chronic and persistent mental illness. *Unit head:* Ann Polcari, Psychiatric Graduate Program Coordinator, 617-373-7571, E-mail: a.polcari@neu.edu. *Application contact:* Margaret Schnabel, Director of Graduate Admissions, 617-373-2708, E-mail: bouvegrad@neu.edu. Web site: http://www.northeastern.edu/bouve/programs/cppsychealthnurse.html.

Oregon Health & Science University, School of Nursing, Program in Mental Health Nursing, Portland, OR 97239-3098. Offers MN, MS, Post Master's Certificate. *Accreditation:* AACN. *Degree requirements:* For master's, thesis optional. *Entrance requirements:* For master's, GRE General Test, bachelor's degree in nursing, minimum undergraduate GPA of 3.0, previous course work in statistics; for Post Master's Certificate, master's degree in nursing.

Pontifical Catholic University of Puerto Rico, College of Sciences, Department of Nursing, Program in Mental Health and Psychiatric Nursing, Ponce, PR 00717-0777. Offers MSN. Part-time and evening/weekend programs available. *Degree requirements:* For master's, comprehensive exam (for some programs), thesis, clinical research paper. *Entrance requirements:* For master's, GRE General Test, 2 letters of recommendation, interview, minimum GPA of 2.75. Electronic applications accepted.

Rivier University, School of Graduate Studies, Division of Nursing, Nashua, NH 03060. Offers adult psychiatric/mental health practitioner (MS); family nurse practitioner (MS); nursing education (MS). *Accreditation:* NLN. Part-time and evening/weekend programs available. *Entrance requirements:* For master's, GRE, MAT. Electronic applications accepted.

Rush University, College of Nursing, Department of Community Systems and Mental Health Nursing, Chicago, IL 60612-3832. Offers community and mental health nursing (DNP, PhD); family nurse practitioner (MSN, Post-Master's Certificate); psychiatric clinical specialist (MSN); psychiatric nurse practitioner - adult (MSN); psychiatric nurse practitioner - family (MSN); psychiatric-mental health clinical specialist (Post-Master's Certificate); psychiatric-mental health nurse practitioner (Post-Master's Certificate); public health nursing (MSN). *Accreditation:* AACN. Part-time programs available. Postbaccalaureate distance learning degree programs offered (minimal on-campus study). Terminal master's awarded for partial completion of doctoral program. *Degree requirements:* For master's, capstone project; for doctorate, thesis/dissertation, DNP leadership project. *Entrance requirements:* For master's, GRE General Test (waived if nursing GPA is above 3.0 or cumulative GPA is above 3.25), interview; for doctorate, GRE General Test, interview, course work in statistics (DN Sc). Electronic applications accepted. *Faculty research:* Immigrant mental health, de-escalation strategies, caregiver interventions, parent-teacher training, restraint use.

Rutgers, The State University of New Jersey, Newark, Graduate School, Program in Nursing, Newark, NJ 07102. Offers nursing (MS), including acute care of adults and aged, advanced practice in pediatric nursing, advanced practice with childbearing families, community health nursing, family nurse practitioner, primary care of adults and aged, psychiatric/mental health nursing. *Accreditation:* AACN. Part-time programs available. *Degree requirements:* For master's, comprehensive exam. *Entrance requirements:* For master's, GRE General Test, RN license, minimum B average, BS in nursing. Additional exam requirements/recommendations for international students: Required—TOEFL. Electronic applications accepted. *Faculty research:* HIV/AIDS, quality of life: MS and breast cancer, sleep patterns of cardiac patients.

Sage Graduate School, School of Health Sciences, Department of Nursing, Program in Psychiatric Mental Health Nurse Practitioner, Troy, NY 12180-4115. Offers psychiatric mental health (MS, Post Master's Certificate). *Accreditation:* AACN. Part-time and evening/weekend programs available. *Faculty:* 5 full-time (all women), 9 part-time/adjunct (all women). *Students:* 7 full-time (all women), 24 part-time (22 women); includes 3 minority (1 American Indian or Alaska Native, non-Hispanic/Latino; 1 Asian, non-Hispanic/Latino; 1 Hispanic/Latino). Average age 44. 16 applicants, 44% accepted, 7 enrolled. In 2011, 5 master's, 2 other advanced degrees awarded. *Degree requirements:* For master's, thesis or alternative. *Entrance requirements:* For master's, BS in nursing, minimum GPA of 2.75, resume, 2 letters of recommendation. Additional exam requirements/recommendations for international students: Required—TOEFL (minimum score 550 paper-based; 213 computer-based). *Application deadline:* Applications are processed on a rolling basis. Application fee: $40. *Expenses: Tuition:* Full-time $11,880; part-time $660 per credit hour. Tuition and fees vary according to program. *Financial support:* Fellowships, research assistantships, teaching assistantships, Federal Work-Study, scholarships/grants, and unspecified assistantships available. Support available to part-time students. Financial award application deadline: 3/1; financial award applicants required to submit FAFSA. *Unit head:* Dr. Esther Haskevitz, Dean, School of Health Sciences, 518-244-2296, Fax: 518-244-4571, E-mail: haskve@sage.edu. *Application contact:* Arlene Pericak, Director, 518-244-2012, Fax: 518-244-2009, E-mail: perica@sage.edu.

Saint Francis Medical Center College of Nursing, Graduate Programs, Peoria, IL 61603-3783. Offers child and family nurse practitioner (MSN); clinical nurse leader (MSN); family nurse practitioner (MSN); family psychiatric mental health nurse practitioner (MSN); medical-surgical nursing (MSN); neonatal nurse practitioner (MSN); nurse clinician (Post-Graduate Certificate); nurse educator (MSN, Post-Graduate Certificate); nursing (DNP); nursing management leadership (MSN). *Accreditation:* NLN. Part-time programs available. Postbaccalaureate distance learning degree programs offered (minimal on-campus study). *Faculty:* 6 full-time (all women), 5 part-time/adjunct (all women). *Students:* 26 full-time (25 women), 174 part-time (166 women); includes 19 minority (8 Black or African American, non-Hispanic/Latino; 1 American Indian or Alaska Native, non-Hispanic/Latino; 3 Asian, non-Hispanic/Latino; 6 Hispanic/Latino; 1 Native Hawaiian or other Pacific Islander, non-Hispanic/Latino). Average age 37. 123 applicants, 93% accepted, 93 enrolled. In 2011, 29 degrees awarded. *Degree requirements:* For master's, research experience, portfolio, practicum; for doctorate, practicum hours. *Entrance requirements:* For master's, nursing research, health assessment, graduate course work in statistics, RN license; for doctorate, master's degree in nursing, professional portfolio, graduate statistics, transcripts, RN license. Additional exam requirements/recommendations for international students: Required—TOEFL. *Application deadline:* For fall admission, 6/1 priority date for domestic students, 6/1 for international students; for spring admission, 11/15 priority date for domestic students, 11/15 for international students. Applications are processed on a rolling basis. Application fee: $50. Electronic applications accepted. *Expenses: Tuition:* Full-time $6120; part-time $510 per semester hour. *Required fees:* $300. *Financial support:* In 2011–12, 3 students received support. Scholarships/grants and tuition waivers (partial) available. Support available to part-time students. Financial award application deadline: 6/15; financial award applicants required to submit FAFSA. *Faculty research:* Outcome and curriculum planning, health promotion, NCLEX-RN results, decision-making program evaluation. *Unit head:* Dr. Patti A. Stockert, President of the College, 309-655-4124, Fax: 309-624-8973, E-mail: patricia.a.stockert@osfhealthcare.org. *Application contact:* Dr. Janice F. Boundy, Dean, 309-655-2230, Fax: 309-624-8973, E-mail: jan.f.boundy@osfhealthcare.org. Web site: http://www.sfmccon.edu/graduate-programs/.

Seattle University, College of Nursing, Program in Advanced Practice Nursing Immersion, Seattle, WA 98122-1090. Offers adult/gerontological nurse practitioner (MSN); advanced community public health (MSN); certified nurse midwifery (MSN); family nurse practitioner (MSN); psychiatric mental health nurse practitioner (MSN). *Faculty:* 43 full-time, 63 part-time/adjunct. *Students:* 104 full-time (91 women); includes 24 minority (2 Black or African American, non-Hispanic/Latino; 12 Asian, non-Hispanic/Latino; 7 Hispanic/Latino; 3 Two or more races, non-Hispanic/Latino). Average age 30. *Degree requirements:* For master's, thesis or scholarly project. *Entrance requirements:* For master's, GRE, bachelor's degree, minimum GPA of 3.0, professional resume, two recommendations, letter of intent, English proficiency (for non-English speakers). Additional exam requirements/recommendations for international students: Required—TOEFL (minimum score 92 iBT), IELTS. *Application deadline:* For fall admission, 12/1 for domestic and international students. Application fee: $55. Electronic applications accepted. *Financial support:* Scholarships/grants and traineeships available. Financial award applicants required to submit FAFSA. *Unit head:* Dr. Azita Emami, Dean, 206-296-5660. *Application contact:* Janet Shandley, Associate Dean of Graduate Admissions, 206-296-5900, Fax: 206-298-5656, E-mail: grad_admissions@seattleu.edu.

Seattle University, College of Nursing, Program in Nursing, Seattle, WA 98122-1090. Offers adult/gerontological nurse practitioner (MSN); advanced community public health (MSN); psychiatric mental health nurse practitioner (MSN). *Faculty:* 43 full-time, 63 part-time/adjunct. *Students:* 22 full-time (20 women); includes 4 minority (1 Black or African American, non-Hispanic/Latino; 1 Asian, non-Hispanic/Latino; 1 Hispanic/Latino; 1 Two or more races, non-Hispanic/Latino). *Degree requirements:* For master's, thesis or scholarly project. *Entrance requirements:* For master's, GRE, bachelor's degree in nursing or associate degree in nursing with baccalaureate in different major, 5-quarter statistics course, minimum cumulative GPA of 3.0, professional resume, two recommendations, letter of intent, English proficiency (for non-English speakers), copy of current RN license or ability to obtain RN license in WA state. Additional exam requirements/recommendations for international students: Required—TOEFL (minimum score 92 iBT), IELTS. *Application deadline:* For fall admission, 12/1 for domestic and international students. Application fee: $55. Electronic applications accepted. *Financial support:* In 2011–12, 2 teaching assistantships were awarded; scholarships/grants and traineeships also available. Financial award applicants required to submit FAFSA. *Unit head:* Dr. Azita Emami, Dean, 206-296-5660. *Application contact:* Janet Shandley, Associate Dean of Graduate Admissions, 206-296-5900, Fax: 206-298-5656, E-mail: grad_admissions@seattleu.edu.

Shenandoah University, School of Health Professions, Division of Nursing, Winchester, VA 22601-5195. Offers family nurse practitioner (Certificate); nurse-midwifery (Certificate); nurse-midwifery endorsement (Certificate); nursing (MSN, DNP); post-master's in nursing education (Certificate); psychiatric mental health nurse practitioner (Certificate). *Accreditation:* AACN; ACNM/ACME. Part-time programs available. *Faculty:* 11 full-time (all women), 2 part-time/adjunct (both women). *Students:* 40 full-time (34 women), 102 part-time (96 women); includes 32 minority (22 Black or African American, non-Hispanic/Latino; 1 American Indian or Alaska Native, non-Hispanic/Latino; 5 Asian, non-Hispanic/Latino; 3 Hispanic/Latino; 1 Two or more races, non-Hispanic/Latino), 2 international. Average age 39. 69 applicants, 90% accepted, 45 enrolled. In 2011, 15 master's, 2 doctorates, 17 other advanced degrees awarded. *Degree requirements:* For master's, research project, clinical hours; for doctorate and Certificate, clinical hours. *Entrance requirements:* For master's, GRE General Test, previous course work in statistics, community nursing, and physical assessment; RN license; BSN; minimum undergraduate GPA of 3.0; appropriate clinical experience; curriculum vitae; 3 letters of recommendation; for doctorate, MSN, minimum GPA of 3.0, 3 letters of recommendation,

essay, interview; for Certificate, MSN, minimum GPA of 3.0, 3 letters of recommendation, minimum of one year (2,080 hours) clinical nursing experience, interview. Additional exam requirements/recommendations for international students: Required—TOEFL (minimum score 550 paper-based; 213 computer-based; 79 iBT), IELTS (minimum score 6.5), Sakae Institute of Study Abroad (minimum score 550). *Application deadline:* For fall admission, 6/15 priority date for domestic students, 6/15 for international students. Applications are processed on a rolling basis. Application fee: $30. Electronic applications accepted. *Expenses: Tuition:* Full-time $17,952; part-time $748 per credit. *Required fees.* $500 per term. Tuition and fees vary according to course level, course load and program. *Financial support:* In 2011–12, 13 students received support, including 3 teaching assistantships with partial tuition reimbursements available (averaging $4,224 per year); career-related internships or fieldwork, institutionally sponsored loans, scholarships/grants, unspecified assistantships, and federal loans, alternative loans also available. Support available to part-time students. Financial award application deadline: 3/15; financial award applicants required to submit FAFSA. *Faculty research:* Moral reasoning in nurses, improving health care access to under-served rural women, screening for depression and anxiety in the obese in a rural free clinic, health care outcomes among patients in a free clinic setting cared for by nurse practitioners, effects of depression on diabetes as evidenced by the relationship between the patient healthcare questionnaire (PHQ-9) scores and the patient's glycohemoglobin (HbA1c). *Unit head:* Dr. Kathryn Ganske, Director, 540-678-4374, Fax: 540-665-5519, E-mail: kganske@su.edu. *Application contact:* David Anthony, Dean of Admissions, 540-665-4581, Fax: 540-665-4627, E-mail: admit@su.edu. Web site: http://www.su.edu/nurse.

Southeastern Louisiana University, College of Nursing and Health Sciences, School of Nursing, Hammond, LA 70402. Offers adult psychiatric/mental health nurse practitioner/clinical nurse specialist (MSN); education (MSN); nurse executive (MSN); nurse practitioner (MSN). *Accreditation:* AACN. Part-time and evening/weekend programs available. *Faculty:* 12 full-time (11 women), 7 part-time/adjunct (4 women). *Students:* 17 full-time (16 women), 108 part-time (94 women); includes 12 minority (8 Black or African American, non-Hispanic/Latino; 2 Asian, non-Hispanic/Latino; 1 Hispanic/Latino; 1 Two or more races, non-Hispanic/Latino), 1 international. Average age 35. 50 applicants, 100% accepted, 29 enrolled. In 2011, 27 degrees awarded. *Degree requirements:* For master's, thesis. *Entrance requirements:* For master's, GRE (verbal and quantitative), baccalaureate degree in nursing from accredited undergraduate nursing program; minimum GPA of 2.7; all transcripts from undergraduate school and any work attempted at the graduate level; curriculum vitae; valid Louisiana Registered Nurse license; letters of recommendation; letter of intent/statement of purpose. Additional exam requirements/recommendations for international students: Required—TOEFL (minimum score 500 paper-based; 173 computer-based; 61 iBT). *Application deadline:* For fall admission, 7/15 priority date for domestic students, 6/1 for international students; for spring admission, 12/1 priority date for domestic students, 10/1 for international students. Applications are processed on a rolling basis. Application fee: $20 ($30 for international students). Electronic applications accepted. *Expenses:* Tuition, state resident: full-time $3977; part-time $283 per semester hour. Tuition, nonresident: full-time $13,482; part-time $811 per semester hour. *Financial support:* Federal Work-Study, institutionally sponsored loans, scholarships/grants, traineeships, and unspecified assistantships available. Support available to part-time students. Financial award application deadline: 5/1; financial award applicants required to submit FAFSA. *Faculty research:* Gender issues, LGBT issues, occupational health/safety, accelerated students, caring development. *Total annual research expenditures:* $245,268. *Unit head:* Dr. Lorinda Sealy, Graduate Coordinator, 985-549-5045, Fax: 985-549-5087, E-mail: lorinda.sealy@selu.edu. *Application contact:* Sandra Meyers, Graduate Admissions Analyst, 985-549-5620, Fax: 985-549-5632, E-mail: admissions@selu.edu. Web site: http://www.selu.edu/acad_research/depts/nurs.

Southern Arkansas University–Magnolia, Graduate Programs, Magnolia, AR 71754. Offers agriculture (MS); business administration (MBA); computer and information sciences (MS); education (M Ed), including counseling and development, curriculum and instruction, educational administration and supervision, elementary education, middle level, reading, secondary education, TESOL; kinesiology (M Ed); library media and information specialist (M Ed); mental health and clinical counseling (MS); public administration (MPA); school counseling (M Ed); teaching (MAT). *Accreditation:* NCATE. Part-time and evening/weekend programs available. Postbaccalaureate distance learning degree programs offered. *Faculty:* 34 full-time (15 women), 8 part-time/adjunct (5 women). *Students:* 87 full-time (62 women), 320 part-time (224 women); includes 116 minority (111 Black or African American, non-Hispanic/Latino; 2 American Indian or Alaska Native, non-Hispanic/Latino; 2 Asian, non-Hispanic/Latino; 1 Hispanic/Latino), 25 international. Average age 33. 201 applicants, 98% accepted, 156 enrolled. In 2011, 162 master's awarded. *Degree requirements:* For master's, comprehensive exam (for some programs), thesis optional. *Entrance requirements:* For master's, GRE, MAT or GMAT, minimum GPA of 2.5. Additional exam requirements/recommendations for international students: Required—TOEFL (minimum score 173 computer-based). *Application deadline:* For fall admission, 7/15 for domestic and international students; for winter admission, 12/1 for domestic and international students; for spring admission, 12/1 for domestic and international students. Applications are processed on a rolling basis. Application fee: $25 ($35 for international students). Electronic applications accepted. *Expenses:* Tuition, state resident: part-time $232 per credit. Tuition, nonresident: part-time $339 per credit. *Required fees:* $44 per credit. Part-time tuition and fees vary according to course load. *Financial support:* Career-related internships or fieldwork, Federal Work-Study, scholarships/grants, tuition waivers (full), and unspecified assistantships available. Financial award applicants required to submit FAFSA. *Faculty research:* Alternative certification for teachers, supervision of instruction, instructional leadership, counseling. *Unit head:* Dr. Kim Bloss, Dean, School of Graduate Studies, 870-235-4150, Fax: 870-235-5227, E-mail: kkbloss@saumag.edu. *Application contact:* Gaye Calhoun, Admissions Specialist, 870-235-4150, Fax: 870-235-5227, E-mail: glcalhoun@saumag.edu. Web site: http://www.saumag.edu/graduate.

Stony Brook University, State University of New York, Stony Brook University Medical Center, Health Sciences Center, School of Nursing, Program in Mental Health/Psychiatric Nursing, Stony Brook, NY 11794. Offers MS, Certificate. *Accreditation:* AACN. *Degree requirements:* For master's, thesis. *Entrance requirements:* For master's, BSN, minimum GPA of 3.0, course work in statistics.

Uniformed Services University of the Health Sciences, Graduate School of Nursing, Bethesda, MD 20814-4799. Offers family nurse practitioner (MSN); nurse anesthesia (MSN); nursing science (PhD); perioperative clinical nurse specialty (MSN); psychiatric mental health nurse practitioner (MSN). Program available to military officers only. *Accreditation:* AACN; AANA/CANAEP. *Faculty:* 36 full-time (21 women), 2 part-time/adjunct (0 women). *Students:* 71 full-time (35 women); includes 17 minority (11 Black or African American, non-Hispanic/Latino; 3 Asian, non-Hispanic/Latino; 3 Hispanic/Latino). Average age 36. 120 applicants, 59% accepted, 71 enrolled. In 2011, 57 master's, 2 doctorates awarded. *Degree requirements:* For master's, thesis or alternative. *Entrance requirements:* For master's, GRE, BSN, clinical experience, minimum GPA of 3.0, previous course work in science, writing paper; for doctorate, GRE, written papers, articles. *Application deadline:* For fall admission, 7/1 for domestic students; for winter admission, 2/15 for domestic students. Application fee: $0.

Electronic applications accepted. *Faculty research:* Prenatal care, military health care, military readiness, distance learning. *Unit head:* Dr. Carol A. Romano, Associate Dean for Academic Affairs, 301-295-1180, Fax: 301-295-1707, E-mail: carol.romano@usuhs.edu. *Application contact:* Terry Lynn Malavakis, Recording Secretary for Admissions Committee, 301-295-1055, Fax: 301-295-1707, E-mail: terry.malavakis@usuhs.edu. Web site: http://www.usuhs.mil/gsn/.

University at Buffalo, the State University of New York, Graduate School, School of Nursing, Buffalo, NY 14214. Offers adult clinical nurse specialist (DNP); adult nurse practitioner (DNP); family nurse practitioner (DNP); health care systems and leadership (MS); nurse anesthetist (DNP); nursing (PhD); nursing education (Certificate); post-master's track (DNP); psychiatric mental health nurse practitioner (DNP). *Accreditation:* AACN; AANA/CANAEP (one or more programs are accredited). Part-time programs available. Postbaccalaureate distance learning degree programs offered (minimal on-campus study). *Faculty:* 29 full-time (25 women), 18 part-time/adjunct (17 women). *Students:* 101 full-time (76 women), 100 part-time (90 women); includes 19 minority (10 Black or African American, non-Hispanic/Latino; 2 American Indian or Alaska Native, non-Hispanic/Latino; 2 Asian, non-Hispanic/Latino; 2 Hispanic/Latino; 3 Native Hawaiian or other Pacific Islander, non-Hispanic/Latino), 34 international. Average age 34. 342 applicants, 26% accepted, 67 enrolled. In 2011, 51 master's, 3 doctorates awarded. *Median time to degree:* Of those who began their doctoral program in fall 2003, 75% received their degree in 8 years or less. *Degree requirements:* For master's, thesis optional, comprehensive exams or project; for doctorate, comprehensive exam (for some programs), capstone (for DNP), dissertation (for PhD). *Entrance requirements:* For doctorate, GRE or MAT, minimum GPA of 3.0 (3.25 for PhD), RN license, BS or MS in nursing, 3 references, writing sample; for Certificate, interview, minimum GPA of 3.0 or GRE General Test, RN license, MS in nursing. Additional exam requirements/recommendations for international students: Required—TOEFL (minimum score 550 paper-based; 213 computer-based; 79 iBT), IELTS (minimum score 6.5). *Application deadline:* For fall admission, 8/15 for domestic students, 4/1 for international students; for spring admission, 12/15 for domestic students, 10/1 for international students. Application fee: $75. Electronic applications accepted. *Financial support:* In 2011–12, 80 students received support, including 6 fellowships with full tuition reimbursements available (averaging $17,000 per year), 3 research assistantships with full tuition reimbursements available (averaging $10,600 per year), 5 teaching assistantships with full tuition reimbursements available (averaging $10,600 per year); scholarships/grants, traineeships, health care benefits, and unspecified assistantships also available. Financial award application deadline: 3/15; financial award applicants required to submit FAFSA. *Faculty research:* Oncology, palliative care, gerontology, addictions, mental health, community wellness. *Total annual research expenditures:* $1.3 million. *Unit head:* Dr. Marsha L. Lewis, Dean and Professor, 716-829-2533, Fax: 716-829-2566, E-mail: ubnursingdean@buffalo.edu. *Application contact:* Dr. David J. Lang, Director of Student Affairs, 716-829-2537, Fax: 716-829-2067, E-mail: nursing@buffalo.edu. Web site: http://nursing.buffalo.edu/.

University of Alaska Anchorage, College of Health, School of Nursing, Anchorage, AK 99508. Offers family nurse practitioner (Certificate); nursing (MS); nursing education (Certificate); psychiatric nurse practitioner (Certificate). *Accreditation:* NLN. Part-time and evening/weekend programs available. *Degree requirements:* For master's, comprehensive exam, individual project. *Entrance requirements:* For master's, GRE or MAT, BS in nursing, interview, minimum GPA of 3.0, RN license, 1 year of part-time or 6 months of full-time clinical experience. Additional exam requirements/recommendations for international students: Required—TOEFL (minimum score 550 paper-based; 213 computer-based).

University of Cincinnati, Graduate School, College of Nursing, Cincinnati, OH 45221-0038. Offers clinical nurse specialist (MSN), including adult health, community health, neonatal, nursing administration, occupational health, pediatric health, psychiatric nursing, women's health; nurse anesthesia (MSN); nurse midwifery (MSN); nurse practitioner (MSN), including acute care, ambulatory care, family, family/psychiatric, women's health; nursing (PhD); MBA/MSN. *Accreditation:* AACN; AANA/CANAEP (one or more programs are accredited); ACNM/ACME. Part-time programs available. Postbaccalaureate distance learning degree programs offered (no on-campus study). Terminal master's awarded for partial completion of doctoral program. *Degree requirements:* For master's, thesis or alternative; for doctorate, comprehensive exam, thesis/dissertation. *Entrance requirements:* For master's and doctorate, GRE General Test. Additional exam requirements/recommendations for international students: Required—TOEFL (minimum score 520 paper-based; 190 computer-based). Electronic applications accepted. *Faculty research:* Substance abuse, injury and violence, symptom management.

University of Colorado Denver, College of Nursing, Aurora, CO 80045. Offers adult clinical nurse specialist (MS); adult nurse practitioner (MS); family nurse practitioner (MS); family psychiatric mental health nurse practitioner (MS); health care informatics (MS); nurse-midwifery (MS); nursing (DNP, PhD); nursing leadership and health care systems (MS); pediatric nurse practitioner (MS); pediatric nursing leadership (MS); special studies (MS); women's health care (MS); MS/PhD. *Accreditation:* ACNM/ACME (one or more programs are accredited); NLN (one or more programs are accredited). Part-time and evening/weekend programs available. Postbaccalaureate distance learning degree programs offered (minimal on-campus study). *Faculty:* 69 full-time (65 women), 68 part-time/adjunct (64 women). *Students:* 308 full-time (288 women), 134 part-time (118 women); includes 59 minority (11 Black or African American, non-Hispanic/Latino; 8 American Indian or Alaska Native, non-Hispanic/Latino; 10 Asian, non-Hispanic/Latino; 27 Hispanic/Latino; 3 Two or more races, non-Hispanic/Latino), 8 international. Average age 39. 298 applicants, 46% accepted, 110 enrolled. In 2011, 72 master's, 19 doctorates awarded. Terminal master's awarded for partial completion of doctoral program. *Degree requirements:* For master's, thesis optional; for doctorate, comprehensive exam, thesis/dissertation, 42 credits of coursework, 30 credits of dissertation. *Entrance requirements:* For master's, GRE if cumulative undergraduate GPA is less than 3.0, undergraduate nursing degree from NLNAC- or CCNE-accredited school or university; completion of research and statistics courses with minimum grade of C; copy of current and unencumbered nursing license; for doctorate, GRE, bachelor's and/or master's degrees in nursing from NLN- or CCNE-accredited institution; portfolio; minimum undergraduate GPA of 3.0, graduate 3.5; graduate-level intermediate statistics and master's-level nursing theory courses with minimum B grade; interview. Additional exam requirements/recommendations for international students: Required—TOEFL (minimum score 560 paper-based; 220 computer-based; 83 iBT). *Application deadline:* For fall admission, 4/1 for domestic students; for spring admission, 9/1 for domestic students. Application fee: $65. Electronic applications accepted. *Expenses:* Contact institution. *Financial support:* In 2011–12, 40 students received support. Fellowships, research assistantships, teaching assistantships, Federal Work-Study, scholarships/grants, and unspecified assistantships available. Support available to part-time students. Financial award application deadline: 4/1; financial award applicants required to submit FAFSA. *Faculty research:* Biological and behavioral phenomena in pregnancy and postpartum; patterns of glycemia during the insulin resistance of pregnancy; obesity, gestational diabetes, and relationship to neonatal adiposity; men's awareness and knowledge of male breast cancer; cognitive-behavioral therapy for chronic insomnia after breast cancer treatment; massage therapy for the treatment of tension-type

headaches. *Total annual research expenditures:* $5.2 million. *Unit head:* Dr. Patricia Moritz, Dean, 303-724-1679, E-mail: pat.moritz@ucdenver.edu. *Application contact:* Judy Campbell, Graduate Programs Coordinator, 303-724-8503, E-mail: judy.campbell@ucdenver.edu. Web site: http://www.ucdenver.edu/academics/colleges/nursing/Pages/default.aspx.

University of Delaware, College of Health Sciences, School of Nursing, Newark, DE 19716. Offers adult nurse practitioner (MSN, PMC); cardiopulmonary clinical nurse specialist (MSN, PMC); cardiopulmonary clinical nurse specialist/adult nurse practitioner (MSN, PMC); family nurse practitioner (MSN, PMC); gerontology clinical nurse specialist (MSN, PMC); gerontology clinical nurse specialist geriatric nurse practitioner (PMC); gerontology clinical nurse specialist/geriatric nurse practitioner (MSN); health services administration (MSN, PMC); nursing of children clinical nurse specialist (MSN, PMC); nursing of children clinical nurse specialist/pediatric nurse practitioner (MSN, PMC); oncology/immune deficiency clinical nurse specialist (MSN, PMC); oncology/immune deficiency clinical nurse specialist/adult nurse practitioner (MSN, PMC); perinatal/women's health clinical nurse specialist (MSN, PMC); perinatal/women's health clinical nurse specialist/women's health nurse practitioner (MSN, PMC); psychiatric nursing clinical nurse specialist (MSN, PMC). *Accreditation:* AACN; NLN (one or more programs are accredited). Part-time and evening/weekend programs available. Postbaccalaureate distance learning degree programs offered (minimal on-campus study). *Degree requirements:* For master's, thesis optional. *Entrance requirements:* For master's, BSN, interview, RN license. Electronic applications accepted. *Faculty research:* Marriage and chronic illness, health promotion, congestive heart failure patient outcomes, school nursing, diabetes in children, culture, health disparities, cardiovascular, prison nursing, oncology, public policy, child obesity, smoking and teen pregnancy, blood pressure measurements, men's health.

University of Illinois at Chicago, Graduate College, College of Nursing, Program in Nursing, Chicago, IL 60607-7128. Offers acute care clinical nurse specialist (MS); acute care nurse practitioner (MS); administrative studies in nursing (MS); adult nurse practitioner (MS); adult/geriatric nurse practitioner (MS); advanced community health nurse specialist (MS); family nurse practitioner (MS); geriatric clinical nurse specialist (MS); geriatric nurse practitioner (MS); mental health clinical nurse specialist (MS); mental health nurse practitioner (MS); nurse midwifery (MS); occupational health/advanced community health nurse specialist (MS); occupational health/family nurse practitioner (MS); pediatric clinical nurse specialist (MS); pediatric nurse practitioner (MS); perinatal clinical nurse specialist (MS); school/advanced community health nurse specialist (MS); school/family nurse practitioner (MS); women's health nurse practitioner (MS). *Accreditation:* AACN. Part-time programs available. *Degree requirements:* For master's, thesis or alternative. *Entrance requirements:* For master's, GRE General Test, minimum GPA of 2.75. Additional exam requirements/recommendations for international students: Required—TOEFL. Electronic applications accepted.

The University of Kansas, University of Kansas Medical Center, School of Nursing, Kansas City, KS 66160. Offers adult/gerontological clinical nurse specialist (PMC); adult/gerontological nurse practitioner (PMC); clinical research management (PMC); family nurse practitioner (PMC); health care informatics (PMC); health professions educator (PMC); nurse midwife (PMC); nursing (MS, DNP, PhD); organizational leadership (PMC); psychiatric/mental health nurse practitioner (PMC); public health nursing (PMC). *Accreditation:* AACN; ACNM/ACME. Part-time programs available. Postbaccalaureate distance learning degree programs offered (minimal on-campus study). *Faculty:* 80. *Students:* 79 full-time (71 women), 336 part-time (317 women); includes 63 minority (24 Black or African American, non-Hispanic/Latino; 2 American Indian or Alaska Native, non-Hispanic/Latino; 18 Asian, non-Hispanic/Latino; 15 Hispanic/Latino; 4 Two or more races, non-Hispanic/Latino), 6 international. Average age 37. 155 applicants, 82% accepted, 127 enrolled. In 2011, 79 master's, 15 doctorates, 12 other advanced degrees awarded. Terminal master's awarded for partial completion of doctoral program. *Degree requirements:* For master's, comprehensive exam, thesis optional, general oral exam; for doctorate, variable foreign language requirement, thesis/dissertation, comprehensive oral exam (for DNP); comprehensive written and oral exam (for PhD). *Entrance requirements:* For master's, bachelor's degree in nursing, minimum GPA of 3.0, RN license, 1 year of clinical experience, RN license in KS and MO; for doctorate, GRE General Test, master's degree in nursing, minimum GPA of 3.5, RN license in KS and MO; national certification (for some specialties). Additional exam requirements/recommendations for international students: Required—TOEFL. *Application deadline:* For fall admission, 4/1 for domestic and international students; for spring admission, 9/1 for domestic and international students. Application fee: $60. Electronic applications accepted. Tuition and fees vary according to course load, campus/location, program and reciprocity agreements. *Financial support:* Research assistantships with full and partial tuition reimbursements, teaching assistantships with full and partial tuition reimbursements, and traineeships available. Financial award application deadline: 2/14; financial award applicants required to submit FAFSA. *Faculty research:* Breastfeeding practices of teen mothers, national database of nursing quality indicators, caregiving of families of patients using technology in the home, simulation in nursing education, diaphragm fatigue. *Total annual research expenditures:* $6.1 million. *Unit head:* Dr. Karen L. Miller, Dean, 913-588-1601, Fax: 913-588-1660, E-mail: kmiller@kumc.edu. *Application contact:* Dr. Debra J. Ford, Associate Dean, Student Affairs, 913-588-1619, Fax: 913-588-1615, E-mail: dford@kumc.edu. Web site: http://nursing.kumc.edu.

University of Louisville, Graduate School, School of Nursing, Louisville, KY 40202. Offers adult nurse practitioner (MSN); family nurse practitioner (MSN); health professions education (MSN); neonatal nurse practitioner (MSN); nursing research (PhD); psychiatric mental health nurse practitioner (MSN). *Accreditation:* AACN. Part-time programs available. *Faculty:* 24 full-time (22 women), 4 part-time/adjunct (3 women). *Students:* 82 full-time (74 women), 65 part-time (58 women); includes 20 minority (13 Black or African American, non-Hispanic/Latino; 1 American Indian or Alaska Native, non-Hispanic/Latino; 1 Asian, non-Hispanic/Latino; 1 Hispanic/Latino; 4 Two or more races, non-Hispanic/Latino), 2 international. Average age 34. 41 applicants, 56% accepted, 19 enrolled. In 2011, 42 master's, 2 doctorates awarded. Terminal master's awarded for partial completion of doctoral program. *Degree requirements:* For master's, thesis optional; for doctorate, comprehensive exam, thesis/dissertation. *Entrance requirements:* For master's, GRE General Test, bachelor's degree in nursing, minimum GPA of 3.0, RN license; for doctorate, GRE General Test, BSN or MSN with recommended minimum GPA of 3.0. Additional exam requirements/recommendations for international students: Required—TOEFL. *Application deadline:* For fall admission, 4/1 priority date for domestic students, 4/1 for international students. Applications are processed on a rolling basis. Application fee: $50. Electronic applications accepted. *Expenses:* Tuition, state resident: full-time $9692; part-time $539 per credit hour. Tuition, nonresident: full-time $20,168; part-time $1121 per credit hour. Tuition and fees vary according to program and reciprocity agreements. *Financial support:* In 2011–12, 45 students received support, including 6 research assistantships with full tuition reimbursements available (averaging $20,000 per year), 6 teaching assistantships with full tuition reimbursements available (averaging $19,167 per year); fellowships with full tuition reimbursements available, institutionally sponsored loans, scholarships/grants, traineeships, health care benefits, and unspecified assistantships also available. Support available to part-time students. Financial award application deadline: 4/15; financial award applicants required to submit FAFSA. *Faculty research:* Maternal-child/family stress after pregnancy loss, postpartum depression, access to healthcare (underserved populations), quality of life issues, physical activity (impact on chronic/acute conditions). *Total annual research expenditures:* $795,250. *Unit head:* Dr. Marcia J. Hern, Dean, 502-852-8300, Fax: 502-852-5044, E-mail: m.hern@gwise.louisville.edu. *Application contact:* Dr. Lee Ridner, Interim Associate Dean for Academic Affairs and Director of MSN Programs, 502-852-8518, Fax: 502-852-0704, E-mail: romain01@louisville.edu. Web site: http://www.louisville.edu/nursing/.

University of Maryland, Baltimore, Graduate School, School of Nursing, Master's Program in Nursing, Baltimore, MD 21201. Offers community health nursing (MS); gerontological nursing (MS); maternal-child nursing (MS); medical-surgical nursing (MS); nurse-midwifery education (MS); nursing administration (MS); nursing education (MS); nursing health policy (MS); primary care nursing (MS); psychiatric nursing (MS); MS/MBA. MS/MBA offered jointly with University of Baltimore. *Accreditation:* AACN; AANA/CANAEP; NLN (one or more programs are accredited). Part-time programs available. *Students:* 370 full-time (314 women), 480 part-time (441 women); includes 308 minority (176 Black or African American, non-Hispanic/Latino; 2 American Indian or Alaska Native, non-Hispanic/Latino; 70 Asian, non-Hispanic/Latino; 33 Hispanic/Latino; 27 Two or more races, non-Hispanic/Latino), 9 international. Average age 35. 990 applicants, 30% accepted, 204 enrolled. In 2011, 301 master's awarded. *Degree requirements:* For master's, comprehensive exam (for some programs), thesis or alternative. *Entrance requirements:* For master's, minimum GPA of 2.75, course work in statistics, BS in nursing. Additional exam requirements/recommendations for international students: Required—TOEFL (minimum score 550 paper-based; 80 iBT) or IELTS (minimum score 7). *Application deadline:* For fall admission, 2/1 for domestic students, 1/15 for international students. Application fee: $50. Electronic applications accepted. *Financial support:* Fellowships, research assistantships, teaching assistantships, career-related internships or fieldwork, and traineeships available. Support available to part-time students. Financial award application deadline: 2/15; financial award applicants required to submit FAFSA. *Unit head:* Dr. Jane Kapustin, Assistant Dean, 410-706-6741, Fax: 410-706-4231. *Application contact:* Marjorie Fass, Admissions Director, 410-706-0501, Fax: 410-706-7238.

University of Massachusetts Lowell, School of Health and Environment, Department of Nursing, Program in Adult Psychiatric and Mental Health Nursing, Lowell, MA 01854-2881. Offers MS, Graduate Certificate. *Accreditation:* AACN. Part-time programs available. *Degree requirements:* For master's, thesis optional. *Entrance requirements:* For master's, GRE General Test, minimum GPA of 3.0, MA nursing license, interview, 3 letters of recommendation.

University of Michigan, Horace H. Rackham School of Graduate Studies, School of Nursing, Division of Acute, Critical and Long-term Care, Program in Psychiatric Mental Health Nursing, Ann Arbor, MI 48109. Offers psychiatric mental health nurse practitioner (MS); psychiatric mental health nursing- clinical nurse specialist (MS). *Accreditation:* AACN. Part-time programs available. *Degree requirements:* For master's, thesis. *Entrance requirements:* For master's, GRE General Test (if BSN GPA less than 3.25), Michigan licensure, minimum of B average in BSN program. Additional exam requirements/recommendations for international students: Required—TOEFL (minimum score 560 paper-based; 220 computer-based). Electronic applications accepted. *Faculty research:* Clinical specialist roles, depression, eating disorders, care of chronically mentally ill.

University of Minnesota, Twin Cities Campus, Graduate School, School of Nursing, Program in Psychiatric Mental Health Clinical Nurse Specialist, Minneapolis, MN 55455-0213. Offers MS. *Accreditation:* AACN. Part-time programs available. *Entrance requirements:* Additional exam requirements/recommendations for international students: Required—TOEFL (minimum score 586 paper-based; 240 computer-based).

University of Missouri–St. Louis, College of Nursing, St. Louis, MO 63121. Offers adult nurse practitioner (DNP, Post Master's Certificate); clinical nurse specialist (DNP); family mental health nurse practitioner (DNP); family nurse practitioner (MSN, DNP, Post Master's Certificate); neonatal nurse practitioner (MSN); nurse educator (MSN); nurse leader (MSN); nurse practitioner (Post Master's Certificate); nursing (PhD); pediatric clinical nurse specialist (DNP); pediatric nurse practitioner (MSN, DNP, Post Master's Certificate); women's health nurse practitioner (MSN, Post Master's Certificate). *Accreditation:* AACN. Part-time programs available. *Faculty:* 12 full-time (11 women), 14 part-time/adjunct (all women). *Students:* 240 part-time (226 women); includes 30 minority (26 Black or African American, non-Hispanic/Latino; 1 Asian, non-Hispanic/Latino; 2 Hispanic/Latino; 1 Two or more races, non-Hispanic/Latino). Average age 37. 228 applicants, 28% accepted, 53 enrolled. In 2011, 66 master's, 2 doctorates, 2 other advanced degrees awarded. *Degree requirements:* For doctorate, comprehensive exam, thesis/dissertation; for Post Master's Certificate, thesis. *Entrance requirements:* For master's, 2 recommendation letters; minimum GPA of 3.0; BSN; nursing licensure; statement of purpose; course in differential/inferential statistics; for doctorate, GRE, 2 letters of recommendation, MSN, minimum GPA of 3.2, course in differential/inferential statistics; for Post Master's Certificate, 2 recommendation letters; MSN; advanced practice certificate; minimum GPA of 3.0; essay. Additional exam requirements/recommendations for international students: Required—TOEFL (minimum score 550 paper-based; 213 computer-based). *Application deadline:* For fall admission, 2/15 for domestic and international students. Application fee: $35 ($40 for international students). Electronic applications accepted. *Expenses:* Tuition, state resident: full-time $6273; part-time $3866 per year. Tuition, nonresident: full-time $14,969; part-time $9980 per year. *Required fees:* $315 per year. *Financial support:* In 2011–12, 3 research assistantships with full and partial tuition reimbursements (averaging $12,339 per year) were awarded. Financial award application deadline: 4/1; financial award applicants required to submit FAFSA. *Faculty research:* Health promotion and restoration, family disruption, violence, abuse, battered women, health survey methods. *Unit head:* Dr. Nancy Magnuson, Director, 314-516-6066. *Application contact:* 314-516-5458, Fax: 314-516-6996, E-mail: gradadm@umsl.edu. Web site: http://www.umsl.edu/divisions/nursing/.

The University of North Carolina at Chapel Hill, School of Nursing, Chapel Hill, NC 27599-7460. Offers nursing (MSN, PhD, PMC), including adult nurse practitioner (MSN, PMC), children's health advanced practice (MSN, PMC), family nurse practitioner (MSN, PMC), health care systems (MSN, PMC), psychiatric/mental health nursing (MSN, PMC), women's health nursing (MSN, PMC). *Accreditation:* AACN; NLN (one or more programs are accredited). Part-time programs available. *Degree requirements:* For master's, comprehensive exam, thesis; for doctorate, thesis/dissertation, 3 exams. *Entrance requirements:* For master's and doctorate, GRE General Test. *Faculty research:* Chronic illness, parenting, cardiovascular health in children, elderly, HIV-AIDS.

The University of North Carolina at Charlotte, Graduate School, College of Health and Human Services, School of Nursing, Charlotte, NC 28223-0001. Offers administration (Post-Master's Certificate); advanced clinical (MSN, Post-Master's Certificate); anesthesia (MSN, Post-Master's Certificate); community health (MSN); family nurse practitioner (MSN, Post-Master's Certificate); health administration (MSN); mental health (MSN); nurse educator (MSN, Post-Master's Certificate); systems population (MSN). *Accreditation:* AACN. *Faculty:* 20 full-time (19 women), 5 part-time/

adjunct (all women). *Students:* 76 full-time (65 women), 160 part-time (149 women); includes 49 minority (32 Black or African American, non-Hispanic/Latino; 1 American Indian or Alaska Native, non-Hispanic/Latino; 8 Asian, non-Hispanic/Latino; 8 Hispanic/Latino), 1 international. Average age 35. 191 applicants, 42% accepted, 71 enrolled. In 2011, 76 master's, 10 other advanced degrees awarded. *Degree requirements:* For master's, thesis or alternative, practicum. *Entrance requirements:* For master's, GRE General Test, minimum GPA of 3.0 in undergraduate major. Additional exam requirements/recommendations for international students: Required—TOEFL (minimum score 570 paper-based; 220 computer-based; 83 iBT). *Application deadline:* For fall admission, 7/15 for domestic students, 5/1 for international students; for spring admission, 11/15 for domestic students, 10/1 for international students. Application fee: $65 ($75 for international students). *Expenses:* Tuition, state resident: full-time $3689. Tuition, nonresident: full-time $15,226. *Required fees:* $2198. Tuition and fees vary according to course load and program. *Financial support:* In 2011–12, 10 students received support, including 4 research assistantships (averaging $5,284 per year), 6 teaching assistantships (averaging $2,918 per year); career-related internships or fieldwork, institutionally sponsored loans, scholarships/grants, traineeships, unspecified assistantships, and administrative assistanship also available. Support available to part-time students. Financial award application deadline: 4/1; financial award applicants required to submit FAFSA. *Total annual research expenditures:* $955,795. *Unit head:* Dr. Lucille L. Travis, Director, 704-687-7959, Fax: 704-687-6017, E-mail: ltravis1@uncc.edu. *Application contact:* Kathy B. Giddings, Director of Graduate Admissions, 704-687-5503, Fax: 704-687-3279, E-mail: gradadm@uncc.edu. Web site: http://nursing.uncc.edu/.

University of North Dakota, Graduate School, College of Nursing, Grand Forks, ND 58202. Offers advanced public health nursing (MS); family nurse practitioner (MS); gerontological nursing (MS); nurse anesthesia (MS); nursing (MS, PhD); nursing education (MS); psychiatric and mental health (MS). *Accreditation:* AACN; AANA/CANAEP (one or more programs are accredited). Part-time and evening/weekend programs available. Postbaccalaureate distance learning degree programs offered (minimal on-campus study). *Degree requirements:* For master's, thesis or alternative. *Entrance requirements:* For master's, minimum GPA of 3.0; for doctorate, GRE or MAT, minimum GPA of 3.0. Additional exam requirements/recommendations for international students: Required—TOEFL (minimum score 550 paper-based; 213 computer-based; 79 iBT), IELTS (minimum score 6.5). Electronic applications accepted. *Faculty research:* Adult health, anesthesia, rural health, health administration, family nurse practitioner.

University of Pennsylvania, School of Nursing, Psychiatric Mental Health Advanced Practice Nurse Program, Philadelphia, PA 19104. Offers adult and special populations (MSN); child and family (MSN); geropsychiatrics (MSN). *Accreditation:* AACN. Part-time programs available. *Students:* 9 full-time (8 women), 17 part-time (13 women); includes 8 minority (4 Black or African American, non-Hispanic/Latino; 1 Asian, non-Hispanic/Latino; 2 Hispanic/Latino; 1 Two or more races, non-Hispanic/Latino). 49 applicants, 45% accepted, 19 enrolled. In 2011, 11 degrees awarded. *Entrance requirements:* For master's, GRE General Test, BSN, minimum GPA of 3.0, previous course work in statistics. Additional exam requirements/recommendations for international students: Required—TOEFL. *Application deadline:* For fall admission, 2/15 priority date for domestic students. Applications are processed on a rolling basis. Application fee: $70. *Expenses:* Contact institution. *Financial support:* Fellowships, research assistantships, teaching assistantships, career-related internships or fieldwork, Federal Work-Study, and institutionally sponsored loans available. Support available to part-time students. Financial award application deadline: 4/1. *Faculty research:* Use of restraints in psychiatry, victims of trauma, spiritual use of prayer by cancer patients, coping strategies of African-Americans, urban health care. *Unit head:* Assistant Dean of Admissions and Financial Aid, 866-867-6877, Fax: 215-573-8439, E-mail: admissions@nursing.upenn.edu. *Application contact:* Laura Leahy, Associate Director, 215-746-5469, E-mail: leahylgl@nursing.upenn.edu. Web site: http://www.nursing.upenn.edu/psych/Pages/default.aspx.

University of Pittsburgh, School of Nursing, Clinical Nurse Specialist Program, Pittsburgh, PA 15260. Offers medical/surgical clinical nurse specialist (MSN, DNP); psychiatric and mental health clinical nurse specialist (MSN, DNP). *Accreditation:* AACN. Part-time programs available. *Students:* 4 full-time (all women), 20 part-time (18 women); includes 2 minority (both Asian, non-Hispanic/Latino). Average age 43. 18 applicants, 67% accepted, 10 enrolled. In 2011, 5 master's, 2 doctorates awarded. *Degree requirements:* For master's, comprehensive exam, thesis optional. *Entrance requirements:* For master's, GRE or MAT, BSN, RN license, letters of recommendation, resume, course work in statistics, 1-3 years of nursing experience. Additional exam requirements/recommendations for international students: Required—TOEFL (minimum score 550 paper-based; 213 computer-based; 80 iBT). *Application deadline:* For fall admission, 6/1 priority date for domestic students, 6/1 for international students. Applications are processed on a rolling basis. Application fee: $50. Electronic applications accepted. *Expenses:* Tuition, state resident: full-time $18,774; part-time $760 per credit. Tuition, nonresident: full-time $30,736; part-time $1258 per credit. *Required fees:* $740; $200 per term. Tuition and fees vary according to program. *Financial support:* In 2011–12, 2 students received support, including 1 fellowship with full tuition reimbursement available (averaging $22,724 per year), 1 teaching assistantship with partial tuition reimbursement available (averaging $5,596 per year); scholarships/grants, traineeships, health care benefits, and unspecified assistantships also available. Support available to part-time students. *Unit head:* Dr. Sandra Engberg, Associate Dean for Clinical Education, 412-624-3835, Fax: 412-624-8521, E-mail: sje1@pitt.edu. *Application contact:* Laurie Lapsley, Administrator of Graduate Student Services, 412-624-9670, Fax: 412-624-2409, E-mail: lapsleyl@pitt.edu.

University of Pittsburgh, School of Nursing, Nurse Practitioner Program, Pittsburgh, PA 15261. Offers acute care nurse practitioner (MSN, DNP); adult nurse practitioner (MSN, DNP); family nurse practitioner (MSN, DNP); neonatal (MSN, DNP); nursing practice (DNP); pediatric nurse practitioner (MSN, DNP); psychiatric primary care nurse practitioner (MSN, DNP). *Accreditation:* AACN. Part-time programs available. *Students:* 46 full-time (44 women), 135 part-time (123 women); includes 13 minority (6 Black or African American, non-Hispanic/Latino; 1 American Indian or Alaska Native, non-Hispanic/Latino; 6 Asian, non-Hispanic/Latino). Average age 32. 126 applicants, 71% accepted, 70 enrolled. In 2011, 24 master's, 4 doctorates awarded. *Degree requirements:* For master's, comprehensive exam, thesis optional. *Entrance requirements:* For master's, GRE General Test or MAT, BSN, RN license, letters of recommendation, resume, course work in statistics, 1-3 years of nursing experience; for doctorate, GRE General Test, BSN, RN license, minimum GPA of 3.5, 3 letters of recommendation. Additional exam requirements/recommendations for international students: Required—TOEFL (minimum score 550 paper-based; 213 computer-based; 80 iBT). *Application deadline:* Applications are processed on a rolling basis. Application fee: $50. Electronic applications accepted. *Expenses:* Tuition, state resident: full-time $18,774; part-time $760 per credit. Tuition, nonresident: full-time $30,736; part-time $1258 per credit. *Required fees:* $740; $200 per term. Tuition and fees vary according to program. *Financial support:* In 2011–12, 5 students received support, including 1 fellowship with partial tuition reimbursement available (averaging $11,330 per year), 1 research assistantship with full tuition reimbursement available (averaging $35,942 per year), 3 teaching assistantships with full and partial tuition reimbursements available

(averaging $27,470 per year); scholarships/grants, traineeships, health care benefits, and unspecified assistantships also available. Support available to part-time students. *Unit head:* Dr. Sandra Engberg, Associate Dean for Clinical Education, 412-624-3835, Fax: 412-624-8521, E-mail: sje1@pitt.edu. *Application contact:* Laurie Lapsley, Administrator of Graduate Student Services, 412-624-9670, Fax: 412-624-2409, E-mail: lapsleyl@pitt.edu. Web site: http://www.nursing.pitt.edu.

University of Puerto Rico, Medical Sciences Campus, School of Nursing, San Juan, PR 00936-5067. Offers adult and elderly nursing (MSN); child and adolescent nursing (MSN); critical care nursing (MSN); family and community nursing (MSN); family nurse practitioner (MSN); maternity nursing (MSN); mental health and psychiatric nursing (MSN). *Accreditation:* AACN; AANA/CANAEP. *Entrance requirements:* For master's, GRE or EXADEP, interview, Puerto Rico RN license or professional license for international students, general and specific point average, article analysis. Electronic applications accepted. *Faculty research:* HIV, health disparities, teen violence, women and violence, neurological disorders.

University of Rhode Island, Graduate School, College of Nursing, Kingston, RI 02881. Offers administration (MS); clinical nurse leader (MS); clinical specialist in gerontology (MS); clinical specialist in psychiatric/mental health (MS); family nurse practitioner (MS); gerontological nurse practitioner (MS); nursing (DNP, PhD); nursing education (MS). *Accreditation:* AACN; ACNM/ACME (one or more programs are accredited). Part-time programs available. *Faculty:* 29 full-time (28 women), 2 part-time/adjunct (1 woman). *Students:* 33 full-time (30 women), 81 part-time (77 women); includes 6 minority (1 Asian, non-Hispanic/Latino; 5 Hispanic/Latino). In 2011, 17 master's, 6 doctorates awarded. *Degree requirements:* For master's, comprehensive exam; for doctorate, comprehensive exam, thesis/dissertation. *Entrance requirements:* For master's, GRE or MAT, 2 letters of recommendation, scholarly papers; for doctorate, GRE, 3 letters of recommendation, scholarly papers. Additional exam requirements/recommendations for international students: Required—TOEFL (minimum score 550 paper-based; 213 computer-based). *Application deadline:* For fall admission, 4/15 for domestic students, 2/1 for international students; for spring admission, 11/15 for domestic students, 7/15 for international students. Application fee: $65. Electronic applications accepted. *Expenses:* Tuition, state resident: full-time $10,432; part-time $580 per credit hour. Tuition, nonresident: full-time $23,130; part-time $1285 per credit hour. *Required fees:* $1362; $36 per credit hour. $35 per semester. One-time fee: $130. *Financial support:* In 2011–12, 5 teaching assistantships with full and partial tuition reimbursements (averaging $12,596 per year) were awarded. Financial award application deadline: 4/15; financial award applicants required to submit FAFSA. *Faculty research:* Group intervention for grieving women in prison, translating Best Practice in non-drug interventions for postoperative pain management, further development and testing of the pain assessment inventory, preschool motor and functional performance of two cohorts, neuroactivation of brain motor areas in preterm children. *Unit head:* Dr. Dayle Joseph, Dean, 401-874-2766, Fax: 401-874-2061, E-mail: dayle@uri.edu. *Application contact:* Dr. Mary C. Sullivan, Director of Graduate Studies, 401-874-5339, Fax: 401-874-2061, E-mail: mcsullivan@uri.edu. Web site: http://www.uri.edu/nursing/.

University of Rochester, School of Nursing, Rochester, NY 14642. Offers acute care nurse practitioner (MS); adult nurse practitioner (MS); adult/geriatric nurse practitioner (MS); care of children and families/pediatric nurse practitioner (MS); care of children and families/pediatric nurse practitioner/neonatal nurse practitioner (MS); clinical nurse leader (MS); clinical research coordinator (MS); family nurse practitioner (MS); family psychiatric mental health nurse practitioner (MS); health care organization management and leadership (MS); health practice research (PhD); nursing (DNP). *Accreditation:* AACN; NLN (one or more programs are accredited). Part-time programs available. Postbaccalaureate distance learning degree programs offered (minimal on-campus study). *Faculty:* 49 full-time (42 women), 72 part-time/adjunct (60 women). *Students:* 38 full-time (32 women), 196 part-time (181 women); includes 37 minority (20 Black or African American, non-Hispanic/Latino; 9 Asian, non-Hispanic/Latino; 8 Hispanic/Latino), 5 international. Average age 36. 68 applicants, 56% accepted, 26 enrolled. In 2011, 49 master's, 7 doctorates awarded. Terminal master's awarded for partial completion of doctoral program. *Median time to degree:* Of those who began their doctoral program in fall 2003, 40% received their degree in 8 years or less. *Degree requirements:* For doctorate, thesis/dissertation. *Entrance requirements:* For master's, BS in nursing, minimum GPA of 3.0, course work in statistics; for doctorate, GRE General Test, MS in nursing, minimum GPA of 3.5. Additional exam requirements/recommendations for international students: Required—or IELTS (minimum score 6.5); Recommended—TOEFL (minimum score 560 paper-based; 230 computer-based; 88 iBT). *Application deadline:* For fall admission, 4/1 priority date for domestic students, 4/1 for international students; for spring admission, 9/1 for domestic and international students. Application fee: $50. Electronic applications accepted. *Expenses:* Tuition: Full-time $41,040. *Financial support:* In 2011–12, 49 students received support, including 1 fellowship with full and partial tuition reimbursement available (averaging $18,700 per year); scholarships/grants, traineeships, health care benefits, tuition waivers (partial), and unspecified assistantships also available. Support available to part-time students. Financial award application deadline: 6/30. *Faculty research:* Clinical research in aging, managing asthma in children, interventions to improve outcomes in critically ill children and their mothers, nurse home visitation studies, medical device evaluation, critical care clinical studies, high risk behavior and prevention, palliative care, pregnancy-related weight gain. *Total annual research expenditures:* $4.3 million. *Unit head:* Dr. Kathy H. Rideout, Interim Dean, 585-273-8902, Fax: 585-273-1268, E-mail: kathy_rideout@urmc.rochester.edu. *Application contact:* Elaine Andolina, Director of Admissions, 585-275-2375, Fax: 585-756-8299, E-mail: elaine_andolina@urmc.rochester.edu. Web site: http://www.son.rochester.edu.

University of San Diego, Hahn School of Nursing and Health Science, San Diego, CA 92110-2492. Offers adult-gerontology clinical nurse specialist (MSN); adult-gerontology nurse practitioner/family nurse practitioner (MSN); clinical nursing (MSN); entry-level nursing (for non-RNs) (MSN); executive nurse leader (MSN); family nurse practitioner (MSN); family/lifespan psychiatric-mental health nurse practitioner (MSN); healthcare informatics (MS, MSN); nursing (PhD); nursing practice (DNP); pediatric nurse practitioner/family nurse practitioner (MSN). *Accreditation:* AACN. Part-time and evening/weekend programs available. *Faculty:* 23 full-time (21 women), 37 part-time/adjunct (34 women). *Students:* 157 full-time (131 women), 182 part-time (162 women); includes 121 minority (21 Black or African American, non-Hispanic/Latino; 6 American Indian or Alaska Native, non-Hispanic/Latino; 51 Asian, non-Hispanic/Latino; 36 Hispanic/Latino; 2 Native Hawaiian or other Pacific Islander, non-Hispanic/Latino; 5 Two or more races, non-Hispanic/Latino), 7 international. Average age 36. 506 applicants, 47% accepted, 150 enrolled. In 2011, 87 master's, 26 doctorates awarded. *Degree requirements:* For doctorate, thesis/dissertation (for some programs), residency (DNP). *Entrance requirements:* For master's, GRE General Test (entry-level nursing), BSN, current California RN licensure (except for entry-level nursing); minimum GPA of 3.0; for doctorate, minimum GPA of 3.5, MSN, current California RN licensure. Additional exam requirements/recommendations for international students: Required—TOEFL (minimum score 580 paper-based; 237 computer-based; 83 iBT), TWE. *Application deadline:* For fall admission, 3/1 priority date for domestic students, 3/1 for international students; for spring admission, 11/1 priority date for domestic students, 11/1 for international students. Applications are processed on a rolling basis. Application fee: $45. Electronic

applications accepted. *Expenses: Tuition:* Full-time $22,482; part-time $1249 per unit. *Required fees:* $224. Full-time tuition and fees vary according to course load and degree level. *Financial support:* In 2011–12, 232 students received support. Scholarships/grants and traineeships available. Support available to part-time students. Financial award application deadline: 4/1; financial award applicants required to submit FAFSA. *Faculty research:* Palliative and end of life care, maternal/child health, childhood obesity, health care disparities, cognitive functioning. *Unit head:* Dr. Sally Hardin, Dean, 619-260-4550, Fax: 619-260-6814. *Application contact:* Monica Mahon, Associate Director of Graduate Admissions, 619-260-4524, Fax: 619-260-4158, E-mail: grads@sandiego.edu. Web site: http://www.sandiego.edu/academics/nursing/.

University of South Carolina, The Graduate School, College of Nursing, Program in Advanced Practice Nursing in Psychiatric Mental Health, Columbia, SC 29208. Offers MSN, Certificate. Part-time programs available. Postbaccalaureate distance learning degree programs offered (minimal on-campus study). *Entrance requirements:* For master's, master's degree in nursing, RN license; for Certificate, MSN. Additional exam requirements/recommendations for international students: Required—TOEFL (minimum score 570 paper-based; 213 computer-based). Electronic applications accepted. *Faculty research:* Systems research, evidence based practice, breast cancer, violence.

University of South Carolina, The Graduate School, College of Nursing, Program in Community Mental Health and Psychiatric Health Nursing, Columbia, SC 29208. Offers psychiatric/mental health nurse practitioner (MSN); psychiatric/mental health specialist (MSN). *Accreditation:* AACN. Part-time programs available. *Degree requirements:* For master's, thesis or alternative. *Entrance requirements:* For master's, GRE General Test, MAT, BS in nursing, nursing license. Additional exam requirements/recommendations for international students: Required—TOEFL (minimum score 570 paper-based; 230 computer-based). Electronic applications accepted. *Faculty research:* Systems research, evidence based practice, breast cancer, violence.

University of Southern Maine, School of Nursing, Portland, ME 04104-9300. Offers adult health nursing (PMC); adult psychiatric/mental health nurse practitioner (MS); clinical nurse leader (MS); clinical nurse specialist psychiatric-mental health nursing (MS); education (MS); family nursing (PMC); family psychiatric/mental health nurse practitioner (MS); management (MS); medical/surgical nursing (MS); nurse practitioner adult health nursing (MS); nurse practitioner family nursing (MS); nursing (DNP); psychiatric-mental health nursing (PMC); MBA/MSN. *Accreditation:* AACN. Part-time programs available. *Degree requirements:* For master's, thesis optional. *Entrance requirements:* For master's, GRE General Test or MAT, minimum GPA of 3.0; for doctorate, GRE. Additional exam requirements/recommendations for international students: Required—TOEFL (minimum score 550 paper-based; 213 computer-based). Electronic applications accepted. *Faculty research:* Women's health, nursing history, weight control, community services, substance abuse.

University of Southern Mississippi, Graduate School, College of Health, School of Nursing, Hattiesburg, MS 39406-0001. Offers family nurse practitioner (MSN); nursing (DNP, PhD); nursing executive (MSN); psychiatric nurse practitioner (MSN). *Accreditation:* AACN. Part-time and evening/weekend programs available. *Faculty:* 17 full-time (16 women), 1 part-time/adjunct (0 women). *Students:* 115 full-time (98 women), 43 part-time (38 women); includes 42 minority (35 Black or African American, non-Hispanic/Latino; 1 American Indian or Alaska Native, non-Hispanic/Latino; 3 Asian, non-Hispanic/Latino; 3 Two or more races, non-Hispanic/Latino). Average age 40. 128 applicants, 52% accepted, 58 enrolled. In 2011, 42 master's, 2 doctorates awarded. *Degree requirements:* For master's, comprehensive exam, thesis optional; for doctorate, comprehensive exam, thesis/dissertation. *Entrance requirements:* For master's, GRE General Test, minimum GPA of 2.75 during last 60 hours, nursing license, BS in nursing; for doctorate, GRE General Test, master's degree in nursing, minimum GPA of 3.5. Additional exam requirements/recommendations for international students: Required—TOEFL, IELTS. *Application deadline:* For fall admission, 3/15 priority date for domestic students, 5/1 for international students; for spring admission, 1/10 priority date for domestic students, 1/10 for international students. Applications are processed on a rolling basis. Application fee: $50. Electronic applications accepted. *Financial support:* In 2011–12, 14 research assistantships with full tuition reimbursements (averaging $12,577 per year), teaching assistantships (averaging $12,000 per year) were awarded; Federal Work-Study, institutionally sponsored loans, scholarships/grants, traineeships, health care benefits, and unspecified assistantships also available. Financial award application deadline: 3/15; financial award applicants required to submit FAFSA. *Faculty research:* Gerontology, caregivers, HIV, bereavement, pain, nursing leadership. *Unit head:* Dr. Katherine Nugent, Director and Associate Dean, 601-266-5500, Fax: 601-266-5927. *Application contact:* Dr. Sandra Bishop, Graduate Coordinator, 601-266-5500, Fax: 601-266-5927. Web site: http://www.usm.edu/graduateschool/table.php.

The University of Texas at Austin, Graduate School, School of Nursing, Austin, TX 78712-1111. Offers adult -gerontology clinical nurse specialist (MSN); child health (MSN), including administration, public health nursing; child health (MSN), including teaching; family nurse practitioner (MSN); family psychiatric/mental health nurse practitioner (MSN); holistic adult health (MSN), including administration, education; maternity (MSN), including administration, public health nursing; maternity (MSN), including teaching; nursing (PhD); nursing administration and healthcare systems management (MSN); pediatric nurse practitioner (MSN); public health nursing (MSN). *Accreditation:* AACN. Part-time programs available. *Degree requirements:* For master's, thesis optional; for doctorate, thesis/dissertation. *Entrance requirements:* For master's and doctorate, GRE General Test. Additional exam requirements/recommendations for international students: Required—TOEFL (minimum score 550 paper-based; 213 computer-based). *Application deadline:* For fall admission, 12/1 for domestic students. Application fee: $50 ($75 for international students). Electronic applications accepted. *Financial support:* Fellowships, research assistantships, teaching assistantships, scholarships/grants, and traineeships available. Financial award application deadline: 2/1. *Faculty research:* Chronic illness management, memory and aging, health promotion, women's health, adolescent health. *Unit head:* Dr. Alexa Stuifbergen, Dean, 512-471-4100, Fax: 512-471-4910, E-mail: astuifbergen@mail.utexas.edu. Web site: http://www.utexas.edu/nursing/.

The University of Toledo, College of Graduate Studies, College of Nursing, Department of Population and Community Care, Toledo, OH 43606-3390. Offers adult nurse practitioner (Certificate); adult nurse practitioner/clinical nurse specialist (MSN); clinical nurse leader (MSN); family nurse practitioner (MSN, Certificate); nurse educator (MSN, Certificate); pediatric nurse practitioner (MSN, Certificate); psychiatric-mental health clinical nurse specialist (MSN, Certificate). Part-time programs available. *Faculty:* 43. *Students:* 77 full-time (63 women), 198 part-time (180 women); includes 30 minority (14 Black or African American, non-Hispanic/Latino; 1 American Indian or Alaska Native, non-Hispanic/Latino; 4 Asian, non-Hispanic/Latino; 8 Hispanic/Latino; 3 Two or more races, non-Hispanic/Latino; 1 international. Average age 33. 172 applicants, 53% accepted, 82 enrolled. In 2011, 66 master's, 10 other advanced degrees awarded. *Degree requirements:* For master's, thesis or alternative. *Entrance requirements:* For master's, GRE, BS in nursing, minimum undergraduate GPA of 3.0, statement of purpose, three letters of recommendation, transcripts from all prior institutions attended, Nursing CAS application, UT supplemental application; for Certificate, BS in nursing, minimum undergraduate GPA of 3.0, statement of purpose, three letters of

recommendation, transcripts from all prior institutions attended. Additional exam requirements/recommendations for international students: Required—TOEFL (minimum score 550 paper-based; 213 computer-based; 80 iBT), IELTS (minimum score 6.5). Application fee: $45 ($75 for international students). Electronic applications accepted. *Financial support:* Research assistantships, Federal Work-Study, scholarships/grants, traineeships, and tuition waivers (full and partial) available. *Application contact:* Joan Mulligan, Admissions Analyst, 419-383-4168, Fax: 419-383-6140, E-mail: joan.mulligan@utoledo.edu. Web site: http://www.utoledo.edu/nursing/.

University of Virginia, School of Nursing, Charlottesville, VA 22903. Offers acute and specialty care (MSN); acute care nurse practitioner (MSN); clinical nurse leadership (MSN); community-public health leadership (MSN); nursing (DNP, PhD); psychiatric mental health counseling (MSN); MSN/MBA. *Accreditation:* AACN. Part-time programs available. *Faculty:* 44 full-time (43 women), 2 part-time/adjunct (both women). *Students:* 174 full-time (152 women), 151 part-time (139 women); includes 57 minority (28 Black or African American, non-Hispanic/Latino; 1 American Indian or Alaska Native, non-Hispanic/Latino; 14 Asian, non-Hispanic/Latino; 10 Hispanic/Latino; 4 Two or more races, non-Hispanic/Latino), 11 international. Average age 37. 236 applicants, 40% accepted, 74 enrolled. In 2011, 70 master's, 15 doctorates awarded. *Degree requirements:* For doctorate, comprehensive exam (for some programs), capstone project (DNP), dissertation (PhD). *Entrance requirements:* For master's, GRE General Test, MAT; for doctorate, GRE General Test. Additional exam requirements/recommendations for international students: Required—TOEFL, IELTS. *Application deadline:* Applications are processed on a rolling basis. Application fee: $60. Electronic applications accepted. *Expenses:* Contact institution. *Financial support:* Fellowships, research assistantships, teaching assistantships, Federal Work-Study, and scholarships/grants available. Financial award applicants required to submit FAFSA. *Unit head:* Dorrie K. Fontaine, Dean, 434-924-0141, Fax: 434-982-1809. *Application contact:* Clay Hysell, Assistant Dean for Admissions and Financial Services, 434-924-0141, Fax: 434-982-1809, E-mail: nur-osa@virginia.edu. Web site: http://www.nursing.virginia.edu/.

University of Wisconsin–Madison, School of Nursing, Madison, WI 53706-1380. Offers adult/gerontology (DNP); nursing (PhD); pediatrics (DNP); psychiatric mental health (DNP); MS/MPH. *Accreditation:* AACN. Part-time programs available. *Degree requirements:* For doctorate, comprehensive exam, thesis/dissertation. *Entrance requirements:* For doctorate, GRE General Test, 2 samples of scholarly written work, BS in nursing from an accredited program, minimum undergraduate GPA of 3.0 in last 60 credits (for PhD); licensure as professional nurse (for DNP). Additional exam requirements/recommendations for international students: Required—TOEFL (minimum score 600 paper-based; 250 computer-based; 100 iBT). Electronic applications accepted. *Expenses:* Tuition, state resident: full-time $10,296; part-time $643.51 per credit. Tuition, nonresident: full-time $24,054; part-time $1503.40 per credit. *Required fees:* $70.06 per credit. Tuition and fees vary according to course load, campus/location, program and reciprocity agreements. *Faculty research:* Nursing informatics to promote self-care and disease management skills among patients and caregivers; quality of care to frail, vulnerable, and chronically ill populations; study of health-related and health-seeking behaviors; eliminating health disparities; pain and symptom management for patients with cancer.

Vanderbilt University, Vanderbilt University School of Nursing, Nashville, TN 37240. Offers acute care nurse practitioner (MSN), including intensivist; adult-gerontology primary care nurse practitioner (MSN); emergency nurse practitioner (MSN); family nurse practitioner (MSN); family psychiatric and mental health nurse practitioner (MSN); health systems management (MSN); neonatal nurse practitioner (MSN); nurse midwifery (MSN); nurse midwifery/family nurse practitioner (MSN); nursing informatics (MSN); nursing practice (DNP); nursing science (PhD); pediatric acute care nurse practitioner (MSN); pediatric primary care nurse practitioner (MSN); women's health nurse practitioner (MSN), including urogynecology, women's health; women's health nurse practitioner/adult gerontology nurse practitioner (MSN); MSN/M Div; MSN/MTS. *Accreditation:* ACNM/ACME; NLN (one or more programs are accredited). Part-time programs available. Postbaccalaureate distance learning degree programs offered (minimal on-campus study). *Faculty:* 120 full-time (105 women), 415 part-time/adjunct (302 women). *Students:* 570 full-time (503 women), 395 part-time (364 women); includes 107 minority (57 Black or African American, non-Hispanic/Latino; 1 American Indian or Alaska Native, non-Hispanic/Latino; 19 Asian, non-Hispanic/Latino; 19 Hispanic/Latino; 2 Native Hawaiian or other Pacific Islander, non-Hispanic/Latino; 9 Two or more races, non-Hispanic/Latino), 10 international. Average age 32. 1,116 applicants, 56% accepted, 455 enrolled. In 2011, 341 master's, 33 doctorates awarded. *Degree requirements:* For doctorate, comprehensive exam, thesis/dissertation. *Entrance requirements:* For master's, GRE General Test (within the past 5 years), minimum B average in undergraduate course work, 3 letters of recommendation; for doctorate, GRE General Test, interview, 3 letters of recommendation from doctorally-prepared faculty, MSN, essay. Additional exam requirements/recommendations for international students: Required—TOEFL (minimum score 570 paper-based; 88 computer-based), IELTS (minimum score 6.5). *Application deadline:* For fall admission, 12/1 priority date for domestic students, 12/1 for international students. Applications are processed on a rolling basis. Application fee: $50. Electronic applications accepted. *Expenses:* Contact institution. *Financial support:* In 2011–12, 392 students received support. Scholarships/grants and health care benefits available. Support available to part-time students. Financial award application deadline: 3/15; financial award applicants required to submit FAFSA. *Faculty research:* Lymphedema, palliative care and bereavement, health services research including workforce, safety and quality of care, gerontology, better birth outcomes including nutrition. *Total annual research expenditures:* $1.8 million. *Unit head:* Dr. Colleen Conway-Welch, Dean, 615-343-8776, Fax: 615-343-7711, E-mail: colleen.conway-welch@vanderbilt.edu. *Application contact:* Patricia Peerman, Assistant Dean for Enrollment Management, 615-322-3800, Fax: 615-343-0333, E-mail: vusn-admissions@vanderbilt.edu. Web site: http://www.nursing.vanderbilt.edu.

Virginia Commonwealth University, Graduate School, School of Nursing, Richmond, VA 23284-9005. Offers adult health acute nursing (MS); adult health primary nursing (MS); biobehavioral clinical research (PhD); child health nursing (MS); clinical nurse leader (MS); family health nursing (MS); nurse educator (MS); nurse practitioner (MS); nursing (Certificate); nursing administration (MS), including clinical nurse manager; psychiatric-mental health nursing (MS); women's health nursing (MS). *Accreditation:* NLN (one or more programs are accredited). Part-time and evening/weekend programs available. *Degree requirements:* For master's, thesis optional; for doctorate, thesis/dissertation. *Entrance requirements:* For master's, GRE General Test, BSN, minimum GPA of 2.8; for doctorate, GRE General Test. Additional exam requirements/recommendations for international students: Required—TOEFL (minimum score 600 paper-based; 250 computer-based; 100 iBT). Electronic applications accepted. *Expenses:* Tuition, state resident: full-time $9133; part-time $507 per credit. Tuition, nonresident: full-time $18,777; part-time $1043 per credit. *Required fees:* $77 per credit. Tuition and fees vary according to degree level, campus/location, program and student level.

Wayne State University, College of Nursing, Program in Psychiatric Mental Health Nurse Practitioner, Detroit, MI 48202. Offers MSN, Certificate. *Accreditation:* AACN.

Part-time programs available. *Students:* 9 full-time (7 women), 33 part-time (29 women); includes 12 minority (5 Black or African American, non-Hispanic/Latino; 5 Asian, non-Hispanic/Latino; 1 Hispanic/Latino; 1 Two or more races, non-Hispanic/Latino). Average age 41. 11 applicants, 82% accepted, 7 enrolled. In 2011, 2 degrees awarded. *Degree requirements:* For master's, thesis or alternative. *Entrance requirements:* For master's, minimum GPA of 2.8; for Certificate, graduate degree in nursing, current Michigan RN license, three letters of reference, personal goal statement. Additional exam requirements/recommendations for international students: Required—TOEFL (minimum score 550 paper-based; 213 computer-based); Recommended—TWE (minimum score 6). *Application deadline:* For fall admission, 6/1 priority date for domestic students, 5/1 for international students; for winter admission, 10/1 priority date for domestic students, 9/1 for international students; for spring admission, 2/1 priority date for domestic students, 1/1 for international students. Applications are processed on a rolling basis. Application fee: $50. Electronic applications accepted. *Expenses:* Tuition, state resident: part-time $512.85 per credit. Tuition, nonresident: part-time $1132.65 per credit. *Required fees:* $26.60 per credit. $199.65 per semester. Tuition and fees vary according to course load and program. *Financial support:* In 2011–12, 6 students received support. Research assistantships, institutionally sponsored loans, and scholarships/grants available. Support available to part-time students. Financial award applicants required to submit FAFSA. *Faculty research:* Immigrant and minority health, homelessness, HIV/AIDS, promotion of sleep, substance abuse. *Unit head:* Dr. Barbara Redman, Dean, 313-577-4070, Fax: 313-577-4571, E-mail: ae9080@wayne.edu. *Application contact:* Dr. Cynthia Redwine, Assistant Dean for the Office of Student Affairs, 313-577-4082, E-mail: nursinginfo@wayne.edu. Web site: http://www.nursing.wayne.edu/msn/pmhcurriculum.php.

School Nursing

Cambridge College, School of Education, Cambridge, MA 02138-5304. Offers autism specialist (M Ed); autism/behavior analyst (M Ed); behavior analyst (Post-Master's Certificate); behavioral management (M Ed); early childhood teacher (M Ed); education specialist in curriculum and instruction (CAGS); educational leadership (Ed D); elementary teacher (M Ed); English as a second language (M Ed, Certificate); general science (M Ed); health education (Post-Master's Certificate); health/family and consumer sciences (M Ed); history (M Ed); individualized (M Ed); information technology literacy (M Ed); instructional technology (M Ed); interdisciplinary studies (M Ed); library teacher (M Ed); literacy education (M Ed); mathematics (M Ed); mathematics specialist (Certificate); middle school mathematics and science (M Ed); school administration (M Ed, CAGS); school guidance counselor (M Ed); school nurse education (M Ed); school social worker/school adjustment counselor (M Ed); special education administrator (CAGS); special education/moderate disabilities (M Ed); teaching skills and methodologies (M Ed). Part-time and evening/weekend programs available. Postbaccalaureate distance learning degree programs offered (minimal on-campus study). *Degree requirements:* For master's, thesis, internship/practicum (licensure program only); for doctorate, thesis/dissertation; for other advanced degree, thesis. *Entrance requirements:* For master's, interview, resume, documentation of licensure, 2 professional references; for doctorate, official transcripts, interview, resume, documentation of licensure (if any), written personal statement/essay, portfolio of scholarly and professional work, qualifying assessment, 2 professional references, health insurance, immunizations form; for other advanced degree, official transcripts, interview, resume, documentation of licensure (if any), written personal statement/essay, 2 professional references, health insurance, immunizations form. Additional exam requirements/recommendations for international students: Required—TOEFL (minimum score 550 paper-based; 213 computer-based; 79 iBT); Recommended—IELTS (minimum score 6). Electronic applications accepted. *Expenses:* Contact institution. *Faculty research:* Adult education, accelerated learning, mathematics education, brain compatible learning, special education and law.

Eastern Mennonite University, Program in Nursing, Harrisonburg, VA 22802-2462. Offers leadership and management (MSN); leadership/school nursing (MSN). Part-time programs available. Postbaccalaureate distance learning degree programs offered (minimal on-campus study). *Degree requirements:* For master's, clinical hours.

Eastern University, Graduate Education Programs, St. Davids, PA 19087-3696. Offers multicultural education (M Ed); school health services (M Ed); school nurse (Certificate). Part-time programs available. *Entrance requirements:* For master's, minimum GPA of 2.5. Additional exam requirements/recommendations for international students: Required—TOEFL.

Felician College, Program in Education, Lodi, NJ 07644-2117. Offers education (MA); educational leadership (principal/supervision) (MA); educational supervision (PMC); principal (PMC); school nursing and health education (MA, Certificate). *Accreditation:* Teacher Education Accreditation Council. Part-time and evening/weekend programs available. *Students:* 12 full-time (9 women), 93 part-time (83 women); includes 15 minority (5 Black or African American, non-Hispanic/Latino; 1 Asian, non-Hispanic/Latino; 9 Hispanic/Latino), 3 international. Average age 37. 18 applicants, 50% accepted, 9 enrolled. *Degree requirements:* For master's, project. *Entrance requirements:* For master's, MAT, minimum GPA of 3.0, 3 letters of recommendation. Additional exam requirements/recommendations for international students: Recommended—TOEFL (minimum score 550 paper-based; 213 computer-based). *Application deadline:* Applications are processed on a rolling basis. Application fee: $40. *Expenses: Tuition:* Part-time $925 per credit. *Required fees:* $262.50 per semester. Part-time tuition and fees vary according to class time and student level. *Financial support:* Federal Work-Study available. *Unit head:* Dr. Rosemarie Liebmann, Associate Dean, 201-559-3537, E-mail: liebmannr@felician.edu. *Application contact:* Dr. Margaret Smolin, Associate Director, Graduate Admissions, 201-559-6077, Fax: 201-559-6138, E-mail: graduate@felician.edu.

Kean University, College of Natural, Applied and Health Sciences, Program in Nursing, Union, NJ 07083. Offers clinical management (MSN), including transcultural focus; community health nursing (MSN); school nursing (MSN). *Accreditation:* NLN. *Faculty:* 9 full-time (all women). *Students:* 7 full-time (6 women), 95 part-time (86 women); includes 49 minority (40 Black or African American, non-Hispanic/Latino; 5 Asian, non-Hispanic/Latino; 3 Hispanic/Latino; 1 Native Hawaiian or other Pacific Islander, non-Hispanic/Latino). Average age 45. 38 applicants, 97% accepted, 27 enrolled. In 2011, 34 master's awarded. *Degree requirements:* For master's, thesis or alternative, clinical field experience. *Entrance requirements:* For master's, minimum GPA of 3.0; BS in nursing; RN license; 2 letters of recommendation; interview; 1 completed course of the following: basic health assessment and human growth and development across the life span; minimum B grade in prerequisite courses; transcripts. Additional exam requirements/recommendations for international students: Required—TOEFL (minimum score 79 computer-based). *Application deadline:* For fall admission, 6/1 for domestic and international students; for spring admission, 12/1 for domestic and international students. Applications are processed on a rolling basis. Application fee: $75 ($150 for international students). Electronic applications accepted. *Expenses:* Tuition, state resident: full-time $11,302; part-time $550 per credit. Tuition, nonresident: full-time $15,318; part-time $674 per credit. *Required fees:* $2849; $130 per credit. Tuition and fees vary according to degree level. *Financial support:* In 2011–12, 1 research assistantship with full tuition reimbursement (averaging $3,263 per year) was awarded; unspecified assistantships also available. Financial award applicants required to submit FAFSA. *Unit head:* Dr. Minnie Campbell, Program Coordinator, 908-527-3396, E-mail: mcampbel@kean.edu. *Application contact:* Ann-Marie Kay, Assistant Director of Graduate Admissions, 908-737-5922, Fax: 908-737-5925, E-mail: akay@kean.edu. Web site: http://www.kean.edu/KU/School-of-Nursing.

Kutztown University of Pennsylvania, College of Liberal Arts and Sciences, Program in School Nursing, Kutztown, PA 19530-0730. Offers MSN. Part-time and evening/weekend programs available. *Faculty:* 2 full-time (both women). *Students:* 17 part-time (all women). Average age 44. In 2011, 5 master's awarded. *Entrance requirements:* Additional exam requirements/recommendations for international students: Required—TOEFL (minimum score 550 paper-based; 79 iBT). *Application deadline:* For fall admission, 8/1 priority date for domestic students, 8/1 for international students; for spring admission, 12/1 priority date for domestic students, 12/1 for international students. Applications are processed on a rolling basis. Application fee: $35. Electronic applications accepted. *Expenses:* Tuition, state resident: full-time $7488; part-time $416 per credit. Tuition, nonresident: full-time $11,232; part-time $624 per credit. *Financial support:* Career-related internships or fieldwork, Federal Work-Study, scholarships/grants, and unspecified assistantships available. Financial award application deadline: 3/1. *Unit head:* Dr. Mary Ann Dailey, Chairperson, 610-683-4329, Fax: 610-683-4708, E-mail: mdailey@kutztown.edu. *Application contact:* Kelly D. Burr, Associate Director, Graduate Admissions, 610-683-4200, Fax: 610-683-1393, E-mail: graduate@kutztown.edu.

Monmouth University, The Graduate School, The Marjorie K. Unterberg School of Nursing and Health Studies, West Long Branch, NJ 07764-1898. Offers adult nurse practitioner (MSN); adult psychiatric and mental health advanced practice nursing (MSN, Post-Master's Certificate); advanced practice nursing (Post-Master's Certificate); family nurse practitioner (MSN, Post-Master's Certificate); forensic nursing (MSN, Certificate); nursing (MSN); nursing administration (MSN, Post-Master's Certificate); nursing education (MSN, Post-Master's Certificate); nursing practice (DNP); school nursing (MSN, Certificate). *Accreditation:* AACN. Part-time and evening/weekend programs available. *Faculty:* 12 full-time (all women), 2 part-time/adjunct (both women). *Students:* 16 full-time (11 women), 244 part-time (238 women); includes 73 minority (23 Black or African American, non-Hispanic/Latino; 2 American Indian or Alaska Native, non-Hispanic/Latino; 34 Asian, non-Hispanic/Latino; 12 Hispanic/Latino; 1 Native Hawaiian or other Pacific Islander, non-Hispanic/Latino; 1 Two or more races, non-Hispanic/Latino), 1 international. Average age 41. 107 applicants, 92% accepted, 67 enrolled. In 2011, 55 master's awarded. *Degree requirements:* For master's, practicum (for some tracks). *Entrance requirements:* For master's, GRE General Test, RN license, 1 year of work experience, minimum undergraduate GPA of 2.75. Additional exam requirements/recommendations for international students: Required—TOEFL (minimum score 550 paper-based; 213 computer-based; 79 iBT), IELTS (minimum score 5) or Michigan English Language Assessment Battery (minimum score 77), Cambridge A, B, C. *Application deadline:* For fall admission, 7/15 priority date for domestic students, 6/1 for international students; for spring admission, 11/15 priority date for domestic students, 11/1 for international students. Applications are processed on a rolling basis. Application fee: $50. Electronic applications accepted. *Financial support:* In 2011–12, 138 students received support, including 138 fellowships (averaging $1,423 per year), 4 research assistantships (averaging $5,240 per year); career-related internships or fieldwork, scholarships/grants, and unspecified assistantships also available. Support available to part-time students. Financial award applicants required to submit FAFSA. *Faculty research:* Relationship of undergraduate GPA and GRE to succeed in a graduate nursing program. *Unit head:* Dr. Janet Mahoney, Dean, 732-571-3443, Fax: 732-263-5131, E-mail: jmahoney@monmouth.edu. *Application contact:* Kevin Roane, Director, Office of Graduate Admission, 732-571-3452, Fax: 732-263-5123, E-mail: gradadm@monmouth.edu. Web site: http://www.monmouth.edu/nursingschool.

Saint Joseph's University, College of Arts and Sciences, Department of Health Services, Philadelphia, PA 19131-1395. Offers health administration (MS, Post-Master's Certificate); health care ethics (Post-Master's Certificate); health education (MS, Post-Master's Certificate); health informatics (Post-Master's Certificate); healthcare ethics (MS); long-term care administration (MS); nurse anesthesia (MS); school nurse certification (MS). Part-time and evening/weekend programs available. *Faculty:* 9 full-time (1 woman), 21 part-time/adjunct (11 women). *Students:* 76 full-time (53 women), 261 part-time (204 women); includes 106 minority (79 Black or African American, non-Hispanic/Latino; 2 American Indian or Alaska Native, non-Hispanic/Latino; 12 Asian, non-Hispanic/Latino; 10 Hispanic/Latino; 1 Native Hawaiian or other Pacific Islander, non-Hispanic/Latino; 2 Two or more races, non-Hispanic/Latino), 17 international. Average age 35. 143 applicants, 69% accepted, 91 enrolled. In 2011, 67 master's awarded. *Entrance requirements:* For master's, GRE (if GPA less than 2.75), 2 letters of recommendation, minimum GPA of 2.75, resume. Additional exam requirements/recommendations for international students: Required—TOEFL (minimum score 550 paper-based; 213 computer-based; 79 iBT). *Application deadline:* For fall admission, 7/15 priority date for domestic students, 4/15 for international students; for winter admission, 1/15 for international students; for spring admission, 11/15 priority date for domestic students, 10/15 for international students. Applications are processed on a rolling basis. Application fee: $35. Electronic applications accepted. *Expenses: Tuition:* Part-time $735 per credit hour. Tuition and fees vary according to degree level and program. *Financial support:* Career-related internships or fieldwork and unspecified assistantships available. Financial award applicants required to submit FAFSA. *Unit head:* Nakia Henderson, Director, 610-660-2952, E-mail: nakia.henderson@sju.edu. *Application contact:* Kate McConnell, Director, Graduate College of Arts and Sciences Admissions and Retention, 610-660-3184, Fax: 610-660-3230, E-mail: kate.mcconnell@sju.edu.

School Nursing

Seton Hall University, College of Nursing, South Orange, NJ 07079-2697. Offers advanced practice in primary health care (MSN, DNP), including adult/gerontological nurse practitioner, pediatric nurse practitioner; entry into practice (MSN); health systems administration (MSN, DNP); nursing (PhD); nursing case management (MSN); nursing education (MA); school nurse (MSN); MSN/MA. *Accreditation:* AACN. Part-time programs available. Postbaccalaureate distance learning degree programs offered (minimal on-campus study). *Faculty:* 10 full-time (all women), 3 part-time/adjunct (1 woman). *Students:* 12 full-time (11 women), 217 part-time (197 women); includes 38 minority (15 Black or African American, non-Hispanic/Latino; 1 American Indian or Alaska Native, non-Hispanic/Latino; 12 Asian, non-Hispanic/Latino; 10 Hispanic/Latino). 180 applicants, 51% accepted, 82 enrolled. *Degree requirements:* For master's, research project; for doctorate, dissertation or scholarly project. *Entrance requirements:* For doctorate, GRE (waived for students with GPA of 3.5 or higher). Additional exam requirements/recommendations for international students: Required—TOEFL. *Application deadline:* For fall admission, 4/15 priority date for domestic students. Applications are processed on a rolling basis. Electronic applications accepted. *Expenses: Tuition:* Part-time $1033 per credit hour. *Required fees:* $85 per semester. *Financial support:* Institutionally sponsored loans, scholarships/grants, traineeships, tuition waivers (partial), and unspecified assistantships available. Support available to part-time students. Financial award applicants required to submit FAFSA. *Faculty research:* Parent/child, adult, and gerontological nursing; breast cancer; families of children with HIV; parish nursing. *Unit head:* Dr. Phyllis Shanley Hansell, Dean, 973-761-9014, E-mail: phyllis.hansell@shu.edu. *Application contact:* Kristyn Kent Wuillermin, Director of Strategic Alliances, Marketing and Enrollment, 973-761-9291, Fax: 973-761-9607, E-mail: kristyn.kent@shu.edu.

University of Illinois at Chicago, Graduate College, College of Nursing, Program in Nursing, Chicago, IL 60607-7128. Offers acute care clinical nurse specialist (MS); acute care nurse practitioner (MS); administrative studies in nursing (MS); adult nurse practitioner (MS); adult/geriatric nurse practitioner (MS); advanced community health nurse specialist (MS); family nurse practitioner (MS); geriatric clinical nurse specialist (MS); geriatric nurse practitioner (MS); mental health clinical nurse specialist (MS); mental health nurse practitioner (MS); nurse midwifery (MS); occupational health/advanced community health nurse specialist (MS); occupational health/family nurse practitioner (MS); pediatric clinical nurse specialist (MS); pediatric nurse practitioner (MS); perinatal clinical nurse specialist (MS); school/advanced community health nurse specialist (MS); school/family nurse practitioner (MS); women's health nurse practitioner (MS). *Accreditation:* AACN. Part-time programs available. *Degree requirements:* For master's, thesis or alternative. *Entrance requirements:* For master's, GRE General Test, minimum GPA of 2.75. Additional exam requirements/recommendations for international students: Required—TOEFL. Electronic applications accepted.

West Chester University of Pennsylvania, College of Health Sciences, Department of Nursing, West Chester, PA 19383. Offers nursing education (Certificate); public health nursing (MSN), including administration; school nursing (Teaching Certificate). *Accreditation:* AACN. Part-time and evening/weekend programs available. *Faculty:* 1 (woman) full-time, 2 part-time/adjunct (both women). *Students:* 10 full-time (all women), 31 part-time (all women); includes 8 minority (7 Black or African American, non-Hispanic/Latino; 1 Asian, non-Hispanic/Latino), 2 international. Average age 46. 20 applicants, 75% accepted, 13 enrolled. In 2011, 1 degree awarded. *Entrance requirements:* For master's, RN license, BSN or RN with bachelor's degree in another discipline, minimum GPA of 2.8, experience as a nurse providing direct clinical care, two letters of recommendation. Additional exam requirements/recommendations for international students: Required—TOEFL (minimum score 550 paper-based; 213 computer-based; 80 iBT). *Application deadline:* For fall admission, 4/15 priority date for domestic students, 3/15 for international students; for spring admission, 10/15 priority date for domestic students, 9/1 for international students. Applications are processed on a rolling basis. Application fee: $45. Electronic applications accepted. *Expenses:* Tuition, state resident: full-time $7488; part-time $416 per credit. Tuition, nonresident: full-time $11,232; part-time $624 per credit. *Required fees:* $1784.64; $67.59 per credit. Tuition and fees vary according to program. *Financial support:* Unspecified assistantships available. Support available to part-time students. Financial award application deadline: 2/15; financial award applicants required to submit FAFSA. *Unit head:* Dr. Charlotte Mackey, Chair, 610-436-3474, Fax: 610-436-3083, E-mail: cmackey@wcupa.edu. *Application contact:* Dr. Ann Coghlan Stowe, Graduate Coordinator, 610-436-2331, Fax: 610-436-3083, E-mail: astowe@wcupa.edu. Web site: http://www.wcupa.edu/_ACADEMICS/HealthSciences/nursing/.

Wright State University, School of Graduate Studies, College of Nursing and Health, Program in Nursing, Dayton, OH 45435. Offers acute care nurse practitioner (MS); administration of nursing and health care systems (MS); adult health (MS); child and adolescent health (MS); community health (MS); family nurse practitioner (MS); nurse practitioner (MS); school nurse (MS); MBA/MS. *Accreditation:* AACN. Part-time and evening/weekend programs available. *Degree requirements:* For master's, thesis or alternative. *Entrance requirements:* For master's, GRE General Test, BSN from NLN-accredited college, Ohio RN license. Additional exam requirements/recommendations for international students: Required—TOEFL. *Faculty research:* Clinical nursing and health, teaching, caring, pain administration, informatics and technology.

Transcultural Nursing

Augsburg College, Program in Transcultural Community Health Nursing, Minneapolis, MN 55454-1351. Offers MA. *Accreditation:* AACN. *Degree requirements:* For master's, thesis or alternative.

University of Medicine and Dentistry of New Jersey, School of Nursing, Program in Urban Health, Newark, NJ 07107-1709. Offers PhD. Program offered jointly with New Jersey Institute of Technology. Part-time and evening/weekend programs available. *Entrance requirements:* Additional exam requirements/recommendations for international students: Required—TOEFL. Electronic applications accepted.

Women's Health Nursing

Case Western Reserve University, Frances Payne Bolton School of Nursing, Doctor of Nursing Practice Program, Cleveland, OH 44106. Offers acute care nurse practitioner (DNP); adult gerontology nurse practitioner (DNP); educational leadership (DNP); family nurse practitioner (DNP); family systems psychiatric mental health nursing (DNP); midwifery/family nursing (DNP); neonatal nurse practitioner (DNP); pediatric nurse practitioner (DNP); practice leadership (DNP); women's health nurse practitioner (DNP). *Students:* 73 full-time, 194 part-time; includes 11 minority (6 Black or African American, non-Hispanic/Latino; 3 Asian, non-Hispanic/Latino; 2 Hispanic/Latino). 122 applicants, 74% accepted, 49 enrolled. In 2011, 47 doctorates awarded. Terminal master's awarded for partial completion of doctoral program. *Degree requirements:* For doctorate, thesis/dissertation. *Entrance requirements:* For doctorate, GRE General Test or MAT. Additional exam requirements/recommendations for international students: Required—TOEFL (minimum score 577 paper-based; 90 iBT), IELTS (minimum score 7). *Application deadline:* For fall admission, 6/1 priority date for domestic students, 6/1 for international students; for spring admission, 10/1 for domestic and international students. Applications are processed on a rolling basis. Application fee: $75. *Financial support:* In 2011–12, 6 students received support, including 1 teaching assistantship; research assistantships, Federal Work-Study, institutionally sponsored loans, and tuition waivers (partial) also available. Support available to part-time students. Financial award application deadline: 6/30; financial award applicants required to submit FAFSA. *Faculty research:* Clinical nursing, acute care, gerontology, mental health, critical care. *Unit head:* Dr. Donna Dowling, Director, 216-368-1869, Fax: 216-368-3542, E-mail: dad10@case.edu. *Application contact:* Donna Hassik, Admissions Coordinator, 216-368-5253, Fax: 216-368-0124, E-mail: dmh7@case.edu. Web site: http://fpb.case.edu/DNP/.

Case Western Reserve University, Frances Payne Bolton School of Nursing, Master's Programs in Nursing, Nurse Practitioner Program, Cleveland, OH 44106. Offers acute care cardiovascular nursing (MSN); acute care nurse practitioner (MSN); acute care/flight nurse (MSN); adult gerontology nurse practitioner (MSN); family nurse practitioner (MSN); neonatal nurse practitioner (MSN); pediatric nurse practitioner (MSN); women's health nurse practitioner (MSN). *Accreditation:* NLN. Part-time programs available. Postbaccalaureate distance learning degree programs offered (minimal on-campus study). *Faculty:* 54 full-time (50 women), 5 part-time/adjunct (3 women). *Students:* 89 full-time (69 women), 77 part-time (67 women); includes 17 minority (11 Black or African American, non-Hispanic/Latino; 5 Asian, non-Hispanic/Latino; 1 Hispanic/Latino), 17 international. Average age 35. 75 applicants, 84% accepted, 42 enrolled. In 2011, 34 master's awarded. *Degree requirements:* For master's, thesis optional. *Entrance requirements:* For master's, GRE General Test or MAT. Additional exam requirements/recommendations for international students: Required—TOEFL (minimum score 577 paper-based; 90 iBT), IELTS (minimum score 7). *Application deadline:* For fall admission, 6/1 for domestic students; for spring admission, 10/1 for domestic students. Applications are processed on a rolling basis. Application fee: $75. *Financial support:* In 2011–12, 7 teaching assistantships were awarded; research assistantships, institutionally sponsored loans, and tuition waivers (partial) also available. Support available to part-time students. Financial award application deadline: 6/30; financial award applicants required to submit FAFSA. *Faculty research:* Positive and negative mood states in parents of twins, effect of a care path on chronic obstructive pulmonary disease home care. *Unit head:* Dr. Carol Savrin, Director, 216-368-5304, Fax: 216-368-3542, E-mail: cls18@case.edu. *Application contact:* Donna Hassik, Admissions Coordinator, 216-368-5253, Fax: 216-368-0124, E-mail: dmh7@case.edu. Web site: http://fpb.cwru.edu/MSN/majors.shtm.

Columbia University, School of Nursing, Program in Women's Health Nurse Practitioner, New York, NY 10032. Offers Adv C. *Accreditation:* AACN. Part-time programs available. *Entrance requirements:* For degree, MSN. Electronic applications accepted.

Drexel University, College of Nursing and Health Professions, Division of Graduate Nursing, Philadelphia, PA 19104-2875. Offers adult acute care (MSN); adult psychiatric/mental health (MSN); advanced practice nursing (MSN); clinical trials research (MSN); family nurse practitioner (MSN); leadership in health systems management (MSN); nursing education (MSN); pediatric primary care (MSN); women's health (MSN). *Accreditation:* AACN; NLN. Electronic applications accepted.

Emory University, Nell Hodgson Woodruff School of Nursing, Atlanta, GA 30322-1100. Offers adult nurse practitioner (MSN); emergency nurse practitioner (MSN); family nurse practitioner (MSN); family nurse-midwife (MSN); health systems leadership (MSN); nurse-midwifery (MSN); pediatric nurse practitioner acute and primary care (MSN); women's health care (Title X) (MSN); women's health nurse practitioner (MSN); women's health/adult health nurse practitioner (MSN); MSN/MPH. *Accreditation:* AACN; ACNM/ACME (one or more programs are accredited). Part-time programs available. *Faculty:* 30 full-time (29 women), 11 part-time/adjunct (10 women). *Students:* 110 full-time (106 women), 53 part-time (51 women); includes 49 minority (35 Black or African American, non-Hispanic/Latino; 2 American Indian or Alaska Native, non-Hispanic/Latino; 10 Asian, non-Hispanic/Latino; 2 Hispanic/Latino), 4 international. Average age 32. 182 applicants, 63% accepted, 86 enrolled. In 2011, 81 master's awarded. *Entrance requirements:* For master's, GRE General Test or MAT, minimum GPA of 3.0, BS in nursing from an accredited institution, RN license and additional course work, 3 letters of recommendation. Additional exam requirements/recommendations for international students: Required—TOEFL (minimum score 600 paper-based; 100 iBT). *Application deadline:* For fall admission, 1/15 priority date for domestic students, 1/15 for international students; for spring admission, 10/1 priority date for domestic students, 10/1 for international students. Applications are processed on a rolling basis. Application fee: $50. Electronic applications accepted. *Expenses:* Contact institution. *Financial support:* In 2011–12, 14 fellowships (averaging $28,000 per year) were awarded; career-related

internships or fieldwork, Federal Work-Study, institutionally sponsored loans, and scholarships/grants also available. Support available to part-time students. Financial award application deadline: 3/1; financial award applicants required to submit CSS PROFILE or FAFSA. *Faculty research:* Older adult falls and injuries, minority health issues, cardiac symptoms and quality of life, bio-ethics and decision-making, menopausal issues. *Unit head:* Dr. Linda McCauley, Dean, 404-727-7976, Fax: 404-727-9800, E-mail: linda.mccauley@emory.edu. Web site: http://www.nursing.emory.edu/.

Frontier Nursing University, Graduate Programs, Hyden, KY 41749. Offers community-based family nurse practitioner (MSN, Post Master's Certificate); community-based nurse-midwifery education (MSN, Post Master's Certificate); community-based women?s health care nurse practitioner (MSN, Post Master's Certificate). *Accreditation:* ACNM; NLN.

Georgia Southern University, Jack N. Averitt College of Graduate Studies, College of Health and Human Sciences, School of Nursing, Statesboro, GA 30460. Offers nurse practitioner (MSN, Certificate); nursing science (DNP); rural community health nurse practitioner (MSN); rural community health nurse specialist (Certificate); rural family nurse practitioner (MSN, Certificate); women's health nurse practitioner (MSN, Certificate). *Accreditation:* AACN. Part-time programs available. Postbaccalaureate distance learning degree programs offered. *Students:* 3 full-time (all women), 79 part-time (74 women); includes 13 minority (9 Black or African American, non-Hispanic/Latino; 1 Asian, non-Hispanic/Latino; 1 Hispanic/Latino; 1 Native Hawaiian or other Pacific Islander, non-Hispanic/Latino; 1 Two or more races, non-Hispanic/Latino), 1 international. Average age 37. 75 applicants, 57% accepted, 34 enrolled. In 2011, 23 master's, 11 doctorates awarded. *Degree requirements:* For master's, comprehensive exam, thesis optional; for doctorate, clinical immersion project, capstone practicum. *Entrance requirements:* For master's, GRE General Test or MAT, minimum GPA of 3.0, Georgia nursing license, 2 years of clinical experience, CPR certification; for doctorate, GRE, MAT, portfolio, certification, RN licensure, clinical hours; for Certificate, MSN. Additional exam requirements/recommendations for international students: Required—TOEFL (minimum score 550 paper-based; 213 computer-based; 80 iBT). *Application deadline:* For fall admission, 3/1 priority date for domestic students, 3/1 for international students; for spring admission, 10/1 priority date for domestic students, 10/1 for international students. Applications are processed on a rolling basis. Application fee: $50. Electronic applications accepted. *Expenses:* Tuition, state resident: full-time $6300; part-time $263 per semester hour. Tuition, nonresident: full-time $25,174; part-time $1049 per semester hour. *Required fees:* $1872. *Financial support:* In 2011–12, 44 students received support, including research assistantships with partial tuition reimbursements available (averaging $7,200 per year), teaching assistantships with partial tuition reimbursements available (averaging $7,200 per year); career-related internships or fieldwork, Federal Work-Study, scholarships/grants, traineeships, tuition waivers (partial), and unspecified assistantships also available. Support available to part-time students. Financial award application deadline: 4/15; financial award applicants required to submit FAFSA. *Faculty research:* Obesity, diabetes mellitus, vulnerable populations, breast cancer, nursing education, literacy. *Total annual research expenditures:* $50,000. *Unit head:* Dr. Donna Hodnicki, Chair, 912-478-5056, Fax: 912-478-0536, E-mail: dhodnick@georgiasouthern.edu. *Application contact:* Amanda Gilliland, Coordinator for Graduate Student Recruitment, 912-478-5384, Fax: 912-478-0740, E-mail: gradadmissions@georgiasouthern.edu. Web site: http:// www.chhs.georgiasouthern.edu/nursing/.

Georgia State University, College of Health and Human Sciences, Byrdine F. Lewis School of Nursing, Atlanta, GA 30302-3083. Offers adult health (MS); adult health nursing (Certificate); child health (MS); family nurse practitioner (MS, Certificate); health promotion, protection and restoration (PhD); perinatal/women's health (MS); psychiatric mental health nursing (Certificate); psychiatric/mental health (MS); women's health nursing (Certificate). *Accreditation:* AACN. Part-time and evening/weekend programs available. Postbaccalaureate distance learning degree programs offered (minimal on-campus study). *Degree requirements:* For master's, research activity; for doctorate, comprehensive exam, thesis/dissertation. *Entrance requirements:* For master's, MAT (preferred) or GRE, interview, RN license; for doctorate, GRE General Test. Additional exam requirements/recommendations for international students: Required—TOEFL (minimum score 550 paper-based; 213 computer-based). Electronic applications accepted. *Expenses:* Contact institution. *Faculty research:* Breast cancer prevention, sexually compulsive behaviors, health risks in minority youth, asthma treatment strategies, adolescent alcohol-related issues.

Hampton University, Graduate College, School of Nursing, Hampton, VA 23668. Offers advanced adult nursing (MS); community health nursing (MS); community mental health/psychiatric nursing (MS); family nursing (MS); gerontological nursing for the nurse practitioner (MS); pediatric nursing (MS); women's health nursing (MS). *Accreditation:* AACN; NLN. Part-time and evening/weekend programs available. *Degree requirements:* For master's, thesis optional. *Entrance requirements:* For master's, GRE General Test. *Faculty research:* Curriculum development, physical and mental assessment.

Indiana University–Purdue University Fort Wayne, College of Health and Human Services, Department of Nursing, Fort Wayne, IN 46805-1499. Offers adult nursing practitioner (MS); nurse executive (MS); nursing administration (Certificate); nursing education (MS); women's health nurse practitioner (MS). Part-time programs available. *Faculty:* 10 full-time (all women). *Students:* 3 full-time (all women), 33 part-time (31 women); includes 3 minority (1 American Indian or Alaska Native, non-Hispanic/Latino; 1 Asian, non-Hispanic/Latino; 1 Hispanic/Latino). Average age 36. 13 applicants, 92% accepted, 10 enrolled. In 2011, 14 master's awarded. *Entrance requirements:* For master's, GRE Writing Test (if GPA below 3.0), BS in nursing, eligibility for Indiana RN license, minimum GPA of 3.0, essay, copy of resume, three references, undergraduate course work in research and statistics within last 5 years. Additional exam requirements/recommendations for international students: Required—TOEFL (minimum score 550 paper-based; 213 computer-based; 77 iBT); Recommended—TWE. *Application deadline:* For fall admission, 5/1 priority date for domestic students, 5/1 for international students; for spring admission, 11/15 priority date for domestic students. Applications are processed on a rolling basis. Application fee: $55 ($60 for international students). Electronic applications accepted. *Financial support:* In 2011–12, 11 teaching assistantships with partial tuition reimbursements (averaging $12,930 per year) were awarded; scholarships/grants also available. Support available to part-time students. Financial award application deadline: 3/1; financial award applicants required to submit FAFSA. *Faculty research:* Child psychiatric nursing. *Total annual research expenditures:* $296,680. *Unit head:* Dr. Carol Sternberger, Chair, 260-481-5798, Fax: 260-481-5767, E-mail: sternber@ipfw.edu. *Application contact:* Dr. Deborah Poling, Director of Graduate Program, 260-481-6276, Fax: 260-481-5767, E-mail: polingd@ipfw.edu. Web site: http://www.ipfw.edu/nursing/.

Indiana University–Purdue University Indianapolis, School of Nursing, Indianapolis, IN 46202-2896. Offers acute care nurse practitioner (MSN); adult health clinical nurse specialist (MSN); adult health nursing (MSN), including adult clinical nurse specialist; adult nurse practitioner (MSN); adult psychiatric/mental health nursing (MSN); child psychiatric/mental health nursing (MSN); community health nursing (MSN); family nurse practitioner (MSN); neonatal nurse practitioner (MSN); nursing (MSN, DNP), including nursing education (MSN); nursing (MSN), including nursing administration; nursing science (PhD); pediatric clinical nurse specialist (MSN); women's health nurse

practitioner (MSN); MSN/MPA; MSN/MPH. *Accreditation:* AACN; NLN (one or more programs are accredited). Part-time programs available. *Faculty:* 85 full-time (82 women), 60 part-time/adjunct (all women). *Students:* 35 full-time (32 women), 360 part-time (340 women); includes 47 minority (28 Black or African American, non-Hispanic/Latino; 9 Asian, non-Hispanic/Latino; 4 Hispanic/Latino; 1 Native Hawaiian or other Pacific Islander, non-Hispanic/Latino; 5 Two or more races, non-Hispanic/Latino), 5 international. Average age 38. 119 applicants, 76% accepted, 54 enrolled. In 2011, 89 master's, 10 doctorates awarded. Terminal master's awarded for partial completion of doctoral program. *Degree requirements:* For master's, thesis; for doctorate, thesis/dissertation. *Entrance requirements:* For master's, minimum GPA of 3.0, RN license; for doctorate, GRE General Test, minimum GPA of 3.0, MSN, RN license, graduate statistics course with minimum B grade (not older than 3 years). Additional exam requirements/recommendations for international students: Required—TOEFL. *Application deadline:* For fall admission, 2/15 for domestic students; for spring admission, 9/15 for domestic students. Application fee: $55 ($65 for international students). *Financial support:* In 2011–12, 93 students received support, including 9 fellowships with full tuition reimbursements available (averaging $7,039 per year), 7 teaching assistantships with full tuition reimbursements available (averaging $5,300 per year); research assistantships with full tuition reimbursements available, Federal Work-Study, institutionally sponsored loans, scholarships/grants, and tuition waivers (full) also available. Support available to part-time students. Financial award application deadline: 5/1. *Faculty research:* Clinical science, health systems. *Total annual research expenditures:* $3 million. *Unit head:* Associate Dean for Graduate Programs, 317-274-2806, E-mail: nursing@iupui.edu. *Application contact:* Information Contact, 317-274-2806. Web site: http:// nursing.iupui.edu/.

The Johns Hopkins University, School of Nursing, Nurse Practitioner Program, Baltimore, MD 21218-2699. Offers adult acute/critical care (MSN, Certificate); adult and pediatric primary care (MSN); adult or pediatric primary care (Certificate); emergency preparedness/disaster response (Certificate); family primary care (MSN, Certificate); women's health (Certificate). *Accreditation:* AACN; NLN (one or more programs are accredited). Part-time programs available. *Degree requirements:* For master's, thesis optional, scholarly project or portfolio. *Entrance requirements:* For master's, GRE, interview, minimum GPA of 3.0, BSN, Maryland RN license. Additional exam requirements/recommendations for international students: Required—TOEFL (minimum score 550 paper-based; 213 computer-based). Electronic applications accepted. *Expenses:* Contact institution. *Faculty research:* Community outreach, primary care of underserved populations, substance-abusing individuals, childhood violence, women's health.

Kent State University, College of Nursing, Kent, OH 44242-0001. Offers acute care nurse practitioner (MSN); adult nurse practitioner (MSN); clinical nurse specialist (MSN); family nurse practitioner (MSN); geriatric nurse practitioner (MSN); health care management (MSN); nurse educator (MSN); nursing (PhD); nursing practice (DNP); pediatric nurse practitioner (MSN); psychiatric/mental health nurse practitioner (MSN); women's health nurse practitioner (MSN). PhD program offered jointly with The University of Akron. *Accreditation:* AACN. Part-time programs available. *Degree requirements:* For master's, thesis optional; for doctorate, comprehensive exam, thesis/dissertation. *Entrance requirements:* For master's, GRE (if undergraduate GPA less than 3.0), minimum GPA of 2.75; for doctorate, GRE, MSN. Additional exam requirements/recommendations for international students: Required—TOEFL. Electronic applications accepted. *Expenses:* Contact institution. *Faculty research:* Women and violence, methodological specialties, osteoporosis in women, new caregivers and the elderly.

Loyola University Chicago, Graduate School, Marcella Niehoff School of Nursing, Women's Health Nurse Practitioner Program, Chicago, IL 60660. Offers MSN, Certificate. *Accreditation:* AACN. Part-time and evening/weekend programs available. *Students:* 2 full-time (both women), 15 part-time (all women); includes 3 minority (all Black or African American, non-Hispanic/Latino). Average age 30. 11 applicants, 91% accepted, 10 enrolled. In 2011, 3 master's awarded. *Degree requirements:* For master's, comprehensive exam or oral thesis defense. *Entrance requirements:* For master's, BSN, minimum nursing GPA of 3.0, 1000 hours experience before starting clinical, Illinois nursing license, 3 letters of reference. *Application deadline:* Applications are processed on a rolling basis. Application fee: $50. Electronic applications accepted. *Expenses:* Tuition: Full-time $15,660; part-time $870 per credit hour. *Required fees:* $125 per semester. Tuition and fees vary according to course load and program. *Financial support:* Teaching assistantships and traineeships available. Financial award application deadline: 3/1. *Faculty research:* Breast feeding, postpartum depression, pre-term labor toxicity. *Unit head:* Dr. Penny Marzalik, Associate Professor, 708-216-9101, Fax: 708-216-9555, E-mail: pmarzal@luc.edu. *Application contact:* Amy Weatherford, Enrollment Advisor, School of Nursing, 773-508-3249, Fax: 773-508-3241, E-mail: aweatherford@luc.edu. Web site: http://www.luc.edu/nursing/np/.

MGH Institute of Health Professions, School of Nursing, Boston, MA 02129. Offers advanced practice nursing (MSN); gerontological nursing (MSN); nursing (DNP); pediatric nursing (MSN); psychiatric nursing (MSN); teaching and learning for health care education (Certificate); women's health nursing (MSN). *Accreditation:* AACN; NLN (one or more programs are accredited). *Faculty:* 41 full-time (36 women), 14 part-time/adjunct (13 women). *Students:* 418 full-time (365 women), 72 part-time (63 women); includes 51 minority (20 Black or African American, non-Hispanic/Latino; 1 American Indian or Alaska Native, non-Hispanic/Latino; 24 Asian, non-Hispanic/Latino; 5 Hispanic/Latino; 1 Native Hawaiian or other Pacific Islander, non-Hispanic/Latino). Average age 32. 1,041 applicants, 36% accepted, 148 enrolled. In 2011, 85 master's, 12 doctorates, 98 other advanced degrees awarded. *Degree requirements:* For master's, thesis or alternative. *Entrance requirements:* For master's, GRE General Test, bachelor's degree from regionally-accredited college or university. Additional exam requirements/recommendations for international students: Required—TOEFL (minimum score 550 paper-based; 213 computer-based; 80 iBT). *Application deadline:* For fall admission, 1/10 for domestic and international students; for spring admission, 11/1 for domestic and international students. Application fee: $65. Electronic applications accepted. *Expenses:* Tuition: Full-time $12,720; part-time $1060 per credit. *Required fees:* $1725; $430 per semester. One-time fee: $350. *Financial support:* In 2011–12, 75 students received support, including 4 research assistantships (averaging $1,200 per year), 17 teaching assistantships (averaging $1,200 per year); career-related internships or fieldwork, scholarships/grants, traineeships, and unspecified assistantships also available. Support available to part-time students. Financial award application deadline: 4/1; financial award applicants required to submit FAFSA. *Faculty research:* Biobehavioral nursing, HIV/AIDS, gerontological nursing, women's health, vulnerable populations, health systems. *Unit head:* Dr. Laurie Lauzon-Clabo, Dean, 617-643-0605, Fax: 617-726-8022, E-mail: llauzonclabo@mghihp.edu. *Application contact:* Maureen Rika Judd, Director of Admissions, 617-726-6069, Fax: 617-726-8010, E-mail: admissions@mghihp.edu. Web site: http://www.mghihp.edu/academics/nursing/.

Old Dominion University, College of Health Sciences, School of Nursing, Women's Health Nurse Practitioner Emphasis, Norfolk, VA 23529. Offers MSN. Part-time programs available. Postbaccalaureate distance learning degree programs offered (minimal on-campus study). *Students:* 6 full-time (all women), 7 part-time (all women); includes 2 minority (both Black or African American, non-Hispanic/Latino). Average age 37. 13

applicants, 62% accepted, 5 enrolled. In 2011, 4 master's awarded. *Degree requirements:* For master's, comprehensive exam. *Entrance requirements:* For master's, GRE or MAT. Additional exam requirements/recommendations for international students: Required—TOEFL. *Application deadline:* For fall admission, 5/1 priority date for domestic students, 4/15 for international students. Application fee: $50. Electronic applications accepted. *Expenses:* Tuition, state resident: full-time $9096; part-time $379 per credit. Tuition, nonresident: full-time $23,064; part-time $961 per credit. *Required fees:* $127 per semester. One-time fee: $50. *Unit head:* Dr. Kathleen Putnam, Graduate Program Director, 757-683-5256, E-mail: kputnam@odu.edu. *Application contact:* Sue Parker, Coordinator, Graduate Student Services, 757-683-4298, Fax: 757-683-5253, E-mail: sparker@odu.edu. Web site: http://hs.odu.edu/nursing/academics/womens_nurse/womens_nurse.shtml.

Queen's University at Kingston, School of Graduate Studies and Research, Faculty of Health Sciences, School of Nursing, Kingston, ON K7L 3N6, Canada. Offers health and chronic illness (M Sc); nurse scientist (PhD); primary health care nurse practitioner (Certificate); women's and children's health (M Sc). *Degree requirements:* For master's, thesis. *Entrance requirements:* For master's, RN license. Additional exam requirements/recommendations for international students: Required—TOEFL. *Faculty research:* Women and children's health, health and chronic illness.

Rosalind Franklin University of Medicine and Science, College of Health Professions, Department of Interprofessional Healthcare Studies, Women's Healthcare Studies Program, North Chicago, IL 60064-3095. Offers MS, Certificate. Part-time and evening/weekend programs available. Postbaccalaureate distance learning degree programs offered (minimal on-campus study). *Degree requirements:* For master's, thesis optional, project. *Entrance requirements:* For master's, licensure/registration/certification in clinical health field, minimum GPA of 3.0, BS or BA. Additional exam requirements/recommendations for international students: Required—TOEFL.

Stony Brook University, State University of New York, Stony Brook University Medical Center, Health Sciences Center, School of Nursing, Program in Perinatal Women's Health Nursing, Stony Brook, NY 11794. Offers MS, Certificate. *Accreditation:* AACN. Postbaccalaureate distance learning degree programs offered. *Degree requirements:* For master's, thesis. *Entrance requirements:* For master's, BSN, minimum GPA of 3.0, course work in statistics.

Texas Woman's University, Graduate School, College of Nursing, Denton, TX 76201. Offers acute care nurse practitioner (MS); adult health clinical nurse specialist (MS); adult health nurse practitioner (MS); child health clinical nurse specialist (MS); clinical nurse leader (MS); family nurse practitioner (MS); health systems management (MS); nursing education (MS); nursing practice (DNP); nursing science (PhD); pediatric nurse practitioner (MS); women's health clinical nurse specialist (MS); women's health nurse practitioner (MS). *Accreditation:* AACN. Part-time programs available. Postbaccalaureate distance learning degree programs offered. *Faculty:* 70 full-time (69 women), 7 part-time/adjunct (all women). *Students:* 87 full-time (78 women), 870 part-time (815 women); includes 489 minority (235 Black or African American, non-Hispanic/Latino; 5 American Indian or Alaska Native, non-Hispanic/Latino; 169 Asian, non-Hispanic/Latino; 78 Hispanic/Latino; 2 Native Hawaiian or other Pacific Islander, non-Hispanic/Latino), 19 international. Average age 38. 368 applicants, 71% accepted, 205 enrolled. In 2011, 147 master's, 21 doctorates awarded. *Degree requirements:* For master's, comprehensive exam, thesis or alternative; for doctorate, comprehensive exam, thesis/dissertation. *Entrance requirements:* For master's, GRE or MAT, minimum GPA of 3.0 on last 60 hours in undergraduate nursing degree and overall, RN license, BS in nursing, basic statistics course; for doctorate, GRE (preferred minimum score 153 [500 old version] Verbal, 144 [500 old version] Quantitative, 4 Analytical), MS in nursing, minimum preferred GPA of 3.5, RN license, statistics, 2 letters of reference, curriculum vitae, graduate nursing-theory course, graduate research course, statement of professional goals and research interests. Additional exam requirements/recommendations for international students: Required—TOEFL (minimum score 550 paper-based; 213 computer-based; 79 iBT). *Application deadline:* For fall admission, 5/1 priority date for domestic students, 3/1 for international students; for spring admission, 9/15 priority date for domestic students, 7/1 for international students. Applications are processed on a rolling basis. Application fee: $50 ($75 for international students). Electronic applications accepted. *Expenses:* Tuition, state resident: full-time $3834; part-time $213 per credit hour. Tuition, nonresident: full-time $9468; part-time $526 per credit hour. *Required fees:* $213 per credit hour. Tuition and fees vary according to course load. *Financial support:* In 2011–12, 149 students received support, including 10 research assistantships (averaging $12,942 per year), 1 teaching assistantship (averaging $12,942 per year); career-related internships or fieldwork, Federal Work-Study, institutionally sponsored loans, scholarships/grants, traineeships, health care benefits, and unspecified assistantships also available. Support available to part-time students. Financial award application deadline: 3/1; financial award applicants required to submit FAFSA. *Faculty research:* Screening, prevention, and treatment for intimate partner violence; needs of adolescents during childbirth intervention; a network analysis decision tool for nurse managers (Social Network Analysis); support for adolescents with implantable cardioverter defibrillators; informatics: nurse staffing, safety, quality, and financial data as they relate to patient care outcomes; prevention and treatment of obesity; improving infant outcomes related to premature birth. *Total annual research expenditures:* $462,088. *Unit head:* Dr. Patricia Holden-Huchton, Interim Dean, 940-898-2401, Fax: 940-898-2437, E-mail: nursing@twu.edu. *Application contact:* Dr. Samuel Wheeler, Assistant Director of Admissions, 940-898-3188, Fax: 940-898-3081, E-mail: wheelersr@twu.edu. Web site: http://www.twu.edu/nursing/.

University of Cincinnati, Graduate School, College of Nursing, Cincinnati, OH 45221-0038. Offers clinical nurse specialist (MSN), including adult health, community health, neonatal, nursing administration, occupational health, pediatric health, psychiatric nursing, women's health; nurse anesthesia (MSN); nurse midwifery (MSN); nurse practitioner (MSN), including acute care, ambulatory care, family, family/psychiatric, women's health; nursing (PhD); MBA/MSN. *Accreditation:* AACN; AANA/CANAEP (one or more programs are accredited); ACNM/ACME. Part-time programs available. Postbaccalaureate distance learning degree programs offered (no on-campus study). Terminal master's awarded for partial completion of doctoral program. *Degree requirements:* For master's, thesis or alternative; for doctorate, comprehensive exam, thesis/dissertation. *Entrance requirements:* For master's and doctorate, GRE General Test. Additional exam requirements/recommendations for international students: Required—TOEFL (minimum score 520 paper-based; 190 computer-based). Electronic applications accepted. *Faculty research:* Substance abuse, injury and violence, symptom management.

University of Colorado at Colorado Springs, Beth-El College of Nursing and Health Sciences, Colorado Springs, CO 80933-7150. Offers adult health nurse practitioner and clinical specialist (MSN); family practitioner (MSN), including community clinical specialist, forensic clinical specialist, holistic clinical specialist; neonatal nurse practitioner and clinical specialist (MSN); nursing administration (MSN); nursing practice (DNP); women nurse practitioner (MSN). *Accreditation:* AACN. Part-time programs available. Postbaccalaureate distance learning degree programs offered (minimal on-campus study). *Faculty:* 31 full-time (28 women), 6 part-time/adjunct (all women). *Students:* 122 full-time (103 women), 68 part-time (64 women); includes 36 minority (4 Black or African American, non-Hispanic/Latino; 2 American Indian or Alaska Native, non-Hispanic/Latino; 9 Asian, non-Hispanic/Latino; 18 Hispanic/Latino; 3 Two or more races, non-Hispanic/Latino), 5 international. Average age 35. 153 applicants, 71% accepted, 60 enrolled. In 2011, 41 master's, 15 doctorates awarded. *Degree requirements:* For master's, comprehensive exam, thesis optional; for doctorate, capstone project. *Entrance requirements:* For master's, GRE General Test or MAT, BSN, minimum GPA of 3.0, unrestricted RN license; for doctorate, interview; active RN license; MA; minimum GPA of 3.3; National Certification as NP or CNS; portfolio. Additional exam requirements/recommendations for international students: Required—TOEFL. *Application deadline:* For fall admission, 6/15 priority date for domestic students; for spring admission, 11/15 for domestic students. Application fee: $60 ($75 for international students). Electronic applications accepted. *Expenses:* Contact institution. *Financial support:* In 2011–12, 33 students received support, including 1 fellowship (averaging $2,500 per year); career-related internships or fieldwork, Federal Work-Study, and scholarships/grants also available. Support available to part-time students. Financial award application deadline: 3/1; financial award applicants required to submit FAFSA. *Faculty research:* Women's health, uncertainty, empowerment, family experience in chronic illness. *Total annual research expenditures:* $322,604. *Unit head:* Dr. Nancy Smith, Dean, 719-255-4411, Fax: 719-255-4416, E-mail: nsmith2@uccs.edu. *Application contact:* Diane Busch, Director, 719-255-4424, Fax: 719-255-4416, E-mail: dbusch@uccs.edu. Web site: http://www.uccs.edu/~bethel/.

University of Colorado Denver, College of Nursing, Aurora, CO 80045. Offers adult clinical nurse specialist (MS); adult nurse practitioner (MS); family nurse practitioner (MS); family psychiatric mental health nurse practitioner (MS); health care informatics (MS); nurse-midwifery (MS); nursing (DNP, PhD); nursing leadership and health care systems (MS); pediatric nurse practitioner (MS); pediatric nursing leadership (MS); special studies (MS); women's health care (MS); MS/PhD. *Accreditation:* ACNM/ACME (one or more programs are accredited); NLN (one or more programs are accredited). Part-time and evening/weekend programs available. Postbaccalaureate distance learning degree programs offered (minimal on-campus study). *Faculty:* 69 full-time (65 women), 68 part-time/adjunct (64 women). *Students:* 308 full-time (288 women), 134 part-time (118 women); includes 59 minority (11 Black or African American, non-Hispanic/Latino; 8 American Indian or Alaska Native, non-Hispanic/Latino; 10 Asian, non-Hispanic/Latino; 27 Hispanic/Latino; 3 Two or more races, non-Hispanic/Latino), 8 international. Average age 39. 298 applicants, 46% accepted, 110 enrolled. In 2011, 72 master's, 19 doctorates awarded. Terminal master's awarded for partial completion of doctoral program. *Degree requirements:* For master's, thesis optional; for doctorate, comprehensive exam, thesis/dissertation, 42 credits of coursework, 30 credits of dissertation. *Entrance requirements:* For master's, GRE if cumulative undergraduate GPA is less than 3.0, undergraduate nursing degree from NLNAC- or CCNE-accredited school or university; completion of research and statistics courses with minimum grade of C; copy of current and unencumbered nursing license; for doctorate, GRE, bachelor's and/or master's degrees in nursing from NLN- or CCNE-accredited institution; portfolio; minimum undergraduate GPA of 3.0, graduate 3.5; graduate-level intermediate statistics and master's-level nursing theory courses with minimum B grade; interview. Additional exam requirements/recommendations for international students: Required—TOEFL (minimum score 560 paper-based; 220 computer-based; 83 iBT). *Application deadline:* For fall admission, 4/1 for domestic students; for spring admission, 9/1 for domestic students. Application fee: $65. Electronic applications accepted. *Expenses:* Contact institution. *Financial support:* In 2011–12, 40 students received support. Fellowships, research assistantships, teaching assistantships, Federal Work-Study, scholarships/grants, and unspecified assistantships available. Support available to part-time students. Financial award application deadline: 4/1; financial award applicants required to submit FAFSA. *Faculty research:* Biological and behavioral phenomena in pregnancy and postpartum; patterns of glycemia during the insulin resistance of pregnancy; obesity, gestational diabetes, and relationship to neonatal adiposity; men's awareness and knowledge of male breast cancer; cognitive-behavioral therapy for chronic insomnia after breast cancer treatment; massage therapy for the treatment of tension-type headaches. *Total annual research expenditures:* $5.2 million. *Unit head:* Dr. Patricia Moritz, Dean, 303-724-1679, E-mail: pat.moritz@ucdenver.edu. *Application contact:* Judy Campbell, Graduate Programs Coordinator, 303-724-8503, E-mail: judy.campbell@ucdenver.edu. Web site: http://www.ucdenver.edu/academics/colleges/nursing/Pages/default.aspx.

University of Delaware, College of Health Sciences, School of Nursing, Newark, DE 19716. Offers adult nurse practitioner (MSN, PMC); cardiopulmonary clinical nurse specialist (MSN, PMC); cardiopulmonary clinical nurse specialist/adult nurse practitioner (MSN, PMC); family nurse practitioner (MSN, PMC); gerontology clinical nurse specialist (MSN, PMC); gerontology clinical nurse specialist geriatric nurse practitioner (PMC); gerontology clinical nurse specialist/geriatric nurse practitioner (MSN); health services administration (MSN, PMC); nursing of children clinical nurse specialist (MSN, PMC); nursing of children clinical nurse specialist/pediatric nurse practitioner (MSN, PMC); oncology/immune deficiency clinical nurse specialist (MSN, PMC); oncology/immune deficiency clinical nurse specialist/adult nurse practitioner (MSN, PMC); perinatal/women's health clinical nurse specialist (MSN, PMC); perinatal/women's health clinical nurse specialist/women's health nurse practitioner (MSN, PMC); psychiatric nursing clinical nurse specialist (MSN, PMC). *Accreditation:* AACN; NLN (one or more programs are accredited). Part-time and evening/weekend programs available. Postbaccalaureate distance learning degree programs offered (minimal on-campus study). *Degree requirements:* For master's, thesis optional. *Entrance requirements:* For master's, BSN, interview, RN license. Electronic applications accepted. *Faculty research:* Marriage and chronic illness, health promotion, congestive heart failure patient outcomes, school nursing, diabetes in children, culture, health disparities, cardiovascular, prison nursing, oncology, public policy, child obesity, smoking and teen pregnancy, blood pressure measurements, men's health.

University of Illinois at Chicago, Graduate College, College of Nursing, Program in Nursing, Chicago, IL 60607-7128. Offers acute care clinical nurse specialist (MS); acute care nurse practitioner (MS); administrative studies in nursing (MS); adult nurse practitioner (MS); adult/geriatric nurse practitioner (MS); advanced community health nurse specialist (MS); family nurse practitioner (MS); geriatric clinical nurse specialist (MS); geriatric nurse practitioner (MS); mental health clinical nurse specialist (MS); mental health nurse practitioner (MS); nurse midwifery (MS); occupational health/advanced community health nurse specialist (MS); occupational health/family nurse practitioner (MS); pediatric clinical nurse specialist (MS); pediatric nurse practitioner (MS); perinatal clinical nurse specialist (MS); school/advanced community health nurse specialist (MS); school/family nurse practitioner (MS); women's health nurse practitioner (MS). *Accreditation:* AACN. Part-time programs available. *Degree requirements:* For master's, thesis or alternative. *Entrance requirements:* For master's, GRE General Test, minimum GPA of 2.75. Additional exam requirements/recommendations for international students: Required—TOEFL. Electronic applications accepted.

University of Medicine and Dentistry of New Jersey, School of Nursing, Newark, NJ 07107-3001. Offers adult health (MSN); adult occupational health (MSN); advanced practice nursing (MSN, Post Master's Certificate); family nurse practitioner (MSN); nurse anesthesia (MSN); nursing (MSN); nursing informatics (MSN); urban health (PhD); women's health practitioner (MSN). *Accreditation:* AANA/CANAEP; NLN (one or more programs are accredited). Part-time programs available. *Entrance requirements:* For

master's, GRE, RN license; basic life support, statistics, and health assessment experience. Additional exam requirements/recommendations for international students: Required—TOEFL. Electronic applications accepted. *Expenses:* Contact institution. *Faculty research:* HIV/AIDS, diabetes education, learned helplessness, nursing science, psychoeducation.

University of Minnesota, Twin Cities Campus, Graduate School, School of Nursing, Program in Women's Health Nurse Practitioner, Minneapolis, MN 55455-0213. Offers MS. *Accreditation:* AACN. Postbaccalaureate distance learning degree programs offered (minimal on-campus study). *Entrance requirements:* Additional exam requirements/recommendations for international students: Required—TOEFL (minimum score 586 paper-based; 240 computer-based).

University of Missouri–Kansas City, School of Nursing, Kansas City, MO 64110-2499. Offers adult clinical nurse specialist (MSN), including adult nurse practitioner, women's health nurse practitioner; family nurse practitioner (MSN); neonatal nurse practitioner (MSN); nurse educator (MSN); nurse executive (MSN); nursing (PhD); nursing practice (DNP); pediatric nurse practitioner (MSN). *Accreditation:* AACN. Part-time programs available. Postbaccalaureate distance learning degree programs offered (minimal on-campus study). *Faculty:* 40 full-time (35 women), 57 part-time/adjunct (52 women). *Students:* 51 full-time (48 women), 381 part-time (352 women); includes 41 minority (22 Black or African American, non-Hispanic/Latino; 7 Asian, non-Hispanic/Latino; 12 Hispanic/Latino). Average age 37. 195 applicants, 49% accepted, 90 enrolled. In 2011, 78 master's, 19 doctorates awarded. *Degree requirements:* For master's, thesis or alternative. *Entrance requirements:* For master's, minimum undergraduate GPA of 3.2; for doctorate, GRE, 3 letters of reference, interview by invitation. Additional exam requirements/recommendations for international students: Required—TOEFL (minimum score 550 paper-based; 213 computer-based; 80 iBT). *Application deadline:* For fall admission, 2/1 priority date for domestic students, 2/1 for international students; for spring admission, 9/1 priority date for domestic students, 9/1 for international students. Application fee: $45 ($50 for international students). *Expenses:* Tuition, state resident: full-time $5798; part-time $322.10 per credit hour. Tuition, nonresident: full-time $14,969; part-time $831.60 per credit hour. *Required fees:* $93.51 per credit hour. *Financial support:* In 2011–12, 25 teaching assistantships with partial tuition reimbursements (averaging $6,927 per year) were awarded; fellowships, research assistantships, career-related internships or fieldwork, Federal Work-Study, institutionally sponsored loans, and tuition waivers (full and partial) also available. Support available to part-time students. Financial award application deadline: 3/1; financial award applicants required to submit FAFSA. *Faculty research:* Geriatrics/gerontology, children's pain, neonatology, Alzheimer's care, cancer caregivers. *Unit head:* Dr. Lora Lacey-Haun, Dean, 816-235-1700, Fax: 816-235-1701, E-mail: lacey-haunc@umkc.edu. *Application contact:* Leah Wilder, Coordinator for Admissions and Recruitment, 816-235-5768, Fax: 816-235-1701, E-mail: wilderl@umkc.edu. Web site: http://nursing.umkc.edu/.

University of Missouri–St. Louis, College of Nursing, St. Louis, MO 63121. Offers adult nurse practitioner (DNP, Post Master's Certificate); clinical nurse specialist (DNP); family mental health nurse practitioner (DNP); family nurse practitioner (MSN, DNP, Post Master's Certificate); neonatal nurse practitioner (MSN); nurse educator (MSN); nurse leader (MSN); nurse practitioner (Post Master's Certificate); nursing (PhD); pediatric clinical nurse specialist (DNP); pediatric nurse practitioner (MSN, DNP, Post Master's Certificate); women's health nurse practitioner (MSN, Post Master's Certificate). *Accreditation:* AACN. Part-time programs available. *Faculty:* 12 full-time (11 women), 14 part-time/adjunct (all women). *Students:* 240 part-time (226 women); includes 30 minority (26 Black or African American, non-Hispanic/Latino; 1 Asian, non-Hispanic/Latino; 2 Hispanic/Latino; 1 Two or more races, non-Hispanic/Latino). Average age 37. 228 applicants, 28% accepted, 53 enrolled. In 2011, 66 master's, 2 doctorates, 2 other advanced degrees awarded. *Degree requirements:* For doctorate, comprehensive exam, thesis/dissertation; for Post Master's Certificate, thesis. *Entrance requirements:* For master's, 2 recommendation letters; minimum GPA of 3.0; BSN; nursing licensure; statement of purpose; course in differential/inferential statistics; for doctorate, GRE, 2 letters of recommendation, MSN, minimum GPA of 3.2, course in differential/inferential statistics; for Post Master's Certificate, 2 recommendation letters; MSN; advanced practice certificate; minimum GPA of 3.0; essay. Additional exam requirements/recommendations for international students: Required—TOEFL (minimum score 550 paper-based; 213 computer-based). *Application deadline:* For fall admission, 2/15 for domestic and international students. Application fee: $35 ($40 for international students). Electronic applications accepted. *Expenses:* Tuition, state resident: full-time $6273; part-time $3866 per year. Tuition, nonresident: full-time $14,969; part-time $9980 per year. *Required fees:* $315 per year. *Financial support:* In 2011–12, 3 research assistantships with full and partial tuition reimbursements (averaging $12,339 per year) were awarded. Financial award application deadline: 4/1; financial award applicants required to submit FAFSA. *Faculty research:* Health promotion and restoration, family disruption, violence, abuse, battered women, health survey methods. *Unit head:* Dr. Nancy Magnuson, Director, 314-516-6066. *Application contact:* 314-516-5458, Fax: 314-516-6996, E-mail: gradadm@umsl.edu. Web site: http://www.umsl.edu/divisions/nursing/.

The University of North Carolina at Chapel Hill, School of Nursing, Chapel Hill, NC 27599-7460. Offers nursing (MSN, PhD, PMC), including adult nurse practitioner (MSN, PMC), children's health advanced practice (MSN, PMC), family nurse practitioner (MSN, PMC), health care systems (MSN, PMC), psychiatric/mental health nursing (MSN, PMC), women's health nursing (MSN, PMC). *Accreditation:* AACN; NLN (one or more programs are accredited). Part-time programs available. *Degree requirements:* For master's, comprehensive exam, thesis; for doctorate, thesis/dissertation, 3 exams. *Entrance requirements:* For master's and doctorate, GRE General Test. *Faculty research:* Chronic illness, parenting, cardiovascular health in children, elderly, HIV-AIDS.

University of Pennsylvania, School of Nursing, Women's Healthcare Nurse Practitioner Program, Philadelphia, PA 19104. Offers MSN. *Accreditation:* AACN. Part-time programs available. Postbaccalaureate distance learning degree programs offered (minimal on-campus study). *Entrance requirements:* For master's, GRE General Test, BSN, minimum GPA of 3.0, previous course work in statistics, physical assessment experience. Additional exam requirements/recommendations for international students: Required—TOEFL. *Expenses:* Contact institution. *Faculty research:* New mother and infant healthcare follow-up, adequacy of antepartum care, models of healthcare.

University of South Carolina, The Graduate School, College of Nursing, Program in Clinical Nursing, Columbia, SC 29208. Offers acute care clinical specialist (MSN); acute care nurse practitioner (MSN); women's health nurse practitioner (MSN). *Accreditation:* AACN. Part-time programs available. *Degree requirements:* For master's, thesis or alternative. *Entrance requirements:* For master's, GRE General Test or MAT, BS in nursing, RN licensure. Additional exam requirements/recommendations for international students: Required—TOEFL (minimum score 570 paper-based; 230 computer-based). Electronic applications accepted. *Faculty research:* Systems research, evidence based practice, breast cancer, violence.

Vanderbilt University, Vanderbilt University School of Nursing, Nashville, TN 37240. Offers acute care nurse practitioner (MSN), including intensivist; adult-gerontology primary care nurse practitioner (MSN); emergency nurse practitioner (MSN); family nurse practitioner (MSN); family psychiatric and mental health nurse practitioner (MSN); health systems management (MSN); neonatal nurse practitioner (MSN); nurse midwifery (MSN); nurse midwifery/family nurse practitioner (MSN); nursing informatics (MSN); nursing practice (DNP); nursing science (PhD); pediatric acute care nurse practitioner (MSN); pediatric primary care nurse practitioner (MSN); women's health nurse practitioner (MSN), including urogynecology, women's health; women's health nurse practitioner/adult gerontology nurse practitioner (MSN); MSN/M Div; MSN/MTS. *Accreditation:* ACNM/ACME; NLN (one or more programs are accredited). Part-time programs available. Postbaccalaureate distance learning degree programs offered (minimal on-campus study). *Faculty:* 120 full-time (105 women), 415 part-time/adjunct (302 women). *Students:* 570 full-time (503 women), 395 part-time (364 women); includes 107 minority (57 Black or African American, non-Hispanic/Latino; 1 American Indian or Alaska Native, non-Hispanic/Latino; 19 Asian, non-Hispanic/Latino; 19 Hispanic/Latino; 2 Native Hawaiian or other Pacific Islander, non-Hispanic/Latino; 9 Two or more races, non-Hispanic/Latino), 10 international. Average age 32. 1,116 applicants, 56% accepted, 455 enrolled. In 2011, 341 master's, 33 doctorates awarded. *Degree requirements:* For doctorate, comprehensive exam, thesis/dissertation. *Entrance requirements:* For master's, GRE General Test (within the past 5 years), minimum B average in undergraduate course work, 3 letters of recommendation; for doctorate, GRE General Test, interview, 3 letters of recommendation from doctorally-prepared faculty, MSN, essay. Additional exam requirements/recommendations for international students: Required—TOEFL (minimum score 570 paper-based; 88 computer-based), IELTS (minimum score 6.5). *Application deadline:* For fall admission, 12/1 priority date for domestic students, 12/1 for international students. Applications are processed on a rolling basis. Application fee: $50. Electronic applications accepted. *Expenses:* Contact institution. *Financial support:* In 2011–12, 392 students received support. Scholarships/grants and health care benefits available. Support available to part-time students. Financial award application deadline: 3/15; financial award applicants required to submit FAFSA. *Faculty research:* Lymphedema, palliative care and bereavement, health services research including workforce, safety and quality of care, gerontology, better birth outcomes including nutrition . *Total annual research expenditures:* $1.8 million. *Unit head:* Dr. Colleen Conway-Welch, Dean, 615-343-8776, Fax: 615-343-7711, E-mail: colleen.conway-welch@vanderbilt.edu. *Application contact:* Patricia Peerman, Assistant Dean for Enrollment Management, 615-322-3800, Fax: 615-343-0333, E-mail: vusn-admissions@vanderbilt.edu. Web site: http://www.nursing.vanderbilt.edu.

Virginia Commonwealth University, Graduate School, School of Nursing, Richmond, VA 23284-9005. Offers adult health acute nursing (MS); adult health primary nursing (MS); biobehavioral clinical research (PhD); child health nursing (MS); clinical nurse leader (MS); family health nursing (MS); nurse educator (MS); nurse practitioner (MS); nursing (Certificate); nursing administration (MS), including clinical nurse manager; psychiatric-mental health nursing (MS); women's health nursing (MS). *Accreditation:* NLN (one or more programs are accredited). Part-time and evening/weekend programs available. *Degree requirements:* For master's, thesis optional; for doctorate, thesis/dissertation. *Entrance requirements:* For master's, GRE General Test, BSN, minimum GPA of 2.8; for doctorate, GRE General Test. Additional exam requirements/recommendations for international students: Required—TOEFL (minimum score 600 paper-based; 250 computer-based; 100 iBT). Electronic applications accepted. *Expenses:* Tuition, state resident: full-time $9133; part-time $507 per credit. Tuition, nonresident: full-time $18,777; part-time $1043 per credit. *Required fees:* $77 per credit. Tuition and fees vary according to degree level, campus/location, program and student level.

Wayne State University, College of Nursing, Detroit, MI 48202. Offers adult acute care nursing (MSN); adult primary care nursing (MSN); advanced practice nursing with women, neonates and children (MSN); community health nursing (MSN); complementary therapies in healthcare (Certificate); infant mental health (DNP, PhD); nurse-midwifery (Certificate); nursing (PhD); nursing education (MSN, Certificate), including nursing education (Certificate), transcultural nursing; nursing practice (DNP); pediatric nurse practitioner - acute care (Certificate); pediatric nurse practitioner - primary care (Certificate); psychiatric mental health nurse practitioner (MSN, Certificate); women's health nurse practitioner (Certificate). Application deadline for DNP and PhD is January 15. *Accreditation:* AACN. Part-time programs available. *Students:* 136 full-time (124 women), 333 part-time (300 women); includes 127 minority (82 Black or African American, non-Hispanic/Latino; 1 American Indian or Alaska Native, non-Hispanic/Latino; 27 Asian, non-Hispanic/Latino; 12 Hispanic/Latino; 5 Two or more races, non-Hispanic/Latino), 17 international. Average age 37. 180 applicants, 56% accepted, 90 enrolled. In 2011, 95 master's, 6 doctorates, 21 other advanced degrees awarded. Terminal master's awarded for partial completion of doctoral program. *Degree requirements:* For master's, thesis or alternative; for doctorate, thesis/dissertation. *Entrance requirements:* For master's, minimum honor point average of 2.8 in upper-division course work; BA from NLN- or CCNE-accredited program; references; current RN license; personal statement; for doctorate, GRE General Test (for PhD applicants; DNP applicants may choose the GRE exception but must submit a writing sample), minimum GPA of 3.3, bachelor's or master's degree in nursing, current RN license, interview, goals statement, curriculum vitae, reference letters from doctorally-prepared individuals (three for PhD applicants, two for DNP); for Certificate, graduate degree in nursing, current Michigan RN license, three letters of reference, personal goal statement. Additional exam requirements/recommendations for international students: Required—TOEFL (minimum score 550 paper-based; 213 computer-based); Recommended—TWE (minimum score 6). *Application deadline:* For fall admission, 6/1 priority date for domestic students, 5/1 for international students; for winter admission, 10/1 priority date for domestic students, 9/1 for international students; for spring admission, 2/1 priority date for domestic students, 1/1 for international students. Applications are processed on a rolling basis. Application fee: $50. Electronic applications accepted. *Expenses:* Tuition, state resident: part-time $512.85 per credit. Tuition, nonresident: part-time $1132.65 per credit. *Required fees:* $26.60 per credit. $199.65 per semester. Tuition and fees vary according to course load and program. *Financial support:* In 2011–12, 81 students received support, including 2 fellowships with tuition reimbursements available (averaging $13,708 per year), 1 research assistantship with tuition reimbursement available (averaging $17,391 per year), 4 teaching assistantships with tuition reimbursements available (averaging $27,103 per year); Federal Work-Study, institutionally sponsored loans, scholarships/grants, traineeships, and unspecified assistantships also available. Support available to part-time students. Financial award applicants required to submit FAFSA. *Faculty research:* Urban self-care and care-giving, health disparities, healthy functioning across the life-span. *Total annual research expenditures:* $1.2 million. *Unit head:* Dr. Barbara Redman, Dean, 313-577-4070, Fax: 313-577-4571, E-mail: ae9080@wayne.edu. *Application contact:* Dr. Cynthia Redwine, Assistant Dean for the Office of Student Affairs, 313-577-4082, Fax: 313-577-6949, E-mail: nursinginfo@wayne.edu. Web site: http://www.nursing.wayne.edu/.

ADELPHI UNIVERSITY
School of Nursing

Programs of Study

The School of Nursing at Adelphi University offers a Master of Science (M.S.) in adult health practitioner; an M.S. in nursing administration; an M.S. in nursing education; a Ph.D. in nursing; and post-master's certificate programs in adult health practitioner, nursing administration, and nursing education.

The M.S. in adult health practitioner (52 credits) entails in-depth study of adult health nursing. The curriculum integrates theoretical knowledge and practical skills while exploring the issues and forces within the healthcare delivery system that affect the roles of the advanced practice nurse. The program emphasizes scientific inquiry as a tool for building clinical knowledge and testing the validity of the theoretical assumptions underlying nursing practice. Students have opportunities to work with advanced practice nurses and other health professionals in a variety of clinical settings.

The M.S. in nursing administration (45 credits) prepares nurse managers who can function in a variety of healthcare settings. Topics include nursing theories, group dynamics, communication, and professional issues and trends. To prepare to serve as leaders in improving healthcare services, students study leadership roles in the healthcare field. Through the program's research component, students gain practice in analyzing and implementing research findings.

The M.S. in nursing education (46 credits) prepares nurse educators who are competent to function in a variety of educational and healthcare settings. Students will acquire knowledge, skills, and values related to teaching and learning, instructional design, assessment and measurement strategies, curriculum development implementation, and evaluation in nursing education. Seminar and practicum is an opportunity for students to be guided by expert nurse educators and apply their knowledge as nurse educators.

The Ph.D. in nursing program is an innovative 54-credit program designed to advance healthcare teaching, research, and leadership by educating nurses with a master's degree to become nursing scholars and educators. The plan of study offers strong core courses in both nursing science and research. The program may be taken on a full-time (9 to 12 credits) or part-time basis following a progressive program plan. Most of the courses are offered one day a week. Students are admitted only in the fall semester and proceed through the program in cohorts, taking classes together.

The post-master's certificate programs in nursing administration, adult health nurse practitioner, and nursing education are designed for students who already hold a master's degree in nursing and want to specialize in another discipline. The programs aim to strengthen the administrative or clinical capability of master's-prepared nurses who are planning or are already involved in a role expansion or role change. The program is a part-time course of study.

Research Facilities

The Nursing Resource Center features learning laboratories that simulate hospital and clinical settings. A clinical coordinator provides supervision as students gain invaluable practice. One laboratory is set up with all appropriate hospital supplies and equipment, including advanced patient-care mannequins and simulators. The second laboratory is equipped with state-of-the-art nursing tools for complete assessment practice. The computer laboratory offers online learning and practice programs.

The University's primary research holdings are at Swirbul Library and include 600,000 volumes (including bound periodicals and government publications), 806,000 items in microformats, 33,000 audiovisual items, and online access to more than 61,000 electronic journal titles and 221 research databases.

Financial Aid

Adelphi University offers a wide variety of federal aid programs, state grants, scholarship and fellowship programs, on- and off-campus employment, and teaching and research assistantships. More information is available online at ecampus.adelphi.edu/sfs.

Cost of Study

For the 2012–2013 academic year, the tuition rate is $965 per credit. University fees range from $315 to $550 per semester.

Living and Housing Costs

The University assists single and married students in finding suitable accommodations whenever possible. The cost of living depends on the location and number of rooms rented.

Location

Located in historic Garden City, New York, 45 minutes from Manhattan and 20 minutes from Queens, Adelphi's 75-acre suburban campus is known for the beauty of its landscape and architecture. The campus is a short walk from the Long Island Rail Road and is convenient to New York's major airports and several major highways. Off-campus centers are located in Manhattan, Hauppauge, and Poughkeepsie.

The University and The School

Founded in 1896, Adelphi is a fully accredited, private university with nearly 8,000 undergraduate, graduate, and returning-adult students in the arts and sciences, business, clinical psychology, education, nursing, and social work. Students come from forty-three states and forty-five countries. The Princeton Review named Adelphi University a Best College in the Northeastern Region, and the *Fiske Guide to Colleges* recognized Adelphi as a Best Buy in higher education for six years in a row. The University is one of only twenty-five private institutions in the nation to earn this recognition.

The School of Nursing is dedicated to providing students with the skills, knowledge, and specialized training to succeed as qualified caregivers and leaders in the nursing profession. The course of study combines theory, research, clinical practice, and community service. Adelphi's extensive school and community partnerships provide wide-ranging opportunities to gain fieldwork experience. The curricula of the School of Nursing are registered by the New York State Education Department and Division of Professional Education, and are accredited by the Commission on Collegiate Nursing Education (CCNE).

Applying

Each master's degree applicant should have a bachelor's degree in nursing, with a course in basic statistics and be licensed as a professional registered nurse. Students must submit a completed application, a $50 application fee, official college transcripts, and two letters of recommendation. Applications are processed on a rolling basis.

Adelphi University

Applicants for the Ph.D. program must have an M.S. or M.S.N. from an accredited nursing program (CCNE or NLNAC approved) and submit a completed application, three professional letters of reference (from a supervisor, committee chair, former professor, etc.), satisfactory GRE scores (taken within the last five years), licensure as an RN in New York State, a professional writing sample, and an interview with at least 2 members of the School of Nursing. All application materials must be received by March 15 to be considered for the following fall semester for the Ph.D. program.

Correspondence and Information

School of Nursing
Patrick Coonan, Dean
Alumnae Hall, Room 220
Adelphi University
One South Avenue
Garden City, New York 11530
Phone: 516-877-4510
Fax: 516-877-4558
E-mail: coonan@adelphi.edu
Web site: http://nursing.adelphi.edu/

THE FACULTY AND THEIR RESEARCH

Judith Ackerhalt, Ed.D., Columbia. Therapeutic communication.

Deborah Ambrosio-Mawhirter, Ed.D., Dowling. Human assessment: a holistic approach.

Helen Ballestas, Ph.D., Capella. Patient-centered nursing care.

Stefni Bogard, M.S.N., Pennsylvania. Health assessment throughout the lifespan; adult health nursing.

Jacqueline Brandwein, M.A., NYU. Alterations in the holistic integrity of the childbearing family; alterations of holistic integrity of children.

Nancy Cole, M.S., Adelphi. holistic approach to alterations in physiological integrity; nursing care of adults; professionalism in the provision of the holistic care.

Patrick R. Coonan, Ed.D., Columbia Teachers College.

Christine Coughlin, Ed.D., Columbia Teachers College. Patient/family perception of care; leadership qualities of front-line nursing leaders.

Diane Dembicki, Ph.D., Colorado State. Public health/community nutrition; international health and nutrition; cultural diversity; developmental education.

Margo DeSevo, Ph.D., NYU. Genetics and maternity.

Patricia Donohue-Porter, Ph.D. Adelphi. Quality improvement; patient safety; leadership.

Patricia Facquet, Ed.D., Cambridge College. Pediatric palliative care; adolescent medicine; simulation.

Darylann Ficken, D.N.P., Columbia.

Maryann Forbes, Ph.D., Adelphi. Effects of long-term mechanical ventilation on patients and families; nursing care of the COPD patient; simulation in nursing education; gerontology.

Yvonne Gray, M.S., SUNY Downstate. Technology information literacy; professionalism in the provision of holistic care.

Clarilee Hauser, Ph.D., California, San Francisco. Alterations in holistic integrity managed in community; community health nursing; professionalism in the provision of the holistic care.

Beth Heydemann, M.S., Columbia. Cardiovascular and thoracic surgery; adult primary care; case management; patient-centered nursing care.

Stephen Holzemer, Ph.D., Adelphi. Community health; health policy; critical thinking.

William Jacobowitz, Ed.D., Columbia Teachers College. Mental health nursing.

Marilyn Klainberg, Ed.D., Columbia Teachers College. Use of computers to enhance nursing practice and nursing education.

Elizabeth Lee, Ph.D., Connecticut. Adult health nursing; health promotion and disease prevention; health assessment.

Seonah Lee, Ph.D., Illinois. Clinical decision support systems and evaluation criteria for mixed-method research.

Shan Liu, Ph.D., Yale. Pharmacology.

Teresa L. Mascitti, M.S.N., Molloy. Pathophysiology for nurse practitioners; adult health nursing; health assessment.

Andrea McCrink, Ed.D., Dowling. Pediatric nursing; high-risk behaviors in teens and college students.

Ditsapelo McFarland, Ph.D., Boston College. Women's health; cultural diversities in healthcare.

Deborah J. Murphy, M.S., Columbia. Holistic healthcare.

Anne Peirce, Ph.D., Maryland. Professional nursing practice; philosophical foundations of nursing science; dissertation guidance.

Janet Raman, Ed.D., Dowling Pharmacology; academic success of the nursing student.

Maureen Roller, D.N.P., Case Western Reserve. Adult internal medicine; older adults; relationship to exercise adherence.

K. C. Rondello, M.D., St. George's (Grenada). Health management in times of disaster; hospital and healthcare policy and management.

Bayla Samter, M.S., Columbia. Physical assessment of the adult; adult health nursing; health assessment.

Holly K. Shaw, Ph.D., Adelphi. Advanced nursing practice; communication in nursing.

Margaret Silver, M.Ed., Columbia Teachers College. Aging and chronic mental illness.

Yiyuan Sun, D.N.Sc., Yale. Cancer prevention and early detection; symptom management (oncology).

Arlene Trolman, Ed.D., Columbia. Alterations in holistic integrity managed in the community.

Joan Valas, Ph.D., Columbia. Technology and information; ethics; chronic illness; social inequalities.

Thomas J. Virgona, Ph.D., LIU, C.W. Post. Disaster recovery; information security; healthcare informatics.

Jane White, Ph.D., Catholic University. Research (qualitative and quantitative approaches); nursing science and epidemiology.

Adelphi's campus is located in historic Garden City, Long Island, New York.

A registered arboretum, Adelphi is truly a green campus.

BRIGHAM YOUNG UNIVERSITY
College of Nursing

Programs of Study

The Brigham Young University (BYU) College of Nursing offers a Master of Science (M.S.) degree that prepares students as family nurse practitioners (FNP). A post-master's family nurse practitioner degree is available for those who have already received a master's degree in nursing. Graduates are eligible to apply for certification examinations. The program can be completed in six semesters of full-time study.

Research Facilities

The research center offers work space for faculty members and students, research resources, research journals, and eight computer work stations. Current software includes several programs for quantitative and qualitative data analysis, media presentation preparation, scanning, and word processing. Statistical consultation services are available to students with data analysis during the thesis/project process.

Financial Aid

Tuition scholarships are available, along with research and teaching assistantships. Federal monies specific to nurses are available. University loans and Federal Stafford Student Loans are also available.

Cost of Study

Tuition at BYU is charged on the basis of the student's membership or nonmembership in the Church of Jesus Christ of Latter-Day Saints (LDS). Full-time graduate nursing students enrolled in the fall or winter semester pay $2880 if they are LDS members or $5760 if they are nonmembers. Those enrolled in the spring or summer term pay $1440 if they are LDS members or $2880 if they are nonmembers. Part-time tuition per credit hour is $320 for LDS students and $640 for non-LDS students. During fall and winter semesters, full-time study consists of 8.5 or more hours, and for spring and summer terms it consists of at least 4.5 credit hours.

Living and Housing Costs

A variety of on-campus and off-campus housing is available. A large number of off-campus apartments are also available.

Student Groups

There are approximately 30 students in the graduate program. Students gain knowledge and are provided opportunities to develop the commitment to service and lifelong learning. BYU students have a long tradition of a high pass rate on the certification examination, and are highly recruited.

Location

The University is nestled at the foot of the beautifully rugged Wasatch Range of the Rocky Mountains. The campus is the focal point of the Provo/Orem community of 163,000 people. The valley lies 45 miles south of Salt Lake City; it is bounded on the west by Utah Lake and on the east by the Wasatch Mountains. The setting offers a variety of recreational opportunities, including numerous ski resorts, mountain climbing, and spectacular national parks.

The University and The College

Brigham Young University is sponsored and operated by the Church of Jesus Christ of Latter-Day Saints. Founded in 1875, BYU is one of the largest privately owned, church-sponsored universities in the United States, with 1,283 faculty members and 32,955 students. Students represent all fifty states and more than 120 other countries. In keeping with an inscription at the campus entrance—"The world is our campus"—the University offers students many local and international learning experiences. Facilities and programs include a 793-acre research farm, a PBS television station, a 3-million-volume library, and study centers in Washington, D.C.; London; Vienna; and Jerusalem. Programs also extend into South America, the Middle East, Africa, Eastern Europe, and other parts of the world.

The College of Nursing was established in 1952. Following in the footsteps of pioneer nurses and midwives, College alumni have established a legacy of service as clinicians, nurse practitioners, administrators, educators, health and welfare missionaries, and scholars. The University and the College of Nursing endeavor to provide students with the broad-based education and skills necessary for becoming professionals and informed citizens.

Applying

Applicants can obtain application forms from the University Web site or the Office of Graduate Studies, B-356 ASB, Provo, Utah 84602-1339 (telephone: 801-422-4091). Application packages should include a statement of intent for graduate education, official transcripts of previous academic work, standardized test scores, and three letters of recommendation from former instructors or employers. Application may be made online. The deadline for submission of the form and supporting documents is December 1. Entry to both the M.S. program and the post-master's program is restricted to spring semester. A personal interview with faculty members and completion of a short writing exercise are necessary. The application fee is $50.

Correspondence and Information

Stephanie Wilson

Graduate Program

400 Spencer W. Kimball Tower (SWKT)

Brigham Young University

Provo, Utah 84602

United States

Phone: 801-422-4142

Fax: 801-422-0538

E-mail: stephanie_wilson@byu.edu

Web site: http://nursing.byu.edu

Brigham Young University

THE FACULTY AND THEIR RESEARCH

Renea Beckstrand, Associate Professor; Ph.D., Utah, 2001. End of life and critical care.

Ana C. Birkhead, Assistant Professor, Ph.D., California, San Francisco, 2007. Hispanic women's health.

Kent Blad, Associate Teaching Professor; D.N.P., Utah, 2010. Acute care.

Beth Cole, Professor; Ph.D., BYU, 1978. Caring connections: A hope and comfort in grief.

Karen Dearing, Assistant Professor; Ph.D., Utah, 2003. Schizophrenia recovery, nurse-patient relations.

Donna Freeborn, Assistant Professor; Ph.D., Oregon Health Sciences, 2008. Women's issues.

Barbara Heise, Assistant Professor; Ph.D., Virginia, 2006. Adult and gerontological mental health, alcohol and drug abuse.

Jane Lassetter, Associate Professor; Ph.D., Oregon Health & Science, 2008. Culture and health.

Beth Luthy, Assistant Professor; D.N.P., Rush, 2008. Childhood immunizations.

Barbara L. Mandleco, Professor; Ph.D., Brigham Young, 1991. Growth and development, resilience in children.

Erin Maughan, Assistant Professor; Ph.D., Utah, 2006. Community nursing, specializing in school nursing.

Sabrina Jarvis, Assistant Professor; D.N.P., Utah, 2010. Acute care.

Patty Ravert, Associate Professor and Director, Nursing Learning Center; Ph.D., Utah, 2004. Outcomes of simulated learning experiences.

Mary Williams, Associate Professor; Ph.D., Arizona, 1991. Transplant anxiety, instrumentation, qualitative methodology.

D'YOUVILLE COLLEGE
Department of Nursing

Programs of Study

At the graduate level, nursing programs include a Doctor of Nursing Practice (D.N.P.); Master of Science (M.S.) in community health nursing with concentrations in advanced clinical nursing, nursing management, and nursing education; Master of Science in nursing with choice of clinical focus; and Master of Science in family nurse practitioner studies as well as a post-master's certificate in family nurse practitioner studies. A five-year Bachelor of Science in Nursing/Master of Science in nursing (B.S.N./M.S.) degree program, degree-completion programs for nurses who have already received their associate degrees, RN to B.S.N./M.S. program, and an RN to B.S.N./M.S. in community health nursing program are also available.

Innovative class scheduling provides working nursing professionals the opportunity to study full-time by attending only one day per week. This alternative scheduling allows students to continue working in their professions while earning their degrees.

Research Facilities

D'Youville's modern Library Resource Center contains 130,000 volumes, including microtext and software, and subscriptions to 500 periodicals and newspapers. The library has state-of-the-art computer reference capabilities for both in-house and off-site users, including access to over 70 online databases. The multimillion-dollar Health Science Building houses laboratories, including those for anatomy, organic chemistry, quantitative analysis, and computer science. It also houses classrooms, faculty member offices, and development centers, including one for career development.

Financial Aid

D'Youville attempts to provide financial aid for students who would not otherwise be able to attend. Determination of aid is based on the Free Application for Federal Student Aid. Aid is available in the form of grants, loans, and employment on campus. In addition, D'Youville offers scholarships for academic achievement to incoming students.

Graduate students must be matriculated for 6 or more credits in a degree program. Nurse traineeship assistance is available to students enrolled for a minimum of 9 credit hours per semester in the graduate nursing program. Canadian students (citizens and landed immigrants), except those enrolled in the RN degree-completion program, are offered a 20 percent tuition reduction and may also apply for the Ontario Student Assistance Program (OSAP). All students enrolled in the RN degree-completion program are offered a 50 percent tuition reduction.

Cost of Study

Graduate tuition for 2012–13 is $810 per credit hour for master's and advanced certificate programs and $875 per credit hour for doctoral programs. A general College fee of between $50 and $175 is required, based on credit hours taken.

Living and Housing Costs

Marguerite Hall, the residence facility, houses men and women on separate floors and includes a coed floor for graduate and adult students. For 2012–13, room and board costs $5125 per semester. Overnight accommodation is available, space permitting. A residence-apartment complex houses 175 junior, senior, and graduate students in one- and four-bedroom apartments. The resident apartment complex rates are around $4187per semester, based on the type of apartment reserved.

Student Group

Graduate degree programs are enhanced by a 13:1 student-faculty ratio. The current enrollment is 636 full-time and 359 part-time graduate students. Seventy percent of the students are women, 15 percent are members of minority groups, and 16 percent are internationals students. D'Youville's proximity to the Canadian border accounts for the majority of the international student population.

Location

D'Youville is situated on Buffalo's residential west side. The College is within minutes of many social attractions, including the downtown shopping center, the Kleinhans Music hall, the Albright-Knox Art Gallery, two museums, and several theaters that offer stage productions. Seasonal changes in the area offer a variety of recreational opportunities. Buffalo is only 90 minutes from Toronto and 25 minutes from Niagara Falls, making it a gateway to recreation areas in western New York and Ontario. Holiday Valley, a skier's paradise, is an hour's drive away. The city is serviced by the New York State Thruway, Amtrak, Greyhound and Trailways bus lines, and most major airlines.

D'Youville enjoys a diversified interchange with the community due to its affiliations with schools, hospitals, and social agencies in the area. College students in the Buffalo area number more than 60,000.

The College

Commencing in 1942, D'Youville College was the first private college in New York State to offer a four-year Bachelor of Science in Nursing degree program. The College offers six doctoral, thirteen master's-level, and five postbaccalaureate programs as well as baccalaureate and advanced certificate programs. Graduate programs, in addition to nursing, include education (childhood, adolescence, special, and TESOL), health services administration, international business, M.B.A., occupational therapy, and physician assistant studies. Doctoral programs include chiropractic, educational leadership, health policy and health education, pharmacy, and physical therapy. D'Youville offers the undergraduate degrees of Bachelor of Arts (B.A.), Bachelor of Science (B.S.), and Bachelor of Science in Nursing (B.S.N.). Majors include accounting, biology, business management, chiropractic (seven-year B.S./D.C.), dietetics, education (childhood, adolescence, and special), English, exercise and sports studies, global studies, health services, history, information technology, nursing, occupational therapy, philosophy, physical therapy, physician assistant, preprofessional

D'Youville College

studies (dental, law, medicine, pharmacy, and veterinary studies), psychology, and sociology. Five-year combined bachelor's/master's (B.S./M.S.) programs are offered in dietetics, education, information technology (B.S.)/international business (M.S.), nursing, and occupational therapy. A six-year B.S./D.P.T. program is offered in physical therapy.

Applying

A master's degree in advanced practice nursing from an approved or accredited college or university and RN licensure are required for admission to the Doctor of Nursing Practice program.

A baccalaureate degree in nursing from an approved or accredited college or university and RN licensure are required for admission to the graduate nursing programs. Licensure as a registered nurse in New York State and a minimum of one year of experience as a registered nurse are required of candidates applying to the nurse practitioner programs. Admissions to graduate programs are based on an overall evaluation of credentials, including the applicant's undergraduate record, with a minimum 3.0 overall GPA (on a 4.0 scale) and 3.25 for the DNP program. Applicants who do not fulfill admission requirements may be admitted provisionally. Applicants whose native language is not English must submit a minimum TOEFL score of 500. Graduate application files are reviewed on a rolling basis.

Correspondence and Information

Linda E. Fisher
Director of Graduate Admission
D'Youville College
One D'Youville Square
320 Porter Avenue
Buffalo, New York 14201
Phone: 716-829-8400
           800-777-3921 (toll-free)
E-mail: graduateadmissions@dyc.edu
Web site: http://www.dyc.edu

THE FACULTY

Denise Dunford, Assistant Professor and Director of Family Nurse Practitioner Program; D.N.S., SUNY at Buffalo.
Judith Lewis, Dean, School of Nursing; Ed.D., Cincinnati.
Kathleen Mariano, Assistant Professor; D.N.S., SUNY at Buffalo.
Abigail Mitchell; Assistant Professor; D.H.Ed., A. T. Still.
Eileen Nahigian, Assistant Professor; D.N.S., SUNY at Buffalo.
Sharon Mang, Assistant Professor; D.N.P., SUNY at Buffalo.
Shannon McCrory-Churchill, Assistant Professor; D.H.Ed., A. T. Still.
Tina Sinatra-Wilhelm; Assistant Professor; DNP, Chatham University.

FELICIAN COLLEGE

Master of Science in Nursing
Advanced Practice, Education, and Executive Leadership Tracks

Programs of Study

The Master of Science in Nursing (M.S.N.) program at Felician College is designed to prepare the registered nurse with a Bachelor of Science in Nursing (B.S.N.) degree for advanced practice as nurse practitioners in primary-care settings; as administrators in patient care services across the health-care spectrum; and as nurse educators in higher education, staff development and continuing education, and patient and community education settings.

The Advanced Practice track emphasizes nursing care of families or adults, with a specific focus on vulnerable and underserved populations. The Executive Leadership track develops knowledge and skill in key areas such as risk management, administrative practices and principles, and patient quality and safety initiatives. The Education track emphasizes the preparation of leaders in education to support nurses' professional development as well as to coordinate, develop, implement, and evaluate patient, family, and community education programs that promote and restore health and prevent disease.

The Advanced Practice program offers students a choice of either a completely online format or a cohort-based, on-campus model with a hybrid delivery method, blending classroom and e-learning. The Executive Leadership program blends Web-based teaching with traditional classroom and project-based learning experiences. The Nurse Educator track, also cohort based, is offered on campus, with the majority of classes presented as hybrids.

The Adult-Gerontology Nurse Practitioner track requires 43 credits and 600 clinical hours, while the Family Nurse Practitioner track requires 46 credits and 780 clinical hours. Courses are taught on a trimester schedule, with 12-week sessions and terms that start in September, January, and April. Students choosing the on-campus cohort model meet one day per week for each session. Students generally take at least two courses per term and can complete the degree in as little as two years. All students are required to take 28 credits of professional core courses before they complete the course work required for their track of choice. Graduates are eligible to take the advanced practice national certification examination in family or adult health. Graduates are also eligible to apply for admission to doctoral programs.

The Executive Leadership track consists of 36 credits, which can be completed in approximately two years, as well as clinical and practicum hours. The program's eight-week courses are offered one evening per week on the same evening for the duration of the program, allowing students to plan their schedules far in advance. For candidates wishing to enter the M.S.N./Executive Leadership program who hold a bachelor's degree in a field other than nursing, Felician College offers a bridge program to help students develop the core competencies they will need in order to progress through the program.

The Education track requires 42 credits as well as clinical and practicum hours, based on individual course requirements. Courses are taught in a trimester schedule, cohort model, meeting one day per week for twelve-week sessions. Students

take two courses per session and can complete the degree in just over two years. Students take 22 credits of professional core courses before beginning the 20 credits of specialty courses in education. Graduates of the Education track are eligible to take the ANCC Nursing Professional Development Certification Examination and the National League for Nursing Certification in Nurse Educator Examination. Graduates of the program are eligible to apply for admission to doctoral study.

The post-master's certificate program in Advanced Practice prepares a nurse with a master's degree in nursing for primary-care practice in family or adult advanced practice. The credits required for the certificate range from 10 to 31, based on the student's educational background and prerequisite course work. The program consists of four foundation courses, with more courses in the chosen area of specialization, as well as clinical experience. A 22-credit post-master's certificate in Nursing Education is also offered.

Research Facilities

The Nursing Resource and Simulation Center, a multifaceted center of learning for all nursing students, is located on the Lodi campus. The center has a state-of-the-art computer room, where CD-ROM and interactive video programs are used to intensify the learning experience. The Nursing Resource and Simulation Center staff members assist students with clinical competencies through the use of mannequins and other equipment that simulates clinical procedures. Individual tutoring and workshops are offered to enhance theory comprehension.

A center for child care and simulated nursing practice is also available on the Lodi campus. The first floor is devoted to a well-equipped Child Care Center for the convenience of students and faculty members. The upper floor houses the Nursing Resource and Simulation Laboratory, which provides a simulated hospital setting for the clinical training of students in the nursing programs.

The College Library is a two-story building that serves the needs of students, faculty and staff members, and alumni with more than 110,000 books and over 800 periodical subscriptions. This collection is enhanced by large holdings of materials in microform, which can be used on the library's reader/printer equipment. With its computers linked to information services such as DIALOG and OCLC, and as a member of the New Jersey Library Network and VALE, the library locates and obtains information, journal articles, and books not available in its collection from sources all over the country. Computerized databases can also be accessed directly by users through the online First Search workstation, where up-to-date information on 40 million books and an index of 15,000 periodicals is available. The library is also connected to the Internet and has several CD-ROM workstations. Through EBSCOhost, Bell & Howell's Proquest, CINAHL, and other services, students and faculty and staff members have access to numerous online journal indexes—as well as articles from thousands of periodicals—from anywhere on the campus computer network or from their home computers. An experienced staff of professional librarians is available to assist users.

The College's computer facilities include an academic and administrative network, four computerized labs, a computerized learning center, and two computer centers that are available for students, with a total of about 200 computers available for student/faculty member use. All classrooms, offices, and facilities are wired for Internet and e-mail.

Financial Aid

Fellowships and loans are available. To qualify for financial aid, a student must complete the Free Application for Federal Student Aid (FAFSA).

Cost of Study

In 2012–13, graduate tuition is $915 per credit. Fees are additional.

Living and Housing Costs

Students are housed in two residence halls on the Rutherford campus, Milton Court and Elliott Terrace. Both buildings have housing organized around student suites containing semiprivate baths. On-campus room and board is approximately $11,400 per year. On-campus housing is not available to married students.

Student Group

Felician College enrolls approximately 2,300 students. In fall 2011 there were approximately 350 students enrolled in graduate programs.

Location

Felician College's Lodi campus is located on the banks of the Saddle River on a beautifully landscaped campus of 27 acres and offers a collegiate setting in suburban Bergen County, within easy driving distance of New York City. The Felician College Rutherford Campus is set on 10.5 beautifully landscaped acres in the heart of the historic community of Rutherford, New Jersey. Only 15 minutes from the Lodi campus, the Rutherford complex contains student residences, classroom buildings, a student center, and a gymnasium. The campus is a short distance from downtown Rutherford, where there are many shops and businesses of interest to students.

The College

Felician College, a coeducational liberal arts college, is a Catholic, private, independent institution for students representing diverse religious, racial, and ethnic backgrounds. The College operates on two campuses in Lodi and Rutherford, New Jersey. The College is one of the institutions of higher learning conducted by the Felician Sisters in the United States. Its mission is to provide a values-oriented education based in the liberal arts while it prepares students for meaningful

lives and careers in contemporary society. To meet the needs of students and to provide personal enrichment courses to matriculated and nonmatriculated students, Felician College offers day, evening, and weekend programs. The College is accredited by the Middle States Association of Colleges and Schools and carries program accreditation from the National Accrediting Agency for Clinical Laboratory Sciences and the International Assembly for Collegiate Business Education.

Applying

In addition to being licensed as a registered nurse, applicants must have a Bachelor of Science in Nursing degree from a program accredited by a national accrediting agency and approved by the Board of Nursing, with a minimum cumulative GPA of 3.0. The Executive Leadership track requires successful completion of undergraduate courses in nursing research and statistics, while the Education and Advanced Practice tracks require these two courses in addition to pathophysiology, and health assessment. Applicants must submit the completed application, the $40 nonrefundable application fee, all official academic transcripts, and two professional or academic references from persons qualified to judge the applicant's ability to succeed in graduate study. Applicants must also submit copies of all licensure held as a registered professional nurse, including New Jersey, and/or the state of the clinical practicum. The licensee cannot have any pending disciplinary action against their nursing license from any Board of Nursing. International credential requirements are reviewed on an individual basis. Applications are processed on a rolling basis. Applicants for the Advanced Practice curriculum must have at least one year of clinical practice and must be currently employed in professional practice. For students outside of New Jersey, some states require program approval (permission to operate) for students to participate in clinical practice in hospitals and private practice settings within that state. Students are encouraged to check with the Program Associate Dean to identify specific state requirements prior to enrolling in the program.

Correspondence and Information

Office of Graduate Admission
Felician College
262 South Main Street
Lodi, New Jersey 07644-2117
United States
Phone: 201-559-6077
Fax: 201-559-6138
E-mail: graduate@felician.edu
Web site: http://www.felician.edu/

THE FACULTY

Specific information regarding the faculty of Felician College is available on the College's Web site at http://www.felician.edu.

HAWAI'I PACIFIC UNIVERSITY
College of Nursing and Health Sciences

Programs of Study

Hawai'i Pacific University's Master of Science in Nursing (M.S.N.) degree is designed to prepare students to assume enhanced roles in community-based care as advanced practice nurses. With three concentrations, Community Clinical Nurse Specialist (CNS), Community Clinical Nurse Specialist Educator, or Family Nurse Practitioner (FNP), students learn contemporary approaches for delivering cost-effective, qualitative health care, especially to chronically underserved populations such as the poor, elderly, and those in multiethnic communities. The program focuses on those skills needed by nurses to succeed in the constantly changing health-care environment: enhanced critical thinking, assessment, problem solving, continued education of nurses, and effective communication skills.

The RN-M.S.N. pathway allows registered nurses without baccalaureate degrees in nursing to transition into the M.S.N. program. Students entering the RN-M.S.N. pathway are granted provisional admission status until all prerequisites have been completed. Students who successfully complete the program receive an M.S.N. degree.

Hawai'i Pacific University (HPU) offers the joint Master of Science in Nursing and Master of Business Administration (M.S.N./M.B.A.) program to complement a nurse's clinical skills with a solid business foundation. The joint program focuses on skills needed by both health-care and business leaders: analytical reasoning, leadership, and effective communication.

Research Facilities

To support graduate studies, HPU's Meader and Atherton Libraries offer over 110,000 bound volumes, 350,000 microfiche items, and periodical subscriptions to 1,500 print titles and 30,000 electronic journals. Databases of public and state university libraries, legislative information, and business-oriented statistical data are also available in the library or online. Students can access HPU's library databases, course information, their academic information, and an e-mail account through Pipeline, the university's internal Web site for students. The University's accessible on-campus computer center houses more than 420 computers with specialized software to support graduate academic programs. HPU also provides free Wi-Fi so students can have wireless access to Pipeline resources anywhere on campus using laptops. A significant number of online courses are available.

Financial Aid

The University participates in all federal financial aid programs designated for graduate students. These programs provide aid in the form of subsidized (need-based) and unsubsidized (non-need-based) Federal Stafford Student Loans. Through these loans, funds may be available to cover a student's entire cost of education. To apply for aid, students must submit the Free Application for Federal Student Aid (FAFSA) beginning January 1.

The University also offers several types of institutional graduate scholarships to new full-time, degree-seeking students. U.S. citizens, permanent residents, and international students who have a demonstrated financial need may apply. HPU's graduate scholarships include the Graduate Trustee Scholarship of $6000 ($3000/semester), the Graduate Dean Scholarship of $4000 ($2000/semester), and the Graduate Kokua Scholarship of $2000 ($1000/semester). Factors that may be considered when evaluating requests are previous academic record, community involvement and service, and professional work experience and achievement.

In order to be eligible for the best award package, students should apply by HPU's priority deadline of March 1. Applications received after the priority deadline will be awarded on a funds-available basis. Mailing of student award letters usually begins by the end of March. Applicants will be notified by mail as decisions are made.

Cost of Study

Tuition for graduate students enrolled in fall and spring semesters is determined on a per-credit basis; full-time status for a graduate student is 9 credits. Tuition for the optional winter and summer sessions is also determined on a per-credit basis. For the 2012–13 academic year, full-time tuition is $13,590 for most graduate degree programs, including the M.S.N. program. Other expenses, including books, personal expenses, fees, and a student bus pass are estimated at $3285.

Living and Housing Costs

The University has off-campus housing and an apartment referral service for graduate students. The cost of living in off-campus apartments is approximately $12,482 for a double-occupancy room. Further graduate housing information is available online at www.hpu.edu/housing.

Student Group

University enrollment currently stands at more than 8,200. HPU is one of the most culturally diverse universities in America with students from all 50 U.S. states and more than 100 countries.

Student Outcomes

M.S.N. graduates are eligible to sit for certification as Family Nurse Practitioners or Advanced Practice Nurse Educators when they complete their degree. Course work and practicum time in the Clinical Nurse Specialist track can also focus on the nurse educator role.

Location

HPU combines the excitement of an urban, downtown campus with the serenity of a residential campus. The urban campus is ideally located in downtown Honolulu, the business and financial center of the Pacific. The downtown campus comprises seven buildings in the center of Honolulu's business district and is home to the College of Business Administration and the College of Humanities and Social Sciences.

Eight miles away, situated on 135 acres in Kaneohe, the windward Hawai'i Loa campus is the site of the College of Nursing and Health Sciences and the College of Natural and Computational Sciences. The Hawai'i Loa campus has residence halls, dining commons, the Educational Technology Center, a student center, and outdoor recreational facilities, including a soccer field, tennis courts, a softball field, and an exercise room.

Programs of Study

HPU is affiliated with the Oceanic Institute, an aquaculture research facility located on a 56-acre site at Makapu'u Point on the windward coast of Oahu, Hawaii. All three sites are linked by HPU shuttle and also easily accessed by public transportation.

Notably, the downtown campus location is within walking distance of shopping and dining. Iolani Palace, the only royal palace in the United States is a few blocks away, as are the State Capitol, City Hall, and the Blaisdell Concert Hall. The Honolulu Academy of Arts, Museum of Contemporary Art, Waikiki Aquarium, Honolulu Zoo, and many other cultural attractions are located nearby.

The University

HPU is a private, nonprofit university with approximately 8,200 students. Founded in 1965, HPU prides itself on maintaining strong academic programs, small class sizes, individual attention to students, and a diverse faculty and student population. HPU is recognized as a Best in the West college by the Princeton Review and *U.S. News & World Report* and a Best Buy by *Barron's* business magazine. HPU offers more than fifty acclaimed undergraduate programs and fourteen distinguished graduate programs. The University has a faculty of more than 500, a student-faculty ratio of 15:1, and an average class size of fewer than 25 students. A wide range of counseling and other student support services are available. There are more than fifty student organizations on campus, including the Graduate Student Organization.

Applying

Students must have a baccalaureate degree from an accredited college or university in the United States or an equivalent degree from another country. Applicants should complete and forward a graduate admissions application, send in the $50 nonrefundable application fee, have official transcripts sent from all colleges or universities previously attended, and forward two letters of recommendation. A resume and personal statement about the applicant's academic and career goals is required. Applicants who have taken the Graduate Record Examination (GRE) should have their scores sent directly to the Graduate Admissions Office. International students should submit scores of a recognized English proficiency test such as TOEFL. Admissions decisions are made on a rolling basis, and applicants are notified between one and two weeks after all documents have been submitted. Applicants are encouraged to submit their applications online.

Correspondence and Information

Graduate Admissions
Hawai'i Pacific University
1164 Bishop Street, #911
Honolulu, Hawaii 96813
Phone: 808-544-1135
        866-GRAD-HPU (toll-free)
Fax: 808-544-0280
E-mail: graduate@hpu.edu
Web site: http://www.hpu.edu/hpumsn

THE FACULTY

Dale Allison, Acting Dean/Interim Chair, Professor of Nursing; Ph.D., Pennsylvania.
Patricia Burrell, Professor of Nursing; Ph.D., Utah.
Randy Caine, Dean, College of Nursing and Health Sciences; Ed.D., Pepperdine.
Catherine Critz, Associate Professor of Nursing; Ph.D., Syracuse.
ReNel Davis, Professor of Nursing; Ph.D., Colorado.
Hobie Feagai, Associate Professor of Nursing; Ed.D., Argosy.
Patricia Lange-Otsuka, Associate Dean, College of Nursing and Health Sciences; Ed.D., Nova Southeastern.

HOLY FAMILY UNIVERSITY

School of Nursing and Allied Health Professions
Graduate Programs

Holy Family
UNIVERSITY

Programs of Study

Since its founding more than half a century ago, Holy Family University has been a regional leader in the education of registered nurses (RNs). Building on this impressive legacy, the University offers master's degrees in nursing and post-master's certificate programs.

The Master of Science in Nursing (M.S.N.) program includes the following concentrations: community health nursing, nursing administration, and nursing education. Two post-master's certificate programs are offered—one in nursing education and one in nursing administration. The requirement for admission to these programs is the same as for the M.S.N. program.

The program is fully accredited by the Commission on Collegiate Nursing Education.

Research Facilities

Modern facilities in Holy Family's Nurse Education Building fully prepare students for the environments and technologies they're likely to encounter after graduating. Nursing students gain hands-on experience in a nursing simulation center and a newly renovated nursing practice lab. M.S.N. courses are conducted seminar-style with low student-to-faculty ratios.

Financial Aid

Holy Family is committed to helping adults further their education by consistently maintaining competitive tuition rates. Most graduate students are eligible for Federal Stafford Loans when attending with a half-time enrollment status (6 graduate credits) or greater. Students who are committed to teaching full time in a school of nursing after graduation are eligible to apply for the federal Nurse Faculty Loan Program. For more information, students should contact the Financial Aid Office at finaid@holyfamily.edu or 267-341-3233.

Cost of Study

Tuition for Holy Family's traditional graduate programs is $655 per credit hour; clinical courses are $735 per credit hour.

Living and Housing Costs

Holy Family University does not provide graduate student housing; however there are numerous housing options available in the nearby area.

Student Outcomes

Holy Family M.S.N. students have written grants which have been funded; published articles in refereed journals; been co-participants in faculty-student research; and served as adjunct clinical faculty in the baccalaureate nursing program. Graduates have achieved leadership positions in education and healthcare institutions.

Location

The School of Nursing and Allied Health Professions is housed on Holy Family's Northeast Philadelphia campus. Located less than a mile from Bucks County, Holy Family offers the benefits of a big city in a quiet, parklike suburban setting. With easy access to regional rail lines, city bus routes, and nearby expressways, the University is conveniently located for students throughout Greater Philadelphia.

The School of Nursing and Allied Health Professions

The mission of the School of Nursing and Allied Health Professions is to educate students within the university environment, at the graduate and undergraduate levels, to assume a professional role in the delivery of high quality care in nursing and radiologic science and cultivate a sense of responsibility to be actively involved in service to the human family.

The vision of the School of Nursing and Allied Health Professions is to provide exceptional quality nursing and radiologic science education in a caring, collegial, faith-based environment that challenges students and faculty to extend their intellectual horizons.

The mission and vision of the School of Nursing and Allied Health Professions are built upon the core values of Holy Family University: family, respect, integrity, service and responsibility, learning, and vision.

Applying

Applicants to the M.S.N. program must possess a B.S.N. from an NLNAC-accredited or CCNE-accredited nursing program at a regionally accredited institution or an RN from an NLNAC-accredited program with a B.S. or B.A. degree in a related area; have completed an undergraduate statistics course with a grade of C or better and attained an undergraduate grade point average of 3.0 or above on a 4.0 scale; hold licensure as a registered nurse in the United States; and present two professional references, an application along with the $25 fee, official transcripts from all colleges or universities attended, a 250- to 500-word personal statement concerning the student's interest and reason for applying, and a resume.

Applicants who hold a non-nursing B.S. or B.A. degree must complete B.S.N. competencies in community health nursing, research, and leadership as prerequisites to certain M.S.N. courses.

Holy Family University

Correspondence and Information

Graduate Admissions Office
Holy Family University
9801 Frankford Avenue
Philadelphia, Pennsylvania 19114
United States
Phone: 267-341-3327
Fax: 215-637-1478
E-mail: gradstudy@holyfamily.edu
Web site: www.holyfamily.edu

THE FACULTY AND THEIR RESEARCH

Ana Maria Catanzaro, Professor; Ph.D., Catholic University of America. Religion/spirituality and health, public health, health-care ethics, nursing education, research.

Patricia H. Dunn, Associate Professor; Ph.D., Pennsylvania. Obstetrical/neonatal nursing, nursing education.

Kathryn Van Dyke Hayes, Professor; Ph.D., Catholic University of America. Nursing diagnosis, spinal cord injury, nursing theory.

Gloria Kersey-Matusiak, Professor; Ph.D., Temple. Cultural competency, diversity education, English as a second language student issues, organizational development.

Karen Montalto, Associate Professor; Ph.D., Widener. Student stress and social support, NCLEX pass rates, QSEN competencies, simulation.

Mary Wombwell, Professor; Ed.D., Widener. Teaching and learning in nursing education.

Boas Yu, Assistant Professor; Ed.D., Columbia, 2002. Holistic nursing, nursing administration, gerontology.

ST. JOSEPH'S COLLEGE, NEW YORK

Department of Nursing
Master of Science with a Major in Nursing

St. Joseph's College
NEW YORK
SCHOOL OF PROFESSIONAL
AND GRADUATE STUDIES

Programs of Study

St. Joseph's College (SJC) offers the Master of Science degree with a major in nursing. The program, registered with the New York State Education Department, enrolled its first class in 2005. Students pick one of two concentrations—clinical nurse specialist in adult health or nursing education.

The graduate curriculum, consisting of a core and specialty concentrations, builds on the knowledge base and practice competencies of the baccalaureate-prepared nurse and prepares the graduate for advanced professional practice. Graduates of the clinical nurse specialist (CNS) in adult health concentration (38 credits) are prepared to actualize the multifaceted role of the CNS in a variety of health-care settings, reflecting three spheres of relationships—patient and client, nurses and nursing practice, and organizations and systems. Graduates of the nursing education concentration (37 credits) are ready to assume nurse educator positions in either academic or service settings or in patient education.

The program meets the needs of the working professional. Designed for part-time study, the program can be completed in seven semesters. Each class enters as a cohort group, attending classes one day per week during the fall and spring semesters and one summer. Additional hours are required for clinical/practicum courses.

Students acquire the knowledge base and experiences needed to transition into advanced practice nursing and work with diverse populations in a variety of settings.

For instance, graduates of the clinical nurse specialist (CNS) in adult education concentration are well versed in the three areas of CNS practice: patient/client, nurses and nursing practice, and organization/systems. They also acquire the skills needed to consistently improve patient outcomes and nursing care.

Graduates of the nurse education concentration gain the skills needed to work in academic or service settings where they teach and mentor nurses and nursing students or administer patient education programs.

Research Facilities

The Callahan Library at the Long Island Campus is a modern, 25,000-square-foot freestanding facility with seating for more than 300 readers. A curriculum library, seminar rooms, administrative offices, and two classrooms are housed in this building. Holdings include more than 105,000 volumes and 307 periodical titles, and they are supplemented by videos and other instructional aids. Patrons have access to the Internet and to several online academic databases. A fully automated library system, Endeavor, ensures the efficient retrieval and management of all library resources. Other resources include the library at St. Joseph's Brooklyn Campus, with more than 109,000 volumes and membership in the Long Island Library Resources Council. This facilitates cooperative associations with the academic and special libraries on Long Island. Internet access, subscriptions to several online full-text databases, and

membership in the international bibliographic utility OCLC allow almost limitless access to available information.

McEntegart Hall is a fully air-conditioned five-level structure. Three spacious reading areas with a capacity for 300 readers, including individual study carrels and shelf space for 200,000 volumes, provide an excellent environment for research. In addition, McEntegart Hall houses the College archives, a curriculum library, three computer laboratories, a nursing education laboratory, and a videoconference room. There are eight classrooms, a chapel, a cafeteria, and faculty and student lounges.

A high-speed fiber-optic intracampus network connects all offices, instructional facilities, computer laboratories, and libraries on both the Brooklyn and Long Island Campuses. The network provides Internet access to all students and faculty and staff members. An integrated online library system enables students to search for and check out books at either campus. Online databases and other electronic resources are available to students from either campus or from their home computers. Two wireless laptop classrooms with smart-classroom features provide flexible instruction spaces with the latest technologies. Videoconferencing facilities connect the two campuses, allowing for real-time distance learning in a small-group setting.

Financial Aid

Financial aid is available in the form of federal and private loans, scholarships, and work-study programs. Students should contact the Financial Aid Office for more information (Brooklyn Campus, telephone: 718-940-5700; Long Island Campus, telephone: 631-687-2600).

Cost of Study

In 2012–13, tuition was $19,500 or $715 per credit for graduate programs. The College and technology fees per semester for 12 or more credits totaled $200, and the nursing lab fee was $100.

Student Group

The total enrollment for all graduate programs on both campuses is 740.

Location

St. Joseph's College has two campuses—the main campus in the residential Clinton Hill section of Brooklyn and the Long Island branch campus in Patchogue, New York. The main campus offers easy access to all transit lines; to the Long Island Expressway; to all bridges in Brooklyn, Manhattan, and Queens; and to the Verrazano-Narrows Bridge to Staten Island. Within 30 minutes, students leaving St. Joseph's College can find themselves at the Metropolitan Museum of Art, the 42nd Street Library, Carnegie Hall and Lincoln Center, the Broadway theater district, Madison Square Garden, or Shea Stadium. The College itself stands in the center of one of the nation's most

St. Joseph's College, New York

diversified academic communities, consisting of six colleges and universities within a 2-mile radius of each other. The 27-acre Long Island Campus, adjacent to Great Patchogue Lake, is an ideal setting for studying, socializing, and partaking in extracurricular activities. Located just off Sunrise Highway, the Long Island Campus is easily accessible from all parts of Long Island.

The College and The Department

St. Joseph's College is a fully accredited institution that has been dedicated to providing a diverse population of students in the New York metropolitan area with an affordable education rooted in the liberal arts tradition since 1916. Independent and coeducational, the College provides a strong academic and value-oriented education at the undergraduate and graduate levels. For over a decade, the College has consistently been ranked among America's best colleges by *U.S. News & World Report* and *Forbes.*

The mission of the Department of Nursing is to provide professional nursing education that prepares the student to think critically and to utilize nursing theory, related sciences, and humanities to improve their practice; assists the student to internalize professional values and standards of practice; provides learning experiences that acknowledge the needs of a diversified student population with varied nursing practice experience; encourages students to actively participate in all aspects of their educational experiences; and facilitates student development of a spirit of inquiry and an appreciation of learning as a lifelong process.

Applying

Students must possess a B.S. degree with a major in nursing from a nationally accredited nursing program (NLNAC or CCNE). Prerequisite courses include an undergraduate health assessment course and an undergraduate statistics course. Students should have a minimum GPA of 3.0; preference is given to applicants with a GPA of 3.3 or above. One year of professional clinical practice should be completed prior to admission. Applicants must submit the completed application, the application fee, official transcripts, a current curriculum vitae, a personal statement, and two letters of recommendation. In addition, applicants must provide proof of New York State RN licensure, current professional registration, and professional malpractice insurance. An interview is required.

Correspondence and Information

Brooklyn Campus
St. Joseph's College
245 Clinton Avenue
Brooklyn, New York 11205
Phone: 718-940-5800
E-mail: brooklynap@sjcny.edu
Web site: http://www.sjcny.edu/Academics/
     MS-degree-with-a-Major-in-Nursing/250

Long Island Campus
St. Joseph's College
155 West Roe Boulevard
Patchogue, New York 11772
Phone: 631-687-4501
E-mail: suffolkap@sjcny.edu

THE FACULTY

Lorraine Brown, Assistant Professor; M.S.N., Boston University; RN.

Barbara Carlstrom, Assistant Professor; M.S.N., Stony Brook, SUNY; RN.

Maria Fletcher, Associate Professor; Ph.D., Adelphi; RN.

Laurel Janssen-Breen, Assistant Professor; M.A., NYU; RN.

Florence Jerdan, Associate Professor; Ph.D., Adelphi; RN.

Tae Sook Kim, Associate Professor; Ph.D., NYU; RN.

Linda Morgante, Assistant Professor; M.S.N., CUNY, Hunter; RN.

Catherine Pearsall, Assistant Professor; Ph.D., Duquesne; CNE, FNP, ANPC, RN.

Barbara Sands, Professor and Director; Ph.D., Adelphi; RN.

Boas Yu, Assistant Professor; Ed.D., Columbia Teachers College; RN.

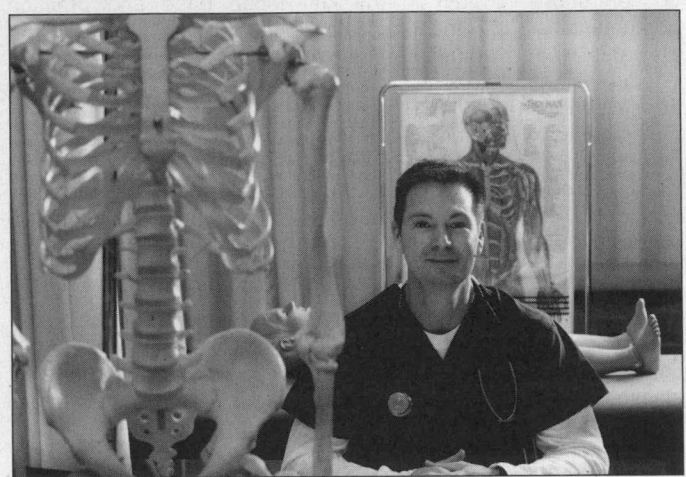

Section 24
Public Health

This section contains a directory of institutions offering graduate work in public health, followed by in-depth entries submitted by institutions that chose to prepare detailed program descriptions. Additional information about programs listed in the directory but not augmented by an in-depth entry may be obtained by writing directly to the dean of a graduate school or chair of a department at the address given in the directory.

For programs offering related work, see also in this book *Allied Health; Biological and Biomedical Sciences; Ecology, Environmental Biology, and Evolutionary Biology; Health Services; Microbiological Sciences; Nursing;* and *Nutrition.* In the other guides in this series:

Graduate Programs in the Humanities, Arts & Social Sciences

See *Family and Consumer Sciences (Gerontology)* and *Sociology, Anthropology, and Archaeology (Demography and Population Studies)*

Graduate Programs in the Physical Sciences, Mathematics, Agricultural Sciences, the Environment & Natural Resources

See *Mathematical Sciences* and *Environmental Sciences and Management*

Graduate Programs in Engineering & Applied Sciences

See *Biomedical Engineering and Biotechnology, Civil and Environmental Engineering, Industrial Engineering, Energy and Power Engineering (Nuclear Engineering),* and *Management of Engineering and Technology*

Graduate Programs in Business, Education, Information Studies, Law & Social Work

See *Education.*

CONTENTS

Program Directories

Displays and Close-Ups

Public Health—General

Adelphi University, University College, Graduate Certificate in Emergency Management Program, Garden City, NY 11530-0701. Offers Certificate. Part-time and evening/weekend programs available. *Faculty:* 1 full-time (0 women), 24 part-time/adjunct (9 women). *Students:* 1 full-time (0 women), 8 part-time (3 women); includes 1 minority (Black or African American, non-Hispanic/Latino). Average age 42. 6 applicants, 50% accepted, 1 enrolled. In 2011, 3 Certificates awarded. *Application deadline:* For fall admission, 5/1 for international students; for spring admission, 12/1 for international students. Applications are processed on a rolling basis. Application fee: $50. Electronic applications accepted. *Expenses: Tuition:* Full-time $29,600; part-time $930 per credit. *Required fees:* $1100. *Financial support:* Research assistantships with partial tuition reimbursements, Federal Work-Study, and institutionally sponsored loans available. *Faculty research:* Emergency nursing, disaster management, disaster preparedness. *Unit head:* Shawn O'Riley, Executive Director, 516-877-3412, E-mail: ucinfo@adelphi.edu. *Application contact:* Christine Murphy, Director of Admissions, 516-877-3050, Fax: 516-877-3039, E-mail: graduateadmissions@adelphi.edu. Web site: http://academics.adelphi.edu/universitycollege/emergency-management-certificate.php.

American Public University System, AMU/APU Graduate Programs, Charles Town, WV 25414. Offers accounting (MBA, MS); administration and supervision (M Ed); criminal justice (MA); emergency and disaster management (MA); entrepreneurship (MBA); environmental policy and management (MS), including environmental planning, environmental sustainability, fish and wildlife management, general (MA, MS), global environmental management; finance (MBA); general (MBA); global business management (MBA); guidance and counseling (M Ed); history (MA), including American history, ancient and classical history, European history, global history, military and diplomatic history, public history; homeland security (MA); homeland security resource allocation (MBA); humanities (MA); information technology (MS), including digital forensics, enterprise software development, information assurance and security, IT project management; information technology management (MBA); intelligence studies (MA), including criminal intelligence, general (MA, MS), homeland security, intelligence analysis, intelligence collection, intelligence operations, terrorism studies; international relations and conflict resolution (MA), including comparative and security issues, conflict resolution, international and transnational security issues, peacekeeping; legal studies (MA); management (MA), including defense management, general (MA, MS), human resource management, organizational leadership, public administration, reverse logistics, strategic consulting; marketing (MBA); military history (MA), including American military history, American revolution, civil war, war since 1946, World War II; military studies (MA), including air warfare, asymmetrical warfare, joint warfare, land warfare, naval warfare, strategic leadership; national security studies (MA), including general (MA, MS), homeland security, regional security studies, security and intelligence analysis, terrorism studies; nonprofit management (MBA); political science (MA), including American politics and government, comparative government and development, public policy; psychology (MA); public administration (MA, MPA), including disaster management (MPA), environmental policy (MA), health policy (MPA), human resources (MPA), national security (MPA), organizational management (MPA), security management (MPA); public health (MA, MPH), including emergency management (MPH), environmental health (MPH), public administration (MA); reverse logistics management (MA); security management (MA); space studies (MS), including aerospace science, planetary science; sports and health sciences (MS); sports management (MS), including coaching theory and strategy, sports administration; teaching (M Ed), including curriculum and instruction for elementary teachers, elementary, elementary reading, English language learners, instructional leadership, online learning, secondary social sciences, special education; transportation and logistics management (MA), including maritime engineering management. Programs offered via distance learning only. Part-time and evening/weekend programs available. Postbaccalaureate distance learning degree programs offered (no on-campus study). *Faculty:* 445 full-time (241 women), 1,360 part-time/adjunct (617 women). *Students:* 688 full-time (338 women), 10,168 part-time (3,706 women); includes 3,130 minority (1,007 Black or African American, non-Hispanic/Latino; 103 American Indian or Alaska Native, non-Hispanic/Latino; 825 Asian, non-Hispanic/Latino; 810 Hispanic/Latino; 51 Native Hawaiian or other Pacific Islander, non-Hispanic/Latino; 334 Two or more races, non-Hispanic/Latino), 134 international. Average age 35. In 2011, 2,386 master's awarded. *Degree requirements:* For master's, comprehensive exam or practicum. *Entrance requirements:* For master's, official transcript showing earned bachelor's degree from institution accredited by recognized accrediting body. Additional exam requirements/recommendations for international students: Required—TOEFL (minimum score 550 paper-based; 213 computer-based), IELTS (minimum score 6.5). *Application deadline:* Applications are processed on a rolling basis. Application fee: $0. Electronic applications accepted. *Expenses: Tuition:* Part-time $325 per credit hour. *Financial support:* Applicants required to submit FAFSA. *Faculty research:* Military history, criminal justice, management performance, national security. *Unit head:* Dr. Karan Powell, Executive Vice President and Provost, 877-468-6268, Fax: 304-724-3780. *Application contact:* Terry Grant, Vice President of Enrollment Management, 877-468-6268, Fax: 304-724-3780, E-mail: info@apus.edu. Web site: http://www.apus.edu.

American University of Beirut, Graduate Programs, Faculty of Health Sciences, Beirut, Lebanon. Offers environmental sciences (MSES), including environmental health; epidemiology (MS); epidemiology and biostatistics (MPH); health management and policy (MPH); health promotion and community health (MPH); population health (MS). Part-time programs available. *Faculty:* 29 full-time (19 women), 5 part-time/adjunct (2 women). *Students:* 63 full-time (52 women), 103 part-time (87 women). Average age 27. 156 applicants, 71% accepted, 56 enrolled. In 2011, 69 master's awarded. *Degree requirements:* For master's, one foreign language, comprehensive exam, thesis (for some programs). *Entrance requirements:* For master's, 2 letters of recommendation, personal statement, transcripts. Additional exam requirements/recommendations for international students: Required—TOEFL (minimum score 600 paper-based; 250 computer-based; 97 iBT), IELTS (minimum score 7). *Application deadline:* For fall admission, 2/20 for domestic and international students; for spring admission, 11/1 for domestic and international students. Application fee: $50. Electronic applications accepted. *Expenses: Tuition:* Full-time $12,780; part-time $710 per credit. Tuition and fees vary according to course load and program. *Financial support:* In 2011–12, 62 students received support. Scholarships/grants, health care benefits, and unspecified assistantships available. Financial award application deadline: 2/20. *Faculty research:* Tobacco control; health of the elderly; youth health; mental health; women's health; reproductive and sexual health, including HIV/AIDS; water quality; health systems; quality in health care delivery; health human resources; health policy; occupational and environmental health; social inequality; social determinants of health; chronic diseases. *Total annual research expenditures:* $722,649. *Unit head:* Iman Adel Nuwayhid, Dean, 961-1340119, Fax: 961-1744470, E-mail: nuwayhid@aub.edu.lb. *Application contact:* Mitra Tauk, Administrative Coordinator, 961-1350000 Ext. 4687, Fax: 961-1744470, E-mail: mt12@aub.edu.lb. Web site: http://fhs.aub.edu.lb.

Argosy University, Atlanta, College of Health Sciences, Atlanta, GA 30328. Offers public health (MPH).

Argosy University, Chicago, College of Health Sciences, Chicago, IL 60601. Offers public health (MPH).

Argosy University, Dallas, College of Health Sciences, Farmers Branch, TX 75244. Offers public health (MPH).

Argosy University, Denver, College of Health Sciences, Denver, CO 80231. Offers public health (MPH).

Argosy University, Hawai`i, College of Health Sciences, Honolulu, HI 96813. Offers public health (MPH).

Argosy University, Inland Empire, College of Health Sciences, San Bernardino, CA 92408. Offers public health (MPH).

Argosy University, Los Angeles, College of Health Sciences, Santa Monica, CA 90045. Offers public health (MPH).

Argosy University, Nashville, College of Health Sciences, Nashville, TN 37214. Offers public health (MPH).

Argosy University, Orange County, College of Health Sciences, Orange, CA 92868. Offers public health (MPH).

Argosy University, Phoenix, College of Health Sciences, Phoenix, AZ 85021. Offers public health (MPH).

Argosy University, Salt Lake City, College of Health Sciences, Draper, UT 84020. Offers public health (MPH).

Argosy University, San Diego, College of Health Sciences, San Diego, CA 92108. Offers public health (MPH).

Argosy University, San Francisco Bay Area, College of Health Sciences, Alameda, CA 94501. Offers public health (MPH).

Argosy University, Sarasota, College of Health Sciences, Sarasota, FL 34235. Offers public health (MPH).

Argosy University, Schaumburg, College of Health Sciences, Schaumburg, IL 60173-5403. Offers public health (MPH).

Argosy University, Seattle, College of Health Sciences, Seattle, WA 98121. Offers public health (MPH).

Argosy University, Tampa, College of Health Sciences, Tampa, FL 33607. Offers public health (MPH).

Argosy University, Twin Cities, College of Health Sciences, Eagan, MN 55121. Offers health services management (MS); public health (MPH).

Argosy University, Washington DC, College of Health Sciences, Arlington, VA 22209. Offers public health (MPH).

Arizona State University, College of Nursing and Health Innovation, Phoenix, AZ 85004. Offers advanced nursing practice (DNP); child/family mental health nurse practitioner (Graduate Certificate); clinical research management (MS); community and public health practice (Graduate Certificate); community health (MS); exercise and wellness (MS), including exercise and wellness; family nurse practitioner (Graduate Certificate); healthcare innovation (MHI); international health for healthcare (Graduate Certificate); kinesiology (MS, PhD); nursing (MS, Graduate Certificate); nursing and healthcare innovation (PhD); nutrition (MS); physical activity nutrition and wellness (PhD), including physical activity, nutrition and wellness; public health (MPH); regulatory science and health safety (MS). *Accreditation:* AACN. Postbaccalaureate distance learning degree programs offered (minimal on-campus study). *Degree requirements:* For master's, comprehensive exam (for some programs), thesis (for some programs), interactive Program of Study (iPOS) submitted before completing 50 percent of required credit hours; for doctorate, comprehensive exam, thesis/dissertation, interactive Program of Study (iPOS) submitted before completing 50 percent of required credit hours. *Entrance requirements:* For master's and doctorate, GRE, minimum GPA of 3.0 or equivalent in last 2 years of work leading to bachelor's degree. Additional exam requirements/recommendations for international students: Required—TOEFL (minimum score 80 iBT), TOEFL, IELTS, or Pearson Test of English. Electronic applications accepted. *Expenses:* Contact institution.

Armstrong Atlantic State University, School of Graduate Studies, Program in Health Science, Savannah, GA 31419-1997. Offers health services administration (MHSA); public health (MPH). *Accreditation:* CAHME; CEPH. Part-time and evening/weekend programs available. Postbaccalaureate distance learning degree programs offered (no on-campus study). *Faculty:* 9 full-time (4 women), 2 part-time/adjunct (1 woman). *Students:* 56 full-time (37 women), 25 part-time (21 women); includes 31 minority (22 Black or African American, non-Hispanic/Latino; 2 American Indian or Alaska Native, non-Hispanic/Latino; 6 Asian, non-Hispanic/Latino; 1 Hispanic/Latino), 5 international. Average age 30. 78 applicants, 49% accepted, 29 enrolled. In 2011, 30 master's awarded. *Degree requirements:* For master's, comprehensive exam, thesis optional, internship. *Entrance requirements:* For master's, GMAT or GRE General Test, MAT, minimum GPA of 2.8, letter of intent, letters of recommendation. Additional exam requirements/recommendations for international students: Required—TOEFL (minimum score 523 paper-based; 193 computer-based). *Application deadline:* For fall admission, 7/1 priority date for domestic students, 5/1 for international students; for spring admission, 11/15 priority date for domestic students, 9/15 for international students. Applications are processed on a rolling basis. Application fee: $30. Electronic applications accepted. *Expenses:* Tuition, state resident: full-time $3402. Tuition, nonresident: full-time $12,636. *Financial support:* In 2011–12, research assistantships with full tuition reimbursements (averaging $5,000 per year) were awarded; career-related internships or fieldwork, Federal Work-Study, scholarships/grants, tuition waivers (full), and unspecified assistantships also available. Support available to part-time students. Financial award applicants required to submit FAFSA. *Faculty research:* Health administration, community health, health education. *Unit head:* Dr. James Streater, Department Head, 912-344-2548, E-mail: sandy.streater@armstrong.edu. *Application contact:* Jill Bell, Director, Graduate Enrollment Services, 912-344-2798, Fax: 912-344-3488, E-mail: graduate@armstrong.edu. Web site: http://www.armstrong.edu/Health_Professions/Health_Sciences/healthsciences_welcome.

A.T. Still University of Health Sciences, School of Health Management, Kirksville, MO 63501. Offers dental emphasis (MPH); health administration (MHA); health education (MH Ed, DH Ed); public health (MPH). Part-time and evening/weekend programs available. Postbaccalaureate distance learning degree programs offered (no on-campus study). *Faculty:* 15 full-time (8 women), 52 part-time/adjunct (27 women). *Students:* 50 full-time (36 women), 391 part-time (245 women); includes 125 minority (48 Black or African American, non-Hispanic/Latino; 4 American Indian or Alaska Native, non-

Hispanic/Latino; 42 Asian, non-Hispanic/Latino; 26 Hispanic/Latino; 5 Two or more races, non-Hispanic/Latino). Average age 32. 121 applicants, 90% accepted, 89 enrolled. In 2011, 156 master's, 38 doctorates awarded. *Degree requirements:* For master's, thesis, integrated terminal project; for doctorate, thesis/dissertation. *Entrance requirements:* For master's, minimum GPA of 3.0, bachelor's degree or equivalent from U.S. institution; for doctorate, minimum GPA of 3.0, master's or terminal degree. Additional exam requirements/recommendations for international students: Required—TOEFL (minimum score 550 paper-based; 213 computer-based; 80 iBT). *Application deadline:* For fall admission, 7/9 for domestic students, 7/6 for international students; for winter admission, 9/28 for domestic and international students; for spring admission, 1/11 for domestic and international students. Application fee: $60. Electronic applications accepted. *Expenses:* Contact institution. *Financial support:* In 2011–12, 72 students received support. Scholarships/grants available. Financial award application deadline: 5/1; financial award applicants required to submit FAFSA. *Faculty research:* Public health: cultural health disparities, emergency preparedness, infectious disease, maternal and child health, environmental health; health education: overweight and obesity; health administration: leadership, strategic thinking, governance, healthcare reform economics, patient-centered care. *Unit head:* Dr. Kimberly O'Reilly, Interim Dean, 660-626-2820, Fax: 660-626-2826, E-mail: koreilley@atsu.edu. *Application contact:* Sarah Spencer, Associate Director, Admissions, 660-626-2820 Ext. 2669, Fax: 660-626-2826, E-mail: sspencer@atsu.edu. Web site: http://www.atsu.edu/shm.

Austin Peay State University, College of Graduate Studies, College of Behavioral and Health Sciences, Department of Health and Human Performance, Clarksville, TN 37044. Offers health leadership (MS). Part-time and evening/weekend programs available. Postbaccalaureate distance learning degree programs offered (no on-campus study). *Faculty:* 6 full-time (3 women). *Students:* 21 full-time (16 women), 45 part-time (32 women); includes 28 minority (19 Black or African American, non-Hispanic/Latino; 6 Hispanic/Latino; 3 Two or more races, non-Hispanic/Latino). Average age 30. 58 applicants, 86% accepted, 38 enrolled. In 2011, 24 master's awarded. *Degree requirements:* For master's, comprehensive exam, thesis optional. *Entrance requirements:* For master's, GRE General Test, 3 letters of recommendation, minimum undergraduate GPA of 2.5. Additional exam requirements/recommendations for international students: Required—TOEFL (minimum score 500 paper-based; 173 computer-based). *Application deadline:* For fall admission, 8/1 priority date for domestic students. Applications are processed on a rolling basis. Application fee: $25. Electronic applications accepted. *Expenses:* Tuition, state resident: part-time $350 per credit hour. Tuition, nonresident: full-time $20,644; part-time $971 per credit hour. *Required fees:* $1224; $61.20 per credit hour. *Financial support:* In 2011–12, research assistantships with full tuition reimbursements (averaging $5,184 per year) were awarded; career-related internships or fieldwork, Federal Work-Study, institutionally sponsored loans, scholarships/grants, and unspecified assistantships also available. Support available to part-time students. Financial award application deadline: 3/1; financial award applicants required to submit FAFSA. *Unit head:* Dr. Marcy Maurer, Chair, 931-221-6105, Fax: 931-221-7040, E-mail: maurerm@apsu.edu. *Application contact:* Kendra Bryant, Graduate Admissions, 800-844-2778, Fax: 931-221-6188, E-mail: admissionsweb@apsu.edu. Web site: http://www.apsu.edu/hhp/.

Barry University, School of Podiatric Medicine, Podiatric Medicine and Surgery Program, Podiatric Medicine/Public Health Option, Miami Shores, FL 33161-6695. Offers DPM/MPH.

Benedictine University, Graduate Programs, Program in Public Health, Lisle, IL 60532-0900. Offers administration of health care institutions (MPH); dietetics (MPH); disaster management (MPH); health education (MPH); health information systems (MPH); MBA/MPH; MPH/MS. Part-time and evening/weekend programs available. Postbaccalaureate distance learning degree programs offered. *Faculty:* 2 full-time (0 women), 8 part-time/adjunct (3 women). *Students:* 85 full-time (61 women), 437 part-time (333 women); includes 217 minority (133 Black or African American, non-Hispanic/Latino; 1 American Indian or Alaska Native, non-Hispanic/Latino; 65 Asian, non-Hispanic/Latino; 18 Hispanic/Latino), 28 international. Average age 33. 172 applicants, 80% accepted, 113 enrolled. In 2011, 116 master's awarded. *Entrance requirements:* For master's, MAT, GRE, or GMAT. Additional exam requirements/recommendations for international students: Required—TOEFL (minimum score 550 paper-based; 213 computer-based). *Application deadline:* For fall admission, 9/1 for domestic students; for winter admission, 12/1 for domestic students; for spring admission, 2/15 for domestic students. Application fee: $40. *Financial support:* Career-related internships or fieldwork and health care benefits available. Support available to part-time students. *Unit head:* Dr. Georgeen Polyak, Director, 630-829-6217, E-mail: gpolyak@ben.edu. *Application contact:* Kari Gibbons, Associate Vice President, Enrollment Center, 630-829-6200, Fax: 630-829-6584, E-mail: kgibbons@ben.edu.

Boise State University, Graduate College, College of Health Science, Boise, ID 83725-0399. Offers MHS. Part-time programs available. *Degree requirements:* For master's, thesis. *Entrance requirements:* For master's, GRE General Test, GMAT or MAT, minimum GPA of 3.0. Electronic applications accepted.

Boston University, Henry M. Goldman School of Dental Medicine, Boston, MA 02118. Offers advanced general dentistry (CAGS); dental public health (MS, MSD, D Sc D, CAGS); dentistry (DMD); endodontics (MSD, D Sc D, CAGS); operative dentistry (MSD, D Sc D, CAGS); oral and maxillofacial surgery (MSD, D Sc D, CAGS); oral biology (MSD, D Sc, D Sc D, PhD); orthodontics (MSD, D Sc D, CAGS); pediatric dentistry (MSD, D Sc D, CAGS); periodontology (MSD, D Sc D, CAGS); prosthodontics (MSD, D Sc D, CAGS). *Accreditation:* ADA (one or more programs are accredited). *Faculty:* 119 full-time (53 women), 83 part-time/adjunct (24 women). *Students:* 802 full-time (386 women); includes 155 minority (6 Black or African American, non-Hispanic/Latino; 2 American Indian or Alaska Native, non-Hispanic/Latino; 110 Asian, non-Hispanic/Latino; 35 Hispanic/Latino; 2 Native Hawaiian or other Pacific Islander, non-Hispanic/Latino), 329 international. Average age 27. In 2011, 17 master's, 173 doctorates, 61 other advanced degrees awarded. *Degree requirements:* For master's and CAGS, thesis; for doctorate, thesis/dissertation (for some programs). *Entrance requirements:* For doctorate, DAT (for DMD), minimum recommended GPA of 3.0 (for DMD); for CAGS, dental degree. Additional exam requirements/recommendations for international students: Required—TOEFL. *Application deadline:* Applications are processed on a rolling basis. Application fee: $75 ($105 for international students). Electronic applications accepted. *Expenses:* Contact institution. *Financial support:* In 2011–12, 480 students received support. Career-related internships or fieldwork, institutionally sponsored loans, and scholarships/grants available. Financial award application deadline: 4/15; financial award applicants required to submit FAFSA. *Faculty research:* Defense mechanisms, bone-cell regulation, protein biochemistry, molecular biology, biomaterials. *Unit head:* Dr. Jeffrey W. Hutter, Dean, 617-638-4780. *Application contact:* Admissions Representative, 617-638-4787, Fax: 617-638-4798, E-mail: sdmadmis@bu.edu. Web site: http://www.bu.edu/dental.

Boston University, School of Public Health, Boston, MA 02118. Offers MA, MPH, MS, Dr PH, PhD, JD/MPH, MBA/MPH, MD/MPH, MPH/MA, MSW/MPH. *Accreditation:* CEPH. Part-time and evening/weekend programs available. *Faculty:* 153 full-time, 271 part-time/adjunct. *Students:* 499 full-time (388 women), 344 part-time (296 women); includes 180 minority (34 Black or African American, non-Hispanic/Latino; 1 American Indian or Alaska Native, non-Hispanic/Latino; 90 Asian, non-Hispanic/Latino; 30 Hispanic/Latino; 3 Native Hawaiian or other Pacific Islander, non-Hispanic/Latino; 22 Two or more races, non-Hispanic/Latino), 69 international. Average age 27. 2,439 applicants, 48% accepted, 337 enrolled. In 2011, 331 master's, 21 doctorates awarded. *Degree requirements:* For master's, comprehensive exam (for some programs), thesis optional, culminating experience, practicum; for doctorate, thesis/dissertation, comprehensive written and oral exams. *Entrance requirements:* For master's, GRE, MCAT, GMAT, LSAT, DAT, U.S. bachelor's degree or international equivalent; for doctorate, GRE, MCAT, GMAT, LSAT, MPH or equivalent. Additional exam requirements/recommendations for international students: Required—TOEFL (minimum score 600 paper-based; 250 computer-based; 100 iBT), IELTS (minimum score 6). *Application deadline:* For fall admission, 2/1 priority date for domestic students, 2/1 for international students; for spring admission, 10/15 priority date for domestic students, 10/15 for international students. Applications are processed on a rolling basis. Application fee: $115. Electronic applications accepted. *Expenses:* Contact institution. *Financial support:* Fellowships, career-related internships or fieldwork, Federal Work-Study, institutionally sponsored loans, scholarships/grants, traineeships, and tuition waivers (partial) available. Support available to part-time students. Financial award application deadline: 3/1; financial award applicants required to submit FAFSA. *Faculty research:* Clinical trials, observational studies, environmental epidemiology, global ecology, environmental sustainability, community health, environmental justice, infectious disease, non-infectious disease, research methods, genetic epi, pharmaceutical assessment, bioethics, health law, human rights, health policy, management, finance and management, family health, disease control in developing countries, child and adolescent health, women's health, health disparities. *Unit head:* Dr. Robert F. Meenan, Dean, 617-638-4640, Fax: 617-638-5299, E-mail: asksph@bu.edu. *Application contact:* LePhan Quan, Associate Director of Admissions, 617-638-4640, Fax: 617-638-5299, E-mail: asksph@bu.edu. Web site: http://sph.bu.edu.

Bowling Green State University, Graduate College, College of Health and Human Services, Program in Public Health, Bowling Green, OH 43403. Offers MPH. *Accreditation:* CEPH. Part-time programs available. *Degree requirements:* For master's, thesis or alternative. *Entrance requirements:* For master's, GRE General Test, minimum GPA of 3.0. Additional exam requirements/recommendations for international students: Required—TOEFL. Electronic applications accepted.

Brooklyn College of the City University of New York, Division of Graduate Studies, Department of Health and Nutrition Science, Program in Public Health, Brooklyn, NY 11210-2889. Offers community-public health (MPH). *Accreditation:* CEPH. *Degree requirements:* For master's, thesis or alternative, 46 credits. *Entrance requirements:* For master's, GRE, 2 letters of recommendation, essay, interview. Electronic applications accepted.

Brown University, Graduate School, Division of Biology and Medicine, Department of Community Health, Program in Public Health, Providence, RI 02912. Offers MPH. *Accreditation:* CEPH. *Entrance requirements:* For master's, GRE General Test or MCAT. Additional exam requirements/recommendations for international students: Required—TOEFL.

California State University, Fresno, Division of Graduate Studies, College of Health and Human Services, Department of Public Health, Fresno, CA 93740-8027. Offers health policy and management (MPH); health promotion (MPH). *Accreditation:* CEPH. Part-time and evening/weekend programs available. *Degree requirements:* For master's, thesis or alternative. *Entrance requirements:* For master's, GRE General Test, minimum GPA of 2.5. Additional exam requirements/recommendations for international students: Required—TOEFL. Electronic applications accepted. *Faculty research:* Foster parent training, geriatrics, tobacco control.

California State University, Fullerton, Graduate Studies, College of Health and Human Development, Department of Health Science, Fullerton, CA 92834-9480. Offers public health (MPH). *Accreditation:* CEPH. Part-time programs available. *Students:* 38 full-time (26 women), 54 part-time (39 women); includes 56 minority (4 Black or African American, non-Hispanic/Latino; 23 Asian, non-Hispanic/Latino; 29 Hispanic/Latino), 3 international. Average age 32. 206 applicants, 29% accepted, 46 enrolled. In 2011, 33 master's awarded. *Entrance requirements:* For master's, minimum GPA of 3.0 in last 60 units attempted. Application fee: $55. *Financial support:* Career-related internships or fieldwork, Federal Work-Study, institutionally sponsored loans, and scholarships/grants available. Support available to part-time students. Financial award application deadline: 3/1; financial award applicants required to submit FAFSA. *Unit head:* Dr. Jessie Jones, Department Head, 657-278-2620. *Application contact:* Admissions/Applications, 657-278-2371.

California State University, Northridge, Graduate Studies, College of Health and Human Development, Department of Health Sciences, Northridge, CA 91330. Offers health administration (MS); public health (MPH). *Accreditation:* CEPH. *Entrance requirements:* For master's, GRE General Test or minimum GPA of 3.0. Additional exam requirements/recommendations for international students: Required—TOEFL. *Faculty research:* Labor market needs assessment, health education products, dental hygiene, independent practice prototype.

California State University, San Bernardino, Graduate Studies, College of Natural Sciences, Program in Health Science, San Bernardino, CA 92407-2397. Offers health science (MS); public health (MPH). *Students:* 14 full-time (13 women), 6 part-time (all women); includes 9 minority (3 Black or African American, non-Hispanic/Latino; 1 Asian, non-Hispanic/Latino; 5 Hispanic/Latino), 2 international. Average age 29. 12 applicants, 42% accepted, 3 enrolled. In 2011, 9 master's awarded. *Expenses:* Tuition, state resident: full-time $7356. Tuition, nonresident: full-time $7356. *Required fees:* $1077. Tuition and fees vary according to program. *Unit head:* Dr. Cynthia Paxton, Assistant Dean, 909-537-5343, Fax: 909-537-7037, E-mail: cpaxton@csusb.edu. *Application contact:* Sandra Kamusikiri, Associate Vice-President/Dean of Graduate Studies, 909-537-5058, E-mail: skamusik@csusb.edu.

Case Western Reserve University, School of Medicine and School of Graduate Studies, Graduate Programs in Medicine, Department of Epidemiology and Biostatistics, Program in Public Health, Cleveland, OH 44106. Offers MPH. *Accreditation:* CEPH. Part-time programs available. *Degree requirements:* For master's, essay, field experience, presentation. *Entrance requirements:* For master's, GRE General Test or MCAT, 3 letters of recommendation. Additional exam requirements/recommendations for international students: Required—TOEFL. Electronic applications accepted. *Faculty research:* Public policy and aging, statistical modeling, behavioral medicine and evaluation, continuous quality improvement; tobacco cessation and prevention.

Charles Drew University of Medicine and Science, College of Science and Health, Los Angeles, CA 90059. Offers urban public health (MPH).

Claremont Graduate University, Graduate Programs, School of Community and Global Health, San Dimas, CA 91773. Offers health promotion science (PhD); public health (MPH). *Faculty:* 10 full-time (4 women). *Students:* 31 full-time (21 women), 7 part-time (5 women); includes 24 minority (4 Black or African American, non-Hispanic/Latino; 7 Asian, non-Hispanic/Latino; 11 Hispanic/Latino; 2 Two or more races, non-Hispanic/Latino), 2 international. Average age 30. In 2011, 2 master's awarded. *Entrance requirements:* For master's and doctorate, GRE. Additional exam requirements/

recommendations for international students: Required—TOEFL (minimum score 550 paper-based; 213 computer-based; 80 iBT). *Application deadline:* For fall admission, 2/1 priority date for domestic students; for spring admission, 11/1 priority date for domestic students. Applications are processed on a rolling basis. Application fee: $60. Electronic applications accepted. *Expenses: Tuition:* Full-time $36,374; part-time $1581 per unit. *Required fees:* $165 per semester. *Financial support:* Fellowships, research assistantships, teaching assistantships, Federal Work-Study, institutionally sponsored loans, and scholarships/grants available. Support available to part-time students. Financial award application deadline: 2/15; financial award applicants required to submit FAFSA. *Unit head:* Andy Johnson, Dean, 909-607-8235, E-mail: andy.johnson@cgu.edu. *Application contact:* E-mail: admiss@cgu.edu. Web site: http://www.cgu.edu/pages/5644.asp.

Cleveland State University, College of Graduate Studies, College of Education and Human Services, Department of Health, Physical Education, Recreation and Dance, Cleveland, OH 44115. Offers community health education (M Ed); exercise science (M Ed); human performance (M Ed); physical education pedagogy (M Ed); public health (MPH); school health education (M Ed); sport and exercise psychology (M Ed); sports management (M Ed). Part-time programs available. *Faculty:* 7 full-time (4 women), 3 part-time/adjunct (2 women). *Students:* 40 full-time (22 women), 91 part-time (48 women); includes 17 minority (15 Black or African American, non-Hispanic/Latino; 1 Asian, non-Hispanic/Latino; 1 Hispanic/Latino), 17 international. Average age 28. 138 applicants, 80% accepted, 60 enrolled. In 2011, 30 master's awarded. *Degree requirements:* For master's, comprehensive exam, thesis optional. *Entrance requirements:* For master's, GRE General Test or MAT (if undergraduate GPA less than 2.75), minimum undergraduate GPA of 2.75. Additional exam requirements/recommendations for international students: Required—TOEFL (minimum score 525 paper-based; 197 computer-based), IELTS (minimum score 6). *Application deadline:* For fall admission, 7/15 priority date for domestic students; for spring admission, 12/15 priority date for domestic students. Applications are processed on a rolling basis. Application fee: $30. Electronic applications accepted. *Expenses:* Tuition, state resident: full-time $6416; part-time $494 per credit hour. Tuition, nonresident: full-time $12,074; part-time $929 per credit hour. *Financial support:* In 2011–12, 6 research assistantships with full and partial tuition reimbursements (averaging $3,480 per year), 1 teaching assistantship with full and partial tuition reimbursement (averaging $3,480 per year) were awarded; career-related internships or fieldwork, tuition waivers (full), and unspecified assistantships also available. Financial award application deadline: 3/15. *Faculty research:* Bone density, marketing fitness centers, motor development of disabled, online learning and survey research. *Unit head:* Dr. Sheila M. Patterson, Chairperson, 216-687-4870, Fax: 216-687-5410, E-mail: s.m.patterson@csuohio.edu. *Application contact:* Deborah L. Brown, Interim Assistant Director, Graduate Admissions, 216-523-7572, Fax: 216-687-5400, E-mail: d.l.brown@csuohio.edu. Web site: http://www.csuohio.edu/coehs/departments/hperd.

Columbia University, Columbia University Mailman School of Public Health, New York, NY 10032. Offers Exec MPH, MPH, MS, Dr PH, PhD, DDS/MPH, MBA/MPH, MD/MPH, MPA/MPH, MPH/MIA, MPH/MOT, MPH/MS, MPH/MSN, MPH/MSSW. PhD offered in cooperation with the Graduate School of Arts and Sciences. *Accreditation:* CEPH (one or more programs are accredited). Part-time and evening/weekend programs available. *Faculty:* 312 full-time (155 women), 284 part-time/adjunct (128 women). *Students:* 681 full-time (564 women), 593 part-time (432 women); includes 426 minority (80 Black or African American, non-Hispanic/Latino; 3 American Indian or Alaska Native, non-Hispanic/Latino; 218 Asian, non-Hispanic/Latino; 91 Hispanic/Latino; 1 Native Hawaiian or other Pacific Islander, non-Hispanic/Latino; 33 Two or more races, non-Hispanic/Latino), 167 international. Average age 29. 2,153 applicants, 60% accepted, 581 enrolled. In 2011, 451 master's, 26 doctorates awarded. *Degree requirements:* For master's, thesis (for some programs); for doctorate, comprehensive exam, thesis/dissertation. *Entrance requirements:* For master's, GRE General Test; for doctorate, GRE General Test, MPH or equivalent (Dr PH). Additional exam requirements/recommendations for international students: Required—TOEFL (minimum score 600 paper-based; 250 computer-based; 100 iBT). *Application deadline:* For fall admission, 1/5 for domestic students, 1/1 for international students. Application fee: $60. Electronic applications accepted. *Expenses:* Contact institution. *Financial support:* In 2011–12, 600 students received support. Fellowships, research assistantships, teaching assistantships, career-related internships or fieldwork, Federal Work-Study, and traineeships available. Support available to part-time students. Financial award application deadline: 2/1; financial award applicants required to submit FAFSA. *Unit head:* Dr. Linda P. Fried, Dean/Professor, 212-305-9300, Fax: 212-305-9342, E-mail: lpfried@columbia.edu. *Application contact:* Dr. Joseph Korevec, Director of Admissions and Financial Aid, 212-305-8698, Fax: 212-342-1861, E-mail: ph-admit@columbia.edu. Web site: http://www.mailman.hs.columbia.edu/.

Dartmouth College, The Dartmouth Institute, Program in Public Health, Hanover, NH 03755. Offers MPH. Degree awarded through Medical School. *Accreditation:* CEPH. Part-time programs available. *Degree requirements:* For master's, research project or practicum. *Entrance requirements:* For master's, GRE or MCAT, 3 letters of recommendation. Additional exam requirements/recommendations for international students: Required—TOEFL.

Davenport University, Sneden Graduate School, Grand Rapids, MI 49512. Offers accounting (MBA); business administration (EMBA); finance (MBA); health care management (MBA); human resources (MBA); information assurance (MS); public health (MPH); strategic management (MBA). Evening/weekend programs available. *Entrance requirements:* For master's, GMAT, minimum undergraduate GPA of 2.75. Additional exam requirements/recommendations for international students: Required—TOEFL. Electronic applications accepted. *Faculty research:* Leadership, management, marketing, organizational culture.

Davenport University, Sneden Graduate School, Warren, MI 48092-5209. Offers accounting (MBA); business administration (EMBA); finance (MBA); health care management (MBA); human resources management (MBA); information assurance (MS); public health (MPH); strategic management (MBA). *Entrance requirements:* For master's, minimum undergraduate GPA of 2.7.

Davenport University, Sneden Graduate School, Dearborn, MI 48126-3799. Offers accounting (MBA); business administration (EMBA); finance (MBA); health care management (MBA); human resources management (MBA); information assurance (MS); marketing (MBA); public health (MPH); strategic management (MBA). Part-time and evening/weekend programs available. Postbaccalaureate distance learning degree programs offered (no on-campus study). *Entrance requirements:* For master's, minimum GPA of 2.7, previous course work in accounting and statistics. *Faculty research:* Accounting, international accounting, social and environmental accounting, finance.

DePaul University, College of Liberal Arts and Sciences, Program in Public Health, Chicago, IL 60604-2287. Offers community health practice (MPH). *Application contact:* Ann Spittle, Director of Graduate Admission, 773-325-7315, Fax: 773-476-3244, E-mail: graduatelas@depaul.edu.

Des Moines University, College of Health Sciences, Program in Public Health, Des Moines, IA 50312-4104. Offers MPH. *Accreditation:* CEPH. Part-time and evening/weekend programs available. *Entrance requirements:* For master's, minimum GPA of 3.0. Additional exam requirements/recommendations for international students: Required—TOEFL (minimum score 600 paper-based). Electronic applications accepted. *Expenses:* Contact institution. *Faculty research:* Quality improvement, women's health, health promotion, patient education.

Drexel University, School of Public Health, Philadelphia, PA 19104-2875. Offers MPH, MS, PhD, Certificate. *Accreditation:* CEPH. *Entrance requirements:* For master's, GMAT, GRE, LSAT, or MCAT, previous course work in statistics and word processing. Additional exam requirements/recommendations for international students: Required—TOEFL. Electronic applications accepted. *Expenses:* Contact institution. *Faculty research:* Epidemiology, behavioral and social sciences, problem-based learning.

East Carolina University, Brody School of Medicine, Program in Public Health, Greenville, NC 27858-4353. Offers MPH, MD/MPH. *Accreditation:* CEPH. Part-time programs available. *Degree requirements:* For master's, field placement professional paper. *Entrance requirements:* For master's, GRE or MCAT. Additional exam requirements/recommendations for international students: Required—TOEFL (minimum score 550 paper-based; 213 computer-based). *Application deadline:* For fall admission, 4/15 for domestic and international students; for spring admission, 10/15 for domestic and international students. Application fee: $50. Electronic applications accepted. *Expenses:* Tuition, state resident: full-time $3557; part-time $444.63 per semester hour. Tuition, nonresident: full-time $14,351; part-time $1793.88 per semester hour. *Required fees:* $2016; $252 per semester hour. Part-time tuition and fees vary according to course load, campus/location and program. *Financial support:* Research assistantships with full tuition reimbursements and unspecified assistantships available. Financial award applicants required to submit FAFSA. *Faculty research:* Public health, disparities in public health. *Unit head:* Dr. Lloyd F. Novick, Chairman, Family Medicine, 252-744-4079, Fax: 252-744-2987, E-mail: novickl@ecu.edu. *Application contact:* Dean of Graduate School, 252-328-6012, Fax: 252-328-6071, E-mail: gradschool@ecu.edu.

East Carolina University, Graduate School, College of Fine Arts and Communication, School of Communication, Greenville, NC 27858-4353. Offers health communication (MA). *Entrance requirements:* For master's, GRE. *Expenses:* Tuition, state resident: full-time $3557; part-time $444.63 per semester hour. Tuition, nonresident: full-time $14,351; part-time $1793.88 per semester hour. *Required fees:* $2016; $252 per semester hour. Part-time tuition and fees vary according to course load, campus/location and program. *Financial support:* Teaching assistantships available. *Unit head:* Dr. Linda Kean, Director, 252-328-4227, E-mail: keanl@ecu.edu. *Application contact:* Dean of Graduate School, 252-328-6012, Fax: 252-328-6071, E-mail: gradschool@ecu.edu. Web site: http://www.ecu.edu/cs-cfac/comm/graduate/index.cfm.

Eastern Virginia Medical School, Master of Public Health Program, Norfolk, VA 23501-1980. Offers MPH. Program offered jointly with Old Dominion University. *Accreditation:* CEPH. Evening/weekend programs available. *Faculty:* 6 full-time (3 women), 31 part-time/adjunct (17 women). *Students:* 110 full-time (80 women); includes 66 minority (43 Black or African American, non-Hispanic/Latino; 22 Asian, non-Hispanic/Latino; 1 Hispanic/Latino). 158 applicants, 51% accepted, 57 enrolled. In 2011, 29 master's awarded. *Degree requirements:* For master's, field practicum. *Entrance requirements:* For master's, GRE General Test. Additional exam requirements/recommendations for international students: Required—TOEFL (minimum score 650 paper-based; 278 computer-based). *Application deadline:* For fall admission, 4/30 for domestic and international students. Applications are processed on a rolling basis. Application fee: $60. Electronic applications accepted. *Expenses:* Contact institution. *Financial support:* Applicants required to submit FAFSA. *Faculty research:* Community-based health research. *Unit head:* Joseph Flannery, Interim Director, 757-466-6120, Fax: 757-446-6121, E-mail: flannejg@evms.edu. *Application contact:* Aileen Litwin, Instructional Technology Support Analyst, 757-446-6029, Fax: 757-446-6121, E-mail: litwinam@evms.edu. Web site: http://www.evms.edu/evms-school-of-health-professions/master-in-public-health.html.

East Stroudsburg University of Pennsylvania, Graduate School, College of Health Sciences, Program in Public Health, East Stroudsburg, PA 18301-2999. Offers community health education (MPH). Part-time and evening/weekend programs available. Postbaccalaureate distance learning degree programs offered (minimal on-campus study). *Degree requirements:* For master's, comprehensive exam, publishable paper, oral comprehensive exam. *Entrance requirements:* For master's, GRE, 3 letters of recommendation. Additional exam requirements/recommendations for international students: Required—TOEFL (minimum score 560 paper-based; 220 computer-based; 83 iBT). Electronic applications accepted. *Faculty research:* Public health infrastructure.

East Tennessee State University, School of Graduate Studies, College of Public Health, Doctor of Public Health Programs, Johnson City, TN 37614. Offers community health (DPH); epidemiology (DPH). *Accreditation:* CEPH. *Students:* 15 full-time (11 women), 7 part-time (4 women); includes 6 minority (3 Black or African American, non-Hispanic/Latino; 3 Asian, non-Hispanic/Latino), 3 international. 11 applicants, 73% accepted, 8 enrolled. In 2011, 1 doctorate awarded. Terminal master's awarded for partial completion of doctoral program. *Degree requirements:* For doctorate, comprehensive exam, thesis/dissertation, culminating experience/practicum. *Entrance requirements:* For doctorate, GRE General Test, SOPHAS application, MPH or equivalent, four letters of recommendation. Additional exam requirements/recommendations for international students: Required—TOEFL (minimum score 550 paper-based; 213 computer-based; 79 iBT). *Application deadline:* For fall admission, 3/1 for domestic and international students. Application fee: $35 ($45 for international students). Electronic applications accepted. *Expenses:* Tuition, state resident: full-time $7312; part-time $350 per credit hour. Tuition, nonresident: full-time $18,490; part-time $621 per credit hour. *Required fees:* $63 per credit hour. Tuition and fees vary according to course load and program. *Financial support:* In 2011–12, 14 students received support, including 13 research assistantships with full tuition reimbursements available (averaging $14,000 per year); career-related internships or fieldwork, institutionally sponsored loans, scholarships/grants, tuition waivers (full), and unspecified assistantships also available. Financial award application deadline: 7/1; financial award applicants required to submit FAFSA. *Faculty research:* Rural health issues, youth and adolescent health, health of the elderly, environmental epidemiology, spatial analysis of data. *Unit head:* Dr. Rob Pack, Associate Dean, 423-439-4243, Fax: 423-439-5238, E-mail: packr@etsu.edu. *Application contact:* Mary Duncan, Graduate Specialist, 423-439-4302, Fax: 423-439-5624, E-mail: duncanm@etsu.edu.

Emory University, Rollins School of Public Health, Atlanta, GA 30322. Offers MPH, MSPH, PhD, JD/MPH, MBA/MPH, MD/MPH, MM Sc/MPH, MSN/MPH. *Accreditation:* CEPH (one or more programs are accredited). Part-time and evening/weekend programs available. Postbaccalaureate distance learning degree programs offered (minimal on-campus study). *Faculty:* 208 full-time (88 women), 275 part-time/adjunct (90 women). *Students:* 358 full-time (277 women); includes 99 minority (42 Black or African American, non-Hispanic/Latino; 44 Asian, non-Hispanic/Latino; 13 Hispanic/Latino), 15 international. Average age 27. In 2011, 302 master's awarded. *Degree requirements:* For master's, variable foreign language requirement, comprehensive exam (for some programs), thesis (for some programs), practicum. *Entrance requirements:* For master's, GRE General Test. Additional exam requirements/recommendations for international students: Required—TOEFL (minimum score 550 paper-based; 213 computer-based;

80 iBT). *Application deadline:* For fall admission, 1/5 priority date for domestic students, 1/5 for international students. Application fee: $95. Electronic applications accepted. *Expenses:* Contact institution. *Financial support:* In 2011–12, 14 fellowships with full and partial tuition reimbursements were awarded; research assistantships, teaching assistantships, career-related internships or fieldwork, Federal Work-Study, institutionally sponsored loans, scholarships/grants, traineeships, health care benefits, and unspecified assistantships also available. Support available to part-time students. Financial award application deadline: 1/5; financial award applicants required to submit FAFSA. *Faculty research:* HIV/AIDS prevention, infectious disease, minority health, health disparities, bioterrorism. *Unit head:* Dr. James W. Curran, Dean, 404-727-8720. *Application contact:* Office of Admissions, 404-727-3956, E-mail: admit@sph.emory.edu. Web site: http://www.sph.emory.edu/.

Florida Agricultural and Mechanical University, Division of Graduate Studies, Research, and Continuing Education, College of Pharmacy and Pharmaceutical Sciences, Institute of Public Health, Tallahassee, FL 32307-3200. Offers MPH. *Accreditation:* CEPH. *Entrance requirements:* Additional exam requirements/recommendations for international students: Required—TOEFL.

Florida International University, Robert Stempel College of Public Health and Social Work, Programs in Public Health, Miami, FL 33199. Offers biostatistics (MPH); environmental and occupational health (MPH, PhD); epidemiology (MPH, PhD); health policy and management (MPH); health promotion and disease prevention (PhD); health promotion and diseases prevention (MPH). Ph D is fall admission only; MPH offered jointly with University of Miami. *Accreditation:* CEPH. Part-time and evening/weekend programs available. Postbaccalaureate distance learning degree programs offered (no on-campus study). *Degree requirements:* For master's, thesis optional; for doctorate, comprehensive exam, thesis/dissertation. *Entrance requirements:* For master's, minimum GPA of 3.0, letters of recommendation; for doctorate, GRE, resume, minimum GPA of 3.0, letters of recommendation, letter of intent. Additional exam requirements/recommendations for international students: Required—TOEFL (minimum score 550 paper-based; 80 iBT). Electronic applications accepted. *Expenses:* Contact institution. *Faculty research:* Drugs/AIDS intervention among migrant workers, provision of services for active/recovering drug users with HIV.

Florida State University, The Graduate School, College of Social Sciences and Public Policy, Public Health Program, Tallahassee, FL 32303. Offers MPH. Part-time programs available. *Faculty:* 6 full-time (1 woman), 2 part-time/adjunct (0 women). *Students:* 24 full-time (13 women), 36 part-time (32 women); includes 25 minority (17 Black or African American, non-Hispanic/Latino; 1 American Indian or Alaska Native, non-Hispanic/Latino; 2 Asian, non-Hispanic/Latino; 4 Hispanic/Latino; 1 Native Hawaiian or other Pacific Islander, non-Hispanic/Latino), 4 international. Average age 26. 87 applicants, 64% accepted, 22 enrolled. In 2011, 18 master's awarded. *Degree requirements:* For master's, internship, research paper. *Entrance requirements:* For master's, GRE General Test, minimum GPA of 3.0. Additional exam requirements/recommendations for international students: Required—TOEFL (minimum score 550 paper-based; 213 computer-based; 80 iBT). *Application deadline:* For fall admission, 7/1 priority date for domestic students, 7/1 for international students; for spring admission, 11/1 for domestic and international students. Applications are processed on a rolling basis. Application fee: $30. Electronic applications accepted. *Expenses:* Tuition, state resident: full-time $9474; part-time $350.88 per credit hour. Tuition, nonresident: full-time $16,236; part-time $601.34 per credit hour. *Required fees:* $630 per semester. One-time fee: $20. Tuition and fees vary according to course load and campus/location. *Financial support:* In 2011–12, 3 students received support, including 3 research assistantships with full tuition reimbursements available (averaging $5,000 per year); fellowships with tuition reimbursements available, career-related internships or fieldwork, Federal Work-Study, institutionally sponsored loans, and unspecified assistantships also available. Financial award application deadline: 2/15. *Faculty research:* Health behavior surveillance, long term care policy, long term care evaluation, HMO's, Medicaid. *Total annual research expenditures:* $1 million. *Unit head:* Dr. William G. Weissert, Director, 850-644-4418, Fax: 850-644-1367, E-mail: william.weissert@fsu.edu. *Application contact:* Kaley Boggs, Academic Program Specialist, 850-644-4418, E-mail: kboggs@fsu.edu. Web site: http://www.coss.fsu.edu/publichealth/.

Fort Valley State University, College of Graduate Studies and Extended Education, Program in Public Health, Fort Valley, GA 31030. Offers environmental health (MPH). *Degree requirements:* For master's, thesis. *Entrance requirements:* For master's, GRE General Test. Additional exam requirements/recommendations for international students: Recommended—TOEFL.

George Mason University, College of Health and Human Services, Department of Global and Community Health, Fairfax, VA 22030. Offers biostatistics (Certificate); epidemiology (Certificate); epidemiology and biostatistics (MS); gerontology (Certificate); global health (MS, Certificate); nutrition (Certificate); public health (MPH, Certificate). *Faculty:* 11 full-time (5 women), 16 part-time/adjunct (12 women). *Students:* 101 full-time (84 women), 114 part-time (92 women); includes 85 minority (43 Black or African American, non-Hispanic/Latino; 30 Asian, non-Hispanic/Latino; 11 Hispanic/Latino; 1 Two or more races, non-Hispanic/Latino), 14 international. Average age 32. 162 applicants, 61% accepted, 53 enrolled. In 2011, 80 master's, 15 other advanced degrees awarded. *Degree requirements:* For master's, comprehensive exam (for some programs), thesis or practicum. *Entrance requirements:* For master's, GRE, 2 official transcripts; expanded goals statement; 3 letters of recommendation; resume; 1 completed course in health science, statistics, natural sciences and social science (for MPH); 6 credits of foreign language if not fluent (for MS in global health); for Certificate, 2 official transcripts; expanded goals statement; 3 letters of recommendation; resume; bachelor's degree from regionally-accredited institution with minimum GPA of 3.0; statistics and college-level algebra with minimum B grade (for Certificate in biostatistics). Additional exam requirements/recommendations for international students: Required—TOEFL (minimum score 575 paper-based; 230 computer-based; 88 iBT), IELTS, Pearson Test of English. *Application deadline:* For fall admission, 4/1 priority date for domestic students; for spring admission, 11/1 priority date for domestic students. Applications are processed on a rolling basis. Application fee: $65 ($80 for international students). Electronic applications accepted. *Expenses:* Tuition, state resident: full-time $8750; part-time $364.58 per credit. Tuition, nonresident: full-time $24,092; part-time $1003.83 per credit. *Required fees:* $2514; $104.75 per credit. *Financial support:* In 2011–12, 14 students received support, including 12 research assistantships with full and partial tuition reimbursements available (averaging $15,000 per year), 2 teaching assistantships with full and partial tuition reimbursements available (averaging $11,781 per year); career-related internships or fieldwork, Federal Work-Study, scholarships/grants, unspecified assistantships, and health care benefits (full-time research and teaching assistantship recipients) also available. Financial award application deadline: 3/1; financial award applicants required to submit FAFSA. *Faculty research:* Providing introductory and advanced degrees in health-related disciplines centered in global and community issues, health issues and the needs of affected populations at the regional and global level. *Total annual research expenditures:* $64,518. *Unit head:* Dr. Carlos Sluzki, Dean, 703-993-1920, Fax: 703-993-1943, E-mail: csluzki@gmu.edu. *Application contact:* Allan Weiss, Office Manager, 703-993-3126, Fax: 703-993-1908, E-mail: aweiss2@gmu.edu. Web site: http://chhs.gmu.edu/gch/index.

Georgetown University, Graduate School of Arts and Sciences, Programs in Biomedical Sciences, Department of Microbiology and Immunology, Washington, DC 20057. Offers biohazardous threat agents and emerging infectious diseases (MS); general microbiology and immunology (MS); global infectious diseases (PhD); microbiology and immunology research (PhD); science policy and advocacy (MS). Part-time programs available. *Degree requirements:* For master's, 30 credit hours of coursework; for doctorate, comprehensive exam, thesis/dissertation. *Entrance requirements:* For master's, GRE General Test, 3 letters of reference, bachelor's degree in related field; for doctorate, GRE General Test, 3 letters of reference, MS/BS in related field. Additional exam requirements/recommendations for international students: Required—TOEFL (minimum score 505 paper-based; 213 computer-based). Electronic applications accepted. *Faculty research:* Pathogenesis and basic biology of the fungus Candida albicans, molecular biology of viral immunopathological mechanisms in Multiple Sclerosis.

The George Washington University, School of Public Health and Health Services, Department of Global Health, Washington, DC 20052. Offers MPH, JD/MPH, LL M/MPH, MD/MPH. *Accreditation:* CEPH. *Faculty:* 9 full-time (7 women), 56 part-time/adjunct (21 women). *Students:* 84 full-time (72 women), 107 part-time (88 women); includes 61 minority (29 Black or African American, non-Hispanic/Latino; 1 American Indian or Alaska Native, non-Hispanic/Latino; 13 Asian, non-Hispanic/Latino; 14 Hispanic/Latino; 4 Two or more races, non-Hispanic/Latino), 12 international. Average age 28. 426 applicants, 68% accepted, 69 enrolled. In 2011, 89 master's awarded. *Degree requirements:* For master's, case study or special project. *Entrance requirements:* For master's, GMAT, GRE General Test, or MCAT. Additional exam requirements/recommendations for international students: Required—TOEFL. *Application deadline:* For fall admission, 4/15 priority date for domestic students, 4/15 for international students; for spring admission, 11/1 for domestic and international students. Applications are processed on a rolling basis. Application fee: $75. *Financial support:* In 2011–12, 24 students received support. Tuition waivers available. Financial award application deadline: 2/15. *Unit head:* Dr. James Sherry, Chair, 202-994-0270, Fax: 202-994-1955, E-mail: sherry@gwu.edu. *Application contact:* Jane Smith, Director of Admissions, 202-994-0248, Fax: 202-994-1860, E-mail: sphhsinfo@gwumc.edu.

The George Washington University, School of Public Health and Health Services, Department of Health Services Management and Leadership, Washington, DC 20052. Offers health management and leadership (MHSA); health policy (MHSA); health services administration (Specialist); public health management (MPH). *Accreditation:* CAHME (one or more programs are accredited). *Faculty:* 8 full-time (2 women), 25 part-time/adjunct (3 women). *Degree requirements:* For master's, internship or residency. *Entrance requirements:* For master's, GMAT or GRE; for Specialist, GMAT or GRE, master's degree in related field. Additional exam requirements/recommendations for international students: Required—TOEFL. *Application deadline:* For fall admission, 5/15 priority date for domestic students; for winter admission, 11/15 for domestic students; for spring admission, 4/1 for domestic students. Applications are processed on a rolling basis. Application fee: $75. *Financial support:* Career-related internships or fieldwork, Federal Work-Study, and institutionally sponsored loans available. Financial award application deadline: 6/1. *Faculty research:* Hospital administration, ambulatory health care, social gerontology, health care financing, health care ethics. *Unit head:* Dr. Robert Burke, Chair, 202-994-5560, Fax: 202-416-0075, E-mail: bobburke@gwu.edu. *Application contact:* Jane Smith, Director of Admissions, 202-994-0248, Fax: 202-994-1860, E-mail: sphhsinfo@gwumc.edu. Web site: http://sphhs.gwumc.edu/departments/healthservicesmanagementleadership.

Georgia Southern University, Jack N. Averitt College of Graduate Studies, Jiann-Ping Hsu College of Public Health, Program in Public Health, Statesboro, GA 30460. Offers biostatistics (MPH, Dr PH); community health behavior and education (Dr PH); community health education (MPH); environmental health sciences (MPH); epidemiology (MPH); health services policy management (MPH); public health leadership (Dr PH). *Accreditation:* CEPH. Part-time programs available. *Students:* 87 full-time (60 women), 39 part-time (25 women); includes 68 minority (58 Black or African American, non-Hispanic/Latino; 6 Asian, non-Hispanic/Latino; 4 Hispanic/Latino), 20 international. Average age 30. 73 applicants, 84% accepted, 42 enrolled. In 2011, 22 master's, 4 doctorates awarded. *Degree requirements:* For master's, thesis optional, practicum; for doctorate, comprehensive exam, thesis/dissertation, practicum. *Entrance requirements:* For master's, GRE General Test, minimum GPA of 2.75, resume, 3 letters of reference; for doctorate, GRE, GMAT, MCAT, LSAT, 3 letters of reference, statement of purpose, resume or curriculum vitae. Additional exam requirements/recommendations for international students: Required—TOEFL (minimum score 550 paper-based; 213 computer-based; 80 iBT). *Application deadline:* For fall admission, 3/1 priority date for domestic students, 3/1 for international students; for spring admission, 10/1 priority date for domestic students, 10/1 for international students. Applications are processed on a rolling basis. Application fee: $50. Electronic applications accepted. *Expenses:* Contact institution. *Financial support:* In 2011–12, 59 students received support, including research assistantships with partial tuition reimbursements available (averaging $7,200 per year), teaching assistantships with partial tuition reimbursements available (averaging $7,200 per year); career-related internships or fieldwork, Federal Work-Study, scholarships/grants, tuition waivers (partial), and unspecified assistantships also available. Support available to part-time students. Financial award application deadline: 4/15; financial award applicants required to submit FAFSA. *Faculty research:* Rural public health best practices, health disparity elimination, community initiatives to enhance public health, cost effectiveness analysis, epidemiology of rural public health, environmental health issues, health care system assessment, rural health care, health policy and healthcare financing. *Unit head:* Dr. Charles Hardy, Dean, 912-478-2674, Fax: 912-478-5811, E-mail: chardy@georgiasouthern.edu. *Application contact:* Amanda Gilliland, Coordinator for Graduate Student Recruitment, 912-478-5384, Fax: 912-478-0740, E-mail: gradadmissions@georgiasouthern.edu. Web site: http://chhs.georgiasouthern.edu/health/.

Georgia State University, Andrew Young School of Policy Studies, Department of Public Management and Policy, Atlanta, GA 30303. Offers disaster management (Certificate); non-profit management (Certificate); planning and economic development (Certificate); public administration (MPA), including criminal justice, management and finance, nonprofit management, planning and economic development, policy analysis and evaluation, public health; public policy (MPP, PhD), including disaster policy (MPP), nonprofit policy (MPP), planning and economic development policy (MPP), public finance policy (MPP), social policy (MPP); JD/MPA. *Accreditation:* NASPAA (one or more programs are accredited). Part-time and evening/weekend programs available. Terminal master's awarded for partial completion of doctoral program. *Degree requirements:* For master's, thesis optional; for doctorate, comprehensive exam, thesis/dissertation. *Entrance requirements:* For master's and doctorate, GRE General Test. Additional exam requirements/recommendations for international students: Required—TOEFL. Electronic applications accepted. *Faculty research:* Public management, policy analysis, public finance, planning and economic development, nonprofit leadership and policy.

Georgia State University, College of Health and Human Sciences, Institute of Public Health, Atlanta, GA 30302-3995. Offers MPH, Certificate. *Accreditation:* CEPH. Part-

Public Health—General

time and evening/weekend programs available. *Degree requirements:* For master's, thesis, practicum. *Entrance requirements:* For master's and Certificate, GRE, GMAT. Additional exam requirements/recommendations for international students: Required—TOEFL (minimum score 550 paper-based; 213 computer-based; 80 iBT). Electronic applications accepted. *Faculty research:* Health promotion and behavior, prevention sciences, health policy and management.

Graduate School and University Center of the City University of New York, Graduate Studies, Program in Public Health, New York, NY 10016-4039. Offers DPH. *Accreditation:* CEPH. Part-time programs available. *Degree requirements:* For doctorate, thesis/dissertation, exams, research seminars. *Entrance requirements:* For doctorate, GRE General Test, MPH, 2 letters of recommendation, curriculum vitae or resume.

Grand Canyon University, College of Nursing and Health Sciences, Phoenix, AZ 85017-1097. Offers addiction counseling (MS); health care administration (MS); health care informatics (MS); marriage and family therapy (MS); professional counseling (MS); public health (MS). Part-time and evening/weekend programs available. Postbaccalaureate distance learning degree programs offered (no on-campus study). *Entrance requirements:* For master's, undergraduate degree with minimum GPA of 2.8. Additional exam requirements/recommendations for international students: Required—TOEFL (minimum score 575 paper-based; 233 computer-based; 90 iBT), IELTS (minimum score 7).

Harvard University, Cyprus International Institute for the Environment and Public Health in Association with Harvard School of Public Health, Cambridge, MA 02138. Offers environmental/public health (PhD); epidemiology and biostatistics (MS). *Entrance requirements:* For master's and doctorate, GRE, resume/curriculum vitae, 3 letters of recommendation, BA or BS (including diploma and official transcripts). Additional exam requirements/recommendations for international students: Required—TOEFL (minimum score 220 computer-based), IELTS (minimum score 7). Electronic applications accepted. *Expenses: Tuition:* Full-time $36,304. *Required fees:* $1186. Full-time tuition and fees vary according to program. *Faculty research:* Air pollution, climate change, biostatistics, sustainable development, environmental management.

Harvard University, Harvard School of Public Health, Boston, MA 02115-6096. Offers MOH, MPH, SM, DPH, PhD, SD, JD/MPH, MD/MPH. SM program offered jointly with Simmons College. *Accreditation:* CEPH (one or more programs are accredited). Part-time programs available. *Faculty:* 337 full-time (100 women), 124 part-time/adjunct (42 women). *Students:* 869 full-time, 313 part-time; includes 213 minority (54 Black or African American, non-Hispanic/Latino; 4 American Indian or Alaska Native, non-Hispanic/Latino; 78 Asian, non-Hispanic/Latino; 48 Hispanic/Latino; 1 Native Hawaiian or other Pacific Islander, non-Hispanic/Latino; 28 Two or more races, non-Hispanic/Latino), 399 international. Average age 31. 2,155 applicants, 33% accepted, 556 enrolled. In 2011, 483 master's, 60 doctorates awarded. Terminal master's awarded for partial completion of doctoral program. *Degree requirements:* For master's, comprehensive exam (for some programs), thesis (for some programs); for doctorate, thesis/dissertation, qualifying exam. *Entrance requirements:* For master's and doctorate, GRE. Additional exam requirements/recommendations for international students: Required—TOEFL (minimum score 590 paper-based; 240 computer-based; 95 iBT); Recommended—IELTS (minimum score 7). *Application deadline:* For fall admission, 12/15 for domestic and international students. Application fee: $115. Electronic applications accepted. *Expenses:* Contact institution. *Financial support:* Fellowships, research assistantships, teaching assistantships, career-related internships or fieldwork, Federal Work-Study, scholarships/grants, traineeships, and unspecified assistantships available. Support available to part-time students. Financial award application deadline: 2/17;

financial award applicants required to submit FAFSA. *Unit head:* Dr. Julio Frenk, Dean of the Faculty, 617-432-1025, Fax: 617-277-5320, E-mail: deansoff@hsph.harvard.edu. *Application contact:* Vincent W. James, Director of Admissions, 617-432-1031, Fax: 617-432-7080, E-mail: admissions@hsph.harvard.edu. Web site: http://www.hsph.harvard.edu/.

See Display below and Close-Up on page 865.

Hofstra University, School of Education, Health, and Human Services, Programs in Health, Hempstead, NY 11549. Offers community health (MS); health administration (MHA); public health (MPH). Part-time and evening/weekend programs available. *Students:* 66 full-time (43 women), 70 part-time (52 women); includes 60 minority (39 Black or African American, non-Hispanic/Latino; 11 Asian, non-Hispanic/Latino; 8 Hispanic/Latino; 2 Two or more races, non-Hispanic/Latino), 4 international. Average age 30. 90 applicants, 83% accepted, 48 enrolled. In 2011, 50 master's awarded. *Degree requirements:* For master's, internship, minimum GPA of 3.0. *Entrance requirements:* For master's, interview, 2 letters of recommendation, essay, resume. Additional exam requirements/recommendations for international students: Required—TOEFL (minimum score 550 paper-based; 213 computer-based; 80 iBT). *Application deadline:* Applications are processed on a rolling basis. Application fee: $70 ($75 for international students). Electronic applications accepted. *Expenses: Tuition:* Full-time $18,990; part-time $1055 per credit hour. *Required fees:* $970. Tuition and fees vary according to program. *Financial support:* In 2011–12, 25 students received support, including 17 fellowships with full and partial tuition reimbursements available (averaging $2,588 per year), 2 research assistantships with full and partial tuition reimbursements available (averaging $14,226 per year); career-related internships or fieldwork, Federal Work-Study, institutionally sponsored loans, scholarships/grants, tuition waivers (full and partial), and unspecified assistantships also available. Support available to part-time students. Financial award applicants required to submit FAFSA. *Faculty research:* Integrated long-term care, health care policy, cost-benefit analysis, chronic illness management, long-term care policy form. *Unit head:* Dr. Liora P. Schmelkin, Chairperson, 516-463-4680, Fax: 516-463-6505, E-mail: prolps@hofstra.edu. *Application contact:* Carol Drummer, Dean of Graduate Admissions, 516-463-4876, Fax: 516-463-4664, E-mail: gradstudent@hofstra.edu. Web site: http://www.hofstra.edu/education/.

Howard University, College of Medicine, Program in Public Health, Washington, DC 20059-0002. Offers MPH.

Hunter College of the City University of New York, Graduate School, Schools of the Health Professions, School of Health Sciences, Programs in Urban Public Health, New York, NY 10021-5085. Offers community health education (MPH); environmental and occupational health education (MS); epidemiology and biostatistics (MPH); health policy management (MPH); nutrition and public health (MPH); MS/MPH. *Accreditation:* CEPH. Part-time programs available. *Faculty:* 23 full-time (12 women), 18 part-time/adjunct (11 women). *Students:* 34 full-time (24 women), 235 part-time (177 women); includes 100 minority (47 Black or African American, non-Hispanic/Latino; 6 American Indian or Alaska Native, non-Hispanic/Latino; 27 Asian, non-Hispanic/Latino; 20 Hispanic/Latino), 16 international. Average age 32. 227 applicants, 58% accepted, 76 enrolled. In 2011, 73 master's awarded. *Degree requirements:* For master's, comprehensive exam. *Entrance requirements:* For master's, GRE General Test, undergraduate major in natural or social sciences, health studies, nutrition or related field; 1 year of work or volunteer experience related to public health, nutrition, environmental health, social services, or community organization. Additional exam requirements/recommendations for international students: Required—TOEFL. *Application deadline:* For fall admission, 4/1 for domestic students, 2/1 for international students; for spring admission, 11/1 for domestic students, 9/1 for international students. Application fee: $125. *Expenses:*

HARVARD

SCHOOL OF PUBLIC HEALTH

Powerful ideas for a healthier world

From advancing scientific discovery to educating national and international leaders, the Harvard School of Public Health has been at the forefront of efforts to benefit the health of populations worldwide. Shaping new ideas in our field and communicating them effectively will continue to be priorities in the years ahead as we serve society's changing health needs.

Degrees offered:

Master of Public Health
Master of Science, specified field
Combined MD/MPH program

Doctor of Philosophy, specified field
Doctor of Public Health
Doctor of Science, specified field

Combined JD/MPH program

For more information, contact:

Admissions Office
Harvard School of Public Health
Phone: 617-432-1031
E-mail: admissions@hsph.harvard.edu

http://www.hsph.harvard.edu/

Tuition, state resident: full-time $8210; part-time $345 per credit. Tuition, nonresident: full-time $15,360; part-time $640 per credit. *Required fees:* $280 per semester. One-time fee: $125. Tuition and fees vary according to class time, campus/location and program. *Financial support:* Application deadline: 3/1. *Unit head:* Bernice Rumala, Director of Recruitment and Student Support Services, 212-481-3478, Fax: 212-481-5260, E-mail: brumala@hunter.cuny.edu. *Application contact:* Michael Goldstein, Assistant Director for Graduate Admissions, 212-772-4288, Fax: 212-650-3336, E-mail: admissions@hunter.cuny.edu. Web site: http://www.hunter.cuny.edu/uph/grad-test.

Idaho State University, Office of Graduate Studies, College of Education, Department of Educational Foundations, Pocatello, ID 83209-8059. Offers child and family studies (M Ed); curriculum leadership (M Ed); education (M Ed); educational administration (M Ed); educational foundations (5th Year Certificate); elementary education (M Ed), including K-12 education, literacy, secondary education. Part-time programs available. *Degree requirements:* For master's, comprehensive exam, thesis optional, oral exam, written exam; for 5th Year Certificate, comprehensive exam, thesis (for some programs), oral exam, written exam. *Entrance requirements:* For master's, GRE General Test or MAT, minimum undergraduate GPA of 3.0; for 5th Year Certificate, GRE General Test, minimum undergraduate GPA of 3.0, master's degree. Additional exam requirements/recommendations for international students: Required—TOEFL (minimum score 550 paper-based; 213 computer-based; 80 iBT). Electronic applications accepted. *Faculty research:* Child and families studies; business education; special education; math, science, and technology education.

Idaho State University, Office of Graduate Studies, Kasiska College of Health Professions, Department of Health and Nutrition Sciences, Program in Public Health, Pocatello, ID 83209-8109. Offers MPH. *Accreditation:* CEPH. Part-time programs available. *Degree requirements:* For master's, comprehensive exam, thesis. *Entrance requirements:* For master's, GRE General Test, minimum GPA of 3.0 for upper division classes, 2 letters of recommendation. Additional exam requirements/recommendations for international students: Required—TOEFL (minimum score 600 paper-based; 213 computer-based). Electronic applications accepted.

Independence University, Program in Public Health, Salt Lake City, UT 84107. Offers MPH. Part-time and evening/weekend programs available. Postbaccalaureate distance learning degree programs offered (no on-campus study). *Degree requirements:* For master's, final project or thesis.

Indiana University Bloomington, School of Health, Physical Education and Recreation, Department of Applied Health Science, Bloomington, IN 47405-7000. Offers biostatistics (MPH); environmental health (MPH, PhD); epidemiology (MPH, PhD); health behavior (PhD); health promotion (MS); human development/family studies (MS); nutrition science (MS); public health administration (MPH); safety management (MS); school and college health programs (MS); social, behavioral and community health (MPH). *Accreditation:* CEPH (one or more programs are accredited). *Faculty:* 24 full-time (12 women). *Students:* 169 full-time (126 women), 25 part-time (17 women); includes 56 minority (39 Black or African American, non-Hispanic/Latino; 2 American Indian or Alaska Native, non-Hispanic/Latino; 4 Asian, non-Hispanic/Latino; 9 Hispanic/Latino; 2 Two or more races, non-Hispanic/Latino), 29 international. Average age 30. 170 applicants, 74% accepted, 79 enrolled. In 2011, 52 master's, 9 doctorates awarded. *Degree requirements:* For master's, thesis optional; for doctorate, thesis/dissertation. *Entrance requirements:* For master's, GRE (MS in nutrition science), 3 recommendations; for doctorate, GRE, 3 recommendations. Additional exam requirements/recommendations for international students: Required—TOEFL (minimum score 550 paper-based; 213 computer-based; 79 iBT). *Application deadline:* For fall admission, 4/30 priority date for domestic students, 12/1 for international students; for spring admission, 11/15 priority date for domestic students, 9/1 for international students. Application fee: $55 ($65 for international students). *Financial support:* Fellowships, research assistantships with full and partial tuition reimbursements, teaching assistantships with full and partial tuition reimbursements, career-related internships or fieldwork, Federal Work-Study, institutionally sponsored loans, scholarships/grants, tuition waivers (partial), and fee remissions available. Financial award application deadline: 3/1. *Faculty research:* Cancer education, HIV/AIDS and drug education, public health, parent-child interactions, safety education. *Total annual research expenditures:* $2.8 million. *Unit head:* Dr. David K. Lohrmann, Chair, 812-856-5101, Fax: 812-855-3936, E-mail: dlohrman@indiana.edu. *Application contact:* Dr. Susan Middlestadt, Associate Professor and Graduate Coordinator, 812-856-5768, Fax: 812-855-3936, E-mail: semiddle@indiana.edu. Web site: http://www.indiana.edu/~aphealth/.

Indiana University–Purdue University Indianapolis, Indiana University School of Medicine, Department of Public Health, Indianapolis, IN 46202-2896. Offers behavioral health science (MPH); epidemiology (MPH); health policy and management (MPH). *Accreditation:* CEPH. *Students:* 134 full-time (86 women), 134 part-time (93 women); includes 53 minority (25 Black or African American, non-Hispanic/Latino; 1 American Indian or Alaska Native, non-Hispanic/Latino; 14 Asian, non-Hispanic/Latino; 10 Hispanic/Latino; 3 Two or more races, non-Hispanic/Latino), 13 international. Average age 30. 236 applicants, 58% accepted, 106 enrolled. In 2011, 81 master's awarded. Application fee: $55 ($65 for international students). *Expenses:* Contact institution. *Financial support:* In 2011–12, teaching assistantships (averaging $14,058 per year) were awarded. *Unit head:* Dr. Carole Kacius, Director, 317-274-3126. *Application contact:* Robert M. Stump, Jr., Director of Admissions, 317-274-3772, E-mail: inmedadm@iupui.edu.

The Johns Hopkins University, Bloomberg School of Public Health, Baltimore, MD 21205. Offers MHA, MHS, MPH, Sc M, Dr PH, PhD, Sc D, JD/MPH, MBA/MPH, MHS/MA, MSN/MPH, MSW/MPH. *Accreditation:* CEPH (one or more programs are accredited). Part-time and evening/weekend programs available. Postbaccalaureate distance learning degree programs offered (minimal on-campus study). *Faculty:* 547 full-time (289 women), 28 part-time/adjunct (9 women). *Students:* 1,437 full-time (1,060 women), 488 part-time (311 women); includes 574 minority (144 Black or African American, non-Hispanic/Latino; 2 American Indian or Alaska Native, non-Hispanic/Latino; 304 Asian, non-Hispanic/Latino; 71 Hispanic/Latino; 4 Native Hawaiian or other Pacific Islander, non-Hispanic/Latino; 49 Two or more races, non-Hispanic/Latino), 439 international. Average age 30. 3,274 applicants, 51% accepted, 716 enrolled. In 2011, 563 master's, 133 doctorates awarded. *Degree requirements:* For master's, comprehensive exam (for some programs), thesis (for some programs); for doctorate, comprehensive exam, thesis/dissertation. *Entrance requirements:* For master's and doctorate, GRE General Test, 3 letters of recommendation, resume. Additional exam requirements/recommendations for international students: Required—TOEFL (minimum score 600 paper-based; 250 computer-based). *Application deadline:* Applications are processed on a rolling basis. Application fee: $45. Electronic applications accepted. *Financial support:* In 2011–12, 1,256 students received support, including 38 fellowships (averaging $34,333 per year), 59 research assistantships (averaging $23,525 per year), 11 teaching assistantships (averaging $3,126 per year), career-related internships or fieldwork, Federal Work-Study, institutionally sponsored loans, scholarships/grants, traineeships, health care benefits, and stipends also available. Support available to part-time students. Financial award application deadline: 3/15; financial award applicants required to submit FAFSA. *Faculty research:* Biodefense

studies, infectious/chronic disease, human nutrition, environmental hazards, genetics. *Total annual research expenditures:* $372.9 million. *Unit head:* Dr. Michael J. Klag, Dean, 410-955-3540, Fax: 410-955-0121, E-mail: mklag@jhsph.edu. *Application contact:* Leslie K. Vink, Director of Recruitment, Communications and Special Projects, 410-955-3543, Fax: 410-955-0464, E-mail: lvink@jhsph.edu. Web site: http://www.jhsph.edu/.

Laurentian University, School of Graduate Studies and Research, Interdisciplinary Program in Rural and Northern Health, Sudbury, ON P3E 2C6, Canada. Offers PhD.

Loma Linda University, School of Public Health, Loma Linda, CA 92350. Offers MBA, MHA, MPH, MSPH, Dr PH, Postbaccalaureate Certificate. *Accreditation:* CEPH (one or more programs are accredited). Part-time programs available. *Degree requirements:* For doctorate, thesis/dissertation. *Entrance requirements:* For master's, GRE General Test, baccalaureate degree, minimum 3.0 GPA; for doctorate, GRE General Test, minimum GPA of 3.2. Additional exam requirements/recommendations for international students: Required—TOEFL (minimum score 550 paper-based, 213 computer-based) or Michigan English Language Assessment Battery. Electronic applications accepted. *Faculty research:* Lifestyle and health, nutrition and cancer, nutrition and cardiovascular disease, smoking and health, aging and longevity.

Louisiana State University Health Sciences Center, School of Public Health, New Orleans, LA 70112. Offers behavioral and community health sciences (MPH); biostatistics (MPH, MS, PhD); community health sciences (PhD); environmental and occupational health sciences (MPH); epidemiology (MPH, PhD); health policy and systems management (MPH). Part-time programs available. *Entrance requirements:* For master's, GRE General Test.

Louisiana State University in Shreveport, College of Business, Education, and Human Development, Program in Public Health, Shreveport, LA 71115-2399. Offers MPH. Program offered jointly with Louisiana State University Health Sciences Center at Shreveport. Part-time and evening/weekend programs available. *Students:* 17 full-time (14 women), 6 part-time (4 women); includes 6 minority (5 Black or African American, non-Hispanic/Latino; 1 Hispanic/Latino), 4 international. Average age 31. 18 applicants, 100% accepted, 10 enrolled. In 2011, 13 master's awarded. *Entrance requirements:* For master's, GRE or MCAT, 3 letters of recommendation, professional statement, personal interview. Additional exam requirements/recommendations for international students: Required—TOEFL (minimum score 550 paper-based; 213 computer-based; 80 iBT). *Application deadline:* For fall admission, 6/30 for domestic and international students; for spring admission, 11/30 for domestic and international students. Application fee: $10 ($20 for international students). *Unit head:* Dr. Rosevelt Jacobs, Program Director, 318-797-5218, E-mail: rosevelt.jacobs@lsus.edu. *Application contact:* Christianne Wojcik, Director of Academic Services, 318-797-5247, Fax: 318-798-4120, E-mail: christianne.wojcik@lsus.edu.

Loyola University Chicago, Graduate School, Public Health Program, Chicago, IL 60660. Offers MPH. *Students:* 18 full-time (12 women), 14 part-time (10 women); includes 14 minority (4 Black or African American, non-Hispanic/Latino; 7 Asian, non-Hispanic/Latino; 2 Hispanic/Latino; 1 Two or more races, non-Hispanic/Latino), 1 international. Average age 35. 52 applicants, 58% accepted, 21 enrolled. In 2011, 5 master's awarded. *Expenses: Tuition:* Full-time $15,660; part-time $870 per credit hour. *Required fees:* $125 per semester. Tuition and fees vary according to course load and program. *Unit head:* Izlze Berzins, Administrative Coordinator, 708-327-9224, Fax: 708-327-9090, E-mail: iberzin@lumc.edu. *Application contact:* Izlze Berzins, Administrative Coordinator, 708-327-9224, Fax: 708-327-9090, E-mail: iberzin@lumc.edu.

Medical College of Wisconsin, Graduate School of Biomedical Sciences, Department of Population Health, Program in Public Health, Milwaukee, WI 53226-0509. Offers public and community health (PhD); public health (MPH, Graduate Certificate). *Entrance requirements:* For master's, doctorate, and Graduate Certificate, GRE, official transcripts, three letters of recommendation. Additional exam requirements/recommendations for international students: Required—TOEFL.

Medical College of Wisconsin, Graduate School of Biomedical Sciences, Program in Public and Community Health, Milwaukee, WI 53226-0509. Offers PhD, MD/PhD. *Degree requirements:* For doctorate, comprehensive exam, thesis/dissertation. *Entrance requirements:* For doctorate, GRE, official transcripts, three letters of recommendation. Additional exam requirements/recommendations for international students: Required—TOEFL (minimum score 580 paper-based; 273 computer-based; 100 iBT). Electronic applications accepted. *Expenses:* Contact institution. *Faculty research:* Community-academic partnerships, community-based participatory research, injury prevention, health policy, women's health, emergency medical services.

Michigan State University, College of Human Medicine and The Graduate School, Graduate Programs in Human Medicine, Program in Public Health, East Lansing, MI 48824. Offers MPH.

Missouri State University, Graduate College, College of Health and Human Services, Program in Public Health, Springfield, MO 65897. Offers MPH. *Faculty:* 4 full-time (2 women). *Students:* 10 full-time (6 women), 16 part-time (10 women); includes 6 minority (4 Black or African American, non-Hispanic/Latino; 2 Asian, non-Hispanic/Latino), 7 international. Average age 29. 22 applicants, 77% accepted, 9 enrolled. In 2011, 15 master's awarded. *Degree requirements:* For master's, comprehensive exam, thesis or alternative. *Entrance requirements:* For master's, GRE, minimum GPA of 3.0, 1 year work experience. Additional exam requirements/recommendations for international students: Required—TOEFL (minimum score 550 paper-based; 213 computer-based; 79 iBT). *Application deadline:* For fall admission, 7/20 priority date for domestic students, 5/1 for international students; for spring admission, 12/20 priority date for domestic students, 9/1 for international students. Applications are processed on a rolling basis. Application fee: $35 ($50 for international students). Electronic applications accepted. *Expenses:* Tuition, state resident: full-time $4086; part-time $227 per credit hour. Tuition, nonresident: full-time $8172; part-time $454 per credit hour. *Required fees:* $275 per semester. Tuition and fees vary according to course load, campus/location and program. *Financial support:* Federal Work-Study, institutionally sponsored loans, scholarships/grants, and unspecified assistantships available. Financial award application deadline: 3/31; financial award applicants required to submit FAFSA. *Unit head:* Dr. Vickie Sanchez, Program Director, 417-836-6304, E-mail: vickiesanchez@missouristate.edu. *Application contact:* Misty Stewart, Coordinator of Graduate Recruitment, 417-836-6079, Fax: 417-836-6200, E-mail: mistystewart@missouristate.edu.

Montclair State University, The Graduate School, College of Education and Human Services, Department of Health and Nutrition Sciences, Program in Public Health, Montclair, NJ 07043-1624. Offers MPH. Part-time and evening/weekend programs available. *Students:* 13 full-time (all women), 22 part-time (18 women); includes 13 minority (6 Black or African American, non-Hispanic/Latino; 2 Asian, non-Hispanic/Latino; 5 Hispanic/Latino). Average age 31. 67 applicants, 22% accepted, 12 enrolled. In 2011, 5 master's awarded. *Degree requirements:* For master's, comprehensive exam, thesis or alternative. *Entrance requirements:* For master's, GRE General Test, essay, 2 letters of recommendation. Additional exam requirements/recommendations for international students: Required—TOEFL (minimum score 83 iBT), IELTS (minimum score 6.5). *Application deadline:* Applications are processed on a rolling basis.

Application fee: $60. Electronic applications accepted. *Financial support:* In 2011–12, 4 research assistantships with full tuition reimbursements (averaging $7,000 per year) were awarded; Federal Work-Study, scholarships/grants, and unspecified assistantships also available. Support available to part-time students. Financial award application deadline: 3/1; financial award applicants required to submit FAFSA. *Unit head:* Dr. Eva Goldfarb, Chairperson, 973-655-4154. *Application contact:* Amy Aiello, Executive Director of The Graduate School, 973-655-5147, Fax: 973-655-7869, E-mail: graduate.school@montclair.edu. Web site: http://cehs.montclair.edu/academic/hns/programs/master_publichealth.shtml.

Morehouse School of Medicine, Master of Public Health Program, Atlanta, GA 30310-1495. Offers epidemiology (MPH); health administration, management and policy (MPH); health education/health promotion (MPH); international health (MPH). *Accreditation:* CEPH. Part-time programs available. *Degree requirements:* For master's, thesis, practicum, public health leadership seminar. *Entrance requirements:* For master's, GRE General Test, writing test, public health or human service experience. Additional exam requirements/recommendations for international students: Required—TOEFL (minimum score 550 paper-based; 200 computer-based). Electronic applications accepted. *Expenses:* Contact institution. *Faculty research:* Women's and adolescent health, violence prevention, cancer epidemiology/disparities, substance abuse prevention.

Morgan State University, School of Graduate Studies, School of Community Health and Policy, Baltimore, MD 21251. Offers nursing (MS, PhD); public health (MPH, Dr PH). *Accreditation:* CEPH. *Degree requirements:* For doctorate, thesis/dissertation. *Entrance requirements:* For doctorate, GRE, minimum GPA of 3.0. Additional exam requirements/recommendations for international students: Required—TOEFL (minimum score 550 paper-based; 213 computer-based).

National University, Academic Affairs, School of Health and Human Services, Department of Community Health, La Jolla, CA 92037-1011. Offers health informatics (MS); healthcare administration (MHA); public health (MPH). Part-time and evening/weekend programs available. Postbaccalaureate distance learning degree programs offered. *Degree requirements:* For master's, thesis. *Entrance requirements:* Additional exam requirements/recommendations for international students: Required—TOEFL (minimum score 550 paper-based; 213 computer-based; 79 iBT). Application fee: $60 ($65 for international students). *Financial support:* Career-related internships or fieldwork, institutionally sponsored loans, and scholarships/grants available. Support available to part-time students. Financial award application deadline: 6/30; financial award applicants required to submit FAFSA. *Unit head:* Dr. Gina Piane, 858-309-3474, E-mail: gpiane@nu.edu. *Application contact:* Dominick Giovanniello, Associate Regional Dean, 800-NAT-UNIV, Fax: 858-541-7792, E-mail: dgiovann@nu.edu. Web site: http://www.nu.edu/OurPrograms/SchoolOfHealthAndHumanServices/CommunityHealth.html.

New Mexico State University, Graduate School, College of Health and Social Services, Department of Public Health Sciences, Las Cruces, NM 88003-8001. Offers community health education (MPH). Part-time programs available. Postbaccalaureate distance learning degree programs offered (minimal on-campus study). *Students:* 38 full-time (35 women), 38 part-time (28 women); includes 32 minority (2 Black or African American, non-Hispanic/Latino; 7 American Indian or Alaska Native, non-Hispanic/Latino; 1 Asian, non-Hispanic/Latino; 21 Hispanic/Latino; 1 Two or more races, non-Hispanic/Latino), 7 international. Average age 35. 48 applicants, 58% accepted, 17 enrolled. In 2011, 28 master's awarded. *Degree requirements:* For master's, thesis optional. *Entrance requirements:* For master's, GRE. Additional exam requirements/recommendations for international students: Required—TOEFL (minimum score 550 paper-based; 79 iBT), IELTS (minimum score 6.5). *Application deadline:* For fall admission, 2/15 for domestic and international students. Application fee: $40 ($50 for international students). Electronic applications accepted. *Expenses:* Tuition, state resident: full-time $5004; part-time $208.50 per credit. Tuition, nonresident: full-time $17,446; part-time $726.90 per credit. *Financial support:* In 2011–12, 1 research assistantship (averaging $24,744 per year), 17 teaching assistantships (averaging $15,256 per year) were awarded; fellowships, career-related internships or fieldwork, and health care benefits also available. Financial award application deadline: 4/1. *Faculty research:* Community health education, health issues of U. S.-Mexico border, health policy and management, victims of violence, environmental and occupational health issues. *Unit head:* Dr. Mark J. Kittleson, Head, 575-646-4300, Fax: 575-646-4343, E-mail: kittle@nmsu.edu. *Application contact:* Dr. James Robinson, III, Graduate Coordinator, 575-646-7431, E-mail: jrobin3@nmsu.edu. Web site: http://publichealth.nmsu.edu.

New York Medical College, School of Health Sciences and Practice, Valhalla, NY 10595-1691. Offers MPH, MS, DPT, Dr PH, Graduate Certificate. *Accreditation:* CEPH. Part-time and evening/weekend programs available. Postbaccalaureate distance learning degree programs offered (no on-campus study). *Faculty:* 47 full-time (28 women), 195 part-time/adjunct (109 women). *Students:* 200 full-time (150 women), 287 part-time (192 women); includes 170 minority (69 Black or African American, non-Hispanic/Latino; 1 American Indian or Alaska Native, non-Hispanic/Latino; 70 Asian, non-Hispanic/Latino; 30 Hispanic/Latino), 10 international. Average age 32. 355 applicants, 66% accepted, 160 enrolled. In 2011, 150 master's, 16 doctorates awarded. *Degree requirements:* For master's, thesis; for doctorate, comprehensive exam, thesis/dissertation, project (DPT only). *Entrance requirements:* For master's, minimum undergraduate GPA of 3.0; for doctorate, GRE, minimum graduate GPA of 3.2. Additional exam requirements/recommendations for international students: Required—TOEFL (minimum score 637 paper-based; 250 computer-based; 110 iBT), IELTS (minimum score 7). *Application deadline:* For fall admission, 8/1 priority date for domestic students, 5/15 for international students; for spring admission, 12/1 priority date for domestic students, 10/15 for international students. Applications are processed on a rolling basis. Application fee: $50 ($100 for international students). Electronic applications accepted. *Expenses:* Contact institution. *Financial support:* In 2011–12, 230 students received support. Research assistantships with full and partial tuition reimbursements available, teaching assistantships with full and partial tuition reimbursements available, career-related internships or fieldwork, Federal Work-Study, institutionally sponsored loans, health care benefits, tuition waivers (partial), and tuition reimbursements available. Support available to part-time students. Financial award applicants required to submit FAFSA. *Faculty research:* Disaster preparedness, autism, health literacy, adolescent HIV, health disparities, women's health issues, tobacco control, sexual trauma, homelessness, workplace health promotion and stress management. *Total annual research expenditures:* $932,000. *Unit head:* Dr. Robert W. Amler, Dean, 914-594-4843, Fax: 914-594-4292. *Application contact:* Pamela Suett, Director of Recruitment, 914-594-4510, Fax: 914-594-4292, E-mail: shsp_admissions@nymc.edu. Web site: http://www.nymc.edu/sph/.

New York Medical College, School of Health Sciences and Practice, Department of Epidemiology and Community Health, Program in Behavioral Sciences and Health Promotion, Valhalla, NY 10595-1691. Offers behavioral sciences and health promotion (MPH); public health (Graduate Certificate). Part-time and evening/weekend programs available. *Faculty:* 4 full-time, 16 part-time/adjunct. *Students:* 35 full-time, 50 part-time. Average age 32. 37 applicants, 68% accepted, 21 enrolled. In 2011, 25 master's awarded. *Degree requirements:* For master's, thesis. *Entrance requirements:* For master's, minimum undergraduate GPA of 3.0. Additional exam requirements/recommendations for international students: Required—TOEFL (minimum score 637 paper-based; 250 computer-based; 110 iBT), IELTS (minimum score 7). *Application deadline:* For fall admission, 8/1 priority date for domestic students, 5/15 for international students; for spring admission, 12/1 priority date for domestic students, 10/15 for international students. Applications are processed on a rolling basis. Application fee: $50 ($100 for international students). Electronic applications accepted. *Financial support:* Career-related internships or fieldwork, Federal Work-Study, institutionally sponsored loans, health care benefits, and tuition reimbursements available. Support available to part-time students. Financial award applicants required to submit FAFSA. *Unit head:* Dr. Martin K. Diner, Assistant Professor, 914-594-4804, Fax: 914-594-3481, E-mail: martin_diner@nymc.edu. *Application contact:* Pamela Suett, Director of Recruitment, 914-594-4510, Fax: 914-594-4292, E-mail: shsp_admissions@nymc.edu. Web site: http://www.nymc.edu/shsp.

New York University, Steinhardt School of Culture, Education, and Human Development, Department of Nutrition, Food Studies, and Public Health, Program in Community Public Health, New York, NY 10012-1019. Offers PhD. *Accreditation:* CEPH. Part-time programs available. *Entrance requirements:* For doctorate, GRE General Test, interview. Additional exam requirements/recommendations for international students: Required—TOEFL. Electronic applications accepted. *Faculty research:* Social epidemiology, primary health care, global health, immigrants and health, infectious disease prevention, HIV/AIDS.

Northeastern University, Bouvé College of Health Sciences, Program in Exercise Science, Boston, MA 02115-5096. Offers physical activity and public health (MS). Part-time and evening/weekend programs available. *Students:* 26 full-time (17 women). 36 applicants, 69% accepted, 13 enrolled. In 2011, 8 master's awarded. *Degree requirements:* For master's, comprehensive exam, thesis optional. *Entrance requirements:* For master's, GRE General Test. Additional exam requirements/recommendations for international students: Required—TOEFL (minimum score 100 iBT). *Application deadline:* For fall admission, 6/1 for domestic students. Applications are processed on a rolling basis. Application fee: $50. Electronic applications accepted. *Financial support:* Research assistantships with tuition reimbursements, teaching assistantships with tuition reimbursements, career-related internships or fieldwork, Federal Work-Study, scholarships/grants, tuition waivers (partial), and unspecified assistantships available. Support available to part-time students. Financial award application deadline: 3/1; financial award applicants required to submit FAFSA. *Faculty research:* Exercise in cardiovascular pulmonary and metabolic diseases, mechanisms related to lactate and ventilation threshold, body composition assessment techniques. *Unit head:* Prof. Carmen C. Sceppa, Director, Graduate Program in Exercise Science, 617-373-5543, Fax: 617-373-2968, E-mail: c.sceppa@neu.edu. *Application contact:* Margaret Schnabel, Director of Graduate Admissions, 617-373-2708, E-mail: bouvegrad@neu.edu. Web site: http://www.northeastern.edu/graduate/programs/exercise-science/.

Northeastern University, Bouvé College of Health Sciences, Program in Urban Public Health, Boston, MA 02115-5096. Offers urban health (MPH). Part-time programs available. *Students:* 33 full-time, 14 part-time. 65 applicants, 69% accepted, 17 enrolled. In 2011, 6 master's awarded. *Degree requirements:* For master's, capstone project. *Entrance requirements:* For master's, GRE, minimum undergraduate GPA of 3.0, 3 letters of recommendation. Additional exam requirements/recommendations for international students: Required—TOEFL (minimum score 100 iBT). *Application deadline:* For fall admission, 5/1 for domestic students; for spring admission, 10/1 for domestic students. Applications are processed on a rolling basis. Application fee: $50. Electronic applications accepted. *Financial support:* Scholarships/grants available. *Unit head:* Dr. Shan Mohammed, Program Director, 617-373-7729, E-mail: s.mohammed@neu.edu. *Application contact:* Margaret Schnabel, Director of Graduate Admissions, 617-373-2708, E-mail: bouvegrad@neu.edu. Web site: http://www.northeastern.edu/bouve/programs/MPH/mpubhealth.html.

Northern Arizona University, Graduate College, College of Health and Human Services, Program in Clinical and Translational Sciences, Flagstaff, AZ 86011. Offers Certificate. *Entrance requirements:* Additional exam requirements/recommendations for international students: Required—TOEFL (minimum score 550 paper-based; 213 computer-based; 80 iBT), IELTS (minimum score 7). Application fee: $65. *Expenses:* Tuition, state resident: full-time $7190; part-time $355 per credit hour. Tuition, nonresident: full-time $18,092; part-time $1005 per credit hour. *Required fees:* $818; $328 per semester. *Financial support:* Applicants required to submit FAFSA. *Unit head:* Kelly Harris, Program and Education Coordinator, 928-523-1331, Fax: 928-523-9135, E-mail: kelly.harris@nau.edu. *Application contact:* April Sandoval, Coordinator, 928-523-4348, Fax: 928-523-8950, E-mail: april.sandoval@nau.edu. Web site: http://www4.nau.edu/academiccatalog/2010/Educational_Programs/Health_Professions/Interdisciplinary_Health_Policy_Institute/CertClinTranScience.htm.

Northern Illinois University, Graduate School, College of Health and Human Sciences, School of Nursing and Health Studies, De Kalb, IL 60115-2854. Offers nursing (MS); public health (MPH). *Accreditation:* AACN. Part-time programs available. *Faculty:* 12 full-time (11 women), 1 (woman) part-time/adjunct. *Students:* 28 full-time (21 women), 232 part-time (214 women); includes 61 minority (20 Black or African American, non-Hispanic/Latino; 24 Asian, non-Hispanic/Latino; 14 Hispanic/Latino; 3 Two or more races, non-Hispanic/Latino), 9 international. Average age 35. 118 applicants, 40% accepted, 20 enrolled. In 2011, 77 master's awarded. *Degree requirements:* For master's, thesis optional, internship. *Entrance requirements:* For master's, minimum GPA of 3.0 in last 60 hours, BA in nursing, nursing license. Additional exam requirements/recommendations for international students: Required—TOEFL (minimum score 550 paper-based; 213 computer-based). *Application deadline:* For fall admission, 6/1 for domestic students, 5/1 for international students; for spring admission, 11/1 for domestic students, 10/1 for international students. Applications are processed on a rolling basis. Application fee: $40. Electronic applications accepted. *Financial support:* In 2011–12, 7 research assistantships with full tuition reimbursements, 16 teaching assistantships with full tuition reimbursements were awarded; fellowships with full tuition reimbursements, career-related internships or fieldwork, Federal Work-Study, scholarships/grants, tuition waivers (full), and unspecified assistantships also available. Support available to part-time students. Financial award applicants required to submit FAFSA. *Faculty research:* Neonatal intensive care, stress and coping, refugee and immigrant issues, older adults, autoimmune disorders. *Unit head:* Dr. Brigid Lusk, Chair, 815-753-6550, Fax: 815-753-0814, E-mail: blusk@niu.edu. *Application contact:* Graduate School Office, 815-753-0395, E-mail: gradsch@niu.edu. Web site: http://www.chhs.niu.edu/nursing/.

Northwestern University, The Graduate School, Program in Public Health, Evanston, IL 60208. Offers MPH. *Accreditation:* CEPH. Part-time and evening/weekend programs available. *Entrance requirements:* For master's, GRE General Test. Additional exam requirements/recommendations for international students: Required—TOEFL. *Faculty research:* Cardiovascular epidemiology, cancer epidemiology, nutritional interventions for the prevention of cardiovascular disease and cancer, women's health, outcomes research.

Nova Southeastern University, Health Professions Division, College of Osteopathic Medicine, Fort Lauderdale, FL 33314-7796. Offers biomedical informatics (MS, Graduate Certificate), including biomedical informatics (MS), clinical informatics (Graduate Certificate), public health informatics (Graduate Certificate); disaster and emergency preparedness (MS); osteopathic medicine (DO); public health (MPH). *Accreditation:* AOsA. *Faculty:* 86 full-time (38 women), 1,072 part-time/adjunct (232 women). *Students:* 952 full-time (377 women), 18 part-time (5 women); includes 323 minority (24 Black or African American, non-Hispanic/Latino; 2 American Indian or Alaska Native, non-Hispanic/Latino; 175 Asian, non-Hispanic/Latino; 91 Hispanic/Latino; 31 Native Hawaiian or other Pacific Islander, non-Hispanic/Latino), 22 international. Average age 28. 3,628 applicants, 17% accepted, 241 enrolled. In 2011, 75 master's, 213 doctorates awarded. *Entrance requirements:* For master's, GRE, licensed healthcare professional or GRE; for doctorate, MCAT, biology, chemistry, organic chemistry, physics (all with labs), and English. *Application deadline:* For fall admission, 1/15 for domestic students. Applications are processed on a rolling basis. Application fee: $50. Electronic applications accepted. *Expenses:* Contact institution. *Financial support:* In 2011–12, 80 students received support, including 6 fellowships with full tuition reimbursements available (averaging $40,000 per year); research assistantships, teaching assistantships, career-related internships or fieldwork, Federal Work-Study, institutionally sponsored loans, and scholarships/grants also available. Financial award application deadline: 6/1; financial award applicants required to submit FAFSA. *Faculty research:* Teaching strategies, simulated patient use, HIV-AIDS education, minority health issues, managed care education. *Unit head:* Dr. Anthony J. Silavgni, Dean, 954-262-1407, E-mail: silvagni@hpd.nova.edu. *Application contact:* Anastasia Leveille, College of Medicine Admissions Counselor, 866-817-4068. Web site: http://www.medicine.nova.edu/.

The Ohio State University, College of Public Health, Columbus, OH 43210. Offers MHA, MPH, MS, PhD, JD/MHA, MHA/MBA, MHA/MD, MHA/MPA, MHA/MS, MPH/JD, MPH/MD, OD/MPH. *Accreditation:* CAHME; CEPH. *Faculty:* 40. *Students:* 208 full-time (143 women), 100 part-time (71 women); includes 56 minority (25 Black or African American, non-Hispanic/Latino; 22 Asian, non-Hispanic/Latino; 7 Hispanic/Latino; 2 Two or more races, non-Hispanic/Latino), 18 international. Average age 29. In 2011, 73 master's, 7 doctorates awarded. *Degree requirements:* For master's, thesis optional, practicum. *Entrance requirements:* For master's, GRE. Additional exam requirements/recommendations for international students: Required—TOEFL (minimum score 550 paper-based; 79 iBT), Michigan English Language Assessment Battery (minimum score 82). *Application deadline:* Applications are processed on a rolling basis. Application fee: $40 ($50 for international students). Electronic applications accepted. *Expenses:* Tuition, state resident: full-time $11,400. Tuition, nonresident: full-time $28,125. Tuition and fees vary according to course load, degree level, campus/location and program. *Financial support:* Fellowships and research assistantships available. *Unit head:* Stanley Lemeshow, Dean, 614-247-8196, E-mail: lemeshow.1@osu.edu. *Application contact:* Judy Dawson, Coordinator of Admissions and Recruitment, 614-292-8350, Fax: 614-247-0013, E-mail: jdawson@cph.osu.edu. Web site: http://cph.osu.edu/.

Ohio University, Graduate College, College of Health Sciences and Professions, Department of Social and Public Health, Athens, OH 45701-2979. Offers early child development and family life (MS); family studies (MS); health administration (MHA); public health (MPH); social work (MSW). *Accreditation:* CEPH. Part-time and evening/weekend programs available. Postbaccalaureate distance learning degree programs offered (no on-campus study). *Students:* 17 full-time (15 women), 380 part-time (259 women); includes 64 minority (38 Black or African American, non-Hispanic/Latino; 1 American Indian or Alaska Native, non-Hispanic/Latino; 14 Asian, non-Hispanic/Latino; 8 Hispanic/Latino; 3 Two or more races, non-Hispanic/Latino), 10 international. 114 applicants, 83% accepted, 72 enrolled. In 2011, 63 master's awarded. *Degree requirements:* For master's, capstone (MPH). *Entrance requirements:* For master's, GMAT, GRE General Test, previous course work in accounting, management, and statistics, previous public health background (MHA, MPH). Additional exam requirements/recommendations for international students: Required—TOEFL (minimum score 550 paper-based; 80 iBT) or IELTS (minimum score 6.5). *Application deadline:* Applications are processed on a rolling basis. Application fee: $50 ($55 for international students). Electronic applications accepted. *Expenses:* Contact institution. *Financial support:* Research assistantships with full tuition reimbursements, career-related internships or fieldwork, Federal Work-Study, institutionally sponsored loans, and unspecified assistantships available. Financial award applicants required to submit FAFSA. *Faculty research:* Health care management, health policy, managed care, health behavior, disease prevention. *Unit head:* Dr. Matthew Adeyanju, School Director, 740-593-1849, Fax: 740-593-0555, E-mail: adeyanju@ohio.edu. *Application contact:* Dr. Ruth Ann Althaus, Graduate Coordinator, Master of Health Administration Program, 740-597-2981, E-mail: althaus@ohio.edu. Web site: http://www.ohio.edu/chsp/sph/.

Old Dominion University, College of Health Sciences, ODU/EVMS Joint Program for the Master of Public Health, Norfolk, VA 23529. Offers environmental health (MPH); health promotion (MPH). Program offered jointly with Eastern Virginia Medical School. *Accreditation:* CEPH. Part-time and evening/weekend programs available. *Faculty:* 7 full-time (4 women), 6 part-time/adjunct (3 women). *Students:* 1 (woman) full-time, 49 part-time (34 women); includes 18 minority (9 Black or African American, non-Hispanic/Latino; 3 Asian, non-Hispanic/Latino; 5 Hispanic/Latino; 1 Two or more races, non-Hispanic/Latino), 1 international. Average age 29. 67 applicants, 60% accepted, 30 enrolled. In 2011, 28 master's awarded. *Degree requirements:* For master's, field practicum, capstone project. *Entrance requirements:* For master's, GRE, MCAT, minimum GPA of 2.75. Additional exam requirements/recommendations for international students: Required—TOEFL (minimum score 650 paper-based; 278 computer-based). *Application deadline:* For fall admission, 5/31 priority date for domestic students, 4/30 for international students. Application fee: $50 ($100 for international students). Electronic applications accepted. *Expenses:* Tuition, state resident: full-time $9096; part-time $379 per credit. Tuition, nonresident: full-time $23,064; part-time $961 per credit. *Required fees:* $127 per semester. One-time fee: $50. *Financial support:* In 2011–12, 3 teaching assistantships with partial tuition reimbursements (averaging $10,000 per year) were awarded; career-related internships or fieldwork, institutionally sponsored loans, and scholarships/grants also available. Financial award application deadline: 5/1; financial award applicants required to submit FAFSA. *Faculty research:* Community-based health research, public health research in environmental health and health promotion. *Total annual research expenditures:* $150,133. *Unit head:* Associate Director, 757-683-4259, Fax: 757-446-6121. *Application contact:* William Heffelfinger, Director of Graduate Admissions, 757-683-5554, Fax: 757-683-3255, E-mail: gradadmit@odu.edu. Web site: http://www.evms.edu/hlthprof/mph.

Old Dominion University, College of Health Sciences, Program in Community Health and Environmental Health, Norfolk, VA 23529. Offers MS. Part-time and evening/weekend programs available. Postbaccalaureate distance learning degree programs offered (no on-campus study). *Faculty:* 4 full-time (1 woman), 3 part-time/adjunct (1 woman). *Students:* 3 full-time (0 women), 12 part-time (4 women); includes 5 minority (2 Black or African American, non-Hispanic/Latino; 2 Asian, non-Hispanic/Latino; 1 Hispanic/Latino). Average age 30. 10 applicants, 80% accepted, 7 enrolled. In 2011, 5 master's awarded. *Degree requirements:* For master's, comprehensive exam, oral exam, written exam, practicum or thesis. *Entrance requirements:* For master's, GRE General Test, minimum GPA of 2.75. Additional exam requirements/recommendations for international students: Required—TOEFL (minimum score 650 paper-based; 278 computer-based). *Application deadline:* For fall admission, 8/1 priority date for domestic students, 7/1 for international students; for winter admission, 11/1 priority date for domestic students, 10/1 for international students; for spring admission, 4/1 priority date for domestic students, 3/1 for international students. Applications are processed on a rolling basis. Application fee: $50. Electronic applications accepted. *Expenses:* Tuition, state resident: full-time $9096; part-time $379 per credit. Tuition, nonresident: full-time $23,064; part-time $961 per credit. *Required fees:* $127 per semester. One-time fee: $50. *Financial support:* In 2011–12, 5 research assistantships with tuition reimbursements (averaging $14,000 per year), 2 teaching assistantships with partial tuition reimbursements (averaging $10,000 per year) were awarded; career-related internships or fieldwork, institutionally sponsored loans, scholarships/grants, and tuition waivers (partial) also available. Financial award applicants required to submit FAFSA. *Faculty research:* Toxicology, occupational health, environmental hazards. *Total annual research expenditures:* $150,133. *Unit head:* Dr. Anna Jeng, Graduate Program Director, 757-683-4594, Fax: 757-683-4410, E-mail: chpgpd@odu.edu. *Application contact:* William Heffelfinger, Director of Graduate Admissions, 757-683-5554, Fax: 757-683-3255, E-mail: gradadmit@odu.edu. Web site: http://hs.odu.edu/commhealth/.

Penn State Hershey Medical Center, College of Medicine, Graduate School Programs in the Biomedical Sciences, Graduate Program in Public Health, Hershey, PA 17033. Offers MPH. Part-time and evening/weekend programs available. *Students:* 13 full-time (12 women); includes 6 minority (4 Black or African American, non-Hispanic/Latino; 1 Asian, non-Hispanic/Latino; 1 Hispanic/Latino), 2 international. 47 applicants, 30% accepted, 13 enrolled. *Degree requirements:* For master's, thesis or alternative. *Entrance requirements:* Additional exam requirements/recommendations for international students: Required—TOEFL (minimum score 550 paper-based; 213 computer-based; 80 iBT). *Application deadline:* For fall admission, 1/31 for domestic students, 2/1 for international students. Applications are processed on a rolling basis. Application fee: $65. Electronic applications accepted. *Financial support:* Fellowships available. Financial award applicants required to submit FAFSA. *Unit head:* Dr. Roger T. Anderson, Director, 717-531-7178, E-mail: rta11@psu.edu. *Application contact:* Amanda Perry, Program Coordinator, 717-531-1502, Fax: 717-531-4359, E-mail: mphprogram@phs.psu.edu. Web site: http://med.psu.edu/web/phs/program/mph.

Penn State Hershey Medical Center, College of Medicine, Graduate School Programs in the Biomedical Sciences, Graduate Program in Public Health Sciences, Hershey, PA 17033. Offers MS. Part-time programs available. *Students:* 17 full-time (11 women); includes 5 minority (1 Black or African American, non-Hispanic/Latino; 2 Asian, non-Hispanic/Latino; 1 Hispanic/Latino; 1 Two or more races, non-Hispanic/Latino), 1 international. 47 applicants, 30% accepted, 13 enrolled. In 2011, 9 master's awarded. *Degree requirements:* For master's, thesis or alternative. *Entrance requirements:* Additional exam requirements/recommendations for international students: Required—TOEFL (minimum score 550 paper-based). *Application deadline:* For fall admission, 1/31 priority date for domestic students, 2/1 for international students. Applications are processed on a rolling basis. Application fee: $65. Electronic applications accepted. *Financial support:* Fellowships available. Financial award applicants required to submit FAFSA. *Faculty research:* Clinical trials, statistical methods in genetic epidemiology, genetic factors in nicotine dependence and dementia syndromes, health economics, cancer. *Unit head:* Dr. Douglas Leslie, Chair, 717-531-7178, Fax: 717-531-5779, E-mail: hes-grad-hmc@psu.edu. *Application contact:* Mardi Sawyer, Program Administrator, 717-531-7178, Fax: 717-531-5779, E-mail: hes-grad-hmc@psu.edu. Web site: http://www.pennstatehershey.org/web/phs/programs.

Ponce School of Medicine & Health Sciences, Program in Public Health, Ponce, PR 00732-7004. Offers epidemiology (Dr PH); public health (MPH). *Degree requirements:* For master's, one foreign language, comprehensive exam, thesis. *Entrance requirements:* For master's, GRE General Test or EXADEP, proficiency in Spanish and English, minimum GPA of 2.7, 3 letters of recommendation; for doctorate, GRE, proficiency in Spanish and English, minimum GPA of 3.0, letter of recommendation.

Portland State University, Graduate Studies, College of Urban and Public Affairs, School of Community Health, Portland, OR 97207-0751. Offers aging (Certificate); health education (MA, MS); health education and health promotion (MPH); health studies (MPA, MPH), including health administration. MPH offered jointly with Oregon State University, Oregon Health and Science University. *Accreditation:* CEPH. Part-time programs available. *Degree requirements:* For master's, oral and written exams. *Entrance requirements:* For master's, GRE General Test, 3 letters of recommendation, minimum GPA of 3.0. Additional exam requirements/recommendations for international students: Required—TOEFL (minimum score 550 paper-based; 213 computer-based).

Purdue University, Graduate School, College of Health and Human Sciences, Department of Nutrition Science, West Lafayette, IN 47907. Offers animal health (MS, PhD); biochemical and molecular nutrition (MS, PhD); growth and development (MS, PhD); human and clinical nutrition (MS, PhD); public health and education (MS, PhD). *Faculty:* 17 full-time (10 women), 14 part-time/adjunct (12 women). *Students:* 35 full-time (33 women), 2 part-time (both women); includes 3 minority (1 Black or African American, non-Hispanic/Latino; 2 Asian, non-Hispanic/Latino), 17 international. Average age 28. 120 applicants, 18% accepted, 11 enrolled. In 2011, 5 master's, 8 doctorates awarded. *Degree requirements:* For master's, thesis; for doctorate, thesis/dissertation. *Entrance requirements:* For master's and doctorate, GRE General Test, scores in verbal and quantitative areas must be greater than 1000 or 300 if the GRE was taken August 1, 2011 or after, minimum undergraduate GPA of 3.0 or equivalent. Additional exam requirements/recommendations for international students: Required—TOEFL (minimum score 600 paper-based; 77 iBT). *Application deadline:* For fall admission, 1/15 for domestic and international students. Applications are processed on a rolling basis. Application fee: $60 ($75 for international students). Electronic applications accepted. *Financial support:* Fellowships, research assistantships, and teaching assistantships available. Support available to part-time students. Financial award applicants required to submit FAFSA. *Faculty research:* Nutrient requirements, nutrient metabolism, nutrition and disease prevention. *Unit head:* Dr. Connie M. Weaver, Head, 765-494-8237, Fax: 765-494-0674, E-mail: weavercm@purdue.edu. *Application contact:* Marilyn McCammack, Graduate Secretary, 765-476-7492, E-mail: mccammac@purdue.edu. Web site: http://www.cfs.purdue.edu/fn/.

Purdue University, School of Veterinary Medicine and Graduate School, Graduate Programs in Veterinary Medicine, Department of Comparative Pathobiology, West Lafayette, IN 47907-2027. Offers comparative epidemiology and public health (MS); comparative epidemiology and public heath (PhD); comparative microbiology and immunology (MS, PhD); comparative pathobiology (MS, PhD); interdisciplinary studies (PhD), including microbial pathogenesis, molecular signaling and cancer biology, molecular virology; lab animal medicine (MS); veterinary anatomic pathology (MS); veterinary clinical pathology (MS). Terminal master's awarded for partial completion of doctoral program. *Degree requirements:* For master's, thesis (for some programs); for doctorate, thesis/dissertation. *Entrance requirements:* For master's and doctorate, GRE General Test. Additional exam requirements/recommendations for international students: Required—TOEFL (minimum score 575 paper-based; 232 computer-based), IELTS (minimum score 6.5), TWE (minimum score 4). Electronic applications accepted.

Public Health—General

Queen's University at Kingston, School of Graduate Studies and Research, Faculty of Health Sciences, Department of Community Health and Epidemiology, Kingston, ON K7L 3N6, Canada. Offers epidemiology (PhD); epidemiology and population health (M Sc); health services (M Sc); policy research and clinical epidemiology (M Sc); public health (MPH). Part-time programs available. *Degree requirements:* For master's, thesis. *Entrance requirements:* For master's, GRE General Test (strongly recommended). Additional exam requirements/recommendations for international students: Required—TOEFL (minimum score 600 paper-based; 250 computer-based). *Faculty research:* Cancer epidemiology, clinical trials, biostatistics health services research, health policy.

Rutgers, The State University of New Jersey, New Brunswick, Edward J. Bloustein School of Planning and Public Policy, Program in Public Health, Piscataway, NJ 08854-8097. Offers MPH, Dr PH, PhD, MBA/MPH, MD/MPH. MPH, Dr PH, PhD, MD/MPH, MBA/MPH offered jointly wtih University of Medicine and Dentistry of New Jersey. *Accreditation:* CEPH. Part-time and evening/weekend programs available. *Degree requirements:* For master's, internship; for doctorate, thesis/dissertation. *Entrance requirements:* For master's, GMAT, GRE General Test; for doctorate, GRE General Test, MPH (Dr PH). Additional exam requirements/recommendations for international students: Required—TOEFL. *Expenses:* Contact institution. *Faculty research:* Epidemiology, risk perception, statistical research design, health care utilization, health promotion.

St. Catherine University, Graduate Programs, Program in Holistic Health Studies, St. Paul, MN 55105. Offers MA. Part-time programs available. *Degree requirements:* For master's, thesis optional. *Entrance requirements:* For master's, 1 course in anatomy, physiology and psychology. Additional exam requirements/recommendations for international students: Required—TOEFL (minimum score 600 paper-based; 250 computer-based; 100 iBT). *Expenses:* Contact institution.

Saint Louis University, Graduate Education, School of Public Health and Graduate Education, Department of Health Management and Policy, St. Louis, MO 63103-2097. Offers health administration (MHA); health policy (MPH); public health studies (PhD). *Accreditation:* CAHME. Part-time programs available. *Degree requirements:* For master's, comprehensive exam, internship. *Entrance requirements:* For master's, GMAT or GRE General Test, LSAT, MCAT, letters of recommendation, resume. Additional exam requirements/recommendations for international students: Required—TOEFL (minimum score 525 paper-based; 194 computer-based). *Faculty research:* Management of HIV/AIDS, rural health services, prevention of asthma, genetics and health services use, health insurance and access to care.

Salus University, College of Health Sciences, Elkins Park, PA 19027-1598. Offers physician assistant (MMS); public health (MPH). *Accreditation:* ARC-PA. *Entrance requirements:* For master's, GRE (recommended). Additional exam requirements/recommendations for international students: Required—TOEFL. Electronic applications accepted.

San Diego State University, Graduate and Research Affairs, College of Health and Human Services, Graduate School of Public Health, San Diego, CA 92182. Offers environmental health (MPH); epidemiology (MPH, PhD), including biostatistics (MPH); global emergency preparedness and response (MS); global health (PhD); health behavior (PhD); health promotion (MPH); health services administration (MPH); toxicology (MS); MPH/MA; MSW/MPH. *Accreditation:* ABET (one or more programs are accredited); CAHME (one or more programs are accredited); CEPH (one or more programs are accredited). Part-time programs available. *Degree requirements:* For master's, comprehensive exam (for some programs), thesis (for some programs); for doctorate, thesis/dissertation. *Entrance requirements:* For master's, GMAT (MPH in health services administration), GRE General Test; for doctorate, GRE General Test. Additional exam requirements/recommendations for international students: Required—TOEFL. *Faculty research:* Evaluation of tobacco, AIDS prevalence and prevention, mammography, infant death project, Alzheimer's in elderly Chinese.

San Francisco State University, Division of Graduate Studies, College of Health and Human Services, Department of Health Education, San Francisco, CA 94132-1722. Offers MPH. *Accreditation:* CEPH. Part-time programs available. *Students:* Average age 36. *Application deadline:* Applications are processed on a rolling basis. *Unit head:* Dr. Mary Beth Love, Chair, 415-338-1413, E-mail: love@sfsu.edu. *Application contact:* Sally Geisse, Assistant Graduate Coordinator, 415-338-1413, E-mail: sgeisse@sfsu.edu. Web site: http://healthed.sfsu.edu/.

San Jose State University, Graduate Studies and Research, College of Applied Sciences and Arts, Department of Health Science, San Jose, CA 95192-0001. Offers applied social gerontology (Certificate); community health education (MPH). *Accreditation:* CEPH (one or more programs are accredited). Postbaccalaureate distance learning degree programs offered. *Entrance requirements:* For master's, GRE General Test. Electronic applications accepted. *Faculty research:* Behavioral science in occupational and health care settings, epidemiology in health care settings.

Sarah Lawrence College, Graduate Studies, Program in Health Advocacy, Bronxville, NY 10708-5999. Offers MA. Part-time programs available. *Degree requirements:* For master's, fieldwork. *Entrance requirements:* For master's, previous course work in biology and microeconomics, minimum B average in undergraduate course work. Additional exam requirements/recommendations for international students: Required—TOEFL (minimum score 600 paper-based). *Expenses:* Contact institution.

Simon Fraser University, Graduate Studies, Faculty of Health Sciences, Burnaby, BC V5A 1S6, Canada. Offers population and public health (M Sc). *Degree requirements:* For master's, thesis, practicum or project.

Southern Connecticut State University, School of Graduate Studies, School of Health and Human Services, Department of Public Health, New Haven, CT 06515-1355. Offers MPH. *Accreditation:* CEPH. Part-time and evening/weekend programs available. *Faculty:* 10 full-time (7 women), 1 (woman) part-time/adjunct. *Students:* 21 full-time (15 women), 27 part-time (24 women); includes 19 minority (10 Black or African American, non-Hispanic/Latino; 3 Asian, non-Hispanic/Latino; 5 Hispanic/Latino; 1 Two or more races, non-Hispanic/Latino), 2 international. 174 applicants, 16% accepted, 13 enrolled. In 2011, 19 master's awarded. *Degree requirements:* For master's, thesis or alternative. *Entrance requirements:* For master's, minimum undergraduate QPA of 3.0 in graduate major field or 2.5 overall, interview. *Application deadline:* For fall admission, 3/15 for domestic students. Application fee: $50. Electronic applications accepted. *Expenses:* Tuition, state resident: full-time $5137; part-time $413 per credit. *Required fees:* $4008; $55 per term. *Financial support:* In 2011–12, 1 teaching assistantship was awarded; career-related internships or fieldwork also available. Financial award application deadline: 4/15; financial award applicants required to submit FAFSA. *Unit head:* Dr. William Faraclas, Chairperson, 203-392-6950, Fax: 203-392-6965, E-mail: faraclas@southernct.edu. *Application contact:* Dr. Deborah Flynn, Graduate Coordinator, 203-392-6969, Fax: 203-392-6965, E-mail: flynnd1@southernct.edu.

State University of New York Downstate Medical Center, College of Medicine, Program in Public Health, Brooklyn, NY 11203-2098. Offers urban and immigrant health (MPH); MD/MPH. *Accreditation:* CEPH. Part-time programs available. *Degree requirements:* For master's, practicum. *Entrance requirements:* For master's, GRE, MCAT or OAT, 2 letters of recommendation, minimum undergraduate GPA of 3.0. Additional exam requirements/recommendations for international students: Required—TOEFL (minimum score 550 paper-based).

Stony Brook University, State University of New York, Stony Brook University Medical Center, Health Sciences Center, School of Medicine, Program in Public Health, Stony Brook, NY 11794. Offers community health (MPH); evaluation sciences (MPH); family violence (MPH); health economics (MPH); population health (MPH); substance abuse (MPH). *Accreditation:* CEPH. *Entrance requirements:* For master's, GRE, 3 references. Additional exam requirements/recommendations for international students: Required—TOEFL. Electronic applications accepted. *Faculty research:* Population health, health service research, health economics.

Syracuse University, Maxwell School of Citizenship and Public Affairs, Program in Public Health, Syracuse, NY 13244. Offers CAS. *Students:* 10 full-time (8 women), 7 part-time (5 women); includes 2 minority (1 Asian, non-Hispanic/Latino; 1 Two or more races, non-Hispanic/Latino). Average age 33. *Expenses: Tuition:* Part-time $1206 per credit. *Unit head:* Dr. Michael Wasylenko, Interim Dean, 315-443-4000, Fax: 315-443-3385. *Application contact:* Diana Hahn, Associate Director, Graduate Recruitment and Retention, 315-443-4492, Fax: 315-443-3423, E-mail: grad@syr.edu.

Teachers College, Columbia University, Graduate Faculty of Education, Department of Health and Behavior Studies, Program in Nutrition and Public Health, New York, NY 10027-6696. Offers MS, Ed D. *Unit head:* Prof. Isobel R. Contento, Program Coordinator, 212-678-3950. *Application contact:* Elizabeth Puleio, Admissions Contact, 212-678-3710.

Temple University, Health Sciences Center, College of Health Professions and Social Work, Department of Public Health, Philadelphia, PA 19122-6096. Offers environmental health (MS); epidemiology (MS); public health (MPH, PhD); school health education (Ed M). *Accreditation:* CEPH (one or more programs are accredited). Part-time and evening/weekend programs available. *Faculty:* 15 full-time (8 women). *Students:* 62 full-time (44 women), 28 part-time (25 women); includes 24 minority (14 Black or African American, non-Hispanic/Latino; 5 Asian, non-Hispanic/Latino; 5 Hispanic/Latino), 7 international. Average age 29. 92 applicants, 68% accepted, 29 enrolled. In 2011, 30 master's, 4 doctorates awarded. Terminal master's awarded for partial completion of doctoral program. *Degree requirements:* For doctorate, thesis/dissertation. *Entrance requirements:* For master's and doctorate, minimum undergraduate GPA of 3.0. Additional exam requirements/recommendations for international students: Required—TOEFL (minimum score 550 paper-based; 213 computer-based; 79 iBT). Application fee: $50. Electronic applications accepted. *Expenses:* Tuition, state resident: full-time $12,366; part-time $687 per credit hour. Tuition, nonresident: full-time $17,298; part-time $961 per credit hour. *Required fees:* $590; $213 per year. *Financial support:* Fellowships with tuition reimbursements, research assistantships with tuition reimbursements, teaching assistantships with tuition reimbursements, career-related internships or fieldwork, Federal Work-Study, institutionally sponsored loans, scholarships/grants, and tuition waivers (partial) available. Financial award application deadline: 1/15; financial award applicants required to submit FAFSA. *Faculty research:* Program development and evaluation in HIV prevention, violence prevention, women's health policy, psychosocial aspects of disability. *Unit head:* Dr. Alice J. Hausman, Chair, 215-204-5112, Fax: 215-204-1854, E-mail: publichealth@temple.edu. *Application contact:* Tara Schumacher, Coordinator of Outreach, 215-204-6575, Fax: 215-204-8781, E-mail: tara.schumacher@temple.edu. Web site: http://chpsw.temple.edu/publichealth/.

Texas A&M Health Science Center, School of Rural Public Health, College Station, TX 77840. Offers environmental/occupational health (MPH); epidemiology/biostatistics (MPH); health policy/management (MPH); social and behavioral health (MPH). *Accreditation:* CEPH. Part-time programs available. Postbaccalaureate distance learning degree programs offered (no on-campus study). *Degree requirements:* For master's, thesis optional. *Entrance requirements:* For master's, GRE General Test, minimum undergraduate GPA of 3.0. Electronic applications accepted. *Faculty research:* Tobacco cessation, youth health risk.

Texas A&M University, College of Veterinary Medicine and Biomedical Sciences, Department of Veterinary Integrative Biosciences, College Station, TX 77843. Offers epidemiology (MS); food safety/toxicology/environmental health (MS); science and technology journalism (MS); veterinary public health (MS). *Faculty:* 23. *Students:* 34 full-time (18 women), 12 part-time (9 women); includes 10 minority (2 Black or African American, non-Hispanic/Latino; 5 Asian, non-Hispanic/Latino; 3 Hispanic/Latino), 19 international. Average age 30. Terminal master's awarded for partial completion of doctoral program. *Degree requirements:* For master's, comprehensive exam, thesis. *Entrance requirements:* For master's, GRE General Test, minimum undergraduate GPA of 3.0. Additional exam requirements/recommendations for international students: Required—TOEFL. *Application deadline:* For fall admission, 7/15 priority date for domestic students, 4/1 for international students; for spring admission, 10/1 priority date for domestic students, 9/15 for international students. Applications are processed on a rolling basis. Application fee: $50 ($75 for international students). Electronic applications accepted. *Expenses:* Tuition, state resident: full-time $5437; part-time $226.55 per credit hour. Tuition, nonresident: full-time $12,949; part-time $539.55 per credit hour. *Required fees:* $2741. *Financial support:* In 2011–12, fellowships (averaging $18,000 per year), research assistantships (averaging $15,600 per year), teaching assistantships (averaging $15,600 per year) were awarded; institutionally sponsored loans, unspecified assistantships, and clinical associateships also available. Financial award application deadline: 7/15; financial award applicants required to submit FAFSA. *Faculty research:* Metal toxicology, reproductive biology, genetics of neural development, developmental biology, environmental toxicology. *Unit head:* Dr. Evelyn Tiffany-Castiglioni, Head, 979-458-1077, E-mail: c-tiffany@tamu.edu. *Application contact:* Graduate Admissions, 979-845-1044, E-mail: admissions@tamu.edu. Web site: http://vetmed.tamu.edu/vibs.

Thomas Jefferson University, Jefferson School of Population Health, Program in Public Health, Philadelphia, PA 19107. Offers MPH, Certificate. *Accreditation:* CEPH. Part-time and evening/weekend programs available. Postbaccalaureate distance learning degree programs offered (minimal on-campus study). Terminal master's awarded for partial completion of doctoral program. *Degree requirements:* For master's, capstone project or thesis. *Entrance requirements:* For master's, GRE or other graduate examination, 2 letters of recommendation, interview, curriculum vitae. Additional exam requirements/recommendations for international students: Required—TOEFL (minimum score 250 computer-based; 100 iBT). Electronic applications accepted.

Touro College, School of Health Sciences, Bay Shore, NY 11706. Offers occupational therapy (MS); Oriental medicine (MSOM); physical therapy (DPT); public health (MPH); speech-language pathology (MS). *Faculty:* 20 full-time, 94 part-time/adjunct. *Students:* 136. *Expenses:* Contact institution. *Financial support:* Fellowships available. *Unit head:* Dr. Louis Primavera, Dean, 516-673-3200. *Application contact:* Dean, School of Health Sciences, 516-673-3200.

Touro University, Graduate Programs, Vallejo, CA 94592. Offers education (MA); medical health sciences (MS); osteopathic medicine (DO); pharmacy (Pharm D); public health (MPH). *Accreditation:* AOsA; ARC-PA. Part-time and evening/weekend programs available. *Faculty:* 93 full-time (52 women), 55 part-time/adjunct (28 women). *Students:* 1,402 full-time (851 women). 6,914 applicants, 12% accepted, 503 enrolled. *Degree*

requirements: For master's, comprehensive exam, thesis; for doctorate, comprehensive exam. *Entrance requirements:* For doctorate, BS/BA. *Application deadline:* For fall admission, 3/15 for domestic students; for winter admission, 12/1 for domestic students. Applications are processed on a rolling basis. Application fee: $100. Electronic applications accepted. *Expenses: Tuition:* Full-time $25,000; part-time $575 per credit. *Required fees:* $250 per year. Tuition and fees vary according to course level, course load, degree level and program. *Financial support:* Fellowships, research assistantships, teaching assistantships, Federal Work-Study, and scholarships/grants available. Support available to part-time students. Financial award applicants required to submit FAFSA. *Faculty research:* Cancer, heart disease. *Application contact:* Steve Davis, Associate Director of Admissions, 707-638-5270, Fax: 707-638-5250, E-mail: steven.davis@tu.edu.

Trident University International, College of Health Sciences, Cypress, CA 90630. Offers MS, PhD, Certificate. Part-time and evening/weekend programs available. Postbaccalaureate distance learning degree programs offered (no on-campus study). *Degree requirements:* For doctorate, comprehensive exam, thesis/dissertation. *Entrance requirements:* For master's, minimum GPA of 2.5 (students with GPA 3.0 or greater may transfer up to 30% of graduate level credits); for doctorate, minimum GPA of 3.4. Additional exam requirements/recommendations for international students: Required—TOEFL. Electronic applications accepted.

Trinity Washington University, School of Professional Studies, Washington, DC 20017-1094. Offers business administration (MBA); communication (MA); international security studies (MA); organizational management (MSA), including federal program management, human resource management, nonprofit management, organizational development, public and community health. Part-time and evening/weekend programs available. *Degree requirements:* For master's, thesis (for some programs), capstone project (MSA). *Entrance requirements:* For master's, minimum GPA of 2.5. Additional exam requirements/recommendations for international students: Required—TOEFL (minimum score 550 paper-based; 213 computer-based).

Tufts University, School of Medicine, Public Health and Professional Degree Programs, Boston, MA 02111. Offers biomedical sciences (MS); health communication (MS); pain research, education and policy (MS); public health (MPH). MS programs offered jointly with Emerson College. *Accreditation:* CEPH (one or more programs are accredited). Part-time and evening/weekend programs available. *Faculty:* 70 full-time (27 women), 35 part-time/adjunct (15 women). *Students:* 271 full-time (153 women), 69 part-time (57 women); includes 121 minority (21 Black or African American, non-Hispanic/Latino; 66 Asian, non-Hispanic/Latino; 20 Hispanic/Latino; 3 Native Hawaiian or other Pacific Islander, non-Hispanic/Latino; 11 Two or more races, non-Hispanic/Latino), 10 international. Average age 27. 906 applicants, 54% accepted, 199 enrolled. In 2011, 152 master's awarded. *Degree requirements:* For master's, thesis (for some programs). *Entrance requirements:* For master's, GRE General Test, MCAT, GMAT. Additional exam requirements/recommendations for international students: Required—TOEFL (minimum score 270 computer-based; 110 iBT). *Application deadline:* For fall admission, 1/15 priority date for domestic students, 1/15 for international students; for spring admission, 10/25 priority date for domestic students, 10/25 for international students. Applications are processed on a rolling basis. Application fee: $70. Electronic applications accepted. *Expenses:* Contact institution. *Financial support:* In 2011–12, 17 students received support, including 1 fellowship (averaging $3,000 per year), 35 teaching assistantships (averaging $1,700 per year); Federal Work-Study and scholarships/grants also available. Support available to part-time students. Financial award application deadline: 2/4; financial award applicants required to submit FAFSA. *Faculty research:* Environmental and occupational health, nutrition, epidemiology, health communication, health services management and policy, biostatics, protein interaction, mRNA processing, vascular pathology. *Unit head:* Dr. Aviva Must, Dean, 617-636-0935, Fax: 617-636-0898, E-mail: aviva.must@tufts.edu. *Application contact:* Emily Keily, Director of Admissions, 617-636-0935, Fax: 617-636-0898, E-mail: med-phpd@tufts.edu. Web site: http://publichealth.tufts.edu.

Tulane University, School of Public Health and Tropical Medicine, New Orleans, LA 70118-5669. Offers MHA, MMM, MPH, MPHTM, MS, MSPH, Dr PH, PhD, Sc D, Diploma, JD/MHA, JD/MSPH, MD/MPH, MD/MPHTM, MD/MSPH, MD/PhD, MSW/MPH. MS, PhD offered through the Graduate School. *Accreditation:* CAHME (one or more programs are accredited); CEPH (one or more programs are accredited). Part-time and evening/weekend programs available. Postbaccalaureate distance learning degree programs offered (no on-campus study). Terminal master's awarded for partial completion of doctoral program. *Degree requirements:* For master's, comprehensive exam (for some programs); for doctorate, comprehensive exam, thesis/dissertation. *Entrance requirements:* For master's and doctorate, GRE General Test. Additional exam requirements/recommendations for international students: Required—TOEFL. Electronic applications accepted. *Expenses:* Contact institution.

Uniformed Services University of the Health Sciences, School of Medicine, Graduate Programs in the Biomedical Sciences and Public Health, Bethesda, MD 20814. Offers emerging infectious diseases (PhD); medical and clinical psychology (PhD), including clinical psychology, medical and clinical psychology, medical psychology; molecular and cell biology (MS, PhD); neuroscience (PhD); preventive medicine and biometrics (MPH, MS, MSPH, MTMH, Dr PH, PhD), including environmental health sciences (PhD), healthcare administration and policy (MS), medical zoology (PhD), public health (MPH, MSPH, Dr PH), tropical medicine and hygiene (MTMH). *Faculty:* 372 full-time (119 women), 4,044 part-time/adjunct (908 women). *Students:* 176 full-time (96 women); includes 31 minority (6 Black or African American, non-Hispanic/Latino; 4 American Indian or Alaska Native, non-Hispanic/Latino; 14 Asian, non-Hispanic/Latino; 7 Hispanic/Latino), 11 international. Average age 28. 278 applicants, 20% accepted, 47 enrolled. In 2011, 36 master's, 17 doctorates awarded. Terminal master's awarded for partial completion of doctoral program. *Degree requirements:* For master's, comprehensive exam, thesis or alternative; for doctorate, comprehensive exam, thesis/dissertation, qualifying exam. *Entrance requirements:* For master's, GRE General Test; for doctorate, GRE General Test, minimum GPA of 3.0. Additional exam requirements/recommendations for international students: Required—TOEFL. *Application deadline:* For fall admission, 1/1 priority date for domestic students, 1/1 for international students. Applications are processed on a rolling basis. Application fee: $0. Electronic applications accepted. *Financial support:* In 2011–12, fellowships with full tuition reimbursements (averaging $26,000 per year), research assistantships with full tuition reimbursements (averaging $26,000 per year) were awarded; career-related internships or fieldwork, scholarships/grants, health care benefits, and tuition waivers (full) also available. *Unit head:* Dr. Eleanor S. Metcalf, Associate Dean, 301-295-1104, E-mail: emetcalf@usuhs.edu. *Application contact:* Elena Marina Sherman, Program Administrative Specialist, 301-295-3913, Fax: 301-295-6772, E-mail: elena.sherman@usuhs.mil. Web site: http://www.usuhs.mil/graded.

Uniformed Services University of the Health Sciences, School of Medicine, Graduate Programs in the Biomedical Sciences and Public Health, Department of Preventive Medicine and Biometrics, Program in Public Health, Bethesda, MD 20814-4799. Offers MPH, MSPH, Dr PH. *Accreditation:* CEPH (one or more programs are accredited). *Faculty:* 43 full-time (14 women), 143 part-time/adjunct (25 women). *Students:* 52 full-time (17 women); includes 12 minority (1 Black or African American, non-Hispanic/Latino; 3 American Indian or Alaska Native, non-Hispanic/Latino; 6 Asian, non-Hispanic/Latino; 2 Hispanic/Latino), 9 international. Average age 30. 71 applicants, 63% accepted, 32 enrolled. In 2011, 37 master's, 2 doctorates awarded. *Degree requirements:* For master's, comprehensive exam; for doctorate, thesis/dissertation, qualifying exam. *Entrance requirements:* For master's, GRE General Test; for doctorate, GRE General Test, minimum GPA of 3.0. Additional exam requirements/recommendations for international students: Required—TOEFL. *Application deadline:* For fall admission, 1/1 priority date for domestic students. Applications are processed on a rolling basis. Application fee: $0. *Financial support:* In 2011–12, fellowships with full tuition reimbursements (averaging $26,000 per year) were awarded; scholarships/grants, health care benefits, and tuition waivers (full) also available. *Faculty research:* Epidemiology, biostatistics, health services administration, environmental and occupational health, tropical public health. *Unit head:* Dr. David Cruess, Director, 301-295-3465, Fax: 301-295-1933, E-mail: dcruess@usuhs.mil. *Application contact:* Elena Marina Sherman, Program Administrative Specialist, 301-295-3913, Fax: 301-295-6772, E-mail: elena.sherman@usuhs.mil. Web site: http://www.usuhs.mil/pmb.

Université de Montréal, Faculty of Arts and Sciences, Program in Societies, Public Policies and Health, Montréal, QC H3C 3J7, Canada. Offers DESS.

Université de Montréal, Faculty of Medicine, Program in Communal and Public Health, Montréal, QC H3C 3J7, Canada. Offers community health (M Sc, DESS); public health (PhD). *Accreditation:* CEPH. Part-time programs available. Terminal master's awarded for partial completion of doctoral program. *Degree requirements:* For master's, thesis; for doctorate, thesis/dissertation, general exam. *Entrance requirements:* For master's and doctorate, proficiency in French, knowledge of English; for DESS, proficiency in French. Electronic applications accepted. *Faculty research:* Epidemiology, health services utilization, health promotion and education, health behaviors, poverty and child health.

University at Albany, State University of New York, School of Public Health, Program in Public Health, Rensselaer, NY 12144. Offers MPH, Dr PH. *Degree requirements:* For master's, thesis; for doctorate, thesis/dissertation. *Entrance requirements:* For master's and doctorate, GRE General Test. Additional exam requirements/recommendations for international students: Required—TOEFL (minimum score 550 paper-based; 213 computer-based). Electronic applications accepted.

University at Buffalo, the State University of New York, Graduate School, School of Public Health and Health Professions, Department of Social and Preventive Medicine, Buffalo, NY 14214. Offers epidemiology (MS, PhD); public health (MPH). Part-time programs available. *Faculty:* 13 full-time (7 women), 6 part-time/adjunct (3 women). *Students:* 41 full-time (27 women), 15 part-time (13 women); includes 7 minority (3 Black or African American, non-Hispanic/Latino; 4 Asian, non-Hispanic/Latino), 10 international. Average age 29. 111 applicants, 50% accepted, 18 enrolled. In 2011, 18 master's, 3 doctorates awarded. Terminal master's awarded for partial completion of doctoral program. *Degree requirements:* For master's, comprehensive exam, thesis; for doctorate, comprehensive exam, thesis/dissertation. *Entrance requirements:* For master's and doctorate, GRE General Test. Additional exam requirements/recommendations for international students: Required—TOEFL (minimum score 600 paper-based; 250 computer-based; 100 iBT). *Application deadline:* For fall admission, 1/15 priority date for domestic students, 1/15 for international students. Applications are processed on a rolling basis. Application fee: $50. Electronic applications accepted. *Financial support:* In 2011–12, 17 students received support, including 5 fellowships with full tuition reimbursements available (averaging $22,000 per year), 7 research assistantships with full tuition reimbursements available (averaging $20,000 per year); teaching assistantships with full tuition reimbursements available, career-related internships or fieldwork, Federal Work-Study, institutionally sponsored loans, health care benefits, and unspecified assistantships also available. Financial award application deadline: 2/1; financial award applicants required to submit FAFSA. *Faculty research:* Epidemiology of cancer, nutrition, infectious diseases, epidemiology of environmental, women's health and CVD research. *Unit head:* Dr. Jo Freudenheim, Chair, 716-829-5375, Fax: 716-829-2979, E-mail: jfreuden@buffalo.edu. *Application contact:* Dr. Carl Li, Director of Graduate Studies, 716-829-5382, Fax: 716-829-2979, E-mail: carlli@buffalo.edu. Web site: http://sphhp.buffalo.edu/spm/.

See Display on page 846 and Close-Up on page 867.

The University of Akron, Graduate School, College of Nursing, Akron, OH 44325. Offers nursing (MSN, PhD); public health (MPH). PhD offered jointly with Kent State University. *Accreditation:* AACN; AANA/CANAEP (one or more programs are accredited). Part-time programs available. *Faculty:* 41 full-time (40 women), 60 part-time/adjunct (58 women). *Students:* 68 full-time (59 women), 287 part-time (252 women); includes 32 minority (20 Black or African American, non-Hispanic/Latino; 5 Asian, non-Hispanic/Latino; 3 Hispanic/Latino; 4 Two or more races, non-Hispanic/Latino), 5 international. Average age 34. 202 applicants, 72% accepted, 85 enrolled. In 2011, 87 master's, 1 doctorate awarded. *Degree requirements:* For doctorate, one foreign language, thesis/dissertation, qualifying exam. *Entrance requirements:* For master's, current Ohio state license as registered nurse, three letters of reference, 300-word essay, interview with program coordinator; for doctorate, GRE, minimum GPA of 3.0, MSN, nursing license or eligibility for licensure, writing sample, letters of recommendation, interview, resume, personal statement of research interests and career goals. Additional exam requirements/recommendations for international students: Required—TOEFL (minimum score 550 paper-based; 213 computer-based; 79 iBT). *Application deadline:* For fall admission, 7/15 for domestic and international students. Applications are processed on a rolling basis. Application fee: $30 ($40 for international students). Electronic applications accepted. *Expenses:* Tuition, state resident: full-time $7038; part-time $391 per credit hour. Tuition, nonresident: full-time $12,051; part-time $670 per credit hour. *Required fees:* $1274; $34 per credit hour. *Financial support:* In 2011–12, 10 teaching assistantships with full tuition reimbursements were awarded; career-related internships or fieldwork and Federal Work-Study also available. *Faculty research:* Health promotion and chronic disease prevention; mental health and psychosocial resilience; gerontological health, trauma and violence; gut oxygenation during shock and trauma, simulation and the pedagogy of teaching and learning. *Total annual research expenditures:* $618,835. *Unit head:* Dr. Roberta DePompei, Interim Dean, 330-972-6114, E-mail: rdepom1@uakron.edu. *Application contact:* Dr. Marlene Huff, Graduate Director, 330-972-7555, E-mail: mhuff@uakron.edu. Web site: http://www.uakron.edu/nursing/.

The University of Alabama at Birmingham, School of Public Health, Program in Public Health, Birmingham, AL 35294. Offers MPH, MSPH, DPH. *Accreditation:* CEPH. *Expenses:* Tuition, state resident: full-time $5922; part-time $309 per hour. Tuition, nonresident: full-time $13,428; part-time $726 per hour. Tuition and fees vary according to program. *Unit head:* Dr. Peter Ginter, Chair, 205-975-8970, Fax: 205-975-5484.

University of Alaska Anchorage, College of Health, Department of Health Sciences, Anchorage, AK 99508. Offers public health practice (MPH). *Accreditation:* CEPH. Part-time programs available. *Degree requirements:* For master's, comprehensive exam, thesis. *Entrance requirements:* For master's, writing sample. Additional exam requirements/recommendations for international students: Required—TOEFL (minimum score 550 paper-based; 213 computer-based).

Public Health—General

University of Alberta, School of Public Health, Department of Public Health Sciences, Edmonton, AB T6G 2E1, Canada. Offers clinical epidemiology (M Sc, MPH); environmental and occupational health (MPH); environmental health sciences (M Sc); epidemiology (M Sc); global health (M Sc, MPH); health policy and management (MPH); health policy research (M Sc); health technology assessment (MPH); occupational health (M Sc); population health (M Sc); public health leadership (MPH); public health sciences (PhD); quantitative methods (MPH). *Accreditation:* CEPH (one or more programs are accredited). Terminal master's awarded for partial completion of doctoral program. *Degree requirements:* For master's, thesis (for some programs); for doctorate, thesis/dissertation. *Entrance requirements:* For master's, GMAT or GRE General Test. Additional exam requirements/recommendations for international students: Required—TOEFL (minimum score 550 paper-based; 213 computer-based) or IELTS (minimum score 6). Electronic applications accepted. *Faculty research:* Biostatistics, health promotion and socio-behavioral health science.

The University of Arizona, Mel and Enid Zuckerman College of Public Health, Tucson, AZ 85724. Offers MPH, MS, Dr PH, PhD. *Accreditation:* CEPH. *Faculty:* 21 full-time (12 women), 9 part-time/adjunct (6 women). *Students:* 235 full-time (169 women), 106 part-time (82 women); includes 119 minority (16 Black or African American, non-Hispanic/Latino; 12 American Indian or Alaska Native, non-Hispanic/Latino; 16 Asian, non-Hispanic/Latino; 38 Hispanic/Latino; 37 Two or more races, non-Hispanic/Latino), 29 international. Average age 32. 483 applicants, 41% accepted, 62 enrolled. In 2011, 71 master's, 8 doctorates awarded. *Entrance requirements:* Additional exam requirements/recommendations for international students: Required—TOEFL (minimum score 550 paper-based; 213 computer-based; 79 iBT). *Application deadline:* For fall admission, 1/1 for domestic and international students. Applications are processed on a rolling basis. Application fee: $75. Electronic applications accepted. *Expenses:* Tuition, state resident: full-time $10,840. Tuition, nonresident: full-time $25,802. *Financial support:* In 2011–12, 26 research assistantships with full tuition reimbursements (averaging $23,100 per year), 41 teaching assistantships with full tuition reimbursements (averaging $18,327 per year) were awarded; health care benefits and unspecified assistantships also available. *Total annual research expenditures:* $11.7 million. *Unit head:* Dr. Iman Hakim, Interim Dean, 520-626-7083, E-mail: ihakim@email.arizona.edu. *Application contact:* Lorraine Varela, Special Assistant to the Dean, 520-626-3201, E-mail: varelal@coph.arizona.edu. Web site: http://www.publichealth.arizona.edu/.

The University of British Columbia, Faculty of Medicine, School of Population and Public Health, Vancouver, BC V6T 1Z3, Canada. Offers health administration (MHA); health care and epidemiology (MH Sc, PhD); public health (MPH). *Accreditation:* CEPH (one or more programs are accredited). Postbaccalaureate distance learning degree programs offered (minimal on-campus study). *Degree requirements:* For master's, thesis (for some programs), major paper (MH Sc), research project (MHA); for doctorate, thesis/dissertation. *Entrance requirements:* For master's, GRE General Test or GMAT, PCAT, MCAT (MHA), MD or equivalent (for MH Sc); 4-year undergraduate degree from accredited university with minimum B+ overall academic average and in math or statistics course at undergraduate level (for MPH); 4-year undergraduate degree from accredited university with minimum B+ overall academic average plus work experience (for MHA); for doctorate, master's degree from accredited university with minimum B+ overall academic average and in math or statistics course at undergraduate level. Additional exam requirements/recommendations for international students: Required—TOEFL. Electronic applications accepted. *Faculty research:* Population and public health, clinical epidemiology, epidemiology and biostatistics, global health and vulnerable populations, health care services and systems, occupational and environmental health, public health emerging threats and rapid response, social and life course determinants of health, health administration.

University of California, Berkeley, Graduate Division, Haas School of Business and School of Public Health, Concurrent MBA/MPH Program, Berkeley, CA 94720-1500. Offers MBA/MPH. *Accreditation:* AACSB; CEPH. *Faculty:* 77 full-time (18 women), 152 part-time/adjunct (24 women). *Students:* 37 full-time (23 women); includes 15 minority (13 Asian, non-Hispanic/Latino; 1 Hispanic/Latino; 1 Two or more races, non-Hispanic/Latino), 9 international. Average age 28. *Entrance requirements:* Additional exam requirements/recommendations for international students: Required—TOEFL. Application fee: $200. Electronic applications accepted. *Financial support:* Fellowships with tuition reimbursements, teaching assistantships with tuition reimbursements, career-related internships or fieldwork, scholarships/grants, and unspecified assistantships available. Financial award applicants required to submit FAFSA. *Unit head:* Prof. Kristi Raube, Director, Health Services Management Program, 510-642-5023, Fax: 510-643-6659, E-mail: raube@haas.berkeley.edu. *Application contact:* Lee Forgue, Student Affairs Officer, 510-642-5023, Fax: 510-643-6659, E-mail: eilis@haas.berkeley.edu. Web site: http://www.haas.berkeley.edu/.

University of California, Berkeley, Graduate Division, School of Public Health, Group in Environmental Health Sciences, Berkeley, CA 94720-1500. Offers MPH, MS, Dr PH, PhD. *Degree requirements:* For master's, comprehensive exam (MPH), project or thesis (MS); for doctorate, thesis/dissertation, departmental and qualifying exams. *Entrance requirements:* For master's, GRE General Test, minimum GPA of 3.0; previous course work in biology, calculus, and chemistry; 3 letters of recommendation; for doctorate, GRE General Test, master's degree in relevant scientific discipline or engineering; minimum GPA of 3.0; previous course work in biology, calculus, and chemistry; 3 letters of recommendation. Additional exam requirements/recommendations for international students: Required—TOEFL. *Faculty research:* Toxicology, industrial hygiene, exposure assessment, risk assessment, ergonomics.

University of California, Berkeley, Graduate Division, School of Public Health, Group in Epidemiology, Berkeley, CA 94720-1500. Offers epidemiology (MS, PhD); infectious diseases (MPH, PhD). *Accreditation:* CEPH (one or more programs are accredited). *Degree requirements:* For master's, comprehensive exam; for doctorate, thesis/dissertation, oral and written exam. *Entrance requirements:* For master's, GRE General Test, minimum GPA of 3.0; MD, DDS, DVM, or PhD in biomedical science (MPH); for doctorate, GRE General Test, minimum GPA of 3.0.

University of California, Berkeley, Graduate Division, School of Public Health, Programs in Public Health, Berkeley, CA 94720-1500. Offers MPH, Dr PH. *Accreditation:* CEPH. Postbaccalaureate distance learning degree programs offered (minimal on-campus study). *Degree requirements:* For doctorate, thesis/dissertation, exam. *Entrance requirements:* For doctorate, GRE General Test, minimum GPA of 3.0.

University of California, Irvine, College of Health Sciences, Program in Public Health, Irvine, CA 92697. Offers MPH, PhD. *Students:* 18 full-time (15 women), 7 part-time (3 women); includes 11 minority (8 Asian, non-Hispanic/Latino; 1 Hispanic/Latino; 2 Two or more races, non-Hispanic/Latino), 2 international. Average age 25. 157 applicants, 39% accepted, 10 enrolled. In 2011, 9 master's awarded. Application fee: $80 ($100 for international students). *Unit head:* Oladele A. Ogunseitan, Chair, 949-824-6350, Fax: 949-824-2056, E-mail: oladele.ogunseitan@uci.edu. *Application contact:* Stephanie Uiga, Graduate Student Affairs Officer, 949-824-7095, E-mail: suiga@uci.edu. Web site: http://publichealth.uci.edu/.

University of California, Irvine, School of Social Ecology, Programs in Social Ecology, Irvine, CA 92697. Offers environmental analysis and design (PhD); epidemiology and public health (PhD); social ecology (PhD). *Students:* 10 full-time (9 women), 1 (woman) part-time; includes 2 minority (1 Asian, non-Hispanic/Latino; 1 Hispanic/Latino), 1 international. Average age 34. 19 applicants, 11% accepted, 2 enrolled. In 2011, 1 doctorate awarded. Application fee: $80 ($100 for international students). *Unit head:* Valerie Jenness, Dean, 949-824-6094, Fax: 949-824-1845, E-mail: jenness@uci.edu. *Application contact:* Maria Victoria Dela Cruz, Director, Graduate Services, 949-824-5918, Fax: 949-824-1845, E-mail: mvdelacr@uci.edu. Web site: http://socialecology.uci.edu/core/graduate-se-core-programs.

University of California, Los Angeles, Graduate Division, School of Public Health, Los Angeles, CA 90095. Offers MPH, MS, D Env, Dr PH, PhD, JD/MPH, MA/MPH, MBA/MPH, MD/MPH, MD/PhD, MSW/MPH. *Accreditation:* CAHME (one or more programs are accredited); CEPH (one or more programs are accredited). *Degree requirements:* For doctorate, thesis/dissertation, oral and written qualifying exams. *Entrance requirements:* For master's, GRE General Test, minimum GPA of 3.0; for doctorate, GRE General Test, minimum undergraduate GPA of 3.0. Electronic applications accepted.

University of California, San Diego, Office of Graduate Studies, Program in Public Health and Epidemiology, La Jolla, CA 92093. Offers PhD. Program offered jointly with San Diego State University. Electronic applications accepted.

University of Colorado Denver, Colorado School of Public Health, Program in Public Health, Aurora, CO 80045. Offers community and behavioral health (MPH, Dr PH); environmental and occupational health (MPH); epidemiology (MPH); health systems, management and policy (MPH). *Accreditation:* CEPH. Part-time and evening/weekend programs available. *Students:* 216 full-time (177 women), 47 part-time (38 women); includes 48 minority (10 Black or African American, non-Hispanic/Latino; 5 American Indian or Alaska Native, non-Hispanic/Latino; 14 Asian, non-Hispanic/Latino; 17 Hispanic/Latino; 1 Native Hawaiian or other Pacific Islander, non-Hispanic/Latino; 1 Two or more races, non-Hispanic/Latino), 7 international. Average age 33. 670 applicants, 51% accepted, 160 enrolled. In 2011, 83 degrees awarded. *Degree requirements:* For master's, thesis or alternative, 42 credit hours; for doctorate, comprehensive exam, thesis/dissertation, 67 credit hours. *Entrance requirements:* For master's, GRE, baccalaureate degree or equivalent; minimum GPA of 3.0; transcripts; references; resume; essay; for doctorate, GRE, MPH or master's or higher degree in related field or equivalent; 2 years previous work experience in public health, essay, resume. Additional exam requirements/recommendations for international students: Required—TOEFL (minimum score 550 paper-based; 213 computer-based). *Application deadline:* For fall admission, 2/1 for domestic students. Application fee: $65. Electronic applications accepted. *Expenses:* Contact institution. *Financial support:* Fellowships, research assistantships, Federal Work-Study, scholarships/grants, and unspecified assistantships available. Support available to part-time students. Financial award application deadline: 3/15; financial award applicants required to submit FAFSA. *Faculty research:* Cancer prevention by nutrition, cancer survivorship outcomes, social and cultural factors related to health. *Unit head:* Dr. Jack Barnette, Program Director, 303-724-4472, E-mail: jack.barnette@ucdenver.edu. *Application contact:* Jennifer Pacheco, Admissions Specialist, 303-724-5585, E-mail: jennifer.pacheco@ucdenver.edu. Web site: http://www.ucdenver.edu/academics/colleges/PublicHealth/departments/CommunityBehavioralHealth/Pages/CommunityBehavioralHealth.aspx.

University of Connecticut, Graduate School, University of Connecticut Health Center, Field of Public Health, Storrs, CT 06269. Offers MPH, JD/MPH. *Degree requirements:* For master's, comprehensive exam. *Entrance requirements:* Additional exam requirements/recommendations for international students: Required—TOEFL (minimum score 550 paper-based; 213 computer-based). Electronic applications accepted.

University of Connecticut Health Center, Graduate School, Program in Public Health, Farmington, CT 06030. Offers MPH, DMD/MPH, MD/MPH. *Accreditation:* CEPH. Part-time and evening/weekend programs available. *Degree requirements:* For master's, thesis optional. *Entrance requirements:* For master's, GRE. Additional exam requirements/recommendations for international students: Required—TOEFL (minimum score 600 paper-based; 250 computer-based). Electronic applications accepted. *Faculty research:* Cancer epidemiology, birth defects, gerontology, health manpower, health services.

University of Florida, College of Medicine, Program in Clinical Investigation, Gainesville, FL 32611. Offers clinical investigation (MS); epidemiology (MS); public health (MPH). Part-time programs available. *Entrance requirements:* For master's, GRE, MD, PhD, DMD/DDS or Pharm D.

University of Florida, Graduate School, College of Public Health and Health Professions, Programs in Public Health, Gainesville, FL 32611. Offers biostatistics (MPH); environmental health (MPH); epidemiology (MPH); public health management and policy (MPH); public health practice (MPH); social and behavioral sciences (MPH). *Accreditation:* CEPH. Postbaccalaureate distance learning degree programs offered. *Students:* 76 full-time (57 women), 21 part-time (13 women); includes 33 minority (15 Black or African American, non-Hispanic/Latino; 12 Asian, non-Hispanic/Latino; 6 Hispanic/Latino), 7 international. Average age 30. 313 applicants, 49% accepted, 63 enrolled. In 2011, 66 master's awarded. *Degree requirements:* For master's, internship. *Entrance requirements:* For master's, GRE General Test, minimum GPA of 3.0. Additional exam requirements/recommendations for international students: Required—TOEFL (minimum score 550 paper-based; 213 computer-based; 80 iBT), IELTS (minimum score 6). Application fee: $30. *Financial support:* In 2011–12, 14 students received support, including 1 fellowship, 11 research assistantships, 2 teaching assistantships. Financial award applicants required to submit FAFSA. *Unit head:* Mary Peoples Sheps, Senior Associate Dean for Public Health, 352-273-6084, Fax: 352-273-6448, E-mail: mpeoplessheps@phhp.ufl.edu. Web site: http://www.mph.ufl.edu/.

University of Georgia, College of Public Health, Doctor of Public Health Program, Athens, GA 30602. Offers Dr PH. *Faculty:* 23 full-time (9 women), 3 part-time/adjunct (1 woman). *Students:* 179 full-time (121 women), 24 part-time (18 women); includes 64 minority (37 Black or African American, non-Hispanic/Latino; 18 Asian, non-Hispanic/Latino; 4 Hispanic/Latino; 5 Two or more races, non-Hispanic/Latino), 19 international. Average age 28. 368 applicants, 54% accepted, 73 enrolled. *Application contact:* Joel M. Lee, Graduate Coordinator, 706-542-3709, Fax: 706-542-6730, E-mail: joellee@uga.edu. Web site: http://www.publichealth.uga.edu/academics/drph.

University of Hawaii at Manoa, John A. Burns School of Medicine, Department of Public Health Sciences and Epidemiology, Honolulu, HI 96822. Offers epidemiology (PhD); global health and population studies (Graduate Certificate); public health (MPH, MS, Dr PH). *Accreditation:* CEPH. Part-time programs available. *Entrance requirements:* Additional exam requirements/recommendations for international students: Required—TOEFL (minimum score 550 paper-based; 213 computer-based; 79 iBT), IELTS (minimum score 5).

University of Illinois at Chicago, Graduate College, School of Public Health, Chicago, IL 60607-7128. Offers MHA, MPH, MS, Dr PH, PhD, DDS/MPH, MBA/MPH, MD/PhD, MPH/MS. *Accreditation:* CEPH (one or more programs are accredited). Part-time programs available. Terminal master's awarded for partial completion of doctoral program. *Degree requirements:* For master's, thesis, field practicum; for doctorate, thesis/dissertation, independent research, internship. *Entrance requirements:* For

master's and doctorate, GRE General Test, minimum GPA of 2.75. Additional exam requirements/recommendations for international students: Required—TOEFL. Electronic applications accepted.

University of Illinois at Springfield, Graduate Programs, College of Public Affairs and Administration, Program in Public Health, Springfield, IL 62703-5407. Offers MPH. Part-time and evening/weekend programs available. Postbaccalaureate distance learning degree programs offered (no on-campus study). *Faculty:* 5 full-time (3 women), 1 part-time/adjunct (0 women). *Students:* 33 full-time (23 women), 44 part-time (31 women); includes 16 minority (8 Black or African American, non-Hispanic/Latino; 1 American Indian or Alaska Native, non-Hispanic/Latino; 5 Asian, non-Hispanic/Latino; 1 Hispanic/Latino; 1 Two or more races, non-Hispanic/Latino), 4 international. Average age 33. 59 applicants, 49% accepted, 18 enrolled. In 2011, 23 master's awarded. *Degree requirements:* For master's, comprehensive exam, internship. *Entrance requirements:* For master's, GRE, minimum undergraduate GPA of 3.0, 3 letters of recommendation, statement of personal goals. Additional exam requirements/recommendations for international students: Required—TOEFL (minimum score 500 paper-based; 176 computer-based; 61 iBT). *Application deadline:* Applications are processed on a rolling basis. Application fee: $50 ($60 for international students). Electronic applications accepted. *Expenses:* Tuition, state resident: full-time $6978; part-time $290.75 per credit hour. Tuition, nonresident: full-time $15,282; part-time $636.75 per credit hour. *Required fees:* $2106; $87.75 per credit hour. *Financial support:* In 2011–12, fellowships with full tuition reimbursements (averaging $8,550 per year), research assistantships with full tuition reimbursements (averaging $8,550 per year), teaching assistantships with full tuition reimbursements (averaging $8,550 per year) were awarded; career-related internships or fieldwork, Federal Work-Study, scholarships/grants, health care benefits, and unspecified assistantships also available. Support available to part-time students. Financial award application deadline: 11/15; financial award applicants required to submit FAFSA. *Unit head:* Dr. Sharron Lafollette, Program Administrator, 217-206-7894, Fax: 217-206-7279, E-mail: slafo1@uis.edu. *Application contact:* Dr. Lynn Pardie, Office of Graduate Studies, 800-252-8533, Fax: 217-206-7623, E-mail: lpard1@uis.edu. Web site: http://www.uis.edu/publichealth/.

University of Illinois at Urbana–Champaign, Graduate College, College of Applied Health Sciences, Department of Kinesiology and Community Health, Champaign, IL 61820. Offers community health (MS, MSPH, PhD); kinesiology (MS, PhD); public health (MPH); rehabilitation (MS). *Faculty:* 25 full-time (12 women). *Students:* 137 full-time (83 women), 10 part-time (8 women); includes 35 minority (16 Black or African American, non-Hispanic/Latino; 14 Asian, non-Hispanic/Latino; 3 Hispanic/Latino; 2 Two or more races, non-Hispanic/Latino), 38 international. 167 applicants, 40% accepted, 45 enrolled. In 2011, 22 master's, 11 doctorates awarded. *Entrance requirements:* For master's, GRE, minimum GPA of 3.0; for doctorate, GRE, minimum graduate GPA of 3.5. Additional exam requirements/recommendations for international students: Required—TOEFL. *Application deadline:* Applications are processed on a rolling basis. Application fee: $75 ($90 for international students). Electronic applications accepted. *Financial support:* In 2011–12, 15 fellowships, 37 research assistantships, 71 teaching assistantships were awarded; tuition waivers (full and partial) also available. *Unit head:* Wojciech Chodzko-Zajko, Head, 217-244-0823, Fax: 217-244-7322, E-mail: wojtek@illinois.edu. *Application contact:* Tina M. Candler, Office Manager, 217-333-1083, Fax: 217-244-7322, E-mail: tcandler@illinois.edu. Web site: http://www.kch.illinois.edu/.

The University of Iowa, College of Dentistry and Graduate College, Graduate Programs in Dentistry, Department of Preventive and Community Dentistry, Iowa City, IA 52242-1316. Offers dental public health (MS). *Degree requirements:* For master's, thesis. *Entrance requirements:* For master's, GRE, DDS. Additional exam requirements/recommendations for international students: Required—TOEFL.

The University of Iowa, Graduate College, College of Public Health, Iowa City, IA 52242-1316. Offers MHA, MPH, MS, PhD, Certificate, DVM/MPH, JD/MHA, JD/MPH, MBA/MHA, MD/MPH, MHA/MA, MHA/MS, MS/MA, MS/MS, MSN/MPH, Pharm D/MPH. *Accreditation:* CEPH. *Degree requirements:* For master's, exam; for doctorate, comprehensive exam, thesis/dissertation. *Entrance requirements:* For master's and doctorate, GRE General Test, minimum GPA of 3.0. Additional exam requirements/recommendations for international students: Required—TOEFL. Electronic applications accepted. *Expenses:* Contact institution.

The University of Kansas, University of Kansas Medical Center, School of Medicine, Department of Preventive Medicine and Public Health, Kansas City, KS 66160. Offers biostatistics (MPH); clinical research (MS); environmental health sciences (MPH); epidemiology (MPH); public health management (MPH); social and behavioral health (MPH); MD/MPH; MPH/MSN; PhD/MPH. Part-time programs available. *Faculty:* 76. *Students:* 51 full-time (32 women), 74 part-time (53 women); includes 35 minority (10 Black or African American, non-Hispanic/Latino; 4 American Indian or Alaska Native, non-Hispanic/Latino; 9 Asian, non-Hispanic/Latino; 8 Hispanic/Latino; 4 Two or more races, non-Hispanic/Latino), 6 international. Average age 33. 77 applicants, 69% accepted, 45 enrolled. In 2011, 25 master's awarded. *Degree requirements:* For master's, thesis, capstone practicum defense. *Entrance requirements:* For master's, GRE, MCAT, LSAT, GMAT or other equivalent graduate professional exam. Additional exam requirements/recommendations for international students: Required—TOEFL. *Application deadline:* For fall admission, 3/1 for domestic and international students. Applications are processed on a rolling basis. Application fee: $60. Tuition and fees vary according to course load, campus/location, program and reciprocity agreements. *Financial support:* In 2011–12, 21 research assistantships (averaging $10,200 per year) were awarded; career-related internships or fieldwork, Federal Work-Study, scholarships/grants, and unspecified assistantships also available. Financial award application deadline: 2/14; financial award applicants required to submit FAFSA. *Faculty research:* Cancer screening and prevention, smoking cessation, obesity and physical activity, health services/outcomes research. *Total annual research expenditures:* $8 million. *Unit head:* Dr. Edward F. Ellerbeck, Chairman, 913-588-2774, Fax: 913-588-2780, E-mail: eellerbe@kumc.edu. *Application contact:* Tanya Honderick, Assistant Director, KU-MPH, 913-588-2720, Fax: 913-588-8505, E-mail: thonderick@kumc.edu. Web site: http://ph.kumc.edu/.

University of Kentucky, Graduate School, College of Public Health, Program in Public Health, Lexington, KY 40506-0032. Offers MPH. *Entrance requirements:* For master's, GRE General Test, minimum undergraduate GPA of 2.75. Additional exam requirements/recommendations for international students: Required—TOEFL (minimum score 550 paper-based; 213 computer-based). Electronic applications accepted.

University of Louisville, Graduate School, School of Public Health and Information Sciences, Department of Environmental and Occupational Health Sciences, Louisville, KY 40202. Offers environmental and occupational health sciences (MPH); public health (PhD), including environmental health. *Accreditation:* CEPH. *Degree requirements:* For doctorate, comprehensive exam, thesis/dissertation. *Entrance requirements:* For doctorate, GRE (50th percentile), official transcripts, statement of purpose, resume/curriculum vitae, master's degree or better, 3 letters of recommendation, minimum GPA of 3.0. Additional exam requirements/recommendations for international students: Required—TOEFL (minimum score 600 paper-based; 250 computer-based; 100 iBT). Electronic applications accepted. *Expenses:* Tuition, state resident: full-time $9692;

part-time $539 per credit hour. Tuition, nonresident: full-time $20,168; part-time $1121 per credit hour. Tuition and fees vary according to program and reciprocity agreements.

The University of Manchester, School of Dentistry, Manchester, United Kingdom. Offers basic dental sciences (cancer studies) (M Phil, PhD); basic dental sciences (molecular genetics) (M Phil, PhD); basic dental sciences (stem cell biology) (M Phil, PhD); biomaterials sciences and dental technology (M Phil, PhD); dental public health/community dentistry (M Phil, PhD); dental science (clinical) (PhD); endodontology (M Phil, PhD); fixed and removable prosthodontics (M Phil, PhD); operative dentistry (M Phil, PhD); oral and maxillofacial surgery (M Phil, PhD); oral radiology (M Phil, PhD); orthodontics (M Phil, PhD); restorative dentistry (M Phil, PhD).

University of Maryland, College Park, Academic Affairs, School of Public Health, College Park, MD 20742. Offers MA, MHA, MPH, MS, PhD. Part-time and evening/weekend programs available. *Faculty:* 112 full-time (67 women), 48 part-time/adjunct (32 women). *Students:* 177 full-time (121 women), 49 part-time (40 women); includes 76 minority (40 Black or African American, non-Hispanic/Latino; 1 American Indian or Alaska Native, non-Hispanic/Latino; 23 Asian, non-Hispanic/Latino; 9 Hispanic/Latino; 3 Two or more races, non-Hispanic/Latino), 32 international. 652 applicants, 19% accepted, 60 enrolled. In 2011, 36 master's, 11 doctorates awarded. *Degree requirements:* For doctorate, thesis/dissertation. *Entrance requirements:* For master's and doctorate, GRE General Test, minimum GPA of 3.0, 3 letters of recommendation. Additional exam requirements/recommendations for international students: Required—TOEFL. *Application deadline:* For fall admission, 1/15 for domestic students, 2/1 for international students; for spring admission, 6/1 for international students. Applications are processed on a rolling basis. Application fee: $75. Electronic applications accepted. *Expenses:* Tuition, state resident: part-time $525 per credit hour. Tuition, nonresident: part-time $1131 per credit hour. *Required fees:* $386.31 per term. Tuition and fees vary according to program. *Financial support:* In 2011–12, 16 fellowships with full and partial tuition reimbursements (averaging $17,012 per year), 13 research assistantships (averaging $16,048 per year), 84 teaching assistantships (averaging $16,015 per year) were awarded; career-related internships or fieldwork, Federal Work-Study, and scholarships/grants also available. Support available to part-time students. Financial award applicants required to submit FAFSA. *Total annual research expenditures:* $11.7 million. *Unit head:* Dr. Robert Gold, Dean, 301-405-2437, Fax: 301-314-9167, E-mail: rsgold@umd.edu. *Application contact:* Dr. Charles A. Carmello, Dean of Graduate School, 301-405-0358, Fax: 301-314-9305.

University of Massachusetts Amherst, Graduate School, Interdisciplinary Programs, Dual Degree Program in Public Health and Public Policy and Administration, Amherst, MA 01003. Offers MPH/MPPA. *Students:* 1 applicant, 100% accepted, 0 enrolled. *Entrance requirements:* Additional exam requirements/recommendations for international students: Required—TOEFL (minimum score 600 paper-based; 250 computer-based; 100 iBT), IELTS (minimum score 7). *Application deadline:* For fall admission, 2/1 for domestic and international students. Applications are processed on a rolling basis. Application fee: $50 ($65 for international students). Electronic applications accepted. Tuition and fees vary according to course load, campus/location and program. *Financial support:* Career-related internships or fieldwork, Federal Work-Study, scholarships/grants, traineeships, health care benefits, tuition waivers, and unspecified assistantships available. Support available to part-time students. Financial award application deadline: 2/1; financial award applicants required to submit FAFSA. *Unit head:* Dr. M. V. Lee Badgett, Director, 413-545-2714. *Application contact:* Lindsay DeSantis, Interim Supervisor of Admissions, 413-545-0722, Fax: 413-577-0010, E-mail: gradadm@grad.umass.edu. Web site: http://www.masspolicy.org/acad_mppa_health.html.

University of Massachusetts Amherst, Graduate School, School of Public Health and Health Sciences, Department of Public Health, Amherst, MA 01003. Offers biostatistics (MPH, MS, PhD); community health education (MPH, MS, PhD); environmental health sciences (MPH, MS, PhD); epidemiology (MPH, MS, PhD); health policy and management (MPH, MS, PhD); nutrition (MPH, PhD); public health practice (MPH); MPH/MPPA. *Accreditation:* CEPH (one or more programs are accredited). Part-time and evening/weekend programs available. Postbaccalaureate distance learning degree programs offered (no on-campus study). *Faculty:* 46 full-time (26 women). *Students:* 118 full-time (88 women), 249 part-time (183 women); includes 75 minority (28 Black or African American, non-Hispanic/Latino; 21 Asian, non-Hispanic/Latino; 20 Hispanic/Latino; 6 Two or more races, non-Hispanic/Latino), 55 international. Average age 36. 377 applicants, 67% accepted, 91 enrolled. In 2011, 83 master's, 4 doctorates awarded. Terminal master's awarded for partial completion of doctoral program. *Degree requirements:* For master's, thesis (for some programs); for doctorate, comprehensive exam, thesis/dissertation. *Entrance requirements:* For master's and doctorate, GRE General Test. Additional exam requirements/recommendations for international students: Required—TOEFL (minimum score 550 paper-based; 213 computer-based; 80 iBT), IELTS (minimum score 6.5). *Application deadline:* For fall admission, 2/1 for domestic and international students. Applications are processed on a rolling basis. Application fee: $40 ($65 for international students). Electronic applications accepted. Tuition and fees vary according to course load, campus/location and program. *Financial support:* Fellowships with full and partial tuition reimbursements, research assistantships with full and partial tuition reimbursements, teaching assistantships with full and partial tuition reimbursements, career-related internships or fieldwork, Federal Work-Study, scholarships/grants, traineeships, health care benefits, tuition waivers (full and partial), and unspecified assistantships available. Support available to part-time students. Financial award application deadline: 2/1. *Unit head:* Dr. Paula Stamps, Graduate Program Director, 413-545-2861, Fax: 413-545-1645. *Application contact:* Lindsay DeSantis, Interim Supervisor of Admissions, 413-545-0722, Fax: 413-577-0010, E-mail: gradadm@grad.umass.edu. Web site: http://www.umass.edu/sphhs/public_health/.

University of Massachusetts Lowell, School of Health and Environment, Department of Clinical Laboratory and Nutritional Sciences, Lowell, MA 01854-2881. Offers clinical laboratory sciences (MS); clinical pathology (Graduate Certificate); nutritional sciences (Graduate Certificate); public health laboratory sciences (Graduate Certificate). *Accreditation:* NAACLS. Part-time programs available. Postbaccalaureate distance learning degree programs offered. *Degree requirements:* For master's, thesis optional. *Entrance requirements:* For master's, GRE General Test, minimum GPA of 3.0, letters of recommendation. *Faculty research:* Cardiovascular disease, lipoprotein metabolism, micronutrient evaluation, alcohol metabolism, mycobacterial drug resistance.

University of Medicine and Dentistry of New Jersey, UMDNJ–School of Public Health (UMDNJ, Rutgers, NJIT) Newark Campus, Newark, NJ 07107-1709. Offers clinical epidemiology (Certificate); dental public health (MPH); general public health (Certificate); public policy and oral health services administration (Certificate); quantitative methods (MPH); urban health (MPH); DMD/MPH; MD/MPH; MS/MPH. *Accreditation:* CEPH. Part-time and evening/weekend programs available. *Degree requirements:* For master's, thesis, internship. *Entrance requirements:* For master's, GRE General Test. Additional exam requirements/recommendations for international students: Required—TOEFL. Electronic applications accepted.

University of Medicine and Dentistry of New Jersey, UMDNJ–School of Public Health (UMDNJ, Rutgers, NJIT) Piscataway/New Brunswick Campus, Piscataway, NJ

08854. Offers biostatistics (MPH, MS, Dr PH, PhD); clinical epidemiology (Certificate); environmental and occupational health (MPH, Dr PH, PhD, Certificate); epidemiology (MPH, Dr PH, PhD); general public health (Certificate); health education and behavioral science (MPH, Dr PH, PhD); health systems and policy (MPH, PhD); public health preparedness (Certificate); DO/MPH; JD/MPH; MD/MPH; MPH/MBA; MPH/MSPA; MS/MPH; Psy D/MPH. *Accreditation:* CEPH. Part-time and evening/weekend programs available. *Degree requirements:* For master's, thesis, internship; for doctorate, comprehensive exam, thesis/dissertation. *Entrance requirements:* For master's, GRE General Test; for doctorate, GRE General Test, MPH (Dr PH); MA, MPH, or MS (PhD). Additional exam requirements/recommendations for international students: Required—TOEFL. Electronic applications accepted.

University of Medicine and Dentistry of New Jersey, UMDNJ–School of Public Health (UMDNJ, Rutgers, NJIT) Stratford/Camden Campus, Stratford, NJ 08084. Offers general public health (Certificate); health systems and policy (MPH); DO/MPH. *Accreditation:* CEPH. Part-time and evening/weekend programs available. *Degree requirements:* For master's, thesis, internship. *Entrance requirements:* For master's, GRE General Test. Additional exam requirements/recommendations for international students: Required—TOEFL. Electronic applications accepted.

University of Memphis, Graduate School, School of Public Health, Memphis, TN 38152. Offers biostatistics (MPH); environmental health (MPH); epidemiology (MPH); health systems management (MPH); public health (MHA); social and behavioral sciences (MPH). Part-time and evening/weekend programs available. Postbaccalaureate distance learning degree programs offered. *Degree requirements:* For master's, comprehensive exam, thesis. *Entrance requirements:* For master's, GRE, letters of recommendation. Additional exam requirements/recommendations for international students: Required—TOEFL. Electronic applications accepted. *Faculty research:* Health and medical savings accounts, adoption rates, health informatics, Telehealth technologies, biostatistics, environmental health, epidemiology, health systems management, social and behavioral sciences.

University of Miami, Graduate School, Miller School of Medicine, Graduate Programs in Medicine, Department of Epidemiology and Public Health, Coral Gables, FL 33124. Offers epidemiology (PhD); public health (MPH, MSPH); JD/MPH; MD/MPH; MD/PhD; MPA/MPH; MPH/MAIA. *Accreditation:* CEPH (one or more programs are accredited). Part-time programs available. *Degree requirements:* For master's, thesis (for some programs), project, practicum; for doctorate, comprehensive exam, thesis/dissertation. *Entrance requirements:* For master's, GRE General Test, minimum GPA of 3.0, 3 letters of recommendation; for doctorate, GRE General Test, minimum GPA of 3.0, course work in epidemiology and statistics, 3 letters of recommendation. Additional exam requirements/recommendations for international students: Required—TOEFL (minimum score 550 paper-based; 213 computer-based; 59 iBT). Electronic applications accepted. *Faculty research:* Behavioral epidemiology, substance abuse, AIDS, cardiovascular diseases, women's health.

University of Michigan, School of Public Health, Ann Arbor, MI 48109. Offers MHSA, MPH, MS, PhD, JD/MHSA, MD/MPH, MHSA/MBA, MHSA/MNA, MHSA/MPP, MHSA/MSIOE, MPH/JD, MPH/MA, MPH/MBA, MPH/MPP, MPH/MS, MPH/MSW. MS and PhD offered through the Horace H. Rackham School of Graduate Studies. *Accreditation:* CAHME (one or more programs are accredited); CEPH (one or more programs are accredited). Part-time and evening/weekend programs available. Terminal master's awarded for partial completion of doctoral program. *Degree requirements:* For doctorate, oral defense of dissertation, preliminary exam. *Entrance requirements:* For master's and doctorate, GRE General Test. Additional exam requirements/recommendations for international students: Required—TOEFL (minimum score 560 paper-based; 220 computer-based; 100 iBT). Electronic applications accepted.

University of Minnesota, Twin Cities Campus, School of Public Health, Minneapolis, MN 55455. Offers MHA, MPH, MS, PhD, Certificate, DVM/MPH, JD/MS, JD/PhD, MD/MPH, MD/PhD, MPH/JD, MPH/MS, MPH/MSN, MPP/MS. *Accreditation:* CEPH (one or more programs are accredited). Part-time programs available. Postbaccalaureate distance learning degree programs offered (minimal on-campus study). Terminal master's awarded for partial completion of doctoral program. *Degree requirements:* For doctorate, thesis/dissertation. *Entrance requirements:* For master's and doctorate, GRE General Test. Additional exam requirements/recommendations for international students: Required—TOEFL. Electronic applications accepted. *Expenses:* Contact institution.

University of Missouri, Graduate School, Master of Public Health Program, Columbia, MO 65211. Offers health promotion and policy (MPH); public health (Graduate Certificate); veterinary public health (MPH); DVM/MPH; MPH/MA; MPH/MPA. *Accreditation:* CEPH. *Students:* 86 full-time (61 women), 68 part-time (49 women); includes 36 minority (20 Black or African American, non-Hispanic/Latino; 7 Asian, non-Hispanic/Latino; 4 Hispanic/Latino; 5 Two or more races, non-Hispanic/Latino), 16 international. Average age 29. 99 applicants, 85% accepted, 64 enrolled. In 2011, 44 master's, 34 other advanced degrees awarded. *Entrance requirements:* Additional exam requirements/recommendations for international students: Required—TOEFL (minimum score 550 paper-based; 215 computer-based; 80 iBT). Application fee: $55 ($75 for international students). *Expenses:* Tuition, state resident: full-time $5881. Tuition, nonresident: full-time $15,183. *Required fees:* $952. Tuition and fees vary according to campus/location and program. *Faculty research:* Health professions, health care equality, global health, communicable diseases, public health; zoonosis and infectious diseases, medical education, inquiry-based learning, social determinants of health, violence against women, health disparities, breast cancer screening, epigenetic, nursing, environmental health, cancer and chronic diseases, environmental exposures with metals, geographical information systems, substance use disorders/addictions, mental health. *Unit head:* Dr. Kristofer Hagglund, Associate Dean, 573-884-7050, E-mail: hagglundk@missouri.edu. *Application contact:* Lise Saffran, 573-884-6844, E-mail: saffranl@missouri.edu. Web site: http://publichealth.missouri.edu/.

University of Missouri, School of Medicine, Program in Public Health, Columbia, MO 65211. Offers MS. *Accreditation:* CEPH. *Students:* 8 full-time (5 women); includes 4 minority (2 Hispanic/Latino; 2 Two or more races, non-Hispanic/Latino), 1 international. Average age 32. 4 applicants, 100% accepted, 4 enrolled. In 2011, 44 master's awarded. *Entrance requirements:* For master's, 3 letters of recommendation; personal statement; curriculum vitae or resume; verification from medical school and residency program; official transcripts. Additional exam requirements/recommendations for international students: Required—TOEFL (minimum score 500 paper-based). *Expenses:* Tuition, state resident: full-time $5881. Tuition, nonresident: full-time $15,183. *Required fees:* $952. Tuition and fees vary according to campus/location and program. *Unit head:* Dr. Steven C. Zweig, Chair, Department of Family and Community Medicine, 573-884-7411. *Application contact:* Ashley Granger, Administrative Assistant, 573-884-7060, E-mail: grangeran@health.missouri.edu. Web site: http://www.fcm.missouri.edu.

The University of Montana, Graduate School, College of Health Professions and Biomedical Sciences, School of Public and Community Health Sciences, Missoula, MT 59812-0002. Offers public health (MPH, CPH). Part-time programs available. Postbaccalaureate distance learning degree programs offered.

University of Nebraska Medical Center, Graduate Studies, Program in Public Health, Omaha, NE 68198. Offers MPH. *Accreditation:* CEPH. Part-time programs available. Postbaccalaureate distance learning degree programs offered (minimal on-campus study). *Degree requirements:* For master's, service-learning capstone course. *Entrance requirements:* Additional exam requirements/recommendations for international students: Required—TOEFL (minimum score 550 paper-based; 213 computer-based). Electronic applications accepted. *Faculty research:* Ethics, environmental health, cultural influence on health, rural health policy, cancer prevention.

University of Nevada, Las Vegas, Graduate College, School of Community Health Sciences, Department of Environmental and Occupational Health, Las Vegas, NV 89154-3064. Offers public health (MPH, PhD). *Faculty:* 12 full-time (5 women), 11 part-time/adjunct (3 women). *Students:* 41 full-time (31 women), 58 part-time (35 women); includes 34 minority (8 Black or African American, non-Hispanic/Latino; 2 American Indian or Alaska Native, non-Hispanic/Latino; 12 Asian, non-Hispanic/Latino; 7 Hispanic/Latino; 1 Native Hawaiian or other Pacific Islander, non-Hispanic/Latino; 4 Two or more races, non-Hispanic/Latino), 7 international. Average age 34. 45 applicants, 64% accepted, 19 enrolled. In 2011, 37 master's awarded. *Entrance requirements:* Additional exam requirements/recommendations for international students: Required—TOEFL (minimum score 550 paper-based; 213 computer-based; 80 iBT), IELTS (minimum score 7). *Application deadline:* For fall admission, 4/1 priority date for domestic students, 5/1 for international students; for spring admission, 11/1 priority date for domestic students, 10/1 for international students. Applications are processed on a rolling basis. Application fee: $60 ($95 for international students). Electronic applications accepted. *Financial support:* In 2011–12, 28 students received support, including 24 research assistantships with partial tuition reimbursements available (averaging $8,725 per year), 3 teaching assistantships (averaging $10,973 per year); institutionally sponsored loans, scholarships/grants, health care benefits, and unspecified assistantships also available. Financial award application deadline: 3/1. *Faculty research:* Environmental health: micro (mold) to macro (Lake Mead ecosystem). *Total annual research expenditures:* $473,431. *Unit head:* Dr. Shawn Gerstenberger, Chair/Associate Professor, 702-895-1565, Fax: 702-895-5573, E-mail: shawn.gerstenberger@unlv.edu. *Application contact:* Graduate College Admissions Evaluator, 702-895-3320, Fax: 702-895-4180, E-mail: gradcollege@unlv.edu. Web site: http://publichealth.unlv.edu/EOH_welcome.html.

University of Nevada, Reno, Graduate School, Division of Health Sciences, Department of Public Health, Reno, NV 89557. Offers MPH, PhD, MPH/MSN. *Accreditation:* CEPH. Terminal master's awarded for partial completion of doctoral program. *Degree requirements:* For master's, thesis optional, culminating experience; for doctorate, thesis/dissertation. *Entrance requirements:* For master's, GRE General Test, GMAT, LSAT, MCAT or DAT, minimum GPA of 2.75; for doctorate, GRE General Test, GMAT, LSAT, MCAT or DAT, minimum GPA of 3.0. Additional exam requirements/recommendations for international students: Required—TOEFL (minimum score 500 paper-based; 173 computer-based; 61 iBT), IELTS (minimum score 6). Electronic applications accepted. *Faculty research:* Biomechanics and basic fundamentals of skiing, social psychology in sports and recreation, fitness and aging, elementary physical education, body fat evaluation.

University of New England, College of Graduate Studies, Program in Public Health, Biddeford, ME 04005-9526. Offers MPH, Certificate. Part-time programs available. Postbaccalaureate distance learning degree programs offered. *Faculty:* 2 full-time, 3 part-time/adjunct. *Students:* 61 full-time (45 women), 16 part-time (14 women). In 2011, 13 master's, 1 other advanced degree awarded. *Degree requirements:* For Certificate, practicum. *Entrance requirements:* For degree, undergraduate course work in math and science. Additional exam requirements/recommendations for international students: Required—TOEFL (minimum score 550 paper-based; 213 computer-based). *Application deadline:* Applications are processed on a rolling basis. Electronic applications accepted. *Expenses:* Contact institution. *Financial support:* Available to part-time students. Application deadline: 5/1; applicants required to submit FAFSA. *Unit head:* Denise Bisaillon, Director, 207-221-4464, E-mail: dbisaillon@une.edu. *Application contact:* Stacy Gato, Director of Graduate Admissions, 207-221-4225, Fax: 207-221-4898, E-mail: gradadmissions@une.edu.

University of New Hampshire, Graduate School Manchester Campus, Manchester, NH 03101. Offers business administration (MBA); counseling (M Ed); education (M Ed, MAT); educational administration and supervision (M Ed, Ed S); information technology (MS); management of technology (MS); public administration (MPA); public health (MPH, Certificate); social work (MSW); software systems engineering (Certificate). Part-time and evening/weekend programs available. *Students:* 78 full-time (50 women), 130 part-time (65 women); includes 11 minority (2 Black or African American, non-Hispanic/Latino; 5 Asian, non-Hispanic/Latino; 4 Hispanic/Latino), 4 international. Average age 34. 132 applicants, 55% accepted, 57 enrolled. In 2011, 66 master's, 9 other advanced degrees awarded. *Degree requirements:* For master's, thesis or alternative. *Entrance requirements:* Additional exam requirements/recommendations for international students: Required—TOEFL (minimum score 550 paper-based; 213 computer-based; 80 iBT). *Application deadline:* For fall admission, 6/1 for domestic students, 4/1 for international students; for spring admission, 12/1 for domestic students. Applications are processed on a rolling basis. Application fee: $65. Electronic applications accepted. *Expenses:* Tuition, state resident: full-time $12,360; part-time $687 per credit hour. Tuition, nonresident: full-time $25,680; part-time $1058 per credit hour. *International tuition:* $29,550 full-time. *Required fees:* $1666; $833 per course. $416.50 per semester. Tuition and fees vary according to course load and degree level. *Financial support:* In 2011–12, 11 students received support, including 2 teaching assistantships; fellowships, research assistantships, Federal Work-Study, scholarships/grants, health care benefits, and unspecified assistantships also available. Support available to part-time students. Financial award application deadline: 3/1; financial award applicants required to submit FAFSA. *Unit head:* Candice Brown, Director, 603-641-4313, E-mail: unhm.gradcenter@unh.edu. *Application contact:* Graduate Admissions Office, 603-862-3000, Fax: 603-862-0275, E-mail: grad.school@unh.edu. Web site: http://www.gradschool.unh.edu/manchester/.

University of New Hampshire, Graduate School, School of Health and Human Services, Department of Health Management and Policy, Durham, NH 03824. Offers public health (MPH, Postbaccalaureate Certificate). Part-time and evening/weekend programs available. *Faculty:* 15 full-time (3 women). *Students:* 23 full-time (19 women), 31 part-time (24 women); includes 8 minority (6 Black or African American, non-Hispanic/Latino; 1 Asian, non-Hispanic/Latino; 1 Hispanic/Latino). Average age 36. 46 applicants, 70% accepted, 17 enrolled. In 2011, 20 master's, 5 other advanced degrees awarded. *Entrance requirements:* For master's, GMAT or GRE General Test. Additional exam requirements/recommendations for international students: Required—TOEFL (minimum score 550 paper-based; 213 computer-based; 80 iBT). *Application deadline:* For fall admission, 6/1 priority date for domestic students, 4/1 for international students; for spring admission, 12/1 for domestic students. Applications are processed on a rolling basis. Application fee: $65. Electronic applications accepted. *Expenses:* Contact institution. *Financial support:* In 2011–12, 4 students received support. Fellowships, research assistantships, teaching assistantships, and scholarships/grants available. Financial award application deadline: 2/15. *Unit head:* Dr. Jim Lewis, Chairperson, 603-

862-3413. *Application contact:* Ann-Marie Matteucci, Administrative Assistant, 603-862-2733, E-mail: masterof.publichealth@unh.edu. Web site: http://chhs.unh.edu/hmp/index.

University of New Mexico, Health Sciences Center Graduate Programs, Program in Public Health, Albuquerque, NM 87131-5196. Offers community health (MPH); epidemiology (MPH); generalist (MPH). *Accreditation:* CEPH. Part-time programs available. Postbaccalaureate distance learning degree programs offered. *Faculty:* 11 full-time (8 women), 2 part-time/adjunct (1 woman). *Students:* 18 full-time (15 women), 26 part-time (21 women); includes 17 minority (3 American Indian or Alaska Native, non-Hispanic/Latino; 13 Hispanic/Latino; 1 Two or more races, non-Hispanic/Latino), 1 international. Average age 37. 34 applicants, 59% accepted, 11 enrolled. In 2011, 11 degrees awarded. *Degree requirements:* For master's, thesis. *Entrance requirements:* For master's, GRE, MCAT, 2 years of experience in health field. Additional exam requirements/recommendations for international students: Required—TOEFL. *Application deadline:* For fall admission, 2/1 for domestic students. Application fee: $50. *Financial support:* Fellowships, research assistantships with tuition reimbursements, and Federal Work-Study available. Financial award application deadline: 12/15; financial award applicants required to submit FAFSA. *Faculty research:* Epidemiology, rural health, environmental health, Native American health issues. *Total annual research expenditures:* $1 million. *Unit head:* Dr. Kristine Tollestrup, Director, 505-272-4173, Fax: 505-272-4494, E-mail: ktollestrup@salud.unm.edu. *Application contact:* Gayle Garcia, Education Coordinator, 505-272-3982, Fax: 505-272-4494, E-mail: garciag@salud.unm.edu. Web site: http://hsc.unm.edu/som/fcm/mph/mphindex.shtml.

The University of North Carolina at Chapel Hill, Graduate School, School of Public Health, Chapel Hill, NC 27599. Offers MHA, MPH, MS, MSCR, MSEE, MSPH, Dr PH, PhD, DDS/MPH, JD/MPH, MBA/MHA, MBA/MSPH, MD/MPH, MD/MSPH, MHA/MBA, MHA/MCRP, MHA/MSIS, MHA/MSLS, MPH/MCRP, MPH/MSW, MSPH/M Ed, MSPH/MCRP, MSPH/MSIS, MSPH/MSLS, MSPH/MSW. *Accreditation:* CAHME (one or more programs are accredited); CEPH (one or more programs are accredited). Part-time programs available. Postbaccalaureate distance learning degree programs offered (minimal on-campus study). Terminal master's awarded for partial completion of doctoral program. *Degree requirements:* For master's, comprehensive exam, thesis, paper, capstone; for doctorate, comprehensive exam, thesis/dissertation. *Entrance requirements:* For master's and doctorate, GRE General Test, minimum GPA of 3.0 (recommended). Additional exam requirements/recommendations for international students: Required—TOEFL. Electronic applications accepted. *Faculty research:* Infection disease, health promotion and disease prevention, injury prevention, international health, environmental studies, occupational health studies.

The University of North Carolina at Charlotte, Graduate School, College of Health and Human Services, Department of Public Health Sciences, Charlotte, NC 28223-0001. Offers community health (Certificate); health administration (MHA); health services research (PhD); public health (MSPH). *Accreditation:* CAHME. Part-time programs available. *Faculty:* 16 full-time (10 women), 2 part-time/adjunct (1 woman). *Students:* 80 full-time (67 women), 40 part-time (30 women); includes 30 minority (22 Black or African American, non-Hispanic/Latino; 3 Asian, non-Hispanic/Latino; 5 Hispanic/Latino), 10 international. Average age 28. 171 applicants, 57% accepted, 46 enrolled. In 2011, 53 master's, 3 doctorates, 5 other advanced degrees awarded. Terminal master's awarded for partial completion of doctoral program. *Degree requirements:* For master's, thesis or comprehensive exam; for doctorate, thesis/dissertation. *Entrance requirements:* For master's, GRE or MAT (public health), GRE or GMAT (health administration), minimum GPA of 3.0 during previous 2 years, 2.75 overall. Additional exam requirements/recommendations for international students: Required—TOEFL (minimum score 557 paper-based; 220 computer-based; 83 iBT) *Application deadline:* For fall admission, 7/1 for domestic students, 5/1 for international students; for spring admission, 11/1 for domestic students, 10/1 for international students. Applications are processed on a rolling basis. Application fee: $65 ($75 for international students). Electronic applications accepted. *Expenses:* Tuition, state resident: full-time $3689. Tuition, nonresident: full-time $15,226. *Required fees:* $2198. Tuition and fees vary according to course load and program. *Financial support:* In 2011–12, 21 students received support, including 5 research assistantships (averaging $9,974 per year), 15 teaching assistantships (averaging $8,502 per year); career-related internships or fieldwork, Federal Work-Study, institutionally sponsored loans, scholarships/grants, unspecified assistantships, and administrative assistantship also available. Support available to part-time students. Financial award application deadline: 4/1; financial award applicants required to submit FAFSA. *Faculty research:* Pediatric asthma self-management, reproductive epidemiology, social aspects of injury prevention, chronic illness self-care, competency-based professional education. *Total annual research expenditures:* $405,550. *Unit head:* Dr. Andrew R. Harver, Chair, 704-687-8680, Fax: 704-687-6122, E-mail: arharver@uncc.edu. *Application contact:* Kathy B. Giddings, Director of Graduate Admissions, 704-687-5503, Fax: 704-687-3279, E-mail: gradadm@uncc.edu. Web site: http://publichealth.uncc.edu/.

University of Northern Colorado, Graduate School, College of Natural and Health Sciences, School of Human Sciences, Program in Public Health, Greeley, CO 80639. Offers public health education (MPH). *Accreditation:* CEPH. *Degree requirements:* For master's, comprehensive exam, thesis or alternative. *Entrance requirements:* For master's, GRE General Test, 2 letters of recommendation. Electronic applications accepted.

University of North Florida, Brooks College of Health, Department of Public Health, Jacksonville, FL 32224. Offers aging services (Certificate); community health (MPH); geriatric management (MSH); health administration (MHA); rehabilitation counseling (MS). *Accreditation:* CEPH. Part-time and evening/weekend programs available. *Faculty:* 15 full-time (10 women), 3 part-time/adjunct (2 women). *Students:* 106 full-time (77 women), 55 part-time (36 women); includes 28 minority (10 Black or African American, non-Hispanic/Latino; 2 American Indian or Alaska Native, non-Hispanic/Latino; 9 Asian, non-Hispanic/Latino; 5 Hispanic/Latino; 2 Two or more races, non-Hispanic/Latino), 7 international. Average age 30. 209 applicants, 38% accepted, 51 enrolled. In 2011, 65 master's awarded. *Degree requirements:* For master's, thesis optional. *Entrance requirements:* For master's, GRE General Test (MSH, MS, MPH); GMAT or GRE General Test (MHA), minimum GPA of 3.0 in last 60 hours. Additional exam requirements/recommendations for international students: Required—TOEFL (minimum score 500 paper-based; 173 computer-based). *Application deadline:* For fall admission, 7/1 priority date for domestic students, 5/1 for international students; for spring admission, 11/1 priority date for domestic students, 10/1 for international students. Applications are processed on a rolling basis. Application fee: $30. Electronic applications accepted. *Expenses:* Tuition, state resident: full-time $8793; part-time $366.38 per credit hour. Tuition, nonresident: full-time $23,502; part-time $979.24 per credit hour. *Required fees:* $1384; $57.66 per credit hour. Tuition and fees vary according to course load and program. *Financial support:* In 2011–12, 60 students received support. Research assistantships, teaching assistantships, career-related internships or fieldwork, Federal Work-Study, scholarships/grants, and tuition waivers (partial) available. Support available to part-time students. Financial award application deadline: 4/1; financial award applicants required to submit FAFSA. *Faculty research:* Dietary supplements; alcohol, tobacco, and other drug use prevention; turnover among

health professionals; aging; psychosocial aspects of disabilities. *Total annual research expenditures:* $197,732. *Unit head:* Dr. JoAnn Nolin, Chair, 904-620-2840, Fax: 904-620-2848, E-mail: jnolin@unf.edu. *Application contact:* Heather Kenney, Director of Advising, 904-620-2810, Fax: 904-620-1030, E-mail: heather.kenney@unf.edu. Web site: http://www.unf.edu/brooks/public_health/.

University of North Texas Health Science Center at Fort Worth, School of Public Health, Fort Worth, TX 76107-2699. Offers biostatistics (MPH); community health (MPH); disease control and prevention (Dr PH); environmental and occupational health sciences (MPH); epidemiology (MPH); health administration (MHA); health policy and management (MPH, Dr PH); DO/MPH; MS/MPH; MSN/MPH. MPH offered jointly with University of North Texas; DO/MPH with Texas College of Osteopathic Medicine. *Accreditation:* CEPH. Part-time and evening/weekend programs available. *Degree requirements:* For master's, thesis or alternative, supervised internship; for doctorate, thesis/dissertation, supervised internship. *Entrance requirements:* For master's, GRE General Test. Additional exam requirements/recommendations for international students: Required—TOEFL. Electronic applications accepted.

University of Oklahoma Health Sciences Center, Graduate College, College of Public Health, Program in General Public Health, Oklahoma City, OK 73190. Offers MPH, Dr PH.

University of Oklahoma Health Sciences Center, Graduate College, College of Public Health, Program in Preparedness and Terrorism, Oklahoma City, OK 73190. Offers MPH.

University of Ottawa, Faculty of Graduate and Postdoctoral Studies, Interdisciplinary Programs, Program in Population Health, Ottawa, ON K1N 6N5, Canada. Offers PhD. *Degree requirements:* For doctorate, comprehensive exam, thesis/dissertation. Electronic applications accepted. *Faculty research:* Population health.

University of Pennsylvania, Perelman School of Medicine, Master of Public Health Program, Philadelphia, PA 19129. Offers environmental health (MPH); generalist (MPH); global health (MPH); DMD/MPH; JD/MPH; MD/MPH; MPH/MBE; MSCE/MPH; MSN/MPH; MSW/MPH; PhD/MPH. Part-time and evening/weekend programs available. *Faculty:* 30 full-time (18 women), 35 part-time/adjunct (19 women). *Students:* 34 full-time (29 women), 28 part-time (24 women); includes 11 minority (3 Black or African American, non-Hispanic/Latino; 6 Asian, non-Hispanic/Latino; 2 Hispanic/Latino), 2 international. 182 applicants, 25% accepted, 27 enrolled. In 2011, 18 master's awarded. *Entrance requirements:* For master's, GRE. Additional exam requirements/recommendations for international students: Recommended—TOEFL. *Application deadline:* For spring admission, 4/30 for domestic and international students. Application fee: $70. *Expenses:* Tuition: Full-time $26,660; part-time $4944 per course. *Required fees:* $2318; $291 per course. Tuition and fees vary according to course load, degree level and program. *Financial support:* In 2011–12, 4 teaching assistantships with partial tuition reimbursements were awarded; fellowships, scholarships/grants, and tuition waivers (partial) also available. Financial award application deadline: 4/30. *Faculty research:* Health disparities, health behaviors, obesity, global health, epidemiology and prevention research. *Unit head:* Dr. Jennifer A. Pinto-Martin, Director, 215-898-4726, E-mail: pinto@nursing.upenn.edu. *Application contact:* Karen Kelly, Admission Coordinator, 215-573-0917, Fax: 215-573-9025, E-mail: kakelly@mail.med.upenn.edu. Web site: http://www.publichealth.med.upenn.edu/.

University of Pittsburgh, Graduate School of Public Health, Pittsburgh, PA 15260. Offers MHA, MPH, MS, Dr PH, PhD, Certificate, JD/MPH, MD/MPH, MD/PhD, MID/MPH, MPH/MPA, MPH/MSW, MPH/PhD. *Accreditation:* CEPH (one or more programs are accredited). Part-time programs available. *Faculty:* 163 full-time (76 women), 252 part-time/adjunct (101 women). *Students:* 458 full-time (317 women), 181 part-time (136 women); includes 126 minority (49 Black or African American, non-Hispanic/Latino; 45 Asian, non-Hispanic/Latino; 14 Hispanic/Latino; 18 Two or more races, non-Hispanic/Latino), 146 international. Average age 30. 1,478 applicants, 59% accepted, 187 enrolled. In 2011, 147 master's, 43 doctorates awarded. Terminal master's awarded for partial completion of doctoral program. *Degree requirements:* For master's, comprehensive exam (for some programs); thesis; for doctorate, comprehensive exam, thesis/dissertation. *Entrance requirements:* For master's, GRE; for doctorate and Certificate, GRE, bachelor's degree, recommendations, professional statement, transcripts. Additional exam requirements/recommendations for international students: Required—TOEFL (minimum score 550 paper-based; 80 iBT) or IELTS (minimum score 6.5). *Application deadline:* For fall admission, 1/4 priority date for domestic students, 1/4 for international students; for winter admission, 11/1 priority date for domestic students, 8/1 for international students; for spring admission, 3/1 priority date for domestic students, 2/1 for international students. Applications are processed on a rolling basis. Application fee: $115. Electronic applications accepted. *Expenses:* Tuition, state resident: full-time $18,774; part-time $760 per credit. Tuition, nonresident: full-time $30,736; part-time $1258 per credit. *Required fees:* $740; $200 per term. Tuition and fees vary according to program. *Financial support:* In 2011–12, 243 students received support, including 48 fellowships (averaging $6,534 per year), 175 research assistantships (averaging $11,323 per year), 20 teaching assistantships (averaging $10,475 per year); career-related internships or fieldwork, scholarships/grants, traineeships, health care benefits, tuition waivers (full and partial), and unspecified assistantships also available. Support available to part-time students. Financial award applicants required to submit FAFSA. *Faculty research:* Statistical genetics, genetic epidemiology, community-based participatory research, occupational and pulmonary medicine, Epstein-Barr virus. *Total annual research expenditures:* $77.4 million. *Unit head:* Dr. Donald S. Burke, Dean, 412-624-3001, E-mail: donburke@pitt.edu. *Application contact:* Karrie Presutti, Admissions Manager, E-mail: stuaff@pitt.edu. Web site: http://www.publichealth.pitt.edu/.

University of Rochester, School of Medicine and Dentistry, Graduate Programs in Medicine and Dentistry, Department of Community and Preventive Medicine, Programs in Public Health and Clinical Investigation, Rochester, NY 14627. Offers clinical investigation (MS); public health (MPH); MBA/MPH; MD/MPH; MPH/MS; MPH/PhD. *Accreditation:* CEPH. *Entrance requirements:* For master's, GRE General Test. *Expenses:* Tuition: Full-time $41,040.

University of San Francisco, School of Nursing and Health Professions, Program in Public Health, San Francisco, CA 94117-1080. Offers MPH. *Faculty:* 2 part-time/adjunct (both women). *Students:* 22 full-time (21 women); includes 9 minority (1 Black or African American, non-Hispanic/Latino; 3 Asian, non-Hispanic/Latino; 2 Hispanic/Latino; 3 Two or more races, non-Hispanic/Latino). Average age 27. 52 applicants, 62% accepted, 22 enrolled. *Application deadline:* For fall admission, 6/15 for domestic students; for spring admission, 10/15 for domestic students. *Expenses:* Tuition: Full-time $20,070; part-time $1115 per unit. Tuition and fees vary according to course load, campus/location and program. *Unit head:* Dr. Kia James, Coordinator, 415-422-5555. *Application contact:* Information Contact, 415-422-4723, Fax: 415-422-2217. Web site: http://www.usfca.edu/nursing/mph/.

University of South Africa, College of Human Sciences, Pretoria, South Africa. Offers adult education (M Ed); African languages (MA, PhD); African politics (MA, PhD); Afrikaans (MA, PhD); ancient history (MA, PhD); ancient Near Eastern studies (MA, PhD); anthropology (MA, PhD); applied linguistics (MA); Arabic (MA, PhD); archaeology

(MA); art history (MA); Biblical archaeology (MA); Biblical studies (M Th, D Th, PhD); Christian spirituality (M Th, D Th); church history (M Th, D Th); classical studies (MA, PhD); clinical psychology (MA); communication (MA, PhD); comparative education (M Ed, Ed D); consulting psychology (D Admin, D Com, PhD); curriculum studies (M Ed, Ed D); development studies (M Admin, MA, D Admin, PhD); didactics (M Ed, Ed D); education (M Tech); education management (M Ed, Ed D); educational psychology (M Ed); English (MA); environmental education (M Ed); French (MA, PhD); German (MA, PhD); Greek (MA); guidance and counseling (M Ed); health studies (MA, PhD), including health sciences education (MA), health services management (MA), medical and surgical nursing science (critical care general) (MA), midwifery and neonatal nursing science (MA), trauma and emergency care (MA); history (MA, PhD); history of education (Ed D); inclusive education (M Ed, Ed D); information and communications technology policy and regulation (MA); information science (MA, MIS, PhD); international politics (MA, PhD); Islamic studies (MA, PhD); Italian (MA, PhD); Judaica (MA, PhD); linguistics (MA, PhD); mathematical education (M Ed); mathematics education (MA); missiology (M Th, D Th); modern Hebrew (MA, PhD); musicology (MA, MMus, D Mus, PhD); natural science education (M Ed); New Testament (M Th, D Th); Old Testament (D Th); pastoral therapy (M Th, D Th); philosophy (MA); philosophy of education (M Ed, Ed D); politics (MA, PhD); Portuguese (MA, PhD); practical theology (M Th, D Th); psychology (MA, MS, PhD); psychology of education (M Ed, Ed D); public health (MA); religious studies (MA, D Th, PhD); Romance languages (MA); Russian (MA, PhD); Semitic languages (MA, PhD); social behavior studies in HIV/AIDS (MA); social science (mental health) (MA); social science in development studies (MA); social science in psychology (MA); social science in social work (MA); social science in sociology (MA); social work (MSW, DSW, PhD); socio-education (M Ed, Ed D); sociolinguistics (MA); sociology (MA, PhD); Spanish (MA, PhD); systematic theology (M Th, D Th); TESOL (teaching English to speakers of other languages) (MA); theological ethics (M Th, D Th); theory of literature (MA, PhD); urban ministries (D Th); urban ministry (M Th).

University of South Carolina, The Graduate School, Arnold School of Public Health, Program in General Public Health, Columbia, SC 29208. Offers MPH. *Accreditation:* CEPH. Part-time programs available. *Degree requirements:* For master's, comprehensive exam, practicum. *Entrance requirements:* For master's, DAT or MCAT, GRE General Test, previously earned MD or doctoral degree. Additional exam requirements/recommendations for international students: Required—TOEFL (minimum score 570 paper-based; 230 computer-based). Electronic applications accepted.

University of South Carolina, The Graduate School, Arnold School of Public Health, Program in Physical Activity and Public Health, Columbia, SC 29208. Offers MPH. *Accreditation:* CEPH. Part-time programs available. *Degree requirements:* For master's, comprehensive exam, practicum. *Entrance requirements:* For master's, GRE. Additional exam requirements/recommendations for international students: Required—TOEFL (minimum score 570 paper-based; 230 computer-based). Electronic applications accepted.

University of South Carolina, The Graduate School, College of Nursing, Program in Nursing and Public Health, Columbia, SC 29208. Offers MPH/MSN. *Accreditation:* AACN; CEPH. Part-time programs available. *Entrance requirements:* Additional exam requirements/recommendations for international students: Required—TOEFL (minimum score 570 paper-based; 230 computer-based). Electronic applications accepted. *Faculty research:* System research, evidence based practice, breast cancer, violence.

University of Southern California, Keck School of Medicine and Graduate School, Graduate Programs in Medicine, Department of Preventive Medicine, Program in Health Behavior Research, Los Angeles, CA 90032. Offers PhD. *Faculty:* 21 full-time (13 women). *Students:* 24 full-time (18 women); includes 6 minority (1 American Indian or Alaska Native, non-Hispanic/Latino; 5 Asian, non-Hispanic/Latino), 2 international. Average age 32. 33 applicants, 30% accepted, 6 enrolled. In 2011, 5 doctorates awarded. *Degree requirements:* For doctorate, comprehensive exam, thesis/dissertation. *Entrance requirements:* For doctorate, GRE General Test, minimum GPA of 3.0. Additional exam requirements/recommendations for international students: Required—TOEFL (minimum score 600 paper-based; 250 computer-based; 100 iBT). *Application deadline:* For fall admission, 12/1 priority date for domestic students, 12/1 for international students. Application fee: $85. Electronic applications accepted. *Financial support:* In 2011–12, 23 students received support, including 7 fellowships with full tuition reimbursements available (averaging $31,037 per year), 10 research assistantships with full and partial tuition reimbursements available (averaging $31,037 per year), 8 teaching assistantships with full and partial tuition reimbursements available (averaging $31,037 per year); institutionally sponsored loans, scholarships/grants, traineeships, health care benefits, and unspecified assistantships also available. Financial award application deadline: 5/4; financial award applicants required to submit CSS PROFILE or FAFSA. *Faculty research:* Obesity prevention; etiology and prevention of substance abuse, other addictive behaviors, and chronic diseases; health disparities; translational research. *Total annual research expenditures:* $3.4 million. *Unit head:* Dr. Jennifer Unger, Director, 323-442-8234, E-mail: unger@usc.edu. *Application contact:* Marny Barovich, Program Manager, 323-442-8299, E-mail: barovich@hsc.usc.edu. Web site: http://phdhbr.usc.edu.

University of Southern Mississippi, Graduate School, College of Health, Department of Community Health Sciences, Hattiesburg, MS 39406-0001. Offers epidemiology and biostatistics (MPH); health education (MPH); health policy/administration (MPH); occupational/environmental health (MPH); public health nutrition (MPH). *Accreditation:* CEPH. Part-time and evening/weekend programs available. *Faculty:* 8 full-time (4 women), 1 part-time/adjunct (0 women). *Students:* 81 full-time (66 women), 17 part-time (13 women); includes 49 minority (43 Black or African American, non-Hispanic/Latino; 1 Asian, non-Hispanic/Latino; 2 Hispanic/Latino; 3 Two or more races, non-Hispanic/Latino), 7 international. Average age 32. 70 applicants, 94% accepted, 43 enrolled. In 2011, 45 degrees awarded. *Degree requirements:* For master's, comprehensive exam, thesis (for some programs). *Entrance requirements:* For master's, GRE General Test, minimum GPA of 2.75 in last 60 hours. Additional exam requirements/recommendations for international students: Required—TOEFL, IELTS. *Application deadline:* For fall admission, 3/1 priority date for domestic students, 3/1 for international students; for spring admission, 1/10 priority date for domestic students, 1/10 for international students. Applications are processed on a rolling basis. Application fee: $50. Electronic applications accepted. *Financial support:* In 2011–12, 5 research assistantships with full tuition reimbursements (averaging $7,000 per year), 1 teaching assistantship with full tuition reimbursement (averaging $8,263 per year) were awarded; career-related internships or fieldwork, Federal Work-Study, institutionally sponsored loans, scholarships/grants, health care benefits, and unspecified assistantships also available. Financial award application deadline: 3/15; financial award applicants required to submit FAFSA. *Faculty research:* Rural health care delivery, school health, nutrition of pregnant teens, risk factor reduction, sexually transmitted diseases. *Unit head:* Dr. Emanual Ahua, Interim Chair, 601-266-5437, Fax: 601-266-5043. *Application contact:* Shonna Breland, Manager of Graduate Admissions, 601-266-6563, Fax: 601-266-5138. Web site: http://www.usm.edu/chs.

University of South Florida, Graduate School, College of Public Health, Tampa, FL 33612. Offers MHA, MPH, MSPH, Dr PH, PhD. *Accreditation:* CEPH (one or more programs are accredited). Part-time and evening/weekend programs available.

Postbaccalaureate distance learning degree programs offered (minimal on-campus study). *Degree requirements:* For master's, comprehensive exam, thesis (for some programs); for doctorate, comprehensive exam, thesis/dissertation. *Entrance requirements:* For master's, GRE General Test, minimum GPA of 3.0 in upper-level course work, 3 professional letters of recommendation, resume/curriculum vitae; for doctorate, GRE General Test, minimum GPA of 3.0 in upper-level course work, goal statement letter, three professional letters of recommendation, resume/curriculum vitae, writing sample. Additional exam requirements/recommendations for international students: Required—TOEFL (minimum score 550 paper-based; 213 computer-based; 79 iBT). Electronic applications accepted.

The University of Tennessee, Graduate School, College of Education, Health and Human Sciences, Program in Public Health, Knoxville, TN 37996. Offers community health education (MPH); gerontology (MPH); health planning/administration (MPH); MS/MPH. *Accreditation:* CEPH. *Degree requirements:* For master's, thesis optional. *Entrance requirements:* For master's, minimum GPA of 2.7. Additional exam requirements/recommendations for international students: Required—TOEFL. Electronic applications accepted. *Expenses:* Tuition, state resident: full-time $8332; part-time $464 per credit hour. Tuition, nonresident: full-time $25,174; part-time $1400 per credit hour. *Required fees:* $1162; $56 per credit hour. Tuition and fees vary according to program.

The University of Texas Health Science Center at Houston, The University of Texas School of Public Health, Houston, TX 77030. Offers MPH, MS, Dr PH, PhD, Certificate, JD/MPH, MD/MPH, MS/MPH, MSN/MPH, MSW/MPH, PhD/MPH. JD/MPH and MSW/MPH offered jointly with University of Houston. *Accreditation:* CEPH. Part-time programs available. *Degree requirements:* For master's, thesis; for doctorate, comprehensive exam, thesis/dissertation. *Entrance requirements:* For master's and doctorate, GRE General Test. Additional exam requirements/recommendations for international students: Required—TOEFL (minimum score 565 paper-based; 225 computer-based; 86 iBT). Electronic applications accepted. *Faculty research:* Big-security and public health preparedness, health promotion and prevention research, health services research, infectious diseases, environmental and occupational health.

The University of Texas Medical Branch, Graduate School of Biomedical Sciences, Program in Preventive Medicine and Community Health, Program in Public Health, Galveston, TX 77555. Offers MPH. *Accreditation:* CEPH. *Degree requirements:* For master's, thesis. *Entrance requirements:* For master's, GRE, United States Medical Licensing Exam (USMLE) or NBE, preventive medicine residency. Additional exam requirements/recommendations for international students: Required—TOEFL (minimum score 550 paper-based; 213 computer-based). Electronic applications accepted.

University of the Sciences in Philadelphia, College of Graduate Studies, Mayes College of Healthcare Business and Policy, Program in Public Health, Philadelphia, PA 19104-4495. Offers MPH.

University of the Sciences in Philadelphia, College of Graduate Studies, Program in Health Policy and Public Health, Philadelphia, PA 19104-4495. Offers health policy (MPH, MS); public health (MPH). Part-time and evening/weekend programs available. *Degree requirements:* For doctorate, comprehensive exam, thesis/dissertation. *Entrance requirements:* For master's and doctorate, GRE General Test. Additional exam requirements/recommendations for international students: Required—TOEFL, TWE. *Expenses:* Contact institution. *Faculty research:* Managed care, pharmacoeconomics, health law and regulation, rehabilitation, genetic technologies.

The University of Toledo, College of Graduate Studies, College of Medicine and Life Sciences, Department of Public Health and Preventative Medicine, Toledo, OH 43606-3390. Offers biostatistics and epidemiology (Certificate); contemporary gerontological practice (Certificate); environmental and occupational health and safety (MPH); epidemiology (MPH, Certificate); global public health (Certificate); health administration (MPH); health promotion (MPH); medical health and science education (Certificate); nutrition (MPH); occupational health (MSOH, Certificate); public health and emergency response (Certificate); MD/MPH. Part-time and evening/weekend programs available. *Faculty:* 6. *Students:* 95 full-time (74 women), 66 part-time (45 women); includes 37 minority (21 Black or African American, non-Hispanic/Latino; 11 Asian, non-Hispanic/Latino; 3 Hispanic/Latino; 2 Two or more races, non-Hispanic/Latino), 6 international. Average age 29. 132 applicants, 75% accepted, 70 enrolled. In 2011, 60 master's, 26 other advanced degrees awarded. *Degree requirements:* For master's, thesis or alternative. *Entrance requirements:* For master's, GRE, minimum undergraduate GPA of 3.0, three letters of recommendation, statement of purpose, transcripts from all prior institutions attended, resume; for Certificate, minimum undergraduate GPA of 3.0, three letters of recommendation, statement of purpose, transcripts from all prior institutions attended, resume. Additional exam requirements/recommendations for international students: Required—TOEFL (minimum score 550 paper-based; 213 computer-based; 80 iBT), IELTS (minimum score 6.5). *Application deadline:* For fall admission, 3/15 for domestic and international students. Applications are processed on a rolling basis. Application fee: $45 ($75 for international students). Electronic applications accepted. *Financial support:* In 2011–12, 15 research assistantships with full tuition reimbursements (averaging $10,000 per year) were awarded; Federal Work-Study, institutionally sponsored loans, scholarships/grants, tuition waivers (full and partial), and unspecified assistantships also available. *Unit head:* Dr. Sheryl A. Milz, Chair, 419-383-3976, Fax: 419-383-6140, E-mail: sheryl.milz@utoledo.edu. *Application contact:* Joan Mulligan, Admissions Analyst, 419-383-4186, Fax: 419-383-6140, E-mail: joan.mulligan@utoledo.edu. Web site: http://nocphmph.org/.

University of Toronto, School of Graduate Studies, Dalla Lana School of Public Health, Toronto, ON M5S 1A1, Canada. Offers biostatistics (M Sc, PhD); community health (M Sc); epidemiology (MPH, PhD); health and behavioral science (PhD); health promotion (MPH); social science and health (PhD). *Accreditation:* CAHME (one or more programs are accredited); CEPH (one or more programs are accredited). Part-time programs available. *Degree requirements:* For master's, thesis (for some programs), practicum; for doctorate, comprehensive exam, thesis/dissertation, oral thesis defense. *Entrance requirements:* For master's, 2 letters of reference, relevant professional/research experience, minimum B average in final year; for doctorate, 2 letters of reference, relevant professional/research experience, minimum B+ average. Additional exam requirements/recommendations for international students: Required—TOEFL (minimum score 580 paper-based; 93 iBT), TWE (minimum score 5). Electronic applications accepted. *Expenses:* Contact institution.

University of Utah, School of Medicine and Graduate School, Graduate Programs in Medicine, Programs in Public Health, Salt Lake City, UT 84112-1107. Offers biostatistics (M Stat); public health (MPH, MSPH, PhD). *Accreditation:* CEPH (one or more programs are accredited). Part-time programs available. *Degree requirements:* For master's, comprehensive exam, thesis or project (MSPH); for doctorate, comprehensive exam, thesis/dissertation. *Entrance requirements:* For master's and doctorate, GRE General Test, 3 letters of reference, in-person interviews, minimum GPA of 3.0. Additional exam requirements/recommendations for international students: Required—TOEFL (minimum score 550 paper-based; 175 computer-based). Electronic applications accepted. *Faculty research:* Health services, health policy, epidemiology of chronic disease, infectious disease epidemiology, cancer epidemiology.

University of Virginia, School of Medicine, Department of Public Health Sciences, Program in Public Health, Charlottesville, VA 22903. Offers MPH. *Accreditation:* CEPH. *Students:* 49 full-time (32 women), 5 part-time (3 women); includes 17 minority (11 Black or African American, non-Hispanic/Latino; 5 Asian, non-Hispanic/Latino; 1 Two or more races, non-Hispanic/Latino), 3 international. Average age 26. 85 applicants, 42% accepted, 23 enrolled. In 2011, 14 master's awarded. *Degree requirements:* For master's, written or oral comprehensive exam or thesis. *Entrance requirements:* For master's, GRE, MCAT, LSAT or GMAT, 2 letters of recommendation. Additional exam requirements/recommendations for international students: Required—TOEFL. *Application deadline:* For fall admission, 3/30 for domestic and international students. Applications are processed on a rolling basis. Application fee: $60. Electronic applications accepted. *Financial support:* Applicants required to submit FAFSA. *Unit head:* Dr. Ruth Gaare Bernheim, Chair, 434-924-8430, Fax: 434-924-8437. *Application contact:* Tracey L. Brookman, Academic Programs Administrator, 434-924-8430, Fax: 434-924-8437, E-mail: ms-hes@virginia.edu. Web site: http://www.healthsystem.virginia.edu/internet/phs/wdc-lib/phs_home.cfm?flush-1.

University of Virginia, School of Nursing, Charlottesville, VA 22903. Offers acute and specialty care (MSN); acute care nurse practitioner (MSN); clinical nurse leadership (MSN); community-public health leadership (MSN); nursing (DNP, PhD); psychiatric mental health counseling (MSN); MSN/MBA. *Accreditation:* AACN. Part-time programs available. *Faculty:* 44 full-time (43 women), 2 part-time/adjunct (both women). *Students:* 174 full-time (152 women), 151 part-time (139 women); includes 57 minority (28 Black or African American, non-Hispanic/Latino; 1 American Indian or Alaska Native, non-Hispanic/Latino; 14 Asian, non-Hispanic/Latino; 10 Hispanic/Latino; 4 Two or more races, non-Hispanic/Latino), 11 international. Average age 37. 236 applicants, 40% accepted, 74 enrolled. In 2011, 70 master's, 15 doctorates awarded. *Degree requirements:* For doctorate, comprehensive exam (for some programs), capstone project (DNP), dissertation (PhD). *Entrance requirements:* For master's, GRE General Test, MAT; for doctorate, GRE General Test. Additional exam requirements/recommendations for international students: Required—TOEFL, IELTS. *Application deadline:* Applications are processed on a rolling basis. Application fee: $60. Electronic applications accepted. *Expenses:* Contact institution. *Financial support:* Fellowships, research assistantships, teaching assistantships, Federal Work-Study, and scholarships/grants available. Financial award applicants required to submit FAFSA. *Unit head:* Dorrie K. Fontaine, Dean, 434-924-0141, Fax: 434-982-1809. *Application contact:* Clay Hysell, Assistant Dean for Admissions and Financial Services, 434-924-0141, Fax: 434-982-1809, E-mail: nur-osa@virginia.edu. Web site: http://www.nursing.virginia.edu/.

University of Waterloo, Graduate Studies, Faculty of Applied Health Sciences, School of Public Health and Health Systems, Program in Public Health, Waterloo, ON N2L 3G1, Canada. Offers MPH. Part-time programs available. Postbaccalaureate distance learning degree programs offered (minimal on-campus study). *Degree requirements:* For master's, practicum. *Entrance requirements:* For master's, honour's degree, minimum B average, resume, 1 year work experience. Additional exam requirements/recommendations for international students: Required—TOEFL, TWE. Electronic applications accepted. *Faculty research:* Public health, population health, health communication, health promotion and disease prevention, environmental health.

University of West Florida, College of Arts and Sciences: Sciences, School of Allied Health and Life Sciences, Program in Public Health, Pensacola, FL 32514-5750. Offers MPH. *Accreditation:* CEPH. Part-time and evening/weekend programs available. *Faculty:* 4 full-time (3 women), 8 part-time/adjunct (3 women). *Students:* 38 full-time (26 women), 53 part-time (37 women); includes 21 minority (15 Black or African American, non-Hispanic/Latino; 4 Asian, non-Hispanic/Latino; 2 Two or more races, non-Hispanic/Latino), 3 international. Average age 36. 63 applicants, 78% accepted, 34 enrolled. In 2011, 11 master's awarded. *Entrance requirements:* For master's, GRE (minimum score: verbal 450, quantitative 550), GMAT (minimum score 465), or MCAT (minimum score 25), official transcripts; two personal writing samples (e.g., written reports completed by applicant or other representative samples of professional writing skills); basic computer competency; three letters of recommendation. Additional exam requirements/recommendations for international students: Required—TOEFL (minimum score 550 paper-based; 213 computer-based). *Application deadline:* For fall admission, 6/1 for domestic and international students; for spring admission, 10/1 for domestic and international students. Applications are processed on a rolling basis. Application fee: $30. *Expenses:* Tuition, state resident: full-time $5729; part-time $302 per credit hour. Tuition, nonresident: full-time $20,059; part-time $961 per credit hour. *Required fees:* $1509; $63 per credit hour. *Financial support:* In 2011–12, 4 research assistantships with partial tuition reimbursements (averaging $6,560 per year) were awarded. Financial award application deadline: 4/15; financial award applicants required to submit FAFSA. *Unit head:* Dr. George L. Stewart, Chairperson, 850-474-2748. *Application contact:* Terry McCray, Assistant Director of Graduate Studies, 850-473-7718, Fax: 850-474-7714, E-mail: gradadmissions@uwf.edu. Web site: http://uwf.edu/sahls/masters-ph/.

University of Wisconsin–La Crosse, Office of University Graduate Studies, College of Science and Health, Department of Health Education and Health Promotion, La Crosse, WI 54601-3742. Offers community health education (MPH, MS); school health education (MS). *Accreditation:* CEPH (one or more programs are accredited). Part-time and evening/weekend programs available. *Faculty:* 7 full-time (4 women), 1 (woman) part-time/adjunct. *Students:* 19 full-time (15 women), 14 part-time (10 women); includes 3 minority (2 Asian, non-Hispanic/Latino; 1 Hispanic/Latino), 5 international. Average age 28. 29 applicants, 72% accepted, 10 enrolled. In 2011, 12 master's awarded. *Degree requirements:* For master's, thesis (for some programs), community health education preceptorship. *Entrance requirements:* For master's, GRE General Test, GRE Subject Test (MPH). Additional exam requirements/recommendations for international students: Required—TOEFL (minimum score 550 paper-based; 213 computer-based). Application fee: $56. Electronic applications accepted. *Expenses:* Tuition, state resident: full-time $8391; part-time $481.17 per credit. Tuition, nonresident: full-time $17,850; part-time $1006.68 per credit. *Required fees:* $2 per credit. $18.25 per semester. Tuition and fees vary according to course load, program, reciprocity agreements and student level. *Financial support:* In 2011–12, 3 research assistantships with partial tuition reimbursements (averaging $6,682 per year) were awarded; Federal Work-Study, scholarships/grants, health care benefits, and tuition waivers (partial) also available. Support available to part-time students. Financial award application deadline: 3/15; financial award applicants required to submit FAFSA. *Faculty research:* Stress management, wellness inventories, needs assessment, health promotion, drug and alcohol use, education, school curriculum. *Unit head:* Dr. Dan Duquette, Chair, 608-785-8161, Fax: 608-785-6792, E-mail: duquette.rode@uwlax.edu. *Application contact:* Kathryn Kiefer, Director of Admissions, 608-785-8939, E-mail: admissions@uwlax.edu. Web site: http://www.uwlax.edu/sah/hehp/.

University of Wisconsin–Milwaukee, Graduate School, College of Nursing, Milwaukee, WI 53201-0413. Offers family nursing practitioner (Post Master's Certificate); health professional education (Certificate); nursing (MS, PhD); public health (Certificate). *Accreditation:* AACN. Part-time programs available. *Faculty:* 30 full-time (29 women), 2 part-time/adjunct (both women). *Students:* 125 full-time (114 women), 122 part-time (108 women); includes 34 minority (15 Black or African American, non-Hispanic/Latino; 1 American Indian or Alaska Native, non-Hispanic/Latino; 7 Asian, non-Hispanic/Latino; 1 Hispanic/Latino; 10 Two or more races, non-Hispanic/Latino), 6 international. Average age 39. 128 applicants, 49% accepted, 41 enrolled. In 2011, 52 master's, 16 doctorates awarded. *Degree requirements:* For master's, thesis; for doctorate, thesis/dissertation. *Entrance requirements:* For master's, GRE General Test or MAT, autobiographical sketch; for doctorate, GRE, minimum GPA of 3.2. Additional exam requirements/recommendations for international students: Required—TOEFL (minimum score 550 paper-based; 79 iBT), IELTS (minimum score 6.5). *Application deadline:* For fall admission, 1/1 priority date for domestic students; for spring admission, 9/1 for domestic students. Applications are processed on a rolling basis. Application fee: $56 ($96 for international students). Electronic applications accepted. One-time fee: $506.10 full-time. Tuition and fees vary according to course load and reciprocity agreements. *Financial support:* In 2011–12, 3 fellowships, 1 research assistantship, 9 teaching assistantships were awarded; career-related internships or fieldwork, Federal Work-Study, health care benefits, unspecified assistantships, and project assistantships also available. Support available to part-time students. Financial award application deadline: 4/15; financial award applicants required to submit FAFSA. *Total annual research expenditures:* $3.3 million. *Unit head:* Dr. Sally Lundeen, Dean, 414-229-4189, E-mail: slundeen@uwm.edu. *Application contact:* Kim Litwack, Representative, 414-229-5098. Web site: http://www.uwm.edu/Dept/Nursing/.

University of Wisconsin–Milwaukee, Graduate School, Zilber School of Public Health, Department of Public Health, Milwaukee, WI 53201-0413. Offers community and behavioral health promotion (PhD); public health (MPH, Graduate Certificate). *Students:* 5 full-time (3 women), 8 part-time (7 women); includes 1 minority (Black or African American, non-Hispanic/Latino), 1 international. Average age 30. 22 applicants, 59% accepted, 11 enrolled. One-time fee: $506.10 full-time. Tuition and fees vary according to course load and reciprocity agreements. *Total annual research expenditures:* $1.3 million. *Unit head:* Paul Florsheim, Department Chair, 414-229-2490, E-mail: paulf@uwm.edu. *Application contact:* Darcie K. G. Warren, Graduate Program Manager, 414-229-5633, E-mail: darcie@uwm.edu.

Vanderbilt University, Graduate School, Center for Medicine, Health, and Society, Nashville, TN 37240-1001. Offers MA, MD/MA. *Students:* 5 full-time (all women). Average age 25. 8 applicants, 63% accepted, 4 enrolled. In 2011, 2 degrees awarded. *Degree requirements:* For master's, comprehensive exam (for some programs), thesis (for some programs). *Entrance requirements:* Additional exam requirements/recommendations for international students: Required—TOEFL (minimum score 570 paper-based; 230 computer-based; 88 iBT). *Application deadline:* For fall admission, 1/15 for domestic and international students. Electronic applications accepted. *Financial support:* Federal Work-Study, scholarships/grants, and health care benefits available. Financial award application deadline: 1/15; financial award applicants required to submit CSS PROFILE or FAFSA. *Faculty research:* Cultural history of health and disease, the rise of scientific medicine, scientific and medical constructions of gender and sexuality, integrative medicine, domestic and international public health, healthcare administration. *Unit head:* Dr. Jonathan Metzl, Director for Center for Medicine, Health and Society and Director of Graduate Studies, E-mail: jonathan.metzl@vanderbilt.edu. Web site: http://www.vanderbilt.edu/mhs/.

Vanderbilt University, School of Medicine, Program in Public Health, Nashville, TN 37240-1001. Offers MPH. *Degree requirements:* For master's, thesis, project. *Entrance requirements:* For master's, curriculum vitae.

Virginia Commonwealth University, Medical College of Virginia-Professional Programs, School of Medicine, School of Medicine Graduate Programs, Department of Epidemiology and Community Health, Richmond, VA 23284-9005. Offers epidemiology (MPH, PhD); public health practice (MPH); social and behavioral science (MPH); MD/MPH; MSW/MPH. *Accreditation:* CEPH. Part-time programs available. *Degree requirements:* For doctorate, comprehensive exam, thesis/dissertation. *Entrance requirements:* For master's, GRE; for doctorate, GRE General Test, interview, 3 letters of recommendation, minimum graduate GPA of 3.0, master's degree in public health or related field including epidemiology and biostatistics. Additional exam requirements/recommendations for international students: Required—TOEFL (minimum score 600 paper-based; 250 computer-based; 100 iBT). Electronic applications accepted. *Expenses:* Tuition, state resident: full-time $9133; part-time $507 per credit. Tuition, nonresident: full-time $18,777; part-time $1043 per credit. *Required fees:* $77 per credit. Tuition and fees vary according to degree level, campus/location, program and student level. *Faculty research:* Sickle cell anemia, breast cancer, HIV/AIDS, hospital epidemiology, infectious diseases.

Virginia Polytechnic Institute and State University, Virginia-Maryland Regional College of Veterinary Medicine, Master of Public Health Program, Blacksburg, VA 24061. Offers MPH. *Degree requirements:* For master's, comprehensive exam (for some programs), thesis (for some programs). *Entrance requirements:* For master's, GRE. Additional exam requirements/recommendations for international students: Required—TOEFL (minimum score 550 paper-based; 213 computer-based). *Application deadline:* For fall admission, 7/1 for domestic and international students; for spring admission, 12/1 for domestic and international students. Applications are processed on a rolling basis. Application fee: $65. Electronic applications accepted. *Expenses:* Tuition, state resident: full-time $10,048; part-time $558.25 per credit hour. Tuition, nonresident: full-time $19,497; part-time $1083.25 per credit hour. *Required fees:* $405 per semester. Tuition and fees vary according to course load, campus/location and program. *Financial support:* Career-related internships or fieldwork, Federal Work-Study, scholarships/grants, health care benefits, and unspecified assistantships available. *Unit head:* Dr. Francois C. Elvinger, Unit Head, 540-231-3532, E-mail: elvinger@vt.edu. *Application contact:* Kerry Redican, Information Contact, 540-231-5743, E-mail: kredican@vt.edu. Web site: http://mph.vetmed.vt.edu/.

Walden University, Graduate Programs, School of Counseling and Social Service, Minneapolis, MN 55401. Offers career counseling (MS); counselor education and supervision (PhD), including consultation, counseling and social change, forensic mental health counseling, general program, nonprofit management and leadership, trauma and crisis; human services (PhD), including clinical social work, criminal justice, disaster, crisis and intervention, family studies and intervention strategies, general program, human services administration, public health, social policy analysis and planning; marriage, couple, and family counseling (MS), including forensic counseling, trauma and crisis counseling; mental health counseling (MS), including forensic counseling, trauma and crisis counseling. Part-time and evening/weekend programs available. Postbaccalaureate distance learning degree programs offered (minimal on-campus study). *Faculty:* 26 full-time (19 women), 252 part-time/adjunct (178 women). *Students:* 3,089 full-time (2,614 women), 1,044 part-time (907 women); includes 2,109 minority (1,718 Black or African American, non-Hispanic/Latino; 31 American Indian or Alaska Native, non-Hispanic/Latino; 43 Asian, non-Hispanic/Latino; 236 Hispanic/Latino; 2 Native Hawaiian or other Pacific Islander, non-Hispanic/Latino; 79 Two or more races, non-Hispanic/Latino), 55 international. Average age 39. In 2011, 180 master's, 15 doctorates awarded. *Degree requirements:* For master's, residency (for some programs); for doctorate, thesis/dissertation, residency. *Entrance requirements:* For master's, bachelor's degree or equivalent in related field, minimum GPA of 2.5; for doctorate, master's degree or equivalent in related field; minimum GPA of 3.0; official

transcripts; three years' related professional/academic experience (preferred); access to computer and Internet. Additional exam requirements/recommendations for international students: Required—TOEFL (minimum score 550 paper-based; 213 computer-based), IELTS (minimum score 6.5), or Michigan English Language Assessment Battery (minimum score 82). *Application deadline:* Applications are processed on a rolling basis. Application fee: $50. Electronic applications accepted. *Financial support:* Federal Work-Study, scholarships/grants, unspecified assistantships, and family tuition reduction, active duty/veteran tuition reduction, group tuition reduction, interest-free payment plans, employee tuition reduction available. Support available to part-time students. Financial award applicants required to submit FAFSA. *Unit head:* Dr. Savitri Dixon-Saxon, Associate Dean, 800-925-3368. *Application contact:* Jennifer Hall, Vice President of Enrollment Management, 866-4-WALDEN, E-mail: info@waldenu.edu. Web site: http://www.waldenu.edu/Colleges-and-Schools/College-of-Social-and-Behavioral-Sciences/School-of-Counseling-and-Social-Service.htm.

Walden University, Graduate Programs, School of Health Sciences, Minneapolis, MN 55401. Offers clinical research administration (MS, Postbaccalaureate Certificate); health informatics (MS); health services (PhD), including community health education and advocacy, general program, healthcare administration, leadership, public health policy, self-designed; healthcare administration (MHA); public health (MPH, PhD), including community health and education (PhD), epidemiology (PhD). Part-time and evening/weekend programs available. Postbaccalaureate distance learning degree programs offered (minimal on-campus study). *Faculty:* 20 full-time (13 women), 175 part-time/adjunct (81 women). *Students:* 2,777 full-time (2,158 women), 1,350 part-time (1,038 women); includes 2,379 minority (1,935 Black or African American, non-Hispanic/Latino; 33 American Indian or Alaska Native, non-Hispanic/Latino; 173 Asian, non-Hispanic/Latino; 180 Hispanic/Latino; 9 Native Hawaiian or other Pacific Islander, non-Hispanic/Latino; 49 Two or more races, non-Hispanic/Latino), 247 international. Average age 40. In 2011, 528 master's, 79 doctorates, 1 other advanced degree awarded. *Degree requirements:* For doctorate, thesis/dissertation, residency. *Entrance requirements:* For master's, bachelor's degree or equivalent in related field, minimum GPA of 2.5; for doctorate, master's degree or equivalent in related field; minimum GPA of 3.0; official transcripts; three years of related professional/academic experience (preferred); access to computer and Internet. Additional exam requirements/recommendations for international students: Required—TOEFL (minimum score 550 paper-based; 213 computer-based), IELTS (minimum score 6.5), or Michigan English Language Assessment Battery (minimum score 82). *Application deadline:* Applications are processed on a rolling basis. Application fee: $50. Electronic applications accepted. *Financial support:* Federal Work-Study, scholarships/grants, unspecified assistantships, and family tuition reduction, active duty/veteran tuition reduction, group tuition reduction, interest-free payment plans, employee tuition reduction available. Support available to part-time students. Financial award applicants required to submit FAFSA. *Unit head:* Dr. Jorg Westermann, Associate Dean, 800-925-3368. *Application contact:* Jennifer Hall, Vice President of Enrollment Management, 866-4-WALDEN, E-mail: info@waldenu.edu. Web site: http://www.waldenu.edu/Colleges-and-Schools/College-of-Health-Sciences/School-of-Health-Sciences.htm.

Washington University in St. Louis, George Warren Brown School of Social Work, St. Louis, MO 63130-4899. Offers public health (MPH); social work (MSW, PhD); JD/MSW; M Arch/MSW; MBA/MSW; MPH/MBA; MSW/M Div; MSW/MAPS; MSW/MJCS; MSW/MPH. MSW/M Div and MSW/MAPS offered jointly with Eden Theological Seminary. *Accreditation:* CSWE (one or more programs are accredited). *Faculty:* 46 full-time, 82 part-time/adjunct. *Students:* 574 full-time (490 women); includes 127 minority (55 Black or African American, non-Hispanic/Latino; 6 American Indian or Alaska Native, non-Hispanic/Latino; 31 Asian, non-Hispanic/Latino; 12 Hispanic/Latino; 23 Two or more races, non-Hispanic/Latino), 98 international. Average age 27. 746 applicants, 63% accepted, 234 enrolled. In 2011, 235 master's, 6 doctorates awarded. *Degree requirements:* For master's, 60 credit hours (MSW), 45 credit hours (MPH); practicum; for doctorate, comprehensive exam, thesis/dissertation. *Entrance requirements:* For master's, GRE, GMAT, LSAT, or MCAT (public health), minimum GPA of 3.0; for doctorate, GRE, MA or MSW. Additional exam requirements/recommendations for international students: Required—TOEFL (minimum score 575 paper-based; 233 computer-based; 90 iBT). *Application deadline:* For fall admission, 12/15 priority date for domestic students, 12/15 for international students. Applications are processed on a rolling basis. Application fee: $40. Electronic applications accepted. *Expenses:* Contact institution. *Financial support:* In 2011–12, 486 students received support. Federal Work-Study, institutionally sponsored loans, scholarships/grants, health care benefits, tuition waivers (partial), and research assistantships, partial tuition waivers available. Support available to part-time students. Financial award applicants required to submit FAFSA. *Faculty research:* Mental health services, social development, child welfare, at-risk teens, autism, environmental health, health policy, health communications, obesity, violence and injury prevention, chronic disease prevention, poverty, public health, productive aging/gerontology, social work, civic engagement, school social work, program evaluation, health disparities. *Unit head:* Dr. Edward F. Lawlor, Dean/Professor, 314-935-6693, Fax: 314-935-8511, E-mail: elawlor@wustl.edu. *Application contact:* Richard Sigg, Director of Admissions and Recruiting, 314-935-6676, Fax: 314-935-4859, E-mail: rsigg@wustl.edu. Web site: http://gwbweb.wustl.edu/.

Wayne State University, School of Medicine, Department of Family Medicine and Public Health Sciences, Detroit, MI 48202. Offers public health (MPH), including occupational and environmental health, public health practice; public health practice (Certificate). *Students:* 19 full-time (14 women), 23 part-time (13 women); includes 19 minority (3 Black or African American, non-Hispanic/Latino; 14 Asian, non-Hispanic/Latino; 2 Hispanic/Latino), 10 international. Average age 34. 121 applicants, 26% accepted, 18 enrolled. In 2011, 3 master's, 4 other advanced degrees awarded. *Degree requirements:* For master's, thesis (for some programs), project or thesis. *Entrance requirements:* For master's, GRE, undergraduate work in mathematics, natural science, and social science; experience in health-related position; for Certificate, background in a health-related field; background of course work or experience in the areas of mathematics, social science, natural science, and computer usage. Additional exam requirements/recommendations for international students: Required—TOEFL (minimum score 550 paper-based; 213 computer-based; 100 iBT); Recommended—TWE (minimum score 6). *Application deadline:* For fall admission, 2/15 for domestic students, 1/1 for international students. Application fee: $50. Electronic applications accepted. *Expenses:* Tuition, state resident: part-time $512.85 per credit. Tuition, nonresident: part-time $1132.65 per credit. *Required fees:* $26.60 per credit. $199.65 per semester. Tuition and fees vary according to course load and program. *Financial support:* In 2011–12, 11 students received support. Scholarships/grants available. *Faculty research:* Urban health disparities, community health promotion, substance abuse etiology and prevention, HIV/AIDS, interpersonal violence. *Unit head:* Dr. Richard Severson, Program Director, 313-577-1051. *Application contact:* Dr. Kimberly Campbell-Voytal, Graduate Student Officer, 313-577-1051, E-mail: mphprogram@med.wayne.edu. Web site: http://www.med.wayne.edu/fam/.

West Chester University of Pennsylvania, College of Health Sciences, Department of Health, West Chester, PA 19383. Offers emergency preparedness (Certificate); health care management (MPH, Certificate), including health care management (Certificate), integrative (MPH); school health (M Ed). *Accreditation:* CEPH. Part-time and evening/weekend programs available. *Faculty:* 2 full-time (both women), 15 part-time/adjunct (11 women). *Students:* 112 full-time (85 women), 94 part-time (76 women); includes 82 minority (64 Black or African American, non-Hispanic/Latino; 2 American Indian or Alaska Native, non-Hispanic/Latino; 12 Asian, non-Hispanic/Latino; 3 Hispanic/Latino; 1 Two or more races, non-Hispanic/Latino), 16 international. Average age 29. 149 applicants, 65% accepted, 73 enrolled. In 2011, 34 master's, 3 other advanced degrees awarded. *Degree requirements:* For master's, thesis (for some programs), minimum GPA of 3.0. *Entrance requirements:* For master's, one-page statement of career objectives, two letters of reference. Additional exam requirements/recommendations for international students: Required—TOEFL (minimum score 550 paper-based; 213 computer-based; 80 iBT). *Application deadline:* For fall admission, 4/15 priority date for domestic students, 3/15 for international students; for spring admission, 10/15 priority date for domestic students, 9/1 for international students. Applications are processed on a rolling basis. Application fee: $45. Electronic applications accepted. *Expenses:* Tuition, state resident: full-time $7488; part-time $416 per credit. Tuition, nonresident: full-time $11,232; part-time $624 per credit. *Required fees:* $1784.64; $67.59 per credit. Tuition and fees vary according to program. *Financial support:* Unspecified assistantships available. Support available to part-time students. Financial award application deadline: 2/15; financial award applicants required to submit FAFSA. *Faculty research:* Health school communities, community health issues and evidence-based programs, environment and health, nutrition and health, integrative health. *Unit head:* Dr. Bethann Cinelli, Chair, 610-436-2267, E-mail: bcinelli@wcupa.edu. *Application contact:* Dr. Lynn Carson, Graduate Coordinator, 610-436-2138, E-mail: lcarson@wcupa.edu. Web site: http://www.wcupa.edu/_ACADEMICS/HealthSciences/health/.

Western Kentucky University, Graduate Studies, College of Health and Human Services, Department of Public Health, Bowling Green, KY 42101. Offers healthcare administration (MHA); public health (MPH). *Accreditation:* CEPH. Part-time and evening/weekend programs available. *Degree requirements:* For master's, comprehensive exam, thesis or alternative. *Entrance requirements:* For master's, GRE General Test, minimum GPA of 2.75. Additional exam requirements/recommendations for international students: Required—TOEFL (minimum score 555 paper-based; 213 computer-based; 79 iBT). *Faculty research:* Health education training, driver traffic safety, community readiness, occupational injuries, local health departments.

Westminster College, School of Nursing and Health Sciences, Salt Lake City, UT 84105-3697. Offers family nurse practitioner (MSN); nurse anesthesia (MSNA); nurse education (MSNED); nursing (MSN); public health (MPH). *Accreditation:* AACN; AANA/CANAEP. *Faculty:* 13 full-time (7 women), 7 part-time/adjunct (4 women). *Students:* 102 full-time (54 women), 16 part-time (12 women); includes 9 minority (2 Black or African American, non-Hispanic/Latino; 1 American Indian or Alaska Native, non-Hispanic/Latino; 5 Asian, non-Hispanic/Latino; 1 Hispanic/Latino), 1 international. Average age 34. 106 applicants, 64% accepted, 38 enrolled. In 2011, 53 master's awarded. *Degree requirements:* For master's, clinical practicum, 504 clinical practice hours. *Entrance requirements:* For master's, GRE, resume, Utah RN license in good standing, minimum GPA of 3.0, 3 letters of reference, BSN from accredited nursing program, proof of clear state and federal background check, drug test results, personal interview, current PALS certification, current ACLS certification. Additional exam requirements/recommendations for international students: Required—TOEFL (minimum score 600 paper-based; 250 computer-based; 100 iBT), IELTS (minimum score 7). *Application deadline:* Applications are processed on a rolling basis. Application fee: $50. Electronic applications accepted. *Expenses:* Contact institution. *Financial support:* In 2011–12, 11 students received support. Career-related internships or fieldwork and tuition reimbursement, tuition remission available. Support available to part-time students. Financial award applicants required to submit FAFSA. *Faculty research:* Collaborative testing in nursing: student outcomes and perspectives, Implementing New Educational Paradigms into Pre-Licensure Nursing Curricula conference presentation. *Unit head:* Dr. Sheryl Steadman, Dean, 801-832-2164, Fax: 801-832-3110, E-mail: ssteadman@westminstercollege.edu. *Application contact:* Dr. Gary Daynes, Vice President for Strategic Outreach and Enrollment, 801-832-2200, Fax: 801-832-3101, E-mail: admission@westminstercollege.edu. Web site: http://www.westminstercollege.edu/msn.

West Virginia University, School of Medicine, Department of Community Medicine, Program in Public Health, Morgantown, WV 26506. Offers community health/preventative medicine (MPH). *Accreditation:* CEPH. Part-time programs available. Postbaccalaureate distance learning degree programs offered (minimal on-campus study). *Degree requirements:* For master's, practicum, project. *Entrance requirements:* For master's, GRE General Test, MCAT, medical degree, medical internship. *Expenses:* Contact institution. *Faculty research:* Occupational health, environmental health, clinical epidemiology, health care management, prevention.

Wright State University, School of Medicine, Program in Public Health, Dayton, OH 45435. Offers health promotion and education (MPH); public health management (MPH); public health nursing (MPH). *Accreditation:* CEPH.

Yale University, School of Medicine, Yale School of Public Health, New Haven, CT 06520. Offers applied biostatistics and epidemiology (APMPH); biostatistics (MPH, MS, PhD), including global health (MPH); chronic disease epidemiology (MPH, PhD), including global health (MPH); environmental health sciences (MPH, PhD), including global health (MPH); epidemiology of microbial diseases (MPH, PhD), including global health (MPH); global health (APMPH); health management (MPH), including global health; health policy (MPH), including global health; health policy and administration (APMPH, PhD); occupational and environmental medicine (APMPH); preventive medicine (APMPH); social and behavioral sciences (APMPH, MPH), including global health (MPH); JD/MPH;- M Div/MPH; MBA/MPH; MD/MPH; MEM/MPH; MFS/MPH; MM Sc/MPH; MPH/MA; MSN/MPH. MS and PhD offered through the Graduate School. *Accreditation:* CEPH. Part-time programs available. Terminal master's awarded for partial completion of doctoral program. *Degree requirements:* For master's, thesis, summer internship; for doctorate, comprehensive exam, thesis/dissertation, residency. *Entrance requirements:* For master's, GMAT, GRE, or MCAT, two years of undergraduate coursework in math and science; for doctorate, GRE General Test. Additional exam requirements/recommendations for international students: Required—TOEFL (minimum score 100 iBT). Electronic applications accepted. *Expenses:* Contact institution. *Faculty research:* Genetic and emerging infections epidemiology, virology, cost/quality, vector biology, quantitative methods, aging, asthma, cancer.

Community Health

Adelphi University, Ruth S. Ammon School of Education, Program in Health Studies, Garden City, NY 11530-0701. Offers community health education (MA, Certificate); school health education (MA). Part-time and evening/weekend programs available. *Students:* 11 full-time (9 women), 43 part-time (26 women); includes 6 minority (2 Black or African American, non-Hispanic/Latino; 3 Hispanic/Latino; 1 Two or more races, non-Hispanic/Latino), 3 international. Average age 27. In 2011, 30 master's awarded. *Degree requirements:* For master's, internship. *Entrance requirements:* For master's, 3 letters of recommendation, resume, minimum cumulative GPA of 2.75. Additional exam requirements/recommendations for international students: Required—TOEFL (minimum score 550 paper-based; 213 computer-based; 80 iBT). *Application deadline:* For fall admission, 4/1 for international students; for spring admission, 11/1 for international students. Applications are processed on a rolling basis. Application fee: $50. Electronic applications accepted. *Expenses: Tuition:* Full-time $29,600; part-time $930 per credit. *Required fees:* $1100. *Financial support:* Fellowships, research assistantships with partial tuition reimbursements, teaching assistantships, career-related internships or fieldwork, Federal Work-Study, institutionally sponsored loans, and tuition waivers (full) available. Support available to part-time students. Financial award application deadline: 2/15; financial award applicants required to submit FAFSA. *Faculty research:* Alcohol abuse, tobacco cessation, drug abuse, healthy family lives, healthy personal living. *Unit head:* Dr. Ronald Feingold, Director, 516-877-4764, E-mail: feingold@adelphi.edu. *Application contact:* Christine Murphy, Director of Admissions, 516-877-3050, Fax: 516-877-3039, E-mail: graduateadmissions@adelphi.edu.

American University of Beirut, Graduate Programs, Faculty of Health Sciences, Beirut, Lebanon. Offers environmental sciences (MSES), including environmental health; epidemiology (MS); epidemiology and biostatistics (MPH); health management and policy (MPH); health promotion and community health (MPH); population health (MS). Part-time programs available. *Faculty:* 29 full-time (19 women), 5 part-time/ adjunct (2 women). *Students:* 63 full-time (52 women), 103 part-time (87 women). Average age 27. 156 applicants, 71% accepted, 56 enrolled. In 2011, 69 master's awarded. *Degree requirements:* For master's, one foreign language, comprehensive exam, thesis (for some programs). *Entrance requirements:* For master's, 2 letters of recommendation, personal statement, transcripts. Additional exam requirements/ recommendations for international students: Required—TOEFL (minimum score 600 paper-based; 250 computer-based; 97 iBT), IELTS (minimum score 7). *Application deadline:* For fall admission, 2/20 for domestic and international students; for spring admission, 11/1 for domestic and international students. Application fee: $50. Electronic applications accepted. *Expenses: Tuition:* Full-time $12,780; part-time $710 per credit. Tuition and fees vary according to course load and program. *Financial support:* In 2011–12, 62 students received support. Scholarships/grants, health care benefits, and unspecified assistantships available. Financial award application deadline: 2/20. *Faculty research:* Tobacco control; health of the elderly; youth health; mental health; women's health; reproductive and sexual health, including HIV/AIDS; water quality; health systems; quality in health care delivery; health human resources; health policy; occupational and environmental health; social inequality; social determinants of health; chronic diseases. *Total annual research expenditures:* $722,649. *Unit head:* Iman Adel Nuwayhid, Dean, 961-1340119, Fax: 961-1744470, E-mail: nuwayhid@aub.edu.lb. *Application contact:* Mitra Tauk, Administrative Coordinator, 961-1350000 Ext. 4687, Fax: 961-1744470, E-mail: mt12@aub.edu.lb. Web site: http://fhs.aub.edu.lb.

Arcadia University, Graduate Studies, Department of Medical Science and Community Health, Glenside, PA 19038-3295. Offers MM Sc, MPH, MSHE, MSPH, MM Sc/MAHE, MM Sc/MSPH. *Students:* 209 full-time (174 women), 18 part-time (16 women); includes 15 minority (3 Black or African American, non-Hispanic/Latino; 8 Asian, non-Hispanic/ Latino; 4 Two or more races, non-Hispanic/Latino), 2 international. Average age 27. In 2011, 124 master's awarded. *Entrance requirements:* For master's, GRE General Test or MCAT. Additional exam requirements/recommendations for international students: Required—TOEFL. *Application deadline:* For fall admission, 1/5 priority date for domestic students. Application fee: $50. *Expenses:* Contact institution. *Financial support:* Tuition waivers (partial) available. *Unit head:* Michael Dryer, Chair and Program Director, 215-572-2083. *Application contact:* 215-572-2910, Fax: 215-572-4041, E-mail: admiss@arcadia.edu.

Arizona State University, College of Nursing and Health Innovation, Phoenix, AZ 85004. Offers advanced nursing practice (DNP); child/family mental health nurse practitioner (Graduate Certificate); clinical research management (MS); community and public health practice (Graduate Certificate); community health (MS); exercise and wellness (MS), including exercise and wellness; family nurse practitioner (Graduate Certificate); healthcare innovation (MHI); international health for healthcare (Graduate Certificate); kinesiology (MS, PhD); nursing (MS, Graduate Certificate); nursing and healthcare innovation (PhD); nutrition (MS); physical activity nutrition and wellness (PhD), including physical activity, nutrition and wellness; public health (MPH); regulatory science and health safety (MS). *Accreditation:* AACN. Postbaccalaureate distance learning degree programs offered (minimal on-campus study). *Degree requirements:* For master's, comprehensive exam (for some programs), thesis (for some programs), interactive Program of Study (iPOS) submitted before completing 50 percent of required credit hours; for doctorate, comprehensive exam, thesis/dissertation, interactive Program of Study (iPOS) submitted before completing 50 percent of required credit hours. *Entrance requirements:* For master's and doctorate, GRE, minimum GPA of 3.0 or equivalent in last 2 years of work leading to bachelor's degree. Additional exam requirements/recommendations for international students: Required—TOEFL (minimum score 80 iBT), TOEFL, IELTS, or Pearson Test of English. Electronic applications accepted. *Expenses:* Contact institution.

Austin Peay State University, College of Graduate Studies, College of Behavioral and Health Sciences, Department of Health and Human Performance, Clarksville, TN 37044. Offers health leadership (MS). Part-time and evening/weekend programs available. Postbaccalaureate distance learning degree programs offered (no on-campus study). *Faculty:* 6 full-time (3 women). *Students:* 21 full-time (16 women), 45 part-time (32 women); includes 28 minority (19 Black or African American, non-Hispanic/Latino; 6 Hispanic/Latino; 3 Two or more races, non-Hispanic/Latino). Average age 30. 58 applicants, 86% accepted, 38 enrolled. In 2011, 24 master's awarded. *Degree requirements:* For master's, comprehensive exam, thesis optional. *Entrance requirements:* For master's, GRE General Test, 3 letters of recommendation, minimum undergraduate GPA of 2.5. Additional exam requirements/recommendations for international students: Required—TOEFL (minimum score 500 paper-based; 173 computer-based). *Application deadline:* For fall admission, 8/1 priority date for domestic students. Applications are processed on a rolling basis. Application fee: $25. Electronic applications accepted. *Expenses:* Tuition, state resident: part-time $350 per credit hour. Tuition, nonresident: full-time $20,644; part-time $971 per credit hour. *Required fees:* $1224; $61.20 per credit hour. *Financial support:* In 2011–12, research assistantships

with full tuition reimbursements (averaging $5,184 per year) were awarded; career-related internships or fieldwork, Federal Work-Study, institutionally sponsored loans, scholarships/grants, and unspecified assistantships also available. Support available to part-time students. Financial award application deadline: 3/1; financial award applicants required to submit FAFSA. *Unit head:* Dr. Marcy Maurer, Chair, 931-221-6105, Fax: 931-221-7040, E-mail: maurerm@apsu.edu. *Application contact:* Kendra Bryant, Graduate Admissions, 800-844-2778, Fax: 931-221-6188, E-mail: admissionsweb@apsu.edu. Web site: http://www.apsu.edu/hhp/.

Bloomsburg University of Pennsylvania, School of Graduate Studies, College of Science and Technology, Department of Nursing, Bloomsburg, PA 17815-1301. Offers adult and family nurse practitioner (MSN); adult health and illness (MSN); community health (MSN); nursing (MSN); nursing administration (MSN). *Accreditation:* AACN; AANA/CANAEP. *Degree requirements:* For master's, thesis. *Entrance requirements:* For master's, minimum QPA of 3.0. Additional exam requirements/recommendations for international students: Required—TOEFL. Electronic applications accepted. *Faculty research:* Cardiopulmonary nursing, cancer topics, women's health.

Brooklyn College of the City University of New York, Division of Graduate Studies, Department of Health and Nutrition Science, Program in Community Health, Brooklyn, NY 11210-2889. Offers community health education (MA); computer science and health science (MS); health care management (MPH); health care policy and administration (MPH); thanatology (MA). *Accreditation:* CEPH. *Degree requirements:* For master's, thesis or alternative. *Entrance requirements:* For master's, 2 letters of recommendation, essay. Additional exam requirements/recommendations for international students: Required—TOEFL. Electronic applications accepted. *Faculty research:* Diet restriction, religious practices in bereavement, diabetes, stress management, palliative care.

Brooklyn College of the City University of New York, Division of Graduate Studies, Department of Health and Nutrition Science, Program in Public Health, Brooklyn, NY 11210-2889. Offers community-public health (MPH). *Accreditation:* CEPH. *Degree requirements:* For master's, thesis or alternative, 46 credits. *Entrance requirements:* For master's, GRE, 2 letters of recommendation, essay, interview. Electronic applications accepted.

Brown University, Graduate School, Division of Biology and Medicine, Department of Community Health, Providence, RI 02912. Offers health services research (MS, PhD); public health (MPH); statistical science (MS, PhD), including biostatistics, epidemiology; MD/PhD. *Accreditation:* CEPH. *Degree requirements:* For doctorate, thesis/dissertation, preliminary exam. *Entrance requirements:* For master's and doctorate, GRE General Test. Additional exam requirements/recommendations for international students: Required—TOEFL.

Canisius College, Graduate Division, Office of Professional Studies, Buffalo, NY 14208-1098. Offers applied nutrition (MS); community and school health (MS). Postbaccalaureate distance learning degree programs offered (no on-campus study). *Faculty:* 9 part-time/adjunct (7 women). *Students:* 17 full-time (15 women), 6 part-time (5 women); includes 3 minority (1 Black or African American, non-Hispanic/Latino; 1 Asian, non-Hispanic/Latino; 1 Two or more races, non-Hispanic/Latino), 2 international. Average age 32. 35 applicants, 74% accepted, 20 enrolled. *Entrance requirements:* Additional exam requirements/recommendations for international students: Required—TOEFL. *Application deadline:* Applications are processed on a rolling basis. Application fee: $25. Electronic applications accepted. *Financial support:* Career-related internships or fieldwork, Federal Work-Study, scholarships/grants, and unspecified assistantships available. Support available to part-time students. Financial award application deadline: 4/30; financial award applicants required to submit FAFSA. *Faculty research:* Nutrition, community and school health. *Unit head:* Dr. Khalid Bibi, Executive Director, 716-888-8296. *Application contact:* Donna Shaffner, Dean of Admissions, 716-888-2200, Fax: 716-888-3230, E-mail: admissions@canisius.edu. Web site: http://www.canisius.edu/professional-studies/.

Clemson University, Graduate School, College of Health, Education, and Human Development, Eugene T. Moore School of Education, Program in Counselor Education, Clemson, SC 29634. Offers clinical mental health counseling (M Ed); community mental health (M Ed); school counseling (K-12) (M Ed); student affairs (higher education) (M Ed). *Accreditation:* ACA; NCATE. Part-time and evening/weekend programs available. *Students:* 127 full-time (101 women), 28 part-time (19 women); includes 23 minority (14 Black or African American, non-Hispanic/Latino; 3 Asian, non-Hispanic/Latino; 2 Hispanic/Latino; 1 Native Hawaiian or other Pacific Islander, non-Hispanic/Latino; 3 Two or more races, non-Hispanic/Latino), 1 international. Average age 28. 186 applicants, 58% accepted, 45 enrolled. In 2011, 66 master's awarded. *Degree requirements:* For master's, comprehensive exam. *Entrance requirements:* For master's, GRE General Test. Additional exam requirements/recommendations for international students: Required—TOEFL; Recommended—IELTS. *Application deadline:* For fall admission, 2/1 priority date for domestic students; for spring admission, 10/1 for domestic students. Applications are processed on a rolling basis. Application fee: $70 ($80 for international students). Electronic applications accepted. *Expenses:* Contact institution. *Financial support:* In 2011–12, 74 students received support, including 10 research assistantships with partial tuition reimbursements available (averaging $8,402 per year), 1 teaching assistantship with partial tuition reimbursement available (averaging $12,528 per year); institutionally sponsored loans, health care benefits, and unspecified assistantships also available. Financial award application deadline: 6/1; financial award applicants required to submit FAFSA. *Faculty research:* At-risk youth, ethnic identity development across the life span, postsecondary transitions and college readiness, distance and distributed learning environments, the student veteran experience in college, student development theory. *Unit head:* Dr. Michael J. Padilla, Director/Associate Dean, 864-656-4444, Fax: 864-656-0311, E-mail: padilla@clemson.edu. *Application contact:* Dr. David Fleming, Graduate Coordinator, 864-656-1881, Fax: 864-656-0311, E-mail: dflemin@clemson.edu.

The College at Brockport, State University of New York, School of Health and Human Performance, Department of Health Science, Brockport, NY 14420-2997. Offers health education (MS Ed), including community health education, health education K-12. *Students:* 11 full-time (9 women), 19 part-time (13 women); includes 6 minority (4 Black or African American, non-Hispanic/Latino; 1 American Indian or Alaska Native, non-Hispanic/Latino; 1 Asian, non-Hispanic/Latino). 35 applicants, 43% accepted, 8 enrolled. In 2011, 2 master's awarded. *Degree requirements:* For master's, thesis or alternative. *Entrance requirements:* For master's, minimum GPA of 3.0, letters of recommendation. Additional exam requirements/recommendations for international students: Required—TOEFL (minimum score 550 paper-based; 213 computer-based; 79 iBT). *Application deadline:* For fall admission, 4/1 priority date for domestic students, 4/1 for international students; for spring admission, 11/1 priority date for domestic students, 11/1 for international students. Application fee: $80. Electronic applications accepted. *Financial*

support: In 2011–12, 1 teaching assistantship with full tuition reimbursement (averaging $6,000 per year) was awarded; Federal Work-Study, scholarships/grants, and unspecified assistantships also available. Support available to part-time students. Financial award application deadline: 3/15; financial award applicants required to submit FAFSA. *Faculty research:* Nutrition, substance use, HIV/AIDS, bioethics, worksite health. *Unit head:* Dr. Patti Follensbee, Chairperson, 585-395-5483, Fax: 585-395-5246, E-mail: pfallons@brockport.edu. *Application contact:* Dr. Patti Follansbee, Admissions Coordinator, 585-395-5483, Fax: 585-395-5246, E-mail: pfollans@brockport.edu. Web site: http://www.brockport.edu/graduate/.

Columbia University, Columbia University Mailman School of Public Health, Division of Sociomedical Sciences, New York, NY 10032. Offers MPH, Dr PH, PhD. PhD offered in cooperation with the Graduate School of Arts and Sciences. *Accreditation:* CEPH (one or more programs are accredited). Part-time programs available. *Students:* 182 full-time (160 women), 108 part-time (90 women); includes 99 minority (20 Black or African American, non-Hispanic/Latino; 47 Asian, non-Hispanic/Latino; 21 Hispanic/Latino; 11 Two or more races, non-Hispanic/Latino), 24 international. Average age 29. 546 applicants, 48% accepted, 121 enrolled. In 2011, 88 master's, 5 doctorates awarded. *Degree requirements:* For master's, thesis; for doctorate, thesis/dissertation. *Entrance requirements:* For master's, GRE General Test; for doctorate, GRE General Test, MPH or equivalent (Dr PH). Additional exam requirements/recommendations for international students: Required—TOEFL (minimum score 600 paper-based; 250 computer-based; 100 iBT). *Application deadline:* For fall admission, 1/5 for domestic students. Application fee: $60. Electronic applications accepted. *Financial support:* Research assistantships, teaching assistantships, career-related internships or fieldwork, and Federal Work-Study available. Support available to part-time students. Financial award application deadline: 2/1; financial award applicants required to submit FAFSA. *Faculty research:* Social and cultural factors in health and health care, health services delivery and utilization, health promotion and disease prevention, AIDS. *Unit head:* Dr. Amy Fairchild, Chair, 212-305-5656. *Application contact:* Dr. Joseph Korevec, Director of Admissions and Financial Aid, 212-305-8698, Fax: 212-342-1861, E-mail: ph-admit@columbia.edu. Web site: http://www.mailman.hs.columbia.edu/sms/index.html.

Dalhousie University, Faculty of Medicine, Department of Community Health and Epidemiology, Halifax, NS B3H 4R2, Canada. Offers M Sc. *Degree requirements:* For master's, thesis. *Entrance requirements:* Additional exam requirements/recommendations for international students: Required—1 of 5 approved tests: TOEFL, IELTS, CANTEST, CAEL, Michigan English Language Assessment Battery. Electronic applications accepted. *Expenses:* Contact institution. *Faculty research:* Population health, health promotion and disease prevention, health services utilization, chronic disease epidemiology.

DePaul University, College of Liberal Arts and Sciences, Program in Public Health, Chicago, IL 60604-2287. Offers community health practice (MPH). *Application contact:* Ann Spittle, Director of Graduate Admission, 773-325-7315, Fax: 773-476-3244, E-mail: graduatelas@depaul.edu.

Duquesne University, School of Education, Department of Counseling, Psychology, and Special Education, Program in Special Education, Pittsburgh, PA 15282-0001. Offers cognitive, behavior, physical/health disabilities (MS Ed); community mental health/special education support (MS Ed). Part-time and evening/weekend programs available. *Faculty:* 7 full-time (all women), 1 part-time/adjunct (0 women). *Students:* 28 full-time (26 women), 3 part-time (2 women); includes 1 minority (Black or African American, non-Hispanic/Latino). Average age 25. 15 applicants, 67% accepted, 6 enrolled. In 2011, 21 degrees awarded. *Degree requirements:* For master's, thesis optional. *Entrance requirements:* For master's, bachelor's degree. Additional exam requirements/recommendations for international students: Required—TOEFL (minimum score 550 paper-based; 80 computer-based), IELTS (minimum score 7). *Application deadline:* For fall admission, 9/1 for domestic students; for spring admission, 1/1 for domestic students. Applications are processed on a rolling basis. Application fee: $0. Electronic applications accepted. Application fee is waived when completed online. *Expenses: Tuition:* Full-time $16,596; part-time $922 per credit. *Required fees:* $1584; $88 per credit. Tuition and fees vary according to program. *Financial support:* In 2011–12, 1 research assistantship was awarded. Support available to part-time students. *Unit head:* Dr. Lisa Vernon-Dotson, Assistant Professor, 412-396-1103, Fax: 412-396-1340, E-mail: vernonl@duq.edu. *Application contact:* Michael Dolinger, Director of Student and Academic Services, 412-396-6647, Fax: 412-396-5585, E-mail: dolingerm@duq.edu. Web site: http://www.duq.edu/education.

East Carolina University, Graduate School, Thomas Harriot College of Arts and Sciences, Department of Political Science, Greenville, NC 27858-4353. Offers community health administration (Certificate); public administration (MPA). *Accreditation:* NASPAA. Part-time and evening/weekend programs available. *Degree requirements:* For master's, one foreign language, comprehensive exam. *Entrance requirements:* For master's, GRE General Test. Additional exam requirements/recommendations for international students: Required—TOEFL. *Application deadline:* For fall admission, 6/1 priority date for domestic students; for spring admission, 10/15 for domestic students. Applications are processed on a rolling basis. Application fee: $50. *Expenses:* Tuition, state resident: full-time $3557; part-time $444.63 per semester hour. Tuition, nonresident: full-time $14,351; part-time $1793.88 per semester hour. *Required fees:* $2016; $252 per semester hour. Part-time tuition and fees vary according to course load, campus/location and program. *Financial support:* Research assistantships with partial tuition reimbursements, teaching assistantships with partial tuition reimbursements, and Federal Work-Study available. Support available to part-time students. Financial award application deadline: 6/1. *Unit head:* Dr. Brad Lockerbie, Chair, 252-328-1066, Fax: 252-328-4134, E-mail: lockerbieb@ecu.edu. *Application contact:* Dean of Graduate School, 252-328-6012, Fax: 252-328-6071, E-mail: gradschool@ecu.edu. Web site: http://www.ecu.edu/polsci/mpa/index.html.

Eastern Kentucky University, The Graduate School, College of Health Sciences, Department of Health Promotion and Administration, Richmond, KY 40475-3102. Offers community health (MPH). *Degree requirements:* For master's, comprehensive exam, thesis optional. *Entrance requirements:* For master's, GRE or MAT, letters of recommendation. *Faculty research:* Risk behavior, health systems, injury control, nutrition.

East Stroudsburg University of Pennsylvania, Graduate School, College of Health Sciences, Program in Public Health, East Stroudsburg, PA 18301-2999. Offers community health education (MPH). Part-time and evening/weekend programs available. Postbaccalaureate distance learning degree programs offered (minimal on-campus study). *Degree requirements:* For master's, comprehensive exam, publishable paper, oral comprehensive exam. *Entrance requirements:* For master's, GRE, 3 letters of recommendation. Additional exam requirements/recommendations for international students: Required—TOEFL (minimum score 560 paper-based; 220 computer-based; 83 iBT). Electronic applications accepted. *Faculty research:* Public health infrastructure.

East Tennessee State University, School of Graduate Studies, College of Public Health, Doctor of Public Health Programs, Johnson City, TN 37614. Offers community health (DPH); epidemiology (DPH). *Accreditation:* CEPH. *Students:* 15 full-time (11 women), 7 part-time (4 women); includes 6 minority (3 Black or African American, non-Hispanic/Latino; 3 Asian, non-Hispanic/Latino), 3 international. 11 applicants, 73% accepted, 8 enrolled. In 2011, 1 doctorate awarded. Terminal master's awarded for partial completion of doctoral program. *Degree requirements:* For doctorate, comprehensive exam, thesis/dissertation, culminating experience/practicum. *Entrance requirements:* For doctorate, GRE General Test, SOPHAS application, MPH or equivalent, four letters of recommendation. Additional exam requirements/recommendations for international students: Required—TOEFL (minimum score 550 paper-based; 213 computer-based; 79 iBT). *Application deadline:* For fall admission, 3/1 for domestic and international students. Application fee: $35 ($45 for international students). Electronic applications accepted. *Expenses:* Tuition, state resident: full-time $7312; part-time $350 per credit hour. Tuition, nonresident: full-time $18,490; part-time $621 per credit hour. *Required fees:* $63 per credit hour. Tuition and fees vary according to course load and program. *Financial support:* In 2011–12, 14 students received support, including 13 research assistantships with full tuition reimbursements available (averaging $14,000 per year); career-related internships or fieldwork, institutionally sponsored loans, scholarships/grants, tuition waivers (full), and unspecified assistantships also available. Financial award application deadline: 7/1; financial award applicants required to submit FAFSA. *Faculty research:* Rural health issues, youth and adolescent health, health of the elderly, environmental epidemiology, spatial analysis of data. *Unit head:* Dr. Rob Pack, Associate Dean, 423-439-4243, Fax: 423-439-5238, E-mail: packr@etsu.edu. *Application contact:* Mary Duncan, Graduate Specialist, 423-439-4302, Fax: 423-439-5624, E-mail: duncanm@etsu.edu.

East Tennessee State University, School of Graduate Studies, College of Public Health, Master of Public Health Programs, Johnson City, TN 37614. Offers biostatistics (MPH); community health (MPH); environmental health (MPH); epidemiology (MPH); public health administration (MPH). Part-time programs available. Postbaccalaureate distance learning degree programs offered (no on-campus study). *Students:* 45 full-time (27 women), 31 part-time (21 women); includes 14 minority (8 Black or African American, non-Hispanic/Latino; 3 Asian, non-Hispanic/Latino; 2 Hispanic/Latino; 1 Two or more races, non-Hispanic/Latino), 11 international. 92 applicants, 45% accepted, 40 enrolled. In 2011, 24 master's awarded. *Degree requirements:* For master's, comprehensive exam, field experience. *Entrance requirements:* For master's, GRE General Test, SOPHAS application, minimum GPA of 2.75, letters of recommendation. Additional exam requirements/recommendations for international students: Required—TOEFL (minimum score 550 paper-based; 213 computer-based; 79 iBT). *Application deadline:* For fall admission, 3/1 for domestic and international students. Application fee: $35 ($45 for international students). Electronic applications accepted. *Expenses:* Tuition, state resident: full-time $7312; part-time $350 per credit hour. Tuition, nonresident: full-time $18,490; part-time $621 per credit hour. *Required fees:* $63 per credit hour. Tuition and fees vary according to course load and program. *Financial support:* In 2011–12, 31 students received support, including 14 research assistantships with full tuition reimbursements available (averaging $6,000 per year), 2 teaching assistantships with full tuition reimbursements available (averaging $6,000 per year); career-related internships or fieldwork, institutionally sponsored loans, scholarships/grants, and unspecified assistantships also available. Financial award application deadline: 7/1; financial award applicants required to submit FAFSA. *Faculty research:* Rural health issues, youth and adolescent health, health of the elderly, environmental epidemiology, spatial analysis of data. *Unit head:* Dr. Brian Martin, Graduate Program Coordinator, 423-439-4429, Fax: 423-439-6491, E-mail: martinb@etsu.edu. *Application contact:* Mary Duncan, Graduate Specialist, 423-439-4302, Fax: 423-439-5624, E-mail: duncanm@etsu.edu. Web site: http://www.etsu.edu/cph/academics/graduate/MPHHome.aspx.

George Mason University, College of Health and Human Services, Department of Global and Community Health, Fairfax, VA 22030. Offers biostatistics (Certificate); epidemiology (Certificate); epidemiology and biostatistics (MS); gerontology (Certificate); global health (MS, Certificate); nutrition (Certificate); public health (MPH, Certificate). *Faculty:* 11 full-time (5 women), 16 part-time/adjunct (12 women). *Students:* 101 full-time (84 women), 114 part-time (92 women); includes 85 minority (43 Black or African American, non-Hispanic/Latino; 30 Asian, non-Hispanic/Latino; 11 Hispanic/Latino; 1 Two or more races, non-Hispanic/Latino), 14 international. Average age 32. 162 applicants, 61% accepted, 53 enrolled. In 2011, 80 master's, 15 other advanced degrees awarded. *Degree requirements:* For master's, comprehensive exam (for some programs), thesis or practicum. *Entrance requirements:* For master's, GRE, 2 official transcripts; expanded goals statement; 3 letters of recommendation; resume; 1 completed course in health science, statistics, natural sciences and social science (for MPH); 6 credits of foreign language if not fluent (for MS in global health); for Certificate, 2 official transcripts; expanded goals statement; 3 letters of recommendation; resume; bachelor's degree from regionally-accredited institution with minimum GPA of 3.0; statistics and college-level algebra with minimum B grade (for Certificate in biostatistics). Additional exam requirements/recommendations for international students: Required—TOEFL (minimum score 575 paper-based; 230 computer-based; 88 iBT), IELTS, Pearson Test of English. *Application deadline:* For fall admission, 4/1 priority date for domestic students; for spring admission, 11/1 priority date for domestic students. Applications are processed on a rolling basis. Application fee: $65 ($80 for international students). Electronic applications accepted. *Expenses:* Tuition, state resident: full-time $8750; part-time $364.58 per credit. Tuition, nonresident: full-time $24,092; part-time $1003.83 per credit. *Required fees:* $2514; $104.75 per credit. *Financial support:* In 2011–12, 14 students received support, including 12 research assistantships with full and partial tuition reimbursements available (averaging $15,000 per year), 2 teaching assistantships with full and partial tuition reimbursements available (averaging $11,781 per year); career-related internships or fieldwork, Federal Work-Study, scholarships/grants, unspecified assistantships, and health care benefits (full-time research and teaching assistantship recipients) also available. Financial award application deadline: 3/1; financial award applicants required to submit FAFSA. *Faculty research:* Providing introductory and advanced degrees in health-related disciplines centered in global and community issues, health issues and the needs of affected populations at the regional and global level. *Total annual research expenditures:* $64,518. *Unit head:* Dr. Carlos Sluzki, Dean, 703-993-1920, Fax: 703-993-1943, E-mail: csluzki@gmu.edu. *Application contact:* Allan Weiss, Office Manager, 703-993-3126, Fax: 703-993-1908, E-mail: aweiss2@gmu.edu. Web site: http://chhs.gmu.edu/gch/index.

Georgetown University, Graduate School of Arts and Sciences, School of Continuing Studies, Washington, DC 20057. Offers American studies (MALS); Catholic studies (MALS); classical civilizations (MALS); disability studies (MPS); ethics and the professions (MALS); human resources management (MPS); humanities (MALS); individualized study (MALS); international affairs (MALS); Islam and Muslim-Christian relations (MALS); journalism (MPS); liberal studies (DLS); literature and society (MALS); medieval and early modern European studies (MALS); public relations and corporate communications (MPS); real estate (MPS); religious studies (MALS); social and public policy (MALS); sports industry management (MPS); the theory and practice of American democracy (MALS); visual culture (MALS). *Entrance requirements:* Additional exam requirements/recommendations for international students: Required—TOEFL.

Georgia Southern University, Jack N. Averitt College of Graduate Studies, Jiann-Ping Hsu College of Public Health, Program in Public Health, Statesboro, GA 30460. Offers biostatistics (MPH, Dr PH); community health behavior and education (Dr PH);

community health education (MPH); environmental health sciences (MPH); epidemiology (MPH); health services policy management (MPH); public health leadership (Dr PH). *Accreditation:* CEPH. Part-time programs available. *Students:* 87 full-time (60 women), 39 part-time (25 women); includes 68 minority (58 Black or African American, non-Hispanic/Latino; 6 Asian, non-Hispanic/Latino; 4 Hispanic/Latino), 20 international. Average age 30. 73 applicants, 84% accepted, 42 enrolled. In 2011, 22 master's, 4 doctorates awarded. *Degree requirements:* For master's, thesis optional, practicum; for doctorate, comprehensive exam, thesis/dissertation, practicum. *Entrance requirements:* For master's, GRE General Test, minimum GPA of 2.75, resume, 3 letters of reference; for doctorate, GRE, GMAT, MCAT, LSAT, 3 letters of reference, statement of purpose, resume or curriculum vitae. Additional exam requirements/recommendations for international students: Required—TOEFL (minimum score 550 paper-based; 213 computer-based; 80 iBT). *Application deadline:* For fall admission, 3/1 priority date for domestic students, 3/1 for international students; for spring admission, 10/1 priority date for domestic students, 10/1 for international students. Applications are processed on a rolling basis. Application fee; $50. Electronic applications accepted. *Expenses:* Contact institution. *Financial support:* In 2011–12, 59 students received support, including research assistantships with partial tuition reimbursements available (averaging $7,200 per year), teaching assistantships with partial tuition reimbursements available (averaging $7,200 per year); career-related internships or fieldwork, Federal Work-Study, scholarships/grants, tuition waivers (partial), and unspecified assistantships also available. Support available to part-time students. Financial award application deadline: 4/15; financial award applicants required to submit FAFSA. *Faculty research:* Rural public health best practices, health disparity elimination, community initiatives to enhance public health, cost effectiveness analysis, epidemiology of rural public health, environmental health issues, health care system assessment, rural health care, health policy and healthcare financing. *Unit head:* Dr. Charles Hardy, Dean, 912-478-2674, Fax: 912-478-5811, E-mail: chardy@georgiasouthern.edu. *Application contact:* Amanda Gilliland, Coordinator for Graduate Student Recruitment, 912-478-5384, Fax: 912-478-0740, E-mail: gradadmissions@georgiasouthern.edu. Web site: http://chhs.georgiasouthern.edu/health/.

Hofstra University, School of Education, Health, and Human Services, Programs in Health, Hempstead, NY 11549. Offers community health (MS); health administration (MHA); public health (MPH). Part-time and evening/weekend programs available. *Students:* 66 full-time (43 women), 70 part-time (52 women); includes 60 minority (39 Black or African American, non-Hispanic/Latino; 11 Asian, non-Hispanic/Latino; 8 Hispanic/Latino; 2 Two or more races, non-Hispanic/Latino), 4 international. Average age 30. 90 applicants, 83% accepted, 48 enrolled. In 2011, 50 master's awarded. *Degree requirements:* For master's, internship, minimum GPA of 3.0. *Entrance requirements:* For master's, interview, 2 letters of recommendation, essay, resume. Additional exam requirements/recommendations for international students: Required—TOEFL (minimum score 550 paper-based; 213 computer-based; 80 iBT). *Application deadline:* Applications are processed on a rolling basis. Application fee: $70 ($75 for international students). Electronic applications accepted. *Expenses: Tuition:* Full-time $18,990; part-time $1055 per credit hour. *Required fees:* $970. Tuition and fees vary according to program. *Financial support:* In 2011–12, 25 students received support, including 17 fellowships with full and partial tuition reimbursements available (averaging $2,588 per year), 2 research assistantships with full and partial tuition reimbursements available (averaging $14,226 per year); career-related internships or fieldwork, Federal Work-Study, institutionally sponsored loans, scholarships/grants, tuition waivers (full and partial), and unspecified assistantships also available. Support available to part-time students. Financial award applicants required to submit FAFSA. *Faculty research:* Integrated long-term care, health care policy, cost-benefit analysis, chronic illness management, long-term care policy form. *Unit head:* Dr. Liora P. Schmelkin, Chairperson, 516-463-4680, Fax: 516-463-6505, E-mail: prolps@hofstra.edu. *Application contact:* Carol Drummer, Dean of Graduate Admissions, 516-463-4876, Fax: 516-463-4664, E-mail: gradstudent@hofstra.edu. Web site: http://www.hofstra.edu/education/.

Hunter College of the City University of New York, Graduate School, Schools of the Health Professions, School of Health Sciences, Programs in Urban Public Health, Program in Community Health Education, New York, NY 10021-5085. Offers MPH. *Accreditation:* CEPH. Part-time and evening/weekend programs available. *Faculty:* 10 full-time (5 women), 9 part-time/adjunct (4 women). *Students:* 15 full-time (14 women), 62 part-time (60 women); includes 24 minority (11 Black or African American, non-Hispanic/Latino; 1 American Indian or Alaska Native, non-Hispanic/Latino; 7 Asian, non-Hispanic/Latino; 5 Hispanic/Latino), 4 international. Average age 32. 83 applicants, 58% accepted, 19 enrolled. In 2011, 18 master's awarded. *Degree requirements:* For master's, comprehensive exam, thesis optional, internship. *Entrance requirements:* For master's, GRE General Test, previous course work in calculus and statistics. Additional exam requirements/recommendations for international students: Required—TOEFL. *Application deadline:* For fall admission, 4/1 for domestic students; for spring admission, 11/1 for domestic students. Application fee: $125. *Expenses:* Tuition, state resident: full-time $8210; part-time $345 per credit. Tuition, nonresident: full-time $15,360; part-time $640 per credit. *Required fees:* $280 per semester. One-time fee: $125. Tuition and fees vary according to class time, campus/location and program. *Financial support:* In 2011–12, 6 fellowships were awarded; career-related internships or fieldwork, Federal Work-Study, institutionally sponsored loans, and tuition waivers (partial) also available. Support available to part-time students. Financial award application deadline: 3/1. *Unit head:* Beatrice Krauss, Director, Center of Community and Urban Health, 212-481-4283, Fax: 212-481-5260, E-mail: bkrauss@hunter.cuny.edu. *Application contact:* William Zlata, Director of Graduate Admissions, 212-772-4482, Fax: 212-650-3336, E-mail: admissions@hunter.cuny.edu. Web site: http://www.hunter.cuny.edu/uph/grad-test/community-health-education-1.

Idaho State University, Office of Graduate Studies, Kasiska College of Health Professions, Department of Family Medicine, Pocatello, ID 83209-8357. Offers Post-Master's Certificate. *Degree requirements:* For Post-Master's Certificate, comprehensive exam, thesis optional, 3 year residency program. *Entrance requirements:* For degree, GRE General Test, MD or DO. Additional exam requirements/recommendations for international students: Required—TOEFL (minimum score 600 paper-based; 213 computer-based). Electronic applications accepted. *Faculty research:* Health disparities in primary care, cardiovascular risk reduction (particularly in dyslipidemia, diabetes, hypertension), health application of geographic information systems, mechanisms for increasing quality in primary care, collaborative care models for improving health.

Independence University, Program in Health Services, Salt Lake City, UT 84107. Offers community health (MSHS); wellness promotion (MSHS). Part-time and evening/weekend programs available. Postbaccalaureate distance learning degree programs offered (no on-campus study). *Degree requirements:* For master's, fieldwork, internship, final project (wellness promotion). *Entrance requirements:* For master's, previous course work in psychology.

Indiana State University, College of Graduate and Professional Studies, College of Nursing, Health and Human Services, Department of Health, Safety, and Environmental Health Sciences, Terre Haute, IN 47809. Offers community health promotion (MA, MS);

health and safety education (MA, MS); occupational safety management (MA, MS). *Accreditation:* NCATE (one or more programs are accredited). *Degree requirements:* For master's, thesis or alternative. *Entrance requirements:* For master's, GRE General Test. Electronic applications accepted.

Indiana University Bloomington, School of Health, Physical Education and Recreation, Department of Applied Health Science, Bloomington, IN 47405-7000. Offers biostatistics (MPH); environmental health (MPH, PhD); epidemiology (MPH, PhD); health behavior (PhD); health promotion (MS); human development/family studies (MS); nutrition science (MS); public health administration (MPH); safety management (MS); school and college health programs (MS); social, behavioral and community health (MPH). *Accreditation:* CEPH (one or more programs are accredited). *Faculty:* 24 full-time (12 women). *Students:* 169 full-time (126 women), 25 part-time (17 women); includes 56 minority (39 Black or African American, non-Hispanic/Latino; 2 American Indian or Alaska Native, non-Hispanic/Latino; 4 Asian, non-Hispanic/Latino; 9 Hispanic/Latino; 2 Two or more races, non-Hispanic/Latino), 29 international. Average age 30. 170 applicants, 74% accepted, 79 enrolled. In 2011, 52 master's, 9 doctorates awarded. *Degree requirements:* For master's, thesis optional; for doctorate, thesis/dissertation. *Entrance requirements:* For master's, GRE (MS in nutrition science), 3 recommendations; for doctorate, GRE, 3 recommendations. Additional exam requirements/recommendations for international students: Required—TOEFL (minimum score 550 paper-based; 213 computer-based; 79 iBT). *Application deadline:* For fall admission, 4/30 priority date for domestic students, 12/1 for international students; for spring admission, 11/15 priority date for domestic students, 9/1 for international students. Application fee: $55 ($65 for international students). *Financial support:* Fellowships, research assistantships with full and partial tuition reimbursements, teaching assistantships with full and partial tuition reimbursements, career-related internships or fieldwork, Federal Work-Study, institutionally sponsored loans, scholarships/grants, tuition waivers (partial), and fee remissions available. Financial award application deadline: 3/1. *Faculty research:* Cancer education, HIV/AIDS and drug education, public health, parent-child interactions, safety education. *Total annual research expenditures:* $2.8 million. *Unit head:* Dr. David K. Lohrmann, Chair, 812-856-5101, Fax: 812-855-3936, E-mail: dlohrman@indiana.edu. *Application contact:* Dr. Susan Middlestadt, Associate Professor and Graduate Coordinator, 812-856-5768, Fax: 812-855-3936, E-mail: semiddle@indiana.edu. Web site: http://www.indiana.edu/~aphealth/.

The Johns Hopkins University, Bloomberg School of Public Health, Department of Health, Behavior and Society, Baltimore, MD 21218-2699. Offers genetic counseling (Sc M); health education and health communication (MHS); social and behavioral sciences (Dr PH, PhD, Sc D); social factors in health (MHS). *Degree requirements:* For master's, comprehensive exam (for some programs), thesis (for some programs); for doctorate, comprehensive exam, thesis/dissertation. *Entrance requirements:* For master's, GRE, curriculum vitae, 3 letters of recommendation; for doctorate, GRE, transcripts, curriculum vitae, 3 recommendation letters. Additional exam requirements/recommendations for international students: Required—TOEFL (minimum score 600 paper-based; 250 computer-based; 100 iBT). Electronic applications accepted. *Faculty research:* Social determinants of health and structural and community-level inventions to improve health, communication and health education, behavioral and social aspects of genetic counseling.

Long Island University–Brooklyn Campus, School of Health Professions, Department of Community Health, Brooklyn, NY 11201-8423. Offers community mental health (MS); family health (MS); health management (MS). Part-time and evening/weekend programs available. *Entrance requirements:* For master's, 2 letters of recommendation. Additional exam requirements/recommendations for international students: Required—TOEFL (minimum score 500 paper-based; 173 computer-based). Electronic applications accepted.

Louisiana State University Health Sciences Center, School of Public Health, New Orleans, LA 70112. Offers behavioral and community health sciences (MPH); biostatistics (MPH, MS, PhD); community health sciences (PhD); environmental and occupational health sciences (MPH); epidemiology (MPH, PhD); health policy and systems management (MPH). Part-time programs available. *Entrance requirements:* For master's, GRE General Test.

Massachusetts College of Pharmacy and Health Sciences, Graduate Studies, Program in Community Oral Health, Boston, MA 02115-5896. Offers MS. Part-time programs available. Postbaccalaureate distance learning degree programs offered (minimal on-campus study). *Students:* 3 part-time (all women). Average age 45. 12 applicants, 100% accepted, 3 enrolled. *Entrance requirements:* For master's, 2 years of work experience in health care. Additional exam requirements/recommendations for international students: Required—TOEFL (minimum score 550 paper-based; 213 computer-based; 79 iBT). *Application deadline:* For fall admission, 7/1 priority date for domestic students. Application fee: $70. *Expenses: Tuition:* Full-time $30,200; part-time $945 per credit hour. *Unit head:* Becky DeSpain Eden, Assistant Dean of Graduate Studies, 617-735-1594, E-mail: becky.eden@mcphs.edu. *Application contact:* Brian Barilone, Coordinator of Graduate Admission, 617-879-5032, E-mail: admissions@mcphs.edu.

Massachusetts School of Professional Psychology, Graduate Programs, Boston, MA 02132. Offers applied psychology in higher education student personnel administration (MA); clinical psychology (Psy D); counseling psychology (MA); counseling psychology and community mental health (MA); counseling psychology and global mental health (MA); executive coaching (Graduate Certificate); forensic and counseling psychology (MA); leadership psychology (Psy D); organizational psychology (MA); primary care psychology (MA); respecialization in clinical psychology (Certificate); school psychology (Psy D); MA/CAGS. *Accreditation:* APA. *Degree requirements:* For master's, comprehensive exam (for some programs); for doctorate, thesis/dissertation (for some programs). Electronic applications accepted.

McGill University, Faculty of Graduate and Postdoctoral Studies, Faculty of Medicine, Department of Epidemiology and Biostatistics, Montréal, QC H3A 2T5, Canada. Offers community health (M Sc); environmental health (M Sc); epidemiology and biostatistics (M Sc, PhD, Diploma); health care evaluation (M Sc); medical statistics (M Sc). *Accreditation:* CEPH (one or more programs are accredited).

Medical College of Wisconsin, Graduate School of Biomedical Sciences, Department of Population Health, Program in Public Health, Milwaukee, WI 53226-0509. Offers public and community health (PhD); public health (MPH, Graduate Certificate). *Entrance requirements:* For master's, doctorate, and Graduate Certificate, GRE, official transcripts, three letters of recommendation. Additional exam requirements/recommendations for international students: Required—TOEFL.

Medical College of Wisconsin, Graduate School of Biomedical Sciences, Program in Public and Community Health, Milwaukee, WI 53226-0509. Offers PhD, MD/PhD. *Degree requirements:* For doctorate, comprehensive exam, thesis/dissertation. *Entrance requirements:* For doctorate, GRE, official transcripts, three letters of recommendation. Additional exam requirements/recommendations for international students: Required—TOEFL (minimum score 580 paper-based; 273 computer-based; 100 iBT). Electronic applications accepted. *Expenses:* Contact institution. *Faculty*

Community Health

research: Community-academic partnerships, community-based participatory research, injury prevention, health policy, women's health, emergency medical services.

Meharry Medical College, School of Graduate Studies, Division of Community Health Sciences, Nashville, TN 37208-9989. Offers occupational medicine (MSPH); public health administration (MSPH). *Accreditation:* CEPH. Part-time and evening/weekend programs available. *Degree requirements:* For master's, thesis, externship. *Entrance requirements:* For master's, GRE General Test, GMAT. *Expenses:* Contact institution. *Faculty research:* Policy and management, health care financing, health education and promotion.

Memorial University of Newfoundland, Faculty of Medicine and School of Graduate Studies, Graduate Programs in Medicine, Division of Community Health and Humanities, St. John's, NL A1C 5S7, Canada. Offers community health (M Sc, PhD, Diploma). Part-time programs available. *Degree requirements:* For master's, thesis; for doctorate, comprehensive exam, thesis/dissertation, oral defense of thesis. *Entrance requirements:* For master's, MD or B Sc; for doctorate, MD or M Sc; for Diploma, bachelor's degree in health-related field. Additional exam requirements/recommendations for international students: Required—TOEFL. *Faculty research:* Health care delivery and administration, health services, psychosocial, aging.

Minnesota State University Mankato, College of Graduate Studies, College of Allied Health and Nursing, Department of Health Science, Mankato, MN 56001. Offers community health education (MS); school health education (MS, Postbaccalaureate Certificate). Part-time programs available. *Students:* 10 full-time (5 women), 31 part-time (26 women). *Degree requirements:* For master's, comprehensive exam, thesis or alternative. *Entrance requirements:* For master's, minimum GPA of 3.0 during previous 2 years; for Postbaccalaureate Certificate, teaching license. Additional exam requirements/recommendations for international students: Required—TOEFL (minimum score 500 paper-based; 173 computer-based; 61 iBT). *Application deadline:* For fall admission, 7/1 for domestic students, 5/1 for international students; for spring admission, 11/1 for domestic students, 10/1 for international students. Applications are processed on a rolling basis. Application fee: $40. Electronic applications accepted. *Financial support:* Research assistantships with full tuition reimbursements, teaching assistantships with full tuition reimbursements, career-related internships or fieldwork, and Federal Work-Study available. Support available to part-time students. Financial award application deadline: 3/15; financial award applicants required to submit FAFSA. *Faculty research:* Teaching methods, stress prophylaxis and management, effects of alcohol. *Unit head:* Dr. Dawn Larsen, Graduate Coordinator, 507-389-2113. *Application contact:* 507-389-2321, E-mail: grad@mnsu.edu. Web site: http://ahn.mnsu.edu/health/.

Mount Sinai School of Medicine, Graduate School of Biological Sciences, New York, NY 10029-6504. Offers biomedical sciences (MS, PhD); clinical research education (MS, PhD); community medicine (MPH); genetic counseling (MS); neurosciences (PhD); MD/PhD. Terminal master's awarded for partial completion of doctoral program. *Degree requirements:* For master's, thesis; for doctorate, comprehensive exam, thesis/dissertation. *Entrance requirements:* For master's, GRE General Test; for doctorate, GRE General Test, GRE Subject Test, 3 years of college pre-med course work. Additional exam requirements/recommendations for international students: Required—TOEFL. Electronic applications accepted. *Faculty research:* Cancer, genetics and genomics, immunology, neuroscience, developmental and stem cell biology, translational research.

National University, Academic Affairs, School of Health and Human Services, Department of Community Health, La Jolla, CA 92037-1011. Offers health informatics (MS); healthcare administration (MHA); public health (MPH). Part-time and evening/weekend programs available. Postbaccalaureate distance learning degree programs offered. *Degree requirements:* For master's, thesis. *Entrance requirements:* Additional exam requirements/recommendations for international students: Required—TOEFL (minimum score 550 paper-based; 213 computer-based; 79 iBT). Application fee: $60 ($65 for international students). *Financial support:* Career-related internships or fieldwork, institutionally sponsored loans, and scholarships/grants available. Support available to part-time students. Financial award application deadline: 6/30; financial award applicants required to submit FAFSA. *Unit head:* Dr. Gina Piane, 858-309-3474, E-mail: gpiane@nu.edu. *Application contact:* Dominick Giovanniello, Associate Regional Dean, 800-NAT-UNIV, Fax: 858-541-7792, E-mail: dgiovann@nu.edu. Web site: http://www.nu.edu/OurPrograms/SchoolOfHealthAndHumanServices/CommunityHealth.html.

New Jersey City University, Graduate Studies and Continuing Education, College of Professional Studies, Department of Health Sciences, Jersey City, NJ 07305-1597. Offers community health education (MS); health administration (MS); school health education (MS). Part-time and evening/weekend programs available. *Students:* 6 full-time (5 women), 45 part-time (37 women); includes 19 minority (13 Black or African American, non-Hispanic/Latino; 4 Asian, non-Hispanic/Latino; 2 Hispanic/Latino), 2 international. Average age 41. In 2011, 16 master's awarded. *Degree requirements:* For master's, thesis or alternative, internship. *Entrance requirements:* Additional exam requirements/recommendations for international students: Required—TOEFL. *Application deadline:* For fall admission, 8/1 priority date for domestic students; for spring admission, 12/1 for domestic students. Applications are processed on a rolling basis. Application fee: $0. *Expenses:* Tuition, state resident: part-time $494 per credit. Tuition, nonresident: part-time $911.30 per credit. *Required fees:* $95.90 per year. *Financial support:* Career-related internships or fieldwork and unspecified assistantships available. *Unit head:* Dr. Lilliam Rosado, Chairperson, 201-200-3431, E-mail: lrosado@njcu.edu. *Application contact:* Dr. William Bajor, Dean of Graduate Studies, 201-200-3409, Fax: 201-200-3411, E-mail: wbajor@njcu.edu.

New Mexico State University, Graduate School, College of Health and Social Services, Department of Public Health Sciences, Las Cruces, NM 88003-8001. Offers community health education (MPH). Part-time programs available. Postbaccalaureate distance learning degree programs offered (minimal on-campus study). *Students:* 38 full-time (35 women), 38 part-time (28 women); includes 32 minority (2 Black or African American, non-Hispanic/Latino; 7 American Indian or Alaska Native, non-Hispanic/Latino; 1 Asian, non-Hispanic/Latino; 21 Hispanic/Latino; 1 Two or more races, non-Hispanic/Latino), 7 international. Average age 35. 48 applicants, 58% accepted, 17 enrolled. In 2011, 28 master's awarded. *Degree requirements:* For master's, thesis optional. *Entrance requirements:* For master's, GRE. Additional exam requirements/recommendations for international students: Required—TOEFL (minimum score 550 paper-based; 79 iBT), IELTS (minimum score 6.5). *Application deadline:* For fall admission, 2/15 for domestic and international students. Application fee: $40 ($50 for international students). Electronic applications accepted. *Expenses:* Tuition, state resident: full-time $5004; part-time $208.50 per credit. Tuition, nonresident: full-time $17,446; part-time $726.90 per credit. *Financial support:* In 2011–12, 1 research assistantship (averaging $24,744 per year), 17 teaching assistantships (averaging $15,256 per year) were awarded; fellowships, career-related internships or fieldwork, and health care benefits also available. Financial award application deadline: 4/1. *Faculty research:* Community health education, health issues of U.S.-Mexico border, health policy and management, victims of violence, environmental and occupational health issues. *Unit head:* Dr. Mark J. Kittleson, Head, 575-646-4300, Fax: 575-646-4343, E-mail: kittle@nmsu.edu. *Application contact:* Dr. James Robinson, III, Graduate

Coordinator, 575-646-7431, E-mail: jrobin3@nmsu.edu. Web site: http://publichealth.nmsu.edu.

New York University, Steinhardt School of Culture, Education, and Human Development, Department of Nutrition, Food Studies, and Public Health, Program in Community Public Health, New York, NY 10012-1019. Offers PhD. *Accreditation:* CEPH. Part-time programs available. *Entrance requirements:* For doctorate, GRE General Test, interview. Additional exam requirements/recommendations for international students: Required—TOEFL. Electronic applications accepted. *Faculty research:* Social epidemiology, primary health care, global health, immigrants and health, infectious disease prevention, HIV/AIDS.

Northwest Nazarene University, Graduate Studies, Program in Social Work, Nampa, ID 83686-5897. Offers addiction studies (MSW); clinical gerontological practice with mature and older adults (MSW); community mental health practice (MSW); management, community planning and social administration (MSW). *Accreditation:* CSWE. Part-time programs available. Postbaccalaureate distance learning degree programs offered (no on-campus study). *Faculty:* 10 full-time (7 women), 4 part-time/adjunct (2 women). *Students:* 117 full-time (89 women), 15 part-time (11 women); includes 17 minority (2 American Indian or Alaska Native, non-Hispanic/Latino; 1 Asian, non-Hispanic/Latino; 14 Hispanic/Latino). Average age 36. 70 applicants, 93% accepted, 54 enrolled. In 2011, 42 master's awarded. *Degree requirements:* For master's, comprehensive exam. *Application deadline:* Applications are processed on a rolling basis. Application fee: $25. Electronic applications accepted. *Unit head:* Dr. Mary Curran, Director, 208-467-8679, E-mail: msw@nnu.edu. *Application contact:* Nancy Gibson, Program Assistant, 208-467-8679, Fax: 208-467-8879, E-mail: nkgibson@nnu.edu.

Quinnipiac University, School of Nursing, Care of Populations Track, Hamden, CT 06518-1940. Offers DNP. *Faculty:* 6 full-time (5 women), 7 part-time/adjunct (4 women). *Students:* 4 part-time (all women), 1 international. 6 applicants, 83% accepted, 4 enrolled. *Expenses: Tuition:* Part-time $855 per credit. *Required fees:* $35 per credit. *Unit head:* Dr. Jeanne LeVasseur, Director of Graduate Admissions, 203-582-3484, Fax: 203-582-3230, E-mail: jeanne.levasseur@quinnipiac.edu. *Application contact:* Kristin Parent, Assistant Director of Graduate Health Sciences Admissions, 800-462-1944, Fax: 203-582-3443, E-mail: kristin.parent@quinnipiac.edu.

Sage Graduate School, School of Health Sciences, Department of Psychology, Troy, NY 12180-4115. Offers community psychology (MA), including child care and children's services, community counseling, community health education, community psychology, general psychology; counseling and community psychology (MA). Part-time and evening/weekend programs available. *Faculty:* 4 full-time (3 women), 2 part-time/adjunct (1 woman). *Students:* 31 full-time (29 women), 57 part-time (55 women); includes 12 minority (8 Black or African American, non-Hispanic/Latino; 2 Hispanic/Latino; 2 Two or more races, non-Hispanic/Latino). Average age 28. 81 applicants, 36% accepted, 16 enrolled. In 2011, 23 master's awarded. *Degree requirements:* For master's, thesis or alternative. *Entrance requirements:* For master's, GRE General Test. Additional exam requirements/recommendations for international students: Required—TOEFL (minimum score 550 paper-based; 213 computer-based). *Application deadline:* Applications are processed on a rolling basis. Application fee: $40. *Expenses: Tuition:* Full-time $11,880; part-time $660 per credit hour. Tuition and fees vary according to program. *Financial support:* Fellowships, research assistantships, Federal Work-Study, scholarships/grants, and unspecified assistantships available. Support available to part-time students. Financial award application deadline: 3/1; financial award applicants required to submit FAFSA. *Faculty research:* Effectiveness of arts integration programs in elementary/secondary schools, literacy-based substance abuse program, outcome evaluation of program to increase college entry among urban youth. *Unit head:* Dr. Esther Haskevitz, Interim Dean, School of Health Sciences, 518-244-2296, Fax: 518-244-4571, E-mail: haskve@sage.edu. *Application contact:* Dr. Jean Poppei, Chair, 518-244-2076, Fax: 518-244-4545, E-mail: poppej@sage.edu.

Saint Louis University, Graduate Education, School of Public Health and Graduate Education, Department of Community Health, St. Louis, MO 63103-2097. Offers MPH, MS, MSPH. *Accreditation:* CEPH. Part-time programs available. Postbaccalaureate distance learning degree programs offered (no on-campus study). *Degree requirements:* For master's, comprehensive exam. *Entrance requirements:* For master's, GRE General Test, LSAT, GMAT or MCAT, letters of recommendation, resume. Additional exam requirements/recommendations for international students: Required—TOEFL (minimum score 525 paper-based; 194 computer-based). Electronic applications accepted. *Faculty research:* Obesity prevention, health disparities, health policy, child health.

Simon Fraser University, Graduate Studies, Faculty of Health Sciences, Burnaby, BC V5A 1S6, Canada. Offers population and public health (M Sc). *Degree requirements:* For master's, thesis, practicum or project.

Southern Illinois University Carbondale, Graduate School, College of Education and Human Services, Department of Health Education and Recreation, Program in Community Health Education, Carbondale, IL 62901-4701. Offers MPH. *Students:* 29 full-time (24 women), 4 part-time (all women); includes 12 minority (8 Black or African American, non-Hispanic/Latino; 1 Asian, non-Hispanic/Latino; 3 Hispanic/Latino), 3 international. 37 applicants, 65% accepted, 16 enrolled. In 2011, 8 master's awarded. *Unit head:* Dr. David Birch, Chair, 618-453-2777, Fax: 618-453-1829, E-mail: dabirch@siu.edu. *Application contact:* Carol Reynolds, Administrative Assistant, 618-453-2415, Fax: 618-453-1829, E-mail: creynolds@siu.edu.

Southern New Hampshire University, School of Liberal Arts, Manchester, NH 03106-1045. Offers clinical services for adults psychiatric disabilities (Certificate); clinical services for children and adolescents with psychiatric disabilities (Certificate); clinical services for persons with co-occurring substance abuse and psychiatric disabilities (Certificate); community mental health (MS); fiction writing (MFA); non-fiction writing (MFA); teaching English as a foreign language (MS). Part-time and evening/weekend programs available. *Degree requirements:* For master's, one foreign language, thesis. *Entrance requirements:* For master's, minimum GPA of 2.75: MS-TEFL, 3.0: MFA. Additional exam requirements/recommendations for international students: Required—TOEFL (minimum score 550 paper-based; 213 computer-based; 79 iBT), IELTS (minimum score 6.5), TWE (minimum score 5). Electronic applications accepted. *Expenses:* Contact institution. *Faculty research:* Action research, state of the art practice in behavioral health services, wraparound approaches to working with youth, learning styles.

State University of New York Downstate Medical Center, College of Medicine, Program in Public Health, Brooklyn, NY 11203-2098. Offers urban and immigrant health (MPH); MD/MPH. *Accreditation:* CEPH. Part-time programs available. *Degree requirements:* For master's, practicum. *Entrance requirements:* For master's, GRE, MCAT or OAT, 2 letters of recommendation, minimum undergraduate GPA of 3.0. Additional exam requirements/recommendations for international students: Required—TOEFL (minimum score 550 paper-based).

Stony Brook University, State University of New York, Stony Brook University Medical Center, Health Sciences Center, School of Medicine, Program in Population Health and Clinical Outcomes Research, Stony Brook, NY 11794. Offers PhD.

Stony Brook University, State University of New York, Stony Brook University Medical Center, Health Sciences Center, School of Medicine, Program in Public Health, Stony Brook, NY 11794. Offers community health (MPH); evaluation sciences (MPH); family violence (MPH); health economics (MPH); population health (MPH); substance abuse (MPH). *Accreditation:* CEPH. *Entrance requirements:* For master's, GRE, 3 references. Additional exam requirements/recommendations for international students: Required—TOEFL. Electronic applications accepted. *Faculty research:* Population health, health service research, health economics.

Syracuse University, Falk College of Sport and Human Dynamics, Program in Child and Family Health in the Global Community, Syracuse, NY 13244. Offers MS. Part-time programs available. *Students:* 7 full-time (6 women), 3 part-time (all women); includes 2 minority (1 Black or African American, non-Hispanic/Latino; 1 Asian, non-Hispanic/Latino), 1 international. Average age 28. 14 applicants, 79% accepted, 10 enrolled. *Entrance requirements:* For master's, GRE. Additional exam requirements/recommendations for international students: Required—TOEFL (minimum score 100 iBT). *Application deadline:* For fall admission, 3/15 priority date for domestic students, 3/15 for international students. Application fee: $75. Electronic applications accepted. *Expenses: Tuition:* Part-time $1206 per credit. *Financial support:* Fellowships with full tuition reimbursements, research assistantships with partial tuition reimbursements, and teaching assistantships with partial tuition reimbursements available. Financial award application deadline: 1/15. *Unit head:* Dr. Diane Lyden Murphy, Dean, 315-443-5582, Fax: 315-443-2562. *Application contact:* Felecia Otero, Director, College Relations, 315-443-5555, Fax: 315-443-2562, E-mail: falk@syr.edu. Web site: http://humanecology.syr.edu/.

Universidad de Ciencias Medicas, Graduate Programs, San Jose, Costa Rica. Offers dermatology (SP); family health (MS); health service center administration (MHA); human anatomy (MS); medical and surgery (MD); occupational medicine (MS); pharmacy (Pharm D). Part-time programs available. *Degree requirements:* For master's, thesis; for doctorate and SP, comprehensive exam. *Entrance requirements:* For master's, MD or bachelor's degree; for doctorate, admissions test; for SP, admissions test, MD.

Université de Montréal, Faculty of Medicine, Program in Communal and Public Health, Montréal, QC H3C 3J7, Canada. Offers community health (M Sc, DESS); public health (PhD). *Accreditation:* CEPH. Part-time programs available. Terminal master's awarded for partial completion of doctoral program. *Degree requirements:* For master's, thesis; for doctorate, thesis/dissertation, general exam. *Entrance requirements:* For master's and doctorate, proficiency in French, knowledge of English; for DESS, proficiency in French. Electronic applications accepted. *Faculty research:* Epidemiology, health services utilization, health promotion and education, health behaviors, poverty and child health.

Université Laval, Faculty of Medicine, Graduate Programs in Medicine, Department of Social and Preventive Medicine, Program in Community Health, Québec, QC G1K 7P4, Canada. Offers M Sc, PhD. Part-time programs available. Terminal master's awarded for partial completion of doctoral program. *Degree requirements:* For master's, thesis (for some programs); for doctorate, comprehensive exam, thesis/dissertation. *Entrance requirements:* For master's, knowledge of French, comprehension of written English; for doctorate, French exam, comprehension of French, written comprehension of English. Electronic applications accepted.

Université Laval, Faculty of Medicine, Post-Professional Programs in Medical Studies, Québec, QC G1K 7P4, Canada. Offers anatomy–pathology (DESS); anesthesiology (DESS); cardiology (DESS); care of older people (Diploma); clinical research (DESS); community health (DESS); dermatology (DESS); diagnostic radiology (DESS); emergency medicine (Diploma); family medicine (DESS); general surgery (DESS); geriatrics (DESS); hematology (DESS); internal medicine (DESS); maternal and fetal medicine (Diploma); medical biochemistry (DESS); medical microbiology and infectious diseases (DESS); medical oncology (DESS); nephrology (DESS); neurology (DESS); neurosurgery (DESS); obstetrics and gynecology (DESS); ophthalmology (DESS); orthopedic surgery (DESS); oto-rhino-laryngology (DESS); palliative medicine (Diploma); pediatrics (DESS); plastic surgery (DESS); psychiatry (DESS); pulmonary medicine (DESS); radiology–oncology (DESS); thoracic surgery (DESS); urology (DESS). *Degree requirements:* For other advanced degree, comprehensive exam. *Entrance requirements:* For degree, knowledge of French. Electronic applications accepted.

University at Buffalo, the State University of New York, Graduate School, School of Public Health and Health Professions, Department of Community Health and Health Behavior, Buffalo, NY 14214. Offers MPH, PhD. Part-time programs available. *Faculty:* 7 full-time (3 women). *Students:* 21 full-time (18 women), 3 part-time (1 woman); includes 4 minority (3 Black or African American, non-Hispanic/Latino; 1 Asian, non-Hispanic/Latino), 3 international. Average age 26. 53 applicants, 66% accepted, 10 enrolled. In 2011, 5 degrees awarded. *Degree requirements:* For master's, thesis; for doctorate, comprehensive exam, thesis/dissertation. *Entrance requirements:* For master's and doctorate, GRE. Additional exam requirements/recommendations for international students: Required—TOEFL (minimum score 213 computer-based; 79 iBT). *Application deadline:* For fall admission, 1/15 priority date for domestic students, 2/1 for international students. Applications are processed on a rolling basis. Application fee: $50. Electronic applications accepted. *Financial support:* In 2011–12, 6 students received support, including 2 fellowships with full tuition reimbursements available (averaging $4,000 per year), 2 research assistantships with full tuition reimbursements available (averaging $21,000 per year). Financial award application deadline: 3/15; financial award applicants required to submit FAFSA. *Unit head:* Dr. Gary A. Giovino, Chair, 716-829-6952, E-mail: ggiovino@buffalo.edu. *Application contact:* Barbara L. Sen, Graduate Program Coordinator, 716-829-6956, Fax: 716-829-6040, E-mail: bsen@buffalo.edu. Web site: http://sphhp.buffalo.edu/chhb/.

The University of Alabama, Graduate School, College of Human Environmental Sciences, Program in Human Environmental Science, Tuscaloosa, AL 35487. Offers family financial planning and counseling (MS); interactive technology (MS); quality management (MS); restaurant and meeting management (MS); rural community health (MS); sport management (MS). *Faculty:* 1 full-time (0 women). *Students:* 80 full-time (53 women), 93 part-time (55 women); includes 51 minority (42 Black or African American, non-Hispanic/Latino; 3 American Indian or Alaska Native, non-Hispanic/Latino; 3 Hispanic/Latino; 3 Two or more races, non-Hispanic/Latino), 1 international. Average age 33. 118 applicants, 79% accepted, 75 enrolled. In 2011, 83 degrees awarded. *Degree requirements:* For master's, comprehensive exam. *Entrance requirements:* For master's, GRE (for some specializations), minimum GPA of 3.0. Additional exam requirements/recommendations for international students: Required—TOEFL. *Application deadline:* Applications are processed on a rolling basis. Application fee: $50 ($60 for international students). Electronic applications accepted. *Expenses:* Tuition, state resident: full-time $8600. Tuition, nonresident: full-time $21,900. *Faculty research:* Hospitality management, sports medicine education, technology and education. *Unit head:* Dr. Milla D. Boschung, Dean, 205-348-6250, Fax: 205-348-1786, E-mail: mboschun@ches.ua.edu. *Application contact:* Dr. Stuart Usdan, Associate Dean, 205-348-6150, Fax: 205-348-3789, E-mail: susdan@ches.ua.edu.

University of Alberta, School of Public Health, Department of Public Health Sciences, Edmonton, AB T6G 2E1, Canada. Offers clinical epidemiology (M Sc, MPH); environmental and occupational health (MPH); environmental health sciences (M Sc); epidemiology (M Sc); global health (M Sc, MPH); health policy and management (MPH); health policy research (M Sc); health technology assessment (MPH); occupational health (M Sc); population health (M Sc); public health leadership (MPH); public health sciences (PhD); quantitative methods (MPH). *Accreditation:* CEPH (one or more programs are accredited). Terminal master's awarded for partial completion of doctoral program. *Degree requirements:* For master's, thesis (for some programs); for doctorate, thesis/dissertation. *Entrance requirements:* For master's, GMAT or GRE General Test. Additional exam requirements/recommendations for international students: Required—TOEFL (minimum score 550 paper-based; 213 computer-based) or IELTS (minimum score 6). Electronic applications accepted. *Faculty research:* Biostatistics, health promotion and socio-behavioral health science.

University of Calgary, Faculty of Graduate Studies, Faculty of Education, Graduate Division of Educational Research, Calgary, AB T2N 1N4, Canada. Offers community rehabilitation and disability studies (M Ed, M Sc, Ed D, PhD, Graduate Certificate, Graduate Diploma); curriculum, teaching and learning (M Ed, M Sc, MA, Ed D, PhD, Graduate Certificate, Graduate Diploma); educational contexts (M Ed, MA, Ed D, PhD, Graduate Certificate, Graduate Diploma); educational leadership (M Ed, MA, Ed D, PhD, Graduate Certificate, Graduate Diploma); educational technology (M Ed, M Sc, MA, Ed D, PhD, Graduate Certificate, Graduate Diploma); gifted education (M Sc, MA, Ed D, PhD, Graduate Certificate, Graduate Diploma); higher education administration (Ed D); interpretive studies in education (M Ed, M Sc, MA, Ed D, PhD, Graduate Certificate, Graduate Diploma); second language teaching (M Ed, Ed D, PhD, Graduate Certificate, Graduate Diploma); teaching English as a second language (M Ed, M Sc, MA, Ed D, PhD, Graduate Certificate, Graduate Diploma); workplace and adult learning (M Ed, MA, Ed D, PhD, Graduate Certificate, Graduate Diploma). Ed D in both higher education administration and educational leadership offered via distance delivery. Part-time and evening/weekend programs available. Postbaccalaureate distance learning degree programs offered (minimal on-campus study). *Degree requirements:* For master's, thesis (for some programs); for doctorate, thesis/dissertation, candidacy exam. *Entrance requirements:* For master's, minimum GPA of 3.0, 3 letters of reference; for doctorate, minimum GPA of 3.5, 3 letters of reference; for other advanced degree, minimum GPA of 3.0. Additional exam requirements/recommendations for international students: Required—TOEFL, IELTS. Electronic applications accepted. *Faculty research:* Curriculum, leadership, technology, contexts, gifted, second language teaching, work place and adult learning.

University of Calgary, Faculty of Medicine and Faculty of Graduate Studies, Department of Community Health Sciences, Calgary, AB T2N 1N4, Canada. Offers M Sc, MCM, PhD. *Degree requirements:* For master's, thesis; for doctorate, thesis/dissertation, candidacy exam. *Entrance requirements:* For master's and doctorate, minimum GPA of 3.2. Additional exam requirements/recommendations for international students: Required—TOEFL (minimum score 600 paper-based; 250 computer-based). Electronic applications accepted. *Faculty research:* Epidemiology, health research, biostatistics, health economics, health policy.

University of California, Los Angeles, Graduate Division, School of Public Health, Department of Community Health Sciences, Los Angeles, CA 90095. Offers public health (MPH, MS, Dr PH, PhD); JD/MPH; MA/MPH; MD/MPH; MSW/MPH. *Degree requirements:* For master's, comprehensive exam or thesis; for doctorate, thesis/dissertation, oral and written qualifying exams. *Entrance requirements:* For master's, GRE General Test, minimum GPA of 3.0; for doctorate, GRE General Test, minimum undergraduate GPA of 3.0. Electronic applications accepted.

University of Colorado Denver, College of Liberal Arts and Sciences, Program in Humanities, Denver, CO 80217. Offers community health science (MSS); humanities (MH); international studies (MSS); society and the environment (MSS); women's and gender studies (MSS). Part-time and evening/weekend programs available. *Students:* 41 full-time (28 women), 42 part-time (26 women); includes 13 minority (1 Black or African American, non-Hispanic/Latino; 2 American Indian or Alaska Native, non-Hispanic/Latino; 2 Asian, non-Hispanic/Latino; 8 Hispanic/Latino). Average age 33. 30 applicants, 60% accepted, 10 enrolled. In 2011, 19 master's awarded. *Degree requirements:* For master's, thesis or alternative, 36 credit hours, project or thesis. *Entrance requirements:* For master's, writing sample, statement of purpose/letter of intent. Additional exam requirements/recommendations for international students: Required—TOEFL (minimum score 525 paper-based; 197 computer-based; 71 iBT). *Application deadline:* For fall admission, 5/15 for domestic and international students; for spring admission, 10/15 for domestic and international students. Application fee: $50 ($75 for international students). Electronic applications accepted. *Financial support:* Federal Work-Study and scholarships/grants available. Financial award application deadline: 4/1; financial award applicants required to submit FAFSA. *Faculty research:* Women and gender in the classical Mediterranean, communication theory and democracy, relationship between psychology and philosophy. *Unit head:* Myra Bookman, Associate Director of Humanities and Social Science, 303-556-2496, Fax: 303-556-8100, E-mail: myra.bookman@ucdenver.edu. *Application contact:* Catherine Osmundson, Program Assistant, 303-556-2305, E-mail: catherine.osmundson@ucdenver.edu. Web site: http://www.ucdenver.edu/academics/colleges/CLAS/Programs/HumanitiesSocialSciences/Programs/Pages/Admissions.aspx.

University of Colorado Denver, Colorado School of Public Health, Program in Public Health, Aurora, CO 80045. Offers community and behavioral health (MPH, Dr PH); environmental and occupational health (MPH); epidemiology (MPH); health systems, management and policy (MPH). *Accreditation:* CEPH. Part-time and evening/weekend programs available. *Students:* 216 full-time (177 women), 47 part-time (38 women); includes 48 minority (10 Black or African American, non-Hispanic/Latino; 5 American Indian or Alaska Native, non-Hispanic/Latino; 14 Asian, non-Hispanic/Latino; 17 Hispanic/Latino; 1 Native Hawaiian or other Pacific Islander, non-Hispanic/Latino; 1 Two or more races, non-Hispanic/Latino), 7 international. Average age 33. 670 applicants, 51% accepted, 160 enrolled. In 2011, 83 degrees awarded. *Degree requirements:* For master's, thesis or alternative, 42 credit hours; for doctorate, comprehensive exam, thesis/dissertation, 67 credit hours. *Entrance requirements:* For master's, GRE, baccalaureate degree or equivalent; minimum GPA of 3.0; transcripts; references; resume; essay; for doctorate, GRE, MPH or master's or higher degree in related field or equivalent; 2 years previous work experience in public health, essay, resume. Additional exam requirements/recommendations for international students: Required—TOEFL (minimum score 550 paper-based; 213 computer-based). *Application deadline:* For fall admission, 2/1 for domestic students. Application fee: $65. Electronic applications accepted. *Expenses:* Contact institution. *Financial support:* Fellowships, research assistantships, Federal Work-Study, scholarships/grants, and unspecified assistantships available. Support available to part-time students. Financial award application deadline: 3/15; financial award applicants required to submit FAFSA. *Faculty research:* Cancer prevention by nutrition, cancer survivorship outcomes, social and cultural factors related to health. *Unit head:* Dr. Jack Barnette, Program Director, 303-724-4472, E-mail: jack.barnette@ucdenver.edu. *Application contact:* Jennifer Pacheco, Admissions Specialist, 303-724-5585, E-mail: jennifer.pacheco@ucdenver.edu. Web

Community Health

site: http://www.ucdenver.edu/academics/colleges/PublicHealth/departments/CommunityBehavioralHealth/Pages/CommunityBehavioralHealth.aspx.

University of Colorado Denver, School of Medicine, Physician Assistant Program, Aurora, CO 80045. Offers child health associate (MPAS), including global health, leadership, education, advocacy, development, and scholarship, rural health, urban/underserved populations. *Accreditation:* ARC-PA. *Students:* 124 full-time (107 women), 2 part-time (both women); includes 12 minority (1 American Indian or Alaska Native, non-Hispanic/Latino; 6 Asian, non-Hispanic/Latino; 5 Hispanic/Latino). Average age 26. 274 applicants, 17% accepted, 44 enrolled. In 2011, 37 master's awarded. *Degree requirements:* For master's, comprehensive exam, successful completion of all coursework and rotations. *Entrance requirements:* For master's, GRE General Test, minimum GPA of 2.8, 3 letters of recommendation, prerequisite courses in chemistry, biology, general genetics, psychology and statistics, interviews for the finalists. Additional exam requirements/recommendations for international students: Required—TOEFL (minimum score 550 paper-based; 213 computer-based). *Application deadline:* For fall admission, 10/1 for domestic students. Application fee: $170. Electronic applications accepted. *Expenses:* Contact institution. *Financial support:* Career-related internships or fieldwork and scholarships/grants available. Financial award application deadline: 3/15; financial award applicants required to submit FAFSA. *Faculty research:* Clinical genetics and genetic counseling, evidence-based medicine, pediatric allergy and asthma, childhood diabetes, standardized patient assessment. *Unit head:* Jonathan Bowser, Interim Program Director, 303-724-1349, E-mail: jonathan.bowser@ucdenver.edu. *Application contact:* Kay Denler, Director of Admissions, 303-724-1340, E-mail: kay.denler@ucdenver.edu. Web site: http://www.ucdenver.edu/academics/colleges/medicalschool/education/degree_programs/PAProgram/Pages/Home.aspx.

University of Illinois at Chicago, Graduate College, School of Public Health, Division of Community Health Sciences, Chicago, IL 60607-7128. Offers MPH, MS, Dr PH, PhD. *Accreditation:* CEPH (one or more programs are accredited). Part-time programs available. Terminal master's awarded for partial completion of doctoral program. *Degree requirements:* For master's, thesis, field practicum; for doctorate, thesis/dissertation, independent research, internship. *Entrance requirements:* For master's and doctorate, GRE General Test, minimum GPA of 2.75. Additional exam requirements/recommendations for international students: Required—TOEFL. Electronic applications accepted.

University of Illinois at Urbana–Champaign, Graduate College, College of Applied Health Sciences, Department of Kinesiology and Community Health, Champaign, IL 61820. Offers community health (MS, MSPH, PhD); kinesiology (MS, PhD); public health (MPH); rehabilitation (MS). *Faculty:* 25 full-time (12 women). *Students:* 137 full-time (83 women), 10 part-time (8 women); includes 35 minority (16 Black or African American, non-Hispanic/Latino; 14 Asian, non-Hispanic/Latino; 3 Hispanic/Latino; 2 Two or more races, non-Hispanic/Latino), 38 international. 167 applicants, 40% accepted, 45 enrolled. In 2011, 22 master's, 11 doctorates awarded. *Entrance requirements:* For master's, GRE, minimum GPA of 3.0; for doctorate, GRE, minimum graduate GPA of 3.5. Additional exam requirements/recommendations for international students: Required—TOEFL. *Application deadline:* Applications are processed on a rolling basis. Application fee: $75 ($90 for international students). Electronic applications accepted. *Financial support:* In 2011–12, 15 fellowships, 37 research assistantships, 71 teaching assistantships were awarded; tuition waivers (full and partial) also available. *Unit head:* Wojciech Chodzko-Zajko, Head, 217-244-0823, Fax: 217-244-7322, E-mail: wojtek@illinois.edu. *Application contact:* Tina M. Candler, Office Manager, 217-333-1083, Fax: 217-244-7322, E-mail: tcandler@illinois.edu. Web site: http://www.kch.illinois.edu/.

The University of Iowa, Graduate College, College of Public Health, Department of Community and Behavioral Health, Iowa City, IA 52242-1316. Offers MS, PhD. *Accreditation:* CEPH. *Degree requirements:* For master's, thesis; for doctorate, comprehensive exam, thesis/dissertation. *Entrance requirements:* For master's and doctorate, GRE General Test, minimum GPA of 3.0. Additional exam requirements/recommendations for international students: Required—TOEFL (minimum score 600 paper-based; 250 computer-based; 100 iBT). Electronic applications accepted.

University of Louisville, Graduate School, College of Education and Human Development, Department of Health and Sport Sciences, Louisville, KY 40292-0001. Offers community health education (M Ed); exercise physiology (MS); health and physical education (MAT); sport administration (MS). Part-time and evening/weekend programs available. *Entrance requirements:* For master's, GRE General Test. Additional exam requirements/recommendations for international students: Required—TOEFL (minimum score 560 paper-based; 210 computer-based; 83 iBT). Electronic applications accepted. *Expenses:* Tuition, state resident: full-time $9692; part-time $539 per credit hour. Tuition, nonresident: full-time $20,168; part-time $1121 per credit hour. Tuition and fees vary according to program and reciprocity agreements. *Faculty research:* Impact of sports and sport marketing on society, factors associated with school and community health, cardiac and pulmonary rehabilitation, impact of participation in activities on student retention and graduation, strength and conditioning.

University of Manitoba, Faculty of Medicine and Faculty of Graduate Studies, Graduate Programs in Medicine, Department of Community Health Sciences, Winnipeg, MB R3T 2N2, Canada. Offers M Sc, MPH, PhD, G Dip. Part-time programs available. *Degree requirements:* For master's, thesis; for doctorate, thesis/dissertation. *Entrance requirements:* For master's and doctorate, minimum GPA of 3.0. *Faculty research:* Health services, aboriginal health, health policy, epidemiology, international health.

University of Massachusetts Amherst, Graduate School, School of Public Health and Health Sciences, Department of Public Health, Amherst, MA 01003. Offers biostatistics (MPH, MS, PhD); community health education (MPH, MS, PhD); environmental health sciences (MPH, MS, PhD); epidemiology (MPH, MS, PhD); health policy and management (MPH, MS, PhD); nutrition (MPH, PhD); public health practice (MPH); MPH/MPPA. *Accreditation:* CEPH (one or more programs are accredited). Part-time and evening/weekend programs available. Postbaccalaureate distance learning degree programs offered (no on-campus study). *Faculty:* 46 full-time (26 women). *Students:* 118 full-time (88 women), 249 part-time (183 women); includes 75 minority (28 Black or African American, non-Hispanic/Latino; 21 Asian, non-Hispanic/Latino; 20 Hispanic/Latino; 6 Two or more races, non-Hispanic/Latino), 55 international. Average age 36. 377 applicants, 67% accepted, 91 enrolled. In 2011, 83 master's, 4 doctorates awarded. Terminal master's awarded for partial completion of doctoral program. *Degree requirements:* For master's, thesis (for some programs); for doctorate, comprehensive exam, thesis/dissertation. *Entrance requirements:* For master's and doctorate, GRE General Test. Additional exam requirements/recommendations for international students: Required—TOEFL (minimum score 550 paper-based; 213 computer-based; 80 iBT), IELTS (minimum score 6.5). *Application deadline:* For fall admission, 2/1 for domestic and international students. Applications are processed on a rolling basis. Application fee: $40 ($65 for international students). Electronic applications accepted. Tuition and fees vary according to course load, campus/location and program. *Financial support:* Fellowships with full and partial tuition reimbursements, research assistantships with full and partial tuition reimbursements, teaching assistantships with full and partial tuition reimbursements, career-related internships or fieldwork, Federal Work-Study, scholarships/grants, traineeships, health care benefits, tuition waivers (full and partial), and unspecified assistantships available. Support available to part-time students. Financial award application deadline: 2/1. *Unit head:* Dr. Paula Stamps, Graduate Program Director, 413-545-2861, Fax: 413-545-1645. *Application contact:* Lindsay DeSantis, Interim Supervisor of Admissions, 413-545-0722, Fax: 413-577-0010, E-mail: gradadm@grad.umass.edu. Web site: http://www.umass.edu/sphhs/public_health/.

University of Minnesota, Twin Cities Campus, School of Public Health, Major in Community Health Education, Minneapolis, MN 55455-0213. Offers MPH. *Accreditation:* CEPH. Part-time programs available. *Degree requirements:* For master's, fieldwork, project. *Entrance requirements:* For master's, GRE General Test. Additional exam requirements/recommendations for international students: Required—TOEFL. Electronic applications accepted. *Faculty research:* Assessing population behavior, designing community-wide prevention and treatment, preventing alcohol and drug abuse, influencing health policies.

University of Nevada, Las Vegas, Graduate College, School of Community Health Sciences, Las Vegas, NV 89154-3063. Offers M Ed, MHA, MPH, PhD. *Faculty:* 20 full-time (7 women). *Students:* 68 full-time (48 women), 102 part-time (69 women); includes 61 minority (19 Black or African American, non-Hispanic/Latino; 2 American Indian or Alaska Native, non-Hispanic/Latino; 16 Asian, non-Hispanic/Latino; 10 Hispanic/Latino; 3 Native Hawaiian or other Pacific Islander, non-Hispanic/Latino; 11 Two or more races, non-Hispanic/Latino), 14 international. Average age 33. 85 applicants, 61% accepted, 37 enrolled. In 2011, 47 master's awarded. *Entrance requirements:* Additional exam requirements/recommendations for international students: Required—TOEFL, IELTS (minimum score 7). *Application deadline:* For fall admission, 5/1 for international students; for spring admission, 10/1 for international students. Application fee: $60 ($95 for international students). Electronic applications accepted. *Financial support:* In 2011–12, 31 students received support, including 28 research assistantships with partial tuition reimbursements available (averaging $8,788 per year), 3 teaching assistantships (averaging $10,973 per year); institutionally sponsored loans, scholarships/grants, health care benefits, and unspecified assistantships also available. Financial award application deadline: 3/1. *Faculty research:* Environmental health: micro (mold) to macro (Lake Mead ecosystem); health promotion and disease prevention: asthma, diabetes, cancer, HIV/AIDS, substance abuse, injury, hospital-acquired infections; health management and policy; health disparities/health equity; health information systems. *Total annual research expenditures:* $1.7 million. *Unit head:* Dr. Mary Guinan, Dean, 702-895-5090, Fax: 702-895-5184, E-mail: mary.guinan@unlv.edu. *Application contact:* Graduate College Admissions Evaluator, 702-895-3320, Fax: 702-895-4180, E-mail: gradcollege@unlv.edu. Web site: http://publichealth.unlv.edu/.

University of New Mexico, Graduate School, College of Education, Department of Health, Exercise and Sports Sciences, Program in Health Education, Albuquerque, NM 87131-2039. Offers community health education (MS). *Accreditation:* NCATE. Part-time programs available. *Students:* 24 full-time (21 women), 15 part-time (11 women); includes 21 minority (5 Black or African American, non-Hispanic/Latino; 2 American Indian or Alaska Native, non-Hispanic/Latino; 1 Asian, non-Hispanic/Latino; 12 Hispanic/Latino; 1 Two or more races, non-Hispanic/Latino), 3 international. Average age 32. 23 applicants, 87% accepted, 14 enrolled. In 2011, 12 degrees awarded. *Degree requirements:* For master's, comprehensive exam, thesis optional. *Entrance requirements:* For master's, 3 letters of reference, resume, minimum cumulative GPA of 3.0 in last 2 years of bachelor's degree, letter of intent. Additional exam requirements/recommendations for international students: Required—TOEFL (minimum score 550 paper-based; 213 computer-based). *Application deadline:* For fall admission, 6/15 priority date for domestic students; for spring admission, 11/1 priority date for domestic students. Applications are processed on a rolling basis. Application fee: $50. Electronic applications accepted. *Financial support:* In 2011–12, 23 students received support, including 2 fellowships (averaging $2,290 per year), 3 teaching assistantships with full tuition reimbursements available (averaging $11,911 per year); career-related internships or fieldwork, institutionally sponsored loans, scholarships/grants, and health care benefits also available. Financial award application deadline: 3/1; financial award applicants required to submit FAFSA. *Faculty research:* Alcohol and families, health behaviors and sexuality, multicultural health behavior, health promotion policy, school/community-based prevention, health and aging. *Total annual research expenditures:* $91,910. *Unit head:* Dr. Elias Duryea, Coordinator, 505-277-5151, Fax: 505-277-6227, E-mail: duryea@unm.edu. *Application contact:* Carol Catania, Graduate Coordinator, 505-277-5151, Fax: 505-277-6227, E-mail: catania@unm.edu. Web site: http://coe.unm.edu/departments/hess/health-education/health-education-ms.html.

University of New Mexico, Health Sciences Center Graduate Programs, Program in Public Health, Albuquerque, NM 87131-5196. Offers community health (MPH); epidemiology (MPH); generalist (MPH). *Accreditation:* CEPH. Part-time programs available. Postbaccalaureate distance learning degree programs offered. *Faculty:* 11 full-time (8 women), 2 part-time/adjunct (1 woman). *Students:* 18 full-time (15 women), 26 part-time (21 women); includes 17 minority (3 American Indian or Alaska Native, non-Hispanic/Latino; 13 Hispanic/Latino; 1 Two or more races, non-Hispanic/Latino), 1 international. Average age 37. 34 applicants, 59% accepted, 11 enrolled. In 2011, 11 degrees awarded. *Degree requirements:* For master's, thesis. *Entrance requirements:* For master's, GRE, MCAT, 2 years of experience in health field. Additional exam requirements/recommendations for international students: Required—TOEFL. *Application deadline:* For fall admission, 2/1 for domestic students. Application fee: $50. *Financial support:* Fellowships, research assistantships with tuition reimbursements, and Federal Work-Study available. Financial award application deadline: 12/15; financial award applicants required to submit FAFSA. *Faculty research:* Epidemiology, rural health, environmental health, Native American health issues. *Total annual research expenditures:* $1 million. *Unit head:* Dr. Kristine Tollestrup, Director, 505-272-4173, Fax: 505-272-4494, E-mail: ktollestrup@salud.unm.edu. *Application contact:* Gayle Garcia, Education Coordinator, 505-272-3982, Fax: 505-272-4494, E-mail: garciag@salud.unm.edu. Web site: http://hsc.unm.edu/som/fcm/mph/mphindex.shtml.

The University of North Carolina at Charlotte, Graduate School, College of Health and Human Services, Department of Public Health Sciences, Charlotte, NC 28223-0001. Offers community health (Certificate); health administration (MHA); health services research (PhD); public health (MSPH). *Accreditation:* CAHME. Part-time programs available. *Faculty:* 16 full-time (10 women), 2 part-time/adjunct (1 woman). *Students:* 80 full-time (67 women), 40 part-time (30 women); includes 30 minority (22 Black or African American, non-Hispanic/Latino; 3 Asian, non-Hispanic/Latino; 5 Hispanic/Latino), 10 international. Average age 28. 171 applicants, 57% accepted, 46 enrolled. In 2011, 53 master's, 3 doctorates, 5 other advanced degrees awarded. Terminal master's awarded for partial completion of doctoral program. *Degree requirements:* For master's, thesis or comprehensive exam; for doctorate, thesis/dissertation. *Entrance requirements:* For master's, GRE or MAT (public health), GRE or GMAT (health administration), minimum GPA of 3.0 during previous 2 years, 2.75 overall. Additional exam requirements/recommendations for international students: Required—TOEFL (minimum score 557 paper-based; 220 computer-based; 83 iBT). *Application deadline:* For fall admission, 7/1 for domestic students, 5/1 for international students; for spring admission, 11/1 for domestic students, 10/1 for international students. Applications are processed on a rolling basis. Application fee: $65 ($75 for international students). Electronic applications accepted. *Expenses:* Tuition, state

resident: full-time $3689. Tuition, nonresident: full-time $15,226. *Required fees:* $2198. Tuition and fees vary according to course load and program. *Financial support:* In 2011–12, 21 students received support, including 5 research assistantships (averaging $9,974 per year), 15 teaching assistantships (averaging $8,502 per year); career-related internships or fieldwork, Federal Work-Study, institutionally sponsored loans, scholarships/grants, unspecified assistantships, and administrative assistantship also available. Support available to part-time students. Financial award application deadline: 4/1; financial award applicants required to submit FAFSA. *Faculty research:* Pediatric asthma self-management, reproductive epidemiology, social aspects of injury prevention, chronic illness self-care, competency-based professional education. *Total annual research expenditures:* $405,550. *Unit head:* Dr. Andrew R. Harver, Chair, 704-687-8680, Fax: 704-687-6122, E-mail: arharver@uncc.edu. *Application contact:* Kathy B. Giddings, Director of Graduate Admissions, 704-687-5503, Fax: 704-687-3279, E-mail: gradadm@uncc.edu. Web site: http://publichealth.uncc.edu/.

The University of North Carolina at Charlotte, Graduate School, College of Health and Human Services, School of Nursing, Charlotte, NC 28223-0001. Offers administration (Post-Master's Certificate); advanced clinical (MSN, Post-Master's Certificate); anesthesia (MSN, Post-Master's Certificate); community health (MSN); family nurse practitioner (MSN, Post-Master's Certificate); health administration (MSN); mental health (MSN); nurse educator (MSN, Post-Master's Certificate); systems population (MSN). *Accreditation:* AACN. *Faculty:* 20 full-time (19 women), 5 part-time/adjunct (all women). *Students:* 76 full-time (65 women), 160 part-time (149 women); includes 49 minority (32 Black or African American, non-Hispanic/Latino; 1 American Indian or Alaska Native, non-Hispanic/Latino; 8 Asian, non-Hispanic/Latino; 8 Hispanic/Latino), 1 international. Average age 35. 191 applicants, 42% accepted, 71 enrolled. In 2011, 76 master's, 10 other advanced degrees awarded. *Degree requirements:* For master's, thesis or alternative, practicum. *Entrance requirements:* For master's, GRE General Test, minimum GPA of 3.0 in undergraduate major. Additional exam requirements/recommendations for international students: Required—TOEFL (minimum score 570 paper-based; 220 computer-based; 83 iBT). *Application deadline:* For fall admission, 7/15 for domestic students, 5/1 for international students; for spring admission, 11/15 for domestic students, 10/1 for international students. Application fee: $65 ($75 for international students). *Expenses:* Tuition, state resident: full-time $3689. Tuition, nonresident: full-time $15,226. *Required fees:* $2198. Tuition and fees vary according to course load and program. *Financial support:* In 2011–12, 10 students received support, including 4 research assistantships (averaging $5,284 per year), 6 teaching assistantships (averaging $2,918 per year); career-related internships or fieldwork, institutionally sponsored loans, scholarships/grants, traineeships, unspecified assistantships, and administrative assistanship also available. Support available to part-time students. Financial award application deadline: 4/1; financial award applicants required to submit FAFSA. *Total annual research expenditures:* $955,795. *Unit head:* Dr. Lucille L. Travis, Director, 704-687-7959, Fax: 704-687-6017, E-mail: ltravis1@uncc.edu. *Application contact:* Kathy B. Giddings, Director of Graduate Admissions, 704-687-5503, Fax: 704-687-3279, E-mail: gradadm@uncc.edu. Web site: http://nursing.uncc.edu/.

The University of North Carolina at Greensboro, Graduate School, School of Health and Human Performance, Department of Public Health Education, Greensboro, NC 27412-5001. Offers community health education (MPH, Dr PH). *Accreditation:* CEPH; NCATE. *Degree requirements:* For master's, comprehensive exam, thesis or alternative. *Entrance requirements:* For master's, GRE General Test or MAT. Additional exam requirements/recommendations for international students: Required—TOEFL. Electronic applications accepted. *Faculty research:* Peer facilitator training, innovative health education approaches.

University of Northern British Columbia, Office of Graduate Studies, Prince George, BC V2N 4Z9, Canada. Offers business administration (Diploma); community health science (M Sc); disability management (MA); education (M Ed); first nations studies (MA); gender studies (MA); history (MA); interdisciplinary studies (MA); international studies (MA); mathematical, computer and physical sciences (M Sc); natural resources and environmental studies (M Sc, MA, MNRES, PhD); political science (MA); psychology (M Sc, PhD); social work (MSW). Part-time and evening/weekend programs available. Postbaccalaureate distance learning degree programs offered (no on-campus study). *Degree requirements:* For master's, thesis; for doctorate, thesis/dissertation. *Entrance requirements:* For master's, GRE, minimum B average in undergraduate course work; for doctorate, candidacy exam, minimum A average in graduate course work.

University of Northern Iowa, Graduate College, College of Education, School of Health, Physical Education, and Leisure Services, Division of Health Promotion and Education, Cedar Falls, IA 50614. Offers community health education (Ed D); health education (MA). Part-time and evening/weekend programs available. *Students:* 15 full-time (10 women), 14 part-time (13 women); includes 5 minority (4 Black or African American, non-Hispanic/Latino; 1 Hispanic/Latino), 4 international. 27 applicants, 81% accepted, 8 enrolled. In 2011, 9 master's awarded. *Degree requirements:* For master's, comprehensive exam, thesis or alternative; for doctorate, thesis/dissertation. *Entrance requirements:* For master's, minimum GPA of 3.0; for doctorate, GRE, minimum GPA of 3.5. Additional exam requirements/recommendations for international students: Required—TOEFL (minimum score 500 paper-based; 180 computer-based; 61 iBT). *Application deadline:* For fall admission, 8/1 priority date for domestic students. Applications are processed on a rolling basis. Application fee: $50 ($70 for international students). Electronic applications accepted. *Expenses:* Tuition, state resident: full-time $7476. Tuition, nonresident: full-time $16,410. *Required fees:* $942. *Financial support:* Career-related internships or fieldwork, Federal Work-Study, and tuition waivers (full and partial) available. Support available to part-time students. Financial award application deadline: 2/1. *Unit head:* Dr. Diane Depken, Coordinator, 319-273-7287, Fax: 319-273-5958, E-mail: diane.depken@uni.edu. *Application contact:* Laurie S. Russell, Record Analyst, 319-273-2623, Fax: 319-273-2885, E-mail: laurie.russell@uni.edu. Web site: http://www.uni.edu/coe/hpels/HealthPromotion&Ed/.

University of North Florida, Brooks College of Health, Department of Public Health, Jacksonville, FL 32224. Offers aging services (Certificate); community health (MPH); geriatric management (MSH); health administration (MHA); rehabilitation counseling (MS). *Accreditation:* CEPH. Part-time and evening/weekend programs available. *Faculty:* 15 full-time (10 women), 3 part-time/adjunct (2 women). *Students:* 106 full-time (77 women), 55 part-time (36 women); includes 28 minority (10 Black or African American, non-Hispanic/Latino; 2 American Indian or Alaska Native, non-Hispanic/Latino; 9 Asian, non-Hispanic/Latino; 5 Hispanic/Latino; 2 Two or more races, non-Hispanic/Latino), 7 international. Average age 30. 209 applicants, 38% accepted, 51 enrolled. In 2011, 65 master's awarded. *Degree requirements:* For master's, thesis optional. *Entrance requirements:* For master's, GRE General Test (MSH, MS, MPH); GMAT or GRE General Test (MHA), minimum GPA of 3.0 in last 60 hours. Additional exam requirements/recommendations for international students: Required—TOEFL (minimum score 500 paper-based; 173 computer-based). *Application deadline:* For fall admission, 7/1 priority date for domestic students, 5/1 for international students; for spring admission, 11/1 priority date for domestic students, 10/1 for international students. Applications are processed on a rolling basis. Application fee: $30. Electronic applications accepted. *Expenses:* Tuition, state resident: full-time $8793; part-time $366.38 per credit hour. Tuition, nonresident: full-time $23,502; part-time $979.24 per credit hour. *Required fees:* $1384; $57.66 per credit hour. Tuition and fees vary according to course load and program. *Financial support:* In 2011–12, 60 students received support. Research assistantships, teaching assistantships, career-related internships or fieldwork, Federal Work-Study, scholarships/grants, and tuition waivers (partial) available. Support available to part-time students. Financial award application deadline: 4/1; financial award applicants required to submit FAFSA. *Faculty research:* Dietary supplements; alcohol, tobacco, and other drug use prevention; turnover among health professionals; aging; psychosocial aspects of disabilities. *Total annual research expenditures:* $197,732. *Unit head:* Dr. JoAnn Nolin, Chair, 904-620-2840, Fax: 904-620-2848, E-mail: jnolin@unf.edu. *Application contact:* Heather Kenney, Director of Advising, 904-620-2810, Fax: 904-620-1030, E-mail: heather.kenney@unf.edu. Web site: http://www.unf.edu/brooks/public_health/.

University of North Texas, Toulouse Graduate School, College of Public Affairs and Community Service, Department of Sociology, Denton, TX 76203. Offers global and comparative (PhD); health and illness (PhD); social stratification and inequality (PhD); sociology (MA, MS). Terminal master's awarded for partial completion of doctoral program. *Degree requirements:* For master's, variable foreign language requirement, comprehensive exam, thesis (for some programs); for doctorate, variable foreign language requirement, comprehensive exam, thesis/dissertation. *Entrance requirements:* For master's, GRE General Test, 4 letters of recommendation; for doctorate, GRE General Test, master's degree, 4 letters of recommendation. Additional exam requirements/recommendations for international students: Required—TOEFL (minimum score 550 paper-based; 213 computer-based; 79 iBT). Electronic applications accepted. *Expenses:* Tuition, state resident: part-time $100 per credit hour. Tuition, nonresident: part-time $413 per credit hour. *Faculty research:* Health and illness, social inequality, globalization and development, family.

University of North Texas Health Science Center at Fort Worth, School of Public Health, Fort Worth, TX 76107-2699. Offers biostatistics (MPH); community health (MPH); disease control and prevention (Dr PH); environmental and occupational health sciences (MPH); epidemiology (MPH); health administration (MHA); health policy and management (MPH, Dr PH); DO/MPH; MS/MPH; MSN/MPH. MPH offered jointly with University of North Texas; DO/MPH with Texas College of Osteopathic Medicine. *Accreditation:* CEPH. Part-time and evening/weekend programs available. *Degree requirements:* For master's, thesis or alternative, supervised internship; for doctorate, thesis/dissertation, supervised internship. *Entrance requirements:* For master's, GRE General Test. Additional exam requirements/recommendations for international students: Required—TOEFL. Electronic applications accepted.

University of Ottawa, Faculty of Graduate and Postdoctoral Studies, Faculty of Medicine, Department of Epidemiology and Community Medicine, Ottawa, ON K1N 6N5, Canada. Offers epidemiology (M Sc), including health technology assessment. *Degree requirements:* For master's, thesis. *Entrance requirements:* For master's, honors degree or equivalent, minimum B average. Electronic applications accepted. *Faculty research:* Epidemiologic concepts and methods, health technology assessment.

University of Ottawa, Faculty of Graduate and Postdoctoral Studies, Interdisciplinary Programs, Ottawa, ON K1N 6N5, Canada. Offers e-business (Certificate); e-commerce (Certificate); finance (Certificate); health services and policies research (Diploma); population health (PhD); population health risk assessment and management (Certificate); public management and governance (Certificate); systems science (Certificate).

University of Phoenix–Birmingham Campus, College of Health and Human Services, Birmingham, AL 35244. Offers education (MHA); gerontology (MHA); health administration (MHA); health care management (MBA); informatics (MHA); nursing (MSN); nursing/health care education (MSN); MSN/MBA; MSN/MHA.

University of Phoenix–Central Valley Campus, College of Nursing, Fresno, CA 93720-1562. Offers education (MHA); gerontology (MHA); health administration (MHA); nursing (MSN); MSN/MBA.

University of Phoenix–Chattanooga Campus, College of Nursing, Chattanooga, TN 37421-3707. Offers education (MHA); gerontology (MHA); health administration (MHA).

University of Phoenix–Hawaii Campus, College of Nursing, Honolulu, HI 96813-4317. Offers education (MHA); family nurse practitioner (MSN); gerontology (MHA); health administration (MHA); nursing (MSN); nursing/health care education (MSN); MSN/MBA. Evening/weekend programs available. *Degree requirements:* For master's, thesis (for some programs). *Entrance requirements:* For master's, minimum undergraduate GPA of 2.5, 3 years of work experience, RN license. Additional exam requirements/recommendations for international students: Required—TOEFL (minimum score 550 paper-based; 213 computer-based; 79 iBT). Electronic applications accepted.

University of Pittsburgh, Graduate School of Public Health, Department of Behavioral and Community Health Science, Pittsburgh, PA 15260. Offers behavioral and community health sciences (MPH, Dr PH); community-based participatory research and practice (Certificate); lesbian, gay, bisexual and transgender health and wellness (Certificate); minority health and health disparities (Certificate); program evaluation (Certificate); public health preparedness (Certificate); MID/MPH; MPH/MPA; MPH/MSW; MPH/PhD. *Accreditation:* CAHME (one or more programs are accredited). Part-time programs available. *Faculty:* 15 full-time (7 women), 38 part-time/adjunct (15 women). *Students:* 80 full-time (64 women), 33 part-time (28 women); includes 28 minority (16 Black or African American, non-Hispanic/Latino; 5 Asian, non-Hispanic/Latino; 5 Hispanic/Latino; 2 Two or more races, non-Hispanic/Latino), 7 international. Average age 31. 286 applicants, 63% accepted, 25 enrolled. In 2011, 38 master's, 2 doctorates awarded. *Degree requirements:* For master's, thesis; for doctorate, comprehensive exam, thesis/dissertation, preliminary exams. *Entrance requirements:* For master's and Certificate, GRE; for doctorate, GRE, master's degree in public health or related field. Additional exam requirements/recommendations for international students: Required—TOEFL (minimum score 550 paper-based, 80 iBT) or IELTS (minimum score 6.5). *Application deadline:* For fall admission, 5/1 priority date for domestic students, 4/1 for international students; for winter admission, 9/1 for international students; for spring admission, 10/1 priority date for domestic students, 2/1 for international students. Applications are processed on a rolling basis. Application fee: $115. Electronic applications accepted. *Expenses:* Tuition, state resident: full-time $18,774; part-time $760 per credit. Tuition, nonresident: full-time $30,736; part-time $1258 per credit. *Required fees:* $740; $200 per term. Tuition and fees vary according to program. *Financial support:* In 2011–12, 21 students received support, including 10 fellowships with full and partial tuition reimbursements available (averaging $4,081 per year), 11 research assistantships with full and partial tuition reimbursements available (averaging $7,841 per year), 3 teaching assistantships with full and partial tuition reimbursements available (averaging $9,460 per year); unspecified assistantships also available. *Faculty research:* Maternal and child health, community-based participatory research, minority health and health disparities, aging. *Total annual research expenditures:* $2.6 million. *Unit head:* Dr. Ronald D. Stall, Chairman, 412-624-7933, Fax: 412-648-5975, E-mail: rstall@pitt.edu. *Application contact:* Natalie C. Arnold,

Recruitment and Academic Affairs Administrator, 412-624-3107, Fax: 412-624-5510, E-mail: narnold@pitt.edu. Web site: http://www.bchs.pitt.edu/.

University of Pittsburgh, Graduate School of Public Health, Department of Infectious Diseases and Microbiology, Pittsburgh, PA 15260. Offers bioscience of infectious diseases (MPH); community and behavioral intervention of infectious diseases (MPH); infectious diseases and microbiology (MS, PhD); LGBT health and wellness (Certificate). Part-time programs available. *Faculty:* 21 full-time (6 women), 24 part-time/adjunct (7 women). *Students:* 57 full-time (44 women), 13 part-time (9 women); includes 15 minority (4 Black or African American, non-Hispanic/Latino; 9 Asian, non-Hispanic/Latino; 2 Hispanic/Latino), 7 international. Average age 27. 157 applicants, 56% accepted, 29 enrolled. In 2011, 13 master's, 3 doctorates awarded. Terminal master's awarded for partial completion of doctoral program. *Degree requirements:* For master's, one foreign language, comprehensive exam (for some programs), thesis; for doctorate, one foreign language, comprehensive exam, thesis/dissertation. *Entrance requirements:* For master's and doctorate, GRE General Test, MCAT, or DAT. Additional exam requirements/recommendations for international students: Required—TOEFL (minimum score 550 paper-based; 80 iBT) or IELTS (minimum score 6.5). *Application deadline:* For fall admission, 1/4 priority date for domestic students, 1/4 for international students. Applications are processed on a rolling basis. Application fee: $115. Electronic applications accepted. *Expenses:* Tuition, state resident: full-time $18,774; part-time $760 per credit. Tuition, nonresident: full-time $30,736; part-time $1258 per credit. *Required fees:* $740; $200 per term. Tuition and fees vary according to program. *Financial support:* In 2011–12, 31 students received support, including 12 fellowships (averaging $7,248 per year), 19 research assistantships with full and partial tuition reimbursements available (averaging $5,448 per year). Financial award applicants required to submit FAFSA. *Faculty research:* HIV, Epstein-Barr virus, virology, immunology, malaria. *Total annual research expenditures:* $15.6 million. *Unit head:* Dr. Charles R. Rinaldo, Jr., Chairman, 412-624-3928, Fax: 412-624-4953, E-mail: rinaldo@pitt.edu. *Application contact:* Dr. Jeremy Martinson, Assistant Professor, 412-624-5646, Fax: 412-383-8926, E-mail: jmartins@pitt.edu. Web site: http://www.idm.pitt.edu/.

University of Saskatchewan, College of Medicine, Department of Community Health and Epidemiology, Saskatoon, SK S7N 5A2, Canada. Offers M Sc, PhD. *Degree requirements:* For master's, thesis; for doctorate, thesis/dissertation. *Entrance requirements:* Additional exam requirements/recommendations for international students: Required—TOEFL.

University of South Florida, Graduate School, College of Public Health, Department of Community and Family Health, Tampa, FL 33620-9951. Offers MPH, MSPH, Dr PH, PhD. *Accreditation:* CEPH (one or more programs are accredited). Part-time and evening/weekend programs available. *Degree requirements:* For master's, comprehensive exam, thesis (for some programs); for doctorate, comprehensive exam, thesis/dissertation. *Entrance requirements:* For master's, GRE General Test, minimum GPA of 3.0 in upper-level course work, goal statement letter, two professional letters of recommendation, resume/curriculum vitae; for doctorate, GRE General Test, minimum GPA of 3.0 in upper-level course work, goal statement letter, three professional letters of recommendation, resume/curriculum vitae, writing sample. Additional exam requirements/recommendations for international students: Required—TOEFL (minimum score 550 paper-based; 213 computer-based; 79 iBT). Electronic applications accepted. *Faculty research:* Family violence, high-risk infants, medical material and child health, healthy start, social marketing, adolescent health, high-risk behaviors.

The University of Tennessee, Graduate School, College of Education, Health and Human Sciences, Program in Human Ecology, Knoxville, TN 37996. Offers child and family studies (PhD); community health (PhD); nutrition science (PhD); retailing and consumer sciences (PhD); textile science (PhD). *Degree requirements:* For doctorate, thesis/dissertation. *Entrance requirements:* For doctorate, GRE General Test, minimum GPA of 2.7. Additional exam requirements/recommendations for international students: Required—TOEFL. Electronic applications accepted. *Expenses:* Tuition, state resident: full-time $8332; part-time $464 per credit hour. Tuition, nonresident: full-time $25,174; part-time $1400 per credit hour. *Required fees:* $1162; $56 per credit hour. Tuition and fees vary according to program.

The University of Tennessee, Graduate School, College of Education, Health and Human Sciences, Program in Public Health, Knoxville, TN 37996. Offers community health education (MPH); gerontology (MPH); health planning/administration (MPH); MS/MPH. *Accreditation:* CEPH. *Degree requirements:* For master's, thesis optional. *Entrance requirements:* For master's, minimum GPA of 2.7. Additional exam requirements/recommendations for international students: Required—TOEFL. Electronic applications accepted. *Expenses:* Tuition, state resident: full-time $8332; part-time $464 per credit hour. Tuition, nonresident: full-time $25,174; part-time $1400 per credit hour. *Required fees:* $1162; $56 per credit hour. Tuition and fees vary according to program.

The University of Texas Medical Branch, Graduate School of Biomedical Sciences, Program in Preventive Medicine and Community Health, Galveston, TX 77555. Offers MPH, MS, PhD. *Accreditation:* CEPH. *Degree requirements:* For master's, thesis; for doctorate, thesis/dissertation. *Entrance requirements:* For master's, GRE General Test or MAT; for doctorate, GRE General Test. Additional exam requirements/recommendations for international students: Required—TOEFL (minimum score 550 paper-based; 213 computer-based). Electronic applications accepted.

University of Virginia, School of Nursing, Charlottesville, VA 22903. Offers acute and specialty care (MSN); acute care nurse practitioner (MSN); clinical nurse leadership (MSN); community-public health leadership (MSN); nursing (DNP, PhD); psychiatric mental health counseling (MSN); MSN/MBA. *Accreditation:* AACN. Part-time programs available. *Faculty:* 44 full-time (43 women), 2 part-time/adjunct (both women). *Students:* 174 full-time (152 women), 151 part-time (139 women); includes 57 minority (28 Black or African American, non-Hispanic/Latino; 1 American Indian or Alaska Native, non-Hispanic/Latino; 14 Asian, non-Hispanic/Latino; 10 Hispanic/Latino; 4 Two or more races, non-Hispanic/Latino), 11 international. Average age 37. 236 applicants, 40% accepted, 74 enrolled. In 2011, 70 master's, 15 doctorates awarded. *Degree requirements:* For doctorate, comprehensive exam (for some programs), capstone project (DNP), dissertation (PhD). *Entrance requirements:* For master's, GRE General Test, MAT; for doctorate, GRE General Test. Additional exam requirements/recommendations for international students: Required—TOEFL, IELTS. *Application deadline:* Applications are processed on a rolling basis. Application fee: $60. Electronic applications accepted. *Expenses:* Contact institution. *Financial support:* Fellowships, research assistantships, teaching assistantships, Federal Work-Study, and scholarships/grants available. Financial award applicants required to submit FAFSA. *Unit head:* Dorrie K. Fontaine, Dean, 434-924-0141, Fax: 434-982-1809. *Application contact:* Clay Hysell, Assistant Dean for Admissions and Financial Services, 434-924-0141, Fax: 434-982-1809, E-mail: nur-osa@virginia.edu. Web site: http://www.nursing.virginia.edu/.

University of Washington, Graduate School, School of Public Health, Department of Health Services, Seattle, WA 98195. Offers bioinformatics (PhD); cancer prevention and control (PhD); clinical research (MS); community-oriented public health practice (MPH); economics or finance (PhD); evaluation sciences (PhD); health behavior and health promotion (PhD); health policy research (PhD); health services (MS, PhD); health services administration (EMHA, MHA); health systems policy (MPH); maternal and child health (MPH, PhD); occupational health (PhD); population health and social determinants (PhD); social and behavioral sciences (MPH); sociology and demography (PhD); JD/MHA; MHA/MBA; MHA/MD; MHA/MPA; MPH/JD; MPH/MD; MPH/MN; MPH/MPA; MPH/MS; MPH/MSD; MPH/MSW; MPH/PhD. Part-time and evening/weekend programs available. Postbaccalaureate distance learning degree programs offered (minimal on-campus study). *Faculty:* 40 full-time (23 women), 62 part-time/adjunct (25 women). *Students:* 98 full-time (78 women), 86 part-time (64 women); includes 49 minority (7 Black or African American, non-Hispanic/Latino; 3 American Indian or Alaska Native, non-Hispanic/Latino; 28 Asian, non-Hispanic/Latino; 11 Hispanic/Latino), 3 international. Average age 32. 374 applicants, 49% accepted, 104 enrolled. In 2011, 43 master's, 5 doctorates awarded. Terminal master's awarded for partial completion of doctoral program. *Degree requirements:* For master's, thesis (for some programs), practicum (MPH); for doctorate, comprehensive exam, thesis/dissertation. *Entrance requirements:* For master's and doctorate, GRE General Test, minimum GPA of 3.0. Additional exam requirements/recommendations for international students: Required—TOEFL (minimum score 580 paper-based; 237 computer-based; 92 iBT), IELTS (minimum score 7). *Application deadline:* For fall admission, 1/1 for domestic students, 11/1 for international students. Application fee: 75 Albanian leks. Electronic applications accepted. *Financial support:* In 2011–12, 47 students received support, including 10 fellowships with full and partial tuition reimbursements available (averaging $22,000 per year), 10 research assistantships with full and partial tuition reimbursements available (averaging $18,700 per year), 3 teaching assistantships with full and partial tuition reimbursements available (averaging $4,575 per year); institutionally sponsored loans, traineeships, and health care benefits also available. Financial award application deadline: 2/28; financial award applicants required to submit FAFSA. *Faculty research:* Public health practice, health promotion and disease prevention, maternal and child health, organizational behavior and culture, health policy. *Unit head:* Dr. Larry Kessler, Chair, 206-543-2930. *Application contact:* Kitty A. Andert, MPH/MS/PhD Programs Manager, 206-616-2926, Fax: 206-543-3964, E-mail: kitander@u.washington.edu. Web site: http://depts.washington.edu/hserv/.

University of West Florida, College of Professional Studies, Department of Health, Leisure, and Exercise Science, Community Health Education Program, Pensacola, FL 32514-5750. Offers aging studies (MS); health promotion and worksite wellness (MS); psychosocial (MS). Part-time and evening/weekend programs available. *Faculty:* 3 full-time (1 woman). *Students:* 10 full-time (9 women), 7 part-time (6 women); includes 4 minority (2 Black or African American, non-Hispanic/Latino; 1 Asian, non-Hispanic/Latino; 1 Hispanic/Latino), 1 international. Average age 28. 7 applicants, 71% accepted, 4 enrolled. In 2011, 9 master's awarded. *Degree requirements:* For master's, thesis or alternative. *Entrance requirements:* For master's, GRE or MAT, official transcripts; minimum GPA of 3.0; letter of intent; three personal references. Additional exam requirements/recommendations for international students: Required—TOEFL (minimum score 550 paper-based; 213 computer-based). *Application deadline:* For fall admission, 6/1 for domestic and international students; for spring admission, 10/1 for domestic and international students. Applications are processed on a rolling basis. Application fee: $30. *Expenses:* Tuition, state resident: full-time $5729; part-time $302 per credit hour. Tuition, nonresident: full-time $20,059; part-time $961 per credit hour. *Required fees:* $1509; $63 per credit hour. *Financial support:* Research assistantships, teaching assistantships, and unspecified assistantships available. *Unit head:* Dr. John Todorovich, Chairperson, 850-473-7248, Fax: 850-474-2106. *Application contact:* Terry McCray, Assistant Director of Graduate Admissions, 850-473-7718, Fax: 850-473-7714, E-mail: gradadmissions@uwf.edu.

University of Wisconsin–La Crosse, Office of University Graduate Studies, College of Science and Health, Department of Health Education and Health Promotion, Program in Community Health Education, La Crosse, WI 54601-3742. Offers MPH, MS. *Accreditation:* CEPH. *Faculty:* 7 full-time (4 women), 1 (woman) part-time/adjunct. *Students:* 19 full-time (15 women), 11 part-time (8 women); includes 3 minority (2 Asian, non-Hispanic/Latino; 1 Hispanic/Latino), 5 international. Average age 28. 28 applicants, 71% accepted, 9 enrolled. In 2011, 9 master's awarded. *Degree requirements:* For master's, thesis. *Entrance requirements:* For master's, GRE General Test, GRE Subject Test (MPH), 3 letters of recommendation. Additional exam requirements/recommendations for international students: Required—TOEFL (minimum score 550 paper-based; 213 computer-based; 79 iBT). Application fee: $56. Electronic applications accepted. *Expenses:* Tuition, state resident: full-time $8391; part-time $481.17 per credit. Tuition, nonresident: full-time $17,850; part-time $1006.68 per credit. *Required fees:* $2 per credit. $18.25 per semester. Tuition and fees vary according to course load, program, reciprocity agreements and student level. *Financial support:* In 2011–12, 3 research assistantships with partial tuition reimbursements (averaging $6,682 per year) were awarded; Federal Work-Study, scholarships/grants, health care benefits, and tuition waivers (partial) also available. Support available to part-time students. Financial award applicants required to submit FAFSA. *Unit head:* Dr. Gary Gilmore, Director, 608-785-8163, E-mail: gilmore.gary@uwlax.edu. *Application contact:* Kathryn Kiefer, Director of Admissions, 608-785-8939, E-mail: admissions@uwlax.edu. Web site: http://www.uwlax.edu/sah/hehp/html/grad.htm.

University of Wisconsin–Madison, School of Medicine and Public Health and Graduate School, Graduate Programs in Medicine, Madison, WI 53705. Offers biomolecular chemistry (MS, PhD); cancer biology (PhD); genetics and medical genetics (MS, PhD), including genetics (PhD), medical genetics (MS); medical physics (MS, PhD), including health physics (MS), medical physics; microbiology (PhD); molecular and cellular pharmacology (PhD); pathology and laboratory medicine (PhD); physiology (PhD); population health sciences (MPH, MS, PhD), including clinical research (MS, PhD), epidemiology (MS, PhD), health services research (MS, PhD), population health sciences (MPH), social and behavioral health sciences (MS, PhD); DPT/MPH; DVM/MPH; MD/MPH; MD/PhD; MPA/MPH; MS/MPH; Pharm D/MPH. Part-time programs available. Postbaccalaureate distance learning degree programs offered (minimal on-campus study). Terminal master's awarded for partial completion of doctoral program. Application fee: $45. Electronic applications accepted. *Expenses:* Contact institution. *Financial support:* Fellowships with full tuition reimbursements, research assistantships with full tuition reimbursements, teaching assistantships with full tuition reimbursements, scholarships/grants, traineeships, and tuition waivers (full) available. *Unit head:* Dr. Richard L. Moss, Senior Associate Dean for Basic Research, Biotechnology and Graduate Studies, 608-265-0523, Fax: 608-265-0522, E-mail: rlmoss@wisc.edu. *Application contact:* Information Contact, 608-262-2433, Fax: 608-262-5134, E-mail: gradadmiss@mail.bascom.wisc.edu. Web site: http://www.med.wisc.edu.

University of Wyoming, College of Education, Programs in Counselor Education, Laramie, WY 82070. Offers community mental health (MS); counselor education and supervision (PhD); school counseling (MS); student affairs (MS). *Accreditation:* ACA (one or more programs are accredited). *Degree requirements:* For master's, comprehensive exam (for some programs), thesis optional; for doctorate, thesis/dissertation, video demonstration. *Entrance requirements:* For master's, interview, background check; for doctorate, video tape session, interview, writing sample, master's degree, background check. Additional exam requirements/recommendations for international students: Required—TOEFL. *Faculty research:* Wyoming SAGE

photovoice project; accountable school counseling programs; GLBT issues; addictions; play therapy-early childhood mental health.

Virginia Commonwealth University, Medical College of Virginia-Professional Programs, School of Medicine, School of Medicine Graduate Programs, Department of Epidemiology and Community Health, Richmond, VA 23284-9005. Offers epidemiology (MPH, PhD); public health practice (MPH); social and behavioral science (MPH); MD/MPH; MSW/MPH. *Accreditation:* CEPH. Part-time programs available. *Degree requirements:* For doctorate, comprehensive exam, thesis/dissertation. *Entrance requirements:* For master's, GRE; for doctorate, GRE General Test, interview, 3 letters of recommendation, minimum graduate GPA of 3.0, master's degree in public health or related field including epidemiology and biostatistics. Additional exam requirements/recommendations for international students: Required—TOEFL (minimum score 600 paper-based; 250 computer-based; 100 iBT). Electronic applications accepted. *Expenses:* Tuition, state resident: full-time $9133; part-time $507 per credit. Tuition, nonresident: full-time $18,777; part-time $1043 per credit. *Required fees:* $77 per credit. Tuition and fees vary according to degree level, campus/location, program and student level. *Faculty research:* Sickle cell anemia, breast cancer, HIV/AIDS, hospital epidemiology, infectious diseases.

Virginia Polytechnic Institute and State University, Graduate School, College of Agriculture and Life Sciences, Department of Human Nutrition, Foods and Exercise, Blacksburg, VA 24061. Offers behavioral and community science (MS, PhD); clinical physiology and metabolism (MS, PhD); molecular and cellular science (MS, PhD). *Degree requirements:* For master's, comprehensive exam (for some programs), thesis (for some programs); for doctorate, comprehensive exam (for some programs), thesis/dissertation (for some programs). *Entrance requirements:* For master's and doctorate, GRE. Additional exam requirements/recommendations for international students: Required—TOEFL (minimum score 550 paper-based; 213 computer-based). *Application deadline:* For fall admission, 7/1 for domestic and international students; for spring admission, 12/1 for domestic and international students. Applications are processed on a rolling basis. Application fee: $65. Electronic applications accepted. *Expenses:* Tuition, state resident: full-time $10,048; part-time $558.25 per credit hour. Tuition, nonresident: full-time $19,497; part-time $1083.25 per credit hour. *Required fees:* $405 per semester. Tuition and fees vary according to course load, campus/location and program. *Financial support:* Fellowships with full tuition reimbursements, research assistantships with full tuition reimbursements, teaching assistantships with full tuition reimbursements, career-related internships or fieldwork, Federal Work-Study, scholarships/grants, health care benefits, and unspecified assistantships available. Financial award application deadline: 1/15. *Faculty research:* Nutrition and food science research. *Unit head:* Dr. Susan M. Hutson, Unit Head, 540-231-8766, Fax: 540-231-3916, E-mail: susanh5@vt.edu. *Application contact:* Robert Grange, Information Contact, 540-231-2725, Fax: 540-231-3916, E-mail: rgrange@vt.edu. Web site: http://www.hnfe.vt.edu/.

Virginia State University, School of Graduate Studies, Research, and Outreach, School of Engineering, Science and Technology, Department of Psychology, Petersburg, VA 23806-0001. Offers behavioral and community health sciences (PhD); clinical health psychology (PhD); clinical psychology (MS); general psychology (MS). *Degree requirements:* For master's, one foreign language, thesis. *Entrance requirements:* For master's, GRE General Test.

Walden University, Graduate Programs, School of Health Sciences, Minneapolis, MN 55401. Offers clinical research administration (MS, Postbaccalaureate Certificate); health informatics (MS); health services (PhD), including community health education and advocacy, general program, healthcare administration, leadership, public health policy, self-designed; healthcare administration (MHA); public health (MPH, PhD), including community health and education (PhD), epidemiology (PhD). Part-time and evening/weekend programs available. Postbaccalaureate distance learning degree programs offered (minimal on-campus study). *Faculty:* 20 full-time (13 women), 175 part-time/adjunct (81 women). *Students:* 2,777 full-time (2,158 women), 1,350 part-time (1,038 women); includes 2,379 minority (1,935 Black or African American, non-Hispanic/Latino; 33 American Indian or Alaska Native, non-Hispanic/Latino; 173 Asian, non-Hispanic/Latino; 180 Hispanic/Latino; 9 Native Hawaiian or other Pacific Islander, non-Hispanic/Latino; 49 Two or more races, non-Hispanic/Latino), 247 international. Average age 40. In 2011, 528 master's, 79 doctorates, 1 other advanced degree awarded. *Degree requirements:* For doctorate, thesis/dissertation, residency. *Entrance requirements:* For master's, bachelor's degree or equivalent in related field, minimum GPA of 2.5; for doctorate, master's degree or equivalent in related field; minimum GPA of 3.0; official transcripts; three years of related professional/academic experience (preferred); access to computer and Internet. Additional exam requirements/recommendations for international students: Required—TOEFL (minimum score 550 paper-based; 213 computer-based), IELTS (minimum score 6.5), or Michigan English Language Assessment Battery (minimum score 82). *Application deadline:* Applications are processed on a rolling basis. Application fee: $50. Electronic applications accepted. *Financial support:* Federal Work-Study, scholarships/grants, unspecified assistantships, and family tuition reduction, active duty/veteran tuition reduction, group tuition reduction, interest-free payment plans, employee tuition reduction available. Support available to part-time students. Financial award applicants required to submit FAFSA. *Unit head:* Dr. Jorg Westermann, Associate Dean, 800-925-3368. *Application contact:* Jennifer Hall, Vice President of Enrollment Management, 866-4-WALDEN, E-mail: info@waldenu.edu. Web site: http://www.waldenu.edu/Colleges-and-Schools/College-of-Health-Sciences/School-of-Health-Sciences.htm.

West Virginia University, School of Medicine, Department of Community Medicine, Program in Public Health, Morgantown, WV 26506. Offers community health/preventative medicine (MPH). *Accreditation:* CEPH. Part-time programs available. Postbaccalaureate distance learning degree programs offered (minimal on-campus study). *Degree requirements:* For master's, practicum, project. *Entrance requirements:* For master's, GRE General Test, MCAT, medical degree, medical internship. *Expenses:* Contact institution. *Faculty research:* Occupational health, environmental health, clinical epidemiology, health care management, prevention.

Environmental and Occupational Health

American Public University System, AMU/APU Graduate Programs, Charles Town, WV 25414. Offers accounting (MBA, MS); administration and supervision (M Ed); criminal justice (MA); emergency and disaster management (MA); entrepreneurship (MBA); environmental policy and management (MS), including environmental planning, environmental sustainability, fish and wildlife management, general (MA, MS), global environmental management; finance (MBA); general (MBA); global business management (MBA); guidance and counseling (M Ed); history (MA), including American history, ancient and classical history, European history, global history, military and diplomatic history, public history; homeland security (MA); homeland security resource allocation (MBA); humanities (MA); information technology (MS), including digital forensics, enterprise software development, information assurance and security, IT project management; information technology management (MBA); intelligence studies (MA), including criminal intelligence, general (MA, MS), homeland security, intelligence analysis, intelligence collection, intelligence operations, terrorism studies; international relations and conflict resolution (MA), including comparative and security issues, conflict resolution, international and transnational security issues, peacekeeping; legal studies (MA); management (MA), including defense management, general (MA, MS), human resource management, organizational leadership, public administration, reverse logistics, strategic consulting; marketing (MBA); military history (MA), including American military history, American revolution, civil war, war since 1946, World War II; military studies (MA), including air warfare, asymmetrical warfare, joint warfare, land warfare, naval warfare, strategic leadership; national security studies (MA), including general (MA, MS), homeland security, regional security studies, security and intelligence analysis, terrorism studies; nonprofit management (MBA); political science (MA), including American politics and government, comparative government and development, public policy; psychology (MA); public administration (MA, MPA), including disaster management (MPA), environmental policy (MA), health policy (MPA), human resources (MPA), national security (MPA), organizational management (MPA), security management (MPA); public health (MA, MPH), including emergency management (MPH), environmental health (MPH), public administration (MA); reverse logistics management (MA); security management (MA); space studies (MS), including aerospace science, planetary science; sports and health sciences (MS); sports management (MS), including coaching theory and strategy, sports administration; teaching (M Ed), including curriculum and instruction for elementary teachers, elementary, elementary reading, English language learners, instructional leadership, online learning, secondary social sciences, special education; transportation and logistics management (MA), including maritime engineering management. Programs offered via distance learning only. Part-time and evening/weekend programs available. Postbaccalaureate distance learning degree programs offered (no on-campus study). *Faculty:* 445 full-time (241 women), 1,360 part-time/adjunct (617 women). *Students:* 688 full-time (338 women), 10,168 part-time (3,706 women); includes 3,130 minority (1,007 Black or African American, non-Hispanic/Latino; 103 American Indian or Alaska Native, non-Hispanic/Latino; 825 Asian, non-Hispanic/Latino; 810 Hispanic/Latino; 51 Native Hawaiian or other Pacific Islander, non-Hispanic/Latino; 334 Two or more races, non-Hispanic/Latino), 134 international. Average age 35. In 2011, 2,386 master's awarded. *Degree requirements:* For master's, comprehensive exam or practicum. *Entrance requirements:* For master's, official transcript showing earned bachelor's degree from institution accredited by recognized accrediting body. Additional exam requirements/recommendations for international students: Required—TOEFL (minimum score 550 paper-based; 213 computer-based), IELTS (minimum score 6.5). *Application deadline:* Applications are processed on a rolling basis. Application fee: $0. Electronic applications accepted. *Expenses: Tuition:* Part-time $325 per credit hour. *Financial support:* Applicants required to submit FAFSA. *Faculty research:* Military history, criminal justice, management performance, national security. *Unit head:* Dr. Karan Powell, Executive Vice President and Provost, 877-468-6268, Fax: 304-724-3780. *Application contact:* Terry Grant, Vice President of Enrollment Management, 877-468-6268, Fax: 304-724-3780, E-mail: info@apus.edu. Web site: http://www.apus.edu.

American University of Beirut, Graduate Programs, Faculty of Health Sciences, Beirut, Lebanon. Offers environmental sciences (MSES), including environmental health; epidemiology (MS); epidemiology and biostatistics (MPH); health management and policy (MPH); health promotion and community health (MPH); population health (MS). Part-time programs available. *Faculty:* 29 full-time (19 women), 5 part-time/adjunct (2 women). *Students:* 63 full-time (52 women), 103 part-time (87 women). Average age 27. 156 applicants, 71% accepted, 56 enrolled. In 2011, 69 master's awarded. *Degree requirements:* For master's, one foreign language, comprehensive exam, thesis (for some programs). *Entrance requirements:* For master's, 2 letters of recommendation, personal statement, transcripts. Additional exam requirements/recommendations for international students: Required—TOEFL (minimum score 600 paper-based; 250 computer-based; 97 iBT), IELTS (minimum score 7). *Application deadline:* For fall admission, 2/20 for domestic and international students; for spring admission, 11/1 for domestic and international students. Application fee: $50. Electronic applications accepted. *Expenses: Tuition:* Full-time $12,780; part-time $710 per credit. Tuition and fees vary according to course load and program. *Financial support:* In 2011–12, 62 students received support. Scholarships/grants, health care benefits, and unspecified assistantships available. Financial award application deadline: 2/20. *Faculty research:* Tobacco control; health of the elderly; youth health; mental health; women's health; reproductive and sexual health, including HIV/AIDS; water quality; health systems; quality in health care delivery; health human resources; health policy; occupational and environmental health; social inequality; social determinants of health; chronic diseases. *Total annual research expenditures:* $722,649. *Unit head:* Iman Adel Nuwayhid, Dean, 961-1340119, Fax: 961-1744470, E-mail: nuwayhid@aub.edu.lb. *Application contact:* Mitra Tauk, Administrative Coordinator, 961-1350000 Ext. 4687, Fax: 961-1744470, E-mail: mt12@aub.edu.lb. Web site: http://fhs.aub.edu.lb.

Anna Maria College, Graduate Division, Program in Occupational and Environmental Health and Safety, Paxton, MA 01612. Offers MS. Part-time and evening/weekend programs available. *Degree requirements:* For master's, thesis. *Entrance requirements:* For master's, minimum GPA of 2.7. Additional exam requirements/recommendations for international students: Required—TOEFL (minimum score 500 paper-based). Electronic applications accepted.

Boston University, School of Public Health, Environmental Health Department, Boston, MA 02118. Offers MPH, MS, PhD. *Accreditation:* CEPH (one or more programs are accredited). Part-time and evening/weekend programs available. *Faculty:* 14 full-time, 20 part-time/adjunct. *Students:* 26 full-time (22 women), 17 part-time (13 women); includes 5 minority (1 Black or African American, non-Hispanic/Latino; 4 Asian, non-Hispanic/Latino), 2 international. Average age 27. 138 applicants, 45% accepted, 18 enrolled. In 2011, 23 master's, 4 doctorates awarded. *Degree requirements:* For master's, comprehensive exam (for some programs), thesis (for some programs); for doctorate, one foreign language, thesis/dissertation, comprehensive written and oral exams. *Entrance requirements:* For master's, GRE, LSAT, GMAT, DAT, or MCAT. U.S.

bachelor's degree or foreign equivalent; for doctorate, GRE, MCAT, MPH or equivalent. Additional exam requirements/recommendations for international students: Required—TOEFL (minimum score 600 paper-based; 250 computer-based; 100 iBT) or IELTS (minimum score 6). *Application deadline:* For fall admission, 2/1 priority date for domestic students, 2/1 for international students; for spring admission, 10/15 priority date for domestic students, 10/15 for international students. Applications are processed on a rolling basis. Application fee: $115. Electronic applications accepted. *Expenses: Tuition:* Full-time $40,848; part-time $1276 per credit hour. *Required fees:* $572; $286 per semester. *Financial support:* Career-related internships or fieldwork, Federal Work-Study, institutionally sponsored loans, and scholarships/grants available. Support available to part-time students. Financial award application deadline: 3/1; financial award applicants required to submit FAFSA. *Unit head:* Dr. Roberta White, Chair, 617-638-4620, E-mail: envhlth@bu.edu. *Application contact:* LePhan Quan, Associate Director of Admissions, 617-638-4640, Fax: 617-638-5299, E-mail: asksph@bu.edu.

California State University, Northridge, Graduate Studies, College of Health and Human Development, Department of Environmental and Occupational Health, Northridge, CA 91330. Offers environmental and occupational health (MS); industrial hygiene (MS). *Degree requirements:* For master's, seminar, field experience, comprehensive exam or thesis. *Entrance requirements:* For master's, GRE General Test or minimum GPA of 3.0. Additional exam requirements/recommendations for international students: Required—TOEFL.

Capella University, School of Public Service Leadership, Minneapolis, MN 55402. Offers criminal justice (MS, PhD); emergency management (MS, PhD); general human services (MS, PhD); general public administration (MPA, DPA); gerontology (MS); health care administration (MS, PhD); health management and policy (MSPH); management of nonprofit agencies (MS, PhD); nurse educator (MS); public safety leadership (MS, PhD); social and community services (MS, PhD); social behavioral sciences (MSPH).

Clemson University, Graduate School, College of Engineering and Science, Department of Environmental Engineering and Earth Sciences, Program in Environmental Health Physics, Clemson, SC 29634. Offers MS. *Unit head:* Dr. Tanju Karanfil, Chair, 864-653-1005, Fax: 864-656-5973, E-mail: tkaranf@clemson.edu. *Application contact:* Jan Young, Graduate Student Services Coordinator, 864-656-3278, Fax: 864-656-5973, E-mail: ej@clemson.edu. Web site: http://www.clemson.edu/ces/eees/gradprog/ehp/.

Colorado State University, College of Veterinary Medicine and Biomedical Sciences, Department of Environmental and Radiological Health Sciences, Fort Collins, CO 80523-1681. Offers environmental health (MS, PhD); radiological health sciences (MS, PhD). Part-time programs available. *Faculty:* 26 full-time (7 women), 3 part-time/adjunct (0 women). *Students:* 105 full-time (66 women), 28 part-time (14 women); includes 20 minority (5 Black or African American, non-Hispanic/Latino; 1 American Indian or Alaska Native, non-Hispanic/Latino; 10 Hispanic/Latino; 4 Two or more races, non-Hispanic/Latino), 7 international. Average age 28. 92 applicants, 82% accepted, 56 enrolled. In 2011, 39 master's, 23 doctorates awarded. Terminal master's awarded for partial completion of doctoral program. *Degree requirements:* For master's, comprehensive exam (for some programs), thesis (for some programs), publishable paper; for doctorate, comprehensive exam, thesis/dissertation, publishable paper. *Entrance requirements:* For master's, GRE General Test, 1 year of course work in biology lab and chemistry lab, 1 semester of course work in organic chemistry, course work in calculus, resume, letters of recommendation; for doctorate, GRE General Test, 1 year of course work in biology lab and chemistry lab, 1 semester of course work in organic chemistry, course work in calculus, resume, letters of recommendation, evidence of research capability. Additional exam requirements/recommendations for international students: Required—TOEFL (minimum score 550 paper-based; 213 computer-based). *Application deadline:* For fall admission, 6/1 for domestic and international students; for spring admission, 11/1 for domestic and international students. Applications are processed on a rolling basis. Application fee: $50. Electronic applications accepted. *Expenses:* Tuition, state resident: full-time $7992. Tuition, nonresident: full-time $19,592. *Required fees:* $1735; $58 per credit. *Financial support:* In 2011–12, 20 students received support, including 5 fellowships with full and partial tuition reimbursements available (averaging $45,693 per year), 13 research assistantships with full and partial tuition reimbursements available (averaging $18,772 per year), 2 teaching assistantships with full and partial tuition reimbursements available (averaging $12,330 per year); career-related internships or fieldwork, Federal Work-Study, institutionally sponsored loans, traineeships, and unspecified assistantships also available. Support available to part-time students. Financial award application deadline: 2/1; financial award applicants required to submit FAFSA. *Faculty research:* Epidemiology, toxicology, industrial hygiene, occupational health, radiation therapy. *Total annual research expenditures:* $7.8 million. *Unit head:* Dr. Jac A. Nickoloff, Head, 970-491-6674, Fax: 970-491-0623, E-mail: j.nickoloff@colostate.edu. *Application contact:* Jeanne A. Brockway, Graduate Program Coordinator, 970-491-5003, Fax: 970-491-0623, E-mail: jeanne.brockway@colostate.edu. Web site: http://www.cvmbs.colostate.edu/erhs/.

Columbia Southern University, College of Safety and Emergency Services, Orange Beach, AL 36561. Offers criminal justice (MS); environmental management (MS); occupational safety and health (MS); occupational safety and health/environmental management (MS). Part-time and evening/weekend programs available. Postbaccalaureate distance learning degree programs offered (no on-campus study). *Entrance requirements:* For master's, bachelor's degree from accredited/approved institution. Additional exam requirements/recommendations for international students: Required—TOEFL. Electronic applications accepted.

Columbia University, Columbia University Mailman School of Public Health, Department of Environmental Health Sciences, New York, NY 10032. Offers MPH, Dr PH, PhD. PhD offered in cooperation with the Graduate School of Arts and Sciences. *Accreditation:* CEPH (one or more programs are accredited). Part-time programs available. *Students:* 42 full-time (36 women), 35 part-time (29 women); includes 22 minority (2 Black or African American, non-Hispanic/Latino; 16 Asian, non-Hispanic/Latino; 3 Hispanic/Latino; 1 Two or more races, non-Hispanic/Latino), 11 international. Average age 29. 126 applicants, 47% accepted, 26 enrolled. In 2011, 24 master's, 4 doctorates awarded. *Degree requirements:* For master's, thesis optional; for doctorate, thesis/dissertation. *Entrance requirements:* For master's, GRE General Test, 1 year of course work in biology, general chemistry, organic chemistry, and mathematics; for doctorate, GRE General Test, MPH or equivalent (Dr PH). Additional exam requirements/recommendations for international students: Required—TOEFL (minimum score 600 paper-based; 250 computer-based; 100 iBT). *Application deadline:* For fall admission, 1/5 for domestic students. Applications are processed on a rolling basis. Application fee: $60. Electronic applications accepted. *Financial support:* Research assistantships, teaching assistantships, career-related internships or fieldwork, and Federal Work-Study available. Support available to part-time students. Financial award application deadline: 2/1; financial award applicants required to submit FAFSA. *Faculty research:* Health effects of environmental and occupational exposure to chemicals and radiation, molecular epidemiology, risk assessment, molecular toxicology, and environmental policy. *Unit head:* Dr. Tomas Guilarte, Chair, 212-305-3466, Fax: 212-305-4012. *Application contact:* Dr. Joseph Korevec, Director of Admissions and Financial Aid, 212-305-8698, Fax: 212-342-1861, E-mail: ph-admit@columbia.edu. Web site: http://mailman.hs.columbia.edu/ehs/index.html.

Duke University, Graduate School, Integrated Toxicology and Environmental Health Program, Durham, NC 27708. Offers PhD, Certificate. *Faculty:* 36 full-time. *Students:* 4 full-time (0 women). 21 applicants, 14% accepted, 2 enrolled. *Entrance requirements:* For doctorate, GRE General Test. Additional exam requirements/recommendations for international students: Required—TOEFL (minimum score 550 paper-based; 213 computer-based; 83 iBT), IELTS (minimum score 7). *Application deadline:* For fall admission, 12/8 priority date for domestic students, 12/8 for international students. Application fee: $75. Electronic applications accepted. *Expenses: Tuition:* Full-time $40,720. *Required fees:* $3107. *Financial support:* Fellowships available. Financial award application deadline: 12/8. *Unit head:* Cynthia Kuhn, Director, 919-613-8078, Fax: 919-668-1799. *Application contact:* Elizabeth Hutton, Director of Admissions, 919-684-3913, Fax: 919-684-2277, E-mail: grad-admissions@duke.edu. Web site: http://toxicology.geneimprint.com/graduate/.

Duke University, Nicholas School of the Environment, Durham, NC 27708-0328. Offers coastal environmental management (MEM); DEL-environmental leadership (MEM); energy and environment (MEM); environmental economics and policy (MEM); environmental health and security (MEM); forest resource management (MF); global environmental change (MEM); resource ecology (MEM); water and air resources (MEM); JD/AM; JD/MEM; JD/MF; MAT/MEM; MBA/MEM; MBA/MF; MEM/MPP; MF/MPP. *Accreditation:* SAF (one or more programs are accredited). Part-time programs available. *Degree requirements:* For master's, thesis. *Entrance requirements:* For master's, GRE General Test, previous course work in biology or ecology, calculus, statistics, and microeconomics; computer familiarity with word processing and data analysis. Additional exam requirements/recommendations for international students: Required—TOEFL (minimum score 550 paper-based; 213 computer-based). Electronic applications accepted. *Expenses:* Contact institution. *Faculty research:* Ecosystem management, conservation ecology, earth systems, risk assessment.

East Carolina University, Graduate School, College of Health and Human Performance, Department of Health Education and Promotion, Greenville, NC 27858-4353. Offers athletic training (MS); environmental health (MS); health education (MA, MA Ed). *Accreditation:* NCATE. *Degree requirements:* For master's, comprehensive exam, thesis optional. *Entrance requirements:* For master's, GRE General Test or MAT. Additional exam requirements/recommendations for international students: Required—TOEFL. *Application deadline:* For fall admission, 6/1 priority date for domestic students. Applications are processed on a rolling basis. Application fee: $50. *Expenses:* Tuition, state resident: full-time $3557; part-time $444.63 per semester hour. Tuition, nonresident: full-time $14,351; part-time $1793.88 per semester hour. *Required fees:* $2016; $252 per semester hour. Part-time tuition and fees vary according to course load, campus/location and program. *Financial support:* Fellowships, research assistantships, teaching assistantships, and career-related internships or fieldwork available. Support available to part-time students. Financial award application deadline: 6/1. *Faculty research:* Community health education, worksite health promotion, school health education, environmental health. *Unit head:* Dr. Tim Kelley, Chair, 252-737-2225, E-mail: kelleyt@ecu.edu. Web site: http://www.ecu.edu/hlth/.

East Carolina University, Graduate School, Thomas Harriot College of Arts and Sciences, Department of Psychology, Program in Health Psychology, Greenville, NC 27858-4353. Offers clinical health psychology (PhD); occupational health psychology (PhD); pediatric school psychology (PhD). *Entrance requirements:* For doctorate, GRE. *Expenses:* Tuition, state resident: full-time $3557; part-time $444.63 per semester hour. Tuition, nonresident: full-time $14,351; part-time $1793.88 per semester hour. *Required fees:* $2016; $252 per semester hour. Part-time tuition and fees vary according to course load, campus/location and program. *Financial support:* Fellowships, research assistantships, and teaching assistantships available. *Unit head:* Dr. Kathleen Row, Chair, 252-328-6492, Fax: 252-328-6283, E-mail: rowk@ecu.edu. Web site: http://www.ecu.edu/psyc/Health-Psychology-Doctoral-Program.cfm.

Eastern Kentucky University, The Graduate School, College of Health Sciences, Department of Clinical Laboratory Science/Environmental Health Science, Richmond, KY 40475-3102. Offers environmental health science (MPH). *Accreditation:* CEPH. *Degree requirements:* For master's, comprehensive exam, thesis optional, practicum, capstone course. *Entrance requirements:* For master's, GRE. *Faculty research:* Water quality, food safety, occupational health, air quality.

East Tennessee State University, School of Graduate Studies, College of Public Health, Department of Environmental Health, Johnson City, TN 37614. Offers administrative (MSEH); environmental health (PhD). Part-time programs available. *Faculty:* 4 full-time (1 woman). *Students:* 7 full-time (4 women), 1 part-time (0 women), 2 international. Average age 31. 8 applicants, 25% accepted, 2 enrolled. In 2011, 1 master's awarded. *Degree requirements:* For master's, comprehensive exam, thesis optional, research project (for non-thesis option), environmental health practice, seminar; for doctorate, comprehensive exam, thesis/dissertation, environmental health practice, seminar. *Entrance requirements:* For master's, GRE General Test, 30 hours of course work in natural and physical sciences, minimum GPA of 3.0, three letters of recommendation; for doctorate, GRE General Test, MPH or MS in related field of study with research-based thesis, three letters of recommendation, curriculum vitae or resume. Additional exam requirements/recommendations for international students: Required—TOEFL (minimum score 550 paper-based; 213 computer-based; 79 iBT). *Application deadline:* For fall admission, 6/1 for domestic students, 4/30 for international students; for spring admission, 11/1 for domestic students, 9/30 for international students. Application fee: $35 ($45 for international students). Electronic applications accepted. *Expenses:* Tuition, state resident: full-time $7312; part-time $350 per credit hour. Tuition, nonresident: full-time $18,490; part-time $621 per credit hour. *Required fees:* $63 per credit hour. Tuition and fees vary according to course load and program. *Financial support:* In 2011–12, 7 students received support, including 6 research assistantships with full tuition reimbursements available (averaging $6,000 per year), 1 teaching assistantship with full tuition reimbursement available (averaging $14,000 per year); career-related internships or fieldwork, institutionally sponsored loans, scholarships/grants, and unspecified assistantships also available. Financial award application deadline: 7/1; financial award applicants required to submit FAFSA. *Faculty research:* Water quality, ecotoxicology, occupational health, indoor air quality and community focused environmental health. *Unit head:* Dr. Phillip R. Scheuerman, Chair, 423-439-7633, Fax: 423-439-5238, E-mail: philsche@etsu.edu. *Application contact:* Mary Duncan, Graduate Specialist, 423-439-4302, Fax: 423-439-5624, E-mail: duncanm@etsu.edu.

East Tennessee State University, School of Graduate Studies, College of Public Health, Master of Public Health Programs, Johnson City, TN 37614. Offers biostatistics (MPH); community health (MPH); environmental health (MPH); epidemiology (MPH); public health administration (MPH). Part-time programs available. Postbaccalaureate distance learning degree programs offered (no on-campus study). *Students:* 45 full-time (27 women), 31 part-time (21 women); includes 14 minority (8 Black or African American, non-Hispanic/Latino; 3 Asian, non-Hispanic/Latino; 2 Hispanic/Latino; 1 Two or more races, non-Hispanic/Latino), 11 international. 92 applicants, 45% accepted, 40 enrolled. In 2011, 24 master's awarded. *Degree requirements:* For master's,

comprehensive exam, field experience. *Entrance requirements:* For master's, GRE General Test, SOPHAS application, minimum GPA of 2.75, letters of recommendation. Additional exam requirements/recommendations for international students: Required—TOEFL (minimum score 550 paper-based; 213 computer-based; 79 iBT). *Application deadline:* For fall admission, 3/1 for domestic and international students. Application fee: $35 ($45 for international students). Electronic applications accepted. *Expenses:* Tuition, state resident: full-time $7312; part-time $350 per credit hour. Tuition, nonresident: full-time $18,490; part-time $621 per credit hour. *Required fees:* $63 per credit hour. Tuition and fees vary according to course load and program. *Financial support:* In 2011–12, 31 students received support, including 14 research assistantships with full tuition reimbursements available (averaging $6,000 per year), 2 teaching assistantships with full tuition reimbursements available (averaging $6,000 per year); career-related internships or fieldwork, institutionally sponsored loans, scholarships/grants, and unspecified assistantships also available. Financial award application deadline: 7/1; financial award applicants required to submit FAFSA. *Faculty research:* Rural health issues, youth and adolescent health, health of the elderly, environmental epidemiology, spatial analysis of data. *Unit head:* Dr. Brian Martin, Graduate Program Coordinator, 423-439-4429, Fax: 423-439-6491, E-mail: martinb@etsu.edu. *Application contact:* Mary Duncan, Graduate Specialist, 423-439-4302, Fax: 423-439-5624, E-mail: duncanm@etsu.edu. Web site: http://www.etsu.edu/cph/academics/graduate/MPHHome.aspx.

Emory University, Rollins School of Public Health, Department of Environmental Health, Atlanta, GA 30322-1100. Offers environmental health (MPH); environmental health and epidemiology (MSPH); environmental health sciences (PhD); global environmental health (MPH). *Accreditation:* CEPH. Part-time programs available. *Students:* 23 full-time. Average age 27. 7 applicants, 100% accepted, 4 enrolled. *Degree requirements:* For master's, thesis, practicum. *Entrance requirements:* For master's, GRE General Test. Additional exam requirements/recommendations for international students: Required—TOEFL. *Application deadline:* For fall admission, 1/3 priority date for domestic students, 1/3 for international students. Application fee: $95. Electronic applications accepted. *Expenses: Tuition:* Full-time $34,800. *Required fees:* $1300. *Financial support:* Fellowships with full and partial tuition reimbursements, career-related internships or fieldwork, Federal Work-Study, institutionally sponsored loans, scholarships/grants, traineeships, health care benefits, and unspecified assistantships available. Support available to part-time students. Financial award application deadline: 1/5; financial award applicants required to submit FAFSA. *Unit head:* Dr. Paige Tolbert, Chair, 404-727-0196, Fax: 404-727-8744, E-mail: ptolber@sph.emory.edu. *Application contact:* Ariadne Switchenberg, Graduate Program Administrator, 404-727-7905, Fax: 404-727-8744, E-mail: ascarl@emory.edu.

Florida International University, Robert Stempel College of Public Health and Social Work, Programs in Public Health, Miami, FL 33199. Offers biostatistics (MPH); environmental and occupational health (MPH, PhD); epidemiology (MPH, PhD); health policy and management (MPH); health promotion and disease prevention (PhD); health promotion and diseases prevention (MPH). Ph D is fall admission only; MPH offered jointly with University of Miami. *Accreditation:* CEPH. Part-time and evening/weekend programs available. Postbaccalaureate distance learning degree programs offered (no on-campus study). *Degree requirements:* For master's, thesis optional; for doctorate, comprehensive exam, thesis/dissertation. *Entrance requirements:* For master's, minimum GPA of 3.0, letters of recommendation; for doctorate, GRE, resume, minimum GPA of 3.0, letters of recommendation, letter of intent. Additional exam requirements/recommendations for international students: Required—TOEFL (minimum score 550 paper-based; 80 iBT). Electronic applications accepted. *Expenses:* Contact institution. *Faculty research:* Drugs/AIDS intervention among migrant workers, provision of services for active/recovering drug users with HIV.

Fort Valley State University, College of Graduate Studies and Extended Education, Program in Public Health, Fort Valley, GA 31030. Offers environmental health (MPH). *Degree requirements:* For master's, thesis. *Entrance requirements:* For master's, GRE General Test. Additional exam requirements/recommendations for international students: Recommended—TOEFL.

Gannon University, School of Graduate Studies, College of Engineering and Business, School of Engineering and Computer Science, Program in Environmental and Occupational Science and Health, Erie, PA 16541-0001. Offers Certificate. Part-time and evening/weekend programs available. *Entrance requirements:* Additional exam requirements/recommendations for international students: Required—TOEFL (minimum score 79 iBT). *Application deadline:* Applications are processed on a rolling basis. Application fee: $25. Electronic applications accepted. *Financial support:* Scholarships/grants available. Financial award application deadline: 7/1; financial award applicants required to submit FAFSA. *Unit head:* Dr. Harry Diz, Chair, 814-871-7633, E-mail: diz001@gannon.edu. *Application contact:* Kara Morgan, Director of Graduate Admissions, 814-871-5831, Fax: 814-871-5827, E-mail: graduate@gannon.edu.

The George Washington University, School of Public Health and Health Services, Department of Environmental and Occupational Health, Washington, DC 20052. Offers environmental health science and policy (MPH); public health (MPH). *Accreditation:* CEPH. *Faculty:* 5 full-time (2 women), 31 part-time/adjunct (19 women). *Students:* 1 (woman) full-time, 12 part-time (10 women); includes 2 minority (1 Asian, non-Hispanic/Latino; 1 Hispanic/Latino). Average age 37. In 2011, 8 master's awarded. *Degree requirements:* For master's, case study or special project. *Entrance requirements:* For master's, GMAT, GRE General Test, or MCAT. Additional exam requirements/recommendations for international students: Required—TOEFL. *Application deadline:* For fall admission, 4/15 priority date for domestic students, 4/15 for international students; for spring admission, 11/1 for domestic and international students. Applications are processed on a rolling basis. Application fee: $75. *Financial support:* In 2011–12, 7 students received support. Tuition waivers available. Financial award application deadline: 2/15. *Unit head:* Dr. David Michaels, Director, 202-994-2461, E-mail: eohdmm@gwumc.edu. *Application contact:* Jane Smith, Director of Admissions, 202-994-0248, Fax: 202-994-1860, E-mail: sphhsinfo@gwumc.edu.

Georgia Southern University, Jack N. Averitt College of Graduate Studies, Jiann-Ping Hsu College of Public Health, Program in Public Health, Statesboro, GA 30460. Offers biostatistics (MPH, Dr PH); community health behavior and education (Dr PH); community health education (MPH); environmental health sciences (MPH); epidemiology (MPH); health services policy management (MPH); public health leadership (Dr PH). *Accreditation:* CEPH. Part-time programs available. *Students:* 87 full-time (60 women), 39 part-time (25 women); includes 68 minority (58 Black or African American, non-Hispanic/Latino; 6 Asian, non-Hispanic/Latino; 4 Hispanic/Latino), 20 international. Average age 30. 73 applicants, 84% accepted, 42 enrolled. In 2011, 22 master's, 4 doctorates awarded. *Degree requirements:* For master's, thesis optional, practicum; for doctorate, comprehensive exam, thesis/dissertation, practicum. *Entrance requirements:* For master's, GRE General Test, minimum GPA of 2.75, resume, 3 letters of reference; for doctorate, GRE, GMAT, MCAT, LSAT, 3 letters of reference, statement of purpose, resume or curriculum vitae. Additional exam requirements/recommendations for international students: Required—TOEFL (minimum score 550 paper-based; 213 computer-based; 80 iBT). *Application deadline:* For fall admission, 3/1 priority date for domestic students, 3/1 for international students; for spring admission,

10/1 priority date for domestic students, 10/1 for international students. Applications are processed on a rolling basis. Application fee: $50. Electronic applications accepted. *Expenses:* Contact institution. *Financial support:* In 2011–12, 59 students received support, including research assistantships with partial tuition reimbursements available (averaging $7,200 per year), teaching assistantships with partial tuition reimbursements available (averaging $7,200 per year); career-related internships or fieldwork, Federal Work-Study, scholarships/grants, tuition waivers (partial), and unspecified assistantships also available. Support available to part-time students. Financial award application deadline: 4/15; financial award applicants required to submit FAFSA. *Faculty research:* Rural public health best practices, health disparity elimination, community initiatives to enhance public health, cost effectiveness analysis, epidemiology of rural public health, environmental health issues, health care system assessment, rural health care, health policy and healthcare financing. *Unit head:* Dr. Charles Hardy, Dean, 912-478-2674, Fax: 912-478-5811, E-mail: chardy@georgiasouthern.edu. *Application contact:* Amanda Gilliland, Coordinator for Graduate Student Recruitment, 912-478-5384, Fax: 912-478-0740, E-mail: gradadmissions@georgiasouthern.edu. Web site: http://chhs.georgiasouthern.edu/health/.

Harvard University, Cyprus International Institute for the Environment and Public Health in Association with Harvard School of Public Health, Cambridge, MA 02138. Offers environmental health (MS); environmental/public health (PhD); epidemiology and biostatistics (MS). *Entrance requirements:* For master's and doctorate, GRE, resume/curriculum vitae, 3 letters of recommendation, BA or BS (including diploma and official transcripts). Additional exam requirements/recommendations for international students: Required—TOEFL (minimum score 220 computer-based), IELTS (minimum score 7). Electronic applications accepted. *Expenses: Tuition:* Full-time $36,304. *Required fees:* $1186. Full-time tuition and fees vary according to program. *Faculty research:* Air pollution, climate change, biostatistics, sustainable development, environmental management.

Harvard University, Harvard School of Public Health, Department of Environmental Health, Boston, MA 02115-6096. Offers environmental health (MOH, SM, DPH, PhD, SD); occupational health (MOH, SM, DPH, SD); physiology (PhD, SD). Part-time programs available. *Faculty:* 43 full-time (8 women), 23 part-time/adjunct (7 women). *Students:* 74 full-time, 3 part-time; includes 14 minority (4 Black or African American, non-Hispanic/Latino; 8 Asian, non-Hispanic/Latino; 2 Hispanic/Latino), 38 international. Average age 29. 88 applicants, 39% accepted, 26 enrolled. In 2011, 15 master's, 12 doctorates awarded. *Degree requirements:* For doctorate, thesis/dissertation, qualifying exam. *Entrance requirements:* For master's and doctorate, GRE. Additional exam requirements/recommendations for international students: Required—TOEFL (minimum score 595 paper-based; 240 computer-based; 95 iBT); Recommended—IELTS (minimum score 7). *Application deadline:* For fall admission, 12/15 for domestic and international students. Application fee: $115. Electronic applications accepted. *Expenses: Tuition:* Full-time $36,304. *Required fees:* $1186. Full-time tuition and fees vary according to program. *Financial support:* Fellowships, research assistantships, teaching assistantships, career-related internships or fieldwork, Federal Work-Study, scholarships/grants, traineeships, and unspecified assistantships available. Support available to part-time students. Financial award application deadline: 2/17; financial award applicants required to submit FAFSA. *Faculty research:* Industrial hygiene and occupational safety, population genetics, indoor and outdoor air pollution, cell and molecular biology of the lungs, infectious diseases. *Unit head:* Dr. Douglas Dockery, Chairman, 617-432-1270, Fax: 617-432-6913. *Application contact:* Vincent W. James, Director of Admissions, 617-432-1031, Fax: 617-432-7080, E-mail: admissions@hsph.harvard.edu. Web site: http://www.hsph.harvard.edu/departments/environmental-health/.

Hunter College of the City University of New York, Graduate School, Schools of the Health Professions, School of Health Sciences, Programs in Urban Public Health, Program in Environmental and Occupational Health Education, New York, NY 10021-5085. Offers MS. *Accreditation:* ABET; CEPH. Part-time and evening/weekend programs available. *Faculty:* 3 full-time (0 women), 1 part-time/adjunct (0 women). *Students:* 4 full-time (3 women), 29 part-time (15 women); includes 17 minority (9 Black or African American, non-Hispanic/Latino; 5 Asian, non-Hispanic/Latino; 3 Hispanic/Latino), 1 international. Average age 32. 14 applicants, 57% accepted, 8 enrolled. In 2011, 12 master's awarded. *Degree requirements:* For master's, comprehensive exam, thesis optional, internship. *Entrance requirements:* For master's, GRE General Test, previous course work in calculus and statistics. Additional exam requirements/recommendations for international students: Required—TOEFL. *Application deadline:* For fall admission, 4/1 for domestic students, 2/1 for international students; for spring admission, 11/1 for domestic students, 9/1 for international students. Application fee: $125. *Expenses:* Tuition, state resident: full-time $8210; part-time $345 per credit. Tuition, nonresident: full-time $15,360; part-time $640 per credit. *Required fees:* $280 per semester. One-time fee: $125. Tuition and fees vary according to class time, campus/location and program. *Financial support:* In 2011–12, 6 fellowships were awarded; career-related internships or fieldwork, Federal Work-Study, institutionally sponsored loans, and tuition waivers (partial) also available. Support available to part-time students. Financial award application deadline: 3/1. *Faculty research:* Hazardous waste, asbestos, lead exposures, worker training, public employees. *Unit head:* Jack Caravanos, Director, 212-481-7569. *Application contact:* William Zlata, Director for Graduate Admissions, 212-772-4482, Fax: 212-650-3336, E-mail: admissions@hunter.cuny.edu. Web site: http://www.hunter.cuny.edu/uph/grad-test/environmental-occupational-health-sciences.

Indiana State University, College of Graduate and Professional Studies, College of Nursing, Health and Human Services, Department of Health, Safety, and Environmental Health Sciences, Terre Haute, IN 47809. Offers community health promotion (MA, MS); health and safety education (MA, MS); occupational safety management (MA, MS). *Accreditation:* NCATE (one or more programs are accredited). *Degree requirements:* For master's, thesis or alternative. *Entrance requirements:* For master's, GRE General Test. Electronic applications accepted.

Indiana University Bloomington, School of Health, Physical Education and Recreation, Department of Applied Health Science, Bloomington, IN 47405-7000. Offers biostatistics (MPH); environmental health (MPH, PhD); epidemiology (MPH, PhD); health behavior (PhD); health promotion (MS); human development/family studies (MS); nutrition science (MS); public health administration (MPH); safety management (MS); school and college health programs (MS); social, behavioral and community health (MPH). *Accreditation:* CEPH (one or more programs are accredited). *Faculty:* 24 full-time (12 women). *Students:* 169 full-time (126 women), 25 part-time (17 women); includes 56 minority (39 Black or African American, non-Hispanic/Latino; 2 American Indian or Alaska Native, non-Hispanic/Latino; 4 Asian, non-Hispanic/Latino; 9 Hispanic/Latino; 2 Two or more races, non-Hispanic/Latino), 29 international. Average age 30. 170 applicants, 74% accepted, 79 enrolled. In 2011, 52 master's, 9 doctorates awarded. *Degree requirements:* For master's, thesis optional; for doctorate, thesis/dissertation. *Entrance requirements:* For master's, GRE (MS in nutrition science), 3 recommendations; for doctorate, GRE, 3 recommendations. Additional exam requirements/recommendations for international students: Required—TOEFL (minimum score 550 paper-based; 213 computer-based; 79 iBT). *Application deadline:* For fall

admission, 4/30 priority date for domestic students, 12/1 for international students; for spring admission, 11/15 priority date for domestic students, 9/1 for international students. Application fee: $55 ($65 for international students). *Financial support:* Fellowships, research assistantships with full and partial tuition reimbursements, teaching assistantships with full and partial tuition reimbursements, career-related internships or fieldwork, Federal Work-Study, institutionally sponsored loans, scholarships/grants, tuition waivers (partial), and fee remissions available. Financial award application deadline: 3/1. *Faculty research:* Cancer education, HIV/AIDS and drug education, public health, parent-child interactions, safety education. *Total annual research expenditures:* $2.8 million. *Unit head:* Dr. David K. Lohrmann, Chair, 812-856-5101, Fax: 812-855-3936, E-mail: dlohrman@indiana.edu. *Application contact:* Dr. Susan Middlestadt, Associate Professor and Graduate Coordinator, 812-856-5768, Fax: 812-855-3936, E-mail: semiddle@indiana.edu. Web site: http://www.indiana.edu/~aphealth/.

Indiana University of Pennsylvania, School of Graduate Studies and Research, College of Health and Human Services, Department of Safety Sciences, Program in Safety Sciences, Indiana, PA 15705-1087. Offers MS. Part-time programs available. *Faculty:* 3 full-time (1 woman). *Students:* 18 full-time (5 women), 35 part-time (9 women); includes 4 minority (2 Black or African American, non-Hispanic/Latino; 2 Hispanic/Latino), 5 international. Average age 31. 79 applicants, 61% accepted, 27 enrolled. *Degree requirements:* For master's, thesis optional. *Entrance requirements:* For master's, 2 letters of recommendation. Additional exam requirements/recommendations for international students: Required—TOEFL (minimum score 540 paper-based; 207 computer-based). *Application deadline:* For fall admission, 4/1 priority date for domestic students. Applications are processed on a rolling basis. Application fee: $50. Electronic applications accepted. *Expenses:* Tuition, state resident: full-time $7488; part-time $416 per credit. Tuition, nonresident: full-time $11,232; part-time $624 per credit. *Required fees:* $2070; $192.20 per credit. $90 per semester. *Financial support:* In 2011–12, 7 research assistantships with full and partial tuition reimbursements (averaging $5,963 per year) were awarded; fellowships also available. Financial award application deadline: 4/15; financial award applicants required to submit FAFSA. *Unit head:* Dr. Chris Janicak, Graduate Coordinator, 724-357-3270. *Application contact:* Dr. Robert Soule, Graduate Coordinator, 724-357-3270, E-mail: bobsoule@iup.edu. Web site: http://www.iup.edu/upper.aspx?id=216.

Indiana University–Purdue University Indianapolis, School of Public and Environmental Affairs, Indianapolis, IN 46202. Offers criminal justice and public safety (MS); homeland security and emergency management (Graduate Certificate); library management (Graduate Certificate); nonprofit management (Graduate Certificate); public affairs (MPA); public management (Graduate Certificate); social entrepreneurship: nonprofit and public benefit organizations (Graduate Certificate); JD/MPA; MLS/NMC; MLS/PMC; MPA/MA. *Accreditation:* CAHME (one or more programs are accredited); NASPAA. Part-time and evening/weekend programs available. Postbaccalaureate distance learning degree programs offered (no on-campus study). *Faculty:* 24 full-time (8 women), 10 part-time/adjunct (2 women). *Students:* 204 full-time (124 women), 109 part-time (74 women); includes 61 minority (45 Black or African American, non-Hispanic/Latino; 1 American Indian or Alaska Native, non-Hispanic/Latino; 7 Asian, non-Hispanic/Latino; 8 Hispanic/Latino), 11 international. Average age 31. 214 applicants, 83% accepted, 147 enrolled. In 2011, 55 master's, 43 other advanced degrees awarded. *Entrance requirements:* For master's, GRE General Test, GMAT or LSAT, minimum GPA of 3.0 (preferred). *Application deadline:* For fall admission, 5/15 priority date for domestic students, 2/1 for international students; for spring admission, 2/15 priority date for domestic students, 9/15 for international students. Applications are processed on a rolling basis. Application fee: $60. Electronic applications accepted. *Financial support:* In 2011–12, 12 research assistantships with full tuition reimbursements (averaging $12,000 per year) were awarded; fellowships, teaching assistantships, career-related internships or fieldwork, Federal Work-Study, institutionally sponsored loans, and scholarships/grants also available. Support available to part-time students. Financial award application deadline: 3/1; financial award applicants required to submit FAFSA. *Faculty research:* Nonprofit and public management, public policy, urban policy, sustainability policy, disaster preparedness and recovery, vehicular safety, homicide, offender rehabilitation and re-entry. *Total annual research expenditures:* $1.6 million. *Unit head:* Dr. Terry L. Baumer, Executive Associate Dean, 317-274-2016, Fax: 317-274-5153, E-mail: tebaumer@iupui.edu. *Application contact:* Luke Bickel, Director of Graduate Programs, 317-274-4656, Fax: 317-278-9668, E-mail: lbickel@iupui.edu. Web site: http://www.spea.iupui.edu/.

The Johns Hopkins University, Bloomberg School of Public Health, Department of Environmental Health Sciences, Baltimore, MD 21218-2699. Offers environmental health engineering (PhD); environmental health sciences (MHS, Dr PH); occupational and environmental health (PhD); occupational and environmental hygiene (MHS, MHS); physiology (PhD); toxicology (PhD). Postbaccalaureate distance learning degree programs offered (minimal on-campus study). *Degree requirements:* For master's, essay, presentation; for doctorate, comprehensive exam, thesis/dissertation, 1 year full-time residency, oral and written exams. *Entrance requirements:* For master's, GRE General Test or MCAT, 3 letters of recommendation, transcripts; for doctorate, GRE General Test or MCAT, 3 letters of recommendation. Additional exam requirements/recommendations for international students: Required—TOEFL (minimum score 600 paper-based; 250 computer-based). Electronic applications accepted. *Faculty research:* Chemical carcinogenesis/toxicology, lung disease, occupational and environmental health, nuclear imaging, molecular epidemiology.

Keene State College, School of Professional and Graduate Studies, Keene, NH 03435. Offers curriculum and instruction (M Ed); education leadership (PMC); educational leadership (M Ed); safety and occupational health applied science (MS); school counselor (M Ed, PMC); special education (M Ed); teacher certification (Postbaccalaureate Certificate). *Accreditation:* NCATE. Part-time and evening/weekend programs available. *Faculty:* 11 full-time (7 women), 15 part-time/adjunct (8 women). *Students:* 36 full-time (32 women), 69 part-time (54 women); includes 1 minority (American Indian or Alaska Native, non-Hispanic/Latino), 1 international. Average age 33. 48 applicants, 83% accepted, 32 enrolled. In 2011, 39 master's, 12 other advanced degrees awarded. *Entrance requirements:* For master's, PRAXIS I, resume; minimum GPA of 2.5. Additional exam requirements/recommendations for international students: Required—TOEFL (minimum score 550 paper-based; 173 computer-based; 61 iBT). *Application deadline:* For fall admission, 4/1 for domestic students; for spring admission, 12/1 for domestic students. Applications are processed on a rolling basis. Application fee: $50. Electronic applications accepted. *Expenses:* Tuition, state resident: part-time $420 per credit. Tuition, nonresident: part-time $460 per credit. Tuition and fees vary according to course load. *Financial support:* Research assistantships, career-related internships or fieldwork, Federal Work-Study, institutionally sponsored loans, and unspecified assistantships available. Support available to part-time students. Financial award application deadline: 3/1; financial award applicants required to submit FAFSA. *Unit head:* Dr. Melinda Treadwell, Dean, 603-358-2220, E-mail: mtreadwe@keene.edu. *Application contact:* Peggy Richmond, Director of Admissions, 603-358-2276, Fax: 603-358-2767, E-mail: admissions@keene.edu. Web site: http://www.keene.edu/ps/.

Lewis University, College of Arts and Sciences, Program in Public Safety Administration, Romeoville, IL 60446. Offers MS. Part-time and evening/weekend programs available. Postbaccalaureate distance learning degree programs offered (no on-campus study). *Faculty:* 3 full-time (0 women), 8 part-time/adjunct (1 woman). *Students:* 9 full-time (2 women), 84 part-time (20 women); includes 28 minority (11 Black or African American, non-Hispanic/Latino; 17 Hispanic/Latino). Average age 37. In 2011, 29 master's awarded. *Entrance requirements:* For master's, bachelor's degree, 2 letters of recommendation. Additional exam requirements/recommendations for international students: Required—TOEFL (minimum score 500 paper-based; 213 computer-based). *Application deadline:* For fall admission, 5/1 for international students; for spring admission, 11/15 for international students. Applications are processed on a rolling basis. Application fee: $40. Electronic applications accepted. *Financial support:* Application deadline: 5/1; applicants required to submit FAFSA. *Unit head:* Dr. Calvin Edwards, Chair of Justice, Law and Public Safety Studies, 815-838-0500, Fax: 815-836-5870, E-mail: koloshsa@lewisu.edu. *Application contact:* Michelle Mega, Coordinator, 815-838-0500 Ext. 5342, Fax: 815-836-5342, E-mail: megami@lewisu.edu.

Loma Linda University, School of Public Health, Programs in Environmental and Occupational Health, Loma Linda, CA 92350. Offers MPH, MSPH. *Accreditation:* CEPH. *Entrance requirements:* Additional exam requirements/recommendations for international students: Required—Michigan English Language Assessment Battery or TOEFL. *Faculty research:* Human exposure to toxins, smog.

Louisiana State University Health Sciences Center, School of Public Health, New Orleans, LA 70112. Offers behavioral and community health sciences (MPH); biostatistics (MPH, MS, PhD); community health sciences (PhD); environmental and occupational health sciences (MPH); epidemiology (MPH, PhD); health policy and systems management (MPH). Part-time programs available. *Entrance requirements:* For master's, GRE General Test.

Loyola University Chicago, Graduate School, Marcella Niehoff School of Nursing, Population-Based Infection Control and Environmental Safety Program, Chicago, IL 60660. Offers population based infection control (MSN, Certificate). Part-time and evening/weekend programs available. *Students:* 12 part-time (11 women). Average age 37. 3 applicants, 100% accepted, 2 enrolled. In 2011, 6 master's awarded. *Entrance requirements:* For master's, Illinois nursing license, 3 letters of recommendation, minimum nursing GPA of 3.0, 1000 hours experience before starting clinical. Application fee: $50. *Expenses: Tuition:* Full-time $15,660; part-time $870 per credit hour. *Required fees:* $125 per semester. Tuition and fees vary according to course load and program. *Financial support:* Traineeships available. *Unit head:* Dr. Ida Androwich, Professor, 708-216-9276, Fax: 708-216-9555, E-mail: iandrow@luc.edu. *Application contact:* Amy Weatherford, Enrollment Advisor, School of Nursing, 773-508-3249, Fax: 773-508-3241, E-mail: aweatherford@luc.edu. Web site: http://luc.edu/nursing/infectionprevention/.

McGill University, Faculty of Graduate and Postdoctoral Studies, Faculty of Medicine, Department of Epidemiology and Biostatistics, Montréal, QC H3A 2T5, Canada. Offers community health (M Sc); environmental health (M Sc); epidemiology and biostatistics (M Sc, PhD, Diploma); health care evaluation (M Sc); medical statistics (M Sc). *Accreditation:* CEPH (one or more programs are accredited).

McGill University, Faculty of Graduate and Postdoctoral Studies, Faculty of Medicine and Department of Epidemiology and Biostatistics, Department of Occupational Health, Montréal, QC H3A 2T5, Canada. Offers M Sc, PhD.

Meharry Medical College, School of Graduate Studies, Division of Community Health Sciences, Nashville, TN 37208-9989. Offers occupational medicine (MSPH); public health administration (MSPH). *Accreditation:* CEPH. Part-time and evening/weekend programs available. *Degree requirements:* For master's, thesis, externship. *Entrance requirements:* For master's, GRE General Test, GMAT. *Expenses:* Contact institution. *Faculty research:* Policy and management, health care financing, health education and promotion.

Mercer University, Graduate Studies, Cecil B. Day Campus, College of Continuing and Professional Studies, Macon, GA 31207-0003. Offers clinical mental health (MS); counselor education and supervision (PhD); public safety leadership (MS); school counseling (MS). *Application contact:* Tracey M. Wofford, Associate Director of Admissions, 678-547-6422, E-mail: wofford_tm@mercer.edu.

Mississippi Valley State University, Department of Natural Science and Environmental Health, Program in Environmental Health, Itta Bena, MS 38941-1400. Offers MS. Evening/weekend programs available.

Murray State University, College of Health Sciences and Human Services, Program in Occupational Safety and Health, Murray, KY 42071. Offers environmental science (MS); industrial hygiene (MS); safety management (MS). *Accreditation:* ABET. Part-time programs available. *Degree requirements:* For master's, comprehensive exam, thesis optional, professional internship. Electronic applications accepted. *Faculty research:* Light effects on plant growth, ergonomics, toxic effects of pets' pesticides, traffic safety.

New York Medical College, School of Health Sciences and Practice, Department of Environmental Health Science, Valhalla, NY 10595-1691. Offers environmental health science (MPH); industrial hygiene (Graduate Certificate). *Accreditation:* CEPH. Part-time and evening/weekend programs available. *Faculty:* 5 full-time, 9 part-time/adjunct. *Students:* 25 full-time, 35 part-time. Average age 32. 35 applicants, 71% accepted, 20 enrolled. In 2011, 15 master's awarded. *Degree requirements:* For master's, thesis. *Entrance requirements:* For master's, minimum undergraduate GPA of 3.0. Additional exam requirements/recommendations for international students: Required—TOEFL (minimum score 637 paper-based; 250 computer-based; 110 iBT), IELTS (minimum score 7). *Application deadline:* For fall admission, 8/1 priority date for domestic students, 5/15 for international students; for spring admission, 12/1 priority date for domestic students, 10/15 for international students. Applications are processed on a rolling basis. Application fee: $50 ($100 for international students). Electronic applications accepted. *Financial support:* Career-related internships or fieldwork, Federal Work-Study, institutionally sponsored loans, health care benefits, tuition waivers (partial), and tuition reimbursement available. Support available to part-time students. Financial award applicants required to submit FAFSA. *Unit head:* Dr. Diane E. Heck, Chair, 914-594-4804, Fax: 914-594-4292, E-mail: diane_heck@nymc.edu. *Application contact:* Pamela Suett, Director of Recruitment, 914-594-4510, Fax: 914-594-4292, E-mail: shsp_admissions@nymc.edu. Web site: http://www.nymc.edu/sph/.

New York University, Graduate School of Arts and Science, Department of Environmental Medicine, New York, NY 10012-1019. Offers environmental health sciences (MS, PhD), including biostatistics (PhD), environmental hygiene (MS), epidemiology (PhD), ergonomics and biomechanics (PhD), exposure assessment and health effects (PhD), molecular toxicology/carcinogenesis (PhD), toxicology. Part-time programs available. *Faculty:* 26 full-time (7 women). *Students:* 62 full-time (43 women), 9 part-time (4 women); includes 12 minority (2 Black or African American, non-Hispanic/Latino; 3 Asian, non-Hispanic/Latino; 7 Hispanic/Latino), 27 international. Average age 30. 70 applicants, 56% accepted, 26 enrolled. In 2011, 9 master's, 8 doctorates awarded. Terminal master's awarded for partial completion of doctoral program. *Degree requirements:* For master's, thesis or alternative; for doctorate, one foreign language, thesis/dissertation, oral and written exams. *Entrance requirements:* For master's and

doctorate, GRE General Test, GRE Subject Test, minimum GPA of 3.0; bachelor's degree in biological, physical, or engineering science. Additional exam requirements/recommendations for international students: Required—TOEFL. *Application deadline:* For fall admission, 12/12 for domestic and international students. Application fee: $90. *Financial support:* Fellowships with tuition reimbursements, teaching assistantships with tuition reimbursements, career-related internships or fieldwork, Federal Work-Study, institutionally sponsored loans, and health care benefits available. Financial award application deadline: 12/12; financial award applicants required to submit FAFSA. *Unit head:* Dr. Max Costa, Chair, 845-731-3661, Fax: 845-351-4510, E-mail: ehs@env.med.nyu.edu. *Application contact:* Dr. Jerome J. Solomon, Director of Graduate Studies, 845-731-3661, Fax: 845-351-4510, E-mail: ehs@env.med.nyu.edu. Web site: http://environmental-medicine.med.nyu.edu/.

North Carolina Agricultural and Technical State University, School of Graduate Studies, School of Technology, Department of Construction Management and Occupational Safety and Health, Greensboro, NC 27411. Offers construction management (MSTM); environmental and occupational safety (MSTM); occupational safety and health (MSTM).

Oakland University, Graduate Study and Lifelong Learning, School of Health Sciences, Program in Safety Management, Rochester, MI 48309-4401. Offers MS.

Old Dominion University, College of Health Sciences, ODU/EVMS Joint Program for the Master of Public Health, Norfolk, VA 23529. Offers environmental health (MPH); health promotion (MPH). Program offered jointly with Eastern Virginia Medical School. *Accreditation:* CEPH. Part-time and evening/weekend programs available. *Faculty:* 7 full-time (4 women), 6 part-time/adjunct (3 women). *Students:* 1 (woman) full-time, 49 part-time (34 women); includes 18 minority (9 Black or African American, non-Hispanic/Latino; 3 Asian, non-Hispanic/Latino; 5 Hispanic/Latino; 1 Two or more races, non-Hispanic/Latino), 1 international. Average age 29. 67 applicants, 60% accepted, 30 enrolled. In 2011, 28 master's awarded. *Degree requirements:* For master's, field practicum, capstone project. *Entrance requirements:* For master's, GRE, MCAT, minimum GPA of 2.75. Additional exam requirements/recommendations for international students: Required—TOEFL (minimum score 650 paper-based; 278 computer-based). *Application deadline:* For fall admission, 5/31 priority date for domestic students, 4/30 for international students. Application fee: $50 ($100 for international students). Electronic applications accepted. *Expenses:* Tuition, state resident: full-time $9096; part-time $379 per credit. Tuition, nonresident: full-time $23,064; part-time $961 per credit. *Required fees:* $127 per semester. One-time fee: $50. *Financial support:* In 2011–12, 3 teaching assistantships with partial tuition reimbursements (averaging $10,000 per year) were awarded; career-related internships or fieldwork, institutionally sponsored loans, and scholarships/grants also available. Financial award application deadline: 5/1; financial award applicants required to submit FAFSA. *Faculty research:* Community-based health research, public health research in environmental health and health promotion. *Total annual research expenditures:* $150,133. *Unit head:* Associate Director, 757-683-4259, Fax: 757-446-6121. *Application contact:* William Heffelfinger, Director of Graduate Admissions, 757-683-5554, Fax: 757-683-3255, E-mail: gradadmit@odu.edu. Web site: http://www.evms.edu/hlthprof/mph.

Old Dominion University, College of Health Sciences, Program in Community Health and Environmental Health, Norfolk, VA 23529. Offers MS. Part-time and evening/weekend programs available. Postbaccalaureate distance learning degree programs offered (no on-campus study). *Faculty:* 4 full-time (1 woman), 3 part-time/adjunct (1 woman). *Students:* 3 full-time (0 women), 12 part-time (4 women); includes 5 minority (2 Black or African American, non-Hispanic/Latino; 2 Asian, non-Hispanic/Latino; 1 Hispanic/Latino). Average age 30. 10 applicants, 80% accepted, 7 enrolled. In 2011, 5 master's awarded. *Degree requirements:* For master's, comprehensive exam, oral exam, written exam, practicum or thesis. *Entrance requirements:* For master's, GRE General Test, minimum GPA of 2.75. Additional exam requirements/recommendations for international students: Required—TOEFL (minimum score 650 paper-based; 278 computer-based). *Application deadline:* For fall admission, 8/1 priority date for domestic students, 7/1 for international students; for winter admission, 11/1 priority date for domestic students, 10/1 for international students; for spring admission, 4/1 priority date for domestic students, 3/1 for international students. Applications are processed on a rolling basis. Application fee: $50. Electronic applications accepted. *Expenses:* Tuition, state resident: full-time $9096; part-time $379 per credit. Tuition, nonresident: full-time $23,064; part-time $961 per credit. *Required fees:* $127 per semester. One-time fee: $50. *Financial support:* In 2011–12, 5 research assistantships with tuition reimbursements (averaging $14,000 per year), 2 teaching assistantships with partial tuition reimbursements (averaging $10,000 per year) were awarded; career-related internships or fieldwork, institutionally sponsored loans, scholarships/grants, and tuition waivers (partial) also available. Financial award applicants required to submit FAFSA. *Faculty research:* Toxicology, occupational health, environmental hazards. *Total annual research expenditures:* $150,133. *Unit head:* Dr. Anna Jeng, Graduate Program Director, 757-683-4594, Fax: 757-683-4410, E-mail: chpgpd@odu.edu. *Application contact:* William Heffelfinger, Director of Graduate Admissions, 757-683-5554, Fax: 757-683-3255, E-mail: gradadmit@odu.edu. Web site: http://hs.odu.edu/commhealth/.

Oregon State University, Graduate School, College of Public Health and Human Sciences, Programs in Public Health, Corvallis, OR 97331. Offers biostatistics (MPH); environmental and occupational health and safety (MPH, PhD); epidemiology (MPH); health management and policy (MPH, PhD); health promotion and health behavior (MPH, PhD); international health (MPH). *Accreditation:* CEPH. Terminal master's awarded for partial completion of doctoral program. *Degree requirements:* For doctorate, one foreign language, thesis/dissertation. *Entrance requirements:* For master's and doctorate, minimum GPA of 3.0 in last 90 hours. Additional exam requirements/recommendations for international students: Required—TOEFL. *Faculty research:* Traffic safety, health safety, injury control, health promotion.

Purdue University, Graduate School, College of Health and Human Sciences, School of Health Sciences, West Lafayette, IN 47907. Offers health physics (MS, PhD); medical physics (MS, PhD); occupational and environmental health science (MS, PhD), including aerosol deposition and lung disease , ergonomics, exposure and risk assessment, indoor air quality and bioaerosols (PhD), liver/lung toxicology; occupational and environmental health science (PhD), including indoor air quality and bioaerosols; radiation biology (PhD); toxicology (PhD); MS/PhD. Part-time programs available. *Faculty:* 10 full-time (3 women), 24 part-time/adjunct (3 women). *Students:* 24 full-time (9 women), 7 part-time (2 women); includes 2 minority (both Asian, non-Hispanic/Latino), 13 international. Average age 30. 49 applicants, 37% accepted, 7 enrolled. In 2011, 18 master's, 5 doctorates awarded. *Degree requirements:* For master's, thesis optional; for doctorate, one foreign language, thesis/dissertation. *Entrance requirements:* For master's and doctorate, GRE General Test, minimum undergraduate GPA of 3.0 or equivalent. Additional exam requirements/recommendations for international students: Required—TOEFL (minimum score 550 computer-based; 77 iBT); Recommended—TWE. *Application deadline:* For fall admission, 5/15 for domestic and international students; for spring admission, 10/15 for domestic and international students. Applications are processed on a rolling basis. Application fee: $60 ($75 for international students). Electronic applications accepted. *Financial support:* In 2011–12, fellowships with tuition reimbursements (averaging $14,400 per year), research assistantships with tuition reimbursements (averaging $12,000 per year), teaching assistantships with tuition reimbursements (averaging $12,000 per year) were awarded; career-related internships or fieldwork and traineeships also available. Support available to part-time students. Financial award applicants required to submit FAFSA. *Faculty research:* Environmental toxicology, industrial hygiene, radiation dosimetry. *Unit head:* Dr. Wei Zheng, Head, 765-494-1419, E-mail: wz18@purdue.edu. *Application contact:* Jennifer S. Franklin, Graduate Contact, 765-494-0248, E-mail: jfranklin@purdue.edu. Web site: http://www.healthsciences.purdue.edu/.

Rochester Institute of Technology, Graduate Enrollment Services, College of Applied Science and Technology, School of Engineering Technology, Department of Civil Engineering Technology, Environmental Management and Safety, Program in Environmental Health and Safety Management, Rochester, NY 14623-5603. Offers MS. Part-time programs available. Postbaccalaureate distance learning degree programs offered (no on-campus study). *Students:* 16 full-time (3 women), 37 part-time (14 women); includes 7 minority (2 Black or African American, non-Hispanic/Latino; 1 American Indian or Alaska Native, non-Hispanic/Latino; 4 Asian, non-Hispanic/Latino), 14 international. Average age 29. 42 applicants, 38% accepted, 10 enrolled. In 2011, 21 degrees awarded. *Degree requirements:* For master's, thesis or project. *Entrance requirements:* Additional exam requirements/recommendations for international students: Required—TOEFL (minimum score 550 paper-based; 213 computer-based; 79 iBT) or IELTS (minimum score 6). *Application deadline:* Applications are processed on a rolling basis. Application fee: $50. Electronic applications accepted. *Expenses: Tuition:* Full-time $34,659; part-time $963 per credit hour. *Required fees:* $228; $76 per quarter. *Faculty research:* Design, implementation and effectiveness of integrated environmental health and safety management systems in industry. *Unit head:* Joseph Rosenbeck, Graduate Program Director, 585-475-6469, E-mail: jmrcem@rit.edu. *Application contact:* Diane Ellison, Assistant Vice President, Graduate Enrollment Services, 585-475-2229, Fax: 585-475-7164, E-mail: gradinfo@rit.edu. Web site: http://www.rit.edu/cast/cetems/ms-in-environmental-health-and-safety-management.php.

Saint Joseph's University, College of Arts and Sciences, Programs in Environmental Protection and Safety Management, Philadelphia, PA 19131-1395. Offers environmental protection and safety management (MS, Post-Master's Certificate). Part-time and evening/weekend programs available. *Faculty:* 8 part-time/adjunct (2 women). *Students:* 2 full-time, 25 part-time (7 women); includes 2 minority (both Black or African American, non-Hispanic/Latino), 1 international. Average age 36. 10 applicants, 80% accepted, 7 enrolled. In 2011, 1 master's awarded. *Entrance requirements:* For master's, GRE (if GPA less than 2.75), minimum GPA of 2.75, 2 letters of recommendation, resume. Additional exam requirements/recommendations for international students: Required—TOEFL (minimum score 550 paper-based; 213 computer-based; 79 iBT). *Application deadline:* For fall admission, 7/15 priority date for domestic students, 4/15 for international students; for winter admission, 1/15 for international students; for spring admission, 11/15 priority date for domestic students, 10/15 for international students. Applications are processed on a rolling basis. Application fee: $35. Electronic applications accepted. *Expenses: Tuition:* Part-time $735 per credit hour. Tuition and fees vary according to degree level and program. *Financial support:* Applicants required to submit FAFSA. *Unit head:* Dr. Sabrina Deturk, Associate Dean and Executive Director Graduate Arts and Sciences, 610-660-1289, E-mail: sdeturk@sju.edu. *Application contact:* Kate McConnell, Director, Graduate College of Arts and Sciences Admissions and Retention, 610-660-3184, Fax: 610-660-3230, E-mail: kate.mcconnell@sju.edu. Web site: http://www.sju.edu/academics/cas/grad/epsm/index.html.

Saint Joseph's University, College of Arts and Sciences, Programs in Public Safety and Management, Philadelphia, PA 19131-1395. Offers homeland security (MS, Certificate); public safety management (MS, Certificate). Part-time and evening/weekend programs available. Postbaccalaureate distance learning degree programs offered. *Faculty:* 1 full-time (0 women), 7 part-time/adjunct (1 woman). *Students:* 10 full-time (2 women), 60 part-time (10 women); includes 11 minority (8 Black or African American, non-Hispanic/Latino; 1 Asian, non-Hispanic/Latino; 2 Hispanic/Latino), 1 international. Average age 36. 27 applicants, 59% accepted, 12 enrolled. In 2011, 16 master's, 1 other advanced degree awarded. *Entrance requirements:* For master's, GRE (if GPA less than 2.75), minimum GPA of 2.75, 2 letters of recommendation, resume. Additional exam requirements/recommendations for international students: Required—TOEFL (minimum score 550 paper-based; 213 computer-based; 79 iBT). *Application deadline:* For fall admission, 7/15 priority date for domestic students, 4/15 for international students; for winter admission, 1/15 for international students; for spring admission, 11/15 priority date for domestic students, 10/15 for international students. Applications are processed on a rolling basis. Application fee: $35. Electronic applications accepted. *Expenses: Tuition:* Part-time $735 per credit hour. Tuition and fees vary according to degree level and program. *Financial support:* Applicants required to submit FAFSA. *Unit head:* Dr. Sabrina Deturk, Associate Dean and Executive Director Graduate Arts and Sciences, 610-660-1289, E-mail: sdeturk@sju.edu. *Application contact:* Kate McConnell, Assistant Director of Graduate Admissions, 610-660-3184, Fax: 610-660-3230, E-mail: kate.mcconnell@sju.edu. Web site: http://www.sju.edu/academics/cas/grad/publicsafety/index.html.

Saint Mary's University of Minnesota, Schools of Graduate and Professional Programs, Graduate School of Business and Technology, Public Safety Administration Program, Winona, MN 55987-1399. Offers MA. *Unit head:* Lora Setter, Director, 612-238-4547, E-mail: llsetter@smumn.edu. *Application contact:* Yasin Alsaidi, Director of Admissions for Graduate and Professional Programs, 612-728-5207, Fax: 612-728-5121, E-mail: yalsaidi@smumn.edu. Web site: http://www.smumn.edu/graduate-home/areas-of-study/graduate-school-of-business-technology/ma-in-public-safety-administration.

San Diego State University, Graduate and Research Affairs, College of Health and Human Services, Graduate School of Public Health, San Diego, CA 92182. Offers environmental health (MPH); epidemiology (MPH, PhD), including biostatistics (MPH); global emergency preparedness and response (MS); global health (PhD); health behavior (PhD); health promotion (MPH); health services administration (MPH); toxicology (MS); MPH/MA; MSW/MPH. *Accreditation:* ABET (one or more programs are accredited); CAHME (one or more programs are accredited); CEPH (one or more programs are accredited). Part-time programs available. *Degree requirements:* For master's, comprehensive exam (for some programs), thesis (for some programs); for doctorate, thesis/dissertation. *Entrance requirements:* For master's, GMAT (MPH in health services administration), GRE General Test; for doctorate, GRE General Test. Additional exam requirements/recommendations for international students: Required—TOEFL. *Faculty research:* Evaluation of tobacco, AIDS prevalence and prevention, mammography, infant death project, Alzheimer's in elderly Chinese.

Southeastern Oklahoma State University, School of Arts and Sciences, Durant, OK 74701-0609. Offers biology (MT); computer information systems (MT); occupational safety and health (MT). Part-time and evening/weekend programs available. *Faculty:* 12 full-time (4 women), 1 part-time/adjunct (0 women). *Students:* 17 full-time (6 women), 45 part-time (8 women); includes 18 minority (1 Black or African American, non-Hispanic/Latino; 15 American Indian or Alaska Native, non-Hispanic/Latino; 2 Hispanic/Latino), 2 international. Average age 28. 19 applicants, 95% accepted, 18 enrolled. *Degree requirements:* For master's, thesis optional. *Entrance requirements:* For master's,

minimum GPA of 3.0 in last 60 hours or 2.75 overall. Additional exam requirements/ recommendations for international students: Required—TOEFL (minimum score 550 paper-based; 213 computer-based; 79 iBT). *Application deadline:* For fall admission, 8/1 for domestic students, 6/1 for international students; for spring admission, 1/5 for domestic students, 11/1 for international students. Application fee: $20 ($55 for international students). Electronic applications accepted. *Expenses:* Tuition, state resident: full-time $3537; part-time $173.95 per credit hour. Tuition, nonresident: full-time $8673; part-time $459.30 per credit hour. *Required fees:* $22.55 per credit hour. *Financial support:* In 2011–12, 8 students received support. Fellowships, research assistantships, teaching assistantships, Federal Work-Study, and institutionally sponsored loans available. Support available to part-time students. Financial award application deadline: 6/15; financial award applicants required to submit FAFSA. *Unit head:* Dr. Teresa Golden, Graduate Coordinator, 580-745-2286, E-mail: tgolden@se.edu. *Application contact:* Carrie Williamson, Graduate Secretary, 580-745-2220, Fax: 580-745-7474, E-mail: cwilliamson@se.edu. Web site: http://www.se.edu/arts-and-sciences/.

Stony Brook University, State University of New York, School of Professional Development, Stony Brook, NY 11794. Offers biology-grade 7-12 (MAT); chemistry-grade 7-12 (MAT); coaching (Graduate Certificate); coaching online (Graduate Certificate); computer integrated engineering (Graduate Certificate); earth science-grade 7-12 (MAT); educational computing (Graduate Certificate); educational leadership (Advanced Certificate); English-grade 7-12 (MAT); environmental management (Graduate Certificate); environmental/occupational health and safety (Graduate Certificate); French-grade 7-12 (MAT); German-grade 7-12 (MAT); human resource management (Graduate Certificate); human resource management online (Graduate Certificate); information systems management (Graduate Certificate); Italian-grade 7-12 (MAT); liberal studies (MA); liberal studies online (MAT); mathematics-grade 7-12 (MAT); operation research (Graduate Certificate); physics-grade 7-12 (MAT); professional studies online (MPS); school administration and supervision (Graduate Certificate); school building leadership (Graduate Certificate); school district administration (Graduate Certificate); school district business leadership (Advanced Certificate); school district leadership (Graduate Certificate); social science and the professions (MPS), including environmental waste management, human resource management; social studies-grade 7-12 (MAT); Spanish-grade 7-12 (MAT); waste management (Graduate Certificate). Part-time and evening/weekend programs available. Postbaccalaureate distance learning degree programs offered. *Degree requirements:* For master's, one foreign language, thesis or alternative.

Temple University, Health Sciences Center, College of Health Professions and Social Work, Department of Public Health, Philadelphia, PA 19122-6096. Offers environmental health (MS); epidemiology (MS); public health (MPH, PhD); school health education (Ed M). *Accreditation:* CEPH (one or more programs are accredited). Part-time and evening/weekend programs available. *Faculty:* 15 full-time (8 women). *Students:* 62 full-time (44 women), 28 part-time (25 women); includes 24 minority (14 Black or African American, non-Hispanic/Latino; 5 Asian, non-Hispanic/Latino; 5 Hispanic/Latino), 7 international. Average age 29. 92 applicants, 68% accepted, 29 enrolled. In 2011, 30 master's, 4 doctorates awarded. Terminal master's awarded for partial completion of doctoral program. *Degree requirements:* For doctorate, thesis/dissertation. *Entrance requirements:* For master's and doctorate, minimum undergraduate GPA of 3.0. Additional exam requirements/recommendations for international students: Required—TOEFL (minimum score 550 paper-based; 213 computer-based; 79 iBT). Application fee: $50. Electronic applications accepted. *Expenses:* Tuition, state resident: full-time $12,366; part-time $687 per credit hour. Tuition, nonresident: full-time $17,298; part-time $961 per credit hour. *Required fees:* $590; $213 per year. *Financial support:* Fellowships with tuition reimbursements, research assistantships with tuition reimbursements, teaching assistantships with tuition reimbursements, career-related internships or fieldwork, Federal Work-Study, institutionally sponsored loans, scholarships/grants, and tuition waivers (partial) available. Financial award application deadline: 1/15; financial award applicants required to submit FAFSA. *Faculty research:* Program development and evaluation in HIV prevention, violence prevention, women's health policy, psychosocial aspects of disability. *Unit head:* Dr. Alice J. Hausman, Chair, 215-204-5112, Fax: 215-204-1854, E-mail: publichealth@temple.edu. *Application contact:* Tara Schumacher, Coordinator of Outreach, 215-204-6575, Fax: 215-204-8781, E-mail: tara.schumacher@temple.edu. Web site: http://chpsw.temple.edu/publichealth/.

Texas A&M Health Science Center, School of Rural Public Health, College Station, TX 77840. Offers environmental/occupational health (MPH); epidemiology/biostatistics (MPH); health policy/management (MPH); social and behavioral health (MPH). *Accreditation:* CEPH. Part-time programs available. Postbaccalaureate distance learning degree programs offered (no on-campus study). *Degree requirements:* For master's, thesis optional. *Entrance requirements:* For master's, GRE General Test, minimum undergraduate GPA of 3.0. Electronic applications accepted. *Faculty research:* Tobacco cessation, youth health risk.

Towson University, Program in Occupational Science, Towson, MD 21252-0001. Offers Sc D. Part-time and evening/weekend programs available. *Students:* 4 full-time (2 women), 14 part-time (13 women); includes 3 minority (all Black or African American, non-Hispanic/Latino), 2 international. *Degree requirements:* For doctorate, thesis/dissertation, comprehensive assessment. *Entrance requirements:* For doctorate, GRE or MAT, NBCOT certification, minimum GPA of 3.25. Additional exam requirements/ recommendations for international students: Required—TOEFL (minimum score 600 paper-based; 250 computer-based). *Application deadline:* For fall admission, 8/15 priority date for domestic students, 8/15 for international students; for winter admission, 11/15 priority date for domestic students, 11/15 for international students; for spring admission, 1/15 priority date for domestic students, 1/15 for international students. Applications are processed on a rolling basis. Application fee: $50. Electronic applications accepted. *Expenses:* Tuition, state resident: part-time $337 per credit. Tuition, nonresident: part-time $709 per credit. *Required fees:* $99 per credit. *Financial support:* Application deadline: 4/1; applicants required to submit FAFSA. *Unit head:* Maggie Reitz, Graduate Program Director, 410-704-2762, E-mail: mreitz@towson.edu.

Trident University International, College of Health Sciences, Program in Health Sciences, Cypress, CA 90630. Offers clinical research administration (MS, Certificate); emergency and disaster management (MS, Certificate); environmental health science (Certificate); health care administration (PhD); health care management (MS), including health informatics; health education (MS, Certificate); health informatics (Certificate); health sciences (PhD); international health (MS); international health: educator or researcher option (PhD); international health: practitioner option (PhD); law and expert witness studies (MS, Certificate); public health (MS); quality assurance (Certificate). Part-time and evening/weekend programs available. Postbaccalaureate distance learning degree programs offered (no on-campus study). *Degree requirements:* For doctorate, comprehensive exam, thesis/dissertation, defense of dissertation. *Entrance requirements:* For master's, minimum GPA of 2.5 (students with GPA 3.0 or greater may transfer up to 30% of graduate level credits); for doctorate, minimum GPA of 3.4, curriculum vitae, course work in research methods or statistics. Additional exam requirements/recommendations for international students: Required—TOEFL. Electronic applications accepted.

Tufts University, Cummings School of Veterinary Medicine, Program in Conservation Medicine, Medford, MA 02155. Offers MS. *Faculty:* 39 part-time/adjunct (21 women). *Students:* 9 full-time (8 women); includes 1 minority (Black or African American, non-Hispanic/Latino), 2 international. 15 applicants, 60% accepted, 9 enrolled. *Degree requirements:* For master's, case study, preceptorship. *Entrance requirements:* For master's, GRE, official transcripts, curriculum vitae. Additional exam requirements/ recommendations for international students: Required—TOEFL or IELTS. *Application deadline:* For fall admission, 4/1 for domestic and international students. Application fee: $70. Electronic applications accepted. *Expenses: Tuition:* Full-time $41,208; part-time $1030 per credit hour. Full-time tuition and fees vary according to degree level, program and student level. Part-time tuition and fees vary according to course load. *Financial support:* Federal Work-Study available. Financial award application deadline: 5/15; financial award applicants required to submit FAFSA. *Faculty research:* Non-invasive saliva collection techniques for free-ranging mountain gorillas and captive eastern gorillas, animal sentinels for infectious diseases. *Unit head:* Dr. Gretchen Kaufman, Director, 508-839-7918, E-mail: gretchen.kaufman@tufts.edu. *Application contact:* Rebecca Russo, Director of Admissions, 508-839-7920, Fax: 508-887-4820, E-mail: vetadmissions@tufts.edu. Web site: http://www.tufts.edu/vet/mcm/.

Tufts University, School of Engineering, Department of Civil and Environmental Engineering, Medford, MA 02155. Offers bioengineering (ME, MS), including environmental technology; civil engineering (ME, MS, PhD), including geotechnical engineering, structural engineering, water diplomacy (PhD); environmental engineering (ME, MS, PhD), including environmental engineering and environmental sciences, environmental geotechnology, environmental health, environmental science and management, hazardous materials management, water diplomacy (PhD), water resources engineering. Part-time programs available. *Faculty:* 18 full-time, 5 part-time/ adjunct. *Students:* 102 full-time (50 women); includes 8 minority (1 Black or African American, non-Hispanic/Latino; 6 Asian, non-Hispanic/Latino; 1 Hispanic/Latino), 37 international. Average age 27. 162 applicants, 59% accepted, 37 enrolled. In 2011, 18 degrees awarded. Terminal master's awarded for partial completion of doctoral program. *Degree requirements:* For master's, thesis or alternative; for doctorate, thesis/ dissertation. *Entrance requirements:* For master's and doctorate, GRE General Test. Additional exam requirements/recommendations for international students: Required—TOEFL (minimum score 550 paper-based; 213 computer-based; 80 iBT). *Application deadline:* For fall admission, 1/15 priority date for domestic students, 12/15 for international students; for spring admission, 10/15 for domestic students, 9/15 for international students. Applications are processed on a rolling basis. Application fee: $75. Electronic applications accepted. *Expenses: Tuition:* Full-time $41,208; part-time $1030 per credit hour. Full-time tuition and fees vary according to degree level, program and student level. Part-time tuition and fees vary according to course load. *Financial support:* Fellowships with full tuition reimbursements, research assistantships with full and partial tuition reimbursements, teaching assistantships with full and partial tuition reimbursements, Federal Work-Study, scholarships/grants, tuition waivers (partial), and unspecified assistantships available. Financial award application deadline: 1/15; financial award applicants required to submit FAFSA. *Faculty research:* Environmental and water resources engineering, environmental health, geotechnical and geoenvironmental engineering, structural engineering and mechanics, water diplomacy. *Unit head:* Dr. Kurt Penell, Chair, 617-627-3211, Fax: 617-627-3994. *Application contact:* Laura Sacco, Information Contact, 617-627-3211, E-mail: ceeinfo@tufts.edu. Web site: http://www.ase.tufts.edu/cee/.

Tulane University, School of Public Health and Tropical Medicine, Department of Environmental Health Sciences, New Orleans, LA 70118-5669. Offers MPH, MSPH, Dr PH, PhD, JD/MSPH. *Accreditation:* ABET (one or more programs are accredited); CEPH (one or more programs are accredited). *Degree requirements:* For doctorate, comprehensive exam, thesis/dissertation. *Entrance requirements:* For master's and doctorate, GRE General Test. Additional exam requirements/recommendations for international students: Required—TOEFL. Electronic applications accepted.

Uniformed Services University of the Health Sciences, School of Medicine, Graduate Programs in the Biomedical Sciences and Public Health, Bethesda, MD 20814. Offers emerging infectious diseases (PhD); medical and clinical psychology (PhD), including clinical psychology, medical and clinical psychology, medical psychology; molecular and cell biology (MS, PhD); neuroscience (PhD); preventive medicine and biometrics (MPH, MS, MSPH, MTMH, Dr PH, PhD), including environmental health sciences (PhD), healthcare administration and policy (MS), medical zoology (PhD), public health (MPH, MSPH, Dr PH), tropical medicine and hygiene (MTMH). *Faculty:* 372 full-time (119 women), 4,044 part-time/adjunct (908 women). *Students:* 176 full-time (96 women); includes 31 minority (6 Black or African American, non-Hispanic/Latino; 4 American Indian or Alaska Native, non-Hispanic/ Latino; 14 Asian, non-Hispanic/Latino; 7 Hispanic/Latino), 11 international. Average age 28. 278 applicants, 20% accepted, 47 enrolled. In 2011, 36 master's, 17 doctorates awarded. Terminal master's awarded for partial completion of doctoral program. *Degree requirements:* For master's, comprehensive exam, thesis or alternative; for doctorate, comprehensive exam, thesis/dissertation, qualifying exam. *Entrance requirements:* For master's, GRE General Test; for doctorate, GRE General Test, minimum GPA of 3.0. Additional exam requirements/recommendations for international students: Required—TOEFL. *Application deadline:* For fall admission, 1/1 priority date for domestic students, 1/1 for international students. Applications are processed on a rolling basis. Application fee: $0. Electronic applications accepted. *Financial support:* In 2011–12, fellowships with full tuition reimbursements (averaging $26,000 per year), research assistantships with full tuition reimbursements (averaging $26,000 per year) were awarded; career-related internships or fieldwork, scholarships/grants, health care benefits, and tuition waivers (full) also available. *Unit head:* Dr. Eleanor S. Metcalf, Associate Dean, 301-295-1104, E-mail: emetcalf@usuhs.edu. *Application contact:* Elena Marina Sherman, Program Administrative Specialist, 301-295-3913, Fax: 301-295-6772, E-mail: elena.sherman@usuhs.mil. Web site: http://www.usuhs.mil/graded.

Uniformed Services University of the Health Sciences, School of Medicine, Graduate Programs in the Biomedical Sciences and Public Health, Department of Preventive Medicine and Biometrics, Program in Environmental Health Sciences, Bethesda, MD 20814-4799. Offers PhD. *Accreditation:* CEPH. *Faculty:* 43 full-time (14 women), 143 part-time/adjunct (25 women). *Students:* 2 full-time (0 women); includes 1 minority (Hispanic/Latino). Average age 30. 1 applicant, 0% accepted. In 2011, 2 doctorates awarded. *Degree requirements:* For doctorate, comprehensive exam, thesis/ dissertation, qualifying exam. *Entrance requirements:* For doctorate, GRE, minimum GPA of 3.0. Additional exam requirements/recommendations for international students: Required—TOEFL. *Application deadline:* For fall admission, 1/1 priority date for domestic students. Applications are processed on a rolling basis. Application fee: $0. *Financial support:* In 2011–12, fellowships with full tuition reimbursements (averaging $26,000 per year) were awarded; tuition waivers (full) also available. *Unit head:* Dr. David Cruess, Director, 301-295-3465, Fax: 301-295-1933, E-mail: dcruess@usuhs.mil. *Application contact:* Elena Marina Sherman, Program Administrative Specialist, 301-295-3913, Fax: 301-295-6772, E-mail: elena.sherman@usuhs.mil.

Universidad Autonoma de Guadalajara, Graduate Programs, Guadalajara, Mexico. Offers administrative law and justice (LL M); advertising and corporate communications (MA); architecture (M Arch); business (MBA); computational science (MCC); education (Ed M, Ed D); English-Spanish translation (MA); entrepreneurship and management (MBA); integrated management of digital animation (MA); international business (MIB); international corporate law (LL M); internet technologies (MS); manufacturing systems (MMS); occupational health (MS); philosophy (MA, PhD); power electronics (MS); quality systems (MQS); renewable energy (MS); social evaluation of projects (MBA); strategic market research (MBA); tax law (MA); teaching mathematics (MA).

Universidad de Ciencias Medicas, Graduate Programs, San Jose, Costa Rica. Offers dermatology (SP); family health (MS); health service center administration (MHA); human anatomy (MS); medical and surgery (MD); occupational medicine (MS); pharmacy (Pharm D). Part-time programs available. *Degree requirements:* For master's, thesis; for doctorate and SP, comprehensive exam. *Entrance requirements:* For master's, MD or bachelor's degree; for doctorate, admissions test; for SP, admissions test, MD.

Université de Montréal, Faculty of Medicine, Department of Environmental and Occupational Health, Montréal, QC H3C 3J7, Canada. Offers M Sc. *Accreditation:* CEPH. *Degree requirements:* For master's, thesis. *Entrance requirements:* For master's, proficiency in French, knowledge of English. Electronic applications accepted. *Faculty research:* Metabolism of chemical substances, toxicity, biological surveillance, risk analysis.

Université du Québec à Montréal, Graduate Programs, Program in Ergonomics in Occupational Health and Safety, Montréal, QC H3C 3P8, Canada. Offers Diploma. Part-time programs available. *Entrance requirements:* For degree, appropriate bachelor's degree or equivalent, proficiency in French.

Université Laval, Faculty of Medicine, Graduate Programs in Medicine, Department of Social and Preventive Medicine, Program in Accident Prevention and Occupational Health and Safety Management, Québec, QC G1K 7P4, Canada. Offers Diploma. Part-time programs available. *Entrance requirements:* For degree, knowledge of French. Electronic applications accepted.

University at Albany, State University of New York, School of Public Health, Department of Environmental Health Sciences, Albany, NY 12222-0001. Offers environmental and analytical chemistry (MS, PhD); environmental and occupational health (MS, PhD); toxicology (MS, PhD). *Degree requirements:* For master's, thesis; for doctorate, comprehensive exam, thesis/dissertation. *Entrance requirements:* For master's and doctorate, GRE General Test, GRE Subject Test, 3 letters of reference. Additional exam requirements/recommendations for international students: Required—TOEFL (minimum score 600 paper-based; 213 computer-based). Electronic applications accepted. *Faculty research:* Xenobiotic metabolism, neurotoxicity of halogenated hydrocarbons, pharmac/toxicogenomics, environmental analytical chemistry.

The University of Alabama at Birmingham, School of Public Health, Program in Environmental Health Sciences, Birmingham, AL 35294. Offers PhD. *Degree requirements:* For doctorate, thesis/dissertation. *Entrance requirements:* For doctorate, GRE General Test. Additional exam requirements/recommendations for international students: Required—TOEFL. *Application deadline:* For fall admission, 4/1 for domestic students. Electronic applications accepted. *Expenses:* Tuition, state resident: full-time $5922; part-time $309 per hour. Tuition, nonresident: full-time $13,428; part-time $726 per hour. Tuition and fees vary according to program. *Financial support:* Fellowships, career-related internships or fieldwork, scholarships/grants, and unspecified assistantships available. *Faculty research:* Aquatic toxicology, virology. *Unit head:* Dr. Michelle Fanucchi, Chair, 205-934-7230, Fax: 205-975-6341. Web site: http://www.uab.edu/PublicHealth/.

University of Alberta, School of Public Health, Department of Public Health Sciences, Edmonton, AB T6G 2E1, Canada. Offers clinical epidemiology (M Sc, MPH); environmental and occupational health (MPH); environmental health sciences (M Sc); epidemiology (M Sc); global health (M Sc, MPH); health policy and management (MPH); health policy research (M Sc); health technology assessment (MPH); occupational health (M Sc); population health (M Sc); public health leadership (MPH); public health sciences (PhD); quantitative methods (MPH). *Accreditation:* CEPH (one or more programs are accredited). Terminal master's awarded for partial completion of doctoral program. *Degree requirements:* For master's, thesis (for some programs); for doctorate, thesis/dissertation. *Entrance requirements:* For master's, GMAT or GRE General Test. Additional exam requirements/recommendations for international students: Required—TOEFL (minimum score 550 paper-based; 213 computer-based) or IELTS (minimum score 6). Electronic applications accepted. *Faculty research:* Biostatistics, health promotion and socio-behavioral health science.

University of Arkansas for Medical Sciences, Graduate School, Occupational and Environmental Health Program, Little Rock, AR 72205-7199. Offers MS, Certificate. Offered jointly with the University of Arkansas at Little Rock and the National Center for Toxicological Research. *Accreditation:* CEPH. *Degree requirements:* For master's, thesis or alternative. *Entrance requirements:* For master's, GRE General Test. Additional exam requirements/recommendations for international students: Required—TOEFL.

The University of British Columbia, School of Environmental Health, Vancouver, BC V6T 1Z1, Canada. Offers M Sc, PhD. Part-time programs available. *Degree requirements:* For master's, comprehensive exam (for some programs), thesis optional; for doctorate, comprehensive exam, thesis/dissertation. *Entrance requirements:* For master's and doctorate, GRE. Additional exam requirements/recommendations for international students: Required—TOEFL (minimum score 600 paper-based; 250 computer-based; 100 iBT); Recommended—TWE. Electronic applications accepted. *Faculty research:* Acoustics, exposure assessment and epidemiology, occupational and environmental respiratory disease, occupational and environmental policy.

University of California, Berkeley, Graduate Division, School of Public Health, Group in Environmental Health Sciences, Berkeley, CA 94720-1500. Offers MPH, MS, Dr PH, PhD. *Degree requirements:* For master's, comprehensive exam (MPH), project or thesis (MS); for doctorate, thesis/dissertation, departmental and qualifying exams. *Entrance requirements:* For master's, GRE General Test, minimum GPA of 3.0; previous course work in biology, calculus, and chemistry; 3 letters of recommendation; for doctorate, GRE General Test, master's degree in relevant scientific discipline or engineering; minimum GPA of 3.0; previous course work in biology, calculus, and chemistry; 3 letters of recommendation. Additional exam requirements/recommendations for international students: Required—TOEFL. *Faculty research:* Toxicology, industrial hygiene, exposure assessment, risk assessment, ergonomics.

University of California, Los Angeles, Graduate Division, School of Public Health, Department of Environmental Health Sciences, Los Angeles, CA 90095. Offers environmental health sciences (MS, PhD); environmental science and engineering (D Env); molecular toxicology (PhD); JD/MPH. *Accreditation:* ABET (one or more programs are accredited). *Degree requirements:* For master's, comprehensive exam or thesis; for doctorate, thesis/dissertation, oral and written qualifying exams. *Entrance requirements:* For master's, GRE General Test, minimum GPA of 3.0; for doctorate, GRE General Test, minimum undergraduate GPA of 3.0. Electronic applications accepted.

University of Central Missouri, The Graduate School, College of Health and Human Services, Warrensburg, MO 64093. Offers criminal justice (MS); industrial hygiene (MS); occupational safety management (MS); physical education/exercise and sport science (MS); rural family nursing (MS); social gerontology (MS); sociology (MA); speech language pathology and audiology (MS). *Accreditation:* NCATE. Part-time programs available. Postbaccalaureate distance learning degree programs offered. *Entrance requirements:* Additional exam requirements/recommendations for international students: Required—TOEFL (minimum score 550 paper-based; 79 computer-based). Electronic applications accepted.

University of Cincinnati, Graduate School, College of Medicine, Graduate Programs in Biomedical Sciences, Department of Environmental Health, Cincinnati, OH 45221. Offers environmental and industrial hygiene (MS, PhD); environmental and occupational medicine (MS); environmental genetics and molecular toxicology (MS, PhD); epidemiology and biostatistics (MS, PhD); occupational safety and ergonomics (MS, PhD). *Accreditation:* ABET (one or more programs are accredited). Terminal master's awarded for partial completion of doctoral program. *Degree requirements:* For master's, thesis; for doctorate, thesis/dissertation, qualifying exam. *Entrance requirements:* For master's, GRE General Test, bachelor's degree in science; for doctorate, GRE General Test. Additional exam requirements/recommendations for international students: Required—TOEFL (minimum score 600 paper-based; 250 computer-based; 100 iBT). Electronic applications accepted. *Faculty research:* Carcinogens and mutagenesis, pulmonary studies, reproduction and development.

University of Colorado Denver, College of Liberal Arts and Sciences, Department of Geography and Environmental Sciences, Denver, CO 80217. Offers environmental sciences (MS), including air quality, ecosystems, environmental health, environmental science education, geo-spatial analysis, hazardous waste, water quality. Part-time and evening/weekend programs available. *Students:* 42 full-time (25 women), 6 part-time (5 women); includes 6 minority (2 Black or African American, non-Hispanic/Latino; 1 Asian, non-Hispanic/Latino; 2 Hispanic/Latino; 1 Two or more races, non-Hispanic/Latino), 10 international. Average age 29. 31 applicants, 68% accepted, 13 enrolled. In 2011, 24 master's awarded. *Degree requirements:* For master's, thesis or alternative, 30 credits including 21 of core requirements and 9 of environmental science electives. *Entrance requirements:* For master's, GRE General Test, BA in one of the natural/physical sciences or engineering (or equivalent background); prerequisite coursework in calculus and physics (one semester each), general chemistry with lab and general biology with lab (two semesters each), three letters of recommendation. Additional exam requirements/recommendations for international students: Required—TOEFL (minimum score 525 paper-based; 197 computer-based). *Application deadline:* For fall admission, 4/1 for domestic and international students; for spring admission, 10/1 for domestic and international students. Application fee: $50 ($75 for international students). Electronic applications accepted. *Financial support:* Research assistantships, teaching assistantships, and Federal Work-Study available. Financial award application deadline: 4/1; financial award applicants required to submit FAFSA. *Faculty research:* Air quality, environmental health, ecosystems, hazardous waste, water quality, geo-spatial analysis and environmental science education. *Unit head:* Dr. Brian K. Page, Department Chair, 303-556-8332, Fax: 303-556-6197, E-mail: john.wyckoff@cudenver.edu. *Application contact:* Sue Eddleman, Program Assistant, 303-556-6197, E-mail: sue.eddleman@ucdenver.edu. Web site: http://www.ucdenver.edu/academics/colleges/CLAS/Departments/ges/Pages/Geography.aspx.

University of Colorado Denver, Colorado School of Public Health, Program in Public Health, Aurora, CO 80045. Offers community and behavioral health (MPH, Dr PH); environmental and occupational health (MPH); epidemiology (MPH); health systems, management and policy (MPH). *Accreditation:* CEPH. Part-time and evening/weekend programs available. *Students:* 216 full-time (177 women), 47 part-time (38 women); includes 48 minority (10 Black or African American, non-Hispanic/Latino; 5 American Indian or Alaska Native, non-Hispanic/Latino; 14 Asian, non-Hispanic/Latino; 17 Hispanic/Latino; 1 Native Hawaiian or other Pacific Islander, non-Hispanic/Latino; 1 Two or more races, non-Hispanic/Latino), 7 international. Average age 33. 670 applicants, 51% accepted, 160 enrolled. In 2011, 83 degrees awarded. *Degree requirements:* For master's, thesis or alternative, 42 credit hours; for doctorate, comprehensive exam, thesis/dissertation, 67 credit hours. *Entrance requirements:* For master's, GRE, baccalaureate degree or equivalent; minimum GPA of 3.0; transcripts; references; resume; essay; for doctorate, GRE, MPH or master's or higher degree in related field or equivalent; 2 years previous work experience in public health, essay, resume. Additional exam requirements/recommendations for international students: Required—TOEFL (minimum score 550 paper-based; 213 computer-based). *Application deadline:* For fall admission, 2/1 for domestic students. Application fee: $65. Electronic applications accepted. *Expenses:* Contact institution. *Financial support:* Fellowships, research assistantships, Federal Work-Study, scholarships/grants, and unspecified assistantships available. Support available to part-time students. Financial award application deadline: 3/15; financial award applicants required to submit FAFSA. *Faculty research:* Cancer prevention by nutrition, cancer survivorship outcomes, social and cultural factors related to health. *Unit head:* Dr. Jack Barnette, Program Director, 303-724-4472, E-mail: jack.barnette@ucdenver.edu. *Application contact:* Jennifer Pacheco, Admissions Specialist, 303-724-5585, E-mail: jennifer.pacheco@ucdenver.edu. Web site: http://www.ucdenver.edu/academics/colleges/PublicHealth/departments/CommunityBehavioralHealth/Pages/CommunityBehavioralHealth.aspx.

University of Connecticut, Graduate School, Center for Continuing Studies, Program in Occupational Safety and Health Management, Storrs, CT 06269. Offers MPS.

University of Denver, University College, Denver, CO 80208. Offers arts and culture (MLS, Certificate), including art, literature, and culture, arts development and program management (Certificate), creative writing; environmental policy and management (MAS, Certificate), including energy and sustainability (Certificate), environmental assessment of nuclear power (Certificate), environmental health and safety (Certificate), environmental management, natural resource management (Certificate); geographic information systems (MAS, Certificate); global affairs (MLS, Certificate), including translation studies, world history and culture; healthcare leadership (MPH, Certificate), including healthcare policy, law, and ethics, medical and healthcare information technologies, strategic management of healthcare; information and communications technology (MCIS, Certificate), including database design and administration (Certificate), geographic information systems (MCIS), information security systems security (Certificate), information systems security (MCIS), project management (MCIS, MPS, Certificate), software design and administration (Certificate), software design and programming (MCIS), technology management, telecommunications technology (MCIS), Web design and development; leadership and organizations (MPS, Certificate), including human capital in organizations, philanthropic leadership, project management (MCIS, MPS, Certificate), strategic innovation and change; organizational and professional communication (MPS, Certificate), including alternative dispute resolution, organizational communication, organizational development and training, public relations and marketing; security management (MAS, Certificate), including emergency planning and response, information security (MAS), organizational security; strategic human

resource management (MPS, Certificate), including global human resources (MPS), human resource management and development (MPS). Part-time and evening/weekend programs available. Postbaccalaureate distance learning degree programs offered (no on-campus study). *Faculty:* 204 part-time/adjunct (80 women). *Students:* 56 full-time (26 women), 1,096 part-time (647 women); includes 196 minority (81 Black or African American, non-Hispanic/Latino; 7 American Indian or Alaska Native, non-Hispanic/Latino; 30 Asian, non-Hispanic/Latino; 66 Hispanic/Latino; 3 Native Hawaiian or other Pacific Islander, non-Hispanic/Latino; 9 Two or more races, non-Hispanic/Latino), 76 international. Average age 36. 572 applicants, 95% accepted, 410 enrolled. In 2011, 404 master's, 123 other advanced degrees awarded. *Degree requirements:* For master's, capstone project. *Entrance requirements:* For master's, two letters of recommendation, personal statement, resume. Additional exam requirements/recommendations for international students: Required—TOEFL (minimum score 550 paper-based; 80 iBT). *Application deadline:* For fall admission, 7/20 priority date for domestic students, 6/8 for international students; for winter admission, 10/26 priority date for domestic students, 9/14 for international students; for spring admission, 2/1 priority date for domestic students, 12/14 for international students. Applications are processed on a rolling basis. Application fee: $75. Electronic applications accepted. *Expenses:* Contact institution. *Financial support:* Applicants required to submit FAFSA. *Unit head:* Dr. James Davis, Dean, 303-871-2291, Fax: 303-871-4047, E-mail: jdavis@du.edu. *Application contact:* Information Contact, 303-871-3155, Fax: 303-871-4047, E-mail: ucolinfo@du.edu. Web site: http://www.universitycollege.du.edu/.

University of Florida, Graduate School, College of Public Health and Health Professions, Programs in Public Health, Gainesville, FL 32611. Offers biostatistics (MPH); environmental health (MPH); epidemiology (MPH); public health management and policy (MPH); public health practice (MPH); social and behavioral sciences (MPH). *Accreditation:* CEPH. Postbaccalaureate distance learning degree programs offered. *Students:* 76 full-time (57 women), 21 part-time (13 women); includes 33 minority (15 Black or African American, non-Hispanic/Latino; 12 Asian, non-Hispanic/Latino; 6 Hispanic/Latino), 7 international. Average age 30. 313 applicants, 49% accepted, 63 enrolled. In 2011, 66 master's awarded. *Degree requirements:* For master's, internship. *Entrance requirements:* For master's, GRE General Test, minimum GPA of 3.0. Additional exam requirements/recommendations for international students: Required—TOEFL (minimum score 550 paper-based; 213 computer-based; 80 iBT), IELTS (minimum score 6). Application fee: $30. *Financial support:* In 2011–12, 14 students received support, including 1 fellowship, 11 research assistantships, 2 teaching assistantships. Financial award applicants required to submit FAFSA. *Unit head:* Mary Peoples Sheps, Senior Associate Dean for Public Health, 352-273-6084, Fax: 352-273-6448, E-mail: mpeoplessheps@phhp.ufl.edu. Web site: http://www.mph.ufl.edu/.

University of Georgia, College of Public Health, Department of Environmental Health Science, Athens, GA 30602. Offers MPH, MSEH. *Accreditation:* CEPH. *Faculty:* 6 full-time (2 women), 1 (woman) part-time/adjunct. *Students:* 19 full-time (11 women), 1 part-time (0 women); includes 3 minority (1 Black or African American, non-Hispanic/Latino; 1 Asian, non-Hispanic/Latino; 1 Two or more races, non-Hispanic/Latino), 7 international. Average age 29. 23 applicants, 35% accepted, 6 enrolled. In 2011, 1 master's awarded. Terminal master's awarded for partial completion of doctoral program. *Degree requirements:* For master's, thesis. *Entrance requirements:* For master's, GRE General Test. Additional exam requirements/recommendations for international students: Required—TOEFL. *Application deadline:* For fall admission, 3/1 priority date for domestic students; for spring admission, 11/15 for domestic students. Application fee: $50. Electronic applications accepted. *Financial support:* Research assistantships with full tuition reimbursements available. *Faculty research:* Risk assessment, environmental toxicology, water quality, air quality. *Unit head:* Dr. Jia-Sheng Wang, Head, 706-542-2454, Fax: 706-542-7472, E-mail: jswang@uga.edu. *Application contact:* Dr. Erin K. Lipp, Graduate Coordinator, 706-543-8138, Fax: 706-542-7472, E-mail: mblack@uga.edu. Web site: http://www.uga.edu/publichealth/ehs/.

University of Illinois at Chicago, Graduate College, School of Public Health, Division of Environmental and Occupational Health Sciences, Chicago, IL 60607-7128. Offers MPH, MS, Dr PH, PhD. *Accreditation:* ABET (one or more programs are accredited); CEPH (one or more programs are accredited). Part-time programs available. Terminal master's awarded for partial completion of doctoral program. *Degree requirements:* For master's, thesis, field practicum; for doctorate, thesis/dissertation, independent research, internship. *Entrance requirements:* For master's and doctorate, GRE General Test, minimum GPA of 2.75. Additional exam requirements/recommendations for international students: Required—TOEFL. Electronic applications accepted.

The University of Iowa, Graduate College, College of Public Health, Department of Occupational and Environmental Health, Iowa City, IA 52242-1316. Offers MS, PhD, Certificate, MS/MA, MS/MS. *Accreditation:* ABET (one or more programs are accredited); CEPH. *Degree requirements:* For master's, thesis optional, exam; for doctorate, comprehensive exam, thesis/dissertation. *Entrance requirements:* For master's and doctorate, GRE General Test, minimum GPA of 3.0. Additional exam requirements/recommendations for international students: Required—TOEFL (minimum score 600 paper-based; 250 computer-based; 100 iBT). Electronic applications accepted.

The University of Kansas, University of Kansas Medical Center, School of Medicine, Department of Preventive Medicine and Public Health, Kansas City, KS 66160. Offers biostatistics (MPH); clinical research (MS); environmental health sciences (MPH); epidemiology (MPH); public health management (MPH); social and behavioral health (MPH); MD/MPH; MPH/MSN; PhD/MPH. Part-time programs available. *Faculty:* 76. *Students:* 51 full-time (32 women), 74 part-time (53 women); includes 35 minority (10 Black or African American, non-Hispanic/Latino; 4 American Indian or Alaska Native, non-Hispanic/Latino; 9 Asian, non-Hispanic/Latino; 8 Hispanic/Latino; 4 Two or more races, non-Hispanic/Latino), 6 international. Average age 33. 77 applicants, 69% accepted, 45 enrolled. In 2011, 25 master's awarded. *Degree requirements:* For master's, thesis, capstone practicum defense. *Entrance requirements:* For master's, GRE, MCAT, LSAT, GMAT or other equivalent graduate professional exam. Additional exam requirements/recommendations for international students: Required—TOEFL. *Application deadline:* For fall admission, 3/1 for domestic and international students. Applications are processed on a rolling basis. Application fee: $60. Tuition and fees vary according to course load, campus/location, program and reciprocity agreements. *Financial support:* In 2011–12, 21 research assistantships (averaging $10,200 per year) were awarded; career-related internships or fieldwork, Federal Work-Study, scholarships/grants, and unspecified assistantships also available. Financial award application deadline: 2/14; financial award applicants required to submit FAFSA. *Faculty research:* Cancer screening and prevention, smoking cessation, obesity and physical activity, health services/outcomes research. *Total annual research expenditures:* $8 million. *Unit head:* Dr. Edward F. Ellerbeck, Chairman, 913-588-2774, Fax: 913-588-2780, E-mail: eellerbe@kumc.edu. *Application contact:* Tanya Honderick, Assistant Director, KU-MPH, 913-588-2720, Fax: 913-588-8505, E-mail: thonderick@kumc.edu. Web site: http://ph.kumc.edu/.

University of Louisville, Graduate School, School of Public Health and Information Sciences, Department of Environmental and Occupational Health Sciences, Louisville, KY 40202. Offers environmental and occupational health sciences (MPH); public health (PhD), including environmental health. *Accreditation:* CEPH. *Degree requirements:* For doctorate, comprehensive exam, thesis/dissertation. *Entrance requirements:* For doctorate, GRE (50th percentile), official transcripts, statement of purpose, resume/curriculum vitae, master's degree or better, 3 letters of recommendation, minimum GPA of 3.0. Additional exam requirements/recommendations for international students: Required—TOEFL (minimum score 600 paper-based; 250 computer-based; 100 iBT). Electronic applications accepted. *Expenses:* Tuition, state resident: full-time $9692; part-time $539 per credit hour. Tuition, nonresident: full-time $20,168; part-time $1121 per credit hour. Tuition and fees vary according to program and reciprocity agreements.

University of Maryland, College Park, Academic Affairs, School of Public Health, MD Institute for Applied Environmental Health, College Park, MD 20742. Offers environmental health sciences (MPH). *Faculty:* 4 full-time (2 women), 1 part-time/adjunct (0 women). *Students:* 15 full-time (11 women), 3 part-time (all women); includes 5 minority (3 Black or African American, non-Hispanic/Latino; 1 Asian, non-Hispanic/Latino; 1 Two or more races, non-Hispanic/Latino), 2 international. 47 applicants, 28% accepted, 6 enrolled. In 2011, 4 master's awarded. *Entrance requirements:* For master's, GRE General Test, 3 letters of recommendation, minimum undergraduate GPA of 3.0, undergraduate transcripts, statement of goals and interests. *Application deadline:* For fall admission, 1/15 for domestic and international students. Applications are processed on a rolling basis. Application fee: $75. Electronic applications accepted. *Expenses:* Tuition, state resident: part-time $525 per credit hour. Tuition, nonresident: part-time $1131 per credit hour. *Required fees:* $386.31 per term. Tuition and fees vary according to program. *Financial support:* In 2011–12, 1 research assistantship (averaging $15,878 per year), 7 teaching assistantships (averaging $16,297 per year) were awarded; fellowships also available. Financial award applicants required to submit FAFSA. *Total annual research expenditures:* $813,413. *Unit head:* Donald Milton, Director, 301-405-0389, E-mail: dmilton@umd.edu. *Application contact:* Dr. Charles A. Caramello, Dean of Graduate School, 301-405-0358, Fax: 301-314-9305. Web site: http://sph.umd.edu/miaeh/.

University of Massachusetts Amherst, Graduate School, School of Public Health and Health Sciences, Department of Public Health, Amherst, MA 01003. Offers biostatistics (MPH, MS, PhD); community health education (MPH, MS, PhD); environmental health sciences (MPH, MS, PhD); epidemiology (MPH, MS, PhD); health policy and management (MPH, MS, PhD); nutrition (MPH, PhD); public health practice (MPH); MPH/MPPA. *Accreditation:* CEPH (one or more programs are accredited). Part-time and evening/weekend programs available. Postbaccalaureate distance learning degree programs offered (no on-campus study). *Faculty:* 46 full-time (26 women). *Students:* 118 full-time (88 women), 249 part-time (183 women); includes 75 minority (28 Black or African American, non-Hispanic/Latino; 21 Asian, non-Hispanic/Latino; 20 Hispanic/Latino; 6 Two or more races, non-Hispanic/Latino), 55 international. Average age 36. 377 applicants, 67% accepted, 91 enrolled. In 2011, 83 master's, 4 doctorates awarded. Terminal master's awarded for partial completion of doctoral program. *Degree requirements:* For master's, thesis (for some programs); for doctorate, comprehensive exam, thesis/dissertation. *Entrance requirements:* For master's and doctorate, GRE General Test. Additional exam requirements/recommendations for international students: Required—TOEFL (minimum score 550 paper-based; 213 computer-based; 80 iBT), IELTS (minimum score 6.5). *Application deadline:* For fall admission, 2/1 for domestic and international students. Applications are processed on a rolling basis. Application fee: $40 ($65 for international students). Electronic applications accepted. Tuition and fees vary according to course load, campus/location and program. *Financial support:* Fellowships with full and partial tuition reimbursements, research assistantships with full and partial tuition reimbursements, teaching assistantships with full and partial tuition reimbursements, career-related internships or fieldwork, Federal Work-Study, scholarships/grants, traineeships, health care benefits, tuition waivers (full and partial), and unspecified assistantships available. Support available to part-time students. Financial award application deadline: 2/1. *Unit head:* Dr. Paula Stamps, Graduate Program Director, 413-545-2861, Fax: 413-545-1645. *Application contact:* Lindsay DeSantis, Interim Supervisor of Admissions, 413-545-0722, Fax: 413-577-0010, E-mail: gradadm@grad.umass.edu. Web site: http://www.umass.edu/sphhs/public_health/.

University of Medicine and Dentistry of New Jersey, UMDNJ–School of Public Health (UMDNJ, Rutgers, NJIT) Piscataway/New Brunswick Campus, Piscataway, NJ 08854. Offers biostatistics (MPH, MS, Dr PH, PhD); clinical epidemiology (Certificate); environmental and occupational health (MPH, Dr PH, PhD, Certificate); epidemiology (MPH, Dr PH, PhD); general public health (Certificate); health education and behavioral science (MPH, Dr PH, PhD); health systems and policy (MPH, PhD); public health preparedness (Certificate); DO/MPH; JD/MPH; MD/MPH; MPH/MBA; MPH/MSPA; MS/MPH; Psy D/MPH. *Accreditation:* CEPH. Part-time and evening/weekend programs available. *Degree requirements:* For master's, thesis, internship; for doctorate, comprehensive exam, thesis/dissertation. *Entrance requirements:* For master's, GRE General Test; for doctorate, GRE General Test, MPH (Dr PH); MA, MPH, or MS (PhD). Additional exam requirements/recommendations for international students: Required—TOEFL. Electronic applications accepted.

University of Memphis, Graduate School, School of Public Health, Memphis, TN 38152. Offers biostatistics (MPH); environmental health (MPH); epidemiology (MPH); health systems management (MPH); public health (MHA); social and behavioral sciences (MPH). Part-time and evening/weekend programs available. Postbaccalaureate distance learning degree programs offered. *Degree requirements:* For master's, comprehensive exam, thesis. *Entrance requirements:* For master's, GRE, letters of recommendation. Additional exam requirements/recommendations for international students: Required—TOEFL. Electronic applications accepted. *Faculty research:* Health and medical savings accounts, adoption rates, health informatics, Telehealth technologies, biostatistics, environmental health, epidemiology, health systems management, social and behavioral sciences.

University of Miami, Graduate School, College of Engineering, Department of Industrial Engineering, Program in Occupational Ergonomics and Safety, Coral Gables, FL 33124. Offers environmental health and safety (MS); occupational ergonomics and safety (MSOES). Part-time programs available. *Degree requirements:* For master's, thesis optional. *Entrance requirements:* For master's, GRE General Test, minimum GPA of 3.0. Additional exam requirements/recommendations for international students: Required—TOEFL (minimum score 550 paper-based; 213 computer-based). Electronic applications accepted. *Faculty research:* Noise, heat stress, water pollution.

University of Michigan, School of Public Health, Department of Environmental Health Sciences, Ann Arbor, MI 48109. Offers environmental health sciences (MS, PhD); environmental quality and health (MPH); human nutrition (MPH); industrial hygiene (MPH, MS); nutritional sciences (MS); occupational and environmental epidemiology (MPH); toxicology (MPH, MS, PhD). *Accreditation:* CEPH (one or more programs are accredited). Part-time programs available. Terminal master's awarded for partial completion of doctoral program. *Degree requirements:* For master's, thesis (for some programs); for doctorate, thesis/dissertation, preliminary exam, oral defense of dissertation. *Entrance requirements:* For master's and doctorate, GRE General Test and/or MCAT. Additional exam requirements/recommendations for international students: Required—TOEFL (minimum score 560 paper-based; 220 computer-based;

100 iBT). Electronic applications accepted. *Faculty research:* Toxicology, occupational hygiene, nutrition, environmental exposure sciences, environmental epidemiology.

University of Minnesota, Twin Cities Campus, School of Public Health, Division of Environmental Health Sciences, Area in Environmental Health Policy, Minneapolis, MN 55455-0213. Offers MPH, MS, PhD. *Accreditation:* CEPH (one or more programs are accredited). *Degree requirements:* For doctorate, thesis/dissertation. *Entrance requirements:* For master's and doctorate, GRE General Test. Electronic applications accepted.

University of Minnesota, Twin Cities Campus, School of Public Health, Division of Environmental Health Sciences, Area in Occupational Medicine, Minneapolis, MN 55455-0213. Offers MPH. *Accreditation:* CEPH. *Entrance requirements:* For master's, GRE General Test. Electronic applications accepted.

University of Minnesota, Twin Cities Campus, School of Public Health, Major in Public Health Practice, Minneapolis, MN 55455-0213. Offers core concepts (Certificate); food safety and biosecurity (Certificate); occupational health and safety (Certificate); preparedness, response and recovery (Certificate); public health practice (MPH); DVM/MPH; MD/MPH. Part-time programs available. Postbaccalaureate distance learning degree programs offered (no on-campus study). *Degree requirements:* For master's, thesis. *Entrance requirements:* For master's, GRE, MCAT, United States Medical Licensing Exam. Additional exam requirements/recommendations for international students: Required—TOEFL (minimum score 600 paper-based; 250 computer-based). Electronic applications accepted.

University of Nevada, Reno, Graduate School, Interdisciplinary Program in Environmental Sciences and Health, Reno, NV 89557. Offers MS, PhD. Terminal master's awarded for partial completion of doctoral program. *Degree requirements:* For master's, thesis; for doctorate, thesis/dissertation. *Entrance requirements:* For master's, GRE General Test, minimum GPA of 2.75; for doctorate, GRE General Test, minimum GPA of 3.0. Additional exam requirements/recommendations for international students: Required—TOEFL (minimum score 500 paper-based; 173 computer-based; 61 iBT), IELTS (minimum score 6). Electronic applications accepted. *Faculty research:* Environmental chemistry, environmental toxicology, ecological toxicology.

University of New Haven, Graduate School, College of Arts and Sciences, Program in Environmental Sciences, West Haven, CT 06516-1916. Offers environmental geoscience (MS); environmental health and management (MS); environmental science (MS); geographical information systems (Certificate). Part-time and evening/weekend programs available. *Students:* 19 full-time (11 women), 15 part-time (6 women); includes 5 minority (2 Black or African American, non-Hispanic/Latino; 1 Asian, non-Hispanic/Latino; 1 Hispanic/Latino; 1 Two or more races, non-Hispanic/Latino), 7 international. 9 applicants, 100% accepted, 5 enrolled. In 2011, 9 master's awarded. *Degree requirements:* For master's, thesis or alternative. *Application deadline:* For fall admission, 5/31 for international students; for winter admission, 10/15 for international students; for spring admission, 1/15 for international students. Applications are processed on a rolling basis. Application fee: $50. Electronic applications accepted. *Expenses: Tuition:* Part-time $750 per credit. *Financial support:* Research assistantships with partial tuition reimbursements, teaching assistantships with partial tuition reimbursements, career-related internships or fieldwork, Federal Work-Study, scholarships/grants, tuition waivers, and unspecified assistantships available. Support available to part-time students. Financial award applicants required to submit FAFSA. *Faculty research:* Mapping and assessing geological and living resources in Long Island Sound, geology, San Salvador Island, Bahamas. *Unit head:* Dr. Roman Zajac, Coordinator, 203-932-7108, E-mail: rzajac@newhaven.edu. *Application contact:* Eloise Gormley, Director of Graduate Admissions, 203-932-7449, Fax: 203-932-7137, E-mail: gradinfo@newhaven.edu. Web site: http://www.newhaven.edu/4728/.

The University of North Carolina at Chapel Hill, Graduate School, School of Public Health, Department of Environmental Sciences and Engineering, Chapel Hill, NC 27599. Offers air, radiation and industrial hygiene (MPH, MS, MSEE, MSPH, PhD); aquatic and atmospheric sciences (MPH, MS, MSPH, PhD); environmental engineering (MPH, MS, MSEE, MSPH, PhD); environmental health sciences (MPH, MS, MSPH, PhD); environmental management and policy (MPH, MS, MSPH, PhD). Terminal master's awarded for partial completion of doctoral program. *Degree requirements:* For master's, comprehensive exam, thesis (for some programs), research paper; for doctorate, comprehensive exam, thesis/dissertation. *Entrance requirements:* For master's and doctorate, GRE General Test, minimum GPA of 3.0. Additional exam requirements/recommendations for international students: Required—TOEFL. Electronic applications accepted. *Faculty research:* Air, radiation and industrial hygiene, aquatic and atmospheric sciences, environmental health sciences, environmental management and policy, water resources engineering.

University of North Texas Health Science Center at Fort Worth, School of Public Health, Fort Worth, TX 76107-2699. Offers biostatistics (MPH); community health (MPH); disease control and prevention (Dr PH); environmental and occupational health sciences (MPH); epidemiology (MPH); health administration (MHA); health policy and management (MPH, Dr PH); DO/MPH; MS/MPH; MSN/MPH. MPH offered jointly with University of North Texas; DO/MPH with Texas College of Osteopathic Medicine. *Accreditation:* CEPH. Part-time and evening/weekend programs available. *Degree requirements:* For master's, thesis or alternative, supervised internship; for doctorate, thesis/dissertation, supervised internship. *Entrance requirements:* For master's, GRE General Test. Additional exam requirements/recommendations for international students: Required—TOEFL. Electronic applications accepted.

University of Oklahoma Health Sciences Center, Graduate College, College of Public Health, Department of Occupational and Environmental Health, Oklahoma City, OK 73190. Offers MPH, MS, Dr PH, PhD, JD/MPH, JD/MS. JD/MPH, JD/MS offered jointly with University of Oklahoma. *Accreditation:* ABET (one or more programs are accredited); CEPH (one or more programs are accredited). Part-time programs available. *Degree requirements:* For master's, comprehensive exam, thesis (for some programs); for doctorate, comprehensive exam, thesis/dissertation. *Entrance requirements:* For master's, GRE General Test (for all except occupational medicine), 3 letters of recommendation, resume; for doctorate, GRE (for all except occupational medicine), 3 letters of recommendation, resume. Additional exam requirements/recommendations for international students: Required—TOEFL (minimum score 570 paper-based; 230 computer-based). *Faculty research:* Environmental safety, accident prevention and injury control.

University of Pennsylvania, Perelman School of Medicine, Master of Public Health Program, Philadelphia, PA 19129. Offers environmental health (MPH); generalist (MPH); global health (MPH); DMD/MPH; JD/MPH; MD/MPH; MPH/MBE; MSCE/MPH; MSN/MPH; MSW/MPH; PhD/MPH. Part-time and evening/weekend programs available. *Faculty:* 30 full-time (18 women), 35 part-time/adjunct (19 women). *Students:* 34 full-time (29 women), 28 part-time (24 women); includes 11 minority (3 Black or African American, non-Hispanic/Latino; 6 Asian, non-Hispanic/Latino; 2 Hispanic/Latino), 2 international. 182 applicants, 25% accepted, 27 enrolled. In 2011, 18 master's awarded. *Entrance requirements:* For master's, GRE. Additional exam requirements/recommendations for international students: Recommended—TOEFL. *Application deadline:* For spring admission, 4/30 for domestic and international students. Application fee: $70. *Expenses: Tuition:* Full-time $26,660; part-time $4944 per course. *Required fees:* $2318; $291 per course. Tuition and fees vary according to course load, degree level and program. *Financial support:* In 2011–12, 4 teaching assistantships with partial tuition reimbursements were awarded; fellowships, scholarships/grants, and tuition waivers (partial) also available. Financial award application deadline: 4/30. *Faculty research:* Health disparities, health behaviors, obesity, global health, epidemiology and prevention research. *Unit head:* Dr. Jennifer A. Pinto-Martin, Director, 215-898-4726, E-mail: pinto@nursing.upenn.edu. *Application contact:* Karen Kelly, Admission Coordinator, 215-573-0917, Fax: 215-573-9025, E-mail: kakelly@mail.med.upenn.edu. Web site: http://www.publichealth.med.upenn.edu/.

University of Pittsburgh, Graduate School of Public Health, Department of Environmental and Occupational Health, Pittsburgh, PA 15260. Offers environmental and occupational health (MPH, MS, Dr PH, PhD); environmental health risk assessment (Certificate); public health preparedness (Certificate). *Accreditation:* CEPH (one or more programs are accredited). Part-time programs available. *Faculty:* 27 full-time (10 women), 19 part-time/adjunct (4 women). *Students:* 27 full-time (13 women), 19 part-time (13 women); includes 2 minority (1 Asian, non-Hispanic/Latino; 1 Two or more races, non-Hispanic/Latino), 14 international. Average age 31. 59 applicants, 63% accepted, 10 enrolled. In 2011, 6 master's, 6 doctorates awarded. Terminal master's awarded for partial completion of doctoral program. *Degree requirements:* For master's, comprehensive exam (for some programs), thesis; for doctorate, comprehensive exam, thesis/dissertation, preliminary exams. *Entrance requirements:* For master's and Certificate, GRE General Test; for doctorate, GRE General Test, minimum GPA of 3.4; background in biology, physics, chemistry and calculus. Additional exam requirements/recommendations for international students: Required—TOEFL (minimum score 550 paper-based; 80 iBT) or IELTS (minimum score 6.5). *Application deadline:* For fall admission, 1/4 priority date for domestic students, 1/4 for international students; for winter admission, 11/1 priority date for domestic students, 8/1 for international students; for spring admission, 3/1 priority date for domestic students, 2/1 for international students. Applications are processed on a rolling basis. Application fee: $115. Electronic applications accepted. *Expenses:* Tuition, state resident: full-time $18,774; part-time $760 per credit. Tuition, nonresident: full-time $30,736; part-time $1258 per credit. *Required fees:* $740; $200 per term. Tuition and fees vary according to program. *Financial support:* In 2011–12, 17 students received support, including 2 fellowships (averaging $2,431 per year), 14 research assistantships (averaging $10,682 per year), 1 teaching assistantship (averaging $11,426 per year); career-related internships or fieldwork, scholarships/grants, traineeships, health care benefits, and unspecified assistantships also available. Support available to part-time students. *Faculty research:* Molecular toxicology, redox signaling, gene environment interaction, progenitor-progeny lineage, occupational and pulmonary medicine. *Total annual research expenditures:* $8.2 million. *Unit head:* Dr. Bruce R. Pitt, Chairman, 412-383-8400, Fax: 412-383-7658, E-mail: brucep@pitt.edu. *Application contact:* Eileen Penny Weiss, Student Affairs Administrator, 412-383-7297, Fax: 412-383-7658, E-mail: pweiss@pitt.edu. Web site: http://www.eoh.pitt.edu/.

University of Puerto Rico, Medical Sciences Campus, Graduate School of Public Health, Department of Environmental Health, Doctoral Program in Environmental Health, San Juan, PR 00936-5067. Offers MS, Dr PH. Part-time programs available. *Expenses:* Contact institution.

University of South Alabama, Graduate School, Program in Environmental Toxicology, Mobile, AL 36688-0002. Offers MS. *Students:* 11 full-time (5 women), 2 part-time (1 woman), 4 international. 11 applicants, 45% accepted, 3 enrolled. In 2011, 4 master's awarded. *Degree requirements:* For master's, thesis. *Entrance requirements:* For master's, GRE. *Application deadline:* For fall admission, 7/15 for domestic students, 6/15 for international students; for spring admission, 12/1 for domestic students, 11/1 for international students. Application fee: $35. *Expenses:* Tuition, state resident: full-time $7968; part-time $332 per credit hour. Tuition, nonresident: full-time $15,936; part-time $664 per credit hour. *Unit head:* Dr. Julio F. Turrens, Director of Graduate Studies, 251-380-2714. *Application contact:* Dr. B. Keith Harrison, Dean of the Graduate School, 251-460-6310, Fax: 251-461-1513, E-mail: kharriso@usouthal.edu.

University of South Carolina, The Graduate School, Arnold School of Public Health, Department of Environmental Health Sciences, Program in Environmental Quality, Columbia, SC 29208. Offers MPH, MS, MSPH, PhD. *Accreditation:* CEPH (one or more programs are accredited). Part-time programs available. *Degree requirements:* For master's, comprehensive exam, thesis (for some programs), practicum (MPH); for doctorate, one foreign language, comprehensive exam, thesis/dissertation. *Entrance requirements:* For master's and doctorate, GRE General Test. Additional exam requirements/recommendations for international students: Required—TOEFL (minimum score 570 paper-based; 230 computer-based). Electronic applications accepted. *Faculty research:* Environmental assessment and planning; environmental toxicology; ecosystems analysis; air quality monitoring and modeling.

University of Southern California, Keck School of Medicine and Graduate School, Graduate Programs in Medicine, Department of Preventive Medicine, Master of Public Health Program, Los Angeles, CA 90032-3628. Offers biostatistics/epidemiology (MPH); child and family health (MPH); environmental health (MPH); global health leadership (MPH); health communication (MPH); health education and promotion (MPH); public health policy (MPH). *Accreditation:* CEPH. Part-time programs available. *Faculty:* 22 full-time (12 women), 3 part-time/adjunct (0 women). *Students:* 148 full-time (115 women), 35 part-time (23 women); includes 100 minority (8 Black or African American, non-Hispanic/Latino; 66 Asian, non-Hispanic/Latino; 26 Hispanic/Latino), 26 international. Average age 24. 218 applicants, 73% accepted, 88 enrolled. In 2011, 91 master's awarded. *Degree requirements:* For master's, practicum, final report, oral presentation. *Entrance requirements:* For master's, GRE General Test, MCAT, GMAT, minimum GPA of 3.0. Additional exam requirements/recommendations for international students: Required—TOEFL (minimum score 600 paper-based; 250 computer-based; 100 iBT). *Application deadline:* For fall admission, 6/1 priority date for domestic students, 6/1 for international students; for spring admission, 11/1 priority date for domestic students, 10/1 for international students. Applications are processed on a rolling basis. Application fee: $85. Electronic applications accepted. *Financial support:* In 2011–12, 148 students received support. Career-related internships or fieldwork, Federal Work-Study, institutionally sponsored loans, and scholarships/grants available. Support available to part-time students. Financial award application deadline: 5/4; financial award applicants required to submit CSS PROFILE or FAFSA. *Faculty research:* Substance abuse prevention, cancer and heart disease prevention, mass media and health communication research, health promotion, treatment compliance. *Unit head:* Dr. Louise A. Rohrbach, Director, 323-442-8237, Fax: 323-442-8297, E-mail: rohrbac@usc.edu. *Application contact:* Chrystal Romero, Admissions Counselor, 323-442-7257, Fax: 323-442-8297, E-mail: ccromero@usc.edu. Web site: http://mph.usc.edu/main.php.

University of Southern Mississippi, Graduate School, College of Health, Department of Community Health Sciences, Hattiesburg, MS 39406-0001. Offers epidemiology and biostatistics (MPH); health education (MPH); health policy/administration (MPH); occupational/environmental health (MPH); public health nutrition (MPH). *Accreditation:* CEPH. Part-time and evening/weekend programs available. *Faculty:* 8 full-time (4 women), 1 part-time/adjunct (0 women). *Students:* 81 full-time (66 women), 17 part-time

(13 women); includes 49 minority (43 Black or African American, non-Hispanic/Latino; 1 Asian, non-Hispanic/Latino; 2 Hispanic/Latino; 3 Two or more races, non-Hispanic/Latino), 7 international. Average age 32. 70 applicants, 94% accepted, 43 enrolled. In 2011, 45 degrees awarded. *Degree requirements:* For master's, comprehensive exam, thesis (for some programs). *Entrance requirements:* For master's, GRE General Test, minimum GPA of 2.75 in last 60 hours. Additional exam requirements/recommendations for international students: Required—TOEFL, IELTS. *Application deadline:* For fall admission, 3/1 priority date for domestic students, 3/1 for international students; for spring admission, 1/10 priority date for domestic students, 1/10 for international students. Applications are processed on a rolling basis. Application fee: $50. Electronic applications accepted. *Financial support:* In 2011–12, 5 research assistantships with full tuition reimbursements (averaging $7,000 per year), 1 teaching assistantship with full tuition reimbursement (averaging $8,263 per year) were awarded; career-related internships or fieldwork, Federal Work-Study, institutionally sponsored loans, scholarships/grants, health care benefits, and unspecified assistantships also available. Financial award application deadline: 3/15; financial award applicants required to submit FAFSA. *Faculty research:* Rural health care delivery, school health, nutrition of pregnant teens, risk factor reduction, sexually transmitted diseases. *Unit head:* Dr. Emanual Ahua, Interim Chair, 601-266-5437, Fax: 601-266-5043. *Application contact:* Shonna Breland, Manager of Graduate Admissions, 601-266-6563, Fax: 601-266-5138. Web site: http://www.usm.edu/chs.

University of South Florida, Graduate School, College of Public Health, Department of Environmental and Occupational Health, Tampa, FL 33620-9951. Offers MPH, MSPH, PhD. *Accreditation:* ABET (one or more programs are accredited); CEPH (one or more programs are accredited). Part-time and evening/weekend programs available. *Degree requirements:* For master's, comprehensive exam, thesis (for some programs); for doctorate, comprehensive exam, thesis/dissertation. *Entrance requirements:* For master's, GRE General Test, minimum GPA of 3.0 in upper-level course work, goal statement letter, two professional letters of recommendation, resume/curriculum vitae; for doctorate, GRE General Test, minimum GPA of 3.0 in upper-level course work, goal statement letter, three professional letters of recommendation, resume/curriculum vitae, writing sample. Additional exam requirements/recommendations for international students: Required—TOEFL (minimum score 550 paper-based; 213 computer-based; 79 iBT). Electronic applications accepted. *Faculty research:* Biomedical assessment/stress test, risk impact, nitrobenzes on mammalism glutathion transferases, lysimeter research management, independent hygiene development.

The University of Texas at Tyler, College of Engineering and Computer Science, Department of Civil Engineering, Tyler, TX 75799-0001. Offers environmental engineering (MS); industrial safety (MS); structural engineering (MS); transportation engineering (MS); water resources engineering (MS). Part-time and evening/weekend programs available. *Degree requirements:* For master's, thesis optional. *Entrance requirements:* For master's, GRE General Test, bachelor's degree in engineering, associated science degree. Additional exam requirements/recommendations for international students: Required—TOEFL (minimum score 79 computer-based). *Faculty research:* Non-destructive strength testing, indoor air quality, transportation routing and signaling, pavement replacement criteria, flood water routing, construction and long-term behavior of innovative geotechnical foundation and embankment construction used in highway construction, engineering education.

University of the Sacred Heart, Graduate Programs, Department of Natural Sciences, Program in Occupational Health and Safety, San Juan, PR 00914-0383. Offers MS.

The University of Toledo, College of Graduate Studies, College of Medicine and Life Sciences, Department of Public Health and Preventative Medicine, Toledo, OH 43606-3390. Offers biostatistics and epidemiology (Certificate); contemporary gerontological practice (Certificate); environmental and occupational health and safety (MPH); epidemiology (MPH, Certificate); global public health (Certificate); health administration (MPH); health promotion (MPH); medical health and science education (Certificate); nutrition (MPH); occupational health (MSOH, Certificate); public health and emergency response (Certificate); MD/MPH. Part-time and evening/weekend programs available. *Faculty:* 6. *Students:* 95 full-time (74 women), 66 part-time (45 women); includes 37 minority (21 Black or African American, non-Hispanic/Latino; 11 Asian, non-Hispanic/Latino; 3 Hispanic/Latino; 2 Two or more races, non-Hispanic/Latino), 6 international. Average age 29. 132 applicants, 75% accepted, 70 enrolled. In 2011, 60 master's, 26 other advanced degrees awarded. *Degree requirements:* For master's, thesis or alternative. *Entrance requirements:* For master's, GRE, minimum undergraduate GPA of 3.0, three letters of recommendation, statement of purpose, transcripts from all prior institutions attended, resume; for Certificate, minimum undergraduate GPA of 3.0, three letters of recommendation, statement of purpose, transcripts from all prior institutions attended, resume. Additional exam requirements/recommendations for international students: Required—TOEFL (minimum score 550 paper-based; 213 computer-based; 80 iBT), IELTS (minimum score 6.5). *Application deadline:* For fall admission, 3/15 for domestic and international students. Applications are processed on a rolling basis. Application fee: $45 ($75 for international students). Electronic applications accepted. *Financial support:* In 2011–12, 15 research assistantships with full tuition reimbursements (averaging $10,000 per year) were awarded; Federal Work-Study, institutionally sponsored loans, scholarships/grants, tuition waivers (full and partial), and unspecified assistantships also available. *Unit head:* Dr. Sheryl A. Milz, Chair, 419-383-3976, Fax: 419-383-6140, E-mail: sheryl.milz@utoledo.edu. *Application contact:* Joan Mulligan, Admissions Analyst, 419-383-4186, Fax: 419-383-6140, E-mail: joan.mulligan@utoledo.edu. Web site: http://nocphmph.org/.

University of Washington, Graduate School, School of Public Health, Department of Environmental and Occupational Health Sciences, Seattle, WA 98195. Offers environmental and occupational health (MPH); environmental and occupational hygiene (PhD); environmental health (MS); occupational and environmental exposure sciences (MS); occupational and environmental medicine (MPH); toxicology (MS, PhD); MPH/MPA; MS/MPA. Part-time programs available. *Faculty:* 31 full-time (4 women), 7 part-time/adjunct (2 women). *Students:* 66 full-time (40 women), 10 part-time (6 women); includes 18 minority (1 Black or African American, non-Hispanic/Latino; 2 American Indian or Alaska Native, non-Hispanic/Latino; 10 Asian, non-Hispanic/Latino; 5 Hispanic/Latino), 4 international. Average age 29. 127 applicants, 36% accepted, 27 enrolled. In 2011, 21 degrees awarded. Terminal master's awarded for partial completion of doctoral program. *Degree requirements:* For master's, comprehensive exam, thesis (for some programs), project or thesis; for doctorate, comprehensive exam, thesis/dissertation. *Entrance requirements:* For master's, GRE General Test, one year each of physics, general chemistry, and biology; two quarters of organic chemistry; one quarter of calculus; for doctorate, GRE General Test, minimum GPA of 3.0, prerequisite course work in biology, chemistry, physics, calculus. Additional exam requirements/recommendations for international students: Required—TOEFL (minimum score 580 paper-based; 237 computer-based; 92 iBT). *Application deadline:* For fall admission, 1/1 for domestic students, 11/1 for international students. Application fee: $75. Electronic applications accepted. *Financial support:* In 2011–12, 72 fellowships with full tuition reimbursements (averaging $42,000 per year), 89 research assistantships with full tuition reimbursements (averaging $42,000 per year), 11 teaching assistantships with full tuition reimbursements (averaging $42,000 per year) were awarded; career-related internships or fieldwork, institutionally sponsored loans, traineeships, health care benefits, and unspecified assistantships also available. Financial award application deadline: 1/1. *Faculty research:* Developmental and behavioral toxicology, biochemical toxicology, exposure assessment, hazardous waste, industrial chemistry. *Unit head:* Dr. David Kalman, Chair, 206-543-6991, Fax: 206-543-0477. *Application contact:* Rory A. Murphy, Manager, Student Services, 206-543-6991, Fax: 206-543-0477, E-mail: ehgrad@u.washington.edu. Web site: http://depts.washington.edu/envhlth/.

University of Washington, Graduate School, School of Public Health, Department of Health Services, Seattle, WA 98195. Offers bioinformatics (PhD); cancer prevention and control (PhD); clinical research (MS); community-oriented public health practice (MPH); economics or finance (PhD); evaluation sciences (PhD); health behavior and health promotion (PhD); health policy research (PhD); health services (MS, PhD); health services administration (EMHA, MHA); health systems policy (MPH); maternal and child health (MPH, PhD); occupational health (PhD); population health and social determinants (PhD); social and behavioral sciences (MPH); sociology and demography (PhD); JD/MHA; MHA/MBA; MHA/MD; MHA/MPA; MPH/JD; MPH/MD; MPH/MN; MPH/MPA; MPH/MS; MPH/MSD; MPH/MSW; MPH/PhD. Part-time and evening/weekend programs available. Postbaccalaureate distance learning degree programs offered (minimal on-campus study). *Faculty:* 40 full-time (23 women), 62 part-time/adjunct (25 women). *Students:* 98 full-time (78 women), 86 part-time (64 women); includes 49 minority (7 Black or African American, non-Hispanic/Latino; 3 American Indian or Alaska Native, non-Hispanic/Latino; 28 Asian, non-Hispanic/Latino; 11 Hispanic/Latino), 3 international. Average age 32. 374 applicants, 49% accepted, 104 enrolled. In 2011, 43 master's, 5 doctorates awarded. Terminal master's awarded for partial completion of doctoral program. *Degree requirements:* For master's, thesis (for some programs), practicum (MPH); for doctorate, comprehensive exam, thesis/dissertation. *Entrance requirements:* For master's and doctorate, GRE General Test, minimum GPA of 3.0. Additional exam requirements/recommendations for international students: Required—TOEFL (minimum score 580 paper-based; 237 computer-based; 92 iBT), IELTS (minimum score 7). *Application deadline:* For fall admission, 1/1 for domestic students, 11/1 for international students. Application fee: 75 Albanian leks. Electronic applications accepted. *Financial support:* In 2011–12, 47 students received support, including 10 fellowships with full and partial tuition reimbursements available (averaging $22,000 per year), 10 research assistantships with full and partial tuition reimbursements available (averaging $18,700 per year), 3 teaching assistantships with full and partial tuition reimbursements available (averaging $4,575 per year); institutionally sponsored loans, traineeships, and health care benefits also available. Financial award application deadline: 2/28; financial award applicants required to submit FAFSA. *Faculty research:* Public health practice, health promotion and disease prevention, maternal and child health, organizational behavior and culture, health policy. *Unit head:* Dr. Larry Kessler, Chair, 206-543-2930. *Application contact:* Kitty A. Andert, MPH/MS/PhD Programs Manager, 206-616-2926, Fax: 206-543-3964, E-mail: kitander@u.washington.edu. Web site: http://depts.washington.edu/hserv/.

University of West Florida, College of Professional Studies, Department of Health, Leisure, and Exercise Science, Community Health Education Program, Pensacola, FL 32514-5750. Offers aging studies (MS); health promotion and worksite wellness (MS); psychosocial (MS). Part-time and evening/weekend programs available. *Faculty:* 3 full-time (1 woman). *Students:* 10 full-time (9 women), 7 part-time (6 women); includes 4 minority (2 Black or African American, non-Hispanic/Latino; 1 Asian, non-Hispanic/Latino; 1 Hispanic/Latino), 1 international. Average age 28. 7 applicants, 71% accepted, 4 enrolled. In 2011, 9 master's awarded. *Degree requirements:* For master's, thesis or alternative. *Entrance requirements:* For master's, GRE or MAT, official transcripts; minimum GPA of 3.0; letter of intent; three personal references. Additional exam requirements/recommendations for international students: Required—TOEFL (minimum score 550 paper-based; 213 computer-based). *Application deadline:* For fall admission, 6/1 for domestic and international students; for spring admission, 10/1 for domestic and international students. Applications are processed on a rolling basis. Application fee: $30. *Expenses:* Tuition, state resident: full-time $5729; part-time $302 per credit hour. Tuition, nonresident: full-time $20,059; part-time $961 per credit hour. *Required fees:* $1509; $63 per credit hour. *Financial support:* Research assistantships, teaching assistantships, and unspecified assistantships available. *Unit head:* Dr. John Todorovich, Chairperson, 850-473-7248, Fax: 850-474-2106. *Application contact:* Terry McCray, Assistant Director of Graduate Admissions, 850-473-7718, Fax: 850-473-7714, E-mail: gradadmissions@uwf.edu.

University of Wisconsin–Milwaukee, Graduate School, Zilber School of Public Health, Department of Environmental and Occupational Health, Milwaukee, WI 53201-0413. Offers PhD. *Students:* 8 full-time (3 women), 2 part-time (1 woman); includes 2 minority (both Asian, non-Hispanic/Latino), 2 international. Average age 38. 15 applicants, 33% accepted, 3 enrolled. One-time fee: $506.10 full-time. Tuition and fees vary according to course load and reciprocity agreements. *Unit head:* Darcie Galowitch, Representative, 414-229-3264, E-mail: darcie@uwm.edu. *Application contact:* Darcie K. G. Warren, Graduate Program Manager, 414-229-5633, E-mail: darcie@uwm.edu.

University of Wisconsin–Whitewater, School of Graduate Studies, College of Education and Professional Studies, Department of Occupational and Environmental Safety, Whitewater, WI 53190-1790. Offers safety (MS). Part-time and evening/weekend programs available. Postbaccalaureate distance learning degree programs offered (no on-campus study). *Students:* 12 full-time (3 women), 15 part-time (6 women); includes 7 minority (3 Black or African American, non-Hispanic/Latino; 1 American Indian or Alaska Native, non-Hispanic/Latino; 2 Asian, non-Hispanic/Latino; 1 Hispanic/Latino). Average age 31. 5 applicants, 80% accepted, 3 enrolled. In 2011, 9 master's awarded. *Degree requirements:* For master's, thesis or alternative. *Entrance requirements:* For master's, 2 letters of recommendation. Additional exam requirements/recommendations for international students: Required—TOEFL (minimum score 550 paper-based; 213 computer-based; 80 iBT), IELTS (minimum score 6). *Application deadline:* For fall admission, 7/15 priority date for domestic students, 7/15 for international students; for spring admission, 12/1 priority date for domestic students, 12/1 for international students. Applications are processed on a rolling basis. Application fee: $56. Electronic applications accepted. *Expenses:* Tuition, state resident: full-time $4088. Tuition, nonresident: full-time $8817. Tuition and fees vary according to program. *Financial support:* Research assistantships, Federal Work-Study, unspecified assistantships, and out-of-state fee waivers available. Support available to part-time students. Financial award application deadline: 3/15; financial award applicants required to submit FAFSA. *Faculty research:* Industrial ergonomics; work, measurement, and design; product design/evaluation. *Unit head:* Dr. Sang Choi, Coordinator, 262-472-5427, Fax: 262-472-1091, E-mail: chios@uww.edu. *Application contact:* Sally A. Lange, School of Graduate Studies, 262-472-1006, Fax: 262-472-5027, E-mail: gradschl@uww.edu.

Wayne State University, Eugene Applebaum College of Pharmacy and Health Sciences, Department of Health Care Sciences, Program in Occupational and Environmental Health Sciences, Detroit, MI 48202. Offers analytical toxicology (Post-Master's Certificate); environmental health and hazardous materials control (Certificate); industrial hygiene (MS); industrial toxicology (MS); occupational safety (Certificate). *Accreditation:* CEPH. *Faculty:* 37 full-time (18 women), 3 part-time/adjunct (0 women). *Students:* 6 full-time (3 women), 15 part-time (8 women); includes 7 minority (4 Black or

African American, non-Hispanic/Latino; 3 Asian, non-Hispanic/Latino), 3 international. Average age 30. 10 applicants, 70% accepted, 5 enrolled. In 2011, 14 master's awarded. *Entrance requirements:* Additional exam requirements/recommendations for international students: Required—TOEFL. *Expenses:* Tuition, state resident: part-time $512.85 per credit. Tuition, nonresident: part-time $1132.65 per credit. *Required fees:* $26.60 per credit. $199.65 per semester. Tuition and fees vary according to course load and program. *Financial support:* Research assistantships available. *Unit head:* Dr. Peter Frade, Chairperson, 313-577-7874, Fax: 313-577-0097, E-mail: ab8123@ wayne.edu. *Application contact:* Peter Warner, Graduate Director, 313-577-1551, E-mail: aa4631@wayne.edu.

Wayne State University, School of Medicine, Department of Family Medicine and Public Health Sciences, Detroit, MI 48202. Offers public health (MPH), including occupational and environmental health, public health practice; public health practice (Certificate). *Students:* 19 full-time (14 women), 23 part-time (13 women); includes 19 minority (3 Black or African American, non-Hispanic/Latino; 14 Asian, non-Hispanic/Latino; 2 Hispanic/Latino), 10 international. Average age 34. 121 applicants, 26% accepted, 18 enrolled. In 2011, 3 master's, 4 other advanced degrees awarded. *Degree requirements:* For master's, thesis (for some programs), project or thesis. *Entrance requirements:* For master's, GRE, undergraduate work in mathematics, natural science, and social science; experience in health-related position; for Certificate, background in a health-related field; background of course work or experience in the areas of mathematics, social science, natural science, and computer usage. Additional exam requirements/recommendations for international students: Required—TOEFL (minimum score 550 paper-based; 213 computer-based; 100 iBT); Recommended—TWE (minimum score 6). *Application deadline:* For fall admission, 2/15 for domestic students, 1/1 for international students. Application fee: $50. Electronic applications accepted. *Expenses:* Tuition, state resident: part-time $512.85 per credit. Tuition, nonresident: part-time $1132.65 per credit. *Required fees:* $26.60 per credit. $199.65 per semester. Tuition and fees vary according to course load and program. *Financial support:* In 2011–12, 11 students received support. Scholarships/grants available. *Faculty research:* Urban health disparities, community health promotion, substance abuse etiology and prevention, HIV/AIDS, interpersonal violence. *Unit head:* Dr. Richard Severson, Program Director, 313-577-1051. *Application contact:* Dr. Kimberly Campbell-

Voytal, Graduate Student Officer, 313-577-1051, E-mail: mphprogram@ med.wayne.edu. Web site: http://www.med.wayne.edu/fam/.

West Virginia University, College of Engineering and Mineral Resources, Department of Industrial and Management Systems Engineering, Program in Occupational Safety and Health, Morgantown, WV 26506. Offers PhD. Part-time programs available. Postbaccalaureate distance learning degree programs offered (minimal on-campus study). *Degree requirements:* For doctorate, comprehensive exam, thesis/dissertation. *Entrance requirements:* For doctorate, GRE General Test, Minimum GPA of 3.5. Additional exam requirements/recommendations for international students: Required—TOEFL. *Faculty research:* Safety management, ergonomics and workplace design, safety and health training, construction safety.

Yale University, School of Medicine, Yale School of Public Health, New Haven, CT 06520. Offers applied biostatistics and epidemiology (APMPH); biostatistics (MPH, MS, PhD), including global health (MPH); chronic disease epidemiology (MPH, PhD), including global health (MPH); environmental health sciences (MPH, PhD), including global health (MPH); epidemiology of microbial diseases (MPH, PhD), including global health (MPH); global health (APMPH); health management (MPH), including global health; health policy (MPH), including global health; health policy and administration (APMPH, PhD); occupational and environmental medicine (APMPH); preventive medicine (APMPH); social and behavioral sciences (APMPH, MPH), including global health (MPH); JD/MPH; M Div/MPH; MBA/MPH; MD/MPH; MEM/MPH; MFS/MPH; MM Sc/MPH; MPH/MA; MSN/MPH. MS and PhD offered through the Graduate School. *Accreditation:* CEPH. Part-time programs available. Terminal master's awarded for partial completion of doctoral program. *Degree requirements:* For master's, thesis, summer internship; for doctorate, comprehensive exam, thesis/dissertation, residency. *Entrance requirements:* For master's, GMAT, GRE, or MCAT, two years of undergraduate coursework in math and science; for doctorate, GRE General Test. Additional exam requirements/recommendations for international students: Required— TOEFL (minimum score 100 iBT). Electronic applications accepted. *Expenses:* Contact institution. *Faculty research:* Genetic and emerging infections epidemiology, virology, cost/quality, vector biology, quantitative methods, aging, asthma, cancer.

Epidemiology

American University of Beirut, Graduate Programs, Faculty of Health Sciences, Beirut, Lebanon. Offers environmental sciences (MSES), including environmental health; epidemiology (MS); epidemiology and biostatistics (MPH); health management and policy (MPH); health promotion and community health (MPH); population health (MS). Part-time programs available. *Faculty:* 29 full-time (19 women), 5 part-time/ adjunct (2 women). *Students:* 63 full-time (52 women), 103 part-time (87 women). Average age 27. 156 applicants, 71% accepted, 56 enrolled. In 2011, 69 master's awarded. *Degree requirements:* For master's, one foreign language, comprehensive exam, thesis (for some programs). *Entrance requirements:* For master's, 2 letters of recommendation, personal statement, transcripts. Additional exam requirements/ recommendations for international students: Required—TOEFL (minimum score 600 paper-based; 250 computer-based; 97 iBT), IELTS (minimum score 7). *Application deadline:* For fall admission, 2/20 for domestic and international students; for spring admission, 11/1 for domestic and international students. Application fee: $50. Electronic applications accepted. *Expenses: Tuition:* Full-time $12,780; part-time $710 per credit. Tuition and fees vary according to course load and program. *Financial support:* In 2011–12, 62 students received support. Scholarships/grants, health care benefits, and unspecified assistantships available. Financial award application deadline: 2/20. *Faculty research:* Tobacco control; health of the elderly; youth health; mental health; women's health; reproductive and sexual health, including HIV/AIDS; water quality; health systems; quality in health care delivery; health human resources; health policy; occupational and environmental health; social inequality; social determinants of health; chronic diseases. *Total annual research expenditures:* $722,649. *Unit head:* Iman Adel Nuwayhid, Dean, 961-1340119, Fax: 961-1744470, E-mail: nuwayhid@aub.edu.lb. *Application contact:* Mitra Tauk, Administrative Coordinator, 961-1350000 Ext. 4687, Fax: 961-1744470, E-mail: mt12@aub.edu.lb. Web site: http://fhs.aub.edu.lb.

Boston University, School of Public Health, Epidemiology Department, Boston, MA 02118. Offers MPH, MS, PhD. *Accreditation:* CEPH (one or more programs are accredited). Part-time and evening/weekend programs available. *Faculty:* 25 full-time, 60 part-time/adjunct. *Students:* 101 full-time (77 women), 76 part-time (60 women); includes 33 minority (4 Black or African American, non-Hispanic/Latino; 22 Asian, non-Hispanic/Latino; 3 Hispanic/Latino; 4 Two or more races, non-Hispanic/Latino), 13 international. Average age 28. 565 applicants, 36% accepted, 65 enrolled. In 2011, 71 master's awarded. *Degree requirements:* For master's, comprehensive exam (for some programs), thesis (for some programs); for doctorate, comprehensive exam, thesis/ dissertation. *Entrance requirements:* For master's, GRE, LSAT, GMAT, DAT or MCAT, U.S. bachelor's degree or foreign equivalent; for doctorate, GRE, MCAT, GMAT, LSAT, MPH or equivalent. Additional exam requirements/recommendations for international students: Required—TOEFL (minimum score 600 paper-based; 250 computer-based; 100 iBT), IELTS (minimum score 6). *Application deadline:* For fall admission, 2/1 priority date for domestic students, 2/1 for international students; for spring admission, 10/15 priority date for domestic students, 10/15 for international students. Applications are processed on a rolling basis. Application fee: $115. Electronic applications accepted. *Expenses: Tuition:* Full-time $40,848; part-time $1276 per credit hour. *Required fees:* $572; $286 per semester. *Financial support:* Career-related internships or fieldwork, Federal Work-Study, institutionally sponsored loans, and scholarships/grants available. Support available to part-time students. Financial award application deadline: 3/1; financial award applicants required to submit FAFSA. *Unit head:* Dr. C. Robert Horsburgh, Jr., Chair, 617-638-7775, E-mail: epi@bu.edu. *Application contact:* LePhan Quan, Associate Director of Admissions, 617-638-4640, Fax: 617-638-5299, E-mail: asksph@bu.edu. Web site: http://sph.bu.edu/epi.

Brown University, Graduate School, Division of Biology and Medicine, Department of Community Health, Providence, RI 02912. Offers health services research (MS, PhD); public health (MPH); statistical science (MS, PhD), including biostatistics, epidemiology; MD/PhD. *Accreditation:* CEPH. *Degree requirements:* For doctorate, thesis/dissertation, preliminary exam. *Entrance requirements:* For master's and doctorate, GRE General Test. Additional exam requirements/recommendations for international students: Required—TOEFL.

Brown University, Graduate School, Division of Biology and Medicine, Department of Community Health, Center for Statistical Sciences, Program in Epidemiology,

Providence, RI 02912. Offers MS, PhD, MD/PhD. *Degree requirements:* For doctorate, thesis/dissertation, preliminary exam. *Entrance requirements:* For master's and doctorate, GRE General Test.

Case Western Reserve University, School of Medicine and School of Graduate Studies, Graduate Programs in Medicine, Department of Epidemiology and Biostatistics, Program in Epidemiology, Cleveland, OH 44106. Offers MS, PhD. *Accreditation:* CEPH. Part-time programs available. Terminal master's awarded for partial completion of doctoral program. *Degree requirements:* For master's, comprehensive exam, thesis; for doctorate, comprehensive exam, thesis/dissertation. *Entrance requirements:* For master's, GRE General Test or MCAT, 3 recommendations; for doctorate, GRE General Test, 3 recommendations. Additional exam requirements/recommendations for international students: Required—TOEFL (minimum score 550 paper-based; 213 computer-based). Electronic applications accepted. *Faculty research:* Cardiovascular epidemiology, cancer risk factors, HIV in underserved populations, effectiveness studies in Medicare patients.

Case Western Reserve University, School of Medicine and School of Graduate Studies, Graduate Programs in Medicine, Department of Epidemiology and Biostatistics, Program in Genetic and Molecular Epidemiology, Cleveland, OH 44106. Offers MS, PhD. *Degree requirements:* For master's, comprehensive exam, thesis; for doctorate, comprehensive exam, thesis/dissertation. *Entrance requirements:* For master's and doctorate, GRE. Additional exam requirements/recommendations for international students: Required—TOEFL (minimum score 550 paper-based; 213 computer-based).

Columbia University, Columbia University Mailman School of Public Health, Department of Epidemiology, New York, NY 10032. Offers MPH, MS, Dr PH, PhD. PhD offered in cooperation with the Graduate School of Arts and Sciences. *Accreditation:* CEPH (one or more programs are accredited). Part-time programs available. *Students:* 127 full-time (94 women), 148 part-time (112 women); includes 92 minority (15 Black or African American, non-Hispanic/Latino; 2 American Indian or Alaska Native, non-Hispanic/Latino; 40 Asian, non-Hispanic/Latino; 24 Hispanic/Latino; 11 Two or more races, non-Hispanic/Latino), 41 international. Average age 29. 449 applicants, 63% accepted, 115 enrolled. In 2011, 69 master's, 14 doctorates awarded. *Degree requirements:* For master's, thesis; for doctorate, thesis/dissertation. *Entrance requirements:* For master's, GRE General Test; for doctorate, GRE General Test, MPH or equivalent (Dr PH). Additional exam requirements/recommendations for international students: Required—TOEFL (minimum score 600 paper-based; 250 computer-based; 100 iBT). *Application deadline:* For fall admission, 1/5 for domestic students. Application fee: $60. Electronic applications accepted. *Financial support:* Research assistantships, teaching assistantships, career-related internships or fieldwork, and Federal Work-Study available. Support available to part-time students. Financial award application deadline: 2/1; financial award applicants required to submit FAFSA. *Faculty research:* Infectious disease epidemiology, chronic disease epidemiology, social epidemiology, psychiatric epidemiology, and neurological epidemiology. *Unit head:* Dr. Sandro Galeo, Chairperson, 212-305-9410. *Application contact:* Dr. Joseph Korevec, Director of Admissions and Financial Aid, 212-305-8698, Fax: 212-342-1861, E-mail: ph-admit@ columbia.edu. Web site: http://www.mailman.hs.columbia.edu/epi/index.html.

Cornell University, Graduate School, Graduate Fields of Comparative Biomedical Sciences, Field of Comparative Biomedical Sciences, Ithaca, NY 14853-0001. Offers cellular and molecular medicine (MS, PhD); developmental and reproductive biology (MS, PhD); infectious diseases (MS, PhD); population medicine and epidemiology (MS, PhD); structural and functional biology (MS, PhD). *Faculty:* 97 full-time (27 women). *Students:* 38 full-time (23 women); includes 5 minority (2 Black or African American, non-Hispanic/Latino; 1 Asian, non-Hispanic/Latino; 2 Hispanic/Latino), 15 international. Average age 30. 45 applicants, 22% accepted, 9 enrolled. In 2011, 2 master's, 7 doctorates awarded. *Degree requirements:* For master's, thesis; for doctorate, comprehensive exam, thesis/dissertation. *Entrance requirements:* For master's and doctorate, GRE General Test, 2 letters of recommendation. Additional exam requirements/recommendations for international students: Required—TOEFL (minimum score 550 paper-based; 213 computer-based; 77 iBT). *Application deadline:* For fall admission, 12/15 for domestic students. Application fee: $95. Electronic applications accepted. *Financial support:* In 2011–12, 12 fellowships with full tuition

reimbursements, 25 research assistantships with full tuition reimbursements were awarded; teaching assistantships with full tuition reimbursements, institutionally sponsored loans, scholarships/grants, health care benefits, tuition waivers (full and partial), and unspecified assistantships also available. Financial award applicants required to submit FAFSA. *Faculty research:* Receptors and signal transduction, viral and bacterial infectious diseases, tumor metastasis, clinical sciences/nutritional disease, developmental/neurological disorders. *Unit head:* Director of Graduate Studies, 607-253-3276, Fax: 607-253-3756. *Application contact:* Graduate Field Assistant, 607-253-3276, Fax: 607-253-3756, E-mail: graduate_edcvm@cornell.edu. Web site: http://www.gradschool.cornell.edu/fields.php?id-64&a-2.

Dalhousie University, Faculty of Medicine, Department of Community Health and Epidemiology, Halifax, NS B3H 4R2, Canada. Offers M Sc. *Degree requirements:* For master's, thesis. *Entrance requirements:* Additional exam requirements/recommendations for international students: Required—1 of 5 approved tests: TOEFL, IELTS, CANTEST, CAEL, Michigan English Language Assessment Battery. Electronic applications accepted. *Expenses:* Contact institution. *Faculty research:* Population health, health promotion and disease prevention, health services utilization, chronic disease epidemiology.

Drexel University, School of Public Health, Department of Epidemiology and Biostatistics, Philadelphia, PA 19104-2875. Offers biostatistics (MS); epidemiology (PhD); epidemiology and biostatistics (Certificate).

East Tennessee State University, School of Graduate Studies, College of Public Health, Doctor of Public Health Programs, Johnson City, TN 37614. Offers community health (DPH); epidemiology (DPH). *Accreditation:* CEPH. *Students:* 15 full-time (11 women), 7 part-time (4 women); includes 6 minority (3 Black or African American, non-Hispanic/Latino; 3 Asian, non-Hispanic/Latino), 3 international. 11 applicants, 73% accepted, 8 enrolled. In 2011, 1 doctorate awarded. Terminal master's awarded for partial completion of doctoral program. *Degree requirements:* For doctorate, comprehensive exam, thesis/dissertation, culminating experience/practicum. *Entrance requirements:* For doctorate, GRE General Test, SOPHAS application, MPH or equivalent, four letters of recommendation. Additional exam requirements/recommendations for international students: Required—TOEFL (minimum score 550 paper-based; 213 computer-based; 79 iBT). *Application deadline:* For fall admission, 3/1 for domestic and international students. Application fee: $35 ($45 for international students). Electronic applications accepted. *Expenses:* Tuition, state resident: full-time $7312; part-time $350 per credit hour. Tuition, nonresident: full-time $18,490; part-time $621 per credit hour. *Required fees:* $63 per credit hour. Tuition and fees vary according to course load and program. *Financial support:* In 2011–12, 14 students received support, including 13 research assistantships with full tuition reimbursements available (averaging $14,000 per year); career-related internships or fieldwork, institutionally sponsored loans, scholarships/grants, tuition waivers (full), and unspecified assistantships also available. Financial award application deadline: 7/1; financial award applicants required to submit FAFSA. *Faculty research:* Rural health issues, youth and adolescent health, health of the elderly, environmental epidemiology, spatial analysis of data. *Unit head:* Dr. Rob Pack, Associate Dean, 423-439-4243, Fax: 423-439-5238, E-mail: packr@etsu.edu. *Application contact:* Mary Duncan, Graduate Specialist, 423-439-4302, Fax: 423-439-5624, E-mail: duncanm@etsu.edu.

East Tennessee State University, School of Graduate Studies, College of Public Health, Master of Public Health Programs, Johnson City, TN 37614. Offers biostatistics (MPH); community health (MPH); environmental health (MPH); epidemiology (MPH); public health administration (MPH). Part-time programs available. Postbaccalaureate distance learning degree programs offered (no on-campus study). *Students:* 45 full-time (27 women), 31 part-time (21 women); includes 14 minority (8 Black or African American, non-Hispanic/Latino; 3 Asian, non-Hispanic/Latino; 2 Hispanic/Latino; 1 Two or more races, non-Hispanic/Latino), 11 international. 92 applicants, 45% accepted, 40 enrolled. In 2011, 24 master's awarded. *Degree requirements:* For master's, comprehensive exam, field experience. *Entrance requirements:* For master's, GRE General Test, SOPHAS application, minimum GPA of 2.75, letters of recommendation. Additional exam requirements/recommendations for international students: Required—TOEFL (minimum score 550 paper-based; 213 computer-based; 79 iBT). *Application deadline:* For fall admission, 3/1 for domestic and international students. Application fee: $35 ($45 for international students). Electronic applications accepted. *Expenses:* Tuition, state resident: full-time $7312; part-time $350 per credit hour. Tuition, nonresident: full-time $18,490; part-time $621 per credit hour. *Required fees:* $63 per credit hour. Tuition and fees vary according to course load and program. *Financial support:* In 2011–12, 31 students received support, including 14 research assistantships with full tuition reimbursements available (averaging $6,000 per year), 2 teaching assistantships with full tuition reimbursements available (averaging $6,000 per year); career-related internships or fieldwork, institutionally sponsored loans, scholarships/grants, and unspecified assistantships also available. Financial award application deadline: 7/1; financial award applicants required to submit FAFSA. *Faculty research:* Rural health issues, youth and adolescent health, health of the elderly, environmental epidemiology, spatial analysis of data. *Unit head:* Dr. Brian Martin, Graduate Program Coordinator, 423-439-4429, Fax: 423-439-6491, E-mail: martinb@etsu.edu. *Application contact:* Mary Duncan, Graduate Specialist, 423-439-4302, Fax: 423-439-5624, E-mail: duncanm@etsu.edu. Web site: http://www.etsu.edu/cph/academics/graduate/MPHHome.aspx.

East Tennessee State University, School of Graduate Studies, College of Public Health, Public Health Certificate Programs, Johnson City, TN 37614. Offers biostatistics (Postbaccalaureate Certificate); epidemiology (Postbaccalaureate Certificate); gerontology (Postbaccalaureate Certificate); health care management (Postbaccalaureate Certificate); rural health (Postbaccalaureate Certificate). Part-time programs available. *Students:* 2 full-time (both women), 5 part-time (all women); includes 4 minority (all Black or African American, non-Hispanic/Latino). 18 applicants, 28% accepted, 5 enrolled. In 2011, 7 Postbaccalaureate Certificates awarded. *Degree requirements:* For Postbaccalaureate Certificate, culminating experience or community-based project. *Entrance requirements:* For degree, minimum GPA of 2.5, 3 letters of recommendation, resume (gerontology). Additional exam requirements/recommendations for international students: Required—TOEFL (minimum score 550 paper-based; 213 computer-based; 79 iBT). *Application deadline:* For fall admission, 6/1 for domestic students, 4/29 for international students; for spring admission, 11/1 for domestic students, 9/30 for international students. Application fee: $35 ($45 for international students). Electronic applications accepted. *Expenses:* Tuition, state resident: full-time $7312; part-time $350 per credit hour. Tuition, nonresident: full-time $18,490; part-time $621 per credit hour. *Required fees:* $63 per credit hour. Tuition and fees vary according to course load and program. *Financial support:* Institutionally sponsored loans and scholarships/grants available. Financial award application deadline: 7/1; financial award applicants required to submit FAFSA. *Faculty research:* Rural health issues, youth and adolescent health, health of the elderly, environmental epidemiology, spatial analysis of data. *Unit head:* Dr. Randy Wykoff, Dean, 423-439-4243, Fax: 423-439-5238, E-mail: wykoff@etsu.edu. *Application contact:* Mary Duncan, Graduate Specialist, 423-439-4302, Fax: 423-439-5624, E-mail: duncanm@etsu.edu.

Emory University, Rollins School of Public Health, Department of Environmental Health, Atlanta, GA 30322-1100. Offers environmental health (MPH); environmental health and epidemiology (MSPH); environmental health sciences (PhD); global environmental health (MPH). *Accreditation:* CEPH. Part-time programs available. *Students:* 23 full-time. Average age 27. 7 applicants, 100% accepted, 4 enrolled. *Degree requirements:* For master's, thesis, practicum. *Entrance requirements:* For master's, GRE General Test. Additional exam requirements/recommendations for international students: Required—TOEFL. *Application deadline:* For fall admission, 1/3 priority date for domestic students, 1/3 for international students. Application fee: $95. Electronic applications accepted. *Expenses: Tuition:* Full-time $34,800. *Required fees:* $1300. *Financial support:* Fellowships with full and partial tuition reimbursements, career-related internships or fieldwork, Federal Work-Study, institutionally sponsored loans, scholarships/grants, traineeships, health care benefits, and unspecified assistantships available. Support available to part-time students. Financial award application deadline: 1/5; financial award applicants required to submit FAFSA. *Unit head:* Dr. Paige Tolbert, Chair, 404-727-0196, Fax: 404-727-8744, E-mail: ptolber@sph.emory.edu. *Application contact:* Ariadne Switchenberg, Graduate Program Administrator, 404-727-7905, Fax: 404-727-8744, E-mail: ascarl@emory.edu.

Emory University, Rollins School of Public Health, Department of Epidemiology, Atlanta, GA 30322-1100. Offers MPH, MSPH, PhD. *Accreditation:* CEPH. Part-time programs available. *Students:* 71 full-time. Average age 27. 132 applicants, 11% accepted, 9 enrolled. *Degree requirements:* For master's, thesis, practicum. *Entrance requirements:* For master's, GRE General Test. Additional exam requirements/recommendations for international students: Required—TOEFL (minimum score 550 paper-based; 213 computer-based; 80 iBT). *Application deadline:* For fall admission, 12/1 priority date for domestic students, 12/1 for international students. Application fee: $95. Electronic applications accepted. *Expenses:* Contact institution. *Financial support:* Fellowships with full and partial tuition reimbursements, career-related internships or fieldwork, Federal Work-Study, institutionally sponsored loans, scholarships/grants, traineeships, health care benefits, and unspecified assistantships available. Support available to part-time students. Financial award application deadline: 1/5; financial award applicants required to submit FAFSA. *Faculty research:* Cancer, infectious diseases, epidemiological methods, environmental/occupational health, women's and children's health. *Unit head:* Dr. Viola Vaccarino, Chair, 404-727-8010, Fax: 404-727-8737. *Application contact:* Jena Black, Graduate Program Administrator, 404-727-8729, Fax: 404-727-8737, E-mail: jena.black@emory.edu.

Emory University, Rollins School of Public Health, Online Program in Public Health, Atlanta, GA 30322-1100. Offers applied epidemiology (MPH); applied public health informatics (MPH); prevention science (MPH). Part-time and evening/weekend programs available. Postbaccalaureate distance learning degree programs offered (minimal on-campus study). *Students:* 35 full-time. Average age 40. *Degree requirements:* For master's, thesis, practicum. *Entrance requirements:* For master's, GRE. Additional exam requirements/recommendations for international students: Required—TOEFL (minimum score 550 paper-based; 213 computer-based; 80 iBT). *Application deadline:* For fall admission, 1/5 priority date for domestic students, 1/5 for international students. Applications are processed on a rolling basis. Application fee: $95. Electronic applications accepted. *Expenses: Tuition:* Full-time $34,800. *Required fees:* $1300. *Financial support:* Fellowships with full and partial tuition reimbursements, career-related internships or fieldwork, Federal Work-Study, institutionally sponsored loans, scholarships/grants, traineeships, health care benefits, and unspecified assistantships available. Support available to part-time students. Financial award application deadline: 1/5; financial award applicants required to submit FAFSA. *Unit head:* Melissa Alperin, Director, 404-727-2928, Fax: 404-727-3996, E-mail: malperi@emory.edu. Web site: http://www.sph.emory.edu/CMPH/.

Florida International University, Robert Stempel College of Public Health and Social Work, Programs in Public Health, Miami, FL 33199. Offers biostatistics (MPH); environmental and occupational health (MPH, PhD); epidemiology (MPH, PhD); health policy and management (MPH); health promotion and disease prevention (PhD); health promotion and diseases prevention (MPH). Ph D is fall admission only; MPH offered jointly with University of Miami. *Accreditation:* CEPH. Part-time and evening/weekend programs available. Postbaccalaureate distance learning degree programs offered (no on-campus study). *Degree requirements:* For master's, thesis optional; for doctorate, comprehensive exam, thesis/dissertation. *Entrance requirements:* For master's, minimum GPA of 3.0, letters of recommendation; for doctorate, GRE, resume, minimum GPA of 3.0, letters of recommendation, letter of intent. Additional exam requirements/recommendations for international students: Required—TOEFL (minimum score 550 paper-based; 80 iBT). Electronic applications accepted. *Expenses:* Contact institution. *Faculty research:* Drugs/AIDS intervention among migrant workers, provision of services for active/recovering drug users with HIV.

George Mason University, College of Health and Human Services, Department of Global and Community Health, Fairfax, VA 22030. Offers biostatistics (Certificate); epidemiology (Certificate); epidemiology and biostatistics (MS); gerontology (Certificate); global health (MS, Certificate); nutrition (Certificate); public health (MPH, Certificate). *Faculty:* 11 full-time (5 women), 16 part-time/adjunct (12 women). *Students:* 101 full-time (84 women), 114 part-time (92 women); includes 85 minority (43 Black or African American, non-Hispanic/Latino; 30 Asian, non-Hispanic/Latino; 11 Hispanic/Latino; 1 Two or more races, non-Hispanic/Latino), 14 international. Average age 32. 162 applicants, 61% accepted, 53 enrolled. In 2011, 80 master's, 15 other advanced degrees awarded. *Degree requirements:* For master's, comprehensive exam (for some programs), thesis or practicum. *Entrance requirements:* For master's, GRE, 2 official transcripts; expanded goals statement; 3 letters of recommendation; resume; 1 completed course in health science, statistics, natural sciences and social science (for MPH); 6 credits of foreign language if not fluent (for MS in global health); for Certificate, 2 official transcripts; expanded goals statement; 3 letters of recommendation; resume; bachelor's degree from regionally-accredited institution with minimum GPA of 3.0; statistics and college-level algebra with minimum B grade (for Certificate in biostatistics). Additional exam requirements/recommendations for international students: Required—TOEFL (minimum score 575 paper-based; 230 computer-based; 88 iBT), IELTS, Pearson Test of English. *Application deadline:* For fall admission, 4/1 priority date for domestic students; for spring admission, 11/1 priority date for domestic students. Applications are processed on a rolling basis. Application fee: $65 ($80 for international students). Electronic applications accepted. *Expenses:* Tuition, state resident: full-time $8750; part-time $364.58 per credit. Tuition, nonresident: full-time $24,092; part-time $1003.83 per credit. *Required fees:* $2514; $104.75 per credit. *Financial support:* In 2011–12, 14 students received support, including 12 research assistantships with full and partial tuition reimbursements available (averaging $15,000 per year), 2 teaching assistantships with full and partial tuition reimbursements available (averaging $11,781 per year); career-related internships or fieldwork, Federal Work-Study, scholarships/grants, unspecified assistantships, and health care benefits (full-time research and teaching assistantship recipients) also available. Financial award application deadline: 3/1; financial award applicants required to submit FAFSA. *Faculty research:* Providing introductory and advanced degrees in health-related disciplines centered in global and community issues, health issues and the needs of affected populations at the regional and global level. *Total annual research expenditures:* $64,518. *Unit head:* Dr. Carlos

Sluzki, Dean, 703-993-1920, Fax: 703-993-1943, E-mail: csluzki@gmu.edu. *Application contact:* Allan Weiss, Office Manager, 703-993-3126, Fax: 703-993-1908, E-mail: aweiss2@gmu.edu. Web site: http://chhs.gmu.edu/gch/index.

Georgetown University, Graduate School of Arts and Sciences, Programs in Biomedical Sciences, Department of Biostatistics, Bioinformatics and Biomathematics, Washington, DC 20057-1484. Offers biostatistics (MS), including bioinformatics, epidemiology. *Entrance requirements:* For master's, GRE General Test. Additional exam requirements/recommendations for international students: Required—TOEFL. *Faculty research:* Occupation epidemiology, cancer.

The George Washington University, Columbian College of Arts and Sciences, Program in Epidemiology, Washington, DC 20052. Offers MS, PhD. Part-time and evening/weekend programs available. *Students:* 4 full-time (3 women), 20 part-time (14 women); includes 8 minority (4 Asian, non-Hispanic/Latino; 4 Hispanic/Latino), 3 international. Average age 31. 25 applicants, 52% accepted. In 2011, 3 doctorates awarded. *Degree requirements:* For master's, comprehensive exam; for doctorate, thesis/dissertation, general exam. *Entrance requirements:* For master's and doctorate, GRE General Test, minimum GPA of 3.0. Additional exam requirements/ recommendations for international students: Required—TOEFL (minimum score 550 paper-based; 213 computer-based; 80 iBT). *Application deadline:* For fall admission, 1/15 priority date for domestic students, 1/15 for international students; for spring admission, 10/1 priority date for domestic students, 9/1 for international students. Applications are processed on a rolling basis. Application fee: $75. Electronic applications accepted. *Financial support:* In 2011–12, 1 student received support. Fellowships with tuition reimbursements available, teaching assistantships, and tuition waivers available. *Unit head:* Dr. Sean D. Cleary, Director, 202-994-5757, Fax: 202-994-0082, E-mail: sphsdc@gwumc.edu. *Application contact:* 202-994-6210, Fax: 202-994-6213, E-mail: askccas@gwu.edu.

The George Washington University, School of Public Health and Health Services, Department of Epidemiology and Biostatistics, Washington, DC 20052. Offers biostatistics (MPH); epidemiology (MPH); microbiology and emerging infectious diseases (MSPH). *Faculty:* 23 full-time (15 women), 26 part-time/adjunct (15 women). *Students:* 62 full-time (54 women), 41 part-time (30 women); includes 37 minority (16 Black or African American, non-Hispanic/Latino; 16 Asian, non-Hispanic/Latino; 3 Hispanic/Latino; 2 Two or more races, non-Hispanic/Latino), 8 international. Average age 27. 298 applicants, 69% accepted, 35 enrolled. In 2011, 49 master's awarded. *Degree requirements:* For master's, case study or special project. *Entrance requirements:* For master's, GMAT, GRE General Test, or MCAT. Additional exam requirements/recommendations for international students: Required—TOEFL. *Application deadline:* For fall admission, 4/15 priority date for domestic students, 4/15 for international students; for spring admission, 11/1 for domestic and international students. Applications are processed on a rolling basis. Application fee: $75. *Financial support:* In 2011–12, 6 students received support. Tuition waivers available. Financial award application deadline: 2/15. *Unit head:* Dr. Alan E. Greenberg, Chair, 202-994-0612, E-mail: aeg1@gwu.edu. *Application contact:* Jane Smith, Director of Admissions, 202-994-0248, Fax: 202-994-1860, E-mail: sphhsinfo@gwumc.edu.

Georgia Southern University, Jack N. Averitt College of Graduate Studies, Jiann-Ping Hsu College of Public Health, Program in Public Health, Statesboro, GA 30460. Offers biostatistics (MPH, Dr PH); community health behavior and education (Dr PH); community health education (MPH); environmental health sciences (MPH); epidemiology (MPH); health services policy management (MPH); public health leadership (Dr PH). *Accreditation:* CEPH. Part-time programs available. *Students:* 87 full-time (60 women), 39 part-time (25 women); includes 68 minority (58 Black or African American, non-Hispanic/Latino; 6 Asian, non-Hispanic/Latino; 4 Hispanic/Latino), 20 international. Average age 30. 73 applicants, 84% accepted, 42 enrolled. In 2011, 22 master's, 4 doctorates awarded. *Degree requirements:* For master's, thesis optional, practicum; for doctorate, comprehensive exam, thesis/dissertation, practicum. *Entrance requirements:* For master's, GRE General Test, minimum GPA of 2.75, resume, 3 letters of reference; for doctorate, GRE, GMAT, MCAT, LSAT, 3 letters of reference, statement of purpose, resume or curriculum vitae. Additional exam requirements/ recommendations for international students: Required—TOEFL (minimum score 550 paper-based; 213 computer-based; 80 iBT). *Application deadline:* For fall admission, 3/1 priority date for domestic students, 3/1 for international students; for spring admission, 10/1 priority date for domestic students, 10/1 for international students. Applications are processed on a rolling basis. Application fee: $50. Electronic applications accepted. *Expenses:* Contact institution. *Financial support:* In 2011–12, 59 students received support, including research assistantships with partial tuition reimbursements available (averaging $7,200 per year), teaching assistantships with partial tuition reimbursements available (averaging $7,200 per year); career-related internships or fieldwork, Federal Work-Study, scholarships/grants, tuition waivers (partial), and unspecified assistantships also available. Support available to part-time students. Financial award application deadline: 4/15; financial award applicants required to submit FAFSA. *Faculty research:* Rural public health best practices, health disparity elimination, community initiatives to enhance public health, cost effectiveness analysis, epidemiology of rural public health, environmental health issues, health care system assessment, rural health care, health policy and healthcare financing. *Unit head:* Dr. Charles Hardy, Dean, 912-478-2674, Fax: 912-478-5811, E-mail: chardy@georgiasouthern.edu. *Application contact:* Amanda Gilliland, Coordinator for Graduate Student Recruitment, 912-478-5384, Fax: 912-478-0740, E-mail: gradadmissions@georgiasouthern.edu. Web site: http://chhs.georgiasouthern.edu/health/.

Harvard University, Cyprus International Institute for the Environment and Public Health in Association with Harvard School of Public Health, Cambridge, MA 02138. Offers environmental health (MS); environmental/public health (PhD); epidemiology and biostatistics (MS). *Entrance requirements:* For master's and doctorate, GRE, resume/ curriculum vitae, 3 letters of recommendation, BA or BS (including diploma and official transcripts). Additional exam requirements/recommendations for international students: Required—TOEFL (minimum score 220 computer-based), IELTS (minimum score 7). Electronic applications accepted. *Expenses: Tuition:* Full-time $36,304. *Required fees:* $1186. Full-time tuition and fees vary according to program. *Faculty research:* Air pollution, climate change, biostatistics, sustainable development, environmental management.

Harvard University, Harvard School of Public Health, Department of Epidemiology, Boston, MA 02115-6096. Offers cancer epidemiology (SM, DPH); cardiovascular epidemiology (SM, DPH, SD); clinical epidemiology (SM, DPH, SD); environmental/ occupational epidemiology (SM, SD); epidemiologic methods (DPH, SD); epidemiology (SM, DPH, SD); epidemiology of aging (SM, DPH, SD); infectious diseases (SM, DPH, SD); molecular/genetic epidemiology (DPH, SD); neuroepidemiology (DPH, SD); nutritional epidemiology (DPH); oral and dental health epidemiology (SM, SD); pharmacoepidemiology (SM, DPH, SD); psychiatric epidemiology (SM, DPH); reproductive epidemiology (SM, SD). Part-time programs available. *Faculty:* 77 full-time (31 women), 21 part-time/adjunct (5 women). *Students:* 125 full-time, 33 part-time; includes 31 minority (2 Black or African American, non-Hispanic/Latino; 1 American Indian or Alaska Native, non-Hispanic/Latino; 18 Asian, non-Hispanic/Latino; 3 Hispanic/ Latino; 7 Two or more races, non-Hispanic/Latino), 69 international. Average age 30. 340 applicants, 27% accepted, 62 enrolled. In 2011, 33 master's, 16 doctorates awarded. *Degree requirements:* For doctorate, thesis/dissertation, qualifying exam. *Entrance requirements:* For master's and doctorate, GRE. Additional exam requirements/recommendations for international students: Required—TOEFL (minimum score 595 paper-based; 240 computer-based; 95 iBT); Recommended—IELTS (minimum score 7). *Application deadline:* For fall admission, 12/15 for domestic and international students. Application fee: $115. Electronic applications accepted. *Expenses: Tuition:* Full-time $36,304. *Required fees:* $1186. Full-time tuition and fees vary according to program. *Financial support:* Fellowships, research assistantships, teaching assistantships, Federal Work-Study, scholarships/grants, traineeships, and unspecified assistantships available. Support available to part-time students. Financial award application deadline: 2/17; financial award applicants required to submit FAFSA. *Faculty research:* Cancer prevention and epidemiology, cardiovascular epidemiology, environmental and occupational epidemiology, pharmacoepidemiology, psychiatric epidemiology. *Unit head:* Dr. Hans-Olov Adami, Chair, 617-432-1050, Fax: 617-432-7805, E-mail: hadami@hsph.harvard.edu. *Application contact:* Vincent W. James, Director of Admissions, 617-432-1031, Fax: 617-432-7080, E-mail: admissions@hsph.harvard.edu. Web site: http://www.hsph.harvard.edu/departments/epidemiology/.

Harvard University, Harvard School of Public Health, Department of Nutrition, Boston, MA 02115-6096. Offers nutrition (DPH, PhD, SD); nutritional epidemiology (DPH, SD); public health nutrition (DPH, SD). *Faculty:* 22 full-time (4 women), 8 part-time/adjunct (2 women). *Students:* 32 full-time; includes 6 minority (1 Black or African American, non-Hispanic/Latino; 1 American Indian or Alaska Native, non-Hispanic/Latino; 1 Asian, non-Hispanic/Latino; 1 Hispanic/Latino; 2 Two or more races, non-Hispanic/Latino), 17 international. Average age 31. 35 applicants, 17% accepted, 5 enrolled. In 2011, 6 doctorates awarded. *Degree requirements:* For doctorate, thesis/dissertation, qualifying exam. *Entrance requirements:* For doctorate, GRE. Additional exam requirements/ recommendations for international students: Required—TOEFL (minimum score 595 paper-based; 240 computer-based; 95 iBT); Recommended—IELTS (minimum score 7). *Application deadline:* For fall admission, 12/15 for domestic and international students. Application fee: $115. Electronic applications accepted. *Expenses: Tuition:* Full-time $36,304. *Required fees:* $1186. Full-time tuition and fees vary according to program. *Financial support:* Fellowships, research assistantships, teaching assistantships, Federal Work-Study, scholarships/grants, traineeships, and unspecified assistantships available. Support available to part-time students. Financial award application deadline: 2/17; financial award applicants required to submit FAFSA. *Faculty research:* Dietary and genetic factors affecting heart diseases in humans; interactions among nutrition, immunity, and infection; role of diet and lifestyle in preventing macrovascular complications in diabetics. *Unit head:* Dr. Walter Willett, Chair, 617-432-1333, Fax: 617-432-2435, E-mail: walter.willett@channing.harvard.edu. *Application contact:* Vincent W. James, Director of Admissions, 617-432-1031, Fax: 617-432-7080, E-mail: admissions@hsph.harvard.edu. Web site: http://www.hsph.harvard.edu/ departments/nutrition/.

Hunter College of the City University of New York, Graduate School, Schools of the Health Professions, School of Health Sciences, Programs in Urban Public Health, Program in Epidemiology and Biostatistics, New York, NY 10021-5085. Offers MPH. *Accreditation:* CEPH. Part-time and evening/weekend programs available. *Faculty:* 6 full-time (4 women), 1 (woman) part-time/adjunct. *Students:* 6 full-time (1 woman), 48 part-time (29 women); includes 22 minority (9 Black or African American, non-Hispanic/ Latino; 11 Asian, non-Hispanic/Latino; 2 Hispanic/Latino), 5 international. Average age 32. 47 applicants, 49% accepted, 12 enrolled. In 2011, 15 master's awarded. *Degree requirements:* For master's, comprehensive exam, thesis optional, internship. *Entrance requirements:* For master's, GRE General Test, previous course work in calculus and statistics. Additional exam requirements/recommendations for international students: Required—TOEFL. *Application deadline:* For fall admission, 4/1 for domestic students; for spring admission, 11/1 for domestic students. Application fee: $125. *Expenses:* Tuition, state resident: full-time $8210; part-time $345 per credit. Tuition, nonresident: full-time $15,360; part-time $640 per credit. *Required fees:* $280 per semester. One-time fee: $125. Tuition and fees vary according to class time, campus/location and program. *Financial support:* In 2011–12, 6 fellowships were awarded; career-related internships or fieldwork, Federal Work-Study, institutionally sponsored loans, and tuition waivers (partial) also available. Support available to part-time students. Financial award application deadline: 3/1. *Unit head:* Victoria Frye, Coordinator, 212-481-7580, Fax: 212-481-5260, E-mail: vfrye@hunter.cuny.edu. *Application contact:* Milena Solo, Director for Graduate Admissions, 212-772-4288, Fax: 212-650-3336, E-mail: milena.solo@hunter.cuny.edu. Web site: http://www.hunter.cuny.edu/uph/grad-test/ epidemiology-biostatistics.

Indiana University Bloomington, School of Health, Physical Education and Recreation, Department of Applied Health Science, Bloomington, IN 47405-7000. Offers biostatistics (MPH); environmental health (MPH, PhD); epidemiology (MPH, PhD); health behavior (PhD); health promotion (MS); human development/family studies (MS); nutrition science (MS); public health administration (MPH); safety management (MS); school and college health programs (MS); social, behavioral and community health (MPH). *Accreditation:* CEPH (one or more programs are accredited). *Faculty:* 24 full-time (12 women). *Students:* 169 full-time (126 women), 25 part-time (17 women); includes 56 minority (39 Black or African American, non-Hispanic/Latino; 2 American Indian or Alaska Native, non-Hispanic/Latino; 4 Asian, non-Hispanic/Latino; 9 Hispanic/ Latino; 2 Two or more races, non-Hispanic/Latino), 29 international. Average age 30. 170 applicants, 74% accepted, 79 enrolled. In 2011, 52 master's, 9 doctorates awarded. *Degree requirements:* For master's, thesis optional; for doctorate, thesis/dissertation. *Entrance requirements:* For master's, GRE (MS in nutrition science), 3 recommendations; for doctorate, GRE, 3 recommendations. Additional exam requirements/recommendations for international students: Required—TOEFL (minimum score 550 paper-based; 213 computer-based; 79 iBT). *Application deadline:* For fall admission, 4/30 priority date for domestic students, 12/1 for international students; for spring admission, 11/15 priority date for domestic students, 9/1 for international students. Application fee: $55 ($65 for international students). *Financial support:* Fellowships, research assistantships with full and partial tuition reimbursements, teaching assistantships with full and partial tuition reimbursements, career-related internships or fieldwork, Federal Work-Study, institutionally sponsored loans, scholarships/grants, tuition waivers (partial), and fee remissions available. Financial award application deadline: 3/1. *Faculty research:* Cancer education, HIV/AIDS and drug education, public health, parent-child interactions, safety education. *Total annual research expenditures:* $2.8 million. *Unit head:* Dr. David K. Lohrmann, Chair, 812-856-5101, Fax: 812-855-3936, E-mail: dlohrman@indiana.edu. *Application contact:* Dr. Susan Middlestadt, Associate Professor and Graduate Coordinator, 812-856-5768, Fax: 812-855-3936, E-mail: semiddle@indiana.edu. Web site: http://www.indiana.edu/ ~aphealth/.

Indiana University–Purdue University Indianapolis, Indiana University School of Medicine, Department of Public Health, Indianapolis, IN 46202-2896. Offers behavioral health science (MPH); epidemiology (MPH); health policy and management (MPH). *Accreditation:* CEPH. *Students:* 134 full-time (86 women), 134 part-time (93 women); includes 53 minority (25 Black or African American, non-Hispanic/Latino; 1 American Indian or Alaska Native, non-Hispanic/Latino; 14 Asian, non-Hispanic/Latino; 10

Hispanic/Latino; 3 Two or more races, non-Hispanic/Latino), 13 international. Average age 30. 236 applicants, 58% accepted, 106 enrolled. In 2011, 81 master's awarded. Application fee: $55 ($65 for international students). *Expenses:* Contact institution. *Financial support:* In 2011–12, teaching assistantships (averaging $14,058 per year) were awarded. *Unit head:* Dr. Carole Kacius, Director, 317-274-3126. *Application contact:* Robert M. Stump, Jr., Director of Admissions, 317-274-3772, E-mail: inmedadm@iupui.edu.

The Johns Hopkins University, Bloomberg School of Public Health, Department of Epidemiology, Baltimore, MD 21205. Offers cancer epidemiology (MHS, Sc M, PhD, Sc D); cardiovascular disease epidemiology (MHS, Sc M, PhD, Sc D); clinical epidemiology (MHS, Sc M, PhD, Sc D); clinical trials (PhD, Sc D); epidemiology (Dr PH); epidemiology (general) (MHS, Sc M, PhD, Sc D); epidemiology of aging (MHS, Sc M, PhD, Sc D); human genetics/genetic epidemiology (MHS, Sc M, PhD, Sc D); infectious disease epidemiology (MHS, Sc M, PhD, Sc D); occupational/environmental epidemiology (MHS, Sc M, PhD, Sc D). Part-time programs available. *Degree requirements:* For master's, comprehensive exam, thesis, 1 year full-time residency; for doctorate, comprehensive exam, thesis/dissertation, 2 years full-time residency, oral and written exams, student teaching. *Entrance requirements:* For master's, GRE General Test or MCAT, 3 letters of recommendation, curriculum vitae; for doctorate, GRE General Test, minimum 1 year of work experience, 3 letters of recommendation, curriculum vitae, academic records from all schools. Additional exam requirements/recommendations for international students: Required—TOEFL (minimum score 600 paper-based; 250 computer-based; 100 iBT); Recommended—IELTS (minimum score 7.5), TWE. Electronic applications accepted. *Faculty research:* Cancer and congenital malformations, nutritional epidemiology, AIDS, tuberculosis, cardiovascular disease, risk assessment.

The Johns Hopkins University, Bloomberg School of Public Health, Department of International Health, Baltimore, MD 21205. Offers global disease epidemiology and control (MHS, PhD); health systems (MHS, PhD); human nutrition (MHS, PhD); international health (Dr PH); social and behavioral interventions (MHS, PhD). *Degree requirements:* For master's, comprehensive exam, thesis (for some programs), 1 year full-time residency, 4-9 month internship; for doctorate, comprehensive exam, thesis/dissertation or alternative, 1.5 years full-time residency, oral and written exams. *Entrance requirements:* For master's, GRE General Test or MCAT, 3 letters of recommendation, resume; for doctorate, GRE General Test or MCAT, 3 letters of recommendation, resume, transcripts. Additional exam requirements/recommendations for international students: Required—TOEFL (minimum score 600 paper-based; 250 computer-based; 100 iBT); Recommended—IELTS (minimum score 7). Electronic applications accepted. *Faculty research:* Nutrition, infectious diseases, health systems, health economics, humanitarian emergencies.

Loma Linda University, School of Public Health, Programs in Epidemiology and Biostatistics, Loma Linda, CA 92350. Offers MPH, MSPH, Dr PH, Postbaccalaureate Certificate. *Entrance requirements:* Additional exam requirements/recommendations for international students: Required—Michigan English Language Assessment Battery or TOEFL.

Louisiana State University Health Sciences Center, School of Public Health, New Orleans, LA 70112. Offers behavioral and community health sciences (MPH); biostatistics (MPH, MS, PhD); community health sciences (PhD); environmental and occupational health sciences (MPH); epidemiology (MPH, PhD); health policy and systems management (MPH). Part-time programs available. *Entrance requirements:* For master's, GRE General Test.

McGill University, Faculty of Graduate and Postdoctoral Studies, Faculty of Medicine, Department of Epidemiology and Biostatistics, Montréal, QC H3A 2T5, Canada. Offers community health (M Sc); environmental health (M Sc); epidemiology and biostatistics (M Sc, PhD, Diploma); health care evaluation (M Sc); medical statistics (M Sc). *Accreditation:* CEPH (one or more programs are accredited).

Medical College of Wisconsin, Graduate School of Biomedical Sciences, Department of Population Health, Milwaukee, WI 53226-0509. Offers bioethics (MA, Graduate Certificate); biostatistics (PhD); epidemiology (MS); public health (MPH, PhD, Graduate Certificate), including public and community health (PhD), public health (MPH). *Entrance requirements:* For master's, doctorate, and Graduate Certificate, GRE, official transcripts, three letters of recommendation. Additional exam requirements/recommendations for international students: Required—TOEFL.

Medical University of South Carolina, College of Graduate Studies, Division of Biostatistics and Epidemiology, Charleston, SC 29425. Offers biostatistics (MS, PhD); epidemiology (MS, PhD); DMD/PhD; MD/PhD. *Faculty:* 21 full-time (14 women), 1 part-time/adjunct (0 women). *Students:* 14 full-time (11 women), 2 part-time (both women); includes 4 minority (3 Black or African American, non-Hispanic/Latino; 1 Hispanic/Latino), 5 international. Average age 29. 36 applicants, 31% accepted, 5 enrolled. In 2011, 4 degrees awarded. Terminal master's awarded for partial completion of doctoral program. *Median time to degree:* Of those who began their doctoral program in fall 2003, 80% received their degree in 8 years or less. *Degree requirements:* For master's, comprehensive exam, thesis (for some programs); for doctorate, comprehensive exam, oral and written exams. *Entrance requirements:* For master's, GRE General Test, two semesters of college-level calculus; for doctorate, GRE General Test, interview, minimum GPA of 3.0, two semesters of college-level calculus. Additional exam requirements/recommendations for international students: Required—TOEFL (minimum score 600 paper-based; 250 computer-based; 100 iBT). *Application deadline:* For fall admission, 1/15 priority date for domestic students, 1/15 for international students. Applications are processed on a rolling basis. Application fee: $0 ($85 for international students). Electronic applications accepted. *Financial support:* In 2011–12, 18 research assistantships with partial tuition reimbursements (averaging $23,000 per year) were awarded; Federal Work-Study and scholarships/grants also available. Support available to part-time students. Financial award application deadline: 3/10; financial award applicants required to submit FAFSA. *Faculty research:* Health disparities, central nervous system injuries, radiation exposure, analysis of clinical trial data, biomedical information. *Unit head:* Dr. Yuko Y. Palesch, Professor/Director, 843-876-1917, Fax: 843-792-6590, E-mail: paleschy@musc.edu. *Application contact:* Dr. Ramesh Ramakrishnan, Associate Professor, 843-876-1140, Fax: 843-876-1126, E-mail: ramakris@musc.edu. Web site: http://www.musc.edu/dbbe/.

Memorial University of Newfoundland, Faculty of Medicine and School of Graduate Studies, Graduate Programs in Medicine, Division of Clinical Epidemiology, St. John's, NL A1C 5S7, Canada. Offers M Sc, PhD, Diploma.

Michigan State University, College of Human Medicine and The Graduate School, Graduate Programs in Human Medicine, Department of Epidemiology, East Lansing, MI 48824. Offers MS, PhD. *Degree requirements:* For master's, oral thesis defense. *Entrance requirements:* Additional exam requirements/recommendations for international students: Required—TOEFL. Electronic applications accepted.

Morehouse School of Medicine, Master of Public Health Program, Atlanta, GA 30310-1495. Offers epidemiology (MPH); health administration, management and policy (MPH); health education/health promotion (MPH); international health (MPH). *Accreditation:* CEPH. Part-time programs available. *Degree requirements:* For master's, thesis, practicum, public health leadership seminar. *Entrance requirements:* For master's, GRE General Test, writing test, public health or human service experience. Additional exam requirements/recommendations for international students: Required—TOEFL (minimum score 550 paper-based; 200 computer-based). Electronic applications accepted. *Expenses:* Contact institution. *Faculty research:* Women's and adolescent health, violence prevention, cancer epidemiology/disparities, substance abuse prevention.

New York Medical College, School of Health Sciences and Practice, Department of Epidemiology and Community Health, Program in Epidemiology, Valhalla, NY 10595-1691. Offers MPH. *Accreditation:* CEPH. Part-time and evening/weekend programs available. *Faculty:* 4 full-time, 14 part-time/adjunct. *Students:* 25 full-time, 40 part-time. Average age 32. 37 applicants, 68% accepted, 18 enrolled. In 2011, 18 master's awarded. *Degree requirements:* For master's, thesis. *Entrance requirements:* For master's, minimum undergraduate GPA of 3.0. Additional exam requirements/recommendations for international students: Required—TOEFL (minimum score 600 paper-based; 250 computer-based; 100 iBT), IELTS (minimum score 7). *Application deadline:* For fall admission, 8/1 priority date for domestic students, 5/15 for international students; for spring admission, 12/1 priority date for domestic students, 12/1 for international students. Applications are processed on a rolling basis. Application fee: $50 ($100 for international students). Electronic applications accepted. *Financial support:* Career-related internships or fieldwork, Federal Work-Study, institutionally sponsored loans, health care benefits, tuition waivers (partial), and tuition reimbursements available. Support available to part-time students. Financial award applicants required to submit FAFSA. *Unit head:* Dr. Jenniferl Calder, Director of MPH Studies, 914-594-4804, Fax: 914-594-4292, E-mail: jennifer_calder@nymc.edu. *Application contact:* Pamela Suett, Director of Recruitment, 914-594-4510, Fax: 914-594-4292, E-mail: shsp_admissions@nymc.edu. Web site: http://www.nymc.edu/shsp.

New York University, Graduate School of Arts and Science, Department of Environmental Medicine, New York, NY 10012-1019. Offers environmental health sciences (MS, PhD), including biostatistics (PhD), environmental hygiene (MS), epidemiology (PhD), ergonomics and biomechanics (PhD), exposure assessment and health effects (PhD), molecular toxicology/carcinogenesis (PhD), toxicology. Part-time programs available. *Faculty:* 26 full-time (7 women). *Students:* 62 full-time (43 women), 9 part-time (4 women); includes 12 minority (2 Black or African American, non-Hispanic/Latino; 3 Asian, non-Hispanic/Latino; 7 Hispanic/Latino), 27 international. Average age 30. 70 applicants, 56% accepted, 26 enrolled. In 2011, 9 master's, 8 doctorates awarded. Terminal master's awarded for partial completion of doctoral program. *Degree requirements:* For master's, thesis or alternative; for doctorate, one foreign language, thesis/dissertation, oral and written exams. *Entrance requirements:* For master's and doctorate, GRE General Test, GRE Subject Test, minimum GPA of 3.0; bachelor's degree in biological, physical, or engineering science. Additional exam requirements/recommendations for international students: Required—TOEFL. *Application deadline:* For fall admission, 12/12 for domestic and international students. Application fee: $90. *Financial support:* Fellowships with tuition reimbursements, teaching assistantships with tuition reimbursements, career-related internships or fieldwork, Federal Work-Study, institutionally sponsored loans, and health care benefits available. Financial award application deadline: 12/12; financial award applicants required to submit FAFSA. *Unit head:* Dr. Max Costa, Chair, 845-731-3661, Fax: 845-351-4510, E-mail: ehs@env.med.nyu.edu. *Application contact:* Dr. Jerome J. Solomon, Director of Graduate Studies, 845-731-3661, Fax: 845-351-4510, E-mail: ehs@env.med.nyu.edu. Web site: http://environmental-medicine.med.nyu.edu/.

North Carolina State University, College of Veterinary Medicine, Program in Comparative Biomedical Sciences, Raleigh, NC 27695. Offers cell biology (MS, PhD); infectious disease (MS, PhD); pathology (MS, PhD); pharmacology (MS, PhD); population medicine (MS, PhD). Part-time programs available. *Degree requirements:* For master's, thesis; for doctorate, thesis/dissertation. *Entrance requirements:* For master's and doctorate, GRE General Test. Additional exam requirements/recommendations for international students: Required—TOEFL (minimum score 550 paper-based; 213 computer-based). Electronic applications accepted. *Expenses:* Contact institution. *Faculty research:* Infectious diseases, cell biology, pharmacology and toxicology, genomics, pathology and population medicine.

Oregon Health & Science University, School of Medicine, Graduate Programs in Medicine, Department of Public Health and Preventive Medicine, Portland, OR 97239-3098. Offers biostatistics (Certificate); epidemiology and biostatistics (MPH). *Accreditation:* CEPH. Part-time programs available. *Faculty:* 17 full-time (13 women). *Students:* 18 full-time (12 women), 59 part-time (44 women); includes 19 minority (3 Black or African American, non-Hispanic/Latino; 2 American Indian or Alaska Native, non-Hispanic/Latino; 13 Asian, non-Hispanic/Latino; 1 Two or more races, non-Hispanic/Latino), 1 international. Average age 33. 45 applicants, 64% accepted, 28 enrolled. In 2011, 20 master's awarded. *Degree requirements:* For master's, thesis, fieldwork/internship. *Entrance requirements:* For master's, GRE General Test (minimum scores: 153 Verbal/148 Quantitative/4.5 Analytical), previous undergraduate course work in statistics. Additional exam requirements/recommendations for international students: Required—TOEFL (minimum score 550 paper-based; 213 computer-based; 87 iBT). *Application deadline:* For fall admission, 2/1 for domestic students. Application fee: $70. Electronic applications accepted. *Financial support:* Health care benefits available. *Faculty research:* Epidemiologic research, biostatistics, health services research, community-based research, health disparities. *Unit head:* Dr. Thomas M. Becker, Professor/Chair, 503-494-8257, Fax: 503-494-4981, E-mail: pmph@ohsu.edu. *Application contact:* Tree Triano, Education Manager, 503-494-2012, Fax: 503-494-4981, E-mail: pmph@ohsu.edu. Web site: http://www.ohsu.edu/public-health.

Oregon State University, Graduate School, College of Public Health and Human Sciences, Programs in Public Health, Program in Epidemiology, Corvallis, OR 97331. Offers MPH.

Ponce School of Medicine & Health Sciences, Program in Public Health, Ponce, PR 00732-7004. Offers epidemiology (Dr PH); public health (MPH). *Degree requirements:* For master's, one foreign language, comprehensive exam, thesis. *Entrance requirements:* For master's, GRE General Test or EXADEP, proficiency in Spanish and English, minimum GPA of 2.7, 3 letters of recommendation; for doctorate, GRE, proficiency in Spanish and English, minimum GPA of 3.0, letter of recommendation.

Purdue University, School of Veterinary Medicine and Graduate School, Graduate Programs in Veterinary Medicine, Department of Comparative Pathobiology, West Lafayette, IN 47907-2027. Offers comparative epidemiology and public health (MS); comparative epidemiology and public heath (PhD); comparative microbiology and immunology (MS, PhD); comparative pathobiology (MS, PhD); interdisciplinary studies (PhD), including microbial pathogenesis, molecular signaling and cancer biology, molecular virology; lab animal medicine (MS); veterinary anatomic pathology (MS); veterinary clinical pathology (MS). Terminal master's awarded for partial completion of doctoral program. *Degree requirements:* For master's, thesis (for some programs); for doctorate, thesis/dissertation. *Entrance requirements:* For master's and doctorate, GRE General Test. Additional exam requirements/recommendations for international students: Required—TOEFL (minimum score 575 paper-based; 232 computer-based), IELTS (minimum score 6.5), TWE (minimum score 4). Electronic applications accepted.

Queen's University at Kingston, School of Graduate Studies and Research, Faculty of Health Sciences, Department of Community Health and Epidemiology, Kingston, ON K7L 3N6, Canada. Offers epidemiology (PhD); epidemiology and population health (M Sc); health services (M Sc); policy research and clinical epidemiology (M Sc); public health (MPH). Part-time programs available. *Degree requirements:* For master's, thesis. *Entrance requirements:* For master's, GRE General Test (strongly recommended). Additional exam requirements/recommendations for international students: Required—TOEFL (minimum score 600 paper-based; 250 computer-based). *Faculty research:* Cancer epidemiology, clinical trials, biostatistics health services research, health policy.

San Diego State University, Graduate and Research Affairs, College of Health and Human Services, Graduate School of Public Health, San Diego, CA 92182. Offers environmental health (MPH); epidemiology (MPH, PhD), including biostatistics (MPH); global emergency preparedness and response (MS); global health (PhD); health behavior (PhD); health promotion (MPH); health services administration (MPH); toxicology (MS); MPH/MA; MSW/MPH. *Accreditation:* ABET (one or more programs are accredited); CAHME (one or more programs are accredited); CEPH (one or more programs are accredited). Part-time programs available. *Degree requirements:* For master's, comprehensive exam (for some programs), thesis (for some programs); for doctorate, thesis/dissertation. *Entrance requirements:* For master's, GMAT (MPH in health services administration), GRE General Test; for doctorate, GRE General Test. Additional exam requirements/recommendations for international students: Required—TOEFL. *Faculty research:* Evaluation of tobacco, AIDS prevalence and prevention, mammography, infant death project, Alzheimer's in elderly Chinese.

Stanford University, School of Medicine, Graduate Programs in Medicine, Division of Epidemiology, Stanford, CA 94305-9991. Offers MS, PhD. *Degree requirements:* For master's, thesis; for doctorate, thesis/dissertation, qualifying examinations. *Entrance requirements:* For doctorate, GRE General Test or MCAT. Additional exam requirements/recommendations for international students: Required—TOEFL. Electronic applications accepted. *Expenses: Tuition:* Full-time $40,050; part-time $890 per credit.

Temple University, Health Sciences Center, College of Health Professions and Social Work, Department of Public Health, Philadelphia, PA 19122-6096. Offers environmental health (MS); epidemiology (MS); public health (MPH, PhD); school health education (Ed M). *Accreditation:* CEPH (one or more programs are accredited). Part-time and evening/weekend programs available. *Faculty:* 15 full-time (8 women). *Students:* 62 full-time (44 women), 28 part-time (25 women); includes 24 minority (14 Black or African American, non-Hispanic/Latino; 5 Asian, non-Hispanic/Latino; 5 Hispanic/Latino), 7 international. Average age 29. 92 applicants, 68% accepted, 29 enrolled. In 2011, 30 master's, 4 doctorates awarded. Terminal master's awarded for partial completion of doctoral program. *Degree requirements:* For doctorate, thesis/dissertation. *Entrance requirements:* For master's and doctorate, minimum undergraduate GPA of 3.0. Additional exam requirements/recommendations for international students: Required—TOEFL (minimum score 550 paper-based; 213 computer-based; 79 iBT). Application fee: $50. Electronic applications accepted. *Expenses:* Tuition, state resident: full-time $12,366; part-time $687 per credit hour. Tuition, nonresident: full-time $17,298; part-time $961 per credit hour. *Required fees:* $590; $213 per year. *Financial support:* Fellowships with tuition reimbursements, research assistantships with tuition reimbursements, teaching assistantships with tuition reimbursements, career-related internships or fieldwork, Federal Work-Study, institutionally sponsored loans, scholarships/grants, and tuition waivers (partial) available. Financial award application deadline: 1/15; financial award applicants required to submit FAFSA. *Faculty research:* Program development and evaluation in HIV prevention, violence prevention, women's health policy, psychosocial aspects of disability. *Unit head:* Dr. Alice J. Hausman, Chair, 215-204-5112, Fax: 215-204-1854, E-mail: publichealth@temple.edu. *Application contact:* Tara Schumacher, Coordinator of Outreach, 215-204-6575, Fax: 215-204-8781, E-mail: tara.schumacher@temple.edu. Web site: http://chpsw.temple.edu/publichealth/.

Texas A&M Health Science Center, School of Rural Public Health, College Station, TX 77840. Offers environmental/occupational health (MPH); epidemiology/biostatistics (MPH); health policy/management (MPH); social and behavioral health (MPH). *Accreditation:* CEPH. Part-time programs available. Postbaccalaureate distance learning degree programs offered (no on-campus study). *Degree requirements:* For master's, thesis optional. *Entrance requirements:* For master's, GRE General Test, minimum undergraduate GPA of 3.0. Electronic applications accepted. *Faculty research:* Tobacco cessation, youth health risk.

Texas A&M University, College of Veterinary Medicine and Biomedical Sciences, Department of Veterinary Integrative Biosciences, College Station, TX 77843. Offers epidemiology (MS); food safety/toxicology/environmental health (MS); science and technology journalism (MS); veterinary public health (MS). *Faculty:* 23. *Students:* 34 full-time (18 women), 12 part-time (9 women); includes 10 minority (2 Black or African American, non-Hispanic/Latino; 5 Asian, non-Hispanic/Latino; 3 Hispanic/Latino), 19 international. Average age 30. Terminal master's awarded for partial completion of doctoral program. *Degree requirements:* For master's, comprehensive exam, thesis. *Entrance requirements:* For master's, GRE General Test, minimum undergraduate GPA of 3.0. Additional exam requirements/recommendations for international students: Required—TOEFL. *Application deadline:* For fall admission, 7/15 priority date for domestic students, 4/1 for international students; for spring admission, 10/1 priority date for domestic students, 9/15 for international students. Applications are processed on a rolling basis. Application fee: $50 ($75 for international students). Electronic applications accepted. *Expenses:* Tuition, state resident: full-time $5437; part-time $226.55 per credit hour. Tuition, nonresident: full-time $12,949; part-time $539.55 per credit hour. *Required fees:* $2741. *Financial support:* In 2011–12, fellowships (averaging $18,000 per year), research assistantships (averaging $15,600 per year), teaching assistantships (averaging $15,600 per year) were awarded; institutionally sponsored loans, unspecified assistantships, and clinical associateships also available. Financial award application deadline: 7/15; financial award applicants required to submit FAFSA. *Faculty research:* Metal toxicology, reproductive biology, genetics of neural development, developmental biology, environmental toxicology. *Unit head:* Dr. Evelyn Tiffany-Castiglioni, Head, 979-458-1077, E-mail: c-tiffany@tamu.edu. *Application contact:* Graduate Admissions, 979-845-1044, E-mail: admissions@tamu.edu. Web site: http://vetmed.tamu.edu/vibs.

Thomas Edison State College, School of Applied Science and Technology, Program in Clinical Trials Management, Trenton, NJ 08608-1176. Offers Graduate Certificate. Part-time programs available. Postbaccalaureate distance learning degree programs offered (no on-campus study). *Students:* 20 part-time (13 women); includes 7 minority (2 Black or African American, non-Hispanic/Latino; 2 Asian, non-Hispanic/Latino; 3 Hispanic/Latino). Average age 42. In 2011, 6 Graduate Certificates awarded. *Entrance requirements:* Additional exam requirements/recommendations for international students: Required—TOEFL (minimum score 550 paper-based; 213 computer-based; 79 iBT). *Application deadline:* For fall admission, 8/15 priority date for domestic students, 8/15 for international students; for winter admission, 11/15 priority date for domestic students, 11/15 for international students; for spring admission, 2/15 priority date for domestic students, 2/18 for international students. Applications are processed on a rolling basis. Application fee: $75. Electronic applications accepted. *Financial support:* Applicants required to submit FAFSA. *Unit head:* Dr. Thomas G. Divine, Dean, School of Applied Science and Technology, 609-984-1130, Fax: 609-984-3898, E-mail: info@tesc.edu. *Application contact:* David Hoftiezer, Director of Admissions, 888-442-8372, Fax: 609-984-8447, E-mail: admissions@tesc.edu. Web site: http://www.tesc.edu/2248.php.

Thomas Jefferson University, Jefferson College of Graduate Studies, Certificate Programs in Clinical Research, Human Clinical Investigation, and Infectious Diseases, Philadelphia, PA 19107. Offers Certificate. *Faculty:* 22 full-time (7 women), 23 part-time/adjunct (6 women). *Students:* 14 part-time (10 women); includes 7 minority (2 Black or African American, non-Hispanic/Latino; 4 Asian, non-Hispanic/Latino; 1 Hispanic/Latino), 3 international. 20 applicants, 75% accepted, 11 enrolled. In 2011, 6 Certificates awarded. *Entrance requirements:* For degree, GRE General Test (recommended). Additional exam requirements/recommendations for international students: Required—TOEFL (minimum score 100 iBT) or IELTS (minimum score 7). *Application deadline:* For fall admission, 8/1 priority date for domestic students, 3/1 for international students; for winter admission, 12/1 priority date for domestic students, 6/1 for international students; for spring admission, 4/1 priority date for domestic students. Applications are processed on a rolling basis. Application fee: $50. Electronic applications accepted. *Financial support:* In 2011–12, 5 students received support. Federal Work-Study and institutionally sponsored loans available. Support available to part-time students. Financial award application deadline: 5/1; financial award applicants required to submit FAFSA. *Faculty research:* Epidemiology, clinical research, statistics, planning and management, disease control. *Unit head:* Dr. Dennis M. Gross, Associate Dean, 215-503-0156, Fax: 215-503-3433, E-mail: dennis.gross@jefferson.edu. *Application contact:* Eleanor M. Gorman, Assistant Coordinator, Graduate Center Programs, 215-503-5799, Fax: 215-503-3433, E-mail: eleanor.gorman@jefferson.edu. Web site: http://www.jefferson.edu/jcgs/cert/.

Thomas Jefferson University, Jefferson School of Population Health, Program in Chronic Care Management, Philadelphia, PA 19107. Offers MS, PhD, Certificate. Postbaccalaureate distance learning degree programs offered (no on-campus study). *Entrance requirements:* For master's, GRE or other graduate examination, 2 letters of recommendation, interview. Additional exam requirements/recommendations for international students: Required—TOEFL. Electronic applications accepted.

Tufts University, Graduate School of Arts and Sciences, Graduate Certificate Programs, Program in Epidemiology, Medford, MA 02155. Offers Certificate. Electronic applications accepted. *Expenses: Tuition:* Full-time $41,208; part-time $1030 per credit hour. Full-time tuition and fees vary according to degree level, program and student level. Part-time tuition and fees vary according to course load.

Tufts University, Sackler School of Graduate Biomedical Sciences, Clinical and Translational Science Program, Medford, MA 02155. Offers MS, PhD. *Faculty:* 33 full-time (9 women). *Students:* 31 full-time (16 women); includes 6 minority (4 Asian, non-Hispanic/Latino; 1 Hispanic/Latino; 1 Two or more races, non-Hispanic/Latino), 13 international. Average age 33. In 2011, 11 degrees awarded. Terminal master's awarded for partial completion of doctoral program. *Degree requirements:* For master's, thesis; for doctorate, thesis/dissertation. *Entrance requirements:* For master's and doctorate, MD or PhD, strong clinical research background. Additional exam requirements/recommendations for international students: Required—TOEFL (minimum score 600 paper-based; 250 computer-based; 100 iBT). *Application deadline:* For fall admission, 12/15 for domestic and international students. Application fee: $70. Electronic applications accepted. *Expenses: Tuition:* Full-time $41,208; part-time $1030 per credit hour. Full-time tuition and fees vary according to degree level, program and student level. Part-time tuition and fees vary according to course load. *Financial support:* Application deadline: 12/15. *Faculty research:* Clinical study design, mathematical modeling, meta analysis, epidemiologic research, coronary heart disease. *Unit head:* Dr. David Kent, Program Director, 617-636-3234, Fax: 617-636-8023, E-mail: dkent@tuftsmedicalcenter.edu. *Application contact:* Kellie Melchin, Associate Director of Admissions, 617-636-6767, Fax: 617-636-0375, E-mail: sackler-school@tufts.edu. Web site: http://sackler.tufts.edu/Academics/Degree-Programs/PhD-Programs/Clinical-and-Translational-Science.

Tulane University, School of Public Health and Tropical Medicine, Department of Epidemiology, New Orleans, LA 70118-5669. Offers MPH, MS, Dr PH, PhD. MS and PhD offered through the Graduate School. *Accreditation:* CEPH (one or more programs are accredited). Part-time programs available. *Degree requirements:* For doctorate, comprehensive exam, thesis/dissertation. *Entrance requirements:* For master's and doctorate, GRE General Test. Additional exam requirements/recommendations for international students: Required—TOEFL. Electronic applications accepted. *Faculty research:* Environment, cancer, cardiovascular epidemiology, women's health.

Université Laval, Faculty of Medicine, Graduate Programs in Medicine, Department of Medicine, Programs in Epidemiology, Québec, QC G1K 7P4, Canada. Offers M Sc, PhD. Terminal master's awarded for partial completion of doctoral program. *Degree requirements:* For master's, thesis; for doctorate, comprehensive exam, thesis/dissertation. *Entrance requirements:* For master's and doctorate, knowledge of French, comprehension of written English. Electronic applications accepted.

University at Albany, State University of New York, School of Public Health, Department of Epidemiology and Biostatistics, Albany, NY 12222-0001. Offers MS, PhD. *Degree requirements:* For master's, thesis; for doctorate, thesis/dissertation. *Entrance requirements:* For master's and doctorate, GRE General Test. Additional exam requirements/recommendations for international students: Required—TOEFL (minimum score 550 paper-based; 213 computer-based). Electronic applications accepted.

University at Buffalo, the State University of New York, Graduate School, School of Public Health and Health Professions, Department of Social and Preventive Medicine, Buffalo, NY 14214. Offers epidemiology (MS, PhD); public health (MPH). Part-time programs available. *Faculty:* 13 full-time (7 women), 6 part-time/adjunct (3 women). *Students:* 41 full-time (27 women), 15 part-time (13 women); includes 7 minority (3 Black or African American, non-Hispanic/Latino; 4 Asian, non-Hispanic/Latino), 10 international. Average age 29. 111 applicants, 50% accepted, 18 enrolled. In 2011, 18 master's, 3 doctorates awarded. Terminal master's awarded for partial completion of doctoral program. *Degree requirements:* For master's, comprehensive exam, thesis; for doctorate, comprehensive exam, thesis/dissertation. *Entrance requirements:* For master's and doctorate, GRE General Test. Additional exam requirements/recommendations for international students: Required—TOEFL (minimum score 600 paper-based; 250 computer-based; 100 iBT). *Application deadline:* For fall admission, 1/15 priority date for domestic students, 1/15 for international students. Applications are processed on a rolling basis. Application fee: $50. Electronic applications accepted. *Financial support:* In 2011–12, 17 students received support, including 5 fellowships with full tuition reimbursements available (averaging $22,000 per year), 7 research assistantships with full tuition reimbursements available (averaging $20,000 per year); teaching assistantships with full tuition reimbursements available, career-related internships or fieldwork, Federal Work-Study, institutionally sponsored loans, health care benefits, and unspecified assistantships also available. Financial award application deadline: 2/1; financial award applicants required to submit FAFSA. *Faculty research:* Epidemiology of cancer, nutrition, infectious diseases, epidemiology of environmental,

Epidemiology

women's health and CVD research. *Unit head:* Dr. Jo Freudenheim, Chair, 716-829-5375, Fax: 716-829-2979, E-mail: jfreuden@buffalo.edu. *Application contact:* Dr. Carl Li, Director of Graduate Studies, 716-829-5382, Fax: 716-829-2979, E-mail: carlli@buffalo.edu. Web site: http://sphhp.buffalo.edu/spm/.

See Display below and Close-Up on page 867.

The University of Alabama at Birmingham, School of Public Health, Program in Epidemiology, Birmingham, AL 35294. Offers PhD. *Degree requirements:* For doctorate, thesis/dissertation. *Entrance requirements:* For doctorate, GRE General Test or MAT, MPH or MSPH. *Expenses:* Tuition, state resident: full-time $5922; part-time $309 per hour. Tuition, nonresident: full-time $13,428; part-time $726 per hour. Tuition and fees vary according to program. *Financial support:* Career-related internships or fieldwork available. *Faculty research:* Biometry. *Unit head:* Dr. Donna K. Arnett, Chair, 205-934-7066, Fax: 205-934-8665, E-mail: arnett@uab.edu. Web site: http://www.uab.edu/publichealth/Epidem.html.

University of Alberta, School of Public Health, Department of Public Health Sciences, Edmonton, AB T6G 2E1, Canada. Offers clinical epidemiology (M Sc, MPH); environmental and occupational health (MPH); environmental health sciences (M Sc); epidemiology (M Sc); global health (M Sc, MPH); health policy and management (MPH); health policy research (M Sc); health technology assessment (MPH); occupational health (M Sc); population health (M Sc); public health leadership (MPH); public health sciences (PhD); quantitative methods (MPH). *Accreditation:* CEPH (one or more programs are accredited). Terminal master's awarded for partial completion of doctoral program. *Degree requirements:* For master's, thesis (for some programs); for doctorate, thesis/dissertation. *Entrance requirements:* For master's, GMAT or GRE General Test. Additional exam requirements/recommendations for international students: Required—TOEFL (minimum score 550 paper-based; 213 computer-based) or IELTS (minimum score 6). Electronic applications accepted. *Faculty research:* Biostatistics, health promotion and socio-behavioral health science.

The University of Arizona, Mel and Enid Zuckerman College of Public Health, Program in Epidemiology, Tucson, AZ 85721. Offers MS, PhD. *Faculty:* 9 full-time (6 women), 1 (woman) part-time/adjunct. *Students:* 17 full-time (10 women), 3 part-time (all women); includes 4 minority (1 Black or African American, non-Hispanic/Latino; 2 Hispanic/Latino; 1 Two or more races, non-Hispanic/Latino), 4 international. Average age 38. 42 applicants, 19% accepted, 1 enrolled. In 2011, 1 master's, 4 doctorates awarded. *Entrance requirements:* Additional exam requirements/recommendations for international students: Required—TOEFL (minimum score 550 paper-based; 213 computer-based; 79 iBT). *Application deadline:* For fall admission, 1/1 for domestic and international students. Applications are processed on a rolling basis. Application fee: $75. Electronic applications accepted. *Expenses:* Tuition, state resident: full-time $10,840. Tuition, nonresident: full-time $25,802. *Financial support:* In 2011–12, 4 research assistantships (averaging $18,151 per year), 14 teaching assistantships (averaging $18,469 per year) were awarded. *Total annual research expenditures:* $4.2 million. *Unit head:* Dr. Iman Hakim, Interim Dean, 520-626-7083, E-mail: ihakim@email.arizona.edu. *Application contact:* Lorraine Varela, Special Assistant to the Dean, 520-626-3201, E-mail: varela@coph.arizona.edu.

The University of British Columbia, Faculty of Medicine, School of Population and Public Health, Vancouver, BC V6T 1Z3, Canada. Offers health administration (MHA); health care and epidemiology (MH Sc, PhD); public health (MPH). *Accreditation:* CEPH (one or more programs are accredited). Postbaccalaureate distance learning degree programs offered (minimal on-campus study). *Degree requirements:* For master's, thesis (for some programs), major paper (MH Sc), research project (MHA); for doctorate, thesis/dissertation. *Entrance requirements:* For master's, GRE General Test or GMAT, PCAT, MCAT (MHA), MD or equivalent (for MH Sc); 4-year undergraduate degree from accredited university with minimum B+ overall academic average and in math or statistics course at undergraduate level (for MPH); 4-year undergraduate degree from accredited university with minimum B+ overall academic average plus work experience (for MHA); for doctorate, master's degree from accredited university with minimum B+ overall academic average and in math or statistics course at undergraduate level. Additional exam requirements/recommendations for international students: Required—TOEFL. Electronic applications accepted. *Faculty research:* Population and public health, clinical epidemiology, epidemiology and biostatistics, global health and vulnerable populations, health care services and systems, occupational and environmental health, public health emerging threats and rapid response, social and life course determinants of health, health administration.

University of Calgary, Faculty of Medicine and Faculty of Graduate Studies, Department of Microbiology and Infectious Diseases, Calgary, AB T2N 1N4, Canada. Offers M Sc, PhD. *Degree requirements:* For master's, thesis, oral thesis exam; for doctorate, thesis/dissertation, candidacy exam, oral thesis exam. *Entrance requirements:* For master's and doctorate, minimum GPA of 3.2. Additional exam requirements/recommendations for international students: Required—TOEFL (minimum score 580 paper-based; 237 computer-based). Electronic applications accepted. *Faculty research:* Bacteriology, virology, parasitology, immunology.

University of California, Berkeley, Graduate Division, School of Public Health, Group in Epidemiology, Berkeley, CA 94720-1500. Offers epidemiology (MS, PhD); infectious diseases (MPH, PhD). *Accreditation:* CEPH (one or more programs are accredited). *Degree requirements:* For master's, comprehensive exam; for doctorate, thesis/dissertation, oral and written exam. *Entrance requirements:* For master's, GRE General Test, minimum GPA of 3.0; MD, DDS, DVM, or PhD in biomedical science (MPH); for doctorate, GRE General Test, minimum GPA of 3.0.

University of California, Davis, Graduate Studies, Graduate Group in Epidemiology, Davis, CA 95616. Offers MS, PhD. Terminal master's awarded for partial completion of doctoral program. *Degree requirements:* For master's, comprehensive exam (for some programs), thesis (for some programs); for doctorate, thesis/dissertation. *Entrance requirements:* For master's and doctorate, GRE General Test, GRE Subject Test (biology), minimum GPA of 3.25. Additional exam requirements/recommendations for international students: Required—TOEFL (minimum score 550 paper-based; 213 computer-based). Electronic applications accepted. *Faculty research:* Environmental/occupational wildlife, reproductive and veterinary epidemiology, infectious/chronic disease epidemiology, public health.

University of California, Irvine, School of Medicine, Department of Epidemiology, Irvine, CA 92697. Offers MS, PhD. *Students:* 4 full-time (3 women); includes 3 minority (2 Asian, non-Hispanic/Latino; 1 Hispanic/Latino). Average age 27. 2 applicants, 100% accepted, 2 enrolled. Terminal master's awarded for partial completion of doctoral program. *Degree requirements:* For master's, comprehensive exam, thesis; for doctorate, comprehensive exam, thesis/dissertation. *Entrance requirements:* For master's, GRE, minimum GPA of 3.0, letters of recommendation; for doctorate, GRE, minimum GPA of 3.0, personal statement, letters of recommendation. Additional exam requirements/recommendations for international students: Required—TOEFL (minimum score 550 paper-based; 213 computer-based; 80 iBT), IELTS (minimum score 7). *Application deadline:* For fall admission, 1/15 priority date for domestic students, 1/15 for international students. Application fee: $60 ($80 for international students). Electronic applications accepted. *Financial support:* In 2011–12, 6 students received support, including fellowships with full tuition reimbursements available (averaging $25,000 per year), research assistantships with full tuition reimbursements available (averaging $46,000 per year), teaching assistantships with full tuition reimbursements available (averaging $33,000 per year); Federal Work-Study,

University at Buffalo
The State University of New York

Department of Social and Preventive Medicine

- M.S. and Ph.D. programs designed for individuals who wish to pursue advanced training in epidemiological research; exciting research opportunities include work in women's health, cancer, genetics, global health and environmental health

- MPH programs provide training for public health practitioners in epidemiology, environmental health sciences or health services administration

- Close collaboration with such facilities as Roswell Park Cancer Institute (National Cancer Institute–designated comprehensive cancer center), health departments, hospitals, and other schools within our own urban research University

- Outstanding and affordable educational educational opportunities with exceptional and varied career options.

For more information, please contact:
Dr. Carl Li, M.D., M.P.H.
Director of Graduate Studies
Department of Social and Preventive Medicine
University at Buffalo (SUNY)
270 Farber Hall
Buffalo, New York 14214-8001
716-829-5382

carlli@buffalo.edu

http://sphhp.buffalo.edu/spm

institutionally sponsored loans, scholarships/grants, traineeships, health care benefits, and unspecified assistantships also available. Financial award application deadline: 1/15; financial award applicants required to submit FAFSA. *Faculty research:* Genetic/molecular epidemiology, cancer epidemiology, biostatistics, environmental health, occupational health. *Total annual research expenditures:* $15 million. *Unit head:* Dr. Hoda Anton-Culver, Chair, 949-824-7401, Fax: 949-824-4773, E-mail: hantoncu@uci.edu. *Application contact:* Julie Strope, Departmental Administrator, 949-824-0306, Fax: 949-824-4773, E-mail: jstrope@uci.edu. Web site: http://www.epi.uci.edu/.

University of California, Irvine, School of Social Ecology, Programs in Social Ecology, Irvine, CA 92697. Offers environmental analysis and design (PhD); epidemiology and public health (PhD); social ecology (PhD). *Students:* 10 full-time (9 women), 1 (woman) part-time; includes 2 minority (1 Asian, non-Hispanic/Latino; 1 Hispanic/Latino), 1 international. Average age 34. 19 applicants, 11% accepted, 2 enrolled. In 2011, 1 doctorate awarded. Application fee: $80 ($100 for international students). *Unit head:* Valerie Jenness, Dean, 949-824-6094, Fax: 949-824-1845, E-mail: jenness@uci.edu. *Application contact:* Maria Victoria Dela Cruz, Director, Graduate Services, 949-824-5918, Fax: 949-824-1845, E-mail: mvdelacr@uci.edu. Web site: http://socialecology.uci.edu/graduate-se-core-programs.

University of California, Los Angeles, Graduate Division, School of Public Health, Department of Epidemiology, Los Angeles, CA 90095. Offers MPH, MS, Dr PH, PhD, MD/MPH. *Degree requirements:* For master's, comprehensive exam or thesis; for doctorate, thesis/dissertation, oral and written qualifying exams. *Entrance requirements:* For master's, GRE General Test, minimum GPA of 3.0; for doctorate, GRE General Test, minimum undergraduate GPA of 3.0. Electronic applications accepted.

University of California, San Diego, Office of Graduate Studies, Program in Public Health and Epidemiology, La Jolla, CA 92093. Offers PhD. Program offered jointly with San Diego State University. Electronic applications accepted.

University of Cincinnati, Graduate School, College of Medicine, Graduate Programs in Biomedical Sciences, Department of Environmental Health, Cincinnati, OH 45221. Offers environmental and industrial hygiene (MS, PhD); environmental and occupational medicine (MS); environmental genetics and molecular toxicology (MS, PhD); epidemiology and biostatistics (MS, PhD); occupational safety and ergonomics (MS, PhD). *Accreditation:* ABET (one or more programs are accredited). Terminal master's awarded for partial completion of doctoral program. *Degree requirements:* For master's, thesis; for doctorate, thesis/dissertation, qualifying exam. *Entrance requirements:* For master's, GRE General Test, bachelor's degree in science; for doctorate, GRE General Test. Additional exam requirements/recommendations for international students: Required—TOEFL (minimum score 600 paper-based; 250 computer-based; 100 iBT). Electronic applications accepted. *Faculty research:* Carcinogens and mutagenesis, pulmonary studies, reproduction and development.

University of Colorado Denver, Colorado School of Public Health, Department of Epidemiology, Aurora, CO 80045. Offers MS, PhD. Part-time programs available. *Students:* 16 full-time (10 women), 7 part-time (3 women); includes 3 minority (1 Black or African American, non-Hispanic/Latino; 1 Hispanic/Latino; 1 Two or more races, non-Hispanic/Latino), 6 international. Average age 35. 30 applicants, 20% accepted, 5 enrolled. In 2011, 3 doctorates awarded. *Degree requirements:* For master's, thesis, 38 credit hours; for doctorate, comprehensive exam, thesis/dissertation, 67 credit hours. *Entrance requirements:* For master's, GRE General Test, baccalaureate degree in scientific field, minimum GPA of 3.0, math course work through integral calculus, two official copies of all academic transcripts, four letters of recommendation/reference, essays describing the applicant's career goals and reasons for applying to the program, resume; for doctorate, GRE or MCAT, bachelor's, master's, or higher degree; minimum undergraduate and graduate GPA of 3.0; coursework in calculus, organic chemistry, epidemiology, biological sciences, and public health; 2 official copies of all academic transcripts; 4 letters of reference; essays. Additional exam requirements/recommendations for international students: Required—TOEFL (minimum score 550 paper-based; 213 computer-based; 80 iBT). *Application deadline:* For fall admission, 2/1 for domestic students, 1/1 for international students. Application fee: $65. Electronic applications accepted. *Expenses:* Contact institution. *Financial support:* Fellowships, research assistantships, Federal Work-Study, scholarships/grants, and unspecified assistantships available. Financial award application deadline: 3/1; financial award applicants required to submit FAFSA. *Faculty research:* Public health practice and practice-based research, reproductive and perinatal epidemiology, obesity, infectious disease epidemiology, diabetes. *Unit head:* Dr. Jill Norris, Chair, 303-724-4428, E-mail: jill.norris@ucdenver.edu. *Application contact:* Dr. Dana Dabelea, Concentration Director, 303-724-4414, E-mail: dana.dabelea@ucdenver.edu. Web site: http://www.ucdenver.edu/academics/colleges/PublicHealth/departments/Epidemiology/Pages/welcome.aspx.

University of Colorado Denver, Colorado School of Public Health, Program in Public Health, Aurora, CO 80045. Offers community and behavioral health (MPH, Dr PH); environmental and occupational health (MPH); epidemiology (MPH); health systems, management and policy (MPH). *Accreditation:* CEPH. Part-time and evening/weekend programs available. *Students:* 216 full-time (177 women), 47 part-time (38 women); includes 48 minority (10 Black or African American, non-Hispanic/Latino; 5 American Indian or Alaska Native, non-Hispanic/Latino; 14 Asian, non-Hispanic/Latino; 17 Hispanic/Latino; 1 Native Hawaiian or other Pacific Islander, non-Hispanic/Latino; 1 Two or more races, non-Hispanic/Latino), 7 international. Average age 33. 670 applicants, 51% accepted, 160 enrolled. In 2011, 83 degrees awarded. *Degree requirements:* For master's, thesis or alternative, 42 credit hours; for doctorate, comprehensive exam, thesis/dissertation, 67 credit hours. *Entrance requirements:* For master's, GRE, baccalaureate degree or equivalent; minimum GPA of 3.0; transcripts; references; resume; essay; for doctorate, GRE, MPH or master's or higher degree in related field or equivalent; 2 years previous work experience in public health, essay, resume. Additional exam requirements/recommendations for international students: Required—TOEFL (minimum score 550 paper-based; 213 computer-based). *Application deadline:* For fall admission, 2/1 for domestic students. Application fee: $65. Electronic applications accepted. *Expenses:* Contact institution. *Financial support:* Fellowships, research assistantships, Federal Work-Study, scholarships/grants, and unspecified assistantships available. Support available to part-time students. Financial award application deadline: 3/15; financial award applicants required to submit FAFSA. *Faculty research:* Cancer prevention by nutrition, cancer survivorship outcomes, social and cultural factors related to health. *Unit head:* Dr. Jack Barnette, Program Director, 303-724-4472, E-mail: jack.barnette@ucdenver.edu. *Application contact:* Jennifer Pacheco, Admissions Specialist, 303-724-5585, E-mail: jennifer.pacheco@ucdenver.edu. Web site: http://www.ucdenver.edu/academics/colleges/PublicHealth/departments/CommunityBehavioralHealth/Pages/CommunityBehavioralHealth.aspx.

University of Florida, College of Medicine, Program in Clinical Investigation, Gainesville, FL 32611. Offers clinical investigation (MS); epidemiology (MS); public health (MPH). Part-time programs available. *Entrance requirements:* For master's, GRE, MD, PhD, DMD/DDS or Pharm D.

University of Florida, Graduate School, College of Public Health and Health Professions, Programs in Public Health, Gainesville, FL 32611. Offers biostatistics (MPH); environmental health (MPH); epidemiology (MPH); public health management and policy (MPH); public health practice (MPH); social and behavioral sciences (MPH). *Accreditation:* CEPH. Postbaccalaureate distance learning degree programs offered. *Students:* 76 full-time (57 women), 21 part-time (13 women); includes 33 minority (15 Black or African American, non-Hispanic/Latino; 12 Asian, non-Hispanic/Latino; 6 Hispanic/Latino), 7 international. Average age 30. 313 applicants, 49% accepted, 63 enrolled. In 2011, 66 master's awarded. *Degree requirements:* For master's, internship. *Entrance requirements:* For master's, GRE General Test, minimum GPA of 3.0. Additional exam requirements/recommendations for international students: Required—TOEFL (minimum score 550 paper-based; 213 computer-based; 80 iBT), IELTS (minimum score 6). Application fee: $30. *Financial support:* In 2011–12, 14 students received support, including 1 fellowship, 11 research assistantships, 2 teaching assistantships. Financial award applicants required to submit FAFSA. *Unit head:* Mary Peoples Sheps, Senior Associate Dean for Public Health, 352-273-6084, Fax: 352-273-6448, E-mail: mpeoplessheps@phhp.ufl.edu. Web site: http://www.mph.ufl.edu/.

University of Guelph, Ontario Veterinary College and Graduate Studies, Graduate Programs in Veterinary Sciences, Department of Population Medicine, Guelph, ON N1G 2W1, Canada. Offers epidemiology (M Sc, DV Sc, PhD); health management (DV Sc); population medicine and health management (M Sc); swine health management (M Sc); theriogenology (M Sc, DV Sc). *Degree requirements:* For master's, thesis; for doctorate, comprehensive exam, thesis/dissertation. *Entrance requirements:* Additional exam requirements/recommendations for international students: Required—TOEFL.

University of Hawaii at Manoa, John A. Burns School of Medicine, Department of Public Health Sciences and Epidemiology, Program in Epidemiology, Honolulu, HI 96822. Offers PhD. Part-time programs available. *Degree requirements:* For doctorate, comprehensive exam, thesis/dissertation. *Entrance requirements:* For doctorate, GRE General Test. Additional exam requirements/recommendations for international students: Required—TOEFL (minimum score 600 paper-based; 250 computer-based; 100 iBT), IELTS (minimum score 7).

University of Illinois at Chicago, Graduate College, School of Public Health, Program in Epidemiology, Chicago, IL 60607-7128. Offers cancer epidemiology (MS, PhD); epidemiology (MPH, MS, Dr PH, PhD). *Accreditation:* CEPH (one or more programs are accredited). Part-time programs available. Terminal master's awarded for partial completion of doctoral program. *Degree requirements:* For master's, thesis, field practicum; for doctorate, thesis/dissertation, independent research, internship. *Entrance requirements:* For master's and doctorate, GRE General Test, minimum GPA of 2.75. Additional exam requirements/recommendations for international students: Required—TOEFL. Electronic applications accepted.

The University of Iowa, Graduate College, College of Public Health, Department of Epidemiology, Iowa City, IA 52242-1316. Offers clinical investigation (MS); epidemiology (MS, PhD). *Accreditation:* CEPH. *Degree requirements:* For master's, thesis optional, exam; for doctorate, comprehensive exam, thesis/dissertation. *Entrance requirements:* For master's and doctorate, GRE General Test, minimum GPA of 3.0. Additional exam requirements/recommendations for international students: Required—TOEFL (minimum score 600 paper-based; 250 computer-based; 100 iBT). Electronic applications accepted.

The University of Kansas, University of Kansas Medical Center, School of Medicine, Department of Preventive Medicine and Public Health, Kansas City, KS 66160. Offers biostatistics (MPH); clinical research (MS); environmental health sciences (MPH); epidemiology (MPH); public health management (MPH); social and behavioral health (MPH); MD/MPH; MPH/MSN; PhD/MPH. Part-time programs available. *Faculty:* 76. *Students:* 51 full-time (32 women), 74 part-time (53 women); includes 35 minority (10 Black or African American, non-Hispanic/Latino; 4 American Indian or Alaska Native, non-Hispanic/Latino; 9 Asian, non-Hispanic/Latino; 8 Hispanic/Latino; 4 Two or more races, non-Hispanic/Latino), 6 international. Average age 33. 77 applicants, 69% accepted, 45 enrolled. In 2011, 25 master's awarded. *Degree requirements:* For master's, thesis, capstone practicum defense. *Entrance requirements:* For master's, GRE, MCAT, LSAT, GMAT or other equivalent graduate professional exam. Additional exam requirements/recommendations for international students: Required—TOEFL. *Application deadline:* For fall admission, 3/1 for domestic and international students. Applications are processed on a rolling basis. Application fee: $60. Tuition and fees vary according to course load, campus/location, program and reciprocity agreements. *Financial support:* In 2011–12, 21 research assistantships (averaging $10,200 per year) were awarded; career-related internships or fieldwork, Federal Work-Study, scholarships/grants, and unspecified assistantships also available. Financial award application deadline: 2/14; financial award applicants required to submit FAFSA. *Faculty research:* Cancer screening and prevention, smoking cessation, obesity and physical activity, health services/outcomes research. *Total annual research expenditures:* $8 million. *Unit head:* Dr. Edward F. Ellerbeck, Chairman, 913-588-2774, Fax: 913-588-2780, E-mail: eellerbe@kumc.edu. *Application contact:* Tanya Honderick, Assistant Director, KU-MPH, 913-588-2720, Fax: 913-588-8505, E-mail: thonderick@kumc.edu. Web site: http://ph.kumc.edu/.

University of Louisville, Graduate School, School of Public Health and Information Sciences, Department of Epidemiology and Population Health, Louisville, KY 40292-0001. Offers epidemiology (MPH, MS, PhD). Part-time programs available. Terminal master's awarded for partial completion of doctoral program. *Degree requirements:* For master's, thesis, 38 credit hours of required and elective coursework; for doctorate, comprehensive exam, thesis/dissertation, 50 credit hours of required and elective coursework beyond master's degree. *Entrance requirements:* For master's, GRE, bachelor's degree in appropriate discipline, official transcripts, statement of purpose, resume/curriculum vitae, letters of recommendation; for doctorate, GRE, master's degree or higher, official transcripts, statement of purpose, resume/curriculum vitae, letters of recommendation. Additional exam requirements/recommendations for international students: Required—TOEFL (minimum score 600 paper-based; 250 computer-based; 100 iBT). Electronic applications accepted. *Expenses:* Tuition, state resident: full-time $9692; part-time $539 per credit hour. Tuition, nonresident: full-time $20,168; part-time $1121 per credit hour. Tuition and fees vary according to program and reciprocity agreements. *Faculty research:* Epidemiology: aging, cancer, cardiovascular diseases, infectious diseases, metabolic/nutritional diseases, other chronic diseases; genetic, molecular and environmental risk factors; population genetics, demographics, epidemiologic methods, biostatistics.

University of Maryland, Baltimore, Graduate School, Graduate Program in Life Sciences, Baltimore, MD 21201. Offers biochemistry and molecular biology (MS, PhD), including biochemistry; epidemiology (PhD); gerontology (PhD); molecular medicine (MS, PhD), including cancer biology (PhD), cell and molecular physiology (PhD), human genetics and genomic medicine (PhD), molecular medicine (MS), molecular toxicology and pharmacology (PhD); molecular microbiology and immunology (PhD); neuroscience (PhD); physical rehabilitation science (PhD); toxicology (MS, PhD); MD/MS; MD/PhD. *Students:* 262 full-time (164 women), 49 part-time (30 women); includes 74 minority (21 Black or African American, non-Hispanic/Latino; 1 American Indian or Alaska Native, non-Hispanic/Latino; 30 Asian, non-Hispanic/Latino; 14 Hispanic/Latino; 8 Two or more races, non-Hispanic/Latino), 46 international. Average age 29. 719 applicants, 22% accepted, 64 enrolled. In 2011, 20 master's, 35 doctorates awarded. *Degree*

requirements: For master's, comprehensive exam (for some programs), thesis (for some programs); for doctorate, comprehensive exam, thesis/dissertation. *Entrance requirements:* For master's and doctorate, GRE. Additional exam requirements/recommendations for international students: Required—TOEFL (minimum score 550 paper-based; 80 iBT); Recommended—IELTS (minimum score 7). *Application deadline:* For fall admission, 1/15 for domestic and international students. Application fee: $50. Electronic applications accepted. *Financial support:* In 2011–12, research assistantships with partial tuition reimbursements (averaging $25,000 per year) were awarded; fellowships, scholarships/grants, health care benefits, and unspecified assistantships also available. Financial award application deadline: 3/1. *Faculty research:* Cancer, reproduction, cardiovascular, immunology. *Unit head:* Dr. Margaret Merryl McCarthy, Assistant Dean for Graduate Studies, 410-706-2655, Fax: 410-706-8341, E-mail: mmccarthy@umaryland.edu. *Application contact:* Keith T. Brooks, Assistant Dean, 410-706-7131, Fax: 410-706-3473, E-mail: kbrooks@umaryland.edu. Web site: http://lifesciences.umaryland.edu.

University of Maryland, Baltimore, Graduate School, Graduate Programs in Pharmacy, Department of Pharmaceutical Health Service Research, Baltimore, MD 21201. Offers epidemiology (MS); pharmacy administration (PhD); Pharm D/PhD. *Degree requirements:* For doctorate, comprehensive exam, thesis/dissertation. *Entrance requirements:* For doctorate, GRE General Test. Additional exam requirements/recommendations for international students: Required—TOEFL, IELTS. Electronic applications accepted. *Faculty research:* Pharmacoeconomics, outcomes research, public health policy, drug therapy and aging.

University of Maryland, Baltimore, School of Medicine, Department of Epidemiology and Public Health, Baltimore, MD 21201. Offers biostatistics (MS); clinical research (MS); epidemiology and preventative medicine (PhD); epidemiology and preventive medicine (MPH, MS); gerontology (PhD); human genetics and genomic (PhD); human genetics and genomic medicine (MS); molecular epidemiology (MS, PhD); toxicology (MS, PhD); JD/MS; MD/PhD; MS/PhD. *Accreditation:* CEPH. Part-time programs available. *Students:* 94 full-time (68 women), 61 part-time (46 women); includes 51 minority (18 Black or African American, non-Hispanic/Latino; 25 Asian, non-Hispanic/Latino; 7 Hispanic/Latino; 1 Two or more races, non-Hispanic/Latino), 21 international. Average age 32. 109 applicants, 32% accepted, 19 enrolled. In 2011, 13 master's, 9 doctorates awarded. *Degree requirements:* For doctorate, comprehensive exam, thesis/dissertation. *Entrance requirements:* For master's and doctorate, GRE General Test. Additional exam requirements/recommendations for international students: Required—TOEFL (minimum score 550 paper-based; 213 computer-based; 80 iBT); Recommended—IELTS (minimum score 7). *Application deadline:* For fall admission, 2/1 for domestic students, 1/15 for international students. Application fee: $50. Electronic applications accepted. *Expenses:* Contact institution. *Financial support:* In 2011–12, research assistantships with partial tuition reimbursements (averaging $25,000 per year) were awarded; fellowships, Federal Work-Study, scholarships/grants, and unspecified assistantships also available. Financial award application deadline: 3/1; financial award applicants required to submit FAFSA. *Unit head:* Dr. Laura Hungerford, Program Director, 410-706-8492, Fax: 410-706-4225. *Application contact:* Danielle Fitzpatrick, Program Coordinator, 410-706-8492, Fax: 410-706-4225, E-mail: dfitzpatrick@epi.umaryland.edu. Web site: http://epidemiology.umaryland.edu/Pages/Home.aspx.

University of Maryland, Baltimore County, Graduate School, College of Arts, Humanities and Social Sciences, Department of Emergency Health Services, Baltimore, MD 21250. Offers administration, planning, and policy (MS); education (MS); emergency health services (MS); emergency management (Postbaccalaureate Certificate); preventive medicine and epidemiology (MS). Part-time and evening/weekend programs available. Postbaccalaureate distance learning degree programs offered (no on-campus study). *Faculty:* 2 full-time (0 women), 7 part-time/adjunct (1 woman). *Students:* 20 full-time (8 women), 21 part-time (10 women); includes 2 minority (both Black or African American, non-Hispanic/Latino), 6 international. Average age 32. 13 applicants, 85% accepted, 10 enrolled. In 2011, 13 master's awarded. *Degree requirements:* For master's, comprehensive exam, thesis (for some programs). *Entrance requirements:* For master's, GRE General Test, minimum GPA of 3.0. Additional exam requirements/recommendations for international students: Required—TOEFL (minimum score 85 iBT). *Application deadline:* For fall admission, 7/1 for domestic students, 4/1 for international students. Applications are processed on a rolling basis. Application fee: $45. Electronic applications accepted. *Financial support:* In 2011–12, 2 students received support, including 1 fellowship with tuition reimbursement available (averaging $70,000 per year), 1 research assistantship with tuition reimbursement available (averaging $21,000 per year); career-related internships or fieldwork, Federal Work-Study, health care benefits, and unspecified assistantships also available. Financial award application deadline: 5/30; financial award applicants required to submit FAFSA. *Faculty research:* EMS management, disaster health services, emergency management. *Total annual research expenditures:* $50,000. *Unit head:* Dr. Bruce Walz, Chairman, 410-455-3223. *Application contact:* Dr. Rick Bissell, Program Director, 410-455-3776, Fax: 410-455-3045, E-mail: bissell@umbc.edu. Web site: http://ehs.umbc.edu/.

University of Maryland, College Park, Academic Affairs, School of Public Health, Department of Epidemiology and Biostatistics, College Park, MD 20742. Offers biostatistics (MPH); epidemiology (MPH, PhD). *Faculty:* 13 full-time (9 women), 6 part-time/adjunct (3 women). *Students:* 18 full-time (12 women), 13 part-time (9 women); includes 11 minority (1 Black or African American, non-Hispanic/Latino; 7 Asian, non-Hispanic/Latino; 1 Hispanic/Latino; 2 Two or more races, non-Hispanic/Latino), 3 international. 173 applicants, 10% accepted, 13 enrolled. In 2011, 6 master's, 1 doctorate awarded. *Application deadline:* For fall admission, 1/15 for domestic and international students. Application fee: $75. *Expenses:* Tuition, state resident: part-time $525 per credit hour. Tuition, nonresident: part-time $1131 per credit hour. *Required fees:* $386.31 per term. Tuition and fees vary according to program. *Financial support:* In 2011–12, 4 fellowships with full and partial tuition reimbursements (averaging $18,850 per year), 7 research assistantships (averaging $16,015 per year), 5 teaching assistantships (averaging $15,969 per year) were awarded. *Total annual research expenditures:* $1.2 million. *Unit head:* Dr. Mei-Ling Lee, Chair, 301-405-4581, E-mail: mltlee@umd.edu. *Application contact:* Dr. Charles A. Caramello, Dean of Graduate School, 301-405-0358, Fax: 301-314-9305. Web site: http://www.sph.umd.edu/epib/.

University of Massachusetts Amherst, Graduate School, School of Public Health and Health Sciences, Department of Public Health, Amherst, MA 01003. Offers biostatistics (MPH, MS, PhD); community health education (MPH, MS, PhD); environmental health sciences (MPH, MS, PhD); epidemiology (MPH, MS, PhD); health policy and management (MPH, MS, PhD); nutrition (MPH, PhD); public health practice (MPH); MPH/MPPA. *Accreditation:* CEPH (one or more programs are accredited). Part-time and evening/weekend programs available. Postbaccalaureate distance learning degree programs offered (no on-campus study). *Faculty:* 46 full-time (26 women). *Students:* 118 full-time (88 women), 249 part-time (183 women); includes 75 minority (28 Black or African American, non-Hispanic/Latino; 21 Asian, non-Hispanic/Latino; 20 Hispanic/Latino; 6 Two or more races, non-Hispanic/Latino), 55 international. Average age 36. 377 applicants, 67% accepted, 91 enrolled. In 2011, 83 master's, 4 doctorates awarded. Terminal master's awarded for partial completion of doctoral program. *Degree requirements:* For master's, thesis (for some programs); for doctorate, comprehensive exam, thesis/dissertation. *Entrance requirements:* For master's and doctorate, GRE General Test. Additional exam requirements/recommendations for international students: Required—TOEFL (minimum score 550 paper-based; 213 computer-based; 80 iBT), IELTS (minimum score 6.5). *Application deadline:* For fall admission, 2/1 for domestic and international students. Applications are processed on a rolling basis. Application fee: $40 ($65 for international students). Electronic applications accepted. Tuition and fees vary according to course load, campus/location and program. *Financial support:* Fellowships with full and partial tuition reimbursements, research assistantships with full and partial tuition reimbursements, teaching assistantships with full and partial tuition reimbursements, career-related internships or fieldwork, Federal Work-Study, scholarships/grants, traineeships, health care benefits, tuition waivers (full and partial), and unspecified assistantships available. Support available to part-time students. Financial award application deadline: 2/1. *Unit head:* Dr. Paula Stamps, Graduate Program Director, 413-545-2861, Fax: 413-545-1645. *Application contact:* Lindsay DeSantis, Interim Supervisor of Admissions, 413-545-0722, Fax: 413-577-0010, E-mail: gradadm@grad.umass.edu. Web site: http://www.umass.edu/sphhs/public_health/.

University of Massachusetts Lowell, School of Health and Environment, Department of Work Environment, Lowell, MA 01854-2881. Offers cleaner production and pollution prevention (MS, Sc D); environmental risk assessment (Certificate); epidemiology (MS, Sc D); ergonomics and safety (MS, Sc D); identification and control of ergonomic hazards (Certificate); job stress and healthy job redesign (Certificate); occupational and environmental hygiene (MS, Sc D); radiological health physics and general work environment protection (Certificate); work environment policy (MS, Sc D). *Accreditation:* ABET (one or more programs are accredited). Part-time programs available. Terminal master's awarded for partial completion of doctoral program. *Degree requirements:* For master's, thesis optional; for doctorate, thesis/dissertation. *Entrance requirements:* For master's and doctorate, GRE General Test. Additional exam requirements/recommendations for international students: Required—TOEFL.

University of Massachusetts Worcester, Graduate School of Biomedical Sciences, Worcester, MA 01655-0115. Offers biochemistry and molecular pharmacology (PhD); bioinformatics and computational biology (PhD); cancer biology (PhD); cell biology (PhD); clinical and population health research (PhD); clinical investigation (MS); immunology and virology (PhD); interdisciplinary graduate program (PhD); molecular genetics and microbiology (PhD); neuroscience (PhD); DVM/PhD; MD/PhD. *Faculty:* 1,427 full-time (526 women), 309 part-time/adjunct (196 women). *Students:* 416 full-time (225 women); includes 47 minority (12 Black or African American, non-Hispanic/Latino; 32 Asian, non-Hispanic/Latino; 3 Hispanic/Latino), 144 international. Average age 29. 623 applicants, 17% accepted, 54 enrolled. In 2011, 5 master's, 63 doctorates awarded. Terminal master's awarded for partial completion of doctoral program. *Degree requirements:* For master's, comprehensive exam, thesis; for doctorate, comprehensive exam, thesis/dissertation. *Entrance requirements:* For master's, bachelor's degree; for doctorate, GRE General Test. Additional exam requirements/recommendations for international students: Required—TOEFL (minimum score 600 paper-based; 250 computer-based; 100 iBT) or IELTS (minimum score 7.5). *Application deadline:* For fall admission, 12/15 for domestic and international students; for spring admission, 5/15 for domestic students. Application fee: $50. Electronic applications accepted. *Expenses:* Contact institution. *Financial support:* In 2011–12, 416 students received support, including 416 research assistantships with full tuition reimbursements available (averaging $29,200 per year); scholarships/grants, health care benefits, tuition waivers (full), and unspecified assistantships also available. Financial award application deadline: 4/16. *Faculty research:* RNA interference, cell biology, bioinformatics, clinical research, infectious disease. *Total annual research expenditures:* $262.7 million. *Unit head:* Dr. Anthony Carruthers, Dean, 508-856-4135, E-mail: anthony.carruthers@umassmed.edu. *Application contact:* Dr. Kendall Knight, Associate Dean and Interim Director of Admissions and Recruitment, 508-856-5628, Fax: 508-856-3659, E-mail: kendall.knight@umassmed.edu. Web site: http://www.umassmed.edu/gsbs/.

University of Medicine and Dentistry of New Jersey, School of Health Related Professions, Department of Health Informatics, Program in Clinical Trials Sciences, Newark, NJ 07107-1709. Offers MS. Part-time programs available. Postbaccalaureate distance learning degree programs offered (no on-campus study). *Degree requirements:* For master's, project. *Entrance requirements:* For master's, two recommendations, personal statement, current resume or curriculum vita, minimum GPA of 2.75. Additional exam requirements/recommendations for international students: Required—TOEFL.

University of Medicine and Dentistry of New Jersey, UMDNJ–School of Public Health (UMDNJ, Rutgers, NJIT) Newark Campus, Newark, NJ 07107-1709. Offers clinical epidemiology (Certificate); dental public health (MPH); general public health (Certificate); public policy and oral health services administration (Certificate); quantitative methods (MPH); urban health (MPH); DMD/MPH; MD/MPH; MS/MPH. *Accreditation:* CEPH. Part-time and evening/weekend programs available. *Degree requirements:* For master's, thesis, internship. *Entrance requirements:* For master's, GRE General Test. Additional exam requirements/recommendations for international students: Required—TOEFL. Electronic applications accepted.

University of Medicine and Dentistry of New Jersey, UMDNJ–School of Public Health (UMDNJ, Rutgers, NJIT) Piscataway/New Brunswick Campus, Piscataway, NJ 08854. Offers biostatistics (MPH, MS, Dr PH, PhD); clinical epidemiology (Certificate); environmental and occupational health (MPH, Dr PH, PhD, Certificate); epidemiology (MPH, Dr PH, PhD); general public health (Certificate); health education and behavioral science (MPH, Dr PH, PhD); health systems and policy (MPH, PhD); public health preparedness (Certificate); DO/MPH; JD/MPH; MD/MPH; MPH/MBA; MPH/MSPA; MS/MPH; Psy D/MPH. *Accreditation:* CEPH. Part-time and evening/weekend programs available. *Degree requirements:* For master's, thesis, internship; for doctorate, comprehensive exam, thesis/dissertation. *Entrance requirements:* For master's, GRE General Test; for doctorate, GRE General Test, MPH (Dr PH); MA, MPH, or MS (PhD). Additional exam requirements/recommendations for international students: Required—TOEFL. Electronic applications accepted.

University of Memphis, Graduate School, School of Public Health, Memphis, TN 38152. Offers biostatistics (MPH); environmental health (MPH); epidemiology (MPH); health systems management (MPH); public health (MHA); social and behavioral sciences (MPH). Part-time and evening/weekend programs available. Postbaccalaureate distance learning degree programs offered. *Degree requirements:* For master's, comprehensive exam, thesis. *Entrance requirements:* For master's, GRE, letters of recommendation. Additional exam requirements/recommendations for international students: Required—TOEFL. Electronic applications accepted. *Faculty research:* Health and medical savings accounts, adoption rates, health informatics, Telehealth technologies, biostatistics, environmental health, epidemiology, health systems management, social and behavioral sciences.

University of Miami, Graduate School, Miller School of Medicine, Graduate Programs in Medicine, Department of Epidemiology and Public Health, Coral Gables, FL 33124. Offers epidemiology (PhD); public health (MPH, MSPH); JD/MPH; MD/MPH; MD/PhD; MPA/MPH; MPH/MAIA. *Accreditation:* CEPH (one or more programs are accredited). Part-time programs available. *Degree requirements:* For master's, thesis (for some

programs), project, practicum; for doctorate, comprehensive exam, thesis/dissertation. *Entrance requirements:* For master's, GRE General Test, minimum GPA of 3.0, 3 letters of recommendation; for doctorate, GRE General Test, minimum GPA of 3.0, course work in epidemiology and statistics, 3 letters of recommendation. Additional exam requirements/recommendations for international students: Required—TOEFL (minimum score 550 paper-based; 213 computer-based; 59 iBT). Electronic applications accepted. *Faculty research:* Behavioral epidemiology, substance abuse, AIDS, cardiovascular diseases, women's health.

University of Michigan, School of Public Health, Department of Epidemiology, Ann Arbor, MI 48109-2029. Offers dental public health (MPH); epidemiological science (PhD); epidemiology (MS); general epidemiology (MPH); hospital and molecular epidemiology (MPH); international health (MPH). PhD and MS offered through the Horace H. Rackham School of Graduate Studies. *Accreditation:* CEPH (one or more programs are accredited). Part-time programs available. Terminal master's awarded for partial completion of doctoral program. *Degree requirements:* For master's, thesis (for some programs); for doctorate, comprehensive exam, thesis/dissertation, oral defense of dissertation, preliminary exam. *Entrance requirements:* For master's and doctorate, GRE General Test, MCAT. Additional exam requirements/recommendations for international students: Required—TOEFL (minimum score 560 paper-based; 220 computer-based; 100 iBT). Electronic applications accepted. *Faculty research:* Molecular virology, infectious diseases, women's health, genetics, social epidemiology.

University of Minnesota, Twin Cities Campus, School of Public Health, Division of Environmental Health Sciences, Area in Environmental and Occupational Epidemiology, Minneapolis, MN 55455-0213. Offers MPH, MS, PhD. *Accreditation:* CEPH (one or more programs are accredited). *Degree requirements:* For doctorate, thesis/dissertation. *Entrance requirements:* For master's and doctorate, GRE General Test. Electronic applications accepted.

University of Minnesota, Twin Cities Campus, School of Public Health, Major in Epidemiology, Minneapolis, MN 55455-0213. Offers MPH, PhD. *Accreditation:* CEPH (one or more programs are accredited). Part-time programs available. Terminal master's awarded for partial completion of doctoral program. *Degree requirements:* For master's, fieldwork, project; for doctorate, comprehensive exam, thesis/dissertation. *Entrance requirements:* For master's, GRE General Test; for doctorate, GRE General Test, master's degree in related field. Additional exam requirements/recommendations for international students: Required—TOEFL. Electronic applications accepted. *Expenses:* Contact institution. *Faculty research:* Prevention of cardiovascular disease, nutrition, genetic epidemiology, behavioral interventions, research methods.

University of New Mexico, Health Sciences Center Graduate Programs, Program in Public Health, Albuquerque, NM 87131-5196. Offers community health (MPH); epidemiology (MPH); generalist (MPH). *Accreditation:* CEPH. Part-time programs available. Postbaccalaureate distance learning degree programs offered. *Faculty:* 11 full-time (8 women), 2 part-time/adjunct (1 woman). *Students:* 18 full-time (15 women), 26 part-time (21 women); includes 17 minority (3 American Indian or Alaska Native, non-Hispanic/Latino; 13 Hispanic/Latino; 1 Two or more races, non-Hispanic/Latino), 1 international. Average age 37. 34 applicants, 59% accepted, 11 enrolled. In 2011, 11 degrees awarded. *Degree requirements:* For master's, thesis. *Entrance requirements:* For master's, GRE, MCAT, 2 years of experience in health field. Additional exam requirements/recommendations for international students: Required—TOEFL. *Application deadline:* For fall admission, 2/1 for domestic students. Application fee: $50. *Financial support:* Fellowships, research assistantships with tuition reimbursements, and Federal Work-Study available. Financial award application deadline: 12/15; financial award applicants required to submit FAFSA. *Faculty research:* Epidemiology, rural health, environmental health, Native American health issues. *Total annual research expenditures:* $1 million. *Unit head:* Dr. Kristine Tollestrup, Director, 505-272-4173, Fax: 505-272-4494, E-mail: ktollestrup@salud.unm.edu. *Application contact:* Gayle Garcia, Education Coordinator, 505-272-3982, Fax: 505-272-4494, E-mail: garciag@salud.unm.edu. Web site: http://hsc.unm.edu/som/fcm/mph/mphindex.shtml.

The University of North Carolina at Chapel Hill, Graduate School, School of Public Health, Department of Epidemiology, Chapel Hill, NC 27599. Offers MPH, MSCR, PhD. *Accreditation:* CEPH (one or more programs are accredited). Terminal master's awarded for partial completion of doctoral program. *Degree requirements:* For master's, comprehensive exam, major paper; for doctorate, comprehensive exam, thesis/dissertation. *Entrance requirements:* For master's and doctorate, GRE General Test, minimum GPA of 3.0. Additional exam requirements/recommendations for international students: Required—TOEFL. Electronic applications accepted. *Faculty research:* Chronic disease: cancer, cardiovascular, nutritional; environmental/occupational injury; infectious diseases; reproductive diseases; healthcare.

The University of North Carolina at Chapel Hill, School of Dentistry and Graduate School, Graduate Programs in Dentistry, Chapel Hill, NC 27599. Offers dental hygiene (MS); endodontics (MS); epidemiology (PhD); operative dentistry (MS); oral and maxillofacial pathology (MS); oral and maxillofacial radiology (MS); oral biology (PhD); orthodontics (MS); pediatric dentistry (MS); periodontology (MS); prosthodontics (MS). *Faculty:* 82 full-time (28 women). *Students:* 90 full-time (46 women); includes 20 minority (7 Black or African American, non-Hispanic/Latino; 10 Asian, non-Hispanic/Latino; 3 Hispanic/Latino), 30 international. Average age 28. 475 applicants, 7% accepted, 31 enrolled. In 2011, 20 master's, 2 doctorates awarded. *Degree requirements:* For master's, thesis; for doctorate, thesis/dissertation. *Entrance requirements:* For master's, GRE General Test (for orthodontics and oral biology only); National Dental Board Part I (Part II if available), dental degree (for all except dental hygiene); for doctorate, GRE General Test. Additional exam requirements/recommendations for international students: Required—TOEFL (minimum score 550 paper-based; 213 computer-based; 79 iBT). Application fee: $78. Electronic applications accepted. *Expenses:* Contact institution. *Financial support:* In 2011–12, research assistantships with partial tuition reimbursements (averaging $22,000 per year), teaching assistantships with partial tuition reimbursements (averaging $6,420 per year) were awarded; fellowships also available. Financial award application deadline: 3/1; financial award applicants required to submit FAFSA. *Faculty research:* Clinical research, inflammation, immunology, neuroscience, molecular biology. *Total annual research expenditures:* $6 million. *Unit head:* Dr. Ceib Phillips, Assistant Dean for Advanced Education and Graduate Studies, 919-966-2763, Fax: 919-843-8864, E-mail: ceib_phillips@dentistry.unc.edu. *Application contact:* Koyah Rivera, Graduate Registrar, 919-537-3347, Fax: 919-966-5795, E-mail: koyah_rivera@dentistry.unc.edu. Web site: http://www.dentistry.unc.edu/.

University of North Texas Health Science Center at Fort Worth, School of Public Health, Fort Worth, TX 76107-2699. Offers biostatistics (MPH); community health (MPH); disease control and prevention (Dr PH); environmental and occupational health sciences (MPH); epidemiology (MPH); health administration (MHA); health policy and management (MPH, Dr PH); DO/MPH; MS/MPH; MSN/MPH. MPH offered jointly with University of North Texas; DO/MPH with Texas College of Osteopathic Medicine. *Accreditation:* CEPH. Part-time and evening/weekend programs available. *Degree requirements:* For master's, thesis or alternative, supervised internship; for doctorate, thesis/dissertation, supervised internship. *Entrance requirements:* For master's, GRE General Test. Additional exam requirements/recommendations for international students: Required—TOEFL. Electronic applications accepted.

University of Oklahoma Health Sciences Center, Graduate College, College of Public Health, Program in Biostatistics and Epidemiology, Oklahoma City, OK 73190. Offers biostatistics (MPH, MS, Dr PH, PhD); epidemiology (MPH, MS, Dr PH, PhD). *Accreditation:* CEPH (one or more programs are accredited). Part-time programs available. *Degree requirements:* For master's, comprehensive exam, thesis (for some programs); for doctorate, comprehensive exam, thesis/dissertation. *Entrance requirements:* For master's, 3 letters of recommendation, resume; for doctorate, GRE General Test, letters of recommendation. Additional exam requirements/recommendations for international students: Required—TOEFL (minimum score 570 paper-based; 230 computer-based), TWE. *Faculty research:* Statistical methodology, applied statistics, acute and chronic disease epidemiology.

University of Ottawa, Faculty of Graduate and Postdoctoral Studies, Faculty of Medicine, Department of Epidemiology and Community Medicine, Ottawa, ON K1N 6N5, Canada. Offers epidemiology (M Sc), including health technology assessment. *Degree requirements:* For master's, thesis. *Entrance requirements:* For master's, honors degree or equivalent, minimum B average. Electronic applications accepted. *Faculty research:* Epidemiologic concepts and methods, health technology assessment.

University of Pennsylvania, Perelman School of Medicine, Center for Clinical Epidemiology and Biostatistics, Philadelphia, PA 19104. Offers clinical epidemiology (MSCE); epidemiology (PhD). PhD offered through the School of Arts and Sciences. *Accreditation:* CEPH. Part-time programs available. *Faculty:* 72 full-time (27 women), 119 part-time/adjunct (40 women). *Students:* 94 full-time (50 women), 4 part-time (3 women); includes 41 minority (7 Black or African American, non-Hispanic/Latino; 27 Asian, non-Hispanic/Latino; 7 Hispanic/Latino). Average age 30. 50 applicants, 84% accepted, 35 enrolled. In 2011, 30 master's awarded. *Degree requirements:* For master's, comprehensive exam, thesis. *Entrance requirements:* For master's, GRE General Test or MCAT, advanced degree, clinical experience. Additional exam requirements/recommendations for international students: Required—TOEFL. *Application deadline:* For fall admission, 12/1 priority date for domestic students, 12/1 for international students. Applications are processed on a rolling basis. Application fee: $0. Electronic applications accepted. *Expenses:* Contact institution. *Financial support:* In 2011–12, 70 students received support, including 65 fellowships with full and partial tuition reimbursements available (averaging $45,500 per year); career-related internships or fieldwork, scholarships/grants, health care benefits, and unspecified assistantships also available. Financial award application deadline: 11/15. *Faculty research:* Health services research, pharmacoepidemiology, women's health, cancer epidemiology, genetic epidemiology. *Total annual research expenditures:* $45.9 million. *Unit head:* Dr. Harold I. Feldman, Director, 215-573-0901, Fax: 215-573-2265, E-mail: hfeldman@mail.med.upenn.edu. *Application contact:* Jennifer E. Kuklinski, Associate Director for Graduate Training in Epidemiology, 215-573-2382, Fax: 215-573-5315, E-mail: jkuklins@mail.med.upenn.edu. Web site: http://www.cceb.upenn.edu/.

University of Pittsburgh, Graduate School of Public Health, Department of Epidemiology, Pittsburgh, PA 15260. Offers MPH, MS, Dr PH, PhD, MD/PhD. *Accreditation:* CEPH (one or more programs are accredited). Part-time programs available. *Faculty:* 47 full-time (30 women), 94 part-time/adjunct (50 women). *Students:* 90 full-time (65 women), 41 part-time (30 women); includes 22 minority (8 Black or African American, non-Hispanic/Latino; 6 Asian, non-Hispanic/Latino; 4 Hispanic/Latino; 4 Two or more races, non-Hispanic/Latino), 24 international. Average age 32. 362 applicants, 46% accepted, 34 enrolled. In 2011, 24 master's, 18 doctorates awarded. Terminal master's awarded for partial completion of doctoral program. *Degree requirements:* For master's, comprehensive exam (for some programs), thesis (for some programs), internship experience (MPH); for doctorate, comprehensive exam, thesis/dissertation, teaching practicum. *Entrance requirements:* For master's, GRE General Test, DAT, MCAT, 3 credits each of course work in human biology and algebra or higher mathematics, 6 in behavioral science (MPH); minimum GPA of 3.0; for doctorate, GRE General Test, DAT, MCAT, 3 credits of course work in biology and math, minimum GPA of 3.0. Additional exam requirements/recommendations for international students: Required—TOEFL (minimum score 550 paper-based; 80 iBT) or IELTS (minimum score 6.5). *Application deadline:* For fall admission, 1/5 priority date for domestic students, 1/5 for international students; for spring admission, 11/1 priority date for domestic students, 8/1 for international students. Applications are processed on a rolling basis. Application fee: $115. Electronic applications accepted. *Expenses:* Tuition, state resident: full-time $18,774; part-time $760 per credit. Tuition, nonresident: full-time $30,736; part-time $1258 per credit. *Required fees:* $740; $200 per term. Tuition and fees vary according to program. *Financial support:* In 2011–12, 57 students received support, including 18 fellowships with full tuition reimbursements available (averaging $8,366 per year), 38 research assistantships with full tuition reimbursements available (averaging $14,707 per year), 1 teaching assistantship with full tuition reimbursement available (averaging $850 per year); career-related internships or fieldwork, scholarships/grants, and traineeships also available. Support available to part-time students. Financial award applicants required to submit FAFSA. *Faculty research:* Aging, cardiovascular, clinical trials, diabetes, psychiatric, women's health, genetics, alcohol. *Total annual research expenditures:* $36.5 million. *Unit head:* Dr. Anne B. Newman, Chair, 412-624-3056, Fax: 412-624-3737, E-mail: newmana@edc.pitt.edu. *Application contact:* Lori S. Smith, Student Affairs Manager, 412-383-5269, E-mail: smithl@edc.pitt.edu. Web site: http://www.epidemiology.pitt.edu/.

University of Prince Edward Island, Atlantic Veterinary College, Graduate Program in Veterinary Medicine, Charlottetown, PE C1A 4P3, Canada. Offers anatomy (M Sc, PhD); bacteriology (M Sc, PhD); clinical pharmacology (M Sc, PhD); clinical sciences (M Sc, PhD); epidemiology (M Sc, PhD), including reproduction; fish health (M Sc, PhD); food animal nutrition (M Sc, PhD); immunology (M Sc, PhD); microanatomy (M Sc, PhD); parasitology (M Sc, PhD); pathology (M Sc, PhD); pharmacology (M Sc, PhD); physiology (M Sc, PhD); toxicology (M Sc, PhD); veterinary science (M Vet Sc); virology (M Sc, PhD). Part-time programs available. *Degree requirements:* For master's, thesis; for doctorate, thesis/dissertation. *Entrance requirements:* For master's, DVM, B Sc honors degree, or equivalent; for doctorate, M Sc. Additional exam requirements/recommendations for international students: Required—TOEFL (minimum score 550 paper-based; 213 computer-based; 80 iBT). *Expenses:* Contact institution. *Faculty research:* Animal health management, infectious diseases, fin fish and shellfish health, basic biomedical sciences, ecosystem health.

University of Puerto Rico, Medical Sciences Campus, Graduate School of Public Health, Department of Social Sciences, Program in Epidemiology, San Juan, PR 00936-5067. Offers MPH, MS. *Accreditation:* CEPH (one or more programs are accredited). Part-time programs available. *Entrance requirements:* For master's, GRE, previous course work in biology, chemistry, physics, mathematics, and social sciences. *Expenses:* Contact institution.

University of Rochester, School of Medicine and Dentistry, Graduate Programs in Medicine and Dentistry, Department of Community and Preventive Medicine, Program in Epidemiology, Rochester, NY 14627. Offers PhD. *Degree requirements:* For doctorate, thesis/dissertation, qualifying exam. *Entrance requirements:* For doctorate, GRE General Test. *Expenses:* Tuition: Full-time $41,040.

University of Saskatchewan, College of Medicine, Department of Community Health and Epidemiology, Saskatoon, SK S7N 5A2, Canada. Offers M Sc, PhD. *Degree*

requirements: For master's, thesis; for doctorate, thesis/dissertation. *Entrance requirements:* Additional exam requirements/recommendations for international students: Required—TOEFL.

University of South Carolina, The Graduate School, Arnold School of Public Health, Department of Epidemiology and Biostatistics, Program in Epidemiology, Columbia, SC 29208. Offers MPH, MSPH, Dr PH, PhD. *Accreditation:* CEPH (one or more programs are accredited). Part-time programs available. *Degree requirements:* For master's, comprehensive exam, thesis (for some programs), practicum (MPH); for doctorate, comprehensive exam, thesis/dissertation (for some programs), practicum. *Entrance requirements:* For master's, GRE General Test; for doctorate, GRE General Test, master's degree. Additional exam requirements/recommendations for international students: Required—TOEFL (minimum score 570 paper-based; 230 computer-based; 88 iBT). Electronic applications accepted. *Faculty research:* Cancer epidemiology, mental health epidemiology, health effects of physical activity, environmental epidemiology, genetic epidemiology, asthma epidemiology.

University of Southern California, Keck School of Medicine and Graduate School, Graduate Programs in Medicine, Department of Preventive Medicine, Division of Biostatistics, Los Angeles, CA 90089. Offers applied biostatistics/epidemiology (MS); biostatistics (MS, PhD); epidemiology (PhD); genetic epidemiology and statistical genetics (PhD); molecular epidemiology (MS, PhD). *Faculty:* 71 full-time (30 women). *Students:* 97 full-time (51 women); includes 24 minority (18 Asian, non-Hispanic/Latino; 3 Hispanic/Latino; 3 Two or more races, non-Hispanic/Latino), 56 international. Average age 29. 68 applicants, 62% accepted, 17 enrolled. In 2011, 7 master's, 8 doctorates awarded. Terminal master's awarded for partial completion of doctoral program. *Degree requirements:* For master's, thesis; for doctorate, thesis/dissertation. *Entrance requirements:* For master's and doctorate, GRE General Test, GRE Subject Test, minimum GPA of 3.0. Additional exam requirements/recommendations for international students: Required—TOEFL (minimum score 600 paper-based; 300 computer-based; 100 iBT). *Application deadline:* For fall admission, 12/1 priority date for domestic students, 12/1 for international students. Application fee: $85. Electronic applications accepted. *Financial support:* In 2011–12, 3 fellowships with full tuition reimbursements (averaging $29,100 per year), 43 research assistantships with full tuition reimbursements (averaging $29,100 per year), 22 teaching assistantships with full and partial tuition reimbursements (averaging $14,550 per year) were awarded; career-related internships or fieldwork, Federal Work-Study, institutionally sponsored loans, scholarships/grants, traineeships, health care benefits, and unspecified assistantships also available. Financial award application deadline: 5/4; financial award applicants required to submit CSS PROFILE or FAFSA. *Faculty research:* Clinical trials in ophthalmology and cancer research, methods of analysis for epidemiological studies, genetic epidemiology. *Total annual research expenditures:* $1.3 million. *Unit head:* Dr. William Gauderman, Director, 323-442-2633, Fax: 323-442-2993, E-mail: mtrujill@usc.edu. *Application contact:* Mary L. Trujillo, Student Adviser, 323-442-2633, Fax: 323-442-2993, E-mail: mtrujill@usc.edu. Web site: http://keck.usc.edu/Education/Academic_Department_and_Divisions/Department_of_Preventive_Medicine/Divisions/Biostatistics.aspx.

University of Southern California, Keck School of Medicine and Graduate School, Graduate Programs in Medicine, Department of Preventive Medicine, Master of Public Health Program, Los Angeles, CA 90032-3628. Offers biostatistics/epidemiology (MPH); child and family health (MPH); environmental health (MPH); global health leadership (MPH); health communication (MPH); health education and promotion (MPH); public health policy (MPH). *Accreditation:* CEPH. Part-time programs available. *Faculty:* 22 full-time (12 women), 3 part-time/adjunct (0 women). *Students:* 148 full-time (115 women), 35 part-time (23 women); includes 100 minority (8 Black or African American, non-Hispanic/Latino; 66 Asian, non-Hispanic/Latino; 26 Hispanic/Latino), 26 international. Average age 24. 218 applicants, 73% accepted, 88 enrolled. In 2011, 91 master's awarded. *Degree requirements:* For master's, practicum, final report, oral presentation. *Entrance requirements:* For master's, GRE General Test, MCAT, GMAT, minimum GPA of 3.0. Additional exam requirements/recommendations for international students: Required—TOEFL (minimum score 600 paper-based; 250 computer-based; 100 iBT). *Application deadline:* For fall admission, 6/1 priority date for domestic students, 6/1 for international students; for spring admission, 11/1 priority date for domestic students, 10/1 for international students. Applications are processed on a rolling basis. Application fee: $85. Electronic applications accepted. *Financial support:* In 2011–12, 148 students received support. Career-related internships or fieldwork, Federal Work-Study, institutionally sponsored loans, and scholarships/grants available. Support available to part-time students. Financial award application deadline: 5/4; financial award applicants required to submit CSS PROFILE or FAFSA. *Faculty research:* Substance abuse prevention, cancer and heart disease prevention, mass media and health communication research, health promotion, treatment compliance. *Unit head:* Dr. Louise A. Rohrbach, Director, 323-442-8237, Fax: 323-442-8297, E-mail: rohrbac@usc.edu. *Application contact:* Chrystal Romero, Admissions Counselor, 323-442-7257, Fax: 323-442-8297, E-mail: ccromero@usc.edu. Web site: http://mph.usc.edu/main.php.

University of Southern Mississippi, Graduate School, College of Health, Department of Community Health Sciences, Hattiesburg, MS 39406-0001. Offers epidemiology and biostatistics (MPH); health education (MPH); health policy/administration (MPH); occupational/environmental health (MPH); public health nutrition (MPH). *Accreditation:* CEPH. Part-time and evening/weekend programs available. *Faculty:* 8 full-time (4 women), 1 part-time/adjunct (0 women). *Students:* 81 full-time (66 women), 17 part-time (13 women); includes 49 minority (43 Black or African American, non-Hispanic/Latino; 1 Asian, non-Hispanic/Latino; 2 Hispanic/Latino; 3 Two or more races, non-Hispanic/Latino), 7 international. Average age 32. 70 applicants, 94% accepted, 43 enrolled. In 2011, 45 degrees awarded. *Degree requirements:* For master's, comprehensive exam, thesis (for some programs). *Entrance requirements:* For master's, GRE General Test, minimum GPA of 2.75 in last 60 hours. Additional exam requirements/recommendations for international students: Required—TOEFL, IELTS. *Application deadline:* For fall admission, 3/1 priority date for domestic students, 3/1 for international students; for spring admission, 1/10 priority date for domestic students, 1/10 for international students. Applications are processed on a rolling basis. Application fee: $50. Electronic applications accepted. *Financial support:* In 2011–12, 5 research assistantships with full tuition reimbursements (averaging $7,000 per year), 1 teaching assistantship with full tuition reimbursement (averaging $8,263 per year) were awarded; career-related internships or fieldwork, Federal Work-Study, institutionally sponsored loans, scholarships/grants, health care benefits, and unspecified assistantships also available. Financial award application deadline: 3/15; financial award applicants required to submit FAFSA. *Faculty research:* Rural health care delivery, school health, nutrition of pregnant teens, risk factor reduction, sexually transmitted diseases. *Unit head:* Dr. Emanual Ahua, Interim Chair, 601-266-5437, Fax: 601-266-5043. *Application contact:* Shonna Breland, Manager of Graduate Admissions, 601-266-6563, Fax: 601-266-5138. Web site: http://www.usm.edu/chs.

University of South Florida, Graduate School, College of Public Health, Department of Epidemiology and Biostatistics, Tampa, FL 33620-9951. Offers MPH, MSPH, PhD. *Accreditation:* CEPH (one or more programs are accredited). Part-time and evening/weekend programs available. *Degree requirements:* For master's, comprehensive exam, thesis (for some programs); for doctorate, comprehensive exam, thesis/dissertation. *Entrance requirements:* For master's, GRE General Test, minimum GPA of 3.0 in upper-level course work, goal statement letter, two professional letters of recommendation, resume/curriculum vitae; for doctorate, GRE General Test, minimum GPA of 3.0 in upper-level course work, 3 professional letters of recommendation, resume/curriculum vitae, writing sample. Additional exam requirements/recommendations for international students: Required—TOEFL (minimum score 550 paper-based; 213 computer-based; 79 iBT). Electronic applications accepted. *Faculty research:* Dementia, mental illness, mental health preventative trails, rural health outreach, clinical and administrative studies.

The University of Toledo, College of Graduate Studies, College of Medicine and Life Sciences, Department of Public Health and Preventive Medicine, Toledo, OH 43606-3390. Offers biostatistics and epidemiology (Certificate); contemporary gerontological practice (Certificate); environmental and occupational health and safety (MPH); epidemiology (MPH, Certificate); global public health (Certificate); health administration (MPH); health promotion (MPH); medical health and science education (Certificate); nutrition (MPH); occupational health (MSOH, Certificate); public health and emergency response (Certificate); MD/MPH. Part-time and evening/weekend programs available. *Faculty:* 6. *Students:* 95 full-time (74 women), 66 part-time (45 women); includes 37 minority (21 Black or African American, non-Hispanic/Latino; 11 Asian, non-Hispanic/Latino; 3 Hispanic/Latino; 2 Two or more races, non-Hispanic/Latino), 6 international. Average age 29. 132 applicants, 75% accepted, 70 enrolled. In 2011, 60 master's, 26 other advanced degrees awarded. *Degree requirements:* For master's, thesis or alternative. *Entrance requirements:* For master's, GRE, minimum undergraduate GPA of 3.0, three letters of recommendation, statement of purpose, transcripts from all prior institutions attended, resume; for Certificate, minimum undergraduate GPA of 3.0, three letters of recommendation, statement of purpose, transcripts from all prior institutions attended, resume. Additional exam requirements/recommendations for international students: Required—TOEFL (minimum score 550 paper-based; 213 computer-based; 80 iBT), IELTS (minimum score 6.5). *Application deadline:* For fall admission, 3/15 for domestic and international students. Applications are processed on a rolling basis. Application fee: $45 ($75 for international students). Electronic applications accepted. *Financial support:* In 2011–12, 15 research assistantships with full tuition reimbursements (averaging $10,000 per year) were awarded; Federal Work-Study, institutionally sponsored loans, scholarships/grants, tuition waivers (full and partial), and unspecified assistantships also available. *Unit head:* Dr. Sheryl A. Milz, Chair, 419-383-3976, Fax: 419-383-6140, E-mail: sheryl.milz@utoledo.edu. *Application contact:* Joan Mulligan, Admissions Analyst, 419-383-4186, Fax: 419-383-6140, E-mail: joan.mulligan@utoledo.edu. Web site: http://nocphmph.org/.

University of Toronto, School of Graduate Studies, Dalla Lana School of Public Health, Toronto, ON M5S 1A1, Canada. Offers biostatistics (M Sc, PhD); community health (M Sc); epidemiology (MPH, PhD); health and behavioral science (PhD); health promotion (MPH); social science and health (PhD). *Accreditation:* CAHME (one or more programs are accredited); CEPH (one or more programs are accredited). Part-time programs available. *Degree requirements:* For master's, thesis (for some programs), practicum; for doctorate, comprehensive exam, thesis/dissertation, oral thesis defense. *Entrance requirements:* For master's, 2 letters of reference, relevant professional/research experience, minimum B average in final year; for doctorate, 2 letters of reference, relevant professional/research experience, minimum B+ average. Additional exam requirements/recommendations for international students: Required—TOEFL (minimum score 580 paper-based; 93 iBT), TWE (minimum score 5). Electronic applications accepted. *Expenses:* Contact institution.

University of Washington, Graduate School, School of Public Health, Department of Epidemiology, Seattle, WA 98195. Offers clinical research (MS); epidemiology (MPH, MS, PhD); global health (MPH); maternal/child health (MPH); nutritional sciences (MPH, MS, PhD); public health genetics (MPH, MS, PhD), including genetic epidemiology (MS), public health genetics (MPH, PhD); MPH/JD; MPH/MPA; MS/MPA. *Accreditation:* CEPH (one or more programs are accredited). *Faculty:* 62 full-time (35 women), 45 part-time/adjunct (22 women). *Students:* 135 full-time (93 women), 37 part-time (23 women); includes 37 minority (6 Black or African American, non-Hispanic/Latino; 1 American Indian or Alaska Native, non-Hispanic/Latino; 23 Asian, non-Hispanic/Latino; 7 Hispanic/Latino), 17 international. Average age 32. 291 applicants, 35% accepted, 58 enrolled. In 2011, 45 master's, 16 doctorates awarded. *Degree requirements:* For master's, comprehensive exam (for some programs), thesis; for doctorate, comprehensive exam, thesis/dissertation. *Entrance requirements:* For master's, GRE General Test (except for those holding PhD, MD, DDS, DVM, DO or equivalent from U.S. schools); for doctorate, GRE. Additional exam requirements/recommendations for international students: Required—TOEFL (minimum score 580 paper-based; 237 computer-based; 92 iBT) or IELTS (minimum score 7). *Application deadline:* For fall admission, 12/1 for domestic students, 11/1 for international students. Application fee: $75. Electronic applications accepted. *Expenses:* Contact institution. *Financial support:* In 2011–12, 152 students received support, including 75 fellowships with partial tuition reimbursements available, 49 research assistantships with partial tuition reimbursements available, 4 teaching assistantships with partial tuition reimbursements available; career-related internships or fieldwork, Federal Work-Study, traineeships, health care benefits, and unspecified assistantships also available. Support available to part-time students. Financial award applicants required to submit FAFSA. *Faculty research:* Chronic disease, health disparities and social determinants of health, aging and neuroepidemiology, maternal and child health, molecular and genetic epidemiology. *Unit head:* Dr. Scott Davis, Chair, 206-543-1065, Fax: 206-543-8525. *Application contact:* Kate O'Brien, Student Services Manager, 206-543-1065, Fax: 206-543-8525, E-mail: epi@u.washington.edu. Web site: http://depts.washington.edu/epidem/.

The University of Western Ontario, Faculty of Graduate Studies, Biosciences Division, Department of Epidemiology and Biostatistics, London, ON N6A 5B8, Canada. Offers M Sc, PhD. *Accreditation:* CEPH (one or more programs are accredited). Part-time programs available. *Degree requirements:* For master's, thesis; for doctorate, comprehensive exam, thesis proposal defense. *Entrance requirements:* For master's, BA or B Sc honors degree, minimum B+ average in last 10 courses; for doctorate, M Sc or equivalent, minimum B+ average in last 10 courses. *Faculty research:* Chronic disease epidemiology, clinical epidemiology.

University of Wisconsin–Madison, School of Medicine and Public Health and Graduate School, Graduate Programs in Medicine, Department of Population Health Sciences, Madison, WI 53726. Offers epidemiology (MS, PhD); population health (MS, PhD), including clinical research, epidemiology, health services research, social and behavioral health sciences; public health (MPH); DPT/MPH; DVM/MPH; JD/MPH; MD/MPH; MPA/MPH; MS/MPH; Pharm D/MPH. *Accreditation:* CEPH. Part-time programs available. *Faculty:* 104 full-time (54 women), 2 part-time/adjunct (0 women). *Students:* 69 full-time (50 women), 13 part-time (9 women); includes 19 minority (8 Black or African American, non-Hispanic/Latino; 8 Asian, non-Hispanic/Latino; 3 Hispanic/Latino), 15 international. Average age 31. 96 applicants, 41% accepted, 26 enrolled. In 2011, 5 master's, 6 doctorates awarded. Terminal master's awarded for partial completion of doctoral program. *Degree requirements:* For master's, thesis, defense; for doctorate, comprehensive exam, thesis/dissertation, qualifying exam, preliminary exam,

dissertation defense. *Entrance requirements:* For master's and doctorate, GRE (MCAT or LSAT acceptable for those with doctoral degrees) taken within the last 5 years, minimum GPA of 3.0, quantitative preparation (calculus, statistics, or other) with minimum B average. Additional exam requirements/recommendations for international students: Required—TOEFL (minimum score 580 paper-based; 237 computer-based; 92 iBT). *Application deadline:* For fall admission, 1/15 for domestic and international students. Application fee: $56. Electronic applications accepted. *Expenses:* Tuition, state resident: full-time $10,296; part-time $643.51 per credit. Tuition, nonresident: full-time $24,054; part-time $1503.40 per credit. *Required fees:* $70.06 per credit. Tuition and fees vary according to course load, campus/location, program and reciprocity agreements. *Financial support:* Fellowships with full tuition reimbursements, research assistantships with full tuition reimbursements, teaching assistantships with full tuition reimbursements, scholarships/grants, traineeships, health care benefits, and unspecified assistantships available. Support available to part-time students. *Faculty research:* Epidemiology (cancer, environmental, aging, infectious and genetic disease), determinants of population health, health services research, social and behavioral health sciences, biostatistics. *Total annual research expenditures:* $11.4 million. *Unit head:* Kathy Rutlin, MS/PhD Programs Coordinator, 608-265-8108, Fax: 608-263-2820, E-mail: karutlin@wisc.edu. *Application contact:* Quinn H. Fullenkamp, MS/PhD Assistant Programs Coordinator, 608-263-6583, Fax: 608-263-2820, E-mail: qhfullen@wisc.edu. Web site: http://www.pophealth.wisc.edu.

Virginia Commonwealth University, Medical College of Virginia-Professional Programs, School of Medicine, School of Medicine Graduate Programs, Department of Epidemiology and Community Health, Richmond, VA 23284-9005. Offers epidemiology (MPH, PhD); public health practice (MPH); social and behavioral science (MPH); MD/MPH; MSW/MPH. *Accreditation:* CEPH. Part-time programs available. *Degree requirements:* For doctorate, comprehensive exam, thesis/dissertation. *Entrance requirements:* For master's, GRE; for doctorate, GRE General Test, interview, 3 letters of recommendation, minimum graduate GPA of 3.0, master's degree in public health or related field including epidemiology and biostatistics. Additional exam requirements/recommendations for international students: Required—TOEFL (minimum score 600 paper-based; 250 computer-based; 100 iBT). Electronic applications accepted. *Expenses:* Tuition, state resident: full-time $9133; part-time $507 per credit. Tuition, nonresident: full-time $18,777; part-time $1043 per credit. *Required fees:* $77 per credit. Tuition and fees vary according to degree level, campus/location, program and student level. *Faculty research:* Sickle cell anemia, breast cancer, HIV/AIDS, hospital epidemiology, infectious diseases.

Walden University, Graduate Programs, School of Health Sciences, Minneapolis, MN 55401. Offers clinical research administration (MS, Postbaccalaureate Certificate); health informatics (MS); health services (PhD), including community health education and advocacy, general program, healthcare administration, leadership, public health policy, self-designed; healthcare administration (MHA); public health (MPH, PhD), including community health and education (PhD), epidemiology (PhD). Part-time and evening/weekend programs available. Postbaccalaureate distance learning degree programs offered (minimal on-campus study). *Faculty:* 20 full-time (13 women), 175 part-time/adjunct (81 women). *Students:* 2,777 full-time (2,158 women), 1,350 part-time (1,038 women); includes 2,379 minority (1,935 Black or African American, non-Hispanic/Latino; 33 American Indian or Alaska Native, non-Hispanic/Latino; 173 Asian, non-Hispanic/Latino; 180 Hispanic/Latino; 9 Native Hawaiian or other Pacific Islander, non-Hispanic/Latino; 49 Two or more races, non-Hispanic/Latino), 247 international. Average age 40. In 2011, 528 master's, 79 doctorates, 1 other advanced degree awarded. *Degree requirements:* For doctorate, thesis/dissertation, residency. *Entrance*

requirements: For master's, bachelor's degree or equivalent in related field, minimum GPA of 2.5; for doctorate, master's degree or equivalent in related field; minimum GPA of 3.0; official transcripts; three years of related professional/academic experience (preferred); access to computer and Internet. Additional exam requirements/recommendations for international students: Required—TOEFL (minimum score 550 paper-based; 213 computer-based), IELTS (minimum score 6.5), or Michigan English Language Assessment Battery (minimum score 82). *Application deadline:* Applications are processed on a rolling basis. Application fee: $50. Electronic applications accepted. *Financial support:* Federal Work-Study, scholarships/grants, unspecified assistantships, and family tuition reduction, active duty/veteran tuition reduction, group tuition reduction, interest-free payment plans, employee tuition reduction available. Support available to part-time students. Financial award applicants required to submit FAFSA. *Unit head:* Dr. Jorg Westermann, Associate Dean, 800-925-3368. *Application contact:* Jennifer Hall, Vice President of Enrollment Management, 866-4-WALDEN, E-mail: info@waldenu.edu. Web site: http://www.waldenu.edu/Colleges-and-Schools/College-of-Health-Sciences/School-of-Health-Sciences.htm.

Weill Cornell Medical College, Weill Cornell Graduate School of Medical Sciences, Program in Clinical Epidemiology and Health Services Research, New York, NY 10021. Offers MS. *Faculty:* 22 full-time (7 women). *Students:* 21 full-time (14 women); includes 8 minority (3 Black or African American, non-Hispanic/Latino; 2 Asian, non-Hispanic/Latino; 1 Hispanic/Latino; 2 Native Hawaiian or other Pacific Islander, non-Hispanic/Latino), 3 international. Average age 35. 31 applicants, 42% accepted, 11 enrolled. In 2011, 10 master's awarded. *Degree requirements:* For master's, thesis. *Entrance requirements:* For master's, 3 years of work experience, MD or RN certificate. *Application deadline:* For fall admission, 12/15 for domestic students. Application fee: $60. *Expenses:* Tuition: Full-time $46,001. *Financial support:* Scholarships/grants available. *Faculty research:* Research methodology, biostatistical techniques, data management, decision analysis, health economics. *Unit head:* Dr. Carol Mancuso, Director, 212-746-5454. *Application contact:* Alison Kenny, Administrator of Clinical and Educational Programs, 212-746-1608, Fax: 212-746-7443, E-mail: alh2006@med.cornell.edu. Web site: http://weill.cornell.edu/gradschool/program/ce_courses.html.

Yale University, School of Medicine, Yale School of Public Health, New Haven, CT 06520. Offers applied biostatistics and epidemiology (APMPH); biostatistics (MPH, MS, PhD), including global health (MPH); chronic disease epidemiology (MPH, PhD), including global health (MPH); environmental health sciences (MPH, PhD), including global health (MPH); epidemiology of microbial diseases (MPH, PhD), including global health (MPH); global health (APMPH); health management (MPH), including global health; health policy (MPH), including global health; health policy and administration (APMPH, PhD); occupational and environmental medicine (APMPH); preventive medicine (APMPH); social and behavioral sciences (APMPH, MPH), including global health (MPH); JD/MPH; M Div/MPH; MBA/MPH; MD/MPH; MEM/MPH; MFS/MPH; MM Sc/MPH; MPH/MA; MSN/MPH. MS and PhD offered through the Graduate School. *Accreditation:* CEPH. Part-time programs available. Terminal master's awarded for partial completion of doctoral program. *Degree requirements:* For master's, thesis, summer internship; for doctorate, comprehensive exam, thesis/dissertation, residency. *Entrance requirements:* For master's, GMAT, GRE, or MCAT, two years of undergraduate coursework in math and science; for doctorate, GRE General Test. Additional exam requirements/recommendations for international students: Required—TOEFL (minimum score 100 iBT). Electronic applications accepted. *Expenses:* Contact institution. *Faculty research:* Genetic and emerging infections epidemiology, virology, cost/quality, vector biology, quantitative methods, aging, asthma, cancer.

Health Promotion

American University, College of Arts and Sciences, School of Education, Teaching, and Health, Program in Health Promotion Management, Washington, DC 20016-8001. Offers MS, Certificate. *Students:* 20 full-time (17 women), 30 part-time (23 women); includes 5 minority (2 Black or African American, non-Hispanic/Latino; 1 Asian, non-Hispanic/Latino; 1 Hispanic/Latino; 1 Two or more races, non-Hispanic/Latino), 1 international. Average age 28. 35 applicants, 69% accepted, 15 enrolled. In 2011, 11 master's awarded. *Degree requirements:* For master's, comprehensive exam, thesis or alternative, tools of research. *Entrance requirements:* For master's, GRE, interview (recommended). Application fee: $80. *Expenses:* Tuition: Full-time $24,264; part-time $1348 per credit hour. *Required fees:* $430. Tuition and fees vary according to course load and program. *Unit head:* Dr. Sarah Irvine-Belson, Director, 202-885-3714, Fax: 202-885-1187, E-mail: educate@american.edu. *Application contact:* Kathleen Clowery, Director, Graduate Admissions, 202-885-3621, Fax: 202-885-1505, E-mail: clowery@american.edu. Web site: http://www.american.edu/cas/seth/.

American University of Beirut, Graduate Programs, Faculty of Health Sciences, Beirut, Lebanon. Offers environmental sciences (MSES), including environmental health; epidemiology (MS); epidemiology and biostatistics (MPH); health management and policy (MPH); health promotion and community health (MPH); population health (MS). Part-time programs available. *Faculty:* 29 full-time (19 women), 5 part-time/adjunct (2 women). *Students:* 63 full-time (52 women), 103 part-time (87 women). Average age 27. 156 applicants, 71% accepted, 56 enrolled. In 2011, 69 master's awarded. *Degree requirements:* For master's, one foreign language, comprehensive exam, thesis (for some programs). *Entrance requirements:* For master's, 2 letters of recommendation, personal statement, transcripts. Additional exam requirements/recommendations for international students: Required—TOEFL (minimum score 600 paper-based; 250 computer-based; 97 iBT), IELTS (minimum score 7). *Application deadline:* For fall admission, 2/20 for domestic and international students; for spring admission, 11/1 for domestic and international students. Application fee: $50. Electronic applications accepted. *Expenses:* Tuition: Full-time $12,780; part-time $710 per credit. Tuition and fees vary according to course load and program. *Financial support:* In 2011–12, 62 students received support. Scholarships/grants, health care benefits, and unspecified assistantships available. Financial award application deadline: 2/20. *Faculty research:* Tobacco control; health of the elderly; youth health; mental health; women's health; reproductive and sexual health, including HIV/AIDS; water quality; health systems; quality in health care delivery; health human resources; health policy; occupational and environmental health; social inequality; social determinants of health; chronic diseases. *Total annual research expenditures:* $722,649. *Unit head:* Iman Adel Nuwayhid, Dean, 961-1340119, Fax: 961-1744470, E-mail: nuwayhid@aub.edu.lb. *Application contact:* Mitra Tauk, Administrative Coordinator, 961-1350000 Ext. 4687, Fax: 961-1744470, E-mail: mt12@aub.edu.lb. Web site: http://fhs.aub.edu.lb.

Auburn University, Graduate School, College of Education, Department of Kinesiology, Auburn University, AL 36849. Offers exercise science (M Ed, MS, PhD); health promotion (M Ed, MS); kinesiology (PhD); physical education/teacher education (M Ed, MS, Ed D, Ed S). *Accreditation:* NCATE. Part-time programs available. *Faculty:* 15 full-time (8 women). *Students:* 60 full-time (30 women), 33 part-time (15 women); includes 17 minority (14 Black or African American, non-Hispanic/Latino; 1 Asian, non-Hispanic/Latino; 2 Hispanic/Latino), 6 international. Average age 27. 116 applicants, 61% accepted, 41 enrolled. In 2011, 48 master's, 4 doctorates awarded. *Degree requirements:* For master's, thesis (for some programs); for doctorate, thesis/dissertation; for Ed S, exam, field project. *Entrance requirements:* For master's, GRE General Test; for doctorate and Ed S, GRE General Test, interview, master's degree. *Application deadline:* For fall admission, 7/7 for domestic students; for spring admission, 11/24 for domestic students. Applications are processed on a rolling basis. Application fee: $50 ($60 for international students). Electronic applications accepted. *Expenses:* Tuition, state resident: full-time $7290; part-time $405 per credit hour. Tuition, nonresident: full-time $21,870; part-time $1215 per credit hour. *International tuition:* $22,000 full-time. *Required fees:* $1402. *Financial support:* Research assistantships, teaching assistantships, and Federal Work-Study available. Support available to part-time students. Financial award application deadline: 3/15; financial award applicants required to submit FAFSA. *Faculty research:* Biomechanics, exercise physiology, motor skill learning, school health, curriculum development. *Unit head:* Dr. Mary E. Rudisill, Head, 334-844-1458. *Application contact:* Dr. George Flowers, Dean of the Graduate School, 334-844-2125.

Ball State University, Graduate School, College of Applied Science and Technology, Fisher Institute for Wellness and Gerontology, Interdepartmental Program in Wellness Management, Muncie, IN 47306-1099. Offers MA, MS. *Faculty:* 1. *Students:* 11 full-time (6 women), 2 part-time (1 woman); includes 4 minority (1 Black or African American, non-Hispanic/Latino; 2 Hispanic/Latino; 1 Two or more races, non-Hispanic/Latino). Average age 25. 12 applicants, 58% accepted, 6 enrolled. In 2011, 12 degrees awarded. *Entrance requirements:* For master's, GRE General Test, interview. Application fee: $25 ($35 for international students). Tuition and fees vary according to program and reciprocity agreements. *Financial support:* In 2011–12, 14 students received support, including 13 teaching assistantships (averaging $10,629 per year); research assistantships with full tuition reimbursements available and career-related internships or fieldwork also available. Financial award application deadline: 3/1. *Unit head:* Dr. Jane Ellery, Head, 765-285-8259, E-mail: jellery@bsu.edu. *Application contact:* Dr. Robert Morris, Associate Provost for Research and Dean of the Graduate School, 765-285-5723, Fax: 765-285-1328, E-mail: rmorris@bsu.edu. Web site: http://www.bsu.edu/wellness/.

Benedictine University, Graduate Programs, Program in Nutrition and Wellness, Lisle, IL 60532-0900. Offers MS. *Students:* 27 full-time (all women), 7 part-time (all women);

includes 1 minority (Asian, non-Hispanic/Latino). 43 applicants, 81% accepted, 15 enrolled. In 2011, 15 degrees awarded. *Entrance requirements:* Additional exam requirements/recommendations for international students: Required—TOEFL (minimum score 550 paper-based; 213 computer-based). *Application deadline:* For fall admission, 9/1 for domestic students; for winter admission, 12/1 for domestic students; for spring admission, 2/15 for domestic students. Applications are processed on a rolling basis. Application fee: $40. Electronic applications accepted. *Financial support:* Career-related internships or fieldwork and health care benefits available. Support available to part-time students. *Faculty research:* Community and corporate wellness risk assessment, health behavior change, self-efficacy, evaluation of health program impact and effectiveness. *Total annual research expenditures:* $8,335. *Unit head:* Catherine Arnold, Director, 630-829-6534, E-mail: carnold@ben.edu. *Application contact:* Kari Gibbons, Associate Vice President, Enrollment Center, 630-829-6200, Fax: 630-829-6584, E-mail: kgibbons@ben.edu.

Boston University, School of Public Health, Social and Behavioral Sciences Department, Boston, MA 02118. Offers Dr PH. *Accreditation:* CEPH. Part-time and evening/weekend programs available. *Students:* 52 full-time (45 women), 53 part-time (49 women); includes 26 minority (6 Black or African American, non-Hispanic/Latino; 10 Asian, non-Hispanic/Latino; 7 Hispanic/Latino; 1 Native Hawaiian or other Pacific Islander, non-Hispanic/Latino; 2 Two or more races, non-Hispanic/Latino), 4 international. Average age 28. 361 applicants, 59% accepted, 55 enrolled. *Degree requirements:* For doctorate, thesis/dissertation. *Entrance requirements:* For doctorate, GRE, GMAT. Additional exam requirements/recommendations for international students: Required—TOEFL (minimum score 600 paper-based; 250 computer-based; 100 iBT) or IELTS (minimum score 6). *Application deadline:* For fall admission, 2/1 priority date for domestic students, 2/1 for international students; for spring admission, 10/15 priority date for domestic students, 10/15 for international students. Applications are processed on a rolling basis. Application fee: $115. Electronic applications accepted. *Expenses: Tuition:* Full-time $40,848; part-time $1276 per credit hour. *Required fees:* $572; $286 per semester. *Financial support:* Career-related internships or fieldwork, Federal Work-Study, institutionally sponsored loans, scholarships/grants, and tuition waivers (partial) available. Support available to part-time students. Financial award application deadline: 3/1; financial award applicants required to submit FAFSA. *Unit head:* Dr. Deborah Bowen, Chair, Community Health Sciences, 617-638-5160, E-mail: asksb@bu.edu. *Application contact:* LePhan Quan, Associate Director of Admissions, 617-638-4640, Fax: 617-638-5299, E-mail: asksph@bu.edu. Web site: http://sph.bu.edu/sb.

Bridgewater State University, School of Graduate Studies, School of Education and Allied Studies, Department of Movement Arts, Health Promotion, and Leisure Studies, Program in Health Promotion, Bridgewater, MA 02325-0001. Offers M Ed. Part-time and evening/weekend programs available. *Entrance requirements:* For master's, GRE General Test.

Brigham Young University, Graduate Studies, College of Life Sciences, Department of Exercise Sciences, Provo, UT 84602. Offers athletic training (MS); exercise physiology (MS, PhD); exercise science (MS); health promotion (MS, PhD); physical medicine and rehabilitation (PhD). *Faculty:* 21 full-time (3 women), 3 part-time/adjunct (0 women). *Students:* 17 full-time (10 women), 35 part-time (20 women); includes 4 minority (2 Asian, non-Hispanic/Latino; 1 Hispanic/Latino; 1 Native Hawaiian or other Pacific Islander, non-Hispanic/Latino), 1 international. Average age 29. 28 applicants, 43% accepted, 7 enrolled. In 2011, 14 master's, 1 doctorate awarded. *Degree requirements:* For master's, thesis, oral defense; for doctorate, comprehensive exam, thesis/dissertation, oral defense, oral and written exams. *Entrance requirements:* For master's, GRE General Test, minimum GPA of 3.2 in last 60 hours of course work; for doctorate, GRE General Test, minimum GPA of 3.5 in last 60 hours of course work. Additional exam requirements/recommendations for international students: Required—TOEFL (minimum score 580 paper-based; 237 computer-based; 85 iBT), IELTS (minimum score 7). *Application deadline:* For fall admission, 2/1 for domestic and international students. Application fee: $50. Electronic applications accepted. *Expenses: Tuition:* Full-time $5760; part-time $320 per credit. Tuition and fees vary according to student's religious affiliation. *Financial support:* In 2011–12, 52 students received support, including 15 research assistantships with partial tuition reimbursements available (averaging $5,615 per year), 34 teaching assistantships with partial tuition reimbursements available (averaging $10,106 per year); fellowships, career-related internships or fieldwork, institutionally sponsored loans, scholarships/grants, tuition waivers (partial), unspecified assistantships, and 10 PhD fulltTuition scholarships also available. Financial award application deadline: 3/1. *Faculty research:* Injury prevention and rehabilitation, human skeletal muscle adaptation, cardiovascular health and fitness, lifestyle modification and health promotion. *Total annual research expenditures:* $2,888. *Unit head:* Dr. Gary Mack, Chair, 801-422-2466, Fax: 801-422-0555, E-mail: gary_mack@byu.edu. *Application contact:* Dr. Jeffrey Brent Feland, Graduate Coordinator, 801-422-1182, Fax: 801-422-0555, E-mail: brent_feland@byu.edu. Web site: http://www.exsc.byu.edu.

California State University, Fresno, Division of Graduate Studies, College of Health and Human Services, Department of Public Health, Fresno, CA 93740-8027. Offers health policy and management (MPH); health promotion (MPH). *Accreditation:* CEPH. Part-time and evening/weekend programs available. *Degree requirements:* For master's, thesis or alternative. *Entrance requirements:* For master's, GRE General Test, minimum GPA of 2.5. Additional exam requirements/recommendations for international students: Required—TOEFL. Electronic applications accepted. *Faculty research:* Foster parent training, geriatrics, tobacco control.

Claremont Graduate University, Graduate Programs, School of Community and Global Health, San Dimas, CA 91773. Offers health promotion science (PhD); public health (MPH). *Faculty:* 10 full-time (4 women). *Students:* 31 full-time (21 women), 7 part-time (5 women); includes 24 minority (4 Black or African American, non-Hispanic/Latino; 7 Asian, non-Hispanic/Latino; 11 Hispanic/Latino; 2 Two or more races, non-Hispanic/Latino), 2 international. Average age 30. In 2011, 2 master's awarded. *Entrance requirements:* For master's and doctorate, GRE. Additional exam requirements/recommendations for international students: Required—TOEFL (minimum score 550 paper-based; 213 computer-based; 80 iBT). *Application deadline:* For fall admission, 2/1 priority date for domestic students; for spring admission, 11/1 priority date for domestic students. Applications are processed on a rolling basis. Application fee: $60. Electronic applications accepted. *Expenses: Tuition:* Full-time $36,374; part-time $1581 per unit. *Required fees:* $165 per semester. *Financial support:* Fellowships, research assistantships, teaching assistantships, Federal Work-Study, institutionally sponsored loans, and scholarships/grants available. Support available to part-time students. Financial award application deadline: 2/15; financial award applicants required to submit FAFSA. *Unit head:* Andy Johnson, Dean, 909-607-8235, E-mail: andy.johnson@cgu.edu. *Application contact:* E-mail: admiss@cgu.edu. Web site: http://www.cgu.edu/pages/5644.asp.

Cleveland Chiropractic College–Kansas City Campus, Program in Health Promotion, Overland Park, KS 66210. Offers MSHP. *Faculty:* 1 (woman) full-time, 2 part-time/adjunct. *Students:* 3 full-time (1 woman); includes 1 minority (Two or more races, non-Hispanic/Latino). Average age 37. 5 applicants, 20% accepted, 0 enrolled. *Entrance requirements:* For master's, GRE, minimum GPA of 3.0, BS/BA. Additional exam requirements/recommendations for international students: Required—TOEFL (minimum score 550 paper-based; 213 computer-based; 79 iBT). *Application deadline:* For fall admission, 7/1 for domestic and international students; for winter admission, 10/1 for domestic and international students. Applications are processed on a rolling basis. Application fee: $50. Electronic applications accepted. *Expenses:* Contact institution. *Financial support:* Applicants required to submit FAFSA. *Unit head:* Karen Doyle, Dean, 913-234-0646, Fax: 913-234-0906, E-mail: karen.doyle@cleveland.edu. *Application contact:* Melissa Denton, Director of Admissions, 913-234-0744, Fax: 913-234-0906, E-mail: kc.admissions@cleveland.edu.

Concord University, Graduate Studies, Athens, WV 24712-1000. Offers educational leadership and supervision (M Ed); geography (M Ed); health promotion (M Ed); reading specialist (M Ed). Part-time and evening/weekend programs available. Postbaccalaureate distance learning degree programs offered (no on-campus study). *Entrance requirements:* For master's, GRE or MAT, baccalaureate degree with minimum GPA of 2.5 from regionally-accredited institution; teaching license; 2 letters of recommendation; completed disposition assessment form. Electronic applications accepted.

Eastern Kentucky University, The Graduate School, College of Health Sciences, Department of Exercise and Sport Science, Richmond, KY 40475-3102. Offers exercise and sport science (MS); exercise and wellness (MS); sports administration (MS). Part-time programs available. *Entrance requirements:* For master's, GRE General Test (minimum score 700 verbal and quantitative), minimum GPA of 2.5 (for most), minimum GPA of 3.0 (analytical writing). *Faculty research:* Nutrition and exercise.

Eastern Michigan University, Graduate School, College of Health and Human Services, School of Health Promotion and Human Performance, Ypsilanti, MI 48197. Offers MS, Graduate Certificate. Part-time and evening/weekend programs available. Postbaccalaureate distance learning degree programs offered (minimal on-campus study). *Faculty:* 27 full-time (10 women). *Students:* 72 full-time (45 women), 116 part-time (51 women); includes 31 minority (21 Black or African American, non-Hispanic/Latino; 3 American Indian or Alaska Native, non-Hispanic/Latino; 1 Asian, non-Hispanic/Latino; 4 Hispanic/Latino; 1 Native Hawaiian or other Pacific Islander, non-Hispanic/Latino; 1 Two or more races, non-Hispanic/Latino), 8 international. Average age 28. 190 applicants, 67% accepted, 77 enrolled. In 2011, 75 master's, 2 other advanced degrees awarded. *Entrance requirements:* For master's, MAT (orthotics and prosthetics). Additional exam requirements/recommendations for international students: Required—TOEFL. *Application deadline:* For fall admission, 8/1 for domestic students, 5/1 for international students; for winter admission, 12/1 for domestic students, 10/1 for international students; for spring admission, 4/15 for domestic students, 3/1 for international students. Applications are processed on a rolling basis. Application fee: $35. *Expenses:* Tuition, state resident: full-time $10,367; part-time $432 per credit hour. Tuition, nonresident: full-time $20,435; part-time $851 per credit hour. *Required fees:* $39 per credit hour. $46 per semester. One-time fee: $100. Tuition and fees vary according to course level, degree level and reciprocity agreements. *Financial support:* Fellowships, research assistantships with full tuition reimbursements, teaching assistantships with full tuition reimbursements, career-related internships or fieldwork, Federal Work-Study, institutionally sponsored loans, scholarships/grants, tuition waivers (partial), and unspecified assistantships available. Support available to part-time students. Financial award applicants required to submit FAFSA. *Unit head:* Dr. Christine Karshin, Director, 734-487-0090, Fax: 734-487-2024, E-mail: christine.karshin@emich.edu. *Application contact:* Dr. Brenda Riemer, Chair, Graduate Programs, 734-487-0090 Ext. 2745, Fax: 734-487-2024, E-mail: briemer@emich.edu.

Emory University, Rollins School of Public Health, Online Program in Public Health, Atlanta, GA 30322-1100. Offers applied epidemiology (MPH); applied public health informatics (MPH); prevention science (MPH). Part-time and evening/weekend programs available. Postbaccalaureate distance learning degree programs offered (minimal on-campus study). *Students:* 35 full-time. Average age 40. *Degree requirements:* For master's, thesis, practicum. *Entrance requirements:* For master's, GRE. Additional exam requirements/recommendations for international students: Required—TOEFL (minimum score 550 paper-based; 213 computer-based; 80 iBT). *Application deadline:* For fall admission, 1/5 priority date for domestic students, 1/5 for international students. Applications are processed on a rolling basis. Application fee: $95. Electronic applications accepted. *Expenses: Tuition:* Full-time $34,800. *Required fees:* $1300. *Financial support:* Fellowships with full and partial tuition reimbursements, career-related internships or fieldwork, Federal Work-Study, institutionally sponsored loans, scholarships/grants, traineeships, health care benefits, and unspecified assistantships available. Support available to part-time students. Financial award application deadline: 1/5; financial award applicants required to submit FAFSA. *Unit head:* Melissa Alperin, Director, 404-727-2928, Fax: 404-727-3996, E-mail: malperi@emory.edu. Web site: http://www.sph.emory.edu/CMPH/.

Fairmont State University, Programs in Education, Fairmont, WV 26554. Offers digital media, new literacies and learning (M Ed); education (MAT); exercise science, fitness and wellness (M Ed); leadership studies (M Ed); online learning (M Ed); professional studies (M Ed); reading (M Ed); special education (M Ed). *Accreditation:* NCATE. Part-time and evening/weekend programs available. Postbaccalaureate distance learning degree programs offered. *Faculty:* 16 part-time/adjunct (10 women). *Students:* 103 full-time (72 women), 142 part-time (103 women); includes 11 minority (2 Black or African American, non-Hispanic/Latino; 1 American Indian or Alaska Native, non-Hispanic/Latino; 6 Hispanic/Latino; 2 Two or more races, non-Hispanic/Latino), 2 international. Average age 33. 71 applicants, 85% accepted. In 2011, 58 master's awarded. *Entrance requirements:* For master's, GRE. *Application deadline:* For fall admission, 5/1 for domestic and international students. Applications are processed on a rolling basis. Application fee: $40. *Expenses:* Tuition, state resident: full-time $5900. Tuition, nonresident: full-time $12,596. *Unit head:* Dr. Van O. Dempsey, III, Dean, School of Education, 304-367-4241, Fax: 304-367-4599, E-mail: vdempsey@fairmontstate.edu. Web site: http://www.fairmontstate.edu/graduatestudies/default.asp.

Florida Atlantic University, College of Education, Department of Exercise Science and Health Promotion, Boca Raton, FL 33431-0991. Offers MS. Part-time and evening/weekend programs available. *Faculty:* 9 full-time (3 women), 14 part-time/adjunct (10 women). *Students:* 43 full-time (21 women), 20 part-time (9 women); includes 12 minority (5 Black or African American, non-Hispanic/Latino; 1 Asian, non-Hispanic/Latino; 4 Hispanic/Latino; 2 Two or more races, non-Hispanic/Latino), 2 international. Average age 26. 78 applicants, 51% accepted, 7 enrolled. In 2011, 23 master's awarded. *Degree requirements:* For master's, comprehensive exam, thesis optional. *Entrance requirements:* For master's, GRE General Test, minimum GPA of 3.0 during last 60 hours of course work. Additional exam requirements/recommendations for international students: Required—TOEFL (minimum score 500 paper-based). *Application deadline:* For fall admission, 7/1 priority date for domestic students, 2/15 for international students; for spring admission, 11/1 priority date for domestic students, 7/15 for international students. Applications are processed on a rolling basis. Application fee: $30. *Expenses: Tuition, area resident:* Part-time $343.02 per credit hour. Tuition, state resident: full-time $8232. Tuition, nonresident: full-time $23,931; part-time $997.14 per credit hour. *Financial support:* Research assistantships with partial tuition

reimbursements, teaching assistantships with partial tuition reimbursements, and career-related internships or fieldwork available. *Faculty research:* Pulmonary limitations during exercise, metabolism regulation, determinants of performance, age-related change in functional mobility and geriatric exercise, behavioral change aimed at promoting active lifestyles. *Unit head:* Dr. Sue Graves, Chair, 954-236-1261, Fax: 954-236-1259. *Application contact:* Dr. Joseph A. O'Kroy, Graduate Coordinator, 954-236-1266, Fax: 954-236-1259, E-mail: okroy@fau.edu. Web site: http://www.coe.fau.edu/academicdepartments/eshp/.

Florida International University, Robert Stempel College of Public Health and Social Work, Programs in Public Health, Miami, FL 33199. Offers biostatistics (MPH); environmental and occupational health (MPH, PhD); epidemiology (MPH, PhD); health policy and management (MPH); health promotion and disease prevention (PhD); health promotion and diseases prevention (MPH). Ph D is fall admission only; MPH offered jointly with University of Miami. *Accreditation:* CEPH. Part-time and evening/weekend programs available. Postbaccalaureate distance learning degree programs offered (no on-campus study). *Degree requirements:* For master's, thesis optional; for doctorate, comprehensive exam, thesis/dissertation. *Entrance requirements:* For master's, minimum GPA of 3.0, letters of recommendation; for doctorate, GRE, resume, minimum GPA of 3.0, letters of recommendation, letter of intent. Additional exam requirements/recommendations for international students: Required—TOEFL (minimum score 550 paper-based; 80 iBT). Electronic applications accepted. *Expenses:* Contact institution. *Faculty research:* Drugs/AIDS intervention among migrant workers, provision of services for active/recovering drug users with HIV.

George Mason University, College of Education and Human Development, School of Recreation, Health and Tourism, Manassas , VA 20110. Offers exercise, fitness, and health promotion (MS); sport and recreation studies (MS). *Faculty:* 34 full-time (15 women), 59 part-time/adjunct (32 women). *Students:* 18 full-time (10 women), 25 part-time (11 women); includes 5 minority (2 Black or African American, non-Hispanic/Latino; 1 Asian, non-Hispanic/Latino; 1 Hispanic/Latino; 1 Two or more races, non-Hispanic/Latino). Average age 29. 58 applicants, 60% accepted, 22 enrolled. In 2011, 7 degrees awarded. *Degree requirements:* For master's, thesis (for some programs). *Entrance requirements:* For master's, GRE General Test or MAT, 3 letters of recommendation; official transcripts; expanded goals statement; undergraduate course in statistics and minimum GPA of 3.0 in last 60 credit hours and overall (for MS in sport and recreation studies); baccalaureate degree related to kinesiology, exercise science or athletic training (for MS in exercise, fitness and health promotion). Additional exam requirements/recommendations for international students: Required—TOEFL (minimum score 570 paper-based; 230 computer-based; 88 iBT), IELTS, Pearson Test of English. *Application deadline:* For fall admission, 4/1 priority date for domestic students; for spring admission, 11/1 priority date for domestic students. Application fee: $65 ($80 for international students). Electronic applications accepted. *Expenses:* Tuition, state resident: full-time $8750; part-time $364.58 per credit. Tuition, nonresident: full-time $24,092; part-time $1003.83 per credit. *Required fees:* $2514; $104.75 per credit. *Financial support:* In 2011–12, 7 students received support, including 7 research assistantships with full and partial tuition reimbursements available (averaging $6,675 per year); career-related internships or fieldwork, Federal Work-Study, scholarships/grants, unspecified assistantships, and health care benefits (full-time research or teaching assistantship recipients) also available. Support available to part-time students. Financial award application deadline: 3/1; financial award applicants required to submit FAFSA. *Faculty research:* Informing policy; promoting economic development; advocating stewardship of natural resources; improving the quality of life of individuals, families, and communities at the local, national and international levels. *Total annual research expenditures:* $553,053. *Unit head:* David Wiggins, Director, 703-993-2057, Fax: 703-993-2025, E-mail: dwiggin1@gmu.edu. *Application contact:* Dr. Pierre Rodgers, Associate Professor/Co-Coordinator of Graduate Programs, 703-993-8317, Fax: 703-993-2025, E-mail: prodgers@gmu.edu. Web site: http://rht.gmu.edu/grad/.

Georgetown University, Graduate School of Arts and Sciences, Programs in Biomedical Sciences, Department of Microbiology and Immunology, Washington, DC 20057. Offers biohazardous threat agents and emerging infectious diseases (MS); general microbiology and immunology (MS); global infectious diseases (PhD); microbiology and immunology research (PhD); science policy and advocacy (MS). Part-time programs available. *Degree requirements:* For master's, 30 credit hours of coursework; for doctorate, comprehensive exam, thesis/dissertation. *Entrance requirements:* For master's, GRE General Test, 3 letters of reference, bachelor's degree in related field; for doctorate, GRE General Test, 3 letters of reference, MS/BS in related field. Additional exam requirements/recommendations for international students: Required—TOEFL (minimum score 505 paper-based; 213 computer-based). Electronic applications accepted. *Faculty research:* Pathogenesis and basic biology of the fungus Candida albicans, molecular biology of viral immunopathological mechanisms in Multiple Sclerosis.

Georgia College & State University, Graduate School, College of Health Sciences, Department of Kinesiology, Milledgeville, GA 31061. Offers health promotion (M Ed); human performance (M Ed); kinesiology (MAT); outdoor education (M Ed). *Accreditation:* NCATE (one or more programs are accredited). Part-time and evening/weekend programs available. *Students:* 31 full-time (13 women), 11 part-time (7 women); includes 8 minority (6 Black or African American, non-Hispanic/Latino; 2 Hispanic/Latino), 1 international. Average age 27. 32 applicants, 69% accepted, 16 enrolled. In 2011, 12 master's awarded. *Degree requirements:* For master's, comprehensive exam, thesis optional. *Entrance requirements:* For master's, GRE General Test or MAT, minimum GPA of 2.75 in upper-level undergraduate courses, 2 letters of reference. Additional exam requirements/recommendations for international students: Recommended—TOEFL (minimum score 550 paper-based; 213 computer-based; 79 iBT). *Application deadline:* For fall admission, 7/1 priority date for domestic students, 4/1 for international students; for spring admission, 11/15 priority date for domestic students, 9/1 for international students. Applications are processed on a rolling basis. Application fee: $40. Electronic applications accepted. *Expenses:* Tuition, state resident: full-time $4006; part-time $267 per credit hour. Tuition, nonresident: full-time $17,802; part-time $989 per credit hour. *Required fees:* $936 per semester. Tuition and fees vary according to course load and campus/location. *Financial support:* In 2011–12, 25 research assistantships with full tuition reimbursements were awarded; career-related internships or fieldwork and unspecified assistantships also available. Support available to part-time students. Financial award applicants required to submit FAFSA. *Unit head:* Dr. Lisa Griffin, Interim Chair, 478-445-4072, Fax: 478-445-1790, E-mail: lisa.griffin@gcsu.edu. *Application contact:* 800-342-0471, E-mail: grad-admit@gcsu.edu.

Georgia State University, College of Health and Human Sciences, Byrdine F. Lewis School of Nursing, Atlanta, GA 30302-3083. Offers adult health (MS); adult health nursing (Certificate); child health (MS); family nurse practitioner (MS, Certificate); health promotion, protection and restoration (PhD); perinatal/women's health (MS); psychiatric mental health nursing (Certificate); psychiatric/mental health (MS); women's health nursing (Certificate). *Accreditation:* AACN. Part-time and evening/weekend programs available. Postbaccalaureate distance learning degree programs offered (minimal on-campus study). *Degree requirements:* For master's, research activity; for doctorate,

comprehensive exam, thesis/dissertation. *Entrance requirements:* For master's, MAT (preferred) or GRE, interview, RN license; for doctorate, GRE General Test. Additional exam requirements/recommendations for international students: Required—TOEFL (minimum score 550 paper-based; 213 computer-based). Electronic applications accepted. *Expenses:* Contact institution. *Faculty research:* Breast cancer prevention, sexually compulsive behaviors, health risks in minority youth, asthma treatment strategies, adolescent alcohol-related issues.

Goddard College, Graduate Division, Master of Arts in Health Arts and Sciences Program, Plainfield, VT 05667-9432. Offers MA. *Degree requirements:* For master's, thesis. *Entrance requirements:* For master's, 3 letters of recommendation, study plan and resource list, interview. Electronic applications accepted.

Harvard University, Harvard School of Public Health, Department of Society, Human Development and Health, Boston, MA 02115-6096. Offers SM, DPH, SD. Part-time programs available. *Faculty:* 31 full-time (18 women), 18 part-time/adjunct (10 women). *Students:* 92 full-time, 9 part-time; includes 31 minority (7 Black or African American, non-Hispanic/Latino; 12 Asian, non-Hispanic/Latino; 10 Hispanic/Latino; 2 Two or more races, non-Hispanic/Latino), 17 international. Average age 29. 192 applicants, 31% accepted, 35 enrolled. In 2011, 21 master's, 8 doctorates awarded. *Degree requirements:* For doctorate, thesis/dissertation, qualifying exam. *Entrance requirements:* For master's and doctorate, GRE. Additional exam requirements/recommendations for international students: Required—TOEFL (minimum score 590 paper-based; 240 computer-based; 95 iBT); Recommended—IELTS (minimum score 7). *Application deadline:* For fall admission, 12/15 for domestic and international students. Application fee: $115. Electronic applications accepted. *Expenses: Tuition:* Full-time $36,304. *Required fees:* $1186. Full-time tuition and fees vary according to program. *Financial support:* Fellowships, research assistantships, teaching assistantships, Federal Work-Study, scholarships/grants, traineeships, and unspecified assistantships available. Support available to part-time students. Financial award application deadline: 2/17; financial award applicants required to submit FAFSA. *Faculty research:* Social determinants of health, program design and planned social change, health and social policy, heath care and community-based interventions, health effects and prevention of gender-based violence. *Unit head:* Dr. Ichiro Kawachi, Chair, 617-432-1135, Fax: 617-432-3123, E-mail: ikawachi@hsph.harvard.edu. *Application contact:* Vincent W. James, Director of Admissions, 617-432-1031, Fax: 617-432-7080, E-mail: admissions@hsph.harvard.edu. Web site: http://www.hsph.harvard.edu/departments/society-human-development-and-health/.

Independence University, Program In Health Services, Salt Lake City, UT 84107. Offers community health (MSHS); wellness promotion (MSHS). Part-time and evening/weekend programs available. Postbaccalaureate distance learning degree programs offered (no on-campus study). *Degree requirements:* For master's, fieldwork, internship, final project (wellness promotion). *Entrance requirements:* For master's, previous course work in psychology.

Independence University, Program in Nursing, Salt Lake City, UT 84107. Offers community health (MSN); gerontology (MSN); nursing administration (MSN); wellness promotion (MSN).

Indiana State University, College of Graduate and Professional Studies, College of Nursing, Health and Human Services, Department of Health, Safety, and Environmental Health Sciences, Terre Haute, IN 47809. Offers community health promotion (MA, MS); health and safety education (MA, MS); occupational safety management (MA, MS). *Accreditation:* NCATE (one or more programs are accredited). *Degree requirements:* For master's, thesis or alternative. *Entrance requirements:* For master's, GRE General Test. Electronic applications accepted.

Indiana University Bloomington, School of Health, Physical Education and Recreation, Department of Applied Health Science, Bloomington, IN 47405-7000. Offers biostatistics (MPH); environmental health (MPH, PhD); epidemiology (MPH, PhD); health behavior (PhD); health promotion (MS); human development/family studies (MS); nutrition science (MS); public health administration (MPH); safety management (MS); school and college health programs (MS); social, behavioral and community health (MPH). *Accreditation:* CEPH (one or more programs are accredited). *Faculty:* 24 full-time (12 women). *Students:* 169 full-time (126 women), 25 part-time (17 women); includes 56 minority (39 Black or African American, non-Hispanic/Latino; 2 American Indian or Alaska Native, non-Hispanic/Latino; 4 Asian, non-Hispanic/Latino; 9 Hispanic/Latino; 2 Two or more races, non-Hispanic/Latino), 29 international. Average age 30. 170 applicants, 74% accepted, 79 enrolled. In 2011, 52 master's, 9 doctorates awarded. *Degree requirements:* For master's, thesis optional; for doctorate, thesis/dissertation. *Entrance requirements:* For master's, GRE (MS in nutrition science), 3 recommendations; for doctorate, GRE, 3 recommendations. Additional exam requirements/recommendations for international students: Required—TOEFL (minimum score 550 paper-based; 213 computer-based; 79 iBT). *Application deadline:* For fall admission, 4/30 priority date for domestic students, 12/1 for international students; for spring admission, 11/15 priority date for domestic students, 9/1 for international students. Application fee: $55 ($65 for international students). *Financial support:* Fellowships, research assistantships with full and partial tuition reimbursements, teaching assistantships with full and partial tuition reimbursements, career-related internships or fieldwork, Federal Work-Study, institutionally sponsored loans, scholarships/grants, tuition waivers (partial), and fee remissions available. Financial award application deadline: 3/1. *Faculty research:* Cancer education, HIV/AIDS and drug education, public health, parent-child interactions, safety education. *Total annual research expenditures:* $2.8 million. *Unit head:* Dr. David K. Lohrmann, Chair, 812-856-5101, Fax: 812-855-3936, E-mail: dlohrman@indiana.edu. *Application contact:* Dr. Susan Middlestadt, Associate Professor and Graduate Coordinator, 812-856-5768, Fax: 812-855-3936, E-mail: semiddle@indiana.edu. Web site: http://www.indiana.edu/~aphealth/.

Indiana University Bloomington, School of Health, Physical Education and Recreation, Department of Kinesiology, Bloomington, IN 47405-7000. Offers adapted physical education (MS); applied sport science (MS); athletic administration/sport management (MS); athletic training (MS); biomechanics (MS); ergonomics (MS); exercise physiology (MS); human performance (PhD), including adapted physical education, biomechanics, exercise physiology, motor learning/control, sport management; motor learning/control (MS); physical activity, fitness and wellness (MS). Part-time programs available. *Faculty:* 28 full-time (11 women). *Students:* 150 full-time (59 women), 22 part-time (9 women); includes 20 minority (12 Black or African American, non-Hispanic/Latino; 1 American Indian or Alaska Native, non-Hispanic/Latino; 1 Asian, non-Hispanic/Latino; 4 Hispanic/Latino; 2 Two or more races, non-Hispanic/Latino), 33 international. Average age 28. 211 applicants, 60% accepted, 62 enrolled. In 2011, 67 master's, 7 doctorates awarded. Terminal master's awarded for partial completion of doctoral program. *Degree requirements:* For master's, thesis optional; for doctorate, variable foreign language requirement, thesis/dissertation. *Entrance requirements:* For master's, GRE General Test, minimum GPA of 2.8; for doctorate, GRE General Test, minimum graduate GPA of 3.5, undergraduate 3.0. *Application deadline:* For fall admission, 1/1 for international students; for spring admission, 9/1 for international students. Applications are processed on a rolling basis. Application fee: $55 ($65 for international students). *Financial support:* Fellowships,

research assistantships with full tuition reimbursements, teaching assistantships with full tuition reimbursements, career-related internships or fieldwork, Federal Work-Study, institutionally sponsored loans, scholarships/grants, tuition waivers (partial), and fee remissions available. Financial award application deadline: 3/1. *Faculty research:* Exercise physiology and biochemistry, sports biomechanics, human motor control, adaptation of fitness and exercise to special populations. *Unit head:* Dr. David M. Koceja, Chairperson, 812-855-5523, Fax: 812-855-3193, E-mail: koceja@indiana.edu. *Application contact:* Kristine M. Wasson, Administrative Assistant for Graduate Studies, 812-855-5523, Fax: 812-855-3193, E-mail: ktanksle@indiana.edu. Web site: http://www.indiana.edu/~kines/.

Instituto Tecnologico de Santo Domingo, Graduate School, Area of Health Sciences, Santo Domingo, Dominican Republic. Offers bioethics (M Bioethics); clinical bioethics (Certificate); clinical nutrition (Certificate); comprehensive health and the adolescent (Certificate); comrehensive adloescent health (MS); health and social security (M Mgmt).

Kent State University, Graduate School of Education, Health, and Human Services, School of Health Sciences, Program in Health Education and Promotion, Kent, OH 44242-0001. Offers M Ed, MA, PhD. *Accreditation:* NCATE. *Faculty:* 7 full-time (6 women), 4 part-time/adjunct (all women). *Students:* 22 full-time (19 women), 20 part-time (16 women); includes 8 minority (all Black or African American, non-Hispanic/Latino). 21 applicants, 43% accepted. In 2011, 12 master's, 2 doctorates awarded. *Degree requirements:* For doctorate, comprehensive exam, thesis/dissertation. *Entrance requirements:* For master's, 2 letters of reference, goals statement; for doctorate, GRE General Test, goals statement, resume, interview. Additional exam requirements/recommendations for international students: Required—TOEFL (minimum score 550 paper-based; 213 computer-based; 80 iBT). *Application deadline:* Applications are processed on a rolling basis. Application fee: $30 ($60 for international students). Electronic applications accepted. *Expenses:* Tuition, state resident: full-time $8136; part-time $452 per credit hour. Tuition, nonresident: full-time $14,292; part-time $794 per credit hour. *Financial support:* In 2011–12, 6 fellowships with full tuition reimbursements (averaging $10,250 per year) were awarded; research assistantships with full tuition reimbursements, teaching assistantships with full tuition reimbursements, Federal Work-Study, scholarships/grants, and unspecified assistantships also available. Financial award application deadline: 4/1; financial award applicants required to submit FAFSA. *Faculty research:* Substance use/abuse, sexuality, community health assessment, epidemiology, HIV/AIDS. *Unit head:* Dr. Kele Ding, Coordinator, 330-672-0688, E-mail: kding@kent.edu. *Application contact:* Nancy Miller, Academic Program Coordinator, Office of Graduate Student Services, 330-672-2586, Fax: 330-672-9162, E-mail: ogs@kent.edu. Web site: http://www.kent.edu/ehhs/Schools/hs/programs/hedp/.

Lehman College of the City University of New York, Division of Natural and Social Sciences, Department of Health Sciences, Program in Health Education and Promotion, Bronx, NY 10468-1589. Offers MA. *Accreditation:* CEPH; NCATE. Part-time and evening/weekend programs available. *Degree requirements:* For master's, thesis or alternative. *Entrance requirements:* For master's, minimum GPA of 2.7.

Loma Linda University, School of Public Health, Programs in Health Promotion and Education, Loma Linda, CA 92350. Offers MPH, Dr PH. *Accreditation:* CEPH (one or more programs are accredited). *Degree requirements:* For doctorate, thesis/dissertation. *Entrance requirements:* For doctorate, GRE General Test. Additional exam requirements/recommendations for international students: Required—Michigan English Language Assessment Battery or TOEFL.

Louisiana State University in Shreveport, College of Business, Education, and Human Development, Program in Kinesiology and Wellness, Shreveport, LA 71115-2399. Offers MS. Part-time and evening/weekend programs available. *Students:* 5 full-time (2 women), 2 part-time (1 woman); includes 2 minority (both Asian, non-Hispanic/Latino), 1 international. Average age 26. 3 applicants, 100% accepted, 0 enrolled. In 2011, 4 master's awarded. *Entrance requirements:* For master's, GRE, baccalaureate degree with minimum GPA of 2.5 or 2.75 on last 60 credit hours attempted in degree program. Additional exam requirements/recommendations for international students: Required—TOEFL (minimum score 550 paper-based; 213 computer-based; 80 iBT). *Application deadline:* For fall admission, 6/30 for domestic and international students; for spring admission, 11/30 for domestic and international students. Application fee: $10 ($20 for international students). *Financial support:* Unspecified assistantships available. Financial award applicants required to submit FAFSA. *Unit head:* Dr. Timothy P. Winter, Program Director, 318-797-5264, Fax: 318-797-5386, E-mail: timothy.winter@lsus.edu. *Application contact:* Christianne Wojcik, Director of Academic Services, 318-797-5247, Fax: 318-798-4120, E-mail: christianne.wojcik@lsus.edu.

Marymount University, School of Health Professions, Program in Health Promotion Management, Arlington, VA 22207-4299. Offers MS. Part-time and evening/weekend programs available. *Faculty:* 2 full-time (1 woman), 1 (woman) part-time/adjunct. *Students:* 12 full-time (all women), 20 part-time (19 women); includes 13 minority (10 Black or African American, non-Hispanic/Latino; 1 Asian, non-Hispanic/Latino; 2 Hispanic/Latino), 3 international. Average age 31. 15 applicants, 100% accepted, 13 enrolled. In 2011, 14 master's awarded. *Entrance requirements:* For master's, GRE or MAT, 2 letters of recommendation, interview, resume. Additional exam requirements/recommendations for international students: Required—TOEFL (minimum score 600 paper-based; 250 computer-based; 96 iBT), IELTS (minimum score 6.5). *Application deadline:* For fall admission, 7/1 for international students. Applications are processed on a rolling basis. Application fee: $40. Electronic applications accepted. *Expenses: Tuition:* Part-time $770 per credit hour. *Required fees:* $8 per credit hour. One-time fee: $180 full-time. *Financial support:* In 2011–12, 4 students received support. Research assistantships with full tuition reimbursements available, career-related internships or fieldwork, Federal Work-Study, scholarships/grants, and unspecified assistantships available. Support available to part-time students. Financial award applicants required to submit FAFSA. *Unit head:* Dr. Michael Nordvall, Chair, 703-526-6876, Fax: 703-284-3819, E-mail: michael.nordvall@marymount.edu. *Application contact:* Francesca Reed, Director, Graduate Admissions, 703-284-5901, Fax: 703-527-3815, E-mail: grad.admissions@marymount.edu. Web site: http://www.marymount.edu/academics/programs/healthPromo.

Marywood University, Academic Affairs, College of Health and Human Services, Department of Nutrition and Dietetics, Scranton, PA 18509-1598. Offers dietetic internship (Certificate); human development (PhD), including health promotion; nutrition (MS); sports nutrition and exercise science (MS). *Entrance requirements:* Additional exam requirements/recommendations for international students: Required—TOEFL (minimum score 550 paper-based; 213 computer-based; 79 iBT). Application fee: $35. Electronic applications accepted. *Financial support:* Career-related internships or fieldwork, scholarships/grants, and unspecified assistantships available. Support available to part-time students. Financial award application deadline: 6/30; financial award applicants required to submit FAFSA. *Faculty research:* Community nutrition and the environment, wellness, human performance and sports nutrition, dietary regimens, food systems management. *Unit head:* Dr. Lee Harrison, Chairperson, 570-348-6211 Ext. 2303, E-mail: harrisonl@marywood.edu. Web site: http://www.marywood.edu/nutrition/graduate-programs/.

McNeese State University, Doré School of Graduate Studies, Burton College of Education, Department of Health and Human Performance, Lake Charles, LA 70609. Offers exercise physiology (MS); health promotion (MS); nutrition and wellness (MS). *Accreditation:* NCATE. Evening/weekend programs available. *Faculty:* 5 full-time (2 women). *Students:* 42 full-time (28 women), 11 part-time (8 women); includes 14 minority (11 Black or African American, non-Hispanic/Latino; 1 Asian, non-Hispanic/Latino; 1 Hispanic/Latino; 1 Two or more races, non-Hispanic/Latino), 5 international. In 2011, 23 master's awarded. *Entrance requirements:* For master's, GRE, undergraduate major or minor in health and human performance or related field of study. *Application deadline:* For fall admission, 5/15 priority date for domestic students, 5/15 for international students; for spring admission, 10/15 priority date for domestic students, 10/15 for international students. Applications are processed on a rolling basis. Application fee: $20 ($30 for international students). *Expenses:* Tuition, state resident: part-time $519 per credit hour. Tuition and fees vary according to course load. *Financial support:* Application deadline: 5/1. *Unit head:* Dr. Michael Soileau, Head, 337-475-5374, Fax: 337-475-5947, E-mail: msoileau@mcneese.edu. *Application contact:* Dr. George F. Mead, Jr., Interim Dean of Dore' School of Graduate Studies, 337-475-5396, Fax: 337-475-5397, E-mail: admissions@mcneese.edu.

Mississippi State University, College of Agriculture and Life Sciences, Department of Food Science, Nutrition and Health Promotion, Mississippi State, MS 39762. Offers food science and technology (MS, PhD); health promotion (MS); nutrition (MS, PhD). Postbaccalaureate distance learning degree programs offered (no on-campus study). *Faculty:* 9 full-time (3 women), 3 part-time/adjunct (1 woman). *Students:* 45 full-time (33 women), 38 part-time (31 women); includes 15 minority (8 Black or African American, non-Hispanic/Latino; 2 American Indian or Alaska Native, non-Hispanic/Latino; 1 Asian, non-Hispanic/Latino; 2 Hispanic/Latino; 1 Native Hawaiian or other Pacific Islander, non-Hispanic/Latino; 1 Two or more races, non-Hispanic/Latino), 18 international. Average age 30. 132 applicants, 28% accepted, 26 enrolled. In 2011, 27 master's, 3 doctorates awarded. *Degree requirements:* For master's, comprehensive exam, thesis; for doctorate, comprehensive exam, thesis/dissertation. *Entrance requirements:* For master's, GRE General Test, minimum GPA of 2.8; for doctorate, GRE General Test, minimum GPA of 3.0. Additional exam requirements/recommendations for international students: Required—TOEFL (minimum score 475 paper-based; 153 computer-based; 53 iBT); Recommended—IELTS (minimum score 4.5). *Application deadline:* For fall admission, 7/1 for domestic students, 5/1 for international students; for spring admission, 11/1 for domestic students, 9/1 for international students. Applications are processed on a rolling basis. Application fee: $40. Electronic applications accepted. *Expenses:* Tuition, state resident: full-time $5805; part-time $322.50 per credit hour. Tuition, nonresident: full-time $14,670; part-time $815 per credit hour. *Financial support:* In 2011–12, 8 research assistantships with full tuition reimbursements (averaging $13,126 per year), 4 teaching assistantships with full tuition reimbursements (averaging $12,741 per year) were awarded; Federal Work-Study, institutionally sponsored loans, scholarships/grants, and unspecified assistantships also available. Financial award application deadline: 4/1; financial award applicants required to submit FAFSA. *Faculty research:* Food preservation, food chemistry, food safety, food processing, product development. *Unit head:* Dr. Juan Silva, Professor and Interim Head, 662-325-3200, Fax: 662-325-8728, E-mail: jls@ra.msstate.edu. Web site: http://www.fsnhp.msstate.edu.

Missouri State University, Graduate College, College of Health and Human Services, Department of Health, Physical Education, and Recreation, Springfield, MO 65897. Offers health promotion and wellness management (MS); secondary education (MS Ed), including physical education. Part-time programs available. *Faculty:* 12 full-time (5 women). *Students:* 11 full-time (8 women), 8 part-time (5 women); includes 2 minority (1 Black or African American, non-Hispanic/Latino; 1 Asian, non-Hispanic/Latino). Average age 28. 14 applicants, 100% accepted, 9 enrolled. In 2011, 10 master's awarded. *Degree requirements:* For master's, comprehensive exam, thesis or alternative. *Entrance requirements:* For master's, GRE (MS), minimum GPA of 2.8 (MS); 9-12 teaching certification (MS Ed). Additional exam requirements/recommendations for international students: Required—TOEFL (minimum score 550 paper-based; 213 computer-based; 79 iBT). *Application deadline:* For fall admission, 7/20 priority date for domestic students, 5/1 for international students; for spring admission, 12/20 priority date for domestic students, 9/1 for international students. Applications are processed on a rolling basis. Application fee: $35 ($50 for international students). Electronic applications accepted. *Expenses:* Tuition, state resident: full-time $4086; part-time $227 per credit hour. Tuition, nonresident: full-time $8172; part-time $454 per credit hour. *Required fees:* $275 per semester. Tuition and fees vary according to course load, campus/location and program. *Financial support:* In 2011–12, 7 teaching assistantships with full tuition reimbursements (averaging $8,988 per year) were awarded; Federal Work-Study, institutionally sponsored loans, scholarships/grants, and unspecified assistantships also available. Financial award application deadline: 3/31; financial award applicants required to submit FAFSA. *Unit head:* Dr. Sarah McCallister, Acting Head, 417-836-6582, Fax: 417-836-5371, E-mail: sarahmccallister@missouristate.edu. *Application contact:* Misty Stewart, Coordinator of Graduate Admissions and Recruitment, 417-836-6079, Fax: 417-836-6200, E-mail: mistystewart@missouristate.edu. Web site: http://www.missouristate.edu/HPER/.

Morehouse School of Medicine, Master of Public Health Program, Atlanta, GA 30310-1495. Offers epidemiology (MPH); health administration, management and policy (MPH); health education/health promotion (MPH); international health (MPH). *Accreditation:* CEPH. Part-time programs available. *Degree requirements:* For master's, thesis, practicum, public health leadership seminar. *Entrance requirements:* For master's, GRE General Test, writing test, public health or human service experience. Additional exam requirements/recommendations for international students: Required—TOEFL (minimum score 550 paper-based; 200 computer-based). Electronic applications accepted. *Expenses:* Contact institution. *Faculty research:* Women's and adolescent health, violence prevention, cancer epidemiology/disparities, substance abuse prevention.

National University, Academic Affairs, School of Health and Human Services, Department of Health Sciences, La Jolla, CA 92037-1011. Offers clinical affairs (MS); clinical regulatory affairs (MS); health coaching (Certificate). Part-time and evening/weekend programs available. Postbaccalaureate distance learning degree programs offered. *Degree requirements:* For master's, thesis. *Entrance requirements:* For master's, interview, minimum GPA of 2.5. Additional exam requirements/recommendations for international students: Required—TOEFL (minimum score 550 paper-based; 213 computer-based; 79 iBT). Application fee: $60 ($65 for international students). *Financial support:* Career-related internships or fieldwork, institutionally sponsored loans, and scholarships/grants available. Support available to part-time students. Financial award application deadline: 6/30; financial award applicants required to submit FAFSA. *Unit head:* Dr. Patric Schiltz, Chair, 858-309-3476, Fax: 858-309-3480, E-mail: pschiltz@nu.edu. *Application contact:* Dominick Giovanniello, Associate Regional Dean, 800-NAT-UNIV, Fax: 858-541-7792, E-mail: dgiovann@nu.edu. Web site: http://www.nu.edu/OurPrograms/SchoolOfHealthAndHumanServices.html.

Nebraska Methodist College, Program in Health Promotion Management, Omaha, NE 68114. Offers MS. Evening/weekend programs available. Postbaccalaureate distance

learning degree programs offered (no on-campus study). *Degree requirements:* For master's, thesis or alternative, capstone project. *Entrance requirements:* For master's, interview. Additional exam requirements/recommendations for international students: Required—TOEFL (minimum score 550 paper-based; 213 computer-based; 80 iBT). *Faculty research:* Congregational health promotion, fitness testing with elderly, educational assessment, statistics instruction, resilience.

New York Medical College, School of Health Sciences and Practice, Department of Epidemiology and Community Health, Program in Behavioral Sciences and Health Promotion, Valhalla, NY 10595-1691. Offers behavioral sciences and health promotion (MPH); public health (Graduate Certificate). Part-time and evening/weekend programs available. *Faculty:* 4 full-time, 16 part-time/adjunct. *Students:* 35 full-time, 50 part-time. Average age 32. 37 applicants, 68% accepted, 21 enrolled. In 2011, 25 master's awarded. *Degree requirements:* For master's, thesis. *Entrance requirements:* For master's, minimum undergraduate GPA of 3.0. Additional exam requirements/recommendations for international students: Required—TOEFL (minimum score 637 paper-based; 250 computer-based; 110 iBT), IELTS (minimum score 7). *Application deadline:* For fall admission, 8/1 priority date for domestic students, 5/15 for international students; for spring admission, 12/1 priority date for domestic students, 10/15 for international students. Applications are processed on a rolling basis. Application fee: $50 ($100 for international students). Electronic applications accepted. *Financial support:* Career-related internships or fieldwork, Federal Work-Study, institutionally sponsored loans, health care benefits, and tuition reimbursements available. Support available to part-time students. Financial award applicants required to submit FAFSA. *Unit head:* Dr. Martin K. Diner, Assistant Professor, 914-594-4804, Fax: 914-594-3481, E-mail: martin_diner@nymc.edu. *Application contact:* Pamela Suett, Director of Recruitment, 914-594-4510, Fax: 914-594-4292, E-mail: shsp_admissions@nymc.edu. Web site: http://www.nymc.edu/shsp.

New York University, Steinhardt School of Culture, Education, and Human Development, Department of Applied Psychology, Program in Counseling, New York, NY 10012-1019. Offers counseling and guidance (MA; Advanced Certificate), including bilingual school counseling (MA); school counseling (MA); counseling for mental health and wellness (MA); counseling psychology (PhD). *Accreditation:* APA (one or more programs are accredited). Part-time programs available. *Faculty:* 9 full-time (6 women). *Students:* 157 full-time (120 women), 54 part-time (46 women); includes 88 minority (30 Black or African American, non-Hispanic/Latino; 1 American Indian or Alaska Native, non-Hispanic/Latino; 19 Asian, non-Hispanic/Latino; 33 Hispanic/Latino; 5 Two or more races, non-Hispanic/Latino), 21 international. Average age 26. 891 applicants, 32% accepted, 91 enrolled. In 2011, 76 master's, 5 doctorates awarded. *Degree requirements:* For master's, thesis (for some programs); for doctorate, thesis/dissertation. *Entrance requirements:* For doctorate, GRE General Test, interview. Additional exam requirements/recommendations for international students: Required—TOEFL. *Application deadline:* For fall admission, 12/1 priority date for domestic students, 12/1 for international students. Applications are processed on a rolling basis. Application fee: $75. Electronic applications accepted. *Financial support:* Fellowships with full and partial tuition reimbursements, research assistantships, teaching assistantships with partial tuition reimbursements, career-related internships or fieldwork, Federal Work-Study, institutionally sponsored loans, scholarships/grants, tuition waivers (partial), and unspecified assistantships available. Support available to part-time students. Financial award application deadline: 2/1; financial award applicants required to submit FAFSA. *Faculty research:* Cross-cultural counseling; group dynamics; culture, race and ethnicity; religiosity and psychological development; well-being and mental health. *Unit head:* 212-998-5555, Fax: 212-995-4358. *Application contact:* 212-998-5030, Fax: 212-995-4328, E-mail: steinhardt.gradadmissions@nyu.edu. Web site: http://steinhardt.nyu.edu/appsych/counseling.

Oakland University, Graduate Study and Lifelong Learning, School of Health Sciences, Program in Complimentary Medicine and Wellness, Rochester, MI 48309-4401. Offers Certificate.

Old Dominion University, College of Health Sciences, ODU/EVMS Joint Program for the Master of Public Health, Norfolk, VA 23529. Offers environmental health (MPH); health promotion (MPH). Program offered jointly with Eastern Virginia Medical School. *Accreditation:* CEPH. Part-time and evening/weekend programs available. *Faculty:* 7 full-time (4 women), 6 part-time/adjunct (3 women). *Students:* 1 (woman) full-time, 49 part-time (34 women); includes 18 minority (9 Black or African American, non-Hispanic/Latino; 3 Asian, non-Hispanic/Latino; 5 Hispanic/Latino; 1 Two or more races, non-Hispanic/Latino), 1 international. Average age 29. 67 applicants, 60% accepted, 30 enrolled. In 2011, 28 master's awarded. *Degree requirements:* For master's, field practicum, capstone project. *Entrance requirements:* For master's, GRE, MCAT, minimum GPA of 2.75. Additional exam requirements/recommendations for international students: Required—TOEFL (minimum score 650 paper-based; 278 computer-based). *Application deadline:* For fall admission, 5/31 priority date for domestic students, 4/30 for international students. Application fee: $50 ($100 for international students). Electronic applications accepted. *Expenses:* Tuition, state resident: full-time $9096; part-time $379 per credit. Tuition, nonresident: full-time $23,064; part-time $961 per credit. *Required fees:* $127 per semester. One-time fee: $50. *Financial support:* In 2011–12, 3 teaching assistantships with partial tuition reimbursements (averaging $10,000 per year) were awarded; career-related internships or fieldwork, institutionally sponsored loans, and scholarships/grants also available. Financial award application deadline: 5/1; financial award applicants required to submit FAFSA. *Faculty research:* Community-based health research, public health research in environmental health and health promotion. *Total annual research expenditures:* $150,133. *Unit head:* Associate Director, 757-683-4259, Fax: 757-446-6121. *Application contact:* William Heffelfinger, Director of Graduate Admissions, 757-683-5554, Fax: 757-683-3255, E-mail: gradadmit@odu.edu. Web site: http://www.evms.edu/hlthprof/mph.

Old Dominion University, Darden College of Education, Program in Physical Education, Exercise and Wellness Emphasis, Norfolk, VA 23529. Offers MS Ed. Part-time and evening/weekend programs available. *Faculty:* 7 full-time (4 women). *Students:* 22 full-time (16 women), 9 part-time (all women); includes 8 minority (5 Black or African American, non-Hispanic/Latino; 1 American Indian or Alaska Native, non-Hispanic/Latino; 1 Asian, non-Hispanic/Latino; 1 Two or more races, non-Hispanic/Latino), 3 international. Average age 27. 12 applicants, 100% accepted, 10 enrolled. In 2011, 13 master's awarded. *Degree requirements:* For master's, comprehensive exam, thesis or alternative, internship, research project. *Entrance requirements:* For master's, GRE, minimum GPA of 2.8 overall, 3.0 in major. Additional exam requirements/recommendations for international students: Required—TOEFL (minimum score 550 paper-based; 200 computer-based; 79 iBT). *Application deadline:* For fall admission, 7/1 for domestic students; for spring admission, 11/1 for domestic students. Applications are processed on a rolling basis. Application fee: $40. *Expenses:* Tuition, state resident: full-time $9096; part-time $379 per credit. Tuition, nonresident: full-time $23,064; part-time $961 per credit. *Required fees:* $127 per semester. One-time fee: $50. *Financial support:* In 2011–12, 1 teaching assistantship (averaging $9,000 per year) was awarded; career-related internships or fieldwork and scholarships/grants also available. Financial award application deadline: 4/15. *Faculty research:* Diabetes, exercise prescription, gait and balance. *Total annual research expenditures:* $105,000. *Unit*

head: Dr. David Swain, Graduate Program Director, 757-683-6028, E-mail: dswain@odu.edu. *Application contact:* William Heffelfinger, Director of Graduate Admissions, 757-683-5554, Fax: 757-683-3255, E-mail: gradadmit@odu.edu. Web site: http://education.odu.edu/esper/academics/exsci/graduate.shtml.

Oregon State University, Graduate School, College of Public Health and Human Sciences, Programs in Public Health, Corvallis, OR 97331. Offers biostatistics (MPH); environmental and occupational health and safety (MPH, PhD); epidemiology (MPH); health management and policy (MPH, PhD); health promotion and health behavior (MPH, PhD); international health (MPH). *Accreditation:* CEPH. Terminal master's awarded for partial completion of doctoral program. *Degree requirements:* For doctorate, one foreign language, thesis/dissertation. *Entrance requirements:* For master's and doctorate, minimum GPA of 3.0 in last 90 hours. Additional exam requirements/recommendations for international students: Required—TOEFL. *Faculty research:* Traffic safety, health safety, injury control, health promotion.

Portland State University, Graduate Studies, College of Urban and Public Affairs, School of Community Health, Portland, OR 97207-0751. Offers aging (Certificate); health education (MA, MS); health education and health promotion (MPH); health studies (MPA, MPH), including health administration. MPH offered jointly with Oregon State University, Oregon Health and Science University. *Accreditation:* CEPH. Part-time programs available. *Degree requirements:* For master's, oral and written exams. *Entrance requirements:* For master's, GRE General Test, 3 letters of recommendation, minimum GPA of 3.0. Additional exam requirements/recommendations for international students: Required—TOEFL (minimum score 550 paper-based; 213 computer-based).

Rocky Mountain University of Health Professions, PhD Program in Health Promotion and Wellness, Provo, UT 84606. Offers PhD. *Degree requirements:* For doctorate, thesis/dissertation.

Rowan University, Graduate School, College of Education, Department of Health and Exercise Science, Glassboro, NJ 08028-1701. Offers health promotion management (MA). *Degree requirements:* For master's, comprehensive exam, thesis. *Entrance requirements:* For master's, GRE General Test, GRE Subject Test, interview, minimum GPA of 2.8. Additional exam requirements/recommendations for international students: Required—TOEFL. Electronic applications accepted.

St. Catharine College, School of Graduate Studies, St. Catharine, KY 40061-9499. Offers leadership (MA), including community and regional studies, health promotion and leadership. *Entrance requirements:* For master's, GRE, LSAT, MCAT or GMAT, official transcripts. Additional exam requirements/recommendations for international students: Required—TOEFL, IELTS, or Michigan English Language Assessment Battery. Electronic applications accepted.

San Diego State University, Graduate and Research Affairs, College of Health and Human Services, Graduate School of Public Health, San Diego, CA 92182. Offers environmental health (MPH); epidemiology (MPH, PhD), including biostatistics (MPH); global emergency preparedness and response (MS); global health (PhD); health behavior (PhD); health promotion (MPH); health services administration (MPH); toxicology (MS); MPH/MA; MSW/MPH. *Accreditation:* ABET (one or more programs are accredited); CAHME (one or more programs are accredited); CEPH (one or more programs are accredited). Part-time programs available. *Degree requirements:* For master's, comprehensive exam (for some programs), thesis (for some programs); for doctorate, thesis/dissertation. *Entrance requirements:* For master's, GMAT (MPH in health services administration), GRE General Test; for doctorate, GRE General Test. Additional exam requirements/recommendations for international students: Required—TOEFL. *Faculty research:* Evaluation of tobacco, AIDS prevalence and prevention, mammography, infant death project, Alzheimer's in elderly Chinese.

Springfield College, Graduate Programs, Programs in Exercise Science and Sport Studies, Springfield, MA 01109-3797. Offers athletic training (MS); exercise physiology (MS), including clinical exercise physiology, science and research; exercise science and sport studies (PhD); health promotion and disease prevention (MS); sport psychology (MS). Part-time programs available. Terminal master's awarded for partial completion of doctoral program. *Degree requirements:* For master's, comprehensive exam, research project or thesis; for doctorate, comprehensive exam, thesis/dissertation. *Entrance requirements:* For master's and doctorate, GRE General Test. Additional exam requirements/recommendations for international students: Required—TOEFL (minimum score 550 paper-based; 213 computer-based). Electronic applications accepted.

Texas A&M University—Commerce, Graduate School, College of Education and Human Services, Department of Health and Human Performance, Commerce, TX 75429-3011. Offers exercise physiology (MS); health and human performance (M Ed); health promotion (MS); health, kinesiology and sports studies (Ed D); motor performance (MS); sport studies (MS). Part-time programs available. *Degree requirements:* For master's, comprehensive exam, thesis (for some programs). *Entrance requirements:* For master's, GRE General Test. Electronic applications accepted. *Faculty research:* Teaching, physical fitness.

Union Institute & University, Master of Arts Program–Online, Montpelier, VT 05602. Offers creativity studies (MA); education (MA); health and wellness (MA); history and culture (MA); leadership, public policy, and social issues (MA); literature and writing (MA); psychology (MA). Part-time programs available. Postbaccalaureate distance learning degree programs offered (no on-campus study). *Degree requirements:* For master's, thesis. Electronic applications accepted.

Union Institute & University, Programs in Psychology and Counseling, Brattleboro, VT 05301. Offers clinical mental health counseling (MA); clinical psychology (Psy D); counseling psychology (MA); counselor education and supervision (CAGS); developmental psychology (MA); educational psychology (MA); human development and wellness (CAGS); organizational psychology (MA); psychology education (CAGS). Psy D offered in Ohio and Vermont. Postbaccalaureate distance learning degree programs offered (minimal on-campus study). *Degree requirements:* For master's, thesis, internship (depending on concentration); for doctorate, thesis/dissertation, internship, practicum. Electronic applications accepted.

Universidad del Turabo, Graduate Programs, Programs In Education, Program in Wellness, Gurabo, PR 00778-3030. Offers MPHE. *Students:* 13 full-time (3 women), 1 part-time (0 women); all minorities (all Hispanic/Latino). Average age 31. 7 applicants, 100% accepted, 7 enrolled. In 2011, 9 master's awarded. *Unit head:* Angela Candelario, Dean, 787-743-7979 Ext. 4126. *Application contact:* Virginia Gonzalez, Admissions Officer, 787-746-3009.

The University of Alabama, Graduate School, College of Human Environmental Sciences, Department of Health Science, Tuscaloosa, AL 35487-0311. Offers health education and promotion (PhD); health studies (MA). Part-time programs available. Postbaccalaureate distance learning degree programs offered (no on-campus study). *Faculty:* 8 full-time (5 women). *Students:* 27 full-time (21 women), 86 part-time (71 women); includes 37 minority (28 Black or African American, non-Hispanic/Latino; 1 American Indian or Alaska Native, non-Hispanic/Latino; 4 Asian, non-Hispanic/Latino; 2 Hispanic/Latino; 2 Two or more races, non-Hispanic/Latino). Average age 32. 111 applicants, 76% accepted, 48 enrolled. In 2011, 47 master's, 4 doctorates awarded. *Median time to degree:* Of those who began their doctoral program in fall 2003, 100%

received their degree in 8 years or less. *Degree requirements:* For master's, comprehensive exam, thesis optional; for doctorate, one foreign language, comprehensive exam, thesis/dissertation. *Entrance requirements:* For master's, minimum GPA of 3.0; for doctorate, GRE General Test, minimum GPA of 3.0, prerequisites in health education. Additional exam requirements/recommendations for international students: Required—TOEFL. *Application deadline:* For fall admission, 3/15 priority date for domestic students, 3/15 for international students. Applications are processed on a rolling basis. Application fee: $50 ($60 for international students). Electronic applications accepted. *Expenses:* Tuition, state resident: full-time $8600. Tuition, nonresident: full-time $21,900. *Financial support:* In 2011–12, 2 research assistantships with full tuition reimbursements (averaging $10,500 per year), 6 teaching assistantships with full tuition reimbursements (averaging $10,500 per year) were awarded; career-related internships or fieldwork, Federal Work-Study, institutionally sponsored loans, health care benefits, and unspecified assistantships also available. Financial award application deadline: 4/14. *Faculty research:* Program planning, substance abuse prevention, obesity prevention, nutrition, physical activity, athletic training, osteoporosis, health behavior. *Total annual research expenditures:* $106,620. *Unit head:* Dr. Lori W. Turner, Department Head and Professor, 205-348-2956, Fax: 205-348-7568, E-mail: lwturner@ches.ua.edu. *Application contact:* Dr. Stuart Usdan, Associate Professor and Doctoral Program Coordinator, 205-348-8373, Fax: 205-348-7568, E-mail: susdan@ches.ua.edu. Web site: http://ches.ua.edu/.

The University of Alabama at Birmingham, College of Arts and Sciences, School of Education, Program in Health Education and Promotion, Birmingham, AL 35294. Offers PhD. Program offered jointly with The University of Alabama (Tuscaloosa). *Accreditation:* NCATE. *Degree requirements:* For doctorate, thesis/dissertation. *Entrance requirements:* For doctorate, GRE General Test, MAT, minimum GPA of 3.25. Electronic applications accepted. *Expenses:* Tuition, state resident: full-time $5922; part-time $309 per hour. Tuition, nonresident: full-time $13,428; part-time $726 per hour. Tuition and fees vary according to program. *Unit head:* Dr. Kristi Menear, Chair, 205-975-7409, Fax: 205-975-8040, E-mail: kmenear@uab.edu. Web site: http://www.uab.edu/humanstudies/healthedphd.

The University of Alabama at Birmingham, School of Public Health, Program in Health Education and Promotion, Birmingham, AL 35294. Offers PhD. Program offered jointly with The University of Alabama (Tuscaloosa). *Expenses:* Tuition, state resident: full-time $5922; part-time $309 per hour. Tuition, nonresident: full-time $13,428; part-time $726 per hour. Tuition and fees vary according to program. *Unit head:* Dr. Jalie Tucker, Chair, 205-934-6020, Fax: 205-975-5484.

University of Alberta, School of Public Health, Centre for Health Promotion Studies, Edmonton, AB T6G 2E1, Canada. Offers health promotion (M Sc, Postgraduate Diploma). Part-time programs available. Postbaccalaureate distance learning degree programs offered.

University of Arkansas for Medical Sciences, Graduate School, Program in Health Promotion and Prevention Research, Little Rock, AR 72205-7199. Offers PhD.

University of Central Oklahoma, College of Graduate Studies and Research, College of Education and Professional Studies, Department of Kinesiology and Health Studies, Edmond, OK 73034-5209. Offers athletic training (MS); wellness management (MS). *Students:* 48 full-time (28 women), 39 part-time (28 women); includes 29 minority (11 Black or African American, non-Hispanic/Latino; 5 American Indian or Alaska Native, non-Hispanic/Latino; 3 Asian, non-Hispanic/Latino; 5 Hispanic/Latino; 5 Two or more races, non-Hispanic/Latino), 11 international. Average age 29. In 2011, 18 master's awarded. *Expenses:* Tuition, state resident: full-time $3901; part-time $218.30 per credit hour. Tuition, nonresident: full-time $9198; part-time $511.20 per credit hour. Tuition and fees vary according to program. *Unit head:* Jeff McKibbin, Program Director, 405-974-2959, Fax: 405-974-3805, E-mail: jmckibbin@uco.edu. *Application contact:* Dr. Richard Bernard, Dean, Graduate College, 405-974-3493, Fax: 405-974-3852, E-mail: gradcoll@uco.edu. Web site: http://www.ucogradat.net.

University of Chicago, Division of Biological Sciences, Program in Health Studies, Chicago, IL 60637-1513. Offers MS, PhD. Part-time programs available. *Degree requirements:* For master's, thesis; for doctorate, comprehensive exam, thesis/dissertation, ethics class, 2 teaching assistantships. *Entrance requirements:* For doctorate, GRE General Test. Additional exam requirements/recommendations for international students: Required—TOEFL (minimum score 600 paper-based; 250 computer-based; 104 iBT), IELTS (minimum score 7). Electronic applications accepted.

University of Colorado at Colorado Springs, College of Letters, Arts and Sciences, Master of Sciences Program, Colorado Springs, CO 80933-7150. Offers applied science - bioscience (M Sc); applied science - physics (M Sc); biology (M Sc); chemistry (M Sc); health promotion (M Sc); mathematics (M Sc); physics (M Sc); sports medicine (M Sc); sports nutrition (M Sc). Part-time programs available. *Students:* 13 full-time (5 women), 11 part-time (6 women); includes 3 minority (2 Asian, non-Hispanic/Latino; 1 Hispanic/Latino). Average age 33. 15 applicants, 53% accepted, 3 enrolled. In 2011, 39 degrees awarded. *Degree requirements:* For master's, thesis or alternative. *Entrance requirements:* For master's, minimum GPA of 2.75. Additional exam requirements/recommendations for international students: Recommended—TOEFL. *Application deadline:* For fall admission, 6/1 priority date for domestic students; for spring admission, 12/1 for domestic students. Application fee: $60 ($75 for international students). *Expenses:* Contact institution. *Financial support:* In 2011–12, 5 students received support. Fellowships, research assistantships, teaching assistantships, career-related internships or fieldwork, Federal Work-Study, and scholarships/grants available. Support available to part-time students. Financial award application deadline: 3/1; financial award applicants required to submit FAFSA. *Faculty research:* Biomechanics and physiology of elite athletic training, genetic engineering in yeast and bacteria including phage display and DNA repair, immunology and cell biology, synthetic organic chemistry. *Unit head:* Dr. Tom Christensen, Dean, 719-255-4550, Fax: 719-255-4200, E-mail: tchriste@uccs.edu. *Application contact:* Taryn Bailey, Information Contact, 719-255-3702, Fax: 719-255-3037, E-mail: gradinfo@uccs.edu.

University of Delaware, College of Health Sciences, Department of Behavioral Health and Nutrition, Newark, DE 19716. Offers health promotion (MS); human nutrition (MS). Part-time programs available. *Degree requirements:* For master's, thesis. *Entrance requirements:* For master's, GRE General Test, interview, minimum GPA of 3.0. Additional exam requirements/recommendations for international students: Required—TOEFL (minimum score 550 paper-based; 213 computer-based). Electronic applications accepted. *Faculty research:* Sport biomechanics, rehabilitation biomechanics, vascular dynamics.

University of Georgia, College of Public Health, Department of Health Promotion and Behavior, Athens, GA 30602. Offers MPH, PhD. *Accreditation:* CEPH; NCATE (one or more programs are accredited). *Faculty:* 8 full-time (6 women). *Students:* 22 full-time (20 women), 8 part-time (6 women); includes 11 minority (8 Black or African American, non-Hispanic/Latino; 2 Asian, non-Hispanic/Latino; 1 Hispanic/Latino), 4 international. Average age 32. 33 applicants, 21% accepted, 3 enrolled. In 2011, 3 doctorates awarded. *Degree requirements:* For master's, thesis (MA); for doctorate, thesis/dissertation. *Entrance requirements:* For master's, GRE General Test or MAT; for doctorate, GRE General Test. *Application deadline:* For fall admission, 7/1 priority date for domestic students; for spring admission, 11/15 for domestic students. Application fee: $50. Electronic applications accepted. *Financial support:* Fellowships, research assistantships, teaching assistantships, and unspecified assistantships available. *Unit head:* Dr. Mark G. Wilson, Head, 706-542-4364, Fax: 706-542-4956, E-mail: mwilson@uga.edu. *Application contact:* Dr. Marsha Davis, Graduate Coordinator, 706-542-4369, Fax: 706-542-4956, E-mail: davism@uga.edu. Web site: http://www.publichealth.uga.edu/hpb/.

University of Kentucky, Graduate School, College of Education, Program in Kinesiology and Health Promotion, Lexington, KY 40506-0032. Offers exercise science (PhD); kinesiology (MS, Ed D). Terminal master's awarded for partial completion of doctoral program. *Degree requirements:* For master's, comprehensive exam, thesis optional; for doctorate, comprehensive exam, thesis/dissertation. *Entrance requirements:* For master's, GRE General Test, minimum undergraduate GPA of 2.75; for doctorate, GRE General Test, minimum graduate GPA of 3.0. Additional exam requirements/recommendations for international students: Required—TOEFL (minimum score 550 paper-based; 213 computer-based). Electronic applications accepted.

University of Louisville, Graduate School, School of Public Health and Information Sciences, Department of Health Promotion and Behavioral Sciences, Louisville, KY 40202. Offers health promotion (PhD). *Accreditation:* CEPH. Part-time programs available. *Degree requirements:* For doctorate, comprehensive exam, thesis/dissertation. *Entrance requirements:* For doctorate, GRE or equivalent, official transcripts, statement of purpose, resume/curriculum vitae, letters of recommendation. Additional exam requirements/recommendations for international students: Required—TOEFL (minimum score 600 paper-based; 250 computer-based; 100 iBT). Electronic applications accepted. *Expenses:* Tuition, state resident: full-time $9692; part-time $539 per credit hour. Tuition, nonresident: full-time $20,168; part-time $1121 per credit hour. Tuition and fees vary according to program and reciprocity agreements. *Faculty research:* Infectious disease control, emergency preparedness, health equity, evaluation methods, tobacco prevention policy.

University of Massachusetts Lowell, School of Health and Environment, Department of Nursing, Program in Nursing, Lowell, MA 01854-2881. Offers PhD. *Accreditation:* AACN. *Degree requirements:* For doctorate, thesis/dissertation, qualifying examination. *Entrance requirements:* For doctorate, GRE General Test, master's degree in nursing with minimum GPA of 3.3, current MA RN license, 2 years of professional nursing experience, 3 letters of recommendation.

University of Memphis, Graduate School, College of Education, Department of Health and Sport Sciences, Memphis, TN 38152. Offers clinical nutrition (MS); exercise and sport science (MS); health promotion (MS); physical education teacher education (MS), including teacher education; sport and leisure commerce (MS). Part-time and evening/weekend programs available. *Degree requirements:* For master's, comprehensive exam, thesis. *Entrance requirements:* For master's, GRE General Test or GMAT (sport and leisure commerce). *Faculty research:* Sport marketing and consumer analysis, health psychology, smoking cessation, psychosocial aspects of cardiovascular disease, global health promotion.

University of Michigan, School of Public Health, Department of Health Behavior and Health Education, Ann Arbor, MI 48109. Offers MPH, PhD, MPH/MSW. PhD offered through the Horace H. Rackham School of Graduate Studies. *Accreditation:* CEPH (one or more programs are accredited). Terminal master's awarded for partial completion of doctoral program. *Degree requirements:* For doctorate, oral defense of dissertation, preliminary exam. *Entrance requirements:* For master's, GRE General Test (preferred); MCAT; for doctorate, GRE General Test. Additional exam requirements/recommendations for international students: Required—TOEFL (minimum score 560 paper-based; 220 computer-based; 100 iBT). Electronic applications accepted. *Faculty research:* Empowerment theory; structure, culture, and health; health disparities; community-based participatory research; health and medical decision-making.

University of Missouri, Graduate School, Master of Public Health Program, Columbia, MO 65211. Offers health promotion and policy (MPH); public health (Graduate Certificate); veterinary public health (MPH); DVM/MPH; MPH/MA; MPH/MPA. *Accreditation:* CEPH. *Students:* 86 full-time (61 women), 68 part-time (49 women); includes 36 minority (20 Black or African American, non-Hispanic/Latino; 7 Asian, non-Hispanic/Latino; 4 Hispanic/Latino; 5 Two or more races, non-Hispanic/Latino), 16 international. Average age 29. 99 applicants, 85% accepted, 64 enrolled. In 2011, 44 master's, 34 other advanced degrees awarded. *Entrance requirements:* Additional exam requirements/recommendations for international students: Required—TOEFL (minimum score 550 paper-based; 215 computer-based; 80 iBT). Application fee: $55 ($75 for international students). *Expenses:* Tuition, state resident: full-time $5881. Tuition, nonresident: full-time $15,183. *Required fees:* $952. Tuition and fees vary according to campus/location and program. *Faculty research:* Health professions, health care equality, global health, communicable diseases, public health; zoonosis and infectious diseases, medical education, inquiry-based learning, social determinants of health, violence against women, health disparities, breast cancer screening, epigenetic, nursing, environmental health, cancer and chronic diseases, environmental exposures with metals, geographical information systems, substance use disorders/addictions, mental health. *Unit head:* Dr. Kristofer Hagglund, Associate Dean, 573-884-7050, E-mail: hagglundk@missouri.edu. *Application contact:* Lise Saffran, 573-884-6844, E-mail: saffranl@missouri.edu. Web site: http://publichealth.missouri.edu/.

The University of Montana, Graduate School, Phyllis J. Washington College of Education and Human Sciences, Department of Health and Human Performance, Missoula, MT 59812-0002. Offers exercise science (MS); health and human performance (MS); health promotion (MS). Part-time programs available. *Entrance requirements:* For master's, GRE General Test. Additional exam requirements/recommendations for international students: Required—TOEFL. *Faculty research:* Exercise physiology, performance psychology, nutrition, pre-employment physical screening, program evaluation.

University of Nebraska–Lincoln, Graduate College, College of Education and Human Sciences, Department of Nutrition and Health Sciences, Lincoln, NE 68588. Offers community nutrition and health promotion (MS); nutrition (MS, PhD); nutrition and exercise (MS); nutrition and health sciences (MS, PhD). *Degree requirements:* For master's, thesis optional. *Entrance requirements:* For master's, GRE General Test. Additional exam requirements/recommendations for international students: Required—TOEFL (minimum score 550 paper-based; 213 computer-based). Electronic applications accepted. *Faculty research:* Foods/food service administration, community nutrition science, diet-health relationships.

University of Nevada, Las Vegas, Graduate College, School of Community Health Sciences, Department of Health Promotion, Las Vegas, NV 89154-3050. Offers health care promotion (M Ed). Part-time and evening/weekend programs available. *Faculty:* 5 full-time (3 women), 5 part-time/adjunct (2 women). *Students:* 1 (woman) full-time, 12 part-time (10 women); includes 7 minority (3 Black or African American, non-Hispanic/Latino; 1 Native Hawaiian or other Pacific Islander, non-Hispanic/Latino; 3 Two or more races, non-Hispanic/Latino). Average age 34. 6 applicants, 0% accepted, 0 enrolled. In 2011, 12 master's awarded. *Degree requirements:* For master's, comprehensive exam (for some programs), project. *Entrance requirements:* Additional exam requirements/

recommendations for international students: Required—TOEFL (minimum score 550 paper-based; 213 computer-based; 80 iBT), IELTS (minimum score 7). *Application deadline:* For fall admission, 5/1 for international students; for spring admission, 10/1 for international students. Applications are processed on a rolling basis. Application fee: $60 ($95 for international students). Electronic applications accepted. *Financial support:* In 2011–12, 2 students received support, including 2 research assistantships with partial tuition reimbursements available (averaging $10,834 per year); institutionally sponsored loans, scholarships/grants, health care benefits, and unspecified assistantships also available. Financial award application deadline: 3/1. *Faculty research:* Health promotion; disease prevention: asthma, diabetes, cancer, HIV/AIDS, substance abuse; injury prevention; prevention of hospital-acquired infections. *Total annual research expenditures:* $76,014. *Unit head:* Dr. Shawn Gerstenberger, Chair/Associate Professor, 702-895-1565, Fax: 702-895-3979, E-mail: shawn.gerstenberger@unlv.edu. *Application contact:* Graduate College Admissions Evaluator, 702-895-3320, Fax: 702-895-4180, E-mail: gradcollege@unlv.edu. Web site: http://publichealth.unlv.edu/.

University of North Alabama, College of Education, Department of Health, Physical Education, and Recreation, FLORENCE, AL 35632-0001. Offers health and human performance (MS), including exercise science, kinesiology, wellness and health promotion; P-12 physical education (MA Ed). *Faculty:* 3 full-time (2 women), 2 part-time/adjunct (0 women). *Students:* 11 full-time (4 women), 4 part-time (1 woman); includes 3 minority (2 Black or African American, non-Hispanic/Latino; 1 Two or more races, non-Hispanic/Latino), 2 international. Average age 24. In 2011, 4 master's awarded. *Unit head:* Dr. Thomas E. Coates, Chair, 256-765-4377. *Application contact:* Kim Mauldin, Director of Admissions, 256-765-4608, Fax: 256-765-4960, E-mail: komauldin@una.edu. Web site: http://www.una.edu/hper/docs/HPERThesisGuideliens.pdf.

The University of North Carolina at Chapel Hill, Graduate School, School of Public Health, Public Health Leadership Program, Chapel Hill, NC 27599. Offers health care and prevention (MPH); leadership (MPH); occupational health nursing (MPH); public health nursing (MS). Part-time programs available. Postbaccalaureate distance learning degree programs offered (minimal on-campus study). *Degree requirements:* For master's, comprehensive exam, thesis (MS), paper (MPH). *Entrance requirements:* For master's, GRE General Test, minimum GPA of 3.0, public health experience. Additional exam requirements/recommendations for international students: Required—TOEFL. Electronic applications accepted. *Faculty research:* Occupational health issues, clinical outcomes, prenatal and early childcare, adolescent health, effectiveness of home visiting, issues in occupational health nursing, community-based interventions.

University of Oklahoma, College of Arts and Sciences, Department of Health and Exercise Science, Norman, OK 73019. Offers health and exercise science (MS, PhD), including exercise physiology, general (MS), health promotion. *Faculty:* 8 full-time (2 women). *Students:* 35 full-time (15 women), 3 part-time (all women); includes 5 minority (1 Black or African American, non-Hispanic/Latino; 1 American Indian or Alaska Native, non-Hispanic/Latino; 1 Hispanic/Latino; 2 Two or more races, non-Hispanic/Latino), 8 international. Average age 28. 33 applicants, 33% accepted, 4 enrolled. In 2011, 8 master's, 4 doctorates awarded. *Degree requirements:* For master's, comprehensive exam (for some programs), thesis. *Entrance requirements:* For master's, GRE General Test, minimum GPA of 3.0 in last 60 hours of undergraduate course work, interview, 3 letters of recommendation; for doctorate, GRE General Test, 3 letters of recommendation, curriculum vitae. Additional exam requirements/recommendations for international students: Required—TOEFL (minimum score 550 paper-based; 79 iBT). *Application deadline:* For fall admission, 4/1 priority date for domestic students, 3/1 for international students; for spring admission, 11/1 for domestic students, 9/1 for international students. Applications are processed on a rolling basis. Application fee: $40 ($90 for international students). Electronic applications accepted. *Expenses:* Tuition, state resident: full-time $4087; part-time $170.30 per credit hour. Tuition, nonresident: full-time $14,875; part-time $619.80 per credit hour. *Required fees:* $2659; $100.25 per credit hour. Tuition and fees vary according to course load and degree level. *Financial support:* In 2011–12, 38 students received support, including 35 teaching assistantships with partial tuition reimbursements available (averaging $13,224 per year); career-related internships or fieldwork, scholarships/grants, health care benefits, and unspecified assistantships also available. Financial award applicants required to submit FAFSA. *Faculty research:* Neuromuscular function and performance, aging, bone health and endocrine function, childhood obesity, physical performance. *Total annual research expenditures:* $387,349. *Unit head:* Michael Bemben, Chair, 405-325-5211, Fax: 405-325-0594, E-mail: mgbemben@ou.edu. *Application contact:* Dr. Laurette Taylor, Graduate Liaison, 405-325-1372, Fax: 405-325-0594, E-mail: eltaylr@ou.edu. Web site: http://hes.ou.edu.

University of Oklahoma Health Sciences Center, Graduate College, College of Public Health, Department of Health Promotion Sciences, Oklahoma City, OK 73190. Offers MPH, MS, Dr PH, PhD. *Accreditation:* CEPH (one or more programs are accredited). Part-time programs available. *Degree requirements:* For master's, comprehensive exam, thesis (for some programs); for doctorate, 2 foreign languages, comprehensive exam, thesis/dissertation. *Entrance requirements:* For master's, letters of recommendation, resume; for doctorate, GRE, letters of recommendation. Additional exam requirements/recommendations for international students: Required—TOEFL (minimum score 570 paper-based; 230 computer-based). *Faculty research:* Health education, school health, health behavior, American Indian health.

University of Pittsburgh, Graduate School of Public Health, Department of Infectious Diseases and Microbiology, Pittsburgh, PA 15260. Offers bioscience of infectious diseases (MPH); community and behavioral intervention of infectious diseases (MPH); infectious diseases and microbiology (MS, PhD); LGBT health and wellness (Certificate). Part-time programs available. *Faculty:* 21 full-time (6 women), 24 part-time/adjunct (7 women). *Students:* 57 full-time (44 women), 13 part-time (9 women); includes 15 minority (4 Black or African American, non-Hispanic/Latino; 9 Asian, non-Hispanic/Latino; 2 Hispanic/Latino), 7 international. Average age 27. 157 applicants, 56% accepted, 29 enrolled. In 2011, 13 master's, 3 doctorates awarded. Terminal master's awarded for partial completion of doctoral program. *Degree requirements:* For master's, one foreign language, comprehensive exam (for some programs), thesis; for doctorate, one foreign language, comprehensive exam, thesis/dissertation. *Entrance requirements:* For master's and doctorate, GRE General Test, MCAT, or DAT. Additional exam requirements/recommendations for international students: Required—TOEFL (minimum score 550 paper-based; 80 iBT) or IELTS (minimum score 6.5). *Application deadline:* For fall admission, 1/4 priority date for domestic students, 1/4 for international students. Applications are processed on a rolling basis. Application fee: $115. Electronic applications accepted. *Expenses:* Tuition, state resident: full-time $18,774; part-time $760 per credit. Tuition, nonresident: full-time $30,736; part-time $1258 per credit. *Required fees:* $740; $200 per term. Tuition and fees vary according to program. *Financial support:* In 2011–12, 31 students received support, including 12 fellowships (averaging $7,248 per year), 19 research assistantships with full and partial tuition reimbursements available (averaging $5,448 per year). Financial award applicants required to submit FAFSA. *Faculty research:* HIV, Epstein-Barr virus, virology, immunology, malaria. *Total annual research expenditures:* $15.6 million. *Unit head:* Dr. Charles R. Rinaldo, Jr., Chairman, 412-624-3928, Fax: 412-624-4953, E-mail: rinaldo@

pitt.edu. *Application contact:* Dr. Jeremy Martinson, Assistant Professor, 412-624-5646, Fax: 412-383-8926, E-mail: jmartins@pitt.edu. Web site: http://www.idm.pitt.edu/.

University of Pittsburgh, School of Health and Rehabilitation Sciences, Master's Programs in Health and Rehabilitation Sciences, Pittsburgh, PA 15260. Offers health and rehabilitation sciences (MS), including clinical dietetics and nutrition, health care supervision and management, health information systems, occupational therapy, physical therapy, rehabilitation counseling, rehabilitation science and technology, sports medicine, wellness and human performance. *Accreditation:* APTA. Part-time and evening/weekend programs available. *Faculty:* 22 full-time (16 women), 4 part-time/adjunct (2 women). *Students:* 144 full-time (91 women), 35 part-time (23 women); includes 23 minority (8 Black or African American, non-Hispanic/Latino; 8 Asian, non-Hispanic/Latino; 3 Hispanic/Latino; 4 Two or more races, non-Hispanic/Latino), 74 international. Average age 28. 399 applicants, 61% accepted, 121 enrolled. In 2011, 86 master's awarded. *Degree requirements:* For master's, comprehensive exam (for some programs), thesis optional. *Entrance requirements:* For master's, minimum GPA of 3.0. Additional exam requirements/recommendations for international students: Required—TOEFL (minimum score 550 paper-based; 213 computer-based; 80 iBT), IELTS (minimum score 6.5). *Application deadline:* For fall admission, 3/1 for international students; for spring admission, 7/31 for international students. Applications are processed on a rolling basis. Application fee: $50. Electronic applications accepted. *Expenses:* Contact institution. *Financial support:* Research assistantships, teaching assistantships, Federal Work-Study, institutionally sponsored loans, traineeships, and unspecified assistantships available. Financial award applicants required to submit FAFSA. *Faculty research:* Assistive technology, seating and wheeled mobility, cellular neurophysiology, low back syndrome, augmentative communication. *Total annual research expenditures:* $7.8 million. *Unit head:* Dr. Clifford E. Brubaker, Dean, 412-383-6560, Fax: 412-383-6535, E-mail: cliffb@pitt.edu. *Application contact:* Shameem Gangjee, Director of Admissions, 412-383-6558, Fax: 412-383-6535, E-mail: admissions@shrs.pitt.edu. Web site: http://www.shrs.pitt.edu/.

University of Puerto Rico, Medical Sciences Campus, Graduate School of Public Health, Department of Human Development, Program in School Health Promotion, San Juan, PR 00936-5067. Offers Certificate.

University of South Carolina, The Graduate School, Arnold School of Public Health, Department of Health Promotion, Education, and Behavior, Columbia, SC 29208. Offers health education (MAT); health promotion, education, and behavior (MPH, MS, MSPH, Dr PH, PhD); school health education (Certificate); MSW/MPH. MAT offered in cooperation with the College of Education. *Accreditation:* CEPH (one or more programs are accredited); NCATE (one or more programs are accredited). Part-time programs available. *Degree requirements:* For master's, comprehensive exam, thesis or alternative, practicum (MPH), project (MS); for doctorate, comprehensive exam, thesis/dissertation. *Entrance requirements:* For master's and doctorate, GRE General Test. Additional exam requirements/recommendations for international students: Required—TOEFL (minimum score 570 paper-based; 230 computer-based; 75 iBT). Electronic applications accepted. *Faculty research:* Health disparities and inequalities in communities, global health and nutrition, cancer and HIV/AIDS prevention, health communication, policy and program design.

University of South Carolina, The Graduate School, Arnold School of Public Health, Program in Physical Activity and Public Health, Columbia, SC 29208. Offers MPH. *Accreditation:* CEPH. Part-time programs available. *Degree requirements:* For master's, comprehensive exam, practicum. *Entrance requirements:* For master's, GRE. Additional exam requirements/recommendations for international students: Required—TOEFL (minimum score 570 paper-based; 230 computer-based). Electronic applications accepted.

University of Southern California, Keck School of Medicine and Graduate School, Graduate Programs in Medicine, Department of Preventive Medicine, Master of Public Health Program, Los Angeles, CA 90032-3628. Offers biostatistics/epidemiology (MPH); child and family health (MPH); environmental health (MPH); global health leadership (MPH); health communication (MPH); health education and promotion (MPH); public health policy (MPH). *Accreditation:* CEPH. Part-time programs available. *Faculty:* 22 full-time (12 women), 3 part-time/adjunct (0 women). *Students:* 148 full-time (115 women), 35 part-time (23 women); includes 100 minority (8 Black or African American, non-Hispanic/Latino; 66 Asian, non-Hispanic/Latino; 26 Hispanic/Latino), 26 international. Average age 24. 218 applicants, 73% accepted, 88 enrolled. In 2011, 91 master's awarded. *Degree requirements:* For master's, practicum, final report, oral presentation. *Entrance requirements:* For master's, GRE General Test, MCAT, GMAT, minimum GPA of 3.0. Additional exam requirements/recommendations for international students: Required—TOEFL (minimum score 600 paper-based; 250 computer-based; 100 iBT). *Application deadline:* For fall admission, 6/1 priority date for domestic students, 6/1 for international students; for spring admission, 11/1 priority date for domestic students, 10/1 for international students. Applications are processed on a rolling basis. Application fee: $85. Electronic applications accepted. *Financial support:* In 2011–12, 148 students received support. Career-related internships or fieldwork, Federal Work-Study, institutionally sponsored loans, and scholarships/grants available. Support available to part-time students. Financial award application deadline: 5/4; financial award applicants required to submit CSS PROFILE or FAFSA. *Faculty research:* Substance abuse prevention, cancer and heart disease prevention, mass media and health communication research, health promotion, treatment compliance. *Unit head:* Dr. Louise A. Rohrbach, Director, 323-442-8237, Fax: 323-442-8297, E-mail: rohrbac@usc.edu. *Application contact:* Chrystal Romero, Admissions Counselor, 323-442-7257, Fax: 323-442-8297, E-mail: ccromero@usc.edu. Web site: http://mph.usc.edu/main.php.

The University of Tennessee, Graduate School, College of Education, Health and Human Sciences, Program in Health Promotion and Health Education, Knoxville, TN 37996. Offers MS. *Accreditation:* CEPH. Part-time programs available. *Degree requirements:* For master's, thesis optional. *Entrance requirements:* For master's, minimum GPA of 2.7. Additional exam requirements/recommendations for international students: Required—TOEFL. Electronic applications accepted. *Expenses:* Tuition, state resident: full-time $8332; part-time $464 per credit hour. Tuition, nonresident: full-time $25,174; part-time $1400 per credit hour. *Required fees:* $1162; $56 per credit hour. Tuition and fees vary according to program.

University of the Incarnate Word, School of Graduate Studies and Research, School of Mathematics, Science, and Engineering, Program in Nutrition, San Antonio, TX 78209-6397. Offers administration (MS); medical nutrition therapy (MS); nutrition education and health promotion (MS); nutrition services administration (MS). Part-time and evening/weekend programs available. *Faculty:* 3 full-time (2 women), 1 (woman) part-time/adjunct. *Students:* 7 full-time (all women), 16 part-time (15 women); includes 8 minority (1 Black or African American, non-Hispanic/Latino; 2 Asian, non-Hispanic/Latino; 5 Hispanic/Latino), 1 international. Average age 25. 26 applicants, 92% accepted, 9 enrolled. In 2011, 5 master's awarded. *Degree requirements:* For master's, comprehensive exam, thesis or alternative. *Entrance requirements:* For master's, two letters of recommendation. Additional exam requirements/recommendations for international students: Required—TOEFL (minimum score 560 paper-based; 220 computer-based; 83 iBT). *Application deadline:* Applications are processed on a rolling basis. Application fee: $20. Electronic applications accepted. *Expenses: Tuition:* Part-

time $725 per credit hour. Tuition and fees vary according to degree level. *Financial support:* In 2011–12, research assistantships (averaging $5,000 per year) were awarded; Federal Work-Study and scholarships/grants also available. Financial award applicants required to submit FAFSA. *Faculty research:* Nutrition. *Total annual research expenditures:* $109,000. *Unit head:* Dr. Beth Senne-Duff, Associate Professor, 210-829-3165, Fax: 210-829-3153, E-mail: beths@uiwtx.edu. *Application contact:* Andrea Cyterski-Acosta, Dean of Enrollment, 210-829-6005, Fax: 210-829-3921, E-mail: admis@uiwtx.edu. Web site: http://www.uiw.edu/nutrition/nutrition3.htm.

The University of Toledo, College of Graduate Studies, College of Medicine and Life Sciences, Department of Public Health and Preventative Medicine, Toledo, OH 43606-3390. Offers biostatistics and epidemiology (Certificate); contemporary gerontological practice (Certificate); environmental and occupational health and safety (MPH); epidemiology (MPH, Certificate); global public health (Certificate); health administration (MPH); health promotion (MPH); medical health and science education (Certificate); nutrition (MPH); occupational health (MSOH, Certificate); public health and emergency response (Certificate); MD/MPH. Part-time and evening/weekend programs available. *Faculty:* 6. *Students:* 95 full-time (74 women), 66 part-time (45 women); includes 37 minority (21 Black or African American, non-Hispanic/Latino; 11 Asian, non-Hispanic/Latino; 3 Hispanic/Latino; 2 Two or more races, non-Hispanic/Latino), 6 international. Average age 29. 132 applicants, 75% accepted, 70 enrolled. In 2011, 60 master's, 26 other advanced degrees awarded. *Degree requirements:* For master's, thesis or alternative. *Entrance requirements:* For master's, GRE, minimum undergraduate GPA of 3.0, three letters of recommendation, statement of purpose, transcripts from all prior institutions attended, resume; for Certificate, minimum undergraduate GPA of 3.0, three letters of recommendation, statement of purpose, transcripts from all prior institutions attended, resume. Additional exam requirements/recommendations for international students: Required—TOEFL (minimum score 550 paper-based; 213 computer-based; 80 iBT), IELTS (minimum score 6.5). *Application deadline:* For fall admission, 3/15 for domestic and international students. Applications are processed on a rolling basis. Application fee: $45 ($75 for international students). Electronic applications accepted. *Financial support:* In 2011–12, 15 research assistantships with full tuition reimbursements (averaging $10,000 per year) were awarded; Federal Work-Study, institutionally sponsored loans, scholarships/grants, tuition waivers (full and partial), and unspecified assistantships also available. *Unit head:* Dr. Sheryl A. Milz, Chair, 419-383-3976, Fax: 419-383-6140, E-mail: sheryl.milz@utoledo.edu. *Application contact:* Joan Mulligan, Admissions Analyst, 419-383-4186, Fax: 419-383-6140, E-mail: joan.mulligan@utoledo.edu. Web site: http://nocphmph.org/.

The University of Toledo, College of Graduate Studies, College of Nursing, Department of Health Promotions, Outcomes, Systems, and Policy, Toledo, OH 43606-3390. Offers DNP. *Accreditation:* CEPH. Postbaccalaureate distance learning degree programs offered (no on-campus study). *Faculty:* 43. *Students:* 10 part-time (all women); includes 1 minority (Hispanic/Latino). Average age 48. 12 applicants, 67% accepted, 8 enrolled. In 2011, 6 degrees awarded. *Degree requirements:* For doctorate, thesis/dissertation or alternative, evidence-based project. *Entrance requirements:* For doctorate, GRE (taken within the past 5 years), personal statement, resume/curriculum vitae, letters of recommendation, documented supervised clinical hours in master's program, Nursing CAS application, UT supplemental application. Additional exam requirements/recommendations for international students: Required—TOEFL (minimum score 550 paper-based; 213 computer-based; 80 iBT), IELTS (minimum score 6.5). Application fee: $45 ($75 for international students). Electronic applications accepted. *Financial support:* Tuition waivers (full and partial) available. *Unit head:* Dr. Dianne Smolen, Chair. *Application contact:* College of Graduate Studies - HSC, 419-383-4112, Fax: 419-383-6140, E-mail: joan.mulligan@utoledo.edu. Web site: http://www.utoledo.edu/nursing/.

The University of Toledo, College of Graduate Studies, Judith Herb College of Education, Health Science and Human Service, Department of Health and Recreation, Toledo, OH 43606-3390. Offers health education (ME, PhD); health promotions and education (MPH); recreation and leisure studies (MA). Part-time programs available. *Students:* 20 full-time (16 women), 30 part-time (21 women); includes 5 minority (4 Black or African American, non-Hispanic/Latino; 1 Asian, non-Hispanic/Latino), 2 international. Average age 34. 26 applicants, 65% accepted, 12 enrolled. In 2011, 11 master's, 5 doctorates awarded. *Degree requirements:* For master's, comprehensive exam, thesis; for doctorate, thesis/dissertation. *Entrance requirements:* For master's and doctorate, minimum cumulative GPA of 2.7 for all previous academic work, letters of recommendation. Additional exam requirements/recommendations for international students: Required—TOEFL (minimum score 550 paper-based; 213 computer-based; 80 iBT), IELTS (minimum score 6.5). *Application deadline:* For fall admission, 1/15 priority date for domestic students, 1/15 for international students. Applications are processed on a rolling basis. Application fee: $45 ($75 for international students). Electronic applications accepted. *Financial support:* In 2011–12, 11 teaching assistantships with full and partial tuition reimbursements (averaging $9,682 per year) were awarded; career-related internships or fieldwork, Federal Work-Study, institutionally sponsored loans, scholarships/grants, tuition waivers (full and partial), and unspecified assistantships also available. Support available to part-time students. *Unit head:* Joseph Dake, Chair, 419-530-2767, E-mail: joseph.dake@utoledo.edu. *Application contact:* Graduate School Office, 419-530-4723, Fax: 419-530-4724, E-mail: grdsch@utnet.utoledo.edu. Web site: http://www.utoledo.edu/eduhshs/.

University of Toronto, School of Graduate Studies, Dalla Lana School of Public Health, Toronto, ON M5S 1A1, Canada. Offers biostatistics (M Sc, PhD); community health (M Sc); epidemiology (MPH, PhD); health and behavioral science (PhD); health promotion (MPH); social science and health (PhD). *Accreditation:* CAHME (one or more programs are accredited); CEPH (one or more programs are accredited). Part-time programs available. *Degree requirements:* For master's, thesis (for some programs), practicum; for doctorate, comprehensive exam, thesis/dissertation, oral thesis defense. *Entrance requirements:* For master's, 2 letters of reference, relevant professional/research experience, minimum B average in final year; for doctorate, 2 letters of reference, relevant professional/research experience, minimum B+ average. Additional exam requirements/recommendations for international students: Required—TOEFL (minimum score 580 paper-based; 93 iBT), TWE (minimum score 5). Electronic applications accepted. *Expenses:* Contact institution.

University of Utah, Graduate School, College of Health, Department of Health Promotion and Education, Salt Lake City, UT 84112. Offers M Phil, MS, Ed D, PhD. Part-time and evening/weekend programs available. *Faculty:* 6 full-time (3 women), 1 part-time/adjunct (0 women). *Students:* 36 full-time (25 women), 15 part-time (10 women); includes 7 minority (2 Asian, non-Hispanic/Latino; 4 Hispanic/Latino; 1 Two or more races, non-Hispanic/Latino), 5 international. Average age 32. 38 applicants, 58% accepted, 18 enrolled. In 2011, 15 master's, 4 doctorates awarded. Terminal master's awarded for partial completion of doctoral program. *Median time to degree:* Of those who began their doctoral program in fall 2003, 100% received their degree in 8 years or less. *Degree requirements:* For master's, comprehensive exam, thesis or alternative, field experience; for doctorate, comprehensive exam, thesis/dissertation, field experience. *Entrance requirements:* For master's, GRE (for thesis option), minimum GPA of 3.0; for doctorate, GRE General Test, minimum GPA of 3.2. Additional exam requirements/recommendations for international students: Required—TOEFL (minimum score 500 paper-based; 173 computer-based). *Application deadline:* For fall admission, 10/15 for domestic and international students; for spring admission, 2/15 for domestic and international students. Applications are processed on a rolling basis. Application fee: $55 ($65 for international students). Electronic applications accepted. *Financial support:* In 2011–12, 14 students received support, including 3 research assistantships with full tuition reimbursements available (averaging $12,000 per year), 6 teaching assistantships with full tuition reimbursements available (averaging $12,000 per year); career-related internships or fieldwork, Federal Work-Study, institutionally sponsored loans, and scholarships/grants also available. Financial award application deadline: 2/15; financial award applicants required to submit FAFSA. *Faculty research:* Health behavior and counseling, health service administration, evaluation of health programs. *Total annual research expenditures:* $119,213. *Unit head:* Leslie K. Chatelain, Department Chair, 801-581-4512, Fax: 801-585-3646, E-mail: les.chatelain@utah.edu. *Application contact:* Dr. Glenn E. Richardson, Director of Graduate Studies, 801-581-8039, Fax: 801-585-3646, E-mail: glenn.richardson@health.utah.edu. Web site: http://www.health.utah.edu/healthed/index.htm.

University of Wisconsin–Milwaukee, Graduate School, Zilber School of Public Health, Department of Public Health, Milwaukee, WI 53201-0413. Offers community and behavioral health promotion (PhD); public health (MPH, Graduate Certificate). *Students:* 5 full-time (3 women), 8 part-time (7 women); includes 1 minority (Black or African American, non-Hispanic/Latino), 1 international. Average age 30. 22 applicants, 59% accepted, 11 enrolled. One-time fee: $506.10 full-time. Tuition and fees vary according to course load and reciprocity agreements. *Total annual research expenditures:* $1.3 million. *Unit head:* Paul Florsheim, Department Chair, 414-229-2490, E-mail: paulf@uwm.edu. *Application contact:* Darcie K. G. Warren, Graduate Program Manager, 414-229-5633, E-mail: darcie@uwm.edu.

University of Wisconsin–Stevens Point, College of Professional Studies, School of Health Promotion and Human Development, Stevens Point, WI 54481-3897. Offers human and community resources (MS); nutritional sciences (MS). Part-time programs available. *Degree requirements:* For master's, thesis or alternative. *Entrance requirements:* For master's, minimum GPA of 2.75.

University of Wyoming, College of Health Sciences, Division of Kinesiology and Health, Laramie, WY 82070. Offers MS. *Accreditation:* NCATE. Part-time programs available. Postbaccalaureate distance learning degree programs offered (no on-campus study). *Degree requirements:* For master's, comprehensive exam (for some programs), thesis (for some programs). *Entrance requirements:* For master's, GRE General Test, minimum GPA of 3.0. Additional exam requirements/recommendations for international students: Required—TOEFL. Electronic applications accepted. *Faculty research:* Teacher effectiveness, effects of exercising on heart function, physiological responses of overtraining, psychological benefits of physical activity, health behavior.

Walden University, Graduate Programs, School of Health Sciences, Minneapolis, MN 55401. Offers clinical research administration (MS, Postbaccalaureate Certificate); health informatics (MS); health services (PhD), including community health education and advocacy, general program, healthcare administration, leadership, public health policy, self-designed; healthcare administration (MHA); public health (MPH, PhD), including community health and education (PhD), epidemiology (PhD). Part-time and evening/weekend programs available. Postbaccalaureate distance learning degree programs offered (minimal on-campus study). *Faculty:* 20 full-time (13 women), 175 part-time/adjunct (81 women). *Students:* 2,777 full-time (2,158 women), 1,350 part-time (1,038 women); includes 2,379 minority (1,935 Black or African American, non-Hispanic/Latino; 33 American Indian or Alaska Native, non-Hispanic/Latino; 173 Asian, non-Hispanic/Latino; 180 Hispanic/Latino; 9 Native Hawaiian or other Pacific Islander, non-Hispanic/Latino; 49 Two or more races, non-Hispanic/Latino), 247 international. Average age 40. In 2011, 528 master's, 79 doctorates, 1 other advanced degree awarded. *Degree requirements:* For doctorate, thesis/dissertation, residency. *Entrance requirements:* For master's, bachelor's degree or equivalent in related field, minimum GPA of 2.5; for doctorate, master's degree or equivalent in related field; minimum GPA of 3.0; official transcripts; three years of related professional/academic experience (preferred); access to computer and Internet. Additional exam requirements/recommendations for international students: Required—TOEFL (minimum score 550 paper-based; 213 computer-based), IELTS (minimum score 6.5), or Michigan English Language Assessment Battery (minimum score 82). *Application deadline:* Applications are processed on a rolling basis. Application fee: $50. Electronic applications accepted. *Financial support:* Federal Work-Study, scholarships/grants, unspecified assistantships, and family tuition reduction, active duty/veteran tuition reduction, group tuition reduction, interest-free payment plans, employee tuition reduction available. Support available to part-time students. Financial award applicants required to submit FAFSA. *Unit head:* Dr. Jorg Westermann, Associate Dean, 800-925-3368. *Application contact:* Jennifer Hall, Vice President of Enrollment Management, 866-4-WALDEN, E-mail: info@waldenu.edu. Web site: http://www.waldenu.edu/Colleges-and-Schools/College-of-Health-Sciences/School-of-Health-Sciences.htm.

West Virginia University, School of Medicine, Department of Community Medicine, Morgantown, WV 26506. Offers public health (MPH), including community health/preventative medicine; public health sciences (PhD). *Accreditation:* CEPH. Part-time and evening/weekend programs available. Postbaccalaureate distance learning degree programs offered (minimal on-campus study). *Degree requirements:* For master's, thesis (for some programs). *Entrance requirements:* For master's, minimum GPA of 3.0. Additional exam requirements/recommendations for international students: Required—TOEFL. *Faculty research:* Adolescent smoking cessation, cardiovascular disease, women's health, worker's health.

Wilfrid Laurier University, Faculty of Graduate and Postdoctoral Studies, Faculty of Science, Department of Kinesiology and Physical Education, Waterloo, ON N2L 3C5, Canada. Offers physical activity and health (M Sc). *Degree requirements:* For master's, thesis. *Entrance requirements:* For master's, honours degree in kinesiology, health, physical education with a minimum B+ in kinesiology and health-related courses. Additional exam requirements/recommendations for international students: Required—TOEFL (minimum score 89 iBT). Electronic applications accepted. *Faculty research:* Biomechanics, health, exercise physiology, motor control, sport psychology.

Wright State University, School of Medicine, Program in Public Health, Dayton, OH 45435. Offers health promotion and education (MPH); public health management (MPH); public health nursing (MPH). *Accreditation:* CEPH.

Industrial Hygiene

California State University, Northridge, Graduate Studies, College of Health and Human Development, Department of Environmental and Occupational Health, Northridge, CA 91330. Offers environmental and occupational health (MS); industrial hygiene (MS). *Degree requirements:* For master's, seminar, field experience, comprehensive exam or thesis. *Entrance requirements:* For master's, GRE General Test or minimum GPA of 3.0. Additional exam requirements/recommendations for international students: Required—TOEFL.

Montana Tech of The University of Montana, Graduate School, Department of Industrial Hygiene, Butte, MT 59701-8997. Offers MS. *Accreditation:* ABET. Part-time programs available. Postbaccalaureate distance learning degree programs offered (no on-campus study). *Faculty:* 7 full-time (2 women). *Students:* 11 full-time (5 women), 39 part-time (18 women); includes 7 minority (2 Black or African American, non-Hispanic/Latino; 1 American Indian or Alaska Native, non-Hispanic/Latino; 4 Hispanic/Latino), 1 international. 31 applicants, 32% accepted, 10 enrolled. In 2011, 8 master's awarded. *Degree requirements:* For master's, comprehensive exam (for some programs), thesis. *Entrance requirements:* For master's, GRE (or 5 years' work experience for online program), minimum GPA of 3.0. Additional exam requirements/recommendations for international students: Required—TOEFL (minimum score 525 paper-based; 195 computer-based; 71 iBT). *Application deadline:* For fall admission, 4/1 priority date for domestic students; for spring admission, 10/1 priority date for domestic students. Applications are processed on a rolling basis. Application fee: $30. Electronic applications accepted. *Financial support:* In 2011–12, 15 students received support, including 9 teaching assistantships with partial tuition reimbursements available (averaging $2,400 per year); research assistantships with partial tuition reimbursements available, career-related internships or fieldwork, institutionally sponsored loans, and tuition waivers (full and partial) also available. Financial award application deadline: 4/1; financial award applicants required to submit FAFSA. *Faculty research:* Ergonomics, metal bioavailability, aerosols, particulate sizing, respiration protection. *Unit head:* Dr. Terry Spear, Head, 406-496-4445, Fax: 406-496-4650, E-mail: tspear@mtech.edu. *Application contact:* Fred Sullivan, Administrator, Graduate School, 406-496-4304, Fax: 406-496-4710, E-mail: fsullivan@mtech.edu. Web site: http://www.mtech.edu/academics/gradschool/degreeprograms/degrees-industrial-hygiene.htm.

Murray State University, College of Health Sciences and Human Services, Program in Occupational Safety and Health, Murray, KY 42071. Offers environmental science (MS); industrial hygiene (MS); safety management (MS). *Accreditation:* ABET. Part-time programs available. *Degree requirements:* For master's, comprehensive exam, thesis optional, professional internship. Electronic applications accepted. *Faculty research:* Light effects on plant growth, ergonomics, toxic effects of pets' pesticides, traffic safety.

New York Medical College, School of Health Sciences and Practice, Department of Environmental Health Science, Graduate Certificate Program in Industrial Hygiene, Valhalla, NY 10595-1691. Offers Graduate Certificate. *Faculty:* 5 full-time, 16 part-time/adjunct. *Students:* 13 full-time, 19 part-time. Average age 32. 15 applicants, 67% accepted, 7 enrolled. *Entrance requirements:* Additional exam requirements/recommendations for international students: Required—TOEFL (minimum score 637 paper-based; 110 iBT), IELTS (minimum score 7). *Application deadline:* For fall admission, 8/1 for domestic students; for spring admission, 12/1 for domestic students. Applications are processed on a rolling basis. Application fee: $50. Electronic applications accepted. *Unit head:* Dr. Diane E. Heck, Chair, 914-594-3383, Fax: 914-594-4292, E-mail: diane_heck@nymc.edu. *Application contact:* Pamela Suett, Director of Recruitment, 914-594-4510, Fax: 914-594-4292, E-mail: shsp_admissions@nymc.edu. Web site: http://www.nymc.edu/shsp.

University of Central Missouri, The Graduate School, College of Health and Human Services, Warrensburg, MO 64093. Offers criminal justice (MS); industrial hygiene (MS); occupational safety management (MS); physical education/exercise and sport science (MS); rural family nursing (MS); social gerontology (MS); sociology (MA); speech language pathology and audiology (MS). *Accreditation:* NCATE. Part-time programs available. Postbaccalaureate distance learning degree programs offered. *Entrance requirements:* Additional exam requirements/recommendations for international students: Required—TOEFL (minimum score 550 paper-based; 79 computer-based). Electronic applications accepted.

University of Cincinnati, Graduate School, College of Medicine, Graduate Programs in Biomedical Sciences, Department of Environmental Health, Cincinnati, OH 45221. Offers environmental and industrial hygiene (MS, PhD); environmental and occupational medicine (MS); environmental genetics and molecular toxicology (MS, PhD); epidemiology and biostatistics (MS, PhD); occupational safety and ergonomics (MS, PhD). *Accreditation:* ABET (one or more programs are accredited). Terminal master's awarded for partial completion of doctoral program. *Degree requirements:* For master's, thesis; for doctorate, thesis/dissertation, qualifying exam. *Entrance requirements:* For master's, GRE General Test, bachelor's degree in science; for doctorate, GRE General Test. Additional exam requirements/recommendations for international students: Required—TOEFL (minimum score 600 paper-based; 250 computer-based; 100 iBT). Electronic applications accepted. *Faculty research:* Carcinogens and mutagenesis, pulmonary studies, reproduction and development.

University of Massachusetts Lowell, School of Health and Environment, Department of Work Environment, Lowell, MA 01854-2881. Offers cleaner production and pollution prevention (MS, Sc D); environmental risk assessment (Certificate); epidemiology (MS, Sc D); ergonomics and safety (MS, Sc D); identification and control of ergonomic hazards (Certificate); job stress and healthy job redesign (Certificate); occupational and environmental hygiene (MS, Sc D); radiological health physics and general work environment protection (Certificate); work environment policy (MS, Sc D). *Accreditation:* ABET (one or more programs are accredited). Part-time programs available. Terminal master's awarded for partial completion of doctoral program. *Degree requirements:* For master's, thesis optional; for doctorate, thesis/dissertation. *Entrance requirements:* For master's and doctorate, GRE General Test. Additional exam requirements/recommendations for international students: Required—TOEFL.

University of Michigan, School of Public Health, Department of Environmental Health Sciences, Ann Arbor, MI 48109. Offers environmental health sciences (MS, PhD); environmental quality and health (MPH); human nutrition (MPH); industrial hygiene (MPH, MS); nutritional sciences (MS); occupational and environmental epidemiology (MPH); toxicology (MPH, MS, PhD). *Accreditation:* CEPH (one or more programs are accredited). Part-time programs available. Terminal master's awarded for partial completion of doctoral program. *Degree requirements:* For master's, thesis (for some programs); for doctorate, thesis/dissertation, preliminary exam, oral defense of dissertation. *Entrance requirements:* For master's and doctorate, GRE General Test and/or MCAT. Additional exam requirements/recommendations for international students: Required—TOEFL (minimum score 560 paper-based; 220 computer-based; 100 iBT). Electronic applications accepted. *Faculty research:* Toxicology, occupational hygiene, nutrition, environmental exposure sciences, environmental epidemiology.

University of Minnesota, Twin Cities Campus, School of Public Health, Division of Environmental Health Sciences, Area in Industrial Hygiene, Minneapolis, MN 55455-0213. Offers MPH, MS, PhD. *Accreditation:* ABET (one or more programs are accredited); CEPH (one or more programs are accredited). *Degree requirements:* For doctorate, thesis/dissertation. *Entrance requirements:* For master's and doctorate, GRE General Test. Electronic applications accepted.

The University of North Carolina at Chapel Hill, Graduate School, School of Public Health, Department of Environmental Sciences and Engineering, Chapel Hill, NC 27599. Offers air, radiation and industrial hygiene (MPH, MS, MSEE, MSPH, PhD); aquatic and atmospheric sciences (MPH, MS, MSPH, PhD); environmental engineering (MPH, MS, MSEE, MSPH, PhD); environmental health sciences (MPH, MS, MSPH, PhD); environmental management and policy (MPH, MS, MSPH, PhD). Terminal master's awarded for partial completion of doctoral program. *Degree requirements:* For master's, comprehensive exam, thesis (for some programs), research paper; for doctorate, comprehensive exam, thesis/dissertation. *Entrance requirements:* For master's and doctorate, GRE General Test, minimum GPA of 3.0. Additional exam requirements/recommendations for international students: Required—TOEFL. Electronic applications accepted. *Faculty research:* Air, radiation and industrial hygiene, aquatic and atmospheric sciences, environmental health sciences, environmental management and policy, water resources engineering.

University of Puerto Rico, Medical Sciences Campus, Graduate School of Public Health, Department of Environmental Health, Program in Industrial Hygiene, San Juan, PR 00936-5067. Offers MS. Part-time programs available. *Degree requirements:* For master's, thesis. *Entrance requirements:* For master's, GRE, previous course work in biology, chemistry, mathematics, and physics. *Expenses:* Contact institution.

University of South Carolina, The Graduate School, Arnold School of Public Health, Department of Environmental Health Sciences, Program in Industrial Hygiene, Columbia, SC 29208. Offers MPH, MSPH, PhD. *Accreditation:* ABET (one or more programs are accredited); CEPH (one or more programs are accredited). *Degree requirements:* For master's, comprehensive exam, thesis (for some programs), practicum (MPH); for doctorate, one foreign language, comprehensive exam, thesis/dissertation. *Entrance requirements:* Additional exam requirements/recommendations for international students: Required—TOEFL (minimum score 570 paper-based; 230 computer-based). Electronic applications accepted. *Faculty research:* Sampling and calibration method development, exposure and risk assessment, respirator and dermal protective equipment, ergonomics, air cleaning methods and devices.

University of Wisconsin–Stout, Graduate School, College of Technology, Engineering, and Management, MS Program in Risk Control, Menomonie, WI 54751. Offers MS. Part-time programs available. *Degree requirements:* For master's, thesis. *Entrance requirements:* For master's, minimum GPA of 3.0. Additional exam requirements/recommendations for international students: Required—TOEFL (minimum score 500 paper-based; 173 computer-based; 61 iBT). Electronic applications accepted. *Faculty research:* Environmental microbiology, water supply safety, facilities planning, industrial ventilation, bioterrorist.

West Virginia University, College of Engineering and Mineral Resources, Department of Industrial and Management Systems Engineering, Program in Industrial Hygiene, Morgantown, WV 26506. Offers MS. *Accreditation:* ABET. Part-time programs available. *Degree requirements:* For master's, thesis or alternative. *Entrance requirements:* For master's, GRE General Test, minimum GPA of 3.0. Additional exam requirements/recommendations for international students: Required—TOEFL. *Faculty research:* Safety management, ergonomics and workplace design, safety and health training, construction safety.

International Health

Arizona State University, College of Liberal Arts and Sciences, School of Human Evolution and Social Change, Tempe, AZ 85287-2402. Offers anthropology (PhD); anthropology (archaeology) (PhD); anthropology (bioarchaeology) (PhD); anthropology (museum studies) (MA); anthropology (physical) (PhD); applied mathematics for the life and social sciences (PhD); environmental social science (PhD); environmental social science (urbanism) (PhD); global health (MA); global health (health and culture) (PhD); global health (urbanism) (PhD); immigration studies (Graduate Certificate). Terminal master's awarded for partial completion of doctoral program. *Degree requirements:* For master's, thesis or alternative, interactive Program of Study (iPOS) submitted before completing 50 percent of required credit hours; for doctorate, comprehensive exam, thesis/dissertation, interactive Program of Study (iPOS) submitted before completing 50 percent of required credit hours. *Entrance requirements:* For master's and doctorate, GRE, minimum GPA of 3.0 or equivalent in last 2 years of work leading to bachelor's degree. Additional exam requirements/recommendations for international students: Required—TOEFL (minimum score 80 iBT), TOEFL, IELTS, or Pearson Test of English. Electronic applications accepted.

Arizona State University, College of Nursing and Health Innovation, Phoenix, AZ 85004. Offers advanced nursing practice (DNP); child/family mental health nurse practitioner (Graduate Certificate); clinical research management (MS); community and public health practice (Graduate Certificate); community health (MS); exercise and

wellness (MS), including exercise and wellness; family nurse practitioner (Graduate Certificate); healthcare innovation (MHI); international health for healthcare (Graduate Certificate); kinesiology (MS, PhD); nursing (MS, Graduate Certificate); nursing and healthcare innovation (PhD); nutrition (MS); physical activity nutrition and wellness (PhD), including physical activity, nutrition and wellness; public health (MPH); regulatory science and health safety (MS). *Accreditation:* AACN. Postbaccalaureate distance learning degree programs offered (minimal on-campus study). *Degree requirements:* For master's, comprehensive exam (for some programs), thesis (for some programs), interactive Program of Study (iPOS) submitted before completing 50 percent of required credit hours; for doctorate, comprehensive exam, thesis/dissertation, interactive Program of Study (iPOS) submitted before completing 50 percent of required credit hours. *Entrance requirements:* For master's and doctorate, GRE, minimum GPA of 3.0 or equivalent in last 2 years of work leading to bachelor's degree. Additional exam requirements/recommendations for international students: Required—TOEFL (minimum score 80 iBT), TOEFL, IELTS, or Pearson Test of English. Electronic applications accepted. *Expenses:* Contact institution.

Boston University, School of Public Health, International Health Department, Boston, MA 02118. Offers MPH, Dr PH. *Accreditation:* CEPH (one or more programs are accredited). Part-time and evening/weekend programs available. *Faculty:* 29 full-time, 37 part-time/adjunct. *Students:* 147 full-time (116 women), 79 part-time (74 women); includes 52 minority (13 Black or African American, non-Hispanic/Latino; 26 Asian, non-Hispanic/Latino; 7 Hispanic/Latino; 6 Two or more races, non-Hispanic/Latino), 22 international. Average age 27. 656 applicants, 54% accepted, 108 enrolled. *Degree requirements:* For doctorate, thesis/dissertation. *Entrance requirements:* For master's, GRE, DAT, MCAT, GMAT, LSAT; for doctorate, GRE, GMAT. Additional exam requirements/recommendations for international students: Required—TOEFL (minimum score 600 paper-based; 250 computer-based; 100 iBT) or IELTS (minimum score 6). *Application deadline:* For fall admission, 2/1 priority date for domestic students, 2/1 for international students; for spring admission, 10/15 priority date for domestic students, 10/15 for international students. Applications are processed on a rolling basis. Application fee: $115. Electronic applications accepted. *Expenses: Tuition:* Full-time $40,848; part-time $1276 per credit hour. *Required fees:* $572; $286 per semester. *Financial support:* Research assistantships with full tuition reimbursements, career-related internships or fieldwork, Federal Work-Study, institutionally sponsored loans, and scholarships/grants available. Financial award application deadline: 3/1; financial award applicants required to submit FAFSA. *Unit head:* Dr. Jonathon Simon, Chair, 617-638-5234, E-mail: ih@bu.edu. *Application contact:* LePhan Quan, Associate Director of Admissions, 617-638-4640, Fax: 617-638-5299, E-mail: asksph@bu.edu. Web site: http://sph.bu.edu/ih.

Brandeis University, The Heller School for Social Policy and Management, Program in International Health Policy and Management, Waltham, MA 02454-9110. Offers MS. *Students:* 28 full-time (9 women), 1 (woman) part-time; includes 4 minority (all Black or African American, non-Hispanic/Latino), 22 international. Average age 31. 171 applicants, 63% accepted, 24 enrolled. In 2011, 28 master's awarded. *Entrance requirements:* For master's, 3 letters of recommendation, curriculum vitae or resume, 5 years of international health experience. Additional exam requirements/recommendations for international students: Required—TOEFL (minimum score 600 paper-based; 250 computer-based; 100 iBT). *Application deadline:* For fall admission, 3/15 for domestic and international students. Applications are processed on a rolling basis. Application fee: $55. Electronic applications accepted. *Financial support:* In 2011–12, 29 students received support, including 1 fellowship with full and partial tuition reimbursement available (averaging $10,000 per year); scholarships/grants and tuition waivers (partial) also available. Financial award application deadline: 3/15; financial award applicants required to submit FAFSA. *Faculty research:* International development, health financing, and health systems. *Unit head:* Dr. A. K. Nandakumar,, Program Director, 781-736-3926, E-mail: aknkumar@brandeis.edu. *Application contact:* Elizabeth Cole, Admissions Officer, 781-736-2647, Fax: 781-736-2774, E-mail: elcole@brandeis.edu.

Brandeis University, The Heller School for Social Policy and Management, Program in Social Policy, Waltham, MA 02454-9110. Offers assets and inequalities (PhD); children, youth and families (PhD); global health and development (PhD); health and behavioral health (PhD). *Students:* 132 full-time (107 women), 12 part-time (9 women); includes 18 minority (8 Black or African American, non-Hispanic/Latino; 5 Asian, non-Hispanic/Latino; 5 Hispanic/Latino), 18 international. Average age 32. 115 applicants, 47% accepted, 23 enrolled. In 2011, 15 doctorates awarded. *Degree requirements:* For doctorate, comprehensive exam, thesis/dissertation, qualifying paper, 2-year residency. *Entrance requirements:* For doctorate, GRE General Test, 3 letters of recommendation, statement of purpose, writing sample, at least 3-5 years of professional experience. Additional exam requirements/recommendations for international students: Required—TOEFL (minimum score 600 paper-based; 250 computer-based; 100 iBT). *Application deadline:* For fall admission, 1/2 for domestic and international students. Application fee: $55. Electronic applications accepted. *Financial support:* In 2011–12, 15 fellowships with full tuition reimbursements (averaging $20,000 per year) were awarded; scholarships/grants, traineeships, health care benefits, tuition waivers (full and partial), and unspecified assistantships also available. Financial award application deadline: 1/2. *Faculty research:* Health; mental health; substance abuse; children, youth, and families; aging; international and community development; disabilities; work and inequality; hunger and poverty. *Unit head:* Dr. Susan Parish, Program Director, 781-736-3928, E-mail: slp@brandeis.edu. *Application contact:* Elizabeth Cole, Assistant Director for Admissions and Financial Aid, 781-736-2647, E-mail: elcole@brandeis.edu. Web site: http://heller.brandeis.edu/academic/phd.html.

Central Michigan University, Central Michigan University Global Campus, Program in Health Administration, Mount Pleasant, MI 48859. Offers health administration (DHA); international health (Certificate); nutrition and dietetics (MS). Part-time and evening/weekend programs available. Postbaccalaureate distance learning degree programs offered (minimal on-campus study). Electronic applications accepted. *Financial support:* Scholarships/grants available. Support available to part-time students. Financial award applicants required to submit FAFSA. *Unit head:* Steven D. Berkshire, Director, 989-774-1640, E-mail: berks1sd@cmich.edu. *Application contact:* Off-Campus Programs Call Center, 877-268-4636, E-mail: cmuoffcampus@cmich.edu.

Duke University, Graduate School, Duke Global Health Institute, Durham, NC 27708-0586. Offers MS. *Faculty:* 49 full-time. *Students:* 53 full-time (35 women); includes 14 minority (4 Black or African American, non-Hispanic/Latino; 1 American Indian or Alaska Native, non-Hispanic/Latino; 9 Asian, non-Hispanic/Latino), 9 international. 79 applicants, 67% accepted, 29 enrolled. In 2011, 7 master's awarded. *Degree requirements:* For master's, thesis. *Entrance requirements:* For master's, GRE General Test or MCAT. Additional exam requirements/recommendations for international students: Required—TOEFL (minimum score 550 paper-based; 213 computer-based; 83 iBT), IELTS (minimum score 7). *Application deadline:* For fall admission, 1/30 priority date for domestic students, 1/30 for international students. Application fee: $75. *Expenses: Tuition:* Full-time $40,720. *Required fees:* $3107. *Unit head:* Dr. Christopher Woods, Director of Graduate Studies, 919-681-7916, Fax: 919-681-7748, E-mail: s.martin@duke.edu. *Application contact:* Elizabeth Hutton, Director of Admissions, 919-684-3913, Fax: 919-684-2277, E-mail: grad-admissions@duke.edu. Web site: http://globalhealth.duke.edu/.

Emory University, Rollins School of Public Health, Hubert Department of Global Health, Atlanta, GA 30322-1100. Offers global health (MPH); public nutrition (MSPH). *Accreditation:* CEPH. *Students:* 73 full-time. Average age 27. *Degree requirements:* For master's, thesis, practicum. *Entrance requirements:* For master's, GRE General Test. Additional exam requirements/recommendations for international students: Required—TOEFL (minimum score 550 paper-based; 213 computer-based; 80 iBT). *Application deadline:* For fall admission, 1/5 priority date for domestic students, 1/5 for international students. Application fee: $95. Electronic applications accepted. *Expenses: Tuition:* Full-time $34,800. *Required fees:* $1300. *Financial support:* Fellowships with full and partial tuition reimbursements, career-related internships or fieldwork, Federal Work-Study, institutionally sponsored loans, scholarships/grants, traineeships, health care benefits, and unspecified assistantships available. Support available to part-time students. Financial award application deadline: 1/5; financial award applicants required to submit FAFSA. *Unit head:* Dr. Carlos Del Rio, Chair, 404-727-1557, Fax: 404-727-1278, E-mail: cdelrio@emory.edu. Web site: http://www.sph.emory.edu/gh.

George Mason University, College of Health and Human Services, Department of Global and Community Health, Fairfax, VA 22030. Offers biostatistics (Certificate); epidemiology (Certificate); epidemiology and biostatistics (MS); gerontology (Certificate); global health (MS, Certificate); nutrition (Certificate); public health (MPH, Certificate). *Faculty:* 11 full-time (5 women), 16 part-time/adjunct (12 women). *Students:* 101 full-time (84 women), 114 part-time (92 women); includes 85 minority (43 Black or African American, non-Hispanic/Latino; 30 Asian, non-Hispanic/Latino; 11 Hispanic/Latino; 1 Two or more races, non-Hispanic/Latino), 14 international. Average age 32. 162 applicants, 61% accepted, 53 enrolled. In 2011, 80 master's, 15 other advanced degrees awarded. *Degree requirements:* For master's, comprehensive exam (for some programs), thesis or practicum. *Entrance requirements:* For master's, GRE, 2 official transcripts; expanded goals statement; 3 letters of recommendation; resume; 1 completed course in health science, statistics, natural sciences and social science (for MPH); 6 credits of foreign language if not fluent (for MS in global health); for Certificate, 2 official transcripts; expanded goals statement; 3 letters of recommendation; resume; bachelor's degree from regionally-accredited institution with minimum GPA of 3.0; statistics and college-level algebra with minimum B grade (for Certificate in biostatistics). Additional exam requirements/recommendations for international students: Required—TOEFL (minimum score 575 paper-based; 230 computer-based; 88 iBT), IELTS, Pearson Test of English. *Application deadline:* For fall admission, 4/1 priority date for domestic students; for spring admission, 11/1 priority date for domestic students. Applications are processed on a rolling basis. Application fee: $65 ($80 for international students). Electronic applications accepted. *Expenses:* Tuition, state resident: full-time $8750; part-time $364.58 per credit. Tuition, nonresident: full-time $24,092; part-time $1003.83 per credit. *Required fees:* $2514; $104.75 per credit. *Financial support:* In 2011–12, 14 students received support, including 12 research assistantships with full and partial tuition reimbursements available (averaging $15,000 per year), 2 teaching assistantships with full and partial tuition reimbursements available (averaging $11,781 per year); career-related internships or fieldwork, Federal Work-Study, scholarships/grants, unspecified assistantships, and health care benefits (full-time research and teaching assistantship recipients) also available. Financial award application deadline: 3/1; financial award applicants required to submit FAFSA. *Faculty research:* Providing introductory and advanced degrees in health-related disciplines centered in global and community issues, health issues and the needs of affected populations at the regional and global level. *Total annual research expenditures:* $64,518. *Unit head:* Dr. Carlos Sluzki, Dean, 703-993-1920, Fax: 703-993-1943, E-mail: csluzki@gmu.edu. *Application contact:* Allan Weiss, Office Manager, 703-993-3126, Fax: 703-993-1908, E-mail: aweiss2@gmu.edu. Web site: http://chhs.gmu.edu/gch/index.

George Mason University, College of Humanities and Social Sciences, Program in Global Affairs, Fairfax, VA 22030. Offers MA. *Expenses:* Tuition, state resident: full-time $8750; part-time $364.58 per credit. Tuition, nonresident: full-time $24,092; part-time $1003.83 per credit. *Required fees:* $2514; $104.75 per credit. *Application contact:* Laura Layland, Graduate Admissions Assistant, 703-993-2409, E-mail: llayland@gmu.edu.

George Mason University, School of Public Policy, Program in Health and Medical Policy, Fairfax, VA 22030. Offers global medical policy (Certificate); health and medical policy (MS). *Expenses:* Tuition, state resident: full-time $8750; part-time $364.58 per credit. Tuition, nonresident: full-time $24,092; part-time $1003.83 per credit. *Required fees:* $2514; $104.75 per credit. *Application contact:* Tennille Haegele, Director of Graduate Admissions, School of Public Policy, 703-993-3183, Fax: 703-993-4876, E-mail: thaegele@gmu.edu.

Georgetown University, Law Center, Washington, DC 20001. Offers global health law (LL M); individualized study (LL M); international business and economic law (LL M); law (JD, SJD); national security law (LL M); securities and financial regulation (LL M); taxation (LL M); JD/LL M; JD/MA; JD/MBA; JD/MPH; JD/PhD. *Accreditation:* ABA. Part-time and evening/weekend programs available. *Degree requirements:* For master's, thesis; for doctorate, thesis/dissertation (for some programs). *Entrance requirements:* For master's, JD, LL B, or first law degree earned in country of origin; for doctorate, LSAT (for JD). Additional exam requirements/recommendations for international students: Required—TOEFL. *Expenses:* Contact institution. *Faculty research:* Constitutional law, legal history, jurisprudence.

The George Washington University, School of Public Health and Health Services, Department of Global Health, Washington, DC 20052. Offers MPH, JD/MPH, LL M/MPH, MD/MPH. *Accreditation:* CEPH. *Faculty:* 9 full-time (7 women), 56 part-time/adjunct (21 women). *Students:* 84 full-time (72 women), 107 part-time (88 women); includes 61 minority (29 Black or African American, non-Hispanic/Latino; 1 American Indian or Alaska Native, non-Hispanic/Latino; 13 Asian, non-Hispanic/Latino; 14 Hispanic/Latino; 4 Two or more races, non-Hispanic/Latino), 12 international. Average age 28. 426 applicants, 68% accepted, 69 enrolled. In 2011, 89 master's awarded. *Degree requirements:* For master's, case study or special project. *Entrance requirements:* For master's, GMAT, GRE General Test, or MCAT. Additional exam requirements/recommendations for international students: Required—TOEFL. *Application deadline:* For fall admission, 4/15 priority date for domestic students, 4/15 for international students; for spring admission, 11/1 for domestic and international students. Applications are processed on a rolling basis. Application fee: $75. *Financial support:* In 2011–12, 24 students received support. Tuition waivers available. Financial award application deadline: 2/15. *Unit head:* Dr. James Sherry, Chair, 202-994-0270, Fax: 202-994-1955, E-mail: sherry@gwu.edu. *Application contact:* Jane Smith, Director of Admissions, 202-994-0248, Fax: 202-994-1860, E-mail: sphhsinfo@gwumc.edu.

Harvard University, Harvard School of Public Health, Department of Global Health and Population, Boston, MA 02115-6096. Offers SM, DPH, SD. Part-time programs available. *Faculty:* 38 full-time (8 women), 12 part-time/adjunct (4 women). *Students:* 92 full-time, 1 part-time; includes 8 minority (1 Black or African American, non-Hispanic/Latino; 4 Asian, non-Hispanic/Latino; 1 Hispanic/Latino; 2 Two or more races, non-Hispanic/Latino), 37 international. Average age 28. 218 applicants, 25% accepted, 33 enrolled. In 2011, 26 master's, 4 doctorates awarded. *Degree requirements:* For

master's, thesis; for doctorate, thesis/dissertation, qualifying exam. *Entrance requirements:* For master's and doctorate, GRE. Additional exam requirements/recommendations for international students: Required—TOEFL (minimum score 595 paper-based; 240 computer-based; 95 iBT); Recommended—IELTS (minimum score 7). *Application deadline:* For fall admission, 12/15 for domestic and international students. Application fee: $115. Electronic applications accepted. *Expenses: Tuition:* Full-time $36,304. *Required fees:* $1186. Full-time tuition and fees vary according to program. *Financial support:* Fellowships, research assistantships, teaching assistantships, Federal Work-Study, scholarships/grants, traineeships, and unspecified assistantships available. Support available to part-time students. Financial award application deadline: 2/17; financial award applicants required to submit FAFSA. *Faculty research:* International health policy, economics, reproductive health, ecology. *Unit head:* Dr. David Bloom, Chair, 617-432-1232, Fax: 617-432-6733, E-mail: dbloom@hsph.harvard.edu. *Application contact:* Vincent W. James, Director of Admissions, 617-432-1031, Fax: 617-432-7080, E-mail: admissions@hsph.harvard.edu. Web site: http://www.hsph.harvard.edu/departments/global-health-and-population/.

The Johns Hopkins University, Bloomberg School of Public Health, Department of International Health, Baltimore, MD 21205. Offers global disease epidemiology and control (MHS, PhD); health systems (MHS, PhD); human nutrition (MHS, PhD); international health (Dr PH); social and behavioral interventions (MHS, PhD). *Degree requirements:* For master's, comprehensive exam, thesis (for some programs), 1 year full-time residency, 4-9 month internship; for doctorate, comprehensive exam, thesis/dissertation or alternative, 1.5 years full-time residency, oral and written exams. *Entrance requirements:* For master's, GRE General Test or MCAT, 3 letters of recommendation, resume; for doctorate, GRE General Test or MCAT, 3 letters of recommendation, resume, transcripts. Additional exam requirements/recommendations for international students: Required—TOEFL (minimum score 600 paper-based; 250 computer-based; 100 iBT); Recommended—IELTS (minimum score 7). Electronic applications accepted. *Faculty research:* Nutrition, infectious diseases, health systems, health economics, humanitarian emergencies.

Loma Linda University, School of Public Health, Programs in Global Health, Loma Linda, CA 92350. Offers MPH. *Accreditation:* CEPH. *Entrance requirements:* Additional exam requirements/recommendations for international students: Required—Michigan English Language Assessment Battery or TOEFL.

Massachusetts School of Professional Psychology, Graduate Programs, Boston, MA 02132. Offers applied psychology in higher education student personnel administration (MA); clinical psychology (Psy D); counseling psychology (MA); counseling psychology and community mental health (MA); counseling psychology and global mental health (MA); executive coaching (Graduate Certificate); forensic and counseling psychology (MA); leadership psychology (Psy D); organizational psychology (MA); primary care psychology (MA); respecialization in clinical psychology (Certificate); school psychology (Psy D); MA/CAGS. *Accreditation:* APA. *Degree requirements:* For master's, comprehensive exam (for some programs); for doctorate, thesis/dissertation (for some programs). Electronic applications accepted.

Medical University of South Carolina, College of Health Professions, Department of Health Professions, Program in Health Administration-Global, Charleston, SC 29425. Offers MHA. *Entrance requirements:* Additional exam requirements/recommendations for international students: Required—TOEFL. *Unit head:* Dr. Emily L. Moore, Program Director, 843-792-4840, E-mail: mooreemi@musc.edu. *Application contact:* Melissa Freeland, Director of Student Services, 843-792-8510, Fax: 843-792-3327, E-mail: freelan@musc.edu.

Morehouse School of Medicine, Master of Public Health Program, Atlanta, GA 30310-1495. Offers epidemiology (MPH); health administration, management and policy (MPH); health education/health promotion (MPH); international health (MPH). *Accreditation:* CEPH. Part-time programs available. *Degree requirements:* For master's, thesis, practicum, public health leadership seminar. *Entrance requirements:* For master's, GRE General Test, writing test, public health or human service experience. Additional exam requirements/recommendations for international students: Required—TOEFL (minimum score 550 paper-based; 200 computer-based). Electronic applications accepted. *Expenses:* Contact institution. *Faculty research:* Women's and adolescent health, violence prevention, cancer epidemiology/disparities, substance abuse prevention.

New York Medical College, School of Health Sciences and Practice, Department of Health Policy and Management, Graduate Certificate Program in Global Health, Valhalla, NY 10595-1691. Offers Graduate Certificate. *Accreditation:* CEPH. Part-time and evening/weekend programs available. *Faculty:* 2 full-time, 3 part-time/adjunct. *Students:* 15 full-time, 25 part-time. 35 applicants, 71% accepted, 20 enrolled. *Entrance requirements:* Additional exam requirements/recommendations for international students: Required—TOEFL (minimum score 637 paper-based; 250 computer-based; 110 iBT), IELTS (minimum score 7). *Application deadline:* For fall admission, 8/1 priority date for domestic students, 5/15 for international students; for spring admission, 12/1 priority date for domestic students, 10/15 for international students. Applications are processed on a rolling basis. Application fee: $50 ($100 for international students). Electronic applications accepted. *Financial support:* Research assistantships, teaching assistantships, career-related internships or fieldwork, Federal Work-Study, institutionally sponsored loans, health care benefits, and tuition waivers (partial) available. Support available to part-time students. Financial award applicants required to submit FAFSA. *Unit head:* Dr. Padmini Murthy, Director, 914-594-3480, Fax: 914-594-3481, E-mail: mini_murthy@nymc.edu. *Application contact:* Pamela Suett, Director of Recruitment, 914-594-4510, Fax: 914-594-4292, E-mail: shsp_admissions@nymc.edu. Web site: http://www.nymc.edu/sph/.

Oregon State University, Graduate School, College of Public Health and Human Sciences, Programs in Public Health, Program in International Health, Corvallis, OR 97331. Offers MPH.

San Diego State University, Graduate and Research Affairs, College of Health and Human Services, Graduate School of Public Health, San Diego, CA 92182. Offers environmental health (MPH); epidemiology (MPH, PhD), including biostatistics (MPH); global emergency preparedness and response (MS); global health (PhD); health behavior (PhD); health promotion (MPH); health services administration (MPH); toxicology (MS); MPH/MA; MSW/MPH. *Accreditation:* ABET (one or more programs are accredited); CAHME (one or more programs are accredited); CEPH (one or more programs are accredited). Part-time programs available. *Degree requirements:* For master's, comprehensive exam (for some programs), thesis (for some programs); for doctorate, thesis/dissertation. *Entrance requirements:* For master's, GMAT (MPH in health services administration), GRE General Test; for doctorate, GRE General Test. Additional exam requirements/recommendations for international students: Required—TOEFL. *Faculty research:* Evaluation of tobacco, AIDS prevalence and prevention, mammography, infant death project, Alzheimer's in elderly Chinese.

Syracuse University, Falk College of Sport and Human Dynamics, Program in Global Health, Syracuse, NY 13244. Offers CAS. *Expenses: Tuition:* Part-time $1206 per credit. *Unit head:* Dr. Diane Lyden Murphy, Dean, 315-443-5582, Fax: 315-443-2562. *Application contact:* Felecia Otero, Director of College Admissions, 315-443-5555, Fax: 315-443-2562, E-mail: falk@syr.edu. Web site: http://falk.syr.edu/HealthWellness/GlobalHealth_CAS.aspx.

Trident University International, College of Health Sciences, Program in Health Sciences, Cypress, CA 90630. Offers clinical research administration (MS, Certificate); emergency and disaster management (MS, Certificate); environmental health science (Certificate); health care administration (PhD); health care management (MS), including health informatics; health education (MS, Certificate); health informatics (Certificate); health sciences (PhD); international health (MS); international health: educator or researcher option (PhD); international health: practitioner option (PhD); law and expert witness studies (MS, Certificate); public health (MS); quality assurance (Certificate). Part-time and evening/weekend programs available. Postbaccalaureate distance learning degree programs offered (no on-campus study). *Degree requirements:* For doctorate, comprehensive exam, thesis/dissertation, defense of dissertation. *Entrance requirements:* For master's, minimum GPA of 2.5 (students with GPA 3.0 or greater may transfer up to 30% of graduate level credits); for doctorate, minimum GPA of 3.4, curriculum vitae, course work in research methods or statistics. Additional exam requirements/recommendations for international students: Required—TOEFL. Electronic applications accepted.

Tufts University, Fletcher School of Law and Diplomacy, Medford, MA 02155. Offers LL M, MA, MALD, MIB, PhD, DVM/MA, JD/MALD, MALD/MA, MALD/MBA, MALD/MS, MD/MA. Postbaccalaureate distance learning degree programs offered (minimal on-campus study). *Degree requirements:* For master's, one foreign language, thesis; for doctorate, one foreign language, comprehensive exam, thesis/dissertation, dissertation defense. *Entrance requirements:* For master's and doctorate, GMAT or GRE General Test. Additional exam requirements/recommendations for international students: Required—TOEFL (minimum score 600 paper-based; 250 computer-based; 100 iBT), IELTS (minimum score 7). Electronic applications accepted. *Expenses:* Contact institution. *Faculty research:* Negotiation and conflict resolution, international organizations, international business and economic law, security studies, development economics.

Tulane University, School of Public Health and Tropical Medicine, Department of International Health and Development, New Orleans, LA 70118-5669. Offers MPH, Dr PH, PhD, MSW/MPH. *Accreditation:* CEPH (one or more programs are accredited). Part-time programs available. Terminal master's awarded for partial completion of doctoral program. *Degree requirements:* For master's, one foreign language; for doctorate, one foreign language, comprehensive exam, thesis/dissertation. *Entrance requirements:* For master's and doctorate, GRE General Test. Additional exam requirements/recommendations for international students: Required—TOEFL. Electronic applications accepted. *Faculty research:* Reproductive health, HIV/AIDS, nutrition and food security, health financing, program evaluation.

Uniformed Services University of the Health Sciences, School of Medicine, Graduate Programs in the Biomedical Sciences and Public Health, Bethesda, MD 20814. Offers emerging infectious diseases (PhD); medical and clinical psychology (PhD), including clinical psychology, medical and clinical psychology, medical psychology; molecular and cell biology (MS, PhD); neuroscience (PhD); preventive medicine and biometrics (MPH, MS, MSPH, MTMH, Dr PH, PhD), including environmental health sciences (PhD), healthcare administration and policy (MS), medical zoology (PhD), public health (MPH, MSPH, Dr PH), tropical medicine and hygiene (MTMH). *Faculty:* 372 full-time (119 women), 4,044 part-time/adjunct (908 women). *Students:* 176 full-time (96 women); includes 31 minority (6 Black or African American, non-Hispanic/Latino; 4 American Indian or Alaska Native, non-Hispanic/Latino; 14 Asian, non-Hispanic/Latino; 7 Hispanic/Latino), 11 international. Average age 28. 278 applicants, 20% accepted, 47 enrolled. In 2011, 36 master's, 17 doctorates awarded. Terminal master's awarded for partial completion of doctoral program. *Degree requirements:* For master's, comprehensive exam, thesis or alternative; for doctorate, comprehensive exam, thesis/dissertation, qualifying exam. *Entrance requirements:* For master's, GRE General Test; for doctorate, GRE General Test, minimum GPA of 3.0. Additional exam requirements/recommendations for international students: Required—TOEFL. *Application deadline:* For fall admission, 1/1 priority date for domestic students, 1/1 for international students. Applications are processed on a rolling basis. Application fee: $0. Electronic applications accepted. *Financial support:* In 2011–12, fellowships with full tuition reimbursements (averaging $26,000 per year), research assistantships with full tuition reimbursements (averaging $26,000 per year) were awarded; career-related internships or fieldwork, scholarships/grants, health care benefits, and tuition waivers (full) also available. *Unit head:* Dr. Eleanor S. Metcalf, Associate Dean, 301-295-1104, E-mail: emetcalf@usuhs.edu. *Application contact:* Elena Marina Sherman, Program Administrative Specialist, 301-295-3913, Fax: 301-295-6772, E-mail: elena.sherman@usuhs.mil. Web site: http://www.usuhs.mil/graded.

Uniformed Services University of the Health Sciences, School of Medicine, Graduate Programs in the Biomedical Sciences and Public Health, Department of Preventive Medicine and Biometrics, Program in Tropical Medicine and Hygiene, Bethesda, MD 20814-4799. Offers MTMH. *Accreditation:* CEPH. *Faculty:* 43 full-time (14 women), 143 part-time/adjunct (25 women). *Students:* 4 full-time (0 women); includes 2 minority (1 Black or African American, non-Hispanic/Latino; 1 Hispanic/Latino). Average age 30. 10 applicants, 70% accepted. In 2011, 3 master's awarded. *Degree requirements:* For master's, comprehensive exam. *Entrance requirements:* For master's, GRE General Test, MD, U.S. citizenship. *Application deadline:* For fall admission, 1/1 priority date for domestic students. Applications are processed on a rolling basis. Application fee: $0. *Financial support:* Health care benefits available. *Faculty research:* Epidemiology, biostatistics, tropical public health. *Unit head:* Dr. David Cruess, Director, 301-295-3465, Fax: 301-295-1933, E-mail: dcruess@usuhs.mil. *Application contact:* Elena Marina Sherman, Program Administrative Specialist, 301-295-3913, Fax: 301-295-6772, E-mail: elena.sherman@usuhs.mil. Web site: http://www.usuhs.mil/pmb.

University of Alberta, School of Public Health, Department of Public Health Sciences, Edmonton, AB T6G 2E1, Canada. Offers clinical epidemiology (M Sc, MPH); environmental and occupational health (MPH); environmental health sciences (M Sc); epidemiology (M Sc); global health (M Sc, MPH); health policy and management (MPH); health policy research (M Sc); health technology assessment (MPH); occupational health (M Sc); population health (M Sc); public health leadership (MPH); public health sciences (PhD); quantitative methods (MPH). *Accreditation:* CEPH (one or more programs are accredited). Terminal master's awarded for partial completion of doctoral program. *Degree requirements:* For master's, thesis (for some programs); for doctorate, thesis/dissertation. *Entrance requirements:* For master's, GMAT or GRE General Test. Additional exam requirements/recommendations for international students: Required—TOEFL (minimum score 550 paper-based; 213 computer-based) or IELTS (minimum score 6). Electronic applications accepted. *Faculty research:* Biostatistics, health promotion and socio-behavioral health science.

University of Colorado Denver, Business School, Master of Business Administration Program, Denver, CO 80217. Offers business intelligence (MBA); business strategy (MBA); business to business marketing (MBA); business to consumer marketing (MBA); change management (MBA); corporate financial management (MBA); enterprise technology management (MBA); entrepreneurship (MBA); health administration (MBA),

including financial management, health administration, health information technologies, international health management and policy; human resources management (MBA); investment management (MBA); managing for sustainability (MBA); services management (MBA); sports and entertainment management (MBA). *Accreditation:* AACSB. Part-time and evening/weekend programs available. Postbaccalaureate distance learning degree programs offered (no on-campus study). *Students:* 784 full-time (306 women), 203 part-time (81 women); includes 135 minority (18 Black or African American, non-Hispanic/Latino; 5 American Indian or Alaska Native, non-Hispanic/Latino; 50 Asian, non-Hispanic/Latino; 58 Hispanic/Latino; 4 Two or more races, non-Hispanic/Latino), 38 international. Average age 31. 433 applicants, 76% accepted, 212 enrolled. In 2011, 326 master's awarded. *Degree requirements:* For master's, 48 semester hours, including 30 of core courses, 3 in international business, and 15 in electives from over 50 other graduate business courses. *Entrance requirements:* For master's, GMAT, resume, official transcripts, essay, two letters of recommendation, financial statements (for international applicants). Additional exam requirements/recommendations for international students: Required—TOEFL (minimum score 560 paper-based; 197 computer-based; 83 iBT). *Application deadline:* For fall admission, 4/15 priority date for domestic students, 3/15 for international students; for spring admission, 10/15 priority date for domestic students, 10/1 for international students. Applications are processed on a rolling basis. Application fee: $50 ($75 for international students). Electronic applications accepted. *Expenses:* Contact institution. *Financial support:* Scholarships/grants available. Support available to part-time students. Financial award application deadline: 4/1; financial award applicants required to submit FAFSA. *Faculty research:* Marketing, management, entrepreneurship, finance, health administration. *Unit head:* Elizabeth Cooperman, Professor of Finance and Managing for Sustainability/MBA Program Director, 303-315-8422, E-mail: elizabeth.cooperman@ucdenver.edu. *Application contact:* Shelly Townley, Admissions Director, Graduate Programs, 303-315-8202, E-mail: shelly.townley@ucdenver.edu. Web site: http://www.ucdenver.edu/academics/colleges/business/degrees/ms/accounting/Pages/Accounting.aspx.

University of Colorado Denver, School of Medicine, Physician Assistant Program, Aurora, CO 80045. Offers child health associate (MPAS), including global health, leadership, education, advocacy, development, and scholarship, rural health, urban/underserved populations. *Accreditation:* ARC-PA. *Students:* 124 full-time (107 women), 2 part-time (both women); includes 12 minority (1 American Indian or Alaska Native, non-Hispanic/Latino; 6 Asian, non-Hispanic/Latino; 5 Hispanic/Latino). Average age 26. 274 applicants, 17% accepted, 44 enrolled. In 2011, 37 master's awarded. *Degree requirements:* For master's, comprehensive exam, successful completion of all coursework and rotations. *Entrance requirements:* For master's, GRE General Test, minimum GPA of 2.8, 3 letters of recommendation, prerequisite courses in chemistry, biology, general genetics, psychology and statistics, interviews for the finalists. Additional exam requirements/recommendations for international students: Required—TOEFL (minimum score 550 paper-based; 213 computer-based). *Application deadline:* For fall admission, 10/1 for domestic students. Application fee: $170. Electronic applications accepted. *Expenses:* Contact institution. *Financial support:* Career-related internships or fieldwork and scholarships/grants available. Financial award application deadline: 3/15; financial award applicants required to submit FAFSA. *Faculty research:* Clinical genetics and genetic counseling, evidence-based medicine, pediatric allergy and asthma, childhood diabetes, standardized patient assessment. *Unit head:* Jonathan Bowser, Interim Program Director, 303-724-1349, E-mail: jonathan.bowser@ucdenver.edu. *Application contact:* Kay Denler, Director of Admissions, 303-724-1340, E-mail: kay.denler@ucdenver.edu. Web site: http://www.ucdenver.edu/academics/colleges/medicalschool/education/degree_programs/PAProgram/Pages/Home.aspx.

University of Denver, Josef Korbel School of International Studies, Denver, CO 80210. Offers conflict resolution (MA); global finance, trade and economic integration (MA); global health affairs (Certificate); homeland security (Certificate); humanitarian assistance (Certificate); international administration (MA); international development (MA); international human rights (MA); international security (MA); international studies (MA, PhD). Part-time programs available. *Faculty:* 41 full-time (14 women), 33 part-time/adjunct (8 women). *Students:* 440 full-time (270 women), 38 part-time (22 women); includes 54 minority (6 Black or African American, non-Hispanic/Latino; 2 American Indian or Alaska Native, non-Hispanic/Latino; 16 Asian, non-Hispanic/Latino; 20 Hispanic/Latino; 1 Native Hawaiian or other Pacific Islander, non-Hispanic/Latino; 9 Two or more races, non-Hispanic/Latino), 35 international. Average age 27. 940 applicants, 75% accepted, 256 enrolled. In 2011, 257 master's, 7 doctorates, 43 other advanced degrees awarded. *Degree requirements:* For master's, one foreign language, thesis (for some programs); for doctorate, one foreign language, comprehensive exam, thesis/dissertation, two extended research papers. *Entrance requirements:* For master's, GRE General Test, Official transcript from each undergraduate institution, two letters of recommendation, statement of purpose, resume/curriculum vitae; for doctorate, GRE General Test, official transcript from each undergraduate institution, three letters of recommendation, statement of purpose, resume/curriculum vitae; for Certificate, official transcript from each undergraduate institution, two letters of recommendation, statement of purpose, resume/curriculum vitae. Additional exam requirements/recommendations for international students: Required—TOEFL (minimum score 587 paper-based; 95 iBT). *Application deadline:* For fall admission, 1/15 priority date for domestic students, 12/15 for international students. Application fee: $60. Electronic applications accepted. *Financial support:* In 2011–12, 261 students received support, including 3 teaching assistantships with partial tuition reimbursements available (averaging $5,222 per year); career-related internships or fieldwork, Federal Work-Study, institutionally sponsored loans, scholarships/grants, and unspecified assistantships also available. Support available to part-time students. Financial award application deadline: 2/15; financial award applicants required to submit FAFSA. *Faculty research:* Human rights and international security, international politics and economics, economic-social and political development, international technology analysis and management. *Unit head:* Christopher R. Hill, Dean, 303-871-2359, Fax: 303-871-2456, E-mail: christopher.r.hill@du.edu. *Application contact:* Brad Miller, Director of Graduate Admissions, 303-871-2989, Fax: 303-871-2124, E-mail: brad.miller@du.edu. Web site: http://www.du.edu/korbel/.

University of Michigan, School of Public Health, Department of Epidemiology, Ann Arbor, MI 48109-2029. Offers dental public health (MPH); epidemiological science (PhD); epidemiology (MS); general epidemiology (MPH); hospital and molecular epidemiology (MPH); international health (MPH). PhD and MS offered through the Horace H. Rackham School of Graduate Studies. *Accreditation:* CEPH (one or more programs are accredited). Part-time programs available. Terminal master's awarded for partial completion of doctoral program. *Degree requirements:* For master's, thesis (for some programs); for doctorate, comprehensive exam, thesis/dissertation, oral defense of dissertation, preliminary exam. *Entrance requirements:* For master's and doctorate, GRE General Test, MCAT. Additional exam requirements/recommendations for international students: Required—TOEFL (minimum score 560 paper-based; 220 computer-based; 100 iBT). Electronic applications accepted. *Faculty research:* Molecular virology, infectious diseases, women's health, genetics, social epidemiology.

University of Minnesota, Twin Cities Campus, School of Public Health, Division of Environmental Health Sciences, Minneapolis, MN 55455-0213. Offers environmental

and occupational epidemiology (MPH, MS, PhD); environmental chemistry (MS, PhD); environmental health policy (MPH, MS, PhD); environmental infectious diseases (MPH, MS, PhD); environmental toxicology (MPH, MS, PhD); exposure sciences (MS); general environmental health (MPH, MS); global environmental health (MPH, MS, PhD); industrial hygiene (MPH, MS, PhD); occupational health nursing (MPH, MS, PhD); occupational medicine (MPH); MPH/MS. *Accreditation:* CEPH (one or more programs are accredited). Part-time programs available. *Degree requirements:* For master's, thesis optional; for doctorate, thesis/dissertation. *Entrance requirements:* For master's and doctorate, GRE General Test. Additional exam requirements/recommendations for international students: Required—TOEFL (minimum score 600 paper-based; 250 computer-based; 100 iBT). Electronic applications accepted. *Faculty research:* Behavior/measurement of airborne particles, toxicity mechanisms of environmental contaminants, health and safety interventions, foodborne disease surveillance, measuring pesticide exposures in children.

University of Pennsylvania, Perelman School of Medicine, Master of Public Health Program, Philadelphia, PA 19129. Offers environmental health (MPH); generalist (MPH); global health (MPH); DMD/MPH; JD/MPH; MD/MPH; MPH/MBE; MSCE/MPH; MSN/MPH; MSW/MPH; PhD/MPH. Part-time and evening/weekend programs available. *Faculty:* 30 full-time (18 women), 35 part-time/adjunct (19 women). *Students:* 34 full-time (29 women), 28 part-time (24 women); includes 11 minority (3 Black or African American, non-Hispanic/Latino; 6 Asian, non-Hispanic/Latino; 2 Hispanic/Latino), 2 international. 182 applicants, 25% accepted, 27 enrolled. In 2011, 18 master's awarded. *Entrance requirements:* For master's, GRE. Additional exam requirements/recommendations for international students: Recommended—TOEFL. *Application deadline:* For spring admission, 4/30 for domestic and international students. Application fee: $70. *Expenses: Tuition:* Full-time $26,660; part-time $4944 per course. *Required fees:* $2318; $291 per course. Tuition and fees vary according to course load, degree level and program. *Financial support:* In 2011–12, 4 teaching assistantships with partial tuition reimbursements were awarded; fellowships, scholarships/grants, and tuition waivers (partial) also available. Financial award application deadline: 4/30. *Faculty research:* Health disparities, health behaviors, obesity, global health, epidemiology and prevention research. *Unit head:* Dr. Jennifer A. Pinto-Martin, Director, 215-898-4726, E-mail: pinto@nursing.upenn.edu. *Application contact:* Karen Kelly, Admission Coordinator, 215-573-0917, Fax: 215-573-9025, E-mail: kakelly@mail.med.upenn.edu. Web site: http://www.publichealth.med.upenn.edu/.

University of Phoenix–Online Campus, College of Nursing, Phoenix, AZ 85034-7209. Offers informatics (MSN); international (MSN); nurse practitioner (MSN); nursing (MSN); nursing/health care education (MSN); MSN/Certificate; MSN/MBA; MSN/MHA. *Accreditation:* AACN. Evening/weekend programs available. Postbaccalaureate distance learning degree programs offered. *Students:* 5,257 full-time (4,805 women); includes 1,381 minority (803 Black or African American, non-Hispanic/Latino; 36 American Indian or Alaska Native, non-Hispanic/Latino; 271 Asian, non-Hispanic/Latino; 188 Hispanic/Latino; 51 Native Hawaiian or other Pacific Islander, non-Hispanic/Latino; 32 Two or more races, non-Hispanic/Latino), 244 international. Average age 43. *Entrance requirements:* Additional exam requirements/recommendations for international students: Required—TOEFL, TOEIC (Test of English as an International Communication), Berlitz Online English Proficiency Exam, Pearson Test of English, or IELTS. *Application deadline:* Applications are processed on a rolling basis. Application fee: $45. Electronic applications accepted. *Expenses:* Contact institution. *Financial support:* Scholarships/grants available. Financial award applicants required to submit FAFSA. *Application contact:* 866-766-0766. Web site: http://www.phoenix.edu/colleges_divisions/nursing.html.

University of Southern California, Keck School of Medicine and Graduate School, Graduate Programs in Medicine, Department of Preventive Medicine, Master of Public Health Program, Los Angeles, CA 90032-3628. Offers biostatistics/epidemiology (MPH); child and family health (MPH); environmental health (MPH); global health leadership (MPH); health communication (MPH); health education and promotion (MPH); public health policy (MPH). *Accreditation:* CEPH. Part-time programs available. *Faculty:* 22 full-time (12 women), 3 part-time/adjunct (0 women). *Students:* 148 full-time (115 women), 35 part-time (23 women); includes 100 minority (8 Black or African American, non-Hispanic/Latino; 66 Asian, non-Hispanic/Latino; 26 Hispanic/Latino), 26 international. Average age 24. 218 applicants, 73% accepted, 88 enrolled. In 2011, 91 master's awarded. *Degree requirements:* For master's, practicum, final report, oral presentation. *Entrance requirements:* For master's, GRE General Test, MCAT, GMAT, minimum GPA of 3.0. Additional exam requirements/recommendations for international students: Required—TOEFL (minimum score 600 paper-based; 250 computer-based; 100 iBT). *Application deadline:* For fall admission, 6/1 priority date for domestic students, 6/1 for international students; for spring admission, 11/1 priority date for domestic students, 10/1 for international students. Applications are processed on a rolling basis. Application fee: $85. Electronic applications accepted. *Financial support:* In 2011–12, 148 students received support. Career-related internships or fieldwork, Federal Work-Study, institutionally sponsored loans, and scholarships/grants available. Support available to part-time students. Financial award application deadline: 5/4; financial award applicants required to submit CSS PROFILE or FAFSA. *Faculty research:* Substance abuse prevention, cancer and heart disease prevention, mass media and health communication research, health promotion, treatment compliance. *Unit head:* Dr. Louise A. Rohrbach, Director, 323-442-8237, Fax: 323-442-8297, E-mail: rohrbac@usc.edu. *Application contact:* Chrystal Romero, Admissions Counselor, 323-442-7257, Fax: 323-442-8297, E-mail: ccromero@usc.edu. Web site: http://mph.usc.edu/main.php.

University of South Florida, Graduate School, College of Public Health, Department of Global Health, Tampa, FL 33620-9951. Offers MPH, MSPH, Dr PH, PhD. Part-time and evening/weekend programs available. *Degree requirements:* For master's, comprehensive exam, thesis (for some programs), minimum GPA of 3.0; for doctorate, comprehensive exam, thesis/dissertation. *Entrance requirements:* For master's, GRE General Test, minimum GPA of 3.0 in upper-level course work, goal statement letter, two professional letters of recommendation, resume/curriculum vitae; for doctorate, GRE General Test, minimum GPA of 3.0 in upper-level course work, goal statement letter, three professional letters of recommendation, resume/curriculum vitae, writing sample. Additional exam requirements/recommendations for international students: Required—TOEFL (minimum score 550 paper-based; 213 computer-based; 79 iBT). Electronic applications accepted.

The University of Toledo, College of Graduate Studies, College of Medicine and Life Sciences, Department of Public Health and Preventative Medicine, Toledo, OH 43606-3390. Offers biostatistics and epidemiology (Certificate); contemporary gerontological practice (Certificate); environmental and occupational health and safety (MPH); epidemiology (MPH, Certificate); global public health (Certificate); health administration (MPH); health promotion (MPH); medical health and science education (Certificate); nutrition (MPH); occupational health (MSOH, Certificate); public health and emergency response (Certificate); MD/MPH. Part-time and evening/weekend programs available. *Faculty:* 6. *Students:* 95 full-time (74 women), 66 part-time (45 women); includes 37 minority (21 Black or African American, non-Hispanic/Latino; 11 Asian, non-Hispanic/Latino; 3 Hispanic/Latino; 2 Two or more races, non-Hispanic/Latino), 6 international. Average age 29. 132 applicants, 75% accepted, 70 enrolled. In 2011, 60 master's, 26

other advanced degrees awarded. *Degree requirements:* For master's, thesis or alternative. *Entrance requirements:* For master's, GRE, minimum undergraduate GPA of 3.0, three letters of recommendation, statement of purpose, transcripts from all prior institutions attended, resume; for Certificate, minimum undergraduate GPA of 3.0, three letters of recommendation, statement of purpose, transcripts from all prior institutions attended, resume. Additional exam requirements/recommendations for international students: Required—TOEFL (minimum score 550 paper-based; 213 computer-based; 80 iBT), IELTS (minimum score 6.5). *Application deadline:* For fall admission, 3/15 for domestic and international students. Applications are processed on a rolling basis. Application fee: $45 ($75 for international students). Electronic applications accepted. *Financial support:* In 2011–12, 15 research assistantships with full tuition reimbursements (averaging $10,000 per year) were awarded; Federal Work-Study, institutionally sponsored loans, scholarships/grants, tuition waivers (full and partial), and unspecified assistantships also available. *Unit head:* Dr. Sheryl A. Milz, Chair, 419-383-3976, Fax: 419-383-6140, E-mail: sheryl.milz@utoledo.edu. *Application contact:* Joan Mulligan, Admissions Analyst, 419-383-4186, Fax: 419-383-6140, E-mail: joan.mulligan@utoledo.edu. Web site: http://nocphmph.org/.

University of Washington, Graduate School, School of Public Health, Department of Epidemiology, Seattle, WA 98195. Offers clinical research (MS); epidemiology (MPH, MS, PhD); global health (MPH); maternal/child health (MPH); nutritional sciences (MPH, MS, PhD); public health genetics (MPH, MS, PhD), including genetic epidemiology (MS), public health genetics (MPH, PhD); MPH/JD; MPH/MPA; MS/MPA. *Accreditation:* CEPH (one or more programs are accredited). *Faculty:* 62 full-time (35 women), 45 part-time/adjunct (22 women). *Students:* 135 full-time (93 women), 37 part-time (23 women); includes 37 minority (6 Black or African American, non-Hispanic/Latino; 1 American Indian or Alaska Native, non-Hispanic/Latino; 23 Asian, non-Hispanic/Latino; 7 Hispanic/Latino), 17 international. Average age 32. 291 applicants, 35% accepted, 58 enrolled. In 2011, 45 master's, 16 doctorates awarded. *Degree requirements:* For master's, comprehensive exam (for some programs), thesis; for doctorate, comprehensive exam, thesis/dissertation. *Entrance requirements:* For master's, GRE General Test (except for those holding PhD, MD, DDS, DVM, DO or equivalent from U.S. schools); for doctorate, GRE. Additional exam requirements/recommendations for international students: Required—TOEFL (minimum score 580 paper-based; 237 computer-based; 92 iBT) or IELTS (minimum score 7). *Application deadline:* For fall admission, 12/1 for domestic students, 11/1 for international students. Application fee: $75. Electronic applications accepted. *Expenses:* Contact institution. *Financial support:* In 2011–12, 152 students received support, including 75 fellowships with partial tuition reimbursements available, 49 research assistantships with partial tuition reimbursements available, 4 teaching assistantships with partial tuition reimbursements available; career-related internships or fieldwork, Federal Work-Study, traineeships, health care benefits, and unspecified assistantships also available. Support available to part-time students. Financial award applicants required to submit FAFSA. *Faculty research:* Chronic disease, health disparities and social determinants of health, aging and neuroepidemiology, maternal and child health, molecular and genetic epidemiology. *Unit head:* Dr. Scott Davis, Chair, 206-543-1065, Fax: 206-543-8525. *Application contact:* Kate O'Brien, Student Services

Manager, 206-543-1065, Fax: 206-543-8525, E-mail: epi@u.washington.edu. Web site: http://depts.washington.edu/epidem/.

University of Washington, Graduate School, School of Public Health, Department of Global Health, Seattle, WA 98195. Offers global health (MPH); global health - peace corps international (MPH); health metrics and evaluation (MPH); leadership, policy and management (MPH); pathobiology (PhD); MPH/MAIS; MPH/MD; MPH/MN; MPH/MPA; MPH/MSW; MPH/PhD. Part-time programs available. *Faculty:* 43 full-time (16 women), 20 part-time/adjunct (12 women). *Students:* 25 full-time (15 women), 22 part-time (16 women); includes 11 minority (4 Black or African American, non-Hispanic/Latino; 4 Asian, non-Hispanic/Latino; 3 Hispanic/Latino), 8 international. Average age 29. 259 applicants, 22% accepted, 38 enrolled. In 2011, 26 master's awarded. *Degree requirements:* For master's, thesis, practicum. *Entrance requirements:* For master's, GRE. Additional exam requirements/recommendations for international students: Required—TOEFL (minimum score 500 paper-based; 173 computer-based; 61 iBT), IELTS (minimum score 6). *Application deadline:* For fall admission, 12/1 for domestic students, 11/1 for international students. Application fee: $75. Electronic applications accepted. *Financial support:* In 2011–12, 1 student received support, including 5 research assistantships with full tuition reimbursements available (averaging $35,600 per year), 7 teaching assistantships with full tuition reimbursements available (averaging $17,800 per year); tuition waivers also available. Financial award application deadline: 6/30; financial award applicants required to submit FAFSA. *Faculty research:* AIDS and STDs, international health, reproductive health, tuberculosis, infectious disease. *Unit head:* Dr. King K. Holmes, Chair, 206-744-8493, Fax: 206-744-3694. *Application contact:* Katie Wakefield, Program Coordinator, 206-897-1804, Fax: 206-744-3694, E-mail: katiew74@u.washington.edu. Web site: http://depts.washington.edu/deptgh.

Yale University, School of Medicine, Yale School of Public Health, New Haven, CT 06520. Offers applied biostatistics and epidemiology (APMPH); biostatistics (MPH, MS, PhD), including global health (MPH); chronic disease epidemiology (MPH, PhD), including global health (MPH); environmental health sciences (MPH, PhD), including global health (MPH); epidemiology of microbial diseases (MPH, PhD), including global health (MPH); global health (APMPH); health management (MPH), including global health; health policy (MPH), including global health; health policy and administration (APMPH, PhD); occupational and environmental medicine (APMPH); preventive medicine (APMPH); social and behavioral sciences (APMPH, MPH), including global health (MPH); JD/MPH; M Div/MPH; MBA/MPH; MD/MPH; MEM/MPH; MFS/MPH; MM Sc/MPH; MPH/MA; MSN/MPH. MS and PhD offered through the Graduate School. *Accreditation:* CEPH. Part-time programs available. Terminal master's awarded for partial completion of doctoral program. *Degree requirements:* For master's, thesis, summer internship; for doctorate, comprehensive exam, thesis/dissertation, residency. *Entrance requirements:* For master's, GMAT, GRE, or MCAT, two years of undergraduate coursework in math and science; for doctorate, GRE General Test. Additional exam requirements/recommendations for international students: Required—TOEFL (minimum score 100 iBT). Electronic applications accepted. *Expenses:* Contact institution. *Faculty research:* Genetic and emerging infections epidemiology, virology, cost/quality, vector biology, quantitative methods, aging, asthma, cancer.

Maternal and Child Health

Bank Street College of Education, Graduate School, Program in Child Life, New York, NY 10025. Offers MS. *Students:* 22 full-time (all women), 5 part-time (all women); includes 4 minority (1 Black or African American, non-Hispanic/Latino; 1 Asian, non-Hispanic/Latino; 2 Two or more races, non-Hispanic/Latino). Average age 25. 32 applicants, 53% accepted, 11 enrolled. In 2011, 13 master's awarded. *Degree requirements:* For master's, thesis. *Entrance requirements:* For master's, interview, essays, 100 hours of volunteer experience in a child life setting. Additional exam requirements/recommendations for international students: Required—TOEFL (minimum score 600 paper-based; 250 computer-based; 100 iBT), IELTS (minimum score 7). *Application deadline:* For fall admission, 2/15 priority date for domestic students, 2/15 for international students; for spring admission, 11/1 priority date for domestic students, 11/1 for international students. Applications are processed on a rolling basis. Application fee: $65. *Expenses: Required fees:* $1240 per credit. $100 per term. One-time fee: $250 part-time. *Financial support:* Career-related internships or fieldwork, Federal Work-Study, scholarships/grants, and unspecified assistantships available. Support available to part-time students. Financial award application deadline: 4/15; financial award applicants required to submit FAFSA. *Faculty research:* Therapeutic play in child life setting, child advocacy, psychosocial and educational intervention with care of sick children. *Unit head:* Troy Pinkney-Ragsdale, Director, 212-875-4473, Fax: 212-875-4753, E-mail: tpinkneyragsdale@bankstreet.edu. *Application contact:* Seena Berg, Associate Director of Graduate Admissions, 212-875-4402, Fax: 212-875-4678, E-mail: sberg@bankstreet.edu. Web site: http://bankstreet.edu/graduate-school/academics/programs/child-life/.

Bank Street College of Education, Graduate School, Program in Infant and Family Development and Early Intervention, New York, NY 10025. Offers infant and family development (MS Ed); infant and family early childhood special and general education (MS Ed); infant and family/early childhood special education (Ed M). *Students:* 15 full-time (14 women), 19 part-time (18 women); includes 13 minority (6 Black or African American, non-Hispanic/Latino; 1 Asian, non-Hispanic/Latino; 3 Hispanic/Latino; 3 Two or more races, non-Hispanic/Latino), 1 international. Average age 28. 31 applicants, 74% accepted, 15 enrolled. In 2011, 15 master's awarded. *Degree requirements:* For master's, thesis. *Entrance requirements:* For master's, interview, essays. Additional exam requirements/recommendations for international students: Required—TOEFL (minimum score 600 paper-based; 250 computer-based; 100 iBT), IELTS (minimum score 7). *Application deadline:* For fall admission, 2/15 priority date for domestic students, 2/15 for international students; for spring admission, 11/1 priority date for domestic students, 11/1 for international students. Applications are processed on a rolling basis. Application fee: $65. Electronic applications accepted. *Expenses: Required fees:* $1240 per credit. $100 per term. One-time fee: $250 part-time. *Financial support:* Career-related internships or fieldwork, Federal Work-Study, scholarships/grants, and unspecified assistantships available. Support available to part-time students. Financial award application deadline: 4/15; financial award applicants required to submit FAFSA. *Faculty research:* Early intervention, early attachment practice in infant and toddler childcare, parenting skills in adolescents. *Unit head:* Dr. Virginia Casper, Director, 212-875-4703, Fax: 212-875-4753, E-mail: vcasper@bankstreet.edu. *Application contact:* Ann Morgan, Director of Graduate Admissions, 212-875-4403, Fax: 212-875-4678, E-mail: amorgan@bankstreet.edu. Web site: http://bankstreet.edu/graduate-school/academics/programs/infant-and-family-development-programs-overview/.

Boston University, School of Public Health, Maternal and Child Health Department, Boston, MA 02118. Offers maternal and child health (MPH, Dr PH). Part-time and evening/weekend programs available. *Students:* 60 full-time (55 women), 28 part-time (all women); includes 16 minority (4 Black or African American, non-Hispanic/Latino; 4 Asian, non-Hispanic/Latino; 3 Hispanic/Latino; 5 Two or more races, non-Hispanic/Latino), 8 international. Average age 27. 215 applicants, 52% accepted, 37 enrolled. In 2011, 28 master's, 1 doctorate awarded. *Degree requirements:* For doctorate, thesis/dissertation. *Entrance requirements:* For master's, GRE, DAT, MCAT, LSAT, or GMAT; for doctorate, GRE, GMAT. Additional exam requirements/recommendations for international students: Required—TOEFL (minimum score 600 paper-based; 250 computer-based; 100 iBT) or IELTS (minimum score 6). *Application deadline:* For fall admission, 2/1 priority date for domestic students, 2/1 for international students; for spring admission, 10/15 priority date for domestic students, 10/15 for international students. Applications are processed on a rolling basis. Application fee: $115. Electronic applications accepted. *Expenses: Tuition:* Full-time $40,848; part-time $1276 per credit hour. *Required fees:* $572; $286 per semester. *Financial support:* In 2011–12, 10 fellowships were awarded; career-related internships or fieldwork, Federal Work-Study, institutionally sponsored loans, scholarships/grants, traineeships, and tuition waivers (partial) also available. Financial award application deadline: 3/1; financial award applicants required to submit FAFSA. *Unit head:* Dr. Deborah Bowen, Chair, Community Health Sciences, 617-638-5205, E-mail: askmch@bu.edu. *Application contact:* LePhan Quan, Associate Director of Admissions, 617-638-4640, Fax: 617-638-5299, E-mail: asksph@bu.edu. Web site: http://sph.bu.edu/mch.

Columbia University, Columbia University Mailman School of Public Health, Department of Population and Family Health, New York, NY 10032. Offers MPH. *Accreditation:* CEPH. Part-time programs available. *Students:* 101 full-time (94 women), 35 part-time (34 women); includes 42 minority (9 Black or African American, non-Hispanic/Latino; 16 Asian, non-Hispanic/Latino; 13 Hispanic/Latino; 1 Native Hawaiian or other Pacific Islander, non-Hispanic/Latino; 3 Two or more races, non-Hispanic/Latino), 14 international. Average age 27. 222 applicants, 70% accepted, 68 enrolled. In 2011, 73 master's awarded. *Entrance requirements:* For master's, GRE General Test. Additional exam requirements/recommendations for international students: Required—TOEFL (minimum score 600 paper-based; 250 computer-based; 100 iBT). *Application deadline:* For fall admission, 1/5 for domestic students. Application fee: $60. *Financial support:* Research assistantships, career-related internships or fieldwork, and Federal Work-Study available. Financial award application deadline: 2/1; financial award applicants required to submit FAFSA. *Faculty research:* Child and adolescent health, global health systems, health and human rights, humanitarian disasters, sexual and reproductive health. *Unit head:* Dr. John Santelli, Chairperson, 212-304-5200. *Application contact:* Dr. Joseph Korevec, Director of Admissions and Financial Aid, 212-305-8698, Fax: 212-342-1861, E-mail: ph-admit@columbia.edu. Web site: http://www.mailman.hs.columbia.edu/popfam/index.html.

East Carolina University, Graduate School, Thomas Harriot College of Arts and Sciences, Department of Psychology, Program in Health Psychology, Greenville, NC 27858-4353. Offers clinical health psychology (PhD); occupational health psychology (PhD); pediatric school psychology (PhD). *Entrance requirements:* For doctorate, GRE. *Expenses:* Tuition: state resident: full-time $3557; part-time $444.63 per semester hour. Tuition, nonresident: full-time $14,351; part-time $1793.88 per semester hour. *Required*

fees: $2016; $252 per semester hour. Part-time tuition and fees vary according to course load, campus/location and program. *Financial support:* Fellowships, research assistantships, and teaching assistantships available. *Unit head:* Dr. Kathleen Row, Chair, 252-328-6492, Fax: 252-328-6283, E-mail: rowk@ecu.edu. Web site: http://www.ecu.edu/psyc/Health-Psychology-Doctoral-Program.cfm.

Future Generations Graduate School, Program in Applied Community Change and Conservation, Franklin, WV 26807. Offers MA.

Instituto Tecnologico de Santo Domingo, Graduate School, Area of Health Sciences, Santo Domingo, Dominican Republic. Offers bioethics (M Bioethics); clinical bioethics (Certificate); clinical nutrition (Certificate); comprehensive health and the adolescent (Certificate); comrehensive adloescent health (MS); health and social security (M Mgmt).

Oakland University, Graduate Study and Lifelong Learning, School of Health Sciences, Program in Physical Therapy, Rochester, MI 48309-4401. Offers neurological rehabilitation (Certificate); orthopedic manual physical therapy (Certificate); orthopedic physical therapy (Certificate); pediatric rehabilitation (Certificate); physical therapy (MSPT, DPT, Dr Sc PT); teaching and learning for rehabilitation professionals (Certificate). *Accreditation:* APTA. *Degree requirements:* For master's, thesis (for some programs). *Entrance requirements:* For master's, acceptance in the 2-year preparatory post-baccalaureate program, minimum GPA of 3.0; for doctorate, GRE General Test. Additional exam requirements/recommendations for international students: Required—TOEFL (minimum score 550 paper-based; 213 computer-based). *Expenses:* Contact institution.

Syracuse University, Falk College of Sport and Human Dynamics, Program in Child and Family Health in the Global Community, Syracuse, NY 13244. Offers MS. Part-time programs available. *Students:* 7 full-time (6 women), 3 part-time (all women); includes 2 minority (1 Black or African American, non-Hispanic/Latino; 1 Asian, non-Hispanic/Latino), 1 international. Average age 28. 14 applicants, 79% accepted, 10 enrolled. *Entrance requirements:* For master's, GRE. Additional exam requirements/recommendations for international students: Required—TOEFL (minimum score 100 iBT). *Application deadline:* For fall admission, 3/15 priority date for domestic students, 3/15 for international students. Application fee: $75. Electronic applications accepted. *Expenses: Tuition:* Part-time $1206 per credit. *Financial support:* Fellowships with full tuition reimbursements, research assistantships with partial tuition reimbursements, and teaching assistantships with partial tuition reimbursements available. Financial award application deadline: 1/15. *Unit head:* Dr. Diane Lyden Murphy, Dean, 315-443-5582, Fax: 315-443-2562. *Application contact:* Felecia Otero, Director, College Relations, 315-443-5555, Fax: 315-443-2562, E-mail: falk@syr.edu. Web site: http://humanecology.syr.edu/.

Troy University, Graduate School, College of Health and Human Services, Program in Nursing, Troy, AL 36082. Offers adult health (MSN); clinical nurse specialist adult health (DNP); clinical nurse specialist maternal infant (DNP); family nurse practitioner (MSN, DNP, PMC); informatics specialist (MSN); maternal infant (MSN). *Accreditation:* NLN. Part-time and evening/weekend programs available. *Faculty:* 11 full-time (10 women), 7 part-time/adjunct (4 women). *Students:* 58 full-time (43 women), 181 part-time (165 women); includes 91 minority (76 Black or African American, non-Hispanic/Latino; 8 American Indian or Alaska Native, non-Hispanic/Latino; 1 Asian, non-Hispanic/Latino; 3 Hispanic/Latino; 1 Native Hawaiian or other Pacific Islander, non-Hispanic/Latino; 2 Two or more races, non-Hispanic/Latino). Average age 38. 144 applicants, 63% accepted, 73 enrolled. In 2011, 35 master's, 8 doctorates awarded. *Degree requirements:* For master's, comprehensive exam, minimum GPA of 3.0, candidacy; for doctorate, minimum GPA of 3.0, submission of approved comprehensive e-portfolio, completion of residency synthesis project, minimum of 1000 hours of clinical practice, score of 80% or better on qualifying exam. *Entrance requirements:* For master's, MAT (minimum score 396) or GRE (minimum score 850), minimum GPA of 3.0, BSN, current RN licensure; 2 letters of reference; for doctorate, GRE (minimum score of 850), BSN or MSN, minimum GPA of 3.0, 2 letters of reference, current RN licensure, essay. Additional exam requirements/recommendations for international students: Required—TOEFL (minimum score 523 paper-based; 193 computer-based; 70 iBT), IELTS (minimum score 6), or ACT COMPASS ESL (minimum listening, reading, and grammar score 270). *Application deadline:* Applications are processed on a rolling basis. Application fee: $50. Electronic applications accepted. *Expenses:* Tuition, state resident: full-time $6960; part-time $290 per credit hour. Tuition, nonresident: full-time $13,920; part-time $580 per credit hour. *Required fees:* $386 per term. *Financial support:* Available to part-time students. Applicants required to submit FAFSA. *Unit head:* Dr. Bernita K. Hamilton, Director, School of Nursing, 334-670-3428, Fax: 334-670-3743, E-mail: bernitah@troy.edu. *Application contact:* Brenda K. Campbell, Director of Graduate Admissions, 334-670-3178, Fax: 334-670-3733, E-mail: bcamp@troy.edu.

Tulane University, School of Public Health and Tropical Medicine, Department of Community Health Sciences, Program in Maternal and Child Health, New Orleans, LA 70118-5669. Offers MPH, Dr PH, MSW/MPH. *Accreditation:* CEPH (one or more programs are accredited). *Degree requirements:* For doctorate, comprehensive exam, thesis/dissertation. *Entrance requirements:* For master's and doctorate, GRE General Test. Additional exam requirements/recommendations for international students: Required—TOEFL.

University of California, Davis, Graduate Studies, Program in Maternal and Child Nutrition, Davis, CA 95616. Offers MAS. *Degree requirements:* For master's, comprehensive exam. *Entrance requirements:* Additional exam requirements/recommendations for international students: Required—TOEFL (minimum score 550 paper-based; 213 computer-based).

University of Maryland, College Park, Academic Affairs, School of Public Health, Department of Family Science, College Park, MD 20742. Offers family studies (PhD); marriage and family therapy (MS); maternal and child health (PhD). *Accreditation:* AAMFT/COAMFTE. Part-time and evening/weekend programs available. *Faculty:* 20 full-time (17 women), 15 part-time/adjunct (14 women). *Students:* 45 full-time (37 women), 4 part-time (3 women); includes 17 minority (11 Black or African American, non-Hispanic/Latino; 3 Asian, non-Hispanic/Latino; 3 Hispanic/Latino), 5 international. 129 applicants, 12% accepted, 12 enrolled. In 2011, 9 master's, 6 doctorates awarded. *Degree requirements:* For master's, thesis or alternative; for doctorate, comprehensive exam, thesis/dissertation, oral defense. *Entrance requirements:* For master's, GRE General Test, minimum GPA of 3.0, 3 letters of recommendation; for doctorate, GRE General Test, minimum GPA of 3.0, 3 letters of recommendation, research sample. *Application deadline:* For fall admission, 12/15 for domestic and international students. Applications are processed on a rolling basis. Application fee: $75. Electronic applications accepted. *Expenses:* Tuition, state resident: part-time $525 per credit hour. Tuition, nonresident: part-time $1131 per credit hour. *Required fees:* $386.31 per term. Tuition and fees vary according to program. *Financial support:* In 2011–12, 2 fellowships with full tuition reimbursements (averaging $20,000 per year), 1 research assistantship (averaging $17,125 per year), 30 teaching assistantships (averaging $16,061 per year) were awarded; career-related internships or fieldwork, Federal Work-Study, and scholarships/grants also available. Support available to part-time students. Financial award applicants required to submit FAFSA. *Faculty research:* Family life quality, interracial couples, child support, homeless families, family and child well-being. *Total annual research expenditures:* $1.2 million. *Unit head:* Elaine Anderson, Chair, 301-405-4009, Fax: 301-314-9161, E-mail: eanders@umd.edu. *Application contact:* Dr. Charles A. Caramello, Dean of Graduate School, 301-405-0358, Fax: 301-314-9305. Web site: http://www.sph.umd.edu/fmsc/.

University of Minnesota, Twin Cities Campus, School of Public Health, Major in Maternal and Child Health, Minneapolis, MN 55455-0213. Offers MPH. *Accreditation:* CEPH. Part-time programs available. *Degree requirements:* For master's, fieldwork, project. *Entrance requirements:* For master's, GRE General Test, 1 year of relevant experience. Additional exam requirements/recommendations for international students: Required—TOEFL. Electronic applications accepted. *Expenses:* Contact institution. *Faculty research:* Reproductive and perinatal health, family planning, child adolescent and family health, risk reduction and resiliency, child and family adaptation to chronic health conditions.

University of Mississippi Medical Center, School of Graduate Studies in the Health Sciences, Department of Maternal-Fetal Medicine, Jackson, MS 39216-4505. Offers MS. *Degree requirements:* For master's, thesis. *Entrance requirements:* For master's, status as obstetrician-gynecologist in the Department of Obstetrics and Gynecology's Maternal-Fetal Medicine Fellowship Program.

The University of North Carolina at Chapel Hill, Graduate School, School of Public Health, Department of Maternal and Child Health, Chapel Hill, NC 27599. Offers MPH, MSPH, Dr PH, PhD, MD/MSPH, MPH/MSW, MSPH/M Ed, MSPH/MSW. *Accreditation:* CEPH (one or more programs are accredited). *Degree requirements:* For master's, comprehensive exam, major paper; for doctorate, comprehensive exam, thesis/dissertation. *Entrance requirements:* For master's, GRE General Test or MCAT, minimum GPA of 3.0, paid MHCH-related work experience (preferred); for doctorate, GRE General Test, minimum GPA of 3.0, paid MHCH-related work experience (preferred). Additional exam requirements/recommendations for international students: Required—TOEFL. Electronic applications accepted. *Faculty research:* Women's health, prenatal health, family planning, program evaluation, child health policy and priorities.

University of Puerto Rico, Medical Sciences Campus, Graduate School of Public Health, Department of Human Development, Program in Maternal and Child Health, San Juan, PR 00936-5067. Offers MPH. Part-time and evening/weekend programs available. *Entrance requirements:* For master's, GRE, previous course work in algebra.

University of Washington, Graduate School, School of Public Health, Department of Epidemiology, Seattle, WA 98195. Offers clinical research (MS); epidemiology (MPH, MS, PhD); global health (MPH); maternal/child health (MPH); nutritional sciences (MPH, MS, PhD); public health genetics (MPH, MS, PhD), including genetic epidemiology (MS), public health genetics (MPH, PhD); MPH/JD; MPH/MPA; MS/MPA. *Accreditation:* CEPH (one or more programs are accredited). *Faculty:* 62 full-time (35 women), 45 part-time/adjunct (22 women). *Students:* 135 full-time (93 women), 37 part-time (23 women); includes 37 minority (6 Black or African American, non-Hispanic/Latino; 1 American Indian or Alaska Native, non-Hispanic/Latino; 23 Asian, non-Hispanic/Latino; 7 Hispanic/Latino), 17 international. Average age 32. 291 applicants, 35% accepted, 58 enrolled. In 2011, 45 master's, 16 doctorates awarded. *Degree requirements:* For master's, comprehensive exam (for some programs), thesis; for doctorate, comprehensive exam, thesis/dissertation. *Entrance requirements:* For master's, GRE General Test (except for those holding PhD, MD, DDS, DVM, DO or equivalent from U.S. schools); for doctorate, GRE. Additional exam requirements/recommendations for international students: Required—TOEFL (minimum score 580 paper-based; 237 computer-based; 92 iBT) or IELTS (minimum score 7). *Application deadline:* For fall admission, 12/1 for domestic students, 11/1 for international students. Application fee: $75. Electronic applications accepted. *Expenses:* Contact institution. *Financial support:* In 2011–12, 152 students received support, including 75 fellowships with partial tuition reimbursements available, 49 research assistantships with partial tuition reimbursements available, 4 teaching assistantships with partial tuition reimbursements available; career-related internships or fieldwork, Federal Work-Study, traineeships, health care benefits, and unspecified assistantships also available. Support available to part-time students. Financial award applicants required to submit FAFSA. *Faculty research:* Chronic disease, health disparities and social determinants of health, aging and neuroepidemiology, maternal and child health, molecular and genetic epidemiology. *Unit head:* Dr. Scott Davis, Chair, 206-543-1065, Fax: 206-543-8525. *Application contact:* Kate O'Brien, Student Services Manager, 206-543-1065, Fax: 206-543-8525, E-mail: epi@u.washington.edu. Web site: http://depts.washington.edu/epidem/.

University of Washington, Graduate School, School of Public Health, Department of Health Services, Seattle, WA 98195. Offers bioinformatics (PhD); cancer prevention and control (PhD); clinical research (MS); community-oriented public health practice (MPH); economics or finance (PhD); evaluation sciences (PhD); health behavior and health promotion (PhD); health policy research (PhD); health services (MS, PhD); health services administration (EMHA, MHA); health systems policy (MPH); maternal and child health (MPH, PhD); occupational health (PhD); population health and social determinants (PhD); social and behavioral sciences (MPH); sociology and demography (PhD); JD/MHA; MHA/MBA; MHA/MD; MHA/MPA; MPH/JD; MPH/MD; MPH/MN; MPH/MPA; MPH/MS; MPH/MSD; MPH/MSW; MPH/PhD. Part-time and evening/weekend programs available. Postbaccalaureate distance learning degree programs offered (minimal on-campus study). *Faculty:* 40 full-time (23 women), 62 part-time/adjunct (25 women). *Students:* 98 full-time (78 women), 86 part-time (64 women); includes 49 minority (7 Black or African American, non-Hispanic/Latino; 3 American Indian or Alaska Native, non-Hispanic/Latino; 28 Asian, non-Hispanic/Latino; 11 Hispanic/Latino), 3 international. Average age 32. 374 applicants, 49% accepted, 104 enrolled. In 2011, 43 master's, 5 doctorates awarded. Terminal master's awarded for partial completion of doctoral program. *Degree requirements:* For master's, thesis (for some programs), practicum (MPH); for doctorate, comprehensive exam, thesis/dissertation. *Entrance requirements:* For master's and doctorate, GRE General Test, minimum GPA of 3.0. Additional exam requirements/recommendations for international students: Required—TOEFL (minimum score 580 paper-based; 237 computer-based; 92 iBT), IELTS (minimum score 7). *Application deadline:* For fall admission, 1/1 for domestic students, 11/1 for international students. Application fee: 75 Albanian leks. Electronic applications accepted. *Financial support:* In 2011–12, 47 students received support, including 10 fellowships with full and partial tuition reimbursements available (averaging $22,000 per year), 10 research assistantships with full and partial tuition reimbursements available (averaging $18,700 per year), 3 teaching assistantships with full and partial tuition reimbursements available (averaging $4,575 per year); institutionally sponsored loans, traineeships, and health care benefits also available. Financial award application deadline: 2/28; financial award applicants required to submit FAFSA. *Faculty research:* Public health practice, health promotion and disease prevention, maternal and child health, organizational behavior and culture, health policy. *Unit head:* Dr. Larry Kessler, Chair, 206-543-2930. *Application contact:* Kitty A. Andert, MPH/MS/PhD Programs Manager, 206-616-2926, Fax: 206-543-3964, E-mail: kitander@u.washington.edu. Web site: http://depts.washington.edu/hserv/.

HARVARD UNIVERSITY
School of Public Health

HARVARD
SCHOOL OF PUBLIC HEALTH

Programs of Study

The Harvard School of Public Health (HSPH) offers programs leading to the graduate degrees of Master of Public Health (M.P.H.), Doctor of Public Health (D.P.H.), Master of Science in a specified field (S.M. in that field), and Doctor of Science in a specified field (S.D. in that field). Doctor of Philosophy (Ph.D.) degrees are offered in specific fields of study through the Graduate School of Arts and Sciences. Programs are offered in biostatistics; environmental health; epidemiology; genetics and complex diseases; global health and population; health policy and management; immunology and infectious diseases; nutrition; and society, human development, and health. Some programs are designed for physicians, lawyers, managers, and other health-care professionals; some for college graduates who wish to train for health careers; and others for individuals who hold graduate degrees in medicine, law, business, government, education, and other fields who wish to apply their special skills to public health problems. Special programs include the Master of Science in maternal and child health nursing, administered jointly by HSPH and Simmons College; the combined M.D./M.P.H. program, offered in conjunction with medical schools; and the J.D./M.P.H. joint-degree program offered by HSPH and Harvard Law School. The School offers residency training leading to certification by the American Board of Preventive Medicine in occupational medicine.

Research Facilities

The main buildings of the School are the Sebastian S. Kresge Educational Facilities Building at 677 Huntington Avenue, the François-Xavier Bagnoud Building at 651 Huntington Avenue, and the Health Sciences Laboratories at 665 Huntington Avenue. The School maintains well-equipped research laboratories containing sophisticated instrumentation and supporting animal facilities. Computing and data processing resources are also available to students through the Instructional Computing Facility. The Francis A. Countway Library serves the library needs of the School. It holds more than 630,000 volumes, subscribes to 3,500 current journal titles, and houses over 10,000 noncurrent biomedical journal titles in addition to its extensive collection of historical materials, making it the largest library in the country serving a medical and health-related school.

Financial Aid

Financial aid at the School of Public Health can come from a variety of sources. Some departments have training grants that offer students full tuition plus a stipend. Through need-based and merit-based programs at the School and University levels, other students are offered grants that range from half to full tuition. To supplement other aid, many students borrow through one or more of the federal educational loan programs and work at part-time jobs at Harvard and in the community.

Cost of Study

Master's program students are assessed tuition at $992 per credit. Students in a one-year master's program are required to take a minimum of 42.5 credits at $42,160, while students in multiple-year master's programs typically take 40 credits their first year at $37,600. Doctoral students are assessed a flat tuition rate. The full-time rate for 2012–13 for students in their first or second year is $37,600. Health insurance, health services, and registration fees are required, and total costs are $3,348. Books and supplies cost approximately $1,384 in 2012–13.

Living and Housing Costs

For the academic year 2012–13, it is estimated that a single student needs a minimum of $18,216 for housing and living costs: $10,710 for rent and utilities and $7,506 for other expenses. Limited housing is available in the Shattuck International House, with preference given to international students. Most students arrange for housing in the adjacent communities.

Student Group

There were 1,182 graduate students (718 women and 464 men) enrolled in 2011–12. Sixty-one nations were represented.

Student Outcomes

Graduates of the Harvard School of Public Health find employment in a variety of settings. It depends in part upon their previous experience and in part upon department and degree programs from which they graduate. Recent graduates have found positions in research institutes, with pharmaceutical companies and governmental and nongovernmental agencies, within the health-care industry, and as faculty members of universities.

Location

Boston is a heterogeneous metropolis rich in history and charm. Athletic, cultural, and recreational activities are abundant. The School is within walking distance of museums, colleges and universities, waterways, and parks.

The University and The School

Harvard College was founded in 1636; until the establishment of professorships in medicine in 1782, it composed the whole of the institution now called Harvard University. In addition to the college, ten graduate schools are now part of the University.

Activity in professional education in the field of public health had been steadily increasing at Harvard University for more than two decades before the actual founding of the School in 1922. The primary mission of the School is to carry out teaching and research aimed at improving the health of population groups throughout the world. The School emphasizes not only the development and implementation of disease prevention and treatment programs but also the planning and management of systems involved in the delivery of health services in this country and abroad. The School cooperates with the Medical School in teaching and research and has close ties with other Harvard faculties. The School has more than 431 full-time and part-time faculty members and nine academic departments representing major biomedical and social disciplines.

Applying

HSPH participates in the Schools of Public Health Application Service (SOPHAS), which is an online, common application service designed to provide a more efficient application process. Students should visit the SOPHAS Web site at http://www.sophas.org for more specific information and for access to the application for admission. All applicants to the School are required to submit scores from the GRE (ETS school code: 3456); applicants are urged to take the test no later than November, since applications are not considered without the scores. Applicants may submit the DAT, GMAT, or MCAT, as appropriate to the applicant's background, in lieu of the GRE. Lawyers applying to the M.P.H. program may submit LSAT scores. Applicants with prior test scores may submit them with their application materials. In addition, applicants must persuade the Committee on Admissions and Degrees of their ability to meet academic standards and of their overall qualifications to undertake advanced study at a graduate level. Students should visit the School's Web site (http://www.hsph.harvard.edu/) for information concerning the deadline to apply for admission and to apply online.

As a matter of policy, law, and commitment, Harvard University does not discriminate against applicants or students in admission, educational policies, or scholarship and loan programs on the basis of race, religion, sex, sexual orientation, marital or parental status, veteran status, national origin, color, creed, handicap, or age. Members of minority groups are strongly encouraged to apply.

Correspondence and Information

Catalogs and applications:
Admissions Office
Harvard School of Public Health
158 Longwood Avenue
Boston, Massachusetts 02115-5810
United States
Phone: 617-432-1031
Fax: 617-432-7080
E-mail: admissions@hsph.harvard.edu
Web site: http://www.hsph.harvard.edu/

Counseling and program information:
Vincent W. James, Director
Kerri Noonan, Associate Director
Admissions Office
Harvard School of Public Health
158 Longwood Avenue
Boston, Massachusetts 02115-5810
United States
Phone: 617-432-1031
E-mail: admissions@hsph.harvard.edu

Harvard University

FACULTY CHAIRS AND DEPARTMENTAL ACTIVITIES

Biostatistics (617-432-1056, biostat_admissions@hsph.harvard.edu)
Chair: Victor De Gruttola, S.D. The program combines both theory and application of statistical science to analyze public health problems and further biomedical research. Students are prepared for academic and private-sector research careers. Faculty research spans both methodological developments on new statistical techniques and important subject-matter applications that lead to significant advances in the health sciences. Current departmental research on statistical and computing methods for observational studies and clinical trials includes survival analysis, missing-data problems, and causal inference. Other areas of investigation include environmental research; clinical aspects of the study of AIDS and cancer; quantitative problems in health-risk analysis, technology assessment, and clinical decision making; statistical methodology in psychiatric research and in genetic studies; and statistical genetics and computational biology.

Environmental Health (617-432-1270, envhlth@hsph.harvard.edu)
Chair: Douglas Dockery, S.D. The mission of the Department of Environmental Health is to advance the health of all people around the world through research and training in environmental health. The department emphasizes the role of air, water, the built environment, and the workplace as critical determinants of health. Faculty members in the department study the pathogenesis and prevention of environmentally produced illnesses and act as catalysts for scientifically based public health advances. Research approaches range from the molecular studies to policy evaluation. Teaching and research activities of the department are carried out through three concentrations: exposure, epidemiology, and risk; occupational health; and molecular and integrative physiological sciences.

Epidemiology (617-432-1050, epidept@hsph.harvard.edu)
Chair: Michelle Williams, Sc.D. Epidemiology, the study of the frequency, distribution, and determinants of disease in humans, is a fundamental science of public health. Epidemiologists use many approaches, but the ultimate aim of epidemiologic research is the prevention or effective control of human disease. Current research involves the role of viruses in the etiology of cancer; the connection between diet and risk of cancer, cardiovascular disease, and other major chronic diseases; the relationship between exposure to chemicals in the workplace and the development of cancer; the epidemiology of infectious disease; factors in early life predisposing individuals to chronic diseases; and the health effects of drugs and medical devices.

Genetics and Complex Diseases
(617-432-0054, dhasting@hsph.harvard.edu)
Chair: Gökhan Hotamisligil, M.D., Ph.D. The complex interplay of biological processes with environmental factors as they apply to chronic, multigenic, and multifactorial diseases is the emphasis of the Department of Genetics and Complex Diseases. Research programs in the department focus on molecular mechanisms of adaptive responses to environmental signals to elucidate the mechanisms underlying the intricate interaction between genetic determinants and their divergent responses to stress signals. Alterations in these integrated adaptive mechanisms have a major impact on the health of human populations. The diseases under study include nutritional and metabolic diseases (obesity, diabetes, and cardiovascular diseases), inflammatory bowel disease, cancer, and aging.

Global Health and Population
(617-432-1232, bheil@hsph.harvard.edu)
Chair: Wafaie Fawzi, M.B.B.S., D.P.H. The department seeks to improve global health through education, research, and service from a population-based perspective. Research interests span a wide spectrum of topics, including social and economic development, health policy, and demography; design and financing of health-care systems; women's health and children's health; and prevention and control of infectious and chronic diseases. The department has a special concern with questions of health equity and human rights, particularly in relation to health and population issues in developing countries.

Health Policy and Management (617-432-1090, hpm@hsph.harvard.edu)
Chair: Arnold Epstein, M.D. The department is mission oriented in its concern with improving the health-care delivery system and mitigating public health risks in the United States and abroad. It is dedicated to resolving major management and health policy problems through original research, advanced training, and dispute resolution. Research priorities are organized into seven broad areas: decision science, health care management, health economics. law and public health, quality and access, political policy, and public health policy.

Immunology and Infectious Diseases
(617-432-1023, asabarof@hsph.harvard.edu)
Chair: Dyann Wirth, Ph.D. The department focuses on the biological, immunological, epidemiological, and ecological aspects of viral, bacterial, protozoan, and helminthic diseases of animals and humans and the vectors that transmit some of these infectious agents. Emphasis is on research identifying basic pathogenic mechanisms that may lead to better diagnostic tools and the development of vaccines as well as the identification of new targets for antiviral and antiparasitic drugs.

Nutrition (617-432-1333, pbrown@hsph.harvard.edu)
Chair: Walter C. Willett, M.D., M.P.H., D.P.H. The department's mission is to improve human health through research aimed at understanding how diet influences health, the dissemination of new knowledge about nutrition to health professionals and the public, the development of nutritional strategies, and the education of researchers and practitioners. Department research ranges from molecular biology to human studies of cancer and heart disease, including the conduct of population-based intervention trials. Current research covers a wide range of topics, including large prospective studies of dietary factors in relation to heart disease, cancer, diabetes, and ophthalmologic disease; development of methods to assess nutritional status by analysis of body tissue; the interaction of nutritional factors with genetic determinants of disease; and the interaction of nutritional factors and infectious agents.

Society, Human Development, and Health
(617-432-1135, esolomon@hsph.harvard.edu)
Chair: Ichiro Kawachi, M.D., Ph.D. The mission of the Department of Society, Human Development, and Health is to improve health throughout the lifespan, including a special emphasis on children and adolescents. This mission is achieved through research to identify the social and behavioral determinants of health, development and evaluation of interventions and policies leading to the improvement of population health, and the preparation of professionals and researchers who fill leadership positions in advocacy and public service. The department's educational mission is to train both scholars and practitioners: scholars whose research illuminates basic social determinants of health and who identify and test innovative social policy and service interventions and practitioners who are skilled in designing, implementing, and evaluating health-enhancing interventions in action settings.

Division of Biological Sciences (617-432-4470, bph@hsph.harvard.edu)
Director: Marianne Wessling-Resnick, Ph.D. The Division of Biological Sciences is an umbrella organization encompassing the HSPH Departments of Environmental Health, Genetics and Complex Diseases, Immunology and Infectious Diseases, and Nutrition. In most of these departments, two doctoral degrees are offered: the Doctor of Philosophy (Ph.D.) and the Doctor of Science (S.D.). The Ph.D. programs generally center on laboratory-based investigation in the biological sciences, whereas the S.D. programs emphasize epidemiological analysis. The Ph.D. programs are administered by the Division of Biological Sciences.

Master of Public Health Program
(617-432-0090, roberta@hsph.harvard.edu)
Director: Murray Mittleman, M.D.C.M., M.P.H., D.P.H. The program is designed to provide both a general background and flexibility of specialization in public health. The seven areas of concentration are clinical effectiveness, global health, health and social behavior, health care management and policy, law and public health, occupational and environmental health, and quantitative methods.

UNIVERSITY AT BUFFALO, THE STATE UNIVERSITY OF NEW YORK

Program in Epidemiology

Programs of Study

The Department of Social and Preventive Medicine of the University at Buffalo (UB) offers the following programs of study:

Ph.D. in epidemiology: This degree provides the highest level of training in epidemiology with opportunities for research that include epidemiology of cancer, infectious diseases, osteoporosis, eye diseases, cardiovascular diseases, women's health, and environmental and occupational epidemiology. Included in this work is evaluation of factors such as nutrition, physical activity and physical fitness, stress, genetic factors, hormones, and hand hygiene in relation to risk of chronic and infectious diseases. Financial aid for Ph.D. in epidemiology students includes salary, tuition, and research support. Within the Ph.D. in epidemiology, there is a specialized track in cancer epidemiology, prevention, and control. This program provides interdisciplinary training with mentors and research experiences in both the Department of Social and Preventive Medicine in the School of Public Health and Health Professions and at Roswell Park Cancer Institute (a National Cancer Institute–designated comprehensive cancer center). The individualized curriculum provides training in cancer epidemiology, cancer biology, and pathology as well as interdisciplinary research opportunities.

M.S. in epidemiology: This degree program is designed for individuals who wish to pursue advanced training in epidemiological research and clinical epidemiology. It provides students with the skills and knowledge needed to design and conduct epidemiologic studies of the etiology and distribution of diseases, the control and prevention of diseases, and the promotion of health.

Master of Public Health (M.P.H.) with concentrations in epidemiology, environmental health, or health services administration: These degree programs provide training for public health practitioners. Training in the epidemiology concentration includes the study of epidemiologic research methods; biostatistics; survey methods; and understanding the biological, behavioral, and social determinants of disease and health outcomes. Training in environmental health focuses on an understanding of the sources and physiologic effects of physical, chemical, and biologic agents that persist in the environment. The program includes training in risk assessment and air pollution. The health services administration program trains students in program planning and evaluation, and health policy.

The School of Public Health and Health Professions is accredited by the Council on Education in Public Health. The University at Buffalo is accredited by the Middle States Commission on Higher Education.

There is close collaboration with Roswell Park Cancer Institute (New York State Department of Health's National Cancer Institute–designated comprehensive cancer center), Erie County and Niagara County Health Departments, local hospitals, other local health organizations, and other schools within the urban research university.

Research Facilities

The University at Buffalo library system, the largest in the State University of New York (SUNY) system, provides support for research and graduate studies through collections and digital resources in ten libraries, including the Health Sciences Library. The Health Sciences Library provides services to meet the information needs of the instructional, research, and clinical programs in the Schools of Dental Medicine, Medicine and Biomedical Sciences, Nursing, Pharmacy and Pharmaceutical Sciences, and Public Health and Health Professions. The Information Technology Service Center supports the research, academic, service, and administrative activities in the School of Public Health and Health Professions by providing a strong information technology infrastructure for the School's faculty, staff, and students. The Department of Social and Preventive Medicine includes facilities for research in epidemiology including a state-of-the-art biological specimen bank, facilities for biological specimen processing, other laboratory facilities, interview facilities, and computer labs.

Financial Aid

Financial aid is offered for Ph.D. students. Graduate student assistantships are competitive and awarded on the basis of merit. Assistantships provide a stipend of $20,000 per year plus full-tuition scholarship. In addition, employer-paid health care insurance is provided.

Students interested in the cancer epidemiology track may be eligible for a cancer predoctoral fellowship funded by an NCI R25T education grant. Fellows receive a stipend of $22,000 per year plus full tuition, as well as funds for other research-related activities (books, attendance at scientific meetings, memberships).

Students are also supported with research assistantships or research grants.

Cost of Study

Tuition for graduate programs for 2012–13 is $5616 (including fees) per semester for New York State residents and $9271 (including fees) per semester for non–New York State residents. Credit hour charges for part-time students (less than 12 credit hours per semester) are $390 per credit hour for New York State residents and $695 per credit hour for non–New York State residents. Tuition and fees are subject to change.

Living and Housing Costs

The University at Buffalo has four apartment complexes that house graduate students. Flickinger Court is a two-bedroom townhouse complex that houses only graduate and married students; it is off campus but is part of the University housing system. All its apartments are furnished with appliances and most have bedroom furniture. Creekside Village is an on-campus, two-bedroom townhouse complex that houses only graduate students. These apartments are fully furnished. Flint Village and South Lake Village are apartment complexes located on campus with fully furnished units. They house both graduate and undergraduate students in four-bedroom, two-bedroom, single, and studio apartments. Prospective students can visit http://www.student-affairs.buffalo.edu/housing for current, detailed information.

Student Group

The total enrollment of 28,860 at the University at Buffalo in 2011–12 included 9,757 graduate students. The student body included representatives from more than 100 countries.

Student Outcomes

Career opportunities in epidemiology and public health are remarkably diverse. Opportunities for graduates include work in academia, national and international health agencies, local and

University at Buffalo, The State University of New York

state health departments, pharmaceutical companies, health-care organizations, and nonprofit research institutions. Some graduates work in the delivery of public health services while others conduct research, all with the goal of improving public health.

Graduates from the Department of Social and Preventive Medicine academic programs hold leadership positions in national health agencies such as the National Institute of Child Health and Human Development, the National Cancer Institute, the National Institute for Occupational Safety and Health, the Centers for Disease Control and Prevention, and the Environmental Protection Agency. Some graduates have taken research, faculty, and administrative positions in the U.S. and around the world at institutions such as George Washington University, the University of Georgia, and McMaster University. Others work in research institutions like Roswell Park Cancer Institute, local and state health departments around the U.S., and for nonprofit organizations such as Doctors Without Borders and the American Cancer Society. Recent graduates have also taken positions as Presidential Management Fellows, Epidemic Intelligence Service officers with the Centers for Disease Control and Prevention, and postdoctoral fellows at the National Cancer Institute.

Location

University at Buffalo, the State University of New York, is located in the second-largest city in New York State. The city is conveniently located near outstanding boating, swimming, hiking, camping, and skiing areas. The cities of Toronto and Niagara Falls are just a short drive away. Also nearby is the world-famous Stratford (Canada) Shakespeare Festival.

The cultural attractions of Buffalo include the Albright-Knox Art Gallery, the Buffalo Philharmonic Orchestra, science and historical museums, several permanent professional theater companies, and numerous amateur theater groups. Buffalo also has several professional sports teams, including football, hockey, and minor-league Triple-A baseball.

The University

Founded in 1846, the University at Buffalo is a member of the Association of American Universities, the leading research universities in the United States and Canada. It is a research-intensive public university that spends more than $348.2 million annually on groundbreaking research relating to new cures, faster computers, smarter software, and other life improvements.

The University has a high percentage of international students, and is ranked second among the country's public research universities and seventeenth among American colleges in its percentage of international enrollment.

Among the university's most notable graduates are astronaut Ellen Schulman Baker; Wilson Greatbatch, inventor of the implantable battery-operated cardiac pacemaker; and CNN journalist Wolf Blitzer.

Applying

Applications should be submitted online by selecting the desired degree at http://sphhp.buffalo.edu.

Correspondence and Information

Dr. Carl Li, M.D., M.P.H.
Director of Graduate Studies
Department of Social and Preventive Medicine
University at Buffalo (SUNY)
270 Farber Hall
Buffalo,, New York 14214
United States
Phone: 716-829-5382
E-mail: carlli@buffalo.edu
Web site: http://sphhp.buffalo.edu/spm

Marcia Wopperer
Program Coordinator
Department of Social and Preventative Medicine
University at Buffalo (SUNY)
270 Farber Hall
Buffalo, New York 14214
United States
Phone: 716-829-5364
E-mail: mwoppere@buffalo.edu

THE FACULTY

The Department of Social and Preventive Medicine has a faculty with highly active research programs in diverse areas. Faculty focus on research including work on environmental epidemiology, genetic epidemiology, molecular epidemiology, and the epidemiology of cancer, women's health, eye diseases, and cardiovascular diseases. Faculty members have expertise in nutrition and physical activity, global health, and stress. For more information regarding faculty, please see http://sphhp.buffalo.edu/spm/research/index.php.

Squire Hall, on the South Campus of the University at Buffalo. Set in an urban environment, UB is an outstanding research institution. The region is characterized by a diverse population with a small town warmth and friendliness.

ACADEMIC AND PROFESSIONAL PROGRAMS IN THE MEDICAL PROFESSIONS AND SCIENCES

Section 25
Acupuncture and Oriental Medicine

This section contains a directory of institutions offering graduate work in acupuncture and oriental medicine. Additional information about programs listed in the directory but not augmented by an in-depth entry may be obtained by writing directly to the dean of a graduate school or chair of a department at the address given in the directory.

CONTENTS

Acupuncture and Oriental Medicine

Academy for Five Element Acupuncture, Graduate Program, Hallandale, FL 33009. Offers M Ac. *Accreditation:* ACAOM.

Academy of Chinese Culture and Health Sciences, Program in Traditional Chinese Medicine, Oakland, CA 94612. Offers MS. *Accreditation:* ACAOM. Part-time and evening/weekend programs available. *Degree requirements:* For master's, comprehensive exam, thesis. *Entrance requirements:* Additional exam requirements/recommendations for international students: Required—TOEFL (minimum score 500 paper-based; 173 computer-based). *Faculty research:* Herbs, acupuncture.

Academy of Oriental Medicine at Austin, Master of Acupuncture and Oriental Medicine Program, Austin, TX 78757. Offers MAcOM. *Accreditation:* ACAOM. *Faculty:* 10 full-time (3 women), 19 part-time/adjunct (11 women). *Students:* 149 full-time (109 women), 53 part-time (36 women); includes 43 minority (4 Black or African American, non-Hispanic/Latino; 21 Asian, non-Hispanic/Latino; 18 Hispanic/Latino). Average age 35. 43 applicants, 88% accepted, 32 enrolled. In 2011, 52 master's awarded. *Degree requirements:* For master's, comprehensive exam, clinical rotations (40.5 credits). *Entrance requirements:* For master's, BA or higher or minimum of 90 credits at baccalaureate level from regionally-accredited institution with 30 credits of general education coursework; minimum GPA of 2.5. Additional exam requirements/recommendations for international students: Required—TOEFL (minimum score 85 iBT). *Application deadline:* For fall admission, 7/19 priority date for domestic students; for winter admission, 11/1 priority date for domestic students; for spring admission, 5/15 priority date for domestic students. Applications are processed on a rolling basis. Application fee: $75. Electronic applications accepted. *Financial support:* Scholarships/grants available. Financial award applicants required to submit FAFSA. *Faculty research:* Acupuncture, Chinese herbal medicine, integrative medicine, pulse diagnosis. *Unit head:* Dr. William R. Morris, President, 512-454-1188, Fax: 512-454-7001, E-mail: info@aoma.edu. *Application contact:* Justine Meccio, Director of Admissions, 512-492-3017, Fax: 512-454-7001, E-mail: admissions@aoma.edu. Web site: https://aoma.edu/patients.

Acupuncture & Integrative Medicine College, Berkeley, Program in Oriental Medicine, Berkeley, CA 94704. Offers MS. *Accreditation:* ACAOM. Part-time and evening/weekend programs available. *Degree requirements:* For master's, comprehensive exam. *Entrance requirements:* For master's, interview, minimum GPA of 2.5, 60 semester units of course work at the baccalaureate level. Additional exam requirements/recommendations for international students: Required—TOEFL (minimum score 500 paper-based; 173 computer-based). *Faculty research:* Stimulus therapy, oxygen hemoglobin, acupuncture needling, classical Chinese medicine.

Acupuncture and Massage College, Program in Oriental Medicine, Miami, FL 33176. Offers MOM. *Accreditation:* ACAOM.

American College of Acupuncture and Oriental Medicine, Graduate Studies, Houston, TX 77063. Offers MAOM. *Accreditation:* ACAOM. Part-time programs available. *Entrance requirements:* For master's, 60 undergraduate credit hours. Additional exam requirements/recommendations for international students: Required—TOEFL.

American College of Traditional Chinese Medicine, Graduate Programs, San Francisco, CA 94107. Offers acupuncture and Oriental medicine (DAOM); dermatology (Certificate); shiatsu massage (Certificate); traditional Chinese medicine (MSTCM); tui na massage (Certificate). *Accreditation:* ACAOM. Part-time programs available. *Faculty:* 20 full-time (10 women), 58 part-time/adjunct (25 women). *Students:* 206 full-time (146 women), 84 part-time (69 women); includes 85 minority (3 Black or African American, non-Hispanic/Latino; 65 Asian, non-Hispanic/Latino; 17 Hispanic/Latino), 7 international. 60 applicants, 95% accepted, 40 enrolled. *Degree requirements:* For master's, one foreign language, comprehensive exam, internship; for doctorate, thesis/dissertation, clinical experience. *Entrance requirements:* For master's, minimum of 90 semester or 135 quarter units from an accredited institution, minimum GPA of 3.0, interview; for doctorate, MSTCM or equivalent, interview, state or national license. Additional exam requirements/recommendations for international students: Required—TOEFL (minimum score 550 paper-based; 213 computer-based; 79 iBT); Recommended—IELTS (minimum score 6.5). *Application deadline:* For fall admission, 9/1 for domestic and international students; for winter admission, 12/1 for domestic and international students; for spring admission, 3/1 for domestic and international students. Applications are processed on a rolling basis. Application fee: $100 ($150 for international students). *Expenses: Tuition:* Full-time $14,000; part-time $237 per contact hour. *Required fees:* $30 per quarter. *Financial support:* Teaching assistantships, Federal Work-Study, institutionally sponsored loans, and scholarships/grants available. Support available to part-time students. Financial award applicants required to submit FAFSA. *Unit head:* Lixin Huang, President, 415-282-7600 Ext. 12, Fax: 415-282-0856, E-mail: lixinhuang@actcm.edu. *Application contact:* Gina Rossi, Admissions Counselor, 415-282-7600 Ext. 14, Fax: 415-282-0856, E-mail: admissions@actcm.edu. Web site: http://www.actcm.edu/.

Arizona School of Acupuncture and Oriental Medicine, Graduate Programs, Tucson, AZ 85712. Offers M Ac, M Ac OM. *Accreditation:* ACAOM.

Atlantic Institute of Oriental Medicine, Graduate Program, Fort Lauderdale, FL 33301. Offers MS. *Accreditation:* ACAOM. Evening/weekend programs available. *Entrance requirements:* Additional exam requirements/recommendations for international students: Required—TOEFL (minimum score 500 paper-based).

Bastyr University, School of Acupuncture and Oriental Medicine, Kenmore, WA 98028-4966. Offers acupuncture (MS); acupuncture and Oriental medicine (MS, DAOM); Chinese herbal medicine (Certificate). *Accreditation:* ACAOM. Evening/weekend programs available. *Students:* 111 full-time (86 women), 23 part-time (17 women); includes 48 minority (3 Black or African American, non-Hispanic/Latino; 32 Asian, non-Hispanic/Latino; 2 Hispanic/Latino; 11 Two or more races, non-Hispanic/Latino), 20 international. Average age 32. In 2011, 45 master's, 2 doctorates, 2 other advanced degrees awarded. *Entrance requirements:* For master's, course work in biology, chemistry, intermediate algebra and psychology; for doctorate, MS in acupuncture or certificate and 10 years clinical experience. Additional exam requirements/recommendations for international students: Required—TOEFL (minimum score 550 paper-based; 213 computer-based; 79 iBT). *Application deadline:* For fall admission, 3/15 priority date for domestic students, 3/15 for international students. Applications are processed on a rolling basis. Application fee: $75. Electronic applications accepted. *Expenses: Tuition:* Full-time $27,653; part-time $6440 per quarter. *Required fees:* $75; $75. One-time fee: $375. Tuition and fees vary according to course load, degree level, program and student level. *Financial support:* In 2011–12, 57 students received support, including 14 teaching assistantships (averaging $2,000 per year); career-related internships or fieldwork, Federal Work-Study, and scholarships/grants also available. Support available to part-time students. Financial award application deadline: 4/15; financial award applicants required to submit FAFSA. *Faculty research:* Integrative oncology, acupuncture and chemotherapy-induced peripheral neuropathy (CIPN), traditional Chinese medicine and stroke rehabilitation, acupuncture and prevention and wellness, electroacupuncture. *Unit head:* Dr. Kyo Mitchell, Interim Associate Dean and Assistant Professor, 425-602-3151, Fax: 425-823-6222, E-mail: kmitchell@bastyr.edu. *Application contact:* Admissions Office, 425-602-3330, Fax: 425-602-3090, E-mail: admissions@bastyr.edu. Web site: http://www.bastyr.edu/academics/areas-study/acupuncture-oriental-medicine.

Canadian Memorial Chiropractic College, Certificate Programs, Toronto, ON M2H 3J1, Canada. Offers chiropractic clinical sciences (Certificate); chiropractic radiology (Certificate); chiropractic sports sciences (Certificate); clinical acupuncture (Certificate). *Degree requirements:* For Certificate, thesis. *Entrance requirements:* For degree, DC, board certification. *Faculty research:* Theories and concepts of chiropractic, sciences related to chiropractic, assessments of the efficacy and efficiency of chiropractic.

Colorado School of Traditional Chinese Medicine, Graduate Program, Denver, CO 80206-2127. Offers acupuncture (MS); traditional Chinese medicine (MS). *Accreditation:* ACAOM. Part-time programs available. *Faculty:* 52 part-time/adjunct (20 women). *Students:* 131 full-time (97 women), 9 part-time (6 women). Average age 33. 62 applicants, 100% accepted, 62 enrolled. In 2011, 25 master's awarded. *Entrance requirements:* For master's, 60 semester credits or 90 quarter credits from an accredited college. Additional exam requirements/recommendations for international students: Required—TOEFL (minimum score 500 paper-based; 173 computer-based; 61 iBT). *Application deadline:* For fall admission, 8/20 for domestic and international students; for winter admission, 12/24 for domestic and international students; for spring admission, 4/23 for domestic and international students. Applications are processed on a rolling basis. Application fee: $50. Part-time tuition and fees vary according to class time, course load and program. *Financial support:* Scholarships/grants available. Financial award applicants required to submit FAFSA. *Unit head:* Vladimir Dibrigida, Administrative Director, 303-329-6355 Ext. 11, Fax: 303-388-8165, E-mail: director@cstcm.edu. *Application contact:* Will Wallin, Registrar, 303-329-6355 Ext. 12, Fax: 303-388-8165, E-mail: registrar@cstcm.edu. Web site: http://www.cstcm.edu.

Dongguk University Los Angeles, Program in Oriental Medicine, Los Angeles, CA 90020. Offers MS. *Accreditation:* ACAOM. Part-time and evening/weekend programs available.

East West College of Natural Medicine, Graduate Programs, Sarasota, FL 34234. Offers MSOM. *Accreditation:* ACAOM.

Emperor's College of Traditional Oriental Medicine, Graduate Programs, Santa Monica, CA 90403. Offers MTOM, DAOM. *Accreditation:* ACAOM. Part-time and evening/weekend programs available. *Entrance requirements:* For master's, minimum 2 years of undergraduate course work, interview; for doctorate, CA acupuncture licensure. *Faculty research:* Menopause, dysmenorrhea.

Five Branches University: Graduate School of Traditional Chinese Medicine, Program in Traditional Chinese Medicine, Santa Cruz, CA 95062. Offers MTCM. *Accreditation:* ACAOM. *Degree requirements:* For master's, comprehensive exam. *Entrance requirements:* For master's, 6 units in anatomy and physiology, 9 units in basic sciences, minimum GPA of 2.5. Electronic applications accepted.

Florida College of Integrative Medicine, Graduate Program, Orlando, FL 32809. Offers MSOM. *Accreditation:* ACAOM. Evening/weekend programs available. *Entrance requirements:* For master's, minimum 60 semester hours of undergraduate coursework. Electronic applications accepted.

Institute of Clinical Acupuncture and Oriental Medicine, Program in Oriental Medicine, Honolulu, HI 96817. Offers MSOM. *Accreditation:* ACAOM.

Midwest College of Oriental Medicine, Graduate Programs, Racine, WI 53403-9747. Offers acupuncture (Certificate); oriental medicine (MSOM). *Accreditation:* ACAOM. Part-time and evening/weekend programs available. *Degree requirements:* For master's and Certificate, comprehensive exam, thesis. *Entrance requirements:* For master's and Certificate, 60 semester credit hours from accredited school, 2 letters of recommendation, interview. Additional exam requirements/recommendations for international students: Required—TOEFL. *Faculty research:* Pharmacology.

Midwest College of Oriental Medicine, Graduate Programs-Chicago, Chicago, IL 60613. Offers acupuncture (Certificate); oriental medicine (MSOM). *Accreditation:* ACAOM. Part-time and evening/weekend programs available. *Degree requirements:* For master's and Certificate, comprehensive exam, thesis. *Entrance requirements:* For master's and Certificate, 60 semester credit hours from accredited school, 2 letters of recommendation, interview. Additional exam requirements/recommendations for international students: Required—TOEFL.

National College of Natural Medicine, School of Classical Chinese Medicine, Portland, OR 97201. Offers M Ac, MSOM. *Accreditation:* ACAOM. Evening/weekend programs available. *Faculty:* 12 full-time (3 women), 15 part-time/adjunct (6 women). *Students:* 189. Average age 28. *Degree requirements:* For master's, thesis. *Entrance requirements:* Additional exam requirements/recommendations for international students: Recommended—TOEFL. *Application deadline:* For fall admission, 11/1 priority date for domestic students, 11/1 for international students; for winter admission, 2/1 priority date for domestic students, 2/1 for international students. Applications are processed on a rolling basis. Application fee: $75. *Expenses:* Contact institution. *Financial support:* Federal Work-Study and scholarships/grants available. Financial award application deadline: 4/30; financial award applicants required to submit FAFSA. *Faculty research:* Cases on herbs and acupuncture for asthma, diabetes, depression associated with menopause; Qi Gong to maintain weight loss. *Unit head:* Dr. Laurie Regan, Dean, 503-552-1775, Fax: 503-499-0027, E-mail: admissions@ncnm.edu. *Application contact:* Hang Nguyen, Admissions Coordinator, 503-552-1660, Fax: 503-499-0027, E-mail: admissions@ncmn.edu.

National University of Health Sciences, College of Professional Studies, Lombard, IL 60148-4583. Offers acupuncture (MSAC); chiropractic medicine (DC); naturopathic medicine (ND); Oriental medicine (MSOM). *Accreditation:* CCE. *Degree requirements:* For master's and doctorate, comprehensive exam, internship, community service. *Entrance requirements:* For master's, bachelor's degree, character references, undergraduate transcripts; for doctorate, bachelor's degree, character references, undergraduate transcripts, written essay. Additional exam requirements/recommendations for international students: Required—TOEFL (minimum score 550 paper-based; 79 iBT). Electronic applications accepted. *Faculty research:* Discipline/whole practice research (including practice-based research networks), mechanisms of action, clinical trials, and evidence-based practice of CAM therapies; educational research in CAM teaching institutions.

New England School of Acupuncture, Program in Acupuncture and Oriental Medicine, Newton, MA 02458. Offers acupuncture (M Ac); acupuncture and Oriental

medicine (MAOM). *Accreditation:* ACAOM (one or more programs are accredited). Part-time programs available. *Degree requirements:* For master's, comprehensive exam. *Entrance requirements:* For master's, previous course work in anatomy, biology, physiology, and psychology. Additional exam requirements/recommendations for international students: Required—TOEFL (minimum score 550 paper-based; 213 computer-based). *Faculty research:* Acupuncture and women's health, acupuncture and stroke rehabilitation, tai chi and cardiovascular health, tai chi and balance, cancer.

New York Chiropractic College, Acupuncture and Oriental Medicine Programs, Seneca Falls, NY 13148-0800. Offers acupuncture (MS); acupuncture and oriental medicine (MS). *Accreditation:* ACAOM. *Degree requirements:* For master's, clinical internship. *Entrance requirements:* For master's, interview, minimum GPA of 2.5, writing example, references. Additional exam requirements/recommendations for international students: Recommended—TOEFL (minimum score 550 paper-based; 213 computer-based). Electronic applications accepted. *Faculty research:* Chinese herbal medicine, traditional Chinese medicine, cancer, gait and posture, obesity.

New York College of Health Professions, Graduate School of Oriental Medicine, Syosset, NY 11791-4413. Offers acupuncture (MS); Oriental medicine (MS). *Accreditation:* ACAOM. Part-time programs available. *Degree requirements:* For master's, thesis. *Entrance requirements:* For master's, minimum GPA of 2.5, 60 semester credits in undergraduate course work. Additional exam requirements/recommendations for international students: Required—TOEFL. *Faculty research:* Breast cancer, diabetic neuropathy hemolysis.

New York College of Traditional Chinese Medicine, Graduate Programs, Mineola, NY 11501. Offers oriental medicine (MAOM). *Accreditation:* ACAOM.

Northwestern Health Sciences University, College of Acupuncture and Oriental Medicine, Bloomington, MN 55431-1599. Offers acupuncture (M Ac); oriental medicine (MOM). *Accreditation:* ACAOM. *Students:* 97 full-time (81 women), 18 part-time (17 women). Average age 33. In 2011, 26 master's awarded. *Entrance requirements:* For master's, 60 semester credits of course work with minimum GPA of 2.5. Additional exam requirements/recommendations for international students: Required—TOEFL (minimum score 540 paper-based; 207 computer-based; 76 iBT). *Application deadline:* For fall admission, 5/1 priority date for domestic students, 5/1 for international students; for winter admission, 9/1 priority date for domestic students, 9/1 for international students. Applications are processed on a rolling basis. Application fee: $50. Electronic applications accepted. *Financial support:* Career-related internships or fieldwork, Federal Work-Study, and scholarships/grants available. Support available to part-time students. *Unit head:* Mark McKenzie, Dean, 952-888-4777 Ext. 274, Fax: 952-889-1398, E-mail: mmckenzie@nwhealth.edu. *Application contact:* Kate DiAna, Director of Admissions, 952-888-4777 Ext. 273, Fax: 952-888-6713, E-mail: admit@nwhealth.edu. Web site: http://www.nwhealth.edu/acupuncture-oriental-medicine/.

Oregon College of Oriental Medicine, Graduate Program in Acupuncture and Oriental Medicine, Portland, OR 97216. Offers M Ac OM, MAcOM, DAOM. *Accreditation:* ACAOM. Part-time programs available. *Entrance requirements:* For master's, minimum 3 years of college; course work in chemistry, biology, and psychology; for doctorate, documentation of clinical practice, 3 years of clinical experience. Additional exam requirements/recommendations for international students: Required—TOEFL (minimum score 550 paper-based).

Pacific College of Oriental Medicine, Graduate Program, San Diego, CA 92108. Offers MSTOM, DAOM. *Accreditation:* ACAOM. Part-time and evening/weekend programs available. *Entrance requirements:* For master's, 2 letters of reference, interviews, minimum GPA of 3.0. *Faculty research:* PMS, acupuncture, herbs, Tai Ji Quan, sports medicine.

Pacific College of Oriental Medicine-Chicago, Graduate Program, Chicago, IL 60613. Offers MTOM. *Accreditation:* ACAOM. Part-time and evening/weekend programs available. *Entrance requirements:* For master's, 2 letters of reference, interview, minimum GPA of 3.0. *Faculty research:* AIDS, cancer, mental health, clinical counseling.

Pacific College of Oriental Medicine-New York, Graduate Program, New York, NY 10010. Offers MSTOM. *Accreditation:* ACAOM. Part-time and evening/weekend programs available. *Entrance requirements:* For master's, 2 letters of reference, interview, minimum GPA of 3.0. *Faculty research:* Energy medicine, acupuncture in the treatment of neurological disorders.

Samra University of Oriental Medicine, Program in Oriental Medicine, Los Angeles, CA 90015. Offers MS, DAOM. Part-time and evening/weekend programs available. *Degree requirements:* For master's, comprehensive exam. *Entrance requirements:* For master's, 60 semester (90 quarter) units with a "C" average in general education from an accredited college. *Faculty research:* Herbal therapy; alleviation of AIDS symptoms, cancer, colds, flu.

Seattle Institute of Oriental Medicine, Graduate Program, Seattle, WA 98115. Offers M Ac OM. *Accreditation:* ACAOM. *Degree requirements:* For master's, one foreign language, comprehensive exam. *Entrance requirements:* For master's, course work in biology, psychology, chemistry, anatomy, physiology; CPR/first aid certification; 3 years (90 semester credits) post secondary coursework.. Additional exam requirements/recommendations for international students: Recommended—TOEFL (minimum score 500 paper-based).

South Baylo University, Program in Oriental Medicine and Acupuncture, Anaheim, CA 92801-1701. Offers MS. *Accreditation:* ACAOM. Evening/weekend programs available. *Degree requirements:* For master's, 3 foreign languages, comprehensive exam. *Entrance requirements:* Additional exam requirements/recommendations for international students: Required—TOEFL (minimum score 500 paper-based; 173 computer-based). Electronic applications accepted. *Faculty research:* Effectiveness of acupuncture therapy.

Southern California University of Health Sciences, College of Acupuncture and Oriental Medicine, Whittier, CA 90609-1166. Offers MAOM. *Accreditation:* ACAOM. Part-time and evening/weekend programs available. *Faculty:* 14 full-time (6 women), 14 part-time/adjunct (3 women). *Students:* 2 full-time (1 woman), 154 part-time (91 women); includes 90 minority (4 Black or African American, non-Hispanic/Latino; 1 American Indian or Alaska Native, non-Hispanic/Latino; 66 Asian, non-Hispanic/Latino; 12 Hispanic/Latino; 7 Native Hawaiian or other Pacific Islander, non-Hispanic/Latino). Average age 42. 94 applicants, 48% accepted, 30 enrolled. In 2011, 31 master's awarded. *Entrance requirements:* For master's, 60 semester hours or 90 quarter credits of undergraduate course work, interview. Additional exam requirements/recommendations for international students: Required—TOEFL (minimum score 500 paper-based; 173 computer-based). *Application deadline:* Applications are processed on a rolling basis. Application fee: $50. Electronic applications accepted. *Financial support:* In 2011–12, 30 students received support. Federal Work-Study, scholarships/grants, and International Student Work Program available. Financial award applicants required to submit FAFSA. *Faculty research:* Hypertension, low back pain, smoking cessation, sports medicine. *Unit head:* Dr. Wen-Shuo Wu, Dean, 562-947-8755 Ext. 7028, E-mail: wen-shuowu@scuhs.edu. *Application contact:* Tracy Nieto, Assistant Director of Admissions, 562-902-3319, Fax: 562-902-3321, E-mail: tracynieto@scuhs.edu.

Southwest Acupuncture College, Program in Oriental Medicine, Albuquerque Campus, Albuquerque, NM 87109, Armenia. Offers MS. *Accreditation:* ACAOM. Part-time programs available. *Entrance requirements:* For master's, minimum 2 years of college general education. Additional exam requirements/recommendations for international students: Required—TOEFL (minimum score 500 paper-based; 173 computer-based). Electronic applications accepted.

Southwest Acupuncture College, Program in Oriental Medicine, Boulder Campus, Boulder, CO 80301. Offers MS. *Accreditation:* ACAOM. Part-time programs available. *Entrance requirements:* For master's, minimum 2 years of college general education.

Southwest Acupuncture College, Program in Oriental Medicine, Santa Fe Campus, Santa Fe, NM 87505. Offers MS. *Accreditation:* ACAOM. Part-time programs available. *Entrance requirements:* For master's, minimum 2 years of college general education. Additional exam requirements/recommendations for international students: Required—TOEFL (minimum score 500 paper-based; 173 computer-based). Electronic applications accepted.

Swedish Institute, College of Health Sciences, Graduate Program, New York, NY 10001-6700. Offers acupuncture (MS). *Accreditation:* ACAOM. Part-time and evening/weekend programs available. *Entrance requirements:* Additional exam requirements/recommendations for international students: Required—TOEFL (minimum score 72 iBT).

Tai Sophia Institute, Chinese Herb Certificate Program, Laurel, MD 20723. Offers Certificate. Part-time and evening/weekend programs available. *Entrance requirements:* Additional exam requirements/recommendations for international students: Required—TOEFL.

Tai Sophia Institute, Program in Acupuncture, Laurel, MD 20723. Offers M Ac. *Accreditation:* ACAOM. *Degree requirements:* For master's, comprehensive exam, 500 clinical hours, oral exams. *Entrance requirements:* Additional exam requirements/recommendations for international students: Required—TOEFL. *Faculty research:* Philosophical roots of oriental medicine, meridian pathways, points, pulses.

Tai Sophia Institute, Program in Applied Healing Arts, Laurel, MD 20723. Offers MA. *Entrance requirements:* Additional exam requirements/recommendations for international students: Required—TOEFL. *Faculty research:* Healing habits of mind and heart, an expanded vision, bringing of one's vision and practices to a special arena.

Tai Sophia Institute, Program in Herbal Medicine, Laurel, MD 20723. Offers MS. *Entrance requirements:* Additional exam requirements/recommendations for international students: Required—TOEFL. *Faculty research:* Philosophical roots of holistic healing, botany, herbal pharmacology; materia medica, holistic healing.

Texas College of Traditional Chinese Medicine, Program in Acupuncture and Oriental Medicine, Austin, TX 78702. Offers MAOM. *Accreditation:* ACAOM. *Entrance requirements:* For master's, 60 hours applicable to bachelor's degree. Additional exam requirements/recommendations for international students: Required—TOEFL (minimum score 500 paper-based; 173 computer-based), TWE. Electronic applications accepted.

Touro College, School of Health Sciences, Bay Shore, NY 11706. Offers occupational therapy (MS); Oriental medicine (MSOM); physical therapy (DPT); public health (MPH); speech-language pathology (MS). *Faculty:* 20 full-time, 94 part-time/adjunct. *Students:* 136. *Expenses:* Contact institution. *Financial support:* Fellowships available. *Unit head:* Dr. Louis Primavera, Dean, 516-673-3200. *Application contact:* Dean, School of Health Sciences, 516-673-3200.

Traditional Chinese Medical College of Hawaii, Graduate Programs, Kamuela, HI 96743-2288. Offers MSOM. *Accreditation:* ACAOM.

Tri-State College of Acupuncture, Program in Acupuncture, New York, NY 10011. Offers acupuncture (MS); oriental medicine (MS); traditional Chinese herbology (Certificate). *Accreditation:* ACAOM. Evening/weekend programs available. *Entrance requirements:* Additional exam requirements/recommendations for international students: Recommended—TOEFL.

University of Bridgeport, Acupuncture Institute, Bridgeport, CT 06604. Offers MS. *Accreditation:* ACAOM. Part-time programs available. *Faculty:* 2 full-time (1 woman), 8 part-time/adjunct (2 women). *Students:* 14 full-time (13 women), 9 part-time (8 women); includes 7 minority (2 Black or African American, non-Hispanic/Latino; 1 American Indian or Alaska Native, non-Hispanic/Latino; 2 Asian, non-Hispanic/Latino; 1 Hispanic/Latino; 1 Two or more races, non-Hispanic/Latino), 3 international. Average age 44. 28 applicants, 79% accepted, 6 enrolled. In 2011, 8 master's awarded. *Entrance requirements:* Additional exam requirements/recommendations for international students: Recommended—TOEFL (minimum score 550 paper-based; 213 computer-based; 80 iBT), IELTS (minimum score 6.5). *Application deadline:* For fall admission, 8/1 priority date for domestic students, 8/1 for international students; for spring admission, 12/1 priority date for domestic students, 12/1 for international students. Applications are processed on a rolling basis. Application fee: $50. Electronic applications accepted. *Expenses:* Contact institution. *Unit head:* Dr. Jennifer Brett, Director, 203-576-4122, Fax: 203-576-4107, E-mail: acup@bridgeport.edu. *Application contact:* Leanne Proctor, Director of Health Sciences Admission, 203-576-4352, Fax: 203-576-4941, E-mail: acup@bridgeport.edu.

WON Institute of Graduate Studies, Acupuncture Studies Program, Glenside, PA 19038. Offers M Ac. *Accreditation:* ACAOM. *Entrance requirements:* For master's, 6 prerequisite credits in anatomy and physiology, 2 letters of recommendation, essay. Additional exam requirements/recommendations for international students: Required—TOEFL (minimum score 550 paper-based; 213 computer-based; 79 iBT), TSE (minimum score 40). Electronic applications accepted. *Faculty research:* Meditation and pulse taking, acupuncture and apprehension.

World Medicine Institute of Acupuncture and Herbal Medicine, Program in Acupuncture and Oriental Medicine, Honolulu, HI 96828. Offers M Ac OM. *Accreditation:* ACAOM. Part-time and evening/weekend programs available. *Entrance requirements:* For master's, minimum 60 college credits.

Yo San University of Traditional Chinese Medicine, Program in Acupuncture and Traditional Chinese Medicine, Los Angeles, CA 90066. Offers MATCM. *Accreditation:* ACAOM. Part-time programs available. Postbaccalaureate distance learning degree programs offered (no on-campus study). *Degree requirements:* For master's, observation and practice internships, exam. *Entrance requirements:* For master's, minimum 2 years of college, interview, minimum GPA of 2.5.

Section 26
Chiropractic

This section contains a directory of institutions offering graduate work in chiropractic. Additional information about programs listed in the directory but not augmented by an in-depth entry may be obtained by writing directly to the dean of a graduate school or chair of a department at the address given in the directory.

CONTENTS

Chiropractic

Canadian Memorial Chiropractic College, Certificate Programs, Toronto, ON M2H 3J1, Canada. Offers chiropractic clinical sciences (Certificate); chiropractic radiology (Certificate); chiropractic sports sciences (Certificate); clinical acupuncture (Certificate). *Degree requirements:* For Certificate, thesis. *Entrance requirements:* For degree, DC, board certification. *Faculty research:* Theories and concepts of chiropractic, sciences related to chiropractic, assessments of the efficacy and efficiency of chiropractic.

Canadian Memorial Chiropractic College, Professional Program, Toronto, ON M2H 3J1, Canada. Offers DC. *Entrance requirements:* For doctorate, 3 full years of university (15 full courses or 90 hours). *Faculty research:* Theories and concepts of chiropractic, sciences related to chiropractic, assessment of the efficacy and efficiency of chiropractic.

Cleveland Chiropractic College–Kansas City Campus, Professional Program, Overland Park, KS 66210. Offers DC. *Accreditation:* CCE. Part-time programs available. *Faculty:* 38 full-time (6 women), 7 part-time/adjunct (3 women). *Students:* 458 full-time (163 women), 9 part-time (4 women); includes 51 minority (6 Black or African American, non-Hispanic/Latino; 5 American Indian or Alaska Native, non-Hispanic/Latino; 8 Asian, non-Hispanic/Latino; 16 Hispanic/Latino; 16 Two or more races, non-Hispanic/Latino), 3 international. Average age 33. 179 applicants, 55% accepted, 66 enrolled. In 2011, 103 doctorates awarded. *Degree requirements:* For doctorate, comprehensive exam. *Entrance requirements:* For doctorate, 90 semester hours of pre-professional study. Additional exam requirements/recommendations for international students: Required—TOEFL (minimum score 550 paper-based; 213 computer-based; 79 iBT). *Application deadline:* For fall admission, 7/1 priority date for domestic students, 7/1 for international students; for winter admission, 11/1 priority date for domestic students, 11/1 for international students; for spring admission, 3/1 priority date for domestic students, 3/1 for international students. Applications are processed on a rolling basis. Application fee: $50. Electronic applications accepted. *Expenses: Tuition:* Full-time $23,700. *Required fees:* $140. *Financial support:* In 2011–12, 43 students received support. Federal Work-Study and scholarships/grants available. Financial award applicants required to submit FAFSA. *Faculty research:* Effectiveness and efficacy of chiropractic care. *Unit head:* Dr. Paul Barlett, Academic Dean, 913-234-0643. *Application contact:* Melissa Denton, Director of Admissions, 913-234-0744, Fax: 913-234-0906, E-mail: kc.admissions@cleveland.edu.

D'Youville College, Department of Chiropractic, Buffalo, NY 14201-1084. Offers DC. *Accreditation:* CCE. *Faculty:* 10 full-time (2 women), 23 part-time/adjunct (6 women). *Students:* 73 full-time (26 women), 7 part-time (2 women); includes 9 minority (3 Black or African American, non-Hispanic/Latino; 1 American Indian or Alaska Native, non-Hispanic/Latino; 3 Asian, non-Hispanic/Latino; 1 Hispanic/Latino; 1 Two or more races, non-Hispanic/Latino), 18 international. Average age 27. 56 applicants, 46% accepted, 7 enrolled. In 2011, 13 doctorates awarded. *Entrance requirements:* For doctorate, minimum GPA of 2.5, 90 undergraduate credits. *Application deadline:* Applications are processed on a rolling basis. Application fee: $25. Electronic applications accepted. *Expenses:* Contact institution. *Faculty research:* Radiology diagnosis, chiropractic treatment and diagnosis. *Unit head:* Dr. Kathleen Linaker, Executive Director, Chiropractic Department, 716-829-7725 Ext. 7793, Fax: 716-829-7893. *Application contact:* Linda Fisher, Graduate Admissions Director, 716-829-8400, Fax: 716-829-7900, E-mail: graduateadmissions@dyc.edu.

Institut Franco-Europen de Chiropratique, Professional Program, 94200 Ivry-sur-Seine, France. Offers DC.

Life Chiropractic College West, Professional Program, Hayward, CA 94545. Offers DC. *Accreditation:* CCE. *Faculty:* 29 full-time (11 women), 33 part-time/adjunct (9 women). *Students:* 272 full-time (118 women), 48 part-time (17 women). *Entrance requirements:* For doctorate, minimum GPA of 2.5. Additional exam requirements/recommendations for international students: Required—TOEFL (minimum score 550 paper-based). *Application deadline:* For fall admission, 8/1 priority date for domestic students, 7/1 for international students; for winter admission, 10/1 priority date for domestic students, 10/1 for international students; for spring admission, 2/1 priority date for domestic students, 1/1 for international students. Applications are processed on a rolling basis. Application fee: $45. *Expenses: Tuition:* Full-time $22,650; part-time $377.50 per credit hour. One-time fee: $45 full-time. *Financial support:* Research assistantships, teaching assistantships, career-related internships or fieldwork, Federal Work-Study, and scholarships/grants available. Financial award application deadline: 4/1; financial award applicants required to submit FAFSA. *Faculty research:* Imaging, ergonomics, upper cervical adjusting, academics. *Total annual research expenditures:* $2,500. *Unit head:* Dr. Brian Kelly, President, 800-788-4476 Ext. 2350, E-mail: bkelly@lifewest.edu. *Application contact:* Carlos Alicea, Executive Director of Enrollment, 800-788-4476 Ext. 2520, Fax: 510-780-4525, E-mail: admissions@lifewest.edu. Web site: http://www.lifewest.edu/.

Life University, College of Chiropractic, Marietta, GA 30060-2903. Offers DC. *Accreditation:* CCE. Part-time programs available. *Degree requirements:* For doctorate, comprehensive exam, thesis/dissertation or alternative. *Entrance requirements:* For doctorate, minimum 3 years of college; course work in biology, chemistry, physics, humanities, psychology, and English; minimum GPA of 2.5. Additional exam requirements/recommendations for international students: Required—TOEFL (minimum score 500 paper-based; 173 computer-based). *Application deadline:* Applications are processed on a rolling basis. Application fee: $50. Electronic applications accepted. *Financial support:* Research assistantships, Federal Work-Study, institutionally sponsored loans, scholarships/grants, and tuition waivers (partial) available. Support available to part-time students. Financial award application deadline: 9/1; financial award applicants required to submit FAFSA. *Faculty research:* Chiropractic clinical trial, spinal modeling, biomechanics, clinical evaluation studies, chiropractic technique development, sports performance. *Unit head:* Dr. Leslie King, Dean of Instruction, 770-426-2757, E-mail: lesliek@life.edu. *Application contact:* Dr. Deborah Heairlston, Director of New Student Development, 770-426-2884, Fax: 770-426-2895, E-mail: drdeb@life.edu. Web site: http://www.life.edu/Chiropractic_College.

Logan University–College of Chiropractic, Chiropractic Program, Chesterfield, MO 63006-1065. Offers DC. *Accreditation:* CCE. *Faculty:* 47 full-time (17 women), 41 part-time/adjunct (25 women). *Students:* 796 full-time (303 women), 68 part-time (27 women); includes 71 minority (26 Black or African American, non-Hispanic/Latino; 2 American Indian or Alaska Native, non-Hispanic/Latino; 16 Asian, non-Hispanic/Latino; 16 Hispanic/Latino; 11 Two or more races, non-Hispanic/Latino), 17 international. Average age 26. 209 applicants, 95% accepted, 129 enrolled. In 2011, 264 doctorates awarded. *Degree requirements:* For doctorate, comprehensive exam. *Entrance requirements:* For doctorate, 90 hours of pre-chiropractic including biology, chemistry, physics, and social sciences; minimum GPA of 2.5. Additional exam requirements/recommendations for international students: Required—TOEFL (minimum score 79 iBT). *Application deadline:* For fall admission, 7/15 priority date for domestic students, 7/15 for international students; for winter admission, 11/15 priority date for domestic students, 11/15 for international students; for spring admission, 3/15 priority date for domestic students, 3/15 for international students. Applications are processed on a rolling basis. Application fee: $50. Electronic applications accepted. *Financial support:* In 2011–12, 100 students received support. Federal Work-Study and scholarships/grants available. Support available to part-time students. Financial award applicants required to submit FAFSA. *Faculty research:* Effects of injury on proprioception as measured by joint position sense, interventions for older adults with low back pain, interventions affecting heart rate variability, finite element computer modeling of spinal biomechanics, electrophysiological diagnosis of common neuromusculoskeletal conditions, the effects of spinal manipulation on posture and postural control. *Unit head:* Dr. Carl W. Saubert, IV, Acting Vice President, Academic Affairs, 636-227-2100 Ext. 1745, Fax: 636-207-2431, E-mail: carl.saubert@logan.edu. *Application contact:* Steve Held, Director of Admissions, 636-227-2100 Ext. 1752, Fax: 636-207-2425, E-mail: loganadm@logan.edu.

Logan University–College of Chiropractic, University Programs, Chesterfield, MO 63006-1065. Offers nutrition and human performance (MS); sports science and rehabilitation (MS). *Faculty:* 10 full-time (6 women), 16 part-time/adjunct (6 women). *Students:* 27 full-time (12 women), 39 part-time (10 women); includes 12 minority (7 Black or African American, non-Hispanic/Latino; 4 Asian, non-Hispanic/Latino; 1 Hispanic/Latino). Average age 26. 45 applicants, 98% accepted, 34 enrolled. In 2011, 51 master's awarded. *Degree requirements:* For master's, comprehensive exam. *Entrance requirements:* For master's, GRE or National Board of Chiropractic Examiners test, minimum GPA of 2.5. Additional exam requirements/recommendations for international students: Required—TOEFL (minimum score 79 iBT). *Application deadline:* For fall admission, 7/15 priority date for domestic students, 7/15 for international students; for winter admission, 11/15 priority date for domestic students, 11/15 for international students; for spring admission, 3/15 priority date for domestic students, 3/15 for international students. Application fee: $50. *Expenses:* Contact institution. *Financial support:* In 2011–12, 35 students received support. Federal Work-Study and scholarships/grants available. Support available to part-time students. Financial award applicants required to submit FAFSA. *Faculty research:* Ankle injury prevention in high school athletes, low back pain in college football players, short arc banding and low back pain, the effects of enzymes on inflammatory blood markers, gait analysis in high school and college athletes. *Unit head:* Dr. Elizabeth A. Goodman, Dean, 636-227-2100, Fax: 636-207-2431, E-mail: elizabeth.goodman@logan.edu. *Application contact:* Steve Held, Director of Admissions, 636-227-2100 Ext. 1754, Fax: 636-207-2425, E-mail: loganadm@logan.edu.

National University of Health Sciences, Chiropractic Program in Florida, Seminole, FL 33772. Offers DC. *Degree requirements:* For doctorate, comprehensive exam, internship, community service. *Entrance requirements:* For doctorate, bachelor's degree, character references, undergraduate transcripts, written essay. Additional exam requirements/recommendations for international students: Required—TOEFL (minimum score 550 paper-based; 79 iBT). Electronic applications accepted.

National University of Health Sciences, College of Professional Studies, Lombard, IL 60148-4583. Offers acupuncture (MSAC); chiropractic medicine (DC); naturopathic medicine (ND); Oriental medicine (MSOM). *Accreditation:* CCE. *Degree requirements:* For master's and doctorate, comprehensive exam, internship, community service. *Entrance requirements:* For master's, bachelor's degree, character references, undergraduate transcripts; for doctorate, bachelor's degree, character references, undergraduate transcripts, written essay. Additional exam requirements/recommendations for international students: Required—TOEFL (minimum score 550 paper-based; 79 iBT). Electronic applications accepted. *Faculty research:* Discipline/whole practice research (including practice-based research networks), mechanisms of action, clinical trials, and evidence-based practice of CAM therapies; educational research in CAM teaching institutions.

New York Chiropractic College, Doctor of Chiropractic Program, Seneca Falls, NY 13148-0800. Offers DC. *Accreditation:* CCE. *Degree requirements:* For doctorate, internship in health center (clinic). *Entrance requirements:* For doctorate, 24 credit hours of course work in science (90 credit hours with minimum GPA of 2.5), references, interview. Additional exam requirements/recommendations for international students: Recommended—TOEFL (minimum score 550 paper-based; 213 computer-based). Electronic applications accepted. *Faculty research:* Anatomy, pathophysiology, neurophysiology biomechanics, musculoskeletal pain syndrome, nutrition.

Northwestern Health Sciences University, College of Chiropractic, Bloomington, MN 55431-1599. Offers DC. *Accreditation:* CCE. *Students:* 583 full-time (263 women), 33 part-time (17 women). Average age 26. In 2011, 174 doctorates awarded. *Entrance requirements:* For doctorate, 90 semester hours of course work in health or science, minimum GPA of 2.5. Additional exam requirements/recommendations for international students: Required—TOEFL (minimum score 540 paper-based; 207 computer-based; 76 iBT). *Application deadline:* For fall admission, 5/1 priority date for domestic students, 5/1 for international students; for winter admission, 9/1 priority date for domestic students, 9/1 for international students. Applications are processed on a rolling basis. Application fee: $50. Electronic applications accepted. *Financial support:* Career-related internships or fieldwork, Federal Work-Study, and scholarships/grants available. Support available to part-time students. *Faculty research:* Headache, low back pain, neck pain, sciatica, rehabilitative exercise. *Unit head:* Dr. Renee DeVries, Dean, 952-888-4777 Ext. 411, Fax: 952-888-6713, E-mail: rdevries@nwhealth.edu. *Application contact:* Kate DiAna, Director of Admissions, 952-888-4777 Ext. 273, Fax: 952-888-6713, E-mail: admit@nwhealth.edu. Web site: http://www.nwhealth.edu/college-of-chiropractic/.

Palmer College of Chiropractic, Professional Program, Davenport, IA 52803-5287. Offers DC. *Accreditation:* CCE. Part-time programs available. *Entrance requirements:* For doctorate, minimum GPA of 2.5, 90 hours of prerequisite coursework. Additional exam requirements/recommendations for international students: Required—TOEFL (minimum score 500 paper-based; 61 iBT). Electronic applications accepted. *Faculty research:* Studies to advance the understanding of chiropractic.

Palmer College of Chiropractic, Professional Program–Florida Campus, Davenport, IA 52803-5287. Offers DC. *Accreditation:* CCE. Part-time programs available. *Degree requirements:* For doctorate, clinical internship. *Entrance requirements:* For doctorate, minimum GPA of 2.5, 90 hours of prerequisite coursework. Additional exam requirements/recommendations for international students: Recommended—TOEFL (minimum score 500 paper-based; 61 iBT).

Palmer College of Chiropractic, Professional Program–West Campus, San Jose, CA 95134-1617. Offers DC. *Accreditation:* CCE. Part-time programs available. *Degree requirements:* For doctorate, clinical internship. *Entrance requirements:* For doctorate, minimum GPA of 2.5. Additional exam requirements/recommendations for international

students: Required—TOEFL. Electronic applications accepted. *Faculty research:* Low back pain complaints, spinal manipulation therapy, cervical biomechanics, clinical trials, practice guidelines.

Parker University, Doctor of Chiropractic Program, Dallas, TX 75229-5668. Offers DC. *Accreditation:* CCE. Part-time programs available. *Entrance requirements:* For doctorate, minimum GPA of 2.65. Additional exam requirements/recommendations for international students: Required—TOEFL (minimum score 550 paper-based; 213 computer-based). Electronic applications accepted. *Faculty research:* Arterial tonometry, bioenergetics, outcome assessment for clinical care.

Sherman College of Chiropractic, Professional Program, Spartanburg, SC 29304-1452. Offers DC. *Accreditation:* CCE. Electronic applications accepted. *Faculty research:* Chiropractic effect of immune response, biomechanics, videofluoroscopy, dynamic motion.

Southern California University of Health Sciences, Los Angeles College of Chiropractic, Whittier, CA 90609-1166. Offers DC. *Accreditation:* CCE. *Faculty:* 31 full-time (12 women), 17 part-time/adjunct (7 women). *Students:* 164 full-time (58 women), 369 part-time (138 women); includes 233 minority (21 Black or African American, non-Hispanic/Latino; 5 American Indian or Alaska Native, non-Hispanic/Latino; 110 Asian, non-Hispanic/Latino; 70 Hispanic/Latino; 16 Native Hawaiian or other Pacific Islander, non-Hispanic/Latino; 11 Two or more races, non-Hispanic/Latino). Average age 31. 358 applicants, 70% accepted, 205 enrolled. In 2011, 102 doctorates awarded. *Degree requirements:* For doctorate, clinical internship. *Entrance requirements:* For doctorate, minimum GPA of 2.5, 90 incoming units in prerequisite coursework. Additional exam requirements/recommendations for international students: Required—TOEFL (minimum score 500 paper-based; 173 computer-based). *Application deadline:* Applications are processed on a rolling basis. Application fee: $50. Electronic applications accepted. *Financial support:* In 2011–12, 91 students received support. Career-related internships or fieldwork, Federal Work-Study, scholarships/grants, and International Student Work Program available. Financial award applicants required to submit FAFSA. *Faculty research:* Low back pain, smoking cessation, sports medicine. *Unit head:* Dr. Michael Sackett, Dean, 562-947-8755 Ext. 522, Fax: 562-947-5724, E-mail: mikesackett@scuhs.edu. *Application contact:* Tracy Nieto, Assistant Director of Admissions, 562-947-8755 Ext. 319, Fax: 562-902-3321, E-mail: tracynieto@scuhs.edu.

Texas Chiropractic College, Professional Program, Pasadena, TX 77505-1699. Offers DC. *Accreditation:* CCE. *Entrance requirements:* For doctorate, 90 semester hours at regionally-accredited college or university, minimum GPA of 2.5. Additional exam requirements/recommendations for international students: Required—TOEFL. *Faculty research:* Range of motion comparison male vs. female student stress levels.

Université du Québec à Trois-Rivières, Graduate Programs, Program in Chiropractic, Trois-Rivières, QC G9A 5H7, Canada. Offers DC.

University of Bridgeport, College of Chiropractic, Bridgeport, CT 06604. Offers DC. *Accreditation:* CCE. *Faculty:* 20 full-time (4 women), 16 part-time/adjunct (5 women). *Students:* 177 full-time (72 women), 2 part-time (0 women); includes 57 minority (18 Black or African American, non-Hispanic/Latino; 15 Asian, non-Hispanic/Latino; 13 Hispanic/Latino; 11 Two or more races, non-Hispanic/Latino), 16 international. Average age 29. 114 applicants, 39% accepted, 17 enrolled. In 2011, 33 doctorates awarded. *Degree requirements:* For doctorate, thesis/dissertation, National Board of Chiropractic Exam Parts I and II. *Entrance requirements:* Additional exam requirements/recommendations for international students: Recommended—TOEFL (minimum score 550 paper-based; 213 computer-based; 80 iBT), IELTS (minimum score 6.5). *Application deadline:* For fall admission, 4/1 priority date for domestic students, 4/1 for international students; for spring admission, 11/1 priority date for domestic students, 11/1 for international students. Applications are processed on a rolling basis. Application fee: $75. Electronic applications accepted. *Expenses:* Contact institution. *Financial support:* In 2011–12, 170 students received support. Federal Work-Study and institutionally sponsored loans available. Support available to part-time students. Financial award application deadline: 6/1; financial award applicants required to submit FAFSA. *Unit head:* Dr. Francis A. Zolli, Dean, 203-576-4279, E-mail: zolli@bridgeport.edu. *Application contact:* Leanne Proctor, Director of Health Science Admissions, 203-576-4352, Fax: 203-576-4941, E-mail: chiro@bridgeport.edu.

University of Western States, Professional Program, Portland, OR 97230-3099. Offers DC. *Accreditation:* CCE. *Degree requirements:* For doctorate, comprehensive exam, internship. *Entrance requirements:* For doctorate, 3 years of pre-chiropractic study in biological sciences, minimum GPA of 2.5. *Faculty research:* Low back pain.

Section 27
Dentistry and Dental Sciences

This section contains a directory of institutions offering graduate work in dentistry and dental sciences, followed by an in-depth entry submitted by an institution that chose to prepare a detailed program description. Additional information about programs listed in the directory but not augmented by an in-depth entry may be obtained by writing directly to the dean of a graduate school or chair of a department at the address given in the directory.

For programs offering related work, see also in this book *Allied Health.*

CONTENTS

Dentistry

Boston University, Henry M. Goldman School of Dental Medicine, Boston, MA 02118. Offers advanced general dentistry (CAGS); dental public health (MS, MSD, D Sc D, CAGS); dentistry (DMD); endodontics (MSD, D Sc D, CAGS); operative dentistry (MSD, D Sc D, CAGS); oral and maxillofacial surgery (MSD, D Sc D, CAGS); oral biology (MSD, D Sc, D Sc D, PhD); orthodontics (MSD, D Sc D, CAGS); pediatric dentistry (MSD, D Sc D, CAGS); periodontology (MSD, D Sc D, CAGS); prosthodontics (MSD, D Sc D, CAGS). *Accreditation:* ADA (one or more programs are accredited). *Faculty:* 119 full-time (53 women), 83 part-time/adjunct (24 women). *Students:* 802 full-time (386 women); includes 155 minority (6 Black or African American, non-Hispanic/Latino; 2 American Indian or Alaska Native, non-Hispanic/Latino; 110 Asian, non-Hispanic/Latino; 35 Hispanic/Latino; 2 Native Hawaiian or other Pacific Islander, non-Hispanic/Latino), 329 international. Average age 27. In 2011, 17 master's, 173 doctorates, 61 other advanced degrees awarded. *Degree requirements:* For master's and CAGS, thesis; for doctorate, thesis/dissertation (for some programs). *Entrance requirements:* For doctorate, DAT (for DMD), minimum recommended GPA of 3.0 (for DMD); for CAGS, dental degree. Additional exam requirements/recommendations for international students: Required—TOEFL. *Application deadline:* Applications are processed on a rolling basis. Application fee: $75 ($105 for international students). Electronic applications accepted. *Expenses:* Contact institution. *Financial support:* In 2011–12, 480 students received support. Career-related internships or fieldwork, institutionally sponsored loans, and scholarships/grants available. Financial award application deadline: 4/15; financial award applicants required to submit FAFSA. *Faculty research:* Defense mechanisms, bone-cell regulation, protein biochemistry, molecular biology, biomaterials. *Unit head:* Dr. Jeffrey W. Hutter, Dean, 617-638-4780. *Application contact:* Admissions Representative, 617-638-4787, Fax: 617-638-4798, E-mail: sdmadmis@bu.edu. Web site: http://www.bu.edu/dental.

Case Western Reserve University, School of Dental Medicine, Professional Program in Dentistry, Cleveland, OH 44106. Offers DMD. *Accreditation:* ADA. *Degree requirements:* For doctorate, thesis/dissertation. *Entrance requirements:* For doctorate, DAT. Additional exam requirements/recommendations for international students: Required—TOEFL (minimum score 550 paper-based; 213 computer-based). *Expenses:* Contact institution. *Faculty research:* Periodontal disease; overall health; natural antibodies; obesity and periodontal disease; 3D cone beam computerized tomography.

Columbia University, College of Dental Medicine, Professional Program in Dental and Oral Surgery, New York, NY 10032. Offers DDS, DDS/MBA, DDS/MPH. *Accreditation:* ADA. *Entrance requirements:* For doctorate, DAT, previous course work in biology, organic chemistry, inorganic chemistry, physics, and English.

Creighton University, School of Dentistry, Omaha, NE 68178-0001. Offers DDS. *Accreditation:* ADA. *Entrance requirements:* For doctorate, DAT. *Expenses:* Contact institution. *Faculty research:* Dental implants, bone calcification, dental materials, laser usage in dentistry.

Georgia Health Sciences University, College of Dental Medicine, Augusta, GA 30912. Offers DMD, DMD/MS, DMD/PhD. *Accreditation:* ADA. *Faculty:* 53 full-time (10 women), 14 part-time/adjunct (4 women). *Students:* 282 full-time (130 women), 1 part-time (0 women); includes 77 minority (32 Black or African American, non-Hispanic/Latino; 1 American Indian or Alaska Native, non-Hispanic/Latino; 29 Asian, non-Hispanic/Latino; 9 Hispanic/Latino; 6 Two or more races, non-Hispanic/Latino). Average age 26. 309 applicants, 26% accepted, 70 enrolled. In 2011, 61 doctorates awarded. *Degree requirements:* For doctorate, comprehensive exam. *Entrance requirements:* For doctorate, DAT, previous course work in biology, English, organic chemistry, and general chemistry; 1 semester of course work in physics. Additional exam requirements/recommendations for international students: Required—TOEFL (minimum score 100 iBT). *Application deadline:* For fall admission, 10/15 for domestic students. Application fee: $30. Electronic applications accepted. *Expenses:* Contact institution. *Financial support:* Federal Work-Study and scholarships/grants available. Financial award application deadline: 5/1; financial award applicants required to submit FAFSA. *Faculty research:* Biocompatibility, dentin bonding, oral cancer, ceramic strengthening, resin polymerization. *Total annual research expenditures:* $1.2 million. *Unit head:* Dr. Connie Drisko, Dean, 706-721-2117, Fax: 706-721-6276, E-mail: cdrisko@georgiahealth.edu. *Application contact:* Dr. Carole M. Hanes, Associate Dean for Student and Alumni Affairs, 706-721-3587, Fax: 706-721-6276, E-mail: chanes@georgiahealth.edu. Web site: http://www.georgiahealth.edu/dentalmedicine/index.html.

Harvard University, School of Dental Medicine, Advanced Graduate Programs in Dentistry, Cambridge, MA 02138. Offers advanced general dentistry (Certificate); dental public health (Certificate); endodontics (Certificate); general practice residency (Certificate); oral biology (M Med Sc, D Med Sc); oral implantology (Certificate); oral medicine (Certificate); oral pathology (Certificate); oral surgery (Certificate); orthodontics (Certificate); pediatric dentistry (Certificate); periodontics (Certificate); prosthodontics (Certificate). *Expenses: Tuition:* Full-time $36,304. *Required fees:* $1186. Full-time tuition and fees vary according to program.

Harvard University, School of Dental Medicine, Professional Program in Dental Medicine, Cambridge, MA 02138. Offers DMD. *Accreditation:* ADA. *Entrance requirements:* For doctorate, DAT, 1 year each: biology, general chemistry, organic chemistry, physics, calculus, English. *Expenses: Tuition:* Full-time $36,304. *Required fees:* $1186. Full-time tuition and fees vary according to program.

Howard University, College of Dentistry, Washington, DC 20059-0002. Offers advanced education program general dentistry (Certificate); dentistry (DDS); general dentistry (Certificate); oral and maxillofacial surgery (Certificate); orthodontics (Certificate); pediatric dentistry (Certificate). *Accreditation:* ADA (one or more programs are accredited). *Degree requirements:* For doctorate, comprehensive exam, didactic and clinical exams. *Entrance requirements:* For doctorate, DAT, 8 semester hours of course work in each biology, inorganic chemistry, organic chemistry. *Expenses:* Contact institution. *Faculty research:* Epidemiological, biomaterial, molecular genetic, behavioral modification, and clinical trial studies.

Idaho State University, Office of Graduate Studies, Kasiska College of Health Professions, Department of Dental Sciences, Pocatello, ID 83209-8088. Offers advanced general dentistry (Post-Doctoral Certificate). First year of Idaho Dental Education Program available in conjunction with Creighton University's School of Dentistry. *Degree requirements:* For Post-Doctoral Certificate, comprehensive exam, thesis optional, 1-year residency. *Entrance requirements:* For degree, DAT, 3 dental application forms. Additional exam requirements/recommendations for international students: Required—TOEFL (minimum score 600 paper-based; 213 computer-based). Electronic applications accepted. *Expenses:* Contact institution.

Indiana University–Purdue University Indianapolis, School of Dentistry, Indianapolis, IN 46202-2896. Offers MS, MSD, DDS, PhD, Certificate. *Accreditation:* ADA (one or more programs are accredited). *Faculty:* 96 full-time (28 women). *Students:* 480 full-time (204 women), 44 part-time (18 women); includes 81 minority (10 Black or African American, non-Hispanic/Latino; 1 American Indian or Alaska Native, non-Hispanic/Latino; 45 Asian, non-Hispanic/Latino; 20 Hispanic/Latino; 5 Two or more races, non-Hispanic/Latino), 60 international. Average age 28. In 2011, 29 master's, 140 doctorates awarded. *Degree requirements:* For master's, thesis or manuscript, qualifying exam; for doctorate, thesis/dissertation (for some programs), completion of all coursework with a passing grade; minimum GPA of 3.0 and qualifying examination (for PhD); minimum GPA of 2.0 and passing scores for Part I and II of National Board of Dental Examinations (for DDS); for Certificate, completion of all coursework with passing grades, minimum GPA of 3.0. *Entrance requirements:* For master's, DDS or DMD; for doctorate, GRE (for PhD); DAT (for DDS), DDS or DMD. Additional exam requirements/recommendations for international students: Required—TOEFL (minimum score 550 paper-based; 213 computer-based). *Application deadline:* For winter admission, 11/1 for domestic and international students. Applications are processed on a rolling basis. Application fee: $55 ($65 for international students). Electronic applications accepted. *Expenses:* Contact institution. *Financial support:* In 2011–12, 43 students received support, including 25 fellowships (averaging $9,864 per year); research assistantships, teaching assistantships, Federal Work-Study, institutionally sponsored loans, and scholarships/grants also available. Financial award application deadline: 3/1; financial award applicants required to submit FAFSA. *Faculty research:* Caries research: early caries detection and management, secondary caries, remineralization, oral biofilms, fluoride, dental erosion; oral biology: molecular biology and immunobiology of streptococcus mutans, oral biofilms, infection control, actinobaccillus actinomycetemcomitans; orthodontics and oral facial genetics: orthodontics biomechanics; oral pathology and immunology: chronic inflammation and autoimmunity, innate immunity in oral pathology; periodontal disease and implants. *Total annual research expenditures:* $7.8 million. *Unit head:* John N. Williams, Dean, 317-274-7461. *Application contact:* Pamela Clark, Associate Dean for Student Affairs and Director of Admissions, 317-278-1758, Fax: 317-278-9066, E-mail: pamelac@iupui.edu. Web site: http://www.iusd.iupui.edu/.

Loma Linda University, School of Dentistry, Loma Linda, CA 92350. Offers MS, DDS, Certificate, DDS/MS, DDS/PhD, MS/Certificate. *Accreditation:* ADA. *Entrance requirements:* For master's, GRE, minimum GPA of 3.0; for doctorate, DAT. Additional exam requirements/recommendations for international students: Required—TOEFL (minimum score 550 paper-based; 213 computer-based). *Expenses:* Contact institution.

Louisiana State University Health Sciences Center, School of Dentistry, New Orleans, LA 70112-2223. Offers DDS. *Accreditation:* ADA. *Entrance requirements:* For doctorate, DAT, interview. *Expenses:* Contact institution. *Faculty research:* HIV/AIDS, implants, metallurgy, lipids, DNA.

Marquette University, School of Dentistry, Professional Program in Dentistry, Milwaukee, WI 53201-1881. Offers DDS. *Accreditation:* ADA. *Faculty:* 35 full-time (10 women), 122 part-time/adjunct (32 women). *Students:* 321 full-time (137 women); includes 60 minority (13 Black or African American, non-Hispanic/Latino; 3 American Indian or Alaska Native, non-Hispanic/Latino; 18 Asian, non-Hispanic/Latino; 22 Hispanic/Latino; 1 Native Hawaiian or other Pacific Islander, non-Hispanic/Latino; 3 Two or more races, non-Hispanic/Latino), 6 international. Average age 25. 2,544 applicants, 5% accepted, 80 enrolled. In 2011, 82 doctorates awarded. *Degree requirements:* For doctorate, National Board Dental Ecam Part 1 and 2, regional licensure exam. *Entrance requirements:* For doctorate, DAT, 1 year course work in each biology, inorganic chemistry, organic chemistry, physics, and English. Additional exam requirements/recommendations for international students: Required—TOEFL. *Application deadline:* For fall admission, 1/1 for domestic and international students. Applications are processed on a rolling basis. Application fee: $45. *Expenses:* Contact institution. *Financial support:* In 2011–12, 292 students received support. Institutionally sponsored loans and scholarships/grants available. Financial award applicants required to submit FAFSA. *Faculty research:* Biomaterials, wound healing, diabetes, biocompatibility, cancer, aging, lasers. *Unit head:* Dr. Denis Lynch, Associate Dean for Academic Affairs, 414-288-7267, Fax: 414-288-3586, E-mail: denis.lynch@marquette.edu. *Application contact:* Brian Trecek, Assistant to the Dean and Director of Admissions, 414-288-3532, Fax: 414-288-3586, E-mail: brian.trecek@marquette.edu. Web site: http://www.marquette.edu/dentistry.

McGill University, Faculty of Graduate and Postdoctoral Studies, Faculty of Dentistry, Montréal, QC H3A 2T5, Canada. Offers forensic dentistry (Certificate); oral and maxillofacial surgery (M Sc, PhD).

McGill University, Professional Program in Dentistry, Montréal, QC H3A 2T5, Canada. Offers DMD. *Accreditation:* ADA. Electronic applications accepted.

Medical University of South Carolina, College of Dental Medicine, Charleston, SC 29425. Offers DMD, DMD/PhD. *Accreditation:* ADA. *Faculty:* 51 full-time (14 women), 35 part-time/adjunct (8 women). *Students:* 279 full-time (122 women); includes 38 minority (9 Black or African American, non-Hispanic/Latino; 3 American Indian or Alaska Native, non-Hispanic/Latino; 23 Asian, non-Hispanic/Latino; 3 Hispanic/Latino). Average age 26. 793 applicants, 9% accepted, 70 enrolled. In 2011, 56 doctorates awarded. *Degree requirements:* For doctorate, National Board of Dental Examinations Part I and II. *Entrance requirements:* For doctorate, DAT, interview, 52 hours of specific pre-dental course work. Additional exam requirements/recommendations for international students: Required—TOEFL (minimum score 600 paper-based; 250 computer-based). *Application deadline:* For spring admission, 1/15 for domestic and international students. Application fee: $95. Electronic applications accepted. *Expenses:* Contact institution. *Financial support:* In 2011–12, 52 students received support. Federal Work-Study, scholarships/grants, and tuition waivers (partial) available. Support available to part-time students. Financial award application deadline: 3/10; financial award applicants required to submit FAFSA. *Faculty research:* South Carolina oral health, genetics, health disparities, Chlamydia, oral cancer. *Unit head:* Dr. John J. Sanders, Dean, 843-792-3811, Fax: 843-792-1376, E-mail: sandersjj@musc.edu. *Application contact:* William H. Liner, Dental Admissions Counselor, 843-792-4892, Fax: 843-792-6615, E-mail: linerw@musc.edu. Web site: http://www.musc.edu/dentistry/.

Meharry Medical College, School of Dentistry, Nashville, TN 37208-9989. Offers DDS. *Accreditation:* ADA. *Entrance requirements:* For doctorate, DAT.

Midwestern University, Downers Grove Campus, College of Dental Medicine-Illinois, Downers Grove, IL 60515-1235. Offers DMD. *Students:* 131 full-time (48 women); includes 38 minority (1 Black or African American, non-Hispanic/Latino; 35 Asian, non-Hispanic/Latino; 1 Hispanic/Latino; 1 Two or more races, non-Hispanic/Latino), 9 international. Average age 25. 1,962 applicants, 16% accepted, 131 enrolled. *Entrance requirements:* For doctorate, DAT, bachelor's degree, minimum overall GPA of 2.75, three letters of recommendation. *Application contact:* Michael Laken, Director of Admissions, 630-515-6171, Fax: 630-971-6086, E-mail: admissil@midwestern.edu. Web site: http://www.midwestern.edu/Programs_and_Admission/IL_Dental_Medicine.html.

Midwestern University, Glendale Campus, College of Dental Medicine, Glendale, AZ 85308. Offers DMD. *Accreditation:* ADA. *Faculty:* 18 full-time (6 women), 2 part-time/adjunct (0 women). *Students:* 442 full-time (195 women); includes 85 minority (7 Black or African American, non-Hispanic/Latino; 3 American Indian or Alaska Native, non-Hispanic/Latino; 52 Asian, non-Hispanic/Latino; 12 Hispanic/Latino; 3 Native Hawaiian or other Pacific Islander, non-Hispanic/Latino; 8 Two or more races, non-Hispanic/Latino), 17 international. Average age 27. 2,769 applicants, 9% accepted, 111 enrolled. *Unit head:* Dr. Richard Simonsen, Dean, 623-572-3801. *Application contact:* James Walter, Director of Admissions, 888-247-9277, Fax: 623-572-3229, E-mail: admissaz@midwestern.edu.

New York University, College of Dentistry, Advanced Placement DDS Program, New York, NY 10010. Offers DDS. *Faculty:* 242 full-time (85 women), 689 part-time/adjunct (186 women). *Students:* 741 applicants, 24% accepted, 126 enrolled. *Entrance requirements:* For doctorate, National Dental Board Exam. Additional exam requirements/recommendations for international students: Required—TOEFL (minimum score 230 computer-based; 90 iBT). *Application deadline:* For fall admission, 12/1 for domestic and international students. Applications are processed on a rolling basis. Application fee: $100. Electronic applications accepted. *Unit head:* Dr. Charles Bertolami, Dean, 212-998-9898, Fax: 212-995-4240, E-mail: charles.bertolami@nyu.edu. *Application contact:* Dr. Anthony M. Palatta, Assistant Dean for Student Affairs and Admissions, 212-998-9918, Fax: 212-995-4240, E-mail: ap16@nyu.edu. Web site: http://www.nyu.edu/dental/academicprograms/ddsap/index.html.

New York University, College of Dentistry, Professional Program in Dentistry, New York, NY 10010. Offers DDS. *Accreditation:* ADA. *Faculty:* 242 full-time (85 women), 689 part-time/adjunct (186 women). *Students:* 1,318 full-time (635 women); includes 703 minority (34 Black or African American, non-Hispanic/Latino; 1 American Indian or Alaska Native, non-Hispanic/Latino; 604 Asian, non-Hispanic/Latino; 64 Hispanic/Latino). Average age 25. 4,842 applicants, 14% accepted, 245 enrolled. In 2011, 327 doctorates awarded. *Entrance requirements:* For doctorate, DAT, BA or 90 credit equivalent. *Application deadline:* For fall admission, 1/4 for domestic and international students. Applications are processed on a rolling basis. Application fee: $75. Electronic applications accepted. *Financial support:* In 2011–12, 106 students received support. Application deadline: 3/1; applicants required to submit FAFSA. *Unit head:* Dr. Anthony Palatta, Assistant Dean for Admissions and Student Affairs, 212-998-9918, Fax: 212-995-4240, E-mail: ap16@nyu.edu. *Application contact:* Dr. Eugenia Mejia, Director for Admissions, 212-998-5333, Fax: 212-995-4302, E-mail: ak96@nyu.edu. Web site: http://www.nyu.edu/dental/.

Nova Southeastern University, Health Professions Division, College of Dental Medicine, Fort Lauderdale, FL 33314-7796. Offers dental medicine (DMD); dentistry (MS, Graduate Certificate). *Accreditation:* ADA. *Faculty:* 83 full-time (23 women), 168 part-time/adjunct (36 women). *Students:* 498 full-time (273 women); includes 212 minority (10 Black or African American, non-Hispanic/Latino; 91 Asian, non-Hispanic/Latino; 100 Hispanic/Latino; 4 Native Hawaiian or other Pacific Islander, non-Hispanic/Latino; 7 Two or more races, non-Hispanic/Latino), 57 international. Average age 27. 2,774 applicants, 6% accepted, 115 enrolled. In 2011, 1 master's, 128 doctorates, 35 other advanced degrees awarded. *Degree requirements:* For master's, thesis. *Entrance requirements:* For doctorate, DAT, minimum GPA of 3.0. Additional exam requirements/recommendations for international students: Required—TOEFL (minimum score 550 paper-based; 225 computer-based). *Application deadline:* For fall admission, 1/15 for domestic students, 2/15 for international students. Applications are processed on a rolling basis. Application fee: $50. *Expenses:* Contact institution. *Financial support:* In 2011–12, 372 students received support, including 1 fellowship with full tuition reimbursement available, 11 teaching assistantships with full tuition reimbursements available. Financial award application deadline: 4/1; financial award applicants required to submit FAFSA. *Faculty research:* Tissue engineering, dental materials. *Unit head:* Dr. Robert A. Uchin, Dean, 954-262-7312, Fax: 954-262-1782, E-mail: ruchin@nova.edu. *Application contact:* Su-Ann Zarrett, Associate Director, 954-262-1108, Fax: 954-262-2282, E-mail: zarrett@nsu.nova.edu.

The Ohio State University, College of Dentistry, Columbus, OH 43210. Offers dentistry (MS, DDS); oral biology (PhD); DDS/PhD. *Accreditation:* ADA (one or more programs are accredited). *Faculty:* 80. *Students:* 501 full-time (214 women), 18 part-time (4 women); includes 99 minority (19 Black or African American, non-Hispanic/Latino; 3 American Indian or Alaska Native, non-Hispanic/Latino; 53 Asian, non-Hispanic/Latino; 20 Hispanic/Latino; 4 Two or more races, non-Hispanic/Latino), 25 international. Average age 27. In 2011, 21 master's, 104 doctorates awarded. Terminal master's awarded for partial completion of doctoral program. *Degree requirements:* For master's, thesis; for doctorate, thesis/dissertation (for some programs). *Entrance requirements:* For doctorate, DAT (for DDS). Additional exam requirements/recommendations for international students: Required—TOEFL (minimum score 550 paper-based; 79 iBT), Michigan English Language Assessment Battery (minimum score 82). *Application deadline:* Applications are processed on a rolling basis. Electronic applications accepted. *Expenses:* Contact institution. *Financial support:* In 2011–12, 7 fellowships with tuition reimbursements, 13 research assistantships with tuition reimbursements (averaging $11,000 per year), 78 teaching assistantships with tuition reimbursements (averaging $12,000 per year) were awarded; Federal Work-Study and institutionally sponsored loans also available. Financial award application deadline: 3/1. *Faculty research:* Neurobiology, inflammation and immunity, materials science, bone biology. Total annual research expenditures: $3.4 million. *Unit head:* Dr. Patrick M. Lloyd, Dean, 614-292-9755. *Application contact:* Georgia Paletta, Interim Director, 614-292-9444, Fax: 614-292-3656, E-mail: paletta.4@osu.edu. Web site: http://www.dent.ohio-state.edu/.

Oregon Health & Science University, School of Dentistry, Professional Program in Dentistry, Portland, OR 97239-3098. Offers dentistry (DMD); oral and maxillofacial surgery (Certificate); MD/DMD. *Accreditation:* ADA. *Entrance requirements:* For doctorate, DAT. Electronic applications accepted. *Faculty research:* Dentin permeability, tooth sensations, fluoride metabolism, immunology of periodontal disease, craniofacial growth.

Saint Louis University, Graduate Education, Center for Advanced Dental Education, St. Louis, MO 63103-2097. Offers endodontics (MSD); orthodontics (MSD); periodontics (MSD). *Degree requirements:* For master's, comprehensive exam, thesis, teaching practicum. *Entrance requirements:* For master's, GRE General Test, NBDE (National Board Dental Exam), DDS or DMD, interview, letters of recommendation. Additional exam requirements/recommendations for international students: Required—TOEFL (minimum score 525 paper-based; 194 computer-based). Electronic applications accepted. *Faculty research:* Craniofacial growth.

Southern Illinois University Edwardsville, School of Dental Medicine, Alton, IL 62002. Offers DMD. *Accreditation:* ADA. *Faculty:* 21 full-time (4 women). *Students:* 196 full-time (77 women); includes 24 minority (3 Black or African American, non-Hispanic/Latino; 1 American Indian or Alaska Native, non-Hispanic/Latino; 7 Asian, non-Hispanic/Latino; 8 Hispanic/Latino; 2 Native Hawaiian or other Pacific Islander, non-Hispanic/Latino; 3 Two or more races, non-Hispanic/Latino). Average age 25. In 2011, 46 doctorates awarded. *Entrance requirements:* For doctorate, DAT. *Application deadline:* For fall admission, 6/1 priority date for domestic students, 6/1 for international students. Application fee: $20. Electronic applications accepted. *Expenses:* Contact institution. *Financial support:*

Application deadline: 3/1; applicants required to submit FAFSA. *Unit head:* Dr. Bruce Rotter, Interim Dean, 618-474-7000, E-mail: sdmapps@siue.edu. *Application contact:* Michelle Robinson, Coordinator of Graduate Recruitment, 618-650-2811, Fax: 618-650-3523, E-mail: michero@siue.edu. Web site: http://www.siue.edu/dentalmedicine.

Stony Brook University, State University of New York, Stony Brook University Medical Center, Health Sciences Center, School of Dental Medicine, Professional Program in Dental Medicine, Stony Brook, NY 11794. Offers dental medicine (DDS); endodontics (Certificate); orthodontics (Certificate); periodontics (Certificate). *Accreditation:* ADA (one or more programs are accredited). *Entrance requirements:* For doctorate, DAT.

Temple University, Health Sciences Center, Kornberg School of Dentistry, Professional Program in Dentistry, Philadelphia, PA 19122-6096. Offers DMD, DMD/MBA. *Accreditation:* ADA. *Entrance requirements:* For doctorate, DAT, 6 credits of course work in each biology, chemistry, organic chemistry, physics, and English. *Expenses:* Contact institution.

Texas A&M Health Science Center, Baylor College of Dentistry, Professional Program in Dentistry, College Station, TX 77840. Offers DDS. *Entrance requirements:* For doctorate, DAT. *Expenses:* Contact institution. *Faculty research:* Bleaching, implants, craniofacial growth, oral oncology, pulp biology.

Tufts University, School of Dental Medicine, International Student Program in Dental Medicine, Medford, MA 02155. Offers DMD. *Accreditation:* ADA. *Entrance requirements:* For doctorate, National Dental Hygiene Board Exam Part I, BDS, DDS, or equivalent. Additional exam requirements/recommendations for international students: Required—TOEFL. *Expenses:* Tuition: Full-time $41,208; part-time $1030 per credit hour. Full-time tuition and fees vary according to degree level, program and student level. Part-time tuition and fees vary according to course load.

Tufts University, School of Dental Medicine, Professional Program in Dental Medicine, Medford, MA 02155. Offers DMD, DMD/PhD. *Accreditation:* ADA. *Entrance requirements:* For doctorate, DAT. *Expenses:* Tuition: Full-time $41,208; part-time $1030 per credit hour. Full-time tuition and fees vary according to degree level, program and student level. Part-time tuition and fees vary according to course load.

Universidad Central del Este, School of Dentistry, San Pedro de Macoris, Dominican Republic. Offers DMD.

Universidad Iberoamericana, Graduate School, Santo Domingo D.N., Dominican Republic. Offers business administration (MBA, PMBA); constitutional law (LL M); dentistry (DMD); educational management (MA); integrated marketing communication (MA); psychopedagogical intervention (M Ed); real estate law (LL M); strategic management of human talent (MM).

Universidad Nacional Pedro Henriquez Urena, School of Dentistry, Santo Domingo, Dominican Republic. Offers DDS.

Université Laval, Faculty of Dentistry, Professional Programs in Dentistry, Québec, QC G1K 7P4, Canada. Offers DMD. *Accreditation:* ADA. *Entrance requirements:* For doctorate, visual perception exam, manual dexterity exam, interview, knowledge of French. Electronic applications accepted.

University at Buffalo, the State University of New York, Graduate School, School of Dental Medicine, Graduate Programs in Dental Medicine, Buffalo, NY 14260. Offers advanced education in general dentistry (Certificate); combined prosthodontics (Certificate); endodontics (Certificate); general practice residency (Certificate); oral and maxillofacial pathology (Certificate); oral and maxillofacial surgery (Certificate); oral biology (PhD); oral sciences (MS); orthodontics (MS, Certificate); pediatric dentistry (Certificate); periodontics (Certificate); temporomandibular disorders and oralfacial pain (Certificate). *Degree requirements:* For master's, thesis; for doctorate, thesis/dissertation; for Certificate, comprehensive exam (for some programs). *Entrance requirements:* For doctorate, GRE General Test, GRE Subject Test in biology or DDS; for Certificate, DDS, DMD or equivalent. Additional exam requirements/recommendations for international students: Required—TOEFL (minimum score 79 iBT). Electronic applications accepted. *Expenses:* Contact institution. *Faculty research:* Immunology and microbiology of dental disease, surface science, saliva biochemistry, bone biology.

University at Buffalo, the State University of New York, Graduate School, School of Dental Medicine, Professional Program in Dental Medicine, Buffalo, NY 14260. Offers DDS. *Accreditation:* ADA. *Degree requirements:* For doctorate, National Dental Board Exams. *Entrance requirements:* For doctorate, DAT.

The University of Alabama at Birmingham, School of Dentistry, Professional Program in Dentistry, Birmingham, AL 35294. Offers DMD. *Accreditation:* ADA. *Entrance requirements:* For doctorate, DAT. Electronic applications accepted. *Expenses:* Tuition, state resident: full-time $5922; part-time $309 per hour. Tuition, nonresident: full-time $13,428; part-time $726 per hour. Tuition and fees vary according to program. *Financial support:* Fellowships and Federal Work-Study available. *Faculty research:* Etiology and pathogenesis of dental diseases, dental biomaterials, therapy of dental diseases. *Unit head:* Dr. Huw F. Thomas, Dean, 205-934-4720, Fax: 205-934-9283. *Application contact:* Dr. Steven J. Filler, Director of Dentistry Admissions, 205-934-5424, Fax: 205-975-6519, E-mail: sfiller@uab.edu.

University of Alberta, Faculty of Medicine and Dentistry, Department of Dentistry, Professional Program in Dentistry, Edmonton, AB T6G 2E1, Canada. Offers DDS. *Accreditation:* ADA. *Entrance requirements:* For doctorate, DAT (Canadian version), interview. Additional exam requirements/recommendations for international students: Required—TOEFL. Electronic applications accepted. *Faculty research:* Oral biology, biochemistry of connective tissues, preventive dentistry, applied clinical orthodontics, biomaterials.

The University of British Columbia, Faculty of Dentistry, Professional Program in Dentistry, Vancouver, BC V6T 1Z1, Canada. Offers DMD. *Accreditation:* ADA. *Entrance requirements:* For doctorate, DAT, ACFD Eligibility Exam, interview, psychomotor assessment. Additional exam requirements/recommendations for international students: Required—IELTS. Electronic applications accepted. *Expenses:* Contact institution.

University of California, Los Angeles, School of Dentistry, Professional Program in Dentistry, Los Angeles, CA 90095. Offers DDS, Certificate, DDS/MS, DDS/PhD, MS/Certificate, PhD/Certificate. *Accreditation:* ADA (one or more programs are accredited). *Students:* 370 full-time (167 women); includes 130 minority (7 Black or African American, non-Hispanic/Latino; 1 American Indian or Alaska Native, non-Hispanic/Latino; 95 Asian, non-Hispanic/Latino; 13 Hispanic/Latino; 14 Two or more races, non-Hispanic/Latino), 17 international. Average age 26. 1,732 applicants, 8% accepted, 88 enrolled. In 2011, 99 doctorates awarded. *Entrance requirements:* For doctorate, DAT. Application fee: $60. *Financial support:* In 2011–12, 18 fellowships, 1 teaching assistantship were awarded; research assistantships, Federal Work-Study, institutionally sponsored loans, scholarships/grants, tuition waivers (full and partial), and unspecified assistantships also available. Financial award application deadline: 3/1. *Unit head:* Dr. No Hee Park, Acting Division Chair, 310-206-6063, E-mail: nhpark@dentistry.ucla.edu. *Application contact:* School of Dentistry Admissions, 310-794-7971, E-mail: dds_admissions@dentistry.ucla.edu. Web site: http://www.dentistry.ucla.edu.

Dentistry

University of California, San Francisco, School of Dentistry, San Francisco, CA 94143-0150. Offers DDS. *Accreditation:* ADA. *Entrance requirements:* For doctorate, DAT. *Expenses:* Contact institution.

University of Colorado Denver, School of Dental Medicine, Aurora, CO 80045. Offers dental surgery (DDS); orthodontics (MS); periodontics (MS). *Accreditation:* ADA. *Faculty:* 73 full-time (26 women), 40 part-time/adjunct (14 women). *Students:* 361 full-time (154 women), 2 part-time (0 women); includes 82 minority (10 Black or African American, non-Hispanic/Latino; 2 American Indian or Alaska Native, non-Hispanic/Latino; 40 Asian, non-Hispanic/Latino; 29 Hispanic/Latino; 1 Two or more races, non-Hispanic/Latino), 37 international. Average age 30. 110 applicants, 97% accepted, 95 enrolled. In 2011, 16 master's, 73 doctorates awarded. *Entrance requirements:* For master's, GRE, National Board Dental Exam Part I and II, three letters of recommendation, personal essay; for doctorate, DAT, prerequisite courses in microbiology, general biochemistry and English composition (1 semester each); general chemistry/lab, organic chemistry/lab, general biology/lab and general physics/lab (2 semesters each), interview, letters of recommendation, letter/essay. Additional exam requirements/recommendations for international students: Required—TOEFL (minimum score 580 paper-based; 237 computer-based). *Application deadline:* For fall admission, 12/31 for domestic students. Application fee: $75. Electronic applications accepted. *Expenses:* Contact institution. *Financial support:* In 2011–12, 64 students received support. Application deadline: 4/1; applicants required to submit FAFSA. *Faculty research:* Pain control, materials research, geriatric dentistry, restorative dentistry, periodontic. *Total annual research expenditures:* $6.1 million. *Unit head:* Dr. Denise K. Kassebaum, Dean, 303-724-7100, Fax: 303-724-7109, E-mail: denise.kassebaum@ucdenver.edu. *Application contact:* Dr. Randy L. Kluender, Assistant Dean for Admissions and Student Affairs, 303-724-7120, E-mail: randy.kluender@ucdenver.edu. Web site: http://ucdenver.edu/academics/colleges/dentalmedicine/Pages/DentalMedicine.aspx.

University of Connecticut Health Center, School of Dental Medicine, Professional Program in Dental Medicine, Farmington, CT 06030. Offers DMD, Certificate. *Accreditation:* ADA. *Entrance requirements:* For doctorate, National Board Dental Examination. Additional exam requirements/recommendations for international students: Required—TOEFL (minimum score 550 paper-based; 215 computer-based).

University of Detroit Mercy, School of Dentistry, Professional Program in Dentistry, Detroit, MI 48221. Offers DDS. *Accreditation:* ADA. *Entrance requirements:* For doctorate, DAT. *Faculty research:* Peer evaluation in teaching, evaluation of restorative materials, HIV and periodontal disease.

University of Florida, College of Dentistry, Professional Programs in Dentistry, Gainesville, FL 32611. Offers dentistry (DMD); foreign trained dentistry (Certificate). *Degree requirements:* For Certificate, National Dental Boards Parts I and II. *Entrance requirements:* For doctorate, DAT, interview; for Certificate, interview. Additional exam requirements/recommendations for international students: Required—TOEFL (minimum score 550 paper-based; 213 computer-based). *Faculty research:* Actinobacillus, critical thinking, DNA adenine, methylase, LJP.

University of Illinois at Chicago, College of Dentistry, Professional Program in Dentistry, Chicago, IL 60607-7128. Offers DDS, DDS/MPH, DDS/PhD. *Accreditation:* ADA. *Entrance requirements:* For doctorate, DAT. Additional exam requirements/recommendations for international students: Required—TOEFL. Electronic applications accepted.

The University of Iowa, College of Dentistry and Graduate College, Graduate Programs in Dentistry, Iowa City, IA 52242-1316. Offers endodontics (MS, Certificate); operative dentistry (MS, Certificate); oral and maxillofacial surgery (MS, Certificate); oral pathology, radiology and medicine (MS, Certificate), including oral and maxillofacial pathology (Certificate), oral and maxillofacial radiology (Certificate), stomatology (MS); oral science (MS, PhD); orthodontics (MS, Certificate); pediatric dentistry (Certificate); periodontics (MS, Certificate); preventive and community dentistry (MS), including dental public health; prosthodontics (MS, Certificate). *Accreditation:* ADA. *Degree requirements:* For master's, thesis; for doctorate, thesis/dissertation. *Entrance requirements:* For master's, GRE, DDS; for Certificate, DDS. Additional exam requirements/recommendations for international students: Required—TOEFL. *Expenses:* Contact institution.

The University of Iowa, College of Dentistry, Professional Program in Dentistry, Iowa City, IA 52242-1316. Offers DDS. *Accreditation:* ADA. *Entrance requirements:* For doctorate, DAT, minimum 90 semester hours with minimum GPA of 2.5.

University of Kentucky, College of Dentistry, Lexington, KY 40536-0297. Offers MS, DMD. *Accreditation:* ADA (one or more programs are accredited). *Faculty:* 70 full-time (25 women), 46 part-time/adjunct (11 women). *Students:* 229 full-time (110 women); includes 43 minority (20 Black or African American, non-Hispanic/Latino; 18 Asian, non-Hispanic/Latino; 5 Hispanic/Latino), 1 international. Average age 28. 1,464 applicants, 6% accepted, 57 enrolled. In 2011, 51 degrees awarded. *Median time to degree:* Of those who began their doctoral program in fall 2003, 98% received their degree in 8 years or less. *Degree requirements:* For master's, comprehensive exam, thesis optional. *Entrance requirements:* For doctorate, DAT. *Application deadline:* For fall admission, 12/1 priority date for domestic students. Applications are processed on a rolling basis. Application fee: $65. Electronic applications accepted. *Financial support:* In 2011–12, 65 students received support. Fellowships, research assistantships, teaching assistantships, career-related internships or fieldwork, Federal Work-Study, institutionally sponsored loans, and scholarships/grants available. Support available to part-time students. Financial award application deadline: 4/15; financial award applicants required to submit FAFSA. *Faculty research:* Herpes virus reactivation, chronic oral infection and inflammation of periodontal disease, prevention and control programs, orofacial pain, craniofacial bone biology. *Total annual research expenditures:* $2.5 million. *Unit head:* Dr. Sharon P. Turner, Dean, 859-323-1884, Fax: 859-323-1042. *Application contact:* Melissa D. Lockard, Admissions Coordinator, 859-323-6071, Fax: 859-257-5550, E-mail: mlock2@email.uky.edu. Web site: http://www.mc.uky.edu/Dentistry/.

University of Louisville, School of Dentistry, Louisville, KY 40202. Offers dentistry (DMD); oral biology (MS). *Accreditation:* ADA (one or more programs are accredited). Part-time programs available. *Degree requirements:* For master's, thesis; for doctorate, National Board exams. *Entrance requirements:* For master's, DAT, GRE General Test, or National Board Dental Exam, minimum GPA of 2.75; for doctorate, DAT, 32 hours of course work in science. Additional exam requirements/recommendations for international students: Required—TOEFL (minimum score 100 iBT). Electronic applications accepted. *Expenses:* Contact institution. *Faculty research:* Inflammation and periondontitis, birth defects and developmental biology, biomaterials, oral infections, digital imaging.

The University of Manchester, School of Dentistry, Manchester, United Kingdom. Offers basic dental sciences (cancer studies) (M Phil, PhD); basic dental sciences (molecular genetics) (M Phil, PhD); basic dental sciences (stem cell biology) (M Phil, PhD); biomaterials sciences and dental technology (M Phil, PhD); dental public health/community dentistry (M Phil, PhD); dental science (clinical) (PhD); endodontology (M Phil, PhD); fixed and removable prosthodontics (M Phil, PhD); operative dentistry (M Phil, PhD); oral and maxillofacial surgery (M Phil, PhD); oral radiology (M Phil, PhD); orthodontics (M Phil, PhD); restorative dentistry (M Phil, PhD).

University of Manitoba, Faculty of Dentistry, Professional Program in Dentistry, Winnipeg, MB R3T 2N2, Canada. Offers DMD. *Accreditation:* ADA. *Entrance requirements:* For doctorate, DAT, interview. *Faculty research:* Oral physiology, microbiology, and biochemistry of the oral cavity in health and disease; application of clinical research.

University of Maryland, Baltimore, Professional and Advanced Education Programs in Dentistry, Baltimore, MD 21201-1627. Offers advanced general dentistry (Certificate); dentistry (DDS); endodontics (Certificate); oral-maxillofacial surgery (Certificate); orthodontics (Certificate); pediatric dentistry (Certificate); periodontics (Certificate); prosthodontics (Certificate); DDS/MBA; DDS/PhD. *Accreditation:* ADA. *Students:* 583 full-time (295 women), 3 part-time (1 woman); includes 198 minority (33 Black or African American, non-Hispanic/Latino; 2 American Indian or Alaska Native, non-Hispanic/Latino; 121 Asian, non-Hispanic/Latino; 31 Hispanic/Latino; 11 Two or more races, non-Hispanic/Latino), 20 international. Average age 26. In 2011, 128 doctorates, 31 Certificates awarded. *Entrance requirements:* For doctorate, DAT, coursework in science; for Certificate, National Dental Board Exams, DDS. Additional exam requirements/recommendations for international students: Required—TOEFL (minimum score 550 paper-based; 213 computer-based; 80 iBT). *Application deadline:* Applications are processed on a rolling basis. Application fee: $85. Electronic applications accepted. *Expenses:* Contact institution. *Financial support:* Career-related internships or fieldwork, Federal Work-Study, scholarships/grants, and traineeships available. Financial award application deadline: 3/1; financial award applicants required to submit FAFSA. *Faculty research:* Pain/neuroscience, oncology/molecular and cell biology, infectious disease/microbiology, bio-material studies, health promotion and disparities. *Unit head:* Dr. Christian S. Stohler, Dean, 410-706-7461. *Application contact:* Dr. Patricia Meehan, Assistant Dean for Admissions, 410-706-7472, Fax: 410-706-0945, E-mail: ddsadmissions@umaryland.edu. Web site: http://www.dental.umaryland.edu/.

University of Medicine and Dentistry of New Jersey, New Jersey Dental School, Newark, NJ 07101-1709. Offers dental science (MS); dentistry (DMD); endodontics (Certificate); oral medicine (Certificate); orthodontics (Certificate); pediatric dentistry (Certificate); periodontics (Certificate); prosthodontics (Certificate); DMD/MPH; DMD/PhD; MD/Certificate; MS/Certificate. DMD/MPH offered jointly with New Jersey Institute of Technology, Rutgers, The State University of New Jersey, Camden. *Accreditation:* ADA (one or more programs are accredited). *Entrance requirements:* For doctorate, DAT. Electronic applications accepted. *Expenses:* Contact institution.

University of Michigan, School of Dentistry, Professional Program in Dentistry, Ann Arbor, MI 48109. Offers DDS. *Accreditation:* ADA. *Students:* 442 full-time (202 women); includes 102 minority (21 Black or African American, non-Hispanic/Latino; 66 Asian, non-Hispanic/Latino; 11 Hispanic/Latino; 4 Two or more races, non-Hispanic/Latino), 17 international. Average age 26. 2,148 applicants, 10% accepted, 108 enrolled. In 2011, 111 doctorates awarded. *Entrance requirements:* For doctorate, DAT, 6 credits of course work in English; 8 credits of course work each in chemistry, organic chemistry, biology, and physics; 3 credits of biochemistry, microbiology, psychology, sociology. *Application deadline:* For fall admission, 12/1 for domestic students. Applications are processed on a rolling basis. Application fee: $65. Electronic applications accepted. *Expenses:* Contact institution. *Financial support:* In 2011–12, 364 students received support. Fellowships, research assistantships, teaching assistantships, and scholarships/grants available. Financial award applicants required to submit FAFSA. *Unit head:* Dr. Marilyn Woolfolk, Assistant Dean for Student Services, 734-763-3313, Fax: 734-764-1922, E-mail: ddsadmissions@umich.edu. *Application contact:* Patricia Katcher, Associate Director of Admissions, 734-763-3316, Fax: 734-764-1922, E-mail: ddsadmissions@umich.edu. Web site: http://www.dent.umich.edu.

University of Minnesota, Twin Cities Campus, School of Dentistry, Professional Program in Dentistry, Minneapolis, MN 55455-0213. Offers DDS. *Accreditation:* ADA. *Entrance requirements:* For doctorate, DAT. Additional exam requirements/recommendations for international students: Required—TOEFL.

University of Mississippi Medical Center, School of Dentistry, Jackson, MS 39216-4505. Offers MS, DMD, PhD. *Accreditation:* ADA. *Entrance requirements:* For doctorate, DAT (for DMD). *Expenses:* Contact institution. *Faculty research:* Bone growth factors, salivary markers of disease, biomaterial synthesis and evaluation, metabolic bone disease, periodontal disease.

University of Missouri–Kansas City, School of Dentistry, Kansas City, MO 64110-2499. Offers advanced education in dentistry (Graduate Dental Certificate); dental hygiene education (MS); dentistry (DDS); endodontics (Graduate Dental Certificate); oral and maxillofacial surgery (Graduate Dental Certificate); oral biology (MS, PhD); orthodontics and dentofacial orthopedics (Graduate Dental Certificate); pediatric dentistry (Graduate Dental Certificate); periodontics (Graduate Dental Certificate). PhD (interdisciplinary) offered through the School of Graduate Studies. *Accreditation:* ADA (one or more programs are accredited). *Faculty:* 95 full-time (41 women), 62 part-time/adjunct (18 women). *Students:* 420 full-time (182 women), 44 part-time (26 women); includes 67 minority (7 Black or African American, non-Hispanic/Latino; 2 American Indian or Alaska Native, non-Hispanic/Latino; 45 Asian, non-Hispanic/Latino; 11 Hispanic/Latino; 2 Two or more races, non-Hispanic/Latino), 2 international. Average age 27. 511 applicants, 23% accepted, 115 enrolled. In 2011, 9 master's, 98 doctorates, 17 other advanced degrees awarded. *Degree requirements:* For master's, thesis; for doctorate, thesis/dissertation (for some programs). *Entrance requirements:* For master's, DAT, letters of evaluation, personal interview; for doctorate, DAT (for DDS); for Graduate Dental Certificate, DDS. Additional exam requirements/recommendations for international students: Required—TOEFL (minimum score 550 paper-based; 213 computer-based; 80 iBT). *Application deadline:* For fall admission, 2/1 for domestic and international students. Application fee: $45 ($50 for international students). *Expenses:* Contact institution. *Financial support:* In 2011–12, 3 fellowships (averaging $59,417 per year), 3 research assistantships (averaging $19,471 per year) were awarded; career-related internships or fieldwork, Federal Work-Study, institutionally sponsored loans, and tuition waivers (full and partial) also available. Support available to part-time students. Financial award application deadline: 3/1; financial award applicants required to submit FAFSA. *Faculty research:* Biomaterials, dental use of lasers, effectiveness of periodontal treatments, temporomandibular joint dysfunction. *Unit head:* Dr. Marsha Pyle, Dean, 816-235-2010. *Application contact:* Dr. John Killip, Associate Dean for Student Programs, 816-235-2080. Web site: http://dentistry.umkc.edu/.

University of Nebraska Medical Center, College of Dentistry, Professional Program in Dentistry, Omaha, NE 68198. Offers DDS. *Accreditation:* ADA. *Entrance requirements:* For doctorate, DAT. *Expenses:* Contact institution.

University of Nebraska Medical Center, College of Dentistry, Program in Dentistry, Omaha, NE 68198. Offers MS, PhD, Certificate. *Accreditation:* ADA. *Degree requirements:* For Certificate, thesis or alternative. *Entrance requirements:* For degree, GRE or National Board Dental Exam, DDS or DMD.

The University of North Carolina at Chapel Hill, School of Dentistry, Professional Program in Dentistry, Chapel Hill, NC 27599-7450. Offers DDS, DDS/PhD. *Accreditation:* ADA. *Faculty:* 104 full-time, 421 part-time/adjunct. *Students:* 319 full-time

(163 women); includes 93 minority (38 Black or African American, non-Hispanic/Latino; 4 American Indian or Alaska Native, non-Hispanic/Latino; 35 Asian, non-Hispanic/Latino; 16 Hispanic/Latino). Average age 25. 1,421 applicants, 6% accepted, 81 enrolled. In 2011, 76 degrees awarded. *Entrance requirements:* For doctorate, DAT, interview. Additional exam requirements/recommendations for international students: Required—TOEFL (minimum score 550 paper-based; 213 computer-based). *Application deadline:* For fall admission, 11/1 for domestic and international students. Application fee: $80. Electronic applications accepted. *Expenses:* Contact institution. *Financial support:* In 2011–12, 6 fellowships (averaging $1,800 per year) were awarded; Federal Work-Study, institutionally sponsored loans, and scholarships/grants also available. Financial award application deadline: 3/1; financial award applicants required to submit FAFSA. *Unit head:* Dr. Janet M. Guthmiller, Associate Dean for Academic Affairs, 919-537-3347, Fax: 919-966-5795, E-mail: janet_guthmiller@dentistry.unc.edu. *Application contact:* Dr. Aldridge D. Wilder, Jr., Assistant Dean for Admissions and Student Affairs, 919-537-3347, Fax: 919-966-5795, E-mail: aldridge_wilder@dentistry.unc.edu. Web site: http://www.dentistry.unc.edu/portals/prospectivestudents/.

University of Oklahoma Health Sciences Center, College of Dentistry, Advanced Education in General Dentistry Program, Oklahoma City, OK 73190. Offers Certificate. *Accreditation:* ADA. Electronic applications accepted.

University of Oklahoma Health Sciences Center, College of Dentistry, Professional Program in Dentistry, Oklahoma City, OK 73190. Offers DDS. *Accreditation:* ADA. *Degree requirements:* For doctorate, National Board Dental Exam Part I and Part II. *Entrance requirements:* For doctorate, DAT, minimum GPA of 2.5; course work in English, general psychology, biology, general chemistry, organic chemistry, physics, and biochemistry. Additional exam requirements/recommendations for international students: Required—TOEFL (minimum score 570 paper-based; 230 computer-based). Electronic applications accepted. *Faculty research:* Dental caries, microwave sterilization, dental care delivery systems, dental materials, oral health of Native Americans.

University of Pennsylvania, School of Dental Medicine, Philadelphia, PA 19104. Offers DMD, DMD/MS Ed. *Accreditation:* ADA. *Faculty:* 70 full-time (21 women), 330 part-time/adjunct (88 women). *Students:* 525 full-time (293 women); includes 262 minority (17 Black or African American, non-Hispanic/Latino; 1 American Indian or Alaska Native, non-Hispanic/Latino; 224 Asian, non-Hispanic/Latino; 20 Hispanic/Latino). Average age 24. 2,207 applicants, 12% accepted, 121 enrolled. *Entrance requirements:* For doctorate, DAT. *Application deadline:* For fall admission, 12/1 for domestic and international students. Applications are processed on a rolling basis. Application fee: $60. *Expenses:* Contact institution. *Financial support:* In 2011–12, 222 students received support. Federal Work-Study, scholarships/grants, and Health Professions loans, Perkins loans, federal Direct loans and federal Grad Plus loans available. Financial award application deadline: 5/15; financial award applicants required to submit FAFSA. *Faculty research:* Bone, teeth and extracellular matrix; craniofacial genetic anomalies; infection and host response; periodonatal diseases; stem cells; improvement of tempormandibular function. *Unit head:* Dr. Denis Kinane, Dean, 215-898-8941, Fax: 215-573-4075. *Application contact:* Corky Cacas, Director of Admissions, 215-898-8943, Fax: 215-573-9648, E-mail: dental-admissions@dental.upenn.edu. Web site: http://www.dental.upenn.edu/.

University of Pittsburgh, School of Dental Medicine, Professional Program in Dental Medicine, Pittsburgh, PA 15260. Offers DMD. *Accreditation:* ADA. *Faculty:* 91 full-time (42 women), 188 part-time/adjunct (50 women). *Students:* 319 full-time (121 women); includes 104 minority (10 Black or African American, non-Hispanic/Latino; 79 Asian, non-Hispanic/Latino; 13 Hispanic/Latino; 2 Two or more races, non-Hispanic/Latino), 13 international. Average age 26. 2,149 applicants, 10% accepted, 80 enrolled. In 2011, 81 degrees awarded. *Entrance requirements:* For doctorate, DAT, minimum GPA of 3.2 (science and non-science). Additional exam requirements/recommendations for international students: Required—TOEFL (minimum score 100 iBT). *Application deadline:* For fall admission, 12/1 for domestic and international students. Applications are processed on a rolling basis. Application fee: $35 ($50 for international students). Electronic applications accepted. *Expenses:* Contact institution. *Financial support:* In 2011–12, 88 students received support. Fellowships, teaching assistantships with full tuition reimbursements available, and scholarships/grants available. Financial award application deadline: 4/30; financial award applicants required to submit FAFSA. *Faculty research:* Human genetics, tissue engineering, public health, periodontal disease, cariology. *Total annual research expenditures:* $5.8 million. *Unit head:* Dr. Kenneth Etzel, Associate Dean for Student Services and Admissions, 412-648-8422, Fax: 412-648-9751, E-mail: kre@pitt.edu. *Application contact:* Rosemary Mangold, Assistant Director of Admissions, 412-648-8437, Fax: 412-648-9571, E-mail: mangold@pitt.edu. Web site: http://www.dental.pitt.edu.

University of Pittsburgh, School of Dental Medicine, Residency Programs in Dental Medicine, Advanced Education Program in General Practice Residency, Pittsburgh, PA 15260. Offers Certificate. *Accreditation:* ADA. *Faculty:* 3 full-time (1 woman), 5 part-time/adjunct (2 women). *Students:* 3 full-time (all women); includes 2 minority (1 Black or African American, non-Hispanic/Latino; 1 Asian, non-Hispanic/Latino). Average age 28. 17 applicants, 18% accepted, 3 enrolled. In 2011, 3 Certificates awarded. *Application deadline:* For fall admission, 10/15 for domestic students. Application fee: $0. Electronic applications accepted. *Expenses:* Tuition, state resident: full-time $18,774; part-time $760 per credit. Tuition, nonresident: full-time $30,736; part-time $1258 per credit. *Required fees:* $740; $200 per term. Tuition and fees vary according to program. *Financial support:* Fellowships, research assistantships, and teaching assistantships available. *Unit head:* Dr. Mary Ellen Cuccaro, Program Director, 412-648-6730, Fax: 412-648-6798, E-mail: mec11@pitt.edu. *Application contact:* Andrea M. Ford, Residency Coordinator, 412-648-6801, Fax: 412-648-6835, E-mail: fordam@upmc.edu.

University of Pittsburgh, School of Dental Medicine, Residency Programs in Dental Medicine, Department of Pediatric Dentistry, Pittsburgh, PA 15260. Offers MDS, Certificate. *Accreditation:* ADA. *Faculty:* 3 full-time (all women), 3 part-time/adjunct (2 women). *Students:* 4 full-time (2 women); includes 1 minority (Hispanic/Latino). Average age 28. 65 applicants, 3% accepted, 2 enrolled. *Degree requirements:* For Certificate, clinical research project. *Entrance requirements:* For degree, National Dental Board Exam Parts I and II, U.S. or Canadian dental degree. *Application deadline:* For fall admission, 10/1 for domestic students. Application fee: $35. Electronic applications accepted. *Expenses:* Tuition, state resident: full-time $18,774; part-time $760 per credit. Tuition, nonresident: full-time $30,736; part-time $1258 per credit. *Required fees:* $740; $200 per term. Tuition and fees vary according to program. *Financial support:* In 2011–12, 4 students received support. Stipends ($24,000) available. Financial award application deadline: 7/30; financial award applicants required to submit FAFSA. *Faculty research:* Sports dentistry, behavior management, special needs populations, adolescent oral health, infant oral health, genetics, and cariology. *Unit head:* Dr. Deborah A. Studen-Pavlovich, Chair and Professor, 412-648-8183, Fax: 412-648-8435, E-mail: das12@pitt.edu. *Application contact:* Sharon A. Hohman, Departmental Secretary, 412-648-8416, Fax: 412-648-8435, E-mail: sah10@pitt.edu. Web site: http://www.dental.pitt.edu.

University of Pittsburgh, School of Dental Medicine, Residency Programs in Dental Medicine, Program in Advanced Education in General Dentistry, Pittsburgh, PA 15260. Offers Certificate. *Accreditation:* ADA. *Faculty:* 4 part-time/adjunct (1 woman). *Students:* 3 full-time (1 woman); includes 1 minority (Asian, non-Hispanic/Latino). Average age 27. 35 applicants, 9% accepted, 3 enrolled. In 2011, 3 Certificates awarded. *Entrance requirements:* For degree, National Dental Board Parts I and II, American or Canadian DDS or DMD. *Application deadline:* For fall admission, 12/15 for domestic students. Applications are processed on a rolling basis. Application fee: $50. Electronic applications accepted. *Expenses:* Tuition, state resident: full-time $18,774; part-time $760 per credit. Tuition, nonresident: full-time $30,736; part-time $1258 per credit. *Required fees:* $740; $200 per term. Tuition and fees vary according to program. *Financial support:* In 2011–12, 3 students received support, including 3 fellowships (averaging $23,000 per year). *Unit head:* Dr. Maribeth Krzesinski, Director, 412-648-8093, Fax: 412-383-7796, E-mail: mbk3@pitt.edu. *Application contact:* Pamela A. Edwards, Administrator, Office of Resident Education, 412-648-8406, Fax: 412-648-8219, E-mail: pae3@pitt.edu. Web site: http://www.dental.pitt.edu/students/residency_programs.php.

University of Puerto Rico, Medical Sciences Campus, School of Dental Medicine, Professional Program in Dentistry, San Juan, PR 00936-5067. Offers DMD. *Accreditation:* ADA. *Entrance requirements:* For doctorate, DAT, interview. *Expenses:* Contact institution. *Faculty research:* Analgesic drugs, anti-inflammatory drugs, saliva cytoanalysis, dental material and cariology, oral health condition of school-age population.

University of Saskatchewan, College of Dentistry, Saskatoon, SK S7N 5A2, Canada. Offers DMD. *Accreditation:* ADA. *Entrance requirements:* For doctorate, DAT. Additional exam requirements/recommendations for international students: Required—TOEFL (minimum score 550 paper-based; 213 computer-based; 80 iBT), IELTS (minimum score 6.5), Michigan English Language Assessment Battery (85); CanTEST (4.0); CAEL (60); CPE (C). Electronic applications accepted. *Expenses:* Contact institution. *Faculty research:* Protein structure, oral cavity, immunology, bone densitometry, biological sciences.

University of Southern California, Graduate School, Herman Ostrow School of Dentistry, Professional Program in Dentistry, Los Angeles, CA 90089. Offers DDS, DDS/MBA, DDS/MS. *Accreditation:* ADA (one or more programs are accredited).

The University of Tennessee Health Science Center, College of Dentistry, Memphis, TN 38163-0002. Offers dentistry (DDS); oral and maxillofacial surgery (Certificate); orthodontics (MS); pediatric dentistry (MS, Certificate); periodontics (MS); prosthodontics (Certificate). *Accreditation:* ADA (one or more programs are accredited). *Degree requirements:* For master's, thesis. *Entrance requirements:* For master's, GRE, interviews; for doctorate, DAT, interview, pre-professional evaluation. Additional exam requirements/recommendations for international students: Required—TOEFL (minimum score 275 computer-based). Electronic applications accepted. *Expenses:* Contact institution. *Faculty research:* Oral cancer, proteomics, inflammation mechanisms, defensins, periopathogens, dental material.

The University of Texas Health Science Center at Houston, The University of Texas School of Dentistry at Houston, Houston, TX 77225-0036. Offers MS, DDS. *Accreditation:* ADA. *Entrance requirements:* For doctorate, DAT, 90 semester hours of prerequisite courses. Electronic applications accepted. *Faculty research:* Salivary diagnostics, autoimmune disease, mucosal immunity, craniofacial anomalies, molecular imaging, bioengineering.

The University of Texas Health Science Center at San Antonio, Dental School, San Antonio, TX 78229-3900. Offers MS, DDS, Certificate, DDS/PhD. *Accreditation:* ADA (one or more programs are accredited). *Faculty:* 117 full-time (34 women), 76 part-time/adjunct (18 women). *Students:* 398 full-time (198 women); includes 213 minority (3 Black or African American, non-Hispanic/Latino; 1 American Indian or Alaska Native, non-Hispanic/Latino; 141 Asian, non-Hispanic/Latino; 60 Hispanic/Latino; 8 Two or more races, non-Hispanic/Latino), 7 international. Average age 23. 1,204 applicants, 15% accepted, 98 enrolled. In 2011, 106 degrees awarded. *Median time to degree:* Of those who began their doctoral program in fall 2003, 93% received their degree in 8 years or less. *Degree requirements:* For master's, thesis; for doctorate, comprehensive exam. *Entrance requirements:* For master's, GRE General Test, DDS; for doctorate, DAT; for Certificate, DDS. *Application deadline:* For fall admission, 10/1 for domestic students. Application fee: $75. Electronic applications accepted. *Financial support:* In 2011–12, 382 students received support. Teaching assistantships, institutionally sponsored loans, and scholarships/grants available. Financial award application deadline: 3/1; financial award applicants required to submit FAFSA. *Faculty research:* Neuropharmacology, periodontal disease, biomaterials, bone mineralization, caries prevention. *Total annual research expenditures:* $16.4 million. *Unit head:* Dr. D. Adriana Segura, Associate Dean for Student Affairs, 210-567-3180, Fax: 210-567-4776, E-mail: seguraa@uthscsa.edu. *Application contact:* E-mail: dsadmissions@uthscsa.edu. Web site: http://dental.uthscsa.edu/.

University of the Pacific, Arthur A. Dugoni School of Dentistry, Stockton, CA 95211-0197. Offers MSD, DDS, Certificate. *Accreditation:* ADA (one or more programs are accredited). *Faculty:* 73 full-time (21 women), 177 part-time/adjunct (59 women). *Students:* 516 full-time (266 women); includes 245 minority (5 Black or African American, non-Hispanic/Latino; 1 American Indian or Alaska Native, non-Hispanic/Latino; 215 Asian, non-Hispanic/Latino; 24 Hispanic/Latino), 32 international. Average age 26. 3,043 applicants, 7% accepted, 141 enrolled. In 2011, 5 master's, 141 doctorates awarded. *Degree requirements:* For master's, comprehensive exam, thesis. *Entrance requirements:* For master's, GRE General Test; for doctorate, National Board Dental Exam Part I, DAT, foreign dental degree (for international students); for Certificate, DDS/DMD. Additional exam requirements/recommendations for international students: Required—TOEFL. *Application deadline:* For fall admission, 9/15 for international students. Applications are processed on a rolling basis. Electronic applications accepted. *Expenses:* Contact institution. *Financial support:* Institutionally sponsored loans, scholarships/grants, and stipends available. Support available to part-time students. Financial award application deadline: 3/2; financial award applicants required to submit FAFSA. *Faculty research:* Cell kinetics, cell membrane transport, orthodontics, virus cell membrane fusion, bioenergy transduction. *Unit head:* Dr. Arthur A. Dugoni, Dean, 415-929-6424. *Application contact:* Dr. Craig S. Yarborough, Associate Dean for Institutional Advancement and Student Services, 415-929-6491. Web site: http://dental.pacific.edu/.

University of Toronto, School of Graduate Studies, Faculty of Dentistry, Professional Program in Dentistry, Toronto, ON M5S 1A1, Canada. Offers DDS. *Accreditation:* ADA. *Entrance requirements:* For doctorate, Canadian DAT or equivalent, minimum GPA of 3.0; completion of at least 2 courses in life sciences and 1 course in humanities or social sciences. Additional exam requirements/recommendations for international students: Required—TOEFL (minimum score 600 paper-based; 100 iBT), TWE (minimum score 5). Electronic applications accepted. *Expenses:* Contact institution.

University of Washington, Graduate School, School of Dentistry, Program in Dental Surgery, Seattle, WA 98195. Offers DDS. *Accreditation:* ADA. *Entrance requirements:* For doctorate, DAT.

The University of Western Ontario, Schulich School of Medicine and Dentistry, School of Dentistry, Professional Program in Dentistry, London, ON N6A 5B8, Canada. Offers

DDS. *Accreditation:* ADA. *Entrance requirements:* For doctorate, DAT (Canadian version), minimum B average.

Virginia Commonwealth University, Medical College of Virginia-Professional Programs, School of Dentistry, Richmond, VA 23284-9005. Offers MS, DDS, DDS/MS, DDS/PhD. *Accreditation:* ADA. *Entrance requirements:* For master's, National Board Dental Exam; for doctorate, DAT. Electronic applications accepted. *Expenses:* Contact institution.

Western University of Health Sciences, College of Dental Medicine, Pomona, CA 91766-1854. Offers DMD. *Accreditation:* ADA. *Faculty:* 26 full-time (13 women), 14 part-time/adjunct (3 women). *Students:* 211 full-time (85 women); includes 114 minority (4 Black or African American, non-Hispanic/Latino; 4 American Indian or Alaska Native, non-Hispanic/Latino; 92 Asian, non-Hispanic/Latino; 10 Hispanic/Latino; 4 Two or more races, non-Hispanic/Latino), 4 international. Average age 27. 2,510 applicants, 10% accepted, 74 enrolled. *Entrance requirements:* For doctorate, DAT, minimum 30 hours of dental-related work experience; minimum 90 semester or 135 quarter units of undergraduate/graduate coursework; letters of recommendation. Additional exam requirements/recommendations for international students: Required—TOEFL. *Application deadline:* For fall admission, 12/1 for domestic students. Applications are processed on a rolling basis. Application fee: $60. Electronic applications accepted. *Unit head:* Dr. James J. Koelbl, Dean, 909-706-3504, E-mail: jkoelbl@westernu.edu. *Application contact:* Marie Anderson, Director of Admissions, 909-469-5485, Fax: 909-469-5570, E-mail: admissions@westernu.edu. Web site: http://www.westernu.edu/xp/edu/dentistry/welcome.xml.

West Virginia University, School of Dentistry, Professional Program in Dentistry, Morgantown, WV 26506. Offers DDS. *Accreditation:* ADA. *Degree requirements:* For doctorate, comprehensive exam. *Entrance requirements:* For doctorate, DAT, letters of recommendation, interview. Additional exam requirements/recommendations for international students: Required—TOEFL (minimum score 500 paper-based; 173 computer-based).

Oral and Dental Sciences

A.T. Still University of Health Sciences, Arizona School of Dentistry and Oral Health, Mesa, AZ 85206. Offers dental medicine (DMD); orthodontics (Certificate). *Faculty:* 29 full-time (12 women), 137 part-time/adjunct (43 women). *Students:* 289 full-time (143 women), 1 part-time (0 women); includes 103 minority (10 Black or African American, non-Hispanic/Latino; 11 American Indian or Alaska Native, non-Hispanic/Latino; 55 Asian, non-Hispanic/Latino; 19 Hispanic/Latino; 8 Two or more races, non-Hispanic/Latino). Average age 28. 3,181 applicants, 4% accepted, 76 enrolled. In 2011, 58 doctorates, 4 Certificates awarded. *Degree requirements:* For doctorate, National Board Exams I and II. *Entrance requirements:* For doctorate, DAT, minimum GPA of 2.5 overall and in science. *Application deadline:* For fall admission, 12/1 for domestic and international students. Applications are processed on a rolling basis. Application fee: $70. Electronic applications accepted. *Expenses:* Contact institution. *Financial support:* In 2011–12, 60 students received support. Federal Work-Study and scholarships/grants available. Financial award application deadline: 5/1; financial award applicants required to submit FAFSA. *Faculty research:* EBD in clinical practice, xerostomia and malnutrition in assisted living settings, medical screening in the dental office: patient attitudes, rapid oral HIV screening in the dental setting, dental public health: early childhood caries, low level laser use. *Unit head:* Dr. Jack Dillenberg, Dean, 480-219-6000, Fax: 480-219-6110, E-mail: jdillenberg@atsu.edu. *Application contact:* Donna Sparks, Associate Director, Admissions Processing, 660-626-2117, Fax: 660-626-2969, E-mail: admissions@atsu.edu. Web site: http://www.atsu.edu/asdoh.

A.T. Still University of Health Sciences, School of Health Management, Kirksville, MO 63501. Offers dental emphasis (MPH); health administration (MHA); health education (MH Ed, DH Ed); public health (MPH). Part-time and evening/weekend programs available. Postbaccalaureate distance learning degree programs offered (no on-campus study). *Faculty:* 15 full-time (8 women), 52 part-time/adjunct (27 women). *Students:* 50 full-time (36 women), 391 part-time (245 women); includes 125 minority (48 Black or African American, non-Hispanic/Latino; 4 American Indian or Alaska Native, non-Hispanic/Latino; 42 Asian, non-Hispanic/Latino; 26 Hispanic/Latino; 5 Two or more races, non-Hispanic/Latino). Average age 32. 121 applicants, 90% accepted, 89 enrolled. In 2011, 156 master's, 38 doctorates awarded. *Degree requirements:* For master's, thesis, integrated terminal project; for doctorate, thesis/dissertation. *Entrance requirements:* For master's, minimum GPA of 3.0, bachelor's degree or equivalent from U.S. institution; for doctorate, minimum GPA of 3.0, master's or terminal degree. Additional exam requirements/recommendations for international students: Required—TOEFL (minimum score 550 paper-based; 213 computer-based; 80 iBT). *Application deadline:* For fall admission, 7/9 for domestic students, 7/6 for international students; for winter admission, 9/28 for domestic and international students; for spring admission, 1/11 for domestic and international students. Application fee: $60. Electronic applications accepted. *Expenses:* Contact institution. *Financial support:* In 2011–12, 72 students received support. Scholarships/grants available. Financial award application deadline: 5/1; financial award applicants required to submit FAFSA. *Faculty research:* Public health: cultural health disparities, emergency preparedness, infectious disease, maternal and child health, environmental health; health education: overweight and obesity; health administration: leadership, strategic thinking, governance, healthcare reform economics, patient-centered care. *Unit head:* Dr. Kimberly O'Reilly, Interim Dean, 660-626-2820, Fax: 660-626-2826, E-mail: koreilley@atsu.edu. *Application contact:* Sarah Spencer, Associate Director, Admissions, 660-626-2820 Ext. 2669, Fax: 660-626-2826, E-mail: sspencer@atsu.edu. Web site: http://www.atsu.edu/shm.

Boston University, Henry M. Goldman School of Dental Medicine, Boston, MA 02118. Offers advanced general dentistry (CAGS); dental public health (MS, MSD, D Sc D, CAGS); dentistry (DMD); endodontics (MSD, D Sc D, CAGS); operative dentistry (MSD, D Sc D, CAGS); oral and maxillofacial surgery (MSD, D Sc D, CAGS); oral biology (MSD, D Sc, D Sc D, PhD); orthodontics (MSD, D Sc D, CAGS); pediatric dentistry (MSD, D Sc D, CAGS); periodontology (MSD, D Sc D, CAGS); prosthodontics (MSD, D Sc D, CAGS). *Accreditation:* ADA (one or more programs are accredited). *Faculty:* 119 full-time (53 women), 83 part-time/adjunct (24 women). *Students:* 802 full-time (386 women); includes 155 minority (6 Black or African American, non-Hispanic/Latino; 2 American Indian or Alaska Native, non-Hispanic/Latino; 110 Asian, non-Hispanic/Latino; 35 Hispanic/Latino; 2 Native Hawaiian or other Pacific Islander, non-Hispanic/Latino), 329 international. Average age 27. In 2011, 17 master's, 173 doctorates, 61 other advanced degrees awarded. *Degree requirements:* For master's and CAGS, thesis; for doctorate, thesis/dissertation (for some programs). *Entrance requirements:* For doctorate, DAT (for DMD), minimum recommended GPA of 3.0 (for DMD); for CAGS, dental degree. Additional exam requirements/recommendations for international students: Required—TOEFL. *Application deadline:* Applications are processed on a rolling basis. Application fee: $75 ($105 for international students). Electronic applications accepted. *Expenses:* Contact institution. *Financial support:* In 2011–12, 480 students received support. Career-related internships or fieldwork, institutionally sponsored loans, and scholarships/grants available. Financial award application deadline: 4/15; financial award applicants required to submit FAFSA. *Faculty research:* Defense mechanisms, bone-cell regulation, protein biochemistry, molecular biology, biomaterials. *Unit head:* Dr. Jeffrey W. Hutter, Dean, 617-638-4780. *Application contact:* Admissions Representative, 617-638-4787, Fax: 617-638-4798, E-mail: sdmadmis@bu.edu. Web site: http://www.bu.edu/dental.

Boston University, School of Medicine, Division of Graduate Medical Sciences, Program in Oral Biology, Boston, MA 02215. Offers PhD. *Faculty:* 16 full-time (1 woman), 2 part-time/adjunct (1 woman). *Students:* 25 full-time (11 women); includes 2 minority (1 Asian, non-Hispanic/Latino; 1 Hispanic/Latino), 19 international. Average age 29. 9 applicants, 33% accepted, 2 enrolled. In 2011, 3 doctorates awarded. *Degree requirements:* For doctorate, thesis/dissertation. *Entrance requirements:* For doctorate, GRE. Additional exam requirements/recommendations for international students: Required—TOEFL. *Application deadline:* For fall admission, 1/15 priority date for domestic students; for spring admission, 10/15 priority date for domestic students. Application fee: $75. Electronic applications accepted. *Expenses:* *Tuition:* Full-time $40,848; part-time $1276 per credit hour. *Required fees:* $572; $286 per semester. *Financial support:* In 2011–12, fellowships (averaging $30,500 per year), research assistantships (averaging $30,500 per year) were awarded. Financial award applicants required to submit FAFSA. *Unit head:* Dr. Phillip Trackman, Director, 617-638-4942, E-mail: trackman@bu.edu. *Application contact:* Alicia Ruff, Assistant Director of Admissions, 617-638-4733, E-mail: aruff@bu.edu. Web site: http://www.bu.edu/academics/sdm/programs/oral-biology/phd/.

Case Western Reserve University, School of Dental Medicine and School of Graduate Studies, Advanced Specialty Education Programs in Dentistry, Cleveland, OH 44106. Offers advanced general dentistry (Certificate); endodontics (MSD, Certificate); oral surgery (Certificate); orthodontics (MSD, Certificate); pedodontics (MSD, Certificate); periodontics (MSD, Certificate). *Degree requirements:* For master's, thesis. *Entrance requirements:* For master's, National Dental Board Exam, DDS, minimum GPA of 3.0; for Certificate, DDS. Additional exam requirements/recommendations for international students: Required—TOEFL (minimum score 550 paper-based; 213 computer-based; 79 iBT). *Expenses:* Contact institution. *Faculty research:* Natural antibiotics, obesity and periodontal disease, perioninfection and CV disease, periodontal disease and overall health, 3D cone beam computerized tomography.

Columbia University, College of Dental Medicine and Graduate School of Arts and Sciences, Programs in Dental Specialties, New York, NY 10027. Offers advanced education in general dentistry (Certificate); biomedical informatics (MA, PhD); endodontics (Certificate); orthodontics (MS, Certificate); periodontics (MS, Certificate); prosthodontics (MS, Certificate); science education (MA). *Degree requirements:* For master's, thesis, presentation of seminar. *Entrance requirements:* For master's, GRE General Test, DDS or equivalent. *Expenses:* Contact institution. *Faculty research:* Analysis of growth/form, pulpal microcirculation, implants, microbiology of oral environment, calcified tissues.

Dalhousie University, Faculty of Dentistry, Department of Oral and Maxillofacial Surgery, Halifax, NS B3H 3J5, Canada. Offers MD/M Sc. Electronic applications accepted. *Expenses:* Contact institution. *Faculty research:* Cleft lip/palate, jaw biomechanics.

Georgia Health Sciences University, College of Graduate Studies, Program in Oral Biology and Maxillofacial Pathology, Augusta, GA 30912. Offers MS, PhD. Part-time programs available. *Faculty:* 14 full-time (2 women), 3 part-time/adjunct (0 women). *Students:* 17 full-time (10 women), 11 part-time (4 women); includes 9 minority (3 Asian, non-Hispanic/Latino; 5 Hispanic/Latino; 1 Two or more races, non-Hispanic/Latino), 6 international. Average age 33. 15 applicants, 53% accepted, 2 enrolled. In 2011, 8 master's awarded. *Degree requirements:* For master's, thesis; for doctorate, thesis/dissertation. *Entrance requirements:* For master's and doctorate, GRE General Test or DAT, DDS, DMD, or equivalent degree. Additional exam requirements/recommendations for international students: Required—TOEFL (minimum score 550 paper-based; 213 computer-based; 79 iBT). *Application deadline:* For fall admission, 5/1 for domestic students, 3/1 for international students. Application fee: $50. Electronic applications accepted. *Financial support:* In 2011–12, 1 student received support. Federal Work-Study, institutionally sponsored loans, scholarships/grants, and tuition waivers available. Support available to part-time students. Financial award application deadline: 5/31; financial award applicants required to submit FAFSA. *Faculty research:* Oral cancer and chemoprevention, properties of biomaterials including oxidative stress, mechanical stress and shear stress responses, taurine and blood pressure in diabetes, bone and dentin biology, induction of periodontal regeneration. *Total annual research expenditures:* $1 million. *Unit head:* Dr. Mahmood Mozaffari, Interim Chair and Professor, 706-721-2991, Fax: 706-721-3392, E-mail: mmozaff@georgiahealth.edu. *Application contact:* Dr. Jill Lewis, Professor and Program Director, 706-721-2991, Fax: 706-721-3392, E-mail: jillewis@georgiahealth.edu. Web site: http://www.georgiahealth.edu/sod/oralbio/programs.html.

Harvard University, Graduate School of Arts and Sciences, Program in Biological Sciences in Dental Medicine, Cambridge, MA 02138. Offers PhD. *Expenses:* *Tuition:* Full-time $36,304. *Required fees:* $1186. Full-time tuition and fees vary according to program.

Harvard University, School of Dental Medicine, Advanced Graduate Programs in Dentistry, Cambridge, MA 02138. Offers advanced general dentistry (Certificate); dental public health (Certificate); endodontics (Certificate); general practice residency (Certificate); oral biology (M Med Sc, D Med Sc); oral implantology (Certificate); oral medicine (Certificate); oral pathology (Certificate); oral surgery (Certificate); orthodontics (Certificate); pediatric dentistry (Certificate); periodontics (Certificate); prosthodontics (Certificate). *Expenses:* *Tuition:* Full-time $36,304. *Required fees:* $1186. Full-time tuition and fees vary according to program.

Howard University, College of Dentistry, Washington, DC 20059-0002. Offers advanced education program general dentistry (Certificate); dentistry (DDS); general dentistry (Certificate); oral and maxillofacial surgery (Certificate); orthodontics

(Certificate); pediatric dentistry (Certificate). *Accreditation:* ADA (one or more programs are accredited). *Degree requirements:* For doctorate, comprehensive exam, didactic and clinical exams. *Entrance requirements:* For doctorate, DAT, 8 semester hours of course work in each biology, inorganic chemistry, organic chemistry. *Expenses:* Contact institution. *Faculty research:* Epidemiological, biomaterial, molecular genetic, behavioral modification, and clinical trial studies.

Idaho State University, Office of Graduate Studies, Kasiska College of Health Professions, Department of Dental Sciences, Pocatello, ID 83209-8088. Offers advanced general dentistry (Post-Doctoral Certificate). First year of Idaho Dental Education Program available in conjunction with Creighton University's School of Dentistry. *Degree requirements:* For Post-Doctoral Certificate, comprehensive exam, thesis optional, 1-year residency. *Entrance requirements:* For degree, DAT, 3 dental application forms. Additional exam requirements/recommendations for international students: Required—TOEFL (minimum score 600 paper-based; 213 computer-based). Electronic applications accepted. *Expenses:* Contact institution.

Jacksonville University, School of Orthodontics, Jacksonville, FL 32211. Offers Certificate. *Entrance requirements:* Additional exam requirements/recommendations for international students: Required—TOEFL. *Expenses:* Contact institution.

Loma Linda University, School of Dentistry, Program in Endodontics, Loma Linda, CA 92350. Offers MS, Certificate, MS/Certificate. *Degree requirements:* For master's, thesis. *Entrance requirements:* For master's, GRE General Test, DDS or DMD, minimum GPA of 3.0, National Boards. Additional exam requirements/recommendations for international students: Required—TOEFL (minimum score 550 paper-based; 213 computer-based).

Loma Linda University, School of Dentistry, Program in Implant Dentistry, Loma Linda, CA 92350. Offers MS, Certificate, MS/Certificate. *Degree requirements:* For master's, thesis. *Entrance requirements:* For master's, GRE General Test, DDS or DMD, minimum GPA of 3.0.

Loma Linda University, School of Dentistry, Program in Oral and Maxillofacial Surgery, Loma Linda, CA 92350. Offers MS, Certificate, MS/Certificate. *Degree requirements:* For master's, thesis. *Entrance requirements:* For master's, GRE General Test, DDS or DMD, minimum GPA of 3.0.

Loma Linda University, School of Dentistry, Program in Orthodontics, Loma Linda, CA 92350. Offers MS, Certificate, MS/Certificate. *Degree requirements:* For master's, thesis. *Entrance requirements:* For master's, GRE General Test, DDS or DMD, minimum GPA of 3.0. Additional exam requirements/recommendations for international students: Required—TOEFL (minimum score 550 paper-based; 213 computer-based).

Loma Linda University, School of Dentistry, Program in Periodontics, Loma Linda, CA 92350. Offers MS. *Degree requirements:* For master's, thesis. *Entrance requirements:* For master's, GRE General Test, DDS or DMD, minimum GPA of 3.0. Additional exam requirements/recommendations for international students: Required—TOEFL (minimum score 550 paper-based; 213 computer-based).

Marquette University, School of Dentistry and Graduate School, Graduate Programs in Dentistry, Program in Advanced Training in General Dentistry, Milwaukee, WI 53201-1881. Offers MS, Certificate. *Faculty:* 2 full-time (1 woman), 2 part-time/adjunct (0 women). *Students:* 2 full-time (1 woman); includes 1 minority (Hispanic/Latino). Average age 30. 31 applicants, 13% accepted, 2 enrolled. In 2011, 4 other advanced degrees awarded. *Entrance requirements:* For master's, National Board Dental Exams I and II, DDS or equivalent. Additional exam requirements/recommendations for international students: Required—TOEFL. *Application deadline:* For fall admission, 10/1 for domestic students, 9/1 for international students. Application fee: $50. *Expenses: Tuition:* Full-time $17,010; part-time $945 per credit hour. Tuition and fees vary according to program. *Financial support:* In 2011–12, fellowships with partial tuition reimbursements (averaging $35,000 per year) were awarded; institutionally sponsored loans also available. Financial award application deadline: 9/1; financial award applicants required to submit FAFSA. *Unit head:* Dr. Joseph Vitolo, Director, 414-288-3640, Fax: 414-288-3586, E-mail: joseph.vitolo@marquette.edu. *Application contact:* Arthur Hefti, Associate Dean for Research and Graduate Studies, 414-288-3532, E-mail: arthur.hefti@marquette.edu. Web site: http://www.marquette.edu/dentistry/admissions/AEGD.shtml.

Marquette University, School of Dentistry and Graduate School, Graduate Programs in Dentistry, Program in Dental Biomaterials, Milwaukee, WI 53201-1881. Offers MS. Part-time programs available. *Faculty:* 1 full-time (0 women). *Students:* 2 part-time (both women). Average age 31. 12 applicants, 17% accepted, 2 enrolled. In 2011, 1 master's awarded. *Degree requirements:* For master's, thesis. *Entrance requirements:* For master's, GRE General Test. Additional exam requirements/recommendations for international students: Required—TOEFL. *Application deadline:* For spring admission, 3/1 priority date for domestic students, 3/1 for international students. Applications are processed on a rolling basis. Application fee: $50. *Expenses: Tuition:* Full-time $17,010; part-time $945 per credit hour. Tuition and fees vary according to program. *Financial support:* Fellowships, career-related internships or fieldwork, institutionally sponsored loans, and tuition waivers (partial) available. Financial award application deadline: 9/1. *Faculty research:* Metallurgy, ceramics, polymers, mechanical behavior, cements. *Unit head:* Dr. David Berzins, Director, 414-288-5690, Fax: 414-288-3586, E-mail: david.berzins@marquette.edu. *Application contact:* Arthur Hefti, Associate Dean for Research and Graduate Studies, 414-288-3532, E-mail: arthur.hefti@marquette.edu. Web site: http://www.marquette.edu/dentistry/admissions/DentalBiomaterials.shtml.

Marquette University, School of Dentistry and Graduate School, Graduate Programs in Dentistry, Program in Endodontics, Milwaukee, WI 53201-1881. Offers MS, Certificate. *Faculty:* 1 full-time (0 women), 6 part-time/adjunct (1 woman). *Students:* 6 full-time (0 women); includes 1 minority (Asian, non-Hispanic/Latino), 1 international. Average age 29. 67 applicants, 4% accepted, 3 enrolled. In 2011, 3 master's awarded. *Degree requirements:* For master's, research thesis or acceptance of a paper in a peer-reviewed journal. *Entrance requirements:* For master's, National Board Dental Exams I and II, DDS or equivalent. Additional exam requirements/recommendations for international students: Required—TOEFL. *Application deadline:* For fall admission, 9/1 priority date for domestic students, 9/1 for international students. Application fee: $50. *Expenses:* Contact institution. *Financial support:* Fellowships, institutionally sponsored loans, and tuition waivers (partial) available. Financial award application deadline: 9/1; financial award applicants required to submit FAFSA. *Faculty research:* Properties of NiTi files, prevention of post-endodontic pain. *Unit head:* Dr. James Bahcall, Director, 414-288-6517, Fax: 414-288-3586, E-mail: james.bahcall@marquette.edu. *Application contact:* Arthur Hefti, Associate Dean for Research and Graduate Studies, 414-288-3532, E-mail: arthur.hefti@marquette.edu. Web site: http://www.marquette.edu/dentistry/admissions/Endodontics.shtml.

Marquette University, School of Dentistry and Graduate School, Graduate Programs in Dentistry, Program in Orthodontics, Milwaukee, WI 53201-1881. Offers MS, Certificate. *Faculty:* 3 full-time (0 women), 11 part-time/adjunct (0 women). *Students:* 10 full-time (3 women); includes 2 minority (both Asian, non-Hispanic/Latino), 1 international. Average age 29. 145 applicants, 3% accepted, 5 enrolled. In 2011, 11 master's, 4 other advanced degrees awarded. *Degree requirements:* For master's, thesis. *Entrance requirements:* For master's, National Board Dental Exams I and II, DDS or equivalent.

Additional exam requirements/recommendations for international students: Required—TOEFL. *Application deadline:* For fall admission, 9/1 priority date for domestic students, 9/1 for international students. Application fee: $50. *Expenses:* Contact institution. *Financial support:* Fellowships, institutionally sponsored loans, and tuition waivers (partial) available. Financial award application deadline: 9/1; financial award applicants required to submit FAFSA. *Faculty research:* In vitro and in vivo behavior of orthodontic wires, effect of orthodontic treatment on facial esthetics. *Total annual research expenditures:* $50,000. *Unit head:* Dr. Thomas G. Bradley, Director, 414-288-5480, Fax: 414-288-3586, E-mail: thomas.bradley@marquette.edu. *Application contact:* Arthur Hefti, Associate Dean for Research and Graduate Studies, 414-288-3532, E-mail: arthur.hefti@marquette.edu. Web site: http://www.marquette.edu/dentistry/admissions/Mission_000.shtml.

Marquette University, School of Dentistry and Graduate School, Graduate Programs in Dentistry, Program in Prosthodontics, Milwaukee, WI 53201-1881. Offers MS, Certificate. *Faculty:* 2 full-time (1 woman), 2 part-time/adjunct (0 women). *Students:* 6 full-time (3 women); includes 1 minority (Asian, non-Hispanic/Latino), 2 international. Average age 27. 28 applicants, 11% accepted, 3 enrolled. In 2011, 2 master's awarded. *Degree requirements:* For master's, thesis or alternative. *Entrance requirements:* For master's, National Board Dental Exams I and II, DDS or equivalent. Additional exam requirements/recommendations for international students: Required—TOEFL. *Application deadline:* For fall admission, 9/1 priority date for domestic students, 9/1 for international students. Application fee: $50. *Expenses: Tuition:* Full-time $17,010; part-time $945 per credit hour. Tuition and fees vary according to program. *Financial support:* Fellowships, institutionally sponsored loans, and tuition waivers (partial) available. Financial award application deadline: 9/1; financial award applicants required to submit FAFSA. *Faculty research:* Properties of ceramic materials. *Unit head:* Dr. Gerald Ziebert, Director, 414-288-5555, Fax: 414-288-3586, E-mail: gerald.ziebert@marquette.edu. *Application contact:* Arthur Hefti, Associate Dean for Research and Graduate Studies, 414-288-3532, E-mail: arthur.hefti@marquette.edu. Web site: http://www.marquette.edu/dentistry/admissions/Prosthodontics.shtml.

Massachusetts College of Pharmacy and Health Sciences, Graduate Studies, Program in Community Oral Health, Boston, MA 02115-5896. Offers MS. Part-time programs available. Postbaccalaureate distance learning degree programs offered (minimal on-campus study). *Students:* 3 part-time (all women). Average age 45. 12 applicants, 100% accepted, 3 enrolled. *Entrance requirements:* For master's, 2 years of work experience in health care. Additional exam requirements/recommendations for international students: Required—TOEFL (minimum score 550 paper-based; 213 computer-based; 79 iBT). *Application deadline:* For fall admission, 7/1 priority date for domestic students. Application fee: $70. *Expenses: Tuition:* Full-time $30,200; part-time $945 per credit hour. *Unit head:* Becky DeSpain Eden, Assistant Dean of Graduate Studies, 617-735-1594, E-mail: becky.eden@mcphs.edu. *Application contact:* Brian Barilone, Coordinator of Graduate Admission, 617-879-5032, E-mail: admissions@mcphs.edu.

McGill University, Faculty of Graduate and Postdoctoral Studies, Faculty of Dentistry, Montréal, QC H3A 2T5, Canada. Offers forensic dentistry (Certificate); oral and maxillofacial surgery (M Sc, PhD).

Metropolitan State University, College of Health, Community and Professional Studies, St. Paul, MN 55106-5000. Offers advanced dental therapy (MS); leadership and management (MSN); nursing (DNP); psychology (MA). *Accreditation:* AACN. Part-time programs available. *Students:* 26 full-time (24 women), 160 part-time (158 women); includes 20 minority (7 Black or African American, non-Hispanic/Latino; 2 American Indian or Alaska Native, non-Hispanic/Latino; 2 Asian, non-Hispanic/Latino; 2 Hispanic/Latino; 7 Two or more races, non-Hispanic/Latino), 7 international. Average age 36. *Degree requirements:* For master's, thesis or alternative; for doctorate, thesis/dissertation or alternative. *Entrance requirements:* For master's, GRE General Test, minimum GPA of 3.0, RN license, BS/BAN; for doctorate, minimum GPA of 3.0; RN license, MSN. Additional exam requirements/recommendations for international students: Required—TOEFL (minimum score 550 paper-based; 213 computer-based). *Application deadline:* For fall admission, 1/15 for domestic students; for winter admission, 1/15 for international students. Application fee: $20. *Expenses:* Tuition, state resident: full-time $5799.06; part-time $322.17 per credit. Tuition, nonresident: full-time $11,411; part-time $633.92 per credit. Tuition and fees vary according to degree level, program and reciprocity agreements. *Financial support:* Fellowships, career-related internships or fieldwork, Federal Work-Study, institutionally sponsored loans, and traineeships available. Financial award applicants required to submit FAFSA. *Faculty research:* Women's health, gerontology. *Unit head:* Ann Leja, Interim Dean, 651-793-1402, Fax: 651-793-1382, E-mail: ann.leja@metrostate.edu. *Application contact:* Lynda Zimmerman, Academic Advisor, 651-793-1378, Fax: 651-793-1382, E-mail: lynda.zimmerman@metrostate.edu. Web site: http://www.metrostate.edu/cnhs/.

New York University, College of Dentistry, Postgraduate Programs in Dentistry, New York, NY 10010. Offers endodontics (Advanced Certificate); oral and maxillofacial surgery (Advanced Certificate); orthodontics (Advanced Certificate); pediatric dentistry (Advanced Certificate); periodontics (Advanced Certificate); prosthodontics (Advanced Certificate); prosthodontics (implantology) (Advanced Certificate). *Faculty:* 242 full-time (85 women), 689 part-time/adjunct (186 women). *Students:* 116 full-time (58 women); includes 61 minority (5 Black or African American, non-Hispanic/Latino; 47 Asian, non-Hispanic/Latino; 9 Hispanic/Latino). Average age 31. 537 applicants, 8% accepted, 38 enrolled. In 2011, 35 Advanced Certificates awarded. *Entrance requirements:* For degree, National Dental Boards Exam Part I, DDS. Additional exam requirements/recommendations for international students: Required—TOEFL (minimum score 587 paper-based; 230 computer-based; 95 iBT). *Application deadline:* For fall admission, 12/1 for domestic students. Application fee: $100. Electronic applications accepted. *Financial support:* Scholarships/grants and unspecified assistantships available. Financial award application deadline: 3/1; financial award applicants required to submit FAFSA. *Unit head:* Dr. David Sirois, Dean, College of Dentistry, 212-998-9540, Fax: 212-995-4240, E-mail: david.sirois@nyu.edu. *Application contact:* Dr. Anthony M. Palatta, Assistant Dean for Student Affairs and Admissions, 212-998-9918, Fax: 212-995-4240, E-mail: ap16@nyu.edu. Web site: http://www.nyu.edu/dental/.

New York University, Graduate School of Arts and Science, Department of Biology, New York, NY 10012-1019. Offers biology (PhD); biomedical journalism (MS); cancer and molecular biology (PhD); computational biology (PhD); computers in biological research (MS); developmental genetics (PhD); general biology (MS); immunology and microbiology (PhD); molecular genetics (PhD); neurobiology (PhD); oral biology (MS); plant biology (PhD); recombinant DNA technology (MS); MS/MBA. Part-time programs available. *Faculty:* 24 full-time (5 women). *Students:* 146 full-time (90 women), 54 part-time (36 women); includes 49 minority (1 Black or African American, non-Hispanic/Latino; 33 Asian, non-Hispanic/Latino; 12 Hispanic/Latino; 3 Two or more races, non-Hispanic/Latino), 89 international. Average age 27. 394 applicants, 62% accepted, 82 enrolled. In 2011, 68 master's, 6 doctorates awarded. Terminal master's awarded for partial completion of doctoral program. *Degree requirements:* For master's, thesis or alternative, qualifying paper; for doctorate, comprehensive exam, thesis/dissertation. *Entrance requirements:* For master's, GRE General Test; for doctorate, GRE General Test, GRE Subject Test. Additional exam requirements/recommendations for

international students: Required—TOEFL. *Application deadline:* For fall admission, 12/1 priority date for domestic students, 12/1 for international students. Application fee: $90. *Financial support:* Fellowships with tuition reimbursements, research assistantships with tuition reimbursements, teaching assistantships with tuition reimbursements, career-related internships or fieldwork, Federal Work-Study, institutionally sponsored loans, scholarships/grants, health care benefits, and unspecified assistantships available. Financial award application deadline: 12/1; financial award applicants required to submit FAFSA. *Faculty research:* Genomics, molecular and cell biology, development and molecular genetics, molecular evolution of plants and animals. *Unit head:* Stephen Small, Chair, 212-998-8200, Fax: 212-995-4015, E-mail: biology@nyu.edu. *Application contact:* Justin Blau, Director of Graduate Studies, 212-998-8200, Fax: 212-995-4015, E-mail: biology@nyu.edu. Web site: http://biology.as.nyu.edu/.

New York University, Graduate School of Arts and Science and College of Dentistry, Department of Biomaterials and Biomimetics, New York, NY 10012-1019. Offers biomaterials science (MS). *Faculty:* 5 full-time (2 women). *Students:* 16 full-time (10 women), 10 part-time (6 women), 17 international. Average age 32. 14 applicants, 79% accepted, 7 enrolled. In 2011, 5 master's awarded. *Degree requirements:* For master's, thesis. *Entrance requirements:* For master's, DDS or DMD. Additional exam requirements/recommendations for international students: Required—TOEFL. *Application deadline:* For fall admission, 5/1 for domestic and international students; for spring admission, 10/1 for domestic and international students. Application fee: $90. *Financial support:* Application deadline: 5/1; applicants required to submit FAFSA. *Faculty research:* Calcium phosphate, composite restoratives, surfactants, dental metallurgy, impression materials. *Unit head:* Dr. John L. Ricci, Director of Graduate Studies, 212-998-9703, Fax: 212-995-4244, E-mail: gsas.graduate.biomaterials@nyu.edu. *Application contact:* Carmen Chilsom, Department Administrator, 212-998-9703, Fax: 212-995-4244, E-mail: graduate.biomaterials@nyu.edu. Web site: http://www.nyu.edu/gsas/program/biomaterials/.

The Ohio State University, College of Dentistry, Columbus, OH 43210. Offers dentistry (MS, DDS); oral biology (PhD); DDS/PhD. *Accreditation:* ADA (one or more programs are accredited). *Faculty:* 80. *Students:* 501 full-time (214 women), 18 part-time (4 women); includes 99 minority (19 Black or African American, non-Hispanic/Latino; 3 American Indian or Alaska Native, non-Hispanic/Latino; 53 Asian, non-Hispanic/Latino; 20 Hispanic/Latino; 4 Two or more races, non-Hispanic/Latino), 25 international. Average age 27. In 2011, 21 master's, 104 doctorates awarded. Terminal master's awarded for partial completion of doctoral program. *Degree requirements:* For master's, thesis; for doctorate, thesis/dissertation (for some programs). *Entrance requirements:* For doctorate, DAT (for DDS). Additional exam requirements/recommendations for international students: Required—TOEFL (minimum score 550 paper-based; 79 iBT), Michigan English Language Assessment Battery (minimum score 82). *Application deadline:* Applications are processed on a rolling basis. Electronic applications accepted. *Expenses:* Contact institution. *Financial support:* In 2011–12, 7 fellowships with tuition reimbursements, 13 research assistantships with tuition reimbursements (averaging $11,000 per year), 78 teaching assistantships with tuition reimbursements (averaging $12,000 per year) were awarded; Federal Work-Study and institutionally sponsored loans also available. Financial award application deadline: 3/1. *Faculty research:* Neurobiology, inflammation and immunity, materials science, bone biology. *Total annual research expenditures:* $3.4 million. *Unit head:* Dr. Patrick M. Lloyd, Dean, 614-292-9755. *Application contact:* Georgia Paletta, Interim Director, 614-292-9444, Fax: 614-292-3656, E-mail: paletta.4@osu.edu. Web site: http://www.dent.ohio-state.edu/.

Oregon Health & Science University, School of Dentistry, Graduate Programs in Dentistry, Department of Endodontics, Portland, OR 97239-3098. Offers Certificate. *Entrance requirements:* For degree, GRE General Test. Additional exam requirements/recommendations for international students: Required—TOEFL.

Oregon Health & Science University, School of Dentistry, Graduate Programs in Dentistry, Department of Orthodontics, Portland, OR 97239-3098. Offers MS, Certificate. *Degree requirements:* For master's, thesis. *Entrance requirements:* For master's and Certificate, GRE General Test, DMD/DDS. Additional exam requirements/recommendations for international students: Required—TOEFL.

Oregon Health & Science University, School of Dentistry, Graduate Programs in Dentistry, Department of Pediatric Dentistry, Portland, OR 97239-3098. Offers Certificate.

Oregon Health & Science University, School of Dentistry, Graduate Programs in Dentistry, Department of Periodontology, Portland, OR 97239-3098. Offers MS, Certificate. *Degree requirements:* For master's, thesis. *Entrance requirements:* For master's and Certificate, GRE General Test, DMD/DDS. Additional exam requirements/recommendations for international students: Required—TOEFL.

Oregon Health & Science University, School of Dentistry, Graduate Programs in Dentistry, Department of Restorative Dentistry, Division of Biomaterials and Biomechanics, Portland, OR 97239-3098. Offers MS.

Oregon Health & Science University, School of Dentistry, Graduate Programs in Dentistry, Program in Oral Molecular Biology, Portland, OR 97239-3098. Offers MS.

Oregon Health & Science University, School of Dentistry, Professional Program in Dentistry, Portland, OR 97239-3098. Offers dentistry (DMD); oral and maxillofacial surgery (Certificate); MD/DMD. *Accreditation:* ADA. *Entrance requirements:* For doctorate, DAT. Electronic applications accepted. *Faculty research:* Dentin permeability, tooth sensations, fluoride metabolism, immunology of periodontal disease, craniofacial growth.

Roseman University of Health Sciences, College of Dental Medicine, Henderson, NV 89014. Offers advanced education in orthodontics and dentofacial orthopedics (MAIA). *Degree requirements:* For master's, comprehensive exam, thesis or alternative. *Entrance requirements:* For master's, National Board Dental Examination 1 and 2, graduation from U.S. or Canadian dental school, Nevada dental license. *Expenses:* Contact institution.

Saint Louis University, Graduate Education, Center for Advanced Dental Education, St. Louis, MO 63103-2097. Offers endodontics (MSD); orthodontics (MSD); periodontics (MSD). *Degree requirements:* For master's, comprehensive exam, thesis, teaching practicum. *Entrance requirements:* For master's, GRE General Test, NBDE (National Board Dental Exam), DDS or DMD, interview, letters of recommendation. Additional exam requirements/recommendations for international students: Required—TOEFL (minimum score 525 paper-based; 194 computer-based). Electronic applications accepted. *Faculty research:* Craniofacial growth.

Seton Hill University, Orthodontics Certificate Program, Greensburg, PA 15601. Offers Certificate. *Faculty:* 2 full-time (0 women), 8 part-time/adjunct (1 woman). *Students:* 16 full-time (4 women); includes 1 minority (Asian, non-Hispanic/Latino). *Entrance requirements:* For degree, U.S. National Dental Board Exams (Part 1 & 2), eligibility for PA licensure, DDS/DMD, minimum GPA of 3.0, transcripts, personal statement. Additional exam requirements/recommendations for international students: Required—TOEFL (minimum score 650 paper-based; 280 computer-based; 114 iBT), IELTS (minimum score 7). *Application deadline:* For fall admission, 9/15 priority date for domestic students, 9/15 for international students. *Expenses: Tuition:* Full-time $13,446; part-time $747 per credit. *Required fees:* $700; $25 per credit. $50 per term. *Faculty research:* Device for tooth movement, occlusion, evaluation of "text messaging" to reduce pain and anxiety in orthodontics, smile esthetics, temporomandibular disorders. *Total annual research expenditures:* $1,500. *Unit head:* Dr. Donald Rinchuse, Director, 724-652-2950, E-mail: rinchuse@setonhill.edu. *Application contact:* Meghan Kennedy, Orthodontic Center Business Manager, 724-652-2997, E-mail: mkennedy@setonhill.edu.

Stony Brook University, State University of New York, Stony Brook University Medical Center, Health Sciences Center, School of Dental Medicine and Graduate School, Department of Oral Biology and Pathology, Stony Brook, NY 11794. Offers MS, PhD. *Entrance requirements:* For doctorate, GRE General Test. Additional exam requirements/recommendations for international students: Required—TOEFL. *Expenses:* Contact institution. *Faculty research:* Collagen metabolism, periodontal disease and diabetes, salivary antimicrobial proteins, dental plaque metabolism and dental caries.

Stony Brook University, State University of New York, Stony Brook University Medical Center, Health Sciences Center, School of Dental Medicine, Professional Program in Dental Medicine, Stony Brook, NY 11794. Offers dental medicine (DDS); endodontics (Certificate); orthodontics (Certificate); periodontics (Certificate). *Accreditation:* ADA (one or more programs are accredited). *Entrance requirements:* For doctorate, DAT.

Temple University, Health Sciences Center, Kornberg School of Dentistry and Graduate School, Graduate Programs in Dentistry, Philadelphia, PA 19122-6096. Offers advanced education in general dentistry (Certificate); endodontology (Certificate); oral biology (MS); orthodontics (Certificate); periodontology (Certificate). *Degree requirements:* For master's, thesis; for Certificate, comprehensive exam. *Entrance requirements:* For master's, GRE; for Certificate, National Boards Parts I and II, DMD or DDS, 3 letters of recommendation. Additional exam requirements/recommendations for international students: Required—TOEFL (minimum score 650 paper-based). *Expenses:* Contact institution. *Faculty research:* Saliva and salivary glands, implantology, material science, periodontal disease, geriatric dentistry.

Texas A&M Health Science Center, Baylor College of Dentistry, Department of Diagnostic Sciences, College Station, TX 77840. Offers oral and maxillofacial pathology (MS, PhD, Certificate). Part-time programs available. Terminal master's awarded for partial completion of doctoral program. *Degree requirements:* For master's, thesis; for doctorate, thesis/dissertation. *Entrance requirements:* For master's and doctorate, GRE General Test, DDS or DMD; for Certificate, GRE General Test, National Board Dental Examination, DDS or DMD. Additional exam requirements/recommendations for international students: Required—TOEFL. *Faculty research:* Oral cancer and precancer, odontogenic tumors, stomatology.

Texas A&M Health Science Center, Baylor College of Dentistry, Department of Endodontics, College Station, TX 77840. Offers endodontics (PhD, Certificate); health professions education (MS); oral biology (MS). *Degree requirements:* For master's, thesis; for doctorate, thesis/dissertation. *Entrance requirements:* For master's and Certificate, GRE General Test, National Board Dental Examination, DDS or DMD; for doctorate, GRE General Test, DDS or DMD. Additional exam requirements/recommendations for international students: Required—TOEFL. *Faculty research:* Periradicular healing in response to a biologically inductive root-end filling material.

Texas A&M Health Science Center, Baylor College of Dentistry, Department of Oral and Maxillofacial Surgery, College Station, TX 77840. Offers MD, Certificate. MD offered jointly with Texas Tech University. *Degree requirements:* For Certificate, thesis. *Entrance requirements:* For doctorate, DAT, MCAT; for Certificate, GRE General Test, National Board Dental Examination, DDS or DMD. Additional exam requirements/recommendations for international students: Required—TOEFL. *Faculty research:* Dental implants, temporomandibular joint, recombinant BMP-2.

Texas A&M Health Science Center, Baylor College of Dentistry, Department of Orthodontics, College Station, TX 77840. Offers MS, Certificate. *Degree requirements:* For master's and Certificate, thesis. *Entrance requirements:* For master's and Certificate, GRE General Test, National Board Dental Examination, DDS or DMD. Additional exam requirements/recommendations for international students: Required—TOEFL. *Faculty research:* Craniofacial biology, distraction osteogenesis, clinical orthodontics, function and shape memory alloys.

Texas A&M Health Science Center, Baylor College of Dentistry, Department of Pediatric Dentistry, College Station, TX 77840. Offers MS, Certificate. Part-time programs available. *Degree requirements:* For master's and Certificate, thesis. *Entrance requirements:* For master's and Certificate, GRE General Test, National Board Dental Examination, DDS or DMD. Additional exam requirements/recommendations for international students: Required—TOEFL. *Faculty research:* Pulp biology, pharmacological methods of behavior management.

Texas A&M Health Science Center, Baylor College of Dentistry, Department of Periodontics, College Station, TX 77840. Offers MS, Certificate. Part-time programs available. *Degree requirements:* For master's and Certificate, thesis. *Entrance requirements:* For master's and Certificate, GRE General Test, National Board Dental Examination, DDS or DMD. Additional exam requirements/recommendations for international students: Required—TOEFL. *Faculty research:* Dental implants, quantification of &ITcandida albicans&RO in adult periodontitis: a survey, smoking, wound healing, stomatology, gingival overgrowth, diabetes mellitus.

Texas A&M Health Science Center, Baylor College of Dentistry, Department of Restorative Sciences, Field of Prosthodontics, College Station, TX 77840. Offers MS, Certificate. Part-time programs available. *Degree requirements:* For master's, thesis. *Entrance requirements:* For master's and Certificate, GRE General Test, National Board Dental Examination, DDS or DMD. Additional exam requirements/recommendations for international students: Required—TOEFL. *Faculty research:* Biomaterials, implants.

Tufts University, School of Dental Medicine, Advanced Education Programs in Dental Medicine, Medford, MA 02155. Offers dentistry (Certificate), including endodontics, oral and maxillofacial surgery, orthodontics, pediatric dentistry, periodontology, prosthodontics. *Entrance requirements:* Additional exam requirements/recommendations for international students: Required—TOEFL. *Expenses:* Contact institution.

Tufts University, School of Dental Medicine, Graduate Programs in Dental Medicine, Medford, MA 02155. Offers MS. *Degree requirements:* For master's, thesis. *Entrance requirements:* For master's, DDS, DMD, or equivalent; minimum B average. Additional exam requirements/recommendations for international students: Required—TOEFL. *Expenses:* Contact institution. *Faculty research:* Periodontal research, dental materials, salivary research, epidemiology, bone biology.

Université de Montréal, Faculty of Dental Medicine, Program in Multidisciplinary Residency, Montréal, QC H3C 3J7, Canada. Offers Certificate. Electronic applications accepted.

Université de Montréal, Faculty of Dental Medicine, Program in Oral and Dental Sciences, Montréal, QC H3C 3J7, Canada. Offers M Sc. Electronic applications accepted.

Université de Montréal, Faculty of Dental Medicine, Program in Orthodontics, Montréal, QC H3C 3J7, Canada. Offers M Sc. Electronic applications accepted.

Université de Montréal, Faculty of Dental Medicine, Program in Pediatric Dentistry, Montréal, QC H3C 3J7, Canada. Offers M Sc. Electronic applications accepted.

Université de Montréal, Faculty of Dental Medicine, Program in Prosthodontics Rehabilitation, Montréal, QC H3C 3J7, Canada. Offers M Sc. Electronic applications accepted.

Université Laval, Faculty of Dentistry, Diploma Program in Buccal and Maxillofacial Surgery, Québec, QC G1K 7P4, Canada. Offers DESS. *Degree requirements:* For DESS, comprehensive exam. *Entrance requirements:* For degree, interview, knowledge of French. Electronic applications accepted.

Université Laval, Faculty of Dentistry, Diploma Program in Gerodontology, Québec, QC G1K 7P4, Canada. Offers DESS. Part-time programs available. *Entrance requirements:* For degree, interview, good knowledge of French. Electronic applications accepted.

Université Laval, Faculty of Dentistry, Diploma Program in Multidisciplinary Dentistry, Québec, QC G1K 7P4, Canada. Offers DESS. *Entrance requirements:* For degree, interview, knowledge of French. Electronic applications accepted.

Université Laval, Faculty of Dentistry, Diploma Program in Periodontics, Québec, QC G1K 7P4, Canada. Offers DESS. *Entrance requirements:* For degree, interview, knowledge of French. Electronic applications accepted.

Université Laval, Faculty of Dentistry, Graduate Program in Dentistry, Québec, QC G1K 7P4, Canada. Offers M Sc. *Degree requirements:* For master's, thesis (for some programs). Electronic applications accepted.

University at Buffalo, the State University of New York, Graduate School, School of Dental Medicine, Graduate Programs in Dental Medicine, Department of Oral Biology, Buffalo, NY 14260. Offers PhD. *Degree requirements:* For doctorate, thesis/dissertation. *Entrance requirements:* For doctorate, GRE General Test, GRE Subject Test in biology or DDS. Additional exam requirements/recommendations for international students: Required—TOEFL (minimum score 79 iBT). Electronic applications accepted. *Faculty research:* Oral immunology and microbiology, bone physiology, biochemistry, molecular genetics, neutrophil biology.

University at Buffalo, the State University of New York, Graduate School, School of Dental Medicine, Graduate Programs in Dental Medicine, Department of Oral Diagnostic Sciences, Buffalo, NY 14260. Offers biomaterials (MS). Part-time programs available. *Degree requirements:* For master's, thesis. *Entrance requirements:* Additional exam requirements/recommendations for international students: Required—TOEFL (minimum score 79 iBT). Electronic applications accepted. *Faculty research:* Bioengineering, surface science, bioadhesion, regulatory sterilization.

University at Buffalo, the State University of New York, Graduate School, School of Dental Medicine, Graduate Programs in Dental Medicine, Department of Orthodontics, Buffalo, NY 14260. Offers MS, Certificate. *Degree requirements:* For master's, thesis. *Entrance requirements:* For master's, DDS or equivalent. Additional exam requirements/recommendations for international students: Required—TOEFL (minimum score 500 paper-based; 79 iBT). Electronic applications accepted. *Faculty research:* Stem cell, clinical respiration, growth and development.

University at Buffalo, the State University of New York, Graduate School, School of Dental Medicine, Graduate Programs in Dental Medicine, Program in Oral Sciences, Buffalo, NY 14260. Offers MS. *Degree requirements:* For master's, thesis. *Entrance requirements:* For master's, DDS, DMD or equivalent foreign degree. Additional exam requirements/recommendations for international students: Required—TOEFL (minimum score 79 iBT). Electronic applications accepted. *Faculty research:* Oral biology and pathology, behavioral sciences, neuromuscular physiology, facial pain, oral microbiology.

The University of Alabama at Birmingham, School of Dentistry, Graduate Programs in Dentistry, Birmingham, AL 35294. Offers MS. *Degree requirements:* For master's, thesis. *Expenses:* Tuition, state resident: full-time $5922; part-time $309 per hour. Tuition, nonresident: full-time $13,428; part-time $726 per hour. Tuition and fees vary according to program. *Unit head:* Dr. Huw F. Thomas, Dean, 205-934-4720, Fax: 205-934-9283. *Application contact:* Dr. Steven J. Filler, Director of Dentistry Admissions, 205-934-5424, Fax: 205-975-6519, E-mail: sfiller@uab.edu. Web site: http://www.dental.uab.edu/.

University of Alberta, Faculty of Medicine and Dentistry, Department of Dentistry, Program in Orthodontics, Edmonton, AB T6G 2E1, Canada. Offers M Sc, PhD. *Degree requirements:* For master's, thesis; for doctorate, thesis/dissertation. *Entrance requirements:* Additional exam requirements/recommendations for international students: Required—TOEFL (minimum score 580 paper-based; 237 computer-based). Electronic applications accepted.

The University of British Columbia, Faculty of Dentistry and Faculty of Graduate Studies, Graduate/Postgraduate and Professional Specialty Programs in Dentistry, Vancouver, BC V6T 1Z1, Canada. Offers dental science (M Sc, PhD); periodontics (Diploma). *Degree requirements:* For master's, thesis; for doctorate, comprehensive exam, thesis/dissertation. *Entrance requirements:* For degree, dental license, interview. Additional exam requirements/recommendations for international students: Required—TOEFL (minimum score 580 paper-based; 237 computer-based). Electronic applications accepted. *Expenses:* Contact institution. *Faculty research:* Cell biology, oral physiology, microbiology, immunology, biomaterials.

University of California, Los Angeles, Graduate Division, College of Letters and Science and David Geffen School of Medicine, UCLA ACCESS to Programs in the Molecular, Cellular and Integrative Life Sciences, Los Angeles, CA 90095. Offers biochemistry and molecular biology (PhD); biological chemistry (PhD); cellular and molecular pathology (PhD); human genetics (PhD); microbiology, immunology, and molecular genetics (PhD); molecular biology (PhD); molecular toxicology (PhD); molecular, cellular and integrative physiology (PhD); neurobiology (PhD); oral biology (PhD); physiology (PhD). *Students:* 44 full-time (30 women); includes 18 minority (11 Asian, non-Hispanic/Latino; 6 Hispanic/Latino; 1 Two or more races, non-Hispanic/Latino), 9 international. Average age 25. 495 applicants, 18% accepted, 41 enrolled. *Degree requirements:* For doctorate, thesis/dissertation, oral and written qualifying exams. *Entrance requirements:* For doctorate, GRE General Test, minimum undergraduate GPA of 3.0. Additional exam requirements/recommendations for international students: Required—TOEFL. *Application deadline:* For fall admission, 12/15 for domestic and international students. Application fee: $70 ($90 for international students). Electronic applications accepted. *Financial support:* In 2011–12, 51 fellowships with full and partial tuition reimbursements, 9 research assistantships with full and partial tuition reimbursements were awarded; teaching assistantships with full and partial tuition reimbursements, Federal Work-Study, institutionally sponsored loans, scholarships/grants, health care benefits, tuition waivers (full and partial), and

unspecified assistantships also available. Financial award application deadline: 3/1; financial award applicants required to submit FAFSA. *Faculty research:* Molecular, cellular, and developmental biology; immunology; microbiology; integrative biology. *Unit head:* Jody Spillane, Project Coordinator, 310-206-1845, E-mail: jspillane@mednet.ucla.edu. *Application contact:* UCLA ACCESS Admissions, 310-206-1845, E-mail: uclaaccess@mednet.ucla.edu. Web site: https://www.uclaaccess.ucla.edu/.

University of California, Los Angeles, School of Dentistry and Graduate Division, Graduate Programs in Dentistry, Program in Oral Biology, Los Angeles, CA 90095. Offers MS, PhD, DDS/MS, DDS/PhD, MD/PhD, MS/Certificate, PhD/Certificate. *Students:* 52 full-time (25 women); includes 18 minority (1 Black or African American, non-Hispanic/Latino; 15 Asian, non-Hispanic/Latino; 1 Hispanic/Latino; 1 Two or more races, non-Hispanic/Latino), 10 international. Average age 28. 49 applicants, 43% accepted, 18 enrolled. In 2011, 17 master's, 2 doctorates awarded. *Degree requirements:* For master's, thesis; for doctorate, thesis/dissertation, oral and written qualifying exams. *Entrance requirements:* For doctorate, GRE General Test. *Application deadline:* For fall admission, 2/15 for domestic students. Application fee: $70 ($90 for international students). Electronic applications accepted. *Financial support:* In 2011–12, 21 students received support, including 11 fellowships, 4 research assistantships; teaching assistantships, Federal Work-Study, institutionally sponsored loans, and tuition waivers (full and partial) also available. Financial award application deadline: 3/1. *Faculty research:* Neurophysiology, immunology of periodontal disease. *Unit head:* Dr. Cun-Yu Wang, Director, 310-825-4415, E-mail: cwang@dentistry.ucla.edu. *Application contact:* Dr. Francesco Chiappelli, Advisor, 310-794-6625, E-mail: fchiappelli@dentistry.ucla.edu.

University of California, San Francisco, Graduate Division, Program in Oral and Craniofacial Sciences, San Francisco, CA 94143. Offers MS, PhD. Terminal master's awarded for partial completion of doctoral program. *Degree requirements:* For master's, thesis; for doctorate, thesis/dissertation. *Entrance requirements:* For master's and doctorate, GRE General Test.

University of Colorado Denver, School of Dental Medicine, Aurora, CO 80045. Offers dental surgery (DDS); orthodontics (MS); periodontics (MS). *Accreditation:* ADA. *Faculty:* 73 full-time (26 women), 40 part-time/adjunct (14 women). *Students:* 361 full-time (154 women), 2 part-time (0 women); includes 82 minority (10 Black or African American, non-Hispanic/Latino; 2 American Indian or Alaska Native, non-Hispanic/Latino; 40 Asian, non-Hispanic/Latino; 29 Hispanic/Latino; 1 Two or more races, non-Hispanic/Latino), 37 international. Average age 30. 110 applicants, 97% accepted, 95 enrolled. In 2011, 16 master's, 73 doctorates awarded. *Entrance requirements:* For master's, GRE, National Board Dental Exam Part I and II, three letters of recommendation, personal essay; for doctorate, DAT, prerequisite courses in microbiology, general biochemistry and English composition (1 semester each); general chemistry/lab, organic chemistry/lab, general biology/lab and general physics/lab (2 semesters each), interview, letters of recommendation, letter/essay. Additional exam requirements/recommendations for international students: Required—TOEFL (minimum score 580 paper-based; 237 computer-based). *Application deadline:* For fall admission, 12/31 for domestic students. Application fee: $75. Electronic applications accepted. *Expenses:* Contact institution. *Financial support:* In 2011–12, 64 students received support. Application deadline: 4/1; applicants required to submit FAFSA. *Faculty research:* Pain control, materials research, geriatric dentistry, restorative dentistry, periodontic. *Total annual research expenditures:* $6.1 million. *Unit head:* Dr. Denise K. Kassebaum, Dean, 303-724-7100, Fax: 303-724-7109, E-mail: denise.kassebaum@ucdenver.edu. *Application contact:* Dr. Randy L. Kluender, Assistant Dean for Admissions and Student Affairs, 303-724-7120, E-mail: randy.kluender@ucdenver.edu. Web site: http://ucdenver.edu/academics/colleges/dentalmedicine/Pages/DentalMedicine.aspx.

University of Connecticut, Graduate School, University of Connecticut Health Center, Field of Dental Science, Storrs, CT 06269. Offers M Dent Sc. *Degree requirements:* For master's, comprehensive exam. *Entrance requirements:* For master's, GRE General Test. Additional exam requirements/recommendations for international students: Required—TOEFL (minimum score 550 paper-based; 213 computer-based). Electronic applications accepted.

University of Connecticut Health Center, Graduate School, Programs in Biomedical Sciences, Combined Degree Programs in Oral Biology, Farmington, CT 06030. Offers DMD/PhD. *Entrance requirements:* Additional exam requirements/recommendations for international students: Required—TOEFL (minimum score 600 paper-based; 250 computer-based).

University of Connecticut Health Center, Graduate School, Programs in Biomedical Sciences, Program in Skeletal, Craniofacial and Oral Biology, Farmington, CT 06030. Offers PhD, DMD/PhD, MD/PhD. *Degree requirements:* For doctorate, comprehensive exam, thesis/dissertation. *Entrance requirements:* For doctorate, GRE General Test. Additional exam requirements/recommendations for international students: Required—TOEFL (minimum score 600 paper-based; 250 computer-based). Electronic applications accepted. *Faculty research:* Skeletal development and patterning, bone biology, connective tissue biology, neurophysiology of taste and smell, microbiological aspects of caries.

See Display on next page and Close-Up on page 893.

University of Connecticut Health Center, School of Dental Medicine, Program in Dental Science, Farmington, CT 06030. Offers MDS. Part-time programs available. *Degree requirements:* For master's, comprehensive exam, thesis. *Entrance requirements:* For master's, National Board Dental Examination Parts I and II. *Expenses:* Contact institution.

University of Detroit Mercy, School of Dentistry, Department of Endodontics, Detroit, MI 48221. Offers MS, Certificate. *Degree requirements:* For master's, thesis. *Entrance requirements:* For master's, DDS or DMD; for Certificate, DAT, DDS or DMD. *Faculty research:* Roof and filling materials, cavity preparations, pulp biology.

University of Detroit Mercy, School of Dentistry, Department of Orthodontics, Detroit, MI 48221. Offers MS, Certificate. *Degree requirements:* For master's, thesis. *Entrance requirements:* For master's, DDS or DMD; for Certificate, DAT, DDS or DMD. *Faculty research:* Changes in oral flora due to fixed orthodontic appliances, cranioskeletal osteogenesis.

University of Detroit Mercy, School of Dentistry, Department of Periodontology and Dental Hygiene, Detroit, MI 48221. Offers periodontics (MS, Certificate).

University of Florida, College of Dentistry and Graduate School, Graduate Programs in Dentistry, Department of Endodontics, Gainesville, FL 32611. Offers MS, Certificate. *Entrance requirements:* For master's, DAT, GRE General Test, National Board Dental Examination Parts I and II, minimum GPA of 3.0, interview; for Certificate, DAT. Additional exam requirements/recommendations for international students: Required—TOEFL (minimum score 550 paper-based; 213 computer-based). *Faculty research:* Canal cleanliness, antibiotics, resilon, lasers, microbes.

University of Florida, College of Dentistry and Graduate School, Graduate Programs in Dentistry, Department of Oral Biology, Gainesville, FL 32611. Offers PhD. *Degree requirements:* For doctorate, thesis/dissertation. *Entrance requirements:* For doctorate,

GRE General Test, minimum GPA of 3.0. Additional exam requirements/recommendations for international students: Required—TOEFL. Electronic applications accepted. *Faculty research:* Bacterial genetics, cell adhesion, salivary glands, cell proliferation.

University of Florida, College of Dentistry and Graduate School, Graduate Programs in Dentistry, Department of Orthodontics, Gainesville, FL 32611. Offers MS, Certificate. *Degree requirements:* For master's, thesis. *Entrance requirements:* For master's, DAT, GRE General Test, National Board Dental Examination Parts I and II, minimum GPA of 3.0, interview. Additional exam requirements/recommendations for international students: Required—TOEFL (minimum score 550 paper-based; 213 computer-based). *Faculty research:* Bone biology, osteoclasts, clinical research, root resorption, pain control.

University of Florida, College of Dentistry and Graduate School, Graduate Programs in Dentistry, Department of Periodontology, Gainesville, FL 32611. Offers MS, Certificate. *Degree requirements:* For master's, thesis. *Entrance requirements:* For master's, DAT, GRE General Test, National Board Dental Examination Parts I and II, minimum GPA of 3.0, interview. Additional exam requirements/recommendations for international students: Required—TOEFL (minimum score 550 paper-based; 213 computer-based). *Faculty research:* Gingival grafting, periodontal plastic surgery, regenerative periodontal surgery, dental implant complications, osteogenic fibroma.

University of Florida, College of Dentistry and Graduate School, Graduate Programs in Dentistry, Department of Prosthodontics, Gainesville, FL 32611. Offers MS, Certificate. *Degree requirements:* For master's, thesis. *Entrance requirements:* For master's, DAT, GRE General Test, National Board Dental Examination Parts I and II, minimum GPA of 3.0, interview. Additional exam requirements/recommendations for international students: Required—TOEFL (minimum score 550 paper-based; 213 computer-based). *Faculty research:* Computer panograph, dental implants, resin provisional materials wear rate, implant surface variation, Sjorgen's Syndrome.

University of Illinois at Chicago, College of Dentistry and Graduate College, Graduate Programs in Oral Sciences, Chicago, IL 60607-7128. Offers MS, PhD. *Degree requirements:* For master's, thesis. *Entrance requirements:* For master's, GRE General Test, DDS, DVM, or MD. Additional exam requirements/recommendations for international students: Required—TOEFL. Electronic applications accepted. *Expenses:* Contact institution.

The University of Iowa, College of Dentistry and Graduate College, Graduate Programs in Dentistry, Iowa City, IA 52242-1316. Offers MS, Certificate. *Degree requirements:* For master's, thesis. *Entrance requirements:* For master's, GRE, DDS; for Certificate, DDS. Additional exam requirements/recommendations for international students: Required—TOEFL.

The University of Iowa, College of Dentistry and Graduate College, Graduate Programs in Dentistry, Department of Operative Dentistry, Iowa City, IA 52242-1316. Offers MS, Certificate. *Degree requirements:* For master's, thesis. *Entrance requirements:* For master's, GRE, DDS; for Certificate, DDS. Additional exam requirements/recommendations for international students: Required—TOEFL.

The University of Iowa, College of Dentistry and Graduate College, Graduate Programs in Dentistry, Department of Oral and Maxillofacial Surgery, Iowa City, IA 52242-1316. Offers MS, Certificate. *Degree requirements:* For master's, thesis. *Entrance requirements:* For master's, GRE, DDS; for Certificate, DDS.

The University of Iowa, College of Dentistry and Graduate College, Graduate Programs in Dentistry, Department of Oral Pathology, Radiology and Medicine, Iowa City, IA 52242-1316. Offers oral and maxillofacial pathology (Certificate); oral and maxillofacial radiology (Certificate); stomatology (MS). *Degree requirements:* For

master's, thesis. *Entrance requirements:* For master's, GRE, DDS, minimum GPA of 2.7. Additional exam requirements/recommendations for international students: Required—TOEFL.

The University of Iowa, College of Dentistry and Graduate College, Graduate Programs in Dentistry, Department of Orthodontics, Iowa City, IA 52242-1316. Offers MS, Certificate. *Degree requirements:* For master's, thesis. *Entrance requirements:* For master's, GRE, DDS; for Certificate, DDS. Additional exam requirements/recommendations for international students: Required—TOEFL.

The University of Iowa, College of Dentistry and Graduate College, Graduate Programs in Dentistry, Department of Pediatric Dentistry, Iowa City, IA 52242-1316. Offers Certificate. *Entrance requirements:* For degree, DDS. Additional exam requirements/recommendations for international students: Required—TOEFL.

The University of Iowa, College of Dentistry and Graduate College, Graduate Programs in Dentistry, Department of Periodontics, Iowa City, IA 52242-1316. Offers MS, Certificate. *Degree requirements:* For master's, thesis. *Entrance requirements:* For master's, GRE, DDS; for Certificate, DDS. Additional exam requirements/recommendations for international students: Required—TOEFL.

The University of Iowa, College of Dentistry and Graduate College, Graduate Programs in Dentistry, Department of Preventive and Community Dentistry, Iowa City, IA 52242-1316. Offers dental public health (MS). *Degree requirements:* For master's, thesis. *Entrance requirements:* For master's, GRE, DDS. Additional exam requirements/recommendations for international students: Required—TOEFL.

The University of Iowa, College of Dentistry and Graduate College, Graduate Programs in Dentistry, Department of Prosthodontics, Iowa City, IA 52242-1316. Offers MS, Certificate. *Degree requirements:* For master's, thesis. *Entrance requirements:* For master's, GRE, DDS; for Certificate, DDS. Additional exam requirements/recommendations for international students: Required—TOEFL.

The University of Iowa, College of Dentistry and Graduate College, Graduate Programs in Dentistry, Oral Science Graduate Program, Iowa City, IA 52242-1316. Offers MS, PhD. *Degree requirements:* For master's, thesis; for doctorate, thesis/dissertation. *Entrance requirements:* For master's, GRE, DDS. Additional exam requirements/recommendations for international students: Required—TOEFL.

University of Kentucky, Graduate School, Graduate Program in Dentistry, Lexington, KY 40506-0032. Offers MS. *Degree requirements:* For master's, comprehensive exam, thesis. *Entrance requirements:* For master's, GRE General Test, minimum undergraduate GPA of 2.5. Additional exam requirements/recommendations for international students: Required—TOEFL (minimum score 550 paper-based; 213 computer-based). Electronic applications accepted.

University of Louisville, School of Dentistry, Louisville, KY 40202. Offers dentistry (DMD); oral biology (MS). *Accreditation:* ADA (one or more programs are accredited). Part-time programs available. *Degree requirements:* For master's, thesis; for doctorate, National Board exams. *Entrance requirements:* For master's, DAT, GRE General Test, or National Board Dental Exam, minimum GPA of 2.75; for doctorate, DAT, 32 hours of course work in science. Additional exam requirements/recommendations for international students: Required—TOEFL (minimum score 100 iBT). Electronic applications accepted. *Expenses:* Contact institution. *Faculty research:* Inflammation and periondontitis, birth defects and developmental biology, biomaterials, oral infections, digital imaging.

The University of Manchester, School of Dentistry, Manchester, United Kingdom. Offers basic dental sciences (cancer studies) (M Phil, PhD); basic dental sciences (molecular genetics) (M Phil, PhD); basic dental sciences (stem cell biology) (M Phil, PhD); biomaterials sciences and dental technology (M Phil, PhD); dental public health/

University of Connecticut Health Center

UCHC offers you exceptional research opportunities spanning **Cell Analysis and Modeling; Cell Biology; Genetics and Developmental Biology; Immunology; Molecular Biology and Biochemistry; Neuroscience;** and **Skeletal, Craniofacial and Oral Biology**.

Key features of our program include:

❖ Integrated admissions with access to more than 100 laboratories.

❖ Flexible educational program tailored to the interests of each student.

❖ Excellent education in a stimulating, cutting edge research environment.

❖ Competitive stipend ($28,000 for 2012–13 year), tuition waiver, and availability of student health plan.

❖ State-of-the-art research facilities, including the new Cell and Genome Sciences Building, which houses the UConn Stem Cell Institute, the Center for Cell Analysis and Modeling, and the Department of Genetics and Developmental Biology.

For more information, please contact:
Stephanie Rauch, Biomedical Science Admissions Coordinator
University of Connecticut Health Center
263 Farmington Ave., MC 3906
Farmington, CT 06030
BiomedSciAdmissions@uchc.edu
http://grad.uchc.edu/prospective/programs/phd_biosci/index.html

community dentistry (M Phil, PhD); dental science (clinical) (PhD); endodontology (M Phil, PhD); fixed and removable prosthodontics (M Phil, PhD); operative dentistry (M Phil, PhD); oral and maxillofacial surgery (M Phil, PhD); oral radiology (M Phil, PhD); orthodontics (M Phil, PhD); restorative dentistry (M Phil, PhD).

University of Manitoba, Faculty of Dentistry and Faculty of Graduate Studies, Graduate Programs in Dentistry, Department of Dental Diagnostic and Surgical Sciences, Winnipeg, MB R3T 2N2, Canada. Offers oral and maxillofacial surgery (M Dent); periodontology (M Dent). *Entrance requirements:* For master's, dental degree. *Faculty research:* Implantology, clinical trials, tobacco use, periodontal disease.

University of Manitoba, Faculty of Dentistry and Faculty of Graduate Studies, Graduate Programs in Dentistry, Department of Oral Biology, Winnipeg, MB R3T 2N2, Canada. Offers M Sc, PhD. *Degree requirements:* For master's, thesis; for doctorate, comprehensive exam, thesis/dissertation. *Entrance requirements:* For master's, B Sc or pre-M Sc. Additional exam requirements/recommendations for international students: Required—TOEFL (minimum score 250 computer-based). *Faculty research:* Oral bacterial ecology and metabolism, biofilms, saliva and oral health, secretory mechanisms.

University of Manitoba, Faculty of Dentistry and Faculty of Graduate Studies, Graduate Programs in Dentistry, Department of Preventive Dental Science, Winnipeg, MB R3T 2N2, Canada. Offers orthodontics (M Sc). *Degree requirements:* For master's, thesis. *Entrance requirements:* For master's, dental degree. Electronic applications accepted.

University of Maryland, Baltimore, Graduate School, Graduate Programs in Dentistry, Department of Oral Pathology, Baltimore, MD 21201. Offers MS, PhD. *Students:* 4 full-time (0 women), all international. Average age 30. 13 applicants, 15% accepted, 1 enrolled. In 2011, 2 doctorates awarded. *Degree requirements:* For master's, thesis or alternative; for doctorate, comprehensive exam, thesis/dissertation. *Entrance requirements:* For master's and doctorate, GRE General Test, DDS, DMD. Additional exam requirements/recommendations for international students: Required—TOEFL (minimum score 550 paper-based; 80 iBT) or IELTS (minimum score 7). *Application deadline:* For fall admission, 5/1 for domestic students, 1/15 for international students. Application fee: $50. Electronic applications accepted. *Financial support:* Fellowships, research assistantships, and teaching assistantships available. Support available to part-time students. Financial award application deadline: 2/15. *Faculty research:* Histopathology, epidemiology of oral lesions, embryology. *Unit head:* Dr. Christian S. Stohler, Dean and Professor, 410-706-7461, Fax: 410-706-0193, E-mail: cstohler@umaryland.edu. *Application contact:* Dr. Mark Scheper, Director, 410-706-7936, Fax: 410-706-0193, E-mail: mscheper@umaryland.edu.

University of Maryland, Baltimore, Graduate School, Graduate Programs in Dentistry, Graduate Program in Biomedical Sciences - Dental School, Baltimore, MD 21201. Offers MS, PhD, DDS/PhD. *Students:* 3 full-time (all women); includes 1 minority (Two or more races, non-Hispanic/Latino), 2 international. Average age 34. In 2011, 13 master's, 1 doctorate awarded. *Degree requirements:* For master's, thesis optional; for doctorate, comprehensive exam, thesis/dissertation. *Entrance requirements:* For master's and doctorate, GRE General Test. Additional exam requirements/recommendations for international students: Required—TOEFL (minimum score 550 paper-based; 80 iBT) or IELTS (minimum score 7). *Application deadline:* For fall admission, 5/1 for domestic students, 1/15 for international students. Application fee: $50. Electronic applications accepted. *Financial support:* In 2011–12, research assistantships with full tuition reimbursements (averaging $23,000 per year) were awarded. *Faculty research:* Neuroscience, molecular and cell biology, infectious diseases. *Unit head:* Dr. Ronald Dubner, Professor and Chair, 410-706-0860, Fax: 410-706-0865, E-mail: rdubner@dental.umaryland.edu. *Application contact:* Dr. Sharon Gordon, Graduate Program Director, 410-706-1656, Fax: 410-706-0865, E-mail: sgordon@umaryland.edu.

University of Maryland, Baltimore, Professional and Advanced Education Programs in Dentistry, Baltimore, MD 21201-1627. Offers advanced general dentistry (Certificate); dentistry (DDS); endodontics (Certificate); oral-maxillofacial surgery (Certificate); orthodontics (Certificate); pediatric dentistry (Certificate); periodontics (Certificate); prosthodontics (Certificate); DDS/MBA; DDS/PhD. *Accreditation:* ADA. *Students:* 583 full-time (295 women), 3 part-time (1 woman); includes 198 minority (33 Black or African American, non-Hispanic/Latino; 2 American Indian or Alaska Native, non-Hispanic/Latino; 121 Asian, non-Hispanic/Latino; 31 Hispanic/Latino; 11 Two or more races, non-Hispanic/Latino), 20 international. Average age 26. In 2011, 128 doctorates, 31 Certificates awarded. *Entrance requirements:* For doctorate, DAT, coursework in science; for Certificate, National Dental Board Exams, DDS. Additional exam requirements/recommendations for international students: Required—TOEFL (minimum score 550 paper-based; 213 computer-based; 80 iBT). *Application deadline:* Applications are processed on a rolling basis. Application fee: $85. Electronic applications accepted. *Expenses:* Contact institution. *Financial support:* Career-related internships or fieldwork, Federal Work-Study, scholarships/grants, and traineeships available. Financial award application deadline: 3/1; financial award applicants required to submit FAFSA. *Faculty research:* Pain/neuroscience, oncology/molecular and cell biology, infectious disease/microbiology, bio-material studies, health promotion and disparities. *Unit head:* Dr. Christian S. Stohler, Dean, 410-706-7461. *Application contact:* Dr. Patricia Meehan, Assistant Dean for Admissions, 410-706-7472, Fax: 410-706-0945, E-mail: ddsadmissions@umaryland.edu. Web site: http://www.dental.umaryland.edu/.

University of Medicine and Dentistry of New Jersey, New Jersey Dental School, Newark, NJ 07101-1709. Offers dental science (MS); dentistry (DMD); endodontics (Certificate); oral medicine (Certificate); orthodontics (Certificate); pediatric dentistry (Certificate); periodontics (Certificate); prosthodontics (Certificate); DMD/MPH; DMD/PhD; MD/Certificate; MS/Certificate. DMD/MPH offered jointly with New Jersey Institute of Technology, Rutgers, The State University of New Jersey, Camden. *Accreditation:* ADA (one or more programs are accredited). *Entrance requirements:* For doctorate, DAT. Electronic applications accepted. *Expenses:* Contact institution.

University of Michigan, School of Dentistry and Horace H. Rackham School of Graduate Studies, Graduate Programs in Dentistry, Endodontics Program, Ann Arbor, MI 48109-1078. Offers MS. *Students:* 10 full-time (1 woman); includes 3 minority (1 American Indian or Alaska Native, non-Hispanic/Latino; 1 Asian, non-Hispanic/Latino; 1 Hispanic/Latino). 29 applicants, 10% accepted, 3 enrolled. In 2011, 3 master's awarded. *Degree requirements:* For master's, thesis. *Entrance requirements:* For master's, DDS. Additional exam requirements/recommendations for international students: Required—TOEFL (minimum score 84 iBT). *Application deadline:* For fall admission, 9/1 for domestic and international students. Applications are processed on a rolling basis. Application fee: $65 ($75 for international students). Electronic applications accepted. *Unit head:* Dr. Neville McDonald, Program Director, 734-647-3722, E-mail: somerled@umich.edu. *Application contact:* Patricia Katcher, Associate Admissions Director, 734-763-1068, Fax: 734-764-1922, E-mail: graddentinquiry@umich.edu. Web site: http://www.dent.umich.edu/crse/graduateprogram/endodontics.

University of Michigan, School of Dentistry and Horace H. Rackham School of Graduate Studies, Graduate Programs in Dentistry, Orthodontics Program, Ann Arbor, MI 48109-1078. Offers MS. Part-time and evening/weekend programs available. Postbaccalaureate distance learning degree programs offered (minimal on-campus study). *Students:* 21 full-time (11 women); includes 6 minority (4 Asian, non-Hispanic/Latino; 2 Hispanic/Latino). 174 applicants, 4% accepted, 7 enrolled. In 2011, 6 master's awarded. Terminal master's awarded for partial completion of doctoral program. *Degree requirements:* For master's, thesis. *Entrance requirements:* For master's, GRE, National Dental Board Exam, DDS. Additional exam requirements/recommendations for international students: Required—TOEFL (minimum score 84 iBT). *Application deadline:* For fall admission, 9/1 for domestic and international students. Application fee: $65 ($75 for international students). Electronic applications accepted. *Unit head:* Dr. Sunil Kapila, Program Director, 734-764-1080, E-mail: skapila@umich.edu. *Application contact:* Patricia Katcher, Associate Admissions Director, 734-763-1068, Fax: 734-764-1922, E-mail: graddentinquiry@umich.edu. Web site: http://www.dent.umich.edu/opd/graduateprograms/ortho/about.

University of Michigan, School of Dentistry and Horace H. Rackham School of Graduate Studies, Graduate Programs in Dentistry, Pediatric Dentistry Program, Ann Arbor, MI 48109-1078. Offers MS. Part-time and evening/weekend programs available. Postbaccalaureate distance learning degree programs offered (minimal on-campus study). *Students:* 18 full-time (17 women); includes 5 minority (4 Asian, non-Hispanic/Latino; 1 Hispanic/Latino). 100 applicants, 6% accepted, 6 enrolled. In 2011, 4 master's awarded. Terminal master's awarded for partial completion of doctoral program. *Degree requirements:* For master's, thesis. *Entrance requirements:* For master's, DDS. Additional exam requirements/recommendations for international students: Required—TOEFL (minimum score 84 iBT). *Application deadline:* For fall admission, 9/17 for domestic students, 10/1 for international students. Application fee: $65 ($75 for international students). Electronic applications accepted. *Unit head:* Dr. James Boynton, Program Director, 734-764-1522, E-mail: jboynton@umich.edu. *Application contact:* Patricia Katcher, Associate Admissions Director, 734-763-1068, Fax: 734-764-1922, E-mail: graddentinquiry@umich.edu. Web site: http://www.dent.umich.edu/opd/graduateprograms/ped/aboutus.

University of Michigan, School of Dentistry and Horace H. Rackham School of Graduate Studies, Graduate Programs in Dentistry, Periodontics Program, Ann Arbor, MI 48109-1078. Offers MS. *Students:* 13 full-time (5 women); includes 7 minority (1 Black or African American, non-Hispanic/Latino; 5 Asian, non-Hispanic/Latino; 1 Hispanic/Latino). 42 applicants, 12% accepted, 5 enrolled. In 2011, 4 master's awarded. *Degree requirements:* For master's, thesis. *Entrance requirements:* For master's, DDS. Additional exam requirements/recommendations for international students: Required—TOEFL (minimum score 84 iBT). *Application deadline:* For fall admission, 8/1 for domestic and international students. Applications are processed on a rolling basis. Application fee: $65 ($75 for international students). Electronic applications accepted. *Unit head:* Dr. Hom-Lay Wang, Program Director, 734-764-1948, E-mail: homlay@umich.edu. *Application contact:* Patricia Katcher, Associate Admissions Director, 734-763-1068, Fax: 734-764-1922, E-mail: graddentinquiry@umich.edu.

University of Michigan, School of Dentistry and Horace H. Rackham School of Graduate Studies, Graduate Programs in Dentistry, Prosthodontics Program, Ann Arbor, MI 48109-1078. Offers MS. Part-time and evening/weekend programs available. Postbaccalaureate distance learning degree programs offered (minimal on-campus study). *Students:* 11 full-time (4 women); includes 1 minority (Asian, non-Hispanic/Latino). 45 applicants, 7% accepted, 3 enrolled. In 2011, 1 master's awarded. Terminal master's awarded for partial completion of doctoral program. *Degree requirements:* For master's, thesis. *Entrance requirements:* For master's, DDS. Additional exam requirements/recommendations for international students: Required—TOEFL (minimum score 84 iBT). *Application deadline:* For fall admission, 10/1 for domestic and international students. Applications are processed on a rolling basis. Application fee: $65 ($75 for international students). Electronic applications accepted. *Unit head:* Dr. Michael Razzoog, Program Director, 734-647-1369, E-mail: merim@umich.edu. *Application contact:* Patricia Katcher, Associate Admissions Director, 734-763-1068, Fax: 734-764-1922, E-mail: graddentinquiry@umich.edu. Web site: http://www.dent.umich.edu/bms/gradstudentsprosgradprog.

University of Michigan, School of Dentistry and Horace H. Rackham School of Graduate Studies, Graduate Programs in Dentistry, Restorative Dentistry Program, Ann Arbor, MI 48109-1078. Offers MS. Part-time programs available. *Students:* 13 full-time (8 women); includes 5 minority (3 Asian, non-Hispanic/Latino; 2 Hispanic/Latino). 33 applicants, 15% accepted, 5 enrolled. In 2011, 7 master's awarded. *Degree requirements:* For master's, thesis. *Entrance requirements:* Additional exam requirements/recommendations for international students: Required—TOEFL (minimum score 84 iBT). *Application deadline:* For fall admission, 10/1 for domestic and international students. Applications are processed on a rolling basis. Application fee: $65 ($75 for international students). Electronic applications accepted. *Unit head:* Dr. Peter Yaman, Program Director, 734-647-3722, E-mail: pyam@umich.edu. *Application contact:* Patricia Katcher, Associate Admissions Director, 734-763-1068, Fax: 734-764-1922, E-mail: graddentinquiry@umich.edu. Web site: http://www.dent.umich.edu/crse/graduateprograms/restorativedentistry.

University of Michigan, School of Dentistry, Oral Health Sciences PhD Program, Ann Arbor, MI 48109-1078. Offers PhD. *Faculty:* 32 full-time (8 women). *Students:* 14 full-time (9 women); includes 7 minority (4 Asian, non-Hispanic/Latino; 3 Hispanic/Latino), 2 international. Average age 30. 19 applicants, 16% accepted, 2 enrolled. In 2011, 3 doctorates awarded. *Degree requirements:* For doctorate, thesis/dissertation, preliminary exam, oral defense of dissertation. *Entrance requirements:* For doctorate, GRE. Additional exam requirements/recommendations for international students: Required—TOEFL. *Application deadline:* For fall admission, 1/5 priority date for domestic students, 1/5 for international students. Applications are processed on a rolling basis. Application fee: $65 ($75 for international students). Electronic applications accepted. *Financial support:* In 2011–12, 12 fellowships with full tuition reimbursements (averaging $22,000 per year), 2 research assistantships with full tuition reimbursements (averaging $22,000 per year) were awarded; scholarships/grants, traineeships, and health care benefits also available. *Faculty research:* Craniofacial development, oral and pharyngeal cancer, mineralized tissue biology and musculoskeletal disorders, tissue engineering and regeneration, oral infectious and immunologic diseases, oral sensory systems and central circuits. *Total annual research expenditures:* $19.9 million. *Unit head:* Dr. Jan Hu, Associate Dean for Research and Training, 734-615-1970, E-mail: ohsphd@umich.edu. *Application contact:* Patricia E. Schultz, Training Manager, 734-615-1970, E-mail: ohsphd@umich.edu.

University of Minnesota, Twin Cities Campus, School of Dentistry and Graduate School, Graduate Programs in Dentistry, Advanced Education Program in Periodontology, Minneapolis, MN 55455-0213. Offers MS. *Degree requirements:* For master's, comprehensive exam, thesis. *Entrance requirements:* For master's, DDS/DMD, letter from Dental Dean, specific GGP/class rank, two letters of recommendation. Additional exam requirements/recommendations for international students: Required—TOEFL (minimum score 590 paper-based; 243 computer-based). *Faculty research:* Periodontitis, risk factors, regenerating, diabetes immunology.

University of Minnesota, Twin Cities Campus, School of Dentistry and Graduate School, Graduate Programs in Dentistry, Division of Endodontics, Minneapolis, MN 55455-0213. Offers MS, Certificate. *Degree requirements:* For master's, thesis.

Oral and Dental Sciences

Entrance requirements: Additional exam requirements/recommendations for international students: Required—TOEFL. *Faculty research:* Pain, inflammation, neuropharmacology, neuropeptides, cytokines.

University of Minnesota, Twin Cities Campus, School of Dentistry and Graduate School, Graduate Programs in Dentistry, Division of Orthodontics, Minneapolis, MN 55455-0213. Offers MS. *Degree requirements:* For master's, thesis. *Entrance requirements:* Additional exam requirements/recommendations for international students: Required—TOEFL (minimum score 587 paper-based; 240 computer-based). *Faculty research:* Bone biology, 3-D imaging.

University of Minnesota, Twin Cities Campus, School of Dentistry and Graduate School, Graduate Programs in Dentistry, Division of Pediatric Dentistry, Minneapolis, MN 55455-0213. Offers MS. *Degree requirements:* For master's, thesis. *Entrance requirements:* Additional exam requirements/recommendations for international students: Required—TOEFL. *Faculty research:* Molecular genetics of facial growth, dental material/adhesion, expanded functions dental auxiliary utilization.

University of Minnesota, Twin Cities Campus, School of Dentistry and Graduate School, Graduate Programs in Dentistry, Division of Prosthodontics, Minneapolis, MN 55455-0213. Offers MS. *Degree requirements:* For master's, thesis, clinical. *Entrance requirements:* Additional exam requirements/recommendations for international students: Required—TOEFL.

University of Minnesota, Twin Cities Campus, School of Dentistry and Graduate School, Graduate Programs in Dentistry, Program in Oral Biology, Minneapolis, MN 55455-0213. Offers MS, PhD. *Degree requirements:* For master's, thesis. *Faculty research:* Microbiology, neuroscience, biomaterials, biochemistry, cancer biology.

University of Minnesota, Twin Cities Campus, School of Dentistry and Graduate School, Graduate Programs in Dentistry, Program in Oral Health Services for Older Adults (Geriatrics), Minneapolis, MN 55455-0213. Offers MS, Certificate. *Degree requirements:* For master's, thesis (for some programs). *Entrance requirements:* For master's, DDS degree or equivalent. Additional exam requirements/recommendations for international students: Required—TOEFL (minimum score 560 paper-based; 233 computer-based). Electronic applications accepted. *Faculty research:* Geriatrics dental care, long-term care dental services, oral-systemic health relationships, utilization of care by older adults.

University of Minnesota, Twin Cities Campus, School of Dentistry and Graduate School, Graduate Programs in Dentistry, Program in Temporomandibular Joint Disorders, Minneapolis, MN 55455-0213. Offers MS. *Degree requirements:* For master's, comprehensive exam, thesis. *Entrance requirements:* Additional exam requirements/recommendations for international students: Required—TOEFL. Electronic applications accepted. *Faculty research:* Clinical trials, TMJ mechanicals, diagnostic criteria, biomarkers, genetics.

University of Mississippi Medical Center, School of Dentistry, Department of Craniofacial and Dental Research, Jackson, MS 39216-4505. Offers MS, PhD.

University of Missouri–Kansas City, School of Dentistry, Kansas City, MO 64110-2499. Offers advanced education in dentistry (Graduate Dental Certificate); dental hygiene education (MS); dentistry (DDS); endodontics (Graduate Dental Certificate); oral and maxillofacial surgery (Graduate Dental Certificate); oral biology (MS, PhD); orthodontics and dentofacial orthopedics (Graduate Dental Certificate); pediatric dentistry (Graduate Dental Certificate); periodontics (Graduate Dental Certificate). PhD (interdisciplinary) offered through the School of Graduate Studies. *Accreditation:* ADA (one or more programs are accredited). *Faculty:* 95 full-time (41 women), 62 part-time/adjunct (18 women). *Students:* 420 full-time (182 women), 44 part-time (26 women); includes 67 minority (7 Black or African American, non-Hispanic/Latino; 2 American Indian or Alaska Native, non-Hispanic/Latino; 45 Asian, non-Hispanic/Latino; 11 Hispanic/Latino; 2 Two or more races, non-Hispanic/Latino), 2 international. Average age 27. 511 applicants, 23% accepted, 115 enrolled. In 2011, 9 master's, 98 doctorates, 17 other advanced degrees awarded. *Degree requirements:* For master's, thesis; for doctorate, thesis/dissertation (for some programs). *Entrance requirements:* For master's, DAT, letters of evaluation, personal interview; for doctorate, DAT (for DDS); for Graduate Dental Certificate, DDS. Additional exam requirements/recommendations for international students: Required—TOEFL (minimum score 550 paper-based; 213 computer-based; 80 iBT). *Application deadline:* For fall admission, 2/1 for domestic and international students. Application fee: $45 ($50 for international students). *Expenses:* Contact institution. *Financial support:* In 2011–12, 3 fellowships (averaging $59,417 per year), 3 research assistantships (averaging $19,471 per year) were awarded; career-related internships or fieldwork, Federal Work-Study, institutionally sponsored loans, and tuition waivers (full and partial) also available. Support available to part-time students. Financial award application deadline: 3/1; financial award applicants required to submit FAFSA. *Faculty research:* Biomaterials, dental use of lasers, effectiveness of periodontal treatments, temporomandibular joint dysfunction. *Unit head:* Dr. Marsha Pyle, Dean, 816-235-2010. *Application contact:* Dr. John Killip, Associate Dean for Student Programs, 816-235-2080. Web site: http://dentistry.umkc.edu/.

The University of North Carolina at Chapel Hill, School of Dentistry and Graduate School, Graduate Programs in Dentistry, Chapel Hill , NC 27599. Offers dental hygiene (MS); endodontics (MS); epidemiology (PhD); operative dentistry (MS); oral and maxillofacial pathology (MS); oral and maxillofacial radiology (MS); oral biology (PhD); orthodontics (MS); pediatric dentistry (MS); periodontology (MS); prosthodontics (MS). *Faculty:* 82 full-time (28 women). *Students:* 90 full-time (46 women); includes 20 minority (7 Black or African American, non-Hispanic/Latino; 10 Asian, non-Hispanic/Latino; 3 Hispanic/Latino), 30 international. Average age 28. 475 applicants, 7% accepted, 31 enrolled. In 2011, 20 master's, 2 doctorates awarded. *Degree requirements:* For master's, thesis; for doctorate, thesis/dissertation. *Entrance requirements:* For master's, GRE General Test (for orthodontics and oral biology only); National Dental Board Part I (Part II if available), dental degree (for all except dental hygiene); for doctorate, GRE General Test. Additional exam requirements/recommendations for international students: Required—TOEFL (minimum score 550 paper-based; 213 computer-based; 79 iBT). Application fee: $78. Electronic applications accepted. *Expenses:* Contact institution. *Financial support:* In 2011–12, research assistantships with partial tuition reimbursements (averaging $22,000 per year), teaching assistantships with partial tuition reimbursements (averaging $6,420 per year) were awarded; fellowships also available. Financial award application deadline: 3/1; financial award applicants required to submit FAFSA. *Faculty research:* Clinical research, inflammation, immunology, neuroscience, molecular biology. *Total annual research expenditures:* $6 million. *Unit head:* Dr. Ceib Phillips, Assistant Dean for Advanced Education and Graduate Studies, 919-966-2763, Fax: 919-843-8864, E-mail: ceib_phillips@dentistry.unc.edu. *Application contact:* Koyah Rivera, Graduate Registrar, 919-537-3347, Fax: 919-966-5795, E-mail: koyah_rivera@dentistry.unc.edu. Web site: http://www.dentistry.unc.edu/.

University of Oklahoma Health Sciences Center, College of Dentistry and Graduate College, Graduate Programs in Dentistry, Department of Orthodontics, Oklahoma City, OK 73190. Offers MS. *Degree requirements:* For master's, thesis. *Entrance requirements:* For master's, minimum GPA of 3.0, DDS/DMD. Additional exam requirements/recommendations for international students: Required—TOEFL. Electronic applications accepted. *Faculty research:* Craniofacial growth and development, biomechanical principles in orthodontics.

University of Oklahoma Health Sciences Center, College of Dentistry and Graduate College, Graduate Programs in Dentistry, Department of Periodontics, Oklahoma City, OK 73190. Offers MS. *Degree requirements:* For master's, thesis. *Entrance requirements:* For master's, DDS/DMD, minimum GPA of 3.0. Additional exam requirements/recommendations for international students: Required—TOEFL (minimum score 550 paper-based; 213 computer-based). Electronic applications accepted.

University of Pittsburgh, School of Dental Medicine, Residency Programs in Dental Medicine, Advanced Education Program in Prosthodontics, Pittsburgh, PA 15261. Offers MDS, Certificate. *Faculty:* 2 full-time (0 women), 4 part-time/adjunct (0 women). *Students:* 9 full-time (2 women); includes 1 minority (Asian, non-Hispanic/Latino). Average age 27. 44 applicants, 7% accepted, 3 enrolled. *Degree requirements:* For master's, comprehensive exam, thesis. *Entrance requirements:* Additional exam requirements/recommendations for international students: Required—TOEFL. *Application deadline:* For fall admission, 10/30 for domestic and international students. Applications are processed on a rolling basis. Application fee: $50. Electronic applications accepted. *Expenses:* Tuition, state resident: full-time $18,774; part-time $760 per credit. Tuition, nonresident: full-time $30,736; part-time $1258 per credit. *Required fees:* $740; $200 per term. Tuition and fees vary according to program. *Financial support:* In 2011–12, 7 students received support. Stipends available. *Faculty research:* Implant dentistry, occlusion, biomechanics, genetics, biomaterials. *Unit head:* Dr. Mohsen Azarbal, Associate Professor/Director, 412-648-8453, Fax: 412-648-8850, E-mail: moa5@pitt.edu. *Application contact:* Pamela A. Edwards, Administrator, Office of Resident Education, 412-648-8406, Fax: 412-648-8219, E-mail: pae3@pitt.edu.

University of Pittsburgh, School of Dental Medicine, Residency Programs in Dental Medicine, Department of Dental Anesthesiology, Pittsburgh, PA 15260. Offers Certificate. *Faculty:* 4 full-time (0 women), 5 part-time/adjunct (1 woman). *Students:* 8 full-time (0 women). Average age 35. 27 applicants, 15% accepted, 4 enrolled. In 2011, 2 Certificates awarded. *Entrance requirements:* For degree, National Board Dental Exam Parts I and II, DMD or DDS. *Application deadline:* For fall admission, 10/1 for domestic students. Application fee: $50. Electronic applications accepted. *Expenses:* Tuition, state resident: full-time $18,774; part-time $760 per credit. Tuition, nonresident: full-time $30,736; part-time $1258 per credit. *Required fees:* $740; $200 per term. Tuition and fees vary according to program. *Financial support:* In 2011–12, 8 fellowships (averaging $36,000 per year) were awarded; health care benefits also available. *Faculty research:* Clinical pharmacology and random controlled trials. *Unit head:* Dr. Michael A. Cuddy, Program Director, 412-648-8609, Fax: 412-648-2591, E-mail: mc2@pitt.edu. *Application contact:* Lisa R. Lehman, Department Administrator, 412-648-8609, Fax: 412-648-2591, E-mail: lrl12@pitt.edu. Web site: http://www.dental.pitt.edu/.

University of Pittsburgh, School of Dental Medicine, Residency Programs in Dental Medicine, Department of Endodontics, Pittsburgh, PA 15260. Offers MDS, Certificate. *Faculty:* 2 full-time (1 woman), 6 part-time/adjunct (1 woman). *Students:* 6 full-time (1 woman); includes 2 minority (1 Black or African American, non-Hispanic/Latino; 1 Asian, non-Hispanic/Latino). Average age 27. 62 applicants, 5% accepted, 3 enrolled. In 2011, 3 Certificates awarded. *Degree requirements:* For master's, comprehensive exam, thesis. *Entrance requirements:* For master's and Certificate, National Boards Part 1 and 2. *Application deadline:* For fall admission, 9/15 for domestic students. Application fee: $50. *Expenses:* Tuition, state resident: full-time $18,774; part-time $760 per credit. Tuition, nonresident: full-time $30,736; part-time $1258 per credit. *Required fees:* $740; $200 per term. Tuition and fees vary according to program. *Financial support:* Application deadline: 4/15. *Faculty research:* Pulpal neurobiology, root canal therapy, root fracture/resorption repair, osseous grafts related to endodontics, endodontic surge. *Total annual research expenditures:* $10,000. *Unit head:* Dr. Herbert L. Ray, Jr., Director, 412-648-8647, Fax: 412-383-7796, E-mail: skipp@pitt.edu. *Application contact:* Pamela A. Edwards, Administrator, Office of Resident Education, 412-648-8406, Fax: 412-648-8219, E-mail: pae3@pitt.edu. Web site: http://www.dental.pitt.edu/.

University of Pittsburgh, School of Dental Medicine, Residency Programs in Dental Medicine, Department of Oral and Maxillofacial Surgery, Pittsburgh, PA 15260. Offers craniofacial and maxillofacial surgery (Certificate); oral and maxillofacial surgery (Certificate). *Faculty:* 12 full-time (3 women). *Students:* 13 full-time (0 women); includes 1 minority (Asian, non-Hispanic/Latino). Average age 25. 111 applicants. In 2011, 4 Certificates awarded. *Degree requirements:* For Certificate, comprehensive exam. *Entrance requirements:* For degree, National Boards Part I, U.S. or Canadian dental degree (DDS or DMD). *Application deadline:* For fall admission, 10/15 for domestic students. Applications are processed on a rolling basis. Application fee: $0. Electronic applications accepted. *Expenses:* Contact institution. *Financial support:* In 2011–12, 8 students received support, including 4 fellowships with partial tuition reimbursements available (averaging $36,000 per year); scholarships/grants, health care benefits, and tuition waivers also available. *Faculty research:* Clefts, craniofacial anomalies, facial trauma, head and neck cancer, pain management. *Total annual research expenditures:* $2 million. *Unit head:* Dr. Bernard J. Costello, Program Director, 412-648-6801, Fax: 412-648-6835. *Application contact:* Andrea M. Ford, Residency and Fellowship Coordinator, 412-648-6801, Fax: 412-648-6835, E-mail: fordam@upmc.edu. Web site: http://www.dental.p.h.edu/.

University of Pittsburgh, School of Dental Medicine, Residency Programs in Dental Medicine, Department of Orthodontics and Dentofacial Orthopedics, Pittsburgh, PA 15261. Offers MDS, Certificate. *Faculty:* 1 full-time (0 women), 8 part-time/adjunct (2 women). *Students:* 12 full-time (4 women); includes 4 minority (all Asian, non-Hispanic/Latino). Average age 27. 181 applicants, 2% accepted. In 2011, 2 master's awarded. *Degree requirements:* For master's, comprehensive exam, thesis; for Certificate, comprehensive exam. *Entrance requirements:* For master's and Certificate, National Boards Parts I and II. *Application deadline:* For fall admission, 10/1 for domestic students. *Expenses:* Tuition, state resident: full-time $18,774; part-time $760 per credit. Tuition, nonresident: full-time $30,736; part-time $1258 per credit. *Required fees:* $740; $200 per term. Tuition and fees vary according to program. *Faculty research:* Facial form, orthodontic outcomes. *Unit head:* Dr. Joseph F. A. Petrone, Chair, Department of Orthodontics and Dentofacial Orthopedics, 412-648-8638, Fax: 412-648-8817, E-mail: jfap@pitt.edu. *Application contact:* Lauren M. Breskovich, Department Administrator, 412-648-8419, Fax: 412-648-8817, E-mail: lmb111@pitt.edu. Web site: http://www.dental.pitt.edu/orthodontics/index.php.

University of Pittsburgh, School of Dental Medicine, Residency Programs in Dental Medicine, Department of Periodontics, Pittsburgh, PA 15261. Offers MDS, Certificate. *Faculty:* 4 full-time (2 women), 8 part-time/adjunct (2 women). *Students:* 9 full-time (2 women); includes 2 minority (1 Black or African American, non-Hispanic/Latino; 1 Asian, non-Hispanic/Latino), 3 international. Average age 28. 36 applicants, 8% accepted, 3 enrolled. *Degree requirements:* For master's, comprehensive exam, thesis. *Entrance requirements:* For degree, DMD, DDS. *Application deadline:* For fall admission, 8/15 priority date for domestic students, 8/15 for international students. Applications are processed on a rolling basis. Application fee: $50. *Expenses:* Tuition, state resident: full-time $18,774; part-time $760 per credit. Tuition, nonresident: full-time $30,736; part-time $1258 per credit. *Required fees:* $740; $200 per term. Tuition and fees vary

according to program. *Financial support:* Stipends available. *Faculty research:* Bone tissue engineering, transcriptional regulation, periodontics, implantology, gene delivery. *Total annual research expenditures:* $50,000. *Unit head:* Dr. Pouran Famili, Director/Chair, 412-648-8598, Fax: 412-648-8594, E-mail: pof@pitt.edu. *Application contact:* Pamela A. Edwards, Administrator, Office of Resident Education, 412-648-8406, Fax: 412-648-8219, E-mail: pae3@pitt.edu.

University of Puerto Rico, Medical Sciences Campus, School of Dental Medicine, Graduate Programs in Dentistry, San Juan, PR 00936-5067. Offers general dentistry (Certificate); oral and maxillofacial surgery (Certificate); orthodontics (Certificate); pediatric dentistry (Certificate); prosthodontics (Certificate). *Degree requirements:* For Certificate, comprehensive exam (for some programs). *Entrance requirements:* For degree, National Board Dental Exam I, National Board Dental Exam II, DDS or DMD, interview. Electronic applications accepted. *Expenses:* Contact institution. *Faculty research:* Analgesic drugs, anti-inflammatory drugs, saliva cytoanalysis, dental materials, oral epidemiology and dental caries.

University of Rochester, School of Medicine and Dentistry, Graduate Programs in Medicine and Dentistry, Center for Oral Biology, Rochester, NY 14627. Offers dental science (MS). *Degree requirements:* For master's, thesis. *Entrance requirements:* For master's, GRE General Test, DDS or equivalent. *Expenses: Tuition:* Full-time $41,040.

University of Southern California, Graduate School, Herman Ostrow School of Dentistry and Graduate School, Department of Craniofacial Biology, Los Angeles, CA 90089. Offers MS, PhD, Graduate Certificate. Terminal master's awarded for partial completion of doctoral program. *Degree requirements:* For master's, comprehensive exam, thesis; for doctorate, comprehensive exam, thesis/dissertation. *Entrance requirements:* For master's and doctorate, GRE, undergraduate degree. Additional exam requirements/recommendations for international students: Required—TOEFL. Electronic applications accepted. *Faculty research:* Orthodontics, periodontics, tooth development, oral biology, stem cell biology.

The University of Tennessee Health Science Center, College of Dentistry, Memphis, TN 38163-0002. Offers dentistry (DDS); oral and maxillofacial surgery (Certificate); orthodontics (MS); pediatric dentistry (MS, Certificate); periodontics (MS); prosthodontics (Certificate). *Accreditation:* ADA (one or more programs are accredited). *Degree requirements:* For master's, thesis. *Entrance requirements:* For master's, GRE, interviews; for doctorate, DAT, interview, pre-professional evaluation. Additional exam requirements/recommendations for international students: Required—TOEFL (minimum score 275 computer-based). Electronic applications accepted. *Expenses:* Contact institution. *Faculty research:* Oral cancer, proteomics, inflammation mechanisms, defensins, periopathogens, dental material.

The University of Toledo, College of Graduate Studies, College of Medicine and Life Sciences, Department of Surgery, Toledo, OH 43606-3390. Offers oral biology (MSBS). *Faculty:* 8. *Students:* 5 full-time (2 women). Average age 30. 2 applicants, 100% accepted, 2 enrolled. In 2011, 2 master's awarded. *Degree requirements:* For master's, thesis or alternative. *Entrance requirements:* For master's, DAT, minimum undergraduate GPA of 3.0, three letters of recommendation, statement of purpose, transcripts from all prior institutions attended, acceptance into Pediatric Dental Residency Program at UT. Additional exam requirements/recommendations for international students: Required—TOEFL (minimum score 550 paper-based; 213 computer-based; 80 iBT), IELTS (minimum score 6.5). *Application deadline:* Applications are processed on a rolling basis. Application fee: $45 ($75 for international students). Electronic applications accepted. *Financial support:* Federal Work-Study, institutionally sponsored loans, tuition waivers, and tuition paid as part of the residency program available. *Faculty research:* Oral biology-tissue cultures. *Unit head:* Dr. Michael Nedley, Chair, 419-383-3504, E-mail: michael.nedley@utoledo.edu. *Application contact:* Brandi Hendrickson, Program Coordinator, 419-383-3504, E-mail: brandi.hendrickson@utoledo.edu. Web site: http://www.utoledo.edu/med/grad/.

University of Toronto, School of Graduate Studies, Faculty of Dentistry, Graduate Programs in Dentistry, Toronto, ON M5S 1A1, Canada. Offers M Sc, PhD. Part-time programs available. Terminal master's awarded for partial completion of doctoral program. *Degree requirements:* For master's, thesis; for doctorate, thesis/dissertation. *Entrance requirements:* For master's, honors B Sc, minimum B average, 2 letters of reference; for doctorate, M Sc, minimum B+ average. Additional exam requirements/recommendations for international students: Required—Michigan English Language Assessment Battery, IELTS, TOEFL or COPE. Electronic applications accepted. *Expenses:* Contact institution. *Faculty research:* Plaque, periodontal biology, biomaterials/dental implants, community dentistry, growth and development.

University of Toronto, School of Graduate Studies, Faculty of Dentistry, Specialty Master's Programs, Toronto, ON M5S 1A1, Canada. Offers dental anesthesia (M Sc); dental public health (M Sc); endodontics (M Sc); oral and maxillofacial surgery and anesthesia (M Sc); oral pathology (M Sc); oral radiology (M Sc); orthodontics (M Sc); pediatric dentistry (M Sc); periodontology (M Sc); prosthodontics (M Sc). *Degree requirements:* For master's, thesis. *Entrance requirements:* For master's, completion of professional degree of DDS/BDS, DMD, minimum B average, 2 letters of reference. Additional exam requirements/recommendations for international students: Required—TOEFL (minimum score 600 paper-based; 100 iBT), TWE (minimum score 5). *Expenses:* Contact institution. *Faculty research:* Plaque and periodontal biology, biomaterials/dental implants, community dentistry, growth development, neurophysiology.

University of Washington, Graduate School, School of Dentistry and Graduate School, Graduate Programs in Dentistry, Department of Endodontics, Seattle, WA 98195. Offers MSD, Certificate.

University of Washington, Graduate School, School of Dentistry and Graduate School, Graduate Programs in Dentistry, Department of Orthodontics, Seattle, WA 98195. Offers MSD, Certificate.

University of Washington, Graduate School, School of Dentistry, Program in Dental Surgery, Seattle, WA 98195. Offers DDS. *Accreditation:* ADA. *Entrance requirements:* For doctorate, DAT.

The University of Western Ontario, Schulich School of Medicine and Dentistry, School of Dentistry, Program in Graduate Orthodontics, London, ON N6A 5B8, Canada. Offers M Cl D. *Degree requirements:* For master's, thesis. *Entrance requirements:* For master's, GRE General Test, minimum B average, 1 year of general practice preferred. Additional exam requirements/recommendations for international students: Required—TOEFL (minimum score 600 paper-based; 250 computer-based).

West Virginia University, School of Dentistry, Division of Dental Hygiene, Morgantown, WV 26506. Offers MS. Part-time programs available. *Degree requirements:* For master's, thesis. *Entrance requirements:* For master's, GRE, MAT, BS in dental hygiene or equivalent, minimum GPA of 2.75. Additional exam requirements/recommendations for international students: Required—TOEFL. *Faculty research:* Curriculum and instruction, infection control, special patient care, diversity and cultural sensitivity, oral health disparities.

West Virginia University, School of Dentistry, Graduate Programs in Dentistry, Morgantown, WV 26506. Offers endodontics (MS); orthodontics (MS); prosthodontics (MS). *Degree requirements:* For master's, thesis. *Entrance requirements:* For master's, National Dental Board Exam Parts I and II, DDS/DMD from accredited U.S. or Canadian Dental School, minimum GPA of 3.0. Additional exam requirements/recommendations for international students: Required—TOEFL. *Expenses:* Contact institution. *Faculty research:* Growth and development, cephalographics, endodontic interpretation and therapy.

UNIVERSITY OF CONNECTICUT HEALTH CENTER

Graduate Program in Skeletal, Craniofacial, and Oral Biology

Programs of Study

The Graduate Program in Skeletal, Craniofacial, and Oral Biology provides students with interdisciplinary research training in the areas of skeletal, craniofacial, and oral biology, emphasizing contemporary research technologies in cell, molecular, and developmental biology; genetics; and biochemistry. Trainees may enter a Ph.D. program or a combined D.M.D./Ph.D., M.D./Ph.D., or dental residency/Ph.D. program. The program prepares trainees for academic or industrial careers in the basic biomedical sciences or for academic careers in medicine or dental medicine.

Areas of research include regulation of the formation, outgrowth, and patterning of the developing limb; control of cartilage differentiation, endochondral ossification, osteogenesis, and joint formation; molecular regulation of gene expression in bone; homeobox gene regulation of osteoblast differentiation; gene therapy of bone diseases; hormonal and cytokine regulation of bone growth, formation, and remodeling; control of craniofacial skeletogenesis and tooth development; signal transduction and intracellular signaling pathways; cellular and molecular aspects of the pathogenesis of inflammatory disease; microbiology, pathogenesis, and immunology of caries and periodontal disease; neural structure and function in the gustatory system; biomaterial development for tissue engineering; bone cell–implant interactions; differentiation of human embryonic stem cells into skeletal tissues; and analysis of oral and mucosal function and disease.

Research Facilities

The University complex provides excellent physical facilities for research in both basic and clinical sciences. The Health Center Library is well equipped with extensive journal and book holdings and rapid electronic access to database searching, the World Wide Web, and library holdings. The library also contains the Computer Education Center and the End User Support Center. The Center for Laboratory Animal Care contains a transgenic mouse production facility fully equipped for gene targeting studies and with special facilities for housing immunodeficient animals. Facilities include the Center for Biomaterials, the General Clinical Research Center, the Center for Cell Analysis and Modeling (confocal microscopy, low light level microscopy, two photon microscopy), the Center for Bone Histology and Histomorphometry; the Molecular Imaging Laboratory, the Fluorescence Flow Cytometry Facility, the Electron Microscopy Facility, Gene Targeting and Transgenic Facility, the Microarray Core Facility, the Molecular Core Facility, NMR Structural Biology Facility, National Resource for Cell Analysis and Modeling, and the Center for Molecular Medicine (laser capture microdissection).

Financial Aid

Support for doctoral students engaged in full-time degree programs at the Health Center is provided on a competitive basis. Graduate research assistantships for 2012–13 provide a stipend of $28,000 per year, which includes a waiver of tuition/University fees for the fall and spring semesters and a student health-insurance plan. While financial aid is offered competitively, the Health Center makes every possible effort to address the financial needs of all students during their period of training.

Cost of Study

For 2012–13, tuition is $10,836 per year for full-time students who are Connecticut residents and $28,116 per year for full-time students who are out-of-state residents. General University fees are added to the cost of tuition for students who do not receive a tuition waiver. These costs are usually met by traineeships or research assistantships for doctoral students.

Living and Housing Costs

There is a wide range of affordable housing options in the Greater Hartford area within easy commuting distance of the campus, including an extensive complex that is adjacent to the Health Center. Costs range from $600 to $900 per month for a one-bedroom unit; two or more students sharing an apartment usually pay less. University housing is not available at the Health Center.

Student Group

The Program in Skeletal, Craniofacial, and Oral Biology has approximately 20 trainees. At the Health Center there are about 500 students in the Schools of Medicine and Dental Medicine, 150 Ph.D. students, and about 50 postdoctoral fellows. Graduate students are represented on various administrative committees concerned with curricular affairs. A graduate student organization fosters social contact among graduate students in the Health Center and represents graduate students' needs and concerns to the faculty and administration.

Location

The Health Center is located in the historic town of Farmington, Connecticut. Set in the beautiful New England countryside, on a hill overlooking the Farmington Valley, it is close to ski areas, hiking trails, and facilities for boating, fishing, and swimming. Connecticut's capital city of Hartford, 7 miles east of Farmington, is the center of an urban region of approximately 800,000 people. The beaches of the Long Island Sound are about 50 minutes away to the south, and the beautiful Berkshires are a short drive to the northwest. New York City and Boston can be reached within 2½ hours by car.

Hartford is the home of the acclaimed Hartford Stage Company, TheatreWorks, the Hartford Symphony and Chamber orchestras, two ballet companies, an opera company, the Wadsworth Atheneum (the oldest public art museum in the nation), the Mark Twain house, the Hartford Civic Center, and many other interesting cultural and recreational facilities. The area is also home to several branches of the University of Connecticut, Trinity College, and the University of Hartford, which includes the Hartt School of Music. Bradley International Airport (about 30 minutes from campus) serves the Hartford/Springfield area with frequent airline connections to major cities in this country and abroad. Frequent bus and rail service is also available from Hartford.

The Health Center

The 200-acre Health Center campus at Farmington houses a division of the University of Connecticut Graduate School, as well as the Schools of Medicine and Dental Medicine. The campus also includes the John Dempsey Hospital, associated clinics, and extensive medical research facilities, all in a centralized facility with more than 1 million square feet of floor space. The Health Center's newest research addition, the Academic Research Building, opened in 1999. This impressive eleven-story structure provides 170,000 square feet of state-of-the-art laboratory space. The faculty at the center includes more than 260 full-time members. The institution has a strong commitment to graduate study within an environment that promotes social and intellectual interaction among the various educational programs. Graduate students are represented on various administrative committees concerned with curricular affairs, and the Graduate Student Organization (GSO) represents graduate students' needs and concerns to the faculty and administration, in addition to fostering social contact among graduate students in the Health Center.

Applying

Applications for admission should be submitted via the online application system and should be filed together with transcripts, three letters of recommendation, a personal statement, and recent results from the General Test of the Graduate Record Examinations. International students must take the Test of English as a Foreign Language (TOEFL) to satisfy Graduate School requirements.

The deadline for completed applications and receipt of all supplemental materials is **December 1**. Please note that GRE and TOEFL exams taken after the due date will not be accepted for consideration for admission.

Deadlines and application procedures for combined programs vary depending on the program. For further information on combined programs, prospective students should contact Dr. Mina Mina in the Department of Reconstructive Sciences.

In accordance with the laws of the state of Connecticut and of the United States, the University of Connecticut Health Center does not discriminate against any person in its educational and employment activities on the grounds of race, color, creed, national origin, sex, age, or physical disability.

Correspondence and Information

Graduate Admissions Office
Ph.D. in Biomedical Science Program
University of Connecticut Health Center
263 Farmington Ave., MC 3906
Farmington, Connecticut 06030-3906
United States
Phone: 860-679-4509
E-mail: BiomedSciAdmissions@uchc.edu
Web site: http://grad.uchc.edu/prospective/programs/phd_biosci/index.html

University of Connecticut Health Center

THE FACULTY AND THEIR RESEARCH

Andrew Arnold, Professor of Medicine and Murray-Heilig Chair in Molecular Medicine; M.D., Harvard. The molecular genetic underpinnings of tumors of the endocrine glands, role of the cyclin D1 oncogene, animal modeling of hyperparathyroidism.

Dashzeveg Bayarsaihan, Assistant Professor; Ph.D. TFII-I family proteins.

Caroline N. Dealy, Associate Professor of Reconstructive Sciences, Center for Regenerative Medicine and Skeletal Development; Ph.D., Connecticut. Roles of various growth factors and signaling molecules, particularly IGF-I and insulin, in the regulation of chick limb development.

Anne Delany, Assistant Professor of Medicine; Ph.D., Dartmouth. Study of noncollagenous matrix proteins and metalloproteinases important in bone remodeling, including investigation of function and posttranscriptional regulation of osteonectin or SPARC in bone and function and regulation of the metastasis-associated metalloproteinase, stromelysyin-3, in bone.

Patricia I. Diaz, Assistant Professor; Ph.D., Adelaide (Australia); D.D.S., Universidad CES (Colombia). Interspecies interactions in oral microbial communities that determine oral biofilm formation; shifts in the oral microbiome composition associated with oral diseases such as mucositis during cancer chemotherapy and periodontal diseases; interaction of oral microbial communities with the host.

Anna Dongari-Bagtzoglou, Assistant Professor, Department of Oral Health and Diagnostic Sciences, Division of Periodontology; D.D.S., Ph.D., Texas Health Science Center at San Antonio. Host-pathogen interactions, with emphasis on the pathogenesis of inflammation and the innate immune functions of oral mucosal cells.

Hicham Drissi, Associate Professor of Orthopaedic Surgery; Ph.D., University of Paris V. Molecular pathways of bone and cartilage repair.

Paul M. Epstein, Associate Professor of Cell Biology; Ph.D., Yeshiva (Einstein). Second messengers and signal transduction, with particular focus on cyclic nucleotide metabolism and protein phosphorylation, with emphasis on analysis of cyclic nucleotide phosphodiesterase (PDE).

Marion Frank, Professor of Oral Health and Diagnostic Sciences and Director, Center for Neurosciences; Ph.D., Brown. Study of the sense of taste, using basic and clinical research; development of a fundamental understanding of gustatory systems in mammals at all levels from receptors to cerebral cortex; application of basic knowledge of gustatory systems to the diagnosis and treatment of taste disorders in humans.

A. Jon Goldberg, Professor of Reconstructive Sciences, Center for Regenerative Medicine and Skeletal Development; Ph.D., Michigan. Biomaterials, with studies involving structure-property relationships, development of novel systems, clinical evaluations, and surface analysis.

Gloria Gronowicz, Professor of Surgery; Ph.D., Columbia. Effects of hormones and growth factors on the production of extracellular matrix (ECM) proteins, on the regulation of integrins (receptors for ECM proteins), and on apoptosis in bone; response of bone cells to implant biomaterials.

Arthur R. Hand, Professor of Craniofacial Sciences, Division of Pediatric Dentistry; D.D.S., UCLA. Study of gene expression in rodent salivary glands during normal growth and development and in various experimental conditions employing morphological, immunological, and biochemical methodology.

Marc Hansen, Professor of Medicine, Center for Molecular Medicine; Ph.D., Cincinnati. Molecular genetics of osteosarcoma and related bone diseases.

Marja M. Hurley, Associate Professor of Medicine; M.D., Connecticut. Molecular mechanisms regulating the expression of fibroblast growth factors in bone, mechanisms of signal transduction by growth factors in bone cells, and role of fibroblast growth factors in bone remodeling.

Ivo Kalajzic, Assistant Professor, Department of Reconstructive Sciences and Department of Genetics and Developmental Biology; M.D., Zagreb (Croatia); Ph.D., Split (Croatia). Bone biology, differentiation of the osteoblast lineage cells.

Barbara E. Kream, Professor of Medicine; Ph.D., Yale. Hormonal regulation of bone remodeling.

Liisa T. Kuhn, Assistant Professor of Reconstructive Sciences, Center for Regenerative Medicine and Skeletal Development; Ph.D., California, Santa Barbara. Biomaterials for drug delivery and bone regeneration and repair.

Sangamesh Kumbar, Assistant Professor of Orthopedic Surgery; Ph.D., Karnatak (India). Synthesis and characterization of novel biomaterials/ polymers for tissue engineering and drug delivery applications.

Marc Lalande, Professor and Head, Department of Genetics and Developmental Biology; Ph.D., Toronto. Genomic imprinting of human chromosome 15q.

Sun-Kyeong Lee, Assistant Professor of Medicine; Ph.D., Connecticut. Osteoclast biology and molecular and cellular regulation by cytokines in osteoclastogenesis.

Leo Lefrancois, Professor of Immunology; Ph.D., Wake Forest. T-lymphocyte development, mucosal immunology, intestinal intraepithelial T lymphocytes, gamma/delta T cells.

Alexander Lichtler, Associate Professor of Reconstructive Sciences, Center for Regenerative Medicine and Skeletal Development; Ph.D., Florida. Hormone regulation of bone collagen synthesis.

Alan G. Lurie, Professor of Oral Health and Diagnostic Sciences and Chairperson, Division of Oral and Maxillofacial Radiology; D.D.S., UCLA; Ph.D., Rochester. Actions and interactions of radiation and chemical carcinogens during epithelial carcinogenesis, DNA mutagenesis and repair by gamma radiation in lymphoblasts from both normal and ataxia telangiectatic humans, clinical research digital imaging.

Peter Maye, Assistant Professor of Reconstructive Sciences, Ph.D., Wesleyan. Isolation, characterization, and differentiation of embryonic and adult skeletal stem cells down the osteogenic lineage.

Mina Mina, Professor of Craniofacial Sciences; Chairperson, Division of Pediatric Dentistry; and Director, Skeletal, Craniofacial, and Oral Biology Graduate Program; D.M.D., National University of Iran; Ph.D., Connecticut Health Center. Development of the mandibular arch, including the elongation and polarized outgrowth of the mandibular primordia and subsequent differentiation of the skeletal tissues in spatially defined patterns; characterization of genetic and epigenetic influences involved in the pattern formation and skeletogenesis of the chick mandible and mouse tooth germ; regulation of patterning in the developing mandible and developing teeth by mandibular epithelium, extracellular matrix molecules, growth factors, and transcription factors.

Lakshmi Nair, Assistant Professor of Orthopedic Surgery and Chemical, Materials, and Biomolecular Engineering; Ph.D., SCTIMST (India). Design and development of regenerative biomaterials to favorably modulate the responses of a variety of cell types involved in tissue regeneration and repair.

Syam P. Nukavarapu, Assistant Professor of Orthopaedic Surgery and Chemical, Materials, and Biomolecular Engineering. Ph.D, Indian Institute of Science. Scaffold-based bone-tissue engineering.

Carol C. Pilbeam, Professor of Medicine; Ph.D., Yale. Mechanisms of regulation of bone formation and resorption.

Justin D. Radolf, Professor of Medicine and Center for Microbial Pathogenesis; M.D., California, San Francisco. Molecular pathogenesis and immunobiology of spirochetal infections.

Ernst Reichenberger, Assistant Professor of Reconstructive Sciences, Center for Regenerative Medicine and Skeletal Development; Ph.D., Erlangen (Germany). Study of complex processes required for generating and maintaining the skin and bones through characterization of human genetic disorders in which they are disrupted, including aplasia cutis congenita (ACC), cherubism, and craniometaphyseal dysplasia (CMD).

Blanka Rogina, Assistant Professor of Genetics and Developmental Biology; Ph.D., Zagreb (Croatia). Molecular and genetic mechanisms underlying aging and cost of reproduction.

Edward F. Rossomando, Professor of Craniofacial Sciences; D.D.S., Pennsylvania; Ph.D., Rockefeller; M.S. (management), Rensselaer. Translational research, strategic management, entrepreneurship, management of innovation and technology, strategic management in the health-care industry.

David W. Rowe, Professor of Reconstructive Sciences and Director, Center for Regenerative Medicine and Skeletal Development; M.D., Vermont. Genetic and hormonal control of type I collagen production, development of strategies for somatic gene therapy for heritable diseases of bone built upon the structural and regulatory principles of collagen production.

Sunil Wadhwa, Assistant Professor of Craniofacial Sciences, Division of Orthodontics; D.D.S., Columbia; Ph.D., Connecticut. Bone biology and temporomandibular joint development and function.

Section 28
Medicine

This section contains a directory of institutions offering graduate work in medicine, followed by an in-depth entry submitted by an institution that chose to prepare a detailed program description. Additional information about programs listed in the directory but not augmented by an in-depth entry may be obtained by writing directly to the dean of a graduate school or chair of a department at the address given in the directory.

CONTENTS

Allopathic Medicine

Albany Medical College, Professional Program, Albany, NY 12208-3479. Offers MD. *Accreditation:* LCME/AMA. *Degree requirements:* For doctorate, United States Medical Licensing Exam Steps 1 and 2, clinical skills. *Entrance requirements:* For doctorate, MCAT, letters of recommendation, interview. Electronic applications accepted. *Expenses:* Contact institution.

Albert Einstein College of Medicine, Professional Program in Medicine, Bronx, NY 10461. Offers MD, MD/PhD. *Accreditation:* LCME/AMA. *Degree requirements:* For doctorate, independent scholars project. *Entrance requirements:* For doctorate, MCAT, interview. *Faculty research:* Cancer, diabetes mellitus, liver disease, infectious disease, neuroscience.

American University of Beirut, Graduate Programs, Faculty of Medicine, Beirut, Lebanon. Offers anatomy, cell biology and human morphology (MS); biochemistry and medical genetics (MS); biomedical sciences (PhD); experimental pathology, immunology and microbiology (MS); medicine (MD); neuroscience (MS); pharmacology and toxicology (MS). Part-time programs available. *Faculty:* 232 full-time (58 women), 68 part-time/adjunct (7 women). *Students:* 346 full-time (135 women), 69 part-time (57 women). Average age 23. In 2011, 20 master's, 82 doctorates awarded. *Degree requirements:* For master's, one foreign language, comprehensive exam, thesis (for some programs). *Entrance requirements:* For master's, letter of recommendation; for doctorate, MCAT, bachelor's degree. Additional exam requirements/recommendations for international students: Required—TOEFL (minimum score 600 paper-based; 250 computer-based; 100 iBT), IELTS (minimum score 7.5). *Application deadline:* For fall admission, 4/30 for domestic and international students; for spring admission, 11/1 for domestic and international students. Application fee: $50. *Expenses: Tuition:* Full-time $12,780; part-time $710 per credit. Tuition and fees vary according to course load and program. *Financial support:* In 2011–12, 19 students received support. Career-related internships or fieldwork, institutionally sponsored loans, scholarships/grants, health care benefits, and unspecified assistantships available. Financial award application deadline: 2/2. *Faculty research:* Cancer research (targeted therapy, mechanisms of leukemogenesis, tumor cell extravasation and metastasis, cancer stem cells); stem cell research (regenerative medicine, drug discovery); genetic research (neurogenetics, hereditary cardiomyopathy, hemoglobinopathies, pharmacogenomics, proteomics); neuroscience research (pain, neurodegenerative disorder); metabolism (inflammation and metabolism, metabolic disorder, diabetes mellitus); vascular and renal biology, signal transduction. *Total annual research expenditures:* $2.3 million. *Unit head:* Dr. Mohamed Sayegh, Dean, 961-1350000 Ext. 4700, Fax: 961-1744464, E-mail: msayegh@aub.edu.lb. *Application contact:* Dr. Salim Kanaan, Director, Admissions Office, 961-1350000 Ext. 2594, Fax: 961-1750775, E-mail: sk00@aub.edu.lb. Web site: http://www.aub.edu.lb/fm/fm_home/Pages/index.aspx.

Baylor College of Medicine, Medical School, Professional Program in Medicine, Houston, TX 77030-3498. Offers MD. *Accreditation:* LCME/AMA. *Students:* 728 full-time (339 women); includes 426 minority (34 Black or African American, non-Hispanic/Latino; 13 American Indian or Alaska Native, non-Hispanic/Latino; 275 Asian, non-Hispanic/Latino; 104 Hispanic/Latino), 2 international. Average age 24. 4,835 applicants, 7% accepted, 186 enrolled. In 2011, 157 doctorates awarded. *Entrance requirements:* For doctorate, MCAT, 90 hours of pre-med course work. *Application deadline:* For fall admission, 11/1 for domestic students. Applications are processed on a rolling basis. Application fee: $90. Electronic applications accepted. *Expenses:* Contact institution. *Financial support:* In 2011–12, 518 students received support. Federal Work-Study, institutionally sponsored loans, and scholarships/grants available. Financial award application deadline: 5/11; financial award applicants required to submit FAFSA. *Unit head:* Dr. Stephen B. Greenberg, Dean of Medical Education, 713-798-8878, Fax: 713-798-3096, E-mail: stepheng@bcm.edu. *Application contact:* Dr. Lloyd H. Michael, Interim Senior Associate Dean of the Medical School, 713-798-4842, Fax: 713-798-5563, E-mail: lmichael@bcm.edu. Web site: http://www.bcm.edu/.

Boston University, School of Medicine, Division of Graduate Medical Sciences, MD/PhD Program, Boston, MA 02215. Offers MD/PhD. *Students:* 76 full-time (29 women); includes 11 minority (2 Black or African American, non-Hispanic/Latino; 8 Asian, non-Hispanic/Latino; 1 Hispanic/Latino), 3 international. Average age 28. 223 applicants, 13% accepted, 6 enrolled. *Application deadline:* For fall admission, 11/1 for domestic students. Application fee: $110. *Expenses: Tuition:* Full-time $40,848; part-time $1276 per credit hour. *Required fees:* $572; $286 per semester. *Financial support:* In 2011–12, 76 students received support. Applicants required to submit CSS PROFILE or FAFSA. *Unit head:* Dr. John Schwartz, Director, 617-638-7321, E-mail: jhsch@bu.edu. *Application contact:* Julie Shine, Administrator, 617-638-5255, E-mail: jshine@bu.edu. Web site: http://www.bumc.bu.edu/gms/academics/phd-and-mdphd/mdphd-combined-degree-program/.

Boston University, School of Medicine, Professional Program in Medicine, Boston, MA 02215. Offers MD, MD/MBA, MD/MPH, MD/PhD. *Accreditation:* LCME/AMA. *Students:* 691 full-time (347 women), 36 part-time (23 women); includes 365 minority (60 Black or African American, non-Hispanic/Latino; 205 Asian, non-Hispanic/Latino; 71 Hispanic/Latino; 2 Native Hawaiian or other Pacific Islander, non-Hispanic/Latino; 27 Two or more races, non-Hispanic/Latino), 22 international. Average age 25. In 2011, 158 doctorates awarded. *Application deadline:* For fall admission, 11/1 for domestic students. Application fee: $95. *Expenses: Tuition:* Full-time $40,848; part-time $1276 per credit hour. *Required fees:* $572; $286 per semester. *Financial support:* Federal Work-Study available. Support available to part-time students. *Unit head:* Dr. Karen H. Antman, Dean, 617-638-5300. *Application contact:* Dr. Robert Witzburg, Associate Dean for Admissions, 617-638-4630.

Brown University, Program in Medicine, Providence, RI 02912. Offers MD, MD/PhD. *Accreditation:* LCME/AMA. *Expenses:* Contact institution.

Case Western Reserve University, School of Medicine, Professional Program in Medicine, Cleveland, OH 44106. Offers MD, MD/JD, MD/MA, MD/MBA, MD/MPH, MD/MS, MD/PhD. *Accreditation:* LCME/AMA. *Entrance requirements:* For doctorate, MCAT, interview. Electronic applications accepted.

Charles Drew University of Medicine and Science, Professional Program in Medicine, Los Angeles, CA 90059. Offers MD. *Entrance requirements:* For doctorate, MCAT.

Columbia University, College of Physicians and Surgeons, Professional Program in Medicine, New York, NY 10032. Offers MD, MD/DDS, MD/MPH, MD/MS, MD/PhD. *Accreditation:* LCME/AMA. Part-time programs available. *Entrance requirements:* For doctorate, MCAT.

Columbia University, School of Continuing Education, Program in Narrative Medicine, New York, NY 10027. Offers MS. Electronic applications accepted.

Creighton University, School of Medicine, Professional Program in Medicine, Omaha, NE 68178-0001. Offers MD, MD/PhD. *Accreditation:* LCME/AMA. *Entrance requirements:* For doctorate, MCAT. Electronic applications accepted. *Expenses: Tuition:* Full-time $12,672; part-time $704 per credit hour. *Required fees:* $1410; $136 per semester. Tuition and fees vary according to campus/location and reciprocity agreements. *Faculty research:* Hereditary cancer, osteoporosis, diabetes, immunology, microbiology.

Dalhousie University, Faculty of Medicine, Halifax, NS B3H 4H7, Canada. Offers M Sc, MD, PhD, M Sc/PhD, MD/M Sc, MD/PhD. *Accreditation:* LCME/AMA. *Entrance requirements:* For master's, MCAT; for doctorate, MCAT (for MD). Electronic applications accepted.

Dartmouth College, Dartmouth Medical School, Hanover, NH 03755. Offers MD, MD/MBA, MD/PhD. *Accreditation:* LCME/AMA.

Drexel University, College of Medicine, Professional Program in Medicine, Philadelphia, PA 19104-2875. Offers MD, MD/PhD. *Accreditation:* LCME/AMA. *Degree requirements:* For doctorate, National Board Exam Parts I and II. *Entrance requirements:* For doctorate, MCAT. Electronic applications accepted.

Duke University, School of Medicine, Professional Program in Medicine, Durham, NC 27708-0586. Offers MD, MD/JD, MD/MALS, MD/MBA, MD/MHS, MD/MLS, MD/MMCi, MD/MPH, MD/MPP, MD/MSIS, MD/PhD. *Accreditation:* LCME/AMA. *Faculty:* 1,458 full-time (472 women). *Students:* 410 full-time (204 women); includes 200 minority (71 Black or African American, non-Hispanic/Latino; 5 American Indian or Alaska Native, non-Hispanic/Latino; 106 Asian, non-Hispanic/Latino; 18 Hispanic/Latino), 15 international. Average age 26. 4,581 applicants, 5% accepted, 102 enrolled. In 2011, 104 doctorates awarded. *Entrance requirements:* For doctorate, MCAT. *Application deadline:* For fall admission, 11/1 for domestic students. Application fee: $85. Electronic applications accepted. *Expenses:* Contact institution. *Financial support:* In 2011–12, 211 students received support. Institutionally sponsored loans and scholarships/grants available. Financial award application deadline: 5/1; financial award applicants required to submit FAFSA. *Unit head:* Dr. Edward G. Buckley, Vice Dean, Medical Education, 919-668-3381, Fax: 919-660-7040, E-mail: buckl002@mc.duke.edu. *Application contact:* Dr. Brenda E. Armstrong, Director of Admissions, 919-684-2985, Fax: 919-684-8893, E-mail: medadm@mc.duke.edu. Web site: http://www.dukemed.duke.edu/.

East Carolina University, Brody School of Medicine, Professional Program in Medicine, Greenville, NC 27858-4353. Offers MD. *Accreditation:* LCME/AMA. *Entrance requirements:* For doctorate, MCAT, pre-med courses, interviews, faculty evaluations. *Application deadline:* For fall admission, 11/15 for domestic students. Applications are processed on a rolling basis. Application fee: $60. Electronic applications accepted. *Expenses:* Tuition, state resident: full-time $3557; part-time $444.63 per semester hour. Tuition, nonresident: full-time $14,351; part-time $1793.88 per semester hour. *Required fees:* $2016; $252 per semester hour. Part-time tuition and fees vary according to course load, campus/location and program. *Financial support:* Institutionally sponsored loans and scholarships/grants available. *Faculty research:* Diabetes, cardiovascular disease, cancer, neurological disorders. *Unit head:* Dr. Paul Cunningham, Dean, 252-744-2201, E-mail: cunninghamp@ecu.edu. *Application contact:* Contact Center, 252-744-1020, E-mail: somadmissions@ecu.edu.

Eastern Virginia Medical School, Professional Program in Medicine, Norfolk, VA 23501-1980. Offers MD, MD/MPH. *Accreditation:* LCME/AMA. *Students:* 497 full-time (222 women); includes 169 minority (36 Black or African American, non-Hispanic/Latino; 126 Asian, non-Hispanic/Latino; 7 Hispanic/Latino). 4,958 applicants, 118 enrolled. In 2011, 104 doctorates awarded. *Entrance requirements:* For doctorate, MCAT, bachelor's degree or equivalent, course work in sciences. *Application deadline:* For fall admission, 11/15 priority date for domestic students. Applications are processed on a rolling basis. Application fee: $95. Electronic applications accepted. *Financial support:* Applicants required to submit FAFSA. *Unit head:* Dr. Ronald W. Flenner, Associate Dean for Medicine, 757-446-5829, Fax: 757-446-5896, E-mail: flennerw@evms.edu. *Application contact:* Susan Castora, Director of Admissions, 757-446-5812, Fax: 757-446-5896, E-mail: castorsl@evms.edu. Web site: http://www.evms.edu/md-admissions/evms-md-admissions-information.html.

East Tennessee State University, James H. Quillen College of Medicine, Professional Programs in Medicine, Johnson City, TN 37614. Offers MD. *Accreditation:* LCME/AMA. *Faculty:* 115 full-time (36 women), 35 part-time/adjunct (8 women). *Students:* 269 full-time (122 women); includes 44 minority (6 Black or African American, non-Hispanic/Latino; 1 American Indian or Alaska Native, non-Hispanic/Latino; 27 Asian, non-Hispanic/Latino; 3 Hispanic/Latino; 7 Two or more races, non-Hispanic/Latino). Average age 26. 1,144 applicants, 9% accepted, 60 enrolled. In 2011, 60 doctorates awarded. *Entrance requirements:* For doctorate, MCAT. Additional exam requirements/recommendations for international students: Required—TOEFL (minimum score 550 paper-based; 213 computer-based). *Application deadline:* For fall admission, 12/1 for domestic students. Applications are processed on a rolling basis. Application fee: $25. *Expenses:* Tuition, state resident: full-time $7312; part-time $350 per credit hour. Tuition, nonresident: full-time $18,490; part-time $621 per credit hour. *Required fees:* $63 per credit hour. Tuition and fees vary according to course load and program. *Financial support:* Career-related internships or fieldwork, Federal Work-Study, institutionally sponsored loans, and scholarships/grants available. Financial award application deadline: 5/10; financial award applicants required to submit FAFSA. *Total annual research expenditures:* $2 million. *Unit head:* Dr. Philip Bagnell, Dean, 423-439-6316, Fax: 423-439-8090, E-mail: bagnell@etsu.edu. *Application contact:* E. Doug Taylor, Assistant Dean for Admissions and Records, 423-439-2033, Fax: 423-439-2110, E-mail: dougt@etsu.edu.

Emory University, School of Medicine, Professional Program in Medicine, Atlanta, GA 30322-4510. Offers MD, MD/MPH, MD/MSCR, MD/PhD. *Accreditation:* LCME/AMA. *Faculty:* 2,154 full-time (775 women), 1,194 part-time/adjunct (463 women). *Students:* 531 full-time (286 women); includes 154 minority (41 Black or African American, non-Hispanic/Latino; 91 Asian, non-Hispanic/Latino; 16 Hispanic/Latino; 6 Two or more races, non-Hispanic/Latino), 14 international. Average age 25. 4,926 applicants, 7% accepted, 136 enrolled. In 2011, 124 doctorates awarded. *Degree requirements:* For doctorate, United States Medical Licensing Exam Step 1 and 2. *Entrance requirements:* For doctorate, MCAT. *Application deadline:* For fall admission, 10/15 for domestic and international students. Applications are processed on a rolling basis. Application fee: $100. Electronic applications accepted. *Expenses:* Contact institution. *Financial support:* In 2011–12, 379 students received support. Institutionally sponsored loans and scholarships/grants available. Financial award application deadline: 3/1; financial award applicants required to submit CSS PROFILE or FAFSA. *Faculty research:* Immunology and pathogenesis of chronic viral infections, immunological memory and vaccine development, development of antiviral agents to treat infections caused by human immunodeficiency and hepatitis viruses, development of therapeutic and diagnostic approaches to improve outcomes after transplantation genetic mechanisms of neuropsychiatric disease, Fragile X Syndrome, immune system ontogeny and

phylogeny. *Total annual research expenditures:* $316.3 million. *Unit head:* Dr. John William Eley, Executive Associate Dean, Medical Education and Student Affairs, 404-727-5655, Fax: 404-727-0045, E-mail: jeley@emory.edu. *Application contact:* Dr. Ira K. Schwartz, Associate Dean of Medical Education and Student Affairs/Director of Admissions, 404-727-5660, Fax: 404-727-5456, E-mail: medadmiss@emory.edu. Web site: http://www.med.emory.edu.

Florida Atlantic University, Charles E. Schmidt College of Medicine, Boca Raton, FL 33431-0991. Offers biomedical science (MS); integrative biology (PhD); medicine (MD). *Faculty:* 17 full-time (7 women), 4 part-time/adjunct (0 women). *Students:* 89 full-time (45 women), 11 part-time (6 women); includes 33 minority (3 Black or African American, non-Hispanic/Latino; 11 Asian, non-Hispanic/Latino; 15 Hispanic/Latino; 4 Two or more races, non-Hispanic/Latino), 4 international. Average age 24. 1,583 applicants, 7% accepted, 75 enrolled. In 2011, 26 master's awarded. *Degree requirements:* For master's, thesis (for some programs). *Entrance requirements:* For master's, GRE, minimum GPA of 3.0. *Application deadline:* For fall admission, 5/1 for domestic students, 3/15 for international students; for spring admission, 10/1 for domestic and international students. Application fee: $30. *Expenses: Tuition, area resident:* Part-time $343.02 per credit hour. Tuition, state resident: full-time $8232. Tuition, nonresident: full-time $23,931; part-time $997.14 per credit hour. *Financial support:* Fellowships and research assistantships available. *Faculty research:* Protein engineering, biology of mind-body interaction, neuroendocrinology, gene expression, methodologies of correction of gynecomastia. *Unit head:* Dr. David J. Bjorkman, Dean, 561-297-4341. *Application contact:* Julie Sivigny, Academic Program Specialist for Graduate Studies, 561-297-2216, E-mail: jsivigny@fau.edu. Web site: http://med.fau.edu/medicine.

Florida International University, Herbert Wertheim College of Medicine, Miami, FL 33199. Offers MD. *Entrance requirements:* For doctorate, MCAT (minimum score of 25), minimum overall GPA of 3.0; 3 letters of recommendation, 2 from basic science faculty (biology, chemistry, physics, math) and 1 from any other faculty member. Electronic applications accepted. *Expenses:* Contact institution.

Georgetown University, School of Medicine, Washington, DC 20057. Offers MD, MD/MBA, MD/PhD. *Accreditation:* LCME/AMA. *Entrance requirements:* For doctorate, MCAT, minimum 90 credit hours with 1 year of course work in biology, organic chemistry, inorganic chemistry, physics, mathematics, and English. *Expenses:* Contact institution.

The George Washington University, School of Medicine and Health Sciences, Professional Program in Medicine, Washington, DC 20052. Offers MD, MD/MPH, MD/PhD. *Accreditation:* LCME/AMA. *Faculty:* 138 full-time (66 women), 383 part-time/adjunct (89 women). *Students:* 714 full-time (392 women), 2 part-time (1 woman); includes 283 minority (74 Black or African American, non-Hispanic/Latino; 1 American Indian or Alaska Native, non-Hispanic/Latino; 180 Asian, non-Hispanic/Latino; 21 Hispanic/Latino; 2 Native Hawaiian or other Pacific Islander, non-Hispanic/Latino; 5 Two or more races, non-Hispanic/Latino), 16 international. Average age 26. 10,625 applicants, 3% accepted, 178 enrolled. In 2011, 161 doctorates awarded. *Entrance requirements:* For doctorate, MCAT, minimum 90 undergraduate semester hours, specific pre-med courses equal to 38 semester hours. *Application deadline:* For fall admission, 12/1 for domestic students. Applications are processed on a rolling basis. Application fee: $80. *Financial support:* Career-related internships or fieldwork, Federal Work-Study, and institutionally sponsored loans available. *Unit head:* Dr. Alan Wasserman, Chair, 202-741-2302. *Application contact:* Diane P. McQuail, Director of Admissions, 202-994-3507, E-mail: maeve@gwu.edu.

Georgia Health Sciences University, Medical College of Georgia, Augusta, GA 30912. Offers MD, MD/PhD. *Accreditation:* LCME/AMA. *Faculty:* 438 full-time (133 women), 80 part-time/adjunct (37 women). *Students:* 800 full-time (354 women), 2 part-time (0 women); includes 284 minority (56 Black or African American, non-Hispanic/Latino; 188 Asian, non-Hispanic/Latino; 23 Hispanic/Latino; 17 Two or more races, non-Hispanic/Latino). Average age 25. 2,055 applicants, 15% accepted, 190 enrolled. In 2011, 178 doctorates awarded. *Degree requirements:* For doctorate, comprehensive exam. *Entrance requirements:* For doctorate, MCAT, minimum GPA of 3.6 in sciences, 3.64 overall. *Application deadline:* For fall admission, 11/1 for domestic students. Applications are processed on a rolling basis. Application fee: $0. *Expenses:* Contact institution. *Financial support:* Fellowships with tuition reimbursements, career-related internships or fieldwork, Federal Work-Study, institutionally sponsored loans, and scholarships/grants available. Support available to part-time students. Financial award application deadline: 5/1; financial award applicants required to submit FAFSA. *Faculty research:* Cancer, cardiovascular diseases, diabetes, neurological diseases, infection and inflammation. *Total annual research expenditures:* $59.1 million. *Unit head:* Dr. Peter Buckley, Dean, 706-721-2231, Fax: 706-721-7035, E-mail: pbuckley@georgiahealth.edu. *Application contact:* Dr. Geoffrey H. Young, Associate Dean for Admissions, 706-721-3186, Fax: 706-721-0959, E-mail: geyoung@georgiahealth.edu. Web site: http://www.georgiahealth.edu/medicine/.

Harvard University, Harvard Medical School and Graduate School of Arts and Sciences, Division of Health Sciences and Technology, Program in Medical Sciences, Cambridge, MA 02138. Offers MD. Program offered jointly with Massachusetts Institute of Technology. *Accreditation:* LCME/AMA. *Students:* 192 full-time (73 women); includes 102 minority (4 Black or African American, non-Hispanic/Latino; 85 Asian, non-Hispanic/Latino; 10 Hispanic/Latino; 3 Two or more races, non-Hispanic/Latino), 12 international. Average age 26. 1,012 applicants, 3% accepted, 30 enrolled. In 2011, 20 doctorates awarded. *Degree requirements:* For doctorate, thesis/dissertation. *Entrance requirements:* For doctorate, MCAT. *Application deadline:* For fall admission, 10/15 for domestic students. Application fee: $85. Electronic applications accepted. *Expenses:* Contact institution. *Financial support:* In 2011–12, 66 students received support, including 3 fellowships with partial tuition reimbursements available (averaging $53,667 per year), 45 research assistantships with partial tuition reimbursements available (averaging $11,654 per year), 21 teaching assistantships with partial tuition reimbursements available (averaging $4,170 per year); career-related internships or fieldwork, scholarships/grants, health care benefits, and unspecified assistantships also available. Financial award application deadline: 10/15; financial award applicants required to submit FAFSA. *Unit head:* Dr. David Earl Cohen, Director of Health Sciences and Technology, 617-726-5576. *Application contact:* Zara Smith, MD Admissions Coordinator, 617-432-7195, E-mail: hstadmissions@hms.harvard.edu.

Harvard University, Harvard Medical School, Professional Program in Medicine, Cambridge, MA 02138. Offers MD, PhD, MD/MBA, MD/MM Sc, MD/MPH, MD/MPP, MD/PhD. *Accreditation:* LCME/AMA. Electronic applications accepted. *Expenses: Tuition:* Full-time $36,304. *Required fees:* $1186. Full-time tuition and fees vary according to program.

Hofstra University, School of Medicine, Hempstead, NY 11549. Offers medicine (MD); molecular basis of medicine (PhD); MD/PhD. *Accreditation:* LCME/AMA. *Faculty:* 8 full-time (3 women). *Students:* 43 full-time (22 women); includes 16 minority (3 Black or African American, non-Hispanic/Latino; 6 Asian, non-Hispanic/Latino; 2 Hispanic/Latino; 2 Native Hawaiian or other Pacific Islander, non-Hispanic/Latino; 3 Two or more races, non-Hispanic/Latino). Average age 25. *Entrance requirements:* For doctorate, MCAT. Additional exam requirements/recommendations for international students: Required—TOEFL (minimum score 600 paper-based; 250 computer-based; 100 iBT). *Application deadline:* For fall admission, 12/1 priority date for domestic students. Application fee: $100. Electronic applications accepted. *Expenses:* Contact institution. *Financial support:* In 2011–12, 43 students received support, including 43 fellowships with full and partial tuition reimbursements available (averaging $31,287 per year); research assistantships with full and partial tuition reimbursements available, Federal Work-Study, institutionally sponsored loans, scholarships/grants, and tuition waivers (full and partial) also available. Support available to part-time students. Financial award applicants required to submit FAFSA. *Faculty research:* Pathogenesis of sepsis, autoimmune disease, pathogenesis of schizophrenia and movement disorder, pathogenesis and treatment of chronic leukemia, population health: healthcare quality and effectiveness. *Unit head:* Dr. Lawrence Smith, Dean, 516-463-7577, Fax: 516-463-5631, E-mail: medlgs@hofstra.edu. *Application contact:* Carol Drummer, Dean of Graduate Admissions, 516-463-4876, Fax: 516-463-4664, E-mail: gradstudent@hofstra.edu. Web site: http://medicine.hofstra.edu/.

Howard University, College of Medicine, Professional Program in Medicine, Washington, DC 20059-0002. Offers MD, PhD, MD/PhD. *Accreditation:* LCME/AMA. *Faculty research:* Infectious diseases, protein modeling, neuropsychopharmacology.

Indiana University–Purdue University Indianapolis, Indiana University School of Medicine, Indianapolis, IN 46202-5114. Offers MPH, MS, MD, PhD, MD/MA, MD/MBA, MD/MS, MD/PhD. *Accreditation:* LCME/AMA. *Faculty:* 270 full-time (56 women). *Students:* 1,594 full-time (764 women), 227 part-time (142 women); includes 374 minority (110 Black or African American, non-Hispanic/Latino; 5 American Indian or Alaska Native, non-Hispanic/Latino; 169 Asian, non-Hispanic/Latino; 64 Hispanic/Latino; 1 Native Hawaiian or other Pacific Islander, non-Hispanic/Latino; 25 Two or more races, non-Hispanic/Latino), 118 international. Average age 26. 1,007 applicants, 45% accepted, 419 enrolled. In 2011, 123 master's, 323 doctorates awarded. *Degree requirements:* For doctorate, thesis/dissertation (for some programs). *Entrance requirements:* For master's, GRE General Test; for doctorate, GRE General Test (for PhD); MCAT (for MD). Additional exam requirements/recommendations for international students: Required—TOEFL. *Application deadline:* For fall admission, 8/1 priority date for domestic students. Applications are processed on a rolling basis. Application fee: $55 ($65 for international students). *Expenses:* Contact institution. *Financial support:* Fellowships with full and partial tuition reimbursements, research assistantships with full and partial tuition reimbursements, teaching assistantships with full tuition reimbursements, Federal Work-Study, institutionally sponsored loans, scholarships/grants, tuition waivers (full and partial), and stipends available. Support available to part-time students. *Total annual research expenditures:* $94.3 million. *Unit head:* Dr. D. Craig Brater, Dean, 317-274-5000, Fax: 317-278-5211. *Application contact:* Robert M. Stump, Jr., Director of Admissions, 317-274-3772, E-mail: inmedadm@iupui.edu. Web site: http://www.medicine.iu.edu/.

Instituto Tecnologico de Santo Domingo, School of Medicine, Santo Domingo, Dominican Republic. Offers M Bioethics, MD.

The Johns Hopkins University, School of Medicine, Professional Program in Medicine, Baltimore, MD 21218-2699. Offers MD, MD/PhD. *Accreditation:* LCME/AMA. *Entrance requirements:* For doctorate, MCAT. Electronic applications accepted.

Loma Linda University, School of Medicine, Loma Linda, CA 92350. Offers MS, MD, PhD. *Accreditation:* LCME/AMA. *Degree requirements:* For master's, thesis optional; for doctorate, thesis/dissertation (for some programs). *Entrance requirements:* For doctorate, MCAT (for MD). Additional exam requirements/recommendations for international students: Required—TOEFL (minimum score 550 paper-based; 213 computer-based). *Expenses:* Contact institution.

Louisiana State University Health Sciences Center, School of Medicine in New Orleans, New Orleans, LA 70112-2223. Offers MPH, MD, MD/PhD. Open only to Louisiana residents. *Accreditation:* LCME/AMA. *Entrance requirements:* For doctorate, MCAT. Electronic applications accepted. *Expenses:* Contact institution. *Faculty research:* Medical and basic sciences.

Louisiana State University Health Sciences Center at Shreveport, School of Medicine, Shreveport, LA 71130-3932. Offers MD, MD/PhD. *Accreditation:* LCME/AMA. *Entrance requirements:* For doctorate, MCAT. *Expenses:* Contact institution. *Faculty research:* Biomedical science, molecular biology, cardiovascular science.

Loyola University Chicago, Stritch School of Medicine, Maywood, IL 60153. Offers MD. *Accreditation:* LCME/AMA. *Degree requirements:* For doctorate, passing scores on U. S. Medical Licensing Exam Step 1, Step 2CS, and Step 2CK. *Entrance requirements:* For doctorate, MCAT, 1 full academic year of general biology or zoology, organic chemistry, physics and inorganic chemistry all with labs. *Expenses:* Contact institution. *Faculty research:* Cardiovascular pathophysiology, cancer biology, neuroscience, burn injury, infectious disease.

Marshall University, Joan C. Edwards School of Medicine, Professional Program in Medicine, Huntington, WV 25755. Offers MD. *Accreditation:* LCME/AMA. *Degree requirements:* For doctorate, U.S. Medical Licensing Exam, Steps 1 and 2. *Entrance requirements:* For doctorate, MCAT, 1 year of course work in biology, physics, chemistry, organic chemistry, English, and social or behavioral sciences. *Expenses:* Contact institution.

Mayo Medical School, Professional Program, Rochester, MN 55905. Offers MD, MD/Certificate, MD/PhD. MD offered through the Mayo Foundation's Division of Education; MD/PhD, MD/Certificate with Mayo Graduate School. *Accreditation:* LCME/AMA. *Entrance requirements:* For doctorate, MCAT, previous undergraduate course work in biology, chemistry, physics, and biochemistry. Electronic applications accepted.

McGill University, Faculty of Graduate and Postdoctoral Studies, Faculty of Medicine, Department of Surgery, Montréal, QC H3A 2T5, Canada. Offers M Sc, PhD.

McGill University, Professional Program in Medicine, Montréal, QC H3A 2T5, Canada. Offers MD/CM, MD/MBA, MD/PhD. *Accreditation:* LCME/AMA.

Medical College of Wisconsin, Medical School, Professional Program in Medicine, Milwaukee, WI 53226-0509. Offers MD, MD/MA, MD/MS, MD/PhD. *Accreditation:* LCME/AMA. *Entrance requirements:* For doctorate, GRE, official transcripts, three letters of recommendation. Additional exam requirements/recommendations for international students: Required—TOEFL.

Medical University of South Carolina, College of Medicine, Charleston, SC 29425. Offers MD, MD/MBA, MD/MHA, MD/MPH, MD/MSCR, MD/PhD. *Accreditation:* LCME/AMA. *Faculty:* 1,110 full-time (429 women), 182 part-time/adjunct (76 women). *Students:* 695 full-time (288 women); includes 178 minority (87 Black or African American, non-Hispanic/Latino; 4 American Indian or Alaska Native, non-Hispanic/Latino; 65 Asian, non-Hispanic/Latino; 22 Hispanic/Latino), 8 international. Average age 26. 3,188 applicants, 6% accepted, 158 enrolled. In 2011, 136 doctorates awarded. *Degree requirements:* For doctorate, Steps 1 and 2 of Clinical Performance Exam and U.S. Medical Licensing Examination. *Entrance requirements:* For doctorate, MCAT, interview. *Application deadline:* For fall admission, 12/1 for domestic students. Applications are processed on a rolling basis. Application fee: $85. Electronic applications accepted. *Expenses:* Contact institution. *Financial support:* In 2011–12,

676 students received support. Federal Work-Study and scholarships/grants available. Financial award application deadline: 3/10; financial award applicants required to submit FAFSA. *Faculty research:* Cardiovascular proteomics, translational cancer research, diabetes mellitus, neurodegenerative diseases, addiction. *Total annual research expenditures:* $114 million. *Unit head:* Dr. Etta D. Pisano, Dean, 843-792-2842, Fax: 843-792-2967, E-mail: pisanoe@musc.edu. *Application contact:* Joan M. Graesch, Admissions Counselor, 843-792-3283, Fax: 843-792-0204, E-mail: jmg26@musc.edu. Web site: http://www.musc.edu/com1.

Meharry Medical College, School of Medicine, Nashville, TN 37208-9989. Offers MD. *Accreditation:* LCME/AMA. *Entrance requirements:* For doctorate, MCAT. Electronic applications accepted. *Faculty research:* Signal transduction, membrane biology, neurophysiology, tropical medicine.

Mercer University, School of Medicine, Macon, GA 31207. Offers MFT, MPH, MSA, MD. *Accreditation:* AAMFT/COAMFTE; LCME/AMA (one or more programs are accredited). *Entrance requirements:* Additional exam requirements/recommendations for international students: Required—TOEFL. *Faculty research:* Anatomy, biochemistry/nutrition, genetics, microbiology/immunology, neuroscience.

Michigan State University, College of Human Medicine, Professional Program in Human Medicine, East Lansing, MI 48824. Offers human medicine (MD); human medicine/medical scientist training program (MD). *Accreditation:* LCME/AMA. *Entrance requirements:* Additional exam requirements/recommendations for international students: Required—TOEFL, Michigan State University ELT (minimum score 85), Michigan Michigan English Language Assessment Battery (minimum score 83). Electronic applications accepted.

Morehouse School of Medicine, Professional Program, Atlanta, GA 30310-1495. Offers MD, MD/MPH. *Accreditation:* LCME/AMA. *Degree requirements:* For doctorate, U.S. Medical Licensing Exam Steps 1 and 2. *Entrance requirements:* For doctorate, MCAT. Electronic applications accepted. *Expenses:* Contact institution. *Faculty research:* Cardiovascular disease and related sequela, infectious diseases/HIV-AIDS, neurological diseases, cancer.

Mount Sinai School of Medicine, Department of Medical Education, New York, NY 10029-6504. Offers MD, MD/PhD. *Accreditation:* LCME/AMA. *Degree requirements:* For doctorate, comprehensive exam, United States Medical Licensing Examination Steps 1 and 2. *Entrance requirements:* For doctorate, MCAT. Additional exam requirements/recommendations for international students: Required—TOEFL. Electronic applications accepted. *Expenses:* Contact institution. *Faculty research:* Academic medicine, translational research.

New York Medical College, Professional Program, Vahalla, NY 10595-1691. Offers MD, MD/MPH, MD/PhD. *Accreditation:* LCME/AMA. *Entrance requirements:* For doctorate, MCAT, 2 semesters of course work in general biology, general chemistry, organic chemistry, physics, and English. Electronic applications accepted. *Expenses:* Contact institution. *Faculty research:* Vascular function, hormonal regulation of blood pressure, physiological and molecular control of heart failure, neuroscience, adult stem cells.

New York University, School of Medicine, Professional Program in Medicine, New York, NY 10012-1019. Offers MD, MD/MA, MD/MPA, MD/PhD. *Accreditation:* LCME/AMA. *Entrance requirements:* For doctorate, MCAT. *Expenses:* Contact institution. *Faculty research:* Vascular biology, cancer genetics, molecular pathogenesis, epithelial pathobiology, microbial pathogenesis/host defense.

Northeastern Ohio Medical University, College of Medicine, Rootstown, OH 44272-0095. Offers MD. *Accreditation:* LCME/AMA. *Degree requirements:* For doctorate, U.S. Medical Licensing Exam Step 1. *Entrance requirements:* For doctorate, MCAT, 2 semesters of course work in organic chemistry and physics. Electronic applications accepted. *Expenses:* Contact institution. *Faculty research:* Lipid metabolism/cardiovascular disease, bone diseases/skeletal biology, virology/infectious diseases, clinical outcomes, sensory neurobiology.

Northwestern University, Northwestern University Feinberg School of Medicine, Combined MD/PhD Medical Scientist Training Program, Evanston, IL 60208. Offers MD/PhD. Application must be made to both The Graduate School and the Medical School. *Accreditation:* LCME/AMA. Electronic applications accepted. *Faculty research:* Cardiovascular epidemiology, cancer epidemiology, nutritional interventions for the prevention of cardiovascular disease and cancer, women's health, outcomes research.

The Ohio State University, College of Medicine, School of Biomedical Science, Professional Program in Medicine, Columbus, OH 43210. Offers MD. *Accreditation:* LCME/AMA. *Entrance requirements:* For doctorate, MCAT. Electronic applications accepted. *Expenses:* Tuition, state resident: full-time $11,400. Tuition, nonresident: full-time $28,125. Tuition and fees vary according to course load, degree level, campus/location and program. *Faculty research:* Molecular genetics, stress and the immune system, molecular cardiology, transplantation biology.

Oregon Health & Science University, School of Medicine, Professional Program in Medicine, Portland, OR 97239-3098. Offers MD, MD/DMD, MD/MPH, MD/PhD. *Accreditation:* LCME/AMA. *Faculty:* 2,045. *Students:* 503 full-time (262 women); includes 119 minority (3 Black or African American, non-Hispanic/Latino; 2 American Indian or Alaska Native, non-Hispanic/Latino; 82 Asian, non-Hispanic/Latino; 14 Hispanic/Latino; 1 Native Hawaiian or other Pacific Islander, non-Hispanic/Latino; 17 Two or more races, non-Hispanic/Latino). Average age 28. 4,835 applicants, 5% accepted, 128 enrolled. In 2011, 107 doctorates awarded. *Degree requirements:* For doctorate, National Board Exam Parts I and II. *Entrance requirements:* For doctorate, MCAT, 1 year of course work in biology, English, social science and physics; 2 years of course work in chemistry and genetics. *Application deadline:* For fall admission, 10/15 for domestic students. Applications are processed on a rolling basis. Application fee: $100. *Financial support:* Fellowships, research assistantships, Federal Work-Study, institutionally sponsored loans, scholarships/grants, and health care benefits available. Financial award application deadline: 3/1; financial award applicants required to submit FAFSA. *Unit head:* Dr. Molly Osborne, Associate Dean for Students and Educational Affairs, 503-494-8220, Fax: 503-494-3400. *Application contact:* Debbie Melton, Director, Admissions, 503-494-8220, Fax: 503-494-3400. Web site: http://www.ohsu.edu/som/.

Penn State Hershey Medical Center, College of Medicine, Hershey, PA 17033. Offers MPH, MS, MD, PhD, MD/PhD, PhD/MBA. *Accreditation:* LCME/AMA. Terminal master's awarded for partial completion of doctoral program. *Degree requirements:* For master's, thesis optional; for doctorate, comprehensive exam (for some programs), thesis/dissertation (for some programs), minimum GPA of 3.0 (for PhD). *Entrance requirements:* For master's, GRE; for doctorate, GRE (for PhD); MCAT (for MD). Additional exam requirements/recommendations for international students: Required—TOEFL (minimum score 560 paper-based; 220 computer-based). *Application deadline:* Applications are processed on a rolling basis. Application fee: $65. Electronic applications accepted. *Expenses:* Contact institution. *Financial support:* In 2011–12, 99 students received support, including research assistantships with full tuition reimbursements available (averaging $22,260 per year); fellowships with full tuition reimbursements available, career-related internships or fieldwork, scholarships/grants, health care benefits, and unspecified assistantships also available. *Unit head:* Dr. Michael Verderame, Assistant Dean for Graduate Studies, 717-531-8892, Fax: 717-531-0786, E-mail: grad-hmc@psu.edu. *Application contact:* Dr. Michael F. Verderame, Associate Dean of Graduate Studies, 717-531-8892, Fax: 717-531-0786, E-mail: grad-hmc@psu.edu. Web site: http://www.pennstatehershey.org/web/gsa/home.

Ponce School of Medicine & Health Sciences, Professional Program, Ponce, PR 00732-7004. Offers MD. *Accreditation:* LCME/AMA. *Degree requirements:* For doctorate, one foreign language, comprehensive exam, United States Medical Licensing Exam. *Entrance requirements:* For doctorate, MCAT, coursework in Spanish language, proficiency in Spanish/English, 3 letters of recommendation, criminal background check. Additional exam requirements/recommendations for international students: Required—TOEFL. Electronic applications accepted.

Pontificia Universidad Catolica Madre y Maestra, Department of Medicine, Santiago, Dominican Republic. Offers MD.

Queen's University at Kingston, School of Medicine, Professional Program in Medicine, Kingston, ON K7L 3N6, Canada. Offers MD. *Accreditation:* LCME/AMA. *Entrance requirements:* For doctorate, MCAT.

Rosalind Franklin University of Medicine and Science, The Chicago Medical School, North Chicago, IL 60064-3095. Offers MD, MD/MS, MD/PhD. *Accreditation:* LCME/AMA. *Degree requirements:* For doctorate, clerkship, step 1 and step 2 exams. *Entrance requirements:* For doctorate, MCAT, 3 years of course work with lab in biology, physics, inorganic chemistry, and organic chemistry. *Expenses:* Contact institution. *Faculty research:* Neurosciences, structural biology, cancer biology, cell biology, developmental biology.

Rush University, Rush Medical College, Chicago, IL 60612. Offers MD, MD/PhD. *Accreditation:* LCME/AMA. *Faculty:* 870 full-time (340 women). *Students:* 549 full-time (282 women); includes 178 minority (18 Black or African American, non-Hispanic/Latino; 3 American Indian or Alaska Native, non-Hispanic/Latino; 98 Asian, non-Hispanic/Latino; 50 Hispanic/Latino; 2 Native Hawaiian or other Pacific Islander, non-Hispanic/Latino; 7 Two or more races, non-Hispanic/Latino). 4,155 applicants, 6% accepted, 129 enrolled. In 2011, 121 degrees awarded. *Entrance requirements:* For doctorate, MCAT, in-person interview. *Application deadline:* For fall admission, 11/1 for domestic students. Applications are processed on a rolling basis. Application fee: $75. Electronic applications accepted. *Expenses:* Contact institution. *Financial support:* In 2011–12, 320 students received support. Federal Work-Study and institutionally sponsored loans available. Financial award application deadline: 5/1; financial award applicants required to submit FAFSA. *Unit head:* Dr. Cynthia E. Boyd, Assistant Dean, Admissions, 312-942-6915, Fax: 312-942-6840, E-mail: rmc_admissions@rush.edu. *Application contact:* Jill M. Volk, Director of Recruitment and Special Programs, 312-942-6915, Fax: 312-942-6840, E-mail: rmc_admissions@rush.edu. Web site: http://www.rushu.rush.edu/medcol.

Saint Louis University, Graduate Education, School of Medicine, Program in Medicine, St. Louis, MO 63103-2097. Offers MD. *Accreditation:* LCME/AMA. *Degree requirements:* For doctorate, U.S. Medical Licensing Exam Steps 1 and 2. *Entrance requirements:* For doctorate, MCAT, photograph, letters of recommendation, interview. Additional exam requirements/recommendations for international students: Required—TOEFL (minimum score 525 paper-based; 199 computer-based). Electronic applications accepted. *Expenses:* Contact institution. *Faculty research:* Geriatric medicine, organ transplantation, chronic disease prevention, vaccine research.

San Juan Bautista School of Medicine, Professional Program, Caguas, PR 00726-4968. Offers MD. *Accreditation:* LCME/AMA. *Degree requirements:* For doctorate, comprehensive exam, United States Medical Licensing Exam Steps I and II. *Entrance requirements:* For doctorate, MCAT, interview. *Faculty research:* Protein structure, CI tissue inflammations, bacterial metabolism, human hormone.

Stanford University, School of Medicine, Professional Program in Medicine, Stanford, CA 94305-9991. Offers MD. *Accreditation:* LCME/AMA. *Entrance requirements:* For doctorate, MCAT. Electronic applications accepted. *Expenses:* Contact institution.

State University of New York Downstate Medical Center, College of Medicine, Brooklyn, NY 11203-2098. Offers MPH, MD, MD/MPH, MD/PhD. *Accreditation:* LCME/AMA. *Entrance requirements:* For doctorate, MCAT. *Expenses:* Contact institution. *Faculty research:* AIDS epidemiology, virus/host interaction, molecular genetics, developmental neurobiology, prostate cancer.

State University of New York Downstate Medical Center, School of Graduate Studies, MD/PhD Program, Brooklyn, NY 11203-2098. Offers MD/PhD. *Entrance requirements:* Additional exam requirements/recommendations for international students: Recommended—TOEFL.

State University of New York Upstate Medical University, College of Medicine, Syracuse, NY 13210-2334. Offers MD, MD/PhD. *Accreditation:* LCME/AMA. *Degree requirements:* For doctorate, comprehensive exam. *Entrance requirements:* For doctorate, MCAT. Additional exam requirements/recommendations for international students: Required—TOEFL. Electronic applications accepted. *Expenses:* Contact institution.

Stony Brook University, State University of New York, Stony Brook University Medical Center, Health Sciences Center, School of Medicine, Medical Scientist Training Program, Stony Brook, NY 11794. Offers MD/PhD.

Stony Brook University, State University of New York, Stony Brook University Medical Center, Health Sciences Center, School of Medicine, Professional Program in Medicine, Stony Brook, NY 11794. Offers MD, MD/PhD. *Accreditation:* LCME/AMA. *Entrance requirements:* For doctorate, MCAT, interview.

Temple University, Health Sciences Center, School of Medicine, Doctor of Medicine Program, Philadelphia, PA 19140. Offers MD, MD/MPH, MD/PhD. *Accreditation:* LCME/AMA. *Faculty:* 481 full-time (142 women), 39 part-time/adjunct (9 women). *Students:* 778 full-time (362 women); includes 298 minority (59 Black or African American, non-Hispanic/Latino; 4 American Indian or Alaska Native, non-Hispanic/Latino; 170 Asian, non-Hispanic/Latino; 62 Hispanic/Latino; 3 Native Hawaiian or other Pacific Islander, non-Hispanic/Latino). Average age 25. 10,318 applicants, 5% accepted, 211 enrolled. In 2011, 181 doctorates awarded. *Degree requirements:* For doctorate, United States Medical Licensing Exam Step 1, Step 2CK, Step 2CS. *Entrance requirements:* For doctorate, MCAT. *Application deadline:* For fall admission, 12/15 for domestic students. Applications are processed on a rolling basis. Application fee: $75. Electronic applications accepted. *Expenses:* Contact institution. *Financial support:* In 2011–12, 341 students received support, including 11 fellowships with full tuition reimbursements available (averaging $15,600 per year), 12 research assistantships with full tuition reimbursements available (averaging $26,500 per year); Federal Work-Study, institutionally sponsored loans, and scholarships/grants also available. Financial award application deadline: 3/1; financial award applicants required to submit FAFSA. *Faculty research:* Translational medicine, molecular biology and immunology of autoimmune diseases and cancer, cardiovascular and pulmonary disease pathophysiology, biology of substance abuse, causes and consequences of obesity, molecular mechanisms of neurological dysfunction. *Total annual research expenditures:* $66.5 million. *Unit head:* Dr. Larry R. Kaiser, Dean, 215-707-8773, E-mail: larry.kaiser@temple.edu. *Application*

contact: Information Contact, 215-707-3656, E-mail: medadmissions@temple.edu. Web site: http://www.temple.edu/medicine/.

Texas Tech University Health Sciences Center, School of Medicine, Lubbock, TX 79430-0002. Offers MD, JD/MD, MD/MBA, MD/PhD. Open only to residents of Texas, eastern New Mexico, and southwestern Oklahoma; MD/PhD offered jointly with Texas Tech University; JD/MD with School of Law. *Accreditation:* LCME/AMA. *Entrance requirements:* For doctorate, MCAT. Additional exam requirements/recommendations for international students: Required—TOEFL. Electronic applications accepted. *Expenses:* Contact institution.

Thomas Jefferson University, Jefferson College of Graduate Studies, MD/PhD Program, Philadelphia, PA 19107. Offers MD/PhD. *Students:* 16 full-time (10 women); includes 1 minority (Asian, non-Hispanic/Latino), 1 international. 138 applicants, 12% accepted, 5 enrolled. *Entrance requirements:* Additional exam requirements/ recommendations for international students: Required—TOEFL (minimum score 250 computer-based; 100 iBT) or IELTS. *Application deadline:* For fall admission, 11/1 for domestic and international students. Applications are processed on a rolling basis. Application fee: $0. Electronic applications accepted. *Financial support:* In 2011–12, 16 fellowships with full tuition reimbursements were awarded; Federal Work-Study and institutionally sponsored loans also available. Financial award application deadline: 5/1; financial award applicants required to submit FAFSA. *Faculty research:* Signal transduction, tumorigenesis, apoptosis, molecular immunology, structural biology. *Unit head:* Dr. Scott A. Waldman, Academic Director, 215-955-6086, Fax: 215-955-5681, E-mail: scott.waldman@jefferson.edu. *Application contact:* Marc E. Stearns, Director of Admissions, 215-503-0155, Fax: 215-503-9920, E-mail: jcgs-info@jefferson.edu. Web site: http://www.jefferson.edu/jcgs/mdphd/.

Thomas Jefferson University, Jefferson Medical College, Philadelphia, PA 19107. Offers MD, MD/PhD. *Accreditation:* LCME/AMA. *Faculty:* 779 full-time (236 women), 46 part-time/adjunct (23 women). *Students:* 1,054 full-time (536 women); includes 315 minority (9 Black or African American, non-Hispanic/Latino; 2 American Indian or Alaska Native, non-Hispanic/Latino; 240 Asian, non-Hispanic/Latino; 64 Hispanic/Latino), 56 international. Average age 23. 9,912 applicants, 5% accepted, 260 enrolled. In 2011, 256 doctorates awarded. *Entrance requirements:* For doctorate, MCAT. *Application deadline:* For fall admission, 11/15 for domestic and international students. Applications are processed on a rolling basis. Application fee: $80. Electronic applications accepted. *Expenses:* Contact institution. *Financial support:* In 2011–12, 849 students received support. Federal Work-Study, institutionally sponsored loans, and scholarships/grants available. Financial award application deadline: 3/1; financial award applicants required to submit FAFSA. *Faculty research:* Translational medicine, Alzheimer's research, pancreatic cancer, oncology and endocrinology. *Total annual research expenditures:* $64.1 million. *Unit head:* Dr. Mark Tykowcinski, Interim Dean, 215-955-6980, Fax: 215-923-6939. *Application contact:* Dr. Clara Callahan, Dean for Admissions, 215-955-6983, Fax: 215-955-5151, E-mail: clara.callahan@jefferson.edu. Web site: http://www.jefferson.edu/jmc/.

Tufts University, School of Medicine, Professional Program in Medicine, Medford, MA 02155. Offers MD, MD/MA, MD/MBA, MD/MPH, MD/MSE, MD/PhD. MD/PhD offered jointly with Sackler School of Graduate Biomedical Sciences; MD/MBA with Brandeis University. *Accreditation:* LCME/AMA. *Students:* 799 full-time (365 women), 1 part-time (0 women); includes 248 minority (27 Black or African American, non-Hispanic/Latino; 157 Asian, non-Hispanic/Latino; 36 Hispanic/Latino; 1 Native Hawaiian or other Pacific Islander, non-Hispanic/Latino; 27 Two or more races, non-Hispanic/Latino), 2 international. Average age 26. 8,885 applicants, 7% accepted, 201 enrolled. In 2011, 175 doctorates awarded. *Entrance requirements:* For doctorate, MCAT. *Application deadline:* For fall admission, 1/15 for domestic students. Applications are processed on a rolling basis. Application fee: $105. Electronic applications accepted. *Expenses:* Contact institution. *Financial support:* Federal Work-Study, institutionally sponsored loans, and scholarships/grants available. Financial award application deadline: 3/30; financial award applicants required to submit FAFSA. *Unit head:* Dr. Harris Berman, Dean, 617-636-6565. *Application contact:* Thomas Slavin, Director of Admissions, 617-636-6571, E-mail: med-admissions@tufts.edu. Web site: http://md.tufts.edu/.

Tulane University, School of Medicine, Professional Programs in Medicine, New Orleans, LA 70118-5669. Offers MD, MD/MBA, MD/MPH, MD/MPHTM, MD/MSPH, MD/PhD. *Accreditation:* LCME/AMA. *Entrance requirements:* For doctorate, MCAT.

Universidad Autonoma de Guadalajara, School of Medicine, Guadalajara, Mexico. Offers MD.

Universidad Central del Caribe, School of Medicine, Bayamón, PR 00960-6032. Offers MA, MS, MD, PhD. *Accreditation:* LCME/AMA. *Degree requirements:* For doctorate, variable foreign language requirement. *Entrance requirements:* For doctorate, MCAT (for MD). *Faculty research:* Membrane neurotransmitter receptors, brain neurotransmission, cocaine toxicology, membrane transport, antimetabolite pharmacology.

Universidad Central del Este, Medical School, San Pedro de Macoris, Dominican Republic. Offers MD.

Universidad de Ciencias Medicas, Graduate Programs, San Jose, Costa Rica. Offers dermatology (SP); family health (MS); health service center administration (MHA); human anatomy (MS); medical and surgery (MD); occupational medicine (MS); pharmacy (Pharm D). Part-time programs available. *Degree requirements:* For master's, thesis; for doctorate and SP, comprehensive exam. *Entrance requirements:* For master's, MD or bachelor's degree; for doctorate, admissions test; for SP, admissions test, MD.

Universidad de Iberoamerica, Graduate School, San Jose, Costa Rica. Offers clinical neuropsychology (PhD); clinical psychology (M Psych); educational psychology (M Psych); forensic psychology (M Psych); hospital management (MHA); intensive care nursing (MN); medicine (MD).

Universidad Iberoamericana, School of Medicine, Santo Domingo D.N., Dominican Republic. Offers MD.

Universidad Nacional Pedro Henriquez Urena, School of Medicine, Santo Domingo, Dominican Republic. Offers MD.

Université de Montréal, Faculty of Medicine, Professional Program in Medicine, Montréal, QC H3C 3J7, Canada. Offers MD. Open only to Canadian residents. *Accreditation:* LCME/AMA. *Entrance requirements:* For doctorate, proficiency in French. Electronic applications accepted.

Université de Sherbrooke, Faculty of Medicine and Health Sciences, Professional Program in Medicine, Sherbrooke, QC J1K 2R1, Canada. Offers MD. *Accreditation:* LCME/AMA. Electronic applications accepted.

Université Laval, Faculty of Medicine, Post-Professional Programs in Medical Studies, Québec, QC G1K 7P4, Canada. Offers anatomy–pathology (DESS); anesthesiology (DESS); cardiology (DESS); care of older people (Diploma); clinical research (DESS); community health (DESS); dermatology (DESS); diagnostic radiology (DESS); emergency medicine (Diploma); family medicine (DESS); general surgery (DESS); geriatrics (DESS); hematology (DESS); internal medicine (DESS); maternal and fetal

medicine (Diploma); medical biochemistry (DESS); medical microbiology and infectious diseases (DESS); medical oncology (DESS); nephrology (DESS); neurology (DESS); neurosurgery (DESS); obstetrics and gynecology (DESS); ophthalmology (DESS); orthopedic surgery (DESS); oto-rhino-laryngology (DESS); palliative medicine (Diploma); pediatrics (DESS); plastic surgery (DESS); psychiatry (DESS); pulmonary medicine (DESS); radiology–oncology (DESS); thoracic surgery (DESS); urology (DESS). *Degree requirements:* For other advanced degree, comprehensive exam. *Entrance requirements:* For degree, knowledge of French. Electronic applications accepted.

Université Laval, Faculty of Medicine, Professional Program in Medicine, Québec, QC G1K 7P4, Canada. Offers MD. *Accreditation:* LCME/AMA. *Entrance requirements:* For doctorate, interview, proficiency in French. Electronic applications accepted.

University at Buffalo, the State University of New York, Graduate School, School of Medicine and Biomedical Sciences, Professional Program in Medicine, Buffalo, NY 14260. Offers MD, MD/MBA, MD/MPH, MD/PhD. *Accreditation:* LCME/AMA. *Students:* 591 full-time (273 women); includes 149 minority (16 Black or African American, non-Hispanic/Latino; 4 American Indian or Alaska Native, non-Hispanic/Latino; 127 Asian, non-Hispanic/Latino; 2 Hispanic/Latino). Average age 26. 4,512 applicants, 9% accepted, 140 enrolled. In 2011, 131 doctorates awarded. *Entrance requirements:* For doctorate, MCAT, interview. *Application deadline:* For fall admission, 11/15 for domestic students. Applications are processed on a rolling basis. Application fee: $65. Electronic applications accepted. *Financial support:* In 2011–12, 551 students received support. Career-related internships or fieldwork, Federal Work-Study, and institutionally sponsored loans available. Financial award application deadline: 3/1; financial award applicants required to submit FAFSA. *Faculty research:* Microbial pathogenesis, neuronal plasticity, structural biology of ion channels, structural development, cell biology of development. *Unit head:* Dr. Charles Severin, Dean for Admissions, 716-829-2803, Fax: 716-829-2798, E-mail: severin@buffalo.edu. *Application contact:* James J. Rosso, Admissions Advisor, 716-829-3466, Fax: 716-829-3849, E-mail: jjrosso@buffalo.edu. Web site: http://medicine.buffalo.edu/education/md.html.

The University of Alabama at Birmingham, School of Medicine, Birmingham, AL 35294. Offers MD. *Accreditation:* LCME/AMA. *Entrance requirements:* For doctorate, MCAT, interview. *Expenses:* Contact institution. *Financial support:* Fellowships and career-related internships or fieldwork available. Financial award application deadline: 5/1; financial award applicants required to submit FAFSA. *Unit head:* Dr. Ray L. Watts, Vice President/Dean, School of Medicine, 205-934-1111, Fax: 205-934-0333. Web site: http://www.uab.edu/uasom/.

The University of Arizona, College of Medicine, Professional Programs in Medicine, Tucson, AZ 85721. Offers MD, MD/PhD. MD program open only to state residents. *Accreditation:* LCME/AMA. *Faculty:* 155 full-time (39 women), 43 part-time/adjunct (9 women). *Students:* 658 full-time (330 women); includes 164 minority (10 Black or African American, non-Hispanic/Latino; 1 American Indian or Alaska Native, non-Hispanic/Latino; 44 Asian, non-Hispanic/Latino; 44 Hispanic/Latino; 65 Two or more races, non-Hispanic/Latino), 3 international. Average age 28. 502 applicants, 23% accepted. In 2011, 128 doctorates awarded. *Entrance requirements:* For doctorate, MCAT, previous course work in general chemistry, organic chemistry, biology/zoology, physics, and English. Application fee: $0. *Expenses:* Tuition, state resident: full-time $10,840. Tuition, nonresident: full-time $25,802. *Financial support:* Fellowships, research assistantships, teaching assistantships, career-related internships or fieldwork, Federal Work-Study, institutionally sponsored loans, and tuition waivers (full and partial) available. *Faculty research:* Developmental biology, cellular structure and function, immunology, clinical cancer research, heart and respiratory disease. *Total annual research expenditures:* $196.5 million. *Unit head:* Dr. Thomas Boyer, Dean, 520-626-6349, E-mail: tboyer@deptofmed.arizona.edu. *Application contact:* Dr. Shirley Nickols Fahey, Associate Dean for Admissions, 520-621-2211.

University of Arkansas for Medical Sciences, College of Medicine, Little Rock, AR 72205-7199. Offers MD, MD/PhD. *Accreditation:* LCME/AMA. *Entrance requirements:* For doctorate, MCAT. *Expenses:* Contact institution.

The University of British Columbia, Faculty of Medicine, Department of Surgery, Vancouver, BC V6T 1Z1, Canada. Offers M Sc. Part-time programs available. *Degree requirements:* For master's, thesis. *Entrance requirements:* Additional exam requirements/recommendations for international students: Required—TOEFL. Electronic applications accepted. *Faculty research:* Photodynamic therapy, transplantation immunobiology, isolated cell culture, neurophysiology.

The University of British Columbia, Faculty of Medicine, Professional Program in Medicine, Vancouver, BC V6T 1Z1, Canada. Offers MD, MD/PhD. *Accreditation:* LCME/AMA. *Entrance requirements:* For doctorate, MCAT.

University of Calgary, Faculty of Medicine, MD Program, Calgary, AB T2N 4N1, Canada. Offers MD. *Accreditation:* LCME/AMA. *Students:* 518 full-time (263 women). Average age 26. 2,132 applicants, 16% accepted, 170 enrolled. In 2011, 153 doctorates awarded. *Entrance requirements:* For doctorate, MCAT. *Application deadline:* For fall admission, 10/15 for domestic students. Application fee: $150. Electronic applications accepted. *Financial support:* Career-related internships or fieldwork available. *Unit head:* Dr. Bruce Wright, Associate Dean, Medical Education, 403-220-3843, Fax: 403-270-2681, E-mail: umeadm4@ucalgary.ca. *Application contact:* Adele Meyers, Coordinator, Admissions and Student Affairs, 403-220-4357, Fax: 403-210-8148, E-mail: meyers@ucalgary.ca. Web site: http://medicine.ucalgary.ca.

University of California, Berkeley, Graduate Division, School of Public Health, Group in Health and Medical Sciences, Berkeley, CA 94720-1500. Offers MD/MS. Program offered jointly with University of California, San Francisco.

University of California, Davis, School of Medicine, Sacramento, CA 95817. Offers MD, MD/MBA, MD/MPH, MD/MS, MD/PhD. *Accreditation:* LCME/AMA. *Faculty:* 699 full-time (232 women), 115 part-time/adjunct (49 women). *Students:* 405 full-time (230 women); includes 237 minority (21 Black or African American, non-Hispanic/Latino; 3 American Indian or Alaska Native, non-Hispanic/Latino; 129 Asian, non-Hispanic/Latino; 59 Hispanic/Latino; 3 Native Hawaiian or other Pacific Islander, non-Hispanic/Latino; 22 Two or more races, non-Hispanic/Latino), 2 international. Average age 27. 4,792 applicants, 4% accepted, 100 enrolled. In 2011, 8 doctorates awarded. *Degree requirements:* For doctorate, comprehensive exam. *Entrance requirements:* For doctorate, MCAT, 1 year each of English, biological science (lower-division with lab), general chemistry (with lab), organic chemistry (with lab), physics, and college-level math. *Application deadline:* For fall admission, 10/1 for domestic and international students. Applications are processed on a rolling basis. Application fee: $70. Electronic applications accepted. *Expenses:* Contact institution. *Financial support:* In 2011–12, 390 students received support, including 11 fellowships with full tuition reimbursements available (averaging $22,367 per year), 10 research assistantships with partial tuition reimbursements available (averaging $26,005 per year), 4 teaching assistantships with partial tuition reimbursements available (averaging $1,923 per year); institutionally sponsored loans and scholarships/grants also available. Support available to part-time students. Financial award application deadline: 3/1; financial award applicants required to submit FAFSA. *Faculty research:* Cancer biology, cardiovascular disease, clinical and translational research, neuroscience, regenerative medicine. *Total annual research*

expenditures: $160.8 million. *Unit head:* Dr. Claire Pomeroy, Dean/Vice Chancellor, Human Health Sciences, 916-734-7131, Fax: 916-734-7055, E-mail: claire.pomeroy@ucdmc.ucdavis.edu. *Application contact:* Joanna Garcia, Director of Admissions and Outreach, 916-734-4663, Fax: 916-734-4050, E-mail: joanna.garcia@ucdmc.ucdavis.edu. Web site: http://www.ucdmc.ucdavis.edu/medschool/.

University of California, Irvine, School of Medicine, Professional Program in Medicine, Irvine, CA 92697. Offers MD, MD/MBA, MD/MPH, MD/PhD. *Accreditation:* LCME/AMA. *Students:* 411 full-time (196 women), 33 part-time (14 women); includes 142 minority (9 Black or African American, non-Hispanic/Latino; 2 American Indian or Alaska Native, non-Hispanic/Latino; 96 Asian, non-Hispanic/Latino; 32 Hispanic/Latino; 3 Native Hawaiian or other Pacific Islander, non-Hispanic/Latino). Average age 26. *Entrance requirements:* For doctorate, MCAT. Additional exam requirements/recommendations for international students: Required—TOEFL (minimum score 550 paper-based; 213 computer-based). *Application deadline:* For fall admission, 11/1 for domestic students. Application fee: $70 ($90 for international students). Electronic applications accepted. *Financial support:* Fellowships, institutionally sponsored loans, traineeships, health care benefits, and unspecified assistantships available. Financial award application deadline: 3/1; financial award applicants required to submit FAFSA. *Unit head:* Dr. Ralph Victor Clayman, Dean and Professor, 949-824-5926, Fax: 949-824-2676, E-mail: rclayman@uci.edu. *Application contact:* Prof. Alan L. Goldin, Associate Dean and Professor, 949-824-5334, 8508, Fax: 949-824-8504, E-mail: agoldin@uci.edu.

University of California, Los Angeles, David Geffen School of Medicine, Professional Program in Medicine, Los Angeles, CA 90095. Offers MD, MD/MBA, MD/PhD. *Accreditation:* LCME/AMA. *Students:* 652 full-time (312 women); includes 197 minority (19 Black or African American, non-Hispanic/Latino; 119 Asian, non-Hispanic/Latino; 48 Hispanic/Latino; 11 Two or more races, non-Hispanic/Latino), 2 international. Average age 25. 6,703 applicants, 4% accepted, 158 enrolled. In 2011, 161 doctorates awarded. *Entrance requirements:* For doctorate, MCAT. Application fee: $70. *Financial support:* In 2011–12, 91 fellowships, 2 research assistantships were awarded; teaching assistantships, Federal Work-Study, institutionally sponsored loans, scholarships/grants, and tuition waivers (full and partial) also available. Financial award application deadline: 3/1. *Unit head:* Dr. A. Eugene Washington, Vice Chancellor, Health Sciences/Dean, School of Medicine, 310-825-5687, E-mail: ewashington@mednet.ucla.edu. *Application contact:* School of Medicine Admissions, 310-825-6081. Web site: http://www.mednet.ucla.edu/som/.

University of California, San Diego, School of Medicine, Professional Program in Medicine, La Jolla, CA 92093. Offers MD, MD/PhD. *Accreditation:* LCME/AMA. *Entrance requirements:* For doctorate, MCAT.

University of California, San Francisco, School of Medicine, San Francisco, CA 94143-0410. Offers MD, PhD, MD/MPH, MD/MS, MD/PhD. *Accreditation:* LCME/AMA (one or more programs are accredited). *Faculty:* 2,031 full-time (678 women), 128 part-time/adjunct (41 women). *Students:* 634 full-time (354 women); includes 331 minority (44 Black or African American, non-Hispanic/Latino; 124 Asian, non-Hispanic/Latino; 100 Hispanic/Latino; 24 Native Hawaiian or other Pacific Islander, non-Hispanic/Latino; 39 Two or more races, non-Hispanic/Latino). Average age 24. 6,767 applicants, 4% accepted, 149 enrolled. In 2011, 163 doctorates awarded. *Entrance requirements:* For doctorate, MCAT (for MD), interview (for MD). *Application deadline:* For fall admission, 10/15 for domestic students. Applications are processed on a rolling basis. Application fee: $60 ($80 for international students). Electronic applications accepted. *Expenses:* Contact institution. *Financial support:* In 2011–12, 543 students received support. Federal Work-Study, institutionally sponsored loans, scholarships/grants, and tuition waivers (partial) available. Financial award application deadline: 2/1; financial award applicants required to submit FAFSA. *Faculty research:* Neurosciences, human genetics, developmental biology, social/behavioral/policy sciences, immunology. *Total annual research expenditures:* $414.4 million. *Unit head:* Dr. Sam Hawgood, Dean, 415-476-2342, Fax: 415-476-0689, E-mail: sam.hawgood@ucsf.edu. *Application contact:* Hallen Chung, Director of Admissions, 415-476-8090, Fax: 415-476-5490, E-mail: chungh@medsch.ucsf.edu. Web site: http://www.medschool.ucsf.edu/.

University of Central Florida, College of Medicine, Orlando, FL 32816. Offers MS, MD, PhD. *Accreditation:* LCME/AMA. *Expenses:* Tuition, state resident: part-time $277.08 per credit hour. Tuition, nonresident: part-time $277.08 per credit hour. Part-time tuition and fees vary according to degree level and program. *Financial support:* Fellowships, research assistantships, and teaching assistantships available. *Unit head:* Dr. Deborah C. German, Vice President for Medical Affairs and Dean, 407-266-1000, E-mail: deborah.german@ucf.edu. *Application contact:* Barbara Rodriguez, Director, Admissions and Registration, 407-823-2766, Fax: 407-823-6442, E-mail: gradadmissions@ucf.edu. Web site: http://www.med.ucf.edu.

University of Chicago, Pritzker School of Medicine, Chicago, IL 60637-1513. Offers MD, MD/PhD. *Accreditation:* LCME/AMA. *Entrance requirements:* For doctorate, MCAT, one year of each with lab: chemistry, physics, biology and organic chemistry. Electronic applications accepted. *Faculty research:* Human genetics, diabetes, developmental biology, structural biology, neurobiology.

University of Cincinnati, Graduate School, College of Allied Health Sciences, Program in Transfusion and Transplantation Sciences, Cincinnati, OH 45221. Offers blood transfusion medicine (MS); cellular therapies (MS). *Degree requirements:* For master's, comprehensive exam, thesis. *Entrance requirements:* For master's, GRE General Test. Additional exam requirements/recommendations for international students: Required—TOEFL (minimum score 570 paper-based). Electronic applications accepted. *Faculty research:* Preservation of red cells, red cell oxidation and delivery to tissues, cellular therapies, coagulopathies.

University of Cincinnati, Graduate School, College of Medicine, Physician Scientist Training Program, Cincinnati, OH 45221. Offers MD/PhD. *Entrance requirements:* Additional exam requirements/recommendations for international students: Required—TOEFL. Electronic applications accepted.

University of Cincinnati, Graduate School, College of Medicine, Professional Program in Medicine, Cincinnati, OH 45221. Offers MD. *Accreditation:* LCME/AMA. *Entrance requirements:* For doctorate, MCAT. Electronic applications accepted. *Faculty research:* Molecular genetics, environmental health, neuroscience and cell biology, cardiovascular science, developmental biology.

University of Colorado Denver, School of Medicine, Professional Program in Medicine, Aurora, CO 80045. Offers MD, MD/MBA, MD/PhD. *Students:* 634 full-time (305 women), 1 (woman) part-time; includes 125 minority (16 Black or African American, non-Hispanic/Latino; 6 American Indian or Alaska Native, non-Hispanic/Latino; 56 Asian, non-Hispanic/Latino; 47 Hispanic/Latino), 6 international. Average age 27. 7,246 applicants, 2% accepted, 159 enrolled. In 2011, 143 doctorates awarded. *Entrance requirements:* For doctorate, MCAT, application completed through both AMCAS and the Colorado Med school program, essay, interviews for the finalists, prerequisite coursework in biology (with lab), general chemistry (with lab), organic chemistry (with lab), general physics (with lab), English literature/composition, college-level mathematics (algebra and above). Additional exam requirements/recommendations for international students: Required—TOEFL (minimum score 550 paper-based). *Application deadline:* For fall admission, 11/1 for domestic students, 10/1 for international students. Application fee: $100 ($125 for international students). Electronic applications accepted. *Expenses:* Contact institution. *Financial support:* Application deadline: 4/1; applicants required to submit FAFSA. *Unit head:* Dr. Richard Krugman, Dean, 303-724-0882, E-mail: richard.krugman@ucdenver.edu. *Application contact:* Ashley Ehlers, Office of Admissions Medical Program Assistant, 303-724-8025, E-mail: somadmin@ucdenver.edu. Web site: http://www.ucdenver.edu/academics/colleges/medicalschool/education/Pages/default.aspx.

University of Connecticut Health Center, School of Medicine, Farmington, CT 06030. Offers MD, MD/MBA, MD/MPH, MD/PhD. *Accreditation:* LCME/AMA. *Entrance requirements:* For doctorate, MCAT. Electronic applications accepted. *Expenses:* Contact institution.

University of Florida, College of Medicine, Professional Program in Medicine, Gainesville, FL 32611. Offers MD, MD/PhD. *Accreditation:* LCME/AMA. *Entrance requirements:* For doctorate, MCAT, 8 semester hours of course work in biology, general chemistry, and general physics; 4 semester hours of course work in geochemistry and organic chemistry. Electronic applications accepted. *Faculty research:* Neurobiology, gene therapy and genetic imaging technologies, diabetes and autoimmune diseases, transplantation.

University of Hawaii at Manoa, John A. Burns School of Medicine, Professional Program in Medicine, Honolulu, HI 96822. Offers MD. *Accreditation:* LCME/AMA. *Entrance requirements:* For doctorate, MCAT. Electronic applications accepted. *Expenses:* Contact institution.

University of Illinois at Chicago, College of Medicine, Professional Program in Medicine, Chicago, IL 60607-7128. Offers MD, MD/MS, MD/PhD. Part-time programs available. *Entrance requirements:* For doctorate, MCAT. Electronic applications accepted. *Faculty research:* Biomedical and clinical sciences.

University of Illinois at Urbana–Champaign, Graduate College, Medical Scholars Program, Urbana, IL 61801. Offers MD/MBA, MD/PhD. *Students:* 138 full-time (65 women); includes 45 minority (2 Black or African American, non-Hispanic/Latino; 33 Asian, non-Hispanic/Latino; 10 Hispanic/Latino). 105 applicants, 22% accepted, 17 enrolled. *Application deadline:* For fall admission, 12/31 for domestic students. Application fee: $0. Electronic applications accepted. *Expenses:* Contact institution. *Financial support:* In 2011–12, 26 fellowships with full tuition reimbursements (averaging $10,000 per year), 25 research assistantships with full tuition reimbursements (averaging $14,000 per year), 23 teaching assistantships with full tuition reimbursements (averaging $14,000 per year) were awarded; traineeships, health care benefits, and unspecified assistantships also available. Financial award applicants required to submit FAFSA. *Unit head:* Dr. James Hall, Associate Dean, 217-333-8146, Fax: 217-333-2640. *Application contact:* Jenni Crum, Coordinator, 217-333-8146, Fax: 217-333-2640, E-mail: jlcrum@illinois.edu. Web site: https://www.med.illinois.edu/mdphd/.

The University of Iowa, Roy J. and Lucille A. Carver College of Medicine, Professional Program in Medicine, Iowa City, IA 52242-1316. Offers MD, MD/JD, MD/MBA, MD/MPH, MD/PhD. *Accreditation:* LCME/AMA. *Faculty:* 891 full-time (254 women). *Students:* 586 full-time (271 women); includes 143 minority (25 Black or African American, non-Hispanic/Latino; 2 American Indian or Alaska Native, non-Hispanic/Latino; 70 Asian, non-Hispanic/Latino; 29 Hispanic/Latino; 1 Native Hawaiian or other Pacific Islander, non-Hispanic/Latino; 16 Two or more races, non-Hispanic/Latino). Average age 26. 3,555 applicants, 9% accepted, 148 enrolled. In 2011, 146 doctorates awarded. *Degree requirements:* For doctorate, U.S. Medical Licensing Examination Steps 1 and 2. *Entrance requirements:* For doctorate, MCAT, course work in biology, chemistry, physics, mathematics, English, and social sciences; bachelor's degree. *Application deadline:* For fall admission, 11/1 for domestic students. Applications are processed on a rolling basis. Application fee: $60. Electronic applications accepted. *Expenses:* Contact institution. *Financial support:* In 2011–12, 351 students received support. Institutionally sponsored loans, scholarships/grants, and unspecified assistantships available. Support available to part-time students. Financial award applicants required to submit FAFSA. *Unit head:* Dr. Christopher Cooper, Associate Dean, 319-335-8435, Fax: 319-335-8643. *Application contact:* Kathi J. Huebner, Director of Admissions, 319-335-6703, Fax: 319-335-8049, E-mail: medical-admissions@uiowa.edu. Web site: http://www.medicine.uiowa.edu/md/.

The University of Kansas, University of Kansas Medical Center, School of Medicine, MD/PhD Program, Kansas City, KS 66160. Offers MD/PhD. *Students:* 34 full-time (16 women); includes 6 minority (1 Black or African American, non-Hispanic/Latino; 4 Asian, non-Hispanic/Latino; 1 Two or more races, non-Hispanic/Latino). Average age 27. 47 applicants, 15% accepted, 4 enrolled. *Application deadline:* For fall admission, 11/15 priority date for domestic students. Applications are processed on a rolling basis. Application fee: $35. Electronic applications accepted. Tuition and fees vary according to course load, campus/location, program and reciprocity agreements. *Financial support:* Fellowships with full tuition reimbursements, research assistantships with full tuition reimbursements, and teaching assistantships with full tuition reimbursements available. Financial award application deadline: 2/14; financial award applicants required to submit FAFSA. *Faculty research:* Neuroscience, cancer biology, stem cell biology, reproductive biology. *Unit head:* Dr. Timothy A. Fields, Director, 913-588-7169, E-mail: tfields@kumc.edu. *Application contact:* Janice Fletcher, Administrative Manager, 913-588-5241, Fax: 913-945-6848, E-mail: jfletcher@kumc.edu. Web site: http://www3.kumc.edu/mdphd/.

The University of Kansas, University of Kansas Medical Center, School of Medicine, MD Program, Lawrence, KS 66045. Offers MD. *Faculty:* 890. *Students:* 708 full-time (317 women); includes 146 minority (39 Black or African American, non-Hispanic/Latino; 1 American Indian or Alaska Native, non-Hispanic/Latino; 57 Asian, non-Hispanic/Latino; 34 Hispanic/Latino; 15 Two or more races, non-Hispanic/Latino). Average age 26. 2,519 applicants, 9% accepted, 187 enrolled. In 2011, 166 doctorates awarded. *Degree requirements:* For doctorate, comprehensive exam. *Entrance requirements:* For doctorate, MCAT, bachelor's degree. *Application deadline:* For fall admission, 10/15 for domestic students. Applications are processed on a rolling basis. Application fee: $50. Electronic applications accepted. Tuition and fees vary according to course load, campus/location, program and reciprocity agreements. *Faculty research:* Reproductive biology (fertility, ovulation, embryo implantation, pregnancy maintenance), multidisciplinary research on the basic mechanisms of cancer, renal research, neurological research, liver research. *Total annual research expenditures:* $28.3 million. *Application contact:* Amy Meara, Director, Premed Programs, 913-588-5280, Fax: 913-588-5259, E-mail: premedinfo@kumc.edu. Web site: http://medicine.kumc.edu/.

University of Kentucky, College of Medicine, Professional Program in Medicine, Lexington, KY 40506-0032. Offers MD, MD/PhD. *Accreditation:* LCME/AMA. *Entrance requirements:* For doctorate, MCAT. Electronic applications accepted.

University of Louisville, School of Medicine, Professional Programs in Medicine, Louisville, KY 40292-0001. Offers MD, MD/MBA, MD/MS, MD/PhD. *Accreditation:* LCME/AMA. *Entrance requirements:* For doctorate, MCAT. *Expenses:* Tuition, state resident: full-time $9692; part-time $539 per credit hour. Tuition, nonresident: full-time $20,168; part-time $1121 per credit hour. Tuition and fees vary according to program and reciprocity agreements.

University of Maryland, Baltimore, School of Medicine, Professional Program in Medicine, Baltimore, MD 21201. Offers MD, MD/PhD. *Accreditation:* LCME/AMA. *Students:* 640 full-time (359 women), 11 part-time (10 women); includes 220 minority (54 Black or African American, non-Hispanic/Latino; 136 Asian, non-Hispanic/Latino; 12 Hispanic/Latino; 18 Two or more races, non-Hispanic/Latino), 1 international. Average age 25. In 2011, 150 doctorates awarded. *Entrance requirements:* For doctorate, MCAT, AMCAS application, science coursework. *Application deadline:* For fall admission, 11/1 for domestic students. Applications are processed on a rolling basis. Application fee: $70. Electronic applications accepted. *Expenses:* Contact institution. *Financial support:* Federal Work-Study and scholarships/grants available. Financial award application deadline: 3/15; financial award applicants required to submit FAFSA. *Unit head:* Dr. E. Albert Reece, Dean and Vice President for Medical Affairs, 410-706-7410, Fax: 410-706-0235, E-mail: deanmed@som.umaryland.edu. *Application contact:* Dr. Milford M. Foxwell, Jr., Associate Dean for Admissions, 410-706-7478, Fax: 410-706-0467, E-mail: admissions@som.umaryland.edu.

University of Massachusetts Worcester, School of Medicine, Worcester, MA 01655-0115. Offers MD, MD/PhD. *Accreditation:* LCME/AMA. *Faculty:* 1,427 full-time (526 women), 309 part-time/adjunct (196 women). *Students:* 514 full-time (276 women); includes 114 minority (23 Black or African American, non-Hispanic/Latino; 1 American Indian or Alaska Native, non-Hispanic/Latino; 78 Asian, non-Hispanic/Latino; 11 Hispanic/Latino; 1 Native Hawaiian or other Pacific Islander, non-Hispanic/Latino). Average age 27. 972 applicants, 21% accepted, 125 enrolled. In 2011, 86 doctorates awarded. *Degree requirements:* For doctorate, U.S. Medical Licensing Examination Step 1. *Entrance requirements:* For doctorate, MCAT, state residency (MD only)/ bachelor's degree. *Application deadline:* For fall admission, 12/15 for domestic students. Applications are processed on a rolling basis. Application fee: $75. Electronic applications accepted. *Expenses:* Contact institution. *Financial support:* In 2011–12, 449 students received support. Institutionally sponsored loans, scholarships/grants, health care benefits, tuition waivers (partial), and unspecified assistantships available. Financial award application deadline: 4/18; financial award applicants required to submit FAFSA. *Faculty research:* RNA interference, cell dynamics, immunology and virology, chemical biology, stem cell research. *Total annual research expenditures:* $262.7 million. *Unit head:* Dr. Terence R. Flotte, Dean/Provost/Executive Deputy Chancellor, 508-856-8000. *Application contact:* Karen Lawton, Director of Admissions, 508-856-2323, Fax: 508-856-3629, E-mail: admissions@umassmed.edu. Web site: http:// www.umassmed.edu/som.

University of Medicine and Dentistry of New Jersey, New Jersey Medical School, Newark, NJ 07101-1709. Offers MD, MD/Certificate, MD/JD, MD/MBA, MD/MPH, MD/ PhD. *Accreditation:* LCME/AMA. *Entrance requirements:* For doctorate, MCAT. Additional exam requirements/recommendations for international students: Required— TOEFL. Electronic applications accepted. *Expenses:* Contact institution.

University of Medicine and Dentistry of New Jersey, Robert Wood Johnson Medical School, Piscataway, NJ 08822. Offers MD, MD/JD, MD/MBA, MD/MPH, MD/MS, MD/ MSJ, MD/PhD. *Accreditation:* LCME/AMA (one or more programs are accredited). *Entrance requirements:* For doctorate, MCAT. Additional exam requirements/ recommendations for international students: Required—TOEFL. Electronic applications accepted. *Expenses:* Contact institution.

University of Miami, Graduate School, Miller School of Medicine, Professional Program in Medicine, Coral Gables, FL 33124. Offers MD. *Accreditation:* LCME/AMA. *Entrance requirements:* For doctorate, MCAT, 90 pre-med semester hours. Electronic applications accepted. *Faculty research:* AIDS, cancer, diabetes, neuroscience, wound healing.

University of Michigan, Medical School and Horace H. Rackham School of Graduate Studies, Medical Scientist Training Program, Ann Arbor, MI 48109. Offers MD/PhD. *Accreditation:* LCME/AMA. *Students:* 86 full-time (28 women); includes 35 minority (3 Black or African American, non-Hispanic/Latino; 31 Asian, non-Hispanic/Latino; 1 Hispanic/Latino). 276 applicants, 15% accepted, 13 enrolled. *Application deadline:* For fall admission, 10/15 for domestic students. Applications are processed on a rolling basis. Application fee: $150. Electronic applications accepted. *Financial support:* In 2011–12, 86 students received support, including 69 fellowships with full tuition reimbursements available (averaging $26,500 per year), 15 research assistantships with full tuition reimbursements available (averaging $26,500 per year), 2 teaching assistantships with full tuition reimbursements available (averaging $26,500 per year); scholarships/grants, traineeships, and health care benefits also available. *Unit head:* Dr. Ronald J. Koenig, Director, 734-764-6176, Fax: 734-764-8180, E-mail: rkoenig@ umich.edu. *Application contact:* Laurie Koivupalo, Administrative Associate, 734-764-6176, Fax: 734-764-8180, E-mail: lkoivupl@umich.edu. Web site: http:// www.med.umich.edu/medschool/mstp/.

University of Michigan, Medical School, Professional Program in Medicine, Ann Arbor, MI 48109. Offers medicine (MD); MD/MA Edu; MD/MBA; MD/MPH; MD/MPP; MD/MS; MD/MSI; MD/PhD. *Accreditation:* LCME/AMA. *Faculty:* 2,128 full-time, 1,102 part-time/ adjunct. *Students:* 704 full-time (348 women); includes 255 minority (32 Black or African American, non-Hispanic/Latino; 6 American Indian or Alaska Native, non-Hispanic/ Latino; 178 Asian, non-Hispanic/Latino; 39 Hispanic/Latino). Average age 26. 5,267 applicants, 8% accepted, 171 enrolled. In 2011, 180 degrees awarded. *Median time to degree:* Of those who began their doctoral program in fall 2003, 98% received their degree in 8 years or less. *Entrance requirements:* For doctorate, MCAT. *Application deadline:* For fall admission, 11/30 for domestic students. Applications are processed on a rolling basis. Application fee: $85. Electronic applications accepted. *Financial support:* In 2011–12, 403 students received support. Institutionally sponsored loans and scholarships/grants available. Financial award application deadline: 3/31; financial award applicants required to submit FAFSA. *Unit head:* Dr. James O. Woolliscroft, Dean, 734-764-8175, Fax: 734-734-763-4936, E-mail: woolli@umich.edu. *Application contact:* Robert F. Ruiz, Director of Admissions, 734-764-6317, Fax: 734-936-3510, E-mail: rfruiz@umich.edu. Web site: http://www.med.umich.edu/medschool/index.htm.

University of Minnesota, Duluth, Medical School, Professional Program in Medicine, Duluth, MN 55812-2496. Offers MD. Program offered jointly with University of Minnesota, Twin Cities Campus. *Entrance requirements:* For doctorate, MCAT. Electronic applications accepted.

University of Minnesota, Twin Cities Campus, Medical School, Professional Program in Medicine, Minneapolis, MN 55455-0213. Offers MD, JD/MD, MD/MBA, MD/MHI, MD/ MPH, MD/MS, MD/PhD. *Accreditation:* LCME/AMA. *Entrance requirements:* For doctorate, MCAT, 1 semester each of biology, chemistry, 4 other life sciences, and a humanity or social science. Electronic applications accepted. *Expenses:* Contact institution.

University of Mississippi Medical Center, School of Medicine, Jackson, MS 39216-4505. Offers MD, MD/PhD. *Accreditation:* LCME/AMA. *Entrance requirements:* For doctorate, MCAT. *Faculty research:* Cardiovascular physiology (computer simulation), transplant immunology, reproductive endocrinology, protein structure, neurotransmitter vesicle structure.

University of Missouri, School of Medicine, Professional Program in Medicine, Columbia, MO 65211. Offers MD, MD/MS, MD/PhD. *Accreditation:* LCME/AMA. *Faculty:* 330 full-time (88 women), 78 part-time/adjunct (15 women). *Students:* 387 full-time (188

women); includes 58 minority (18 Black or African American, non-Hispanic/Latino; 5 American Indian or Alaska Native, non-Hispanic/Latino; 33 Asian, non-Hispanic/Latino; 2 Hispanic/Latino), 1 international. Average age 25. In 2011, 93 degrees awarded. *Entrance requirements:* For doctorate, MCAT, minimum GPA of 3.49, specified pre-med courses. *Application deadline:* For fall admission, 11/1 for domestic students. Applications are processed on a rolling basis. *Expenses:* Tuition, state resident: full-time $5881. Tuition, nonresident: full-time $15,183. *Required fees:* $952. Tuition and fees vary according to campus/location and program. *Financial support:* In 2011–12, 361 students received support. Career-related internships or fieldwork, institutionally sponsored loans, and scholarships/grants available. Financial award application deadline: 8/15; financial award applicants required to submit FAFSA. *Faculty research:* Basic and clinical biomedical sciences. *Unit head:* Dr. Robert Churchill, Interim Dean, 573-884-9080, E-mail: churchillr@missouri.edu. *Application contact:* Marivern Easton, Enrollment Specialist, Admissions, Recruitment and Records, 573-882-8047, E-mail: eastonm@missouri.edu. Web site: http://som.missouri.edu/.

University of Missouri–Kansas City, School of Medicine, Kansas City, MO 64110-2499. Offers anesthesia (MS); bioinformatics (MS); medicine (MD); MD/PhD. *Accreditation:* LCME/AMA. *Faculty:* 38 full-time (13 women), 15 part-time/adjunct (4 women). *Students:* 424 full-time (224 women), 11 part-time (7 women); includes 230 minority (25 Black or African American, non-Hispanic/Latino; 1 American Indian or Alaska Native, non-Hispanic/Latino; 190 Asian, non-Hispanic/Latino; 12 Hispanic/Latino; 2 Two or more races, non-Hispanic/Latino), 2 international. Average age 23. 821 applicants, 15% accepted, 107 enrolled. In 2011, 4 master's, 101 doctorates awarded. *Degree requirements:* For doctorate, one foreign language, United States Medical Licensing Exam Step 1 and 2. *Entrance requirements:* For doctorate, interview. *Application deadline:* For fall admission, 11/15 for domestic and international students. Application fee: $50. *Expenses:* Contact institution. *Financial support:* Career-related internships or fieldwork, Federal Work-Study, institutionally sponsored loans, scholarships/grants, and tuition waivers (partial) available. Financial award application deadline: 3/1; financial award applicants required to submit FAFSA. *Faculty research:* Cardiovascular disease, women's and children's health, trauma and infectious diseases, neurological, metabolic disease. *Unit head:* Dr. Betty Drees, Dean, 816-235-1808, E-mail: dreesb@umkc.edu. *Application contact:* Kelly Kasper-Cushman, Interim Admissions Coordinator, 816-235-1870, Fax: 816-235-6579, E-mail: kasperkm@ umkc.edu. Web site: http://www.med.umkc.edu/.

University of Nebraska Medical Center, College of Medicine, Omaha, NE 68198-5527. Offers MD, Certificate, MD/MPH, MD/PhD. *Accreditation:* LCME/AMA. *Entrance requirements:* For doctorate, MCAT. Electronic applications accepted. *Expenses:* Contact institution.

University of New Mexico, Health Sciences Center Graduate Programs, Professional Program in Medicine, Albuquerque, NM 87131-2039. Offers MD. *Faculty:* 1,012 full-time (454 women), 202 part-time/adjunct (91 women). *Students:* 341 full-time (186 women); includes 148 minority (8 Black or African American, non-Hispanic/Latino; 13 American Indian or Alaska Native, non-Hispanic/Latino; 23 Asian, non-Hispanic/Latino; 103 Hispanic/Latino; 1 Two or more races, non-Hispanic/Latino). Average age 28. 225 applicants, 52% accepted, 94 enrolled. In 2011, 77 doctorates awarded. *Degree requirements:* For doctorate, research. *Entrance requirements:* For doctorate, MCAT, general biology, general chemistry, organic chemistry, biochemistry and physics; minimum GPA of 3.0. *Application deadline:* For fall admission, 11/15 for domestic students. Applications are processed on a rolling basis. Application fee: $75. *Expenses:* Contact institution. *Financial support:* In 2011–12, 229 students received support. Institutionally sponsored loans and scholarships/grants available. Financial award application deadline: 5/1; financial award applicants required to submit FAFSA. *Faculty research:* Cancer, infectious disease, brain and behavioral illness, children's health, cardiovascular and metabolic disease. *Total annual research expenditures:* $75 million. *Unit head:* Dr. Robert Sapien, Associate Dean of Admissions, 505-272-4766, Fax: 505-272-8239, E-mail: rsapien@salud.unm.edu. *Application contact:* Dr. Marlene Ballejos, Assistant Dean of Admissions, 505-272-4766, Fax: 505-272-8239, E-mail: mballejos@ salud.unm.edu. Web site: http://hsc.unm.edu/som/admissions.

The University of North Carolina at Chapel Hill, School of Medicine, Professional Program in Medicine, Chapel Hill, NC 27599. Offers MD, MD/MPH, MD/PhD. *Accreditation:* LCME/AMA. *Entrance requirements:* For doctorate, MCAT.

University of North Dakota, School of Medicine and Health Sciences, Professional Program in Medicine, Grand Forks, ND 58202. Offers MD, MD/PhD. *Accreditation:* LCME/AMA. *Entrance requirements:* For doctorate, MCAT, minimum GPA of 3.0. Additional exam requirements/recommendations for international students: Required— TOEFL (minimum score 550 paper-based; 213 computer-based; 79 iBT), IELTS (minimum score 6.5). Electronic applications accepted.

University of Oklahoma Health Sciences Center, College of Medicine, Professional Program in Medicine, Oklahoma City, OK 73190. Offers MD, MD/PhD. *Accreditation:* LCME/AMA. *Entrance requirements:* For doctorate, MCAT. *Faculty research:* Behavior and drugs, structure and function of endothelium, genetics and behavior, gene structure and function, action of antibiotics.

University of Ottawa, Faculty of Graduate and Postdoctoral Studies, Faculty of Medicine, Ottawa, ON K1N 6N5, Canada. Offers M Sc, MD, PhD. *Accreditation:* LCME/ AMA. *Degree requirements:* For master's, thesis; for doctorate, thesis/dissertation (for some programs). *Entrance requirements:* For master's, honors degree or equivalent, minimum B average. Electronic applications accepted.

University of Pennsylvania, Perelman School of Medicine, Professional Program in Medicine, Philadelphia, PA 19104. Offers MD, MD/JD, MD/MBA, MD/MBE, MD/MS, MD/ MSCE, MD/PhD. *Accreditation:* LCME/AMA. *Faculty:* 2,496 full-time (899 women), 1,205 part-time/adjunct (541 women). *Students:* 767 full-time (357 women); includes 290 minority (56 Black or African American, non-Hispanic/Latino; 145 Asian, non-Hispanic/Latino; 64 Hispanic/Latino; 25 Two or more races, non-Hispanic/Latino), 14 international. Average age 25. 6,157 applicants, 4% accepted, 166 enrolled. In 2011, 147 doctorates awarded. *Entrance requirements:* For doctorate, MCAT. *Application deadline:* For fall admission, 10/15 for domestic and international students. Application fee: $80. Electronic applications accepted. *Expenses:* Tuition: Full-time $26,660; part-time $4944 per course. *Required fees:* $2318; $291 per course. Tuition and fees vary according to course load, degree level and program. *Financial support:* In 2011–12, 650 students received support. Fellowships, research assistantships, teaching assistantships, career-related internships or fieldwork, Federal Work-Study, institutionally sponsored loans, and scholarships/grants available. Financial award application deadline: 5/1; financial award applicants required to submit FAFSA. *Unit head:* Dr. Gail Morrison, Vice Dean, 215-898-8034, E-mail: morrisog@ mail.med.upenn.edu. *Application contact:* Gaye Sheffler, Director, Admissions, 215-898-8001, Fax: 215-898-0833, E-mail: sheffler@mail.med.upenn.edu.

University of Pittsburgh, School of Medicine, Professional Program in Medicine, Pittsburgh, PA 15261. Offers MD. *Accreditation:* LCME/AMA. *Faculty:* 2,201 full-time (739 women), 64 part-time/adjunct (36 women). *Students:* 604 full-time (273 women); includes 275 minority (48 Black or African American, non-Hispanic/Latino; 169 Asian, non-Hispanic/Latino; 38 Hispanic/Latino; 1 Native Hawaiian or other Pacific Islander,

non-Hispanic/Latino; 19 Two or more races, non-Hispanic/Latino). Average age 24. 5,003 applicants, 7% accepted, 146 enrolled. In 2011, 150 doctorates awarded. *Degree requirements:* For doctorate, U.S. Medical Licensing Examination Steps 1 and 2. *Entrance requirements:* For doctorate, MCAT, at least one full-year of undergraduate education in the United States or Canada. Additional exam requirements/ recommendations for international students: Required—TOEFL (minimum score 600 paper-based; 100 iBT), IELTS. *Application deadline:* For fall admission, 10/15 for domestic students. Applications are processed on a rolling basis. Application fee: $85. Electronic applications accepted. *Expenses:* Contact institution. *Financial support:* In 2011–12, 396 students received support. Institutionally sponsored loans and scholarships/grants available. Financial award application deadline: 4/15; financial award applicants required to submit FAFSA. *Faculty research:* Drug discovery and vaccine development; regenerative medicine; artificial organ and medical device development; psychiatry and neuroscience; structural, computational and developmental biology. *Total annual research expenditures:* $539.8 million. *Unit head:* Dr. Beth Piraino, Associate Dean, 412-648-9891, Fax: 412-648-8768, E-mail: admissions@medschool.pitt.edu. *Application contact:* Cynthia May Bonetti, Executive Director for Admissions and Financial Aid, 412-648-9891, Fax: 412-648-8768, E-mail: admissions@medschool.pitt.edu. Web site: http://www.medschool.pitt.edu/.

University of Puerto Rico, Medical Sciences Campus, School of Medicine, Professional Program in Medicine, San Juan, PR 00936-5067. Offers MD. *Accreditation:* LCME/AMA. *Degree requirements:* For doctorate, one foreign language. *Entrance requirements:* For doctorate, MCAT, minimum GPA of 2.5, computer literacy.

University of Rochester, School of Medicine and Dentistry, Professional Program in Medicine, Rochester, NY 14627. Offers MD, MD/MPH, MD/MS, MD/PhD. *Accreditation:* LCME/AMA. *Entrance requirements:* For doctorate, MCAT. *Expenses: Tuition:* Full-time $41,040.

University of Saskatchewan, College of Medicine, Professional Program in Medicine, Saskatoon, SK S7N 5A2, Canada. Offers MD. *Accreditation:* LCME/AMA.

University of South Alabama, College of Medicine, Professional Program in Medicine, Mobile, AL 36688. Offers MD, MD/PhD. *Accreditation:* LCME/AMA. *Faculty:* 45 full-time (10 women), 1 part-time/adjunct (0 women). *Students:* 303 full-time (137 women); includes 42 minority (16 Black or African American, non-Hispanic/Latino; 1 American Indian or Alaska Native, non-Hispanic/Latino; 22 Asian, non-Hispanic/Latino; 3 Native Hawaiian or other Pacific Islander, non-Hispanic/Latino). In 2011, 69 doctorates awarded. *Entrance requirements:* For doctorate, MCAT. Additional exam requirements/ recommendations for international students: Required—TOEFL (minimum score 173 computer-based). *Application deadline:* For fall admission, 11/15 for domestic and international students. Application fee: $75. Electronic applications accepted. *Expenses:* Tuition, state resident: full-time $7968; part-time $332 per credit hour. Tuition, nonresident: full-time $15,936; part-time $664 per credit hour. *Financial support:* Scholarships/grants available. Financial award applicants required to submit FAFSA. *Unit head:* Mark Scott, Dean, USA College of Medicine, 251-460-7176, E-mail: mscott@usouthal.edu. *Application contact:* Peggy Terrell, Academic Advisor/Director of Admissions, 251-460-7176, Fax: 251-461-1513, E-mail: mscott@usouthal.edu.

University of South Carolina, School of Medicine, Professional Program in Medicine, Columbia, SC 29208. Offers MD, MD/MPH, MD/PhD. *Accreditation:* LCME/AMA. *Entrance requirements:* For doctorate, MCAT. Electronic applications accepted. *Faculty research:* Cardiovascular diseases, oncology, reproductive biology, vision, neuroscience.

The University of South Dakota, Graduate School, School of Medicine, Professional Program in Medicine, Vermillion, SD 57069-2390. Offers MD. *Accreditation:* LCME/AMA. *Degree requirements:* For doctorate, U.S. Medical Licensing Exam-Step 1 & 2, CK OSCE. *Entrance requirements:* For doctorate, MCAT, previous course work in biology, chemistry, organic chemistry, mathematics and physics. Electronic applications accepted. *Expenses:* Tuition, state resident: full-time $3118.50; part-time $173.25 per credit hour. Tuition, nonresident: full-time $6601; part-time $366.70 per credit hour. *Required fees:* $2268; $126 per credit hour. Tuition and fees vary according to program.

University of Southern California, Keck School of Medicine, Professional Program in Medicine, Los Angeles, CA 90089. Offers MD, MD/MBA, MD/MPH, MD/PhD. *Accreditation:* LCME/AMA. *Faculty:* 1,396 full-time (537 women), 173 part-time/adjunct (85 women). *Students:* 701 full-time (340 women); includes 352 minority (30 Black or African American, non-Hispanic/Latino; 2 American Indian or Alaska Native, non-Hispanic/Latino; 185 Asian, non-Hispanic/Latino; 89 Hispanic/Latino; 4 Native Hawaiian or other Pacific Islander, non-Hispanic/Latino; 42 Two or more races, non-Hispanic/Latino), 10 international. Average age 24. 6,737 applicants, 5% accepted, 180 enrolled. In 2011, 162 doctorates awarded. *Entrance requirements:* For doctorate, MCAT, 2 semesters or 3 quarters of course work in biology, chemistry, organic chemistry, physics (all with lab); 1 course in molecular biology; 30 units of course work in social sciences. *Application deadline:* For fall admission, 11/1 for domestic and international students. Applications are processed on a rolling basis. Application fee: $90. Electronic applications accepted. *Expenses:* Contact institution. *Financial support:* In 2011–12, 148 students received support, including 7 research assistantships (averaging $22,000 per year); institutionally sponsored loans and scholarships/grants also available. Financial award application deadline: 4/15; financial award applicants required to submit FAFSA. *Unit head:* Dr. Raquel Arias, Interim Associate Dean for Admissions/Associate Dean for Educational Affairs, 323-442-2552, Fax: 323-442-2433, E-mail: medadmit@usc.edu. *Application contact:* Director of Admissions, 323-442-2552, Fax: 323-442-2433, E-mail: medadmit@usc.edu. Web site: http://keck.usc.edu/.

University of South Florida, Graduate School, College of Medicine, Tampa, FL 33620-9951. Offers MABMH, MS, MSB, MSBCB, MSMS, DPT, MD, PhD. *Accreditation:* LCME/AMA. Part-time programs available. *Faculty:* 186 full-time (57 women), 56 part-time/adjunct (16 women). *Students:* 533 full-time (310 women), 613 part-time (302 women); includes 485 minority (121 Black or African American, non-Hispanic/Latino; 7 American Indian or Alaska Native, non-Hispanic/Latino; 206 Asian, non-Hispanic/Latino; 138 Hispanic/Latino; 13 Two or more races, non-Hispanic/Latino), 24 international. Average age 27. 1,209 applicants, 60% accepted, 541 enrolled. In 2011, 167 master's, 158 doctorates awarded. Terminal master's awarded for partial completion of doctoral program. *Degree requirements:* For master's, comprehensive exam, thesis; for doctorate, comprehensive exam (for some programs), thesis/dissertation (for some programs). *Entrance requirements:* Additional exam requirements/recommendations for international students: Required—TOEFL (minimum score 550 paper-based; 213 computer-based). *Application deadline:* For fall admission, 2/15 for domestic students, 1/2 for international students. Application fee: $30. Electronic applications accepted. *Total annual research expenditures:* $4.3 million. *Unit head:* Michael Barber, Director, 813-974-9702, Fax: 813-974-3886, E-mail: mbarber@health.usf.edu. *Application contact:* Francisco Vera, Assistant Director for Admissions, 813-974-8800, E-mail: fvera@usf.edu. Web site: http://health.usf.edu/nocms/medicine/graduatestudies/.

The University of Tennessee Health Science Center, College of Medicine, Memphis, TN 38163-0002. Offers MS, MD, PhD, MD/PhD. *Accreditation:* LCME/AMA. *Entrance requirements:* For doctorate, MCAT (for MD). Electronic applications accepted. *Expenses:* Contact institution.

The University of Texas Health Science Center at Houston, University of Texas Medical School at Houston, Houston, TX 77225-0036. Offers MD, MD/MPH, MD/PhD. *Accreditation:* LCME/AMA. *Entrance requirements:* For doctorate, MCAT. Electronic applications accepted. *Expenses:* Contact institution. *Faculty research:* Stroke, infectious diseases, cardiovascular disease, neoplastic disease (cancer), molecular medicine for the prevention of diseases.

The University of Texas Health Science Center at San Antonio, School of Medicine, San Antonio, TX 78229-3900. Offers MPH, MD. *Accreditation:* LCME/AMA. *Entrance requirements:* For doctorate, MCAT. *Expenses:* Contact institution. *Faculty research:* Geriatrics, diabetes, cancer, AIDS, obesity.

The University of Texas Medical Branch, School of Medicine, Galveston, TX 77555. Offers MD. *Accreditation:* LCME/AMA. *Entrance requirements:* For doctorate, MCAT. *Expenses:* Contact institution.

The University of Texas Southwestern Medical Center, Southwestern Medical School, Dallas, TX 75390. Offers MD, MD/PhD. *Accreditation:* LCME/AMA. *Entrance requirements:* For doctorate, MCAT. Electronic applications accepted. *Expenses:* Contact institution. *Faculty research:* Endocrinology, molecular biology, immunology, cancer biology, neuroscience.

University of Toronto, Faculty of Medicine, Toronto, ON M5S 1A1, Canada. Offers M Sc, M Sc BMC, M Sc OT, M Sc PT, MH Sc, MD, PhD, MD/PhD. *Accreditation:* LCME/AMA. *Entrance requirements:* For doctorate, MCAT (for MD). Electronic applications accepted. *Expenses:* Contact institution.

University of Utah, School of Medicine, MD/PhD Program in Medicine, Salt Lake City, UT 84112-1107. Offers MD/PhD. Part-time programs available. Electronic applications accepted. *Faculty research:* Molecular biology, biochemistry, cell biology, immunology, bioengineering.

University of Utah, School of Medicine, Professional Program in Medicine, Salt Lake City, UT 84112-1107. Offers MD. *Accreditation:* LCME/AMA. *Entrance requirements:* For doctorate, MCAT, 2 years chemistry with lab, 1 year physics with lab, writing/ speech, 2 courses biology, 1 course cell biology or biochemistry, 1 course humanities, 1 course diversity, 1 course social science. Electronic applications accepted. *Expenses:* Contact institution. *Faculty research:* Molecular biology, genetics, immunology, cardiology, endocrinology.

University of Vermont, College of Medicine, Professional Program in Medicine, Burlington, VT 05405. Offers MD, MD/MS, MD/PhD. *Accreditation:* LCME/AMA. *Students:* 443 (226 women); includes 120 minority (10 Black or African American, non-Hispanic/Latino; 59 Asian, non-Hispanic/Latino; 36 Hispanic/Latino; 15 Two or more races, non-Hispanic/Latino), 7 international. 5,860 applicants, 4% accepted, 114 enrolled. In 2011, 112 doctorates awarded. *Entrance requirements:* For doctorate, MCAT. Additional exam requirements/recommendations for international students: Required—TOEFL (minimum score 550 paper-based; 213 computer-based; 80 iBT). *Application deadline:* For fall admission, 11/1 for domestic and international students. Applications are processed on a rolling basis. Application fee: $95. Electronic applications accepted. *Expenses:* Contact institution. *Financial support:* In 2011–12, 340 students received support. Institutionally sponsored loans and scholarships/grants available. Support available to part-time students. Financial award application deadline: 2/28; financial award applicants required to submit FAFSA. *Unit head:* Dr. G. Scott Waterman, Associate Dean for Student Affairs, 802-656-2150, Fax: 802-656-9377. *Application contact:* Janice M. Gallant, Associate Dean for Admissions, 802-656-2150.

University of Virginia, School of Medicine, Charlottesville, VA 22903. Offers MPH, MS, MD, PhD, JD/MPH, MD/PhD. *Accreditation:* LCME/AMA. *Faculty:* 934 full-time (300 women), 79 part-time/adjunct (48 women). *Students:* 951 full-time (446 women), 20 part-time (12 women); includes 298 minority (71 Black or African American, non-Hispanic/ Latino; 3 American Indian or Alaska Native, non-Hispanic/Latino; 128 Asian, non-Hispanic/Latino; 78 Hispanic/Latino; 18 Two or more races, non-Hispanic/Latino), 69 international. Average age 26. 5,296 applicants, 11% accepted, 269 enrolled. In 2011, 44 master's, 182 doctorates awarded. *Entrance requirements:* For doctorate, MCAT (for MD). Additional exam requirements/recommendations for international students: Required—TOEFL. *Application deadline:* Applications are processed on a rolling basis. Application fee: $80. Electronic applications accepted. *Financial support:* Institutionally sponsored loans and scholarships/grants available. Financial award applicants required to submit FAFSA. *Unit head:* Steven T. DeKosky, Vice President and Dean, 434-924-5118, E-mail: slh2m@virginia.edu. *Application contact:* Lesley L. Thomas, Director, Admissions Office, 434-924-5571, Fax: 434-982-2586, E-mail: medsch-adm@virginia.edu. Web site: http://www.med.virginia.edu/schools/medschl.html.

University of Washington, Graduate School, School of Medicine, Professional Program in Medicine, Seattle, WA 98195. Offers MD, MD/MPH, MD/PhD. *Accreditation:* LCME/AMA. *Entrance requirements:* For doctorate, MCAT or GRE, minimum 3 years of college. Electronic applications accepted.

The University of Western Ontario, Faculty of Graduate Studies, Biosciences Division, Department of Family Medicine, London, ON N6A 5B8, Canada. Offers M Cl Sc. *Accreditation:* LCME/AMA. Part-time programs available. Postbaccalaureate distance learning degree programs offered (minimal on-campus study). *Degree requirements:* For master's, thesis. *Entrance requirements:* For master's, medical degree, minimum B average. Additional exam requirements/recommendations for international students: Required—TOEFL. *Faculty research:* Family medicine education, dietary counseling, alcohol problems, palliative care support, multicultural health care.

The University of Western Ontario, Schulich School of Medicine and Dentistry, Professional Program in Medicine, London, ON N6A 5B8, Canada. Offers MD. *Accreditation:* LCME/AMA.

University of Wisconsin–Madison, School of Medicine and Public Health, Professional Program in Medicine, Madison, WI 53705. Offers MD. *Accreditation:* LCME/AMA. *Expenses:* Tuition, state resident: full-time $10,296; part-time $643.51 per credit. Tuition, nonresident: full-time $24,054; part-time $1503.40 per credit. *Required fees:* $70.06 per credit. Tuition and fees vary according to course load, campus/location, program and reciprocity agreements. *Unit head:* Dr. Robert N. Golden, Dean, 608-263-4910, Fax: 608-265-3286, E-mail: rngolden@wisc.edu. *Application contact:* Information Contact, 608-265-6344. Web site: http://www.med.wisc.edu/education/main/100.

Vanderbilt University, School of Medicine, Nashville, TN 37240-1001. Offers MDE, MMP, MPH, MS, MSCI, Au D, DMP, MD, PhD, MD/PhD. *Accreditation:* LCME/AMA (one or more programs are accredited). *Entrance requirements:* For doctorate, MCAT (for MD). Electronic applications accepted. *Expenses:* Contact institution.

Virginia Commonwealth University, Medical College of Virginia-Professional Programs, School of Medicine, Professional Program in Medicine, Richmond, VA 23284-9005. Offers MD, MD/MHA, MD/MPH, MD/PhD. *Accreditation:* LCME/AMA. *Entrance requirements:* For doctorate, MCAT. Electronic applications accepted. *Expenses:* Contact institution.

Wake Forest University, School of Medicine, Professional Program in Medicine, Winston-Salem, NC 27109. Offers MD, MD/MA, MD/MBA, MD/MS, MD/PhD. *Accreditation:* LCME/AMA. *Entrance requirements:* For doctorate, MCAT, 32 hours of

course work in science. Electronic applications accepted. *Faculty research:* Cancer, stroke, infectious diseases, membrane biology, nutrition.

Washington University in St. Louis, School of Medicine, Professional Program in Medicine, St. Louis, MO 63130-4899. Offers MD, MD/MA, MD/MS, MD/PhD. *Accreditation:* LCME/AMA. *Faculty:* 1,773 full-time (564 women), 134 part-time/adjunct (78 women). *Students:* 614 full-time (297 women), 4 part-time (3 women); includes 241 minority (45 Black or African American, non-Hispanic/Latino; 1 American Indian or Alaska Native, non-Hispanic/Latino; 174 Asian, non-Hispanic/Latino; 21 Hispanic/Latino), 11 international. Average age 23. 4,045 applicants, 8% accepted, 121 enrolled. In 2011, 115 doctorates awarded. *Entrance requirements:* For doctorate, MCAT. *Application deadline:* For fall admission, 12/31 for domestic and international students. Applications are processed on a rolling basis. Application fee: $65. Electronic applications accepted. *Expenses:* Contact institution. *Financial support:* Career-related internships or fieldwork and institutionally sponsored loans available. *Unit head:* Dr. Larry Shapiro, Dean, 314-362-6827. *Application contact:* Dr. W. Edwin Dodson, Associate Dean, 314-362-6848, Fax: 314-362-4658, E-mail: wumscoa@msnotes.wustl.edu.

Wayne State University, School of Medicine, Professional Program in Medicine, Detroit, MI 48202. Offers pediatric global health (Certificate); MD/MPH; MD/PhD. *Accreditation:* LCME/AMA. Part-time programs available. *Students:* 1,179 full-time (533 women), 47 part-time (23 women); includes 357 minority (74 Black or African American, non-Hispanic/Latino; 3 American Indian or Alaska Native, non-Hispanic/Latino; 240 Asian, non-Hispanic/Latino; 11 Hispanic/Latino; 11 Native Hawaiian or other Pacific Islander, non-Hispanic/Latino; 18 Two or more races, non-Hispanic/Latino), 63 international. Average age 25. 4,135 applicants, 12% accepted, 310 enrolled. In 2011, 308 doctorates awarded. *Entrance requirements:* For doctorate, MCAT, interview. Additional exam requirements/recommendations for international students: Required—TOEFL (minimum score 600 paper-based; 250 computer-based; 100 iBT); Recommended—TWE (minimum score 6). *Application deadline:* For fall admission, 12/15 for domestic and international students. Application fee: $50. Electronic applications accepted. *Expenses:* Tuition, state resident: part-time $512.85 per credit. Tuition, nonresident: part-time $1132.65 per credit. *Required fees:* $26.60 per credit. $199.65 per semester. Tuition and fees vary according to course load and program. *Financial support:* In 2011–12, 462 students received support. Scholarships/grants available. *Unit head:* Dr. Valerie M. Parisi, Dean, 313-577-7742, E-mail: vparisi@med.wayne.edu. *Application contact:* E-mail: officeofthedean@med.wayne.edu. Web site: http://home.med.wayne.edu/.

West Virginia University, School of Medicine, Professional Program in Medicine, Morgantown, WV 26506. Offers MD, MD/PhD. *Accreditation:* LCME/AMA. *Entrance requirements:* For doctorate, MCAT.

Wright State University, School of Medicine, Professional Program in Medicine, Dayton, OH 45435. Offers MD. *Accreditation:* LCME/AMA. *Entrance requirements:* For doctorate, MCAT.

Yale University, School of Medicine, Professional Program in Medicine, New Haven, CT 06510. Offers MD. *Accreditation:* LCME/AMA. *Degree requirements:* For doctorate, thesis/dissertation. *Entrance requirements:* For doctorate, MCAT. Electronic applications accepted.

Bioethics

Albany Medical College, Alden March Bioethics Institute, Albany, NY 12208. Offers bioethics (MS); clinical ethics (Certificate); clinical ethics consultation (Certificate). Part-time and evening/weekend programs available. Postbaccalaureate distance learning degree programs offered (no on-campus study). *Faculty:* 7 full-time (3 women), 23 part-time/adjunct (13 women). *Students:* 5 full-time (4 women), 38 part-time (27 women); includes 4 minority (3 Black or African American, non-Hispanic/Latino; 1 Asian, non-Hispanic/Latino), 2 international. Average age 40. 29 applicants, 97% accepted, 22 enrolled. In 2011, 12 master's, 2 other advanced degrees awarded. *Degree requirements:* For master's, thesis. *Entrance requirements:* For master's and Certificate, GRE, GMAT, LSAT, or MCAT (if no graduate degree), essay, official transcripts, 2 letters of reference. Additional exam requirements/recommendations for international students: Recommended—TOEFL. *Application deadline:* Applications are processed on a rolling basis. Application fee: $100. Electronic applications accepted. *Expenses:* Contact institution. *Financial support:* In 2011–12, 15 students received support. Scholarships/grants, tuition waivers (full and partial), and employee discounts available. *Faculty research:* Ethics in nanotechnology, ethics in genetics, ethics in transplants, philosophy and bioethics, the states and bioethics. *Total annual research expenditures:* $25,000. *Unit head:* Dr. Bruce D. White, Director, 518-262-6082, Fax: 518-262-6856, E-mail: whiteb@mail.amc.edu. *Application contact:* Hayley A. Dittus-Doria, Coordinator of Graduate Studies, 518-262-2639, Fax: 518-262-6856, E-mail: dittush@mail.amc.edu. Web site: http://www.amc.edu/bioethics.

Boston University, School of Public Health, Health Law, Bioethics and Human Rights Department, Boston, MA 02118. Offers MPH. Part-time and evening/weekend programs available. *Faculty:* 5 full-time, 16 part-time/adjunct. *Students:* 10 full-time (8 women), 8 part-time (all women); includes 5 minority (1 Black or African American, non-Hispanic/Latino; 1 Asian, non-Hispanic/Latino; 1 Hispanic/Latino; 1 Native Hawaiian or other Pacific Islander, non-Hispanic/Latino; 1 Two or more races, non-Hispanic/Latino). Average age 28. 86 applicants, 56% accepted, 9 enrolled. *Entrance requirements:* For master's, GRE, MCAT, LSAT, GMAT, DAT. Additional exam requirements/recommendations for international students: Required—TOEFL (minimum score 600 paper-based; 250 computer-based; 100 iBT) or IELTS (minimum score 6). *Application deadline:* For fall admission, 2/1 priority date for domestic students, 2/1 for international students; for spring admission, 10/15 priority date for domestic students, 10/15 for international students. Applications are processed on a rolling basis. Application fee: $115. Electronic applications accepted. *Expenses: Tuition:* Full-time $40,848; part-time $1276 per credit hour. *Required fees:* $572; $286 per semester. *Financial support:* In 2011–12, 1 fellowship was awarded; career-related internships or fieldwork, Federal Work-Study, institutionally sponsored loans, scholarships/grants, and tuition waivers (partial) also available. Support available to part-time students. Financial award application deadline: 3/1; financial award applicants required to submit FAFSA. *Unit head:* Prof. George Annas, Chair, 617-638-4626, E-mail: hld@bu.edu. *Application contact:* LePhan Quan, Associate Director of Admissions, 617-638-4640, Fax: 617-638-5299, E-mail: asksph@bu.edu. Web site: http://sph.bu.edu.

Case Western Reserve University, Frances Payne Bolton School of Nursing, Nursing/Bioethics Program, Cleveland, OH 44106. Offers MSN/MA. *Application deadline:* For fall admission, 6/1 for domestic and international students; for spring admission, 10/1 for domestic and international students. Applications are processed on a rolling basis. Application fee: $75. *Financial support:* Fellowships, research assistantships, and teaching assistantships available. Financial award application deadline: 6/30; financial award applicants required to submit FAFSA. *Unit head:* Dr. Barbara Daly, Head, 216-368-5994, E-mail: barbara.daly@case.edu. *Application contact:* Donna Hassik, Admissions Coordinator, 216-368-5253, Fax: 216-368-0124, E-mail: dmh7@case.edu. Web site: http://fpb.case.edu/MSN/.

Case Western Reserve University, School of Medicine and School of Graduate Studies, Graduate Programs in Medicine, Department of Bioethics, Cleveland, OH 44106. Offers MA, JD/MA, MA/MD, MA/MPH, MA/PhD, MSN/MA, MSSA/MA. *Entrance requirements:* For master's, GRE General Test or MCAT or MAT or LSAT or GMAT. Additional exam requirements/recommendations for international students: Required—TOEFL (minimum score 550 paper-based). Electronic applications accepted. *Faculty research:* Ethical issues in genetics, conflicts of interest, organ donation, end-of-life decision making, clinical ethics consultation.

Cleveland State University, College of Graduate Studies, College of Liberal Arts and Social Sciences, Department of Philosophy, Cleveland, OH 44115. Offers bioethics (MA, Certificate), including bioethics (MA); philosophy (MA), including philosophy. Part-time and evening/weekend programs available. *Faculty:* 4 full-time (3 women), 2 part-time/adjunct (1 woman). *Students:* 2 full-time (1 woman), 11 part-time (4 women); includes 3 minority (2 Black or African American, non-Hispanic/Latino; 1 Two or more races, non-Hispanic/Latino). Average age 32. 18 applicants, 72% accepted, 6 enrolled. In 2011, 2 master's, 1 other advanced degree awarded. *Degree requirements:* For master's, comprehensive exam, thesis optional. *Entrance requirements:* For master's, BA or BS or equivalent degree with minimum GPA of 2.75. Additional exam requirements/recommendations for international students: Required—TOEFL (minimum score 525 paper-based; 197 computer-based). *Application deadline:* For fall admission, 5/1 priority date for domestic students, 5/1 for international students. Applications are processed on a rolling basis. Application fee: $30. *Expenses:* Tuition, state resident: full-time $6416; part-time $494 per credit hour. Tuition, nonresident: full-time $12,074; part-time $929 per credit hour. *Financial support:* In 2011–12, 6 students received support, including research assistantships with full tuition reimbursements available (averaging $3,480 per year), 6 teaching assistantships with full tuition reimbursements available (averaging $3,480 per year); health care benefits, tuition waivers (full), and unspecified assistantships also available. *Faculty research:* Ethics, history of philosophy, bioethics, social and political philosophy, history of women philosophers. *Unit head:* Dr. Mary Ellen Waithe, Chairperson, 216-687-3900, Fax: 216-523-7482, E-mail: m.waithe@csuohio.edu. *Application contact:* Dr. Giannina Pianalto, Director of Graduate Admissions, 216-687-5599, Fax: 216-687-5400, E-mail: g.pianalto@csuohio.edu. Web site: http://www.csuohio.edu/philosophy/.

Columbia University, School of Continuing Education, Program in Bioethics, New York, NY 10027. Offers MS. Part-time programs available. *Degree requirements:* For master's, thesis. Electronic applications accepted.

Drew University, Caspersen School of Graduate Studies, Program in Medical Humanities, Madison, NJ 07940-1493. Offers MMH, DMH, CMH. Part-time and evening/weekend programs available. *Degree requirements:* For master's, thesis; for doctorate, thesis/dissertation. *Entrance requirements:* For master's and doctorate, transcripts, writing sample, personal statement, recommendations. Additional exam requirements/recommendations for international students: Required—TOEFL (minimum score 585 paper-based; 240 computer-based; 95 iBT), TWE (minimum score 4). *Expenses:* Contact institution. *Faculty research:* Biomedical ethics, medical narrative, history of medicine, medicine and the arts.

Duquesne University, Graduate School of Liberal Arts, Program in Health Care Ethics, Pittsburgh, PA 15282-0001. Offers MA, DHCE, PhD, Certificate. Part-time programs available. Postbaccalaureate distance learning degree programs offered (no on-campus study). *Faculty:* 2 full-time (0 women), 2 part-time/adjunct (both women). *Students:* 47 full-time (26 women), 7 part-time (4 women); includes 8 minority (7 Black or African American, non-Hispanic/Latino; 1 Asian, non-Hispanic/Latino), 13 international. Average age 39. 19 applicants, 84% accepted, 9 enrolled. In 2011, 1 master's, 1 doctorate awarded. Terminal master's awarded for partial completion of doctoral program. *Degree requirements:* For doctorate, 2 foreign languages, comprehensive exam, thesis/dissertation. *Entrance requirements:* For master's, GRE General Test; for doctorate, GRE General Test, master's degree in health care ethics. Additional exam requirements/recommendations for international students: Required—TOEFL. *Application deadline:* For fall admission, 8/1 for domestic students, 5/1 for international students. Applications are processed on a rolling basis. Electronic applications accepted. *Expenses: Tuition:* Full-time $16,596; part-time $922 per credit. *Required fees:* $1584; $88 per credit. Tuition and fees vary according to program. *Financial support:* In 2011–12, 6 research assistantships with full and partial tuition reimbursements (averaging $18,000 per year) were awarded; Federal Work-Study and tuition waivers (full and partial) also available. Support available to part-time students. Financial award application deadline: 5/1. *Unit head:* Dr. Henk ten Have, Director. *Application contact:* Linda L. Rendulic, Assistant to the Dean, 412-396-6400, Fax: 412-396-5265, E-mail: rendulic@duq.edu.

Emory University, Laney Graduate School, Emory Center for Ethics, Atlanta, GA 30322-1100. Offers bioethics (MA). Part-time programs available. *Students:* 14 applicants, 43% accepted, 3 enrolled. *Degree requirements:* For master's, practicum experience, capstone project. *Application deadline:* For fall admission, 3/1 priority date for domestic students, 3/1 for international students. *Expenses: Tuition:* Full-time $34,800. *Required fees:* $1300. *Unit head:* Dr. Paul Root Wolpe, Center Director, 404-727-3150. *Application contact:* Toby Schonfeld, Graduate Program Director, 404-727-1752, E-mail: toby.schonfeld@emory.edu. Web site: http://www.ethics.emory.edu/.

Indiana University–Purdue University Indianapolis, School of Liberal Arts, Department of Philosophy, Indianapolis, IN 46202-2896. Offers American philosophy (Certificate); bioethics (Certificate); philosophy (MA); JD/MA; MD/MA. Part-time programs available. *Faculty:* 13 full-time (2 women), 1 part-time/adjunct (0 women). *Students:* 8 full-time (5 women), 14 part-time (8 women); includes 3 minority (1 Black or African American, non-Hispanic/Latino; 1 Asian, non-Hispanic/Latino; 1 Two or more races, non-Hispanic/Latino). Average age 32. 15 applicants, 47% accepted, 6 enrolled. In 2011, 7 degrees awarded. *Degree requirements:* For master's, thesis optional. *Entrance requirements:* For master's, GRE. Additional exam requirements/

recommendations for international students: Required—TOEFL. *Application deadline:* For fall admission, 3/1 priority date for domestic students, 3/1 for international students; for spring admission, 11/15 for domestic and international students. Applications are processed on a rolling basis. Application fee: $55 ($65 for international students). Electronic applications accepted. *Financial support:* In 2011–12, fellowships (averaging $1,000 per year), teaching assistantships (averaging $4,330 per year) were awarded; research assistantships with full tuition reimbursements also available. Financial award application deadline: 1/15; financial award applicants required to submit FAFSA. *Faculty research:* American philosophy, Peirce bioethics, metaphysics, ethical theory. *Unit head:* Dr. John Tilley, Associate Professor and Chair, 317-274-4690, Fax: 317-278-4579, E-mail: jtilley@iupui.edu. *Application contact:* Dr. Jason Thomas Eberl, Assistant Professor and Graduate Co-Director, 317-278-9239, Fax: 317-278-4579, E-mail: jeberl@iupui.edu. Web site: http://www.iupui.edu/~philosop/.

Instituto Tecnologico de Santo Domingo, Graduate School, Area of Health Sciences, Santo Domingo, Dominican Republic. Offers bioethics (M Bioethics); clinical bioethics (Certificate); clinical nutrition (Certificate); comprehensive health and the adolescent (Certificate); comrehensive adloescent health (MS); health and social security (M Mgmt).

The Johns Hopkins University, Bloomberg School of Public Health, Department of Health Policy and Management, Baltimore, MD 21205-1996. Offers bioethics and policy (PhD); health and public policy (PhD); health care management and leadership (Dr PH); health economics (MHS); health economics and policy (PhD); health finance and management (MHA); health policy (MHS); health services research and policy (PhD). *Accreditation:* CAHME (one or more programs are accredited). Part-time programs available. *Degree requirements:* For master's, thesis (for some programs), internship (for some programs); for doctorate, comprehensive exam, thesis/dissertation, 1 year full-time residency (for some programs), oral and written exams. *Entrance requirements:* For master's, GRE General Test or GMAT, 3 letters of recommendation, curriculum vitae/resume; for doctorate, GRE General Test or GMAT, 3 letters of recommendation, curriculum vitae, transcripts. Additional exam requirements/recommendations for international students: Recommended—TOEFL (minimum score 600 paper-based; 250 computer-based; 100 iBT), IELTS. Electronic applications accepted. *Faculty research:* Quality of care and health outcomes, health care finance and technology, health disparities and vulnerable populations, injury prevention, health policy and health care policy.

Kansas City University of Medicine and Biosciences, College of Biosciences, Kansas City, MO 64106-1453. Offers bioethics (MA); biomedical sciences (MS). Part-time programs available. *Degree requirements:* For master's, comprehensive exam, thesis (for some programs). *Entrance requirements:* For master's, MCAT, GRE.

Loma Linda University, Faculty of Religion, Program in Biomedical and Clinical Ethics, Loma Linda, CA 92350. Offers MA, Certificate. *Degree requirements:* For master's, comprehensive exam, thesis optional. *Entrance requirements:* For master's, GRE General Test, baccalaureate degree. Additional exam requirements/recommendations for international students: Required—TOEFL. Electronic applications accepted.

Loyola Marymount University, College of Liberal Arts, The Bioethics Institute, Program in Bioethics, Los Angeles, CA 90045. Offers MA. Part-time programs available. *Faculty:* 3 full-time (1 woman). *Students:* 3 full-time (0 women), 6 part-time (5 women); includes 2 minority (1 Black or African American, non-Hispanic/Latino; 1 Two or more races, non-Hispanic/Latino), 1 international. Average age 49. In 2011, 10 master's awarded. *Entrance requirements:* For master's, GRE or MAT, personal statement, interview, letters of recommendation. Additional exam requirements/recommendations for international students: Required—TOEFL (minimum score 600 paper-based; 250 computer-based; 100 iBT). *Application deadline:* For fall admission, 3/1 for domestic students; for spring admission, 10/1 for domestic students. Applications are processed on a rolling basis. Application fee: $50. Electronic applications accepted. *Financial support:* In 2011–12, 9 students received support. Scholarships/grants and unspecified assistantships available. Support available to part-time students. Financial award application deadline: 6/1; financial award applicants required to submit FAFSA. *Unit head:* Robert V. Doyle, Program Director, 310-258-2621, E-mail: robert.doyle@lmu.edu. *Application contact:* Chake H. Kouyoumjian, Associate Dean of the Graduate Division, 310-338-2721, E-mail: ckouyoum@lmu.edu. Web site: http://bellarmine.lmu.edu/bioethics.htm.

Loyola University Chicago, Graduate School, Program in Bioethics, Chicago, IL 60660. Offers D Be. Postbaccalaureate distance learning degree programs offered (minimal on-campus study). *Students:* 27 part-time (11 women); includes 2 minority (1 Black or African American, non-Hispanic/Latino; 1 Two or more races, non-Hispanic/Latino), 1 international. Average age 49. 14 applicants, 93% accepted, 12 enrolled. *Entrance requirements:* For doctorate, master's degree in bioethics or health care ethics. *Expenses: Tuition:* Full-time $15,660; part-time $870 per credit hour. *Required fees:* $125 per semester. Tuition and fees vary according to course load and program. *Unit head:* Dr. Samuel Attoh, Dean, 773-508-3459, Fax: 773-508-2460, E-mail: sattoh@luc.edu. *Application contact:* Ron Martin, Assistant Director of Enrollment Management, 312-915-8950, Fax: 312-915-8905, E-mail: gradapp@luc.edu.

Loyola University Chicago, Graduate School, Program in Bioethics and Health Policy, Chicago, IL 60660. Offers Certificate, MD/MA. Postbaccalaureate distance learning degree programs offered (no on-campus study). *Students:* 2 full-time (1 woman), 92 part-time (49 women); includes 11 minority (6 Black or African American, non-Hispanic/Latino; 1 Asian, non-Hispanic/Latino; 2 Hispanic/Latino; 2 Two or more races, non-Hispanic/Latino), 2 international. 43 applicants, 86% accepted, 30 enrolled. *Expenses: Tuition:* Full-time $15,660; part-time $870 per credit hour. *Required fees:* $125 per semester. Tuition and fees vary according to course load and program. *Financial support:* Scholarships/grants available. *Unit head:* Dr. Samuel Attoh, Dean, 773-508-3459, Fax: 773-508-2460, E-mail: sattoh@luc.edu. *Application contact:* Ron Martin, Assistant Director of Enrollment Management, 312-915-8950, Fax: 312-915-8905, E-mail: gradapp@luc.edu.

McGill University, Faculty of Graduate and Postdoctoral Studies, Faculty of Arts, Department of Philosophy, Montréal, QC H3A 2T5, Canada. Offers bioethics (MA); philosophy (PhD).

McGill University, Faculty of Graduate and Postdoctoral Studies, Faculty of Law, Montréal, QC H3A 2T5, Canada. Offers air and space law (LL M, DCL, Graduate Certificate); bioethics (LL M); comparative law (LL M, DCL, Graduate Certificate); law (LL M, DCL). Applications for LL M with specialization in bioethics are made initially through the Biomedical Ethics Unit in the Faculty of Medicine.

McGill University, Faculty of Graduate and Postdoctoral Studies, Faculty of Medicine, Department of Medicine, Montréal, QC H3A 2T5, Canada. Offers experimental medicine (M Sc, PhD), including bioethics (M Sc), experimental medicine.

Medical College of Wisconsin, Graduate School of Biomedical Sciences, Department of Population Health, Program in Bioethics, Milwaukee, WI 53226-0509. Offers MA, Graduate Certificate. Part-time programs available. *Degree requirements:* For master's, thesis. *Entrance requirements:* For master's and Graduate Certificate, GRE, official transcripts, three letters of recommendation. Additional exam requirements/recommendations for international students: Required—TOEFL. *Faculty research:* Ethics committees and consultation, ethics of managed care, discussion of code status by physicians.

Mount Sinai School of Medicine, The Bioethics Program, New York, NY 10029-6504. Offers MS. Program offered jointly with Union Graduate College.

New York University, Graduate School of Arts and Science, Program in Bioethics, New York, NY 10012-1019. Offers MA. Part-time programs available. *Students:* 15 full-time (12 women), 11 part-time (9 women); includes 4 minority (1 Black or African American, non-Hispanic/Latino; 3 Hispanic/Latino), 6 international. Average age 27. 17 applicants, 100% accepted, 8 enrolled. In 2011, 26 master's awarded. *Degree requirements:* For master's, one foreign language. *Entrance requirements:* For master's, GRE General Test. Additional exam requirements/recommendations for international students: Required—TOEFL. *Application deadline:* For fall admission, 5/1 priority date for domestic students, 5/1 for international students; for spring admission, 11/1 priority date for domestic students, 11/1 for international students. Application fee: $90. *Financial support:* Application deadline: 5/1. *Unit head:* Dale Jamieson, Acting Director, 212-992-7999, Fax: 212-995-4157, E-mail: bioethics@nyu.edu. *Application contact:* Zahra Ali, Program Coordinator, 212-992-7999, Fax: 212-995-4157, E-mail: bioethics@nyu.edu.

Rush University, College of Health Sciences, Program in Healthcare Ethics, Chicago, IL 60612-3832. Offers MA, Graduate Certificate. Part-time programs available. *Degree requirements:* For master's, oral presentation of thesis. *Entrance requirements:* For master's, GRE General Test, minimum GPA of 3.0. Electronic applications accepted. *Faculty research:* Daily spirituality in the disease process, training psychiatry residents in spirituality, defining and screening for spiritual struggle.

Saint Louis University, Graduate Education, Center for Health Care Ethics, St. Louis, MO 63103-2097. Offers clinical health care ethics (Certificate); health care ethics (PhD). *Degree requirements:* For doctorate, comprehensive exam, thesis/dissertation. *Entrance requirements:* For doctorate, GRE General Test, master's degree in ethics or a field related to health care, basic competencies in philosophical and applied ethics, transcripts. Additional exam requirements/recommendations for international students: Required—TOEFL (minimum score 525 paper-based; 194 computer-based). Electronic applications accepted. *Faculty research:* Health policy, clinical ethics, research ethics, empirical bioethics, ethics education and assessment.

Trinity International University, Trinity Graduate School, Deerfield, IL 60015-1284. Offers bioethics (MA); communication and culture (MA); counseling psychology (MA); instructional leadership (M Ed); teaching (MA). Part-time and evening/weekend programs available. Postbaccalaureate distance learning degree programs offered (minimal on-campus study). *Degree requirements:* For master's, comprehensive exam. *Entrance requirements:* For master's, GRE General Test or MAT, minimum undergraduate GPA of 3.0. Additional exam requirements/recommendations for international students: Required—TOEFL (minimum score 580 paper-based; 237 computer-based), TWE (minimum score 4). Electronic applications accepted.

Union Graduate College, Center for Bioethics and Clinical Leadership, Schenectady, NY 12308-3107. Offers bioethics (MS); clinical ethics (AC); clinical leadership in health management (MS); health, policy and law (AC). Part-time and evening/weekend programs available. Postbaccalaureate distance learning degree programs offered (minimal on-campus study). *Faculty:* 2 full-time (0 women), 10 part-time/adjunct (7 women). *Students:* 7 full-time (4 women), 92 part-time (52 women); includes 38 minority (6 Black or African American, non-Hispanic/Latino; 26 Asian, non-Hispanic/Latino; 4 Hispanic/Latino; 2 Two or more races, non-Hispanic/Latino), 3 international. Average age 32. 32 applicants, 78% accepted, 21 enrolled. In 2011, 21 master's, 3 other advanced degrees awarded. *Entrance requirements:* For master's, letters of recommendation. Additional exam requirements/recommendations for international students: Required—TOEFL (minimum score 550 paper-based; 213 computer-based). *Application deadline:* Applications are processed on a rolling basis. Application fee: $60. Electronic applications accepted. *Expenses:* Contact institution. *Financial support:* In 2011–12, 10 students received support. Federal Work-Study, scholarships/grants, health care benefits, and tuition waivers (partial) available. Support available to part-time students. Financial award applicants required to submit FAFSA. *Faculty research:* Bioethics education, clinical ethics consultation, research ethics, history of biomedical ethics, international bioethics/research ethics. *Unit head:* Dr. Robert B. Baker, Director, 518-631-9860, Fax: 518-631-9903, E-mail: bakerr@union.edu. *Application contact:* Ann Nolte, Assistant Director, 518-631-9860, Fax: 518-631-9903, E-mail: noltea@uniongraduatecollege.edu.

Université de Montréal, Faculty of Medicine, Programs in Bioethics, Montréal, QC H3C 3J7, Canada. Offers MA, DESS. Electronic applications accepted.

Université de Montréal, Faculty of Theology and Sciences of Religions, Montréal, QC H3C 3J7, Canada. Offers health, spirituality and bioethics (DESS); practical theology (MA, PhD); religious sciences (MA, PhD); theology (MA, D Th, PhD, L Th); theology-Biblical studies (PhD). *Degree requirements:* For master's, one foreign language; for doctorate, 2 foreign languages, thesis/dissertation, general exam. Electronic applications accepted.

University of Pennsylvania, Perelman School of Medicine, Department of Medical Ethics and Health Policy, Philadelphia, PA 19104. Offers MBE, DMD/MBE, JD/MBE, LL M/MBE, MD/MBE, MS Ed/MBE, MSN/MBE, MSW/MBE, PhD/MBE. Part-time and evening/weekend programs available. *Faculty:* 4 full-time (1 woman), 5 part-time/adjunct (3 women). *Students:* 38 full-time (19 women), 120 part-time (73 women); includes 55 minority (15 Black or African American, non-Hispanic/Latino; 18 Asian, non-Hispanic/Latino; 4 Hispanic/Latino; 18 Two or more races, non-Hispanic/Latino), 2 international. Average age 31. 51 applicants, 92% accepted, 46 enrolled. In 2011, 40 master's awarded. *Degree requirements:* For master's, thesis. *Application deadline:* Applications are processed on a rolling basis. Application fee: $70. *Expenses: Tuition:* Full-time $26,660; part-time $4944 per course. *Required fees:* $2318; $291 per course. Tuition and fees vary according to course load, degree level and program. *Unit head:* Dr. Autumn Fiester, Director, 215-573-2602. *Application contact:* Dr. Nora L. Jones, Associate Director, 215-573-4042, Fax: 215-573-3036, E-mail: noralj@mail.med.upenn.edu. Web site: http://www.med.upenn.edu/mbe/.

University of Pittsburgh, Dietrich School of Arts and Sciences, Center for Bioethics and Health Law, Pittsburgh, PA 15213. Offers bioethics (MA). Part-time programs available. *Faculty:* 4 full-time (1 woman), 3 part-time/adjunct (1 woman). *Students:* 2 full-time (0 women), 11 part-time (5 women); includes 1 minority (Asian, non-Hispanic/Latino), 1 international. Average age 35. 11 applicants, 64% accepted, 6 enrolled. In 2011, 1 master's awarded. *Degree requirements:* For master's, thesis. *Entrance requirements:* For master's, GRE General Test, letters of recommendation, writing sample. Additional exam requirements/recommendations for international students: Required—TOEFL. *Application deadline:* For fall admission, 2/1 priority date for domestic students, 6/30 for international students. Applications are processed on a rolling basis. Application fee: $50. Electronic applications accepted. *Expenses:* Tuition, state resident: full-time $18,774; part-time $760 per credit. Tuition, nonresident: full-time $30,736; part-time $1258 per credit. *Required fees:* $740; $200 per term. Tuition and fees vary according to program. *Financial support:* Tuition waivers (partial) available. *Faculty research:* End of life care, ethics and genetics, health law and policy, organ

donation and transplantation, research ethics. *Unit head:* Dr. Lisa S. Parker, Director of Graduate Education, 412-647-5780, Fax: 412-647-5877, E-mail: lisap@pitt.edu. *Application contact:* Janet E. Malis, Administrative Assistant, 412-647-5785, Fax: 412-647-5877, E-mail: bioethic@pitt.edu. Web site: http://www.pitt.edu/~bioethic/.

University of South Florida, Graduate School, College of Medicine and Graduate School, Graduate Programs in Medical Sciences, Tampa, FL 33620-9951. Offers bioethics and medical humanities (MABMH); bioinformatics and computational biology (MSBCB); biotechnology (MSB); medical sciences (MSMS, PhD). *Students:* 439 full-time (235 women), 111 part-time (65 women); includes 258 minority (82 Black or African American, non-Hispanic/Latino; 2 American Indian or Alaska Native, non-Hispanic/Latino; 85 Asian, non-Hispanic/Latino; 77 Hispanic/Latino; 12 Two or more races, non-Hispanic/Latino), 24 international. Average age 27. 1,032 applicants, 53% accepted, 364 enrolled. In 2011, 167 master's, 14 doctorates awarded. Terminal master's awarded for partial completion of doctoral program. *Degree requirements:* For master's, comprehensive exam, thesis; for doctorate, comprehensive exam, thesis/dissertation. *Entrance requirements:* For master's, GRE, MCAT, or GMAT, minimum GPA of 3.0 in last 60 hours of coursework; for doctorate, GRE, minimum GPA of 3.0 in last 60 hours of coursework, three letters of recommendation, personal statement, interview. Additional exam requirements/recommendations for international students: Required—TOEFL (minimum score 550 paper-based; 213 computer-based; 79 iBT) or IELTS (minimum score 6.5). *Application deadline:* For fall admission, 2/15 for domestic students, 1/2 for international students. Application fee: $30. *Expenses:* Contact institution. *Unit head:* Dr. Michael Barber, Program Director, 813-974-9702, Fax: 813-974-4317, E-mail: mbarber@health.usf.edu. *Application contact:* Francisco Vera, Assistant Director for Admissions, 813-974-8800, E-mail: fvera@usf.edu. Web site: http://health.usf.edu/medicine/graduatestudies.

The University of Tennessee, Graduate School, College of Arts and Sciences, Department of Philosophy, Knoxville, TN 37996. Offers medical ethics (MA, PhD); philosophy (MA, PhD); religious studies (MA). Part-time programs available. *Degree requirements:* For master's, thesis or alternative; for doctorate, one foreign language, thesis/dissertation. *Entrance requirements:* For master's and doctorate, GRE General Test, minimum GPA of 2.7. Additional exam requirements/recommendations for international students: Required—TOEFL. Electronic applications accepted. *Expenses:* Tuition, state resident: full-time $8332; part-time $464 per credit hour. Tuition, nonresident: full-time $25,174; part-time $1400 per credit hour. *Required fees:* $1162; $56 per credit hour. Tuition and fees vary according to program.

University of Toronto, Faculty of Medicine, Institute of Medical Science, Toronto, ON M5S 1A1, Canada. Offers bioethics (MH Sc); biomedical communications (M Sc BMC); medical radiation science (MH Sc); medical science (M Sc, PhD). *Degree requirements:* For master's, thesis; for doctorate, thesis/dissertation, thesis defense. *Entrance requirements:* For master's, minimum GPA of 3.7 in 3 of 4 years (M Sc), interview; for doctorate, M Sc or equivalent, defended thesis, minimum A- average, interview. Additional exam requirements/recommendations for international students: Required—TOEFL (minimum score 600 paper-based; 93 iBT), TWE (minimum score 5). Electronic applications accepted.

University of Virginia, College and Graduate School of Arts and Sciences, Center for Biomedical Ethics, Charlottesville, VA 22903. Offers bioethics (MA). *Degree requirements:* For master's, thesis. *Entrance requirements:* For master's, GRE General Test. *Application deadline:* Applications are processed on a rolling basis. Application fee: $60. Electronic applications accepted. *Financial support:* Applicants required to submit FAFSA. *Unit head:* Daniel Becker, Director, 434-924-5974, E-mail: dmb2y@virginia.edu. *Application contact:* Associate Dean of Graduate Programs.

University of Washington, Graduate School, School of Medicine, Graduate Programs in Medicine, Department of Medical History and Ethics, Seattle, WA 98195. Offers bioethics (MA).

Naturopathic Medicine

Bastyr University, School of Naturopathic Medicine, Kenmore, WA 98028-4966. Offers ND. *Accreditation:* CNME; MEAC. Part-time programs available. *Students:* 441 full-time (350 women), 11 part-time (10 women); includes 97 minority (8 Black or African American, non-Hispanic/Latino; 2 American Indian or Alaska Native, non-Hispanic/Latino; 50 Asian, non-Hispanic/Latino; 12 Hispanic/Latino; 1 Native Hawaiian or other Pacific Islander, non-Hispanic/Latino; 24 Two or more races, non-Hispanic/Latino), 27 international. Average age 30. In 2011, 98 doctorates awarded. *Degree requirements:* For doctorate, comprehensive exam. *Entrance requirements:* For doctorate, 1 year of course work in biology, chemistry, organic chemistry and physics. Additional exam requirements/recommendations for international students: Required—TOEFL (minimum score 550 paper-based; 213 computer-based; 79 iBT). *Application deadline:* For fall admission, 2/1 priority date for domestic students, 2/1 for international students. Applications are processed on a rolling basis. Application fee: $75. Electronic applications accepted. *Expenses: Tuition:* Full-time $27,653; part-time $6440 per quarter. *Required fees:* $75; $75. One-time fee: $375. Tuition and fees vary according to course load, degree level, program and student level. *Financial support:* In 2011–12, 252 students received support, including 6 research assistantships (averaging $2,500 per year), 122 teaching assistantships (averaging $2,000 per year); career-related internships or fieldwork, Federal Work-Study, and scholarships/grants also available. Support available to part-time students. Financial award application deadline: 4/15; financial award applicants required to submit FAFSA. *Faculty research:* Integrative oncology, integrative care for neurodegenerative diseases, vitamin D supplementation, sauna (hyperthermia-based) detoxification, intranasal glutathione (nasal spray) for Parkinson's disease. *Unit head:* Dr. Jane Guiltinan, Dean, 425-823-1300, Fax: 425-823-6222. *Application contact:* Alexis Rush, Associate Director of Admissions, 425-602-3330, Fax: 425-602-3090, E-mail: ndadvise@bastyr.edu. Web site: http://www.bastyr.edu/academics/areas-study/study-naturopathic-medicine/.

Canadian College of Naturopathic Medicine, Doctor of Naturopathic Medicine Program, Toronto, ON M2K 1E2, Canada. Offers ND. *Accreditation:* CNME. *Entrance requirements:* Additional exam requirements/recommendations for international students: Recommended—TOEFL (minimum score 580 paper-based; 257 computer-based). *Faculty research:* Natural health products for lung cancer: a series of 10 systematic reviews, the use of habanero chili pepper for cancer: a systematic review, melatonin as an anticancer agent with and without chemotherapy: systematic review and meta-analysis, interactions between natural health products and pharmaceuticals: a systematic review, the use of selenium for patients with HIV/AIDS: a systematic review and meta-analysis.

See Display on next page and Close-Up on page 909.

National College of Natural Medicine, School of Naturopathic Medicine, Portland, OR 97201. Offers integrative medicine research (MS); naturopathic medicine (ND). *Accreditation:* CNME. *Faculty:* 22 full-time (10 women), 59 part-time/adjunct (40 women). *Students:* 447. Average age 28. *Entrance requirements:* For master's, GRE. Additional exam requirements/recommendations for international students: Recommended—TOEFL. *Application deadline:* For fall admission, 11/1 priority date for domestic students, 11/1 for international students; for winter admission, 2/1 priority date for domestic students, 2/1 for international students. Applications are processed on a rolling basis. Application fee: $75. *Expenses: Tuition:* Full-time $24,795; part-time $375 per credit. *Financial support:* Federal Work-Study and scholarships/grants available. Financial award application deadline: 4/30; financial award applicants required to submit FAFSA. *Faculty research:* Diet and diabetes, whole practice research, cruciferous vegetables and cancer, natural medicine and immune function, taraxacum and diuretics. *Total annual research expenditures:* $375,000. *Unit head:* Dr. Margot Longenecker, Dean, 503-552-1697, Fax: 503-499-0022, E-mail: mlongenecker@ncnm.edu. *Application contact:* Hang Nguyen, Admissions Coordinator, 503-552-1660, Fax: 503-499-0027, E-mail: admissions@ncnm.edu.

National University of Health Sciences, College of Professional Studies, Lombard, IL 60148-4583. Offers acupuncture (MSAC); chiropractic medicine (DC); naturopathic medicine (ND); Oriental medicine (MSOM). *Accreditation:* CCE. *Degree requirements:* For master's and doctorate, comprehensive exam, internship, community service. *Entrance requirements:* For master's, bachelor's degree, character references, undergraduate transcripts; for doctorate, bachelor's degree, character references, undergraduate transcripts, written essay. Additional exam requirements/recommendations for international students: Required—TOEFL (minimum score 550 paper-based; 79 iBT). Electronic applications accepted. *Faculty research:* Discipline/whole practice research (including practice-based research networks), mechanisms of action, clinical trials, and evidence-based practice of CAM therapies; educational research in CAM teaching institutions.

Southwest College of Naturopathic Medicine and Health Sciences, Program in Naturopathic Medicine, Tempe, AZ 85282. Offers ND. *Accreditation:* CNME. *Faculty:* 30 full-time (18 women), 58 part-time/adjunct (40 women). *Students:* 370 full-time (271 women), 13 part-time (12 women); includes 130 minority (47 Black or African American, non-Hispanic/Latino; 22 Asian, non-Hispanic/Latino; 38 Hispanic/Latino; 6 Native Hawaiian or other Pacific Islander, non-Hispanic/Latino; 17 Two or more races, non-Hispanic/Latino), 23 international. Average age 31. 191 applicants, 72% accepted, 85 enrolled. In 2011, 69 doctorates awarded. *Entrance requirements:* For doctorate, minimum GPA of 3.0, letters of recommendation. Additional exam requirements/recommendations for international students: Required—TOEFL or IELTS. *Application deadline:* For fall admission, 2/1 priority date for domestic students; for spring admission, 11/1 priority date for domestic students. Applications are processed on a rolling basis. Application fee: $65 ($90 for international students). *Expenses: Tuition:* Full-time $25,460; part-time $268 per credit. *Required fees:* $22 per quarter. One-time fee: $815. Tuition and fees vary according to course load and student level. *Financial support:* Federal Work-Study and scholarships/grants available. Support available to part-time students. Financial award application deadline: 7/1; financial award applicants required to submit FAFSA. *Faculty research:* Autism, environmental toxicology, microbial infection, diabetes, homeopathy. *Unit head:* Dr. Christine Girard, Executive Vice President of Academic and Clinical Affairs, 480-858-9100 Ext. 241, E-mail: c.girard@scnm.edu. *Application contact:* Eve Bilotas, Assistant Director of Admissions, 480-858-9100 Ext. 213, Fax: 480-222-9413, E-mail: e.bilotas@scnm.edu. Web site: http://www.scnm.edu.

Universidad del Turabo, Graduate Programs, School of Health Sciences, Program in Naturopathy, Gurabo, PR 00778-3030. Offers ND. *Students:* 29 full-time (20 women); includes 24 minority (all Hispanic/Latino). Average age 31. 17 applicants, 82% accepted, 12 enrolled. *Unit head:* David Mendez, Head, 787-743-7979. *Application contact:* Virginia Gonzalez, Admissions Officer, 787-746-3009.

University of Bridgeport, College of Naturopathic Medicine, Bridgeport, CT 06604. Offers ND. *Accreditation:* CNME. *Faculty:* 6 full-time (3 women), 19 part-time/adjunct (7 women). *Students:* 96 full-time (78 women), 4 part-time (all women); includes 40 minority (13 Black or African American, non-Hispanic/Latino; 2 American Indian or Alaska Native, non-Hispanic/Latino; 10 Asian, non-Hispanic/Latino; 8 Hispanic/Latino; 7 Two or more races, non-Hispanic/Latino), 2 international. Average age 32. 140 applicants, 32% accepted, 28 enrolled. In 2011, 15 doctorates awarded. *Degree requirements:* For doctorate, NPLEX Part I. *Entrance requirements:* For doctorate, minimum GPA of 2.5. Additional exam requirements/recommendations for international students: Recommended—TOEFL (minimum score 550 paper-based; 213 computer-based; 80 iBT), IELTS. *Application deadline:* For fall admission, 8/1 priority date for domestic students, 8/1 for international students; for spring admission, 12/1 for domestic students, 2/1 for international students. Applications are processed on a rolling basis. Application fee: $75. Electronic applications accepted. *Expenses: Tuition:* Full-time $22,880; part-time $700 per credit. *Required fees:* $1870; $95 per semester. Tuition and fees vary according to course load and program. *Financial support:* In 2011–12, 80 students received support. Federal Work-Study, institutionally sponsored loans, and scholarships/grants available. Financial award application deadline: 4/1; financial award applicants required to submit FAFSA. *Unit head:* Dr. Elizabeth W. Pimentel, Dean, 203-576-4110, Fax: 203-574-4107, E-mail: gkhalsa@bridgeport.edu. *Application contact:* Leanne Proctor, Director of Health Science Admissions, 203-576-4352, Fax: 203-576-4941, E-mail: natmed@bridgeport.edu.

Osteopathic Medicine

A.T. Still University of Health Sciences, Kirksville College of Osteopathic Medicine, Kirksville, MO 63501. Offers biomedical sciences (MS); osteopathic medicine (DO). *Accreditation:* AOsA. *Faculty:* 43 full-time (9 women), 21 part-time/adjunct (3 women). *Students:* 706 full-time (285 women), 14 part-time (6 women); includes 116 minority (12 Black or African American, non-Hispanic/Latino; 1 American Indian or Alaska Native, non-Hispanic/Latino; 69 Asian, non-Hispanic/Latino; 19 Hispanic/Latino; 15 Two or more races, non-Hispanic/Latino), 12 international. Average age 27. 3,556 applicants, 11% accepted, 172 enrolled. In 2011, 13 master's, 176 doctorates awarded. *Degree requirements:* For master's, thesis; for doctorate, Level 1 and 2 COMLEX-PE and CE exams. *Entrance requirements:* For master's, GRE, MCAT, or DAT, minimum undergraduate GPA of 2.5 (cumulative and science); for doctorate, MCAT, bachelor's degree with minimum GPA of 2.5 (cumulative and science) or 90 semester hours with minimum GPA of 3.5 (cumulative and science) and minimum MCAT score of 28. Additional exam requirements/recommendations for international students: Recommended—TOEFL. *Application deadline:* For fall admission, 2/1 for domestic and international students. Applications are processed on a rolling basis. Application fee: $70. Electronic applications accepted. *Expenses:* Contact institution. *Financial support:* In 2011–12, 192 students received support, including 20 fellowships with full tuition reimbursements available (averaging $16,000 per year); Federal Work-Study and scholarships/grants also available. Financial award application deadline: 5/1; financial award applicants required to submit FAFSA. *Faculty research:* Ion channels controlling neuronal excitability, osteopathic palpatory procedures, gene array studies of pain remediation, thoracic lymphatic pump techniques, animal models of manual medicine, melanoma metastasis, exercise science, orthopedics, practice-based research network, antibiotic resistance, staphylococcus aureus, bacterial virulence and environmental survival. *Total annual research expenditures:* $394,713. *Unit head:* Dr. Margaret Wilson, Dean, 660-626-2354, Fax: 660-626-2080, E-mail: jsuzewits@atsu.edu. *Application contact:* Donna Sparks, Associate Director, Admissions Processing, 660-626-2117, Fax: 660-626-2969, E-mail: admissions@atsu.edu. Web site: http://www.atsu.edu/kcom/.

A.T. Still University of Health Sciences, School of Osteopathic Medicine in Arizona, Mesa, AZ 85206. Offers DO. *Accreditation:* AOsA. *Faculty:* 36 full-time (14 women), 36 part-time/adjunct (10 women). *Students:* 416 full-time (204 women); includes 163 minority (7 Black or African American, non-Hispanic/Latino; 6 American Indian or Alaska Native, non-Hispanic/Latino; 94 Asian, non-Hispanic/Latino; 36 Hispanic/Latino; 2 Native Hawaiian or other Pacific Islander, non-Hispanic/Latino; 18 Two or more races, non-Hispanic/Latino). Average age 28. 3,680 applicants, 7% accepted, 108 enrolled. In 2011, 91 doctorates awarded. *Degree requirements:* For doctorate, Level 1 and 2 COMLEX-PE and CE exams. *Entrance requirements:* For doctorate, MCAT, minimum undergraduate GPA of 2.5 (cumulative and science) with bachelor's degree. *Application deadline:* For fall admission, 3/1 for domestic students. Applications are processed on a rolling basis. Application fee: $70. Electronic applications accepted. *Financial support:* In 2011–12, 26 students received support, including 1 fellowship; Federal Work-Study and scholarships/grants also available. Financial award application deadline: 5/1; financial award applicants required to submit FAFSA. *Faculty research:* Medical education research, osteopathic medicine research, practice-based research network. *Total annual research expenditures:* $307. *Unit head:* Dr. Thomas McWilliams, Interim Dean, 480-219-6000, Fax: 480-219-6110, E-mail: tmcwilliams@atsu.edu. *Application*

contact: Donna Sparks, Associate Director for Admissions, 660-626-2117, Fax: 660-626-2969, E-mail: admissions@atsu.edu. Web site: http://www.atsu.edu/soma.

Des Moines University, College of Osteopathic Medicine, Des Moines, IA 50312-4104. Offers DO. *Accreditation:* AOsA. *Degree requirements:* For doctorate, National Board of Osteopathic Medical Examiners Exam Level 1 and 2. *Entrance requirements:* For doctorate, MCAT, minimum GPA of 3.0; 8 hours of course work in biology, chemistry, organic chemistry, and physics; 3 hours of biochemistry; 6 hours of course work in English; interview. Electronic applications accepted. *Expenses:* Contact institution. *Faculty research:* Cardiovascular, infectious disease, cancer immunology, cell signaling nociception.

Edward Via College of Osteopathic Medicine–Virginia Campus, Graduate Program, Blacksburg, VA 24060. Offers DO. *Accreditation:* AOsA. *Faculty:* 67 full-time (23 women), 894 part-time/adjunct (182 women). *Students:* 757 full-time (352 women). Average age 25. *Degree requirements:* For doctorate, thesis/dissertation. *Entrance requirements:* For doctorate, MCAT, 8 hours of biology, general chemistry, and organic chemistry; 6 hours each of additional science and English; minimum overall science GPA of 2.75. *Application deadline:* For fall admission, 2/1 for domestic and international students. Applications are processed on a rolling basis. Application fee: $85. *Expenses: Tuition:* Full-time $37,080. *Required fees:* $830. *Financial support:* Scholarships/grants available. *Faculty research:* Nanobiology of aging, calcium transport regulation, prescription drug abuse, oxidative stress and inflammation, immune protection. *Application contact:* Tyler Corvin, Director of Admissions, 540-231-6138, Fax: 540-231-5252, E-mail: admissions@vcom.vt.edu.

Edward Via College of Osteopathic Medicine–Carolinas Campus, Graduate Program, Spartanburg, SC 29303. Offers DO. *Accreditation:* AOsA. *Faculty:* 67 full-time (23 women), 894 part-time/adjunct (182 women). *Students:* 162 full-time (82 women). *Expenses: Tuition:* Full-time $37,080. *Required fees:* $830. *Application contact:* Mattie Bendall, Director of Admissions, 864-327-9805, Fax: 864-804-6986, E-mail: mbendall@carolinas.vcom.edu.

Georgia Campus–Philadelphia College of Osteopathic Medicine, Program in Osteopathic Medicine, Suwanee, GA 30024. Offers DO. *Accreditation:* AOsA.

Kansas City University of Medicine and Biosciences, College of Osteopathic Medicine, Kansas City, MO 64106-1453. Offers DO, DO/MA, DO/MBA. *Accreditation:* AOsA. *Degree requirements:* For doctorate, comprehensive exam, National Board Exam - COMLEX. *Entrance requirements:* For doctorate, MCAT, on-campus interview. *Faculty research:* 2-Chloroadenine in DNA use in controlling leukemia, dietary isoprenoids role in tumor cell control, preventive medicine and public health research of maternal and child health, nonenzymatic glycosylation in cardiac tissue.

Lake Erie College of Osteopathic Medicine, Professional Programs, Erie, PA 16509-1025. Offers biomedical sciences (Postbaccalaureate Certificate); medical education (MS); osteopathic medicine (DO); pharmacy (Pharm D). *Accreditation:* ACPE; AOsA. *Degree requirements:* For doctorate, comprehensive exam, National Osteopathic Medical Licensing Exam, Levels 1 and 2; for Postbaccalaureate Certificate, comprehensive exam, North American Pharmacist Licensure Examination (NAPLEX). *Entrance requirements:* For doctorate, MCAT, minimum GPA of 3.2, letters of recommendation; for Postbaccalaureate Certificate, PCAT, letters of recommendation, minimum GPA of 3.5. Electronic applications accepted. *Faculty research:* Cardiac

Change the future of health care

There's more to healing and wellness than a prescription or a five-minute consultation. Teaching people how to live well goes a long way towards disease prevention and building a strong, healthy society.

Get excited about being part of a sustainable health-care system in Canada

The Canadian College of Naturopathic Medicine is Canada's premier institute for education and research in naturopathic medicine. CCNM brings new thinking, new research and new approaches to health care, harnessing science to unleash the healing power of nature.

For more information on becoming a naturopathic doctor, visit www.ccnm.edu or call 1-866-241-2266.

ccnm
CANADIAN COLLEGE OF
NATUROPATHIC MEDICINE

smooth and skeletal muscle mechanics, chemotherapeutics and vitamins, osteopathic manipulation.

Lincoln Memorial University, DeBusk College of Osteopathic Medicine, Harrogate, TN 37752-1901. Offers DO. *Accreditation:* AOsA. *Entrance requirements:* For doctorate, MCAT. Additional exam requirements/recommendations for international students: Required—TOEFL (minimum score 600 paper-based; 250 computer-based; 100 iBT).

Michigan State University, College of Osteopathic Medicine, Professional Program in Osteopathic Medicine, East Lansing, MI 48824. Offers DO. *Accreditation:* AOsA. Electronic applications accepted.

Midwestern University, Downers Grove Campus, Chicago College of Osteopathic Medicine, Downers Grove, IL 60515-1235. Offers DO. *Accreditation:* AOsA. *Faculty:* 37 full-time (15 women), 30 part-time/adjunct (11 women). *Students:* 768 full-time (361 women), 2 part-time (both women); includes 210 minority (3 Black or African American, non-Hispanic/Latino; 181 Asian, non-Hispanic/Latino; 9 Hispanic/Latino; 5 Native Hawaiian or other Pacific Islander, non-Hispanic/Latino; 12 Two or more races, non-Hispanic/Latino), 6 international. Average age 26. 5,695 applicants, 8% accepted, 204 enrolled. In 2011, 178 doctorates awarded. *Entrance requirements:* For doctorate, MCAT, 1 year course work each in organic chemistry, general chemistry, biology, physics, and English. *Application deadline:* For fall admission, 1/1 for domestic students. Applications are processed on a rolling basis. Application fee: $50. *Expenses:* Contact institution. *Financial support:* In 2011–12, 568 students received support. Fellowships with partial tuition reimbursements available, career-related internships or fieldwork, Federal Work-Study, institutionally sponsored loans, and tuition waivers (full and partial) available. Financial award application deadline: 6/1; financial award applicants required to submit FAFSA. *Faculty research:* Cadmium toxicity, amino acid transport, metabolic actions of vanadium, diabetes and obesity. *Total annual research expenditures:* $1.2 million. *Unit head:* Dr. Karen J. Nichols, Dean, 630-515-6159, E-mail: knicho@ midwestern.edu. *Application contact:* Michael Laken, Director of Admissions, 630-515-6171, Fax: 630-971-6086, E-mail: admissil@midwestern.edu. Web site: http:// www.midwestern.edu/Programs_and_Admission/IL_Osteopathic_Medicine.html.

Midwestern University, Glendale Campus, Arizona College of Osteopathic Medicine, Glendale, AZ 85308. Offers DO. *Accreditation:* AOsA. *Faculty:* 43 full-time (14 women), 12 part-time/adjunct (5 women). *Students:* 997 full-time (359 women), 13 part-time (4 women); includes 256 minority (5 Black or African American, non-Hispanic/Latino; 1 American Indian or Alaska Native, non-Hispanic/Latino; 191 Asian, non-Hispanic/Latino; 31 Hispanic/Latino; 6 Native Hawaiian or other Pacific Islander, non-Hispanic/Latino; 22 Two or more races, non-Hispanic/Latino), 19 international. Average age 27. 3,746 applicants, 15% accepted, 257 enrolled. In 2011, 135 doctorates awarded. *Entrance requirements:* For doctorate, MCAT. *Application deadline:* For fall admission, 11/1 priority date for domestic students; for winter admission, 2/1 for domestic students. Applications are processed on a rolling basis. Application fee: $50. Electronic applications accepted. *Expenses:* Contact institution. *Financial support:* Fellowships with partial tuition reimbursements, career-related internships or fieldwork, Federal Work-Study, institutionally sponsored loans, and tuition waivers (full and partial) available. Financial award application deadline: 6/12; financial award applicants required to submit FAFSA. *Unit head:* Dr. Lori Kemper, Dean, 623-572-3202. *Application contact:* James Walter, Director of Admissions, 888-247-9277, Fax: 623-572-3229, E-mail: admissaz@midwestern.edu.

New York Institute of Technology, New York College of Osteopathic Medicine, Old Westbury, NY 11568-8000. Offers DO, DO/MBA, DO/MS. *Accreditation:* AOsA. *Students:* 1,186 full-time (625 women); includes 524 minority (63 Black or African American, non-Hispanic/Latino; 392 Asian, non-Hispanic/Latino; 67 Hispanic/Latino; 1 Native Hawaiian or other Pacific Islander, non-Hispanic/Latino; 1 Two or more races, non-Hispanic/Latino). Average age 27. In 2011, 265 doctorates awarded. *Degree requirements:* For doctorate, comprehensive exam. *Entrance requirements:* For doctorate, MCAT, 6 hours of course work in biology, English, general chemistry, organic chemistry, and physics; minimum GPA of 2.75. *Application deadline:* For fall admission, 2/1 for domestic students. Application fee: $60. *Expenses:* Contact institution. *Financial support:* Fellowships with partial tuition reimbursements and tuition waivers (full and partial) available. Financial award application deadline: 4/1; financial award applicants required to submit FAFSA. *Faculty research:* Osteopathic manipulation therapy, paleodiet of fossil horses, effect of OMT on range motion of arthritic knee, osteopathic treatment of muscle with compromised innervation, cycling smooth muscle crossbridges as substrates for myosin light chain kinase and phosphatase. *Unit head:* Dr. Thomas Scandalis, Dean, 516-686-3722, Fax: 516-686-3830, E-mail: tscandal@nyit.edu. *Application contact:* Rodika Zaika, Director of NYCOM Admissions, 516-686-3792, Fax: 516-686-3831, E-mail: rzaika@nyit.edu. Web site: http://www.nyit.edu/nycom/.

Nova Southeastern University, Health Professions Division, College of Osteopathic Medicine, Fort Lauderdale, FL 33314-7796. Offers biomedical informatics (MS, Graduate Certificate), including biomedical informatics (MS), clinical informatics (Graduate Certificate); public health informatics (Graduate Certificate); disaster and emergency preparedness (MS); osteopathic medicine (DO); public health (MPH). *Accreditation:* AOsA. *Faculty:* 86 full-time (38 women), 1,072 part-time/adjunct (232 women). *Students:* 952 full-time (377 women), 18 part-time (5 women); includes 323 minority (24 Black or African American, non-Hispanic/Latino; 2 American Indian or Alaska Native, non-Hispanic/Latino; 175 Asian, non-Hispanic/Latino; 91 Hispanic/Latino; 31 Native Hawaiian or other Pacific Islander, non-Hispanic/Latino), 22 international. Average age 28. 3,628 applicants, 17% accepted, 241 enrolled. In 2011, 75 master's, 213 doctorates awarded. *Entrance requirements:* For master's, GRE, licensed healthcare professional or GRE; for doctorate, MCAT, biology, chemistry, organic chemistry, physics (all with labs), and English. *Application deadline:* For fall admission, 1/15 for domestic students. Applications are processed on a rolling basis. Application fee: $50. Electronic applications accepted. *Expenses:* Contact institution. *Financial support:* In 2011–12, 80 students received support, including 6 fellowships with full tuition reimbursements available (averaging $40,000 per year); research assistantships, teaching assistantships, career-related internships or fieldwork, Federal Work-Study, institutionally sponsored loans, and scholarships/grants also available. Financial award application deadline: 6/1; financial award applicants required to submit FAFSA. *Faculty research:* Teaching strategies, simulated patient use, HIV-AIDS education, minority health issues, managed care education. *Unit head:* Dr. Anthony J. Silavgni, Dean, 954-262-1407, E-mail: silvagni@hpd.nova.edu. *Application contact:* Anastasia Leveille, College of Medicine Admissions Counselor, 866-817-4068. Web site: http://www.medicine.nova.edu/.

Ohio University, Heritage College of Osteopathic Medicine, Athens, OH 45701-2979. Offers DO, DO/MA, DO/MBA, DO/MHA, DO/MS, DO/PhD. *Accreditation:* AOsA. *Degree requirements:* For doctorate, comprehensive exam, thesis/dissertation (for some programs), National Board Exam Parts I and II, COMLEX-PE. *Entrance requirements:* For doctorate, MCAT, interview; course work in English, physics, biology, general chemistry, organic chemistry, and behavioral sciences. Electronic applications accepted. *Expenses:* Contact institution. *Faculty research:* Diabetes and cancer research, cardiovascular disease, drug development, biomechanics, international medicine.

Oklahoma State University Center for Health Sciences, College of Osteopathic Medicine, Tulsa, OK 74107-1898. Offers DO, DO/MS, DO/PhD. *Accreditation:* AOsA. *Faculty:* 25 full-time (6 women), 2 part-time/adjunct (1 woman). *Students:* 374 full-time (175 women); includes 101 minority (17 Black or African American, non-Hispanic/Latino; 41 American Indian or Alaska Native, non-Hispanic/Latino; 29 Asian, non-Hispanic/Latino; 14 Hispanic/Latino). Average age 28. 1,860 applicants, 8% accepted, 63 enrolled. In 2011, 89 doctorates awarded. *Entrance requirements:* For doctorate, MCAT (minimum score 21), interview, minimum 90 hours of college course work, minimum GPA of 3.0. Additional exam requirements/recommendations for international students: Required—TOEFL. *Application deadline:* For fall admission, 2/1 for domestic students. Applications are processed on a rolling basis. Application fee: $40. *Financial support:* In 2011–12, 328 students received support. Federal Work-Study, institutionally sponsored loans, scholarships/grants, and tuition waivers available. Financial award application deadline: 3/31; financial award applicants required to submit FAFSA. *Faculty research:* Neuroscience, artificial vision, mechanisms of hormone action, vaccines and immunotherapy, pathogenic free-living amoebae. *Total annual research expenditures:* $1.7 million. *Unit head:* Dr. Kayse Shrum, Provost and Dean, Center for Health Sciences, 918-561-8201, Fax: 918-561-8413, E-mail: lana.rusch@okstate.edu. *Application contact:* Lindsey Kirkpatrick, Assistant Director of Admissions and Recruitment, 800-677-1972, Fax: 918-561-8243, E-mail: lindsey.kirkpatrick@ okstate.edu.

Philadelphia College of Osteopathic Medicine, Graduate and Professional Programs, Program in Osteopathic Medicine, Philadelphia, PA 19131-1694. Offers DO, DO/MBA, DO/MPH, DO/PhD. DO/MBA offered jointly with Saint Joseph's University; DO/MPH with Temple University, DO/PhD with University of the Sciences in Philadelphia. *Accreditation:* AOsA. *Entrance requirements:* For doctorate, MCAT, minimum GPA of 3.2; course work in biology, chemistry, English, and physics. *Faculty research:* Alzheimer's disease, non-human stem cells, inflammatory diseases, pain management, physical activity.

Touro University, Graduate Programs, Vallejo, CA 94592. Offers education (MA); medical health sciences (MS); osteopathic medicine (DO); pharmacy (Pharm D); public health (MPH). *Accreditation:* AOsA; ARC-PA. Part-time and evening/weekend programs available. *Faculty:* 93 full-time (52 women), 55 part-time/adjunct (28 women). *Students:* 1,402 full-time (851 women). 6,914 applicants, 12% accepted, 503 enrolled. *Degree requirements:* For master's, comprehensive exam, thesis; for doctorate, comprehensive exam. *Entrance requirements:* For doctorate, BS/BA. *Application deadline:* For fall admission, 3/15 for domestic students; for winter admission, 12/1 for domestic students. Applications are processed on a rolling basis. Application fee: $100. Electronic applications accepted. *Expenses:* Tuition: Full-time $25,000; part-time $575 per credit. *Required fees:* $250 per year. Tuition and fees vary according to course level, course load, degree level and program. *Financial support:* Fellowships, research assistantships, teaching assistantships, Federal Work-Study, and scholarships/grants available. Support available to part-time students. Financial award applicants required to submit FAFSA. *Faculty research:* Cancer, heart disease. *Application contact:* Steve Davis, Associate Director of Admissions, 707-638-5270, Fax: 707-638-5250, E-mail: steven.davis@tu.edu.

University of Medicine and Dentistry of New Jersey, School of Osteopathic Medicine, Stratford, NJ 08084-1501. Offers DO, DO/MPA, DO/MPH, DO/PhD, JD/DO. *Accreditation:* AOsA. *Entrance requirements:* For doctorate, MCAT. Electronic applications accepted. *Expenses:* Contact institution.

University of New England, College of Osteopathic Medicine, Program in Osteopathic Medicine, Biddeford, ME 04005-9526. Offers DO. *Faculty:* 36 full-time, 19 part-time/adjunct. *Students:* 510 full-time (283 women). In 2011, 113 doctorates awarded. *Entrance requirements:* For doctorate, MCAT, interview. *Application deadline:* For fall admission, 3/1 for domestic students. *Expenses:* Contact institution. *Financial support:* Fellowships, institutionally sponsored loans, and scholarships/grants available. Financial award application deadline: 5/1; financial award applicants required to submit FAFSA. *Unit head:* Dr. Marc Hahn, Interim Dean, 207-602-2340, Fax: 207-878-2434, E-mail: deanunecom@une.edu. *Application contact:* Stacy Gato, Director, Graduate Admissions, 207-221-4225 Ext. 2292, Fax: 207-221-4898, E-mail: gradadmissions@ une.edu.

University of North Texas Health Science Center at Fort Worth, Texas College of Osteopathic Medicine, Fort Worth, TX 76107-2699. Offers osteopathic medicine (DO); physician assistant studies (MPAS); DO/MPH; DO/MS; DO/PhD; MPAS/MPH. DO/MPH offered jointly with University of North Texas. *Accreditation:* AOsA. *Entrance requirements:* For doctorate, MCAT, 1 year course work in each biology, physics and English; 2 years course work in chemistry. Electronic applications accepted. *Faculty research:* Tuberculosis, aging, cardiovascular disease, cancer.

University of Pikeville, School of Osteopathic Medicine, Pikeville, KY 41501. Offers DO. *Accreditation:* AOsA. In 2011, 59 doctorates awarded. *Application deadline:* For fall admission, 2/1 for domestic students. Applications are processed on a rolling basis. *Expenses:* Tuition: Full-time $6000. Tuition and fees vary according to degree level and program. *Financial support:* In 2011–12, 167 students received support, including 3 fellowships (averaging $27,000 per year); scholarships/grants also available. Financial award application deadline: 8/1; financial award applicants required to submit FAFSA. *Faculty research:* Primary care in medically underserved areas. *Unit head:* Dr. John A. Strosnider, Dean, 606-218-5411, Fax: 606-218-8442. *Application contact:* Stephen M. Payson, Associate Dean for Student Affairs, 606-218-5408, Fax: 606-218-5442, E-mail: spayson@pc.edu.

Western University of Health Sciences, College of Osteopathic Medicine of the Pacific, Pomona, CA 91766-1854. Offers DO. *Accreditation:* AOsA. *Faculty:* 59 full-time (16 women), 8 part-time/adjunct (3 women). *Students:* 989 full-time (467 women); includes 417 minority (4 Black or African American, non-Hispanic/Latino; 2 American Indian or Alaska Native, non-Hispanic/Latino; 378 Asian, non-Hispanic/Latino; 29 Hispanic/Latino; 1 Native Hawaiian or other Pacific Islander, non-Hispanic/Latino; 3 Two or more races, non-Hispanic/Latino), 18 international. Average age 27. 5,988 applicants, 10% accepted, 319 enrolled. In 2011, 206 doctorates awarded. *Entrance requirements:* For doctorate, MCAT, minimum GPA of 3.3, interview, letters of recommendation. *Application deadline:* For fall admission, 4/15 for domestic students. Applications are processed on a rolling basis. Application fee: $65. *Financial support:* Fellowships, research assistantships, teaching assistantships, institutionally sponsored loans, scholarships/grants, tuition waivers (full), unspecified assistantships, and veterans educational benefits available. Financial award application deadline: 3/2; financial award applicants required to submit FAFSA. *Unit head:* Dr. Clinton Adams, Dean, 909-469-5423, Fax: 909-469-5535, E-mail: aclinton@westernu.edu. *Application contact:* Susan Hanson, Director of Admissions, 909-469-5329, Fax: 909-469-5570, E-mail: admissions@westernu.edu. Web site: http://www.westernu.edu/xp/edu/comp/ deans_philosophy.xml.

West Virginia School of Osteopathic Medicine, Professional Program, Lewisburg, WV 24901-1196. Offers DO. *Accreditation:* AOsA. *Faculty:* 54 full-time (24 women), 1 part-time/adjunct (0 women). *Students:* 813 full-time (374 women); includes 172 minority (13 Black or African American, non-Hispanic/Latino; 4 American Indian or Alaska Native,

non-Hispanic/Latino; 133 Asian, non-Hispanic/Latino; 22 Hispanic/Latino). Average age 27. 3,520 applicants, 12% accepted, 210 enrolled. In 2011, 192 degrees awarded. *Median time to degree:* Of those who began their doctoral program in fall 2003, 98% received their degree in 8 years or less. *Degree requirements:* For doctorate, comprehensive exam, Comlex Level 1 and 2 (PE and CE). *Entrance requirements:* For doctorate, MCAT, 3 hours of English; 8 hours each of biology, physics, inorganic chemistry, and organic chemistry. *Application deadline:* For fall admission, 2/15 for domestic students. Applications are processed on a rolling basis. Application fee: $80. Electronic applications accepted. *Expenses:* Tuition, state resident: full-time $19,950. Tuition, nonresident: full-time $49,950. *Required fees:* $200. *Financial support:* In 2011–12, 27 students received support, including 10 teaching assistantships with full tuition reimbursements available (averaging $34,950 per year); Federal Work-Study, scholarships/grants, tuition waivers (full), and unspecified assistantships also available. Financial award application deadline: 4/1; financial award applicants required to submit FAFSA. *Faculty research:* Niacin and ischemia reperfusion injury, medial tibia stress syndrome, prevention of ischemia reperfusion injury, the role of ATP depletion in ediating susceptibility to ischemia-induced ventricular fibrillation, dental health in health care, role of homocysteine in ovarian function and female fertility. *Total annual research expenditures:* $201,105. *Unit head:* Dr. Michael D. Adelman, President, 304-645-6295, Fax: 304-645-4859, E-mail: madelman@osteo.wvsom.edu. *Application contact:* Donna S. Varney, Director of Admissions, 304-647-6373, Fax: 304-647-6384, E-mail: dvarney@wvsom.edu.

Podiatric Medicine

Barry University, School of Podiatric Medicine, Podiatric Medicine and Surgery Program, Miami Shores, FL 33161-6695. Offers DPM, DPM/MBA, DPM/MPH. *Accreditation:* APMA. *Entrance requirements:* For doctorate, MCAT, GRE General Test, previous course work in science and English. Additional exam requirements/recommendations for international students: Required—TOEFL. Electronic applications accepted. *Expenses:* Contact institution.

California School of Podiatric Medicine at Samuel Merritt University, Professional Program, Oakland, CA 94609. Offers DPM. *Accreditation:* APMA. *Faculty:* 18 full-time (4 women), 7 part-time/adjunct (1 woman). *Students:* 168 full-time (70 women), 4 part-time (3 women); includes 93 minority (10 Black or African American, non-Hispanic/Latino; 1 American Indian or Alaska Native, non-Hispanic/Latino; 66 Asian, non-Hispanic/Latino; 10 Hispanic/Latino; 6 Two or more races, non-Hispanic/Latino). Average age 27. 375 applicants, 30% accepted, 47 enrolled. In 2011, 35 doctorates awarded. *Entrance requirements:* For doctorate, MCAT (less than 3 years old), at least 90 semester hours of undergraduate course work; 1 year of course work in organic chemistry or biochemistry, inorganic chemistry, physics, biological sciences (all courses must come with a lab), and English/communications. *Application deadline:* For fall admission, 4/1 priority date for domestic students, 4/1 for international students. Applications are processed on a rolling basis. Application fee: $50. *Expenses:* Contact institution. *Financial support:* In 2011–12, 85 students received support. Federal Work-Study, institutionally sponsored loans, and scholarships/grants available. Financial award application deadline: 3/2; financial award applicants required to submit FAFSA. *Faculty research:* Glycation in diabetes and protein dysfunction, lower extremity biomechanics, diabetic wound care, plantar warts among HIV-infected patients, interdisciplinary equity and inclusion issues. *Unit head:* Irma Walker-Adame, Associate Dean for Administrative Affairs, 510-869-8742, E-mail: iadame@samuelmerritt.edu. *Application contact:* Dr. David Tran, Assistant Director of Admission, 510-869-6789, Fax: 510-869-6525, E-mail: dtran@samuelmerritt.edu.

Des Moines University, College of Podiatric Medicine and Surgery, Des Moines, IA 50312-4104. Offers DPM. *Accreditation:* APMA. *Entrance requirements:* For doctorate, MCAT, interview; minimum GPA of 2.5; 1 year of organic chemistry, inorganic chemistry, physics, biology, and English. Electronic applications accepted. *Expenses:* Contact institution. *Faculty research:* Physics of equines, gait analysis.

Midwestern University, Glendale Campus, College of Health Sciences, Arizona Campus, Program in Podiatric Medicine, Glendale, AZ 85308. Offers DPM. *Accreditation:* APMA. *Faculty:* 9 full-time (3 women), 1 part-time/adjunct (0 women). *Students:* 121 full-time (23 women), 1 part-time (0 women); includes 21 minority (2 American Indian or Alaska Native, non-Hispanic/Latino; 9 Asian, non-Hispanic/Latino; 8 Hispanic/Latino; 1 Native Hawaiian or other Pacific Islander, non-Hispanic/Latino; 1 Two or more races, non-Hispanic/Latino), 1 international. Average age 27. 393 applicants, 13% accepted, 30 enrolled. *Entrance requirements:* For doctorate, MCAT or PCAT, 90 semester hours at an accredited college or university, minimum GPA of 2.75. *Application deadline:* For fall admission, 6/1 for domestic students. Applications are processed on a rolling basis. Application fee: $50. *Expenses:* Contact institution. *Unit head:* Jeffrey C. Page, Director, 623-572-3451. *Application contact:* James Walter, Director of Admissions, 888-247-9277, Fax: 623-572-3229, E-mail: admissaz@midwestern.edu.

New York College of Podiatric Medicine, Professional Program, New York, NY 10035. Offers DPM, DPM/MPH. *Accreditation:* APMA. *Degree requirements:* For doctorate, comprehensive exam. *Entrance requirements:* For doctorate, MCAT or DAT, 1 year course work in biology, physics, English, and general and organic chemistry. Additional exam requirements/recommendations for international students: Required—TOEFL.

Ohio College of Podiatric Medicine, Professional Program, Independence, OH 44131. Offers DPM. *Accreditation:* APMA. *Faculty:* 16 full-time (7 women), 9 part-time/adjunct (4 women). *Students:* 426 full-time (172 women), 1 part-time (0 women); includes 115 minority (36 Black or African American, non-Hispanic/Latino; 4 American Indian or Alaska Native, non-Hispanic/Latino; 59 Asian, non-Hispanic/Latino; 16 Hispanic/Latino), 8 international. Average age 27. 468 applicants, 44% accepted, 113 enrolled. In 2011, 105 doctorates awarded. *Entrance requirements:* For doctorate, MCAT, satisfactory course work in biology, chemistry, English and physics. Additional exam requirements/recommendations for international students: Recommended—TOEFL (minimum score 81 iBT). *Application deadline:* For fall admission, 4/1 priority date for domestic students. Applications are processed on a rolling basis. Application fee: $50. Electronic applications accepted. *Expenses: Tuition:* Full-time $31,000; part-time $1550 per semester hour. *Required fees:* $2409; $956 per semester. *Financial support:* In 2011–12, 86 students received support. Career-related internships or fieldwork, Federal Work-Study, institutionally sponsored loans, and scholarships/grants available. Financial award applicants required to submit FAFSA. *Unit head:* Dr. Thomas Melillo, President, 216-231-3300. *Application contact:* Lois Lott, Dean of Student Affairs, 216-231-3300 Ext. 7486, Fax: 216-447-0210, E-mail: llott@ocpm.edu. Web site: http://www.ocpm.edu/

Rosalind Franklin University of Medicine and Science, The Dr. William M. Scholl College of Podiatric Medicine, North Chicago, IL 60064-3095. Offers DPM. *Accreditation:* APMA. *Entrance requirements:* For doctorate, MCAT (or GRE on approval), 12 semester hours of biology; 8 semester hours of inorganic chemistry, organic chemistry and physics; 6 semester hours of English. Additional exam requirements/recommendations for international students: Required—TOEFL.

Temple University, Health Sciences Center, School of Podiatric Medicine, Philadelphia, PA 19107-2496. Offers DPM, DPM/MBA, DPM/PhD. DPM/PhD offered jointly with Drexel University, University of Pennsylvania. *Accreditation:* APMA. *Degree requirements:* For doctorate, National Board Exam. *Entrance requirements:* For doctorate, MCAT, GRE, or DAT, interview, 8 hours of organic chemistry, inorganic chemistry, physics, biology. *Expenses: Tuition,* state resident: full-time $12,366; part-time $687 per credit hour. Tuition, nonresident: full-time $17,298; part-time $961 per credit hour. *Required fees:* $590; $213 per year. *Faculty research:* Gait analysis, infectious diseases, diabetic neuropathy, peripheral vascular disease.

THE CANADIAN COLLEGE OF NATUROPATHIC MEDICINE

Doctor of Naturopathic Medicine Program

Programs of Study

The Canadian College of Naturopathic Medicine (CCNM) is Canada's premier institute for education and research in naturopathic medicine. Naturopathic doctors are highly educated primary-care providers who integrate standard medical diagnostics with a broad range of natural therapies. CCNM offers a rigorous four-year, full-time Doctor of Naturopathic Medicine (N.D.) program. CCNM is also home to the Robert Schad Naturopathic Clinic, a dynamic naturopathic teaching clinic where senior clinicians and N.D. supervisors conduct more than 25,000 patient visits per year. CCNM's intensive four-year program involves more than 4,200 hours (classroom and clinic) and is accredited by the Council on Naturopathic Medical Education (CNME), which is the North American accrediting agency for naturopathic programs recognized by the U.S. Department of Education. CCNM is a member of the Association of Accredited Naturopathic Medical Colleges.

The N.D. curriculum involves three major areas of study: basic sciences, clinical sciences, and naturopathic disciplines. Students take courses in the basic sciences of anatomy, histopathology, physiology, biochemistry, microbiology, and immunology. Development of problem-solving skills in applied basic life sciences is achieved through lectures, case discussion, tutorial groups, and clinical simulations. Some of these courses have a laboratory component. Laboratory resources include diagnostic test kits and access to human cadavers for gross anatomy study. A variety of audiovisual resources are also available.

Clinical science disciplines include physical and clinical diagnosis, differential and laboratory diagnosis, advanced imaging, physical assessment, health psychology, primary care, and pathology. The principles and philosophy of naturopathic medicine form the bridgework between the academic and clinical parts of the curriculum. Six major disciplines define the areas of naturopathic practice: acupuncture/traditional Chinese medicine (TCM), botanical medicine, physical medicine (massage, hydrotherapy, etc.), clinical nutrition, homeopathic medicine, and lifestyle counseling.

Research Facilities

CCNM has collaborated with many major medical research institutions, including McMaster University, University of Oxford, the Hospital for Sick Children, the University of Toronto, the Ottawa Regional Cancer Centre, the Ottawa General Hospital, the Centre for Addiction and Mental Health, the Mayo Clinic, and the Johns Hopkins University, to advance the state of knowledge in naturopathic medicine. Researchers from CCNM have published numerous systematic reviews and research articles on naturopathic therapies in a wide variety of peer-reviewed journals, including *BMJ, JAMA, Lancet Oncology, the Archives of Internal Medicine,* and *PloS One*. CCNM is a leader in the conduct of clinical trials investigating naturopathic medical approaches for the diagnosis and treatment of disease, including studies on melatonin for non-small-cell lung cancer, cinnamon for type 2 diabetes, and naturopathic interventions for chronic low-back pain, anxiety, rotator cuff dysfunction, and risk for cardiovascular disease. The Scientific Review Board and Research Ethics Board at CCNM provide expert review on the conduct of research in complementary and alternative medicines.

CCNM's Ottawa Integrative Cancer Centre (OICC), which opened in 2011, is a model multidisciplinary flagship centre providing whole-person integrative care to people with cancer, cancer survivors, and those seeking both primary and secondary cancer prevention. The OICC is the first integrative oncology and research centre in Eastern Canada to provide care, advocacy, and education for the use of whole-person care to the cancer community and health-care practitioners, regionally and nationally.

The Learning Resources Centre houses more than 11,000 resources on naturopathic and complementary health care. CCNM's Department of Research and Clinical Epidemiology is advancing the state of medicine through a better understanding of complementary and alternative medical science. Research department faculty members educate students in their first years in epidemiology, encouraging them to investigate evidence-based medicine throughout their years at the college and to consider a research project of their own. This commitment to evidence-based medicine cultivates research initiatives within the CCNM community, including student and faculty initiatives, through teaching, experiential learning, and mentorship. By fostering this culture of research, CCNM has become a leader in naturopathic and complementary medicine worldwide, investigating topics that not only improve naturopathic treatment practices but also have widespread relevance and international impact.

Financial Aid

Canadian students enrolled in the Doctor of Naturopathic Medicine program may be eligible for federal and provincial financial assistance. Students must apply in their province of residence and submit a new loan application each year. Students should apply as early as possible. For more information, students can contact their provincial loan office or Student Services. Students may also be eligible for scholarships and bursaries and should contact Student Services for more information.

American students attending CCNM may be eligible for U.S.-based financial assistance such as unsubsidized Direct Loans.

Bank loans through the Canadian Imperial Bank of Commerce (CIBC) are another possibility. Students enrolled in the N.D. program at CCNM can apply for a professional line of credit without the need of a co-signatory. The four-year program limit is Can$140,000. (Note: This information was correct at the time of publication. As policies at financial institutions are subject to change, students should contact their institution of choice to confirm details).

Cost of Study

In-state and out-of-state tuition for the 2012–13 academic year is Can$20,100; international tuition is Can$21,990. Books, materials, and miscellaneous expenses cost approximately Can$1500–$3000.

Living and Housing Costs

On-campus residence is $475 per month.

Student Group

Currently, over 550 students are enrolled at CCNM. Students come from every province in Canada; with significant numbers from the United States and abroad. The ratio of women to men at CCNM is approximately 4:1. Student ages range from 20 to 50 years and older.

Student Outcomes

Upon graduation, many naturopathic doctors open their own practice. CCNM graduates are building successful practices throughout North America, including remote areas. Some graduates, however, choose to partner with existing naturopathic practices, multidisciplinary clinics, wellness centres, fitness centres, spas, or corporate wellness programs. Many naturopathic doctors conduct special lectures and workshops, represent natural health product companies as spokespeople, develop natural health products, and perform medical and scientific research.

Location

CCNM's 4.43-acre, 176,000-square-foot campus is conveniently located in Toronto's North York region at the Leslie subway station. It is also close to major highways. Toronto is Canada's largest city, with a population of 4.4 million. Toronto is well maintained, with excellent public transportation and comparatively low living costs. Rated the safest large North American city, Toronto is a welcoming multicultural mosaic. Toronto offers students a wealth of entertainment, leisure, and cultural activities. Whether tastes lead to exotic cuisines, multicultural festivals, sports events, or the theatre district, there is always something to capture interest in Toronto.

The College

Naturopathic medical education began in Canada in 1978 with the founding of the Ontario College of Naturopathic Medicine in Toronto. In 1992, the college became the Canadian College of Naturopathic Medicine to better reflect its mandate to educate students from across Canada.

Applying

CCNM is committed to excellence in naturopathic education and to the success of its graduates. All candidates for admission are evaluated based on their academic history and personal interview, as well as their motivation for becoming a naturopathic doctor, leadership skills, problem-solving and critical-thinking skills, and specific personal qualities and characteristics. The admission decision is based primarily on the applicant's undergraduate grade point average, but additional criteria may include the applicant's academic history, essay, references, autobiographical sketch, and interview. Historically, the average cumulative GPA of accepted students has been 3.3 on a 4.0 scale, encompassing a range of 2.7 to 4.0

Applicants must have completed a baccalaureate degree. Prerequisite courses include biology, organic chemistry, psychology, physiology, and humanities, as well as recommended courses in anatomy, environmental science, microbiology, physics, sociology, and statistics.

Correspondence and Information

Student Services
The Canadian College of Naturopathic Medicine
1255 Sheppard Avenue East
Toronto, Ontario M2K 1E2
Canada
Phone: 416-498-1255 Ext. 245
866-241-2266 Ext. 245 (toll-free)
E-mail: info@ccnm.edu
Web site: http://www.ccnm.edu

The Canadian College of Naturopathic Medicine

THE FACULTY AND THEIR RESEARCH

Nadia Bakir, N.D., FCAH, DHANP; Associate Professor, Clinic Supervisor, and Coordinator, Robert Schad Naturopathic Clinic (RSNC) Homeopathy Shifts. Nadia Bakir designed, developed, and implemented the Homeopathy Specialty Clinic at the Robert Schad Naturopathic Clinic, which is now an integral part of the RSNC curriculum. She has committed herself to updating and improving the College's homeopathic curriculum and coordinates an annual student trip to India to study homeopathy. Bakir believes that maintaining a private practice in addition to her position at CCNM enriches her contribution to students.

Kimberlee Blyden-Taylor, N.D.; Assistant Professor and Clinic Supervisor. Kimberlee Blyden-Taylor supervises fourth-year clinic interns and the RSNC's homeopathic medicine specialty groups. In addition to working within the RSNC, Blyden-Taylor teaches and facilitates group studies for a number of CCNM's academic courses. She is also the founder and director of Redhawk Healing Arts in Toronto, where she runs her private practice.

Jasmine Carino, N.D.; Associate Dean of the Curriculum and Residency Program. Jasmine Carino is a graduate of Laurentian University and CCNM.

Nick De Groot, N.D.; Dean. Nick De Groot is responsible for overseeing the day-to-day operations of the clinic. In addition to monitoring and developing the quality of patient care, De Groot supervises the clinical education of students in every stage of the naturopathic program.

Shehab El-hashemy, M.B.Ch.B, N.D.; Associate Dean of Academic Delivery. Shehab El-hashemy is a graduate of Cairo University (Egypt), Lakehead University, and CCNM.

Chris Habib, N.D.; Chris Habib is a naturopathic doctor who graduated from CCNM in 2010. Prior to this, he completed his Honours Bachelor of Science at the University of Toronto with a double major in life science and psychology. He has previously done research at the Hospital for Sick Kids in the field of diabetes. Habib has given lectures on various health topics, most notably relating to kidney health; shadowed extensively at a cancer treatment clinic; and volunteered in a clinic that focuses on treating patients with HIV/AIDS. He currently holds a position at CCNM as the Research Resident and he also teaches. He has gained extensive clinical experience by treating patients for a year during his clinical internship and was recognized for superior patient management. Since then, Habib has continued to see patients and supervise interns, both at the student clinic and at a community health clinic in Toronto.

Jennifer Hillier, N.D.; Assistant Professor. An enthusiastic member of the clinic faculty, Jennifer Hillier supervises fourth-year interns in their care of patients at the RSNC and at Anishnawbe Health Toronto, an interdisciplinary satellite clinic dedicated to improving the health and well-being of aboriginal people. She works with second- and third-year students in physical and clinical diagnosis tutorials and primary-care analysis. Hillier has a family practice in Mississauga, with a focus on family medicine and traditional Asian therapies. Inspired by inner-city need, she has also established a free HIV clinic in Vancouver, along with a community-based research project investigating the efficacy of alternative medicine in the treatment of HIV.

Hal Huff, N.D., Clinic Faculty and Head Supervisor, Sherbourne Health Centre, Naturopathic HIV/AIDS Clinic. Hal Huff directs the College's HIV/AIDS specialty clinic and frequently lectures on the use of naturopathic medicine for the treatment of HIV and hepatitis C. He participates in several Ontario government-funded initiatives to investigate the use of complementary and alternative medicine to treat HIV/AIDS. Huff also participates in CCNM's institutional review board (IRB), established to set and enforce the ethical standards of CCNM's research activities.

Deborah Kennedy, M.B.A., N.D.; Research Fellow. Deborah Kennedy is a resident naturopathic doctor at the RSNC. Kennedy supervises fourth-year interns at the RSNC and Sherbourne Health Centre satellite clinic, as well as the RSNC second-year clinical rotations in hydrotherapy and massage. She also assists second-year students with their skills development. Kennedy operates a general naturopathic practice from the RSNC.

Afsoun Khalili, N.D.; Clinic Faculty. Afsoun Khalili teaches, observes, and evaluates fourth-year student interns during their clinic shifts, both at the Robert Schad Naturopathic Clinic and the Sherbourne Health Centre. Khalili is the creator and coordinator of Be Your Best Self, an RSNC support-group program that helps clinic patients lose weight and maintain their weight loss with healthy lifestyle habits. In addition, Khalili promotes CCNM's corporate wellness program, delivering presentations explaining the bottom-line benefits of institutionalized health strategies. Khalili maintains a private practice located in the Robert Schad Naturopathic Clinic.

Nellie Pachkovskaja, M.D., Ph.D., CMS; Professor, Clinical Sciences, and Associate Dean, Academics. Dr. Nellie Pachkovskaja designs, develops, reviews, and delivers academic curriculum content, course structure, and program-related learning materials. In addition, Dr. Pachkovskaja monitors the program's overall integration and consistency, prepares timetables and exam schedules, and monitors student academic performance. She acts as an academic liaison between students and faculty members.

Jonathan Prousky, N.D., FRSH; Associate Professor of Clinical Nutrition and Chief Naturopathic Medical Officer. In addition to ensuring the delivery of safe and effective naturopathic medical care, Jonathan Prousky develops clinical curriculum for the N.D. program and coordinates educational activities and operations within the Robert Schad Naturopathic Clinic to ensure the competency of all graduates. He coordinates the monthly grand rounds program and supervises the postgraduate residency program in naturopathic medicine. Prousky has also been published in numerous lay publications and peer-reviewed medical journals.

Paul Saunders, N.D., Ph.D., DHANP, CCH; Adjunct Faculty. After earning a Ph.D. in plant ecology from Duke University, Paul Saunders graduated from the Ontario (now the Canadian) College of Naturopathic Medicine and then earned an additional N.D. diploma at National College of Naturopathic Medicine, Portland, Oregon. Dr. Saunders introduced the practice of peer reviewing during his tenure as editor of the *Canadian Journal of Herbalism* (2000–02). He has participated in numerous conferences, delivered lectures for prominent groups, and been honoured with various awards and distinctions. Dr. Saunders currently teaches botanical medicine, parenteral therapy, venipuncture, and art and practice of naturopathic medicine. He currently runs a private practice in Dundas, Ontario.

Dugald Seely, N.D.; Assistant Professor and Research Fellow. As a research fellow in CCNM's Department of Clinical Epidemiology, Dugald Seely is involved in developing clinical trials and research methodology to assess natural health products and therapies used by naturopathic doctors. He also secures funding for conducting and disseminating research projects at CCNM and in collaboration with other institutions. As Assistant Professor, Seely teaches the principles of research and clinical epidemiology and assists student research initiatives.

Ljubisa Terzic, M.D.; Associate Professor. Ljubisa Terzic practised as a resident neurosurgeon in the University Medical Centre in Sarajevo while completing a postgraduate program in ear, nose, and throat (ENT) and maxillofacial surgery at the University of Zagreb and teaching anatomy and general surgery at the local university. Having relocated to Canada, Dr. Terzic teaches anatomy, embryology, and minor surgical procedures at CCNM. A favourite with students, he has been presented with several teaching awards. Dr. Terzic has authored and coauthored a number of published articles and textbooks.

CURRENT RESEARCH PROJECTS

Clinical trial to assess the effect of melatonin on lung cancer recurrence and mortality. This study was funded by the Lotte and John Hecht Memorial Foundation.

Clinical trial to test the efficacy of cinnamon as an aid in diabetes to reduce blood sugar levels.

Clinical trial to compare the effectiveness of two naturopathic-based treatments on shoulder pain in workers at Canada Post.

When time permits and when funding initiatives dictate, the department is also involved in conducting and publishing secondary research in the form of systematic reviews. Current work in this area includes a comparison of trials that have tested *Panax ginseng* for diabetes from a Western-versus-Eastern medicine perspective, a systematic review of all clinical trials that assess for the effect of melatonin on chemotherapy toxicity, and a systematic review of English and Chinese language studies that assess acupuncture as a treatment aid for poststroke rehabilitation.

Section 29
Optometry and Vision Sciences

This section contains a directory of institutions offering graduate work in optometry and vision sciences. Additional information about programs listed in the directory but not augmented by an in-depth entry may be obtained by writing directly to the dean of a graduate school or chair of a department at the address given in the directory.

In the other guides in this series:
Graduate Programs in the Humanities, Arts & Social Sciences
See *Psychology and Counseling*
Graduate Programs in the Physical Sciences, Mathematics, Agricultural Sciences, the Environment & Natural Resources
See *Physics*

Graduate Programs in Engineering & Applied Sciences
See *Biomedical Engineering* and *Biotechnology*

CONTENTS

Program Directories

Optometry

Ferris State University, Michigan College of Optometry, Big Rapids, MI 49307. Offers OD. *Accreditation:* AOA. *Faculty:* 18 full-time (4 women), 91 part-time/adjunct (32 women). *Students:* 145 full-time (85 women); includes 6 minority (3 Asian, non-Hispanic/Latino; 3 Two or more races, non-Hispanic/Latino), 10 international. Average age 24. 33 applicants, 100% accepted, 28 enrolled. In 2011, 33 doctorates awarded. *Degree requirements:* For doctorate, comprehensive exam, senior research project. *Entrance requirements:* For doctorate, OAT. Additional exam requirements/recommendations for international students: Required—TOEFL (minimum score 500 paper-based; 173 computer-based; 61 iBT). *Application deadline:* For fall admission, 2/1 for domestic and international students. Applications are processed on a rolling basis. Application fee: $30. Electronic applications accepted. *Financial support:* Career-related internships or fieldwork, Federal Work-Study, and scholarships/grants available. Financial award application deadline: 3/15; financial award applicants required to submit FAFSA. *Faculty research:* Corneal reshaping, spatial vision and vision science, reading disabilities, vision development, vision care access. *Unit head:* Dr. Michael Cron, Dean, 231-591-3706, Fax: 231-591-2394, E-mail: cronm@ferris.edu. *Application contact:* Colleen Olson, Assistant to the Associate Dean, 231-591-3703, Fax: 231-591-2394, E-mail: olsonc@ferris.edu. Web site: http://www.ferris.edu/mco/.

Illinois College of Optometry, Professional Program, Chicago, IL 60616-3878. Offers OD. *Accreditation:* AOA. *Entrance requirements:* For doctorate, OAT. Electronic applications accepted. *Faculty research:* Eye disease treatment, binocular vision, cataract development, pediatric vision, genetic eye disease.

Indiana University Bloomington, School of Optometry, Bloomington, IN 47405-3680. Offers MS, OD, PhD. *Accreditation:* AOA (one or more programs are accredited). *Faculty:* 36 full-time (11 women), 7 part-time/adjunct (5 women). *Students:* 327 full-time (196 women), 14 part-time (8 women); includes 46 minority (13 Black or African American, non-Hispanic/Latino; 2 American Indian or Alaska Native, non-Hispanic/Latino; 23 Asian, non-Hispanic/Latino; 4 Hispanic/Latino; 4 Two or more races, non-Hispanic/Latino), 28 international. Average age 25. 401 applicants, 44% accepted, 89 enrolled. In 2011, 79 degrees awarded. Terminal master's awarded for partial completion of doctoral program. *Degree requirements:* For master's, thesis; for doctorate, comprehensive exam, thesis/dissertation. *Entrance requirements:* For master's, GRE, BA in science; for doctorate, GRE; OAT (for OD), BA in science (master's degree preferred). Additional exam requirements/recommendations for international students: Required—TOEFL (minimum score 550 paper-based; 213 computer-based; 80 iBT). *Application deadline:* For fall admission, 1/15 for domestic students; for winter admission, 2/1 for domestic and international students; for spring admission, 9/1 for domestic students. Applications are processed on a rolling basis. Application fee: $55 ($65 for international students). Electronic applications accepted. *Expenses:* Contact institution. *Financial support:* Fellowships with full tuition reimbursements, research assistantships with full tuition reimbursements, Federal Work-Study, institutionally sponsored loans, scholarships/grants, and health care benefits available. Support available to part-time students. Financial award application deadline: 12/1; financial award applicants required to submit FAFSA. *Faculty research:* Corneal physiology, contact lenses, adaptive optics, dry eye, low vision, refractive anomalies, ophthalmic imaging, glaucoma, ocular physiology, infant vision, retinal disease. *Total annual research expenditures:* $5.6 million. *Unit head:* Dr. P. Sarita Soni, Interim Dean, 812-855-4440, Fax: 812-855-8664, E-mail: sonip@indiana.edu. *Application contact:* Patricia Reyes, Associate Director of Student Services, 812-855-1292, Fax: 812-855-4389, E-mail: patreyes@indiana.edu. Web site: http://www.opt.indiana.edu/.

Inter American University of Puerto Rico School of Optometry, Professional Program, Bayamn, PR 00957. Offers OD. *Accreditation:* AOA. *Degree requirements:* For doctorate, thesis/dissertation, research project. *Entrance requirements:* For doctorate, OAT, interview, minimum GPA of 2.5, 2 letters of recommendation. Electronic applications accepted. *Expenses:* Contact institution. *Faculty research:* Visual characteristics of special populations, contact lenses, refraction and diabetes.

Midwestern University, Glendale Campus, Arizona College of Optometry, Glendale, AZ 85308. Offers OD. *Accreditation:* AOA. *Faculty:* 4 full-time (0 women). *Students:* 143 full-time (61 women), 3 part-time (1 woman); includes 50 minority (2 Black or African American, non-Hispanic/Latino; 30 Asian, non-Hispanic/Latino; 9 Hispanic/Latino; 9 Two or more races, non-Hispanic/Latino), 9 international. Average age 26. 723 applicants, 13% accepted, 49 enrolled. *Entrance requirements:* For doctorate, OAT, bachelor's degree, minimum overall cumulative and science GPA of 2.75, 2 letters of recommendation. *Unit head:* Hector Santiago, Dean, 623-572-3901, Fax: 623-572-3911, E-mail: azoptometry@midwestern.edu. *Application contact:* James Walter, Director of Admissions, 888-247-9277, Fax: 623-572-3229, E-mail: admissaz@midwestern.edu.

The New England College of Optometry, Graduate and Professional Programs, Boston, MA 02115-1100. Offers optometry (OD); vision science (MS). *Accreditation:* AOA. *Entrance requirements:* For doctorate, OAT. Electronic applications accepted.

Northeastern State University, College of Optometry, Tahlequah, OK 74464. Offers OD. Applicants must be a resident of Oklahoma, Arkansas, Kansas, Colorado, New Mexico, Missouri, Texas, or Nebraska. *Accreditation:* AOA. *Faculty:* 109 full-time (56 women), 1 (woman) part-time/adjunct. *Students:* 109 full-time (56 women); includes 17 minority (2 Black or African American, non-Hispanic/Latino; 3 American Indian or Alaska Native, non-Hispanic/Latino; 8 Asian, non-Hispanic/Latino; 4 Hispanic/Latino). Average age 26. 112 applicants, 35% accepted, 28 enrolled. In 2011, 26 doctorates awarded. *Degree requirements:* For doctorate, research project. *Entrance requirements:* For doctorate, OAT. *Application deadline:* For fall admission, 2/1 for domestic students. Applications are processed on a rolling basis. Application fee: $45. *Expenses:* Contact institution. *Financial support:* In 2011–12, 83 students received support. Federal Work-Study, institutionally sponsored loans, scholarships/grants, tuition waivers (partial), and residencies available. Financial award application deadline: 5/1; financial award applicants required to submit FAFSA. *Faculty research:* Extended-wear and bifocal contact lenses, methods of vision therapy, glaucoma, low vision, diabetes. *Total annual research expenditures:* $73,778. *Application contact:* Natalie Batt, Student and Alumni Affairs, 918-456-5511 Ext. 4036, Fax: 918-458-2104, E-mail: batt@nsuok.edu. Web site: http://www.optometry.nsuok.edu.

Nova Southeastern University, Health Professions Division, College of Optometry, Fort Lauderdale, FL 33328. Offers clinical vision research (MS); optometry (OD). *Accreditation:* AOA. Postbaccalaureate distance learning degree programs offered (no on-campus study). *Faculty:* 48 full-time (32 women), 11 part-time/adjunct (10 women). *Students:* 380 full-time (242 women), 14 part-time (5 women); includes 169 minority (16 Black or African American, non-Hispanic/Latino; 1 American Indian or Alaska Native, non-Hispanic/Latino; 107 Asian, non-Hispanic/Latino; 40 Hispanic/Latino; 3 Native Hawaiian or other Pacific Islander, non-Hispanic/Latino; 2 Two or more races, non-Hispanic/Latino), 15 international. Average age 26. 1,070 applicants, 21% accepted,

102 enrolled. In 2011, 1 master's, 97 doctorates awarded. *Degree requirements:* For master's, comprehensive exam (for some programs), thesis. *Entrance requirements:* For master's, OAT or GRE, BA; for doctorate, OAT, minimum GPA of 3.0. Additional exam requirements/recommendations for international students: Required—TOEFL (minimum score 79 iBT). *Application deadline:* For fall admission, 4/1 for domestic and international students. Applications are processed on a rolling basis. Application fee: $50. Electronic applications accepted. *Expenses:* Contact institution. *Financial support:* In 2011–12, 393 students received support. Federal Work-Study, institutionally sponsored loans, and scholarships/grants available. Financial award applicants required to submit FAFSA. *Faculty research:* Retinal disease, low vision, binocular vision, contact lenses, accommodation. *Unit head:* Dr. David Loshin, Dean, 954-262-1404, Fax: 954-262-1818. *Application contact:* Shavanah Moya, Admissions Counselor, 954-262-1132, Fax: 954-262-2282, E-mail: smoya1@nova.edu. Web site: http://optometry.nova.edu/.

The Ohio State University, College of Optometry, Columbus, OH 43210. Offers optometry (OD); vision science (MS, PhD); OD/MS. *Accreditation:* AOA (one or more programs are accredited). *Faculty:* 22. *Students:* 254 full-time (142 women), 8 part-time (5 women); includes 30 minority (1 Black or African American, non-Hispanic/Latino; 1 American Indian or Alaska Native, non-Hispanic/Latino; 22 Asian, non-Hispanic/Latino; 5 Hispanic/Latino; 1 Two or more races, non-Hispanic/Latino), 2 international. Average age 26. In 2011, 8 master's, 60 doctorates awarded. *Degree requirements:* For master's, thesis; for doctorate, thesis/dissertation. *Entrance requirements:* Additional exam requirements/recommendations for international students: Required—TOEFL (minimum score 600 paper-based; 250 computer-based; 79 iBT), Michigan English Language Assessment Battery (minimum score 82). *Application deadline:* For fall admission, 8/15 priority date for domestic students, 7/1 for international students; for winter admission, 12/1 priority date for domestic students, 11/1 for international students; for spring admission, 3/1 priority date for domestic students, 2/1 for international students. Applications are processed on a rolling basis. Electronic applications accepted. *Expenses:* Contact institution. *Financial support:* Research assistantships with full tuition reimbursements, teaching assistantships with full tuition reimbursements, Federal Work-Study, institutionally sponsored loans, and scholarships/grants available. Financial award application deadline: 2/1; financial award applicants required to submit FAFSA. *Unit head:* Dr. Melvin Shipp, Dean, 614-292-3246, E-mail: shipp.25@osu.edu. *Application contact:* Graduate Admissions, 614-292-9444, Fax: 614-292-3895, E-mail: domestic.grad@osu.edu. Web site: http://www.optometry.ohio-state.edu/.

Salus University, College of Optometry, Elkins Park, PA 19027-1598. Offers OD, OD/MS. *Accreditation:* AOA. *Degree requirements:* For doctorate, comprehensive exam (for some programs). *Entrance requirements:* For doctorate, OAT, interview. Additional exam requirements/recommendations for international students: Required—TOEFL. Electronic applications accepted. *Faculty research:* Vision research, visual perception, ocular motility, electrodiagnosis, photobiology glaucoma, myopia, keratoconus.

Southern California College of Optometry, Graduate and Professional Programs, Fullerton, CA 92831-1615. Offers optometry (OD); vision science (MS). *Accreditation:* AOA. *Degree requirements:* For doctorate, thesis/dissertation. *Entrance requirements:* For doctorate, OAT. Electronic applications accepted. *Faculty research:* Structure and function of the human visual system.

Southern College of Optometry, Professional Program, Memphis, TN 38104-2222. Offers OD. *Accreditation:* AOA. *Degree requirements:* For doctorate, clinical experience. *Entrance requirements:* For doctorate, OAT, 3 years of undergraduate pre-optometry course work.

State University of New York College of Optometry, Professional Program, New York, NY 10036. Offers OD, OD/MS, OD/PhD. *Accreditation:* AOA. *Entrance requirements:* For doctorate, OAT. Additional exam requirements/recommendations for international students: Required—TOEFL (minimum score 550 paper-based; 220 computer-based; 80 iBT). Electronic applications accepted. *Faculty research:* Optometry, vision research.

Université de Montréal, School of Optometry, Professional Program in Optometry, Montréal, QC H3C 3J7, Canada. Offers OD. Open only to Canadian residents. *Accreditation:* AOA. *Degree requirements:* For doctorate, thesis/dissertation. Electronic applications accepted.

The University of Alabama at Birmingham, School of Optometry, Professional Program in Optometry, Birmingham, AL 35294. Offers OD. *Entrance requirements:* For doctorate, OAT, interview. *Expenses:* Tuition, state resident: full-time $5922; part-time $309 per hour. Tuition, nonresident: full-time $13,428; part-time $726 per hour. Tuition and fees vary according to program. *Financial support:* Application deadline: 5/1. *Unit head:* Dr. William J. Benjamin, Chair, 205-934-6753, E-mail: eyesert@uab.edu. *Application contact:* Dr. Gerald Simon, Director, Optometry Student Affairs, 205-996-4923, Fax: 205-934-6758, E-mail: gsimonod@uab.edu.

University of California, Berkeley, School of Optometry, Berkeley, CA 94720-1500. Offers OD, Certificate. *Accreditation:* AOA. *Entrance requirements:* For doctorate, OAT. Additional exam requirements/recommendations for international students: Required—TOEFL (minimum score 570 paper-based; 230 computer-based). Electronic applications accepted. *Faculty research:* Low vision, spatial vision, psychophysics of vision, clinical optics, patient care.

University of Houston, College of Optometry, Professional Program in Optometry, Houston, TX 77204. Offers OD. *Accreditation:* AOA. *Faculty research:* Refractive error development, corneal physiology, low vision, binocular vision.

The University of Manchester, Faculty of Life Sciences, Manchester, United Kingdom. Offers adaptive organismal biology (M Phil, PhD); animal biology (M Phil, PhD); biochemistry (M Phil, PhD); bioinformatics (M Phil, PhD); biomolecular sciences (M Phil, PhD); biotechnology (M Phil, PhD); cell biology (M Phil, PhD); cell matrix research (M Phil, PhD); channels and transporters (M Phil, PhD); developmental biology (M Phil, PhD); Egyptology (M Phil, PhD); environmental biology (M Phil, PhD); evolutionary biology (M Phil, PhD); gene expression (M Phil, PhD); genetics (M Phil, PhD); history of science, technology and medicine (M Phil, PhD); immunology (M Phil, PhD); integrative neurobiology and behavior (M Phil, PhD); membrane trafficking (M Phil, PhD); microbiology (M Phil, PhD); molecular and cellular neuroscience (M Phil, PhD); molecular biology (M Phil, PhD); molecular cancer studies (M Phil, PhD); neuroscience (M Phil, PhD); ophthalmology (M Phil, PhD); optometry (M Phil, PhD); organelle function (M Phil, PhD); pharmacology (M Phil, PhD); physiology (M Phil, PhD); plant sciences (M Phil, PhD); stem cell research (M Phil, PhD); structural biology (M Phil, PhD); systems neuroscience (M Phil, PhD); toxicology (M Phil, PhD).

University of Missouri–St. Louis, College of Optometry, Professional Program in Optometry, St. Louis, MO 63121. Offers OD. *Accreditation:* AOA. *Faculty:* 23 full-time (6 women), 14 part-time/adjunct (4 women). *Students:* 173 full-time (106 women); includes

24 minority (6 Black or African American, non-Hispanic/Latino; 16 Asian, non-Hispanic/Latino; 2 Hispanic/Latino), 4 international. Average age 23. 375 applicants, 30% accepted, 40 enrolled. In 2011, 43 doctorates awarded. *Entrance requirements:* For doctorate, OAT, 90 hours of undergraduate course work. *Application deadline:* For fall admission, 2/15 for domestic and international students. Applications are processed on a rolling basis. Application fee: $50. Electronic applications accepted. *Expenses:* Tuition, state resident: full-time $6273; part-time $3866 per year. Tuition, nonresident: full-time $14,969; part-time $9980 per year. *Required fees:* $315 per year. *Financial support:* In 2011–12, 140 students received support, including 3 research assistantships (averaging $500 per year), 3 teaching assistantships (averaging $500 per year); Federal Work-Study, institutionally sponsored loans, and scholarships/grants also available. Financial award application deadline: 4/1; financial award applicants required to submit FAFSA. *Faculty research:* Visual psychophysics and perception, noninvasive assessment of visual processing, aging and Alzheimer's disease, orthokeratology. *Unit head:* Dr. Edward S. Bennett, Director, Student Services, 314-516-6263, Fax: 314-516-6708, E-mail: optstuaff@umsl.edu. *Application contact:* Linda L. Stein, Administrative Assistant, 314-516-5905, Fax: 314-516-6708, E-mail: linda_stein@umsl.edu. Web site: http://www.umsl.edu/divisions/optometry/Academic%20Programs/opt_curric.html.

University of the Incarnate Word, School of Optometry, San Antonio, TX 78209-6397. Offers OD. *Accreditation:* AOA. *Faculty:* 20 full-time (8 women), 7 part-time/adjunct (2 women). *Students:* 183 full-time (105 women); includes 85 minority (5 Black or African American, non-Hispanic/Latino; 69 Asian, non-Hispanic/Latino; 11 Hispanic/Latino), 18 international. Average age 25. 111 applicants, 100% accepted, 64 enrolled. *Degree requirements:* For doctorate, clinical contact hours. *Entrance requirements:* For doctorate, OAT, 90 credit hours of prerequisite course work; letters of recommendation; interview. Additional exam requirements/recommendations for international students: Required—TOEFL (minimum score 560 paper-based; 220 computer-based; 83 iBT). *Application deadline:* For fall admission, 7/15 for domestic students. Applications are processed on a rolling basis. Application fee: $50. Electronic applications accepted. *Expenses:* Contact institution. *Financial support:* In 2011–12, 5 fellowships (averaging $4,000 per year) were awarded; Federal Work-Study and scholarships/grants also available. Financial award applicants required to submit FAFSA. *Faculty research:*

Computer-based color vision, contrast sensitivity, and Amsler grid testing; response time in color deficiency; binocular enhancement of color vision; interactive instructional tools for teaching gross anatomy. *Total annual research expenditures:* $130,000. *Unit head:* Dr. Andrew Buzzelli, Founding Dean, 210-883-1195, Fax: 210-283-6890, E-mail: buzzelli@uiwtx.edu. *Application contact:* Kristine Benne, Director of Admissions and Student Services, School of Optometry, 210-883-1190, Fax: 210-883-1191, E-mail: optometry@uiwtx.edu. Web site: http://optometry.uiw.edu/.

University of Waterloo, Graduate Studies, Faculty of Science, School of Optometry, Waterloo, ON N2L 3G1, Canada. Offers optometry (OD); vision science (M Sc, PhD). *Accreditation:* AOA. Part-time programs available. *Degree requirements:* For master's, thesis; for doctorate, thesis/dissertation. *Entrance requirements:* For master's, honors degree, minimum B average; for doctorate, master's degree, minimum B average. Additional exam requirements/recommendations for international students: Required—TOEFL (minimum score 580 paper-based; 237 computer-based), TWE (minimum score 4). Electronic applications accepted. *Faculty research:* Vision science, fundamental and clinical vision, physiological optics, psycho-physics, perception.

Western University of Health Sciences, College of Optometry, Pomona, CA 91766-1854. Offers OD. *Accreditation:* AOA. *Faculty:* 25 full-time (10 women), 2 part-time/adjunct (both women). *Students:* 248 full-time (170 women); includes 155 minority (4 Black or African American, non-Hispanic/Latino; 131 Asian, non-Hispanic/Latino; 9 Hispanic/Latino; 11 Two or more races, non-Hispanic/Latino), 15 international. Average age 26. 794 applicants, 22% accepted, 86 enrolled. *Degree requirements:* For doctorate, comprehensive exam (for some programs). *Entrance requirements:* For doctorate, OAT, letters of recommendation; BS or BA (recommended). Additional exam requirements/recommendations for international students: Required—TOEFL. *Application deadline:* For fall admission, 5/1 for domestic and international students. Application fee: $65. Electronic applications accepted. *Unit head:* Dr. Elizabeth Hoppe, Dean, 909-706-3497, E-mail: ehoppe@westernu.edu. *Application contact:* Marie Anderson, Director of Admissions, 909-469-5485, Fax: 909-469-5570, E-mail: admissions@westernu.edu. Web site: http://www.westernu.edu/xp/edu/optometry/welcome.xml.

Vision Sciences

Eastern Virginia Medical School, Ophthalmic Technology Program, Norfolk, VA 23501-1980. Offers Certificate. *Faculty:* 1 (woman) full-time, 1 (woman) part-time/adjunct. *Students:* 9 full-time (5 women); includes 1 minority (Asian, non-Hispanic/Latino). 10 applicants, 80% accepted, 6 enrolled. *Application deadline:* For fall admission, 4/1 for domestic students. Applications are processed on a rolling basis. Application fee: $60. Electronic applications accepted. *Expenses:* Contact institution. *Unit head:* Lori J. Wood, Director, 757-446-5104, Fax: 757-446-6179, E-mail: optech@evms.edu. *Application contact:* Rose Mwayungu, Admissions and Enrollment Manager, 757-446-7153, Fax: 757-446-6179, E-mail: mwayunra@evms.edu. Web site: http://www.evms.edu/evms-school-of-health-professions/ophthalmic-technology.html.

The New England College of Optometry, Graduate and Professional Programs, Boston, MA 02115-1100. Offers optometry (OD); vision science (MS). *Accreditation:* AOA. *Entrance requirements:* For doctorate, OAT. Electronic applications accepted.

Nova Southeastern University, Health Professions Division, College of Optometry, Fort Lauderdale, FL 33328. Offers clinical vision research (MS); optometry (OD). *Accreditation:* AOA. Postbaccalaureate distance learning degree programs offered (no on-campus study). *Faculty:* 48 full-time (32 women), 11 part-time/adjunct (10 women). *Students:* 380 full-time (242 women), 14 part-time (5 women); includes 169 minority (16 Black or African American, non-Hispanic/Latino; 1 American Indian or Alaska Native, non-Hispanic/Latino; 107 Asian, non-Hispanic/Latino; 40 Hispanic/Latino; 3 Native Hawaiian or other Pacific Islander, non-Hispanic/Latino; 2 Two or more races, non-Hispanic/Latino), 15 international. Average age 26. 1,070 applicants, 21% accepted, 102 enrolled. In 2011, 1 master's, 97 doctorates awarded. *Degree requirements:* For master's, comprehensive exam (for some programs), thesis. *Entrance requirements:* For master's, OAT or GRE, BA; for doctorate, OAT, minimum GPA of 3.0. Additional exam requirements/recommendations for international students: Required—TOEFL (minimum score 79 iBT). *Application deadline:* For fall admission, 4/1 for domestic and international students. Applications are processed on a rolling basis. Application fee: $50. Electronic applications accepted. *Expenses:* Contact institution. *Financial support:* In 2011–12, 393 students received support. Federal Work-Study, institutionally sponsored loans, and scholarships/grants available. Financial award applicants required to submit FAFSA. *Faculty research:* Retinal disease, low vision, binocular vision, contact lenses, accommodation. *Unit head:* Dr. David Loshin, Dean, 954-262-1404, Fax: 954-262-1818. *Application contact:* Shavanah Moya, Admissions Counselor, 954-262-1132, Fax: 954-262-2282, E-mail: smoya1@nova.edu. Web site: http://optometry.nova.edu/.

Salus University, College of Education and Rehabilitation, Elkins Park, PA 19027-1598. Offers education of children and youth with visual and multiple impairments (M Ed, Certificate); low vision rehabilitation (MS, Certificate); orientation and mobility therapy (MS, Certificate); vision rehabilitation therapy (MS, Certificate); OD/MS. Part-time programs available. Postbaccalaureate distance learning degree programs offered. *Entrance requirements:* For master's, GRE or MAT, letters of reference (3), interviews (2). Additional exam requirements/recommendations for international students: Required—TOEFL, TWE. *Expenses:* Contact institution. *Faculty research:* Knowledge utilization, technology transfer.

Southern California College of Optometry, Graduate and Professional Programs, Fullerton, CA 92831-1615. Offers optometry (OD); vision science (MS). *Accreditation:* AOA. *Degree requirements:* For doctorate, thesis/dissertation. *Entrance requirements:* For doctorate, OAT. Electronic applications accepted. *Faculty research:* Structure and function of the human visual system.

State University of New York College of Optometry, Graduate Programs, New York, NY 10036. Offers PhD, OD/MS, OD/PhD. Part-time programs available. Terminal master's awarded for partial completion of doctoral program. *Degree requirements:* For doctorate, comprehensive exam, thesis/dissertation, specialty exam. *Entrance requirements:* For doctorate, GRE General Test. Additional exam requirements/recommendations for international students: Required—TOEFL (minimum score 550 paper-based; 220 computer-based; 80 iBT). *Expenses:* Contact institution. *Faculty research:* Oculomotor systems, perception, physiological optics, ocular biochemistry, accommodation, color and motion.

Université de Montréal, School of Optometry, Graduate Programs in Optometry, Montréal, QC H3C 3J7, Canada. Offers vision sciences (M Sc); visual impairment

intervention-orientation and mobility (DESS); visual impairment intervention-readaptation (DESS). Part-time programs available. *Degree requirements:* For master's, thesis. *Entrance requirements:* For master's, OD or appropriate bachelor's degree, minimum GPA of 2.7. Electronic applications accepted. *Faculty research:* Binocular vision, visual electrophysiology, eye movements, corneal metabolism, glare sensitivity.

The University of Alabama at Birmingham, School of Optometry, Graduate Program in Vision Science, Birmingham, AL 35294. Offers MS, PhD. Terminal master's awarded for partial completion of doctoral program. *Degree requirements:* For master's, thesis; for doctorate, thesis/dissertation. *Entrance requirements:* For master's and doctorate, GRE General Test, OAT, interview. *Expenses:* Tuition, state resident: full-time $5922; part-time $309 per hour. Tuition, nonresident: full-time $13,428; part-time $726 per hour. Tuition and fees vary according to program. *Unit head:* Dr. Paul D. Gamlin, Department Chair, 205-934-0322, E-mail: pgamlin@uab.edu. *Application contact:* Dr. Gerald Simon, Director, Optometry Student Affairs, 205-996-4923, Fax: 205-934-6758, E-mail: gsimonod@uab.edu. Web site: http://icare.opt.uab.edu/.

University of Alberta, Faculty of Medicine and Dentistry and Faculty of Graduate Studies and Research, Graduate Programs in Medicine, Department of Ophthalmology, Edmonton, AB T6G 2E1, Canada. Offers M Sc, PhD. Part-time programs available. Terminal master's awarded for partial completion of doctoral program. *Degree requirements:* For master's, thesis; for doctorate, comprehensive exam, thesis/dissertation. *Faculty research:* Ocular genetics.

University of California, Berkeley, Graduate Division, Group in Vision Science, Berkeley, CA 94720-1500. Offers MS, PhD. *Degree requirements:* For master's, thesis; for doctorate, thesis/dissertation. *Entrance requirements:* For master's and doctorate, GRE General Test, GRE Subject Test, minimum GPA of 3.0, 3 letters of recommendation. *Faculty research:* Visual neuroscience, bioengineering, computational vision, molecular cell biology, basic and clinical psychophysics.

University of Chicago, Division of Biological Sciences, Department of Ophthalmology and Visual Science, Chicago, IL 60637-1513. Offers PhD. *Degree requirements:* For doctorate, thesis/dissertation, ethics class, 2 teaching assistantships. *Entrance requirements:* For doctorate, GRE General Test. Additional exam requirements/recommendations for international students: Required—TOEFL (minimum score 600 paper-based; 250 computer-based; 104 iBT), IELTS (minimum score 7). *Faculty research:* Visual psychophysics, visual molecular biology, immunology, transplantation, infections.

University of Guelph, Ontario Veterinary College and Graduate Studies, Graduate Programs in Veterinary Sciences, Department of Clinical Studies, Guelph, ON N1G 2W1, Canada. Offers anesthesiology (M Sc, DV Sc); cardiology (DV Sc, Diploma); clinical studies (Diploma); dermatology (M Sc); diagnostic imaging (M Sc, DV Sc); emergency/critical care (M Sc, DV Sc, Diploma); medicine (M Sc, DV Sc); neurology (M Sc, DV Sc); ophthalmology (M Sc, DV Sc); surgery (M Sc, DV Sc). *Degree requirements:* For master's, thesis; for doctorate, comprehensive exam, thesis/dissertation. *Entrance requirements:* Additional exam requirements/recommendations for international students: Required—TOEFL (minimum score 550 paper-based; 213 computer-based), IELTS (minimum score 6.5). Electronic applications accepted. *Faculty research:* Orthopedics, respirology, oncology, exercise physiology, cardiology.

University of Houston, College of Optometry, Program in Physiological Optics/Vision Science, Houston, TX 77204. Offers physiological optics (MS, PhD). *Faculty research:* Space perception, amblyopia, binocular vision, development of visual skills, strabismus, visual cell biology, refractive error.

The University of Manchester, Faculty of Life Sciences, Manchester, United Kingdom. Offers adaptive organismal biology (M Phil, PhD); animal biology (M Phil, PhD); biochemistry (M Phil, PhD); bioinformatics (M Phil, PhD); biomolecular sciences (M Phil, PhD); biotechnology (M Phil, PhD); cell biology (M Phil, PhD); cell matrix research (M Phil, PhD); channels and transporters (M Phil, PhD); developmental biology (M Phil, PhD); Egyptology (M Phil, PhD); environmental biology (M Phil, PhD); evolutionary biology (M Phil, PhD); gene expression (M Phil, PhD); genetics (M Phil, PhD); history of science, technology and medicine (M Phil, PhD); immunology (M Phil, PhD); integrative neurobiology and behavior (M Phil, PhD); membrane trafficking (M Phil, PhD); microbiology (M Phil, PhD); molecular and cellular neuroscience (M Phil, PhD);

Vision Sciences

molecular biology (M Phil, PhD); molecular cancer studies (M Phil; PhD); neuroscience (M Phil, PhD); ophthalmology (M Phil, PhD); optometry (M Phil, PhD); organelle function (M Phil, PhD); pharmacology (M Phil, PhD); physiology (M Phil, PhD); plant sciences (M Phil, PhD); stem cell research (M Phil, PhD); structural biology (M Phil, PhD); systems neuroscience (M Phil, PhD); toxicology (M Phil, PhD).

University of Missouri–St. Louis, College of Optometry and Graduate School, Program in Vision Science, St. Louis, MO 63121. Offers MS, PhD. *Faculty:* 11 full-time (1 woman). *Students:* 3 full-time (1 woman), 1 (woman) part-time; includes 3 minority (1 Black or African American, non-Hispanic/Latino; 2 Asian, non-Hispanic/Latino). Average age 29. 9 applicants, 11% accepted, 1 enrolled. *Degree requirements:* For master's, thesis; for doctorate, comprehensive exam, thesis/dissertation. *Entrance requirements:* For master's and doctorate, GRE General Test. Additional exam requirements/recommendations for international students: Required—TOEFL (minimum score 570 paper-based). *Application deadline:* For fall admission, 3/15 for domestic and international students. Applications are processed on a rolling basis. Application fee: $25 ($40 for international students). Electronic applications accepted. *Expenses:* Contact institution. *Financial support:* In 2011–12, 1 research assistantship with full tuition reimbursement (averaging $23,000 per year), 3 teaching assistantships with full tuition reimbursements (averaging $23,000 per year) were awarded; fellowships with full tuition reimbursements, Federal Work-Study, institutionally sponsored loans, and unspecified assistantships also available. Financial award application deadline: 3/15; financial award applicants required to submit FAFSA. *Faculty research:* Theoretical and applied optics, theoretical and applied psychophysics, eye movements, binocular vision, contact lenses. *Unit head:* Dr. Carl J. Bassi, Director, Research and Graduate Studies, 314-516-6029, Fax: 314-516-5150, E-mail: bassi@umsl.edu. *Application contact:* Dr. Edward S. Bennett, Director, Student Services, 314-516-6263, Fax: 314-516-6708, E-mail: optstuaff@umsl.edu. Web site: http://www.umsl.edu/divisions/optometry/programs/physoptic.html.

University of Waterloo, Graduate Studies, Faculty of Science, School of Optometry, Waterloo, ON N2L 3G1, Canada. Offers optometry (OD); vision science (M Sc, PhD). *Accreditation:* AOA. Part-time programs available. *Degree requirements:* For master's, thesis; for doctorate, thesis/dissertation. *Entrance requirements:* For master's, honors degree, minimum B average; for doctorate, master's degree, minimum B average. Additional exam requirements/recommendations for international students: Required—TOEFL (minimum score 580 paper-based; 237 computer-based), TWE (minimum score 4). Electronic applications accepted. *Faculty research:* Vision science, fundamental and clinical vision, physiological optics, psycho-physics, perception.

Section 30
Pharmacy and Pharmaceutical Sciences

This section contains a directory of institutions offering graduate work in pharmacy and pharmaceutical sciences, followed by in-depth entries submitted by institutions that chose to prepare detailed program descriptions. Additional information about programs listed in the directory but not augmented by an in-depth entry may be obtained by writing directly to the dean of a graduate school or chair of a department at the address given in the directory.

For programs offering related work, see also in this book *Allied Health, Biochemistry, Biological and Biomedical Sciences, Nutrition, Pharmacology and Toxicology,* and *Physiology.* In the other guides in this series:

Graduate Programs in the Physical Sciences, Mathematics, Agricultural Sciences, the Environment & Natural Resources

See *Chemistry*

Graduate Programs in Engineering & Applied Sciences

See *Biomedical Engineering and Biotechnology,* and *Chemical Engineering*

CONTENTS

Medicinal and Pharmaceutical Chemistry

Cleveland State University, College of Graduate Studies, College of Sciences and Health Professions, Department of Chemistry, Cleveland, OH 44115. Offers analytical chemistry (MS); clinical chemistry (MS); clinical/bioanalytical chemistry (PhD), including cellular and molecular medicine, clinical chemistry, clinical/bioanalytical chemistry; environmental chemistry (MS); inorganic chemistry (MS); pharmaceutical/organic chemistry (MS); physical chemistry (MS). Part-time and evening/weekend programs available. *Faculty:* 12 full-time (0 women). *Students:* 17 full-time (8 women), 87 part-time (36 women); includes 6 minority (5 Black or African American, non-Hispanic/Latino; 1 Asian, non-Hispanic/Latino), 74 international. Average age 27. 143 applicants, 59% accepted, 22 enrolled. In 2011, 14 master's, 10 doctorates awarded. *Median time to degree:* Of those who began their doctoral program in fall 2003, 67% received their degree in 8 years or less. *Degree requirements:* For master's, thesis optional; for doctorate, comprehensive exam, thesis/dissertation. *Entrance requirements:* For master's and doctorate, GRE General Test. Additional exam requirements/recommendations for international students: Required—TOEFL (minimum score 525 paper-based; 197 computer-based; 65 iBT). *Application deadline:* For fall admission, 1/15 priority date for domestic students, 1/15 for international students. Applications are processed on a rolling basis. Application fee: $30. Electronic applications accepted. *Expenses:* Tuition, state resident: full-time $6416; part-time $494 per credit hour. Tuition, nonresident: full-time $12,074; part-time $929 per credit hour. *Financial support:* In 2011–12, 44 students received support, including 5 fellowships with full tuition reimbursements available (averaging $30,000 per year), 13 research assistantships with full tuition reimbursements available (averaging $20,000 per year), 24 teaching assistantships with full tuition reimbursements available (averaging $18,500 per year); scholarships/grants and unspecified assistantships also available. Financial award application deadline: 1/15. *Faculty research:* Bioanalytical techniques and molecular diagnostics, glycoproteomics and antithrombotic agents, drug discovery and innovation, analytical pharmacology, inflammatory disease research. *Total annual research expenditures:* $3 million. *Unit head:* Dr. David J. Anderson, Interim Chair, 216-687-2467, Fax: 216-687-9298, E-mail: d.anderson@csuohio.edu. *Application contact:* Richelle P. Emery, Administrative Coordinator, 216-687-2457, Fax: 216-687-9298, E-mail: r.emery@csuohio.edu. Web site: http://www.csuohio.edu/chemistry/.

Duquesne University, Mylan School of Pharmacy, Graduate School of Pharmaceutical Sciences, Program in Medicinal Chemistry, Pittsburgh, PA 15282-0001. Offers MS, PhD. *Faculty:* 4 full-time (0 women). *Students:* 24 full-time (9 women), all international. Average age 27. 52 applicants, 12% accepted, 3 enrolled. In 2011, 1 degree awarded. *Degree requirements:* For master's, thesis; for doctorate, comprehensive exam, thesis/dissertation. *Entrance requirements:* For master's and doctorate, GRE General Test. Additional exam requirements/recommendations for international students: Required—TOEFL. *Application deadline:* For fall admission, 2/1 priority date for domestic students, 2/1 for international students; for spring admission, 10/1 priority date for domestic students, 10/1 for international students. Applications are processed on a rolling basis. Application fee: $50. Electronic applications accepted. *Expenses:* Tuition: Full-time $16,596; part-time $922 per credit. *Required fees:* $1584; $88 per credit. Tuition and fees vary according to program. *Financial support:* In 2011–12, 22 students received support, including 12 research assistantships with full tuition reimbursements available, 10 teaching assistantships with full tuition reimbursements available. *Unit head:* Dr. Aleem Gangjee, Head, 412-396-6070. *Application contact:* Information Contact, 412-396-1172, E-mail: gsps-adm@duq.edu. Web site: http://www.duq.edu/pharmacy/graduate.cfm.

Florida Agricultural and Mechanical University, Division of Graduate Studies, Research, and Continuing Education, College of Pharmacy and Pharmaceutical Sciences, Graduate Programs in Pharmaceutical Sciences, Tallahassee, FL 32307-3200. Offers environmental toxicology (PhD); medicinal chemistry (MS, PhD); pharmaceutics (MS, PhD); pharmacology/toxicology (MS, PhD); pharmacy administration (MS). *Accreditation:* CEPH. *Degree requirements:* For master's, comprehensive exam, thesis, publishable paper; for doctorate, comprehensive exam, thesis/dissertation, publishable paper. *Entrance requirements:* For master's and doctorate, GRE General Test, minimum GPA of 3.0 in last 60 hours. Additional exam requirements/recommendations for international students: Required—TOEFL. *Faculty research:* Anticancer agents, anti-inflammatory drugs, chronopharmacology, neuroendocrinology, microbiology.

Idaho State University, Office of Graduate Studies, College of Pharmacy, Department of Biomedical and Pharmaceutical Sciences, Pocatello, ID 83209-8334. Offers biopharmaceutical analysis (PhD); drug delivery (PhD); medicinal chemistry (PhD); pharmaceutical sciences (MS); pharmacology (PhD). Part-time programs available. *Degree requirements:* For master's, one foreign language, comprehensive exam, thesis, thesis research, classes in speech and technical writing; for doctorate, comprehensive exam, thesis/dissertation, written and oral exams, classes in speech and technical writing. *Entrance requirements:* For master's, GRE General Test, minimum GPA of 3.0, 3 letters of recommendation; for doctorate, GRE General Test, BS in pharmacy or related field, minimum GPA of 3.0, 3 letters of recommendation. Additional exam requirements/recommendations for international students: Required—TOEFL (minimum score 550 paper-based; 213 computer-based; 80 iBT). Electronic applications accepted. *Expenses:* Contact institution. *Faculty research:* Metabolic toxicity of heavy metals, neuroendocrine pharmacology, cardiovascular pharmacology, cancer biology, immunopharmacology.

Long Island University–C. W. Post Campus, School of Health Professions and Nursing, Department of Biomedical Sciences, Brookville, NY 11548-1300. Offers cardiovascular perfusion (MS); clinical laboratory management (MS); medical biology (MS), including hematology, immunology, medical biology, medical chemistry, medical microbiology. Part-time and evening/weekend programs available. Postbaccalaureate distance learning degree programs offered. *Degree requirements:* For master's, thesis. *Entrance requirements:* For master's, minimum GPA of 2.75 in major. Electronic applications accepted.

Medical University of South Carolina, College of Graduate Studies, Department of Pharmaceutical and Biomedical Sciences, Charleston, SC 29425. Offers cell injury and repair (PhD); drug discovery (PhD); medicinal chemistry (PhD); toxicology (PhD); DMD/PhD; MD/PhD; Pharm D/PhD. *Faculty:* 8 full-time (1 woman), 1 part-time/adjunct (0 women). *Students:* 26 full-time (12 women), 7 international. Average age 29. In 2011, 3 doctorates awarded. *Degree requirements:* For doctorate, thesis/dissertation, oral and written exams, teaching and research seminar. *Entrance requirements:* For doctorate, GRE General Test, interview, minimum GPA of 3.0. Additional exam requirements/recommendations for international students: Required—TOEFL (minimum score 600 paper-based; 250 computer-based; 100 iBT). *Application deadline:* For fall admission, 1/15 priority date for domestic students, 1/15 for international students. Applications are processed on a rolling basis. Application fee: $0 ($85 for international students). Electronic applications accepted. *Financial support:* In 2011–12, 7 students received

support, including 17 research assistantships with partial tuition reimbursements available (averaging $23,000 per year); Federal Work-Study, scholarships/grants, and traineeships also available. Support available to part-time students. Financial award application deadline: 3/10; financial award applicants required to submit FAFSA. *Faculty research:* Drug discovery, toxicology, metabolomics, cell stress and injury. *Unit head:* Dr. Rick Schnellmann, Eminent Scholar, Professor and Chair, 843-792-3754, Fax: 843-792-6590, E-mail: schnell@musc.edu. *Application contact:* Dr. Craig C. Beeson, Associate Professor, 843-876-5091, Fax: 843-792-6590, E-mail: beesonc@musc.edu. Web site: http://www.musc.edu/psci/index.html.

New Jersey Institute of Technology, Office of Graduate Studies, College of Science and Liberal Arts, Department of Chemistry and Environmental Science, Program in Pharmaceutical Chemistry, Newark, NJ 07102. Offers MS. *Students:* 41 full-time (15 women), 13 part-time (8 women); includes 13 minority (3 Black or African American, non-Hispanic/Latino; 9 Asian, non-Hispanic/Latino; 1 Hispanic/Latino), 36 international. Average age 25. 97 applicants, 73% accepted, 19 enrolled. In 2011, 12 master's awarded. *Entrance requirements:* Additional exam requirements/recommendations for international students: Required—TOEFL (minimum score 550 paper-based; 213 computer-based; 79 iBT). *Application deadline:* For fall admission, 6/1 priority date for domestic students, 5/1 for international students; for spring admission, 11/15 priority date for domestic students, 11/15 for international students. Applications are processed on a rolling basis. Application fee: $65. Electronic applications accepted. *Expenses:* Tuition, state resident: full-time $7980; part-time $867 per credit. Tuition, nonresident: full-time $11,336; part-time $1196 per credit. *Required fees:* $230 per credit. *Financial support:* Application deadline: 1/15. *Unit head:* Dr. Somenath Mitra, Chair, 973-596-5611, E-mail: mitra@njit.edu. *Application contact:* Kathryn Kelly, Director of Admissions, 973-596-3300, Fax: 973-596-3461, E-mail: admissions@njit.edu. Web site: http://chemistry.njit.edu/academics/graduate/pharmchem/index.php.

Purdue University, College of Pharmacy and Pharmacal Sciences and Graduate School, Graduate Programs in Pharmacy and Pharmacal Sciences, West Lafayette, IN 47907. Offers industrial and physical pharmacy (MS, PhD, Certificate), including pharmaceutics (PhD), regulatory quality compliance (MS, Certificate); medicinal chemistry and molecular pharmacology (MS, PhD), including analytical medicinal chemistry (PhD), biophysical and computational chemistry (PhD), cancer research (PhD), immunology and infectious disease (PhD), medicinal and bioorganic chemistry (PhD), medicinal biochemistry and molecular biology (PhD), medicinal chemistry and chemical biology (PhD), molecular pharmacology (PhD), natural products and pharmacognosy (PhD), neuropharmacology, neurodegeneration, and neurotoxicology (PhD), nuclear pharmacy (MS), radiopharmaceutical chemistry and nuclear pharmacy (PhD), systems biology and functional genomics (PhD); pharmacy practice (MS, PhD), including clinical pharmacy, pharmacy administration, Part-time programs available. *Faculty:* 47 full-time (9 women), 46 part-time/adjunct (10 women). *Students:* 89 full-time (43 women), 29 part-time (18 women); includes 18 minority (3 Black or African American, non-Hispanic/Latino; 10 Asian, non-Hispanic/Latino; 5 Hispanic/Latino), 51 international. Average age 31. 371 applicants, 15% accepted, 25 enrolled. In 2011, 12 master's, 15 doctorates, 13 other advanced degrees awarded. Terminal master's awarded for partial completion of doctoral program. *Degree requirements:* For doctorate, thesis/dissertation. *Entrance requirements:* For master's and doctorate, GRE General Test, minimum undergraduate GPA of 3.0. Additional exam requirements/recommendations for international students: Required—TOEFL. *Application deadline:* Applications are processed on a rolling basis. Application fee: $60 ($75 for international students). Electronic applications accepted. *Financial support:* Fellowships, research assistantships, teaching assistantships, career-related internships or fieldwork, and traineeships available. Support available to part-time students. Financial award applicants required to submit FAFSA. *Faculty research:* Medicinal chemistry and pharmaceutics, cancer research, monoclonal antibodies. *Unit head:* Dr. C. K. Svensson, Dean, 765-494-1368, E-mail: svensson@purdue.edu. *Application contact:* Dr. G. Marc Loudon, Associate Dean for Graduate Programs, 765-494-1362.

Rutgers, The State University of New Jersey, New Brunswick, Ernest Mario School of Pharmacy, Program in Medicinal Chemistry, Piscataway, NJ 08854-8097. Offers MS, PhD. Part-time programs available. *Degree requirements:* For master's, comprehensive exam, thesis; for doctorate, comprehensive exam, thesis/dissertation. *Entrance requirements:* For master's and doctorate, GRE General Test. Additional exam requirements/recommendations for international students: Required—TOEFL (minimum score 600 paper-based; 250 computer-based; 90 iBT). Electronic applications accepted. *Faculty research:* Synthesis and design of anticancer drugs, synthesis of pro-drugs for prostate cancer, natural product synthesis, natural product isolation and structure elucidation, computational chemistry.

Temple University, Health Sciences Center, School of Pharmacy, Department of Pharmaceutical Sciences, Philadelphia, PA 19122-6096. Offers medicinal chemistry (MS, PhD); pharmaceutics (MS, PhD); pharmacodynamics (MS, PhD); quality assurance/regulatory affairs (MS). Part-time programs available. Postbaccalaureate distance learning degree programs offered. *Faculty:* 13 full-time (2 women). *Students:* 24 full-time (16 women), 12 part-time (6 women); includes 1 minority (Black or African American, non-Hispanic/Latino), 23 international. Average age 30. 48 applicants, 75% accepted, 24 enrolled. In 2011, 76 master's, 2 doctorates awarded. *Degree requirements:* For master's, thesis; for doctorate, 2 foreign languages, thesis/dissertation. *Entrance requirements:* For master's, GRE General Test, minimum undergraduate GPA of 3.0; for doctorate, GRE General Test, minimum GPA of 3.0. Additional exam requirements/recommendations for international students: Required—TOEFL (minimum score 550 paper-based; 213 computer-based; 79 iBT). *Application deadline:* For fall admission, 1/15 for domestic students, 12/15 for international students. Application fee: $50. Electronic applications accepted. *Expenses:* Contact institution. *Financial support:* Fellowships with tuition reimbursements, research assistantships with tuition reimbursements, and teaching assistantships with tuition reimbursements available. Financial award application deadline: 1/15; financial award applicants required to submit FAFSA. *Faculty research:* Pharmacokinetics, synthesis of medicinals, protein research, biopharm-formulation. *Unit head:* Dr. Daniel Canney, Interim Chair, 215-707-6924, E-mail: daniel.canney@temple.edu. *Application contact:* Tara Schumacher, Coordinator of Outreach, 215-204-6575, Fax: 215-204-8781, E-mail: tara.schumacher@temple.edu.

University at Buffalo, the State University of New York, Graduate School, College of Arts and Sciences, Department of Chemistry, Buffalo, NY 14260. Offers chemistry (MA, PhD); medicinal chemistry (MS, PhD). Part-time programs available. *Faculty:* 30 full-time (4 women), 1 (woman) part-time/adjunct. *Students:* 142 full-time (54 women); includes 17 minority (8 Black or African American, non-Hispanic/Latino; 4 Asian, non-Hispanic/Latino; 5 Hispanic/Latino), 43 international. Average age 26. 235 applicants, 25% accepted, 24 enrolled. In 2011, 11 master's, 15 doctorates awarded. Terminal master's awarded for partial completion of doctoral program. *Median time to degree:* Of

those who began their doctoral program in fall 2003, 100% received their degree in 8 years or less. *Degree requirements:* For master's, thesis or alternative, project; for doctorate, thesis/dissertation, synopsis proposal. *Entrance requirements:* For master's and doctorate, GRE General Test. Additional exam requirements/recommendations for international students: Required—TOEFL (minimum score 550 paper-based; 213 computer-based; 79 iBT). *Application deadline:* For fall admission, 3/1 priority date for domestic students, 3/1 for international students; for spring admission, 11/1 priority date for domestic students. Applications are processed on a rolling basis. Application fee: $75. Electronic applications accepted. *Financial support:* In 2011–12, 3 students received support, including 3 fellowships with full tuition reimbursements available (averaging $22,080 per year), 34 research assistantships with full tuition reimbursements available (averaging $22,080 per year), 83 teaching assistantships with full tuition reimbursements available (averaging $22,080 per year); Federal Work-Study, institutionally sponsored loans, and unspecified assistantships also available. Financial award application deadline: 6/15; financial award applicants required to submit FAFSA. *Faculty research:* Synthesis, measurements, structure theory, translation. *Total annual research expenditures:* $1.8 million. *Unit head:* Dr. Luis A. Colon, Chairman, 716-645-6824, Fax: 716-645-6963, E-mail: chechair@buffalo.edu. *Application contact:* Dr. Steven T. Diver, Director of Graduate Studies, 716-645-4208, Fax: 716-645-6963, E-mail: diver@buffalo.edu. Web site: http://www.chem.buffalo.edu/.

University of California, Irvine, College of Health Sciences, Program in Medicinal Chemistry and Pharmacology, Irvine, CA 92697. Offers PhD. *Students:* 11 full-time (7 women); includes 8 minority (1 Black or African American, non-Hispanic/Latino; 4 Asian, non-Hispanic/Latino; 2 Hispanic/Latino; 1 Two or more races, non-Hispanic/Latino). Average age 26. 60 applicants, 20% accepted, 9 enrolled. Application fee: $80 ($100 for international students). *Unit head:* Richard Chamberlin, Chair, 949-824-7089, Fax: 949-824-9920, E-mail: richard.chamberlin@uci.edu. *Application contact:* Sheree McPeak, Graduate Division, 949-824-4611, Fax: 949-824-9096, E-mail: ogsfront@uci.edu. Web site: http://www.pharmsci.uci.edu/graduate/index.php.

University of California, San Francisco, School of Pharmacy and Graduate Division, Chemistry and Chemical Biology Graduate Program, San Francisco, CA 94143. Offers PhD. *Faculty:* 45 full-time (11 women). *Students:* 52 full-time (30 women); includes 17 minority (4 Black or African American, non-Hispanic/Latino; 8 Asian, non-Hispanic/Latino; 5 Hispanic/Latino), 4 international. Average age 27. 95 applicants, 23% accepted, 7 enrolled. In 2011, 7 degrees awarded. *Median time to degree:* Of those who began their doctoral program in fall 2003, 100% received their degree in 8 years or less. *Degree requirements:* For doctorate, thesis/dissertation. *Entrance requirements:* For doctorate, GRE General Test, GRE Subject Test, minimum GPA of 3.0. Additional exam requirements/recommendations for international students: Required—TOEFL (minimum score 550 paper-based; 213 computer-based; 80 iBT). *Application deadline:* For fall admission, 12/1 for domestic and international students. Applications are processed on a rolling basis. Application fee: $80 ($100 for international students). Electronic applications accepted. *Financial support:* In 2011–12, 52 students received support, including 9 fellowships with full tuition reimbursements available (averaging $29,500 per year), 43 research assistantships with full tuition reimbursements available (averaging $29,500 per year); teaching assistantships with partial tuition reimbursements available, institutionally sponsored loans, scholarships/grants, traineeships, and tuition waivers (full) also available. Financial award application deadline: 5/15. *Faculty research:* Biochemistry, macromolecular structure, cellular and molecular pharmacology, physical chemistry and computational biology, synthetic chemistry. *Unit head:* Dr. Charles S. Craik, Director, 415-476-8146, E-mail: craik@cgl.ucsf.edu. *Application contact:* Julia Molla, Senior Administrative Analyst, 415-476-1914, Fax: 415-514-1546, E-mail: julia.molla@ucsf.edu. Web site: http://ccb.ucsf.edu/.

University of Connecticut, Graduate School, School of Pharmacy, Department of Pharmaceutical Sciences, Program in Medicinal Chemistry, Storrs, CT 06269. Offers MS, PhD. Terminal master's awarded for partial completion of doctoral program. *Degree requirements:* For master's, comprehensive exam, thesis; for doctorate, thesis/dissertation. *Entrance requirements:* Additional exam requirements/recommendations for international students: Required—TOEFL (minimum score 550 paper-based; 213 computer-based). Electronic applications accepted.

University of Florida, Graduate School, College of Pharmacy and Graduate School, Graduate Programs in Pharmacy, Department of Medicinal Chemistry, Gainesville, FL 32611. Offers MSP, PhD. Part-time and evening/weekend programs available. Postbaccalaureate distance learning degree programs offered (minimal on-campus study). *Faculty:* 7 full-time (2 women). *Students:* 34 full-time (20 women), 166 part-time (114 women); includes 35 minority (11 Black or African American, non-Hispanic/Latino; 4 American Indian or Alaska Native, non-Hispanic/Latino; 5 Asian, non-Hispanic/Latino; 15 Hispanic/Latino), 14 international. Average age 33. 51 applicants, 6% accepted, 3 enrolled. In 2011, 100 master's, 1 doctorate awarded. Terminal master's awarded for partial completion of doctoral program. *Degree requirements:* For master's, thesis optional; for doctorate, comprehensive exam, thesis/dissertation. *Entrance requirements:* For master's and doctorate, GRE General Test, minimum GPA of 3.0. Additional exam requirements/recommendations for international students: Required—TOEFL (minimum score 550 paper-based; 213 computer-based; 80 iBT), IELTS (minimum score 6). *Application deadline:* For fall admission, 5/1 priority date for domestic students, 5/1 for international students; for winter admission, 10/1 for domestic and international students. Applications are processed on a rolling basis. Application fee: $30. Electronic applications accepted. *Financial support:* In 2011–12, 5 students received support, including 1 fellowship, 4 teaching assistantships; research assistantships also available. Financial award application deadline: 4/15; financial award applicants required to submit FAFSA. *Faculty research:* Drug metabolism and toxicology, discovery of biologically active natural products, chelator chemistry and biochemistry, anti-cancer drug and prodrug discovery, discovery of neuroactive drugs. *Total annual research expenditures:* $2.3 million. *Unit head:* Dr. Margaret O. James, Chair, 352-273-7707, Fax: 352-392-9455, E-mail: mojames@ufl.edu. *Application contact:* Dr. Raymond J. Bergeron, Graduate Coordinator, 352-273-7725, Fax: 352-392-9455, E-mail: rayb@ufl.edu. Web site: http://www.cop.ufl.edu/mc/.

The University of Kansas, Graduate Studies, School of Pharmacy, Department of Medicinal Chemistry, Lawrence, KS 66045. Offers MS, PhD. *Faculty:* 14 full-time (5 women). *Students:* 36 full-time (14 women); includes 2 minority (both Asian, non-Hispanic/Latino), 17 international. Average age 27. 87 applicants, 26% accepted, 12 enrolled. In 2011, 3 master's, 3 doctorates awarded. Terminal master's awarded for partial completion of doctoral program. *Degree requirements:* For master's, comprehensive exam, thesis (for some programs); for doctorate, comprehensive exam, thesis/dissertation, cumulative exams. *Entrance requirements:* For master's and doctorate, GRE General Test. Additional exam requirements/recommendations for international students: Required—TOEFL. *Application deadline:* For fall admission, 2/1 priority date for domestic students, 2/1 for international students. Applications are processed on a rolling basis. Application fee: $55 ($65 for international students). Electronic applications accepted. Tuition and fees vary according to course load, campus/location, program and reciprocity agreements. *Financial support:* Fellowships with full tuition reimbursements, research assistantships with full tuition reimbursements, teaching assistantships with full tuition reimbursements, health care benefits, and unspecified assistantships available. Financial award application deadline: 3/1. *Faculty research:* Drug design and synthesis, natural products chemistry, drug metabolism and toxicity, enzyme mechanism and inhibition, antiinfective and chemotherapeutic agents. *Unit head:* Prof. Barbara Timmermann, Professor/Chair, 785-864-4495, Fax: 785-864-5326, E-mail: btimmer@ku.edu. *Application contact:* Prof. Apurba Dutta, Director of Graduate Studies, 785-864-4495, Fax: 785-864-5326, E-mail: medchem@ku.edu. Web site: http://www.medchem.ku.edu/.

The University of Kansas, Graduate Studies, School of Pharmacy, Department of Pharmaceutical Chemistry, Lawrence, KS 66047. Offers MS, PhD. Part-time and evening/weekend programs available. Postbaccalaureate distance learning degree programs offered (no on-campus study). *Faculty:* 15 full-time (2 women). *Students:* 43 full-time (16 women), 17 part-time (13 women); includes 11 minority (2 Black or African American, non-Hispanic/Latino; 6 Asian, non-Hispanic/Latino; 2 Hispanic/Latino; 1 Two or more races, non-Hispanic/Latino), 23 international. Average age 29. 90 applicants, 13% accepted, 11 enrolled. In 2011, 9 master's, 10 doctorates awarded. Terminal master's awarded for partial completion of doctoral program. *Degree requirements:* For master's, thesis, qualifying exam; for doctorate, comprehensive exam, thesis/dissertation, qualifying exam. *Entrance requirements:* For master's, GRE General Test, bachelor's degree in biological sciences, chemical engineering, chemistry, or pharmacy; for doctorate, GRE General Test. Additional exam requirements/recommendations for international students: Required—TOEFL. *Application deadline:* For fall admission, 1/15 priority date for domestic students, 1/15 for international students. Applications are processed on a rolling basis. Application fee: $55 ($65 for international students). Electronic applications accepted. Tuition and fees vary according to course load, campus/location, program and reciprocity agreements. *Financial support:* Fellowships with full tuition reimbursements, research assistantships with full and partial tuition reimbursements, career-related internships or fieldwork, scholarships/grants, traineeships, and unspecified assistantships available. Financial award application deadline: 1/15. *Faculty research:* Drug delivery, drug analysis, biotechnology, nanomaterials, protein structure. *Unit head:* Dr. Christian Schoneich, Chair, 785-864-4880, Fax: 785-864-5736, E-mail: schoneic@ku.edu. *Application contact:* Dr. John Stobaugh, Graduate Director, 785-864-3996, Fax: 785-864-5736, E-mail: stobaugh@ku.edu. Web site: http://www.pharmchem.ku.edu/.

University of Michigan, College of Pharmacy and University of Michigan, Department of Medicinal Chemistry, Ann Arbor, MI 48109. Offers PhD. *Degree requirements:* For doctorate, oral defense of dissertation, preliminary exam. *Entrance requirements:* For doctorate, GRE. Additional exam requirements/recommendations for international students: Required—TOEFL or IELTS. *Expenses:* Contact institution.

University of Minnesota, Twin Cities Campus, College of Pharmacy and Graduate School, Graduate Programs in Pharmacy, Graduate Program in Medicinal Chemistry, Minneapolis, MN 55455. Offers MS, PhD. *Faculty:* 27 full-time (4 women), 6 part-time/adjunct (2 women). *Students:* 43 full-time (20 women); includes 5 minority (1 Black or African American, non-Hispanic/Latino; 3 Asian, non-Hispanic/Latino; 1 Two or more races, non-Hispanic/Latino), 21 international. Average age 26. 74 applicants, 19% accepted, 8 enrolled. In 2011, 1 master's, 3 doctorates awarded. Terminal master's awarded for partial completion of doctoral program. *Median time to degree:* Of those who began their doctoral program in fall 2003, 100% received their degree in 8 years or less. *Degree requirements:* For master's, comprehensive exam, thesis; for doctorate, comprehensive exam, thesis/dissertation. *Entrance requirements:* For doctorate, GRE General Test, BS in biology, chemistry, or pharmacy. Additional exam requirements/recommendations for international students: Required—TOEFL (minimum score 550 paper-based; 80 computer-based). *Application deadline:* For fall admission, 12/15 for domestic and international students. Application fee: $75 ($95 for international students). Electronic applications accepted. *Financial support:* In 2011–12, 43 students received support, including 28 fellowships with full and partial tuition reimbursements available (averaging $8,000 per year), 24 research assistantships with full tuition reimbursements available (averaging $24,970 per year), 7 teaching assistantships with full tuition reimbursements available (averaging $15,171 per year); health care benefits and unspecified assistantships also available. Financial award application deadline: 12/15. *Faculty research:* Drug design and synthesis, molecular modeling, chemical aspects of drug metabolism and toxicity. *Total annual research expenditures:* $5.1 million. *Unit head:* Dr. Gunda I. Georg, Department Head of Medicinal Chemistry, 612-626-6320, Fax: 612-626-3114, E-mail: georg@umn.edu. Web site: http://www.pharmacy.umn.edu/medchem/graduate/.

University of Mississippi, Graduate School, School of Pharmacy, Graduate Programs in Pharmacy, Oxford, University, MS 38677. Offers medicinal chemistry (PhD); pharmaceutical sciences (MS); pharmaceutics (PhD); pharmacognosy (PhD); pharmacology (PhD); pharmacy administration (PhD). *Students:* 96 full-time (33 women), 11 part-time (3 women); includes 11 minority (4 Black or African American, non-Hispanic/Latino; 5 Asian, non-Hispanic/Latino; 1 Hispanic/Latino; 1 Two or more races, non-Hispanic/Latino), 68 international. In 2011, 8 master's, 10 doctorates awarded. *Unit head:* Dr. Barbara G. Wells, Dean, 662-915-7265, Fax: 662-915-5704, E-mail: pharmacy@olemiss.edu. *Application contact:* Dr. Christy M. Wyandt, Associate Dean, 662-915-7474, Fax: 662-915-7577, E-mail: cwyandt@olemiss.edu.

University of Rhode Island, Graduate School, College of Pharmacy, Department of Biomedical and Pharmaceutical Sciences, Kingston, RI 02881. Offers medicinal chemistry and pharmacognosy (MS, PhD); pharmaceutics and pharmacokinetics (MS, PhD); pharmacology and toxicology (MS, PhD). Part-time programs available. *Faculty:* 20 full-time (6 women), 2 part-time/adjunct (1 woman). *Students:* 41 full-time (21 women), 16 part-time (7 women); includes 8 minority (1 Black or African American, non-Hispanic/Latino; 6 Asian, non-Hispanic/Latino; 1 Two or more races, non-Hispanic/Latino), 24 international. In 2011, 4 master's, 3 doctorates awarded. *Entrance requirements:* For master's and doctorate, GRE, 2 letters of recommendation. Additional exam requirements/recommendations for international students: Required—TOEFL (minimum score 550 paper-based; 213 computer-based). Application fee: $65. Electronic applications accepted. *Expenses:* Tuition, state resident: full-time $10,432; part-time $580 per credit hour. Tuition, nonresident: full-time $23,130; part-time $1285 per credit hour. *Required fees:* $1362; $36 per credit hour. $35 per semester. One-time fee: $130. *Financial support:* In 2011–12, 8 research assistantships with partial tuition reimbursements (averaging $9,529 per year), 11 teaching assistantships with full and partial tuition reimbursements (averaging $9,807 per year) were awarded. Financial award applicants required to submit FAFSA. *Faculty research:* Chemical carcinogenesis with a major emphasis on the structural and synthetic aspects of DNA-adduct formation, drug-drug/herb interaction, drug-genetic interaction, signaling of nuclear receptors, transcriptional regulation, oncogenesis. *Unit head:* Dr. Clinton O. Chichester, Chair, 401-874-5034, Fax: 401-874-5787, E-mail: chichester@uri.edu. *Application contact:* Dr. David C. Rowley, Graduate Coordinator, 401-874-9228, Fax: 401-874-2516, E-mail: drowley@uri.edu. Web site: http://www.uri.edu/pharmacy/departments/bps/index.shtml.

The University of Texas at Austin, Graduate School, College of Pharmacy, Graduate Programs in Pharmacy, Austin, TX 78712-1111. Offers health outcomes and pharmacy practice (PhD); health outcomes and pharmacy practice (MS); medicinal chemistry (PhD); pharmaceutics (PhD); pharmacology and toxicology (PhD); pharmacotherapy (MS, PhD); translational science (PhD). PhD in translational science offered jointly with

The University of Texas Health Science Center at San Antonio and The University of Texas at San Antonio. *Degree requirements:* For master's, thesis; for doctorate, thesis/dissertation. *Entrance requirements:* For master's and doctorate, GRE General Test. *Application deadline:* For fall admission, 1/15 priority date for domestic students, 1/15 for international students; for spring admission, 10/1 for domestic students. Applications are processed on a rolling basis. Application fee: $50 ($75 for international students). Electronic applications accepted. *Financial support:* Fellowships, research assistantships, teaching assistantships with partial tuition reimbursements, Federal Work-Study, scholarships/grants, health care benefits, and unspecified assistantships available. Financial award application deadline: 2/1; financial award applicants required to submit FAFSA. *Faculty research:* Synthetic medical chemistry, synthetic molecular biology, bio-organic chemistry, pharmacoeconomics, pharmacy practice. *Unit head:* Dr. M. Lynn Crismon, Dean, 512-471-3718, E-mail: lynn.crismon@austin.utexas.edu.

University of the Sciences in Philadelphia, College of Graduate Studies, Program in Chemistry, Biochemistry and Pharmacognosy, Philadelphia, PA 19104-4495. Offers biochemistry (MS, PhD); chemistry (MS, PhD); pharmacognosy (MS, PhD). Part-time programs available. *Degree requirements:* For master's, thesis, qualifying exams; for doctorate, comprehensive exam, thesis/dissertation, qualifying exams. *Entrance requirements:* For master's and doctorate, GRE General Test, GRE Subject Test. Additional exam requirements/recommendations for international students: Required—TOEFL, TWE. *Expenses:* Contact institution. *Faculty research:* Organic and medicinal synthesis, mass spectroscopy use in protein analysis, study of analogues of taxol, cholesteryl esters.

The University of Toledo, College of Graduate Studies, College of Pharmacy and Pharmaceutical Sciences, Program in Medicinal and Biological Chemistry, Toledo, OH 43606-3390. Offers MS, PhD. Terminal master's awarded for partial completion of doctoral program. *Degree requirements:* For master's, thesis; for doctorate, thesis/dissertation. *Entrance requirements:* For master's and doctorate, GRE General Test. Additional exam requirements/recommendations for international students: Required—TOEFL (minimum score 550 paper-based; 213 computer-based; 80 iBT). Electronic applications accepted. *Faculty research:* Neuroscience, molecular modeling, immunotoxicology, organic synthesis, peptide biochemistry.

University of Utah, Graduate School, College of Pharmacy, Department of Medicinal Chemistry, Salt Lake City, UT 84112-5820. Offers MS, PhD. *Faculty:* 9 full-time (1 woman). *Students:* 6 full-time (2 women), 3 part-time (0 women), 4 international. Average age 30. 2 applicants, 100% accepted, 1 enrolled. In 2011, 1 master's, 6 doctorates awarded. *Entrance requirements:* For doctorate, GRE, minimum GPA of 3.0. Additional exam requirements/recommendations for international students: Required—TOEFL (minimum score 61 iBT). *Application deadline:* For fall admission, 1/15 priority date for domestic students, 12/15 for international students. Application fee: $55 ($65 for international students). Electronic applications accepted. *Financial support:* In 2011–12, 11 students received support, including 1 fellowship with full tuition reimbursement available (averaging $15,000 per year), 10 research assistantships with full tuition reimbursements available (averaging $26,000 per year); teaching assistantships and unspecified assistantships also available. *Faculty research:* Anticancer and anti-infective drug discovery, assays for high-throughput screening, neuroactive peptides, bioinorganic chemistry, structure-based drug design and modeling. *Total annual research expenditures:* $3.4 million. *Unit head:* Dr. Darrell R. Davis, Chair, 801-581-7063, Fax: 801-581-7087, E-mail: darrell.davis@utah.edu. *Application contact:* Dr. Thomas E. Cheatham, Director of Graduate Studies, 801-587-9652, Fax: 801-581-7087, E-mail: tom.cheatham@pharm.utah.edu. Web site: http://www.pharmacy.utah.edu/medchem/.

University of Utah, Graduate School, College of Pharmacy, Department of Pharmaceutics and Pharmaceutical Chemistry, Salt Lake City, UT 84112. Offers MS, PhD. *Faculty:* 9 full-time (1 woman), 2 part-time/adjunct (0 women). *Students:* 28 full-time (16 women), 7 part-time (3 women); includes 1 minority (Asian, non-Hispanic/Latino), 21 international. Average age 28. 68 applicants, 6% accepted, 4 enrolled. In 2011, 5 degrees awarded. Terminal master's awarded for partial completion of doctoral program. *Median time to degree:* Of those who began their doctoral program in fall 2003, 98% received their degree in 8 years or less. *Degree requirements:* For master's, thesis; for doctorate, comprehensive exam, thesis/dissertation, peer-reviewed scientific publications and oral presentations. *Entrance requirements:* For master's and doctorate, GRE. Additional exam requirements/recommendations for international students: Required—TOEFL (minimum score 550 paper-based; 100 computer-based). *Application deadline:* For fall admission, 12/1 priority date for domestic students, 12/1 for international students. Applications are processed on a rolling basis. Application fee: $55 ($65 for international students). Electronic applications accepted. *Financial support:* In 2011–12, 37 students received support, including 3 fellowships (averaging $2,500 per year), 36 research assistantships (averaging $25,000 per year); teaching assistantships, scholarships/grants, health care benefits, tuition waivers (full), and unspecified assistantships also available. *Faculty research:* Drug delivery, biopharmaceutics, nano medicine, pharmacokinetics, polymeric biomaterials. *Total annual research expenditures:* $2.1 million. *Unit head:* Dr. David W. Grainger, Chairperson, 801-581-7831, Fax: 801-581-3674, E-mail: phceu@pharm.utah.edu. *Application contact:* Office of Admissions, 801-581-7281, Fax: 801-585-3034, E-mail: admissionweb_grad@saff.utah.edu. Web site: http://www.pharmacy.utah.edu/pharmaceutics/.

University of Washington, School of Pharmacy, Department of Medicinal Chemistry, Seattle, WA 98195. Offers PhD, Pharm D/PhD. *Faculty:* 8 full-time (1 woman). *Students:* 24 full-time (12 women); includes 7 minority (1 Black or African American, non-Hispanic/Latino; 5 Asian, non-Hispanic/Latino; 1 Hispanic/Latino), 4 international. 52 applicants, 13% accepted, 3 enrolled. In 2011, 5 doctorates awarded. *Degree requirements:* For doctorate, thesis/dissertation. *Entrance requirements:* For doctorate, GRE General Test, minimum GPA of 3.0, 3 letters of recommendation, statement of purpose, transcripts, resume. Additional exam requirements/recommendations for international students: Required—TOEFL. *Application deadline:* For fall admission, 12/15 for domestic and international students. Application fee: $75. Electronic applications accepted. *Financial support:* Fellowships, research assistantships, Federal Work-Study, and institutionally sponsored loans available. *Faculty research:* Chemical and molecular aspects of drug action, metabolism and drug toxicity, theoretical studies on protein folding, NMR of macromolecules and biomedical mass spectrometry. *Unit head:* Dr. Allan E. Rettie, Chairman, 206-685-0615, E-mail: rettie@uw.edu. *Application contact:* Meg Running, Graduate Program Assistant, 206-543-2224, E-mail: medchem@uw.edu. Web site: http://sop.washington.edu/medchem.

Virginia Commonwealth University, Medical College of Virginia-Professional Programs, School of Pharmacy, Department of Pharmaceutics, Richmond, VA 23284-9005. Offers medicinal chemistry (MS); pharmaceutical sciences (PhD); pharmaceutics (MS); pharmacotherapy and pharmacy administration (MS). Terminal master's awarded for partial completion of doctoral program. *Degree requirements:* For master's, thesis; for doctorate, thesis/dissertation. *Entrance requirements:* For master's and doctorate, GRE General Test. Additional exam requirements/recommendations for international students: Required—TOEFL. Electronic applications accepted. *Expenses:* Tuition, state resident: full-time $9133; part-time $507 per credit. Tuition, nonresident: full-time $18,777; part-time $1043 per credit. *Required fees:* $77 per credit. Tuition and fees vary according to degree level, campus/location, program and student level. *Faculty research:* Drug delivery systems, drug development.

Wayne State University, Eugene Applebaum College of Pharmacy and Health Sciences, Department of Pharmaceutical Sciences, Detroit, MI 48202. Offers medicinal chemistry (MS, PhD); pharmaceutics (MS, PhD); pharmacology/toxicology (MS, PhD). *Accreditation:* ACPE (one or more programs are accredited). Part-time programs available. *Students:* 15 full-time (6 women), 4 part-time (3 women); includes 2 minority (1 Black or African American, non-Hispanic/Latino; 1 Asian, non-Hispanic/Latino), 11 international. Average age 27. 234 applicants, 3% accepted, 7 enrolled. In 2011, 1 degree awarded. *Degree requirements:* For master's, thesis; for doctorate, thesis/dissertation. *Entrance requirements:* For master's, GRE General Test, bachelor's degree with minimum GPA of 3.0, three letters of recommendation, personal statement; for doctorate, GRE General Test, bachelor's degree with minimum GPA of 3.0, three letters of recommendation. Additional exam requirements/recommendations for international students: Required—TOEFL (minimum score 550 paper-based; 213 computer-based); Recommended—TWE (minimum score 6). *Application deadline:* For fall admission, 3/1 for domestic and international students. Application fee: $50. Electronic applications accepted. *Expenses:* Tuition, state resident: part-time $512.85 per credit. Tuition, nonresident: part-time $1132.65 per credit. *Required fees:* $26.60 per credit. $199.65 per semester. Tuition and fees vary according to course load and program. *Financial support:* In 2011–12, 1 fellowship with tuition reimbursement (averaging $1,800 per year), 11 research assistantships with full tuition reimbursements (averaging $23,682 per year) were awarded; career-related internships or fieldwork, scholarships/grants, health care benefits, and unspecified assistantships also available. Support available to part-time students. *Faculty research:* Mechanisms of resistance of bacteria to anti-microbial agents, drug metabolism and disposition in children, treatment strategies for stroke/neurovascular disease, prevalence and treatment of diabetes in Arab-Americans, ethnic variability in development of osteoporosis. *Unit head:* Dr. George B. Corcoran, Chair, 313-577-1737, Fax: 313-577-2033, E-mail: corcoran@wayne.edu. *Application contact:* 313-577-1047, E-mail: pscgrad@wayne.edu. Web site: http://www.cphs.wayne.edu/psc/index.php.

West Virginia University, School of Pharmacy, Program in Pharmaceutical and Pharmacological Sciences, Morgantown, WV 26506. Offers administrative pharmacy (PhD); behavioral pharmacy (MS, PhD); biopharmaceutics/pharmacokinetics (MS, PhD); industrial pharmacy (MS); medicinal chemistry (MS, PhD); pharmaceutical chemistry (MS, PhD); pharmaceutics (MS, PhD); pharmacology and toxicology (MS); pharmacy (MS); pharmacy administration (MS). Part-time programs available. Terminal master's awarded for partial completion of doctoral program. *Degree requirements:* For master's, thesis; for doctorate, one foreign language, comprehensive exam, thesis/dissertation. *Entrance requirements:* For master's and doctorate, GRE General Test, minimum GPA of 2.75. Additional exam requirements/recommendations for international students: Required—TOEFL; Recommended—TWE. Electronic applications accepted. *Expenses:* Contact institution. *Faculty research:* Pharmaceutics, medicinal chemistry, biopharmaceutics/pharmacokinetics, health outcomes research.

Pharmaceutical Administration

Columbia University, Graduate School of Business, MBA Program, New York, NY 10027. Offers accounting (MBA); decision, risk, and operations (MBA); entrepreneurship (MBA); finance and economics (MBA); healthcare and pharmaceutical management (MBA); human resource management (MBA); international business (MBA); leadership and ethics (MBA); management (MBA); marketing (MBA); media (MBA); private equity (MBA); real estate (MBA); social enterprise (MBA); value investing (MBA); DDS/MBA; JD/MBA; MBA/MIA; MBA/MPH; MBA/MS; MD/MBA. *Entrance requirements:* For master's, GMAT, 2 letters of recommendation. Additional exam requirements/recommendations for international students: Required—TOEFL. Electronic applications accepted. *Expenses:* Contact institution. *Faculty research:* Human decision making and behavioral research; real estate market and mortgage defaults; financial crisis and corporate governance; international business; security analysis and accounting.

Duquesne University, Mylan School of Pharmacy, Graduate School of Pharmaceutical Sciences, Program in Pharmaceutical Administration, Pittsburgh, PA 15282-0001. Offers pharmacy administration (MS). *Faculty:* 4 full-time (1 woman). *Students:* 7 full-time (6 women), 6 international. Average age 25. 46 applicants, 2% accepted, 1 enrolled. *Degree requirements:* For master's, thesis. *Entrance requirements:* For master's, GRE General Test. Additional exam requirements/recommendations for international students: Required—TOEFL. *Application deadline:* For fall admission, 2/1 priority date for domestic students, 2/1 for international students. Applications are processed on a rolling basis. Application fee: $50. Electronic applications accepted. *Expenses: Tuition:* Full-time $16,596; part-time $922 per credit. *Required fees:* $1584; $88 per credit. Tuition and fees vary according to program. *Financial support:* In 2011–12, 4 students received support, including 4 teaching assistantships with full tuition reimbursements available. *Unit head:* Dr. Khalid Kamal, Head, 412-396-1926. *Application contact:* Information Contact, 412-396-1172, E-mail: gsps-adm@duq.edu. Web site: http://www.duq.edu/pharmacy/graduate.cfm.

Emmanuel College, Graduate and Professional Programs, Graduate Programs in Management, Boston, MA 02115. Offers biopharmaceutical leadership (MSM); human resource management (MSM, Graduate Certificate); management (MSM); management and leadership (Graduate Certificate); research administration (MSM, Graduate Certificate). Part-time and evening/weekend programs available. Postbaccalaureate distance learning degree programs offered (no on-campus study). *Faculty:* 60 part-time/adjunct (24 women). *Students:* 6 full-time (4 women), 216 part-time (155 women); includes 53 minority (28 Black or African American, non-Hispanic/Latino; 1 American Indian or Alaska Native, non-Hispanic/Latino; 10 Asian, non-Hispanic/Latino; 14 Hispanic/Latino). Average age 34. 61 applicants, 75% accepted, 39 enrolled. In 2011, 76 master's, 29 other advanced degrees awarded. *Degree requirements:* For master's,

thesis or alternative, 36 credits, including a 6-credit capstone project. *Entrance requirements:* For master's, interview, essay, resume, 2 letters of recommendation, bachelor's degree; for Graduate Certificate, transcripts from all regionally-accredited institutions attended (showing proof of bachelor's degree completion), 2 letters of recommendation, essay, resume, interview. Additional exam requirements/ recommendations for international students: Required—TOEFL (minimum score 600 paper-based; 250 computer-based; 106 iBT) or IELTS (minimum score 6.5). *Application deadline:* For fall admission, 7/31 priority date for domestic students; for spring admission, 11/30 priority date for domestic students. Applications are processed on a rolling basis. Application fee: $0. Electronic applications accepted. *Expenses: Tuition:* Part-time $2139 per course. Tuition and fees vary according to program and reciprocity agreements. *Financial support:* Applicants required to submit FAFSA. *Unit head:* Dr. Joyce DeLeo, Vice President of Academic Affairs, 617-735-9700, Fax: 617-507-0434, E-mail: gpp@emmanuel.edu. *Application contact:* Enrollment Counselor, 617-735-9700, Fax: 617-507-0434, E-mail: gpp@emmanuel.edu. Web site: http://gpp.emmanuel.edu.

Fairleigh Dickinson University, Metropolitan Campus, Silberman College of Business, Program in Pharmaceutical Studies, Teaneck, NJ 07666-1914. Offers chemical studies (Certificate); pharmaceutical studies (MBA, Certificate).

Florida Agricultural and Mechanical University, Division of Graduate Studies, Research, and Continuing Education, College of Pharmacy and Pharmaceutical Sciences, Graduate Programs in Pharmaceutical Sciences, Tallahassee, FL 32307-3200. Offers environmental toxicology (PhD); medicinal chemistry (MS, PhD); pharmaceutics (MS, PhD); pharmacology/toxicology (MS, PhD); pharmacy administration (MS). *Accreditation:* CEPH. *Degree requirements:* For master's, comprehensive exam, thesis, publishable paper; for doctorate, comprehensive exam, thesis/dissertation, publishable paper. *Entrance requirements:* For master's and doctorate, GRE General Test, minimum GPA of 3.0 in last 60 hours. Additional exam requirements/recommendations for international students: Required—TOEFL. *Faculty research:* Anticancer agents, anti-inflammatory drugs, chronopharmacology, neuroendocrinology, microbiology.

Idaho State University, Office of Graduate Studies, College of Pharmacy, Department of Pharmacy Practice and Administrative Sciences, Pocatello, ID 83209-8333. Offers pharmacy (Pharm D); pharmacy administration (MS, PhD). *Accreditation:* ACPE (one or more programs are accredited). Part-time programs available. *Degree requirements:* For master's, one foreign language, comprehensive exam, thesis, thesis research, speech and technical writing classes; for doctorate, comprehensive exam, thesis/dissertation, oral and written exams, speech and technical writing classes. *Entrance requirements:* For master's, GRE General Test, minimum GPA of 3.0, 3 letters of recommendation; for doctorate, GRE General Test, BS in pharmacy or related field, minimum GPA of 3.0, 3 letters of recommendation. Additional exam requirements/recommendations for international students: Required—TOEFL (minimum score 550 paper-based; 213 computer-based; 80 iBT). Electronic applications accepted. *Expenses:* Contact institution. *Faculty research:* Pharmaceutical care outcomes, drug use review, pharmacoeconomics.

Long Island University–Brooklyn Campus, Arnold and Marie Schwartz College of Pharmacy and Health Sciences, Graduate Programs in Pharmacy, Division of Social and Administrative Sciences, Brooklyn, NY 11201-8423. Offers drug regulatory affairs (MS); pharmacy administration (MS). Part-time and evening/weekend programs available. *Degree requirements:* For master's, thesis optional. *Entrance requirements:* For master's, minimum GPA of 3.0.

New Jersey Institute of Technology, Office of Graduate Studies, Newark College of Engineering, Department of Mechanical Engineering, Program in Pharmaceutical Systems Management, Newark, NJ 07102. Offers MS. Part-time programs available. *Students:* 12 full-time (7 women), 7 part-time (4 women); includes 4 minority (1 Black or African American, non-Hispanic/Latino; 3 Asian, non-Hispanic/Latino), 11 international. Average age 28. 28 applicants, 86% accepted, 9 enrolled. In 2011, 8 master's awarded. *Entrance requirements:* Additional exam requirements/recommendations for international students: Required—TOEFL (minimum score 550 paper-based; 213 computer-based; 79 iBT). *Application deadline:* For fall admission, 6/1 priority date for domestic students, 5/1 for international students; for spring admission, 11/15 priority date for domestic students, 11/15 for international students. Applications are processed on a rolling basis. Application fee: $65. Electronic applications accepted. *Expenses:* Tuition, state resident: full-time $7980; part-time $867 per credit. Tuition, nonresident: full-time $11,336; part-time $1196 per credit. *Required fees:* $230 per credit. *Financial support:* Application deadline: 1/15. *Unit head:* Dr. Rajpal S. Sodhi, Interim Chair, 973-596-3333, E-mail: rajpal.s.sodhi@njit.edu. *Application contact:* Kathryn Kelly, Director of Admissions, 973-596-3300, Fax: 973-596-3461, E-mail: admissions@njit.edu. Web site: http://mechanical.njit.edu/academics/graduate/ms-pharmaceutical.php.

The Ohio State University, College of Pharmacy, Columbus, OH 43210. Offers MS, PhD, Pharm D. *Accreditation:* ACPE (one or more programs are accredited). Part-time programs available. *Faculty:* 47. *Students:* 567 full-time (329 women), 29 part-time (15 women); includes 141 minority (18 Black or African American, non-Hispanic/Latino; 1 American Indian or Alaska Native, non-Hispanic/Latino; 104 Asian, non-Hispanic/Latino; 12 Hispanic/Latino; 6 Two or more races, non-Hispanic/Latino), 58 international. Average age 27. In 2011, 5 master's, 135 doctorates awarded. *Degree requirements:* For doctorate, thesis/dissertation (for some programs). *Entrance requirements:* For master's, GRE General Test, minimum GPA of 3.0; for doctorate, GRE General Test; PCAT (for Pharm D), minimum GPA of 3.0. Additional exam requirements/ recommendations for international students: Required—TOEFL, Michigan English Language Assessment Battery (minimum score 82). *Application deadline:* For fall admission, 1/1 priority date for domestic students. Application fee: $40 ($50 for international students). Electronic applications accepted. *Expenses:* Contact institution. *Financial support:* Fellowships with full tuition reimbursements, research assistantships with full tuition reimbursements, teaching assistantships with full tuition reimbursements, career-related internships or fieldwork, Federal Work-Study, institutionally sponsored loans, scholarships/grants, and traineeships available. *Unit head:* Dr. Robert W. Brueggemeier, Dean, 614-292-5711, Fax: 614-292-2588, E-mail: odmail@pharmacy.ohio-state.edu. *Application contact:* Graduate Program Coordinator, 614-292-6822, Fax: 614-292-2588, E-mail: gradprogram@pharmacy.ohio-state.edu. Web site: http://www.pharmacy.ohio-state.edu.

Purdue University, College of Pharmacy and Pharmacal Sciences and Graduate School, Graduate Programs in Pharmacy and Pharmacal Sciences, Department of Industrial and Physical Pharmacy, West Lafayette, IN 47907. Offers pharmaceutics (PhD); regulatory quality compliance (MS, Certificate). *Faculty:* 9 full-time (3 women), 33 part-time/adjunct (4 women). *Students:* 26 full-time (17 women), 27 part-time (16 women); includes 13 minority (2 Black or African American, non-Hispanic/Latino; 9 Asian, non-Hispanic/Latino; 2 Hispanic/Latino), 15 international. Average age 35. 59 applicants, 32% accepted, 11 enrolled. In 2011, 7 master's, 3 doctorates awarded. *Degree requirements:* For doctorate, thesis/dissertation. *Entrance requirements:* For doctorate, GRE General Test, minimum B average; BS in biology, chemistry, or pharmacy. Additional exam requirements/recommendations for international students: Required—TOEFL. *Application deadline:* For fall admission, 1/1 for domestic and international students. Applications are processed on a rolling basis. Application fee: $55. Electronic applications accepted. *Financial support:* Fellowships, research assistantships, teaching assistantships, and traineeships available. Support available to part-time students. Financial award applicants required to submit FAFSA. *Faculty research:* Controlled drug delivery systems, liposomes, antacids, coating technology. *Unit head:* Dr. S. R. Byrn, Graduate Head, 765-494-1460. *Application contact:* Dr. Kenneth R. Morris, Graduate Committee Chair, 765-496-3387, E-mail: morris@pharmacy.purdue.edu.

St. John's University, College of Pharmacy and Health Sciences, Graduate Programs in Pharmacy, Program in Pharmacy Administration, Queens, NY 11439. Offers MS. Part-time and evening/weekend programs available. *Students:* 20 full-time (10 women), 11 part-time (3 women); includes 1 minority (Asian, non-Hispanic/Latino), 28 international. Average age 25. 83 applicants, 47% accepted, 3 enrolled. In 2011, 18 master's awarded. *Degree requirements:* For master's, comprehensive exam, thesis optional, one-year residency. *Entrance requirements:* For master's, GRE General Test, bachelor's degree in pharmacy, minimum GPA of 3.0, 2 letters of recommendation. Additional exam requirements/recommendations for international students: Required—TOEFL (minimum score 600 paper-based; 250 computer-based; 100 iBT), IELTS (minimum score 5.5). *Application deadline:* For fall admission, 3/1 priority date for domestic students, 5/1 for international students; for spring admission, 11/1 priority date for domestic students, 11/1 for international students. Applications are processed on a rolling basis. Application fee: $70. Electronic applications accepted. *Expenses:* Contact institution. *Financial support:* Fellowships, research assistantships, and career-related internships or fieldwork available. Support available to part-time students. Financial award application deadline: 3/1; financial award applicants required to submit FAFSA. *Unit head:* Dr. Wenchen Wu, Chair, 718-990-5690, E-mail: wuw@stjohns.edu. *Application contact:* Robert Medrano, Director of Graduate Admissions, 718-990-1601, E-mail: gradhelp@stjohns.edu.

San Diego State University, Graduate and Research Affairs, College of Sciences, Program in Regulatory Affairs, San Diego, CA 92182. Offers MS. *Degree requirements:* For master's, thesis. *Entrance requirements:* For master's, GRE General Test, 3 letters of recommendation, employment/volunteer experience list. Additional exam requirements/recommendations for international students: Required—TOEFL. Electronic applications accepted.

Temple University, Fox School of Business, MBA Programs, Philadelphia, PA 19122-6096. Offers accounting (MBA); business management (MBA); financial management (MBA); healthcare and life sciences innovation (MBA); human resource management (MBA); international business (IMBA); IT management (MBA); marketing management (MBA); pharmaceutical management (MBA); strategic management (EMBA, MBA). EMBA offered in Philadelphia, PA and Tokyo, Japan. *Accreditation:* AACSB. Part-time and evening/weekend programs available. Postbaccalaureate distance learning degree programs offered (minimal on-campus study). *Entrance requirements:* For master's, GMAT, minimum undergraduate GPA of 3.0. Additional exam requirements/ recommendations for international students: Required—TOEFL (minimum score 600 paper-based; 250 computer-based; 100 iBT), IELTS (minimum score 7.5). *Expenses:* Tuition, state resident: full-time $12,366; part-time $687 per credit hour. Tuition, nonresident: full-time $17,298; part-time $961 per credit hour. *Required fees:* $590; $213 per year.

University of Arkansas for Medical Sciences, College of Pharmacy, Program in Pharmaceutical Evaluation and Policy, Little Rock, AR 72205-7199. Offers MS. *Degree requirements:* For master's, thesis. *Entrance requirements:* For master's, GRE, 3 letters of recommendation, resume. Additional exam requirements/recommendations for international students: Required—TOEFL.

University of Florida, Graduate School, College of Pharmacy and Graduate School, Graduate Programs in Pharmacy, Department of Pharmaceutical Outcomes and Policy, Gainesville, FL 32611. Offers MSP, PhD. Part-time programs available. Postbaccalaureate distance learning degree programs offered (minimal on-campus study). *Faculty:* 11 full-time (6 women). *Students:* 29 full-time (20 women), 142 part-time (84 women); includes 59 minority (26 Black or African American, non-Hispanic/Latino; 3 American Indian or Alaska Native, non-Hispanic/Latino; 22 Asian, non-Hispanic/Latino; 8 Hispanic/Latino), 14 international. Average age 37. 171 applicants, 42% accepted, 57 enrolled. In 2011, 72 master's, 3 doctorates awarded. *Degree requirements:* For doctorate, thesis/dissertation. *Entrance requirements:* For master's and doctorate, GRE General Test (minimum score of 1000), minimum GPA of 3.0. Additional exam requirements/recommendations for international students: Required—TOEFL (minimum score 550 paper-based; 213 computer-based; 80 iBT), IELTS (minimum score 6). *Application deadline:* For fall admission, 1/15 priority date for domestic students. Applications are processed on a rolling basis. Application fee: $30. Electronic applications accepted. *Financial support:* In 2011–12, 12 students received support, including 2 fellowships, 4 research assistantships, 6 teaching assistantships; tuition waivers (full) also available. Financial award applicants required to submit FAFSA. *Faculty research:* Pharmaceutical care, drug use systems, drug-related morbidity. *Unit head:* Dr. Richard Segal, Chair, 352-273-6268, Fax: 352-273-6270, E-mail: segal@cop.health.ufl.edu. *Application contact:* Dr. Carole Kimberlin, Graduate Coordinator, 352-273-6263, Fax: 352-273-6270, E-mail: kimber@cop.ufl.edu. Web site: http://www.cop.ufl.edu/education/graduate-programs/pharmaceutical-outcomes-and-policy/.

University of Houston, College of Pharmacy, Houston, TX 77204. Offers pharmaceutics (MSPHR, PhD); pharmacology (MSPHR, PhD); pharmacy (Pharm D); pharmacy administration (MSPHR, PhD). *Accreditation:* ACPE. Part-time programs available. Terminal master's awarded for partial completion of doctoral program. *Entrance requirements:* For doctorate, PCAT (for Pharm D). Additional exam requirements/recommendations for international students: Required—TOEFL. Electronic applications accepted. *Faculty research:* Drug screening and design, cardiovascular pharmacology, infectious disease, asthma research, herbal medicine.

University of Illinois at Chicago, College of Pharmacy and Graduate College, Graduate Programs in Pharmacy, Chicago, IL 60607-7128. Offers biopharmaceutical sciences (PhD); forensic science (MS); medicinal chemistry (MS, PhD); pharmacognosy (MS, PhD); pharmacy administration (MS, PhD). Terminal master's awarded for partial completion of doctoral program. *Degree requirements:* For master's, variable foreign language requirement, thesis; for doctorate, variable foreign language requirement, thesis/dissertation. *Entrance requirements:* For master's and doctorate, GRE General Test. Additional exam requirements/recommendations for international students: Required—TOEFL. Electronic applications accepted. *Expenses:* Contact institution.

University of Maryland, Baltimore, Graduate School, Graduate Programs in Pharmacy, Department of Pharmaceutical Health Service Research, Baltimore, MD 21201. Offers epidemiology (MS); pharmacy administration (PhD); Pharm D/PhD. *Degree requirements:* For doctorate, comprehensive exam, thesis/dissertation. *Entrance requirements:* For doctorate, GRE General Test. Additional exam requirements/recommendations for international students: Required—TOEFL, IELTS. Electronic applications accepted. *Faculty research:* Pharmacoeconomics, outcomes research, public health policy, drug therapy and aging.

University of Michigan, College of Pharmacy and Horace H. Rackham School of Graduate Studies, Department of Social and Administrative Sciences, Ann Arbor, MI

48109. Offers PhD. Terminal master's awarded for partial completion of doctoral program. *Degree requirements:* For doctorate, oral defense of dissertation, preliminary exam. *Entrance requirements:* For doctorate, GRE General Test. Additional exam requirements/recommendations for international students: Required—TOEFL or IELTS. Electronic applications accepted.

University of Minnesota, Twin Cities Campus, College of Pharmacy and Graduate School, Graduate Programs in Pharmacy, Graduate Program in Social and Administrative Pharmacy, Minneapolis, MN 55455-0213. Offers MS, PhD. Part-time programs available. *Faculty:* 24 full-time (8 women), 18 part-time/adjunct (6 women). *Students:* 21 full-time (8 women), 7 part-time (4 women); includes 11 minority (3 Black or African American, non-Hispanic/Latino; 5 Asian, non-Hispanic/Latino; 3 Hispanic/Latino). Average age 28. 44 applicants, 14% accepted, 4 enrolled. In 2011, 2 master's, 2 doctorates awarded. Terminal master's awarded for partial completion of doctoral program. *Degree requirements:* For master's, thesis (for some programs); for doctorate, thesis/dissertation. *Entrance requirements:* For master's, GRE General Test, BS in science; for doctorate, GRE General Test or Pharm D. Additional exam requirements/recommendations for international students: Required—TOEFL (minimum score 100 iBT). *Application deadline:* For fall admission, 2/1 priority date for domestic students, 2/1 for international students. Applications are processed on a rolling basis. Application fee: $75 ($95 for international students). Electronic applications accepted. *Financial support:* In 2011–12, 3 fellowships with full tuition reimbursements (averaging $15,000 per year), 3 research assistantships with full tuition reimbursements (averaging $15,000 per year), 7 teaching assistantships with full tuition reimbursements (averaging $15,000 per year) were awarded; career-related internships or fieldwork, scholarships/grants, traineeships, health care benefits, and unspecified assistantships also available. *Faculty research:* Pharmaceutical economics, pharmaceutical policy, pharmaceutical social/behavioral sciences. *Total annual research expenditures:* $507,493. *Unit head:* Dr. Jon C. Schommer, Director of Graduate Studies, 612-626-9915, Fax: 612-625-9931, E-mail: schom010@umn.edu. *Application contact:* Valorie Cremin, Executive Secretary, 612-624-2973, Fax: 612-625-9931, E-mail: cremi001@umn.edu. Web site: http://www.pharmacy.umn.edu/.

University of Mississippi, Graduate School, School of Pharmacy, Graduate Programs in Pharmacy, Oxford, University, MS 38677. Offers medicinal chemistry (PhD); pharmaceutical sciences (MS); pharmaceutics (PhD); pharmacognosy (PhD); pharmacology (PhD); pharmacy administration (PhD). *Students:* 96 full-time (33 women), 11 part-time (3 women); includes 11 minority (4 Black or African American, non-Hispanic/Latino; 5 Asian, non-Hispanic/Latino; 1 Hispanic/Latino; 1 Two or more races, non-Hispanic/Latino), 68 international. In 2011, 8 master's, 10 doctorates awarded. *Unit head:* Dr. Barbara G. Wells, Dean, 662-915-7265, Fax: 662-915-5704, E-mail: pharmacy@olemiss.edu. *Application contact:* Dr. Christy M. Wyandt, Associate Dean, 662-915-7474, Fax: 662-915-7577, E-mail: cwyandt@olemiss.edu.

University of the Sciences in Philadelphia, College of Graduate Studies, Program in Pharmaceutical Business, Philadelphia, PA 19104-4495. Offers MBA. Part-time and evening/weekend programs available. *Entrance requirements:* Additional exam requirements/recommendations for international students: Required—TOEFL, TWE. *Expenses:* Contact institution.

University of the Sciences in Philadelphia, College of Graduate Studies, Program in Pharmacy Administration, Philadelphia, PA 19104-4495. Offers MS. Part-time programs available. *Entrance requirements:* Additional exam requirements/recommendations for international students: Required—TOEFL, TWE. *Expenses:* Contact institution. *Faculty research:* Cost-effect analysis, pharmaceutical economics, pharmaceutical care, marketing research, health communications.

The University of Toledo, College of Graduate Studies, College of Pharmacy and Pharmaceutical Sciences, Program in Pharmaceutical Sciences, Toledo, OH 43606-3390. Offers administrative pharmacy (MSPS); industrial pharmacy (MSPS); pharmacology toxicology (MSPS). *Degree requirements:* For master's, thesis. *Entrance requirements:* For master's, GRE General Test. Additional exam requirements/recommendations for international students: Required—TOEFL (minimum score 550 paper-based; 213 computer-based; 80 iBT). Electronic applications accepted.

University of West Florida, College of Professional Studies, Department of Applied Science, Technology and Administration, Program in Administration, Pensacola, FL 32514-5750. Offers acquisition and contract administration (MSA); biomedical/pharmaceutical (MSA); criminal justice administration (MSA); database administration (MSA); education leadership (MSA); healthcare administration (MSA); human performance technology (MSA); leadership (MSA); nursing administration (MSA); public administration (MSA); software engineering administration (MSA). Part-time and evening/weekend programs available. Postbaccalaureate distance learning degree programs offered (no on-campus study). *Students:* 36 full-time (28 women), 158 part-time (95 women); includes 61 minority (31 Black or African American, non-Hispanic/Latino; 4 American Indian or Alaska Native, non-Hispanic/Latino; 4 Asian, non-Hispanic/Latino; 17 Hispanic/Latino; 2 Native Hawaiian or other Pacific Islander, non-Hispanic/Latino; 3 Two or more races, non-Hispanic/Latino), 1 international. Average age 34. 102 applicants, 59% accepted, 40 enrolled. In 2011, 62 master's awarded. *Entrance requirements:* For master's, GRE General Test, letter of intent, names of references. Additional exam requirements/recommendations for international students: Required—TOEFL (minimum score 550 paper-based; 213 computer-based). *Application deadline:* For fall admission, 6/1 for domestic and international students; for spring admission, 10/1 for domestic and international students. Applications are processed on a rolling basis. Application fee: $30. *Expenses:* Tuition, state resident: full-time $5729; part-time $302 per credit hour. Tuition, nonresident: full-time $20,059; part-time $961 per credit hour. *Required fees:* $1509; $63 per credit hour. *Financial support:* Unspecified assistantships available. Financial award application deadline: 4/15; financial award applicants required to submit FAFSA. *Unit head:* Dr. Karen Rasmussen, Chairperson, 850-474-2301, Fax: 850-474-2804, E-mail: krasmuss@uwf.edu. *Application contact:* Terry McCray, Assistant Director of Graduate Admissions, 850-473-7718, Fax: 850-473-7714, E-mail: gradadmissions@uwf.edu. Web site: http://uwf.edu/msaprogram/.

University of West Florida, College of Professional Studies, Department of Research and Applied Studies, Pensacola, FL 32514-5750. Offers administration (MSA), including acquisition and contract administration, biomedical/pharmaceutical, criminal justice administration, database administration, education leadership, healthcare administration, human performance technology, leadership, nursing administration, public administration, software engineering and administration; college student personnel administration (M Ed), including college personnel administration, guidance and counseling; curriculum and instruction (M Ed, Ed S); educational leadership (M Ed); middle and secondary level education and ESOL (M Ed). Part-time and evening/weekend programs available. *Faculty:* 2 full-time (both women), 3 part-time/adjunct (2 women). *Students:* 26 full-time (15 women), 13 part-time (9 women); includes 6 minority (4 Black or African American, non-Hispanic/Latino; 1 Hispanic/Latino; 1 Two or more races, non-Hispanic/Latino), 1 international. Average age 26. 51 applicants, 51% accepted, 16 enrolled. In 2011, 17 master's, 49 Ed Ss awarded. *Entrance requirements:* For master's, GRE or MAT, official transcripts; minimum undergraduate GPA of 3.0; letter of intent; three letters of recommendation; resume. Additional exam requirements/recommendations for international students: Required—TOEFL (minimum score 550 paper-based; 213 computer-based). *Application deadline:* For fall admission, 6/1 for domestic and international students; for spring admission, 10/1 for domestic and international students. Applications are processed on a rolling basis. Application fee: $30. *Expenses:* Tuition, state resident: full-time $5729; part-time $302 per credit hour. Tuition, nonresident: full-time $20,059; part-time $961 per credit hour. *Required fees:* $1509; $63 per credit hour. *Financial support:* In 2011–12, 33 fellowships (averaging $860 per year), 10 research assistantships (averaging $3,280 per year), 2 teaching assistantships (averaging $3,760 per year) were awarded; unspecified assistantships also available. Financial award application deadline: 4/15; financial award applicants required to submit FAFSA. *Unit head:* Dr. Joyce Nichols, Chairperson, 850-857-6042, E-mail: jcoleman0@uwf.edu. *Application contact:* Terry McCray, Assistant Director of Graduate Admissions, 850-473-7718, Fax: 850-473-7714, E-mail: gradadmissions@uwf.edu. Web site: http://uwf.edu/pcl/.

University of Wisconsin–Madison, School of Pharmacy and Graduate School, Graduate Programs in Pharmacy, Madison, WI 53706-1380. Offers pharmaceutical sciences (PhD); social and administrative sciences in pharmacy (MS, PhD). Terminal master's awarded for partial completion of doctoral program. *Degree requirements:* For master's, thesis (for some programs); for doctorate, comprehensive exam (for some programs), thesis/dissertation. *Entrance requirements:* For master's and doctorate, GRE. Additional exam requirements/recommendations for international students: Required—TOEFL. Electronic applications accepted. *Expenses:* Contact institution.

Virginia Commonwealth University, Medical College of Virginia-Professional Programs, School of Pharmacy, Department of Pharmaceutics, Richmond, VA 23284-9005. Offers medicinal chemistry (MS); pharmaceutical sciences (PhD); pharmaceutics (MS); pharmacotherapy and pharmacy administration (MS). Terminal master's awarded for partial completion of doctoral program. *Degree requirements:* For master's, thesis; for doctorate, thesis/dissertation. *Entrance requirements:* For master's and doctorate, GRE General Test. Additional exam requirements/recommendations for international students: Required—TOEFL. Electronic applications accepted. *Expenses:* Tuition, state resident: full-time $9133; part-time $507 per credit. Tuition, nonresident: full-time $18,777; part-time $1043 per credit. *Required fees:* $77 per credit. Tuition and fees vary according to degree level, campus/location, program and student level. *Faculty research:* Drug delivery systems, drug development.

West Virginia University, School of Pharmacy, Program in Pharmaceutical and Pharmacological Sciences, Morgantown, WV 26506. Offers administrative pharmacy (PhD); behavioral pharmacy (MS, PhD); biopharmaceutics/pharmacokinetics (MS, PhD); industrial pharmacy (MS); medicinal chemistry (MS, PhD); pharmaceutical chemistry (MS, PhD); pharmaceutics (MS, PhD); pharmacology and toxicology (MS); pharmacy (MS); pharmacy administration (MS). Part-time programs available. Terminal master's awarded for partial completion of doctoral program. *Degree requirements:* For master's, thesis; for doctorate, one foreign language, comprehensive exam, thesis/dissertation. *Entrance requirements:* For master's and doctorate, GRE General Test, minimum GPA of 2.75. Additional exam requirements/recommendations for international students: Required—TOEFL; Recommended—TWE. Electronic applications accepted. *Expenses:* Contact institution. *Faculty research:* Pharmaceutics, medicinal chemistry, biopharmaceutics/pharmacokinetics, health outcomes research.

Pharmaceutical Sciences

Albany College of Pharmacy and Health Sciences, School of Pharmacy and Pharmaceutical Sciences, Albany, NY 12208. Offers pharmaceutical sciences (MS), including pharmaceutics, pharmacology; pharmacy (Pharm D). *Accreditation:* ACPE. *Faculty:* 66 full-time (30 women), 11 part-time/adjunct (6 women). *Students:* 510 full-time (313 women), 3 part-time (2 women); includes 114 minority (21 Black or African American, non-Hispanic/Latino; 1 American Indian or Alaska Native, non-Hispanic/Latino; 69 Asian, non-Hispanic/Latino; 12 Hispanic/Latino; 11 Two or more races, non-Hispanic/Latino), 47 international. Average age 23. 1,477 applicants, 14% accepted, 106 enrolled. In 2011, 3 master's, 230 doctorates awarded. *Degree requirements:* For master's, thesis; for doctorate, practice experience. *Entrance requirements:* For master's, GRE, minimum GPA of 3.0; for doctorate, PCAT, minimum GPA of 2.5. Additional exam requirements/recommendations for international students: Required—TOEFL (minimum score 474 paper-based; 84 iBT). *Application deadline:* For fall admission, 3/1 for domestic and international students. Applications are processed on a rolling basis. Application fee: $100. Electronic applications accepted. *Expenses: Tuition:* Full-time $29,100; part-time $855 per credit hour. *Required fees:* $1230; $680. Tuition and fees vary according to degree level. *Financial support:* In 2011–12, 20 students received support. Federal Work-Study and scholarships/grants available. Support available to part-time students. Financial award application deadline: 3/1; financial award applicants required to submit FAFSA. *Faculty research:* Therapeutic use of drugs, pharmacokinetics, drug delivery and design. *Unit head:* Dr. Mehdi Boroujerdi, Provost, 518-694-7212, Fax: 518-694-7063. *Application contact:* Donna Myers, Director of Pharmacy and Graduate Admissions, 518-694-7186, Fax: 518-694-7929, E-mail: graduate@acphs.edu. Web site: http://www.acphs.edu/.

See Display on page 927 and Close-Up on page 935.

Auburn University, Harrison School of Pharmacy and Graduate School, Graduate Program in Pharmacy, Auburn University, AL 36849. Offers pharmacal sciences (MS, PhD); pharmaceutical sciences (PhD); pharmacy care systems (MS, PhD). Part-time programs available. *Faculty:* 14 full-time (1 woman). *Students:* 19 full-time (10 women), 8 part-time (4 women), 20 international. Average age 28. 134 applicants, 5% accepted, 6 enrolled. In 2011, 5 doctorates awarded. *Degree requirements:* For master's, thesis; for doctorate, thesis/dissertation. *Entrance requirements:* For master's and doctorate, GRE General Test. *Application deadline:* For fall admission, 7/7 for domestic students; for spring admission, 11/24 for domestic students. Applications are processed on a rolling basis. Application fee: $50 ($60 for international students). Electronic applications

accepted. *Expenses:* Tuition, state resident: full-time $7290; part-time $405 per credit hour. Tuition, nonresident: full-time $21,870; part-time $1215 per credit hour. *International tuition:* $22,000 full-time. *Required fees:* $1402. *Financial support:* Fellowships, research assistantships, and teaching assistantships available. *Faculty research:* Communications, facilities design, substance abuse. *Total annual research expenditures:* $600,000. *Unit head:* Dr. R. Lee Evans, Dean and Professor, Harrison School of Pharmacy, 334-844-8348, Fax: 334-844-8353. *Application contact:* Dr. George Flowers, Dean of the Graduate School, 334-844-2125.

Boston University, School of Medicine, Division of Graduate Medical Sciences, Department of Pharmacology and Experimental Therapeutics, Boston, MA 02118. Offers MA, PhD, MD/PhD. *Faculty:* 11 full-time (4 women), 16 part-time/adjunct (4 women). *Students:* 9 full-time (8 women), 5 part-time (4 women); includes 4 minority (1 Black or African American, non-Hispanic/Latino; 2 Asian, non-Hispanic/Latino; 1 Hispanic/Latino). Average age 30. 46 applicants, 17% accepted, 2 enrolled. In 2011, 3 doctorates awarded. Terminal master's awarded for partial completion of doctoral program. *Degree requirements:* For master's, thesis; for doctorate, thesis/dissertation. *Entrance requirements:* For master's and doctorate, GRE General Test, GRE Subject Test. Additional exam requirements/recommendations for international students: Required—TOEFL. *Application deadline:* For fall admission, 1/15 priority date for domestic students; for spring admission, 10/15 priority date for domestic students. *Application fee:* $75. Electronic applications accepted. *Expenses: Tuition:* Full-time $40,848; part-time $1276 per credit hour. *Required fees:* $572; $286 per semester. *Financial support:* In 2011–12, 1 fellowship (averaging $30,500 per year), research assistantships (averaging $30,500 per year) were awarded; Federal Work-Study, scholarships/grants, traineeships, tuition waivers, and research stipends also available. Financial award applicants required to submit FAFSA. *Faculty research:* Molecular pharmacology, neuropharmacology, peptide receptors, psychopharmacology. *Unit head:* Dr. David H. Farb, Chairman, 617-638-4300, Fax: 617-638-4329, E-mail: dfarb@bu.edu. *Application contact:* Dr. Carol T. Walsh, Graduate Director, 617-638-4326, Fax: 617-638-4329, E-mail: ctwalsh@bu.edu. Web site: http://www.bumc.bu.edu/.

Butler University, College of Pharmacy and Health Sciences, Indianapolis, IN 46208-3485. Offers pharmaceutical science (MS, Pharm D); physician assistance studies (MS). *Accreditation:* ACPE (one or more programs are accredited). Part-time and evening/weekend programs available. *Faculty:* 18 full-time (10 women), 1 (woman) part-time/adjunct. *Students:* 273 full-time (178 women), 18 part-time (14 women); includes 20 minority (4 Black or African American, non-Hispanic/Latino; 11 Asian, non-Hispanic/Latino; 4 Hispanic/Latino; 1 Two or more races, non-Hispanic/Latino), 14 international. Average age 24. 58 applicants, 7% accepted, 4 enrolled. In 2011, 47 master's, 115 doctorates awarded. *Degree requirements:* For master's, research paper or thesis. *Application deadline:* For fall admission, 8/1 priority date for domestic students; for spring admission, 12/15 for domestic students. Applications are processed on a rolling basis. *Application fee:* $35. Electronic applications accepted. *Expenses:* Contact institution. *Financial support:* Applicants required to submit FAFSA. *Faculty research:* Anti-seizure drugs, casein kinase inhibitors, speech recognition interface for prescribing drugs, pharmacoeconomics. *Total annual research expenditures:* $92,000. *Unit head:* Dr. Mary Andritz, Dean, 317-940-9451, Fax: 317-940-6172, E-mail: mandritz@butler.edu. *Application contact:* Dr. Bruce Clayton, Professor, 317-940-9830, E-mail: bclayton@butler.edu. Web site: http://www.butler.edu/pharmacy-pa/.

Campbell University, Graduate and Professional Programs, School of Pharmacy, Buies Creek, NC 27506. Offers clinical research (MS); pharmaceutical science (MS); pharmacy (Pharm D). *Accreditation:* ACPE. Part-time and evening/weekend programs available. *Entrance requirements:* For master's, MCAT, PCAT, GRE, bachelor's degree in health sciences or related field; for doctorate, PCAT. Additional exam requirements/recommendations for international students: Required—TOEFL (minimum score 550 paper-based; 213 computer-based; 79 iBT). Electronic applications accepted. *Expenses:* Contact institution. *Faculty research:* Immunology, medicinal chemistry, pharmaceutics, applied pharmacology.

Creighton University, School of Medicine and Graduate School, Graduate Programs in Medicine, Department of Pharmacology, Omaha, NE 68178-0001. Offers pharmaceutical sciences (MS); pharmacology (MS, PhD); Pharm D/MS. Terminal master's awarded for partial completion of doctoral program. *Degree requirements:* For master's, comprehensive exam, thesis; for doctorate, comprehensive exam, thesis/dissertation, oral and written preliminary exams. *Entrance requirements:* For master's and doctorate, GRE General Test, minimum GPA of 3.0, undergraduate degree in sciences. Additional exam requirements/recommendations for international students: Required—TOEFL. Electronic applications accepted. *Expenses: Tuition:* Full-time $12,672; part-time $704 per credit hour. *Required fees:* $1410; $136 per semester. Tuition and fees vary according to campus/location and reciprocity agreements. *Faculty research:* Pharmacology secretion, cardiovascular-renal pharmacology, adrenergic receptors, signal transduction, genetic regulation of receptors.

Creighton University, School of Pharmacy and Health Professions and Department of Pharmacology, Program in Pharmaceutical Sciences, Omaha, NE 68178-0001. Offers MS, Pharm D/MS. *Degree requirements:* For master's, thesis. *Entrance requirements:* For master's, GRE, three recommendations. Additional exam requirements/recommendations for international students: Required—TOEFL (minimum score 550 paper-based; 213 computer-based; 80 iBT). Electronic applications accepted. *Expenses: Tuition:* Full-time $12,672; part-time $704 per credit hour. *Required fees:* $1410; $136 per semester. Tuition and fees vary according to campus/location and reciprocity agreements.

Dartmouth College, Program in Experimental and Molecular Medicine, Molecular Pharmacology, Toxicology and Experimental Therapeutics Track, Hanover, NH 03755. Offers PhD.

Drexel University, College of Medicine, Biomedical Graduate Programs, Program in Drug Discovery and Development, Philadelphia, PA 19104-2875. Offers MS. *Degree requirements:* For master's, thesis.

Duquesne University, Mylan School of Pharmacy, Graduate School of Pharmaceutical Sciences, Program in Pharmaceutics, Pittsburgh, PA 15282-0001. Offers MS, PhD, MBA/MS. *Faculty:* 7 full-time (1 woman). *Students:* 21 full-time (8 women); includes 1 minority (Asian, non-Hispanic/Latino), 14 international. Average age 28. 164 applicants, 2% accepted, 3 enrolled. In 2011, 2 degrees awarded. *Degree requirements:* For master's, thesis; for doctorate, comprehensive exam, thesis/dissertation. *Entrance requirements:* For master's and doctorate, GRE General Test. Additional exam requirements/recommendations for international students: Required—TOEFL. *Application deadline:* For fall admission, 2/1 priority date for domestic students, 2/1 for international students; for spring admission, 10/1 priority date for domestic students, 10/1 for international students. Applications are processed on a rolling basis. *Application fee:* $50. Electronic applications accepted. *Expenses: Tuition:* Full-time $16,596; part-time $922 per credit. *Required fees:* $1584; $88 per credit. Tuition and fees vary according to program. *Financial support:* In 2011–12, 18 students received support, including 2 research assistantships with full tuition reimbursements available, 16 teaching assistantships with full tuition reimbursements available; unspecified assistantships also available. *Unit head:* Dr. Wilson S. Meng, Head, 412-396-6366.

Application contact: Information Contact, 412-396-1172, E-mail: gsps-adm@duq.edu. Web site: http://www.duq.edu/pharmacy/graduate.cfm.

East Tennessee State University, James H. Quillen College of Medicine, Biomedical Science Graduate Program, Johnson City, TN 37614. Offers anatomy and cell biology (PhD); biochemistry and molecular biology (PhD); microbiology (PhD); pharmaceutical sciences (PhD); pharmacology (PhD); physiology (PhD); quantitative biosciences (PhD). *Faculty:* 33 full-time (6 women). *Students:* 29 full-time (15 women), 2 part-time (both women); includes 4 minority (1 Black or African American, non-Hispanic/Latino; 1 Asian, non-Hispanic/Latino; 2 Hispanic/Latino), 6 international. Average age 29. 76 applicants, 12% accepted, 7 enrolled. In 2011, 1 doctorate awarded. *Degree requirements:* For doctorate, thesis/dissertation, comprehensive qualifying exam. *Entrance requirements:* For doctorate, GRE General Test, GRE Subject Test. Additional exam requirements/recommendations for international students: Required—TOEFL (minimum score 550 paper-based; 213 computer-based; 79 iBT). *Application deadline:* For fall admission, 3/15 priority date for domestic students, 3/1 for international students. *Application fee:* $35 ($45 for international students). Electronic applications accepted. *Expenses:* Contact institution. *Financial support:* In 2011–12, 29 students received support, including 29 research assistantships with full tuition reimbursements available (averaging $19,000 per year); career-related internships or fieldwork, institutionally sponsored loans, scholarships/grants, and unspecified assistantships also available. Financial award application deadline: 7/1; financial award applicants required to submit FAFSA. *Faculty research:* Cardiovascular biology, neuroscience, infectious disease, cancer, inflammatory disease. *Total annual research expenditures:* $3.6 million. *Unit head:* Dr. Mitchell E. Robinson, Associate Dean/Program Director, 423-439-2031, Fax: 423-439-2140, E-mail: robinson@etsu.edu. *Application contact:* Shella Bennett, Graduate Specialist, 423-439-4708, Fax: 423-439-5624, E-mail: bennetsg@etsu.edu.

Florida Agricultural and Mechanical University, Division of Graduate Studies, Research, and Continuing Education, College of Pharmacy and Pharmaceutical Sciences, Graduate Programs in Pharmaceutical Sciences, Tallahassee, FL 32307-3200. Offers environmental toxicology (PhD); medicinal chemistry (MS, PhD); pharmaceutics (MS, PhD); pharmacology/toxicology (MS, PhD); pharmacy administration (MS). *Accreditation:* CEPH. *Degree requirements:* For master's, comprehensive exam, thesis, publishable paper; for doctorate, comprehensive exam, thesis/dissertation, publishable paper. *Entrance requirements:* For master's and doctorate, GRE General Test, minimum GPA of 3.0 in last 60 hours. Additional exam requirements/recommendations for international students: Required—TOEFL. *Faculty research:* Anticancer agents, anti-inflammatory drugs, chronopharmacology, neuroendocrinology, microbiology.

Idaho State University, Office of Graduate Studies, College of Pharmacy, Department of Biomedical and Pharmaceutical Sciences, Pocatello, ID 83209-8334. Offers biopharmaceutical analysis (PhD); drug delivery (PhD); medicinal chemistry (PhD); pharmaceutical sciences (MS); pharmacology (PhD). Part-time programs available. *Degree requirements:* For master's, one foreign language, comprehensive exam, thesis, thesis research, classes in speech and technical writing; for doctorate, comprehensive exam, thesis/dissertation, written and oral exams, classes in speech and technical writing. *Entrance requirements:* For master's, GRE General Test, minimum GPA of 3.0, 3 letters of recommendation; for doctorate, GRE General Test, BS in pharmacy or related field, minimum GPA of 3.0, 3 letters of recommendation. Additional exam requirements/recommendations for international students: Required—TOEFL (minimum score 550 paper-based; 213 computer-based; 80 iBT). Electronic applications accepted. *Expenses:* Contact institution. *Faculty research:* Metabolic toxicity of heavy metals, neuroendocrine pharmacology, cardiovascular pharmacology, cancer biology, immunopharmacology.

The Johns Hopkins University, Zanvyl Krieger School of Arts and Sciences, Advanced Academic Programs, Program in Bioscience Regulatory Affairs, Baltimore, MD 21218-2699. Offers MS. *Degree requirements:* For master's, practicum. *Entrance requirements:* For master's, undergraduate degree in the life sciences or engineering from a four-year college with minimum GPA of 3.0.

Long Island University–Brooklyn Campus, Arnold and Marie Schwartz College of Pharmacy and Health Sciences, Graduate Programs in Pharmacy, Division of Pharmaceutical Sciences, Brooklyn, NY 11201-8423. Offers cosmetic science (MS); industrial pharmacy (MS); pharmaceutics (PhD); pharmacology/toxicology (MS). Part-time and evening/weekend programs available. Terminal master's awarded for partial completion of doctoral program. *Degree requirements:* For master's, thesis optional; for doctorate, thesis/dissertation, candidacy exam. *Entrance requirements:* For master's and doctorate, minimum GPA of 3.0.

Long Island University–Hudson at Rockland, Graduate School, Program in Pharmaceutics, Orangeburg, NY 10962. Offers cosmetic science (MS); industrial pharmacy (MS). Part-time programs available. *Entrance requirements:* For master's, college transcripts, 2 letters of recommendation. Additional exam requirements/recommendations for international students: Required—TOEFL.

Massachusetts College of Pharmacy and Health Sciences, Graduate Studies, Program in Pharmaceutics/Industrial Pharmacy, Boston, MA 02115-5896. Offers MS, PhD. *Students:* 22 full-time (15 women), 2 part-time (1 woman); includes 3 minority (all Asian, non-Hispanic/Latino), 18 international. Average age 30. 48 applicants, 15% accepted, 4 enrolled. In 2011, 2 master's, 1 doctorate awarded. Terminal master's awarded for partial completion of doctoral program. *Degree requirements:* For master's, thesis, oral defense of thesis; for doctorate, one foreign language, comprehensive exam, thesis/dissertation, oral defense of dissertation, qualifying exam. *Entrance requirements:* For master's and doctorate, GRE General Test, minimum QPA of 3.0. Additional exam requirements/recommendations for international students: Required—TOEFL (minimum score 550 paper-based; 213 computer-based; 79 iBT). *Application deadline:* For fall admission, 2/1 priority date for domestic students, 2/1 for international students. *Application fee:* $70. *Expenses: Tuition:* Full-time $30,200; part-time $945 per credit hour. *Financial support:* Fellowships with partial tuition reimbursements, research assistantships with partial tuition reimbursements, teaching assistantships with full tuition reimbursements, tuition waivers (partial), and library assistantships available. Financial award application deadline: 3/15. *Faculty research:* Pharmacokinetics and drug metabolism, pharmaceutics and physical pharmacy, dosage forms. *Unit head:* Dr. Eman Atef, Assistant Professor, Pharmaceutics, 617-732-2980, E-mail: eman.atef@mcphs.edu. *Application contact:* Brian Barilone, Associate Director of Transfer and Graduate Admission, 617-879-5032, E-mail: admissions@mcphs.edu.

Memorial University of Newfoundland, School of Graduate Studies, School of Pharmacy, St. John's, NL A1C 5S7, Canada. Offers MSCPharm, PhD. Part-time programs available. *Degree requirements:* For master's, thesis, seminar; for doctorate, comprehensive exam, thesis/dissertation, oral defense of thesis. *Entrance requirements:* For master's, B Sc in pharmacy or related area. Electronic applications accepted. *Faculty research:* Pharmaceutics, medicinal chemistry, physical pharmacy, pharmacology, toxicology.

Mercer University, Graduate Studies, Cecil B. Day Campus, College of Pharmacy and Health Sciences, Macon, GA 31207-0003. Offers medical sciences/physician assistant studies (MM Sc); pharmaceutical sciences (PhD); pharmacology (PhD); pharmacy

(Pharm D); physical therapy (DPT); Pharm D/MBA; Pharm D/PhD. *Accreditation:* ACPE (one or more programs are accredited). *Faculty:* 28 full-time (17 women), 4 part-time/adjunct (3 women). *Students:* 747 full-time (487 women), 7 part-time (2 women); includes 232 minority (79 Black or African American, non-Hispanic/Latino; 136 Asian, non-Hispanic/Latino; 8 Hispanic/Latino; 9 Two or more races, non-Hispanic/Latino), 50 international. Average age 26. 1,895 applicants, 18% accepted, 176 enrolled. In 2011, 31 master's, 155 doctorates awarded. *Degree requirements:* For doctorate, comprehensive exam (for some programs), thesis/dissertation (for some programs). *Entrance requirements:* For master's, GRE, minimum GPA of 3.0 (preferred); for doctorate, GRE; PCAT (for Pharm D), Pharm D or BS in pharmacy or science, minimum GPA of 3.0. Additional exam requirements/recommendations for international students: Required—TOEFL. *Application deadline:* Applications are processed on a rolling basis. Electronic applications accepted. *Expenses:* Contact institution. *Financial support:* In 2011–12, 350 students received support. Teaching assistantships with tuition reimbursements available, career-related internships or fieldwork, Federal Work-Study, institutionally sponsored loans, scholarships/grants, tuition waivers, and unspecified assistantships available. Support available to part-time students. Financial award application deadline: 5/1; financial award applicants required to submit FAFSA. *Faculty research:* Stability and compatibility of steroids, synthesis of antihypertensives, disposition of cyclosporine, DUZ-drug research, synthesis of enzyme inhibitors. *Unit head:* Dr. Hewitt W. Matthews, Dean, 678-547-6306, Fax: 678-547-6315, E-mail: matthews_h@mercer.edu. *Application contact:* Dr. James W. Bartling, Associate Dean for Student Affairs and Admissions, 678-547-6181, Fax: 678-547-6518, E-mail: bartling_jw@mercer.edu. Web site: http://www.cophs.mercer.edu.

North Dakota State University, College of Graduate and Interdisciplinary Studies, College of Pharmacy, Nursing and Allied Sciences, Department of Pharmaceutical Sciences, Fargo, ND 58108. Offers MS, PhD. *Accreditation:* ACPE. Part-time programs available. *Faculty:* 10 full-time (1 woman). *Students:* 19 full-time (10 women), 6 part-time (3 women), 22 international. Average age 25. 73 applicants, 5% accepted, 3 enrolled. In 2011, 1 doctorate awarded. Terminal master's awarded for partial completion of doctoral program. *Degree requirements:* For master's, thesis; for doctorate, thesis/dissertation. *Entrance requirements:* For master's and doctorate, GRE General Test. Additional exam requirements/recommendations for international students: Required—TOEFL. *Application deadline:* For fall admission, 3/15 priority date for domestic students; for spring admission, 11/15 priority date for domestic students. Applications are processed on a rolling basis. Application fee: $35. Electronic applications accepted. *Financial support:* In 2011–12, 19 research assistantships with full tuition reimbursements (averaging $14,000 per year) were awarded; institutionally sponsored loans also available. Financial award application deadline: 4/15. *Faculty research:* Subcellular pharmacokinetics, cancer, cardiovascular drug design, iontophoresis, neuropharmacology. *Unit head:* Dr. Jagdish Singh, Chair, 701-231-7943, E-mail: jagdishsingh@ndsu.edu. *Application contact:* Assistant Professor. Web site: http://www.ndsu.nodak.edu/pharmsci/.

Northeastern University, Bouvé College of Health Sciences, School of Pharmacy, Boston, MA 02115-5096. Offers MS, PhD. Students enter program as undergraduates. *Accreditation:* ACPE. *Students:* 125 full-time, 10 part-time. 304 applicants, 34% accepted, 56 enrolled. In 2011, 39 master's, 19 doctorates awarded. *Degree requirements:* For doctorate, comprehensive exam, thesis/dissertation. *Entrance requirements:* For master's and doctorate, GRE. Additional exam requirements/recommendations for international students: Required—TOEFL (minimum score 100 iBT). *Application deadline:* For fall admission, 3/1 for domestic students, 6/1 for international students. Electronic applications accepted. *Financial support:* In 2011–12, 17 research assistantships, 18 teaching assistantships were awarded; scholarships/grants also available. *Unit head:* John R. Reynolds, Dean, 617-373-3380, Fax: 617-373-7655, E-mail: schoolofpharmacy@neu.edu. *Application contact:* Margaret Schnabel, Director of Graduate Admission, 617-373-2708, Fax: 617-373-8780, E-mail: admissions@neu.edu. Web site: http://www.northeastern.edu/bouve/programs/dpharmacy.html.

Oregon State University, College of Pharmacy, Corvallis, OR 97331. Offers MS, PhD, Pharm D. *Accreditation:* ACPE (one or more programs are accredited). Part-time programs available. Terminal master's awarded for partial completion of doctoral program. *Degree requirements:* For master's, thesis; for doctorate, thesis/dissertation (for some programs). *Entrance requirements:* For master's, GRE General Test, minimum GPA of 3.0 in last 90 hours. Additional exam requirements/recommendations for international students: Required—TOEFL. *Faculty research:* Pharmacology/toxicology, pharmacokinetics, biopharmaceutics, neuroscience, natural products.

Purdue University, College of Pharmacy and Pharmacal Sciences and Graduate School, Graduate Programs in Pharmacy and Pharmacal Sciences, Department of Pharmacy Practice, West Lafayette, IN 47907. Offers clinical pharmacy (MS, PhD); pharmacy administration (MS, PhD). *Faculty:* 16 full-time (4 women), 13 part-time/adjunct (4 women). *Students:* 14 full-time (8 women), 2 part-time (both women); includes 2 minority (1 Black or African American, non-Hispanic/Latino; 1 Hispanic/Latino), 10 international. Average age 29. 51 applicants, 8% accepted, 2 enrolled. In 2011, 3 master's, 1 doctorate awarded. Terminal master's awarded for partial completion of doctoral program. *Degree requirements:* For master's, thesis optional; for doctorate, thesis/dissertation. *Entrance requirements:* For master's, GRE General Test, minimum undergraduate GPA of 3.0 or equivalent; for doctorate, GRE General Test, minimum undergraduate GPA of 3.0 or equivalent; master's degree with minimum GPA of 3.0 or equivalent. Additional exam requirements/recommendations for international students: Required—TOEFL (minimum score 550 paper-based; 77 iBT), TWE, TWE recommended for MS, required for Ph D. *Application deadline:* Applications are processed on a rolling basis. Application fee: $60 ($75 for international students). Electronic applications accepted. *Financial support:* In 2011–12, teaching assistantships with tuition reimbursements (averaging $20,000 per year) were awarded; fellowships, research assistantships, career-related internships or fieldwork, and traineeships also available. Support available to part-time students. Financial award applicants required to submit FAFSA. *Faculty research:* Clinical drug studies, pharmacy education advancement, administrative studies. *Unit head:* Dr. James E. Tisdale, Interim Head, 317-613-2315 Ext. 306, E-mail: jtisdale@purdue.edu. *Application contact:* Dr. Janine C. Mott, Graduate Contact, 765-494-1362, E-mail: jmott@purdue.edu.

Queen's University at Kingston, School of Graduate Studies and Research, Faculty of Health Sciences, Department of Anatomy and Cell Biology, Kingston, ON K7L 3N6, Canada. Offers biology of reproduction (M Sc, PhD); cancer (M Sc, PhD); cardiovascular pathophysiology (M Sc, PhD); cell and molecular biology (M Sc, PhD); drug metabolism (M Sc, PhD); endocrinology (M Sc, PhD); motor control (M Sc, PhD); neural regeneration (M Sc, PhD); neurophysiology (M Sc, PhD). Part-time programs available. *Degree requirements:* For master's, thesis; for doctorate, one foreign language, comprehensive exam, thesis/dissertation. *Entrance requirements:* Additional exam requirements/recommendations for international students: Required—TOEFL. Electronic applications accepted. *Faculty research:* Human kinetics, neuroscience, reproductive biology, cardiovascular.

Rush University, Graduate College, Division of Pharmacology, Chicago, IL 60612-3832. Offers clinical research (MS); pharmacology (MS, PhD); MD/PhD. Terminal master's awarded for partial completion of doctoral program. *Degree requirements:* For master's, thesis; for doctorate, thesis/dissertation. *Entrance requirements:* For master's and doctorate, GRE General Test, interview. Additional exam requirements/recommendations for international students: Required—TOEFL (minimum score 550 paper-based; 213 computer-based). *Faculty research:* Dopamine neurobiology and Parkinson's disease; cardiac electrophysiology and clinical pharmacology; neutrophil motility, apoptosis, and adhesion; angiogenesis; pulmonary vascular physiology.

Rutgers, The State University of New Jersey, New Brunswick, Ernest Mario School of Pharmacy, Program in Pharmaceutical Science, Piscataway, NJ 08854-8097. Offers MS, PhD. Part-time programs available. Terminal master's awarded for partial completion of doctoral program. *Degree requirements:* For master's, thesis; for doctorate, thesis/dissertation. *Entrance requirements:* For master's and doctorate, GRE General Test, 3 letters of recommendation. Additional exam requirements/recommendations for international students: Required—TOEFL (minimum score 550 paper-based; 213 computer-based; 83 iBT). Electronic applications accepted. *Faculty research:* Drug delivery, drug transport and drug metabolism; pharmacokinetics and pharmacodynamics; cancer chemoprevention and dietary phytochemicals; pharmacogenomics and personalized medicine; bioinformatics and computational pharmaceutical sciences.

St. John's University, College of Pharmacy and Health Sciences, Graduate Programs in Pharmacy, Program in Pharmaceutical Sciences, Queens, NY 11439. Offers MS, PhD. Part-time and evening/weekend programs available. *Students:* 68 full-time (29 women), 106 part-time (56 women); includes 18 minority (3 Black or African American, non-Hispanic/Latino; 12 Asian, non-Hispanic/Latino; 1 Hispanic/Latino; 2 Two or more races, non-Hispanic/Latino), 141 international. Average age 27. 451 applicants, 37% accepted, 53 enrolled. In 2011, 37 master's, 7 doctorates awarded. Terminal master's awarded for partial completion of doctoral program. *Degree requirements:* For master's, comprehensive exam, thesis optional, one-year residency; for doctorate, comprehensive exam, thesis/dissertation, qualifying exams, residency. *Entrance requirements:* For master's, GRE General Test, minimum GPA of 3.0, 2 letters of recommendation, statement of goals; for doctorate, GRE General Test, minimum GPA of 3.5 (undergraduate), 3.0 (graduate); 2 letters of recommendation. Additional exam requirements/recommendations for international students: Required—TOEFL (minimum score 600 paper-based; 250 computer-based; 100 iBT), IELTS (minimum score 5.5). *Application deadline:* For fall admission, 3/1 priority date for domestic students, 5/1 for international students; for spring admission, 11/1 priority date for domestic students, 11/1 for international students. Applications are processed on a rolling basis. Application fee: $70. Electronic applications accepted. *Expenses:* Contact institution. *Financial support:* Fellowships, research assistantships, career-related internships or fieldwork, and scholarships/grants available. Support available to part-time students. Financial award application deadline: 3/1; financial award applicants required to submit FAFSA. *Faculty research:* Neurotoxicology, biochemical toxicology, molecular pharmacology, neuropharmacology, intermediary metabolism. *Unit head:* Dr. Louis Trombetta, Chair, 718-990-6025, E-mail: trombetl@stjohns.edu. *Application contact:* Robert Medrano, Director of Graduate Admission, 718-990-1601, Fax: 718-990-5686, E-mail: gradhelp@stjohns.edu.

South Dakota State University, Graduate School, College of Pharmacy, Department of Pharmaceutical Sciences, Brookings, SD 57007. Offers biological science (MS); pharmaceutical sciences (PhD). *Degree requirements:* For master's, thesis, oral exam; for doctorate, comprehensive exam, thesis/dissertation, oral exam. *Entrance requirements:* For master's and doctorate, GRE General Test. Additional exam requirements/recommendations for international students: Required—TOEFL (minimum score 550 paper-based; 213 computer-based). *Faculty research:* Drugs of abuse, anti-cancer drugs, sustained drug delivery, drug metabolism.

Stevens Institute of Technology, Graduate School, Charles V. Schaefer Jr. School of Engineering, Department of Mechanical Engineering, Program in Pharmaceutical Manufacturing, Hoboken, NJ 07030. Offers M Eng, MS, Certificate.

Stevens Institute of Technology, Graduate School, Wesley J. Howe School of Technology Management, Program in Business Administration, Hoboken, NJ 07030. Offers engineering management (MBA); financial engineering (MBA); information management (MBA); information technology in financial services (MBA); information technology in the pharmaceutical industry (MBA); information technology outsourcing (MBA); pharmaceutical management (MBA); project management (MBA); technology management (MBA); telecommunications management (MBA).

Temple University, Health Sciences Center, School of Pharmacy, Department of Pharmaceutical Sciences, Program in Quality Assurance/Regulatory Affairs, Philadelphia, PA 19122-6096. Offers MS. Part-time and evening/weekend programs available. Postbaccalaureate distance learning degree programs offered (minimal on-campus study). *Students:* 4 full-time (3 women), 103 part-time (66 women); includes 25 minority (6 Black or African American, non-Hispanic/Latino; 13 Asian, non-Hispanic/Latino; 5 Hispanic/Latino; 1 Two or more races, non-Hispanic/Latino). Average age 37. 21 applicants, 100% accepted, 15 enrolled. In 2011, 75 master's awarded. *Degree requirements:* For master's, thesis. *Entrance requirements:* For master's, GRE or GMAT, minimum undergraduate GPA of 3.0. Additional exam requirements/recommendations for international students: Required—TOEFL (minimum score 550 paper-based; 213 computer-based; 79 iBT). *Application deadline:* For fall admission, 8/1 for domestic students, 12/15 for international students; for spring admission, 12/15 for domestic students, 8/1 for international students. Applications are processed on a rolling basis. Application fee: $50. Electronic applications accepted. *Expenses:* Tuition, state resident: full-time $12,366; part-time $687 per credit hour. Tuition, nonresident: full-time $17,298; part-time $961 per credit hour. *Required fees:* $590; $213 per year. *Financial support:* Application deadline: 1/15; applicants required to submit FAFSA. *Unit head:* Dr. Daniel Canney, Director of Graduate Studies, 215-707-4948, E-mail: canney@temple.edu. *Application contact:* Tara Schumacher, Coordinator of Outreach, 215-204-6575, Fax: 215-204-8781, E-mail: tara.schumacher@temple.edu. Web site: http://www.temple.edu/pharmacy_QARA.

Texas Tech University Health Sciences Center, Graduate School of Biomedical Sciences, Department of Pharmaceutical Sciences, Lubbock, TX 79430. Offers MS, PhD. *Accreditation:* ACPE. Terminal master's awarded for partial completion of doctoral program. *Degree requirements:* For master's, thesis; for doctorate, thesis/dissertation. *Entrance requirements:* For master's and doctorate, GRE General Test, minimum GPA of 3.0. Additional exam requirements/recommendations for international students: Required—TOEFL (minimum score 550 paper-based; 213 computer-based; 79 iBT). Electronic applications accepted. *Faculty research:* Drug design and delivery, pharmacology, pharmacokinetics, drug receptor modeling, molecular and reproductive biology.

Université de Montréal, Faculty of Pharmacy, Montréal, QC H3C 3J7, Canada. Offers drugs development (DESS); pharmaceutical care (DESS); pharmaceutical practice (M Sc); pharmaceutical sciences (M Sc, PhD); pharmacist-supervisor teacher (DESS). Part-time programs available. Terminal master's awarded for partial completion of doctoral program. *Degree requirements:* For master's, thesis; for doctorate, thesis/dissertation. *Entrance requirements:* For master's and doctorate, proficiency in French.

Electronic applications accepted. *Faculty research:* Novel drug delivery systems, immunoassay development, medicinal chemistry of CNS compounds, pharmacokinetics and biopharmaceutical compounds.

Université Laval, Faculty of Pharmacy, Program in Hospital Pharmacy, Québec, QC G1K 7P4, Canada. Offers M Sc. *Entrance requirements:* For master's, knowledge of French, interview. Electronic applications accepted.

Université Laval, Faculty of Pharmacy, Programs in Community Pharmacy, Québec, QC G1K 7P4, Canada. Offers DESS. Part-time programs available. *Entrance requirements:* For degree, knowledge of French. Electronic applications accepted.

Université Laval, Faculty of Pharmacy, Programs in Pharmacy, Québec, QC G1K 7P4, Canada. Offers M Sc, PhD. Part-time programs available. Terminal master's awarded for partial completion of doctoral program. *Degree requirements:* For master's, thesis; for doctorate, comprehensive exam, thesis/dissertation. *Entrance requirements:* For master's and doctorate, knowledge of French. Electronic applications accepted.

University at Buffalo, the State University of New York, Graduate School, School of Pharmacy and Pharmaceutical Sciences, Department of Pharmaceutical Sciences, Buffalo, NY 14260. Offers MS, PhD, Pharm D/MS, Pharm D/PhD. *Faculty:* 14 full-time (2 women), 1 part-time/adjunct (0 women). *Students:* 62 full-time (37 women), 9 part-time (5 women); includes 16 minority (13 Asian, non-Hispanic/Latino; 3 Two or more races, non-Hispanic/Latino), 32 international. Average age 25. 446 applicants, 4% accepted, 15 enrolled. In 2011, 5 master's, 7 doctorates awarded. Terminal master's awarded for partial completion of doctoral program. *Degree requirements:* For master's, comprehensive exam (for some programs), thesis optional, project; for doctorate, comprehensive exam, thesis/dissertation. *Entrance requirements:* For master's, GRE, BS, B Eng, or Pharm D; for doctorate, GRE, BS, MS, B Eng, M Eng, or Pharm D. Additional exam requirements/recommendations for international students: Required—TOEFL (minimum score 550 paper-based; 213 computer-based; 79 iBT). *Application deadline:* For fall admission, 2/15 for domestic and international students. Applications are processed on a rolling basis. Application fee: $50. Electronic applications accepted. *Financial support:* In 2011–12, 38 students received support, including 38 research assistantships with full tuition reimbursements available (averaging $23,500 per year); health care benefits and unspecified assistantships also available. Financial award application deadline: 3/1; financial award applicants required to submit FAFSA. *Faculty research:* Pharmacokinetics, biopharmaceutics, drug delivery systems, pharmacodynamics, drug metabolism and analysis. *Total annual research expenditures:* $3.5 million. *Unit head:* Dr. William J. Jusko, Chair, 716-645-2855 Ext. 225, Fax: 716-645-3693, E-mail: wjjusko@acsu.buffalo.edu. *Application contact:* Dr. Murali Ramanathan, Director of Graduate Studies, 716-645-4846, Fax: 716-645-3690, E-mail: murali@buffalo.edu. Web site: http://pharmacy.buffalo.edu/pages/16/Pharmaceutical-Sciences-Admissions.html.

University of Alberta, Faculty of Graduate Studies and Research, Department of Pharmacy and Pharmaceutical Sciences, Edmonton, AB T6G 2E1, Canada. Offers M Sc, PhD. Terminal master's awarded for partial completion of doctoral program. *Degree requirements:* For master's, thesis; for doctorate, thesis/dissertation. *Entrance requirements:* Additional exam requirements/recommendations for international students: Required—Michigan English Language Assessment Battery or IELTS. Electronic applications accepted. *Faculty research:* Radiopharmacy, pharmacokinetics, bionucleonics, medicinal chemistry, microbiology.

The University of Arizona, College of Pharmacy, Program in Pharmaceutical Sciences, Tucson, AZ 85721. Offers medicinal and natural products chemistry (MS, PhD); pharmaceutical economics (MS, PhD); pharmaceutics and pharmacokinetics (MS, PhD). *Faculty:* 10 full-time (2 women), 2 part-time/adjunct (0 women). *Students:* 35 full-time (19 women), 5 part-time (4 women); includes 12 minority (2 Black or African American, non-Hispanic/Latino; 5 Asian, non-Hispanic/Latino; 4 Hispanic/Latino; 1 Two or more races, non-Hispanic/Latino), 7 international. Average age 31. 89 applicants, 13% accepted, 12 enrolled. In 2011, 3 master's, 5 doctorates awarded. *Degree requirements:* For master's, thesis; for doctorate, one foreign language, thesis/dissertation. *Entrance requirements:* For master's, GRE General Test, 3 letters of recommendation, bachelor's degree in related field; for doctorate, GRE General Test, 3 letters of recommendation, statement of purpose, bachelor's degree in related field. Additional exam requirements/recommendations for international students: Required—TOEFL (minimum score 550 paper-based; 213 computer-based; 79 iBT). *Application deadline:* For fall admission, 1/1 for domestic students, 12/1 for international students. Applications are processed on a rolling basis. Application fee: $65. Electronic applications accepted. *Expenses:* Tuition, state resident: full-time $10,840. Tuition, nonresident: full-time $25,802. *Financial support:* In 2011–12, 45 research assistantships with full tuition reimbursements (averaging $24,034 per year) were awarded; scholarships/grants, health care benefits, tuition waivers (full), and unspecified assistantships also available. Financial award application deadline: 3/1. *Faculty research:* Drug design, natural products isolation, biological applications of NMR and mass spectrometry, drug formulation and delivery, pharmacokinetics. *Total annual research expenditures:* $2 million. *Unit head:* Dr. Terrence Monks, Department Head, 520-626-9906, Fax: 520-626-4063, E-mail: monks@pharmacy.arizona.edu. *Application contact:* Nancy F. Colbert, Information Contact, 520-626-7265, Fax: 520-626-2466, E-mail: colbert@pharmacy.arizona.edu. Web site: http://grad.arizona.edu/live/programs/description/129.

University of Arkansas for Medical Sciences, College of Pharmacy, Program in Pharmaceutical Evaluation and Policy, Little Rock, AR 72205-7199. Offers MS. *Degree requirements:* For master's, thesis. *Entrance requirements:* For master's, GRE, 3 letters of recommendation, resume. Additional exam requirements/recommendations for international students: Required—TOEFL.

The University of British Columbia, Faculty of Pharmaceutical Sciences, Vancouver, BC V6T 1Z3, Canada. Offers M Sc, PhD, Pharm D. *Degree requirements:* For master's, thesis, seminar; for doctorate, comprehensive exam (for some programs), thesis/dissertation (for some programs), seminar (for PhD). *Entrance requirements:* Additional exam requirements/recommendations for international students: Required—TOEFL (minimum score 600 paper-based; 250 computer-based; 100 iBT). Electronic applications accepted. *Faculty research:* Biopharmaceutics, pharmaceutical chemistry, pharmacology, toxicology, formulation.

University of California, San Francisco, School of Pharmacy and Graduate Division, Pharmaceutical Sciences and Pharmacogenomics Graduate Group, San Francisco, CA 94158-0775. Offers PhD. *Faculty:* 52 full-time (14 women). *Students:* 48 full-time (24 women); includes 16 minority (15 Asian, non-Hispanic/Latino; 1 Hispanic/Latino). Average age 23. 92 applicants, 15% accepted, 8 enrolled. In 2011, 7 doctorates awarded. *Degree requirements:* For doctorate, comprehensive exam, thesis/dissertation. *Entrance requirements:* For doctorate, GRE General Test, minimum GPA of 3.0. Additional exam requirements/recommendations for international students: Required—TOEFL. *Application deadline:* For fall admission, 12/1 for domestic and international students. Application fee: $70 ($90 for international students). Electronic applications accepted. *Financial support:* In 2011–12, 6 fellowships with full tuition reimbursements (averaging $28,000 per year), 34 research assistantships with full tuition reimbursements (averaging $28,000 per year), 8 teaching assistantships with full tuition reimbursements (averaging $28,000 per year) were awarded; career-related internships or fieldwork, institutionally sponsored loans, scholarships/grants, traineeships, tuition waivers (full), and unspecified assistantships also available. Financial award application deadline: 4/6. *Faculty research:* Drug development, drug delivery, molecular pharmacology. *Unit head:* Deanna L. Kroetz, Program Director, 415-476-1159, Fax: 415-476-6022, E-mail: deanna.kroetz@ucsf.edu. *Application contact:* Debbie Acoba-Idlebi, Program Coordinator, 415-476-1947, Fax: 415-476-6022, E-mail: debbie.acoba@ucsf.edu. Web site: http://bts.ucsf.edu/pspg/.

University of Cincinnati, College of Pharmacy, Division of Pharmaceutical Sciences, Cincinnati, OH 45221. Offers MS, PhD. *Degree requirements:* For master's, thesis; for doctorate, thesis/dissertation. *Entrance requirements:* For master's and doctorate, GRE General Test, minimum GPA of 3.0. Additional exam requirements/recommendations for international students: Required—TOEFL.

University of Colorado Denver, School of Pharmacy, Doctor of Pharmacy Program, Aurora, CO 80045. Offers Pharm D. Postbaccalaureate distance learning degree programs offered (no on-campus study). *Students:* 637 full-time (382 women), 211 part-time (127 women); includes 291 minority (52 Black or African American, non-Hispanic/Latino; 4 American Indian or Alaska Native, non-Hispanic/Latino; 189 Asian, non-Hispanic/Latino; 44 Hispanic/Latino; 2 Two or more races, non-Hispanic/Latino), 34 international. Average age 31. 440 applicants, 86% accepted, 358 enrolled. In 2011, 156 doctorates awarded. *Degree requirements:* For doctorate, final-year experience in pharmacy setting. *Entrance requirements:* For doctorate, PCAT, minimum GPA of 2.5, 2.75 in the sciences; prerequisite coursework in general chemistry with lab, organic chemistry with lab, general biology with lab, microbiology with lab, biochemistry, human anatomy and physiology with lab, general physics, calculus, English composition, public speaking, microeconomics. Additional exam requirements/recommendations for international students: Required—TOEFL (minimum score 550 paper-based; 213 computer-based). *Application deadline:* For fall admission, 12/1 for domestic students. Application fee: $150. Electronic applications accepted. *Expenses:* Contact institution. *Financial support:* Career-related internships or fieldwork, Federal Work-Study, and scholarships/grants available. Support available to part-time students. Financial award application deadline: 3/15; financial award applicants required to submit FAFSA. *Faculty research:* Mechanistic studies of viral assembly, synthetic gene delivery systems for use in gene therapy, mechanisms of toxicity, pulmonary drug delivery. *Unit head:* Ralpha Altiere, Dean, 303-724-2631, E-mail: ralph.altiere@ucdenver.edu. *Application contact:* Admissions, 303-724-2882, E-mail: pharmd.info@ucdenver.edu. Web site: http://www.ucdenver.edu/academics/colleges/pharmacy/AcademicPrograms/PharmDProgram/Pages/PharmDProgram.aspx.

University of Colorado Denver, School of Pharmacy, Program in Pharmaceutical Sciences, Aurora, CO 80045. Offers clinical pharmaceutical sciences (PhD); pharmaceutical biotechnology (PhD); pharmaceutical outcomes research (PhD). *Students:* 30 full-time (14 women); includes 4 minority (all Asian, non-Hispanic/Latino), 11 international. Average age 29. 35 applicants, 11% accepted, 4 enrolled. *Degree requirements:* For doctorate, comprehensive exam, thesis/dissertation, minimum 60 credit hours of upper-level courses, 30 of which are thesis research, research rotations and thesis defense. *Entrance requirements:* For doctorate, GRE, minimum undergraduate GPA of 3.0; prior coursework in general chemistry, organic chemistry, calculus, biology, and physics. Additional exam requirements/recommendations for international students: Required—TOEFL. *Application deadline:* For fall admission, 1/15 for domestic students. Application fee: $50 ($75 for international students). Electronic applications accepted. *Expenses:* Contact institution. *Financial support:* Fellowships, research assistantships, teaching assistantships, Federal Work-Study, scholarships/grants, health care benefits, tuition waivers (full), unspecified assistantships, and stipend available. Support available to part-time students. Financial award application deadline: 3/15; financial award applicants required to submit FAFSA. *Faculty research:* Pharmaceutical biotechnology, molecular toxicology, cancer pharmacology, drug discovery, clinical and translational sciences. *Unit head:* Dr. David Ross, Chair/Professor of Toxicology, 303-724-7265, E-mail: david.ross@ucdenver.edu. *Application contact:* Jackie Milowski, Graduate Admissions, 303-724-7263, E-mail: jackie.milowski@ucdenver.edu. Web site: http://www.ucdenver.edu/academics/colleges/pharmacy/Pages/SchoolofPharmacy.aspx.

University of Connecticut, Graduate School, School of Pharmacy, Department of Pharmaceutical Sciences, Program in Pharmaceutics, Storrs, CT 06269. Offers MS, PhD. Terminal master's awarded for partial completion of doctoral program. *Degree requirements:* For master's, comprehensive exam, thesis; for doctorate, thesis/dissertation. *Entrance requirements:* For master's and doctorate, GRE General Test. Additional exam requirements/recommendations for international students: Required—TOEFL (minimum score 550 paper-based; 213 computer-based). Electronic applications accepted.

University of Florida, Graduate School, College of Pharmacy and Graduate School, Graduate Programs in Pharmacy, Department of Pharmaceutics, Gainesville, FL 32611. Offers pharmaceutical sciences (PhD). *Faculty:* 6 full-time (1 woman). *Students:* 32 full-time (16 women), 5 part-time (4 women); includes 2 minority (1 Asian, non-Hispanic/Latino; 1 Hispanic/Latino), 26 international. Average age 32. 236 applicants, 48% accepted, 110 enrolled. In 2011, 4 degrees awarded. *Median time to degree:* Of those who began their doctoral program in fall 2003, 100% received their degree in 8 years or less. *Degree requirements:* For doctorate, comprehensive exam, thesis/dissertation. *Entrance requirements:* For doctorate, GRE General Test, minimum GPA of 3.0. Additional exam requirements/recommendations for international students: Required—TOEFL (minimum score 550 paper-based; 213 computer-based; 80 iBT), IELTS (minimum score 6). *Application deadline:* For fall admission, 2/1 priority date for domestic students, 2/1 for international students; for spring admission, 9/1 for domestic students, 10/1 for international students. Applications are processed on a rolling basis. Application fee: $30. Electronic applications accepted. *Financial support:* In 2011–12, 1 research assistantship, 7 teaching assistantships were awarded; fellowships, tuition waivers (full), and unspecified assistantships also available. Financial award applicants required to submit FAFSA. *Faculty research:* Basic, applied, and clinical investigations in pharmacokinetics/biopharmaceutics; pharmaceutical analysis, pharmaceutical biotechnology and drug delivery; herbal medicine. *Total annual research expenditures:* $961,059. *Unit head:* Dr. Hartmut Derendorf, Chair, 352-273-7856, Fax: 352-392-4447, E-mail: hartmut@ufl.edu. *Application contact:* Dr. Anthony Palmieri, III, Graduate Coordinator, 352-273-7868, Fax: 352-392-4447, E-mail: palmieri@cop.ufl.edu. Web site: http://www.cop.ufl.edu/pc/.

University of Florida, Graduate School, College of Pharmacy and Graduate School, Graduate Programs in Pharmacy, Department of Pharmacotherapy and Translational Research, Gainesville, FL 32611. Offers MSP. *Faculty:* 6 full-time (1 woman). *Entrance requirements:* Additional exam requirements/recommendations for international students: Required—TOEFL (minimum score 550 paper-based; 213 computer-based; 80 iBT), IELTS (minimum score 6). *Application deadline:* For fall admission, 1/15 for domestic and international students. Application fee: $30. Electronic applications accepted. *Financial support:* Application deadline: 1/15; applicants required to submit FAFSA. *Faculty research:* Understanding genetic and non-genetic factors that contribute to variability in drug response, cardiology, transplant/immunology, asthma/pulmonary,

Pharmaceutical Sciences

psychiatry, clinical pharmacology/drug metabolism. *Unit head:* Dr. Julie Johnson, Chair, 352-273-6007, E-mail: johnson@cop.ufl.edu. *Application contact:* Dr. Reginald F. Frye, Graduate Coordinator, 352-273-5453, E-mail: frye@cop.ufl.edu. Web site: http://www.cop.ufl.edu/research/pharmacotherapy-and-translational-research/.

University of Georgia, College of Pharmacy, Athens, GA 30602. Offers MS, PhD, Pharm D, Certificate. *Accreditation:* ACPE (one or more programs are accredited). *Faculty:* 39 full-time (12 women), 4 part-time/adjunct (0 women). *Students:* 60 full-time (29 women), 31 part-time (23 women); includes 17 minority (8 Black or African American, non-Hispanic/Latino; 4 Asian, non-Hispanic/Latino; 3 Hispanic/Latino; 2 Two or more races, non-Hispanic/Latino), 32 international. Average age 31. 226 applicants, 14% accepted, 15 enrolled. In 2011, 5 master's, 3 doctorates, 121 other advanced degrees awarded. *Degree requirements:* For doctorate, variable foreign language requirement, thesis/dissertation (for some programs). *Entrance requirements:* For master's, GRE General Test, minimum GPA of 3.0; for doctorate, GRE General Test (for PhD), minimum GPA of 3.0 (for PhD). Additional exam requirements/recommendations for international students: Required—TOEFL (minimum score 80 iBT). *Application deadline:* For fall admission, 7/1 priority date for domestic students; for spring admission, 11/15 for domestic students. Application fee: $50. Electronic applications accepted. *Expenses:* Contact institution. *Financial support:* Fellowships, research assistantships, teaching assistantships, career-related internships or fieldwork, Federal Work-Study, institutionally sponsored loans, tuition waivers, and unspecified assistantships available. Support available to part-time students. Financial award application deadline: 2/15. *Unit head:* Dr. Svein Oie, Dean, 706-542-1914, Fax: 706-542-5269, E-mail: soie@rx.uga.edu. *Application contact:* Dr. Melissa Barry, Assistant Dean of The Graduate School, 706-425-2934, Fax: 706-425-3093, E-mail: mjb14@uga.edu. Web site: http://www.rx.uga.edu/.

University of Houston, College of Pharmacy, Houston, TX 77204. Offers pharmaceutics (MSPHR, PhD); pharmacology (MSPHR, PhD); pharmacy (Pharm D); pharmacy administration (MSPHR, PhD). *Accreditation:* ACPE. Part-time programs available. Terminal master's awarded for partial completion of doctoral program. *Entrance requirements:* For doctorate, PCAT (for Pharm D). Additional exam requirements/recommendations for international students: Required—TOEFL. Electronic applications accepted. *Faculty research:* Drug screening and design, cardiovascular pharmacology, infectious disease, asthma research, herbal medicine.

University of Illinois at Chicago, College of Pharmacy and Graduate College, Graduate Programs in Pharmacy, Chicago, IL 60607-7128. Offers biopharmaceutical sciences (PhD); forensic science (MS); medicinal chemistry (MS, PhD); pharmacognosy (MS, PhD); pharmacy administration (MS, PhD). Terminal master's awarded for partial completion of doctoral program. *Degree requirements:* For master's, variable foreign language requirement, thesis; for doctorate, variable foreign language requirement, thesis/dissertation. *Entrance requirements:* For master's and doctorate, GRE General Test. Additional exam requirements/recommendations for international students: Required—TOEFL. Electronic applications accepted. *Expenses:* Contact institution.

The University of Kansas, Graduate Studies, School of Pharmacy, Department of Pharmacy Practice, Lawrence, KS 66047. Offers MS. *Faculty:* 7 full-time (2 women), 13 part-time/adjunct (8 women). *Students:* 6 full-time (2 women). Average age 26. 3 applicants, 100% accepted, 3 enrolled. In 2011, 2 degrees awarded. *Degree requirements:* For master's, thesis. *Entrance requirements:* For master's, GRE General Test, Pharm D, Kansas pharmacy license, ASHP Resident Matching Program. Additional exam requirements/recommendations for international students: Recommended—TOEFL. *Application deadline:* For fall admission, 2/1 priority date for domestic students. Application fee: $55 ($65 for international students). Electronic applications accepted. Tuition and fees vary according to course load, campus/location, program and reciprocity agreements. *Financial support:* Fellowships with partial tuition reimbursements, health care benefits, and residencies available. Financial award application deadline: 2/15. *Faculty research:* Drug trials, drug stability, pharmacoeconomics, education, outcomes. *Total annual research expenditures:* $42,000. *Unit head:* David Henry, Chair, 785-864-6066, Fax: 785-864-2399, E-mail: dhenry@kumc.edu. *Application contact:* Dr. Dennis Grauer, Graduate Director, 785-864-3262, Fax: 785-864-2399, E-mail: dgrauer@kumc.edu. Web site: http://pharmpractice.ku.edu/.

University of Kentucky, Graduate School, Graduate Programs in Pharmaceutical Sciences, Lexington, KY 40506-0032. Offers MS, PhD. Terminal master's awarded for partial completion of doctoral program. *Degree requirements:* For master's, thesis optional; for doctorate, comprehensive exam, thesis/dissertation. *Entrance requirements:* For master's, GRE General Test, minimum undergraduate GPA of 3.2; for doctorate, GRE General Test, minimum graduate GPA of 3.2. Additional exam requirements/recommendations for international students: Required—TOEFL (minimum score 550 paper-based; 213 computer-based; 79 iBT). Electronic applications accepted. *Faculty research:* Drug development, biotechnology, medicinal chemistry, cardiology, pharmacokinetics, CNS pharmacology, clinical pharmacology, pharmacotherapy and health outcomes, pharmaceutical policy.

The University of Manchester, School of Pharmacy and Pharmaceutical Sciences, Manchester, United Kingdom. Offers M Phil, PhD.

University of Manitoba, Faculty of Graduate Studies, Faculty of Pharmacy, Winnipeg, MB R3T 2N2, Canada. Offers M Sc, PhD. *Degree requirements:* For master's, one foreign language, thesis.

University of Maryland, Baltimore, Graduate School, Graduate Programs in Pharmacy, Department of Pharmaceutical Sciences, Baltimore, MD 21201. Offers PhD. *Degree requirements:* For doctorate, comprehensive exam, thesis/dissertation. *Entrance requirements:* For doctorate, GRE General Test. Additional exam requirements/recommendations for international students: Required—TOEFL (minimum score 600 paper-based; 260 computer-based), IELTS. Electronic applications accepted. *Faculty research:* Drug delivery, cellular and biological chemistry, clinical pharmaceutical sciences, biopharmaceutics, neuroscience.

University of Michigan, College of Pharmacy and Horace H. Rackham School of Graduate Studies, Department of Pharmaceutical Sciences, Ann Arbor, MI 48109. Offers PhD. Terminal master's awarded for partial completion of doctoral program. *Degree requirements:* For doctorate, oral defense of dissertation, preliminary exam. *Entrance requirements:* For doctorate, GRE General Test. Additional exam requirements/recommendations for international students: Required—TOEFL or IELTS. Electronic applications accepted. *Faculty research:* New drug design, new drug delivery systems, new biotechnology, pharmacy and the public sector.

University of Minnesota, Twin Cities Campus, College of Pharmacy and Graduate School, Graduate Programs in Pharmacy, Graduate Program in Experimental and Clinical Pharmacology, Minneapolis, MN 55455-0213. Offers MS, PhD. *Degree requirements:* For doctorate, thesis/dissertation.

University of Minnesota, Twin Cities Campus, College of Pharmacy and Graduate School, Graduate Programs in Pharmacy, Graduate Program in Pharmaceutics, Minneapolis, MN 55455. Offers PhD. *Faculty:* 8 full-time (2 women), 11 part-time/adjunct (2 women). *Students:* 19 full-time (10 women), 1 part-time (0 women); includes 1

minority (Asian, non-Hispanic/Latino), 14 international. Average age 27. 61 applicants, 10% accepted, 3 enrolled. In 2011, 3 doctorates awarded. Terminal master's awarded for partial completion of doctoral program. *Degree requirements:* For doctorate, comprehensive exam, thesis/dissertation. *Entrance requirements:* For doctorate, GRE General Test (preferred minimum scores: Quantitative 80%, Analytical Writing 4.5), bachelor's degree. Additional exam requirements/recommendations for international students: Required—TOEFL (minimum score 100 iBT). *Application deadline:* For fall admission, 12/31 priority date for domestic students, 12/31 for international students. Application fee: $75 ($95 for international students). Electronic applications accepted. *Financial support:* In 2011–12, 20 students received support, including 3 fellowships with full tuition reimbursements available (averaging $22,500 per year), 11 research assistantships with full tuition reimbursements available (averaging $22,500 per year), 6 teaching assistantships with full tuition reimbursements available (averaging $22,500 per year); career-related internships or fieldwork, traineeships, health care benefits, unspecified assistantships, and summer internships with pharmaceutical companies also available. Financial award application deadline: 12/31. *Faculty research:* Drug delivery, drug metabolism, molecular biopharmaceutics, pharmacokinetics and pharmacodynamics, crystal engineering, biophysical chemistry. *Total annual research expenditures:* $2.2 million. *Unit head:* Dr. Timothy S. Wiedmann, Director of Graduate Studies, 612-624-5457, Fax: 612-626-2125, E-mail: wiedm001@umn.edu. *Application contact:* Candice McDermott, Executive Secretary, 612-624-5153, Fax: 612-626-2125, E-mail: mcder002@umn.edu. Web site: http://www.pharmacy.umn.edu/pharmaceutics/.

University of Mississippi, Graduate School, School of Pharmacy, Graduate Programs in Pharmacy, Oxford, University, MS 38677. Offers medicinal chemistry (PhD); pharmaceutical sciences (MS); pharmaceutics (PhD); pharmacognosy (PhD); pharmacology (PhD); pharmacy administration (PhD). *Students:* 96 full-time (33 women), 11 part-time (3 women); includes 11 minority (4 Black or African American, non-Hispanic/Latino; 5 Asian, non-Hispanic/Latino; 1 Hispanic/Latino; 1 Two or more races, non-Hispanic/Latino), 68 international. In 2011, 8 master's, 10 doctorates awarded. *Unit head:* Dr. Barbara G. Wells, Dean, 662-915-7265, Fax: 662-915-5704, E-mail: pharmacy@olemiss.edu. *Application contact:* Dr. Christy M. Wyandt, Associate Dean, 662-915-7474, Fax: 662-915-7577, E-mail: cwyandt@olemiss.edu.

University of Missouri–Kansas City, School of Pharmacy, Kansas City, MO 64110-2499. Offers pharmaceutical sciences (PhD); pharmacology and toxicology (PhD); pharmacy (Pharm D). PhD offered through School of Graduate Studies. *Accreditation:* ACPE (one or more programs are accredited). Postbaccalaureate distance learning degree programs offered (minimal on-campus study). *Faculty:* 54 full-time (22 women), 6 part-time/adjunct (3 women). *Students:* 364 full-time (233 women); includes 39 minority (10 Black or African American, non-Hispanic/Latino; 1 American Indian or Alaska Native, non-Hispanic/Latino; 24 Asian, non-Hispanic/Latino; 2 Hispanic/Latino; 2 Two or more races, non-Hispanic/Latino), 4 international. Average age 25. 419 applicants, 40% accepted, 162 enrolled. In 2011, 113 doctorates awarded. *Degree requirements:* For doctorate, comprehensive exam (for some programs), thesis/dissertation (for some programs). *Entrance requirements:* For doctorate, PCAT (for Pharm D). Additional exam requirements/recommendations for international students: Required—TOEFL (minimum score 550 paper-based; 213 computer-based; 80 iBT). *Application deadline:* For fall admission, 3/1 for domestic and international students. Applications are processed on a rolling basis. Application fee: $45 ($50 for international students). Electronic applications accepted. *Expenses:* Contact institution. *Financial support:* In 2011–12, 31 research assistantships with full and partial tuition reimbursements (averaging $9,797 per year), 23 teaching assistantships with full tuition reimbursements (averaging $11,995 per year) were awarded; career-related internships or fieldwork, Federal Work-Study, institutionally sponsored loans, tuition waivers (full and partial), and unspecified assistantships also available. Financial award application deadline: 3/1; financial award applicants required to submit FAFSA. *Faculty research:* Bio-organic and medicinal chemistry, drug delivery, pharmaceutics, molecular neurobiology, neurology. *Unit head:* Dr. Russell B. Melchert, Dean, 816-235-1609, Fax: 816-235-5190, E-mail: melchertr@umkc.edu. *Application contact:* Shelly M. Janasz, Director, Student Services, 816-235-2400, Fax: 816-235-5190, E-mail: janaszs@umkc.edu. Web site: http://pharmacy.umkc.edu/.

The University of Montana, Graduate School, College of Health Professions and Biomedical Sciences, Skaggs School of Pharmacy, Department of Biomedical and Pharmaceutical Sciences, Missoula, MT 59812-0002. Offers biomedical sciences (PhD); neuroscience (MS, PhD); pharmaceutical sciences (MS); toxicology (MS, PhD). *Accreditation:* ACPE. *Degree requirements:* For master's, oral defense of thesis; for doctorate, research dissertation defense. *Entrance requirements:* For master's and doctorate, GRE General Test. Additional exam requirements/recommendations for international students: Required—TOEFL (minimum score 540 paper-based; 210 computer-based). Electronic applications accepted. *Faculty research:* Cardiovascular pharmacology, medicinal chemistry, neurosciences, environmental toxicology, pharmacogenetics, cancer.

University of Nebraska Medical Center, Graduate Studies, Department of Pharmaceutical Sciences, Omaha, NE 68198. Offers MS, PhD. Terminal master's awarded for partial completion of doctoral program. *Degree requirements:* For master's, thesis; for doctorate, comprehensive exam, thesis/dissertation. *Entrance requirements:* For master's, GRE General Test; for doctorate, GRE. Additional exam requirements/recommendations for international students: Required—TOEFL (minimum score 550 paper-based; 213 computer-based). Electronic applications accepted. *Faculty research:* Pharmaceutics, medicinal chemistry, toxicology, chemical carcinogenesis, pharmacokinetics.

University of New Mexico, Graduate School, College of Pharmacy, Graduate Programs in Pharmaceutical Sciences, Albuquerque, NM 87131-2039. Offers MS, PhD. Part-time programs available. *Faculty:* 9 full-time (3 women), 1 (woman) part-time/adjunct. *Students:* 6 full-time (2 women), 5 part-time (3 women); includes 1 minority (Hispanic/Latino), 7 international. Average age 32. 55 applicants, 7% accepted, 3 enrolled. In 2011, 4 master's, 1 doctorate awarded. *Degree requirements:* For master's, comprehensive exam, thesis; for doctorate, comprehensive exam, thesis/dissertation. *Entrance requirements:* For master's and doctorate, GRE General Test (for some concentrations), 3 letters of recommendation, letter of intent, resume. Additional exam requirements/recommendations for international students: Required—TOEFL (minimum score 580 paper-based; 237 computer-based; 93 iBT). *Application deadline:* For fall admission, 2/1 for domestic and international students. Application fee: $50. Electronic applications accepted. *Financial support:* In 2011–12, 6 students received support, including 6 research assistantships (averaging $9,569 per year); health care benefits and residencies also available. Financial award application deadline: 3/1; financial award applicants required to submit FAFSA. *Faculty research:* Pharmaceutical research, cancer research, pharmacy administration, radiopharmacy, toxicology. *Total annual research expenditures:* $2 million. *Unit head:* Lynda Welage, Dean, 505-272-3241, Fax: 505-272-8324, E-mail: lswelage@salud.unm.edu. *Application contact:* Nicole Bingham, Graduate Admissions and Recruitment Advisor, 505-272-4992, Fax: 505-272-8324, E-mail: nicluna@salud.unm.edu. Web site: http://hsc.unm.edu/pharmacy/.

The University of North Carolina at Chapel Hill, Eshelman School of Pharmacy, Chapel Hill, NC 27599. Offers MS, PhD. *Accreditation:* ACPE (one or more programs

are accredited). Part-time programs available. Postbaccalaureate distance learning degree programs offered (minimal on-campus study). Terminal master's awarded for partial completion of doctoral program. *Degree requirements:* For master's, comprehensive exam, thesis; for doctorate, comprehensive exam, thesis/dissertation. *Entrance requirements:* For master's and doctorate, GRE General Test, minimum GPA of 3.0. Additional exam requirements/recommendations for international students: Required—TOEFL (minimum score 550 paper-based; 213 computer-based). Electronic applications accepted. *Faculty research:* Health services research, pharmacokinetics, molecular modeling, infectious disease, genomics/proteomics, translational research.

University of Oklahoma Health Sciences Center, College of Pharmacy and Graduate College, Graduate Programs in Pharmacy, Oklahoma City, OK 73190. Offers MS, PhD, MS/MBA. MS/MBA offered jointly with Oklahoma State University, University of Oklahoma. Terminal master's awarded for partial completion of doctoral program. *Degree requirements:* For master's, comprehensive exam, thesis; for doctorate, comprehensive exam, thesis/dissertation. *Entrance requirements:* For master's and doctorate, GRE General Test. Additional exam requirements/recommendations for international students: Required—TOEFL. *Faculty research:* Medicinal chemistry, pharmacokinetics/biopharmaceutics, nuclear pharmacy, pharmacy administration, pharmacodynamics and toxicology.

University of Pittsburgh, School of Pharmacy, Graduate Program in Pharmaceutical Sciences, Pittsburgh, PA 15260. Offers MS, PhD. Part-time programs available. *Faculty:* 26 full-time (5 women). *Students:* 48 full-time (16 women), 1 part-time (0 women); includes 2 minority (1 Black or African American, non-Hispanic/Latino; 1 Asian, non-Hispanic/Latino), 36 international. Average age 30. 195 applicants, 15% accepted, 18 enrolled. In 2011, 2 master's, 3 doctorates awarded. Terminal master's awarded for partial completion of doctoral program. *Degree requirements:* For master's, comprehensive exam (for some programs), thesis, 30 credits; for doctorate, comprehensive exam, thesis/dissertation, 72 credits. *Entrance requirements:* For master's and doctorate, GRE General Test. Additional exam requirements/recommendations for international students: Required—TOEFL (minimum score 550 paper-based; 213 computer-based; 80 iBT). *Application deadline:* For fall admission, 1/15 priority date for domestic students, 1/15 for international students. Applications are processed on a rolling basis. Application fee: $50. Electronic applications accepted. *Expenses:* Contact institution. *Financial support:* In 2011–12, 38 students received support, including 4 fellowships with full tuition reimbursements available (averaging $24,000 per year), 4 research assistantships with full tuition reimbursements available (averaging $24,500 per year), 16 teaching assistantships with full tuition reimbursements available (averaging $23,280 per year); career-related internships or fieldwork, scholarships/grants, health care benefits, and unspecified assistantships also available. Financial award application deadline: 1/15. *Faculty research:* Drug delivery and targeting, neuroendocrine pharmacology, genomics, proteomics and drug discovery, clinical pharmaceutical sciences. *Total annual research expenditures:* $6.9 million. *Unit head:* Dr. M. Maggie Folan, Chair, Graduate Program Council, 412-648-8555, Fax: 412-383-9996, E-mail: folanm@pitt.edu. *Application contact:* Lori M. Schmotzer, Graduate Program Coordinator, 412-648-1014, Fax: 412-383-9996, E-mail: schmotze@pitt.edu. Web site: http://www.pharmacy.pitt.edu.

University of Puerto Rico, Medical Sciences Campus, School of Pharmacy, San Juan, PR 00936-5067. Offers industrial pharmacy (MS); pharmaceutical sciences (MS); pharmacy (Pharm D). The MS in Pharmacy program is not admitting students in the academic year 2010-2011. *Accreditation:* ACPE. Part-time and evening/weekend programs available. *Degree requirements:* For master's, thesis; for doctorate, portfolio, research project. *Entrance requirements:* For master's, GRE, interview; for doctorate, PCAT, interview. Electronic applications accepted. *Expenses:* Contact institution. *Faculty research:* Controlled release, solid dosage form, screening of anti-HIV drugs, pharmacokinetic/pharmacodynamic of drugs.

University of Rhode Island, Graduate School, College of Pharmacy, Department of Biomedical and Pharmaceutical Sciences, Kingston, RI 02881. Offers medicinal chemistry and pharmacognosy (MS, PhD); pharmaceutics and pharmacokinetics (MS, PhD); pharmacology and toxicology (MS, PhD). Part-time programs available. *Faculty:* 20 full-time (6 women), 2 part-time/adjunct (1 woman). *Students:* 41 full-time (21 women), 16 part-time (7 women); includes 8 minority (1 Black or African American, non-Hispanic/Latino; 6 Asian, non-Hispanic/Latino; 1 Two or more races, non-Hispanic/Latino), 24 international. In 2011, 4 master's, 3 doctorates awarded. *Entrance requirements:* For master's and doctorate, GRE, 2 letters of recommendation. Additional exam requirements/recommendations for international students: Required—TOEFL (minimum score 550 paper-based; 213 computer-based). Application fee: $65. Electronic applications accepted. *Expenses:* Tuition, state resident: full-time $10,432; part-time $580 per credit hour. Tuition, nonresident: full-time $23,130; part-time $1285 per credit hour. *Required fees:* $1362; $36 per credit hour. $35 per semester. One-time fee: $130. *Financial support:* In 2011–12, 8 research assistantships with partial tuition reimbursements (averaging $9,529 per year), 11 teaching assistantships with full and partial tuition reimbursements (averaging $9,807 per year) were awarded. Financial award applicants required to submit FAFSA. *Faculty research:* Chemical carcinogenesis with a major emphasis on the structural and synthetic aspects of DNA-adduct formation, drug-drug/herb interaction, drug-genetic interaction, signaling of nuclear receptors, transcriptional regulation, oncogenesis. *Unit head:* Dr. Clinton O. Chichester, Chair, 401-874-5034, Fax: 401-874-5787, E-mail: chichester@uri.edu. *Application contact:* Dr. David C. Rowley, Graduate Coordinator, 401-874-9228, Fax: 401-874-2516, E-mail: drowley@uri.edu. Web site: http://www.uri.edu/pharmacy/departments/bps/index.shtml.

University of Rhode Island, Graduate School, College of Pharmacy, Department of Pharmacy Practice, Kingston, RI 02881. Offers pharmaceutical sciences (MS, PhD), including pharmacoepidemiology and pharmacoeconomics; MS/PhD; PhD/MBA. *Accreditation:* ACPE. *Faculty:* 26 full-time (20 women), 1 part-time/adjunct (0 women). *Students:* 657 full-time (384 women), 3 part-time (2 women); includes 104 minority (20 Black or African American, non-Hispanic/Latino; 56 Asian, non-Hispanic/Latino; 22 Hispanic/Latino; 6 Two or more races, non-Hispanic/Latino), 26 international. In 2011, 89 doctorates awarded. *Entrance requirements:* For master's and doctorate, 2 letters of recommendation. Additional exam requirements/recommendations for international students: Required—TOEFL (minimum score 550 paper-based; 213 computer-based). Application fee: $65. Electronic applications accepted. *Expenses:* Tuition, state resident: full-time $10,432; part-time $580 per credit hour. Tuition, nonresident: full-time $23,130; part-time $1285 per credit hour. *Required fees:* $1362; $36 per credit hour. $35 per semester. One-time fee: $130. *Financial support:* Applicants required to submit FAFSA. *Faculty research:* Treatment, virulence inhibition (toxin and biofilm), colonization and control of methicillin-resistant Staphylococcus aureus (MRSA); investigating activity of catheter lock solutions against biofilm producing bacteria. *Unit head:* Dr. Marilyn Barbour, Chair, 401-874-5842, Fax: 401-874-2181, E-mail: mbarbourri@aol.com. *Application contact:* Nasser H. Zawia, Dean of the Graduate School, 401-874-5909, Fax: 401-874-5787, E-mail: nzawia@uri.edu. Web site: http://www.uri.edu/pharmacy/departments/php/index.shtml.

University of Saskatchewan, College of Graduate Studies and Research, College of Pharmacy and Nutrition, Saskatoon, SK S7N 5A2, Canada. Offers M Sc, PhD. *Degree requirements:* For master's, thesis; for doctorate, thesis/dissertation. *Entrance requirements:* Additional exam requirements/recommendations for international students: Required—TOEFL.

University of South Carolina, South Carolina College of Pharmacy and The Graduate School, Department of Basic Pharmaceutical Sciences, Columbia, SC 29208. Offers MS, PhD. PhD offered jointly with Medical University of South Carolina. Part-time programs available. Terminal master's awarded for partial completion of doctoral program. *Degree requirements:* For master's, one foreign language, comprehensive exam, thesis; for doctorate, one foreign language, comprehensive exam, thesis/dissertation. *Entrance requirements:* For master's, GRE General Test, BS in biology, chemistry, pharmacy, or related field; for doctorate, GRE General Test, BS in biology, chemistry, or related field. Additional exam requirements/recommendations for international students: Required—TOEFL. Electronic applications accepted. *Faculty research:* Cancer treatment and prevention, Ion channels, DNA damage repair, inflammation.

University of Southern California, Graduate School, School of Pharmacy, Department of Pharmacology and Pharmaceutical Sciences, Los Angeles, CA 90089. Offers MS, PhD. Terminal master's awarded for partial completion of doctoral program. *Degree requirements:* For master's, comprehensive exam, thesis, 24 units of formal course work, excluding research and seminar courses; for doctorate, comprehensive exam, thesis/dissertation, 24 units of formal course work, excluding research and seminar courses. *Entrance requirements:* For master's and doctorate, GRE. Additional exam requirements/recommendations for international students: Required—TOEFL (minimum score 603 paper-based; 250 computer-based; 100 iBT). Electronic applications accepted. *Faculty research:* Drug design, drug delivery, pharmaceutical sciences.

University of Southern California, Graduate School, School of Pharmacy, Graduate Programs in Pharmaceutical Economics and Policy, Los Angeles, CA 90033. Offers MS, PhD. Terminal master's awarded for partial completion of doctoral program. *Degree requirements:* For master's, comprehensive exam, thesis, 24 units of formal course work, excluding research and seminar courses; for doctorate, comprehensive exam, thesis/dissertation, 24 units of formal course work, excluding research and seminar courses. *Entrance requirements:* For master's and doctorate, GRE. Additional exam requirements/recommendations for international students: Required—TOEFL (minimum score 603 paper-based; 250 computer-based; 100 iBT). Electronic applications accepted. *Faculty research:* Cost-effective analyses/modeling, retrospective data analysis of comparative effectiveness, quality of life measurement, competitive pricing systems in health care.

University of Southern California, Graduate School, School of Pharmacy, Program in Clinical and Experimental Therapeutics, Los Angeles, CA 90089. Offers PhD. Terminal master's awarded for partial completion of doctoral program. *Degree requirements:* For doctorate, comprehensive exam, thesis/dissertation, 24 units of course work, excluding research and dissertation courses. *Entrance requirements:* For doctorate, GRE, minimum overall GPA of 3.0, three letters of recommendation. Additional exam requirements/recommendations for international students: Required—TOEFL (minimum score 625 paper-based; 250 computer-based; 100 iBT). Electronic applications accepted. *Faculty research:* Pharmacology and therapeutics: inflammation, tissue regeneration, myelosuppression, bacterial resistance and virulence, alcoholism, CNS disorders, metabolomics and lipidomics.

University of Southern California, Graduate School, School of Pharmacy, Regulatory Science Programs, Los Angeles, CA 90089. Offers clinical research design and management (Graduate Certificate); food safety (Graduate Certificate); patient and product safety (Graduate Certificate); preclinical drug development (Graduate Certificate); regulatory and clinical affairs (Graduate Certificate); regulatory science (MS, DRSc). Part-time and evening/weekend programs available. Postbaccalaureate distance learning degree programs offered (minimal on-campus study). Terminal master's awarded for partial completion of doctoral program. *Degree requirements:* For master's, thesis optional; for doctorate, comprehensive exam, thesis/dissertation. *Entrance requirements:* For master's, GRE. Additional exam requirements/recommendations for international students: Required—TOEFL (minimum score 603 paper-based; 250 computer-based; 100 iBT). Electronic applications accepted.

The University of Texas at Austin, Graduate School, College of Pharmacy, Graduate Programs in Pharmacy, Austin, TX 78712-1111. Offers health outcomes and pharmacy practice (PhD); health outcomes and pharmacy practice (MS); medicinal chemistry (PhD); pharmaceutics (PhD); pharmacology and toxicology (PhD); pharmacotherapy (MS, PhD); translational science (PhD). PhD in translational science offered jointly with The University of Texas Health Science Center at San Antonio and The University of Texas at San Antonio. *Degree requirements:* For master's, thesis; for doctorate, thesis/dissertation. *Entrance requirements:* For master's and doctorate, GRE General Test. *Application deadline:* For fall admission, 1/15 priority date for domestic students, 1/15 for international students; for spring admission, 10/1 for domestic students. Applications are processed on a rolling basis. Application fee: $50 ($75 for international students). Electronic applications accepted. *Financial support:* Fellowships, research assistantships, teaching assistantships with partial tuition reimbursements, Federal Work-Study, scholarships/grants, health care benefits, and unspecified assistantships available. Financial award application deadline: 2/1; financial award applicants required to submit FAFSA. *Faculty research:* Synthetic medical chemistry, synthetic molecular biology, bio-organic chemistry, pharmacoeconomics, pharmacy practice. *Unit head:* Dr. M. Lynn Crismon, Dean, 512-471-3718, E-mail: lynn.crismon@austin.utexas.edu.

University of the Pacific, Thomas J. Long School of Pharmacy and Health Sciences, Pharmaceutical and Chemical Sciences Graduate Program, Stockton, CA 95211-0197. Offers MS, PhD. *Faculty:* 9 full-time (1 woman). *Students:* 4 full-time (1 woman), 45 part-time (25 women); includes 7 minority (all Asian, non-Hispanic/Latino), 38 international. Average age 27. 94 applicants, 14% accepted, 10 enrolled. In 2011, 1 master's, 3 doctorates awarded. *Entrance requirements:* Additional exam requirements/recommendations for international students: Required—TOEFL (minimum score 475 paper-based; 150 computer-based). Application fee: $75. *Expenses: Tuition:* Full-time $18,900; part-time $1181 per unit. *Required fees:* $949. *Financial support:* Application deadline: 3/1; applicants required to submit FAFSA. *Unit head:* Dr. Xiaolin Li, Head, 209-946-3162, E-mail: bjasti@pacific.edu. *Application contact:* Cyndi Porter, Outreach Officer, 209-946-3957, Fax: 209-946-2410, E-mail: cporter@pacific.edu.

University of the Sciences in Philadelphia, College of Graduate Studies, Program in Pharmaceutics, Philadelphia, PA 19104-4495. Offers MS, PhD. Part-time programs available. Terminal master's awarded for partial completion of doctoral program. *Degree requirements:* For master's, thesis (for some programs); for doctorate, comprehensive exam, thesis/dissertation, oral defense. *Entrance requirements:* For master's and doctorate, GRE General Test. Additional exam requirements/recommendations for international students: Required—TOEFL, TWE. *Faculty research:* Pharmacodynamics, disperse systems, peptide-biomembranes interactions, in vitro/in vivo correlations, cellular drug delivery.

The University of Toledo, College of Graduate Studies, College of Pharmacy and Pharmaceutical Sciences, Program in Pharmaceutical Sciences, Toledo, OH 43606-3390. Offers administrative pharmacy (MSPS); industrial pharmacy (MSPS); pharmacology toxicology (MSPS). *Degree requirements:* For master's, thesis. *Entrance*

requirements: For master's, GRE General Test. Additional exam requirements/recommendations for international students: Required—TOEFL (minimum score 550 paper-based; 213 computer-based; 80 iBT). Electronic applications accepted.

University of Toronto, School of Graduate Studies, Leslie Dan Faculty of Pharmacy, Toronto, ON M5S 1A1, Canada. Offers M Sc, PhD, Pharm D. Part-time programs available. *Degree requirements:* For master's, thesis, poster presentation, oral thesis defense; for doctorate, thesis/dissertation (for some programs). *Entrance requirements:* For master's, minimum B average in last 2 years of full-time study, 3 letters of reference, resume. Additional exam requirements/recommendations for international students: Required—TOEFL (600 paper-based, 250 computer-based), Michigan English Language Assessment Battery (88) or IELTS (7); GRE General Test. Electronic applications accepted.

University of Utah, Graduate School, College of Pharmacy, Department of Pharmacotherapy, Salt Lake City, UT 84112. Offers MS, PhD. *Faculty:* 19 full-time (11 women), 30 part-time/adjunct (14 women). *Students:* 6 full-time (3 women), 4 part-time (0 women); includes 1 minority (Asian, non-Hispanic/Latino), 6 international. Average age 28. 30 applicants, 20% accepted, 5 enrolled. In 2011, 3 degrees awarded. Terminal master's awarded for partial completion of doctoral program. *Degree requirements:* For master's, comprehensive exam, thesis or alternative; for doctorate, comprehensive exam, thesis/dissertation. *Entrance requirements:* For doctorate, GRE. Additional exam requirements/recommendations for international students: Required—TOEFL (minimum score 550 paper-based; 213 computer-based; 80 iBT). *Application deadline:* For fall admission, 1/10 for domestic students, 12/15 for international students. Application fee: $55 ($65 for international students). *Financial support:* In 2011–12, 4 students received support, including 3 research assistantships with full tuition reimbursements available (averaging $21,000 per year); health care benefits also available. Financial award application deadline: 12/15. *Faculty research:* Outcomes in pharmacy, pharmacotherapy. *Total annual research expenditures:* $131,217. *Unit head:* Dr. Diana I. Brixner, Department Chair and Professor, 801-581-6731. *Application contact:* Sara Ray, Academic Program Manager, 801-581-5984, Fax: 801-585-6160, E-mail: sara.ray@pharm.utah.edu. Web site: http://www.pharmacy.utah.edu/pharmacotherapy/.

University of Washington, School of Pharmacy, Department of Pharmaceutics, Seattle, WA 98195. Offers MS, PhD, Pharm D/PhD. *Faculty:* 15 full-time (6 women). *Students:* 19 full-time (12 women), 2 part-time (1 woman); includes 12 minority (10 Asian, non-Hispanic/Latino; 2 Hispanic/Latino). Average age 29. 66 applicants, 17% accepted, 6 enrolled. In 2011, 7 degrees awarded. Terminal master's awarded for partial completion of doctoral program. *Median time to degree:* Of those who began their doctoral program in fall 2003, 100% received their degree in 8 years or less. *Degree requirements:* For master's, thesis; for doctorate, thesis/dissertation. *Entrance requirements:* For master's and doctorate, GRE General Test. Additional exam requirements/recommendations for international students: Required—TOEFL. *Application deadline:* For fall admission, 1/15 for domestic and international students. Application fee: $75. Electronic applications accepted. *Financial support:* In 2011–12, 19 students received support, including 5 fellowships with full tuition reimbursements available (averaging $27,348 per year), 14 research assistantships with full tuition reimbursements available (averaging $27,348 per year); institutionally sponsored loans, scholarships/grants, health care benefits, and tuition waivers (partial) also available. *Faculty research:* Pharmacokinetics, drug delivery, drug metabolism, pharmacogenetics, transporters. *Unit head:* Dr. Kenneth E. Thummel, Chair, 206-543-9434, Fax: 206-543-3204, E-mail: thummel@u.washington.edu. *Application contact:* Kathy Homson, Program Coordinator, 206-616-2797, Fax: 206-543-3204, E-mail: pceut@u.washington.edu. Web site: http://sop.washington.edu/pharmaceutics.

University of Wisconsin–Madison, School of Pharmacy and Graduate School, Graduate Programs in Pharmacy, Pharmaceutical Sciences Division, Madison, WI 53706-1380. Offers PhD. Terminal master's awarded for partial completion of doctoral program. *Degree requirements:* For doctorate, comprehensive exam, thesis/dissertation. *Entrance requirements:* For doctorate, GRE. Additional exam requirements/recommendations for international students: Required—TOEFL. Electronic applications accepted. *Expenses:* Tuition, state resident: full-time $10,296; part-time $643.51 per credit. Tuition, nonresident: full-time $24,054; part-time $1503.40 per credit. *Required fees:* $70.06 per credit. Tuition and fees vary according to course load, campus/location, program and reciprocity agreements. *Faculty research:* Drug action, drug delivery, drug discovery.

University of Wisconsin–Madison, School of Pharmacy and Graduate School, Graduate Programs in Pharmacy, Social and Administrative Sciences in Pharmacy Division, Madison, WI 53706-1380. Offers MS, PhD. Terminal master's awarded for partial completion of doctoral program. *Degree requirements:* For master's, comprehensive exam (for some programs), thesis optional; for doctorate, comprehensive exam, thesis/dissertation. *Entrance requirements:* For master's and doctorate, GRE. Additional exam requirements/recommendations for international students: Required—TOEFL. Electronic applications accepted. *Expenses:* Tuition, state resident: full-time $10,296; part-time $643.51 per credit. Tuition, nonresident: full-time $24,054; part-time $1503.40 per credit. *Required fees:* $70.06 per credit. Tuition and fees vary according to course load, campus/location, program and reciprocity agreements. *Faculty research:* Patient-provider communication, economics, patient care systems.

Virginia Commonwealth University, Medical College of Virginia-Professional Programs, School of Pharmacy, Department of Pharmaceutics, Richmond, VA 23284-9005. Offers medicinal chemistry (MS); pharmaceutical sciences (PhD); pharmaceutics (MS); pharmacotherapy and pharmacy administration (MS). Terminal master's awarded for partial completion of doctoral program. *Degree requirements:* For master's, thesis; for doctorate, thesis/dissertation. *Entrance requirements:* For master's and doctorate, GRE General Test. Additional exam requirements/recommendations for international students: Required—TOEFL. Electronic applications accepted. *Expenses:* Tuition, state resident: full-time $9133; part-time $507 per credit. Tuition, nonresident: full-time $18,777; part-time $1043 per credit. *Required fees:* $77 per credit. Tuition and fees vary according to degree level, campus/location, program and student level. *Faculty research:* Drug delivery systems, drug development.

Wayne State University, Eugene Applebaum College of Pharmacy and Health Sciences, Department of Pharmaceutical Sciences, Detroit, MI 48202. Offers medicinal chemistry (MS, PhD); pharmaceutics (MS, PhD); pharmacology/toxicology (MS, PhD). *Accreditation:* ACPE (one or more programs are accredited). Part-time programs available. *Students:* 15 full-time (6 women), 4 part-time (3 women); includes 2 minority (1 Black or African American, non-Hispanic/Latino; 1 Asian, non-Hispanic/Latino), 11 international. Average age 27. 234 applicants, 3% accepted, 7 enrolled. In 2011, 1 degree awarded. *Degree requirements:* For master's, thesis; for doctorate, thesis/dissertation. *Entrance requirements:* For master's, GRE General Test, bachelor's degree with minimum GPA of 3.0, three letters of recommendation, personal statement; for doctorate, GRE General Test, bachelor's degree with minimum GPA of 3.0, three letters of recommendation. Additional exam requirements/recommendations for international students: Required—TOEFL (minimum score 550 paper-based; 213 computer-based); Recommended—TWE (minimum score 6). *Application deadline:* For fall admission, 3/1 for domestic and international students. Application fee: $50. Electronic applications accepted. *Expenses:* Tuition, state resident: part-time $512.85 per credit. Tuition, nonresident: part-time $1132.65 per credit. *Required fees:* $26.60 per credit. $199.65 per semester. Tuition and fees vary according to course load and program. *Financial support:* In 2011–12, 1 fellowship with tuition reimbursement (averaging $1,800 per year), 11 research assistantships with full tuition reimbursements (averaging $23,682 per year) were awarded; career-related internships or fieldwork, scholarships/grants, health care benefits, and unspecified assistantships also available. Support available to part-time students. *Faculty research:* Mechanisms of resistance of bacteria to anti-microbial agents, drug metabolism and disposition in children, treatment strategies for stroke/neurovascular disease, prevalence and treatment of diabetes in Arab-Americans, ethnic variability in development of osteoporosis. *Unit head:* Dr. George B. Corcoran, Chair, 313-577-1737, Fax: 313-577-2033, E-mail: corcoran@wayne.edu. *Application contact:* 313-577-1047, E-mail: pscgrad@wayne.edu. Web site: http://www.cphs.wayne.edu/psc/index.php.

Western University of Health Sciences, College of Pharmacy, Program in Pharmaceutical Sciences, Pomona, CA 91766-1854. Offers MS. *Faculty:* 11 full-time (3 women). *Students:* 13 full-time (6 women), 1 part-time (0 women); includes 5 minority (1 Black or African American, non-Hispanic/Latino; 3 Asian, non-Hispanic/Latino; 1 Hispanic/Latino), 6 international. Average age 27. 70 applicants, 9% accepted, 6 enrolled. In 2011, 8 master's awarded. *Entrance requirements:* For master's, GRE, minimum overall GPA of 2.5; BS in pharmacy, chemistry, biology or related scientific area. Additional exam requirements/recommendations for international students: Required—TOEFL (minimum score 550 paper-based; 213 computer-based; 89 iBT). *Application deadline:* For fall admission, 3/1 for domestic and international students; for spring admission, 11/1 for domestic and international students. Application fee: $40. Electronic applications accepted. *Expenses:* Contact institution. *Financial support:* Institutionally sponsored loans and scholarships/grants available. Financial award application deadline: 3/2; financial award applicants required to submit FAFSA. *Unit head:* Stephen O'Barr, Chair, 909-469-5643, Fax: 909-469-5539. *Application contact:* Kathryn Ford, Director of Admissions, 909-469-5542, Fax: 909-469-5570, E-mail: admissions@westernu.edu. Web site: http://www.westernu.edu/pharmacy-dpp_message.

West Virginia University, School of Medicine, Graduate Programs at the Health Sciences Center, Interdisciplinary Graduate Programs in Biomedical Sciences, Program in Pharmaceutical and Pharmacological Sciences, Morgantown, WV 26506. Offers MS, PhD, MD/PhD. *Degree requirements:* For doctorate, comprehensive exam, thesis/dissertation. *Entrance requirements:* For doctorate, GRE General Test, minimum GPA of 3.0. Additional exam requirements/recommendations for international students: Required—TOEFL. Electronic applications accepted. *Faculty research:* Medicinal chemistry, pharmacokinetics, nano-pharmaceutics, polymer-based drug delivery, molecular therapeutics.

West Virginia University, School of Pharmacy, Program in Pharmaceutical and Pharmacological Sciences, Morgantown, WV 26506. Offers administrative pharmacy (PhD); behavioral pharmacy (MS, PhD); biopharmaceutics/pharmacokinetics (MS, PhD); industrial pharmacy (MS); medicinal chemistry (MS, PhD); pharmaceutical chemistry (MS, PhD); pharmaceutics (MS, PhD); pharmacology and toxicology (MS); pharmacy (MS); pharmacy administration (MS). Part-time programs available. Terminal master's awarded for partial completion of doctoral program. *Degree requirements:* For master's, thesis; for doctorate, one foreign language, comprehensive exam, thesis/dissertation. *Entrance requirements:* For master's and doctorate, GRE General Test, minimum GPA of 2.75. Additional exam requirements/recommendations for international students: Required—TOEFL; Recommended—TWE. Electronic applications accepted. *Expenses:* Contact institution. *Faculty research:* Pharmaceutics, medicinal chemistry, biopharmaceutics/pharmacokinetics, health outcomes research.

Pharmacy

Albany College of Pharmacy and Health Sciences, School of Pharmacy and Pharmaceutical Sciences, Albany, NY 12208. Offers pharmaceutical sciences (MS), including pharmaceutics, pharmacology; pharmacy (Pharm D). *Accreditation:* ACPE. *Faculty:* 66 full-time (30 women), 11 part-time/adjunct (6 women). *Students:* 510 full-time (313 women), 3 part-time (2 women); includes 114 minority (21 Black or African American, non-Hispanic/Latino; 1 American Indian or Alaska Native, non-Hispanic/Latino; 69 Asian, non-Hispanic/Latino; 12 Hispanic/Latino; 11 Two or more races, non-Hispanic/Latino), 47 international. Average age 23. 1,477 applicants, 14% accepted, 106 enrolled. In 2011, 3 master's, 230 doctorates awarded. *Degree requirements:* For master's, thesis; for doctorate, practice experience. *Entrance requirements:* For master's, GRE, minimum GPA of 3.0; for doctorate, PCAT, minimum GPA of 2.5. Additional exam requirements/recommendations for international students: Required—TOEFL (minimum score 474 paper-based; 84 iBT). *Application deadline:* For fall admission, 3/1 for domestic and international students. Applications are processed on a rolling basis. Application fee: $100. Electronic applications accepted. *Expenses: Tuition:* Full-time $29,100; part-time $855 per credit hour. *Required fees:* $1230; $680. Tuition and fees vary according to degree level. *Financial support:* In 2011–12, 20 students received support. Federal Work-Study and scholarships/grants available. Support available to part-time students. Financial award application deadline: 3/1; financial award applicants required to submit FAFSA. *Faculty research:* Therapeutic use of drugs, pharmacokinetics, drug delivery and design. *Unit head:* Dr. Mehdi Boroujerdi, Provost, 518-694-7212, Fax: 518-694-7063. *Application contact:* Donna Myers, Director of Pharmacy and Graduate Admissions, 518-694-7186, Fax: 518-694-7929, E-mail: graduate@acphs.edu. Web site: http://www.acphs.edu/.

See Display on next page and Close-Up on page 935.

Auburn University, Harrison School of Pharmacy, Professional Program in Pharmacy, Auburn University, AL 36849. Offers Pharm D. *Accreditation:* ACPE. Part-time programs

available. *Faculty:* 5 full-time (3 women). *Students:* 549 full-time (373 women), 45 part-time (32 women); includes 104 minority (46 Black or African American, non-Hispanic/Latino; 9 American Indian or Alaska Native, non-Hispanic/Latino; 45 Asian, non-Hispanic/Latino; 4 Hispanic/Latino), 7 international. Average age 24. 747 applicants, 26% accepted, 148 enrolled. In 2011, 132 doctorates awarded. Application fee: $0. *Expenses:* Contact institution. *Financial support:* Federal Work-Study available. Support available to part-time students. Financial award applicants required to submit FAFSA. *Unit head:* Dr. R. Lee Evans, Dean and Professor, Harrison School of Pharmacy, 334-844-8348, Fax: 334-844-8353. *Application contact:* Dr. George Flowers, Dean of the Graduate School, 334-844-2125.

Belmont University, College of Pharmacy, Nashville, TN 37212-3757. Offers Pharm D. *Faculty:* 25 full-time (17 women). *Students:* 293 full-time (184 women), 1 (woman) part-time; includes 65 minority (21 Black or African American, non-Hispanic/Latino; 1 American Indian or Alaska Native, non-Hispanic/Latino; 34 Asian, non-Hispanic/Latino; 8 Hispanic/Latino; 1 Two or more races, non-Hispanic/Latino), 4 international. Average age 25. 1,246 applicants, 14% accepted, 76 enrolled. *Degree requirements:* For doctorate, comprehensive exam. *Entrance requirements:* For doctorate, PCAT. Additional exam requirements/recommendations for international students: Required—TOEFL. *Application deadline:* For fall admission, 8/31 priority date for domestic students; for spring admission, 3/1 for domestic students. Applications are processed on a rolling basis. Application fee: $50. Electronic applications accepted. *Expenses: Tuition:* Full-time $28,500; part-time $900 per hour. *Required fees:* $790; $165 per semester. Tuition and fees vary according to course level, degree level and program. *Financial support:* In 2011–12, 8 students received support. Applicants required to submit FAFSA. *Faculty research:* Academic innovation, cultural competency, medication errors, patient safety. *Unit head:* Dr. Phil Johnston, Dean, 615-460-6746, Fax: 615-460-6741, E-mail: phil.johnston@belmont.edu. *Application contact:* Dr. Elinor Gray, Dean of Enrollment Services, 615-460-6747, Fax: 615-460-6741, E-mail: elinor.gray@belmont.edu. Web site: http://www.belmont.edu/pharmacy.

Butler University, College of Pharmacy and Health Sciences, Indianapolis, IN 46208-3485. Offers pharmaceutical science (MS, Pharm D); physician assistance studies (MS). *Accreditation:* ACPE (one or more programs are accredited). Part-time and evening/weekend programs available. *Faculty:* 18 full-time (10 women), 1 (woman) part-time/adjunct. *Students:* 273 full-time (178 women), 18 part-time (14 women); includes 20 minority (4 Black or African American, non-Hispanic/Latino; 11 Asian, non-Hispanic/Latino; 4 Hispanic/Latino; 1 Two or more races, non-Hispanic/Latino), 14 international. Average age 24. 58 applicants, 7% accepted, 4 enrolled. In 2011, 47 master's, 115 doctorates awarded. *Degree requirements:* For master's, research paper or thesis. *Application deadline:* For fall admission, 8/1 priority date for domestic students; for spring admission, 12/15 for domestic students. Applications are processed on a rolling basis. Application fee: $35. Electronic applications accepted. *Expenses:* Contact institution. *Financial support:* Applicants required to submit FAFSA. *Faculty research:* Anti-seizure drugs, casein kinase inhibitors, speech recognition interface for prescribing drugs, pharmacoeconomics. *Total annual research expenditures:* $92,000. *Unit head:* Dr. Mary Andritz, Dean, 317-940-9451, Fax: 317-940-6172, E-mail: mandritz@butler.edu. *Application contact:* Dr. Bruce Clayton, Professor, 317-940-9830, E-mail: bclayton@butler.edu. Web site: http://www.butler.edu/pharmacy-pa/.

Campbell University, Graduate and Professional Programs, School of Pharmacy, Buies Creek, NC 27506. Offers clinical research (MS); pharmaceutical science (MS); pharmacy (Pharm D). *Accreditation:* ACPE. Part-time and evening/weekend programs available. *Entrance requirements:* For master's, MCAT, PCAT, GRE, bachelor's degree in health sciences or related field; for doctorate, PCAT. Additional exam requirements/recommendations for international students: Required—TOEFL (minimum score 550 paper-based; 213 computer-based; 79 iBT). Electronic applications accepted.

Expenses: Contact institution. *Faculty research:* Immunology, medicinal chemistry, pharmaceutics, applied pharmacology.

Creighton University, School of Pharmacy and Health Professions, Professional Program in Pharmacy, Omaha, NE 68178-0001. Offers Pharm D. *Accreditation:* ACPE. Postbaccalaureate distance learning degree programs offered (no on-campus study). *Entrance requirements:* For doctorate, PCAT. Electronic applications accepted. *Expenses: Tuition:* Full-time $12,672; part-time $704 per credit hour. *Required fees:* $1410; $136 per semester. Tuition and fees vary according to campus/location and reciprocity agreements. *Faculty research:* Patient safety in health services research, health information technology and health services research, nanotechnology and drug development, pharmacy practice outcomes research, cross-cultural care of patients in pharmacy practice.

Drake University, College of Pharmacy and Health Sciences, Des Moines, IA 50311-4516. Offers pharmacy (Pharm D); Pharm D/JD; Pharm D/MBA; Pharm D/MPA. *Faculty:* 34 full-time (22 women), 4 part-time/adjunct (all women). *Students:* 726 full-time (489 women), 8 part-time (5 women); includes 100 minority (4 Black or African American, non-Hispanic/Latino; 1 American Indian or Alaska Native, non-Hispanic/Latino; 77 Asian, non-Hispanic/Latino; 6 Hispanic/Latino; 12 Two or more races, non-Hispanic/Latino), 9 international. Average age 22. 307 applicants, 46% accepted, 132 enrolled. In 2011, 103 doctorates awarded. *Degree requirements:* For doctorate, rotations. *Entrance requirements:* For doctorate, PCAT, interview. Additional exam requirements/recommendations for international students: Required—TOEFL. *Application deadline:* For fall admission, 2/1 priority date for domestic students. Application fee: $135. Electronic applications accepted. *Expenses:* Contact institution. *Financial support:* In 2011–12, 10 teaching assistantships (averaging $3,200 per year) were awarded; career-related internships or fieldwork, Federal Work-Study, institutionally sponsored loans, and scholarships/grants also available. Support available to part-time students. Financial award application deadline: 3/1; financial award applicants required to submit FAFSA. *Faculty research:* Cost-benefit and cost-analysis of pharmaceutical products and services, patient satisfaction, community health planning and development, nutrition, ambulatory care. *Total annual research expenditures:* $163,164. *Unit head:* Dr. Raylene Rospond, Dean, 515-271-1814, Fax: 515-271-4171, E-mail: raylene.rospond@drake.edu. *Application contact:* Dr. Renae J. Chesnut, Associate Dean for Student Affairs, 515-271-3018, Fax: 515-271-4171, E-mail: renae.chesnut@drake.edu. Web site: http://pharmacy.drake.edu/.

Duquesne University, Mylan School of Pharmacy, Professional Program in Pharmacy, Pittsburgh, PA 15282. Offers Pharm D. Students enter program as first-year undergraduates. *Accreditation:* ACPE. Evening/weekend programs available. *Faculty:* 48 full-time (20 women), 2 part-time/adjunct (0 women). *Students:* 798 full-time (508 women), 12 part-time (8 women); includes 48 minority (14 Black or African American, non-Hispanic/Latino; 1 American Indian or Alaska Native, non-Hispanic/Latino; 24 Asian, non-Hispanic/Latino; 9 Hispanic/Latino), 10 international. Average age 23. 990 applicants, 55% accepted, 172 enrolled. In 2011, 181 doctorates awarded. *Entrance requirements:* For doctorate, PCAT (for professional phase). Additional exam requirements/recommendations for international students: Required—TOEFL. *Application deadline:* For fall admission, 12/1 priority date for domestic students, 12/1 for international students. Applications are processed on a rolling basis. Application fee: $50. Electronic applications accepted. *Expenses: Tuition:* Full-time $16,596; part-time $922 per credit. *Required fees:* $1584; $88 per credit. Tuition and fees vary according to program. *Financial support:* Federal Work-Study and scholarships/grants available. Financial award application deadline: 5/1; financial award applicants required to submit FAFSA. *Unit head:* Dr. Thomas J. Mattei, Associate Dean for Professional Programs, 412-396-6393. *Application contact:* Admissions/Recruitment Coordinator, 412-396-

Albany College of Pharmacy
AND HEALTH SCIENCES

EST. 1881

Founded in 1881, Albany College of Pharmacy and Health Sciences is a private, independent institution committed to the advancement of health care. The College provides an array of graduate and professional degree programs in a personalized learning environment. Students may pursue a Doctor of Pharmacy (Pharm.D.) degree on the Albany Campus or the Colchester, Vermont, Campus, or they may choose a graduate degree program in one of the following areas: Pharmaceutical Sciences, Health Outcomes Research, Biotechnology, and Cytotechnology & Molecular Cytology. Opportunities also exist for students in each of these programs to work side-by-side with faculty on research projects involving a variety of disease states. For more information, please visit www.acphs.edu.

For more information, please contact:
Donna S. Myers, Director of Pharmacy and Graduate Admissions
Office of Graduate Admissions
Albany College of Pharmacy and Health Sciences
106 New Scotland Avenue
Albany, NY 12208
graduate@acphs.edu
www.acphs.edu

6393, Fax: 412-396-4375, E-mail: pharmadmission@duq.edu. Web site: http://www.duq.edu/pharmacy.

D'Youville College, School of Pharmacy, Buffalo, NY 14201-1084. Offers Pharm D. *Accreditation:* ACPE. *Students:* 129 full-time (60 women); includes 21 minority (7 Black or African American, non-Hispanic/Latino; 10 Asian, non-Hispanic/Latino; 3 Hispanic/Latino; 1 Two or more races, non-Hispanic/Latino), 5 international. Average age 24. 1 applicant, 100% accepted, 1 enrolled. *Expenses: Tuition:* Full-time $18,960; part-time $790 per credit hour. *Required fees:* $310. Tuition and fees vary according to degree level and program. *Unit head:* Dr. Canio Marasco, Assistant Dean of Faculty and Student Affairs, 716-829-7846, Fax: 716-829-7760, E-mail: pharmacyadmissions@dyc.edu. *Application contact:* Linda Fisher, Graduate Admissions Director, 716-829-8400, Fax: 716-829-7900, E-mail: graduateadmissions@dyc.edu. Web site: http://www.dyc.edu/academics/pharmacy/.

East Tennessee State University, College of Pharmacy, Johnson City, TN 37614. Offers Pharm D. *Accreditation:* ACPE. *Students:* 315 full-time (174 women), 4 part-time (2 women); includes 35 minority (11 Black or African American, non-Hispanic/Latino; 13 Asian, non-Hispanic/Latino; 5 Hispanic/Latino; 2 Native Hawaiian or other Pacific Islander, non-Hispanic/Latino; 4 Two or more races, non-Hispanic/Latino). Average age 25. In 2011, 72 doctorates awarded. *Expenses:* Tuition, state resident: full-time $7312; part-time $350 per credit hour. Tuition, nonresident: full-time $18,490; part-time $621 per credit hour. *Required fees:* $63 per credit hour. Tuition and fees vary according to course load and program. *Unit head:* Dr. Larry D. Calhoun, Dean, 423-439-2068, Fax: 423-439-6310, E-mail: calhoun@etsu.edu. *Application contact:* Admissions and Records Office, 423-439-6300, Fax: 423-439-6320, E-mail: pharmacy@etsu.edu.

Ferris State University, College of Pharmacy, Big Rapids, MI 49307. Offers Pharm D. *Accreditation:* ACPE. *Faculty:* 36 full-time (20 women), 4 part-time/adjunct (3 women). *Students:* 501 full-time (269 women), 28 part-time (19 women); includes 53 minority (10 Black or African American, non-Hispanic/Latino; 31 Asian, non-Hispanic/Latino; 7 Hispanic/Latino; 5 Two or more races, non-Hispanic/Latino), 21 international. Average age 24. 146 applicants, 89% accepted, 98 enrolled. In 2011, 147 doctorates awarded. *Degree requirements:* For doctorate, 8 clerkships during 4th professional year which equals 1,520 hours of clerkship. *Entrance requirements:* For doctorate, PCAT, 2 years or more of pre-pharmacy course work. *Application deadline:* For fall admission, 12/1 for domestic and international students. Application fee: $150. *Expenses:* Contact institution. *Financial support:* Career-related internships or fieldwork, Federal Work-Study, institutionally sponsored loans, and scholarships/grants available. Financial award applicants required to submit FAFSA. *Faculty research:* Diabetes, rural health education, managed care practice, antimicrobial pharmacotherapy, medicinal flora. *Unit head:* Dr. Stephen Durst, Dean, 231-591-2254, Fax: 231-591-3829, E-mail: dursts@ferris.edu. *Application contact:* Tara M. Lee, Administrative Specialist, Admissions, 231-591-3780, Fax: 231-591-3829, E-mail: leet@ferris.edu. Web site: http://www.ferris.edu/college/pharmacy/.

Florida Agricultural and Mechanical University, Division of Graduate Studies, Research, and Continuing Education, College of Pharmacy and Pharmaceutical Sciences, Professional Program in Pharmacy and Pharmaceutical Sciences, Tallahassee, FL 32307-3200. Offers Ex Doc, Pharm D. *Accreditation:* ACPE. *Entrance requirements:* Additional exam requirements/recommendations for international students: Required—TOEFL.

Georgia Campus–Philadelphia College of Osteopathic Medicine, School of Pharmacy, Suwanee, GA 30024. Offers Pharm D.

Hampton University, School of Pharmacy, Hampton, VA 23668. Offers Pharm D. *Accreditation:* ACPE.

Harding University, College of Pharmacy, Searcy, AR 72147-2230. Offers Pharm D. *Faculty:* 27 full-time (13 women), 1 part-time/adjunct (0 women). *Students:* 232 full-time (120 women), 1 part-time (0 women); includes 72 minority (22 Black or African American, non-Hispanic/Latino; 4 American Indian or Alaska Native, non-Hispanic/Latino; 43 Asian, non-Hispanic/Latino; 1 Hispanic/Latino; 2 Two or more races, non-Hispanic/Latino), 4 international. Average age 27. 330 applicants, 29% accepted, 55 enrolled. *Degree requirements:* For doctorate, licensure as a pharmacy intern in AR, completion of 300 hours of introductory pharmacy practice experience and 1,440 hours of advanced pharmacy practice experience. *Entrance requirements:* For doctorate, PCAT, 90 semester hours of undergraduate work. Additional exam requirements/recommendations for international students: Required—TOEFL (minimum score 550 paper-based). *Application deadline:* For fall admission, 3/1 priority date for domestic students, 3/1 for international students. Applications are processed on a rolling basis. Application fee: $50. Electronic applications accepted. *Expenses:* Contact institution. *Financial support:* In 2011–12, 35 students received support. Scholarships/grants available. Financial award applicants required to submit FAFSA. *Faculty research:* Field stable molecular diagnostics reagent development; the impact of UGT2B17 genetic polymorphisms on the disposition and action exemestane in healthy volunteers; optimization of 5-FU cancer chemotherapy, evaluation of issues associated with pediatric eosing; exploration of the physiologic impact of salmonella toxins; clinical study evaluating a novel point of care device as compared to the current industry standard for measurement of prothrombin time. *Total annual research expenditures:* $77,324. *Unit head:* Dr. Julie Ann Hixson-Wallace, Dean, 501-279-5205, Fax: 501-279-5525, E-mail: jahixson@harding.edu. *Application contact:* Carol Jones, Director of Admissions, 501-279-5523, Fax: 501-279-5525, E-mail: ccjones@harding.edu. Web site: http://www.harding.edu/pharmacy/.

Howard University, College of Pharmacy, Washington, DC 20059-0002. Offers Pharm D, Pharm D/MBA. *Accreditation:* ACPE. Postbaccalaureate distance learning degree programs offered (minimal on-campus study). *Degree requirements:* For doctorate, comprehensive exam. *Entrance requirements:* For doctorate, PCAT, minimum GPA of 2.5. Electronic applications accepted. *Expenses:* Contact institution. *Faculty research:* Kinetics of drug absorption, stealth liposomes, synthesis, opiate analgesics.

Idaho State University, Office of Graduate Studies, College of Pharmacy, Department of Pharmacy Practice and Administrative Sciences, Pocatello, ID 83209-8333. Offers pharmacy (Pharm D); pharmacy administration (MS, PhD). *Accreditation:* ACPE (one or more programs are accredited). Part-time programs available. *Degree requirements:* For master's, one foreign language, comprehensive exam, thesis, thesis research, speech and technical writing classes; for doctorate, comprehensive exam, thesis/dissertation, oral and written exams, speech and technical writing classes. *Entrance requirements:* For master's, GRE General Test, minimum GPA of 3.0, 3 letters of recommendation; for doctorate, GRE General Test, BS in pharmacy or related field, minimum GPA of 3.0, 3 letters of recommendation. Additional exam requirements/recommendations for international students: Required—TOEFL (minimum score 550 paper-based; 213 computer-based; 80 iBT). Electronic applications accepted. *Expenses:* Contact institution. *Faculty research:* Pharmaceutical care outcomes, drug use review, pharmacoeconomics.

Lake Erie College of Osteopathic Medicine, Professional Programs, Erie, PA 16509-1025. Offers biomedical sciences (Postbaccalaureate Certificate); medical education (MS); osteopathic medicine (DO); pharmacy (Pharm D). *Accreditation:* ACPE; AOsA. *Degree requirements:* For doctorate, comprehensive exam, National Osteopathic Medical Licensing Exam, Levels 1 and 2; for Postbaccalaureate Certificate, comprehensive exam, North American Pharmacist Licensure Examination (NAPLEX). *Entrance requirements:* For doctorate, MCAT, minimum GPA of 3.2, letters of recommendation; for Postbaccalaureate Certificate, PCAT, letters of recommendation, minimum GPA of 3.5. Electronic applications accepted. *Faculty research:* Cardiac smooth and skeletal muscle mechanics, chemotherapeutics and vitamins, osteopathic manipulation.

Lebanese American University, School of Pharmacy, Beirut, Lebanon. Offers Pharm D. *Accreditation:* ACPE.

Lipscomb University, College of Pharmacy, Nashville, TN 37204-3951. Offers Pharm D. *Faculty:* 25 full-time (11 women). *Students:* 299 full-time (175 women), 2 part-time (both women); includes 38 minority (13 Black or African American, non-Hispanic/Latino; 2 American Indian or Alaska Native, non-Hispanic/Latino; 20 Asian, non-Hispanic/Latino; 3 Hispanic/Latino). Average age 26. 750 applicants, 19% accepted, 75 enrolled. *Entrance requirements:* For doctorate, PCAT (minimum 45th percentile), 66 pre-professional semester hours, minimum GPA of 2.5, interview. Additional exam requirements/recommendations for international students: Required—TOEFL (minimum score 570 paper-based; 230 computer-based). *Application deadline:* For fall admission, 2/7 for domestic students. Applications are processed on a rolling basis. Application fee: $50 ($75 for international students). Electronic applications accepted. *Expenses: Tuition:* Full-time $16,830; part-time $935 per credit hour. Tuition and fees vary according to degree level and program. *Financial support:* Application deadline: 2/15; applicants required to submit FAFSA. *Unit head:* Dr. Roger Davis, Dean/Professor of Pharmacy Practice, 615-966-1000. *Application contact:* Kathryne Chanell, Administrative Assistant, 615-966-7176, E-mail: kathryne.channell@lipscomb.edu. Web site: http://pharmacy.lipscomb.edu/.

Loma Linda University, School of Pharmacy, Loma Linda, CA 92350. Offers Pharm D. *Accreditation:* ACPE. *Degree requirements:* For doctorate, intern pharmacist license.

Marshall University, School of Pharmacy, Huntington, WV 25755. Offers Pharm D. *Unit head:* Dr. Kevin W. Yingling, Founding Dean, 304-696-7302, E-mail: pharmacy@marshall.edu. *Application contact:* Dr. Tammy Johnson, Graduate Admissions, 304-746-1900, Fax: 304-746-1902, E-mail: services@marshall.edu. Web site: http://www.marshall.edu/wpmu/pharmacy/.

Massachusetts College of Pharmacy and Health Sciences, Graduate Studies, Doctoral Programs in Pharmacy–Boston, Postbaccalaureate Doctor of Pharmacy Pathway Program, Boston, MA 02115-5896. Offers Pharm D. Part-time programs available. Postbaccalaureate distance learning degree programs offered (minimal on-campus study). *Students:* 83 part-time (55 women); includes 27 minority (4 Black or African American, non-Hispanic/Latino; 21 Asian, non-Hispanic/Latino; 2 Hispanic/Latino), 9 international. Average age 40. 98 applicants, 60% accepted, 59 enrolled. In 2011, 39 doctorates awarded. *Entrance requirements:* For doctorate, registered pharmacist status in the U.S.; working at or have access to a site that provides opportunities to practice pharmaceutical care; curriculum vitae; letter of recommendation. Additional exam requirements/recommendations for international students: Required—TOEFL (minimum score 550 paper-based; 213 computer-based; 79 iBT). *Application deadline:* For fall admission, 5/1 priority date for domestic students. Applications are processed on a rolling basis. Application fee: $70. Electronic applications accepted. *Expenses: Tuition:* Full-time $30,200; part-time $945 per credit hour. *Unit head:* Kathy Grams, Director, 617-732-2830, E-mail: kathy.grams@mcphs.edu. *Application contact:* Brian Barilone, Associate Director of Transfer and Graduate Admission, 617-879-5032, E-mail: admissions@mcphs.edu.

Massachusetts College of Pharmacy and Health Sciences, Graduate Studies, Doctoral Programs in Pharmacy–Boston, Program in Pharmacy, Boston, MA 02115-5896. Offers Pharm D. Postbaccalaureate distance learning degree programs offered. *Students:* 1,916 full-time (1,172 women), 45 part-time (28 women); includes 709 minority (59 Black or African American, non-Hispanic/Latino; 3 American Indian or Alaska Native, non-Hispanic/Latino; 605 Asian, non-Hispanic/Latino; 29 Hispanic/Latino; 1 Native Hawaiian or other Pacific Islander, non-Hispanic/Latino; 12 Two or more races, non-Hispanic/Latino), 130 international. Average age 21. 2,465 applicants, 55% accepted, 504 enrolled. In 2011, 248 doctorates awarded. *Entrance requirements:* For doctorate, SAT (if fewer than 30 semester hours completed), minimum GPA of 2.5, interview. Additional exam requirements/recommendations for international students: Required—TOEFL (minimum score 550 paper-based; 213 computer-based; 79 iBT). *Application deadline:* For fall admission, 2/1 priority date for domestic students, 2/1 for international students. Application fee: $70. Electronic applications accepted. *Expenses: Tuition:* Full-time $30,200; part-time $945 per credit hour. *Financial support:* Application deadline: 3/15. *Unit head:* Dr. Douglas Pisano, Dean, School of Pharmacy, 617-732-2781. *Application contact:* Kathleen Ryan, Coordinator of Transfer Admissions, Pharmacy and Nursing, 617-732-5042.

Massachusetts College of Pharmacy and Health Sciences, School of Pharmacy–Worcester/Manchester, Boston, MA 02115-5896. Offers Pharm D. *Students:* 789 full-time (458 women), 10 part-time (2 women); includes 145 minority (42 Black or African American, non-Hispanic/Latino; 93 Asian, non-Hispanic/Latino; 7 Hispanic/Latino; 3 Native Hawaiian or other Pacific Islander, non-Hispanic/Latino), 71 international. Average age 27. 2,340 applicants, 22% accepted, 406 enrolled. In 2011, 201 doctorates awarded. *Entrance requirements:* Additional exam requirements/recommendations for international students: Required—TOEFL (minimum score 550 paper-based; 213 computer-based; 79 iBT). Application fee: $70. *Expenses: Tuition:* Full-time $30,200; part-time $945 per credit hour. *Unit head:* Dr. Michael Malloy, Dean, 508-373-5603, E-mail: michael.malloy@mcphs.edu. *Application contact:* Bryan Witham, Director of Admissions, Worcester and Manchester, 508-373-5623, E-mail: bryan.witham@mcphs.edu.

Medical University of South Carolina, South Carolina College of Pharmacy, Charleston, SC 29425. Offers Pharm D. *Accreditation:* ACPE. *Faculty:* 36 full-time (15 women), 3 part-time/adjunct (2 women). *Students:* 314 full-time (202 women), 2 part-time (0 women); includes 49 minority (20 Black or African American, non-Hispanic/Latino; 1 American Indian or Alaska Native, non-Hispanic/Latino; 18 Asian, non-Hispanic/Latino; 10 Hispanic/Latino), 3 international. Average age 25. 526 applicants, 43% accepted, 192 enrolled. In 2011, 78 doctorates awarded. *Entrance requirements:* For doctorate, PCAT, 2 years pre-professional course work, interview, minimum GPA of 2.5. Additional exam requirements/recommendations for international students: Required—TOEFL (minimum score 600 paper-based; 250 computer-based). *Application deadline:* For fall admission, 1/1 for domestic and international students. Application fee: $85. Electronic applications accepted. *Expenses:* Contact institution. *Financial support:* Career-related internships or fieldwork, Federal Work-Study, institutionally sponsored loans, and scholarships/grants available. Financial award application deadline: 3/10; financial award applicants required to submit FAFSA. *Faculty research:* Rational and computer aided drug design; drug metabolism and transport; molecular immunology and cellular toxicology; cell injury, death and regeneration; outcome sciences. *Unit head:* Dr. Joseph T. DiPiro, Executive Dean, 843-792-8452, Fax: 843-792-9081, E-mail: jdipiro@

sccp.sc.edu. *Application contact:* Dr. Philip D. Hall, Associate Dean, 843-792-8979, Fax: 843-792-9081, E-mail: hallpd@sccp.sc.edu. Web site: http://www.sccp.sc.edu.

Mercer University, Graduate Studies, Cecil B. Day Campus, College of Pharmacy and Health Sciences, Macon, GA 31207-0003. Offers medical sciences/physician assistant studies (MM Sc); pharmaceutical sciences (PhD); pharmacology (PhD); pharmacy (Pharm D); physical therapy (DPT); Pharm D/MBA; Pharm D/PhD. *Accreditation:* ACPE (one or more programs are accredited). *Faculty:* 28 full-time (17 women), 4 part-time/adjunct (3 women). *Students:* 747 full-time (487 women), 7 part-time (2 women); includes 232 minority (79 Black or African American, non-Hispanic/Latino; 136 Asian, non-Hispanic/Latino; 8 Hispanic/Latino; 9 Two or more races, non-Hispanic/Latino), 50 international. Average age 26. 1,895 applicants, 18% accepted, 176 enrolled. In 2011, 31 master's, 155 doctorates awarded. *Degree requirements:* For doctorate, comprehensive exam (for some programs), thesis/dissertation (for some programs). *Entrance requirements:* For master's, GRE, minimum GPA of 3.0 (preferred); for doctorate, GRE; PCAT (for Pharm D), Pharm D or BS in pharmacy or science, minimum GPA of 3.0. Additional exam requirements/recommendations for international students: Required—TOEFL. *Application deadline:* Applications are processed on a rolling basis. Electronic applications accepted. *Expenses:* Contact institution. *Financial support:* In 2011–12, 350 students received support. Teaching assistantships with tuition reimbursements available, career-related internships or fieldwork, Federal Work-Study, institutionally sponsored loans, scholarships/grants, tuition waivers, and unspecified assistantships available. Support available to part-time students. Financial award application deadline: 5/1; financial award applicants required to submit FAFSA. *Faculty research:* Stability and compatibility of steroids, synthesis of antihypertensives, disposition of cyclosporine, DUZ-drug research, synthesis of enzyme inhibitors. *Unit head:* Dr. Hewitt W. Matthews, Dean, 678-547-6306, Fax: 678-547-6315, E-mail: matthews_h@mercer.edu. *Application contact:* Dr. James W. Bartling, Associate Dean for Student Affairs and Admissions, 678-547-6181, Fax: 678-547-6518, E-mail: bartling_jw@mercer.edu. Web site: http://www.cophs.mercer.edu.

Midwestern University, Downers Grove Campus, Chicago College of Pharmacy, Downers Grove, IL 60515-1235. Offers Pharm D. *Accreditation:* ACPE. Part-time programs available. Postbaccalaureate distance learning degree programs offered (minimal on-campus study). *Faculty:* 50 full-time (35 women). *Students:* 817 full-time (487 women), 10 part-time (2 women); includes 375 minority (14 Black or African American, non-Hispanic/Latino; 2 American Indian or Alaska Native, non-Hispanic/Latino; 308 Asian, non-Hispanic/Latino; 29 Hispanic/Latino; 3 Native Hawaiian or other Pacific Islander, non-Hispanic/Latino; 19 Two or more races, non-Hispanic/Latino), 11 international. Average age 25. 2,499 applicants, 19% accepted, 201 enrolled. In 2011, 217 doctorates awarded. *Entrance requirements:* For doctorate, PCAT. *Application deadline:* For fall admission, 2/3 for domestic students. Application fee: $50. *Expenses:* Contact institution. *Financial support:* Federal Work-Study and institutionally sponsored loans available. Support available to part-time students. Financial award applicants required to submit FAFSA. *Unit head:* Dr. Nancy Fjortoft, Dean, 630-971-6408. *Application contact:* Michael Laken, Director of Admissions, 630-515-6171, Fax: 630-971-6086, E-mail: admissil@midwestern.edu. Web site: http://www.midwestern.edu/Programs_and_Admission/IL_Pharmacy.html.

Midwestern University, Glendale Campus, College of Pharmacy-Glendale, Glendale, AZ 85308. Offers Pharm D. *Accreditation:* ACPE. *Faculty:* 36 full-time (27 women), 1 (woman) part-time/adjunct. *Students:* 427 full-time (215 women), 6 part-time (1 woman); includes 194 minority (10 Black or African American, non-Hispanic/Latino; 1 American Indian or Alaska Native, non-Hispanic/Latino; 151 Asian, non-Hispanic/Latino; 20 Hispanic/Latino; 5 Native Hawaiian or other Pacific Islander, non-Hispanic/Latino; 7 Two or more races, non-Hispanic/Latino), 8 international. Average age 28. 1,716 applicants, 16% accepted, 154 enrolled. In 2011, 133 doctorates awarded. *Entrance requirements:*

For doctorate, PCAT. *Application deadline:* For fall admission, 2/1 for domestic students. Application fee: $50. *Expenses:* Contact institution. *Financial support:* Applicants required to submit FAFSA. *Unit head:* Dr. Dennis McCallian, Interim Dean, 623-572-3501. *Application contact:* James Walter, Director of Admissions, 888-247-9277, Fax: 623-572-3229, E-mail: admissaz@midwestern.edu. Web site: http://www.midwestern.edu/Programs_and_Admission/AZ_Pharmacy.html.

Northeastern Ohio Medical University, College of Pharmacy, Rootstown, OH 44272-0095. Offers Pharm D. *Entrance requirements:* For doctorate, PCAT. Electronic applications accepted. *Expenses:* Contact institution.

Nova Southeastern University, Health Professions Division, College of Pharmacy, Fort Lauderdale, FL 33314-7796. Offers PhD, Pharm D. *Accreditation:* ACPE. Postbaccalaureate distance learning degree programs offered (minimal on-campus study). *Faculty:* 52 full-time (32 women), 9 part-time/adjunct (3 women). *Students:* 922 full-time (572 women), 42 part-time (30 women); includes 606 minority (73 Black or African American, non-Hispanic/Latino; 2 American Indian or Alaska Native, non-Hispanic/Latino; 148 Asian, non-Hispanic/Latino; 377 Hispanic/Latino; 1 Native Hawaiian or other Pacific Islander, non-Hispanic/Latino; 5 Two or more races, non-Hispanic/Latino), 104 international. Average age 27. 1,343 applicants, 31% accepted, 209 enrolled. In 2011, 244 doctorates awarded. *Degree requirements:* For doctorate, comprehensive exam (for some programs), thesis/dissertation (for some programs). *Entrance requirements:* For doctorate, PCAT (for Pharm D); GRE (for PhD). Additional exam requirements/recommendations for international students: Required—TOEFL (minimum score 550 paper-based; 213 computer-based) or IELTS. *Application deadline:* For fall admission, 3/1 for domestic students, 2/1 for international students. Applications are processed on a rolling basis. Application fee: $50. Electronic applications accepted. *Expenses:* Contact institution. *Financial support:* In 2011–12, 5 teaching assistantships were awarded; career-related internships or fieldwork, Federal Work-Study, institutionally sponsored loans, and scholarships/grants also available. Financial award application deadline: 4/15; financial award applicants required to submit FAFSA. *Faculty research:* Neovascularization, health care delivery, pharmacoeconomics, cardiovascular/metabolic metastasis. *Total annual research expenditures:* $526,388. *Unit head:* Dr. Andres Malave, Dean, 954-262-1304, Fax: 954-262-2278, E-mail: copdean@nova.edu. *Application contact:* Brittney Lyda, Admissions Counselor, 954-262-1112, Fax: 954-262-2282, E-mail: bl541@nova.edu. Web site: http://pharmacy.nova.edu/.

See Display below and Close-Up on page 937.

Ohio Northern University, Raabe College of Pharmacy, Ada, OH 45810-1599. Offers Pharm D. Students enter the program as undergraduates. *Accreditation:* ACPE. *Faculty:* 33 full-time (13 women), 2 part-time/adjunct (0 women). *Students:* 1,021 full-time (640 women), 9 part-time (2 women); includes 76 minority (17 Black or African American, non-Hispanic/Latino; 1 American Indian or Alaska Native, non-Hispanic/Latino; 39 Asian, non-Hispanic/Latino; 5 Hispanic/Latino; 14 Two or more races, non-Hispanic/Latino), 37 international. Average age 21. 914 applicants, 38% accepted, 195 enrolled. In 2011, 164 doctorates awarded. *Degree requirements:* For doctorate, 9 clinical rotations, capstone course. *Entrance requirements:* For doctorate, ACT or SAT. Additional exam requirements/recommendations for international students: Required—TOEFL (minimum score 550 paper-based; 213 computer-based; 80 iBT). *Expenses:* Contact institution. *Financial support:* Federal Work-Study, institutionally sponsored loans, and scholarships/grants available. Financial award applicants required to submit FAFSA. *Faculty research:* Alcohol and substance abuse, women in pharmacy, non-traditional education, continuing pharmaceutical education, medicinal chemistry. *Unit head:* Dr. Jon E. Sprague, Dean, 419-772-2275, Fax: 419-772-3554, E-mail: j-sprague@onu.edu. *Application contact:* Dr. Robert McCurdy, Assistant Dean and

---

NOVA SOUTHEASTERN UNIVERSITY

College of Pharmacy

An Innovative Program of Graduate Study, Research, and Service

Attain your Ph.D. degree in one of three distinct sequences: Drug Discovery; Drug Development (Pharmaceutics); and Determinants of Drug Use (Social and Administrative Pharmacy)

Also available: Doctor of Pharmacy/Master of Business Administration (Pharm.D./M.B.A.)

*NSU is the only U.S. college of pharmacy with a full-service community pharmacy (on the main campus) and a full-service hospital pharmacy.

*College of Pharmacy programs are taught by multilingual, multicultural, full-time faculty members engaged in practice.

*Clinical and applied research is delivered at sites in Florida at Fort Lauderdale and West Palm Beach and in Ponce, Puerto Rico.

For more information, please contact:
Dr. Hugh M. McLean, Associate Dean, Research and Graduate Education
Health Professions Division
College of Pharmacy
Nova Southeastern University
Fort Lauderdale, FL 33328-2018
954-262-1101 or 877-640-0218(toll-free)
E-mail: hugh.mclean@nova.edu
http://pharmacy.nova.edu/

Pharmacy

Director of Pharmacy Student Services, 419-772-2278, Fax: 419-772-3554, E-mail: r-mccurdy@onu.edu. Web site: http://www.onu.edu/pharmacy/.

The Ohio State University, College of Pharmacy, Columbus, OH 43210. Offers MS, PhD, Pharm D. *Accreditation:* ACPE (one or more programs are accredited). Part-time programs available. *Faculty:* 47. *Students:* 567 full-time (329 women), 29 part-time (15 women); includes 141 minority (18 Black or African American, non-Hispanic/Latino; 1 American Indian or Alaska Native, non-Hispanic/Latino; 104 Asian, non-Hispanic/Latino; 12 Hispanic/Latino; 6 Two or more races, non-Hispanic/Latino), 58 international. Average age 27. In 2011, 5 master's, 135 doctorates awarded. *Degree requirements:* For doctorate, thesis/dissertation (for some programs). *Entrance requirements:* For master's, GRE General Test, minimum GPA of 3.0; for doctorate, GRE General Test; PCAT (for Pharm D), minimum GPA of 3.0. Additional exam requirements/recommendations for international students: Required—TOEFL, Michigan English Language Assessment Battery (minimum score 82). *Application deadline:* For fall admission, 1/1 priority date for domestic students. Application fee: $40 ($50 for international students). Electronic applications accepted. *Expenses:* Contact institution. *Financial support:* Fellowships with full tuition reimbursements, research assistantships with full tuition reimbursements, teaching assistantships with full tuition reimbursements, career-related internships or fieldwork, Federal Work-Study, institutionally sponsored loans, scholarships/grants, and traineeships available. *Unit head:* Dr. Robert W. Brueggemeier, Dean, 614-292-5711, Fax: 614-292-2588, E-mail: odmail@pharmacy.ohio-state.edu. *Application contact:* Graduate Program Coordinator, 614-292-6822, Fax: 614-292-2588, E-mail: gradprogram@pharmacy.ohio-state.edu. Web site: http://www.pharmacy.ohio-state.edu.

Oregon State University, College of Pharmacy, Corvallis, OR 97331. Offers MS, PhD, Pharm D. *Accreditation:* ACPE (one or more programs are accredited). Part-time programs available. Terminal master's awarded for partial completion of doctoral program. *Degree requirements:* For master's, thesis; for doctorate, thesis/dissertation (for some programs). *Entrance requirements:* For master's, GRE General Test, minimum GPA of 3.0 in last 90 hours. Additional exam requirements/recommendations for international students: Required—TOEFL. *Faculty research:* Pharmacology/toxicology, pharmacokinetics, biopharmaceutics, neuroscience, natural products.

Pacific University, School of Pharmacy, Forest Grove, OR 97116-1797. Offers Pharm D. *Accreditation:* ACPE. *Entrance requirements:* Additional exam requirements/recommendations for international students: Required—TOEFL (minimum score 600 paper-based; 250 computer-based). Electronic applications accepted. *Expenses:* Contact institution. *Faculty research:* Informatics, enzyme metabolism, apostosis/cell cycle, neurophysiology of chronic pain, neurophysiology of Alzheimer's.

Palm Beach Atlantic University, Gregory School of Pharmacy, West Palm Beach, FL 33416-4708. Offers Pharm D. *Accreditation:* ACPE. *Faculty:* 22 full-time (16 women), 3 part-time/adjunct (2 women). *Students:* 300 full-time (179 women), 10 part-time (8 women); includes 133 minority (23 Black or African American, non-Hispanic/Latino; 1 American Indian or Alaska Native, non-Hispanic/Latino; 58 Asian, non-Hispanic/Latino; 48 Hispanic/Latino; 2 Native Hawaiian or other Pacific Islander, non-Hispanic/Latino; 1 Two or more races, non-Hispanic/Latino), 17 international. Average age 26. 439 applicants, 38% accepted, 76 enrolled. In 2011, 61 doctorates awarded. *Entrance requirements:* For doctorate, PCAT, minimum GPA of 3.4. Additional exam requirements/recommendations for international students: Required—TOEFL (minimum score 550 paper-based; 213 computer-based; 79 iBT). *Application deadline:* For fall admission, 5/31 priority date for domestic students, 5/31 for international students. Applications are processed on a rolling basis. Application fee: $150. Electronic applications accepted. *Expenses:* Contact institution. *Financial support:* Unspecified assistantships available. Financial award applicants required to submit FAFSA. *Unit head:* Dr. Mary Ferrill, Dean, 561-803-2700, E-mail: mary_ferrill@pba.edu. *Application contact:* Lucas Whittaker, Director of Pharmacy Admissions, 561-803-2750. Web site: http://www.pba.edu.

Purdue University, College of Pharmacy and Pharmacal Sciences, Professional Program in Pharmacy and Pharmacal Sciences, West Lafayette, IN 47907. Offers Pharm D. *Accreditation:* ACPE. *Students:* 623 full-time (399 women), 12 part-time (8 women); includes 113 minority (29 Black or African American, non-Hispanic/Latino; 1 American Indian or Alaska Native, non-Hispanic/Latino; 69 Asian, non-Hispanic/Latino; 11 Hispanic/Latino; 3 Two or more races, non-Hispanic/Latino), 27 international. Average age 24. 1,156 applicants, 16% accepted, 157 enrolled. *Entrance requirements:* For doctorate, minimum 2 years of pre-pharmacy course work, interview. *Application deadline:* For fall admission, 12/3 for domestic and international students. Application fee: $60 ($75 for international students). *Expenses:* Contact institution. *Financial support:* Career-related internships or fieldwork, Federal Work-Study, and scholarships/grants available. Financial award application deadline: 3/15; financial award applicants required to submit FAFSA. *Faculty research:* Medicinal chemistry, pharmacology, pharmaceutics, clinical pharmacy, pharmacy administration. *Unit head:* Dr. C. L. Svensson, Dean, 765-494-1368, Fax: 765-494-7880, E-mail: svensson@purdue.edu. Web site: http://www.pharmacy.purdue.edu/.

Regis University, Rueckert-Hartman College for Health Professions, Denver, CO 80221-1099. Offers family nurse practitioner (MSN); health informatics (Postbaccalaureate Certificate); health services administration (MS); leadership in healthcare systems (MSN); neonatal nurse practitioner (MSN); nursing (MSN); pharmacy (Pharm D); physical therapy (DPT, TDPT). *Entrance requirements:* Additional exam requirements/recommendations for international students: Required—TOEFL (minimum score 550 paper-based; 213 computer-based; 82 iBT). Electronic applications accepted. *Expenses:* Contact institution. *Faculty research:* Normal and pathological balance and gait research, normal/pathological upper limb motor control/biomechanics, exercise energy/metabolism research, optical treatment protocols for therapeutic modalities.

Roosevelt University, Graduate Division, College of Pharmacy, Chicago, IL 60605. Offers Pharm D. *Accreditation:* ACPE.

Roseman University of Health Sciences, College of Pharmacy, Henderson, NV 89014. Offers Pharm D. *Accreditation:* ACPE. *Degree requirements:* For doctorate, comprehensive exam. *Entrance requirements:* For doctorate, PCAT.

Rutgers, The State University of New Jersey, New Brunswick, Ernest Mario School of Pharmacy, Piscataway, NJ 08854-8097. Offers medicinal chemistry (MS, PhD); pharmaceutical science (MS, PhD); pharmacy (Pharm D). *Accreditation:* ACPE. *Degree requirements:* For doctorate, variable foreign language requirement. *Entrance requirements:* For doctorate, SAT or PCAT (for Pharm D), interview, criminal background check (for Pharm D). Additional exam requirements/recommendations for international students: Recommended—TOEFL (minimum score 550 paper-based; 213 computer-based). Electronic applications accepted. *Expenses:* Contact institution. *Faculty research:* Pharmacokinetics, cancer prevention, cardiology, neurology, pharmacodynamics.

St. John Fisher College, Wegmans School of Pharmacy, Doctor of Pharmacy Program, Rochester, NY 14618-3597. Offers Pharm D. *Accreditation:* ACPE. *Faculty:* 29 full-time (21 women), 2 part-time/adjunct (1 woman). *Students:* 300 full-time (157 women), 2 part-time (1 woman); includes 58 minority (8 Black or African American, non-Hispanic/Latino; 39 Asian, non-Hispanic/Latino; 7 Hispanic/Latino; 4 Two or more races, non-Hispanic/Latino), 8 international. Average age 25. 862 applicants, 19% accepted, 80 enrolled. In 2011, 60 doctorates awarded. *Degree requirements:* For doctorate, advanced pharmacy practice experience. *Entrance requirements:* For doctorate, PCAT, 2 letters of recommendation, interview, minimum of 62 credit hours of specific undergraduate courses. Additional exam requirements/recommendations for international students: Required—TOEFL (minimum score 575 paper-based; 233 computer-based; 80 iBT). *Application deadline:* For fall admission, 3/1 for domestic students. Applications are processed on a rolling basis. Application fee: $50. Electronic applications accepted. *Expenses:* Contact institution. *Financial support:* In 2011–12, 39 students received support. Scholarships/grants available. Financial award applicants required to submit FAFSA. *Faculty research:* Opioid pharmacology, heavy metal toxicology. *Unit head:* Dr. Scott A. Swigart, Dean of the School of Pharmacy, 585-385-8201, Fax: 585-385-8453, E-mail: sswigart@sjfc.edu. *Application contact:* Jose Perales, Director of Graduate Admissions, 585-385-8067, E-mail: jperales@sjfc.edu. Web site: http://www.sjfc.edu/pharmacy/.

St. John's University, College of Pharmacy and Health Sciences, Professional Program in Pharmacy, Queens, NY 11439. Offers Pharm D. *Accreditation:* ACPE. *Students:* 478 full-time (278 women), 11 part-time (3 women); includes 355 minority (11 Black or African American, non-Hispanic/Latino; 1 American Indian or Alaska Native, non-Hispanic/Latino; 316 Asian, non-Hispanic/Latino; 15 Hispanic/Latino; 8 Native Hawaiian or other Pacific Islander, non-Hispanic/Latino; 4 Two or more races, non-Hispanic/Latino), 17 international. Average age 23. In 2011, 246 doctorates awarded. *Degree requirements:* For doctorate, comprehensive exam, 1-year residency. *Entrance requirements:* For doctorate, bachelor's degree from an ACPE-accredited program or BS in pharmacy and license, clinical experience, interview. Additional exam requirements/recommendations for international students: Required—TOEFL (minimum score 600 paper-based; 250 computer-based; 100 iBT), IELTS (minimum score 5.5). *Application deadline:* For fall admission, 3/1 priority date for domestic students, 5/1 for international students; for spring admission, 11/1 priority date for domestic students, 11/1 for international students. Applications are processed on a rolling basis. Application fee: $70. Electronic applications accepted. *Expenses:* Contact institution. *Financial support:* Research assistantships, career-related internships or fieldwork, and unspecified assistantships available. Support available to part-time students. Financial award application deadline: 3/1; financial award applicants required to submit FAFSA. *Faculty research:* Patient outcomes, drug-drug-infections, pharmacokinetics, pharmacodynamics. *Unit head:* Dr. Candace Smith, Chair, 718-990-5374, E-mail: smithc@stjohns.edu. *Application contact:* Robert Medrano, Director of Graduate Admission, 718-990-1601, Fax: 718-990-5686, E-mail: gradhelp@stjohns.edu.

St. Louis College of Pharmacy, Professional Program, St. Louis, MO 63110-1088. Offers Pharm D. *Accreditation:* ACPE. *Entrance requirements:* For doctorate, PCAT, 2 letters of recommendation. Additional exam requirements/recommendations for international students: Required—TOEFL (minimum score 550 paper-based; 220 computer-based). Electronic applications accepted. *Faculty research:* Geriatrics, cardiology, psychobiology, infectious diseases.

Samford University, McWhorter School of Pharmacy, Birmingham, AL 35229. Offers Pharm D. *Accreditation:* ACPE. *Faculty:* 39 full-time (25 women), 1 part-time/adjunct (0 women). *Students:* 510 full-time (332 women), 4 part-time (2 women); includes 54 minority (20 Black or African American, non-Hispanic/Latino; 3 American Indian or Alaska Native, non-Hispanic/Latino; 21 Asian, non-Hispanic/Latino; 8 Hispanic/Latino; 2 Two or more races, non-Hispanic/Latino), 6 international. Average age 24. 752 applicants, 17% accepted, 129 enrolled. In 2011, 117 doctorates awarded. *Entrance requirements:* For doctorate, PCAT, minimum GPA of 2.75. Additional exam requirements/recommendations for international students: Required—TOEFL (minimum score 550 paper-based; 213 computer-based; 80 iBT). *Application deadline:* For fall admission, 2/1 for domestic students. Applications are processed on a rolling basis. Application fee: $50. Electronic applications accepted. *Expenses:* Contact institution. *Financial support:* In 2011–12, 143 students received support. Career-related internships or fieldwork, Federal Work-Study, and institutionally sponsored loans available. Financial award application deadline: 5/2; financial award applicants required to submit FAFSA. *Faculty research:* Biotechnology, transdermal drug delivery, vaccines, human skin models, genetic mapping of disease, determination of pharmacokinetics of new drug candidates, impact of herbal supplements on orally administered chemotherapeutic prodrugs. *Unit head:* Dr. Charles D. Sands, III, Dean, 205-726-2820, Fax: 205-726-2759, E-mail: ccsands@samford.edu. *Application contact:* C. Bruce Foster, Director of External Relations and Pharmacy Admissions, 205-726-2982, Fax: 205-726-4141, E-mail: cbfoster@samford.edu. Web site: http://pharmacy.samford.edu.

Shenandoah University, School of Pharmacy, Winchester, VA 22601-5195. Offers Pharm D. *Accreditation:* ACPE. Part-time programs available. Postbaccalaureate distance learning degree programs offered (minimal on-campus study). *Faculty:* 20 full-time (11 women), 3 part-time/adjunct (2 women). *Students:* 315 full-time (176 women), 141 part-time (88 women); includes 125 minority (27 Black or African American, non-Hispanic/Latino; 92 Asian, non-Hispanic/Latino; 5 Hispanic/Latino; 1 Two or more races, non-Hispanic/Latino), 21 international. Average age 31. 690 applicants, 38% accepted, 150 enrolled. In 2011, 135 doctorates awarded. *Degree requirements:* For doctorate, clerkship. *Entrance requirements:* For doctorate, PCAT (minimum composite score 60th percentile), interview, minimum GPA of 2.5, 3 letters of recommendation. Additional exam requirements/recommendations for international students: Required—TOEFL (minimum score 550 paper-based; 213 computer-based; 79 iBT), IELTS (minimum score 6.5), Sakae Institute of Study Abroad (minimum score 550). *Application deadline:* For fall admission, 2/1 for domestic and international students. Applications are processed on a rolling basis. Application fee: $30. Electronic applications accepted. *Expenses:* Contact institution. *Financial support:* In 2011–12, 10 students received support. Career-related internships or fieldwork, institutionally sponsored loans, scholarships/grants, and federal loans, alternative loans available. Support available to part-time students. Financial award application deadline: 3/15; financial award applicants required to submit FAFSA. *Faculty research:* Drug metabolism, pharmacogenomics, pharmacokinetics, natural products, gene expression. *Total annual research expenditures:* $5,973. *Unit head:* Dr. Alan McKay, Dean, 540-665-1282, Fax: 540-665-1283, E-mail: amckay@su.edu. *Application contact:* David Anthony, Dean of Admissions, 540-665-4581, Fax: 540-665-4627, E-mail: admit@su.edu. Web site: http://pharmacy.su.edu.

South Dakota State University, Graduate School, College of Pharmacy, Professional Program in Pharmacy, Brookings, SD 57007. Offers Pharm D. *Accreditation:* ACPE. *Entrance requirements:* For doctorate, ACT or PCAT, bachelor's degree in pharmacy. Additional exam requirements/recommendations for international students: Required—TOEFL (minimum score 550 paper-based; 213 computer-based). *Faculty research:* Geriatric medicine, drugs of abuse, anti-cancer drugs, drug metabolism, sustained drug delivery.

Southern Illinois University Edwardsville, School of Pharmacy, Edwardsville, IL 62026-0001. Offers Pharm D. *Accreditation:* ACPE. *Faculty:* 21 full-time (4 women). *Students:* 322 full-time (192 women); includes 40 minority (9 Black or African American, non-Hispanic/Latino; 14 Asian, non-Hispanic/Latino; 13 Hispanic/Latino; 4 Two or more

races, non-Hispanic/Latino). Average age 26. In 2011, 78 doctorates awarded. *Entrance requirements:* For doctorate, PCAT. *Application deadline:* For fall admission, 11/1 for domestic and international students. Application fee: $40. Electronic applications accepted. Tuition and fees vary according to course load and program. *Financial support:* Career-related internships or fieldwork, Federal Work-Study, institutionally sponsored loans, scholarships/grants, and traineeships available. Support available to part-time students. Financial award application deadline: 3/1; financial award applicants required to submit FAFSA. *Unit head:* Dr. Gireesh V. Gupchup, Dean, 618-650-5150, E-mail: pharmacy@siue.edu. *Application contact:* Michelle Robinson, Coordinator of Graduate Recruitment, 618-650-2811, Fax: 618-650-3523, E-mail: michero@siue.edu. Web site: http://www.siue.edu/pharmacy.

South University, Graduate Programs, School of Pharmacy, Savannah, GA 31406. Offers Pharm D/MBA. *Accreditation:* ACPE.

See Close-Up on page 941.

South University, Program in Pharmacy, Columbia, SC 29203. Offers Pharm D. Web site: http://www.southuniversity.edu/school-of-pharmacy/columbia-pharmacy-pharmd-245712.aspx.

See Close-Up on page 939.

Southwestern Oklahoma State University, College of Pharmacy, Weatherford, OK 73096-3098. Offers Pharm D. *Accreditation:* ACPE. *Entrance requirements:* For doctorate, PCAT.

Temple University, Health Sciences Center, School of Pharmacy, Professional Program in Pharmacy, Philadelphia, PA 19122-6096. Offers Pharm D. *Accreditation:* ACPE. *Students:* 606 full-time (373 women); includes 280 minority (58 Black or African American, non-Hispanic/Latino; 1 American Indian or Alaska Native, non-Hispanic/Latino; 210 Asian, non-Hispanic/Latino; 10 Hispanic/Latino; 1 Two or more races, non-Hispanic/Latino), 38 international. In 2011, 152 doctorates awarded. *Entrance requirements:* For doctorate, PCAT. *Expenses:* Contact institution. *Unit head:* Dr. Michael Mancano, Interim Chair of the Department of Pharmacy Practice, 215-707-4936, E-mail: michael.mancano@temple.edu. *Application contact:* Tara Schumacher, Coordinator of Outreach, 215-204-6575, Fax: 215-204-8781, E-mail: tara.schumacher@temple.edu. Web site: http://www.temple.edu/pharmacy/programs/PharmD.html.

Texas A&M Health Science Center, Irma Lerma Rangel College of Pharmacy, College Station, TX 77840. Offers Pharm D. *Entrance requirements:* For doctorate, PCAT, minimum GPA of 2.75, transcripts from each college/university attended.

Texas Southern University, College of Pharmacy and Health Sciences, Houston, TX 77004-4584. Offers MS, PhD, Pharm D. *Accreditation:* ACPE. Postbaccalaureate distance learning degree programs offered. *Entrance requirements:* For master's, PCAT; for doctorate, GRE General Test, PCAT (for Pharm D). Electronic applications accepted. *Faculty research:* Basic and clinical pharmacokinetics, metabolism studies, diabetes, hypertension, sickle cell.

Thomas Jefferson University, Jefferson School of Pharmacy, Philadelphia, PA 19107. Offers Pharm D.

Touro University, Graduate Programs, Vallejo, CA 94592. Offers education (MA); medical health sciences (MS); osteopathic medicine (DO); pharmacy (Pharm D); public health (MPH). *Accreditation:* AOsA; ARC-PA. Part-time and evening/weekend programs available. *Faculty:* 93 full-time (52 women), 55 part-time/adjunct (28 women). *Students:* 1,402 full-time (851 women). 6,914 applicants, 12% accepted, 503 enrolled. *Degree requirements:* For master's, comprehensive exam, thesis; for doctorate, comprehensive exam. *Entrance requirements:* For doctorate, BS/BA. *Application deadline:* For fall admission, 3/15 for domestic students; for winter admission, 12/1 for domestic students. Applications are processed on a rolling basis. Application fee: $100. Electronic applications accepted. *Expenses: Tuition:* Full-time $25,000; part-time $575 per credit. *Required fees:* $250 per year. Tuition and fees vary according to course level, course load, degree level and program. *Financial support:* Fellowships, research assistantships, teaching assistantships, Federal Work-Study, and scholarships/grants available. Support available to part-time students. Financial award applicants required to submit FAFSA. *Faculty research:* Cancer, heart disease. *Application contact:* Steve Davis, Associate Director of Admissions, 707-638-5270, Fax: 707-638-5250, E-mail: steven.davis@tu.edu.

Universidad de Ciencias Medicas, Graduate Programs, San Jose, Costa Rica. Offers dermatology (SP); family health (MS); health service center administration (MHA); human anatomy (MS); medical and surgery (MD); occupational medicine (MS); pharmacy (Pharm D). Part-time programs available. *Degree requirements:* For master's, thesis; for doctorate and SP, comprehensive exam. *Entrance requirements:* For master's, MD or bachelor's degree; for doctorate, admissions test; for SP, admissions test, MD.

University at Buffalo, the State University of New York, Graduate School, School of Pharmacy and Pharmaceutical Sciences, Professional Program in Pharmacy, Buffalo, NY 14260. Offers Pharm D, Pharm D/JD, Pharm D/MBA, Pharm D/MPH, Pharm D/MS, Pharm D/PhD. *Accreditation:* ACPE. *Faculty:* 24 full-time (10 women), 8 part-time/adjunct (4 women). *Students:* 354 full-time (221 women); includes 109 minority (12 Black or African American, non-Hispanic/Latino; 1 American Indian or Alaska Native, non-Hispanic/Latino; 89 Asian, non-Hispanic/Latino; 7 Hispanic/Latino), 15 international. Average age 24. 918 applicants, 14% accepted, 124 enrolled. In 2011, 110 doctorates awarded. *Degree requirements:* For doctorate, project. *Entrance requirements:* For doctorate, PCAT. *Application deadline:* For fall admission, 2/1 priority date for domestic students, 2/1 for international students. Applications are processed on a rolling basis. Application fee: $50. Electronic applications accepted. *Financial support:* In 2011–12, 308 students received support, including 9 fellowships; scholarships/grants and health care benefits also available. Financial award application deadline: 3/1; financial award applicants required to submit FAFSA. *Faculty research:* Pharmacokinetics, pharmacoepidemiology, AIDS, renal transplant, Attention Deficit Hyperactivity Disorder (ADHD), HIV/AIDS, oncology, critical care, PKPD, renal transplantation, pharmacometrics. *Total annual research expenditures:* $3.4 million. *Unit head:* Dr. Edward M. Bednarczyk, Chairman, 716-645-2828 Ext. 357, Fax: 716-645-2886, E-mail: eb@buffalo.edu. *Application contact:* Dr. Jennifer M. Hess, Assistant Dean, 716-645-2825 Ext. 1, Fax: 716-645-3688, E-mail: pharm-admin@buffalo.edu. Web site: http://pharmacy.buffalo.edu/pages/3/PharmD-Program.html.

University of Alberta, Faculty of Graduate Studies and Research, Department of Pharmacy and Pharmaceutical Sciences, Edmonton, AB T6G 2E1, Canada. Offers M Sc, PhD. Terminal master's awarded for partial completion of doctoral program. *Degree requirements:* For master's, thesis; for doctorate, thesis/dissertation. *Entrance requirements:* Additional exam requirements/recommendations for international students: Required—Michigan English Language Assessment Battery or IELTS. Electronic applications accepted. *Faculty research:* Radiopharmacy, pharmacokinetics, bionucleonics, medicinal chemistry, microbiology.

The University of Arizona, College of Pharmacy, Pharmacy Professional Program, Tucson, AZ 85721. Offers Pharm D. *Accreditation:* ACPE. Part-time programs available. *Faculty:* 38 full-time (7 women). *Students:* 388 full-time (242 women), 4 part-time (0 women); includes 162 minority (8 Black or African American, non-Hispanic/Latino; 1 American Indian or Alaska Native, non-Hispanic/Latino; 43 Asian, non-Hispanic/Latino; 31 Hispanic/Latino; 79 Two or more races, non-Hispanic/Latino), 8 international. Average age 29. In 2011, 87 doctorates awarded. *Entrance requirements:* For doctorate, PCAT, 4-6 months of pharmacy experience. Additional exam requirements/recommendations for international students: Required—TOEFL (minimum score 550 paper-based; 213 computer-based; 79 iBT). Application fee: $75. Electronic applications accepted. *Expenses:* Tuition, state resident: full-time $10,840. Tuition, nonresident: full-time $25,802. *Financial support:* In 2011–12, 11 research assistantships (averaging $20,700 per year) were awarded; career-related internships or fieldwork, scholarships/grants, health care benefits, and unspecified assistantships also available. *Faculty research:* Health/service administrative pharmacy education, geriatric pharmacy, social and behavioral pharmacy management and economics. *Total annual research expenditures:* $1.8 million. *Unit head:* Dr. Marie A. Chisholm-Burns, Head, 520-626-2298, E-mail: chilholm@pharmacy.arizona.edu. *Application contact:* General Information Contact, 520-626-4311, E-mail: admissionsinfo@pharmacy.arizona.edu. Web site: http://www.pharmacy.arizona.edu/programs/pharmd-program.

University of Arkansas for Medical Sciences, College of Pharmacy, Little Rock, AR 72205-7199. Offers MS, Pharm D. *Accreditation:* ACPE (one or more programs are accredited). *Degree requirements:* For master's, thesis. *Entrance requirements:* For master's, GRE; for doctorate, PCAT. Additional exam requirements/recommendations for international students: Required—TOEFL. *Expenses:* Contact institution.

The University of British Columbia, Faculty of Pharmaceutical Sciences, Vancouver, BC V6T 1Z3, Canada. Offers M Sc, PhD, Pharm D. *Degree requirements:* For master's, thesis, seminar; for doctorate, comprehensive exam (for some programs), thesis/dissertation (for some programs), seminar (for PhD). *Entrance requirements:* Additional exam requirements/recommendations for international students: Required—TOEFL (minimum score 600 paper-based; 250 computer-based; 100 iBT). Electronic applications accepted. *Faculty research:* Biopharmaceutics, pharmaceutical chemistry, pharmacology, toxicology, formulation.

University of California, San Diego, School of Pharmacy and Pharmaceutical Sciences, La Jolla, CA 92093. Offers Pharm D. *Accreditation:* ACPE.

University of California, San Francisco, School of Pharmacy, Program in Pharmacy, San Francisco, CA 94143. Offers Pharm D. *Accreditation:* ACPE. *Faculty:* 89 full-time (42 women), 15 part-time/adjunct (2 women). *Students:* 480 full-time (327 women); includes 295 minority (11 Black or African American, non-Hispanic/Latino; 1 American Indian or Alaska Native, non-Hispanic/Latino; 248 Asian, non-Hispanic/Latino; 35 Hispanic/Latino). Average age 25. 1,528 applicants, 9% accepted, 122 enrolled. In 2011, 122 doctorates awarded. *Degree requirements:* For doctorate, comprehensive exam, supervised practice experience. *Entrance requirements:* For doctorate, 2 years of preparatory course work in basic sciences. *Application deadline:* For fall admission, 11/1 for domestic and international students. Application fee: $60 ($80 for international students). Electronic applications accepted. *Financial support:* In 2011–12, 457 students received support. Teaching assistantships, career-related internships or fieldwork, Federal Work-Study, institutionally sponsored loans, and scholarships/grants available. Financial award application deadline: 2/1; financial award applicants required to submit FAFSA. *Faculty research:* Drug delivery, drug metabolism and chemical toxicology, macromolecular structure, molecular parasitology, pharmacokinetics. *Unit head:* Cynthia B. Watchmaker, Associate Dean/Director, Office of Student and Curricular Affairs, 415-476-8025, Fax: 415-476-6805, E-mail: watchmakerc@pharmacy.ucsf.edu. *Application contact:* Joel Gonzales, Admissions Director, 415-502-5368, Fax: 415-476-6805, E-mail: osaca@pharmacy.ucsf.edu. Web site: http://pharmacy.ucsf.edu/.

University of Charleston, School of Pharmacy, Charleston, WV 25304-1099. Offers Pharm D. *Accreditation:* ACPE. *Degree requirements:* For doctorate, passing grade in all coursework, minimum cumulative GPA of 2.3 for all courses. *Entrance requirements:* For doctorate, PCAT (taken within 2 years of the date of application), minimum undergraduate GPA of 2.75, completion of 66 credit hours of pre-pharmacy prerequisite course work, criminal background check, immunization records. Additional exam requirements/recommendations for international students: Required—TOEFL. *Application deadline:* For fall admission, 2/1 priority date for domestic students, 2/1 for international students. Applications are processed on a rolling basis. Electronic applications accepted. *Financial support:* Application deadline: 3/1; applicants required to submit FAFSA. *Unit head:* Dr. Michelle Easton, Dean, 304-357-4889, Fax: 304-357-4868, E-mail: michelleeaston@ucwv.edu. *Application contact:* Jamie Bero, Director of Student Affairs, School of Pharmacy, 304-720-6685, Fax: 304-357-4868, E-mail: jamiebero@ucwv.edu. Web site: http://www.ucwv.edu/Pharmacy/.

University of Cincinnati, College of Pharmacy, Division of Pharmacy Practice, Cincinnati, OH 45221. Offers Pharm D. *Accreditation:* ACPE. *Entrance requirements:* For doctorate, GRE General Test, BS in pharmacy or equivalent, minimum GPA of 3.0. Additional exam requirements/recommendations for international students: Required—TOEFL.

University of Connecticut, Graduate School, School of Pharmacy, Professional Program in Pharmacy, Storrs, CT 06269. Offers Pharm D.

The University of Findlay, Graduate and Professional Studies, College of Pharmacy, Findlay, OH 45840-3653. Offers Pharm D. *Accreditation:* ACPE. *Faculty:* 19 full-time (7 women), 3 part-time/adjunct (0 women). *Students:* 105 full-time (73 women), 3 part-time (1 woman); includes 11 minority (3 Black or African American, non-Hispanic/Latino; 6 Asian, non-Hispanic/Latino; 2 Hispanic/Latino), 5 international. Average age 25. 52 applicants, 100% accepted, 50 enrolled. In 2011, 60 doctorates awarded. *Entrance requirements:* For doctorate, bachelor's degree from accredited institution, minimum cumulative GPA of 3.0, minimum C grade in all required courses. Additional exam requirements/recommendations for international students: Required—TOEFL (minimum score 550 paper-based; 213 computer-based; 80 iBT). *Application deadline:* Applications are processed on a rolling basis. Electronic applications accepted. *Expenses: Tuition:* Full-time $6300; part-time $700 per semester hour. *Required fees:* $35 per semester hour. One-time fee: $25. Tuition and fees vary according to course load, degree level and program. *Financial support:* In 2011–12, 2 teaching assistantships (averaging $3,600 per year) were awarded; Federal Work-Study, health care benefits, and unspecified assistantships also available. Financial award application deadline: 4/1; financial award applicants required to submit FAFSA. *Unit head:* Dr. Donald Stansloski, Dean, 419-434-5327, Fax: 419-434-4822. *Application contact:* Heather Riffle, Assistant Director, Graduate and Professional Studies, 419-434-4640, Fax: 419-434-5517, E-mail: riffle@findlay.edu. Web site: http://www.findlay.edu/academics/colleges/cphm/.

University of Florida, Graduate School, College of Pharmacy and Graduate School, Graduate Programs in Pharmacy, Gainesville, FL 32611. Offers medicinal chemistry (MS, MSP, PhD), including pharmaceutical chemistry (MS); pharmaceutical outcomes and policy (MSP, PhD); pharmaceutics (PhD), including pharmaceutical sciences; pharmacodynamics (MSP, PhD); pharmacology (PhD); pharmacotherapy and translational research (MSP, PhD), including clinical pharmaceutical sciences (PhD), clinical pharmacy (MSP), medication therpay management (MSP); pharmacy

(Pharm D); Pharm D/PhD. Part-time programs available. Terminal master's awarded for partial completion of doctoral program. *Degree requirements:* For master's, thesis; for doctorate, thesis/dissertation. *Entrance requirements:* For master's and doctorate, GRE General Test, minimum GPA of 3.0. Additional exam requirements/recommendations for international students: Required—TOEFL. Electronic applications accepted. *Faculty research:* Drug discovery, outcomes research, toxicology, drug design, pharmacodynamic modeling.

University of Florida, Graduate School, College of Pharmacy, Professional Program in Pharmacy, Gainesville, FL 32611. Offers Pharm D, MBA/Pharm D, Pharm D/MPH, Pharm D/PhD. *Accreditation:* ACPE. Part-time programs available. Postbaccalaureate distance learning degree programs offered (no on-campus study). *Entrance requirements:* For doctorate, PCAT, minimum GPA of 2.5. Additional exam requirements/recommendations for international students: Required—TOEFL. Electronic applications accepted. *Faculty research:* Drug discovery, drug delivery, pharmacodynamics, socioeconomics of pharmacy, neurobiology of aging.

University of Georgia, College of Pharmacy, Athens, GA 30602. Offers MS, PhD, Pharm D, Certificate. *Accreditation:* ACPE (one or more programs are accredited). *Faculty:* 39 full-time (12 women), 4 part-time/adjunct (0 women). *Students:* 60 full-time (29 women), 31 part-time (23 women); includes 17 minority (8 Black or African American, non-Hispanic/Latino; 4 Asian, non-Hispanic/Latino; 3 Hispanic/Latino; 2 Two or more races, non-Hispanic/Latino), 32 international. Average age 31. 226 applicants, 14% accepted, 15 enrolled. In 2011, 5 master's, 3 doctorates, 121 other advanced degrees awarded. *Degree requirements:* For doctorate, variable foreign language requirement, thesis/dissertation (for some programs). *Entrance requirements:* For master's, GRE General Test, minimum GPA of 3.0; for doctorate, GRE General Test (for PhD), minimum GPA of 3.0 (for PhD). Additional exam requirements/recommendations for international students: Required—TOEFL (minimum score 80 iBT). *Application deadline:* For fall admission, 7/1 priority date for domestic students; for spring admission, 11/15 for domestic students. Application fee: $50. Electronic applications accepted. *Expenses:* Contact institution. *Financial support:* Fellowships, research assistantships, teaching assistantships, career-related internships or fieldwork, Federal Work-Study, institutionally sponsored loans, tuition waivers, and unspecified assistantships available. Support available to part-time students. Financial award application deadline: 2/15. *Unit head:* Dr. Svein Oie, Dean, 706-542-1914, Fax: 706-542-5269, E-mail: soie@rx.uga.edu. *Application contact:* Dr. Melissa Barry, Assistant Dean of The Graduate School, 706-425-2934, Fax: 706-425-3093, E-mail: mjb14@uga.edu. Web site: http://www.rx.uga.edu/.

University of Houston, College of Pharmacy, Houston, TX 77204. Offers pharmaceutics (MSPHR, PhD); pharmacology (MSPHR, PhD); pharmacy (Pharm D); pharmacy administration (MSPHR, PhD). *Accreditation:* ACPE. Part-time programs available. Terminal master's awarded for partial completion of doctoral program. *Entrance requirements:* For doctorate, PCAT (for Pharm D). Additional exam requirements/recommendations for international students: Required—TOEFL. Electronic applications accepted. *Faculty research:* Drug screening and design, cardiovascular pharmacology, infectious disease, asthma research, herbal medicine.

University of Illinois at Chicago, College of Pharmacy, Center for Pharmaceutical Biotechnology, Chicago, IL 60607-7173. Offers PhD.

University of Illinois at Chicago, College of Pharmacy, Professional Program in Pharmacy, Chicago, IL 60607-7128. Offers Pharm D. *Accreditation:* ACPE. *Entrance requirements:* For doctorate, PCAT.

The University of Iowa, College of Pharmacy, Iowa City, IA 52242-1316. Offers MS, PhD, Pharm D/MPH. *Accreditation:* ACPE (one or more programs are accredited). *Degree requirements:* For master's, thesis optional, exam; for doctorate, comprehensive exam, thesis/dissertation. *Entrance requirements:* For master's and doctorate, GRE General Test, minimum GPA of 3.0. Additional exam requirements/recommendations for international students: Required—TOEFL (minimum score 550 paper-based; 213 computer-based; 81 iBT). Electronic applications accepted.

University of Kentucky, College of Pharmacy, Professional Program in Pharmacy, Lexington, KY 40506-0032. Offers Pharm D. *Accreditation:* ACPE. *Entrance requirements:* For doctorate, PCAT, interview, minimum GPA of 2.5. Additional exam requirements/recommendations for international students: Required—TOEFL (minimum score 550 paper-based; 213 computer-based). *Expenses:* Contact institution. *Faculty research:* Cardiology, pharmacokinetics, pediatrics, critical care, nutrition, infectious disease.

University of Louisiana at Monroe, Graduate School, College of Pharmacy, Program in Pharmacy, Monroe, LA 71209-0001. Offers PhD. *Accreditation:* ACPE. *Faculty:* 18 full-time (4 women), 21 part-time/adjunct (3 women). *Students:* 345 full-time (208 women), 5 part-time (2 women); includes 74 minority (20 Black or African American, non-Hispanic/Latino; 1 American Indian or Alaska Native, non-Hispanic/Latino; 43 Asian, non-Hispanic/Latino; 7 Hispanic/Latino; 3 Two or more races, non-Hispanic/Latino), 31 international. Average age 25. 51 applicants, 29% accepted, 12 enrolled. In 2011, 96 doctorates awarded. *Degree requirements:* For doctorate, comprehensive exam, thesis/dissertation. *Entrance requirements:* For doctorate, GRE General Test or GMAT. Additional exam requirements/recommendations for international students: Required—TOEFL (minimum score 500 paper-based; 173 computer-based; 61 iBT). *Application deadline:* For fall admission, 8/24 priority date for domestic students, 7/1 for international students; for winter admission, 12/14 priority date for domestic students; for spring admission, 1/19 priority date for domestic students, 11/1 for international students. Applications are processed on a rolling basis. Application fee: $20 ($30 for international students). Electronic applications accepted. *Expenses:* Tuition, state resident: full-time $3436; part-time $240 per credit hour. Tuition, nonresident: full-time $3436; part-time $240 per credit hour. *International tuition:* $10,733 full-time. *Required fees:* $1460.90. *Financial support:* In 2011–12, 26 research assistantships with full tuition reimbursements (averaging $6,032 per year) were awarded; Federal Work-Study and unspecified assistantships also available. Financial award application deadline: 4/1; financial award applicants required to submit FAFSA. *Unit head:* Dr. Benny L. Blaylock, Dean, 318-342-1600, Fax: 318-342-1606, E-mail: blaylock@ulm.edu. *Application contact:* Dr. Paul W. Sylvester, Director, Research and Graduate Studies, 318-342-1958, Fax: 318-342-1606, E-mail: sylvester@ulm.edu. Web site: http://rxweb.ulm.edu/pharmacy/.

The University of Manchester, School of Pharmacy and Pharmaceutical Sciences, Manchester, United Kingdom. Offers M Phil, PhD.

University of Maryland, Baltimore, Graduate School, Graduate Programs in Pharmacy, Baltimore, MD 21201. Offers pharmaceutical health service research (MS, PhD), including epidemiology (MS), pharmacy administration (PhD); pharmaceutical sciences (PhD); Pharm D/PhD. *Accreditation:* ACPE (one or more programs are accredited). *Degree requirements:* For doctorate, comprehensive exam, thesis/dissertation. *Entrance requirements:* For doctorate, GRE General Test. Additional exam requirements/recommendations for international students: Required—TOEFL (minimum score 550 paper-based; 215 computer-based), IELTS. Electronic applications accepted. *Faculty research:* Drug discovery, pharmacokinetics, drug delivery, pharmaceutical outcomes and policy, pharmaceutical sciences.

University of Maryland, Baltimore, Professional Program in Pharmacy, Baltimore, MD 21201. Offers Pharm D, JD/Pharm D, Pharm D/MBA, Pharm D/MPH, Pharm D/PhD. *Accreditation:* ACPE. *Faculty:* 86 full-time (44 women), 57 part-time/adjunct (12 women). *Students:* 643 full-time (417 women); includes 401 minority (78 Black or African American, non-Hispanic/Latino; 4 American Indian or Alaska Native, non-Hispanic/Latino; 313 Asian, non-Hispanic/Latino; 5 Hispanic/Latino; 1 Native Hawaiian or other Pacific Islander, non-Hispanic/Latino). Average age 25. 1,220 applicants, 14% accepted, 165 enrolled. In 2011, 65 doctorates awarded. *Entrance requirements:* For doctorate, PCAT, 65 hours in pre-pharmacy course work, on-site interview. Additional exam requirements/recommendations for international students: Required—TOEFL (minimum score 550 paper-based; 213 computer-based; 80 iBT). *Application deadline:* For fall admission, 1/5 for domestic and international students. Application fee: $45. Electronic applications accepted. *Financial support:* In 2011–12, 225 students received support. Career-related internships or fieldwork, Federal Work-Study, institutionally sponsored loans, and scholarships/grants available. Support available to part-time students. Financial award application deadline: 3/1; financial award applicants required to submit FAFSA. *Faculty research:* Pharmaceutics, molecular biology, pharmacology, pharmacoepidemiology, pharmacoeconomics. Total annual research expenditures: $16.5 million. *Unit head:* Dr. Jill Morgan, Associate Dean for Student Affairs, 410-706-4332, Fax: 410-706-2158, E-mail: jmorgan@rx.umaryland.edu. *Application contact:* Patrice Sharp, Admissions Officer, 410-706-0732, Fax: 410-706-2158, E-mail: pharmdhelp@umaryland.edu. Web site: http://www.pharmacy.umaryland.edu.

University of Michigan, College of Pharmacy, Professional Program in Pharmacy, Ann Arbor, MI 48109. Offers Pharm D, Pharm D/PhD. *Accreditation:* ACPE. *Entrance requirements:* For doctorate, PCAT.

University of Minnesota, Duluth, Medical School, Department of Biochemistry, Molecular Biology and Biophysics, Duluth, MN 55812-2496. Offers biochemistry, molecular biology and biophysics (MS); biology and biophysics (PhD); social, administrative, and clinical pharmacy (MS, PhD); toxicology (MS, PhD). Terminal master's awarded for partial completion of doctoral program. *Degree requirements:* For master's, comprehensive exam, thesis; for doctorate, comprehensive exam, thesis/dissertation. *Entrance requirements:* For master's and doctorate, GRE General Test. Additional exam requirements/recommendations for international students: Required—TOEFL. Electronic applications accepted. *Faculty research:* Intestinal cancer biology; hepatotoxins and mitochondriopathies; toxicology; cell cycle regulation in stem cells; neurobiology of brain development, trace metal function and blood-brain barrier; hibernation biology.

University of Minnesota, Twin Cities Campus, College of Pharmacy, Professional Program in Pharmacy, Minneapolis, MN 55455-0213. Offers Pharm D. *Accreditation:* ACPE. *Faculty:* 52 full-time (16 women), 4 part-time/adjunct (1 woman). *Students:* 640 full-time (270 women). In 2011, 66 doctorates awarded. *Degree requirements:* For doctorate, paper and seminar presentation. *Entrance requirements:* For doctorate, 2 years of pharmacy-related course work. *Application deadline:* For fall admission, 2/1 for domestic students. Application fee: $50. *Financial support:* Career-related internships or fieldwork, Federal Work-Study, and institutionally sponsored loans available. Support available to part-time students. Financial award applicants required to submit FAFSA. *Unit head:* Wendy L. St. Peter, Associate Dean, 612-624-9490, Fax: 612-624-2974, E-mail: pharosaa@tc.umn.edu. *Application contact:* Information Contact, 612-625-3014, Fax: 612-625-6002, E-mail: gsquest@umn.edu. Web site: http://www.pharmacy.umn.edu/.

University of Mississippi, Graduate School, School of Pharmacy, Professional Program in Pharmacy, Oxford, University, MS 38677. Offers Pharm D. *Accreditation:* ACPE. *Students:* 257 full-time (161 women), 1 (woman) part-time; includes 34 minority (16 Black or African American, non-Hispanic/Latino; 1 American Indian or Alaska Native, non-Hispanic/Latino; 13 Asian, non-Hispanic/Latino; 1 Hispanic/Latino; 3 Two or more races, non-Hispanic/Latino), 1 international. In 2011, 98 doctorates awarded. *Application deadline:* For fall admission, 4/1 for domestic students. Applications are processed on a rolling basis. Application fee: $25. *Expenses:* Contact institution. *Financial support:* Scholarships/grants available. Financial award application deadline: 3/1; financial award applicants required to submit FAFSA. *Unit head:* Dr. David Allen, Dean, 662-915-7265, Fax: 662-915-5704, E-mail: pharmacy@olemiss.edu. *Application contact:* Dr. Christy M. Wyandt, Associate Dean, 662-915-7474, Fax: 662-915-7577, E-mail: cwyandt@olemiss.edu.

University of Missouri–Kansas City, School of Pharmacy, Kansas City, MO 64110-2499. Offers pharmaceutical sciences (PhD); pharmacology and toxicology (PhD); pharmacy (Pharm D). PhD offered through School of Graduate Studies. *Accreditation:* ACPE (one or more programs are accredited). Postbaccalaureate distance learning degree programs offered (minimal on-campus study). *Faculty:* 54 full-time (22 women), 6 part-time/adjunct (3 women). *Students:* 364 full-time (233 women); includes 39 minority (10 Black or African American, non-Hispanic/Latino; 1 American Indian or Alaska Native, non-Hispanic/Latino; 24 Asian, non-Hispanic/Latino; 2 Hispanic/Latino; 2 Two or more races, non-Hispanic/Latino), 4 international. Average age 25. 419 applicants, 40% accepted, 162 enrolled. In 2011, 113 doctorates awarded. *Degree requirements:* For doctorate, comprehensive exam (for some programs), thesis/dissertation (for some programs). *Entrance requirements:* For doctorate, PCAT (for Pharm D). Additional exam requirements/recommendations for international students: Required—TOEFL (minimum score 550 paper-based; 213 computer-based; 80 iBT). *Application deadline:* For fall admission, 3/1 for domestic and international students. Applications are processed on a rolling basis. Application fee: $45 ($50 for international students). Electronic applications accepted. *Expenses:* Contact institution. *Financial support:* In 2011–12, 31 research assistantships with full and partial tuition reimbursements (averaging $9,797 per year), 23 teaching assistantships with full tuition reimbursements (averaging $11,995 per year) were awarded; career-related internships or fieldwork, Federal Work-Study, institutionally sponsored loans, tuition waivers (full and partial), and unspecified assistantships also available. Financial award application deadline: 3/1; financial award applicants required to submit FAFSA. *Faculty research:* Bio-organic and medicinal chemistry, drug delivery, pharmaceutics, molecular neurobiology, neurology. *Unit head:* Dr. Russell B. Melchert, Dean, 816-235-1609, Fax: 816-235-5190, E-mail: melchertr@umkc.edu. *Application contact:* Shelly M. Janasz, Director, Student Services, 816-235-2400, Fax: 816-235-5190, E-mail: janaszs@umkc.edu. Web site: http://pharmacy.umkc.edu/.

The University of Montana, Graduate School, College of Health Professions and Biomedical Sciences, Skaggs School of Pharmacy, Missoula, MT 59812-0002. Offers biomedical and pharmaceutical sciences (MS, PhD), including biomedical sciences (PhD), neuroscience, pharmaceutical sciences (MS), toxicology; pharmacy (Pharm D). Electronic applications accepted. *Faculty research:* Neuroendocrinology, neuropharmacology, molecular biochemistry, cardiovascular pharmacology, pharmacognosy.

University of Nebraska Medical Center, College of Pharmacy, Omaha, NE 68198-6000. Offers Pharm D. *Accreditation:* ACPE. *Faculty:* 31 full-time (7 women), 12 part-time/adjunct (9 women). *Students:* 233 full-time (150 women), 2 part-time (1 woman); includes 29 minority (4 Black or African American, non-Hispanic/Latino; 23 Asian, non-Hispanic/Latino; 2 Hispanic/Latino). Average age 23. 137 applicants, 44% accepted, 60

enrolled. In 2011, 60 degrees awarded. *Entrance requirements:* For doctorate, PCAT, 90 semester hours of pre-pharmacy work. *Application deadline:* For fall admission, 12/1 for domestic and international students. Applications are processed on a rolling basis. Application fee: $45. Electronic applications accepted. *Expenses:* Contact institution. *Financial support:* Career-related internships or fieldwork, Federal Work-Study, institutionally sponsored loans, scholarships/grants, and tuition waivers (full and partial) available. Financial award application deadline: 4/1; financial award applicants required to submit FAFSA. *Faculty research:* Biopharmaceutics, nanomedicine, drug design, pharmaceutics, pharmacokinetics. *Unit head:* Dr. Courtney V. Fletcher, Dean, 402-559-4333, Fax: 402-559-5060, E-mail: cfletcher@unmc.edu. *Application contact:* Dr. Charles H. Krobot, Associate Dean for Student Affairs, 402-559-4333, Fax: 402-559-5060, E-mail: ckrobot@unmc.edu. Web site: http://www.unmc.edu/pharmacy/.

University of New England, College of Pharmacy, Biddeford, ME 04005-9526. Offers Pharm D. *Accreditation:* ACPE. *Faculty:* 29 full-time, 3 part-time/adjunct. *Students:* 293 full-time (185 women). *Unit head:* Gayle A. Brazeau, Dean, 207-221-4500, Fax: 207-523-1927, E-mail: gbrazeau@une.edu. *Application contact:* Stacy Gato, Assistant Director of Graduate Admissions, 207-221-4225, Fax: 207-221-4898, E-mail: gradadmissions@une.edu. Web site: http://www.une.edu/pharmacy/.

University of New Mexico, Graduate School, College of Pharmacy, Professional Program in Pharmacy, Albuquerque, NM 87131-2039. Offers Pharm D. *Accreditation:* ACPE. *Students:* 352 full-time (210 women), 2 part-time (both women); includes 190 minority (10 Black or African American, non-Hispanic/Latino; 12 American Indian or Alaska Native, non-Hispanic/Latino; 56 Asian, non-Hispanic/Latino; 106 Hispanic/Latino; 6 Two or more races, non-Hispanic/Latino), 3 international. Average age 29. 450 applicants, 22% accepted, 88 enrolled. In 2011, 85 degrees awarded. *Entrance requirements:* For doctorate, PCAT, 3 letters of recommendation, interview, 91 credit hours of prerequisites, letter of intent, Pharmcas application. *Application deadline:* For fall admission, 1/1 for domestic students. Applications are processed on a rolling basis. Application fee: $50. Electronic applications accepted. *Expenses:* Contact institution. *Financial support:* In 2011–12, 325 students received support. Federal Work-Study, institutionally sponsored loans, and scholarships/grants available. Financial award application deadline: 3/1; financial award applicants required to submit FAFSA. *Total annual research expenditures:* $107,864. *Unit head:* Dr. Lynda Welage, Dean, 505-272-3241, Fax: 505-272-8324, E-mail: lswelage@salud.unm.edu. *Application contact:* Krystal McCutchen, Coordinator, Student Advisement, 505-272-0583, Fax: 505-272-8324, E-mail: kmccutchen@salud.unm.edu. Web site: http://hsc.unm.edu/pharmacy/.

University of Oklahoma Health Sciences Center, College of Pharmacy, Professional Program in Pharmacy, Oklahoma City, OK 73190. Offers Pharm D. *Accreditation:* ACPE.

University of Pittsburgh, School of Pharmacy, Professional Program in Pharmacy, Pittsburgh, PA 15260. Offers Pharm D. *Accreditation:* ACPE. *Faculty:* 70 full-time (37 women), 96 part-time/adjunct (47 women). *Students:* 429 full-time (257 women); includes 54 minority (16 Black or African American, non-Hispanic/Latino; 1 American Indian or Alaska Native, non-Hispanic/Latino; 33 Asian, non-Hispanic/Latino; 4 Hispanic/Latino), 2 international. Average age 22. 798 applicants, 15% accepted, 107 enrolled. In 2011, 104 doctorates awarded. *Entrance requirements:* For doctorate, PCAT. *Application deadline:* For fall admission, 12/3 for domestic students. Application fee: $215. Electronic applications accepted. *Expenses:* Contact institution. *Financial support:* In 2011–12, 128 students received support. Career-related internships or fieldwork, Federal Work-Study, and scholarships/grants available. Financial award application deadline: 10/1. *Faculty research:* Drug delivery and targeting; neuroendocrine pharmacology; genomics, proteomics, and drug discovery; clinical pharmaceutical sciences. *Total annual research expenditures:* $6.9 million. *Unit head:* Dr. Sharon Corey, Assistant Dean of Students, 412-648-9157, Fax: 412-383-9996, E-mail: coreys@pitt.edu. *Application contact:* Marcia L. Borrelli, Director of Student Services, 412-383-9000, Fax: 412-383-9996, E-mail: borrelli@pitt.edu. Web site: http://www.pharmacy.pitt.edu.

University of Puerto Rico, Medical Sciences Campus, School of Pharmacy, San Juan, PR 00936-5067. Offers industrial pharmacy (MS); pharmaceutical sciences (MS); pharmacy (Pharm D). The MS in Pharmacy program is not admitting students in the academic year 2010-2011. *Accreditation:* ACPE. Part-time and evening/weekend programs available. *Degree requirements:* For master's, thesis; for doctorate, portfolio, research project. *Entrance requirements:* For master's, GRE, interview; for doctorate, PCAT, interview. Electronic applications accepted. *Expenses:* Contact institution. *Faculty research:* Controlled release, solid dosage form, screening of anti-HIV drugs, pharmacokinetic/pharmacodynamic of drugs.

University of Rhode Island, Graduate School, College of Pharmacy, Department of Pharmacy Practice, Kingston, RI 02881. Offers pharmaceutical sciences (MS, PhD), including pharmacoepidemiology and pharmacoeconomics; MS/PhD; PhD/MBA. *Accreditation:* ACPE. *Faculty:* 26 full-time (20 women), 1 part-time/adjunct (0 women). *Students:* 657 full-time (384 women), 3 part-time (2 women); includes 104 minority (20 Black or African American, non-Hispanic/Latino; 56 Asian, non-Hispanic/Latino; 22 Hispanic/Latino; 6 Two or more races, non-Hispanic/Latino), 26 international. In 2011, 89 doctorates awarded. *Entrance requirements:* For master's and doctorate, 2 letters of recommendation. Additional exam requirements/recommendations for international students: Required—TOEFL (minimum score 550 paper-based; 213 computer-based). Application fee: $65. Electronic applications accepted. *Expenses:* Tuition, state resident: full-time $10,432; part-time $580 per credit hour. Tuition, nonresident: full-time $23,130; part-time $1285 per credit hour. *Required fees:* $1362; $36 per credit hour. $35 per semester. One-time fee: $130. *Financial support:* Applicants required to submit FAFSA. *Faculty research:* Treatment, virulence inhibition (toxin and biofilm), colonization and control of methicillin-resistant Staphylococcus aureus (MRSA); investigating activity of catheter lock solutions against biofilm producing bacteria. *Unit head:* Dr. Marilyn Barbour, Chair, 401-874-5842, Fax: 401-874-2181, E-mail: mbarbourri@aol.com. *Application contact:* Nasser H. Zawia, Dean of the Graduate School, 401-874-5909, Fax: 401-874-5787, E-mail: nzawia@uri.edu. Web site: http://www.uri.edu/pharmacy/departments/php/index.shtml.

University of Saint Joseph, School of Pharmacy, West Hartford, CT 06117-2700. Offers Pharm D. *Students:* 67 full-time (46 women); includes 35 minority (8 Black or African American, non-Hispanic/Latino; 24 Asian, non-Hispanic/Latino; 2 Hispanic/Latino; 1 Two or more races, non-Hispanic/Latino), 1 international. Average age 26. *Application deadline:* Applications are processed on a rolling basis. Electronic applications accepted. *Expenses:* Tuition: Part-time $670 per credit. *Required fees:* $40 per credit. Tuition and fees vary according to course load, degree level, campus/location and program. *Financial support:* Career-related internships or fieldwork available. *Unit head:* Dr. Joseph R. Ofosu, Dean, 860-231-5858. *Application contact:* Graduate Admissions Office, 860-231-5261, E-mail: graduate@usj.edu.

University of South Carolina, South Carolina College of Pharmacy, Professional Program in Pharmacy, Columbia, SC 29208. Offers Pharm D. *Accreditation:* ACPE. *Degree requirements:* For doctorate, one foreign language. *Entrance requirements:* For doctorate, PCAT, 2 years of preprofessional study, interview. Electronic applications

accepted. *Faculty research:* Cancer treatment and prevention, Ion channels, DNA damage repair, inflammation.

University of Southern California, Graduate School, School of Pharmacy, Professional Program in Pharmacy, Los Angeles, CA 90089. Offers Pharm D, Pharm D/MBA, Pharm D/MS, Pharm D/PhD. *Accreditation:* ACPE. Electronic applications accepted. *Faculty research:* Infectious diseases, health services research, geriatric pharmacology, clinical psychopharmacology.

The University of Tennessee Health Science Center, College of Pharmacy, Memphis, TN 38163-0002. Offers MS, PhD, Pharm D, Pharm D/PhD. *Accreditation:* ACPE (one or more programs are accredited). Terminal master's awarded for partial completion of doctoral program. *Degree requirements:* For master's, thesis; for doctorate, thesis/dissertation (for some programs). *Entrance requirements:* For master's, GRE General Test, minimum GPA of 3.0; for doctorate, GRE General Test (for PhD); PCAT (for Pharm D), minimum GPA of 3.0. Additional exam requirements/recommendations for international students: Required—TOEFL. Electronic applications accepted. *Expenses:* Contact institution.

The University of Texas at Austin, Graduate School, College of Pharmacy, Professional Program in Pharmacy, Austin, TX 78712-1111. Offers Pharm D, Pharm D/PhD. Program offered jointly with The University of Texas Health Science Center at San Antonio. *Accreditation:* ACPE. *Entrance requirements:* For doctorate, GRE General Test. *Application deadline:* For fall admission, 1/15 for domestic students. Application fee: $50 ($75 for international students). *Financial support:* Application deadline: 2/1. *Unit head:* Dr. M. Lynn Crismon, Dean, 512-471-3718, E-mail: lynn.crismon@austin.utexas.edu.

University of the Incarnate Word, Feik School of Pharmacy, San Antonio, TX 78209-6397. Offers Pharm D. *Accreditation:* ACPE. *Faculty:* 36 full-time (24 women). *Students:* 396 full-time (277 women), 3 part-time (all women); includes 271 minority (37 Black or African American, non-Hispanic/Latino; 1 American Indian or Alaska Native, non-Hispanic/Latino; 109 Asian, non-Hispanic/Latino; 120 Hispanic/Latino; 1 Native Hawaiian or other Pacific Islander, non-Hispanic/Latino; 3 Two or more races, non-Hispanic/Latino), 8 international. Average age 27. 121 applicants, 100% accepted, 105 enrolled. In 2011, 86 doctorates awarded. *Entrance requirements:* For doctorate, PCAT, 80 hours of documented pharmacy observational experience; on-site interview (if selected); critical thinking assessment and writing sample during interview process; minimum GPA of 2.5 and 64 hours (71 hours for financial aid) in accredited pre-pharmacy course. Additional exam requirements/recommendations for international students: Required—TOEFL (minimum score 560 paper-based). *Application deadline:* For fall admission, 1/5 for domestic students. Application fee: $100. *Expenses:* Contact institution. *Financial support:* Federal Work-Study and scholarships/grants available. Financial award applicants required to submit FAFSA. *Unit head:* Dr. Arcelia Johnson-Fannin, Founding Dean, 210-883-1015, Fax: 210-822-1516, E-mail: johnsonf@uiwtx.edu. *Application contact:* Dr. Kevin Lord, Assistant Dean, Student Affairs and Assistant Professor, Pharmaceutical Sciences, 210-883-1060, Fax: 210-822-1521, E-mail: lord@uiwtx.edu. Web site: http://www.uiw.edu/pharmacy.

University of the Pacific, Thomas J. Long School of Pharmacy and Health Sciences, Professional Program in Pharmacy, Stockton, CA 95211-0197. Offers Pharm D. *Accreditation:* ACPE. *Faculty:* 34 full-time (17 women), 13 part-time/adjunct (7 women). *Students:* 626 full-time (401 women), 14 part-time (6 women); includes 467 minority (13 Black or African American, non-Hispanic/Latino; 2 American Indian or Alaska Native, non-Hispanic/Latino; 436 Asian, non-Hispanic/Latino; 16 Hispanic/Latino), 8 international. Average age 24. 2,031 applicants, 15% accepted, 209 enrolled. In 2011, 202 doctorates awarded. *Entrance requirements:* Additional exam requirements/recommendations for international students: Required—TOEFL. *Application deadline:* For fall admission, 2/1 for domestic students. Application fee: $75. *Expenses:* Tuition: Full-time $18,900; part-time $1181 per unit. *Required fees:* $949. *Financial support:* Career-related internships or fieldwork, Federal Work-Study, institutionally sponsored loans, and tuition waivers (partial) available. Support available to part-time students. Financial award application deadline: 3/1; financial award applicants required to submit FAFSA. *Unit head:* Dr. Philip Oppenheimer, Dean, 209-946-2561, Fax: 209-946-2410. *Application contact:* Cyndi Porter, Outreach Officer, 209-946-3957, Fax: 209-946-2410, E-mail: cporter@pacific.edu. Web site: http://www.pacific.edu/pharmacy/.

University of the Sciences in Philadelphia, Philadelphia College of Pharmacy, Philadelphia, PA 19104-4495. Offers MS, PhD, Pharm D. *Faculty research:* Pharmacokinetics, oncology, critical care, pediatrics, cardiology.

University of Utah, Graduate School, College of Pharmacy, Professional Program in Pharmacy, Salt Lake City, UT 84112-5820. Offers Pharm D. *Accreditation:* ACPE. *Students:* 219 full-time (101 women), 2 part-time (0 women); includes 40 minority (3 Black or African American, non-Hispanic/Latino; 1 American Indian or Alaska Native, non-Hispanic/Latino; 26 Asian, non-Hispanic/Latino; 7 Hispanic/Latino; 1 Native Hawaiian or other Pacific Islander, non-Hispanic/Latino; 2 Two or more races, non-Hispanic/Latino). Average age 28. 290 applicants, 23% accepted, 65 enrolled. In 2011, 52 doctorates awarded. *Entrance requirements:* For doctorate, PCAT. Additional exam requirements/recommendations for international students: Required—TOEFL (minimum score 100 iBT). *Application deadline:* For fall admission, 12/1 for domestic and international students. Application fee: $55 ($65 for international students). Electronic applications accepted. *Expenses:* Contact institution. *Financial support:* Teaching assistantships available. *Faculty research:* Pain management, pharmacokinetic aspects of antiarrhythmics and anticoagulants, patient compliance. *Total annual research expenditures:* $5 million. *Unit head:* Dr. Chris M. Ireland, Dean, 801-581-6731. *Application contact:* Sarah Lindsey, Academic Advisor/Program Coordinator, 801-581-5384, E-mail: pharmd.admissions@pharm.utah.edu. Web site: http://www.pharmacy.utah.edu/.

University of Washington, School of Pharmacy and Graduate School, Department of Pharmacy, Seattle, WA 98195-7630. Offers MS, PhD. *Faculty:* 14 full-time (4 women), 3 part-time/adjunct (1 woman). *Students:* 20 full-time (11 women); includes 5 minority (all Asian, non-Hispanic/Latino), 2 international. 55 applicants, 9% accepted, 5 enrolled. In 2011, 3 master's, 3 doctorates awarded. Terminal master's awarded for partial completion of doctoral program. *Degree requirements:* For master's, thesis; for doctorate, thesis/dissertation. *Entrance requirements:* For master's and doctorate, GRE General Test. Additional exam requirements/recommendations for international students: Required—TOEFL. *Application deadline:* For winter admission, 1/1 priority date for domestic students, 1/1 for international students. Application fee: $75 ($100 for international students). Electronic applications accepted. *Financial support:* In 2011–12, 8 students received support, including 2 fellowships with full tuition reimbursements available (averaging $14,751 per year), 8 research assistantships with full tuition reimbursements available (averaging $14,751 per year), 2 teaching assistantships with full tuition reimbursements available (averaging $14,751 per year); institutionally sponsored loans, scholarships/grants, and tuition waivers (full) also available. *Faculty research:* Pharmacoeconomics, pharmacoepidemiology, drug policy, outcomes research. *Total annual research expenditures:* $1.2 million. *Unit head:* Dr. Peggy Odegard, Chair, 206-543-6788, Fax: 206-543-3835, E-mail: podegard@uw.edu.

Application contact: Dr. David Veenstra, Director, 206-543-6788, Fax: 206-543-3835, E-mail: veenstra@uw.edu. Web site: http://sop.washington.edu/porpp.

University of Washington, School of Pharmacy, Professional Program in Pharmacy, Seattle, WA 98195-7631. Offers Pharm D, Pharm D/Certificate, Pharm D/PhD. *Accreditation:* ACPE. *Students:* 352 full-time (229 women); includes 181 minority (2 Black or African American, non-Hispanic/Latino; 3 American Indian or Alaska Native, non-Hispanic/Latino; 161 Asian, non-Hispanic/Latino; 6 Hispanic/Latino; 1 Native Hawaiian or other Pacific Islander, non-Hispanic/Latino; 8 Two or more races, non-Hispanic/Latino). Average age 25. 354 applicants, 33% accepted, 94 enrolled. In 2011, 87 doctorates awarded. *Entrance requirements:* For doctorate, PCAT. *Application deadline:* For fall admission, 1/7 for domestic and international students. Application fee: $45. Electronic applications accepted. *Financial support:* In 2011–12, 152 students received support. Fellowships, career-related internships or fieldwork, scholarships/grants, and tuition waivers (partial) available. Financial award application deadline: 7/13; financial award applicants required to submit FAFSA. *Unit head:* Dr. Nanci Murphy, Associate Dean, Academic and Student Programs, 206-685-2715, Fax: 206-616-2740, E-mail: pharminf@u.washington.edu. *Application contact:* Admissions Coordinator, 206-543-6100, Fax: 206-616-2740, E-mail: pharminf@u.washington.edu. Web site: http://sop.washington.edu/students.

University of Wisconsin–Madison, School of Pharmacy, Professional Program in Pharmacy, Madison, WI 53706-1380. Offers Pharm D. *Accreditation:* ACPE. *Expenses:* Tuition, state resident: full-time $10,296; part-time $643.51 per credit. Tuition, nonresident: full-time $24,054; part-time $1503.40 per credit. *Required fees:* $70.06 per credit. Tuition and fees vary according to course load, campus/location, program and reciprocity agreements.

University of Wyoming, College of Health Sciences, School of Pharmacy, Laramie, WY 82070. Offers Pharm D. *Accreditation:* ACPE. *Entrance requirements:* For doctorate, PCAT. Additional exam requirements/recommendations for international students: Required—TOEFL.

Virginia Commonwealth University, Medical College of Virginia-Professional Programs, School of Pharmacy, Professional Program in Pharmacy, Richmond, VA 23284-9005. Offers Pharm D, Pharm D/MBA, Pharm D/MPH, Pharm D/PhD. *Accreditation:* ACPE. Part-time programs available. *Degree requirements:* For doctorate, research project. *Entrance requirements:* For doctorate, PCAT. Electronic applications accepted. *Expenses:* Tuition, state resident: full-time $9133; part-time $507 per credit. Tuition, nonresident: full-time $18,777; part-time $1043 per credit. *Required fees:* $77 per credit. Tuition and fees vary according to degree level, campus/location, program and student level. *Faculty research:* Oncology, cardiology, infectious diseases, epilepsy, connective tissue.

Washington State University, Graduate School, College of Pharmacy, Department of Pharmaceutical Sciences, Pullman, WA 99164. Offers PhD, Pharm D. *Accreditation:* ACPE. *Students:* 13 full-time (10 women); includes 3 minority (2 Asian, non-Hispanic/Latino; 1 Hispanic/Latino), 7 international. Average age 27. 47 applicants, 28% accepted, 7 enrolled. In 2011, 3 doctorates awarded. *Entrance requirements:* For doctorate, GRE (for PhD). *Application deadline:* For fall admission, 2/1 for domestic students; for spring admission, 9/1 for domestic students. Applications are processed on a rolling basis. Application fee: $75. *Financial support:* Fellowships, career-related internships or fieldwork, Federal Work-Study, and scholarships/grants available. Financial award application deadline: 4/1. *Faculty research:* Enzymes, quality assurance, practices, tumor biology of metastasis, heart disease, anxiety and pain control. *Unit head:* Dr. Raymond M. Quock, Chair, 509-335-5956, Fax: 509-335-5902. *Application contact:* Graduate School Admissions, 800-GRAD-WSU, Fax: 509-335-1949, E-mail: gradsch@wsu.edu. Web site: http://www.pharmacy.wsu.edu/pharmsci.

Washington State University Spokane, Program in Pharmacy, Spokane, WA 99210-1495. Offers Pharm D. *Faculty:* 39. *Degree requirements:* For doctorate, comprehensive exam, thesis/dissertation. *Entrance requirements:* For doctorate, GRE, 3 letters of recommendation, supplemental pharmacy CAS form, interview. *Application deadline:* For fall admission, 1/10 priority date for domestic students, 1/10 for international students; for spring admission, 7/1 priority date for domestic students, 7/1 for international students. Applications are processed on a rolling basis. Application fee: $75. *Expenses:* Contact institution. *Financial support:* Career-related internships or fieldwork, Federal Work-Study, and scholarships/grants available. Financial award application deadline: 2/15. *Faculty research:* Infectious disease, neuropsychopharmacology, biotechnology/gene therapy. *Total annual research expenditures:* $5.2 million. *Unit head:* Dr. William Campbell, Interim Dean, 509-335-4750, E-mail: vburnham@wsu.edu. *Application contact:* Teresa Woolverton, Academic Coordinator, 509-335-2356, E-mail: twool@wsu.edu. Web site: http://www.pharmacy.wsu.edu/futurestudents/pharmd/index.html.

Wayne State University, Eugene Applebaum College of Pharmacy and Health Sciences, Department of Pharmaceutical Sciences, Detroit, MI 48202. Offers medicinal chemistry (MS, PhD); pharmaceutics (MS, PhD); pharmacology/toxicology (MS, PhD). *Accreditation:* ACPE (one or more programs are accredited). Part-time programs available. *Students:* 15 full-time (6 women), 4 part-time (3 women); includes 2 minority (1 Black or African American, non-Hispanic/Latino; 1 Asian, non-Hispanic/Latino), 11 international. Average age 27. 234 applicants, 3% accepted, 7 enrolled. In 2011, 1 degree awarded. *Degree requirements:* For master's, thesis; for doctorate, thesis/dissertation. *Entrance requirements:* For master's, GRE General Test, bachelor's degree with minimum GPA of 3.0, three letters of recommendation, personal statement; for doctorate, GRE General Test, bachelor's degree with minimum GPA of 3.0, three letters of recommendation. Additional exam requirements/recommendations for international students: Required—TOEFL (minimum score 550 paper-based; 213 computer-based); Recommended—TWE (minimum score 6). *Application deadline:* For fall admission, 3/1 for domestic and international students. Application fee: $50. Electronic applications accepted. *Expenses:* Tuition, state resident: part-time $512.85 per credit. Tuition, nonresident: part-time $1132.65 per credit. *Required fees:* $26.60 per credit. $199.65 per semester. Tuition and fees vary according to course load and program. *Financial support:* In 2011–12, 1 fellowship with tuition reimbursement (averaging $1,800 per year), 11 research assistantships with full tuition reimbursements (averaging $23,682 per year) were awarded; career-related internships or fieldwork, scholarships/grants, health care benefits, and unspecified assistantships also available. Support available to part-time students. *Faculty research:* Mechanisms of resistance of bacteria to anti-microbial agents, drug metabolism and disposition in children, treatment strategies for stroke/neurovascular disease, prevalence and treatment of diabetes in Arab-Americans, ethnic variability in development of osteoporosis. *Unit head:* Dr. George B. Corcoran, Chair, 313-577-1737, Fax: 313-577-2033, E-mail: corcoran@wayne.edu. *Application contact:* 313-577-1047, E-mail: pscgrad@wayne.edu. Web site: http://www.cphs.wayne.edu/psc/index.php.

Wayne State University, Eugene Applebaum College of Pharmacy and Health Sciences, Department of Pharmacy Practice, Detroit, MI 48202. Offers pharmacy (Pharm D); Pharm D/PhD. *Students:* 305 full-time (188 women), 35 part-time (20 women); includes 46 minority (4 Black or African American, non-Hispanic/Latino; 42 Asian, non-Hispanic/Latino), 38 international. Average age 25. 399 applicants, 30% accepted, 100 enrolled. In 2011, 120 doctorates awarded. Terminal master's awarded for partial completion of doctoral program. *Entrance requirements:* For doctorate, PharmCAS application. Additional exam requirements/recommendations for international students: Required—TOEFL (minimum score 550 paper-based; 213 computer-based); Recommended—TWE (minimum score 6). *Application deadline:* For fall admission, 11/1 for domestic and international students. Application fee: $50. Electronic applications accepted. *Expenses:* Tuition, state resident: part-time $512.85 per credit. Tuition, nonresident: part-time $1132.65 per credit. *Required fees:* $26.60 per credit. $199.65 per semester. Tuition and fees vary according to course load and program. *Financial support:* In 2011–12, 29 students received support. Fellowships, research assistantships with tuition reimbursements available, and scholarships/grants available. Support available to part-time students. *Faculty research:* Pharmacodynamics and pharmacokinetics of anti-infective agents, efficacy of drug treatments for traumatic head injury and stroke, cultural difference in Arab-Americans related to diabetes treatment and prevention, drug disposition and effect in pediatrics, evaluation of anticoagulation regimens. *Unit head:* Dr. Lloyd Y. Young, Dean, 313-577-1574, E-mail: youngl@wayne.edu. *Application contact:* Dr. Mary K. Clark, Assistant Dean for Student and Alumni Affairs, 313-577-1716, E-mail: cphsinfo@wayne.edu. Web site: http://www.cphs.wayne.edu/practice/index.php.

Western University of Health Sciences, College of Pharmacy, Program in Pharmacy, Pomona, CA 91766-1854. Offers Pharm D. *Accreditation:* ACPE. *Faculty:* 23 full-time (9 women), 2 part-time/adjunct (1 woman). *Students:* 533 full-time (398 women); includes 343 minority (14 Black or African American, non-Hispanic/Latino; 2 American Indian or Alaska Native, non-Hispanic/Latino; 309 Asian, non-Hispanic/Latino; 16 Hispanic/Latino; 2 Two or more races, non-Hispanic/Latino), 28 international. Average age 27. 1,671 applicants, 14% accepted, 140 enrolled. In 2011, 139 doctorates awarded. *Degree requirements:* For doctorate, comprehensive exam (for some programs). *Entrance requirements:* For doctorate, minimum GPA of 2.75, interview, letters of recommendation; BS in pharmacy or equivalent (recommended). Additional exam requirements/recommendations for international students: Required—TOEFL (minimum score 550 paper-based; 213 computer-based; 79 iBT). *Application deadline:* For fall admission, 11/1 for domestic and international students. Application fee: $65. Electronic applications accepted. *Expenses:* Contact institution. *Financial support:* Institutionally sponsored loans and scholarships/grants available. Financial award application deadline: 3/2; financial award applicants required to submit FAFSA. *Unit head:* Dr. Daniel Robinson, Dean, 909-469-5581, Fax: 909-469-5539. *Application contact:* Jeanene White, Information Contact, 909-469-5541, Fax: 909-469-5570, E-mail: admissions@westernu.edu. Web site: http://www.westernu.edu/pharmacy-dpp_message.

West Virginia University, School of Pharmacy, Professional Program in Pharmacy, Morgantown, WV 26506. Offers clinical pharmacy (Pharm D). Students enter program as undergraduates. *Accreditation:* ACPE. *Degree requirements:* For doctorate, 100 hours of community service. *Entrance requirements:* For doctorate, PCAT, minimum GPA of 3.1. Electronic applications accepted.

West Virginia University, School of Pharmacy, Program in Pharmaceutical and Pharmacological Sciences, Morgantown, WV 26506. Offers administrative pharmacy (PhD); behavioral pharmacy (MS, PhD); biopharmaceutics/pharmacokinetics (MS, PhD); industrial pharmacy (MS); medicinal chemistry (MS, PhD); pharmaceutical chemistry (MS, PhD); pharmaceutics (MS, PhD); pharmacology and toxicology (MS); pharmacy (MS); pharmacy administration (MS). Part-time programs available. Terminal master's awarded for partial completion of doctoral program. *Degree requirements:* For master's, thesis; for doctorate, one foreign language, comprehensive exam, thesis/dissertation. *Entrance requirements:* For master's and doctorate, GRE General Test, minimum GPA of 2.75. Additional exam requirements/recommendations for international students: Required—TOEFL; Recommended—TWE. Electronic applications accepted. *Expenses:* Contact institution. *Faculty research:* Pharmaceutics, medicinal chemistry, biopharmaceutics/pharmacokinetics, health outcomes research.

Wilkes University, College of Graduate and Professional Studies, Nesbitt College of Pharmacy and Nursing, School of Pharmacy, Wilkes-Barre, PA 18766-0002. Offers Pharm D. *Students:* 276 full-time (169 women), 3 part-time (2 women); includes 12 minority (2 Black or African American, non-Hispanic/Latino; 7 Asian, non-Hispanic/Latino; 1 Hispanic/Latino; 2 Two or more races, non-Hispanic/Latino), 2 international. Average age 22. In 2011, 70 doctorates awarded. *Entrance requirements:* For doctorate, PCAT. Additional exam requirements/recommendations for international students: Required—TOEFL (minimum score 550 paper-based; 213 computer-based; 79 iBT). *Financial support:* Application deadline: 3/1; applicants required to submit FAFSA. *Unit head:* Dr. Bernard Graham, Dean, 570-408-4280, Fax: 570-408-7729, E-mail: bernard.graham@wilkes.edu. *Application contact:* Erin Sutzko, Director of Extended Learning, 570-408-4253, Fax: 570-408-7846, E-mail: erin.sutzko@wilkes.edu. Web site: http://www.wilkes.edu/pages/390.asp.

Wingate University, School of Pharmacy, Wingate, NC 28174-0159. Offers Pharm D. *Accreditation:* ACPE. *Faculty:* 38 full-time (25 women). *Students:* 321 full-time (186 women); includes 17 minority (4 Black or African American, non-Hispanic/Latino; 9 Asian, non-Hispanic/Latino; 4 Hispanic/Latino), 4 international. Average age 25. In 2011, 62 doctorates awarded. *Degree requirements:* For doctorate, comprehensive exam. *Entrance requirements:* For doctorate, PCAT. *Application deadline:* For fall admission, 2/1 for domestic and international students. Applications are processed on a rolling basis. Application fee: $0. Electronic applications accepted. *Expenses:* Contact institution. *Financial support:* In 2011–12, 182 students received support. Fellowships, research assistantships, teaching assistantships, career-related internships or fieldwork, and scholarships/grants available. Financial award application deadline: 5/30. *Faculty research:* Stress response in aging, arthritis therapy educational processes, professional development, sarcopenia in aging, geriatric-psych drug therapy. *Unit head:* Dr. Robert Supernaw, Vice President for Graduate Education, 704-233-8015, Fax: 704-233-8332, E-mail: supernaw@wingate.edu. *Application contact:* Jean Tarlton, Coordinator of Pharmacy Admissions, 704-233-8324, Fax: 704-233-8332, E-mail: jtarlton@wingate.edu. Web site: http://pharmacy.wingate.edu/.

Xavier University of Louisiana, College of Pharmacy, New Orleans, LA 70125-1098. Offers Pharm D. *Accreditation:* ACPE. *Entrance requirements:* Additional exam requirements/recommendations for international students: Required—TOEFL. Electronic applications accepted. *Expenses:* Contact institution.

ALBANY COLLEGE OF PHARMACY AND HEALTH SCIENCES

Programs of Study

Albany College of Pharmacy and Health Sciences (ACPHS) offers a range of master's degree programs in the health sciences, spanning areas that include pharmaceutics, diagnostics, and laboratory research.

Students interested in these disciplines may pursue graduate degrees in the following areas: biotechnology, cytotechnology and molecular cytology, health outcomes research, and pharmaceutical sciences. Each of these master's degree programs may be completed in two years by full-time students, although options exist for working professionals interested in pursuing a degree program on a part-time basis.

Regardless of the program, students have opportunities to work side-by-side with faculty members on a wide range of projects. Whether it is discovering and developing new drugs, conducting molecular clinical case studies, or examining how people will pay for health care in the future, ACPHS has experts and resources to help students gain the knowledge necessary to succeed in their chosen careers.

The graduate programs at ACPHS are further differentiated from those of many other colleges and universities by small class sizes and the individualized attention afforded to each student. This environment allows students to work with faculty members who are most closely aligned with their interests and who are able to help them reach their goals.

Graduates of these programs are well positioned to accelerate their current career paths, transition to new careers in the health sciences, advance into executive level positions, or gain the academic foundation needed to pursue a Ph.D. or M.D.

Research Facilities

The Pharmaceutical Research Institute at Albany College of Pharmacy and Health Sciences (PRI) is a research and development institute dedicated to cutting-edge research, pharmaceutical services, and education.

ACPHS students benefit from the knowledge and experience of PRI Chairman and Vice Provost for Research Shaker A. Mousa, Ph.D. Dr. Mousa is a former senior researcher at DuPont Pharmaceuticals Company who holds 30 U.S. patents and 200 international patents. His work has been reported in more than 700 publications.

PRI's primary objective is to enrich and advance pharmaceutical education by providing hands-on access to the full spectrum of drug development. The institute strives to demonstrate how medicines advance from the bench to the bedside, presenting students with a deeper understanding of the drug development process and the array of career opportunities available in the field.

The Bioscience Research Building houses the Department of Pharmaceutical Sciences. Dedicated laboratory space, including an animal research facility, exists for conducting research in pharmacology, pharmaceutics, and related areas.

The Research Institute for Health Outcomes (RIHO) conducts research and disseminates findings in the areas of health outcomes, comparative effectiveness, pharmacoeconomics, and health technology assessment. Outcomes research is a type of study that measures the results of various medical interventions and options including drug treatments, therapies, health-care services, and diagnostic tools in actual clinical practice situations. The results of outcomes research can guide health-care decision makers in

selecting and utilizing the most appropriate treatment strategies to optimize patient care.

The College also has interdepartmental groups of faculty members dedicated to the study of infectious disease and nephrology.

Financial Aid

Students may apply for financial aid through the federal student financial aid program as well as alternative lending sources. Students performing research for funded faculty members have opportunities to secure additional financial support. International students seeking loans through a U.S. lender must have a sponsor or cosigner who is a U.S. citizen.

Cost of Study

For the 2012–13 academic year, full-time tuition for M.S. students is $9000 per semester or $900 per credit hour. General fees, including the meal plan, are $4500 per year. Cost of books will vary depending on the program.

Living and Housing Costs

Although most graduate students live off-campus, a limited amount of housing exists for graduate students on campus. For on-campus housing information, students should contact the Office of Residence Life at 518-694-7155. Requests for on-campus housing should be made no later than February for the fall semester. Students may contact the Office of Graduate Admissions at 518-694-7149 for off-campus housing information.

Student Group

The College has more than 1,600 undergraduate and graduate students enrolled full-time at its Albany and Vermont campuses. ACPHS has a diverse student body, with international students representing approximately 10 percent of the student population. ACPHS encourages individuals from all races, religions, national origin, sex and sexual preference, marital status, disability, and age to apply for admission to the College.

Location

The College's main campus is located in Albany, New York. Albany has recently garnered several honors as an excellent place to live. These include being ranked by *Business Week* magazine as one of the top 20 cities for Generation Y based on its high percentage of creative workers and high income growth; being ranked fifteenth on *Forbes'* list of America's most innovative cities; and being ranked eighteenth by Portfolio.com for quality of life among the largest U.S. metro areas. The city's location—situated at the crossroads of the Northeast—puts it within a 3- to 4-hour drive from New York City, Montreal, Boston, and Philadelphia.

The ACPHS satellite campus in Colchester, Vermont, is 3 hours away.

The College

Founded in 1881, Albany College of Pharmacy and Health Sciences is a private, independent institution committed to graduating the best health care minds in the world. ACPHS offers five bachelor's programs and four graduate programs in the health sciences, in addition to its doctor of pharmacy program. The College's main

Albany College of Pharmacy and Health Sciences

campus is located in Albany, New York; its satellite campus is in Colchester, Vermont.

Applying

The deadline for application is April 15 for the fall semester and November 1 for the spring. Students should contact the Office of Graduate Admissions to confirm if a particular program allows spring admission. As with most graduate programs, admission is competitive and space is limited. Serious applicants should apply early and submit a complete application.

Students must submit the graduate admissions application along with a $75 application fee, GRE scores, transcripts, and a personal statement. International applicants must also include a WES or ECE evaluation for international transcripts and a TOEFL score. Highly qualified applicants will be invited for an in-person or telephone interview. All admissions materials should be sent to the Office of Graduate Admissions or e-mailed to graduate@acphs.edu.

Correspondence and Information

Albany College of Pharmacy and Health Sciences
Office of Graduate Admissions
106 New Scotland Avenue
Albany, New York 12208-3492
United States
Phone: 518-694-7149
        888-203-8010 (toll-free)
E-mail: graduate@acphs.edu
Web site: http://www.acphs.edu

FACULTY HEADS AND PROGRAMS

John Denio, M.S., M.B.A., Interim Provost
Shaker A. Mousa, Ph.D., Vice Provost for Research
Martha Hass, Ph.D., Interim Dean, School of Graduate Studies
Hassan El-Fawal, Ph.D., Dean, School of Health Sciences
William Millington, Ph.D., Chair, Department of Pharmaceutical Sciences (Albany Campus)
Stefan Balaz, Ph.D., Chair, Department of Pharmaceutical Sciences (Vermont Campus)

M.S. in Pharmaceutical Sciences: The M.S. in Pharmaceutical Sciences program educates students in the scientific disciplines required for the discovery, development, and evaluation of new drugs and other pharmaceutical products. The thesis option trains students in basic and translational research under the supervision of a thesis advisor and committee of research faculty. This path is ideal for students interested in working as research scientists or pursuing a Ph.D. or M.D. The nonthesis option is geared toward individuals in the pharmaceutical or biomedical industry who would like to accelerate their careers with a graduate degree but who are not necessarily interested in laboratory research. The M.S. in Pharmaceutical Sciences degree may be pursued on either the Albany or Vermont Campus.

M.S. in Biotechnology: Designed to meet the needs of laboratory diagnosticians or basic research scientists, the M.S. in Biotechnology program integrates the basic sciences and laboratory innovation. Graduates of this program will improve their opportunity for advancement in their current field, in addition to gaining flexibility to pursue careers in areas such as molecular diagnostics, oncology research, forensic science, and environmental toxicology.

M.S. in Health Outcomes Research: The M.S. in Health Outcomes Research program provides the knowledge and skills necessary for evaluating outcomes of commonly prescribed therapies in order to guide the selection of the most effective treatments. This field is playing an increasingly important role in finding better ways to provide the best care at the lowest cost.

M.S. in Cytotechnology and Molecular Cytology: The M.S. in Cytotechnology and Molecular Cytology program is designed to train students and diagnosticians to become leaders in the field of tissue and cell-based diagnostics. Students who enter this program learn to utilize traditional and innovative technologies such as image analysis, flow cytometry, and immunohistochemistry to diagnose cancer and other diseases in their early stages.

The ACPHS Student Center is home to lecture halls, the bookstore, student lounge, and dining hall. Dining options include offerings from Tim Horton's, Au Bon Pain, and Cold Stone Creamery.

Small class sizes at ACPHS allow students to work closely with faculty members.

NOVA SOUTHEASTERN UNIVERSITY

College of Pharmacy

Programs of Study

Nova Southeastern University (NSU) offers an innovative program of graduate study and research leading to the Doctor of Philosophy degree (Ph.D.). Students can choose to pursue the Ph.D. degree in one of three distinct sequences: Molecular Medicine and Pharmacogenomics (Drug Discovery), Drug Development (Pharmaceutics), or Social and Administrative Pharmacy (Determinants of Drug Use). Also available is the dual degree, Doctor of Pharmacy/Master of Business Administration (Pharm.D./M.B.A.).

At the completion of the Ph.D. sequences, students are able to demonstrate the knowledge base expected at the Ph.D. level in a pharmacy specialty; design and conduct independent research that adds to the understanding of their pharmacy specialty; prepare and defend rational and structured proposals seeking support for research efforts; and prepare and present lucid reports on their own research, as well as the research of others.

Programs in the College of Pharmacy (COP) are taught primarily by multilingual, multicultural, full-time faculty members. Clinical and applied research is delivered at sites in Fort Lauderdale and West Palm Beach, Florida, and Ponce, Puerto Rico. Both live and online lectures are used.

Research Facilities

NSU is the only college of pharmacy in the United States with a full-service community pharmacy (on the main campus) and a full-service hospital pharmacy.

The research laboratories in COP occupy approximately 3,000 square feet of the Library/Research Building in the Health Professions Division (HPD). Each individual laboratory space ranges from 300 to 750 square feet and is equipped with general biochemistry and/or tissue culture equipment. Some laboratories include specialized equipment for pharmaceutical preparations, radioligand binding assays, molecular biological applications, and proteomics applications. There are also common laboratory facilities for shared equipment. Two FluorChem E digital darkroom systems are available for use, along with a fully equipped darkroom and a fully equipped laboratory designed for studies using radioactive chemicals. All common use laboratories are located in close proximity to the College of Pharmacy laboratories and are fully accessible to all HPD researchers.

The animal facility is also located within the research area of the Library/ Laboratory Building, and it complies with the minimum standards for use of rats and mice. The College of Pharmacy also has access to an OLAW approved animal facility at the Rumbaugh-Goodwin Institute for Cancer Research (RGICR), located near the main campus. This facility has two holding rooms to house rodents and separate cage wash and storage areas. The RGICR animal facility is maintained by a full-time caretaker who also oversees the animal rooms in the HPD Library and Research Building. Both facilities are governed by an Institutional Animal Care and Use Committee (IACUC). The RGICR facility is fully compliant with OLAW standards and is available for use by all NSU researchers. A consulting veterinarian is responsible for oversight of the health of animals in both facilities.

NSU maintains an extensive information technology network for teaching, learning, research, and administrative computing. Comprehensive fiber-optic and wireless networks provide connectivity for user access. A dedicated wide area network (WAN) supports high-speed connections from all campuses. The research facility has Pentium personal computers (PC) for data collection, data processing and analysis. The COP researchers all have access to modern Dell and IBM computers in their offices as well as in their laboratories, equipped with the necessary software for word processing, routine data analysis, and photo processing. Researchers also have easy access to the NSU's four computer labs that house more than 200 Pentium 200 MHz PCs with ready access to the Internet and Ovid online database.

Financial Aid

Top candidates are eligible for scholarships, which consist of a tuition waiver and teaching assistantships. Non-scholarship students can apply for a variety of loans.

Cost of Study

Tuition for 2012–13 is $25,875 (subject to change by the board of trustees without notice). An HPD general access fee of $145 is required each year. An NSU student services fee of $900 is also required annually.

Living and Housing Costs

The Rolling Hills Graduate Apartments, which opened in 2008, are approximately 1 mile west of the NSU main campus and offer housing for approximately 373 students. Each single and quad room is fully furnished and features a kitchen, bathroom, and living room. Married housing is available.

Costs range between $3353 and $6494 per semester or between $8071 and $15,609 for a twelve-month contract. All rates include unlimited laundry, NSU-secured wireless Internet, furnishings, utilities, air conditioning, cable TV, and local telephone service. More information about student housing is available at http://www.nova.edu/reslife/.

Student Group

NSU's College of Pharmacy has consistently led the nation in the level of enrollment of Hispanic doctoral pharmacy students. Students are actively involved in local, national, and international community-based health clinics; the legislative processes; and humanitarian missions in countries abroad.

Student Outcomes

Graduate passing rates for NSU students on pharmacy licensing exams are at rates near or above 90 percent, consistent with national pass rates.

Location

Davie, a city of more than 80,000, maintains a sense of small-town intimacy while its location between major highways is near both an international airport and a seaport, which offers access to the state's metropolitan centers. The area is famous for its wide expanses of sandy beaches and its tropical climate. Nearby Fort Lauderdale is home to numerous museums, art galleries, and a performing arts center.

NSU's main campus consists of 300 acres with general-purpose athletic fields and NCAA-qualifying soccer and baseball fields. The residence halls on the main campus serve undergraduate, graduate, health professions, and law students. The College of Pharmacy also has branch campuses in West Palm Beach, Florida and Ponce, Puerto Rico.

The University and The College

Founded in 1964 as Nova University, the institution merged with Southeastern University of the Health Sciences in 1994, creating Nova Southeastern University. NSU offers a wide range of undergraduate, graduate, and professional degree programs to more than 29,000 students every year. It is the seventh-largest independent institution in the nation and the largest independent not-for-profit university in the Southeast. NSU is experiencing a sustained period of academic growth, fiscal strength, and commitment to the challenges of the twenty-first century.

The NSU College of Pharmacy has experienced the fastest growth among colleges of pharmacy. Since 1986, it has graduated more than 2,700 pharmacists.

Applying

Students are recruited for the Ph.D. program from the NSU College of Pharmacy; other U.S. schools/colleges of pharmacy; and graduates with degrees in fields related to social, economic, behavioral, and administrative pharmacy, as well as chemistry, biology, and other related scientific fields. Students are also recruited from international institutions, especially pharmacy graduates from India, Saudi Arabia, China, Europe, Canada, Latin America and the Caribbean. Successful applicants, whether foreign or domestic, are required to comply with the following guidelines. All applicants must have an earned baccalaureate degree, with a GPA equivalent to a B or better, from an accredited institution of higher education in pharmacy or a related scientific area or in a discipline related to social, economic, behavioral, or administrative pharmacy. Application materials must include GRE results, proof of proficiency in English, a formal application form, three letters of reference, transcripts received directly from the degree granting institution, and a brief written essay on the goals of the applicant.

Applicants may apply for matriculation into the fall semester. The Office of Admissions processes applications on a rolling admissions basis; therefore, it is in the best interest of the applicant to apply as early as possible. To be considered for admission, students must complete the application form and submit supporting documents and a nonrefundable fee of $50 by March 1. Official transcripts of all work attempted at all colleges and universities must be forwarded by the institutions attended to Enrollment Processing Services (EPS), College of Pharmacy, Office of Admissions, 3301 College Ave, P.O. Box 299000, Ft. Lauderdale, FL 33329-9905. It is the responsibility of the applicant to ensure that arrangements are made for these transcripts to be sent. A final transcript covering all of the applicant's work must be forwarded to EPS prior to matriculation. Three individual letters of evaluation from professors or supervisors in the applicant's major field of study are required. All applicants are required to submit official Graduate Record Examination (GRE) scores. The NSU code is 5522. GRE scores must be less than five years old prior to the candidate's matriculation. Undergraduate course work taken at an international institution must be evaluated for U.S. institution

equivalence. It is the applicant's responsibility to have the course work evaluated by either World Education Services, Josef Silney & Associates, or Educational Credential Evaluators, Inc. A complete course-by-course evaluation must be sent to the Office of Admissions.

Upon receipt of the completed application and required credentials, the Ph.D. Committee on Admissions selects those applicants to receive personal interviews on the NSU Fort Lauderdale campus or via telephone. The Office of Admissions notifies those who are selected of the interview date and time. Being granted an interview does not guarantee admission.

Applications forms are available and can be submitted online at http://www. nova.edu/apply/index.html. Applicants may also have an application mailed to them by request.

Correspondence and Information

Dr. Hugh M. McLean
Associate Dean, Research and Graduate Education
Health Professions Division
College of Pharmacy
Nova Southeastern University
Fort Lauderdale, Florida 78249
United States
E-mail: hugh.mclean@nova.edu

Health Professions Admissions Office
Attention: Jessie Sutton
Nova Southeastern University
Phone: 954-262-1101
          877-640-0218 (toll-free)
Web site: http://www.nova.edu

THE FACULTY AND THEIR RESEARCH

Hugh M. McLean, Associate Dean, Research and Graduate Education; Pharm.D., Creighton, 2007; Ph.D., Florida A&M, 1991. Development of potent yet safer novel anti-inflammatory steroids via the mutual-prodrug approach; synthesis and pharmacological evaluations of antedrugs, prodrugs, and mutual prodrugs.

Appu Rathinavelu, Associate Dean, Institutional Planning and Development; Ph.D., Madras (India), 1985. Gene expression analysis in highly metastatic tumors, understanding intracellular pathway regulating angiogenesis, ANP receptor regulation and cardiovascular function.

Drug Development and Molecular Medicine and Pharmacogenomics (Drug Discovery) Sequences

Michelle A. Clark, Associate Professor and Chairperson, Department of Pharmaceutical Sciences; Ph.D., South Florida, 1996. Central signaling pathways for blood pressure regulation and control, role of the central renin angiotensin system in the regulation of cardiovascular and other diseases.

Rais A. Ansari, Assistant Professor, Pharmaceutical Sciences; Ph.D., Kanpur (India), 1985. Mechanism of alcohol-mediated hypertension, transcriptional regulation of human angiotensinogen gene after ethanol and environmental toxicants exposure.

Ana Maria Castejon, Associate Professor, Pharmaceutical Sciences; Ph.D., Central University (Venezuela), 1997. Oxidative stress and autism, diabetes mellitus, effects of statins in vascular smooth muscle cells, genetics of salt sensitivity in human subjects, developing an insulin resistance model to test for abnormal insulin pancreatic secretion in prediabetic subjects, intravenous microdialysis in human patients.

Luigi Cubeddu, Professor, Pharmaceutical Sciences; M.D., Central University (Venezuela); Ph.D., Colorado. Mechanisms and treatment of hypertension associated with obesity, salt-sensitive hypertension, early detection of insulin resistance and abnormalities in glucose metabolism, statin withdrawal syndrome.

Stephen G. Grant, Visiting Associate Professor, Pharmaceutical Sciences; Ph.D., Toronto, 1985. Somatic mutation as a predictive biomarker of carcinogenesis; epigenetic mechanisms in carcinogenesis; biomonitoring and biodosimetry of genotoxic cancer therapy; in vitro and in silico development of genotoxic and pseudo-genotoxic anti-cancer agents.

Young M. Kwon, Assistant Professor, Pharmaceutical Sciences, Ph.D., Utah, 2003. Targeted delivery and triggered release system for therapeutic macromolecules; bioconjugate chemistry and PEGylation; nonviral gene carriers and intracellular drug delivery; protein stability and release from biodegradable polymer.

Jean J. Latimer, Associate Professor, Pharmaceutical Sciences; Ph.D., Buffalo, SUNY, 1989. Loss of DNA repair as causative factor in cancer formation; breast tissue engineering; ancestral disparity in breast cancer development and pharmacogenomics; drug resistance (via cancer stem cells) in childhood leukemia.

Anastasios Lymperopoulos, Assistant Professor, Pharmaceutical Sciences; Ph.D., Patras (Greece), 2004. Cardiovascular biology/pharmacology and gene therapy, with a focus on adrenergic system regulation in heart failure; novel roles of G-protein coupled receptor kinases and their cofactors, beta-arrestins, in regulation of various important cardiovascular G-protein coupled receptors; roles of G-protein coupled receptor kinases and their cofactors, beta-arrestins, in adrenal gland physiology and biology.

Enrique A. Nieves, Assistant Professor, Pharmaceutical Sciences; Ph.D., Florida, 1982. Applications of nanotechnology in drug product development and pharmaceutical process designs, development of co-excipients for improved drug formulations, nanotechnology applications in the extraction and isolation of new drugs from natural sources.

Hamid Omidian, Associate Professor, Pharmaceutical Sciences; Ph.D., Brunel (London), 1997. Hydrogels for pharmaceutical and biomedical applications, hydrogel-based controlled delivery systems and technologies, hydrogel-based gastroretentive drug delivery platforms, hydrogel-based platforms for cell culture and proliferation.

Mutasem Rawas-Qalaji, Assistant Professor, Pharmaceutical Sciences; Ph.D., Manitoba (Canada), 2006. Enhancing the permeability and the relative bioavailability of poorly absorbed drugs by nanotechnology, formulation and delivery of drug-loaded nanoparticles through noninvasive and user-friendly routes of administration, formulation and evaluation of sublingual ODT tablets as an alternative noninvasive dosage form.

Syed A. A. Rizvi, Assistant Professor, Pharmaceutical Sciences; Ph.D., Mercer, 2010. Cocrystallization and formulation strategies for low bioavailability drugs; micellar electrokinetic chromatography.

Edwin Santini, Assistant Professor, Pharmaceutical Sciences; Ph.D., Ponce (Puerto Rico), 2004; Cellular mechanisms underlying conditioned fear expression and extinction, research techniques: patch-clamp recordings and Pavlovian fear conditioning.

Robert C. Speth, Professor, Pharmaceutical Sciences; Ph.D., Vanderbilt, 1976. Brain renin-angiotensin system pharmacology and functionality.

Social and Administrative Pharmacy (Determinants of Drug Use) Sequence

Manuel J. Carvajal, Professor and Chairperson, Department of Sociobehavioral and Administrative Pharmacy; Ph.D., Florida, 1974. Applied econometrics geared to problem solving; various areas of human capital including fertility, migration, poverty, and discrimination; gender and ethnic differences in labor market outcomes and job satisfaction.

Catherine A. Harrington, Associate Professor, Sociobehavioral and Administrative Pharmacy; Ph.D., Michigan, 1993; Pharm.D., Michigan, 1987. Developing databases and information systems that assist in evaluation of drug therapy, use of meta-analysis techniques to obtain evidence from literature.

Nile M. Khanfar, Assistant Professor, Sociobehavioral and Administrative Pharmacy; Ph.D., Louisiana at Monroe, 2005; M.B.A., Louisiana at Monroe, 2001. Management leadership, strategic management/marking business cases, direct-to-consumer advertising of prescription medication and its influence on consumer behavior.

L. Leanne Lai, Professor, Sociobehavioral and Administrative Pharmacy; Ph.D., Maryland, Baltimore, 1996. Pharmacoeconomics and outcomes research, pharmacoepidemiology and secondary data analysis, international education.

Ioana Popovici, Assistant Professor, Sociobehavioral and Administrative Pharmacy; Ph.D., Florida International, 2007. Economic evaluation of substance abuse treatment interventions, relationship between addictive substance use or abuse and its economic consequences.

Sylvia E. Rabionet, Associate Professor, Sociobehavioral and Administrative Pharmacy; Ed.D., Harvard, 2002. Health disparities, public health issues.

Jesus Sanchez, Assistant Professor, Sociobehavioral and Administrative Pharmacy; Ph.D., Miami (Florida), 2001. HIV reduction among high-risk migrant workers; building capacity and infrastructure in the migrant farm worker communities in South Florida; prevalence of HIV, hepatitis B and C, and associated risk factors among Hispanic injection drug users.

SOUTH UNIVERSITY

Columbia Campus
School of Pharmacy
Doctor of Pharmacy

Program of Study

The South University School of Pharmacy, accredited by the Accreditation Council for Pharmacy Education (ACPE), is one of only three schools of pharmacy in the state of South Carolina and one of a few ACPE-accredited Doctor of Pharmacy degree programs in the United States to offer an accelerated three-year curriculum. The goal of the South University School of Pharmacy is to prepare graduates for the practice of pharmaceutical care and life-long learning with special emphasis on the community environment in which the majority of healthcare and patient-care services will be provided in the future.

The School of Pharmacy program was developed using a visionary approach that employs carefully structured curriculum designed to prepare graduates for both high standards of contemporary pharmacy practice and the evolution of the profession. Seasoned and energetic faculty members offer students the benefit of teaching basic sciences and practice in a setting of collaborative learning and teamwork.

Following acceptance into the program, Pharm.D. students begin an accelerated, full-time, twelve-quarter schedule designed to provide four academic years of study within three calendar years. This accelerated pace is only available at a handful of institutions across the country. South University's program was designed to meet the increasing demand for well-trained pharmacists and is tailored to accentuate the future of the pharmacy profession while also developing pharmacists who are familiar with contemporary practice. The curriculum is structured to educate and prepare competent pharmaceutical practitioners who can provide care in a variety of institutional, community, and other settings. Students learn the skills needed to assess, monitor, initiate, or adjust drug therapy programs. In those roles, they are prepared to educate patients on the proper use of pharmaceuticals, develop drug therapy plans through data evaluation, and partner with other healthcare providers to contribute to a patient's well-being.

Research Facilities

In June of 2010, South University opened the doors of its South Carolina Doctor of Pharmacy program. The school occupies a new building in Columbia, South Carolina, on the existing South University campus. Students in the School of Pharmacy enjoy access to a practice lab and mock pharmacy where they study to develop dispensing, compounding, and intravenous admixture skills. In addition, an onsite Drug Information Center provides information to consumers and healthcare professionals while also serving as an advanced rotation site for students.

Financial Aid

A range of financial aid options is available to students who qualify. The Columbia campus of South University offers access to federal and state programs, including grants, loans, and work-study programs. Eligible students may apply for veterans' educational benefits and are encouraged to investigate the availability of grants and scholarships through community resources. As a first step, students should complete the Free Application for Federal Student Aid (FAFSA). Students may apply electronically at http://www.fafsa.ed.gov or through the program.

Cost of Study

Tuition information for the Doctor of Pharmacy program may be obtained by contacting the School of Pharmacy via the South University website at http://www.southuniversity.edu.

Living and Housing Costs

South University does not offer or operate student housing. Pharmacy students typically live in apartments in the Columbia area. Students who commute from long distances can arrange to stay at nearby hotels that offer long-term rates. More information may be obtained by contacting the Admissions Department.

Student Group

The Columbia campus of South University has a diverse student body enrolled in both day and evening classes. Students are primarily commuters who live within 50 miles of the city.

Student Outcomes

The South University Career Services Department has been established to assist currently enrolled students in developing their career plans and reaching their employment goals. Career services include, but are not limited to, one-on-one career counseling, special career-related workshops and programs, coaching for resume and cover letter development, and resume referral to employers.

Location

South University's Columbia campus is located in the Carolina Research Park in northeast Columbia. The campus features spacious classrooms, multiple computer labs, a fully equipped medical lab, and a student lounge. The campus is located just minutes from downtown off I-77 at Farrow Road and Park Lane.

The campus surroundings are highlighted by a natural wooded landscape and vast green space featuring a tranquil campus courtyard. Convenient to malls, shopping, and the growing east side of Columbia, the new campus location provides easier access to students throughout the greater Columbia area.

The University

The School of Pharmacy is accredited by the American Council on Pharmaceutical Education (ACPE). South University is accredited by the Southern Association of Colleges and Schools Commission on Colleges to award associate, baccalaureate, masters, and doctorate degrees. Contact the Commission on Colleges at 1866 Southern Lane, Decatur, Georgia 30033-4097

or call 404-679-4500 for questions about the accreditation of South University.

Applying

Students are accepted into the Doctor of Pharmacy program once each year, in June. Entrance into the program is gained through a formal application review and assessment of the applicant's potential for professional and academic achievement. Prospective students must complete a minimum of two years of pre-pharmacy course requirements at an acceptable accredited collegiate institution. A grade of C (2.0) or better must be earned in each prerequisite course. Applicants also must take the Pharmacy College Admissions Test (PCAT) no later than January of the year of admission. Additional requirements for the Doctor of Pharmacy program can be found in the South University catalog or by visiting the South University website http://www.southuniversity.edu.

The South University School of Pharmacy utilizes the Pharmacy College Application Service (PharmCAS), a centralized application service for prospective students applying to colleges and schools of pharmacy. Only those applications submitted through PharmCAS will be accepted. In addition, a supplemental application is required to complete the application process, no later than February 1. The application is available at http://www.southuniversity.edu/Pharmacy.

Correspondence and Information

Applications for admission to the South University Doctor of Pharmacy program are available by contacting:

School of Pharmacy
South University
9 Science Court
Columbia, South Carolina 29203
United States
Phone: 803-799-9082
      866-629-3031 (toll-free)
Fax: 803-935-4382
E-mail: pharmd@southuniversity.edu
Website: http://www.southuniversity.edu/pharmacy

See suprograms.info for program duration; tuition, fees, and other costs; median debt; federal salary data; alumni success; and other important information. http://www.southuniversity.edu/programs-info/form/

THE FACULTY

One of the most outstanding aspects of South University's Doctor of Pharmacy program is the dedication of the faculty members and their ability to cultivate a supportive learning environment. Faculty members are committed to their roles as mentors, teachers, and co-learners. They are also dedicated to the training of students who can assume positions of leadership within the field of pharmacy. A current list of program faculty members is available at the South University website (http://www.southuniversity.edu/pharmacy).

South University's School of Pharmacy is one of only a few schools in the country to offer an accelerated three-year Doctor of Pharmacy degree program.

SOUTH UNIVERSITY

Savannah Campus
School of Pharmacy
Doctor of Pharmacy

Program of Study

The South University School of Pharmacy, accredited by the Accreditation Council for Pharmacy Education (ACPE), is one of only four schools of pharmacy in the state of Georgia and one of a few ACPE-accredited Doctor of Pharmacy degree programs in the U.S. to offer an accelerated three-year curriculum. The goal of the South University School of Pharmacy is to prepare graduates for the practice of pharmaceutical care and life-long learning with special emphasis on the community environment in which the majority of healthcare and patient-care services will be provided in the future.

The School of Pharmacy program was developed using a visionary approach that employs a carefully structured curriculum designed to prepare graduates for both high standards of contemporary pharmacy practice and the evolution of the profession. Seasoned and energetic faculty members offer students the benefit of teaching basic sciences and practice in a setting of collaborative learning and teamwork.

Following acceptance into the program, Pharm.D. students begin an accelerated, full-time, twelve-quarter schedule designed to provide four academic years of study within three calendar years. This accelerated pace is only available at a handful of institutions across the country. South University's program was designed to meet the increasing demand for well-trained pharmacists and is tailored to accentuate the future of the pharmacy profession while also developing pharmacists who are familiar with contemporary practice. The curriculum is structured to educate and prepare competent pharmaceutical practitioners who can provide care in a variety of institutional, community, and other settings. Students learn the skills needed to assess, monitor, initiate, or adjust drug therapy programs. In those roles, they are prepared to educate patients on the proper use of pharmaceuticals, develop drug therapy plans through data evaluation, and partner with other healthcare providers to contribute to a patient's well-being.

Research Facilities

South University's Savannah campus is home to the College of Arts and Sciences, College of Business, the College of Health Professions, the College of Nursing, and the School of Pharmacy. The campus houses classroom and laboratory facilities for the health sciences and pharmacy programs. Specifically, the South University School of Pharmacy in Savannah occupies 40,000-square-feet of a freestanding facility designed to house a modern pharmacy school. This facility provides wireless instructional, laboratory, and office facilities for pharmacy students, faculty members, and administrators. In addition to eight small classrooms, two large modern lecture halls, and a number of smaller classrooms, the building also houses a General Purpose Laboratory that includes rooms for patient counseling practice and teaching physical assessment along with a sterile products room and a model pharmacy. There is also a 32-station Analytical Chemistry Laboratory that is used for chemistry, pharmaceutics, and professional laboratory courses. Practice sites to provide both intermediate and advanced practice experiences include community pharmacies, hospitals, managed-care facilities, pharmaceutical companies, and other venues that have been recruited to support the experiential component of the curriculum. South University's facilities are designed to offer personalized and technically sophisticated instructional delivery.

The campus library provides comfortable study space for students, wireless Internet capabilities for laptop network connectivity, a separate computer lab, and reference and interlibrary loan services.

Financial Aid

A range of financial aid options is available to students who qualify. The Savannah campus of South University offers access to federal and state programs, including grants, loans, and work-study programs. Eligible students may apply for veterans' educational benefits and are encouraged to investigate the availability of grants and scholarships through community resources. As a first step, students should complete the Free Application for Federal Student Aid (FAFSA). Students may apply electronically at http://www.fafsa.ed.gov or through the program.

Cost of Study

Tuition information for the Doctor of Pharmacy program may be obtained by contacting the School of Pharmacy via the South University website at http://www.southuniversity.edu.

Living and Housing Costs

South University offers school-sponsored student housing at its Savannah campus in conjunction with a local apartment complex. Due to the full-time nature of the program, pharmacy students typically live in rental homes or apartments in the Savannah area. More information may be obtained by contacting the Director of Student Housing at 912-201-8000.

Student Group

The Savannah campus of South University has a diverse student body enrolled in both day and evening classes. Students are primarily commuters who live within 50 miles of the city.

Student Outcomes

The South University Career Services Department has been established to assist currently enrolled students in developing their career plans and reaching their employment goals. Career services include, but are not limited to, one-on-one career counseling, special career-related workshops and programs, coaching for resume and cover letter development, and resume referral to employers.

South University

Location

Located on the south side of the historic city of Savannah, the campus is situated on nine acres of land. It is convenient to the city's bustling midtown section and a full range of educational and cultural activities. The Atlantic Ocean and recreational amenities of Tybee Island, including beaches and numerous outdoor activities, are just minutes away. In addition, the campus is located just a short drive from Hilton Head Island and Charleston, South Carolina.

The University

The School of Pharmacy is accredited by the American Council on Pharmaceutical Education (ACPE). South University is accredited by the Southern Association of Colleges and Schools Commission on Colleges to award associate, baccalaureate, masters, and doctorate degrees. Contact the Commission on Colleges at 1866 Southern Lane, Decatur, Georgia 30033-4097 or call 404-679-4500 for questions about the accreditation of South University.

Applying

Students are accepted into the Doctor of Pharmacy program once each year, in June. Entrance into the program is gained through a formal application review and assessment of the applicant's potential for professional and academic achievement. Prospective students must complete a minimum of two years of pre-pharmacy course requirements at an acceptable accredited collegiate institution. A grade of C (2.0) or better must be earned in each prerequisite course. Applicants also must take the Pharmacy College Admissions Test (PCAT) no later than January of the year of admission. Additional requirements for the Doctor of Pharmacy program can be found in the South University catalog or by visiting the South University website: http://www.southuniversity.edu.

The South University School of Pharmacy utilizes the Pharmacy College Application Service (PharmCAS), a centralized application service for prospective students applying to colleges and schools of pharmacy. Only those applications submitted through PharmCAS will be accepted. In addition, a supplemental application is required to complete the application process, along with a fee of $50 no later than February 1. The application is available at http://www.southuniversity.edu/Pharmacy.

Correspondence and Information

Applications for admission to the South University Doctor of Pharmacy program are available by contacting:

School of Pharmacy
South University
709 Mall Boulevard
Savannah, Georgia 31406-4805
United States
Phone: 912-201-8120
      866-629-2901 (toll-free)
Fax: 912-201-8070
E-mail: pharmd@southuniversity.edu
Website: http://www.southuniversity.edu/pharmacy

See suprograms.info for program duration; tuition, fees, and other costs; median debt; federal salary data; alumni success; and other important information. http://www.southuniversity.edu/programs-info/form/

THE FACULTY

One of the most outstanding aspects of South University's Doctor of Pharmacy program is the dedication of the faculty members and their ability to cultivate a supportive learning environment. Faculty members are committed to their roles as mentors, teachers, and co-learners. They are also dedicated to the training of students who can assume positions of leadership within the field of pharmacy. A current list of program faculty members is available at the South University website (http://www.southuniversity.edu/pharmacy).

South University's School of Pharmacy is one of only a few schools in the country to offer an accelerated three-year Doctor of Pharmacy degree program.

Section 31
Veterinary Medicine and Sciences

This section contains a directory of institutions offering graduate work in veterinary medicine and sciences. Additional information about programs listed in the directory may be obtained by writing directly to the dean of a graduate school or chair of a department at the address given in the directory.

For programs offering related work, see also in this book *Biological and Biomedical Sciences* and *Zoology*. In the other guides in this series:

Graduate Programs in the Humanities, Arts & Social Sciences
See *Economics (Agricultural Economics and Agribusiness)*
Graduate Programs in the Physical Sciences, Mathematics, Agricultural Sciences, the Environment & Natural Resources
See *Agricultural and Food Sciences, Marine Sciences and Oceanography,* and *Natural Resources*

Graduate Programs in Engineering & Applied Sciences
See *Agricultural Engineering and Bioengineering* and *Biomedical Engineering and Biotechnology*

CONTENTS

Program Directories

Veterinary Medicine

Auburn University, College of Veterinary Medicine, Professional Program in Veterinary Medicine, Auburn University, AL 36849. Offers DVM, DVM/MS. *Accreditation:* AVMA. *Faculty:* 100 full-time (40 women), 5 part-time/adjunct (1 woman). *Students:* 393 full-time (288 women), 31 part-time (24 women); includes 16 minority (6 Black or African American, non-Hispanic/Latino; 2 American Indian or Alaska Native, non-Hispanic/Latino; 4 Asian, non-Hispanic/Latino; 4 Hispanic/Latino), 2 international. Average age 25. 810 applicants, 120 enrolled. In 2011, 91 doctorates awarded. *Degree requirements:* For doctorate, preceptorship. *Application deadline:* For fall admission, 7/7 for domestic students; for spring admission, 11/24 for domestic students. Applications are processed on a rolling basis. Application fee: $50 ($60 for international students). *Expenses:* Contact institution. *Financial support:* Fellowships available. Financial award application deadline: 3/15; financial award applicants required to submit FAFSA. *Unit head:* Dr. Calvin Johnson, Dean, 334-844-4546. *Application contact:* Dr. George Flowers, Interim Dean of the Graduate School, 334-844-2125.

Colorado State University, College of Veterinary Medicine and Biomedical Sciences, Professional Program in Veterinary Medicine, Fort Collins, CO 80523-1601. Offers DVM, DVM/PhD, MBA/DVM. *Accreditation:* AVMA. *Students:* 548 full-time (437 women); includes 88 minority (1 Black or African American, non-Hispanic/Latino; 2 American Indian or Alaska Native, non-Hispanic/Latino; 19 Asian, non-Hispanic/Latino; 47 Hispanic/Latino; 19 Two or more races, non-Hispanic/Latino), 1 international. Average age 27. 1,501 applicants, 10% accepted, 137 enrolled. In 2011, 137 doctorates awarded. *Entrance requirements:* For doctorate, GRE General Test. Additional exam requirements/recommendations for international students: Required—TOEFL. *Application deadline:* For fall admission, 10/3 for domestic and international students. Application fee: $60. Electronic applications accepted. *Expenses:* Tuition, state resident: full-time $7992. Tuition, nonresident: full-time $19,592. *Required fees:* $1735; $58 per credit. *Financial support:* In 2011–12, 3 fellowships (averaging $42,008 per year) were awarded; research assistantships and teaching assistantships also available. Financial award application deadline: 3/1; financial award applicants required to submit FAFSA. *Faculty research:* Animal reproduction, infectious diseases, cancer biology, musculoskeletal research, neurobiology. *Total annual research expenditures:* $1.3 million. *Unit head:* Dr. Peter Hellyer, Associate Dean, 970-491-2009, E-mail: peter.hellyer@colostate.edu. *Application contact:* Dr. Sherry Stewart, Assistant Dean of Admissions and Student Affairs, 970-491-7054, Fax: 970-491-2250, E-mail: sherry.stewart@colostate.edu. Web site: http://www.cvmbs.colostate.edu/.

Cornell University, College of Veterinary Medicine, Ithaca, NY 14853-0001. Offers veterinary medicine (DVM). *Accreditation:* AVMA. *Faculty:* 179 full-time (66 women). *Students:* 360 full-time (282 women); includes 60 minority (9 Black or African American, non-Hispanic/Latino; 2 American Indian or Alaska Native, non-Hispanic/Latino; 20 Asian, non-Hispanic/Latino; 22 Hispanic/Latino; 7 Two or more races, non-Hispanic/Latino). Average age 26. 917 applicants, 13% accepted, 102 enrolled. In 2011, 87 doctorates awarded. *Entrance requirements:* For doctorate, GRE General Test or MCAT, animal or veterinary experience, letters of recommendation. Additional exam requirements/recommendations for international students: Required—TOEFL. *Application deadline:* For fall admission, 10/1 for domestic and international students. Application fee: $65. Electronic applications accepted. *Expenses:* Contact institution. *Financial support:* In 2011–12, 322 students received support. Federal Work-Study, institutionally sponsored loans, and scholarships/grants available. Financial award application deadline: 2/1; financial award applicants required to submit CSS PROFILE or FAFSA. *Faculty research:* Biomedical research, comparative cancer, infectious diseases/host response, reproductive biology, genetics/epigenetics. *Total annual research expenditures:* $53.4 million. *Unit head:* Dr. Michael Kotlikoff, Dean, 607-253-3771, Fax: 607-253-3701. *Application contact:* Jennifer A. Mailey, Director of Admissions, 607-253-3700, Fax: 607-253-3709, E-mail: jam333@cornell.edu. Web site: http://www.vet.cornell.edu/.

Iowa State University of Science and Technology, Department of Veterinary Diagnostic and Production Animal Medicine, Ames, IA 50011-1250. Offers veterinary preventative medicine (MS). *Degree requirements:* For master's, thesis or alternative. *Entrance requirements:* For master's, GRE General Test. Additional exam requirements/recommendations for international students: Required—TOEFL (minimum score 550 paper-based; 79 iBT), IELTS (minimum score 6.5). *Application deadline:* For fall admission, 2/1 for domestic and international students. Applications are processed on a rolling basis. Application fee: $40 ($90 for international students). Electronic applications accepted. *Financial support:* Scholarships/grants available. *Unit head:* Dr. H. Scott Hurd, Director of Graduate Education, 515-294-1761, Fax: 515-294-1072, E-mail: llayman@iastate.edu. *Application contact:* Lori Layman, Application Contact, 515-294-1761, Fax: 515-294-1072, E-mail: llayman@iastate.edu. Web site: http://vetmed.iastate.edu/vdpam/.

Iowa State University of Science and Technology, Professional Program in Veterinary Medicine, Ames, IA 50011. Offers DVM. *Accreditation:* AVMA.

Louisiana State University and Agricultural and Mechanical College, School of Veterinary Medicine, Professional Program in Veterinary Medicine, Baton Rouge, LA 70803. Offers DVM. Enrollment limited to state and contract students and a limited number of highly qualified out-of-state applicants. *Students:* 335 full-time (254 women), 1 (woman) part-time; includes 33 minority (5 Black or African American, non-Hispanic/Latino; 2 Asian, non-Hispanic/Latino; 24 Hispanic/Latino; 2 Two or more races, non-Hispanic/Latino). Average age 26. 91 applicants, 100% accepted, 84 enrolled. In 2011, 81 doctorates awarded. *Entrance requirements:* For doctorate, GRE General Test or MCAT. Additional exam requirements/recommendations for international students: Required—TOEFL. *Application deadline:* For fall admission, 3/1 priority date for domestic students. Applications are processed on a rolling basis. *Expenses:* Contact institution. *Financial support:* In 2011–12, 294 students received support. Fellowships with full and partial tuition reimbursements available, research assistantships with full and partial tuition reimbursements available, teaching assistantships with full and partial tuition reimbursements available, Federal Work-Study, institutionally sponsored loans, health care benefits, tuition waivers (full and partial), and unspecified assistantships available. Financial award applicants required to submit FAFSA. *Faculty research:* Veterinary microbiology, pathology, immunology, anatomy, epidemiology. *Unit head:* Dr. Peter Haynes, Dean, 225-578-9903, E-mail: pfhaynes@vetmed.lsu.edu. *Application contact:* Dr. James E. Miller, Associate Dean, 225-578-9652, E-mail: jmille1@lsu.edu. Web site: http://www.vetmed.lsu.edu/.

Michigan State University, College of Veterinary Medicine, Professional Program in Veterinary Medicine, East Lansing, MI 48824. Offers veterinary medicine (DVM); veterinary medicine/medical scientist training program (DVM). *Accreditation:* AVMA. *Entrance requirements:* Additional exam requirements/recommendations for international students: Required—TOEFL. Electronic applications accepted. *Expenses:* Contact institution.

Mississippi State University, College of Veterinary Medicine, Professional Program in Veterinary Medicine, Mississippi State, MS 39762. Offers DVM. *Accreditation:* AVMA. *Entrance requirements:* For doctorate, VCAT, GRE, minimum GPA of 3.5 in math and science coursework and overall; letter of recommendation. Additional exam requirements/recommendations for international students: Required—TOEFL (minimum score 213 computer-based). *Application deadline:* For fall admission, 10/1 for domestic students. Application fee: $40. Electronic applications accepted. *Expenses:* Contact institution. *Faculty research:* Veterinary education, advancing research in veterinary medicine and biomedical fields. *Unit head:* Dr. Margaret Kern, Associate Dean for Academic Affairs, 662-325-1326, Fax: 662-325-8714, E-mail: kern@cvm.msstate.edu. *Application contact:* Missy Hadaway, Admissions Coordinator, 662-325-9065, Fax: 662-325-8714, E-mail: hadaway@cvm.msstate.edu. Web site: http://www.cvm.msstate.edu/

North Carolina State University, College of Veterinary Medicine, Professional Program, Raleigh, NC 27695. Offers DVM. *Entrance requirements:* For doctorate, GRE. Additional exam requirements/recommendations for international students: Required—TOEFL.

North Carolina State University, College of Veterinary Medicine, Program in Specialized Veterinary Medicine, Raleigh, NC 27695. Offers MSpVM. *Accreditation:* AVMA. *Degree requirements:* For master's, thesis optional. *Entrance requirements:* For master's, GRE General Test. Additional exam requirements/recommendations for international students: Required—TOEFL (minimum score 550 paper-based; 213 computer-based). Electronic applications accepted. *Faculty research:* Cell biology, infectious diseases, pharmacology and toxicology, genomics, pathology and population medicine.

North Carolina State University, College of Veterinary Medicine, Program in Veterinary Public Health, Raleigh, NC 27695. Offers MVPH. *Degree requirements:* For master's, thesis optional. Electronic applications accepted.

Oklahoma State University, Center for Veterinary Health Sciences, Professional Program in Veterinary Medicine, Stillwater, OK 74078. Offers DVM. *Accreditation:* AVMA. *Entrance requirements:* For doctorate, GRE General Test, GRE Subject Test (biology). Electronic applications accepted. *Expenses:* Tuition, state resident: full-time $4044; part-time $168.50 per credit hour. Tuition, nonresident: full-time $16,008; part-time $667 per credit hour. *Required fees:* $2122; $88.45 per credit hour. One-time fee: $50. Tuition and fees vary according to course load and campus/location. *Faculty research:* Infectious diseases, physiology, toxicology, biomedical lasers, clinical studies.

Oregon State University, College of Veterinary Medicine, Veterinary Medicine Professional Program, Corvallis, OR 97331. Offers DVM. Program admissions open only to residents of Oregon and other states participating in the Western Interstate Commission for Higher Education. *Accreditation:* AVMA. *Entrance requirements:* For doctorate, VCAT and/or GRE, minimum GPA of 3.3 during previous 2 years, 3.2 overall.

Purdue University, School of Veterinary Medicine, Professional Program in Veterinary Medicine, West Lafayette, IN 47907. Offers DVM, DVM/MS, DVM/PhD. *Accreditation:* AVMA. *Entrance requirements:* For doctorate, GRE General Test. Additional exam requirements/recommendations for international students: Required—TOEFL. Electronic applications accepted.

Texas A&M University, College of Veterinary Medicine and Biomedical Sciences, Department of Large Animal Clinical Sciences, College Station, TX 77843. Offers MS. *Faculty:* 3. *Students:* 6 full-time (4 women), 4 part-time (all women), 1 international. Average age 30. *Degree requirements:* For master's, thesis (for some programs). *Entrance requirements:* For master's, GRE General Test. Additional exam requirements/recommendations for international students: Required—TOEFL. Application fee: $50 ($75 for international students). *Expenses:* Tuition, state resident: full-time $5437; part-time $226.55 per credit hour. Tuition, nonresident: full-time $12,949; part-time $539.55 per credit hour. *Required fees:* $2741. *Financial support:* In 2011–12, fellowships with tuition reimbursements (averaging $37,500 per year), research assistantships (averaging $30,700 per year), teaching assistantships (averaging $37,500 per year) were awarded. Financial award application deadline: 4/1; financial award applicants required to submit FAFSA. *Faculty research:* Epidemiology, including environmental and food safety; veterinary clinical studies. *Unit head:* Dr. William Moyer, Head, 979-845-9127, Fax: 979-847-8863, E-mail: wmoyer@tamu.edu. *Application contact:* Dr. James A. Thompson, Graduate Advisor, 979-845-3541, Fax: 979-847-8863, E-mail: jthompson@cvm.tamu.edu. Web site: http://vetmed.tamu.edu/vlcs.

Texas A&M University, College of Veterinary Medicine and Biomedical Sciences, Professional Programs in Veterinary Medicine, College Station, TX 77843. Offers DVM, DVM/PhD. *Accreditation:* AVMA. *Faculty:* 1. *Students:* 551 full-time (417 women), 1 (woman) part-time; includes 80 minority (6 Black or African American, non-Hispanic/Latino; 2 American Indian or Alaska Native, non-Hispanic/Latino; 19 Asian, non-Hispanic/Latino; 50 Hispanic/Latino; 3 Two or more races, non-Hispanic/Latino), 6 international. Average age 24. In 2011, 3 doctorates awarded. *Entrance requirements:* For doctorate, GRE. *Application deadline:* For fall admission, 9/1 for domestic students. Application fee: $100. *Expenses:* Contact institution. *Financial support:* Application deadline: 4/1; applicants required to submit FAFSA. *Faculty research:* Reproductive biology, theriogenology, genetics, endocrinology, animal behavior. *Unit head:* Dr. Eleanor Green, Dean, 979-845-5053, E-mail: emgreen@tamu.edu. *Application contact:* Yolanda Brinkman, Academic Coordinator, 979-458-0379, Fax: 979-845-5088, E-mail: ymbrinkman@cvm.tamu.edu. Web site: http://www.cvm.tamu.edu/dcvm/admissions/index.shtml.

Tufts University, Cummings School of Veterinary Medicine, North Grafton, MA 01536. Offers animals and public policy (MS); biomedical sciences (PhD), including digestive diseases, infectious diseases, neuroscience and reproductive biology, pathology; conservation medicine (MS); veterinary medicine (DVM); DVM/MPH, DVM/MS. *Accreditation:* AVMA (one or more programs are accredited). *Faculty:* 93 full-time (42 women), 14 part-time/adjunct (7 women). *Students:* 381 full-time (326 women); includes 47 minority (3 Black or African American, non-Hispanic/Latino; 4 American Indian or Alaska Native, non-Hispanic/Latino; 23 Asian, non-Hispanic/Latino; 16 Hispanic/Latino; 1 Two or more races, non-Hispanic/Latino), 7 international. Average age 25. 762 applicants, 33% accepted, 122 enrolled. In 2011, 8 master's, 80 doctorates awarded. *Degree requirements:* For master's, thesis (for some programs); for doctorate, comprehensive exam, thesis/dissertation (for some programs). *Entrance requirements:* For master's and doctorate, GRE General Test. Additional exam requirements/recommendations for international students: Required—TOEFL or IELTS. *Application deadline:* For fall admission, 11/1 for domestic and international students. Application fee: $70. Electronic applications accepted. *Expenses:* Contact institution. *Financial support:* In 2011–12, 245 students received support, including 6 research assistantships with full tuition reimbursements available (averaging $25,000 per year), 4 teaching assistantships (averaging $5,000 per year); career-related internships or

fieldwork, Federal Work-Study, institutionally sponsored loans, scholarships/grants, and institutional aid awards; health care benefits for PhD students also available. Financial award application deadline: 5/15; financial award applicants required to submit FAFSA. *Faculty research:* Oncology, veterinary ethics, international veterinary medicine, veterinary genomics, pathogenesis of Clostridium difficile, wildlife fertility control. *Unit head:* Dr. Deborah T. Kochevar, Dean, 508-839-5302, Fax: 508-839-2953, E-mail: deborah.kochevar@tufts.edu. *Application contact:* Rebecca Russo, Director of Admissions, 508-839-7920, Fax: 508-887-4820, E-mail: vetadmissions@tufts.edu. Web site: http://www.tufts.edu/.

Tuskegee University, Graduate Programs, College of Veterinary Medicine, Nursing and Allied Health, School of Veterinary Medicine, Tuskegee, AL 36088. Offers MS, DVM. *Faculty:* 62 full-time (6 women). *Students:* 287 full-time (216 women), 8 part-time (7 women); includes 210 minority (183 Black or African American, non-Hispanic/Latino; 2 American Indian or Alaska Native, non-Hispanic/Latino; 1 Asian, non-Hispanic/Latino; 24 Hispanic/Latino), 9 international. Average age 31. 281 applicants, 26% accepted. In 2011, 6 master's, 59 doctorates awarded. *Degree requirements:* For master's, thesis. *Entrance requirements:* For master's, GRE General Test; for doctorate, VCAT. Additional exam requirements/recommendations for international students: Required—TOEFL (minimum score 500 paper-based; 69 computer-based). *Application deadline:* For fall admission, 7/15 for domestic students. Applications are processed on a rolling basis. Application fee: $25 ($35 for international students). *Expenses: Tuition:* Full-time $17,070; part-time $705 per credit hour. *Financial support:* Application deadline: 4/15. *Unit head:* Dr. Tsegaye Habtemariam, Dean, 334-727-8174, Fax: 334-727-8177. *Application contact:* Dr. Robert L. Laney, Jr., Vice President/Director of Admissions and Enrollment Management, 334-727-8580, Fax: 334-727-5750, E-mail: planey@tuskegee.edu.

Université de Montréal, Faculty of Veterinary Medicine, Professional Program in Veterinary Medicine, Montréal, QC H3C 3J7, Canada. Offers DES. Open only to Canadian residents. *Accreditation:* AVMA. Part-time programs available. Electronic applications accepted. *Faculty research:* Animal reproduction, infectious diseases of swine, physiology of exercise in horses, viral diseases of cattle, health management and epidemiology.

University of California, Davis, School of Veterinary Medicine, Program in Veterinary Medicine, Davis, CA 95616. Offers DVM, DVM/MPVM. *Accreditation:* AVMA. *Entrance requirements:* For doctorate, GRE General Test. Additional exam requirements/recommendations for international students: Required—TOEFL. Electronic applications accepted.

University of Florida, College of Veterinary Medicine, Professional Program in Veterinary Medicine, Gainesville, FL 32611. Offers DVM. *Accreditation:* AVMA. *Entrance requirements:* For doctorate, GRE General Test.

University of Georgia, College of Veterinary Medicine, Athens, GA 30602. Offers MAM, MFAM, MS, DVM, PhD. *Accreditation:* AVMA (one or more programs are accredited). *Faculty:* 111 full-time (44 women), 11 part-time/adjunct (2 women). *Students:* 156 full-time (99 women), 5 part-time (2 women); includes 14 minority (6 Asian, non-Hispanic/Latino; 2 Hispanic/Latino; 6 Two or more races, non-Hispanic/Latino), 47 international. Average age 30. 120 applicants, 35% accepted, 23 enrolled. In 2011, 11 master's, 15 doctorates awarded. *Degree requirements:* For doctorate, variable foreign language requirement, thesis/dissertation (for some programs). *Entrance requirements:* For master's, GRE General Test; for doctorate, GRE General Test; GRE Subject Test in biology (for DVM). *Application deadline:* For fall admission, 7/1 priority date for domestic students; for spring admission, 11/15 for domestic students. Application fee: $50. Electronic applications accepted. *Expenses:* Contact institution. *Financial support:* Fellowships, research assistantships, teaching assistantships, Federal Work-Study, scholarships/grants, and unspecified assistantships available. Financial award applicants required to submit FAFSA. *Unit head:* Dr. Sheila W. Allen, Dean, 706-542-3461, Fax: 706-542-8254, E-mail: sallen01@uga.edu. *Application contact:* Malik McKinley, Director of Graduate Admissions, 706-542-5727, E-mail: dvmadmit@uga.edu. Web site: http://www.vet.uga.edu.

University of Guelph, Ontario Veterinary College and Graduate Studies, Graduate Programs in Veterinary Sciences, Department of Clinical Studies, Guelph, ON N1G 2W1, Canada. Offers anesthesiology (M Sc, DV Sc); cardiology (DV Sc, Diploma); clinical studies (Diploma); dermatology (M Sc); diagnostic imaging (M Sc, DV Sc); emergency/critical care (M Sc, DV Sc, Diploma); medicine (M Sc, DV Sc); neurology (M Sc, DV Sc); ophthalmology (M Sc, DV Sc); surgery (M Sc, DV Sc). *Degree requirements:* For master's, thesis; for doctorate, comprehensive exam, thesis/dissertation. *Entrance requirements:* Additional exam requirements/recommendations for international students: Required—TOEFL (minimum score 550 paper-based; 213 computer-based), IELTS (minimum score 6.5). Electronic applications accepted. *Faculty research:* Orthopedics, respirology, oncology, exercise physiology, cardiology.

University of Illinois at Urbana–Champaign, College of Veterinary Medicine, Professional Program in Veterinary Medicine, Champaign, IL 61820. Offers veterinary medical science (DVM). *Accreditation:* AVMA. *Faculty:* 49 full-time (24 women), 5 part-time/adjunct (2 women). *Students:* 490 full-time (391 women), 3 part-time (2 women); includes 52 minority (6 Black or African American, non-Hispanic/Latino; 1 American Indian or Alaska Native, non-Hispanic/Latino; 15 Asian, non-Hispanic/Latino; 24 Hispanic/Latino; 6 Two or more races, non-Hispanic/Latino), 1 international. 245 applicants, 88% accepted, 132 enrolled. In 2011, 116 doctorates awarded. *Entrance requirements:* For doctorate, GRE. Application fee: $75 ($90 for international students). Electronic applications accepted. *Expenses:* Contact institution. *Financial support:* In 2011–12, 3 fellowships, 1 research assistantship, 1 teaching assistantship were awarded; tuition waivers (full and partial) also available. *Unit head:* Herbert Whiteley, Dean, 217-333-2760, Fax: 217-333-4628, E-mail: hwhitele@illinois.edu. *Application contact:* Mary Anna Kelm, Assistant Dean for Academic and Student Affairs, 217-333-1192, Fax: 217-333-4628, E-mail: marykelm@illinois.edu. Web site: http://vetmed.illinois.edu/.

University of Maryland, College Park, Academic Affairs, College of Agriculture and Natural Resources, Maryland Campus of VA/MD Regional College of Veterinary Medicine, Professional Program in Veterinary Medicine, College Park, MD 20742. Offers DVM. *Accreditation:* AVMA. *Students:* 115 full-time (96 women); includes 20 minority (1 Black or African American, non-Hispanic/Latino; 11 Asian, non-Hispanic/Latino; 7 Hispanic/Latino; 1 Native Hawaiian or other Pacific Islander, non-Hispanic/Latino). 30 applicants, 97% accepted, 27 enrolled. In 2011, 25 doctorates awarded. *Degree requirements:* For doctorate, thesis/dissertation, oral exam, public seminar. Application fee: $75. *Expenses: Tuition,* state resident: part-time $525 per credit hour. *Tuition,* nonresident: part-time $1131 per credit hour. *Required fees:* $386.31 per term. Tuition and fees vary according to program. *Unit head:* Dr. Siba K. Samal, Chair, 301-314-6813, Fax: 301-314-6855, E-mail: ssamal@umd.edu. *Application contact:* Dr. Charles A. Caramello, Dean of Graduate School, 301-405-0358, Fax: 301-314-9305.

University of Minnesota, Twin Cities Campus, College of Veterinary Medicine, Professional Program in Veterinary Medicine, Minneapolis, MN 55455-0213. Offers DVM, DVM/PhD. *Accreditation:* AVMA. *Entrance requirements:* For doctorate, GRE General Test. Electronic applications accepted. *Expenses:* Contact institution. *Faculty*

research: Infectious toxic diseases of animals, zoonotic animal models of human disease, epidemiologic and preventive medicine.

University of Missouri, College of Veterinary Medicine, Professional Program in Veterinary Medicine, Columbia, MO 65211. Offers DVM. *Accreditation:* AVMA. *Faculty:* 113 full-time (37 women), 8 part-time/adjunct (3 women). *Students:* 322 full-time (250 women); includes 13 minority (1 Black or African American, non-Hispanic/Latino; 1 American Indian or Alaska Native, non-Hispanic/Latino; 4 Asian, non-Hispanic/Latino; 7 Hispanic/Latino). Average age 24. 334 applicants, 34% accepted, 111 enrolled. In 2011, 69 degrees awarded. *Entrance requirements:* For doctorate, VCAT, minimum GPA of 2.5 for state residents, 3.0 for nonresidents. *Application deadline:* For fall admission, 11/1 for domestic students. Electronic applications accepted. *Expenses:* Tuition, state resident: full-time $5881. Tuition, nonresident: full-time $15,183. *Required fees:* $952. Tuition and fees vary according to campus/location and program. *Financial support:* In 2011–12, 58 students received support. Fellowships, research assistantships, career-related internships or fieldwork, institutionally sponsored loans, tuition waivers (full), and research associateships available. *Faculty research:* Cardiovascular physiology, food safety, infectious diseases, laboratory animal medicine, ophthalmology. *Total annual research expenditures:* $4 million. *Unit head:* Dr. Neil C. Olson, Dean, E-mail: olsonne@missouri.edu. *Application contact:* Dr. C. B. Chastain, Associate Dean of Academic Affairs, E-mail: chastainc@missouri.edu. Web site: http://vetmed.missouri.edu/.

University of Pennsylvania, School of Veterinary Medicine, Philadelphia, PA 19104. Offers VMD, VMD/MBA, VMD/PhD. *Accreditation:* AVMA. *Faculty:* 125 full-time (56 women), 28 part-time/adjunct (11 women). *Students:* 458 full-time (346 women), 24 part-time (21 women); includes 46 minority (6 Black or African American, non-Hispanic/Latino; 1 American Indian or Alaska Native, non-Hispanic/Latino; 20 Asian, non-Hispanic/Latino; 16 Hispanic/Latino; 3 Two or more races, non-Hispanic/Latino), 2 international. Average age 24. 1,295 applicants, 14% accepted, 116 enrolled. In 2011, 112 degrees awarded. *Entrance requirements:* For doctorate, GRE. Additional exam requirements/recommendations for international students: Required—TOEFL. *Application deadline:* For fall admission, 10/1 for domestic students. Application fee: $0. *Expenses:* Contact institution. *Financial support:* Career-related internships or fieldwork, Federal Work-Study, and institutionally sponsored loans available. *Total annual research expenditures:* $25 million. *Unit head:* Dr. Joan C. Hendricks, Dean, 215-898-8841, Fax: 215-573-8837, E-mail: vetdean@vet.upenn.edu. *Application contact:* Malcolm Keiter, Assistant Dean for Admissions, 215-898-5434, Fax: 215-573-8819, E-mail: admissions@vet.upenn.edu. Web site: http://www.vet.upenn.edu/.

University of Prince Edward Island, Atlantic Veterinary College, Professional Program in Veterinary Medicine, Charlottetown, PE C1A 4P3, Canada. Offers DVM. *Accreditation:* AVMA. *Entrance requirements:* For doctorate, GRE. Additional exam requirements/recommendations for international students: Required—TOEFL (minimum score 550 paper-based; 213 computer-based; 80 iBT), Canadian Academic English Language Assessment, Michigan English Language Assessment Battery, Canadian Test of English for Scholars and Trainees. *Faculty research:* Shellfish toxicology, animal nutrition, fish health, toxicology, animal health management.

University of Saskatchewan, Western College of Veterinary Medicine and College of Graduate Studies and Research, Graduate Programs in Veterinary Medicine, Department of Large Animal Clinical Sciences, Saskatoon, SK S7N 5A2, Canada. Offers M Sc, M Vet Sc, PhD. *Degree requirements:* For master's, thesis (for some programs); for doctorate, comprehensive exam (for some programs), thesis/dissertation. *Entrance requirements:* Additional exam requirements/recommendations for international students: Required—TOEFL (minimum score 80 iBT); Recommended—IELTS (minimum score 6.5). Electronic applications accepted. *Faculty research:* Reproduction, infectious diseases, epidemiology, food safety.

University of Saskatchewan, Western College of Veterinary Medicine and College of Graduate Studies and Research, Graduate Programs in Veterinary Medicine, Department of Small Animal Clinical Sciences, Saskatoon, SK S7N 5A2, Canada. Offers small animal clinical sciences (M Sc, PhD); veterinary anesthesiology, radiology and surgery (M Vet Sc); veterinary internal medicine (M Vet Sc). *Degree requirements:* For master's, thesis (for some programs); for doctorate, comprehensive exam (for some programs), thesis/dissertation. *Entrance requirements:* Additional exam requirements/recommendations for international students: Required—TOEFL (minimum score 80 iBT); Recommended—IELTS (minimum score 6.5). Electronic applications accepted. *Faculty research:* Orthopedics, wildlife, cardiovascular exercise/myelopathy, ophthalmology.

University of Saskatchewan, Western College of Veterinary Medicine, Professional Program in Veterinary Medicine, Saskatoon, SK S7N 5A2, Canada. Offers DVM. *Accreditation:* AVMA. *Degree requirements:* For doctorate, thesis/dissertation.

The University of Tennessee, Graduate School, College of Veterinary Medicine, Knoxville, TN 37996. Offers DVM. *Accreditation:* AVMA. *Entrance requirements:* For doctorate, VCAT, interview, minimum GPA of 2.7. Additional exam requirements/recommendations for international students: Required—TOEFL. *Expenses:* Contact institution.

University of Wisconsin–Madison, School of Veterinary Medicine, Madison, WI 53706-1380. Offers MS, DVM, PhD. *Accreditation:* AVMA (one or more programs are accredited). Terminal master's awarded for partial completion of doctoral program. *Degree requirements:* For master's, thesis; for doctorate, thesis/dissertation (for some programs). *Entrance requirements:* For doctorate, GRE General Test (for DVM). *Expenses:* Contact institution. *Faculty research:* Infectious disease, ophthalmology, orthopedics, food animal production, oncology, cardio-respiratory.

Virginia Polytechnic Institute and State University, Virginia-Maryland Regional College of Veterinary Medicine, Professional Programs in Veterinary Medicine, Blacksburg, VA 24061. Offers DVM. *Accreditation:* AVMA. *Entrance requirements:* Additional exam requirements/recommendations for international students: Required—TOEFL (minimum score 550 paper-based; 213 computer-based). *Application deadline:* For fall admission, 7/1 for domestic and international students; for spring admission, 12/1 for domestic and international students. Applications are processed on a rolling basis. Application fee: $65. Electronic applications accepted. *Expenses:* Contact institution. *Financial support:* Career-related internships or fieldwork, Federal Work-Study, scholarships/grants, health care benefits, and unspecified assistantships available. *Unit head:* Dr. Roger J. Avery, Unit Head, 540-231-5649, Fax: 540-231-7367, E-mail: avery@vt.edu. *Application contact:* Becky Jones, Information Contact, 540-231-4992, Fax: 540-231-7367, E-mail: vmsgrad@vt.edu. Web site: http://www.vetmed.vt.edu/acad/dvm/.

Washington State University, College of Veterinary Medicine, Professional Program in Veterinary Medicine, Pullman, WA 99164. Offers DVM, DVM/MS, DVM/PhD. *Accreditation:* AVMA. *Faculty:* 39 full-time (6 women), 19 part-time/adjunct (6 women). *Students:* 390 full-time (306 women); includes 43 minority (8 American Indian or Alaska Native, non-Hispanic/Latino; 19 Asian, non-Hispanic/Latino; 13 Hispanic/Latino; 3 Two or more races, non-Hispanic/Latino). Average age 25. 1,086 applicants, 14% accepted, 91 enrolled. In 2011, 96 doctorates awarded. *Entrance requirements:* For doctorate, GRE General Test. Additional exam requirements/recommendations for international students: Required—TOEFL. *Application deadline:* For fall admission, 10/3 for domestic

and international students. Application fee: $60. Electronic applications accepted. *Financial support:* In 2011–12, 326 students received support. Research assistantships, teaching assistantships, career-related internships or fieldwork, Federal Work-Study, institutionally sponsored loans, scholarships/grants, traineeships, and tuition waivers (partial) available. Support available to part-time students. Financial award application deadline: 2/15; financial award applicants required to submit FAFSA. *Faculty research:* Biotechnology, immunology, pathology, neurosciences, clinical sciences. *Unit head:* Dr. Patricia Talcott, Director of Admissions, 509-355-1532. *Application contact:* Barbara Hodson, Program Coordinator, 509-335-1532, Fax: 509-335-6133, E-mail: bhodson@vetmed.wsu.edu. Web site: http://www.vetmed.wsu.edu/.

Western University of Health Sciences, College of Veterinary Medicine, Pomona, CA 91766-1854. Offers DVM. *Accreditation:* AVMA. *Faculty:* 54 full-time (25 women), 3 part-time/adjunct (1 woman). *Students:* 399 full-time (317 women); includes 107 minority (5 Black or African American, non-Hispanic/Latino; 7 American Indian or Alaska Native, non-Hispanic/Latino; 58 Asian, non-Hispanic/Latino; 29 Hispanic/Latino; 4 Native Hawaiian or other Pacific Islander, non-Hispanic/Latino; 4 Two or more races, non-Hispanic/Latino), 6 international. Average age 27. 735 applicants, 24% accepted, 101 enrolled. In 2011, 97 doctorates awarded. *Degree requirements:* For doctorate, comprehensive exam (for some programs). *Entrance requirements:* For doctorate, MCAT or GRE General Test, minimum GPA of 2.75, letters of recommendation, interview. Additional exam requirements/recommendations for international students: Required—TOEFL (minimum score 550 paper-based; 213 computer-based). *Application deadline:* For fall admission, 10/1 for domestic students. Application fee: $50. Electronic applications accepted. *Expenses:* Contact institution. *Financial support:* Institutionally sponsored loans, scholarships/grants, and veterans educational benefits available. Financial award application deadline: 3/2; financial award applicants required to submit FAFSA. *Unit head:* Dr. Phil Nelson, Dean, 909-469-5637, Fax: 909-469-5635. *Application contact:* Karen Hutton-Lopez, Director of Admissions, 909-469-5650, Fax: 909-469-5570, E-mail: admissions@westernu.edu. Web site: http://www.westernu.edu/veterinary.

Veterinary Sciences

Auburn University, College of Veterinary Medicine and Graduate School, Graduate Programs in Veterinary Medicine, Auburn University, AL 36849. Offers biomedical sciences (MS, PhD), including anatomy, physiology and pharmacology (MS), biomedical sciences (PhD), clinical sciences (MS), large animal surgery and medicine (MS), pathobiology (MS), radiology (MS), small animal surgery and medicine (MS); DVM/MS. Part-time programs available. *Faculty:* 100 full-time (40 women), 5 part-time/adjunct (1 woman). *Students:* 17 full-time (13 women), 59 part-time (33 women); includes 6 minority (1 Black or African American, non-Hispanic/Latino; 3 Asian, non-Hispanic/Latino; 2 Hispanic/Latino), 30 international. Average age 30. 36 applicants, 69% accepted, 11 enrolled. In 2011, 19 master's awarded. *Degree requirements:* For doctorate, thesis/dissertation. *Entrance requirements:* For master's, GRE General Test; for doctorate, GRE General Test, GRE Subject Test. *Application deadline:* For fall admission, 7/7 for domestic students; for spring admission, 11/24 for domestic students. Applications are processed on a rolling basis. Application fee: $50 ($60 for international students). Electronic applications accepted. *Expenses:* Tuition, state resident: full-time $7290; part-time $405 per credit hour. Tuition, nonresident: full-time $21,870; part-time $1215 per credit hour. *International tuition:* $22,000 full-time. *Required fees:* $1402. *Financial support:* Research assistantships, teaching assistantships, and Federal Work-Study available. Support available to part-time students. Financial award application deadline: 3/15; financial award applicants required to submit FAFSA. *Unit head:* Dr. Calvin Johnson, Acting Dean, 334-844-2650. *Application contact:* Dr. George Flowers, Dean of the Graduate School, 334-844-2125.

Clemson University, Graduate School, College of Agriculture, Forestry and Life Sciences, Department of Animal and Veterinary Sciences, Clemson, SC 29634. Offers animal and veterinary sciences (MS, PhD). *Faculty:* 10 full-time (5 women), 1 part-time/adjunct (0 women). *Students:* 9 full-time (6 women), 1 (woman) part-time; includes 1 minority (Black or African American, non-Hispanic/Latino), 1 international. Average age 29. 11 applicants, 45% accepted, 2 enrolled. In 2011, 3 doctorates awarded. *Degree requirements:* For doctorate, thesis/dissertation. *Entrance requirements:* For master's and doctorate, GRE General Test. Additional exam requirements/recommendations for international students: Required—TOEFL. *Application deadline:* For fall admission, 4/15 for international students; for spring admission, 9/15 for international students. Applications are processed on a rolling basis. Application fee: $70 ($80 for international students). Electronic applications accepted. *Expenses:* Contact institution. *Financial support:* In 2011–12, 8 students received support, including 6 research assistantships with partial tuition reimbursements available (averaging $12,667 per year), 4 teaching assistantships with partial tuition reimbursements available (averaging $14,750 per year); fellowships with full and partial tuition reimbursements available, career-related internships or fieldwork, Federal Work-Study, institutionally sponsored loans, scholarships/grants, and unspecified assistantships also available. Financial award applicants required to submit FAFSA. *Total annual research expenditures:* $1.1 million. *Unit head:* Dr. Susan K. Duckett, Chair, 864-656-2570, Fax: 864-656-3131, E-mail: sducket@clemson.edu. *Application contact:* Dr. Denzil Maurice, 864-656-4023, E-mail: dmrc@clemson.edu. Web site: http://www.clemson.edu/avs.

Colorado State University, College of Veterinary Medicine and Biomedical Sciences, Department of Clinical Sciences, Fort Collins, CO 80523-1678. Offers MS, PhD. Part-time programs available. *Faculty:* 59 full-time (22 women), 2 part-time/adjunct (1 woman). *Students:* 15 full-time (10 women), 50 part-time (32 women); includes 5 minority (2 Asian, non-Hispanic/Latino; 3 Hispanic/Latino), 17 international. Average age 33. 24 applicants, 79% accepted, 16 enrolled. In 2011, 16 master's, 2 doctorates awarded. *Degree requirements:* For master's, comprehensive exam (for some programs), thesis (for some programs), exam; for doctorate, comprehensive exam, thesis/dissertation, exam. *Entrance requirements:* For master's, minimum GPA of 3.0, DVM or other equivalent medical degree, 3 letters of recommendation; for doctorate, DVM or other equivalent medical degree, 3 letters of recommendation, biographical statement. Additional exam requirements/recommendations for international students: Recommended—TOEFL (minimum score 550 paper-based; 213 computer-based; 80 iBT). *Application deadline:* For fall admission, 6/1 priority date for domestic students, 4/1 for international students; for spring admission, 11/1 for domestic students, 9/1 for international students. Applications are processed on a rolling basis. Application fee: $50. Electronic applications accepted. *Expenses:* Tuition, state resident: full-time $7992. Tuition, nonresident: full-time $19,592. *Required fees:* $1735; $58 per credit. *Financial support:* In 2011–12, 28 students received support, including 13 fellowships (averaging $31,180 per year), 13 research assistantships with full and partial tuition reimbursements available (averaging $27,107 per year), 2 teaching assistantships (averaging $4,381 per year); Federal Work-Study, institutionally sponsored loans, and unspecified assistantships also available. Financial award application deadline: 2/15; financial award applicants required to submit FAFSA. *Faculty research:* Orthopedics, oncology, epidemiology, critical care/emergency medicine, equine medicine. *Total annual research expenditures:* $9.6 million. *Unit head:* Dr. D. Paul Lunn, Head, 970-297-1274, Fax: 970-297-1275, E-mail: david.lunn@colostate.edu. *Application contact:* Morna J. Mynard, Information Contact, 970-297-4030, Fax: 970-297-1275, E-mail: morna.mynard@colostate.edu. Web site: http://www.cvmbs.colostate.edu/clinsci/.

Drexel University, College of Medicine, Biomedical Graduate Programs, Program in Laboratory Animal Science, Philadelphia, PA 19104-2875. Offers MLAS. Part-time programs available. *Degree requirements:* For master's, comprehensive exam. *Entrance requirements:* For master's, GRE General Test, minimum GPA of 3.0. Additional exam requirements/recommendations for international students: Required—TOEFL. Electronic applications accepted. *Faculty research:* Laboratory animal medicine, experimental surgery, development of animal models for human diseases.

Iowa State University of Science and Technology, Department of Veterinary Clinical Sciences, Ames, IA 50011. Offers MS. *Degree requirements:* For master's, thesis or alternative. *Entrance requirements:* For master's, GRE. Additional exam requirements/recommendations for international students: Required—TOEFL (minimum score 550 paper-based; 79 iBT), IELTS (minimum score 6.5). Application fee: $40 ($90 for international students). Electronic applications accepted. *Faculty research:* Theriogenology, veterinary medicine, veterinary surgery, extracorporeal shock waves, therapy, orthopedic research in animals. *Unit head:* Dr. Albert Jergens, Director of Graduate Education, 515-294-6411, Fax: 515-294-9281, E-mail: dgilloon@iastate.edu. *Application contact:* Diane Gilloon, Application Contact, 515-294-6411, Fax: 515-294-9281, E-mail: dgilloon@iastate.edu. Web site: http://vetmed.iastate.edu/vcs/.

Iowa State University of Science and Technology, Department of Veterinary Microbiology and Preventive Medicine, Ames, IA 50011-1250. Offers veterinary microbiology (MS, PhD). *Entrance requirements:* For master's and doctorate, GRE General Test. Additional exam requirements/recommendations for international students: Required—TOEFL (minimum score 550 paper-based; 79 iBT), IELTS (minimum score 6.5). *Application deadline:* For fall admission, 2/1 priority date for domestic students, 2/1 for international students. Applications are processed on a rolling basis. Application fee: $40 ($90 for international students). Electronic applications accepted. *Faculty research:* Bacteriology, immunology, virology, public health and food safety. *Unit head:* Dr. Qijing Zhang, Director of Graduate Education, 515-294-5776, Fax: 515-294-8500, E-mail: vetmicro@iastate.edu. *Application contact:* Liz Westberg, Application Contact, 515-294-5776, Fax: 515-294-8500, E-mail: vetmicro@iastate.edu. Web site: http://vetmed.iastate.edu/vmpm.

Kansas State University, College of Veterinary Medicine, Department of Clinical Sciences, Manhattan, KS 66506. Offers MPH. *Faculty:* 31 full-time (12 women), 7 part-time/adjunct (6 women). *Students:* 42 full-time (27 women), 29 part-time (21 women); includes 12 minority (7 Black or African American, non-Hispanic/Latino; 2 Hispanic/Latino; 3 Two or more races, non-Hispanic/Latino), 9 international. Average age 29. 46 applicants, 65% accepted, 22 enrolled. In 2011, 9 master's awarded. *Degree requirements:* For master's, thesis. *Entrance requirements:* For master's, GRE, DVM. Additional exam requirements/recommendations for international students: Required—TOEFL (minimum score 550 paper-based; 213 computer-based). *Application deadline:* For fall admission, 2/1 priority date for domestic students, 2/1 for international students; for spring admission, 8/1 priority date for domestic students, 8/1 for international students. Applications are processed on a rolling basis. Application fee: $40 ($55 for international students). Electronic applications accepted. *Financial support:* In 2011–12, 11 research assistantships (averaging $30,118 per year) were awarded; institutionally sponsored loans and scholarships/grants also available. Financial award application deadline: 3/1; financial award applicants required to submit FAFSA. *Faculty research:* Clinical trials, equine gastrointestinal ulceration, leptospirosis, food animal pharmacology, equine immunology, diabetes. *Total annual research expenditures:* $1.5 million. *Unit head:* Dr. Michael Cates, Director and Professor, 785-532-2042, E-mail: cates@ksu.edu. *Application contact:* Barta Stevenson, Program Assistant, 785-532-2042, E-mail: bstevens@vet.k-state.edu. Web site: http://www.vet.k-state.edu/depts/ClinicalSciences/.

Louisiana State University and Agricultural and Mechanical College, School of Veterinary Medicine and Graduate School, Department of Comparative Biomedical Sciences, Baton Rouge, LA 70803. Offers MS, PhD. *Faculty:* 14 full-time (1 woman). *Students:* 12 full-time (3 women), 2 part-time (both women), 9 international. Average age 31. 5 applicants, 60% accepted, 3 enrolled. In 2011, 3 degrees awarded. *Degree requirements:* For master's, thesis; for doctorate, thesis/dissertation, final exam. *Entrance requirements:* For master's and doctorate, GRE, minimum GPA of 3.0. Additional exam requirements/recommendations for international students: Required—TOEFL (minimum score 550 paper-based; 213 computer-based; 79 iBT) or IELTS (minimum score 6.5). *Application deadline:* For fall admission, 5/15 for international students; for spring admission, 10/15 for international students. Electronic applications accepted. *Financial support:* In 2011–12, 13 students received support, including 3 fellowships with full and partial tuition reimbursements available (averaging $23,086 per year), 8 research assistantships with full and partial tuition reimbursements available (averaging $22,000 per year); teaching assistantships, Federal Work-Study, institutionally sponsored loans, scholarships/grants, health care benefits, and unspecified assistantships also available. Support available to part-time students. Financial award applicants required to submit FAFSA. *Faculty research:* Gene therapy, metastasis, DNA repair, cytokines in cardiovascular function, aquatic toxicology. *Total annual research expenditures:* $1.6 million. *Unit head:* Dr. George Strain, Chair, 225-578-9758, Fax: 225-578-9895, E-mail: strain@lsu.edu. *Application contact:* Dr. George M. Strain, Graduate Adviser, 225-578-9758, Fax: 225-578-9895, E-mail: strain@lsu.edu. Web site: http://www.vetmed.lsu.edu/van/.

Louisiana State University and Agricultural and Mechanical College, School of Veterinary Medicine and Graduate School, Department of Pathobiological Sciences, Baton Rouge, LA 70803. Offers MS, PhD. *Faculty:* 27 full-time (6 women). *Students:* 24 full-time (10 women), 12 part-time (8 women); includes 4 minority (3 Asian, non-Hispanic/Latino; 1 Hispanic/Latino), 15 international. Average age 31. 18 applicants, 39% accepted, 5 enrolled. In 2011, 5 degrees awarded. *Degree requirements:* For doctorate, thesis/dissertation. *Entrance requirements:* Additional exam requirements/

recommendations for international students: Required—TOEFL (minimum score 550 paper-based; 213 computer-based; 79 iBT) or IELTS (minimum score 6.5). *Application deadline:* For fall admission, 5/15 for international students; for spring admission, 10/15 for international students. Application fee: $50 ($70 for international students). Electronic applications accepted. *Financial support:* In 2011–12, 36 students received support, including 3 fellowships with full tuition reimbursements available (averaging $25,501 per year), 25 research assistantships with full and partial tuition reimbursements available (averaging $22,540 per year); teaching assistantships with full and partial tuition reimbursements available, Federal Work-Study, scholarships/grants, health care benefits, and unspecified assistantships also available. Support available to part-time students. Financial award applicants required to submit FAFSA. *Faculty research:* Infectious disease, host-pathogen interaction, vaccinology. *Total annual research expenditures:* $5.3 million. *Unit head:* Dr. Ronald Thune, Head, 225-578-9680, Fax: 225-578-9701, E-mail: thune@mail.vetmed.lsu.edu. *Application contact:* Dr. Kevin Macaluso, Graduate Adviser, 225-578-9677, Fax: 225-578-9701, E-mail: kmacaluso@vetmed.lsu.edu, Web site: http://www.vetmed.lsu.edu/pbs/.

Louisiana State University and Agricultural and Mechanical College, School of Veterinary Medicine and Graduate School, Department of Veterinary Clinical Sciences, Baton Rouge, LA 70803. Offers MS, PhD. *Faculty:* 33 full-time (15 women). *Students:* 7 full-time (5 women), 6 part-time (2 women); includes 1 minority (Hispanic/Latino), 8 international. Average age 30. In 2011, 2 degrees awarded. *Entrance requirements:* For master's and doctorate, GRE, DVM or equivalent degree. Additional exam requirements/recommendations for international students: Required—TOEFL (minimum score 550 paper-based; 213 computer-based; 79 iBT) or IELTS (minimum score 6.5). *Application deadline:* For fall admission, 5/15 for domestic and international students; for spring admission, 10/15 for international students. Application fee: $50 ($70 for international students). Electronic applications accepted. *Financial support:* In 2011–12, 13 students received support, including 7 research assistantships with full and partial tuition reimbursements available (averaging $23,263 per year); fellowships, teaching assistantships, Federal Work-Study, institutionally sponsored loans, scholarships/grants, health care benefits, and unspecified assistantships also available. Support available to part-time students. Financial award applicants required to submit FAFSA. *Faculty research:* Urology/nephrology, equine arthroscopy orthopedics and laser surgery, physical rehabilitation on companion animals, cardiology, gastroenterology, infectious diseases, medical oncology, mare infertility. *Total annual research expenditures:* $502,435. *Unit head:* Dr. Dale Paccamonti, Head, 225-578-9551, Fax: 225-578-9559, E-mail: pacc@lsu.edu. *Application contact:* Dr. Susan Eades, Graduate Adviser, 225-578-9512, Fax: 225-578-9559, E-mail: sceades@vetmed.lsu.edu. Web site: http://www.vetmed.lsu.edu/vcs/.

Michigan State University, College of Veterinary Medicine and The Graduate School, Graduate Programs in Veterinary Medicine, East Lansing, MI 48824. Offers comparative medicine and integrative biology (MS, PhD), including comparative medicine and integrative biology, comparative medicine and integrative biology–environmental toxicology (PhD); food safety and toxicology (MS), including food safety; integrative toxicology (PhD), including animal science–environmental toxicology, biochemistry and molecular biology–environmental toxicology, chemistry–environmental toxicology, crop and soil sciences–environmental toxicology, environmental engineering–environmental toxicology, environmental geosciences–environmental toxicology, fisheries and wildlife–environmental toxicology, food science–environmental toxicology, forestry–environmental toxicology, genetics–environmental toxicology, human nutrition–environmental toxicology, microbiology–environmental toxicology, pharmacology and toxicology–environmental toxicology, zoology–environmental toxicology; large animal clinical sciences (MS, PhD); microbiology and molecular genetics (MS, PhD), including industrial microbiology, microbiology, microbiology and molecular genetics, microbiology–environmental toxicology (PhD); pathobiology and diagnostic investigation (MS, PhD), including pathology, pathology–environmental toxicology (PhD); pharmacology and toxicology (MS, PhD); pharmacology and toxicology–environmental toxicology (PhD); physiology (MS, PhD); small animal clinical sciences (MS). Electronic applications accepted. *Faculty research:* Molecular genetics, food safety/toxicology, comparative orthopedics, airway disease, population medicine.

Mississippi State University, College of Veterinary Medicine, Office of Research and Graduate Studies, Mississippi State, MS 39762. Offers environmental toxicology (PhD); veterinary medical sciences (MS, PhD). Part-time programs available. *Faculty:* 91 full-time (28 women), 14 part-time/adjunct (6 women). *Students:* 53 full-time (34 women), 42 part-time (23 women); includes 10 minority (8 Black or African American, non-Hispanic/Latino; 1 Asian, non-Hispanic/Latino; 1 Hispanic/Latino), 25 international. Average age 31. 18 applicants, 61% accepted, 11 enrolled. In 2011, 10 master's, 4 doctorates awarded. Terminal master's awarded for partial completion of doctoral program. *Degree requirements:* For master's, thesis (for some programs); for doctorate, thesis/dissertation. *Entrance requirements:* For master's, minimum undergraduate GPA of 3.0, bachelor's degree; for doctorate, minimum undergraduate GPA of 3.0. Additional exam requirements/recommendations for international students: Required—TOEFL (minimum score 550 paper-based; 213 computer-based; 79 iBT); Recommended—IELTS (minimum score 6.5). *Application deadline:* For fall admission, 7/1 priority date for domestic students, 5/1 for international students; for spring admission, 11/1 priority date for domestic students, 9/1 for international students. Applications are processed on a rolling basis. Application fee: $40. Electronic applications accepted. *Expenses:* Contact institution. *Financial support:* In 2011–12, 36 research assistantships with partial tuition reimbursements (averaging $18,945 per year) were awarded; career-related internships or fieldwork, institutionally sponsored loans, scholarships/grants, and unspecified assistantships also available. Financial award application deadline: 4/1; financial award applicants required to submit FAFSA. *Faculty research:* Food animal health (poultry and warm-water aquaculture) using immunology, microbiology, molecular biology, parasitology, pathology, pharmacology, and environmental toxicology. *Unit head:* Dr. Mark L. Lawrence, Associate Dean of Research and Graduate Studies, 662-325-1205, Fax: 662-325-1193, E-mail: lawrence@cvm.msstate.edu. *Application contact:* Barbara E. Perrigin, Coordinator, Graduate Studies, 662-325-1417, Fax: 662-325-1193, E-mail: bperrigin@cvm.msstate.edu. Web site: http://www.cvm.msstate.edu/research/graduate.html.

North Carolina State University, College of Veterinary Medicine, Program in Comparative Biomedical Sciences, Raleigh, NC 27695. Offers cell biology (MS, PhD); infectious disease (MS, PhD); pathology (MS, PhD); pharmacology (MS, PhD); population medicine (MS, PhD). Part-time programs available. *Degree requirements:* For master's, thesis; for doctorate, thesis/dissertation. *Entrance requirements:* For master's and doctorate, GRE General Test. Additional exam requirements/recommendations for international students: Required—TOEFL (minimum score 550 paper-based; 213 computer-based). Electronic applications accepted. *Expenses:* Contact institution. *Faculty research:* Infectious diseases, cell biology, pharmacology and toxicology, genomics, pathology and population medicine.

North Dakota State University, College of Graduate and Interdisciplinary Studies, College of Agriculture, Food Systems, and Natural Resources, Department of Veterinary and Microbiological Sciences, Fargo, ND 58108. Offers food safety (MS); microbiology (MS); molecular pathogenesis (PhD). Part-time programs available. *Faculty:* 8 full-time (6 women). *Students:* 15 full-time (5 women), 5 part-time (3 women), 9 international. 24 applicants, 46% accepted, 3 enrolled. In 2011, 1 master's, 1 doctorate awarded. *Degree requirements:* For master's, thesis; for doctorate, thesis/dissertation, oral and written preliminary exams. *Entrance requirements:* For master's and doctorate, GRE. Additional exam requirements/recommendations for international students: Required—TOEFL (minimum score 525 paper-based; 197 computer-based; 71 iBT). *Application deadline:* For fall admission, 2/15 priority date for domestic students. Applications are processed on a rolling basis. Application fee: $35. *Financial support:* Fellowships with full tuition reimbursements, research assistantships with full tuition reimbursements, teaching assistantships with full tuition reimbursements, Federal Work-Study, and institutionally sponsored loans available. Financial award application deadline: 4/15. *Faculty research:* Bacterial gene regulation, antibiotic resistance, molecular virology, mechanisms of bacterial pathogenesis, immunology of animals. *Unit head:* Dr. Charlene Wolf-Hall, Head, 701-231-7667, E-mail: charlene.hall@ndsu.edu. *Application contact:* Dr. John McEvoy, Associate Professor, 701-231-8530, Fax: 701-231-7514, E-mail: eugene.berry@ndsu.edu. Web site: http://vetmicro.ndsu.nodak.edu/.

The Ohio State University, College of Veterinary Medicine, Program in Comparative and Veterinary Medicine, Columbus, OH 43210. Offers MS, PhD. *Faculty:* 113. *Students:* 77 full-time (49 women), 15 part-time (12 women); includes 3 minority (1 American Indian or Alaska Native, non-Hispanic/Latino; 2 Hispanic/Latino), 36 international. Average age 30. In 2011, 14 master's, 2 doctorates awarded. *Entrance requirements:* For master's and doctorate, GRE (for graduates of institutions not accredited by the AVMA). Additional exam requirements/recommendations for international students: Required—TOEFL (minimum score 550 paper-based; 250 computer-based; 79 iBT), Michigan English Language Assessment Battery (minimum score 82). *Application deadline:* Applications are processed on a rolling basis. Application fee: $40 ($50 for international students). Electronic applications accepted. *Expenses:* Tuition, state resident: full-time $11,400. Tuition, nonresident: full-time $28,125. Tuition and fees vary according to course load, degree level, campus/location and program. *Unit head:* Lonnie King, Dean, 614-688-8749, Fax: 614-292-3544, E-mail: king.1518@osu.edu. *Application contact:* Graduate Admissions, 614-292-6031, Fax: 614-292-3656, E-mail: gradadmissions@osu.edu. Web site: http://vet.osu.edu/education/graduate-programs.

Oklahoma State University, Center for Veterinary Health Sciences and Graduate College, Graduate Program in Veterinary Biomedical Sciences, Stillwater, OK 74078. Offers MS, PhD. Postbaccalaureate distance learning degree programs offered (no on-campus study). Terminal master's awarded for partial completion of doctoral program. *Degree requirements:* For master's, thesis; for doctorate, comprehensive exam, thesis/dissertation. *Entrance requirements:* For master's and doctorate, GRE General Test. Additional exam requirements/recommendations for international students: Required—TOEFL (minimum score 80 iBT). Electronic applications accepted. *Expenses:* Contact institution. *Faculty research:* Infectious and parasitic diseases, physiology, toxicology, biomedical lasers, clinical studies.

Oregon State University, College of Veterinary Medicine, Program in Comparative Veterinary Medicine, Corvallis, OR 97331. Offers MS. *Degree requirements:* For master's, one foreign language, thesis. *Entrance requirements:* For master's, minimum GPA of 3.0 in last 90 hours of course work. Additional exam requirements/recommendations for international students: Required—TOEFL. *Faculty research:* Microbiology, virology, toxicology.

Penn State Hershey Medical Center, College of Medicine, Graduate School Programs in the Biomedical Sciences, Graduate Program in Laboratory Animal Medicine, Hershey, PA 17033. Offers MS. *Students:* 5 full-time (3 women); includes 1 minority (Black or African American, non-Hispanic/Latino), 2 international. 2 applicants, 100% accepted, 2 enrolled. In 2011, 1 master's awarded. *Degree requirements:* For master's, thesis or alternative. *Entrance requirements:* For master's, GRE, DVM. Additional exam requirements/recommendations for international students: Required—TOEFL (minimum score 550 paper-based; 213 computer-based). *Application deadline:* For fall admission, 1/31 priority date for domestic students, 2/1 for international students. Applications are processed on a rolling basis. Application fee: $65. Electronic applications accepted. *Financial support:* In 2011–12, 2 students received support. Fellowships with full tuition reimbursements available, research assistantships with full tuition reimbursements available, scholarships/grants, traineeships, health care benefits, and unspecified assistantships available. Financial award applicants required to submit FAFSA. *Faculty research:* Veterinary pathology; pain, analgesia and anesthesia of lab animals; genetically modified animal models of cancer; transgenic animals. *Unit head:* Dr. Ronald P. Wilson, Chair, 717-531-8460, Fax: 717-531-5001, E-mail: grad-hmc@psu.edu. *Application contact:* Nannette Kirst, Program Aide, 717-531-8460, Fax: 717-531-5001, E-mail: nkirst@psu.edu. Web site: http://www.pennstatehershey.org/web/comparativemedicine/programs.

Penn State University Park, Graduate School, College of Agricultural Sciences, Department of Veterinary and Biomedical Sciences, State College, University Park, PA 16802-1503. Offers pathobiology (MS, PhD). *Unit head:* Dr. Bruce A. McPheron, Dean, 814-865-2541, Fax: 814-865-3103, E-mail: bam10@psu.edu. *Application contact:* Cynthia E. Nicosia, Director of Graduate Enrollment Services, 814-865-1834, E-mail: cey1@psu.edu. Web site: http://vbs.psu.edu/.

Purdue University, School of Veterinary Medicine and Graduate School, Graduate Programs in Veterinary Medicine, Department of Basic Medical Sciences, West Lafayette, IN 47907. Offers anatomy (MS, PhD); pharmacology (MS, PhD); physiology (MS, PhD). Part-time programs available. Terminal master's awarded for partial completion of doctoral program. *Degree requirements:* For master's, thesis; for doctorate, thesis/dissertation. *Entrance requirements:* For master's and doctorate, GRE General Test. Additional exam requirements/recommendations for international students: Required—TOEFL. Electronic applications accepted. *Faculty research:* Development and regeneration, tissue injury and shock, biomedical engineering, ovarian function, bone and cartilage biology, cell and molecular biology.

Purdue University, School of Veterinary Medicine and Graduate School, Graduate Programs in Veterinary Medicine, Department of Comparative Pathobiology, West Lafayette, IN 47907-2027. Offers comparative epidemiology and public health (MS); comparative epidemiology and public heath (PhD); comparative microbiology and immunology (MS, PhD); comparative pathobiology (MS, PhD); interdisciplinary studies (PhD), including microbial pathogenesis, molecular signaling and cancer biology, molecular virology; lab animal medicine (MS); veterinary anatomic pathology (MS); veterinary clinical pathology (MS). Terminal master's awarded for partial completion of doctoral program. *Degree requirements:* For master's, thesis (for some programs); for doctorate, thesis/dissertation. *Entrance requirements:* For master's and doctorate, GRE General Test. Additional exam requirements/recommendations for international students: Required—TOEFL (minimum score 575 paper-based; 232 computer-based), IELTS (minimum score 6.5), TWE (minimum score 4). Electronic applications accepted.

Purdue University, School of Veterinary Medicine and Graduate School, Graduate Programs in Veterinary Medicine, Department of Veterinary Clinical Sciences, West Lafayette, IN 47907. Offers MS, PhD. Degrees offered are post-DVM. Terminal master's awarded for partial completion of doctoral program. *Degree requirements:* For master's,

thesis (for some programs); for doctorate, thesis/dissertation. *Entrance requirements:* For master's and doctorate, DVM. *Faculty research:* Flow cytometry, chemotherapy, biologic response modifiers, broncho-alveolar lavage, lithotripsy.

South Dakota State University, Graduate School, College of Agriculture and Biological Sciences, Department of Veterinary and Biomedical Sciences, Brookings, SD 57007. Offers biological sciences (MS, PhD). Part-time and evening/weekend programs available. *Degree requirements:* For master's, thesis (for some programs), oral exam; for doctorate, comprehensive exam, thesis/dissertation, preliminary oral and written exams. *Entrance requirements:* Additional exam requirements/recommendations for international students: Required—TOEFL (minimum score 525 paper-based; 197 computer-based; 71 iBT). *Faculty research:* Infectious disease, food animal, virology, immunology.

Texas A&M University, College of Veterinary Medicine and Biomedical Sciences, Department of Veterinary Small Animal Medicine and Surgery, College Station, TX 77843. Offers MS. *Faculty:* 3. *Students:* 8 full-time (2 women); includes 2 minority (both Hispanic/Latino), 6 international. Average age 25. *Degree requirements:* For master's, thesis. *Entrance requirements:* For master's, GRE General Test. Additional exam requirements/recommendations for international students: Required—TOEFL. Application fee: $50 ($75 for international students). *Expenses:* Tuition, state resident: full-time $5437; part-time $226.55 per credit hour. Tuition, nonresident: full-time $12,949; part-time $539.55 per credit hour. *Required fees:* $2741. *Financial support:* In 2011–12, research assistantships with full tuition reimbursements (averaging $13,800 per year) were awarded; fellowships and teaching assistantships also available. Financial award application deadline: 3/1; financial award applicants required to submit FAFSA. *Faculty research:* Gastroenterology, anesthesiology, nephrology and urology, cardiology, nutrition. *Unit head:* Dr. Sandee Hartsfield, Head, 979-845-9051, Fax: 979-845-6978, E-mail: shartsfield@tamu.edu. *Application contact:* Graduate Admissions, 979-845-1044, E-mail: admissions@tamu.edu. Web site: http://vetmed.tamu.edu/vscs/.

Tuskegee University, Graduate Programs, College of Veterinary Medicine, Nursing and Allied Health, School of Veterinary Medicine, Tuskegee, AL 36088. Offers MS, DVM. *Faculty:* 62 full-time (6 women). *Students:* 287 full-time (216 women), 8 part-time (7 women); includes 210 minority (183 Black or African American, non-Hispanic/Latino; 2 American Indian or Alaska Native, non-Hispanic/Latino; 1 Asian, non-Hispanic/Latino; 24 Hispanic/Latino), 9 international. Average age 31. 281 applicants, 26% accepted. In 2011, 6 master's, 59 doctorates awarded. *Degree requirements:* For master's, thesis. *Entrance requirements:* For master's, GRE General Test; for doctorate, VCAT. Additional exam requirements/recommendations for international students: Required—TOEFL (minimum score 500 paper-based; 69 computer-based). *Application deadline:* For fall admission, 7/15 for domestic students. Applications are processed on a rolling basis. Application fee: $25 ($35 for international students). *Expenses: Tuition:* Full-time $17,070; part-time $705 per credit hour. *Financial support:* Application deadline: 4/15. *Unit head:* Dr. Tsegaye Habtemariam, Dean, 334-727-8174, Fax: 334-727-8177. *Application contact:* Dr. Robert L. Laney, Jr., Vice President/Director of Admissions and Enrollment Management, 334-727-8580, Fax: 334-727-5750, E-mail: planey@tuskegee.edu.

Université de Montréal, Faculty of Veterinary Medicine and Faculty of Graduate Studies, Graduate Programs in Veterinary Sciences, Montréal, QC H3C 3J7, Canada. Offers M Sc, PhD. *Degree requirements:* For master's, one foreign language, thesis optional. Electronic applications accepted. *Faculty research:* Animal reproduction, infectious diseases of swine, physiology of exercise in horses, viral diseases of cattle, health management and epidemiology.

University of California, Davis, School of Veterinary Medicine and Graduate Studies, Program in Preventive Veterinary Medicine, Davis, CA 95616. Offers MPVM, DVM/MPVM. Part-time programs available. *Degree requirements:* For master's, thesis. *Entrance requirements:* For master's, DVM or equivalent. Additional exam requirements/recommendations for international students: Required—TOEFL (minimum score 550 paper-based; 213 computer-based). *Faculty research:* Epidemiology, zoonoses, veterinary public health, wildlife and ecosystem health.

University of California, Davis, School of Veterinary Medicine, Residency Training Program, Davis, CA 95616. Offers Certificate. *Entrance requirements:* For degree, DVM or equivalent, 1 year of related experience. *Faculty research:* Small animal and large animal medicine, surgery, infectious diseases, pathology.

University of Florida, College of Veterinary Medicine, Graduate Program in Veterinary Medical Sciences, Gainesville, FL 32611. Offers forensic toxicology (Certificate); veterinary medical sciences (MS, PhD), including forensic toxicology (MS). Postbaccalaureate distance learning degree programs offered (no on-campus study). Terminal master's awarded for partial completion of doctoral program. *Degree requirements:* For master's, thesis; for doctorate, thesis/dissertation. *Entrance requirements:* For master's and doctorate, GRE General Test, minimum GPA of 3.0. Additional exam requirements/recommendations for international students: Required—TOEFL (minimum score 550 paper-based; 213 computer-based). Electronic applications accepted. *Expenses:* Contact institution.

University of Georgia, College of Veterinary Medicine, Department of Large Animal Medicine, Athens, GA 30602. Offers MS. *Faculty:* 8 full-time (3 women). *Students:* 11 full-time (8 women). Average age 29. 2 applicants, 100% accepted, 1 enrolled. Application fee is waived when completed online. *Unit head:* Dr. Andrew Hugh Parks, Head, 706-542-6372, E-mail: parksa@uga.edu. *Application contact:* Dr. John Peroni, Graduate Coordinator, 706-542-9321, Fax: 706-542-8833, E-mail: jperoni@uga.edu. Web site: http://www.vet.uga.edu/lam/index.php.

University of Georgia, College of Veterinary Medicine, Department of Population Health, Athens, GA 30602. Offers food animal medicine (MFAM); population health (MAM). *Faculty:* 23 full-time (6 women), 2 part-time/adjunct (0 women). *Students:* 5 full-time (2 women); includes 1 minority (Black or African American, non-Hispanic/Latino), 2 international. Average age 31. 1 applicant. In 2011, 2 master's awarded. *Entrance requirements:* For master's, GRE General Test. *Application deadline:* For fall admission, 7/1 priority date for domestic students; for spring admission, 11/15 for domestic students. Application fee: $50. Electronic applications accepted. *Financial support:* Fellowships, research assistantships, teaching assistantships, and unspecified assistantships available. *Unit head:* Dr. Mark W. Jackwood, Head, 706-542-5475, Fax: 706-542-5630, E-mail: mjackwoo@uga.edu. *Application contact:* Dr. Charles Hofacre, Graduate Coordinator, 706-542-5653, Fax: 706-542-5630, E-mail: chofacre@uga.edu. Web site: http://www.vet.uga.edu/populationhealth/.

University of Georgia, College of Veterinary Medicine, Department of Small Animal Medicine and Surgery, Athens, GA 30602. Offers MS. *Faculty:* 17 full-time (7 women). *Students:* 24 full-time (15 women); includes 1 minority (Asian, non-Hispanic/Latino), 2 international. Average age 30. 7 applicants, 86% accepted, 4 enrolled. *Unit head:* Dr. Spencer Johnston, 706-542-4622, Fax: 706-542-6460, E-mail: spencerj@uga.edu. *Application contact:* Dr. Scott Brown, Graduate Coordinator, 706-542-8121, E-mail: sbrown01@uga.edu. Web site: http://www.vet.uga.edu/SAMS/index.php.

University of Guelph, Ontario Veterinary College and Graduate Studies, Graduate Programs in Veterinary Sciences, Guelph, ON N1G 2W1, Canada. Offers M Sc, DV Sc, PhD, Diploma. *Accreditation:* AVMA (one or more programs are accredited). *Degree requirements:* For master's, thesis; for doctorate, comprehensive exam, thesis/dissertation. *Entrance requirements:* Additional exam requirements/recommendations for international students: Required—TOEFL. *Faculty research:* Veterinary and comparative medicine, biomedical sciences, population medicine, pathology, microbiology.

University of Idaho, College of Graduate Studies, College of Agricultural and Life Sciences, Department of Animal and Veterinary Science, Moscow, ID 83843-2330. Offers animal physiology (PhD); animal science (MS), including production. *Faculty:* 1 full-time, 1 part-time/adjunct. *Students:* 13 full-time, 17 part-time. Average age 30. In 2011, 8 master's, 1 doctorate awarded. *Degree requirements:* For doctorate, thesis/dissertation. *Entrance requirements:* For master's, GRE General Test, minimum GPA of 2.8; for doctorate, minimum undergraduate GPA of 2.8, graduate 3.0. *Application deadline:* For fall admission, 8/1 for domestic students; for spring admission, 12/15 for domestic students. Applications are processed on a rolling basis. Application fee: $60. Electronic applications accepted. *Expenses:* Tuition, state resident: full-time $3874; part-time $334 per credit hour. Tuition, nonresident: full-time $16,394; part-time $861 per credit hour. *Required fees:* $2808; $99 per credit hour. Tuition and fees vary according to program. *Financial support:* Research assistantships and teaching assistantships available. Financial award applicants required to submit FAFSA. *Faculty research:* Reproductive biology, muscle and growth physiology, meat science, aquaculture, ruminant nutrition. *Unit head:* Dr. Carl W. Hunt, Head, 208-885-6345, E-mail: avs-students@uidaho.edu. *Application contact:* Erick Larson, Director of Graduate Admissions, 208-885-4723, E-mail: gadms@uidaho.edu. Web site: http://www.uidaho.edu/cals/avs.

University of Illinois at Urbana–Champaign, College of Veterinary Medicine, Department of Comparative Biosciences, Urbana, IL 61802. Offers comparative biosciences (MS, PhD); DVM/PhD. *Faculty:* 11 full-time (7 women), 2 part-time/adjunct (1 woman). *Students:* 10 full-time (5 women), 5 part-time (4 women); includes 3 minority (2 Asian, non-Hispanic/Latino; 1 Hispanic/Latino), 5 international. 4 applicants, 50% accepted, 1 enrolled. In 2011, 2 degrees awarded. *Degree requirements:* For doctorate, thesis/dissertation. *Entrance requirements:* For master's and doctorate, GRE, minimum GPA of 3.0. Additional exam requirements/recommendations for international students: Required—TOEFL (minimum score 600 paper-based; 250 computer-based). *Application deadline:* Applications are processed on a rolling basis. Application fee: $75 ($90 for international students). Electronic applications accepted. *Financial support:* In 2011–12, 2 fellowships, 9 research assistantships, 1 teaching assistantship were awarded; tuition waivers (full and partial) also available. *Unit head:* Dr. Duncan Ferguson, Head, 217-333-2506, Fax: 217-244-1652, E-mail: dcf@illinois.edu. *Application contact:* Peggy Olsen, Administrative Aide, 217-244-4182, Fax: 217-244-1652, E-mail: pfolsen@illinois.edu. Web site: http://vetmed.illinois.edu/vb/.

University of Illinois at Urbana–Champaign, College of Veterinary Medicine, Department of Pathobiology, Urbana, IL 61802. Offers MS, PhD, DVM/PhD. Part-time programs available. *Faculty:* 18 full-time (6 women). *Students:* 8 full-time (5 women), 7 part-time (1 woman); includes 1 minority (Asian, non-Hispanic/Latino), 7 international. 17 applicants, 6% accepted, 1 enrolled. In 2011, 1 degree awarded. Terminal master's awarded for partial completion of doctoral program. *Degree requirements:* For doctorate, thesis/dissertation. *Entrance requirements:* For master's and doctorate, GRE, minimum GPA of 3.0. Additional exam requirements/recommendations for international students: Required—TOEFL (minimum score 590 paper-based; 243 computer-based). *Application deadline:* Applications are processed on a rolling basis. Application fee: $75 ($90 for international students). Electronic applications accepted. *Financial support:* In 2011–12, 2 fellowships, 7 research assistantships, 5 teaching assistantships were awarded; tuition waivers (full and partial) also available. *Faculty research:* Epidemiology, immunology, microbiology, parasitology, clinical pathology. *Unit head:* Mark S. Kuhlenschmidt, Head, 217-333-9039, Fax: 217-244-7421, E-mail: kuhlensc@illinois.edu. *Application contact:* Paula Moxley, Administrative Aide, 217-244-8924, Fax: 217-244-7421, E-mail: pkm@illinois.edu. Web site: http://vetmed.illinois.edu/path/.

University of Illinois at Urbana–Champaign, College of Veterinary Medicine, Department of Veterinary Clinical Medicine, Urbana, IL 61801. Offers MS, PhD, DVM/PhD. *Faculty:* 19 full-time (10 women). *Students:* 26 full-time (20 women), 4 part-time (3 women); includes 1 minority (Black or African American, non-Hispanic/Latino), 8 international. 11 applicants, 82% accepted, 8 enrolled. In 2011, 11 master's, 2 doctorates awarded. *Degree requirements:* For doctorate, thesis/dissertation. *Entrance requirements:* For master's and doctorate, GRE (if applicant does not have a DVM), minimum GPA of 3.0. Additional exam requirements/recommendations for international students: Required—TOEFL (minimum score 550 paper-based; 213 computer-based). *Application deadline:* Applications are processed on a rolling basis. Application fee: $75 ($90 for international students). Electronic applications accepted. *Financial support:* In 2011–12, 1 fellowship, 4 research assistantships were awarded; teaching assistantships and tuition waivers (full and partial) also available. *Unit head:* Karen L. Campbell, Head, 217-333-5310, Fax: 217-244-1475, E-mail: klcampbe@illinois.edu. *Application contact:* Theresa Schafroth, Office Manager, 217-244-7434, Fax: 217-244-1475, E-mail: schafrot@illinois.edu. Web site: http://vetmed.illinois.edu/vcm/.

University of Kentucky, Graduate School, College of Agriculture, Program in Veterinary Science, Lexington, KY 40506-0032. Offers MS, PhD. *Degree requirements:* For master's, comprehensive exam, thesis; for doctorate, comprehensive exam, thesis/dissertation. *Entrance requirements:* For master's, GRE General Test, minimum undergraduate GPA of 2.75; for doctorate, GRE General Test, minimum graduate GPA of 3.0. Additional exam requirements/recommendations for international students: Required—TOEFL (minimum score 550 paper-based; 213 computer-based). Electronic applications accepted. *Faculty research:* Microbiology, reproductive physiology, genetics, pharmacology/toxicology, parasitology.

University of Maryland, College Park, Academic Affairs, College of Agriculture and Natural Resources, Maryland Campus of VA/MD Regional College of Veterinary Medicine, Veterinary Medical Sciences Program, College Park, MD 20742. Offers MS, PhD. *Students:* 17 full-time (8 women), 1 (woman) part-time, 10 international. 12 applicants, 50% accepted, 5 enrolled. In 2011, 1 master's, 5 doctorates awarded. *Degree requirements:* For master's, thesis, oral exam; for doctorate, thesis/dissertation, oral exam, public seminar. *Entrance requirements:* For doctorate, GRE General Test. *Application deadline:* For fall admission, 5/1 for domestic students, 2/1 for international students; for spring admission, 9/1 for domestic students, 6/1 for international students. Applications are processed on a rolling basis. Application fee: $75. Electronic applications accepted. *Expenses:* Tuition, state resident: part-time $525 per credit hour. Tuition, nonresident: part-time $1131 per credit hour. *Required fees:* $386.31 per term. Tuition and fees vary according to program. *Financial support:* In 2011–12, 1 fellowship (averaging $10,000 per year), 4 research assistantships (averaging $18,636 per year), 12 teaching assistantships (averaging $17,607 per year) were awarded. *Unit head:* Dr. Xiaoping Zhu Zhu, Director, 301-314-6814, Fax: 301-314-6855, E-mail: xzhu1@umd.edu. *Application contact:* Dr. Charles A. Caramello, Dean of Graduate School, 301-405-0358, Fax: 301-314-9305, E-mail: ccaramel@umd.edu.

University of Minnesota, Twin Cities Campus, College of Veterinary Medicine and Graduate School, Graduate Programs in Veterinary Medicine, Program in Comparative

and Molecular Bioscience, Minneapolis, MN 55455-0213. Offers MS, PhD, DVM/PhD. Terminal master's awarded for partial completion of doctoral program. *Degree requirements:* For master's, comprehensive exam, thesis; for doctorate, comprehensive exam, thesis/dissertation. *Entrance requirements:* For master's and doctorate, GRE. Additional exam requirements/recommendations for international students: Required—TOEFL (minimum score 550 paper-based; 213 computer-based; 79 iBT). Electronic applications accepted. *Faculty research:* Molecular regulation of immunity; mechanisms of bacterial, viral, and parasite pathogenesis; structural and functional comparative physiology and pathology.

University of Minnesota, Twin Cities Campus, College of Veterinary Medicine and Graduate School, Graduate Programs in Veterinary Medicine, Program in Veterinary Medicine, Minneapolis, MN 55455-0213. Offers MS, PhD, DVM/PhD. Terminal master's awarded for partial completion of doctoral program. *Degree requirements:* For master's, comprehensive exam, thesis; for doctorate, comprehensive exam, thesis/dissertation. *Entrance requirements:* Additional exam requirements/recommendations for international students: Required—TOEFL (minimum score 550 paper-based; 213 computer-based; 79 iBT). Electronic applications accepted. *Faculty research:* Infectious diseases, internal medicine, population medicine, surgery/radiology/anesthesiology, theriogenology.

University of Missouri, College of Veterinary Medicine and Graduate School, Graduate Programs in Veterinary Medicine, Columbia, MO 65211. Offers veterinary biomedical sciences (MS, PhD), including biomedical sciences, comparative medicine (MS); veterinary medicine and surgery (MS); veterinary pathobiology (MS, PhD), including comparative medicine (MS), pathobiology; DVM/MS; DVM/PhD. *Faculty:* 112 full-time (41 women), 12 part-time/adjunct (4 women). *Students:* 40 full-time (18 women), 38 part-time (25 women); includes 5 minority (1 Asian, non-Hispanic/Latino; 4 Hispanic/Latino), 12 international. Average age 31. 65 applicants, 42% accepted, 24 enrolled. In 2011, 26 master's, 11 doctorates awarded. *Degree requirements:* For master's, thesis; for doctorate, 2 foreign languages, comprehensive exam, thesis/dissertation. *Entrance requirements:* For master's and doctorate, GRE General Test, minimum GPA of 3.0. Additional exam requirements/recommendations for international students: Required—TOEFL (minimum score 600 paper-based; 250 computer-based; 100 iBT). Application fee: $55 ($75 for international students). Electronic applications accepted. *Expenses:* Contact institution. *Financial support:* Fellowships with full tuition reimbursements, research assistantships with full tuition reimbursements, teaching assistantships with full tuition reimbursements, and institutionally sponsored loans available. *Faculty research:* Exercise physiology, cardiovascular science, comparative medicine, biodefense-related organisms, vector borne infectious diseases. *Unit head:* Dr. Ronald Terjung, Associate Dean for Research and Postdoctoral Studies, 573-882-2635, E-mail: terjungr@missouri.edu. *Application contact:* Brenda Klemme, Office Support Staff III, 573-882-7305, E-mail: klemmeb@missouri.edu. Web site: http://vetmed.missouri.edu/departments.htm.

University of Nebraska–Lincoln, Graduate College, College of Agricultural Sciences and Natural Resources, School of Veterinary Medicine and Biomedical Sciences, Lincoln, NE 68588. Offers veterinary science (MS). MS, PhD offered jointly with University of Nebraska Medical Center. Postbaccalaureate distance learning degree programs offered (minimal on-campus study). *Degree requirements:* For master's, thesis optional; for doctorate, comprehensive exam, thesis/dissertation. *Entrance requirements:* For master's, GRE General Test; for doctorate, GRE General Test, MCAT, or VCAT. Additional exam requirements/recommendations for international students: Required—TOEFL (minimum score 550 paper-based; 213 computer-based). Electronic applications accepted. *Faculty research:* Virology, immunobiology, molecular biology, mycotoxins, ocular degeneration.

University of Prince Edward Island, Atlantic Veterinary College, Graduate Program in Veterinary Medicine, Charlottetown, PE C1A 4P3, Canada. Offers anatomy (M Sc, PhD); bacteriology (M Sc, PhD); clinical pharmacology (M Sc, PhD); clinical sciences (M Sc, PhD); epidemiology (M Sc, PhD), including reproduction; fish health (M Sc, PhD); food animal nutrition (M Sc, PhD); immunology (M Sc, PhD); microanatomy (M Sc, PhD); parasitology (M Sc, PhD); pathology (M Sc, PhD); pharmacology (M Sc, PhD); physiology (M Sc, PhD); toxicology (M Sc, PhD); veterinary science (M Vet Sc); virology (M Sc, PhD). Part-time programs available. *Degree requirements:* For master's, thesis; for doctorate, thesis/dissertation. *Entrance requirements:* For master's, DVM, B Sc honors degree, or equivalent; for doctorate, M Sc. Additional exam requirements/recommendations for international students: Required—TOEFL (minimum score 550 paper-based; 213 computer-based; 80 iBT). *Expenses:* Contact institution. *Faculty research:* Animal health management, infectious diseases, fin fish and shellfish health, basic biomedical sciences, ecosystem health.

University of Saskatchewan, Western College of Veterinary Medicine and College of Graduate Studies and Research, Graduate Programs in Veterinary Medicine, Saskatoon, SK S7N 5A2, Canada. Offers large animal clinical sciences (M Sc, M Vet Sc, PhD); small animal clinical sciences (M Sc, M Vet Sc, PhD), including small animal clinical sciences (M Sc, PhD), veterinary anesthesiology, radiology and surgery (M Vet Sc), veterinary internal medicine (M Vet Sc); veterinary biomedical sciences (M Sc, M Vet Sc, PhD), including veterinary anatomy (M Sc), veterinary biomedical sciences (M Vet Sc), veterinary physiological sciences (M Sc, PhD); veterinary medicine (M Sc, PhD); veterinary microbiology (M Sc, M Vet Sc, PhD); veterinary pathology (M Sc, M Vet Sc, PhD). *Degree requirements:* For master's, comprehensive exam, thesis (for some programs); for doctorate, comprehensive exam, thesis/dissertation. *Entrance requirements:* Additional exam requirements/recommendations for international students: Required—TOEFL (minimum score 80 iBT) or IELTS (minimum score 6.5). Electronic applications accepted. *Expenses:* Contact institution. *Faculty research:* Reproduction, toxicology, wildlife diseases, food animal medicine, equine health.

University of Washington, Graduate School, School of Medicine, Graduate Programs in Medicine, Department of Comparative Medicine, Seattle, WA 98195. Offers MS.

University of Wisconsin–Madison, School of Veterinary Medicine, Madison, WI 53706-1380. Offers MS, DVM, PhD. *Accreditation:* AVMA (one or more programs are accredited). Terminal master's awarded for partial completion of doctoral program. *Degree requirements:* For master's, thesis; for doctorate, thesis/dissertation (for some programs). *Entrance requirements:* For doctorate, GRE General Test (for DVM). *Expenses:* Contact institution. *Faculty research:* Infectious disease, ophthalmology, orthopedics, food animal production, oncology, cardio-respiratory.

Utah State University, School of Graduate Studies, College of Agriculture, Department of Animal, Dairy and Veterinary Sciences, Logan, UT 84322. Offers animal science (MS, PhD); bioveterinary science (MS, PhD); dairy science (MS). Part-time programs available. *Degree requirements:* For master's, thesis (for some programs); for doctorate, comprehensive exam, thesis/dissertation. *Entrance requirements:* For master's and doctorate, GRE General Test, minimum GPA of 3.0. Additional exam requirements/recommendations for international students: Required—TOEFL. Electronic applications accepted. *Faculty research:* Monoclonal antibodies, antiviral chemotherapy, management systems, biotechnology, rumen fermentation manipulation.

Virginia Polytechnic Institute and State University, Virginia-Maryland Regional College of Veterinary Medicine and Graduate School, Graduate Programs in Biomedical and Veterinary Sciences, Blacksburg, VA 24061. Offers biomedical and veterinary sciences (MS, PhD); translational medicine and research (Certificate). Part-time programs available. *Degree requirements:* For master's, comprehensive exam (for some programs), thesis (for some programs); for doctorate, comprehensive exam (for some programs), thesis/dissertation (for some programs). *Entrance requirements:* For master's and doctorate, GRE. Additional exam requirements/recommendations for international students: Required—TOEFL (minimum score 550 paper-based; 213 computer-based). *Application deadline:* For fall admission, 7/1 for domestic and international students; for spring admission, 12/1 for domestic and international students. Applications are processed on a rolling basis. Application fee: $65. Electronic applications accepted. *Expenses:* Contact institution. *Financial support:* Career-related internships or fieldwork, Federal Work-Study, scholarships/grants, health care benefits, and unspecified assistantships available. Financial award application deadline: 1/15. *Faculty research:* Infectious diseases, nanotechnology and neuroscience, immunology, nutrition, toxicology and pharmacology. *Unit head:* Dr. Roger J. Avery, Unit Head, 540-231-5649, Fax: 540-231-7367, E-mail: avery@vt.edu. *Application contact:* Becky Jones, Information Contact, 540-231-4992, Fax: 540-231-7367, E-mail: vmsgrad@vt.edu. Web site: http://www.vetmed.vt.edu.

Washington State University, College of Veterinary Medicine and Graduate School, Graduate Programs in Veterinary Science, Department of Veterinary and Comparative Anatomy, Pharmacology, and Physiology, Pullman, WA 99164-6520. Offers neuroscience (MS, PhD); veterinary science (MS, PhD). Part-time programs available. *Faculty:* 24 full-time (7 women), 1 part-time/adjunct (0 women). *Students:* 4 full-time (2 women), 3 international. Average age 30. 1 applicant, 100% accepted, 1 enrolled. *Degree requirements:* For master's, thesis, written exam; for doctorate, thesis/dissertation, written exam, oral exam. *Entrance requirements:* For master's and doctorate, GRE General Test or MCAT, minimum GPA of 3.0. Additional exam requirements/recommendations for international students: Required—TOEFL (minimum score 550 paper-based; 213 computer-based; 80 iBT). *Application deadline:* For fall admission, 12/31 priority date for domestic students, 12/31 for international students; for spring admission, 8/1 for domestic and international students. Applications are processed on a rolling basis. Application fee: $50. Electronic applications accepted. *Financial support:* In 2011–12, 1 student received support, including fellowships with full tuition reimbursements available (averaging $28,000 per year), 3 research assistantships with full tuition reimbursements available (averaging $21,588 per year), teaching assistantships with full tuition reimbursements available (averaging $21,588 per year); Federal Work-Study, scholarships/grants, health care benefits, and unspecified assistantships also available. Financial award application deadline: 4/15. *Faculty research:* Addiction, sleep and performance, body weight and energy balance, emotion and well being, learning and memory, reproduction, vision, movement. *Total annual research expenditures:* $5.5 million. *Unit head:* Dr. Steven K. Simasko, Chair, 509-335-6624, Fax: 509-335-4650, E-mail: simasko@vetmed.wsu.edu. *Application contact:* Bobbi Sauer, Office Assistant II, 509-335-7675, Fax: 509-335-4650, E-mail: grad.neuro@vetmed.wsu.edu. Web site: http://www.vetmed.wsu.edu/depts-vcapp/.

Washington State University, College of Veterinary Medicine and Graduate School, Graduate Programs in Veterinary Science, Department of Veterinary Clinical Sciences, Pullman, WA 99164. Offers MS. Part-time programs available. *Faculty:* 25 full-time (3 women). *Students:* 32 full-time (21 women), 12 international. Average age 30. 6 applicants, 100% accepted, 6 enrolled. In 2011, 8 degrees awarded. *Degree requirements:* For master's, thesis, oral exam. *Entrance requirements:* For master's, GRE General Test, minimum GPA of 3.0, DVM or equivalent. *Application deadline:* For fall admission, 12/31 priority date for domestic students. Application fee: $75. Electronic applications accepted. *Financial support:* In 2011–12, research assistantships with full tuition reimbursements (averaging $20,800 per year) were awarded. Financial award application deadline: 3/1. *Faculty research:* Oncology, mastitis, nuclear medicine, neuroanesthesia, exercise physiology. *Total annual research expenditures:* $500,000. *Unit head:* Dr. William Dernell, Chair, 509-335-0738, Fax: 509-335-0880. *Application contact:* Theresa A. Pfaff, Administrative Manager, 509-335-0723, Fax: 509-335-0880, E-mail: tpfaff@vetmed.wsu.edu. Web site: http://www.vetmed.wsu.edu/.

Washington State University, College of Veterinary Medicine and Graduate School, Graduate Programs in Veterinary Science, Department of Veterinary Microbiology and Pathology, Pullman, WA 99164. Offers veterinary science (MS, PhD). *Faculty:* 23 full-time (4 women), 10 part-time/adjunct (4 women). *Students:* 49 full-time (25 women); includes 3 minority (2 Black or African American, non-Hispanic/Latino; 1 Hispanic/Latino), 27 international. Average age 31. 62 applicants, 19% accepted, 9 enrolled. In 2011, 3 master's, 3 doctorates awarded. Terminal master's awarded for partial completion of doctoral program. *Degree requirements:* For master's, thesis, oral exam; for doctorate, thesis/dissertation, oral exam. *Entrance requirements:* For master's and doctorate, minimum GPA of 3.0. Additional exam requirements/recommendations for international students: Required—TOEFL (minimum score 550 paper-based; 213 computer-based; 80 iBT). *Application deadline:* Applications are processed on a rolling basis. Application fee: $75. Electronic applications accepted. *Financial support:* In 2011–12, 12 fellowships, 32 research assistantships were awarded; institutionally sponsored loans, scholarships/grants, traineeships, health care benefits, and unspecified assistantships also available. Financial award application deadline: 3/1. *Faculty research:* Microbial pathogenesis, veterinary and wildlife parasitology, laboratory animal pathology, immune responses to infectious diseases. *Unit head:* Dr. David J. Prieur, Chair, 509-335-6030, Fax: 509-335-8529, E-mail: dprieur@vetmed.wsu.edu. *Application contact:* Dr. Guy Palmer, Professor, 509-335-6033, Fax: 509-335-8529, E-mail: gpalmer@vetmed.wsu.edu. Web site: http://www.vetmed.wsu.edu/depts-vmp/.

APPENDIXES

Peterson's Graduate Programs in the Physical Sciences, Mathematics,
Agricultural Sciences, the Environment & Natural Resources 2013

Institutional Changes
Since the 2012 Edition

Following is an alphabetical listing of institutions that have recently closed, merged with other institutions, or changed their names or status. In the case of a name change, the former name appears first, followed by the new name.

Adams State College (Alamosa, CO): name changed to Adams State University

Andrew Jackson University (Birmingham, AL): name changed to New Charter University

The Art Institute of Atlanta (Atlanta, GA): no longer offers graduate degrees

The Art Institute of Boston at Lesley University (Boston, MA): merged into a single entry for Lesley University (Cambridge, MA)

The Art Institute of California–San Francisco (San Francisco, CA): name changed to The Art Institute of California, a college of Argosy University, San Francisco

Atlantic Union College (South Lancaster, MA): currently not accepting applications

Babel University School of Translation (Honolulu, HI): name changed to Babel University Professional School of Translation

Baldwin-Wallace College (Berea, OH): name changed to Baldwin Wallace University

Baltimore International College (Baltimore, MD): name changed to Stratford University

Bethany University (Scotts Valley, CA): closed

Bethesda Christian University (Anaheim, CA): name changed to Bethesda University of California

Broadview University (West Jordan, UT): name changed to Broadview University–West Jordan

City of Hope National Medical Center/Beckman Research Institute (Duarte, CA): name changed to Irell & Manella Graduate School of Biological Sciences

City University of New York School of Law at Queens College (Flushing, NY): name changed to City University of New York School of Law

Cleveland Chiropractic College–Los Angeles Campus (Los Angeles, CA): closed

College of Notre Dame of Maryland (Baltimore, MD): name changed to Notre Dame of Maryland University

College of the Humanities and Sciences, Harrison Middleton University (Tempe, AZ): name changed to Harrison Middleton University

Colorado Technical University Denver (Greenwood Village, CO): name changed to Colorado Technical University Denver South

Concordia University (Ann Arbor, MI): name changed to Concordia University Ann Arbor

Cornell University, Joan and Sanford I. Weill Medical College and Graduate School of Medical Sciences (New York, NY): name changed to Weill Cornell Medical College

Daniel Webster College–Portsmouth Campus (Portsmouth, NH): closed

Edward Via Virginia College of Osteopathic Medicine (Blacksburg, VA): name changed to Edward Via College of Osteopahtic Medicine–Virginia Campus

Evangelical Theological Seminary (Myerstown, PA): name changed to Evangelical Seminary

Everest University (Lakeland, FL): no longer offers graduate degrees

Faith Evangelical Lutheran Seminary (Tacoma, WA): name changed to Faith Evangelical College & Seminary

Franklin Pierce Law Center (Concord, NH): name changed to University of New Hampshire School of Law

Frontier School of Midwifery and Family Nursing (Hyden, KY): name changed to Frontier Nursing University

Globe University (Woodbury, MN): name changed to Globe University–Woodbury

Harding University Graduate School of Religion (Memphis, TN): name changed to Harding School of Theology

Kol Yaakov Torah Center (Monsey, NY): closed

Long Island University at Riverhead (Riverhead, NY): name changed to Long Island University–Riverhead

Long Island University, Brentwood Campus (Brentwood, NY): name changed to Long Island University–Brentwood Campus

Long Island University, Brooklyn Campus (Brooklyn, NY): name changed to Long Island University–Brooklyn Campus

Long Island University, C.W. Post Campus (Brookville, NY): name changed to Long Island University–C. W. Post Campus

Long Island University, Rockland Graduate Campus (Orangeburg, NY): name changed to Long Island University–Hudson at Rockland

Long Island University, Westchester Graduate Campus (Purchase, NY): name changed to Long Island University–Hudson at Westchester

Lourdes College (Sylvania, OH): name changed to Lourdes University

Lutheran Theological Seminary (Saskatoon, SK, Canada): name changed to Lutheran Theological Seminary Saskatoon

Mars Hill Graduate School (Seattle, WA): name changed to The Seattle School of Theology and Psychology

Mesa State College (Grand Junction, CO): name changed to Colorado Mesa University

Michigan Theological Seminary (Plymouth, MI): name changed to Moody Theological Seminary–Michigan

Midwest University (Wentzville, MO): no longer accredited by agency recognized by USDE or CHEA

National Defense Intelligence College (Washington, DC): name changed to National Intelligence University

National-Louis University (Chicago, IL): name changed to National Louis University

National Theatre Conservatory (Denver, CO): closed

The New School: A University (New York, NY): name changed to The New School

Northeastern Ohio Universities Colleges of Medicine and Pharmacy (Rootstown, OH): name changed to Northeastern Ohio Medical University

Northwest Baptist Seminary (Tacoma, WA): name changed to Corban University School of Ministry

Northwood University (Midland, MI): name changed to Northwood University, Michigan Campus

OGI School of Science & Engineering at Oregon Health & Science University (Beaverton, OR): merged into a single entry for Oregon Health & Science University (Portland, OR) by request from the institution

Parker College of Chiropractic (Dallas, TX): name changed to Parker University

Philadelphia Biblical University (Langhorne, PA): name changed to Cairn University

Piedmont Baptist College and Graduate School (Winston-Salem, NC): name changed to Piedmont International University

Pikeville College (Pikeville, KY): name changed to University of Pikeville

Polytechnic Institute of NYU (Brooklyn, NY): name changed to Polytechnic Institute of New York University

Ponce School of Medicine (Ponce, PR): name changed to Ponce School of Medicine & Health Sciences

Rivier College (Nashua, NH): name changed to Rivier University

Saint Bernard's School of Theology and Ministry (Rochester, NY): name changed to St. Bernard's School of Theology and Ministry

St. Charles Borromeo Seminary, Overbrook (Wynnewood, PA): name changed to Saint Charles Borromeo Seminary, Overbrook

Saint Francis Seminary (St. Francis, WI): name changed to Saint Francis de Sales Seminary

Saint Joseph College (West Hartford, CT): name changed to University of Saint Joseph

Saint Vincent de Paul Regional Seminary (Boynton Beach, FL): name changed to St. Vincent de Paul Regional Seminary

Schiller International University (London, United Kingdom): closed

Silver Lake College (Manitowoc, WI): name changed to Silver Lake College of the Holy Family

Trinity (Washington) University (Washington, DC): name changed to Trinity Washington University

TUI University (Cypress, CA): name changed to Trident University International

University of Phoenix (Phoenix, AZ): name changed to University of Phoenix–Online Campus

University of Phoenix–Phoenix Campus (Phoenix, AZ): name changed to University of Phoenix–Phoenix Main Campus

The University of Tennessee–Oak Ridge National Laboratory Graduate School of Genome Science and Technology (Oak Ridge, TN): name changed to The University of Tennessee–Oak Ridge National Laboratory

The University of Texas Southwestern Medical Center at Dallas (Dallas, TX): name changed to The University of Texas Southwestern Medical Center

University of Trinity College (Toronto, ON, Canada): name changed to Trinity College

Washington Theological Union (Washington, DC): closed

West Virginia University Institute of Technology (Montgomery, WV): no longer offers graduate degrees.

Abbreviations Used in the Guides

The following list includes abbreviations of degree names used in the profiles in the 2013 edition of the guides. Because some degrees (e.g., Doctor of Education) can be abbreviated in more than one way (e.g., D.Ed. or Ed.D.), and because the abbreviations used in the guides reflect the preferences of the individual colleges and universities, the list may include two or more abbreviations for a single degree.

DEGREES

A Mus D	Doctor of Musical Arts
AC	Advanced Certificate
AD	Artist's Diploma
	Doctor of Arts
ADP	Artist's Diploma
Adv C	Advanced Certificate
Adv M	Advanced Master
AGC	Advanced Graduate Certificate
AGSC	Advanced Graduate Specialist Certificate
ALM	Master of Liberal Arts
AM	Master of Arts
AMBA	Accelerated Master of Business Administration
	Aviation Master of Business Administration
AMRS	Master of Arts in Religious Studies
APC	Advanced Professional Certificate
APMPH	Advanced Professional Master of Public Health
App Sc	Applied Scientist
App Sc D	Doctor of Applied Science
AstE	Astronautical Engineer
Au D	Doctor of Audiology
B Th	Bachelor of Theology
CAES	Certificate of Advanced Educational Specialization
CAGS	Certificate of Advanced Graduate Studies
CAL	Certificate in Applied Linguistics
CALS	Certificate of Advanced Liberal Studies
CAMS	Certificate of Advanced Management Studies
CAPS	Certificate of Advanced Professional Studies
CAS	Certificate of Advanced Studies
CASPA	Certificate of Advanced Study in Public Administration
CASR	Certificate in Advanced Social Research
CATS	Certificate of Achievement in Theological Studies
CBHS	Certificate in Basic Health Sciences
CBS	Graduate Certificate in Biblical Studies
CCJA	Certificate in Criminal Justice Administration
CCSA	Certificate in Catholic School Administration
CCTS	Certificate in Clinical and Translational Science
CE	Civil Engineer
CEM	Certificate of Environmental Management
CET	Certificate in Educational Technologies
CGS	Certificate of Graduate Studies
Ch E	Chemical Engineer
CM	Certificate in Management
CMH	Certificate in Medical Humanities
CMM	Master of Church Ministries
CMS	Certificate in Ministerial Studies
CNM	Certificate in Nonprofit Management
CPASF	Certificate Program for Advanced Study in Finance
CPC	Certificate in Professional Counseling
	Certificate in Publication and Communication
CPH	Certificate in Public Health
CPM	Certificate in Public Management
CPS	Certificate of Professional Studies
CScD	Doctor of Clinical Science
CSD	Certificate in Spiritual Direction
CSS	Certificate of Special Studies
CTS	Certificate of Theological Studies
CURP	Certificate in Urban and Regional Planning
D Admin	Doctor of Administration
D Arch	Doctor of Architecture
D Be	Doctor in Bioethics
D Com	Doctor of Commerce
D Couns	Doctor of Counseling
D Div	Doctor of Divinity
D Ed	Doctor of Education
D Ed Min	Doctor of Educational Ministry
D Eng	Doctor of Engineering
D Engr	Doctor of Engineering
D Ent	Doctor of Enterprise
D Env	Doctor of Environment
D Law	Doctor of Law
D Litt	Doctor of Letters
D Med Sc	Doctor of Medical Science
D Min	Doctor of Ministry
D Miss	Doctor of Missiology
D Mus	Doctor of Music
D Mus A	Doctor of Musical Arts
D Phil	Doctor of Philosophy
D Prof	Doctor of Professional Studies
D Ps	Doctor of Psychology
D Sc	Doctor of Science
D Sc D	Doctor of Science in Dentistry
D Sc IS	Doctor of Science in Information Systems
D Sc PA	Doctor of Science in Physician Assistant Studies
D Th	Doctor of Theology
D Th P	Doctor of Practical Theology
DA	Doctor of Accounting
	Doctor of Arts
DA Ed	Doctor of Arts in Education
DAH	Doctor of Arts in Humanities
DAOM	Doctorate in Acupuncture and Oriental Medicine
DAT	Doctorate of Athletic Training
DATH	Doctorate of Art Therapy
DBA	Doctor of Business Administration
DBH	Doctor of Behavioral Health
DBL	Doctor of Business Leadership
DBS	Doctor of Buddhist Studies
DC	Doctor of Chiropractic
DCC	Doctor of Computer Science
DCD	Doctor of Communications Design
DCL	Doctor of Civil Law
	Doctor of Comparative Law
DCM	Doctor of Church Music
DCN	Doctor of Clinical Nutrition
DCS	Doctor of Computer Science
DDN	Diplôme du Droit Notarial
DDS	Doctor of Dental Surgery
DE	Doctor of Education
	Doctor of Engineering
	Doctor of Economic Development
DED	Doctor of Educational Innovation and Technology
DEIT	Doctor of Executive Leadership
DEL	Doctor of Educational Ministry
DEM	Diplôme d'Études Spécialisées
DEPD	Doctor of Engineering Science
DES	Diplôme d'Études Supérieures Spécialisées
DESS	Doctor of Fine Arts
DFA	Diploma in Graduate and Professional Studies
DGP	Doctor of Health Education
DH Ed	Doctor of Health Sciences
DH Sc	Doctor of Health Administration
DHA	Doctor of Health Care Ethics
DHCE	Doctor of Hebrew Letters
DHL	Doctor of Hebrew Literature
	Doctor of Health Science
DHS	Doctor of Health Science
DHSc	Diploma in Christian Studies
Dip CS	Doctor of Industrial Technology
DIT	Doctor of Jewish Education
DJ Ed	Doctor of Jewish Studies
DJS	Doctor of Liberal Studies
DLS	Doctor of Management
DM	Doctor of Music
	Doctor of Musical Arts
DMA	Doctor of Dental Medicine
DMD	Doctor of Music Education
DME	Doctor of Music Education
DMEd	Doctor of Marital and Family Therapy
DMFT	Doctor of Medical Humanities
DMH	Doctor of Modern Languages
DML	Doctorate in Medical Physics
DMP	

DMPNA	Doctor of Management Practice in Nurse Anesthesia	IM Acc	Integrated Master of Accountancy
DN Sc	Doctor of Nursing Science	IMA	Interdisciplinary Master of Arts
DNAP	Doctor of Nurse Anesthesia Practice	IMBA	International Master of Business Administration
DNP	Doctor of Nursing Practice	IMES	International Master's in Environmental Studies
DNP-A	Doctor of Nursing PracticeAnesthesia	Ingeniero	Engineer
DNS	Doctor of Nursing Science	JCD	Doctor of Canon Law
DO	Doctor of Osteopathy	JCL	Licentiate in Canon Law
DOT	Doctor of Occupational Therapy	JD	Juris Doctor
DPA	Doctor of Public Administration	JSD	Doctor of Juridical Science
DPC	Doctor of Pastoral Counseling		Doctor of Jurisprudence
DPDS	Doctor of Planning and Development Studies		Doctor of the Science of Law
DPH	Doctor of Public Health	JSM	Master of Science of Law
DPM	Doctor of Plant Medicine	L Th	Licenciate in Theology
	Doctor of Podiatric Medicine	LL B	Bachelor of Laws
DPPD	Doctor of Policy, Planning, and Development	LL CM	Master of Laws in Comparative Law
DPS	Doctor of Professional Studies	LL D	Doctor of Laws
DPT	Doctor of Physical Therapy	LL M	Master of Laws
DPTSc	Doctor of Physical Therapy Science	LL M in Tax	Master of Laws in Taxation
Dr DES	Doctor of Design	LL M CL	Master of Laws (Common Law)
Dr NP	Doctor of Nursing Practice	M Ac	Master of Accountancy
Dr PH	Doctor of Public Health		Master of Accounting
Dr Sc PT	Doctor of Science in Physical Therapy		Master of Acupuncture
DRSc	Doctor of Regulatory Science	M Ac OM	Master of Acupuncture and Oriental Medicine
DS	Doctor of Science	M Acc	Master of Accountancy
DS Sc	Doctor of Social Science		Master of Accounting
DSJS	Doctor of Science in Jewish Studies	M Acct	Master of Accountancy
DSL	Doctor of Strategic Leadership		Master of Accounting
DSW	Doctor of Social Work	M Accy	Master of Accountancy
DTL	Doctor of Talmudic Law	M Actg	Master of Accounting
DV Sc	Doctor of Veterinary Science	M Acy	Master of Accountancy
DVM	Doctor of Veterinary Medicine	M Ad	Master of Administration
DWS	Doctor of Worship Studies	M Ad Ed	Master of Adult Education
EAA	Engineer in Aeronautics and Astronautics	M Adm	Master of Administration
EASPh D	Engineering and Applied Science Doctor of Philosophy	M Adm Mgt	Master of Administrative Management
		M Admin	Master of Administration
ECS	Engineer in Computer Science	M ADU	Master of Architectural Design and Urbanism
Ed D	Doctor of Education	M Adv	Master of Advertising
Ed DCT	Doctor of Education in College Teaching	M Aero E	Master of Aerospace Engineering
Ed L D	Doctor of Education Leadership	M AEST	Master of Applied Environmental Science and Technology
Ed M	Master of Education	M Ag	Master of Agriculture
Ed S	Specialist in Education	M Ag Ed	Master of Agricultural Education
Ed Sp	Specialist in Education	M Agr	Master of Agriculture
EDB	Executive Doctorate in Business	M Anesth Ed	Master of Anesthesiology Education
EDM	Executive Doctorate in Management	M App Comp Sc	Master of Applied Computer Science
EE	Electrical Engineer	M App St	Master of Applied Statistics
EJD	Executive Juris Doctor	M Appl Stat	Master of Applied Statistics
EMBA	Executive Master of Business Administration	M Aq	Master of Aquaculture
EMFA	Executive Master of Forensic Accounting	M Arc	Master of Architecture
EMHA	Executive Master of Health Administration	M Arch	Master of Architecture
EMIB	Executive Master of International Business	M Arch I	Master of Architecture I
EML	Executive Master of Leadership	M Arch II	Master of Architecture II
EMPA	Executive Master of Public Administration	M Arch E	Master of Architectural Engineering
EMS	Executive Master of Science	M Arch H	Master of Architectural History
EMTM	Executive Master of Technology Management	M Bioethics	Master in Bioethics
Eng	Engineer	M Biomath	Master of Biomathematics
Eng Sc D	Doctor of Engineering Science	M Ch	Master of Chemistry
Engr	Engineer	M Ch E	Master of Chemical Engineering
Ex Doc	Executive Doctor of Pharmacy	M Chem	Master of Chemistry
Exec Ed D	Executive Doctor of Education	M Cl D	Master of Clinical Dentistry
Exec MBA	Executive Master of Business Administration	M Cl Sc	Master of Clinical Science
Exec MPA	Executive Master of Public Administration	M Comp	Master of Computing
Exec MPH	Executive Master of Public Health	M Comp Sc	Master of Computer Science
Exec MS	Executive Master of Science	M Coun	Master of Counseling
G Dip	Graduate Diploma	M Dent	Master of Dentistry
GBC	Graduate Business Certificate	M Dent Sc	Master of Dental Sciences
GCE	Graduate Certificate in Education	M Des	Master of Design
GDM	Graduate Diploma in Management	M Des S	Master of Design Studies
GDPA	Graduate Diploma in Public Administration	M Div	Master of Divinity
GDRE	Graduate Diploma in Religious Education	M Ec	Master of Economics
GEMBA	Global Executive Master of Business Administration	M Econ	Master of Economics
		M Ed	Master of Education
GEMPA	Gulf Executive Master of Public Administration	M Ed T	Master of Education in Teaching
GM Acc	Graduate Master of Accountancy	M En	Master of Engineering
GMBA	Global Master of Business Administration		Master of Environmental Science
GP LL M	Global Professional Master of Laws	M En S	Master of Environmental Sciences
GPD	Graduate Performance Diploma	M Eng	Master of Engineering
GSS	Graduate Special Certificate for Students in Special Situations	M Eng Mgt	Master of Engineering Management
		M Engr	Master of Engineering
IEMBA	International Executive Master of Business Administration	M Ent	Master of Enterprise

M Env	Master of Environment	MA Islamic	Master of Arts in Islamic Studies
M Env Des	Master of Environmental Design	MA Min	Master of Arts in Ministry
M Env E	Master of Environmental Engineering	MA Miss	Master of Arts in Missiology
M Env Sc	Master of Environmental Science	MA Past St	Master of Arts in Pastoral Studies
M Fin	Master of Finance	MA Ph	Master of Arts in Philosophy
M Geo E	Master of Geological Engineering	MA Psych	Master of Arts in Psychology
M Geoenv E	Master of Geoenvironmental Engineering	MA Sc	Master of Applied Science
M Geog	Master of Geography	MA Sp	Master of Arts (Spirituality)
M Hum	Master of Humanities	MA Th	Master of Arts in Theology
M Hum Svcs	Master of Human Services	MA-R	Master of Arts (Research)
M IBD	Master of Integrated Building Delivery	MAA	Master of Administrative Arts
M IDST	Master's in Interdisciplinary Studies		Master of Applied Anthropology
M Kin	Master of Kinesiology		Master of Applied Arts
M Land Arch	Master of Landscape Architecture		Master of Arts in Administration
M Litt	Master of Letters	MAAA	Master of Arts in Arts Administration
M Mat SE	Master of Material Science and Engineering	MAAAP	Master of Arts Administration and Policy
M Math	Master of Mathematics	MAAE	Master of Arts in Art Education
M Mech E	Master of Mechanical Engineering	MAAT	Master of Arts in Applied Theology
M Med Sc	Master of Medical Science		Master of Arts in Art Therapy
M Mgmt	Master of Management	MAB	Master of Agribusiness
M Mgt	Master of Management	MABC	Master of Arts in Biblical Counseling
M Min	Master of Ministries		Master of Arts in Business Communication
M Mtl E	Master of Materials Engineering	MABE	Master of Arts in Bible Exposition
M Mu	Master of Music	MABL	Master of Arts in Biblical Languages
M Mus	Master of Music	MABM	Master of Agribusiness Management
M Mus Ed	Master of Music Education	MABMH	bioethics and medical humanities
M Music	Master of Music	MABS	Master of Arts in Biblical Studies
M Nat Sci	Master of Natural Science	MABT	Master of Arts in Bible Teaching
M Oc E	Master of Oceanographic Engineering	MAC	Master of Accountancy
M Pet E	Master of Petroleum Engineering		Master of Accounting
M Pharm	Master of Pharmacy		Master of Arts in Communication
M Phil	Master of Philosophy		Master of Arts in Counseling
M Phil F	Master of Philosophical Foundations	MACC	Master of Arts in Christian Counseling
M Pl	Master of Planning		Master of Arts in Clinical Counseling
M Plan	Master of Planning	MACCM	Master of Arts in Church and Community Ministry
M Pol	Master of Political Science	MACCT	Master of Accounting
M Pr Met	Master of Professional Meteorology	MACD	Master of Arts in Christian Doctrine
M Prob S	Master of Probability and Statistics	MACE	Master of Arts in Christian Education
M Psych	Master of Psychology	MACFM	Master of Arts in Children's and Family Ministry
M Pub	Master of Publishing	MACH	Master of Arts in Church History
M Rel	Master of Religion	MACI	Master of Arts in Curriculum and Instruction
M Sc	Master of Science	MACIS	Master of Accounting and Information Systems
M Sc A	Master of Science (Applied)	MACJ	Master of Arts in Criminal Justice
M Sc AC	Master of Science in Applied Computing	MACL	Master of Arts in Christian Leadership
M Sc AHN	Master of Science in Applied Human Nutrition	MACM	Master of Arts in Christian Ministries
M Sc BMC	Master of Science in Biomedical Communications		Master of Arts in Christian Ministry
M Sc CS	Master of Science in Computer Science		Master of Arts in Church Music
M Sc E	Master of Science in Engineering		Master of Arts in Counseling Ministries
M Sc Eng	Master of Science in Engineering	MACN	Master of Arts in Counseling
M Sc Engr	Master of Science in Engineering	MACO	Master of Arts in Counseling
M Sc F	Master of Science in Forestry	MAcOM	Master of Acupuncture and Oriental Medicine
M Sc FE	Master of Science in Forest Engineering	MACP	Master of Arts in Christian Practice
M Sc Geogr	Master of Science in Geography		Master of Arts in Counseling Psychology
M Sc N	Master of Science in Nursing	MACS	Master of Applied Computer Science
M Sc OT	Master of Science in Occupational Therapy		Master of Arts in Catholic Studies
M Sc P	Master of Science in Planning		Master of Arts in Christian Studies
M Sc Pl	Master of Science in Planning	MACSE	Master of Arts in Christian School Education
M Sc PT	Master of Science in Physical Therapy	MACT	Master of Arts in Christian Thought
M Sc T	Master of Science in Teaching		Master of Arts in Communications and Technology
M SEM	Master of Sustainable Environmental Management	MAD	Master in Educational Institution Administration
M Serv Soc	Master of Social Service		Master of Art and Design
M Soc	Master of Sociology	MAD-Crit	Master of Arts in Design Criticism
M Sp Ed	Master of Special Education	MADR	Master of Arts in Dispute Resolution
M Stat	Master of Statistics	MADS	Master of Animal and Dairy Science
M Sys E	Master of Systems Engineering		Master of Applied Disability Studies
M Sys Sc	Master of Systems Science	MAE	Master of Aerospace Engineering
M Tax	Master of Taxation		Master of Agricultural Economics
M Tech	Master of Technology		Master of Agricultural Education
M Th	Master of Theology		Master of Architectural Engineering
M Tox	Master of Toxicology		Master of Art Education
M Trans E	Master of Transportation Engineering		Master of Arts in Education
M Urb	Master of Urban Planning		Master of Arts in English
M Vet Sc	Master of Veterinary Science	MAEd	Master of Arts Education
MA	Master of Accounting	MAEL	Master of Arts in Educational Leadership
	Master of Administration	MAEM	Master of Arts in Educational Ministries
	Master of Arts	MAEN	Master of Arts in English
MA Comm	Master of Arts in Communication	MAEP	Master of Arts in Economic Policy
MA Ed	Master of Arts in Education	MAES	Master of Arts in Environmental Sciences
MA Ed Ad	Master of Arts in Educational Administration	MAET	Master of Arts in English Teaching
MA Ext	Master of Agricultural Extension	MAF	Master of Arts in Finance

MAFE	Master of Arts in Financial Economics	
MAFLL	Master of Arts in Foreign Language and Literature	
MAFM	Master of Accounting and Financial Management	
MAFS	Master of Arts in Family Studies	
MAG	Master of Applied Geography	
MAGU	Master of Urban Analysis and Management	
MAH	Master of Arts in Humanities	
MAHA	Master of Arts in Humanitarian Assistance	
	Master of Arts in Humanitarian Studies	
MAHCM	Master of Arts in Health Care Mission	
MAHG	Master of American History and Government	
MAHL	Master of Arts in Hebrew Letters	
MAHN	Master of Applied Human Nutrition	
MAHSR	Master of Applied Health Services Research	
MAIA	Master of Arts in International Administration	
	Master of Arts in International Affairs	
MAIB	Master of Arts in International Business	
MAIDM	Master of Arts in Interior Design and Merchandising	
MAIH	Master of Arts in Interdisciplinary Humanities	
MAIOP	Master of Arts in Industrial/Organizational Psychology	
MAIPCR	Master of Arts in International Peace and Conflict Management	
MAIS	Master of Arts in Intercultural Studies	
	Master of Arts in Interdisciplinary Studies	
	Master of Arts in International Studies	
MAIT	Master of Administration in Information Technology	
	Master of Applied Information Technology	
MAJ	Master of Arts in Journalism	
MAJ Ed	Master of Arts in Jewish Education	
MAJCS	Master of Arts in Jewish Communal Service	
MAJE	Master of Arts in Jewish Education	
MAJPS	Master of Arts in Jewish Professional Studies	
MAJS	Master of Arts in Jewish Studies	
MAL	Master in Agricultural Leadership	
MALA	Master of Arts in Liberal Arts	
MALD	Master of Arts in Law and Diplomacy	
MALER	Master of Arts in Labor and Employment Relations	
MALM	Master of Arts in Leadership Evangelical Mobilization	
MALP	Master of Arts in Language Pedagogy	
MALPS	Master of Arts in Liberal and Professional Studies	
MALS	Master of Arts in Liberal Studies	
MAM	Master of Acquisition Management	
	Master of Agriculture and Management	
	Master of Applied Mathematics	
	Master of Arts in Ministry	
	Master of Arts Management	
	Master of Avian Medicine	
MAMB	Master of Applied Molecular Biology	
MAMC	Master of Arts in Mass Communication	
	Master of Arts in Ministry and Culture	
	Master of Arts in Ministry for a Multicultural Church	
	Master of Arts in Missional Christianity	
MAME	Master of Arts in Missions/Evangelism	
MAMFC	Master of Arts in Marriage and Family Counseling	
MAMFCC	Master of Arts in Marriage, Family, and Child Counseling	
MAMFT	Master of Arts in Marriage and Family Therapy	
MAMHC	Master of Arts in Mental Health Counseling	
MAMI	Master of Arts in Missions	
MAMS	Master of Applied Mathematical Sciences	
	Master of Arts in Ministerial Studies	
	Master of Arts in Ministry and Spirituality	
MAMT	Master of Arts in Mathematics Teaching	
MAN	Master of Applied Nutrition	
MANT	Master of Arts in New Testament	
MAOL	Master of Arts in Organizational Leadership	
MAOM	Master of Acupuncture and Oriental Medicine	
	Master of Arts in Organizational Management	
MAOT	Master of Arts in Old Testament	
MAP	Master of Applied Psychology	
	Master of Arts in Planning	
	Master of Psychology	
	Master of Public Administration	
MAP Min	Master of Arts in Pastoral Ministry	
MAPA	Master of Arts in Public Administration	
MAPC	Master of Arts in Pastoral Counseling	

	Master of Arts in Professional Counseling	
MAPE	Master of Arts in Political Economy	
MAPM	Master of Arts in Pastoral Ministry	
	Master of Arts in Pastoral Music	
	Master of Arts in Practical Ministry	
MAPP	Master of Arts in Public Policy	
MAPPS	Master of Arts in Asia Pacific Policy Studies	
MAPS	Master of Arts in Pastoral Counseling/Spiritual Formation	
	Master of Arts in Pastoral Studies	
	Master of Arts in Public Service	
MAPT	Master of Practical Theology	
MAPW	Master of Arts in Professional Writing	
MAR	Master of Arts in Reading	
	Master of Arts in Religion	
Mar Eng	Marine Engineer	
MARC	Master of Arts in Rehabilitation Counseling	
MARE	Master of Arts in Religious Education	
MARL	Master of Arts in Religious Leadership	
MARS	Master of Arts in Religious Studies	
MAS	Master of Accounting Science	
	Master of Actuarial Science	
	Master of Administrative Science	
	Master of Advanced Study	
	Master of Aeronautical Science	
	Master of American Studies	
	Master of Applied Science	
	Master of Applied Statistics	
	Master of Archival Studies	
MASA	Master of Advanced Studies in Architecture	
MASD	Master of Arts in Spiritual Direction	
MASE	Master of Arts in Special Education	
MASF	Master of Arts in Spiritual Formation	
MASJ	Master of Arts in Systems of Justice	
MASLA	Master of Advanced Studies in Landscape Architecture	
MASM	Master of Aging Services Management	
	Master of Arts in Specialized Ministries	
MASP	Master of Applied Social Psychology	
	Master of Arts in School Psychology	
MASPAA	Master of Arts in Sports and Athletic Administration	
MASS	Master of Applied Social Science	
	Master of Arts in Social Science	
MAST	Master of Arts in Science Teaching	
MASW	Master of Aboriginal Social Work	
MAT	Master of Arts in Teaching	
	Master of Arts in Theology	
	Master of Athletic Training	
	Master's in Administration of Telecommunications	
Mat E	Materials Engineer	
MATCM	Master of Acupuncture and Traditional Chinese Medicine	
MATDE	Master of Arts in Theology, Development, and Evangelism	
MATDR	Master of Territorial Management and Regional Development	
MATE	Master of Arts for the Teaching of English	
MATESL	Master of Arts in Teaching English as a Second Language	
MATESOL	Master of Arts in Teaching English to Speakers of Other Languages	
MATF	Master of Arts in Teaching English as a Foreign Language/Intercultural Studies	
MATFL	Master of Arts in Teaching Foreign Language	
MATH	Master of Arts in Therapy	
MATI	Master of Administration of Information Technology	
MATL	Master of Arts in Teacher Leadership	
	Master of Arts in Teaching of Languages	
	Master of Arts in Transformational Leadership	
MATM	Master of Arts in Teaching of Mathematics	
MATS	Master of Arts in Theological Studies	
	Master of Arts in Transforming Spirituality	
MATSL	Master of Arts in Teaching a Second Language	
MAUA	Master of Arts in Urban Affairs	
MAUD	Master of Arts in Urban Design	
MAURP	Master of Arts in Urban and Regional Planning	
MAWSHP	Master of Arts in Worship	
MAYM	Master of Arts in Youth Ministry	
MB	Master of Bioinformatics	

	Master of Biology
MBA	Master of Business Administration
MBA-AM	Master of Business Administration in Aviation Management
MBA-EP	Master of Business AdministrationNExperienced Professionals
MBA/MGPS	Master of Business Administration/Master of Global Policy Studies
MBAA	Master of Business Administration in Aviation
MBAE	Master of Biological and Agricultural Engineering
	Master of Biosystems and Agricultural Engineering
MBAH	Master of Business Administration in Health
MBAi	Master of Business AdministrationNInternational
MBAICT	Master of Business Administration in Information and Communication Technology
MBATM	Master of Business Administration in Technology Management
MBC	Master of Building Construction
MBE	Master of Bilingual Education
	Master of Bioengineering
	Master of Bioethics
	Master of Biological Engineering
	Master of Biomedical Engineering
	Master of Business and Engineering
	Master of Business Economics
	Master of Business Education
MBEE	Master in Biotechnology Enterprise and Entrepreneurship
MBET	Master of Business, Entrepreneurship and Technology
MBIOT	Master of Biotechnology
MBiotech	Master of Biotechnology
MBL	Master of Business Law
	Master of Business Leadership
MBLE	Master in Business Logistics Engineering
MBMI	Master of Biomedical Imaging and Signals
MBMSE	Master of Business Management and Software Engineering
MBOE	Master of Business Operational Excellence
MBS	Master of Biblical Studies
	Master of Biological Science
	Master of Biomedical Sciences
	Master of Bioscience
	Master of Building Science
	Master of Business and Science
MBST	Master of Biostatistics
MBT	Master of Biblical and Theological Studies
	Master of Biomedical Technology
	Master of Biotechnology
	Master of Business Taxation
MC	Master of Communication
	Master of Counseling
	Master of Cybersecurity
MC Ed	Master of Continuing Education
MC Sc	Master of Computer Science
MCA	Master of Arts in Applied Criminology
	Master of Commercial Aviation
MCAM	Master of Computational and Applied Mathematics
MCC	Master of Computer Science
MCCS	Master of Crop and Soil Sciences
MCD	Master of Communications Disorders
	Master of Community Development
MCE	Master in Electronic Commerce
	Master of Christian Education
	Master of Civil Engineering
	Master of Control Engineering
MCEM	Master of Construction Engineering Management
MCH	Master of Chemical Engineering
MCHE	Master of Chemical Engineering
MCIS	Master of Communication and Information Studies
	Master of Computer and Information Science
	Master of Computer Information Systems
MCIT	Master of Computer and Information Technology
MCJ	Master of Criminal Justice
MCJA	Master of Criminal Justice Administration
MCL	Master in Communication Leadership
	Master of Canon Law
	Master of Comparative Law
MCM	Master of Christian Ministry
	Master of Church Music
	Master of City Management
	Master of Communication Management
	Master of Community Medicine
	Master of Construction Management
	Master of Contract Management
	Master of Corporate Media
MCMP	Master of City and Metropolitan Planning
MCMS	Master of Clinical Medical Science
MCN	Master of Clinical Nutrition
MCOL	Master of Arts in Community and Organizational Leadership
MCP	Master of City Planning
	Master of Community Planning
	Master of Counseling Psychology
	Master of Cytopathology Practice
	Master of Science in Quality Systems and Productivity
MCPC	Master of Arts in Chaplaincy and Pastoral Care
MCPD	Master of Community Planning and Development
MCR	Master in Clinical Research
MCRP	Master of City and Regional Planning
MCRS	Master of City and Regional Studies
MCS	Master of Christian Studies
	Master of Clinical Science
	Master of Combined Sciences
	Master of Communication Studies
	Master of Computer Science
	Master of Consumer Science
MCSE	Master of Computer Science and Engineering
MCSL	Master of Catholic School Leadership
MCSM	Master of Construction Science/Management
MCST	Master of Science in Computer Science and Information Technology
MCTP	Master of Communication Technology and Policy
MCTS	Master of Clinical and Translational Science
MCVS	Master of Cardiovascular Science
MD	Doctor of Medicine
MDA	Master of Development Administration
	Master of Dietetic Administration
MDB	Master of Design-Build
MDE	Master of Developmental Economics
	Master of Distance Education
	Master of the Education of the Deaf
MDH	Master of Dental Hygiene
MDM	Master of Design Methods
	Master of Digital Media
MDP	Master in Sustainable Development Practice
	Master of Development Practice
MDR	Master of Dispute Resolution
MDS	Master of Dental Surgery
	Master of Design Studies
ME	Master of Education
	Master of Engineering
	Master of Entrepreneurship
	Master of Evangelism
ME Sc	Master of Engineering Science
MEA	Master of Educational Administration
	Master of Engineering Administration
MEAP	Master of Environmental Administration and Planning
MEBT	Master in Electronic Business Technologies
MEC	Master of Electronic Commerce
MECE	Master of Electrical and Computer Engineering
Mech E	Mechanical Engineer
MED	Master of Education of the Deaf
MEDS	Master of Environmental Design Studies
MEE	Master in Education
	Master of Electrical Engineering
	Master of Energy Engineering
	Master of Environmental Engineering
MEEM	Master of Environmental Engineering and Management
MEENE	Master of Engineering in Environmental Engineering
MEEP	Master of Environmental and Energy Policy
MEERM	Master of Earth and Environmental Resource Management
MEH	Master in Humanistic Studies
	Master of Environmental Horticulture
MEHP	Master of Education in the Health Professions
MEHS	Master of Environmental Health and Safety
MEIM	Master of Entertainment Industry Management

MEL — Master of Educational Leadership
Master of English Literature
MELP — Master of Environmental Law and Policy
MEM — Master of Ecosystem Management
Master of Electricity Markets
Master of Engineering Management
Master of Environmental Management
Master of Marketing
MEME — Master of Engineering in Manufacturing Engineering
Master of Engineering in Mechanical Engineering
MENG — Master of Arts in English
MENVEGR — Master of Environmental Engineering
MEP — Master of Engineering Physics
MEPC — Master of Environmental Pollution Control
MEPD — Master of EducationNProfessional Development
Master of Environmental Planning and Design
MER — Master of Employment Relations
MERE — Master of Entrepreneurial Real Estate
MES — Master of Education and Science
Master of Engineering Science
Master of Environment and Sustainability
Master of Environmental Science
Master of Environmental Studies
Master of Environmental Systems
Master of Special Education
MESM — Master of Environmental Science and Management
MET — Master of Educational Technology
Master of Engineering Technology
Master of Entertainment Technology
Master of Environmental Toxicology
METM — Master of Engineering and Technology Management
MEVE — Master of Environmental Engineering
MF — Master of Finance
Master of Forestry
MFA — Master of Fine Arts
MFAM — Master in Food Animal Medicine
MFAS — Master of Fisheries and Aquatic Science
MFAW — Master of Fine Arts in Writing
MFC — Master of Forest Conservation
MFCS — Master of Family and Consumer Sciences
MFE — Master of Financial Economics
Master of Financial Engineering
Master of Forest Engineering
MFG — Master of Functional Genomics
MFHD — Master of Family and Human Development
MFM — Master of Financial Management
Master of Financial Mathematics
MFMS — Master's in Food Microbiology and Safety
MFPE — Master of Food Process Engineering
MFR — Master of Forest Resources
MFRC — Master of Forest Resources and Conservation
MFS — Master of Food Science
Master of Forensic Sciences
Master of Forest Science
Master of Forest Studies
Master of French Studies
MFST — Master of Food Safety and Technology
MFT — Master of Family Therapy
Master of Food Technology
MFWB — Master of Fishery and Wildlife Biology
MFWCB — Master of Fish, Wildlife and Conservation Biology
MFWS — Master of Fisheries and Wildlife Sciences
MFYCS — Master of Family, Youth and Community Sciences
MG — Master of Genetics
MGA — Master of Global Affairs
Master of Governmental Administration
MGC — Master of Genetic Counseling
MGD — Master of Graphic Design
MGE — Master of Geotechnical Engineering
MGEM — Master of Global Entrepreneurship and Management
MGIS — Master of Geographic Information Science
Master of Geographic Information Systems
MGM — Master of Global Management
MGP — Master of Gestion de Projet
MGPS — Master of Global Policy Studies
MGPS/MA — Master of Global Policy Studies/Master of Arts
MGPS/MPH — Master of Global Policy Studies/Master of Public Health

MGREM — Master of Global Real Estate Management
MGS — Master of Gerontological Studies
Master of Global Studies
MH — Master of Humanities
MH Ed — Master of Health Education
MH Sc — Master of Health Sciences
MHA — Master of Health Administration
Master of Healthcare Administration
Master of Hospital Administration
Master of Hospitality Administration
MHAD — Master of Health Administration
MHB — Master of Human Behavior
MHCA — Master of Health Care Administration
MHCI — Master of Health Care Informatics
Master of Human-Computer Interaction
MHCL — Master of Health Care Leadership
MHE — Master of Health Education
Master of Human Ecology
MHE Ed — Master of Home Economics Education
MHEA — Master of Higher Education Administration
MHHS — Master of Health and Human Services
MHI — Master of Health Informatics
Master of Healthcare Innovation
MHIIM — Master of Health Informatics and Information Management
MHIS — Master of Health Information Systems
MHK — Master of Human Kinetics
MHL — Master of Hebrew Literature
MHM — Master of Healthcare Management
MHMS — Master of Health Management Systems
MHP — Master of Health Physics
Master of Heritage Preservation
Master of Historic Preservation
MHPA — Master of Heath Policy and Administration
MHPE — Master of Health Professions Education
MHR — Master of Human Resources
MHRD — Master in Human Resource Development
MHRIR — Master of Human Resources and Industrial Relations
MHRLR — Master of Human Resources and Labor Relations
MHRM — Master of Human Resources Management
MHS — Master of Health Science
Master of Health Sciences
Master of Health Studies
Master of Hispanic Studies
Master of Human Services
Master of Humanistic Studies
MHSA — Master of Health Services Administration
MHSM — Master of Health Systems Management
MI — Master of Information
Master of Instruction
MI Arch — Master of Interior Architecture
MIA — Master of Interior Architecture
Master of International Affairs
MIAA — Master of International Affairs and Administration
MIAM — Master of International Agribusiness Management
MIAPD — Master of Interior Architecture and Product Design
MIB — Master of International Business
MIBA — Master of International Business Administration
MICM — Master of International Construction Management
MID — Master of Industrial Design
Master of Industrial Distribution
Master of Interior Design
Master of International Development
MIDC — Master of Integrated Design and Construction
MIE — Master of Industrial Engineering
MIH — Master of Integrative Health
MIHTM — Master of International Hospitality and Tourism Management
MIJ — Master of International Journalism
MILR — Master of Industrial and Labor Relations
MiM — Master in Management
MIM — Master of Industrial Management
Master of Information Management
Master of International Management
MIMLAE — Master of International Management for Latin American Executives
MIMS — Master of Information Management and Systems
Master of Integrated Manufacturing Systems
MIP — Master of Infrastructure Planning
Master of Intellectual Property

	Master of International Policy		Master of Mass Communications
MIPA	Master of International Public Affairs		Master of Music Conducting
MIPER	Master of International Political Economy of Resources	MMCM	Master of Music in Church Music
MIPP	Master of International Policy and Practice	MMCSS	Master of Mathematical Computational and Statistical Sciences
	Master of International Public Policy	MME	Master of Manufacturing Engineering
MIPS	Master of International Planning Studies		Master of Mathematics Education
MIR	Master of Industrial Relations		Master of Mathematics for Educators
	Master of International Relations		Master of Mechanical Engineering
MIRHR	Master of Industrial Relations and Human Resources		Master of Medical Engineering
			Master of Mining Engineering
MIS	Master of Industrial Statistics		Master of Music Education
	Master of Information Science	MMF	Master of Mathematical Finance
	Master of Information Systems	MMFT	Master of Marriage and Family Therapy
	Master of Integrated Science	MMG	Master of Management
	Master of Interdisciplinary Studies	MMH	Master of Management in Hospitality
	Master of International Service		Master of Medical Humanities
	Master of International Studies	MMI	Master of Management of Innovation
MISE	Master of Industrial and Systems Engineering	MMIS	Master of Management Information Systems
MISKM	Master of Information Sciences and Knowledge Management	MMM	Master of Manufacturing Management
			Master of Marine Management
MISM	Master of Information Systems Management		Master of Medical Management
MIT	Master in Teaching	MMME	Master of Metallurgical and Materials Engineering
	Master of Industrial Technology	MMP	Master of Management Practice
	Master of Information Technology		Master of Marine Policy
	Master of Initial Teaching		Master of Medical Physics
	Master of International Trade		Master of Music Performance
	Master of Internet Technology	MMPA	Master of Management and Professional Accounting
MITA	Master of Information Technology Administration		
MITM	Master of Information Technology and Management	MMQM	Master of Manufacturing Quality Management
		MMR	Master of Marketing Research
MITO	Master of Industrial Technology and Operations	MMRM	Master of Marine Resources Management
MJ	Master of Journalism	MMS	Master of Management Science
	Master of Jurisprudence		Master of Management Studies
MJ Ed	Master of Jewish Education		Master of Manufacturing Systems
MJA	Master of Justice Administration		Master of Marine Studies
MJM	Master of Justice Management		Master of Materials Science
MJS	Master of Judicial Studies		Master of Medical Science
	Master of Juridical Science		Master of Medieval Studies
MKM	Master of Knowledge Management	MMSE	Master of Manufacturing Systems Engineering
ML	Master of Latin		Multidisciplinary Master of Science in Engineering
ML Arch	Master of Landscape Architecture	MMSM	Master of Music in Sacred Music
MLA	Master of Landscape Architecture	MMT	Master in Marketing
	Master of Liberal Arts		Master of Music Teaching
MLAS	Master of Laboratory Animal Science		Master of Music Therapy
	Master of Liberal Arts and Sciences		Master's in Marketing Technology
MLAUD	Master of Landscape Architecture in Urban Development	MMus	Master of Music
		MN	Master of Nursing
MLD	Master of Leadership Development		Master of Nutrition
MLE	Master of Applied Linguistics and Exegesis	MN NP	Master of Nursing in Nurse Practitioner
MLER	Master of Labor and Employment Relations	MNA	Master of Nonprofit Administration
MLHR	Master of Labor and Human Resources		Master of Nurse Anesthesia
MLI Sc	Master of Library and Information Science	MNAL	Master of Nonprofit Administration and Leadership
MLIS	Master of Library and Information Science	MNAS	Master of Natural and Applied Science
	Master of Library and Information Studies	MNCM	Master of Network and Communications Management
MLM	Master of Library Media		
MLRHR	Master of Labor Relations and Human Resources	MNE	Master of Network Engineering
MLS	Master of Leadership Studies		Master of Nuclear Engineering
	Master of Legal Studies	MNL	Master in International Business for Latin America
	Master of Liberal Studies	MNM	Master of Nonprofit Management
	Master of Library Science	MNO	Master of Nonprofit Organization
	Master of Life Sciences	MNPL	Master of Not-for-Profit Leadership
MLSP	Master of Law and Social Policy	MNpS	Master of Nonprofit Studies
MLT	Master of Language Technologies	MNR	Master of Natural Resources
MLTCA	Master of Long Term Care Administration	MNRES	Master of Natural Resources and Environmental Studies
MM	Master of Management		
	Master of Ministry	MNRM	Master of Natural Resource Management
	Master of Missiology	MNRS	Master of Natural Resource Stewardship
	Master of Music	MNS	Master of Natural Science
MM Ed	Master of Music Education	MO	Master of Oceanography
MM Sc	Master of Medical Science	MOD	Master of Organizational Development
MM St	Master of Museum Studies	MOGS	Master of Oil and Gas Studies
MMA	Master of Marine Affairs	MOH	Master of Occupational Health
	Master of Media Arts	MOL	Master of Organizational Leadership
	Master of Musical Arts	MOM	Master of Oriental Medicine
MMAE	Master of Mechanical and Aerospace Engineering	MOR	Master of Operations Research
MMAL	Master of Maritime Administration and Logistics	MOT	Master of Occupational Therapy
MMAS	Master of Military Art and Science	MP	Master of Physiology
MMB	Master of Microbial Biotechnology		Master of Planning
MMBA	Managerial Master of Business Administration	MP Ac	Master of Professional Accountancy
MMC	Master of Manufacturing Competitiveness		

MP Acc	Master of Professional Accountancy	MRLS	Master of Resources Law Studies
	Master of Professional Accounting	MRM	Master of Resources Management
	Master of Public Accounting	MRP	Master of Regional Planning
MP Aff	Master of Public Affairs	MRS	Master of Religious Studies
MP Aff/MPH	Master of Public Affairs/Master of Public Health	MRSc	Master of Rehabilitation Science
MP Th	Master of Pastoral Theology	MS	Master of Science
MPA	Master of Physician Assistant	MS Cmp E	Master of Science in Computer Engineering
	Master of Professional Accountancy	MS Kin	Master of Science in Kinesiology
	Master of Professional Accounting	MS Acct	Master of Science in Accounting
	Master of Public Administration	MS Accy	Master of Science in Accountancy
	Master of Public Affairs	MS Aero E	Master of Science in Aerospace Engineering
MPAC	Master of Professional Accounting	MS Ag	Master of Science in Agriculture
MPAID	Master of Public Administration and International Development	MS Arch	Master of Science in Architecture
		MS Arch St	Master of Science in Architectural Studies
MPAP	Master of Physician Assistant Practice	MS Bio E	Master of Science in Bioengineering
	Master of Public Affairs and Politics		Master of Science in Biomedical Engineering
MPAS	Master of Physician Assistant Science	MS Bm E	Master of Science in Biomedical Engineering
	Master of Physician Assistant Studies	MS Ch E	Master of Science in Chemical Engineering
MPC	Master of Pastoral Counseling	MS Chem	Master of Science in Chemistry
	Master of Professional Communication	MS Cp E	Master of Science in Computer Engineering
	Master of Professional Counseling	MS Eco	Master of Science in Economics
MPCU	Master of Planning in Civic Urbanism	MS Econ	Master of Science in Economics
MPD	Master of Product Development	MS Ed	Master of Science in Education
	Master of Public Diplomacy	MS El	Master of Science in Educational Leadership and Administration
MPDS	Master of Planning and Development Studies		
MPE	Master of Physical Education	MS En E	Master of Science in Environmental Engineering
	Master of Power Engineering	MS Eng	Master of Science in Engineering
MPEM	Master of Project Engineering and Management	MS Engr	Master of Science in Engineering
MPH	Master of Public Health	MS Env E	Master of Science in Environmental Engineering
MPHE	Master of Public Health Education	MS Exp Surg	Master of Science in Experimental Surgery
MPHTM	Master of Public Health and Tropical Medicine	MS Int A	Master of Science in International Affairs
MPI	Master of Product Innovation	MS Mat E	Master of Science in Materials Engineering
MPIA	Master in International Affairs	MS Mat SE	Master of Science in Material Science and Engineering
	Master of Public and International Affairs		
MPM	Master of Pastoral Ministry	MS Met E	Master of Science in Metallurgical Engineering
	Master of Pest Management	MS Mgt	Master of Science in Management
	Master of Policy Management	MS Min	Master of Science in Mining
	Master of Practical Ministries	MS Min E	Master of Science in Mining Engineering
	Master of Project Management	MS Mt E	Master of Science in Materials Engineering
	Master of Public Management	MS Otal	Master of Science in Otalrynology
MPNA	Master of Public and Nonprofit Administration	MS Pet E	Master of Science in Petroleum Engineering
MPO	Master of Prosthetics and Orthotics	MS Phys	Master of Science in Physics
MPOD	Master of Positive Organizational Development	MS Poly	Master of Science in Polymers
MPP	Master of Public Policy	MS Psy	Master of Science in Psychology
MPPA	Master of Public Policy Administration	MS Pub P	Master of Science in Public Policy
	Master of Public Policy and Administration	MS Sc	Master of Science in Social Science
MPPAL	Master of Public Policy, Administration and Law	MS Sp Ed	Master of Science in Special Education
MPPM	Master of Public and Private Management	MS Stat	Master of Science in Statistics
	Master of Public Policy and Management	MS Surg	Master of Science in Surgery
MPPPM	Master of Plant Protection and Pest Management	MS Tax	Master of Science in Taxation
MPRTM	Master of Parks, Recreation, and Tourism Management	MS Tc E	Master of Science in Telecommunications Engineering
MPS	Master of Pastoral Studies	MS-R	Master of Science (Research)
	Master of Perfusion Science	MS/CAGS	Master of Science/Certificate of Advanced Graduate Studies
	Master of Planning Studies		
	Master of Political Science	MSA	Master of School Administration
	Master of Preservation Studies		Master of Science Administration
	Master of Professional Studies		Master of Science in Accountancy
	Master of Public Service		Master of Science in Accounting
MPSA	Master of Public Service Administration		Master of Science in Administration
MPSRE	Master of Professional Studies in Real Estate		Master of Science in Aeronautics
MPT	Master of Pastoral Theology		Master of Science in Agriculture
	Master of Physical Therapy		Master of Science in Anesthesia
	Master of Practical Theology		Master of Science in Architecture
MPVM	Master of Preventive Veterinary Medicine		Master of Science in Aviation
MPW	Master of Professional Writing		Master of Sports Administration
	Master of Public Works	MSA Phy	Master of Science in Applied Physics
MQM	Master of Quality Management	MSAA	Master of Science in Astronautics and Aeronautics
MQS	Master of Quality Systems	MSAAE	Master of Science in Aeronautical and Astronautical Engineering
MR	Master of Recreation		
	Master of Retailing	MSABE	Master of Science in Agricultural and Biological Engineering
MRA	Master in Research Administration		
MRC	Master of Rehabilitation Counseling	MSAC	Master of Science in Acupuncture
MRCP	Master of Regional and City Planning	MSACC	Master of Science in Accounting
	Master of Regional and Community Planning	MSAE	Master of Science in Aeronautical Engineering
MRD	Master of Rural Development		Master of Science in Aerospace Engineering
MRE	Master of Real Estate		Master of Science in Applied Economics
	Master of Religious Education		Master of Science in Applied Engineering
MRED	Master of Real Estate Development		Master of Science in Architectural Engineering
MREM	Master of Resource and Environmental Management	MSAH	Master of Science in Allied Health
		MSAL	Master of Sport Administration and Leadership

MSAM	Master of Science in Applied Mathematics	MSCRP/MP Aff	Master of Science in Community and Regional Planning/Master of Public Affairs
MSANR	Master of Science in Agriculture and Natural Resources Systems Management	MSCRP/MSSD	Master of Science in Community and Regional Planning/Master of Science in Sustainable Design
MSAPM	Master of Security Analysis and Portfolio Management	MSCRP/MSUD	Master of Science in Community and Regional Planning/Masters of Science in Urban Design
MSAS	Master of Science in Applied Statistics	MSCS	Master of Science in Clinical Science
	Master of Science in Architectural Studies		Master of Science in Computer Science
MSAT	Master of Science in Accounting and Taxation	MSCSD	Master of Science in Communication Sciences and Disorders
	Master of Science in Advanced Technology	MSCSE	Master of Science in Computer Science and Engineering
	Master of Science in Athletic Training		
MSB	Master of Science in Bible	MSCTE	Master of Science in Career and Technical Education
	Master of Science in Biotechnology		
	Master of Science in Business	MSD	Master of Science in Dentistry
	Master of Sustainable Business		Master of Science in Design
MSBA	Master of Science in Business Administration		Master of Science in Dietetics
	Master of Science in Business Analysis	MSE	Master of Science Education
MSBAE	Master of Science in Biological and Agricultural Engineering		Master of Science in Economics
			Master of Science in Education
	Master of Science in Biosystems and Agricultural Engineering		Master of Science in Engineering
			Master of Science in Engineering Management
MSBC	Master of Science in Building Construction		Master of Software Engineering
MSBCB	bioinformatics and computational biology		Master of Special Education
MSBE	Master of Science in Biological Engineering		Master of Structural Engineering
	Master of Science in Biomedical Engineering	MSECE	Master of Science in Electrical and Computer Engineering
MSBENG	Master of Science in Bioengineering		
MSBIT	Master of Science in Business Information Technology	MSED	Master of Sustainable Economic Development
		MSEE	Master of Science in Electrical Engineering
MSBM	Master of Sport Business Management		Master of Science in Environmental Engineering
MSBME	Master of Science in Biomedical Engineering	MSEH	Master of Science in Environmental Health
MSBMS	Master of Science in Basic Medical Science	MSEL	Master of Science in Educational Leadership
MSBS	Master of Science in Biomedical Sciences	MSEM	Master of Science in Engineering Management
MSC	Master of Science in Commerce		Master of Science in Engineering Mechanics
	Master of Science in Communication		Master of Science in Environmental Management
	Master of Science in Computers	MSENE	Master of Science in Environmental Engineering
	Master of Science in Counseling		
	Master of Science in Criminology	MSEO	Master of Science in Electro-Optics
MSCC	Master of Science in Christian Counseling	MSEP	Master of Science in Economic Policy
	Master of Science in Community Counseling	MSEPA	Master of Science in Economics and Policy Analysis
MSCD	Master of Science in Communication Disorders	MSES	Master of Science in Embedded Software Engineering
	Master of Science in Community Development		
MSCE	Master of Science in Civil Engineering		Master of Science in Engineering Science
	Master of Science in Clinical Epidemiology		Master of Science in Environmental Science
	Master of Science in Computer Engineering		Master of Science in Environmental Studies
	Master of Science in Continuing Education	MSESM	Master of Science in Engineering Science and Mechanics
MSCEE	Master of Science in Civil and Environmental Engineering		
		MSET	Master of Science in Educational Technology
MSCF	Master of Science in Computational Finance		Master of Science in Engineering Technology
MSCH	Master of Science in Chemical Engineering	MSEV	Master of Science in Environmental Engineering
MSChE	Master of Science in Chemical Engineering	MSEVH	Master of Science in Environmental Health and Safety
MSCI	Master of Science in Clinical Investigation		
	Master of Science in Curriculum and Instruction	MSF	Master of Science in Finance
MSCIS	Master of Science in Computer and Information Systems		Master of Science in Forestry
			Master of Spiritual Formation
	Master of Science in Computer Information Science	MSFA	Master of Science in Financial Analysis
		MSFAM	Master of Science in Family Studies
	Master of Science in Computer Information Systems	MSFCS	Master of Science in Family and Consumer Science
		MSFE	Master of Science in Financial Engineering
MSCIT	Master of Science in Computer Information Technology	MSFOR	Master of Science in Forestry
		MSFP	Master of Science in Financial Planning
MSCJ	Master of Science in Criminal Justice	MSFS	Master of Science in Financial Sciences
MSCJA	Master of Science in Criminal Justice Administration		Master of Science in Forensic Science
		MSFSB	Master of Science in Financial Services and Banking
MSCJS	Master of Science in Crime and Justice Studies		
MSCLS	Master of Science in Clinical Laboratory Studies	MSFT	Master of Science in Family Therapy
MSCM	Master of Science in Church Management	MSGC	Master of Science in Genetic Counseling
	Master of Science in Conflict Management	MSH	Master of Science in Health
	Master of Science in Construction Management		Master of Science in Hospice
MScM	Master of Science in Management	MSHA	Master of Science in Health Administration
MSCM	Master of Supply Chain Management	MSHCA	Master of Science in Health Care Administration
MSCNU	Master of Science in Clinical Nutrition	MSHCI	Master of Science in Human Computer Interaction
MSCP	Master of Science in Clinical Psychology	MSHCPM	Master of Science in Health Care Policy and Management
	Master of Science in Community Psychology		
	Master of Science in Computer Engineering	MSHE	Master of Science in Health Education
	Master of Science in Counseling Psychology	MSHES	Master of Science in Human Environmental Sciences
MSCPE	Master of Science in Computer Engineering		
MSCPharm	Master of Science in Pharmacy	MSHFID	Master of Science in Human Factors in Information Design
MSCPI	Master in Strategic Planning for Critical Infrastructures		
		MSHFS	Master of Science in Human Factors and Systems
MSCR	Master of Science in Clinical Research	MSHI	Master of Science in Health Informatics
MSCRP	Master of Science in City and Regional Planning	MSHP	Master of Science in Health Professions
	Master of Science in Community and Regional Planning		Master of Science in Health Promotion

MSHR	Master of Science in Human Resources	MSMAE	Master of Science in Materials Engineering
MSHRL	Master of Science in Human Resource Leadership	MSMC	Master of Science in Mass Communications
MSHRM	Master of Science in Human Resource Management	MSME	Master of Science in Mathematics Education
			Master of Science in Mechanical Engineering
MSHROD	Master of Science in Human Resources and Organizational Development	MSMFE	Master of Science in Manufacturing Engineering
		MSMFT	Master of Science in Marriage and Family Therapy
MSHS	Master of Science in Health Science	MSMIS	Master of Science in Management Information Systems
	Master of Science in Health Services		
	Master of Science in Health Systems	MSMIT	Master of Science in Management and Information Technology
	Master of Science in Homeland Security		
MSHT	Master of Science in History of Technology	MSMLS	Master of Science in Medical Laboratory Science
MSI	Master of Science in Information	MSMOT	Master of Science in Management of Technology
	Master of Science in Instruction	MSMS	Master of Science in Management Science
	Master of System Integration		Master of Science in Medical Sciences
MSIA	Master of Science in Industrial Administration	MSMSE	Master of Science in Manufacturing Systems Engineering
	Master of Science in Information Assurance and Computer Security		Master of Science in Material Science and Engineering
MSIB	Master of Science in International Business		Master of Science in Mathematics and Science Education
MSIDM	Master of Science in Interior Design and Merchandising		
MSIDT	Master of Science in Information Design and Technology	MSMT	Master of Science in Management and Technology
		MSMus	Master of Sacred Music
MSIE	Master of Science in Industrial Engineering	MSN	Master of Science in Nursing
	Master of Science in International Economics	MSN-R	Master of Science in Nursing (Research)
MSIEM	Master of Science in Information Engineering and Management	MSNA	Master of Science in Nurse Anesthesia
		MSNE	Master of Science in Nuclear Engineering
MSIID	Master of Science in Information and Instructional Design	MSNED	Master of Science in Nurse Education
		MSNM	Master of Science in Nonprofit Management
MSIM	Master of Science in Information Management	MSNS	Master of Science in Natural Science
	Master of Science in International Management		Master of Science in Nutritional Science
MSIMC	Master of Science in Integrated Marketing Communications	MSOD	Master of Science in Organizational Development
		MSOEE	Master of Science in Outdoor and Environmental Education
MSIR	Master of Science in Industrial Relations		
MSIS	Master of Science in Information Science	MSOES	Master of Science in Occupational Ergonomics and Safety
	Master of Science in Information Studies		
	Master of Science in Information Systems	MSOH	Master of Science in Occupational Health
	Master of Science in Interdisciplinary Studies	MSOL	Master of Science in Organizational Leadership
MSIS/MA	Master of Science in Information Studies/Master of Arts	MSOM	Master of Science in Operations Management
			Master of Science in Oriental Medicine
MSISE	Master of Science in Infrastructure Systems Engineering	MSOR	Master of Science in Operations Research
		MSOT	Master of Science in Occupational Technology
MSISM	Master of Science in Information Systems Management		Master of Science in Occupational Therapy
MSISPM	Master of Science in Information Security Policy and Management	MSP	Master of Science in Pharmacy
			Master of Science in Planning
			Master of Science in Psychology
MSIST	Master of Science in Information Systems Technology		Master of Speech Pathology
MSIT	Master of Science in Industrial Technology	MSPA	Master of Science in Physician Assistant
	Master of Science in Information Technology		Master of Science in Professional Accountancy
	Master of Science in Instructional Technology	MSPAS	Master of Science in Physician Assistant Studies
MSITM	Master of Science in Information Technology Management	MSPC	Master of Science in Professional Communications
			Master of Science in Professional Counseling
MSJ	Master of Science in Journalism	MSPE	Master of Science in Petroleum Engineering
	Master of Science in Jurisprudence	MSPG	Master of Science in Psychology
MSJC	Master of Social Justice and Criminology	MSPH	Master of Science in Public Health
MSJE	Master of Science in Jewish Education	MSPHR	Master of Science in Pharmacy
MSJFP	Master of Science in Juvenile Forensic Psychology	MSPM	Master of Science in Professional Management
MSJJ	Master of Science in Juvenile Justice		Master of Science in Project Management
MSJPS	Master of Science in Justice and Public Safety	MSPNGE	Master of Science in Petroleum and Natural Gas Engineering
MSJS	Master of Science in Jewish Studies		
MSK	Master of Science in Kinesiology	MSPS	Master of Science in Pharmaceutical Science
MSL	Master of School Leadership		Master of Science in Political Science
	Master of Science in Leadership		Master of Science in Psychological Services
	Master of Science in Limnology	MSPT	Master of Science in Physical Therapy
	Master of Strategic Leadership	MSpVM	Master of Specialized Veterinary Medicine
	Master of Studies in Law	MSR	Master of Science in Radiology
MSLA	Master of Science in Landscape Architecture		Master of Science in Reading
	Master of Science in Legal Administration	MSRA	Master of Science in Recreation Administration
MSLD	Master of Science in Land Development	MSRC	Master of Science in Resource Conservation
MSLFS	Master of Science in Life Sciences	MSRE	Master of Science in Real Estate
MSLP	Master of Speech-Language Pathology		Master of Science in Religious Education
MSLS	Master of Science in Library Science	MSRED	Master of Science in Real Estate Development
MSLSCM	Master of Science in Logistics and Supply Chain Management	MSRLS	Master of Science in Recreation and Leisure Studies
MSLT	Master of Second Language Teaching	MSRMP	Master of Science in Radiological Medical Physics
MSM	Master of Sacred Ministry	MSRS	Master of Science in Rehabilitation Science
	Master of Sacred Music	MSS	Master of Science in Software
	Master of School Mathematics		Master of Security Studies
	Master of Science in Management		Master of Social Science
	Master of Science in Organization Management		Master of Social Services
	Master of Security Management		Master of Software Systems
MSMA	Master of Science in Marketing Analysis		Master of Sports Science

	Master of Strategic Studies	MUEP	Master of Urban and Environmental Planning
MSSA	Master of Science in Social Administration	MUP	Master of Urban Planning
MSSCP	Master of Science in Science Content and Process	MUPDD	Master of Urban Planning, Design, and Development
MSSD	Master of Science in Sustainable Design	MUPP	Master of Urban Planning and Policy
MSSE	Master of Science in Software Engineering	MUPRED	Master of Urban Planning and Real Estate Development
	Master of Science in Space Education		
	Master of Science in Special Education	MURP	Master of Urban and Regional Planning
MSSEM	Master of Science in Systems and Engineering Management		Master of Urban and Rural Planning
MSSI	Master of Science in Security Informatics	MURPL	Master of Urban and Regional Planning
	Master of Science in Strategic Intelligence	MUS	Master of Urban Studies
MSSL	Master of Science in School Leadership	MUSA	Master of Urban Spatial Analytics
	Master of Science in Strategic Leadership	MVM	Master of VLSI and Microelectronics
MSSLP	Master of Science in Speech-Language Pathology	MVP	Master of Voice Pedagogy
MSSM	Master of Science in Sports Medicine	MVPH	Master of Veterinary Public Health
MSSP	Master of Science in Social Policy	MVS	Master of Visual Studies
MSSPA	Master of Science in Student Personnel Administration	MWC	Master of Wildlife Conservation
		MWE	Master in Welding Engineering
MSSS	Master of Science in Safety Science	MWPS	Master of Wood and Paper Science
	Master of Science in Systems Science	MWR	Master of Water Resources
MSST	Master of Science in Security Technologies	MWS	Master of Women's Studies
MSSW	Master of Science in Social Work		Master of Worship Studies
MSSWE	Master of Science in Software Engineering	MZS	Master of Zoological Science
MST	Master of Science and Technology	Nav Arch	Naval Architecture
	Master of Science in Taxation	Naval E	Naval Engineer
	Master of Science in Teaching	ND	Doctor of Naturopathic Medicine
	Master of Science in Technology	NE	Nuclear Engineer
	Master of Science in Telecommunications	Nuc E	Nuclear Engineer
	Master of Science Teaching	OD	Doctor of Optometry
MSTC	Master of Science in Technical Communication	OTD	Doctor of Occupational Therapy
	Master of Science in Telecommunications	PBME	Professional Master of Biomedical Engineering
MSTCM	Master of Science in Traditional Chinese Medicine	PC	Performer's Certificate
MSTE	Master of Science in Telecommunications Engineering	PD	Professional Diploma
		PGC	Post-Graduate Certificate
	Master of Science in Transportation Engineering	PGD	Postgraduate Diploma
MSTM	Master of Science in Technical Management	Ph L	Licentiate of Philosophy
	Master of Science in Technology Management	Pharm D	Doctor of Pharmacy
	Master of Science in Transfusion Medicine	PhD	Doctor of Philosophy
MSTOM	Master of Science in Traditional Oriental Medicine	PhD Otal	Doctor of Philosophy in Otalrynology
MSUD	Master of Science in Urban Design	PhD Surg	Doctor of Philosophy in Surgery
MSW	Master of Social Work	PhDEE	Doctor of Philosophy in Electrical Engineering
MSWE	Master of Software Engineering	PMBA	Professional Master of Business Administration
MSWREE	Master of Science in Water Resources and Environmental Engineering	PMC	Post Master Certificate
		PMD	Post-Master's Diploma
MSX	Master of Science in Exercise Science	PMS	Professional Master of Science
MT	Master of Taxation		Professional Master's
	Master of Teaching	Post-Doctoral MS	Post-Doctoral Master of Science
	Master of Technology	Post-MSN Certificate	Post-Master of Science in Nursing Certificate
	Master of Textiles	PPDPT	Postprofessional Doctor of Physical Therapy
MTA	Master of Tax Accounting	Pro-MS	Professional Science Master's
	Master of Teaching Arts	PSM	Professional Master of Science
	Master of Tourism Administration		Professional Science Master's
MTCM	Master of Traditional Chinese Medicine	Psy D	Doctor of Psychology
MTD	Master of Training and Development	Psy M	Master of Psychology
MTE	Master in Educational Technology	Psy S	Specialist in Psychology
MTESOL	Master in Teaching English to Speakers of Other Languages	Psya D	Doctor of Psychoanalysis
		Rh D	Doctor of Rehabilitation
MTHM	Master of Tourism and Hospitality Management	S Psy S	Specialist in Psychological Services
MTI	Master of Information Technology	Sc D	Doctor of Science
MTIM	Master of Trust and Investment Management	Sc M	Master of Science
MTL	Master of Talmudic Law	SCCT	Specialist in Community College Teaching
MTM	Master of Technology Management	ScDPT	Doctor of Physical Therapy Science
	Master of Telecommunications Management	SD	Doctor of Science
	Master of the Teaching of Mathematics		Specialist Degree
MTMH	Master of Tropical Medicine and Hygiene	SJD	Doctor of Juridical Science
MTOM	Master of Traditional Oriental Medicine	SLPD	Doctor of Speech-Language Pathology
MTP	Master of Transpersonal Psychology	SM	Master of Science
MTPC	Master of Technical and Professional Communication	SM Arch S	Master of Science in Architectural Studies
		SMACT	Master of Science in Art, Culture and Technology
MTR	Master of Translational Research	SMBT	Master of Science in Building Technology
MTS	Master of Theatre Studies	SP	Specialist Degree
	Master of Theological Studies	Sp C	Specialist in Counseling
MTSC	Master of Technical and Scientific Communication	Sp Ed	Specialist in Education
MTSE	Master of Telecommunications and Software Engineering	Sp LIS	Specialist in Library and Information Science
		SPA	Specialist in Arts
MTT	Master in Technology Management	SPCM	Specialist in Church Music
MTX	Master of Taxation	Spec	Specialist's Certificate
MUA	Master of Urban Affairs	Spec M	Specialist in Music
MUCD	Master of Urban and Community Design	SPEM	Specialist in Educational Ministries
MUD	Master of Urban Design	Spt	Specialist Degree
MUDS	Master of Urban Design Studies		

ABBREVIATIONS USED IN THE GUIDES

SPTH	Specialist in Theology	TDPT	Transitional Doctor of Physical Therapy
SSP	Specialist in School Psychology	Th D	Doctor of Theology
STB	Bachelor of Sacred Theology	Th M	Master of Theology
STD	Doctor of Sacred Theology	VMD	Doctor of Veterinary Medicine
STL	Licentiate of Sacred Theology	WEMBA	Weekend Executive Master of Business Administration
STM	Master of Sacred Theology	XMA	Executive Master of Arts

INDEXES

Displays and Close-Ups

Directories and Subject Areas

Following is an alphabetical listing of directories and subject areas. Also listed are cross-references for subject area names not used in the directory structure of the guides, for example, "City and Regional Planning (*see* Urban and Regional Planning)."

Graduate Programs in the Humanities, Arts & Social Sciences

Addictions/Substance Abuse Counseling
Administration (*see* Arts Administration; Public Administration)
African-American Studies
African Languages and Literatures (*see* African Studies)
African Studies
Agribusiness (*see* Agricultural Economics and Agribusiness)
Agricultural Economics and Agribusiness
Alcohol Abuse Counseling (*see* Addictions/Substance Abuse Counseling)
American Indian/Native American Studies
American Studies
Anthropology
Applied Arts and Design—General
Applied Behavior Analysis
Applied Economics
Applied History (*see* Public History)
Applied Psychology
Applied Social Research
Arabic (*see* Near and Middle Eastern Languages)
Arab Studies (*see* Near and Middle Eastern Studies)
Archaeology
Architectural History
Architecture
Archives Administration (*see* Public History)
Area and Cultural Studies (*see* African-American Studies; African Studies; American Indian/Native American Studies; American Studies; Asian-American Studies; Asian Studies; Canadian Studies; Cultural Studies; East European and Russian Studies; Ethnic Studies; Folklore; Gender Studies; Hispanic Studies; Holocaust Studies; Jewish Studies; Latin American Studies; Near and Middle Eastern Studies; Northern Studies; Pacific Area/ Pacific Rim Studies; Western European Studies; Women's Studies)
Art/Fine Arts
Art History
Arts Administration
Arts Journalism
Art Therapy
Asian-American Studies
Asian Languages
Asian Studies
Behavioral Sciences (*see* Psychology)
Bible Studies (*see* Religion; Theology)
Biological Anthropology
Black Studies (*see* African-American Studies)
Broadcasting (*see* Communication; Film, Television, and Video Production)
Broadcast Journalism
Building Science
Canadian Studies
Celtic Languages
Ceramics (*see* Art/Fine Arts)
Child and Family Studies
Child Development
Chinese
Chinese Studies (*see* Asian Languages; Asian Studies)
Christian Studies (*see* Missions and Missiology; Religion; Theology)
Cinema (*see* Film, Television, and Video Production)
City and Regional Planning (*see* Urban and Regional Planning)
Classical Languages and Literatures (*see* Classics)
Classics
Clinical Psychology
Clothing and Textiles
Cognitive Psychology (*see* Psychology—General; Cognitive Sciences)
Cognitive Sciences
Communication—General
Community Affairs (*see* Urban and Regional Planning; Urban Studies)
Community Planning (*see* Architecture; Environmental Design; Urban and Regional Planning; Urban Design; Urban Studies)
Community Psychology (*see* Social Psychology)
Comparative and Interdisciplinary Arts
Comparative Literature

Composition (*see* Music)
Computer Art and Design
Conflict Resolution and Mediation/Peace Studies
Consumer Economics
Corporate and Organizational Communication
Corrections (*see* Criminal Justice and Criminology)
Counseling (*see* Counseling Psychology; Pastoral Ministry and Counseling)
Counseling Psychology
Crafts (*see* Art/Fine Arts)
Creative Arts Therapies (*see* Art Therapy; Therapies—Dance, Drama, and Music)
Criminal Justice and Criminology
Cultural Anthropology
Cultural Studies
Dance
Decorative Arts
Demography and Population Studies
Design (*see* Applied Arts and Design; Architecture; Art/Fine Arts; Environmental Design; Graphic Design; Industrial Design; Interior Design; Textile Design; Urban Design)
Developmental Psychology
Diplomacy (*see* International Affairs)
Disability Studies
Drama Therapy (*see* Therapies—Dance, Drama, and Music)
Dramatic Arts (*see* Theater)
Drawing (*see* Art/Fine Arts)
Drug Abuse Counseling (*see* Addictions/Substance Abuse Counseling)
Drug and Alcohol Abuse Counseling (*see* Addictions/Substance Abuse Counseling)
East Asian Studies (*see* Asian Studies)
East European and Russian Studies
Economic Development
Economics
Educational Theater (*see* Theater; Therapies—Dance, Drama, and Music)
Emergency Management
English
Environmental Design
Ethics
Ethnic Studies
Ethnomusicology (*see* Music)
Experimental Psychology
Family and Consumer Sciences—General
Family Studies (*see* Child and Family Studies)
Family Therapy (*see* Child and Family Studies; Clinical Psychology; Counseling Psychology; Marriage and Family Therapy)
Filmmaking (*see* Film, Television, and Video Production)
Film Studies (*see* Film, Television, and Video Production)
Film, Television, and Video Production
Film, Television, and Video Theory and Criticism
Fine Arts (*see* Art/Fine Arts)
Folklore
Foreign Languages (*see* specific language)
Foreign Service (*see* International Affairs; International Development)
Forensic Psychology
Forensic Sciences
Forensics (*see* Speech and Interpersonal Communication)
French
Gender Studies
General Studies (*see* Liberal Studies)
Genetic Counseling
Geographic Information Systems
Geography
German
Gerontology
Graphic Design
Greek (*see* Classics)
Health Communication
Health Psychology
Hebrew (*see* Near and Middle Eastern Languages)
Hebrew Studies (*see* Jewish Studies)
Hispanic and Latin American Languages
Hispanic Studies
Historic Preservation
History
History of Art (*see* Art History)
History of Medicine
History of Science and Technology

Holocaust and Genocide Studies
Home Economics (*see* Family and Consumer Sciences—General)
Homeland Security
Household Economics, Sciences, and Management (*see* Family and
   Consumer Sciences—General)
Human Development
Humanities
Illustration
Industrial and Labor Relations
Industrial and Organizational Psychology
Industrial Design
Interdisciplinary Studies
Interior Design
International Affairs
International Development
International Economics
International Service (*see* International Affairs; International Development)
International Trade Policy
Internet and Interactive Multimedia
Interpersonal Communication (*see* Speech and Interpersonal
   Communication)
Interpretation (*see* Translation and Interpretation)
Islamic Studies (*see* Near and Middle Eastern Studies; Religion)
Italian
Japanese
Japanese Studies (*see* Asian Languages; Asian Studies; Japanese)
Jewelry (*see* Art/Fine Arts)
Jewish Studies
Journalism
Judaic Studies (*see* Jewish Studies; Religion)
Labor Relations (*see* Industrial and Labor Relations)
Landscape Architecture
Latin American Studies
Latin (*see* Classics)
Law Enforcement (*see* Criminal Justice and Criminology)
Liberal Studies
Lighting Design
Linguistics
Literature (*see* Classics; Comparative Literature; specific language)
Marriage and Family Therapy
Mass Communication
Media Studies
Medical Illustration
Medieval and Renaissance Studies
Metalsmithing (*see* Art/Fine Arts)
Middle Eastern Studies (*see* Near and Middle Eastern Studies)
Military and Defense Studies
Mineral Economics
Ministry (*see* Pastoral Ministry and Counseling; Theology)
Missions and Missiology
Motion Pictures (*see* Film, Television, and Video Production)
Museum Studies
Music
Musicology (*see* Music)
Music Therapy (*see* Therapies—Dance, Drama, and Music)
National Security
Native American Studies (*see* American Indian/Native American Studies)
Near and Middle Eastern Languages
Near and Middle Eastern Studies
Near Environment (*see* Family and Consumer Sciences)
Northern Studies
Organizational Psychology (*see* Industrial and Organizational Psychology)
Oriental Languages (*see* Asian Languages)
Oriental Studies (*see* Asian Studies)
Pacific Area/Pacific Rim Studies Painting (*see* Art/Fine Arts)
Pastoral Ministry and Counseling
Philanthropic Studies
Philosophy
Photography
Playwriting (*see* Theater; Writing)
Policy Studies (*see* Public Policy)
Political Science
Population Studies (*see* Demography and Population Studies)
Portuguese
Printmaking (*see* Art/Fine Arts)
Product Design (*see* Industrial Design)
Psychoanalysis and Psychotherapy Psychology—General
Public Administration
Public Affairs
Public History
Public Policy
Public Speaking (*see* Mass Communication; Rhetoric; Speech and
   Interpersonal Communication)
Publishing

Regional Planning (*see* Architecture; Urban and Regional Planning; Urban
   Design; Urban Studies)
Rehabilitation Counseling
Religion
Renaissance Studies (*see* Medieval and Renaissance Studies)
Rhetoric
Romance Languages
Romance Literatures (*see* Romance Languages)
Rural Planning and Studies
Rural Sociology
Russian
Scandinavian Languages
School Psychology
Sculpture (*see* Art/Fine Arts)
Security Administration (*see* Criminal Justice and Criminology)
Slavic Languages
Slavic Studies (*see* East European and Russian Studies; Slavic
   Languages)
Social Psychology
Social Sciences
Sociology
Southeast Asian Studies (*see* Asian Studies)
Soviet Studies (*see* East European and Russian Studies; Russian)
Spanish
Speech and Interpersonal Communication
Sport Psychology
Studio Art (*see* Art/Fine Arts)
Substance Abuse Counseling (*see* Addictions/Substance Abuse
   Counseling)
Survey Methodology
Sustainable Development
Technical Communication
Technical Writing
Telecommunications (*see* Film, Television, and Video Production)
Television (*see* Film, Television, and Video Production)
Textile Design
Textiles (*see* Clothing and Textiles; Textile Design)
Thanatology
Theater
Theater Arts (*see* Theater)
Theology
Therapies—Dance, Drama, and Music
Translation and Interpretation
Transpersonal and Humanistic Psychology
Urban and Regional Planning
Urban Design
Urban Planning (*see* Architecture; Urban and Regional Planning; Urban
   Design; Urban Studies)
Urban Studies
Video (*see* Film, Television, and Video Production)
Visual Arts (*see* Applied Arts and Design; Art/Fine Arts; Film, Television,
   and Video Production; Graphic Design; Illustration; Photography)
Western European Studies
Women's Studies
World Wide Web (*see* Internet and Interactive Multimedia)
Writing

Graduate Programs in the Biological/Biomedical Sciences & Health Related/Medical Professions

Acupuncture and Oriental Medicine
Acute Care/Critical Care Nursing Administration (*see* Health Services
   Management and Hospital Administration; Nursing and Healthcare
   Administration; Pharmaceutical Administration)
Adult Nursing
Advanced Practice Nursing (*see* Family Nurse Practitioner Studies)
Allied Health—General
Allied Health Professions (*see* Clinical Laboratory Sciences/Medical
   Technology; Clinical Research; Communication Disorders; Dental
   Hygiene; Emergency Medical Services; Occupational Therapy; Physical
   Therapy; Physician Assistant Studies; Rehabilitation Sciences)
Allopathic Medicine
Anatomy
Anesthesiologist Assistant Studies
Animal Behavior
Bacteriology
Behavioral Sciences (*see* Biopsychology; Neuroscience; Zoology)
Biochemistry
Bioethics
Biological and Biomedical Sciences—General Biological Chemistry (*see*
   Biochemistry)

Biological Oceanography (*see* Marine Biology)
Biophysics
Biopsychology
Botany
Breeding (*see* Botany; Plant Biology; Genetics)
Cancer Biology/Oncology
Cardiovascular Sciences
Cell Biology
Cellular Physiology (*see* Cell Biology; Physiology)
Child-Care Nursing (*see* Maternal and Child/Neonatal Nursing)
Chiropractic
Clinical Laboratory Sciences/Medical Technology
Clinical Research
Community Health
Community Health Nursing
Computational Biology
Conservation (*see* Conservation Biology; Environmental Biology)
Conservation Biology
Crop Sciences (*see* Botany; Plant Biology)
Cytology (*see* Cell Biology)
Dental and Oral Surgery (*see* Oral and Dental Sciences)
Dental Assistant Studies (*see* Dental Hygiene)
Dental Hygiene
Dental Services (*see* Dental Hygiene)
Dentistry
Developmental Biology Dietetics (*see* Nutrition)
Ecology
Embryology (*see* Developmental Biology)
Emergency Medical Services
Endocrinology (*see* Physiology)
Entomology
Environmental Biology
Environmental and Occupational Health
Epidemiology
Evolutionary Biology
Family Nurse Practitioner Studies
Foods (*see* Nutrition)
Forensic Nursing
Genetics
Genomic Sciences
Gerontological Nursing
Health Physics/Radiological Health
Health Promotion
Health-Related Professions (*see* individual allied health professions)
Health Services Management and Hospital Administration
Health Services Research
Histology (*see* Anatomy; Cell Biology)
HIV/AIDS Nursing
Hospice Nursing
Hospital Administration (*see* Health Services Management and Hospital Administration)
Human Genetics
Immunology
Industrial Hygiene
Infectious Diseases
International Health
Laboratory Medicine (*see* Clinical Laboratory Sciences/Medical Technology; Immunology; Microbiology; Pathology)
Life Sciences (*see* Biological and Biomedical Sciences)
Marine Biology
Maternal and Child Health
Maternal and Child/Neonatal Nursing
Medical Imaging
Medical Microbiology
Medical Nursing (*see* Medical/Surgical Nursing)
Medical Physics
Medical/Surgical Nursing
Medical Technology (*see* Clinical Laboratory Sciences/Medical Technology)
Medical Sciences (*see* Biological and Biomedical Sciences)
Medical Science Training Programs (*see* Biological and Biomedical Sciences)
Medicinal and Pharmaceutical Chemistry
Medicinal Chemistry (*see* Medicinal and Pharmaceutical Chemistry)
Medicine (*see* Allopathic Medicine; Naturopathic Medicine; Osteopathic Medicine; Podiatric Medicine)
Microbiology
Midwifery (*see* Nurse Midwifery)
Molecular Biology
Molecular Biophysics
Molecular Genetics
Molecular Medicine
Molecular Pathogenesis
Molecular Pathology
Molecular Pharmacology
Molecular Physiology

Molecular Toxicology
Naturopathic Medicine
Neural Sciences (*see* Biopsychology; Neurobiology; Neuroscience)
Neurobiology
Neuroendocrinology (*see* Biopsychology; Neurobiology; Neuroscience; Physiology)
Neuropharmacology (*see* Biopsychology; Neurobiology; Neuroscience; Pharmacology)
Neurophysiology (*see* Biopsychology; Neurobiology; Neuroscience; Physiology)
Neuroscience
Nuclear Medical Technology (*see* Clinical Laboratory Sciences/ Medical Technology)
Nurse Anesthesia
Nurse Midwifery
Nurse Practitioner Studies (*see* Family Nurse Practitioner Studies)
Nursing Administration (*see* Nursing and Healthcare Administration)
Nursing and Healthcare Administration
Nursing Education
Nursing—General
Nursing Informatics
Nutrition
Occupational Health (*see* Environmental and Occupational Health; Occupational Health Nursing)
Occupational Health Nursing
Occupational Therapy
Oncology (*see* Cancer Biology/Oncology)
Oncology Nursing
Optometry
Oral and Dental Sciences
Oral Biology (*see* Oral and Dental Sciences)
Oral Pathology (*see* Oral and Dental Sciences)
Organismal Biology (*see* Biological and Biomedical Sciences; Zoology)
Oriental Medicine and Acupuncture (*see* Acupuncture and Oriental Medicine)
Orthodontics (*see* Oral and Dental Sciences)
Osteopathic Medicine
Parasitology
Pathobiology
Pathology
Pediatric Nursing
Pedontics (*see* Oral and Dental Sciences)
Perfusion
Pharmaceutical Administration
Pharmaceutical Chemistry (*see* Medicinal and Pharmaceutical Chemistry)
Pharmaceutical Sciences
Pharmacology
Pharmacy
Photobiology of Cells and Organelles (*see* Botany; Cell Biology; Plant Biology)
Physical Therapy
Physician Assistant Studies
Physiological Optics (*see* Vision Sciences)
Podiatric Medicine
Preventive Medicine (*see* Community Health and Public Health)
Physiological Optics (*see* Physiology)
Physiology
Plant Biology
Plant Molecular Biology
Plant Pathology
Plant Physiology
Pomology (*see* Botany; Plant Biology)
Psychiatric Nursing
Public Health—General
Public Health Nursing (*see* Community Health Nursing)
Psychiatric Nursing
Psychobiology (*see* Biopsychology)
Psychopharmacology (*see* Biopsychology; Neuroscience; Pharmacology)
Radiation Biology
Radiological Health (*see* Health Physics/Radiological Health)
Rehabilitation Nursing
Rehabilitation Sciences
Rehabilitation Therapy (*see* Physical Therapy)
Reproductive Biology
School Nursing
Sociobiology (*see* Evolutionary Biology)
Structural Biology
Surgical Nursing (*see* Medical/Surgical Nursing)
Systems Biology
Teratology
Therapeutics
Theoretical Biology (*see* Biological and Biomedical Sciences)
Therapeutics (*see* Pharmaceutical Sciences; Pharmacology; Pharmacy)
Toxicology

Transcultural Nursing
Translational Biology
Tropical Medicine (*see* Parasitology)
Veterinary Medicine
Veterinary Sciences
Virology
Vision Sciences
Wildlife Biology (*see* Zoology)
Women's Health Nursing
Zoology

Graduate Programs in the Physical Sciences, Mathematics, Agricultural Sciences, the Environment & Natural Resources

Acoustics
Agricultural Sciences
Agronomy and Soil Sciences
Analytical Chemistry
Animal Sciences
Applied Mathematics
Applied Physics
Applied Statistics
Aquaculture
Astronomy
Astrophysical Sciences (*see* Astrophysics; Atmospheric Sciences; Meteorology; Planetary and Space Sciences)
Astrophysics
Atmospheric Sciences
Biological Oceanography (*see* Marine Affairs; Marine Sciences; Oceanography)
Biomathematics
Biometry
Biostatistics
Chemical Physics
Chemistry
Computational Sciences
Condensed Matter Physics
Dairy Science (*see* Animal Sciences)
Earth Sciences (*see* Geosciences)
Environmental Management and Policy
Environmental Sciences
Environmental Studies (*see* Environmental Management and Policy)
Experimental Statistics (*see* Statistics)
Fish, Game, and Wildlife Management
Food Science and Technology
Forestry
General Science (*see* specific topics)
Geochemistry
Geodetic Sciences
Geological Engineering (*see* Geology)
Geological Sciences (*see* Geology)
Geology
Geophysical Fluid Dynamics (*see* Geophysics)
Geophysics
Geosciences
Horticulture
Hydrogeology
Hydrology
Inorganic Chemistry
Limnology
Marine Affairs
Marine Geology
Marine Sciences
Marine Studies (*see* Marine Affairs; Marine Geology; Marine Sciences; Oceanography)
Mathematical and Computational Finance
Mathematical Physics
Mathematical Statistics (*see* Applied Statistics; Statistics)
Mathematics
Meteorology
Mineralogy
Natural Resource Management (*see* Environmental Management and Policy; Natural Resources)
Natural Resources
Nuclear Physics (*see* Physics)
Ocean Engineering (*see* Marine Affairs; Marine Geology; Marine Sciences; Oceanography)
Oceanography
Optical Sciences

Optical Technologies (*see* Optical Sciences)
Optics (*see* Applied Physics; Optical Sciences; Physics)
Organic Chemistry
Paleontology
Paper Chemistry (*see* Chemistry)
Photonics
Physical Chemistry
Physics
Planetary and Space Sciences
Plant Sciences
Plasma Physics
Poultry Science (*see* Animal Sciences)
Radiological Physics (*see* Physics)
Range Management (*see* Range Science)
Range Science
Resource Management (*see* Environmental Management and Policy; Natural Resources)
Solid-Earth Sciences (*see* Geosciences)
Space Sciences (*see* Planetary and Space Sciences)
Statistics
Theoretical Chemistry
Theoretical Physics
Viticulture and Enology
Water Resources

Graduate Programs in Engineering & Applied Sciences

Aeronautical Engineering (*see* Aerospace/Aeronautical Engineering)
Aerospace/Aeronautical Engineering
Aerospace Studies (*see* Aerospace/Aeronautical Engineering)
Agricultural Engineering
Applied Mechanics (*see* Mechanics)
Applied Science and Technology
Architectural Engineering
Artificial Intelligence/Robotics
Astronautical Engineering (*see* Aerospace/Aeronautical Engineering)
Automotive Engineering
Aviation
Biochemical Engineering
Bioengineering Bioinformatics
Biological Engineering (*see* Bioengineering)
Biomedical Engineering
Biosystems Engineering
Biotechnology
Ceramic Engineering (*see* Ceramic Sciences and Engineering)
Ceramic Sciences and Engineering
Ceramics (*see* Ceramic Sciences and Engineering)
Chemical Engineering
Civil Engineering
Computer and Information Systems Security
Computer Engineering
Computer Science
Computing Technology (*see* Computer Science)
Construction Engineering
Construction Management
Database Systems
Electrical Engineering
Electronic Materials
Electronics Engineering (*see* Electrical Engineering)
Energy and Power Engineering
Energy Management and Policy
Engineering and Applied Sciences
Engineering and Public Affairs (*see* Technology and Public Policy)
Engineering and Public Policy (*see* Energy Management and Policy; Technology and Public Policy)
Engineering Design
Engineering Management
Engineering Mechanics (*see* Mechanics)
Engineering Metallurgy (*see* Metallurgical Engineering and Metallurgy)
Engineering Physics
Environmental Design (*see* Environmental Engineering)
Environmental Engineering
Ergonomics and Human Factors
Financial Engineering
Fire Protection Engineering
Food Engineering (*see* Agricultural Engineering)
Game Design and Development
Gas Engineering (*see* Petroleum Engineering)
Geological Engineering
Geophysics Engineering (*see* Geological Engineering)
Geotechnical Engineering
Hazardous Materials Management

Health Informatics
Health Systems (*see* Safety Engineering; Systems Engineering)
Highway Engineering (*see* Transportation and Highway Engineering)
Human-Computer Interaction
Human Factors (*see* Ergonomics and Human Factors)
Hydraulics
Hydrology (*see* Water Resources Engineering)
Industrial Engineering (*see* Industrial/Management Engineering)
Industrial/Management Engineering
Information Science
Internet Engineering
Macromolecular Science (*see* Polymer Science and Engineering)
Management Engineering (*see* Engineering Management; Industrial/
    Management Engineering)
Management of Technology
Manufacturing Engineering
Marine Engineering (*see* Civil Engineering)
Materials Engineering
Materials Sciences
Mechanical Engineering
Mechanics
Medical Informatics
Metallurgical Engineering and Metallurgy
Metallurgy (*see* Metallurgical Engineering and Metallurgy)
Mineral/Mining Engineering
Modeling and Simulation
Nanotechnology
Nuclear Engineering
Ocean Engineering
Operations Research
Paper and Pulp Engineering
Petroleum Engineering
Pharmaceutical Engineering
Plastics Engineering (*see* Polymer Science and Engineering)
Polymer Science and Engineering
Public Policy (*see* Energy Management and Policy; Technology and Public
    Policy)
Reliability Engineering
Robotics (*see* Artificial Intelligence/Robotics)
Safety Engineering
Software Engineering
Solid-State Sciences (*see* Materials Sciences)
Structural Engineering
Surveying Science and Engineering
Systems Analysis (*see* Systems Engineering)
Systems Engineering
Systems Science
Technology and Public Policy
Telecommunications
Telecommunications Management
Textile Sciences and Engineering
Textiles (*see* Textile Sciences and Engineering)
Transportation and Highway Engineering
Urban Systems Engineering (*see* Systems Engineering)
Waste Management (*see* Hazardous Materials Management)
Water Resources Engineering

Graduate Programs in Business, Education, Information Studies, Law & Social Work

Accounting
Actuarial Science
Adult Education
Advertising and Public Relations
Agricultural Education
Alcohol Abuse Counseling (*see* Counselor Education)
Archival Management and Studies
Art Education
Athletics Administration (*see* Kinesiology and Movement Studies)
Athletic Training and Sports Medicine
Audiology (*see* Communication Disorders)
Aviation Management
Banking (*see* Finance and Banking)
Business Administration and Management—General
Business Education
Communication Disorders
Community College Education
Computer Education
Continuing Education (*see* Adult Education)
Counseling (*see* Counselor Education)
Counselor Education

Curriculum and Instruction
Developmental Education
Distance Education Development
Drug Abuse Counseling (*see* Counselor Education)
Early Childhood Education
Educational Leadership and Administration
Educational Measurement and Evaluation
Educational Media/Instructional Technology
Educational Policy
Educational Psychology
Education—General
Education of the Blind (*see* Special Education)
Education of the Deaf (*see* Special Education)
Education of the Gifted
Education of the Hearing Impaired (*see* Special Education)
Education of the Learning Disabled (*see* Special Education)
Education of the Mentally Retarded (*see* Special Education)
Education of the Physically Handicapped (*see* Special Education)
Education of Students with Severe/Multiple Disabilities
Education of the Visually Handicapped (*see* Special Education)
Electronic Commerce
Elementary Education
English as a Second Language
English Education
Entertainment Management
Entrepreneurship
Environmental Education
Environmental Law
Exercise and Sports Science
Exercise Physiology (*see* Kinesiology and Movement Studies)
Facilities and Entertainment Management
Finance and Banking
Food Services Management (*see* Hospitality Management)
Foreign Languages Education
Foundations and Philosophy of Education
Guidance and Counseling (*see* Counselor Education)
Health Education
Health Law
Hearing Sciences (*see* Communication Disorders)
Higher Education
Home Economics Education
Hospitality Management
Hotel Management (*see* Travel and Tourism)
Human Resources Development
Human Resources Management
Human Services
Industrial Administration (*see* Industrial and Manufacturing Management)
Industrial and Manufacturing Management
Industrial Education (*see* Vocational and Technical Education)
Information Studies
Instructional Technology (*see* Educational Media/Instructional Technology)
Insurance
Intellectual Property Law
International and Comparative Education
International Business
International Commerce (*see* International Business)
International Economics (*see* International Business)
International Trade (*see* International Business)
Investment and Securities (*see*   Business Administration and
    Management; Finance and Banking; Investment Management)
Investment Management
Junior College Education (*see* Community College Education)
Kinesiology and Movement Studies
Law
Legal and Justice Studies
Leisure Services (*see* Recreation and Park Management)
Leisure Studies
Library Science
Logistics
Management (*see* Business Administration and Management)
Management Information Systems
Management Strategy and Policy
Marketing
Marketing Research
Mathematics Education
Middle School Education
Movement Studies (*see* Kinesiology and Movement Studies)
Multilingual and Multicultural Education
Museum Education
Music Education
Nonprofit Management
Nursery School Education (*see* Early Childhood Education)
Occupational Education (*see* Vocational and Technical Education)
Organizational Behavior
Organizational Management

Parks Administration (*see* Recreation and Park Management)
Personnel (*see* Human Resources Development; Human Resources Management; Organizational Behavior; Organizational Management; Student Affairs)
Philosophy of Education (*see* Foundations and Philosophy of Education)
Physical Education
Project Management
Public Relations (*see* Advertising and Public Relations)
Quality Management
Quantitative Analysis
Reading Education
Real Estate
Recreation and Park Management
Recreation Therapy (*see* Recreation and Park Management)
Religious Education
Remedial Education (*see* Special Education)
Restaurant Administration (*see* Hospitality Management)
Science Education
Secondary Education
Social Sciences Education
Social Studies Education (*see* Social Sciences Education)
Social Work
Special Education

Speech-Language Pathology and Audiology (*see* Communication Disorders)
Sports Management
Sports Medicine (*see* Athletic Training and Sports Medicine)
Sports Psychology and Sociology (*see* Kinesiology and Movement Studies)
Student Affairs
Substance Abuse Counseling (*see* Counselor Education)
Supply Chain Management
Sustainability Management
Systems Management (*see* Management Information Systems)
Taxation
Teacher Education (*see* specific subject areas)
Teaching English as a Second Language (*see* English as a Second Language)
Technical Education (*see* Vocational and Technical Education)
Transportation Management
Travel and Tourism
Urban Education
Vocational and Technical Education
Vocational Counseling (*see* Counselor Education)

Directories and Subject Areas in This Book

College Portraits
No rankings, no spin... just the facts!

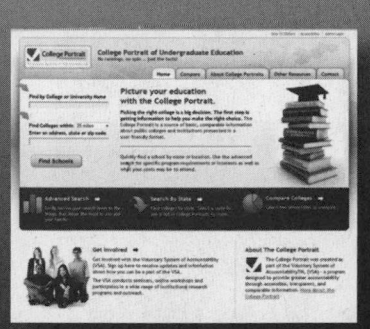

Free access and use—no fees, no log in required!

Visit a website with reliable and user-friendly information on more than 300 public colleges and universities:

>> Learn about the student experience on campus

>> Compare admissions, majors, campus life, class size, and more

>> Calculate your cost to attend a participating university

>> Search by state, distance from home, size, and more

>> Find links and contact information for each campus

Sponsored by the Association of Public and Land-grant Universities and the American Association of State Colleges and Universities

www.collegeportraits.org

Save 10% on the cost of college

Visit
simpletuition.com/smarterstudent
to find out how!

simpletuition
plan · pay less · pay back

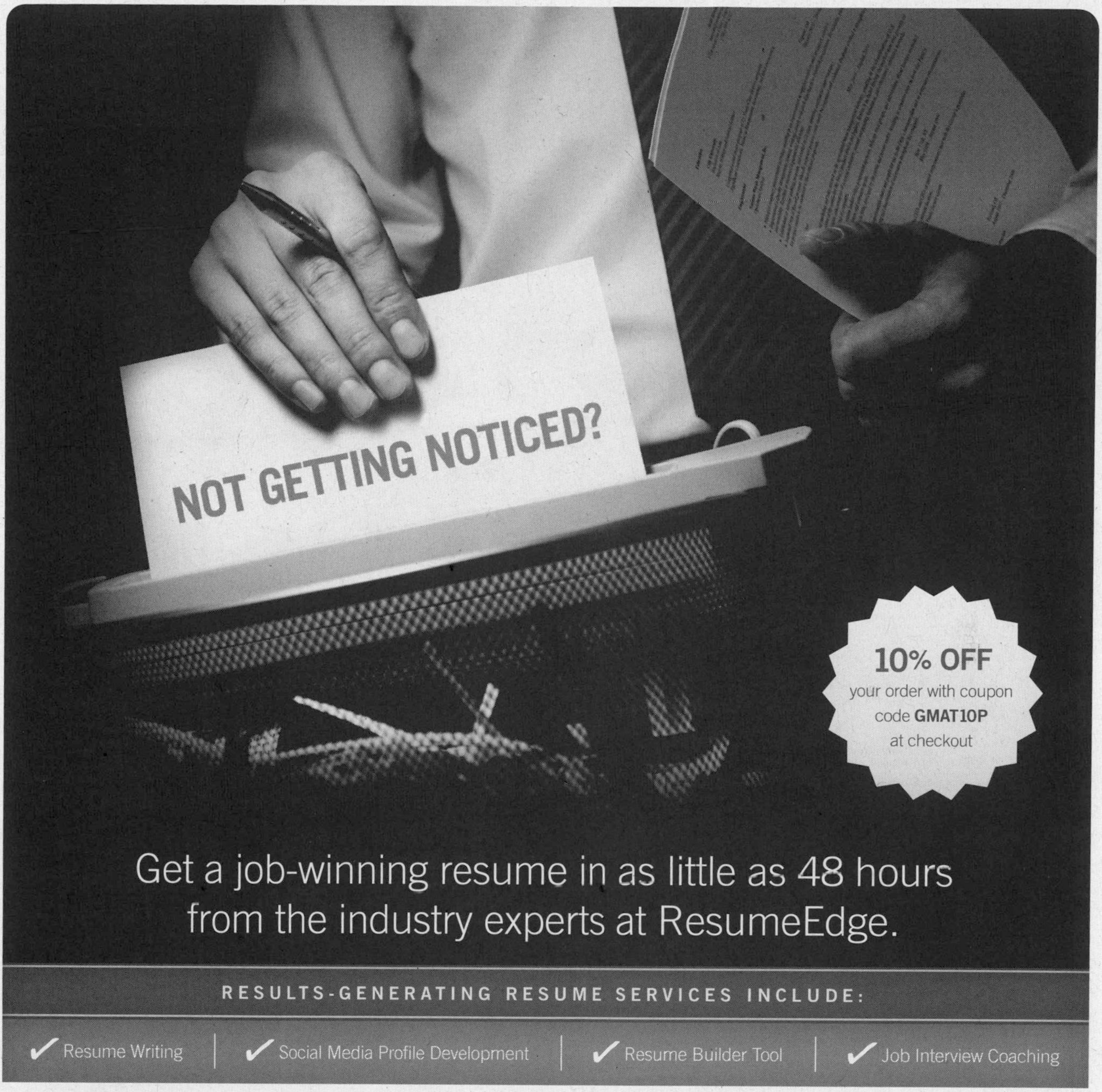

NOT GETTING NOTICED?

10% OFF your order with coupon code **GMAT10P** at checkout

Get a job-winning resume in as little as 48 hours from the industry experts at ResumeEdge.

RESULTS-GENERATING RESUME SERVICES INCLUDE:

✔ Resume Writing ✔ Social Media Profile Development ✔ Resume Builder Tool ✔ Job Interview Coaching

The ResumeEdge Difference

- Certified Professional Resume Writers
- One-on-one contact with your writer
- 98% customer satisfaction rating
- Experts in more than 40 industries
- As little as 48-hour turnaround for most orders
- An established business since 2001
- Resume writing partner to leading sites such as **Dice.com**

"I received calls from every potential employer that I sent my resume to. ***I was offered a fantastic position*** *and feel that it was due, in no small part, to the great resume that [my editor] put together for me!"* —N.G.

LEARN MORE—visit ResumeEdge.com or call 888.438.2633

ResumeEdge
A nelnet SERVICE

NOTES